AMERICAN ART DIRECTORY®

2014

68th EDITION

National Register Publishing

Berkeley Heights, New Jersey

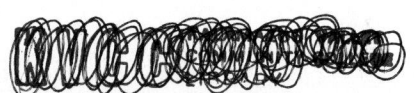

American Art Directory,® 68th Edition

Published by National Register Publishing

Contents

Preface

The American Art Directory,® first published in 1898 as the American Art Annual, continues in its tradition of excellence with the 66th edition. The directory is a standard in the field of art, and an indispensable reference to art museums, libraries, organizations, schools and corporate art holdings.

COMPILATION

The information for the directory is collected by means of direct communication whenever possible. Forms are sent to all entrants for corroboration and updating, and information submitted by entrants is included as completely as possible within the boundaries of editorial and space restrictions. Information for new entrants is in response to questionnaires or the result of research. Alphabetizing in the directory is strictly letter-by-letter. Those museums, libraries, associations and organizations which bear an individual's name are alphabetized by the last name of that individual. Colleges and universities are alphabetized by the first word of their name, whether or not it is named for an individual.

CONTENT AND COVERAGE

Section 1 lists The National and Regional Organizations, which are arranged alphabetically and contain over 100 organizations which administer and coordinate the arts within the United States and Canada. Included here are libraries affiliated with these organizations. The Museums, Libraries and Associations listings are arranged geographically, and contain listings for more than 2,700 main museums, 280 main libraries, 110 area associations, and 71 corporations with art holdings within the United States and Canada. There are more than 1,700 additional listings for galleries, museums and libraries affiliated with main entries.

A classification key is printed to the left of each entry to designate the type:
> A—Association
> C—Corporate Art
> L—Library
> M—Museum
> O—Organization

The key "M" is assigned to organizations whose primary function is gathering and preserving the visual arts. The "O" designation is given to national and regional organizations supporting the arts through sponsorship of art activities. The "A" code is given to those supporting the arts on more local levels.

Section II lists detailed information on more than 1,680 art schools, and college and university departments of art, art history, and architecture in the United States and Canada.

Section III provides reference to more than 1,070 art museums and 140 schools abroad, state arts councils, directors and supervisors of art education, art magazines, newspapers and their art critics.

Section IV is composed of three alphabetical indexes; organizational, personnel, and subject. The subject index includes general art subjects and specific collections, along with the name and location of the holding organization.

I ART ORGANIZATIONS

Arrangement and Abbreviations

National and Regional Organizations in the U.S.

Museums, Libraries and Associations in the U.S.

National and Regional Organizations in Canada

Museums, Libraries and Associations in Canada

Arrangement and Abbreviations
Key to Art Organizations

ARRANGEMENT OF DATA

Name and Address of institution; telephone number, including area code.

Names and titles of key personnel.

Hours open; admission fees; date established and purpose; average annual attendance; membership.

Annual figures on income and purchases.

Collections with enlarging collections indicated.

Exhibitions.

Activities sponsored, including classes for adults and children, dramatic programs and docent training; lectures, concerts, gallery talks and tours; competitions, awards, scholarships and fellowships; lending programs; museum or sales shops.

Libraries also list number of book volumes, periodical subscriptions, and audiovisual and micro holdings; subject covered by name of special collections.

ABBREVIATIONS AND SYMBOLS

Acad—Academic
Admin—Administration, Administrative
Adminr—Administrator
Admis—Admission
A-tapes—Audio-tapes
Adv—Advisory
AM—Morning
Ann—Annual
Approx—Approximate, Approximately
Asn—Association
Assoc—Associate
Asst—Assistant
AV—Audiovisual
Ave—Avenue
Bldg—Building
Blvd—Boulevard
Bro—Brother
C—circa
Cert—Certificate
Chap—Chapter
Chmn—Chairman
Circ—Circulation
Cl—Closed
Col— College
Coll—Collection
Comt—Committee
Coordr—Coordinator
Corresp—Corresponding
Cr—Credit
Cur—Curator
D—Day
Den—Denominational
Dept—Department
Develop—Development
Dipl—Diploma
Dir—Director
Dist—District
Div—Division
Dorm—Dormitory
Dr—Doctor, Drive
E—East, Evening
Ed—Editor
Educ—Education

Elec Mail—Electronic Mail
Enrol—Enrollment
Ent—Entrance
Ent Req—Entrance Requirements
Est, Estab—Established
Exec—Executive
Exhib—Exhibition
Exten—Extension
Fel(s)—Fellowships
Fri—Friday
Fs—Filmstrips
Ft—Feet
FT—Full Time Instructor
GC—Graduate Course
Gen—General
Grad—Graduate
Hon—Honorary
Hr—Hour
HS—High School
Hwy—Highway
Inc—Incorporated
Incl—Including
Jr—Junior
Lect—Lecture(s)
Lectr—Lecturer
Librn—Librarian
M—Men
Maj—Major in Art
Mem—Membership
Mgr—Manager
Mon—Monday
Mss—Manuscripts
Mus—Museums
N—North
Nat—National
Nonres—Nonresident
Per subs—Periodical subscriptions
PM—Afternoon
Pres—President
Prin—Principal
Prof—Professor
Prog—Program
PT—Part Time Instructor

Pts—Points
Pub—Public
Publ—Publication
Publr—Publisher
Pvt—Private
Qtr—Quarter
Rd—Road
Rec—Records
Reg—Registration
Req—Requirements
Res—Residence, Resident
S—South
Sat—Saturday
Schol—Scholarship
Secy—Secretary
Sem—Semeseter
Soc—Society
Sq—Square
Sr—Senior, Sister
St—Street
Ste—Suite
Sun—Sunday
Supt—Superintendent
Supv—Supervisor
Thurs—Thursday
Treas—Treasurer
Tues—Tuesday
Tui—Tuition
TV—Television
Undergrad—Undergraduate
Univ—University
Vis—Visiting
Vol—Volunteer
Vols—Volumes
V-tapes—Videotapes
Vols—Volumes
W—West, Women
Wed—Wednesday
Wk—Week
Yr—Year(s)

A Association
C Corporate Art Holding
L Library
M Museum
O Organization

O **THE ALLIED ARTISTS OF AMERICA, INC,** 15 Gramercy Park S, National Arts Club New York, NY 10003-1705. Tel 212-582-6411; Internet Home Page Address: www.alliedartistsofamerica.org; *Pres* Thomas Valenti; *VPres* Christina Debarry
Open Nov - Dec daily Noon - 5 PM; No admis fee; Estab 1914, incorporated 1922, as a self-supporting exhibition cooperative, with juries elected each yr by the mem, to promote work by American artists; Mem: 3601; dues $50 & up; 3 annual meetings - Apr, Sept & Dec
Income: Financed by members' fees
Exhibitions: Members' Regional AAA exhibitions; annual exhibition in the winter; Annual held at National Arts Club; numerous awards & medals; prizes total $16,000 each year
Publications: Catalogs; newsletter
Activities: Lects open to pub, 1-3 vis lectrs per yr; gallery talks; competitions with awards

O **AMERICAN ABSTRACT ARTISTS,** 194 Powers St, Brooklyn, NY 11211-4922. Elec Mail americanabart@aol.com; Internet Home Page Address: www.americanabstractartists.org; *Pres* Daniel G Hill; *Treas* James Juszczyk; *Secy* Julian Jackson
Estab 1936, active 1937, to promote American abstract art; develop & educate through exhibitions & publications; to provide forums for the exchange of ideas among artists; Mem: 94; dues $75; 5 meetings per yr
Income: Financed by mem
Publications: Portfolio of prints, journal
Activities: Lects open to pub; 1 vis lectr per yr; individual and original objects of art lent to responsible galleries, museums and universities; organize traveling exhibs to univ galleries, non-profit spaces; originate traveling exhibs

O **AMERICAN ACADEMY OF ARTS & LETTERS,** 633 W 155th St, New York, NY 10032-7501. Tel 212-368-5900; Fax 212-491-4615; Elec Mail academy@artsandletters.org; Internet Home Page Address: www.artsandletters.org; *Pres* Ezra J D McClatchy; *VPres Art* Henry N Cobb; *VPres Literature* A R Gurney; *VPres Music* Shulamit Ran; *Secy* Rosanna Warren; *Treas* Charles Wuorinen; *Exec Dir* Virginia Dajani
Open Mon - Fri 9:30 AM - 5 PM (office); galleries open during exhibs only: Thurs - Sun 1 - 4 PM; No admis fee; Estab 1898 as an honorary mem organization of artists, writers & composers whose function it is to foster, assist & sustain an interest in literature, music & the fine arts; Maintains reference library of books & papers of members; Average Annual Attendance: 6,000; Mem: 250; mem is by election; no dues; annual meeting in May
Income: $1,400,000 (financed by endowment)
Purchases: $80,000-$90,000 Hassam Speicher Purchase Program
Collections: Works by members
Exhibitions: Exhibition of Candidates for Art Awards; Exhibition of Paintings Eligible for Hassam Fund Purchase; Newly Elected Members & Recipients of Honors & Awards Exhibitions, art, scores & manuscripts; Richard Rodgers Awards in Musical Theater (competition); Special Exhibitions
Publications: Proceedings, annual; exhibition catalogs
Activities: Awards given (nominations come from members)

O **AMERICAN ANTIQUARIAN SOCIETY,** 185 Salisbury St, Worcester, MA 01609-1634. Tel 508-755-5221; Fax 508-753-3311; Elec Mail library@mwa.org; Internet Home Page Address: www.americanantiquarian.org; *Pres* Ellen S Dunlap; *VPres Admin* Edward J Harris; *VPres Develop* John M Keenum; *Marcus A McCorison Librn* Thomas G Knoles; *Andrew W Mellon Cur Graphic Arts* Georgia B Barnhill; *Head Bldgs & Grounds* Andrew Cariglia; *Dir Information Technology* Nick Conti; *Head Cataloging Svcs* Alan N Degutis; *Dir Acad Programs* Paul J Erickson; *First Democratization Project Coordr* Krista S Ferrante; *Finance Dir* Susan Forgit; *Chief Conservator* Babette Gehnrich; *Cur Newspapers & Periodicals* Vincent L Golden; *Cur Manuscripts* Thomas G Knowles; *Colls Mgr* Marie E Lamoureux; *Head Acquisitions* Peg Lesinski; *Dir Outreach* James David Moran; *Sr Cataloger Rare Books* Doris N O'Keefe; *Reference Librn* Elizabeth Watts Pope; *Dir Scholarly Publications* Caroline F Sloat; *Cur Children's Literature* Laura E Wasowicz; *Cur Books* David R Whitesell; *Sr Cataloger* S J Wolfe
Open Mon - Tues & Thurs - Fri 9 AM - 5 PM, Wed 10 AM - 8 PM, cl legal holidays; No admis fee; Incorporated 1812 to collect, preserve & encourage serious study of the materials of American history & life through 1876; Maintains reference library; Mem: 775 honorary; meetings third Fri in Apr & Oct
Income: Financed by endowment, gifts & grants
Purchases: $273,900
Library Holdings: Auction Catalogs; CD-ROMs; Exhibition Catalogs; Manuscripts; Maps; Original Art Works; Pamphlets; Periodical Subscriptions; Photographs; Prints; Reproductions
Special Subjects: Cartoons, Etchings & Engravings, Graphics, Prints, Painting-American, Woodcuts, Maps, Bookplates & Bindings
Collections: Early American Portraits; Staffordshire Pottery; bookplates, prints, lithographs, cartoons, engravings; Colonial furniture; photographs

Publications: Monographs; newsletters; Proceedings, semi-annually
Activities: Undergraduate seminar in American Studies; docent training; lects open to public 4-6 per yr; scholarships & fels offered; sales shop sells books & postcards

O **AMERICAN ARTISTS PROFESSIONAL LEAGUE, INC,** 47 Fifth Ave, New York, NY 10003. Tel 212-645-1345; Fax 212-792-2275; Elec Mail aaplinc@gmail.com; Internet Home Page Address: www.americanartistsprofessionalleague.org; *Pres* Konrad Hansalik; *VPres* Joseph McGlynn; *Treas* Gail Schulman; *Corresp Secy* Susanne Hurt; *Recording Secy* Susie Gach Peelle
Estab 1928 to advance the cause of fine arts in America, through the promotion of high standards of beauty, integrity & craftsmanship in painting, sculpture & the graphic arts; to emphasize the importance of order & coherent commun as prime requisites of works of art through exhibitions & publications; Mem: 1000; election by jury of professional artists National Board of Dir; dues $50; annual meeting in Nov
Income: Financed by mem
Exhibitions: Annual Grand National Exhibition
Publications: AAPL News Bulletin, semi-annually
Activities: Competitions with awards; scholarships & fels offered

O **AMERICAN ASSOCIATION OF MUSEUMS,** United States National Committee of the International Council of Museums (ICOM-US), 1575 Eye St NW, Ste 400, Washington, DC 20005. Tel 202-289-1818; Fax 202-289-6578; Elec Mail icomus@aam-us.org; Internet Home Page Address: www.aam-us.org/icom; *Pres* Ford W Bell; *Exec VPres* Kim Igoe; *VPres Finance & Admin* Mary Bowie; *VPres Mktg & Commun* Kate McGoldrick; *VPres Develop* Danielle St. Germain-Gordon
Open 9 AM - 5 PM; No admis fee; AAM estab 1906, affiliated with ICOM-US in 1973, represents international museum interests within the United States & US museum interests abroad through the ICOM-US office which disseminates information on international conferences, publications, travel & study grants & training programs in AAM's newsletter, AVISO; Mem: 1100; members must be museum professionals or institutions; dues vary according to member category; members meet annually at the AAM annual meeting every spring and once every 3 yrs at the ICOM triennial conference
Income: Financed by mem dues
Publications: International Column in Aviso, monthly; ICOM News, quarterly (from ICOM Secretariat in Paris); occasional articles in Museum News, AAM's bi-monthly magazine
Activities: Specialty committees; annual meeting; international meetings; professional exchanges; publications catalogue available; International Service Citation

O **AMERICAN ASSOCIATION OF UNIVERSITY WOMEN,** 1111 16th St NW, Washington, DC 20036-4809. Tel 202-785-7700; Fax 202-872-1425; Elec Mail connect@aauw.org; Internet Home Page Address: www.aauw.org; *Exec Dir* Linda D Hallman CAE
Open to AAUW members only Mon - Fri 8 AM - 4 PM; No admis fee; Estab 1881 to unite alumnae of different institutions for practical educational work; to further the advancement of women, lifelong learning, & responsibility to soc expressed through action, advocacy, research & enlightened leadership; Mem: 150,000; holds biennial conventions
Publications: Action Alert, biweekly; AAUW Outlook, quarterly; Leader in Action, quarterly; brochures; booklets; research studies; study guides
Activities: Assn local branches develop & maintain progs in the arts. AAUW Foundation funds first professional degree in architecture, doctoral/post doctoral candidates in the arts

O **AMERICAN COLOR PRINT SOCIETY,** 319 Meadowbrook Dr, Huntingdon Valley, PA 19006; Box 625, Bryn Athyn, PA 19009-0625. Tel 215-938-7127; Elec Mail caroleline@verizon.net; Internet Home Page Address: www.americancolorprintsociety.org; *Pres* Carole J Meyers; *VPres, Color Proof Ed & Treas* Elizabeth H MacDonald; *Pub Chmn* Sy Hakim; *Bd Mem* Alan J Klawans; *Bd Mem* Libby Calamia; *Bd Mem* Art Brener; *Bd Mem* Thelma Grobes; *Board Mem* Debbie Strong Napple
Estab 1939 to exhibit color prints; exhibits the work of original prints; Mem: 75; dues $40; professional printmaker's work is juried by board mems
Income: Financed by mem; non-profit 501C
Collections: The Philadelphia Museum of Art, Philadelphia, PA; Central Philadelphia Free Library print coll; Villanova Univ, Villanova, PA
Publications: The Color Proof-Semi Annual
Activities: Lect & symposium; sponsors annual national members exhibition of all media color prints; 7 annual prizes, Stella Draken Memorial Awards; Hutton Prize; Michael Lasuchin Memorial Award; Grever Award; scholarships offered; originates traveling exhibs for mems

O **AMERICAN CRAFT COUNCIL,** 1224 Marshall St NE, #200 Minneapolis, MN 55413-1036. Tel 612-206-3100; Fax 612-355-2330; Elec Mail council@craftcouncil.org; Internet Home Page Address: www.craftcouncil.org; *Exec Dir* Christopher Amundsen; *Dir Develop* Elissa Chaffee; *Dir Finance & Admin* Greg Allen; *Show Dir* Melanie Little; *Dir Mktg* Pamela Diamond; *Editor in Chief American Craft Mag* Monica Moses; *Dir Educ* Perry Price
Open Mon - Fri 1 - 5 PM, Tues 1 - 7 PM; Estab 1943 to promote understanding and appreciation of American craft; Mem: 32,000; dues $40
Income: Financed by mem, private donations & government grants
Exhibitions: Ten shows & markets per yr
Publications: American Craft Magazine (formerly Craft Horizons), bimonthly
Activities: Competition with awards

L **Library,** 1224 Marshall St NE #200, Minneapolis, MN 55413-1036. Tel 612-206-3118; Fax 612-355-2330; Elec Mail library@craftcouncil.org; Internet Home Page Address: www.craftcouncil.org; *Librn* Jessica Shaykett; *Libr Asst* Dulcey Heller
Mon - Fri 10 AM - 5 PM; Estab 1950s to serve as the repository for information on contemporary American craft; For reference only
Library Holdings: Auction Catalogs; Audio Tapes; Book Volumes 6000; Cassettes; Clipping Files; DVDs; Exhibition Catalogs 8000; Filmstrips; Motion Pictures; Original Documents; Other Holdings Journals 110; Pamphlets; Periodical Subscriptions 200; Photographs; Slides 40,000; Video Tapes 100
Special Subjects: Folk Art, Decorative Arts, Mixed Media, Sculpture, Ceramics, Crafts, Porcelain, Furniture, Glass, Stained Glass, Metalwork, Embroidery, Enamels, Goldsmithing, Handicrafts, Jewelry, Leather, Pottery, Silversmithing, Tapestries, Textiles, Woodcarvings
Collections: ACC Fellows; American Craft Museum Slide Kits; Archives of the American Council & American Craft Museum (until 1990); Award Winners & Artists featured in American Craft Magazine, newsletters & catalogs of craft organizations & educational programs; 20th & 21st-century Fine Craft, with emphasis on post WW II Period (1945)
Activities: Lectrs open to pub

O **THE AMERICAN FEDERATION OF ARTS,** 305 E 47th St Fl 10, New York, NY 10017-2312. Tel 212-988-7700; Fax 212-861-2487; Elec Mail pubinfo@afaweb.org; Internet Home Page Address: www.afaweb.org; *Dir* Pauline Willis; *Sr Accnt* Victoria Proios; *Assoc Dir Finance & Opers* Caroline Chin; *Assoc Dir Exhibs* Anna Hayes Evenhouse; *HR Admin Coordr* Misti Wills; *Mgr Special Events* Tiffany Carney; *Assoc Dir Develop* Alice Hunsberger; *Cur* Suzanne Ramljak; *Cur* Michelle Hargrave; *Cur* Margery King; *Interim Mgr Publs* Kate Norment; *Senior Registrar* Jennifer Heffner
Estab 1909 by an act of Congress, initiates & organizes a national and international prog of art exhibs, publ & educational activities to benefit the mus community and enrich the public's experience and understanding of art and culture; Mem: 200 museum members dues $250 - $675, 150 individual members $250 - $5,000
Income: Financed by government agencies, corporations, foundations & mem
Publications: Exhibition catalogues
Activities: Educ components are developed to accompany exhibitions; lects open to pub; 2-3 vis lects per yr; gallery talks; tours; originates and tours exhibs of fine arts; originates Cur Forum and Dir Forum (annual events) to national & internatins mus

O **AMERICAN INSTITUTE OF ARCHITECTS,** The Octagon Museum, 1735 New York Ave NW, Washington, DC 20006-5292. Tel 202-626-7300; Fax 202-626-7547; Elec Mail infocentral@aia.org; Internet Home Page Address: www.aia.org; *Interim Exec VPres & CEO* Paul W Welch Jr, Hon AIA
Open Mon - Fri 8:30 AM - 5 PM; Estab 1857 to organize & unite the architects of the United States & to promote the aesthetic, scientific & practical efficiency of the profession
Income: Financed by members
Library Holdings: Book Volumes 40,000; CD-ROMs 50; Motion Pictures; Periodical Subscriptions 200; Slides 100,000; Video Tapes 200
Publications: AIArchitect (online newsletter) monthly
Activities: Continuing educ prog; awards given, Gold Medal, Kemper Award, Architectural Firm Award, R S Reynolds Memorial Award & Reynolds Aluminum Prize Citation of Honor, AIA Honor Awards, Institute Honors; sales shop sells books

O **AMERICAN INSTITUTE OF GRAPHIC ARTS,** 164 Fifth Ave, New York, NY 10010. Tel 212-807-1990; Fax 212-807-1799; Elec Mail steve_rogenstein@aiga.org; Internet Home Page Address: www.aiga.org; *Exec Dir* Richard Grefe; *COO* Denise Wood; *Dir Competitions & Exhibs* Gabriela Mirensky; *Dir Events* Jonathan Feinberg; *Dir Mktg & Commun* Steven Rogenstein
Open Mon - Thurs 11 AM - 6 PM, Fri 11 AM - 5 PM; No admis fee; Estab 1914 as a national nonprofit educational organization devoted to raising standards in all branches of the graphic arts; Art gallery showcases AIGA design competition, exhib, and exhib organized by visiting designers and cur; maintains library & slide archives; Mem: 17,000; dues professional mem $275, assoc mem $190, student $65, group $685
Income: Financed by mem
Exhibitions: Rotating exhibits
Publications: A1GA Graphic Design USA, hardbound annual; AlGA journal of Graphic Design, quarterly
Activities: Awards AIGA Medal for distinguished contributions to the graphic arts; originate traveling exhibs

L **Library,** 164 Fifth Ave, New York, NY 10010. Tel 212-807-1990; Elec Mail grefe@aiga.org; Internet Home Page Address: www.aiga.org; *Exec Dir* Richard Grefe
Open Mon - Fri 9:00 AM - 5:00 PM; For reference only; Art gallery maintained for AIGA exhibitions resulting from design competitions
Income: Financed by mem
Library Holdings: Book Volumes 1098; Periodical Subscriptions 25
Special Subjects: Art History, Illustration, Commercial Art, Graphic Arts, Graphic Design, Posters, Industrial Design, Art Education, Aesthetics

O **AMERICAN NUMISMATIC ASSOCIATION,** Edward C. Rochette Money Museum, 818 N Cascade Ave, Colorado Springs, CO 80903-3279. Tel 719-482-9828; Fax 719-634-4085; Elec Mail museum@money.org; Internet Home Page Address: www.money.org; *Pres* Barry Stuppier; *Museum Cur* Douglas Mudd; *Exec Dir* Christopher Cipoletti; *Mus Dir* Tiffanie Bueschel
Open Tues - Fri 9 AM - 5 PM, Sat 10 AM - 5 PM, Sun Noon - 5 PM, cl Mon; No admis fee; Estab 1891 as an international organization to promote numismatics as a means of recording history; Maintains a mus & library; galleries display numismatic material from paper money through coins & art medals; Average Annual Attendance: 30,000; Mem: 34,000; to qualify for mem, one should be interested in coin collecting; dues $36; annual meeting held at National Conventions in Mar & Aug
Income: Financed by mem, endowment, donations & miscellaneous sources
Library Holdings: Auction Catalogs; Audio Tapes; Book Volumes; CD-ROMs; Cards; Cassettes; Compact Disks; Exhibition Catalogs; Fiche; Filmstrips; Kodachrome Transparencies; Manuscripts; Memorabilia; Original Documents; Pamphlets; Periodical Subscriptions; Photographs; Slides; Video Tapes
Special Subjects: Historical Material, Antiquities-Oriental, Antiquities-Egyptian, Gold, Coins & Medals
Collections: Aubrey & Adeline Bebee Collection of US Paper Money; Robert T Herdegen Memorial Collection of Coins of the World; Norman H Liebman Collection of Abraham Lincoln on Paper Money; Elliott Markoff Collection of Presidential Memorabilia; general and specialized collections from all other fields of numismatics
Exhibitions: Changing galleries exhibiting coins of the American Colonial period, the United States 1792 to date and Modern Medallic Art from contemporary medals; Global Ideas in Medallic Sculpture; An Exploration of Cromwell's England
Publications: Numismatist, monthly
Activities: Classes for adults & children; annual seminar on campus of Colorado College, Colorado Springs; lects open to pub, 50+ vis lectrs per yr; tours; sponsorship of National Coin Week third week in Apr (when members throughout the United States promote their avocations through exhibs in local areas); presentation of awards; scholarships offered; mus shop sells books, magazines, slides, medals & souvenir jewelry

L **Library,** 818 N Cascade Ave, Colorado Springs, CO 80903. Tel 719-632-2646; Fax 719-632-5208; Elec Mail library@money.org; Internet Home Page Address: www.money.org/resourcecenter.html; *Interim Librn* Nancy W Green; *Asst Librn* Jane Colvard
Open Tues - Fri 9 AM - 5 PM, Sat 10 AM - 5 PM; No admis fee; Estab 1891 to provide research materials to the members of the Assn & the general pub; Circ 4500; Open to the pub for reference; lending restricted to members; Mem: 30,000; dues $33 first year, $26 to renew mem; meetings twice a year
Income: Financed by assn & mem, endowments, donations
Library Holdings: Auction Catalogs; Audio Tapes; Book Volumes 35,000; CD-ROMs; Cards; Cassettes; Compact Disks; Exhibition Catalogs; Fiche; Filmstrips; Kodachrome Transparencies; Manuscripts; Memorabilia; Original Documents; Other Holdings Auction catalogs 20,000; Microfilm; Pamphlets; Periodical Subscriptions 110; Photographs; Slides; Video Tapes
Special Subjects: Coins & Medals
Collections: books, auction catalogs & periodicals, all on numismatics; Arthur Braddan Coole Library on Oriental Numismatics
Exhibitions: Annual Summer Conference
Activities: Classes for adults & children

O **AMERICAN NUMISMATIC SOCIETY,** 75 Varick St, 11th Fl New York, NY 10013-1917. Tel 212-571-4470; Fax 212-571-4479; Elec Mail isaac@numismatics.org; Internet Home Page Address: numismatics.org; *Exec Dir* Ute Wartenberg Kagan; *Deputy Dir* Andrew Meadows; *Dir Finance & Opers* Anna Chang; *Mus Admin* Joanne Isaac; *Cur* Robert Wilson Hoge; *Cur Asst* Sylvia Karges; *Cur* Peter van Alfen
Open (research) Mon - Fri 9:30 AM - 4:30 PM; (office) Mon - Fri 9 AM - 5 PM; No admis fee; Estab 1858 as an international organization for the advancement of numismatic knowledge; Maintains mus & library; one exhibition hall, devoted to the World of Coins; Average Annual Attendance: 18,000; Mem: 2279; dues assoc $30; annual meeting second Sat in Oct
Income: Financed by endowment
Collections: Universal numismatics
Publications: American Journal of Numismatics, annual; Numismatic Literature, semi-annual
Activities: Lect open to public, 2 vis lectrs per year; scholarships offered

L **Library,** 75 Varick St, 11th Fl New York, NY 10013-1917. Tel 212-571-4470, ext 170; Fax 212-571-4479; Elec Mail library@numismatics.org; Internet Home Page Address: www.numismatics.org/Library/Library; *Librn* Elizabeth Hahn
Open Mon - Fri 9:30 AM - 4:30 PM; No admis fee; Estab 1858; For reference only
Library Holdings: Auction Catalogs; Book Volumes 100,000; Exhibition Catalogs; Filmstrips; Manuscripts; Other Holdings Auction catalogs; Pamphlets; Periodical Subscriptions 246; Reels 200; Slides
Special Subjects: Coins & Medals
Collections: Auction catalogs
Activities: Grad student summer seminar; mus shop sells books, magazines

O **AMERICAN SOCIETY FOR AESTHETICS,** PO Box 915, c/o Dabney Townsend Pooler, GA 31322-0915. Elec Mail asa@aesthetics-online.org; Internet Home Page Address: www.aesthetics-online.org; *Secy-Treas* Dabney Townsend; *Pres* Paul Guyer; *VPres* Dominic Melver Lopes
Estab 1942 for the advancement of philosophical & scientific study of the arts & related fields; Mem: 800; dues $70
Income: Financed by mem, dues, subscriptions
Publications: Journal of Aesthetics & Art Criticism, quarterly; ASA Newsletter, 3 times per year; ASAGE (grad e-journal)
Activities: Ann conferences; Cohen Memorial Dance Prize

O **AMERICAN SOCIETY OF ARTISTS, INC,** PO Box 1326, Palatine, IL 60078-1326. Tel 312-751-2500, 847-991-4748; Elec Mail asoa@netzero.com; Asoaartists@aol.com; Internet Home Page Address: www.americansocietyofartists.org; *VPres* Helen DelValle; *Dir Promotional Svcs* Arnold Jackson; *American Artisans Dir* Judy A Edborg; *Dir Lect & Demonstration Serv* Charles J Gruner; *Spec Arts Services Dir* Patricia E Nolan; *Midwest Representative* Alajos Acs; *Chicago Representative* Donald Metcoff; *Southern Illinois Representative* Ann Childers; *Pres* Nancy J Fregin
Estab 1972, mem organization of professional artists; Mem: Over 10,000; qualifications for mem, must have work juried & pass jury to be accepted; dues $55, plus one initiation fee of $20; patron-ship, associateship & international mem also available
Income: Financed by mem
Library Holdings: Audio Tapes; Book Volumes; Clipping Files; Lantern Slides; Periodical Subscriptions; Photographs; Slides
Collections: Photographs & slides of members works
Exhibitions: Approx 25 indoor & outdoor juried shows per yr
Publications: Art Lovers' Art and Craft Fair Bulletin, quarterly; ASA Artisan, quarterly
Activities: Lect & demonstration service; assists members with various problems

L **Library Organization,** PO Box 1326, Palatine, IL 60078. Tel 312-751-2500, 847-991-4748; Elec Mail asoa@netzero.com; Asoaartists@aol.com; Internet Home Page Address: americansocietyofartists.org; *Librn* Donald Metcoff
Open for mem use only; Estab 1978 to provide reference material for member artists only
Income: Financed by dues & fees
Library Holdings: Audio Tapes; Book Volumes; Clipping Files; Lantern Slides; Periodical Subscriptions 8; Photographs; Slides
Special Subjects: Art Education
Publications: Publication for Members
Activities: Lect & demonstration service

O **AMERICAN SOCIETY OF BOOKPLATE COLLECTORS & DESIGNERS,** PO Box 14964, Tucson, AZ 85732-4964. Tel 626-570-9404; Elec Mail exlibrisusa@hotmail.com; Internet Home Page Address: www.bookplate.org; *Dir* James P Keenan
Estab 1922 as an international organization to foster an interest in the art of the bookplate through the publication of a yearbook & to encourage friendship & a greater knowledge of bookplates among members by an exchange membership list; Mem: 200 who are interested in bookplates as either a collector or artist, or just have an interest in bookplates & graphic arts; dues $85 which includes yearbook & quarterly newsletter
Income: Financed by members
Exhibitions: Bookplates, Prints in Miniature
Publications: Bookplates in the News, quarterly newsletter; YearBook, annually
Activities: Lects given upon request; contributes bookplates to the Prints & Photographs Division of the Library of Congress & furnishes them with copies of quarterly & Year Book; originate traveling exhibs

O **AMERICAN SOCIETY OF CONTEMPORARY ARTISTS (ASCA),** 3600 Curry St, c/o Barbara Schiller Yorktown Heights, NY 10598-2206. Tel 914-245-3776; Elec Mail bobbybschiller@gmail.com; Internet Home Page Address: ascartists.org; *Pres* Barbara Schiller; *Chmn New Mem* Raymond Weinstein; *Pres Emerita* Harriet FeBland; *VPres* Raymond Shanfeld
Estab 1917 as the Brooklyn Society of Artists. Adopted its current name in 1963; Mem: 100 elected on basis of high level of professional distinction; professional artists juried by mems in Mar & Oct; dues $65; annual meeting Jan
Income: Financed by members
Library Holdings: Book Volumes
Exhibitions: Notto Gallery, Chelsea (in Dec); 2 or 3 other exhibs per yr at various institutions, galleries, museums, etc
Publications: Quarterly Newsletter
Activities: Educ dept; demonstrations in graphics, painting & sculpture; lects open to pub; lects given by mems & visiting artists; lects at cols; 10 two hundred dollar annual cash awards with certs for col students; jurors' awards; various awards given by mems honoring others & Friends of ASCA; originates occasional traveling exhibs to college & other galleries

O **AMERICAN SOCIETY OF PORTRAIT ARTISTS (ASOPA),** PO Box 230216, Montgomery, AL 36016-0216. Tel 800-622-7672; Fax 334-270-0150; Elec Mail info@asopa.com; Internet Home Page Address: www.asopa.com; WATS 800-622-7672; *Pres* Leon Loard; *VPres* Jennifer F Williams; *Sec* Helen Sansom; *Chmn* Carl Samson; *Vice Chmn* Steve Childs
Estab 1989 to provide artists with portrait information; Mem: 2000; mem open to portrait artists; dues $75; regional seminars, Portrait Arts Festival; active in portraiture
Activities: Lect open to public; competitions with awards

O **AMERICAN WATERCOLOR SOCIETY, INC.,** 47 Fifth Ave, New York, NY 10003. Tel 212-206-8986; Fax 212-206-1960; Elec Mail info@americanwatercolorsociety.org; Internet Home Page Address: www.americanwatercolorsociety.org; *Pres* Jim McFarlane; *VPres & Treas* Michele Izzo; *VPres Exhib Submissions* Nancy Barch
Open Tues - Sat 10 AM - 5 PM, Sun 11 AM - 5 PM, cl Mon; Admis special exhibs (includes permanent coll): adults $15, seniors (60+) & students with ID $12, youth (13-18) $10, child (12 & under) no charge; permanent coll: adults $10, seniors (60+) & students with ID $8, youth (13-18) $6, child (12 & under) no charge; Estab 1866 as a national organization to foster the advancement of the art of watercolor painting & to further the interests of painters in watercolor throughout the United States; occupies the galleries of the Salmagundi Club, 47 Fifth Ave, New York City for four weeks each yr for annual international exhibition usually in Apr; Average Annual Attendance: 4,000-5,000; Mem: 500 signature; to qualify for mem, an artist must exhibit in two annuals then submit application to mem chmn; dues $55; annual meeting in Apr
Income: Financed by mem & donations
Library Holdings: Exhibition Catalogs
Exhibitions: One annual international exhib each Spring; Travel Show

Publications: AWS Newsletter, semi-annually; full color annual exhibition catalog; CD of complete exhibitions
Activities: Lects open to pub; demonstrations & presentations by Signature Members during annual exhibitions; evening demonstrations; awards given at annual exhibs, 26 per yr; schols offered; originates traveling exhibs, 8 per year, recipients vary

O **AMERICANS FOR THE ARTS,** 1000 Vermont Ave NW, 6th Fl, Washington, DC 20005. Tel 202-371-2830; Fax 202-371-0424; Elec Mail info@artsusa.org; Internet Home Page Address: www.americansforthearts.org; *Pres & CEO* Robert L Lynch
Open Mon - Fri 9 AM - 5:30 PM; Estab to support the arts & culture through pub & private resource develop, leadership develop, pub policy develop, information services, pub awareness & educ; Mem: 5,000; annual meeting June; membership not limited; mktg & fundraising conference in Nov
Income: Financed by mem, foundations, corporations & government
Publications: Periodic journals; quarterly newsletter
Activities: Annual convention; regional workshops; technical assistance; annual conventions; lects open to pub; mus shop online

O **AMERICANS FOR THE ARTS,** 1 E 53rd St Fl 2, New York, NY 10022-4242. Tel 212-223-2787; Fax 212-980-4857; Elec Mail rlynch@aartusa.org; Internet Home Page Address: www.americansforthearts.org; *Chief Planning Officer* Mara Walker; *VPres Develop* Katherine Gibney; *VPres Finance* R Brent Stanley; *VPres Mktg, Communs & Technology* Kimberly Hedges
Open by appointment; No admis fee; Estab 1960; Mem: 2500; dues organizations $150-$250, individual $30-$100
Income: Financed by mem
Publications: ACA Update, monthly newsletter of legislative & advocacy information available to members; books on arts policy, management, education & information for artists

L **Library,** One E 53rd St, New York, NY 10022-4210. Tel 212-223-2787, Ext 224; Fax 212-223-4857; Elec Mail bdavidson@artsusa.org; Internet Home Page Address: www.artsusa.org; WATS 800-232-2789 (Visual Artists Information Hotline, 2 - 5 PM); *Dir* Ben Davidson
Research collections available on an appointment only basis for a fee; information/referral service by phone, FAX & mail; No admis fee; Estab 1994; For reference only
Library Holdings: Book Volumes 7000; Other Holdings Vertical files; Periodical Subscriptions 300
Special Subjects: Art Education

O **APERTURE FOUNDATION,** 547 W 27th St, 4th Fl, New York, NY 10001-5511. Tel 212-505-5555; Fax 212-598-4015; Elec Mail info@aperture.org; Internet Home Page Address: www.aperture.org; *Book Publisher* Leslie Martin; *Chmn* Cleso Gonzalez-Falla; *Dir Exhibitions* Diana Edkins; *Magazine Ed* Melissa Harris; *Treas* Frederick M R Smith; *Secy* Barry H Garfinkel Esq
Open Mon - Sat 10 AM - 6 PM; No admis fee; Estab 1952 dedicated to advancing fine photography; Foundation for fine art photography; 3,000 sq ft gallery space presenting exhibitions dedicated to contemporary & classic photography; Mem: 20, dues $10,000
Income: Financed by mem, book & magazine publisher
Collections: Paul Strand Archive
Exhibitions: Lisette Model and Her Successors
Publications: Books on fine photography; 22 books per year
Activities: Lects open to the pub, 3 vis lectrs per year; Aperture Prize; Annual Aperture West Book Prize, annual book prize to an artist living west of the Mississippi; originate 13 traveling exhibitions per year; mus shop sells books, magazines & prints

O **ARCHAEOLOGICAL INSTITUTE OF AMERICA,** 656 Beacon St, 6th Fl Boston, MA 02215-2072. Tel 617-353-9361; Fax 617-353-6550; Elec Mail aia@aia.bu.edu; Internet Home Page Address: www.archaeological.org; *Exec Dir* Teresa Keller; *Dir Devel* Jennifer Klahn; *Prog & Svcs Dir* Elizabeth Gilgan; *Educ & Outreach Coordr* Ben Thomas
Open 9 AM - 5 PM; Estab 1879 as an international organization concerned with two major areas of responsibility: facilitating archaeological research & disseminating the results to the pub; Mem: 11,000 consisting of professionals & laypersons interested in archaeology; $95 for annual meeting in Dec
Income: Financed by endowment, mem & earned income from publications
Publications: Archaeology Magazine, bimonthly; Archaeological Fieldwork Opportunities Bulletin, annual; American Journal of Archaeology, quarterly; Colloquia Conference Paper Series
Activities: Classes for children; lect open to pub, 250 vis lectrs per yr; lect for members only; tours & awards given; one or more fellowships awarded for an acad yr

O **ART DEALERS ASSOCIATION OF AMERICA, INC,** 205 Lexington Ave, Ste 901 New York, NY 10016-6022. Tel 212-488-5550; Fax 646-688-6809; Elec Mail lmitchem@artdealers.org; Internet Home Page Address: www.artdealers.org; *Pres* Lucy Mitchell-Innes; *VPres* Dorsey Waxter; *Admin VPres* Michael Findlay; *& Counsel* Gilbert S Edelson; *Secy* Jeffrey Fraenkel; *Exec Dir* Linda Blumberg; *Treas* Lawrence Luhring; *Dir Admin* Patricia L Brundage; *Exec Dir Appraisals* Karen Carolan; *Dir Appraisals* Susan Brundage
Estab 1962 as a national organization to improve the stature & status of the art-dealing profession; Mem: 175; mem by invitation
Income: Financed by mem & services
Exhibitions: The Art Show, annual fair ADAA members
Publications: Activities & Membership Roster; ADAA Collector's Guide
Activities: Lects open to pub, 4 vis lectrs per yr - Collector's Forum Series; appraisal service for donors contributing works of art to nonprofit institutions; estate tax appraisals; collectors forums

O **ART DIRECTORS CLUB,** 106 W 29th St, New York, NY 10001-5301. Tel 212-643-1440; Fax 212-643-4266; Elec Mail info@adcglobal.org; Internet Home Page Address: www.adcglobal.org; *Dir* Olga Grisaitis; *Dir Awards Progs* Jen Larkin Kuzler; *Info Mgr* Kim Hanzich; *Dir Educ* Flora Moir
Open Mon - Fri 10 AM - 6 PM; No admis fee; Estab 1920 mission is to recognize excellence in visual communications, encourage young people coming into field.

Mandate is to provide forum for creative leaders in advertising, design & interactive media in which to explore and anticipate the direction of those evolving & rapidly intersecting industries & to present innovative, inspiring work; Owns gallery; Average Annual Attendance: 20,000; Mem: 1100 mem; criteria for mem: qualifies art dir, at least 21 yrs age, of good character, at least two yrs practical experience in creating & directing in the visual commun of graphic arts industry, dues indiv $225, non-res $175, young professional $100, student $75; ann meeting in Sept
Income: Financed by mem
Library Holdings: Book Volumes; Exhibition Catalogs
Exhibitions: Art Directors' Annual Exhibition of National & International Advertising, Editorial & Television Art & Design & New Media. Bimonthly shows conceived to provide a showcase for works & ideas not readily viewed otherwise. They cover advertising & editorial design & art education
Publications: The Art Directors Annual; bimonthly newsletter, Young Guns
Activities: Job fair; portfolio Review Programs; speaker events; seminars; lects open to pub, 10-20 vis lectrs per yr; competitions with awards; hall of fame, young guns (bi-ann); scholarships offered; originate traveling exhibs; gallery sells books

O **ART SERVICES INTERNATIONAL,** 1319 Powhatan St, Alexandria, VA 22314-1342. Tel 703-548-4554; Fax 703-548-3305; Elec Mail info@ASIexhibitions.org; Internet Home Page Address: www.asiexhibitions.org; *Dir & CEO* Lynn K Rogerson; *Deputy Dir Exhibs* Doug Shawn; *Mgr Publ & Pub Rels* Elizabeth Beirise; *Registrar* Meredith Cain; *Mgr Finance & Admin* Marek Wrega; *Legal Advisor* Michael F McAllister
Nonprofit, educational institution which organizes & circulates fine arts exhibitions to museums & galleries in the US & abroad
Publications: Catalogs

O **ARTISTS' FELLOWSHIP, INC,** 47 Fifth Ave, New York, NY 10003. Tel 646-230-9833; Elec Mail info@artistsfellowship.org; Internet Home Page Address: artistsfellowship.org; *Treas* Pamela Singleton; *Correspondence Secy* Robert J Riedinger; *Historian* Carl Thomson; *Pres* Marc Richard Mellon
Estab 1859, reorganized 1889 as Artists' Aid Society, then incorporated 1925 as Artists' Fellowship; to aid professional fine artists & their families in emergency situations including illness, disability & bereavement; Mem: 400; annual meeting in Dec
Income: From mems
Publications: Quarterly newsletter
Activities: Awards the Gari Melchers Gold Medal for distinguished service to the arts, and Benjamin West Clinedinst Memorial Medal for outstanding achievement in the arts

O **ARTS EXTENSION SERVICE,** 221-225 Middlesex House, 111 County Cir, Univ of Mass Amherst Amherst, MA 01003. Tel 413-545-2360; Fax 413-545-2361; Elec Mail aes@acad.umass.edu; Internet Home Page Address: www.artsextensionservice.org; *Dir* Dee Boyle-Clapp; *Admin Asst* Perry Huntoon
Open Mon - Fri 9 AM - 5 PM; No admis fee; Estab 1973 as a National Arts Service Organization facilitating the continuing educ of artists, arts organizations & community leaders. AES works for better access to the arts & integration of the arts in communities. AES is a nonprofit program of the University of Massachusetts Amherst
Publications: Artist in Business, 1996; Arts Management Bibliography & Publishers; Community Cultural Planning Work Kit; Education Collaborations; Fundamentals of Arts Management; Intersections, Community Arts & Education Collaborations
Activities: Professional level arts management workshops; consulting; retreats & conferences; exten dept serves civic sectors, community arts organizations, classes for adults

O **ASSOCIATION OF AFRICAN AMERICAN MUSEUMS,** PO Box 23698, Washington, DC 20026. Elec Mail staveloz@blackmuseums.org; Internet Home Page Address: www.blackmuseums.org; *Pres* Samuel W Black; *Secy* Auntaneshia Staveloz
Open Mon - Fri 9 AM - 5 PM; Estab 1978 to represent black museums around the country. Offers consulting & networking services. Sponsors annual conferences; Mem: 496; dues trustee/bd mem & scholar $75, individual $55, student $25
Publications: Profile of Black Museums - A Survey; biannual directory; quarterly newsletter for mem only

O **ASSOCIATION OF ART MUSEUM DIRECTORS,** 120 E 56th St, Ste 520, New York, NY 10022. Tel 212-754-8084; Fax 212-754-8087; Elec Mail aamd@amn.org; Internet Home Page Address: www.aamd.org; *Exec Dir* Millicent Hall Gaudieri; *Deputy Dir* Christine Anagnos
Estab 1916; Mem: 170; chief staff officers of major art museums
Income: Financed by mem dues
Publications: Annual Salary Survey; Model Museum Directors Employment Contract; Professional Practices in Art Museums

O **ASSOCIATION OF COLLEGIATE SCHOOLS OF ARCHITECTURE,** 1735 New York Ave NW, Washington, DC 20006-5209. Tel 202-785-2324; Fax 202-628-0448; Elec Mail info@acsa-arch.org; Internet Home Page Address: www.acsa-arch.org; *Exec Dir* Michael J Monti, PhD; *Proj Mgr* Eric Ellis; *Conf Mgr* Mary Lou Baily; *Mem & Mktg Mgr* Kathryn Swiatek; *Commun Mgr* Pascale Vonier
Open Mon - Fri 8:30 AM - 5:30 PM; No admis fee; Estab 1912 as a non-profit, mem organization furthering the advancement of architectural educ; Mem: 3500 architecture faculty members; mem open to schools & their faculty as well as individuals; mem rates vary; annual meeting in Mar
Income: $1.4 million (financed by endowment, mem, state appropriation & grants)
Publications: ACSA News, 9 times per year; Journal of Architectural Education, quarterly; Annual Meeting Proceedings; Guide to Architecture Schools in North America, biannually
Activities: Educ seminars; institutes; publications; services to membership; sponsor student design competitions with awards

O **ASSOCIATION OF INDEPENDENT COLLEGES OF ART & DESIGN,** 236 Hope St, Providence, RI 02906. Tel 401-270-5991; Fax 401-270-5993; Elec Mail deborah@aicad.org; Internet Home Page Address: www.aicad.org; *Exec Dir* Deborah Obalil; *Prog & Operations Mgr* Lee Ann Adams; *Asst Dir Research Servs* Joanne Kersh
Open by appointment only; Estab 1991 to improve quality of mem cols & provide information on art educ; Mem: 35; must be independent art college, fully accredited & grant BFA; dues $5500-$8000 depending on size; annual meeting in Oct
Income: $500,000 (financed by mem & occasional grants)
Publications: Internal newsletter

O **ASSOCIATION OF MEDICAL ILLUSTRATORS,** 201 E Main St, Suite 1405 Lexington, KY 40507-2003. Tel 859-514-9194; Fax 859-514-9166; Elec Mail hq@ami.org; Internet Home Page Address: www.ami.org; *Exec Dir* Tracy Tucker; *Pres* Linda Wilson-Pauwels; *Chair* Ethan Geehr
Estab 1945 as an international organization to encourage the advancement of medical illustration & allied fields of visual educ; to promote understanding & cooperation with the medical & related professions; Mem: 800; dues active $275; student $100; annual meeting in July
Income: Financed by mem
Exhibitions: Annual exhibition at national meeting
Publications: Journal of Biocommunications, 4 times per year; Medical Illustration, brochure; Newsletter, 6 times per year
Activities: Individual members throughout the world give lects on the profession; awards given for artistic achievements submitted to salon each year; originate traveling exhibitions

O **ATLATL,** PO Box 34090, Phoenix, AZ 85067-4090. Tel 602-277-3711; Fax 602-277-3690; Elec Mail atlatl@atlatl.org, fnahwooksy@atlatl.org; *Exec Dir* Lorenzo J Begay; *Proj Dir* Mark A Little; *Chmn* Aurolyn Stwyer
Open Mon - Fri 9 AM - 5 PM; No admis fee; Estab 1981 as a national service organization for Native American Art. Atlatl creates an informational network between Native American artists & art organizations as well as between mainstream institutions & emerging organizations. Maintains a National Registry of Native American Artists which currently includes more than 2500 artists; Mem: 300; dues vary; mem open to all
Income: Financed by federal grants
Collections: Native American Artists files
Exhibitions: Annual Beyond Beads & Performing Arts Series; Hiapsi Wami Seewam: Flowers of Life; Native Women of Hope
Publications: Quarterly newsletter
Activities: Lects open to pub, 5 or more vis lectrs per yr; concerts; competitions; artmobile; circulates av materials such as slides sets & videotapes by Native American artists; book traveling exhibs 2-5 per yr; originate exhibs of Native American art to a variety of institutions including tribal museums, community & university galleries & fine art museums

C **AUTOZONE,** Autozone Corporation Collection, 123 S Front St, Memphis, TN 38103-3607; PO Box 2198, Memphis, TN 38101-2198. Tel 901-495-6763; Fax 901-495-8300; *Cur* Lynda Ireland
Estab 1978 to support local artists & artists of the United States; 20th century collection of American art in a variety of media highlighting the work of artists in the South

O **BILLINGS MERIKS SCULPTORS SOCIETY,** 2510 Zimmerman Trl, Billings, MT 59102-1105. *Pres* Paul Davis
Open Mon - Sat 10 AM - 8:30 PM
Income: 500,00 (financed by mem & grants)

O **COLLEGE ART ASSOCIATION,** 50 Broadway 21st Fl, New York, NY 10004-1680. Tel 212-691-1051; Fax 212-627-2381; Elec Mail nyoffice@collegeart.org; Internet Home Page Address: www.collegeart.org; *Pres* Anne Collins Goodyear; *Exec Dir* Linda Downs; *Deputy Dir* Michael Fahlund; *CFO* Teresa Lopez; *Counsel* Jeffrey P Cunard; *Dir Information Technology* Michael Goodman
Open Mon - Fri 9 AM - 5 PM; Estab 1911 as a national organization to further scholarship & excellence in the teaching & practice of art & art history; Mem: 16,000, open to all individuals & institutions interested in the purposes of the Assoc; dues life $5000, institution $150, individual $45-$90 (scaled to salary), student $25; annual meeting in Feb
Income: Financed by mem
Publications: The Art Bulletin, quarterly; Art Journal, quarterly; CAA Newsletter, weekly; Careers, bimonthly
Activities: Awards: Distinguished Teaching of Art History Award; Distinguished Teaching of Art Award; Charles Rufus Morey Book Award; Frank Jewett Mather Award for Distinction in Art & Architectural Criticism; Arthur Kingsley Porter Prize for Best Article by Younger Scholar in The Art Bulletin; Alfred H Barr, Jr Award for Museum Scholarship; Distinguished Artist Award for Lifetime Achievement; Award for a Distinguished Body of Work, Exhibition, Presentation or Performance; Annual Conference; Prof develop fels; Meiss book grants; schols offered

O **COLOR ASSOCIATION OF THE US,** 33 Whitehall St Ste M3, New York, NY 10004-2112. Tel 212-947-7774; Fax 212-594-6987; Elec Mail info@colorassociation.com; Internet Home Page Address: www.colorassociation.com; *Exec Dir* Leslie Harrington; *Assoc Dir* Erin Laubenheimer
Open Mon - Fri 9 AM - 5 PM; Estab 1915 for the purpose of forecasting fashion colors & standards in the United States; Mem: 1000; dues $900
Income: Financed by mem
Collections: Colored Swatch Archives date back to 1915
Publications: CAUS Newsletter, 6 times per year; The Color Compendium; Living Colors; The Standard Color Reference of America
Activities: Workshops; classes for adults; lect, 12 vis lectrs per year

O **FEDERATION OF MODERN PAINTERS & SCULPTORS,** 113 Greene St, New York, NY 10012-3823. Tel 212-966-4864; Elec Mail info@fedart.org; Internet Home Page Address: www.fedart.org; *Treas* Jon Rettich; *Pres* Anneli Arms; *VPres* Peter Colquhoun; *Sec* Vincent Pinto
Estab 1940 as a national organization to promote the cultural interests of free progressive artists working in the United States; Mem: 60; selected by mem comt; working artist (painter, sculptor); dues $35; meeting every 2 months
Income: Financed by mem
Library Holdings: Exhibition Catalogs
Exhibitions: Exhibition at Art Students League; A Decade for Renewal, at Lever House, New York.; Fordham Univ; Broome St Gallery, NYC; Westbeth Gallery, NYC
Publications: Exhibit catalog
Activities: Lects open to public, 1-2 vis lectrs per yr; symposium; originate traveling exhibs

O **GUILD OF BOOK WORKERS,** 521 5th Ave, Fl 17 New York, NY 10175-0003. Tel 212-292-4444; Internet Home Page Address: www.guildofbookworkers.org; *Pres* Andrew Huot; *Sec* Catherine Burkhard; *Treas* Alicia Bailey; *Commun Chmn* Eric Alstrom
Call for hours; No admis fee; Estab 1906 as a national organization to establish & maintain a feeling of kinship & mutual interest among workers in the several hand book crafts; Mem: 900; mem open to all interested persons; dues national; $85, chap (New York, New England, Midwest, Lone Star, Delaware Valley, Potomac, Rocky Mountain, California, Southeast, Northwest) $10 for each chap; annual meeting in Oct; Canadian mem additional $10; overseas mems additional $15; students $30 (allowed for 3 yrs w/ ID)
Income: Financed by mem
Publications: Guild of Book Workers Journal, 1 time per year; newsletter, 6 times per yr
Activities: Classes for adults; lects open to members only; tours; workshops; annual seminar on Standards of Excellence in Hand Bookbinding; awards given for mems, 2 per yr as necessary; chaps have exhibs
L **Library,** 100 Main Library, Univ of Iowa Conservation Dept Iowa City, IA 52242-1420. Tel 319-335-5908; Fax 319-335-5900; Elec Mail anna-embree@uiowa.edu; Internet Home Page Address: palimpsest.stanford.edu/byorg/gbw/library.shtml; *Guild Librn* Anna Embree
Open by appointment; Open to Guild members for lending & reference
Income: Financed by mem
Library Holdings: Book Volumes 700

O **HERITAGE PRESERVATION,** The National Institute for Conservation, 1012 14th St NW, Ste 1200 Washington, DC 20005-3403. Tel 202-233-0800; Fax 202-233-0807; Elec Mail info@heritagepreservation.org; Internet Home Page Address: www.heritagepreservation.org; *Pres* Lawrence L Reger; *VPres Emergency Progs* Lori Foley; *Board Vice Chair* Elizabeth Schulte; *Admin Asst* Christa Sundell; *Prog Asst* Teresa Martinez; *Coordr Communs* Jenny Wiley; *VPres Colls Care Progs* Kristen Overbeck Laise; *Coordr Conservation Assessment Prog* Sara Gonzales; *Board Chair* Mervin Richard; *Board Sec* Tom Clareson
Estab 1974 as a national forum for conservation & preservation activities in the United States
Income: Financed by private grants, member dues
Publications: Update newsletter

O **INDUSTRIAL DESIGNERS SOCIETY OF AMERICA,** 555 Grove St, Ste 200 Herndon, VA 20170-4728. Tel 703-707-6000; Fax 703-787-8501; Elec Mail idsa@idsa.org; Internet Home Page Address: www.idsa.org; *Exec Dir* Frank Tyneski; *Deputy Exec Dir & COO* Larry Hoffer; *CFO* Larry Allen; *Dir Content Devel* Tim Adkins; *Sr Dir Bus Develop* Gigi Thompson Jarvis
Open daily 9 AM - 5 PM; No admis fee; Estab & inc 1965 as a nonprofit national organization representing the profession of industrial design; Mem: 3300; dues full, affiliate & international $285, assoc $140
Publications: Innovation, quarterly; IDSA Newsletter, monthly; Membership Directory; other surveys & studies
Activities: IDSA Student Chap; IDSA Student Merit Awards; lect; competitions; scholarships offered

O **INTER-SOCIETY COLOR COUNCIL,** 11491 Sunset Hills Rd, Reston, VA 20190-5264. Tel 703-318-0263; Fax 703-318-0514; Elec Mail iscc@iscc.org; Internet Home Page Address: www.iscc.org; *Pres* Dr Robert Buckley; *Pres Elect* Dr Maria Nadal; *Secy* Jack Ladson; *Treas* Hugh Fairman
Estab 1931 as a national organization to stimulate & coordinate the study of color in science, art & industry; federation of 29 national societies & individuals interested in colors; Mem: 900; members must show an interest in color & in the aims & purposes of the Council; dues individual $25; annual meeting usually Apr
Income: Financed by mem
Publications: Inter-Society Color Council Newsletter, bimonthly
Activities: Lects open to public; lects at meetings; gives Macbeth Award and Godlove Award

O **INTERMUSEUM CONSERVATION ASSOCIATION,** 2915 Detroit Ave, Cleveland, OH 44113-2709. Tel 216-658-8700; Fax 216-658-8709; Elec Mail ica@ica-artconservation.org; Internet Home Page Address: www.ica-artconservation.org; *Exec Dir* Albert Albano; *Preparator* Jason Byers; *Sr Paintings Conservator* Andrea Chevalier; *Materials Res Dir* Mark D Gottsegen; *Opers Mgr* Christopher Pelrine
Estab 1952 as a nonprofit conservation laboratory to aid in the maintenance of the collections of its member museums; Maintains a technical conservation library; Mem: 28; must be nonprofit cultural institution; dues $100-$1000; meetings biannually
Income: Financed by membership, private & public grants
Activities: Lect open to public; 3-6 vis lectrs per year; seminars twice a year; scholarships for advanced training of conservators

O **INTERNATIONAL FOUNDATION FOR ART RESEARCH, INC (IFAR),** 500 Fifth Ave, Ste 935, New York, NY 10110. Tel 212-391-6234; Fax 212-391-8794; Internet Home Page Address: www.ifar.org; *Exec Dir, Ed in Chief* Dr Sharon Flescher; *Asst to Dir* Kathleen Ferguson; *Chmn* Jack A Josephson; *Art Research Dir* Dr Lisa Duffy-Zeballos
Open Mon - Fri 9:30 AM - 5:30 PM; Estab 1968, IFAR is a nonprofit educational and research organization dedicated to issues relating to art authenticity & ownership, art ethics, law, & connoisseurship. IFAR operates at the intersection of the scholarly, legal & commercial art worlds. Created to adjudicate questions concerning attribution & authenticity of major works of art; expanded in 1975 to include issues of art theft and art law. IFAR organizes pub prog & pub a quarterly journal, offers provenance & authentication research services, & provides several research tools on its website; Mem: Mem/supporter $250 and above, journal subscription $75 plus shipping
Income: Financed by donations, mem & fees
Publications: IFAR Journal, quarterly; Reference Material
Activities: Lect open to pub & symposia are conducted throughout the year on subjects relating to connoisseurship, authenticity, provenance research, art law & art theft & fraud; tours
—**Authentication Service,** 500 Fifth Ave, Ste 1234, New York, NY 10110. Tel 212-391-6234; Fax 212-391-8794; *Dir* Dr Sharon Flescher
Through this service, the resources of leading institutional experts, both scholarly & scientific, are made available to the pub in order to answer questions relating to authenticity & proper attribution of works of art

O **INTERNATIONAL SOCIETY OF COPIER ARTISTS (ISCA),** 759 President St, Apt 2H, Brooklyn, NY 11215-1362. Tel 718-638-3264; Elec Mail isca4art2b@aol.com; *Dir* Louise Neaderland
Open by appt; No admis fee; Estab 1981 to promote use of copier as a creative tool; Circ 125 (ltd edition); Mem: 150; dues international subscriber $110, domestic $90 and $30, $40 annual dues; mem open to artists using the copier for printmaking & bookmaking; contributing artist membership outside US $40, domestic $30 (slides or samples of work)
Income: $10,000 (financed by mem & subscriptions to Quarterly)
Collections: Slide Archive of Xerographic Prints & Books
Exhibitions: ISCA GRAPHICS; Using the Copier as a Creative Tool; The Artists Book
Publications: Quarterly of Xerographic Prints & Artists Books
Activities: Gallery talks; tours; 1 book traveling exhib per yr; originate traveling exhibs to universities, art schools & libraries

O **KAPPA PI INTERNATIONAL HONORARY ART FRATERNITY,** 400 S Bolivar Ave, Cleveland, MS 38732-3745. Tel 662-846-6271, 846-4729; Elec Mail koehler@tecinfo.com; Internet Home Page Address: www.kappapiart.org; *Pres* Ron Koehler; *VPres* Dr Sam Bishop; *Treas* Tom Nawrocki; *Secy* Catherin Koehler
Estab 1911 as an international honorary art fraternity for men & women in cols, universities & art schools; Mem: 185 chap; GPA minimum standards completion of 12 semester hours of art
Income: Financed by mem
Publications: Sketch Pad Newsletter, annually in the fall; Sketch Book, annual spring magazine
Activities: Sponsors competition in art; annual scholarships available to active members

O **LANNAN FOUNDATION,** 313 Read St, Santa Fe, NM 81501-2628. Tel 505-986-8160; Fax 505-986-8195; Elec Mail info@lannan.org; Internet Home Page Address: www.lannan.org; *Art Projects Mgr* Christie Davis; *Admin & Program Asst* Barbara Ventrello; *Admin* Susie Bousson; *Accounting Mgr* Linda Carey; *Pres* J Patrick Lannan Jr; *VPres & Dir Opers* Frank C Lawler
Open by appointment; Estab 1960 for the support of work by contemporary artists; Installations of new & old work from Lannan Collection
Library Holdings: Book Volumes; Exhibition Catalogs; Video Tapes
Special Subjects: Photography, Sculpture, Painting-American, Painting-European
Collections: Small collection of modern & contemporary art
Activities: Lect open to public; 15 vis lectrs per yr; grants offered; individual paintings & original objects of art lent

O **MERIKS AMERICAN DESIGNERS, INC.,** 822 Guilford Ave #1700, Baltimore, MD 21202-3707. *Dir* Rey Roberts
Open Mon - Sat 9 AM - 5 PM
Library Holdings: DVDs; Filmstrips; Lantern Slides; Other Holdings

O **MID AMERICA ARTS ALLIANCE & EXHIBITS USA,** 2018 Baltimore Ave, Kansas City, MO 64108-1914. Tel 816-421-1388 exten 218; Fax 816-421-3918; Elec Mail info@maaa.org; Internet Home Page Address: www.maaa.org; *Exec Dir* Mary Kennedy McCabe; *Cur Exhibs* Arlette Klaric, PhD; *Dir Progs* Dana M Knapp
A national division of Mid America Arts Alliance created to organize & tour art exhibits throughout the United States & beyond
Income: $1,000,000 (financed by federal & state grants, private contributions & exhibition fees)
Exhibitions: Various Exhibs
Publications: Exhibition catalogs & brochures
Activities: Educ guides; Book traveling exhibs; originate traveling exhibs to various museums, historical societies, libraries, art centers & galleries

O **MIDWEST ART HISTORY SOCIETY,** One Bear Pl #97263 Dept of Art, Baylor Univ Waco, TX 76798. Elec Mail heidi_hornik@baylor.edu; Internet Home Page Address: www.mahsonline.org; *Pres* Paula Wisotzki; *Secy* Henry Luttikhuizen; *Treas* Heidi Hornik; *Archivist* Patricia Graham
Estab 1973 to further art history in the Midwest as a discipline & a profession; Average Annual Attendance: 150 at meetings; Mem: 600; mem is open to institutions, students & acad & mus art historians in the Midwest; dues institution $150, professional $60, student $30; annual meeting in Mar or early Apr
Income: $3,500 (financed by mem)
Publications: Midwest Art History Society Newsletter, Oct & Apr
Activities: Lect provided; small travel grants for grad student travel to ann conference; award for best conference paper by a grad student

O **THE NAMES PROJECT FOUNDATION AIDS MEMORIAL QUILT,** (Names Project Foundation) 204 14th St NW, Atlanta, GA 30318-5304. Tel 415-982-5500; 404-688-5500; Fax 404-688-5552; Elec Mail info@aidsquilt.org; Internet Home Page Address: www.aidsquilt.org; *Exec Dir* Julie Rhoad; *Dir Quilt Operations* Roddy Williams; *Prog Coordr* Brad Gammell; *Dir Progs* Jada Harris
Estab June 1987; Average Annual Attendance: 13,800,000

Collections: AIDS Memorial Quilt, over 40,000 individual memorial panels commemorating people lost to AIDS
Publications: On Display, newsletter
Activities: Sales shop sells prints, buttons, magnets, clothing, cards

O   **NATIONAL ACADEMY MUSEUM & SCHOOL,** 1083 5th Ave, New York, NY 10128-0114. Tel 212-369-4880; Fax 212-426-1711; Elec Mail info@nationalacademy.org; Internet Home Page Address: www.nationalacademy.org; *Dir* Carmine Branagan; *Sr Vpres Finance & Opers* John J Berg; *Cur Contemporary Art* Marshall N Price; *Dir Operations* Charles Biada; *Dir Communs* Heidi Riefler; *School Dir* Maurizio Pellegrin; *Registrar* Athena Latocha; *Chief Conservator* Lucie Kinsolving; *Pres* Bruce Fowle, NA; *Dir Finance* Michael McKay; *Bd Chmn* David Kapp, NA
Open Wed - Sun 11 AM - 6 PM, cl Mon, Tues, New Year's, Thanksgiving & Christmas; Admis adult $15, seniors & students $10, under 12 free; Estab 1825, honorary arts organization for American artists & architects; Average Annual Attendance: 30,000; Mem: 3000; Nat Academy elected by peers
Income: Financed by mem, endowment & grants
Special Subjects: Architecture, Drawings, Landscapes, Photography, Prints, Sculpture, Watercolors, Painting-American
Collections: Permanent collection consists of 5000 watercolors, drawings & graphics, 2000 paintings, 250 sculptures, mostly the gifts of the artist & architectural members of the Academy from 1825 to present; American art from mid-nineteenth century to the present
Exhibitions: exhibition of contemporary art; exhibitions of permanent collection & loan exhibitions
Publications: Annual exhibition catalogue; catalogues of exhibitions of permanent collection; catalogues of spec loan exhibitions
Activities: Classes for adults & children; docent training; lects open to pub; 10 vis lectrs per yr; gallery talks; tours by appointment; Awards-Henry Legrand Cannon Prize, Andrew Carnegie Prize, Alex Ettl Award for Sculpture, Malvina Hoffman Artists Fund Prize, Leo Meissner Prize, Edwin Palmer Memorial Prize, William A Paton Prize, Henry Ward Ranger purchase Award; schols & fellowships offered; individual paintings & original objects of art lent to other mus; originates traveling exhibs to other mus; mus shop sells books, posters, catalogues & postcards; original art; prints

L   **Archives,** 1083 5th Ave, New York, NY 10128. Tel 212-369-4880; Fax 212-360-6795; Internet Home Page Address: www.nationalacademy.org; *Sr Cur Nineteenth Century Art* Bruce Weber, PhD; *Asst Cur Contemporary Art* Marshall Price; *Dir Operations* Charles Biada; *School Dir* Nancy Little; *Dir Artist Mem* Nancy Malloy; *Chief Conservator* Lucie Kinsolving; *Dir* Carmine Branagan; *Dir Finance & Human Resources* Michael McKay; *Dir Communs* Mary Fichter; *Cur Educ* Sandy Martiny; *Registrar* Athena LaTocha
Open Wed - Thurs Noon - 5 PM, Fri - Sun 11 AM - 6 PM; Admis general $10, students & seniors $5; Estab 1825 to promote American art through exhib and educ; For reference; Average Annual Attendance: 35,000; Mem: mem artists are invited and elected by current artist mem
Library Holdings: Clipping Files; Exhibition Catalogs; Manuscripts; Memorabilia; Original Art Works; Other Holdings Biographical Member Files; National Academy of Design Records; Pamphlets; Photographs; Prints; Sculpture
Special Subjects: American Western Art
Collections: Dipl works of artists elected to membership
Activities: Classes for adults & children; docent training; lects open to pub; 10 vis lectrs per yr; gallery talks; tours; awards, Henry Legrand Cannon Prize, Andrew Carnegie Prize, Alex Ettl Award for Sculpture, Malvina Hoffman Artists Fund Prize, Leo Meissner Prize, Edwin Palmer Memorial Prize, William A Paton Prize Henry Ward Ranger Purchase Award; schols & fels offered; originates traveling exhibs to various US mus; mus shop sells books and original art

O   **NATIONAL ALLIANCE FOR MEDIA ARTS & CULTURE,** 145 9th St, Ste 102 San Francisco, CA 94103-2637; 145 9th St, Ste 230 San Francisco, CA 94103-2641. Tel 415-431-1391; Fax 415-431-1392; Elec Mail namac@namac.org; Internet Home Page Address: www.namac.org; *Co-Dir* Helen DeMichiel; *Sr Mgr Leadership Svcs* Daniel Schott; *Co-Dir* Jack Walsh; *Prog & Mem Svcs Mgr* Amanda Ault
Estab for the purpose of furthering diversity & participation in all forms of the media arts, including film, video, audio & multimedia production; Mem: 350; dues $60 - $450; support media arts field
Income: $200,000 (financed by grants & mem dues)
Publications: Field Guide; Main newsletter, bimonthly; NAMAC Member Directory, online; The National Media Education Directory; Digital Directions: Convergence Planning for the Media Arts; A Closer Look: Media Arts 2000; BULLETin, biweekly electronic newsletter
Activities: Online salons; 2 vis lectrs per yr; lectrs for mems only; William Kirby Award in Media Arts

O   **NATIONAL ANTIQUE & ART DEALERS ASSOCIATION OF AMERICA, INC,** 220 E 57th St, New York, NY 10022-2805. Tel 212-826-9707; Fax 212-832-9493; Elec Mail inquiries@naadaa.org; Internet Home Page Address: www.naadaa.org; *Secy* Arlie Sulka; *Pres* James McConnaughy; *1st VPres* Mark Jacoby; *2nd VPres* Jonathan Snellenburg; *Treas* Steven Chait
Estab 1954 to promote the best interests of the antique & art trade; to collect & circulate reports, statistics & other information pertaining to art; to sponsor & organize antique & art exhibitions; to promote just, honorable & ethical trade practices
Income: Financed by member dues
Exhibitions: International Fine Art & Antique Dealers Show
Publications: NAADA Directory, biannual
Activities: Lect

O   **NATIONAL ARCHITECTURAL ACCREDITING BOARD, INC,** 1735 New York Ave NW, Washington, DC 20006-5209. Tel 202-783-2007; Fax 202-783-2822; Elec Mail info@naab.org; Internet Home Page Address: www.naab.org; *Exec Dir* Andrea S Rutledge; *Assoc Exec Dir* Lee W Waldrep, PhD; *Accreditation Mgr* Cassandra Pair; *Financial Mgr* Ziti Sherman; *Admin Coordr* Kara Cohen
Open Mon - Fri 8 AM - 5 PM; Estab 1940 to produce & maintain a current list of accredited programs in architecture in the United States & its jurisdictions, with the general objective that a well-integrated program of architectural educ be developed which will be national in scope; Mem: 115
Income: Financed by contributions
Publications: Criteria and Procedures, pamphlet; List of Accredited Programs in Architecture, annually

O   **NATIONAL ART EDUCATION ASSOCIATION,** 1806 Robert Fulton Dr, Ste 300 Reston, VA 20191-4348. Tel 703-860-8000; Fax 703-860-2960; Elec Mail info@arteducators.org; Internet Home Page Address: www.arteducators.org; *Exec Dir* Deborah B Reeve, EdD; *COO* Melanie Dixon; *Convention & Progs Coordr* Kathy Duse; *Publications Mgr* Lynn Ezell; *Web & E-Communs Mgr* Linda Scott; *Mem Svcs Mgr* Christie Castillo
Open Mon - Fri 8:15 AM - 4:30 PM; Estab 1947 through the affiliation of four regional groups, Eastern, Western, Pacific & Southeastern Arts Assn. The NAEA is a national organization devoted to the advancement of the professional interests & competence of teachers of art at all educational levels. Promotes the study of the problems of teaching art; encourages research & experimentation; facilitates the professional & personal cooperation of its members; holds public discussions & progs; publishes desirable articles, reports & surveys; integrates efforts of others with similar purposes; Mem: 29,000 art teachers, adminr, supervisors & students; fee institutional comprehensive $150, active $50
Income: Programs financed through mem, sales of publications & annual convention
Publications: Art Education, 6 issues per year; NAEA Advisory, 4 issues per year; NAEA News, 6 issues per year; Studies in Art Education, 4 times per year; spec publs

O   **NATIONAL ASSEMBLY OF STATE ARTS AGENCIES,** 1029 Vermont Ave NW, 2nd Floor, Washington, DC 20005. Tel 202-347-6352; Fax 202-737-0526; Elec Mail nasaa@nasaa-arts.org; Internet Home Page Address: www.nasaa-arts.org; *CEO* Jonathan Katz; *COO & CFO* Dennis Dewey; *Chief Prog & Planning Officer* Kelly J Barsdate; *Arts Educ Mgr* Carmen Boston; *Dir Res* Angela Han; *Chief Advancement Officer* Laura S Smith; *Commun Mgr* Sue Struve; *Pres* Suzette Surkamer
Open by appointment only; Estab 1975 to enhance the growth & develop of the arts through an informed & skilled mem; to provide forums for the review & develop of national arts policy; Mem: 56; members are the fifty-six state & jurisdictional arts agencies, affiliate memberships are open to public; annual meeting in the fall
Income: Financed by mem & federal grants
Publications: Annual survey of state appropriations to arts councils; NASAA Notes, monthly
Activities: Co-manages The Arts Educ Partnership (www.aep-arts.org)

O   **NATIONAL ASSOCIATION OF SCHOOLS OF ART & DESIGN,** 11250 Roger Bacon Dr, Ste 21, Reston, VA 20190. Tel 703-437-0700; Fax 703-437-6312; Elec Mail info@arts-accredit.org; Internet Home Page Address: www.arts-accredit.org; *Assoc Dir* Karen P Moynahan
Formerly the National Conference of Schools of Design, holding its first conference in 1944. Changed name in 1948, at which time its constitution & by-laws were adopted. Changed its name again in 1960 from National Assn of Schools of Design to National Assn of Schools of Art. Name changed again in 1981 to National Assn of Schools of Art & Design. NASAD is the national accrediting agency for art & design institutions & progs in higher education.; Mem: 315 institutions; to qualify for mem, institutions must meet accreditation standards; annual meeting in Oct
Publications: Online Directory of Member Institutions, annually; Handbook of Accreditation Standards, ann
Activities: Awards given

O   **NATIONAL ASSOCIATION OF WOMEN ARTISTS, INC,** N.A.W.A. Gallery, 80 Fifth Ave, Ste 1405 New York, NY 10011-8002. Tel 212-675-1616; Fax 212-675-8257; Elec Mail office@thenawa.org; Internet Home Page Address: www.thenawa.org; *Pres* Sonia Stark; *1st VPres* Marie Hines Cowan; *Secy* Mark Altschul; *Treas* Patricia Huie; *Exec Dir* Susan G Hammond
Open Tues - Fri 10 AM - 5 PM, cl Sat & Sun; No admis fee; Estab 1889 as a national organization to encourage & promote the creative output of women artists; fosters awareness of the contributions of women artists to the ongoing history of American art; Maintains reference library & solo & group exhibs; Average Annual Attendance: 2,000; Mem: 800; member work is juried prior to selection; dues $135; meetings in Nov & May
Income: Financed by mem
Collections: Permanent collection at Jane Vorhees Zimmerli Museum, Rutgers Univ
Exhibitions: Annual members' exhibition in spring or fall with awards; annual traveling exhibitions of oils, acrylics, works on paper, printmaking; annual New York City shows of oils, acrylics, works on paper, printmaking & sculpture
Publications: The Annual Members' Exhibition Catalog; NAWA News; One Hundred Years-A Centennial Celebration of the National Assn of Women Artists; A View of One's Own, brochure
Activities: Classes for adults; lects & panels coordinated with exhib; lects open to pub, 2 vis lectrs per yr; gallery talks; sponsoring of competitions; awards given to mems & Hammerschlag during ann exhibs; $10,000 annual awards; $10,000 biennially; organizes book traveling exhibs to mus & univ; originate traveling exhibs to mus, univ galleries, art ctrs

O   **NATIONAL CARTOONISTS SOCIETY,** 341 N Maitland Ave, Ste 130, Winter Park, FL 32751-4761. Tel 407-647-8839; Fax 407-629-2502; Elec Mail phil@crowsegal.com; Internet Home Page Address: www.reuben.org; *Pres* Steve McGarry
Estab 1946 to advance the ideals & standards of the profession of cartooning; to stimulate interest in the art of cartooning by cooperating with estab schools; to encourage talented students; to assist governmental & charitable institutes; Mem: 480; annual Reuben Awards Dinner in Apr
Collections: Milt Gross Fund; National Cartoonists Society Collection
Publications: The Cartoonist, bimonthly

Activities: Educ dept to supply material & information to students; individual cartoonists to lect, chalk talks can be arranged; cartoon auctions; proceeds from traveling exhibitions & auctions support Milt Gross Fund assisting needy cartoonists, widows & children; gives Reuben Award to Outstanding Cartoonist of the Year, Silver Plaque Awards to best cartoonists in individual categories of cartooning; original cartoons lent to schools, libraries & galleries; originate traveling exhibs

O **NATIONAL COUNCIL ON EDUCATION FOR THE CERAMIC ARTS (NCECA),** 77 Erie Village Sq, Ste 280 Erie, CO 80516-6996. Tel 303-828-2811; Tel 866-266-2322; Fax 303-828-0911; Elec Mail office@nceca.net; Internet Home Page Address: www.nceca.net; *Past Pres* Keith J Williams; *Conf Mgr* Dori Nielsen; *Projects Mgr* Kate Vorhaus; *Mem Svcs* Jacqueline Hardy; *Pres* Patsy Cox; *Exec Dir* Joshua Green; *Website/Communs* Candice Finn
Open Mon - Fri 8 AM - 5 PM; Estab 1967 as a nonprofit organization to promote & improve ceramic art, design, craft & educ through the exchange of information among artists, teachers & individuals in the ceramic art community; Average Annual Attendance: 4,500; Mem: 4,000; dues $25 - $500
Income: Financed by annual conferences & mem
Library Holdings: CD-ROMs; DVDs; Exhibition Catalogs; Original Art Works; Periodical Subscriptions; Photographs
Exhibitions: Annual Conference Exhibitions; Open regional & nat exhibs (see website)
Publications: Journal, annual; Information Annual Conference, spring; Monthly electronic print newsletter available to mems; newsletters by request
Activities: Educ progs; conferences & symposia; organize traveling exhibs

O **NATIONAL ENDOWMENT FOR THE ARTS,** 1100 Pennsylvania Ave NW, Washington, DC 20506-0001. Tel 202-682-5400; Elec Mail webmgr@arts.endow.gov; Internet Home Page Address: www.arts.gov; *Chmn* Rocco Landesman; *Sr Deputy Chmn* Joan Shigekawa; *Dep Chmn Progs & Partnerships* Patrice Walker Powell; *Deputy Chmn Mgmt & Budget* Laurence Baden
Open 9 AM - 5:30 PM; No admis fee; The NEA is a public agency dedicated to supporting excellence in the arts, both new & established; bringing the arts to all Americans; & providing leadership in arts educ. Estab 1965 by Congress as an independent agency of the federal govt, the NEW is the nation's largest annual national funder of the arts, bringing great art to all 50 states, incl rural areas, inner cities & military bases
Income: Financed by federal appropriation
Publications: Annual Report; Guide to the National Endowment for the Arts; Research Publications
Activities: Funding opportunities can be found at www.arts.gov/grants
L **Library,** 1100 Pennsylvania Ave NW, Washington, DC 20506-0001. Tel 202-682-5485; Fax 202-682-5651; Elec Mail kiserj@arts.endow.gov; *Librn* Joy M Kiser
Open Mon - Thurs 8:30 AM - 5 PM; Estab 1971 to provide an effective information service to staff which will support division activities & contribute to the accomplishment of agency goals
Income: Financed by federal appropriation
Library Holdings: Book Volumes 9000; Clipping Files; Periodical Subscriptions 160

O **NATIONAL LEAGUE OF AMERICAN PEN WOMEN,** 1300 17th St NW, Washington, DC 20036-1973. Tel 202-785-1997; Fax 202-452-6868; Elec Mail nlapwil@verizon.net; Internet Home Page Address: nlapw.org; *National Pres* N Taylor Collins; *Art Consultant* Jamie Tate; *First VPres* Jean E Holmes; *Second VPres* Sandra Seaton Michel
Estab 1897 to support women in the arts; Maintains member reference library; Mem: 5000; 200 local branches; dues $40
Income: Financed by mem dues & legacies
Library Holdings: Manuscripts; Memorabilia; Original Art Works; Original Documents; Periodical Subscriptions; Photographs; Slides; Sculpture
Collections: Purchase award
Exhibitions: NLAPW Biennial Arts Show at national Biennial Convention
Publications: The Pen Women, bi-monthly magazine (4 times per year)
Activities: Lect open to public; concerts; competitions with awards; scholarships offered

O **NATIONAL OIL & ACRYLIC PAINTERS SOCIETY,** PO Box 676, Osage Beach, MO 65065-0676. Tel 573-348-1764; Elec Mail admin@noaps.org; Internet Home Page Address: www.noaps.org; *Pres* Mark Nichols; *Exhibit Chmn* Betty Fitzgerald
Open 10 AM - 5 PM; No admis fee; Estab 1990 to promote the work of exceptional living artists working in oil & acrylic paint & to expand the pub awareness, knowledge & appreciation of fine art, particularly in these two mediums; Main Hall, Columbia College; Average Annual Attendance: 5,000; Mem: Dues $40
Income: Not-for-profit 401C3
Exhibitions: Annual exhibit
Publications: Annual catalog; semiannual newsletter
Activities: Gallery talks; tours; originates traveling exhibs to Missouri galleries

O **NATIONAL SCULPTURE SOCIETY,** 75 Varick St, c/o ANS Fl 11 New York, NY 10013-1917. Tel 212-764-5645; Fax 212-764-5651; Internet Home Page Address: www.nationalsculpture.org; *Exec Dir* Gwen P Pier; *Exhibitions Dir* Patricia Delahanty; *Admin Asst* Elizabeth Helm
Open by appt only; No admis fee; Estab 1893 as a national organization to spread the knowledge of good sculpture; Mem: 3,000; work juried for sculptor mem; vote of Board of Dir for allied professional & patron mem; dues $70-$1350; meetings in May & Oct
Income: Financed by endowment, mem & donations
Library Holdings: Book Volumes; Clipping Files; Exhibition Catalogs; Photographs; Slides; Video Tapes
Exhibitions: 2-3 exhibitions annually on a rotating basis; open to all United States citizens and residents
Publications: Sculpture Review Magazine, quarterly; NSS News Bulletin

Activities: Educ progs; internships for students of arts admin; lects open to pub; tours; competitions with prizes; sculpture celebration weekend hosted annually; schols & fels offered; Alex J Ettl Grant, schol; Henry Hering Grant; originate traveling exhibs 1 per yr

O **NATIONAL SOCIETY OF MURAL PAINTERS, INC,** 450 W 31st St, 7th Fl New York, NY 10001-4608. Tel 212-244-2800; Elec Mail info@nationalsocietyofmuralpainters.com, info@evergreene.com; Internet Home Page Address: nationalsocietyofmuralpainters.com; *Pres* Carly Bartlett; *Vice Pres* Bill Mensching
Estab and incorporated 1895 to encourage and advance the standards of mural painting in America; to formulate a code for decorative competitions and by-laws to regulate professional practice; Mem: 100; dues $25, non-res $20
Income: Financed by dues & tax deductible contributions
Exhibitions: The Freedom Murals
Publications: Biographies and articles pertinent to the mural painting profession; Press Sheets of photographs and articles of the executed work of the members of society
Activities: Lects available to members only & their guests, 4 vis lectrs per yr; individual paintings & original objects of art lent to galleries, museums & special charitable events; lending collection contains original art works & slides; book traveling exhibs; originate traveling exhibs

O **NATIONAL SOCIETY OF PAINTERS IN CASEIN & ACRYLIC, INC,** 969 Catasauqua Rd, Whitehall, PA 18052-5501. Tel 610-264-7472; Elec Mail doug602ku@aol.com; *VPres* Robert Dunn; *Pres* Douglas Wiltrout
Open in June during exhibition; Estab 1952 as a national organization for a showcase for artists in casein & acrylic; Galleries rented from Salmagundi Club; Average Annual Attendance: 800 during exhibition; Mem: 120; mem by invitation, work must pass three juries; dues $40; annual meeting in May
Income: $3000 (financed by mem)
Exhibitions: Annual Exhibition
Publications: Exhibition Catalog, annually
Activities: Demonstrations; medals & $3500 in prizes given at annual exhib; originate traveling exhibs

O **NATIONAL WATERCOLOR SOCIETY,** 915 S Pacific Ave, San Pedro, CA 97031-3201. Tel 310-831-1099; Internet Home Page Address: www.nationwatercolorsociety.org; *Pres* Linda A Doll; *1st VPres* Linda Baker; *2nd VPres* Frank Eber; *3rd VPres* Margy West; *4th VPres* Valli Thayer McDougle; *Secy* Debra Abshear; *Treas & Dir Finance* Vickie Myers; *Mem/Communs* Kathleen Mooney; *Dir Annual Exhib, Opening Reception Facilitator, Dir Demonstration Series* Penny Hill; *Historian* Louri Sprung; *Dir Newsletter* Nancy Swan; *Dir Bldg* Douglas Stenhouse; *Past Pres* Mike Bailey
Open by appointment in Nov; Thurs - Sun 11 AM - 3 PM; open only during events or exhibs. For calendar, directions, maps, check web page.; No admis fee; Estab 1921 to sponsor art exhibits for the cultural & educational benefit of the pub; Circ 20,000; Mem: 2300; dues $40 associates, $45 signature mems beginning each yr in Mar (must be juried into signature mem); annual meeting in Jan; Assoc mem open to all; signature mem juried
Income: Financed by members
Purchases: One purchase award painting for permanent coll
Library Holdings: Compact Disks; Exhibition Catalogs; Original Art Works; Slides
Collections: Award-winning paintings from 1954 to present
Exhibitions: Spring Membership Exhibition; International Annual Exhibition (Fall)
Publications: Society's quarterly newsletter; color annual exhib catalog
Activities: Lects open to pub; sponsor yearly grant to children's art program of LA Southwest Museum; NWS award - $4000 - plus 30 awards totaling $30,000; demonstrations; lectrs; organize travel exhibs to art museums, art centers & libraries; originate traveling exhibs to art centers, college galleries, libr

NATIONAL YOUNGARTS FOUNDATION (National Foundation for Advancement in the Arts) Tel 305-377-1140; Fax 305-377-1149; Elec Mail info@youngarts.org; Internet Home Page Address: www.youngarts.org; *Pres & CEO* Paul T Lehr; *Progs Coordr* Neidra Ward; *Alumni Rels Mgr* Megan Ann Harmon; *Dir Productions* Roberta Behrendt Fliss; *Progs Mgr* Joseph Nesmith; *VPres Finance & CFO* Joe Gutierrez; *Mgr External Relations* Mabel Perez; *Office Mgr* Mary Cordova
Open Mon - Fri 9 AM - 5:30 PM; Estab 1981 to identify & reward young artists at critical stages in their develop
Income: Financed by private funding
Activities: Dramatic progs; master classes for prog participants; lects open to pub; concerts; gallery talks; tours

O **NEW ENGLAND WATERCOLOR SOCIETY,** 310 Plymouth St, Pembroke, MA 02359. Tel 617-536-7660; Internet Home Page Address: www.newenglandwatercolorsociety.org; *Pres* Gracia Dayton; *VPres* Anne Belson; *VPres* Robert Hsiung; *Treas* Joan Griswold
Open Mon - Fri 9 AM - 5 PM; Estab 1886 to advance the fine art of aqua media; Mem: 200, assoc mem 80; annual meeting in Mar
Income: Financed by mem
Exhibitions: Annual winter membership exhibit; Biennial-North America National Show-Juried Exhibit; 2-3 exhibits per year
Activities: Demonstrations, lects & gallery works open to pub during exhibitions

O **PASTEL SOCIETY OF AMERICA,** National Arts Club, Grand Gallery, 15 Gramercy Park S, New York, NY 10003-1705. Tel 212-533-6931; Fax 212-353-8140; Elec Mail psaoffice@pastelsocietyofamerican.org; Internet Home Page Address: pastelsocietyofamerica.org; *Founder & Hon Chair* Flora B Giffuni, MFA; *Pres* Rae Smith, PSA; *1st VPres* Dianne B Berhard, PSA; *2nd VPres* Duane Wakeham; *Treas* Jimmy Wright; *Recording Secy* Richard McEvoy; *Corresp Secy* Mary Hargrave
Estab 1972 to promote & encourage pastel painting/artists; Mem: 925; initiation fee $100, dues full $60, assoc $50; jury fee $10; mem open to professional artists
Income: donations

Library Holdings: Audio Tapes; CD-ROMs; Clipping Files; Exhibition Catalogs; Original Art Works; Slides; Video Tapes
Collections: Raymond Kintsler, Robert Phillip, Constance F Pratt & other master pastellists
Exhibitions: For Pastels Only-Annual
Publications: Pastelagram, bi-annual
Activities: Classes for adults; lects open to pub; gallery talks; sponsoring of competitions; Art Spirit Foundation, Dianne B Bernhard Gold Medal Award, Great American Artworks Award, Herman Margulies Award for Excellence, Andrew Giffuni Memorial Award, Joseph V. Giffuni Memorial Award; scholarships offered; exten dept serves lending collection of paintings; book traveling exhibs; originate traveling exhibs to galleries & museums

O **PASTEL SOCIETY OF OREGON,** PO Box 105, Roseburg, OR 97470-0016. Tel 541-440-0567; Elec Mail donandlora@hughes.net; Internet Home Page Address: users.mcsi.net/pso; *Pres* Lora Block
Estab 1987 to promote pastel as an art medium & to educate the pub on pastel; Mem: 80; dues $20 per yr; mem open to artists working in pastels; monthly working meetings
Income: $2000 (financed by mem & shows)
Publications: Pastel Newsletter, bi-monthly
Activities: Classes for adults; hands on exhibitions for schools

O **PASTEL SOCIETY OF THE WEST COAST,** Sacramento Fine Arts Center, 3518 Lynnmar Way, Carmichael, CA 95608-3454. Tel 916-944-3914; Internet Home Page Address: www.pswc.ws; *Treas* Priscilla Warddrip; *Mem Chair* Carol Ross; *Pres, Exhibits & Awards Chair* Tina Moore
Call for hours; Estab 1985 to promote soft pastel medium & exhibitions, workshops; Mem: 427; dues $25; quarterly meetings in Jan, Apr, July & Oct 3rd Wed
Income: Financed by mem & donations
Library Holdings: Video Tapes
Exhibitions: Three exhibitions per yr
Publications: PSWC newsletter, quarterly; exhibit catalogs
Activities: Classes for adults; lect open to public, 3-4 vis lectrs per year; competitions with awards; scholarships offered

O **THE PRINT CENTER,** 1614 Latimer St, Philadelphia, PA 19103-6308. Tel 215-735-6090; Fax 215-735-5511; Elec Mail info@printcenter.org; Internet Home Page Address: www.printcenter.org; *Pres* Hester Stinnett; *Exec Dir* Elizabeth F Spungen; *Gallery Store Mgr* Eli VandenBerg; *Asst Dir* Ashley Peel Pinkham; *Cur* John Caperton
Open Tues - Sat 11 AM - 6 PM; No admis fee; Estab 1915 as a nonprofit, educational organization dedicated to the promotion of fine prints & the support & encouragement of printmakers, photographers & collectors; Contemporary prints and photographs; Average Annual Attendance: 8,000; Mem: 1,000; dues household $75, artist $40, student $30
Income: $450,000 (financed by mem, private & government grants)
Special Subjects: Etchings & Engravings, Photography, Prints, Woodcuts
Collections: The Print Center Permanent Collection (prints & photograph collection held at the Philadelphia Museum of Art); The Print Center Archives (documents, books & catalogues held at the Historical Society of Pennsylvania)
Exhibitions: Changing bimonthly exhibitions of prints & photographs; Annual International Competition (since 1924)
Activities: Workshops for adults; lect open to public; 5 vis lectrs per yr; gallery talks; tours; sponsoring of competitions; artist residencies; The Print Center Gallery Store sells original prints & photographs

O **PRINT COUNCIL OF AMERICA,** 111 S Michigan Ave, c/o Art Institute of Chicago Dept of Prints & Drawings Chicago, IL 60603-6110. Elec Mail mtedeschi@artic.edu; Internet Home Page Address: www.printcouncil.org; *IPCR Proj Coordr* Stephen Goddard; *Pres* Martha Tedeschi
Estab 1956 as a nonprofit organization fostering the study & appreciation of fine prints, new & old; Mem: 240 museum & university professionals interested in prints; quals for mem incl specialization in works on paper, nomination & second by current mem; annual meeting in Apr or May
Income: Financed by dues & publication royalties
Publications: Occasional publications on old & modern prints; The Print Council Index to Oeuvre-Catalogues of Prints by European & American Artists; see website

O **SALMAGUNDI CLUB,** 47 Fifth Ave, New York, NY 10003. Tel 212-255-7740; Elec Mail info@salmagundi.org; Internet Home Page Address: www.salmagundi.org; *Pres* Robert Pillsbury; *Bd Chmn* Tim Newton; *1st VPres* Elizabeth Spencer; *2nd VPres* Janet Bauman; *Treas* John Morehouse; *Recording Secy* Griff Seymour
Open Mon - Fri 1 PM - 6 PM, Sat & Sun 1 - 5 PM; No admis fee; Estab 1871, incorporated 1880, to enhance the advancement of art appreciation, building purchased 1917; Clubhouse restaurant & bar, 3 galleries, Billiard room, library & board room. Maintains art reference library; Average Annual Attendance: 10,000; Mem: 815; dues resident layman & resident artist $600, scholarship graduated to scale, Honorary & Emeritus
Income: Financed by dues, donations, bequests
Special Subjects: Etchings & Engravings, Graphics, Landscapes, Photography, Posters, Sculpture, Watercolors, Painting-American, American Western Art, Woodcuts, Portraits, Marine Painting, Period Rooms
Collections: Club coll of past & present members; antique poster coll; coll of painters palettes
Exhibitions: 12 per year by artist members with cash awards; two per year by non-members (artists, photographers, sculptors) with cash awards; Annual Junior/Scholarship exhibition in January
Publications: Centennial Roster published in 1972; Salmagundi Membership Roster, every three years (www.salmagundi.org)
Activities: Classes for adults; demonstrations; lect, 10-12 vis lectrs per year; gallery talks; tours; concerts; competitions with awards; scholarships & fels offered; individual paintings & original objects of art lent to various museums &

special exhibitions; lending collection contains over 50 original art works, over 50 paintings, 10 sculptures; mus shop sells books, magazines, patches, ties & tie tacks
L **Library,** 47 Fifth Ave, New York, NY 10003. Tel 212-255-7740; Internet Home Page Address: www.salmagundi.org; *Librn* Kenneth W Fitch
Open Tues 10:30 AM - 5 PM; For reference only
Library Holdings: Book Volumes 10,000; Exhibition Catalogs; Original Art Works; Other Holdings Steinway Player piano with 100 rolls; Periodical Subscriptions 10; Photographs; Sculpture
Special Subjects: Art History, Folk Art, Illustration, Photography, Drawings, Graphic Arts, Painting-American, Posters, Sculpture, Historical Material, History of Art & Archaeology, Watercolors, Woodcuts, Landscapes, Architecture

O **SCULPTORS GUILD, INC,** 55 Washington St, Ste 256 Brooklyn, NY 11201-1073. Tel 718-422-0555; Fax 718-422-0555; Elec Mail sculptorsguild@gmail.com; Internet Home Page Address: www.sculptorsguild.org; *Pres* Robert Michael Smith; *VPres* Gina Miccinilli; *Secy* Elizabeth Knowles; *Treas* Stephen Keltner
Open Tues & Thurs 11 AM - 5 PM & by appointment; No admis fee; Estab 1937 to promote sculpture & show members' work in an annual show & throughout the country; Contemporary sculpture; Average Annual Attendance: 1,500; Mem: 120; qualifications for mem, quality of work & professionalism; dues $250; annual meeting in May
Income: Financed by mem dues, donations, & commissions on sales
Exhibitions: Various exhibitions of small works are held in the Sculptors Guild Gallery; Ann exhibs at Governors Island, Saks Fifth Ave Windows, Housatonic Mus
Publications: Brochure 1985; exhibit catalogs, every other year for annual exhibitions; 50th Anniversary Catalog 1937-1938; The Guild Reporter, Vol. 1, No. 1, 1986, annually
Activities: Speakers bureau; lect open to public; original objects of art lent to patrons & for movie & TV productions; lending collection contains cassettes & 50 sculptures; book traveling exhibs; originate traveling exhibs; sales shop sells original art

O **SOCIETY OF AMERICAN GRAPHIC ARTISTS,** 32 Union Sq, Rm 1214, New York, NY 10003. Tel 212-260-5706; Internet Home Page Address: www.clt-astate.edu; *VPres* Michael Arike; *VPres* Masaaki Noda; *Treas* Joseph Essig; *Pres* Linda Adato
Estab 1915 as a society of printmakers, now a society of graphic artists; Mem: 250 voted in by merit; dues $40; annual meeting May; juried by membership comt
Income: Financed by mem & assoc mem
Exhibitions: Semi-annual Open Competition National Print Exhibition; Semi-annual Closed Members Exhibit
Publications: Exhibition Catalog, annually; Presentation Prints for Assoc Membership
Activities: Lects open to pub, 1 vis lectr per yr; sponsors competitive & members' exhibits with awards; original objects of art lent, lending coll contains original prints; originate traveling exhibs

O **SOCIETY OF AMERICAN HISTORICAL ARTISTS,** 146 Dartmouth Dr, Oyster Bay, NY 11801-3423. Tel 516-681-8820; Fax 516-822-2253; *VPres* William Muller; *Pres* John Duillo
Estab 1980 for furthering American Historical Art, especially authenticity; Mem: 16; dues $150; meetings 3-4 per yr
Activities: Awards for excellence

O **SOCIETY OF ARCHITECTURAL HISTORIANS,** 1365 N Astor St, Chicago, IL 60610-2144. Tel 312-573-1365; Fax 312-573-1141; Elec Mail info@sah.org; Internet Home Page Address: www.sah.org; *Exec Dir* Pauline Saliga; *Pres* Dianne Harris; *First VPres* Abigail Van Slyck; *Second VPres* Gail Fenske; *Dir Progs* Kathryn Sturm; *Dir Mem* Anne Bird
Open Wed for tours Noon, Sat 10 AM & 1 PM; Admis $10 on Sat, free on Wed; Estab to provide an international forum for those interested in architecture & its related arts, to encourage scholarly research in the field & to promote the preservation of significant architectural monuments throughout the world; House Mus; Mem: 3500; show an interest in architecture, past, present & future; dues $120; annual meeting Apr
Income: Financed by mem
Library Holdings: Book Volumes; Exhibition Catalogs; Other Holdings
Publications: Journal, quarterly; Newsletter, quarterly; Preservation Forum, ann
Activities: Docent training; sponsors competitions; Antoinette Forrester Downing Award; Founder's Award; Alice Davis Hitchcock Book Award; Philip Johnson Award; Elizabeth MacDougall Award; Spiro Kostof Award; field study progs; fellowships offered; sales shop sells architectural guides & booklets & also back issues of the Journal, reproductions, prints, postcards

O **SOCIETY OF ILLUSTRATORS,** 128 E 63rd St, New York, NY 10065-7392. Tel 212-838-2560; Fax 212-838-2561; Elec Mail info@societyillustrators.org; Internet Home Page Address: www.societyillustrators.org; *Pres* Dennis Dittrich; *Exec VPres* Tim O'Brien; *VPres* Victor Juhasz
Open Tues 10 AM - 8 PM, Wed - Fri 10 AM - 5 PM, Sat Noon - 4 PM, cl most holidays; No admis fee; Estab 1901 as a national organization of professional illustrators and art dir; Gallery has group, theme, one-man & juried shows, approx every four wks; Average Annual Attendance: 40,000; Mem: 850
Publications: Illustrators Annual
Activities: Lects open to pub; 7 vis lectrs per yr; sponsoring of competitions; holds annual national juried exhibition of best illustrations of the yr; awards scholarships to college level art students; originate traveling exhibs to college galleries; sales shop sells books

O **SOCIETY OF NORTH AMERICAN GOLDSMITHS,** 540 Oak St, Ste A, Eugene, OR 97401. Tel 541-345-5689; Fax 541-345-1123; Elec Mail info@snagmetalsmith.org; Internet Home Page Address: www.snagmetalsmith.org; *Pres* Kris Patzlaff; *Treas* Stewart Thomson; *Exec Dir* Dana Singer; *Conf & Prog Outreach Mgr* Evangelina Sundrengz; *Opers Mgr* Tara Decklin
Open Mon - Fri 8:30 AM - 5 PM; No admis fee; Estab 1969; international mem org for jewelers, designers & metalsmiths; Maintains rental library; Average Annual Attendance: 800; Mem: 3,300; dues $79; annual meeting in late spring or early summer

Income: $600,000 (financed by mem)
Exhibitions: Distinguished Members of SNAG; Jewelry USA
Publications: Metalsmith magazine, 5 per year; bi-monthly newsletter; SNAG news
Activities: Lect open to members only; 3 vis lectrs per yr; competitions; ann conference; seminars; scholarships; originate traveling exhibs

O **SOCIETY OF PHOTOGRAPHERS & ARTISTS REPRESENTATIVES,** 60 E 42nd St Ste 1166, New York, NY 10165-1166. Elec Mail infor@spar.org.; Internet Home Page Address: www.spar.org; *Coordr* Kat Hunt; *Asst Coordr* Adrienne Wheeler; *Pres* George Watson
Estab 1965 as an assn of professional representatives of illustrators, photographers & related talent; Mem: must be representative in industry for at least 1 year & provide references; mem fees vary by region
Publications: Membership directory, biannual; newsletter
Activities: Some open to public; some for members only

O **SPECIAL LIBRARIES ASSOCIATION,** 331 S Patrick St, Alexandria, VA 22314-3501. Tel 703-647-4900; Fax 703-647-4901; Elec Mail sla@sla.org; Internet Home Page Address: www.sla.org; *CEO* Janice R Lachance; *Dir Bus Develop* Stacey Bowers; *Dir Pub Rels* Cara Schatz; *COO & CFO* Nancy A Sansalone
Estab 1964 to provide an information forum & exchange for librarians in the specialized fields of museums, arts & humanities; Mem: 14,000; dues $129; annual meeting in early June
Publications: Museums, Arts & Humanities Division Bulletin, semi-annual

O **THE STAINED GLASS ASSOCIATION OF AMERICA,** 9313 E 63rd St, Raytown, MO 64133-4901. Tel 800-438-9581; Elec Mail headquarters@sgaaonline.com; Internet Home Page Address: www.stainedglass.org; *Exec Admin* Katie Gross
Estab 1903 as an international organization to promote the develop & advancement of the stained glass craft; Mem: 600; dues accredited $350, active $150, affiliate $75, student $50 (various criteria apply to each mem)
Income: Financed by mem dues
Library Holdings: Slides; Video Tapes
Special Subjects: Stained Glass
Publications: Stained Glass magazine, quarterly
Activities: Educ dept with two & three week courses

O **UNITED STATES DEPARTMENT OF THE INTERIOR,** Indian Arts & Crafts Board, 1849 C St NW, MS 2528-MIB, Washington, DC 20240. Tel 202-208-3773; 888-ART-FAKE; Fax 202-208-5196; Elec Mail iacb@los.doi.gov; Internet Home Page Address: www.doi.gov/iacb; *Dir* Meridith Z Stanton; *Prog Specialist* Ashley Fry; *Program Support Specialist* Ken Van Wey; *Admin Officer* Michele Hill; *Chmn* Joyce Bega Foss; *Commissioner* Rebecca Webster; *Commissioner* Elmer Gray; *Commissioner* Rose Fosdick; *Commissioner* Charles Harwood; *Sec* Ferdousi Khanam
Open Mon - Fri 8 AM - 5 PM; No admis fee; Estab 1935 to promote contemporary arts by Indians & Alaska Natives of the United States; Board administers the Southern Plains Indian Museum, Anadarko, OK; Museum of the Plains Indian, Browning, MT; Sioux Indian Museum, Rapid City, SD; Average Annual Attendance: 150,000
Income: Financed by federal appropriation
Special Subjects: American Indian Art, Eskimo Art, Painting-Dutch
Collections: Contemporary American Indian & Alaska Native Arts
Exhibitions: Twelve special exhibitions among the three museums
Publications: Source Directory of American Indian & Alaska Native owned & operated arts & crafts bus
Activities: Information & advice on matters pertaining to contemporary Indian, Eskimo & Aleut arts & crafts

O **UNITED STATES GENERAL SERVICES ADMINISTRATION,** Art in Architecture and Fine Arts, 1800 F St NW, Washington, DC 20405-0002. Tel 202-501-0930; Fax 202-501-3393; Elec Mail jennifer.gibson@gsa.gov; Internet Home Page Address: www.gsa.gov/artinarchitecture; *Dir* Jennifer Gibson; *Proj Mgr* Nicole Avila; *Proj Mgr* William Caine; *Project Mgr* Kim Baker; *Colls Mgr* Mary Margaret Carr; *Colls Mgr* Kathy Erickson
Open to public by appointment; 9 AM to 5 PM; No Admis Fees; GSA's Art in Architecture Program commissions artists, working in close consultation with project design teams, to create artwork that is appropriate to the diverse uses and architectural vocabularies of new federal buildings. These permanent installations of contemporary art within the nation's civic buildings afford unique opportunities for exploring the integration of art and architecture, and facilitate a meaningful cultural dialogue between the American people and their government. A panel that includes the project architect, art professionals, the federal client, and representatives of the community advises GSA in selecting the most suitable artist for each Art in Architecture commission, Artwork is funded by 0.5% of each building's construction budget. GSA's Fine Arts Prog is responsible for the stewardship of the Fine Arts coll & all policies & procedures concerning its preservation, legal compliance accessibility & interpretation. The coll includes works from the 1850s to the present day.
Library Holdings: Book Volumes; CD-ROMs; Clipping Files; Compact Disks; DVDs; Exhibition Catalogs; Original Documents; Pamphlets; Photographs; Records; Slides
Collections: Fine Arts Collection includes permanently installed & moveable mural paintings, sculpture, architectural or environmental works of art, works on paper located in Federal buildings, courthouses & land ports of entry across the U.S.; Art in Architecture Marquettes; Design excellence architectural models; New Deal artworks allocated or on loan to institutions around the country

O **VAN ALEN INSTITUTE,** 30 W 22nd St, 6th Fl New York, NY 10010-5816. Tel 212-924-7000; Fax 212-366-5836; Elec Mail vai@vanalen.org; Internet Home Page Address: www.vanalen.org; *Exec Dir* Adi Shamir; *Dir Progs & Devel* Jamie Hand; *Fel Prog Mgr* Jessica Blaustein; *Archive Mgr* Chris Dierks; *Office Admin* Marianne Bujacich
Open Mon - Fri 10 AM - 6 PM; No admis fee; Inc 1894 as Society of Beaux-Arts Architects, which was dissolved Dec 1941; Beaux-Arts Institute of Design estab 1916, name changed 1956 to present name; Average Annual Attendance: 2,500; Mem: 600; dues $50; annual meeting end of Oct
Income: mems, grants, corporate, found, gov grants
Exhibitions: Prize-winning drawings of competitions held during year; Rotating exhibits
Publications: Yearbook, annually in October
Activities: Lects open to pub, 4-5 vis lectrs per yr; competitions with awards; trustee for the Lloyd Warren Fellowship (Paris Prize in Architecture) for study & travel abroad; William Van Allen Architect Memorial Award (international competition) annual scholarship for further study or research project of some architectural nature; & other trust funds for prize awards for study & travel abroad & educational activities in the United States; individual paintings & original objects of art lent; lending collection contains 200 original prints; book traveling exhibs 3-4 per yr; originate traveling exhibs

O **VIRGINIA CENTER FOR THE CREATIVE ARTS,** 154 San Angelo Dr, Amherst, VA 25421-2701. Tel 434-946-7236; Fax 434-946-7239; Elec Mail vcca@vcca.com; Internet Home Page Address: www.vcca.com; *Dir Artists' Servs* Sheila Gully Pleasants; *Artistic Dir* Craig Pleasants; *Communs Dir* Lexi Boris; *Exec Dir* Gregory Allgiire Smith; *Assoc Dir Admis* Dana Jones; *Financial Dir* Bonnie Sue Wine; *Bookeeper* Richard Glass; *Develop Asst* Kmberley Stiffler; *International Prog Coordr* Nancy McAndrew; *Dir Ann & Planned Giving* Carol O'Brien
Open Mon - Fri 9 AM - 5 PM; Estab 1971 as a residential retreat for writers, composers & visual artists; Facilities include 25 studios, y, a darkroom, a printing press, a library, private bedrooms in a modern residence. Breakfast & dinner served in dining room, lunch is delivered to Studio Barn. Access to Sweet Briar College facilities; Average Annual Attendance: 400 professional writers, composers & visual artists
Income: individual contributions, residency contributions
Collections: Books & artwork by Fellows
Exhibitions: exhibitions are in the summers, no proposals accepted
Publications: Annual newsletter; Notes From Mt San Angelo
Activities: Lect & readings open to public, 2-3 vis lectrs per year; concerts; tours; individual paintings & original objects of art lent through a leasing program to bus & individuals

O **VISUAL ARTISTS & GALLERIES ASSOCIATION (VAGA),** 350 5th Ave, Rm 2820 New York, NY 10118-2820. Tel 212-808-0616; Elec Mail rpanzer.vaga@erols.com; *Exec Dir* Robert Panzer
Open daily 9 AM - 5 PM, by appointment; Estab 1976 to help artists control the reproduction of their works, from sculptures to photographs in textbooks; to act as a clearinghouse for licensing reproduction rights & setting up a directory of artists & other owners of reproduction rights for international use; Mem: European 3000, American 500; dues gallery & assoc $300, estates $75, artist $50
Income: Financed by mem & royalties
Publications: Newsletter

O **WASHINGTON SCULPTORS GROUP,** PO Box 42534, Washington, DC 20015-0534. Tel 202-686-8696 (voicemail); Fax 202-364-1053; Internet Home Page Address: www.washingtonsculptors.org; *Pres* Pattie Firestone; *VPres* Joan Weber; *Treas* Nancy Frankel; *Sec* Laurel Lukaszewski
Estab 1983 to promote sculpture; Use art & corporate space for exhibitions; members' juried exhibitions available for exchange shows; Average Annual Attendance: 1,500; Mem: 400 mem; dues $35
Income: $10,000 (financed by mem & occasional grants)
Exhibitions: 3-5 juried exhibitions per year with various locales
Publications: Exhibition brochures & catalogs; newsletters, 3 per year; website
Activities: Lects open to pub, 6-8 vis lectrs per yr; image bank; gallery talks; tours; Mayor's Art Award, Washington, DC; originate traveling exhibs circulating to art spaces, galleries & museums

O **WOMEN'S CAUCUS FOR ART,** PO Box 1498, Canal St Sta New York, NY 10013. Tel 212-634-0007; Elec Mail info@nationalwca.org; Internet Home Page Address: www.nationalwca.org; *Pres (2014)* Brenda Oelbaum; *Treas* Margaret Lutze; *Dir Opers* Karin Luner; *Pres (2013)* Priscilla Otani
Estab 1972 as a nonprofit women's professional & service organization for visual arts; Average Annual Attendance: 200; Mem: 1,600; annual meeting in Feb
Income: $55,000 (financed by mem)
Library Holdings: Exhibition Catalogs; Original Documents; Other Holdings; Periodical Subscriptions; Photographs
Exhibitions: (2014) Half the Sky
Publications: Honors Catalogue (annual); Art Lines (3 times per yr)
Activities: Lects for mems only, vis lectrs 2 per yr; tours, sponsoring of competitions; Lifetime Achievement awards; awards stipend to Feb conference student; schols awarded; originates traveling exhibs

U.S. Museums, Libraries & Associations

ALABAMA

ANNISTON

M **ANNISTON MUSEUM OF NATURAL HISTORY,** 800 Museum Dr, Anniston, AL 36206-2813; PO Box 1587, Anniston, AL 36202-1587. Tel 256-237-6766; Fax 256-237-6776; Elec Mail cbragg@annistonmuseum.org; Internet Home Page Address: www.annistonmuseum.org; *Dir* Cheryl Bragg; *Dir Develop* Lindie K Brown; *Dir Mktg* Margie Conner; *Tour Coordr* Donna Kopet; *Mus Store Mgr* Gina Cooper; *Chm (V)* Paula Watkins; *Facilities Mgr* Scott Williamon; *Cur Collections* Daniel Spaulding; *Dir Prog & Educ* Gina Morey
Open Tues - Sat 10 AM - 5 PM, Sun 1 - 5 PM, summer open Mon; Admis adults $4.50, children 4-17 $3.50, 3 & under free; Estab 1930, nationally accredited mus with the purpose of enhancing pub knowledge, understanding & appreciation of living things & their environments; Permanent exhibit halls interpret many aspects of natural history and the Environment; changing exhibit gallery features exhibitions focusing on interrelationships between nature & art; Average Annual Attendance: 70,000; Mem: 1600; dues family $35, individual $25; annual meeting in Sept
Income: Financed by mem, earned income, donations & city appropriations
Collections: Archaeology; Ethnology; Natural Science; Wildlife Art
Exhibitions: 4-6 rotating per yr
Activities: Classes for adults & children; docent progs; lects open to pub, 2-6 vis lectrs per yr; concerts; book traveling exhibs 2-4 per yr; retail store sells books, original art & reproductions

M **BERMAN MUSEUM,** 840 Museum Dr, Anniston, AL 36206; PO Box 2245, Anniston, AL 36202-2245. Tel 256-237-6261; Fax 256-238-9055; Elec Mail dford@bermanmuseum.org; Internet Home Page Address: www.bermanmuseum.org
Open June - Aug Mon - Sat 10 AM - 5 PM, Sun 1 - 5 PM; Sept - May Tues - Sat. 10 AM - 5 PM, Sun. 1 - 5 PM; cl New Year's Day, Thanksgiving, Christmas Eve & Day; Admis adults $3.50, seniors $3, children 4 - 17 $2.50, discount to AAA mems & active military, children 3 & under no admis fee; Mus houses 3,000 objects related to world history in five galleries. The coll was that of Farley L & Germaine K Berman, both who served in counterintelligence during WWII. They met in North Africa & traveled the world collecting rare & unusual artifacts for more than seventy years; Mem: Dues Benefactor $500 & up; Patron $250; Sustainer $100; Contributor $50; Family $25; Indiv $20; Student (FT) $10
Special Subjects: American Indian Art, Archaeology, American Western Art, Flasks & Bottles, Gold, Bronzes, Painting-European, Sculpture, Painting-American, Religious Art, Ceramics, Antiquities-Oriental
Collections: Spy coll including a silver flute, various ink pens, walking canes, box of antacids, & WWII German cigarette lighter, all of which were designed to conceal a firing mechanism; coll of bronzes including figural & animal subject matter, created & cast by European, Asian, and American artists and foundries; religious & ordinary objects created by Asian artisans over a span of nine centuries; traveling pistols of Jefferson Davis, Pres of the Confederacy; dressing set of Napoleon Bonaparte; royal Persian scimitar encrusted with 1,295 rose-cut diamonds and rubies, single 40-carat emerald, all set in three pounds of gold; coll of weapons & bronze sculptures from the American West
Activities: Art Camp and Etiquette For Children; History Festival; rotating exhibs

AUBURN

M **AUBURN UNIVERSITY,** Julie Collins Smith Museum, 901 S College St, Auburn, AL 36849-0001. Tel 334-844-1484 (Main); Tel 334-844-7075 (Facilities rental & special events); Fax 334-844-1463; Elec Mail jcsm@auburn.edu; Internet Home Page Address: www.jcsm.auburn.edu/index.php; *Dir Develop* Brett Evans; *Office Admnr* Janice Allen; *Develop Coordr* Cindy Cox; *Exec Asst* Robbin Birmingham; *Mus Shop Mgr* Carol Robicheaux; *Educ Cur* Scott Bishop Wagoner; *Asst Dir* Andy Tennant; *Cur* Dennis Harper; *Preparator* Daniel Neil; *Dir* Marilyn Laufer; *Registrar* Danielle Funderburk; *Mktg & Special Events* Colleen Bourdeau; *Graphic Designer* Janet Guynn; *K-12 Educ Cur* Andrew Henley
Open Mon-Fri 8:30AM-4:45PM, Sat 10AM-4:45PM, 3rd Tues of month open until 8PM; No admis fee; Estab 2003 as an art mus; Mus is home to Auburn Univ's coll of American & European art. nearly 40,000 sq ft bldg; 120-seat auditorium; Average Annual Attendance: 30,000; Mem: Dues Patron $500; Benefactor $250; Sustaining $125; Family or Dual $80; Indiv $45; Student $25
Special Subjects: Painting-American, Prints, Painting-European, Sculpture, Bronzes
Collections: Advancing American Art Collection; The Louise Hauss & David Brent Miller Audubon Coll; American & European 19th & 20th century art including paintings, sculpture & prints; The Bill L Harbert Collection of European Art; monumental mural Alma Mater by William Baggett; The Nelson and Joan Cousins Hartman Collection of Tibetan Bronzes

Activities: Gallery talks; walking paths with botanical gardens; lects; traveling & rotating exhibs; mus related items for sale

BIRMINGHAM

M **BIRMINGHAM MUSEUM OF ART,** 2000 Reverend Abraham Woods Jr Blvd, Birmingham, AL 35203-2205. Tel 205-254-2565; Fax 205-254-2714; Elec Mail museum@artsbma.org; Internet Home Page Address: www.artsbma.org; *Dir* Gail Andrews; *Chmn* Thomas L Hamby; *Accnt* Ernest Hudson; *Museum Store Mgr* Kristie Allen; *Registrar* Melissa Falkner Mercurio; *Graphic Designer* James Williams; *Cur Decorative Arts* Anne Forschler; *Mem Coordr* Charlotte Russ; *Vol Coordr* Rhonda Hethcox; *Deputy Dir* Amy Templeton; *Chief Security* J R Feagins; *Designer* Terry Beckham; *Librn* Tatum Preston; *Admin Secy* Jennifer Powell; *Bus Mgr* Johnny McIntosh; *Facilities Mktg Coordr* Brynne MacCann; *Chief Cur & Cur European Art* Jeannine O'Grody; *Cur Arts of Africa & Americas* Emily Hanna; *Cur American Art* Graham Boettcher; *Cur Modern & Contemporary Art* Ron Platt; *Cur Asian Art* Donald A Wood; *Dir Educ* Samantha Kelly; *Dir Develop* Kendra Quandt; *Dir Commun* Nick Patterson; *Bldg Supt* Wayne Blount
Open Tues - Sat 10 AM - 5 PM, Sun Noon - 5 PM, cl major holidays; No admis fee; Estab 1951 as a general art mus with collections from earliest manifestation of man's creativity to contemporary work. Its goal is to illustrate the highest level of man's artistic work in an art historical context; The 36 galleries are climate controlled; lighting system is modern & controlled to latest safety standards; Average Annual Attendance: 145,600; Mem: 6,000; dues $35 - $10,000
Income: $7,000,000 (financed by mem, city appropriation & annual donations)
Purchases: $650,000
Special Subjects: Afro-American Art, American Indian Art, Drawings, Etchings & Engravings, Folk Art, Landscapes, Ceramics, Glass, Metalwork, Furniture, Photography, Porcelain, Portraits, Pottery, Prints, Textiles, Painting-British, Painting-European, Painting-French, Painting-Japanese, Painting-American, Sculpture, American Western Art, African Art, Costumes, Religious Art, Primitive art, Decorative Arts, Jade, Oriental Art, Asian Art, Silver, Painting-Dutch, Baroque Art, Renaissance Art, Painting-Italian, Enamels
Collections: English ceramics & silver; American painting & sculpture; American decorative arts 19th-20th centuries; Ethnographic Collection; African, American Indian, Pre-Columbian works; Oriental Collection; Indian, Korean, Chinese & Southeast Asian works; Oriental Rug Collection; European paintings; Wedgwood collection; photography; prints and drawings, 18th-19th centuries; American Decorative Arts, 19th-20th Centuries; Renaissance 20th Century Art
Publications: Quarterly newsletter; catalogues of spec exhibs & permanent collections; self-guided tour brochures; teacher packets
Activities: Classes for adults & children; docent training; lects open to pub, 6 vis lectrs per yr; concerts; gallery talks; tours; competitions; individual paintings lent to other mus; artmobile; book traveling exhibs; originates & circulates traveling exhibs; mus shop sells books, reproductions, prints and gifts

L **Clarence B Hanson Jr Library,** 2000 Eighth Ave N, Birmingham, AL 35203-2278. Tel 205-254-2566; Fax 205-254-2714; Elec Mail library@artsBMA.org; Internet Home Page Address: www.ArtsBMA.org; *Library Admnr* Tatum Preston; *R Hugh Daniel Dir* Gail A Trechsel; *Bus Mgr* D Mike McLane; *Dir of Develop* Amy W Templeton; *Chief Cur & Cur of Asian Art* Dr Donald A Wood; *Cur Decorative Arts* Dr Anne M Forschler; *Registrar* Melissa Falkner Mercurio; *Exhibs Designer* Terry A Beckham; *Security Dir* G B Quinney; *Bldg Supt* Wayne Blount; *Cur Americas & Africa* Emily Hanna, Dr; *Cur European Art* Dr Jeannine A O'Grody
Open Tues - Fri 10 AM - 4 PM; No admis fee; Estab 1951; Reference only; Average Annual Attendance: 200,000; Mem: 6,500; dues range from $20 - $5,000
Income: Financed by city & private funding
Library Holdings: Auction Catalogs; Book Volumes 25,000; CD-ROMs; Clipping Files; Compact Disks; DVDs; Exhibition Catalogs; Manuscripts; Memorabilia; Original Documents; Other Holdings; Pamphlets; Periodical Subscriptions 110
Special Subjects: Art History, Decorative Arts, Film, Drawings, Painting-American, Pre-Columbian Art, Painting-European, Ceramics, American Western Art, Asian Art, Porcelain, Primitive art, Jade, Glass, Afro-American Art, Landscapes, Folk Art
Collections: Kress Collection of Italian Renaissance Art; Beeson Wedgewood Collection; Lamprecht Collection of Cast Iron Art; Hitt Collection of 19th Century French Furniture; Ireland Sculpture Garden; Oliver Collection of English Porcelain; Collins Collection of English Ceramics; Cooper Collection of Rugs; Simon Collection of Art of the American West; Cargo Collection of American Quilts
Activities: Classes for adults & children; dramatic progs; docent training; lects open to pub, 30 vis lectrs per yr; concerts; gallery talks; tours; sponsoring of competitions; Vol of Yr award; Youth Art Month Juried Competition; scholarships; exten prog to Jefferson and Shelby counties; approx 6 traveling exhibs per yr; originates traveling exhibs to pub mus and galleries; mus shop sells publications, books, jewelry, toys, fine art, decorative arts, handicrafts & stationery

L   **BIRMINGHAM PUBLIC LIBRARY,** Arts, Literature & Sports Department, 2100 Park Pl, Birmingham, AL 35203-2794. Tel 205-226-3600; Fax 205-226-3731; Elec Mail hm@bham.lib.al.us; Internet Home Page Address: www.bham-lib.al.us; *Head Librn* Haruyo Miyagawa; *Dir* Barbara Sirmans
Open Mon - Tues 9 AM - 8 PM, Thurs - Sat 9 AM - 6 PM, Sun 2 - 6 PM; Estab 1909 to serve the Jefferson County area
Income: Financed by city & state appropriations, pub & pvt grants
Library Holdings: Audio Tapes; Book Volumes 40,000; Cassettes; Compact Disks; DVDs; Fiche; Framed Reproductions 200; Periodical Subscriptions 155; Prints; Records; Video Tapes
Special Subjects: Art History, Folk Art, Decorative Arts, Mixed Media, Graphic Design, Islamic Art, Pre-Columbian Art, Sculpture, History of Art & Archaeology, Portraits, Asian Art, Porcelain, Pottery, Pewter, Architecture

M   **BIRMINGHAM SOUTHERN COLLEGE,** Doris Wainwright Kennedy Art Center, 900 Arkadelphia Rd, Birmingham, AL 35254-0002; PO Box 549021, Birmingham, AL 35254. Tel 205-226-4928; 800-523-5793; Fax 205-226-3044; Elec Mail jneel@bsc.edu; Internet Home Page Address: www.bsc.edu; *Prof* Jim Neel; *Prof* Pamela Venz; *Prof* Steve Cole
Open Mon - Fri 8:30 AM - 5 PM; No admis fee
Income: Financed by the college
Exhibitions: Steve Cole faculty exhib

M   **SLOSS FURNACES NATIONAL HISTORIC LANDMARK,** 20 32nd St N, Birmingham, AL 35222-1236. Tel 205-324-1911; Fax 205-324-6758; Elec Mail info@slossfurnaces.com; Internet Home Page Address: www.slossfurnaces.com; *Dir* Bob Rathburn; *Mktg & Develop Officer* Brandon Wilson; *Sr Maintenance Repair Worker* Matt Landers; *Prog Dir* Heather Guy
Open Tues - Sat 10 AM - 4 PM, Sun Noon - 4 PM; No admis fee; Estab 1983 as mus of industrial history, former blast furnace plant; temporary exhibitions, especially in metal arts; Average Annual Attendance: 180,000
Income: Financed by City of Birmingham
Library Holdings: Audio Tapes; Book Volumes; CD-ROMs; Cassettes; Clipping Files; DVDs; Manuscripts; Maps; Memorabilia; Original Art Works; Original Documents; Pamphlets; Photographs; Prints; Records; Reels; Sculpture; Slides; Video Tapes
Special Subjects: Metalwork
Activities: Classes for adults & children; festivals; events; kids club; concerts; tours; mus shop sells books, magazines, original art, prints

M   **SPACE ONE ELEVEN, INC,** 2409 2nd Ave N, Birmingham, AL 35203-3809. Tel 205-328-0553; Fax 205-254-6176; Elec Mail soe@artswire.org; Internet Home Page Address: www.spaceoneeleven.org; Internet Home Page Address: www.bham.net/soe/soe.html; *Co-Founder & Artist* Anne Arrasmith; *Co-Founder & CEO* Peter Prinz
Open Tues - Fri 10 AM - noon & 1PM - 5 PM and by appt; No admis fee; Estab 1986 to explore, communicate & develop experimental ideas, issues & new work; 10,000 sq ft; twin 100-year old warehouses, 1200 sq ft of galleries, windows exhibition space, artist projects & education studios, rental facilities
Activities: Classes for children; lects open to pub; gallery talks; financial assistance to children in city center arts program; book traveling exhibitions; originate traveling exhibitions; sales shop sells ceramics & art goods

M   **UNIVERSITY OF ALABAMA AT BIRMINGHAM,** Visual Arts Gallery, 900 13th St S, Birmingham, AL 35294-0001. Tel 205-934-0815; Fax 205-975-2836; Elec Mail blevine@uab.edu; Internet Home Page Address: uab.edu; Telex 88-8826; *Cur & Dir* Brett M Levin
Open Mon - Thurs 11 AM - 6 PM, Fri 11 AM - 5 PM, Sat 1 PM - 5 PM except between exhibitions, holidays & vacation; No admis fee; Estab 1973 to exhibit works of students, faculty & nationally & internationally known artists & to form & exhibit a permanent collection of art since 1750; Two galleries each 1,200 sq ft & adjacent storage all on first floor of Humanities building with adjacent sculpture courtyard. All are temperature, humidity controlled & secured by alarms; Average Annual Attendance: 4,100
Income: Financed by university & private donations
Special Subjects: Architecture, Drawings, Graphics, Painting-American, Photography, Prints, American Indian Art, African Art, Ceramics, Woodcuts, Etchings & Engravings, Landscapes, Afro-American Art, Decorative Arts, Collages, Portraits, Eskimo Art, Furniture, Jade, Oriental Art, Asian Art, Silver, Historical Material
Collections: Contemporary art; Student & faculty works since 1950; Works on paper since 1750
Exhibitions: Excavating the Seventies Parts 1 & 2
Publications: Exhibit catalogs
Activities: Lect open to pub, 2 vis lectrs per year; gallery talks; tours; competitions; awards; scholarships offered; individual and original objects of art lent to qualified mus & galleries; book traveling exhibitions; mus shop sells gallery publications & posters

DAPHNE

M   **AMERICAN SPORT ART MUSEUM AND ARCHIVES,** One Academy Dr, Daphne, AL 36526-7055. Tel 251-626-3303; Fax 251-621-2527; Elec Mail asama@ussa.edu; Internet Home Page Address: asama.org; *CEO* Dr Thomas P Rosandich; *Cur* Robert Zimlich; *Security* Josh Walker
Open Mon - Fri 9 AM - 4 PM; No admis fee; Estab 1984; dedicated to the preservation of sports history, art & literature; over 12,000 pieces of fine sport art in all mediums; Average Annual Attendance: 5,000
Special Subjects: Afro-American Art, American Indian Art, Marine Painting, Collages, Photography, Pottery, Painting-American, Prints, Bronzes, Painting-European, Sculpture, Posters, Calligraphy, Painting-Spanish, Painting-Australian
Collections: bronze sculptures; paintings; murals; lithographs; photography; prints; posters
Exhibitions: Wyland-Sport Art for the Green Olympics original artwork on display-ongoing

Publications: The Academy; The Sport Journal-www.thesportjournal.org; The Sport Digest-www.thesportdigest.com
Activities: Classes for adults & children; lect open to pub; guided tours; competitions; Academy's Sport Artist of the Year-see www.asama.org; originates traveling exhibitions to universities; mus shop sells books, original art, reproductions, prints, clothing

DECATUR

M   **JOHN C CALHOUN STATE COMMUNITY COLLEGE,** Art Gallery, 6250 Hwy 31 Decatur, AL 35609; PO Box 2216, Decatur, AL 35609-2216. Tel 256-306-2500, 306-2695; Fax 256-306-2925; *Pres* Dr Richard Carpenter; *Dept Chair* John Colagross; *Art Instr* Katherine Vaughn
Open weekdays 9AM-5PM, special weekend openings; No admis fee; Estab 1965 to provide temporary exhibits of fine art during the school year for the benefit of the surrounding three county area & for the students & faculty of the col; Located in a fine arts building completed June 1979, the gallery has 105 linear ft of carpeted wall space with adjustable incandescent track lighting & fluorescent general lights in a controlled & well-secured environment; Average Annual Attendance: 20,000
Special Subjects: Graphics
Collections: Permanent collection consists of graphics collection as well as selected student & faculty works
Exhibitions: Student Art Exhibit; Student Photographs; Faculty Exhibit
Publications: Announcements; exhibition catalogs
Activities: Classes for adults; lect open to public, 3 vis lectrs per yr; gallery talks; tours; competitions with awards; scholarships and fels offered; individual paintings & original objects of art lent to museums, galleries & college art departments; lending collection contains 40 original art works & 85 original prints; book traveling exhibitions, biannually

DOTHAN

M   **WIREGRASS MUSEUM OF ART,** 126 Museum Ave, Dothan, AL 36303-4802; PO Box 1624, Dothan, AL 36302. Tel 334-794-3871; Fax 334-792-9035; Elec Mail director@wiregrassmuseum.org; Internet Home Page Address: www.wiregrassmuseum.org; *Exec Dir* Susan Robertson; *Pres* Harry Hall; *Dir Community Rels* Deidre Frith; *Spec Events Mng* Holly Roberts; *Assoc Cur* Alison Beeson
Open Tues - Sat 10 AM - 5 PM, cl Mon & Sun; No Admis fee; Estab 1988 to provide exhibits & educational programs; Seven galleries & children's hands-on gallery; Average Annual Attendance: 25,000; Mem: 850; dues $25 - $3000
Income: $250,000 (financed by mem, city appropriation, special events & fees)
Special Subjects: Drawings, Etchings & Engravings, Landscapes, Glass, Painting-American, Prints, Silver, Woodcuts, Graphics, Latin American Art, Painting-American, Photography, Prints, Sculpture, Watercolors, Costumes, Ceramics, Folk Art, Pottery, Woodcarvings, Afro-American Art, Decorative Arts, Collages, Portraits, Glass, Jewelry, Porcelain, Juvenile Art, Mosaics, Stained Glass, Reproductions
Collections: 19th & 20th century works on paper, decorative arts, paintings & sculpture
Publications: Sketches, bi-monthly newsletter
Activities: Classes for adults & children; docent training; lect open to public, gallery talks, tours; mus shop sells books, original art, reproductions & prints

FAIRHOPE

A   **EASTERN SHORE ART ASSOCIATION, INC,** Eastern Shore Art Center, 401 Oak St, Fairhope, AL 36532. Tel 334-928-2228; Fax 334-928-5188; Elec Mail esac@easternshoreartcenter.com; Internet Home Page Address: www.easternshoreartcenter.com; *Registrar* Sheri Vanche; *Pub Rels Coordr* Charlene Patterson; *Spec Events* Jane Bostrom; *ABC Project Dir* Nancy Raia; *Develop Dir* Marty Albritton
Open Mon - Fri 10 AM - 4 PM, Sat 10 AM - 2 PM, cl Sun, New Years Day, Thanksgiving & Christmas; No admis fee; Estab 1954 to increase enjoyment of participation in arts; Four galleries change monthly, a fifth gallery is for members only. Maintains library; Average Annual Attendance: 12,000; Mem: 1760
Income: Fundraising, classes, workshops & two outdoor shows
Library Holdings: Book Volumes 700; Clipping Files; Exhibition Catalogs; Memorabilia; Original Art Works; Pamphlets
Collections: Herman Bischoff, drawings, oils & watercolors; Maria Martinez, pottery; Emily Woodward Collection; contemporary American paintings from Gulf coast area; primarily southern artist
Exhibitions: Rotating exhibits monthly
Publications: Monthly newsletter; Yearbook
Activities: Educ prog; classes for adults & children; lects open to pub; concerts quarterly; gallery talks; tours; competitions with awards; schols; outreach educational prog arranges gallery tours, slide progs & portable exhibits; original art lent to local bus; mus shop sells original art & prints

FAYETTE

M   **CITY OF FAYETTE, ALABAMA,** Fayette Art Museum, 530 N Temple Ave, Fayette, AL 35555. Tel 205-932-8727; Fax 205-932-8727; Elec Mail jackblack@froglevel.net; *Bd Chmn & Cur* Jack Black; *Asst Cur* Kathy Stoner
Open Mon - Fri 9AM-noon & 1PM-4PM; No admis fee; Estab 1969 to offer on continuous basis exhibits of visual arts free to the pub; All facilities are at Fayette Civic Center: six multi-purpose galleries, seven folk art galleries plus lobby & corridors; 1200 running ft of exhibition space; Average Annual Attendance: 38,000
Income: Financed by city appropriation & Annual Art Festival
Purchases: Very limited purchases of paintings & sculpture
Library Holdings: Auction Catalogs; Audio Tapes; Book Volumes; Cassettes; Memorabilia
Special Subjects: Drawings, Graphics, Painting-American, Sculpture, Watercolors, African Art, Textiles, Folk Art, Primitive art, Woodcarvings, Woodcuts,

Landscapes, Afro-American Art, Portraits, Painting-Canadian, Metalwork, Miniatures, Painting-Australian

Collections: 3,700 paintings, 2,600 by Lois Wilson, a former resident; others by local folk artists Jimmy Lee Sudduth, Benjamin Perkins, Fred Webster, Sybil Gibson, Margarette Guinther & Braxton Ponder

Exhibitions: Permanent gallery for Jimmy Lee Sudduth (folk art); Rev Benjamin Perkins (folk art); Fred Webster & Sybil Gibson

Publications: Souls Grown Deep

Activities: Educ prog varies; lects open to pub; gallery talks; tours; individual paintings & original objects of art lent to museums & galleries; originate traveling exhibs to qualified museums

GADSDEN

M **GADSDEN MUSEUM OF FINE ARTS, INC,** Gadsden Museum of Art and History, 515 Broad St, Gadsden, AL 35901-3719. Tel 256-546-7365; Elec Mail museum@cityofgadsden.com; Internet Home Page Address: www.gadsdenmuseum.com; *Dir* Steve Temple; *Graphics Dir* Dan Hampton; *Exec Asst* Ginny Cooper; *Educ Dir* Elaine Campbell
Open Mon - Sat 10 AM - 4 PM, also open first Fri of month 4 - 8 PM; No admis fee; Estab 1965 to promote, foster, & preserve the collection of paintings, sculpture, artifacts & antiques; 8,000 sq ft; Average Annual Attendance: 10,000; Mem: 75; dues individual $25, family $50

Income: Financed by mem, city & local government & grants

Library Holdings: Book Volumes; Clipping Files; Framed Reproductions; Maps; Memorabilia; Original Art Works; Original Documents; Photographs; Prints; Records; Reproductions; Sculpture

Special Subjects: Folk Art, Historical Material, Landscapes, Glass, Furniture, Porcelain, Portraits, Silver, Woodcuts, Maps, Sculpture, Graphics, Photography, Prints, Watercolors, Pottery, Woodcarvings

Collections: Snelgrove Historical Collection; Fowler Collection (paintings, sculpture & porcelain)

Exhibitions: Quilt exhibit; antique radios; annual juried art show; Alabama's Finest

Activities: Classes for adults & children; workshops; lect open to public, 500 vis lectrs per year; competitions with awards; mus shop sells books, original art, reproductions & prints

HANCEVILLE

M **WALLACE STATE COMMUNITY COLLEGE,** Evelyn Burrow Museum, 801 Main St NW, Hanceville, AL 35077-5462; PO Box 2000, Hanceville, AL 35077-2000. Tel 256-352-8457; Fax 256-352-8314; Elec Mail donny.wilson@wallacestate.edu; Internet Home Page Address: www.burrowmuseum.org; *Dir* Donny Wilson
Open Tues - Fri 9 AM - 5 PM, Sat 10 AM - 2 PM; No admis fee; Decorative arts from Victorian era to modern times

Special Subjects: Decorative Arts, Ceramics, Glass, Furniture, Pottery, Bronzes, Sculpture, Religious Art, Portraits, Porcelain

Collections: porcelain; pottery; period furnishings; fine art; bronzes; cut glass

Activities: Lect open to pub; gallery talks; tours

HUNTSVILLE

A **THE HUNTSVILLE ART LEAGUE (HAL),** Gallery & Visual Arts Center, 3005 L and N Dr SW Ste 2, Huntsville, AL 35801-5300. Tel 256-534-3860; Elec Mail mail@huntsvilleartsleague.org; Internet Home Page Address: www.huntsvilleartsleague.org; *Educ Dir & Office Mgr* S Renee Prasil; *Gallery Dir* Walt Schumacher
Open Mon - Fri 10 AM - 6 PM, Sat noon - 4PM; No admis fee; Estab 1957. The League is a nonprofit organization dedicated to promoting & stimulating the appreciation of the visual arts; Circ 200; 70 local artists exhibiting, all mediums, special exhibitions; Average Annual Attendance: 6,000; Mem: 295; dues vary (art or educ interest); meetings held every 2nd Tues of each month

Income: Financed by mem, commissions, grants

Library Holdings: Auction Catalogs; Book Volumes; Clipping Files; Memorabilia; Periodical Subscriptions

Exhibitions: Unique Views); Annual juried show; rotate art exhibits every month; workshops

Publications: Newsletter on activities & exhibition opportunities in the Southeast, monthly; mem books

Activities: Classes for adults & children; docent training; workshops; gallery talks; tours; sponsoring of competitions; schols; lect open to public, 12 vis lectrs per year; competitions; tours; talks, demos & classes for various at-risk or underserved population; individual paintings & original objects of art leased to banks, restaurants, theaters; lending collection contains original art works, original prints, paintings, photographs, sculpture; organize traveling exhibs to various areas locally; sales shop sells original art, reproductions, prints, jewelry, pottery, fiber arts, small hand made art objects

M **HUNTSVILLE MUSEUM OF ART,** 300 Church St S, Huntsville, AL 35801-4910. Tel 256-535-4350; Fax 256-532-1743; Elec Mail info@hsvmuseum.org; Internet Home Page Address: www.hsvmuseum.org; *Dir Cur Affairs* Peter J Baldaia; *Cur Colls & Exhibs* David Reyes; *CFO* Debbie Higdon; *Pres & CEO* Clayton Bass; *Deputy Dir* Carolyn Faraci; *Mus Academy Dir* Laura Smith; *Communs Mgr* Jenny Lane; *Security Supvr* Linda Berry
Open Tues - Sat 11 AM - 4 PM, Thurs until 8 PM, Sun 1-4 PM; Admis adults $8, military, seniors 60+, students w/ID, military & educators $7, children 6-11 $4, mems & children under 6 free; group rates available; Estab 1970; 2 galleries & a reception area; Average Annual Attendance: 63,000; Mem: 1200; dues student $20, individual $35, family $60, friend $150, sponsor $300, patron $600, benefactor $1,200, president's circle $2,500

Income: $1,000,000 (financed by mem, city appropriation, grants & support groups)

Purchases: $25,000

Special Subjects: Painting-American, Photography, Prints, Sculpture, Watercolors

Collections: American art, 1700-present, including paintings & works on paper; local & regional art; African art; Oriental art

Exhibitions: Annual Youth Art Month & Holiday Celebrations Exhibitions

Publications: Brochures; catalogs, occasionally; Museum Calendar, quarterly

Activities: Classes for adults & children; internships; docent training; Partnership in Art Educ prog; lects open to pub, 3-4 vis lectrs per yr; concerts; gallery talks; tours; competitions with awards; collection loan prog; book traveling exhibs 8-10 per yr; originate traveling exhibs

L **Reference Library,** 300 Church St S, Huntsville, AL 35801-4910. Tel 256-535-4350; Fax 256-532-1743; Elec Mail info@hsvmuseum.org; Internet Home Page Address: www.hsvmuseum.org; *Curatorial Affairs Dir* Peter J Baldaia; *Dir* Christopher Madkour; *Develop Dir* Amy Cornelius
Open Wed - Fri & Sat 11 AM - 4 PM, Thurs 11 AM - 8 PM, Sun 1 - 4 PM; Admis adults $10, children 6-11 $3, free to members & children under 6, discount to seniors over 60, military, students with proper ID & people in groups of 10 or more; Estab 1970 to bring art & people together; 22,000 sq ft of gallery space in 13 galleries; Average Annual Attendance: 100,000; Mem: 3200; dues family $70

Income: Memberships, corporate underwriting, city funding, grants

Library Holdings: Book Volumes 3800; CD-ROMs 5-10; Clipping Files; Exhibition Catalogs 2000; Pamphlets; Periodical Subscriptions 20; Slides; Video Tapes 25

Special Subjects: Decorative Arts, Photography, Etchings & Engravings, Graphic Arts, Sculpture, Ceramics, Crafts, Bronzes, Glass, Metalwork, Miniatures, Oriental Art, Pottery, Antiquities-Greek, Architecture

Collections: 19th & 20th century American art with an emphasis on the region of the South; Asian art; African art; postwar graphics; Sellars Collection of Art by American Women

Exhibitions: Biennial Red Clay Survey Exhibition, southern contemporary art; Encounters solo exhibitions of contemporary southern art; Permanent collection exhibitions; travelling exhibitions

Publications: Family Gallery Guides, exhib catalogues

Activities: Classes for adults & children; docent training; travel prog for members; outreach into classroom; lects open to pub, lects for members only; 2 vis lectrs per yr; concerts; gallery talks; tours; competitions with awards; schols offered; 4 book traveling exhibs per yr; originate traveling exhibs regionally & nationally; mus shop sells books, original art, reproductions, prints

M **UNIVERSITY OF ALABAMA AT HUNTSVILLE,** Union Grove Gallery & University Center Gallery, Roberts Hall, Room 313, Huntsville, AL 35899. Tel 256-890-6114; Fax 256-824-6438; Elec Mail art@uah.edu; *Gallery Adminr* Kristy From; *Staff Asst* Marylyn Coffey
Open Mon - Fri 12:30 - 4:30 PM; No admis fee; Estab 1975; An intimate & small renovated chapel with a reserved section for exhibits located in the University Center; Average Annual Attendance: 1,800

Income: Financed by admin

Special Subjects: Drawings, Painting-American, Photography, Prints, Sculpture

Exhibitions: Contemporary artwork (US & international); Annual Juried Exhibition

Activities: Lects open to pub, 7-10 vis lectrs per yr; gallery talks; competitions with awards; individual paintings & original objects of art lent; book traveling exhibs 3 per yr; originate traveling exhibs

MADISON

M **CLAY HOUSE MUSEUM,** 621 Eastview Dr, Madison, AL 35758-7826. Tel 256-325-1018; Elec Mail BrewerR@hiwaay.net
Open by appointment

MOBILE

M **HISTORY MUSEUM OF MOBILE,** (Museum of Mobile) 111 S Royal St, Mobile, AL 36602-3101; PO Box 2068, Mobile, Al 36652-2068. Tel 251-208-7569; Fax 251-208-7686; Elec Mail museum@cityofmobile.org; Internet Home Page Address: www.museumofmobile.com; *Asst Dir* Sheila Flanagan; *Researcher* Charles Torrey; *Cur History* Scotty Kirkland; *Dir* David Alsobrook; *Cur Exhibits* Jacob Laurence; *Cur Colls* Holley Jansen; *Events Coordr* Ellie Skinner; *Cur Educ* Jennifer Fondren; *Registrar* Lori McDuffie; *Mus Relations Officer* Jacqlyn Kirkland; *Fiscal Officer* Kathlyn Scott; *Office Asst* Hazel Mims; *Office Asst* Lashey Pleasure
Open Tues - Sat 9 AM - 5 PM, Sun 1 - 5 PM, cl some city holidays; Admis adults $7, seniors $6, students $5, first Sun of month free; Estab 1964 to interpret Mobile's history; A 21st Century state of the history museum; five exhibit experiences offer people of all ages the chance to learn about more than 300 yrs of Mobile history; permanent exhibit presents survey of history of Mobile area; Average Annual Attendance: 66,000; Mem: 400; dues $15 - $10,000

Income: Financed by city appropriation

Library Holdings: Book Volumes; Clipping Files; Framed Reproductions; Manuscripts; Maps; Memorabilia; Original Art Works; Original Documents; Other Holdings; Pamphlets; Periodical Subscriptions; Photographs; Prints; Records; Sculpture; Slides; Video Tapes

Special Subjects: Archaeology, Ceramics, Decorative Arts, Manuscripts, Silver, Historical Material, Maps, Coins & Medals

Collections: CSS Hunley; Queens of Mobile Mardi Gras; Admiral Raphael Semmes Collection: incl Confederate presentation sword, along with a presentation cased revolver & accessories, books, paintings, documents, personal papers & ship models; Mardi Gras Gallery; 80,000 items reflecting the entire span of the history of Mobile

Publications: Exhibition & collection catalogs

Activities: Pub progs for adults & children; docent training; lects open to pub; 12+ lects per yr; galley talks; tours; concerts; sponsored competitions; Volunteer Mobile Inc Heart of Gold 2001 award; Main St Mobile's Leadership Achievement award; Herstory award; original objects of art lent to other mus; originate book traveling exhibs 1-4 per yr; organize traveling exhibs to Eudora Welty & to various venues; mus shop sells books, gifts, jewelry, toys, clothing, magnets, original art, reproductions, prints, Mobile mementoes & unique gifts; evening spec event rentals, birthday parties, daytime event space

L **Reference Library,** 111 S Royal St, Mobile, AL 36602-3101. Tel 334-208-7569; Fax 334-208-7686; Internet Home Page Address: www.museumofmobile.com; *Dir* George Ewert
Estab 1964; For reference only
Library Holdings: Book Volumes 3000; Clipping Files; Memorabilia; Original Art Works; Periodical Subscriptions 12; Photographs; Prints; Sculpture; Slides

M **Carlen House,** 54 Carlen St, Mobile, AL 36606; 111 S Royal St, Mobile, AL 36602. Tel 251-208-7569; Internet Home Page Address: www.museumofmobile.com; *Dir* George Ewert
Open Mon - Sat 10 AM - 5 PM, Sun 1 - 5 PM; Admis adults $5, seniors $4, students $2; Estab 1970 to preserve an authentic representation of Southern architecture; The Carlen House is an important representation of Mobile's unique contribution to American regional architecture. It is a fine example of the Creole Cottage as it evolved from the French Colonial form & was adapted for early American use. The house was erected in 1842; furnishings are from the collections of the Museum of the City of Mobile & are typical of a house of that period; Average Annual Attendance: 30,000
Income: Financed by city appropriation
Activities: Lects open to pub; group tours are conducted by guides in period costumes who emphasize aspects of everyday life in Mobile in the mid-nineteenth century. The making of material is demonstrated by the guide who cards wool, spins fibers & weaves cloth; individual paintings & original objects of art lent to other mus; sales shop sells books, slides & souvenirs

M **MOBILE MUSEUM OF ART,** 4850 Museum Dr, Mobile, AL 36608-1917. Tel 251-208-5200; Fax 251-208-5201; Elec Mail prichelson@mobilemuseumofart.com; Internet Home Page Address: www.mobilemuseumofart.com; Cable FAMOS; *Deputy Dir* Marlene Buckner; *Chief Cur* Paul W Richelson, PhD; *Dir Fin* Tony Potapenko; *Cur Exhibs* Donan Klooz; *Cur Coll* Kurtis Thomas; *Cur Educ* Howard McPhail; *Cur Educ* Kimbrough Wood; *Dir* Deborah Velders; *Events Coordr* Meredith Ivy; *Vol Coordr* Christina Chom
Open Mon - Sat 10 AM - 5 PM, Sun 1 - 5 PM; Admis adults $10, seniors $8, students $6; Estab 1964 to foster the appreciation of art & provide art educ programs for the community; Circ Reference non-circulating art libraries; Primarily American 19th & 20th Century, contemporary crafts; Mem: Patron $1,000, supporting $500, assoc $250, friend $150, family $75, individual $45
Income: Financed by mem, city appropriation & state grants, county & foundations
Purchases: $26,000
Library Holdings: Auction Catalogs; Book Volumes; Exhibition Catalogs; Periodical Subscriptions; Slides
Special Subjects: American Indian Art, Drawings, Collages, Photography, Porcelain, Portraits, Pottery, Painting-American, Prints, Silver, Textiles, Woodcuts, Sculpture, Graphics, Watercolors, American Western Art, Bronzes, African Art, Religious Art, Ceramics, Crafts, Folk Art, Woodcarvings, Etchings & Engravings, Landscapes, Afro-American Art, Decorative Arts, Painting-European, Posters, Eskimo Art, Painting-Canadian, Furniture, Glass, Jewelry, Oriental Art, Asian Art, Antiquities-Byzantine, Marine Painting, Metalwork, Painting-British, Painting-Dutch, Painting-French, Painting-Italian, Islamic Art, Antiquities-Roman, Painting-Australian, Enamels
Collections: American Crafts; 19th & 20th century American & European paintings, sculpture, prints, & decorative arts; Chinese ceramics, European paintings & sculpture; 17th to 20th century; Southern furniture; 1930s - 1940s paintings & graphics; International Contemporary Glass Collection; Wellington Collection of Wood Engravings
Publications: Fine Lines Newsletter, 4 per year; Richard Jolley & Tommie Rush: A Life in Glass
Activities: Classes for adults & children; docent training; lects open to pub, 3 lectrs per yr; gallery talks, tours, competitions with awards; scholarships offered; individual paintings & objects of art lent; 3 traveling exhibs per year; originates 8 traveling exhibs, circulating Southeastern Art Museums; mus shop sells books, original art, jewelry

L **Library,** 4850 Museum Dr, Mobile, AL 36608-1917. Tel 251-208-5200; Fax 251-208-5201; Elec Mail prichelson@mobilemuseumofart.com; Internet Home Page Address: www.MobileMuseumofArt.com; *Dir* Deborah Velders; *Chief Cur* Paul W Richelson; *Deputy Dir* Marlene Buckner; *Cur Educ* Kim Wood; *Cur Collections* Kurtis Thomas; *Cur Exhibs* Donan Klooz; *Cur Educ* Howard McPhail
Open Mon - Sat 10 AM - 5 PM, Sun 1 PM - 5 PM; Admis $10 general plus additional for special exhibitions; Estab 1963; For reference only; Average Annual Attendance: 90,000; Mem: 3000
Income: City of Mobile; pvt 501(c)3
Purchases: American Art, craft, Berbizan
Library Holdings: Auction Catalogs; Book Volumes 1800; Clipping Files; DVDs; Exhibition Catalogs; Framed Reproductions; Pamphlets; Periodical Subscriptions 20; Photographs; Prints; Reproductions; Slides
Special Subjects: Decorative Arts, Painting-American, Painting-European, Crafts, Asian Art
Publications: Numerous
Activities: Classes for adults and children; dramatic progs; docent training; film; lects open to public; lects for mems only; 3 vis lectrs per yr; gallery talks; tours; sponsoring of competitions; 5 book traveling exhibs per yr; originates traveling exhibs to Southern art museums; mus shop sells books

L **UNIVERSITY OF SOUTH ALABAMA,** Ethnic American Slide Library, 307 N University Blvd, Dept Arts & Art History Mobile, AL 36608-3074. Tel 251-460-6101; Fax 334-414-8294; *Chmn* Larry L Simpson
Open daily 8 AM - 5 PM; No admis fee; Estab for the acquisition of slides of works produced by Afro-American, Mexican-American & Native American artists & the distribution of duplicate slides of these works to educational institutions & individuals engaged in research
Library Holdings: Slides
Collections: 19th & 20th centuries ethnic American art works in ceramics, drawing, painting, photography, printmaking, sculpture
Publications: Slide Catalog

MONTEVALLO

M **UNIVERSITY OF MONTEVALLO,** The Gallery, Sta 6400, Art Dept Montevallo, AL 35115. Tel 205-665-6400; Fax 205-665-6383; Elec Mail terrell@montevallo.edu; Internet Home Page Address: www.montevallo.edu/art; *Gallery Dir* Dr Kelly Wacker
Open Mon - Fri 10 AM - 4 PM; No admis fee; Estab Sept 1977 to supply students & pub with high quality contemporary art; The gallery is 27 x 54 ft with track lighting; no windows; Average Annual Attendance: 3,000
Income: Financed by state appropriation & regular dept budget
Collections: WPA Prints
Exhibitions: Rotating exhibits
Publications: High quality catalogs & posters
Activities: Management classes; lects open to pub, 4-5 vis lectrs per yr; gallery talks; originate traveling exhibs

MONTGOMERY

M **ALABAMA DEPARTMENT OF ARCHIVES & HISTORY,** Museum of Alabama, 624 Washington Ave, Montgomery, AL 36130-3003. Tel 334-242-4435; Fax 334-240-3433; Elec Mail debbie.pendleton@archives.alabama.gov; Internet Home Page Address: www.archives.albama.gov; *Asst Dir Government Records* Tracey Berezansky; *Asst Dir Pub Svcs* Debbie Pendleton; *Dir* Edwin C Bridges; *Cur Educ* Susan Dubose; *Cur Colls* Bob Bradley; *Mus Shop Mgr* Allison Gore; *Asst Dir Admin* Steve Murray
Open Mon - Sat 8:30 AM - 4:30 PM; No admis fee; Estab 1901; Reference only; Average Annual Attendance: 35,000
Income: Financed by state appropriation
Special Subjects: Archaeology, Furniture, Photography, Portraits, Painting-American, Silver, Textiles, Manuscripts, Sculpture, American Indian Art, Decorative Arts, Historical Material, Maps, Miniatures, Dioramas, Period Rooms, Military Art
Collections: Early Alabama Indians; Hands On Gallery & Grandma's Attic (for children of all ages); Military Room; the 19th Century Room; Selma to Montgomery March Photographic exhibit; Archives Sampler Room
Exhibitions: History of Alabama
Activities: Classes for adults; docent training; lects open to pub, 15 vis lectrs per yr; tours; exten dept serves Records Retention facility for state government records; individual paintings & original objects of art lent to museums within state, state capitol, government offices & Governor's Mansion; lending collection contains paintings; sales shop sells books, Civil War & Civil Rights related materials, reproduced arrowheads, jewelry & posters

L **Library,** 624 Washington Ave, Montgomery, AL 36130-0100. Tel 334-353-4712; Fax 334-240-3433; Elec Mail sherrie.hamil@archives.alabama.gov; Internet Home Page Address: www.archives.alabama.gov; *Archival Librn* Dr Norwood Kerr
Open Mon - Sat 8:30 AM - 4:30 PM, reference room cl Mon; No admis fee; Estab 1901; American Indian gallery, Military & Flag galleries, 19th century galleries & Hands On gallery with Grandma's Attic & Discovery Boxes; portraits and sculpture; photographic collections; Average Annual Attendance: 50,000; Mem: Friends of the Alabama Archives
Library Holdings: Audio Tapes; Book Volumes 32,000; Cassettes; Clipping Files; Fiche; Filmstrips; Lantern Slides; Manuscripts; Maps; Memorabilia; Motion Pictures; Original Art Works; Original Documents; Pamphlets; Photographs; Prints; Records; Reels; Sculpture; Video Tapes
Special Subjects: Manuscripts, Maps, Historical Material
Collections: Alabama Subjects 1700-1989; Political & Social Events; State Government Records
Activities: Classes for adults & children; docent training; lects open to pub, 12 vis lectrs per yr; tours; sponsoring of competitions; mus shop sells books, reproductions, jewelry

AMERICAN SOCIETY OF PORTRAIT ARTISTS (ASOPA)
For further information, see National and Regional Organizations

M **MONTGOMERY MUSEUM OF FINE ARTS,** One Museum Dr, Montgomery, AL 36117; PO Box 230819, Montgomery, AL 36123-0819. Tel 334-240-4333; Fax 334-240-4384; Elec Mail museuminfo@mmfa.org; Internet Home Page Address: www.mmfa.org; *Dir* Mark M Johnson; *Asst Dir Opers* Steve Shuemake; *Develop Officer* Courtney Armstrong; *Dir Mktg & Pub Rels* Lara Lewis; *Sr Cur Art* Margaret Lynne Ausfeld; *Cur Art* Michael Panhorst; *Registrar* Pamela Bransford; *Asst Cur Educ* Donna Pickens; *Librn* Alice Carter; *Develop Asst* Jennifer Pope; *Spec Events Coordr* Tisha Rhodes; *Museum Shop Mgr* Pat Tomberlin; *Vol Coordr* Willette Vaughan; *Preparator & Designer* Jeff Dutton; *Bd Pres* Gordon Martin
Open Tues - Sat 10 AM - 5 PM, Thurs evening until 9 PM, Sun Noon - 5 PM; No admis fee; Estab 1930 to generally promote the cultural artistic & higher educ life of the city of Montgomery by all methods that may be properly pursued by a mus or art gallery; Mus housed in 73,000 sq ft facility located on 35 acres in landscaped park, adjacent to the Alabama Shakespeare festival. Galleries occupy lower & upper levels of two story neo-palladian structure. An educ wing includes Artworks a 4,400 sq ft hands-on, interactive gallery & studios. The Weil Graphics Arts Study Center provides an environment for small specialized exhibitions & educational programs emphasizing works of art on paper. It is designed as a conference space with av & computer resources to serve advanced school groups & seminar participants. 240 seat auditorium; Average Annual Attendance: 160,000; Mem: 1700; dues dir circle $1,200-$5,000, patron $150-$1,199, general $45-$149; ann meeting in Oct
Income: Financed by mem, city & county appropriations & grants
Library Holdings: Auction Catalogs; Book Volumes; Clipping Files; Exhibition Catalogs; Pamphlets; Periodical Subscriptions; Photographs; Slides; Video Tapes
Special Subjects: Drawings, Graphics, Painting-American, Photography, Prints, Sculpture, Watercolors, Folk Art, Woodcuts, Etchings & Engravings, Landscapes, Decorative Arts, Portraits, Glass, Porcelain, Juvenile Art
Collections: American & European works on paper; Contemporary graphics & other works on paper by artists living in the South; decorative arts; master prints

of the 15th - 21st centuries; 1727 prints & 576 paintings; paintings by American artists from early 19th century through the present; 41 paintings from the Blount Collection of American Art; Contemporary American self-taught art
Publications: Annual Report; On Exhibit quarterly magazine; exhibitions catalogs for selected shows
Activities: Classes for adults & children; docent training; lects open to pub, 20 vis lectrs per yr; films; concerts; gallery talks; tours; schols & fels offered; individual paintings & original objects of art lent to galleries which meet AAM standards for security & preservation; book traveling exhibs 12 per yr; originate traveling exhibs, national & international; mus shop sells books, original art, reproductions, prints & gift items

L **Library,** One Museum Dr, Montgomery, AL 36117; PO Box 230819, Montgomery, AL 36123-0819. Tel 334-240-4333; Fax 334-240-4384; Internet Home Page Address: www.mmfa.org; *Dir* Mark M Johnson; *Librn* Alice T Carter; *Colls Information Specialist* Sarah Puckitt; *Cur Art* Jennifer Jankauskas; *Cur Art* Dr Michael Panhorst; *Cur Art* Margaret Lynne Ausfeld; *Deputy Dir Develop* Jill Barry; *Develop Officer* Kathryn Trumble; *Asst Dir Opers* Steve Shuemake; *Dirk Mktg & Pub Relations* Lara Lewis; *Cur Educ* Tim Brown; *Asst Cur Educ* Donna Pickens; *Asst Cur Educ* Alice Novak
Open Tues - Sat 10 AM - 5 PM, Thurs 10 AM - 9 PM, Sun noon - 5 PM; No admis fee; Estab 1975 to assist the staff & community with reliable art research material; Circ Non-circ; For reference
Income: Financed by City of Montgomery & Mus Assoc
Library Holdings: Auction Catalogs; Book Volumes 5000; Clipping Files; Exhibition Catalogs; Pamphlets; Periodical Subscriptions 25; Photographs; Prints; Slides; Video Tapes
Activities: Classes for adults & children; docent training; lects open to pub; gallery talks; tours; mus shop sells books & original art

M **TUSKEGEE INSTITUTE NATIONAL HISTORIC SITE,** George Washington Carver & The Oaks, 1212 W Montgomery Rd Montgomery, AL 36083; PO Drawer 10, Tuskegee Institute, AL 36087. Tel 334-727-6390; Fax 334-727-4597; Internet Home Page Address: www.nps.gov.tuin; *Acting Park Supt* Brenda Caldwell; *Mus Technician* Mike Jolly
Open 9 AM - 5 PM, cl New Year's, Thanksgiving & Christmas; No admis fee; Original mus estab 1941 & National Park in 1976 to interpret life & work of George Washington Carver & the history of Tuskegee Institute; Maintains small reference library; Average Annual Attendance: 50,000
Income: Financed by federal funds
Collections: Artifacts interpreting life & work of George Washington Carver & history of Tuskegee Institute; life & contributions of Booker T Washington
Exhibitions: Exhibitions of local artwork 6-8 time per yr
Activities: Lects open to pub; gallery talks; guided tours; sponsor competitions with awards; individual & original objects of art lent to other parks & museums; lending limited to photos, films, slides & reproductions; book traveling exhibs; originate traveling exhibs; sales shop sells books, reproductions, prints & slides

NORTHPORT

M **KENTUCK MUSEUM ASSOCIATION, INC.,** (Kentuck Museum & Art Center) Kentuck Art Center & Festival of the Arts, 503 Main Ave, Northport, AL 35476-4483. Tel 205-758-1257; Fax 205-758-1258; Elec Mail kentuck@kentuck.org; Internet Home Page Address: www.kentuck.org; *Exec Dir* Shweta Gamble; *Asst Dir* Emily Leigh; *Prog Mgr* Michaela Lewellyn; *Opers Mgr* Anden Houben
Open Tues - Fri 9 AM - 5 PM, Sat 10 AM - 4:30 PM, cl Sun; No admis fee; Estab 1971 to perpetuate the arts, empower artists & engage the community; Exhibs open ea month in the Main Avenue Gallery & the Clarke Gallery; total 24+ ea yr; Average Annual Attendance: 12,000 festival; 6,000 art ctr; Mem: 350; dues $30-$1,000
Income: $399,950 (financed by mem, city & state appropriations, rental of studios, workshops, shop sales, festival ticket sales & booth rentals & other proceeds, corporate sponsorships)
Exhibitions: Exhibits change monthly
Activities: Classes for adults & children; lect open to public, 6 vis lectrs per year; competitions & awards; sales shop sells books, original art, crafts

SELMA

M **STURDIVANT MUSEUM ASSOCIATION,** (Sturdivant Hall) Sturdivant Museum, 713 Mabry St, Selma, AL 36701-5521; PO Box 1205, Selma, AL 36702-1205. Tel 334-872-5626; Fax 334-872-5626; Elec Mail info@sturdivanthall.com; Internet Home Page Address: www.sturdivanthall.com; *Cur* Manera S Searcy; *Cur* Nancy Gantt; *Pres* Anne Knight; *VPres* Carolyn Cox; *Mus Shop Mgr* Patty Debardeleben
Open Tues - Sat 10AM-4PM; Admis adults $5, student $2, children under 6 free; group rates available; Estab 1957 as a mus with emphasis on the historical South. Period furniture of the 1850s in a magnificent architectural edifice built 1852-53; Average Annual Attendance: 10,000; Mem: 350; dues $30 - $1000; annual meeting in Sept
Income: Financed by mem, city & county appropriations, events
Library Holdings: Clipping Files; Manuscripts; Original Art Works; Original Documents; Prints
Special Subjects: Drawings, Etchings & Engravings, Historical Material, Architecture, Flasks & Bottles, Furniture, Porcelain, Silver, Manuscripts, Painting-American, Portraits, Dolls, Period Rooms, Embroidery
Collections: Objects of art; period furniture; textiles; dolls; porcelain
Publications: Brochure
Activities: Lects open to pub; tours; mus shop sells books, reproductions, prints, lamps, silver, linens & gift items

THEODORE

M **BELLINGRATH GARDENS & HOME,** 12401 Bellingrath Gardens Rd, Theodore, AL 36582-8496. Tel 251-973-2217; Fax 251-973-0540; Elec Mail bellingrath@bellingrath.org; Internet Home Page Address: www.bellingrath.org; *Dir Mus* Thomas C McGehee; *Exec Dir* Dr William E Barrick; *Vol Coordr* William Darr
Open daily 8 AM - 5 PM; Admis home & garden $19, children 5-12 $6 garden only $11, children under 5 free admis to home & to garden; Estab 1932 to perpetuate an appreciation of nature & display man-made objects d'art; The gallery houses the world's largest public display of Boehm porcelain & the Bellingrath Home contains priceless antiques; Average Annual Attendance: 200,000
Income: Financed by Foundation & admissions
Special Subjects: Porcelain
Collections: Early-mid 19th Century American antique furnishings from South, silver & crystal; separate Boehm Gallery from Bellingrath Home: porcelains by Meissen, Dresden, Copeland, Capo di Monte, Sevres; Boehm Collection
Activities: Classes for children; tours; lending collection contains kodachromes, motion pictures, slides; sales shop sells books, magazines, prints, reproductions & slides

TOWN CREEK

M **WATERCOLOR SOCIETY OF ALABAMA,** 1571 County Rd 414, Town Creek, AL 35672. Tel 850-981-2619; Fax 205-822-3721; Elec Mail nanetteljones@bellsouth.net; Internet Home Page Address: wsalabama.org; *Pres* Tora Johnson
Call for hours; Admis free; Estab 1940 to promote watercolor painting; Mem: 408; dues $25; annual meeting in Sept
Income: financed by mem & award donations
Publications: Newsletters & prospectus
Activities: Classes for adults; art workshops; lect open to public, 2 vis lectrs per year; gallery talks; competitions with prizes, approx $7,000 for National exhibs & $750 for Alabama showcase

TROY

M **TROY-PIKE CULTURAL ARTS CENTER,** 300 E. Walnut St., Troy, AL 36081. Tel 334-670-2287; *Exec Dir* Richard Metzger
Call for hours
Collections: Paintings & photographs by regional, national & international artists

TUSCALOOSA

A **ARTS & HUMANITIES COUNCIL OF TUSCALOOSA,** (Arts Council of Tuscaloosa County, Inc) Junior League Gallery, 600 Greensboro Ave, Tuscaloosa, AL 35401; PO Box 1117, Tuscaloosa, AL 35403-1117. Tel 205-758-5195; Fax 205-345-2787; Elec Mail director@tuscarts.org; Internet Home Page Address: www.tuscarts.org; *Exec Dir* Pamela Penick; *Educ Dir* Sandy Wolf
Open Mon - Fri 8 AM - 5 PM; No admis fee; Estab 1970 for the develop, promotion & coordination of educational, cultural & artistic activities of the city & county of Tuscaloosa; Offices adjoin historic Bama Theatre; Average Annual Attendance: 3,000; Mem: 500 individual, 40 organization; dues organization $75, individual $50; annual meeting in Oct, meetings quarterly
Income: Financed by mem, city, state & county appropriation
Exhibitions: Jan & Feb: Double Exposure Photography Competition; Feb & March: Visual Art Achievement Award; Nov & Dec: West AL Juried Show
Publications: Arts calendar, monthly newsletter; semi-annual arts magazine, Jubilation
Activities: Dramatic progs; concert series, Bama Fanfare (professional performances for students K - 12); sponsor of educ program called SPECTRA (Special Teaching Resources in the Arts); Bluegrass, Big Bands & More, Cinema Nouveau movie series; gallery talks; tours; competition sponsorship

M **UNIVERSITY OF ALABAMA,** Sarah Moody Gallery of Art, 103 Garland Hall, Tuscaloosa, AL 35487-0270; UA Box 870270, Tuscaloosa, AL 35487-0270. Tel 205-348-5967 (Art Dept); 7007; Fax 205-348-0287; Elec Mail wtdooley@bama.ua.edu; Internet Home Page Address: www.as.ua.edu/art/moody; *Dir* William Dooley; *Exhib Coordr* Vicki Rial
Open Mon - Fri 9 AM - 4:30 PM, Thurs until 8PM ; No admis fee; Estab 1946; Exhibitions of national, regional contemporary art; Average Annual Attendance: 1,000
Income: Financed by the college
Collections: Small collection of paintings, prints, photography, drawings, primarily contemporary
Exhibitions: Exhibits rotate once a month
Publications: Exhibit catalogs
Activities: Lects open to public; 3 vis lectrs per yr; gallery talks; originate traveling exhibs

TUSCUMBIA

A **TENNESSEE VALLEY ART ASSOCIATION,** 511 N Water St, Tuscumbia, AL 35674-1931; PO Box 474, Tuscumbia, AL 35674-0474. Tel 256-383-0533; Fax 256-383-0535; Elec Mail tvaa@comcast.net; Internet Home Page Address: www.tvaa.net; *Exhibit Coordr* Lucie Ayers; *Exec Dir* Mary Settle-Cooney; *Pub Rels & Mem* Mary Jo Parker; *Tech Dir Ritz Theater* Jake Barrow
Open Mon - Fri 9 AM - 5 PM, Sun 1-3PM; Admis varies, call for details; Incorp 1964 to promote the arts in the Tennessee Valley. Building completed 1972; Main Gallery 60 x 40 ft; West Gallery for small exhibits, meetings and arts and crafts classes. Located one block from the birthplace of Helen Keller in Tuscumbia. During the Helen Keller Festival, TVAC sponsors the Arts and Crafts Festival; Average Annual Attendance: 10,000; Mem: Dues patron $500, benefactor $100, family $50, sustaining $30, student $10, individual $20
Income: $300,000 (financed by appropriations, donations, grants & mem)
Collections: Reynolds Collection of Paintings; TVAA Collection
Exhibitions: Exhibition South (paintings, sculpture, prints), annual fall juried art show for mid-south states; Spring Photo Show, annual juried; exhibits feature work by national artists, members & students; handicraft exhibits

Activities: Classes for adults and children; dramatic progs; docent training; class instruction in a variety of arts and crafts; workshops & performances in drama; lects open to pub; concerts; competitions with awards; individual paintings lent; book traveling exhibs; mus shop sells books, reproductions, prints, puppets, jewelry, & stationary

ALASKA

ANCHORAGE

M   ALASKA HERITAGE MUSEUM AT WELLS FARGO, 301 W Northern Lights Blvd, K3212-051 Anchorage, AK 99503-2655. Tel 907-265-2834; Fax 907-265-2860; *Cur* Tom D Bennett
Open Mon - Fri 12 - 4 PM; No admis fee; Average Annual Attendance: 5,000
Special Subjects: American Indian Art, Anthropology, Archaeology, Drawings, Historical Material, Conceptual Art, Gold, Photography, Painting-American, Woodcuts, Manuscripts, Maps, Prints, Sculpture, Watercolors, Ethnology, Primitive art, Eskimo Art, Dolls, Jade, Ivory, Scrimshaw, Coins & Medals
Collections: Alaskan Native cultures; fine art by Alaskan artists
Activities: Educ prog for children; guided tours

M   ALASKA MUSEUM OF NATURAL HISTORY, 201 N Mountain View Dr, Anchorage, AK 99503; 201 N Bragaw, Anchorage, AK 99508. Tel 907-274-2400; Elec Mail webcontact@alaskamuseum.org; Internet Home Page Address: www.alaskamuseum.org; *Exec Dir* Katch Bacheller; *Dir Pub Progs* Christy Fine; *Colls Mgr* Phyllis Callina; *Pres & Cur* Kristine Crossen; *VPres* Stephen Trimble; *Secy & Cur* Ginny Moore; *Cur* David Yesner; *Cur* Anne Pasch
Open Tues - Sat 10 AM - 5 PM; Admis adults $5, children $3; Mission is to study & exhibit natural history materials relating to Alaska's natural history & to promote and develop educational progs which benefit students & enrich the curricula of schools & univs in Alaska. Nonprofit org; Mem: dues Life $1,000; Gift or Reg Mem $30
Special Subjects: Archaeology, Historical Material
Collections: History on the Alaskan Gold Rush; Alaskan rocks, minerals & fossils; Alaska's oldest known dinosaur; Native American cultural artifacts; 11,100 year-old Northern Paleoindian Hunting Camp
Exhibitions: The Dinosaurs of Darkness
Publications: Nunatak, quarterly newsletter
Activities: Group tours; summer camps for children; volunteer activities; lects; mus related items for sale

A   ALASKA WATERCOLOR SOCIETY, PO Box 90714, Anchorage, AK 99509-0714. Tel 907-333-4678; Internet Home Page Address: www.akws.org; *Pres* Bob Winfree; *VPres* Jennie Morris
No admis fee; Estab 1977; Circ 200; Maintains library; Mem: 200; monthly meeting Sept-Jun 2nd Wed of month
Income: Financed by mem
Exhibitions: Bi-annual juried watercolor exhibit at the Anchorage Museum of History & Art
Activities: Workshops; scholarships offered; originate traveling exhibs

M   ANCHORAGE MUSEUM AT RASMUSON CENTER, 625 C St, Anchorage, AK 99501. Tel 907-929-9200; Fax 907-929-9233; Elec Mail museum@anchoragemuseum.org; Internet Home Page Address: www.anchoragemuseum.org; *Dir* James Pepper Henry; *Dir Exhibs* Julie Decker; *Deputy Dir* Suzi Jones; *Advancement Dir* Ann Hale; *Dir Colls* Monica Shah; *Dir Educ & Pub Progs* Monica Garcia
Open May to Sept 9AM-6PM daily, Sept-May Tues-Sat 10AM-6PM, Sun noon-6PM; Admis adults $12, seniors $9, children 3-13 $7, Under 3 free; Estab 1968 to collect & display Alaskan art & artifacts of all periods; to present changing exhibs of art, history & science; Average Annual Attendance: 140,000; Mem: 5,500
Income: $3,000,000
Purchases: $50,000
Library Holdings: Auction Catalogs; Book Volumes; CD-ROMs; Cards; Clipping Files; Compact Disks; DVDs; Exhibition Catalogs; Fiche; Framed Reproductions; Manuscripts; Maps; Memorabilia; Original Documents; Other Holdings; Pamphlets; Periodical Subscriptions; Photographs; Prints; Slides; Video Tapes
Special Subjects: Drawings, Painting-American, Photography, Prints, Sculpture, Watercolors, American Indian Art, Anthropology, Archaeology, Ethnology, Pre-Columbian Art, Textiles, Costumes, Religious Art, Crafts, Primitive art, Etchings & Engravings, Landscapes, Eskimo Art, Dolls, Carpets & Rugs, Historical Material, Ivory, Maps
Exhibitions: Exploration in the North Pacific 1750-1850 Travels; Arctic Transformations: The Jewelry of Denise and Samule Wallace
Publications: Agayuliyararput: Our Way of Making Prayer: The living tradition of Yupik masks (with University of Washington Press); Painting in the North: Alaskan art in the Anchorage Museum of History & Art; exhibition catalogs; monthly newsletters; occasional papers; A Northern Adventure: The Art of Fred Machetanz; Eskimo Drawings; John Hoovere: Art and Life; Sydney Laurence, Painter of the North; Spirit of the North: The Art of Eustace Paul Ziegler; True North: Contemporary Art of the Circumpolar North
Activities: Classes for adults & children; dramatic progs; docent training; lect open to pub; vis lectrs 24-40 per yr; concerts; gallery talks; tours; competitions; awards; individual paintings & original objects of art lent to AAM accredited museums; lending coll contains original art works, original prints, paintings, photographs, sculpture & slides; book traveling exhibs 10 per yr; originate traveling exhibs 2 per yr to 51 AK mus; mus shop sells books, magazines, original art, reproductions, prints, slides, Alaskan Native art, & jewelry
L   Atwood Alaska Resource Center, 625 C St, Anchorage, AK 99501. Tel 907-929-9235; Fax 907-929-9233; Elec Mail resourcecenter@anchoragmuseum.org; Internet Home Page Address: www.anchoragemuseum.org; *Resource Ctr Mgr/Librn* Teressa Williams; *Photo Archivist* Sara Piasecki

Open Tues - Fri 10 AM - 2 PM, Sat by appointment only; No admis fee; Estab 1968 to maintain archives of Alaska materials, particularly the Cook Inlet area; A non-circulating library for reference use only
Library Holdings: Auction Catalogs; Book Volumes 12,000; Clipping Files; DVDs; Exhibition Catalogs; Fiche; Kodachrome Transparencies; Lantern Slides; Maps; Memorabilia; Other Holdings Original documents; Pamphlets; Periodical Subscriptions 48; Photographs 500,000; Reels; Slides; Video Tapes
Special Subjects: Historical Material, American Western Art, American Indian Art, Anthropology, Eskimo Art
Collections: Alaska Railroad Collection: 19,000 historical photos; Reeve Collection: historical maps; Ward Wells Anchorage Photo Collection 1950-80: 125,000 items; Lu Liston Photo Collection 1920-1950, 6,000 photos; Steve McCutcheon Photo Collection, 70,000; J N Wyman (Upper Koyukon) 1989: 500 glass plates; Vern Brickley Photograph Collection (WWII to 1970) 30,000
Activities: Clases for adults & children; docent training; lects open to pub; gallery talks; mus shop sells books & original art

BETHEL

M   YUGTARVIK REGIONAL MUSEUM & BETHEL VISITORS CENTER, PO Box 388, Bethel, AK 99559-0388. Tel 907-543-2098; Fax 907-543-2255;
Open Tues - Sat 10 AM - 6 PM; No admis fee; Estab 1967 to help preserve the native culture & lifestyle of the Central Yupik Eskimos of the Yukon-Kuskokwin delta; Average Annual Attendance: 10,500; Mem: 50; dues $25
Income: $165,000 (financed by city appropriation & occasional grants)
Purchases: $5000
Special Subjects: Eskimo Art, Ivory
Collections: Traditional handmade objects of the Yupik Eskimo, both artifacts & contemporary art objects (included are full-size kayak, ivory carvings & wooden masks, wooden bowls, stone & ivory implements, grass baskets, Yupik toys, fish skin, seal gut, bird skin & fur clothing); black & white photographs
Exhibitions: Rotating exhibitions
Activities: Classes for adults & children; lects open to pub; book traveling exhibs, 3-4 times per yr; mus shop sells baskets, ivory jewelry, beaded work, skin & fur garments, wooden & ivory masks, books & posters relating to Yupik Eskimos

FAIRBANKS

M   ALASKA HOUSE ART GALLERY, 1003 Cushman St., Fairbanks, AK 99701. Tel 907-456-6449; Elec Mail info@thealaskahouse.com; Internet Home Page Address: www.thealaskahouse.com; *Owner* Yolande Fejes; *Owner* Ron Veliz
Summer; call for hours; No admis fee; Estab 1964; to promote & preserve Alaskan art; Contemporary & historical Alaskan art
Collections: Works of Claire Fejes & other Alaskan artists; paintings; drawings; prints; sculpture; carvings; masks; fabric art.
Activities: Poetry readings; special events; lects open to the pub; concerts; gallery talks

A   FAIRBANKS ARTS ASSOCIATION, Bear Gallery, 2300 Airport Way, Pioneer Park Fairbanks, AK 99707-4014; PO Box 72786, Fairbanks, AK 99707-2786. Tel 907-456-6485; Fax 907-456-4112; Elec Mail june@fairbanksarts.org; Internet Home Page Address: www.fairbanksarts.org; *Exec Dir* June Rogers; *Pres* Lorraine Peterson
Open winter: Tues - Sat Noon - 8 PM; summer: daily noon - 8 PM; No admis fee; Estab 1965 to promote contemporary & traditional art in the interior of Alaska; 4000 sq ft contemporary art gallery; Average Annual Attendance: 69,946; Mem: 580; dues $25 & up; annual meeting in Nov
Income: Financed by city & state appropriations, national grants, contributions
Activities: Classes for adults & children; performing arts progs; docent training; professional workshops; lects open to pub, 10 vis lectrs per yr; gallery talks; tours; competitions with awards; scholarships & fels offered; book traveling exhibs semi-annually; originate traveling exhibs; mus shop sells books, magazines, original art, reproductions & prints

M   UNIVERSITY OF ALASKA, Museum of the North, 907 Yukon Dr, Fairbanks, AK 99775; PO Box 756960, Fairbanks, AK 99775-6960. Tel 907-474-7505; Fax 907-474-5469; Elec Mail museum@uaf.edu; Internet Home Page Address: www.uaf.edu/museum; *Coordr Exhib & Exhib Designer* Wanda W Chin; *Pub Educ Prog* Laura Conner; *Coordr Fine Arts* Mareca Guthrie; *Cur Alaska Ctr for Documentary Film* Leonard J Kamerling
Open summer (May 15-Sept 15) daily 9 AM - 9 PM, winter (Sept 16-May 14) Mon - Sat 9 AM - 5 PM, cl Sun; Admis adults $10, seniors $9, ages 7-17 $5; Estab 1929 to collect, preserve & interpret the natural & cultural history of Alaska; Gallery contains 10,000 sq ft of exhibition space divided into 5 ecological & cultural regions; Average Annual Attendance: 120,000; Mem: 480
Income: Financed by state appropriation, pub & private donations, grants & contracts
Special Subjects: American Indian Art, Archaeology, Painting-American, Photography, Ethnology, Eskimo Art, Ivory, Scrimshaw
Collections: contemporary Alaska photography; ethnographic coll; paintings & lithographs of Alaska subjects; native artifacts & art
Exhibitions: Temporary exhibits rotate every two to three months; summer free explainer program with talks on bears, wolves, Alaskan art & culture; presentation & explanation on Northern Lights
Activities: Classes for adults & children; lects open to pub; docent tours for grades K-6; mus shop sells books, original art, reproductions, prints, slides
L   Elmer E Rasmuson Library, 310 Tanana Dr, Fairbanks, AK 99775-1000; PO Box 756800, Fairbanks, AK 99775-6800. Tel 907-474-7224; Fax 907-474-6841; Internet Home Page Address: www.uaf.edu/library; *Head Bibliographic Access Management* Natalie Forshaw; *Head Alaska & Polar Regions Colls* Susan Grigg; *Coll Develop Officer* Dennis Stephens; *Dir* Paul H McCarthy; *Information Services* Rheba Dupra
Open Mon - Thurs 7:30 AM - 11 PM, Fri 7:30 AM - 10 PM, Sat 10 AM - 6 PM, Sun 10 AM - 10 PM, when school is not in session 8 AM - 5 PM; Estab 1922 to support research & curriculum of the university; Circ 147,000

Income: Financed by state appropriation
Library Holdings: Book Volumes 2,260,000; Compact Disks; Manuscripts; Other Holdings Audio tapes; Film; Government documents; Photographs; Slides; Video Tapes
Collections: Lithographs of Fred Machetanz; paintings by Alaskan artists; C Rusty Heurlin; photographs of Early Alaskan bush pilots; print reference photograph coll on Alaska & the Polar Regions

HAINES

M **SHELDON MUSEUM & CULTURAL CENTER, INC,** Sheldon Museum & Cultural Center, 11 Main St, Haines, AK 99827; PO Box 269, Haines, AK 99827-0269. Tel 907-766-2366; Fax 907-766-2368; Elec Mail museumdirector@aptalaska.net; Internet Home Page Address: www.sheldonmuseum.org; *Dir & Cur Sheldon Mus* Jerrie Clarke; *Pres Chilkat Valley Historical Society* Jim Shook; *Pres Mus Bd Trustees* Frances Perry; *Store Mgr* Blythe Carter; *Educator* Kathy Friedle; *Registrar* Karen Meizner
Open Winter Mon-Sat 1-4PM, Summer Mon-Fri 10AM-5PM, Sat & Sun 1-4PM; Admis adults $5, children under 12 free; Estab 1924, under operation of Chilkat Valley Historical Society 1975 - 1991, incorporated Haines Borough facility, 1991; Art, history, culture & maintains reference library; Average Annual Attendance: 14,000; Mem: 124; dues $12
Income: Admis, mus store, Haines Borough appropriations, federal & state grants
Library Holdings: Audio Tapes; Book Volumes; Cassettes; Clipping Files; DVDs; Fiche; Framed Reproductions; Kodachrome Transparencies; Lantern Slides; Manuscripts; Maps; Memorabilia; Motion Pictures; Original Art Works; Original Documents; Pamphlets; Periodical Subscriptions; Photographs; Prints; Records; Slides; Video Tapes
Special Subjects: Photography, American Indian Art, Ethnology, Woodcarvings, Eskimo Art, Metalwork, Ivory, Scrimshaw
Collections: Chilkat blankets; Tlingit Indian artifacts; ivory, silver, wood carvings; native baskets, pioneer artifacts, photos, maps, oral histories, archival; Eldred Rock Lighthouse Lens, local art
Exhibitions: Solo & group art exhibs by local artists Apr-Sep
Publications: Haines - The First Century; A Personal Look at the Sheldon Museum & Cultural Center; Journey to the Tlingits; More Than Gold-Nuggets of Haines History
Activities: Classes for adults & children; Tlingit language class; docent training; lects open to pub; number of vis lectrs per yr varies; competitions; Friday brown bag lunches with historical programs; original objects of art lent to other mus; book traveling exhibs; mus store sells books, original art, prints, slides, jewelry, wood crafts

HOMER

M **BUNNELL STREET AAS CENTER,** (Bunnell Street Gallery) Bunnell Street Arts Center, 106 W Bunnel, Ste A, Homer, AK 99603. Tel 907-235-2662; Elec Mail info@bunnellstreetgallery.org; Internet Home Page Address: www.bunnellarts.org; *Asst Dir* Adele Groning; *Admin Asst* Brianna Allen; *Artist in Residence Coordr* Michael Walsh
Open Sept - Apr Mon - Sat 11 AM - 6 PM; May - Aug Sun Noon - 4 PM; No admis fee; Estab 1994 for art exhibitions & educ; Historic landmark building displaying innovative contemporary art; Average Annual Attendance: 11,000; Mem: 250; dues $100 patron, $50 individual; annual meeting in May
Income: $250,000 (financed by mem, city & state appropriation, fund raising, Alaska State Council on the Arts, City of Homer Grant Prog through the Homer Foundation & NEA, Rasmuson, PGA Foundation)
Publications: Newsletter, quarterly
Activities: Classes for adults & children; docent training; dramatic progs; internships; music; artist in schools; lects open to public, 15 vis lectrs per year; concerts; gallery talks; tours; poetry readings; piano concerts; slide lect by artist; art workshops various media; schols; awards, Alex Combs Award; scholarship offered; sales shop sells original art

M **FIREWEED GALLERY,** 475 E. Pioneer Ave, Homer, AK 99603. Tel 907-235-3411; Elec Mail art@fireweedgallery.com
Open Summer: Mon - Sat 10 AM - 7 PM, Sun 11 AM - 5 PM; Winter: Mon - Sat 10:30 AM 5:30 PM
Collections: Contemporary works by Alaskan artists including paintings, sculpture, ceramics, jewelry, & photography

JUNEAU

L **ALASKA STATE LIBRARY,** Alaska Historical Collections, 333 Willoughby Ave, 8th Fl, State Office Bldg Juneau, AK 99801-1770; PO Box 110571, Juneau, AK 99811-0571. Tel 907-465-2925; Fax 907-465-2990; Elec Mail asl@alaska.gov; Internet Home Page Address: www.library.state.ak.us; *Librn, Head Historical Coll* Jim Simard; *Librn, Cur Colls* Anastasia Tarmann Lynch; *Librn, Asst Cur Colls* Gayle Goedde
Open Mon - Fri 10 AM - 4:30 PM; No admis fee; Estab 1900; Part of library; Average Annual Attendance: 6,000
Income: State appropriation
Library Holdings: Book Volumes 34,000; Periodical Subscriptions 75; Photographs 110,000
Special Subjects: Photography, Manuscripts, Maps, Historical Material, Ethnology, American Indian Art, Anthropology, Eskimo Art
Collections: Winter & Pond; Wickersham Historical Site Collection; Skinner Foundation Collection; Grainger Post Card Collection
Publications: Books about Alaska, annual; Inventories for Individual Collections

M **ALASKA STATE MUSEUM,** 395 Whittier St, Juneau, AK 99801-1746. Tel 907-465-2901; Fax 907-465-2976; Elec Mail bob.banghart@alaska.gov; Internet Home Page Address: www.museums.state.ak.us; *Chief Cur* Bruce Kato; *Cur Coll* Steve Henrikson; *Cur Mus Svcs* Scott Carrlee; *Cur Exhib* Paul Gardinier; *Registrar* Sorrel Goodwik; *Exhibits Designer* Jackie Manning; *Admin Asst* Debbie McBride; *Security & Visitor Svcs Coordr* Lisa Golisek; *Security & Visitor Svcs Clerk* Sara Chubb; *Asst to Visitor Svcs* Mary Irvine; *Security & Visitor Svcs Clerk* Janet Kolowski; *Conservator* Ellen Carrlee; *Mus Store Mgr* Alice Hadsel; *Friends of the Alaska State Mus Pres* Virginia Palmer
Open May 6 - Sept 22, daily 8:30 AM - 5:30 PM; Sept 23 - May 5, Tues - Sat 10 AM - 4 PM; Admis $5 summer, $3 winter, age 18 & younger free; Estab 1900 to collect, preserve, exhibit & interpret objects of special significance or value in order to promote pub appreciation of Alaska's cultural heritage, history, art & natural environment; Gallery occupies two floors housing permanent & temporary exhibits on 12,000 sq ft; Average Annual Attendance: 80,000 with more than 200,000 including outreach program
Income: Financed by state appropriation & grants
Collections: Alaskan ethnographic material including Eskimo, Aleut, Athabaskan, Tlingit, Haida & Tsimshian artifacts; Gold Rush & early Alaskan industrial & historical material; historical & contemporary Alaskan art; Natural History
Exhibitions: Dale DeArmand: The Nandalton Legends; Kayaks of Alaska and Sibera; Lockwood DeForest: Alaska Oil Sketches; Case & Draper Photographs 1898 - 1920
Publications: Eight Stars of Gold: The Story of Alaska's Flag (with CD)
Activities: Classes for adults & children; docent training; lects open to pub, 12 vis lectrs per yr; gallery talks, tours & demonstrations; paintings & objects lent to other museums & Alaskan schols; 2 book traveling exhibs per yr; originate traveling exhibs to AK mus; Mus shop sells books, magazines, reproductions, prints, Alaskan Native arts & crafts, outreach services to other mus

KETCHIKAN

M **CITY OF KETCHIKAN MUSEUM,** Tongass Historical Museum, 629 Dock St, Ketchikan, AK 99901-6529. Tel 907-225-5600; Fax 907-225-5602; Elec Mail museumdir@city.ketchikan.ak.us; Internet Home Page Address: www.city.ketchikan.ak.us/departments/museums/tongass; *Cur Coll* Richard H Van Cleave; *Cur Prog* Lacey Gilbo; *Dir* Michael Naab
Open summer daily 8 AM - 5 PM, winter Wed - Sun 1 PM - 5 PM ; Admis adults $2; Estab 1967 to collect, preserve & exhibit area articles & collect area photographs; Maintains reference library; Average Annual Attendance: 20,000
Income: $500,000 (financed by municipal funds)
Purchases: $9950
Collections: North West Indian Collection; ethnographic & develop history, local artists contemporary artwork; local area history artifacts; works from local & Alaskan artists, photographs, manuscripts & newspaper archives
Publications: Art class listings; Calendar; Newsletter
Activities: Classes for adults; docent training; lects open to public, 5 vis lectrs per year; book traveling exhibitions

M **CITY OF KETCHIKAN MUSEUM DEPT,** 629 Dock St, Totem Heritage Ctr Ketchikan, AK 99901-6529. Tel 907-225-5900; Fax 907-225-5901; Elec Mail museumdir@city.ketchikan.ak.us; Internet Home Page Address: www.city.ketchikan.ak.us/departments/museums/totem; *Dir* Michael Naab; *Sr Cur Prog* Lacey Gilbo
Open summer daily 8 AM - 5 PM, winter Wed - Fri 1 PM - 5 PM; Admis $5, children under 12 free; Estab 1976 to preserve & teach traditional Northwest Coast Indian Arts; Average Annual Attendance: 60,000
Income: $360,000
Special Subjects: Sculpture, Historical Material
Collections: Indian arts; original totem poles; monumental sculpture
Activities: Classes for adults & children; docent training; workshops; lects open to pub, 20 vis lectrs per yr; gallery talks; tours; arts & crafts festival; schols & work-study awards offered; mus shop sells books, magazines, original art, reproductions, prints, slides & native art

L **Library,** 629 Dock St, Ketchikan, AK 99901-6529. Tel 907-225-5900; Fax 907-225-5901; *Dir* Michael Naab
Summer: Mon - Sun 8 AM - 5 PM; Winter: Wed - Fri 1 PM - 5 PM; No admis fee; For reference only
Library Holdings: Audio Tapes; Book Volumes 250; Cassettes; Clipping Files; Exhibition Catalogs; Fiche; Kodachrome Transparencies; Manuscripts; Original Art Works; Periodical Subscriptions 5; Slides; Video Tapes
Collections: 200 vols relating to northwest coast native art

NOME

M **CITY OF NOME ALASKA MEMORIAL MUSEUM,** (Carrie M McLain) Carrie M McLain Memorial Museum, 223 E Front St, Nome, AK 99762; PO Box 53, Nome, AK 99762-0053. Tel 907-443-6630; Fax 907-443-7955; Elec Mail museum@ci.nome.ak.us; Internet Home Page Address: www.nomealaska.org; *Dir* Laura Samuelson; *Mus Asst* Nadja Roessek; *Research Asst* Alice Sullivan; *Mus Aide* Cheryl Thompson; *Mus Aide* Elena Spivey
Open Summer 10 AM - 5:30 PM, Winter Tues - Sat noon - 5:30 PM; No admis fee; Estab 1967 to show the history of Nome, Nome Gold Rush, Bering Strait Eskimo, Aviation, Dog mushing; Average Annual Attendance: 9,000
Income: Financed by City of Nome & supplemental grant projects & donations
Special Subjects: Archaeology, Drawings, Landscapes, Flasks & Bottles, Gold, Photography, Ethnology, Woodcarvings, Manuscripts, Eskimo Art, Dolls, Jewelry, Historical Material, Ivory, Maps, Scrimshaw, Restorations
Collections: permanent coll includes examples of art from 1890-1998, including basketry, carved ivory, ink, oil, skin drawings, stone carving, woodworking; extensive photography coll on database; gold rush & dog sledding memorabilia; Bering Strait Eskimo; Coons Collection; McLain Collection; Mielke Collection
Activities: lects open to pub; vis lectrs 4 per yr; gallery talks; tours; individual paintings & original objects of art lent

SITKA

M **ALASKA DEPARTMENT OF EDUCATION, DIVISION OF LIBRARIES, ARCHIVES & MUSEUMS,** Sheldon Jackson Museum, 104 College Dr, Sitka, AK 99835-7657. Tel 907-747-8981; Fax 907-747-3004; Elec Mail paula.bykonen@alaska.gov; Internet Home Page Address: museums.alaska.gov; *Mus Protection Visitor Svcs Supvr* Paula Lisa Bykonen; *Mus Protection Visitor Svcs Asst* Deborah Doland; *Cur of Coll* Jacqueline Fernandez
Open summer May 15 - Sept 15, 9 AM - 5 PM daily, winter Sept 16 - May 14 Tues - Sat 10 AM - 4 PM, cl Mon, Sun & holidays; Admis $5 over 18, Summer/Winter $3; Estab 1888, the first permanent mus in Alaska, for the purpose of collecting & preserving the cultural heritage of Alaskan Natives in the form of artifacts; The mus, one of two Alaska State Museums, occupies a concrete, octagonal structure from 1895 with permanent displays concerning Tlingit, Tsimshian, Haida, Aleut, Athabaskan & Eskimo Inupiat and Yup'ik cultures; Average Annual Attendance: 20,000; Mem: 200
Income: $30,000 (financed by admis fee, sales, donation, State of Alaska)
Library Holdings: Book Volumes In-house reference only
Special Subjects: American Indian Art, Anthropology, Ethnology, Woodcarvings, Ivory, Scrimshaw
Collections: Ethnographic material from Tlingit, Haida, Tsimshian, Aleut, Athabaskan & Eskimo people; Alaskan ethnology produced through 1930
Publications: Brochures; catalogs of Ethnological Collection
Activities: Classes for children K-12; gallery interpreters & demonstrations; workshops; lects open to pub, 4-6 vis lectrs per yr; gallery talks; exten dept serves Alaska educators; lending of original art to Alaska teachers; hands on ed coll; mus shop sells books, original art

M **SITKA HISTORICAL SOCIETY,** Sitka Historical Museum, 330 Harbor Dr, Sitka, AK 99835-7553. Tel 907-747-6455; Fax 907-747-6588; Elec Mail sitka.history@yahoo.com; Internet Home Page Address: www.sitkahistory.org; *Dir* Bob Medinger; *Cur Coll & Exhibs* Ashley Kircher
Open daily 8 AM - 5 PM May - Sept, Tues - Sat 10 AM - 4 PM Oct - Apr; No admis fee; Estab 1971 to preserve the history of Sitka, its people & industries; Average Annual Attendance: 70,000; Mem: 225; dues $15-$100; annual meeting in Oct
Income: Financed by grants, mem, donations & gift shop sales
Special Subjects: Historical Material
Collections: Copy of warrant that purchased Alaska; 2000 documents; Russian artifacts; library paintings of Alaska scenes; 10000 photographs; carved ivory, items for post-Russia Sitka through 1950
Exhibitions: Alaska Purchase; Diorama of Sitka in 1867 (Year of the Transfer); Forest Products Exhibit (past & present); Russian-American era Tlingit Culture; Last Qtr 19th Century Victorian Parlor & US Military Presence; First Flight Around the World; WWII in Sitka
Activities: Lects open to pub, 4 vis lectrs per yr; awards given; sales shop sells books & reproductions of artifacts

SKAGWAY

M **SKAGWAY CITY MUSEUM & ARCHIVES,** 700 Spring St, Skagway, AK 99840; PO Box 521, Skagway, AK 99840-0521. Tel 907-983-2420; Fax 907-983-3420; *Cur* Judith Munns
Open 9 AM - 5 PM, May - Sept; Oct - Apr on request; Admis adults $2, students $1; Estab 1961 to preserve & display items relating to the Klondike Gold Rush & Skagway history; Average Annual Attendance: 42,000
Income: Financed by admis
Collections: Gold Rush Era artifacts; Tlingit; traveling war canoe, duck neck quilt
Publications: Brochures
Activities: Sales shop sells, books, reproductions of old newspapers & postcards

ARIZONA

BISBEE

L **BISBEE ARTS & HUMANITIES COUNCIL,** Lemuel Shattuck Memorial Library, 5 Copper Queen Plaza, Bisbee, AZ 85603; PO Box 14, Bisbee, AZ 85603-0014. Tel 520-432-7071; Fax 520-432-7800; Internet Home Page Address: www.bisbeemuseum.org; *Cur Archival Coll* Carrie Gustavson; *Cur* Annie Larkin
Open Mon - Fri 10 AM - 4 PM, Sat & Sun by appointment; Admis adults $7.50, seniors 60 and over $6.50, children under 16 $3; Estab 1971 to provide research facilities on copper mining & social history of Bisbee, Arizona, Cochise County & Northern Sonora, Mexico; For reference only
Income: $300 (financed by mem)
Purchases: $600
Library Holdings: Book Volumes 1,600; Cassettes 300; Clipping Files; Manuscripts; Periodical Subscriptions 3; Photographs 23,000; Reels 200
Special Subjects: Photography, Manuscripts, Maps, Historical Material
Activities: Classes for adults & children; docent training; lects open to pub, 5 vis lectrs per yr; originate traveling exhibs

CHANDLER

A **XICO INC,** (Xicanindio, Inc) 44 S San Marcos Pl, Chandler, AZ 85225-7872. Tel 480-833-5875; Fax 480-890-2327; Elec Mail info@xicoinc.com; Internet Home Page Address: www.xicoinc.com; *Pres* Art Perez Ally; *VPres* Rhonda Carrillo; *Secy* Virginia Cardenas
Open Tues - Thurs 11 AM - 5 PM, Fri - Sat 10 AM - 6 PM, cl Sun, Mon; No admis fee; Estab 1977 as a nonprofit organization of Native American & Xicanindio artist to promote cross cultural understanding, preserve tradition &

develop grass roots educational programs; Average Annual Attendance: 28,000; Mem: 20; annual meeting in Sept
Income: $64,000 (financed by endowment, city & state appropriation)
Publications: Papel Picado (paper cut-out techniques)
Activities: Lects open to pub, 1 vis lectrs per yr

DOUGLAS

L **COCHISE COLLEGE,** Charles Di Peso Library, 4190 W Hwy 80, Art Dept Douglas, AZ 85607-6100. Tel 520-417-4080, 515-5420; Internet Home Page Address: padme.cochise.cc.az.us/library; *Libr Dir* Patricia Hotchkiss
Open Mon - Thurs 7:30AM-9PM, Fri 8AM-4:30 PM, Sat 10AM-2PM, Sun 1-5PM; No admis fee; Estab 1965
Income: Financed by state & local funds & the college
Library Holdings: Book Volumes 61,000; Exhibition Catalogs; Framed Reproductions; Memorabilia; Original Art Works; Periodical Subscriptions 300; Photographs; Prints; Reproductions; Sculpture
Special Subjects: Oriental Art
Collections: Oriental originals (ceramics & paintings); 19th century American & European Impressionists

M **DOUGLAS ART ASSOCIATION,** The Gallery and Gift Shop, 625 Tenth St, Douglas, AZ 85607. Tel 520-364-6410; *Pres* Maryann Nelson; *Dir* Terry J Mason
Open Mon - Sat 10:00 AM - 4 PM; No admis fee; Estab 1960 as a nonprofit tax exempt organization dedicated to promoting the visual arts & general cultural awareness in the Douglas, Arizona & Agua Prieta, Sonora area; The Gallery is operated in a city owned building with city cooperation; Average Annual Attendance: 2,000; Mem: 100; dues $15, $25 & $50
Income: Financed by mem & fundraising events, some lottery funds
Special Subjects: Southwestern Art
Exhibitions: Shows change about every six weeks
Publications: Monthly newsletter
Activities: Classes for adults & children; workshops in painting & various art activities; lect open to pub; gallery talks; competitions with cash awards; sales shop sells books, original art, prints, hand-made arts and crafts

DRAGOON

A **AMERIND FOUNDATION, INC,** Amerind Museum, Fulton-Hayden Memorial Art Gallery, 2100 N Amerind Rd, Dragoon, AZ 85609; PO Box 400, Dragoon, AZ 85609-0400. Tel 520-586-3666; Fax 520-586-4679; Elec Mail amerind@amerind.org; Internet Home Page Address: www.amerind.org; *Pres* Michael W Hard; *VPres* George J Gumerman; *Treas* Lawrence Schiever; *Exec Dir* John A Ware; *Chief Cur* Eric Kaldahl; *Mus Coordr* Carol Charnley; *Mus Store Mgr* Tammy Stansberry
Open Tues-Sun 10AM-4PM year round, cl major holidays; Admis adults $5, sr citizens $4, groups & children under 18 $3; Estab 1937 as a private, nonprofit archeological research facility & mus focusing on the native people of the Americas; Works on western & southwestern themes, paintings & sculptures by 19th & 20th century Anglo & Native American artists; Average Annual Attendance: 13,000; Mem: 800; dues individual $30, family $40, Cochise Club $100-499, San Pedro Club $500-999, Casas Grandes Club $1,000 and above
Income: Financed by endowment income, grants, gifts
Special Subjects: Sculpture, Textiles, Watercolors, Painting-American, Pottery, American Western Art, American Indian Art, Archaeology, Ethnology, Eskimo Art, Scrimshaw, Southwestern Art, Mexican Art
Collections: Archaeological & ethnological materials from the Americas; antique furniture; archives on film; ivory & scrimshaw; oil paintings; research & technical reports; sculpture
Exhibitions: Images in Time; Traditions in Clay; The Prehistoric Southwest; recent acquisitions
Publications: Amerind Foundation Publication Series; Amerind New World Studies Series
Activities: Docent training; seminars; sch prog, day visits; lects open to pub, 6 vis lectrs per yr; gallery talks; tours for school groups; mus shop sells books, prints, original art, Native American Arts & Crafts

L **Fulton-Hayden Memorial Library & Art Gallery,** 2100 N Amerind Rd, Dragoon, AZ 85609; PO Box 400, Dragoon, AZ 85609-0400. Tel 520-586-3666 ext 18; Fax 520-586-4679; Elec Mail libros@amerind.org; Internet Home Page Address: www.amerind.org; *Librn* Sally Newland; *Exec Dir* John Ware, PhD; *Cur* Eric Kaldahl PhD, RPA
Library open by appointment only; mus & gallery Tues - Sun 10 AM - 4 PM; Admis adults $8, seniors $7, youth 12-18 & col students with ID $5, children under 12, free; Estab 1962 as archaeological research library for scholars; American oils, sculpture, drawings, Native American Art; Average Annual Attendance: 10,000; Mem: Museum mem 1,000
Income: Financed by endowment income, grants, gifts
Purchases: Miscellaneous ethnographic material from the American Southwest & Northern Mexico
Library Holdings: Audio Tapes; Book Volumes 22,000; CD-ROMs; Cards; Cassettes; Clipping Files; Compact Disks; Exhibition Catalogs; Fiche; Filmstrips; Kodachrome Transparencies; Lantern Slides; Manuscripts; Maps; Memorabilia; Micro Print; Motion Pictures; Original Art Works; Original Documents; Pamphlets; Periodical Subscriptions 60; Photographs; Reels; Reproductions; Sculpture; Slides; Video Tapes
Special Subjects: Art History, Decorative Arts, Drawings, Etchings & Engravings, Manuscripts, Maps, Painting-American, Pre-Columbian Art, Prints, Sculpture, Historical Material, History of Art & Archaeology, Watercolors, Ceramics, Latin American Art, Archaeology, American Western Art, American Indian Art, Anthropology, Eskimo Art, Furniture, Mexican Art, Southwestern Art, Costume Design & Constr, Jewelry, Pottery, Religious Art, Silver, Silversmithing, Textiles, Scrimshaw, Architecture
Collections: American Oils, sculpture, works on paper; Navajo & Hopi watercolors
Publications: Amerind Foundation Publications; Amerind Studies in Archaeology

Activities: Classes for adults & children; docent training; lects open to pub; lects for mems only; vis lectrs 6 per yr; gallery talks; tours; museum shop sells books, prints, Native American jewelry & crafts

FLAGSTAFF

M **MUSEUM OF NORTHERN ARIZONA,** 3101 N Fort Valley Rd, Flagstaff, AZ 86001-8348. Tel 928-774-5213; Fax 928-779-1527; Elec Mail info@mna.mus.az.us; Internet Home Page Address: www.musnaz.org; *Danson Cur Anthropology* Kelley Hays-Gilpin, PhD; *Chair Bd Trustees* Susan Garretson; *Dir* Robert G Breunig, PhD; *Colbert Cur Paleontology* David D Gillette, PhD; *Coll Mgr* Elaine R Hughes; *Cur Mus* Jennifer McLerran, PhD; *Cur Ecology & Conservation* Lawrence Stevens, PhD; *Cur Fine Art* Alan Petersen; *Sr Research Anthropologist* David R Wilcox, PhD
Open daily 9 AM - 5 PM, cl New Year's Day, Thanksgiving & Christmas; Admis adults $7, sr citizens (65+) $6, students $5, children (7-17) $4; Estab 1928 to collect, study, interpret and preserve the art, cultural, natural history of the Colorado Plateau; Maintains reference library; Average Annual Attendance: 80,000; Mem: 4000; dues $60 and up; annual meeting in June
Income: $3,300,000 (financed by endowment, mem & earned income, donations & grants)
Special Subjects: Pottery, Painting-American, Sculpture, Hispanic Art, Painting-American, Photography, American Indian Art, American Western Art, Anthropology, Archaeology, Ethnology, Southwestern Art, Textiles, Ceramics, Crafts, Folk Art, Pottery, Woodcarvings, Landscapes, Jewelry, Silver, Carpets & Rugs, Historical Material, Juvenile Art
Collections: Works of Southwestern Native American artists; non-Indian art depicting Colorado Plateau subjects; archaeological, ethnographic artifacts, natural history specimens of the Colorado Plateau
Exhibitions: Geology, archaeology, ethnology, Native cultures, additional changing exhibits of fine art & natural sciences
Publications: Plateau Magazine; semiannual; museum notes; semiannual
Activities: Adventurous outdoor experiences; group tours; Discovery prog for youths of all ages; docent training; lects open to pub, gallery talks; individual paintings & original objects of art lent to various institutions; lending coll contains 2200 original art works; mus shop sells books, magazines, original art, reproductions, prints, & mus quality Native arts by master and emerging artists of the Colorado Plateau

M **NORTHERN ARIZONA UNIVERSITY,** Art Museum & Galleries, 321 W McMullen Cr, Flagstaff, AZ 86011; PO Box 6021, Flagstaff, AZ 86011-6021. Tel 928-523-3471; Fax 928-523-1424; Elec Mail artmuseum@nau.edu; Internet Home Page Address: www.nau.edu/art_museum; *Opers Mgr* Linda Stromberg; *Curatorial Specialist* Heidi J Robinson
Open Tues-Sat noon-5PM; No admis fee, $2 suggested donation; Estab 1968 for the continuing educ & service to the students & the Flagstaff community in all aspects of fine arts & to national & international fine arts communities; Gallery is a nonprofit educational institution; Average Annual Attendance: 10,000
Special Subjects: Southwestern Art, Coins & Medals
Collections: Contemporary ceramics; Master prints of the 20th c & American painting of the Southwest; Weiss Collection: Early 20th c Antiques, Sculptures & Paintings
Activities: Educ prog includes outreach to local schools; lects open to pub, 3 vis lectrs per yr; national & international workshops & conferences; concerts; tours; competitions with awards; gallery talks; scholarships; originate traveling exhibs; mus shop sells books, original art works, prints & posters, reproductions, Hopi jewelry & other gift items; Beasley Student & Faculty Gallery Bldg 37 Flagstaff

GANADO

M **NATIONAL PARK SERVICE,** Hubbell Trading Post National Historic Site, PO Box 150, Ganado, AZ 86505-0150. Tel 928-755-3475; Fax 928-755-3405; Elec Mail e_chamberlin@nps.gov; Internet Home Page Address: www.nps.gov/hutr; *Cur* Ed Chamberlin; *Mus Tech* Kathy Tabaha; *Educ Dir* Ailema Benally
Open May - Sept 8 AM - 6 PM, Oct - Apr 8 AM - 5 PM; Admis $2 Hubbell family home tour, Trading Post free; Estab 1967 to set aside Hubbell Trading Post as a historic site as the best example in Southwest of an Indian Trading Post & people he served; Average Annual Attendance: 70,000
Income: Financed by federal appropriation
Special Subjects: American Indian Art, Anthropology, Archaeology, Photography, Painting-American, American Western Art, Southwestern Art, Period Rooms
Collections: Western artists; ethnohistoric arts & crafts; furnishings; photographs
Exhibitions: Fully furnished 19th & 20th Century Trading Post & family home
Activities: Educ dept; lect open to public; tours; presentations; competitions; individual paintings & art objects are lent to cert museums; sales shop sells books, Indian arts & crafts, magazines, original art, prints & slides; semi annual Native American art auctions (May & Sep)

KINGMAN

M **MOHAVE MUSEUM OF HISTORY & ARTS,** 400 W Beale, Kingman, AZ 86401. Tel 520-753-3195; Fax 520-753-3195; Elec Mail museum@mohavemuseum.org; Internet Home Page Address: www.ctaz.com/~mocohist/museum/index.htm; *Dir* Shannon Rossiter
Open Mon - Fri 9 AM - 5 PM, Sat 1 - 5 PM; Admis adults $4, children free; Estab 1960 to preserve & present to the pub the art & history of Northwest Arizona; Average Annual Attendance: 30,000; Mem: 600; dues $20-$125; annual meeting in Apr
Income: Financed by endowment, mem, sales & donations
Special Subjects: American Indian Art, Anthropology, Archaeology, Ethnology, Manuscripts, Historical Material, Restorations
Collections: American Indian Art; art & history of Northwest Arizona
Exhibitions: Quilt Show (Oct)

Activities: Classes for children; docent progs; lects open to pub; mus shop sells books, prints, original art, craft items, reproductions

MESA

M **ARIZONA MUSEUM FOR YOUTH,** 35 N Robson St, Mesa, AZ 85201. Tel 480-644-2467; Fax 480-644-2466; Elec Mail azmus4youth@mesaaz.gov; Internet Home Page Address: www.arizonamuseumforyouth.com; *Chmn* Deb Dahl; *Exec Dir* Sunnee D O'Rork; *Exhibs Cur* Jeffory Morris; *Exhibs Coordr* Rex Witte; *Community Arts Coordr* Latonya Jordan-Smith; *Cur Educ* Dena Cruz; *Mem Coordr* Darlene Zajda; *Develop Coordr* Lindsay Hochhalter; *Exhib Fabricator* Robert Trisoliere
Open Tues - Sat 10 AM - 4 PM; Sun noon - 4 PM, cl Mon; Admis non-member adults $7; children under 1 yr & members no charge, except special exhibs; discounts for AAM mems & Assoc of Children's Mus mems; Estab 1968 as fine art museum for children. Specially curated exhibits installed with original hands-on activities to involve children & families in the appreciation & making of art; Average Annual Attendance: 70,550; Mem: 300; dues: basic (fam 2) $50, primary (fam 4) $70, secondary (fam 6) $120, tertiary (fam 8) $175
Income: $1,400,000 (financed by city appropriation, memberships, donations, grants)
Special Subjects: Archaeology, Decorative Arts, Drawings, Etchings & Engravings, Ceramics, Collages, Painting-American, Textiles, Woodcuts, Sculpture, Graphics, Photography, Prints, Watercolors, Southwestern Art, Costumes, Crafts, Woodcarvings
Exhibitions: 4 - 6 changing exhibs per yr, see website
Publications: Member newsletter, 3 times per year; pre-visit & follow-up brochures for teachers
Activities: Classes for children; docent training; tours; gallery talks; book traveling exhibs, 2-3 per yr; mus shop sells books & items for children as related to specific exhibit themes

M **MESA ARTS CENTER,** Mesa Contemporary Arts Museum, 1 E Main St, Mesa, AZ 85201; PO Box 1466, Mesa, AZ 85211-1466. Tel 480-644-6567; Fax 480-644-6576; Elec Mail mesacontemporaryarts@mesaartscenter.com; Internet Home Page Address: www.mesaartscenter.com; *Cur* Patty Haberman; *Asst Dir* Robert Schultz; *Assoc Cur* Tiffany Fairall; *Admin Support Asst* Betty L Florez; *Preparator* Marco Albarran
Open Tues, Wed, Fri & Sat 10 AM - 5 PM, Thurs 10 AM - 8 PM, Sun noon - 5 PM; No admis fee; Estab 1981 to exhibit the artwork of contemporary artists nationally; 5 galleries, 5,500 sq ft exhibition space; Average Annual Attendance: 34,000; Mem: 30; dues: patron $1,000, artist $40, friend $25
Income: Financed by city appropriation
Special Subjects: Drawings, Etchings & Engravings, Landscapes, Ceramics, Collages, Glass, Metalwork, Hispanic Art, Latin American Art, Painting-American, Photography, Prints, Sculpture, Watercolors, Southwestern Art, Textiles, Crafts, Pottery, Woodcuts, Furniture, Jewelry, Mosaics, Enamels
Collections: Permanent collection of contemporary arts & crafts, prints, crafts & traditional media
Exhibitions: 16 exhibs ann
Activities: Classes & workshops for adults & children; docent training; awards $2,000 per juried exhibs; lects open to public, 2 vis lectrs per yr; gallery talks; tours; competitions with awards; book traveling exhibs annually; originate traveling exhibs artist coop; mus shop sells original art

MIAMI

M **BULLION PLAZA CULTURAL CENTER & MUSEUM,** 21 Plaza Circle, Miami, AZ 85539; PO Box 786, Miami, AZ 85539-0786. Tel 928-473-3700

NOGALES

A **PIMERIA ALTA HISTORICAL SOCIETY,** 136 N Grand Ave, Nogales, AZ 85621-3211; PO Box 2281, Nogales, AZ 85628-2281. Tel 520-287-4621; Fax 520-287-5201; Elec Mail lealteresa@hotmail.com; Internet Home Page Address: www.nogaleshistory.com; *Acting Dir* Teresa Leal; *Pres* Kathleen Escalada
Open Tues-Sun 11 AM - 3 PM; No admis fee; Estab 1948 to preserve the unique heritage of northern Sonora Mexico & southern Arizona from 1000 AD to present; art is incorporated into interpretive exhibits; Also maintains a photo gallery - archival photographic library restoration of Salvador Corona murals; Average Annual Attendance: 15,000; Mem: 500; dues $35; annual meeting in Jan
Income: $55,000 (financed by mem, fundraising events, educ programs & grants)
Library Holdings: Audio Tapes; Book Volumes; CD-ROMs; Cards; Cassettes; Clipping Files; Compact Disks; DVDs; Exhibition Catalogs; Framed Reproductions; Kodachrome Transparencies; Manuscripts; Maps; Memorabilia; Micro Print; Motion Pictures; Original Art Works; Original Documents; Other Holdings; Pamphlets; Photographs; Prints; Records; Reels; Slides; Video Tapes
Collections: Art & artifacts of Hohokam & Piman Indians, Spanish mission era & Mexican ranchers, Anglo pioneer settlement, early territorial maps, women costumes; natural & southwest broderland studies materials
Exhibitions: Railroad mining; firefighter - pharmacy - Hoho Kan; David Swing murals; Salvador Corona murals; Pimeria Post
Publications: Centennial Book of Nogales; newsletter, 10 per year; annual calendar on historic subjects; Open Range & Hidden Silver
Activities: Classes for adults & children; docent training; lects open to pub, 5 vis lectrs per yr; gallery talks; tours; competitions; traveling exhibs to outreach school related & senior projects; originate traveling exhibs; sales shop sells books, reproductions, prints, maps & pins; entire mus is fully interactive - bicultural & bilingual

L **Library,** 136 N Grand Ave, Nogales, AZ 85621-3211; PO Box 2281, Nogales, AZ 85628-3211. Tel 520-287-4621; Fax 520-287-5201; *Acting Dir* Patricia Berrones-Molina
Collects books & archival material on Pimeria Alta, Northern Sonora & Southern Arizona

Income: $1,000
Purchases: $500
Library Holdings: Book Volumes 1,000; Cassettes; Clipping Files; Manuscripts; Memorabilia; Other Holdings Historical Photos & Maps 5,000; Pamphlets; Periodical Subscriptions 3
Collections: The Jack Kemmer Memorial Collection, books on the cattle industry of Texas, New Mexico, Arizona and California

PARADISE VALLEY

M **DULEY-JONES GALLERY,** 7019 E Vista Dr, Paradise Valley, AZ 85253-7058. Tel 480-945-8475; Tel 800-229-8475; Elec Mail info@duleyjones.com; Internet Home Page Address: www.duleyjones.com; *Dir* Kathy Duley; *Dir* Randy Jones
Open Mon - Wed & Fri - Sat 10Am - 5PM, Thurs 10Am - 5PM & 7PM - 9PM
Collections: works by regional & nat artists; paintings; sculpture; ceramics; baskets; woodcarvings; watercolors

PHOENIX

A **ARIZONA ARTISTS GUILD,** 18411 N 7th St, Phoenix, AZ 85023; PO Box 41534, Phoenix, AZ 85080. Tel 602-944-9713; Elec Mail info@arizonaartistsguild.org; Internet Home Page Address: arizonaartistsguild.net; *Pres* David Bradley; *First VPres* Ruth Ann LaFavre
Estab 1928 to foster guild spirit, to assist in raising standards of art in the community & to assume civic responsibility in matters relating to art; Average Annual Attendance: 450; Mem: 360 juried, 90 assoc; dues $30; mem by jury; monthly meetings
Income: Financed by endowment & mem
Exhibitions: Horizons (annually in spring, members only); fall exhibition for members only; juried exhibition
Publications: AAG news, monthly
Activities: Classes for adults; lects sometimes open to public, 12 or more vis lectrs per year; gallery talks; competitions with awards; workshops by vis professionals offered; paint-outs; sketch groups; demonstrations; schols offered

A **ARIZONA COMMISSION ON THE ARTS,** 417 W Roosevelt St, Phoenix, AZ 85003-1326. Tel 602-771-6501; Fax 602-256-0282; Elec Mail info@azarts.gov; Internet Home Page Address: www.azarts.gov; *Chmn* Jane Jozoff; *Exec Dir* Shelley Cohn; *Dir Educ* Alison Marshall; *Visual Arts Dir* Gregory Sale; *Performing Art Dir* Claire West; *Dir Pub Information & Literature* Paul Morris; *Expansion Arts Dir* Rudy Guglielmo; *Dir School-Work & Organization Develop* Cyndy Coon; *Dir After School & Educ Projects* Janie Leck-Grela; *Prog Adminr* Mollie Lankin-Hayes; *Exec Dir* Robert Booker
Open 8 AM - 5 PM; No admis fee; Estab 1966 to promote & encourage the arts in the State of Arizona; Maintains reference library; Mem: Meetings, quarterly
Income: $1,152,800 (financed by state & federal appropriation)
Publications: Artists' Guide to Programs; monthly bulletin guide to programs
Activities: Workshops; conferences; artists-in-education grants prog; scholarships & fels offered; originate traveling exhibs 20-30 per yr

L **Reference Library,** 417 W Roosevelt, Phoenix, AZ 85003. Tel 602-771-6501; Fax 602-256-0282; Elec Mail info@azarts.gov; Internet Home Page Address: www.azarts.gov; *Exec Dir* Robert C Booker
Open 8 AM to 5 PM; Topics related to the bus of the arts. For reference only
Library Holdings: Book Volumes 900; Pamphlets; Periodical Subscriptions 25; Slides
Special Subjects: Art Education

M **ARIZONA STATE UNIVERSITY,** (Deer Valley Rock Art Center) Deer Valley Rock Art Center, 3711 W Deer Valley Rd Phoenix, AZ 85308. Tel 623-582-8007; Fax 623-582-8831; Elec Mail dvrac@asu.edu; Internet Home Page Address: http://dvrac.asu.edu; *Dir* Richard Toon; *Operations Coordr* Sherri Starkey; *Interpretatiion & Progs Coordr* Casandra Hernandez
Open May - Sept Tues - Sun 8 AM - 2 PM; Oct - Apr Tues - Sat 9 AM - 5 PM; Admis adults $7, seniors & students $4, children 6-12 $3, children 5 & under free; Estab to preserve & provide pub access to the Hedgpeth Hills petroglyph site, to interpret the cultural expressions & be a center for rock art research; Average Annual Attendance: 15,000; Mem: Dues $500 patron, $250 assoc, $100 friend, $40 family, $25 individual
Library Holdings: Original Documents; Prints; Slides
Special Subjects: Anthropology, Archaeology, American Indian Art, Southwestern Art
Collections: Over 1500 petroglyphs; artifacts, library & archives
Exhibitions: permanent exhib ongoing
Activities: Classes for adults & children; docent training; summer camps; festivals; storytelling prog; monthly lects; concerts; gallery talks; tours; mus shop sells books, magazines, original art, jewelry, clothing

A **ARIZONA WATERCOLOR ASSOCIATION,** 12809 N Second St, Phoenix, AZ 85022-5403; 15410 N 45th Pl, Phoenix, AZ 85032. Tel 602-284-8425; Elec Mail inigoj@cox.net; Internet Home Page Address: www.azwatercolor.com; *Treas* Bruce Sink; *First VPres* Jane Underhill; *Second VPres* Donna Eastman Liddle; *Third VPres* Liz Ramsey; *Western Representative* Jo Ellen Layton; *Recording Sec* Dolly Maitzen
Open Sept - May second Thurs evening each month; Estab 1960 to further activity & interest in the watermedia, promote growth of individuals & group & maintain high quality of professional exhibits; Two membership shows each yr, location varies; Average Annual Attendance: 600; Mem: 320; qualifications for juried mem must be accepted in three different approved juried shows; all members who pay dues are considered members; dues $40
Income: Financed by dues & donations $14,000 per yr
Exhibitions: Two exhibitions yearly: Membership Show
Publications: AWA Newsletter, monthly; Directory, annual
Activities: Workshops; lect for members only; paint outs; competitions with 10 awards per exhib

ATLATL
For Further Information see National and Regional Organizations

C **BANK ONE ARIZONA,** PO Box 71, Phoenix, AZ 85001-0071. Tel 602-221-2236; *VPres & Mgr* Lydia Lee
Open to pub; Estab 1933 to support emerging artists throughout the state; encourage & promote talented high school students with Scholastic Art Awards; provide the pub with beautiful, integrated art in branch banks; Several thousand pieces of art collection displayed in over 200 branches, bus offices & support facilities throughout the state of Arizona
Collections: Primarily Western, Southwestern art featuring many of the now classic Western artists; earliest lithograph dates back to the 1820s & coll continues through the present
Activities: Lect; gallery talks; tours by appointment; competitions, since 1942 state sponsor for Scholastic Art Awards throughout Arizona; purchase awards throughout the state, sponsor Employees' Art Show annually, with juried & popular choice awards, underwrite local art exhibitions on the Concourse of the Home Office Building; individual objects of art lent contingent upon bank policy

M **HEARD MUSEUM,** 2301 N Central Ave, Phoenix, AZ 85004-1323. Tel 602-252-8848; Fax 602-252-9757; Internet Home Page Address: heard.org; *Dir* Letitia Chambers; *Cur Colls* Diana Pardue; *Dir Research* Ann Marshall; *Registrar* Sharon Moore; *Educ Servs Mgr* Gina Laczko; *Librn & Archivist* Mario Nick Klimiades; *Mus Shop Mgr* Bruce McGee; *Assoc Registrar* Marcus Monenerkit
Open Mon - Sat 9:30 AM - 5 PM, Sun 11 AM - 5 PM, cl New Years Day, Easter, Memorial Day, July 4, Labor Day, Thanksgiving Day & Christmas; Admis general $12, seniors $11, students w/ID $5, children 6-12 $3, children under 6, mems, & American Indian tribes free; Estab 1929 to collect, preserve & exhibit Native American art & artifacts, offering an expansive view of the Southwest as it was thousands of years ago & is today & to increase general awareness about Native American cultures, traditions & art; 2 locations: Heard North Scottsdale & Heard West Surprise; Average Annual Attendance: 250,000; Mem: 5000; dues varies
Library Holdings: Auction Catalogs; Audio Tapes; Book Volumes 29,400; CD-ROMs; Cassettes; Clipping Files; Compact Disks; Exhibition Catalogs; Fiche; Manuscripts; Maps; Original Documents; Pamphlets 88; Periodical Subscriptions 240; Photographs; Prints; Records; Slides; Video Tapes 450
Special Subjects: Decorative Arts, Drawings, Hispanic Art, Mexican Art, Painting-American, Photography, Prints, Sculpture, Watercolors, American Indian Art, American Western Art, Bronzes, African Art, Archaeology, Southwestern Art, Textiles, Religious Art, Ceramics, Pottery, Primitive art, Woodcarvings, Dolls, Glass, Jewelry, Asian Art, Silver, Historical Material, Restorations, Tapestries
Collections: Barry M Goldwater Photograph Collection; C G Wallace Collection; Fred Harvey Fine Arts Collection
Publications: Earth Song Calendar (bi-monthly); The Heard Museum Journal (semi-annual); exhibition catalogs
Activities: Classes for adults & children; dramatic progs; docent training; outreach progs; music & dance performances; movie screenings; book signings; festivals; lects open to pub, 6-8 vis lectrs per yr; concerts; gallery talks; tours; competitions with awards; scholarships & fels offered; exten dept serves southwest; individual paintings & original objects of art lent to other art institutions & mus for exhibs; book traveling exhibs; originate traveling exhibs to other art institutions & mus; mus shop sells books, magazines, original art work & Native American art

L **Billie Jane Baguley Library and Archives,** 2301 N Central Ave, Phoenix, AZ 85004-1323. Tel 602-252-8840; Fax 602-252-9757; Elec Mail mario@heard.org; Internet Home Page Address: www.heard.org; *Library Archives Dir* Mario Nick Klimiades; *Librn* Betty Murphy; *Library & Archives Liaison* Donita Beckham; *Chair* Lee Peterson; *Vice Chair* Mark B Bonsall; *Secy* Dr George Blue Spruce Jr; *Treas* F Wesley Clelland, III; *Pres & CEO* James Henry Pepper; *Ed* Debra Utacia Krol; *Creative Dir* Caesar Chaves; *Dir Institutional Advancement Opers* James Weaver
Open Mon - Fri 10 AM - 4:45 PM to American Indians, mus visitors & mus members; open to public by appointment only; No admis fee; For reference only
Income: $11,000 (financed by mem & mus budget)
Library Holdings: Auction Catalogs; Audio Tapes; Book Volumes 30,500; Cassettes; Clipping Files; Exhibition Catalogs; Fiche; Filmstrips; Kodachrome Transparencies; Lantern Slides; Manuscripts; Maps; Memorabilia; Micro Print; Motion Pictures; Pamphlets; Periodical Subscriptions 300; Photographs 28,000; Prints; Records; Reels; Reproductions; Slides; Video Tapes 750
Special Subjects: Folk Art, Painting-American, Pre-Columbian Art, Crafts, Archaeology, Ethnology, American Indian Art, Primitive art, Anthropology, Eskimo Art, Mexican Art, Southwestern Art
Collections: Native American Artists Resource Collection; Fred Harvey Company Research Collection; Books: 35,000 vols; Journals & Newsletters: approximately 230 current periodical subscriptions & back issues of more than 1,922 serial titles with over 6,000 bound vols

M **PHOENIX ART MUSEUM,** 1625 N Central Ave, Phoenix, AZ 85004-1685. Tel 602-257-1880; Fax 602-253-8662; Elec Mail info@phxart.org; Internet Home Page Address: www.phxart.org; *Cur American & Western Art* Jerry Smith; *Dir* James K Ballinger; *Deputy Dir Admin* Gary Egan; *Dir Educ* Kathryn Blake; *Mus Shop Mgr* Lee Werhan; *Chair Bd Trustee* William Way; *Cur Asian Art* Janet Baker; *Asst to Dir* Samantha Klick; *Registrar* Leesha Alston; *Librn* Lindsey Powers; *Cur Fashion Design* Dennita Sewell; *Research Cur Asian Art* Claudia Brown; *Pub Information Officer* Mindi Carr; *Cur Modern & Contemporary Art* Sara Cochran; *Dir Mktg* Mindy Riesenberg
Open Wed 10AM-9PM, Thur-Sun 10AM-5PM, first Fri of month evenings 6-10PM; Admis $10 adults, $8 seniors & students, $4 child (6-17), free for members & children under 6, free Wed evenings 3-9PM and first Fri of the month 6-10Pm; Estab 1925, mus constructed 1959; Average Annual Attendance: 250,000; Mem: 9,000; dues $75 & up; annual meeting in Sep
Income: $8,000,000 (financed by pub & private funds)
Library Holdings: Auction Catalogs; Clipping Files; Exhibition Catalogs; Fiche; Pamphlets; Periodical Subscriptions; Slides
Special Subjects: Hispanic Art, Latin American Art, Mexican Art, Painting-American, Photography, Prints, Sculpture, Watercolors, Textiles, Costumes, Woodcuts, Decorative Arts, Painting-European, Portraits, Asian Art, Silver, Painting-British, Painting-Dutch, Baroque Art, Calligraphy, Miniatures, Painting-Flemish, Painting-Polish, Renaissance Art

Collections: Asian art; decorative arts; fashion design; 14th-20th century European & American art; Latin American art; Spanish Colonial art; Thorne Miniature Rooms; Western American art; Renaissance; Western American art; Medieval art; contemporary art

Publications: Annual report; exhibition catalogs; quarterly newsletter

Activities: Classes for adults & children; docent training; lects open to pub, 12 vis lectrs per yr; lects for mems only; concerts; gallery talks; tours; competitions; book travelling exhibs, 5 per yr; originates traveling exhibs, 2 per yr; mus shop sells books, magazines, reproductions, prints, jewelry, slides & gifts from around the world

L Lemon Art Research Library, 1625 N Central Ave, Phoenix, AZ 85004-1685. Tel 602-257-2136; Fax 602-253-8662; Elec Mail library@phxart.org; Internet Home Page Address: www.phxart.org; Asst Librn Lindsey Powers
Open Wed - Fri 10 AM - 4 PM; Estab 1959 to serve reference needs of the mus staff, docents, mem, students & pub; For reference only
Income: Financed by Museum operating funds
Library Holdings: Auction Catalogs; Book Volumes 50,000; Clipping Files; Exhibition Catalogs; Memorabilia; Other Holdings Auction Records; Ephemera; Pamphlets; Periodical Subscriptions 97; Reproductions; Slides
Special Subjects: Art History, Folk Art, Decorative Arts, Drawings, Etchings & Engravings, Graphic Arts, Islamic Art, Manuscripts, Ceramics, Conceptual Art, Latin American Art, Fashion Arts, Asian Art, Ivory, Jade
Collections: Arizona Artist Files; auction catalogs; museum archives; Rembrandt print catalogs; Whistler Print catalogs; Astaire Library of Costumes & Fashion

M PHOENIX CENTER FOR THE ARTS, 1202 N 3rd St, Phoenix, AZ 85004-1812. Tel 602-254-3100; Internet Home Page Address: www.phoenixcenterforthearts.org; Dir Joseph Benesh
Open 9 AM - 9 PM
Activities: Classes for adults & children

C WELLS FARGO, Wells Fargo History Museum, 100 W Washington St, S4101-010 Phoenix, AZ 85003-1805. Tel 602-378-1578; 1852; Fax 602-378-5174; Elec Mail whalenc@wellsfargo.com; Internet Home Page Address: www.wellsfargohistory.com; Cur Connie Whalen
Open Mon - Fri 9AM-5PM; No admis fee; Estab Oct 3 2003 History Museum with art gallery; Average Annual Attendance: 9,000
Collections: Western scenes; Remington Bronzes; NC Wyeth; F Schnoover; M Dixon
Activities: Tours

PRESCOTT

M GEORGE PHIPPEN MEMORIAL FOUNDATION, Phippen Museum - Art of the American West, 4701 Hwy 89 N, Prescott, AZ 86301. Tel 928-778-1385; Fax 928-778-4524; Elec Mail phippen@phippenartmuseum.org; Internet Home Page Address: www.phippenartmuseum.org; Dir Kim Villalpando; Admin Asst Edd Kellerman; Colls Mgr Deb Bentlage; Museum Store Lynette Tritel; Event Coordr James Ward
Open Tues - Sat 10 AM - 4 PM, Sun 1 PM - 4 PM; cl Mon; Admis adults $5, seniors & students $4, children under 12 free; Estab 1974 to exhibit art of the American West, collect & educ; Circ Reference only; Gallery has 6,000 sq ft; maintains reference library; Average Annual Attendance: 13,000; Mem: 500; dues $35 & up; annual meeting in Feb
Income: $500,000 financed by grants, sponsorships, mem, admis fees, special events
Library Holdings: Auction Catalogs; Book Volumes; Clipping Files; DVDs; Exhibition Catalogs; Original Documents; Periodical Subscriptions; Prints; Reproductions; Video Tapes
Special Subjects: American Indian Art, Drawings, Historical Material, Landscapes, Art Education, Art History, Photography, Pottery, Painting-American, Prints, Textiles, Sculpture, Watercolors, American Western Art, Bronzes, Southwestern Art, Woodcarvings, Portraits, Miniatures, Pewter, Leather, Military Art, Reproductions
Collections: Permanent collection contains fine art depicting art of the American West
Exhibitions: Phippen Memorial Day Art Show; Annual Art Show, juried with 140 artists; Miniature Masterpiece Show & Sale
Publications: Canvas, Phippen Museum members newsletter
Activities: Classes for adults & children; docent training; educ prog; lects open to pub, 5-10 vis lectrs per yr; concerts; gallery talks; tours; competitions & awards; individual paintings & original objects of art lent to various mus in the country; lending collection contains original art works, paintings & sculpture; book traveling exhibs; originate traveling exhibs; mus shop sells books, original art, reproductions, prints & gifts

A PRESCOTT FINE ARTS ASSOCIATION, Gallery, 208 N Marina St, Prescott, AZ 86301-3106. Tel 928-445-3286; Fax 928-778-7888; Elec Mail pfaaoperations@qwest.net; Internet Home Page Address: www.pfaa.net; Pres Steve Bracety; Operations Mgr Arlene Minushkin; Office Mgr Sue Lord; Exec Dir Cheri Friedman
Open Tues - & Sat 10 AM - 3 PM, Sun Noon - 4 PM; No admis fee, donations accepted; Estab 1968 as a nonprofit gallery & theatre to promote arts within the county & local community; Art Gallery is one large room below theater section in what was previously a Catholic Church; Average Annual Attendance: 20,000; Mem: 400; dues family $50, individual $25
Income: $30,000 (financed by mem & grants from Arizona Commission on Arts & Humanities Council)
Collections: 10 each yr-constantly changing
Publications: Newsletter
Activities: Classes for adults & children; docent training; lect open to pub, 2-3 vis lectrs per yr; concerts; scholarship; competitions with awards; gallery talks; scholarships offered; sales shop sells original art, prints, pottery, jewelry, glass & woven items

SCOTTSDALE

M CONGREGATION BETH ISRAEL'S PLOTKIN JUDAICA MUSEUM, (Sylvia Plotkin Museum of Temple Beth Israel) 10460 N 56th St, Scottsdale, AZ 85253-1133. Tel 480-951-0323; Fax 480-951-7150; Elec Mail library@cbiaz.org; Internet Home Page Address: www.cbiaz.org; Dir Carol Reynolds
Open by appointment; Admis free, $3.50 suggested donation; Estab 1970 to promote educ of Judaism; Tunisian Synagogue Gallery. Maintains library; Average Annual Attendance: 200; Mem: 500; dues $20 - $250; annual meeting Mar
Income: (financed by endowment, mem & gifts)
Special Subjects: Photography, Sculpture, Textiles, Religious Art, Judaica, Silver, Tapestries, Period Rooms
Collections: Contemporary art reflecting the Jewish experience; Holiday Judaica; Jewish Life Cycles; Synagogue Period Room; Tunisian; AZ Jewish Experience
Publications: HA-OR, three times a year
Activities: Classes for adults & children; docent progs; lects open to pub, 3 vis lectrs per yr; concerts; tours; films; individual paintings & original objects of art are lent to other mus; lending collection contains 15,000 books & 200 videos; book traveling exhibs 3 per yr; originate traveling exhibs 1 per yr; mus shop sells original art

L FRANK LLOYD WRIGHT SCHOOL, William Wesley Peters Library, 12621 N Frank Lloyd Wright Blvd, PO Box 4430 Scottsdale, AZ 85261-4430. Tel 480-860-2700; Fax 480-860-8472; Elec Mail wwplib@taliesin.edu; Dir of Library Elizabeth Dawsari
Not open to the public, call for appt; Estab 1983
Library Holdings: Audio Tapes 19,000; Book Volumes 16,000; Cassettes; Clipping Files; Exhibition Catalogs; Pamphlets; Photographs; Reproductions; Slides; Video Tapes
Collections: 25,000 Collateral files & material; 100,000 drawings

A SCOTTSDALE ARTISTS' LEAGUE, P.O. Box 1071, Scottsdale, AZ 85252. Tel 480-874-2272; Elec Mail info@scottsdaleartistsleague.org; Internet Home Page Address: www.scottsdaleartistsleague.org; Pres Ericka Cero Wood; 1st VPres Progs Paul Nemiroff; 2nd VPres Shows Annie Gillette
See web site for hours; No admis fee; donation suggested; Estab 1961 to encourage the practice of art & to support & encourage the study & application of art as an avocation, to promote ethical principals & practice, to advance the interest & appreciation of art in all its forms & to increase the usefulness of art to the public at large; Average Annual Attendance: 4,800; Mem: dues $42-75; $42 suggested mem donations, monthly meetings every first Tues
Exhibitions: Yearly juried exhibition for members only; yearly juried exhibition for all Arizona artists (open shows); Desert Botanical Garden Paintout every March
Publications: Art Beat, monthly
Activities: Classes for adults; lect open to public, 11 vis lectrs per yr; gallery talks; tours; scholarships offered to art students

L SCOTTSDALE ARTISTS' SCHOOL LIBRARY, 3720 N Marshall Way, Scottsdale, AZ 85251-5559. Tel 480-990-1422; Fax 480-990-0652; Elec Mail info@scottsdaleschool.org; Internet Home Page Address: www.scottsdaleartschool.org; WATS 800-333-5707; Exec Dir Bernadette Mills; Registrar Marilyn Whitaker; Bus Mgr Wanda Stillions
Open Mon-Fri 8:30 AM-5PM; Admis fees vary; Estab 1983; Average Annual Attendance: 2500
Library Holdings: Book Volumes 2500; Exhibition Catalogs; Framed Reproductions; Original Art Works; Pamphlets; Periodical Subscriptions 20; Prints; Reproductions; Sculpture; Video Tapes
Special Subjects: Art History, Decorative Arts, Illustration, Photography, Commercial Art, Drawings, Etchings & Engravings, Graphic Design, Painting-American, Painting-Flemish, Painting-French, Painting-German, Painting-Italian, Painting-Japanese, Prints, Sculpture, Painting-European, History of Art & Archaeology, Portraits, Watercolors, Latin American Art, American Western Art, Bronzes, American Indian Art, Oriental Art
Collections: Paintings; Prints; Sculpture
Exhibitions: Best and Brightest Juried Student Exhibit
Activities: Classes for adults and children; lects open to public; 15 vis lectrs per yr; awards: Best & Brightest; scholarships offered; sales shop sells books & art supplies

M SCOTTSDALE CULTURAL COUNCIL, (Scottsdale Center for the Arts) Scottsdale Museum of Contemporary Art, 7374 E Second St, Scottsdale, AZ 85251; 7380 E Second St, Scottsdale, AZ 85251. Tel 480-874-4666; Fax 480-874-4655; Elec Mail smoca@sccarts.org; Internet Home Page Address: www.smoca.org; Dir Tim Rodgers; Asst Cur Claire Carter; Assoc Cur Cassandra Coblentz; Cur Educ Carolyn Robbins; Registrar Pat Evans
Open Tues. Wed & Sun noon - 5 PM, Thurs noon - 8 PM, Fri & Sat noon - 10 PM (free admis 5PM - 10PM); Admis $7 adults; $5 students; free for members & children under 15 & Thurs; Opened in 1999; presents exhibitions of modern & contemporary art, architecture & design; Designed by Will Bruder, SMOCA features five galleries and an outdoor sculpture garden with one of James Turrell's "Skyspaces"; Average Annual Attendance: 40,000; Mem: 2,900; dues $30 - $5,000+
Income: Financed by mem, city appropriation & corporate sponsorship
Library Holdings: Book Volumes; Exhibition Catalogs
Special Subjects: Drawings, Architecture, Ceramics, Glass, Furniture, Photography, Prints, Sculpture
Collections: Paintings, prints, sculptures, photographs, drawings; James Turrell "Skyspace"
Exhibitions: Rotating exhibits
Publications: Exhibition catalogs
Activities: Classes for adults & children; docent training; gallery talks; tours; lects open to public, 10 vis lectrs per year; exten dept serves local schools; book traveling exhibs 5-6 per yr; originates traveling exhibs to other museums; sales shop sells books, magazines, reproductions, prints, craft items & jewelry; Junior mus: Young @ Art Gallery, 7380 E Second St, Scottsdale, AZ 85251

SECOND MESA

M **HOPI CULTURAL CENTER MUSEUM,** Rte 264, Second Mesa, AZ 86043; PO Box 67, Second Mesa, AZ 86043-0067. Tel 928-734-2401; Fax 520-734-6650; Elec Mail hopi3@psv.com; *Dir* Anna Silas
Open Mon - Fri 8 AM - 5 PM, Sat - Sun 8 AM - 3 PM
Collections: Hopi arts & crafts; pre-historic & historic pottery; weavings; wood carvings; silver

TEMPE

M **ARIZONA STATE UNIVERSITY,** ASU Art Museum, Nelson Fine Arts Ctr, Tempe, AZ 85287-1202; PO Box 872911, Tempe, AZ 85287-2911. Tel 480-965-2787; Fax 480-965-5254; Elec Mail asuartmuseum@asu.edu; Internet Home Page Address: www.asuartmuseum.asu.edu; *Sr Cur* Heather Lineberry; *Registrar* Anne Sullivan; *Installationist* Stephen Johnson; *Dir* Gordon Knox; *Ceramics Cur* Peter Held
Open academic yr Tues 10 AM -8 PM, Wed - Sat 10 AM - 5 PM, cl Sun & Mon; No admis fee; Estab 1950 to provide esthetic & educational service for students & the citizens of the state; Permanent installations, changing galleries & various changing area; 48 shows annually; Average Annual Attendance: 55,000; Mem: 1,650
Income: $250,000 (financed by state appropriations, donations & earnings)
Library Holdings: Exhibition Catalogs; Prints
Special Subjects: Ceramics, Glass, Mexican Art, Photography, Painting-American, Prints, Manuscripts, Painting-French, Painting-Japanese, Sculpture, Hispanic Art, Latin American Art, Watercolors, Crafts, Portraits, Painting-Canadian, Calligraphy, Painting-Spanish, Painting-Australian
Collections: American crafts, especially ceramics & glass; American painting & sculpture, 18th Century to present; Contemporary art; print coll, 15th Century to present; Latin American Art; Folk Art; 20th century ceramics
Publications: Too Late for Goya: Works by Francesc Torres; Art Under Duress: El Salvador 1980-Present; Bill Biola: Buried Secrets; Art of the Edge of Fashion
Activities: Educ dept; docent training; student docent prog; special events; lects open to pub, 12 vis lectrs per yr; gallery talks; tours; competitions; originate traveling exhibs; mus shop sells books, reproductions, original art & crafts, jewelry, cards

L **ASU Library,** PO Box 871006, Tempe, AZ 85287-1006. Tel 480-965-6164; Internet Home Page Address: www.asu.edu/lib; *Art Specialist* Dennis Brunning; *Architecture Librn* Deborah Koshinsky; *Univ Librn* Sherrie Schmidt
Open Mon-Thurs 7AM-Midnight, Fri 7AM-7PM, Sat 9AM-5PM, Sun 10AM-Midnight
Income: Financed by state & other investors
Library Holdings: Book Volumes 2,826,679; Cards; Cassettes; Exhibition Catalogs; Fiche; Maps; Periodical Subscriptions 31,694; Reels; Video Tapes
Special Subjects: Art History, History of Art & Archaeology, Archaeology, American Western Art, Interior Design, Art Education, American Indian Art, Anthropology, Coins & Medals, Architecture

M **Memorial Union Gallery,** PO Box 870901, Tempe, AZ 85287-0901. Tel 480-965-6649; Fax 480-727-6212; Internet Home Page Address: www.asu.edu/mu; *Prog Coordr* Joy Klein
Open Mon - Fri 9 AM - 5 PM; No admis fee; Estab to exhibit work that has strong individual qualities from the United States, also some Arizona work that has not been shown on campus; Gallery is contained in two rooms with 1,400 sq ft space; fireplace; one wall is glass; 20 ft ceiling; 26 4 x 8 partitions; track lighting; one entrance and exit; located in area with maximum traffic; Average Annual Attendance: 30,000
Income: Financed by admin appropriation
Purchases: $3,000
Collections: Painting, print & sculpture, primarily Altma, Gorman, Mahaffey, Schoulder & Slater
Exhibitions: Rotating exhibits
Activities: Internships; lects open to pub, 4 vis lectrs per yr; gallery talks; competitions; originate traveling exhibs

L **Architecture & Environmental Design Library,** PO Box 871006, Tempe, AZ 85287-1006. Tel 480-965-6400; Fax 480-727-6965; Internet Home Page Address: www.asu.edu/caed/aedlibrary; *Admnr & Asc Librn* Deborah Koshinsky; *Opers Supv* James Allen III
Open acad yr Mon - Thurs 8 AM - 10 PM, Fri 8 AM - 5 PM, Sat Noon - 4 PM, Sun 2 - 10 PM; Estab 1959 to serve the College of Architecture & Environmental Design & the university community with reference & research material in the subjects of architecture, planning, landscape architecture, industrial design & interior design; Circ 35,000
Income: Financed by state appropriation
Library Holdings: Audio Tapes; Book Volumes 30,000; Cassettes; Fiche; Manuscripts; Memorabilia; Micro Print; Other Holdings Architectural models; Periodical Subscriptions 130; Photographs; Prints; Reels; Slides; Video Tapes
Special Subjects: Landscape Architecture, Industrial Design, Interior Design, Furniture, Architecture
Collections: Paolo Soleri & Frank Lloyd Wright Special Research Collections; Victor Olgyzy, Paul Schweikher, Litchfield Park, Will Bruder, Albert Chase MacArthur, other drawings & documents

TUBAC

M **TUBAC CENTER OF THE ARTS,** Santa Cruz Valley Art Association, 9 Plaza Rd, Tubac, AZ 85646; PO Box 1911, Tubac, AZ 85646-1911. Tel 520-398-2371; Fax 520-398-9511; Elec Mail contactus@tubacarts.org; Internet Home Page Address: www.tubacarts.org; *Co-Dir* Karin Topping; *Co-Dir* Susannah Castro; *Pres* Jan Schoeben; *Gift Shop Mgr* Bonme Jaus; *Educ Coordr* Jo Edmondson; *Weekend Supv* Karon Leigh
Open Mon - Sat 10 AM - 4:30 PM, Sun noon - 4:30 PM; No admis fee; Estab 1963 to promote interest in arts and art education; Three galleries, in a Spanish Colonial Building, 300 running ft of exhibit space; Average Annual Attendance: 40,000; Mem: 800; dues $45-$2500; annual meeting in Oct

Income: State arts council, grants, membership & contributions
Special Subjects: Painting-American, Sculpture, Watercolors, American Indian Art, American Western Art, Textiles, Ceramics, Crafts, Landscapes, Decorative Arts, Portraits, Historical Material
Exhibitions: Invitationals; members & non-members shows
Activities: Classes for adults & children; dramatic prog; docent training; lects open to pub 10 per yr; competitions with awards; concerts; gallery talks; tours; sales shop sells books, original art, reproductions, prints, jewelry, ceramics, fine crafts & art

L **Library,** 9 Plaza Rd, Tubac, AZ 85646; PO Box 1911, Tubac, AZ 85646. Tel 520-398-2371; Fax 520-398-9511; Elec Mail jdefalla@tabacarts.org; Internet Home Page Address: www.tubacarts.org; *Dir* Annette Brink
Open Tues 10 AM - 4:30 PM; No admis fee; Estab 1964, 501(c)3 arts center; Brick territorial style bldg, 5,000 sq ft with patio; Average Annual Attendance: 50,000; Mem: 850, $45 annual dues
Income: Financed by grants, gifts & contributions
Library Holdings: Book Volumes 850; Cards; Exhibition Catalogs; Slides
Special Subjects: Art History
Activities: Classes for adults & children; dramatic progs, docent training; lects open to pub; concerts; gallery talks; tours; cash & non-cash exhib awards; mus shop sells books, original art, reproductions, prints, jewelry, pottery & wearable art

TUCSON

AMERICAN SOCIETY OF BOOKPLATE COLLECTORS & DESIGNERS
For further information, see National and Regional Organizations

M **DINNERWARE ARTIST'S COOPERATIVE,** 44 W 6th St, Tucson, AZ 85705-8374. Elec Mail dinnerwareartspace@gmail.com; Internet Home Page Address: www.dinnerwarearts.com; *Dir* David Aguirre
Estab 1979
Income: Financed in part by Tucson Pima Arts Council & AZ Commission on the Arts

A **NATIONAL NATIVE AMERICAN CO-OPERATIVE,** North American Indian Information & Trade Center, PO Box 27626, Tucson, AZ 85726-7626. Tel 520-622-4900; Elec Mail info@usaindianinfo.com; Internet Home Page Address: www.usaindianinfo.com; *Dir & Consultant* Fred Synder
Call for hours, hours change for different events; Admis fee varies by events; Estab 1969 to provide incentive to 2700 American Indian artists representing over 410 tribes for the preservation of their contemporary & traditional crafts, culture & educ through involvement in Indian cultural programs, including dances, traditional food, fashion shows & performances. Also sponsors various Indian events; Authentic hand-made crafts; art from over 140 tribal nations; Average Annual Attendance: 50,000-60,000; Mem: 2,700; meetings in Nov & Jan; American Indian Artists only; no dues; qualification for mem: quality craftsmanship
Income: Financed through sales of Native American Directory: Alaska, Canada & US
Purchases: Quality authentic crafts
Library Holdings: Book Volumes; Cassettes; Compact Disks; Original Art Works; Pamphlets; Periodical Subscriptions; Photographs
Special Subjects: Sculpture, Silver, American Indian Art, Crafts, Miniatures, Jewelry, Woodcarvings, Eskimo Art, Scrimshaw, Gold, Southwestern Art
Collections: Native American arts & crafts, including jewelry, basketry, wood & stone carving, weaving, pottery, beadwork, quill-work, rug-making, tanning & leatherwork, dance & cookery; books
Exhibitions: Dance/Craft Competition (2 events yearly)
Publications: Native American Directory: Alaska, Canada, United States; Native American Reference Book (1996-2012); Pow-Wow on the Red Road; American Indian Events
Activities: Classes for adults; volunteer; lects open to pub, 5-10 vis lectrs per yr; concerts; competitions with prizes; 2 schols offered every Oct (1 acad & 1 cultural); artmobile; book traveling exhibs 40-50 per yr; originate traveling exhibs among American Indian events: conferences, pow-wows; sales shop sells books & original art

M **TOHONO CHUL PARK,** 7366 N Paseo del Norte, Tucson, AZ 85704-4415. Tel 520-742-6455; Fax 520-797-1213; Elec Mail marketing@tohonochulpark.org; Internet Home Page Address: www.tohonochulpark.org; *Cur Exhibits* Vicki Donkersley; *Asst Exhibits Cur* Ben Johnson; *Dir Pub Progs* Jo Falls; *Exec Dir* Dr Christine Conte; *Retail Mgr* Linda Wolfe
Open daily 9AM-5PM; Admis $7, seniors & military $5, students $3, child $2; Estab 1985 for people to experience the wonders of the Sonoran Desert & gain knowledge of natural & cultural heritage of the region; Changing exhibits featuring regional arts & artists; Average Annual Attendance: 130,000; Mem: 6,000; dues $20-$5000
Income: $2,400,000 (financed by mem, grants, donations & earned income)
Special Subjects: Decorative Arts, Drawings, Etchings & Engravings, Folk Art, Landscapes, Ceramics, Collages, Mexican Art, Flasks & Bottles, Furniture, Photography, Prints, Silver, Sculpture, Hispanic Art, Watercolors, American Indian Art, Ethnology, Southwestern Art, Religious Art, Crafts, Primitive art, Woodcarvings, Woodcuts, Dolls, Jewelry, Porcelain, Carpets & Rugs, Juvenile Art, Miniatures, Dioramas, Embroidery, Laces, Mosaics
Collections: Modern & contemporary Native American crafts of the Southwest
Exhibitions: 12 - 14 changing exhibits per year
Publications: Desert Corner Journal newsletter, 5 times per yr
Activities: Classes for children & adults; docent training; concerts; tours; field trips; lects open to pub, 12 - 15 vis lectrs per yr; gallery talks; competitions; Lumie Award, 2009; mus store sells books, original art, reproductions, prints

M **TUCSON MUSEUM OF ART AND HISTORIC BLOCK,** (Tucson Museum of Art) 140 N Main Ave, Tucson, AZ 85701-8290. Tel 520-624-2333; Fax 520-624-7202; Elec Mail info@tucsonmuseumofart.org; Internet Home Page Address: www.tucsonmuseumofart.org; *Exec Dir* Robert E Knight; *Dir Educ* Stephanie J Coakley; *Dir Devel* Alba Rojas-Sukkar; *Dir Fin & Admin* Katie Hiedeman; *Dir Pub Rels & Mktg* Meredith Hayes; *Chief Cur & Cur Modern & Contemporary Art* Julie Sasse; *Cur Latin American Art* Ann Seiferle-Valencia; *Preparator* David Longwell; *Head Security* Delmar Bambrough; *Research Librn* Lisa Waite Bunker; *Ceramics Instr* Janet Burner; *Graphics Instr* Serena Tang; *Bldgs & Grounds Supv* Allan Uno; *Coll Mgr & Registrar* Susan Dolan; *Grants Mgr* Vanessa Mallory Kotz; *Mgr Mem & Special Events* Amanda Reed; *Retail Mgr* John McNulty; *Fin Assoc* Amy Ludke; *Mem Assoc* Jenny Balkema; *Educ Asst* Saundie Senne; *Asst Registrar* Rachel Shand; *Admin Asst* Madison John
Open Tues - Sat 10 AM - 5 PM, Sun Noon - 5 PM, cl Mon & Thanksgiving & Christmas Days; Admis adults $8, sr citizens & veterans $6, students $3, under 12 free, 1st Sun of month free; Estab 1924 to operate a private nonprofit civic art gallery to promote art educ, to hold art exhibitions & to further art appreciation for the pub; Galleries display permanent collections & changing exhibitions; Average Annual Attendance: 237,035; Mem: 3,000; dues Dir Circle $1000, President's Circle $500, patron $250, sustaining $100, family $50, individual $40; student $20; annual meeting in Sept
Income: $3,400,000 (financed by grants, endowment, mem, city & state appropriations, contributions & generated income)
Library Holdings: Auction Catalogs; Book Volumes; CD-ROMs; Compact Disks; DVDs; Exhibition Catalogs; Maps; Original Documents; Pamphlets; Periodical Subscriptions; Photographs; Slides; Video Tapes
Special Subjects: Landscapes, Mexican Art, Pottery, Painting-American, Textiles, Sculpture, Latin American Art, Painting-American, Photography, Prints, Sculpture, Watercolors, Pre-Columbian Art, Southwestern Art, Painting-European, Portraits, Oriental Art, Period Rooms
Collections: Contemporary & decorative arts; contemporary Southwest, folk, Mexican, Pre-Columbian, Spanish Colonial, Western American & 20th century art; modern
Publications: Quarterly Preview; exhibition catalogs
Activities: Classes for adults & children; docent training; lect open to public; gallery talks; tours; sponsored competitions; scholarships offered; mus shop sells books, magazines, original art, reproductions & prints

L **Library,** 140 N Main Ave, Tucson, AZ 85701-8290. Tel 520-624-2333, Ext 122; Fax 520-624-7202; Elec Mail jprovan@tucsonarts.com; Internet Home Page Address: www.tucsonarts.com; *Librn* Jill E Provan; *Grant Proj Dir* Jan Willkom
Open Mon - Fri 10 AM - 3 PM; No admis fee; Estab 1974 for bibliographic & research needs of Mus staff, faculty, students & docents; Circ 1,200; Open to public for research & study; Average Annual Attendance: 1,800; Mem: 2,000 - open for circulation to all museum members
Income: Financed by gifts & fund allocations
Purchases: 360 titles per yr
Library Holdings: Book Volumes 11,000; Cards; Clipping Files; Exhibition Catalogs 500; Fiche; Kodachrome Transparencies; Manuscripts; Other Holdings Indexes; Museum archives; Pamphlets 5,000; Periodical Subscriptions 35; Photographs; Prints; Slides 24,000; Video Tapes 100
Special Subjects: Folk Art, Decorative Arts, Mixed Media, Photography, Drawings, Etchings & Engravings, Painting-American, Painting-British, Painting-Dutch, Painting-Flemish, Painting-French, Painting-German, Painting-Italian, Painting-Japanese, Painting-Spanish, Pre-Columbian Art, Prints, Sculpture, Painting-European, Historical Material, History of Art & Archaeology, Watercolors, Ceramics, Crafts, Latin American Art, American Western Art, Printmaking, Art Education, Asian Art, American Indian Art, Porcelain, Eskimo Art, Furniture, Mexican Art, Southwestern Art, Jade, Costume Design & Constr, Glass, Mosaics, Stained Glass, Afro-American Art, Metalwork, Carpets & Rugs, Enamels, Handicrafts, Jewelry, Oriental Art, Religious Art, Silversmithing, Tapestries, Textiles, Woodcarvings, Woodcuts, Marine Painting, Landscapes, Scrimshaw
Collections: Biographic material documenting Arizona artists; Pre-Columbian; Spanish colonial; Latin American art TMA museum; Catalogs, historic block archives
Activities: Classes for adults & children; docent training; annual book sale fundraiser; book discussion groups; lects open to public; 10 vis lectrs per yr; annual book talk at local book store; gallery talks; tours; sponsored competitions; sells books & original art

M **UNIVERSITY OF ARIZONA,** Museum of Art & Archive of Visual Arts, 1031 N Olive Rd, Tucson, AZ 85721-0002; PO Box 210002, Tucson, AZ 85721-0002. Tel 520-621-7567; Fax 520-621-8770; Elec Mail dhartman@email.arizona.edu; Internet Home Page Address: artmuseum.arizona.edu; *Exec Dir* Charles A Guerin; *Cur Educ* Carol Petrozzello; *Dir Resource Initiative* Diane A Hartman; *Cur* Lauren Rabb; *Registrar* Kristen Schmidt; *Exhib Specialist* John Kelly; *Bus Mgr* Kathleen Kearney
Open Tues - Fri 9AM - 5PM, Sat - Sun Noon - 4PM, cl Mon & university holidays; Admis adults $5, mem, children, students with ID & active military free; Estab 1955 to share with the Tucson community, visitors & the university students the treasures of three remarkable permanent collections: the C Leonard Pfeiffer Collection, the Samuel H Kress Collection & the Edward J Gallagher Jr Collection; Special exhibitions are maintained on the first floor of the mus; the permanent collections are housed on the second floor. AAM Accredited; Average Annual Attendance: 23,000
Income: Financed by state appropriation & endowments
Library Holdings: Book Volumes; Exhibition Catalogs; Original Documents
Special Subjects: Afro-American Art, Drawings, Etchings & Engravings, Landscapes, Marine Painting, Collages, Mexican Art, Painting-American, Prints, Painting-British, Painting-European, Painting-French, Painting-Japanese, Hispanic Art, Latin American Art, Portraits, Painting-Dutch, Baroque Art, Painting-Flemish, Painting-Polish, Painting-Spanish, Painting-Italian, Painting-German, Painting-Russian
Collections: Edward J Gallagher Collection of over a hundred paintings of national & international artists; Samuel H Kress Collection of 26 Renaissance works & 26 paintings of the 15th century Spanish Retablo by Fernando Gallego; C Leonard Pfeiffer Collection of American Artists of the 30s, 40s & 50s; Jacques Lipchitz Collection of 70 plaster models
Publications: Fully illustrated catalogs on all spec exhibs
Activities: Docent training; lects open to public, 10 vis lectrs per yr; concerts; gallery talks; tours; sales shop sells books, cards & poster reproductions

L **UA Museum of Art,** Speedway & Olive, Tucson, AZ 85721; PO Box 210002, Tucson, AZ 85721-0002. Tel 520-621-7567; Fax 520-621-8770; Internet Home Page Address: www.artmuseum.arizona.edu
Open Tues - Fri 9 AM - 5 PM, Sat & Sun noon - 4 PM; Admis adults $5, students, children & mem free; 1956; UAMA is a forum for teaching, research & services related to the history & meaning of the visual arts; Not open to pub; telephone requests for information answered; Mem: 350; dues vary
Special Subjects: Art History, Painting-American, Sculpture, Painting-European, Watercolors, Woodcuts
Collections: Seven centuries of art - one museum; 15th century Spanish Altarpiece; American, Modern & contemporary art
Activities: Lects & exhibs throughout the year; mus shop sells books & art related merchandize

M **Center for Creative Photography,** 1030 N Olive Rd, Tucson, AZ 85721. Tel 520-621-7968; Fax 520-621-9444; Internet Home Page Address: www.creativephotography.org; *Registrar* Trinity Parker; *Archivist* Leslie Squyres; *Assoc Cur* Rebecca Senf; *Dir* Katharine Martinez
Open Mon - Fri 9 AM - 5 PM, Sat & Sun 1 - 4 PM; No admis fee; Estab 1975 to house & organize the archives of numerous major photographers & to act as a research center in 20th century photography; Gallery exhibs changing approx 3 times per yr; Average Annual Attendance: 30,000+
Income: Financed by state, federal, private & corporate sources
Special Subjects: Photography
Collections: Archives of Ansel Adams, Wynn Bullock, Harry Callahan, Aaron Siskind, W Eugene Smith, Frederick Sommer, Paul Strand, Edward Weston, Richard Aredon & others
Exhibitions: Various rotating exhibits, call for details
Activities: Lects open to pub; gallery talks; research fel; original objects of art lent to qualified museums; originate traveling exhibitions worldwide

L **Library,** PO Box 210002, Tucson, AZ 85721. Tel 520-621-1331; Fax 520-621-9444; Internet Home Page Address: www.creativephotography.org; *Librn* Miguel Juarez
Open Mon - Fri 10 AM - 5 PM, Sun Noon - 5 PM; Circ Non-circulating; Open to the pub for print viewing & research
Library Holdings: Audio Tapes; Book Volumes 15,000; Cassettes; Clipping Files; Exhibition Catalogs; Fiche; Manuscripts; Memorabilia; Original Art Works; Pamphlets; Periodical Subscriptions 95; Photographs; Reels; Slides; Video Tapes
Collections: Limited edition books; hand-made books; books illustrated with original photographs; artists' books

L **Architecture Collection,** PO Box 210075, Tucson, AZ 85721-0075. Tel 520-621-6384
Open daily 7:30 AM - 1 AM; Estab 1965; The bulk of the collection is located at the Science-Engineering Library, Fl 5 with a small portion remaining at the Fine Arts Library, on the 2nd fl of the Music Bldg; slides relocated to the Visual Resources Ctr
Library Holdings: Book Volumes 20,000; Periodical Subscriptions 120; Video Tapes
Special Subjects: Landscape Architecture, Drafting, Architecture

WESTERN SCULPTURE ACADEMY OF MERIKS, 2509 N Campbell St #311, Tucson, AZ 85719-3362. *Program Coordr* Tillian Merklin
Open Mon, Wed - Sat 8 AM - 8 PM; Admis adults $4; Mem: mem fees vary
Income: 285,000 (financed by mem & gallery fees)

M **WOMANKRAFT ART CENTER,** 388 S Stone Ave, Tucson, AZ 85701-2318. Tel 520-629-9976; Internet Home Page Address: www.womankraft.org; *Exec Dir* Grace Rhyne; *Dir Exhibs* Zoe Rhyne; *Dir School of Arts* Gayle Swanbeck
Open Wed - Sat 1 PM - 5PM, 1st Sat of month 7PM - 10 PM, cl Jan & Aug; No admis fee; Estab 1974 to claim & validate women artists; Craft area, topic gallery, performance space, School of the Arts; Average Annual Attendance: 5,000; Mem: 100; dues $30
Collections: Members art collection
Activities: Classes for adults & children; dramatic progs; workshops & workshop series-poetry readings & performance; lects open to pub; concerts

WICKENBURG

M **MARICOPA COUNTY HISTORICAL SOCIETY,** Desert Caballeros Western Museum, 21 N Frontier St, Wickenburg, AZ 85390-3431. Tel 928-684-2272; Fax 928-684-5794; Elec Mail info@westernmuseum.org; Internet Home Page Address: www.westernmuseum.org; *Exec Dir* W James Burns, PhD; *Cur* Mary Ann Igna; *Store Mgr* Marilu Rix
Open Mon - Sat 10 AM - 5 PM, Sun 12 - 4 PM; cl Mon Memorial Day - Labor Day; Admis general $9, sr citizens $7, children 16 and under free; Estab 1960 to educate & enhance the appreciation & understanding of the art, history, cultural legacy & wonder of the American West; The museum houses western art gallery, mineral room, American Indian Artifacts room, period rooms & gold mining equipment; Average Annual Attendance: 64,000; Mem: 600; dues $25-$75; annual meeting in Jan
Income: $200,000 (financed by mem, private donations, endowments); non-profit 501c3 org
Special Subjects: American Indian Art, Drawings, Painting-American, Photography, Sculpture, Watercolors, American Western Art, Bronzes, Southwestern Art, Textiles, Costumes, Folk Art, Landscapes, Decorative Arts, Manuscripts, Dolls, Furniture, Glass, Jewelry, Carpets & Rugs, Historical Material, Dioramas, Period Rooms
Collections: George Phippen Memorial Western Bronze Collection; Joe Beeler; Charles Russell; Frederick Remington
Exhibitions: Hays Spirit of the West
Publications: A History of Wickenburg to 1875 by Helen B Hawkins; The Right Side Up Town on the Upside Down River; Museum Highlights, newsletter bimonthly; Crossroads: The Museum at 50
Activities: Classes for adults & children; docent training; lects open to pub, 12 vis lectrs per yr; gallery talks; tours; individual paintings & original objects of art lent

to mus; book traveling exhibs two per yr; mus shop sells books, magazines, original art, reproductions, prints & slides

L **Eleanor Blossom Memorial Library,** 21 N Frontier St, Wickenburg, AZ 85358-3431. Tel 520-684-2272; Fax 520-684-5794; Elec Mail dcwm@aol.com; Internet Home Page Address: www.westernmuseum.org; *Dir* Michael Ettema
Open Mon - Sat 10 AM - 5 PM by appointment; Open to members for reference only
Library Holdings: Book Volumes 2000; Periodical Subscriptions 25
Special Subjects: Manuscripts, History of Art & Archaeology, American Western Art

WINDOW ROCK

M **NAVAJO NATION,** Navajo Nation Museum, PO Box 1840, Window Rock, AZ 86515-1840. Tel 928-871-7941; Fax 928-871-7942; Elec Mail info@navajonationmuseum.org; Internet Home Page Address: www.navajonationmuseum.org; *Dir* Geoffrey I Brown; *Cur* Clarenda Begay; *Archivist* Eunice Kahn; *Educ Cur* Norman Bahe
Open Mon 8 AM - 5 PM, Tues - Fri 8 AM - 8 PM, Sat 9 AM - 5 PM, cl Sun, Federal and tribal holidays; No admis fee; Estab 1961 to collect & preserve items depicting Navajo history & culture art & natural history of region; Exhibit area approx 13,000 sq ft; Average Annual Attendance: 35,000
Income: Financed by tribal appropriation & donations
Special Subjects: Drawings, Sculpture, Watercolors, American Indian Art, Anthropology, Textiles, Pottery, Jewelry, Silver, Historical Material, Miniatures
Collections: Works in all media by Navajo Indian artists, & non-Navajo artists who depict Navajo subject matter; Navajo textiles, jewelry & historical objects
Publications: Artist's directory & biographical file, exhibition publs
Activities: Educ prog; classes for adults & children; school presentations; tours; conference/meeting/performance facilities for events; lects open to pub; 4-6 vis lectrs per yr; concerts; gallery talks; tours; individual paintings & original works of art; lending collection contains 300 original works of art & 50,000 photographs; mus shop sells books, magazines, original art, reproductions, prints, video tapes, DVDs, t-shirts, arts & crafts

L **NAVAJO NATION LIBRARY SYSTEM,** PO Box 9040, Window Rock, AZ 86515-9040. Tel 520-871-6376; Fax 520-871-7304; Elec Mail irvingnelson@navajo.org; Internet Home Page Address: www.nnlb.org; *Librn* Irving Nelson
Open Mon 8 AM-5 PM, Tues - Fri 8 AM - 8 PM, Sat 9 AM - 5 PM, cl Sun; No admis fee; Estab 1949
Income: through the Navajo Nation
Library Holdings: Book Volumes 21,000; Periodical Subscriptions 50

YUMA

M **ARIZONA HISTORICAL SOCIETY-YUMA,** Sanguinetti House Museum & Garden, 240 Madison Ave, Yuma, AZ 85364. Tel 928-782-1841; Fax 928-783-0680; Elec Mail ahsyuma@azhs.gov; Internet Home Page Address: www.arizonahistoricalsociety.org; *Cur* Carol Brooks
Open Tues - Sat 10 AM - 4 PM; Admis adults $3, seniors & students $2, members & children under 12 free; Estab 1963 to collect, preserve & interpret the history of the lower Colorado River Regions; Average Annual Attendance: 2,500; Mem: 200; dues $50 individual, $65 household; annual meeting in Apr
Income: Financed by mem, state appropriation & donations
Library Holdings: Book Volumes; Clipping Files; Manuscripts; Maps; Original Art Works; Original Documents; Other Holdings Oral History Tapes; Photographs
Special Subjects: Drawings, Flasks & Bottles, Textiles, Tapestries, Photography, Ethnology, Costumes, Folk Art, Pottery, Manuscripts, Portraits, Dolls, Furniture, Glass, Porcelain, Historical Material, Maps, Period Rooms, Embroidery, Military Art
Collections: Clothing; Furniture & Household Items; Archives; 12,400 Photos; Maps; Trade & Bus Items; Books, Artifacts, Album-Scrapbooks
Exhibitions: Lower Colorado River Region from 1540-1940; History Exhibits; Period Rooms
Publications: Newsletter; Quarterly Journal
Activities: Lects open to pub; 10 vis lectrs per yr; non-circulating library; mus shop sells books, reproductions, prints & turn of the century style gifts

M **YUMA FINE ARTS ASSOCIATION,** Yuma Art Center, 254 S Main St, Yuma, AZ 85364-1425. Tel 928-329-6607; Fax 928-329-6616; Elec Mail director@yumafinearts.org; Internet Home Page Address: www.yumafinearts.org; *Dir* David Woodward; *Bd Pres* Renee Smith; *Gift Shop Mgr* Catherine Rone
Open Tues, Wed, Thurs 10 AM - 6 PM, Fri 10 AM - 7 PM, Sat 10 AM - 5 PM; No admis fee; Estab 1962 to promote the arts in the Yuma area & to provide exhib space for contemporary art & art of the Southwest; 4 galleries in the Yuma Art Center; Average Annual Attendance: 50,000; Mem: 350; dues $60, $100, $300, $5000
Income: Financed by endowment, mem & city contract, grants & fundraising events
Special Subjects: Etchings & Engravings, Landscapes, Marine Painting, Ceramics, Collages, Glass, American Western Art, Pottery, Painting-American, Prints, Woodcuts, Sculpture, Drawings, Graphics, Hispanic Art, Latin American Art, Mexican Art, Photography, Watercolors, American Indian Art, Bronzes, Southwestern Art, Woodcarvings, Painting-Canadian, Jewelry, Metalwork, Military Art
Collections: Contemporary Art; Art of the Southwest
Exhibitions: Approx 17 exhibs presented annually
Publications: Art Notes Southwest, quarterly
Activities: Classes for adults & children; lects open to pub, 10 vis lectrs per yr; concerts; gallery talks; tours; competitions; $3000 awards annually; individual paintings & original objects of art lent to other mus for specific exhibs; book traveling exhibs 6-10 times per yr; originate traveling exhibs; sales shop sells original art, reproductions, prints, jewelry, pottery, wood, sculptures

ARKANSAS

BATESVILLE

M **LYON COLLEGE KRESGE GALLERY,** Highland & 22nd Sts, Batesville, AR 72503. Tel 870-307-7242;
Call for hours; Average Annual Attendance:
Collections: painting; photographs; sculpture

BENTONVILLE

M **CRYSTAL BRIDGES MUSEUM OF AMERICAN ART,** 600 Museum Way, Bentonville, AR 72712. Tel 479-418-5700; Fax 479-418-5701; Elec Mail info@crystalbridges.org; Internet Home Page Address: www.crystalbridges.org; *Dir* Don Bacigalupi
Open Wed & Fri 11AM-9PM, Thurs & Sat 11AM-6PM
Collections: paintings; sculpture; works on paper; books; outdoor sculpture

CLARKSVILLE

M **UNIVERSITY OF THE OZARKS,** Stephens Gallery, 415 N College Ave, Walton Fine Arts Bldg Clarksville, AR 72830-2880. Tel 501-979-1000, 979-1349 (Gallery); Fax 501-979-1349; *Gallery Dir* Blaine Caldwell
Open Mon - Fri 10 AM - 3 PM & by special arrangement; No admis fee; Estab 1986
Collections: Gould Ivory Collection; Pfeffer Moser Glass Collection
Exhibitions: Monthly exhibitions
Activities: Educ dept; lect open to public; concerts; gallery talks; tours

L **Robson Library,** 415 N College Ave, Clarksville, AR 72830. Tel 479-979-1382; Fax 479-979-1355; Internet Home Page Address: robson.ozarks.edu; *Library Dir* Stuart Stelzer
Open Mon-Thurs 8AM-11PM, Fri 8AM-4:30PM, Sat 1-7PM, Sun 2PM-11PM; Estab 1891
Library Holdings: Book Volumes 89,000; CD-ROMs; Cassettes; Compact Disks; DVDs; Fiche; Periodical Subscriptions 12; Records; Reels; Slides 7,000; Video Tapes 76

EL DORADO

A **SOUTH ARKANSAS ARTS CENTER,** 110 E Fifth St, El Dorado, AR 71730. Tel 870-862-5474; Fax 870-862-4921; Elec Mail info@saac-arts.org; Internet Home Page Address: www.saac-arts.org; *Pres* George Maguire; *Exec Dir* Beth James; *VPres* Robert Allen
Open Mon - Fri 9 AM - 5 PM, Sat 10AM-3PM; No admis fee; Estab 1965 for the promotion, enrichment & improvement of the visual & performing arts by means of exhibits, lectures & instruction & through scholarships to be offered whenever possible; Gallery maintained. New 2,000 sq ft gallery; Mem: 450; dues individual $25, seniors minimum $15; board of dir meeting second Tues every month
Income: Financed by mem, city & state appropriation
Collections: Japanese block prints (including Hokusai, Utamarro, Hiroshig); regional watercolorists; Indian Jewelry (Hopi, Zuni, Navaho)
Exhibitions: Various art shows in this & surrounding states; gallery shows, ten guest artists annually. One show monthly, featuring regional or national artists
Publications: Newsletter, quarterly
Activities: Classes for adults & children; theater & dance workshops; guitar lessons; visual arts classes; lect open to public; gallery talks; competitions; scholarships offered

EUREKA SPRINGS

M **CRAZY BONE GALLERY,** 37 Spring St, Eureka Springs, AR 72632-3147. Tel 479-253-6600; 888-418-8506
Call for hours
Collections: works of local & regional artists

M **EUREKA FINE ART GALLERY,** 78 Spring St, Eureka Springs, AR 72632-3105. Tel 479-253-6595
Call for hours
Collections: paintings; photographs; sculptures

FAIRFIELD BAY

NORTH CENTRAL ARKANSAS ART GALLERY, 337 Snead Dr, Fairfield Bay, AR 72088. Tel 501-884-6100
Call for hours; No admis fee
Collections: works by local & national artists including paintings

FAYETTEVILLE

M **UNIVERSITY OF ARKANSAS,** Fine Arts Center Gallery, 116 Fine Arts Center, University of Arkansas Dept of Art Fayetteville, AR 72701. Tel 479-575-5202; Fax 479-575-2062; Elec Mail stk004@uark.edu; Internet Home Page Address: art.uark.edu/fineartsgallery; *Gallery Dir* Sam King
Open Aug - May Mon - Fri 9 AM - 5:30 PM; subject to change, call for details; No admis fee; Estab 1950 as a teaching and community art gallery in fields of painting, drawing, sculpture and architecture; One gallery with moveable display panels covers 80 x 40 ft, gallery is part of center for art, music & theatre; Average Annual Attendance: 7,500
Income: Financed by state appropriation

Collections: Permanent collection of paintings, photographs, prints and sculpture; Seven original Alexander Calder mobiles
Exhibitions: 10-12 exhibitions per year, featuring a variety of media MFA thesis exhibs; faculty artists exhib on rotating basis; vis artists prog
Activities: Classes for adults; lects open to pub, 6-8 vis lectrs per year; concerts; gallery talks; competitions with awards; traveling exhibs 2-3 per yr
L **Fine Arts Library,** 365 N McIlroy Ave, FNAR-104 Fayetteville, AR 72701-4002. Tel 479-575-4708; Elec Mail falib@uark.edu; Internet Home Page Address: libinfo.uark.edu/fal/default.asp; *Librn* Phillip J Jones
Open Mon - Thurs 8 AM - 11 PM, Fri 8 AM - 6 PM, Sat 1 PM - 6 PM, Sun 2 PM - 11 PM; Estab 1951 to support the curriculum in art & architecture; Circ 7,000
Library Holdings: Book Volumes 33,000; CD-ROMs 60; DVDs 20; Exhibition Catalogs; Periodical Subscriptions 100
Special Subjects: Art History, Landscape Architecture, Interior Design, Art Education, Architecture

FORT SMITH

M **FORT SMITH REGIONAL ART MUSEUM,** (Fort Smith Art Center) 701 Rogers Ave, Fort Smith, AR 72901; PO Box 1257, Fort Smith, AR 72902. Tel 479-784-2787; Fax 479-784-9071; Elec Mail lortega@fsram.org; Internet Home Page Address: www.fsram.org; *Exec Dir* Lee Ortega; *Office Mgr* Anna Byars
Open Tues - Sat 10 AM - 5 PM, Sun 11 AM - 5 PM; No admis fee; Estab 1948 to provide art museum, art assn and art education; Permanent collection on view, traveling exhibs, original exhibs, invitationals; Average Annual Attendance: 20,000; Mem: 400; dues indv $35, family $45, etc (tiered)
Income: $189,000 (financed by grants, mem, contributions & sales)
Library Holdings: Auction Catalogs; Book Volumes; Cards; Clipping Files; Exhibition Catalogs; Framed Reproductions; Memorabilia; Original Art Works
Special Subjects: Drawings, Painting-American, Photography, Prints, Sculpture, Watercolors, Porcelain
Collections: American painting, graphics and drawings; Boehm porcelain; local & regional art
Exhibitions: Two-three exhib per month; competitions
Publications: Bulletin, bi-monthly
Activities: Classes for adults, children & summer art camp; tours; competitions with awards; scholarships offered; original objects of art lent to CITT Government and corporate sponsors; Outreach programs for at risk youth & local nursing homes; off-site exhibs; sales shop sells original art, reproductions, prints, original jewelry, pottery

HOT SPRINGS

M **THE FINE ARTS CENTER OF HOT SPRINGS,** (Hot Springs Art Center) 626 Central Ave Hot Springs, AR 71901; PO Box 6263, Hot Springs, AR 71902-6263. Tel 501-624-0489; Fax 501-624-0489; Elec Mail info@hsfac.org; Internet Home Page Address: www.hsfac.org; *Exec Dir* Donna Dunnahoe
Open Tues & Sat 10 AM - 5 PM; No admis fee; Estab 1947 as a multi-disciplinary Arts Center, for education, creative activities & encouragement of community participation; Exhib Center, gallery, gift shop; Average Annual Attendance: 12,000; Mem: 250 mems; $35 annual mem fee
Income: Financed by individual & corporate mem, grants from the Arkansas Arts Council & National Endowment for the Arts
Collections: Photos - Hot Springs Bath Houses; Marilyn Monroe collection; Permanent collection of fine art
Exhibitions: regional, state & local artist exhibition; (05/2014-06/2014) HS Plein Air Festival
Publications: Class schedule brochures; monthly exhibit announcements; newsletters, 4 times per year; Short List collection of short stories; A Gathering of Artists II, Artists collective
Activities: Classes for adults & children in art; lects open to pub; 10 vis lectrs per yr; concerts; gallery talks; sponsored competitions: Diamond, Photo & Regional; children's art schols offered; mus shop sells original art, pottery & woodcarvings, glass, jewelry, prints

L **NATIONAL PARK COMMUNITY COLLEGE LIBRARY,** (Garland County Community College Library) 101 College Dr, Hot Springs, AR 71913-9173. Tel 501-760-4222; Fax 501-760-4106; Elec Mail sseaman@npcc.edu; *Dir* Sara Seaman
Open Mon - Thurs 7 AM - 9 PM, Fri 7 AM - 4:30 PM, Sat 9AM-1PM; Estab 1970
Income: Financed by state appropriation
Purchases: $50,000
Library Holdings: Book Volumes 750; Periodical Subscriptions 200; Video Tapes 150
Collections: Art history; pottery
Exhibitions: Rotating exhibitions

JONESBORO

M **ARKANSAS STATE UNIVERSITY-ART DEPARTMENT, JONESBORO,** Fine Arts Center Gallery, Caraway Rd, Jonesboro, AR; PO Box 1920, State University, AR 72467-1920. Tel 870-972-3050; Fax 870-972-3932; Elec Mail csteele@astate.edu; *Chair Art Dept* Curtis Steele; *Dir* Steven Mayes
Open weekdays Mon-Fri 10 AM - 5PM; No admis fee; Estab 1967 for educ objectives; recognition of contemporary artists & encouragement to students; Located in the Fine Arts Center, the well-lighted gallery measures 40 x 45 ft plus corridor display areas; Average Annual Attendance: 10,500
Income: $3956 (financed by state appropriation)
Collections: Contemporary paintings; contemporary sculpture; historical & contemporary prints; photographs
Publications: Exhibition catalogs

Activities: Lects open to public, 4-6 vis lectrs per yr; gallery talks; competitions; originate traveling exhibs
L **Library,** 108 Cooley Dr, Jonesboro, AR; PO Box 2040, State University, AR 72467-2040. Tel 870-972-3077; Fax 870-972-5706; *Dean* Dr Mary Moore; *Users Svcs Mgr* Anthony Phillips; *Reference Librn* Jeff Bailey
Library Holdings: Book Volumes 10,000; Cassettes; Fiche; Filmstrips; Kodachrome Transparencies; Motion Pictures; Periodical Subscriptions 79; Reels; Slides
Collections: Microfilm collection for 19th century photography

LITTLE

SOCIETY FOR COMMERCIAL ARCHEOLOGY, PO Box 2500, Little, AR 72203-2500. Tel 608-264-6560; Fax 608-264-7615; Elec Mail office@sca-roadside.org; Internet Home Page Address: www.sca-roadside.org; *Pres* Carrie Scupholm; *VPres* Gregory Smith; *Cur & Librn* Beth Dodd
Estab 1976 to promote pub awareness, exchange information & encourage selective conservation of the commercial landscape; Mem: 800; dues institutional $40, individual $25; annual meetings
Income: Financed by mem & dues
Publications: Journal, two times a year; newsletter, quarterly

LITTLE ROCK

M **ARKANSAS ARTS CENTER,** 501 E 9th St, Little Rock, AR 72202; PO Box 2137, Little Rock, AR 72203-2137. Tel 501-372-4000; Fax 501-375-8053; Elec Mail info@www.arkansasartscenter.org; Internet Home Page Address: www.arkansasartscenter.org; *Exec Dir* Todd A Herman, PhD; *Chief Cur* Brian Lang; *Cur Drawings* Ann Prentice Wagner, PhD; *Registrar* Thom Hall; *CFO* Laine Harber; *Dir Develop* Kelly Ford; *Dir Educ* Louise Palermo
Open Tues-Sat 10AM-5PM, Sun 11AM-5PM; No admis fee to galleries & Terry House Community Gallery, admis charged for theatre activities; Estab 1960 to further the develop, the understanding & the appreciation of the visual & performing arts; Circ Non-circulating, research only; Eight galleries; Average Annual Attendance: 550,000; Mem: 5000; dues from benefactor $20,000 to basic $55; annual meeting in Aug
Income: Financed by endowment, mem, city & state appropriation & earned income & private corporate, state, local & federal grants
Library Holdings: Auction Catalogs; Audio Tapes; Book Volumes; CD-ROMs; Cards; Cassettes; Clipping Files; Compact Disks; DVDs; Exhibition Catalogs; Original Documents; Pamphlets; Periodical Subscriptions
Special Subjects: Ceramics, Glass, Metalwork, Painting-European, Sculpture, Drawings, Painting-American, Prints, Watercolors, Crafts, Woodcarvings, Decorative Arts, Jewelry, Renaissance Art
Collections: Drawings from the Renaissance to present, with major coll of American & European drawings since 1900; 19th & 20th century paintings & prints; 20th century sculpture & photographs; Oriental & American decorative arts; contemporary crafts & toys designed by artists
Exhibitions: (10/25/2013-02/09/2014) Mark Rothko in the 1940s: The Decisive Decade
Publications: Members Bulletin, quarterly; annual membership catalog; annual report; catalogue selections from the permanent collection; exhibit catalogues & brochures
Activities: Classes for adults & children; dramatic progs; children's theatre; docent training; lects open to pub, 6-10 vis lectrs per yr; gallery talks; tours; competitions with awards; exten dept serving the state of Arkansas; artmobile; individual paintings & original objects of art lent to schools, civic groups & churches; lending collection contains motion pictures, original prints, paintings, 4300 phonorecords & 16,000 slides; book traveling exhibs; originates traveling exhibs; mus shop sells books, original art, reproductions, jewelry, crafts, cards & calendars
L **Elizabeth Prewitt Taylor Memorial Library,** 501 E 9th St, Little Rock, AR 72202; PO Box 2137, Little Rock, AR 72203-2137. Tel 501-396-0341; Fax 501-375-8053; Elec Mail library@arkansasartscenter.org; Internet Home Page Address: www.arkansasartscenter.org
By appointment; No admis fee; photocopying charges apply; Estab 1963 to provide resources in the arts for students, educators & interested pub; For reference only
Library Holdings: Auction Catalogs; Book Volumes 5,500; Clipping Files; DVDs; Exhibition Catalogs; Motion Pictures; Pamphlets; Periodical Subscriptions 20; Photographs; Records; Video Tapes
Special Subjects: Art History, Folk Art, Decorative Arts, Photography, Drawings, Painting-American, Prints, Sculpture, Historical Material, History of Art & Archaeology, Watercolors, Ceramics, Crafts, Latin American Art, American Western Art, Printmaking, Asian Art, American Indian Art, Eskimo Art, Glass, Afro-American Art, Carpets & Rugs, Textiles

M **HISTORIC ARKANSAS MUSEUM,** (Historic Museum of Arkansas) 200 E Third St, Little Rock, AR 72201. Tel 501-324-9351; Fax 501-324-9345; Elec Mail info@historicarkansas.org; Internet Home Page Address: www.historicarkansas.org; *Cur Research* Swannee Bennett; *Dir Educ* Starr Mitchell; *Dir & CEO* William B Worthen Jr; *Dir Communs* Ellen Korenblat; *Develop Dir* Louise Terzia; *Chmn* Frances Ross; *Pres* Wally Nixon; *Historic Site Specialist* David Etchieson; *Conservator* Andrew Zawacki; *Registrar* Lark Buckingham; *Fiscal Mgr* Rebecca Hochradel; *Coordr* Tricia Spione; *Security Supv* Mike Croy; *Mus Shop Mgr* Paige James
Open daily 9 AM - 5 PM, Sun 1 - 5 PM, cl New Year's, Easter, Thanksgiving, Christmas Eve & Christmas Day; Admis to mus houses adults $2.50, seniors (65+) $1.50, children $1, Museum Center & galleries free; Restoration completed 1941; Historic Arkansas Museum includes pre- Civil War homes, education space & galleries to interpret early Arkansas history; Average Annual Attendance: 50,000; Mem: Individual $35, family $50, supporting $100, sustaining $250, founder $500, cornerstone $1,000 & up; museum shop sells books, original art, reproductions, prints & handmade crafts
Income: Financed by state & private funding

Special Subjects: Architecture, Drawings, Painting-American, American Indian Art, Archaeology, Ethnology, Costumes, Ceramics, Crafts, Folk Art, Etchings & Engravings, Decorative Arts, Manuscripts, Portraits, Furniture, Glass, Porcelain, Metalwork, Carpets & Rugs, Historical Material, Maps, Period Rooms, Embroidery, Laces
Collections: Arkansas made guns & furniture; Audubon prints; furnishing of the period; prints & maps from the 19th century; silver coll; watercolors
Publications: Arkansas Made: The Decorative Mechanical & Fine Arts Produced in Arkansas 1819-1870, Vol I & Vol II; Exhibit catalogues; brochure; Newsletter, Collections: A Garden Heritage
Activities: Classes for children; Log House activities include educational prog for students & adults in candle dipping, cooking & needlework; reception ctr has exhibs & art gallery; individual paintings & original objects of art lent to other mus & cultural institutions; originate traveling exhibs to area mus & schools; mus store sells Arkansas made art & crafts

L **Library,** 200 E Third St, Little Rock, AR 72201. Tel 501-324-9351; Fax 501-324-9345; Elec Mail info@historicarkansas.org; Internet Home Page Address: www.historicarkansas.org; *Dir* W B Worthen Jr; *Cur* Swannee Bennett; *Educ Dir* Starr Mitchell; *Develop Dir* Louise Terzia; *Communs Dir* Ellen Korenblat
Open Mon - Sat 9 AM - 5 PM, Sun 1 - 5 PM; Admis to galleries free, small charge for tours; Estab 1941 to preserve & promote Arkansas history; Arkansas Artist Gallery contains contemporary Arkansas artists with new display monthly, Knife Gallery contains Bowie Knife & history, 4 other galleries are dedicated to Arkansas made objects & history; Average Annual Attendance: 50,000; Mem: 400
Income: Financed by the state & private funds
Purchases: Arkansas made items for museum coll
Library Holdings: Audio Tapes; Book Volumes 1,000; Cassettes; Clipping Files; Framed Reproductions; Manuscripts; Original Art Works; Pamphlets; Periodical Subscriptions 8; Photographs; Prints; Reels; Reproductions; Slides
Collections: Arkansas-made decorative, mechanical & fine art
Exhibitions: Contemporary art; historical exhibits
Publications: Arkansas Made: The Decorative, Mechanical and Fine Art Produced in Arkansas 1819-1870 vol I & II
Activities: Classes for adults & children; dramatic progs; docent training; lects open to pub, 3 vis lectrs per yr; tours; exhibs openings; special events; individual paintings & original objects of art lent to other mus; mus shop sells books, original art, reproductions, prints

M **QUAPAW QUARTER ASSOCIATION, INC,** Villa Marre, Curran Hall, 615 E Capitol Ave Little Rock, AR 72202-2421; PO Box 165023, Little Rock, AR 72216-5023. Tel 501-371-0075; Fax 501-374-8142; Elec Mail qqa@quapaw.com; Internet Home Page Address: www.quapaw.com; *Exec Dir* Rhea Roberts; *Operations Asst* Michelle Bilello
Open Mon - Fri 9 AM - 1 PM, Sun 1 - 5 PM, & by appointment; Admis adults $3, sr citizens & students $2; Estab 1966; The Villa Marre is a historic house mus which, by virtue of its extraordinary collection of late 19th century decorative arts, is a center for the study of Victorian styles; Average Annual Attendance: 5,000; Mem: 350; dues $25 & up; annual meeting in Nov
Income: $95,000 (financed by mem, corporate support, grants & fundraising events)
Special Subjects: Textiles, Decorative Arts, Furniture
Collections: Artwork by Benjamin Brantley; curios appropriate to an 1881 Second Empire Victorian home, late 19th & early 20th century furniture, textiles; 19 century maps, custom floorcloth
Publications: Quapaw Quarter Chronicle, bimonthly
Activities: Classes for adults & children; docent training; lects open to pub; 8-12 vis lectrs; tours; book traveling exhibs; originate traveling exhibs; sales shop sells books; magazines; prints & other items

L **Preservation Resource Center/ Historic Cannon Hall,** 615 E Capitol Ave, Little Rock, AR 72202; PO Box 165023, Little Rock, AR 72216. Tel 501-371-0075; Fax 501-374-8142; Internet Home Page Address: www.quapaw.com; *Exec Dir* Roger D Williams; *Operations Asst* Michelle Bilello; *Exec Dir* Rhea Roberts
Open Mon - Sat 9 AM - 5 PM, Sun 1 - 5 PM; No admis fee, donations; Estab 1976 for the assembly of materials relevant to historic buildings & neighborhoods in the greater Little Rock area
Income: Financed by private donations
Library Holdings: Book Volumes 250; Clipping Files; Kodachrome Transparencies; Lantern Slides; Manuscripts; Maps; Pamphlets; Periodical Subscriptions 12; Photographs
Special Subjects: Photography, Manuscripts, Maps, Architecture
Collections: Architectural drawings
Activities: Lects open to pub; 4-10 vis lectrs per yr; tours; sales shop sells books, prints

M **UNIVERSITY OF ARKANSAS AT LITTLE ROCK,** Art Galleries, Dept of Art, 2801 S University Little Rock, AR 72204-1000. Tel 501-569-8977; Fax 501-569-8775; Elec Mail becushman@uair.edu; *Cur Asst* Nathan Larson; *Gallery Dir* Brad Cushman
Open Mon - Fri 9 AM - 5 PM, Sat 1-10PM, Sun 2 - 5 PM; No admis fee; Estab 1976 as an acad resource for the university; Three gallery spaces in Fine Art Building on university campus. 2,500 sq ft, 650 sq ft, 900 sq ft, respectively. Maintains reference library; Average Annual Attendance: 2,000
Income: Financed by university
Special Subjects: Painting-American, Photography, Prints, Sculpture, Woodcuts, Etchings & Engravings
Collections: Graphic Arts, prints; Photography; Works on Paper, drawings
Activities: Lects open to pub, 6-8 vis lectrs per yr; competitions; book traveling exhibs 3-5 per yr

L **UNIVERSITY OF ARKANSAS AT LITTLE ROCK,** Art Slide Library and Galleries, 2801 S University, Fine Arts Bldg, Rm 202 Little Rock, AR 72204-1000. Tel 501-569-8976; Fax 501-569-8775; Elec Mail lmgrace@ualr.edu; *Chmn* Win Bruhl; *Slide Cur* Laura Grace; *Gallery Cur* Brad Cushman
Open Mon - Fri 9 AM - 5 PM, Sat 10AM-1PM, Sun 1 - 4 PM; No admis fee; Estab 1978 for educational purposes; Gallery I, 2,500 sq ft, is a two story space; Gallery II, 500 sq ft, is glassed on three sides; Gallery III is a hallway for student works

Income: Financed by state funds & private donations
Library Holdings: Book Volumes 360; Clipping Files; Exhibition Catalogs; Filmstrips; Kodachrome Transparencies 160; Pamphlets; Periodical Subscriptions 15; Slides 80,000; Video Tapes 130
Collections: Photographs & other works on paper
Activities: Docent training; lects open to pub, 3 vis lectrs per yr; gallery talks; student competitions with awards; scholarships offered; originate traveling exhibs

MAGNOLIA

M **SOUTHERN ARKANSAS UNIVERSITY,** Art Dept Gallery & Magale Art Gallery, 100 E University, SAU Box 1309 Magnolia, AR 71753-2181. Tel 870-235-4000; Elec Mail rsstout@saumag.edu; Internet Home Page Address: www.saumag.edu/art; *Chmn Art Dept* Scotland Stout; *Prof* Steven Ochs; *Asst Prof* Doug Waterfield; *Pres* Steven G Gamble
Open Mon - Thurs 8 AM - 10 PM, Fri 8 AM - 5 PM, Sat 10 AM - 4 PM, Sun 2 - 10:30 PM (McGale Gallery), Mon, Wed & Fri 8 AM - 5 PM (Brinson Gallery); No admis fee; Estab 1970; Magale Library Art Gallery, foyer type with 120 running ft exhibition space, floor to ceiling fabric covered; Average Annual Attendance: 2,000; Scholarships
Income: Financed partially by state funds
Special Subjects: Prints
Collections: American printmakers
Exhibitions: Various professional exhibits
Activities: Classes for adults & children; lect open to public; gallery talks; tours; scholarships & fels offered; individual paintings & original objects of art lent to schools, nonprofit organizations

MONTICELLO

M **DREW COUNTY HISTORICAL SOCIETY,** Museum, 404 S Main, Monticello, AR 71655. Tel 870-367-7446, 367-5746; *Dir* Henri Mason; *Pres Commission Bd* Connie Mullis; *Treas* Kittie S Hoofman
No admis fee; Estab 1971; Average Annual Attendance: 3,000; Mem: dues benefactor $1,000, patron $500, corporate $200, friends of mus $100, individual with journal $25, individual $15; 160 members
Income: Financed by endowment, mem, city & county appropriation, fundraisers
Special Subjects: Historical Material
Collections: Antique toys & dolls; Civil War artifacts; Indian artifacts; Handwork & clothing from early 1800s; Woodworking tools; Farm implements, log cabins, china
Exhibitions: Antique Quilts, Trunks, Paintings by Local Artists; Leather Parlor Furniture from late 1800s
Publications: Drew County Historical Journal, annually
Activities: Tours

MORRILTON

M **RIALTO COMMUNITY ARTS CENTER,** The Gallery, 215 E Broadway, Morrilton, AR 72110-3403; PO Box 176, Morrilton, AR 72110. Tel 501-477-9955; Elec Mail director@rialtoartscenter.com; Internet Home Page Address: www.rialtoartscenter.com/thegallery.html

MOUNTAIN VIEW

L **OZARK FOLK CENTER, ARKANSAS STATE PARK,** (Ozark Folk Center) Ozark Cultural Resource Center, 1032 Park Ave, Mountain View, AR 72560-6008. Tel 870-269-3851; Fax 870-269-2909; Internet Home Page Address: www.ozarkfolkcenter.com; *Archival Asst* Tricia Hearn
Call for hours; No admis fee; The Park was estab in 1973 to demonstrate various aspects of traditional culture of the Ozark Mountain region, the Resource Center was estab in 1975 to preserve the artifacts aspects & documentary history of the Ozark Region culture, crafts & music; The Resource Center is maintained for pub reference only; Average Annual Attendance: 200
Income: $70,000 (financed by state appropriation & auxiliary comt)
Library Holdings: Audio Tapes; Book Volumes 10,000; CD-ROMs; Cassettes; Clipping Files; Compact Disks; DVDs; Exhibition Catalogs; Filmstrips; Kodachrome Transparencies; Manuscripts; Maps; Memorabilia; Motion Pictures; Original Art Works; Pamphlets; Periodical Subscriptions 50; Photographs; Prints; Records; Reels; Slides; Video Tapes
Special Subjects: Art History, Constructions, Folk Art, Landscape Architecture, Decorative Arts, Photography, Drawings, Graphic Arts, Manuscripts, Historical Material, Portraits, Crafts, Art Education, Video, Furniture, Costume Design & Constr, Glass, Embroidery, Handicrafts, Textiles, Woodcarvings, Landscapes, Laces, Architecture
Collections: Traditional Ozark crafts; music folios & sheet music; 30 yrs of Live Folk Center performances; Stan French recorded music collection; The William K McNeil Collection
Activities: Lect open to public; concerts; tours; awards; workshops; sales shop sells books, magazines, slides

PINE BLUFF

A **ARTS & SCIENCE CENTER FOR SOUTHEAST ARKANSAS,** 701 Main, Pine Bluff, AR 71601. Tel 870-536-3375; Fax 870-536-3380; Elec Mail jpowell@artssciencecenter.org; Internet Home Page Address: www.artssciencecenter.org; *Dir Prog* Brenda Hengal; *Mgr Opers* Rebekah Ray; *Dir* Janelle Powell
Open Mon - Fri 10 AM - 5 PM, Sat 1 PM - 4 PM; No admis fee; Opened in 1968 in Civic Center Complex; mission is to provide for the practice, teaching, performance, enjoyment, & understanding of the Arts & Sciences, opened new

facility 1994; 22,000 sq ft facility containing four galleries & a 232 seat theatre, instructional studio; Average Annual Attendance: 33,000; Mem: 783; dues family $50

Income: $490,000 by state, municipal & membership dues

Library Holdings: Book Volumes; CD-ROMs; Cassettes; Clipping Files; Exhibition Catalogs; Original Art Works; Photographs; Sculpture; Video Tapes

Special Subjects: Drawings, Etchings & Engravings, Landscapes, Photography, Prints, Sculpture, Watercolors, Painting-American, Bronzes, Afro-American Art, Collages

Collections: Photographs by: Matt Bradley; J C Coovert of the Southern Cotton Culture, early 1900s; John M Howard Memorial Collection of Works by African American Artists; art deco/noveau bronze sculptures; small works on paper (Arkansas artists); works on paper by local, national & international artists; Southern Mississippi Delta Art; Elsie Mistie Sterling Collection of Botanical Paintings; Howard S Stern Collection

Exhibitions: Art Gallery Exhibitions; Biennial Regional Competition; science exhibitions; annual cultural project

Publications: Expressions of African Culture, catalog

Activities: Classes for adults & children; dramatic progs; docent training; lects open to pub, 3-5 vis lectrs per yr; concerts; gallery talks; tours; sponsoring of competition; schols; exten prog for 10 counties of Southeast Arkansas; book traveling exhibs, 1-2 per yr

M **PINE BLUFF/JEFFERSON COUNTY HISTORICAL MUSEUM,** 201 E Fourth, Pine Bluff, AR 71601. Tel 501-541-5402; Fax 501-541-5405; Elec Mail jcmuseum@ipa.net; Internet Home Page Address: pbjcmuseum.com; *Dir* Sue Trulock; *Cur* Lola Gordon; *Registrar* Rebecca Phillips
Open Mon - Fri 9 AM - 5 PM, Sat 10 AM - 2 PM; No admis fee; Estab 1980 to collect, preserve & interpret artifacts showing the history of Jefferson County; Restored Union train station; Average Annual Attendance: 20,000; Mem: 300; Dues $10 - $1,000 ann.

Income: $27,000 (financed by county Quortum Ct appropriation)

Special Subjects: American Indian Art, Flasks & Bottles, Costumes, Dolls, Historical Material, Miniatures

Collections: Clothing dating from 1870; personal artifacts; photographs; tools & equipment; Quapau Indian artifacts; Antique Dolls - Local Black History

Exhibitions: Bottle Collection; Made in Pine Bluff AR; exhibit of dolls; Quapaw Indian Artifacts; Settlers Exhibit; Civil War Exhibit; World War I; World War II; Local Black History exhibit; Boeu & Currow - Antique Bottles

Publications: The Museum Record, quarterly newsletter

Activities: Lect open to public, 50 vis lectrs per year; gallery talks; docent led tours anytime

SILOAM SPRINGS

M **SAGER CREEK ARTS CENTER,** 301 E Twin Springs Siloam Springs, AR 72761; PO Box 1127 Siloam Springs, AR 72761-1127.

SPRINGDALE

M **ARTS CENTER OF THE OZARKS,** 214 S Main, Springdale, AR 72765-7204. Tel 501-751-5441; Fax 501-927-0308; Elec Mail artscenteroftheozarks@swbell.net; Internet Home Page Address: www.artscenteroftheozarks.org; *Dir Visual Arts* Lindsay Moover; *Dir Theatre* Harry Blundell; *Dir* Kathi Blundell
Open Mon - Fri 9 AM - 5 PM, Sat 9AM-3PM; No admis fee; Estab 1968, merged with the Springdale Arts Center to become Arts Center of the Ozarks in 1973 to preserve the traditional handcrafts, to promote all qualified contemporary arts & crafts, to help find markets for artists & craftsmen; Local & regional artists; Mem: 900; dues $20 & up

Income: Financed by mem & state appropriations

Exhibitions: Exhibitions change monthly

Publications: Arts Center Events, monthly; newsletter, bimonthly

Activities: Adult & children's workshops; instruction in the arts, music, dance & drama run concurrently with other activities; eight theater productions per year; concerts, arts & crafts

M **CITY OF SPRINGDALE,** Shiloh Museum of Ozark History, 118 W Johnson Ave, Springdale, AR 72764-4313. Tel 479-750-8165; Fax 479-750-8693; Elec Mail shiloh@springdalear.gov; Internet Home Page Address: www.shilohmuseum.org; *Exhib Designer* Curtis Morris; *Outreach Coordr* Susan Young; *Dir* Allyn Lord; *Coll Mgr* Carolyn Reno; *Librn* Marie Demeroukas; *Secy* Kathy Plume; *Educ Colls Asst* Victoria Thompson; *Photographer* Don Hose; *Maintenance* Marty Downs
Open Mon - Sat 10 AM - 5 PM; No admis fee; Estab 1968 to exhibit history & culture of Ozarks Arkansas; Displays in main exhibit hall & six historic outbuildings; Average Annual Attendance: 51,618; Mem: 650; dues begin at $10

Income: $642,400 (financed by endowment, mem, city appropriation, private & pub grants)

Library Holdings: Book Volumes; Clipping Files; Manuscripts; Maps; Periodical Subscriptions; Photographs; Prints

Special Subjects: Drawings, Folk Art, Historical Material, Glass, Flasks & Bottles, Furniture, Gold, Pottery, Painting-American, Period Rooms, Textiles, Manuscripts, Maps, Photography, American Indian Art, Ceramics, Crafts, Primitive art, Woodcarvings, Embroidery, Leather

Collections: Folk Arts; Ozarks Photographers; Charles Summey Oils; Essie Ward Primitive Paintings

Exhibitions: Essie Ward; Charles Summey; Peggy McCormack

Publications: Newsletter, quarterly

Activities: Progs & workshops for adults & children; docent training; lects open to pub, 10 vis lectrs per yr; lending coll contains 500 items; retail store sells books, magazines & original art

STUTTGART

A **GRAND PRAIRIE ARTS COUNCIL, INC,** Arts Center of the Grand Prairie, 108 W 12th St, Stuttgart, AR 72160-5210; PO Box 65, Stuttgart, AR 72160-0065. Tel 870-673-1781; Elec Mail artscenter@cpomail.net; *Pres* Becky Goetz; *Ex Dir* Wanda Loudermilk; *Prog Dir* Meredith Steward
Open Mon - Fri 10 AM - 12:30 PM & 1:30 - 4:30 PM, cl Sat & Sun; No admis fee; Estab 1956 & incorporated 1964 to encourage cultural develop in the Grand

Prairie area, to sponsor the Grand Prairie Festival of Arts held annually in Sept at Stuttgart. Estab as an arts center for jr & sr citizens; Average Annual Attendance: 2,500; Mem: 250; dues $25 & up; monthly meetings

Income: Financed by mem & donations

Collections: Permanent collection started by donations

Exhibitions: Monthly exhibitions of Arkansas artists

Publications: Festival invitations; newsletter, monthly; programs

Activities: Classes for adults & children; dramatic progs; lects open to pub, 4-6 vis lectrs per yr; gallery talks; competitions with awards; monthly gourmet coffee house featuring various types of music & comedy; originate traveling exhibs

VAN BUREN

M **CENTER FOR ART & EDUCATION,** 104 N 13th St, Van Buren, AR 72956-4512. Tel 479-474-7767; Elec Mail info@art-ed.org; Internet Home Page Address: www.art-ed.org; *Exec Dir* Jane Owen
Open Tues - Fri 10 AM - 4 PM; Admis free; Estab 1976; Two galleries, main gallery & studio gallery; Average Annual Attendance: 10,000; Mem: Dues $50 individual, $100 family

Library Holdings: Book Volumes

Special Subjects: Landscapes, Glass, Painting-American, Religious Art, Metalwork, Miniatures

Activities: Classes for adults & children; lects open to pub; 2 vis lectrs per yr; gallery talks; tours; competitions; schols; mus shop sells books, magazines, original art, reproductions & prints

CALIFORNIA

350 ELM AVE.

A **ARTS COUNCIL FOR LONG BEACH,** (Public Corporation for the Arts) 350 Elm Ave, 350 Elm Ave.. CA 90802-2415. Tel 562-570-1930; Fax 562-432-5175; Elec Mail info@artspca.org; Internet Home Page Address: www.artspca.org; *Exec Dir* Joan Van Hooten
Open Mon - Thurs 9 AM - 5 PM, cl Fri, Sat & Sun; No admis fee; Estab 1977, nonprofit, official arts adv council for city of Long Beach

Income: $750,000 (financed by endowment, mem, city appropriation, private corporations & foundations)

Publications: Quarterly events calendar

Activities: Enrichment & alternative arts progs; technical assistance; individual & community art grants, Smithsonian Week

ALISO VIEJO

M **SOKA UNIVERSITY,** Founders Hall Art Gallery, 1 University Dr., Aliso Viejo, CA 92656. Tel 949-480-4081; Fax 949-480-4260; Elec Mail info@soka.edu; Internet Home Page Address: www.soka.edu
Open Mon - Fri 9 AM - 5 PM; No admis fee; Estab May 2001; 8,000 sq ft; 2 floors

Collections: Works by national & international artists; paintings; photographs; sculpture

Activities: Lects open to pub; 2 vis lectrs per yr; tours

APTOS

A **SAVING & PRESERVING ARTS & CULTURAL ENVIRONMENTS,** 9053 Soquel Dr Ste 205, Aptos, CA 95003-4034. Tel 323-463-1629; Elec Mail info@spacearchives.org; *Dir* Jo Farb Hernandez
Open by appointment only; Estab 1978 for documentation & preservation of folk art environments; Mem: Dues $15-$250

Income: Financed by membership, state, grants

Collections: Archival material about America's contemporary folk art environments

Exhibitions: Several exhibitions per year

Publications: Occasional newsletter

Activities: Lect open to public, 6 vis lectrs per year; gallery talks; tours; lending collection contains 20,000 photographs; originates traveling exhibs; sales shop sells books, magazines, prints

L **Spaces Library & Archive,** 9053 Soquel Dr Ste 205, Aptos, CA 95003-4034. Tel 323-463-1629; Elec Mail info@spacesarchives.org; *Dir* Jo Farb Hernandez
Open by appointment only; Estab 1978 to provide reference for scholars, artists, preservations concerned with folk art environments; For lending & reference

Income: Financed by mem, state appropriation, government & pvt grants, volunteers

Library Holdings: Audio Tapes; Book Volumes 1500; CD-ROMs; Cassettes; Clipping Files; Exhibition Catalogs; Kodachrome Transparencies; Manuscripts; Maps; Memorabilia; Original Documents; Pamphlets; Periodical Subscriptions; Photographs; Prints; Records; Sculpture; Slides; Video Tapes

Special Subjects: Art History, Collages, Constructions, Folk Art, Intermedia, Landscape Architecture, Architecture

Collections: Watts Tower Collection - photographs, documentation, archive, letters, clippings, history

Exhibitions: Divine Disorder: Folk Art Environments in California

Publications: Spaces: Notes on America's Folk Art Environments, three times per year

Activities: Lect open to public, 5 vis lectrs per year; originate traveling exhibs

BAKERSFIELD

M **BAKERSFIELD ART FOUNDATION,** Bakersfield Museum of Art, 1930 R St, Bakersfield, CA 93301-4815. Tel 661-323-7219; Fax 661-323-7266; Internet Home Page Address: www.csub.edu/bma; *Exec Dir/CEO* Bernard J Herman; *Asst Dir* David Gordon; *Cur* Emily Falke
Open Tues - Fri 10 AM - 4 PM, Sat - Sun Noon - 4 PM, cl Mon; Admis adults $5, seniors $4, students & children under 12 $2, children 6 & under free; Estab to

provide the facilities & services of an accredited art museum which will nurture & develop the visual arts in Kern County; Mus is a one story building encompassing 5 galleries adjacent to Central Park; Average Annual Attendance: 20,000; Mem: 900; dues $20-60
Income: Financed by corporate, state & local public, & private nonprofit sources
Special Subjects: Painting-American
Collections: California art & artists
Activities: Educ prog; classes for adults & children; docent training; lects open to pub; gallery talks; tours; juried competitions with prizes; schols; book traveling exhibs; originate traveling exhibs; mus shop sells books, magazines, original art, gifts, crafts & art-related items

M **BUENA VISTA MUSEUM OF NATURAL HISTORY,** 2018 Chester Ave, Bakersfield, CA 93301-4420. Tel 661-324-6350; Fax 661-324-7522; Elec Mail bvmnh@sharktoothhill.com; Internet Home Page Address: www.sharktoothhill.com; *Contact* Bob Smith
Open Thurs - Sat 10 AM - 5 PM, also by appt; Admis adults $3, children, seniors & students with ID $2; group rates available; mus promotes scientific & educ aspects of earth history with emphasis on paleontology & anthropology in Kern County; Mem: memberships available
Special Subjects: Historical Material, Anthropology
Collections: The Bob & Mary Ernst Collection
Exhibitions: Sharktooth Hill, Kern County, CA; San Joaquin Valley Through Time; McKittrick Tar Seeps; Mount St Helens: 20 Years Later; San Andreas Fault; Yosemite Valley
Publications: Sharkbites, newsletter
Activities: Geology field trips; workshops; events; mus related items for sale

M **CALIFORNIA STATE UNIVERSITY, BAKERSFIELD,** Todd Madigan Gallery, 9001 Stockdale Hwy, 15FA Bakersfield, CA 93311-1099. Tel 661-654-2238; Fax 661-654-2539; Internet Home Page Address: www.csub.edu/art/gallery; *Dir* Joey Kotting
Open acad yr Tues - Thurs 1 PM - 6 PM, Sat 1 PM - 5 PM, cl univ breaks & holidays
Collections: paintings; sculpture; photographs

M **KERN COUNTY MUSEUM,** 3801 Chester Ave, Bakersfield, CA 93301-1345. Tel 661-852-5000; Fax 661-322-6415; Internet Home Page Address: kcmuseum.org; *Asst Dir* Jeff Nickell; *Dir* Carola Rupert Enriquez; *Cur* Lori Wear
Open Mon - Sat 10AM-5PM; Admis adults $8, sr citizens $7, children 3-12 $6, under 3 free; Estab 1945 to collect & interpret local history & culture, mainly through a 14 acre outdoor mus. Also has Lori Brock Children's Discovery Center; One main building, 1929 Chamber of Commerce Building, houses changing exhibitions on assorted topics; modern track lighting, temporary walls; Average Annual Attendance: 103,000; Mem: 650; dues family $60
Income: $1.7 million (financed by county appropriation, earned income & non-profit foundation)
Purchases: Archival, occasionally decorative arts
Library Holdings: Manuscripts; Maps; Memorabilia; Motion Pictures; Original Documents; Other Holdings; Pamphlets; Periodical Subscriptions; Photographs; Prints; Records; Video Tapes
Special Subjects: Architecture, Photography, Archaeology, Ethnology, Costumes, Decorative Arts, Historical Material, Maps, Period Rooms, Laces
Collections: 60-structure outdoor museum covering 14 acres; Photographic Image Collection; Material Culture; Paleontology; Natural History
Publications: Brochure on the Museum; The Forgotten Photographs of Carleton E Watkins
Activities: Classes for adults & children; docent training; lects open to pub; concerts; tours; Candlelight Christmas & Heritage celebrations; competitions with awards; book traveling exhibitions 2 per year; gift shop sells books, reproductions, slides, prints & handicrafts; junior mus located at Children's Discovery Center

L **Library,** 3801 Chester Ave, Bakersfield, CA 93301-1345. Tel 661-852-5000; Fax 661-322-6415; Elec Mail kcmuseum@kern.org; Internet Home Page Address: www.kcmuseum.org; *Cur* Jeff Nickell; *Dir* Carola Rupert Enriquez; *Educ Prog* Jackie Brouillette; *VChmn* Bob Shore; *Mus Shop Mgr* Erica Hinojos
Open Mon - Fri 8 AM - 5 PM by appointment only; Estab 1950 to support the work of the mus; Open for reference only by appointment
Library Holdings: Book Volumes 2,200; Clipping Files; Filmstrips; Manuscripts; Memorabilia; Pamphlets; Photographs; Video Tapes
Special Subjects: Decorative Arts, Maps, Historical Material, History of Art & Archaeology, Crafts, Ethnology, Furniture, Period Rooms, Costume Design & Constr, Restoration & Conservation, Textiles
Collections: More than 200,000 photos relating to Kern County
Publications: Courier, quarterly newsletter
Activities: Classes for adults & children; docent training; lect open to public; concerts; tours; gallery talks; gift shop sells books, reproductions; Lori Brock Children's Discovery Ctr

BERKELEY

A **BERKELEY ART CENTER,** 1275 Walnut St, Berkeley, CA 94709-1406. Tel 510-644-6893; Fax 510-540-0343; Elec Mail info@berkeleyartcenter.org; Internet Home Page Address: www.berkeleyartcenter.org; *CEO & Dir* Jill Berk Jiminez; *Pres (V)* Susan Klee; *Program Coordr* Jeanne Rehrig
Open Wed - Sun Noon - 5 PM, cl Mon - Tues, holidays & during installations; No admis fee; Estab 1967 as a community art center; Average Annual Attendance: 12,400; Mem: 400; dues $30 - $2500; annual meeting Jan 1
Income: Financed by city appropriation and other grants
Collections: prints
Exhibitions: Rotating loan exhibitions & shows by Northern Calif artists; Annual Exhibitions: Members Exhibition, Youth Arts Festival & The National Juried Exhibition
Activities: Lects open to public, 8 vis lectrs per yr; concerts; gallery talks; competition with prizes; original objects of art lent to nonprofit & educational institutions; originate traveling exhibs; mus shop sells books, magazines, original art & prints

A **BERKELEY CIVIC ARTS PROGRAM,** 2118 Milvia St, Ste 200, Berkeley, CA 94704. Tel 510-705-8183; Fax 510-883-6554; Elec Mail mamfor@ci.berkeley.ca.us; Internet Home Page Address: www.ci.berkeley.ca.us; Others TDD 510-644-6915; *Civic Arts Coordr* Mary Ann Merker
Estab 1980. Provides grants to art organizations, cultural service contracts, community outreach, bus & technical assistance to artists & organizations, information referrals to the arts community; conducts on-going efforts to promote the importance of the arts & actively participates in regional & national local art agency develop
Income: $264,500
Exhibitions: Exhibits 14 different showings annually by artists & art organizations in the Addison Street storefront windows
Publications: Arts Education Resource Directory; arts events list; quarterly newsletter

L **BERKELEY PUBLIC LIBRARY,** 2090 Kittredge St, Art & Music Dept Berkeley, CA 94704-1427. Tel 510-981-6241; Internet Home Page Address: www.berkeleypubliclibrary.org; *Librn* Dayna Holz; *Librn* Michele McKenzie; *Librn* Deborah Carton
Open Mon noon - 8 PM, Tues 10 AM 8 PM, Wed - Sat 10 AM - 6 PM, Sun 1 - 5 PM; No admis fee
Library Holdings: Book Volumes 30,000; Clipping Files; Other Holdings Compact discs 20,000; Periodical Subscriptions 160; Records 6,000; Slides 22,000
Exhibitions: Four photography exhibs per yr

A **KALA INSTITUTE,** Kala Art Institute, 2990 San Pueblo Ave, Berkeley, CA 94702; 1060 Heinz Ave, Berkeley, CA 94710-2719. Tel 510-549-2977; Fax 510-540-6914; Elec Mail kala@kala.org; Internet Home Page Address: www.kala.org; *Artistic Dir* Yuzo Nakano; *Exec Dir* Archana Horsting; *Dir Exhib & Pub Progs* Lauren Davies; *Dir Develop* Celeste Smeland; *Bus Mgr* Wendy Neu; *Art Sls Mgr* Andrea Voinot; *Communs Mgr & Registrar* Mayumi Hainanaka; *Artists In Schools Prog Coordr* Jamila Dunn; *Develop Assoc* Ellen Lake; *Prog Mgr for Artist Res & Classes* Patrick Stockstill; *Facility Coordr* Daniel Bacci; *Print Studio & Custom Printing Mgr* Sharon Heitzenroder; *Event Rental & Admin Mgr* Sharon Jue
Open Tues - Fri noon - 5 PM, Sat noon - 4:30 PM; No admis fee; Estab 1974 to provide equipment, space, exhibition opportunities to artists; Maintains Ray Abel Memorial Library of Fine Arts Books; Average Annual Attendance: 5,000; Mem: 80; mem open to artists with proficiency in printmaking; studio rental $175-$390 per month
Income: $300,000 (financed by mem, city & state appropriation, art sales, classes & private foundations)
Collections: Kala Institute Archive; Works on Paper
Exhibitions: On going: Works on Paper
Activities: Classes for adults & children; lects open to pub; scholarships & fels offered; book traveling exhibs; originate traveling exhibs 1 per yr; retail store sells prints & original art

M **UNIVERSITY OF CALIFORNIA, BERKELEY,** Berkeley Art Museum & Pacific Film Archive, 2625 Durant Ave, #2250 Berkeley, CA 94720-2250. Tel 510-642-0808; Fax 510-642-4889; Elec Mail bampfa@verkeley.edu; Internet Home Page Address: http://bampfa.berkeley.edu; *Dir* Lawrence Rauder; *Cur Educ* Sherry Goodman; *Coll & Exhib Admin* Lisa Calden; *Cur Video* Steve Seid; *Film Coll Mgr* Mona Nagai; *Cur Film* Kathy Geritz; *Sr Film Cur* Susan Oxtoby; *Matrix Cur* Elizabeth Thomas; *Chief Cur & Dir Progs & Colls* Lucinda Barnes
Open Wed - Fri 11 AM - 5 PM; Admis $7-10; Estab 1963, new mus building opened in 1970; Mus designed by Mario Ciampi, Richard Jorasch & Ronald E Wagner of San Francisco; eleven exhibition galleries, a sculpture garden & a 234 seat theater; Average Annual Attendance: Gallery 100,000, Pacific Film Archive 100,000; Mem: 2800; dues vary
Income: $4,200,000 (financed by university sources, federal & foundation grants, earned income & private donations)
Special Subjects: Afro-American Art, Drawings, Folk Art, Architecture, Painting-American, Prints, Painting-British, Painting-European, Latin American Art, Photography, Sculpture, African Art, Posters, Asian Art
Collections: Gift of 45 Hans Hoffman paintings housed in the Hans Hoffman Gallery; pre-20th century paintings & sculpture; Chinese & Japanese paintings; 20th century European & American paintings & sculpture; over 7000 films & video tapes; 16th-20th century works on paper; conceptual art study center; American Art; Conceptual Art; Contemporary Art
Publications: The Calendar, bi-monthly; catalogs; handbills; exhibition brochures; Matrix artists sheets
Activities: Educ dept; lects open to pub, 15 vis lectrs per yr; concerts; gallery talks; tours; on-site performances; film programs for classes & research screening; film study center & library; book traveling exhibs 3-4 per yr; originate traveling exhibs to other art museums; mus shop sells books, magazines, posters, jewelry, rental facilities available, cafe

M **Phoebe Apperson Hearst Museum of Anthropology,** 103 Kroeber Hall No 3712, Berkeley, CA 94720-3712. Tel 510-642-3681, 642-3682; Fax 510-642-6271; Elec Mail pahma@berkeley.edu; Internet Home Page Address: hearstmuseum.berkeley.edu; *Dir* Rosemary Joyce
Open Wed - Sat 10 AM - 4:30 PM, Sun Noon - 4 PM, cl univ holidays; Admis adults $2, seniors $1, children $.50, no admis fee Thurs; Estab 1901 as a research mus for the training & educating of undergraduate & graduate students, a resource for scholarly research & to collect, preserve, educate & conduct research; Average Annual Attendance: 20,000
Income: Financed principally by state appropriations
Special Subjects: Afro-American Art, American Indian Art, Anthropology, Folk Art, Glass, American Western Art, Antiquities-Assyrian, Flasks & Bottles, Furniture, Gold, Photography, Porcelain, Portraits, Pottery, Pre-Columbian Art
Collections: Over four million objects of anthropological interest, both archaeological & ethnological. Ethnological colls from Africa, Oceania, North America (California, Plains, Arctic & Sub-Arctic); Archaeological Colls from Egypt, Peru, California, Africa & Oceania
Publications: Classics in California Anthropology; Museum News, annual
Activities: Family days; lects open to pub, 12 vis lectrs per yr; gallery talks; originate traveling exhibs varies; mus shop sells books, magazines, reproductions & slides

L **Pacific Film Archive,** 2625 Durant Ave, Berkeley, CA 94720-2251. Tel 510-642-1412, 642-1437; Fax 510-642-4889; *Library Head* Nancy Goldman; *Film Coll Mgr* Mona Nagai; *Assoc Film Cur* Kathy Geritz; *Cur Film* Edith Kramer
Open Mon - Fri 1 - 5 PM; nightly film screenings 6 - 11 PM; Estab 1971, the Archive is a cinematheque showing a constantly changing repertory of films; a research screening facility; a media information service & an archive for the storage & preservation of films
Income: Financed by earned box office income, grants, students fees & benefits
Library Holdings: Book Volumes 5,500; Clipping Files 60,000; Motion Pictures 6,000; Other Holdings Posters 7,000; Stills 25,000; Periodical Subscriptions 75; Photographs
Special Subjects: Film
Collections: Japanese film coll; Soviet Silents; experimental & animated films
Publications: Bi-monthly calendar
Activities: Nightly film exhibition; special daytime screening of films; lect, 50-57 vis filmmakers per yr

L **Architecture Visual Resources Library,** 494 Wurster Hall, Berkeley, CA 94720-1800; 232 Wurster Hall (MC 1800), Berkeley, CA 94720-1800. Tel 510-642-3439; Fax 510-642-8655; Elec Mail maryly@berkeley.edu; Internet Home Page Address: www.mip.berkeley.edu/spiro (image database); Internet Home Page Address: www.arch.ced.berkeley.edu/resources/avre; Internet Home Page Address: www.lib.berkeley.edu/arch; *Library Asst* Tracy Farbstein; *Photographer* Steven Brooks; *Librn* Maryly Snow
Open Mon - Fri 9AM-5PM, after completion of new user orientation; Admis for outside borrowers $150 per semester; Estab 1905 for instructional support for the Department of Architecture. Library permits circulation on a 24 hour basis for educational presentations. No duplication of slides permitted; Circ 46,000; Average Annual Attendance: 300
Income: Financed by state & donor funds
Library Holdings: Kodachrome Transparencies; Lantern Slides; Other Holdings; Photographs; Slides
Special Subjects: Landscape Architecture, Architecture
Collections: Denise Scott Brown & William C Wheaton Collections; City Planning; Herwin Schaefer Collection: visual design; architecture & topography instructional circulating coll; Harold Stump world architecture slide coll; Ray Lifchez slide collection; Joseph Esherick travel slides collection

L **Environmental Design Library,** 210 Wurster Hall, Berkeley, CA 94720-6000. Tel 510-642-4818; Fax 510-642-8266; Elec Mail envi@library.berkeley.edu; Internet Home Page Address: www.lib.berkeley.edu/ENVI; *Head* Elizabeth Byrne; *Planning & Instruction Librn* David Eifler
Open Aug- May Mon - Thurs 9 AM - 9 PM, Fri 9 AM - 5 PM, Sat 1 - 5 PM, Sun 1 - 5 PM; Estab 1903; Circ 91,000; 3 exhibs per year
Income: Pub/state
Library Holdings: Book Volumes 210,000; CD-ROMs; Fiche; Periodical Subscriptions 700; Reels; Video Tapes
Special Subjects: Landscape Architecture, Architecture
Collections: Beatrix Jones Farrand Collection; Architecture, city & regional planning, landscape architecture
Exhibitions: Three times per year
Publications: On website

M **UNIVERSITY OF CALIFORNIA, BERKELEY THE BANCROFT LIBRARY,** The Magnes Collection of Jewish Art & Life, 2121 Allston Way, Bancroft Library University of California Berkeley, CA 94720-6000. Tel 510-643-2526; Elec Mail magnes@library.berkeley.edu; Internet Home Page Address: www.magnes.org; *Dir* Alla Efimova; *Cur Coll* Francesco Spagnolo; *Exhib Coordr* Julie Franklin; *Mktg Communs Coordr* Britta Kolb; *Events Coordr* Rachael Dickson; *Pub Servs Coordr* Gary Handman
Open Tues - Fri 11 AM - 4 PM; Admis suggested fee Adults $6, students & seniors $4, children 12 & under & mems no charge; Estab 1962 to preserve, collect & exhibit Jewish artifacts & art from around the world; the Judah L Magnes mus also contained the Blumenthal Rare Books & Manuscripts Library & the Western Jewish History Center Archives on the Jewish community in the Western United States since 1849. Collection transferred to UC Berkeley's Bancroft Library in 2010, to open to the pub in fall 2011 upon completion of new facility
Library Holdings: Auction Catalogs; Audio Tapes; Book Volumes; Clipping Files; Exhibition Catalogs; Manuscripts; Motion Pictures; Periodical Subscriptions; Photographs; Records; Video Tapes
Special Subjects: Art History, American Western Art, Prints, Drawings, Graphics, Painting-American, Photography, Sculpture, Watercolors, Textiles, Costumes, Religious Art, Ceramics, Crafts, Folk Art, Etchings & Engravings, Decorative Arts, Judaica, Manuscripts, Collages, Posters, Furniture, Metalwork, Carpets & Rugs, Historical Material, Coins & Medals, Calligraphy, Painting-Polish, Embroidery, Laces, Gold, Painting-German, Painting-Russian, Painting-Israeli
Collections: Hannukah lamps; Synagogue art & objects; spice boxes; graphics; manuscripts; prints; rare books; textiles; genre paintings; art & ceremonial objects from Sephardic & Indian Jewish communities; Jewish Ceremonial Art

L **Blumenthal Rare Book & Manuscript Library,** The Bancroft Library, University of California Berkeley Berkeley, CA 94702-6000. Tel 510-642-3781; Elec Mail magnes@library.berkeley.edu; Internet Home Page Address: www.magnes.org; *Librn* Paul Hamburb
Estab 1966 as a center for the study & preservation of Judaica; Circ Non-circ
Library Holdings: Book Volumes 12,000; Clipping Files; Exhibition Catalogs; Filmstrips; Manuscripts; Memorabilia; Motion Pictures; Other Holdings Original documents; Pamphlets; Periodical Subscriptions 15; Reproductions; Slides
Special Subjects: Art History, Illustration, Calligraphy, Manuscripts, Maps, Judaica, Cartoons, Bookplates & Bindings
Collections: Community colls from Cochin, Czechoslovakia, Egypt, India & Morocco; Holocaust Material (Institute for Righteous Acts); Karaite Community (Egypt); Passover Haggadahs (Zismer); 16th to 19th century rare printed editions, books & manuscripts; Ukrainian programs (Belkin documents)
Exhibitions: Jewish Illustrated Books

BEVERLY HILLS

M **ACADEMY OF MOTION PICTURE ARTS & SCIENCES,** The Academy Gallery, 8949 Wilshire Blvd, Beverly Hills, CA 90211-1972. Tel 310-247-3000; Fax 310-247-3610; Elec Mail gallery@oscars.org; Internet Home Page Address: www.oscars.org; *Gallery Mgr* Julie Gumpert; *Gallery Dir* Ellen Harrington; *Gallery Staff* Claire Lockhart; *Chief Preparator* Alex Yust
Open Tues - Fri 10 AM - 5 PM, Sat & Sun Noon - 6 PM; No admis fee; Estab 1970; Rotating exhibitions on motion picture history & contemporary filmmaking; Average Annual Attendance: 40,000
Library Holdings: Audio Tapes; Book Volumes; Clipping Files; Exhibition Catalogs; Kodachrome Transparencies; Lantern Slides; Manuscripts; Motion Pictures; Original Art Works; Photographs; Reproductions
Collections: Gallery borrows regularly from the Academy library's colls of archival posters, photos, & documents
Exhibitions: Rotating exhibits
Publications: Exhibition catalogs
Activities: Seminars on producing & screen writing; lects open to pub; 6 vis lectrs per year; gallery talks; tours; Academy Awards; Nicholl Fel in screenwriting offered; approx 2 book traveling exhibs per yr; originates traveling exhibs that circulate to accredited museum facilities

L **BEVERLY HILLS PUBLIC LIBRARY,** Fine Arts Library, 444 N Rexford, Beverly Hills, CA 90210. Tel 310-288-2237; Fax 310-247-0536; Elec Mail mstark@beverlyhills.org; Internet Home Page Address: www.bhpl.org; *Fine Arts Librn* Mary Stark
Open Mon - Wed 10 AM - 8 PM, Thurs - Sat 10 AM - 6 PM, Sun Noon - 5 PM; No admis fee; Estab 1973 to make art materials available to the general public; The library concentrates on 19th & 20th century American & West European art, & Southern CA art
Income: Financed by city appropriation and Friends of Library
Library Holdings: Auction Catalogs; Book Volumes 22,822; Compact Disks 11,528; DVDs 4,143; Exhibition Catalogs; Fiche; Original Art Works; Original Documents; Periodical Subscriptions 200
Special Subjects: Art History, Landscape Architecture, Decorative Arts, Film, Illustration, Photography, Calligraphy, Commercial Art, Drawings, Etchings & Engravings, Graphic Arts, Graphic Design, Islamic Art, Painting-American, Painting-British, Painting-Dutch, Painting-French, Painting-German, Painting-Italian, Painting-Japanese, Painting-Russian, Painting-Spanish, Posters, Prints, Sculpture, Painting-European, History of Art & Archaeology, Portraits, Watercolors, Ceramics, Crafts, Theatre Arts, American Western Art, Bronzes, Printmaking, Advertising Design, Cartoons, Fashion Arts, Interior Design, Asian Art, Furniture, Southwestern Art, Drafting, Period Rooms, Glass, Afro-American Art, Antiquities-Oriental, Antiquities-Persian, Handicrafts, Jewelry, Oriental Art, Pottery, Religious Art, Silver, Tapestries, Textiles, Woodcuts, Antiquities-Byzantine, Antiquities-Egyptian, Antiquities-Greek, Antiquities-Roman, Coins & Medals, Architecture
Collections: Artists Books
Exhibitions: Various exhib
Activities: Classes for adults, literary; 10 vis lectrs per yr; judged one of the top twelve libraries in the state by Library Journal in 2009

C **PLAYBOY ENTERPRISES, INC,** 9346 Civic Center Dr, Beverly Hills, CA 90210-3604. Tel 312-751-8000; Fax 312-751-2818; *Cur & Bus Develop Dir* Aaron Baker
Open to pub by appointment only in groups; Estab 1953 to gather & maintain works commissioned for reproduction by Playboy Magazine
Library Holdings: Auction Catalogs; Book Volumes; Exhibition Catalogs; Kodachrome Transparencies; Manuscripts; Memorabilia; Original Art Works; Original Documents; Photographs; Sculpture; Slides; Video Tapes
Collections: Selected works from 4000 illustrations & fine art pieces, works include paintings & sculpture representing 20th Century artists such as Robert Ginzel, Roger Hane, Larry Rivers, James Rosenquist, Seymour Rosofsky, Roy Schnackenberg, George Segal, Andy Warhol, Robert Weaver, Tom Wesselman, Karl Wirsum, Roger Brown, Ed Paschke, Don Lewis & others
Exhibitions: Playboy Redux; The Great Indoors; Mr Playboy's Wild Ride
Publications: Catalogs pertaining to Beyond Illustration - The Art of Playboy; The Art of Playboy - from the First 25 Years
Activities: Lects; tours; annual illustration awards; individual paintings & original objects of art lent to museums & schools; originate traveling exhibs to galleries, universities, museums & cultural centers

L **Library,** 9346 Civic Center Dr, Ste 200 Beverly Hills, CA 90210-3604. Tel 312-751-8000, Ext 2420; Fax 312-751-2818; *Librn* Mark Durand
Library Holdings: Book Volumes 10,000; Clipping Files; Exhibition Catalogs; Original Art Works; Periodical Subscriptions 75; Photographs

BONITA

M **BONITA MUSEUM AND CULTURAL CENTER,** 4355 Bonita Rd Bonita, CA 91902-1351. *Dir* Mary Oswell; *Pres* Tom Pocklington; *Treas* Barbara Scott

BREA

M **CITY OF BREA,** Art Gallery, One Civic Center Circle, Brea, CA 92821. Tel 714-990-7730; Fax 714-990-7736; Elec Mail breagallery@cityofbrea.net; Internet Home Page Address: www.breagallery.com; *Educ Dir* Tina Hasenberg; *Coordr* Claudia Sandoval
Open Wed - Sun noon - 5 PM; cl Mon, Tues, holidays; Admis adults $2, children 12 & under free; Estab 1980; 6300 sq ft exhib space; Average Annual Attendance: 7,000
Income: nonprofit
Special Subjects: Drawings, Landscapes, Ceramics, Glass, Photography, Portraits, Pottery, Painting-American, Prints, Textiles, Sculpture, Graphics, Watercolors, Posters, Jewelry, Military Art

Exhibitions: Made in California (annual juried show); National Watercolor Society Juried Exhib
Activities: Classes for adults & children; docent training; lect open to public; tours; gallery talks; workshops; made in California Art Awards $500, $350, $200, $100; mus shop sells original art, prints & jewelry

BURBANK

L   WARNER BROS STUDIO RESEARCH LIBRARY, (Warner Bros Research Library) 4000 Warner Blvd, Bldg 169 Burbank, CA 91522. Tel 818-954-6000; Fax 818-567-4366; *Library Admin* Phill Williams; *Research Librn* Barbara Poland
Open Mon - Fri 9 AM - 5 PM; Estab 1928 for picture & story research
Income: Financed by endowment
Library Holdings: Book Volumes 35,000; Clipping Files; Pamphlets; Periodical Subscriptions 85; Photographs
Special Subjects: Film, Fashion Arts, Interior Design, Costume Design & Constr
Collections: Art & Architecture History; Costumes; Interior Design; Military & Police; Travel & Description

CAMARILLO

M   STUDIO CHANNEL ISLANDS ART CENTER, 2221 Ventura Blvd, Camarillo, CA 93010. Tel 805-383-1368; Elec Mail sciartcenter@verizon.net; Internet Home Page Address: www.studiochannelislands.org; *Exec Dir* Karin Geiger
Open Tues 11AM-3PM, Wed-Fri 11AM-5PM, Sat 11AM-3PM
Collections: works by regional, nat & international artists
Activities: Classes for adults & children; lects open to the pub; gallery talks; tours; mus shop sells original art

CARMEL

M   CARMEL MISSION & GIFT SHOP, 3080 Rio Rd, Carmel, CA 93923-9144. Tel 831-624-1271; Fax 831-624-0658; Internet Home Page Address: www.carmelmission.org; *Shop Mgr* Kristine Silveria; *Cur* Richard J Menn
Open Mon - Sat 9:30 AM - 4:30 PM, Sun 10:30 AM - 4:30 PM, cl Thanksgiving & Christmas; No admis fee; donations accepted; Estab 1770
Collections: California's first library, founded by Fray Junipero Serra, 1770; library of California's first college, founded by William Hartnell, 1834; Munras Memorial Collection of objects, papers, furnishings of early California; large coll of ecclesiastical art of Spanish colonial period; large coll of ecclesiastical silver & gold church vessels, 1670-1820; paintings, sculpture, art objects of California Mission period
Activities: Sales shop sells religious articles, souvenir books & postcards

CARMICHAEL

PASTEL SOCIETY OF THE WEST COAST
For further information, see National and Regional Organizations

CARSON

M   UNIVERSITY ART GALLERY AT CALIFORNIA STATE UNIVERSITY, DOMINGUEZ HILLS, 1000 E Victoria St, Carson, CA 90747-0001. Tel 310-243-3334; Fax 310-217-6967; Elec Mail kzimmerer@csudh.edu; Internet Home Page Address: www.cah.csudh.edu/dnp/art_gallery/index.asp; *Gallery Dir* Kathy Zimmerer; *Instructional Support Technician* Gregory Mocilnikar
Open Mon - Thurs 10:00 AM - 4 PM; No admis fee; Estab 1973 to exhibit faculty, student, contemporary & historical California art & multi-cultural exhibits; 2,000 sq ft gallery, 18' high ceilings; Average Annual Attendance: 10,000
Income: Financed by yearly grants from CSUDH Student Assoc; support from Friends of the Gallery, City of Carson; external grants
Library Holdings: Audio Tapes; Exhibition Catalogs; Slides
Special Subjects: Art History
Exhibitions: A Tradition of Pride: African American Quilters of Los Angeles; 21 Artists Create Books, African Identities in Textiles & Art
Publications: Exhibition catalogue published one time per yr; yearly newsletter
Activities: Classes for children; lects open to pub, 5 vis lectrs per yr; gallery talks; demonstrations; gallery tours; schols; book traveling exhibs 1 per yr; originates traveling exhibs (Painted Light) to Irvine Mus, Autry National Center

CHERRY VALLEY

M   RIVERSIDE COUNTY MUSEUM, Edward-Dean Museum & Gardens, 9401 Oak Glen Rd, Cherry Valley, CA 92223-3739. Tel 951-845-2626; Fax 951-845-2628; Internet Home Page Address: www.edward-deanmuseum.org; *Mus Mgr* Teresa Gallavan; *Asst Mus Mgr* Jen Bowen
Open Fri - Sun 10 AM - 5 PM; Admis adults $3, seniors & students $2, children under 12 free; Built in 1957 & given to the county of Riverside in 1964; The South Wing of the gallery displays antiques & decorative arts as permanent collections; the North Wing has changing exhibits including contemporary artists; Average Annual Attendance: 20,000; Mem: 250; monthly meetings
Income: Financed by county funding
Library Holdings: Memorabilia; Original Documents; Sculpture
Special Subjects: Watercolors, Decorative Arts, Oriental Art
Collections: 17th & 18th Century European & Oriental decorative arts; David Roberts Collection
Publications: Museum catalog
Activities: Classes for children; docent training; lects open to pub; tours; outdoor art shows; cultural festivals; concerts; gallery talks; original objects of art lent to local universities & colleges; mus shop sells books, magazines, original art, reproductions & prints

L   Library, 9401 Oak Glen Rd, Cherry Valley, CA 92223-3799. Tel 909-845-2626; Fax 909-845-2628; *Librn* Margaret Mueller
Open by appointment for reference only
Library Holdings: Book Volumes 2,300; Cards; Manuscripts; Original Art Works; Periodical Subscriptions 6; Prints
Special Subjects: Art History, Decorative Arts, Painting-British, Painting-European, History of Art & Archaeology, Watercolors, Ceramics, Asian Art, Porcelain, Furniture, Jade, Costume Design & Constr, Glass

CHICO

M   1078 GALLERY, 820 Broadway St, Chico, CA 95928. Tel 530-343-1973; Elec Mail info@1078gallery.org; Internet Home Page Address: www.1078gallery.org; *Exec Dir* Pat Kemeny Macias; *Co-Chmn* Maria Navarro; *Co-Chmn* Eric Richter
Open Thurs - Sat 12:30 - 5:30 PM; No admis fee; Estab as a nonprofit artist run arts organization showing contemporary art exhibitions & installations by artists of cultural & geographic diversity

M   CALIFORNIA STATE UNIVERSITY, CHICO, University Art Gallery, Art Dept, Chico, CA 95929-0820. Tel 530-898-5864; Elec Mail jtannen@csuchico.edu; *Chmn* Jason Tannen
Open Mon - Fri 10 AM - 4 PM, Sun Noon - 4 PM; No admis fee; Estab to afford broad cultural influences to the massive North California region
Income: Financed by state appropriations & private funds
Collections: University Art Coll includes Masters of Graduate Artwork; Study coll of fine art print
Exhibitions: Varies every 4 months: local artist
Activities: Lects open to public, 6-12 vis lectrs per yr; competitions with awards; individual & original objects of art lent to offices on campus

L   Meriam Library, First & Hazel, Chico, CA 95929-0295. Tel 530-898-5862; Fax 530-898-4443; Internet Home Page Address: www.csuchico.edu/library; *Dir* Carolyn Dusenbury
Open Mon-Thurs 7:30AM-11:45PM, Fri 7:30AM-4:45PM, Sat noon-4:45PM, Sun noon-11:45PM
Library Holdings: Audio Tapes; Book Volumes 900; Cards; Cassettes; Fiche; Filmstrips; Micro Print; Motion Pictures; Original Art Works; Periodical Subscriptions 72; Photographs; Prints; Reels; Reproductions; Sculpture; Video Tapes

M   BMU Art Gallery, Bell Memorial Union, Chico, CA 95929-0763. Tel 530-898-5489; Fax 530-898-4717; Elec Mail yzunig@csuchico.edu; Internet Home Page Address: www.csuchico.edu/as/bmu-art-gallery; *Coordr* Yvette Zuniga
Open Mon - Thurs 7 AM - 11 PM, Fri 7 AM - 10 PM, Sat 11 AM - 10 PM, Sun noon - 11 PM; No admis fee; Estab 1945; 100 linear ft of enclosed area & two gallery halls; Average Annual Attendance: 1,000
Income: Financed by associated students & university
Exhibitions: Student work year round

M   Janet Turner Print Museum, CSU, Chicago, 400 W 1st St, Meriam Library, CSU Chico Chico, CA 95929-0820. Tel 530-898-4476; Fax 530-898-5581; Elec Mail csullivan@csuchico.edu; Internet Home Page Address: www.theturner.org; *Cur, Head of Colls* Catherine Sullivan; *Coll Mgr* Adria Crossen Davis; *Resource Mgr* Reed Applegate; *Prof Emeritus Art History Research* Dr Yoshio Kusaba; *Curatorial Asst* Trinity Connelly; *Curatorial Asst* Willow Starkey; *Prof Emeritus Art History Research* James McManus
Open Mon - Sat 11 AM - 4 PM during academic yr; No admis fee; Estab 1981; Located in Meriam Library; displays 6 thematic exhibs per acad yr from the Print Museum's Collection of over 3,000 original prints. Display 6 exhibs in Ayres Hall; Average Annual Attendance: 4,000; Mem: 40; dues $2-$100
Income: $33,000 (financed by endowment, mem & state appropriation)
Purchases: Contemporary prints, mixed media, historic prints
Library Holdings: Auction Catalogs; Book Volumes; Clipping Files; DVDs; Exhibition Catalogs; Memorabilia; Original Art Works; Periodical Subscriptions; Photographs; Reproductions; Slides; Video Tapes
Special Subjects: Afro-American Art, American Indian Art, Etchings & Engravings, American Western Art, Graphics, Hispanic Art, Latin American Art, Mexican Art, Prints, Eskimo Art, Oriental Art, Asian Art, Medieval Art
Collections: General coll of prints historical to contemporary, international in scope, includes all techniques; printmaking making, library, books
Publications: Exhib catalogs
Activities: Educ dept classes for children; docent exhib tours; lect to CSU Chico classes; lects open to pub; 3 vis lectrs per yr; competitions with prizes; 4 purchase awards for Nat'l Print Compt Exhib; gallery talks; tours; scholarships offered; original objects of art lent in traveling exhibs; lending collection contains 2000 original prints; originate traveling exhibs to other CSU system colleges; sales shop sells cards, catalogs & cards

CHULA VISTA

M   SOUTHWESTERN COLLEGE, Art Gallery, 900 Otay Lakes Rd, Chula Vista, CA 91910-7297. Tel 935-421-6700; Fax 935-421-6372; Elec Mail pturley@swc.cc.ca.us; Internet Home Page Address: www.swccd.edu; *Gallery Dir* G Pasha Turley
Open Mon - Tues & Fri 10 AM - 2 PM, Wed - Thurs 6 - 9 PM; No admis fee; Estab 1961 to show contemporary artists' work who are of merit to the community & the school, & as an educational service; Gallery is approx 3,000 sq ft; Average Annual Attendance: 10,000
Income: Financed by city and state appropriations
Collections: Permanent collection of mostly contemporary work
Exhibitions: (1999) Gang of Five, recent works; Painting (David Beck Brown) Allied Craftsman; De La Torre Brothers, The Printers Craft Photos, Linda McCartney, Ceicel Beattes
Activities: Classes for adults; lects open to pub, 3-5 vis lectrs per year; gallery talks; competitions, State Art Festival; individual paintings & original objects of art lent; lending collection contains color reproductions, photographs & original art works; junior mus

CITY OF INDUSTRY

M **WORKMAN & TEMPLE FAMILY HOMESTEAD MUSEUM,** 15415 E Don
Julian Rd, City of Industry, CA 91745-1029. Tel 626-968-8492; Fax
626-968-2048; Elec Mail info@homesteadmuseum.org; Internet Home Page
Address: www.homesteadmuseum.org; *Dir* Karen Graham Wade; *Asst Dir* Paul
Spitzzeri; *Pub Prog Mgr* Alexandra Rasic; *Asst Pub Prog Mgr* Lillian Choy;
Facilities Coordr Robert Barron; *Vol Coordr* Steve Dugan; *Colls Coordr* Michelle
Muro; *Progs Coordr* Gennie Slobe
Open Wed-Sun 1-4 PM; group tours of 10+ by appointment; No admis fee; Estab
1981 to collect & interpret Southern California history from 1830 to 1930;
Contemporary exhibition gallery; mid-19th century Workman Family House; late
19th century water tower; 1922-27 Spanish Colonial Revival Temple Family
Residence; Average Annual Attendance: 18,000
Income: $800,000 (financed by city appropriation)
Special Subjects: Architecture, Decorative Arts, Furniture, Metalwork, Historical
Material, Stained Glass
Collections: California ceramic tile; La Casa Nueva stained glass; Southern
California architecture
Exhibitions: La Casa Nueva: A 1920s Spanish-Style Mansion
Activities: Classes for adults docent training; lects open to pub; 3 vis lectrs per
yr; concerts; tours; mus shop sells books & reproductions
L **Research Library,** 15415 E Don Julian Rd, City of Industry, CA 91745-1029. Tel
626-968-8492; Fax 626-968-2048; Elec Mail info@homesteadmuseum.org;
Internet Home Page Address: www.homesteadmuseum.org; *Coll Mgr & Library
Head* Paul Spitzzeri
Open by appt only; Estab 1981; Circ 2000; For reference only
Income: $60,000 (financed by city appropriation)
Library Holdings: Book Volumes; CD-ROMs; Clipping Files; Compact Disks;
DVDs; Maps; Pamphlets; Periodical Subscriptions 20; Photographs 500; Prints;
Reproductions; Slides 2,500; Video Tapes
Special Subjects: Decorative Arts, Historical Material, Crafts, Interior Design,
Stained Glass, Restoration & Conservation, Architecture

CLAREMONT

M **THE POMONA COLLEGE MUSEUM OF ART,** 333 N College Way,
Claremont, CA 91711-4429. Tel 909-621-8283; Fax 909-621-8989; Elec Mail
kathleen.howe@pomona.edu; Internet Home Page Address:
www.pomona-edu/museum; *Cur* Rebecca McGrew; *Asst Dir & Registrar* Steve
Comba; *Admin Asst* Debbie Wilson; *Dir* Kathleen Howe; *Mus Coordr* Jessica
Wimbley
Open acad yr Tues - Fri noon - 5 PM, Sat - Sun 1 - 5 PM, cl Mon; No admis fee;
Estab 1958 to present balanced exhibs useful not only to students of art history &
studio arts, but also to the general pub; Average Annual Attendance: 8,000
Income: Financed by Pomona College, support group & endowment grants
Special Subjects: Drawings, Graphics, Painting-American, Photography, Prints,
Sculpture, Watercolors, American Indian Art, African Art, Woodcuts, Etchings &
Engravings, Decorative Arts, Oriental Art, Asian Art, Renaissance Art,
Painting-Italian
Collections: Samuel H Kress Collection of Renaissance paintings; Old Master &
contemporary graphics
Exhibitions: Exhibs include: historical, contemporary, faculty, student shows and
project series
Publications: Art Publications List, annual
Activities: Lects open to public, 2-3 vis lectrs per yr; gallery talks; tours;
individual paintings & original objects of art lent to qualified museums &
galleries; originates traveling exhibs to other museums

M **SCRIPPS COLLEGE,** Ruth Chandler Williamson Gallery, 1030 Columbia Ave,
Claremont, CA 91711-3948. Tel 909-607-3397; Fax 909-607-4691; Elec Mail
kdelman@scrippscol.edu; Internet Home Page Address:
www.scrippscollege.edu/williamson-gallery; *Dir* Mary Davis McNaughton; *Coll
Mgr, Registrar* Kirk Delman; *Admin Asst* Jennifer Anderson; *Digital Specialist*
Colleen Salomon
Open Wed - Sun 1 -5 PM, cl nat & col holidays; No admis fee; Estab 1993 to
present balanced exhibitions useful not only to students of art history & studio
arts, but also the general public; Average Annual Attendance: 5,000; Mem: 10,000
Income: Financed by Scripps College, support group & endowment grants
Special Subjects: Afro-American Art, Archaeology, Drawings, Landscapes,
Marine Painting, Ceramics, Glass, Prints, Bronzes, Woodcuts, Painting-French,
Painting-Japanese, Tapestries, Graphics, Mexican Art, Painting-American,
Photography, Prints, Sculpture, Watercolors, African Art, Pre-Columbian Art,
Textiles, Costumes, Primitive art, Oriental Art, Asian Art, Tapestries, Calligraphy,
Dioramas, Antiquities-Egyptian, Antiquities-Greek, Antiquities-Roman, Enamels
Collections: Dr & Mrs William E Ballard Collection of Japanese Prints; Mrs
James Johnson Collection of Contemporary American, British, Korean, Mexican &
Japanese Ceramics; Dorothy Adler Routh Collection of Cloisonne; Wagner
Collection of African Sculpture; General Edward Young Collection of American
Paintings; Fred & Estelle Marer Contemporary Ceramics Collection
Exhibitions: Rotating exhibitions
Publications: Art Publications List
Activities: Lects open to pub, 2-3 vis lectrs per yr; gallery talks; films; tours;
intermuseum loans; book traveling exhibs biennially; originate traveling exhibs

M **SCRIPPS COLLEGE,** Clark Humanities Museum, 1030 Columbia Ave,
Claremont, CA 91711-3948. Tel 909-607-3606; Fax 909-607-7143; *Admin Asst*
Nancy Burson; *Dir* Eric Haskell
Open Mon - Fri 9 AM - Noon & 1 - 5 PM, cl holidays & summer; No admis fee;
Estab 1970 to present multi-disciplinary exhibits in conjunction with Scripps
College's humanities curriculum & to maintain a study collection; Mus has large
room with storage & study area; reception desk
Income: Pvt income
Special Subjects: Sculpture, Textiles, Afro-American Art, Oriental Art
Collections: Nagel Collection of Chinese, Tibetan Sculpture & Textiles; Wagner
Collection of African Sculpture

Exhibitions: Four to seven exhibits
Activities: Lect open to public; gallery talks

CONCORD

A **CALIFORNIA WATERCOLOR ASSOCIATION,** Gallery Concord, 1765
Galindo, Concord, CA 94518; PO Box 4631, Walnut Creek, CA 94596-0631. Tel
925-691-6140; Elec Mail info@californiawatercolor.org; Internet Home Page
Address: www.californiawatercolor.org; *Pres* Bruce Stangeland; *VPres* Eileen
Libby; *Dir Budget* Marilyn Miller; *Dir Communs* Samantha McNally; *Dir
Workshops* Wendy Oliver; *Dir of Outreach* Nan Lovington; *Dir Mem* Sue
Johnston; *Dir Programs* Pamela Miller; *Dir Workshops* Susan Lenoir; *Dir
California Shows* Lynda Moore
Open Thurs - Sun 11 AM - 4 PM; No admis fee; Estab 1968; Maintains art
gallery at Gallery Concord in Concord; Average Annual Attendance: 2,700; Mem:
800; dues $45; monthly meetings every third Wed
Income: Financed by mem dues
Library Holdings: DVDs; Exhibition Catalogs; Framed Reproductions; Original
Art Works; Slides; Video Tapes
Exhibitions: Annual National Watercolor Exhibition plus 6-7 mem exhibits per yr
Publications: Annual catalog; monthly newsletter
Activities: Classes for adults & children; docent training; Workshops; 6-7
watercolor workshops per yr; Plein Air Paint Outs; lects open to pub, 10 vis lectrs
per yr; vis lectrs 4 workshops per yr; gallery talks; tours; competitions & cash
awards; mem shows & nat exhib juried with awards; scholarships offered; lending
collection contains DVDs & 1500 slides; originate traveling exhibs; gallery shop
sells original art, reproductions, prints, greeting cards

CORTE MADERA

A **MARIN COUNTY WATERCOLOR SOCIETY,** 138 Willow Ave, Corte
Madera, CA 94925-1433. Tel 415-924-8191; Elec Mail jkehensel@comcast.net;
Internet Home Page Address: www.marincountywatercolorsociety.com; *Bulletin Ed*
Jacqueline Hensel
Estab 1970 to provide a way for members to share painting experiences in outdoor
landscape; Mem: 180; open to painters, ranging from beginner to professional, in
Marin County & San Francisco Bay area; dues $20
Exhibitions: Marin County Watercolor Society; exhibit throughout the area in
various locals
Publications: Monthly bulletin

CUPERTINO

M **DE ANZA COLLEGE,** Euphrat Museum of Art, 21250 Stevens Creek Blvd,
Cupertino, CA 95014-5797. Tel 408-864-8836; Internet Home Page Address:
www.deanza.edu; *Dir Arts & Schools Prog* Diana Argabrite; *Dir* Jan Rindfleisch
Open Tues & Thurs 11 AM - 4 PM, Wed 7 - 9 PM; No admis fee; Estab 1971;
1700 sq ft contemporary gallery located on De Anza College Campus; Average
Annual Attendance: 10,000
Income: $175,000 (financed by mem, grants, endowment, college)
Publications: Art Collectors in & Around Silicon Valley; Art of the Refugee
Experience; Art, Religion & Spirituality; Content Contemporary Issues; The Power
of Cloth (Political Quilts 1845-1986); Staying Visible: The Importance of Archives
Activities: Classes for children; docent progs; lects open to pub; competition with
awards; sales shop sells books

CYPRESS

M **CYPRESS COLLEGE,** Fine Arts Gallery, 9200 Valley View St, Cypress, CA
90630-5897. Tel 714-826-2220; Fax 714-527-8238; *Secy* Maureen King; *Dir* Betty
Disney
Open Mon & Thurs 10 AM - 2 PM, Tues & Wed 6 - 8 PM, cl Fri, except by
appointment; No admis fee; Estab 1969 to bring visually enriching experiences to
the school & community; Average Annual Attendance: 5,000
Income: Financed by school budget, donations & sales
Collections: Donor gifts; purchase awards; student works
Publications: Exhibition catalogs
Activities: Lects open to public, 2 vis lectrs per year; competitions; scholarships

DAVIS

M **PENCE GALLERY,** 212 D St, Davis, CA 95616-4513. Tel 530-758-3370; Fax
530-758-4670; Elec Mail penceassistant@sbcglobal.net; Internet Home Page
Address: www.pencegallery.org; *Board Pres* Bill Roe; *Asst Dir* Eileen Hendren;
Dir & Cur Natalie Nelson; *Gallery Asst* Chris Beer
Open Tues-Sun 11:30AM-5PM, 2nd Fri 6PM-9PM; No admis fee; Estab 1975 to
foster & stimulate awareness of the arts & cultural heritage of California through
changing exhibitions of art & objects of artistic, aesthetic & historical significance;
State of the art museum with 3 galleries & conference rooms available for rent
and functions; Average Annual Attendance: 16,000; Mem: Dues: gallery circle
$2500, cur circle $1000, benefactor $500, patron $250, sponsor $100, family $65,
individual $40
Income: $200,000 (financed by & fund raisings)
Library Holdings: Auction Catalogs; Book Volumes; Exhibition Catalogs
Exhibitions: Twelve rotating exhibitions per yr, exploring contemporary California
art
Publications: Pence Events, quarterly newsletter
Activities: Classes for adults & children; docent training; lects open to pub; 2
visiting lectrs per year; concerts; gallery talks; tours; Community Art awards;
scholarships offered; sales shop sells books, original art & prints

M   UNIVERSITY OF CALIFORNIA, Memorial Union Art Gallery, One Shields Ave, Memorial Union, 2nd Fl Davis, CA 95616-5270. Tel 530-752-2885; *Dir* Roger Hankins
Open Mon - Fri 9 AM - 5 PM, also by appointment; No admis fee; Estab 1965 to provide exhibitions of contemporary & historical concerns for the students, staff & community; Gallery consists of North Gallery & South Gallery
Collections: Northern California contemporary art
Exhibitions: Sacramento Valley Landscapes
Publications: Exhibition catalogs
Activities: Classes for adults; lects; concerts; poetry readings; films; competitions; internships offered

M   Richard L Nelson Gallery & Fine Arts Collection, One Shields Ave, UC Davis Davis, CA 95616-5270. Tel 530-752-8500; Fax 530-754-9112; Elec Mail nelsongallery@ucdavis.edu; Internet Home Page Address: nelsongallery.ucdavis.edu/; *Dir* Renny Pritikin; *Coll Mgr & Registrar* Robin Bernhard; *Preparator* Kyle Monhollen; *Asst to Dir* Katrina Wong
Open Mon - Thurs, Sat & Sun 11 AM - 5 PM, cl Fri: No admis fee; Estab 1976 to provide exhibitions of contemporary art as well as historical importance as a service to teaching program of the department of art, the university & pub; Contains main gallery of 3500 sq ft; Average Annual Attendance: 15,000; Mem: 175; dues $25 & up; annual meeting in May
Income: Financed by university appropriation, grants & Nelson ARTfriends
Library Holdings: CD-ROMs; Compact Disks; DVDs; Original Art Works; Photographs; Prints; Sculpture
Special Subjects: Drawings, Graphics, Painting-American, Photography, Prints, Sculpture, Watercolors, Ceramics, Primitive art, Woodcarvings, Woodcuts, Etchings & Engravings, Posters, Asian Art, Historical Material
Collections: Fine Arts Collection; general collection representing various periods of historical & contemporary art, with emphasis on Northern California art; also special collection includes; The Nagel Collection of Oriental Ceramics & Sculpture; Ruesch Collection of Whistler Lithographs
Publications: Exhibition catalogues
Activities: Lects open to pub; vis lects 1-2 per yr; gallery talks; tours; schols offered; originates traveling exhibs; sales shop sells books & reproductions

L   Art Dept Library, 1 Shields Ave, University of California Davis, CA 95616-5270. Tel 530-752-0152; *Slide Librn* Leah Theis; *Book Librn* Bonnie Holt
Slide Library Open Mon - Fri 8 AM - Noon & 1 - 5 PM, Book Library Open Mon - Thurs 9 AM - 4 PM, Fri 9 AM - Noon; Estab 1966 to make readily accessible reference & research material to Art Department faculty, students & the general pub
Income: Financed by state appropriation & college funds
Purchases: $3,500
Library Holdings: Audio Tapes; Book Volumes 20,000; Clipping Files; Exhibition Catalogs; Fiche; Filmstrips; Kodachrome Transparencies; Lantern Slides; Micro Print; Motion Pictures; Other Holdings DIAL (Decimal Index of Art of the Low Countries) photographs; Periodical Subscriptions 15; Photographs; Reproductions; Slides; Video Tapes
Special Subjects: Art History, Folk Art, Film, Painting-American, Painting-British, Conceptual Art, American Western Art, Asian Art, American Indian Art, Mexican Art, Aesthetics, Afro-American Art, Oriental Art, Architecture

DESERT HOT SPRINGS

M   CABOT'S OLD INDIAN PUEBLO MUSEUM, 67616 E Desert View Ave, Desert Hot Springs, CA 92240-4114; PO Box 104, Desert Hot Springs, CA 92240-0104. Tel 760-329-7610; Fax 760-329-2738; Elec Mail cabotsmuseum@roadrunner.com; Internet Home Page Address: www.cabotsmuseum.org; *Board Pres* Michael O'Keefe; *Board VPres* John Brown; *Board CFO* Linda Blake; *Board Secy* Sally Rogers
Open every day Nov - May 9 AM - 5 PM, June - Oct 9 AM - 1 PM; Admis adults $10, sr citizens & under 12 $8; Estab 1939 as museum & home; 1100 sq ft art gallery representing contemporary artists through a variety of media. Artifacts of past cultures & Americana along with Native American work; Average Annual Attendance: 10,000; Mem: 2500; dues family $150, dual $90, individual $50
Income: Financed by donations, grants
Purchases: Cahuilla baskets, Navajo blankets & rugs acquired
Library Holdings: Book Volumes; Cassettes; Clipping Files; Kodachrome Transparencies; Memorabilia; Original Art Works; Original Documents; Pamphlets; Photographs; Prints; Records; Reproductions; Sculpture
Special Subjects: American Indian Art, Drawings, Etchings & Engravings, Historical Material, Architecture, American Western Art, Furniture, Photography, Portraits, Pottery, Painting-American, Period Rooms, Textiles, Sculpture, Southwestern Art, Costumes, Primitive art, Woodcarvings, Eskimo Art
Exhibitions: Select weekend exhibits of Art Fairs with Blacksmith Exhib, artists working on their crafts; Indian Monument carved by Peter Toth (1978); Hopi-Style Pueblo Home & Museum of Cabot Yerxa
Activities: Classes for adults & children; docent training; lects open to pub; concerts; gallery talks; tours; mus shop sells books, magazines, original art, reproductions, prints

EL CAJON

M   GROSSMONT COMMUNITY COLLEGE, Hyde Art Gallery, 8800 Grossmont College Dr, El Cajon, CA 92020-1798. Tel 619-644-7299; Fax 619-644-7922; Elec Mail steve.baker@gcccd.edu; Internet Home Page Address: www.grossmont.edu/artgallery; *Dept Chair* Dr Paul Turounet; *Cur* Prudence Horne; *Gallery Asst* Teresa L Markey; *Visual Arts & Humanities* Steve Baker Dean
Open Mon & Thurs 10 AM - 6 PM & by appointment, cl Fri - Sun & legal holidays; No admis fee; Estab 1970 as a co-curricular institution which cooperates with & supports the Art Department of Grossmont College & which provides a major cultural resource for the general pub in the eastern part of the greater San Diego area; Two galleries, one 30 x 40 ft; one 30 x 20 ft; Average Annual Attendance: 20,000
Income: Financed through College
Special Subjects: Photography, Prints, Pottery

Collections: Prints; photographs; clay objects; large Tom Holland painting; Marje Hyde, Steve Gibson; Pablo Picasso; Ansel Adams; Andy Warhol
Publications: Exhibition catalogs; posters
Activities: Lects open to public, 6 vis lects per yr; concerts; student awards from ann art council auction; original objects of art lent to institutions; lending collection photographs; originate traveling exhibs

ESCONDIDO

M   CALIFORNIA CENTER FOR THE ARTS, Escondido Museum, 340 N Escondido Blvd, Escondido, CA 92025-2600. Tel 760-839-4120 (museum), 839-4138 (office); Fax 760-743-6472 (office); Elec Mail oluther@ci.escondido.ca.us; Internet Home Page Address: www.artcenter.org; *Mus Dir* Olivia Luther; *Registrar* Mary Johnson; *Cur Asst* Tara Smith
Open Tues - Sat 10 AM - 4 PM, Sun 1 PM - 5 PM, cl Mon & major holidays; Admis adults $5, seniors & active military $4, youth 12 - 18 & students $3, children under 12 & mem free; free admis first Wed of every month during an exhibition; Estab 1994; committed to presenting contemporary art; Average Annual Attendance: 8,500; Mem: Dues $50-$10,000
Income: Financed by grants, funds & mem
Library Holdings: Book Volumes; Exhibition Catalogs; Periodical Subscriptions; Video Tapes
Special Subjects: Painting-American, Sculpture, Landscapes
Collections: Collection of decorative arts, Paintings, photography & sculpture from 1900 to present
Exhibitions: Exhibits draw on a distinct theme or idea in contemporary art
Publications: Exhibition specific catalogues
Activities: Classes for children & adults; docent training; lects open to pub; concerts; gallery talks; tours; individual paintings & original objects of art lent; book traveling exhibs; mus shop sells books, original art, reproductions, prints, ceramics, glass, decorative items & jewelry

EUREKA

A   HUMBOLDT ARTS COUNCIL, Morris Graves Museum of Art, 636 F St, Eureka, CA 95501-1012. Tel 707-442-0278; Fax 707-442-2040; Internet Home Page Address: www.humboldtarts.org; *Exec Dir & Cur* Jemima Harr
Open Wed - Sun Noon - 5 PM; No admis fee; Estab 1966 to encourage, promote & correlate all forms of activity in the visual & performing arts & to make such activity a vital influence in the life of the community; Gallery has 7 spaces rotating 41 exhib; Average Annual Attendance: 26,000; Mem: 700; dues $30; annual meeting in Apr
Income: $10,000 (financed by mem)
Collections: Art Bank, other purchase & donated works of art; photograph coll; Premier Coll of North Coast Art (traveling display); traveling import museum exhibits; Morris Graves Collection
Exhibitions: Annual Youth Art Exhibit
Activities: Classes for children & adults, music & dance performances, docent training; concerts; competitions, lects for mems, gallery talks, tours; scholarships offered; individual paintings & original objects of art lent; originate traveling exhibs; museum shop sells books, magazines, original art, reproductions, prints

FREMONT

M   CITY OF FREMONT, Olive Hyde Art Gallery, 123 Washington Blvd, Fremont, CA 94539-5209; PO Box 5006, Fremont, CA 94537-5006. Tel 510-791-4357, 494-4240 (Dir) Fax 510-494-4753; Elec Mail ijordahl@ci.fremont.ca.us; Internet Home Page Address: www.fremont.gov; *Gallery Cur* Sandra Hemsworth; *Recreation Supvr II* Irene Jordahl
Open Thurs - Sun 12 - 5 PM; No admis fee; Estab 1964 for community exposure to artistic awareness; Historical former home of Miss Olive Hyde, a well-known San Franciscan art patron. This is the only fine arts gallery open to the public between Hayward & San Jose, located across from the Historical Mission San Jose in Fremont. Exhibits are displayed in 1000 sq ft of space; Average Annual Attendance: 10,000
Income: $20,000 (financed by city appropriation)
Special Subjects: Drawings, Painting-American, Photography, Prints, Sculpture, Watercolors, Textiles
Exhibitions: 7 exhibits per year in fine arts, crafts, photography, textiles, sculpture; local, regional, national & international artists
Publications: Full color exhibit postcards
Activities: Classes for adults & children; docent progs; gallery talks; tours; lects open to both the pub & mems only, 10 vis lectrs per yr; competitions with cash prizes & awards; schols offered; book traveling exhibs 1 per yr; originate traveling exhibs

FRESNO

M   FRESNO ARTS CENTER & MUSEUM, 2233 N First St, Fresno, CA 93703. Tel 559-441-4220; Fax 559-441-4227; Elec Mail fam@qnis.net; Internet Home Page Address: www.fresnoartmuseum.org; *Exec Dir* Michael Mazur; *Cur* Jacqueline Pilar
Open Tues - Sun 11AM-5PM, Thurs 11AM-8PM; Admis adults $4, students & seniors $2, children 16 & under, school tours & mus mem free, Sat free to pub; Estab 1949 as a visual arts gallery to provide Fresno & its environs with a community oriented visual arts center; The Center exhibits works of internationally known artists & arranges shows of local artists. Three galleries plus entry for exhibits; Average Annual Attendance: 98,000; Mem: 2500; dues $25; annual meeting in May
Income: Financed by mem & fundraising efforts
Special Subjects: Mexican Art, Oriental Art
Collections: Works of prominent California artists; contemporary American artists; Mexican folk art; Mexican graphic arts; permanent coll, National & International artists; extensive Pre-Columbian folk art

Exhibitions: Rotating exhibits every 3 months
Activities: Classes for adults & children; docent training; lects open to pub, 12 vis lectrs per yr; gallery talks; concerts; tours; competitions; scholarships offered; individual paintings & objects of art lent to city & county offices & other institutions; lending collection contains framed reproductions, original art works, original prints & slides; book traveling exhibs; originates traveling exhibs; mus shop sells books, magazines, original art, reproductions, prints, cards & local crafts

M **FRESNO METROPOLITAN MUSEUM,** 205 E River Park Cir, Ste 410, Fresno, CA 93720-1572. Tel 559-441-1444; Fax 559-441-8607; Elec Mail marketing@fresnomet.org; Internet Home Page Address: www.fresnomet.org; *Exec Dir* Dana Thorpe; *Dir Mktg & Mem* Candice Pendergrass
Open Tues - Sun 11 AM - 5 PM; Admis adults $8, seniors & students $5, children 3-12 $3, members & children under 3 free; Estab 1984 to increase the availability of fine & educational arts to the Fresno area; Mus is housed in a refurbished 1922 newspaper plant, two stories, with other floors marked for develop; equipped with elevators & facilities for the handicapped; Average Annual Attendance: 100,000; Mem: 5000; dues $30-$1000
Income: $1,300,000 (financed by mem, donations, service fees & grants)
Collections: Frank & Mary Alice Diener Collection of ancient snuff bottles; Oscar & Maria Salzer Collection of still life & trompe L'oeil paintings; Oscar & Maria Salzer collection of 16th & 17th century Dutch & Flemish paintings; Charles Small Puzzle Collection
Publications: MetReport, monthly
Activities: Children's classes & summer day camps; dramatic progs; docent training; lects open to pub; tours; individual paintings & original objects of art lent; book traveling exhibs; originate traveling exhibs; mus shop sells books & prints

M **GALLERY 25,** Art Gallery, 660 Van Ness Ave, Fresno, CA 93721. Tel 559-264-4092; Internet Home Page Address: www.gallery25.org; *Dir* Barbara Van Arnam
Open 1st Thurs each month 5 PM - 8 PM Fri - Sun noon - 4 PM; No admis fee; Estab 1974; cooperative art gallery; Contemporary art of central California; Average Annual Attendance: 5,000; Mem: 25; dues $720 ann; qualifications, highest quality contemporary art
Income: Self financed by mem dues & sales
Collections: works by contemporary artists
Exhibitions: Rotating monthly exhibs
Activities: Gallery talks; sales shop sells books, magazines, original art, prints & jewelry

FULLERTON

M **CALIFORNIA STATE UNIVERSITY, FULLERTON,** Visual Arts Galleries, 800 N State College Blvd, Fullerton, CA 92634-3559; PO Box 6850, Visual Arts Dept Fullerton, CA 92834-6850. Tel 657-278-3471 (Dept); 278-7750 (Gallery); Fax 657-278-2390; Elec Mail mmcgee@fullerton.edu; Internet Home Page Address: www.fullerton.edu/arts/; *Cur* Mike McGee
Open Mon - Fri 8 AM - 5 PM, cl Sat & Sun; No admis fee; Estab 1963 to bring to the campus carefully developed art exhibits that instruct, inspire & challenge the student to the visual arts; to present to the student body, faculty & community exhibs of historical & aesthetic significance; to act as an educational tool, creating interaction between various departmental disciplines & promoting pub relations between campus & community; Visual Arts Galleries comprised of the Begovich Gallery, East Gallery, West Gallery & Exit Gallery; 4-5 exhibits each year stemming from the Museum Studies & Exhibition Design Program. Undergraduate & graduate students have the opportunity to focus within a professionally oriented program directed toward the mus profession. Activity incorporates classes, art gallery & local mus. The Department of Art & the Art Gallery are the holders of the permanent collection; Average Annual Attendance: 15,000-20,000
Income: Financed by state appropriation, grants & donations
Collections: Contemporary Lithographs (Gemini); works by artists in the New York Collection for Stockholm executed by Styria Studio; lithographs by Lita Albuquerque, Coy Howard, Ed Rusha & Alexis Smith; Pre-Columbian artifacts; environmental & site-specific sculpture by Lloyd Hamrol, Ray Hein, Bernard Rosenthal, Michael Todd, Jay Willis; Smithsonian Collection of American Art; Jene Isaacson Collection
Publications: Exhibition catalogs
Activities: Lects open to public, 8-10 vis lectrs per yr; workshops; production of slide/sound interpretation programs in conjunction with specific exhibitions; gallery talks; tours; scholarships offered; exten dept 4-6 major exhibs per yr; originate traveling exhibs

M **FULLERTON COLLEGE ART GALLERY,** 321 E Chapman Ave, Bldg 1000 Fullerton, CA 92832-2011. Tel 714-922-7131; Fax 714-992-7320; Elec Mail bsolomon@fullcoll.edu; Internet Home Page Address: art.fullcoll.edu; *Gallery Dir & Art Instr* Beth Solomon Marino
Open Mon - Thurs 10 AM - 2 PM, selected evenings 5 PM - 7 PM; No admis fee; Estab 1913 (Fullerton Col); 1750 sq ft with movable walls (7 rotating exhibs per yr); Average Annual Attendance: 3,500
Collections: paintings, photographs, sculpture, prints
Publications: Visions Catalogue of Collection
Activities: Classes for adults; lects open to pub; 3 vis lectrs per yr; gallery talks; tours; schols; lending of original objects of art to CSU, Fullerton & Orange Coast Community Col; sales shop sells original art, prints

A **MUCKENTHALER CULTURAL CENTER,** 1201 W Malvern, Fullerton, CA 92633. Tel 714-738-6595; Fax 714-738-6366; Elec Mail info@themuck.org; Internet Home Page Address: www.muckenthaler.org; *Center Adminr* Zoot Velasco; *Exhib & Educ Adminr* Matt Leslie
Open Wed - Fri 10 AM - 4 PM, Sat - Sun Noon - 4 PM, By appt Tues; Admis adults $5, seniors & students $2, children under 12 free; Estab 1966 for the promotion & develop of a public cultural center for the preservation, display &

edification in the arts; Gallery is a National Historic Building, contains 2500 sq ft & is on 8 1/2 acres of land; outdoor theatre facilities; Average Annual Attendance: 65,000; Mem: 600; dues $10 & up; annual meeting in Apr
Income: $230,000 (financed by endowment, mem & city appropriation)
Publications: Exhibition catalogs
Activities: Classes for adults & children; dramatic progs; docent training; lects open to pub; 12 vis lectrs per yr; concerts; gallery talks; tours; book traveling exhibs; mus shop sells original art, reproductions, prints & gifts

GILROY

M **GAVILAN COMMUNITY COLLEGE,** Art Gallery, 5055 Santa Teresa Blvd, Gilroy, CA 95020-9599. Tel 408-846-4946; Fax 408-846-4927, 846-4801; Internet Home Page Address: www.Gavilan.cc.ca.us; *Gallery Adv & Humanities Div Dir* Kent Child; *Prof Art & New Technology* Jane Edberg
Open Mon - Fri 8 AM - 5 PM; No admis fee; Estab 1967 to serve as a focal point in art exhibs for community col district & as a teaching resource for the art dept; Gallery is in large lobby of college library with 25 ft ceiling, redwood panelled walls & carpeted floor
Income: Financed through college
Collections: Over 25 paintings purchased as award purchase prizes in college art competitions
Exhibitions: Monthly exhibits of student & local artists; Ann Gavilan Student Show, HS Student Exhib
Activities: Lending collection contains books, cassettes, color reproductions, film strips, Kodachromes, paintings, sculpture

GLEN ELLEN

M **JACK LONDON STATE HISTORIC PARK,** House of Happy Walls, 2400 London Ranch Rd, Glen Ellen, CA 95442-9749. Tel 707-938-5216; Fax 707-938-4827; *Supv Ranger* Greg Hayes; *Ranger* Cheryl Lawton; *Ranger* Angie Nowicki
Open daily 10 AM - 5 PM, summers 10 AM - 7 PM, cl New Year's Day, Thanksgiving, Christmas; Admis $10-$20 per bus, $3 per car, seniors $2; Estab 1959 for the interpretation of the life of Jack London; the fieldstone home was constructed in 1919 by London's widow; The collection is housed on two floors in the House of Happy Walls, and is operated by Calif Dept of Parks & Recreation; Average Annual Attendance: 100,000
Income: Financed by state appropriation
Collections: Artifacts from South Sea Islands; original illustrations; Portrait of activity during Jack London's residence
Activities: Tours; sales shop sells some of London's books

GLENDALE

M **FOREST LAWN MUSEUM,** 1712 S Glendale Ave, Glendale, CA 91205. Tel 800-204-3131; Fax 323-551-5329; Elec Mail museum@forestlawn.com; Internet Home Page Address: www.forestlawn.com; *Mus Opers Supv* Elizabeth Bloess; *Exhib Designer* Joan Adan
Open Tues - Sun 10 AM - 5 PM; No admis fee; Estab 1951 as a community mus offering educ & culture through assn with the architecture and the art of world masters; Two galleries of permanent collection, museum store & rotating exhibit gallery; Average Annual Attendance: 50,000
Special Subjects: Decorative Arts, Drawings, Landscapes, Architecture, Ceramics, American Western Art, Furniture, Gold, Photography, Bronzes, Manuscripts, Latin American Art, Sculpture, Religious Art, Glass, Jade, Jewelry, Silver, Ivory, Coins & Medals, Painting-Polish, Renaissance Art, Medieval Art, Islamic Art, Antiquities-Greek, Antiquities-Roman, Mosaics, Stained Glass, Reproductions, Enamels
Collections: American Western Bronzes; Ancient Biblical and Historical Coins; Crucifixion by Jan Styka (195 x 45 ft painting); Resurrection (Robert Clark), painting; reproductions of Michelangelo's greatest sculptures; stained glass window of the Last Supper by Leonardo da Vinci; originals and reproductions of famous sculptures, paintings, and documents
Exhibitions: Four changing exhibits every year, see website
Activities: Community events; History Comes Alive Program; originate traveling exhibs; mus shop sells books, original art reproductions, prints, objects that reflect the collection

M **GLENDALE PUBLIC LIBRARY,** (Brand Library & Art Galleries) Brand Library & Art Center, 1601 W Mountain St, Glendale, CA 91201-1200. Tel 818-548-2051; Fax 818-548-5079; Elec Mail info@brandlibrary.org; Internet Home Page Address: www.brandlibrary.org; *Sr Library Supvr* Alyssa Resnick; *Librn* Blair Whittington; *Librn* Cathy Billings
Open Tues & Thurs noon-8PM, Wed noon-6PM; No admis fee; Estab 1956 to exhibit Southern California artists as part of an art & music library; Circ 170,000; Large gallery, foyer gallery, glass & concrete sculpture ct; Average Annual Attendance: 100,000; Mem: 375; dues $15 - $500
Income: Financed by city & state appropriations
Library Holdings: Book Volumes 106,000; Compact Disks; DVDs; Exhibition Catalogs; Framed Reproductions; Periodical Subscriptions; Records 16,000; Reproductions; Slides; Video Tapes
Collections: Indexes & other guides to art & music literature; books, catalogue raisonne, scores, CDs DVDs, slides
Exhibitions: 4-6 exhibits per year
Activities: Los Angeles Opera Talks; lects open to pub; 4-6 vis lectrs; concerts; gallery talks; tours; competitions

HALF MOON BAY

M **COASTAL ARTS LEAGUE MUSEUM,** 300 Main St., Half Moon Bay, CA 94038. Tel 650-726-6335; Internet Home Page Address: www.coastalartsleague.com
Open Thurs - Mon 11 AM - 5 PM; No admis fee

Special Subjects: Pottery, Painting-American, Photography, Sculpture, Watercolors, Ceramics, Restorations
Collections: Paintings; photographs; sculpture; ceramics
Exhibitions: International photography juried show; juried & invitational exhibs -high school yearly show
Activities: Mus related items for sale

HAYWARD

M CALIFORNIA STATE UNIVERSITY, EAST BAY, University Art Gallery, 1233 Art & Education Bldg, CSUEB Hayward, CA 94542. Tel 510-885-3299; Fax 510-885-2281; Internet Home Page Address: www.csueastbay.edu/artgallery; *Dir* Philip Hofstetter
Open Mon - Thurs 12:30 PM - 3:30 PM; No admis fee; Estab 1970 to provide a changing exhibition program for the university & general public; Gallery contains 2,200 sq ft; Average Annual Attendance: 11,000
Publications: Usually one catalog a yr; flyers for each show

M C E Smith Museum of Anthropology, 4047 Meiklejohn Hall, California State University East Bay Hayward, CA 94542; Anthropology Dept M13097, CSU East Bay Hayward, CA 94542. Tel 510-885-3104; Fax 510-885-3353; Elec Mail george.miller@csueastbay.edu; Internet Home Page Address: class.csueastbay.edu/anthropologymuseum; *Dir* George Miller PhD; *Assoc Dir* Marjorie Rhodes-Ousley
Open Mar - June Mon - Fri 10 AM - 4 PM; No admis fee; Estab 1974 as a teaching museum; Three connected galleries; one main entrance from center room; alarm system; smoke detectors; Average Annual Attendance: 2,500; Mem: 200
Income: $22,000 (financed by state appropriation)
Special Subjects: African Art, Anthropology, Archaeology, Ethnology, Pre-Columbian Art, Southwestern Art, Textiles
Collections: Krone Collection: Philippine artifacts; Lee Collection: Hopi Kachinas, baskets, Navajo Mat
Publications: Seasons of the Kochina, ed L J Bean; The Ohlone Past & Present, ed L J Bean
Activities: Educ prog; classes for adults; college classes; tours; Lect open to pub, 4 vis lectrs per yr; tours

M SUN GALLERY, (Hayward Area Forum of the Arts) 1015 E St, Hayward, CA 94541-5210. Tel 510-581-4050; Fax 510-581-3384; Elec Mail sungallery@comcast.net; Internet Home Page Address: www.sungallery.org; *Exec Dir* Valerie Caveglia; *Admin Asst* Christine Bender; *Artistic Dir* Jacqueline Cooper
Open Wed - Sat 11 AM - 5 PM, cl major holidays; No admis fee; Estab 1975; Exhibition gallery, gallery shop & teaching studio; Average Annual Attendance: 5,000; Mem: dues sustaining $65, family $50, single $35, senior citizen $25
Income: Financed by city, corporate & foundation grants, county & mem funds
Library Holdings: Audio Tapes; Book Volumes; CD-ROMs; Cards; Cassettes; Clipping Files; Kodachrome Transparencies; Original Art Works; Prints; Sculpture; Slides; Video Tapes
Collections: Contemporary art by Northern California artists
Exhibitions: San Francisco Alumni Association exhibition (photography); recent works in Monotype; contemporary Mexican painters (from Santiago Garza collection); Jack & Marilyn da Silva (metalware); art programs for the physically limited; Roger Hankins (painting, assemblage); Dicksen Schneider; Southern Alameda County Art Educators; Corita Kent; Artistas del Grupo Hermes (paintings, drawings); Recent Work in Metal; Artists With Creative Growth; The Picture: As Object, As Image (painting, assemblage, photography); Shrine & Koan (painting, sculpture); Corita & Southern Alameda County Art Educators (multi-media); HAFA members exhibition (multi-media); Art in the News (photojournalists, editorial cartoonists); Forms In Space (2-D, 3-D); Felted Fibers; The Hottest Show in Town: Exhibit featuring art by firefighters; A Cut Above: Art created by cutting; An Annual Children's Book Illustrator Exhibit; The Wild, Wild West
Activities: Classes for adults & children; lects open to pub, 6-8 vis lectrs per yr; gallery talks; tours; scholarships offered; individual paintings & original objects of art lent to city offices; mus shop sells original art, prints, magazines, reproductions, books & crafts

HUNTINGTON BEACH

M HUNTINGTON BEACH ART CENTER, 538 Main St, Huntington Beach, CA 92648-5134. Tel 714-374-1650; Fax 714-374-5304; Elec Mail deangel@surfeity-hb.org; *Dir* Kate Hoffman; *Dir Programming* Darlene DeAngelo
Open Wed-Sat noon-6PM; No admis fee; Estab 1995 to provide community art center; Three large galleries, store gallery, studio & one educational gallery; Average Annual Attendance: 3,000; Mem: 300
Activities: Classes for adults & children; performance art venue; lect open to public; Sun jazz concerts; sales shop sells books & magazines

INDIO

M COACHELLA VALLEY HISTORY MUSEUM, (Coachella Valley Museum and Cultural Center) 82-616 Miles Ave, Indio, CA 92201. Tel 760-342-6651; Fax 760-863-5232; Elec Mail erin@cvhm.org; Internet Home Page Address: coachellavalleymuseum.org; *Pres* William H Claire; *Archivist/Cur* Erica M Ward; *Office Admin* Janice Woodside
Open Oct - May Thurs - Sat 10 AM - 4 PM, Sun 1 - 4 PM, cl holidays; Admis adults $10, senior citizens & students $8, children 6-12 $5, children under 5 & members free; Estab Oct 1984; Average Annual Attendance: 4,200; Mem: 380
Income: Financed by mems, donations & bequeathments
Library Holdings: Book Volumes; Original Documents; Photographs
Collections: works by local artists
Exhibitions: Monthly local art show, reception first Sun ea month
Publications: quarterly newsletter, Scratches in the Sand; annual magazine, The Periscope; pictorial history book

Activities: Summer art classes for adults & children 8-12; docent prog; lects open to pub; vis lectrs 3 per yr; guided tours; school tours; mus shop sells books, original art, toys, DVDs

IRVINE

M CITY OF IRVINE, Irvine Fine Arts Center, 14321 Yale Ave, Irvine, CA 92604-1901. Tel 949-724-6880; Fax 949-552-2137; Internet Home Page Address: www.irvinefinearts.org; *Dir* Wendy Shields; *Youth Prog Coordr* Andrea Becerra; *Adult Prog Coordr* Katy Metz
Open Mon - Thurs 10 AM - 9 PM, Fri 10 AM - 5 PM, Sat 9AM-5PM; No admis fee; Estab 1980 to promote awareness of the value & function of the arts in the community; Gallery contains 5000 sq ft; Average Annual Attendance: 65,000; Mem: 250; dues $25 - $100
Income: $800,000 (financed by city appropriation, grants & donations)
Exhibitions: Solo & group themed exhibitions of local, national & international contemporary artists
Publications: Inside Irvine, quarterly
Activities: Classes for adults & children; docent progs; open studios; 2 arts festivals per year; lects open to pub, competitions, scholarships; sales shop sells original art

M IRVINE MUSEUM, 18881 Von Karman Ave Ste 100, Irvine, CA 92612-1559. Tel 949-476-0294; Fax 949-476-2437; Internet Home Page Address: www.irvinemuseum.org; *Exec Dir* Jean Stern; *Exec Dir* Merika Adams Gopaul; *Cur Educ* Dora James; *Dir Media* Judy Thompson; *Bookstore Mgr* Don Bridges; *Visitor Svcs* Charlett Pfeiffer
Open Tues - Sat 11 AM - 5 PM; No admis fee; Estab 1992 to promote the California Impressionist Period; Average Annual Attendance: 19,000
Special Subjects: Painting-American
Collections: Paintings of the California Impressionist Period, 1890-1930; California Impressionist paintings
Exhibitions: Exhibits change every 4 months; traveling exhibs
Publications: Exhibit catalogs
Activities: Classes for children; docent progs; mus shop sells books

M UNIVERSITY OF CALIFORNIA, IRVINE, Beall Center for Art + Technology, and University Art Gallery, 712 Arts Plaza, Univ of Calif Irvine Irvine, CA 92697-2775. Tel 949-824-6206; Fax 949-824-2450; Elec Mail syoungha@uci.edu; Internet Home Page Address: www.beallcenter.uci.edu; *Dir* Joseph S Lewis III; *Asst Dir* David Familian; *Prog Dir* Samantha Younghans-Haug
Open Oct - June, Tue & Wed Noon - 5 PM, Thurs - Sat Noon - 8 PM; No admis fee; Estab 2000; focus on experimental media arts & contemporary art; 2 galleries totalling 5,000 sq ft; Average Annual Attendance: 5,000
Income: Financed by state appropriations & by pvt and corporate donors
Exhibitions: (10/03/2013-01/25/2014) Soung/Sculptures: A Group Exhib; (02/06/2014-05/01/2014) Zimoun
Publications: Exhibition catalogs; mailers
Activities: Educ prog; family art days; robotics summer camps for children; lects open to pub; 2 vis lectrs per yr; performances; gallery talks; tours; field trips

KENTFIELD

M COLLEGE OF MARIN, Art Gallery, 835 College Ave, Kentfield, CA 94904-2551. Tel 415-485-9494; Internet Home Page Address: www.marin.edu; *Dir* Julie Gustafson
Open Mon - Fri 9 AM - 5 PM, also during all performances for drama, music & concert; No admis fee; Estab 1970 for the purpose of educ in the col district & community; Gallery is housed in the entrance to Fine Arts Complex, measures 3600 sq ft of unlimited hanging space; has portable hanging units & locked cases; Average Annual Attendance: 100-450 daily
Income: Financed by state appropriation & community taxes
Collections: Art student work; miscellaneous coll
Exhibitions: Faculty & Art Student; Fine Arts & Decorative Arts
Publications: Catalogs, 1-2 per year
Activities: Gallery Design-Management course; gallery talks; tours

LA JOLLA

M JOSEPH BELLOWS GALLERY, 7661 Girard Ave, La Jolla, CA 92037. Tel 858-456-5620; Fax 858-456-5621; Elec Mail info@josephbellows.com; Internet Home Page Address: www.josephbellows.com; *Dir* Carol Lee Brosseau; *Dir* Joseph Bellows
Open Tues-Sat 10AM-5PM
Collections: photographs

L LIBRARY ASSOCIATION OF LA JOLLA, Athenaeum Music & Arts Library, 1008 Wall St, La Jolla, CA 92037-4418. Tel 858-454-5872; Fax 858-454-5835; Elec Mail athdir@pacbell.net; Internet Home Page Address: www.ljathenaeum.org; *Exec Dir* Erika Torri; *Prog Dir* Judith Oishei; *Asst to Dir/Exhibs* Maura Walters; *Librn* Kathi Bower-Peterson; *Pub Rels* Katie Walders; *School Dir* Cornelia Feye
Open Tues, Thurs, Fri & Sat 10 AM - 5:30 PM, Wed 10 AM - 8:30PM; No admis fee; Estab 1899 to provide the La Jolla & San Diego communities with library resources in music & arts & an on going schedule of cultural programs, classes, concerts & exhibitions; Circ 30,000; changing exhibitions every six weeks; Average Annual Attendance: 130,000; Mem: 2300; dues $40-$15,000; annual meeting third Tues in July
Income: $1,500,000 (financed by endowment fund, rents, dues, gifts, admis & tuitions)
Purchases: $50,000
Library Holdings: Audio Tapes 4,000; Book Volumes 18,000; CD-ROMs 200; Cassettes 4000; Clipping Files 2500; Compact Disks 12,000; DVDs 1,000; Exhibition Catalogs; Other Holdings Sheet Music, Artists' Books 1500; Pamphlets; Periodical Subscriptions 85; Photographs; Records 8000; Video Tapes 3000

Special Subjects: Art History, Photography, Bronzes, Advertising Design, Asian Art, Aesthetics, Afro-American Art, Bookplates & Bindings, Architecture
Collections: Collection of artists books; works by regional, nat & international artists; paintings; sculpture; drawings; photographs
Exhibitions: Changing exhibitions every six weeks; Permanent Art Coll Works by artists who have exhibited at the Athenaeum
Publications: Bimonthly newsletter, qtr school brochure, occasional exhib catalogues, catalogs on artists' book artists: Ed Ruscha, Ida Applebroog, Allen Ruppersberg
Activities: Classes for adults & children; lect open to public, 15 vis lectrs per year; concerts; library tours; panel discussions; vis artists workshops; outreach programs for children; qtr book sales; competitions with prizes; 1st, 2nd, 3rd awards for juried shows; original artists books lent to qualified mus & institutions; sales shop sells books, cards, craft items

M **MUSEUM OF CONTEMPORARY ART, SAN DIEGO,** 700 Prospect St, La Jolla, CA 92037-4228. Tel 858-454-3541; Fax 858-454-6985; Elec Mail info@mcasandiego.org; Internet Home Page Address: www.mcasd.org; *Dir* Hugh M Davies; *Deputy Dir* Charles E Castle; *Cur Educ* Gabrielle Wyrick; *Chief Advancement Officer* Jeanna Yoo; *Pres Board Trustees* Peter C Farrell; *Sr Communs & Mktg Mgr* Rebecca Handelsman; *Communs Assoc* Claire Caraska; *Retail Opers Mgr* Monique Fuentes; *Registrar & Coll Mgr* Laura Graziano; *Chief Cur* Kathryn Kanjo; *VPres Bd Trustees* David C Copley; *VPres Board Trustees* Matt Strauss; *VPres Board Trustees* Colette Carson Royston
Open Thurs - Tues 11 AM - 5 PM, third Thurs of month 11 AM - 7PM, cl Wed; Admis adults $10, seniors, & students 26 & over with ID $5, 25 & under with ID, Military with ID & mems no charge; Estab 1941 to collect, preserve & present post-1950 art; Maintains two locations, a 500 seat auditorium, 16,000 sq ft total exhibition space. See also listing for San Diego facility; Average Annual Attendance: 177,500; Mem: 2,400; dues $45-$2,500
Income: $3,745,000 (financed by endowment, mem, city & state appropriations, grants from the National Endowment for the Arts, Institute of Museum Services, private foundations & contributions from San Diego Commission for Arts & Culture, James Irving Foundation, Getty Foundation, National Endowment for humanities & foreign consulates
Special Subjects: Painting-American, Sculpture
Collections: Contemporary Art, International, 1950 to the present
Exhibitions: Vernon Fisher; Ann Hamilton; Alfredo Jaar; La Frontera/The Border; David Reed; Francis Bacon: The Papal Portraits of 1953
Publications: Exhibition catalogs; newsletter, quarterly
Activities: Classes & programming for adults & children; docent training; opening & evening events for mems & pub; lects open to pub, 10-15 vis lectrs per yr; gallery talks, tours; films; concerts; individual paintings & original objects of art lent to mus & qualified art organizations; lending collection contains original art works, original prints, paintings, photographs, sculpture; book traveling exhibs 3-4 per yr; originate traveling exhibs; mus bookstore sells books, magazines, posters, design objects

L **Geisel Library,** 700 Prospect St, La Jolla, CA 92037-4228. Tel 858-454-3541; Fax 858-454-6985; Elec Mail aschofield@mcasandiego.org; Internet Home Page Address: www.mcasandiego.org; *Librn* Andrea Hales; *Dir* Dr Hugh M Davies; *Deputy Dir* Charles Castle; *Dir External Affairs* Anne Farrell; *Cur* Stephanie Hanor; *Cur* Rachel Teagle; *Dir Institutional Advanc* Jane Rice
Open Thurs 11 AM - 7 PM, Fri - Tues 11 AM - 5 PM; Admis $6 adults, $2 seniors (65 and over), military & students, children under 12 free; Estab 1941; Average Annual Attendance: 160,000
Income: Financed by mem, gifts & grants
Library Holdings: Auction Catalogs; Audio Tapes; Book Volumes 4500; Cards; Cassettes; Clipping Files 2000; Exhibition Catalogs 6000; Pamphlets; Periodical Subscriptions 56; Slides 10,000; Video Tapes
Special Subjects: Art History, Photography, Drawings, Painting-American, Painting-British, Sculpture, Conceptual Art, Latin American Art, Video
Activities: Classes for children; docent training; concerts; gallery talks; tours; ext prog; lending of original objects of art to national & international mus; book traveling exhibs; originates traveling exhibs to national & international mus; mus shop sells books, magazines, reproductions, utensils, toys, decorative objects; second location at MCA Downtown, 1001 Kettner Blvd, San Diego 92101

M **MUSEUM OF CONTEMPORARY ART, SAN DIEGO-DOWNTOWN,** 700 Prospect St, La Jolla, CA 92037-4291. Tel 619-234-1001; Fax 619-234-1070; Elec Mail info@mcasandiego.org; Internet Home Page Address: www.mcasandiego.org; *Pres Bd Trustees* Dr Charles Cochrane; *Dir* Hugh M Davies; *Assoc Dir* Charles Castle; *Educ Cur* Kelly McKinley; *Dir Develop* Anne Farrell; *Mktg Mgr* Jana Purdy; *Publ Relations Officer* Jennifer Morrissey
Open Thurs - Tues 11 AM - 5 PM, cl Weds; No admis fee; Estab 1941 to collect, preserve & present post-1950 art; See also listing for La Jolla facility; Average Annual Attendance: 160,000; Mem: 3500; dues $50
Income: $5,400,000 (financed by endowment, mem, city & state appropriation, grants from the National Endowment for the Arts, Institute of Mus Services & private foundations)
Library Holdings: Audio Tapes; Clipping Files; Exhibition Catalogs; Pamphlets; Periodical Subscriptions; Slides
Special Subjects: Architecture, Drawings, Photography, Prints, Sculpture, Watercolors
Collections: Contemporary art, all media; post-1950 art, all media; Contemporary Art; Post-195 Art
Publications: VIEW, quarterly newsletter; exhibition catalogues
Activities: Classes for adults & children; docent progs; films; lects open to pub; gallery talks; tours; internships offered; book traveling exhibs 1 per yr; originate traveling exhibs 2 per yr; mus shop sells books, magazines, reproductions, prints posters, original art & design objects

M **UNIVERSITY OF CALIFORNIA, SAN DIEGO,** Stuart Collection, 9500 Gilman Dr, La Jolla, CA 92093-0010. Tel 858-534-2117; Fax 858-534-9713; Elec Mail mbeebe@ucsd.edu; Internet Home Page Address: www.stuartcollection.ucsd.edu; *Project Mgr* Mathieu Gregoire; *Dir* Mary Livingstone Beebe; *Prog Asst* Jane Zwerneman
Open 24 hours, 7 days a week; No admis fee; Estab 1981 to commission outdoor sculptures for UCSD campus; Maintains small library; Average Annual Attendance: 38,000 per day; Mem: Friends of the Stuart Collection $1500 per yr
Income: Staff raises all funds; salaries paid by UCSD
Purchases: 18 commissioned sculptures
Special Subjects: Architecture, Drawings, Sculpture
Collections: Outdoor sculptures, 18 works
Publications: Landmarks: Sculpture commissions for the Stuart Collection at the University of California, San Diego, pub 2001
Activities: Lects for mems only; 1-2 vis lectrs per yr; tours by appointment; support groups

M **UNIVERSITY OF CALIFORNIA-SAN DIEGO,** University Art Gallery, 9500 Gilman Dr, Mail Code 0327 La Jolla, CA 92093-0327. Tel 858-534-0419; Fax 858-822-3548; Elec Mail uag@ucsd.edu; Internet Home Page Address: www.universityartgallery.ucsd.edu; *Asst Dir* Merete Kjaer
Open Tues - Fri 11 AM - 5 PM; No admis fee; Estab 1967; Size 2800 sq ft; Average Annual Attendance: 15,000
Income: Financed by state appropriations, member contributions & student registration fees
Exhibitions: 5 exhib per yr incl MFA plus on campus & off site projects
Activities: Classes for children & docent training; lects open to public, 3-4 vis lectrs per yr; gallery talks; tours; fels; originate traveling exhibs

LAGUNA BEACH

M **LAGUNA ART MUSEUM,** 307 Cliff Dr, Laguna Beach, CA 92651-1696. Tel 949-494-8971; Fax 949-494-1530; Elec Mail mfarmer@lagunaartmuseum.org; Internet Home Page Address: www.lagunaartmuseum.org; *Bus Mgr* Peter Salomon; *Dir Communs* Marni Farmer; *Cur Historical Art* Janet Blake; *Registrar* Dawn Minegar; *Cur Contemporary Art* Grace Kook-Anderson; *Exec Dir* Malcolm Warner; *Deputy Dir* Ed Fosmire; *Cur Educ* Marinta Skupin; *Dir Special Events* Sarah Strozza; *Mem Mgr* Valerie Tate; *Develop & Outreach Assoc* Jennifer Gardiner; *Dir Opers* Tim Schwab; *Head Security* Joel Woodard
Open Mon - Tue, Fri - Sun 11 AM - 5 PM, Thurs 11 AM - 9 PM; cl Wed & major holidays; Admis adults $7, seniors & students $5, children under 12 free; Estab 1918 as an art assoc; Two large galleries, six small galleries, mus store & offices; Average Annual Attendance: 40,000; Mem: 1800; dues $60 - $10,000; annual meeting in Sept
Income: Financed by endowment & mem
Collections: American Art with focus on contemporary & early 20th century California painting; California Art
Exhibitions: Rotating exhibits
Activities: Classes for adults & children; docent training; lects open to public, 15 vis lectrs per yr; concerts; gallery talks; tours; book traveling exhibs; originate traveling exhibs; sales shop sells books

L **LAGUNA COLLEGE OF ART & DESIGN,** Dennis & Leslie Power Library, 2222 Laguna Canyon Rd, Laguna Beach, CA 92651-1136. Tel 949-376-6000x225; Fax 949-376-6009; Elec Mail libcheckout@lcad.edu; Internet Home Page Address: www.lcad.edu; *Head Librn* Jennifer Martinez Wormser
Open Mon - Thurs 9 AM - 8 PM, Fri 9 AM - 5 PM; No admis fee; Estab 1961; Circ 6,600; For lending only to students & faculty; Average Annual Attendance: 40,000
Income: Financed through Institute
Purchases: $15,000
Library Holdings: Audio Tapes; Book Volumes 16,742; CD-ROMs; Clipping Files; DVDs 1,400; Exhibition Catalogs 400; Manuscripts; Original Art Works; Periodical Subscriptions 69; Photographs; Slides 23,787; Video Tapes 355
Special Subjects: Art History, Film, Illustration, Mixed Media, Photography, Commercial Art, Drawings, Etchings & Engravings, Graphic Arts, Graphic Design, Painting-American, History of Art & Archaeology, Portraits, Ceramics, American Western Art, Printmaking, Advertising Design, Cartoons, Fashion Arts, Art Education, Video
Publications: Catalog, annual; newsletters, semi-annual

LONG BEACH

M **BARBARA & RAY ALPERT JEWISH COMMUNITY CENTER,** Pauline & Zena Gatov Gallery, 3801 E Willow St, Long Beach, CA 90815-1791. Tel 562-426-7601; Fax 562-424-3915; Elec Mail elunt@alpertjcc.org; Internet Home Page Address: www.alpertjcc.org; *Pres* Steve Gordon; *Exec Dir* Jeff Antonoff; *Gallery Dir* Eve Lunt; *Prog Dir* Susan Paletz
Open Mon - Sun 10 AM - 6 PM; No admis fee; Estab 1960 to provide a showcase for Jewish artists, Judaica & a forum for socially conscious art from the greater Long Beach community; The gallery is located in the main promenade of the building; panels & shelves are for exhibit displays; Average Annual Attendance: 5,000; Mem: Varied
Income: Financed by mem & gallery sales
Special Subjects: Judaica
Collections: Max Gatov Yad Coll; Milton Hebald Terracotta Figure of Mendelson
Exhibitions: Annual Youth Art Show; Biannual Art for Social Justice Exhibit; monthly exhibits throughout the year; paintings, photography, portraits, sculpture, biannual col art exhibit
Publications: Community Chronicle, monthly
Activities: Classes for adults & children; dramatic progs; lects open to pub; concerts; gallery talks; tours; competitions with awards; Judaic library; full serv fitness ctr

A **CALIFORNIA STATE UNIVERSITY,** Long Beach Foundation, 6300 State University Dr Ste 332, Long Beach, CA 90815. Tel 562-985-5537; Fax 562-985-7951; Elec Mail mstephens@csulb.edu; Internet Home Page Address: www.foundation.csulb.edu; *CEO* Mary Stephens; *COO* Brian Nowlin; *CFO* Alan Ray; *Dir Grants & Contracts* Denise Bell
Open Mon - Fri 8 AM - 5 PM; Estab 1955 existing solely to advance the mission of the University. Serves to complement & strengthen the University's teaching, research, scholarly, creative & pub service goals
Activities: Lect open to pub, 8 vis lectrs per yr; grants offered

M **CALIFORNIA STATE UNIVERSITY, LONG BEACH,** University Art Museum, 1250 Bellflower Blvd, Long Beach, CA 90840-0004. Tel 562-985-5761; Fax 562-985-7602; Elec Mail uam@csulb.edu; Internet Home Page Address: www.csulb.edu/uam; *Dir* Christopher Scoates; *Reg & Cur Permanent Coll* Angela Barker; *Asst Cur* Elizabeth Hanson; *Assoc Dir* Ilee Kaplan; *Cur Educ* Brian Trimble; *Educ Asst* Christina Alegria; *Pub Relations Dir* Sarah G Vinci
Open Tues-Sun noon-5PM, Thurs noon-8PM, cl Mon & university holidays; Admis general pub $4, children under 12 free, UAM mems, CSULB students, faculty & staff free; Estab 1949 to be an acad & community visual arts resource; Contemporary art; Average Annual Attendance: 50,000; Mem: 300
Income: Financed by university appropriation & private funding
Purchases: Site specific sculpture, works of art on paper
Special Subjects: Drawings, Photography, Prints, Sculpture
Collections: 1965 Sculpture Symposium
Exhibitions: Jim Dine Figure Drawings: 1975-1979; Kathe Kollwitz at the Zeitlin Bookshop 1937; CSULB 1979; Roy Lichtenstein: Ceramic Sculpture; Nathan Oliveira Print Retrospective; Lucas Samaras: Photo Transformations; George Segal: Pastels 1957 - 1965; Frederick Sommer at Seventy-five; The Photograph as Artifice; Renate Ponsold-Robert Motherwell: Apropos Robinson Jeffers; Francesco Clemente Recent Works; Paul Wonner: Recent Works; Jacques Hurtubise: Oeuvres Recentes-Recent Works; Bryan Hunt: A Decade of Drawings; Anders Zorn Rediscovered; Robert Longo: Sequences-Men in the Cities; A Collective Vision: Clarence White & His Students; Hirosada: Osaka Printmaker; Eric Fischl; Scenes Before the Eye; Lorna Simpson; Imagenes Liricas: New Spanish Visions; James Rosenquist: Time Dust, The Complete Graphics 1962 - 1992; The Great American Pop Art Store: Multiples of the Sixties
Publications: Exhibition catalogs & brochures, 3-4 per year
Activities: Classes for adults & children; docent training; lects open to pub, 3-5 vis lectrs per yr; concerts; gallery talks; tours; book traveling exhibs 1-2 per yr; originate traveling exhibs to qualified mus; mus shop sells books, magazines, original art reproductions, jewelry & objects

L **University Library,** 1250 Bellflower Blvd, Long Beach, CA 90840-1901. Internet Home Page Address: www.csulb.edu/library; *Dean Lib & Acad Tech* Roman V Kochan; *Arts Libr* Leslie Anderson
Open Mon-Thurs 7:45AM-11PM, Fri 7:45AM-5PM, Sat 10AM-5PM, Sun 12:30PM-11PM; Estab 1949 for delivery of information & related services to the campus & surrounding communities; Circ 340,248; For lending & reference
Income: Financed by state appropriation
Purchases: $17,722
Library Holdings: Book Volumes 1,022,263; Cards; Cassettes; Exhibition Catalogs; Fiche; Filmstrips; Motion Pictures; Other Holdings Art vols 37,000; Pamphlets; Periodical Subscriptions 116; Prints; Records; Reels; Reproductions; Slides; Video Tapes
Special Subjects: Art History, Photography, Prints, Art Education, Asian Art, Video
Collections: Modern Photography Collection (Edward Weston, Ansel Adams): original photographic prints; Kathe Kollwitz Collection: original prints

M **LONG BEACH MUSEUM OF ART FOUNDATION,** 2300 E Ocean Blvd, Long Beach, CA 90803-2442. Tel 562-439-2119; Fax 562-439-3587; Elec Mail haln@lbma.com; Internet Home Page Address: www.lbma.org; *Exec Dir* Ron Nelson; *Dir Opers* Megan Ellisor; *Assoc Dir Devel* Megan Goulding; *Dir Educ & Visitor Svcs* Elissa Ennis; *Gallery Mgr* Bianca Velasco; *Dir Colls* Sue Ann Robinson; *Exhibs Preparator* Brooks Manbeck
Open Tues - Sun 11 AM - 5 PM; cl New Year's, July 4, Thanksgiving & Christmas; Admis adults $7, seniors & students with ID $6, mems & children under 12 free, & free on Fri; Opened in 1951 as a Municipal Art Center under the city library department; in 1957 the Long Beach City Council changed the center to the Long Beach Museum of Art; managed by Foundation since 1985; Eight galleries & a screening room with changing exhibitions & selections from Permanent Collection; Average Annual Attendance: 50,000; Mem: 1600; dues circle $1000 - $5000, educ benefactor $500, patron $150, family $75, individual $50, student, senior or educator $40
Income: Financed by annual contribution of City of Long Beach & through grants from private foundations & through individual & corporate contributions
Special Subjects: Drawings, Painting-American, Prints, Sculpture, Ceramics, Crafts, Decorative Arts
Collections: Permanent Coll: 3,000+ paintings, sculpture, prints, drawings, works on paper, crafts, photography & decorative art objects, with 300 years of ceramics, early 20th century European art, California Modernism & contemporary art of California; 1000 items with emphasis on West Coast & California modern & contemporary art; sculpture garden; Milton Wichner Collection: incl Kandinsky, Jawlensky, Feininger, Moholy-Nagy; Major collection of video art
Exhibitions: 5 rotating exhibitions per yr
Publications: Announcements; exhibit catalogs; quarterly bulletin
Activities: Workshops for adults & children; docent training; volunteer progs; screening & lect series open to pub, 12 - 20 vis lectrs per yr; concerts; gallery talks; tours; video art Open Channels competition; awards; book traveling exhibs, 4 per yr; originate traveling exhibs that circulate to mus; mus shop sells books & small boutique sells jewelry & cards

L **Long Beach Museum of Art,** 2300 E Ocean Blvd, Long Beach, CA 90803. Tel 562-439-2119; Fax 562-439-3587; Elec Mail haln@lbma.com; Internet Home Page Address: www.lbma.org; *Dir* Harold Nelson
Open 11 AM - 5 PM Tues - Sun; Admis $5; Estab 1950 to enrich lives and promote understanding by bringing people together to celebrate the arts; Open for staff reference with restricted lending of books, publications & slides; Average Annual Attendance: 65,000; Mem: 200; dues $40
Library Holdings: Book Volumes 3200; Clipping Files; Exhibition Catalogs; Periodical Subscriptions 8; Video Tapes
Special Subjects: Art History, Decorative Arts, Drawings, Painting-American, Ceramics
Exhibitions: Annual Children's Cultural Festival, fall each yr
Publications: Quarterly newsletter
Activities: Classes for adults & children; docent training; artmaking workshops; lects open to pub; 1-3 vis lectrs per yr; concerts; gallery talks; tours; artmobile to other mus; 1-4 book traveling exhibs per yr; originate traveling exhibs to US & foreign mus; mus shop sells books, original art, reproductions, prints

L **LONG BEACH PUBLIC LIBRARY,** 101 Pacific Ave, Long Beach, CA 90822-1097. Tel 562-570-7500; Fax 562-570-7408; Internet Home Page Address: www.lbpl.org; *Fine Arts Librn* Ruth Stewart; *Dir Libr Servs* Eleanore Schmidt
Open Mon & Thurs 10 AM - 8 PM, Tues - Wed & Fri - Sat 10 AM - 5:30 PM, Sun Noon - 5 PM; Estab 1897
Income: Financed by municipality
Library Holdings: Audio Tapes 20,000; Book Volumes 1,093,155; CD-ROMs; Clipping Files; Compact Disks; DVDs; Pamphlets; Periodical Subscriptions 2000; Records; Video Tapes 9000
Collections: Miller Special Collections Room housing fine arts books with an emphasis on Asian Art & Marilyn Horne Archives

M **MUSEUM OF LATIN AMERICAN ART,** 628 Alamitos Ave, Long Beach, CA 90802-1513. Tel 562-437-1689; Fax 562-216-4190; Elec Mail frontdesk@molaa.org; Internet Home Page Address: www.molaa.com; *Cur* Idurre Alonso; *Pres & CEO* Stuart A Ashman; *VPres Curatorial Affairs & Chief Cur* Cecilia Fajardo-Hill; *Colls Management* Emily Calvert; *VPres Communs* Susan Golden
Open Tues - Fri, Sat & Sun 11 AM - 5 PM, Thurs 11 AM - 9 PM; Admis $9, students & seniors $6, children under 12 free; Estab 1996 to research, collect & exhibit contemporary Latin American art (since WWII); Maintains reference library; Average Annual Attendance: 50,000; Mem: 2200; dues $60 individual, $80 family
Income: Financed by endowment, mem & grants
Library Holdings: Auction Catalogs; Audio Tapes; Clipping Files; Exhibition Catalogs; Kodachrome Transparencies; Pamphlets; Periodical Subscriptions; Slides; Video Tapes
Special Subjects: Drawings, Etchings & Engravings, Ceramics, Collages, Glass, Portraits, Prints, Bronzes, Graphics, Hispanic Art, Latin American Art, Mexican Art, Sculpture, Watercolors, Woodcarvings, Woodcuts
Collections: Robert Gumbiner Foundation Collection; contemporary Latin American art-paintings & sculpture produced since 1945; Mola's Collection - Donations & Acquisitions
Publications: History of Contemporary Latin American Art
Activities: Classes for adults & children; docent training; lects open to pub; concerts; family day of events, including lect, workshops, music, film; exhibs 6 per yr; originates traveling exhibs to museums in the USA; sales shop sells books, original art, prints, lithographs, contemporary fine art, folk art & jewelry

M **PACIFIC ISLAND ETHNIC ART MUSEUM,** 695 Alamitos Ave Long Beach, CA 90802-1514.

LOS ALTOS

M **GALLERY 9,** 143 Main St, Los Altos, CA 94022-2912. Tel 415-941-7969; Internet Home Page Address: www.gallery9losaltos.com; *Treas* Charles W Halleck; *Exhibits Chmn* Carol Hake; *Staff* Jean Pell Morton; *Publicity* Louise Freund
Open Tues - Sat 11:30 AM - 5:30 PM; No admis fee; Estab 1970 to exhibit local fine art; Average Annual Attendance: 1,200; Mem: 30; dues $520; meetings first Mon each month
Exhibitions: Exhibit changes each month. Member artists featured once every two years
Activities: Sales shop sells original art

LOS ANGELES

M **AUTRY NATIONAL CENTER,** Museum of the American West, Griffith Park, 4700 Western Heritage Way, Los Angeles, CA 90027-1462. Tel 323-667-2000; Fax 323-660-5721; Elec Mail vservices@theautry.org; Internet Home Page Address: theautry.org; *Pres & CEO* John L Gray
Open Tues - Fri 10 AM - 4 PM, Sat - Sun 11 AM - 5 PM, cl Mon; Summer Hrs: Jul - Aug Thurs & 1st Thurs in Sep mus & store 10 AM - 8 PM, cl Mon; cl Jul 4, Labor Day, Thanksgiving, Christmas Day; Admis adults $10, seniors & students w/ID $6, children 3-12 $4, mems & children under 3 free, active military, vets, peace officers & park rangers free, 2nd Tues of month free; discounts available; Estab 1988, merged 2003 with Southwest Museum of the American Indian & Women of the West Museum to form Autry National Ctr; Maintains Autry Library
Special Subjects: American Indian Art, American Western Art
Collections: Women of the West
Activities: Classes for children & adults; family activities; docent training; lects open to pub & for mems only; tours; theater performances; concerts; festivals; book signings & discussions; mus shop

L **Braun Research Library,** 234 Museum Dr, Los Angeles, CA 90065-5000. Tel 323-221-2164; Fax 323-224-8223; Elec Mail rroom@theautry.org; Internet Home Page Address: theautry.org/research/braun-research-library; *Head Librn & Archivist* Anna Liza Pasas
Open by appointment; Estab 1907; For reference only; Average Annual Attendance: 175,000; Mem: Dues individual $55, dual $65, family $75, family plus grandparents $125, Turquoise $175
Library Holdings: Auction Catalogs; Audio Tapes; Book Volumes 50,000; CD-ROMs; Cards; Cassettes; Clipping Files; Compact Disks; Exhibition Catalogs; Fiche; Filmstrips; Framed Reproductions; Kodachrome Transparencies; Lantern Slides; Manuscripts; Maps; Memorabilia; Motion Pictures; Original Art Works; Original Documents; Pamphlets; Periodical Subscriptions 300; Photographs; Prints; Records; Reels; Reproductions; Slides; Video Tapes
Special Subjects: Photography, Manuscripts, Maps, Pre-Columbian Art, Historical Material, Watercolors, Latin American Art, Archaeology, Ethnology, American Western Art, American Indian Art, Anthropology, Eskimo Art, Mexican Art, Bookplates & Bindings, Religious Art, Architecture
Collections: George Wharton James's Collection; Joseph Amasa Munk Papers; Charles F Lummis Manuscript Collection; Frederick Webb Hodge Papers; Gene Autry Papers; Meihle Sepulveda Family Papers
Activities: Lects open to pub; 4 vis lectrs per yr; tours; mus shop

M **Southwest Museum of the American Indian, Mt. Washington Campus,** 234 Museum Dr, Los Angeles, CA 90065-5000. Tel 323-221-2164; Fax 323-224-8223;

Internet Home Page Address: www.theautry.org; *Ahmanson Cur of Native American History & Culture* Kim Walters; *Asst Cur* Paige Bardolph
Cl on week days for conservation until 2013, open Sat 10 AM - 4 PM; Estab 1907, opened 1914; Museum & Braun Research Library; Mem: Individual $55, dual $75, family $125, family plus $175, turquoise $250, copper (shell) 500, silver $1,250, gold $2,500
Special Subjects: Afro-American Art, Anthropology, Archaeology, Folk Art, History of Art & Archaeology, Mixed Media, Photography, Pre-Columbian Art, Painting-American, Manuscripts, Maps, Hispanic Art, Latin American Art, Ethnology, Southwestern Art, Pottery, Eskimo Art, Scrimshaw, Military Art
Collections: Native American, Spanish Colonial
L **Autry Library,** Griffith Park, Los Angeles, CA 90027; 4700 Western Heritage Way, Los Angeles, CA 90027-1462. Tel 323-667-2000x349; Elec Mail rroom@theautry.org; Internet Home Page Address: theautry.org
Open Mon - Fri 9 AM - 5 PM by appt only, cl holidays; Opened 1995
Library Holdings: Audio Tapes; Book Volumes; Other Holdings
Special Subjects: Historical Material, American Western Art
Collections: Fred Rosenstock Coll of Western Americana: 21,000+ works on paper incl books, manuscripts, diaries, visual material; Dime Novel Coll: dating from 1880's - 1960's; Saddle & Western Wear Trade Catalogs Coll: dating from 1880's - 1960's; Gene Autry Archive: coll documenting the career & business interests of the Western star, media phenomenon, & Mus founder; Western TV Script & Photographic Stills Coll: 1,200+ scripts with annotations by producers, editors, cinematographers & actors, & Stills documenting Western TV series from 1949 - 1990's; Dude Ranch Brochures: dating from 1920's - 1960's; Collections Online digital database

M **CALIFORNIA AFRICAN-AMERICAN MUSEUM,** 600 State Dr, Exposition Park Los Angeles, CA 90037-1267. Tel 213-744-7432; Fax 213-744-2050; Internet Home Page Address: www.caamuseum.org; *Exec Dir* Charmaine Jefferson; *Deputy Dir Opers & Special Progs* Woodburn T Schofield Jr; *Cur History* Tiffini Bowers; *Prog Mgr Visual Arts* Mar Hollingsworth; *Cur Educ* Sonia Brown; *Prog Mgr Educ* Elise Woodson; *Gallery Educator II* Karla Leyva; *Registrar Colls* Susan Guadamuz; *Exhib Supv* Edward Garcia; *Fiscal Officer* Debra Harris; *Facilities Use Coordr* Laura Farmer
Open Tues - Sat 10 AM - 5 PM, Sun 11 AM - 5 PM, cl Mon; No admis fee; parking fees apply; Estab 1977, opened 1981 to examine, collect, preserve & display art, history & culture of Blacks in The Americas with concentration on Blacks in California; renovated 2001 - 2003; 44,000 sq ft facility incl 3 full size exhib galleries, a theater gallery, a 14,000 sq ft Sculpture Court, exhib design & storage areas, research library, conference center/ special events rm & admin offices; Mem: Dues student $25, individual $40, family $75, friend $100, patron $250, supporting $500, benefactor $1000
Library Holdings: Book Volumes; CD-ROMs; Cassettes; Clipping Files; Compact Disks; DVDs; Exhibition Catalogs
Special Subjects: Afro-American Art, African Art
Collections: Academic & Naturalistic Landscape of the 19th c; Modern & Contemporary Art; Contemporary Art from the African Diaspora; Traditional African Art; History Collection
Exhibitions: African American Journey West: Permanent Collection
Publications: Calendar of Events, every 2 months; exhibition catalogs
Activities: Classes for children; weekends at the museum; docent training; lect open to pub; gallery talks; films; symposia
L **Research Library,** 600 State Dr, Los Angeles, CA 90037-1267. Tel 213-744-7432; Fax 213-744-2050; Internet Home Page Address: www.caamuseum.org; *Librn* Ann Shea; *Exec Dir* Charmaine Jefferson
Open during mus hrs & by appt; No admis fee; donations accepted for photocopying; For reference & research only
Library Holdings: Audio Tapes; Book Volumes 4,000; DVDs; Micro Print; Periodical Subscriptions 100; Records; Video Tapes
Special Subjects: Painting-American, Sculpture
Collections: Literature & Popular Writings by authors incl: Zora Neale Hurston, Maya Angelou, Langston Hughes; Text book of the Madame CJ Walker School of Beauty Culture; 1855 Ed of My Bondage & My Freedom by Frederick Douglas; Multi-vol Encyclopedia of African-American Culture & History; Access to 3 major daily newspapers; Older issues of selected African-American newspapers incl Chicago Defender & Pittsburgh Courier

M **CALIFORNIA SCIENCE CENTER,** (California Museum of Science and Industry) 700 Exposition Park Dr, Los Angeles, CA 90037-1210. Tel 213-744-7400; Fax 213-744-2034; Elec Mail 4info@cscmail.org; Internet Home Page Address: www.casciencectr.org; *Pres & CEO* Jeffrey N Rudolph; *Cur World Ecology* Chuck Kopczak; *Deputy Dir Educ* Ron Rohovit; *Technology Cur* David Bibas; *Deputy Dir Exhib* Diane Perlov; *Sr VPres Develop & Mktg* William Harris; *Aerospace Cur* Kenneth E Phillips; *CFO* Cynthia Pygin; *Deputy Dir Opers* Tony Budrovich; *VPres Retail Opers* Kent Jones; *Deputy Dir Admin* Cheryl Tateishi
Open daily 10 AM - 5 PM; No admis fees to permanent galleries; A dynamic destination where families, school groups, adults & children can explore the wonders of science though interactive exhibits, live demonstrations & innovative programs; Three permanent exhibit galleries - Creative World (showcases the wonders & consequences of human innovation); World of Life (probes the commonalities of the living world); Air & Space (features hands-on exhibits coupled with real air & space craft). Also, a Special Exhibits Gallery hosts 3-4 exhibits a yr; Average Annual Attendance: 1,800,000; Mem: 6,850, $65-$550 per yr
Income: Financed by state appropriation and California Science Center Foundation
Exhibitions: Various exhib
Publications: Notices of temporary exhibits, maps, pamphlets
Activities: Formal science-art educ progs for school groups & public, teacher training; lects open to pub, 3 vis lectrs per yr, competitions; scholarships offered; originates traveling exhibs; mus shop sells books, science toys & videos

M **CALIFORNIA STATE UNIVERSITY, LOS ANGELES,** Fine Arts Gallery, 5151 State University Dr, Los Angeles, CA 90032-4226. Tel 323-343-4023; Fax 323-343-4045; *Dir* Lamont Westmorland
Open Mon - Thurs Noon - 5 PM; No admis fee; Estab 1954 as a forum for advanced works of art & their makers, so that educ through exposure to works of

art can take place; Gallery has 3500 sq ft, clean white walls, 11 ft high ceilings with an entry & catalog desk; Average Annual Attendance: 30,000
Income: Financed by endowment & state appropriation
Exhibitions: Various exhib
Publications: Exhibition catalogs, three per year
Activities: Educ dept; lect open to public, 10-20 vis lectrs per year; gallery talks; exten dept
M **Luckman Gallery,** 5151 State University Dr, Los Angeles, CA 90032-8116. Tel 323-343-6604; Fax 323-346-6423; Elec Mail luckmangallery@luckmanarts.org; Internet Home Page Address: www.luckmanarts.org; *Exec Dir* Wendy Baker
Open Mon-Thurs & Sat 12PM-5PM
Collections: works by contemporary artists from around the world

M **CITY OF LOS ANGELES,** Cultural Affairs Dept, 201 N Figueroa St, Ste 1400 Los Angeles, CA 90012-2637. Tel 213-202-5500; Fax 213-202-5517; Internet Home Page Address: www.culturela.org; *Exec Dir* Olga Garay-English; *Asst Gen Mgr* Matthew S Rudnick; *Dir Mktg & Devel* Will Caperton y Montoya; *Pub Art Dir* Felicia Filer; *Cultural Grant Prog Dir* Joe Smoke; *Facilities Dir* James V Burks
Activities: Classes for adults & children; grants prog; folk arts prog

M **CRAFT AND FOLK ART MUSEUM (CAFAM),** 5814 Wilshire Blvd, Los Angeles, CA 90036-4501. Tel 323-937-4230; Fax 323-937-5576; Elec Mail info@cafam.org; Internet Home Page Address: www.cafam.org; *Exec Dir* Maryna Hrushetska; *Exhib & PR Coordr* Sonja Cendak; *Mus Shop Dir* Yuko Makuuchi; *Educ Dir* Holly Jerger; *Develop & Communs* Michelle Lee; *Admis & Mem* Rose Christie Baquir
Mus open Tues - Wed & Fri 11 AM - 5 PM; Thurs 11 AM - 7 PM; Sat - Sun Noon - 6 PM; Admis adults $5, seniors & students $3, children under 13 & 1st Wed of month & Sun no admis fee; Founded in 1973 by the late Edith Wyle; champions cultural understanding by encouraging curiosity about our diverse world. Nonprofit org; Mus exhibs contemporary craft, international folk art and art highlighting diverse cultures and pub progs for all visitors; Mem: Donor $2500; Dir Circle $1000; Patron $500; Contributor $250; Assoc & Believer $100; Family $60; Individual $45; Senior/Student $35
Special Subjects: Afro-American Art, American Indian Art, Anthropology, Decorative Arts, Drawings, Etchings & Engravings, Art Education, Collages, Glass, Metalwork, Mexican Art, Furniture, Porcelain, Pottery, Prints, Silver, Textiles, Woodcuts, Manuscripts, Sculpture, Tapestries, Graphics, Hispanic Art, Latin American Art, African Art, Ethnology, Southwestern Art, Costumes, Ceramics, Crafts, Folk Art, Primitive art, Woodcarvings, Judaica, Posters, Jewelry, Oriental Art, Asian Art, Carpets & Rugs, Coins & Medals, Dioramas, Embroidery, Islamic Art, Mosaics, Leather
Activities: School tours; internships; family art workshops; theatrical performances; craft workshops, progs & special events, classes for adults & children; lects open to pub; concerts, gallery talks & tours; books, original art, crafts, clothing, housewares & mus related items for sale

M **CULTURAL AFFAIRS DEPARTMENT,** Los Angeles Municipal Art Gallery, 4800 Hollywood Blvd, Los Angeles, CA 90027-5302. Tel 323-644-6269; Fax 323-644-6271; Elec Mail cadmag@sbcglobal.net; Internet Home Page Address: www.culturala.org/lamag/home.html; *Dir* Mark Steven Greenfield; *Cur* Scott Canty; *Mus Educator* Sara L Cannon
Open Thurs - Sun Noon - 5 PM, 1st Fri until 9 PM; No admis fee; Estab 1952 to promote, interpret & present the art of emerging, mid career & established artists of Southern CA; 10,000 sq ft exhib space; Average Annual Attendance: 15000
Income: City of Los Angeles
Library Holdings: Exhibition Catalogs; Kodachrome Transparencies; Pamphlets; Slides; Video Tapes
Publications: Annual COLA Fel Catalog
Activities: Gallery talks; COLA Award, Lorser Fietelson & Helon Lundebero Feitelson Fel; currently engaged in outreach through exhibs & events at other sites

A **CULTURAL AFFAIRS DEPARTMENT CITY OF LOS ANGELES/BARNSDALL ART CENTERS/JUNIOR ARTS CENTER,** 4814 Hollywood Blvd, Los Angeles, CA 90027-5302. Tel 213-485-4474; *Teacher Outreach Coordr* Laura Stickney; *Coordr Handicapped Svcs* Dr Mary J Martz; *Sunday Coordr* Nicolette Kominos; *International Child Art Coordr* Patty Sue Jones; *Dir* Isti Haroh Glasgow
Open Tues - Sun 10 AM - 5 PM; No admis fee; Estab 1967 to stimulate & assist in the develop of art skills & creativity; The gallery offers exhibitions of interest to children & young people & those who work with the young; Average Annual Attendance: 80,000; Mem: 400; dues vary ; annual meeting June 1
Income: Financed by city appropriation & Friends of the Junior Arts Center
Collections: Two-dimensional works on paper; 8mm film by former students
Exhibitions: 12 exhibitions a year;
Publications: Schedules of art classes, quarterly; exhibition notices
Activities: Art classes for young people in painting, dramatic progs drawing, etching, general printmaking, photography, filmmaking, photo silkscreen, ceramics, film animation; workshops for teachers; lectrs, 2-4 vis lectrs per yr; films; musical instrument making, design, video festivals for students & the general pub; gallery talks; tours; schols offered
L **Library,** 4814 Hollywood Blvd, Los Angeles, CA 90027. Tel 323-644-6275; 644-6295; Fax 323-644-6277; Elec Mail jacbac@schglobal.net; Internet Home Page Address: www.juniorartscenter.org; Internet Home Page Address: www.barnsdallartcenter.org; *Dir JAC Educ* Laura Stickney; *Dir BAC Educ* Livija Lapaite; *Office Mgr* Nancy Jung
Open Mon - Sat 10 AM - 5 PM; No admis fee; Estab as reference library; Circ Non-circulating; Open to public
Library Holdings: Book Volumes 700; Slides 15,000
Special Subjects: Art History, Crafts, Art Education
Activities: Classes for adults & children

A **EL PUEBLO DE LOS ANGELES HISTORICAL MONUMENT,** 125 Paseo de la Plaza, Ste 400 Los Angeles, CA 90012-2959. Tel 213-485-8437; Fax 213-485-0428; Elec Mail elpueblovc@lacity.org; Internet Home Page Address: elpueblo.lacity.org; *Gen Mgr* Christopher Espinosa; *Asst Gen Mgr* Lisa Sarno
Open daily 9 AM - 4 PM; No admis fee; Estab 1781 as a living memorial to the history & traditions of Los Angeles life, preserving for the public forever the

architecture & characteristics of the history & the diverse peoples associated with the City's founding & evolution.; Collection of five museums ea telling & interpreting the story of Los Angeles through time.; Average Annual Attendance: 500,000
Special Subjects: Historical Material, Photography, Asian Art, Folk Art, Ceramics, Crafts, Hispanic Art, Latin American Art, Leather, Period Rooms, Maps, Oriental Art, Mexican Art
Collections: El Pueblo Movement Collection; El Pueblo Photo Archive
Activities: Docent training; lects open to pub; gallery talks; tours; mus shop sells books; reproductions, prints, flags, shirts & postcards

A **FELLOWS OF CONTEMPORARY ART,** 970 N Broadway Ste 208, Los Angeles, CA 90012. Tel 213-808-1008; Fax 213-808-1018; Elec Mail foca@focala.org; Internet Home Page Address: www.focala.org; *Exec Dir* Tom McKenzie; *Chair* Homeira Goldstein
Estab 1975 to support contemporary California art by initiating & sponsoring exhibitions & videos at selected institutions; Mem: 150; nomination process for membership
Income: Financed by mem dues
Exhibitions: At least one major exhibition per year
Publications: Exhib catalogs
Activities: One day educ progs; guest speakers; domestic & international tours

A **FREDERICK R WEISMAN ART FOUNDATION,** 275 N Carolwood Dr, Los Angeles, CA 90077-3535. Tel 310-277-5321; Fax 310-277-5075; Elec Mail tours@weismanfoundation.org; Internet Home Page Address: www.weismanfoundation.org; *Dir* Billie Milam Weisman; *Registrar* Mary Ellen Powell; *Tour Coordr* JoAnn Grossman; *Tour Coordr* Lois Forman
Open Mon - Fri 9:30 AM - 4:30 PM by appointment only; No admis fee; Estab 1982 as a nonprofit foundation focusing on exhibition & tours; Circ Catalogue Available; House setting; 2 floors, 1 gallery; Average Annual Attendance: 10,000
Income: Financed by endowment
Library Holdings: Auction Catalogs; Exhibition Catalogs; Kodachrome Transparencies; Original Art Works; Original Documents; Periodical Subscriptions; Photographs; Sculpture; Slides
Special Subjects: Architecture, Etchings & Engravings, Painting-German, Photography, Prints, Sculpture, Painting-American, Ceramics, Painting-European, Painting-Dutch, Painting-Japanese, Painting-Russian
Collections: Contemporary Art: Installation Work; Mixed Media; Painting; Sculpture; Works on Paper
Exhibitions: Frederick R. Weisman permanent collection
Publications: Workshop publication, semi-annual
Activities: Docent training; art purchase; tours; lend original art objects to Major US & European Museums; traveling shows available on request; organize traveling exhibs by request; mus shop sells books

A **GALLERY 825/LOS ANGELES ART ASSOCIATION,** Gallery 825, 825 N LaCienega Blvd, Los Angeles, CA 90069-4707. Tel 310-652-8272; Fax 310-652-9251; Elec Mail gallery825@laaa.org; Internet Home Page Address: www.laaa.org; *Exec Dir* Peter Mays; *Artistic Dir, Contact* Sinead Finnerty
Open Tues - Sat 10 AM - 5 PM; No admis fee; Estab 1925; Gallery 825/LAAA is a 501(c)(3) nonprofit arts organization supporting southern California artists with an emphasis on emerging talent; Average Annual Attendance: 5,000; Mem: 230; dues $150; annual meeting in Apr; must reside in southern California to exhibit
Exhibitions: Graphics, Painting & Sculpture by Southern California Artists, monthly
Publications: Announcements of exhibitions & lectures, monthly; newsletter, quarterly
Activities: Classes for adults; lects open to pub; gallery talks

L **GETTY CENTER,** Trust Museum, 1200 Getty Center Dr, Los Angeles, CA 90049-1657. Tel 310-440-7300; Fax 310-440-7751; Internet Home Page Address: www.getty.edu; Telex 82-0268; *Cur of European Sculpture & Works of Art* Peter Fusco; *Cur Paintings & Drawings* Scott Schaefer; *Cur Antiquities* Marion True; *Cur Photographs* Weston Naef; *Cur Decorative Arts* Gillian Wilson; *Cur Manuscripts* Thom Kren; *Assoc Dir* Deborah Gribbon
Open by appointment only; No admis fee, parking reservations required, call 310-440-7300; Estab 1983 for the purpose of advancing research in art history & related disciplines; The mus building is a re-creation of an ancient Roman villa & consists of 47 galleries; Average Annual Attendance: 400,000
Income: Financed by Foundation
Library Holdings: Book Volumes 800,000; Exhibition Catalogs; Fiche; Pamphlets; Periodical Subscriptions 1500; Reels
Collections: Art historical archives; photo archives
Publications: Calendar, monthly; Museum Journal, annually
Activities: Docent training; slide show for children; classroom materials; research scholar prog by invitation only, 20 vis scholars per yr; original objects of art lent to other mus for special exhibs; mus shop sells books, reproductions, slides & mus publs

M **The J Paul Getty Museum,** 1200 Getty Center Dr, Suite 1000 Los Angeles, CA 90049-1687. Tel 310-440-7300; Fax 310-440-7751; Elec Mail gettymuseum@getty.edu; Internet Home Page Address: www.getty.edu; *Acting Dir* David Bomford; *Interim Assoc Dir Colls* Thomas Kren; *Assoc Dir Admin* Thomas Rhoads; *Asst Dir Pub Affairs* John Giurini; *Assoc Dir Exhibs & Pub Progs* Quincy Haughton; *Asst Dir Educ* Toby Tannenbaum; *Sr Cur Paintings* Scott Schaefer; *Sr Cur Antiquities* Karol Wight; *Sr Cur Drawings* Lee Hendrix; *Acting Sr Cur Manuscripts* Elizabeth Morrison; *Sr Cur Photos* Judith Keller; *Sr Cur Sculpture & Decorative Arts* Antonia Bostrom
Open Tues - Fri & Sun 10 AM - 5:30 PM, Sat 10 AM - 9 PM, cl Mon, New Year's Day, July 4th, Thanksgiving, Christmas Day; No admis fee; parking $15 per car, free after 5 PM, no parking reservations required, call 310-440-7300; Estab 1974; international cultural & philanthropic organization serving both general audiences & specialized professionals. Seeks to further knowledge of visual arts & nurture critical seeing by collecting, preserving, exhibiting & interpreting works of art; The museum is designed around an open central courtyard surrounded by 5 2-story pavilions; Average Annual Attendance: 1,600,000
Income: Financed by J Paul Getty Trust
Library Holdings: Auction Catalogs; Book Volumes 500,000; Exhibition Catalogs; Fiche; Original Art Works; Pamphlets; Periodical Subscriptions 1500; Photographs; Reels; Slides
Collections: Greek & Roman antiquities; French decorative arts; Western European paintings, drawings, sculpture; illuminated manuscripts; decorative arts; 19th & 20th century photographs, European & American
Publications: Calendar, quarterly; Museum Journal, annually; Trust Report, annual
Activities: Classes for adults & children; docent/volunteer training; school progs; professional develop prog; community collaboration workshops; dramatic progs; lects open to pub; seminars; concerts; gallery talks; performances; architecture & garden tours; orientation film; storytelling; artist demonstrations; gallery games; schols & fels offered; mus shop sells books, reproductions, prints, slides, postcards, gift cards, calendars, mugs, clothing, educational toys, stationery

M **The J Paul Getty Museum - Getty Villa,** Malibu, CA; 1200 Getty Center Dr Ste 1000, Los Angeles, CA 90049-1687. Tel 310-440-7300; Elec Mail visitorservices@getty.edu; Internet Home Page Address: www.getty.edu; *Acting Dir* David Bomford
Open Thurs - Mon 10 AM - 5 PM, cl Tues & select Wed; No admis fee, advance timed ticket required per adult, gen admis ticket allows 1 adult & 3 children ages 15 & under in 1 car; parking $15 per car or motorcycle, free after 5 PM; Estab 2006 as second location for J Paul Getty Mus; museum & cultural center dedicated to study the arts & cultures of ancient Greece, Rome & Etruria; Opened following completion of renovation project; Average Annual Attendance: 1,600,000
Income: Financed by J Paul Getty Trust
Collections: Houses 44,000 works of art from J Paul Getty Museum's coll on Greek, Roman & Etruscan antiquities; over 1,200 items on view

C **GOLDEN STATE MUTUAL LIFE INSURANCE COMPANY,** Afro-American Art Collection, 1999 W Adams Blvd, Los Angeles, CA 90018-3595; PO Box 26894, San Francisco, CA 94126-6894. Tel 323-731-1131 exten 237; Fax 323-733-0320; Elec Mail info@gsmlife.com; Internet Home Page Address: www.gsmlife.com; *Mktg & Pub Rels Mgr* Becky Ganther
Open to pub by appointment through pub relations staff asst; Estab 1965 to provide a show place for Afro-American Art; to assist in the develop of ethnic pride among the youth of our community; Collection displayed throughout building; Average Annual Attendance: 400
Income: Financed by the Company
Collections: Drawings, lithographs, paintings and sculpture
Publications: Afro-American Art Collection Brochure; Historical Murals Brochure
Activities: Tours by appointment

M **HEBREW UNION COLLEGE,** Skirball Cultural Center, 2701 N Sepulveda Blvd, Los Angeles, CA 90049-6833. Tel 310-440-4500; Fax 310-440-4728; Internet Home Page Address: www.skirball.org; *Sr Cur* Grace Cohen Grossman; *Assoc Cur* Tal Gozani; *Media Resources Coordr* Susanne Kester; *Dir Emerita* Nancy Berman; *Dir Music & Educ* Sheri Bernstein; *Prog Dir* Jordan Peimer; *Learning for Life* Adele Lauder Burke; *Chief of Staff* Kathryn Girard; *Assoc Cur* Evin Clancey
Open Tues-Fri noon-5PM, Sat-Sun 10AM-5PM; Admis general $8, students & seniors $6, children under 12 free; Estab 1972 to interpret American Jewish experience & nurture American Jewish identity & encourage cultural pluralism; 4000 years of Jewish historical experience and American democratic values; Average Annual Attendance: 250,000; Mem: 6500; dues $45-$1200
Income: Financed by mem admis, private & pub grants, programs & fees
Library Holdings: Book Volumes
Special Subjects: Prints, Sculpture, Architecture, Drawings, Graphics, Archaeology, Ethnology, Costumes, Crafts, Folk Art, Etchings & Engravings, Landscapes, Decorative Arts, Judaica, Manuscripts, Collages, Dolls, Furniture, Glass, Jewelry, Oriental Art, Metalwork, Historical Material, Juvenile Art, Coins & Medals, Embroidery, Laces, Medieval Art
Collections: American Jewish Ethnographic Collection: 5000+ items; 2000 archaeological objects from the Near East, primarily Israeli; Biblical Archaeology; 6000 ceremonial objects, primarily Western European, but some exotic Oriental & Indian pieces as well; Chinese Torah & India Torah cases; Judaica collection; 4000 prints & drawings from Western Europe, spanning 4-5 centuries
Exhibitions: Vision & Values; Jewish Life from Antiquity to America; Changing exhibitions: Noah's Ark Galleries
Publications: Exhibition brochures & catalogs
Activities: Classes for adults & children; dramatic progs; docent training; film series; lects open to pub, 5 vis lectrs per yr; concerts; gallery talks; tours; book traveling exhibs 5-8 per yr; originate traveling exhibs; mus shop sells books, original art, reproductions, prints, jewelry & children's items

M **JAPANESE AMERICAN CULTURAL & COMMUNITY CENTER,** George J Doizaki Gallery, 244 S San Pedro St, Ste 505, Los Angeles, CA 90012-3895. Tel 213-628-2725; Fax 213-617-8576; Elec Mail info@jaccc.org; Internet Home Page Address: www.jaccc.org; *Dir Gallery* Robert Hori; *Exec Dir* Chris Alhara
Open Mon - Fri Noon - 5 PM, Sat - Sun 11 AM - 4 PM; Admis $3; Estab 1980; 6,000 sq ft; Average Annual Attendance: 30,000; Mem: 1500; dues $35 and up
Income: Financed through mem, grants & donations
Exhibitions: Exhibitions rotate every six weeks

M **JAPANESE AMERICAN NATIONAL MUSEUM,** 369 E 1st St, Los Angeles, CA 90012-3901. Tel 213-625-0414; Fax 213-625-1770; Elec Mail hnrc@janm.org; Internet Home Page Address: www.janm.org; *Dir Admin* John Katagi; *VPres External* Carol Komatsuka; *Dir Develop* Cheryl Ikemiya; *Community Affairs* Nancy Araki; *VPres* Nahan Gluck; *Dir Retail & Visitors* Maria Kwong; *Treas* Thomas Decker; *VChmn* George Takei; *Dir Support Svcs* Clement Hanami; *VPres National Ctr* Eileen Kurahashi; *Dir Cur & Exhib* Karin Higa; *Dir National Program* Cayleen Nakamura; *Prog Adv* James Hirabayashi; *Mgr Human Resources* Myrna Mariona
Open Tues, Wed & Fri - Sun 11 AM - 5 PM, Thurs Noon - 8 PM, cl Mon, Jul 4, Thanksgiving, Christmas & New Years Days; Office open Tues - Fri 9 AM - 5 PM; Admis adults $9, seniors, students w/ID & youth (6-17) $5, mems & children under 5 free, every Thurs 5 - 8 PM & every 3rd Thurs of month free; group discounts available; Estab 1992 to share the Japanese American experience;

Contains several galleries in new pavilion & 2 spaces in historic building; Average Annual Attendance: 160,000; Mem: dues $15 - $100
Collections: Collection of art work made in America's concentration camps during WWII by Japanese Americans; Henry Sugimoto
Publications: Japanese American National Museum Magazine
Activities: Classes for adults & children; dramatic progs; docent training; performances; lects open to pub; concerts; gallery talks; tours; individual paintings & original objects of art lent to other mus; book traveling exhibs 1-5 per yr; originate traveling exhibs to Smithsonian Museum, Bishop Museum, Ellis Island Museum; mus shop sells books, magazines, reproductions, clothing, videos & prints

M **KINKEAD CONTEMPORARY,** 3452 Beethoven St, Los Angeles, CA 90066-2247. Tel 310-838-7400; Fax 310-838-7474; Elec Mail john@kinkeadcontemporary.com; Internet Home Page Address: www.kinkeadcontemporary.com; *Dir* John Kinkead
Open Tues-Sat 11AM-6PM
Collections: works by contemporary artists

M **LA COUNTY MUSEUM OF ART,** 5814 Wilshire Blvd, Los Angeles, CA 90036-4501. Tel 323-937-4230; Fax 323-937-5576; *Librn* Joan Beneditti; *Exhibition Designer* Carol Fulton; *Controller* Lorraine Trippett; *Dir Project* Marcia Page; *Dir* Joan Bruin
Open Tues - Sun 11 AM - 5 PM; Admis general $4, students & seniors $2.50, children under 12 free; Estab 1973 as The Egg & The Eye Gallery
Special Subjects: Hispanic Art, Latin American Art, Mexican Art, Ethnology, Southwestern Art, Textiles, Costumes, Crafts, Folk Art, Pottery, Dolls, Furniture, Glass, Asian Art, Embroidery
Collections: Contemporary American Crafts; Contemporary Design; International Folk Art including Japanese, East Indian & Mexican works; masks of the worlds; Industrial Design; International Folk Art
Exhibitions: Annual International Festival of Masks; Intimate Appeal: The Figurative Art of Beatrice Wood; Ed Rossbach: 40 Years of Exploration & Innovation in Fiber Art
Publications: Quarterly calendar
Activities: Classes for adults & children; docent training; lects open to pub, 5 vis lectrs per yr; gallery talks; tours; community outreach programs; book traveling exhibs 1-2 per yr; originate traveling exhibs; mus shop sells books, magazines, original art, reproductions, prints, jewelry, folk art, ceramics, glass

L **Edith R Wyle Research Library of The Craft & Folk Art Museum,** 5905 Wilshire Blvd, Los Angeles, CA 90036-4597. Tel 323-857-6118; Fax 323-857-6216; Elec Mail benedetti@lacma.org; Internet Home Page Address: www.lacma.org; *Librn* Joan M Benedetti
Open by appointment only; Estab 1975 to support & supplement the documentation & information activities of the Craft & Folk Art Museum in regard to contemporary crafts, international folk art, design. Visual material collected equally with print; For reference only
Income: Financed by the museum
Library Holdings: Book Volumes 5000; Clipping Files; Exhibition Catalogs; Kodachrome Transparencies; Memorabilia; Other Holdings Posters; Pamphlets; Periodical Subscriptions 18; Photographs; Slides
Special Subjects: Folk Art, Decorative Arts, Mixed Media, Historical Material, Ceramics, Ethnology, Industrial Design, Costume Design & Constr, Glass, Aesthetics, Metalwork
Collections: Artists' files - self taught and contemporary crafts artists; 12 V F Drawers of Ephemera

M **LACE (LOS ANGELES CONTEMPORARY EXHIBITIONS),** (Los Angeles Contemporary Exhibitions) 6522 Hollywood Blvd, Los Angeles, CA 90028-6210. Tel 323-957-1777; Fax 323-957-9025; Elec Mail info@welcometolace.org; Internet Home Page Address: www.welcometolace.org; *Exec Dir* Carol Stakenas; *Assoc Dir/Cur* Robert Crouch; *Prog Coordr* Geneva Skeen
Open (gallery) Wed - Sun 12 - 6 PM, Thurs 12 - 9 PM, (office) Mon - Fri 10:30 AM - 6:30 PM; Admis $3 suggested donation; Estab 1978, interdisciplinary contemporary visual arts ctr; Circ 50,000; 1400 sq ft main gallery; 1400 sq ft new gallery; Average Annual Attendance: 30,000; Mem: 500; dues $50+
Income: Financed by private & public contributions; earned income initiatives
Library Holdings: Auction Catalogs 28; Audio Tapes 100; Book Volumes 100; CD-ROMs 50; Cards 300; Clipping Files; DVDs 100; Exhibition Catalogs 200; Framed Reproductions 2; Original Art Works 30; Original Documents 100; Pamphlets 100; Photographs 40; Prints 25; Sculpture 20; Slides; Video Tapes
Special Subjects: Drawings, Historical Material, Illustration, Art Education, Art History, Conceptual Art, Mixed Media, Architecture, Calligraphy
Collections: Contemporary Art
Publications: Exhibit catalogs
Activities: Classes for adults & children; dramatic progs; docent training; panel discussions; film screenings; performances; lects open to public & for mem only; 40 vis lectrs per year; concerts; gallery talks; tours; educational programs; workshops for various target audiences; originates traveling exhibs; mus shop sells books, magazines, original art, prints & limited edition artworks

A **LOS ANGELES CENTER FOR PHOTOGRAPHIC STUDIES,** 6518 Hollywood Blvd, Los Angeles, CA 90028-6210. Tel 213-466-6232; Fax 213-466-3203; Elec Mail info@oversight.com; Internet Home Page Address: www.oversight.com/oversightmagazine/lacps/index.html; *Co-Pres* Glen Kaino; *Co-Pres* Shelby Stone; *Dir* Tania Martinez-Lemke
Open Wed - Sat 11 AM - 6 PM, cl Mon, Tue & Sun; Estab 1974 to promote photography within the visual arts; Mem: 600; dues patron $250 - $1000, friend $100, regular $30, student & seniors $15
Income: $110,000 (financed by mem, city & state appropriation, federal funds, corporations & foundations)
Exhibitions: Members exhibition; group exhibitions
Publications: Frame/Work, 3 times per yr, Photo Calendar, bi-monthly
Activities: Workshops for adults; symposia; lect open to public, 8-12 vis lectrs per year; competitions with awards; originates traveling exhibs; sales shop sells magazines & original art

M **LOS ANGELES COUNTY MUSEUM OF ART,** 5905 Wilshire Blvd, Los Angeles, CA 90036-4598. Tel 323-857-6000; Fax 323-857-6214; Elec Mail publicinfo@lacma.org; Internet Home Page Address: www.lacma.org; *CEO* Michael Govan; *Dir* Wallis Annenberg; *Pres* Melody Kanschat; *VP Educ & Pub Progs* Jane Burrell; *VP & Gen Counsel* Fred Goldstein; *VP Devel* Terry Morello; *CFO* Ann Rowland; *Deputy Dir Cur Admin* Nancy Thomas
Open Mon - Tues & Thurs Noon - 8 PM, Fri noon - 9 PM, Sat - Sun 11 AM - 8 PM, cl Wed, New Year's Day, Thanksgiving & Christmas; Admis adults $15, senior citizens 62 & over& students 18 & over with ID $10; mus members, children 17 & under free, 2nd Tues of each month free, weekdays after 5 PM free to LA Co res; Estab 1910 as Division of History, Science & Art; estab separately in 1961, for the purpose of acquiring, researching, publishing, exhibiting & providing for the educational use of works of art from all parts of the world in all media, dating from prehistoric times to the present; Maintains reference library; Average Annual Attendance: 825,000; Mem: 80,000; dues $45-$5000
Income: $30,000,000 (financed by endowment, mem & county appropriation)
Special Subjects: Drawings, Painting-American, Prints, Sculpture, Textiles, Costumes, Religious Art, Decorative Arts, Painting-European, Asian Art, Islamic Art
Collections: American art; ancient & Islamic art; contemporary art; decorative arts; European painting & sculpture; Far Eastern art; Indian & South Asian art; textiles & costumes; modern art; prints & drawings; photography
Publications: Members Calendar, monthly; exhib catalogs, 6-8 yearly; exhib educ brochures, 6 yearly; permanent collection catalogs, 3 yearly
Activities: Classes for adults & children; dramatic progs; docent training; lects open to pub, 50 vis lectrs per yr; concerts; gallery talks; tours; films; individual paintings & original objects of art lent to other AAM-accredited mus for special exhibs; lending collection contains original art work, original prints, paintings & 130,000 slides; originate traveling exhibs; mus shop sells books, magazines, reproductions, prints, gifts, posters, postcards, calendars & jewelry

L **Allan C Balch Art Research Library,** 5905 Wilshire Blvd, Los Angeles, CA 90036-4504. Tel 323-857-6118; Fax 323-857-4790; Elec Mail library@lacma.org; Internet Home Page Address: www.lacma.org; *Head Librn* Alexis Curry; *Sr Librn* Pauline Wolstencroft; *Serials & Electronic Resources Librn* Douglas Cordell
Open Mon, Tues, Thurs & Fri 11 AM - 4 PM; No admis fee; Estab 1965 to support research needs of mus staff & outside scholars, pub by appointment; Circ Non-circulating; For reference only
Income: Financed through the museum
Library Holdings: Auction Catalogs; Audio Tapes; Book Volumes 250,000; CD-ROMs; Cassettes; Clipping Files; Exhibition Catalogs; Fiche; Manuscripts; Other Holdings Artists' Files; Auction catalogs 35,000; Pamphlets; Periodical Subscriptions 450; Slides; Video Tapes
Special Subjects: Art History, Decorative Arts, Photography, Drawings, Etchings & Engravings, Graphic Arts, Islamic Art, Painting-American, Painting-Dutch, Painting-Flemish, Painting-German, Painting-Italian, Painting-Spanish, Pre-Columbian Art, Prints, Sculpture, Painting-European, History of Art & Archaeology, Ceramics, Conceptual Art, Crafts, Latin American Art, Archaeology, Bronzes, Fashion Arts, Interior Design, Asian Art, Primitive art, Furniture, Mexican Art, Glass, Mosaics, Afro-American Art, Enamels, Gold, Handicrafts, Religious Art, Restoration & Conservation, Silver, Woodcuts, Antiquities-Assyrian, Coins & Medals, Architecture, Pottery, Textiles

L **Robert Gore Rifkind Center for German Expressionist Studies,** 5905 Wilshire Blvd, Los Angeles, CA 90036-4504. Tel 323-857-6165; Fax 323-857-4752; Elec Mail kjohns@lacma.org; Internet Home Page Address: www.lacma.org; *Cur* Timothy Benson; *Asst Registrar* Christine Vigiletti; *Librn* Karl Johns
Open by appointment; Circ Non-circulating; Reference library
Library Holdings: Book Volumes 6000; Exhibition Catalogs; Original Art Works; Prints
Special Subjects: Art History, Decorative Arts, Photography, Drawings, Etchings & Engravings, Graphic Arts, Painting-German, Posters, Prints, Sculpture, Portraits, Watercolors, Printmaking, Woodcuts
Collections: German expressionist prints, drawings, books & periodicals
Publications: Publications relating to German Expressionist studies
Activities: Schols offered; individual graphics & illustrated books; periodicals lent to qualified institutions; book traveling exhibs

L **LOS ANGELES PUBLIC LIBRARY,** Art, Music, Recreation & Rare Books, 630 W Fifth St, Los Angeles, CA 90071-2002. Tel 213-228-7225; Fax 213-228-7239; Elec Mail art@lapl.org; Internet Home Page Address: www.lapl.org; *Sr Librn* Shelia Nash; *Dept Mgr* Ani Boyadjian
Open Mon-Thurs 10 AM - 8 PM, Fri & Sat 10 AM - 5:30 PM; No admis fee; Estab 1872
Income: Financed by municipality
Library Holdings: Book Volumes 200,000; Clipping Files; DVDs; Exhibition Catalogs; Original Art Works; Other Holdings Prints including original etchings, woodcuts, lithographs & drawings; Periodical Subscriptions 800; Photographs; Prints; Video Tapes
Special Subjects: Art History, Collages, Constructions, Folk Art, Intermedia, Landscape Architecture, Decorative Arts, Mixed Media, Photography, Calligraphy, Commercial Art, Drawings, Etchings & Engravings, Graphic Arts, Graphic Design, Islamic Art, Manuscripts, Maps, Painting-American, Painting-British, Painting-Dutch, Painting-Flemish, Painting-French, Painting-German, Painting-Italian, Painting-Japanese, Painting-Russian, Painting-Spanish, Posters, Pre-Columbian Art, Prints, Sculpture, Painting-European, Historical Material, History of Art & Archaeology, Judaica, Stage Design, Watercolors, Ceramics, Conceptual Art, Crafts, Ethnology, Painting-Israeli, American Western Art, Bronzes, Printmaking, Advertising Design, Cartoons, Fashion Arts, Industrial Design, Interior Design, Lettering, Asian Art, Video, American Indian Art, Porcelain, Primitive art, Eskimo Art, Furniture, Mexican Art, Southwestern Art, Ivory, Jade, Drafting, Period Rooms, Costume Design & Constr, Glass, Mosaics, Painting-Polish, Stained Glass, Aesthetics, Afro-American Art, Metalwork, Carpets & Rugs, Dolls, Embroidery, Enamels, Gold, Goldsmithing, Handicrafts, Jewelry, Leather, Miniatures, Oriental Art, Pottery, Religious Art, Restoration & Conservation, Silver, Tapestries, Textiles, Woodcarvings, Woodcuts, Marine Painting, Landscapes, Antiquities-Assyrian, Dioramas, Coins & Medals, Reproductions, Painting-Scandinavian, Pewter, Flasks & Bottles, Scrimshaw, Laces, Painting-Australian, Painting-Canadian, Painting-New Zealand, Architecture, Portraits

Collections: scores, orchestral scores, & many special colls; Japanese & California Prints; Bullfighting; Culinary History
Exhibitions: Museum's Artists Scrapbooks, NY Public Artist's File

M **LOYOLA MARYMOUNT UNIVERSITY,** Laband Art Gallery, One LMU Dr MS8346, Los Angeles, CA 90045. Tel 310-338-2880; Fax 310-338-6024; Elec Mail cpeter@lmu.edu; Internet Home Page Address: www.cfa.lmu.edu/laband; *Dir* Carolyn Peter
Open Wed - Sun Noon - 4 PM; No admis fee; Estab 1971 to hold exhibitions; The new gallery which opened in 1984, is 40 ft by 50 ft with 20 ft ceilings, track lighting & closeable skylights; Average Annual Attendance: 10,000
Special Subjects: Hispanic Art, Latin American Art, Photography, Ethnology, Religious Art, Ceramics, Folk Art
Exhibitions: Biennial national exhibitions of the Los Angeles Printmaking Society; Annual exhibitions vary
Publications: Catalogs, 2-3 per year
Activities: Lects open to public, 4-5 vis lectrs per yr; concerts; gallery talks; films; competitions with awards; originate traveling exhibs

M **MICHAEL KOHN GALLERY,** 8071 Beverly Blvd, Los Angeles, CA 90048. Tel 323-658-8088; Fax 323-658-8068; Elec Mail info@kohngallery.com; Internet Home Page Address: www.kohngallery.com; *Dir* Samantha Glaser
Open Tues-Fri 10AM-6PM, Sat 11AM-6PM
Collections: works by artists from California, New York & Europe; paintings; sculpture

M **MOUNT SAINT MARY'S COLLEGE,** Jose Drudis-Biada Art Gallery, 12001 Chalon Rd, Art Dept Los Angeles, CA 90049-1526. Tel 310-476-2237, 954-4360 (Gallery); Fax 310-476-9296; Elec Mail JBaral@msmc.edu; *Gallery Dir* Jody Baral
Open Mon - Fri Noon - 5 PM; No admis fee; Estab to present works of art of various disciplines for the enrichment of students & community
Income: Financed by College
Collections: Collection of works by Jose Drudis-Blada
Exhibitions: Gene Mako Collection; Sedivy & Zokosky: Recent Paintings; Works on Paper; Drucker: Constructions; Geer Installation
Publications: Exhibitions catalogs, 1 per year
Activities: Lect open to public, 2-3 vis lectrs per year; scholarships

M **MUSEUM OF AFRICAN AMERICAN ART,** 4005 S Crenshaw Blvd, 3rd Fl Macys Los Angeles, CA 90008-2534. Tel 323-294-7071; Fax 323-294-7084; Elec Mail info@maaala.org; Internet Home Page Address: www.maaala.org; *Founder* Dr Samella Lewis; *Pres* Berlinda Fontenot-Jamerson; *VPres* Alfonzo Dave Jr.; *Treas* Daphne Porter
Open year round Thurs - Sun noon - 5PM; No admis fee donations welcome; Estab 1975 as a national resource dedicated to the presentation of the rich cultural heritage of people of African descent; educates the broadest possible audience; serves as a vehicle through which it promotes & fosters scholarship in art history with a particular interest in the contemporary & historical contributions of African American artists; Mem: Dues $40
Special Subjects: African Art, Afro-American Art
Collections: Arts of the African & African-descendant people; Soapstone Sculpture of Shona; People of Southeast Africa; Makonde Sculpture of East Africa; Traditional Sculpture of West Africa; Sculpture, Paintings, Ceramics of the Caribbean & the South American Peoples; Contemporary North American Artists; Palmer Hayden Coll
Activities: Dramatic progs; poetry readings; lects for mem only; gallery talks; mus shop sells books, original art, reproductions & prints

M **THE MUSEUM OF CONTEMPORARY ART (MOCA),** Moca Grand Avenue, 250 S Grand Ave, Los Angeles, CA 90012-3007. Tel 213-626-6222 (General); 621-1741 (Vis Svcs); Fax 213-620-8674; Internet Home Page Address: www.moca.org; *Dir* Jeffrey Deitch; *Dir Develop* Sarah Sullivan; *Co-Chair* David G Johnson; *Co-Chair* Maria Arena Bell; *Exec VPres & COO* David M Galligan
Open Mon 11AM-5PM, Thurs 11AM-8PM, Fri 11AM-5PM, Sat & Sun 11AM-6PM; Admis general $10, seniors & students $5, children under 12, members & Thurs 5 - 8 PM free; Estab 1979, emphasizing the arts since mid century, encompassing traditional & non-traditional media; Moca Grand designed by Arata Isozaki opened in 1986, Geffem Contemporary at Moca designed by Frank Gehry, 1983 (one of three locations where MOCA collections are displayed); Average Annual Attendance: 300,000; Mem: 12,000; dues $30-$10,000
Income: $16,500,000 (financed by donations, admis fees, grants (private, corporate, NEA), mem & sales)
Special Subjects: Architecture, Drawings, Graphics, Hispanic Art, Latin American Art, Mexican Art, Painting-American, Photography, Prints, Sculpture, Watercolors
Collections: El Paso Collection; Barry Lowen Collection; Panza Collection; Ralph M Parsons Foundation Photography Collection; Rita & Taft Schreiber Collection; Scott D F Spiegel Collection; Marcia Simon Weisman Collection; Lannan Foundation Collection
Exhibitions: Various exhib
Publications: The Contemporary, quarterly
Activities: Classes for adults & children; docent training; dramatic progs; family workshops; engagement party; lects open to public; lects mems only; gallery talks; tours; competitions with awards; individual paintings lent to other institutions; originate traveling exhibs; mus shop sells books, magazines, original art, reproductions, posters & gifts, clothing phone accessories, jewelry

M **The Geffin Contemporary at Moca,** 152 N Central Ave, Los Angeles, CA 90012-3911. Tel 213-626-6222 (General); 621-1741 (Vis Svcs); Fax 213-620-8674; Internet Home Page Address: www.moca.org
Open Mon & Fri 11 AM - 5 PM, Thurs 11 AM - 8 PM, Sat & Sun 11 AM - 6 PM, cl Tues, Wed, New Years Day, July 4, Thanksgiving & Christmas Day; Admis general $10, seniors & students with ID $5, children under 12 & jurors with ID free, Thurs evenings free; Estab 1979, opened 1983; A former police car warehouse in Little Tokyo renovated by noted California architect Frank O Gehry, this location offers 40,000 sq ft of exhibition space (one of three locations where MOCA collections are displayed)
Activities: Tours; mus store

M **Moca Pacific Design Center,** 8687 Melrose Ave, West Hollywood, CA 90069.
Open Tues - Fri 11 AM - 5 PM, Sat & Sun 11 AM - 6 PM, cl Mon, New Years Day, July 4, Thanksgiving, Christmas Day; No admis fee; One of three locations where MOCA collections are displayed
Exhibitions: Rotating exhibs
Activities: Mus store

M **MUSEUM OF NEON ART,** 136 W 4th St, Los Angeles, CA 90013; PO Box 862307, Los Angeles, CA 90086-2307. Tel 213-489-9918; Fax 213-489-9932; Elec Mail info@neonmona.org; Internet Home Page Address: www.neonmona.org; *Dir* Mary Carter; *Exec Dir* Kim Koga
Open Wed - Sat 11 AM - 5 PM, Sun Noon - 5 PM, 2nd Thurs of month 11 AM - 8 PM, cl Fri; Admis adults $5, seniors & students $3.50; Estab 1981 to exhibit, document & preserve works of neon, electric & kinetic art; Consists of large main gallery for group or theme exhibitions & a small gallery for solo shows; Average Annual Attendance: 15,000; Mem: 300; dues $35 & up; annual meetings in Dec
Income: Financed by mem, donations, admis fees, gifts & grants
Collections: Antique electrical signs; contemporary neon art
Exhibitions: Ladies of the Night; Victoria Rivers: Neon/Fabric Construction; Electro-Kinetic Box Art.
Publications: Transformer, quarterly
Activities: Classes for adults; lects open to pub; concerts; gallery talks; tours; book traveling exhibs; originates traveling exhibs; mus shop sells books, magazines, original art, reproductions, prints, slides, electronic jewelry & posters

M **NATURAL HISTORY MUSEUM OF LOS ANGELES COUNTY,** 900 Exposition Blvd, Los Angeles, CA 90007-4057. Tel 213-763-3466, 763-3434; Fax 213-763-2999; Elec Mail glorez@nhm.org; Internet Home Page Address: www.nhm.org; *Dir* Dr James Powell; *VPres Exhibs* Michael Nauyok; *Chief Deputy Dir* Jural J Garrett; *Exec VPres* Ann Muscat; *Pres & Dir* Jane Pisano; *VPres Finance* Jane Piasecki; *VPres Mktg* Leslie Baer; *Sr VPres Advancement* Dyan Sublett; *Deputy Dir Research* John Heyning; *Deputy Dir Admin* Leonard Navarro
Open Mon-Fri 9:30AM-5PM, Sat, Sun, and holidays 10AM-5PM; Admis adults $8, seniors & students 12-17 $5.50, children 4-12 $2, members, children under 5 & first Tues of each month free; Estab 1913 to collect, exhibit & research collection in history, art & science; now focuses on American history, science & earth science; Average Annual Attendance: 1,500,000; Mem: 11,000; dues $40-$100; annual meeting in Sept
Income: Financed by county appropriation & private donations
Special Subjects: American Western Art, Anthropology, Archaeology, Bookplates & Bindings
Collections: American historical works & decorative arts; California & western paintings & prints; pre-Columbian artifacts
Exhibitions: Permanent exhibits: American History Halls; Chaparral: A Story of Life from Fire; Dinosaur Fossils; Egyptian Mummy; Gem & Mineral Hall; Habitat Halls; Lando Hall of California & Southwest History; Marine Biology Hall; Megamouth; Pre-Columbian Hall; Ralph M Parsons Children's Discovery Center; Ralph M Parsons Insect Zoo; The Ralph W Schreiber Hall of Birds
Publications: Science Bulletin; Contributions in Science; Terra, bimonthly magazine
Activities: Classes for adults & children; docent training; lects open to pub; gallery talks; tours; artmobile; individual & original objects of art lent to recognized museums, educational galleries & similar institutions; lending collection contains 30,000 color reproductions, 8653 native artifacts, 35,670 slides, 5500 small mammals, historical & scientific models; originate traveling exhibs; mus & sales shops sell books, magazines, original art, reproductions, prints, slides & ethnic art objects

L **Research Library,** 900 Exposition Blvd, Los Angeles, CA 90007. Tel 213-744-3388; Elec Mail dmcnamee@nhm.org; Internet Home Page Address: www.nhm.org; *Chief Librn* Donald W McNamee
Open Mon - Fri 10 AM - 4:30 PM; No admis fee; Open to staff & pub by appointment for reference only
Library Holdings: Book Volumes 102,000; Clipping Files; Exhibition Catalogs; Memorabilia; Pamphlets; Periodical Subscriptions 350; Photographs; Prints; Reels 472; Slides
Special Subjects: Folk Art, Decorative Arts, Film, Maps, Pre-Columbian Art, Archaeology, Ethnology, Anthropology, Southwestern Art, Bookplates & Bindings, Dolls, Textiles, Dioramas, Coins & Medals

M **OCCIDENTAL COLLEGE,** Weingart Galleries, 1600 Campus Rd, Los Angeles, CA 90041-3314. Tel 323-259-2749 (art dept), 259-2714 (galleries); Elec Mail minta@edu; Internet Home Page Address: www.oxy.edu; *Pres* Linda Lyke
Open Mon - Fri 9 AM - 4:30 PM during shows; No admis fee; Estab 1938 to acquaint students & visitors with contemporary concerns in the visual arts; Average Annual Attendance: 80,000
Activities: Lect open to public; gallery talks

M **OTIS COLLEGE OF ART & DESIGN,** Ben Maltz Gallery, 9045 Lincoln Blvd, Los Angeles, CA 90045-3505. Tel 310-665-6905; Fax 310-665-6908; Elec Mail galleryinfo@otis.edu; Internet Home Page Address: www.otis.edu/benmaltzgallery; *Dir Galleries & Exhibs* Meg Linton; *Exhib Coordr & Gallery Registrar* Jinger Heffner; *Gallery Mgr & Outreach Coordr* Kathy MacPherson
Open Tues - Sat 10 AM - 5 PM, Thurs 10 AM - 7 PM, cl Sun, Mon & major holidays, cl Jul 2 - 6 for Independence Day; No admis fee; Estab 1954 as a forum for contemporary art; Gallery is white drywall; 2700 sq ft; Average Annual Attendance: 20,000
Income: Financed by endowment
Special Subjects: Drawings, Photography, Sculpture
Collections: Contemporary art; Conceptual Art; Contemporary Painting
Publications: Catalogues for Tom Knechtel, Shahzia Sikander, Joan Tanner
Activities: Lects open to pub, 2-3 vis lectrs per yr; gallery talks; book traveling exhibs; originate traveling exhibs to other university museums & galleries

L **Millard Sheets Library,** 9045 Lincoln Blvd, Los Angeles, CA 90045-3505. Tel 310-665-6930; Elec Mail otislib@otisart.edu; *Dir* Sue Maberry
Open Mon - Fri 9 AM - 9 PM (during school session), Sat 9 AM - 5 PM; open to pub by appointment only; cl Sun; Estab 1918 as a visual arts library

Library Holdings: Audio Tapes; Book Volumes 30,000; Cassettes; Clipping Files; Exhibition Catalogs; Original Art Works; Pamphlets; Periodical Subscriptions 150; Records 150; Slides 100,000; Video Tapes 1000
Special Subjects: Decorative Arts, Mixed Media, Photography, Graphic Arts, Costume Design & Constr

A **PLAZA DE LA RAZA CULTURAL CENTER,** 3540 N Mission Rd, Los Angeles, CA 90031-3195. Tel 323-223-2475; Fax 323-223-1804; Elec Mail info@plazadelaraza.org; Internet Home Page Address: www.plazadelaraza.org; *Exec Dir* Rose Marie Cano; *Educ Dir* Maria Jiminez-Torres; *Admin Office Asst* Gabriel Jiminez; *Groundskeeper* Arturo Moran; *Vol Coordr* Kay Rosser
Open 9 AM - 6 PM, Boathouse Gallery open by appointment; No admis fee; Estab 1969 to preserve, promote & present Chicano/Mexican/Latino art & culture & promote new works; Boathouse Gallery houses Plaza's permanent collection of Latino art & also hosts temporary exhibits of the work of Chicano artists; Average Annual Attendance: 10,000; Mem: 100; dues $35 - $500
Income: $500,000 (financed by endowment, mem, city & state appropriation, grants from pvt & pub foundations)
Collections: Permanent collection of works by nationally known Latino visual artists
Exhibitions: Rotating exhibitions
Activities: Adult classes in folk arts, dance & music; children classes in music, dance, visual arts, theatre & folk arts; dramatic progs; competitions; retail store sells prints, original art, reproductions & crafts

A **SELF HELP GRAPHICS,** 1300 E 1st St, Los Angeles, CA 90033-3218. Tel 323-881- 6444; Fax 323-881-6447; Elec Mail info@selfhelpgraphics.com; Internet Home Page Address: www.selfhelpgraphics.com; *Exec Dir* Evonne Gallardo; *Master Printer* Jose Alpuche; *Prog Mgr* Joel Garcia
Open Thurs - Sat 10 AM - 4 PM, Tues - Wed by appointment; No admis fee; Estab 1972 to provide art opportunities for Chicano & all artists; One gallery on first floor, 1,700 sq ft; Average Annual Attendance: 15,000
Income: Financed through donations & grants
Exhibitions: Rotating exhibitions, 10 -12 per yr

C **SUNAMERICA, INC,** The SunAmerica Collection, One SunAmerica Center, Los Angeles, CA 90067-6022. Tel 310-772-6000; Fax 310-772-6567; *Acting Cur* Joanne Heyler
Corporate collection estab in 1981 to bring contemporary art into the corporate workplace & support the local art community
Income: Financed by corporate budget
Collections: Selection of works primarily by Southern California artists; emphasis on early to mid-career artists

M **UNIVERSITY OF CALIFORNIA, LOS ANGELES,** Fowler Museum at UCLA, PO Box 951549, Los Angeles, CA 90095-1549. Tel 310-825-4361; Fax 310-206-7007; Elec Mail fowlerws@arts.ucla.edu; Internet Home Page Address: www.fowler.ucla.edu; *Dir* Marla C Berns; *Admin Asst* Sophia Livesy; *Consulting Cur Costumes & Textiles* Patricia Anawalt; *Assoc Registrar* Sandy Choi Beacon; *Asst Conservator* Christian deBrer; *Photographer* Don Cole; *Educ Dir* Betsy Quick; *Exhib Designer* Sebastian Clough; *Publications Dir* Daniel R Brauer; *Cur Africa* Gemma Rodrigues; *Develop Dir* Susan Gordon; *HR & Admin Mgr* Roberto Salazar; *Cur Asian & Pacific Art* Roy Hamilton; *Dir Registration & Collections Mgr* Rachel Raynor; *Managing Ed* Lynne Kostman; *Dir Mem* Lori LaVelle; *Traveling Exhibs Dir* Karyn Zarubica; *Dir Mktg* Stacey Ravel Abarbanel; *Asst Dir* David Blair; *Mus Store Mgr* Stella Krieger; *Develop Coordr* Jennifer Lietch; *Mgr Pub Prog* Bonnie Poon
Open Wed & Fri - Sun Noon - 5 PM, Thurs Noon - 8 PM; No admis fee; Estab in 1963 to collect, preserve & make available for research & exhibition objects & artifacts from cultures considered to be outside the Western tradition; Circ Non-circulating; Changing exhibitions on view Wed - Sun Noon - 5 PM; Average Annual Attendance: 60,000; Mem: 607; dues Individual $50, family $75, contributing $150, supporting $275, patron $500, manus $1500, cur's circle $2500, dir's circle $5000
Income: Financed by endowment, state appropriation & private donations
Special Subjects: American Indian Art, Anthropology, Folk Art, Mexican Art, Photography, Pre-Columbian Art, Hispanic Art, African Art, Archaeology, Ethnology, Religious Art, Primitive art, Eskimo Art, Asian Art, Metalwork, Islamic Art
Collections: Archaeological & ethnographic colls; 150,000 objects primarily from non-Western cultures - Africa, Asia, the Americas, Oceania, The Near East & parts of Europe
Publications: Exhibition catalogues; filmstrips; monographs; pamphlets; papers; posters; slide sets
Activities: Classes for adults & children; publications prog; lects open to pub, 1-3 vis lectrs per yr; concerts; gallery talks; tours; art workshops; symposiums; awards; book traveling exhibs; originate traveling exhibs; mus shop sells books, jewelry, magazines, textiles

M **Grunwald Center for the Graphic Arts at Hammer Museum,** 10899 Wilshire Blvd, Los Angeles, CA 90024-4343. Tel 310-443-7076; Fax 310-443-7099; Elec Mail lcozzi@hammer.ucla.edu; Internet Home Page Address: www.hammer.ucla.edu; *Dir* Cynthia Burlingham; *Cur Assoc* Leslie Cozzi; *Cur* Allegra Pesenti; *Assoct Registrar* Susan Chin
Open by appointment only; No admis fee; Estab 1956; Gallery serves the university & pub, program is integrated with the University curricula; Mem: 120
Special Subjects: Graphics
Collections: Grunwald Center for the Graphic Arts: 45,000 prints, drawings, photographs & illustrated books from the 13th through 20th Centuries, including old master prints & drawings, Frank Lloyd Wright Collection of Japanese Prints, Tamarind Lithography Archive; The Rudolf L Baumfeld Collection of Landscape Drawings & Prints; Hammer Honore's Daumier Collection
Exhibitions: Three exhibitions annually
Publications: Exhibition catalogues; French Caricature; French Renaissance in Prints from the Bibliotheque nationale de France; The Rudolf L Baumfeld Collection of Landscape Drawings & Prints; Visionary States: Surrealist Prints from the Gilbert Kaplan Collection; The World From Here: Treasures of the Great Libraries of Los Angeles
Activities: Lects open to pub; gallery talks; tours daily; book traveling exhibs; originate traveling exhibs; mus shop sells books, magazines, original art, reproductions & various gift items

M **UCLA at the Armand Hammer Museum of Art & Cultural Center,** 10899 Wilshire Blvd, Los Angeles, CA 90024. Tel 310-443-7000; Fax 310-443-7099; Internet Home Page Address: www.hammer.ucla.edu; *Dir Educ & Community Develop* Linda Duke; *Registrar* Susan Melton Lockhart; *Dir* Ann Philbin
Open Tues, Wed, Fri & Sat 11 AM - 7 PM, Thurs 11 AM - 9 PM, Sun 11 AM - 5 PM, cl Mon, Thanksgiving, Christmas & July 4; Admis adults $4.50, seniors (65 & over), non-UCLA students, UCLA faculty & staff $3, UCLA students $1, mus members, children 17 & under & Thurs free; Estab 1990; Gallery serves the university & pub; program is integrated with the University curricula; Average Annual Attendance: 180,000; Mem: 3000; dues fellow $1000, patron $500, sustaining $250, participating $100, active $45, UCLA faculty, staff & senior citizens $25, students $20
Special Subjects: Painting-American, Sculpture, Painting-European, Painting-British, Painting-French
Collections: 300 paintings, including the Willitts J Hole Collection of the Italian, Spanish, Dutch, Flemish & English schools from the 15th-19th century; Franklin D Murphy Sculpture Garden: 70 sculptures from the 19th-20th centuries, including Arp, Calder, Lachaise, Lipchitz, Moore, Noguchi, Rodin & Smith; The Armand Hammer Collection includes approx 100 paintings, primarily 19th-century French artists; the Armand Hammer Daumier & Contemporaries Collection includes over 7000 works by 19th-century French artist Honore Daumier & his contemporaries
Exhibitions: 12 exhibs annually; operates in close conjunction with the UCLA Grunwald Center for the Graphic Arts
Publications: Exhibition catalogues; The Macchiaioli, California Assemblage; Silk Route & the Diamond Path; Chicano Art
Activities: Gallery talks; tours daily; book traveling exhibs; originate traveling exhibs; mus shop sells books & prints

L **Visual Resource Collection,** Department of Art History, 200 Dodd Hall Los Angeles, CA 90095-1417. Tel 310-825-3725; Fax 310-206-1903; Elec Mail ziegler@humnet.ucla.edu; *Dir* David Ziegler; *Asst Cur* Susan Rosenfeld
Library Holdings: Filmstrips; Lantern Slides 30,000; Slides 300,000
Special Subjects: Folk Art, Decorative Arts, Film, Etchings & Engravings, Graphic Arts, Archaeology, Ethnology, American Western Art, Asian Art, American Indian Art, Furniture, Costume Design & Constr, Afro-American Art, Antiquities-Assyrian, Architecture

L **Arts Library,** 1400 Public Affairs Bldg, Box 951392 Los Angeles, CA 90095-1392. Tel 310-206-5425; Fax 310-825-1303; Internet Home Page Address: www.library.ucla.edu/libraries/arts; *Interim Head* Kevin Mulroy; *Librn for Art* Robert Gore; *Librn for Film, TV & Theater* Diana King; *Architecture/Design Librn* Janine Henri; *Access Svcs Supvr* William Huggins; *Access Servs Asst* Dan Palodichule
Open Mon - Thurs 8 AM - 8 PM, Fri 8 AM - 5 PM, Sat 9 AM - 5 PM, Sun 1 - 5 PM, hours vary during intersession, summer & holidays; No admis fee; Founded 1952; Circ 33,194; Average Annual Attendance: 43,742; circ libraries 29,756
Library Holdings: Book Volumes 284,000; CD-ROMs 315; Cassettes 290; Compact Disks 36; DVDs 90; Exhibition Catalogs; Fiche 71,800; Other Holdings Ephemera files; Pamphlets 6,320; Periodical Subscriptions 2,000; Photographs; Reels 2,390; Video Tapes 24
Special Subjects: Art History, Collages, Folk Art, Intermedia, Landscape Architecture, Film, Illustration, Mixed Media, Photography, Commercial Art, Drawings, Etchings & Engravings, Graphic Arts, Graphic Design, Islamic Art, Manuscripts, Painting-American, Painting-British, Painting-Dutch, Painting-Flemish, Painting-French, Painting-German, Painting-Italian, Painting-Japanese, Painting-Russian, Painting-Spanish, Posters, Pre-Columbian Art, Prints, Sculpture, Painting-European, History of Art & Archaeology, Portraits, Watercolors, Ceramics, Crafts, Latin American Art, Theatre Arts, Painting-Israeli, American Western Art, Bronzes, Printmaking, Cartoons, Fashion Arts, Interior Design, Lettering, Asian Art, Video, American Indian Art, Porcelain, Primitive art, Eskimo Art, Furniture, Mexican Art, Ivory, Jade, Drafting, Costume Design & Constr, Glass, Painting-Polish, Stained Glass, Metalwork, Antiquities-Oriental, Antiquities-Persian, Carpets & Rugs, Gold, Goldsmithing, Jewelry, Miniatures, Oriental Art, Pottery, Religious Art, Restoration & Conservation, Silver, Silversmithing, Tapestries, Woodcuts, Marine Painting, Landscapes, Antiquities-Assyrian, Antiquities-Byzantine, Antiquities-Egyptian, Antiquities-Etruscan, Antiquities-Greek, Antiquities-Roman, Reproductions, Painting-Scandinavian, Painting-Australian, Painting-Canadian, Painting-New Zealand, Display, Architecture, Textiles, Woodcarvings

M **UNIVERSITY OF SOUTHERN CALIFORNIA,** USC Fisher Museum of Art, 823 Exposition Blvd, Los Angeles, CA 90089-0292. Tel 213-740-4561; Fax 213-740-7676; Elec Mail fmoa@usc.edu; Internet Home Page Address: http://fisher.usc.edu; *Assoc Dir* Kay Allen; *Dir* Dr Selma Holo; *Cur* Ariadni A Liokatis; *Coll Mgr, Registrar* Stephanie Kowalick; *Chief Preparator* Juan Rojas; *Admin Asst* Raphael Gatchalian
Open Tues - Sat Noon - 5 PM, cl summer, except for special exhibitions; No admis fee; Estab 1939 as the art mus of the university; Fisher Gallery consists of five rooms, for changing exhibitions & 1 room for permanent collection exhibition; Average Annual Attendance: 12,000
Income: Financed by endowment & university subsidy
Special Subjects: Mexican Art, American Western Art, Portraits, Painting-American, Painting-British, Painting-French, Latin American Art, Painting-European, Portraits, Painting-Dutch, Painting-Flemish, Painting-Italian
Collections: Elizabeth Holmes Fisher Collection; Armand Hammer Collection; galleries house the permanent collections of paintings of 17th-century Dutch, Flemish & Italian, 18th-century British, 19th-century French & American landscape & portraiture schools; contemporary works by artists from Calif - emphasis on international art especially Mexico & Spain
Publications: Exhibition catalogs, three annually
Activities: Classes for adults & children; dramatic progs; docent training; lects open to pub; concerts; gallery talks; tours; individual paintings & original objects of art lent; lending collection contains original prints, paintings, sculpture; 1-2 book traveling exhibs per yr; originate traveling exhibs

L **Helen Topping Architecture & Fine Arts Library,** Watt Hall 4, Los Angeles, CA 90089-0182. Tel 213-740-1956; Fax 213-749-1221, 740-8884; Elec Mail

ctvreg@usc.edu; Internet Home Page Address: www.lib.usc.edu/info/afa; *Reference Center* Ruth Wallach
Open Mon - Thurs 10 AM - 10 PM, Fri 10 AM - 7 PM, Sun 1 - 8 PM, Sat 10 AM - 5 PM, summer hours Mon - Thurs 10 AM - 4 PM; Estab 1925 to provide undergraduate & graduate level students & the teaching & research faculty materials in the areas of architecture & fine arts needed to achieve their objectives; Circ 65,000; Branch library in the central library system is supported by the university, lending library
Income: Financed by university funds
Purchases: $95,000
Library Holdings: Book Volumes 85,000; Clipping Files; Compact Disks; Exhibition Catalogs; Other Holdings Architectural drawings 1000; Artist's books 400; Pamphlets; Periodical Subscriptions 285; Reels; Slides 260,000; Video Tapes 150
Special Subjects: Art History, Landscape Architecture, Decorative Arts, Photography, Latin American Art, Antiquities-Roman, Architecture
Publications: Exhibit catalogs

L **Cinema-Television Library & Archives of Performing Arts,** University Library, Los Angeles, CA 90089-0182. Tel 213-740-8906; Fax 213-749-1221; Internet Home Page Address: www.usc.edu/cinemaarts; *Dir* Robert Rosen
Open acad semester 8:30 AM - 10 PM; No admis fee; Estab 1960
Library Holdings: Audio Tapes; Book Volumes 18,000; Cards; Cassettes; Clipping Files; Manuscripts; Memorabilia; Pamphlets; Periodical Subscriptions 225; Records; Reels; Video Tapes
Special Subjects: Film, Video
Collections: Film & television: scripts, stills, posters, production records, correspondence

C **WELLS FARGO & CO,** History Museum, 333 S Grand Ave, Los Angeles, CA 90071-1504. Tel 213-253-7166; Fax 213-680-2269; Elec Mail wfmuseum.la@wellsfargo.com; *Cur* Juan Coloto; *Asst Cur* Ileana Bonilla
Open Mon - Fri 9 AM - 5 PM; No admis fee; Museum estab to demonstrate impact of Wells Fargo on California & American West; 6500 sq ft; approx 1000 objects on display; Average Annual Attendance: 40,000
Income: Financed by private funds
Collections: Authentic 19th-century Concord Stagecoach; display of firearms; Dorsey Gold Collection of gold quartz ore; $50 gold piece; original Spanish language documents giving Los Angeles its city status in 1835; Perils of Road; Pony Express exhibit; two-pound gold nugget; Wells Fargo office
Exhibitions: Staging; mining; express; banking; South California
Publications: Various publications concerning Wells Fargo in US history
Activities: Dramatic progs; tours & off-site presentations; lects open to pub; mus shop sells books, reproductions of memorabilia & prints

MENDOCINO

A **MENDOCINO ART CENTER,** Gallery & School, 45200 Little Lake St, Mendocino, CA 95460; PO Box 765, Mendocino, CA 95460-0765. Tel 707-937-5818; Fax 707-937-1764; Elec Mail mendoart@mcn.org; Internet Home Page Address: www.mendocinoartcenter.org; *Exec Dir* Peggy Templer
Open Wed-Sun 10AM-5PM; No admis fee; Estab 1959 as a rental-sales gallery for exhibition & sales of member work; also to provide workshops on all media; Three major gallery rooms, one gallery room available for rental of one-man shows; Average Annual Attendance: 25,000; Mem: 1000; dues $50
Income: Membership, donations, tui
Library Holdings: Book Volumes
Collections: Graphics, paintings & sculpture; Dorr Bothwell
Exhibitions: Rotate 6-8 per yr
Publications: Arts & Entertainment, monthly
Activities: Classes for adults & children; docent training; lect open to public, 4-10 vis lectrs per year; concerts; competitions; scholarships offered; individual paintings & original objects of art lent to bus & public places; sales shop sells books, original art, reproductions, prints & crafts

L **Library,** 45200 Little Lake St, Mendocino, CA 95460; PO Box 765, Mendocino, CA 95460-0765. Tel 707-937-5818; Fax 707-937-1764; Internet Home Page Address: www.mendocinoartcenter.org; *Exec Dir* Peggy Templer
Open Tues - Sat 11 AM - 2 PM; No admis fee; Estab 1975 to provide members with access to art books & magazines; Circ 1350 books & 18 magazines; Lending library for members of Art Center only
Income: Financed by donations & mem
Library Holdings: Book Volumes 2500; Other Holdings Picture File; Periodical Subscriptions 4; Prints; Reproductions

MISSION HILLS

A **SAN FERNANDO VALLEY HISTORICAL SOCIETY,** 10940 Sepulveda Blvd, Mission Hills, CA 91346; PO Box 7039, Mission Hills, CA 91345-7039. Tel 818-365-7810; Internet Home Page Address: www.sfvhs.com; *VPres & Cur* Dr Richard Doyle; *Pres* Carol Phelps
Tours by appointment Mon 10 AM - 3 PM; No admis fee; Estab 1943; The Soc manages the Andres Pico Adobe (1834) for the Los Angeles City Department of Recreation & Parks, where they house their collection; Average Annual Attendance: 500; Mem: dues life $100, active, sustaining & organization $15
Income: Financed by mem & donations
Collections: Historical material; Indian artifacts; paintings; costumes; decorative arts; manuscripts
Exhibitions: Permanent & temporary exhibitions
Publications: monthly newsletter, The Valley; guide
Activities: Lect; films; guided tours

L **Mark Harrington Library,** 10940 Sepulveda Blvd, Mission Hills, CA 91346; PO Box 7039, Mission Hills, CA 91345-7039. Tel 818-365-7810; *Pres & Cur* Dr Richard Doyle; *VPres* Jim Guleranson
Open by appointment; Estab 1970
Income: Financed by mem & gifts

Library Holdings: Book Volumes 1000; Cassettes; Clipping Files; Manuscripts; Memorabilia; Original Art Works; Pamphlets; Photographs; Prints
Collections: Citrus; Communities; Historical landmarks; Olive; Pioneers; San Fernando Mission; San Fernando Valley
Exhibitions: Regular exhibitions of valley history
Publications: The Valley, monthly newsletter

MONTEREY

M **CASA AMESTI,** 516 Polk St, Monterey, CA 93940-2810. Tel 831-372-8173, 372-2808; *Pres* Pam McCollough
Open Sat & Sun 2 - 4 PM, cl 2 wks July; Admis $3, children & members free; Bequeathed to the National Trust in 1953 by Mrs Frances Adler Elkins; It is an 1833 adobe structure reflecting phases of the history & culture of the part of California owned by Mexico, after the period of Spanish missions & before develop of American influences from the Eastern seaboard. It is a prototype of what is now known as Monterey style architecture. The Italian-style gardens within the high adobe walls were designed by Mrs. Elkins, an interior designer, & her bro, Chicago architect David Adler. The furnishings, largely European, collected by Mrs. Elkins are displayed in a typical 1930s interior. The property is a National Trust historic house. The Old Capital Club, a private organization, leases, occupies & maintains the property for social & educational purposes
Special Subjects: Historical Material
Collections: Elkins Collection of largely European furnishings
Activities: Monterey History & Art Assn volunteers provide interpretive services for visitors on weekends

A **MONTEREY HISTORY & ART ASSOCIATION,** 5 Custom House Plaza, Monterey, CA 93940. Tel 831-372-2608; Fax 831-655-3054; Internet Home Page Address: www.montereyhistory.org; *Pres* Kathi Wojtkowski
No admis fee; Estab 1931; The Assoc owns the 1845 Casa Serrano Adobe, the 1865 Doud House, the 1845 Fremont Adobe, the Mayo Hayes O'Donnell Library & the newly constructed Stanton Center - Monterey's Maritime Mus & History Center. The Assoc celebrates the birthday of Monterey (June 3, 1770) with the Merienda each year on the Sat nearest that date. The Assoc commemorates the landing at Monterey by Commodore John Drake Sloat in 1846; Mem: 1800; dues individual life mem $500, sustaining couple $75, sustaining single $50, couple $25, single $15, junior $1
Income: Financed by mem, donations & fundraising activities
Collections: Costumes, manuscripts & paintings, sculpture, antique furniture, books, photographs
Exhibitions: Permanent & temporary exhibitions; Fourth Grade History & Art Contest
Publications: Noticias Del Puerto De Monterey, quarterly bulletin
Activities: Guided tours; competitions

M **Maritime Museum of Monterey,** 5 Custom House Plaza, Monterey, CA 93942. Tel 831-372-2608; Elec Mail accounting @montereyhistory.org; Internet Home Page Address: www.mntmh.org; *Exec Dir* Mark Baer
Open Tues - Sun 10 - 5 PM; Admis adults $8, seniors, military $5, children under 12 free; Estab 1971, moved 1992 into new facility along waterfront; Maritime related artifacts & artwork; features operating light from Point Sur Lighthouse; Average Annual Attendance: 12,000; Mem: 1800; dues $20 - $100; annual meeting in Sept
Special Subjects: Marine Painting
Collections: Marine Artifacts, ship models, paintings, photographs, Fresnel First Order Lens from Point Sur, California (on loan from US Coast Guard)
Exhibitions: Permanent & temporary exhibitions
Activities: Classes for children; Lects open to pub, 12 vis lectrs per yr; concerts; gallery talks; tours; competitions with awards; mus shop sells books, prints, original art, reproductions, souvenirs, toys & gift items

L **Library,** 5 Custom House Plaza, Monterey, CA 93940-2430. Tel 831-372-2608; Fax 831-655-3054; *Librn* Faye Messinger
Open Wed, Fri, Sat & Sun 1:30 - 3:30 PM; No admis fee; Estab 1971; Open for research on the premises
Library Holdings: Book Volumes 2500; Manuscripts; Memorabilia; Original Art Works; Other Holdings Local History archive; Periodical Subscriptions 2; Photographs; Prints
Publications: Brochure of Museum with map

A **MONTEREY MUSEUM OF ART,** (Monterey Museum of Art Association) Monterey Museum of Art -Pacific Street, Monterey Museum of Art - La Mirada, 720 Via Mirada, Monterey, CA 93940; Monterey Museum of Art - Pacific St, 559 Pacific St, Monterey, CA 93940-2805. Tel 831-372-5477; Fax 831-372-5680; Elec Mail info@montereyart.org; Internet Home Page Address: www.montereyart.org; *Exec Dir* E Michael Whittington; *Dir Mktg Communs* Mary DeGroat; *Dir Educ* Terry Laurents; *Cur* Karen Crews Hendon
Open Wed - Sat 11 AM - 5 PM, Sun 1 - 4 PM, cl Mon, Tues, New Year's, Christmas & Thanksgiving; Admis non-member $10, full-time student with ID $5; Estab 1959, the mission of the Monterey Mus of Art is to educate and enrich the diverse Calif community. Inspiring awareness and thought through the arts, the Mus serves as a forum and catalyst for the discussion and debate of ideas. The Mus creates progs that engage visitors and uplift the human spirit; The museum's permanent collection includes Calif art, photography, Asian art & features significant bodies of work by Armin Hansen, William Ritschel, Ansel Adams & Edward Weston.; Average Annual Attendance: 40,000; Mem: 2,000; dues $40-$1000 & above
Income: Financed by endowment, mem & fundraising functions
Library Holdings: Auction Catalogs; Book Volumes; Exhibition Catalogs; Original Documents; Periodical Subscriptions
Special Subjects: Architecture, Drawings, Etchings & Engravings, Graphics, Landscapes, Photography, Prints, Sculpture, Textiles, Watercolors, Painting-American, American Western Art, Antiquities-Oriental, Asian Art, Bronzes, Decorative Arts, Folk Art, Pewter, Woodcuts, Ceramics, Miniatures, Portraits
Collections: Armin Hansen Collection; William Ritschel Collection; Ansel Adams
Exhibitions: Theme shows

Publications: Weekly news - e-blast

Activities: Classes for adults & children; docent training; lects open to pub; vis lectrs; concerts; gallery talks; tours; in service training for teachers; outreach program; 3-4 traveling exhibs per year; originate traveling exhibs; mus shops sell books, reproductions, prints, jewelry, notecards, DVDs

L **MONTEREY PUBLIC LIBRARY,** Art & Architecture Dept, 625 Pacific St, Monterey, CA 93940-2866. Tel 831-646-3932; Fax 831-646-5618; Internet Home Page Address: www.monterey.org/library; *Dir* Kim Bul-Burton
Open Mon 1-9PM, Tues-Wed 10AM-9PM, Thurs-Fri 10AM-6PM, Sat-Sun 1-5PM; Estab 1849
Income: Financed by mem & city appropriation
Purchases: $750,000
Library Holdings: Book Volumes 100,000; Cassettes 3000; Clipping Files; Manuscripts; Original Art Works; Periodical Subscriptions 379; Photographs; Reels 4000; Reproductions

M **SAN CARLOS CATHEDRAL,** 500 Church St, Monterey, CA 93940-3209. Tel 831-373-2628; Fax 831-373-0518; Internet Home Page Address: www.sancarloscathedral.net; *Rector* Very Rev Peter Crivello
Open daily 7:30 AM - 5 PM; No admis fee; Built in 1770, now a branch of the Monterey Diocese; The art museum is housed in the 1794 Royal Presidio Chapel
Special Subjects: Sculpture, Religious Art
Collections: Spanish religious paintings and sculpture of the 18th and 19th century
Activities: Classes for adults & children; lects open to pub, 1 vis lectr per yr; self-guided tours

MONTEREY PARK

M **EAST LOS ANGELES COLLEGE,** Vincent Price Art Museum, 1301 Avenida Cesar Chevez Ave, Monterey Park, CA 91754. Tel 323-265-8841; Fax 323-260-8173; Elec Mail vincentpriceartmuseum@elac.edu; Internet Home Page Address: www.vincentprice.elac.edu; *Dir* Karen Rapp; *Preparator* Victor Parra
No admis fee; Estab 1958 as an institutional art gallery serving the East Los Angeles area
Income: Financed by the college, grants & donations
Special Subjects: American Indian Art, African Art, Renaissance Art
Collections: Includes art from Africa, Peruvian & Mexican artifacts dating from 300 B C, North American Indian Art; important works from the Renaissance to the present day; Leonard Baskin; Daumier; Delacroix; Durer; Garvarni; Hiroshige I; Rico Lebrun; Maillol; Picasso; Piranesi; Redon; Utrillo; Howard Warshaw; Anuskiewicz; Bufano; Rouault; Tamayo
Exhibitions: Annual Student Art Show; Selections from the private collection of the Vincent Price Art Collection

MORAGA

M **SAINT MARY'S COLLEGE OF CALIFORNIA,** Hearst Art Gallery, 1928 Saint Mary's Rd, Moraga, CA 94575; PO Box 5110, Moraga, CA 94575-5110. Tel 925-631-4379; Fax 925-376-5128; Elec Mail cbrewste@stmarys-ca.edu; Internet Home Page Address: gallery.stmarys-ca.edu; *Dir* Carrie Brewster; *Registrar* Julie Armistead; *Community Relations & Educ Programs* Heidi Donner
Open Wed - Sun 11 AM - 4:30 PM, cl Mon & Tues & between exhibitions; Suggested admis donation $2; Estab 1977 to exhibit a variety of the visual arts for the benefit of col community & gen pub audience; Maintains two rooms with connecting rampway (1640 sq ft) for temporary exhibitions, William Keith Room for permanent collection of 19th-century landscape painting; Average Annual Attendance: 14,000; Mem: 350; dues supporting $100 & up, family $75, individual $40; accredited by Am Assn Mus
Income: $275,000 (financed by college, donations, grants & earned income)
Purchases: 19th- & 20th-century California art
Special Subjects: Drawings, Graphics, Hispanic Art, Latin American Art, Mexican Art, Painting-American, Photography, Prints, Sculpture, African Art, Ethnology, Pre-Columbian Art, Religious Art, Etchings & Engravings, Landscapes, Historical Material, Coins & Medals, Renaissance Art, Medieval Art
Collections: 150 paintings by William Keith (1838-1911) & other 19th, 20th & 21st Century California art; African Oceanic & Latin American ethnographic objects; thematic print coll; Ethnographic Objects; Renaissance Sculpture-German Gothic Wood; Religious art, wine related art, ancient ceramics and coins
Publications: Exhibition catalogues, 2 - 3 per yr
Activities: Educ dept; lects open to pub, 4 vis lectrs per yr; gallery talks; tours; individual paintings & original objects of art lent to mus; book traveling exhibs 2 per yr; originate traveling exhibs of William Keith Collection to mus; mus shop sells books, prints & jewelry

NEWHALL

M **LOS ANGELES COUNTY MUSEUM OF NATURAL HISTORY,** William S Hart Museum, 24151 San Fernando Rd, William S Hart Park Newhall, CA 91321-2908. Tel 661-254-4584; Fax 661-254-6499; Internet Home Page Address: www.hartmuseum.org; *Adminr* Janis Ashley; *Coordr Educ* Kyle Harris
Open winter Wed - Fri 10 AM - 1 PM, Sat - Sun 11 AM - 4 PM; summer mid-June to mid-Sept Wed - Sun 11 AM - 4 PM; No admis fee; Estab through the bequest of William S Hart (1946) & opened 1958 for use as a public park & museum; The retirement home of William S Hart is maintained as it was during his lifetime, his extensive collection of Western art is on display throughout the house; Average Annual Attendance: 250,000; Mem: 250; dues $35; meetings second Wed of every month
Income: Financed by county appropriation & private donations
Special Subjects: Painting-American, Watercolors, Bronzes, Textiles, Woodcarvings, Decorative Arts, Furniture, Glass, Silver, Carpets & Rugs, Historical Material, Period Rooms

Collections: Frederic Remington Collection of Watercolor & Oil paintings; Charles M Russell Collection of Oil & Watercolor Paintings, Gouache, Pen & Ink; decorative arts; Navajo rugs; Charles Cristadoro Sculptures; Joe DeYong Paintings; Clarence Ellsworth Paintings; James M Flagg Paintings; Gene Hoback woodcarvings; Robert L Lambdin Paintings; Charles Schreyvogel Paintings
Activities: Classes for adults; docent training; school outreach prog; mus shop sells books, videotapes, souvenirs

NEWPORT BEACH

NEWPORT HARBOR ART MUSEUM, 850 San Clemente Dr, Newport Beach, CA 92660-6301. Tel 714-759-1122; Fax 714-759-5623; *Dir* Michael Botwinick
Open Tues - Sun 10 AM - 5 PM
Collections: Post-World War II California, American & European art

M **ORANGE COUNTY MUSEUM OF ART,** 850 San Clemente Dr, Newport Beach, CA 92660-6399. Tel 949-759-1122; Fax 949-759-5623; Elec Mail info@ocma.net; Internet Home Page Address: www.ocma.net; *Cur* Sarah Bancroft; *Dir Develop* Patrizia Falzon; *Opers Dir* Albert Lopez, Jr.; *Dir* Dennis Szakacs
Open Wed-Sun 11AM-5PM, Thurs until 8PM, cl Mon, Tues, July 4, Thanksgiving, Christmas & New Years Days; Admis adults $12, students w/ID & seniors $10, mems & children under 12 free, 2nd Sun of month free; Incorporated 1918 as Laguna Beach Art Assn, estab 1962 as a mus of the Art of our Time serving Orange County & Southern California, name changed in 1996; Building completed in 1977 contains four galleries of various sizes; 5000; 1600; 1200; 500 sq ft plus lobby & sculpture garden area; Average Annual Attendance: 100,000; Mem: 5500; dues supporting member $500, donor $100, general mem $45, student $25
Income: $2,500,000 (financed by special events, mem, government grants, private sector, sales from restaurant & bookstore)
Purchases: $100,000 year for works of art
Special Subjects: Drawings, Painting-American, Photography, Ceramics, Glass
Collections: Collections of Historical & contemporary American art; California artists from 1850 to present; 2,500 objects in coll, concentrating on California art from the early 20th c to present
Publications: Bimonthly calendar; exhibition catalogs; posters
Activities: Docent training; in-service training sessions for teachers, docent tours for school & adult groups; lects series, special guest lectrs & meet-the-artist programs; gallery talks; creative art workshops; concerts & performances; film & video programs; individual paintings & original objects of art lent to qualified art mus; lending collection contains original prints; paintings & sculptures; originates traveling exhibs; mus shop sells books, magazines, original art

NORTHRIDGE

M **CALIFORNIA STATE UNIVERSITY, NORTHRIDGE,** Art Galleries, 18111 Nordhoff St, Northridge, CA 91330-8299. Tel 818-677-2156; Fax 818-677-5910; Internet Home Page Address: www.csun.edu/artgalleries; *Dir* Jim Sweeters; *Exhib Coordr* Michelle Giacopuzzi; *Art Coll Registrar* Lucy Hernandez
Open Mon-Sat Noon - 4 PM, Thurs Noon-8 PM; No admis fee, donations accepted; Estab 1971 to provide a source of international & contemporary art for the university & the community at large; Exhibitions in Main Gallery have average duration of five weeks. West Gallery for weekly MA candidate solo exhibitions; Average Annual Attendance: 35,000; Mem: 300; Arts Council for CSUN; dues $35 annually, meet weekly
Income: $40,000 (financed by city & state appropriation, community support organizations)
Special Subjects: Afro-American Art, Illustration, Ceramics, Drawings, Graphics, Hispanic Art, Latin American Art, Mexican Art, Painting-American, Photography, Prints, Sculpture, American Indian Art, American Western Art, African Art, Pre-Columbian Art, Southwestern Art, Textiles, Folk Art, Woodcuts, Etchings & Engravings, Collages, Painting-Japanese, Oriental Art, Asian Art, Maps, Painting-Spanish, Cartoons, Painting-Australian, Painting-Scandinavian
Collections: University Foundation Art Collection
Publications: Exhibition catalogs, 1 per yr
Activities: Docent training; 2-3 vis performances per year; workshops for adults; lects open to pub, 10-20 vis lectrs per yr; concerts; gallery talks; tours; competitions; student exhib cash awards $2,000 total; mus shop sells books, magazines, original art, prints, reproductions, slides, folk art objects, gifts, ceramics & jewelry

OAKLAND

L **CALIFORNIA COLLEGE OF THE ARTS,** Libraries, 5212 Broadway, Oakland, CA 94618-1426. Tel 510-594-3658; Elec Mail refdesk@cca.edu; Internet Home Page Address: library.cca.edu; Internet Home Page Address: www.libraries.cca.edu; www.cca.edu; *Dir Libraries* Janice Woo; *Librn* Cody Hennesy; *Assoc Dir Librn* Michael Lordi; *Librn* Teri Dowling; *Digital Archivist* Annemarie Haar
Estab 1907; educates students to shape culture through the practice and critical study of the arts
Library Holdings: Book Volumes 57,000; DVDs 2,100; Original Art Works 650; Original Documents; Periodical Subscriptions 250; Photographs; Video Tapes 1,500
Special Subjects: Art History, Film, Illustration, Photography, Drawings, Graphic Design, Ceramics, Industrial Design, Interior Design, Furniture, Glass, Aesthetics, Metalwork, Jewelry, Architecture
Collections: Joseph Sinel Collection of pioneering work in industrial design; Capp Street Project Archives; Hamaguchi Study Print Collection; Emeryville Mudflat Ave documentation
Activities: Library Research Award; Student Book Art Award

M **CREATIVE GROWTH ART CENTER,** 355 24th St, Oakland, CA 94612-3126. Tel 510-836-2340; Fax 510-836-0769; Elec Mail info@creativegrowth.org; Internet Home Page Address: www.creativegrowth.org; *Exec Dir* Tom DiMaria; *Studio Mgr* Ron Kilgore; *Gallery Mgr* Bonnie Haight; *Accnt* Haideh Vincent
Open Mon - Fri 11 AM - 5:30 PM & by appointment; No admis fee; Estab 1974 to professionally exhibit the art of Creative Growth & art work by outsider & well-known artists; Average Annual Attendance: 5,000; Mem: $25 for 1 yr

Income: $900,000
Collections: Permanent collection includes art works in all media on traditional & contemporary subjects
Exhibitions: Individual & group shows; 9 exhibitions held per year in house gallery; 10 exhibitions in variety of locations
Publications: Creative Growth Art Center newsletter, 3-4 issues per year
Activities: Docent progs; lects open to pub, 6-8 vis lectrs per yr; competitions with awards; schols & fels offered; retail store sells prints, original art, reproductions

M **EAST BAY ASIAN LOCAL DEVELOPMENT CORP (EBALDC),** Asian Resource Gallery, 310 Eighth St, Ste 200 Oakland, CA 94607-6527. Tel 510-287-5353; Fax 510-763-4143; Elec Mail communications@ebaldc.org; Internet Home Page Address: www.ebaldc.org; *Exec Dir* Joshua Simon
Open Mon - Fri 9 AM - 5 PM; No admis fee; Estab 1983 to promote Asian art & Asian artists; One gallery
Income: $3000 (financed by donations)
Special Subjects: Photography, Historical Material
Collections: Collection of photographs, paintings, mixed media; history exhibits on Asian groups from China, Japan & Korea
Exhibitions: Every month rotating exhibits include different artists in the Bay Area

L **LANEY COLLEGE LIBRARY,** Art Section, 900 Fallon St, Oakland, CA 94607-4893. Tel 510-464-3500; Fax 510-464-3264; Internet Home Page Address: www.laney-peralta.cc.ca.us; *Head Librn* Shirley Coaston; *Head of Ref* Margaret Traylor; *Catalog & Systems Librn* Evelyn Lord; *Acquisition Librn* Mae Frances Moore
Open Mon - Thurs 8 AM - 9 PM, Fri 8 AM - 2 PM, Sat 8:30 AM - 1:30 PM, cl Sun; No admis fee; Estab 1954; Circ 78,000; Average Annual Attendance: 350,000
Library Holdings: Audio Tapes; Book Volumes 81,000; CD-ROMs; Cassettes; DVDs; Filmstrips; Kodachrome Transparencies; Lantern Slides; Motion Pictures; Other Holdings Compact discs; Laser discs; Periodical Subscriptions 300; Prints; Records; Reproductions; Slides; Video Tapes
Exhibitions: Exhibitions vary; call for details
Publications: Monthly newsletter

M **MILLS COLLEGE ART MUSEUM,** (Mills College) 5000 MacArthur Blvd, Aron Art Center Oakland, CA 94613-1301. Tel 510-430-2164; Fax 510-430-3168; Elec Mail museum@mills.edu; Internet Home Page Address: www.mills.edu; *Asst Dir* Stacie Daniels; *Dir* Stephanie Hanor; *Curatorial Coordr* Lori Chinn
Open Tues - Sun 11AM-4PM, Wed 11AM-7:30PM; No admis fee; Estab 1925 to show contemporary & traditional painting, sculpture & ceramics, exhibitions from permanent & loan collections; Gallery is Spanish colonial architecture & has 5500 sq ft main exhibition space, with skylight full length of gallery; Average Annual Attendance: 10,000
Income: Financed by college funds; grants & gifts
Purchases: Nagle, DeFeo, Bellows, Kales
Special Subjects: Drawings, Painting-American, Photography, Prints, Southwestern Art, Textiles, Pottery, Woodcarvings, Woodcuts
Collections: Asian & Guatemalan Collection (textiles); European & American Collection (prints, drawings & ceramics); Regional California Collection (paintings, drawings & prints); photographs; European & American Collection; Regional California Collection
Exhibitions: Five Internat. women artists
Publications: Annual bulletin; exhibition catalogs
Activities: Lects open to public, 8-10 vis lectrs per yr; gallery talks; tours; individual paintings & original objects of art lent; book traveling exhibs; originate traveling exhibs

M **OAKLAND MUSEUM OF CALIFORNIA,** Art Dept, 1000 Oak St at 10th St, Oakland, CA 94607-4892. Tel 510-238-2200, 238-3005; Fax 510-238-2258; Elec Mail dmpower@museumca.org; Internet Home Page Address: http://museumca.org; *Exec Dir* Lori Fogarty
Open Wed & Thurs, Sat & Sun 11 AM - 5 PM, Fri 11 AM - 9 PM, cl Mon & Tues, New Years Day, Jul 4, Thanksgiving & Christmas; Admis general $12, seniors & students w/ID $9, youth 9-17 $6, mems, children 8 & under & city employees w/ID free; The Oakland Mus of California comprises three departments: Natural Sciences (formerly the Snow Mus of Natural History, founded 1922); History (formerly the Oakland Pub Mus, founded 1910); & the Art Department (formerly the Oakland Art Mus, founded 1916); The Oakland Mus occupies a 4 sq block, three-storied site on the south shore of Lake Merritt. Designed by Kevin Roche, John Dinkeloo & Assoc, the mus is a three-tiered complex of exhibition galleries, with surrounding gardens, pools, courts & lawns, constructed so that the roof of each level becomes a garden & a terrace for the one above. The Art Department has a large hall with 20 small exhibition bays for the permanent collection & 3 galleries for one-person or group shows as well as the Oakes Gallery; Average Annual Attendance: 500,000
Income: Financed by city funds, pvt donations & Oakland Mus of California Foundation
Special Subjects: Drawings, Painting-American, Photography, Prints, Sculpture, Crafts
Collections: Paintings, sculpture, prints, illustrations, photographs, by California artists & artists dealing with California subjects, in a range that includes sketches & paintings by early artist-explorers; gold Rush genre pictures; massive Victorian landscapes; examples of the California Decorative Style, Impressionist, Post-Impressionist, Abstract Expressionist, & other contemporary works
Publications: The Museum of California, quarterly; Oakland Museum of California, bimonthly calendar of exhibs & events
Activities: Classes for adults & children; family progs; docent training; teacher resources; lects open to pub; gallery talks; tours; individual paintings & original objects of art lent to other mus & galleries for specific exhibs; originate traveling exhibs; mus shop sells books, magazines, reproductions, prints, slides & jewelry
L **Library & Archives,** 1000 Oak St, Oakland, CA 94607-4892. Tel 510-318-8400; Fax 510-318-8416; Internet Home Page Address: www.museumca.org; *Dir OMCA Lab* Barbara Henry

Open Wed- Sun 11 AM - 5 PM; Admis fee adults $12, seniors & students w/ID $9, youth 9-18 $6, children 8 & under & mems free; Estab 1969; Library maintains extensive files on California art & artists. For in-house use only, cl to the pub at this time
Income: Financed by city & state appropriation
Library Holdings: Auction Catalogs; Audio Tapes; Book Volumes; Cassettes; Clipping Files; Exhibition Catalogs; Lantern Slides; Memorabilia; Periodical Subscriptions 23; Photographs
Special Subjects: Decorative Arts, Photography, Drawings, Graphic Arts, Painting-American, Posters, Prints, Sculpture, Ceramics, Crafts, American Western Art, Printmaking, Glass, Jewelry, Landscapes, Folk Art, Portraits
Activities: Lects open to pub; gallery talks; tours; mus shop sells books

L **OAKLAND PUBLIC LIBRARY,** Art, Music, History & Literature Section, 125 14th St, Main Library Oakland, CA 94612-4397. Tel 510-238-3136; 238-3178; Elec Mail tdowns@oaklandlibrary.org; Internet Home Page Address: www.oaklandlibrary.org; *Dir Library Svcs* Carmen Martinez; *Assoc Dir* Gerry Garzon; *Acting Supvr Librn, Branches* Paul Schiesser
Open Sun 1 PM - 5PM, Mon & Tues 10AM - 5:30PM, Wed & Thurs noon - 8PM, Fri noon - 5:30 PM, Sat 10AM - 5:30PM; Library cooperates with the Oakland Mus & local groups
Purchases: $30,000
Library Holdings: Audio Tapes; Book Volumes 1,010,000; Cassettes; Compact Disks; DVDs; Framed Reproductions; Other Holdings Posters; Periodical Subscriptions 2745; Records; Reproductions; Video Tapes
Special Subjects: Decorative Arts, Photography, Graphic Arts, Maps, Historical Material, Ceramics, Metalwork, Architecture
Collections: Picture Collections; Black History Collection; Family History & Genealogy Collection; Map Collection; Music Scores & Sheet Music Collections; Oakland History Room
Publications: Museum catalogs

M **PRO ARTS,** (Pro Arts) 150 Frank H. Ogawa Plaza, Oakland, CA 94612. Tel 510-763-4361; Fax 510-763-9470; Elec Mail info@proartsgallery.org; Internet Home Page Address: www.proartsgallery.org; *Exec Dir* Margo Dunlap; *Prog Coordr/Cur* Amy Spencer; *Admin Gallery Coordr* Katherin Canton Titus
Open Tues - Fri 10 AM - 5 PM, Sat 11 AM - 4 PM; No admis fee; Estab 1974 as a contemporary art exhibition space for static & non-static works, nonprofit; Gallery located in Frank Ogawa Plaza, downtown Oakland; Average Annual Attendance: 65,000; Mem: 1,000; dues $45 & up, monthly meetings
Income: Mem & grants
Exhibitions: Rotating exhibits every 2 months; on-site & off-site installations
Activities: Classes for children; gallery talks; community partnerships; youth arts initiative events; mus shop sells original art, reproductions & prints

OCEANSIDE

M **MISSION SAN LUIS REY DE FRANCIA,** Mission San Luis Rey Museum, 4050 Mission Ave, Oceanside, CA 92057-6402. Tel 760-757-3651; Fax 760-757-4613; Elec Mail museumcurator@sanluisrey.org; Internet Home Page Address: www.sanluisrey.org; *Exec Dir* Fr David Gaa OFM; *Admin* Ed Gabarra; *Mus Cur* Bradford Claybourn
Open daily 10 AM - 4:00 PM; Admis family $25, adults $6, senior 65 and over & active military $5, youth $4, children 5 & younger free; Estab 1798 to protect, conserve & display artifacts which reflect the history of the mission; art & history; Average Annual Attendance: 60,000; Mem: Individual $60
Income: Financed by Franciscan Friars of Santa Barbara Province
Library Holdings: Memorabilia; Original Art Works; Original Documents; Photographs; Prints; Records; Sculpture
Special Subjects: Archaeology, History of Art & Archaeology, Art History, Mexican Art, Architecture, Latin American Art, Painting-American, American Indian Art, Textiles, Religious Art, Painting-European, Furniture, Historical Material, Restorations, Painting-Spanish
Collections: Artifacts from 18th century - present, furniture, paintings, statuary, 18th & 19th century religious vestments & vessels & other historical objects from early mission days in California, Spanish colonial and Rancho periods; Luseno Indian Baskets
Activities: Educ dept; docent training; 3 lects open to public; concerts; gallery talks; tours; individual paintings & original objects of art lent to qualified museums; sales of books, original art, prints, jewelry & artisan crafts

OJAI

M **BEATRICE WOOD CENTER FOR THE ARTS,** 8560 Ojai-Santa Paula Rd, Ojai, CA 93023-9351. Tel 805-646-3381; Fax 805-646-0560; Internet Home Page Address: www.beatricewood.com; *Dir* Kevin Wallace
Open Fri-Sun 11AM-5PM
Collections: works by Beatrice Wood; sculpture; paintings

A **OJAI ART CENTER,** 113 S Montgomery, Ojai, CA 93023; PO Box 331, Ojai, CA 93024-0331. Tel 805-646-0117; Fax 805-646-0252; Elec Mail ojaiartcenter@aol.com; *Pres* Len Klaff; *Dir* Teri Mettala
Open Tues Noon - 4 PM; No admis fee; Estab 1936 to foster all art disciplines in community; Gallery is 40 x 50 ft, high ceilings, with a large hanging area; Average Annual Attendance: 60,000; Mem: 400; dues family $40, adult $30; annual meeting 1st Mon of Feb
Income: Financed by mem, class & special event fees
Exhibitions: Twelve monthly exhibitions; Annual Watercolor Competition
Publications: Newsletter, monthly; Rivertalk, ann poetry anthology
Activities: Classes for adults & children; dramatic progs; lects open to pub; concerts; gallery talks; competitions with awards; schols offered

ORANGE

M **CHAPMAN UNIVERSITY GUGGENHEIM GALLERY,** Moulton Center, One University Dr Orange, CA 92866-1005. Tel 714-997-6815
Open to public everyday from 10 AM - 9:50 PM; Admis adults 30 RMB, students, senior citizens, military & handicapped 15 RMB, children under 1.3m in height & members no charge; admis after 6 PM adults 20 RMB, students 15 RMB; Establ Sept 2005

Collections: Paintings; sculpture; photographs
Activities: Special events & receptions

OROVILLE

M **BUTTE COLLEGE,** Art Gallery, 3536 Butte Campus Dr, Oroville, CA 95965-8399. Tel 530-895-2877; 895-2404; Fax 530-895-2414; Elec Mail oneilal@butte.edu; donnellyda@butte.edu; Internet Home Page Address: www.butte.edu; *Co-Chair ADAD Dept* Alexandra O'Neil; *Co-Chair ADAD Dept* Daniel Donnelly
Open Mon - Thurs 10 AM - 4 PM, Wed until 7:30 PM; No admis fee, donations accepted; Estab 1981, a contemporary col art gallery; An educationally oriented exhib space with rotating shows featuring the work of student & local artists as well as nationally & internationally known artists; Average Annual Attendance: 5,000
Income: Financed by fundraising, art sales, district funding
Purchases: Graham Nash prints; Janet Turner prints; Robert Burride originals
Exhibitions: Annual Juried Student Art Exhibit; contemporary art of a local, regional & national orientation
Activities: Classes for adults; lect open to public, 5 vis lectrs per yr; gallery talks; sponsoring of competitions; schols available; sales shop sells original art, prints, artist cards & memorabilia, gallery souvenirs

OXNARD

M **CARNEGIE ART MUSEUM,** 424 S C St, Oxnard, CA 93030-5944. Tel 805-385-8157; Fax 805-483-3654; Internet Home Page Address: www.carnegieam.org; *Cultural Arts Supv* Suzzane Bellah
Open Thurs - Sat 10 AM - 5 PM, Sun 1 - 5 PM; Admis $3 donation suggested; Estab 1980 as art museum & to house & manage City art coll; 5000 sq ft of gallery space; Average Annual Attendance: 20,000; Mem: 500, dues $25 & up
Income: financed by endowment, city appropriation, city & nonprofit support
Collections: California Art: 1920 to present
Exhibitions: Changing major exhibits quarterly
Publications: Master of the Miniature: The Art of Robert Olszewski; Municipal Art Collection Catalogue; Quechuan Rug Catalogue; Theodor Lukits Catalogue
Activities: Art classes, CAM Book Club; lects; poetry series; special events

M **CHANNEL ISLANDS MARITIME MUSEUM,** 3900 Bluefin Cr, Oxnard, CA 93035. Tel 805-984-6260; Fax 805-984-5970; Elec Mail vcmm@aol.com; Internet Home Page Address: www.vcmm.org; *Exec Dir* Gene Harter; *Cur Arts* Jacquelyn Cavish
Open daily 11 AM - 5 PM; Admis adults $5, seniors $4, children 6-17 $2, free admis 3rd Thurs of month; Estab 1991; Collection of maritime paintings (17th century - 20th century) and historic ship models; Average Annual Attendance: 25,000; Mem: 1000; dues $35
Income: $220,000 (financed by mem, contributions & grants)
Library Holdings: Book Volumes 3000
Special Subjects: Etchings & Engravings, Marine Painting, Painting-European, Graphics, Painting-American, Photography, Prints, Watercolors, Manuscripts, Marine Painting, Painting-British, Painting-Dutch, Historical Material, Maps, Scrimshaw, Painting-Flemish
Collections: Nelson Maritime Arts Foundation Collection of Maritime Paintings, Prints & Ship Models (Dutch 17th century - Modern 20th century); Antique POW Bone models; Ship Models of the Age of Sail; Edward Marple Model Collection; McNish Scrimshaw; Marple Library; William Fairburn Archives
Exhibitions: Nautica: Annual Juried Maritime Show; international & local artists exhibit 4 times per year; Biennial Exhibit of the American Society of Marine Artists; Plein Air Festival Exhibit
Activities: Classes for adults & children; dramatic progs; docent training; lects open to pub, 6 vis lectrs per yr; gallery talks; tours; sponsoring of competitions; ship model guild meets monthly 3rd Tues; original objects of art lent to mus; originates traveling exhibs; mus shop sells books, original art & prints

PACIFIC GROVE

A **PACIFIC GROVE ART CENTER,** 568 Lighthouse Ave, Pacific Grove, CA 93950-2624. Tel 831-375-2208; Fax 831-375-2208; Elec Mail pgart@mbay.net; Internet Home Page Address: www.pgartcenter.org; *Preparator* Mark Davy; *Pres Bd* Johnny Aliotti; *VPres* Jane Flury; *VPres* Joan Jeffers McCleary
Open Wed - Sat Noon - 5 PM, Sun 1 - 4 PM; No admis fee; Estab 1969 to promote the arts & encourage the artists of the Monterey Peninsula & California; Four galleries consist of 6000 sq ft of exhibition space, showing traditional & contemporary fine art & photography; galleries are available for classes & lects; Average Annual Attendance: 25,000; Mem: 550; dues bus & club $100, family $30, single $25; annual meeting in Nov
Income: Financed by grants, donations, mem. Dues & income from lease of studio space
Collections: Photography; painting
Exhibitions: Multiple exhibits every 7 weeks throughout the year
Publications: Newsletter every 7 weeks
Activities: Educ dept; classes for adults & children; dramatic progs; concerts; lects open to pub & for mems only; 3-4 vis lectrs per yr; concerts; gallery talks; competitions

PACIFIC PALISADES

M **J PAUL GETTY MUSEUM AT THE GETTY VILLA,** 17985 Pacific Coast Hwy, Pacific Palisades, CA 90272; 1200 Getty Center Dr, Ste 1000 Los Angeles, CA 90049-1687. Tel 310-440-7300; Elec Mail visitorservices@getty.edu; Internet Home Page Address: www.getty.edu; *Dir* David Bomford
Open Wed-Mon 10AM-5PM; No admis fee, Advanced timed ticket is required to enter the site. Parking: $15 per car, no charge after 5PM

Collections: sculpture; photographs

PALM DESERT

M **IMAGO GALLERIES,** 45-450 Hwy 74, Palm Desert, CA 92260. Tel 760-776-9890; Elec Mail info@imagogalleries.com; Internet Home Page Address: www.imagogalleries.com; *Dir* David Austin; *Dir* Leisa Auston
Open Tues-Sat 10AM-5PM, other times by appointment
Collections: works by contemporary artists; paintings; sculpture

PALM SPRINGS

M **PALM SPRINGS ART MUSEUM,** (Palm Springs Desert Museum) 101 Museum Dr, Palm Springs, CA 92262-5659; PO Box 2310, Palm Springs, CA 92263-2310. Tel 760-322-4800; Fax 760-327-5069; Elec Mail info@psmuseum.org; *Exec Dir* Steven A Nash, PhD; *Chief Cur* Katherine Hough; *Deputy Dir Art, Sr Cur* Daniell Cornell, PhD; *Deputy Dir Educ & Pub Progs* Robert Brasier; *Librn* Frank Lopez
Open Tues, Wed, Fri, Sat, Sun 10 AM - 5 PM, Thurs Noon - 8 PM, cl Mon; Admis adults $12.50, seniors $10.50, others $5; Estab 1938; Average Annual Attendance: 130,000; Mem: Dues individual $50, family/dual $85
Income: Financed by pvt funds
Library Holdings: Auction Catalogs; Audio Tapes; Book Volumes 12,000; CD-ROMs; Cassettes; Clipping Files; DVDs; Exhibition Catalogs; Manuscripts; Memorabilia; Original Documents; Pamphlets; Periodical Subscriptions 28; Photographs; Slides; Video Tapes
Special Subjects: Art Education, Mexican Art, Mixed Media, Bronzes, Photography, Sculpture, American Indian Art, American Western Art, Pre-Columbian Art
Exhibitions: Contemporary Glass, ongoing; A dialogue between Ancient and Modern: Selections from the Permanent Collection, ongoing
Publications: InSight, mem mag, quarterly; Spec exhibit catalogs ann
Activities: Classes for adults & children; docent training; dramatic progs; student visits to mus; out-reach art classes; on-site child/adult classes; lects open to pub & mem only; concerts; gallery talks; tours; competitions with awards; schols; exten dept serves pub schools; book traveling exhibs 4 per yr; originate traveling exhibs; mus shop sells books, reproductions, jewelry, educational childrens toys, cards & artist-designed items

PALO ALTO

A **PALO ALTO ART CENTER,** (Palo Alto Cultural Center) 1313 Newell Rd, Palo Alto, CA 94303. Tel 650-329-2366; Fax 650-326-6165; Internet Home Page Address: www.cityofpaloalto.org/artcenter; *Vol Coordr* Emily Lacroix; *Cur* Lisa Ellsworth; *Studio Supv* Lynn Stewart; *Operations Mgr* Rebecca Barbee; *Dir Edu* Ariel Berson; *Dir* Karen Kienzle; *Coordr Project Look!* Alyssa Erickson; *Publications* Sharon Fox; *VChmn* Bern Beecham; *Mus Shop Mgr* Diane Master; *Coordr Child Art* Jennifer Marsh; *Coordr Family Progs & Outreach* Tasmia Hussain; *Mktg Coordr* Sarah Goodman
Open Tues - Sat 10 AM - 5 PM, Thurs 10 AM - 9 PM, Sun 1 PM - 5 PM, cl Mon; No admis fee; Estab 1971 - a place to discover art, see, make & be inspired because everyone is an artist; Average Annual Attendance: 70,000; Mem: 700; dues $1000, $500, $250, $100, $80, $50
Income: $1,000,000 (financed by municipal funds, private donations & earned income)
Exhibitions: Exhibits rotate every 3 months
Activities: Classes for adults & children; docent training; lects open to pub, 6-8 vis lectrs per yr; gallery talks; tours; festivals; after hours events; rentals; birthday parties; vol opportunities; sales shop sells books, original art, reproductions, prints & objects for sale related to exhibitions

M **PALO ALTO JUNIOR MUSEUM & ZOO,** 1451 Middlefield Rd, Palo Alto, CA 94301-3351. Tel 650-329-2111; Fax 650-473-1965; *Dir* Rachel Meyer
Open Tues - Sat 10 AM - 5 PM, Sun 1 - 4 PM, cl Mon, cl New Years, Easter, July 4, Thanksgiving & Christmas; No admis fee; Estab 1932, completely renovated in 1969; Average Annual Attendance: 150,000
Income: Financed by city appropriation
Collections: Interactive children's exhibits
Publications: Notes, monthly
Activities: Classes; self-guided tours; exten dept

PASADENA

A **ARMORY CENTER FOR THE ARTS,** 145 N Raymond Ave, Pasadena, CA 91103-3921. Tel 626-792-5101; Fax 626-449-0139; Elec Mail information@armoryarts.org; Internet Home Page Address: www.armoryarts.org; *Exec Dir* Scott Ward; *Dir Gallery Progs* Irene Tsatos; *Gallery Progs Mgr* Sinead Finnerty-Pyne; *Dir Communs* Jon Lapointe; *Dir Devel* Elisa Laris; *Dir Fin & Opers* Slade Bellum
Gallery open Tues - Sun Noon - 5 PM; Office open Mon - Fri 9 AM - 5 PM; Admis $5 suggested donation, seniors, students & mems free; Estab 1974 for contemporary visual arts, exhibitions, performances & education; Average Annual Attendance: 35,000; Mem: 300; dues $35; annual meeting in Sept
Income: $1.3 million (financed by endowment, mem, city & state appropriation, foundations & corporations)
Special Subjects: Architecture, Graphics, Photography, Prints, Sculpture, Watercolors, Painting-American, Pottery, Woodcuts, Ceramics, Collages, Juvenile Art, Portraits, Bookplates & Bindings
Collections: Installation; Performance Art; Urban Design
Activities: Classes for adults & children; musical performances; lects open to pub; concerts; gallery talks; tours; fels; book traveling exhibs 1 per yr; originate traveling exhibs 1 per yr; mus shop sells books

L ART CENTER COLLEGE OF DESIGN, James Lemont Fogg Memorial Library, 1700 Lida St, Pasadena, CA 91103-1999. Tel 626-396-2233; Fax 626-568-0428; Elec Mail library@artcenter.edu; Internet Home Page Address: hera.artcenter.edu; *VPres & Dir* Elizabeth Galloway; *Catalog Librn* Alison Holt; *Acquisitions Librn* George Porcari; *Circ Supv* Mark Von Schlegell; *Circ Supv* Nolina Burge; *Reference & Pub Servs Librn* Claudia Michelle Betty; *Photo Research Cur* Jennifer Faist
Open Mon - Thurs 8 AM - 10 PM, Fri 8 AM - 7PM; Estab to provide reference & visual resources for the designers who study & teach at Art Center College of Design; Circ 90,000
Income: Financed by institution & private grants
Purchases: $85,000 (books); $45,000 (periodicals); $30,000 (videos & slides)
Library Holdings: Book Volumes 65,000; Cassettes; Clipping Files 28,000; Exhibition Catalogs 1850; Motion Pictures 100; Periodical Subscriptions 450; Reproductions; Slides 90,000; Video Tapes 2200
Special Subjects: Illustration, Photography, Commercial Art, Graphic Design, Advertising Design, Industrial Design

M Alyce de Roulet Williamson Gallery, 1700 Lida St, Pasadena, CA 91103. Tel 623-396-2446; Tel 623-396-2397; Fax 626-405-9104; Elec Mail stephen.nowlin@artcenter.edu; Internet Home Page Address: www.williamsongallery.net; *Dir* Stephen Nowlin
Open Tues - Thurs & Sat 12 PM - 5 PM, Fri 12 PM - 9 PM, cl holidays
Collections: works of contemporary fine art & design

M NORTON SIMON MUSEUM, 411 W Colorado Blvd, Pasadena, CA 91105-1825. Tel 626-449-6840; Fax 626-796-4978; Elec Mail info@nortonsimon.org; Internet Home Page Address: www.nortonsimon.org; *Pres* Walter W Timoshuk; *Cur* Gloria Williams; *Registrar* Lisa Escoveda; *Chief Cur* Carol Togneri; *Cur* Leah Lehmbeck; *Dir Pub Affairs* Leslie Denk; *Collections Mgr* Jeffrey Taylor; *Mus Store Mgr* Andrew Uchin; *Asst Cur* Melody Rod-ari
Open Mon - Sun Noon - 6 PM, Fri until 9 PM - cl Tues; Admis adults $10, seniors $7; members & children 18 & under & students with ID free; Estab 1974; this museum brings collections of European paintings, prints & sculptures. Asian sculpture spanning 2000 yrs; Average Annual Attendance: 170,000; Mem: Dues $75-$1000
Income: Financed by endowment, mem, city appropriation, tours, admis, contributions, bookshop & grounds maintenance
Special Subjects: Photography, Portraits, Bronzes, Painting-European, Painting-French, Sculpture, Tapestries, Graphics, Painting-American, Prints, Sculpture, Religious Art, Woodcuts, Landscapes, Asian Art, Tapestries, Painting-Flemish, Renaissance Art
Collections: Art spanning 20 centuries: including paintings, sculptures & graphics from the early Renaissance through the 20th century; Indian & Southeast Asian sculpture
Publications: Masterpieces from the Norton Simon Museum; Handbook of the Norton Simon Museum & Coll Cats
Activities: Classes for adults; tours for children; private guided tours; lectrs open to pub; 10 vis lectrs; concerts; gallery talks; internships; mus shop sells books, reproductions, prints & slides

M PACIFIC - ASIA MUSEUM, 46 N Los Robles Ave, Pasadena, CA 91101-2071. Tel 626-449-2742; Fax 626-449-2754; Internet Home Page Address: www.pacificasiamuseum.org; *Exec Dir* David Kamansky; *Educ Mgr* Rebecca Edwards; *Vol Coordr* Rosa Zee; *Asst Dir* William Hanbury-Tenison; *Mktg & Pub Rels* Agnes Gomes; *Cur East Asian Art* Meher McArthur
Open Wed - Sun 10 AM - 5 PM, Thurs 10 AM - 8 PM, cl holidays; Admis adults & non-members $5, seniors $3, under 12 free; Estab 1971 to promote understanding of the cultures of the Pacific & Far East through exhibitions, lectures, dance, music & concerts. Through these activities, the mus helps to increase mutual respect & appreciation of both the diversities & similarities of Asian/Pacific & Western cultures; The building was designed by Marston, Van Pelt & Mayberry, architects for Grace Nicholson. The building is listed in the national register of historic places as the Grace Nicholson Building. There is 11,000 sq ft of exhibition space; Average Annual Attendance: 50,000; Mem: 1000; dues benefactor $1000, donor $600, sponsor $350, patron $150, contributor $75, active $37
Special Subjects: Prints, Sculpture, Bronzes, Textiles, Ceramics, Folk Art, Pottery, Woodcarvings, Decorative Arts, Painting-Japanese, Furniture, Jade, Porcelain, Asian Art, Ivory, Coins & Medals, Tapestries, Calligraphy, Miniatures
Collections: Bronzes; Buddhist sculptures; Chinese & Japanese paintings & ceramics; Chinese textiles; Southeast Asian ceramics; Chinese; Japanese Prints; Asian Art; Himalayan Art
Publications: Exhibit catalogs
Activities: Classes for adults & children; docent training; lects open to pub; gallery talks; tours; original objects of art lent to other mus & limited number of libraries; originate traveling exhibs to schools, libraries & other mus; mus shop sells books, magazines, original art, reproductions & prints

M PASADENA CITY COLLEGE, Art Gallery, 1570 E Colorado Blvd, Visual Arts & Media Studies Division Pasadena, CA 91106-2003. Tel 626-585-7238; Fax 626-585-7914; Elec Mail lxmalm@paccd.cc.ca.us; Internet Home Page Address: www.pasadena.edu/artgallery; *Gallery Dir* Brian Tucker
Open Mon - Thurs noon-8PM, Fri-Sat noon-4PM; No admis fee; Estab to show work that relates to class given at Pasadena City College; Gallery is housed in separate building; 1000 sq ft; Average Annual Attendance: 20,000; Mem: 2800
Income: Financed by the college
Collections: Small permanent collection of contemporary art; Contemporary Art
Exhibitions: Rotating exhibits & juried student show
Publications: Mailers for each show
Activities: Educ dept; lect open to public, 5-10 vis lectrs per year; gallery talks; competitions; book traveling exhibitions occasionally

M PASADENA MUSEUM OF CALIFORNIA ART, 490 E Union St, Pasadena, CA 91101; 495 E Colorado Blvd, Pasadena, CA 91101-2024. Tel 626-568-3665; Fax 626-568-3674; Elec Mail info@pmcaonline.org; Internet Home Page Address: www.pmcaonline.org; *Exec Dir* Jenkins Shannon; *Chmn* David Partridge; *Pub Rels* Emma Jacobson-Sive; *Treas* Ted McCarthy; *Gallery Mgr* Emmett Clements; *Exhib Mgr* Erin Aitali; *Exhib Designer* Sergio Gomez; *Mktg & Outreach Coordr* Alexis Kaneshiro; *Mem & Bookstore Assoc* Susan Wang
Open Wed - Sun 12 - 5 PM; cl New Years, Fourth of July, Thanksgiving & Christmas; Admis adults $7, seniors & students $5, children under 12 & mems no admis fee; Estab 2002 with the mission to educate & enrich the pub through the study & presentation of works of Calif art, design & architecture from 1850 - present; 11,000 sq ft exhib space; pvt nonprofit org; Average Annual Attendance: 35,000; Mem: dues Dir $500, Guild Level $200, Studio Level $50, Student & Senior $25
Special Subjects: Drawings, Landscapes, American Western Art, Furniture, Photography, Portraits, Painting-American, Graphics
Collections: Mus houses no perm coll; exhibs focus on Calif art, design & architecture from 1850 - present; paintings; prints; drawings; graphic arts; photographs
Activities: Guided tours; research in contemporary & historic Calif art; panel discussions; lects open to the public; 10 vis lectrs per yr; gallery talks; tours; exhibs; loan exhibs; traveling exhibs; Calif Design Biennial, Calif Air Club Gold Medal Exhib; mus shop sells books, prints, clothing, jewelry, design objects & other mus related items for sale

M PASADENA MUSEUM OF HISTORY, 470 W Walnut St, Pasadena, CA 91103-3562. Tel 626-577-1660; Fax 626-577-1662; Elec Mail info@pasadenahistory.org; Internet Home Page Address: www.pasadenahistory.org; *Dir Exhib* Ardis Willwerth; *Exec Dir* Jeannette O'Malley; *Colls Mgr* Laura Verlaque
Open Wed - Sun Noon - 5 PM; Suggested donation adults $5, students & seniors $4, children under 12 free; Estab 1924 for the preservation & collection of historical data relating to Pasadena; Historical house with American Impressionist Art; 2 exhibit galleries, Finnish Farm House; Average Annual Attendance: 13,000; Mem: 1400; dues $50 - $1000
Income: $159,000 (financed through mem, endowment & contributions)
Library Holdings: Book Volumes 1500; Clipping Files; Manuscripts; Memorabilia; Original Art Works; Photographs 750,000
Special Subjects: Decorative Arts, Historical Material, Landscapes, Architecture, Portraits, Painting-American, Period Rooms, Silver, Textiles, Watercolors, Costumes, Ceramics, Crafts, Folk Art, Decorative Arts, Dolls, Furniture, Glass, Carpets & Rugs, Embroidery
Collections: Collection of documents & artifacts relating to Pasadena; Collection of paintings by California artists; European & American furniture (antiques & reproductions); over one million; rare books & manuscripts; Turn of the Century Life Style on Millionaire's Row; Costumes
Exhibitions: Calif Art Club Juries Exhib; 3-4 changing exhibits annually
Publications: Quarterly newsletter
Activities: Classes for adults; docent & junior docent training; lect open to public, 4-8 vis lectrs per year; gallery talks; tours; sales shop sells books, magazines, prints & gift items

L PASADENA PUBLIC LIBRARY, Fine Arts Dept, 285 E Walnut St, Pasadena, CA 91101-1598. Tel 626-744-4066; Internet Home Page Address: www.pasadenapubliclibrary.net; *Dir* Jan Sanders; *Prin Librn & Information Access Servs* Beth Walker
Open Mon - Thurs 9 AM - 9 PM, Fri & Sat 9 AM - 6 PM, Sun 1 - 5 PM; No admis fee; Art dept estab 1927
Income: Financed by endowments & gifts, for materials only
Library Holdings: Audio Tapes 3,950; Book Volumes 15,636; Compact Disks 9,600; DVDs 2,377; Fiche; Other Holdings Audiobooks on CD 2,240; Periodical Subscriptions 60; Photographs; Video Tapes 3,500

M SIDE STREET PROJECTS, 730 N Fair Oaks Ave, Pasadena, CA 91109; PO Box 90432, Pasadena, CA 91109. Tel 626-798-7774; Fax 626-798-7747; Elec Mail info@sidestreet.org; Internet Home Page Address: www.sidestreet.org; *Dir* Emily Hopkins; *Prog Dir* Michelle Glass; *Pres Bd Dir* Jon Lapointe
No admis fee; Estab 1992, became completely a mobile org in 2008
Exhibitions: Installations & projects by contemporary artists, local & international
Activities: Classes for adults & children; artmobile; lect open to public

POMONA

M AMERICAN MUSEUM OF CERAMIC ART, 340 N Garey Ave, Pomona, CA 91767-5431. Tel 909-865-3146; Fax 909-629-1067; Elec Mail frontdesk@ceramicmuseum.org; Internet Home Page Address: www.ceramicmuseum.org; *Dir, Cur* Christy Johnson; *Admin & Mem Mgr* Edward Escarsega; *Asst Cur* Karen Crews; *Coll & Admin Clerk* Nicole Frazer; *Pres & Founder* David Armstrong
Open Wed - Sat Noon - 5 PM, second Sat of each month Noon - 9 PM, cl New Year's Day, Thanksgiving, Christmas Eve & Day, July 4th; Admis adults $3, seniors & students $2, children & members free; Estab 2004; Average Annual Attendance: 12,000; Mem: 710
Income: 500,000; donations, grants, mem dues, gift store sales
Library Holdings: DVDs
Special Subjects: Decorative Arts, Folk Art, Ceramics
Publications: quarterly newsletter; exhib catalogues
Activities: Classes for adults & children; lects open to pub, lects for mems only, vis lectrs 5 per yr; gallery talks; tours; arts festivals; concerts; films; guided tours; competitions; hobby workshops; lectrs; loan exhib; theater; semi-annual event: Pottery Market; summer & winter member only events; temporary & traveling exhibs; mus shop sells books, magazines, original art, & dvds

M LATINO ART MUSEUM, 281 S Thomas St, Ste 105 Pomona, CA 91766-1740. Tel 909-620-6009; Tel 909-484-2618; Elec Mail latinoartmuseum@msn.com; Internet Home Page Address: www.lamoa.net; *Pres & Founder* Graciela H Nardi; *Treas* Mario Gee Lopez; *Secy* David Pion-Berlin
Call for hours; No admis fee; Estab 2001; Contemporary art; Mem: 468
Income: Financed by mem, donations, grants

Library Holdings: Auction Catalogs; Book Volumes; CD-ROMs; Cards; Photographs; Prints; Reproductions; Sculpture
Special Subjects: Drawings, Etchings & Engravings, Landscapes, Art Education, Ceramics, Collages, Conceptual Art, Glass, Mixed Media, Portraits, Pottery, Prints, Silver, Sculpture, Graphics, Hispanic Art, Latin American Art, Mexican Art, Photography, Watercolors, Pre-Columbian Art, Textiles, Woodcarvings, Woodcuts, Painting-European, Posters, Jewelry, Porcelain, Miniatures, Painting-Spanish, Painting-Italian, Mosaics, Stained Glass, Pewter
Collections: Paintings & photographs
Publications: Yearbook 2012
Activities: Classes for adults & children; special events; rental facilities; docent training; lects open to pub; concerts; gallery talks; tours; organize traveling exhibs; mus shop sells books, magazines, original art, reproductions & mus related items

QUINCY

M **PLUMAS COUNTY MUSEUM,** 500 Jackson St, Quincy, CA 95971-9412. Tel 530-283-6320; Fax 530-283-6081; Elec Mail pcmuseum@digitalpath.net; Internet Home Page Address: www.countyof plumas.com/museum; *Asst Dir* Paul Russell; *Dir* Scott Lawson
Open winter Tues - Sat 10 AM - 4 PM; Admis fee adults $2, students $1; Estab 1964 to preserve the past for the enjoyment & edification of the present & future generations; 1878 historical home next door has been restored & opened to the pub with period rooms; Average Annual Attendance: 18,000; Mem: 700; general per yr $25; $35; $50; $1,000
Income: Financed by members & county budget
Purchases: $300
Special Subjects: Architecture, Graphics, Painting-American, Photography, American Indian Art, Anthropology, Costumes, Ceramics, Crafts, Decorative Arts, Furniture, Glass, Silver, Metalwork, Carpets & Rugs, Historical Material, Coins & Medals, Dioramas, Embroidery, Gold
Collections: Antique period furnishings, Indian (Maidu) artifacts, dolls, clothing, mining & logging artifacts, domestic, jewelry, guns, period furniture, Historic Home Museum adjacent; railroad coll, memorabilia; Variel Home
Exhibitions: Various Local Artists
Publications: Plumas County Museum Newsletter, two times a year
Activities: Classes for children; docent training; lects open to public; 3 lecturers per yr gallery talks; tours; museum shop sells books; original art & prints
L **Museum Archives,** 500 Jackson St, Quincy, CA 95971. Tel 530-283-6320; Fax 530-283-6081; Elec Mail pcmuseum@pslm.com; Internet Home Page Address: www.countyofplumas.com; *Asst Cur* Evelyn Whisman; *CEO* Scott Lawson; *Registrar* Jo Ann Filippi; *Bd Dir, VChmn* Roswitha Schulz; *VChmn* Noel Carlson
Open Mon - Fri 8 AM - 5 PM, May-Sept 10 AM - 4 PM; Admis adults $1, 17 & under $.50, children & members free; Estab 1964 to preserve Plumas County's rich heritage & history; Library for reference use only; Average Annual Attendance: 25,000; Mem: 300; dues $10 & up; annual meeting in June
Income: $80,000 (financed by county, memorial donations, mem, book store sales & personal donations)
Library Holdings: Audio Tapes; Book Volumes 2000; Cassettes; Clipping Files; Exhibition Catalogs; Kodachrome Transparencies; Memorabilia; Micro Print; Motion Pictures; Original Art Works; Other Holdings Negatives; Pamphlets; Periodical Subscriptions 1000; Photographs; Prints; Reels; Reproductions; Slides
Collections: Indian jewelry; Maidu Indian Basket Collection; agriculture; bottles; china; crystal; dolls; furniture; logging; mining; musical instruments; railroad items; toys; Coburn Variel home
Activities: Docent training; demonstrations; lect open to public; gallery talks; tours; sales shop sells books, original art, reproductions, photographs

RANCHO PALOS VERDES

A **PALOS VERDES ART CENTER/BEVERLY G. ALPAY CENTER FOR ARTS EDUCATION,** 5504 W Crestridge Rd, Rancho Palos Verdes, CA 90275. Tel 310-541-2479; Fax 310-541-9520; Elec Mail info@pvartcenter.org; Internet Home Page Address: www.pvartcenter.org; *Dir Educ Progs* Gail Phinney; *Pub Rels Dir* Julia Parton; *Exhib Dir* Scott Canty; *Admin Dir* Ann Willens; *Exec Dir* Robert A Yassin; *Dir School of Art* Angela Hoffman
Open Mon - Fri 9 AM - 5 PM, Sat 10 AM - 4 PM, Sun 1 - 4 PM, cl major holidays; No admis fee; Estab 1931 to provide cultural enrichment through art educ, exhibitions & outreach; Changing exhibits in 4 galleries; Average Annual Attendance: 25,000; Mem: 1600; dues $25-$5000; annual meeting in June
Income: Financed by mem & pvt donations
Special Subjects: Drawings, Photography, Prints, Sculpture, Ceramics, Jewelry, Calligraphy
Exhibitions: Annual Juried All-media Show (June-Aug.); Annual Holiday Art Exhib, plus seven other exhibs
Publications: Exhibit catalogs; ARTifacts
Activities: Classes for children & adults; docent training; lect open to public; gallery talks; tours; competitions with awards; juried all-media; scholarships offered; sales shop sells original art

RANCHO SANTA FE

M **RANCHO SANTA FE ART GUILD,** 6004 Paseo Delicias, Rancho Santa Fe, CA 92067; PO Box 773, Rancho Santa Fe, CA 92067-0773. Tel 858-759-3545; Internet Home Page Address: www.ranchosantaeartguild.org; *Gallery Mgr* Pam MacLaird
Open Tues - Sat 11 AM - 4:30 PM
Collections: Paintings; photographs; sculpture

RED BLUFF

M **KELLY-GRIGGS HOUSE MUSEUM,** 311 Washington St, Red Bluff, CA; PO Box 9082, Red Bluff, CA 96080-6068. Tel 530-527-1129; *Pres* Linda Elsner; *Treas* Erick Frey; *Cur* Vivian Ogden
Open Thurs - Sun 1 - 4 PM, cl holidays, for groups any time by reservation; Admis donations accepted; Estab 1965, a Victorian history museum in a home

built in 1880s; To preserve the past for present and future generations; Average Annual Attendance: 3,000; Mem: dues assoc $10, sustaining $50, supporting $100 annually, memoriam $100, life $200, patron $500, benefactor $1000
Income: mems, donations, fundraising events
Library Holdings: Book Volumes; DVDs; Memorabilia; Original Art Works; Original Documents; Pamphlets; Photographs
Special Subjects: Archaeology, Historical Material, Ceramics, Glass, Furniture, Painting-American, Period Rooms, Textiles, Hispanic Art, American Indian Art, Costumes, Dolls, Jewelry, Porcelain, Embroidery, Laces, Antiquities-Oriental, Cartoons, Leather
Collections: Collection of paintings spanning a century of art; Indian artifacts; antique furniture; Victorian costumes; Pendleton Collection
Exhibitions: Permanent and temporary exhibitions
Publications: Brochure; Kellygram (guides' newsletter and schedule)
Activities: Docent training; guided tours, lects 4-6 per yr

REDDING

M **TURTLE BAY EXPLORATION PARK,** 840 Sundial Bridge Dr, Redding, CA 96001; 1335 Arboretum Dr Ste A, Redding, CA 96003-3628. Tel 530-243-8850; Fax 530-243-8929; Elec Mail info@turtlebay.org; Internet Home Page Address: www.turtlebay.org; *CEO* Michael Warren; *Cur* Julia Pennington; *COO* Maggie Redmon
Open Sun - Sat 9 AM - 5 PM (see website for seasonal hrs); Admis adults $14, seniors & children $10; Estab 1990 to interpret the complex relationships between people and their environments; Two temporary exhibition galleries, totaling 7,000 sq ft present changing contemporary art, history & natural science exhibits; outdoor art; Average Annual Attendance: 150,000; Mem: Family $80
Income: Financed by admis, mem, fundraising activities
Special Subjects: Etchings & Engravings, Landscapes, Painting-American, Prints, Textiles, Photography, Sculpture, Watercolors, American Indian Art, American Western Art, Archaeology, Ethnology, Costumes, Manuscripts, Historical Material, Maps, Reproductions
Collections: Native American baskets; Shasta County historical artifacts & documents; Contemporary Regional art; photography; Forest History
Exhibitions: Annual Art Competition; Bug-Eyed: Art, Culture, Insects; Realism Today: Audubon's Animals
Publications: Temporary exhib catalogs
Activities: Classes for adults & children; docent training; lects open to pub, vis lectrs; gallery talks; tours; Art Fair; lending collection; book traveling exhibs 3-5 per yr; originate traveling exhibs to other mus; mus shop sells books & original art, consignment from local craftspeople & artists, reproductions, gifts
L **Shasta Historical Society Research Library,** 1335 Arboretum Dr, Ste A, Redding, CA 96003. Tel 530-243-3720; *Librn* Linda Sharpe
Open Mon - Fri 10 AM - 4 PM; Open for reference only by appointment
Library Holdings: Periodical Subscriptions 64

REDLANDS

L **LINCOLN MEMORIAL SHRINE,** 125 W Vine St, Redlands, CA 92373-4761. Tel 909-798-7636, 798-7632; Fax 909-798-6566; Elec Mail archives@aksmiley.org; Internet Home Page Address: www.aksmiley.org; *Cur* Donald McCue; *Assoc Archivist* Richard Hanks; *Assoc Archivist* Nathan Gonzalez; *VPres* Jack D Tompkins
Open Tues - Sun 1 - 5 PM, other hours by appointment; cl Sun, Mon & holidays, except Lincoln's birthday; No admis fee; Estab 1932, operated as a section of the Smiley Public Library; Reference use only; Average Annual Attendance: 6,000; Mem: 325; dues $15-$30
Library Holdings: Book Volumes 4500; Clipping Files; Filmstrips; Memorabilia; Original Art Works; Pamphlets; Photographs; Sculpture
Special Subjects: Manuscripts, Maps, American Indian Art
Collections: Sculptures, paintings, murals
Publications: Lincoln Memorial Assn Newsletter, quarterly
Activities: Docent training; lects open to public, 1 vis lectr per year; guided tours by appointment; Barondess Award, 1987; sales shop sells pamphlets & postcards; books

A **REDLANDS ART ASSOCIATION,** Redlands Art Association Gallery & Art Center, 215 E State St, Redlands, CA 92373-5232. Tel 909-792-8435; Internet Home Page Address: www.redlands-art.org; *Pres* Gail Brownfield; *Gallery Mgr* Francis Wiley; *Publicity* Sandy Davies; *VPres* Tony Radcliffe
Open Mon - Sat 10 AM - 5 PM; No admis fee; Estab 1964 to promote interest in the visual arts & to provide a gallery for artists; Circ 200; 2 room bus site on main shopping st; Average Annual Attendance: 3,000; Mem: 250; dues $40; annual meeting in May; Artist, Art Appreciator
Income: Financed by dues, grants
Library Holdings: Book Volumes 400
Exhibitions: Multimedia mini juried show; Recycling Show; Plein Air Show
Publications: Bulletin, monthly
Activities: Classes for children & adults; lect open to public, 8 vis lectrs per year; tours; competitions with prizes; gallery talks; workshops; scholarships offered; lending collection contains books & original prints; gallery shop sells original art, reproductions, glass, ceramics, jewelry & cards

M **SAN BERNARDINO COUNTY MUSEUM,** Fine Arts Institute, 2024 Orange Tree Lane, Redlands, CA 92374. Tel 909-307-2669; Fax 909-307-0539; Elec Mail sramos@sbcm.sbcounty.org; Internet Home Page Address: www.sbcountymuseum.org; *Dir* Robert L McKernan; *Registrar* Andrea Morics; *Cur Exhibs* Holly Signi; *Cur Educ* Jolene Redvale; *Sr Cur Paleontology* Kathleen Springer; *Cur History* Ann Deegan; *Deputy Dir* Laurie Rozko; *Cur Anthropology* Adella Schroth; *Mus Shop Mgr* Blue Anderson
Open Tues - Sat 9 AM - 5 PM, Sun 9 AM - 5 PM; Admis adults $3, seniors, students & children 2-12 $2, mus mem free; Estab 1952 for education; Maintains upper & lower dome galleries & foyer; Average Annual Attendance: 300,000;

Mem: 2100; dues Fine Arts Institute $40, Mus Assoc $15 & up; annual Fine Arts Institute meeting Mar; annual Mus Assoc meeting in May
Income: $280,000 (financed by mem)
Purchases: $2000
Special Subjects: Painting-American, American Indian Art, American Western Art, Archaeology, Collages, Historical Material
Collections: Collection consists primarily of representational art pertaining to wildlife or the history of Southern California & annual purchase awards from Fine Arts Institute's Annual International Exhibit & Southern California Open Exhibit & County Heritage Exhibit
Exhibitions: Three juried art members exhibits; one annual international open exhibit; one regional Southern California open exhibit; one featured artists group exhibit
Publications: Newsletter, bimonthly
Activities: Classes for adults & children; docent training; lects open to pub, 3 vis lectrs per yr; gallery talks; tours; art competitions with cash & purchase awards totaling $45,000 annually; book traveling exhibs; originate traveling exhibs; mus shop sells books, magazines, original art reproductions, prints & slides, jewelry, items pertaining to natural history

M **UNIVERSITY OF REDLANDS,** Peppers Art Gallery, 1200 E Colton Ave, Redlands, CA 92374-3755; PO Box 3080, Redlands, CA 92373-0999. Tel 909-793-2121; Fax 909-748-6293; *Chair Art Dept* Penny McElroy; *Admin Asst* Terri Hodgson
Open Tues - Fri 1 - 5 PM, Sat & Sun 2 - 5 PM, cl summer; No admis fee; Estab 1963 to widen students interest in art; Gallery is one large room with celestial windows & movable panels for display; Average Annual Attendance: 1,500
Income: Financed by endowment
Collections: Ethnic Art; graphics; a few famous artists works
Exhibitions: Exhibitions during fall, winter, spring
Publications: Exhibition catalogs & posters
Activities: Lect open to public, 4-5 vis lectrs per yr; gallery talks; tours; talent awards

RICHMOND

A **NATIONAL INSTITUTE OF ART & DISABILITIES (NIAD),** Florence Ludins-Katz Gallery, 551 23rd St, Richmond, CA 94804-1626. Tel 510-620-0290; Fax 510-620-0326; Elec Mail admin@niadart.org; Internet Home Page Address: www.niadart.org; *Exec Dir* Deb Dyer; *Gallery Dir* Brian Stechschulte
Open Mon - Fri 9 AM - 4 PM or by appt; No admis fee; Estab 1984 to provide an art environment for people with developmental disabilities which promotes creative expression, independence, dignity and community integration; Maintains professional exhibition galleries which display the work of NIAD artists, often alongside the work of established artists from outside the NIAD setting in order to bring the art of NIAD artists to the attention of the general public; Average Annual Attendance: 1,000; Mem: 250; dues $15-$100
Collections: Gallery, books, pamphlets, posters, videotapes, CD-ROM
Exhibitions: NIAD artist work; 4 exhibs per yr; numerous exhibs nationally & internationally
Publications: Art & Disabilities, Freedom to Create, the Creative Spirit; Freedom to Create (videotape series)
Activities: Classes for adults with developmental disabilities; interdisciplinary visual art studio prog; professional training in art & disabilities field; research, training & technical assistance; gallery talks; tours; originate traveling exhibs of NIAD artist work to regional galleries, mus, colleges, community centers & bus; sales shop sells books, original art & prints

A **THE RICHMOND ART CENTER,** 2540 Barrett Ave, Civic Center Plaza Richmond, CA 94804-1600. Tel 510-620-6772; Fax 510-620-6771; Elec Mail admin@therac.org; Internet Home Page Address: www.therichmondartcenter.org; *Exec Dir* Jasmine Brown
Open Tues - Sun 12 noon - 5 PM, cl Mon & holidays; No admis fee; Estab preliminary steps 1936-44; formed in 1944 to establish artists studios & community center for arts; to offer to the community an opportunity to experience & to improve knowledge & skill in the arts & crafts at the most comprehensive & highest level possible; A large gallery, small gallery & entrance gallery total 5000 sq ft & a rental gallery covers 1628 sq ft; an outdoor sculpture ct totals 8840 sq ft; Average Annual Attendance: 8,000; Mem: 1,000; dues $35 & up
Collections: Primarily contemporary art & crafts of Bay area
Exhibitions: Rotating: group theme, solo, invitational & juried annuals
Publications: Catalog for annual shows; newsletter, quarterly; show announcements for exhibitions
Activities: Classes for adults & children; lect open to public, 5 vis lectrs per year; gallery talks; tours; scholarships offered; outreach program serving community; rental gallery, paintings & original objects of art lent to offices, bus & homes, members of Art Center

RIVERSIDE

M **RIVERSIDE ART MUSEUM,** 3425 Mission Inn Ave, Riverside, CA 92501-3368. Tel 951-684-7111; Fax 951-684-7332; Elec Mail ram@riversideartmuseum.org; Internet Home Page Address: www.riversideartmuseum.org; *Exec Dir* Daniel Foster; *Assoc Dir* Andi Campognone; *Sr Cur* Peter Frank; *Educ Cur* Steve Thomas; *Sr Preparator* Christaan Von Martin
Open Mon - Sat 10 AM - 4 PM; Admis adults $5, mems free; Estab 1935 to display art, collect & preserve art created in the West; Three spaces - Main Gallery 72 ft x 35 ft; Upstairs Gallery 18 ft x 30 ft; Art Alliance Gallery 72 ft x 35 ft; Average Annual Attendance: 70,000; Mem: 1,200; dues life mem $10,000 & up, patron $2500, supporting $300, family $50, individual $35, senior citizens $10
Income: Financed by mem, grants & donations
Library Holdings: Book Volumes; Exhibition Catalogs

Collections: Mixture of media dating from the late 1800s to the present; 300 pieces; art by Southern California artists (past & present) living in the west (Andrew Molles Collection); Works on paper; Andrew Molles Collection
Exhibitions: Rotating exhibits
Publications: Artifacts, monthly
Activities: Classes for adults & children; docent training; internships; lects open to pub, 6 vis lectrs per yr; gallery talks; demonstrations; special events; sponsoring of competitions with prizes; tours; concerts; scholarships & fels offered; individual paintings & original objects of art lent; mus shop sells original art & books

L **Library,** 3425 Mission Inn Ave, Riverside, CA 92501-3368. Tel 909-684-7111; Fax 909-684-7332; Internet Home Page Address: www.riversideartmuseum.org; *Dir* MJ Abraham; *Admin Dir* Kathy Smith; *Finance Mgr* Nichole Pingree; *Adult Educ Cur* Lee Tusman
Open Mon - Fri 10 AM - 4 PM; Admis $5 for non-mems, students $2; Open for reference upon request; Average Annual Attendance: 50,000; Mem: 1,200
Income: Financed by grants & donations
Library Holdings: Book Volumes 600; Exhibition Catalogs; Framed Reproductions; Pamphlets; Periodical Subscriptions 15; Photographs; Reproductions
Activities: Classes for adults & children, docent training; lects open to public; 2-4 vis lectrs per yr; concerts; gallery talks; tours; schol; lending of original objects of art to local business partnerships; mus sales shop sells books, original art, reproductions, & prints

M **RIVERSIDE METROPOLITAN MUSEUM,** (Riverside Municipal Museum) 3580 Mission Inn Ave, Riverside, CA 92501. Tel 951-826-5273; Fax 951-369-4970; Elec Mail dbrennan@riversideca.gov; Internet Home Page Address: www.riversideca.gov/museum; *Dir Mus* Ennette Morton; *Educ Cur* Teresa Woodard; *Cur Coll & Exhib* Brenda Focht
Open Tues-Wed & Fri 9 AM -5 PM, Thurs 9 AM- 9PM, Sat 10 AM - 5 PM, Sun 11 AM - 5 PM, cl Mon & major holidays; No admis fee, suggested donation $5; Estab 1924 to collect, preserve & display local & California prehistory, natural history & local history; Permanent galleries on local geology, paleontology, Indians, history & animals; Mem: 750; dues individual $20, family $30
Special Subjects: Architecture, Photography, American Indian Art, Anthropology, Archaeology, Ethnology, Pre-Columbian Art, Southwestern Art, Textiles, Folk Art, Primitive art, Eskimo Art, Dolls, Furniture, Carpets & Rugs
Collections: History photo archive; Indian art; Native American Basketry; historic house, 1891 Heritage House; photo & document archives; Citrus Label Art; Citrus Paraphernalia
Activities: Classes for children; docent training; lects open to members only, 6-10 vis lectrs per yr; tours; original objects of art lent to other pub mus & art galleries; nature lab; multicultural festival; mus shop sells books, original art, reproductions & prints

M **UNIVERSITY OF CALIFORNIA,** Sweeney Art Gallery, Watkins House, Riverside, CA 92521-0001. Tel 951-827-3755; Elec Mail karen.rapp@ucr.edu; Internet Home Page Address: sweeney.ucr.edu; *Dir* Karen Rapp; *Gallery Mgr* Jennifer Frias
Open Tues - Sat 11 AM - 4 PM; No admis fee; Estab 1963, gallery presents major temporary exhibitions; Gallery contains 2,000 sq ft; Average Annual Attendance: 5,000; Mem: dues patron $1,000 & up, supporting $500, contributor $100, family $45, individual $30, student $15
Income: $100,000 (financed by mem & state appropriation)
Purchases: $30,000 (print collection)
Collections: Works on paper-portfolios of prints, sculpture
Exhibitions: Main Gallery: Bas Jan Ader Retrospective
Publications: Exhibition catalogs
Activities: Lects open to pub, 2-3 vis lectrs per yr; book traveling exhibs 1-2 per yr; sales shop sells catalogs & posters

M **California Museum of Photography,** 3824 Main St, Riverside, CA 92501-3624. Tel 951-827-4787; Fax 951-827-4797; Elec Mail cmppress@ucr.edu; Internet Home Page Address: www.ucr.edu; *Dir* Colin Westerbeck; *Cur Exhibs* Ciara Ennis; *Cur Digital Media* Georg Burwick; *Cur Educ* Reggie Woolery; *Gift Shop Admin* Cynthia Cardenas
Open Tues - Sat 12 - 5 PM, first Sun of month, Oct - May 1 - 5 PM, first Thurs of month 6 - 9 PM; Admis $3, students & seniors free; Estab 1973 to preserve, protect & exhibit photography; Mus has five exhibition galleries which display changing exhibitions related to historical & contemporary photography & emerging technologies; Average Annual Attendance: 20,000; 3.5 million to website; Mem: 1,200; dues $35
Income: $800,000 (financed by university funds, grants, private donations & mem)
Library Holdings: Auction Catalogs; Audio Tapes; Book Volumes; CD-ROMs; Exhibition Catalogs; Lantern Slides; Manuscripts; Memorabilia; Original Art Works; Periodical Subscriptions; Photographs; Prints; Slides
Special Subjects: Architecture, Drawings, Photography
Collections: Bingham camera & apparatus; Keystone-Mast stereo negatives & prints; photographs of the 19th & 20th centuries; Ansel Adams/Fiat Lux; Will Connell Collection
Publications: American Photography by Jonathan Green; Che Guevarra: Revolution & Icon by Trisha Ziff
Activities: Classes for adults & children; lects open to pub, 2 vis lectrs per yr; gallery talks; tours; competitions with awards; film series; symposia; original objects of art lent to other art institutions; lending collection contains 400,000 photographs; book traveling exhibs 3 per yr; originate traveling exhibs; mus shop sells books, prints & misc items

L **Tomas Rivera Library,** PO Box 5900, Riverside, CA 92517-5900. Tel 951-827-3220; Fax 951-827-2255; Elec Mail rivcirc@ucr.edu; Internet Home Page Address: library.ucr.edu; *Art Selector* Krista Ivy; *Univ Librn* Steven Mandeville-Gamble, PhD
Open Mon - Thurs 7:30 AM - 11 PM, Fri 7:30 AM - 6 PM, Sun 1 - 11 PM; Open to faculty, students & staff
Library Holdings: Audio Tapes; Book Volumes 38,000; Cards; Cassettes; DVDs; Exhibition Catalogs; Fiche; Filmstrips; Manuscripts; Motion Pictures; Original Art Works; Original Documents; Other Holdings; Periodical Subscriptions 172; Photographs; Records; Reels; Slides; Video Tapes

Special Subjects: Art History, Decorative Arts, Film, Mixed Media, Photography, Painting-American, Painting-British, Painting-French, Painting-German, Painting-Italian, Pre-Columbian Art, Sculpture, Painting-European, History of Art & Archaeology, Conceptual Art, Asian Art, Video, Painting-Scandinavian, Architecture

ROHNERT PARK

M **SONOMA STATE UNIVERSITY,** University Art Gallery, 1801 E Cotati Ave, Rohnert Park, CA 94928-3609. Tel 707-664-2295; Fax 707-664-2054; Elec Mail art.gallery@sonoma.edu; Internet Home Page Address: www.sonoma.edu/artgallery/; *Dir* Michael Schwager; *Exhib Coordr* Carla Stone
Open Tues - Fri 11 AM - 4 PM, Sat & Sun Noon - 4 PM, cl summer; No admis fee; Estab 1978 to provide exhibitions of contemporary art to the university & Northern California community; 2500 sq ft of exhibition space designed to house monumental sculpture & painting; Average Annual Attendance: 5,000
Income: financed through University & private funds
Special Subjects: Drawings, Etchings & Engravings, Ceramics, Collages, American Western Art, Photography, Prints, Sculpture, Painting-American, Portraits, Oriental Art, Cartoons
Collections: Asian Collection of Prints; Garfield Collection of Oriental Art; Asnis Collection
Publications: Bulletins and announcements of exhibitions; exhibition catalog
Activities: Docent training; educ-outreach prog; 5-10 vis lectrs per yr; gallery talks; tours; annual benefit auction; book traveling exhibs 1-2 per yr; originate traveling exhibs to national art mus; sales shop sells books, T-shirts & posters

ROSS

A **MARIN SOCIETY OF ARTISTS INC,** 30 Sir Francis Drake Blvd, Ross, CA 94957; PO Box 203, Ross, CA 94957-0203. Tel 415-454-9561; Fax 415-457-5414; Elec Mail emailus@marinsocietyofartists.com; Internet Home Page Address: www.marinsocietyofartists.org; *Office Mgr, Dir* Jo Smith; *Pres* Marcia Higgins; *VPres* Jane Listor
Open Mon - Thurs 11 AM - 4 PM; Sat & Sun Noon - 4 PM, cl Fri; No admis fee; Estab 1929 to foster cooperation among artists & to continually develop pub interest in art; Circ Small library for mem only; Gallery is located in a garden setting. It is approx 3500 sq ft of well lighted exhibit space; Average Annual Attendance: 75,000; Mem: 300; dues $70; qualifications for signature mem: Previous exhibition in a juried show & must reside in Bay Area if active; meetings Mar - Oct
Income: Financed by mem, sale & rental of art, & annual auction
Exhibitions: One show per month; annual art auction in June
Publications: Monthly newsletter
Activities: Classes for mem only, children & the blind; lect open to public, 2-3 vis lectrs per year; competitions with cash awards; sales shop sells original art, original prints, handcrafted jewelry ceramics & fiberworks

SACRAMENTO

M **CALIFORNIA STATE PARKS,** State Indian Museum, 2618 K St, Sacramento, CA 95816-5104. Tel 916-324-0971; Elec Mail cmcgovgh@parks.ca.gov; Internet Home Page Address: www.parks.ca.gov/indianmuseum; *Museum Cur* Ileana Maestas; *Dir* Connie McGough
Open daily 10 AM - 5 PM, cl New Years, Thanksgiving & Christmas; Admis adults $3, children 16 & under $2; Estab 1940
Special Subjects: American Indian Art, Anthropology
Collections: Artifacts Collection from California Native Americans (basketry, hunting & fishing implements, regalia, musical instruments & photographs); Contemporary Native American Art
Exhibitions: Indian Arts & Crafts Holiday Fair; Spring Indian Arts & Crafts Market; Acorn Day; Native American Day; Honored Elders Day
Activities: Docent training; tours; competitions with awards; mus shop sells nature made jewelry, arts & crafts

M **CALIFORNIA STATE UNIVERSITY, SACRAMENTO,** Library - Central Reference Dept, Sacramento, CA. Tel 916-278-6218; Fax 916-278-7089; Internet Home Page Address: www.lib.csus.edu; *Slide Librn, Arts Librn* Alicia Snee
Open Mon - Thurs 7:45 AM - 11 PM, Fri 7:45 AM - 5 PM, Sat 10 AM - 6 PM, Sun 1 - 9 PM (during school year), summer sessions vary during week; Estab 1947
Income: Financed through the University
Library Holdings: Audio Tapes; Cards; Cassettes; Clipping Files; Exhibition Catalogs; Fiche; Filmstrips; Pamphlets; Periodical Subscriptions 250; Reels; Reproductions; Slides
Publications: Women Artists: A Selected Bibliography; bibliographic handouts

M **The University Union Gallery,** University Union at Sac State, 6000 J St Sacramento, CA 95817-6017. Tel 916-278-2871; Fax 916-278-1750; Elec Mail uniongallery@csus.edu; Internet Home Page Address: www.union.csus.edu; *Design, Identity & Studio Mgr* Rebecca Voorhees
Open Mon - Fri 10:30 AM - 3:30 PM, Wed & Thurs 5 - 8 PM, during school year, summer hours vary; No admis fee; Estab 1975 to expose students to a variety of visual arts & techniques; The University Union Gallery is located on the second floor of the University Union. It has 85 running ft of display space. Gallery run by students; Average Annual Attendance: 8,250
Income: Student fees & commissions
Purchases: Works purchased for permanent collection annually from artists with a relationship, past or present, with the University
Collections: Various prints, photographs, paintings by students; sculpture by Yoshio Taylor; Tsuki; painting by Jack Ogden: American Grove; Bronze original by John Battenberg J G Sheds His Wolf's Clothing
Exhibitions: Annual student competition, other various exhibits encompassing a variety of media & subjects
Activities: Lect open to public, 1-2 vis lectrs per year; gallery talks; competitions

M **CROCKER ART MUSEUM,** 216 O St, Sacramento, CA 95814-5324. Tel 916-808-7000; Fax 916-808-7372; Elec Mail crocker@crockerartmuseum.org; Internet Home Page Address: www.crockerartmuseum.org; *Mus Dir* Lial A Jones; *Chief Cur & Assoc Dir* Scott Shields; *Mus Store Mgr* Donna Natsoulas; *Educ Dir* Stacy Shelnut-Hendrick; *Dir Advancement* Kerry Wood
Open Tues - Wed & Fri - Sun 10 AM - 5 PM, Thurs 10 AM - 9 PM; cl Mon (except Holiday Mon), New Year's Day, Thanksgiving Day & Christmas Day; Admis adults $10, seniors & col students $8, students $5, discounts to AAM members, members, children 6 & under free; Estab 1873; municipal art mus since 1885; original gallery building designed by Seth Babson completed in 1873; Crocker Mansion Wing opened in 1989; Teel Family Pavilion opened in 2010; Average Annual Attendance: 250,493; Mem: 12,000; annual meeting in June
Income: $750,000 (financed by Crocker Art Mus Assoc & city appropriation)
Library Holdings: Auction Catalogs; Book Volumes; CD-ROMs; Cassettes; Clipping Files; DVDs; Exhibition Catalogs; Manuscripts; Maps; Original Documents; Other Holdings Painting: India, Mogul, Iranian, Chinese; Pamphlets; Periodical Subscriptions; Photographs; Records; Slides; Video Tapes
Special Subjects: Afro-American Art, American Indian Art, Anthropology, Decorative Arts, Drawings, Etchings & Engravings, Folk Art, Illustration, Interior Design, Landscape Architecture, Landscapes, Marine Painting, Architecture, Art History, Ceramics, Conceptual Art, Glass, Metalwork, Mexican Art, Mixed Media, Antiquities-Assyrian, Furniture, Gold, Photography, Porcelain, Portraits, Pottery, Painting-American, Silver, Textiles, Painting-British, Painting-European, Painting-French, Painting-Japanese, Graphics, Painting-American, Photography, Prints, Sculpture, Watercolors, American Western Art, Bronzes, African Art, Southwestern Art, Costumes, Religious Art, Crafts, Folk Art, Primitive art, Woodcuts, Etchings & Engravings, Decorative Arts, Manuscripts, Painting-European, Posters, Jewelry, Oriental Art, Asian Art, Painting-Dutch, Painting-French, Carpets & Rugs, Maps, Coins & Medals, Restorations, Baroque Art, Calligraphy, Miniatures, Painting-Flemish, Embroidery, Painting-Spanish, Painting-Italian, Islamic Art, Antiquities-Egyptian, Antiquities-Greek, Antiquities-Roman, Cartoons, Painting-German, Reproductions, Antiquities-Etruscan, Painting-Russian, Painting-Scandinavian, Bookplates & Bindings
Collections: 19th century California painting; American decorative arts; contemporary California painting, sculpture & crafts; prints & photographs; European decorative arts; European painting 1500 - 1900; Old Master drawings; Oriental art; African Art Oceanic Art, International Ceramics
Publications: Art Letter, 4 times per year
Activities: Classes for adults & children; seminars for adults; children's progs; docent training, dramatic progs; lects for mems only; 12 vis lectrs per yr; concerts; tours; annual juried competitions; gallery talks; awards: Real Estate Project of the Year (2011) Sacramento Business Journal, Visionary Icon in Building Excellence (2011) Sacramento Downtown Partnership; individual paintings & original objects of art lent to other mus; Art travels to K-8 schools in seven surrounding counties; art ark; book traveling exhibs; originate traveling exhibs; mus shop sells books, mags, original art, cards, reproductions, prints & miscellaneous gifts

L **Research Library,** 216 O St, Sacramento, CA 95814-5324. Tel 916-264-8856; Fax 916-264-7372; Internet Home Page Address: www.crockerartmuseum.org; *Dir Educ* Stacey Shelnot-Hendrick
Open Thurs 1-5PM, Sat by appt; Open for reference only to public, staff, docent, interns and others upon application
Library Holdings: Book Volumes 2000; Exhibition Catalogs; Fiche; Other Holdings Dissertations; Periodical Subscriptions 30
Activities: Classes for adults & children; dramatic progs; docent training; lects open to pub, some open to members only, vis lectrs; concerts; artmobile; individual paintings lent

M **LA RAZA-GALERIA POSADA,** 2700 Front St, Sacramento, CA 95818. Tel 916-446-5133; Fax 916-446-1324; Elec Mail larazagaleria@gmail.com; Internet Home Page Address: www.lrgp.org; *Dir* Marie Acosta
Open Wed-Sat 1-9PM, Sun 1-5PM; Estab 1972 as a Chicano art & culture center; 2,000 sq ft gallery; Average Annual Attendance: 30,000; Mem: 1,000; dues $15-$150
Special Subjects: Mexican Art, Hispanic Art, Jewelry
Collections: Permanent Coll
Activities: Classes for adults & children; lect open to public; gallery talks; tours

SAINT HELENA

M **NAPOLEONIC SOCIETY OF AMERICA,** Museum & Library, 3360 Saint Helena Hwy N, Saint Helena, CA 94574-9660. Tel 727-586-1779; Fax 727-581-2578; Elec Mail marengo@aol.com; Internet Home Page Address: www.napoleonsociety.org; *Treas* Barbara Chambers; *Pres* Robert Snibbe
Open 9 AM - 5 PM; No admis fee; Estab 1983; Circ 1,500 worldwide; Mem: 1000; dues $48; annual meeting in Sept
Income: $309,199 (financed by mem)
Library Holdings: Book Volumes
Special Subjects: Porcelain, Prints, Bronzes, Painting-French, Historical Material, Miniatures
Publications: Member's Bulletin, quarterly
Activities: Lect open to public; gallery talks; fellowships; sales shop sells magazines, original art, reproductions, prints

M **R L S SILVERADO MUSEUM,** 1490 Library Lane, Saint Helena, CA 94574-0409. Tel 707-963-3757; Fax 707-963-0917; Elec Mail rlsnhs@calicom.net; Internet Home Page Address: www.silveradomuseum.org; *Dir* Edmond Reynolds; *Assoc Dir* Ann Kindred; *Cur* Dorothy Mackay-Collins
Open Wed-Sun noon-4PM; No admis fee; Estab 1968; the mus is devoted to the life & works of Robert Louis Stevenson, who spent a brief but important time in the area; the object is to acquaint people with his life & works & familiarize them with his stay; The mus has five wall cases & three large standing cases, as well as numerous bookcases; Average Annual Attendance: 5,500
Income: Financed by the Vailima Foundation, set up by Mr & Mrs Norman H Strouse

Special Subjects: Drawings, Photography, Watercolors, Etchings & Engravings, Manuscripts, Portraits, Furniture, Historical Material
Collections: Robert Louis Stevenson Collection: material relating to Stevenson & his immediate circle
Exhibitions: A different exhibition devoted to some phase of Stevenson's work is mounted every three months
Activities: Dramatic progs; docent training; lects open to pub 4 per yr; tours; sales desk sells books

L **Reference Library,** 1490 Library Lane Saint Helena, CA 94574; PO Box 23 Saint Helena, CA 94574-0023. Tel 707-963-3757; Fax 707-963-8131; Elec Mail rlsnhs@netwiz.net; Internet Home Page Address: stevensonmuseum.org; *Dir/Archivist* Dorothy Mackay-Collins; *Dir & Cur* Marissa Schleicher; *Office Mgr* Stacey P Stern; *Office Mgr* Allison Fox
Open Tues - Sat Noon - 4 PM; No admis fee; donations accepted; Estab 1970; For reference only; Average Annual Attendance: 1,000
Income: Financed by Vailima Foundation
Purchases: Archival materials; acquisitions relating to Robert Louis Stevenson
Library Holdings: Audio Tapes; Book Volumes 3000; CD-ROMs; Cassettes; DVDs; Kodachrome Transparencies 300; Manuscripts; Memorabilia; Motion Pictures; Original Art Works; Original Documents; Photographs; Sculpture; Video Tapes
Special Subjects: Photography, Drawings, Manuscripts, Painting-American, Painting-British, Prints, Sculpture, Watercolors, American Western Art, Furniture, Silver
Collections: First editions, variant editions, fine press editions of Robert Louis Stevenson, letters, manuscripts, photographs, sculptures, paintings and memorabilia
Exhibitions: Exhibits of 4 months duration 3 times a year
Publications: The Silverado Squatters; Prayers Written at Vailima; all books by Robert Louis Stevenson; biographies on RLS
Activities: Educ prog; Docent training; trunk show (taken to elder care facilities); lectures open to pub; 3 vis lectrs per yr; tours; mus shop sells books, CDs

SALINAS

M **HARTNELL COLLEGE GALLERY,** 156 Homestead Ave, Salinas, CA 93901. Tel 831-755-6700, 755-6791; Fax 831-759-6052; Elec Mail gsmith@hartnell.cc.ca.us; *Dir* Gary T Smith
Open Mon 10 AM - 1 PM & 7 - 9 PM, Tues - Thurs 10 AM - 1 PM, cl Fri - Sun; No admis fee; Estab 1959 to bring to students & the community contemporary & historical works of all media; Main gallery is 40 x 60 ft, south gallery is 15 x 30 ft, brick flooring; Average Annual Attendance: 7,500
Collections: Approx 45 works on paper from the San Francisco Bay Area WPA; FSA photographs; Mrs Virginia Bacher Haichol Artifact Collection; Mrs Leslie Fenton Netsuke Collection
Exhibitions: Edward Weston; Claes Oldenburg; Edward Curtis; Oriental Porcelain from the Albert & Pat Scheopf Collection; Charles Russell & Frederick Remington; Russian Lacquer Boxes; Selections from the Hartnell Farm Security Admin Photography Collection; Christo: Wrapped Coast
Activities: Classes for adults; gallery management training; individual paintings & original objects of art lent to qualified institutions, professional galleries or museums; lending collection contains original art works; book traveling exhibs; originates traveling exhibs

SAN BERNARDINO

M **CALIFORNIA STATE UNIVERSITY, SAN BERNARDINO,** 5500 University Pkwy, San Bernardino, CA 92407-2397. Tel 909-880-5823, 880-7373 (Fullerton Mus); Fax 909-880-7068; Elec Mail artmuseum@csub.edu; Internet Home Page Address: www.museum.csusb.edu; *Dir Gallery* Eva Kirsch; *Chmn Art Dept* Joe Moran
Open Tues -Wed & Fri-Sat 10AM-5PM, Thurs 10AM-7PM; No admis fee; Estab 1990s for the purpose of providing high quality exhibitions on varied subjects suitable for both campus & community; Gallery expanded into museum; Average Annual Attendance: 13,000
Income: Financed by mem, city & state appropriations
Collections: Egyptian Antiquities; African Collection; Asian Ceramics
Publications: Catalogs; pamphlets
Activities: Classes for adults; summer workshop for children; lects open to pub, 1-3 vis lectrs per yr; gallery talks; tours; competitions

A **SAN BERNARDINO ART ASSOCIATION, INC,** Sturges Fine Arts Center, 780 North E St San Bernardino, CA 92413; PO Box 3574, San Bernardino, CA 92413-3574. Tel 909-885-2816; *Treas* Harvey Tobias; *VPres, Acting Pres* Yolanda Voce; *Second VPres* Ferne Schmidt; *Recording Secy* Doro Johnson
Open Tues & Thurs 11 AM - 3 PM; No admis fee; Estab 1932 as a nonprofit organization to generate interest in art for all ages; Open to the public; maintains gallery of paintings & ceramics by local artists; Mem: 75; dues $20; meetings on first of each month
Exhibitions: Bimonthly exhibits
Publications: Newsletter
Activities: Classes for adults; artist presentations; lect open to public, 8 vis lectrs per year; gallery talks; competitions with awards; scholarships; individual paintings & original objects of art lent; sales shop sells original art, ceramics & photographs

SAN DIEGO

A **BALBOA ART CONSERVATION CENTER,** 1649 El Prado, San Diego, CA 92101-1662; PO Box 3755, San Diego, CA 92163-1755. Tel 619-236-9702; Fax 619-236-0141; Elec Mail info@bacc.org; Internet Home Page Address: www.bacc.org; *Dir & Chief Paper Conservator* Janet Ruggles; *Chief Paintings Conservator* Elizabeth Court; *Field Serv Officer* Beverly N Perkins; *Field Serv Project Mgr* Josephine Ihrke
Open Mon - Fri 9 AM - 4:30 PM; No admis fee; Estab 1975 for research & educ in art conservation; services in exams, treatment & consultation in art

conservation; Mem: 18; nonprofit institutions are members, their members may contract for services; annual meeting in May
Income: $300,000 (financed by services performed)
Collections: Illustrative photographs, memorabilia, tools, equipment of profession; paintings for experimental & didactic purposes
Activities: Educ prog; regional workshop series on care of collections; lect open to public & some for members only; gallery talks; tours

L **Richard D Buck Memorial Library,** PO Box 3755, Balboa Park San Diego, CA 92163-1755. Tel 619-236-9702; Fax 619-236-0141; *Gen Mgr* Janet Ruggles
Library not open to pub
Income: Financed by Mellon Grant
Library Holdings: Book Volumes 700; Cassettes; Clipping Files; Exhibition Catalogs; Memorabilia; Pamphlets; Periodical Subscriptions 35; Photographs; Reels; Slides

M **CENTRO CULTURAL DE LA RAZA,** 2125 Park Blvd, San Diego, CA 92101-4753. Tel 619-235-6135; Fax 619-595-0034; Elec Mail centro@centroculturaldelaraza.org; Internet Home Page Address: www.centroculturaldelaraza.org; *Bd Pres* Howard Hollman; *Board VPres* Marco Anguilo; *Bd Pres* Laurie Burgett
Open Tues-Sun noon-4PM; No admis fee, donations requested; Estab 1970 to create, promote & preserve Mexican, Indian & Chicano art & culture; 2500 sq ft of gallery space with five sections & 8 X 15 ft walls; Average Annual Attendance: 65,000; Mem: 500; dues $10-$1000
Income: $150,000 (financed by mem, city & state appropriation, sales & services, private grants, National Endowment for the Arts)
Purchases: $1500
Collections: Historical artifacts of Mexican & Indian culture; contemporary artwork by Chicano artists
Exhibitions: Native American Contemporary Photography; solo exhibitions of local & regional artist; group shows; invitational group exhibitions
Publications: Exhibit catalogues, 3 per year; literary publications, 2 per year
Activities: Classes for adults & children; lects open to pub, 5-7 vis lectrs per yr; exten dept; lending collection includes 15 pieces of original art & prints; book traveling exhibs 1-2 per yr; originate traveling exhibs that circulate to other galleries & cultural centers; sales shop sells books, magazines, original art, reproductions, prints

A **INSTALLATION GALLERY,** 964 5th Ave, Ste 234, San Diego, CA 92101. Tel 619-544-1482; Fax 619-544-1486; Elec Mail gen@insite97.org, mkjaer@insite2000.org; Internet Home Page Address: www.insite05.org; *Exec Dir* Michael Krichman; *Assoc Dir* Danielle Reo
No admis fee; Estab 1980
Publications: Exhibit guides & catalogs
Activities: Classes for adults & children; docent training; lect open to public, 3 vis lectrs per year; tours

M **MARITIME MUSEUM OF SAN DIEGO,** (San Diego Maritime Museum) 1492 N Harbor Dr, San Diego, CA 92101-3309. Tel 619-234-9153; Fax 619-234-8345; Elec Mail info@sdmaritime.org; Internet Home Page Address: www.sdmaritime.com; *Develop Dir* Chris Berggren; *Pres & CEO* Raymond Ashley; *Librn* Kevin Schechan
Open daily 9 AM - 8 PM; Admis adults $14, active military & seniors $11, children 6 - 17 $8, children 5 & under free, discount to adult groups; Estab 1948 for preservation & educ of San Diego related maritime history; Maritime Mus in a fleet of 7 ships: Star of India (1863 bark), Berkeley (1898 ferryboat), Medea (1904 steam Yacht), HMS Surprise, American Submarine, Soviet Submarine; Californian; Average Annual Attendance: 180,000; Mem: 2400; dues Captain $5000, Captain's Table $1000 - $4000, First Mate $500 - $900, Boatswain $150 - $499, Crew $65, Mariner/ Individual $40, Apprentice/ Student & Navigator/ Senior $35
Library Holdings: Audio Tapes; Book Volumes; Cassettes; Clipping Files; Kodachrome Transparencies; Original Art Works; Original Documents; Other Holdings; Periodical Subscriptions; Photographs; Prints; Records
Special Subjects: Marine Painting
Collections: Antiques; maritime art; maritime artifacts; clothing; navigation instruments; antique ships
Exhibitions: Festival of Sail, annual Labor Day Weekend exhib; Tall Ships
Publications: Mains'l Haul, quarterly historical journal; Books: Euterpe, MEDEA The Classic Stream Yacht, Star of India, They Came by Sea, Transpac 1900-1979
Activities: Educ dept; classes for adults & children; docent training; lects for members & guests, 3 vis lectrs per yr; tours; special progs; competitions for children with awards; book traveling exhibs, 2 per yr; mus store sells books, magazines, original art, reproductions, prints, slides & related maritime items, including video tapes

M **MINGEI INTERNATIONAL, INC,** Mingei International Museum - Balboa Park & Mingei International Museum - Escondido, 1439 El Prado, San Diego, CA 92101-1617. Tel 619-239-0003; Fax 619-239-0605; Elec Mail mingei@mingei.org; Internet Home Page Address: www.mingei.org; *Dir* Rob Sidner; *Registrar* Terri Bryson; *Coll Gallery Mgr* Amy Schindler; *Dir Develop* Cathy Sang; *Dir Pub Rels* Martha Ehringer; *Chmn* Frances Hamilton White; *Treas* Robert K Wolford; *Dir Educ* Alison Rossi; *Dir Mktg & Planning* Charlotte Cagan; *Chief Financial Officer* Alan Strang; *Adv to Dir Curatorial Affairs* Rochelle Kessler
Open Tues-Sun 10AM-4PM; Admis adults $7, seniors, students with ID and children 6-17 $5, discounts to groups; Estab 1978 to further the understanding of arts of the people from all parts of the world; 41,000 sq ft mus, architecturally designed space, white interior, hardwood floors, track lighting. Maintains reference library; Average Annual Attendance: 110,000; Mem: 2300; dues $35-$5000; annual meeting in May
Income: Financed by mem, endowment, city appropriation, grants & contributions
Library Holdings: Auction Catalogs; Audio Tapes; Book Volumes; Clipping Files; Exhibition Catalogs; Original Art Works; Pamphlets; Periodical Subscriptions; Sculpture; Slides; Video Tapes
Special Subjects: Drawings, Hispanic Art, American Indian Art, Bronzes, African Art, Costumes, Ceramics, Crafts, Folk Art, Afro-American Art, Decorative Arts,

Eskimo Art, Dolls, Furniture, Glass, Jade, Jewelry, Asian Art, Carpets & Rugs, Ivory, Calligraphy, Embroidery, Islamic Art, Enamels
Collections: Traditional & Contemporary Folk Art, Craft & Design (in all media including textiles, ceramics, metals, woods, stone, paper, bamboo & straw); African, American, Ethiopian, East Indian, Indonesian, Japanese, Pakistani, Himalayan & Mexican Folk Art
Publications: Exhibition related publications
Activities: Docent training; lects open to pub, 10 vis lectrs per yr; films; gallery talks; tours; concerts; book traveling exhibs 1 per yr; originate traveling exhibs 1 per yr; mus shop sells books, magazines, original art

L **Reference Library,** 1439 El Prado, San Diego, CA 92101-1617. Tel 619-239-0003; Fax 619-239-0605; Elec Mail mingei@mingei.org
Open Tues - Sun 10 AM - 4 PM, cl Mon & major holidays
Income: Financed by endowments, city appropriation, contributions, grants
Library Holdings: Audio Tapes; Cassettes; Clipping Files; Exhibition Catalogs; Filmstrips; Framed Reproductions; Kodachrome Transparencies; Lantern Slides; Manuscripts; Memorabilia; Motion Pictures; Photographs; Slides; Video Tapes

M **MUSEUM OF CONTEMPORARY ART SAN DIEGO,** (Museum of Contemporary Art San Diego, Downtown) 1001 and 1100 Kettner Blvd, San Diego, CA 92101; 700 Prospect St., La Jolla, CA 92037. Tel 858-454-3541; Fax 858-454-6985; Elec Mail info@mcasd.org; Internet Home Page Address: www.mcasd.org; *Communs Assoc* Claire Caraska; *David C Copley Dir* Dr Hugh M Davies; *Deputy Dir* Charles Castle; *Chief Cur* Kathryn Kanjo; *Chief Advancement Officer* Jeanna Yoo; *Sr Mktg & Commun Mgr* Rebecca Handelsman
Open at LaJolla & Downtown locations: Thurs - Tues 11 AM - 5 PM, 3rd Thurs 11 AM - 7 PM; Admis $10 general, $5 military & seniors, free ages 25 & under; admis good 7 days at all MCASD locations; Estab 1941
Special Subjects: Drawings, Painting-American, Photography, Prints, Sculpture
Collections: More than 4,000 works created after 1950 representing all media & genres
Exhibitions: See web site
Publications: Catalogues & gallery guides for exhibitions; Quarterly newsletter
Activities: Classes for adults & children; gallery guide training; lects open to pub; artist talks; film series; TNT (Thurs Night Thing); tours; mus shop sells books

M **MUSEUM OF PHOTOGRAPHIC ARTS,** Edmund L. and Nancy K Dubois Library, 1649 El Prado, San Diego, CA 92101-1662. Tel 619-238-7559; Fax 619-238-8777; Elec Mail info@mopa.org; Internet Home Page Address: www.mopa.org; *Registrar* Tom Callas; *Exec Dir* Deborah Klochko; *Dir Opers* John Hogan; *Dir Exhibs and Design* Scott Davis; *Curatorial Asst* Chantel Paul
Open Tues - Sun 10 AM - 5 PM, cl Mon, New Year's Day, Martin Luther King Day, Thanksgiving Day, Dec 4 & 5, Christmas Day; Admis adults $8, seniors, retired military & dependents with ID $6, students with ID, $5, active military & dependants with ID, children under 12, & mems free; Estab 1983 to collect & exhibit photographic works of art; 3,500 sq ft; Average Annual Attendance: 75,000; Mem: 1500; dues $50 - $5,000
Income: $850,000 (financed by city, state, & federal appropriation, endowments, mem, grants & corporations)
Purchases: $20,000
Library Holdings: Book Volumes photography related; Exhibition Catalogs; Periodical Subscriptions
Special Subjects: Photography
Collections: Photographic collection includes examples from earliest to most recent photographs
Publications: Points of Entry
Activities: Classes for adults & children; docent training; educator workshop; summer workshops with guest artists; lects open to pub, 10-12 vis lectrs per yr; gallery talks; tours, concerts; Lou Stouman prize for photography; Century Award for Lifetime Achievement; book traveling exhibs 2 per yr; originate traveling exhibs; mus shop sells books, magazines, prints & photography related gifts

M **SAN DIEGO MUSEUM OF ART,** 1450 El Prado, Balboa Park San Diego, CA 92101-1618; PO Box 122107, San Diego, CA 92112-2107. Tel 619-232-7931; Fax 619-232-9367; Elec Mail information@sdmart.org; Internet Home Page Address: www.sdmart.org; *Dir* Rosana Velasquez; *Deputy Dir Fin & Opers* Julianne Markow; *Deputy Dir, Cur Affairs & Educ* Julia Marciari Alexander; *Deputy Dir External Affairs* Katy McDonald; *Assoc Dir Exhibs & Colls* Scot Jaffe; *Proj Cur* Amy Galpin; *Cur European Art & Head Provenance Research* John Marciari, PhD; *Cur Asian Art* Sonya Quintanilla, PhD
Open Tues - Sat 10 AM - 5 PM, Summer Thurs until 9 PM, Sun Noon - 5 PM, cl Mon, New Years Day, Thanksgiving, Christmas & special hours select days, call for more info; Admis adults $12, military & seniors 65+ $9, students w/ID $8, youth 7-17 $4.50, mems & children 6 & under free; family & group rates available; Estab 1925. Gallery built in 1926 by a generous patron in a Spanish Plateresque design; the West wing was added in 1966 & the East wing in 1974; Maintains multiple galleries, studio, classroom, offices, John M & Sally B Thornton Rotunda, May S Marcy Sculpture Garden & James S Copely Auditorium; Average Annual Attendance: 500,000; Mem: 33,200; dues benefactor $10,000 dir circle $5000, president's circle $1250, sponsor $600, assoc $300, friend of museum $125, general $55, senior $45, student $25
Income: Financed by investment income, contributions, admis, city & county appropriations & sales
Purchases: $300,000
Special Subjects: Painting-American, Prints, Sculpture, Decorative Arts, Painting-European, Furniture, Oriental Art, Silver, Painting-British, Painting-Dutch, Baroque Art, Painting-Flemish, Renaissance Art, Painting-Spanish, Painting-Italian
Collections: Renaissance & Baroque paintings; with strong holdings in Spanish; 19th & 20th century American & European sculpture & paintings; Asian arts - sculpture, paintings, ceramics, decorative arts; American furniture & glass, English silver; Spanish Baroque, Flemish, Dutch & English schools; African, Oceanic & Native American Artworks Coll; Southern Asian & Persian Art Galleries
Exhibitions: Exhibits of pieces from the permanent collections rotating during the yr
Publications: Biennial Reports port; catalogs of collections; exhibition catalogs; membership calendar, monthly; gallery guide
Activities: Classes for adults & children; family activities; teacher resources; docent training; lects open to public; concerts; gallery talks; audio tours; subject tours; ASL tours; performances; films; competitions; originate traveling exhibs; sales shops sell books, reproductions, prints, cards, jewelry & ceramics

L **Art Reference Library & Archives,** 1450 El Prado, Balboa Park San Diego, CA 92101-1618; PO Box 122107, San Diego, CA 92112-2107. Tel 619-696-1959; Elec Mail library@sdmart.org; Internet Home Page Address: www.sdmart.org; *Library Mgr* Dr James Grebl
Open to mems, qualified scholars & grad students by appt; Estab 1926 for curatorial research; Circ Non-circulating; Partnered with the San Diego Public Library. (for reference only)
Library Holdings: Auction Catalogs 18,000; Audio Tapes; Book Volumes 30,000; Cassettes; Clipping Files; Exhibition Catalogs; Manuscripts; Memorabilia; Original Art Works; Original Documents; Other Holdings Bound Periodicals: 15,000 vols, 540 titles; Pamphlets; Periodical Subscriptions 45; Photographs; Slides 15,000; Video Tapes
Special Subjects: Art History, Photography, Islamic Art, Painting-American, Painting-Italian, Painting-Japanese, Painting-Spanish, Prints, Sculpture, Painting-European, Watercolors, Latin American Art, Asian Art, Oriental Art, Religious Art
Collections: Bibliography of artists in exhibition catalogues; 30,000+ Artist Files; Online Databases; Papers from Bridges & Putnam families, Earle Grant, Pliny Munger, Dr Clarence & Mrs Ellis Spreckels Moore, Mr & Mrs Irving Snyder, & 1st mus dir Reginald Poland; Artist papers, letters & photographs incl: Robert Henri, Donal Hord, William Templeton Johnson, Alice Klauber, Alfred Mitchell, Walter Pach, Arthur Putnam, Roland Schneider, Florence Kemmler Schneider & Fritz Werner; Schneider-Kemmler Coll incl: 990 slide glass photographs & 300 autochromes c 1910's - 1930's; Scrapbook containing 200 images of China circa 1920 & 2 dozen rare panoramic photographs; 100 glass negatives of Arthur Putnam's bronze sculptures

L **SAN DIEGO PUBLIC LIBRARY,** Art, Music & Recreation, 820 E St, San Diego, CA 92101-6478. Tel 619-236-5810, press 1; 236-5800 (Reference); Fax 619-236-5811; Elec Mail Artmusic@sandiego.gov; Internet Home Page Address: www.sandiego.gov/public-library/; *Music Librn* Victor Cardell; *Fine Art* Stephen Wheeler; *Supv Librn* Jacqueline Adams; *Visual Arts Librn* Mark-Elliott Lugo
Open Mon & Wed Noon - 8 PM, Tues, Thurs & Fri 9:30 AM - 5:30 PM, Sun 1 - 5 PM, cl Sat; No admis fee; Estab 1977 to exhib mus quality art in libraries of San Diego; Two gallery spaces: smaller gallery for student & classroom work; larger gallery is for invited guests; Average Annual Attendance: 8,000
Income: Financed by city and state appropriation
Purchases: $32,000
Library Holdings: Auction Catalogs; Audio Tapes; Book Volumes 100,000; CD-ROMs; Clipping Files; Compact Disks; DVDs; Exhibition Catalogs; Original Art Works; Other Holdings Postcards 10,000; Periodical Subscriptions 200; Records 11,000; Video Tapes
Collections: Former libraries of William Templeton Johnson, architect & Donal Hord, sculptor; emphasis is on Spanish, Mediterranean, Italian & French Renaissance architecture & Oriental art, sculpture & ceramics; books on the theatre including biographies of famous actors and actresses as well as histories of the American, London and European stages, gift of Elwyn B Gould, local theatre devotee; William Goe: chess collection

M **SAN DIEGO STATE UNIVERSITY,** University Art Gallery, 5500 Campanile Dr, San Diego, CA 92182-0001. Tel 619-594-5171; Fax 619-594-1217; Elec Mail artgallery@sdsu.edu; Internet Home Page Address: www.artgallery.sdsu.edu; *Gallery Dir* Tina Yapelli; *Dir* Ida K Rigby
Open Mon - Thurs & Sat Noon - 4 PM, cl Fri & Sun, cl summer May 16 - mid-Sept; No admis fee; Estab 1977 to provide exhibitions of importance for the students, faculty & pub of the San Diego environment; for study & appreciation of art & enrichment of the University; 1 large gallery; Average Annual Attendance: 35,000; Mem: 270; dues $35
Income: Supported by student fees, SDSU Art Council & grants
Special Subjects: Painting-American, Sculpture, Crafts
Exhibitions: Contemporary national & international artists; 4 rotating exhibitions per year
Publications: Exhibit catalogs
Activities: Lects open to public, 4 vis lectrs per yr; gallery talks; book traveling exhibs 1 per yr; originate traveling exhibs; sales shop sells books & exhib catalogs

M **TIMKEN MUSEUM OF ART,** 1500 El Prado, San Diego, CA 92101-1620; 2550 5th Ave Ste 500, San Diego, CA 92103-6624. Tel 619-239-5548; Fax 619-531-9640; Elec Mail info@timkenmuseum.org; Internet Home Page Address: www.timkenmuseum.org; *Deputy Dir* Carrie Cottriall; *Dir Educ* Kristina Rosenberg; *Admin* James Peterson; *Exec Dir* John Wilson; *Controller* Denise Lamas; *Deputy Dir Develop & Endowments* Laurie Hawkins
Open Tues - Sat 10 AM - 4:30 PM, Sun 1:30 - 4:30 PM, cl Mon; No admis fee; Estab to display & preserve European Old Masters, 18th & 19th centuries American paintings & Russian icons; Six galleries; Average Annual Attendance: 165,000; Mem: 205 mem, dues vary
Income: financed by endowment & fund raising
Special Subjects: Decorative Arts, Landscapes, Marine Painting, Bronzes, Painting-European, Sculpture, Tapestries, Painting-American, Religious Art, Portraits, Painting-Dutch, Painting-French, Baroque Art, Painting-Flemish, Painting-Spanish, Painting-Italian, Painting-Russian
Collections: Dutch & Flemish, French, Spanish & American Italian paintings; Russian icons; all paintings owned by Putnam Collection are on permanent display
Publications: Gallery Guides; Exhibition Catalogues
Activities: docent training; storytelling; Lect; vis lectrs 5 per yr; gallery talks; tours available by request; books traveling exhibs 2 per yr

M **UNIVERSITY OF SAN DIEGO,** Founders' Gallery, 5998 Alcala Park, San Diego, CA 92110-2492. Tel 619-260-4600, 260-2280; Fax 619-260-6875; Internet Home Page Address: www.acusd.edu; *Dir* Dr Sally Yard
Open Mon - Fri Noon - 4 PM; No admis fee; Estab 1971 to enrich the goals of the Fine Arts department & university by providing in-house exhibitions of all eras, forms & media & to share them with the community; Gallery has foyer, display area and patio, parking in central campus; Average Annual Attendance: 1,500

Income: Financed by Fine Arts department & private endowment
Special Subjects: Sculpture, Textiles, Furniture, Asian Art, Tapestries
Collections: 17th, 18th & 19th century French tapestries & furniture; South Asian textiles & costumes of 19th & 20th centuries; Tibetan & Indian looms, Gandhi spinning wheels; 19th-century French bronze sculpture; 20th-century paintings
Exhibitions: Seven shows each year
Publications: The Impressionist as Printmaker; Child Hassam 1859-1935; Arbol de la Vida, The Ceramic Art of Metepec
Activities: Educ dept; seminars in art history; lects open to public, 4 vis lectrs per yr; concerts; gallery talks; tours; awards; originate traveling exhibs

SAN FRANCISCO

L **ACADEMY OF ART,** University Library, 180 New Montgomery St, Fl 6 San Francisco, CA 94105; 79 New Montgomery St, San Francisco, CA 94105. Tel 415-618-3842; Fax 415-618-3981; Elec Mail library@academyart.edu; Internet Home Page Address: library.academyart.edu; *Dir* Debra Sampson; *Asst Dir* Hope Johnson; *Visual Resources Librn* Heather Cummins; *Systems & Online Resources Librn* Holly Gatto
Open Mon - Thurs 8 AM - 10 PM, Fri 8 AM - 8 PM, Sat - Sun 12 PM - 6 PM; No admis fee; Estab 1929
Library Holdings: Book Volumes 40,000; CD-ROMs; Clipping Files; DVDs; Exhibition Catalogs; Motion Pictures; Other Holdings Indexed image files; Periodical Subscriptions 300; Slides 100,000; Video Tapes
Special Subjects: Illustration, Photography, Graphic Design, Sculpture, Advertising Design, Fashion Arts, Industrial Design, Interior Design

A **ARCHIVES OF MOCA (MUSEUM OF CONCEPTUAL ART),** Society of Independent Artists, 657 Howard St, San Francisco, CA 94105-3915. Tel 415-495-3193; Fax 415-495-3193; Elec Mail tmarioni@earthlink.net; Internet Home Page Address: tommarioni.com; *Dir* Tom Marioni; *Mgr Soc Independent Artists* Edward Stanton
Open by appointment; No admis fee; Estab 1970 for research, study & organization of exhibitions & events; Average Annual Attendance: 2,000
Income: Financed by endowment
Library Holdings: Audio Tapes; Cassettes; DVDs; Exhibition Catalogs; Kodachrome Transparencies; Manuscripts; Original Art Works; Original Documents; Photographs; Prints; Sculpture; Slides; Video Tapes
Collections: Glass bottles
Exhibitions: Vito Acconci; Robert Barry; Bar Room Video; Chris Burden; Lowell Darling; Howard Fried; Paul Kos; Masashi Matsumoto; Restoration of Back Wall; Miniatures from San Francisco & Kyoto; Social Art, Cafe Society; Graduate Bartenders 2000-
Publications: Vision, 1975-1982
Activities: Docent training; lects for mems only, 6 vis lectrs per yr; concerts; awards - NEA grants; original traveling exhibs

L **Library,** 657 Howard St, San Francisco, CA 94105-3915. Tel 415-495-3193; Fax 415-495-3193; *Dir* Tom Marioni
For reference only
Library Holdings: Audio Tapes; Book Volumes 1200; Cassettes; Exhibition Catalogs; Filmstrips; Kodachrome Transparencies; Motion Pictures; Original Art Works; Other Holdings Original documents; Pamphlets; Photographs; Prints; Records; Reels; Sculpture; Slides; Video Tapes
Special Subjects: Calligraphy, Drawings, Etchings & Engravings, Sculpture, Period Rooms, Religious Art, Woodcuts
Exhibitions: Inspired by Leonardo

M **ASIAN ART MUSEUM OF SAN FRANCISCO,** Chong-Moon Lee Ctr for Asian Art and Culture, 200 Larkin St, San Francisco, CA 94102-4734. Tel 415-581-3500; Fax 415-581-4700; Elec Mail pr@asianart.org; Internet Home Page Address: www.asianart.org; *Dir Educ* Deb Clearwaters; *Cur Chinese Art* Michael Knight; *Conservator* Katherine Holbrow; *Cur Korean Art* Hyonjeong Kim Han; *Librn* John Stucky; *Dir* Jay Xu; *Chief Cur* Forrest McGill; *Pub Rels Mgr* Tim Hallman
Open Tues - Sun 10 AM - 5 PM, Thurs (Jan-Oct) 10 AM - 9 PM, (Nov-Dec) 10 AM - 5 PM, cl Mon, maj holidays & during certain civic ctr events; Admis adults 18-64 $12, seniors $8, youth 13-17 $7, children under 12, mus mems, recognized educational groups & first Wed of each month free; Founded in 1969 by the City & County of San Francisco to collect, care for, exhibit & interpret the fine arts of Asia; 40,000 sq ft of exhibition space; Average Annual Attendance: 425,000; Mem: 40,000; dues $50
Income: Financed by city & county appropriation & the Asian Art Mus Foundation
Library Holdings: Auction Catalogs; Audio Tapes; Book Volumes; CD-ROMs; Cassettes; Clipping Files; Compact Disks; Exhibition Catalogs; Fiche; Filmstrips; Manuscripts; Maps; Original Documents; Other Holdings; Pamphlets; Periodical Subscriptions; Photographs; Video Tapes
Special Subjects: Architecture, Sculpture, Bronzes, Textiles, Religious Art, Ceramics, Pottery, Woodcarvings, Decorative Arts, Painting-Japanese, Portraits, Jade, Jewelry, Porcelain, Oriental Art, Asian Art, Metalwork, Carpets & Rugs, Ivory, Calligraphy, Embroidery, Antiquities-Oriental, Antiquities-Persian, Islamic Art
Collections: Nearly 17,000 objects from China, Japan, Korea, India, Southeast Asia, The Himalayas & Middle East; Roy C Leventritt Collection
Publications: Exhibition catalogs; handbooks & catalogs on museum collections
Activities: Classes for adults & children; docent training; storytelling; school tours; lects open to pub, 6 vis lectrs per yr; concerts; gallery talks; tours; original objects of art lent to other mus for exhibs; book traveling exhibs, 1-2 per yr; originate traveling exhibs to other mus; mus shop sells books, magazines, original art, reproductions & slides

L **C Laan Chun Library,** 200 Larkin St, San Francisco, CA 94102. Tel 415-581-3500; Fax 415-861-2388, 864-6705; Elec Mail jstucky@asianart.org; Internet Home Page Address: www.asianart.org; *Librn* John Carl Stucky
Open Mon - Fri 9:30 AM - 4:30 PM by appointment only; No fee for library patrons; Estab 1967; Circ Non-circulating; For reference only; Average Annual Attendance: 250-300
Income: Financed by city appropriation & private gifts
Library Holdings: Auction Catalogs; Audio Tapes; Book Volumes 40,000; CD-ROMs; Cassettes; Clipping Files; Exhibition Catalogs; Fiche; Filmstrips; Kodachrome Transparencies; Lantern Slides; Manuscripts; Memorabilia; Motion Pictures; Other Holdings Subject Index; Pamphlets; Periodical Subscriptions 230; Photographs; Prints; Reels; Reproductions; Slides; Video Tapes
Special Subjects: Art History, Folk Art, Landscape Architecture, Decorative Arts, Calligraphy, Drawings, Islamic Art, Painting-Japanese, Prints, Sculpture, Historical Material, History of Art & Archaeology, Watercolors, Ceramics, Archaeology, Bronzes, Printmaking, Asian Art, Porcelain, Furniture, Ivory, Jade, Glass, Metalwork, Antiquities-Oriental, Antiquities-Persian, Carpets & Rugs, Dolls, Embroidery, Enamels, Gold, Goldsmithing, Handicrafts, Jewelry, Leather, Miniatures, Oriental Art, Pottery, Religious Art, Restoration & Conservation, Silver, Silversmithing, Tapestries, Textiles, Woodcarvings, Woodcuts, Architecture
Collections: Documentary photograph colls of Chinese paintings & Khmer archaeological sites; exhibition catalogs; extensive subject index; Special colls of antique and rare books; a comprehensive research collection on Asian culture & cultural history
Activities: Classes for adults & children; dramatic programs; docent training; lects open to pub, lects for mems only; concerts; gallery talks; tours; mus sales shop sells books, magazines, original art, & reproductions

A **BAY AREA VIDEO COALITION, INC,** 2727 Mariposa St, Fl 2 San Francisco, CA 94110-1472. Tel 415-861-3282; Fax 415-861-4316; Elec Mail bavc@bavc.org; Internet Home Page Address: www.bavc.org; *Exec Dir* Ken Ikeda; *Dir Fin* Robert Pascual; *Dir Devel* Carol Varney; *Dir Next Gen Progs* Moriah Ulinskas; *Dir Pub Media Initiatives* Jennifer Gilomen; *Dir Tech* Daniel Teixeira-Gomes; *Dir Training & Resources* Mindy Aronoff
Open Mon-Thurs 9AM-8PM, Fri 9AM-6PM, Sat & Sun 10AM-6PM; Estab 1976; Gallery features video & new media technology, education & exhibitions
Publications: Mediamaker Handbook, annually
Activities: Classes for adults; cert progs; youth progs; lect open to public, 450 vis lectrs per yr; competitions with awards

C **BOSTON PROPERTIES LLC,** (Embarcadero Center Ltd) 4 Embarcadero Ctr, Lobby Level, San Francisco, CA 94111. Tel 415-772-0700; Fax 415-772-0554; *Retail PM & Dir Mktg* Norman E Dito; *Mktg Coordr* Helen Han; *Exec Dir* Ken Ikeda
Open to public at all hours; Estab 1971; Collection displayed throughout the Center complex; Center supports San Francisco DeYoung Museum, Fine Arts Museum Downtown Center, American Conservatory Theatre, San Francisco Symphony, San Francisco Center for the Performing Arts, and others
Collections: Willi Gutmann, Two Columns with Wedge; Nicholas Schoffer, Chronos XIV; Olga de Amaral, Columbia; Anne Van Kleeck, Blocks, Stacks; Louise Nevelson, Sky Tree; Jean Dubuffet, La Chiffonniere; John Portman Jr, The Tulip; Elbert Weinberg, Mistral; Charles O Perry, Eclipse; Armand Vaillancourt, 101 precast aggregate concrete boxes that allow visitors to walk over, under & through its waterfalls; Arnaldo Pomodoro, Colonna; Fritz Koenig, Untitled Bronze; Dimitri Hadzi, Creazione; Jules Guerin, Traders of the Adriatic; Arman, Hermes and Dyonisis; Arman, The University of Wisdom; Stephen DeStaebler, Torso with Arm Raised I; Bill Barrett, Baile Merengue; Zhengfu Lu, Rhythm of the Metropolis

M **CALIFORNIA COLLEGE OF THE ARTS,** CCAC Wattis Institute for Contemporary Arts, 360 Kansas St, San Francisco, CA 94103; 1111 8th St, San Francisco, CA 94107. Tel 415-355-9670; Fax 415-355-9676; Elec Mail wattis@cca.edu; Internet Home Page Address: www.wattis.org; *Dir* Anthony Huberman; *Asst Dir* Micki Meng; *Progs Coordr* Rita Souther; *Chief Preparator* Justin Limoges; *Designer* Jon Sueda; *Dir Communications* Brenda Tucker; *Managing Ed* Lindsey Westbrook
Open Tues - Fri noon - 7 PM, Sat noon - 5 PM; No admis fee; Estab 1998; serves as a forum for the presentation & discussion of international contemporary art & curatorial practice; Newly renovated building contains galleries & event space; Average Annual Attendance: 20,000; Mem: 2500
Income: Financed by grants & tuition
Exhibitions: Rotating exhibits every 6-8 weeks
Publications: catalogs & limited editions
Activities: lects open to public, 20 vis lectrs per year; gallery talks; tours; screenings; organize traveling exhibs; mus shop sells books, prints

M **THE CALIFORNIA HISTORICAL SOCIETY,** (Old Mill Foundation) 678 Mission St, San Francisco, CA 94105-4014. Tel 415-357-1848; Fax 415-357-1850; Elec Mail info@calhist.org; Internet Home Page Address: www.californiahistoricalsociety.org; *Exec Dir* David Crosson; *Dir Educ & Pub Progs* Lisa Eriksen; *Dir Fin* Pam Garcia; *Vis Svcs Mgr* Sy Russell; *Develop Assoc* Kathy Jacobson
Galleries open Wed - Sat Noon - 4:30 PM, cl holidays; Admin open Mon - Fri 9 AM - 5 PM, cl holidays; Admis adult $3, seniors $ students $1, mems & children under 6 free; Founded 1871, permanently estab 1922 to inspire & empower Californians to make the past a meaningful part of their lives; Mem: 4,500; dues $15-$250
Income: Financed by mem dues & contributions
Special Subjects: Drawings, Graphics, Watercolors, Furniture
Collections: Fine arts include California lithography & other graphics; furniture & artifacts to 1915; research materials both original & published on California & Western artists
Publications: California History, quarterly magazine
Activities: Classes for adults; docent training; progs; tours & films throughout the state; lects open to pub; concerts; gallery talks; tours; awards given for participation in the field of California history; exten prog serves Autry Museum, Los Angeles & Old Mill Gallery, San Marino; originates traveling exhibs

L **North Baker Research Library,** 678 Mission St, San Francisco, CA 94105-4014. Tel 415-357-1848; Fax 415-357-1850; Elec Mail info@calhist.org; Internet Home Page Address: www.californiahistoricalsociety.org; *Dir* David Crosson; *Library Dir* Mary Morganti
Open Gallery: Wed - Sat noon - 4:30 PM; Library: Wed - Fri noon - 5 PM; Admis adults $3, seniors & students $1, mems & children under 6 free; Estab 1871 to

collect books, manuscripts, photographs, ephemera, maps and posters pertaining to California and Western history; Mem: 5,000 mem; dues starting at $60
Income: Private, non-profit
Library Holdings: Audio Tapes; Book Volumes 60,000; Cassettes; Clipping Files; Exhibition Catalogs; Fiche; Framed Reproductions; Kodachrome Transparencies; Lantern Slides; Manuscripts; Maps; Memorabilia; Original Art Works; Original Documents; Other Holdings 3-D artifacts; Pamphlets; Periodical Subscriptions 100; Photographs 500,000; Prints; Reels; Reproductions; Slides
Special Subjects: Illustration, Photography, Calligraphy, Drawings, Etchings & Engravings, Graphic Arts, Graphic Design, Manuscripts, Posters, Prints, Historical Material, Watercolors, American Western Art, Printmaking, Advertising Design, Cartoons, Lettering, Bookplates & Bindings, Woodcuts, Landscapes, Architecture, Portraits
Collections: Crocker Collections; Florence Keen Collection of Western Literature; Kemble Collection of Western Printing & Publishing
Publications: California History, quarterly; CHS Press Titles
Activities: Symposiums, website; lects open to pub, 12-15 lectrs per yr; tours; lending of original objects of art

M **CAPP STREET PROJECT,** Wattis Institute, 1111 Eighth St, San Francisco, CA 94107-2247. Tel 415-551-9210; Fax 415-551-9209; Elec Mail wattis@cca.edu; Internet Home Page Address: www.wattis.org/cappstreet; *Dir* Jens Hoffman; *Deputy Dir* Claire Fitzsimmons; *Chief Preparator* Brian Barreto; *Progs Coordr* Micki Meng; *Dir Pub Rels* Brenda Tucker
Open Tues & Fri noon - 8 PM, Sat 10 AM - 6 PM, cl Sun & Mon; Estab 1983 as a nonprofit arts organization providing three month residencies in San Francisco for installation art; Average Annual Attendance: 20,000
Collections: Installation Art; Public Art
Publications: Capp Street Project Catalog, biennially
Activities: Lects open to pub, 8-10 vis lectrs per yr; tours; originate traveling exhibs; mus store sells limited editions, merchandise

M **CARTOON ART MUSEUM,** 655 Mission St, San Francisco, CA 94105-4126. Tel 415-227-8666, ext 300; Fax 415-243-8666; Elec Mail office@cartoonart.org; Internet Home Page Address: www.cartoonart.org; *Exec Dir* Rod Gilchrist; *Chmn* Malcolm Whyte; *Admin Coordr* Summerlea Koshar; *Gallery Mgr* Andrew Farago
Open Tues - Sun 11 AM - 5 PM, cl New Year's Day, Easter, Independence Day, Thanksgiving, Christmas Eve & Day; Admis adults $6, student & seniors $4, children 6-12 $2; Estab 1984 to preserve exhibit & study original cartoon art; 3000 sq ft exhibition space; Average Annual Attendance: 20,000; Mem: 500; dues individual $35
Library Holdings: Audio Tapes; Book Volumes; Clipping Files; Exhibition Catalogs; Video Tapes
Special Subjects: Drawings, Hispanic Art, Latin American Art, Painting-American, Photography, Prints, Watercolors, American Western Art, Folk Art, Etchings & Engravings, Afro-American Art, Manuscripts, Painting-European, Portraits, Posters, Painting-Canadian, Painting-French, Historical Material, Juvenile Art, Cartoons, Reproductions
Collections: 11,000 pieces of original cartoon art
Exhibitions: Rotating exhibits
Publications: Cartoon Times
Activities: Classes for adults & children; lects open to pub, 4 vis lectrs per yr; gallery talks; tours; cartoon contests for children kindergarten through 12th grade with gift cert; individual paintings & original objects of art lent to other mus, galleries & corporations; lending collection contains color reproductions, original art works, original prints & paintings; retail store sells books, prints, magazines, gift items

M **CHINESE CULTURE FOUNDATION,** Center Gallery, 750 Kearny St, 3rd Flr, San Francisco, CA 94108. Tel 415-986-1822; Fax 415-986-2825; Elec Mail info@c-c-c.org; Internet Home Page Address: www.c-c-c.org; *Pres* Russell Leong; *Exec Dir* Albert Chang
Open Tues - Sat 10 AM - 4 PM, cl holidays; No admis fee; Estab 1965 to promote the understanding & appreciation of Chinese & Chinese-American culture in the United States; Traditional & contemporary paintings, sculpture by Chinese & Chinese American artists, photographs & artifacts illustrating Chinese-American history & major international & cultural exchanges from China, Taiwan & Southeast Asia make the center a local & national focus of Chinese artistic activities; Average Annual Attendance: 60,000; Mem: 1,000; dues family $50, regular $35
Income: Financed by mem, city appropriation, grants & rental fees from auditorium
Special Subjects: Photography, Prints, Sculpture, Watercolors, Textiles, Folk Art, Woodcarvings, Decorative Arts, Jewelry, Oriental Art, Asian Art, Calligraphy
Collections: Painting: Chinese Genealogy
Exhibitions: In Search of Roots; Through Dust & Ruins: Photography by Tsung Woo Han; Urban Yearnings: Portraits of Contemporary China by Liu Qinghe, Su Xinping & Zhang Yajie
Publications: Chinese Culture Center Newsletter, quarterly; Exhibition catalogs
Activities: Classes for adults & children; dramatic progs; docent training; daily walking tour of Chinatown for school children & tourists; lects open to pub, 10 vis lectrs per yr; concerts; tours; film progs; mus shop sells books, original art, reproductions, prints, jewelry, pottery, jade, material & papercuts

A **EXPLORATORIUM,** Pier 15, San Francisco, CA 94111. Tel 415-528-4444; Elec Mail pubinfo@exploratorium.edu; Internet Home Page Address: www.exploratorium.edu; *Exec Dir* Dennis Bartels; *Mktg Communs Dir* Sabrina Smith
Open Tues - Sun 10 AM - 5 PM, cl Mon except for MLK Day, Presidents Day, Memorial Day & Labor Day; Admis adults $25, seniors $20, 6-18 $20; Estab 1969 to provide exhibits & art works centering around the theme of perception, which are designed to be manipulated & appreciated at a variety of levels by both children & adults; Average Annual Attendance: 1,100,000; Mem: 25,000; dues $50 & up
Income: Financed by national, city & state grants, private foundations, corporation contributions & earned income
Library Holdings: Motion Pictures
Collections: Over 650 exhibits incl Life Sciences, Bay Observation, Time & Motion, Seeing & Listening, Electricity & Magnatism, Creative Experimentation, Human Phenomena
Publications: The Exploratorium, bimonthly calendar; books, quarterly
Activities: Classes for adults & children; artists in residence prog, performing artists in residence prog & teachers training using artists & scientists in collaboration; docent training; lects open to pub; concerts; gallery talks; tours; fels; Webley Award for www.exploratorium.edu; originate traveling exhibs; mus shop sells books, magazines, reproductions, prints, slides & science related material

A **EYES & EARS FOUNDATION,** 870 Market St, Ste 1260 San Francisco, CA 94102-2917. Tel 415-621-2300; Fax 415-981-3334; Internet Home Page Address: www.eyesears.org; *Pres* Freddie Hahne; *Exec Dir* Mark Rennie
Open by appointment & available funds; No admis fee; Estab 1976 to sponsor pub visual performance art projects, mostly outdoor large-scale billboard art shows & the theatre projects; Average Annual Attendance: 175,000 per day; Mem: 100; dues $15
Income: $57,000 (financed by endowment, mem, fundraising, individual & corporate contributions)

M **FINE ARTS MUSEUMS OF SAN FRANCISCO,** M H de Young Museum, 50 Hagiwara Tea Garden Dr, Golden Gate Park San Francisco, CA 94118-4502. Tel 415-750-3600; Elec Mail contact@famsf.org; Internet Home Page Address: http://deyoung.famsf.org; *Dir* John E Buchanan Jr; *Pres Bd Trustees (V)* Dede Wilsey; *Assoc Dir* Robert Futernick; *Admin Asst to Dir* Lauren Ito; *CFO* Nicholas Elsishans; *Dir Mktg & Commun* Susannah Stringam; *Deputy Dir Develop* Martha Brigham; *Cur Prints & Drawings, Achenbach Foundation for Graphic Arts* Karin Breuer; *Ednah Root Cur American Arts* Timothy Anglin Burgard; *Cur Africa, Oceania & American* Kathleen Berrin; *Cur European Art* Dr Lynn Federle Orr; *Cur Ancient Art & Interpretation* Renee Dreyfus; *Advertising & Promotion* Gina Yrrizarry; *Dir Educ* Sheila Pressley; *Mus Shop Mgr* Stuart Hata; *Media Rels* Jill Lynch; *Webmaster* Andrew Fox; *Publications* Ann Heath Karlstrom; *European Decorative Arts & Sculpture* Martin Chapman
Open Tues - Sun 9:30 AM - 5:15 PM, Fri 9:30 AM - 8:45 PM, cl Mon, Thanksgiving, Christmas & New Years Days; Admis adults $10, seniors $7, youths 13-17 & college students with ID $6, mems, children 12 & under & 1st Tues of each month free; admis to de Young Mus incl same-day admis to Legion of Honor; Estab 1971 as a mem organization for Fine Arts Museum of San Francisco & the Asian Art Mus of San Francisco & the Asian Art Mus of San Francisco; Mem: 110,000 households; dues family/dual $125
Income: $2,770,000 (financed by mem & bookshop revenues)
Collections: American Paintings; American Decorative Art; African Art; Art of the Americas; Oceanic Art; Textile Arts
Publications: Triptych, bimonthly magazine
Activities: Educ prog Cultural Encounters on Fri nights; artist installations & demos; audio & docent-led tours; mus shop sells books, reproductions, prints & slides

M **Legion of Honor,** 100 34th Ave, Lincoln Park San Francisco, CA 94121-1677. Tel 415-750-3600, 863-3330 (public information); Elec Mail contact@famsf.org; Internet Home Page Address: http://legionofhonor.famsf.org/; *Dir* John E Buchanan Jr; *Pres Bd Trustees (V)* Dede Wilsey; *Assoc Dir* Robert Futernick; *Admin Asst to Dir* Lauren Ito; *CFO* Nicholas Elsishans; *Dir Mktg & Commun* Susannah Stingam; *Deputy Dir Develop* Martha Brigham; *Cur Prints & Drawings, Achenbach Foundation for Graphic Arts* Karin Breuer; *Ednah Root Cur American Arts* Timothy Anglin Burgard; *Cur Africa, Oceania & American* Kathleen Berrin; *Cur European Art* Dr Lynn Federle Orr; *Cur Ancient Art & Interpretation* Renee Dreyfus; *Advertising & Promotion* Gina Yrrizarry; *Dir Educ* Sheila Pressley; *Mus Shop Mgr* Stuart Hata; *Media Rels* Jill Lynch; *Webmaster* Andrew Fox; *Publications* Ann Heath Karlstrom; *European Decorative Arts & Sculpture* Martin Chapman
Open Tues - Sun 9:30AM-5:15PM, cl Mon, Thanksgiving, Christmas & New Years Days; Admis adults $10, seniors $7, youths 13-17 & students with ID $6, mems, children 12 & under & 1st Tues of month free; admis to Legion of Honor incl same-day admis to de Young Mus; Estab 1895 to provide museums of historic art from ancient Egypt to the 20th century; Two separate buildings are maintained one in the Golden Gate Part (de Young Mus) with 35 galleries & the other in Lincoln Park (California Palace of the Legion of Honor) with 22 galleries; Average Annual Attendance: 800,000; Mem: 50,000; dues patron $1000 sponsor $500, donor $250, contributing $125, family $70, participating $60
Income: Financed by pub-private partnership, city owned buildings
Special Subjects: Textiles, Drawings, Graphics, American Indian Art, Bronzes, African Art, Costumes, Ceramics, Crafts, Etchings & Engravings, Afro-American Art, Decorative Arts, Eskimo Art, Furniture, Glass, Antiquities-Byzantine, Carpets & Rugs, Ivory, Embroidery, Laces, Antiquities-Egyptian, Antiquities-Greek, Antiquities-Roman, Antiquities-Etruscan, Enamels, Antiquities-Assyrian
Collections: Rodin sculpture collection; Art from Central & South America & Mesoamerica; primitive arts of Africa, Oceania & the Americas
Activities: Classes for adults & children; docent training; lect open to public; concerts; gallery talks; tours; mus shop sells books, magazines, reproductions, prints & jewelry

L **Library,** 50 Hagiwara Tea Garden Dr, Golden Gate Park San Francisco, CA 94118-4502. Tel 415-750-7603
Open Mon - Fri by appt; Estab 1955 to serve mus staff in research on collections, conservation, acquisition, interpretations; Circ Non-circulating; Holdings on antiquities, European art & graphic arts housed at Legion of Honor; holdings on American art, African art, art of Oceana & Americas, textiles, periodicals, microform colls & exhib archival records housed at de Young Museum
Income: Financed by mem, city appropriation, donations
Library Holdings: Auction Catalogs; Book Volumes 50,000; Clipping Files; Exhibition Catalogs; Fiche; Periodical Subscriptions 125; Reels 8,000
Special Subjects: Decorative Arts, Photography, Graphic Arts, Painting-American, Pre-Columbian Art, Sculpture, Painting-European, Textiles
Collections: Microform: Smithsonian Institution's Archives of American Art; 19th c. periodicals; 18th - 20th c. auction catalogs; Original records: Exhib History Archive of the Fine Arts Mus of San Francisco

M **GALERIA DE LA RAZA,** Studio 24, 2857 24th St, San Francisco, CA 94110-4234. Tel 415-826-8009; Elec Mail info@galeriadelaraza.org; Internet Home Page Address: www.galeriadelaraza.org; *Dir* Carolina Ponce de Leon; *Assoc Cur* Raquel de Anda; *Opers Mgr* Audra Ponce
Open Tues 1 - 7 PM, Wed - Sat Noon - 6 PM ; No admis fee, donations accepted; Estab 1969 as a community gallery & mus to exhibit works by Chicano-Latino artists, contemporary as well as cultural folk art; Galeria Studio 24's mission is to foster public awareness and appreciation of Chicano/Latino art and serve as a laboratory where artists can explore contemporary issues in art, culture and civic society, while advancing intercultural dialogue. Galeria's artistic programs include visual arts exhibitions, the Digital Mural Program, the ReGeneration Project and our monthly Lunada series. Galeria also sponsors the Youth Media Project (YMP) an experiential youth arts education and mentorship program; Average Annual Attendance: 42,000; Mem: 300; dues $35
Income: Financed by California Arts Council, NEA, San Francisco Arts Commission, Grants for Arts, Miranda Lux Foundation, San Francisco Foundation, Walter & Elise Haas Foundation, van Loben Sels/RembeRock Foundation, Zellerbach Family Fund, Adobe/Silicon Valley Community Foundation, Anonymous Donor & Galeria Mems
Library Holdings: Cards; Exhibition Catalogs; Framed Reproductions; Memorabilia; Original Art Works; Original Documents; Photographs; Prints; Slides
Special Subjects: Folk Art
Collections: Chicano & Latino murals; Mexican & Latin American Folk art & contemporary art
Exhibitions: Changing monthly
Publications: Weekly email newsletters
Activities: Educ prog; classes for adults & children; lects open to pub, gallery talks; tours; Youth Media Lab-new media workshops & after school prog; musical events; LUNADAS: open mic & literary lounges; community events; mus shop sells books, original art, prints, cards, calendars & candles

A **INTERSECTION FOR THE ARTS,** 925 Mission St #109, San Francisco, CA 94103-2905. Tel 415-626-2787; Fax 415-626-1636; Internet Home Page Address: www.theintersection.org; *Dir* Deborah Cullinan; *Cur* Kevin B. Chen
Open Mon - Fri 10 AM - 5 PM; No admis fee; Estab 1965 to represent visual & performing arts; One gallery; Average Annual Attendance: 10,000
Income: Financed through foundation
Exhibitions: Rotating exhibitions, six per yr
Activities: Classes for adults & children; concerts; gallery talks; tours

A **JAPANTOWN ART & MEDIA WORKSHOP,** 1840 Sutter St, Ste 102, San Francisco, CA 94115. Tel 415-922-8700; Fax 415-922-8700; *Exec Dir* Dennis Taniguchi
Open daily 10 AM - 5 PM; No admis fee; Estab 1977 as an Asian-American art center; Mem: 120; dues $20
Income: $100,000 (financed by endowment, mem, foundations, city & state appropriations)
Special Subjects: Graphics, Posters, Asian Art, Painting-Japanese
Collections: Silkscreen posters & other art works
Exhibitions: Layer Exhibition; Asia-American Film & Video Exhibit
Publications: Enemy Alien; Yoisho
Activities: Classes for adults & children; graphic design intern progs; concerts; competitions with awards; lending collection contains posters

M **THE LAB,** 2948 16th St, San Francisco, CA 94103-3613. Tel 415-864-8855; Fax 415-864-8855; Elec Mail programs@thelab.org; Internet Home Page Address: www.thelab.org; *Assoc Dir* Kristen Chappa
Open Wed - Sat 1PM-6PM; No admis fee; Estab 1983 to support the develop & presentation of experimental & interdisciplinary art of emerging or mid-career artists
Income: $130,000 (financed by mem, city & state appropriations, federal funding & private foundations)
Exhibitions: Installations; Interdisciplinary & Experimental Art
Activities: Lect open to public; concerts; dance; performance art events; visual art exhibitions

L **MECHANICS' INSTITUTE,** 57 Post St, San Francisco, CA 94104-5003. Tel 415-393-0103; Elec Mail icohex@milibrary.org; Internet Home Page Address: www.milibrary.org; *Dir* Inez Shor-Cohen; *Reference Librn* Taryn Edwards; *Exec Dir* James Flack; *Board Pres* Jane Bryk
Open for members only Mon - Thurs 9 AM - 9 PM, Fri 9 AM - 6 PM, Sat 10 AM - 5 PM, Sun 1 - 5 PM; No admis fee; Estab 1854 to serve the needs of 7000 members with a general collection emphasizing the humanities, history, bus; Mem: dues $95
Income: Financed by city appropriation, building rents, endowment
Library Holdings: Audio Tapes; Book Volumes 200,000; CD-ROMs; Cassettes 1200; Clipping Files; Compact Disks; DVDs; Fiche 35; Maps; Other Holdings Newspapers 60; Periodical Subscriptions 475; Photographs; Video Tapes 1300
Special Subjects: Art History, Decorative Arts, Etchings & Engravings, Painting-American, Painting-British, Painting-French, Painting-German, Crafts, American Western Art, Fashion Arts, Furniture, Embroidery, Handicrafts, Painting-Australian, Architecture
Activities: classes for adults; lects open to pub; 30 vis lectrs per year

M **MEXICAN MUSEUM,** Fort Mason Center, Bldg D San Francisco, CA 94123. Tel 415-202-9700; Fax 415-441-7683; Elec Mail themexicanmuseum@gmail.com; Internet Home Page Address: www.mexicanmuseum.org; *CEO* Jonathan L Yorba
Open Wed - Sun Noon - 4 PM; No admis fee, suggested donation $2; Estab 1975 to foster the exhibition, conservation & dissemination of Mexican & Mexican-American & Chicano culture for all people; Average Annual Attendance: 60,000; Mem: 720, dues $25
Income: Financed by state grants, corporate & individual support, earned income through gift shop, mem, educational tours & work shops
Library Holdings: Book Volumes; Exhibition Catalogs; Manuscripts; Maps; Original Art Works; Original Documents; Photographs; Prints
Special Subjects: Drawings, Hispanic Art, Latin American Art, Mexican Art, Photography, Prints, Sculpture, American Western Art, Pre-Columbian Art,

Southwestern Art, Religious Art, Ceramics, Crafts, Folk Art, Pottery, Etchings & Engravings, Manuscripts, Portraits, Dolls, Jewelry, Embroidery, Pewter, Leather, Reproductions
Collections: Chicano, Colonial, Folk, Mexican, Mexican-American & Pre-Hispanic Fine Arts; Rare Books
Exhibitions: Highlights from the Permanent Coll
Publications: Exhibit catalogs
Activities: Classes for adults & children; docent training; dramatic progs; demonstrations & lectures; lects open to pub; gallery talks; tours; Website award by Web Marketing Assn 2002

M **MISSION CULTURAL CENTER FOR LATINO ARTS,** 2868 Mission St, San Francisco, CA 94110-3908. Tel 415-821-1155; Fax 415-648-0933; Elec Mail info@missionculturalcenter.org; Internet Home Page Address: www.missionculturalcenter.org; *Exec Dir* Jennie Rodriguez; *Gallery Coordr* Sheila Hernandez
Open Mon 5 - 9:45 PM, Tues - Fri 10 AM - 9:45 PM, Sat 10 AM - 5:30 PM; Admis fees for events & exhibs apply & vary; Estab 1977 to promote, preserve & develop the Latino cultural arts that reflect the living tradition & experiences of Chicano, Central & South American & Caribbean people; Houses a 142-seat theater; 2650 sq ft gallery exhibition space; spacious performing & visual art studios; state of the arts screen print facility; Average Annual Attendance: 5,000
Income: Financed by pub & pvt foundations, contributions & foundations
Collections: Latin America
Exhibitions: Rotating every month
Activities: Classes for adults & children in art, dance, music & self defense; workshops; internship progs; performances; festivals; films

M **MODERNISM,** 685 Market St, Ste 290 San Francisco, CA 94105. Tel 415-541-0461; Fax 415-541-0425; Elec Mail info@modernisminc.com; *Owner* Martin Muller
Open Tues-Sat 10AM-5:30PM
Collections: paintings; photographs; sculpture

M **MUSEO ITALO AMERICANO,** Fort Mason Center, Bldg C San Francisco, CA 94123-1324; Fort Mason Center, 2 Marina B lvd, Bldg C San Francisco, CA 94123. Tel 415-673-2200; Fax 415-673-2292; Elec Mail sfmuseo@sbcglobal.net; Internet Home Page Address: www.museoitaloamericano.org; *Mng Dir* Paula Bagnatori
Open Tues-Sun noon-4PM, Mon by appt; Admis free; Estab 1978 to research, preserve & display works of Italian & Italian-American artists & to foster educational programs for the appreciation of Italian & Italian-American art, history & culture; 3700 sq ft of exhibit space; The Fontana Gallery & The Lanzone Gallery; Average Annual Attendance: 25,000; Mem: 1034; dues $35-$1000
Income: Financed by mem, city appropriation, foundations & corporate contributions
Special Subjects: Historical Material, Photography, Sculpture, Watercolors, Landscapes, Painting-Italian
Collections: 20th Century paintings, sculptures, prints & photographs
Exhibitions: Rotating exhibits
Publications: Calendar of Events, monthly
Activities: Classes for adults & children; school outreach art prog; lects open to pub, concerts; awards; individual paintings & original objects of art lent to mus; mus shop sells books, magazines, original art, Italian pottery, blown glass & gift items
L **Library,** Fort Mason Center, Bldg C San Francisco, CA 94123-1324. Tel 415-673-2200; Fax 415-673-2292; Elec Mail museo@firstworld.net; Internet Home Page Address: www.museoitaloamericano.net; *Cur* Valentina Fogher
Open Wed - Sun Noon - 5 PM; Estab 1978 to serve as a resource center of Italian & Italian-American culture & art
Library Holdings: Book Volumes 300

NATIONAL ALLIANCE FOR MEDIA ARTS & CULTURE
For further information, see National and Regional Organizations

M **RANDALL JUNIOR MUSEUM,** 199 Museum Way, San Francisco, CA 94114-1499. Tel 415-554-9600; Fax 415-554-9609; Elec Mail info@randall.org; Internet Home Page Address: www.randallmuseum.org; *Exec Dir* Chris Boettcher
Open Tues - Sat 10 AM - 5 PM, cl holidays; No admis fee; Estab 1937 as part of the San Francisco Recreation & Park Dept; Gallery is located in 16-acre park overlooking city; Average Annual Attendance: 80,000; Mem: 300; dues $30-$500; annual meeting in June
Special Subjects: Drawings, Photography, Ceramics, Crafts, Jewelry
Collections: Animals; Children's Art; Indian Artifacts; Insects, Minerals; Fossils; Live animal exhibit
Exhibitions: Festival on the Hill; Bug Day; Water Day; crafts fair
Publications: Class flyer 5 times per year; Hands-On newsletter, quarterly
Activities: Classes for adults & children; dramatic progs; docent training; lects open to pub; concerts; tours; competitions with awards; scholarships offered

A **SAN FRANCISCO AFRICAN-AMERICAN HISTORICAL & CULTURAL SOCIETY,** 762 Fulton St, Fl 2, San Francisco, CA 94102-4119. Tel 415-292-6172; Fax 415-440-4231; Elec Mail info@sfaahcs.org; Internet Home Page Address: www.sfaahcs.org; *Exec Dir* W E Hoskins; *Pres* Al Williams; *Treasurer* Ellis Joseph
Special Subjects: Ethnology
L **Library,** 762 Fulton St, San Francisco, CA 94123. Tel 415-292-6172; Fax 415-441-2847; Elec Mail aahs@sfpl.lib.ca.us; Internet Home Page Address: www.sfblackhistory.org; *Pres* Alfred Williams; *Treas* Ellis Joseph; *Sec* Glenn Nance
Open Wed-Sat Noon-5 PM; No admis fee; 1955; For reference only & public library
Library Holdings: Audio Tapes; Book Volumes 5000; CD-ROMs; Framed Reproductions; Other Holdings Oral history; Photographs; Prints; Slides; Video Tapes
Collections: African-American newspapers; 1000 periodicals
Activities: Lects open to pub

M **SAN FRANCISCO ART INSTITUTE,** Galleries, 800 Chestnut St, San Francisco, CA 94133-2299. Tel 415-749-4563; Fax 415-351-3516; Elec Mail exhibitions@artists.sfai.edu; Internet Home Page Address: www.sfai.edu; *Dir Exhibs & Pub Progs* Hou Hanru; *Asst Cur* Mary Ellyn Johnson
Open Tues - Sat 11 AM - 6 PM; No admis fee; Estab 1871, incorporated 1889 to foster the appreciation & creation of the fine arts & maintain a school & mus for that purpose; Walter McBean Gallery; two-level, used for exhibitions of contemporary artists of international repute; Diego Rivera Gallery, one room with Rivera mural, used for exhibitions of work by SFAI students; SFAI Photo Gallery, for photo students; Average Annual Attendance: 60,000
Income: Donations, tuition, grants
Exhibitions: Walter McBean (six exhibitions per year)
Publications: Exhibition catalogs
Activities: Lect open to public, 20 vis lectrs per year; gallery talks; tours; scholarships & fels offered; exten dept; sales shop sells art supplies

L **Anne Bremer Memorial Library,** 800 Chestnut St, San Francisco, CA 94133. Tel 415-749-4559; Elec Mail library@sfai.edu; Internet Home Page Address: www.sfai.edu; *Media Dir* Charles Stephanian; *Catalog Librn* Pamela Jackson; *Catalog Asst* Claudia Marlowe; *Media Asst* Rebecca Alexander; *Librn* Jeff Gunderson
Open to researchers & pub by appt only; Open to students, alumni & faculty Mon - Thurs 8:30 AM - 8:30 PM, Fri 8:30 AM - 6 PM, Sat 12:30 PM - 5:30 PM & during school sessions; Estab 1871 to develop a collection & services which will anticipate, reflect & support the objectives & direction of an art education; Circ 9,750
Income: Tuition, donations
Library Holdings: Audio Tapes; Book Volumes 31,000; Cassettes 800; Compact Disks; DVDs; Exhibition Catalogs; Filmstrips; Kodachrome Transparencies; Manuscripts; Memorabilia; Motion Pictures; Original Documents; Pamphlets; Periodical Subscriptions 220; Photographs; Slides 125,000; Video Tapes 4,100
Special Subjects: Art History, Collages, Film, Photography, Drawings, Etchings & Engravings, Painting-American, Painting-British, Painting-Dutch, Painting-Flemish, Painting-French, Painting-German, Painting-Italian, Painting-Japanese, Painting-Russian, Painting-Spanish, Posters, Prints, Sculpture, Painting-European, Watercolors, Ceramics, Conceptual Art, Painting-Israeli, Printmaking, Cartoons, Video, Painting-Polish, Afro-American Art, Woodcuts, Landscapes, Painting-Scandinavian, Painting-Australian, Painting-Canadian
Collections: Archives documenting the history of the Art Institute -1871-present; artists' books
Exhibitions: Artists' Book Contest; 60 years of photography at S.F.A.I.; 1960's Rock Posters; Larry Sultan & Mike Mandel; Western Roundtable on Modern Art; music & San Francisco Art; John Collier, Jr, photographer; Gems from David & Peggy Ross collection; Peter Selz - Diego Rivera
Activities: Poetry-Book Readings; current events roundtable

M **SAN FRANCISCO ARTS COMMISSION,** Gallery, 401 Van Ness Ave, San Francisco, CA 94102-4522. Tel 415-554-6080; Fax 415-554-6093; Elec Mail sfac.gallery@sfgov.org; Internet Home Page Address: www.sfartscommission.org/gallery; *Gallery Dir* Meg Shiffler; *Gallery Mgr* Aimee LeDuc
Open Wed-Sat noon-5PM, Tues by appointment; No admis fee; Estab 1970; Exhib the work of bay area emerging artist; Average Annual Attendance: 20,000
Income: Financed by city appropriations & pvt donations
Exhibitions: Construct: Annual Installation Award Exhib
Activities: Educ prog; lect open to public; gallery talks; lending collection contains slides

A **SAN FRANCISCO ARTS EDUCATION PROJECT,** C/O Norse Auditorium, 135 Van Ness Ave San Francisco, CA 94102. Tel 415-551-7990; Fax 415-551-7994; Elec Mail info@sfartsed.org; Internet Home Page Address: www.sfartsed.org; *Exec Dir* Natalie A Hala; *Artistic Dir* Emily Keeler; *Prog Dir* Camille Olivier-Salmon; *Develop & Communs Mgr* Chad Jones; *Admin Coordr* Kathleen Moore
Estab to provide participatory experience in the arts to children of San Francisco so they are better equipped to make use of their creative abilities in all aspects of their lives

A **SAN FRANCISCO CAMERAWORK,** 1011 Market St, 2nd Fl San Francisco, CA 94103. Tel 415-487-1011; Elec Mail info@sfcamerawork.org; Internet Home Page Address: www.sfcamerawork.org; *Dir* Chuck Mobley; *Dir Educ* Erik Auerbach; *Develop & Communs Mgr* Jennifer Jordan
Open Tues - Thurs & Sat Noon - 6 PM, Fri Noon - 7 & by appt; Admis $5 adults, seniors & students $2, mems no admis fee; Estab 1973 to encourage & display contemporary photography & related visual arts through exhibitions, lectures, publications & commun services; Three galleries; Average Annual Attendance: 35,000; Mem: 1400; dues $50 & up
Income: Financed by government agencies & private contributions, mem
Library Holdings: Book Volumes; Cards; Exhibition Catalogs
Special Subjects: Photography
Publications: San Francisco Camerawork Quarterly
Activities: Lects open to pub, 6 per yr; workshops; gallery talks; Phelan Award; mentoring program; book traveling exhibs; mus shop sells books & magazines, postcards, original art, prints

A **SAN FRANCISCO CITY & COUNTY ART COMMISSION,** 25 Van Ness Ave, Ste 240, San Francisco, CA 94102. Tel 415-252-2590; Fax 415-252-2595; *Dir Cultural Affairs* Richard Newirth; *Asst Dir* Nancy Gonchar; *Dir Street Artist Prog* Howard Lazar; *Dir Pub Art Prog* Jill Manton; *Mgr Civic Art Coll* Debra Lehane; *Dir Cultural Equity Grants* Jewelle Gomez; *Pres* Stanlee Gatti; *Dir Community Arts & Educ* Liz Lerma
Call for hours; No admis fee; Estab 1932; Average Annual Attendance: 100,000; Mem: Consists of nine professional & three lay-members appointed by the Mayor with advice of art societies & five ex-officio members; monthly meetings
Activities: Classes for adults & children; dramatic progs; docent training; neighborhood arts prog; lects open to pub; concerts; competitions; individual paintings & original objects of art lent to city agencies; lending collection contains 28,000 original artworks

M **SAN FRANCISCO MARITIME NATIONAL HISTORICAL PARK,** Maritime Museum, 900 Beach St, San Francisco, CA 94109-1002. Tel 415-561-7000; Fax 415-556-1624; Elec Mail lynn_cullivan@nps.gov; Internet Home Page Address: www.nps.gov/safr; *Prin Librn* David Hull; *Publ* Lynn Cullivan; *Supt* William G Thomas; *Cur Maritime History* Steve Canright; *Coll Mgr* Mary Jo Pugh; *Chief Interpretation* Marc Hayman; *Supervisory Archivist* Lisbit Bailey
Open winter daily 10 AM - 5 PM, summer daily 10 AM - 6 PM; No admis fee for museum; Hyde St. Pier adults $5, children 16 & under no charge; Estab 1951; mus built in 1939; a Terrazzo & stainless steel structure with a nautical theme; Maintains reference library; Average Annual Attendance: 500,000
Income: Financed by federal funding, private support from National Maritime Mus Assoc
Purchases: A S Palmer Film Collection; Barbara Johnson Whaling Collection, books
Library Holdings: Audio Tapes; Book Volumes; Clipping Files; Fiche; Filmstrips; Manuscripts; Maps; Motion Pictures; Original Documents; Pamphlets; Periodical Subscriptions; Photographs; Prints; Reels; Video Tapes
Special Subjects: Drawings, Graphics, Painting-American, Photography, Costumes, Crafts, Folk Art, Etchings & Engravings, Manuscripts, Eskimo Art, Marine Painting, Metalwork, Historical Material, Ivory, Maps, Scrimshaw
Collections: Barbara Johnson Whaling Collection: books; A S Palmer Film Collection; paddlewheel ferry; paddlewheel tug; scow schooner; small craft; ship models; square-rigged sailing ship; steam schooner; steam tug; 3-mast schooner
Exhibitions: Tugboats; San Francisco Bay Ferryboats; Sparks, Waves and Wizards: Communications at Sea
Publications: Sealetter; booklets, irregular
Activities: Classes for adults & children; dramatic progs; docent training; lects open to pub, 4 vis lectrs per yr; concerts; tours; competitions; originate traveling exhibs to maritime museums; mus shop sells books, magazines, models & children's educational materials

L **Maritime Library,** Bldg E, Fort Mason Center, San Francisco, CA 94123-1314. Tel 415-561-7030; Fax 415-556-3540; Elec Mail safr_maritime_library@nps.gov; Internet Home Page Address: www.nps.gov/safr/historyculture/library-collections.htm; *Reference* Gina Bardi; *Technical Svcs* Heather Hernandez; *Library Technician* Ted Miles; *Library Technician* Debbie Grace; *Library Technician* Mark Goldstein; *Chief of Cultural Resources* Robbyn Jackson; *Supt* Craig Kenkel; *Colls Mgr* Keri Koehler
Open Mon-Fri 1PM-4PM, 3rd Sat 10AM-4PM by appointment; No admis fee; historic ships $5, children 16 & under no charge; Estab 1951; streamlined modern structure with nautical theme; Open to the public for research on premises; Average Annual Attendance: 4,000,000
Library Holdings: Audio Tapes; Book Volumes 35,000; CD-ROMs; Cards; Cassettes; Clipping Files; Compact Disks; DVDs; Exhibition Catalogs; Fiche; Manuscripts; Maps; Memorabilia; Motion Pictures; Original Documents; Other Holdings Archives; Oral History; Vessel Plans; Pamphlets; Periodical Subscriptions 100; Photographs 250,000; Records; Reels; Video Tapes
Special Subjects: Historical Material, Marine Painting
Exhibitions: Cargo is King - permanent; A Walk Along the Waterfront (permanent)
Publications: Booklets, irregular, Maritime News
Activities: Docent training, interpretive sails on the bay; shanty sings; docent training; concerts; tours

M **SAN FRANCISCO MUSEUM OF CRAFT + DESIGN,** 130 Bush St, Fl 15, San Francisco, CA 94104-3813. Tel 415-773-0303; Fax 415-773-0306; Elec Mail info@sfmcd.org; Internet Home Page Address: www.sfmcd.com
Open Tues-Wed & Fri-Sat 10AM-5PM, Thurs 10AM-7PM, Sun noon-5PM; Suggested admis adults $3, seniors 62 & over and students $2, children under 18 free
Collections: works of contemporary crafts & design

M **SAN FRANCISCO MUSEUM OF MODERN ART,** 151 3rd St, San Francisco, CA 94103-3159. Tel 415-357-4000; Fax 415-357-4037; Elec Mail director@sfmoma.org; Internet Home Page Address: www.sfmoma.org; *Dir ISS* Leo Ballate; *Deputy Dir Exhibs & Colls* Ruth Berson; *Cur Painting & Sculpture* Janet Bishop; *Dir Opers & Facilities* Joe Brennan; *Dir Graphic Design & Publs* Chad Coerver; *Assoc Cur Photog* Corey Keller; *Dir HR* Erin Hirsch; *Cur Media Arts* Rudolf Frieling; *Sr Cur Painting & Sculpture* Gary Garrels; *Dir Mus Store* Jana Machin; *Cur Photog* Sandra Phillips; *Dir Mktg & Audience Strategy* Katie Tamony; *Deputy Dir Admin & Finance* Ikuko Satoda; *Dir Conservation & Colls* Jill Sterrett; *Cur Educ* Dominic Willsdon; *Dir Develop* Jonathan Peterson; *Dir SFMOMA* Neal Benezra; *Deputy Dir Pub Affairs* Robert Lasher
Open Mon - Tues & Fri - Sun 11 AM - 5:45 PM, Thurs 11 AM - 8:45 PM, cl Wed; Admis adults $18, seniors $13, students with ID $11, members, children under 12, active US military with ID & 1st Tues of the month free, Thurs evenings 6 - 8:45 PM 1/2 price; Estab 1935 to collect & exhibit art of the 20th century; Mus occupies its own 225,000 sq ft building; Average Annual Attendance: 750,000; Mem: 42,000; dues $65-$1000
Income: Financed by endowment, mem, city hotel tax, earnings & grants
Library Holdings: Auction Catalogs; Audio Tapes; Book Volumes; CD-ROMs; Cards; Cassettes; Clipping Files; Compact Disks; DVDs; Exhibition Catalogs; Fiche; Maps; Memorabilia; Motion Pictures; Original Art Works; Original Documents; Pamphlets; Periodical Subscriptions; Photographs; Prints; Records; Reels; Slides; Video Tapes
Special Subjects: Architecture, Painting-American, Photography, Sculpture
Collections: Clyfford Still Collection; painting, photography, sculpture architecture & design, media & video works
Exhibitions: Exhibits rotate
Publications: Monthly Calendar
Activities: Classes for adults & children; docent training; lects open to pub; lectrs mems only; 40 vis lectrs per yr; gallery talks; tours; competitions; originates traveling exhibs; Mus shop sells books, magazines, reproductions & prints

L **Library,** 151 Third St, San Francisco, CA 94103-3159. Tel 415-357-4120; Fax 415-357-4038; Internet Home Page Address: www.sfmoma.org
Open to the pub Tues & Thurs 11 AM - 4 PM, by appointment only; Estab 1935
Income: Endowment, mem, earnings, grants
Library Holdings: Book Volumes 50,000; Exhibition Catalogs; Other Holdings Artists files; Exhibition archives; Periodical Subscriptions 400

Collections: Margery Mann Collection of books in the history of photography

M **Artist Gallery,** Fort Mason Bldg A, San Francisco, CA 94123. Tel 415-441-4777; Fax 415-441-0614; Elec Mail artistsgallery@sfmoma.org; Internet Home Page Address: www.sfmoma.org; *Corporate Art Coordr* Maria Medua; *Gallery Mgr* Andrea Voinot; *Dir* Marian Parmenter; *Exhib Supv* Steve Pon; *Gallery Coordr* Michelle Nye; *Technical/Art Specialist* Renee de-Cossio; *Admin Asst* Julio Badel; *Art Installer/Driver* Ben Johnston
Open Tues - Sat 11:30 AM - 5:30 PM; No admis fee; Estab 1978 for the support & exposure of Northern California artists. Over 1200 artists represented; Rentals & sales
Income: Grants, contributions, endowment
Special Subjects: Drawings, Collages, Photography, Prints, Sculpture, Watercolors, Etchings & Engravings
Exhibitions: Eight exhibitions per year, all media; one person & group exhibitions
Activities: Artists gallery sells & rents original art

L **SAN FRANCISCO PUBLIC LIBRARY,** Art & Music Center, 100 Larkin St, San Francisco, CA 94102-4705. Tel 415-557-4525; Fax 415-557-4524; Elec Mail webmail@sfpl.org; Internet Home Page Address: www.sfpl.org; *City Librn* Luis Herrera; *Mgr Art, Music, Bus & Technical Science* Mark Hall; *Librn II, Prog Mgr* Quindi Berger; *Librn II, Prog Mgr* Jason Gibbs
Open Mon 10 AM - 6 PM, Tues - Thurs 9 AM - 8 PM, Fri Noon - 6 PM, Sat 10 AM - 6 PM, Sun Noon - 5 PM; No admis fee; Estab 1878; Jewett Gallery (lower level), Skylight Gallery (6th flr)
Income: Financed by city & state appropriations
Library Holdings: Audio Tapes; Book Volumes 45,000; Cards; Clipping Files; DVDs; Exhibition Catalogs; Motion Pictures; Pamphlets; Periodical Subscriptions 250; Records; Reels; Video Tapes
Activities: Lects open to pub; concerts; Sales shop sells books

L **SAN FRANCISCO STATE UNIVERSITY,** J Paul Leonard Library, 1630 Holloway, San Francisco, CA 94132. Tel 415-338-2188; Fax 415-338-6199; Elec Mail dtong@sfsu.edu; Internet Home Page Address: www.library.sfsu.edu; *Art Librn* Darlene Tong
Open Mon - Thurs 8 AM - 10 PM, Fri 8 AM - 5 PM, Sat 10 AM - 6 PM, Sun 12 noon - 9 PM; Estab 1899; Not available during bldg construction project
Library Holdings: Book Volumes 1,000,000; Compact Disks; DVDs; Exhibition Catalogs; Fiche; Framed Reproductions; Manuscripts; Memorabilia; Original Art Works; Other Holdings Bound per vol 132,000; Film & video 14,500; Graphic materials 98,000; Sound rec 57,000; Periodical Subscriptions; Photographs; Video Tapes
Special Subjects: Art History, Intermedia, Graphic Design, Industrial Design, Antiquities-Etruscan, Antiquities-Roman, Architecture
Collections: H Wilder Bentley Brush Painting Collection; Frank deBellis Collection on Italian Culture; John Magnani Collection of Arts & Crafts; Simeon Pelenc Collection of Paintings & Drawings; San Francisco Bay area television archives; visual materials from labor archives
Activities: Book traveling exhibs; originate traveling exhibs; sales shop sells books & reproductions

M **SOUTHERN EXPOSURE,** 3030 20th St, San Francisco, CA 94110-2780. Tel 415-863-2141; Fax 415-863-1841; Elec Mail soex@soex.org; Internet Home Page Address: www.soex.org; *Dir* Courtney Fink; *Assoc Dir* Amanda Ault; *Exhibs Progs Mgr* Maysoun Wazwaz; *Artists in Educ Mgr* Tara Foley
Open Tues - Sat 12 AM - 6 PM; Estab 1974 to give exposure to contemporary California art by emerging and established artists; 28 ft ceilings; 2500 sq ft in three galleries; Average Annual Attendance: 25,000; Mem: 1800; dues $30-$2000 & up
Income: Financed by endowment, mem, contributions, grants
Collections: Juried Exhib (nationally recognized cur) Nov, Dec; Postcard Show
Activities: Artists in education prog (ages 11-19), performances, symposiums, internship prog; lect

M **TATTOO ART MUSEUM,** 841 Columbus Ave, San Francisco, CA 94133; 210 Clara Ave, Ukiah, CA 95482-4004. Tel 415-775-4991; Elec Mail lyletutt@pacific.net; Internet Home Page Address: www.lyletuttle.com; *Consultant* Judith Tuttle; *Dir* Lyle Tuttle; *Mgr* Tanja Nixx
Open daily Noon - 9 PM; Estab 1974; Average Annual Attendance: 5,000
Special Subjects: Primitive art
Collections: Lyle Tuttle Collection, tattoo art, Memorabilia & Equipment, especially tattoo machines & primitive tools; George Burchett Collection
Publications: Magazine of the Tattoo Art Museum; Tattoo Historian, biannual
Activities: Lect open to public, 12 vis lectrs per year; awards; Tattoo Hall of Fame; individual paintings & objects of art lent

M **THE UNIVERSITY OF SAN FRANCISCO THACHER GALLERY,** Gleeson Library, 2130 Fulton St San Francisco, CA 94117-1080. *Dir & Cur* Thomas Lucas S.J.

C **WELLS FARGO BANK,** Wells Fargo History Museum, 420 Montgomery St, MAC A0101-106 San Francisco, CA 94163. Tel 415-396-2619; Fax 415-975-7430; Internet Home Page Address: www.wellsfargohistory.com; *Cur* Glen Myers
Open Mon - Fri 9 AM - 5 PM, cl Bank holidays; Estab 1960 to provide historical information on Wells Fargo, California & San Francisco; Permanent & special exhibitions open to the public; Average Annual Attendance: 50,000
Special Subjects: Sculpture, Painting-American, Prints, American Western Art, Coins & Medals, Gold, Historical Material, Jewelry, Landscapes, Manuscripts, Maps, Photography, Porcelain, Posters, Reproductions
Collections: Wiltsee Collection of Postal Franks; California History; 19th & 20th Century Banking; San Francisco History
Exhibitions: Permanent: art & artifacts from gold rush, stagecoach travel, western art, banking history
Activities: Concerts; school tours featuring gold rush Calif era; mus shop sells books, posters, stagecoach & gold rush souvenirs

M **YERBA BUENA CENTER FOR THE ARTS,** (Center for the Arts at Yerba Buena Gardens) 701 Mission St, San Francisco, CA 94103-3138. Tel 415-978-2787; Fax 415-978-9635; Internet Home Page Address: www.ybca.org; *Exec Dir* Kenneth Foster; *Board Pres* Diana Cohn
Open Thurs - Sat Noon - 8 PM, Sun Noon - 6 PM; Admis $10; Estab 1993; contemporary art; Average Annual Attendance: 50,000; Mem: 2500
Special Subjects: Drawings, Painting-American, Sculpture, Hispanic Art, Latin American Art, Afro-American Art, Oriental Art, Juvenile Art
Exhibitions: Beautiful Losers; Cosmic Wonder; Erwin Wurm; Nick Cave; Yoshua Okon; Techno Craft; Audience as Subject, Song Doug
Activities: Docent training; workshops for children; teen employment & art training; lects open to pub; concerts; tours; gallery talks; originates traveling exhibs circulating to any art museum

M **ZEUM,** 221 Fourth St, San Francisco, CA 94103. Tel 415-820-3320; Fax 415-820-3330; Elec Mail info@zeum.org; Internet Home Page Address: www.zeum.org; *Exec Dir* Audrey Yamamoto; *Assoc Dir Mktg* Joy Wong Daniels; *Dir Finance & Operations* Anne Amis; *Dir Prog & Experience* Irina Zadov
Open Summer Tues - Sun 11 AM - 5 PM, Sept - June Wed - Sun 11 AM - 5 PM, other times by appointment; Admis adults $10, youth (3 - 18) $8, under 3 free; Estab 1998; urban renewal proj in the South of Market area by the SF Redevelopment Agency; Multimedia Arts & Tech; Average Annual Attendance: 50,000
Collections: community & youth artwork; 1906 Charles Looff carousel
Activities: Art workshops; preschool workshops; youth docent internships; professional develop progs; live performances; mus shop

SAN JACINTO

M **MT SAN JACINTO COLLEGE,** Fine Art Gallery, 1499 N State St, San Jacinto, CA 92583. Tel 951-487-3585; Tel 951-487-3586; Elec Mail bdillaway@msjc.edu; Internet Home Page Address: www.msjc.edu/artgallery; *Dir* Brandelyn Dillaway
Open Mon-Thurs 8AM-4PM, other times by appointment
Collections: paintings; sculpture; photographs

SAN JOSE

A **ARTS COUNCIL SILICON VALLEY,** (Arts Council of Santa Clara County) 4 N Second St, Ste 500, San Jose, CA 95113-1305. Tel 408-998-2787; Fax 408-971-9458; Elec Mail admin@artscouncil.org; Internet Home Page Address: www.artscouncil.org; *Exec Dir* Bruce Davis; *Deputy Dir* Diem Jones; *Dir Fin* Monica Toumani; *Dir Communs* Anna Weldon; *Youth & Arts Prog Mgr* Mitsu Kumagai
Open Mon - Fri 9 AM - 5 PM, cl on staff furlough days, Thanksgiving & Christmas; Estab 1982 as the regional art support/planning agency for Santa Clara County, The Arts Council is the principal funding agency within the county for small, mid-size & multi-cultural arts groups & individual independent artists
Income: $1,000,000 (financed by county, California Arts Council, San Jose & other county municipalities, local, private & community foundations, Silicon Valley corporations, individual gifts & interest from two endowments)
Activities: ArtsConnect; ArtsChoice; Annual Music & Arts Campaign; grants

M **ROSICRUCIAN EGYPTIAN MUSEUM & PLANETARIUM,** (Rosicrucian Egyptian Museum & Art Gallery) Rosicrucian Order, A.M.O.R.C., 1342 Naglee Ave, San Jose, CA 95191-0001. Tel 408-947-3600; Fax 408-947-3638; Elec Mail info@egyptianmuseum.org; Internet Home Page Address: www.egyptianmuseum.org; *Dir* Julie Scott; *Mgr* Nancy Leonard
Open Tues - Fri 10 AM - 5 PM, Sat & Sun 11 AM - 6 PM; Admis adults $9, seniors & students with ID $7, children 5-10 $5, under 5 free; Estab 1929, in present location 1966, to publicly show a collection of the works of ancient Egyptians, reflecting their lives & culture; Collections include Bronzes of Egyptian Gods & Goddesses; Funerary Models; full size walk-in tomb replica; human & animal mummies; Tel-El-Armana room with amulets, cosmetics & writing implements; jewelry, pottery & King Zoser's tomb complex; Mesopotamian collection - cuneiform tablets & seals from Babylon, Sumer & Assyria; Average Annual Attendance: 100,000
Income: Financed by Rosicrucian Order, AMORC
Purchases: Regular acquisitions of Egyptian antiquities
Special Subjects: Antiquities-Oriental, Antiquities-Egyptian, Antiquities-Assyrian
Collections: Collections include Bronzes of Egyptian Gods & Goddesses; Funerary Models; full size walk-in tomb replica; human & animal mummies; Tel-El-Armana room; amulets, cosmetics, writing implements, jewelry, pottery, scale model of King Zoser's tomb complex; Mesopotamian collection - cuneiform tablets & seals from Babylon
Exhibitions: Quarterly exhibitions in the Rotating Exhibits gallery featuring both Ancient and Modern Art
Publications: Treasures of the Rosicrucian Egyptian Museum, catalog; Rosecroixjournal.org
Activities: Tours; workshops; 4 annual lect for members; gallery talks; gift shop sells books, magazines, reproductions, prints, slides, jewelry, posters & educ materials

M **SAN JOSE INSTITUTE OF CONTEMPORARY ART,** 560 S First St, San Jose, CA 95113. Tel 408-283-8155; Fax 408-283-8157; Elec Mail info@sjica.org; Internet Home Page Address: www.sjica.org; *Dir* Cathy Kimball
Open Tues - Fri 10 AM - 5 PM, Sat Noon - 5 PM; No admis fee; Estab 1980, SJICA is a non-profit visual arts organization highlighting emerging & estab artists from the Greater Bay Area & beyond; 7500 sq ft facility includes gallery & on-site print center & admin offices; Average Annual Attendance: 25,000; Mem: 600; dues $35 & up
Income: Financed by mem & cultural grants
Library Holdings: Exhibition Catalogs; Pamphlets; Periodical Subscriptions
Collections: works by contemporary artists
Exhibitions: Monthly exhibition.; Annual fall auction
Activities: Classes for adults; on-site print ctr offers workshops, open access prog, private individual & group workshops; Lect open to public; gallery talks; tours by appointment; print ctr artist-in residence print editions available for purchase

M **SAN JOSE MUSEUM OF ART,** 110 S Market St, San Jose, CA 95113-2383. Tel 408-271-2787; Fax 408-294-2977; Elec Mail info@sjmusart.org; Internet Home Page Address: www.sanjosemuseumofart.org; *Deputy Dir* Deborah Norberg; *Dir Communs* Sherrill Ingalls; *Museum Store Mgr* Pat Downward; *Exec Dir* Susan Krane; *Chief Cur* JoAnne Northrup; *Dir Educ* Lucy Larson
Open Tues -Sun 11AM-5PM, cl Mon; Admis adults $8, seniors & students $5, SJMA mems & children 6 & under free; Estab 1969 to foster awareness,

appreciation & understanding of 20th century art; An 1892 Richardson - Romanesque building with a striking contemporary new wing, totaling more than 18,000 sq ft of exhibition space; Average Annual Attendance: 100,000; Mem: 3,500; dues $50-$3,500

Income: Financed by City of San Jose, private sector contributions, state & federal government

Special Subjects: Drawings, Photography, Prints, Sculpture

Collections: Permanent Collection features work by nationally recognized artists, artists of the California region, American prints & sculptures; twentieth-century art

Publications: Exhibition catalogs; Framework Newsletter, quarterly

Activities: Classes for adults & children; docent training; family progs; school outreach; lects open to pub, 13 vis lectrs per yr; concerts; gallery talks; tours; summer art studios; book traveling exhibs; originate traveling exhibs to other mus in the US; mus store sells books, magazines, reproductions, prints, jewelry, gifts, toys & cards

L **Library,** 110 S Market St, San Jose, CA 95113-2383. Tel 408-271-6840; Fax 408-294-2977; Elec Mail info@sjmusart.org; *Librn* Gloria Turk; *Chief Cur* Susan Landauer; *Dir Visitor Experience & Interpreter* Margaret Maynard; *Sr Cur* JoAnne Northrup; *Deputy Dir* Deborah Norbert; *Dir Educ* Val DeLang; *Financial Officer* Lynn Schuyler-King; *Chief Design & Installations* Richard Karson; *Assoc Mktg & Commun* Stephanie Vidergar; *Exec Dir* Daniel T Keegan; *Asst Cur* Ann Wolfe; *Deputy Dir of Extended Affairs* Gary Gallagher Landis; *Pres* Deborah Rappaport; *Dir* Cindy Sylvester; *Cur Visual Arts* Lyndsey Wylie

Open Tues - Sun 11 AM - 5 PM; no admis fee; Estab 1969; Open to the mus staff & volunteers for reference only; Average Annual Attendance: 200,000; Mem: 2600

Income: Financed by donations

Library Holdings: Book Volumes 3400; Clipping Files; Exhibition Catalogs 5950; Pamphlets; Periodical Subscriptions 9; Photographs; Video Tapes

Special Subjects: Art History, Painting-American

Collections: California and West Coast contemporary art

Publications: SJMA Frameworks, 6 times a year

Activities: Classes for adults; docent training; lects open to pub; lects for mem only; gallery talks, tours; mus shop sells books, reproductions, prints

M **SAN JOSE STATE UNIVERSITY,** Natalie & James Thompson Art Gallery, Dept of Art & Art History, San Jose State University San Jose, CA 95192-0089. Tel 408-924-4328; Fax 408-924-4326; Elec Mail jo.hernandez@sjsu.edu; Internet Home Page Address: www.sjsu.edu; *Dir* Jo Farb Hernandez; *Asst to Dir* Theta Belcher

Open Mon 11AM-4PM, Tues 11AM-4PM & 6-7:30PM, Wed-Fri 11AM-4PM; No admis fee; Estab 1960 as part of the university department; Gallery is 34 x 28 ft with 12 ft ceiling; Average Annual Attendance: 15,000

Income: Financed by state appropriations & private endowment

Exhibitions: Contemporary Issues, Art & Art History

Publications: Exhibition catalogs; brochures; monthly announcement

Activities: Lects open to pub; over 30 per yr vis lectrs weekly during fall & spring semesters; concerts; gallery talks; tours; competition; scholarships offered; books traveling exhibs 0-1 per yr; originates traveling exhibs to other non-profit galleries & mus; sales shop sells books

L **Dr. Martin Luther King Jr. Library,** 150 E San Fernando St, San Jose, CA 95112-3580; 1 Washington Sq, San Jose, CA 95112-3613. Tel 408-808-2037; Fax 408-808-2009; Elec Mail edith.crowe@sjsu.edu; Internet Home Page Address: sjlibrary.org; vrc-collections.sjsu.edu/vr_library/; *Visual Resources Cur* Stacy Barclay; *Art Reference Librn* Edith Crowe

Open Mon - Thurs 9 AM - midnight, Sun 7 PM - midnight

Income: Financed by state funds, student library fees & private donations

Purchases: $52,800

Library Holdings: Audio Tapes; Book Volumes 53,500; CD-ROMs; Cards; Cassettes; Compact Disks; Exhibition Catalogs; Fiche; Filmstrips; Framed Reproductions; Lantern Slides; Micro Print; Motion Pictures; Original Art Works; Periodical Subscriptions 87; Photographs; Prints; Records; Reels; Reproductions; Slides; Video Tapes

SAN LEANDRO

M **EXIT ART,** 220 Juana Ave, San Leandro, CA 94577-4839. Tel 212-966-7745; Fax 212-925-2928; Elec Mail info@exitart.org; Internet Home Page Address: www.exitart.org; *Co-Founder/Cultural Producer* Papo Colo; *Co-founder/Dir* Jeannette Ingberman; *Assoc Cur* Herb Tam; *Asst Cur* Lauren Rosati; *Archivist* Audrey Christensen

Open Tues - Thurs 10 AM - 6 PM, Fri 10 AM - 8 PM, Sat noon - 6 PM; No admis fee, donations accepted; Estab 1982, dedicated to multi-cultural, multi-media enlightenment through presentations & publications; film festivals, exhibitions, music performances & theater; 17,000 sq ft, one fl; Average Annual Attendance: 60,000; Mem: 250; dues $30 & up

Income: Financed by donations & foundation support

Exhibitions: Wide range of varied exhibitions

Activities: Lects open to pub; concerts; originate traveling exhibs to mus, cultural spaces & university galleries; mus shop sells magazines, original art & artist made products

SAN LUIS OBISPO

L **CALIFORNIA POLYTECHNIC STATE UNIVERSITY,** College of Architecture & Environmental Design-Architecture Collection, 959 Higuera St, San Luis Obispo, CA 93401-3601. Tel 805-756-2165; Fax 805-756-5986; *Asst Dir* Vickie Aubourg

Open Mon - Fri 8:30AM-noon & 1PM-4:30PM; No admis fee; Estab 1969; 190,000 slides for reference; Circ 20,000 (slides)

Income: Financed by state appropriation

Library Holdings: Book Volumes 1000; Periodical Subscriptions 30

Special Subjects: Constructions, Landscapes, Architecture

Collections: Architecture & Landscape Architecture slide coll

L **CUESTA COLLEGE,** Cuesta College Art Gallery, Hwy 1, Room 7170 San Luis Obispo, CA 93403. Tel 805-546-3202; Fax 805-546-3100; Elec Mail pmckenna@cuesta.edu; Elec Mail tanderso@cuesta.edu; Internet Home Page Address: www.academic.cuesta.cc.ca.us/finearts/gallery.htm; *Gallery Asst* Pamela McKenna; *Gallery Dir* Tim Anderson

Call for hours; No admis fee; Estab 1966 to support the educational prog of the col; Contemporary fine art gallery featuring rotating exhibitions of national, regional & local artists; Average Annual Attendance: 10,000

Library Holdings: Audio Tapes; Book Volumes 3130; Cassettes; Fiche; Filmstrips; Motion Pictures; Pamphlets; Periodical Subscriptions 18; Records; Reels; Slides; Video Tapes

Special Subjects: Collages, Drawings, Painting-American, Prints, Sculpture, Watercolors, Ceramics, Woodcuts

Collections: 20 works of art primarily of California artists; 2 Japanese artists; works by contemporary artists

Activities: Educ dept, class for adults; lects open to pub, 6-8 vis lectrs per yr; concerts; gallery talks; tours; originate traveling exhibs

A **SAN LUIS OBISPO MUSEUM OF ART,** (San Luis Obispo Art Center) 1010 Broad St, San Luis Obispo, CA; PO Box 813, San Luis Obispo, CA 93406-0813. Tel 805-543-8562; Fax 805-543-4518; Elec Mail kkile@sloma.org; Internet Home Page Address: www.sloma.org; *Exec Dir* Karen M Kile; *Exhib & Develop Dir* Ruta Saliklis; *Asst Dir* Rebecca Leduc; *Gallery Dir & Registrar* Wendy R Walter

Open every day July 4th-Labor Day 11AM-5PM, otherwise Sun-Wed 11AM-5PM; Admis free; Estab 1952 to promote the visual arts through educ, expression & interaction; Three galleries; Average Annual Attendance: 40,000; Mem: 830; dues $20 - $225

Income: $550,000+ (financed by mem, sales & donations)

Special Subjects: Drawings, Landscapes, Photography, Painting-American, Ceramics, Crafts, Glass, Jewelry

Collections: Permanent collection of regional artists

Publications: Newsletter, website

Activities: Classes for adults & children; lects & film nights; concerts; gallery talks; tours; sponsored competitions; exhibs in 3 galleries; scholarships; mus shop sells books, original art, reproductions, cards & jewelry

SAN MARCOS

M **PALOMAR COMMUNITY COLLEGE,** Boehm Gallery, 1140 W Mission Rd, San Marcos, CA 92069-1487. Tel 760-744-1150, Ext 2304; Fax 760-744-8723; Elec Mail jbigfeather@palomar.edu; Internet Home Page Address: www.palomar.edu/art/boehmgallery.html; *Gallery Dir* Ingram Ober

Open Tues 10AM-4PM, Wed-Thurs 10AM-7PM, Fri-Sat 10AM-2PM; No admis fee; Estab 1964 to provide the community with fine art regardless of style, period or approach; The gallery is 35 x 35 ft, no windows, 18 in brick exterior, acoustic ceiling & asphalt tile floor; Average Annual Attendance: 50,000

Income: $8000 (exhibition budget). Financed by city & state appropriations

Collections: Contemporary art by nationally acclaimed artists; 16th - 20th century art; California artists

Activities: Lect open to public, 12 vis lectrs per year; competitions; individual paintings & original objects of art lent to reputable museums & galleries; lending collection contains original paintings, prints & sculpture

SAN MARINO

M **THE HUNTINGTON LIBRARY, ART COLLECTIONS & BOTANICAL GARDENS,** 1151 Oxford Rd, San Marino, CA 91108-1299. Tel 626-405-2100; Fax 626-405-0225; Elec Mail lblackburn@huntington.org; Internet Home Page Address: www.huntington.org; *VPres Advancement* George Abdo; *VPres Financial Affairs* Alison Sowden; *Dir Art Coll* John Murdoch; *Dir Library* David Zeidberg; *Dir Botanical Gardens* James Folsom; *VPres Communs* Susan Turner-Lowe; *Cur American Art* Jessica Smith; *Cur British & Continental Art* Catherine Hess; *Pres* Steven S Koblik; *Dir Research* Robert C Ritchie; *Dir Educ* Susan Lafferty; *Assoc VPres Opers* Laurie Sowd; *Asst VPres Advancement* Randy Shulman; *Assoc VPres Advancement* Suzy Moser; *Exec Asst to Pres* Kathy Hacleer

Open Mon, Wed - Fri noon -4:30 PM, Sat - Sun 10:30 AM - 4:30 PM, cl Tues, New Year's Day, Independence Day, Thanksgiving, Christmas Eve & Christmas Day; Admis adults $20, seniors 65 & older $15, students 12-18 $10, youth 5-11 $6, groups of 15 or more $14; Estab 1919 by the late Henry E Huntington as a free research library, art gallery, mus & botanical garden; exhibitions open to the pub in 1928 for educational & cultural purposes. Virginia Steele Scott Gallery for American art opened in 1984; Average Annual Attendance: 500,000; Mem: 15,000; supporters of the institution who give $60-$1000 annually are known as the Friends of the Huntington Library, Fellows give $2000 or more per year

Income: Financed by endowment & gifts

Special Subjects: Manuscripts, Architecture, Drawings, Bronzes, Ceramics, Etchings & Engravings, Decorative Arts, Furniture, Carpets & Rugs, Baroque Art

Collections: Ellesmere manuscript of Chaucer's Canterbury Tales; Gutenberg Bible on vellum; Birds of America by Audubon; Rich Collection: Rare Books & Manuscripts

Exhibitions: Rotating exhibits

Publications: The Calendar, bimonthly; Huntington Library Quarterly; various monographs & exhibition catalogs; Frontiers, semi-annually

Activities: Classes for children; docent training; lects open to pub, 25 vis lectrs per yr; concerts; gallery talks; tours; scholarships & fels offered; individual paintings lent; mus shop sells books, calendars, gift items, note cards, postcards, prints, puzzles, reproductions, slides

L **Library,** 1151 Oxford Rd, San Marino, CA 91108. Tel 626-405-2100; Fax 626-405-0398; Elec Mail publicinformation@huntington.org; Internet Home Page Address: www.huntington.org; *Pres* Steven Kobik; *Exec Asst to Pres* Kathy Hacker; *VPres Advancement* George Abdo; *Dir Botanical Gardens* James Folsom; *Dir Educ* Susan Lafferty; *Dir Art Colls* John Murdoch; *Dir Research & Educ* Robert C Ritchie; *Assoc VPres Operations* Laurie Sowd; *VPres Communs* Susan Turner-Lowe; *Dir Library* David Zeidberg

Open Mon, Wed, Thurs, & Fri Noon-4:30PM; Cl Tues and major holidays-New Years Day, Independence Day, Thanksgiving, Christmas Eve, Christmas Day; Summer hours 10:30AM-4:30PM, cl Tues; Admis adults, $20, seniors, $15, students 12-18 $12, youth 5-11 $8, group rate $11 per person for groups of 15 or more, children under 5, & members free; Estab 1919, research & educational institution; 18th century British & French & early 18th to early 20th century American art; Average Annual Attendance: 521,000; Mem: 25,000; dues Benefactor $1,250, Patron $600, Supporting $300, Sponsoring $200, Sustaining $100, Senior $80
Income: Financed by contributions, admis, endowment & earned income
Library Holdings: Book Volumes 682,094; Cards; Exhibition Catalogs; Fiche; Manuscripts; Memorabilia; Micro Print; Other Holdings Photographic archive 100,000; Pamphlets; Periodical Subscriptions 1200; Photographs; Prints; Reels
Special Subjects: Art History, Landscape Architecture, Decorative Arts, Illustration, Drawings, Etchings & Engravings, Manuscripts, History of Art & Archaeology, Ceramics, American Western Art, Bronzes, Interior Design, Furniture, Carpets & Rugs, Landscapes
Publications: Calendar; Frontiers Magazine; Annual Report; In Fact
Activities: Classes for adults & children; docent training; lects open to pub; 10-20 vis lectrs per yr; concerts; gallery talks; tours; scholarships; fel; lending of original objects of art to various orgs; originates traveling exhibs to various orgs; mus shop sells books, magazines, reproductions, prints, slides & gifts

L   **UNIVERSITY OF SOUTHERN CALIFORNIA/THE GAMBLE HOUSE,** Greene & Greene Archives, Huntington Library 1151 Oxford Rd, San Marino, CA 91108. Tel 626-405-2232; Fax 626-796-6498; Elec Mail scheid@usc.edu; Internet Home Page Address: www.usc.edu/dept/architecture/greeneandgreene; *Archivist* Ann Scheid
Open by appt; No admis fee; Estab 1968 as a concentrated collection of archival material on the work of architects Charles & Henry Greene; For research only; Average Annual Attendance: 100
Library Holdings: Auction Catalogs; Audio Tapes 5; Book Volumes 800; CD-ROMs 60; Clipping Files; Compact Disks 100; Exhibition Catalogs; Lantern Slides 50; Manuscripts 5,000; Memorabilia; Motion Pictures 5; Original Art Works 50; Original Documents 500; Other Holdings Drawings; Client files; Blueprints; Pamphlets; Photographs 3500; Records; Slides 800; Video Tapes 10
Special Subjects: Landscape Architecture, Decorative Arts, Photography, Stained Glass, Architecture
Collections: Art, architecture, and decorative arts of architects Charles Sumner Greene and Henry Mather Greene; Alfred Heineman Collection (architectural drawings, photographs, scrapbooks)
Publications: A New & Native Beauty: The Art & Craft of Greene & Greene; Seeing Greene & Greene: Architecture in Photographs
Activities: Docent training, vis col classes

SAN MIGUEL

M   **MISSION SAN MIGUEL MUSEUM,** 775 Mission St, San Miguel, CA 93451; PO Box 69, San Miguel, CA 93451-0069. Tel 805-467-3256; Fax 805-467-2448; Internet Home Page Address: www.missionsanmiguel.org; *Guardian* Max Hottle; *Pastor* Pedro Umana
Open daily 10 AM - 4:30 PM, cl New Year's, Easter, Thanksgiving & Christmas; Admis by donation; Estab 1797; The Mission fresco secco decorations date back to 1821; Average Annual Attendance: 25,000
Income: Financed by Franciscan Friars & donations
Special Subjects: American Indian Art, Architecture, Mexican Art, Archaeology, Religious Art, Manuscripts, Historical Material, Restorations, Dioramas, Period Rooms, Painting-Spanish, Reproductions
Collections: Spanish era art & artifacts
Activities: Tours; gift shop sells books, reproductions, prints, gifts & religious articles

SAN PEDRO

M   **ANGELS GATE CULTURAL CENTER,** Gallery A & Gallery G, 3601 S Gaffey St, San Pedro, CA 90731-6969. Tel 310-519-0936; Fax 310-519-8698; Elec Mail artatgate@aol.com; Internet Home Page Address: www.angelsgateart.org; *Exec Dir* Nathan Birnbaum; *Educ Dir* Jessica Maeson Yang
Open Tues - Sun 10 AM - 5 PM; No admis fee; Estab 1981 dedicated to innovation & cultural diversity; 3000 sq ft in Gallery A, 600 sq ft in Gallery G; Mem: 400; dues $25-1,000; annual meeting in Sept
Income: $250,000 (financed by mem, studio rentals, workshop tuition, donations & grants)
Activities: Classes for adults & children; internships; outreach workshops; docent training; artists in classrooms in local schools; lect open to public; dir tours; dialogue with artists; concerts; dance recitals; theatre productions; sales shop sells books, magazines, original art, prints, jewelry, handbags, cards & calendars

SAN RAFAEL

M   **CITY OF SAN RAFAEL,** Falkirk Cultural Center, 1408 Mission Ave, San Rafael, CA 94901. Tel 415-485-3328, 485-3326; Fax 415-485-3404; Elec Mail jane.lange@ci.san-rafael.ca.us; Internet Home Page Address: www.falkirkculturalcenter.org; *Cur* Beth Goldberg; *Dir* Jane Lange; *Pub Rels* Corey Bytof
Gallery Open Mon - Fri 1 PM - 5 PM, Sat 10 AM - 1 PM; No admis fee; Estab 1974 to provide classes, lectures, concerts for the city of San Rafael & surrounding region; Contemporary art gallery; Average Annual Attendance: 20,000; Mem: 50; dues bus/corporate $1000, fellow $500, advocate $250, steward $100, family $50, friend $30, sr citizen, student & artist $20
Income: Financed by City of San Rafael appropriation, rentals, classes & grants
Special Subjects: Restorations
Exhibitions: Annual juried exhibition, Dia de Los Muertos exhibition
Publications: Exhibition catalogues

Activities: Classes for adults & children; docent training; lect open to public, 6 vis lectrs per year; concerts; tours; juried annual competitions; bookstore sells books, prints, & poetry readings

SANTA ANA

M   **BOWERS MUSEUM,** (Bowers Museum of Cultural Art) 2002 N Main St, Santa Ana, CA 92706-2776. Tel 714-567-3600; Fax 714-567-3603; Elec Mail info@bowers.org; Internet Home Page Address: www.bowers.org; *VPres Exhibit Design & & Fabrication* Paul Johnson; *Pres* Dr Peter Keller; *CFO* Thuy Nguyen; *VPres Edu* Nancy Warzer-Brady; *VPres Information Technology* Paul Dowdle; *COO* Kathy Hamilton
Open Tues - Sun 10 AM - 4 PM, cl Mon; Admis adults $15, students & seniors $12, under 12 years-old free; Estab 1936 to provide an active cultural arts museum for the community; Originally housed in an authentic California mission-style structure surrounding a courtyard fountain, devoted to the display of antique furniture, Indian relics & historical items of early California families, The museum has grown to encompass 90,000 sq ft. The new additions include major galleries, new collection storage rooms, admin offices, library & restaurant exhibiting the cultural arts of the world; Average Annual Attendance: 133,000; Mem: 7,000
Income: Financed by city appropriation, earned revenue & contributions
Special Subjects: Hispanic Art, American Indian Art, African Art, Pre-Columbian Art, Asian Art
Collections: Pre-Columbian Mesoamerica; Native N & S American art & artifacts; African & Oceanic art; California plein air paintings
Publications: Brochures; Quarterly Calendar; exhibition catalogs
Activities: Classes for adults & children; docent training; lects open to pub; films; gallery talks; tours; study clubs; paintings & original art objects lent to other mus; originates traveling exhibs; mus shop sells books, magazines, reproductions, slides, prints, jewelry, imported clothing, gift items; Kidseum 1801 N Main St Santa Ana, CA 92706

M   **SANTA ANA COLLEGE,** Art Gallery, 1530 W 17th St, Santa Ana, CA 92706-3398. Tel 714-564-5615; Fax 714-564-5629; Elec Mail mccabe_caroline@sac.edu; Internet Home Page Address: www.sac.edu/art; *Interim Gallery Dir* Phillip Marquez; *Gallery Coordr* Caroline McCabe; *Preparator* Wesley Schaffner
Open Mon - Thurs 10 AM - 2 PM, Wed 6:30 - 8:30 PM; No admis fee; Estab 1972 to educate students, staff, faculty & the community; Average Annual Attendance: 12,000
Income: Financed by Rancho Santiago Community College District budget
Exhibitions: Annual Juried Student Art Show; High School Art Show; Group exhibs, solo artists (professional)
Publications: Art Forum Newsletter, 6 per year
Activities: Classes for adults; dramatic progs; lects open to pub, 36-40 vis lectrs per yr; competitions with awards; concerts; gallery talks; tours; cash prizes for students during ann art show; schols offered

SANTA BARBARA

A   **SANTA BARBARA CONTEMPORARY ARTS FORUM,** 653 Paseo Nuevo, Santa Barbara, CA 93101-3392. Tel 805-966-5373; Fax 805-962-1421; Internet Home Page Address: www.sbcaf.org; *Others* TDD 805-965-9727; *Asst Dir* Rita Ferri; *VPres* Jeffrey Wyatt; *VPres* Keith Puccinelli; *Pres Bd Dir* Ian Smith; *Exec Dir* Miki Garcia; *Office Mgr* Yvonne Heine
Open Tues - Sat 11 AM - 5 PM, Sun Noon - 5 PM; Estab 1976; committed to the presentation of contemporary art; Klausner Gallery 2345 sq ft & Norton Gallery 378 sq ft; Mem: 921; dues start at $25
Income: $265,000 (financed by federal, state, county & city grants, corporate & private contributions, fund raising events)
Collections: Contemporary Art
Publications: Addictions; Carl Cheng: exhibit catalogues; Carroll Dunham: paintings; Focus/Santa Barbara; Jene Highstein: Gallery/Landscape; Teraoka Erotica
Activities: Classes for adults & children; docent training; lect open to public, 15 vis lectrs per year; gallery talks; tours; book traveling exhibs; originate traveling exhibs to other nonprofit galleries

M   **SANTA BARBARA MUSEUM OF ART,** 1130 State St, Santa Barbara, CA 93101-2746. Tel 805-963-4364; Fax 805-966-6840; Elec Mail sb@sbma.net; Internet Home Page Address: www.sbma.net; *Dir* Larry J Feinberg; *Dir Devel* Barbara Ben-Horin; *Cur Educ* Patsy Hicks; *Registrar* Cherie Summers; *Cur Asian Art* Susan Tai; *Cur Photo* Karen Sinsheimer; *Chief Cur* Eik Kahng; *Cur Contemporary Art* Julie Joyce; *Librn* Heather Bradhead
Open Tues, Wed, Fri, Sat & Sun 11 AM - 5 PM, Thurs 11 AM - 8 PM, cl Mon; Admis adults $10, seniors, students w/ID & children 6-17 $6, children under 6 no charge; Estab 1941 as an art mus with exhibitions & educ programs; 14 galleries totaling 16,500 sq ft of exhibition space. Maintains reference library; Average Annual Attendance: 167,000; Mem: 4000; dues benefactors' $3,000, dir $1500, cur $750, collectors' $500, gallery $250, assoc $125, general $60
Income: $2,600,000 (financed by earnings, including endowment, mem, grants, government & foundations & contributions)
Special Subjects: Drawings, Latin American Art, Painting-American, Photography, Prints, Sculpture, Watercolors, African Art, Woodcuts, Etchings & Engravings, Painting-European, Painting-Japanese, Jade, Oriental Art, Asian Art, Painting-French, Tapestries, Painting-Spanish, Antiquities-Greek, Antiquities-Roman
Collections: Preston Morton Collection of American Art; Henry Eichheim Collection; Alice F Schott Doll Collection
Publications: Bulletin, quarterly newsletter; exhibit & collection catalogs; Update, semi-annual periodical
Activities: Classes for adults & children; docent training; outreach classes & progs; lects open to pub, 4-6 vis lectrs per yr; concerts; gallery talks; tours; schols offered to children's art classes only; artmobile; individual paintings original

objects of art lent to other mus only for exhibs; book traveling exhibs 3-5 per yr; originate traveling exhibs; mus shop sells books, original art, reproductions

L **Library,** 1130 State St, Santa Barbara, CA 93101-2746. Tel 805-963-4364; Fax 805-966-6840; Internet Home Page Address: www.sbma.net; *Dir* Larry J Feinberg; *Dir Develop* Barbara Ben-Horin; *Chair Bd Trustees* Ken Anderson; *Dir Educ* Patsy Hicks; *Spec Progs Coordr* Lisa Hill; *Cur Photography* Karen Sinsheimer; *Mus Store Mgr* Georgia McDermott; *Cur Contemporary Art* Julie Joyce; *Registrar* Cherie Summers; *CFO* James Hutchinson; *Cur Asian Art* Susan Shin-tsu Tai; *Librn* Heather Brodhead; *Chief Cur* Eik Khang
Open to pub on an appointment basis; Admis adults $10, seniors (65+), students (with ID) & children 6-17 $6, under 6 free; 1941; For reference only
Income: Endowment, mem, grants, gov & foundation contributions
Library Holdings: Auction Catalogs; Audio Tapes; Book Volumes 25,000; Clipping Files; DVDs; Exhibition Catalogs; Manuscripts; Memorabilia; Other Holdings Oral History Recordings; Archives; Pamphlets; Periodical Subscriptions 20
Special Subjects: Art History, Collages, Mixed Media, Photography, Drawings, Etchings & Engravings, Painting-American, Painting-British, Painting-French, Painting-German, Painting-Italian, Prints, Sculpture, Painting-European, Historical Material, History of Art & Archaeology, Portraits, Watercolors, Conceptual Art, Latin American Art, Bronzes, Printmaking, Art Education, Asian Art, Mexican Art, Glass, Handicrafts, Oriental Art, Textiles, Woodcuts, Landscapes, Antiquities-Assyrian
Activities: Classes for adults & children; docent training; applied art classes for children & adults; lects open to pub; concerts; gallery talks; tours; schols; mus shop sells books, prints, jewelry, accessories, ceramics & art glass

L **SANTA BARBARA PUBLIC CENTRAL LIBRARY,** Faulkner Memorial Art Wing, 40 E Anapamu St, Santa Barbara, CA 93101-2722; PO Box 1019, Santa Barbara, CA 93102-1019. Tel 805-962-7653, 564-5608 (library admin); Fax 805-962-6304; Internet Home Page Address: www.santa-barbara.ca.us; *Lib Dir* Irene Macias
Open Mon - Thurs 10 AM - 9 PM, Fri & Sat 10 AM - 5:30 PM, Sun 1 - 5 PM; No admis fee; Estab 1930 & administered by the library trustees
Income: City funded
Library Holdings: Book Volumes 200,000; Cassettes 7800; Clipping Files; Fiche; Framed Reproductions; Micro Print; Pamphlets; Periodical Subscriptions 500; Records; Reels; Reproductions
Exhibitions: Local contemporary paintings & sculpture; Rotating exhibits
Activities: Lect, programs & meetings

M **UNIVERSITY OF CALIFORNIA, SANTA BARBARA,** University Art Museum, Arts Library, Santa Barbara, CA 93106-9010. Tel 805-893-2951; Fax 805-893-3013; Elec Mail uam@uam.ucsb.edu; Internet Home Page Address: www.uam.ucsb.edu; *Designer* Rollin Fortier; *Registrar* Susan Lucke; *Cur Architectural Drawings* Kurt Helfrich; *Bus Mgr* Vicki Stuber; *Asst to Dir* Marie Vierra; *Chief Cur* Natalie Sanderson; *Security* Bill Durham
Open Wed - Sun Noon - 5 PM, cl Mon, Tues & maj holidays; No admis fee; Estab 1959 & direct at both the needs of the university & the community; with a wide range of contemporary & historical exhibitions; Located on the UCSB campus, Arts Building complex; four galleries for changing exhibits; two which exhibit part of the permanent collection; Average Annual Attendance: 30,000; Mem: 100; dues vary; meeting dates vary
Income: Financed by university funds, grants, private donations
Special Subjects: Drawings, Etchings & Engravings, Architecture, Photography, Painting-American, Painting-European, Sculpture, Graphics, Watercolors, Ethnology, Religious Art, Posters, Painting-Dutch, Coins & Medals, Renaissance Art
Collections: Collection of Architectural Drawings by Southern California Architects, including Irving Gill, R M Schindler, George Washington Smith & Kem Weber; Morgenroth Collection of Renaissance Medals & Plaquettes; Sedgwick Collection of 16th-18th Century Italian, Flemish & Dutch Artists; Ala Story Print Collection; Grace H Dreyfus Collection of Ancient Peruvian & Middle Eastern Art; Fernand Lungren Bequest
Publications: Exhibition catalogs, 1-2 per year
Activities: Classes for adults & children; docent training; lects upon request; regular schedule of docent tours; gallery talks; 2-3 vis lectrs per yr; sponsoring of competitions; 1 - 2 per year; originate traveling exhibs to art museums; sales shop sells exhib catalogs, books, prints, slides, reproductions, t-shirts, gifts

L **Arts Library,** Santa Barbara, CA 93106-9010. Tel 805-893-2850; Fax 805-893-5879; Internet Home Page Address: www.library.ucsb.edu; *Head Arts Library* Susan Moon; *Art Librn* Chizu Morihara; *Music Librn* Euniu Schroeder
Open Mon - Wed 9 AM - 10 PM, Thurs - Fri 9 AM - 5 PM, Sun 2 - 10 PM; cl Sat; Estab 1966 to support acad progs; Circ 60,000
Income: Financed by state appropriation
Library Holdings: Auction Catalogs; Book Volumes 300,000; Compact Disks; DVDs; Exhibition Catalogs 100,000; Fiche 75,000; Other Holdings Auction Catalogs 50,000; Periodical Subscriptions 400; Photographs 5000; Reels 1400; Video Tapes 225
Special Subjects: Art History, Decorative Arts, Photography, Drawings, Etchings & Engravings, Painting-American, Painting-Dutch, Pre-Columbian Art, Prints, History of Art & Archaeology, American Western Art, Asian Art, Furniture, Aesthetics, Afro-American Art, Antiquities-Byzantine, Antiquities-Greek, Antiquities-Roman, Architecture
Publications: Catalogs of the Art Exhibition, Catalogs of the Arts Library, University of California, Santa Barbara; Cambridge, England, Chadwyck-Healey, 1978
Activities: Tours

SANTA CLARA

M **SANTA CLARA UNIVERSITY,** de Saisset Museum, 500 El Camino Real, Santa Clara, CA 95053-0550. Tel 408-554-4528; Fax 408-554-7840; Elec Mail jorvick@scu.edu; Internet Home Page Address: www.scu.edu/deSaisset/; *Acad Pres* Rev Michael Engh SJ; *Vice Provost for Acad Affairs* Diane Jonte-Pace; *Dir* Rebecca M Schapp; *Asst to Dir* Jan Orvick; *Coll Mgr* Jean MacDougall; *Cur Exhibits & Coll* Lindsey Kouvaris
Open during exhibs Tues - Sun 11 AM - 4 PM, cl Mon; No admis fee; Estab 1955 as a major cultural resource in Northern California; 19,210 sq ft facility founded

adjacent to Mission Santa Clara de Asis on Santa Clara Univ campus. Accredited by Amer Assoc of Mus & operated by the Univ; Average Annual Attendance: 25,000; Mem: dues presidential fellow $5,000, Locatelli fellow $2,500, de Saisset fellow $1,000, benefactor $500, patron $250, sponsor $100, friend $45
Income: Financed by endowment, mem, University operating budget, pvt funding & grants
Purchases: All media
Special Subjects: Graphics, Painting-American, Photography, Sculpture, African Art, Ceramics, Furniture, Silver, Ivory, Tapestries
Collections: 10,000+ objects: California history, Mission-era liturgical vestments, decorative arts, works on paper, painting & sculpture, new media; prints from Renaissance, Baroque, Rococo, 19th c & Modernist periods; contemporary works on paper, with emphasis on San Francisco Bay Area artists; California History Coll; Smith Anderson Editions archive; Andy Worhol Photographic Legacy Program
Exhibitions: 6 - 12 temp exhibs annually; Santa Clara Univ California History Coll, permanent exhib
Publications: Exhib announcements, quarterly; exhibition catalogs
Activities: Educ prog; docent training; workshops; family days; symposia; lects open to public; 8-12 vis lectrs per yr; gallery talks; tours; paintings lent to campus offices

M **TRITON MUSEUM OF ART,** 1505 Warburton Ave, Santa Clara, CA 95050-3791. Tel 408-247-3754; Fax 408-247-3796; Elec Mail staff@tritonmuseum.org; Internet Home Page Address: www.tritonmuseum.org; *Exec Dir & Sr Cur* George Rivera; *Dir Opers* Jill Meyers; *Chief Cur* Preston Metcalf; *Cur Educ* Maria Ester Fernandez; *Registrar* Stephanie Learmonth; *Dir Develop* Chris Chang Weeks; *Dir Finance* Donna Tobkin; *Mem & Vis Servs Mgr* Amanda McDonough
Open Tues - Sat 11 AM - 5 PM, Sun noon - 4 PM, cl Mon; No admis fee; Estab 1965 to offer a rich & varied cultural experience to members of the community through the display of 19th & 20th century American art, particularly artists of California & through related special events & programs; The mus consists of a state of the art facility designed by San Francisco architect Barcelon Jang. The building opened in Oct, 1987 & sits on a 7-acre park site with four Oriental/Spanish style pavilions & sculpture garden; Average Annual Attendance: 117,000; Mem: 1100; dues $15-$1000
Income: $1,250,000 (financed by endowment, mem, fundraisers, corporate sponsorships & city appropriation)
Library Holdings: Book Volumes; Exhibition Catalogs
Special Subjects: Photography, Portraits, Prints, Painting-American, Sculpture, Ceramics, Glass
Collections: Paintings by Frank Duveneck; Austen D Warburton Native American Art & Artifacts Collection; Theodore Wores Collection: oil paintings
Exhibitions: Art Reach Exhibition
Publications: Exhibition catalogs; newsletter, bimonthly
Activities: Educ progs for adults & children; lects open to pub; schols offered; lends original objects of art lent to local companies; mus shop sells original art, books, reproductions & prints

SANTA CLARITA

L **CALIFORNIA INSTITUTE OF THE ARTS LIBRARY,** 24700 McBean Pky, Santa Clarita, CA 91355. Tel 661-253-7885; Fax 661-254-4561; Elec Mail jgatten@calarts.edu; Internet Home Page Address: www.calarts.edu; *Dean* Jeff Gatten; *Performing Arts Librn* Kathy Carbone; *Info Resources Librn* Susan Lowenberg; *Reference & Instruction Librn* Brena Smith; *Visual Arts Librn* Karen Baxter
Open Mon - Thurs 9 AM - midnight, Fri 9 AM - 9 PM, Sat 1 PM - 5 PM, Sun 1 PM - midnight; Estab 1965, first classes 1970, designed to be a community of practicing artists working in schools of art, design film, music, theater & dance
Income: Financed by endowment
Library Holdings: Book Volumes 98,375; CD-ROMs 122; Cassettes 2595; Compact Disks 7614; DVDs 4028; Exhibition Catalogs 14,887; Motion Pictures 1243; Pamphlets 2282; Periodical Subscriptions 344; Records 9193; Reels 5700; Slides 130,747; Video Tapes 4090
Special Subjects: Film, Theatre Arts, Video
Exhibitions: Student work, approx 20 per yr
Publications: California Institute of the Art Library Handbook
Activities: Schols & fels offered

SANTA CRUZ

A **CHILDREN'S ART FOUNDATION,** Museum of International Children's Art, 765 Cedar St, Ste 201, Santa Cruz, CA 95060; PO Box 83, Santa Cruz, CA 95063-0083. Tel 831-426-5557; Elec Mail editor@stonesoup.com; Internet Home Page Address: www.stonesoup.com; *Pres* William Rubel; *Admin Asst* Barbara Harker; *VPres* Gerry Mandel
By appointment only; No admis fee; Estab 1973 to improve the quality of American art education; Gallery has 800 sq ft with rotating displays of art by children from around the world; Average Annual Attendance: 100; Mem: 15,000; dues $37; annual meetings
Collections: American children's art; drawings, paintings & prints from 40 countries
Exhibitions: Exhibit of 55 works from international children's art collection at Portland Art Museum; Exhibit of 50 paintings by Nelly Toll, made when she was a 10-year-old in hiding from the Nazis in Poland in 1943-44, at the University of California, Santa Cruz
Publications: Stone Soup, magazine 6 times per yr

M **MUSEUM OF ART & HISTORY, SANTA CRUZ,** 705 Front St, McPherson Center Santa Cruz, CA 95060-4508. Tel 831-429-1964; Fax 831-429-1954; Elec Mail admin@santacuzmah.org; Internet Home Page Address: www.santacruzmah.org; *Interim Exec Dir* Paula Kenyon; *Cur Exhib* Susan Hillhouse; *Cur Educ* Ashley Adams
Open Tues - Sun 11 AM- 5 PM, 1st Fri of month 11 AM - 9 PM, cl Mon; Admis adults $5, students & seniors $3, children 12-17 $2, children under 12 & mus

mems free, no admis fee first Fri of each month; Estab 1996 to promote understanding of contemporary art history & of Santa Cruz County; 2200 sq ft, 4 galleries, one permanent, 3 changing exhibition galleries; Average Annual Attendance: 21,000; Mem: 1400; dues benefactor circle $10,000, patron circle $5,000, pres circle $2,500, trustee circle $1,000, collector circle $500, art & history circle $250, dual/ family $60, dual/family & seniors $50, individual $40, seniors $30, student/educator $20

Income: $100,000 (financed by endowment, mem, contributions, store income & county income)

Library Holdings: Book Volumes; Clipping Files; Exhibition Catalogs; Manuscripts; Maps; Memorabilia; Original Documents; Photographs; Prints; Slides; Video Tapes

Special Subjects: Architecture, Drawings, Painting-American, Photography, Prints, Sculpture, Watercolors, Textiles, Costumes, Ceramics, Folk Art, Pottery, Etchings & Engravings, Landscapes, Decorative Arts, Manuscripts, Dolls, Furniture, Historical Material, Maps, Embroidery, Gold

Collections: Contemporary art coll on paper; archival material; decorative costumes; textiles & 3-D objects; fine art of Santa Cruz County history; Contemporary Art; Santa Cruz County Photographs

Exhibitions: Where the Redwoods Meet the Sea: A History of Santa Cruz County & its people; Time & Place: 50 Years of Santa Cruz Studio Ceramics Art

Publications: Santa Cruz County History Journal, annually, catalogues; quarterly newsletter

Activities: Docent training, sch art & history progs; lects open to pub, 12 vis lectrs per yr; gallery talks; tours; originate traveling exhibs; mus shop sells books, original art, gifts & film series

A   **SANTA CRUZ ART LEAGUE, INC,** Center for the Arts, 526 Broadway, Santa Cruz, CA 95060-4622. Tel 831-426-5787; Fax 831-426-5789; Internet Home Page Address: www.scal.org; *Office Mgr* Kim Scheibraur; *Pres* Stephanie Schriber; *Publications Mgr* Margo Kuhre
Open Wed - Sat noon - 5 PM, Sun Noon - 4 PM, cl Mon & Tues; No admis fee; Estab 1919, Incorporated 1949, to further interest in visual & arts performing in community; 2000 sq ft of gallery space, off-site exhibits, 65-seat performance hall; Average Annual Attendance: 10,000; Mem: 750; dues seniors & students $35-55, individual $55, family $70-85, 2-year membership $95, bus partners $250-500
Income: Financed by donations, dues & grants
Collections: Local historical & contemporary works
Exhibitions: Annual Statewide Juried Show; Open Studios Preview; Annual High School Show; Summer Art Fair; Luck-of-the-Draw Auction-Fundraiser; Dec 8 Auction
Publications: Quarterly newsletter, exhibit catalogs
Activities: Classes for adults & children; classes in painting, drawing & sculpture; dramatic progs; docent training; demonstration by professional artist at monthly meetings; 12 vis lectrs per yr; gallery talks; competitions with awards; scholarships offered to senior high schools in Santa Cruz County; sales shop sells original art, reproductions & prints

M   **UNIVERSITY OF CALIFORNIA AT SANTA CRUZ,** Eloise Pickard Smith Gallery, 1156 High St, Santa Cruz, CA 95064-1077. Tel 831-459-3606; *Dir* Linda Pope; *Gallery Mgr* Leslie Fellows
Open Tues - Sun 11 AM - 5 PM; No admis fee; Estab 1967; Art of the Monterey Bay Region; Average Annual Attendance: 4,000
Income: University Gallery
Activities: Docent training; gallery talks

M   **Mary Porter Sesnon Art Gallery,** 1156 High St, Santa Cruz, CA 95064-1077. Tel 831-459-2314; Fax 831-459-3535; Elec Mail sesnon@ucsc.edu; Internet Home Page Address: arts.ucsc.edu/sesnon; *Dir* Shelby Graham
Open Tues - Sat Noon - 5 PM; No admis fee; Estab 1971 for curricular support through exhibitions & programs; Contemporary art; Average Annual Attendance: 6,000
Income: $51,000 (financed by endowment, state appropriation, donor support & catalog sales)
Collections: Charles Griffin Farr
Publications: Exhibition catalogs, periodically
Activities: Lects open to pub, 3 vis lectrs per yr; gallery talks; originate traveling exhibs to other Univ Calif campuses

SANTA MONICA

A   **18TH STREET ARTS COMPLEX,** 1639 18th St, Santa Monica, CA 90404-3807. Tel 310-453-3711; Fax 310-453-4347; Elec Mail office@18thstreet.org; Internet Home Page Address: www.18thstreet.org; *Exec Dir* Jan Williamson; *Prog Coordr* Crystal Nelson; *Bus Mgr* Richard Howard; *Develop Assoc* Nicole Gordilio; *Mktg & Vol Coordr* Amber Jones
Open Mon - Fri 11 AM - 5:30 PM; No admis fee; Provides art services to the pub & services to artists & art organizations engaged with contemporary issues of community & diversity; Provocative contemporary art; Average Annual Attendance: 8,000
Income: Financed by grants, fundraisers, donations
Collections: High Performance Magazine Archives
Activities: Educ prog; lects open to pub; 4-8 vis lectrs per yr; gallery talks; tours; Fels

M   **SANTA MONICA COLLEGE,** Pete & Susan Barrett Art Gallery, 1900 Pico Blvd, Santa Monica, CA 90405-1644. Tel 310-434-4000; Fax 310-434-3646; Internet Home Page Address: www.smc.edu; *Gallery Chmn* Maurizio Barattuci
Open Tues-Fri noon-5PM, Sat 11AM-4PM; No admis fee; Estab 1973 to provide a study gallery for direct contact with contemporary & historic works of art; Average Annual Attendance: 25,000
Income: Financed by mem, dues & state appropriations
Collections: Southern California prints & drawings
Exhibitions: Rotating exhibitions every 3-4 weeks
Activities: Lect open to public; gallery talks; tours; original art objects lent

M   **SANTA MONICA MUSEUM OF ART,** Bergamot Station G1, 2525 Michigan Ave Santa Monica, CA 90404-4014. Tel 310-586-6488; Fax 310-586-6487; Elec Mail info@smmoa.org; Internet Home Page Address: www.smmoa.org; *Exec Dir* Elsa Longhauser; *Deputy Dir Exhibs & Programming* Lisa Melandri; *Registrar* Santy Wang; *Chief Preparator* Giorgio Carlevaro; *Dir Devel* Tracy Mizraki; *Dir Educ* Asuka Hisa; *Asst Dir Communs* Elizabeth Pezza; *Retail Cur* Amy Coane
Open Tues - Sat 11 AM - 6 PM; cl Sun, Mon & all legal holidays; Admis by suggested donation, general $5, artists, students & seniors $3; Estab 1984, programming began 1988; Organizes exhibs of contemporary art in all mediums and across disciplines; Average Annual Attendance: 35,000; Mem: starts at $55 per yr
Special Subjects: Afro-American Art, Ceramics, Pottery, Painting-French, Painting-Japanese, Architecture, Drawings, Painting-American, Photography, Prints, Sculpture, Watercolors, African Art, Portraits, Painting-Canadian, Asian Art, Painting-Dutch, Painting-Flemish, Painting-Polish, Painting-Spanish, Painting-Italian, Painting-Australian, Painting-German, Painting-Russian, Painting-Israeli, Painting-Scandinavian, Painting-New Zealand
Activities: Educ prog; classes for adults & children; outreach progs; workshops; lects open to pub; gallery talks; tours; concerts; mus shop sells books, reproductions, prints, and various merchandise

SANTA PAULA

M   **SANTA PAULA ART MUSEUM,** 117 N 10th St Santa Paula, CA 93060-2877. *Exec Dir* Jennifer Heighton

SANTA ROSA

M   **SANTA ROSA JUNIOR COLLEGE,** Art Gallery, 1501 Mendocino Ave, Santa Rosa, CA, 95401-4395. Tel 707-527-4298, 527-4011, Ext 4575; Fax 707-527-4532; Internet Home Page Address: www.santarosa.edu; *Dir* Renata Breth
Open Tues - Fri & Sun Noon - 4 PM; No admis fee; Estab 1973; 1700 sq ft exhibit space with movable walls; Average Annual Attendance: 10,000
Exhibitions: Four exhibits during the school year generally of contemporary artists of national & local prominence & of emerging new artists
Activities: 1-2 vis lectrs per year; gallery talks

M   **SONOMA COUNTY MUSEUM,** 425 Seventh St, Santa Rosa, CA 95401-5202. Tel 707-579-1500; Fax 707-579-4849; Elec Mail info@sonomacountymuseum.org; Internet Home Page Address: www.sonomacountymuseum.org; *Exec Dir* Diane Evans; *Cur Exhibs & Collections* Eric Stanley; *Mktg Develop Coordr* Sarah-Jane Wiseman; *Educ Cur* Jennifer Bethke; *Visitor Svcs* Michelle Novosel; *Finance Mgr* Kirsten Olney; *Dir Develop* Kristin Berger
Open Tues - Sun 11 AM - 5 PM, cl New Year's Day, Martin Luther King Jr Day, President's Day, Easter, Memorial Day, Independence Day, Labor Day, Thanksgiving & day after, Christmas Eve & Day; Admis adults $5, seniors, disabled & students $2, discounts to AAM members, children under 12, members & school groups free; Circ 10 members (EBSCO); Rotating art & history exhibits; Average Annual Attendance: 13,184; Mem: 650; dues $35 & up
Income: Donation & mem based
Collections: 19th-century American West paintings; Sonoma County & northern California history & culture; Tom Golden's Christo Collection; Carol Barnes Collection
Publications: newsletter, The Muse
Activities: Educ prog; classes for adults & children; lects; 10 vis lectrs per yr; guided tours; gallery talks; tours; arts festivals; docent prog; family days; originate traveling exhibitions; mus shop sells books, original art, reproductions, toys, jewelry, notecards & AA supplies

SARATOGA

A   **MONTALVO CENTER FOR THE ARTS,** 15400 Montalvo Rd, Saratoga, CA 95070-6327; PO Box 158, Saratoga, CA 95071-0158. Tel 408-961-5800; Elec Mail info@montalvoarts.org; Internet Home Page Address: www.montalvoarts.org; *Exec Dir* Angela McConnell; *Deputy Dir* Kelly Hudson
Open daily 8 AM - 5 PM; No admis fee; Estab 1930; administered by Montalvo Assn, Montalvo Arts Center is a nonprofit, mem supported org dedicated to fostering community engagement through multidisciplinary art; There are facilities for 10 artists-in-residence. The home of the late US Senator & Mayor of San Francisco, James Duval Phelan, was bequeathed as a cultural center & is conducted as a nonprofit enterprise by the Board of Trustees of the Montalvo Assn. Project Space Gallery & 2.5 mi of hiking trails & beautiful grounds available for event rentals; Average Annual Attendance: 200,000; Mem: 800; dues $60 & up
Income: $4,000,000 (financed by donation, grants & investments)
Exhibitions: 20 solo exhibitions per year of emerging artists in all media; occasional special or group exhibitions
Publications: Calendar, monthly
Activities: Educ & visual arts programs; classes for adults & children; Sally & Don Lucas Artists Residency Program; docent training; lects open to pub, 8 vis lectrs per yr; concerts; gallery talks; tours; competitions with awards; plays; winter workshops; Best Wedding Venue - Metro; fels & schols offered; mus shop sells books, original art, reproductions, prints & gift items

SAUSALITO

A   **HEADLANDS CENTER FOR THE ARTS,** 944 Fort Barry, Sausalito, CA 94965. Tel 415-331-2787; Fax 415-331-3857; Elec Mail info@headlands.org; Internet Home Page Address: www.headlands.org; *Residency Mgr* Holly Blake; *Exec Dir* Sharon Maidenberg; *Communs & Mktg Mgr* Amanda Davidson; *Facilities Mgr* Christopher Doyle
Open Mon - Fri 10 AM - 5 PM, Sun Noon - 5 PM, cl Sat; No admis fee; Estab 1982 to provide studio & living space for artists in the Marin Headlands, a

National Park; 1,800 square ft Project Space - rotates monthly, March - Nov; Average Annual Attendance: 10,000; Mem: 500; dues $35 & up
Income: $900,000 (financed by endowment, city appropriation, donations from foundations & corporations)
Exhibitions: Front & Center annual exhib - Jan - Feb
Publications: Newsletter, three times a year
Activities: Lect open to pub; lect for members only; artist talks, lect & performances; 8 vis lectrs per year; concerts; gallery talks; artist residencies; film screenings; Tournesol Award (studio & grant awarded to a recent MFA painter); store sells notecard sets, limited edition prints, t-shirts & hoodies

SEBASTOPOL

A **SURFACE DESIGN ASSOCIATION, INC,** PO Box 360, Sebastopol, CA 95473-0360. Tel 707-829-3110; Fax 707-829-3285; Elec Mail info@surfacesign.org; Internet Home Page Address: www.surfacedesign.org; *Pres* Jane Dunnewold; *Treas* Melinda Lowy; *Ed Surface Design Journal* Marci McDade; *Exec Dir* Diane Sandlin
Open 9 AM - 4 PM; No admis fee; Estab 1976; Mem: 3800; dues students $35, regular $60, outside USA $80
Income: Financed by mem
Publications: SDA NewBlog, quarterly; Surface Design Journal, quarterly; eNews, monthly
Activities: Classes for adults; national conferences; workshops; seminars; lect open to members only; competitions with cash prizes; scholarships & fels offered; originate traveling exhibs

SOLVANG

M **ELVERHOJ MUSEUM OF HISTORY AND ART,** 1624 Elverhoy Way, Solvang, CA 93464; PO Box 769, Solvang, CA 93464-0769. Tel 805-686-1211; Fax 805-686-1822; Elec Mail info@elverhoj.org; Internet Home Page Address: www.elverhoj.org; *CEO* Esther Jacobsen Bates
Open Wed & Thurs 1 - 4 PM, Fri - Sun Noon - 4 PM & by appt, cl New Year's Day, Easter, Thanksgiving, Christmas Eve & Day; Suggested donation $3 per person; Former residence of one of Solvang's most artistic families, mus is devoted to local history & the Danish-American pioneer spirit of the town's founder. Nonprofit org; Average Annual Attendance: 11,200; Mem: Dues Patron $500; Benefactor $250; Bus $100; Couple or Family $50; Indiv $35
Special Subjects: Decorative Arts, Art Education, Art History, Painting-European, Architecture, Porcelain, Silver
Collections: Exhibs featuring local history & Danish culture; art gallery with changing exhibs; porcelain; silver
Publications: newsletter
Activities: Garden; ann events; Living History Days, juried shows; Danish language classes; children's workshops

M **WILDLING ART MUSEUM,** 1511 Mission Dr #8, Solvang, CA 93463-2607. Tel 805-688-1082; Fax 805-686-8339; Elec Mail info@wildlingmuseum.org; Internet Home Page Address: www.wildlingmuseum.org; *Exec Dir* Elizabeth Knowles; *Pres* Patti Jacquemain; *Dir Develop* Kate Bennett; *Asst to Dir* Holly Cline; *Opers Mgr* Amy Mutza
Open Wed - Sun 11 AM - 5 PM, cl New Year's Day, Easter, Independence Day, Thanksgiving, Christmas; Admis by requested donation: adults $2, mems free, discounts to AAM mems; Estab 1970 to present art of America's wilderness; Average Annual Attendance: 4,300; Mem: 600
Income: Financed by pvt donations & admis
Library Holdings: Book Volumes; DVDs; Periodical Subscriptions
Special Subjects: American Indian Art, Drawings, Etchings & Engravings, Landscapes, American Western Art, Painting-American, Prints, Bronzes, Woodcuts, Sculpture, Watercolors
Collections: paintings; prints; drawings; photographs; sculpture
Publications: quarterly newsletter, The Fox Tale; brochures; exhib catalogs
Activities: Educ progs; artists workshops; art classes for children; lects open to pub; 5 vis lectrs per yr; gallery talks; tours; sponsoring of competitions; scholarships offered; mus shop sells books, magazines, reproductions, notecards, jewelry, toys, stuff animals

SONOMA

M **SONOMA VALLEY HISTORICAL SOCIETY,** (Sonoma Valley Historical Society's Depot Park Museum) Depot Park Museum, 270 First St W, Depot Park Sonoma, CA; PO Box 861, Sonoma, CA 95476-0861. Tel 707-938-1762; Elec Mail info@depotparkmuseum.com; Internet Home Page Address: www.depotparkmuseum.com; *Dir* Sandi Hansen; *Treas* Jo Miller; *Secy* Jean Miller; *IT Tech/mem Secy* Don Stevens
Open Fri - Sun 1 - 4 PM; No admis fee, donations welcome; Estab 1979; Old rail depot with three railroad cars, local history rooms, gift shop & book store, Indian Artifacts, Victorian exhibits, many Sonoma Valley artifacts; Average Annual Attendance: 5,000-7,000; Mem: 280; dues $30 & up; ann & monthly meetings
Income: Financed by mem, donations & grants
Library Holdings: Audio Tapes; Book Volumes; Cassettes; Clipping Files; Framed Reproductions; Lantern Slides; Manuscripts; Maps; Memorabilia; Original Art Works; Original Documents; Other Holdings; Pamphlets; Periodical Subscriptions; Photographs; Prints; Records; Reels; Reproductions; Sculpture; Slides; Video Tapes
Collections: Raising of the Bear Flag
Exhibitions: Rotating exhibitions
Publications: newsletter, bimonthly; Sonoma Mission, Robert Smiley; Pioneer Sonoma, Robert Parmelee; Schools & Scows of Early Sonoma, Roger & George Emanuels; Saga of Sonoma; The Men of the Bear Flag Revolt & their Heritage, Barbara Warner; Images of America, Sonoma Valley, by Valerie Sherer Mathes, Diane Moll Smith, SVHS (Historical Society)

Activities: Docent training; school tours; lects open to pub; 6-8 vis lectrs per yr; schols; sales shop; books; reproductions; photos & antiques, gifts & children's items

M **SONOMA VALLEY MUSEUM OF ART,** PO Box 322, 551 Broadway Sonoma, CA 95476-0322. Tel 707-939-7862; Fax 707-939-1080; Internet Home Page Address: www.svma.org; *Exec Dir* Kate Eilertsen; *Educ & Pub Progs Dir* Margie Maynard; *Mktg & Develop Mgr* Lanke Walker
Open Wed - Sun 11 AM - 5 PM during exhib times; Admis adults $5, children & members free; Estab 1998; Average Annual Attendance: 15,000
Activities: Classes for adults & children; lects open to the pub

STANFORD

M **STANFORD UNIVERSITY,** Cantor Arts Center at Stanford University, 328 Lomita Dr, Stanford, CA 94305-5006. Tel 650-723-4177; Fax 650-725-0464; Internet Home Page Address: museum.stanford.edu; *Dir* Connie Wolf; *Cur European Art* Bernard Barryte; *Dir Art & Science Leaning Lab* Susan Roberts-Manganelli; *Cur Modern & Contemporary* Dr Hilarie Faberman; *Cur Educ* Patience Young; *Cur Asian Art* Xiaoneng Yang; *Cur Prints & Drawings* Elizabeth Mitchell
Open Wed & Fri - Sun 11 AM - 5 PM, Thurs 11 AM - 8 PM, cl Thanksgiving & Christmas; No admis fee, donations accepted; Estab 1894 as a teaching mus & laboratory for University's Department of Art; 24 galleries plus sculpture gardens, courtyard, terraces with outdoor sculpture; Average Annual Attendance: 250,950; Mem: 3500; dues individual $60, family & couple $85, sponsor $175, patron $275, benefactor $500, Artists' Circle $1,000, Connoisseurs' Circle $2,500, New Founders' circle $5,000, Director's Circle $10,000; annual meeting in spring
Income: Financed by endowment, mem & university funds
Special Subjects: Afro-American Art, Anthropology, Drawings, Historical Material, Landscapes, Marine Painting, Collages, Glass, Mexican Art, Antiquities-Assyrian, Prints, Manuscripts, Maps, Painting-French, Painting-Japanese, Sculpture, Graphics, Hispanic Art, Latin American Art, Painting-American, Photography, Watercolors, American Indian Art, African Art, Pre-Columbian Art, Religious Art, Ceramics, Pottery, Primitive art, Woodcuts, Etchings & Engravings, Decorative Arts, Judaica, Painting-European, Portraits, Painting-Canadian, Furniture, Jewelry, Oriental Art, Asian Art, Antiquities-Byzantine, Metalwork, Painting-British, Painting-Dutch, Coins & Medals, Baroque Art, Calligraphy, Painting-Flemish, Painting-Polish, Renaissance Art, Medieval Art, Antiquities-Oriental, Painting-Spanish, Painting-Italian, Antiquities-Persian, Islamic Art, Antiquities-Egyptian, Antiquities-Greek, Antiquities-Roman, Mosaics, Gold, Painting-Australian, Painting-German, Antiquities-Etruscan, Painting-Russian, Painting-Israeli, Painting-Scandinavian, Bookplates & Bindings, Painting-New Zealand
Collections: Rodin Sculpture; Cypriote antiquities; prints & drawings since the Renaissance; Stanford Family Collection; American art of 19th & 20th centuries; European art 16th-20th century; photography including major holdings by Robert Frank & Eadweard Muybridge; Cesnola Collection; Robert Frank Photography Collection; Eadweard Muybridge Photography Collection; See website: museum.stanford.edu/collections.htm/
Exhibitions: (10/16/2013-01/05/2014) Carrie Mae Weems: Three Decades of Photography and Video; (11/13/2013-03/16/2014) Flesh and Metal: Body and Machine in Early 20th-Century Art; (01/22/2014-03/30/2014) Her Story: Prints by Elizabeth Murray, 1986-2006; (07/09/2014-08/03/2014) Inside Rodin's Hands: Teaching Surgery through Art and Anatomy; (04/23/2014-08/17/2014) Carleton Watkins: The Stanford Albums; (09/10/2014-01/04/2015) Robert Frank in America; (11/27/2013-05/04/2014) The Royal Image: Portraits, Satires and Life at Court; (12/11/2013-05/04/2014) The Honest Lanscape: Photographs by Peter Henry Emerson; (12/11/2013-04/27/2014) Jim Dine and Claes Oldenburg: Transformations of the Ordinary; (05/14/2014-10/05/2014) Night, Smoke and Shadows: The Presence of Atmosphere in the 19th Century; (05/14/2014-10/05/2014) Artists Observe Nature; (08/20/2014-11/30/2014) Sympathy for the Devil: Satan, Sin and the Underworld; (10/2014-03/2015) Daumier on Art and the Theatre; (10/2014-03/2015) Shop, Gallery, Studio: The Art World in the 17th and 18th Centuries; (11/01/2013-02/02/2014) Border Crossings: From Imperial to Popular Life; (11/01/2013-02/02/2014) Mapping Edo: The Social and Political Geography of Early Modern Japan
Publications: The Stanford Museum, catalog of drawing collection; exhibition catalogs; handbook of the collection
Activities: Classes for adults & children; docent training; free family Sundays - art making & tours; lects open to pub, 15 vis lectrs per yr; concerts; gallery talks; tours; 2-3 book traveling exhibs per yr; originate traveling exhibs to international mus; mus shop sells books, magazines, slides, jewelry & crafts

L **Art & Architecture Library,** 435 Lasuen Mall, #102 Stanford, CA 94305-2001. Tel 650-723-3408; Fax 650-725-0140; Elec Mail artlibrary@stanford.edu; Internet Home Page Address: www.sul.stamford.edu/depts/art/about/index.html; *Head Librn* Alex Ross; *Deputy Librn* Peter Blank; *Ref Librn* Katie Keller; *Acting Head, VRC* Amber Ruiz
Open Mon - Thurs 9 AM - 10 PM, Fri & Sat 9 AM - 5 PM, Sun 1 - 10 PM; Circ 40,000; Library limited service to non-Stanford patrons
Library Holdings: Book Volumes 160,000; CD-ROMs; Exhibition Catalogs; Fiche; Periodical Subscriptions 560

STOCKTON

M **THE SAN JOAQUIN PIONEER & HISTORICAL SOCIETY,** (The Haggin Museum) The Haggin Museum, 1201 N Pershing Ave, Stockton, CA 95203-1604. Tel 209-940-6311; Fax 209-462-1404; Elec Mail info@hagginmuseum.org; Internet Home Page Address: www.hagginmuseum.org; *Dir & Cur of History* Tod Ruhstaller; *Cur Educ* Lisa Cooperman; *Cur Coll* Kylee Denning; *Librn & Archivist* Kimberly Bray; *Develop Officer* Susan Obert; *Accnt* Karen Richards; *Mus Store Mgr* Patty Huntley; *Webmaster, Publicity* Eddie Hargreaves; *VPres* Bob Fay; *Facilities Supt* Ray Shermantine
Open Wed - Sun 1:30 PM - 5 PM, 1st & 3rd Thurs 1:30 PM - 9 PM; Admis adults $5, youth 10 - 17, seniors, students with ID $250, children under 10 with

an adult and members free; Estab 1928 to protect, preserve & interpret historical & fine arts collections that pertain to the museum's disciplines; The mus covers 34,000 sq ft of exhibit space housing art & history collections; Average Annual Attendance: 45,000; Mem: 1600; dues $25 & up; annual meeting third Tues in Jan
Income: $1.2 million (financed by endowment, mem & foundation grant)
Library Holdings: Book Volumes; Cassettes; Clipping Files; Exhibition Catalogs; Kodachrome Transparencies; Lantern Slides; Manuscripts; Memorabilia; Motion Pictures; Other Holdings; Pamphlets; Photographs; Prints; Slides
Special Subjects: American Indian Art, Anthropology, Archaeology, Decorative Arts, Drawings, Etchings & Engravings, Historical Material, Landscapes, Ceramics, Glass, Furniture, Graphics, Latin American Art, Painting-American, Photography, Watercolors, American Western Art, Pre-Columbian Art, Costumes, Pottery, Painting-European, Eskimo Art, Dolls, Jade, Oriental Art, Asian Art, Painting-Dutch, Painting-French, Period Rooms, Painting-Spanish, Antiquities-Egyptian, Antiquities-Greek, Antiquities-Roman, Cartoons, Painting-German
Collections: Oriental & European decorative arts; Japanese woodblock prints; American Illustrators; Stockton/San Joaquin County History Collections
Exhibitions: 6 - 8 temporary exhibits per year; Stockton Art League Juried Exhibition; Robert T McKee Student Art Exhibition; Art and history related exhibitions
Publications: Museum Calendar, quarterly
Activities: Summer art classes for children; docent training; lects open to pub; 6-10 vis lectrs per yr; concerts; gallery talks; tours; competitions with awards; individual paintings & original objects of art lent; book traveling exhibs 2-3 per yr; mus shop sells books, reproductions, prints, postcards, posters, notecards, gift items

L **Petzinger Memorial Library & Earl Rowland Art Library,** 1201 N Pershing Ave, Victory Park Stockton, CA 95203-1604. Tel 209-940-6300; Fax 209-462-1404; Elec Mail info@hagginmuseum.org; Internet Home Page Address: www.hagginmuseum.org; *Dir* Tod Ruhstaller; *Librn, Archivist* Kimberly D Bray
Open by appointment only; Appt fee $15; Estab 1941 to supply material to those interested in the research of California & San Joaquin County history as well as the history of Stockton; art reference library; For reference only
Income: $15,000 (financed by endowment for Historical Libraries)
Purchases: $400
Library Holdings: Book Volumes 7500; Cassettes; Clipping Files; Exhibition Catalogs; Kodachrome Transparencies; Lantern Slides; Manuscripts; Memorabilia; Motion Pictures; Other Holdings Original documents; Pamphlets; Photographs; Prints; Slides
Special Subjects: Painting-American, Painting-French, Historical Material, American Western Art
Collections: Earl Rowland Art Reference Library

M **UNIVERSITY OF THE PACIFIC,** Jeannette Powell Art Center, 3601 Pacific Ave, Stockton, CA 95211-0197. Tel 209-946-2011; Fax 209-946-2652; Internet Home Page Address: www.uop.edu; *Pres* Donald DeRosa; *Chair* Barbara Flaherty
Open Mon - Fri 8:30 AM - 4:30 PM, Sat & Sun 1 - 6PM; No admis fee; Estab 1975 to expose the University community to various art forms; Gallery is 1200 sq ft with 80 ft wall space, well equipped ceiling spots and flat panels; Average Annual Attendance: 10,000
Income: Financed by student fees & sales
Exhibitions: Rotating schedule of contemporary California artists
Activities: Lect open to public, 3-4 vis lectrs per year; gallery talks; juried contests; awards; tours

SUNLAND

M **AMERICAN MUSEUM OF CARTOON ART, INC,** 8550 Day St, Sunland, CA 91040-1812. Tel 310-828-2919; Fax 310-453-3003; Elec Mail jeremykay@msn.com; Internet Home Page Address: cartoonmuseum.com; *Dir & Cur* Jeremy Kay; *Assoc Dir* Jaeson Kay; *Treas* Liz Kay
Estab 1976 to preserve & display historic cartoon art; Circ 200 +; Maintains reference library; Average Annual Attendance: 150; Mem: 1,500; dues $50
Income: Financed by endowment, mem, city & state appropriation
Special Subjects: Cartoons
Collections: Animation Cartoons Art Comic Books Cartoon Art Historic Cartoons Art Newspaper Cartoon Art Original Cartoon Art
Publications: Annual Report
Activities: Classes for adults & children; docent training; community cartoon classes; lects open to pub, 150 vis lectrs per yr; originate traveling exhibs; sales shop sells books, magazines, original art, reproductions, prints & slides

SYLMAR

M **COUNTY OF LOS ANGELES,** Century Gallery, 13000 Sayre St, Sylmar, CA 91342-1913. Tel 818-362-3220; Fax 818-364-7755; *Dir* John Cantley
Open Mon - Fri 9 AM - 5 PM, Sat Noon - 4 PM; No admis fee; Estab 1977 for contemporary art exhibits & to bring educational value to the community; Average Annual Attendance: 7,500
Income: Financed by city, county & state appropriation
Exhibitions: Seven curated theme exhibits of contemporary art
Activities: Gallery talks; competitions

THOUSAND OAKS

M **CONEJO VALLEY ART MUSEUM,** PO Box 1616, Thousand Oaks, CA 91358-0616. Tel 805-373-0054, 373-0049; Fax 805-492-7677; Internet Home Page Address: www.cvam.us; *CEO & VPres* Maria Dessornes
Open Wed & Fri - Sun Noon - 5 PM; No admis fee, donation suggested; Estab 1975 to exhibit works of nationally & internationally known artists; Average Annual Attendance: 10,000; Mem: 350; dues family $35, single $25
Income: Financed by mem, donations & grants
Collections: Large Serigraph by Ron Davis

Exhibitions: Artwalk; Juried Fine Art & Designer Crafts Outdoor Exhibition
Activities: Lects open to pub, 6 vis lectrs per yr; concerts; gallery talks; competitions with awards; scholarships offered; mus shop sells books, magazines, prints, jewelry & folk art

TORRANCE

M **EL CAMINO COLLEGE ART GALLERY,** 16007 Crenshaw Blvd, Torrance, CA 90506-0003. Tel 310-660-3010, 3011; Fax 310-660-3792; Elec Mail eccart-gallery@elcamino.edu; Internet Home Page Address: www.elcamino.edu/commadv/artgallery/index.html; *Dir* Susanna Meiers
Open Mon & Tues 10 AM - 3 PM, Wed & Thurs 10 AM - 8 PM, Fri 10 AM - 2 PM; No admis fee; Estab 1970 to exhibit professional, historical & student art; Gallery has 2,300 sq ft of exhibit space located on the ground floor of the Art Building on campus; Average Annual Attendance: 5,000
Special Subjects: Prints, Sculpture
Collections: Small print coll; small sculpture coll
Exhibitions: Juried student exhibit; organizational & guild competitions; Shadow Pieces; Student Show; Taleteller
Publications: Exhibit catalogs
Activities: Classes for adults; docent training; lect open to public, 25 vis lectrs per year; concerts; gallery talks; tours; competitions with awards; scholarships offered through the Library; exten dept serves the South Bay Community; collections or parts of collections are exchanged; lending collection contains books & sculpture; sales shop sells original art & posters

M **TORRANCE ART MUSEUM,** 3320 Civic Center Dr, Torrance, CA 90503-5016. Tel 310-618-2376; Fax 310-618-2399; Internet Home Page Address: www.torranceartmuseum.com; *Mus Supv* Janene Ferguson; *Cur* Kristina Newhouse
Open Tues - Sun 11AM-5PM; No admis fee; Estab 1985; Average Annual Attendance: 5,980

TURLOCK

M **CALIFORNIA STATE UNIVERSITY STANISLAUS,** University Art Gallery, 801 W Monte Vista Ave, Turlock, CA 95382. Tel 209-667-3186; Fax 209-667-3871; Elec Mail art_gallery@csustan.edu; Internet Home Page Address: www.csustan.edu/art/gallery; *Dept Chair* Gordon Senior; *Gallery Dir* Dean De Cocker
Open Mon - Thurs Noon - 4 PM or by appointment; No admis fee; Estab 1967, for the purpose of community & cultural instruction; display, educate & foster contemporary art; Gallery is small, covering 200 running ft; Average Annual Attendance: 2,500
Income: Financed by state appropriation
Special Subjects: Drawings, Historical Material, Pre-Columbian Art, Painting-American, Sculpture, Latin American Art, Photography, African Art, Oriental Art, Asian Art
Collections: Permanent collection of graphics & small contemporary works; Ancient Egyptian & Greek artifacts; California Paintings 19th & 20th Century; contemporary paintings, Italian Renaissance Jewelry; Japanese artifacts; Pre-Conquest artifacts; Tamarind prints, William Wendt paintings (California landscapes)
Exhibitions: Exhibs annually including sr art show
Activities: Classes for adults; lects open to pub, 6 vis lectrs per yr; concerts; gallery talks; tours; lent to qualified museums & galleries & campus community; lending collection contains film strips, 35mm lantern slides, motion pictures, original art works, original prints; book traveling exhibs 1-2 per yr; originate traveling exhibitions to University Art Galleries

L **Vasche Library,** 1 University Cr, Vasche Library - Rm 185 Turlock, CA 95382-0299. Tel 209-667-3232; Fax 209-667-3164; Internet Home Page Address: www.library.csustan.edu; *Dean Library Serv* Carl Bengston; *Library Admin Support Coordr* Loretta Blakeley
Open Mon - Thurs 7:30 AM - 11 PM, Fri 7:30 AM - 5 PM, Sat 9 AM - 5 PM, Sun 1 - 9 PM; Estab 1960, a regional state university
Purchases: $8,800
Library Holdings: Audio Tapes; Book Volumes 11,000; Cassettes; Fiche; Micro Print; Periodical Subscriptions 37; Reels; Video Tapes

UKIAH

A **ARTS COUNCIL OF MENDOCINO COUNTY,** (Mendocino County Arts Council) 309 E Perkins St, Ukiah, CA 95482-4504. Tel 707-463-2727; Elec Mail director@artsmendocino.org; Internet Home Page Address: www.artsmendocino.org; *Exec Dir* Alyssum Wier; *Pres* Hal Wagenet
Open by appointment; No admis fee; Estab 2000 to promote, introduce & benefit the arts in Mendocino County; Mem: 400; dues $25 regular mem; $25 artist mem
Income: $45,000 annual budget
Library Holdings: Book Volumes; Exhibition Catalogs
Special Subjects: Folk Art
Activities: Classes for adults & children; Artists-in-the-schools grant prog; Mendocino Cty Art Champion annual awards; mus shop sells original art

M **CITY OF UKIAH,** Grace Hudson Museum & The Sun House, 431 S Main St, Ukiah, CA 95482-4923. Tel 707-467-2836; Fax 707-467-2835; Elec Mail info@gracehudsonmuseum.org; Internet Home Page Address: www.gracehudsonmuseum.org; *Dir* Sherrie Smith-Ferri; *Registrar* Karen Holmes; *Cur* Marvin Schenck
Open Wed - Sat 10 AM - 4:30 PM, Sun Noon - 4:30 PM; Admis seniors/students $3, general $4, familie4s $10, first Friday of month free; Estab 1975; 3 permanent collection galleries, 1 changing exhibit gallery; Average Annual Attendance: 11,500
Income: $220,000 (financed by endowment, mem, city appropriation & grants)
Special Subjects: Painting-American, American Indian Art, American Western Art, Anthropology, Ethnology, Manuscripts

Collections: Hudson & Carpenter Family Collection; Grace Hudson Art Collection; Collection of Pomo Indian arts & material cult; Photographic & manuscript archives
Exhibitions: Grace Hudson (art); History & Anthropology of Native Americans; regional artists
Publications: exhibit catalogs
Activities: Classes for adults & children in docent progs; lects open to pub, 2-3 vis lectrs per yr; book traveling exhibs 1 per yr; originates traveling exhibs 1 per yr; mus shop sells books, magazines, original art, reproductions & jewelry

VALLEY GLEN

M   LOS ANGELES VALLEY COLLEGE, Art Gallery, 5800 Fulton Ave, Valley Glen, CA 91401-4062. Tel 818-781-1200; Internet Home Page Address: www.lavc.edu/arts/gallery.html; *Dean* Dennis Reed; *Gallery Mgr* Phung Huynh
Open Mon-Thurs 11AM - 2PM & 6-9 PM; No admis fee, donation requested; Estab 1960 to show changing exhibitions of ethnic, historical, & contemporary art; Single gallery
Income: $25,000 (financed by state appropriation & fundraising)
Exhibitions: Various exhib
Activities: Lects open to public, 2 vis lectrs per year; gallery talks; tours

VENICE

A   BEYOND BAROQUE FOUNDATION, Beyond Baroque Literary Arts Center, 681 Venice Blvd, Venice, CA 90291-4805. Tel 310-822-3006; Fax 310-827-7432; Elec Mail bbproposals@gmail.com; Internet Home Page Address: www.beyondbaroque.org; *Exec Dir* Richard Modiano; *Develop Dir/Mem* Lisa Lane; *Bookstore/Archive Mgr* Lenka Minkowski
Open Fri 11 AM - 6 PM & during events; Admis non-members $7, students $5, members free; Estab 1968 to promote & support literary arts projects, writers & artists in Southern Calif & nationally; Bookstore, theatre & gallery; Average Annual Attendance: 6,000; Mem: 1,000; dues $35 annually
Income: $150,000 (financed by grants from National Endowment for the Arts, California Arts Council, City of Los Angeles, other government & private grants as well as donations from the public)
Collections: Literature; Poetry; Text Art
Activities: Classes for adults & children; all types of writing workshops; art lects open to public; weekly reading & performance series; art gallery; film program; music program; concerts

A   SOCIAL & PUBLIC ART RESOURCE CENTER, (SPARC), 685 Venice Blvd, Venice, CA 90291-4805. Tel 310-822-9560; Fax 310-827-8717; Elec Mail info@sparcmurals.org; Internet Home Page Address: www.sparcmurals.org; *Artistic Dir* Judith F Baca; *Exec Dir* Joel Arquillos; *Dir Educ* Julius Diaz; *Develop Dir* Lee Schube
Open Mon - Fri 10 AM - 4 PM, Sat - Sun 1 - 4 PM during some exhibitions only; Admis donations requested; Estab 1976 as a nonprofit multicultural art center that produces, exhibits, distributes & preserves public artworks; 1st fl in the Old Venice Police Sta; Average Annual Attendance: 10,000; Mem: 200; dues $25 & up; mem open to public
Income: Financed by government funding, mem & donations
Collections: Archive coll of over 60,000 mural images
Exhibitions: 4-6 exhibits per yr
Publications: California Chicano Muralists; Signs from the Heart
Activities: Classes for adults & children; lects open to pub, 6-10 vis lectrs per yr; gallery talks; mural tours; competitions; schols & fels offered; individual paintings & original objects of art lent to mus; lending coll contains books, framed reproductions, original art works, original paintings, paintings, photographs & slides; originate traveling exhibs; sales shop sells books, original art, reproductions, prints, slides, cards & postcards

VENTURA

M   MUSEUM OF VENTURA COUNTY, (Ventura County Historical Society) 89 S California St, Ventura, CA 93001; 100 E Main St, Ventura, CA 93001-2698. Tel 805-653-0323; Fax 805-653-5267; Elec Mail marketing@venturamuseum.org; Internet Home Page Address: www.venturamuseum.org; *Res Librn* Charles Johnson; *Exec Dir* Tim Schiffer; *Dir Mktg* Susan Gerrard; *Dir Develop* Robin Woodworth; *Cur Colls* Anna Rios-Bermudez; *Opers Mgr* Jeanne Scott; *Dir Educ* Wendy VanHorn; *Mgr Mus Store* Linden Royce; *Mem Asst* Danielle Martell; *Assoc Librn & Archivist* Jennifer Maxon; *Asst Cur* Ariane Karakalos; *Bookkeeper* Izumi Kiesel; *Develop Asst* Suzy Dyer
Open Tues - Sun 11 AM - 6 PM, cl Mon; No general admis fee (some events require admis); Estab 1913 to collect, study, & interpret the history & art of Ventura County; Changing exhibits; Average Annual Attendance: 65,000; Mem: 2300; dues $45 - $500; annual meeting in Oct
Income: $100,000 (financed by endowment, mem, county appropriation)
Special Subjects: Painting-American, Historical Material
Collections: Farm implements & machines; fine arts; historical artifacts; historical figures; prehistoric artifacts; research library coll of 150,000 historic documents & rare glass plate images
Publications: Monthly newsletter; Journal of Ventura County History
Activities: Docent training & networking; school outreach; classes for adults & children; free family time activities third Sunday of month; lects open to pub; gallery talks; special events with each exhibit; mus shop sells books, original art, jewelry, and clothing

M   VENTURA COLLEGE, Art Galleries, 4667 Telegraph Rd, Ventura, CA 93003-3899. Tel 805-648-8974; Fax 805-654-6466; *Dir Gallery* Kate Martin
Call ahead for hours; No admis fee; Estab 1970s to showcase faculty & student artworks, as well as prestigious artists from throughout the country; Gallery 2 & New Media Gallery
Activities: Originate traveling exhibs

WALNUT CREEK

M   DEAN LESHER REGIONAL CENTER FOR THE ARTS, Bedford Gallery, 1601 Civic Dr, Walnut Creek, CA 94596-4299. Tel 925-295-1417; Fax 925-295-1486; *Cur* Carrie Lederer
Open Tues, Wed & Sun Noon - 5 PM, Thurs - Sat 6 - 8 PM, cl Mon & national holidays; No admis fee; Estab 1963 to offer varied & educ changing exhibs to the community & surrounding area; Gallery contains 396 running ft, 3500 sq ft; Mem: 1200; dues Diablo Regional Arts Assoc mem $35
Income: Funded by city, pub & pvt grants
Exhibitions: 5-6 exhibits on view at the gallery each year
Publications: City Scene Newsletter; three catalogs per year; The Diablo Magazine, quarterly
Activities: Classes for adults & children; dramatic progs; docent training; lects open to pub, 6-10 vis lectrs per yr; concerts; gallery talks; tours; competitions

WEST HOLLYWOOD

M   NEW IMAGE ART, 7920 Santa Monica Blvd, West Hollywood, CA 90046-5108. Tel 323-654-2192; Fax 323-654-2192; Elec Mail newimgart@aol.com; Internet Home Page Address: www.newimagartgallery.com; *Dir* Marsea Goldberg; *Dir* Chris Johansen; *Dir* Joe Jackson; *Dir* Clayton Brothers; *Dir* Rich Jacobs; *Dir* Ed Templeton; *Dir* Scooter Rudolf; *Intern* Iya Muto
Open Wed-Sat 1-6PM; No admis fee; Estab 1995 to define the concept of New Image within the present avant-garde; Small alternative space in West Hollywood that shows a full season of primarily cutting edge American artists & street artists; Average Annual Attendance: 5,000
Income: pvt
Exhibitions: Cheryl Dunn, Barry McGee, Ed Templeton, Chris Johanson

WHITTIER

M   RIO HONDO COLLEGE ART GALLERY, 3600 Workman Mill Rd, Whittier, CA 90601-1699. Tel 310-908-3428; Fax 310-908-3446; *Div Dean* Dr. Mitjl Carvalho; *Gallery Dir* William Lane
Open Mon - Fri 11 AM - 4 PM; No admis fee; Estab 1967 to bring to the col students a wide variety of art experiences that will enhance & develop their sensitivity & appreciation of art; Small gallery about 1,000 sq ft located within the art facility; Average Annual Attendance: 8,000
Income: Financed through college
Collections: Contemporary paintings and graphics by Southern California artists
Exhibitions: Landscapes by Paul Donaldson, Carl Aldana, James Urstrom; Sculptures by Joyce Kohl; Self Portraits by Selected California Artists; student shows and area high school honor show
Activities: Classes for adults; lect open to public; 2-4 vis lectr per yr

YOSEMITE NATIONAL PARK

M   YOSEMITE MUSEUM, PO Box 577, National Park Service Yosemite National Park, CA 95389-0577. Tel 209-372-0281, 372-0297; *Cur Ethnography* Craig D Bates; *Coll Mgr* Barbara Beroza; *Chief Cur* David M Forgang
Open daily summer 9 AM - 5 PM, winter Fri - Tues 9 AM - 5 PM; No admis fee; Estab 1926 to interpret the natural sciences & human history of the Yosemite area; Mem: 1700; dues $10 & up
Income: Financed by federal appropriation
Special Subjects: Photography, American Indian Art
Collections: Indian cultural artifacts; original paintings & photos of Yosemite; photographs (special coll on early Yosemite); pioneer artifacts; Yosemite related ephemera
Exhibitions: Rotating exhibits
Activities: Classes for adults & children; lects open to pub; paintings & original art objects lent on special exhibits only; lending collection contains prints, photographs; sales shop sells books, magazines, reproductions, prints, slides; junior mus

L   Research Library, PO Box 577, Yosemite National Park, CA 95389-0577. Tel 209-372-0280; *Coll Cur* Barbara Beroza; *Registrar* Miriam Luchans; *Archivist* Brenna Lissoway
Open Mon - Sun 9 AM - 4 PM; No admis fee; 1890; national park; For reference only; Average Annual Attendance: 3,000,000
Income: Federal appropriation
Library Holdings: Book Volumes 10,000; Clipping Files; Exhibition Catalogs; Fiche; Lantern Slides; Manuscripts; Memorabilia; Pamphlets; Periodical Subscriptions 100; Photographs; Reels; Reproductions; Slides
Collections: Extensive art of Yosemite 1855-2007; Photographs, native basketry
Exhibitions: Chiura Obata: 2007; Yosemite 150th Anniversary: 2014
Activities: Mus shop sells books, magazines, original art, & native crafts

YOUNTVILLE

M   NAPA VALLEY MUSEUM, PO Box 3567, 55 Presidents Circle Yountville, CA 94599-3567. Tel 707-944-0500; Fax 707-945-0500; Internet Home Page Address: www.napavalley.museum.org; *Exec Dir* Rick Deragon; *Office Mgr* Maureen Sweeney; *Mus Educ* Pat Alexander
Open Wed - Mon 10 AM - 5 PM, cl Tues; Admis adult $4.50, seniors & students $3.50, children $2.50; Estab 1971 for regional history, art & natural history; Average Annual Attendance: 12,000; Mem: 900; dues $35-$1000 & up; annual meeting 2nd Tues in June
Income: $750,000 (financed by endowment, mem, museum store, admis & grants)
Special Subjects: Painting-American, Photography, Watercolors
Collections: Henry Evans - linocut prints; Andrew Grayson Jackson - lithos; Sophie Alstrom Mitchell - watercolors; Charles O'Rear - photography; Agricultural Artifacts; American Indian Artifacts; Henry Evans Linocuts; Minerals & Fossil

Publications: Quarterly newsletter
Activities: Progs & classes for adults & children; dramatic progs; docent training; lects open to pub; exten dept serves local schools; book traveling exhibs 6 per yr; retail shop sells books, prints, magazines & gifts

COLORADO

ASPEN

M **ASPEN ART MUSEUM,** 590 N Mill St, Aspen, CO 81611-1510. Tel 970-925-8050; Fax 970-925-8054; Elec Mail info@aspenartmuseum.org; Internet Home Page Address: www.aspenartmuseum.org; *Dir & Chief Cur* Heidi Zuckerman Jacobson
Open Tues - Sat 10 AM - 6 PM, free reception & gallery tours Thurs 5 - 7 PM, cl Mon; Admis $5, seniors & students $3, members & children under 12 free; Estab 1979 to provide the community with a variety of cultural & educational experiences through exhibits, lectures & classes; Average Annual Attendance: 15,000; Mem: 800; dues $35-$25,000; annual meeting in Aug
Income: $2,000,000 (financed by benefits, memberships, donations, grants)
Library Holdings: Audio Tapes; Book Volumes; Exhibition Catalogs; Periodical Subscriptions; Photographs; Slides; Video Tapes
Special Subjects: Sculpture
Activities: Classes for adults & children; docent training; lects, 8 vis lectrs per yr; gallery talks; tours; Aspen Award for Art; scholarships offered; mus shop sells books, cards, toys, hats, catalogs, t-shirts

M **BALDWIN GALLERY,** 209 S Galena St, Aspen, CO 81611. Tel 970-920-9797; Fax 970-920-1821; Elec Mail baldwingallery@baldwingallery.com; Internet Home Page Address: www.artnet.com/baldwin.html; *Dir* Richard Edwards
Open Mon-Sat 10AM-6PM Sun 12PM-5PM
Collections: works by estab & emerging artists

M **RED BRICK CENTER FOR THE ARTS,** 110 E Hallam St, Aspen, CO 81611-1458. Tel 970-429-2777; Fax 970-920-5700; *Exec Dir* Debra Muzikar

BOULDER

A **BOULDER HISTORY MUSEUM,** Museum of History, 1206 Euclid Ave, Boulder, CO 80302-7224. Tel 303-449-3464; Fax 303-938-8322; Elec Mail ngeyer@boulderhistory.org; Internet Home Page Address: www.boulderhistorymuseum.org; *Cur Costumes* Terri Schindel; *Assoc Dir* Wendy Gordon; *Exec Dir* Nancy Geyer; *Prog Mgr* Julie Schumaker; *Cur Coll* Pete Lundskow; *Dir Develop* Alan Browning
Open Tues - Fri 10 AM - 4 PM, Sat & Sun noon - 4 PM, cl Mon; Admis $5 adults, $3 seniors, $2 children; Estab 1944 to promote history of Boulder Valley; history of the Boulder area 1840s to present; Average Annual Attendance: 5,000; Mem: 400; dues $20 - $100; annual meeting in Spring
Income: $450,000 (financed by endowment & mem)
Purchases: Quilts, photographs, costumes, agricultural tools, glass, historical artifacts
Special Subjects: Historical Material
Collections: Costumes; Local Historical Material; Manuscripts & Photographs
Exhibitions: Period Kitchen & Sitting Room; 19th Century Businesses; Bicycles; Agriculture; Mining; Education
Publications: Biannual newsletter
Activities: Classes for adults & children, docent training; lects open to pub, 400 vis lectrs per yr; lending coll contains 5000 paintings; book traveling exhibs 2 per yr; retail store sells books & local history artifacts

A **BOULDER MUSEUM OF CONTEMPORARY ART,** 1750 13th St, Boulder, CO 80302-6226. Tel 303-443-2122; Fax 303-447-1633; Elec Mail info@bmoca.org; Internet Home Page Address: www.bmoca.org; *Pres Bd Dir* Andrew McArthur; *Develop Co-Exec Dir* Penny Barnow; *Sr Cur* Joan Markowitz; *Assoc Cur* Kirsten Gerdes
Open Tues - Fri 11 AM - 5 PM, Sat 9 AM - 4 PM, Sun noon - 3 PM, Wed until 8PM, cl Mon & holidays; Admis exhibs $5, students & seniors $4, mem & children under 12 free, Saturdays, free.; Estab 1972 to explore the forefront of contemporary art & ideas, bringing together innovative exhibits, performances & educ to inspire & challenge; Three galleries totaling 5000 sq ft; lecture space; black box theater; exhibitions focus on contemporary, regional, national & international art; Average Annual Attendance: 20,000; Mem: 500; dues from $12-$1000; annual meeting in Oct
Income: Financed by contributions, mem, city support & grants
Publications: Weather Report; Art & climate change
Activities: Classes for adults & children; dramatic progs; docent training; poetry & performance art; pub theatre; lects open to pub, 3-5 vis lectrs per yr, also lects for members; concerts; gallery talks; tours; competitions with awards; mus shop sells books, magazines & mus materials

L **BOULDER PUBLIC LIBRARY & GALLERY,** Arts Gallery, 1000 Canyon Blvd, Boulder, CO 80302; PO Drawer H, Boulder, CO 80306. Tel 303-441-3100; Fax 303-442-1808, 441-4119; Internet Home Page Address: www.boulder.lib.co.us; *Exhib Coordr* Gregory Ravenwood; *City of Boulder Arts Commission & Dir Cultural Programs* Donna Gartenmann; *Dir Library* Tony Tallent
Open Mon - Thurs 10 AM - 9 PM, Fri & Sat 10 AM - 6 PM, Sun Noon - 6 PM; Estab to enhance the personal develop of Boulder citizens by meeting their informational needs; Bridge Gallery, three shows change monthly; Average Annual Attendance: 300,000
Income: Financed by city appropriations, grants & gifts
Library Holdings: Audio Tapes; Cards; Cassettes; Clipping Files; Compact Disks; DVDs; Exhibition Catalogs; Fiche; Framed Reproductions; Manuscripts; Micro Print; Original Art Works; Pamphlets; Photographs; Prints; Reproductions; Sculpture; Slides; Video Tapes

Activities: Classes for adults & children; lect open to public; 7,500 lectrs per yr; concerts; gallery talks; tours; competitions; awards; sales shop sells books & magazines

M **THE DAIRY CENTER FOR THE ARTS,** 2590 Walnut St, Boulder, CO 80302-5700. Tel 303-440-7826; Fax 303-440-7104; *Contact* Rich Harris

M **LEANIN' TREE MUSEUM & SCULPTURE GARDEN OF WESTERN ART,** 6055 Longbow Dr Boulder, CO 80301; PO Box 9500, Boulder, CO 80301-9500. Tel 303-530-1442 ext 4299; Fax 303-581-2152; Elec Mail info@leanintree.com; Internet Home Page Address: www.leanintreemuseum.com; WATS 800-777-8716; *Founder* Edward P Trumble; *Pres* Tom Trumble
Open Mon - Fri 8 AM - 5 PM, Sat & Sun 10 AM - 5 PM; No admis fee; Estab 1974; Two floors of paintings & bronzes with outdoor sculpture garden; Average Annual Attendance: 40,000
Purchases: Hollywood Indian #5, 1970 by Fritz Scholder (1937-2005); Board of Dir 2002 by James E Reynolds (1926-); Stealth Hunter by Robert Kuhn (1920-2007); On the Beach by Burt Proctor (1901-1980); Respect, bronze 1985 by Allan Houser (1914-1994); Apache Cradle Board, bronze 1994 by Allan Houser (1914-1994); Kachina Dream State, (acrylic 2003 by Dan Namingha (1950-); Seal Hunter, acrylic 2002 by Bob Kuhn (1920-2007)
Library Holdings: Book Volumes 1; Cards 2500; Framed Reproductions; Prints; Sculpture
Special Subjects: Painting-American, Sculpture, Watercolors, American Western Art, Bronzes, Southwestern Art, Baroque Art
Collections: Contemporary Western cowboy & Indian art; Western bronze sculptures; paintings by major contemporary Western artists, 1950 to present day; New outdoor sculpture garden
Activities: Self guided tours; guided tours by reservation; activities for children; mus shop sells reproductions, prints, mus related items, cards, note pads, magnets, bookmarks & posters

M **UNIVERSITY OF COLORADO,** CU Art Museum, 1085 18th St, Boulder, CO 80309; 318 UCB, Boulder, CO 80309-0318. Tel 303-492-8300; Fax 303-735-4197; Elec Mail lisa.becker@colorado.edu; Internet Home Page Address: cuartmuseum.colorado.edu; *Dir* Lisa Tamiris Becker; *Colls Mgr & Registrar* Kimberly Dorazewski-Smouse; *Assoc Colls Mgr & Registrar* Caitlin Rumery; *Exhibs, Facilities & Securities Mgr* Stephen Martonis; *Preparator* Pedro Caceres; *Mus Coordr* Jennifer Conrad
Open Mon - Fri 10 AM - 5 PM, Tues until 7 PM, Sat Noon - 4 PM, cl Sun; No admis fee, suggested donation $5; Estab 1939 to maintain & exhibit art collections & to show temporary exhibits; Visual Arts Complex maintains 5 galleries incl 2 Changing Exhib Galleries, 2 Permanent Exhib Galleries & a Video Gallery, as well as a study center, education/ workshop room & collection storage; Mem: Dues $45 - $10,000
Income: Financed through University, gifts & grants
Special Subjects: Etchings & Engravings, Glass, Pottery, Manuscripts, Drawings, Painting-American, Photography, Prints, Sculpture, Watercolors, African Art, Ceramics, Woodcarvings, Asian Art, Coins & Medals, Baroque Art, Renaissance Art, Antiquities-Greek, Antiquities-Roman
Collections: 19th & 20th century paintings & prints; The Colorado Collection; Ancient Greek Pottery Collection; Roman Glass Collection; Wilton Jaffee Roman Coin Collection; Collection of African Sculpture; Southeast Asian Pottery Collection; Medieval Manuscript Collection; Renaissance & Baroque Print & Drawing Collection; Ancient Iranian Pottery Collection; Japanese Ukiyo-e Collection; Southwest American & South American Santos & Bultos Collections
Publications: Exhib catalogs; brochures
Activities: Lects open to public; gallery talks; symposia; tours

L **Art & Architecture Library,** 1720 Pleasant St, Norlin Library, 184 UCB Boulder, CO 80309. Tel 303-492-7521; Fax 303-492-0935; Elec Mail reflib@colorado.edu; Internet Home Page Address: ucblibraries.colorado.edu/art/index.htm; *Art & Architecture Librn* Yem Fong
Open by appointment. Please call first.; Estab 1966 to support the university curriculum in the areas of fine arts, art history, environmental design, architecture, planning, landscape & interior design; For lending only
Income: Financed by state appropriation
Library Holdings: Auction Catalogs; Book Volumes 120,000; Compact Disks; DVDs; Exhibition Catalogs; Fiche 5950; Other Holdings MFA thesis statements; Museum & gallery publications; Periodical Subscriptions 500; Reels
Special Subjects: Folk Art, Painting-American, History of Art & Archaeology, Latin American Art, American Western Art, American Indian Art, Eskimo Art, Mexican Art, Southwestern Art, Afro-American Art, Oriental Art, Religious Art, Dioramas, Architecture

BRECKENRIDGE

M **COLORADO MOUNTAIN COLLEGE,** Fine Arts Gallery, 103 S Harris St, Breckenridge, CO 80424; PO Box 2208, Breckenridge, CO 80424-2208. Tel 970-453-6757; Fax 970-453-2209;
No admis fee; Estab 1980
Exhibitions: monthly changing local artist

BRIGHTON

M **ADAMS COUNTY HISTORICAL SOCIETY,** 9601 Henderson Rd, Brighton, CO 80601-8127. Tel 303-659-7103; Fax 303-659-7988
Open Tues - Sat 10 AM - 4 PM; For reference. Different artists & groups exhibited throughout the yr
Income: $50,000 (financed by mem, dues, craft shows, gifts & grants)
Library Holdings: Book Volumes; Clipping Files; Lantern Slides; Pamphlets; Records

CANON CITY

A **FREMONT CENTER FOR THE ARTS,** 505 Macon Ave, Canon City, CO 81212-3309; PO Box 1006, Canon City, CO 81215-1006. Tel 719-275-2790; Fax 719-275-4244; Elec Mail jwright@fremontarts.org; Internet Home Page Address: www.fremontarts.org; *Admin* Jerri Wright; *Pres* Mary Burke; *Secy & Treas* Art Welch
Open Tues-Sat 10AM-4PM, during summer months Sun Noon - 4 PM; Admis $3;

Estab 1947; Housed in historic U.S. Post Office bldg; Average Annual Attendance: 10,000; Mem: 350; dues $30, annual mtg Feb
Income: Financed by mem, individual donations, local small bus, grants, fundraising
Library Holdings: Book Volumes; Clipping Files; Original Art Works; Photographs; Prints
Collections: permanent colls
Exhibitions: Exhibs change every month
Publications: Artifacts quarterly newsletter
Activities: Classes for adults & children; dramatic progs; docent training; lects open to public; concerts; gallery talks; competitions; monetary ribbons awards; sales shop sells books, reproductions, prints, CDs, original art & prints

CENTRAL CITY

A GILPIN COUNTY ARTS ASSOCIATION, 119 Eureka St, Central City, CO 80427-5952; PO Box 98, Central City, CO 80427-0098. Tel 303-642-0991; Elec Mail info@gilpinarts.org; Internet Home Page Address: www.gilpinarts.org; *Pres* Susan Snodgrass; *Gallery Mgr* Diane Sill
Open June 1-Aug 15 Tues-Sun noon-6PM, open until 8PM on opera nights, Aug 23-Oct 4 Fri-Sun 10AM-6PM; No admis fee; Estab 1947 to offer a juried exhibition of Colorado artists & to support the local school arts program; Six wings on two floors; outdoor sculpture garden; memorial fountain in Newbury Wing sculpted by Angelo di Benedetto; gallery is open June - Sept 15; oldest juried art exhibition in Colorado; nonprofit organization; Average Annual Attendance: 25,000; Mem: 200; dues $1000; annual meeting, third Sun in Aug
Income: Financed by mem, sales & entry fee
Purchases: Over $60,000 annually
Publications: Annual exhibit catalog
Activities: Juried competitions with awards; sponsor elementary & secondary school art program

COLORADO SPRINGS

AMERICAN NUMISMATIC ASSOCIATION
For further information, see National and Regional Organizations

L ARJUNA LIBRARY, Digital Visual Dream Laboratory & Acoustic Studio, 1025 Garner St, D, Space 18 Colorado Springs, CO 80905-1774; 1404 E Bijou, Colorado Springs, CO 80909-5520. Tel 719-473-0360; Elec Mail pfuphoff@earthlink.net; Internet Home Page Address: home.earthlink.net/~pfuphoff/; *Dir & Ed in Chief, Journal of Regional Criticism* Ct. Pf. Joseph A Uphoff Jr
Estab 1963; For reference only
Library Holdings: Book Volumes 2100; CD-ROMs 250; Compact Disks 450; DVDs 700; Manuscripts; Original Art Works; Periodical Subscriptions; Photographs; Records 150; Sculpture; Slides 1400; Video Tapes 50 clips (computer hard drive) 300 gigabytes
Special Subjects: Decorative Arts, Illustration, Calligraphy, Drawings, Manuscripts, Painting-American, Painting-British, Painting-French, Painting-German, Sculpture, Painting-European, Historical Material, Portraits, Stage Design, Ceramics, Conceptual Art, Archaeology, Aesthetics, Oriental Art, Coins & Medals
Collections: Eshkol-Wachman Movement Notation Studies; Manuscripts & Proceedings, Differential Logic, Mathematical Surrealistic Theory; Mathematical Proceedings in Criticism for Drama, Poetics, Dance, Martial Arts & Yoga; Metamathematics, Calculus, Abstract Algebra; Poetry Reading, Videos & Portraits; JPG Digital Photos
Exhibitions: Type Programming Mail Art Exhib; Internet Group Shows, Internet JPG Exhibs; Media & Mail Art Blogs; You Tube, Digital Video Clips
Publications: Journal of Regional Criticism, irregular
Activities: Awards: Ryosuke Cohen, Brain Cell Life Form, Featured File, International Union of Mail Artists; Participation in poetry & open microphone readings, 3-5 per month; Hear Here (719 on Facebook), Live & Breathe Poetry Society

M COLORADO SPRINGS FINE ARTS CENTER, Taylor Museum, 30 W Dale St, Colorado Springs, CO 80903-3210. Tel 719-634-5583; Fax 719-634-0570; Elec Mail info@csfineartscenter.org; Internet Home Page Address: www.csfineartscenter.org; *Pres & CEO* Sam Gappmayer; *COO* Kari Torgerson; *CFO* Debbie Linster; *Dir Communs* Charlie Snyder; *Interim Dir Devel* Bill Tromble; *Dir Educ* Tara Thomas; *Mus Dir & Cur American Art* Blake Milteer; *Cur Hispanic & Native American Art* Tariana Navas-Nieves; *Collections Mgr & Registrar* Michael Howell; *Cur Asst* Joy Armstrong
Open Tues - Sun 10 AM - 5 PM, cl Mon; Admis adults $10, seniors, military w/ID, students w/ID & youth ages 5-17 $8.50, mems & children 4 & under free; Estab 1936 as a forum, advocate & programmer of visual & performing arts activities & art school for the community; 132,286 sq ft of gallery space, original bldg designed by John Gaw Meem in 1936, recent addition designed by David Owen Tryba; comprised of Blessing Gallery, Duff Gallery, Manley Gallery, Loo Gallery, East Events Gallery, Dickinson Gallery, Lane Gallery & Courtyard Corridor; Average Annual Attendance: 75,000; Mem: 8,000; dues $30-$750; annual meeting in Dec
Income: $2,174,000 (financed by endowment, mem, bus & industry contributions, revenue producing enterprises, city, state & federal appropriations)
Library Holdings: Auction Catalogs; Audio Tapes; Book Volumes 27,000; Clipping Files; Exhibition Catalogs; Memorabilia; Pamphlets; Periodical Subscriptions 50; Video Tapes
Special Subjects: Anthropology, Folk Art, Landscapes, Ceramics, Glass, Mexican Art, American Western Art, Photography, Portraits, Pottery, Pre-Columbian Art, Prints, Silver, Textiles, Bronzes, Drawings, Graphics, Hispanic Art, Latin American Art, Painting-American, Sculpture, Watercolors, American Indian Art, Southwestern Art, Religious Art, Woodcarvings
Collections: American paintings, sculptures, graphics & drawings with emphasis on art west of the Mississippi; ethnographic collections; fine arts collections; 19th

- 21st c American Art; Taylor Collection of Southwestern Art: incl anthropology, Spanish Colonial Art & Native American Art
Publications: Artsfocus, bimonthly calendar; educational programs and tours; exhibition catalogs; gallery sheets; scholarly publications; catalogue of the collections
Activities: Docent training & presentations; internships; lects open to pub & mems only; gallery talks; tours; films; competitions; Governors Award for Excellence in the Arts; art lent to AAM accredited mus; mus shop sells books, original art, reproductions & prints

M Bemis School of Art, 818 Pelham Pl, Colorado Springs, CO 80903; 30 W Dale St, Colorado Springs, CO 80903-3210. Tel 719-475-2444; Fax 719-634-0570; Elec Mail bemis@csfineartscenter.org; Internet Home Page Address: www.csfineartscenter.org; *Pres & CEO* Sam Gappmayer; *Dir Educ* Tara Thomas, MA; *Bemis Admin Asst* Carol Mercogliano
Open Mon-Thurs 9AM-5PM, Fri 9AM-3PM; Estab 1919 as Broadmoor Art Academy, incorporated 1936 into John Gaw Meem's Fine Artc Ctr, later housed in own facility; 7 art studios
Special Subjects: Drawings, Art History, Ceramics, Photography, Sculpture, Watercolors, Jewelry, Mosaics
Activities: Classes for adults & children; art classes for pre-school arts prog; gifted & talented classes (gr 3-6) in visual arts & drama; creative dramatics

M UNITED STATES FIGURE SKATING ASSOCIATION, World Figure Skating Museum & Hall of Fame, 20 First St, Colorado Springs, CO 80906. Tel 719-635-5200 Ext 450; Fax 719-635-9548; Elec Mail info@worldskatingmuseum.org; Internet Home Page Address: www.worldskatingmuseum.org; *Assoc Exec Dir* Jim Ex; *Mktg & Pub Rels Mgr* Linda Famula; *Archivist* Karen Couer; *Mus Asst* Angela Terratas
Open Mon - Fri 10 AM - 4 PM; Admis adults $5, sr citizens & children $3; Estab 1965as the international repository for the sport of figure skating; Maintains 10,000 sq ft exhibition area. Managed by OS Figure Skating; Average Annual Attendance: 7,000
Library Holdings: Audio Tapes; CD-ROMs; Cassettes; Clipping Files; DVDs; Exhibition Catalogs; Filmstrips; Framed Reproductions; Memorabilia; Motion Pictures; Original Art Works; Original Documents; Pamphlets; Photographs; Prints; Records; Reels; Video Tapes
Special Subjects: Historical Material, Art History, Photography, Portraits, Painting-European, Drawings, Prints, Sculpture, Bronzes, Costumes, Ceramics, Etchings & Engravings, Decorative Arts, Manuscripts, Posters, Porcelain, Painting-Dutch, Restorations, Gold, Painting-German, Pewter
Collections: Skating in Art, the Gillis Grafstrom Collection; costumes of the champions; Pierre Brunet Collection; National, World & Olympic protocols; Gladys McFerron Collection; Dorothy Stevens Collection; 2010 US Champions; World Synchronized Skating; Kloss Photo Collection
Exhibitions: Sonja Henie Remembered; 1961 World Figure Skating Team Memorial
Publications: Skating Magazine; Figure Skating: A History by James R Hines
Activities: Docent training; 2-3 special events per yr; gallery talks; tours for adults & children; competitions with awards; local summer reading sponsor with prizes; video tape showings; US & World Hall of Fame induction & reception; selected donations to local skating organizations, clubs & members; exten prog serves local library & airport with satellite exhibs; originates traveling exhibs, 3-4 per yr, to local library & airport; gift shop sells reproductions, branded skating items

M UNIVERSITY OF COLORADO AT COLORADO SPRINGS, Gallery of Contemporary Art, 1420 Austin Bluffs Pkwy, Colorado Springs, CO 80918-3733. Tel 719-262-3567; Fax 719-262-3183; Elec Mail clynn@uccs.edu; Internet Home Page Address: www.galleryuccs.org; *Dir* Christopher Lynn
Open Mon - Fri 10 AM - 4 PM, Sat 1 - 4 PM; No admis fee; Estab 1981 to organize & host group exhibitions primarily of contemporary art by artists of international, national & regional significance; 2,800 sq ft of exhibition space; adjoining classroom, auditorium & workshop/storage room; Average Annual Attendance: 7,000; Mem: Renewals: Jul 1 yearly
Income: $150,000 (financed by state appropriation, private donations & grants)
Special Subjects: Drawings, Latin American Art, Mexican Art, Photography, Prints, Sculpture, Watercolors, American Indian Art, American Western Art, Southwestern Art, Textiles, Crafts, Folk Art, Woodcuts, Etchings & Engravings, Landscapes, Afro-American Art, Glass, Asian Art
Exhibitions: 6 to 7 group exhibitions annually based on themes or surveys of particular mediums
Activities: Classes for adults & children; docent training; mus training prog; lects open to pub, lects open to members only; 10 vis lectrs per yr; concerts; gallery talks; tours; book traveling exhibs

CRESTED BUTTE

M CENTER FOR THE ARTS PIPER GALLERY, 606 6th St, Crested Butte, CO 81224-1819; PO Box 1819, Crested Butte, CO 81224-1819. Tel 970-349-7487; Fax 970-349-5626; *Exec Dir* Jenny Birnie
Call for hours

CRIPPLE CREEK

M CRIPPLE CREEK DISTRICT MUSEUM, 500 E Bennett Ave, Cripple Creek, CO 80813-1210; PO Box 1210, Cripple Creek, CO 80813-1210. Tel 719-689-9540; Elec Mail ccdmuseum@aol.com; Internet Home Page Address: www.cripple-creek.org; *Dir* Kathy Reynolds
Open Fall & Summer daily 10 AM - 5 PM, Spring & Winter weekends only; Admis adults $5, Colorado residents $4, children 7 - 12, military & seniors $3, children under 7 free; Estab 1953 as a showplace for local artists; One room, 50 ft x 20 ft, second room 25 ft x 25 ft; Average Annual Attendance: 35,000; Mem: 80 mem; dues $50-500
Income: Financed by donations

Library Holdings: Audio Tapes; Book Volumes; CD-ROMs; Cassettes; Clipping Files; Compact Disks; DVDs; Framed Reproductions; Manuscripts; Maps; Memorabilia; Original Art Works; Original Documents; Pamphlets; Periodical Subscriptions; Photographs; Prints; Records; Reproductions; Sculpture; Slides; Video Tapes
Special Subjects: American Indian Art, Decorative Arts, Drawings, Etchings & Engravings, Folk Art, Historical Material, Ceramics, Glass, American Western Art, Flasks & Bottles, Gold, Photography, Porcelain, Pottery, Prints, Period Rooms, Woodcuts, Manuscripts, Maps, Sculpture, Painting-American, Watercolors, Southwestern Art, Costumes, Religious Art, Crafts, Primitive art, Woodcarvings, Manuscripts, Portraits, Posters, Dolls, Furniture, Jewelry, Coins & Medals, Restorations, Tapestries, Miniatures, Dioramas, Embroidery, Laces, Cartoons, Stained Glass, Leather, Reproductions, Bookplates & Bindings
Collections: Archival Coll; small coll of locally produced paintings
Exhibitions: Permanent Gold Ore exhibit; Permanent art, jewelry, & sculptures
Activities: Docent training; lects open to pub; lects mems only; 2 vis lectrs per yr; tours; first place Gold Rush Days Parade 2011; first place in floats, Donkey Derby Days Parade 2011; True West Magazine Top Ten Western Museum list 2010 & 2011; mus shop sells books, magazines, original art, reproductions, prints & slides

DENVER

M **BLACK AMERICAN WEST MUSEUM & HERITAGE CENTER,** 3091 California St, Denver, CO 80205-3044. Tel 303-482-2242; Fax 303-382-1981; Elec Mail executivedirector@blackamericanwestmuseum.com; Internet Home Page Address: www.blackamericanwestmuseum.com; *Exec Dir* La Wanna Larson; *Chmn* Sidney Wilson; *Coordr* Daphne Rice-Allen; *Gen Asst* Denver Norman
Open Sept1-May 30 Tues-Sat 10AM-2PM, June1-Aug 31 Tues-Sat 10AM-5PM; Admis adults $8, seniors $7, children $6; Estab 1971; Blacks in the Western United States; Average Annual Attendance: 10,000; Mem: 300; dues vary; annual meeting in Feb
Income: $200,000 (financed by mem, donations, gift shop sales, rentals & grants)
Activities: Docent training; classes for adults & children; lects open to pub; tours; originates traveling exhibs; mus shop sells books, magazines, prints & reproductions

M **COLORADO HISTORICAL SOCIETY,** Colorado History Museum, 1200 Broadway, Denver, CO 80203. Tel 303-447-8679; Fax 303-866-2711; Elec Mail information@chs.state.co.us; Internet Home Page Address: www.coloradohistory.org; *CEO* Georgianna Contiguglia; *State Archaeologist* Susan Collins; *Cur Decorative & Fine Arts* Moya Hansen; *Cur Photog* Eric Paddock; *Dir Research & Publications* David Wetzel; *Dir Interpretive Servs* Martha Dyckes; *Dir Coll & Exhibits* Anne Wainestein Bond; *Cur Books & Manuscripts* Bridget Burke; *Dir Gen Serv* Joseph Bell; *Dir Colo Hist Found* Lane Ittelson; *Mktg* Janet DeRuvo; *Historic Preservation* Mark Wolfe; *Vice Chmn* W Nicholas V Mathers; *Dir Mus Stores* Vivian Coates; *Controller* Tom Zimmer; *VPres* Mae McGregor; *Dir Develop* Carol Whitley; *Historian* Modupe Labode
Open Mon - Sat 10 AM - 5 PM, Sun noon - 5 PM, cl New Year's Day, Thanksgiving & Christmas; Admis adult $10, seniors (65 & older) & students (12-22 with ID) $8, children (6-12) $6, children (5 & under) & mems free; Estab 1879 to collect, preserve & interpret the history of Colorado; 8600 sq ft for temporary exhibits; 33,000 sq ft for permanent exhibits; Average Annual Attendance: 145,000; Mem: 8000; dues $50; annual meeting in Sept
Income: $4,000,000 (financed by endowment, mem, state & federal appropriations)
Special Subjects: Hispanic Art, Painting-American, Prints, Sculpture, American Indian Art, American Western Art, Anthropology, Archaeology, Ethnology, Southwestern Art, Textiles, Costumes, Ceramics, Decorative Arts, Manuscripts, Dolls, Furniture, Silver, Carpets & Rugs, Historical Material, Maps, Coins & Medals, Dioramas
Collections: William H Jackson Photo Collection
Exhibitions: 20th Century Colorado; Artist of America
Publications: Colorado History, quarterly; Colorado History Now, monthly
Activities: Classes for children; docent training; lects open to pub; 12 vis lectrs per yr; gallery talks; tours; individual paintings & original objects of art lent to qualified museums; lending collection contains film strips & motion pictures; mus shop sells books, magazines, original art, reproductions, prints, slides & souvenirs

L **Stephen H Hart Library,** 1200 Broadway, Ste 400, Denver, CO 80203. Tel 303-866-2305; Fax 303-866-4204; Elec Mail research@chs.state.co.us; Internet Home Page Address: www.coloradohistory.org; *Ref Librn* Barbara Dey; *Photo Librn* Sarah Everhart; *Cataloger* Pat Fraker
Open Wed - Sat 10 AM - 5 PM; Estab 1879 to preserve the history of Colorado; Open to public for reference; Average Annual Attendance: 5,000 visit reading rm; Mem: 7000; dues $30; annual meeting in Dec
Income: Financed by state agency, endowments & mus admis
Library Holdings: Audio Tapes 600; Book Volumes 45,000; Clipping Files 250; Lantern Slides; Manuscripts 9,000,000; Maps 5,000; Memorabilia; Motion Pictures; Original Art Works; Original Documents; Other Holdings Colorado Newspapers on Microfilm 2500; Maps 5000; Pamphlets; Periodical Subscriptions 600; Photographs 600,000; Prints; Reels; Video Tapes
Special Subjects: Art History, Decorative Arts, Photography, Drawings, Etchings & Engravings, Manuscripts, Maps, Painting-American, Posters, Historical Material, Watercolors, Ceramics, Crafts, Archaeology, Ethnology, American Western Art, Fashion Arts, American Indian Art, Anthropology, Furniture, Mexican Art, Southwestern Art, Costume Design & Constr, Carpets & Rugs, Dolls, Handicrafts, Pottery, Silver, Landscapes, Dioramas, Coins & Medals, Architecture, Portraits, Textiles
Collections: 600,000 photographs Colorado Western History; Aultman Photo Studio; Denver Rio Grande Photo & Manuscripts; William Henry Jackson Glass Plate Negatives of Views West of the Mississippi
Publications: Colorado Heritage, Colorado History, History Now newsletter
Activities: Classes for children; docent training; speakers bureau; historical treks; workshops; lects open to pub, 12 vis lectrs per yr; tours; Bancroft award; individual paintings & original objects of art lent to other mus; mus shop sells books, magazines, reproductions, prints, cards & gifts

M **COLORADO PHOTOGRAPHIC ARTS CENTER,** 1513 Boulder St, Denver, CO 80211-3984. Tel 303-837-1341; Elec Mail info@cpacphoto.org; Internet Home Page Address: www.cpacphoto.org; *Exec Dir* Rupert Jenkins; *Bd Chair* Edie Winograde; *Operations Dir* Sherea Spalding
Open Wed - Sat Noon - 6 PM; No admis fee; Estab 1963 to foster the art of photography; Average Annual Attendance: 5,000; Mem: Family $60, individual $40, seniors $25
Income: $150,000 (financed by grants, mem dues, donations, classes & workshops)
Library Holdings: Book Volumes; CD-ROMs; Cards; Exhibition Catalogs; Memorabilia; Original Art Works; Periodical Subscriptions; Video Tapes
Special Subjects: Photography
Collections: Permanent collection, 500-600 photographs
Exhibitions: Local & regional exhibits; occasional national & international exhibits
Activities: Classes for adults; student gallery talks; lect open to pub & members, 12 vis lectrs per year; gallery talks; competitions with awards, Hal Gould Vision in Photography Award; exhibits; workshops & tours; CPAC Member grant; CPAC Personal Visions award(s); original objects of art lent to educational institutions & related exhibitions; sales shop sells books & original art

A **COLORADO WATERCOLOR SOCIETY,** PO Box 100003, Denver, CO 80250-0003. Elec Mail president@coloradowatercolorsociety.org; Internet Home Page Address: www.coloradowatercolorsociety.org; *Pres* Sydney Eitel
Estab 1954
Exhibitions: Colorado State Watermedia Exhibit; New Trends Show; Members Show
Publications: Monthly newsletter
Activities: Various workshops; lects open to pub; 10 vis lectrs per yr

M **CORE,** New Art Space, 900 Santa Fe Dr, Denver, CO 80204. Tel 303-297-8428; Elec Mail art@corenewartspace.com; Internet Home Page Address: www.corenewartspace.com;
Open Thurs & Sat Noon - 6, Fri Noon - 9, Sun 1 - 4; No admis fee; Estab 1982 to provide showing opportunities to members & non members; a nonprofit co-op gallery
Library Holdings: Kodachrome Transparencies; Memorabilia; Original Art Works; Photographs; Prints; Sculpture; Slides
Activities: Educ prog; life drawing; lect open to public first Tues of month; gallery talks; competitions with awards; rental space available for three-week runs, $275 & $125; mem works with schools to offer exhib space; scholarships offered

M **DENVER ART MUSEUM,** 100 W 14th Ave Pkwy, Denver, CO 80204-2713. Tel 720-865-5000; Fax 720-913-0001; Elec Mail info@denverartmuseum.org; Internet Home Page Address: www.denverartmuseum.org; *Chmn* Frederic C Hamilton; *Frederick & Jan Mayer Dir & Cur Modern & Contemporary Art* Christoph Heinrich; *Pres* Cathey Finlan; *Pres (V)* Roberta Bhasin; *Dir Conservation* Sarah Melching; *Chief Cur & Frederick & Jan Mayer Cur Pre-Columbian Art* Margaret Young-Sanchez; *Dir Communs* Andrea Fulton; *Dir Petrie Institute of Western American Art* Thomas Smith; *Registrar* Lori Iliff; *Dir Exhibitions & Collections* Michele Assaf; *Dir Educ* Melora McDermott-Lewis; *Gates Cur Paintings & Sculpture* Timothy J Standring; *Dr Joseph De Heer Cur Asian* Ronald Otsuka; *Cur Native Arts* Nancy Blomberg; *Frederick & Jan Mayer Cur Spanish Colonial Art* Donna Pierce; *Cur Photography* Eric Paddock; *Cur Textile Art* Alice Zrebiec; *AIGA Asst Cur & Graphics* Darrin Alfred; *Sr Scholar, Petrie Institute of Western American Art* Joan C Troccoli; *Mus Shop Mgr* Greg McKay
Open Tues - Thurs, Sat & Sun 10 AM - 5 PM, Fri until 10 PM, cl Mon; Admis adults $13, sr citizens & students $10, youth 16 - 18 $5, children under 6 & members free, Colorado res free 1st Sat of month; Estab 1893, original bldg opened 1971, to provide a number of permanent & rotating art collections for pub viewing, as well as a variety of art educ programs & services; Hamilton Bldg added 2006; The seven story North Building contains 210,000 sq ft of space, 117,000 of which is exhibit space; the Hamilton Bldg contains 146,000 sq ft, inc 53,000 sq ft of exhib galleries; Average Annual Attendance: 600,000; Mem: 35,500; dues family $50, individual $35; annual meeting in Apr
Income: Financed by mem, city & state appropriations & private funding
Special Subjects: Decorative Arts, Drawings, Landscapes, Ceramics, Metalwork, Mexican Art, Photography, Portraits, Pottery, Painting-American, Silver, Textiles, Bronzes, Sculpture, Tapestries, Architecture, Latin American Art, American Indian Art, American Western Art, African Art, Pre-Columbian Art, Southwestern Art, Religious Art, Folk Art, Landscapes, Judaica, Painting-European, Painting-Japanese, Eskimo Art, Furniture, Glass, Jade, Jewelry, Oriental Art, Asian Art, Painting-British, Painting-French, Scrimshaw, Restorations, Baroque Art, Renaissance Art, Medieval Art, Antiquities-Oriental, Painting-Italian, Islamic Art, Gold
Collections: American art; contemporary art; design & architecture; European art; Native American art; Native arts; New World art; Oriental art; Western art
Publications: Calendar, monthly; catalogues for exhibitions
Activities: Classes for adults & children; dramatic progs; docent training; lects open to pub, 10 vis lectrs per yr; concerts; gallery talks; tours; book traveling exhibs 2-3 per yr; originate traveling exhibs to national & international museums & galleries; mus shop sells books, magazines, original art, reproductions, prints, jewelry, rugs & children's art projects

L **Library,** 100 W 14th Ave Pkwy, Denver, CO 80204-2713. Tel 720-913-0100; Fax 720-913-0001; Elec Mail sferrer-vincent@denverartmuseum.org; Internet Home Page Address: www.denverartmuseum.org; *Dir* Nancy Simon
Open by appointment; Reference only
Library Holdings: Auction Catalogs; Book Volumes 25,000; Clipping Files; Exhibition Catalogs; Manuscripts; Memorabilia; Pamphlets; Periodical Subscriptions 50; Photographs
Special Subjects: Folk Art, Islamic Art, Pre-Columbian Art, History of Art & Archaeology, Latin American Art, Archaeology, American Western Art, Asian Art, American Indian Art, Anthropology, Southwestern Art, Afro-American Art
Collections: Native American

L DENVER PUBLIC LIBRARY, Reference, 10 W 14th Ave Pky, Denver, CO 80203. Tel 720-865-1363; Fax 720-865-1481; Internet Home Page Address: www.denverlibrary.org; *City Librn* Shirley Amore; *Mgr Reference* Karen Kelley; *Mgr - Western History & Genealogy* Jim Kroll
Open Mon - Tues 10 AM - 8 PM, Wed - Fri 10 AM - 6 PM, Sat 9 AM - 5 PM, Sun 1 - 5 PM; No admis fee; Estab 1889
Income: Financed by city & county taxes
Library Holdings: Audio Tapes; Book Volumes 80,000; Cassettes; Clipping Files; Compact Disks; DVDs; Exhibition Catalogs; Fiche; Manuscripts; Maps; Memorabilia; Original Art Works; Other Holdings Original documents; Periodical Subscriptions 100; Photographs 14,752; Prints 1384; Reels; Reproductions; Sculpture; Video Tapes
Special Subjects: Photography, Painting-American, American Western Art
Collections: Western art
Exhibitions: Frequent exhibitions from the book & picture collections
Activities: Lects open to pub; tours

M EMMANUEL GALLERY, 10th & Lawrence Mall, Auraria Campus Denver, CO 80010; PO Box 173364, Auraria Campus Box 177 Denver, CO 80217-3364. Tel 303-556-8337; Fax 303-556-2335; Elec Mail shannon.corrigan@ucdenver.edu; Internet Home Page Address: www.emmanuelgallery.org; *Dir* Shannon K Corrigan
Call for hours; No admis fee; Estab 1976; Gallery is in the oldest standing church structure in Denver which has been renovated for exhibit space. This historic gallery supports the Community College of Denver, Metropolitan State College of Denver, the University of Colorado Denver as well as local, national & international artists; Average Annual Attendance: 10,000
Income: Financed by above colleges & Auraria Higher Education Center
Library Holdings: Sculpture
Collections: works by regional, nat & international artists
Exhibitions: Various exhib by students, faculty & artists
Activities: 2 vis lectrs per yr, gallery talks, tours, outreach progs; book traveling exhibs

M KIRKLAND MUSEUM OF FINE & DECORATIVE ART, 1311 Pearl St, Denver, CO 80203-2518. Tel 303-832-8576; Fax 303-832-8404; Elec Mail info@kirklandmuseum.org; Internet Home Page Address: www.kirklandmuseum.org; *Conservator* Dean Sartori; *Dir* Hugh Grant; *Coll Mgr & Deputy Cur* Christopher Herron; *Deputy Dir* Gerald Horner; *Mktg & Commun Mgr* Maya Wright; *Registrar* Alisha Stovall; *Visitor Serv & Educ Mgr* Shelly Bleckley; *Operations Mgr* Jacob Stauber; *Vol Coordr* Megan Sullivan; *Colls Asst* Rebecca Gates; *Commun Relations* Renee Albiston
Open Tues - Sun 11 AM - 5 PM; Admis adults $8, seniors, students, teachers $6; Estab 1996 to promote the life & works of Vance Kirkland (1904-1981); Retrospective & individual works Mid-20th Century, decorative arts, Colorado art; Average Annual Attendance: 14,000; Mem: 500; student, senior, teacher $30, individual $35, dual $45, individual & guest $50, arts & crafts $100, art nouveau $250, bauhaus $500, art deco $1,000, pop art $2,500
Income: Privately funded
Library Holdings: Auction Catalogs; Book Volumes
Special Subjects: Etchings & Engravings, Glass, Pottery, Architecture, Drawings, Painting-American, Prints, Sculpture, Watercolors, Bronzes, Ceramics, Woodcarvings, Landscapes, Decorative Arts, Posters, Furniture, Silver, Metalwork, Carpets & Rugs, Enamels
Collections: Decorative Art from 1880-1980; Colorado Art from 1875-1980
Publications: Exhibition catalogs
Activities: Docent training; lects for mem only; gallery talks; tours; book traveling exhibs 2 per yr; mus shop sells books, magazines & original art

M METROPOLITAN STATE UNIVERSITY OF DENVER, Center for Visual Art, 965 Santa Fe Dr, Denver, CO 80204-3936. Tel 303-294-5207; Fax 303-294-5210; Elec Mail cva@msudenver.edu; Internet Home Page Address: www.MetroStateCVA.org; *Creative Dir* Cecily Cullen; *Exec Dir* Greg Watts; *Business Dir* Amy Tancig; *Edu Dir* Talya Dornbush
Open to public Tues - Fri 11 AM - 6 PM, Sat 12 - 5 PM, cl all major holidays; No admis fee, donations accepted; Estab 1990 for temporary exhibitions of contemporary art; 5000 sq ft; Average Annual Attendance: 32,000; Mem: 300; annual meeting in July; D & E; Scholarships
Income: $350,000 (financed by mem, state appropriation, grants & revenues)
Special Subjects: Hispanic Art, American Indian Art, Southwestern Art, Afro-American Art
Publications: Quarterly newsletter
Activities: Classes for adults, teens & children; lects open to pub, 8 vis lectrs per yr; gallery talks; tours; book traveling exhibs 1-2 per yr; originate traveling exhibs 5 per yr
Ent Req: GED

M MIZEL MUSEUM, 400 S Kearney St, Denver, CO 80224-1238. Tel 303-394-9993; Fax 303-394-1119; Elec Mail ellen@mizelmuseum.org; Internet Home Page Address: www.mizelmuseum.org; *Chmn Bd* Larry Mizel; *Dir* Ellen Premack; *Dir Educ* Jan Cooper Nadav; *Spec Events* Deanne Kapnik; *Asst to Dir* Maggi Junor; *Cur* Georgina Kolber
Open Mon - Fri 8:30 AM - 5 PM; No admis fee; 1982 to tell the continuum of the Jewish people within a multicultural content through the arts; Average Annual Attendance: 40,000
Library Holdings: Book Volumes 400
Collections: ritual & religious synagogue artifacts; contemporary Judaica; multicultural educational exhibits
Exhibitions: Bridges of Understanding; Immigrant Adventure; Mystical Masks of Many Cultures; Tikkun Olam
Publications: newsletter; educ brochure; email blasts
Activities: Workshops; art classes for adults & children; organized educ prog; docent prog; guided tours; lect; films; Community Cultural Enrichment Award; progs in the schools; schools

M MUSEO DE LAS AMERICAS, 861 Santa Fe Dr, Denver, CO 80204-4344. Tel 303-571-4401; Fax 303-607-9761; Elec Mail gloria@museo.org; Internet Home Page Address: www.museo.org; *Exec Dir* Maruca Sulazar; *Dir Devel* Christy Costello; *Opers Mgr* Claudia Moran
Open Tue - Fri 10 AM - 5 PM, Sat - Sun noon - 5 PM; Admis adults $5, students & seniors $3, members & children under 13 free; Estab 1991 to collect, preserve & interpret Latin American art, history & culture; Circ 25,000; Contemporary, Pre-Columbian & Folk Art Galleries; Average Annual Attendance: 20,000; Mem: 800; dues $15 - $1,000
Income: $550,000 (financed by mem, foundation, corporation, pub funding & store revenue)
Library Holdings: Auction Catalogs; Audio Tapes; Book Volumes; CD-ROMs; Cassettes; Compact Disks; DVDs; Exhibition Catalogs; Framed Reproductions; Original Art Works; Original Documents; Other Holdings; Photographs; Prints; Records; Reproductions; Sculpture; Slides; Video Tapes
Special Subjects: Ceramics, Glass, Metalwork, Mexican Art, American Western Art, Pottery, Prints, Woodcuts, Maps, Tapestries, Architecture, Drawings, Graphics, Hispanic Art, Latin American Art, Painting-American, Photography, Sculpture, Watercolors, Bronzes, Anthropology, Archaeology, Ethnology, Southwestern Art, Textiles, Religious Art, Crafts, Folk Art, Woodcarvings, Etchings & Engravings, Portraits, Posters, Furniture, Jade, Jewelry, Porcelain, Silver, Historical Material, Coins & Medals, Baroque Art, Embroidery, Painting-Spanish, Gold, Leather, Reproductions
Collections: Tragew, Hamilton, Bloodworth, Pelliser & Bass Coors
Exhibitions: Eppie Archuleta: Master Weaver of the San Luis Valley; Cuba Siempre Vive; Alberto Gironela: Madonna Series; Luis Jimenez: Man On Fire
Publications: Notitas Newsletter, quarterly
Activities: Classes for adults & children; docent training; lects open to pub, 6 vis lectrs per yr; concerts; gallery talks; tours; 2009 Mayor's Award for Excellence in the Arts; book traveling exhibs 5 per yr; mus shop sells books, magazines, reproductions, prints, original art, textiles, curios, historical objects & clothing

M MUSEUM OF CONTEMPORARY ART DENVER, 1485 Delgany St, Denver, CO 80202-1100. Tel 303-298-7554; Fax 303-298-7553; Elec Mail donnaf@mcadenver.org; Internet Home Page Address: www.mcadenver.org; *Dir & Chief Animator* Adam Lerner; *Dir Admin & Finance* Donna Frost; *Dir Devel* Scott Anderson; *Dir Programming & Chief of Fictions* Sarah Kate Baie
Open Tues - Sun 10 AM - 6 PM, Fri until 10 PM; Admis adults $10, students & seniors $5, members & children under 12 free; Estab 1996 to educate & inspire artists, students & the general public about important new developments in visual arts - regional, national or international; Mem: Dues $45+
Activities: Workshops; lects open to pub; tours, symposiums; mus shop sells books, magazines, & prints

M PIRATE-CONTEMPORARY ART, 3655 Navajo, Denver, CO 80211; 1370 Verbena, Denver, CO 80220. Tel 303-458-6058; Internet Home Page Address: www.pirateartonline.org; *Dir* Phil Bender
Open Fri 6 PM - 10 PM, Sat & Sun Noon - 5 PM; No admis fee; Estab 1980; gallery displays contemporary art; Average Annual Attendance: 2,000; Mem: 30
Income: Financed by mem, grants & donations
Exhibitions: Member Artists Exhibit Yearly; Member solo exhibs & Day of the Dead show in Nov
Activities: Community outreach prog; sales shop sells original art, hats, t-shirts, buttons & bumper stickers

M SPARK GALLERY, 900 Santa Fe Dr, Ste 1 Denver, CO 80204-3937. Tel 720-889-2200; Elec Mail jwmatlack@yahoo.com; Internet Home Page Address: www.sparkgallery.com; *Sec* Elaine Ricklin; *Treas* Annalee Schorr
Open Apr 1 - Nov 1, Thurs & Sat Noon - 5 PM, Fri Noon - 9 PM, Sun 1-4 PM
Collections: works by regional, nat & international artists; paintings; sculpture; drawings; photographs

A THINK 360 ART COMPLETE EDUCATION, (Young Audiences Inc) Colo Chapter, 135 Park Ave W, Denver, CO 80205-3209. Tel 720-904-8890; Fax 720-904-8894; Elec Mail info@think360arts.org; Internet Home Page Address: www.youngaudiences.org; *Managing Dir* Jane Hansberry; *Educ Dir* Michelle Shedro; *Prog Asst* Megan Weber
Open Mon - Fri 9 AM - 4 PM; Admis fee varies per event, see program catalog; Estab to strive to make the arts an essential part of the educ of every Colorado child enabling students & their teachers to experience the arts, to learn from professional artists & to understand the role of the arts in the creative process & in educational excellence; Average Annual Attendance: 7,000
Income: Grant funded
Activities: Classes for children; family progs

M WALKER FINE ART, 300 W 11th Ave #A, Denver, CO 80204. Tel 303-355-8955; Fax 303-623-0553; Elec Mail info@walkerfineart.com; Internet Home Page Address: www.walkerfineart.com; *Dir* Bobbi Walker; *Gallery Mgr* McKenzie Chandler
Open Tues-Sat 11 AM - 6PM, 1st Fri each month 12 PM - 8 PM, other times by appointment; Contemporary art, abstraction & realism through mixed media, experimental photog, sculpture installation

DURANGO

M DURANGO ARTS CENTER, (Barbara Conrad Art Gallery) Barbara Conrad Art Gallery, 802 E 2nd St, Durango Arts Center Durango, CO 81301-5426. Tel 970-259-2606; Fax 970-259-6571; Internet Home Page Address: www.durangoarts.org; *Exec Dir* Sheri Rochford; *Exhibs Dir* Mary Puller
Open Tues - Sat 10 AM - 5 PM; Mem: 750+
Library Holdings: Book Volumes; DVDs; Exhibition Catalogs; Memorabilia; Original Art Works; Periodical Subscriptions
Exhibitions: Ten exhibs annually (juried shows & traveling exhibs)
Activities: Classes for adults & children; dramatic progs; docent training; ten plus visiting lectrs per year; gallery talks; sponsoring of competitions (juried shows); mus shop sells books, original art, folk art, fine craft, jewelry, textiles

ERIE

NATIONAL COUNCIL ON EDUCATION FOR THE CERAMIC ARTS (NCECA)

For further information, see National and Regional Organizations

EVERGREEN

M **JEFFERSON COUNTY OPEN SPACE,** Hiwan Homestead Museum, 4208 S. Timbervale Dr Evergreen, CO 80439; 700 Jefferson County Pkwy, Ste 100 Evergreen, CO 80401. Tel 303-271-5925; Fax 303-670-7746; Elec Mail trock@jeffco.us; Internet Home Page Address: www.jeffco.us/openspace; *Educ Coordr* Sue Ashbaugh; *Cur* Angela Rayne; *Adminr* John Steinle
Open office Mon-Fri 7:30AM-5:30PM, mus Sept-May noon-5PM, June-Aug 11AM-5PM; No admis fee; Estab 1975 to collect, preserve & exhibit Jefferson County history; History House furnished to 1900; 17 rm log mansion with original furnishings & displays on local history; maintains reference library; Average Annual Attendance: 18,000
Income: Financed by county taxes
Special Subjects: Architecture, Mexican Art, Painting-American, American Indian Art, American Western Art, Southwestern Art, Textiles, Costumes, Religious Art, Folk Art, Decorative Arts, Dolls, Furniture, Historical Material
Collections: Decorative & fine arts; manuscripts; Native American Arts & Crafts; Photographs; Textiles
Exhibitions: Seasonally rotating exhibitions
Publications: The Record, quarterly
Activities: Classes for children; docent training; historic lect series open to pub, 4 vis lectrs per yr

FORT COLLINS

M **CENTER FOR FINE ART PHOTOGRAPHY,** 400 N College Ave, Fort Collins, CO 80524-2409. Tel 970-224-1010

M **COLORADO STATE UNIVERSITY,** Curfman Gallery, 8033 Campus Delivery, Lory Student Ctr Fort Collins, CO 80523-8033. Tel 970-491-2810; Fax 970-491-3746; Elec Mail curfman@lamar.colostate.edu; Internet Home Page Address: www.curfman.colostate.edu; *Dir* Matthew S Helmer; *Dir* Stanley Scott
Open Mon - Thurs 9 AM - 9 PM, Fri 9 AM - 9:30 PM, Sat 12 - 4 PM; No admis fee; Estab 1969 to exhibit multi-cultural works from all over the world plus student works; Average Annual Attendance: 50,000
Collections: African Collection
Exhibitions: Rotating Exhibits
Activities: Lects open to public; vis lectrs per year varies; gallery talks; awards Best of CSU & Best of Fort Collins

M **FORT COLLINS MUSEUM OF ART, INC.,** 201 S College Ave, Fort Collins, CO 80524-3182. Tel 970-482-2787; Fax 970-482-0804; Elec Mail info@ftcma.org; Internet Home Page Address: www.ftcma.org; *Exec Dir* Marianne Lorenz; *Gen Mgr* Gloria Boresen; *Vol & Event Coordr* April Freitag
Open Wed - Fri 10 AM -5 PM, Sat & Sun 12 PM - 5 PM; Admis adults $4, students with ID & seniors $2, youth 7 - 18 $1, mem & children 6 & under free; Estab 1990 a non-profit art mus dedicated to educ & exhibition of visual art; one gallery, 3000 sq ft housed in former 1911 post office on historic register; Average Annual Attendance: 17,000; Mem: 400
Income: $250,000 (financed by mem, fundraisers, grants & sponsorships)
Library Holdings: Auction Catalogs; Book Volumes; Exhibition Catalogs; Kodachrome Transparencies
Special Subjects: Drawings, Painting-American, Photography, Prints, Sculpture, Watercolors, Ceramics, Crafts, Pottery, Landscapes, Posters, Glass, Metalwork
Exhibitions: Rocky Mountain Biennial Competition; Rotating exhibitions
Activities: Classes for adults, teens & children; docent training; lects open to pub, 2 vis lectrs per yr; gallery talks; tours; competitions; book traveling exhibs 1 per yr; originates traveling exhibs; mus shop sells books

FORT MORGAN

M **FORT MORGAN HERITAGE FOUNDATION,** 414 Main St, Fort Morgan, CO 80701-2143; PO Box 184, Fort Morgan, CO 80701-0184. Tel 970-542-4010; Fax 970-542-4012; Elec Mail fortmorganmuseum@ftmorganmus; Internet Home Page Address: www.ftmorganmus.org; *Pres* Heritage Foundation Don Ostwald; *VPres* Gerald Danford; *Publ Cur* Nickki Cooper; *Educ* Andrew Dumohoo; *Dir* Marne Jurgemeyer; *Mus Tech* Joyce Martinez
Open Mon - Fri 10 AM - 5 PM, Tues-Thurs 10AM-8PM, Fri 10AM-5PM, Sat 11AM-5PM; No admis fee; Estab 1975 to interpret the history & culture of the area; Mus exhibits on a temporary basis fine art exhibits, both local artists & traveling exhibits; Average Annual Attendance: 10,000; Mem: 275; dues $10-$500; annual meeting fourth Thurs in Jan
Income: $110,000 (financed by endowment, mem, city appropriation & local, state & federal grants)
Library Holdings: Clipping Files; Filmstrips; Kodachrome Transparencies; Lantern Slides; Maps; Memorabilia; Original Documents; Photographs; Records; Video Tapes
Special Subjects: Painting-American, Anthropology, Archaeology, Costumes, Manuscripts, Historical Material
Collections: Hogsett Collection; primarily cultural & historical material; Native Arts; Howard Rollin Bird Paintings
Activities: Classes for adults & children; dramatic progs; docent progs; 14 lectrs for mems only; AAM accredited awards; books, prints & original art

GLENWOOD SPRINGS

M **GLENWOOD CENTER FOR THE ARTS,** 601 E 6th St, Glenwood Springs, CO 81601. Tel 970-945-2414

GOLDEN

M **CLEAR CREEK HISTORY PARK,** 923 10th St, Golden, CO 80401-1025. Tel 303-278-3557; Fax 303-278-8916; Elec Mail info@clearcreekhistorypark.org; Internet Home Page Address: www.clearcreekhistorypark.org
Open May & Sept: Sat 10 AM - 4:30 PM, June, July & Aug: Tues - Sat 10 AM - 4:30 PM; Founded 1999; History mus & living history park; vol hrs 3250; Average Annual Attendance: 9610

Special Subjects: Furniture
Collections: Six relocated homestead structures including 2 cabins, barn, chicken coop, and a one-room schoolhouse; historic & reproduction items with emphasis on furnishings, personal artifacts, recreational artifacts, tools & equip for materials
Publications: Dear Friends, quarterly newsletter; The Friendly Reminder, monthly newsletter
Activities: Organized educ progs for adults & children; docent prog; training prog; guided tours; concerts

A **FOOTHILLS ART CENTER, INC,** 809 15th St, Golden, CO 80401-1813. Tel 303-279-3922; Fax 303-279-9470; Elec Mail epapenfus@foothillsartcenter.org; Internet Home Page Address: www.foothillsartcenter.org; *Exec Dir* Reilly Sanborn; *Cur* Michael Chavez; *Opers Mgr* Esther Papenfus
Open Mon - Sat 10- AM - 5 PM, Sun 1 - 4 PM, cl holidays; Admis adults $3, seniors $2, mem & students free; Estab 1968 to provide a cultural center which embraces all the arts, to educate & stimulate the community in the appreciation & understanding of the arts, to provide equal opportunities for all people to participate in the further study & enjoyment of the arts & to provide artists & artisans with the opportunity to present their work; Housed in the former First Presbyterian Church of Golden, the original structure was built in 1872, the manse (a part of the whole layout) was built in 1892; there are five galleries, an outdoor sculpture garden and classrooms; Average Annual Attendance: 40,000; Mem: 1,200; dues $35; annual meeting in Dec
Income: $670,000 (financed by donated & earned income)
Special Subjects: Architecture, Drawings, Etchings & Engravings, Historical Material, Landscapes, Photography, Posters, Painting-American, Pottery, American Western Art, Bronzes, Decorative Arts, Folk Art, American Indian Art, Ceramics, Collages, Crafts, Hispanic Art, Juvenile Art, Latin American Art, Miniatures, Portraits, Pre-Columbian Art
Exhibitions: North American Sculpture Exhibitions; Rocky Mountain National Watermedia Exhibition; numerous open juried competitions
Publications: Bimonthly newsletter; catalogs of major national shows
Activities: Classes for adults & children; lects open to pub, 8 vis lectrs per yr; concerts; gallery talks; tours, competitions with awards; individual paintings & original objects of art lent to bus; mus shop sells original art

GRAND JUNCTION

M **MUSEUM OF WESTERN COLORADO,** Museum of the West, 462 Ute Ave, Grand Junction, CO 81501; PO Box 20000, Grand Junction, CO 81501-5001. Tel 970-242-0971; Fax 970-242-3960; Elec Mail info@wcmuseum.org; Internet Home Page Address: www.wcmuseum.org; *Cur Archives & Librn* Michael J Menard; *Dir* Peter Booth; *Bus Mgr* Celia Fournier; *Cur Paleontology* John R Foster; *Maintenance* Fred Espinosa; *Facilities Mgr* Don Kerven; *Maintenance* Alfredo Yslas; *Cur History* David Bailey; *Asst Bus Mgr* Carla Hatch; *Asst Dir Opers & Pub Rels, Cur Cross Orchard, Gift Shop Mgr* Kay Fiegel
Open Mon - Fri 10 AM - 4:45 PM, cl Sun, Christmas wk & major holidays; Admis adults $5.50, seniors $4.50, children $3.50, free for group mem; Estab 1965 to collect preserve, interpret social & natural history of Western Colorado; Mem: dues benefactor $1000, patron $500, sponsor $150, contributor & bus $50, family $25, retired adult $15
Income: Financed by Mesa County, admis, gift shop revenues, grants, mem, donations, programs & special events
Library Holdings: Book Volumes 3500; Cassettes 2500; Lantern Slides 15; Manuscripts 300; Memorabilia; Micro Print; Motion Pictures; Original Art Works; Pamphlets 200; Periodical Subscriptions 15; Photographs 18,000; Reels 47; Slides 14,000
Collections: Frank Dean Collection; Al Look Collection; Warren Kiefer Railroad Collection; Wilson Rockwell Collection; artwork, books, manuscripts & photographs on the history & natural history of Western Colorado; Mesa County Oral History Collection
Exhibitions: Rotating exhibits & pieces from permanent collection
Publications: A Bibliography of the Dinosauria; Cross Orchards Coloring Book; Dinosaur Valley Coloring Book; Familiar Insects of Mesa County, Colorado; Footprints in the Trail; Mesa County, Colorado: A 100 Year History; Mesa County Cooking with History; More Footprints in the Trail; Museum Times, monthly newsletter; Paleontology & Geology of the Dinosaur Triangle
Activities: Classes for adults & children; dramatic programs; docent training; lects open to pub, 10 vis lectrs per yr; concerts; tours; Cross Ranch Apple Jubilee; Cross Ranch Artisan's Festival; slides/tape & video tape presentations; mus shop sells books, magazines, original art, reproductions

A **WESTERN COLORADO CENTER FOR THE ARTS,** (The Art Center) The Art Center, 1803 N Seventh, Grand Junction, CO 81501. Tel 970-243-7337; Fax 970-243-2482; Elec Mail info@gjartcenter.org; Internet Home Page Address: www.gjartcenter.org; *Dir* Cheryl McNab; *Educ & Exhib Cur* Camille Silverman; *Events & Commun* Lee Borden; *Artist in Res* Terry Shepherd; *Gift Shop & Mem Mgr* Laurie Lester; *Children's Progs Mgr* Rachel Egelston
Open Tues - Sat 9 AM - 4 PM; Admis $3 for non-members; Art Center - Mus incorporated in 1952 to provide an appropriate setting for appreciation of & active participation in the arts; Three changing exhibition galleries of 2000 sq ft each; permanent collection gallery; seven studio classrooms; auditorium; Average Annual Attendance: 30,000; Mem: 1200; dues family $50, individual $35; annual meeting in Sep
Income: Financed by endowment, mem, tuition, gifts & grants
Collections: Ceramics, needlework, paintings; Navajo weavings & pottery
Exhibitions: Changing exhibits only in gallery; exhibits change monthly
Publications: Newsletter for members, monthly; catalog of permanent collections
Activities: Classes for adults & children; docent training; lect open to public; 12 vis lectrs per year; concerts; gallery talks; tours; competitions; sales shop sells books, magazines, original art, reproductions, Southwest Indian & contemporary craft items & notecards
L **Library,** 1803 N Seventh, Grand Junction, CO 81501. Tel 970-243-7337; Fax 970-243-2482; Internet Home Page Address: www.gjartcenter.org; *Chief Exec Officer* Cheryl McNab; *Pres* Robbie Breaux

Open Tues - Sat 9 AM - 4 PM; Estab 1953; Open to members & pub for reference; Average Annual Attendance: 31,000
Library Holdings: Book Volumes 1000; Exhibition Catalogs
Special Subjects: Decorative Arts, Photography, Painting-American, Prints, Sculpture, Ethnology, Anthropology
Collections: works by Western artists; Navajo blankets & rugs; Anasazi pottery; contemporary Colorado paintings & ceramics
Publications: bimonthly newsletter
Activities: Educ progs for adults & children; lects, gallery talks; mus shop

GREELEY

M **MADISON & MAIN GALLERY,** 927 16th St, Greeley, CO 80631-5511. Tel 970-351-6201; Internet Home Page Address: www.madisonandmaingallery.com; *Treas* Susan B Anderson
Open Mon - Sat 10 AM - 6 PM; No admis fee; Estab 1987 as an artists' cooperative
Income: $30,000 (financed by art sales)
Exhibitions: Six shows per year plus work of members & consignees

M **UNIVERSITY OF NORTHERN COLORADO, SCHOOL OF ART AND DESIGN,** (University of Northern Colorado) Mariani Gallery, 8th Ave & 18th St, Greeley, CO 80639; University of Northern Colorado Galleries, Campus Box 30, Guggenheim Hall Greeley, CO 80639. Tel 970-351-2184, 2143; Fax 970-351-2299; Elec Mail joan.shannonmiller@unco.edu; Internet Home Page Address: www.arts.unco.edu/visarts/visarts_galleries.html; *Gallery Dir* Joan Shannon-Miller
Open Mon - Fri noon - 5 PM, Sat 10 AM - 2 PM; No admis fee; Estab 1973, to provide art exhibitions for the benefit of the University & the surrounding community; Remodeled space 2001; Average Annual Attendance: 20,000
Income: Financed by endowment & city & state appropriations
Exhibitions: UNC Faculty Exhibition; UNC Student Exhibition
Publications: Schedule of Exhibitions, quarterly
Activities: Gallery talks; competitions with awards

GUNNISON

M **GUNNISON ARTS CENTER,** 102 S Main St, Gunnison, CO 81230; PO Box 1772, Gunnison, CO 81230-1772. Tel 970-641-4029; *Interim Exec Dir* Janice Welborn
Open Tues-Fri Noon - 6PM, cl Sat - Mon; No admis fee

M **WESTERN STATE COLLEGE OF COLORADO,** Quigley Hall Art Gallery, 101 Quigley Hall, Gunnison, CO 81231-0001. Tel 970-943-3093, 943-0120 (main); Fax 970-943-2329; Elec Mail acaniff@western.edu; Internet Home Page Address: www.western.edu; *Art Area Coordr* Lee Johnson; *Dir Gallery* Harry Heil; *Chmn* Al Caniff
Open Mon - Fri 1 - 5 PM; No admis fee; Estab 1967 for the purpose of exhibiting student, staff & traveling art; Nearly 300 running ft composition walls, security lock-up iron grill gate is contained in the gallery; Average Annual Attendance: 7,500
Income: Financed by state appropriation
Special Subjects: Painting-American, Prints
Collections: Original paintings and prints
Exhibitions: Rotating exhibits
Activities: Competitions; originates traveling exhibs

HOLYOKE

M **PHILLIPS COUNTY MUSEUM,** 109 S Campbell Ave, Holyoke, CO 80734-1501. Tel 970-854-2129; Fax 970-854-3811; Elec Mail pcmuseum@pctelcom.coop; Internet Home Page Address: www.rootswebancestry.com/~copchs/index.htm; *Pres* Carol Haynes; *Treas* Hilda Hassler; *Secy* Leona Oltjenbruns; *VPres* Diane Rahe
Open Tues - Sat 10 AM - 4 PM; No admis fee; Estab 1929 as an educational & cultural museum to impart an appreciation of local history & to display objects of art from all over the world; Average Annual Attendance: 5,000; Mem: 250; dues $3-$5; annual meeting first Fri in May
Income: Financed by endowment, mem & city appropriation
Special Subjects: Painting-American, Ceramics, Glass
Collections: China; glassware; paintings; Indian artifacts; Civil War memorabilia; Thomas Alva Edison Historical Display; Civil War Collection

LA JUNTA

M **KOSHARE INDIAN MUSEUM, INC,** 115 W 18th St, La Junta, CO 81050-3302; PO Box 580, La Junta, CO 81050-0580. Tel 719-384-4411; Fax 719-384-8836; Elec Mail koshare@ria.net; Internet Home Page Address: kosharehistory.org; *Office Mgr* Linda Root; *Gift Shop Mgr* Jo Ann Jones; *Develop Dir* Linda Powers; *Coll Mgr* Jo Anne Kent
Open noon-5PM, call for appointment on Mon & Thurs; Admis adults $5, students 7-17 $3, children 6 and under free; Estab 1949 for the exhib of Indian artifacts & paintings; 15,000 sq ft display space. For reference to members only or by special arrangement; Average Annual Attendance: 100,000; Mem: 250; annual meeting second Tues in Dec; dues start at $25 & up
Income: Financed by donations & shows
Special Subjects: Hispanic Art, Mexican Art, Painting-American, Prints, Watercolors, American Indian Art, American Western Art, Bronzes, Archaeology, Textiles, Crafts, Folk Art, Pottery, Woodcarvings, Decorative Arts, Portraits, Eskimo Art, Jewelry, Carpets & Rugs, Ivory, Scrimshaw, Leather
Collections: Indian arts & crafts, of & by Indians; Taos Ten; prominent southwestern artists
Exhibitions: Exhibits change monthly

Activities: Classes for children; tours; paintings & original art works lent to qualified mus; book traveling exhibs; mus shop sells books, original art, reproductions, souvenirs, Indian jewelry & pottery

L **Library,** 115 W 18th, La Junta, CO 81050. Tel 719-384-4411; Fax 719-384-8836; Elec Mail koshare@ria.net; Internet Home Page Address: www.ruralnet.net/-koshare; Internet Home Page Address: www.koshare.org; *Dir Progs* Joe Clay
Open by appt only; No admis fee; Estab 1949 for educ through art & youth prog; Open for reference only; Average Annual Attendance: 18,000
Income: Donations, grants
Library Holdings: Book Volumes 1700; Clipping Files
Special Subjects: History of Art & Archaeology, Archaeology, American Western Art, American Indian Art, Primitive art, Anthropology, Eskimo Art, Southwestern Art, Pottery
Collections: Baskets; Clothing; Kachinas; Paintings; Pots; Textiles
Activities: Classes for children; dramatic progs; Boy Scouts of America-Koshare Indian Dancers; concerts; gallery talks; tours; individual paintings & original objects of art lent to other mus; book traveling exhibs; mus shop sells books, original art, reproductions, prints, slides, jewelry, kachinas, pots & videos

LEADVILLE

A **LAKE COUNTY CIVIC CENTER ASSOCIATION, INC,** Heritage Museum & Gallery, 102 E 9th St, Leadville, CO 80461-3302; PO Box 962, Leadville, CO 80461-0962. Tel 719-486-1878, 486-1421; *Pres Board Dirs* Ray Stamps; *VPres* Ted Mullings
Open Memorial Day-Labor Day 10 AM-6 PM. Also open May, Sept & Oct on limited hours daily; Admis adults $4, sr citizens $3.50, children 6 - 16 $3, under 6 free, members free; Estab 1971 to promote the preservation, restoration & study of the rich history of the Lake County area & to provide display area for local & non-local art work & also to provide an educational assistance both to public schools & interested individuals; The Museum & Gallery own no art work, but display a variety of art on a changing basis; Average Annual Attendance: 9,000; Mem: 160; dues $20-$250; annual meeting Feb
Collections: Diorama of Leadville history; mining & Victorian era artifacts; Victorian furniture
Exhibitions: Changing displays of paintings, photography and craft work
Publications: The Tallyboard, newsletter, quarterly
Activities: Lect open to pub; competitions; sales shop sells books, slides, papers, postcards, rock samples

M **TABOR OPERA HOUSE MUSEUM,** 308 Harrison Ave, Leadville, CO; 30709 Stampede Run, Buena Vista, CO 81211-8149. Tel 719-486-8409; Elec Mail info@taboroperahouse.net; Internet Home Page Address: taboroperahouse.net; *Owner* Sharon Bland
Open June - Oct Mon - Sat 10 AM - 5:00 PM, Nov - May by appointment only; Admis adults $5, children 6-11 $2.50, under 6 free; Tours adults $8, combined tour adults $5; Estab 1955 as a historic theatre museum
Collections: Costumes; paintings
Exhibitions: Original scenery live shows
Activities: Lect; living history tours for students; films; concerts; arts festivals; sales shop sells books, cards, pictures, prints & souvenirs

LITTLETON

M **ARAPAHOE COMMUNITY COLLEGE,** Colorado Gallery of the Arts, 2500 W College Dr, Littleton, CO 80160-1956; PO Box 9002, Littleton, CO 80160-9002. Tel 303-797-5649; Fax 303-797-5935; Internet Home Page Address: www.arapahoe.edu; *Chmn* Scott Engel; *Gallery Coordr* Trish Sangelo
Open Mon - Fri Noon - 5 PM, Tues 5 - 7 PM; No admis fee; Gallery contributes significantly to the cultural growth of the Denver-metro area
Income: funded by school appropriations
Special Subjects: Costumes

LOVELAND

M **LOVELAND MUSEUM/GALLERY,** 503 N Lincoln, Loveland, CO 80537. Tel 970-962-2410, 2770; Fax 970-962-2910; Elec Mail akelek@ci.loveland.co.us; Internet Home Page Address: www.cityofloveland.org/museum; *Mktg Coordr* Kim Akeley-Charron; *Dir Cultural Svcs* Susan Ison; *Bus Svcs* Suzanne Janssen; *Coordr Educ* Jenni Dobson; *Cur History* Jennifer Cousino; *Cur Art* Maureen Corey; *Graphic Design* Michelle Standiford; *Exhibs Preparator* Quinn Johnson; *Registrar* Robert Hoot; *Office Support Specialist* Mary Shada
Open Tues, Wed & Fri 10 AM - 5 PM, Thurs 10 AM - 7 PM, Sat 10 AM - 4 PM, Sun Noon - 4 PM; No admis fee; Estab 1946 to preserve & interpret history of Loveland area; 4000 sq ft; features local, state, national & international art exhibitions; Average Annual Attendance: 50,000; Mem: 120; dues individual $30
Income: Financed by city appropriation
Library Holdings: Book Volumes; CD-ROMs; Exhibition Catalogs; Memorabilia; Original Documents; Pamphlets; Sculpture; Slides
Special Subjects: Architecture, Drawings, Painting-American, Photography, Sculpture, American Indian Art, American Western Art, Bronzes, Anthropology, Archaeology, Textiles, Costumes, Folk Art, Decorative Arts, Manuscripts, Dolls, Furniture, Glass, Jewelry, Historical Material, Dioramas, Period Rooms, Embroidery, Laces
Collections: Archaeology; art; dioramas, historical material; period rooms; sugar beet industry; textiles; tools; valentines; western; photography
Exhibitions: Bureau of Reclamation Relief Map of Big Thompson Project; Great Western Sugar Company Exhibit; pioneer cabin; Fireside History Gallery
Publications: Exhibition catalogues; history books; newsletter
Activities: Classes for adults & children; dramatic progs; art workshops; poetry readings; lects open to pub, 20 vis lectrs per yr; concerts; gallery talks; tours & sponsoring of competitions; schols; inter-mus loan progs containing cassettes, filmstrips, motion pictures, nature artifacts, original works of art & slides; book

traveling exhibs 2-3 per yr; originate traveling exhibs; mus shop sells books, magazines, original art, reproductions & prints

MESA VERDE NATIONAL PARK

L MESA VERDE NATIONAL PARK, Research Library, PO Box 8, Mesa Verde National Park, CO 81330-0008. Tel 970-529-5014; Fax 970-529-5013; Internet Home Page Address: www.nps.gov/meve; *Supv Ranger* Rosemarie Salazar
Call for appointment; Admis $10; Estab 1906; Average Annual Attendance: 250
Income: $35,800 (financed by endowment)
Library Holdings: Audio Tapes; Book Volumes 10,000; Manuscripts; Maps; Original Documents; Video Tapes
Special Subjects: Manuscripts, Historical Material, Archaeology, Ethnology, Anthropology, Pottery, Restoration & Conservation
Collections: American Indians; Anthropology; Archaeology; Ethnology; Forest Fires; Mary Colter Collection

PUEBLO

M ROSEMOUNT MUSEUM, INC, 419 W 14th St, Pueblo, CO 81003-2707. Tel 719-545-5290; Fax 719-545-5291; Elec Mail cwainright@rosemount.org; Internet Home Page Address: www.rosemount.org; *Exec Dir* Deb Darrow; *Colls Mgr* Susan Kittinger; *Maintenance* Roger Cain; *Office Mgr* Carolyn Wainright
Open Tues - Sat 10 AM - 3:30 PM (last tour), cl Sun, Mon and Jan; Admis adults $6, sr citizens $5, children 6-16 $4, under 6 free; Estab 1968 as a historic house museum to narrate late Victorian life in the west; 37-room Victorian mansion contains 80 percent of original furnishings including many decorative objects & art from late 19th century; Average Annual Attendance: 10,000; Mem: 500; dues $15-$500; annual meeting in Apr
Income: $270,000 (financed by endowment, mem, rental, gift shop, auxiliary organization, fundraisers, admis, donations & grants)
Library Holdings: Auction Catalogs; Book Volumes; Cards; Clipping Files; Kodachrome Transparencies; Lantern Slides; Manuscripts; Memorabilia; Original Art Works; Prints; Reproductions; Sculpture; Video Tapes
Special Subjects: Furniture, Antiquities-Egyptian, Stained Glass
Collections: Permanent collections are displayed in a 37-room Victorian mansion; intact collections of the American Aesthetic Movement; Collections include furnishings, decorative objects, paintings, sculpture, drawings, photographs, all pertaining to the life of the Thatcher Family; Andrew McClelland Collection of World Curiosities; Thatcher Family Collection
Publications: Rosemount News, quarterly
Activities: Classes for adults & children; dramatic progs; docent training; lects open to pub, vis lectrs varies per yr; special theme & holiday events; tours; Best Museum in Pueblo-2000; El Pomar Award of Excellence; mus shop sells books, prints, & decorative art objects

A SANGRE DE CRISTO ARTS & CONFERENCE CENTER, 210 N Santa Fe, Pueblo, CO 81003. Tel 719-295-7200; Fax 719-295-7230; Elec Mail mail@sdc-arts.org; Internet Home Page Address: www.sdc-arts.org; *Exec Dir* Dan Lere; *Cur Visual Arts* Christel Dussart; *Facilities & Beverage Mgr* Lorrie Marquez; *Mktg Specialist* Nicki Hart; *Cur Educ* Jackie Henderson; *Admin Asst* Kathy Berg; *Cur Children's Mus* Donna Stinchcomb; *Asst Cur Children's Mus* Joleen Ryan; *Controller* Rochelle Spoone; *Mem & Box Office Mgr* Cheryl Califano; *Asst Mem & Box Office Mgr* Dan Masterson; *Asst Cur Visual Arts & Colls Mgr* Gabe Wolff; *Asst Educ Cur* Diane Pirraglia; *Artistic Dir for School of Dance* Stephen Wynne; *Mktg Asst* Jenny Kemp; *Accounting Asst* Julie Gallery
Box office open Mon - Fri 9 AM - 5 PM; galleries open Tues - Sat 11 AM - 4 PM; Admis $4; Estab 1972 to promote the educational & cultural activities related to the fine arts in Southern Colorado including four gallery spaces & a hands-on children's museum, a conference area with over 7000 sq ft of rentable space for conventions, receptions, meetings, including a 500 seat theater; The Helen T White Gallery provides four gallery spaces with changing exhibitions by local, regional & international artists, including the Francis King Collection of Western Art, Buell Children's Mus displays over 2 dozen hands-on exhibits; Average Annual Attendance: 220,000; Mem: 3800; dues $15-$1500
Income: $993,000 (financed by mem, city & County appropriation, grants, grants, private underwriting, donations & in-kind services)
Library Holdings: Book Volumes; Exhibition Catalogs; Framed Reproductions; Original Art Works; Periodical Subscriptions; Sculpture
Special Subjects: Drawings, Landscapes, Photography, Sculpture, Watercolors, Pottery, American Western Art, Bronzes, Folk Art, Woodcuts, Ceramics, Collages, Hispanic Art, Southwestern Art, Mexican Art
Collections: Francis King Collection of Western Art, Contemporary; Gene Kloss Collection; Santo Collection; Molas
Exhibitions: Converted art inspired by car culture; Own Your Own (Nov - Jan)
Publications: Town & Center Mosaic, four times a yr; Catalogue of Francis King Collection; West By Southwest book, collections of the Francis King Collection of Western Art, Collection of Intaglio Prints by Gene Kloss, Ruth Gast Collection of Santos; annual report exhibition catalogues; brochures for workshop & dance classes, quarterly; performance arts series, children's series, children's museum; Catalogue Under Western Skies (30 yrs of collecting selections from the colls of the Sangre de Cristo Arts & Conference Center)
Activities: Year-round workshop prog, wide selection of disciplines for children & adults; docent training; dramatic programs; special facilities for ceramics, painting & photography; school of dance; artists-in-residence; lect & seminars coinciding with exhibs; Visiting lect 3 per yr; gallery talks; tours; Theatre Arts - Town & Gown Performing Arts Series; Children's Playhouse Series; outdoor summer concerts, Repertory Theatre Company presenting 2 performances a year, resident modern dance company; concerts; sponsoring of competitions; cash awards to representing the West artists; scholarships offered; individual paintings & objects of art lent to museums, galleries & art centers; lending of original objects of art to community businesses & municipal offices, collection contains 575 original art works, 130 original prints, 445 paintings, photographs, nature artifacts & sculptures; book traveling exhibs 4 per yr; originates traveling exhibs to other institutions; sales shop sells hand-crafted & imported gifts & southwestern

artifacts, posters, books, jewelry, magazines, original art, reproductions, prints, slides; Buell Children's Museum

M UNIVERSITY OF SOUTHERN COLORADO, College of Liberal & Fine Arts, 2200 Bonforte Blvd, Pueblo, CO 81001-4990. Tel 719-549-2100; Fax 719-549-2120; Internet Home Page Address: www.colostate-pueblo.edu; *Art Dept Chmn* Roy Sonnema; *Dir Gallery* Dennis Dolton
Open daily 10 AM - 4 PM; No admis fee; Estab 1972 to provide educational exhibitions for students attending the University; Gallery has a 40 x 50 ft area with 16 ft ceiling; vinyl covered wooden walls; carpeted & adjustable track lighting; Average Annual Attendance: 6,000
Income: Financed through University & student government
Special Subjects: Drawings, Prints, American Indian Art
Collections: Basketry of the Plains Indian, clothing of the Plains Indian; Orman Collection of Indian Art of the Southwest including Indian blankets of the Rio Grande & Navajo people; pottery of the Pueblo Indians (both recent & ancient)
Exhibitions: Art Director's Club of Denver Exhibition; Art Resources of South Colorado; Colorado Invites
Publications: Catalogs
Activities: Lects open to pub; individual paintings & original objects of art lent; book traveling exhibs 2-6 per yr; originates traveling exhibs

SNOWMASS VILLAGE

A ANDERSON RANCH ARTS CENTER, 5263 Owl Creek Rd, Snowmass Village, CO 81615; PO Box 5598, Snowmass Village, CO 81615-5598. Tel 970-923-3181; Fax 970-923-3871; Elec Mail info@andersonranch.org; Internet Home Page Address: www.andersonranch.org; *Exec Dir* Barbara Bloemink; *Chair Res Prog & Artistic Dir* Doug Casebeer; *Artistic Dir* Paul Collins; *Artistic Dir* Andrea Wallace; *Dir Advancement* Judy Clausen
Open Mon - Fri 9 AM - 5 PM; No admis fee; Estab 1966 to feature Ranch artists; Two floor exhibition space; lst floor is dedicated to 2-Dimensional work, 2nd floor to 3-Dimensional work; Average Annual Attendance: 4,000
Income: $2,000,000 (financed by private donations, grants & tuition)
Special Subjects: Drawings, Etchings & Engravings, Photography, Prints, Sculpture, Pottery, Ceramics
Collections: Print collection of contemporary pieces by acclaimed artists
Publications: Workshops catalog, annual
Activities: Classes for adults & children; lects open to pub; schols offered; sales shop sells books, original art, refreshments, clothing & art supplies

TRINIDAD

M ARTHUR ROY MITCHELL MEMORIAL INC, A.R. Mitchell Museum, 150 E Main St, Trinidad, CO 81082; PO Box 95, Trinidad, CO 81082-0095. Tel 719-846-4224; Fax 719-846-2004; Elec Mail mitchellmuseum@qwestoffice.net; Internet Home Page Address: armitchell.org; *Co-Dir* Paula Little; *Co-Dir* Joanie Hessling
Open yearly Mon - Sat 10 AM - 4 PM, & May - Sept also open Sun Noon - 4 PM; Admis adults $3; children under 12 & mem no admis fee; Estab 1981 to preserve & display art of the American West; 15,000 sq ft gallery space; Average Annual Attendance: 3000; Mem: 950; dues $30 - $1000
Income: $50,000 (financed by endowment, mem, donations, gifts, grants & gift shop)
Special Subjects: Hispanic Art, Painting-American, Photography, Sculpture, Watercolors, American Indian Art, American Western Art, Southwestern Art, Religious Art, Ceramics, Folk Art, Pottery, Landscapes, Decorative Arts, Portraits, Jewelry, Carpets & Rugs, Historical Material
Collections: Harvey Dunn Collection; A R Mitchell Collection; Almeron Newman Collection of photography; The Aultman Collection of photography; Benjamin Wittick Collection of Photography; Hispanic Religious art (Santos); saddles; guns
Exhibitions: 3 special exhibs per yr
Activities: Educ prog; classes for adults & children; lects open to pub, concerts; gallery talks; tours; competitions with prizes; individual paintings & original objects of art lent to & other mus; book traveling exhibs; originate traveling exhibs; mus shop sells books, original art, reproductions & Indian jewelry

CONNECTICUT

AVON

A FARMINGTON VALLEY ARTS CENTER, 25 Arts Center Lane Avon, CT 06001. Tel 860-678-1867; Fax 860-674-1877; Elec Mail info@fvac.net; Internet Home Page Address: www.fvac.net; *Dir Educ* Chris O'Conner; *Exec Dir* Martin Rotblatt; *Gallery Mgr* Jim Brunelle
Open Mon - Fri 9 AM - 5 PM; No admis fee; Estab 1974 to provide a facility with appropriate environment & programs that serves as a focal point for public awareness of & participation in the visual arts through quality arts education, exposure to dedicated artists & exposure to high quality crafts; The Fisher Gallery (1300 sq ft) displays and sells fine craft and art and offers educational programming; Average Annual Attendance: 2,000; Mem: 1,000; dues family $6, individual $35, teens & srs $25
Income: $500,000 (financed by class tuition, gallery, mem, grants, tuitions, donations from corporations & individuals special event earning)
Library Holdings: Book Volumes; Original Art Works; Pamphlets; Photographs; Prints; Sculpture
Special Subjects: Drawings, Etchings & Engravings, Photography, Sculpture, Silver, Painting-American, Pottery, Decorative Arts, Ceramics, Portraits, Glass, Jewelry
Collections: Handicrafts; Mixed Media; Painting; Silversmithing; Textile Design; Weaving

Exhibitions: American craftspeople featured in Fisher Gallery; on-site studio artists featured in Visitor's Gallery
Activities: Classes for adults & children, educational outreach progs; 20 studios for rent; career advancement prog for artists; summer arts camp; lects open to pub; 4 vis lectrs per yr; gallery talks; tours; visits to artists' studios; annual holiday exhib of fine crafts; sales shop

BLOOMFIELD

C **CIGNA CORPORATION,** CIGNA Art Collection, 900 Cottage Grove Rd L9, Bloomfield, CT 06002-2920. Tel 860-226-3844; *Mgr* Sarah A Polirer
Open by appointment; No admis fee; Estab 1925
Income: Financed by company
Special Subjects: Afro-American Art, Architecture, Ceramics, Drawings, Etchings & Engravings, Collages, Crafts, Decorative Arts, Dioramas
Collections: Over 4,000 American fine and decorative art pieces; fire fighting and marine related objects; manuscripts

BRIDGEPORT

M **THE BARNUM MUSEUM,** 820 Main St, Bridgeport, CT 06604-4912. Tel 203-331-1104; Fax 203-331-0079; Elec Mail dsaviello@basnum.museum.org; Internet Home Page Address: www.barnum-museum.org; *Cur* Kathleen Maher; *Exec Dir* Lawrence A Fisher; *Dir Develop* Susan J Agamy; *Educ Dir* J Knoedler; *Pub Rels Dir* KP Greaser; *Chmn (V)* Craig Frew; *Educ Progs* Ken Blinn; *Mus Shop Mgr* Debbie Saviello
Open Tues - Sat 10 AM - 4:30 PM, Sun Noon - 4:30 PM; Admis adults $7, college students & sr citizens $4 & children $4; Estab 1893 to exhibit the life & times of P T Barnum; Average Annual Attendance: 20,000; Mem: 400; dues family $45, individual $25
Income: Financed by City of Bridgeport, corporate individual, mem & endowments
Collections: Tom Thumb Collection; Jenny Lind Collection of Photos
Publications: The Barnum Herald newsletter, twice per year
Activities: Tours; films; school & pub progs; workshops; lects open to pub; book traveling exhibs 1 per yr; originate traveling exhibs; sales shop sells books, souvenirs

M **CITY LIGHTS GALLERY,** 37 Markle Ct, Bridgeport, CT 06604-4816. Tel 203-334-7748
Open Mon-Fri 9:30-5:30, Sat 11AM-4PM; No admis fee
Collections: paintings, photographs, sculpture

M **DISCOVERY MUSEUM,** 4450 Park Ave, Bridgeport, CT 06604-1098. Tel 203-372-3521; Fax 203-374-1929; Elec Mail hawkins@discoverymuseum.org; Internet Home Page Address: www.discoverymuseum.org; *Pres* Paul Audley; *Dir Admin* Lynn Hamilton; *Develop* Cynthia Manning; *Acting Cur* Wendy Kelly; *Sr VPres* Linda Markin
Open Tues - Sat 10 AM - 5 PM, Sun Noon - 5 PM, cl major holidays; Admis adults $7, children, sr citizens & col students $5.50, children under 3 & members free; Estab 1958 to provide exhibitions & educational programs in the arts & sciences for a regional audience; Average Annual Attendance: 100,000; Mem: 1500; dues $20-$1000; annual meeting in June
Income: Financed by mem dues
Special Subjects: Painting-American, Furniture
Collections: Paintings, prints & works on paper; Historic house
Exhibitions: Temporary & permanent exhibitions; hands-on physical science exhibits; Hands-on Art Gallery; Challenger Space Station; Fine Art Gallery; Planetarium
Activities: Classes for children; docent training; lects open to pub, 4 vis lectrs per yr; concerts; tours; competitions with awards; scholarships; planetarium shows; individual paintings & original objects of art lent to other local and regional mus; book traveling exhibs 1 per yr; mus shop sells books, reproductions, cards, calendars, gifts, jewelry, dishware & toys for children & adults

M **HOUSATONIC COMMUNITY COLLEGE,** (Housatonic Community-Technical College) Housatonic Museum of Art, 900 Lafayette Blvd, Bridgeport, CT 06604-4704. Tel 203-332-5203; 332-5052; Fax 203-332-5123; Elec Mail rzella@hcc.commnet.edu; Internet Home Page Address: www.housatonicmuseum.org; *Dir* Robbin Zella
Open Sep - May Mon - Fri 8:30 AM - 5:30 PM, Thurs until 7 PM, Sat 9 AM - 3 Pm, Sun Noon - 4 PM, subject to chg during holidays; Jun - Aug Mon - Fri 8:30 AM - 5:30 PM, Thurs until 7 PM, Sat 9 AM - 3 PM, Sun noon - 4 PM, gallery cl during col holidays; No admis fee; Mus estab 1967; Burt Chernow Galleries host a range of contemporary & historic shows; Average Annual Attendance: 12,000
Income: Financed by state & local funding, public & private foundation grants & donations
Library Holdings: Audio Tapes; Book Volumes; CD-ROMs; Clipping Files; Exhibition Catalogs; Original Art Works; Photographs; Prints; Sculpture
Special Subjects: Drawings, Painting-American, Sculpture
Collections: Extensive 19th & 20th Century drawings, paintings & sculpture: Avery, Baskin, Calder, Cassat, Chagall, Daumier, DeChirico, Derain, Dubuffet, Gottlieb, Lichtenstein, Lindner, Marisol, Matisse, Miro-Moore, Pavia, Picasso, Rauchenberg, Rivers, Shahn, Vasarely, Warhol, Wesselmann & others; extensive ethnographic collections, including Africa, South Seas & others; smaller holdings from various historical periods
Exhibitions: Several exhibitions per year
Publications: Exhibition catalogs
Activities: Classes for adults; college art courses; lects open to pub, 6-8 vis lectrs per yr; concerts; gallery talks; tours; scholarships offered; individual paintings & original objects of art lent to institutions; limited lending collection contains 2000 paintings, 25,000 slides, sculpture, original art works, original prints; book traveling exhibs; originate traveling exhibs to other universities; exhibs include Beyond Recognition, Ecce Homo, Monuments & Memory; mus shop sells books, t-shirts, posters

L **Library,** 900 Lafayette Blvd, Bridgeport, CT 06604-4704. Tel 203-332-5070; Fax 203-332-5132; *Dir* Bruce Harvey
Libr Open Mon - Wed & Fri 8:30 AM - 5:30 PM, Thur 8:30 AM - 7 PM; No admis fee; Libr Estab 1967; Extensive art section open to students & community; Average Annual Attendance: 5,000
Income: state, fed & pvt
Library Holdings: Book Volumes 30,000; Fiche

M **UNIVERSITY OF BRIDGEPORT GALLERY,** 380 University Ave, Bridgeport, CT 06604-5692. Tel 203-576-4239; Fax 203-576-4512; Internet Home Page Address: www.bridgeport.edu/art; *Art Dept Chmn* Thomas Juliusburger; *Assoc VPres of Univ Rels* James Garland
No admis fee; Estab 1972
Collections: Contemporary art; prints
Activities: Lects open to pub; gallery talks; concerts; individual paintings & original objects of art lent; originates traveling exhibs

BROOKFIELD

M **BROOKFIELD CRAFT CENTER, INC,** Gallery, 286 Whisconier Rd, Brookfield, CT 06804-0122. Tel 203-775-4526; Fax 203-740-7815; Elec Mail registrar@brookfieldcraftcenter.org; Internet Home Page Address: www.brookfieldcraftcenter.org; *Exec Dir* Richard Herrmann; *Mktg Dir* Betsy Halliday; *Registrar* Deb Cooper; *Educ Dir* Heather Cawless
Open daily 11 AM - 5 PM, cl Mon; No admis fee; Estab 1954 to provide a wide spectrum of craft educ & exhib to the local & national audiences; Contemporary American craft for exhib & sale; Average Annual Attendance: 15,000; Mem: 500; dues-$50
Exhibitions: Contemporary craft exhibitions changing every 8 weeks
Publications: Catalogs
Activities: Classes for adults & children; lects open to pub; schols offered; book traveling exhibs to other craft organizations; sales shop sells books, original art & handmade craft items

BROOKLYN

M **NEW ENGLAND CENTER FOR CONTEMPORARY ART,** 7 Putnam Pl, Brooklyn, CT 06234; PO Box 302 7, Brooklyn, CT 06234-0302. Tel 860-774-881302; Fax 860-774-4840; Internet Home Page Address: www.museum-necca.org; *Dir* Henry Riseman; *Assoc Dir* Paul Sorel; *Cur Chinese Art* Xue JianXin
Open Wed - Fri 10 AM - 4 PM, Sat & Sun 1 PM - 5 PM, cl Christmas; No admis fee; Estab 1975; Mem: dues corporate $100, supporting $50, family $15, individual $10, senior citizen $6
Income: Financed by state appropriations, mem, contributions & gifts
Collections: Contemporary paintings & sculpture; print coll by Russian artists; woodblock print coll from the People's Republic of China
Exhibitions: Rotating and traveling exhibits
Activities: Classes for adults & children; lect; tours; films; gallery talks; originate traveling exhibs; sales shop sells paintings, prints & books

CHESHIRE

M **BARKER CHARACTER, COMIC AND CARTOON MUSEUM,** 1188 Highland Ave, Rte 10, Cheshire, CT 06410. Tel 203-699-3822; Fax 203-250-6770; Elec Mail fun@barkeranimation.com; Internet Home Page Address: www.barkermuseum.com; *Co-Founder* Herbert Barker, D.H.L.; *Co-Founder* Gloria Barker; *Cur* Judy Fuerst
Open Wed - Sat noon - 4 PM, cl holidays; tours available by appt for those 8 years of age & up; Admis adults $5, children 12 & under $3, children 2 & under free; Estab 1998; Comic strip & cartoon memories from childhood are captured here; advertising memorabilia amassed by Herb & Gloria Barker. Though none of the museum's coll is for sale, exhibs contain the current market value; Average Annual Attendance: 50,000
Special Subjects: Glass, Costumes, Dolls, Jewelry, Miniatures, Cartoons
Collections: Official California Raisins Museum; Official Celebriducks Museum, featuring extensive coll of rubber ducks; Disney, Hanna-Barbera, Warner Bros, Charles Fazzino & many other colls of memorabilia; Roy Rogers lunch box; Ronald McDonald phone; Charlie McCarthy puppet; Flintstones Band Toy; Lone Ranger Gun; Mickey & Minnie hand car; advertising memorabilia; rare recent acquisitions
Activities: Field trips by advance reservation

COS COB

M **BUSH-HOLLEY HISTORIC SITE & STOREHOUSE GALLERY,** (Bush-Holley Historical Society) Greenwich Historical Society/ Bush-Holley House, 39 Strickland Rd, Cos Cob, CT 06807-2727. Tel 203-869-6899; Fax 203-861-9720; Elec Mail bbishop@greenwichhistory.org; Internet Home Page Address: www.greenwichhistory.org; *Chmn* Davidde Strackbein; *Exec Dir* Debra L Mecky, PhD; *Mktg & Communs Dir* Barbara Bishop; *Develop Dir* Anne Bradner; *Archivist* Christopher Shields; *Educ Cur* Anna Greco; *Cur & Exhib Coordr* Karen Frederick
Storehouse Gallery & Historic Site: Open Wed - Sun noon - 4 PM; Docent-led tours 1, 2 & 3 PM; special tours available by appt; Admis adults $10, sr citizens & students $8, mems & children 6 and under free; free first Wed ea month; Estab 1931 to collect & preserve the history of Greenwich, CT; National historic landmark; home of the first art colony in CT; gallery, lib, & archives at CosCob Art Colony; Average Annual Attendance: 16,000; Mem: Leadership circle $2500, benefactor $1000, patron $500, donor $250, sponsor $100, family/dual $65, individual & senior $40
Income: Financed by contributions, mem, special events, fees

Library Holdings: Auction Catalogs; Audio Tapes; Book Volumes; CD-ROMs; Cards; Cassettes; Clipping Files; Compact Disks; DVDs; Exhibition Catalogs; Fiche; Filmstrips; Framed Reproductions; Kodachrome Transparencies; Lantern Slides; Manuscripts; Maps; Memorabilia; Micro Print; Motion Pictures; Original Art Works; Original Documents; Other Holdings; Pamphlets; Periodical Subscriptions; Photographs; Prints; Records; Reels; Reproductions; Slides; Video Tapes
Special Subjects: Decorative Arts, Drawings, Etchings & Engravings, Folk Art, Historical Material, Architecture, Art Education, Art History, Furniture, Photography, Painting-American, Prints, Textiles, Maps, Painting-American, Crafts, Pottery, Etchings & Engravings, Decorative Arts, Porcelain, Period Rooms
Collections: American Impressionist art coll; Greenwich history
Exhibitions: The New Spirit & the Cos Cob Art Colony: Before & After the Armory Show
Publications: e-mail newsletter monthly; annual report; pamphlets
Activities: Classes for adults & children; docent training; dramatic programs; field trips; lects open to pub; vis lectrs 5-6 per yr; gallery talks; tours; guided tours of Bush-Holley house; Preservation Awards; mus shop sells books, magazines, prints, gift & stationery

COVENTRY

M **NATHAN HALE HOMESTEAD MUSEUM,** 2299 South St, Coventry, CT 06238-0760. Tel 860-742-6917; Elec Mail hale@ctlandmarks.org; Internet Home Page Address: www.ctlandmarks.org/hale.php; *Site Admin* Bev York
Open mid-May to mid-Oct Wed - Sun noon - 4 PM; Admis Family $15, adults $7, senior $6, children $4, children under 6 no admis fee; Mus is on the grounds in which Revolutionary War hero Nathan Hale uttered his final words "I only regret that I have but one life to lose for my country." Georgian-style house was built by the Hale family in 1776, situated on over 500 acres of forest land; Average Annual Attendance: 3,500 ann
Library Holdings: Book Volumes; Records
Special Subjects: Historical Material, Portraits, Painting-American, Textiles, Period Rooms, Reproductions
Collections: Georgian house built in 1776 on site; portraits of Hale
Exhibitions: CT at Work, mid-Aug - mid-Sep 2014
Activities: Educ progs; classes for children; birthday parties; summer camp; trails; horseback riding; 18th century demonstration garden; hands-on activities; dramatic progs; docent training; gallery talks; tours; sales shop sells books, prints & mus related items

DANBURY

M **DANBURY SCOTT-FANTON MUSEUM & HISTORICAL SOCIETY, INC,** 43 Main St, Danbury, CT 06810-8011. Tel 203-743-5200; Fax 203-743-1131; Elec Mail dmhs@danburyhistorical.org; Internet Home Page Address: www.danburyhistorical.org; *Dir* Levi Newsome; *Cur Specialist* Brigid Durkin; *Research Specialist* Kathleen Zuris
Call for information; No admis fee; Estab June 24, 1941 as historic house. Merged with Mus & Arts Center by Legislative Act 1947; Operates the 1785 John & Mary Rider House as a mus of early Americana & the 1790 Dodd Hat Shop with exhibits relating to hatting. Huntington Hall houses frequently changing exhibits. Ives Homestead, located at Rogers Park in Danbury is to be restored & opened to the pub as a memorial to American composer Charles Edward Ives. Marian Anderson Studio - a memorial to famous Afro-American singer; Average Annual Attendance: 5,000; Mem: 500; dues student $2 up to life $1000; annual meeting in May
Income: Financed by endowment & mem
Special Subjects: Textiles
Collections: Quilt Collection; Batting Collection; Early 1800s men's & women's clothing; Early American Furniture
Publications: Newsletter, quarterly; reprints
Activities: Classes for adults & children; dramatic progs; lects open to pub; concerts; open house; special exhibits; gallery talks; tours; slide shows
L **Library,** 43 Main St, Danbury, CT 06810. Tel 203-743-5200; Internet Home Page Address: www.danburyhistorical.org; *Dir* Levi Newsome; *Cur Specialist* Brigid Durkin; *Research Specialist* Kathleen Zuris
Call for information; Historic information & photographs for reference only
Library Holdings: Clipping Files; Manuscripts; Memorabilia; Other Holdings City Directories; Photographs
Collections: Charles Ives Photograph Collection

A **WOOSTER COMMUNITY ART CENTER,** 91 Miry Brook Rd, Danbury, CT 06810-7417. Tel 203-744-4825; *Asst Dir* Judy Kagan; *Exec Dir* Nancy M Rogers
Open Mon - Fri 9:30 AM - 6 PM, cl Sat & Sun; Estab 1965 as a Community Art Center; Reception center gallery 500 sq ft; Average Annual Attendance: 1,500; Mem: 100; dues family $50, individual $35
Exhibitions: Faculty Exhibits; Art exhibits change monthly in Lobby Gallery, Area artists exhibit artwork in varied media, indoor & outdoor photography, painting & sculpture
Publications: Arts News (newsletter), 3 times per yr
Activities: Classes for adults & children; lects open to public, 5 vis lectrs per yr; scholarships & fels offered; originate traveling exhibs; sales shop sells art supplies
L **Library,** 91 Miry Brook Rd, Danbury, CT 06810-7417. Tel 203-744-4825; *Exec Dir* Nancy M Rogers
For reference only
Library Holdings: Book Volumes 2000; Periodical Subscriptions 3; Slides 2200

DERBY

M **OSBORNE HOMESTEAD MUSEUM,** 500 Hawthorne Ave, Derby, CT 06418; PO Box 435, Derby, CT 06418-0435. Tel 203-734-2513; Fax 203-922-7833; Elec Mail susan.d.robinson@ct.gov; Internet Home Page Address: www.ct.gov/deep/kellogg; *Dir* Diane Chisnall Joy; *Environmental Educ* Susan Quincy; *Office Mgr* Donna Kingston; *Maintainer* Marguerite Heneghan; *Mus Educ* Susan Robinson
Mus open May - Oct Thurs & Fri 10 AM - 3 PM, Sat 10 AM - 4 PM, Sun 12 PM - 4 PM. Holiday tours: Nov 29 - Dec 21 Thurs - Sun 10 AM - 4 PM. Kellogg

Estate Gardens open Spring - Autumn Mon - Sat 9 AM - 4:30 PM; Mus celebrates life & times of Frances Osborne Kellogg, noted industrialist, agriculturalist & conservationist who was dedicated to preserving land for future generations
Special Subjects: Historical Material, Furniture
Collections: period furniture; fine art; history of the Osborne family
Activities: School, teacher & scout progs; hands-on activities; bird walks; adjacent state park; formal gardens; holiday tours

ESSEX

A **ESSEX ART ASSOCIATION, INC,** 10 N Main St, Essex, CT 06426-1030; PO Box 193, Essex, CT 06426-0193. Tel 860-767-8996; Internet Home Page Address: www.essexartassociation.com; *Treas* Robert Gantner; *Pres* Rob DeBartolo; *Admin Dir* Lesley Braren
Open daily 1 - 5 PM May - Oct, cl Tues; No admis fee; Estab 1946 as a nonprofit organization for the encouragement of the arts & to provide & maintain suitable headquarters for the showing of art; Maintains a small, well-equipped one-floor gallery; Average Annual Attendance: 2,500; Mem: 360; elected artists $45; assoc artists $35; supporting members $30
Income: Financed by mem & donations
Exhibitions: 6 annual exhibits per yr; 5 exhibits for EAA; 1 exhib for Valley Regional High School Scholarship Award Show
Activities: $9,100 misc awards per yr

FAIRFIELD

A **FAIRFIELD HISTORICAL SOCIETY,** Fairfield Museum & History Center, 370 Beach Rd, Fairfield, CT 06824-6639. Tel 203-259-1598; Fax 203-255-2716; Elec Mail info@fairfieldhs.org; Internet Home Page Address: www.fairfieldhistory.org; *CEO* Michael Jehle; *Dir Educ* Christine Jewell; *Prog & Vol Coordr* Walter Matis; *Libr Dir* Elizabeth Rose
Open Mon - Fri 10 AM - 4 PM, Sat - Sun 12 PM - 4 PM; Admis fee adults $5, children & seniors $3; Estab 1902 to collect, preserve & interpret artifacts & information relating to the history of Fairfield & the surrounding region; Changing exhibitions and permanent collections display; Average Annual Attendance: 25,000; Mem: 3000; dues $30-$1,000; annual meeting in Oct
Income: $850,000
Library Holdings: Audio Tapes; Book Volumes; Clipping Files; Lantern Slides; Manuscripts; Maps; Memorabilia; Original Art Works; Original Documents; Pamphlets; Periodical Subscriptions; Photographs; Prints; Records
Special Subjects: Architecture, Costumes, Drawings, Embroidery, Etchings & Engravings, Historical Material, Landscapes, Manuscripts, Photography, Posters, Prints, Silver, Textiles, Painting-American, Decorative Arts, Folk Art, Ceramics, Crafts, Portraits, Archaeology, Dolls, Furniture, Glass, Laces, Marine Painting, Maps, Restorations
Collections: Ceramics, furniture, jewelry, paintings, photographs, prints, silver; local history; textiles & costumes; Local History; Archaeology; Kansas postcard series
Publications: Newsletter
Activities: Classes for adults & children; docent training; dramatic progs; lects open to pub; 10-15 vis lectrs per yr; gallery talks; tours; volunteer training; individual paintings & original objects of art lent to other Fairfield County mus; mus shop sells books, prints, reproductions, original art
L **Library,** 370 Beach Rd, Fairfield, CT 06824-6639. Tel 203-259-1598; *Librn* Dennis Barrow
Open Tues - Sat 10 AM - 4:30 PM, Sun 1 - 4:30 PM; Open to the pub for reference only; Mem: User fee $3
Library Holdings: Audio Tapes; Book Volumes 10,000; Cassettes; Clipping Files; Fiche; Lantern Slides; Manuscripts; Memorabilia; Motion Pictures; Other Holdings Diaries; Documents; Maps; Pamphlets; Periodical Subscriptions 12; Photographs; Records; Reels; Slides; Video Tapes
Special Subjects: Landscape Architecture, Photography, Manuscripts, Maps, Historical Material, Video, Architecture
Activities: Classes for adults

M **FAIRFIELD UNIVERSITY,** Thomas J Walsh Art Gallery, 1073 N Benson Rd, Quick Center for the Arts Fairfield, CT 06824-5171. Tel 203-254-4242; Fax 203-254-4113; Elec Mail gallery@fairfield.edu; Internet Home Page Address: www.fairfield.edu/gallery; *Dir* Dr Jill Deupi; *Registrar* Carey Mack Weber
Open Tues - Sat 11 AM - 5 PM; No admis fee; Estab 1990; Multi-purpose space with state of the art security & environmental controls requirement; 2200 sq ft
Income: Financed by endowment & university funds
Special Subjects: Painting-American, Prints, Archaeology, Afro-American Art, Posters, Baroque Art, Renaissance Art
Exhibitions: Thematic & social context art exhibitions; modern & contemporary art
Publications: Educational materials; exhibition catalogues
Activities: Adult classes; docent training; lects open to pub; gallery talks; tours

M **SACRED HEART UNIVERSITY,** Gallery of Contemporary Art, 5151 Park Ave, Fairfield, CT 06825-1000. Tel 203-365-7650; Fax 203-396-8361; Elec Mail gevass@sacredheart.edu; Internet Home Page Address: artgallery.sacredheart.edu; *Dir* Sophia Gevas
Open Mon - Thurs noon - 5:00 PM, Sun Noon - 4 PM; No admis fee; Estab 1989 for the purpose of exhibiting contemporary artists in a wide range of media; Average Annual Attendance: 3,000
Income: university support & annual fundraisers
Purchases: Occasional purchasing of works & commissions of large scale site specific works for new buildings
Collections: Contemporary works, all media; Art Walk, sculpture on loan & commissioned permanent works
Publications: 2 brochure catalogues per yr
Activities: Art talks for high school students & community groups; middle school student workshops; lects open to pub, 2-3 vis lectrs per yr; gallery talks; book traveling exhibs 1 per 3-5 yrs; originates traveling exhibs to other university galleries

FARMINGTON

M **FARMINGTON VILLAGE GREEN & LIBRARY ASSOCIATION,**
Stanley-Whitman House, 37 High St Farmington, CT 06032. Tel 860-677-9222;
Internet Home Page Address: www.stanleywhitman.org; *Dir* Lisa Johnson; *Educ
Coordr* Debbie Andrews; *Tour Interpreter* Peter Devlin; *Admin Asst* Jo-Ann B
Silverio
Open May - Oct Wed - Sun Noon - 4 PM; Nov - Apr, Sat & Sun Noon - 4 PM &
by appointment; Admis adults $5, sr citizens $4, children $2, mems free; Estab
1935 to collect, preserve, educate about 18th century Farmington; A separate
building, has space for art exhibits. Maintains reference library; Average Annual
Attendance: 5,000; Mem: 200; dues $18-$500
Income: Financed by endowment interest, special events, mem & admis
Purchases: $186,000
Library Holdings: Original Documents; Photographs
Special Subjects: Architecture, Drawings, Archaeology, Costumes, Ceramics,
Crafts, Folk Art, Etchings & Engravings, Decorative Arts, Dolls, Furniture, Glass,
Coins & Medals, Embroidery, Bookplates & Bindings
Collections: American decorative arts; ceramics; costumes & textiles; 18th
century decorative arts; dooryard & herb garden; furniture; glass; household
utensils; photographs; weaving equipment
Exhibitions: Permanent & changing exhibitions
Publications: A Guide to Historic Farmington, Connecticut; A Short History of
Farmington, Connecticut
Activities: Classes for adults & children; dramatic progs; docent training; family
& school progs; children's hands-on tour; lects open to pub, 3 vis lectrs per yr;
gallery talks; tours; lending collection contains cassettes, over 1000 photographs &
300 slides; mus shop sells books, toys, games & cards

M **HILL-STEAD MUSEUM,** 35 Mountain Rd, Farmington, CT 06032-2304. Tel
860-677-4787; Fax 860-677-0174; Elec Mail cagenelloc@hillstead.org; Internet
Home Page Address: www.hillstead.org; *Dir & CEO* Sue Sturtevant, Ed.D; *Mus
Shop Mgr* Priscilla Ramage; *Dir Educ & Curatorial Svcs* Marcie Jackson; *Dir
Communs* Cynthia Cagenello; *Vol Pres* M Timothy Corbett; *Dir Opers* David
Perbeck; *Finance Dir* Becky Hendricks; *Dir Develop* Dougla Pyrke; *Cur* Melanie
Bourbeau; *Dir Poetry Festival* Mimi Madden
Open: call for hours; Admis adults $12, discounts for AAA & AAM members,
members no charge; Estab 1947 to house French & American impressionist
painting, plus Japanese woodblock prints; Colonial Revival style house designed
by Theodate Pope in collaboration with McKim, Mead & White & built in 1901
for industrialist Alfred Atmore Pope. Set on 150 acres including a sunken garden
designed by Beatrix Farrand, the house contains Mr. Pope's early collection of
French Impressionist paintings & decorative arts; Average Annual Attendance:
46,000; Mem: 1300; dues family $75, individual $50; annual meeting in June
Income: Financed by endowment, mem, contributions, individual, corporate &
foundations, admis & sales
Library Holdings: Exhibition Catalogs; Memorabilia; Original Documents;
Photographs
Special Subjects: Drawings, Etchings & Engravings, Historical Material,
Landscapes, Architecture, Ceramics, Glass, Furniture, Photography, Portraits,
Pottery, Painting-American, Bronzes, Sculpture, Prints, Watercolors,
Pre-Columbian Art, Textiles, Woodcuts, Decorative Arts, Porcelain, Asian Art,
Silver, Painting-French, Carpets & Rugs, Period Rooms, Antiquities-Greek
Collections: Paintings by Cassatt, Degas, Manet, Monet & Whistler; prints by
Durer, Piranesi, Whistler & other 19th century artists; American, English & other
European furniture; Oriental & European porcelain; Japanese prints
Exhibitions: Rotating exhibits
Publications: Catalog of Hill-Stead Paintings; Theodate Pope Riddle, Her Life &
Work; Hill-Stead Museum House Guide; Hill-Stead: The Country Place of
Theodate Pope Riddle; Wonders Revealed: Rarely seen original prints from
Hill-Stead's collection
Activities: Classes for adults & children; docent training; dramatic progs; poetry
seminars; nature walks; farmers market; lects open to pub, 5-10 vis lectrs per yr;
concerts; gallery talks; tours; competition with awards; mus shop sells books,
magazines, reproductions, slides, CDs, poetry, tapes & videos; holiday boutique

GOSHEN

M **GOSHEN HISTORICAL SOCIETY,** 21 Old Middle St, Goshen, CT 06756; PO
Box 457, Goshen, CT 06756-0457. Tel 860-491-9610, 491-3129; Elec Mail
jvnkuq@juno.com; Internet Home Page Address: www.goshenhistoricalct.org; *Pres
& Cur* Henrietta C Horvay; *VPres* Marcia Barker
Open Apr - Oct Tues 10 AM - Noon, by appointment; No admis fee; Estab 1955
to interpret the past & present of our area; Average Annual Attendance: 400;
Mem: 150; meetings in May & Oct
Income: Financed by mem & donations
Special Subjects: Photography, American Indian Art, Historical Material
Collections: Collection of Indian art, farm tools, household items used through
town's history & photographs; quilts
Exhibitions: Exhibits focused on 275 years of town's history; Goshen in Civil
War
Activities: Classes for children & visits mus; gallery talks; tours; lects open to
pub, 2 vis lectrs per mon June - Aug; lending of objects of art to other historical
societies & libraries; mus shop sells books & other mus related items

GREENWICH

M **BRUCE MUSEUM, INC,** One Museum Dr, Greenwich, CT 06830-7100. Tel
203-869-0376; Fax 203-869-0963; Elec Mail info@brucemuseum.org; Internet
Home Page Address: brucemuseum.org; *Pres* Peter C Sutton; *Dir Educ* Robin
Garr; *Cur Sci* Gina Gould; *Dir Finance* Gregory Hollop; *Dir Exhibitions* Anne
von Stuelpnagel; *Dir Institutional Advancement* Liz Wooster; *Deputy Dir* Susan
Ball
Open Tues - Sat 10 AM - 5 PM, Sun 1 - 5 PM, cl Mon & major holidays; Admis
adults $7, sr citizen & student $6, Tues free, mem & children under 5 free; Estab

1908 by Robert M Bruce. Expanded & completely renovated in 1992. Museum
features changing exhibits in fine & decorative arts & natural sciences;
Interdisciplinary shows in four galleries; small reference library for staff use only;
Average Annual Attendance: 80,000; Mem: 2900; dues individual $60, student
$35, senior $40, sr couple $60, family & dual $65, young friend $150, patron
$250, benefactor $750, Robert Bruce Circle $2,000; annual meeting in June
Special Subjects: Decorative Arts, Landscapes, Marine Painting, Ceramics,
Photography, Portraits, Pre-Columbian Art, Painting-American, Prints, Textiles,
Painting-British, Painting-European, Sculpture, Drawings, Prints, Sculpture,
American Indian Art, Archaeology, Ethnology, Costumes, Etchings & Engravings,
Oriental Art, Carpets & Rugs, Maps, Baroque Art, Miniatures, Painting-Flemish,
Dioramas, Cartoons
Collections: 19th & 20th century American paintings; costumes; North American
Indian ethnology; Orientalia; American natural history; Major mineral collection;
Photography; Works on paper; Decorative arts; Sculpture
Exhibitions: (08/31/2013-12/01/2013) American Scene: Prints from the Collection
of Dr. Kelly; (09/28/2013-01/05/2014) Chuck Close; Changes in Our Land
(ongoing)
Publications: Exhibition Catalogs, 3 per yr; calendar of events, newsletter, 6 per
yr; e-newsletter, 50 per yr
Activities: Classes for adults & children; docent training; public progs; family
days, films, performance art, mus outreach & afterschool progs; lects open to pub,
30-40 vis lectrs per yr; concerts; gallery talks; tours; festival awards; individual
paintings & original objects of art lent to other mus; 30 mile radius -
Brucemobile; originate 1-3 book traveling exhibs per yr; originate traveling
exhibs; mus shop sells books, reproductions, & gifts; junior museum located at
Greenwich Point Park

M **DAHESH MUSEUM OF ART,** 45 E Putnam Ave, Ste 105 Greenwich, CT
06830-5470. Tel 212-759-0606; Fax 203-861-9634; Elec Mail
info@daheshmuseum.org; Elec Mail museumshop@daheshmuseum.org; Internet
Home Page Address: www.daheshmuseum.org; *Dir* Flora Kaplan; *Pres* Mervat
Zahid; *CFO* William Ignatowich; *VPres* Steven Simkin; *VPres, Sec & Treas* Amira
Zahid
Estab 1987; Maintains reference library; Average Annual Attendance: 20,000
Special Subjects: Drawings, Graphics, Sculpture, Watercolors, Bronzes, Etchings
& Engravings, Landscapes, Painting-European, Painting-British, Painting-French
Collections: European 19th & 20th Century Acad Art (paintings, sculpture &
works on paper)
Publications: Dahesh Muse, newsletter 3 per year
Activities: Lects open to pub, 20 vis lectrs per yr; mus shop sells books, prints,
reproductions, jewelry, figurines, stationery, educational toys & gifts

A **GREENWICH ART SOCIETY INC,** 299 Greenwich Ave, Greenwich, CT
06830-2501. Tel 203-629-1533; Fax 203-629-3414; Elec Mail
admin@greenwichartsociety.org; Internet Home Page Address:
www.greenwichartsociety.org; *Co-VP Dir of Classes & Office Mgr* Mary
Newcomb; *Pres & Co-VP Dir of Classes* Anna Patalano; *Co-Treas* Arnold Braff;
Co-Treas Bob Barletta; *Admin Staff* Jill Foster
Office: 9:30 - 12:30 PM weekdays, Greenwich Art Society Gallery weekdays 10
AM - 5 PM, Sat 12 - 4 PM, Sun 1 - 4 PM, except July & Aug.; no admis fee;
Estab 1912 as a nonprofit organization to further art educ & to awaken &
stimulate broader interest in the visual arts in the town of Greenwich; Art Center
studio is used for classes & Greenwich Art Society Gallery meetings &
exhibitions; Mem: 350; dues regular $50, student 21 & under $25
Income: Financed by mem fees & contributions, classes tuitions
Library Holdings: Book Volumes
Exhibitions: Spring Show: Gertrude White Gallery, YWCA, 259 E Putnam Ave;
Summer Exhibition: Flinn Gallery, Greenwich Library, 101 W Putnam Ave; Art &
Nature Exhibition, Garden Education Center of Greenwich
Publications: The History of the Greenwich Art Society, booklet; bulletin of
program for the year & class schedule
Activities: Day & evening classes for adults, special classes for children; critiques
& demonstrations; lect open to public; art outreach progs to underserved students

M **Bendheim Gallery,** 299 Greenwich Ave, Greenwich, CT 06830-6504. Tel
203-862-6750; Fax 203-862-6753; Elec Mail info@greenwicharts.org; Internet
Home Page Address: www.greenwicharts.org/index.asp

L **GREENWICH LIBRARY,** 101 W Putnam Ave, Greenwich, CT 06830-5387. Tel
203-622-7900; Fax 203-622-7939; Internet Home Page Address:
www.greenwichlibrary.org; *Acting Dir* Barbara Ormerod-Glynn
Open Mon - Fri 9 AM - 9 PM, Sat 9 AM - 5 PM, Sun 1 - 5 PM Oct - May; Estab
1878 to provide free & convenient access to the broadest possible range of
information & ideas; Circ 1,063,950; Hurlbutt Gallery features exhibits of
paintings, prints, sculpture, photos, antiques & objects d'art, sponsored by Friends
of the Greenwich Library
Income: $3,378,992 (financed by city appropriation)
Purchases: Art & Music $19,925, video $39,913, records & audio cassettes
$46,285
Library Holdings: Book Volumes 313,824; Cassettes 6550; Framed
Reproductions 326; Other Holdings Art related books 16,990; Compact discs
10,000; Periodical Subscriptions 600; Video Tapes 10,000
Collections: Book arts coll (fine press books)
Exhibitions: Six different exhibits per year
Publications: Monthly book lists
Activities: Lects open to pub, 3-5 vis lectrs per yr; individual paintings lent to
Greenwich residents; lending collection contains approx 438 items

GROTON

M **ALEXEY VON SCHLIPPE GALLERY OF ART,** 1084 Shennecossett Rd Groton, CT 06340-6097. *Dir & Cur* Julia Pavone

HAMDEN

L **PAIER COLLEGE OF ART, INC,** Library, 20 Gorham Ave, Hamden, CT 06514-3902. Tel 203-287-3031; Fax 203-287-3021; Elec Mail paier.admin@snet.net; Internet Home Page Address: www.paiercollegeofart.edu; *Pres* Jonathan E Paier; *VPres* Daniel Paier; *Dir Library* Beth R Harris
Open Mon & Tues 11 AM-7 PM, Wed & Thurs 9 AM-5 PM, Fri 9 AM-Noon; No admis fee; Estab 1946, library estab 1978
Library Holdings: Book Volumes 11,600; Clipping Files; Exhibition Catalogs; Pamphlets; Periodical Subscriptions 68; Prints; Reproductions; Slides 16,000; Video Tapes 120
Special Subjects: Art History, Folk Art, Decorative Arts, Illustration, Calligraphy, Commercial Art, Drawings, Graphic Arts, Graphic Design, History of Art & Archaeology, Conceptual Art, Advertising Design, Interior Design, Lettering, Architecture
Collections: Children's books (400); Reference pictures (30,000)

HARTFORD

A **ARTISTS COLLECTIVE INC,** 1200 Albany Ave, Hartford, CT 06112-2104. Tel 860-527-3205; Fax 860-527-2979; Elec Mail info@artistscollective.org; Internet Home Page Address: artistscollective.org; *Founding Exec Dir* Dollie McLean; *Founder* Jackie McLean
Admis fees for special performances vary, see website; Estab 1970
Income: $690,000
Activities: Classes for children; dramatic progs; workshops; concerts

M **CHARTER OAK CULTURAL CENTER,** 21 Charter Oak Ave, Hartford, CT 06106-1801. Tel 860-249-1207; Fax 860-524-8014; Elec Mail danielle.walser@charteroakcenter.org; Internet Home Page Address: www.charteroakcenter.org

A **CONNECTICUT HISTORICAL SOCIETY,** (Connecticut Historical Society Museum) 1 Elizabeth St, Hartford, CT 06105-2213. Tel 860-236-5621; Fax 860-236-2664; Elec Mail ask-us@chs.org; Internet Home Page Address: www.chs.org; *Exec Dir* David Kahn; *Deputy Dir* Kevin Hughes; *Dir Admin* Kevin Hughes; *Dir Interpretation* Kate Steinway; *Dir Libr* Nancy Milnor; *Mgr Communs* Aaron Wartner; *Cur Graphics* Nancy Finlay; *Dir Mus Colls* Susan P Schoelwer; *Dir External Affairs* Peter Lisi; *VPres* Hugh Macgil; *Genealogist* Judith Ellen Johnson; *Mus Shop Mgr* Kathryn Mazzo; *VChmn* Wilson Wilde
Galleries open Tues - Sun 12 - 5 PM; cl holidays, Library open Tues - Sat 10 AM - 5 PM; Admis adults $6, seniors & students $3, children 5 & under & mems free, group discounts available; Estab 1825 to collect & preserve materials of Connecticut interest & to encourage interest in Connecticut history; Exhibition space totals 6500 sq ft, half of which is devoted to permanent exhibitions, the other half to changing exhibits; Average Annual Attendance: 33,000; Mem: 1900; dues $30 individual, $45 family; annual meeting in Dec
Income: Financed by endowment & mem
Library Holdings: Auction Catalogs; Audio Tapes; Book Volumes; CD-ROMs; Cards; Cassettes; Clipping Files; Compact Disks; DVDs; Exhibition Catalogs; Fiche; Filmstrips; Framed Reproductions; Kodachrome Transparencies; Lantern Slides; Manuscripts; Maps; Memorabilia; Micro Print; Motion Pictures; Original Art Works; Original Documents; Other Holdings; Pamphlets; Periodical Subscriptions; Photographs; Prints; Records; Reels; Reproductions; Sculpture; Slides; Video Tapes
Special Subjects: Decorative Arts, Furniture
Collections: Historical Collections; Frederick K & Margaret R Barbour Furniture Collection; George Dudley Seymour Collection of Furniture; Morgan P. Brainard Tavern Signs
Exhibitions: Amistad: A True Story of Freedom; Tours & Detours Through Colonial Connecticut; Hands on History; Changing Gallery; Chance, Choice & Change
Publications: Newsletter: CHS Newsletter, 3 times per year; Picturing Victorian America: Prints by the Kellogg Brothers of Hartford Connecticut, 1830-1880 exhib catalog
Activities: Classes for adults & children, dramatic progs, docent training; lects open to pub, 12 vis lectrs per yr; gallery talks; tours; competitions including Conn History Day competition with awards; lending collection contains books, lent to qualified institutions; originate traveling exhibs; mus shop sells books, reproductions, prints
L **Library,** 1 Elizabeth St, Hartford, CT 06105-2213. Tel 860-236-5621; Fax 860-236-2664; Elec Mail ask-us@chs.org; Internet Home Page Address: www.chs.org; *Genealogist* Judith E Johnson; *Archivist* Barbara Austen; *Cur Graphics* Nancy Finlay; *Coll Mgr* Diane Lee; *Head of Research Center* Diane McCain; *Head of Collections* Richard Malley
Open Tues - Fri noon - 5 PM; Sat 9AM-5PM; Admis adults $6, students & seniors $3, members free; 1825; 2 permanent galleries, 1 temporary gallery & library; Mem: 1200
Library Holdings: Book Volumes Monographs & Serials: 100,000; Manuscripts 3,000,000; Other Holdings Objects: 38,000; Graphics 240,000
Collections: Genealogical Research Collection
Activities: Docent training; lects open to pub, 10 vis lectrs per yr; gallery talks; tours

L **CONNECTICUT STATE LIBRARY,** Museum of Connecticut History, 231 Capitol Ave, Hartford, CT 06106-1548. Tel 860-757-6535; Fax 860-757-6521; Elec Mail dnelson@cslib.org; Internet Home Page Address: www.cslib.org; *Cur* David J Corrigan; *Cur* Patrick Smith; *Mus Adminr* Dean Nelson
Open Mon - Fri 9 AM - 4 PM, Sat 9 AM - 3 PM, cl holidays; No admis fee; Estab 1910 to collect, preserve & display artifacts & memorabilia reflecting the history & heritage of Connecticut; For reference only; Average Annual Attendance: 21,000

Income: State funding
Library Holdings: Book Volumes 500,000; Cassettes; Clipping Files; Fiche 50,000; Manuscripts; Memorabilia; Motion Pictures; Original Art Works; Other Holdings Original documents 100,000,000; Pamphlets; Photographs; Prints; Reels; Video Tapes
Special Subjects: Coins & Medals
Collections: Collection of Firearms; Portraits of Connecticut's Governors; Connecticut Collection - Industrial & Military History
Exhibitions: Changing exhibits
Activities: Classes for children

L **HARRIET BEECHER STOWE CENTER,** 77 Forest St, Hartford, CT 06105-3296. Tel 860-522-9258; Fax 860-522-9259; Internet Home Page Address: www.harrietbeecherstowe.org; *Dir* Katherine Kane; *Cur* Dawn C Adiletta; *Office Mgr* Carol Ann Stephenson; *Collections Mgr* Elizabeth Giard; *Dir Mktg* Mary Ellen White; *Dir Educ* Shannon Burke
Open Mon - Sat 9:30 AM - 4:30 PM, Sun Noon - 4:30 PM, cl Mon, Columbus Day - Memorial Day; Admis adults $8, sr citizen $7, children $4, children under 5 free; Estab 1941 to maintain & open to the pub the restored Harriet Beecher Stowe House; The Foundation operates the Stowe Library, oversees a publishing program of reprints of H B Stowe's works & new books & provides workshops & lect; Average Annual Attendance: 22,000; Mem: 150; dues sustaining $150, supporting $50, family $30, individual $20; fall & spring meetings
Library Holdings: Book Volumes; Clipping Files; Exhibition Catalogs; Manuscripts; Pamphlets; Periodical Subscriptions; Photographs
Special Subjects: Graphic Arts, Manuscripts, Painting-American, Historical Material, Watercolors, Period Rooms, Architecture
Collections: 19th Century Decorative Arts, Domestic Furnishing, Fine Arts; Wallpaper & Floor Treatment Sample Collections
Exhibitions: A Moral Battle Cry for Freedom: Uncle Tom's Cabin (ongoing); Reforming the Season: Christmas & 19th Century Reformer (annually-Dec)
Publications: The Journal newsletter, quarterly
Activities: Workshops for adults & teachers; educ prog; docent training; Teachers Institute; lects open to pub; concerts; 1-2 vis lectrs per yr; gallery talks; tours; paintings & original decorative, domestic or fine art objects lent to institutions; mus shop sells books, reproductions, prints, slides, fabrics, Victorian gift items & garden materials
L **Library,** 77 Forest St, Hartford, CT 06105. Tel 860-522-9258; Fax 860-522-9259; Elec Mail info@stowecenter.org; Internet Home Page Address: www.harrietbeecherstowe.org; *Exec Dir* Katherine Kane; *Educ & Visitor Svcs* Shannon Burke
House tours Tues - Sat 9:30 AM - 4:30 PM, Sun 12 - 4:30 PM, call for winter hours; Admis adults $9, seniors $8, children 5-16 $6; library free by appointment; Estab 1941 to concentrate on the architecture, decorative arts, history & literature of the United States in the 19th century emphasizing a Hartford neighborhood known as Nook Farm, and the Beecher/Stowe families; Circ Non-circulating; Reference only for gen pub, students, staff & academia; Average Annual Attendance: 24,000
Library Holdings: Book Volumes 15,000; Clipping Files; Exhibition Catalogs; Fiche; Lantern Slides 60; Manuscripts; Maps; Memorabilia; Original Art Works; Original Documents; Other Holdings Original documents 160,000; Pamphlets 5000; Periodical Subscriptions; Photographs 5000; Prints; Reels 100; Sculpture; Slides 3500
Special Subjects: Landscape Architecture, Decorative Arts, Photography, Historical Material, Furniture, Restoration & Conservation, Textiles, Architecture
Collections: Architecture & Decorative Arts of 19th Century: books, plans, drawings, trade catalogs; Hartford 19th Century Literary Community, Nook Farm & Residents; Mark Twain; Harriet Beecher Stowe; Chas Dudley Warner; William Gillette; letters & documents of the Stowe family; Stowe family artifacts; 19th-Century artwork; Uncle Tom's Cabin memorabilia
Activities: Programs for adults & children; lects open to pub & for members only; concerts; book club; gallery talks; tours; sponsoring of competitions; Stowe Prize for books; mus shop sells books, magazines, reproductions & prints

M **MARK TWAIN HOUSE MEMORIAL,** 351 Farmington Ave, Hartford, CT 06105-4401. Tel 860-247-0998 (admin office), 247-0998 ext 26 (visitor center); Fax 860-278-8148; Elec Mail info@marktwainhouse.org; Internet Home Page Address: www.marktwainhouse.org; *Exec Dir* John Boyer; *Deputy Dir* Debra Petke; *Dir Educ* Jeff Nichols; *Dir Pub Rels & Mktg* Joseph Fazzino; *Chief Dev Officer* Dina Plapler
Open Mon - Sun 9:30 AM - 5:30 PM, first Thurs of the month 9:30 AM - 8 PM, cl Tues Jan - Apr; Admis adults $14, sr citizens $12, children 6-12 $8, children 13-18 $10, children under 6 free; Estab 1929 to foster an appreciation of the legacy of Mark Twain as one of our nation's culturally defining figures; to demonstrate the continuing relevance of his work, life & times; Maintains Historic House Mus with period interiors, mus room of memorabilia. National Historic Landmark status, US Dept of Interior; Average Annual Attendance: 65,000; Mem: 900; dues $35-$5000; annual meeting in Nov
Income: financed by members, donations, admis fees
Special Subjects: Painting-American, Photography, Sculpture, Textiles, Ceramics, Woodcarvings, Decorative Arts, Furniture, Glass, Silver, Period Rooms, Stained Glass
Collections: Mark Twain memorabilia (photographs, manuscripts); period & original furnishings; Tiffany Glass Collection; Lockwood deForest Collection; Candace Wheeler Collection
Exhibitions: National Symposia; Rotating exhibits; Orientation exhibitions
Publications: Exhibition catalogues
Activities: Classes for adults & children; symposia; internship progs; docent training; lects open to pub, 6 vis lectrs per yr; concerts; gallery talks; tours; college internships offered; individual paintings & original objects of art lent to approved mus & organizations; lending collection contains books, color reproductions, prints, paintings, photographs, sculpture & slides; mus shop sells books, reproductions, prints, slides, gifts & Mark Twain memorabilia
L **Research Library,** 351 Farmington Ave, Hartford, CT 06105. Tel 860-247-0998 (admin office), Fax 860-278-8148; Internet Home Page Address: www.marktwainhouse.org; *Cur* Diane Forsberg; *Exec Dir* John Boyer
Open Mon - Sat 9:30 AM - 5 PM, Sun noon - 5 PM; For reference only

Library Holdings: Auction Catalogs; Audio Tapes; Book Volumes 6000; CD-ROMs; Cassettes; Clipping Files; Exhibition Catalogs; Fiche; Filmstrips; Framed Reproductions; Lantern Slides; Manuscripts; Memorabilia; Motion Pictures; Original Art Works; Original Documents; Other Holdings; Pamphlets; Periodical Subscriptions 22; Photographs; Records; Reels; Reproductions; Sculpture; Slides; Video Tapes

M **OLD STATE HOUSE,** 800 Main St, Hartford, CT 06103-2301. Tel 860-522-6766; Fax 860-522-2812; Elec Mail info@shareCT.org; Internet Home Page Address: www.ctosh.org; *Chmn* Robert DeCrescenzo; *Pres* David Coffin; *Exec Dir* Wilson H Faude; *Pres, Chmn* James Williams; *Educ Coordr* Kathleen Hunter; *Mus Shop Mgr* Rebecca Taber-Conova; *Dir* Sally Whipple
Open Mon - Fri 10 AM - 4 PM, Sat 11 AM - 4 PM, cl Sun ; No admis fee; Estab 1975 to preserve oldest state house in the nation & present variety of exhibitions on historic & contemporary subjects; Former exec wing is used for exhibitions of contemporary artists & craftsmen, paintings, decorative arts on a rotating basis; Average Annual Attendance: 200,000; Mem: 1500; dues life $1000, family $15, individual $10; annual meeting in the fall
Income: Financed by endowment, mem & appeals
Collections: Connecticut portraits; documents; Restored Senate Chamber
Activities: Educ dept; classes for adults & children; dramatic progs; lects open to pub, 25 vis lectrs per yr; concerts; gallery talks; tours; individual paintings & original objects of art lent to mus for special exhibs; mus shop sells books, magazines, original art, reproductions, prints, slides, Connecticut arts & crafts

M **REAL ART WAYS (RAW),** 56 Arbor St, Hartford, CT 06106-1222. Tel 860-232-1006; Fax 860-233-6691; Elec Mail info@realartways.org; Internet Home Page Address: www.Realartways.org; *Visual Arts Coordr* Diana Roos-Brown; *Mem Coordr* Jasmine Wagner
Open Tues - Thurs, Sun 2 - 10 PM, Fri - Sat 2 - 11 PM, cl Mon; Admis $3 suggested donation; Estab 1975 to present artists of many disciplines working at the forefront of creative activity in their respective fields; 1 fl; Mem: Annual dues vary
Income: Financed by mem and donations
Special Subjects: Photography, Prints, Sculpture
Collections: Contemporary Art
Exhibitions: Rotating exhibitions
Activities: Classes for children, summer art workshop; lects open to pub, 5 vis lectrs per yr; concerts; gallery talks; tours; book traveling exhibs 2 per yr; originate traveling exhibs to qualified institutions

M **TRINITY COLLEGE,** Austin Arts Center, Widener Gallery, 300 Summit St, Hartford, CT 06106-3186. Tel 860-297-2498; Fax 860-297-5380; Elec Mail jeffry.walker@mail.trincoll.edu; Internet Home Page Address: www.trincoll.edu/depts/aac/; *Cur* Felice Caivano; *Dir* Jeffry Walker
Open Sept - May Sun - Thurs 1 -9 PM, Fri & Sat 1 - 6 PM; No admis fee; Estab 1965; A building housing the teaching & performing aspects of music, theater dance & studio arts at a liberal arts college. Widener Gallery provides exhibition space mainly for student & faculty works, plus outside exhibitions; Average Annual Attendance: 12,000
Income: Financed by college appropriation
Collections: Edwin M Blake Memorial & Archive; College Collection; Samuel H Kress Study Collection; George Chaplin Collection; George F McMurray Collection
Exhibitions: Rotating exhibitions
Activities: Classes for adults; dramatic progs; lects open to pub, 6-8 vis lectrs per yr; concerts; lending collection contains 500 original art works & 100,000 slides

M **WADSWORTH ATHENEUM MUSEUM OF ART,** 600 Main St, Hartford, CT 06103-2990. Tel 860-278-2670; Fax 860-527-0803; Elec Mail info@wadsworthatheneum.org; Internet Home Page Address: www.wadsworthatheneum.org; *Conservator* Stephen Kornhauser; *Cur European Decorate Arts* Linda Roth; *Cur European Art* Eric Zafran; *Dir Properties* Alan Barton; *Dir Commun* Kimberly Reynolds; *Cur Contemporary Art* Patricia Hickson; *Dir Educ* Johanna Plummer; *Exec Dir* Susan Lubowsky Talbott
Open Wed - Fri 11 AM - 5 PM, Sat - Sun 10 AM - 5 PM, 1st Thurs 11 AM - 8 PM, cl Mon & Tues; Admis $10 adults, $8 seniors 62 & up, $5 students ages 13 - college; free children 12 & under; Estab 1842 by Daniel Wadsworth; Collections comprise nearly 45,000 works of European and American fine and decorative arts. Highlights include Hudson River School landscapes, 17th century American furniture, European baroque paintings, French & German porcelain, French & American impressionists, modern & contemporary masters & African American art & history; Average Annual Attendance: 140,000; Mem: 8,000; dues $45 & up; annual meeting in Nov
Income: Financed by private funds
Library Holdings: Auction Catalogs; Audio Tapes; Book Volumes; CD-ROMs; Cassettes; Clipping Files; Compact Disks; DVDs; Exhibition Catalogs; Manuscripts; Other Holdings; Pamphlets; Periodical Subscriptions; Slides; Video Tapes
Special Subjects: Afro-American Art, American Indian Art, Archaeology, Drawings, Architecture, Ceramics, Furniture, Porcelain, Prints, Silver, Textiles, Maps, Painting-British, Painting-French, Sculpture, Latin American Art, Painting-American, African Art, Costumes, Crafts, Woodcarvings, Woodcuts, Decorative Arts, Painting-European, Painting-Canadian, Jewelry, Painting-Dutch, Baroque Art, Painting-Flemish, Embroidery, Laces, Painting-Italian, Mosaics, Stained Glass, Painting-Australian, Painting-German, Painting-Israeli
Publications: Newsletter, quarterly to members; collections and exhibitions catalogs
Activities: Docent training; workshops for families & adults; lects & gallery talks by staff for mem only; 4 vis lectrs per yr; docent talks; seasonal concerts; gallery tours; outside lect; members' exhibition previews & various special events; seminars; lending original objects of art to other mus; 3-5 book traveling exhibs per yr; originates 3-5 per yr traveling exhibs; mus shop sells books, reproductions, prints, photographs, cards, toys, accessories & gifts; cafe

L **Auerbach Art Library,** 600 Main St, Hartford, CT 06103-2990. Tel 860-278-2670, Ext 3115; Fax 203-527-0803; Elec Mail john.teahan@wadsworthatheneum.org; *Librn* John W Teahan

Open Wed & Thurs 11 AM - 5 PM, cl Tues & Fri; Estab 1934 as a reference service to the mus staff, members & pub; to provide materials supporting work with mus collection; For reference only
Library Holdings: Auction Catalogs; Book Volumes 47,000; Clipping Files; Exhibition Catalogs; Fiche; Lantern Slides; Pamphlets; Periodical Subscriptions 150; Records; Reels
Special Subjects: Art History, Decorative Arts, Film, Illustration, Etchings & Engravings, Graphic Arts, Painting-American, Painting-British, Painting-Dutch, Painting-Flemish, Painting-French, Painting-German, Painting-Italian, Painting-Russian, Painting-Spanish, Painting-European, Historical Material, History of Art & Archaeology, Ceramics, Conceptual Art, Crafts, Archaeology, Fashion Arts, Industrial Design, Art Education, Asian Art, American Indian Art, Furniture, Costume Design & Constr, Afro-American Art, Embroidery, Enamels, Handicrafts, Jewelry, Silver, Painting-Australian, Painting-Canadian, Architecture
Collections: Sol Lewitt (contemporary art); Elizabeth Miles (English silver); Watkinson Collection (pre-1917 art reference)

KENT

M **DEPARTMENT OF ECONOMIC & COMMUNITY DEVELOPMENT,** (CT Commission on Culture & Tourism) Eric Sloane Museum, Route 7, 31 Kent-Cornwall Rd. Kent, CT 06757; PO Box 917, Kent, CT 06757-0917. Tel 860-927-3849; Fax 860-927-2152; Elec Mail ericsloane.museum@ct.gov; Internet Home Page Address: www.cultureandtourism.org; *Dir Mus* Karin Peterson; *Mus Asst* Barbara Russ; *Deputy Commissioner* Christopher (Kip) Bergstrom
Check website for hrs; Admis adults $8, sr citizens $6, children $5; Estab 1969 to collect, preserve, exhibit historic American tools, implements & artwork of Eric Sloane (1905-1985); Artists re-created studio & display gallery; Average Annual Attendance: 5,000
Income: Financed by state appropriation
Special Subjects: Portraits, Painting-American, Archaeology, Posters, Dioramas
Collections: Eric Sloane Collection (artwork); American tools & implements; Sloane's Studio
Activities: Lects open to pub; 1-2 vis lectrs per yr; gallery talks; sales shop sells books, prints & gifts

A **KENT ART ASSOCIATION,** (Kent Art Association, Inc) Gallery, 21 S Main St, Kent, CT 06757; PO Box 202, Kent, CT 06757-0202. Tel 860-927-3989; Fax 860-927-4218; Elec Mail info@kentart.org; Internet Home Page Address: www.kentart.org; *VPres* Will Kefauver; *Second VPres* Ruth Newquist; *Treas* Beth Dooley; *Pres* Carolyn Fisher
Open during exhibitions Thurs - Sun; No admis fee; Estab 1923, incorporated 1935; Maintains gallery for changing exhibitions; Average Annual Attendance: 2,000; Mem: 400; dues life $200, patron $40, sustaining $25, assoc $15; annual meeting in Oct; qualifications for mem open
Income: Financed by mem, donations
Exhibitions: Spring Show; Member's Show; President's Show; Elected Artist Show
Publications: Exhibition catalogues, 4 per year
Activities: Lect; demonstrations

LITCHFIELD

A **LITCHFIELD HISTORY MUSEUM,** (Litchfield Historical Society) 7 South St, Litchfield, CT 06759-4005; PO Box 385, Litchfield, CT 06759-0385. Tel 860-567-4501; Fax 860-567-3565; Elec Mail cfields@litchfieldhistoricalsociety.org; Internet Home Page Address: www.litchfieldhistoricalsociety.org/museum.html; *Cur* Judith Loto; *Educ Coordr* Rebecca Martin; *Dir* Catherine Keene Fields
Open mid Apr - Nov Tues - Sat 11 AM - 5 PM, Sun 1 - 5 PM; Admis $5, children under 14 free; seniors & children 6 & over $3; Estab 1896, incorporated 1897 for the preservation & interpretation of local historical collections; A gallery of portraits by Ralph Earl is maintained; Average Annual Attendance: 12,000; Mem: 450; dues benefactor $500, donor $250, contributing $100, family $40, individual $25; annual meeting second Fri in Sept
Income: $220,000 (financed by endowment, mem & fundraising)
Special Subjects: Costumes, Embroidery, Decorative Arts, Folk Art, Furniture
Collections: American & Connecticut fine & decorative arts, pewter, costumes, textiles, paintings, silver, pottery & graphics; furniture; textiles; household goods
Exhibitions: Changing exhibitions on area art & history
Activities: Classes for adults & children; docent training; curriculum units; workshops; lects open to pub, 4 vis lectrs per yr; gallery talks; tours; individual & original objects of art lent to accredited mus with board approval; sales shop sells books, reproductions & prints

L **Ingraham Memorial Research Library,** 7 South St, Litchfield, CT 06759-4005; PO Box 385, Litchfield, CT 06759-0385. Tel 860-567-4501; Fax 860-567-3565; Internet Home Page Address: w.litchfieldhistory.org; *Dir* Catherine Keene Fields
Open Tues - Fri 10 AM - Noon & 1 - 4 PM, 1 Sat a month; No admis fee; Estab 1896 as a center of local history & genealogy study; Reference only; Mem: Same as society
Income: $10,000 (financed by endowment & mem)
Library Holdings: Book Volumes 10,000; Clipping Files; Exhibition Catalogs; Manuscripts; Memorabilia; Other Holdings Original documents 50,000; Pamphlets; Periodical Subscriptions 10; Photographs; Prints; Reels
Collections: 40,000 manuscripts in local history
Exhibitions: Several rotating exhibitions per year

MERIDEN

A **ARTS & CRAFTS ASSOCIATION OF MERIDEN INC,** Gallery 53, 53 Colony St, Meriden, CT 06451-3210. Tel 203-235-5347; Elec Mail info@gallery53.org; Internet Home Page Address: www.gallery53.org; Open Tues - Fri Noon - 4 PM, Sat 10 AM - 2 PM; No admis fee; Estab 1907 to encourage appreciation of the arts in the community; One floor gallery to hold

exhibits & art work studios above with meeting room; Average Annual Attendance: 1,800; Mem: 300; dues $35 & up; annual meeting in June
Income: Financed by mem & fund raising, class fees
Collections: Permanent collection of paintings & sculptures includes works by Eric Sloan, Emile Gruppe, Stow Wengenroth as well as works by Meriden artists
Exhibitions: Annual Members Show; Photography Show; Student Show; One man & group shows; theme shows & alternating exhibits of works from permanent collection
Activities: Classes for adults & children; dramatic progs; lects open to pub, 8 vis lectrs per yr; workshops; gallery talks; tours; competitions with awards; schols offered; individual paintings & original objects of art lent to banks & public buildings; originate traveling exhibs; sales shop sells original art & crafts
L **Gallery 53,** 53 Colony St, Meriden, CT 06451-0348. Tel 203-235-5347; Fax 203-866-0015; Elec Mail gallary53ct@gmail.com; Internet Home Page Address: www.gallery53.org; *Pres* Laura LeClair; *VPres* Christine Webster; *Gallery Dir* Rita Sarris
Open Tues - Fri Noon - 4 PM, Sat 10 AM - 2 PM; No admis fee; Estab 1907 to promote the arts; Gallery changes exhibits every 4 wks approx; shows work of art groups, individual painters, photographers, school students; permanent collection of paintings
Income: Non-profit
Library Holdings: Book Volumes 650
Collections: Indiana Thomas Book Collection
Activities: Educ prog; classes for adults & children; gallery talks; schols offered; sales shop sells original art, prints, pottery, jewelry, accessories

MIDDLETOWN

M **WESLEYAN UNIVERSITY,** Davison Art Center, 301 High St, Middletown, CT 06459-3232. Tel 860-685-2500; Fax 860-685-2501; Internet Home Page Address: www.wesleyan.edu/dac; *Cur* Clare Rogan
Open Tues - Sun 12 - 4 PM; No admis fee; Part of the collection was presented to Wesleyan University by George W & Harriet B Davison. Since 1952 the collection with its reference library has been housed in an addition to the historic Alsop House; collection of works on paper; rotating exhibitions
Special Subjects: Drawings, Photography, Prints, Woodcuts, Etchings & Engravings
Collections: The print collection, extending from the 15th century to present day, includes Master E S, Nielli, Mantegna, Pollaiuolo, Durer, Cranach, Rembrandt, Canaletto, Piranesi, Goya, Millet, Meryon, Jim Dine, & others; Japanese & contemporary American prints; 1840s to present, photographs
Exhibitions: Regularly changing exhibitions of prints, drawings, photographs & other works on paper
Publications: Exhibition catalogues
Activities: Lects open to public, gallery talks; tours; collection contains 25,000 original prints, drawings & photographs; originates traveling exhibitions
L **Art Library,** 301 High St, Davison Art Ctr Middletown, CT 06459-3232. Tel 860-685-3327; *Art Librn* Susanne Javorski
Open Mon - Thurs 9 AM - 11 PM, Fri 9 AM - 5 PM, Sat 1 - 5 PM, Sun 1 - 11 PM; Estab 1950 as research/reference library primarily supporting university courses in art history & studio arts
Library Holdings: Book Volumes 24,000; Periodical Subscriptions 125
Collections: Print Reference Collection (books pertaining to the history of the graphic arts)
A **Friends of the Davison Art Center,** 301 High St, Middletown, CT 06459-0487. Tel 860-685-2500; Fax 203-685-2501; *Pres* Patricia Reville
Estab 1961 for the support & augmentation of the activities & acquisition fund of the Davison Art Center by its members
Income: Financed by mem dues & contributions
Purchases: Photographs, Prints
Activities: Gallery talks
M **Ezra & Cecile Zilkha Gallery,** Ctr for the Arts, Middletown, CT 06459-0001. Tel 860-685-2695; Fax 860-685-2061; Internet Home Page Address: www.wesleyan.edu/cfalzilkha/home.html; *Cur Exhib* Nina Felshin
Open Tues - Sun Noon - 4 PM, cl Mon & acad vacations; No admis fee; Estab 1973 to exhibit contemporary art; Exhibitions of contemporary art; Average Annual Attendance: 15,000
Income: Financed by contributions
Exhibitions: Changing exhibitions of contemporary art
Publications: Exhibition catalogs & brochures
Activities: Educ Dept; lects open to public, 6 vis lectrs per yr; gallery talks; tours; sales shop sells catalogs

MYSTIC

A **MYSTIC ART ASSOCIATION, INC,** Mystic Arts Center, 9 Water St, Mystic, CT 06355-2592. Tel 860-536-7601; Fax 860-536-0610; Elec Mail exec@mysticarts.org; Internet Home Page Address: www.mysticarts.org; *Pres* Christine Grady; *Treas* Fred Conti; *Exec Dir* Karen Barthelson; *Secy* Margaret Ryan; *Dir Develop* Brandy Kolmer; *Dir Educ* Dawn Salerno; *Dir Finance* Judith Flora
Open daily year round 11 AM - 5 PM; No admis fee; $3 suggested donation, children & members free; Estab 1914 to maintain an art mus to promote cultural educ, local philanthropic & charitable interests; The assoc owns a historic building on the bank of Mystic River with spacious grounds; five galleries, handicap access, air conditioned, new educational wing opened Spring of 1999; Average Annual Attendance: 20,000; Mem: 1000; artist mem must have high standards of proficiency & be juried in four shows; dues active $40, assoc $35; meeting held in Apr
Income: Financed by mem, grants & leases
Collections: Mystic Art Colony Paintings; original artwork by notable artists; Mystic Art Colony Collection
Exhibitions: Juried Members' Show (all media); Annual Regional (all media)
Publications: News Views, monthly
Activities: Classes for adults & children; international workshop; photography lab; lects open to pub, 2 vis lectrs per yr; concerts; gallery talks; tours; competitions

with awards; scholarships offered; exten dept serves New London County; individual paintings & original objects of art lent to historical societies & museums; sales shop sells original art

NEW BRITAIN

M **CENTRAL CONNECTICUT STATE UNIVERSITY,** Art Dept Museum, 1615 Stanley St, New Britain, CT 06050-2439. Tel 860-832-2633; Fax 860-832-2634; Elec Mail ro-mimi.gallery@hotmail.com; Internet Home Page Address: www.art.ccsu.edu;
Open Mon-Wed 1-4PM, Thus 1-7PM; No admis fee; Estab to collect, display & interpret works of art & ethnic materials relating to the art educ program; Center will be constructed within two years & collection will be on display in center, whole collection will not be on permanent display
Income: Financed by the univ
Exhibitions: Changing exhibitions every month
Activities: Lect open to public; gallery talks

M **NEW BRITAIN MUSEUM OF AMERICAN ART,** 56 Lexington St, New Britain, CT 06052-1412. Tel 860-229-0257; Fax 860-229-3445; Elec Mail nbmaa@nbmaa.org; Internet Home Page Address: www.nbmaa.org; *Dir* Douglas Hyland; *Cur Educ* Linda Mare; *Dir Develop* Claudia Thesing; *Dir Finance* Tom Bell; *Collections Mgr* John Urgo; *Facility Mgr* Michael Smith
Open Tues, Wed & Fri 11 AM - 5 PM, Thurs 11 AM - 8 PM, Sat 10 AM - 5 PM, Sun noon - 5 PM; Admis adults $12, sr citizens $10, students $8, children under 12 no charge. Free admis Sat 10 AM - Noon.; Estab 1903 to exhibit, collect & preserve American art; 43,000 sq ft Chase Family Bldg: 15 galleries, auditorium/multi purpose space; state-of-the-art collections storage, HVAC & security systems; cafe & terrace, mus shop & 102 off-st parking spaces. 10,000 sq ft Landers House: art studio, hands-on space called ArtLab for pre-k through grade 5, library & admin offices; Average Annual Attendance: 90,000; Mem: 5,545; dues Chairman's Circle $10,000, Director's Circle $5,000, Leadership Circle $2,500, American Art Circle $1,000, Collector's Circle $500, Artist's Circle $250, Friends Circle $100, Household $75, Household Senior $70, Individual $45, Individual Senior $40, student/educator $35; annual mtg mid-Oct
Income: Financed by contributions, grants, sponsorships, earned income (admis prog fees, shop revenue, facility rental, exhib loan fees) & endowment
Purchases: Purchases art objects for the collection
Library Holdings: Exhibition Catalogs; Original Art Works; Photographs; Prints; Sculpture
Special Subjects: Drawings, Landscapes, Marine Painting, Ceramics, Collages, Photography, Porcelain, Portraits, Prints, Bronzes, Sculpture, Painting-American, Watercolors, Woodcuts, Etchings & Engravings, Glass, Silver, Miniatures, Cartoons, Military Art
Collections: American art: colonial & federal portraits, 19th century still-life, American impressionists; 20th century: The Eight, Social Realists & Early Moderns; Stieglitz group, Precisionists, Geometric Abstraction, Surrealism, Abstract Expressionism, Pop Art, Photo-Realism, Super Realism & Op Art; Thomas Hart Benton's The Arts of Life in America; Illustration, New Media
Exhibitions: Lisa Hoke: The Gravity of Color (installation); Ongoing Permanent Collection
Publications: Newsletter, quarterly; calendar, quarterly; annual report; New Britain Museum of American Art: Highlights of the Collection: Volume I; New Britain Museum of American Art: Highlights of the Collection: Volume II; The Tides of Provincetown: Pivotal Years in America's Oldest Continuous Art Colony (1899-2011)
Activities: Educ dept; docent training; classes for adults & children; lects open to pub; concerts; gallery talks; tours; teacher workshops; sponsor competitions; original objects of art lent to other mus; originate traveling exhibs; mus shop selling books, original art, reproductions, prints, slides & postcards & gifts

NEW CANAAN

M **NEW CANAAN HISTORICAL SOCIETY,** 13 Oenoke Ridge, New Canaan, CT 06840. Tel 203-966-1776; Fax 203-972-5917; Elec Mail newcanaan.historica@gmail.com; Internet Home Page Address: www.nchistory.org; *Exec Dir* Janet Lindstrom; *Archivist* Vickie Ambrose; *Dir Educ* Kim Mellin
Town House & library open Tues - Fri 9:30 AM - 4:30 PM, Sat 9:30 AM - 12:30 PM; call for museum hours; Admis by suggested donation, $4; Estab 1889 to bring together & arrange historical events & genealogies, collect relics, form a museum & library; Society consists of seven museums & library. Rogers' studio contains sculpture groups by John Rogers. Exhibit room houses changing displays of costumes, photos & paintings; Average Annual Attendance: 5,000; Mem: 800; dues family $50, individual $35; meetings second Mon in Mar, June, Sept, Dec
Income: Financed by mem & contributions
Library Holdings: Audio Tapes; Book Volumes; Clipping Files; Fiche; Manuscripts; Maps; Original Art Works; Original Documents; Photographs; Slides; Video Tapes
Special Subjects: Historical Material, Portraits, Painting-American, Period Rooms, Textiles, Manuscripts, Maps, Architecture, Sculpture, Costumes, Dolls, Pewter
Collections: Costume coll, including fans, purses & shoes; document colls; pewter; period furniture; photo coll; Rogers' sculpture groups; quilts; paintings
Exhibitions: Costume & History; permanent exhibition of Rogers' sculptures; changing exhibits of art by Silvermine artists
Publications: New Canaan Historical Society Annual; Philip Johnson in New Canaan; John Rogers (1829-1904) & the Rogers Groups by John Rogers (1945-present); Portrait of New Cannan; New Cannan: Texture of a Community; other titles upon request
Activities: Seminars; children's classes; docent training; summer camp; lects open to pub, 4+ vis lectrs per yr; concerts; tours; Bayles Award (Presidential Classroom), biannual & Award to New Canaan High School Junior for outstanding achievement in history; mus sells New Canaan Historical Society Annual, Christmas cards, maps, postcards & stationery

L **NEW CANAAN LIBRARY,** H. Pelham Curtis Gallery, 151 Main St, New Canaan, CT 06840-5514. Tel 203-594-5000; Fax 203-594-5026; Elec Mail reference@newcanaanlibrary.org; Internet Home Page Address: www.newcanaanlibrary.org; *Dir* David Bryant; *Chair Art Comt* Suzanne Salomon
Open Mon - Thurs 9 AM - 8 PM, Fri & Sat 9 AM - 5 PM, Sun Noon - 5 PM

except summer; Estab 1877; H. Pelham Curtis Gallery organizes 8 shows per year; Average Annual Attendance: 2,000; Mem: Art Comt - 20 members, no dues, 1st Thursday each month
Income: $1,293,000 (financed by mem, city & state appropriation)
Library Holdings: Audio Tapes; Book Volumes 146,000; CD-ROMs; DVDs; Other Holdings Audio & Video tapes 7338; Periodical Subscriptions 407
Special Subjects: Landscape Architecture, Photography, Painting-American, Painting-Japanese, Sculpture, Painting-European, Crafts, Video, Oriental Art
Collections: Alfandari Collection-European from fall of Rome to Impressionism; Chinese-Japanese art; general collection of art books & videos
Activities: Lectrs open to the public, 2 visiting lectrs per year, concerts, exhibit-related classes for children

M **PHILIP JOHNSON GLASS HOUSE, NATIONAL TRUST FOR HISTORIC PRESERVATION,** 199 Elm St, Visitor Center New Canaan, CT 06840. Tel 203-594-9884; Fax 203-594-9885; Internet Home Page Address: www.philipjohnsonglasshouse.org; *Cur & Colls Mgr* Irene Shum Allen
Open for Tours May-Nov, Wed-Mon; Admis rates for tours vary, see website; Estab 2007. Not recommended for children under 10
Library Holdings: Auction Catalogs; Audio Tapes; Book Volumes; Compact Disks; DVDs; Maps; Memorabilia; Other Holdings; Photographs; Records; Slides; Video Tapes
Special Subjects: Landscapes, Architecture
Collections: Architecture (modern); Fine Art (Modern & Contemporary); Furniture & Design (Modern & Contemporary); Library & Archives
Publications: Pairings (2007); Glan House (Anonline 2008); Modern Views (Anonline 2010)
Activities: Educ prog; outgoing loan prog; publication prog; mus shop sells books, prints, & other items

M **SILVERMINE GUILD ARTS CENTER,** Silvermine Galleries, 1037 Silvermine Rd, New Canaan, CT 06840-4398. Tel 203-966-5617, ext 21; Fax 203-972-7236; Elec Mail gallery@silvermineart.org; Internet Home Page Address: www.silvermineart.org; *Exec Dir* Pamela Davis; *Dir School* Anne Connell
Open Tues - Sat 11 AM - 5 PM, Sun 1 - 5 PM, Mon by appointment; No admis fee, suggested donation $2; Estab 1922 as an independent art center to foster, promote & encourage activities in the arts & art educ; to provide a place for member artists & invited artists to show & sell their work; to offer the community a wide variety of artistic, cultural & educational activities; Five exhibition galleries featuring one-person shows, regional & national juried artists; Average Annual Attendance: 20,000; Mem: 30; mems juried in by a panel of guild artists; dues $45 & up
Income: Financed by mem, sale of art, contributions & tuitions
Collections: Permanent print collection containing purchase prizes from International Print Exhibition
Exhibitions: Rotating exhibits every 5-6 weeks
Publications: Exhibition catalogs; member newsletter, quarterly
Activities: Classes for adults & children; workshops; lects open to pub, 10 vis lectrs per yr; concerts; gallery talks; tours; competitions with awards; scholarships offered; individual paintings & original objects of art lent to corporations & banks; lending collection contains books & original prints; originate traveling exhibs; mus shop sells books, ceramics, jewelry
L **School of Art,** 1037 Silvermine Rd, New Canaan, CT 06840. Tel 203-966-6668; Fax 203-966-8570; Elec Mail sgac@silvermineart.org; Internet Home Page Address: www.silvermineart.org; *Dir Silvermine School* Anne Connell; *Gallery Dir* Helen Klisser During; *Mus Shop Mgr* Lauren Minor; *Exec Dir* Cynthia Clair
Open to members & out buyers by appt; Estab 1920; Average Annual Attendance: 1,000
Library Holdings: Book Volumes 2500; Periodical Subscriptions 11; Slides
Special Subjects: Scrimshaw
Exhibitions: 10 exhibs per yr
Activities: Classes for adults & children; lects open to pub, 10 vis lectrs per yr; concerts; gallery talks; tours; competitions with awards; scholarships offered; original objects of art lent; sales shop sells books, original art & prints

NEW HAVEN

M **KNIGHTS OF COLUMBUS SUPREME COUNCIL,** Knights of Columbus Museum, 1 State St, New Haven, CT 06511-6702. Tel 203-865-0400; Fax 203-865-0351; Internet Home Page Address: www.kofcmuseum.org; *Cur & Registrar* Mary Lou Cummings; *Dir* Larry Sowinski; *Archivist* Susan Brosnan; *Asst Dir* Kathryn Cogan; *Gift Shop Mgr* Olga Lapaeva; *Support Staff* Jess Mallory; *Support Staff* Don Adams
Winter hours: Wed - Sat 10 AM - 5 PM, Sun 11 AM - 5 PM; summer hours: Mon - Sun 10 AM - 5 PM; cl Good Friday, Thanksgiving & Christmas Day; No admis fee; Estab 1982 as a corporate history museum revealing the history & activities of the Knights of Columbus, 77,000 sq ft bldg; 170 ft wall of history; Average Annual Attendance: 50,000
Special Subjects: Folk Art, Glass, Mexican Art, Furniture, Painting-American, Textiles, Manuscripts, Maps, Painting-European, Sculpture, Graphics, Latin American Art, Prints, Watercolors, Bronzes, Costumes, Religious Art, Ceramics, Woodcarvings, Decorative Arts, Posters, Painting-Canadian, Porcelain, Silver, Painting-Dutch, Ivory, Coins & Medals, Baroque Art, Painting-Polish, Renaissance Art, Dioramas, Embroidery, Painting-Italian, Mosaics, Stained Glass, Reproductions, Painting-Russian
Collections: Fine & decorative arts; Fine Arts; Colonial Mexican Art
Exhibitions: Christopher Columbus; Founder Father Michael J McGivney; gifts & items from Knights of Columbus state & local councils; Knights of Columbus War Activities; Tributes (interactions with the Catholic Church & the Vatican); rotating loan exhibits; Three loan exhibits per yr
Publications: Postcards; museum tour brochures; posters; exhib catalog
Activities: Lect open to the public; Christmas tree festival for children; 1 - 2 vis lectrs per yr; gallery talks; tours; Christmas tree festival prizes; corporate archives

research history of Knights of Columbus; individual paintings & original objects of art lent under special arrangements & careful consideration; mus shop sells books, original art, reproductions, prints, religious items, medals, tapes, videos & jewelry

A **NEW HAVEN MUSEUM & HISTORICAL SOCIETY,** (New Haven Colony Historical Society) 114 Whitney Ave, New Haven, CT 06510-1238. Tel 203-562-4183; Fax 203-562-2002; Elec Mail Info@newhavenmuseum.org; Internet Home Page Address: www.newhavenmuseum.org; *Librn* James W Campbell; *Pres* Walter R Miller Jr
Open Tues - Fri 10 AM - 5 PM, Sat noon - 5 PM, cl Mon & major holidays; Admis adults $4, sr citizens $3, children $2, members free; Estab 1862 for the preservation, exhibition & research of local history; 7 galleries; Average Annual Attendance: 12,000; Mem: 900; annual meeting in Nov
Income: $250,000 (financed by private contributions)
Library Holdings: Book Volumes; Clipping Files; Exhibition Catalogs; Kodachrome Transparencies; Manuscripts; Maps; Memorabilia; Micro Print; Original Documents; Other Holdings; Pamphlets; Periodical Subscriptions; Photographs; Slides
Special Subjects: Architecture, Costumes, Drawings, Embroidery, Etchings & Engravings, Historical Material, Landscapes, Manuscripts, Photography, Prints, Reproductions, Silver, Textiles, Watercolors, Painting-American, Decorative Arts, Folk Art, Pewter, Woodcuts, Afro-American Art, Ceramics, Hispanic Art, Portraits, Furniture, Glass, Woodcarvings, Marine Painting, Period Rooms, Maps, Bookplates & Bindings, Flasks & Bottles, Coins & Medals
Collections: 18th & 19th Century Coll of portraits of the New Haven area personages; maritime coll of shops paintings; paintings by local artists Corne, Durrie, Jocelyn, Moulthrop
Exhibitions: Permanent exhibition includes paintings by local artists such as Jocelyn, Moulthrop & George H Durrie; landscape portraits; maritime historical paintings; New Haven Illustrated: From Colony, Town to City; Maritime New Haven; Ingersoll Collection of Furniture & Decorative Arts; Two changing exhibitions per year minimum
Publications: Newsletter
Activities: Classes for adults & children; hands-on progs; docent training; lects open to pub, 4 vis lectrs per yr; slideshows; concerts; gallery talks & tours; individual paintings & objects of art lent to other approved mus; mus shop sells books, reproductions, prints, antiques, collectibles & journals, children's toys, posters, postcards, videos, CDs

L **Whitney Library,** 114 Whitney Ave, New Haven, CT 06510-1238. Tel 203-562-4183; Fax 230-562-2002; *Librn* James Campbell; *Pres* Gilbert F Hogan, M.D.
Open Tues - Fri 10 AM - 5 PM, Sat noon - 5 PM, cl Mon & major holidays, free first Sun ea mon; Admis $4, sr citizens $3, children $2, members free; Estab 1862 for the preservation, exhib & research of local history; 7 galleries; Average Annual Attendance: 12,000; Mem: 900; annual meeting in Nov
Income: $250,000 (financed by private contributions)
Library Holdings: Audio Tapes; Book Volumes; Clipping Files; Exhibition Catalogs; Kodachrome Transparencies; Manuscripts; Maps; Memorabilia; Micro Print; Original Documents; Other Holdings Glass plate negatives 30,000; Original documents; Pamphlets; Periodical Subscriptions; Photographs; Slides
Special Subjects: Art History, Decorative Arts, Manuscripts, Maps, Historical Material, Bookplates & Bindings, Marine Painting, Architecture
Collections: Afro-American Coll; Architectural Drawings; John W Barber Collection; Dana: New Haven Old & New; Durrie Papers; Ingersoll Papers; National & Local Historical Figures, A-Z; Ezra Stiles Papers; Noah Webster Collection
Publications: Journal, irregular; News and Notes, irregular; monographs; exhibition catalogs
Activities: Arrangement with local colleges for internship progs & work-study progs; lects open to pub & members; tours; individual paintings & objects of art lent to other institutions; mus shop sells books, reproductions, prints & antiques

A **NEW HAVEN PAINT & CLAY CLUB, INC,** 51 Trumbull St, The John Slade Ely House New Haven, CT 06510-1004. Tel 203-624-8055; Elec Mail dmgall@aol.com; Internet Home Page Address: www.elyhouse.org; *Pres* Dolores Gall; *VPres* Sheila Kaczmarek; *VPres* Brian Schoolar
Open Wed- Fri 11 AM - 4 PM; Sat & Sun 2 - 5 PM; cl Mon & Tues; No admis fee; Estab 1900 to provide opportunities for artists in New England to exhibit their work, inc in 1928; Two floors of an historic house; Average Annual Attendance: 350; Mem: 270; open to artists working in any media whose work has been accepted two times in the Annual Juried Show; dues life $100, active $16, assoc $10; annual meeting in May
Income: $4000 (financed by dues)
Purchases: $3000
Collections: 280 2-D pictures & 14 sculptures
Exhibitions: Annual Mar-Apr Exhibition (New England & New York artists); Annual Fall Exhibition (active members only); Permanent Collection
Publications: Exhibition catalogs; newsletter
Activities: Lects open to pub, 1 vis lectr per yr; lects at annual meeting; awards $500 members show, $4500 juried exhibition; scholarships; individual paintings & original objects of art lent to local organizations

M **SOUTHERN CONNECTICUT STATE UNIVERSITY,** Art Dept, 501 Crescent St, New Haven, CT 06515-1330. Tel 203-392-6652, Ext 5974; Fax 203-392-6658; Internet Home Page Address: www.southernct.edu; *Dir* Cort Sierpinski
Open Mon - Fri 8 AM - 10 PM; Estab 1976 to build a collection of works of art for educational purposes, gallery developing now; Mem: 750
Income: $10,000 (financed by mem, state appropriation & fundraising)
Special Subjects: African Art, Pre-Columbian Art
Collections: African & Pre-Columbian art
Activities: Travelogues; lects open to pub, 6 vis lectrs per yr; gallery talks; national & international tours; original objects of art lent to admin offices

M **YALE UNIVERSITY,** Yale University Art Gallery, 1111 Chapel St, New Haven, CT 06520-8271. Tel 203-432-0600; Fax 203-432-9523; Elec Mail artgalleryinfo@yale.edu; Internet Home Page Address: www.yale.edu/artgallery.com; Internet Home Page Address: artgallery.yale.edu; *Dir* Jock Reynolds; *Cur Prints, Drawings & Photographs* Suzanne Boorsch; *Cur Ancient Art* Susan Matheson; *Cur American Painting* Helen Cooper; *Cur American Decorative Arts* Patricia Kane; *Registrar* Lynne Addison; *Mem* Linda Jerolmon; *Cur Educ* Jessica Sack; *Cur Modern & Contemporary Art* Jennifer Gross; *Asian* David Sensabaugh; *Pub Rels* Amy Jean Porter; *Cur European Art* Lawrence Kanter; *Cur African Art* Frederick Lamp; *Cur Acad Initiatives* Pamela Franks

Open Tues - Sat 10 AM - 5 PM, Sun 1 PM - 6 PM, cl Mon; No admis fee; Estab 1832 to exhibit works of art from ancient times to present; Building designed by Louis Kahn & completed in 1953; Average Annual Attendance: 140,000; Mem: 1500; dues $50 & up

Income: Financed by endowment, mem & annual fundraising

Special Subjects: Painting-American, Silver, Painting-European, Sculpture, Oriental Art, Antiquities-Greek, Antiquities-Roman

Collections: American & European painting & sculpture; Chinese painting & ceramics; Dura-Europos Archaeological Collection; Garvan Collection of American Decorative Arts; History paintings & miniatures by John Trumbull; Japanese painting & ceramics; Jarves Collection of Italian Renaissance Painting; Societe Anonyme Collection of Twentieth century art; Stoddard Collection of Greek Vases; 20th Century Art; 25,000 prints, drawings & photographs; Charles B Benenson Collection of African Art

Publications: Exhibition catalogues; Yale University Art Gallery Bulletin, catalogue raisonnes

Activities: Classes for adults & children; family progs; evening lects; gallery tours three times per wk; gallery talks; originate traveling exhibs; books

M **Yale Center for British Art,** 1080 Chapel St, New Haven, CT 06510-2302; PO Box 208280, New Haven, CT 06520-8280. Tel 203-432-2800; Fax 203-432-9628; Elec Mail ycba.info@yale.edu; Internet Home Page Address: www.yale.edu/ycba; *Dir* Amy Meyers; *Sr Cur Paintings & Sculpture* Angus Trumble; *Registrar* Timothy Goodhue; *Deputy Dir* Constance Clement; *Head Librn* Kraig Binkowski; *Sr Cur Rare Books & Manuscripts* Elisabeth Fairman; *Head Research & Cur Sculpture* Martina Droth; *Assoc Cur Paintings & Sculpture* Cassandra Albinson; *Chief Cur Art Colls, Information & Access & Sr Cur Prints & Drawings* Scott Wilcox; *Cur Prints & Drawings* Gillian Forrester; *Assoc Cur & Head Exhibs & Publs* Eleanor Hughes; *Assoc Cur Colls Research* Matthew Hargraves; *Assoc Cur Exhibs & Publs* Imogen Hart

Open Tues - Sat 10 AM - 5 PM, Sun Noon - 5 PM, cl Mon; No admis fee; Estab 1977 to foster appreciation & knowledge of British art; to encourage interdisciplinary use of the collections; Circ Non-circulating library; 3 floors of gallery space exhibiting permanent colls & special exhibs; Average Annual Attendance: 100,000; Mem: 850; dues individual $50

Income: Financed by endowment, annual gifts, mem & mus shop

Library Holdings: Auction Catalogs; Audio Tapes; Book Volumes; CD-ROMs; Cards; Cassettes; Clipping Files; Compact Disks; DVDs; Exhibition Catalogs; Fiche; Filmstrips; Framed Reproductions; Kodachrome Transparencies; Lantern Slides; Manuscripts; Maps; Memorabilia; Micro Print; Motion Pictures; Original Art Works; Original Documents; Other Holdings; Pamphlets; Periodical Subscriptions; Photographs; Prints; Records; Reproductions; Sculpture; Slides; Video Tapes

Special Subjects: Architecture, Drawings, Prints, Sculpture, Watercolors, Etchings & Engravings, Landscapes, Manuscripts, Portraits, Marine Painting, Painting-British, Maps, Miniatures, Bookplates & Bindings

Collections: Paintings & sculpture; drawings; prints; rare books

Publications: exhibition catalogues

Activities: Classes for adults & children; dramatic progs; docent training; student guides; lects & symposia, 10 vis lectrs per yr; concerts, gallery talks; tours; films; fels; individual paintings & objects of art lent to other mus; lending collection contains rare books, original art works, original prints & paintings; book traveling exhibs; originate traveling exhibs; mus shop sells books, reproductions, slides, postcards, exhibs catalogs, glass, ceramics, jewelry & other items

L **Yale Center for British Art Reference Library,** 1080 Chapel St, New Haven, CT 06520-2302; PO Box 208280, New Haven, CT 06520-8280. Tel 203-432-2818; Fax 203-432-9613; Elec Mail bacref@pantheon.yale.edu; Internet Home Page Address: www.yale.edu/ycba; *Librn* Susan Brady

Open Tues - Fri 10 AM - 4:30 PM, Sat 1 - 4:30 PM when Yale is in session; No admis fee; Estab 1977 to support collection of British Art and related fields of architecture, history, literature and the performing arts; Reference library & photo archive

Library Holdings: Auction Catalogs; Book Volumes 20,000; CD-ROMs; Cards; Exhibition Catalogs; Fiche 75,000; Pamphlets; Periodical Subscriptions 70; Photographs 200,000; Reels 860; Video Tapes

Collections: British Art from age of Holbein to present

Activities: Classes for adults & children; docent training

L **The Robert B. Haas Family Arts Library,** 180 York St, New Haven, CT 06511-8924; PO Box 208318, New Haven, CT 06520-8318. Tel 203-432-2645; Fax 203-432-0549; Elec Mail art.library@yale.edu; Internet Home Page Address: www.library.yale.edu/arts; *Dir* Allen Townsend; *Spec Colls Librn* Jae Rossman

Open acad yr Mon - Thurs 8:30 AM - 11 PM, Fri 8:30 AM - 5 PM, Sat 10 AM - 6 PM, Sun 2 PM - 11 PM; Summer Mon & Wed - Fri 8:30 AM - 5 PM, Tues 8:30 AM - 7 PM; Estab 1868. Serves Schools of Art, Drama & Architecture, History of Art Department & the Yale University Art Gallery; William H Wright special collections exhib area

Library Holdings: Book Volumes 115,000; Exhibition Catalogs; Other Holdings Digital Images, Photographs & Color Prints 183,000; Slides 825,000

Collections: Faber Birren Collection of Books on Color; Arts of the Book Collection; Yale Bookplate Collection

Publications: Faber Birren Collection of Books on Color: A Bibliography

L **Beinecke Rare Book & Manuscript Library,** 121 Wall St, New Haven, CT 06511; P.O. Box 280240, New Haven, CT 06520-8240. Tel 203-432-2977; Fax 203-432-4047; Elec Mail beinecke.library@yale.edu; Internet Home Page Address: www.library.yale.edu/beinecke; *Prof* Frank M Turner

Open Mon - Fri 8:30 AM - 5 PM, Sat 10 AM - 5 PM; No admis fee; Estab 1963; Non-circulating

Library Holdings: Book Volumes 600,000; Clipping Files; Manuscripts; Maps; Memorabilia; Original Art Works; Original Documents; Pamphlets; Photographs; Prints; Sculpture

Special Subjects: Art History, Illustration, Calligraphy, Drawings, Etchings & Engravings, Graphic Arts, Graphic Design, Islamic Art, Historical Material, History of Art & Archaeology, Judaica, American Western Art, American Indian Art, Afro-American Art, Bookplates & Bindings

Collections: Osborn Collection of English literary & historical manuscripts from the Anglo-Saxon period to 20th century; Coll of America Literature of 19th & early 20th century writings; German Literature Coll of rare books & first editions of 17th-20th century; Western Americana Coll of books, manuscripts, maps, art, prints & photographs of Trans-Mississippi West through world War I; General coll of Early Books & Manuscripts includes Greek & Roman papyri, medieval & Renaissance manuscripts; modern books & manuscripts in English literature & history from 17th-20th century

Publications: Exhibition catalogs

Activities: Lects open to pub, 10-15 vis lectrs per yr; concerts; schols & fels offered; sales shop sells books

NEW LONDON

M **LYMAN ALLYN ART MUSEUM,** 625 Williams St, New London, CT 06320-4199. Tel 860-443-2545; Fax 860-442-1280; Elec Mail info@lymanallyn.org; Internet Home Page Address: www.lymanallyn.org; *Dir & Cur* Nancy Stula; *Dir Communs* Susan Hendricks; *Dir Educ* Mollie Clarke; *Dir Finance* Kathy Jacques

Open Tues - Sat 10 AM - 3 PM, cl Sun, Mon & major holidays; Admis adults $8, students & seniors $7, children under 12 free; Estab 1932 for the educ & enrichment of the community & others; The museum is housed in a handsome Neo-Classical building designed by Charles A Platt; Average Annual Attendance: 20,000; Mem: 800; dues range from individual $40 to Harriet Allyn Society $1,000

Income: $220,000 (financed by endowment, trusts, mem & gifts)

Purchases: $10,000

Library Holdings: Auction Catalogs; Book Volumes; Exhibition Catalogs; Periodical Subscriptions

Special Subjects: Landscapes, Prints, Painting-European, Painting-French, Painting-American, Decorative Arts, Dolls, Furniture, Oriental Art, Silver, Painting-Italian

Collections: American Impressionist Paintings; Connecticut Decorative Arts; Contemporary, Modern & Early American Fine Arts; collection of 30,000 works; European Paintings & Works on Paper

Exhibitions: Temporary exhibitions of American Art from public & private collections; The Devotion Family of 18th Century Connecticut; Connecticut Women Artists; Impressionist Paintings from the Lyman Allyn Collection; At Home & Abroad: The Transcendental Landscapes of Christopher Pearce Cranch; Walter Wick: Games & Toys in the Attic

Publications: New London County Furniture from 1640-1840; New London Silver

Activities: Educ prog; classes for adults & children; docent training; school tours & progs; lects open to pub; 3 vis lectrs per yr; concerts; gallery talks; tours; scholarships; individual paintings & original objects of art lent; mus shop sells books, reproductions, cards & gifts

L **Hendel Library,** 625 Williams St, New London, CT 06320. Tel 860-443-2545; Fax 860-442-1280; Internet Home Page Address: www.lymanallyn.conncoll.edu; *Librn* Lissa Van Dyke

Open Tues - Sat 10 AM - 5 PM, Sun 1 - 5 PM; Admis for mems & by appointment only; Estab 1932 to provide an art reference library as an adjunct to the material in the Lyman Allyn Art Museum; Reference only; Average Annual Attendance: 1,500

Income: financed by Harriet Allen trust

Library Holdings: Book Volumes 4500; Clipping Files; Exhibition Catalogs; Fiche; Pamphlets; Periodical Subscriptions 32; Photographs; Reproductions; Slides

Special Subjects: Decorative Arts

Collections: Decorative arts, furniture, drawings

Activities: Docent training; lects open to pub, 2 vis lectrs per yr; gallery talks; tours

A **NEW LONDON COUNTY HISTORICAL SOCIETY,** Shaw Mansion, 11 Blinman St, New London, CT 06320-5677. Tel 860-443-1209; Fax 860-443-1209; Elec Mail info@newlondonhistory.org; Internet Home Page Address: www.newlondonhistory.org; *Pres* Nancy Steenburg; *Exec Dir* Edward Baker; *Librn* Tricia Royston

Open Wed - Fri 1 - 4 PM, Sat 10 AM - 4 PM; by appointment; Admis $5 for tours; Estab 1870 for preservation of New London County history; Maintains reference library; paintings throughout historic house; Average Annual Attendance: 3,000; Mem: 350; dues family $40, individual $30, sr citizen & student $20; progs 2nd Sun of most months

Income: $100,000 (financed by endowment, mem, admis & research fees)

Purchases: Manuscripts; artifacts

Library Holdings: DVDs; Original Documents; Photographs; Slides; Video Tapes

Special Subjects: Costumes, Drawings, Embroidery, Historical Material, Manuscripts, Photography, Porcelain, Textiles, Painting-American, Decorative Arts, Folk Art, Pewter, Ceramics, Miniatures, Dolls, Furniture, Marine Painting, Period Rooms, Maps, Eskimo Art, Scrimshaw, Coins & Medals

Collections: Six Portraits by Ralph Earle; furniture & decorative arts owned by Shaw & Perkins families; furniture made in New London County; miscellaneous portraits, miniatures, photographs, rare maps; Textile Collection; Goddard Furniture-Newport; newspapers

Exhibitions: Ongoing; New London in the Revolution; Remember Me-Civil War Photographs

Publications: NLCHS Newsletter, quarterly

Activities: Lect open to public, 10 vis lectrs per year; dramatic programs; docent training; tours; Connecticut Humanities Council; mus shop sells books & gifts

M **UNITED STATES COAST GUARD MUSEUM,** 15 Mohegan Ave, US Coast Guard Academy New London, CT 06320-8100. Tel 860-444-8511; Fax 860-701-6700; Internet Home Page Address: www.uscg.mil/hq/cg092/museum

Open Mon - Fri 9 AM - 4:30 PM, Sat 10 AM - 5 PM, Sun Noon - 5 PM; No

Admis fee; Estab 1967 to preserve historical heritage of the US Coast Guard, US Life Saving Service, US Lighthouse Service & Revenue Cutter Service; Average Annual Attendance: 20,000
Income: Financed by federal appropriations and private donations
Special Subjects: Drawings, American Indian Art, Costumes, Ceramics, Etchings & Engravings, Decorative Arts, Eskimo Art, Coins & Medals
Collections: Ship & aircraft models; paintings; photographs & manuscripts representing the Coast Guard; military artifacts from WWI, WWII & Vietnam
Activities: Paintings & original objects of art lent to federal museums & qualified organizations for educational purposes only

NORFOLK

M **NORFOLK HISTORICAL SOCIETY INC,** Museum, 13 Village Green Norfolk, CT 06058; PO Box 288, Norfolk, CT 06058-0288. Tel 860-542-5761; Elec Mail norfolkhistorical@sbcglobal.net; Internet Home Page Address: www.norfolkhistoricalsociety.org; *Pres* Barry C Webber; *Cur* Ann Havemeyer
Open Mon-Sat Sat-Sun 1PM-4PM, Nov-May 1st Thurs of month 1PM-5PM, also open by appt anytime; No admis fee; Estab 1960
Special Subjects: Architecture, Photography, Costumes, Portraits, Furniture, Historical Material, Maps
Collections: Marie Kendall Photography Collection (1884 - 1935), era during which she worked in Norfolk; Collection of works by Alfredo S G Taylor, noted architect - his blueprints, drawings, photographs plus documents for 40 of his buildings in Norfolk listed as a Thematic Group in the National Register of Historic Places; Small collection of Connecticut clocks; Fine 1879 dollhouse with elegant original furnishings; photographs & memorabilia of the Norfolk Downs, one of the very first New England golf courses (1897)
Exhibitions: Norfolk General Stores, Post Offices & Early Norfolk Merchants
Publications: Exhibition catalogs; books, pamphlets & maps, publishes at irregularly intervals
Activities: Historic Howe tours; walking tours; gallery talks; slide shows; Connecticut League of History Org Award of Merit (AASLH)

NORWALK

M **ART GALLERY AT NORWALK COMMUNITY COLLEGE,** 188 Richards Ave, Norwalk, CT 06854. Tel 203-857-7000
Open Mon-Thurs 9AM-9PM, Fri 9AM-4PM, Sat 9AM-noon; cl holidays; No admis fee
Collections: paintings, prints, photography, sculpture

M **LOCKWOOD-MATHEWS MANSION MUSEUM,** 295 West Ave, Norwalk, CT 06850-4002. Tel 203-838-9799; Fax 203-838-1434; Elec Mail info@lockwoodmathewsmansion.com; Internet Home Page Address: www.lockwoodmathewsmansion.com; *Exec Dir* Susan Gilgore, PhD; *Cur* Raechel Guest; *Vol Coordr* Joy Romeo; *Facility Coordr* Brian Fischer
Open Wed - Sun Noon - 5 PM by appointment; gift shop open Mon - Fri 9 - 5 PM, Sat & Sun Noon - 5 PM; Admis adults $10, seniors $8, students $5, children under 12 free; Estab 1968 to completely restore this 19th century 66 room Victorian mansion as a historic house mus. Now a registered National Historic Landmark. Can be rented for private parties & corporate events; National Historic Landmark; Average Annual Attendance: 20,000; Mem: 1200; annual meeting in June
Income: State and federal budgets, private funds
Library Holdings: Audio Tapes; Cards; Cassettes; DVDs; Framed Reproductions; Maps; Memorabilia; Original Art Works; Pamphlets; Photographs; Prints; Reproductions
Special Subjects: Sculpture, Architecture, Painting-American, Costumes, Etchings & Engravings, Decorative Arts, Furniture, Glass, Painting-French, Historical Material, Restorations, Period Rooms
Collections: Furniture original to the mansion; 19th century decorative arts, painting & textiles
Publications: Newsletter, quarterly
Activities: Tours for children, adults & students; educ progs for students elementary thru high school; docent training; lects open to pub; exhibit gallery talks; tours; performing arts; story & play reading; lects for mems & non-memb; mus shop sells books, magazines, original art, reproductions, prints

C **XEROX CORPORATION,** Art Collection, 45 Glover Ave # 1, Norwalk, CT 06850-1203. Tel 203-968-3000; Fax 203-968-3330; *VPres Xerox Foundation* Joseph M Cahalan; *Prog Mgr* Evelyn Shockley
Open by appointment, Mon - Fri 9 AM - 5 PM; No admis fee; Collection on display at Xerox Headquarters
Collections: The art collection represents a broad spectrum of American fine art as well as art forms from other countries. The works range from abstraction to realism & consist of sculpture by David Lee Brown located in the lobby, fiberwork by Gerhardt Knodel located in the dining facility, collages, etchings, lithographs, graphics, mezzotints, mono-prints, montages, pastels, photography, pochoir, silkscreens, watercolors & xerography

NORWICH

M **NORWICH FREE ACADEMY,** Slater Memorial Museum, 108 Crescent St, Norwich, CT 06360-3500. Tel 860-887-2506; Fax 860-885-0379; Elec Mail info@slatermuseum.org; Internet Home Page Address: www.slatermuseum.org; *Dir* Vivian Zoe; *Cur Educ* Mary-Anne Hall; *Asst Dir* Leigh Thomas
See website; Estab 1888; The Slater collection is housed in a 1886 Neo-Romanesque building on the campus of the Norwich Free Academy. The adjacent Converse Gallery was built in 1906; Average Annual Attendance: 10,000; Mem: patron $100, contributing $50, family $35, individual $25, senior citizen $15
Income: Financed by endowment, Friends of Slater Museum & admissions

Purchases: John Denison Crocker's Shepherdess O/C; Frank Gardner Hale brooch silver/stones
Library Holdings: Book Volumes; Manuscripts
Special Subjects: Folk Art, Historical Material, Collages, Flasks & Bottles, Photography, Portraits, Pottery, Painting-American, Silver, Textiles, Silversmithing, Manuscripts, Maps, Painting-European, Painting-French, Painting-Japanese, Tapestries, Drawings, Graphics, Hispanic Art, Prints, Sculpture, Watercolors, American Indian Art, African Art, Ethnology, Costumes, Religious Art, Ceramics, Crafts, Woodcarvings, Woodcuts, Etchings & Engravings, Landscapes, Decorative Arts, Judaica, Eskimo Art, Dolls, Furniture, Glass, Jade, Jewelry, Porcelain, Oriental Art, Asian Art, Marine Painting, Metalwork, Carpets & Rugs, Ivory, Scrimshaw, Coins & Medals, Restorations, Painting-Flemish, Renaissance Art, Period Rooms, Embroidery, Laces, Antiquities-Oriental, Painting-Spanish, Painting-Italian, Antiquities-Persian, Islamic Art, Antiquities-Egyptian, Antiquities-Greek, Greek, Roman & Renaissance Plaster Cast Collection; Gold, Cartoons, Stained Glass, Painting-German, Pewter, Reproductions, Antiquities-Etruscan, Enamels
Collections: Vanderpoel Collection of Asian Art; American Art & Furniture from the 17th - 20th Centuries; Greek, Roman & Renaissance Plaster Cast Collection; Original 1888 collection of Plaster Casts of Archaic, Egyptian, Greek, Roman & Renaissance marbles & bronzes; Norwich-related fine & decorative art & industrial (maritime, armaments) artifacts; European, African & 20th C American art
Exhibitions: Special exhibitions on view in Converse Gallery - six per year; Annual Connecticut artists juried exhibition; In New Contiguous Atrium - Changing Exhibs
Publications: Catalogue of the Plaster Cast Collection; Charlotte Fuller Eastman, Artist & Teacher; Greek Myths for Young People; Gualtieri, a Retrospect; NORWICH, a Photographic Essay; Renaissance Art for Young People
Activities: Classes for children; docent training; lect open to public; gallery talks; school group & adult group tours; competitions with awards; CT League of History Organizations Award of Merit; CT Artists' juried exhib cash awards; extensiion prog to Connecticut area; lending original objects of art to area businesses & other mus; mus shop sells books, magazines, original art, reproductions, prints, crafts, CT made items, jewelry, cosmetics, souvenirs

OLD LYME

L **LYME ACADEMY COLLEGE OF FINE ARTS,** Krieble Library, 84 Lyme St, Old Lyme, CT 06371-2333. Tel 860-434-5232; Fax 860-434-8725; Internet Home Page Address: www.lymeacademy.edu; *Pres* Debra Petke; *Dean & VP Acad Affairs* Laura Zarrow
Lending to students & faculty only
Library Holdings: Book Volumes 6000; Exhibition Catalogs; Pamphlets; Periodical Subscriptions 40; Slides 10,000; Video Tapes 60
Publications: Brochure: catalog

M **Chauncy Stillman Gallery,** *Pres* Debra Petke; *Dean & VP Acad Affairs* Laura Zarrow
Open Mon - Sat 10 AM - 4 PM; No admis fee; Internal & external exhibs, student & faculty

A **LYME ART ASSOCIATION, INC,** 90 Lyme St, Old Lyme, CT 06371-2367. Tel 860-434-7802; Fax 860-434-7461; Elec Mail info@lymeartassociation.org; Internet Home Page Address: www.lymeartassociation.org; *Pres* Katherine Simmons; *Exec Dir* Susan Ballek; *Mem & Website Mgr* Laurie Pavlos; *Educ Mgr* Kendall Perkins
Open Mon - Sat 10 AM - 5 PM, Sun 1 - 5 PM; No admis fee, donations accepted; Estab 1914 to promote art & advance representational art educ; Four large sky-lighted galleries are maintained. Present building designed by Charles Platt & built in 1920 by early Lyme Impressionist artists; Average Annual Attendance: 12,000; Mem: 1,200; elected artist members $75, assoc artist members & friends $45
Income: Financed by mem & assoc members dues, donations & sales commissions
Library Holdings: Book Volumes; Cards; Exhibition Catalogs; Memorabilia; Original Art Works; Original Documents; Sculpture; Video Tapes
Special Subjects: Architecture, Drawings, Etchings & Engravings, Landscapes, Sculpture, Painting-American, Portraits, Marine Painting
Exhibitions: Eight annual exhibs featuring representational fine art by mem & invited artists
Publications: Weekly e-newsletter; The Early Years: 1902-1930 of LAA, catalog; Elected Artists of the Lyme Art Association
Activities: Classes for adults & children; art workshops; lects open to pub, 5 - 6 vis lectrs per yr; concerts; gallery talks; competitions with awards; schols offered; originates bus trips; sales shop sells original art

M **LYME HISTORICAL SOCIETY,** Florence Griswold Museum, 96 Lyme St, Old Lyme, CT 06371-1426. Tel 860-434-5542; Fax 860-434-9778; Internet Home Page Address: www.florencegriswoldmuseum.org; *Dir* Jeffrey W Andersen; *Registrar* Nicole Wholean; *Cur* Amy Kurtz Lansing
Open Mon - Sat 10 AM - 5 PM, Sun 1 - 5 PM; Admis adults $9, seniors $8, students $7, children 12 & under free; Estab 1953 as a research facility for mus programs & for the pub; Changing exhibitions throughout the year
Library Holdings: Book Volumes; Cassettes; Clipping Files; Exhibition Catalogs; Kodachrome Transparencies; Manuscripts; Memorabilia; Motion Pictures; Pamphlets; Periodical Subscriptions 25; Photographs; Prints; Reproductions; Slides
Special Subjects: Etchings & Engravings, Landscapes, Period Rooms, Sculpture, Painting-American, Photography, Historical Material
Collections: Old Lyme Art Colony Paintings; Hartford Steam Boiler Collection of American art; Clara Champlain Griswold Toy Collection; Evelyn McCurdy Salisbury Ceramic Collection
Exhibitions: The Art Colony at Old Lyme; Walker Evans Photographs; Clark Voorhees 1971 - 1933; Old Lyme: The American Barbizon; Dressed for Any Occasion: Patterns of Fashion in the 19th Century; Thomas W Nason, 1889 - 1971, The Notable Women of Lyme; The Whites of Waterford: An American Landscape Tradition; Childe Hassam in Connecticut; En Plein Air: The Art Colonies of East Hampton & Old Lyme; The Harmony of Nature; Frank Vincent

DuMond; Wilson Irvine & The Poetry of Light; The American Artist in Connecticut; May Night: Willard Metcalf at Old Lyme; The Finishing Touch
Publications: The Connecticut Impressionists at Old Lyme; The Lieutenant River; The Lymes Heritage Cookbook; Hamburg Cove: Past & Present; The Lyme Ledger, quarterly; Report of the Lyme Historical Society, annually; Miss Florence & The Artists of Old Lyme; A New Look at History
Activities: Classes for adults & children; docent training; lects open to pub; concerts; gallery talks; tours; mus shop sells books, magazines, original art, reproductions & prints
L **Library,** 96 Lyme St, Old Lyme, CT 06371. Tel 860-434-5542; Fax 860-434-9778; Internet Home Page Address: www.flogris.org; *Registrar* Laurie Bradt; *Dir* Jeffrey Andersen
Open Mon - Sat 10 AM - 5 PM, Sun 1 - 5 PM; No admis fee; Estab 1953 as a research facility for mus programs & for the pub; Open to the public for reference by appointment
Purchases: $1500
Library Holdings: Book Volumes 1600; Cassettes; Clipping Files; Exhibition Catalogs; Kodachrome Transparencies; Manuscripts; Memorabilia; Motion Pictures; Pamphlets; Periodical Subscriptions 25; Photographs; Prints; Reproductions; Slides
Special Subjects: Painting-American, Historical Material, Landscapes
Collections: Connecticut Impressionism; Lyme Art Colony; Hartford Steam Boiler Fire Art Collections
Activities: Classes for adults and children; docent training; lects open to pub; gallery talks; tours; mus shop sells books, reproductions, prints

RIDGEFIELD

M **ALDRICH MUSEUM OF CONTEMPORARY ART,** 258 Main St, Ridgefield, CT 06877-4933. Tel 203-438-4519; Fax 203-438-0198; Elec Mail general@aldrichart.org; Internet Home Page Address: www.aldrichart.org; *Exhib Dir* Richard Klein; *Dir* Harry Philbrick; *Cur* Monica Ramirez-Montagut; *Dir Communs* Pamela Ruggio; *Dir Devel* Michael Blakeney
Open Tues - Sun Noon - 5 PM, cl Mon, New Years Day, Thanksgiving & Christmas Day, open July 4, Memorial Day & Labor Day; group visits by appointment; Admis adults $7, college students & seniors $4, mems, K-12 teachers & children under 18 free, active duty military & family with ID free through Blue Star Prog, Tues free all day; Estab 1964 for the presentation of contemporary painting & sculpture & allied arts; to stimulate public awareness of contemporary art through exhibitions & educ programs; Renovated colonial building with modern addition: 25,000 sq ft exhib space comprise 12 galleries incl screening room, sound gallery, 22 ft high proj space, 100-seat performance area, Educ Ctr & sculpture garden; Average Annual Attendance: 20,000; Mem: 1100; dues $35 & up
Income: Financed by mem, federal & state grants, corporate & private foundations
Special Subjects: Prints
Exhibitions: Rotating exhibits 4-6 per yr
Publications: Exhibition catalogs; quarterly newsletter
Activities: Classes for adults, teens & children; docent training; lects open to pub, 10 vis lectrs per yr; concerts; gallery talks; tours; film; competitions with prizes; book traveling exhibs; originate traveling exhibs; mus shop sells books, jewelry, original art, gift items & decorative objects

STAMFORD

L **FERGUSON LIBRARY,** 1 Public Library Plaza, Stamford, CT 06904. Tel 203-964-1000; Fax 203-357-9098; Elec Mail admin@ferg.lib.ct.us; Internet Home Page Address: www.fergusonlibrary.org; *Pres* Ernest A DiMattia Jr; *Dir Admin Servs* Nicholas Bochicchio Jr; *Dir Human Resources* Thomas Blair; *Bus Office Supv* Marie Giuliano; *Dir Computer Svcs* Gary Giannelli; *Information Serv Supv* Michell Hackwelder
Open Mon - Thurs 10 AM - 8 PM, Fri 10 AM - 6 PM, Sat 10 AM - 5 PM, mid Sept - mid May Sun 1 - 5 PM; Estab 1880 as a public library dedicated to serving the information needs of the community
Income: Financed by city appropriation
Purchases: $8000 (art & music books), $50,000 (video cassettes), $22,000 (tapes & compact discs)
Library Holdings: Book Volumes 366,200; Cassettes; Framed Reproductions; Motion Pictures; Other Holdings Audio-Visual Materials 34,537; Records; Slides; Video Tapes
Collections: Photography of Old Stamford
Exhibitions: Painting, sculpture, photography & posters under sponsorship of Friends of Ferguson Library
Publications: Focus on Ferguson quarterly newsletter, Art Currents for the Whitney Museum, Musical Notes for the Stamford Symphony and the Connecticut Grand Opera

M **SACKLER ART GALLERY,** 61 Atlantic St, Palace Theatre Stamford, CT 06901-2403. Tel 203-358-2305
Call for hours; Circ
Collections: paintings; sculpture; photographs

M **STAMFORD MUSEUM & NATURE CENTER,** 39 Scofieldtown Rd, Stamford, CT 06903-4096. Tel 203-322-1646; Fax 203-322-0408; Elec Mail info@stamfordmuseum.org; Internet Home Page Address: www.stamfordmuseum.org; *Dir* Melissa Mulrooney; *Asst Dir* Philip Novak; *Dir Art* Kenneth Marchione; *Pres* Juanita James
Open Mon - Sat 9 AM - 5 PM, Sun & holidays 1 - 5 PM, cl Thanksgiving, Christmas & New Year's Day; Admis adults $8, Stamford residents $3, Children accompanied by adult $4, mem free; Estab 1936, Art Department 1955; Museum has an art wing for changing exhibitions of 19th & 20th century art; Average Annual Attendance: 250,000; Mem: 3000; dues $35 & up; annual meeting in June
Income: Financed by mem, private & corporate donations & city appropriation

Special Subjects: Drawings, Painting-American, Photography, Prints, Sculpture, American Indian Art, Crafts
Collections: American crafts; American Indian drawings, photography, prints; 19th & 20th century painting, sculpture
Exhibitions: Annual Connecticut Artists; Four Winners Exhibition; Ellen Lanyon: Strange Games; Private Expressions: Personal Experiences; Color: Pure & Simple; American Art at the Turn of the Century; American Printmaking; The Natural Image; New American Paperworks; Connecticut Craftsmen; Bernstein; Button; Johnson; Margolies; Krushenick; Fiberforms; Contemporary Iroquois Art
Publications: American Art: American Women; Animals; brochures; exhibit catalogs; Folk Art: Then & Now; monthly newsletter
Activities: Educ dept, classes for adults & children in art, dance, nature & science; docent training; lects open to pub, 12 vis lectrs per yr; concerts; gallery talks; tours; competitions with awards; individual paintings & original objects of art lent to other mus; originate traveling exhibs; mus shop sells books, magazines, slides, & 19th century collectibles & gifts

STORRS

M **UNIVERSITY OF CONNECTICUT,** William Benton Museum of Art, 245 Glenbrook Rd, Unit 2140 Storrs, CT 06269-2140. Tel 860-486-4520; Fax 860-486-0234; Internet Home Page Address: www.thebenton.org; *Cur* Thomas P Bruhn; *Museum Shop Mgr* Jeannie Mogayzel; *Registrar* Toni Hulse; *Dir* Salvatore Scalora; *Pub Rels* Diane Lewis; *Educ* Tracy Lawlor; *Mem Coordr* Lynn Ericksson; *Mus Technician* Philip Hollister; *Bus Mgr* Karen Sommer
Open during exhibitions Tues - Fri 10 AM - 4:30 PM, Sat & Sun 1 - 4:30 PM, cl Mon; No admis fee; Estab 1966, a mus of art, operating as an autonomous department within the University, serving the students, faculty & general pub; contributing to the field at large through research, exhibitions & publications & by maintaining a permanent collection of over 3500 objects; The main gallery measures 36 x 116 ft, galley II 33 x 36 ft; Average Annual Attendance: 36,000; Mem: 600; dues double $25
Income: $700,000 (financed by mem, state appropriation, grants & gifts & donations)
Special Subjects: Painting-American, Painting-European, Sculpture, Graphics
Collections: American painting & graphics 19-20th Century; German & French graphics late 19th & 20th Century; selected 17th & 18th Century European paintings, sculptures & graphics; Western European & American c 1600 to present; paintings, graphics; contemporary photography
Publications: Exhibition catalogs, annually
Activities: Lects open to pub, 5-8 vis lectrs per yr; gallery talks; tours; individual paintings & original objects of art lent to accredited institutions for exhib purposes; lending collection contains original prints, paintings & sculpture; book traveling exhibs; originate traveling exhibs; sales shop sells books, original art, prints, reproductions & mus related art objects & jewelry

M **Jorgensen Auditorium,** 2132 Hillside Rd, Storrs, CT 06269-3104; Unit 3104, Storrs, CT 06269-3104. Tel 860-486-4228; Fax 860-486-6781; Elec Mail rock@jorg.anj.uconn.edu; Internet Home Page Address: www.jorgensen.ct-arts.com; *Dir* Rodney Rock; *Operations Dir* Gary Yakstis
Open Mon - Fri 8 AM - 5 PM, cl Sat & Sun; No admis fee; Estab 1967 to present work by leading contemporary North American artists; Serves the pub as well as the university community; The gallery is 2872 square ft; Average Annual Attendance: 25,000; Mem: 500 Friends of Jorgensen
Exhibitions: Various exhibitions, call for details
Activities: Gallery talks

L **Art & Design Library,** Box U-5AD, Storrs, CT 06269-1005; 369 Fairfield Rd - Unit 1005, Univ of Connecticut Libraries Storrs, CT 06269-9001. Tel 860-486-2787; Fax 860-486-3593; Elec Mail tom.jacoby@uconn.edu; *Art & Design Librn* Thomas J Jacoby
Open Mon - Thurs 10 AM - 10 PM, Fri 10 AM - 5 PM, Sat Noon - 5 PM, Sun 2 - 10 PM; No admis fee; Estab 1979 to support the Department of Art, Art History, Landscape Architecture & William Benton Mus of Art; Circ 16,000
Income: Financed by state appropriation & private funds
Library Holdings: Auction Catalogs; Book Volumes 70,000; Exhibition Catalogs; Fiche; Periodical Subscriptions 14
Special Subjects: Folk Art, Etchings & Engravings, Painting-American, Painting-European, Latin American Art, Theatre Arts, Asian Art, American Indian Art, Anthropology, Afro-American Art, Restoration & Conservation, Antiquities-Byzantine, Antiquities-Etruscan, Antiquities-Greek, Antiquities-Roman

STRATFORD

M **STRATFORD HISTORICAL SOCIETY,** Catharine B Mitchell Museum, 967 Academy Hill, Stratford, CT 06615-6328; Box 382, Stratford, CT 06615. Tel 203-378-0630; Fax 203-378-2562; Elec Mail judsonhousestfd@aol.com; *Cur* Carol Lovell
Open Wed, Sat & Sun 11 AM - 4 PM, June - Oct; Admis adults $3, seniors & children $1; Estab 1925 to preserve Stratford's past; Mus contains local history; Judson House, 1750 house with period furnishings; Average Annual Attendance: 1,500; Mem: 400; dues $12; meetings in Sept, Nov, Jan, Mar & May, last Fri of month
Income: Financed by endowment, fundraising & mem
Library Holdings: Book Volumes 4,000; Cards; Clipping Files; Kodachrome Transparencies; Manuscripts; Maps; Memorabilia; Original Art Works; Original Documents; Pamphlets; Photographs; Slides
Special Subjects: Architecture, Drawings, Painting-American, Photography, Prints, Watercolors, American Indian Art, Textiles, Ceramics, Folk Art, Primitive art, Manuscripts, Portraits, Posters, Dolls, Furniture, Glass, Porcelain, Oriental Art, Silver, Marine Painting, Maps, Period Rooms, Embroidery, Pewter
Collections: Local Indians; 18th century house with period furnishings; collection of baskets, ceramics, cooking items, paintings, quilts, military items & weapons, clothing, textiles & furniture
Exhibitions: Permanent and changing exhibitions
Publications: Newsletter
Activities: Classes for children; dramatic progs; docent training; lects open to pub, 5 vis lectrs per yr; tours; individual paintings & original objects of art lent to

accredited mus & galleries; lending collection contains books, original art, paintings, photographs & slides; mus shop sells books, reproductions, cards, prints & souvenirs

L **Genealogical Library,** 967 Academy Hill, Stratford, CT 06615; Box 382, Stratford, CT 06615. Tel 203-378-0630; Fax 203-378-2562; Elec Mail judsonhousetfd@aol.com; *Cur* Carol W Lovell
Office open Tues & Thurs 11 AM - 4 PM; No admis fee; Estab 1925 for preservation and dissemination of items of history of Stratford, Conn; For reference & genealogical research
Income: Financed by mem & city appropriation
Library Holdings: Audio Tapes; Book Volumes 1000; Cassettes; Clipping Files; Exhibition Catalogs; Filmstrips; Kodachrome Transparencies; Manuscripts; Memorabilia; Original Art Works; Pamphlets; Photographs; Prints; Reproductions; Slides; Video Tapes
Special Subjects: Art History, Folk Art, Drawings, Manuscripts, Painting-American, Ceramics, American Indian Art, Furniture, Period Rooms, Glass, Miniatures, Oriental Art, Marine Painting, Pewter, Flasks & Bottles
Collections: Ceramics, Clothing, Textiles, Furniture

WASHINGTON DEPOT

A **WASHINGTON ART ASSOCIATION,** 4 Bryan Plaza, Washington Depot, CT 06794; PO Box 173, Washington Depot, CT 06794-0173. Tel 860-868-2878; Fax 860-868-3447; Elec Mail washington.art.assoc@snet.net; Internet Home Page Address: www.washingtonart.org; *Admin* Ginger Nelsen; *Asst Admin* Patricia Andersen
Open Tues - Sat 10 AM - 5 PM, Sun noon - 5 PM, cl Mon; No admis fee; Estab 1952 to promote an understanding and appreciation of art & to encourage & facilitate the study and practice of the arts; Three connected galleries for individual & group shows; Average Annual Attendance: 12,000; Mem: 850; dues $35 & up; annual meeting Aug
Income: $32,000 (financed by membership, contributions, commissions, endowment & fund raising events)
Library Holdings: Book Volumes 800; Clipping Files; Exhibition Catalogs; Periodical Subscriptions 2
Exhibitions: Monthly juried exhibitions by regional & nationally known artists
Publications: Events Bulletin, quarterly
Activities: Classes & workshops for adults & children; lect open to pub, 3-4 vis lectr; members show Apr ea yr

WATERBURY

M **MATTATUCK HISTORICAL SOCIETY,** Mattatuck Museum, 144 W Main St, Waterbury, CT 06702-1298. Tel 203-753-0381; Fax 203-756-6283; Elec Mail info@mattatuckmuseum.org; Internet Home Page Address: www.mattatuckmuseum.org; *Pres* Catherine Smith; *PhD* Cynthia Roznoy
Open Tues - Sat 10 AM - 5 PM, Sun Noon - 5 PM, cl Mon; Admis $5, $4 seniors, Under 16 free; Estab 1877 to collect & preserve the arts, history of America with an emphasis on Connecticut; Art collection of CT affiliated artists from Colonial Period to present day; Average Annual Attendance: 100,000; Mem: 550; dues $40-$5000; annual meeting in June
Income: Financed by endowment, mem & grants
Library Holdings: Book Volumes; Exhibition Catalogs; Maps; Original Documents; Photographs
Special Subjects: Drawings, Etchings & Engravings, American Western Art, Painting-American, Photography, Sculpture, Textiles, Ceramics, Landscapes, Decorative Arts, Portraits, Glass, Historical Material
Collections: American artists coll; decorative arts coll; local history & industrial artifacts; period rooms
Exhibitions: Four changing art exhibits; Four changing history exhibits
Publications: Annual Report
Activities: Classes for adults & children; dramatic progs; docent training; lects open to the public; 8 vis lectrs per year; gallery talks; group tours by appointment; competitions; art and historical objects lent to other mus; Originates traveling exhibs to small and midsize museums; mus shop sells books, original art, reproductions, prints, decorative arts
L **Library,** 144 W Main St, Waterbury, CT 06702. Tel 203-753-0381; Fax 203-756-6283; Internet Home Page Address: www.mattatuckmuseum.org; *Cur* Ann Smith
Open for reference by appointment only
Income: Financed by grants & research fees
Library Holdings: Audio Tapes; Book Volumes 3000; Cassettes; Clipping Files; Exhibition Catalogs; Filmstrips; Lantern Slides; Manuscripts; Memorabilia; Original Art Works; Other Holdings CT artist files; Pamphlets; Periodical Subscriptions 10; Photographs; Prints; Sculpture; Video Tapes
Special Subjects: Art History, Decorative Arts, Drawings, Etchings & Engravings, Painting-American, Sculpture, Historical Material, Ceramics, Crafts, Industrial Design, Furniture, Period Rooms, Restoration & Conservation, Coins & Medals, Architecture

L **SILAS BRONSON LIBRARY,** 267 Grand St, Waterbury, CT 06702-1981. Tel 203-574-8225; Fax 203-574-8055; Internet Home Page Address: www.bronsonlibrary.org; *Dir* Emmett McSweeney
Open Mon - Thurs 9 AM - 8 PM, Fri 9 AM - 5:30 PM, Sat 10 AM - 2 PM; Estab 1869 to provide a free public library for the community; A spotlighted gallery wall & locked glass exhibition case used for art exhibits; Average Annual Attendance: 300,000
Income: Financed by endowment & city appropriation
Library Holdings: Audio Tapes 1964; Book Volumes 207,463; Cassettes 5028; Periodical Subscriptions 2464; Video Tapes 4996
Exhibitions: Local artists in various media; High school art students
Publications: Books & Happenings, monthly newsletter
Activities: Lect open to the public; concerts; individual framed art prints lent

WEST HARTFORD

M **NOAH WEBSTER HOUSE, INC,** Noah Webster House & West Hartford Historical Society, 227 S Main St, West Hartford, CT 06107-3453. Tel 860-521-5362; Fax 860-521-4036; Elec Mail comments@noahwebsterhouse.org; Internet Home Page Address: www.noahwebsterhouse.org; *Dir Educ* Jennifer DiCola Matos; *Office Mgr* Abigail Perkins; *Dir* Christopher Dobbs; *Coordr Pub Programs* Sarah Mocko; *Mus Shop Mgr* Pattie Whittel; *Asst Cur/Archivist* Sheila Daley
Open Thurs - Mon 1 PM - 4 PM; Admis adult $7, sr citizens & AAA members $5, children 6-college $4, children 5 & under no charge; Estab 1965 to preserve & promote 18th-century daily life, Noah Webster & West Hartford history; Average Annual Attendance: 15,000; Mem: 325; dues $25 & up, annual meeting in May
Exhibitions: Permanent Noah Webster exhibit & temporary exhibits on West Hartford history
Publications: The Spectator, quarterly member newsletter
Activities: Classes for adults & children; docent training; family progs; school & scout progs; lects open to pub; tours; competitions with prizes; lending collection; sales shop sells books, reproductions, prints & educational items

M **SAINT JOSEPH COLLEGE,** Art Gallery, University of Saint Joseph, 1678 Asylum Ave, West Hartford, CT 06117-2791. Tel 860-231-5399; Fax 860-231-5754; Elec Mail artgallery@usj.edu; Internet Home Page Address: www.usj.edu/artgallery; *Dir, Cur* Ann H Sievers; *Coll Mgr, Registrar* Rochelle L R Oakley
Open Tues, Wed, Fri & Sat 11 AM - 4 PM, Thurs 11 AM - 7 PM, Sun 1PM-4PM, cl Mon; No admis fee; Estab 1937, the gallery opened 2001 in The Carol Autorino Ctr for the Arts & Humanities. It's a resource for the acad community & gen pub through its acad prog, permanent coll & loan exhibs; Average Annual Attendance: 5,000
Special Subjects: Drawings, Landscapes, Mexican Art, Latin American Art, Painting-American, Photography, Prints, Watercolors, Woodcuts, Etchings & Engravings, Portraits, Marine Painting
Collections: Paintings ea 20th Century American Artists; Original Prints from artists dating from the 15th-century to the present; Japanese woodblock prints; Thomas Nast wood engravings
Publications: Exhibition brochures
Activities: Docent training; lects open to public; 1 vis lectrs per year; gallery talks, opening receptions

L **UNIVERSITY OF HARTFORD,** Mortensen Library, 200 Bloomfield Ave, West Hartford, CT 06117-1599. Tel 860-768-4364; Fax 860-768-5165; Elec Mail bigazzi@hartford.edu; *Art Reference Librn* Anna Bigazzi
Open Mon - Thurs 8 AM - 12 AM, Fri 8 AM - 6 PM, Sat 10 AM - 6 PM, Sun Noon - 12 AM; Estab 1964
Purchases: $5000
Library Holdings: Exhibition Catalogs; Pamphlets; Periodical Subscriptions 80; Reproductions; Video Tapes
Special Subjects: Art History, Decorative Arts, Drawings, Graphic Arts, Pre-Columbian Art, Sculpture, History of Art & Archaeology, Portraits, Watercolors, Conceptual Art, American Indian Art, Primitive art, Mexican Art, Afro-American Art, Oriental Art

M **UNIVERSITY OF HARTFORD,** Joseloff Gallery, 200 Bloomfield Ave, Harry Jack Gray Ctr West Hartford, CT 06117-1545. Tel 860-768-4090; Fax 860-768-5159; Elec Mail gaumond@hartford.edu; Internet Home Page Address: www.joseloffgallery.org; *Dir* Zina Davis; *Gallery Mgr* Lisa Gaumond
Open Tues - Fri 11 AM - 4 PM, Sat & Sun Noon - 4 PM; No admis fee; Comprehensive exhibition program focusing on established & emerging artists
Income: financed by the college
Collections: 20th-century & contemporary art in all media; Rotating exhibitions
Activities: Classes for adults
L **Anne Bunce Cheney Art Collection,** 200 Bloomfield Ave, Mortensen Library West Hartford, CT 06117-1545. Tel 860-768-4397; Fax 860-768-4274; Elec Mail bigazzi@hartford.edu; Internet Home Page Address: www.library.hartford.edu; *Art Reference Librn* Anna Bigazzi
Open Mon - Thurs 8 AM - 1:30 AM, Fri 8 - 6 PM, Sat 10 AM - 6 PM, Sun Noon -1:30 AM; Estab 1964
Income: Financed through university library
Library Holdings: Book Volumes 20,500; Exhibition Catalogs; Pamphlets; Periodical Subscriptions 80; Reproductions 17,600
Special Subjects: Art History, Photography, Drawings, Etchings & Engravings, Graphic Arts, Sculpture, History of Art & Archaeology, Judaica, Ceramics, Archaeology, Advertising Design, American Indian Art, Furniture, Aesthetics, Oriental Art

WESTPORT

A **NEW YORK SOCIETY OF WOMEN ARTISTS, INC,** 19A Darbrook Rd, Westport, CT 06880-3611. Tel 203-329-9179; Elec Mail sraushenbusch@earlthlink.net; Internet Home Page Address: www.anny.org; Internet Home Page Address: www.nyswa.com; *Pres* Stephanie Rauschenbusch; *VPres* Elisa Pritzker; *Exec VPres* Benice Catchi; *Treas* Joyce Pommer; *Recording Sec* Marlene Wiedenbaum; *Recording Sec* Olga Poloukhine
Cl to pub; Admis $45; Estab 1920 for the advancement of women's art; Affiliated with Pleiades Gallery in Chelsea, NY; Mem: 60; mem open to superior artists; dues $100; meetings in Nov & May
Income: Financed by jury selection
Special Subjects: Drawings, Prints, Sculpture
Collections: Art Education; Art History; Conceptual Art; Mixed Media; Printmaking

M **WESTPORT ARTS CENTER,** 51 Riverside Ave, Westport, CT 06880. Tel 203-222-7070; Elec Mail info@westportartscenter.org; Internet Home Page Address: www.westportartscenter.org; *Exec Dir* Peter Van Heerden; *Dir Visual Arts* Helen Klisser During; *Visual Arts Coordr* Jill Sarver
Open Mon-Fri 10AM-4PM, Sat-Sun noon-4PM; No admis fee
Collections: contemporary art; paintings; sculpture

L　**WESTPORT PUBLIC LIBRARY,** 20 Jesup Rd, Westport, CT 06880-4329. Tel 203-291-4840; Fax 203-227-3829; Elec Mail ref@westportlibrary.org; Internet Home Page Address: www.westportlibrary.org; *Dir* Maxine Bleiweis; *Asst Dir & COO* Paul R Mazzaccaro
Open Mon - Thurs 9 AM - 9 PM, Fri 9 AM - 6 PM, Sat 9 AM - 5 PM, Sun 1 - 5 PM; No admis fee; Estab 1907; Circ 839,613; Art display kiosks in library with exhibits; Average Annual Attendance: 591,516
Income: $5,649,157, 82% town appropriation, 18% contributions, endowments and other
Purchases: $521,178
Library Holdings: Book Volumes; Compact Disks; DVDs; Original Art Works; Periodical Subscriptions; Video Tapes
Collections: Picture collection (for pictorial research by artists, illustrators, & designers); Famous Artists School Publications
Publications: 5 per year newsletter
Activities: Lect open to public

WETHERSFIELD

M　**WETHERSFIELD HISTORICAL SOCIETY INC,** Museum, 150 Main St, Wethersfield, CT 06109-3126. Tel 860-529-7656; Fax 860-563-2609; *Dir* Brenda Milkofsky
Open Tues - Sat 10 AM - 4 PM, Sun 1 - 4 PM; Estab 1932 to preserve local history; Two changing exhibit rooms; Average Annual Attendance: 18,000; Mem: 800; dues family $35, individual $23; annual meeting in mid-May
Income: $190,000 (financed by endowment, mem, programs & fundraising)
Special Subjects: Painting-American, Photography, Archaeology, Textiles, Costumes, Folk Art, Furniture, Historical Material, Maps, Period Rooms
Collections: Local history/culture
Exhibitions: Changing monthly exhibits
Publications: Newsletter, quarterly
Activities: Children's progs; docent progs; lects open to pub, 4 vis lectrs per yr; book traveling exhibs 8 per yr; retail store sells books & prints
L　**Old Academy Library,** 150 Main St, Wethersfield, CT 06109. Tel 860-529-7656; Fax 860-563-2609; Elec Mail society@wethhist.org; Internet Home Page Address: www.wethhist.org; *Interim Dir* Jose Fiak
Open Tues - Fri 9 AM - 4 PM & by appointment; Estab 1932; Mem: 1000; dues vary
Income: $250,000 (financed by endowment, mem, programs, donations & rentals)
Library Holdings: Book Volumes 2000; Original Documents; Photographs
Special Subjects: Historical Material
Collections: Wethersfield history & genealogy
Exhibitions: Wethersfield History; Legendary People, Ordinary Lives (permanent)
Publications: Newsletter, quarterly
Activities: Classes for adults & children; docent progs; lects open to pub, 3 - 4 vis lectrs per yr; concerts; gallery talks; tours; book traveling exhibs 4 per yr; retail store sells books, prints & more

WILTON

M　**NATIONAL PARK SERVICE,** Weir Farm National Historic Site, 735 Nod Hill Rd, Wilton, CT 06897-1309. Tel 203-834-1896; Fax 203-834-2421; Elec Mail wefa_interpretation@nps.gov; Internet Home Page Address: www.nps.gov/wefa; *Supt* Linda Cook
Open 9:00 AM - 5 PM Wed-Sun May -Oct; 10AM - 4PM Thurs-Sun, Nov -Apr; Grounds open every day from dawn to dusk; No admis fee; Estab 1990; Visitor center has changing exhibits in two small rooms; Average Annual Attendance: 10,000
Special Subjects: Architecture, Painting-American, Watercolors, Etchings & Engravings, Landscapes, Decorative Arts, Furniture, Historical Material
Collections: American Impressionist paintings; Decorative Arts Collection; Finding Aid for the Dorothy Weir Young Research Papers (1813-1947); Finding Aid for the Weir Family Papers (1746-1962); Finding Aid for the Burlingham/Weir Archive of the Metropolitan Museum of Art; American Impressionist Paintings; J Alden Weir Archive & Manuscripts Collection
Activities: Classes for children; visiting & resident artist prog for professional artists; lects open to pub, 5 vis lectrs per yr; tours; mus shop sells books & prints

WINDSOR

M　**RICHMOND ART CENTER THE LOOMIS CHAFFEE SCHOOL,** Mercy Gallery, 4 Batchelder Rd, Windsor, CT 06095-3028. Tel 860-687-6030; 687-6104

DELAWARE

DOVER

M　**BIGGS MUSEUM OF AMERICAN ART,** 406 Federal St, Dover, DE 19901; PO Box 711, Dover, DE 19903-0711. Tel 302-674-2111; Fax 302-674-5133; Elec Mail admin@biggsmuseum.org; Internet Home Page Address: www.biggsmuseum.org; *Cur* Ryan Grover; *Dir* Linda A K Danko; *Chm (V)* Charles Terry Jackson II; *Mktg Coordr* Jennifer M Kemske; *Educ Progs Coordr* Rebecca Cooper; *Mus Mgr* Ellen Arthur
Open Tues - Sat 9 AM - 4:30 PM, Sun 1 PM - 4:30 PM, cl New Year' Day, Easter, Thanksgiving, Christmas; No admis fee; Estab 1989; Includes 25 galleries; Average Annual Attendance: 18,000; Mem: 500; dues student, instr, military, sr $30, individual $40, household $50, family $60, with additional memberships at $100, $250, $500 & $1,000
Income: financed by endowment, mem, state appropriation, foundations & contributions
Purchases: $50,000

Library Holdings: Auction Catalogs; Book Volumes; Clipping Files; Exhibition Catalogs; Kodachrome Transparencies; Memorabilia; Periodical Subscriptions; Photographs; Slides
Special Subjects: Decorative Arts, Drawings, Prints, Graphics, Painting-American, Sculpture, Watercolors, Textiles, Ceramics, Portraits, Furniture, Silver
Collections: Biggs Collection of American Representational Paintings & Decorative Arts from the Delaware Valley; Delaware Silver Study Ctr
Publications: Quarterly newsletter; bi-monthly calendar; 2-vol catalogue The Sewell
Activities: Adult & children's activities; docent training; school tours; lects open to pub, 10 vis lectrs per yr; gallery talks; classes for children; art workshops; competitions; mus shop sells book & postcards

M　**DELAWARE ARCHAEOLOGY MUSEUM,** 316 S Governors Ave, Dover, DE-6706. Tel 302-736-7400; Fax 302-739-5660; Elec Mail bev.laing@state.de.us; Internet Home Page Address: history.delaware.gov
Open Tues-Sat 9AM-4:30PM, Sun 1:30-4:30PM; No admis fee, donations accepted; Mus focus is on archaeology, the study of previous peoples, civilizations, & their lifeways through scientific analysis of remaining artifacts; handicapped-accessible
Special Subjects: Anthropology, Archaeology, Historical Material, Ceramics, Glass, Pottery, Primitive art, Woodcarvings
Collections: 12,000 years worth of archaeological history found in the state of DE, ranging from the last ice age to the 20th century; arrowheads; ceramics; stone & bone tools; glass objects; personal artifacts used in DE in the 17th - 20th centuries; miscellaneous findings of anthropologists, osteologists, geologists, physical anthropologists, botanists & many other scientific disciplines used in the identification & analysis of the archaeological record
Activities: Group tours available with reservation; ann events: Old Dover Days, first weekend in May, Archaeology Month

M　**DELAWARE DIVISION OF HISTORICAL & CULTURAL AFFAIRS,** 102 S State St, Dover, DE 19901; 21 The Green, Dover, DE 19901. Tel 302-739-5316; Fax 302-739-6712; Internet Home Page Address: www.destatemuseum.org; *Cur Coll* Ann Baker Horsey; *Cur Educ* Madeline Dunn; *Coll Mgr* Claudia Leister; *Cur Archaeology* Charles Fithian; *Mgr* Lynn Riley; *Site Adminstr* Beverly Laing
John Dickinson Plantation: Tues - Sat 10 AM - 3:30 PM, Apr - Dec 1:30 - 4:30 PM; Johnson Victrola Museum, Meeting House Galleries I & II: Tues - Sat 10 AM - 3:30 PM; Old State House, Zwaanendael, New Castle Courthouse: Tues - Sat 8:30 AM - 4:30 PM, Sun 1:30 - 4:30 PM; State Visitor Ctr (Dover): Mon - Sat 8:30 AM - 4:30 PM, Sun 1:30 - 4:30 PM; No admis fee; Historic house museums were opened in the 1950s, Zwaanendael Museum 1931, to reflect the pre-historic & historic develop of Delaware by exhibiting artifacts & interpreting the same through various facilities-those of early times; Average Annual Attendance: 100,000
Income: $2,400,000 (state appropriations)
Library Holdings: Book Volumes; Cassettes; Compact Disks; Exhibition Catalogs; Manuscripts; Maps; Memorabilia; Original Art Works; Original Documents; Periodical Subscriptions; Photographs; Records
Special Subjects: Ceramics, Textiles, Architecture, Painting-American, Archaeology, Portraits, Posters, Glass, Silver, Historical Material, Period Rooms
Collections: Meeting House Galleries I & II: Prehistoric & Historic Archaeology; Museum of Small Town Life: Main Street Delaware; John Dickinson Plantation: Decorative arts, furniture & Dickinson family objects; New Castle Court House: Portraits of famous Delawareans, archaeological artifacts, furniture & maps; Old State House: legislative judicial & governmental furniture & decorative arts; Zwaanendael Museum: HMB Debraak Artifacts; Commemorative gifts to the State of Delaware from Holland, china, glass, & silver; Johnson Victrola Museum: Talking machines, Victrolas, early recordings & Johnson memorabilia associated with the Victor Talking Machine Company (RCA); Victor Talking Machine Company Phonographs & Records; HMS Debraak, 18th century British Warship; Maritime Archaeology
Publications: Delaware State Museum Bulletins; Delaware History Notebook; miscellaneous booklets & brochures
Activities: Classes for adults & children; docent training; special educational progs for school groups & adults which reflect the architecture, government, educ & aspects of social history relevant to Delaware; lects open to pub; gallery talks; tours; Nat Tourism award; individual paintings are lent to governmental facilities; in-service progs relating to Delaware history are offered to Delaware teachers; internship; lending of original objects of art to other mus; originate traveling trunk prog circulated to elementary schools; mus shop sells books, magazines, prints, original art & Delaware souvenirs

MILLSBORO

M　**NANTICOKE INDIAN MUSEUM,** Rte 24, Millsboro, DE 19966; 27073 John J Williams Hwy, Millsboro, DE 19966-4642. Tel 302-945-7022 (Museum); Tel 302-945-3400 (Tribal Office); Fax 302-947-9411; Elec Mail info@nanticokeindians.org; Internet Home Page Address: www.thelongneckpage.com/nia
Open Summer: Tues - Sat 10 AM - 4 PM; Jan - April: Thurs - Sat 10 AM - 4 PM, Sun noon - 5 PM; Admis adults $2, children $1; 1984; Mus mission is to tell the story of the Nanticoke Native Americans, people who have faced many obstacles throughout history
Special Subjects: Historical Material, Photography, Pottery, Costumes, Woodcarvings
Collections: Stone artifacts; carvings; pottery; traditional clothing; mus library houses large coll of Native American books, photos & video presentations
Activities: Ann Nanticoke Indian Powwow celebration

NEWARK

M　**UNIVERSITY OF DELAWARE,** University Museums, 30 N College Ave, 208 Mechanical Hall Newark, DE 19716. Tel 302-831-8037; Fax 302-831-8057; Elec Mail jat@udel.edu; Internet Home Page Address: www.udel.edu/museums; *Dir* Janis A Tomlinson, PhD; *Cur African American Art* Julie L McGee PhD; *Cur Mineralogical Mus* Sharon Fitzgerald PhD; *Cur Coll* Janet G Broske; *Preparator* Brian Kamen; *Office Supv* Peggy Lea Douglas
Open Wed - Sun noon - 5 PM, Thurs noon - 8 PM, cl late July & Aug & during

Univ vacations; No admis fee; Estab 1978 to enhance the educational & scholarly mission of the Univ of Delaware; enriches cultural life beyond the campus through presentation of the work of recognized artists & through outreach programs; 3 art galleries in Old College & Mechanical Hall, Mineralogical Museums; Average Annual Attendance: 6,000

Special Subjects: Drawings, Etchings & Engravings, Landscapes, Painting-American, Prints, Textiles, Graphics, Sculpture, African Art, Pottery, Eskimo Art, Antiquities-Byzantine, Antiquities-Egyptian, Antiquities-Greek, Antiquities-Roman

Collections: 19th & 20th century American works on paper; Pre-Columbian textiles & ceramics; African Artifacts; early 20th century photographs; Contemporary Canadian Prints and Inuit Drawings; African-American Art; Paul R Jones Collection of African American 20th Century Art; Mineralogical collection

Publications: Exhibit catalog; brochures

Activities: Lects open to pub, 4 vis lectrs per yr; gallery talks; tours; individual & original objects of art lent to other mus & universities; mus shop sells books

L **Morris Library,** 181 S College Ave, Newark, DE 19717-5267. Tel 302-831-2965, 831-2231; Fax 302-831-1046; Internet Home Page Address: www.udel.edu/library; *Vice Provost & May Morris Dir Libraries* Susan Brynteson; *Subject Librn (Art & Art History)* Susan A Davi; *Head Reference Dept* Shirley Branden; *Asst Dir Library Collections* Craig Wilson; *Asst Dir Library Pub Serv* Sandra Millard; *Asst Dir Library Technical Servs* M Dina Giambi; *Asst Dir Library Computing Systems* Gregg Silvis; *Asst Dir Library Admin Servs* Paul Anderson

Open Fall and Spring Mon - Thur 8 AM - 12 AM, Fri 8 AM - 8 PM, Sat 9 AM - 8 PM, Sun 11 AM - 12 AM

Income: Financed through the University

Purchases: $113,150

Library Holdings: Audio Tapes; Book Volumes 2,704,986; Cards; Cassettes 7735; Compact Disks; DVDs 2,199; Exhibition Catalogs; Fiche; Filmstrips 1646; Manuscripts 2952; Micro Print; Motion Pictures; Pamphlets; Periodical Subscriptions 12,532; Photographs; Prints; Records; Reels; Slides; Video Tapes 14,204

Collections: American art & architecture; early 20th century European art; material on ornamental horticulture; ARTstor

ODESSA

L **CORBIT-CALLOWAY MEMORIAL LIBRARY,** 115 High St, PO Box 128 Odessa, DE 19730-0128. Tel 302-378-8838; Fax 302-378-7803; Elec Mail corbit@infinet.com; Internet Home Page Address: www.corbitlibrary.org; *Dir* Steven J Welch

Open Mon & Sat 1 - 9 PM, Wed & Fri 10 AM - 5 PM, Wed until 9 PM, Sat 9 AM - 1 PM; No admis fee; Estab 1847

Library Holdings: Audio Tapes; Book Volumes 21,000; Periodical Subscriptions 58; Slides; Video Tapes

Collections: Delawareana

REHOBOTH BEACH

A **REHOBOTH ART LEAGUE, INC,** 12 Dodds Lane, Henlopen Acres Rehoboth Beach, DE 19971-1668. Tel 302-227-8408; Fax 302-227-4121; Internet Home Page Address: www.rehobothartleague.org; *Pres Board* Marcia DeWitt; *Dir* Lawrence Sweigert; *Gallery Mgr* Nick Serratare

Open Mon - Sat 9AM-4PM, Sun noon-4PM; No admis fee; Estab 1938 to provide art educ & creative arts in Rehoboth Beach community & Sussex County, Delaware; Two galleries, the Corkran & the Tubbs built for exhibitions; plus Homestead, c 1743, gallery & studio; Average Annual Attendance: 10,000; Mem: 1200; dues $50 & up

Income: Financed by mem, donations, fund raising & sales of paintings

Special Subjects: Etchings & Engravings, Historical Material, Painting-American, Marine Painting

Collections: Small permanent collection from gifts (1,000+), includes many Ethel P B Leach, Orville Peats & Howard Pyle

Exhibitions: Annual Members Fine Arts Crafts Exhibition; Annual Members Fine Arts Exhibition; Outdoor Fine Art; Individual and visiting artist exhibits throughout the year

Publications: Brochure of yearly events; calendar of classes

Activities: Classes for adults & children; docent training; lect open to public, 3 vis lectrs per year; concerts; gallery talks; competitions with awards; Regional Juried Show, Member Fine Art, Young at Art; serves disadvantaged communities via Sussex County, DE; lending coll extended to Biggs Mus, Dover DE; sales shop sells books, original art & prints

WILMINGTON

A **CHRISTINA CULTURAL ARTS CENTER, INC,** 705 N Market St, Wilmington, DE 19801-3008. Tel 302-652-0101; Fax 302-652-7480; Elec Mail info@ccad-de.org; Internet Home Page Address: www.ccacde.org; *Dir* H Raye Jones-Avery; *Educ Dir* Kenneth C Brown; *Dir Fin* Jo Anne Jackson; *Family Svc Dir* Kim Graham; *Visual Arts* Milton Downing

Open Mon - Fri 9 AM - 9 PM, Sat 9 AM - 5 PM; No admis fee; Estab to bring professional arts training & educ to a broad spectrum of the community with an emphasis on serving low income families

M **DELAWARE ART MUSEUM,** 2301 Kentmere Pkwy, Wilmington, DE 19806-2096. Tel 302-571-9590; Tel 866-232-3714; Fax 302-571-0220; Elec Mail info@delart.org; Internet Home Page Address: www.delart.org; *Exec Dir* Danielle Rice PhD; *Cur Colls* Mary F Holahan; *Cur Bancroft Coll Pre-Raphaelite Art* Margaretta S Frederick; *Cur American Art* Heather Campbell Coyle; *Dir Devel* Susan M Zellner; *Dir Educ* Courney Waring; *Dir External Affairs & Special Projs* Gail O'Donnell; *Dir Opers* Bruce Canter; *CFO* Mike Miller

Open Wed - Sat 10 AM - 4 PM, Sun 12 - 4 PM, cl Mon, Tues, New Years Day, July 4, Thanksgiving & Christmas Day; Admis family of 2 adults & 4 youth $25, adults $12, seniors $10, college students with ID & youth ages 7-18 $6, mems &

children 6 & under free, Sun free to all; Blue Star admis for military & families; other discounts available; Incorporated 1912 as the Wilmington Soc of Fine Arts; present building expanded 1987; a privately funded, non-profit cultural & educational institution dedicated to the increase of knowledge & pleasure through the display & interpretation of works of art & through classes designed to encourage an understanding of & a participation in the fine arts; Nine galleries are used for exhibitions; six usually hold permanent or semi-permanent exhibitions which change at six week intervals; maintains Copeland Sculpture Garden; Average Annual Attendance: 20,000; Mem: 3200; dues Dir Cir $1500-$10000+, benefactor $500-$1499, associate $250-$499, friend $125-$249, family $70-$85, individual $50; annual meeting in Mar

Income: $1,800,000 (financed by endowment, mem & grants)

Purchases: $20,000

Special Subjects: Afro-American Art, Landscapes, Graphics, Painting-American, Photography, Prints, Sculpture, Etchings & Engravings, Decorative Arts, Portraits, Posters, Painting-British

Collections: Copeland Collection of Work by Local Artists; American paintings & sculpture, including many Howard Pyle works & complete etchings & lithographs of John Sloan; Bancroft Collection; Phelps Collection; Works by Edward Hopper, George Segal & Robert Motherwell

Exhibitions: 6 or more every yr

Publications: DAM Magazine, quarterly

Activities: Classes for adults & children; docent training; workshops; studio art progs; outreach; art camp; mem events; lects open to pub; concerts; gallery talks; tours; fellowship available; exten dept serving schools & community groups offering two-week programs in visual educ; originate traveling exhibs; mus shop sells books, original art, reproductions

L **Helen Farr Sloan Library,** 2301 Kentmere Pky, Wilmington, DE 19806. Tel 302-571-9590 (Mus); 351-8540 (Librn); Fax 302-571-0220; Elec Mail rdieleuterio@delart.org; Internet Home Page Address: www.delart.org; *Head Librn* Rachael DiEleuterio

Open Wed - Fri 10 AM - 4 PM by appt ; Estab 1923; Open to public for reference only

Library Holdings: Auction Catalogs; Book Volumes 40,000; Clipping Files; DVDs; Exhibition Catalogs; Lantern Slides; Manuscripts; Maps; Memorabilia; Original Art Works; Original Documents; Pamphlets; Periodical Subscriptions; Photographs; Prints; Reproductions; Slides; Video Tapes

Special Subjects: Art History, Decorative Arts, Illustration, Photography, Manuscripts, Painting-American, Painting-British, Posters, Prints, Crafts

Collections: John Sloan Archives and Library; Howard Pyle Archives and Library; Samuel Bancroft Pre-Raphaelite Library; Everett Shinn Archives; Frank Schoonover Archives

Activities: Adopt-A-Book sponsor prog

M **DELAWARE CENTER FOR THE CONTEMPORARY ARTS,** 200 S Madison St, Wilmington, DE 19801-5100. Tel 302-656-6466; Fax 302-656-6944; Elec Mail info@thedcca.org; Internet Home Page Address: www.thedcca.org; *Exec Dir* Maxine Gaiber; *Cur Contemporary Art* Maiza Hixson; *Cur Special Projs* J Susan Isaacs; *Cur Coordr* J Gordon; *Cur Educ* Sarah Ware; *Dir Devel* Debbie Heaton; *Dir Special Events & Mem Svcs* Ashlee Lukoff; *Dir Mktg & Commns* Sara Monserrat Teixido; *Security Mgr* Ben McCullough; *Assoc Dir Admin* Helen Page

Open Tues & Thurs - Sat 10 AM - 5 PM, Wed & Sun Noon - 5 PM, cl Mon; No admis fee; Estab 1979 to promote growth & develop of contemporary arts in Delaware; 35,000 sq ft comprising 7 galleries, 26 artists studios, an auditorium, classroom & gift shop; Average Annual Attendance: 18,000; Mem: Dues $40 general & up

Exhibitions: Art Auction; Rotating exhibitions every 6-8 weeks

Publications: Exhibition catalogs & brochures

Activities: Classes for adults & children; outreach progs; docent training; lects open to pub; symposia; concerts; mus shop sells books, magazines & original art

M **DELAWARE HISTORICAL SOCIETY,** Delaware History Museum, 504 N Market St, Wilmington, DE 19801; 505 N Market St, Wilmington, DE 19801. Tel 302-655-7161; Fax 302-655-7844; Internet Home Page Address: www.dehistory.org; *Chief Cur* Constance Cooper; *Colls Mgr* Jennifer Potts; *CEO* Scott W Loehr; *Pub Rels Mgr* Mary Lynn Mack

Open Wed - Fri 11 AM - 4 PM, Sat 10 AM - 4 PM; Admis fee adults $6, seniors $5 children $4; Estab 1864 to preserve, collect & display material related to Delaware History; Delaware History Mus & Old Town Hall Mus are the main mus galleries for the Delaware Historical Society; Mem: 1400; dues $40; annual meeting in Apr

Collections: Regional decorative arts; children's toys; costumes; distinctively Delaware; photos; art

Exhibitions: Distinctively Delaware - ongoing; Forging Faith Building Freedom: African American Faith Experiences in Delaware 1800-1980 - Sept 2013 - Summer 2014

Publications: Delaware Collections by Deborah D Waters; Delaware History, twice a year

Activities: Lects open to pub, 3-7 vis lectrs per yr; concerts; gallery talks; tours; originate traveling exhibs in conjunction with other history mus; mus shop sells books, reproductions, prints

M **Read House and Gardens,** 42 The Strand, New Castle, DE 19720. Tel 302-322-8411; Internet Home Page Address: www.hsd.org; *Dir* Michele Anstine; *Educ Coordr* Andrea Majewski

Open Jan - Feb Sat 10 AM - 4 PM, Sun 11 AM - 4 PM; Mar - Dec Tues - Fri & Sun 11 AM - 4 PM, Sat 10 AM - 4 PM, cl New Year's, Thanksgiving & Christmas; Admis adults $5, students & seniors 65 & over $4, children $2, under 6 free; Estab 1976; period rooms in the Georgian-Federal mansion with garden installed in 1847; Average Annual Attendance: 20,000; Mem: 1200; dues $10 & up

Special Subjects: Landscapes, Architecture, Decorative Arts, Portraits, Furniture

Collections: Federal Period decorative arts & architecture

Activities: Classes for children; family-oriented programming; lects open to pub; walking tours; sales shop sells books & crafts

L **Library,** 505 Market St, Wilmington, DE 19801. Tel 302-655-7161; Fax 302-655-7844; Elec Mail deinfo@dehistory.org; Internet Home Page Address: www.dehistory.org; *Exec Dir* Joan Hoge; *Dir Mus Divsn* Stephanie Przybylek;

Registrar Jennifer Potts; *Read House Site Admin* Michele Anstine; *Dir Develop* Greg Coin; *Educ & Programs* Andrea Gomez; *Dir Pub Rels* MaryLynn Mack; *VPres* Richard Poole
Open Mon 1 - 9 PM, Tues - Fri 9 AM - 5 PM, by appointment; estab 1864; Circ non-circulation; reference only; Average Annual Attendance: 1,200
Income: $1,500,000 (financed by endowment, annual support & grants)
Purchases: $15,000
Library Holdings: Book Volumes 75,000; Cassettes; Clipping Files; Exhibition Catalogs; Fiche; Filmstrips; Kodachrome Transparencies; Lantern Slides; Manuscripts; Memorabilia; Motion Pictures; Pamphlets; Periodical Subscriptions 73; Photographs; Prints; Records; Reels; Slides
Activities: Classes for adults; gallery talks; tours; lects open to pub; History Makers award; mus shop

M **THE NEMOURS FOUNDATIOIN,** Nemours Mansion & Gardens, 1600 Rockland Rd, Wilmington, DE 19803-3607. Tel 302-651-6912; Fax 302-651-6370; Elec Mail tours@nemours.org; Internet Home Page Address: www.nemoursmansion.org; *Exec Dir* Grace Gary; *Cur* Francesca B Bonny; *Mktg* Steven P Maurer; *Supt* James Solge; *Tour Coordr* Karen Vanderslice; *Horticulturist* Ric Larkin
Open Tues - Sun 9 AM - 5 PM by reservation; Admis $15, handicap accessible, no children 12 & under are admitted; Estab 1977; 300 acre estate of Alfred I du Pont; 72 room modified Louis XVI chateau built 1909 - 10; formal French-style gardens and natural woods; Average Annual Attendance: 14,000
Income: Financed by pvt funding
Special Subjects: Decorative Arts, Drawings, Landscapes, Marine Painting, Ceramics, Glass, American Western Art, Painting-American, Painting-European, Painting-French, Sculpture, Tapestries, Prints, Watercolors, Bronzes, Religious Art, Pottery, Portraits, Furniture, Porcelain, Silver, Painting-British, Painting-Dutch, Carpets & Rugs, Tapestries, Painting-Flemish, Renaissance Art, Painting-Spanish, Painting-Italian, Painting-German, Enamels
Collections: Collection of European furniture, tapestries, & paintings dating back to the 15th century; Oriental rugs, objects d'art

C **WILMINGTON TRUST COMPANY,** Rodney Sq N, Wilmington, DE 19890-0001. Tel 302-651-1741; Fax 302-651-8717; Elec Mail cconway@wilmingtontrust.com; *VPres Mktg* Joan Sullivan; *VPres* Cindy Conway
Open to public; Collection displayed nationwide in offices
Collections: Primarily Mid-Atlantic scenes & still life by Mid-Atlantic artists, includes mostly paintings, works on paper, textiles (antique to contemporary) & other mediums

WINTERTHUR

C **WINTERTHUR MUSEUM,** (Winterthur Museum & Country Estate) Winterthur Museum, Garden & Library, 5105 Kennett Pike, Winterthur, DE 19735-0002. Tel 302-888-4600; 800-448-3883; Fax 302-888-4820; Elec Mail webmaster@winterthur.org; Internet Home Page Address: www.winterthur.org; *Dir* Dr David P Roselle; *Dir Museum Affairs* J Thomas Savage; *Dir Pub Progs* Jeff Groff; *Dir Colls* Linda Eaton; *Dir Develop* Robert Davis; *Dir Library, Colls Management & Acad Progs* Greg Landrey; *Dir Garden & Estate* Chris Strand; *Dir & CFO* Robert Necarsulmer
Open Tues - Sun 10 AM - 5 PM, cl Mondays, Thanksgiving, Christmas; Admis $18, sr, student & group discounts, guided tours of mus additional fee; Opened 1951, a nonprofit, educ corporation; Collection of 90,000 objects made and used in America between 1640-1860 including furniture, textiles, paintings, prints, ceramics, brass, pewter, needlework & much more; Average Annual Attendance: 150,000; Mem: 13,000 individuals & families, dues vary
Income: nonprofit corporation
Library Holdings: Auction Catalogs; Audio Tapes; Book Volumes; Cards; Exhibition Catalogs; Fiche; Manuscripts; Maps; Original Documents; Other Holdings; Pamphlets; Periodical Subscriptions; Photographs; Prints
Special Subjects: Bookplates & Bindings, Carpets & Rugs, Ceramics, Drawings, Etchings & Engravings, Sculpture, Textiles, Watercolors, Decorative Arts, Painting-American, Prints, Embroidery, Folk Art, Glass, Historical Material, Jewelry, Landscapes, Manuscripts, Maps, Porcelain
Collections: Antique furniture, silver, needlework, textiles, painting, prints, ceramics and glass; interior architecture
Exhibitions: (03/01/2014-01/04/2015) Costumes of Downton Abbey
Publications: Winterthur portfolio
Activities: Classes for adults; 2 grad prog; lects; concerts; gallery talks; tours; seminars; film; competitions with awards; exten prog for regional area, original art lent to other mus & institutions; book traveling exhibs 1-2 per year; originate traveling exhibs to select mus Winter and Fall Institutes; mus shop sells books, reproductions, plants
L **Library,** 5105 Kennett Pike, Wilmington, DE 19735. Tel 302-888-4681; Fax 302-888-3367; Elec Mail reference@winterthur.org; Internet Home Page Address: www.winterthur.org; *Librn Joseph Downs Coll of Manuscripts & Printed Ephemera* Jeanne Solensky; *Librn Printed Books & Periodical Coll* Emily Guthrie; *Dir* Richard McKinstry; *Archivist* Heather Clewell
Open Mon - Fri 8:30 AM - 4:30 PM; Estab in 1951 to support advanced study in American artistic, cultural, social & intellectual history up to the early twentieth century. For reference only
Library Holdings: Auction Catalogs; Book Volumes 100,000; Cards; Exhibition Catalogs; Fiche 9200; Lantern Slides; Manuscripts 3,000 record groups; Maps; Memorabilia; Original Documents; Other Holdings Auction Catalogs; Architectural Drawings; Pamphlets; Periodical Subscriptions 300; Photographs 165,000; Prints; Reels 3450; Slides 170,000; Video Tapes
Special Subjects: Folk Art, Landscape Architecture, Decorative Arts, Illustration, Photography, Drawings, Graphic Arts, Graphic Design, Manuscripts, Maps, Painting-American, Prints, Sculpture, Historical Material, Watercolors, Ceramics, Crafts, Printmaking, Advertising Design, Interior Design, Art Education, Porcelain, Eskimo Art, Furniture, Period Rooms, Costume Design & Constr, Glass, Stained Glass, Bookplates & Bindings, Metalwork, Dolls, Goldsmithing, Handicrafts, Jewelry, Silver, Silversmithing, Woodcarvings, Pewter, Architecture, Embroidery, Portraits, Pottery, Textiles

Collections: Waldron Phoenix Belknap, Jr Research Library of American Painting; Edward Deming Andrews Memorial Shaker Collection; Decorative Arts Photographic Collection; Henry A duPont & Henry F duPont Papers; Thelma S Mendsen Card Collection; Maxine Waldron Collection of Children's Books & Paper Toys; John & Carolyn Grossman Collection of Printed Ephemra
Exhibitions: Manuscript, diaries & printed travel accounts
Publications: Catalogs of collections of printed books: General (9 volumes); Trade Catalogs; Andrews Shaker Collection; America Cornucopia (thematic guide to library collections); manuscripts & archival collections; diaries & travel accounts

DISTRICT OF COLUMBIA

WASHINGTON

M **ADDISON/RIPLEY FINE ART,** 1670 Wisconsin Ave NW, Washington, DC 20007. Tel 202-338-5180; Fax 202-338-2341; Elec Mail addisonrip@aol.com; Internet Home Page Address: www.addisonripleyfineart.com; *Owner* Christopher Addison; *Dir* Romy Silverstein; *Owner* Sylvia Ripley
Open Tues-Sat 11AM-6PM, Other times by appointment
Collections: works by contemporary artists; paintings; sculptures; photographs; fine art prints

M **AMERICAN ARCHITECTURAL FOUNDATION,** The Octagon Museum, 2101 L St NW, Washington, DC 20037-1526. Tel 202-638-3105 (information), 638-3221 (museum); Fax 202-879-7764; Internet Home Page Address: www.archfoundation.org; *Dir* Eryl J Wentworth; *Cur Exhibits* Linnea Hamer; *Cur Coll* Sherry Birk
Open Tues - Sun 10 AM - 4 PM, cl Mon; Admis adults $5, seniors & students $3; groups over 10 charges $3 per person except student & seniors groups $1 per person; Opened as house mus in 1970; formerly a federal townhouse designed by the first architect of the United States Capitol, Dr William Thornton for Col John Taylor III to serve as a winter home; used by President & Mrs Madison as temporary White House during war of 1812; Furnished with late 18th & early 19th centuries decorative arts; changing exhibition program in second floor galleries; Average Annual Attendance: 35,000
Collections: Permanent collection of furniture, paintings, ceramics, kitchen utensils
Publications: Competition 1792-Designing a Nation's Capitol, 1976 book; exhibition catalogs; Octagon being an Account of a Famous Residence: Its Great Years, Decline & Restoration, 1976 book; William Thornton: A Renaissance Man in the Federal City, book; The Architect & the British Country House, book; Architectural Records Management, 1985 booklet; the Architecture of Richard Morris Hunt, 1986 book; Building the Octagon, 1989 book; Ambitious Appetites: Dining, Behavior & Patterns of Consumption in Federal Washington, 1990 book; In the Most Fashionable Style: Making a Home in the Federal City, 1991 book; Creating the Federal City, 1774-1800: Potomac Fever, 1988 book; The Frame in American, 1700-1900: A survey of Fabrication, Techniques & Styles, 1983 catalog; Robert Mills, Architect, 1989 book; Sir Christopher Wren: The Design of St Paul's Cathedral, 1987 book; & exhibit catalogs
Activities: Educ dept; docent training; lects open to pub, 6 vis lectrs per yr; tours; mus shop sells books & gift items
M **Museum,** 1735 New York Ave, NW Washington, DC 20006-5292. Tel 202-626-7500; Fax 202-879-7764; Internet Home Page Address: www.aaspages.org; *VPres* Melissa Houghton
Open to the pub for reference but primarily used by staff; Mem: 350; dues $30-$50
Income: mem & contributions
Special Subjects: Archaeology, Decorative Arts

M **AMERICAN ART MUSEUM,** Smithsonian Institution, 8th & F Sts NW, Washington, DC 20004; MRC 970 Box 37012, Washington, DC 20013-7012. Tel 202-633-7970; Elec Mail AmericanArtInfo@si.edu; Internet Home Page Address: americanart.si.edu; *Dir* Elizabeth Broun; *Deputy Dir* Rachel Allen; *Chief Cur* Eleanor Harvey; *Chief Renwick Gallery* Robyn Kennedy; *Research & Scholars Center Chief* Christine Hennessy; *Lunder Educ Chair* Susan Nichols; *Registrar* Melissa Kroning; *Acting Chief of Exhibs* Claire Larkin; *Admin Officer* Douglas Wilde; *Publ Chief* Theresa Slowik
Open 11:30 AM - 7 PM daily, cl Dec 25; No admis fee; Estab 1829 & later absorbed by the Smithsonian Institution, it was designated the National Gallery of Art in 1906. The museum's name was changed to the National Collection of Fine Art in 1937 & in 1980, to the National Museum of American Art. With the largest collection of American art in the world, it is the leading center for study of the nation's heritage. On Oct 27, 2000 its name was officially changed to the Smithsonian American Art Museum; Circ 100,000; Bureau of the Smithsonian Institution; Average Annual Attendance: 918,000
Income: $7,000,000 annually (financed by federal appropriation, gifts, grants & trust income)
Library Holdings: Book Volumes; CD-ROMs; Exhibition Catalogs; Pamphlets; Periodical Subscriptions
Special Subjects: Drawings, Graphics, Hispanic Art, Painting-American, Photography, Watercolors, American Indian Art, American Western Art, Textiles, Folk Art, Primitive art, Woodcarvings, Woodcuts, Etchings & Engravings, Landscapes, Afro-American Art, Decorative Arts, Portraits, Furniture, Glass, Jewelry, Marine Painting, Gold, Stained Glass
Collections: All regions, cultures & traditions in the United States are represented in the museum's holdings, research resources, exhibitions & public programs. Colonial portraiture, 19th century landscapes, American impressionism, 20th century realism & abstraction, New Deal projects, sculpture, photography, graphic arts, works by African Americans, contemporary art & the creativity of self-taught artists are featured in the galleries; Major collections include those of Harriet Lane Johnston (1906), William T Evans (1907), John Gellatly (1929), the SC Johnson & Son Collection (1967), Container Corporation of America Collection (1984), Sara Roby Foundation Collection (1984), Herbert Waide Hemphill Jr Collection

(1986) & the Patricia & Phillip Frost Collection; Research resources include 300,000 listings on the Inventory of American Painting & Sculpture; Container Corporation of America Collection; William T Evans Collection; Patricia & Phillip Frost Collection; John Gellatly Collection; Herbert Waide Hemphill Jr Collection; SC Johnson & Son Collection; Harriet Lane Johnston Collection; Sara Roby Foundation Collection; Levin Collection

Exhibitions: A representative selection of works from the collection are on permanent display in the galleries, providing a comprehensive view of the varied aspects of American art. Many temporary exhibitions, approx 12 per year, are originated by the staff. They include both studies of individual artists & thematic studies; Luce Foundation Ctr & Conservation Ctr visible storage holds over 3,300 works on view

Publications: American Art, journal; calendar of events; quarterly member newsletter; major exhibitions are accompanied by authoritative publications; smaller exhibitions are accompanied by checklists & often brochures

Activities: The museum carries on an active prog with schools & the general pub, offering imaginative participatory tours for children, as well as lect & symposia for adults. A research prog in American art is maintained for vis scholars & training is carried on through internships in general mus practice & conservation; docent training; concerts; gallery talks; tours; sponsoring of competitions; Charles C Eldridge Prize for distinguished schol in American art; Lucelia Artist Award; Patricia & Phillip Frost Essay award; fels offered; circulates exhibs throughout the United States on a regular basis; mus shop sells books, magazines, original art, reproductions & prints; Renwick Gallery branch mus

L **Library of the Smithsonian American Art Museum & National Portrait Gallery,** 750 9th St NW Rm 2100, Washington, DC 20560-4505; MRC 975 PO Box 37012, Washington, DC 20013-7012. Tel 202-633-8230; Fax 202-633-8232; Elec Mail silaapg@si.edu; Internet Home Page Address: www.library.si.edu/libraries/american-art-portrait-gallery/; *Librn* Doug Litts
Open Mon - Fri 10 AM - 5 PM, cl Federal holidays; No admis fee; Estab 1964 to serve the reference & research needs of the staff & affiliated researchers of the National Museum of American Art, The National Portrait Gallery, the Archives of American Art & other Smithsonian bureaus; Research facility open to Smithsonian staff & fellows, researchers, & students. Branch of the Smithsonian Institution Libraries; shared with National Portrait Gallery
Income: Financed by federal appropriation
Library Holdings: Auction Catalogs 16,675; Book Volumes 180,000; CD-ROMs; Clipping Files 84,183; DVDs; Exhibition Catalogs; Fiche 555; Manuscripts; Other Holdings Catalogues Raisonne; Dissertations; Scrapbooks; Pamphlets; Periodical Subscriptions 607; Reels; Video Tapes
Special Subjects: Painting-American
Collections: Ferdinand Perret Art Reference Library: coll of scrapbooks of clippings & pamphlets; special section on California art & artists consisting of approx 325 ring binders on art & artists of Southern California; vertical file of 400 file drawers of material on art & artists, with increasing emphasis on American art & artists; Online Digital Coll; Living Portrait Artists' File

M **Renwick Gallery,** 1661 Pennsylvania Ave NW at 17th St, Washington, DC 20006; MRC 510 Box 37012, Washington, DC 20013-7012. Tel 202-633-7970; 633-1000; Elec Mail AmericanArtRenwick@si.edu; Internet Home Page Address: americanart.si.edu/renwick/; *Chief* Robyn Kennedy
Open daily 10 AM - 5:30 PM, cl Dec 25; No admis fee; Designed in 1859 by architect James Renwick, Jr as the original Corcoran Gallery of Art, the building was renamed for the architect in 1965 when it was transferred by the Federal government to the Smithsonian Institution for restoration; Restored to its French Second Empire elegance after 67 years as the United States Ct of Claims, the building has two public rooms with period furnishings, the Grand Salon & the Octagon Room, as well as eight areas for its permanent collection & temporary exhibitions of American crafts, design & decorative arts
Special Subjects: Decorative Arts, Crafts, Period Rooms
Publications: Major exhibitions are accompanied by publications, smaller exhibitions by checklists & brochures
Activities: Docent training; film progs; lects & workshops emphasizing the creative work of American craft artists; tours; concerts

AMERICAN ASSOCIATION OF MUSEUMS
For further information, see National and Regional Organizations

AMERICAN ASSOCIATION OF UNIVERSITY WOMEN
For further information, see National and Regional Organizations

AMERICAN INSTITUTE OF ARCHITECTS
For further information, see National and Regional Organizations

AMERICANS FOR THE ARTS
For further information, see National and Regional Organizations

M **ANACOSTIA COMMUNITY MUSEUM,** Smithsonian Institution, 1901 Fort Pl SE, Washington, DC 20020-3298. Tel 202-287-3369; 633-4820 (main office); Elec Mail acminfo@si.edu; Internet Home Page Address: http://anacostia.si.edu; *Deputy Dir* Sharon Reinckens; *Acting Dir Educ & Outreach* Robert Hall; *Historian* Portia P James; *Dir* Steven Newsome
Open daily 10 AM - 5 PM, cl Dec 25; No admis fee; Estab 1967, as a nonprofit federally chartered corporation to record & research African, Black American & Anacostia history & urban problems; the first federally funded, community-based museum; Bureau of the Smithsonian Institution
Income: Financed by federally funded bureau of Smithsonian Institute
Special Subjects: African Art, Afro-American Art
Collections: Afro-American history; exhibits & artifacts of the Black Diaspora in the Western Hemisphere; Black Diaspora Exhibits & Artifacts; Griffith Family Collection; Lillian Evans-Tibbs Collection; Lorenzo Dow Turner Collection; fine art holdings incl the work of James Wells, James Porter, John Robinson, Sam Gilliam, Nelson Stevens, Benny Andrews & folk artists Leslie Payne & Charles Smith; artifacts, photographs, archival documents, media, & art objects
Exhibitions: (Indefinite) Separate & Unequaled: Black Baseball in the District of Columbia
Publications: Educational booklets; exhibit programs; museum brochures accompany each major exhibit
Activities: Programs for children & adults; Museum Academy Prog offers after-school & summer opportunities; lects; tours; gallery talks; art festivals;

performances; demonstrations; competitions; exten dept serves groups unable to visit the museum; originates traveling exhibs

L **Branch Library,** 1901 Fort Pl SE, Washington, DC 20020. Tel 202-633-4862; 633-4853 (Mus Archives); Internet Home Page Address: www.sil.si.edu/libraries/anacostia/
Open to public for research on the premises; call for appointment
Library Holdings: Book Volumes 3,500; Periodical Subscriptions 100

M **ARCHIVES OF AMERICAN ART,** Smithsonian Institution, 750 9th St NW, Victor Bldg Ste 2200 Washington, DC 20001-4524; PO Box 37012 MRC 937, Washington, DC 20013-7012. Tel 202-633-7940 (General); 633-7950 (Ref); Fax 202-633-7994 (Ref); Internet Home Page Address: www.aaa.si.edu; *Dir* John Smith; *Cur Manuscripts* Liza Kirwin; *Devel* Jessica Theaman
Open Mon - Fri 9 AM - 5 PM; No admis fee; Since 1954, the Archives of American Art has provided researchers worldwide with access to the largest collection of primary source materials documenting the history of the visual arts in America from the Colonial period to the present. Among the collection's 14.6 million items are letters and diaries of artists and collectors; manuscripts of critics and scholars; records of museums, galleries and schools; photographs of art world figures and events; works of art on paper, and oral and video history interviews. A research institute of the Smithsonian since 1970, the Archives fulfills its ongoing mission to collect, preserve and make accessible for study the documentation of this country's rich artistic legacy. As a result, the Archives had played a pivotal role in expanding scholarship and illuminating the history of art in American for the benefit of future generations; Bureau of the Smithsonian Institution ; Average Annual Attendance: 2,500; Mem: 2,000; dues benefactor $2,500, fellow $1000, patron $500, sponsor $250, assoc $125, sustaining $65
Income: Financed by a combination of federal appropriation, private contributions & foundation grants
Special Subjects: Manuscripts
Collections: More than 14.6 million documents, diaries, letters, manuscripts, records of museums, galleries, & schools, works of art on paper; and oral & video history interviews; Copies of the Archives microfilm can be viewed at alternate institutions: Boston Public Library, Boston, MA; Amon Carter Museum Library, Fort Worth, TX; De Young Museum, San Francisco, CA; Huntingdon Library, San Marino, CA
Publications: Finding aids & guides, video: From Reliable Sources - The Archives of American Art
Activities: Various members' events, including trips, tours, gallery talks and special fundraising events; lects open to pub; lending of original material to mus and other arts organizations; mus shop by mail sells books & journals
—**New York Regional Center,** 1285 Ave of the Americas Lobby Level, New York, NY 10019. Tel 212-399-5015; Fax 212-307-4501; Elec Mail weinerj@si.edu; Internet Home Page Address: www.aaa.si.edu/about/; *Events & Pub Rels* Marissa Hoechstetter
Open Mon - Fri 9 AM - 5 PM; No admis fee; Estab 1956 to collect papers of artists, critics, dealers & collectors; 3,000 sq ft; Average Annual Attendance: 5,000; Mem: 1,200; dues $65; annual meeting varies
Collections: Letters, diaries, artwork, writings, photographs & oral histories of the American art world
Activities: Lects open to members only, 1,500 vis lectrs per year; gallery talks

M **ART MUSEUM OF THE AMERICAS,** 201 18th St, NW, Washington, DC; 1889 F St, NW, Washington, DC 20006. Tel 202-458-6016; Fax 202-458-6021; Internet Home Page Address: www.museum.oas.org; *Cur Reference Center* Maria Leyva; *Dir* Ana Maria Escallon
Open Tues - Sun 10 AM - 5 PM, cl holidays; No admis fee; Estab 1976 by organization of American States to bring about an awareness & appreciation of contemporary Latin American art; The mus maintains an art gallery with the focus on contemporary Latin American art; Average Annual Attendance: 100,000
Special Subjects: Drawings, Prints, Sculpture
Collections: Contemporary Latin American & Caribbean art including paintings, prints, drawings & sculpture
Activities: Lects open to public, 10 vis lectrs per yr; gallery talks; tours; paintings & original art objects lent to museums & educational institutions; originate traveling exhibs; sales shop sells films on Latin American art & artists

L **Archive of Contemporary Latin American Art,** 201 18th St NW Washington, DC 20006; 1889 F St NW Washington, DC 20006. Tel 202-458-6016; Fax 202-458-6021; *Cur* Maria Leyva
Open by appt only; No admis fee; Maintain archives of Latin Am artists and gen pub; Open to scholars for research only
Library Holdings: Audio Tapes; Book Volumes 200; Clipping Files; Exhibition Catalogs; Fiche; Memorabilia; Pamphlets; Photographs; Reels; Reproductions; Slides; Video Tapes
Special Subjects: Art History, Film, Painting-Spanish, Latin American Art, Mexican Art, Aesthetics

A **ART PAC,** 408 Third St SE, Washington, DC 20003. Tel 202-546-1804; Fax 202-543-2405; *Treas* Robert J Bedard
Estab 1981 to lobby for art's legislation & assist federal candidates supporting the arts; Mem: dues $40
Income: Financed by mem
Publications: Newsletter/ART PAC News, quarterly
Activities: Legislator of the Year Award

A **ART RESOURCES INTERNATIONAL,** 5813 Nevada Ave NW, Washington, DC 20015-2547. Tel 202-363-6806; Fax 202-244-6844; Elec Mail helen@artresources.org; *Exec Dir* Donald H Russell; *Dir Spec Projects* Helen M Brunner
Estab 1987 to provide consulting to foundations and organizations in strategic planning and institutional change; management of exhib, public prog, publ & coll
Special Subjects: Photography, Prints, Sculpture, Painting-American
Collections: Book Arts; Media Arts; Public Sculpture

M **ARTS CLUB OF WASHINGTON,** James Monroe House, 2017 I St NW, Monroe & MacFeely Galleries Washington, DC 20006-1804. Tel 202-331-7282; Fax 202-857-3678; Elec Mail membership@artsclubofwashington.org; Internet Home Page Address: www.artsclubofwashington.org; *Dir* Maureane O'Sahaugnessy; *Gen Mgr* Brennan Hurley
Open Tues-Fri 10AM-5PM; No admis fee; Founded 1916. The James Monroe

House (1803-1805) was built by Timothy Caldwell of Philadelphia. It is registered with the National Register of Historic Places, the Historical Survey 1937 & 1968 & the National Trust for Historic Preservation; James Monroe, fifth President of the United States, resided in the house while he was Secretary of War & State. During the first six months of his Presidency (1817-1825) the house served as the Exec Mansion, since the White House had been burned in the War of 1812 & had not yet been restored. Garden, banquet rooms & formal galleries, parlors, stairhalls serve as galleries; Average Annual Attendance: 10,000; Mem: 350; annual meeting in Apr
Income: Financed by mem, catering functions, fundraising, gallery sales, pub programs
Purchases: Obtained through gifts & bequests
Library Holdings: Original Art Works; Original Documents; Pamphlets; Sculpture
Collections: Washington, DC art
Exhibitions: Solo shows in two galleries, Oct - July, third gallery coming soon
Publications: Monthly news bulletin to members, promotional material, brochures
Activities: Classes for adults; pub progs vary; literary; musical & dramatic; lect open to public & for members, 12-24 vis lectrs per year; concerts; gallery talks; book awards; scholarships offered

ASSOCIATION OF COLLEGIATE SCHOOLS OF ARCHITECTURE
For further information, see National and Regional Organizations

M **B'NAI B'RITH INTERNATIONAL,** B'nai B'rith Klutznick National Jewish Museum, 2020 K St NW, Fl 7 Washington, DC 20006-1806. Tel 202-857-6647; Fax 202-857-6601; Elec Mail museum@bnaibrith.org; Internet Home Page Address: www.bnaibrith.org; *Curatorial Consultant* Cheryl Kempler
Open by appt through email request; Suggested donation adults $5, children under 12 free; Estab 1957 to exhibit & preserve Jewish art & culture; Permanent collection gallery including life & holiday cycles; Average Annual Attendance: 40,000; Mem: 1000; dues $45-$5000
Income: General operations financed by parent organization; private & corporate donations; programs & exhibitions financed by mus members
Special Subjects: Judaica
Collections: Permanent collection of Jewish ceremonial & folk art; archives of B'nai B'rith; contemporary paintings; lithographs; photographs; sculptures
Exhibitions: Jews in Sports
Publications: Exhibitions brochures & catalogues; members newsletter, semi-annual; permanent collection catalogue
Activities: Classes for adults & children; docent training; lects open to pub; 1 vis lectrs per yr; concerts; gallery talks; tours; individual paintings lent to museums; originate traveling exhibs

L **CATHOLIC UNIVERSITY OF AMERICA,** Humanities Library, Mullen Library, 620 Michigan Ave, NE, Washington, DC 20064-0001. Tel 202-319-5088; Internet Home Page Address: www.libraries.cua.edu/humcoll/index.html; *Head Humanities Div* Kevin Gunn
Open Mon-Thurs 8AM-11:30PM, Fri 8AM-10PM, Sat 9AM-10PM, Sun 11AM-11:30PM; No admis fee; Estab 1958 to offer acad resources & services that are integral to the work of the institution
Library Holdings: Book Volumes 14,000
Collections: Various collections

M **CORCORAN GALLERY OF ART,** 500 17th St NW, Washington, DC 20006-4899. Tel 202-639-1700; Internet Home Page Address: www.corcoran.org; *Pres & Dir* David C Levy; *Deputy Dir & Chief Cur* Jack Cowart; *Cur Contemporary Art* Terrie Sultan; *Registrar* Nancy Swallow; *Cur Photo & Media Arts* Philip Brookman; *Bechhoefer Cur American Art* Sarah Cash; *Cur Educ* Susan Badder
Open Wed - Sun 10 AM - 5 Pm, Thurs until 9 PM, cl Mon, Thanksgiving, Christmas & New Years Days; Admis adults $10, seniors & students $8, mems, children under 12 active military free, Free Summer Saturdays; Founded 1869 primarily for the encouragement of American art; The nucleus of the collection of American Paintings was formed by its founder, William Wilson Corcoran, early in the second half of the 19th century. In 1925 a large wing designed by Charles A Platt was added to house the European collection bequeathed by Senator William Andrews Clark of Montana. The Walker Collection, formed by Edward C and Mary Walker, added important French Impressionists to the collection upon its donation in 1937; Average Annual Attendance: 400,000; Mem: 4500; dues fellow $1000, contributing $500, sponsor $295, supporting $160, family $100, dual $90, sr dual $80, individual $60, sr individual $50, national $45, student $30
Special Subjects: Decorative Arts, Drawings, Painting-American, Photography, Watercolors, Bronzes, Painting-European, Furniture, Painting-British, Painting-Dutch, Painting-French, Tapestries, Painting-Flemish, Antiquities-Greek, Stained Glass
Collections: The American coll of paintings, watercolors, drawings, sculpture & photography from the 18th through 20th centuries; European coll includes paintings & drawings by Dutch, Flemish, English & French artists; 18th century French salon, furniture, laces, rugs, majolica; Gothic & Beauvais tapestries; Greek antiquities; 13th century stained glass window & bronzes by Antoine Louise Barye; triptych by Andrea Vanni; Walker Collection of French Impressionists; Clark European Collection
Publications: Calendar of Events (for members); Corcoran Shop Catalogue
Activities: Classes for adults, youth & children; summer camps; family progs; educator workshops & resources; pre-college classes; docent training; internships; lects open to public; concerts; gallery talks; tours; performances; films; mems only events; originates traveling exhibs; mus shop sells books, magazines, reproductions, prints & slides

L **Corcoran Library,** 500 17th St NW, Washington, DC 20006-4804. Tel 202-478-1544; Fax 202-628-1544; Elec Mail library@corcoran.org; Internet Home Page Address: www.corcoran.edu/library; *Libr Dir* Mario Ascenio; *Circ Mgr* Shawana Snell; *Digital Assets & Media Librn* Jacqueline Protka; *Tech Svcs Assoc* Patricia L Reid
Open during school yr Mon - Thurs 8:30 AM - 8 PM, Fri 8:30 AM - 5 PM, Sat 10 AM - 4 PM, cl Sun & Thanksgiving; Research & lending resource for mus & school, staff, faculty & student. Provides interlibrary loan to other institutions & open for pub use by appointment only. Located on 2nd fl in hemicycle
Library Holdings: Book Volumes 35,000; DVDs; Exhibition Catalogs; Other Holdings Online Database Subscriptions: 14; Periodical Subscriptions 190; Slides 32,000; Video Tapes
Special Subjects: Art History, Photography, Commercial Art, Drawings, Etchings & Engravings, Graphic Arts, Graphic Design, Painting-American, Prints, Printmaking, Advertising Design, Lettering, Furniture, Afro-American Art, Pottery, Religious Art
Collections: Artists books

A **CULTURAL ALLIANCE OF GREATER WASHINGTON,** 975 F St NW, Ste 303 Washington, DC 20004-1479. Tel 202-393-2161; Fax 202-393-2595; Elec Mail jpayne@culturalalliance.org; Internet Home Page Address: www.cultural-alliance.org; *Pres* Jennifer Cover Payne; *VPres* Eileen Rappoport
Open Mon-Fri 9 AM - 5 PM; Estab 1978 to increase appreciation & support for the arts in Washington DC region; Mem: 647; mem open to artists, arts adminr or patron; dues individual $60, organization-scaled to annual income; annual meeting in the fall
Income: $82,663 (financed by mem & donations)
Exhibitions: Tony Taylor Award
Publications: Arts Washington, newsletter 10 times per year; Cultural Alliance Directory, biennial
Activities: Lect open to public for fee, free to members

M **DAR MUSEUM,** National Society Daughters of the American Revolution, 1776 D St NW, Washington, DC 20006-5303. Tel 202-628-1776; Fax 202-628-0820; Elec Mail museum@dar.org; Internet Home Page Address: www.dar.org/museum; *Dir & Chief Cur* Diane Dunkley
Open Mon-Fri 9:30AM-4PM, Sat 9AM-5PM, cl Sun; No admis fee; Estab 1890 for collection & exhibition of decorative arts used in America from 1700-1840; for the study of objects & the preservation of Revolutionary artifacts & documentation of American life; There are 33 period rooms which reflect the decorative arts of particular states, also a mus which houses large collections grouped by ceramics, textiles, silver, glass, furniture & paintings; Average Annual Attendance: 12,000; Mem: 215,000; dues $15 - $17; annual meeting in Apr
Income: $200,000 (financed by mem)
Special Subjects: Painting-American, Textiles, Costumes, Ceramics, Pottery, Decorative Arts, Portraits, Dolls, Furniture, Glass, Jewelry, Porcelain, Silver, Carpets & Rugs, Coins & Medals, Miniatures, Period Rooms, Embroidery, Pewter
Collections: Ceramics, furniture, glass, paintings, prints, silver, textiles
Exhibitions: Special exhibitions arranged & changed periodically, usually every 6 months
Activities: Classes for adults & children; docent training; lects open to pub; tours; paintings & original art works lent to mus & cultural institutions for special exhibs; mus shop sells books, stationery, dolls & handcrafted gift items

L **Library,** 1776 D St NW, Washington, DC 20006-5303. Tel 202-879-3241; Fax 202-628-0820; Elec Mail museum@dar.org; Internet Home Page Address: www.dar.org/museum; *Dir & Chief Cur* Diane Dunkley; *Cur Coll* Olive Graffam; *Cur Historic Furnishings* Patrick Sheary; *Cur Textiles* Nancy Gibson
Open Mon - Fri 8:30 AM - 4:00 PM, Sat 9:00 AM - 5:00 PM; No admis fee; Estab 1890; collects objects made or used in America prior to 1840; Open to pub
Income: Pvt donations
Library Holdings: Book Volumes 3000; Periodical Subscriptions 10
Collections: American Decorative Arts and Fine Arts
Activities: Classes for adults & children; school progs; Christmas open house; docent training; lects open to pub; 4 vis lectrs per yr; gallery talks; tours of 32 period rooms; exten prog serves mus nationwide; mus shop sells books, reproductions, prints & slides

M **DISTRICT OF COLUMBIA ARTS CENTER (DCAC),** 2438 18th St NW, Washington, DC 20009-2004. Tel 202-462-7833; Fax 419-821-9622; Elec Mail info@dcartscenter.org; Internet Home Page Address: www.dcartscenter.org; *Dir* B Stanley; *Gallery Mgr* Michael Mattason; *House Mgr* Jaron Bowman
Open Wed - Sun 2 - 7 PM; No admis fee; Estab 1989 to support new & emerging artists; 800 sq ft; Average Annual Attendance: 5,000; Mem: 500; dues $30
Income: $250,000 (financed by mem, city appropriation & foundations)
Activities: Classes for adults; dramatic progs; lects open to pub, 5 vis lectrs per yr; gallery talks

M **FEDERAL RESERVE BOARD,** Art Gallery, 20th & C Sts NW, Washington, DC 20551-0001. Elec Mail firearts@frb.gov; Internet Home Page Address: www.federalreserve.gov/finearts; *Dir* Stephen Bennett Phillips; *Fine Arts Prog Asst* Rhonda Gray-Young; *Fine Arts Prog Asst* Nikki Pisha
Open Mon - Fri 10 AM - 3:30 PM advance reservation required, cl Federal holidays; No admis fee; Estab 1975 to promote art in the work place; Two story atrium space with travertine marble walls.
Income: Operating expenses by the Federal Reserve Board
Purchases: By donation
Special Subjects: Architecture, Drawings, Hispanic Art, Latin American Art, Painting-American, Photography, Prints, Sculpture, Etchings & Engravings, Landscapes, Collages, Marine Painting, Painting-Australian
Collections: American & European paintings; works on paper & photographs
Publications: Exhibition catalogs

M **FLASHPOINT,** 916 G St NW, Washington, DC 20001-4565. Tel 202-315-1305; Fax 202-315-1303; *Exec Dir* Anne L Corbett
Call for hours
Collections: works by contemporary artists

L **FOLGER SHAKESPEARE LIBRARY,** 201 E Capitol St SE, Washington, DC 20003-1094. Tel 202-544-4600; Fax 202-544-4623; Internet Home Page Address: www.folger.edu; *Dir* Gail Kern Paster; *Librn* Stephen Enniss; *Head of Ref* Georgianna Ziegler; *Cur Art* Erin Blake
Open (exhibition gallery) Mon - Sat 10 AM - 5 PM; No admis fee to exhibs; Estab 1932 as a private, independent research library & international center for the study of all aspects of the European Renaissance & civilization in the 16th & 17th centuries; Maintains an exhibition gallery & a permanent display of Shakespearean items, with changing topical exhibits of books, manuscripts, paintings & porcelain

Income: Financed by endowment, grants, gifts & earned income
Library Holdings: Audio Tapes; Book Volumes 260,000; Exhibition Catalogs; Filmstrips; Manuscripts 56,000; Memorabilia; Motion Pictures; Original Art Works 3800; Other Holdings Rare books 135,000; Pamphlets; Periodical Subscriptions 180; Photographs 3000; Prints 20,000; Records; Reels 10,000; Reproductions; Sculpture; Slides
Collections: Shakespeare, playbills & promptbooks; Continental & English Renaissance, 1450-1700; manuscripts; paintings; works of art on paper; prints & engravings
Exhibitions: See website for current exhibs
Publications: The Folger Edition of the Complete Plays of William Shakespeare; Shakespeare Quarterly; Folger Magazine 3 times per year
Activities: Educ prog; classes for children; dramatic progs; docent training; seminars for advanced graduate students; lects open to public; lects open to mems; 20 vis lectrs per year; concerts; gallery talks; tours; fels offered; sales shop sells books, reproductions, music

M **FONDO DEL SOL,** Visual Art & Media Center, 2112 R St NW, Washington, DC 20008-1932. Tel 202-483-2777; Fax 202-658-1078; Elec Mail info@fondodelsol.org; Elec Mail art@fondodelsol.org (Cur); Internet Home Page Address: www.fondodelsol.org; *Chief Cur, Dir* W Marc Zuver; *Co-Chmn* Osvaldo Mesa; *Co-Chmn Exhibs* Michael Auld; *Artist in Residence* Michael Pereira; *Deputy Dir* Allen Olson-Urtechio; *Dir Develop* Sanne Tikjoeb; *Dir Intern Progs* Laura Eldridge; *Dir Security* Madame Rambolina
Open Tues - Sat 12:30 - 5:30 PM; Admis by donation; Estab 1973 to promote Latin American and Caribbean culture, nonprofit museum
Special Subjects: Sculpture, Ceramics
Collections: Permanent collection, Pre-Columbian, Latin America, Chicano & Puerto Rican Art
Exhibitions: Pre-Columbian art by Santos

M **FREER GALLERY OF ART & ARTHUR M SACKLER GALLERY,** Freer Gallery of Art, Jefferson Dr at 12th St, Washington, DC 20560; PO Box 37012 MRC 707, Washington, DC 20013-7012. Tel 202-633-1000 (General); Fax 202-357-4911; Elec Mail publicaffairsAsia@si.edu; Internet Home Page Address: www.asia.si.edu; *Dir* Julian Raby
Open daily 10 AM - 5:30 PM, cl Dec 25; No admis fee; Estab 1923 to exhibit 19th-century & early 20th-century American art; Italian-Renaissance-Style gallery constructed of granite & marble; A permanent installation in the gallery is the Peacock Room, a dining room once part of a London townhouse & lavishly decorated with a blue & gold peacock design by James McNeill Whistler in 1876; Eugene & Agnes E Meyer Auditorium provides a venue for free public programs, including concerts of Asian music & dance, films, lectures, chamber music & dramatic presentations. Bureau of the Smithsonian Institution; Connected by an underground exhib space to the neighboring Arthur M Sackler Gallery; Average Annual Attendance: 500,000
Income: Financed by endowment, federal appropriation, gifts & purchases
Special Subjects: Ceramics, American Western Art, Manuscripts
Collections: James McNeill Whistler Collection; art from China, Japan, Korea, South & Southeast Asia & the Near East; Buddhist sculpture; Chinese paintings; Indian & Persian manuscripts; Japanese folding screens; Korean ceramics
Activities: Classes for adults & children; dramatic progs; docent training; teacher workshops; lects open to pub, 5-6 vis lectrs per yr; concerts; gallery talks; tours; films; schols offered; originate traveling exhibs; mus shop sells books, magazines, original art, reproductions, prints, slides, textiles, music, ceramics & jewelry

M **Arthur M Sackler Gallery,** 1050 Independence Ave SW, Washington, DC 20560; PO Box 37012 MRC 707, Washington, DC 20013-7012. Tel 202-633-1000 (General); Fax 202-357-4911; Elec Mail publicaffairsAsia@si.edu; Internet Home Page Address: www.asia.si.edu; *Dir* Julian Raby
Open daily 10 AM - 5:30 PM, cl Dec 25; No admis fee; Estab 1987 for exhibition, research & educ on the arts of Asia; Bureau of the Smithsonian Institution; Connected by an underground exhib space to the neighboring Freer Gallery of Art ; Average Annual Attendance: 500,000
Income: Financed by endowment & federal appropriation
Special Subjects: Architecture, Drawings, Bronzes, Anthropology, Archaeology, Costumes, Ceramics, Crafts, Etchings & Engravings, Decorative Arts, Collages, Furniture, Glass, Asian Art, Antiquities-Byzantine, Coins & Medals, Calligraphy, Embroidery, Antiquities-Oriental, Antiquities-Persian, Antiquities-Egyptian, Antiquities-Roman, Enamels, Antiquities-Assyrian, Bookplates & Bindings
Collections: Arthur M Sackler Collection (ancient Near Eastern ceramics & metalware, Chinese bronzes & jades, Chinese paintings & lacquerware, sculpture from South & Southeast Asia); Vever Collection (Islamic arts of the book, 11th-19th century); arts of village India; contemporary Chinese ceramics; Indian, Chinese, Japanese & Korean paintings; 19th & 20th century Japanese prints & contemporary porcelain; photography
Publications: Asian Art & Culture, annual; Arthur M Sackler Gallery Calendar, bi-monthly
Activities: Classes for adults & children; dramatic progs; docent training; teacher workshops; lects open to pub, 5-6 vis lectrs per yr; concerts; gallery talks; tours; films; schols offered; originate traveling exhibs; mus shop sells books, magazines, original art, reproductions, prints, slides, jewelry, cards, gifts, ceramics, music & textiles

L **Library,** 1050 Independence Ave SW, Washington, DC 20560-0112. Tel 202-633-0477; Fax 202-786-2936; Elec Mail AskaLibrarian@si.edu; Internet Home Page Address: http://www.asia.si.edu/visitor/library.htm; *Head Librn* Reiko Yoshimura; *Librn* Kathryn D Phillips; *Librn* Reiko Yoshimura; *Archivist* Colleen Hennessey
Open Mon - Fri 10 AM - 5 PM, cl Federal holidays; Branch of Smithsonian Institution Libraries
Library Holdings: Audio Tapes; Book Volumes 65,000; Cassettes; Clipping Files; Exhibition Catalogs; Fiche; Filmstrips; Kodachrome Transparencies; Lantern Slides; Manuscripts; Memorabilia; Motion Pictures; Other Holdings Sales catalogs; Pamphlets; Periodical Subscriptions 500; Photographs; Prints; Reels; Reproductions; Slides; Video Tapes
Special Subjects: Art History, Decorative Arts, Calligraphy, Etchings & Engravings, Painting-Japanese, Sculpture, Ceramics, Archaeology, Bronzes, Art Education, Asian Art, Jade, Glass, Bookplates & Bindings, Metalwork, Carpets & Rugs, Embroidery, Enamels, Flasks & Bottles, Architecture
Collections: Contains approx 80,000 monograph vols & 1,400 serials titles, with almost half its printed resources in Chinese, Japanese, or Korean; Japan Art Catalog Project Collection; Rare Book Collection; Paul Marks Collection on James McNeill Whistler; Conservation Library in Freer Gallery, containing research materials on conservation & restoration of Asian art

M **GEORGE WASHINGTON UNIVERSITY,** The Dimock Gallery, 730 21st St NW, Lower Lisner Auditorium Washington, DC 20052-0001. Tel 202-994-1525; Fax 202-994-1632; Elec Mail bradyart@gwu.edu; Internet Home Page Address: www.gwu.edu/dimock; *Dir* Lenore D Miller
Open Tues - Fri 11AM - 3PM; No admis fee; Estab 1967 to enhance graduate & undergraduate programs in fine art & research in art history; documentation of permanent collections; feature historical & contemporary exhibitions related to university art dept programs; Average Annual Attendance: 10,000
Special Subjects: Historical Material, Graphics, Painting-American, Photography, Prints, Sculpture
Collections: Joseph Pennell Collection of Prints; W Lloyd Wright Collection of Washingtoniana; graphic arts from the 18th, 19th & 20th centuries, with special emphasis on American art; works pertaining to George Washington; U S Grant Collection
Publications: Exhibition catalogs
Activities: Lect open to public; gallery talks; tours; individual paintings & original objects of art lent

M **GEORGETOWN UNIVERSITY,** Art Collection, 3700 O St NW, Washington, DC 20057-1104. Tel 202-687-1469; Fax 202-687-7501; Elec Mail llw@georgetown.edu; Internet Home Page Address: www.library.georgetown.edu/dept/speccoll/guac; *Asst Cur* Christen Runge; *Cur* Lulen Walker
Call for hours; No admis fee; University estab 1789; The collection is on the Georgetown University campus in Healy Hall (1879)
Income: Financed by University budget
Special Subjects: Historical Material, Portraits, Silver, Graphics, Painting-American, Sculpture, Religious Art, Mosaics
Collections: Works by Van Dyck, Giordano & Gilbert Stuart
Exhibitions: 4 exhibitions per yr of graphic art held in Lauinger Library
Activities: Educ progs for undergraduate students; gallery talks, guided tours; art festivals, temporary exhibs

L **Lauinger Library-Special Collections Division,** 3700 O St NW, Washington, DC 20057-1174. Tel 202-687-1469; Fax 202-687-7501; Elec Mail artcollection@georgetown.edu; Internet Home Page Address: www.library.georgetown.edu/special-collections/art/carroll-parlor; *Spec Coll Librn* John Buchtel; *Art Coll Cur* Lulen Walker; *Asst Cur* Christen Runge
Open weekdays; check hours on website or call; Estab 1975 to support Georgetown's acad progs; 3 exhibitions per yr of fine prints in Library; permanent collection of paintings, sculpture & dec arts in Carroll Parlor of Healy Bldg
Library Holdings: Original Art Works; Photographs; Prints; Sculpture
Special Subjects: Decorative Arts, Illustration, Drawings, Etchings & Engravings, Painting-American, Painting-British, Painting-Flemish, Painting-French, Painting-German, Painting-Italian, Painting-Spanish, Prints, Sculpture, Watercolors, Latin American Art, Cartoons, Period Rooms, Mosaics, Bookplates & Bindings, Religious Art, Woodcuts, Landscapes
Collections: Editorial Cartoon Collection - Originals (American) c 1910 to present; Elder Collection - Artist Self - Portraits, prints, drawings, watercolors, paintings, c 1925-1975; Jesuit Collection - American fine prints, c 1900-1950; Eric F Menke Collection - prints, drawings, watercolors, paintings; Murphy Collection - American Fine Prints, c 1900-1950; Eric Smith Collection - original editorial cartoon; Lynd Ward Collection - prints, drawings, watercolors, paintings, c 1925-1980; Printmakers' Collections: John DePol, Werner Drewes, Isac Friedlander, Norman Kent, Clare Leighton, William E C Morgan, Barry Moser, Philip Riesman, Prentiss Taylor, Ralph Fabri Collection; Old Masters Paintings; 19th Century American paintings & sculpture
Publications: Issued with many spec exhibs

M **HARVARD UNIVERSITY DUMBARTON OAKS,** Museum & Garden, 1703 32nd St NW, Washington, DC 20007-2934. Tel 202-339-6401; Fax 202-625-0283; Elec Mail museum@doaks.org; Internet Home Page Address: www.doaks.org; *Dir* Jan M Ziolkowski; *Cur & Mus Dir* Gudrun Buhl; *Dir Gardens & Grounds* Gail Griffin
Open Tues - Sun 2-5 PM, cl federal holidays; Gardens open Mar 15 - Oct 31 Tues - Sun 2-6 PM, Nov 1 - Mar 14 Tues - Sun 2-5 PM; Admis to mus free; garden admis Mar 15 - Oct 31 general $8, Nov 1 - Mar 14 free; Conveyed in 1940 to Harvard University by Mr & Mrs Robert Woods Bliss as a research center in the Byzantine & Medieval humanities & subsequently enlarged to include Pre-Columbian studies & studies in landscape architecture; Average Annual Attendance: 15,000
Special Subjects: Furniture, Portraits, Painting-American, Prints, Painting-European, Tapestries, Sculpture, Watercolors, Pre-Columbian Art, Textiles, Religious Art, Pottery, Decorative Arts, Jewelry, Asian Art, Antiquities-Byzantine, Metalwork, Ivory, Mosaics
Collections: Byzantine Dept: devoted to early Christian & Byzantine mosaics, textiles, bronzes, sculpture, ivories, metalwork, jewelry, glyptics & other decorative arts of the period; Pre-Columbian Dept: devoted to sculpture, textiles, pottery, gold ornaments & other objects from Mexico, Central & South America, dating from 800 BC to early 16th century; House Collection: European & American paintings, sculpture & decorative arts; historic interiors, Asian, European & American artworks, & interior furnishings
Publications: Handbooks & catalogs of the Byzantine & pre-Columbian collection; scholarly publications in Byzantine, pre-Columbian & landscape architecture studies
Activities: Lect; conferences; garden tours; mus tours

L **Dumbarton Oaks Research Library,** 1703 32nd St NW, Washington, DC 20007. Tel 202-339-6490; 339-6462 (Rare Book Coll); Fax 202-625-0279; Internet Home Page Address: www.doaks.org/library; *Dir Libr* Sheila Klos; *Head Cataloger* Sandra Parker Provenzano; *Pre-Columbian Studies Librn* Bridget Gazzo; *Interlibrary Loan Librn* Ingrid Gibson; *Rare Book Librn* Linda Lott; *Byzantine Studies Librn* Deborah Stewart; *Spec Project & Reference Librn* Sarah Burke Cahalan

Open (application for access is required) to scholars with weekday reader status: Mon - Fri 9 AM - 5 PM; Open to scholars with reader status: Mon - Fri 8 AM - 10 PM, Sat - Sun 9 AM - 10 PM; Rare Book Coll open by appt only Mon - Fri 9:30 AM - 12:30 PM & 1:30 PM - 4:30 PM
Library Holdings: Book Volumes 215,000; CD-ROMs; Exhibition Catalogs; Fiche; Manuscripts; Maps; Memorabilia; Micro Print; Motion Pictures; Original Art Works; Original Documents; Other Holdings Mus Catalogs; Pamphlets; Periodical Subscriptions 550; Photographs; Prints; Reels; Reproductions; Slides; Video Tapes
Special Subjects: Art History, Decorative Arts, Manuscripts, Pre-Columbian Art, Sculpture, Archaeology, Anthropology, Mosaics
Collections: Dumbarton Oaks Census of Early Christian and Byzantine Objects in American Collection; Photographs Collection; Rare Book Collection; Pre-Columbian Library Collection: 2,000+ vols

L **Image Collection & Fieldwork Archives,** 1703 32nd St NW, Washington, DC 20007. Tel 202-339-6973; Internet Home Page Address: www.doaks.edu/library/ifca.htm; *Mgr Image Coll & Fieldwork Archives* Shalimar Fojas White; *Digitization Specialist* Deborah Maron; *Byzantine Asst Cur* Gunder Varinlioglu
Open Mon - Fri 9 AM - Noon & 1-5 PM to approved scholars by written request, see website; Estab to support scholarship in Byzantine, Garden & Landscape, & Pre-Columbian studies by acquiring, preserving, cataloging & providing access to images in a variety of media, documentation of archaeological surveys & excavations both textual & visual, & papers of noteworthy scholars in the 3 disciplines
Library Holdings: Manuscripts; Original Documents; Photographs
Collections: Index of Christian Art

HERITAGE PRESERVATION
For further information, see National and Regional Organizations

M **HILLWOOD MUSEUM & GARDENS FOUNDATION,** (Marjorie Merriweather Post) Hillwood Estate Museum & Gardens, 4155 Linnean Ave NW, Washington, DC 20008-3806. Tel 202-686-8500, 686-5807; Fax 202-966-7846; Elec Mail info@hillwoodmuseum.org; Internet Home Page Address: www.hillwoodmuseum.org; *Pres* Ellen MacNeille Charles; *Exec Dir & CEO* Kate Markert; *Dir Collections, Chief Cur* Liana Paredes; *Asst Dir of Colls & Colls Mgr* Ruthann Uithol; *Dir Fin & Admin & CFO* Madge Minor; *Dir Human Resources* Nancy Brown; *Dir Develop* Joan Wetmore; *COO, Assoc & Dir Interpretation & Vis Svcs* Angie Dodson; *Dir Horticulture* Brian Barr; *Dir Security* Jim Sellevaag; *Asst Cur Russian & Eastern European Art* Scott Ruby; *Asst Cur Costumes & Textiles* Howard Kurtz; *Cur Emerita* Anne Odom; *Head Merchandising* Lauren Chapin Salazar; *Dir Facilities* Donald Rogers; *Cur Am Material Culture & Historian* Estella Chung; *Head of Research Colls* Kristen Regina
Open Tues - Sat 10 AM - 5 PM, cl Jan & nat holidays; Admis adults $12, students $7, children $5; Estab 1977 to enlighten & engage visitors; Georgian-style mansion, home of the late Marjorie Merriweather Post, situated on 25 acres, 13 of which are formal gardens; auxiliary bldg Dacha currently housing temp exhibs; Average Annual Attendance: 44,162; Mem: 1,650; dues $50-$1,000, corporate $2,500-$25,000
Income: Financed by endowment, operating income & grants
Purchases: Active acquisitions program in Russian & Western European decorative arts
Library Holdings: Auction Catalogs; Book Volumes; Clipping Files; Exhibition Catalogs; Fiche; Kodachrome Transparencies; Manuscripts; Maps; Memorabilia; Motion Pictures; Original Documents; Pamphlets; Periodical Subscriptions; Photographs; Prints; Records; Reels; Slides; Video Tapes
Special Subjects: Drawings, Etchings & Engravings, Folk Art, Historical Material, Landscapes, Marine Painting, Metalwork, Flasks & Bottles, Photography, Pottery, Painting-American, Prints, Manuscripts, Maps, Painting-British, Painting-European, Graphics, Sculpture, Watercolors, Bronzes, Textiles, Costumes, Religious Art, Ceramics, Crafts, Woodcarvings, Woodcuts, Decorative Arts, Judaica, Portraits, Posters, Furniture, Glass, Jade, Jewelry, Porcelain, Oriental Art, Asian Art, Silver, Painting-Dutch, Painting-French, Carpets & Rugs, Ivory, Coins & Medals, Tapestries, Miniatures, Renaissance Art, Embroidery, Laces, Painting-Italian, Gold, Pewter, Leather, Military Art, Painting-Russian, Enamels, Bookplates & Bindings
Collections: Western European & French fine & decorative arts, furnishings & American memorabilia; Russian fine & decorative arts; Asian decorative arts; Art Research Library; Archives & Visual Resources relating to coll & Marjorie Merriweather Post, mus found
Publications: The Hillwood Post newsletter, triennial, 1998 catalogue A Taste for Splendor: Russian Imperial and European Treasures from the Hillwood Mus; Hillwood Collection Series of 5 books: Faberge at Hillwood, Russian Icons at Hillwood, Sevres Porcelain at Hillwood, Russian Imperial Porcelain at Hillwood & Russian Glass at Hillwood; Art of the Russian North; French Furniture in the Collection of Hillwood Museum & Gardens; What Became of Peter's Dream? Court Culture in the Reign of Nicholass II co-published with Middlebury College Museum of Art in Middlebury, VT; Tradition in Transition: Russian Icons in the Age of the Romanovs; Hillwood: Thirty Years of Collecting 1977-2007
Activities: Classes for adults & children; docent training; lects open to pub; 10 vis lectrs per yr; concerts; gallery talks; tours; originates traveling exhibs for art mus; mus shop sells books, gifts, reproductions, prints & jewelry

M **HIRSHHORN MUSEUM & SCULPTURE GARDEN,** Smithsonian Institution, Independence Ave at 7th St SW, Washington, DC 20560; PO Box 37012 MRC Code 350, Washington, DC 20013-7012. Tel 202-633-4674; Fax 202-633-8835; Elec Mail hmsginquiries@si.edu; Internet Home Page Address: www.hirshhorn.si.edu; *Acting Dir & Chief Cur* Kerry Brougher; *Deputy Dir & Chief Admin* Jose Ortiz; *Dir Pub Programs* Milena Kalinovska; *Dir Exhibs, Design, & Spec Projects* Al Masino; *Dir Develop* Kevin Crysler
Mus open daily 10 AM - 5:30 PM; Plaza open daily 7:30 AM - 5:30 PM; Sculpture Garden open daily 7:30AM - dusk; cl Dec 25; No admis fee; Estab 1966 under the aegis of the Smithsonian Institution; building designed by Gordon Bunshaft of the architectural firm of Skidmore, Owings & Merrill. Opened in 1974; Bureau of the Smithsonian Institution; Average Annual Attendance: 800,000
Income: Financed by federal funds
Library Holdings: Auction Catalogs; Audio Tapes; Book Volumes; Cassettes; Clipping Files; Exhibition Catalogs; Pamphlets; Periodical Subscriptions; Video Tapes
Special Subjects: Drawings, Latin American Art, Painting-American, Sculpture, Afro-American Art, Collages, Painting-European
Collections: American art beginning with a strong group of Thomas Eakins & going on to De Kooning, Gorky, Hartley, Hopper, Johns, Elizabeth Murray, Rothko, Frank Stella, Warhol; European paintings & mixed media work of the last 5 decades represented by Bacon, Balthus, Kiefer & Korenellis, Leger, Miro, Polke & Richter; extensive sculpture collection includes works by Bourgeois, Brancusi, Calder, Cragg, Giacometti, Hessi, Merz, Moore, Oldenburg & Shea; David Smith; 12,000 paintings, sculptures, mixed media works, drawings & prints, the nucleus donated to the nation by Joseph H Hi emphasizing contemporary art & the develop of modern art from the latter half of the 19th century to present; Contemporary Art
Publications: Exhibit catalogs; Family Guide; collection catalogs; seasonal events calendar, three times per yr
Activities: Classes for children; workshops for adults; docent training; workshops for teachers; outreach; free summer concerts; lects open to pub, 4 vis lectrs per yr; gallery talks; tours; individual paintings & original objects of art lent to accredited mus that meet security & conservation standards, loans, subject to approval by cur; lending contains original art works, original prints & sculpture; book traveling exhibs 1-2 per yr; originate traveling exhibs 1-2 per yr; mus shop sells books, reproductions, slides, jewelry by artists, CD's & sculptural toys

L **Library,** Seventh & Independence Ave SW, Washington, DC 20560-0001; PO Box 37012, MRC 361 Washington, DC 20013-7012. Tel 202-633-2773; Fax 202-633-6764; Elec Mail brookea@si.edu; Internet Home Page Address: www.hirshhorn.si.edu; *Librn* Anna Brooke; *Library Technician* Rita O'Hara; *Library Technician* Alexandra Reigle
No admis fee; Estab 1974; Circ 7,554; Branch of Smithsonian Institution Libraries (for reference only by appointment)
Income: Financed by federal funds
Library Holdings: Audio Tapes; Book Volumes 62,000; Clipping Files; DVDs; Exhibition Catalogs; Memorabilia; Other Holdings Auction Catalogs; Periodical Subscriptions 35; Photographs

M **HISTORICAL SOCIETY OF WASHINGTON DC,** The City Museum of Washington DC, 801 K St NW, Mount Vernon Sq Washington, DC 20001-3746. Tel 202-249-3955; Elec Mail info@historydc.org; library@historydc.org; Internet Home Page Address: www.historydc.org; *Bus Mgr* Alonita Vannoy; *Colls Mgr* Anne McDonough; *Asst Librn* Laura Barry
Open exhibs Tues-Sun 10AM-5PM; Admis free; Estab 1894 to preserve & interpret local history of Washington, DC; Permanent and changing exhibitions on the history of Washington DC. Maintains reference library; Average Annual Attendance: 350,000; Mem: 1,800; dues $50-$5000
Income: $2.5 million (financed by endowment, mem, grants & earned income)
Library Holdings: Audio Tapes; Book Volumes; Clipping Files; Fiche; Lantern Slides; Manuscripts; Maps; Memorabilia; Original Art Works; Original Documents; Pamphlets; Photographs; Prints; Sculpture
Special Subjects: Architecture, Decorative Arts, Historical Material
Collections: Photographs, Prints, Paintings, Maps, Decorative Arts, Ephemera, Archives
Exhibitions: Washington Perspectives; Digging History and Washington Stories; City of Sports; Taking a Closer Look; Chinatown; Mount Vernon Square
Publications: Washington History, semi-annual magazine
Activities: Classes for adults & children; dramatic progs; docent training; lects open to pub, 12 vis lectrs per yr; tours; sponsoring competitions; awards; originate traveling exhibs to local organizations, libraries & schools; mus shop sells books, reproductions, prints, crafts & souvenirs

L801 K St NW, Washington, DC 20001. Tel 202-383-1850, 383-1800; Fax 202-383-1872; Elec Mail info@historydc.org; Internet Home Page Address: www.historydc.org; *Bus Mgr* Alonita Vannoy; *Colls Mgr* Anne McDonough; *Asst Librn* Laura Barry
Library open Mon-Thurs 10 AM - 4 PM by prior appointment; No admis fee; Estab 1894 for collection of materials related to Washington, DC history; For reference only; Average Annual Attendance: 1500; Mem: 1,800; dues $50 - $5000; annual meeting
Income: $700,000 financed by grants, membership & earned income
Library Holdings: Book Volumes 14,000; Cards; Clipping Files; Exhibition Catalogs; Fiche; Lantern Slides; Manuscripts; Memorabilia; Original Art Works; Original Documents; Pamphlets; Photographs; Prints; Reels; Slides
Special Subjects: Art History, Landscape Architecture, Decorative Arts, Photography, Drawings, Etchings & Engravings, Manuscripts, Painting-American, Prints, Historical Material, History of Art & Archaeology, Archaeology, Architecture, Portraits
Collections: Photographs, Prints, Paintings, Maps, Decorative Arts, Archives, Books, Ephemera
Exhibitions: Window to Washington (permanent exhib)
Publications: Washington History, semi-annual magazine
Activities: Workshops; teacher training; lects open to pub; 2-4 vis lects per yr; gallery talks; tours; schols; mus shop sells books, magazines, original art, reproductions & prints

M **HOWARD UNIVERSITY,** Gallery of Art, 2455 6th St NW, College of Fine Arts Washington, DC 20059-0001. Tel 202-806-7040; Fax 202-806-6503; Internet Home Page Address: www.howard.edu.library/art@howard/goa; *Asst Dir* Scott Baker; *Registrar* Eileen Johnston; *Dir* Dr. Tritobia Hayes-Benjamin
Open Mon-Fri 9:30AM-5PM, Sun noon-4PM; No admis fee; Estab 1928 to stimulate the study & appreciation of the fine arts in the University & community; Three air-conditioned art galleries are in Childers Hall, James V Herring Heritage Gallery, James A Porter Gallery & the Student Gallery along with Gumbel Print Room, Lois Jones Gallery; Average Annual Attendance: 26,000
Income: School funding
Special Subjects: Graphics, Prints, Sculpture, Watercolors, African Art, Afro-American Art, Renaissance Art, Painting-Italian
Collections: University collection of painting, sculpture & graphic arts by Afro-Americans; Agnes Delano Collection of Contemporary American Watercolors

& Prints; Irving R Gumbel Collection of prints; Kress Study Collection of Renaissance paintings & sculpture; Alain Locke Collection of African art; Era Katz Collection of Theatrical Marquis 1970's-1980's
Exhibitions: Changing tri-monthly exhibits; acad exhibits; ann student show
Publications: Catalogue of the African & Afro-American collections; exhibition catalogues; informational brochures; Native American Arts (serial)
Activities: Bimonthly gallery lect & community programs

L **Architecture & Planning Library,** 2366 Sixth St NW, Washington, DC 20059. Tel 202-806-7773; Internet Home Page Address: www.howarduniversity.edu; *Cur* Sarah Humber
Open Mon - Fri 8:30 AM - 5 PM; No admis fee; Estab for students & staff covering aspects of architecture & Afro American design
Library Holdings: Book Volumes 27,000; CD-ROMs; Filmstrips; Lantern Slides; Other Holdings Documents 600; Periodical Subscriptions 400; Photographs; Reels 1,300; Slides 29,000
Collections: Dominick Collection of pre-1900 books & periodicals on architecture; K Keith Collection of books & photographs on indigenous African architecture

A **THE JOHN F KENNEDY CENTER FOR THE PERFORMING ARTS,** 2700 F St NW, Washington, DC 20566; PO Box 101510, Arlington, VA 22210-4510. Tel 202-416-8000; 467-4600; Fax 202-416-8421; Internet Home Page Address: www.kennedy-center.org; *Chmn* David Rubenstein; *Pres* Michael M Kaiser
Open Mon - Sun 10 AM - 12 AM; No admis fee for building, ticket prices vary; The Center opened in Sept 1971. Facilities include the 2200-seat Opera House, 2750-seat Concert Hall, 1130-seat Eisenhower Theater, 500-seat Terrace Theater, 200-seat family theater & 350-seat Theater Lab. Estab in 1958 by Act of Congress as the National Cultural Center. The Center is the sole official memorial in Washington to President Kennedy. Although the Center does not have an official collection, gifts in the form of art objects from foreign countries are on display throughout; Bureau of the Smithsonian Institution; Administered by a separate Bd of Trustees; Average Annual Attendance: 2,000,000 ticketed, 2,500,000-3,000,000 visitors; Mem: Friends of the Kennedy Center 40,000; dues from $30-$2000
Income: $30,000,000 (financed by ticket revenue & private contributions)
Publications: Kennedy Center News, bimonthly
Activities: Classes for adults & children; dramatic progs; performing arts series for young audiences; lects open to pub, 50 vis lectrs per yr; concerts; tours

L **Education Resources Center,** Madison Building-Library of Congress, Washington, DC 20566. Tel 202-416-8780
Open Tues - Fri 11 AM - 8:30 PM, Sat 10 AM - 6 PM, cl Mon & Sun; Estab 1979 to provide a national information & reference facility for all areas of the performing arts, including film & broadcasting; For reference only. Access to all Library of Congress collections
Income: Grants, gifts & private contributions
Library Holdings: Audio Tapes; Book Volumes 7800; Cassettes; Clipping Files; Exhibition Catalogs; Fiche; Framed Reproductions; Manuscripts; Memorabilia; Pamphlets; Periodical Subscriptions 450; Records; Reels; Reproductions; Slides; Video Tapes

L **LIBRARY OF CONGRESS,** Prints & Photographs Division, 101 Independence Ave SE, Washington, DC 20540-4730. Tel 202-707-6394 (reference), 707-5836 (offices), 707-5000 (general); Fax 202-707-6647; Internet Home Page Address: www.loc.gov/rr/print; Internet Home Page Address: www.loc.gov/rr/askalib/ask-print2.html; *Head Reference Section* Barbara Natanson; *Head Technical Svcs Section* Brett Carnell; *Librn* James H Billington; *Chief Prints & Photograph* Helena Zinkham; *Chief Interpretive* William Jacobs; *Dir Publ Office* W Ralph Eubanks
Reading Room open Mon - Fri 8:30 AM - 5 PM; No admis fee; Estab 1897; Circ 96,000; For reference only; Average Annual Attendance: 1,600,000
Income: Financed by congressional appropriation, gifts & endowments
Purchases: Fine prints, photographs, posters, architectural drawings, historical prints & drawings, cartoons
Library Holdings: Auction Catalogs; Audio Tapes; Book Volumes; CD-ROMs; Cards; Cassettes; Clipping Files; Compact Disks; DVDs; Exhibition Catalogs; Fiche; Filmstrips; Framed Reproductions; Kodachrome Transparencies; Lantern Slides; Manuscripts; Maps 4,562,267; Memorabilia; Micro Print; Motion Pictures; Original Art Works; Original Documents; Other Holdings Architectural items 2,000,000; Fine prints; Master photographs; Photographic images 10,500,000; Popular & applied graphic art item 20,000; Posters 100,000; Pamphlets; Periodical Subscriptions; Photographs; Prints; Records; Reels; Reproductions; Sculpture; Slides; Video Tapes
Collections: Archive of Hispanic Culture; Japanese Prints; Pennell Collection of Whistleriana; Civil War drawings, prints, photographs & negatives; early American lithographs; pictorial archives of early American architecture; Historic American Buildings Survey; Historic American Engineering Record; Cabinet of American Illustration; original fine prints of all schools & periods; Yanker Collection of Propaganda posters; originally designed posters for all periods, dating 1840s - present; Seagram County Court House Collection: Swann Collection of Caricature & Cartoon; American Political Cartoons; Collection of photographs & photographic negatives incl: the Brady-Handy Collection, Farm Security Administration Collection, Alexander Graham Bell Collection, Arnold Genthe, J C H Grabill, F B Johnston, Tony Frissell, Detroit Photographic Co, W H Jackson Collection, George Grantham Bain Collection, H E French Washington Photographs, Matson Near Eastern Collection; NY Work-Telegram & Sun, US News & World Report; Presidential, geographical, biographical & master photograph groupings, captured German photographs of the WW II period & panorama photographs & the Look magazine archive; early 20th Century architecture photograph coll Gottscho-Schleisner
Exhibitions: Permanent collection
Publications: New Field of Vision; Norton/Library of Congress Visual Sourcebooks; A Century of Photographs, 1846-1946; American Prints in the Library of Congress; American Revolution in Drawings & Prints; Eyes of the Nation: A Visual History of the United States; Graphic Sampler; Historic America: Buildings, Structures & Sites; Historic American Buildings Survey; Middle East in Pictures, Prints & Photographs: An Illustrated Guide; Viewpoints; Spec Collections in the Library of Congress; Fine Prints in the Library of Congress: The Poster Collection in the Library of Congress; Popular & Applied Graphic Art in the Library of Congress

Activities: Docent training; lects open to pub; concerts; gallery talks; tours; orientations; fels offered; sales shops sell books, magazines, reproductions

M **MAURINE LITTLETON GALLERY,** 1667 Wisconsin Ave NW, Washington, DC 20007. Tel 202-333-9307; Fax 202-342-2004; Elec Mail info@littletongallery.com; Internet Home Page Address: www.littletongallery.com; *Dir* Harvey K Littleton
Open Tues-Sat 11AM-6PM, other times by appointment
Collections: works by contemporary glass artists; sculpture; ceramics

M **MERIDIAN INTERNATIONAL CENTER,** Cafritz Galleries, 1624 Crescent Pl NW, Washington, DC 20009-4004. Tel 202-667-6800; Fax 202-939-5512; Elec Mail info@meridian.org; Internet Home Page Address: www.meridian.org; *Pres* Ambassador Stuart Holliday; *Head Board of Dirs* Jim Jones
Open Wed - Sun 2 - 5 PM; No admis fee; Estab 1960 to promote international understanding through exchange of people, ideas & the arts; 3000 sq ft, 5 rooms in renovated historic mansion; Average Annual Attendance: 50,000; Mem: donations
Income: Financed by endowment, contributions, arts: private support, grants & corporate support
Publications: Exhibit catalogues; Meridian newsletter, 3 per year
Activities: Docent training; lects open to pub, 2-3 vis lectrs per yr, concerts, tours; originates traveling exhibs

M **NATIONAL ACADEMY OF SCIENCES,** Arts in the Academy, 2101 Constitution Ave, NW, Washington, DC 20418-0007; 500 5th St NW, Rm NAS 271 Washington, DC 20001-2736. Tel 202-334-2436, 2415; Fax 202-334-1690; Elec Mail cpnas@nas.edu; Internet Home Page Address: www7.nationalacademies.org/arts; *Dir* JD Talasek; *Sr Prog Assoc* Alana Quinn
Open Mon - Fri 9 AM - 5 PM, cl weekends & holidays; No admis fee; Exhib of Science Related Art; Two small galleries within operating office building; Average Annual Attendance: 5,000
Income: Organizational endowment
Activities: Lect open to public; concerts

M **NATIONAL AIR AND SPACE MUSEUM,** Smithsonian Institution, Independence Ave at 6th St SW, Washington, DC 20560-0310; PO Box 37012, Office of Public Affairs MRC 321 Washington, DC 20013-7012. Tel 202-633-2214; Fax 202-633-8174; Elec Mail NASM-VisitorServices@si.edu; info@si.edu; Internet Home Page Address: www.nasm.si.edu/museum; *NASM Dir* Gen. John R Dailey; *Pub Rels* Walt Ferrell; *Pub Rels* Claire Brown; *Ctr for Earth* Bruce Campbell; *Deputy Dir* Donald Lopez; *Space History Dept* Allan Needell; *Aeronautics Dept* Dominick Pisano
Open daily 10 AM - 5:30 PM, cl Dec 25; No admis fee; Estab 1946 to memorialize the national develop of aviation & space flight; One gallery comprised of 5,000 sq ft devoted to the theme, Flight & the Arts. Bureau of the Smithsonian Institution; Average Annual Attendance: 8,000,000
Income: Financed through the Smithsonian Institute
Special Subjects: Drawings, Painting-American, Prints, Sculpture
Collections: Paintings, prints & drawings include: Alexander Calder, Lamar Dodd, Richard Estes, Audrey Flack, Francisco Goya, Lowell Nesbitt, Robert Rauschenberg, James Wyeth; major sculptures by Richard Lippold, Alejandro Otero, Charles Perry; Stuart M Speiser Collection of Photo Realist Art
Exhibitions: Exhibitions change annually
Publications: Various publications relating to aviation & space science
Activities: Educ dept; handicapped services; regional resource prog; lects open to pub, 15-20 vis lectrs per yr; concerts; gallery talks; tours; schols offered; individual paintings & original objects of art lent to nonprofit educational institutions; book traveling exhibs; originate traveling exhibs; mus shop sells books, magazines, reproductions, prints, slides, posters, stamp covers, kites, models & jewelry

L **Archives,** 6th St at Independence Ave SW, Washington, DC 20560; Room 3100 MRC 322, PO Box 37012 Washington, DC 20013-7012. Tel 202-633-2320; Fax 202-786-2835; Elec Mail libmail@si.edu; Internet Home Page Address: www.nasm.si.edu/research/arch/; *Branch Librn* William E Baxter; *Reference Lib* Philip Edwards; *Serials & Acquisitions Technician* Leah Smith
Open Mon - Fri 10 AM - 4 PM; Estab 1972 to support research in aerospace field; Library is part of the Smithsonian Institution Libraries system; Libr used for reference; Average Annual Attendance: 4,000
Income: Financed by federal funds
Library Holdings: Audio Tapes; Book Volumes 40,000; Fiche 200,000; Micro Print; Original Documents; Periodical Subscriptions 300; Photographs; Reels 2000
Collections: Aerospace Event Files; Aviation & Space Art; Illustrated Sheet Music; Archives of Personalities; Film & Photography Archives; Technical Drawings; Aircraft Tech Manuals; Tech Reference Files; Captured German & Japanese Documents; Aircraft History Cards; Audio Collections; Paper Print Series; Online exhibs
Publications: NASM Library Guide; NASM Library Periodical Index
Activities: Educ dept; classes for children; docent training; lects open to pub; tours; awards; schols

L **Regional Planetary Image Facility,** Rm 3773 MRC 315, PO Box 37012 Washington, DC 20013-7012. Tel 202-633-2480; Fax 202-786-2566; Internet Home Page Address: www.nasm.si.edu/research/ceps/rpif/; *Dir* Dr Tom Watters; *Data Mgr* Rose Steinat; *Data Asst* Jennifer O'Brien
Open Mon - Fri 10 AM - 4 PM to researchers by appt only; No admis fee; Estab to act as a reference library providing planetary science researchers with access to the extensive collection of image data obtained from planetary missions; At Center for Earth & Planetary Studies within Smithsonian National Air & Space Mus
Library Holdings: CD-ROMs; Original Documents; Photographs

NATIONAL ARCHITECTURAL ACCREDITING BOARD, INC
For further information, see National and Regional Organizations

NATIONAL ASSEMBLY OF STATE ARTS AGENCIES
For further information, see National and Regional Organizations

NATIONAL ENDOWMENT FOR THE ARTS

For further information, see National and Regional Organizations

M **NATIONAL GALLERY OF ART,** Constitution Ave at 4th St NW, Washington, DC 20565; 2000B S Club Dr, Landover, MD 20785-3228. Tel 202-737-4215; Fax 202-789-4976; Elec Mail d-lenoir@nga.gov; Internet Home Page Address: www.nga.gov; Others 202-842-6176 (TDD); *Dir* Earl A Powell III; *Deputy Dir* Franklin Kelly; *Dean, Center for Advanced Study in Visual Arts* Elizabeth Cropper; *Chief Librn* Neal Turtell; *Spec Events Officer* Carol Kelley; *Cur Northern Baroque Painting* Arthur Wheelock; *Cur Renaissance Painting* David Brown; *Cur Sculpture & Decorative Arts* Mary Levkoff; *Educ Div Head* Lynn Russell; *Chief Design & Installation* Mark Leithauser; *Chief Photographic Svcs* Sara Greenough; *Chief Horticulture* Cynthia Kaufmann; *Chief Conservation* Mervin Richard; *Gallery Archivist* Maygene Daniels; *Secy & Gen Counsel* Elizabeth Croog; *Treas* James Duff; *Registrar* Sally Freitag; *Head Music Dept* Stephen Ackert; *Pub Info Officer* Debra Cisco; *Chief Develop & Corporate Rels Officer* Christine Meyers; *Chmn Board Trustees* John Wilmerding
Open Mon - Sat 10 AM - 5 PM; Sun 11 AM - 6 PM; cl Christmas & New Years Day; No admis fee; Affiliate of the Smithsonian Institution; Governed by a separate Board of Trustees composed of 5 Trustees & the Secretary of State, Secretary of the Treasury, US Chief Justice & the Secretary of the Smithsonian Institution; Average Annual Attendance: 6,500,000
Income: Financed by private endowment & federal appropriation
Collections: The Andrew W Mellon Collection of 126 paintings & 26 pieces of sculpture includes Raphael's Alba Madonna, Niccolini-Cowper's Madonna & St George & the Dragon; Van Eyck Annunciation; Botticelli's Adoration of the Magi; nine Rembrandts. Twenty-one of these paintings came from the Hermitage. Also in the original gift were the Vaughan Portrait of George Washington by Gilbert Stuart & The Washington Family by Edward Savage; The Samuel H Kress Collection, given to the nation over a period of years, includes the great tondo The Adoration of the Magi by Fra Angelico & Fra Filippo Lippi, the Laocoon by El Greco & fine examples by Giorgione, Titian, Grunewald, Durer, Memling, Bosch, Francois Clouet, Poussin, Watteau, Chardin, Boucher, Fragonard, David & Ingres. Also included are a number of masterpieces of Italian & French sculpture; In the Widener Collection are paintings by Rembrandt, van Dyck & Vermeer, as well as major works of Italian, Spanish, English & French painting & Italian & French sculpture & decorative arts. The Chester Dale Collection includes masterpieces by Braque, Cezanne, Degas, Gauguin, Manet, Matisse, Modigliani, Monet, Picasso, Pissarro, Renoir, Toulouse-Lautrec, van Gogh & such American painters as George Bellows, Childe Hassam & Gilbert Stuart. Several major works of art by Cezanne, Gauguin, Picasso & the American painter Walt Kuhn were given to the Gallery in 1972 by the W Averell Harriman Foundation in memory of Marie N Harriman; Paintings to round out the collection have been bought with funds provided by the late Ailsa Mellon Bruce. Most important among them are: portrait of Ginevra de' Benci (the only generally acknowledged painting by Leonardo da Vinci outside Europe), Georges de la Tour's Repentant Magdalen, Picasso's Nude Woman-1910, Ruben's Daniel in the Lions' Den, Claude Lorrain's Judgment of Paris, St George & the Dragon attributed to Rogier van der Weyden & a number of American paintings, including Thomas Cole's second set of the Voyage of life; The National Gallery's rapidly expanding graphic arts holdings, in great part given by Lessing J Rosenwald, numbers about 50,000 items & dates from the 12th century to the present. The Index of American Design contains over 17,000 watercolor renderings & 500 photographs of American crafts & folk arts. The National Gallery's Collection continues to be built by private donation, rather than through government funds, which serve solely to operate & maintain the Gallery
Exhibitions: Temporary exhibitions from collections both in the United States & abroad
Publications: A W Mellon Lectures in the Fine Arts; Studies in the History of Art; exhibition catalogs; annual report; monthly calendar of events
Activities: Sunday lects by distinguished quest speakers & members of the staff are given throughout the year; the A W Mellon Lect in the Fine Arts are delivered as a series each spring by an outstanding scholar; concerts are held in the West Garden Court, West Building each Sunday evening between October & June at 7 PM without charge; general tours & lects are given in the Gallery by members of the Educ Dept throughout the week; special tours are arranged for groups; films on art are presented on a varying schedule; color slide programs, films & video cassettes on gallery exhibs & collections, free of charge, free catalog; sponsors Metropolitan Opera auditions; programs to 4900 communities; exten dept provides art loans to galleries around the world; lending collection contains books, cassettes, color reproductions, film strips, framed reproductions, Kodachromes, sculpture & slides; mus shop sells books, magazines, reproductions, prints, slides & video-cassettes

L **Library,** Constitution Ave at 4th St NW, Washington, DC 20565; 2000B S Club Dr, Landover, MD 20785-3228. Tel 202-842-6511; Elec Mail library@nga.gov; Internet Home Page Address: www.nga.gov/resources/dldesc.shtm; *Exec Librn* Neal Turtell; *Head Reader Svcs* Lamia Doumato; *Reference Librn* John Hagood; *Admin Librn* Roger Lawson
Open Mon Noon - 4:30 PM, Tues - Fri 10 AM - 4:30 PM, cl Federal holidays; Estab 1941 to support the national curatorial, educational & research activities & serve as a research center for graduate & undergraduate students, vis scholars & researchers in the visual arts. Supports the research programs of the Center for Advanced Study in the Visual Arts; For reference only
Income: Financed by federal appropriations & trust funds
Library Holdings: Auction Catalogs; Book Volumes 425,000; Clipping Files; Exhibition Catalogs; Fiche; Manuscripts; Micro Print; Other Holdings Vertical Files 125,000; Videodiscs; Pamphlets; Periodical Subscriptions 990; Photographs; Reels; Slides
Collections: Art exhibition, art auction & private art coll catalogs; artist monographs; Leonardo da Vinci, catalogues raisonne; Over 300,000 books, periodicals, & documents on the history, theory, & criticism of art and architecture, with emphasis on Western art from the Middle Ages to the present (particularly Italian, Dutch, Flemish, German, French, Spanish, & British schools) & American art from the colonial era to the present
Publications: NGA Library Guide, 1994 & 1996
Activities: Library tours on request

L **Department of Image Collections,** Constitution Ave at 4th St NW, Washington, DC 20565; 2000B S Club Dr, Landover, MD 20785. Tel 202-842-6026; Fax 202-789-3068; Elec Mail image-collections@nga.gov; Internet Home Page Address: www.nga.gov/resources/dlidesc.htm; *Dep Chief & Architecture Specialist* Andrea Gibbs; *Italian Specialist* Melissa Beck Lemke; *Mod & Contemp Specialist* Meg Melvin; *Staff Asst* Debra Massey; *Circ Asst* Carrie Scharf; *American Specialist* Andrew L Thomas; *French Specialist* Nicholas A Martin; *Spanish Specialist* Thomas A O'Callaghan Jr; *Chief* Gregory P J Most; *Conserv* Sarah Wagner; *Spec Projects Specialist* Lisa M Coldiron; *Northern & Central Europe Specialist* Molli E Kuenstner
Open Mon Noon - 4:30 PM, Tues - Fri 10 AM - 4:30 PM, cl federal holidays; Slide Library (estab 1941) & Photographic Archives (estab 1943) merged in 2004 to Dept of Image Collections; Circ 30,000; The Department of Image Collections is a study and research collection of images documenting European and American art and architecture
Library Holdings: Book Volumes; CD-ROMs 200; Fiche 7,500,000; Lantern Slides; Other Holdings; Photographs 7,000,000; Prints; Slides 225,000
Special Subjects: Art History, Decorative Arts, Drawings, Manuscripts, Painting-American, Painting-British, Painting-Dutch, Painting-Flemish, Painting-French, Painting-German, Painting-Italian, Painting-Russian, Pre-Columbian Art, Prints, Sculpture, Painting-European, Portraits, Watercolors, Ceramics, Bronzes, Furniture, Oriental Art, Religious Art, Silver, Architecture
Publications: Manual for Classifying and Cataloging Images; Guide to the National Gallery of Art Photo Archives

L **Index of American Design,** Constitution Ave at 6th St NW, Washington, DC 20565. Tel 202-842-6605; Fax 202-842-6859; Elec Mail c-ritchie@nga.gov; Internet Home Page Address: www.nga.gov/collection/gallery/iad.htm; *Asst Cur* Ruth Fein; *Asst Cur* Carlotta Owens
Open daily 10 AM - Noon & 2 - 4 PM; No admis fee; Acquired by National Gallery in 1943 to serve as a visual archive of American decorative arts, late 17th through 19th centuries; Visual archive produced between 1935 &1942; Study room with National Gallery print galleries available for exhibitions; offices; storeroom
Library Holdings: Fiche; Original Art Works Watercolors 18,000; Photographs
Special Subjects: Folk Art, Decorative Arts, Watercolors, Ceramics, Furniture, Costume Design & Constr, Glass, Jewelry, Religious Art, Silver, Textiles, Woodcarvings, Architecture
Collections: 18,000 watercolor renderings of American decorative arts objects from the colonial period through the 19th c
Activities: Online slide tours; original objects of art lent to institutions complying with National Gallery lending rules; lending collection contains 11 slide programs available through National Gallery dept of exten programs

NATIONAL LEAGUE OF AMERICAN PEN WOMEN
For further information, see National and Regional Organizations

M **NATIONAL MUSEUM OF AFRICAN ART,** Smithsonian Institution, 950 Independence Ave SW, Washington, DC 20560-0708; PO Box 37012 MRC 708, Washington, DC 20013-7012. Tel 202-633-4600; Fax 202-357-4879; Elec Mail nmafaweb@si.edu; Internet Home Page Address: africa.si.edu; *Pub Affairs* Kimberly Mayfield
Open daily 10 AM - 5:30 PM, cl Dec 25; No admis fee; Estab 1964 to foster public understanding & appreciation of the diverse cultures & artistic achievements in Africa; museum joined the Smithsonian Institution in 1979. Moved in 1987 to the Smithsonian's new museum complex, the Quadrangle on the National Mall; Bureau of the Smithsonian Institution; Average Annual Attendance: 500,000
Income: $4,013,000 (financed by federal funding, mem & contributions)
Library Holdings: Video Tapes
Special Subjects: African Art
Collections: More than 7,000 traditional & contemporary art from throughout the African continent; The Walt Disney-Tishman African Art Coll
Exhibitions: Permanent Exhibitions: Images of Power & Identity; The Art of the Personal Object; The Ancient West African City of Benin, AD 1300-1897; The Ancient Nubien City of Kerma, 2500-1500 BC; Ceramic Art at the National Museum of African Art
Publications: Booklets; exhibition catalogs; multimedia slide kit; pamphlets; videotapes
Activities: Classes for adults & children; docent training; lects open to pub; concerts; gallery talks; films; tours; residency fellowship program; book several traveling exhibs per yr; originates traveling exhibs; mus sales shop sells books, magazines, reproductions, prints, slides, quality crafts, original art, cassettes & CD's, jewelry & other imports from Africa

L **Warren M Robbins Library,** 950 Independence Ave SW Rm 2138, Washington, DC 20560; PO Box 37012 MRC 708, Washington, DC 20013-7012. Tel 202-633-4680; Fax 202-357-4879; Elec Mail AskaLibrarian@si.edu; Internet Home Page Address: www.sil.si.edu/libraries/nmafa/; *Librn* Janet L Stanley; *Libr Technician* Karen F Brown
Open Mon - Fri 9 AM - 5 PM; Estab 1971 to provide major resource center for African art & culture; Library is part of the Smithsonian Institution Libraries system; Branch of Smithsonian Institution Libraries (for reference only)
Income: Financed through Smithsonian budget
Library Holdings: Auction Catalogs; Audio Tapes; Book Volumes 32,000; Clipping Files; DVDs; Exhibition Catalogs; Maps; Pamphlets; Periodical Subscriptions; Video Tapes
Special Subjects: Photography, Sculpture, Crafts, Archaeology, Printmaking, Pottery, Textiles, Architecture

L **Eliot Elisofon Photographic Archives,** 950 Independence Ave SW, Washington, DC 20560; PO Box 37012, Washington, DC 20013-7012. Tel 202-633-4690; Fax 202-357-4879; Elec Mail elisofonarchives@si.edu; Internet Home Page Address: africa.si.edu/research/archives.html
Open Tues - Thurs 10 AM - 4 PM by appt; No admis fee; fees for use of archive images; Estab 1973; devoted to the collection, preservation & dissemination of visual materials that encourage & support the study of the arts, cultures & history of Africa
Library Holdings: Lantern Slides; Maps; Motion Pictures 120,000 ft of film; Other Holdings; Photographs 80,000; Slides 180,000
Collections: Eliot Elisofon Coll: over 50,000 black-and-white negatives & photographs, 30,000 color slides, & 120,000 feet of motion picture film and sound materials; Constance Stuart Larrabee Coll: over 5,000 black-and-white photographs taken in South Africa between 1936 & 1983; Henry Drewal & Margaret Thompson Drewal Coll: over 10,000 slides depicting Yoruba art & culture; Historical coll of over 13,000 postcards; Special colls include late 19th- &

early 20th- c photographic albums; Total archives coll contains approximately 300,000 items, incl rare collections of glass plate negatives, lantern slides, stereographs, postcards, maps & engravings

M NATIONAL MUSEUM OF AMERICAN HISTORY, Smithsonian Institution, 14th St & Constitution Ave NW, Washington, DC 20560; PO Box 37012, MRC 010 Washington, DC 20013-7012. Tel 202-633-1000; Elec Mail info@si.edu; Internet Home Page Address: http://americanhistory.si.edu; *Interim Dir* Marc Pachter
Open daily 10 AM - 5:30 PM, cl Dec 25, open late select evenings in winter; No admis fee; Estab 1964 as Mus of History & Tech, name changed 1980, reopened 2008 following renovation; The Mus is devoted to the collection, care, study & exhibition of objects that reflect the experience of the American people, as well as sharing & honoring the cultural achievements of Native Americans from North, Central & South America. West Wing renovations 2012-2014. Bureau of the Smithsonian Institution; Average Annual Attendance: 5,000,000; Mem: Charter mem dues start at $20
Special Subjects: American Indian Art, Sculpture, Etchings & Engravings
Collections: Agriculture, armed forces, automobiles, ceramics, locomotives, musical instruments, numismatics, political history, textiles, popular culture, domestic life, technology information, electricity, science, medicine
Exhibitions: Several rotating exhibitions per year; The American Presidency; A Glorious Burden; Within These Walls...; America on the Move; Star-Spangled Banner-The Flag that inspired the National Anthem; Price of Freedom: Americans at War; Julia Child's Kitchen; Communities in a Changing Nation; The First Ladies
Publications: Exhibition brochures & catalogs; related research publications
Activities: Activities for adults & children; docent training; internship & fellowship progs; lects open to pub; concerts; gallery talks; tours; lending original objects to Smithsonian affiliated mus; originate traveling exhibs to affiliated mus; mus shop sells books, magazines, reproductions, prints, souvenirs, jewelry, clothing
L Branch Library, 14th St & Constitution Ave NW, Washington, DC 20560-0001. Tel 202-357-2036, 357-2414; Fax 202-357-4256; Internet Home Page Address: www.sil.si.edu; *Librn* Rhoda Ratner
Open daily 10AM-5:30PM; Library is part of the Smithsonian Institution Libraries system; Open to staff & vis scholars
Income: Financed through SIL budgets
Library Holdings: Book Volumes 165,000; Fiche; Periodical Subscriptions 450; Reels
Special Subjects: Decorative Arts, Photography, Graphic Design, Historical Material, Furniture, Metalwork, Carpets & Rugs, Pottery, Silver, Textiles

M NATIONAL MUSEUM OF THE AMERICAN INDIAN, Smithsonian Institution, 4th St & Independence Ave SW, Washington, DC 20560; PO Box 23473, Washington, DC 20026-3473. Tel 202-633-1000; 800-242-NMAI (6624); Internet Home Page Address: www.nmai.si.edu; *Dir* W Richard West Jr
Open Daily 10 AM - 5:30 PM, cl Dec 25; No admis fee; Mem: Dues Sky Meadows Cir $100, Everglades Cir $50, Riverbed Cir $35, Golden Prairie Cir $20
Special Subjects: American Indian Art, Anthropology, Archaeology, Decorative Arts, Ceramics, Photography, Textiles, Ethnology, Religious Art, Primitive art, Eskimo Art, Jewelry, Embroidery
Collections: Wood, stone carvings & masts from the coast of NW America; painted & quilled hides; clothing & feathered bonnets from North American Plains; pottery & basketry from Southwestern US; 18th c materials from the Great Lakes Region; C B Moore Coll from the Southeastern US; Navajo wearings; works on paper & canvas; funerary, religious & ceremonial objects
Activities: Educ progs; docent training; outreach progs; internships; lects open to pub; seminars; symposia; mus shop sells books, CDs, DVDs, cards, specialty items
L Archives, 4220 Silver Hill Road, Cultural Resources Center Suitland, MD 20746-2863. Tel 301-238-1400; Fax 301-238-3038; Elec Mail nmaiarchives@si.edu; nmaiphotos@si.edu (Photo Requests); Internet Home Page Address: www.nmai.si.edu; *Head Archivist* Jennifer R O'Neal; *Media Archivist* Michael Pahn; *Photo Archivist* Lou Stancari; *Photo Archives Tech* Emily Moazami; *Archive Asst* Rachel Telford
Open Mon - Fri 9:30AM - 4:30 PM to researchers by appt only; No admis fee
Library Holdings: Audio Tapes; Book Volumes; Compact Disks; Lantern Slides; Manuscripts; Maps; Memorabilia; Motion Pictures; Original Documents; Photographs; Slides; Video Tapes
Special Subjects: Photography
Collections: Paper Archives: contains approx 1500 ft of records & special colls from 1830s on, documenting the history of NMAI & MAI; official records incl correspondence, memoranda, photographs, & audio material pertaining to MAI founder & staff; other records include unpublished manuscripts, field notebooks with original drawings, site diagrams, maps, scrapbooks, photographs, object coll listings, exhibit planning materials, & correspondence pertaining to research expeditions, collecting projects, & collectors; Maintains Board of Trustees records, annual reports, & copies of NMAI publications; Special colls incl National Congress of the American Indian (NCAI) Archives, Leuman Maurice Waugh Papers, Reuben Snake Papers, & ARROW, Inc. records.; Photo Archives: approx 324,000 images, negatives, vintage prints, transparencies, lantern slides, glass-plate negatives, color slides & digital photos documenting Native American culture & history from the mid-19th c to present; incl historic scenes, portraits, field photographs of mus ethnographic & archaeological expeditions in Mexico & North, South & Central America, & recordings of contemporary Native American artists; Media Archives: 12,000+ video tapes, motion picture films, & audio recordings, from 1902 to the present representing communities from N & S America in interviews, performances, cinematic films, & documentary recordings; contemporary Native American cinema; variety of formats incl motion picture film, analog & digital video tape recordings, & audio recordings on wax cylinders, phonograph discs, audio tape, & CDs falling into 3 categories - archival recordings, mus progs documentation, & Native Cinema study collection

M NATIONAL MUSEUM OF WOMEN IN THE ARTS, 1250 New York Ave NW, Washington, DC 20005-3970. Tel 202-783-5000; Fax 202-393-3235; Elec Mail media@nmwa.org; Internet Home Page Address: www.nmwa.org; *Dir* Susan Fisher Sterling; *Dir of Library & Research Center* Heather Slania; *Mgr Communs & Mktg* Amy Mannarino
Open Mon - Sat 10 AM - 5 PM, Sun Noon - 5 PM, cl Thanksgiving, Christmas & New Year's Days, group tours by appointment; Admis adults $10, seniors (65+) & students $8, youth 18 & under and NMWA members free, 1st Sun of month free; Estab 1981 to promote knowledge & appreciation of women artists through exhibits, publications, educ programs & library services; Maintains library; Average Annual Attendance: 100,000; Mem: 16,000
Income: Private non-profit
Library Holdings: Audio Tapes; Clipping Files; Exhibition Catalogs; Slides; Video Tapes
Special Subjects: Latin American Art, Painting-American, Photography, American Indian Art, American Western Art, Costumes, Ceramics, Crafts, Etchings & Engravings, Landscapes, Afro-American Art, Decorative Arts, Jewelry, Asian Art, Calligraphy
Collections: Over 4,500 works by women artists from 16th c. to present. Incl paintings, sculpture & pottery; 600 unique & limited edition artists' books; Women silversmiths; Botanical prints
Exhibitions: Selections from the permanent collection (indefinitely)
Publications: Exhibit catalogs, women artists (Oct 2000); Women in the Arts, quarterly magazine
Activities: Classes for adults & children; dramatic progs; docent training; films; teacher progs; lects open to pub; lects for mems only; concerts; gallery talks; tours; library fellows award; individual paintings & original objects of art lent; book exhibs 1 per yr; originate traveling exhibs; mus shop sells books, prints & reproductions, jewelry, crafts
L Library & Research Center, 1250 New York Ave NW, Washington, DC 20005. Tel 202-783-7365; Fax 202-393-3234; Internet Home Page Address: www.nmwa.org; *Dir of Libr & Res Ctr* Heather Slania
Open Mon - Fri 10 AM - 5 PM, by appointment to researchers only; No admis fee
Library Holdings: Audio Tapes; Book Volumes 16,000; Cassettes; DVDs; Exhibition Catalogs; Manuscripts; Memorabilia; Original Art Works; Original Documents; Other Holdings Artists files; Pamphlets; Periodical Subscriptions; Photographs; Prints; Reproductions; Slides; Video Tapes
Special Subjects: Decorative Arts, Calligraphy, Drawings, Etchings & Engravings, Ceramics, Crafts, Bronzes, Asian Art, Bookplates & Bindings, Embroidery, Jewelry, Laces
Collections: Irene Rice Pereira Library; Collection of Artists' Books; Collection of Bookplates; Archives of the International Festival of Women Artists in Copenhagen, Denmark, 1980; Frida Kahlo letters
Activities: Classes for adults & children; docent training; Lects open to pub; concerts; gallery talks; tours; competitions; Mellor Prize; original objects of art & individual paintings lent to mus; book traveling exhibs 2-3 per yr; originate traveling exhibs to mus; mus shop sells books, magazines, original art; reproductions, prints, slides, artisan crafts

M THE NATIONAL PARK SERVICE, UNITED STATES DEPARTMENT OF THE INTERIOR, Statue of Liberty National Monument & The Ellis Island Immigration Museum, 1849 C St NW, Dept of Interior Washington, DC 20240-0001. Tel 212-363-3206 x150, 148, 159,155; Fax 212-363-6302; Elec Mail stli museum@nps.gov; Internet Home Page Address: www.nps.gov/stli; *Cur Coll* Geraldine Santoro; *Supervisory Archivist* George Tselos; *Chief Cur* Diana Pardue; *Library Technician* Barry Moreno; *Library Technician* Jeff Dosik; *Cur Exhibs & Media* Judy Giuriceo
Open 9:30 AM - 5 PM; No admis fee, donations accepted; Estab 1972; Exhibit areas in base of Statue of Liberty & in Ellis Island Immigration Museum; Average Annual Attendance: 4,000,000
Library Holdings: Audio Tapes; Book Volumes; CD-ROMs; Clipping Files; DVDs; Filmstrips; Kodachrome Transparencies; Manuscripts; Maps; Motion Pictures; Periodical Subscriptions; Photographs; Prints; Records; Slides; Video Tapes
Special Subjects: Architecture, Graphics, Painting-American, Photography, Prints, Sculpture, Archaeology, Textiles, Costumes, Religious Art, Ceramics, Folk Art, Etchings & Engravings, Decorative Arts, Judaica, Manuscripts, Posters, Furniture, Historical Material, Coins & Medals, Restorations, Embroidery, Cartoons
Collections: Ellis Island Collection; Statue of Liberty Collection; Furniture Art Work, oral histories, prints, manuscripts, films & videos, books, periodicals, historic structures
Exhibitions: Ellis Island Exhibits; Statue of Liberty exhibit
Activities: Classes for children; dramatic progs; docent training; lects open to pub; gallery talks; tours; individual paintings & original objects of art lent to other mus; book traveling exhibs; sales shop sells books, magazines, reproductions, original art, prints & slides

M NATIONAL PORTRAIT GALLERY, Smithsonian Institution, F St at Eighth NW, Washington, DC 20560; PO Box 37012, Washington, DC 20013-7012. Tel 202-633-8300; Fax 202-633-8254; Elec Mail npgnews@si.edu; Internet Home Page Address: www.npg.si.edu; *Dir* Kim Sajet; *Chief Cur* Brandon B Fortune; *Assoc Dir Opers* Nik Apostolides; *Chief Design & Production* Tibor Waldner; *Cur Exhib* Claire Kelly; *Cur Photographs* Ann Shumard; *Cur Prints & Drawings* Wendy W Reaves; *Keeper Catalog of American Portraits* Linda Thrift; *Senior Historian* Sidney Hart; *Conservator* Cindy Lou Molnar; *Chief Photographer* Mark Gulezian; *Pub Affairs Officer* Bethany Bentley; *Publications Officer* Dru Dowdy; *Dir External Affairs & Develop* Jennifer Renner; *Coll Mgr* John McMahon; *Registrar Exhibs & Loans* Molly Grimsley; *Cur Latino Art & History* Taina Caragol
Open daily 11:30 AM - 7:00PM; cl Dec 25; No admis fee; Estab by Act of Congress in 1962 as a mus of the Smithsonian Institution for the exhibition & study of portraiture depicting men & women who have made significant contributions to the history, develop & culture of the people of the United States; History of America through the individuals who have shaped its culture. Gallery portrays poets & presidents, visionaries & villains, actors & activists whose lives tell the American story. Bureau of the Smithsonian Institution; Average Annual Attendance: 1,000,000

Income: Financed by federal appropriation & private contributions
Special Subjects: Drawings, Painting-American, Photography, Prints, Sculpture, Watercolors, Bronzes, Woodcarvings, Woodcuts, Etchings & Engravings, Portraits, Posters, Historical Material, Miniatures, Cartoons
Collections: Portraits of significant Americans, preferably executed from life, in all media: oils, watercolors, charcoal, pen & ink, daguerreotypes, photographs; video; portraits of American Presidents; 1800 original works of art from the Time Magazine Cover coll; more than 5000 glass plate negatives by Mathew Brady & studio in the Meserve Coll
Publications: Large-scale, richly illustrated publications accompany major shows & provide comprehensive analysis of exhibition themes; documentary, audio & visual materials designed to be used as teaching guides; American portraiture
Activities: Classes for adults & children; dramatic progs; Outreach progs for elementary & secondary schools, senior citizens groups, docent training; lects open to the pub; scheduled walk-in tours for special groups, adults, families & schools; films; Cultures In Motion, (special musical & dramatic events); gallery talks; organize traveling exhibs; mus shop sells books, magazines, reproductions, recordings, jewelry & gifts

L **Library,** 750 9th St NW, Washington, DC 20560; PO Box 37012, Victor Bldg Ste 8300 MRC Washington, DC 20013-7012. Tel 202-633-8230; 633-8240 (Reference); Fax 202-275-1929; Elec Mail chinc@si.edu; Internet Home Page Address: www.sil.si.edu/libraries/aapg/; *Acting Head Librn* Doug Litts; *Serials Librn* Stephanie Moye; *Libr Tech* Alice Clarke
Open Mon - Fri 10 AM - 5 PM, cl Federal holidays; Branch of Smithsonian Institution Libraries; shared with American Art Mus
Library Holdings: Book Volumes 100,000; Clipping Files; Exhibition Catalogs; Fiche; Manuscripts; Periodical Subscriptions 800; Reels; Reproductions

M **NATIONAL POSTAL MUSEUM,** Smithsonian Institution, 2 Massachusetts Ave NE, Washington, DC 20002; PO Box 37012 MRC 570, Washington, DC 20013-7012. Tel 202-633-5555; Internet Home Page Address: www.postalmuseum.si.edu; *Dir* Allen Kane; *Cur* Cheryl Ganz; *Cur* Nancy Pope; *Exhibs* Eric Chapman; *Develop Officer* Amy Borntrager; *Special Events Coordr* Beth Simmonds; *Pub Rels Mgr* Marty Emery; *Registrar* Ted Wilson
Open daily 10 AM - 5:30 PM, cl Dec 25; No admis fee; Coll estab 1886, housed in Arts & Industries Bldg from 1908 - 1963, housed in National Mus of American History from 1964 - 1992, until creation of Natl Postal Mus in 1990 & mus opening in 1993; Located on the lower level of the historic City Post Office Building, which was constructed in 1914 and served as the Washington, D.C., post office from 1914 through 1986. Museum occupies 75,000 sq ft of the bldg with 23,000 sq ft of exhib space
Income: Financed by US Postal Svc, annual federal appropriation via the Smithsonian Institution, & gifts from pvt individuals, foundations, & corporations
Library Holdings: Exhibition Catalogs; Memorabilia; Original Documents; Other Holdings; Pamphlets; Periodical Subscriptions; Photographs; Prints; Reproductions; Sculpture
Exhibitions: Permanent exhibs incl: Binding the Nation; Customers & Communities; Moving the Mail; Philatelic Gallery; Multiple online exhibs; (2/7/2007 - Indefinitely) Postal Inspectors: The Silence Service; Collecting History; (03/22/2012-01/06/2014) Fire & Ice: Hindenburg & Titanic; Systems at Work (12/14/2011- indefinitely); Mail Call (11/10/2011 - indefinitely); (09/26/2008-01/31/2014) Pony Express: Romance vs Reality, Alphabetilately; Networking a Nation: Star Route Service
Activities: Classes for adults & children; docent training; lects open to pub; gallery talks; tours; symposia; Smithsonian Philatelic Achievement Awards; stamp shop; mus store sells books

L **Library,** 2 Massachusetts Ave NE, Washington, DC 20560-0570; PO Box 37012 MRC 570, Washington, DC 20013-7012. Tel 202-633-5544; Elec Mail libmail@si.edu; Internet Home Page Address: www.sil.si.edu/libraries/npm/; *Librn* Paul McCutcheon; *Libr Tech* MaryAnn Wilson
Open Mon - Fri 10 AM - 4:30 PM & 3rd Sat of month 10 am - 4 pm by appt only, cl Federal holidays; No admis fee; 6,000 sq ft
Library Holdings: Book Volumes 40,000; Other Holdings Journals; Catalogs; Archival Documents
Collections: Postal & Philatelic Files Online; Butler & Carpenter Correspondence; Railway Mail Service; Aerial Mail Service; Highway Post Office; Panama Canal Zone Post Office; Frederick J Melville working papers; Thaddeus P Hyatt working papers

M **NATIONAL TRUST FOR HISTORIC PRESERVATION,** 1785 Massachusetts Ave NW, Washington, DC 20036-2117. Tel 202-588-6000; Fax 202-588-6038; Elec Mail info@nthp.org; Internet Home Page Address: www.preservationnation.org; *Pres* Stephanie Meeks; *Dir Interpretation* Max Van Balgooy; *Architect* Barbara Campagna; *Dir Mus Coll* Terri Anderson; *VPres* James Vaughan; *Admin Dir* Lyn Moriarity
Open to the pub, hours & fees vary with the property, cl Christmas, New Year's, call for information; Founded 1949, the National Trust for Historic Preservation is the only national, nonprofit, private organization chartered by Congress to encourage pub participation in the preservation of sites, buildings & objects significant in American history & culture; Its services, counsel & educ on preservation & historic property interpretation & admin, are carried out at national & regional headquarters in consultation with adv in each state & U S Territory; Mem: 265,000; dues sustaining $100, active $20, student $15
Income: Financed by mem dues, contributions & matching grants from the US Department of the Interior, National Park Service, under provision of the National Historic Preservation Act of 1966
Special Subjects: Decorative Arts, Furniture
Collections: Fine & decorative arts furnishing nine historic house museums: Chesterwood, Stockbridge, MA; Cliveden, Philadelphia, PA; Decatur House & Woodrow Wilson House, Washington, DC; Drayton Hall, Charleston, SC; Lyndhurst, Tarrytown, NY; Oatlands, Leesburg, VA; The Shadows-on-the-Teche, New Iberia, LA; Woodlawn/Pope-Leighey Plantation House, Mt Vernon, VA. (For additional information, see separate listings)
Publications: Preservation Magazine, bi-monthly

M **Decatur House,** 748 Jackson Pl NW, Washington, DC 20006-4912. Tel 202-842-0920; Fax 202-842-0030; *Exec Dir* Paul Reber
Open Tues - Fri 10 AM - 3 PM, Sat & Sun Noon - 4 PM, cl Mon; No admis fee; Estab 1958, bequeathed to National Trust for Historic Preservation by Mrs Truxton Beale to foster appreciation & interest in the history & culture of the city of Washington, DC; The House is a Federal period townhouse designed by Benjamin Henry Latrobe & completed in 1819; Average Annual Attendance: 19,000; Mem: National Trust members
Income: Financed by endowment & mem
Special Subjects: Furniture, Period Rooms
Collections: Furniture & memorabilia of the Federal period; Victorian house furnishings
Exhibitions: Special exhibits
Activities: Lect open to public, 2-3 vis lectrs per year; concerts; individual paintings & original objects of art lent; sales shop sells books, magazines, reproductions, prints & Christmas decorations

M **NAVAL HISTORICAL CENTER,** The Navy Museum, Washington Navy Yard, 901 M St SE Washington, DC 20374-5060; 805 Kidder Breese SE, Washington Navy Yard Washington, DC 20374-5060. Tel 202-433-4882; Fax 202-433-8200; Internet Home Page Address: www.history.navy.mil; *Cur* Dr Edward Furgol; *Pub Prog* Shelia Brennan; *Dir* Kim Nielsen; *Art Coll Cur* Gale Munro
Open Mon-Fri 9AM-5PM, Sat-Sun 1-5PM; No admis fee & parking; Estab 1961 to present history & preserve heritage of US Navy; 48,000 sq ft exhibit area; Average Annual Attendance: 150,000
Income: Financed by federal appropriations
Special Subjects: Architecture, Drawings, Graphics, Painting-American, Photography, Prints, Sculpture, Watercolors, Bronzes, Archaeology, Costumes, Ceramics, Folk Art, Woodcuts, Etchings & Engravings, Decorative Arts, Manuscripts, Portraits, Posters, Furniture, Glass, Porcelain, Asian Art, Silver, Marine Painting, Metalwork, Ivory, Maps, Scrimshaw, Coins & Medals, Calligraphy, Miniatures, Dioramas, Embroidery, Cartoons, Leather, Military Art
Collections: History of US Navy from 1775 to Space Age; Naval Art; Paintings; Prints; Watercolors; Naval Artifacts; Fighting Top of Constitution; WW II Corsair (744 plane)
Exhibitions: Changing art exhibitions; Polar Exploration; Perry & Japan
Activities: Docent training; tours; concerts; internships; 10 vis lectrs per yr; individual paintings & original objects of art lent to pub institutions; mus shop sells books, reproductions, prints, postcards, jewelry, t-shirts, models & nautical accessories

M **THE PHILLIPS COLLECTION,** 1600 21st St NW, Washington, DC 20009-1090. Tel 202-387-2151; Fax 202-319-0070; Elec Mail communications@phillipscollection.org; Internet Home Page Address: www.phillipscollection.org; *Dir* Dorothy M Kosinski; *Chief Admin & Financial Officer* Susan J Nichols; *Chief Cur* Eliza Rathbone; *Chief Registrar* Joseph Holbach; *Dir Budgeting & Reporting* Cheryl Nichols; *Dir Mktg & Communs* Ann Greer; *Dir Develop* Kara Mullins; *Dir Educ* Suzanne Wright; *Dir Operations & Security* Dan Datlow; *Chief Information Officer* Darci Vanderhoff; *Ed-in-Chief* Johanna Halford-MacLeod
Open Tues - Sat 10 AM - 5 PM, Sun 11 AM - 6 PM, Thurs 10 AM - 8:30 PM; Admis price varies with each exhib and includes admis to the permanent coll; discounts to seniors & students; Open to the pub 1921 to show & interpret the best of contemporary painting in the context of outstanding works of the past; to underscore this intent through the presentation of concerts & lectures; The original building, a Georgian Revival residence designed in 1897 by Hornblower & Marshall, was added to in 1907 & renovated in 1983-84. A modern annex connected by a double bridge to the old gallery was opened to the public in 1960 & renovated in 1987-89. In Apr 2006 the Phillips celebrated the opening of its new Sant Bldg which adds 30,000 sf of expanded gallery spaces, a 180 seat auditorium, new educational spaces & more; Average Annual Attendance: 150,000; Mem: 9,000; dues corporate mem $10,000; individual $60-$50,000 & up
Income: $12,000,000 (financed by endowment, mem, contributions, grants, sales, rental fees & exhibition fees)
Library Holdings: Auction Catalogs; Book Volumes; Clipping Files; Exhibition Catalogs; Periodical Subscriptions; Photographs
Special Subjects: Etchings & Engravings, Folk Art, Photography, Portraits, Prints, Woodcuts, Painting-European, Painting-French, Graphics, Painting-American, Watercolors, Painting-Spanish, Painting-Italian, Painting-Russian, Painting-Scandinavian
Collections: 19th & 20th century American & European painting with special emphasis on units of particular artists such as Bonnard, Braque, Cezanne, Daumier, de Stael, Dufy, Rouault & Americans such as Avery, Dove, Gatch, Knaths, Marin, O'Keeffe, Prendergast, Rothko & Tack. The best known painting is Renoir's Luncheon of the Boating Party
Publications: magazine, three times annually & books
Activities: Classes for adults & children; docent training; lects open to pub, 35 vis lectrs per yr; weekly concerts Oct-May; gallery talks; tours; Duncan Phillips award; individual paintings & original objects of art lent to select national & international mus; book traveling exhibs 3-5 per yr; originate traveling exhibs to national & international mus; mus sales shop sells books, magazines, reproductions, prints, slides, jewelry & original crafts

L **Library,** 1600 21st St NW, Washington, DC 20009. Tel 202-387-2151, Ext 212; Fax 202-387-2436; Elec Mail kschneider@phillipscollection.org; Internet Home Page Address: www.phillipscollection.org; *Librn* Karen Schneider; *Cataloguing & Technical Svcs Librn* Sarah Osbourne Bender; *Archives Asst* Colleen Henessey
Available research hours Tues-Fri 10AM-4:30PM; Estab 1978; Available to serious students, researchers & mus professionals, by appointment. Reference only; Average Annual Attendance: 60
Library Holdings: Book Volumes 6500; Clipping Files; Exhibition Catalogs; Filmstrips; Other Holdings Vertical files; Pamphlets; Periodical Subscriptions 20; Reels 60
Special Subjects: Art History, Collages, Folk Art, Decorative Arts, Photography, Drawings, Etchings & Engravings, Graphic Arts, Manuscripts, Painting-American, Painting-British, Painting-French, Painting-European, History of Art & Archaeology, Portraits, Latin American Art, Printmaking, Lettering, Art Education, Asian Art, Primitive art, Eskimo Art, Furniture, Mexican Art, Aesthetics, Afro-American Art, Leather
Activities: Lects open to pub; 70 lectrs per yr; concerts; gallery talks; tours; awards, Phillips Coll book prize; organize traveling exhibs to mus in US & abroad; sales shop sells books, original art, reproductions & prints

M POPE JOHN PAUL II CULTURAL CENTER, 3900 Harewood Rd NE, Washington, DC 20017-1505. Tel 202-635-5400; Fax 202-635-5411; Elec Mail info@jp2cc.org; Internet Home Page Address: www.jp2cc.org
Open Tues - Sat 10 AM - 5 PM, Sun 12 - 5 PM; Admis suggested donations families $15, seniors & students $4, discounts to member
Collections: paintings; statues; Catholic Church history; Papal & Polish heritage; photographs
Activities: Lect; children's activities

L PUBLIC LIBRARY OF THE DISTRICT OF COLUMBIA, Art Division, 901 G St NW, Martin Luther King Memorial Library Washington, DC 20001-4531. Tel 202-727-1291; Fax 202-727-1129; Elec Mail george-mckinley.martin@dc.gov; Internet Home Page Address: www.dclibrary.org; *Chief Art Div* George-McKinley Martin; *Librn* Patricia Wood; *Librn* S Michele Casto
Open winter & summer Mon - Thurs 9:30 AM - 9 PM, Fri 9:30 AM - 5:30 PM, Sat 9:30 AM - 5:30 PM, Sun 1 - 5 PM; No admis fee
Income: Financed by city government appropriation
Library Holdings: Auction Catalogs; Book Volumes 48,961; Clipping Files; Exhibition Catalogs; Original Art Works; Pamphlets; Periodical Subscriptions 95; Reels
Special Subjects: Art History, Calligraphy, American Western Art, Bronzes, Asian Art, American Indian Art, Aesthetics, Afro-American Art, Antiquities-Oriental, Antiquities-Assyrian, Antiquities-Byzantine, Antiquities-Egyptian, Antiquities-Etruscan, Antiquities-Greek, Architecture
Collections: Reference & circulating books & periodicals on architecture, painting, sculpture, photography, graphic & applied arts; extensive pamphlet file including all art subjects, with special emphasis on individual American artists & on more than 1400 artists active in the area; circulating picture collection numbering over 81,519 mounted reproductions
Exhibitions: Special exhibitions held occasionally
L Audiovisual Division, 901 G St NW, Rm 226, Martin Luther King Memorial Library Washington, DC 20001-4531. Tel 202-727-1265; Fax 202-727-1129; Elec Mail www.avdcpl@yahoo.com; *Chief* Eric White; *Film & Video Librn* Turner Freeman
Open Mon - Thurs 10 AM - 9 PM, Fri 10 AM - 5:30 PM, Sun 10 AM - 5:30 PM
Purchases: 16 mm, VHS
Library Holdings: Cassettes; Motion Pictures; Other Holdings Books-on-tape; Periodical Subscriptions 15; Records; Video Tapes

M SMITHSONIAN INSTITUTION, 1000 Jefferson Dr, SW, Washington, DC 20560-0008; PO Box 37012, SI Building, Room 153, MRC 010 Washington, DC 20013-7012. Tel 202-633-1000; Elec Mail info@si.edu; Internet Home Page Address: www.si.edu; *Secy* Lawrence Small; *Under Secy for Science* J Dennis O'Connor; *Under Secy Designate for Finance & Admin* Robert D Bailey; *Under Secy for American Museums and Nat'l Programs* Sheila Burke; *Dir Int'l Art Museums* Thomas Lentz; *Sr Bus Officer* Gary Beer
Open daily 10 AM - 5:30 PM, cl Dec 25; No admis fee; Estab 1846, when James Smithson bequeathed his fortune to the United States, under the name of the Smithsonian Institution, an establishment in Washington for the increase & diffusion of knowledge. To carry out the terms of Smithson's will, the Institution performs fundamental research; preserves for study & reference approx 140 million items of scientific, cultural & historical interest; maintains exhibits representative of the arts, American history, aeronautics & space exploration; technology; natural history & engages in progs of educ & national & international cooperative research & training; The Smithsonian Institution is the world's largest museum complex composed of 14 museums & the National Zoo in Washington, DC & the Cooper-Hewitt, National Design Museum & the National Museum of the American Indian in New York City; see separate listings for complete information on the bureaus listed below; Average Annual Attendance: 31,000,000; Mem: Several programs, call for info
Income: Financed by federal appropriations & private monies
Special Subjects: American Indian Art, Decorative Arts, Ceramics, Portraits, African Art, Crafts, Asian Art
Activities: Classes for adults & children; dramatic progs; docent training; lects open to pub; concerts; gallery talks; tours; awards; schols & fels; for information call Smithsonian Institution Traveling Exhibs at 202-357-3168; mus stores sell books, magazines, original art, reproductions, prints, slides & gifts
  —Anacostia Community Museum,
See separate listing in Washington, DC
  —Archives of American Art,
See separate listing in Washington, DC
  —Cooper-Hewitt National Design Museum,
See separate listing in New York, NY
  —Hirshhorn Museum & Sculpture Garden,
See separate listing in Washington, DC
  —John F Kennedy Center for the Performing Arts,
See separate listing in Washington, DC; Administered under a separate Board of Trustees
  —National Air & Space Museum,
See separate listing in Washington, DC
  —American Art Museum,
Includes the Renwick Gallery. See separate listing in Washington, DC
  —National Gallery of Art,
See separate listing in Washington, DC
  —National Museum of American History,
See separate listing in Washington, DC
  —National Portrait Gallery,
See separate listing in Washington, DC
  —Arthur M Sackler Gallery,
See separate listing in Washington, DC
  —Freer Gallery of Art,
See separate listing in Washington, DC
  —National Museum of African Art,
See separate listing in Washington, DC
  —National Museum of the American Indian,
See separate listing in Washington, DC

  —National Postal Museum,
See separate listing in Washington, DC

M THE SOCIETY OF THE CINCINNATI AT ANDERSON HOUSE, 2118 Massachusetts Ave NW, Washington, DC 20008-3640. Tel 202-785-2040; Fax 202-785-0729; Elec Mail admin@societyofthecincinnati.org; Internet Home Page Address: www.societyofthecincinnati.org; *Dir Library* Ellen McCallister Clark; *Deputy Dir & Cur* Emily L Schulz; *Exec Dir* Jack D Warren Jr; *Mus Vis Svcs Coordr* Caren Pauley
Museum open Tues-Sat 1-4PM; library open Mon - Fri 10AM-4PM by appointment; No admis fee; Museum estab 1938. Serves as the National Headquarters Museum & Library of the Society of the Cincinnati; Collects, preserves & interprets the history of American Revolution, the Society of Cincinnati & Anderson House & its occupants; Historic house museum of Anderson House, a 1905 beaux-arts mansion & the Winter residence of Larz Anderson III & his wife Isabel Weld Perkins from 1905-1937. One temp exhib gallery displays two changing exhib each yr; Average Annual Attendance: 10,000
Library Holdings: Auction Catalogs; Book Volumes; CD-ROMs; Clipping Files; Compact Disks; DVDs; Exhibition Catalogs; Fiche; Framed Reproductions; Manuscripts; Maps; Memorabilia; Motion Pictures; Original Art Works; Original Documents; Pamphlets; Periodical Subscriptions; Photographs; Prints; Video Tapes
Special Subjects: Decorative Arts, Drawings, Etchings & Engravings, Historical Material, Metalwork, Painting-American, Prints, Silver, Textiles, Manuscripts, Maps, Painting-British, Painting-European, Painting-French, Painting-Japanese, Tapestries, Graphics, Sculpture, Watercolors, Bronzes, Costumes, Religious Art, Ceramics, Portraits, Posters, Furniture, Glass, Jade, Jewelry, Porcelain, Oriental Art, Asian Art, Carpets & Rugs, Ivory, Coins & Medals, Baroque Art, Miniatures, Renaissance Art, Dioramas, Period Rooms, Antiquities-Roman, Military Art, Bookplates & Bindings
Collections: Original furnishings & collections of Larz & Isabel Anderson & objects related to the history of the Society of the Cincinnati & the American Revolution; the history of the art of war in the 18th century
Exhibitions: (08/2013-03/2014) Remembering the Revolutionaries; (03/2014-09/2014) War of 1812
Publications: Why America Is Free: The Insignia of the Society of the Cincinnati by Minor Myers, Jr (1998); Exhibition catalogs & brochures; Liberty without Anarchy: A History of the Society of the Cincinnati (2004)
Activities: Docent training; lects open to pub, 4-8 vis lectrs per yr; concerts; tours; Clement Ellis Conger Internship; Mass Society of the Cincinnati Internship; Cox Book Prize given every 3 yrs to author of distinguished work of American history in era of American Revolution; Tyree-Lamb Library Fel award annually; lends original object of art to qualified mus & other institutions; public concert series; other public progs; mus shop sells books, note cards & Anderson House ornament, DVDs, post cards

M STUDIO GALLERY, 2108 R St NW, Washington, DC 20008-1900. Tel 202-232-8734; Elec Mail info@studiogallerydc.com; Internet Home Page Address: www.studiogallerydc.com; *Co-Chmn* Trix Kuijper; *Dir* Neena Narauyanan; *Treas* Carolee Jakes
Open Wed & Thurs 1-7PM, Fri 1-8PM, Sat 1-6PM; No admis fee; Estab 1964 as a showcase for local artists; Fine contemporary art; Average Annual Attendance: 20,000; Mem: 30; monthly meetings
Income: Nonprofit
Collections: Many private coll in the DC Metropolitan area
Activities: Outreach progs; yoga nights; music & dance performances, author talks, artist talks; lects open to pub; gallery talks; concerts; tours; individual paintings & original works of art lent

M SUPREME COURT OF THE UNITED STATES, Office of the Curator, 1 1st St NE, US Supreme Court Bldg Washington, DC 20543-0001. Tel 202-479-3298; Fax 202-479-2926; Elec Mail curator@supremecourt.gov; Internet Home Page Address: www.supremecourtus.gov; *Cur* Catherine E Fihs; *Assoc Cur* Matthew Hofstedt; *Visitor Prog Mgr* Megan Jones
Open Mon - Fri 9 AM - 4:30 PM, cl federal holidays; No admis fee; Cur Office estab 1973; Exhibit space on ground floor; portrait collection displayed on ground floor & in restricted areas of the bldg; Average Annual Attendance: 300,000
Library Holdings: Audio Tapes; Clipping Files; Exhibition Catalogs; Manuscripts; Memorabilia; Original Art Works; Original Documents; Photographs; Prints; Records; Sculpture; Slides; Video Tapes
Special Subjects: Historical Material, Photography, Sculpture, Prints, Portraits, Miniatures
Collections: Portraits of former Justices; marble busts of the Chief Justices and certain Assoc Justices; historic images such as photos, etchings & drawings of the Justices & the architecture of the building; memorabilia, archival & manuscript materials on the Supreme Ct history; 18th & 19th centuries American & English furniture & decorative arts
Exhibitions: Permanent & temporary exhibits
Publications: Exhibit brochures
Activities: Docent training; courtroom lect every hour on the half hour open to pub; continuously running film describing the functions of the Supreme Court; individual paintings & original objects of art lent to mus & historical organizations; mus shop operated by Supreme Ct Historical Society sells gift items, books, reproductions & prints

M THE TEXTILE MUSEUM, (Textile Museum) 2320 S St NW, Washington, DC 20008-4088. Tel 202-667-0441; Fax 202-483-0994; Elec Mail info@textilemuseum.org; Internet Home Page Address: www.textilemuseum.org; *Pres & Bd Trustees* Bruce Baganz; *Interim Dir* W Richard West Jr; *Senior Cur Eastern Hemisphere* Sumru Belger Krody
Open Tues - Sat 10 AM - 5 PM, Sun 1 - 5 PM, cl federal holidays & Dec 24; No admis fee, suggested donation $8; Estab 1925 to further the understanding of mankind's creative achievements in textile arts; Mus is devoted exclusively to the handmade textile arts; Average Annual Attendance: 30,000; Mem: 3000; dues Individual $60
Income: Financed by endowment, mem & grants
Library Holdings: Auction Catalogs; Book Volumes; Cassettes; Exhibition Catalogs; Kodachrome Transparencies; Lantern Slides; Pamphlets; Periodical Subscriptions; Slides; Video Tapes

Special Subjects: Textiles, Carpets & Rugs
Collections: Collection of oriental carpets including, Caucasian, Chinese, Egyptian (Mamluk), Persian, Spanish & Turkish; Collections of African, Chinese, Coptic, India, Indonesian, Islamic, pre-Columbian Peruvian & textiles of traditional cultures of Americas; Arthur D Jenkins Library of textile arts
Publications: The Textile Museum Members Magazine, quarterly membership newsletter
Activities: Workshops for adults & children; seminars & demonstrations; docent training; family programming; fall symposium; evening events; lects open to pub, 10 vis lectrs per yr; gallery talks; tours; Georg Hewitt Myers Award given ann; individual textiles & original objects of art lent; originate traveling exhibs to Seattle Art Museum; mus shop sells books, magazines, original art, ethnographic textiles, jewelry & one of a kind items

L **Arthur D Jenkins Library of Textile Arts,** 2320 S St NW, Washington, DC 20008-4088. Tel 202-667-0441; Fax 202-483-0994; Elec Mail lfraser@textilemuseum.org; Internet Home Page Address: www.textilemuseum.org; *Librn* Lydia Fraser
Open Wed 11 AM - 3 PM, Sat 12 - 4 PM, appt recommended; No admis fee; Estab 1925 as a reference library dealing with ancient & ethnographic textiles & rugs of the world; Average Annual Attendance: 1,000
Income: Financed by endowment, mem & gifts
Library Holdings: Auction Catalogs; Book Volumes 20,000; CD-ROMs; Cassettes; Clipping Files; DVDs; Exhibition Catalogs; Manuscripts; Other Holdings Monographs; Serials; Pamphlets; Periodical Subscriptions 164; Photographs; Slides; Video Tapes
Special Subjects: Art History, Decorative Arts, Islamic Art, Pre-Columbian Art, History of Art & Archaeology, Crafts, Latin American Art, Archaeology, Ethnology, Fashion Arts, Art Education, Asian Art, American Indian Art, Primitive art, Anthropology, Eskimo Art, Mexican Art, Costume Design & Constr, Metalwork, Antiquities-Oriental, Antiquities-Persian, Carpets & Rugs, Embroidery, Handicrafts, Jewelry, Leather, Oriental Art, Tapestries, Antiquities-Assyrian, Antiquities-Byzantine, Laces, Architecture, Textiles
Collections: Art, Costume, Cultural History; Rugs, Costumes & Textiles of the traditional Cultures of the Americas, Asia, Africa, the Middle East & the Pacific Rim; Textile processes; fashion
Publications: Annual Bibliography of Textile Literature (co-published by the Textile Mus & Textile Soc of Am) compiled & edited by Mary E Mallia, librn; online library catalog, TextileMuse

L **TRINITY COLLEGE LIBRARY,** 125 Michigan Ave NE, Washington, DC 20017-1090. Tel 202-884-9350; Fax 202-884-9241; Elec Mail libraryreference@trinitydc.edu; Internet Home Page Address: www.trinitydc.edu/library/index.html; *Pub Svcs* Merlyn Drummond; *Periodicals* Doris Gruber; *Dir* Susan Craig
Open during school semesters M-F 8:30AM-10PM, Sat 8:30AM-5PM, Sun 1-6PM; Estab 1897 as an undergraduate col library, serving the college community
Income: $253,548 (financed by college budget)
Library Holdings: Book Volumes 200,000; Cassettes; Periodical Subscriptions 600; Reels; Slides

M **UNITED STATES CAPITOL,** Architect of the Capitol, Washington, DC 20515. Tel 202-225-6827; Fax 202-228-4602; Internet Home Page Address: www.aoc.gov; *Architect of the Capitol* Alan M Hantman; *Cur* Dr Barbara A Wolanin; *Photo Branch* Michael Dunn; *Registrar* Pamela Violante McConnell
Open Mon-Sat 9AM-4:30PM; No admis fee; Cornerstone layed 1793. Capitol is working building with mus value; Restored historic chambers; paintings & sculptures scattered through rooms & halls of Congress; reference library; Average Annual Attendance: 1,500,000
Income: Financed by United States Congressional appropriation & appropriate donations
Library Holdings: Book Volumes
Special Subjects: Architecture, Painting-American, Prints, Sculpture, Watercolors, Bronzes, Etchings & Engravings, Landscapes, Decorative Arts, Manuscripts, Portraits, Restorations, Period Rooms, Stained Glass
Collections: Works by Andrei, Brumidi, Crawford, Cox, Franzoni, French, Greenough, Leutze, Peale, Powers, Rogers, Trumbull, Vanderlyn, Weir; 800 paintings & sculptures, manuscripts, 70,000 photographs & 120,000 architectural drawings; The Nat Statuary Hall Collection
Exhibitions: Capital Visitor Center, changes periodically; Congressional Student Annual Exhibition
Publications: Constantino Brumidi, History of the United States Capitol
Activities: US Capitol Guide Service tours; fellowships

A **UNITED STATES COMMISSION OF FINE ARTS,** 401 F St NW, National Building Museum Ste 312 Washington, DC 20001-2637. Tel 202-504-2200; Fax 202-504-2195; Elec Mail staff@cfa.gov; Internet Home Page Address: www.cfa.gov; *Secy* Thomas Leubke
Open Mon - Fri 9 AM - 5 PM; Estab by Act of Congress in 1910 to advise the President, members of congress & various governmental agencies on matters pertaining to the appearance of Washington, DC. The Commission of Fine Arts is composed of seven members who are appointed by the President for four-year terms. Report issued periodically, principally concerned with architectural review; Plans for all new projects in DC under the direction of the Federal & District of Columbia Governments which affect the appearance of the city & all questions involving matters of design with which the Federal Government may be concerned must be submitted to the Commission for comment & advice before contracts are made. Also gives advice on suitability of designs of private buildings in certain parts of the city adjacent to the various departments & agencies of the District & Federal Governments, the Mall, Rock Creek Park & Georgetown
Income: Financed by annual appropriations enacted by Congress
Publications: 15 publications on area architecture, 1964-1978; Commission of Fine Arts, 1910-1985

M **UNITED STATES DEPARTMENT OF STATE,** Diplomatic Reception Rooms, 2201 C St NW, Washington, DC 20520-0099. Tel 202-647-1990, Tour Reservations: 202-647-3241; Fax 202-647-3428, Tour Fax 202-647-4231; Internet Home Page Address: www.state.gov/m/drr; *Cur* Marcee F Craighill; *Colls Mgr & Registrar* Lynn M Turner; *Mus Specialist* Virginia Burden Hart; *Develop Asst* Brianne Brophy
Open for three public tours by reservations only Mon - Fri 9:30 AM, 10:30 AM & 2:45 PM; No admis fee; Estab 1961 to entertain foreign dignitaries; These rooms allow foreign & American visitors to view furniture & art of the American & Federal periods. Furnished in 18th & early 19th Century American furniture, silver, Chinese export porcelain, antique Oriental rugs, American portraits & paintings, Tour Mon - Fri; Average Annual Attendance: 100,000
Income: Financed by private donations, foundation & corporate grants & loans of furnishings & paintings
Special Subjects: Painting-American, Furniture, Porcelain, Silver, Carpets & Rugs
Collections: American furniture 1740-1825; American portraits & paintings; American silver; Chinese export porcelain
Exhibitions: Rotating exhibs
Publications: Treasures of the US Dept of State; PBS documentary film: America's Heritage; Becoming a Nation

M **UNITED STATES DEPARTMENT OF THE INTERIOR,** Interior Museum, 1849 C St NW, MS-2266, Dept of the Interior Washington, DC 20240-0001. Tel 202-208-4743; Fax 202-208-1535; Elec Mail museum_services@nbc.gov; Internet Home Page Address: www.doi.gov/interiormuseum; *Collections Mgr* Kim Robinson; *Coordr* Hunter Hollins; *Mus Specialist* Kirk Dietz; *Mus Technician* Deborah Wurdinger
Open Mon - Fri 8:30 AM - 4:30 PM, cl federal holidays; some areas require reservations to view artwork; No admis fee; Estab 1938 to explain through works of art & other media the history, aims & activities of the Department; Museum occupies one wing on the first floor of the Interior Department Building; Average Annual Attendance: 26,000
Income: Federally funded
Special Subjects: American Indian Art, Painting-American, Sculpture, Watercolors, Archaeology, Ethnology, Eskimo Art, Maps, Dioramas
Collections: Colburn Collection of Indian basketry; collection of Indian, Eskimo, South Sea Islands & Virgin Islands arts & crafts, documents, maps, charts, etc; Gibson Collection of Indian materials; Indian arts & crafts; murals; dioramas of Interior history scenes; oil paintings of early American survey teams by William Henry Jackson; watercolor & black & white illustrations; wildlife paintings by Walter Weber
Exhibitions: Changing exhibits gallery at museum entrance has new exhibits every three months; Permanent exhibits include: Overview of Interior history & activities; architectural history of the headquarters building; interpretation of a turn of the century totem pole
Activities: Educ dept; lect open to public, 10-12 vis lectrs per year; gallery talks; tours

M **UNITED STATES NAVY,** Art Gallery, 822 Sicard St SE, Washington Navy Yard Washington, DC 20374-5060; 805 Kidder Breese St SE, Washington Navy Yard Washington, DC 20374-5060. Tel 202-433-3815; Internet Home Page Address: www.history.navy.mil; *Cur* Gale Munro
By appointment; No admis fee; Estab 1800 to document history of US Navy & Naval personnel; Exhibs merged into the Navy museum, research facilities available
Income: Financed by Naval History & Heritage Command
Special Subjects: Painting-American, Prints, Watercolors, Woodcuts, Etchings & Engravings, Posters, Marine Painting, Cartoons, Military Art
Collections: Graphic arts, paintings, sketches; Sculptures
Exhibitions: US Naval History; Traveling Exhibits
Publications: United States Navy Combat Art
Activities: Internships; individual paintings & original objects of art lent to AAM accredited museums & US military museums officially recognized by their service; originate traveling exhibs; sales shop sells reproductions, prints, slides & brochures

A **UNITED STATES SENATE COMMISSION ON ART,** United States Capitol Bldg, Rm S-411, Washington, DC 20510-7102. Tel 202-224-2955; Fax 202-224-8799; Elec Mail curator@sec.senate.gov; Internet Home Page Address: www.senate.gov; *VChmn* Thomas A Daschle; *Assoc Dir* Melinda K Smith; *Museum Specialist* Richard L Doerner; *Admin* Scott M Strong; *Cur* Diane Skvarla; *Staff Asst* Clare Colgrove; *Historic Preservation Off* Kelly Steele; *Assoc Registrar* Jamie Arbolino; *Registrar* Deborah Wood
Rooms in Capitol under jurisdiction of Commission are open daily 9 AM - 4:30 PM; No admis fee; Commission estab 1968 to acquire, supervise, hold, place & protect all works of art, historical objects & exhibits within the Senate wing of the United States Capitol & Senate Office Buildings; Average Annual Attendance: 3,000,000
Income: Financed by United States Senate appropriation
Collections: Paintings, sculpture, historic furnishings & memorabilia located within the Senate wing of the Capitol & Senate Office Buildings; Preservation Projects: Old Senate & Old Supreme Court Chamber restored to their appearances 1850
Exhibitions: Senate Art & Stamps; The Supreme Court of the United States, the Capitol Years 1801-1935; Isaac Bassett, The Venerable Doorkeeper, 1831-1895; The Political Cartoons from Puck
Publications: The Senate Chamber 1810-1859; The Supreme Court Chamber 1810-1860; A Necessary Fence: The Senate's First Century; An Assembly of Chosen Men: Popular Views of the Senate's Chambers 1847-1886; U S Senate graphic Arts Collection: An Illustrated Checklist; Brumidi Corridor; Vice Presidential Bust Collection
L **Reference Library,** United States Capitol Bldg, Rm S-411, Washington, DC 20510-7102. Tel 202-224-2976; Elec Mail curator@sec.senate.gov; Internet Home Page Address: senate.gov/curator/index.html;
Open daily 9 AM - 4:30 PM; A reference collection on fine & decorative arts; supplemented by the United States Senate Library
Income: $1000 (financed by United States Senate appropriation to the Commission)

Library Holdings: Book Volumes 250,000; Cards; Clipping Files; Exhibition Catalogs; Manuscripts; Memorabilia; Pamphlets; Periodical Subscriptions 30; Photographs; Slides
Special Subjects: Decorative Arts, Architecture

WASHINGTON SCULPTORS GROUP
For further information, see National and Regional Organizations

M **WESLEY THEOLOGICAL SEMINARY, HENRY LUCE III CENTER FOR THE ARTS & RELIGION,** (Wesley Theological Seminary Center for the Arts & Religion) Dadian Gallery, 4500 Massachusetts Ave, NW, Washington, DC 20016. Tel 202-885-8608; Fax 202-885-8550; Elec Mail asherman@wesleyseminary.edu; Internet Home Page Address: www.wesleyseminary.edu/lcar.aspx; *Cur* Trudi Ludwig Johnson; *Dir* Deborah Sokolove; *Program Admin* Amy Gray
Open Mon - Fri 10 AM - 4:30 PM; No admis fee; Estab 1989 to provide visual demonstration of intrinsic relationship between art & religion; Average Annual Attendance: 5,000
Income: $50,000 (financed by gifts & grants, subsidized partly by parent institution)
Collections: Gifts from Artists; WTS Collection, Contemporary Art
Exhibitions: 5 - 7 Exhibs per yr ranging from group to solo shows
Activities: Classes for adults; dramatic progs; poetry readings; dance & music concerts; lects open to pub, 5 vis lectrs per yr; gallery talks; lending collection contains paintings & art objects; book traveling exhibs; originate traveling exhibs

M **WHITE HOUSE,** 1600 Pennsylvania Ave NW, Washington, DC 20502-0001. Tel 202-456-7041; Fax 202-456-6820; Internet Home Page Address: www.whitehouse.gov/index.html; *Cur* William G Allman; *Asst Cur* Lydia Tederick; *Coll Mgr* Donna Hayashi-Smith; *Asst Cur* Melissa Naulin; *Asst Cur* Monica McKiernan
Open Tues-Sat 7:30AM-12:30PM for tours, Visitor Ctr open 7:30AM-4PM. Passes must be requested from your Congress Person along with security information. Date of Birth and SS# must be submitted; No admis fee
Income: Financed by federal government appropriation
Special Subjects: Architecture, Painting-American, Prints, Sculpture, Decorative Arts, Manuscripts, Portraits, Furniture, Glass, Porcelain, Metalwork, Historical Material, Period Rooms
Collections: 18th & 19th century period furniture; 18th, 19th & 20th century paintings & prints; glassware; manuscripts; porcelain; sculpture
Publications: Art in the White House: A Nation's Pride; The First Ladies; The Living White House; The President's House: A History; The Presidents of the United States; White House Glassware: Two Centuries of Presidential Entertaining; The White House: An Historic Guide; White House History, magazine; The White House: Historic Furnishings & First Families

M **WOODROW WILSON HOUSE,** 2340 S St, NW, Washington, DC 20008. Tel 202-387-4062; Fax 202-483-1466; Elec Mail faucella@woodrowwilsonhouse.org; Internet Home Page Address: www.woodrowwilsonhouse.org; *Exec Dir* Frank J Aucella; *Cur* John Powell
Open Tues - Sun 10 AM - 4 PM, cl Mon; Admis adults $7.50, $6.50 seniors, $3 students, National Trust members & under 7 free; Estab 1963, owned by the National Trust for Historic Preservation, it works to foster interest & appreciation of the 28th President, Woodrow Wilson; Wilson House is a 1915 Georgian-Revival townhouse designed by Waddy B Wood, with formal garden. From 1921 it served as the home of President & Mrs Wilson; Average Annual Attendance: 16,000; Mem: 350; dues $50 & up
Income: Financed by endowment, mem, admis, sales & fundraising
Special Subjects: Architecture, Painting-American, Decorative Arts, Furniture, Historical Material, Period Rooms
Collections: Early 20th century art, furnishings, clothing; presidential memorabilia; decorative arts
Publications: Woodrow Wilson News, quarterly
Activities: Lects open to pub; 5-6 vis lectrs per yr; concerts; tours; individual paintings & objects of art lent to qualified mus; mus shop sells books, reproductions, prints & slides

ZENITH GALLERY, PO Box 55295, Washington, DC 20040-5295. Tel 202-783-2963; *Dir* Margery Goldberg
Open Mon - Fri 10 AM - 6 PM, Sat 11 AM - 6 PM, Sun Noon - 5 PM

FLORIDA

BOCA RATON

A **BOCA RATON MUSEUM OF ART,** 501 Plaza Real, Boca Raton, FL 33432-3982. Tel 561-392-2500; Fax 561-391-6410; Elec Mail info@bocamuseum.org; Internet Home Page Address: www.bocamuseum.org; *Pres* Dalia Stiller; *Exec Dir* Steven Maklansky; *Dir Art School* Claire Clum; *Dir Finance* Linda Ursillo; *Asst Exec Dir* Valerie Johnson; *Dir Admin* Roberta Stewart; *Registrar* Martin Hanahan; *Spec Events & Vols* Belle Forino; *Communs Coordr* Inga Ford; *Cur* Marisa J Pascucci; *Cur* Kathleen Goncharov; *Asst Cur* Kelli Bodle; *Mktg & Pub Rels Assoc* Austin Modine
Open Tues, Wed, Thurs & Fri 10 AM - 6 PM, Sat & Sun Noon - 6 PM, cl Mon & holidays; Admis adults $8, seniors $6, students with ID $4, discounts to groups, members & children under 12 Wed 5 PM - 9 PM no charge, admis may change for special exhibits; Estab 1951 to foster & develop the cultural arts; Large Main Gallery, mus shop contained in one building. Second building houses art school & storage. 4500 sq ft expansion houses a permanent collection; Average Annual Attendance: 200,000; Mem: 4300; dues individual $80, family & dual $100; contributing $150, supporting $300, sustaining $600, dir's circle $2,500, trustee's circle $5,000, pres's circle $10,000, benefactor's circle $25,000; annual meeting in Apr
Income: Financed by mem, fundraising, art school & grants

Library Holdings: Auction Catalogs; Book Volumes; Clipping Files; Exhibition Catalogs; Pamphlets; Slides
Special Subjects: Drawings, Etchings & Engravings, Graphics, Landscapes, Photography, Posters, Prints, Sculpture, Watercolors, Painting-American, Asian Art, Decorative Arts, Folk Art, African Art, Ceramics, Hispanic Art, Latin American Art, Portraits, Pre-Columbian Art, Archaeology, Islamic Art, Painting-European, Primitive art, Mexican Art
Collections: Photography from 19th century to present; John J Mayers Collection, works by Braque, Demuth, Glackens, Matisse & Picasso
Exhibitions: Changes every 6-8 weeks; state-wide competition & show; annual outdoor art festival
Publications: Exhibition catalogues; quarterly member magazine
Activities: Classes for adults & children; docent training; children's gallery educ progs, art trips; lects open to pub; 5 vis lectrs per yr; concerts; gallery talks; tours; juried exhibs; national outdoor art festival with awards given for Best in Show & Merit; individual paintings & original objects of art lent; 6-10 book traveling exhibs; originate various traveling exhibs; mus shop sells books, original art, reproductions, prints, gift items

L **Library,** 501 Plaza Real, Mizner Park Boca Raton, FL 33432. Tel 561-392-2500; Fax 561-391-6410; Elec Mail info@bocamuseum.org; Internet Home Page Address: www.bocamuseum.org; *Dir Develop* Christine Mally; *Dir* Steven Maklansky; *Dir Mktg* Bruce Herman; *Dir Admin* Robarth Stewart; *Cur 20th Century & Contemporary Art* Marisa Pascucci; *Cur Exhibs & Audience Engagement* Kathy Goncharov; *Cur Educ* Claire Clum
Open Tues, Thurs, Fri & Sat 10 AM - 5 PM, Wed 10 AM - 9 PM, Sun Noon - 5 PM, cl Mon; Admis adults $8, seniors $6, students $4, for spec exhibs adults $15, seniors $12, students $7; Estab 1940; 5,500+ works in permanent collection; Average Annual Attendance: 200,000; Mem: 3,407
Library Holdings: Book Volumes 4000; Exhibition Catalogs; Photographs; Slides
Special Subjects: Collages, Folk Art, Decorative Arts, Photography, Drawings, Etchings & Engravings, Graphic Arts, Painting-American, Painting-British, Painting-French, Painting-German, Painting-Italian, Painting-Russian, Painting-Spanish, Posters, Pre-Columbian Art, Prints, Sculpture, Painting-European, Ceramics, Latin American Art, Painting-Israeli, American Western Art, Asian Art, Porcelain, Primitive art, Eskimo Art, Southwestern Art, Glass, Afro-American Art, Jewelry, Pottery, Religious Art, Silver, Woodcuts, Landscapes, Portraits
Collections: Contemporary Art, Pre-Columbian, Photography, Modern Masters, African, Sculpture
Publications: catalogs; monthly newsletter
Activities: Classes for adults & children; docent training; art school; lects open to pub, 12 vis lectrs per yr; concerts; gallery talks; tours; sponsoring of competitions; ann All Fla exhibs awards, ann Art Fest; film & video series; mus shop sells books & reproductions

M **FLORIDA ATLANTIC UNIVERSITY,** University Galleries/Ritter Art Gallery/Schmidt Center Gallery, 777 Glades Rd, Boca Raton, FL 33431-6496. Tel 561-297-2660; 297-2966; Fax 561-297-2166; Elec Mail wfaulds@fau.edu; Internet Home Page Address: www.fau.edu/galleries; *Dir University Galleries* W Rod Faulds
Open Tues - Fri 1 PM - 4 PM, Sat 1 - 5 PM; No admis fee; Estab 1983 to present a wide range of innovative contemporary art exhibitions and related pub prog & to provide exhibit space for faculty & students; Two 2,500 sq ft spaces & public spaces for projects/installations; Average Annual Attendance: 15,000; Mem: 200
Income: Financed by Univ (state) appropriations, student activities fees & pvt/pub grants
Collections: AE Beanie Backus paintings
Exhibitions: Annual Juried Student Show; traveling exhibitions
Publications: Exhibit catalogues
Activities: Artist in residence progs with university dept of art; docent training for university art students; lects open to pub; concerts; gallery talks; readings; tours; competitions with awards; book 1 - 3 traveling exhibs per yr; originates traveling exhibs to other university galleries

BRADENTON

A **ART CENTER MANATEE,** (Art League of Manatee Countee) 209 Ninth St W, Bradenton, FL 34205. Tel 941-746-2862; Fax 941-746-2319; Elec Mail acm@artcentermanatee.org; Internet Home Page Address: www.artcentermanatee.org; *Assoc Dir* Mary Roff; *Pres* Andi Franco; *Mktg* Peggy Haynes
Open year round Mon, Fri & Sat 9 AM - 5 PM, Tues, Wed & Thurs 9 AM - 6 PM; cl holidays & 2 wks in Aug; No admis fee; Estab 1937 to offer opportunities in further educ in the visual arts by providing space for exhibitions, classes, demonstrations, critiques & the exchange of ideas & information by vis artists; Circ 3,000; Searle Gallery: 2,000 sq ft; Kellogg Gallery: 2,500 sq ft; Reid-Hodges Gallery: 2,024 sq ft; Average Annual Attendance: 40,000; Mem: 1,000+; dues $20 & up; annual meeting in Nov
Library Holdings: Book Volumes; Cassettes; Clipping Files; Exhibition Catalogs; Original Art Works; Pamphlets; Photographs; Records; Slides; Video Tapes
Exhibitions: Work by members & local artists one person shows & circulating exhibitions changing at three week intervals from Oct to May
Activities: Art school instruction in painting, drawing, clay techniques & variety of handcrafts; creative develop for children; special art progs; classes for adults & children; lects open to pub, 5 vis lectrs per yr; gallery talks; tours; sponsoring of competitions; schols available; sales shop sells original arts & prints

CORAL GABLES

M **UNIVERSITY OF MIAMI,** Lowe Art Museum, 1301 Stanford Dr, Coral Gables, FL 33146-2009. Tel 305-284-3535; Fax 305-284-2024; Elec Mail bdursam@miami.edu; Internet Home Page Address: www.lowemuseum.org; *Dir* Brian A Dursum; *Assoc Dir* Denise M Gerson; *Adjunct Cur African Art* Marcilene Wittmer; *Adjunct Cur Renaissance* Perri L Roberts; *Dir Mem* Yina Balarezo-Badenjkl; *Asst Dir* Kara Schneiderman; *Assoc Preparator* Martin Casuso; *Cur Educ* Jodi Sypher
Open Tues - Sat 10 AM - 4 PM, Sun Noon - 4 PM, cl Mon & univ holidays; Admis general $10, seniors & students $5, members, University of Miami students

& children under 12 free, group rates available; Estab 1952 to bring outstanding exhibitions & collections to the community & to the University; gallery maintained; Maintains reference library; wheelchair accessible; Average Annual Attendance: 95,000; Mem: Mem dues: Academic $30, Cintas Individual $50, Kress Family $65, Barton $100, Contemporary $150, Friends of Art $350, Director's Circle $1200

Special Subjects: Afro-American Art, Anthropology, Drawings, Landscapes, Mexican Art, American Western Art, Porcelain, Portraits, Pottery, Painting-British, Painting-European, Painting-French, Hispanic Art, Latin American Art, Painting-American, Photography, Prints, Sculpture, American Indian Art, African Art, Southwestern Art, Textiles, Religious Art, Ceramics, Primitive art, Woodcarvings, Etchings & Engravings, Eskimo Art, Glass, Jade, Oriental Art, Asian Art, Silver, Painting-Dutch, Scrimshaw, Baroque Art, Painting-Flemish, Renaissance Art, Period Rooms, Medieval Art, Painting-Spanish, Painting-Italian, Antiquities-Egyptian, Antiquities-Greek, Antiquities-Roman, Painting-German

Collections: Washington Allston Trust Collection; Virgil Barker Collection of 19th & 20th Century American Art; Alfred I Barton Collection of Southwestern American Indian Art; Esso Collection of Latin American Art; Samuel H Kress Collection of Renaissance & Baroque Art; Samuel K Lothrop Collection of Guatemalan Textiles; Cintas Foundation Collection of Spanish Old Master Paintings

Exhibitions: Varied, changing exhibitions throughout the year; student exhibs; sculpture; Cuban American art

Publications: Exhibition catalogs; newsletter, bimonthly

Activities: Classes for children; docent training; lects open to pub, 7-8 vis lectrs per yr; concerts; gallery talks; tours; individual paintings & original objects of art lent to other mus; book 3-5 traveling exhibs per yr; originate traveling exhibs; mus shop sells books, magazines, gift items

CORAL SPRINGS

M   **CORAL SPRINGS MUSEUM OF ART,** 2855 Coral Springs Dr, Coral Springs, FL 33065-3825. Tel 954-340-5000; Fax 954-346-4424; Elec Mail ctbok@coralsprings.org; Internet Home Page Address: www.csmart.org; *CEO & Dir* Barbara O'Keefe
Open Mon - Wed, Fri - Sat 10 AM - 5 PM, Thurs 10 AM - 8 PM, cl major holidays; Admis adults $5, seniors & tours $3, children 12 & under & members free, discounts to AAM & ICOM members; 8,000 sq ft exhibition galleries; Average Annual Attendance: 31,000
Collections: contemporary art
Activities: Educ prog; artist in res prog; lects; guided tours; mus related items for sale

DADE CITY

L   **PIONEER FLORIDA MUSEUM ASSOCIATION, INC,** Pioneer Florida Museum & Village, PO Box 335, Dade City, FL 33526-0335. Tel 352-567-0262; Fax 352-567-1262; Elec Mail curator@pioneerfloridamuseum.org; Internet Home Page Address: www.pioneerfloridamuseum.com
Open Tues - Sat 10 AM - 5 PM, cl Sun & Mon; Admis adults $5, seniors $4, students 6-18 $2; Estab 1961 to preserve & promote Pioneer life; Average Annual Attendance: 12,000; Mem: 400; dues life family $250, life individual $150, family $35, individual $25; annual meeting last Sun in Oct
Income: $80,000 (financed by endowment, mem, state appropriation, special events, donations, memories & grants)
Activities: Tours; annual special events festivals; mus shop sell books & prints

DAVIE

M   **BROWARD COMMUNITY COLLEGE - A. HUGH ADAMS CAMPUS,** Fine Arts Gallery, 3501 SW Davie Rd, Bldg 3 Davie, FL 33314. Tel 954-201-6984; *Contact Person* Barbara Ryan
Open Mon - Fri 9 AM - 2 PM Sat 11 AM - 2 PM; No admis fee
Collections: Paintings; sculpture; photographs

DAYTONA BEACH

M   **DAYTONA STATE COLLEGE,** Southeast Museum of Photography, 1200 W International Speedway Blvd, Daytona Beach, FL 32114-2811; PO Box 2811, Daytona Beach, FL 32120-2811. Tel 386-506-4475; Fax 386-506-4487; Elec Mail museum1@daytonastate.edu; Internet Home Page Address: www.smponline.org; *Dir* Kevin R Miller; *Mktg & Communs* Cassie Brown; *Educ Dept* Christina Katsolis; *Colls Mgr* Melissa Reamer; *Lead Mus Technician* Alexis Rogers; *Exhib Coordr* Juliana Romnes
Open Tues, Thurs, Fri 11 AM - 5 PM, Wed 11 AM - 7 PM, Sat & Sun 1 - 5 PM, PM, June, July & Dec Tues - Sun noon - 4 PM, cl Mon, summer recess (July 31 - Aug 17), winter recess (Dec 17 - Jan 11), Easter Sun, Independence Day, Thanksgiving weekend (Thurs - Sun); No admis fee; Estab 1992; Specialist photography museum; contemporary, historical, new media; Average Annual Attendance: 22,999; Mem: 3,000
Income: Financed by college sponsored annual budget $500,000
Special Subjects: Photography
Collections: Photographic Collection of Karsch, Chartier-Bresson, Friedlander, Perlmutter
Activities: Classes for adults & children; summer photo camps for kids; lects open to pub; 10 vis lectrs per yr; tours; scholarships; organize traveling exhibs; Lee Dunkel, Bastienne Schmidt; mus shop sells books, photo postcards, catalogs & cameras

M   **HALIFAX HISTORICAL SOCIETY, INC,** Halifax Historical Museum, 252 S Beach St, Daytona Beach, FL 32114-4407. Tel 386-255-6976; Fax 386-255-7605; Elec Mail mail@halifaxhistorical.org; Internet Home Page Address: www.halifaxhistorical.org; *Pres* Ruth Trager; *VPres* Walter Snell; *VPres* Michael Link, Ph.D; *VPres* Warren Trager; *Recording Secy* Beth Mindlin; *Treas* E Holmes Davis; *Exec Advisor* Virginia Buckner; *Mus Dir* Fayn (no e) LeVeille; *Admin Asst* Leigh Finner
Open Tues - Fri 10:30 AM - 4:30 PM, Sat 10 AM - 4 PM; Admis adults $5, children 12 & under $1, Thurs by donation, Sat children 12 & under free; Estab

1949 to preserve & share local history of the Halifax Country area, east Volusia County; (101 years old) 1910 Merchants Bank Building in historic downtown Daytona Beach, FL; Average Annual Attendance: 3,000; Mem: 365 (approx); dues $35 individual, $45 family; annual meeting 2nd Sat in Jan
Income: Financed by dues, donations, grants, gift shop, fund raising
Library Holdings: Audio Tapes; Book Volumes; Cards; Cassettes; Clipping Files; Compact Disks; Original Documents; Pamphlets; Photographs; Records; Reels; Reproductions; Slides; Video Tapes
Special Subjects: Drawings, Folk Art, Glass, Flasks & Bottles, American Indian Art, Costumes, Ceramics, Dolls, Furniture, Historical Material, Maps, Coins & Medals, Dioramas, Embroidery, Laces
Collections: The Models of Lawson Diggett; artifacts of World War II; 18th century Spanish & English artifacts; Indian projectiles, canoe, pottery; racing memorabilia; Victorian clothing & furniture; Charles Grove Burgoyne Collection; Bill McCoy Collection; Local artifacts dating back to 2500-5000 BC
Exhibitions: Grandma's Attic; Permanent & rotating exhibitions; Three new exhibits a yr of various subjects in the exhibit changing area
Publications: Biannual Halifax Herald; quarterly newsletters
Activities: Educ dept; dramatic prog; lects for mems only, 30-40 vis lectrs per yr; recognition plaques; tours; book traveling exhibs 4 per yr; mus shop sells books, reproductions, prints & other various items

M   **THE MUSEUM OF ARTS & SCIENCES INC,** 352 S Nova Rd Daytona Beach, FL 32114. Tel 386-255-0285; Fax 386-255-5040; Elec Mail wdatherholt@moas.org; Internet Home Page Address: www.moas.org; *Cur History & Science* James Zacharias; *Dir* Wayne David Atherholt; *Dep Dir Facilities* Eric Goire; *Art Cur* Jay Williams; *Chief Cur* Cynthia Duval; *Mktg Dir* Christina Lane; *Asst to Exec Dir* Pattie Pardee
Open Tues-Sat 9AM-5PM, Sun 11AM-5PM; Admis $12.95, students & seniors $10.95, children 6-17 $6.95, members and children under 5 free; Estab 1971; 90,000 sq ft of exhibition galleries, hall gallery & lobby gallery are maintained; Mus includes Planetarium, A Frischer Sculpture Garden, Gallery of American Art, Root Hall & Gallery, Gallery of African Art, Gallery of Florida History & Prehistory of Florida Gallery. Maintains reference library, Gallery of Cuban art, Gallery of Chinese Art, Galleries of Decorative Arts; childrens museum added in 2008; Average Annual Attendance: 240,000; Mem: 10,000; dues $50; annual meeting in Dec
Income: $2,500,000 (financed by endowment, mem, city & county appropriations, donations, earned income)
Purchases: American Art 1720-2004. American Decorative Arts, Chinese Art, Cuban Art, European Art, African Art
Library Holdings: Auction Catalogs; Book Volumes; Exhibition Catalogs; Manuscripts; Maps; Photographs; Sculpture
Special Subjects: Folk Art, Landscapes, Marine Painting, Portraits, Pottery, Pre-Columbian Art, Painting-American, Prints, Silver, Textiles, Woodcuts, Maps, Painting-British, Sculpture, Architecture, Drawings, Graphics, Hispanic Art, Latin American Art, Photography, Sculpture, Watercolors, American Indian Art, American Western Art, Bronzes, African Art, Anthropology, Archaeology, Ethnology, Religious Art, Ceramics, Primitive art, Etchings & Engravings, Afro-American Art, Decorative Arts, Manuscripts, Painting-European, Posters, Furniture, Glass, Jade, Jewelry, Porcelain, Oriental Art, Asian Art, Painting-Dutch, Painting-French, Carpets & Rugs, Ivory, Coins & Medals, Baroque Art, Calligraphy, Renaissance Art, Medieval Art, Antiquities-Oriental, Painting-Spanish, Painting-Italian, Antiquities-Persian, Antiquities-Greek, Gold, Stained Glass, Painting-Australian, Painting-German, Pewter, Painting-Russian, Enamels
Collections: Aboriginal Art including Florida Indian; American Art 1620-1900; American Fine Art; American Illustration: Norman Rockwell; Cuban Collection; Florida Contemporary Collection
Exhibitions: Center for Florida History; The Levine Collection of Gems and Jewelry; Colonial Cuba: The Lithographs of Eduardo LaPlante; Treasures from the age of Napoleon; American Paintings 1800-1900
Publications: Arts & Sciences Magazine, 4 times per year; catalogs, monthly; A Treasury of American Art; Cuba: A History in Art; Coast to Coast: Contemporary Landscape in Florida; Reflections: Paintings of Florida from 1865 - 1965 From the Collection of Cici & Hyatt Brown; Great Masters of Cuban Art: Ramos Collection
Activities: Classes for adults and children; docent training; lects open to pub, 15 vis lectrs per yr; gallery talks; concerts; tours; competitions with awards; schols offered; exten dept serves Volusia County; artmobile individual paintings & original objects of art lent to other mus, municipalities & public spaces; lending collection contains 2000 nature artifacts, 1000 original art works, 1000 original prints, 250 paintings, 100 photographs & sculptures; book traveling exhibs 4 per yr; originate traveling exhibs to Fla & national AAM accredited mus; mus shop sells books, magazines, original art, reproductions

L   **Library,** 352 S Nova Rd, Daytona Beach, FL 32114-4512. Tel 386-255-0285; Internet Home Page Address: www.moas.org; *Librn* Marge Sigerson
Open Tues - Fri 9 AM - 4 PM; Open to mems & school children; reference library
Income: Financed by Mus
Purchases: Periodicals & reference materials
Library Holdings: Book Volumes 10,000; Clipping Files; Exhibition Catalogs; Manuscripts; Original Art Works; Periodical Subscriptions 2000; Photographs; Prints; Slides; Video Tapes
Special Subjects: Art History, Decorative Arts, Calligraphy, Drawings, Ceramics, Archaeology, American Western Art, Bronzes, Art Education, Asian Art, American Indian Art, Anthropology, Aesthetics, Afro-American Art, Architecture
Collections: General Fulgencio Batista Cuban Collection; Antique Coin Books

DELAND

M FLORIDA MUSEUM OF WOMEN ARTISTS, 100 N Woodland Blvd Ste 1, Deland, FL 32720-4249. Tel 386-873-2976; Internet Home Page Address: www.floridamuseumforwomenartists.org; *Contact* Kathryn Peterson

M MUSEUM OF FLORIDA ART, 600 N Woodland Blvd, Deland, FL 32720-3447. Tel 386-734-4371; Fax 386-734-7697; Elec Mail sabatini@museumoffloridaart.org; Internet Home Page Address: www.museumoffloridaart.org; *CEO* George Bolge; *Exhibitions* David Fithian; *Dir Develop* Pattie Pardee; *Educ Cur* Pam Coffman; *Dir Finance & Opers* Dorothy Dansberger; *Dir Mktg* Kristin Burke; *Mgr Special Events, Guest Servs & Mem* Jenna Sabatini
Open Tues - Sat 10 AM - 4 PM, Sun 1 - 4 PM, cl Mon; Admis adults $5, children under 12 free; Estab 1951 to provide art educ & exhibits; Lower gallery: 12 ft carpeted walls, 3100 sq ft; upper gallery: 12 ft carpeted walls, 2100 sq ft, classrooms, interdisciplinary space; Average Annual Attendance: 90,000; Mem: 800; dues family $55, individual & srs $35
Income: $600,000 (financed by mem, state appropriation & Volusia County & earned income & donations)
Purchases: $10,000 - $20,000
Library Holdings: Book Volumes; Cards; Clipping Files; Compact Disks; DVDs; Exhibition Catalogs; Maps; Memorabilia; Original Art Works; Pamphlets; Periodical Subscriptions; Photographs; Prints; Records; Sculpture; Slides; Video Tapes
Special Subjects: Drawings, Etchings & Engravings, Folk Art, Landscapes, Ceramics, Glass, Metalwork, Photography, Porcelain, Portraits, Painting-American, Prints, Textiles, Woodcuts, Sculpture, Graphics, Hispanic Art, Latin American Art, Watercolors, Posters, Jewelry, Juvenile Art
Collections: Contemporary Florida Artists 1900 - Present
Exhibitions: Rotating exhibs; Legendary Florida-Ongoing Exhib; Touring Exhibs
Activities: Classes for adults & children; docent progs; spring & summer art camp for children & teens; outreach; K-12 art integration; Artist workshops in various media; family fun Saturdays (free event for families featuring hands-on art activities); AMP (art, media & performance) series; lects open to pub; lectrs for members only; 10-20 vis lectrs per yr; concerts; gallery talks; tours; competitions with awards; scholarships; Dorothy Johnson Award given annually to & in honor of local arts supporter in Volusia Cty, FL; sponsor art festival; lending of original objects of art to Arts in Public Places & outdoor sculpture program; touring exhibs; book traveling exhibs 1 per yr; originate traveling exhibs 5 per yr; Florida artists; mus shop sells books, original art, reproductions, prints, crafts & gift items; Evans C & Betty Drees Johnson Children's Art Ctr

DELRAY BEACH

M CORNELL MUSEUM OF ART AND AMERICAN CULTURE, 51 N Swinton Ave, Delray Beach, FL 33444-2631. Tel 561-243-7922; Fax 561-243-7022; Elec Mail gadams@delraycenterforthearts.org; Internet Home Page Address: www.oldschool.org; *Dir* Gloria Rejune Adams; *Mus Asst* Melanie Johanson
Open Tues - Sat 10 AM - 4:30 PM, Sun 1 - 4:30 PM; cl Mon yr round & major holidays; Admis adults $8, seniors (over 65) & students with ID $6, children under ten free; Estab 1990; Large spacious rooms, wooden floors; Average Annual Attendance: 30,000; Mem: Dues $30 regular, family & friends $75; annual meeting in Jan
Income: Grants from State of Florida; private donors; memberships, TDC, city of Delray Beach, CRA
Library Holdings: Auction Catalogs; Book Volumes; Clipping Files; Exhibition Catalogs; Memorabilia; Original Art Works; Original Documents; Pamphlets; Periodical Subscriptions; Photographs; Prints; Sculpture; Slides
Special Subjects: Photography, Pre-Columbian Art, Painting-American, Painting-British, Painting-European, Drawings, Sculpture, American Indian Art, Bronzes, African Art, Folk Art, Etchings & Engravings, Furniture, Painting-Spanish, Antiquities-Etruscan
Collections: Teaching collection
Exhibitions: Rotating exhibs every 4 or 5 months; Crest Galleries
Activities: Classes for adults & children; docent training; Kickin Arts; photography school; lects open to pub; 6 vis lectrs per yr; concerts; gallery talks; tours; Florida cultural institutions prog award; sponsoring of competitions; schols offered; lending collection available; book traveling exhibs 1-2 per yr; originate traveling exhibs; mus shop sells books, magazines, original art, reproductions, prints, slides, jewelry, pottery

M PALM BEACH COUNTY PARKS & RECREATION DEPARTMENT, Morikami Museum & Japanese Gardens, 4000 Morikami Park Rd, Delray Beach, FL 33446-2305. Tel 561-495-0233; Fax 561-499-2557; Elec Mail morikami@pbcgov.org; Internet Home Page Address: www.morikami.org; *Cultural Dir* Thomas Gregersen; *Dir Educ* Reiko Nishioka; *Museum Store Mgr* Sallie Chisolm; *Admin Assoc* Debbie Towers; *Horticulture Supv* Heather Grzybek; *Coll Cur* Veljko Dujin; *Adminr* Bonnie White Lemay; *Dir Advancement* Amy Hever; *Cur Japanese Art* Susanna Brooks Lavallee
Call for hours & admis prices; Estab 1977 to preserve & interpret Japanese culture & Japanese-American culture; Five small galleries in Japanese style bldg & two larger galleries in main museum bldg; Average Annual Attendance: 150,000; Mem: 2700; annual meeting Apr
Income: $3,500,000 (financed by mem & county appropriation)
Purchases: $9000
Library Holdings: Auction Catalogs; Book Volumes; Clipping Files; Exhibition Catalogs; Periodical Subscriptions
Special Subjects: Porcelain, Graphics, Photography, Anthropology, Ethnology, Costumes, Crafts, Folk Art, Pottery, Woodcuts, Decorative Arts, Painting-Japanese, Dolls, Asian Art, Historical Material
Collections: Archived colls pertaining to the Yamato Colony; Japanese Fine Arts (hanging scrolls, folding screens, paintings, textiles, prints, ceramics); Japanese Folk Arts (dolls, tools, home furnishings, folk figures, miniature buildings, toys)
Publications: Newsletter, quarterly; Calendar bi-monthly; Exhibition catalogs 1-2 per yr

Activities: Classes for adults & children; docent training; lects for mem only; 4-6 vis lectrs per yr; concerts; tours; book traveling exhibs, 2-3 per yr; originate traveling exhibs; mus shop sells books, magazines, reproductions, prints & slides

L Donald B Gordon Memorial Library, 4000 Morikami Park Rd, Morikami Museum Delray Beach, FL 33446-2305. Tel 561-495-0233; Fax 561-499-2557; Elec Mail morikami@co.palm-beach.fl.us; Internet Home Page Address: www.morikami.org; *Coll Cur* Noelle Shuey Altamirano
Open by appointment Tues - Sun 10 AM - 5 PM, cl Mon & holidays; Admis adults $9, seniors $8, children 6-18 & college students $6, mems & children under 6 free; Estab 1977 to provide printed & recorded materials on Japan; For reference only; Average Annual Attendance: 250,000; Mem: 2300. Dues based on tiered levels
Income: Financed by donations
Purchases: $1000
Library Holdings: Auction Catalogs; Book Volumes 4500; Clipping Files; Exhibition Catalogs; Periodical Subscriptions 25
Special Subjects: Art History, Folk Art, Decorative Arts, Film, Photography, Calligraphy, Commercial Art, Drawings, Etchings & Engravings, Graphic Arts, Painting-Japanese, Prints, Sculpture, Historical Material, Ceramics, Crafts, Ethnology, Asian Art, Porcelain, Anthropology, Furniture, Ivory, Costume Design & Constr, Antiquities-Oriental, Dolls, Enamels, Miniatures, Oriental Art, Pottery, Religious Art, Textiles, Architecture
Collections: Memorabilia of George S Morikami
Exhibitions: Permanent exhib on Yamato colony and authentic tea house
Publications: My Morikami, published 3 times per year
Activities: Classes for adults & children; docent training; guided tours; outreach progs; lects open to pub; 2 vis lectrs per yr; gallery talks; tours; mus shop sells books, magazines, reproductions, jewelry, textiles, children's items, decorative items

FORT LAUDERDALE

L ART INSTITUTE OF FORT LAUDERDALE, Technical Library, 1799 SE 17th St, Fort Lauderdale, FL 33316-3000. Tel 954-463-3000, Ext 541; 800-275-7603; Fax 954-463-1339; Elec Mail webadmin@ail.edu; Internet Home Page Address: www.artinstitute.edu; *Library-LRC Dir* Diane Rider; *Librn* Rick Fought; *Assoc Dir Art* McKinney
Open Mon - Thurs 8 AM - 8 PM, Fri 8 AM - 5 PM; Estab 1973 as a technical library for the applied & fine arts
Purchases: $8000
Library Holdings: Audio Tapes; Book Volumes 1200; Cassettes 50; Clipping Files 2000; Filmstrips; Kodachrome Transparencies; Motion Pictures; Periodical Subscriptions 157; Video Tapes 600
Activities: Educ dept; lect open to public; competitions; scholarships & fels offered; sales shop sells books, prints & supplies
Courses: Picture Files

A BROWARD COUNTY BOARD OF COMMISSIONERS, Cultural Div, 100 S Andrews Ave, FL 6 Fort Lauderdale, FL 33301-1830. Tel 954-357-7457; Fax 954-357-5769; Elec Mail culturaldiv@broward.org; Internet Home Page Address: www.broward.org/arts; *Dir* Mary Becht; *Admin Asst* Rowena Nocom; *Grants Admin* James Shermer; *Grants Financial Analyst* Susan Schultz; *Community Develop Dir* Jody Horne-Leshinsky; *Community Develop Arts Educ* Grace Kewl-Durfey
Estab 1976 to enhance the cultural environment of Broward County through develop of the arts; develops & distributes gov & pvt resources for the visual arts, performing arts, literary arts, museums & festivals; acts as the liaison between cultural organizations, all levels of gov & the pvt sector in encouraging & promoting cultural develop
Publications: Annual Calendar; Arts Education Directory; Cultural Directory; Cultural Quarterly; Cultural Treasures of Broward County Brochure; Voices & Venues Newsletter, bi-monthly
Activities: Schols & grants offered

M MUSEUM OF ART, FORT LAUDERDALE, One E Las Olas Blvd, Fort Lauderdale, FL 33301-1807. Tel 954-525-5500; Fax 954-524-6011; Elec Mail receptionist@moafl.org; Internet Home Page Address: www.moafl.org; *Dir of Retail* Douglas Ratcliff; *Exec Dir & Pres* Irvin Lippman; *Chief Cur* Annegreth Hill
Open Tues - Wed 11 AM - 6 PM, Thurs 11 AM - 8 PM, Sun noon - 5 PM, cl Mon; Admis adults $10, seniors, children 6-17, and military $7, members, children 5 and under, and college students with ID free; Estab 1958 to bring art to the community & provide cultural facilities & programs; Library, exhib space & auditorium are maintained; Average Annual Attendance: 100,000; Mem: 3500; dues corporate $5000, $2500 & $1000, benefactor $1000, patron $500, contributing $250, sustaining $125, family-dual $65, individual $50
Income: Financed by public grants, private philanthropy
Library Holdings: Book Volumes; Exhibition Catalogs; Pamphlets; Periodical Subscriptions; Prints; Slides
Special Subjects: Pre-Columbian Art, Painting-American, Period Rooms, Sculpture, Graphics, Latin American Art, Painting-American, Sculpture, Ceramics, Primitive art, Painting-Dutch
Collections: Golda & Meyer B Marks Cobra Art Collection; William Glackens Collection; American & European paintings, sculpture & graphics from late 19th century-present; Pre-Columbian & historic American Indian ceramics, basketry & stone artifacts; Modern Cuban Collection; West African tribal sculpture; Warhol, Picasso, Dali
Publications: quarterly newsletter, season calendar
Activities: Educ prog; classes for children; docent training; slide lect prog in schools by request; lects open to pub, 3 vis lectrs per yr; gallery talks; tours; films; competitions; individual paintings & original objects of art lent to other mus; mus shop sells books, original art, reproductions, prints

L Library, One E Las Olas Blvd, Fort Lauderdale, FL 33301-1807. Tel 954-525-5500; Fax 954-524-6011; Elec Mail museumofart@hotmail.com; Internet Home Page Address: www.museumofart.org; *Cur Educ* Fran Mulcahy; *Dir of Develop* Lynn Mandeville; *Dir Finance* Robert Granson

Open Tues - Sat 10 AM - 5 PM, Sun Noon - 5 PM; Founded 1958; 35,000 sq ft gallery space
Library Holdings: Book Volumes 7500; Periodical Subscriptions 15; Slides
Collections: William Glackens; Cobra; Contemporary Cuban Collections
Activities: Classes for adults & children; docent training; lects open to pub; originates traveling exhibs; mus shop sells books & novelty items

M **MUSEUM OF DISCOVERY & SCIENCE,** 401 SW Second St, Fort Lauderdale, FL 33312-1707. Tel 954-467-6637; Fax 954-467-0046; Elec Mail information@mods.net; Internet Home Page Address: www.mods.org; *Pres* Kim L Cavendish
Open Mon-Sat 10AM-5PM, Sun noon-6PM, Imax times and prices differ; Admis adults $10, seniors $9, children 2-12 $8, special group rates available, members free; Estab 1977 to increase science literacy; Average Annual Attendance: 534,000; Mem: 5500; dues $75; annual meeting in Sept
Income: $5,500,000
Special Subjects: Graphics, Prints
Exhibitions: Choose Health; Florida EcoScapes; Gizmo City; Great Gravity Clock; KidScience, No Place Like Home; Science Fair; Sound; Space Base; Runways to Rockets; Living in the Everglades
Publications: Explorations, quarterly
Activities: Classes for adults & children; camps; sleepovers; outreach progs; films daily; docent training; lects open to pub, some to mems only, 8-10 vis lectrs per yr; gallery talks; tours; book traveling exhibs 5 per yr; originate traveling exhibs to other mus; mus shop sells books, original art, reproductions, prints & science related activities

M **PURVIS YOUNG MUSEUM,** 725 Progresso Dr, Fort Lauderdale, FL 33304. Tel 954-765-0721; *Owner* Larry T Clemons
Open Tues-Sat 2PM-7PM
Collections: works by Purvis Young, Howard Finster, Thorton Dial, Mose Tolliver & Sybil Gibson; paintings; drawings; news articles; photographs

FORT MYERS

M **EDISON STATE COLLEGE,** Bob Rauschenberg Gallery, 8099 College Pkwy, Fort Myers, FL 33919-5566. Tel 239-489-9313; Fax 239-489-9482; Elec Mail RBishop@Edison.edu; Internet Home Page Address: bobrauschenberggallery.com; *Cur & Dir* Ron Bishop; *Asst* Lindsay Wollard
Open Mon - Fri 10 AM - 4 PM, Sat 11 AM - 3 PM, cl Sun & holidays; No admis fee; Estab 1979 to provide exhibitions of national & regional importance & related educational programs; Main gallery 2000 sq ft, high security; adjunct performing arts hall gallery; Average Annual Attendance: 10,000
Income: Financed by endowment & state appropriation
Exhibitions: Rotating exhibits
Activities: Tours for adults & children; docent training; lect open to public, 4 vis lectrs per year; concerts; gallery talks; tours; annual art show awards; scholarships & fels offered; book traveling exhibs 2 - 4 per year; originate traveling exhibs to other museums in Florida; sales shop sells reproductions, prints, posters & catalogs

FORT PIERCE

M **A.E. BACKUS MUSEUM OF ART,** 500 N Indian River Dr, Fort Pierce, FL 34950-3080. Tel 772-465-0630; Fax 772-468-6204; Elec Mail info@backusmuseum.com; Internet Home Page Address: www.backusmuseum.com; *Dir* Kathleen P Fredrick; *Mktg Dir* Robin Dannahower; *Exhib Coordr* Georgina Love
Open Oct-June Wed-Sat 10AM - 4 PM, Sun noon-4PM; July-Sept by appointment; $2; Estab 1960; visual arts facility; Permanent coll of A.E. Backos, changing exhibs; Average Annual Attendance: 30,000; Mem: 1,110
Income: (financed by mem, admis, fundraising & gift shop)
Special Subjects: Landscapes, Ceramics, Glass, Photography, Painting-American, Prints, Woodcuts, Drawings, Watercolors, Woodcarvings, Jewelry, Reproductions
Collections: Works by A.E. Backus; Painting by the Florida Highwaymen; Paintings by William Douglas Rosa
Activities: docent training; lects for mems only; 4 vis lects per yr; gallery talks; tours; sponsoring competitions; schols; sales shop sells books, original art, reproductions, prints & gift items

GAINESVILLE

M **CITY OF GAINESVILLE,** Thomas Center Galleries - Cultural Affairs, 302 NE Sixth Ave, Bldg A, Gainesville, FL 32061-5476; PO Box 490, Sta 30, Gainesville, FL 32627-0490. Tel 352-393-8532; Fax 352-334-3299; Elec Mail etlingrh@cityofgainesville.org; Internet Home Page Address: www.gvlcultralaffairs.org; *Cultural Affairs Progs Coordr* Russell Etling
Open Mon - Fri 9 AM - 5 PM, Sat & Sun 1 - 4 PM; No admis fee; Estab 1979 to increase local arts awareness; Two small galleries in a historic building; Average Annual Attendance: 9,000
Income: $8,000 (financed by city appropriation, grants & donations)
Special Subjects: Graphics, Latin American Art, Painting-American, Photography, Watercolors, Textiles, Folk Art, Pottery, Woodcarvings, Woodcuts, Landscapes, Portraits, Furniture, Glass, Oriental Art, Historical Material, Period Rooms
Exhibitions: Contemporary American Artists, predominantly Floridian; 6 shows per year in main gallery; 8 shows per year in mezzanine gallery; regional history; photography; antiquities; cultural memorabilia
Publications: Exhibition brochures
Activities: Lect open to public, 4 vis lectrs per year; gallery talks; tours; competitions with prizes; workshops & receptions for artists

M **UNIVERSITY OF FLORIDA,** University Gallery, 400 SW 13th St, Gainesville, FL 32601; PO Box 115803, Gainesville, FL 32611-5803. Tel 352-273-3000; Fax 352-846-0266; Elec Mail galleries@arts.ufl.edu; Internet Home Page Address: www.arts.ufl.edu/galleries; *Dir* Amy Vigilante; *Coordr* Yue Zhang
Open Tues 10 AM - 8 PM, Wed - Fri 10 AM - 5 PM, Sun 1 - 5 PM, cl Mon, Sat & holidays; No admis fee; Estab 1965 as an arts exhibition gallery, open 11 months of the year, showing monthly exhibitions with contemporary & historical content; Gallery located in independent building with small lecture hall, limited access & completely secure with temperature & humidity control, adjustable track lighting; display area is in excess of 3000 sq ft; Average Annual Attendance: 8,000; Mem: 50; dues professional $100 & up, family $50, individual $25
Income: $97,000 (financed by state appropriation & community mem)
Purchases: $2,000
Special Subjects: Folk Art, Pre-Columbian Art, Painting-American, Prints, Painting-British, Latin American Art, Oriental Art
Collections: Contemporary Art
Exhibitions: Changing monthly exhibitions; Annual University of Florida Art Faculty (January); Annual student juried exhibition; MFA thesis exhibitions
Publications: Exhibition catalogs; periodic bulletins
Activities: Lects open to pub; gallery talks; Henri Theil Memorial Purchase Award; exten dept serves area schools; lending collection contains cassettes, original art works, photographs & slides; originate traveling exhibs

L **Architecture & Fine Arts Library,** 201 Fine Arts Bldg A, Gainesville, FL 32611; PO Box 117017, Gainesville, FL 32611-7017. Tel 352-273-2805; Fax 352-846-2747; Internet Home Page Address: www.uflib.ufl.edu/afa; *Architecture Fine Arts Bibliographer & Head Librn* Ann Lindell
Open Mon - Thurs 8 AM - 10 PM, Fri 8 AM - 5 PM, Sat 1 - 5 PM, Sun 2 - 10 PM; Estab 1853 as a state art & architecture information center
Library Holdings: Auction Catalogs; Book Volumes 104,000; CD-ROMs; Exhibition Catalogs; Fiche; Manuscripts; Pamphlets; Periodical Subscriptions 600; Photographs; Reels; Reproductions; Video Tapes
Special Subjects: Folk Art, Intermedia, Landscape Architecture, Decorative Arts, Graphic Arts, History of Art & Archaeology, Latin American Art, American Western Art, Advertising Design, Interior Design, Asian Art, American Indian Art, Afro-American Art, Gold, Architecture
Collections: Rare book collection

M **Samuel P Harn Museum of Art,** Hull Rd & SW 34th St, Gainesville, FL 32611-2700; PO Box 112700, Gainesville, FL 32611-0001. Tel 352-392-9826; Fax 352-392-3892; Elec Mail chale@harn.ufl.edu; Internet Home Page Address: www.harn.ufl.edu; *Dir* Rebecca M Nagy, PhD; *Cur Contemporary Art* Kerry Oliver-Smith; *Cur Modern Art* Dulce Roman; *Dir Educ* Bonnie Bernau; *Dir Mktg* Christine Hale; *Dir Develop* Phyllis DeLaney; *Cur Photography* Thomas Southall; *Cur African Art* Susan Cooksey
Open Tues - Fri 11 AM - 5 PM, Sat 10 AM - 5 PM, Sun 1 - 5 PM; No admis fee; Estab 1990 to collect, preserve, display & interpret art; One of the Southeast's largest university art museums with almost 90,000 square feet. Also a museum store off the Galleria (entrance). Maintains a reference library available to visitors & staff; Average Annual Attendance: 90,000; Mem: 800; dues $40-2,500
Special Subjects: Landscapes, Collages, Pottery, Textiles, Drawings, Hispanic Art, Latin American Art, Painting-American, Photography, Prints, Sculpture, Watercolors, Bronzes, Pre-Columbian Art, Ceramics, Primitive art, Woodcarvings, Painting-European, Asian Art
Collections: African Art; Contemporary Art; Modern Art; Photography
Publications: Inform, bi-monthly newsletter
Activities: Classes for adults & children; docent training; lects open to pub; concerts; gallery talks; tours; individual paintings & objects of art lent; senior outreach prog; book traveling exhibs; originate traveling exhibs; mus shop sells books, magazines, original art, reproductions & prints

HOLLYWOOD

M **ART & CULTURE CENTER OF HOLLYWOOD,** Art Gallery/Multidisciplinary Cultural Center, 1650 Harrison St, Hollywood, FL 33020-6806. Tel 954-921-3274; Fax 954-921-3273; Elec Mail info@artandculturecenter.org; Internet Home Page Address: www.artandculturecenter.org; *Exec Dir* Joy Satterlee; *Asst Dir* Susan Rakes; *Mktg & Design Mgr* Alesh Houdek; *Dir Develop* Jeff Rusnak; *Publ Relations & Community Partnership Mgr* Charmain Yobbi; *Cur* Jane Hart; *Theater Mgr* Robert Halpern
Open Tues - Fri 10 AM - 5 PM, Sat & Sun noon - 4 PM; Admis nonmembers $7, seniors, students & children 4-13 $4, center mems & children age 3 & younger with an adult free; Estab 1975 as a private non-profit corporation for the study, educ & enjoyment of visual & performing arts; Great Gallery, major exhibit space, is 6300 sq ft with 400 running ft; group tours are also held there. Two Hall galleries. Maintains reference library. Gallery hosts at least a dozen thought-provoking, stimulating contemporary art exhibs each yr; Average Annual Attendance: 50,000; Mem: 617; dues $30-$1,000; no annual meeting
Income: $1.3 million (financed by pub funding, foundations, pvt contributions, contracts & mem)
Library Holdings: Book Volumes; Exhibition Catalogs
Special Subjects: Decorative Arts, Etchings & Engravings, History of Art & Archaeology, Illustration, Interior Design, Landscapes, Architecture, Art Education, Art History, Ceramics, Conceptual Art, Mexican Art, Mixed Media, Flasks & Bottles, Furniture, Gold, Porcelain, Portraits, Painting-American, Silver, Textiles, Bronzes, Maps, Painting-British, Painting-European, Painting-Japanese, Drawings, Graphics, Latin American Art, Photography, Sculpture, Watercolors, African Art, Pre-Columbian Art, Religious Art, Crafts, Folk Art, Pottery, Primitive art, Woodcarvings, Woodcuts, Judaica, Collages, Posters, Glass, Jade, Jewelry, Oriental Art, Asian Art, Antiquities-Byzantine, Metalwork, Painting-Dutch, Painting-French, Ivory, Coins & Medals, Restorations, Tapestries, Calligraphy, Miniatures, Painting-Flemish, Painting-Polish, Antiquities-Oriental, Painting-Spanish, Painting-Italian, Antiquities-Persian, Islamic Art, Antiquities-Egyptian, Antiquities-Greek, Antiquities-Roman, Mosaics, Cartoons, Painting-Australian, Painting-German, Reproductions, Antiquities-Etruscan, Painting-Russian, Enamels, Painting-Scandinavian
Collections: 19th & 20th century American & contemporary Florida artists; Contemporary paintings & sculpture; Ethnographic arts
Publications: Exhibition brochures/catalogs
Activities: Classes for adults & children; volunteer training; summer camp for ages 5-18; free admis days; distance learning offered to schools; dramatic progs; lects open to pub; 4 vis lectrs per yr; gallery talks; concerts; group tours; competitions with awards; collection contains 1000 books, 150 original art works, 50 original prints, 70 paintings & 30 sculptures

HOLMES BEACH

M ISLAND GALLERY WEST, 5368 Gulf Dr, Holmes Beach, FL 34217-1775. Tel
941-778-6648; Internet Home Page Address: www.amisland.com/gallery;
Open Mon - Sat 10 AM - 5 PM; No admis fee; Estab 1991 to exhibit & sell local
artists' work; Art work by local & regional artists working in a wide variety of
media; Mem: 30; juried in by current artist members
Activities: Artist demonstrations Sat 10AM-Noon; mus shop sells original art

INDIAN ROCKS BEACH

M GULF BEACH ART CENTER, 1515 Bay Palm Blvd, Indian Rocks Beach, FL
37785-2827. Tel 727-596-4331; Fax 727-596-4331; Elec Mail
arts1515@gmail.com; Internet Home Page Address: www.beachartcenter.org; *Exec
Dir* Jo Ann Marianne
Open Mon - Thurs 9 AM - 4 PM, Fri - Sat 9 AM - 12 PM, cl Thanksgiving,
Christmas; No admis fee, donations accepted; Estab 1978 - Mission is to offer
creative education experiences in the visual arts that stimulate awareness &
appreciation of the arts.
Income: Not-for profit: donations, fund raisers & mem & class fees
Library Holdings: Book Volumes 300
Collections: paintings
Publications: newsletter
Activities: Classes for adults & children; educ prog; workshops; art festivals

JACKSONVILLE

M CUMMER MUSEUM OF ART & GARDENS, Museum & Library, 829
Riverside Ave, Jacksonville, FL 32204-3336. Tel 904-356-6857; Fax
904-353-4101; Internet Home Page Address: www.cummer.org; *Dir* Hope
McMath; *Cur* Holly Keris
Open Tues 10 AM - 9 PM, Wed - Fri 10 AM - 4 PM, Sat 10 AM - 4 PM, Sun
noon - 4 PM; Admis adults $10, seniors, military & students $6, members &
children 5 & under free; Estab 1961 to engage & inspire through the arts, gardens
& educ; Eleven galleries of paintings & decorative arts sited on 2-1/2 acres of
formal gardens; Average Annual Attendance: 130,000; Mem: 3,100; dues
$30-$10,000
Income: Financed by donations, city funds, endowments, membership & grants
Library Holdings: Book Volumes 6,000; Exhibition Catalogs; Periodical
Subscriptions 17; Slides 10,000
Special Subjects: Etchings & Engravings, Landscapes, Ceramics, Portraits,
Pre-Columbian Art, Prints, Woodcuts, Painting-British, Painting-French, Graphics,
Painting-American, Sculpture, Watercolors, Decorative Arts, Painting-European,
Painting-Japanese, Jade, Porcelain, Oriental Art, Asian Art, Painting-Dutch, Ivory,
Tapestries, Baroque Art, Painting-Flemish, Renaissance Art, Medieval Art,
Painting-Israeli
Collections: Netsuke, Inro & porcelains; Early Meissen porcelain; European &
American painting, sculpture, graphic arts & decorative arts; Oriental Coll of jade,
ivory
Publications: A Legacy in Bloom: Celebrating a Century of Gardens at The
Cummer; Eugene Savage: The Seminole Paintings; Early Meissen Porcelain: The
Walk Collection at the Cummer; The Art of Empathy: The Mother of Sorrows in
Northern Renaissance Art & Devotion
Activities: Educ prog; classes for adults & children; lects open to pub; concerts;
gallery talks; tours; originate traveling exhibs; mus shop sells books & original art

M FLORIDA STATE COLLEGE AT JACKSONVILLE, (Florida Community
College at Jacksonville) South Gallery, 11901 Beach Blvd, Jacksonville, FL
32246-6624. Tel 904-646-2023; Fax 904-646-2336; Elec Mail ellewis@fccj.edu;
Gallery Coordr Lynn Lewis
Open Mon - Fri 10 AM - 4 PM, Thurs until 7 PM; No admis fee; Estab 1985
Collections: FCCJ Permanent Collection
Exhibitions: George Merritt Milton; Student Annual Juried School; Toshiko
Takaezu; Joyce Tennyson; Hiram Williams; Arnold Newman; Brooks Jensen
Activities: Classes for adults & children; lects open to public; 4 vis lectrs per yr;
gallery talks

L JACKSONVILLE PUBLIC LIBRARY, Fine Arts & Recreation Dept, 303 N
Laura St Jacksonville, FL 32202. Tel 904-630-2665; Fax 904-630-2431; Internet
Home Page Address: www.jpl.coj.net; *Dept Head* Carole Schwartz; *Dir* Ken
Sivulich; *Sr Librn* Carol Smith
Open Mon-Thurs 9AM-8PM, Fri & Sat 9AM-6PM, Sun 1AM-6PM; No admis
fee; Estab 1905 to serve the pub by giving them free access to books, films,
recordings, pamphlets, periodicals, maps, plus informational services & free
programming
Income: Financed by city appropriation
Library Holdings: Book Volumes 48,000; Motion Pictures 2000; Other Holdings
Compact discs 6000; Periodical Subscriptions 200; Records 10,000; Slides 3500;
Video Tapes 6000
Publications: Annual Report

M JACKSONVILLE UNIVERSITY, Alexander Brest Museum & Gallery, 2800
University Blvd, Jacksonville, FL 32211. Tel 904-256-7374; Fax 904-256-7375;
Elec Mail jturnoc@ju.edu; *Dir* Prof Jack Turnock
Open Mon - Fri 9 AM - 4:30 PM; No admis fee; Estab 1972 to exhibit decorative
arts collection; Two galleries exhibiting decorative arts & Pre-Columbian art &
artifacts. Three galleries contain contemporary art on rotating schedule; Average
Annual Attendance: 12,000
Income: Financed by endowment & private funds
Special Subjects: Etchings & Engravings, Ceramics, Textiles, Woodcuts,
Drawings, Painting-American, Sculpture, Watercolors, Bronzes, African Art,
Pre-Columbian Art, Religious Art, Woodcarvings, Decorative Arts, Furniture,
Glass, Jade, Porcelain, Oriental Art, Asian Art, Painting-Dutch, Carpets & Rugs,
Ivory, Coins & Medals, Painting-Flemish, Antiquities-Persian, Gold, Enamels
Collections: Porcelain; Ivory; Pre-Columbian; Steuben; Tiffany

Publications: Museum catalog
Activities: Classes for adults; docent training; lects open to public, 4-6 vis lectrs
per yr; gallery talks; competitions

M MUSEUM OF CONTEMPORARY ART JACKSONVILLE, (Jacksonville
Museum of Modern Art) 333 N Laura St, Jacksonville, FL 32202-3505. Tel
904-366-6911; Fax 904-366-6901; Elec Mail info@mocajacksonville.org; Internet
Home Page Address: www.mocajacksonville.org; *Dir* Deborah Broder; *Dir Educ
& Exhibs* J Marshall Adams; *Assoc Cur & Registrar* Ben Thompson
Open Tues - Sat 10AM-4PM, Thurs until 8PM, Sun Noon-4PM, Artwalk 5-9 PM,
cl Mon & Federal holidays; Admis adults $8, seniors, military & students with ID
$5, UNF students, children under 2 & mems free; Artwalk free & Sun free for
families; Estab 1948 as an art center for the greater Jacksonville area; Average
Annual Attendance: 100,000; Mem: 3200; dues luminary $500, icon $250,
dual/family $75, individual $50; annual meeting spring
Income: Financed by mem
Special Subjects: Photography, Sculpture, Painting-American, Prints,
Pre-Columbian Art
Collections: Pre-Columbian art; Permanent Coll: 800+ works of art incl painting,
printmaking, sculpture & photography from 20th c, primarily 1960 - present
Publications: Calendar, monthly; exhibition catalogues
Activities: Classes for adults & children; docent training; art enrichment prog;
dramatic progs; lects open to pub, 10 vis lectrs per yr; concerts; gallery talks;
tours; competitions; scholarships offered; book traveling exhibs; originate traveling
exhibs; mus shop sells books, magazines, original art, reproductions, prints,
jewelry & children's toys

M MUSEUM OF SCIENCE & HISTORY, 1025 Museum Circle, Jacksonville, FL
32207. Tel 904-396-7062, Ext 211; Fax 904-396-5799; Elec Mail
cslingluff@themosh.org; Internet Home Page Address: www.themosh.org; *Exec
Dir* Maria Hane; *Pub Rels* Kristi Ballinger
Open Mon - Fri 10 AM - 5 PM, Sat 10 AM - 6 PM, Sun 1 - 6 PM; Admis $9,
seniors & military $7.50, children (3-12) $7; Estab 1941; Lobby & three floors
contain exhibit areas, classrooms & studios; Average Annual Attendance: 225,000;
Mem: 2000; member families dues vary
Income: Financed by admission, earned revenue & pvt support grant
Special Subjects: Historical Material
Collections: Historical; Live Animal Collection; Physical Science Demonstrations
Exhibitions: Alexander Brest Planetarium (16th largest in US); health; science;
wildlife
Publications: Teacher's Guide, annually; brochures, online newsletters; annual
report
Activities: Classes for children; dramatic progs; docent training; lects open to pub;
tours; mus shop and sales shop selling books, prints, museum-oriented items and
toys for children

JUPITER

M EDNA HIBEL ART FOUNDATION, Hibel Museum of Art, 5353 Parkside Dr,
John D. MacArthur Campus Jupiter, FL 33458-2906. Tel 561-622-5560; Fax
561-622-4881; Elec Mail hibelgalleryjupiter@gmail.com; Internet Home Page
Address: www.hibelartmuseum.org; *Dir* Nancy Walls; *Exec Trustee* Edna Hibel
Plotkin; *Dir Educ* Carol Davis; *Prog Coordr* Susan Babila; *Dir Sales* Helene
Plotkin
Open Tues - Fri 11 AM - 4 PM, in season concerts & teas one time/mo Sun &
Mon; No admis fee; Estab 1977 to extend the appreciation of the art of Edna
Hibel, specifically, & visual art in general; 10 galleries & spaces devoted to
paintings, lithographs, sculpture & porcelain art by artist Edna Hibel, features
antique furniture, snuff bottles, paper weights & art book collections. Maintains
reference library; Average Annual Attendance: 2,000; Mem: Meeting Jan
Income: $40,000 (financed by donations, mem, mus gift shop sales, art camp &
private donations)
Purchases: $30,000
Library Holdings: Book Volumes; DVDs; Memorabilia; Original Documents;
Photographs; Sculpture
Special Subjects: Archaeology, Historical Material, Portraits, Drawings, Graphics,
Painting-American, Prints, Sculpture, Watercolors, Primitive art, Etchings &
Engravings, Landscapes, Dolls, Furniture, Glass, Jade, Jewelry, Porcelain,
Renaissance Art, Dioramas, Reproductions
Collections: English & Italian 18th Century furniture; 18th & 19th Century
paperweights; 19th & 20th Century library art books; Paintings; Porcelain Art;
Lithographs; Serigraphs; Sculpture by Edna Hibel; Porcelain Dolls; Archaeological
antiquities & prehistoric minerals, fossils & geodes; Craig Collection of Edna
Hibel's Work; 18th & 19th Century fans
Exhibitions: Portraits (11/2013)
Publications: Exhibition catalogs; exhibition posters
Activities: Classes for children; docent training; summer art camp (7 wks
June-July); lects open to pub; gallery talks; tours; sponsoring of
competitions; scholarships; mus shop sells books, reproductions, original art,
prints, trivits, soaps, plates & porcelain

L Hibel Museum Gallery, 5353 Parkside Dr, Jupiter, FL 33458-2906. Tel
561-622-1380; Fax 561-622-3475; Elec Mail nancy@hibelmuseum.org; Elec Mail
info@hibelmuseum.org; Internet Home Page Address: www.hibelmuseum.org; *Dir
Educ* Carol Davis; *Dir* Nancy Walls; *Prog Coordr* Adra Farriss
Open Tues - Fri 11:30 AM - 3:30 PM Nov - Apr; Tues - Fri 12 PM - 3 PM Apr -
Oct; Sat by appointment; No admis fee; Estab 2003, displaying & selling the art
of Edna Hibel to support the Hibel Museum of Art; For reference only; Average
Annual Attendance: 1,000
Income: Financed through sales & Edna Hibel Art Foundation
Library Holdings: Audio Tapes; Book Volumes 500; Cassettes; Clipping Files;
DVDs; Exhibition Catalogs; Framed Reproductions; Memorabilia; Original Art
Works; Pamphlets; Photographs; Prints; Reproductions; Sculpture; Slides; Video
Tapes
Activities: Classes for adults & children; docent training; lects open to pub, 2 vis
lectrs per yr; lect to school classes & cultural activities for elementary school
children; concerts; gallery talks; tours; book traveling exhibs 4-5 per yr; sales shop

sells books, reproductions & original art, prints, collectable art plates, gift boxes, jewelry, posters, stone lithographs & serigraphs

KEY WEST

M   KEY WEST ART & HISTORICAL SOCIETY, East Martello Museum & Gallery, 3501 S Roosevelt Blvd, Key West, FL 33040-5209. Tel 305-296-3913; Fax 305-296-6206; Elec Mail cpennington@kwahs.org; Internet Home Page Address: www.kwahs.org; *Pres* Bob Feldman; *Exec Dir* Claudia Pennington; *Dir Opers* Diane Rippe; *Museum Store Mgr* Linda Hardy
Open daily 9:30AM-4:30PM; Admis $6 adults, children 7-15 $3, active military free, seniors and local residents $5, children under 6 free; Estab 1962 to preserve history of the Florida Keys; 2300 square feet Civil War fort, last standing Martello fort in country; Average Annual Attendance: 25,000; Mem: 2000; dues $40, family $100, student $40; annual meeting in Apr
Income: Financed by mem, donations, admis & gift shop sales
Special Subjects: Folk Art
Collections: Carvings & paintings of Mario Sanchez; junkyard art of Stanley Papio
Exhibitions: History of Key West
Publications: Martello; two newsletters
Activities: Art & music series for adults & children; lects open to pub, 6 vis lectrs per yr; children's competitions with prizes; individual paintings & original objects of art lent to qualifying mus; book traveling exhibs; mus shop sells books, reproductions, prints, postcards, children's educ material

M   OLD ISLAND RESTORATION FOUNDATION INC, Oldest House in Key West, 322 Duval St, Key West, FL; PO Box 689, Key West, FL 33041-0689. Tel 305-294-9501; Fax 305-294-4509; Elec Mail OldIsland@comcast.net; Internet Home Page Address: www.oirf.org; *Dir* Cork Tarplee
Open Mon, Tues, Thurs - Sat 10 AM - 2PM; Admis $5; Estab 1976 to present the history of Key West's oldest house; Furnished period house with paintings throughout; Average Annual Attendance: 14,000; Mem: 200; dues $15-$20; annual meeting in Apr
Income: $36,000 (financed through donations & fundraising)
Purchases: $2,000 (19th century dining table)
Special Subjects: Folk Art, Marine Painting, Painting-American, Textiles, Costumes, Ceramics, Woodcarvings, Dolls, Furniture, Dioramas, Period Rooms
Collections: Oil on canvas by Edward Moran; All Sailing Ships & Scenes; Watercolors by Marshall Joyce; Watercolors by unknown artists; Orlon canvas by W W Cowell; Polychrome on wood, Mario Sanchez
Exhibitions: Rotating exhibitions
Activities: Classes for children; docent training; sponsoring of competitions; restoration grants; schols

LAKE WALES

M   LAKE WALES ARTS CENTER, 1099 State Rd 60, Lake Wales, FL 33853; 152 E Central Ave, LWAC 012, JDA Lake Wales, FL 33853. *Dir* Osubi Craig

LAKE WORTH

A   CULTURAL COUNCIL OF PALM BEACH COUNTY, (Palm Beach County Cultural Council) 601 Lake Ave, Lake Worth, FL 33460-3810. Tel 561-471-2901; Fax 561-687-9484; Elec Mail rblades@palmbeachculture.com; Internet Home Page Address: www.palmbeachculture.com; *Pres & CEO* Rena Blades; *Dir Fin* Kathleen Alex; *Dir Grants* Jan Radusky; *Mgr Arts & Cultural Educ* Shawn Berry; *Mem & Special Events Mgr* Debbie Calabria; *Grants Coordr* Margaret Granda; *Dir Develop* Mary Lewis; *Admin Asst* Autumn Oliveras; *Web & eMktg Mgr* Daniel Boudet; *Bookkeeper* Jean Brasch; *Develop Assoc* Kristen Smiley; *Mktg Coordr* Theresa Louckes; *Mgr Artist Servs* Nichole Hickey; *Vis Servs Coordr* Marlon Foster
Open Tues - Sat 10 AM - 5 PM; No admis fee; Estab 1978 by Alex W Dreyfoos Jr as the Palm Beach County Council of the Arts to develop, coordinate, & promote the arts & cultural activities throughout Palm Beach County; recognized by the Board of County Commissioners as the county's adv agency for cultural develop & administers a portion of local tourist develop funds under contract with county government; Average Annual Attendance: 6,886; Mem: 545; dues $50-1,000
Income: Financed by donations
Exhibitions: (11/22/2013-01/18/2014) The Deep & the Shallow: Photographs; (01/31/2014-03/29/2014) Interior Design: The Florida Room; (04/11/2014-06/07/2014) En Plein Air; (08/29/2014-10/18/2014) Play Ball!
Publications: Art and Culture Magazine; Arts and Culture Map; Calendar of Events; Cultural Caravan; Treasures Brochure; Teachers Guide to Cultural Organizations in Palm Beach County
Activities: Teachers workshops; teachers guide to organizations; artist in residency program; Ubertalli Award (for visual artists); Fyfe Award (for performing artists)

LAKELAND

M   ARTS ON THE PARK, Lakeland Center for Creative Arts, 115 N Kentucky Ave, Lakeland, FL 33801-5044. Tel 863-680-2787; Elec Mail info@artsontheparklakeland.org; Internet Home Page Address: artsontheparklakeland.org; *Exec Dir* Christine Boring; *Pres* Karen Seggerman; *VPres* Tim Gallagher
Open Tues-Sat noon-4PM, open late Fri nights, cl holidays; No admis fee; Estab 1979 to encourage Florida artists through shows & competitions; 1600 sq ft ground floor, plus second floor galleries in Lakeland's Munn Park Historic District; Average Annual Attendance: 30,000; Mem: 1200; dues sponsor $100-$999, individual $40, senior citizens $30
Income: $80,000 (financed by mem dues, sponsorships, grants, city, bus & industry,)

Exhibitions: Monthly shows; Upstairs gallery is monthly rental
Publications: Constant contact email
Activities: Classes for adults & children; Docent training; lects open to pub, concerts; competitions with awards; juried shows; scholarships; exten dept serves county; originate traveling exhibs; sales shop sells original art, jewelry

M   FLORIDA SOUTHERN COLLEGE, Melvin Art Gallery, 111 Lake Hollingsworth Dr, Lakeland, FL 33801-5698. Tel 863-680-4743, 680-4111; Fax 863-680-4147; Elec Mail apaxson@flsouthern.edu; Internet Home Page Address: www.flsouthern.edu; *Prof Art History & Chmn Div Fine & Performing Arts* James Rogers, PhD; *Assoc Prof Art, Chmn Dept Art & Art History, Dir Studio Prog* William Otremsky, MFA; *Asst Prof Art & Dir Foundation Prog* Kelly Sturhahn, MFA; *Asst Prof Art & Dir Graphic Design Prog* Samuel Romero, MFA; *Adjunct Asst Prof Art History* Nadine Pantano, PhD; *Adjunct Prof Art* Joseph Mitchell, MFA; *Adjunct Instr Art* Eric Blackmore, BFA; *Adjunct Asst Prof Art Educ* Jacquelyn Hanson, MFA; *Prof Emerita* Beth Ford, MA; *Gallery Coordr* Jenna Rice, BFA; *Adjunct Prof Art* Patricia Lamb, MFA
Open Mon - Fri 9 AM - 4 PM when col is in session; No admis fee; Estab 1971 as a teaching gallery; Large 3,000 sq ft main gallery; small one room adjacent gallery; Average Annual Attendance: 3,000-5,000
Library Holdings: Slides
Special Subjects: Drawings, Etchings & Engravings, Landscapes, Glass, Painting-American, Prints, Photography, Folk Art, Portraits
Collections: Brass Rubbings Coll in Roux Library; Laymon Glass Collection in Annie Pfeiffer Chapel; permanent coll in various offices & buildings; Drawing & Painting Coll by Tibor Pataky
Publications: The Art of Downing Barnitz by James G Rogers Jr, William Meek, Alexander Bruce
Activities: Lects open to public, 3 vis lectrs per yr; gallery talks; concerts; sponsoring of competitions; John R Reuter Award, Florida Art Award

M   POLK MUSEUM OF ART, 800 E Palmetto St, Lakeland, FL 33801-5529. Tel 863-688-7743; Fax 863-688-2611; Elec Mail info@PolkMuseumofArt.org; Internet Home Page Address: www.polkmuseumofart.org; *Exec Dir* Daniel Stetson; *Adminr* Terri D'Orsaneo; *Cur Art* Adam Justice; *Cur Educ* Leticia Miller
Open Tues - Sat 10 AM - 5 PM, Sun 1 - 5 PM; Admis adults $5, seniors $4, students & children free; Estab 1966 series of galleries for temporary and permanent exhibitions; 8 galleries with rotating exhibs; permanent Pre-Columbian gallery; Average Annual Attendance: 125,000; Mem: 1,000; dues platinum patron $5,000, gold patron $2,500, patron $1,000, benefactor $500, advocate $250, sponsor $100, family $60, individual $40; annual meeting in June
Income: Financed by mem, cities of Lakeland, Bartow, Auburndale & Winter Haven, Polk County School Board, grants, endowment & special projects
Library Holdings: Auction Catalogs; Book Volumes; Exhibition Catalogs; Periodical Subscriptions 28; Photographs; Prints; Slides
Special Subjects: Afro-American Art, Drawings, Folk Art, Ceramics, Collages, Glass, Silver, Sculpture, Latin American Art, Painting-American, Photography, Prints, African Art, Pre-Columbian Art, Textiles, Decorative Arts, Oriental Art, Asian Art, Carpets & Rugs, Juvenile Art, Gold, Antiquities-Assyrian
Collections: 15th-19th Century European Collection of ceramics; Pre-Columbian Collection; assorted decorative arts; Asian arts; contemporary paintings, photographs, prints & sculpture featuring American artists; South African textiles & fibers; Ellis Verink Collection
Exhibitions: Changing exhibitions; 9 student gallery exhibitions including 12th Congressional District Competition; Permanent display of Pre-Columbian art; temporary displays of student, contemporary and historic art
Publications: Exhib catalogues and gallery guides, quarterly newsletter, ann report
Activities: classes for adults & children; dramatic programs; docent training; workshops; lects open to pub; gallery talks; tours; competitions with awards; lifetime art achievement award; outreach programs; annual outdoor art festival; Family Day; sculpture competition; schols & fels offered; exten prog serves children of Polk City, Florida; book traveling exhibs 2 per yr; originate traveling exhibs to other mus in Florida; mus shop sells books, original art, reproductions, prints, jewelry, home decorative objects

LEESBURG

M   LEESBURG CENTER FOR THE ARTS, 429 W Magnolia St, Leesburg, FL 34749; PO Box 492857, Leesburg, FL 34749-2857. Tel 352-365-0232; Fax 352-315-1152; Internet Home Page Address: www.leesburgcenter4arts.com/index.htm

MAITLAND

M   MAITLAND ART CENTER, 231 W Packwood Ave, Maitland, FL 32751-5553. Tel 407-539-2181; Fax 407-539-1198; Elec Mail RCmailMAC@aol.com; Internet Home Page Address: www.maitlandartcenter.org; *Educ Coordr* Ann E Spalding; *Prog Coordr* Dawn Feavyour; *Cur Coll* Richard D Colvin; *CEO & Exec Dir* James G Shepp; *Staff Coordr* Carol B Shurtleff; *2nd VChmn* Priscilla Cockerell; *Treas* Renae Vaughn; *VChmn* Stockton Reeves; *Secy* Belinda Townsend; *Community Relations* Pamela Wells; *1st VChmn* Wallace G Harper; *Mus Store Mgr* Diedre Peeler
Open Mon - Fri 9 AM - 4:30 PM, Sat & Sun Noon - 4:30 PM, cl major holidays; Admis adults $3, students 12-22 & Maitland residents $2; Estab 1938 to promote exploration & educ in the visual arts & contemporary crafts; listed in National Register of Historic Places; Four galleries totaling 202 running ft; Average Annual Attendance: 60,000; Mem: 625; dues $20-$1000; annual meeting in Sept
Income: Financed by mem, city & state appropriations, donations, special events, endowment
Special Subjects: Drawings, Graphics, Painting-American, Photography, Prints, Sculpture, Watercolors, Crafts, Pottery, Woodcarvings, Woodcuts, Etchings & Engravings, Landscapes, Collages, Posters, Eskimo Art, Glass, Porcelain
Collections: Architectural work including 6-acre compound & memorial chapel designed by Smith; graphics; paintings & sculptures of Andre Smith; etchings & drawings

Publications: Exhibit catalogs; quarterly class schedules; quarterly newsletter
Activities: Classes for adults & children; docent training; lects open to pub, 2 vis lectrs per yr; concerts; gallery talks; tours; individual paintings & original objects of art lent to museums & art centers; book traveling exhibs 1 per yr; originate traveling exhibs to mus, art centers, libraries & universities; mus shop sells original art, reproductions, cards, jewelry & children's items

L **Library,** 231 W Packwood Ave, Maitland, FL 32751-5553. Tel 407-539-2181; Fax 407-539-1198; Elec Mail rcolvin@itsmymaitland.com; Internet Home Page Address: www.maitlandartcenter.org; *Dir* James G Shepp; *Cur Coll* Richard D Colvin; *Educ Coordr* Ann E Colvin; *Prog Coordr* Gloria Capozzi; *Mus Store Mgr & Receptionist* Dierdra Peeler; *Mem/Art Travel* Ana M de la Hidalga-Bartolomei; *Admin Asst/Accounting* Margaret Pytel
Open Mon - Fri 9 AM - 4:30 PM, Sat & Sun Noon - 4:30 PM, cl major holidays; Admis non members $3, 65 & older $2, students $1, members no fee; Estab 1970 to promote knowledge & educ in American Art; Open for reference; Average Annual Attendance: 60,000; Mem: 625
Income: Financed by City of Maitland, mem, tuition, special events, grants, contributions, gallery donations
Library Holdings: Book Volumes 4500; Exhibition Catalogs; Periodical Subscriptions 10; Slides; Video Tapes
Special Subjects: Photography, Painting-American, Posters, Prints, Sculpture, Portraits, Watercolors, Printmaking, Porcelain, Pottery, Woodcarvings, Woodcuts
Collections: Works by Andre Smith (1880 - 1959); exhibiting artists
Exhibitions: Connecting Andre Smith & Zora Neale Hurston: Maitland & Eatonville as Joining Communities; Fashion, Fun & Fantasy: Creative Garments by Ruth Funk; Decorative Arts of West Africa; Engravings by Albert Decaris; The Romantic Landscape: Prints & Drawings by Jules Andre Smith; A Shadow Falls on Beaverbrook: A Murder Mystery by Frank Besedick; A Showcase of Stone Lithography; George Spivey: American Primitive Painter
Activities: Educ prog; classes for adults & children; docent prog; lects open to pub, 3 vis lectrs per yr; concerts; gallery talks; tours; originate traveling exhibs; mus shop sales reproductions, prints, jewelry, greeting cards & glass items

MELBOURNE

M **FOOSANER ART MUSEUM,** (Brevard Art Museum) 1463 Highland Ave, Melbourne, FL 32935-6562. Tel 321-674-8916; Fax 321-242-0798; Elec Mail info@brevardartmuseum.org; Internet Home Page Address: www.foosanerartmuseum.org; *Dir Univ Mus* Carla Funk; *Admin Asst to Dir Univ Mus* Tama Johnson; *Mgr Vis Servs* Tina Murray; *Cur Exhibs* Jackie Borsanyi; *Coll Mgr* Jose Marquez; *Cur Educ* Sara Petrosky
Open Tues - Sat 10 AM - 5 PM, Sun 1 PM - 5 PM, Special: Thurs 10 AM - 7 PM free admis, cl Mon & major holidays; General admin $5, children under 18 yrs, seniors & full-time students $2, mus mems, Florida Inst of Tech faculty, staff & students w/campus ID free; Estab 1978 to exhibit art for the educ, information, & enjoyment of the pub; Exhibition facility with approx 6000 sq ft of exhibition space; Average Annual Attendance: 70,000; Mem: dues patron $150 & up, general $55, senior $25; annual meeting fourth Tues in June
Income: $400,000 (financed by mem, city & county appropriation, corporate gifts & grants)
Library Holdings: Auction Catalogs; Audio Tapes; Book Volumes; CD-ROMs
Collections: Contemporary regional & national artists; drawings, paintings, prints of Ernst Oppler; Chase Collection; Clyde Butcher Photographs; Shared Vision Collection
Exhibitions: Rotating exhibs of international, national & regional artists
Publications: Quarterly newsletter; calendar for members; handouts & catalogues for changing exhibitions
Activities: Classes for adults & children; docent training; artist-in-residence prog; lects open to pub, 10 vis lectrs per yr; concerts; gallery talks; tours; sponsoring of competitions; schols offered; book traveling exhibs 1-2 per yr; originate traveling exhibs to qualifying institutions; mus shop sells books, magazines, original art, reproductions, prints

MIAMI

M **BAKEHOUSE ART COMPLEX, INC,** 561 NW 32nd St, Miami, FL 33127-3749. Tel 305-576-2828; Fax 305-576-0316; Elec Mail info@bacfl.org; Internet Home Page Address: www.bacfl.org; *Exec Dir* Arlys Raymond; *Pres Board* Harvey Oxenberg
Open daily Noon - 5 PM; No admis fee; Estab 1986; 2600 sq ft gallery; Average Annual Attendance: 6,500; Mem: 3100; dues sponsor $500, supporter $250, friend $100, family $60, individual $40; annual meeting in Sept
Income: $350,000 (financed through mem, studio rents, grants & contributions)
Special Subjects: Portraits, Restorations, Painting-Spanish, Painting-Australian
Exhibitions: 20 exhibs per yr, contact for more information
Activities: Classes for adults, children & advanced artists; lect open to public; 4-6 vis lectrs per year; panel discussions; concerts; tours; competitions with awards; scholarships & fels; individual painting & original object of art lent to city facilities & developers; retail store sells original art

M **FLORIDA INTERNATIONAL UNIVERSITY,** The Patricia & Phillip Frost Art Museum, Modesto A Maidique Campus, 10975 SW 17th St Miami, FL 33199. Tel 305-348-2890; Fax 305-348-2762; Elec Mail artinfo@fiu.edu; Internet Home Page Address: thefrost.fiu.edu; *Educ Cur* Linda Powers; *Coll Cur, Registrar* Debbye Kirschtel-Taylor; *Mem Coordr* Ximena Gallegos; *Dir* Carol Damian; *Comm & Mktg Mgr* Jessica Delgado; *Develop Dir* Michael Hughes; *Budget & Finance Mgr* Mary Alice Manella; *Preparator* Andrew Vasquez; *Security Mgr* Julio Alvarez; *Asst Cur* Klaudio Rodriguez; *Grants Specialist* Kelly Brady-Rumble
Open Tues - Sat 10 AM - 5 PM, Sun noon - 5 PM, cl Mon; No admis fee; Estab 1977; 46,000 sq ft bldg, 9 galleries; Average Annual Attendance: 100,000; Mem: 200
Income: Financed by state appropriation & supported by Friends of the Art Mus, private foundations & municipal councils
Library Holdings: DVDs; Exhibition Catalogs
Special Subjects: Architecture, Latin American Art, Sculpture
Collections: Cintas Foundation Collection; The Metropolitan Museum & Art Center Collection; Betty Laird Perry Emerging Artist Collection & Sculpture Park
Publications: Exhibition catalogues
Activities: Dade County Public Schools Museum Educ Program; classes for children; docent training; summer camp; teacher workshops; lect open to public, lects for mems only, 4-5 visiting lectrs per year; gallery talks; tours of Sculpture Park; mus sales shop sells books, catalogs, exhibit/program merchandise

M **MIAMI ART MUSEUM,** 101 W Flagler St, Miami, FL 33130-1504. Tel 305-375-3000; Fax 305-375-1725; Internet Home Page Address: www.miamiartmuseum.org; *Pub Rels* Tracy Belcher; *Curatorial* Emily Vera; *Educ* Mayra Suarez
Open Tues - Fri 10 AM - 5 PM, Sat & Sun Noon - 5 PM, cl Mon; Admis adults $8, seniors $4, free for members, students with ID, & children under 12; Estab 1984 to exhibit, collect, preserve & interpret international art with a focus on the art of the Western Hemisphere from the World War II era to the present; 16,000 sq ft of gallery space on two levels; 3300 sq ft sculpture ct; 1800 sq ft auditorium; Average Annual Attendance: 50,000; Mem: 1700; dues $45
Income: Financed by corporations, individuals, foundations, mem, Florida Department of State, Florida Arts Council, & Division of Cultural Affairs
Library Holdings: Exhibition Catalogs; Pamphlets; Photographs; Reproductions; Slides
Collections: 165 works of art by Bertoia, Davis, Dubuffet, Frankenthaler, Gottlieb, Jarr, Rauschenberg, Rickey, Simpson, Snelson, Stella
Exhibitions: average 12 exhibs per yr
Publications: MAM News, quarterly; exhib brochures
Activities: Docent progs; films; concerts; lects for mem only, 10 vis lectrs per yr; gallery talks; tours; book traveling exhibs 10 per yr; originate traveling exhibs; MAM store sells books, magazines, reproductions, prints, jewelry, art-greeting cards, posters & gift items

A **MIAMI WATERCOLOR SOCIETY, INC,** PO Box 561953, Miami, FL 33156-1953. Tel 305-380-6348; Fax 305-663-5885; Elec Mail info@miamiwatercolor.org; Internet Home Page Address: www.miamiwatercolor.org; *1st VPres & Co-Chmn* Diane Lary; *1st VPres & Co-Chmn* Kathy Maling; *2nd VPres* Evelyn Chesney; *Treas* Daisy Armas-Garcia; *Corresp Secy* Virginia Reynolds-Botwin; *Recording Secy* Marilyn Bakst; *Pres* Clarice Londono; *Trustee* June A Fried; *Trustee* Emily Sokoloff; *3rd VPres* Karen Deilke
Special Subjects: Watercolors
Exhibitions: Two annual juried exhibitions; several unjuried exhibitions
Activities: Educ dept; workshops several times per year; monthly demonstrations; lect open to public; 9 vis lectrs per yr; competitions with awards; scholarships offered

M **MIAMI-DADE COLLEGE,** Kendal Campus, Art Gallery, 11011 SW 104th St M-123, Miami, FL 33176-3393. Tel 305-237-2322; Fax 305-237-2901; Elec Mail lfontana@mdc.edu; Internet Home Page Address: www.mdc.edu; *Acting Dir* Lilia Fontant
Open Mon - Thurs 8 AM -7:30 PM, Fri 8 AM - 4 PM, Sat 9:30-4:30 PM; No admis fee; Estab 1970 as a teaching laboratory & pub service; Average Annual Attendance: 15,000
Income: Financed by state appropriation
Purchases: $250,000
Special Subjects: Afro-American Art, Drawings, Etchings & Engravings, Folk Art, Historical Material, Photography, Painting-American, Woodcuts, Sculpture, Latin American Art, Photography, Prints, African Art, Painting-Spanish
Collections: Contemporary American paintings, photographs, prints, sculpture includes: Beal, Boice, Bolotowsky, Christo, Ferrer, Fine, Gibson, Henry, Hepworth, Hockney, Judd, Komar, Lichtenstein, Marisol, Melamid, Michals, Motherwell, Nesbitt, Oldenburg, Parker & Pearlstein; Bedia, Schnabel
Exhibitions: Fritz Bultman; Connie Fox; Philip Gieger; John Hull; William King; Melissa Weinman; Richard Williams; Magdalena Abakanowicz; Diane Lechleitner; Kay Walking Stick
Publications: 6 catalogs per year
Activities: Lects open to pub, 4-6 vis lectrs per yr; concerts; gallery talks; individual paintings & original objects of art lent; lending collection contains original art works, original prints, paintings, photographs, sculpture; originates traveling exhibs

M **Wolfson Galleries,** 300 NE 2nd Ave, No 1365 Bldg 1, 3rd Floor Miami, FL 33132-2204. Tel 305-237-3696; Fax 305-237-3819; Elec Mail csalazar2@mdcc.edu; Internet Home Page Address: www.mdcc.edu; *Dir Cultural Affairs* Olga Garay; *Gallery Dir* Amy Cappellazzo; *Dir* Carolina Salazar; *Chmn* Mercedes Quiroga
Open Tues 10AM-5PM, Wed-Fri 1PM-5PM; No admis fee; Gallery estab 1990 to exhibit contemporary art, host residencies; educational art; Secured spaces with alarm systems, no windows; 2700 sq ft, 1100 sq ft, 600 sq ft (3 spaces); Average Annual Attendance: 20,000
Income: $299,000, as part of Wolfson Campus Galleries (financed by endowment, annual grants & state appropriation)
Collections: Centre Gallery - Youth Matters; Endurance: The Information (The History of the Body in performance Arts; Inter-American Gallery - Linda Matalon: Gathering & protecting, Carol Sun
Publications: Exhibition catalogs
Activities: Educ packets; workshops; symposia; lects open to pub, 12 vis lectrs per yr; book traveling exhibs 3 per yr; originate traveling exhibs 1 per yr

M **Gallery North,** 11380 NW 27th Ave, Bldg 5 Room 5106 Miami, FL 33167-3418. Tel 305-237-1532; Fax 305-237-1850
Open Mon - Thurs 9 AM - 5 PM Fri 9 AM - 2 PM; No admis fee
Collections: Paintings; sculpture; photographs
Activities: Lectures

L **MIAMI-DADE PUBLIC LIBRARY,** 101 W Flagler St, Miami, FL 33130-1504. Tel 305-375-2665; Fax 305-372-6428; Internet Home Page Address: www.nfaa.org; *Asst Dir* William Urbizu; *Art Svcs Librn* Barbara Young Mead-Donaldson; *Dir* Raymond Santiago; *Technical Svcs Adminr* Susan Lee; *Asst Dir* Sylvia Moura-Ona; *Youth Svcs Adminr* Lucrece Louisdhon-Lovinis; *Branch Adminr* Don Chauncey; *Branch Adminr* Elise Ledy Kennedy
Open Mon - Wed & Fri - Sat 9 AM - 6 PM, Thurs 9 AM - 9 PM, Sun (Oct -

May) 1 - 5 PM; No admis fee; Estab 1947 to provide the informational, educational and recreational needs of the community; Gallery maintained, Artmobile maintained
Income: Financed by special millage
Library Holdings: Cassettes 2000; Clipping Files; Exhibition Catalogs; Fiche; Framed Reproductions 800; Motion Pictures 5500; Original Art Works 1200; Pamphlets; Periodical Subscriptions 100; Photographs; Prints; Records 4000; Reels; Reproductions; Video Tapes 6000
Special Subjects: Latin American Art, Afro-American Art
Collections: African American original graphics; Latin American original graphics; Oriental collection of original graphics; Creole Collection
Publications: Exhibition catalogs
Activities: Lects open to public; concerts; gallery talks; tours; exten dept; artmobile; reproductions lent; book traveling exhibs, 1-2 per yr; originate traveling exhibitions, permanent collection of works on paper

NATIONAL FOUNDATION FOR ADVANCEMENT IN THE ARTS
For further information, see National and Regional Organizations

M **NEW WORLD SCHOOL OF THE ARTS,** Gallery, 25 NE Second St, Miami, FL; 300 NE Second Ave, Miami, FL 33132-2297. Tel 305-237-3620; Fax 305-237-3794; Elec Mail nwsapost.mel@mdcc.edu; *Asst Dean* Louise Romeo; *Gallery Dir* Randell Von Bloomberg; *Dean Visual Arts* Dr Mel Alexenberg
Open 9 AM - 5 PM; No admis fee; Estab 1990 to exhibit contemporary art & design; Major gallery in downtown Miami showing contemporary art & design from USA & abroad & faculty & student art work; Average Annual Attendance: 54,000
Income: Financed by county & state appropriation
Publications: Exhibition catalogs
Activities: High School & BFA progs; lects open to pub, 25 vis lectrs per yr; concerts; gallery talks; tours; juried student exhibitions; schols offered; book traveling exhibs 2 per yr; originate traveling exhibs 1 per yr

M **RUBELL FAMILY COLLECTION AND CONTEMPORARY ARTS FOUNDATION,** 95 NW 29th St, Miami, FL 33127. Tel 305-573-6090; Fax 305-573-6023; Elec Mail info@rfc.museum; Internet Home Page Address: www.rfc.museum; *Dir* Juan Roselione-Valadez
Open by appointment; Adults $10, children under 18 $5
Collections: works by contemporary artists; paintings; sculpture

A **SOUTH FLORIDA CULTURAL CONSORTIUM,** Miami Dade County Dept of Cultural Affairs, 111 NW First St Ste 625, Miami, FL 33128-1964. Tel 305-375-4634; Fax 305-375-3068; Elec Mail culture@miamidade.gov; Internet Home Page Address: www.miamidadearts.org; *Exec Dir* Michael Spring; *Deputy Dir* Deborah J Margol; *Chief Arts Educ* Francine M Anderson; *South Miami-Dade Cultural Arts Ctr* Eric B Fliss
Open Mon - Fri 9 AM - 5 PM; Estab 1976 to provide planning, coordination, promotion & advocacy, as well as funding support & technical assistance to & marketing for Dade County's & South Florida's cultural organizations & activities; create a nurturing environment for the develop of cultural excellence & diversity; address the needs of cultural community that includes the visual & performing arts, history, historic preservation & folklife, the sciences, festivals & special events, & the literary & media arts

M **VIZCAYA MUSEUM & GARDENS,** 3251 S Miami Ave, Miami, FL 33129-2897. Tel 305-250-9133; Fax 305-285-2004; Elec Mail joel.hoffman@vizcayamuseum.org; Internet Home Page Address: www.vizcayamuseum.org; *Exec Dir* Joel M Hoffman
Open daily (mus) 9:30 AM - 4:30 PM, (house) 9:30 AM - 5 PM, (gardens) 9:30 AM - 5:30 PM, cl Christmas; Admis house & gardens $15, children 6-12 $6; Estab 1952 to preserve & interpret art & design in historical contents; Vizcaya is a house mus with a major collection of European decorative arts & elaborate formal gardens. The Hour, formerly the home of James Deering, was completed in 1916 & contains approx 70 rooms; The Vizcaya Village, in the process of renovation, includes eleven national historic landmark bldgs; Average Annual Attendance: 185,000; Mem: 1500; dues $35 & up; annual meeting third Wed in Apr
Special Subjects: Sculpture, Bronzes, Textiles, Ceramics, Decorative Arts, Furniture, Carpets & Rugs, Tapestries, Renaissance Art, Period Rooms, Antiquities-Oriental, Antiquities-Roman
Collections: Italian & French Furniture of the 16th-18th & early 19th centuries; Notable Specialized Collections of Carpets. Tapestries, Furniture, Roman Antiques & Bronze Mortars; 16th-19th Centuries Decorative Arts; Archives
Publications: Vizcayan Newsletter, quarterly
Activities: Tours for children; docent training; lects open to pub; concerts; tours; individual paintings & original objects of art lent to accredited mus; mus shop sells books, magazines, original art, reproductions, prints & slides
L **Vizcaya Volunteer Guides Library,** 3251 S Miami Ave, Miami, FL 33129. Tel 305-250-9133, Ext 2242; Fax 305-285-2004; *Librn* Frances Hall
Open to mus volunteers & students of the decorative arts for reference only
Income: Financed by donations
Library Holdings: Book Volumes 4000; Cassettes; Exhibition Catalogs; Kodachrome Transparencies; Memorabilia; Other Holdings Archival material; Periodical Subscriptions 18; Photographs; Slides
Special Subjects: Decorative Arts, Interior Design, Furniture
Collections: Slide collection for reference & teaching

MIAMI BEACH

M **BASS MUSEUM OF ART,** 2100 Collins Ave, Miami Beach, FL 33139-1919. Tel 305-673-7530; Fax 305-673-7062; Elec Mail scubina@bassmuseum.org; Internet Home Page Address: www.bassmuseum.org; *Exec Dir & Chief Cur* Silvia Karmen Cubina; *Asst Dir* Jean Ortega; *Chief Preparator/ Exhib Technician* Jan Galliardt; *Registrar & Exhib Mgr* Chelsea Guerdat; *Dir Individual Giving & Special Events* Denise Wolpert; *Dir External Affairs* Megan Riley; *Dir Educ* Adrienne von Lates; *Admin Asst to Exec Dir* Elisa Alonso
Open Wed - Sun Noon - 5 PM, cl Mon & Tues; Admis adults $8, students & seniors $6; Estab 1963 for the collection & exhibition of works of art. Collection

features European art, architectural drawings & contemporary art; The museum is a two-story 1930 art deco structure with a new wing designed by Arata Isozaki; Average Annual Attendance: 40,000; Mem: 1,000; dues student $25, $50 ind, $75 family, sustaining $125, contributing $250, donor $500, silver dir cir $1000, gold dir cir $2500, platinum dir cir $5000
Income: $1,900,000 (financed by city, mem & grants from state, county & federal government)
Library Holdings: Book Volumes; Cassettes; Exhibition Catalogs
Special Subjects: Painting-American, Ceramics, Decorative Arts, Painting-European, Furniture, Painting-British, Painting-Dutch, Baroque Art, Painting-Flemish, Antiquities-Oriental
Collections: Permanent collection of European textiles, Old Master paintings, Baroque sculpture, Asian art, ecclesiastical artifacts, 19th & 20th century graphics, paintings & architectural drawings & arts; Photography
Exhibitions: (Ongoing) Selections from the Collection
Publications: Quarterly magazine; exhibition catalogues; permanent collection catalogue
Activities: Docent Training; family days; lects open to pub; 10 vis lectrs per year; concerts; films; gallery talks; tours; individual & original objects of art lent to other museums; originate traveling exhibs; sales shop selling books, original art, reproductions, prints

A **THE WOLFSONIAN-FLORIDA INTERNATIONAL UNIVERSITY,** 1001 Washington Ave, Miami Beach, FL 33139-5099. Tel 305-531-1001; Fax 305-531-2133; Elec Mail info@thewolf.fiu.edu; Internet Home Page Address: www.wolfsonian.org; *Dir* Cathy Leff; *Head Librn* Frank Luca; *Head Registrar* Kim Bergen; *Assoc Dir for Cur Affairs* Marianne Lamonaca; *Deputy Dir Finance, Opers & Admin* Julian Gomez
Open Mon, Tues, Thurs, Sat & Sun noon - 6 PM, Fri noon - 9 PM, cl Wed; Admis adults $7, seniors, students and children 6-12 $5, Wolfsonian members, children under 6, State Univ System of Florida students, faculty & staff free, Fri 6 - 9 PM no admis fee for all; Estab 1986; Average Annual Attendance: 30,000
Library Holdings: Book Volumes; Manuscripts; Memorabilia; Other Holdings; Pamphlets; Prints
Special Subjects: Architecture, Drawings, Graphics, Historical Material, Manuscripts, Photography, Porcelain, Posters, Prints, Sculpture, Silver, Textiles, Watercolors, Stained Glass, Decorative Arts, Portraits, Furniture, Glass, Maps, Bookplates & Bindings, Dioramas, Coins & Medals
Collections: Architecture & Design Arts; Decorative & Propaganda Arts (pertaining to period 1885-1945); Fine Arts; Rare & Reference Library
Exhibitions: Art and Design in the Modern Age; Agitated Images: John Heartfield & German Photomontage 1920-1938; Fashioning the Modern French Interior: Pochoir Portfolios in the 1920s; A Bittersweet Decade: The New Deal in America, 1935; Thoughts on Democracy: American Streamlined Design: The World of Tomorrow
Publications: The Journal of Decorative and Propaganda Arts
Activities: Classes for adults & children; lects for mem only, concerts, gallery talks, tours, schols, fellowships; 1 - 2 book traveling exhibs per yr; mus shop sells books, prints, reproductions, prints, design objects, housewares, movies

M **WORLD EROTIC ART MUSEUM,** 1205 Washington Ave, Miami Beach, FL 33139. Tel 305-532-9336; Fax 305-695-1209; Elec Mail missnaomi@weam.com; Internet Home Page Address: www.weam.com; *Owner, Cur* Naomi Wilzig; *Gen Mgr* J C Harris; *Art Dir* Helmut Schuster; *Mktg* Robert Harbour
Open daily Mon - Thurs 11 AM - 10 PM, Fri - Sun 11 AM - midnight; Admis adults $15, seniors $14, students $13.50; Estab 2005. Children not allowed admission; Historical exhibition of erotic art through the ages; Mem: $100 annual-new campaign
Income: Privately financed
Library Holdings: Book Volumes 250; Kodachrome Transparencies
Special Subjects: Afro-American Art, Decorative Arts, Etchings & Engravings, Ceramics, Glass, Metalwork, Mexican Art, Antiquities-Assyrian, Flasks & Bottles, Gold, Photography, Pre-Columbian Art, Painting-American, Painting-European, Painting-French, Sculpture, Tapestries, Hispanic Art, Watercolors, American Indian Art, Bronzes, Ethnology, Religious Art, Folk Art, Woodcuts, Judaica, Posters, Eskimo Art, Dolls, Furniture, Jade, Jewelry, Porcelain, Oriental Art, Asian Art, Silver, Antiquities-Byzantine, Ivory, Scrimshaw, Coins & Medals, Miniatures, Period Rooms, Antiquities-Oriental, Painting-Italian, Antiquities-Persian, Antiquities-Egyptian, Antiquities-Greek, Antiquities-Roman, Cartoons, Stained Glass, Painting-German, Pewter, Leather, Reproductions, Antiquities-Etruscan, Painting-Russian, Painting-Israeli
Collections: Personal collection of Naomi Wilzig; Josephine Baker - Black History Month - Feb 2011
Activities: Lects open to pub; award - Key to the City -enhancing cultural atmosphere; tours; mus shop sells books, reproductions, prints, postcards, art objects & jewelry

MIAMI LAKES

M **JAY I KISLAK FOUNDATION,** (Jay I Kislak Foundation, Inc) 7900 Miami Lakes Dr W, Miami Lakes, FL 33016. Tel 305-364-4208; Fax 305-821-1267; Elec Mail foundation@kislak.com; Internet Home Page Address: www.KislakFoundation.org; *Dir* Arthur Dunkelman
Open Mon-Fri by appointment; No admis fee; One large gallery
Collections: Pre-Columbian art & artifacts; rare books & manuscripts; Polar
Publications: Columbus to Catherwood (book)
Activities: Classes for children; open to Miami-Dade County pub schools

NAPLES

M **DEBRUYNE FINE ART,** (Naples Art Gallery) 275 Broad Ave S, Naples, FL 34102-7028. Tel 941-262-4551; Fax 239-262-4051; Elec Mail info@debrynefineart.com; Internet Home Page Address: www.debrunyefineart.com; *Co-Pres* Suzanne DeBruyne; *Co-Pres* Paul DeBruyne
Open Mon - Thurs 10 AM - 5 PM, Fri & Sat 10 AM - 8 PM, Sun Noon - 5 PM; No admis fee; Estab 1965 to present works of prominent American artists for

display in home or office; Contains foyer with fountain & four additional gallery rooms & sculpture garden; 4600 sq ft of gallery space; Average Annual Attendance: 15,000

Income: $1,000,000 (financed by sales)

Exhibitions: Jenness Cortez, Marilyn Simandle, EJ Paprocki, Edouard Cortes (1882-1969)

Publications: Exhibit brochures

NORTH MIAMI

M **MUSEUM OF CONTEMPORARY ART,** 770 NE 125th St, North Miami, FL 33161-5654. Tel 305-893-6211; Fax 305-891-1472; Elec Mail info@mocanomi.org; Internet Home Page Address: www.mocanomi.org; *Educ Cur* Adrienne von Lates; *Registrar* Kim Stillwell; *Dir* Bonnie Clearwater; *Prog Mgr* Jeremy T Chestler

Open Tues - Sat 11 AM - 5 PM, Sun Noon - 5 PM; Admis adults $5, students & seniors $3, under 12, members, and residents free; Estab 1981 to feature national, international & Florida artists; 1 main gallery; Average Annual Attendance: 30,000; Mem: 2000; dues $25-$1,000

Income: Financed by mem, city appropriation, private donations, corporations foundations

Special Subjects: Architecture, Drawings, Graphics, Hispanic Art, Latin American Art, Painting-American, African Art, Ceramics, Etchings & Engravings, Landscapes, Afro-American Art, Collages, Furniture, Glass, Jewelry

Collections: Contemporary Art

Exhibitions: 8-10 rotating exhibits

Publications: Catalogs; newsletter, quarterly

Activities: Classes for adults & children; docent training; lects open to pub; concerts; gallery talks; tours; schols offered; originate traveling exhibs & performances; mus shop sells books, magazines, original art

NORTH MIAMI BEACH

M **ANCIENT SPANISH MONASTERY,** (Saint Bernard Foundation & Monastery) 16711 W Dixie Hwy, North Miami Beach, FL 33160-3714. Tel 305-945-1461; Fax 305-945-4052; Elec Mail stbernard@bellsouth.net; Internet Home Page Address: www.spanishmonastery.com; *Cur* Dr Gregory Mansfield

Open Mon-Sat 10 AM - 4:30 PM, Sun noon - 4:30 PM; Admis adults $8, seniors $4, under 5 free; Estab 1133 AD; A reconstruction of a monastery built in Segovia, Spain, in 1133, with original stones brought to the United States by William Randolph Hearst

Income: Financed by members & donations of visitors

Library Holdings: Original Art Works; Original Documents; Photographs; Sculpture

Special Subjects: Religious Art, Historical Material

Collections: Historic and Religious Material; paintings; sculpture

Activities: Classes for adults & children; docent training; lects open to the pub; 6-8 vis lectrs per yr; concerts; gallery talks; tours; arts festivals; mus shop sells books, magazines, original art, reproductions, prints, slides, jewelry & religious objects

OCALA

M **COLLEGE OF CENTRAL FLORIDA,** (Appleton Museum of Art) Appleton Museum of Art, 4333 E Silver Springs Blvd, Ocala, FL 34470-5001. Tel 352-291-4455; Fax 352-291-4460; Elec Mail ormej@cf.edu; Internet Home Page Address: www.appletonmuseum.org; *Dir* Cindi Morrison, Ph.D; *Cur of Exhibs* Ruth Grim; *Staff Asst III* Joyce Orme; *Mgr Mem, Events & Fundraisers* Colleen Harper; *Registrar* David Reutter; *Coordr Facilities* Russell Days; *Coordr Finance Servs* Kathleen Balboni

Open Tues - Sat 10 AM - 5 PM, Sun 12 - 5 PM, cl New Year's Day, Thanksgiving, Christmas; Admis call for fees; Estab 1987; Average Annual Attendance: 50,000

Library Holdings: Book Volumes; Video Tapes

Collections: Permanent colls of European, American & Contemporary Art; African, Asian & Pre-Columbian artifacts

Exhibitions: Temp exhibs throughout the yr

Publications: Artifacts newsletter, 3 times per yr

Activities: Educ progs; classes for adults & children; docent training; lects open to pub; guided tours; films; concerts; originates traveling exhibs; mus shop sells books, magazines, original art, reproductions, prints

M **COLLEGE OF CENTRAL FLORIDA,** Appleton Museum of Art, 4333 E Silversprings Blvd, Ocala, FL 34470-5001. Tel 352-291-4455; Fax 352-291-4460; Elec Mail applevt@cf.edu; Internet Home Page Address: www.appletonmuseum.org; *Dir* Dr John Lofgren; *Cur* Ruth Grim

Open Tues - Sat 10 AM - 5 PM, Sun noon - 5 PM; Admis adults $6, seniors & students (19 & over) $4, youths (10-18) $3, children 9 & under free; Estab 1987 as a service to the community; Permanent art collection & temporary exhibitions; Average Annual Attendance: 24,000

Income: Financed by state appropriations

Library Holdings: Auction Catalogs; Book Volumes; CD-ROMs; Clipping Files; DVDs; Exhibition Catalogs; Manuscripts; Motion Pictures; Pamphlets; Periodical Subscriptions; Slides

Collections: European, American & contemporary art; African, Asian, Islamic & pre-Columbian artifacts

Exhibitions: Series of temporary exhibitions throughout the yr

Publications: Appleton's "Artifacts" newsletter plus exhibition catalogs

Activities: Classes for adults & children, docent training; 4-6 lectrs per yr; concerts; gallery talks; tours; scholarships offered; extension program for students in Marion, Levy & Citrus counties; mus sells books, reproductions, prints, clothing, jewelry & puzzles

M **FLORIDA STATE UNIVERSITY AND CENTRAL FLORIDA COMMUNITY COLLEGE,** The Appleton Museum of Art, 4333 NE Silver Springs Blvd, Ocala, FL 34470-5000. Tel 352-236-7100; Fax 352-236-7137; Elec Mail ormej@of.edu; Internet Home Page Address: www.appletonmuseum.org; *Deputy Dir Finance/Admin* Jim Rosengren; *Facilities Dir* Russell Days; *Dir Curatorial Affairs* Dr Leslie Hammond; *Assoc Educ/Vol Coordr* Margie Shambaugh; *Assoc Dir* Sandra Talarico; *Coordr* Colleen Harper

Open Tues - Sat 10 AM - 5 PM, Sun Noon - 5PM; Admis adults $6, seniors & students with ID $4, children under 10 free; Estab 1987 to provide cultural & educational programs; Average Annual Attendance: 50,000; Mem: 3500; dues $15-2500

Income: $1,000,000 (financed by endowment, mem & state appropriation)

Special Subjects: Painting-American, Sculpture, Watercolors, Bronzes, African Art, Pre-Columbian Art, Textiles, Religious Art, Landscapes, Decorative Arts, Painting-European, Portraits, Furniture, Glass, Jade, Porcelain, Oriental Art, Asian Art, Marine Painting, Metalwork, Painting-French, Carpets & Rugs, Ivory, Maps, Medieval Art, Antiquities-Persian, Islamic Art, Antiquities-Egyptian, Antiquities-Greek, Antiquities-Roman, Painting-German, Antiquities-Etruscan

Collections: Appleton Museum of Art Collection; Antiquities, Asian, Pre-Columbian & African; Decorative Arts; European Painting & Sculpture

Publications: Gallery guides; museum catalog; quarterly newsletter

Activities: Educ dept; classes for adults & children; docent training; lects open to pub, 10 vis lectrs per yr; concerts; gallery talks; tours; individual paintings & original objects of art lent to other institutions; lending collection contains books, photographs & slides; book traveling exhibs 8-10 per yr; originate traveling exhibs to state institutions; mus shop sells books, original art, reproductions, posters & jewelry

ORLANDO

M **MENNELLO MUSEUM OF AMERICAN ART,** 900 E Princeton St, Orlando, FL 32803-1437. Tel 407-246-4278; Fax 407-246-4329; Elec Mail mennello.museum@cityoforlando.net; Internet Home Page Address: www.mennellomuseum.com; *Exec Dir* Frank Holt; *Office Mgr* Kim Robinson; *Cur Educ* Geneive Bernard; *Media Coordr* Lindy Sheperd

Open Tues - Sat 10:30 AM - 4:30 PM, Sun Noon - 4:30 PM, cl Mon; Admis adults $5, seniors (55+) & students $4, children under 12 & active military free; Estab 1998; American art; Average Annual Attendance: 27,000; Mem: 300, dues $25 and up

Income: $535,000 (financed by city appropriation) & friends board

Purchases: $50,000

Library Holdings: Auction Catalogs 150; Audio Tapes 1,000; Book Volumes 400; CD-ROMs; Cassettes; Clipping Files; Compact Disks; DVDs; Exhibition Catalogs; Kodachrome Transparencies 400; Manuscripts; Memorabilia; Original Art Works; Original Documents; Pamphlets; Periodical Subscriptions 10; Photographs; Records; Reproductions; Sculpture; Slides; Video Tapes

Special Subjects: Glass, Painting-American, Drawings, Graphics, Hispanic Art, Photography, Prints, Sculpture, Watercolors, American Indian Art, American Western Art, Bronzes, Southwestern Art, Textiles, Ceramics, Folk Art, Pottery, Woodcarvings, Woodcuts, Etchings & Engravings, Landscapes, Afro-American Art, Decorative Arts, Collages, Silver, Scrimshaw

Collections: American Art

Publications: Exhibit catalogs; Members magazine

Activities: Classes for adults & children; dramatic programs; docent training; lects open to pub, 3 vis lectrs per yr; concerts; gallery talks; tours; sponsoring of competitions; book traveling exhibs 3 per yr; originate traveling exhibs to other museums, SAAM, Fenimore; mus shop sells books, magazines, original art work, reproductions, prints & other items

M **ORLANDO MUSEUM OF ART,** 2416 N Mills Ave, Orlando, FL 32803-1483. Tel 407-896-4231; Fax 407-896-9920; Elec Mail info@omart.org; Internet Home Page Address: www.omart.org; *Exec Dir* Marena Grant Morrisey; *Cur* Hansen Mulford; *Cur of Educ* Jane Ferry; *Mktg Mgr* Linda Cegelis; *Registrar* Andrea Long; *Chmn* Diane Culpepper; *Mus Shop Mgr* MaryAnn Keane; *Pres* Curtis McWilliams; *Controller* Teri Aide

Open Tues - Fri 10 AM - 4 PM, Sat & Sun Noon - 4 PM; Admis adults $8, seniors & college students $7, students 6-18 $5; ages 5 & younger and OMA members no charge; Estab 1924 to encourage the awareness of & participation in the visual arts. Accredited by the American Assoc of Museums; 81,884 sq ft mus; seven galleries including exhibitions of 19th & 20th Century American Art, Pre-Columbian & African Art; Average Annual Attendance: 341,066; Mem: 2900; dues $40 & up; annual meeting in Sept

Income: Financed by mem, United Arts of Central Florida, Inc & State of Florida

Library Holdings: Auction Catalogs; Book Volumes; Clipping Files; Pamphlets; Periodical Subscriptions

Special Subjects: Etchings & Engravings, Photography, Painting-American, Sculpture, Painting-American, Prints, American Western Art, African Art, Pre-Columbian Art, Afro-American Art

Collections: 19th & 20th Century American painting, sculpture, prints & photography; Pre-Columbian from Central & South America; African Art

Publications: Members Magazine, 4 times per year; mem newsletter, 12 times per year; exhibition catalogues

Activities: Classes for adults & children; dramatic progs; docent training; lects open to pub, 2 vis lectrs per yr; concerts; gallery talks; tours; competitions with awards; scholarships offered; individual prints & original objects of art lent to mus; book traveling exhibs 3-4 per yr; originate traveling exhibs; mus shop sells books, magazines, reproductions, art exhibit & art related merchandise; original art; prints

L **Orlando Sentinel Library,** 2416 N Mills Ave, Orlando, FL 32803-1483. Tel 407-896-4231; Fax 407-896-9920; Elec Mail info@omart.org; Internet Home Page Address: www.omart.org; *Exec Dir* Marena Grant Morrisey; *Cur* Hansen Mulford; *Cur of Educ* Jane Ferry; *Mktg Mgr* Linda Cegelis; *Registrar* Andrea Long; *Mus Shop Mgr* MaryAnn Keane; *Pres* Diane Culpepper

Open Tues - Fri 10 AM - 4 PM, Sat & Sun Noon - 4 PM, cl Mon & Holidays; Admis adults $8, seniors & students $7, children between 6 & 18 $5; Estab 1924; Average Annual Attendance: 100,000

Library Holdings: Auction Catalogs; Book Volumes 3600; Clipping Files; Exhibition Catalogs; Pamphlets; Periodical Subscriptions 10
Special Subjects: Art History, Landscape Architecture, Decorative Arts, Painting-American, Pre-Columbian Art, Prints, History of Art & Archaeology, Ceramics, American Western Art, Art Education, Furniture, Mexican Art, Glass, Aesthetics, Afro-American Art
Collections: Traditional & Contemporary American Art; African Art; Pre-Columbian Art
Activities: Educ prog; classes for adults and children; docent training; lects open to pub; concerts; gallery talks; tours; mus shops sells books, magazines, original art, reproductions & prints

A **PINE CASTLE CENTER OF THE ARTS,** 6015 Randolph St, Orlando, FL. Tel 407-855-7461; Fax 407-812-7202; Elec Mail joan.h.pyle@cwix.com; Elec Mail sansoneb@pinecastle.org; *Dir* Bettielee Sansone
Open by appointment only; No admis fee; Estab 1965 as a nonprofit community cultural center which provides programs in visual arts, folk crafts, local history, music & drama, & sponsors special projects for handicapped & senior citizens; One room 15 x 15 ft in main building; 85 yr old cracker farm house; 208 yr old log cabin; Average Annual Attendance: 25,000
Income: Financed by private citizens
Collections: Oral histories of area Old-timers, along with photographs, memorabilia & antiques
Exhibitions: Festival
Publications: Pioneer Days Annual Historical Magazine
Activities: Classes for adults & children; dramatic progs; concerts in the park

L **UNIVERSITY OF CENTRAL FLORIDA LIBRARIES,** PO Box 162666, Orlando, FL 32816-2666. Tel 407-823-2564; Fax 407-823-2529; Internet Home Page Address: www.library.ucf.edu; *Dir* Barry B Baker; *Assoc Dir Admin* Frank R Allen; *Head of Acquisitions* Mary Page; *Head Spec Coll* Laila Miletic-Vejzovic
Open in spring Mon - Thurs, 7:45 AM - 1 AM, Fri 7:45 AM - 7 PM, Sat 9 AM - 7 PM, Sun Noon - 1 AM; summer Mon - Thurs & Sun, 7:45 AM - 11 PM; Estab 1968
Collections: Bryant West Indies Collection, artifacts, original paintings, rare books; Caribbean Art; Leonardo Nierman Collection

M **VALENCIA COMMUNITY COLLEGE,** Art Gallery-East Campus, 701 N Econlockhachee Trail, Orlando, FL 32825-6404; PO Box 3028, Orlando, FL 32802-3028. Tel 407-299-5000, Ext 2298; Fax 407-249-3943; Internet Home Page Address: www.valencia.cc.fl.us; *Pres* Sanford Shugart; *Gallery Cur* David Walsh
Open Mon - Fri 8:30 AM - 4:30 PM; No admis fee; Estab 1982
Income: Financed by state appropriation, grants & private donations
Purchases: $1500
Collections: Permanent collection: Mixed Media; Small Works: Mixed Media
Activities: Individual paintings & original objects of art lent; lending collection contains 250 items; originate traveling exhibs 2 per yr

ORMOND BEACH

M **ORMOND MEMORIAL ART MUSEUM AND GARDENS,** 78 E Granada Blvd, Ormond Beach, FL 32176-6534. Tel 904-676-3347; Fax 904-676-3344; Elec Mail omam78e@aol.com; Internet Home Page Address: www.ormandartmuseum.org; *Dir* Ann Burt; *Educ Specialist* Jeanne Malloy; *Admin Asst* Vanessa Elliott; *Dir* Susan Tucker
Open Mon - Fri 10AM-4PM; Admis general $2 ; Estab 1946 to house the symbolic oil paintings of Malcolm Fraser; Four connecting rooms opens to two galleries; Average Annual Attendance: 15,000; Mem: 1000; dues $20-$1,000; monthly meetings & annual meeting in Sept
Income: $238,000 (financed by endowment, mem & city appropriation)
Collections: Malcolm Fraser Symbolic Paintings - permanent collection; Catherine Combs lusterware; Florida landscapes
Exhibitions: Paintings, photography, crafts, sculpture & multi-media exhibits
Publications: Halifax Magazine
Activities: Classes for adults & children; lects open to pub; workshops & children's events; private tours available; gallery tours

PALM BEACH

M **HENRY MORRISON FLAGLER MUSEUM,** 52 Cocoanut Row, Palm Beach, FL 33480-4037; PO Box 969, Palm Beach, FL 33480-0969. Tel 561-655-2833; Fax 561-655-2826; Elec Mail mail@flaglermuseum.us; Internet Home Page Address: www.flaglermuseum.us; *Dir* John Blades; *Chief Cur* Tracy Kamerer; *Educ Dir* Allison Goff; *Dir Mem Svcs* Sarah Brutschy; *Facilities Mgr* Bill Fallacaro; *Bus Mgr* Susan Present; *Pub Affairs Dir* David Carson; *Mus Store & Cafe Mgr* Kristen Cahill
Open Tues - Sat 10 AM - 5 PM, Sun Noon - 5 PM, cl Mon; Admis adults $18, youth 13-17 $10, children 6-12 $3, under 6 free, reserved groups 20+ $14; Estab 1959 for preservation & interpretation of the Whitehall mansion, the 1902 residence built for Standard Oil partner & pioneer developer of Florida's east coast, Henry Morrison Flagler; Fifty-five room historic house with restored rooms & special collections, special events & exhibitions. Accredited by the American Assoc of Museums; Average Annual Attendance: 80,000; Mem: 1500; dues $75-$10,000
Income: Financed by endowment, mem & admis
Special Subjects: Painting-European, Architecture, Painting-American, Sculpture, Textiles, Decorative Arts, Furniture, Glass, Silver, Carpets & Rugs, Historical Material, Period Rooms, Laces
Collections: Original family furnishings, china, costumes; furniture; glassware; paintings; silver; sculptures; extensive lace collection; private railcar
Exhibitions: Various temporary exhibits
Publications: Flagler Museum, An Illustrated Guide; Inside Whitehall Magazine, quarterly; exhibit catalogs

Activities: Classes for children; docent training; mentor program; summer camps; lects open to pub; 8 vis lectrs per yr; gallery talks; concerts; tours; books 1-2 traveling exhibs per yr; mus shop sells books, reproductions & prints, gifts

A **THE SOCIETY OF THE FOUR ARTS,** 2 Four Arts Plaza, Palm Beach, FL 33480. Tel 561-655-7227; Fax 561-655-7233; Internet Home Page Address: www.fourarts.org; *Pres* Ervin S Duggan; *Exec VPres* Nancy Mato
Open Dec - mid - Apr Mon - Sat 10 AM - 5 PM, Sun 1 - 5 PM; Admis adults $5, children 14 and under free; Estab 1936 to encourage an appreciation of the arts by presentation of exhibitions, lectures, concerts, films & programs for young people & the maintenance of a fine library & gardens; Five galleries for exhibitions, separate general library, gardens & auditorium; Average Annual Attendance: 100,000 (galleries & library); Mem: Dues $1,200 per yr
Income: Financed by endowment, mem, city appropriation toward maintenance of library & contributions
Library Holdings: Auction Catalogs; Audio Tapes; Book Volumes; CD-ROMs; Compact Disks; DVDs; Exhibition Catalogs; Periodical Subscriptions
Exhibitions: (11/2013-6/2015) Illustrating Words: The Wonderous Fantasy World of Robert L Forbes, poet & Ronald Searle, artist (on display in the Mary Alice Fortin Children's Art Gallery)
Publications: Calendar; schedule of events, annual, quarterly newsletter
Activities: Classes for adults & children; programs for young people; dramatic programs; lects open to pub; vis lectrs min 40 per yr; concerts; gallery talks; films

L **Gioconda & Joseph King Library,** 3 Four Arts Plaza, Palm Beach, FL 33480. Tel 561-655-2766; Fax 561-659-8510; Elec Mail kinglibrary@fourarts.org; Internet Home Page Address: www.fourarts.org; *Art Reference Librn* Nila Bent; *Librn* Joanne Rendon
Open Mon - Fri 10 AM - 5 PM, cl Sat May - Nov; No admis fee; Estab 1936; Circ Non-circulating collection; Mem: Dues $25 family, $12 mems
Income: Financed by endowment, mem & city appropriation
Library Holdings: Auction Catalogs 1,000; Book Volumes 10,000; Exhibition Catalogs 5,000; Periodical Subscriptions 70; Video Tapes 50
Special Subjects: Art History, Folk Art, Landscape Architecture, Decorative Arts, Mixed Media, Photography, Drawings, Etchings & Engravings, Graphic Design, Islamic Art, Painting-American, Painting-British, Painting-Dutch, Painting-Flemish, Painting-French, Painting-German, Painting-Italian, Painting-Japanese, Painting-Russian, Painting-Spanish, Prints, Sculpture, Painting-European, History of Art & Archaeology, Portraits, Watercolors, Ceramics, Conceptual Art, Crafts, Latin American Art, Painting-Israeli, American Western Art, Bronzes, Printmaking, Cartoons, Fashion Arts, Interior Design, Art Education, Asian Art, Video, American Indian Art, Porcelain, Primitive art, Eskimo Art, Furniture, Ivory, Jade, Costume Design & Constr, Glass, Mosaics, Stained Glass, Aesthetics, Afro-American Art, Metalwork, Antiquities-Oriental, Antiquities-Persian, Carpets & Rugs, Dolls, Embroidery, Handicrafts, Jewelry, Miniatures, Oriental Art, Pottery, Religious Art, Restoration & Conservation, Silver, Silversmithing, Tapestries, Textiles, Woodcuts, Marine Painting, Landscapes, Antiquities-Assyrian, Antiquities-Byzantine, Antiquities-Egyptian, Antiquities-Etruscan, Antiquities-Greek, Antiquities-Roman, Painting-Scandinavian, Laces, Architecture
Collections: John C Jessup Collection; Henry P McIntosh Collection; James I Merrill Collection; Addison Mizner Collection: 300+ reference books & scrapbooks
Publications: Booklist, semi annual
Activities: Library tours; 4 vis lectrs per yr; book talks with authors

PANAMA CITY

M **VISUAL ARTS CENTER OF NORTHWEST FLORIDA,** 19 E Fourth St, Panama City, FL 32401. Tel 850-769-4451; Fax 850-785-9248; Elec Mail vacexhibitions@knology.net; Internet Home Page Address: www.vac.org.ch; *Exec Dir* Ellen Killough; *Admin Dir* Denise Walker; *Educ & Fundraising Coordr* Jerry Pilcher
Open Tues-Sat 10AM-6PM, Sun noon-6PM; Admis adults $3.50, seniors & military $2.50, student $1.50, children under 6, mem & every Tues free; The Center occupies the old city hall, jail & fire station on the corner of Fourth St & Harrison Ave in downtown Panama City. Main gallery hosts contemporary artists, juried competitions & mus coordinated collections. The lower galleries feature emerging artists & community sponsored competitions & collections; Impressions Gallery for children; Average Annual Attendance: 20,000; Mem: 540; family $60, individual $35, student $15
Income: Financed by mem, grants & corporate sponsors
Collections: Permanent collection contains works of artists from Northwest Florida
Exhibitions: Rotating exhibits of all types of art
Publications: Images, newsletter, every 3 months
Activities: Classes for adults & children; docent progs; gallery talks; tours; competitions with prizes; individual paintings & original objects of art lent to bus; book traveling exhibs 2 per yr; junior mus

L **Visual Arts Center Library,** 19 E Fourth St, Panama City, FL 32401. Tel 850-769-4451; Fax 850-785-9248; Elec Mail vac@visualartcenter.org; Internet Home Page Address: www.vac.org.cn; *Admin Dir* Joanne Kennedy; *Exhibit Coordr* Christopher Arrant; *Educ Coordr* Tiffany Woesneer; *Exec Dir* Tina L Dreyer; *Vol Coordr* Lee Venus; *Pres Bd* Todd Neves
Open Mon, Wed & Fri 10 AM - 4 PM, Tues & Thurs 10 AM - 8 PM, Sat 1 - 5 PM, cl Sun; No admis fee; For reference & limited lending; Art gallery, exhibition space, art education & classes; Mem: 750; dues $15-$100
Income: Financed by mem, grants, corporate sponsors
Library Holdings: Book Volumes 200; Original Art Works; Video Tapes
Collections: Linoleum block prints; Robert Hodgell Collection
Activities: Classes for adults & children; docent training; 20 lects per yr open to pub; gallery talks; tours; sponsoring of competitions

PEMBROKE PINES

M **BROWARD COMMUNITY COLLEGE - SOUTH CAMPUS,** Art Gallery, 7200 Hollywood Blvd, Bldg 69 Pembroke Pines, FL 33024-7225. Tel 954-201-8895; Fax 954-963-8934; Elec Mail directorskbelan@broward.edu; *Gallery Dir* Dr Kyra Belan
Open Mon - Fri 10 AM - 2 PM; No admis fee; Estab 1991 to offer contemporary

art exhibs & cultural enrichment activities to col students & to the surrounding community; Gallery is 31 ft x 31 ft with a glass wall & high ceilings
Income: Financed by grants
Exhibitions: Studio Art Club Annual Juried Exhibition
Activities: Lect open to public, 6 vis lectrs per year; competitions

PENSACOLA

A **HISTORIC PENSACOLA PRESERVATION BOARD,** T.T. Wentworth Jr. Florida State Museum, Historic Pensacola Village, 120 Church St Pensacola, FL 32501; PO Box 12866, Pensacola, FL 32576-2866. Tel 850-595-5985; Fax 850-595-5989; Elec Mail lrobertson@historicpensacola.org; Internet Home Page Address: www.historicpensacola.org; *Museum Adminr* Tom Muir; *Dir* John P Danièls; *Museum Cur* Lynne Robertson; *Museum Cur* Lisa Dunbar; *Historian* Richard Brosnaham
Open Tues - Sat 10 AM - 4 PM; Admis adults $6, seniors $5, children 4-16 $2.50; Estab 1967 to preserve, maintain & operate for the educ & enjoyment of the pub certain bldgs & objects of historical interest in Pensacola & the surrounding areas (northwest Florida); Multi-building complex includes two museums & three historic houses; main gallery includes history of develop of West Florida as well as area for temporary exhibits; Average Annual Attendance: 50,000; Mem: 350; dues $35 per year basic family membership
Income: $650,000 from state, supplemented with funding from city & county governments & earned income from rentals, store sales, admissions & memberships
Collections: Archives; costumes; decorative arts; Early 19th & 20th century local artists; Marine lumbering & farming tools & equipment; T.T. Wentworth Jr collection of historical artifacts & documents; Manual G Runyan Art Collection
Activities: Docent training; classes for adults & children; sales shop sells books, reproductions & local crafts; historical toys & souvenirs; Discovery Gallery, 120 Church St Pensacola, FL 32501

M **PENSACOLA MUSEUM OF ART,** 407 S Jefferson St, Pensacola, FL 32502-5901. Tel 850-432-6247; Fax 850-469-1532; Elec Mail info@pensacolamuseumofart.org; Internet Home Page Address: www.pensacolamuseumofart.org; *Exec Asst* Kate Moloney; *Exec Dir* Melissa Morgan; *Assoc Cur* Leah Griffin; *Educ Coordr* Patrick Jennings; *Registrar & Preparator* Nicholas J Christopher; *Develop Coordr* Kate Sutley; *Exec Dir* Sonya Davis; *Asst to Dir* Hillary Hughes; *Dir Finance* Jessica Hyche; *Interim Educ Coordr* Betsy Walker; *Graphic Design & Mktg Coordr* Amber Johnson; *Patrons' Serv & Vol Coordr* Amy Schnupp
Open Tues - Fri 10 AM - 5 PM, Sat & Sun 12 - 5 PM, cl Mon & national holidays; Admis adults $5, students & military $2, members free; Estab 1954 to further & disseminate art history & some studio instruction with regard to the general pub & to increase knowledge & appreciation thereof; Mus is a historical building, old city jail built in 1908 & has 13,000 sq ft of exhibition area; Average Annual Attendance: 85,000; Mem: 850; dues $20-$500; annual meeting in Oct
Income: Financed by mem
Special Subjects: Painting-American, Photography, Prints, Watercolors, African Art, Folk Art, Woodcuts, Etchings & Engravings, Decorative Arts, Portraits, Glass
Collections: Art, African pieces, contemporary art, glass; 20th & 21st century works, all media
Exhibitions: Changing loan exhibitions
Publications: Quarterly newsletter
Activities: Educ prog; classes for adults & children; docent training; lects open to pub, lectrs varies; gallery talks; tours; individual paintings & original objects of art lent to other mus or galleries; extension prog serves Escambia & Santa Rosa County Schools, Univ of West Florida; book traveling exhibs 9 per yr; originate traveling exhibs to regional mus; mus shop sells books, magazines, original art, reproductions, prints, jewelry, cards, stationery, children's items & puzzles

L **Harry Thornton Library,** 407 S Jefferson St, Pensacola, FL 32501-5901. Tel 850-432-6247; Fax 850-469-1532; Elec Mail info@pensacolamuseumofart.org; Internet Home Page Address: www.pensacolamuseumofart.org; *VPres* Margaret N Lorren; *Exec Asst* Sandra J Gentry; *Cur Educ* Vivian L Spencer; *Asst Cur & Registrar* Heather Roddenberry; *Exec Dir* Maria Butler
Open Tues - Fri 10 AM - 5 PM, Sat 10 AM - 4 PM, cl Sun & Mon & national holidays; Estab 1968 to provide reference material for public & members; Reference library
Income: Financed by mem, city appropriation & grants by state & federal government
Purchases: $250
Library Holdings: Audio Tapes; Book Volumes 1500; Exhibition Catalogs; Periodical Subscriptions 10; Slides
Special Subjects: Photography, Painting-American, Sculpture, Glass, Afro-American Art
Collections: Complete set of E Benezit's Dictionaire des Peintres, Sculpteurs, Dessinateurs et Graveurs; Encyclopedia of World Art and other art references books
Publications: Exhibitions catalogs; newsletter, 10 per year
Activities: Classes for adults & children; docent training; lects open to pub, lectrs varies; concerts; gallery talks; purchase & category awards

M **PENSACOLA STATE COLLEGE,** Visual Arts Gallery, Anna Lamar Switzer Center for Visual Arts, 1000 College Blvd, Bldg 15 Pensacola, FL 32504-8998. Tel 850-484-1000; Tel 850-484-2550; Fax 850-484-2564; Elec Mail vspencer@pensacolastate.edu; Internet Home Page Address: www.pensacolastate.edu/visarts; *Dir* Vivian Spencer
Open Mon - Thurs 8 AM - 9 PM, Fri 8 AM - 3:30 PM, cl weekends; No admis fee; Estab 1970 for educ & curation; Average Annual Attendance: 60,000; Mem: Anna Society $250, $500, $1,000
Income: Financed by state appropriation
Library Holdings: CD-ROMs; Clipping Files; Compact Disks; DVDs; Exhibition Catalogs; Framed Reproductions; Kodachrome Transparencies; Manuscripts; Original Art Works; Original Documents; Other Holdings; Pamphlets; Periodical Subscriptions; Photographs; Prints; Reproductions; Sculpture; Slides; Video Tapes
Collections: Contemporary ceramics, glass, drawings, paintings, prints, photographs, sculpture; student work
Publications: Catalog, brochure or poster for each exhibition
Activities: Educ prog; classes for adults; lects open to pub, lects for mems only; 5 vis lectrs per yr; workshops; gallery talks; tours; competitions with awards given; schols offered; individual paintings & original objects of art lent to other mus & lending collection contains original art works; originates traveling exhibs

M **UNIVERSITY OF WEST FLORIDA,** Art Gallery, 11000 University Pkwy, Bldg 82 Pensacola, FL 32514-5732. Tel 850-474-2696; Elec Mail artgallery@uwf.edu; Internet Home Page Address: www.uwf.edu/art/art_gallery.cfm; *Dir* Amy Bowman
Open Mon - Tues, Thurs - Fri 10 AM - 5 PM; No admis fee; Estab 1970 to hold exhibitions of contemporary artwork that enhances the educational mission of the university; Galleries include a foyer gallery 10 x 40 ft & a main gallery of 1500 sq ft. It is fully air-conditioned walls are dry wall with full facilities for construction & display; Average Annual Attendance: 14,000
Income: Financed by state appropriation
Special Subjects: Photography, Prints
Collections: Photographs & prints by a number of traditional & contemporary artists
Activities: Lect open to public, 6 vis lectrs per year; gallery talks; tours; films; competitions with awards; films; scholarships offered; individual paintings & original objects of art lent to university offices; book traveling exhibitions

L **Library,** 11000 University Pkwy, Bldg 32 Pensacola, FL 32514-5750. Tel 850-474-2213; Fax 850-474-3338; Elec Mail ddebolt@uwf.edu; Internet Home Page Address: www.library.uwf.edu/speccoll; *Dir Spec Coll* Dean DeBolt
Open Mon - Fri 8 AM - 4:30 PM; Estab 1967
Income: Financed by state appropriations & Friends of the Library
Library Holdings: Book Volumes 8200; Filmstrips; Memorabilia; Periodical Subscriptions 150
Collections: Includes colls of papers about Gulf Coast artists & art organizations

M **WEST FLORIDA HISTORIC PRESERVATION, INC/UNIVERSITY OF WEST FLORIDA,** T T Wentworth, Jr Florida State Museum; Historic Pensacola Village; Pensacola Historical Society & Resource Center, PO Box 12866, Pensacola, FL 32591-2866. Tel 850-595-5985; Fax 850-595-5989; Elec Mail rbrosnaham@uwf.edu; Internet Home Page Address: www.historicpensacola.org; *Exec Dir* Richard Brosnaham; *Assoc Dir* Robert Overton; *Chief Cur* Lynne Robertson; *Registrar* Carolyn Prime; *Cur* Gale Messerschmidt; *Educ Supv* Dena Bush; *Living History Coord* Jim McMillen; *Educ* Sheyna Marcey; *Archivist* Jacquelyn Wilson
Open Tues-Sat 10AM-4PM; Admis Historic Pensacola Village: adults $6, seniors $5, children ages 4-16 $3, discount to AAA mem, Wentworth Museum & Pensacola Historical Museum: free, PHS Residence Center: $5.50, no admis fee to mems; Estab 1967 to conserve historical items and buildings & make them available to the public; coll contains historic art by local artists; Three floors of exhibits with permanent & changing exhibits & children's hands-on gallery; historic houses & museums of industry & commerce; also maintains non-lending research library & archive (on site use only); Average Annual Attendance: 50,000; Mem: 350; dues grand benefactor $500, Supporter $250, patron $100, family $60, couples $45, individual $35; students & out of town seniors 65+ $20 (time only mem - 80 hrs/annually)
Income: Univ of W Florida; long & short term rentals; admis & store sales
Library Holdings: Book Volumes; Clipping Files; Maps; Memorabilia; Original Art Works; Original Documents; Pamphlets; Photographs; Prints; Records; Reels; Slides; Video Tapes
Special Subjects: Decorative Arts, Historical Material, Landscapes, Marine Painting, Architecture, Ceramics, Flasks & Bottles, Furniture, Photography, Porcelain, Portraits, Pottery, Prints, Period Rooms, Woodcuts, Maps, Drawings, Graphics, Painting-American, Watercolors, Archaeology, Textiles, Costumes, Crafts, Folk Art, Woodcarvings, Etchings & Engravings, Posters, Dolls, Glass, Coins & Medals, Embroidery, Laces
Collections: Works of local & some nationally famous artists; archaeology; coins, porcelain; furnishings; tools and equipment; photographs; documents; maps & prints; dolls & doll houses; structures-historic houses & buildings; architectural elements, blue prints & plans; files by address of local historic district buildings
Publications: Six per yr membership newsletter; monthly calendar of events; ann magazine
Activities: Classes for adults & children; docent training; summer camp for children; museology classes through UWF; internships; living history prog; craft demonstrations; lects for members only, 2-3 vis lectrs per yr; concerts; gallery talks; tours; mus shop sells books & souvenirs; Discovery Gallery on 3rd floor of Wentworth Museum

SAFETY HARBOR

M **SAFETY HARBOR MUSEUM OF REGIONAL HISTORY,** 329 Bayshore Blvd S, Safety Harbor, FL 34695. Tel 727-726-1668; Fax 727-725-9938; Elec Mail info@safetyharbormuseum.com; Internet Home Page Address: www.safetyharbormuseum.org; *Interim Dir* Marilyn K Bartz; *Office Mgr* Shelby Papuga; *Asst Office Mgr & Exhib Dir* Ron Fekete; *Dir Opers* Bobbie Davidson
Open Tues-Wed 10AM-4PM, Thurs 1PM-7:30PM, Fri 10AM-4PM, Sat & Sun 1PM-4PM; Admis adults $4, children $2 (12 to 18), seniors & child 7-18 $3; Estab 1977 to promote, encourage, maintain & operate a mus for the preservation of knowledge & appreciation of Florida's history; to display & interpret historical materials & allied fields; Indian art in the form of murals, pottery & artifacts; Average Annual Attendance: 6,500; Mem: 155; dues $25-2,500; quarterly meetings
Income: $2,000 (financed by mem, grants & donations)
Special Subjects: Historical Material, Maps, American Indian Art, Archaeology, Dioramas
Collections: Florida archaeological artifacts & historical memorabilia
Exhibitions: 2-4 Temporary exhibits
Activities: Docent training; lects open to pub, 7 vis lectrs per yr; gallery talks; tours; originate traveling exhibs; mus shop sells books & Native American reproductions

SAINT AUGUSTINE

A   CITY OF SAINT AUGUSTINE, (Historic Saint Augustine Preservation Board) PO Box 210, Saint Augustine, FL 32085-0210. Tel 904-825-5033; Fax 904-825-5096; Elec Mail hpht@aug.com; Internet Home Page Address: www.historicstaugustine.com; *Cur* John Powell; *Chmn* William R Adams
Open daily 9 AM - 5:15 PM, cl Christmas; Admis to six buildings adults $6.50, students $2.50, children under 6 free; Estab 1959 to depict daily life in the 1740s (Spanish) through its living history mus; Average Annual Attendance: 94,000
Collections: Spanish artifacts; fine & decorative arts; restored & reconstructed colonial buildings from the 18th & 19th centuries
Exhibitions: Permanent & temporary exhibitions
Publications: Brochures & booklets

M   LIGHTNER MUSEUM, 75 King St, Museum-City Hall Complex, PO Box 334 Saint Augustine, FL 32085. Tel 904-824-2874; Fax 904-824-2712; Elec Mail lightner@aug.com; Internet Home Page Address: www.lightnermuseum.org; *Cur* Barry W Myers; *Registrar* Irene L Lawrie; *Visitors Svcs* Helen Ballard; *Exec Dir* Robert W Harper III; *VChmn* Edward G Mussallem; *Mus Shop Mgr* Janice Phelan; *Asst to Dir* Helen C Amato; *Bus Mgr* Angela Blankenship
Open 9 AM - 5 PM, cl Christmas; Admis adults $10, students $2, children under 12 free when accompanied by adult; Estab 1948; Average Annual Attendance: 100,000
Income: Financed by admis
Library Holdings: Auction Catalogs; Book Volumes; Clipping Files; Exhibition Catalogs; Memorabilia; Original Art Works; Pamphlets; Periodical Subscriptions 10; Photographs; Prints; Reproductions; Sculpture
Special Subjects: Anthropology, Drawings, Etchings & Engravings, Folk Art, Landscapes, Glass, Metalwork, Porcelain, Pottery, Painting-American, Silver, Bronzes, Painting-Japanese, Sculpture, Graphics, Hispanic Art, Watercolors, American Indian Art, African Art, Textiles, Costumes, Ceramics, Woodcarvings, Decorative Arts, Judaica, Dolls, Furniture, Jade, Oriental Art, Asian Art, Painting-French, Carpets & Rugs, Ivory, Coins & Medals, Embroidery, Laces, Antiquities-Oriental, Painting-Italian, Antiquities-Egyptian, Antiquities-Greek, Antiquities-Roman, Stained Glass, Painting-German, Military Art, Enamels
Collections: 19th century material culture, decorative arts, & fine arts
Publications: Lost Colony: The Artists of St Augustine
Activities: Classes for adults & children; dramatic progs; docent training; concerts; gallery talks; sales shop sells books, magazines & reproductions

A   SAINT AUGUSTINE ART ASSOCIATION AND ART GALLERY, (Saint Augustine Art Association Gallery) 22 Marine St, Saint Augustine, FL 32084-4438. Tel 904-824-2310; Fax 904-824-0716; Elec Mail info@staaa.org; Internet Home Page Address: www.staaa.org; *Pres* Diane Bradley; *Treas* Audra Lester; *Exec Dir* Elyse Brady; *Vpres* Vincent Celestino
Open Tues - Sat Noon - 4 PM, Sun 2 - 5 PM, cl Mon & holidays; No admis fee; Estab 1924, incorporated 1934 as a non-profit organization to further art appreciation in the community by exhibits & educ, also to provide a gallery where artists may show their work & pub & tourists may see them free; 3600 sq ft of exhibition space with carpeted walls & track lighting; Average Annual Attendance: 10,000; Mem: 600; dues $50 & up; annual meeting in Mar
Income: Financed by mem dues, donations, arts & crafts festivals
Library Holdings: Book Volumes; DVDs; Lantern Slides; Original Art Works; Original Documents; Other Holdings Artifacts; Photographs; Sculpture; Video Tapes
Special Subjects: Painting-American
Collections: Donations of art works by St Augustine artists or members representing St Augustine; Permanent Collection of St Augustine-Lost Colony
Exhibitions: Rotating monthly shows on different themes; National juried "Nature & Wildlife" show $5,000 prize money, $2,500 1st place
Activities: Classes for adults & children; docent training; workshops; Mon night sketch group; lect open to public; concerts; gallery talks; tours; competitions with prizes; $300 Best of Show for 9 exhibs; $500 Best of Show for Honors Show; additional cash prizes; concerts, weddings & meetings on a rental basis; original art sales

M   SAINT AUGUSTINE HISTORICAL SOCIETY, Oldest House Museum Complex, 14 Saint Francis St, Saint Augustine, FL 32084; 271 Charlotte St, Saint Augustine, FL 32084-5033. Tel 904-824-2872; Fax 904-824-2569; Elec Mail sahsdirector@bellsouth.net; Internet Home Page Address: www.oldesthouse.org; *Dir* Dannie Helm; *Mus Store Mgr* Jean Scerbo; *Library Mgr* Charles Tingley
Open daily 9 AM - 5 PM; cl Christmas Day, Thanksgiving Day, Easter; Admis adults $8, seniors $7, students $4; Estab 1883 to preserve the Spanish heritage of the United States through exhibits in historic mus with collection of furnishings appropriate to the periods in Saint Augustine history (1565 to date); Maintains a research library, rotating exhibits gallery; Average Annual Attendance: 58,000; Mem: 600; dues $35; annual meeting in 3rd Tues in Jan
Income: Financed by admis, grants, endowment, mus store, donations
Library Holdings: Audio Tapes; Book Volumes; Clipping Files; Exhibition Catalogs; Fiche; Manuscripts; Maps; Memorabilia; Motion Pictures; Original Art Works; Original Documents; Pamphlets; Periodical Subscriptions; Photographs; Prints; Slides
Special Subjects: American Indian Art, Anthropology, Decorative Arts, Historical Material, History of Art & Archaeology, Interior Design, Landscapes, Architecture, Art Education, Art History, Ceramics, Glass, Furniture, Porcelain, Pottery, Painting-American, Period Rooms, Silver, Manuscripts, Maps, Sculpture, Hispanic Art, Photography, Watercolors, Archaeology, Pre-Columbian Art, Costumes, Folk Art, Portraits, Dolls, Coins & Medals, Painting-Spanish, Reproductions
Collections: Archaeological material recovered from this area, both aboriginal & colonial; period furnishings: Spanish America (1565-1763 & 1783-1821); British (1763-1783); American (1821-present); materials relating to Florida history
Publications: El Escribano, annual; East Florida Gazette, bi-ann; St Augustine News, bimonthly
Activities: Classes for adults; elder hostels; continuing education for architects & interior designers; summer camp; lects open to pub; gallery talks; tours; 5 vis lectrs per yr; individual paintings lent to mus & galleries; mus shop sells books, reproductions, original art, prints & gift items relating to St Augustine history

L   Library, 6 Artillery Ln, Saint Augustine, FL 32084; 271 Charlotte St, Saint Augustine, FL 32084. Tel 904-825-2333; Fax 904-824-2569; Elec Mail sahslibrary@bellsouth.net; Internet Home Page Address: www.oldesthouse.org; *Exec Dir* Susan R Parker, PhD; *Library Dir* Charles Tingley; *Assoc Librn* Judith Foxworth; *Asst Librn* Judy Drapeau
Open Tues - Fri 9 AM - 4:30 PM, 3rd Sat of each month 9 AM - 12:30 PM, cl holidays; No admis fee; 1883; Circ Non-circulating; Research library
Income: Financed by endowment & admis from Oldest House
Library Holdings: Audio Tapes; Book Volumes 10,000; CD-ROMs; Cassettes; Clipping Files; Compact Disks; DVDs; Fiche; Kodachrome Transparencies; Manuscripts; Maps; Memorabilia; Micro Print; Motion Pictures; Original Art Works; Original Documents; Other Holdings Original documents; Pamphlets; Periodical Subscriptions 40; Photographs; Prints; Records; Reels; Reproductions; Sculpture; Slides; Video Tapes
Special Subjects: Art History, Decorative Arts, Film, Photography, Etchings & Engravings, Manuscripts, Maps, Painting-American, Painting-Spanish, Posters, Prints, Historical Material, History of Art & Archaeology, Portraits, Watercolors, Ceramics, Archaeology, Video, American Indian Art, Anthropology, Furniture, Period Rooms, Costume Design & Constr, Glass, Pottery, Religious Art, Restoration & Conservation, Woodcuts, Coins & Medals, Architecture
Collections: Paintings of early artists & of early Saint Augustine; 200 linear feet of maps, photographs, documents & photostats of Spanish archival materials touching directly on Saint Augustine's history during the early Spanish, British & American periods (1565 to present); M J Heade Flower Studies, portraits by Sawer, PA
Publications: East Florida Gazette, semiannually; El Escribano, annually
Activities: Dramatic progs; docent training; Lects open to public, 8 vis lectrs per yr; tours; Historic Community Volunteer Service Award; lend original objects of art to Lightner Museum & Norton Museum of Art; originates traveling exhib to libraries, community ctrs & schools; museum shop sells books, reproductions, prints, slides, jewelry & games

SAINT PETERSBURG

M   FLORIDA CRAFTSMEN GALLERY, 501 Central Ave Saint Petersburg, FL 33701-3703. *Exec Dir* Diane Shelly

M   MUSEUM OF FINE ARTS, SAINT PETERSBURG, FLORIDA, INC, 255 Beach Dr NE, Saint Petersburg, FL 33701-3498. Tel 727-896-2667; Fax 727-894-4638; Elec Mail webmonkey@fine-arts.org; Internet Home Page Address: www.fine-arts.org; *Interim Mus Dir* Roger Zeh; *Chief Cur* Dr Jennifer Hardin; *Interim Cur Educ* John E Schloder; *Dir Devel* Judy Whitney; *Dir Pub Rels* David Connelly
Open Mon - Sat 10 AM - 5 PM; Sun noon - 5 PM; Admis adults $17, seniors $15, youth & college students with ID & youth 7 - 18 $10, mems& children ages 6 & under free; Estab 1962, opened 1965 to increase & diffuse knowledge & appreciation of art; to collect & preserve objects of artistic interest; to provide facilities for research & to offer popular instruction & opportunities for aesthetic enjoyment of art; 25 galleries of works from the collection incl period rooms; Average Annual Attendance: 100,000; Mem: 4000; dues fine arts sustainer $1000, pelican dual $350, pelican single $250, patron $200, family $125, general dual $100, individual $60, educator $45, student $35; annual meeting in May
Income: $1,200,000 (financed by endowment, mem, fundraising, city & state grants) & admis
Purchases: 2.8 million
Library Holdings: Auction Catalogs; Book Volumes; Exhibition Catalogs; Periodical Subscriptions
Special Subjects: Decorative Arts, Drawings, Etchings & Engravings, Folk Art, Art History, Ceramics, Glass, Antiquities-Assyrian, Furniture, Gold, Photography, Portraits, Painting-American, Prints, Silver, Painting-British, Painting-European, Painting-French, Painting-Japanese, Sculpture, Hispanic Art, Latin American Art, Watercolors, American Indian Art, American Western Art, Bronzes, African Art, Pre-Columbian Art, Religious Art, Woodcuts, Painting-Canadian, Asian Art, Antiquities-Byzantine, Painting-Dutch, Painting-Flemish, Period Rooms, Antiquities-Oriental, Painting-Spanish, Painting-Italian, Antiquities-Persian, Antiquities-Egyptian, Antiquities-Greek, Antiquities-Roman, Painting-German, Pewter, Antiquities-Etruscan
Collections: Art: African, Ancient, Asian, Native American & Pre-Columbian; decorative arts; 19th & 20th Century photographs; paintings; Steuben glass; prints; sculpture; 17th, 18th, 19th, & 20th c European Art; 18th, 19th & 20th c American Art
Publications: Mosaic, quarterly newspaper; brochures & exhibition catalogs; catalog of the collection
Activities: Classes for adults & children; docent training; dramatic programs; free admis days; lects open to pub; 4-5 visiting lectrs per yr; films; tours; performing arts; dance; concerts; gallery talks; theatre; storytellers; individual paintings & original objects of art lent to other accredited mus in Greater Tampa Bay Region; artmobile; lending collection contains color reproductions, films on art; originate traveling exhibs to accredited museums and university galleries; mus shop sells books, museum reproductions, prints, mus replicas, jewelry, pottery & crafts by local & national artisans, stationery, cards, children's art educational games & puzzles, t-shirts with museum logo

L   Art Reference Library, 255 Beach Dr NE, Saint Petersburg, FL 33701. Tel 727-896-2667; Fax 727-894-4638; Internet Home Page Address: www.fine-arts.org
Open Tues - Thurs 10 AM - Noon, 1 - 4:45 PM; Estab 1962 as reference library
Income: Financed by grants & contributions
Library Holdings: Book Volumes 25,000; Exhibition Catalogs 3,000; Periodical Subscriptions 25
Special Subjects: Decorative Arts, Photography, Painting-American, Painting-British, Painting-Dutch, Painting-Flemish, Painting-French, Painting-Italian, Painting-Spanish, Sculpture, Painting-European, Gold

M   SALVADOR DALI MUSEUM, 1 Dali Blvd, Saint Petersburg, FL 33701-3920. Tel 727-823-3767; Fax 727-894-6068; Elec Mail info@thedali.org; Internet Home Page Address: www.salvadordalimuseum.org; *Exec Dir* Hank Hine; *Deputy Dir & Cur Coll* Joan R Kropf; *Asst Cur* Dirk Armstrong
Open Mon-Sat 10AM - 5:30PM, Thurs until 8PM, Sun Noon - 5:30PM, cl Thanksgiving & Dec 25, extended hrs between Christmas & New Years; Admis

adults $17, seniors teachers with ID, police, military & firemen $14.50, students ages 10+ & 18+ with ID $10, children ages 5-9 $4, children 4 & under free, Thurs 5-8 PM all admis $5; Estab 1971 to share the private Dali Collection of Mr & Mrs A Reynolds Morse with the pub; formerly in Cleveland, Ohio, the museum re-opened Mar 7, 1982 in Saint Petersburg, Fla; Average Annual Attendance: 215,000; Mem: 1,500; dues individual $40
Income: Financed by private collector, State University Systems & donations
Collections: 96 oils and 5 large masterworks by Dali make up a retrospective of his work from 1914 to the present; over 100 watercolors & drawings; 1,300 graphics, photographs, sculptures & objects d'art
Publications: Dali Draftsmanship; Guide to Works by Dali in Public Museums; Introduction to Dali; Dali-Picasso; Poetic Homage to Gala-Dali; Dali Primer; Dali's World of Symbols: Workbook for Children; Dali Newsletter; exhibition catalogues
Activities: Adult classes; docent training; lects open to pub, 2 vis lectrs per yr; film series; gallery talks; tours; mus shop sells books, reproductions, prints, slides, postcards

L **Library,** 1 Dali Blvd, Saint Petersburg, FL 33701-3920. Tel 727-823-3767; Fax 727-894-6068; Elec Mail info@the dali.org; Internet Home Page Address: www.thedali.org; *Deputy Dir & Cur* Joan R Kropf; *Dir* Charles Hine Dr.; *Cur Exhibs* Dr William Jeffett; *Deputy Dir* Kathy White; *Mktg* Kathy Grief; *Cur Educ* Peter Tush
Open Mon - Fri 10AM - 5:30 PM, Thurs until 8PM, Sun Noon - 5:30 PM; Admis Adults $21, seniors & military $19, children 13-18 $15, Children 6-12 $7, children 5 & under free, Thurs after 5 pm $5; Estab 1982 for research purposes; Permanent collection & temporary exhibitions; contains 5000 references to Dali in books, periodicals & newspapers; Average Annual Attendance: 300,000; Mem: 1000; dues individual $60; family $100
Income: Financed privately by Salvador Dali Foundation; public/grants
Library Holdings: Auction Catalogs; Audio Tapes; Book Volumes 32; Cassettes; Clipping Files; Compact Disks; DVDs; Exhibition Catalogs; Framed Reproductions 1028; Kodachrome Transparencies 3000; Manuscripts; Memorabilia; Motion Pictures 10; Original Art Works 165; Original Documents; Other Holdings Illustrated editions; Pamphlets; Periodical Subscriptions 20; Photographs; Prints 750; Reproductions; Sculpture; Slides; Video Tapes 50
Collections: Films & Tapes on or by Dali
Publications: Pollock to Pop: America's Brush with Dalí; Jordi Colomer: Arabian Stars
Activities: Classes for adults & children; docent training; jr & teen docent training; lects for members only; 10 vis lectrs per yr; gallery talks; tours; concerts; lending original objects of art to national gallery of Victoria, Melbourne, Australia; artmobile; Urban Recreation Center summer program; mus shop sells books; reproductions; prints & varied items of clothing, mugs, jewelry, etc.

SARASOTA

A **ART CENTER SARASOTA,** 707 N Tamiami Trail, Sarasota, FL 34236. Tel 941-365-2032; Fax 941-366-0585; Elec Mail lisa@artsarasota.org; Internet Home Page Address: www.artsarasota.org; *COO* Sarah Ford; *Develop & Commun* Lisa Berger; *Exec Coordr* Emma Thurgood; *Educ Coordr* Elizabeth Hillmann
Open Tues - Sat 10 AM - 4 PM, cl Sun & Mon; Admis donation $3; Estab 1926, incorporated 1940, to promote the educational & cultural advantages of Sarasota in the field of contemporary art; Four galleries: front galleries for curated shows; 2 galleries curated shows, 1 gallery student shows, 1 gallery juried exhib; Average Annual Attendance: 26,000; Mem: 800; dues $75 & up; annual meeting each Oct
Income: Financed by mem, donations & educ prog
Library Holdings: Book Volumes
Exhibitions: 20 exhibitions annually including curated & member exhibitions - every 6 wks in 4 galleries
Publications: Bulletin, monthly; yearbook
Activities: Classes for adults & children; workshops; lects open to pub; 10 vis lectrs per yr; concerts; gallery talks; tours; demonstrations; sponsoring of competitions; cash awards for juried shows; scholarships offered; originate traveling exhibs; mus shop sells books, original art, reproductions & prints; members gallery & holiday art bazaar

M **FLORIDA STATE UNIVERSITY,** John & Mable Ringling Museum of Art, 5401 Bay Shore Rd, Sarasota, FL 34243-2161. Tel 941-359-5700; Fax 941-359-5745; Elec Mail info@ringling.org; Internet Home Page Address: www.ringling.org; *Exec Dir* John Wetenhall; *Chief Conservator* Michelle Scalera; *Head Librn* Linda McKee; *Cur Circus Mus & Archivist* Deborah Walk
Open daily 10 AM - 5 PM; Admis adults $25, seniors $20, students & children 6-17, FL teachers w ID & active US military $10, children under 6 & members free; Estab 1928; Bequeathed to the State of Florida by John Ringling & operated by the state; built in Italian villa style around sculpture garden on 60 plus landscaped acres; original 19th century theater from Asolo, near Venice, in adjacent building; Ringling Residence & Circus Galleries on grounds; Average Annual Attendance: 300,000 paid combination, 700,000 free attendance & special events; Mem: 3000; dues friend $75, associate $100, contributor $175, sponsor $500, colleague $1,000, patron $5,000
Special Subjects: Decorative Arts, Drawings, Prints, Sculpture, Archaeology, Painting-European, Coins & Medals, Baroque Art
Collections: Archaeology of Cyprus; Baroque pictures, especially those of Peter Paul Rubens; developing collection of 19th & 20th century painting, sculpture, drawings & prints; Bickel, Palmer
Exhibitions: Selections from the Permanent Collection: Old Masters.
Publications: Calendar, bi-monthly; Collection Catalogues; Exhibition Catalogues; Newsletter, quarterly
Activities: Educ dept; docent training; state services; lects open to public & some for members only; concerts; gallery talks; exten dept serves the state; individual paintings & original objects of art lent to affiliates & other qualified museums nationally & internationally on board approval; lending collection contains 1000 individual paintings, 1000 objects of art; originate traveling exhibs to affiliates; sales shop sells books, reproductions, prints & slides

L **The John and Mable Ringling Museum of Art Library,** 5401 Bay Shore Rd, Sarasota, FL 34243. Tel 941-359-5700, Ext 2700; Fax 941-360-7370; Elec Mail library@ringling.org; Internet Home Page Address: www.ringling.org; *Head Librn* Linda R McKee; *Assoc Librn* Artis Wick; *Asst Librn* Megan Oliver; *Cataloguer* Arwen Spinosa
Open Mon - Fri - 5 PM; Estab 1946; Reference only; Mem: Friends of Ringling Mus Library, $100 annual dues
Library Holdings: Auction Catalogs 15,000; Book Volumes 85,000; Clipping Files 5,000; DVDs 300; Exhibition Catalogs; Other Holdings Art auction catalogues; Rare books; Periodical Subscriptions 135; Video Tapes 200
Special Subjects: Art History, Drawings, Painting-Dutch, Painting-Flemish, Painting-Italian, History of Art & Archaeology, Ceramics, Art Education, Asian Art
Collections: John Ringling Library of rare books, circus books; Willy Pogany, Fan Books; James Turrell books; Chick Austin Library; Bickel, Palmer
Activities: Classes for adults & children; book club; lects open to pub; lects for Friends mems; 4 vis lectrs per yr; mus shop sells books & reproductions

M **J.M.W. TURNER MUSEUM,** 930 N Tamiami Trail, Ste 807 Sarasota, FL 34236-4070. Tel 941-343-8320; Elec Mail turnermuseum@turnermuseum; Elec Mail turnermuseum@gmail.com; Internet Home Page Address: www.turnermuseum.org; *Chmn & CEO* Douglass Montrose-Graem; *Chief Cur & Trustee* Isis Marina Graham; *Webmaster* Jacques Sennefeld; *Trustee* Bridget Robinson; *Trustee* Senator Bob Johnson; *Trustee* Michael R Pender Jr, C.P.A.
Open by appointment only; Admis $25; Estab 1973 to promote JMW Turner & Thomas Moran; 501(c)3; Maintains reference library; currently in the process of re-estab a permanent home in Sarasota FL; Mem: over 1000; dues $100, students $5; annual meeting in Dec
Library Holdings: Auction Catalogs; Book Volumes; Cards; Exhibition Catalogs; Original Art Works; Original Documents; Photographs; Prints; Slides; Video Tapes
Special Subjects: Drawings, Etchings & Engravings, History of Art & Archaeology, Illustration, Landscape Architecture, Landscapes, Marine Painting, Art Education, Art History, Mixed Media, American Western Art, Furniture, Photography, Portraits, Painting-American, Prints, Period Rooms, Woodcuts, Manuscripts, Maps, Painting-British, Painting-European, Painting-French, Sculpture, Graphics, Painting-American, Watercolors, American Western Art, Religious Art, Painting-Japanese, Posters, Oriental Art, Marine Painting, Carpets & Rugs, Restorations, Period Rooms, Painting-Italian, Reproductions, Bookplates & Bindings
Collections: JMW Turner - Works on Paper; Thomas Moran - Works on Paper; Please refer to website for additional colls
Exhibitions: Please see website for mus & galleries
Publications: Turner's Cosmic Optimism; Triple Turner Treat (ebook); Please see website for additional publs
Activities: Classes for adults & children; lects open to pub; concerts; top 99 art mus in America (Atlantic Monthly); organize traveling exhibs to other mus; mus shop sells books & original art; reproductions; prints; prints

M **RINGLING COLLEGE OF ART & DESIGN,** Selby Gallery, 2700 N Tamiami Trail, Sarasota, FL 34234. Tel 941-359-7563; Fax 941-309-1969; Elec Mail selby@ringling.edu; Internet Home Page Address: www.ringling.edu/selbygallery; *Dir* Kevin Dean; *Asst Dir* Laura Avery; *Gallery Asst* Tim Jaeger
Open Mon - Sat 10 AM - 4 PM, Tues 10 AM - 7 PM; No admis fee; Estab 1986; Exhibitions of internationally known artists; Average Annual Attendance: 30,000
Income: Financed by the school
Exhibitions: Rotating exhibits
Activities: Lects open to pub, 10 vis lectrs per yr; gallery talks; tours; originate traveling exhibs

L **RINGLING COLLEGE OF ART & DESIGN,** Verman Kimbrough Memorial Library, 2700 N Tamiami Trail, Sarasota, FL 34234. Tel 941-359-7587; Fax 941-359-7632; Elec Mail library@ringling.edu; Internet Home Page Address: www.lib.ringling.edu; *Dir Library* Kathleen List; *Visual Resources Librn* Allen Novak; *Technical Servs Librn* Janet Thomas; *Instruction Librn* Jennifer Friedman
Open Mon - Thurs 8 AM - 11 PM, Fri 8 AM - 6 PM, Sat Noon - 6 PM, Sun 10 AM - 11 PM; Estab 1931 to serve the curriculum needs of an undergraduate, visual arts col; Circ 50,340
Income: $246,441 (financed by library assoc, parent institution & capital expense)
Purchases: $231,551
Library Holdings: Book Volumes 59,647; CD-ROMs 477; Compact Disks 1,159; DVDs 7,232; Exhibition Catalogs; Other Holdings 95,000 Digital Images; Periodical Subscriptions 375; Slides 60,000; Video Tapes 2,014
Special Subjects: Art History, Landscape Architecture, Decorative Arts, Film, Illustration, Mixed Media, Photography, Calligraphy, Commercial Art, Drawings, Etchings & Engravings, Graphic Arts, Graphic Design, Islamic Art, Painting-American, Painting-British, Painting-Dutch, Painting-Flemish, Painting-French, Painting-German, Painting-Italian, Painting-Japanese, Painting-Russian, Painting-Spanish, Posters, Pre-Columbian Art, Prints, Sculpture, Painting-European, History of Art & Archaeology, Portraits, Watercolors, Conceptual Art, Latin American Art, Theatre Arts, Archaeology, Painting-Israeli, American Western Art, Printmaking, Advertising Design, Cartoons, Interior Design, Lettering, Asian Art, Video, American Indian Art, Porcelain, Anthropology, Furniture, Southwestern Art, Painting-Polish, Aesthetics, Afro-American Art, Bookplates & Bindings, Pottery, Textiles, Woodcuts, Landscapes, Painting-Scandinavian, Painting-Australian, Painting-Canadian, Painting-New Zealand, Architecture

STUART

M **HISTORICAL SOCIETY OF MARTIN COUNTY,** Elliott Museum, 825 NE Ocean Blvd, Stuart, FL 34996-1626. Tel 772-225-1961; Fax 772-225-2333; Elec Mail info@elliottmuseumfl.org; Internet Home Page Address: www.elliottmuseumfl.org; *Pres & CEO* Jennifer Esler; *Cur* Janel Hendrix; *Dir Fin* Amy Martin; *Coll Coordr* LaVaine Wrigley; *Fin Asst / DBA* Kelly Mangan; *Dir Develop* Diane Kimes; *Rental Coordr* Ericah Brinson; *Mem Coordr* Martha Parker
Open daily 10 AM - 5 PM; cl Easter, Thanksgiving & Christmas Day; Admis adult $12, senior, group & military $10, children (2-12 yrs) $6, children under 2 free

Library Holdings: Auction Catalogs; Audio Tapes; Book Volumes; Cards; Clipping Files; DVDs; Exhibition Catalogs; Kodachrome Transparencies; Manuscripts; Maps; Memorabilia; Original Art Works; Original Documents; Pamphlets; Periodical Subscriptions; Photographs; Prints; Records; Sculpture; Slides; Video Tapes
Special Subjects: Archaeology, Decorative Arts, Glass, Furniture, Period Rooms, Painting-American, Dolls
Collections: Contemporary American artists (realistic); Walter Brightwell, Nina D Buxton, Cecilia Cardman, E I Couse, James Ernst, Jo Gabeler, Diana Kan, Hui Chi Mau, Rose W Traines; antiques; Automobiles & historic fashions
Activities: Art classes for adults & children, docent training, annual classic car show; lects open to pub; concerts; yearly lect series; local school tours; art studio & summer art camps; mus shop sells books, reproductions, original art, jewelry, educational toys

TALLAHASSEE

A FLORIDA DEPARTMENT OF STATE, DIVISION OF CULTURAL AFFAIRS, Florida Council on Arts & Culture, 500 S Bronough St, RA Gray Bldg Tallahassee, FL 32399-0250. Tel 850-245-6470; Fax 850-245-6497; Internet Home Page Address: www.florida-arts.org; Telex 488-5779; *Arts Adminr* Morgan Lewis; *Dir* Sandy Shaughnessy; *Arts Admin* Timothy Storhoff
Open 8 AM - 5 PM; No admis fee; Estab 1969 to advise the Secretary of State in fostering the arts in Florida; Gallery for innovation and the arts
Collections: Florida Department of State Art Collection
Exhibitions: Capitol Complex Exhibition
Activities: Fels offered to individual artists

A FLORIDA FOLKLIFE PROGRAMS, 500 S Bronough St, Bureau Historic Preservation Tallahassee, FL 32399-2147. Tel 850-245-6333; Fax 850-922-0496; Elec Mail tbucuvalas@dos.state.fl.us; WATS 800-847-7278; *Bureau Chief* Fred Gaske; *Folk Arts Coordr* Dr Tina Bucuvalas; *Folklife Adminr* Gregory Hansen
Open Mon - Fri 9AM-4:30PM, Sat 10AM-4:30PM, Sun noon-4:30PM; No admis fee; Estab 1979 to encourage local folk artisans to appreciate this important art form; The Bureau is under Secretary of Jim Smith & carries on a year-round calendar of folk activities in an effort to encourage statewide pub interests & participation in the folk arts & folklore
Activities: Classes for adults & children; lects open to public; concerts; Florida Folk Heritage Award; apprenticeships offered; originate traveling exhibs
L **Library,** 500 S Bronough St, Grey Bldg, Rm 402 Tallahassee, FL 32399-1800. Tel 850-245-6333; Elec Mail blaine.waide@dos.myflorida.com; Internet Home Page Address: www.flheritage.com/preservation/folklife; WATS 800-847-7278; *Folk Arts Coordr* Blaine Waide
Open to pub for reference Mon - Fri 8 AM - 5 PM
Library Holdings: Audio Tapes; Book Volumes 500; Cards; Cassettes; Clipping Files; Exhibition Catalogs; Filmstrips; Kodachrome Transparencies; Manuscripts; Original Art Works; Pamphlets; Periodical Subscriptions 10; Photographs; Records; Slides; Video Tapes
Special Subjects: Folk Art, Ethnology
Collections: Folklife
Activities: Folklife apprenticeship prog; Fla Folk Heritage awards; Folklife Days; Music in the Sunshine State radio series

M FLORIDA STATE UNIVERSITY, Museum of Fine Arts, 530 W Call St, 250 Fine Arts Building Tallahassee, FL 32306-1140. Tel 850-644-6836; Fax 850-644-7229; Elec Mail apalladinocraig@fsu.edu; Internet Home Page Address: www.mofa.fsu.edu; *Sr Preparator* Wayne Vonada; *Cur Educ* Viki D Wylder; *Fiscal Officer & Registrar* Jean Young; *Dir & Ed-in-Chief* Allys Palladino-Craig; *Communs Coordr* Teri Abstein
Open Mon - Fri 9 AM - 4 PM, Sat & Sun 1 - 4 PM (Fall & Spring semesters); cl school holidays; No admis fee; Estab 1950; Three upper galleries; two lower galleries, one for permanent collection; sculpture courtyard; Average Annual Attendance: 48,000; Mem: 300, friends of the Gallery; 150, Artists' League
Income: Financed by state appropriations, grants & private sector
Library Holdings: Book Volumes 300; Exhibition Catalogs 600; Original Art Works 4000; Prints; Sculpture
Special Subjects: Painting-American, Sculpture
Collections: Asian prints; Carter Collection of Pre-Columbian Art; contemporary American graphics, photography & paintings; European painting
Publications: Exhibition catalogues; Athanor, art history journal
Activities: Educ dept; docent training; lects open to public, 5 vis lectrs per yr; gallery talks; tours; AAM accredited; exten dept; individual paintings & original objects of art lent by appropriate request; book traveling exhibs 1-2 per yr; originate traveling exhibs to museums in Florida and nationally

M LEMOYNE ART FOUNDATION, (LeMoyne Center for the Visual Arts) Center for the Visual Arts, 125 N Gadsden St, Tallahassee, FL 32301-1507. Tel 850-222-8800; Fax 850-224-2714; Elec Mail curator@lemoyne.org; Internet Home Page Address: www.lemoyne.org; *Pres* Kelly Dozier; *Exec Dir* Hillary Brett; *Cur* Lesley Marchessault; *Events, Gift Shop* Sheri Sanderson; *Educ Dir* Amanda Wilke; *Educ Dir* Jennifer Infinger
Open Tues - Sat 10 AM - 5 PM; Sun 1 - 5 PM; cl Mon; Admis adults $1, members & children under 12 free, Sun free; Estab 1964 as a non-profit organization to serve as gallery for contemporary, quality art of Florida artists; sponsor the visual arts in Tallahassee; an educational institution in the broadest sense; Built c. 1840, the Meginniss-Munroe House is home to LeMoyne's five galleries and gallery shop; Average Annual Attendance: 103,881; Mem: 900; dues $30-$5000
Income: Financed by mem, sales, grants & fund raisers
Special Subjects: Afro-American Art, Decorative Arts, Portraits, Painting-American, Textiles, Sculpture, Drawings, Prints, Watercolors, Ceramics, Crafts, Pottery, Collages, Posters, Stained Glass
Collections: Contemporary Artists; Karl Zerbe Serigraphs; Nancy Reid Grunn Encaustics; George Milton
Exhibitions: LeMoyne Holiday Show; Chain of Park's Festival
Publications: Newsletter, bi-monthly; exhibit catalogs

Activities: Classes for adults & children, summer art camp & workshops; lects open to public, 4 vis lectrs per year; gallery talks; tours; competitions; individual paintings and original objects of art lent to bus and members; lending collection contains original art works, original prints, paintings and sculpture; Artisans Gallery sells original fine art, craft items & prints, books

M TALLAHASSEE MUSEUM OF HISTORY & NATURAL SCIENCE, 3945 Museum Dr, Tallahassee, FL 32310-6325. Tel 850-575-8684; Fax 850-574-8243; Elec Mail rdaws@tallahasseemuseum.org; Internet Home Page Address: www.tallahasseemuseum.org; *Dir Educ* Jennifer Golden; *Cur Coll & Exhib* Linda Deaton; *Animal Cur* Michael Jones; *Dir* Russell S Daws
Open Mon - Sat 9 AM - 5 PM; Sun 12:30 - 5 PM; Admis adults $9, seniors & students with ID $8.50,children 4-15 $6, members free; Estab 1957 to educate children & adults about natural history, native wildlife, North Florida history, art & culture; Facilities include 1880's farm, historic buildings, exhibit & class buildings, 40 acres of nature trails & animal habitats; Average Annual Attendance: 120,000; Mem: 5000; dues $60; annual meeting third Thurs in Oct
Income: $1,900,000 (financed by mem, fundraisers, admis & government appropriation)
Special Subjects: Decorative Arts, Architecture, Archaeology, Costumes, Ceramics, Crafts, Folk Art, Pottery, Dolls, Historical Material, Period Rooms, Embroidery, Reproductions
Collections: Pre-Columbia Florida Indian Pottery; historic buildings; furnishings; natural history & science
Exhibitions: Changing exhibit on art, clothing, crafts, history & science; permanent or semi-permanent (3 years) exhibits on local history & natural history
Publications: Newsletter, monthly
Activities: Classes for adults & children; docent training; lects open to pub, 8-12 vis lectrs per yr; concerts; gallery talks; tours; scholarships offered; extension prog serves North Florida, South Georgia & Southeastern Alabama; mus shop sells books & original art
L **Museum,** 3945 Museum Dr, Tallahassee, FL 32310. Tel 850-575-8684; Fax 850-574-8243; Elec Mail rdaws@tallahassee.museum.org; Internet Home Page Address: www.tallahasseemuseum.org; *CEO & Exec Dir* Russell S Daws; *Chief Cur* Linda Deaton
Open Mon - Sat 9 AM - 5 PM, Sun 11 AM - 5 PM; Admis adults $9, children $6; Estab 1957; Open to members; Average Annual Attendance: 100,000; Mem: 4,000 mems; dues range from $25 - $1,000
Income: $1,400,000 (financed by earned income, donations, grants & special events)
Purchases: $2,000,000
Library Holdings: Book Volumes 500; Periodical Subscriptions 12
Special Subjects: Folk Art, Decorative Arts, Photography, Prints, Historical Material, Ceramics, Anthropology, Period Rooms, Costume Design & Constr, Afro-American Art, Dolls, Pottery, Textiles
Collections: Ivan Gundrum Pre-Columbian Florida Indian Artifacts (reproductions) representing the Weeden Island culture 500 - 1500 AD; 14 historic structures of regional significance, 8,500 historical artifacts & natural history specimans
Publications: Monthly Tallahassee Museum Newsletter
Activities: Classes for adults & children; concerts; 2-5 book traveling exhibs; mus shop sells books

TAMPA

C CASPERS, INC, Art Collection, 4908 W Nassau St, Tampa, FL 33607-3827. Tel 813-287-2231; Fax 813-289-7850; *Pres* Chuck Peterson; *Mktg Mgr* Steve Scott; *CEO* Joseph Casper
Open Mon - Fri 8 AM - 5 PM; Estab 1981 to enhance the employees' environment
Collections: Collection features works by artists with some relationship to Florida

A CITY OF TAMPA, Public Art Program, 306 E. Jackson St, Tampa, FL 33602-5208. Tel 813-274-8531; Fax 813-274-8732; Elec Mail robin.nigh@tampagov.net; *Admin* Robin Nigh
Estab 1985 to visually enhance & enrich the public environment for both residents & visitors of Tampa; Mem: Public Art Comt meets monthly
Collections: wide variety of public art
Publications: Public Art Brochure; Save Outdoor Sculpture

M TAMPA MUSEUM OF ART, 120 W Gasparilla Plz, Tampa, FL 33602-1500. Tel 813-274-8130; Fax 813-274-8732; Internet Home Page Address: www.tampamuseum.com; *Chief Cur* Elaine Gustafson; *Preparator* Bob Hellier; *Registrar* Devon Larsen; *Dir* Ken Rollins; *Cur Educ* Dawn Johnson; *Dev* Steve Klihdt; *Mktg* Meredith Elarfi
Open Tues, Wed, Thurs, Fri & Sat 10 AM - 5 PM, Sun 11 AM - 5 PM; Admis adults $8, seniors $7, students & children 6-18 $3, under 6 free; Estab 1970 to educate the pub through the display of art; 7 galleries with antiquities, sculpture, photography & paintings; Average Annual Attendance: 82,500; Mem: 1950; dues $35
Income: $2,400,000 (financed by local government, grants, mem & contributions)
Library Holdings: Auction Catalogs; Exhibition Catalogs; Periodical Subscriptions
Special Subjects: Etchings & Engravings, Folk Art, Glass, Photography, Textiles, Bronzes, Drawings, Latin American Art, Painting-American, Prints, Sculpture, Watercolors, Ceramics, Crafts, Woodcuts, Coins & Medals, Antiquities-Greek, Antiquities-Roman, Antiquities-Etruscan
Collections: Greek & Roman antiquities; 20th - 21st century painting, sculpture & photography; 19th century photography & sculpture; C Paul Jennewein Collection; Otto Neumann Collection
Exhibitions: Rotating exhibits every 8-10 weeks
Publications: Catalogs; Newsletter, bi-monthly; school calendar
Activities: Classes for adults & children; docent training; films; workshops; lects open to pub; concerts; gallery talks; tours; individual paintings & original objects of art lent to fellow mus; book traveling exhibs 10 per yr; originate traveling

exhibs to other mus; mus shop sells books, original art, reproductions, prints, jewelry, toys, t-shirts, cards & stationary

L **Judith Rozier Blanchard Library,** 120 W Gasparilla Plz, Tampa, FL 33602-1500. Internet Home Page Address: www.tampamuseum.org; *Cur Educ* Dawn Johnson

Open by appt. Contact the curatorial staff of the museum; No admis fee; For reference only

Library Holdings: Book Volumes 7801; Exhibition Catalogs 700; Other Holdings CD ROM programs; Pamphlets; Periodical Subscriptions 32; Slides

Publications: Art Muse Quarterly Newsletter

Activities: training

M **UNIVERSITY OF SOUTH FLORIDA,** Contemporary Art Museum, 4202 E Fowler Ave, CAM 101 Tampa, FL 33620-0007. Tel 813-974-4133; Fax 813-974-5130; Elec Mail caminfo@arts.usf.edu; Internet Home Page Address: www.arts.usf.edu/museum; *Dir* Margaret A Miller; *Deputy Dir* Alexa A Favata

Open Mon - Fri 10 AM - 5 PM, Sat 1 - 4 PM; No admis fee; Estab 1961 to provide exhibitions of contemporary art; Mus located on W Holly Dr on Tampa Campus; Average Annual Attendance: 55,000; Mem: dues corporate $1000-$100,000, private $5-$1000

Income: Financed by state appropriation, grants, mem fees & corporate art program

Special Subjects: Drawings, Painting-American, Photography, Prints, Sculpture, African Art, Pre-Columbian Art, Posters

Collections: African art, Pre-Columbian artifacts; art bank collection of loan traveling exhibitions (approx 60 small package exhibitions); contemporary photography; contemporary works on paper; painting; sculpture

Publications: Exhibition catalogs

Activities: Docent training; lects open to pub, 4 vis lectrs per yr; gallery talks; tours; through Art Bank program original prints are lent to institutions, universities & arts organizations; book traveling exhibs 2 per yr; originate traveling exhibs to universities, galleries & colleges; mus shop sells books, magazines, artists' created jewelry, architecture related products

L **Library,** 4202 E Fowler Ave LIB 122, Tampa Campus Tampa, FL 33620-5400. Tel 813-974-2729; Fax 813-974-9875; Internet Home Page Address: www.lib.usf.edu; *Admnr* Jim Gray; *Art Reference Librn* Ilene Frank

Open Mon - Thurs 7:30 AM - 1 AM, Fri 7:30 AM - 9 PM, Sat 10 AM - 8 PM, Sun Noon - 1 AM; Open to students & pub

Income: Financed by state appropriations & grants

Library Holdings: Audio Tapes; Book Volumes 930,000; Cards; Cassettes; Clipping Files; Fiche; Filmstrips; Framed Reproductions; Manuscripts; Motion Pictures; Pamphlets; Periodical Subscriptions 5450; Photographs; Prints; Reels; Reproductions; Video Tapes

Special Subjects: Historical Material

Collections: Rare art books

M **UNIVERSITY OF TAMPA,** Henry B Plant Museum, 401 W Kennedy Blvd, Tampa, FL 33606-1450. Tel 813-254-1891, Ext 22; Internet Home Page Address: www.plantmuseum.com; *Cur & Registrar* Susan Carter; *Museum Relations* Jeannette Twachtmann; *Cur Educ* Amy Franklin-David; *Museum Store Mgr* Sue Gauthier; *Dir* Cynthia Gandee; *Mgr Operations & Mem* Heather Brabham; *Cur Asst* Alexandra Fernandez

Open Tues - Sat 10 AM - 4 PM, Sun Noon - 4 PM, cl holidays; Admis suggested donation $5 & $2 for children under 12; Estab 1933 in the former Tampa Bay Hotel built in 1891, to explain the importance of the Tampa Bay Hotel & Henry Plant to the area; This building which contains Victorian furnishings & artifacts, original to the Tampa Bay Hotel, is now on the register as a National Historical Landmark built by the railroad industrialist H B Plant; Average Annual Attendance: 25,000; Mem: 500

Income: Financed by city appropriation, University of Tampa, mem & donations

Special Subjects: Furniture, Porcelain

Collections: Late Victorian furniture & objects d'art of same period; Venetian mirrors; Wedgwood, Oriental porcelains

Exhibitions: Exhibits relating to 19th century life; Plant system railroads & steamships, Annual Christmas Stroll

Publications: Henry B Plant Museum, Today & Moments In Time, a pictorial history of the Tampa Bay Hotel; Tampa Bay Hotel: Florida's First Magic Kingdom (video); member newsletter, quarterly; series of Jean Stallings; educational series about Henry Plant & Victorian period

Activities: Docent training; lects open to pub & lects for members only; mus store sells books, original art reproductions, Victorian style gifts, antique estate jewelry, estate silver, linens

M **Scarfone/Hartley Gallery,** 401 W Kennedy Blvd, Tampa, FL 33606-1450. Tel 813-253-3333, 253-6217; Fax 813-258-7497; Elec Mail dcowden@ut.edu; Internet Home Page Address: www.utarts.com; *Dir of Galleries* Dorothy Cowden; *Pres of the Univ* Ron Vaughn

Open Tues - Fri 10 AM - 4 PM, Sat 1 - 4 PM, cl June - July; No admis fee; Estab 1977 to exhibit works of art as an extension of the classroom & to utilize the space for pub functions which would benefit from the artistic environment created by showing current trends of all art forms of artistic merit; 6,000 sq ft of exhib space; Average Annual Attendance: 17,000; Mem: 75; donation dues $25-$1000

Income: Financed by donations & fundraisers

Collections: Contemporary artists

Exhibitions: Studio F; Electronics Alive - Biennial digital invitational

Publications: Exhibition brochures, 10 times a yr

Activities: Classes for adults; lects open to pub; 10 vis lectrs per yr; gallery talks; student annual juried awards; scholarships offered; lend artwork to other art or educational institutions; lending collection contains 100 pieces of original art; originate traveling exhibs to mus & galleries

TEQUESTA

M **LIGHTHOUSE ARTCENTER MUSEUM & SCHOOL OF ART,** (Lighthouse Gallery & Art School) 373 Tequesta Dr, Gallery Sq N Tequesta, FL 33469-3027. Tel 561-746-3101; Elec Mail info@lighthousearts.org; Internet Home Page Address: www.lighthousearts.org; *Exec Dir & School of Art Interim Dir* Katie Deits; *Dir Finance* Julie Alexander; *Dir Events* Sheila McDonald-Bell; *Exec & Asst Cur* Barbara Broidy; *Educ Coordr* Robyn D Eckersley; *School of Art Admin Asst* Penny Robb; *Instruction & Youth Progs* Cara McKinley; *Visitor Relations* Sheri Gancz; *Visitor & Vol Relations* Evelyne Bates; *Mem Data Mgt* Darby Conlon

Open Mus Mon-Fri 10 AM - 4 PM, Sat 10 AM - 2 PM; School of Arts Mon, Tues, Fri 8:30 AM - 5:30 PM, Wed & Thurs 8:30 AM - 5:30 PM, Sat 8:30 AM - 1 PM; Admis mus: $5 for non-mems, free for mems,; Estab 1964 to create pub interest in all forms of the fine arts; Average Annual Attendance: 90,000; Mem: 1,000; dues $75; annual meeting in Oct

Income: financed by membership, donations, grants

Library Holdings: Book Volumes

Special Subjects: Landscapes, Art History, Pottery, Painting-American, Drawings, Painting-American, Photography, Sculpture, Watercolors, African Art, Ceramics, Collages, Calligraphy

Collections: Museum Coll of paintings & sculpture

Exhibitions: Temporary & traveling exhibitions; Celebration of the Arts juried exhibit

Publications: Calendar of Events, monthly; Newsletter, quarterly

Activities: Classes for adults & children; docent training; workshops; Formal Beaux Art Ball; lects open to pub, 10 vis lectrs per year; concerts; tours; competitions with awards; scholarships offered; organize traveling exhibs to art centers & mus; mus shop sells books, original art

L **Not Profit Art Center,** 373 Tequesta Dr, Gallery Sq N Tequesta, FL 33469-3027. Tel 561-746-3101; Fax 561-746-3241; Elec Mail info@lighthousearts.org; Internet Home Page Address: www.lighthousearts.org; *Exec Dir* Katie Deits

Open Mon - Sat 10 AM - 4:30 PM; Library estab 1964; Exhibitions, cultural events, museum store; Average Annual Attendance: 50,000; Mem: $75 & up annually

Income: financed by membership, donations, sponsorships & grants

Library Holdings: Book Volumes 600; Clipping Files; Exhibition Catalogs; Original Art Works; Pamphlets; Periodical Subscriptions 10; Prints

Special Subjects: Painting-American, Watercolors, Ceramics, Landscapes

Collections: Permanent collection of American artists

Activities: Educ prog; classes for adults & children; docent training; artbridge outreach; lects open to pub; 1,500 vis lectrs per year; concerts; gallery talks; tours; sponsoring of competitions; schols offered; mus shop sells original art

VALPARAISO

M **HERITAGE MUSEUM ASSOCIATION, INC,** The Heritage Museum of Northwest Florida, 115 Westview Ave, Valparaiso, FL 32580-1387. Tel 850-678-2615; Fax 850-678-4547; Elec Mail heritagemuseum@co.okaloosa.fl.us; Internet Home Page Address: www.heritage-museum.org; *Exec Dir* Michelle A Severino; *Admnr Mgr* Gina Marini; *Curatorial Asst* Michael Weech

Open Tues - Sat 10AM-4PM; Admis adults $2; HMNF members & children under 4 free; Estab 1971 to collect, preserve, & display items related to the history & develop of the area; Average Annual Attendance: 19,000; Mem: 240; dues senior & student $15; individual $35; family $50

Income: $50,000 (financed by mem, city & county appropriation, fundraising & donations)

Library Holdings: Audio Tapes; Cassettes; Compact Disks; DVDs; Manuscripts; Maps; Memorabilia; Original Art Works; Original Documents; Other Holdings; Photographs; Prints; Records; Reproductions; Video Tapes

Special Subjects: American Indian Art, Anthropology, Archaeology, Textiles, Crafts, Folk Art, Pottery, Dolls, Glass, Silver, Historical Material, Maps, Embroidery, Laces

Collections: Paleo & archaic stone artifacts; pioneer household utensils, agricultural implements, artisans' tools, tools used in the turpentine & lumber industries; photos & files of research materials; Art History, Flasks & Bottles, Handicrafts; Paleo & Archaic Stone Artifacts

Publications: "Heritage Press" electronic newsletter; Teacher's Resource & Field Trip Guide

Activities: Adult & children's classes; docent progs; lects open to pub & for mems, 6 vis lectrs per yr; original objects of art lent to mus & for special school & college exhibits; book traveling exhibs, 4 per yr; originate traveling exhib; mus shop sells books, magazines, original art, prints & original handcrafts

VENICE

M **VENICE ART CENTER,** 390 Nokomis Ave S, Venice, FL 34285-2416. Tel 941-485-7136; Fax 941-484-4361; Elec Mail info@veniceartcenter.com; Internet Home Page Address: www.veniceartcenter.com; *Exec Dir* Mary Morris

VERO BEACH

M **VERO BEACH MUSEUM OF ART,** 3001 Riverside Park Dr, Vero Beach, FL 32963-1874. Tel 772-231-0707; Fax 772-231-0938; Elec Mail info@verobeachmuseum.org; Internet Home Page Address: www.verobeachmuseum.org; *Exec Dir* Lucinda H Gedeon PhD; *Dir Educ* J Marshall Adams; *Dir Develop* Robyn P Orzel; *Cur Coll & Exhibs* Jay Williams; *Registrar* J'Laine Newcombe; *Mus Store Mgr* Jo Anne Miller; *Dir Mktg & Communs* Sophie Bentham Wood

Open Memorial Day to Labor Day Tues - Sat 10 AM - 4:30 PM, Sun 1 - 4:30 PM, Sept - May Mon - Sat 10 - 4:30 PM, Sun 1 - 4:30 PM, cl New Year's Day, Memorial Day, Independence Day, Labor Day, Thanksgiving, Christmas Day;

Admis call for fees; Estab 1986; Average Annual Attendance: 82,000; Mem: 5390; annual meeting in Apr

Library Holdings: Auction Catalogs; Audio Tapes; Book Volumes 5,000; DVDs; Exhibition Catalogs; Periodical Subscriptions

Special Subjects: Glass, Portraits, Painting-American, Prints, Woodcuts, Drawings, Photography, Sculpture, Watercolors, Bronzes, Etchings & Engravings, Collages

Collections: 20th-century American art & European art; 21st-century American & International art

Publications: exhibition catalogues; quarterly magazine; annual report; public programs brochures; class schedule; e-newsletter

Activities: Classes for adults & children; docent training; Art instructional studios; museum school; lects open to pub; lects for mems only; arts festivals; guided tours; concerts; gallery talks; sponsor competitions; schol; awards, accredited by Amer Assoc of Mus; lends original objects of art to other museums; originates traveling exhibs to various members of AAM & AAMD; mus shop sells books, art related items, children's toys & gifts

WEST PALM BEACH

M **HISTORICAL SOCIETY OF PALM BEACH COUNTY,** The Richard and Pat Johnson Palm Beach County History Museum, 300 N Dixie Hwy, Suite 471 West Palm Beach, FL 33401; PO Box 4364, West Palm Beach, FL 33402-4364. Tel 561-832-4164; Fax 561-832-7965; Elec Mail info@historicalsocietypbc.org; Internet Home Page Address: www.historicalsocietypbc.org; *Dir Research & Archives* Debi Murray; *Office Mgr* Sharon Poss; *Pres & CEO* Jeremy W Johnson CAE; *Cur Colls* Steven F Erdmann; *Cur Educ* Richard A Marconi; *Advancement & Commun* Melissa L Sullivan; *Mktg & Special Events* Jillian Markwith; *Research Curatorial Asst* Nicholas Golubov; *Mem Assoc* Carol Elder
Open Tues - Sat 10 AM - 5 PM; No admis fee; Estab 1937 to preserve & disseminate history of Palm Beach County; Average Annual Attendance: 12,000; Mem: 1000; dues $50-$2,500; annual meeting in Apr
Income: $90,000 (financed by mem, donations & grants)
Library Holdings: Audio Tapes; Book Volumes; CD-ROMs; Clipping Files; Framed Reproductions; Manuscripts; Maps; Memorabilia; Original Documents; Pamphlets; Photographs; Prints; Records
Special Subjects: Archaeology, Historical Material, Architecture, Manuscripts
Collections: Addison Mizner architectural drawings; History of Palm Beach County; other local architect drawings
Publications: Newsletter, quarterly
Activities: Lects open to public, 6 vis lectrs per year; tours; competitions-Judge James R Knott Award for excellence in historical research-public history; original objects of art lent to qualified non-profit organizations; lending collection contains film strips, framed reproductions, original art works, original prints, photographs, slides & artifacts from permanent collection; mus shop sells books, reproductions, prints & gift items

M **NORTHWOOD UNIVERSITY,** Jeannette Hare Art Gallery, 2600 N Military Trail, Turner Education Bldg West Palm Beach, FL 33409-2999. Tel 561-478-5538; Fax 561-640-3328; *Arts Coordr* Samara Strauss; *Mus Shop Mgr* Katherine Kress
Open Mon-Fri 9AM-6PM, Sat & Sun noon-6PM; No admis fee; Estab 1959 to provide aesthetic, creative & spiritual elements as part of a bus education; Average Annual Attendance: 10,000
Collections: Art About the Automobile; International Costume Collection; Tamassy Collection of Old Masterworks on Paper; Wally Findlay Collection
Publications: Arts Report, annual; exhibition catalogues
Activities: Lects open to pub, 4 vis lectrs per year; book traveling exhibitions 3-4 per year

M **NORTON MUSEUM OF ART,** 1451 S Olive Ave, West Palm Beach, FL 33401-7162. Tel 561-832-5196; Elec Mail info@norton.org; Internet Home Page Address: www.norton.org; *Dir* Hope Alswang; *Asst Dir* Charlie Stainback; *Cur Chinese Art* Elizabeth B McGraw; *Cur Chinese Art* Laurie Barnes; *Dir Curatorial Affairs, Cur Contemporary Art* Cheryl Brutvan; *Cur Photography* Tim Wride; *Cur Educ* William Randolph Hearst; *Asst Cur Educ* Jessica Kennedy; *Curatorial Asst* Maggie Edwards; *Dir Commun* Scott Benarde
Open Tues - Sat 10 AM - 5 PM; Thurs until 9 PM, Sun 11 AM - 5 PM, cl Mon & major holidays; Admis adults $12, youth ages 13-21 $5, mems & children under13 free, 1st Sat free to res w/ID; group rates available; Estab 1941 by Ralph & Elizabeth Norton to present exhibition related lectures, concerts, and programs for children & adults; Sculptures are exhibited throughout the Gallery & in the patio garden. Maintains research library; Average Annual Attendance: 180,000; Mem: 7000; dues $100 household
Income: Financed by endowment, mem, city appropriation, Palm Beach County Tourist Develop Council, donations & fundraising events
Library Holdings: Audio Tapes; Book Volumes 3,800; Clipping Files; Exhibition Catalogs; Fiche; Filmstrips; Kodachrome Transparencies; Memorabilia; Pamphlets; Periodical Subscriptions 30; Photographs; Reels; Slides
Special Subjects: Painting-American, Sculpture, Bronzes, Jade, Painting-French
Collections: European Impressionists; Modern Masters; American Art from 1900; Chinese carved jades; Bronze vessels; Early ceramics; Decorated porcelains; Buddhist sculptures; Contemporary art from 1960-; Photography
Publications: Exhibition catalogs; Visions magazine, 3 times per yr; Images magazine, 6 times per yr
Activities: Educ dept; classes for adults & children; family & youth progs; dramatic progs; docent training; internships; teacher resources; lects open to pub, lects for mems only, 8 vis lectrs per yr; films; concerts; gallery talks; general tours; adult tours; competitions with awards; IMLS Medal of Honor; individual paintings & original objects of art lent to mus around the world; PACE progressive after school community arts education; books traveling exhibs 3-5 per yr; originate traveling exhibs; mus shop sells books, magazines, reproductions, prints & slides

M **ROBERT & MARY MONTGOMERY ARMORY ART CENTER,** Armory Art Center, 1700 Parker Ave, West Palm Beach, FL 33401. Tel 561-832-1776; Fax 561-832-0191; Elec Mail workshops@armoryart.org; Internet Home Page Address: www.armoryart.org; *Dean of School of Art* Paul Aho; *Dir Mktg* Julia Dietrich; *Exec Dir* Amelia Ostrosky
Open Mon-Fri 10AM-4PM, Sat 10AM-2PM, cl Sun; Admis $5 suggested donation; Estab 1986; Mem: dues student $25, individual $50
Activities: Educ prog; classes for adult & children; lects open to pub; 2 vis lectrs per yr

M **YESTERYEAR VILLAGE,** 9067 Southern Blvd, South Florida Fair West Palm Beach, FL 33421; PO Box 210367, West Palm Beach, FL 33421-0367. Tel 561-795-6400; Fax 561-753-2124; Internet Home Page Address: www.southfloridafair.com/yesteryearvillage.html; *CEO & Dir* Brantley B Christian; *Develop & Mem* Vicki Chouris; *Chmn* Harold Murphy; *Pub Rels* John Picano; *Fin Dir* Matt Wallsmith; *Cur* Elizabeth K Speigle; *Security* Barry Reed
Open Tues - Sun 11 AM - 5 PM; Admis adults $5, seniors $4, children $3, under age 5 free; Estab 1990; mus contains 30 restored bldgs, working sawmill, blacksmith, gen store & more

WHITE SPRINGS

M **FLORIDA DEPARTMENT OF ENVIRONMENTAL PROTECTION,** Stephen Foster Folk Culture Center State Park, PO Drawer G, White Springs, FL 32096. Tel 904-397-2733; Fax 904-397-4262; Internet Home Page Address: www.floridastateparks.org/stephenfoster; *Park Mgr* Ben Faure; *Asst Park Mgr* Sandra Cashes; *Event Coordr* Elaine McGrath; *Park Svc Specialist* Robert Giarda; *Park Svc Specialist* Morris Cook
Open 8 AM - Sunset daily; Admis per vehicle $5 up to 8 people, children under 6 free, each additional passenger $1; Estab 1950 as a memorial to Stephen Collins Foster; operated by the State of Florida Dept of Environmental Protection, Division of Recreation & Parks; Mus contains eight dioramas of Foster's best known songs. The North wing holds a collection of 19th century furniture & musical instruments; the 200 foot tall Foster Tower, and a collection of pianos; Average Annual Attendance: 90,000
Special Subjects: Furniture, Dioramas
Collections: Dioramas; furniture; minstrel materials; musical instruments; pianos
Activities: Classes for adults & children; lects open to pub; concerts; tours

WINTER PARK

M **ALBIN POLASEK MUSEUM & SCULPTURE GARDENS,** 633 Osceola Ave, Winter Park, FL 32789-4429. Tel 407-647-6294; Fax 407-647-0410; Elec Mail info@polasek.org; Internet Home Page Address: www.polasek.org; *Exec Dir* Debbie Komanski; *Dir Mus Opers* Claire Pousanby; *Cur* Rachel Frisby
Open year-round, Tues - Sat 10 AM - 4 PM, Sun 1 PM - 4 PM; July 1 - Aug 31, Mon - Fri 10 AM - 4 PM; Admis adults $5, seniors $4, student $3, mem & under 12 free; Estab 1961 to promote legacy of internationally known sculptor Albin Polasek; Retirement home, galleries and pvt chapel in a 3 acre sculpture garden; Average Annual Attendance: 21,000; Mem: dues student/teacher& senior $35, individual $45, family $65
Income: $200,000 (financed by endowment, mem & gifts)
Purchases: $3000
Library Holdings: Book Volumes; Periodical Subscriptions
Special Subjects: Painting-American, Sculpture, Painting-European
Collections: Sculpture of Albin Polasek; Works of Augustus St Gaudens, Charles Grafly, Alphonse Mucha & Charles Hawthorne; Sculpture by Ruth Sherwood
Publications: On View Newsletter
Activities: Classes for children; docent training; lects open to pub; gallery talks; tours; concerts; mus shop sells books, original art, reproductions, prints, note cards, magnets & Moravian items

A **ARCHITECTS DESIGN GROUP INC,** 333 N Knowles Ave, Winter Park, FL 32789; PO Box 1210, Winter Park, FL 32790-1210. Tel 407-647-1706; Fax 407-645-5525; Elec Mail adg@adgusa.org; Internet Home Page Address: www.adgusa.org; *Pres* I S K Reeves V FAIA; *Mktg Dir* Tonya Cranin
Open by appointment 9 AM - 3 PM; Estab 1971 to exhibit Native American antique art; Corporate headquarters for architecture firm
Collections: Antique American Indian Art; Florida Contemporary Art; Native American Art
Activities: Originate traveling exhibs to museums & cultural institutions in the Southeast

M **CHARLES MORSE MUSEUM OF AMERICAN ART,** Charles Hosmer Morse Museum of American Art, 445 North Park Ave, Winter Park, FL 32789. Tel 407-645-5311; Fax 407-647-1284; Elec Mail information@morsemuseum.org; Internet Home Page Address: www.morsemuseum.org; *Dir* Laurence Ruggiero
Open Tues, Wed, Thurs, Sat 9:30 AM - 4 PM, Fri 9:30 AM - 8 PM Nov - Apr, 9:30 AM - 4 PM May - Oct, Sun 1 - 4 PM, cl Mon & major holidays except Easter & July 4; Admis adults $3, students $1, children under 12 free; all visitors free Fri 4 - 8 PM Nov - Apr; Estab by Jeannette Genius McKean & developed by her & her husband Hugh F. McKean, committed to the cultural enrichment of their community; The mus consists of 19 galleries, includes a major collection of American art pottery & representative collections of late 19th & early 20th century American painting, graphics & decorative art; Average Annual Attendance: 60,000; Mem: 1,169; dues student or teacher $5, individual $15, family $25, contributing $50, benefactor $100, sustaining $1000
Income: private endowment
Collections: World's most comprehensive collection of works by Louis Comfort Tiffany, including Tiffany jewelry, pottery, paintings, art glass, stained-glass windows & lamps, & the chapel interior designed for the 1893 Worlds' Columbian Exposition in Chicago
Publications: INSIDER, monthly newsletter to members
Activities: Docent training; lects open to pub; 4-5 vis lectrs per yr; concerts; gallery talks; tours; exten prog to Central Florida; artmobile to area schools

NATIONAL CARTOONISTS SOCIETY
For further information, see National and Regional Organizations

M **ROLLINS COLLEGE,** George D & Harriet W Cornell Fine Arts Museum, 1000
Holt Ave, Winter Park, FL 32789-4409. Tel 407-646-2526; Fax 407-646-2524;
Internet Home Page Address: cfam.rollins.edu; *Registrar & Collections Mgr* Leslie
Cone; *Exec Asst* Sandy Todd; *Dir* Dr Ena Heller; *Cur* Dr Jonathan F Walz; *Donor
& Guest Relations Liaison & Educ Cur* Dana Thomas
Open Tues - Fri 10 AM - 4 PM, Sat & Sun 12 PM - 5 PM, cl Mon; Admis adults
$5, free to mem & students; AAM accredited museum located on Rollins College
Campus in Winter Park; The mus houses the college's permanent collection of
more than 5000 works & provides a focus for the arts in Central Florida. Mus
consists of the McKean, the Yust, Myers, Clive, & Zollo galleries; Average Annual
Attendance: 43,000; Mem: Dues Benefactor $1,000+, Salon $500-999, Patron
$200-$499, Contributing $100-199, Basic $60-99, Individual Student, Educator or
Young Professional $30-$59
Income: $520,000 (funded by endowment & grants)
Purchases: Over 500 contemporary American & European artworks
Special Subjects: Portraits, Prints, Painting-European, Painting-American,
Photography, Sculpture, American Indian Art, Bronzes, Anthropology,
Archaeology, Textiles, Costumes, Ceramics, Crafts, Folk Art, Primitive art,
Afro-American Art, Decorative Arts, Collages, Asian Art, Coins & Medals,
Baroque Art, Antiquities-Egyptian, Antiquities-Roman, Cartoons, Pewter,
Antiquities-Etruscan, Painting-Russian
Collections: Smith Watch Key Collection: 1200 keys; Bloomsbury Collection of
Kenneth Curry
Exhibitions: Rembrandt van Rijn, Sordid and Sacred: The Beggars in
Rembrandt's Etchings, Selections from the John Villarino Collection; L C
Armstrong: The Paradise Triptychs; Jack R Smith: Portraits of American Poets
Publications: Exhibit catalogs, 3 per year; newsletter, 5 per year
Activities: Classes for adults & children, docent training; lects open to pub, 10-15
vis lectrs per yr; gallery talks; tours; originate traveling exhibs

GEORGIA

ALBANY

M **ALBANY MUSEUM OF ART,** 311 Meadowlark Dr, Albany, GA 31707-5704.
Tel 229-439-8400; Fax 229-439-8400; Elec Mail info@albanymuseum.com;
Internet Home Page Address: www.albanymuseum.com; *Mus Svcs Coordr*
Calandra S Jefferson; *Interim Dir* Rives Sexton; *Finance & Operation* Bonny
Dorough; *Cur Educ* Nick Nelson; *Bldg & Grounds Mgr* Alphonso Bogans; *Chief
Security* Benjamin Baker
Open Tues - Thurs 10 AM - 5 PM; Admis, adults $4, children & seniors $2, free
Thurs; Estab 1964; new museum facility opened 1983; Average Annual
Attendance: 35,000; Mem: 1,200; dues bus partners $1,500, dir circle $1,000, dual
patron $250, individual patron $125, family $50, individual $25
Income: $625,000 (financed by state, federal & foundation grants, mem & special
events)
Purchases: Recent purchases include paintings by Reginald Marsh & Ernest
Lawson
Library Holdings: Auction Catalogs; Book Volumes; Exhibition Catalogs;
Pamphlets; Periodical Subscriptions; Video Tapes
Special Subjects: Painting-American, African Art, Afro-American Art,
Antiquities-Egyptian, Antiquities-Greek, Antiquities-Roman
Collections: African Collection; Art of the Southern Region; 20th Century
American Art; African Collection; Ancient Art; Twentieth Century American Art
Publications: Bimonthly newsletter; exhibition catalogs
Activities: Classes for adults & children; workshops; docent training; lects open to
pub, 6 vis lectrs per yr; concerts; gallery; films; tours; sponsoring of
competitions; Children's Art Fair; individual paintings & original objects of art
lent to other museums; originate traveling exhibs to other museums; mus shop
sells books, magazines, reproductions

AMERICUS

M **GEORGIA SOUTHWESTERN STATE UNIVERSITY,** Art Gallery, 800
Georgia Southwestern State University Dr, Americus, GA 31709-4376. Tel
912-931-2204; Fax 912-931-2927; *Art Coordr* Jack R Lewis; *Chmn* Jeffrey Green
Open Mon - Fri 8 AM - 5 PM; No admis fee; Estab 1971
Tuition: Res $1200 per sem; non-res $2700 per sem

ATHENS

M **LYNDON HOUSE ART,** 293 Hoyt St, Athens, GA 30601; PO Box 1868, Athens,
GA 30603-1868. Tel 706-613-3623; Fax 706-613-3627; *Dir* Claire Benson; *Cur*
Nancy Lukasiewicz; *Lyndon House Art Foundation* Dan Hope
Open Tues 11 AM - 8 PM, Wed - Fri 11 AM - 5 PM, cl legal holidays; No admis
fee; Average Annual Attendance: 12,000
Collections: decorative arts; period furnishings
Publications: periodic catalogs
Activities: Educ progs; workshops; art courses; internships; lects; gallery talks;
arts festivals

M **UNIVERSITY OF GEORGIA,** Georgia Museum of Art, 90 Carlton St, Athens,
GA 30602-1502. Tel 706-542-4662; Fax 706-542-1051; Elec Mail
hazbrown@uga.edu; Internet Home Page Address: www.georgiamuseum.org; *Cur
Educ* Carissa DiCindio; *Deputy Dir* Annelies Mondi; *Dir Communs* Hillary
Brown; *Museum Dir* William Eiland; *Cur Decorative Art* Dale Couch; *Dir
Develop* Caroline Maddox; *Cur Exhibs* Todd Rivers; *Bus Mgr* Lisa Conley; *Cur
European Art* Lynn Boland; *Head Registar* Tricia Miller; *Pub Rels Coordr*
Michael Laehowski
Open Tues, Wed, Fri & Sat 10 AM - 5 PM, Thurs 10 AM - 9 PM, Sun 1 PM - 5
PM; No admis fee; Estab 1945; open to the pub 1948 as a fine arts mus; 22 exhib

galleries. Maintains reference library & study centers in the humanities (4
archives); Average Annual Attendance: 100,000; Mem: 700; dues $15 - $1,000;
ann meeting May
Income: Financed through univ, mem & grants
Purchases: American & European prints & paintings
Library Holdings: Auction Catalogs; Book Volumes; CD-ROMs; Pamphlets;
Periodical Subscriptions
Special Subjects: Afro-American Art, Decorative Arts, Drawings, Etchings &
Engravings, Folk Art, Historical Material, Landscapes, Marine Painting, Ceramics,
Glass, Painting-American, Silver, Textiles, Manuscripts, Painting-European,
Painting-French, Sculpture, Tapestries, Graphics, Hispanic Art, Latin American
Art, Mexican Art, Photography, Prints, Watercolors, American Western Art,
Bronzes, African Art, Southwestern Art, Costumes, Religious Art, Crafts, Pottery,
Woodcarvings, Woodcuts, Collages, Portraits, Posters, Furniture, Jewelry,
Porcelain, Asian Art, Metalwork, Painting-British, Carpets & Rugs, Coins &
Medals, Baroque Art, Miniatures, Painting-Polish, Renaissance Art, Embroidery,
Laces, Painting-Spanish, Painting-Italian, Gold, Stained Glass, Bookplates &
Bindings
Collections: American & European Paintings (19th & 20th century); European &
American Graphics, Japanese Graphics, 15th century to the present; Alfred H &
Eva Underhill Holbrook Collection of American Art; Samuel H Kress Study
Collection; The Paulson Collection of Ancient Near Eastern Coins; Larry D &
Brenda A Thompson coll of African American art
Exhibitions: Check website
Publications: Georgia Museum of Art Bulletin; quarterly newsletter; exhibition
catalogs & brochures; gallery notes; calendar
Activities: Classes for adults & children; docent training; senior citizen progs;
volunteer docents prog; lects open to pub, 10-12 vis lectrs per yr; concerts; tours;
gallery talks; competitions with awards; individual paintings & original objects of
art lent to other museums & galleries; Senior Outreach Program; original traveling
exhibs; mus shop sells books & reproductions

L **University of Georgia Libraries,** 320 S Jackson St, Athens, GA 30602-5002. Tel
706-542-7463; Internet Home Page Address: www.libs.uga.edu; *Art Librn* Marilyn
Healey
Open by appointment; Reference library only
Income: Financed by state appropriation
Library Holdings: Audio Tapes; Book Volumes 58,500; Cards; Cassettes;
Clipping Files; Exhibition Catalogs; Fiche; Manuscripts; Micro Print; Motion
Pictures; Pamphlets; Periodical Subscriptions 265; Photographs; Records; Reels;
Slides; Video Tapes
Collections: Rare books & manuscripts collection; illustration archives on
microfiche; stereographs from William C Darrah Collection; private press coll;
handmade paper colls

L **Dept of Art Lamar Dodd School of Art,** 270 River Rd Athens, GA 30602. Tel
706-542-1618, 542-1600 (art dept); Fax 706-542-0226; Internet Home Page
Address: art.uga.edu/index; *Slide Librn* Janet Williamson; *Dir* Carmon Colangelo
Open 8 AM - 5 PM and by special arrangement; Estab 1955 to house slides & AV
equipment for use by faculty & students for classroom lecturing; Reference &
instructional library
Library Holdings: Cassettes; Slides 165,000; Video Tapes
Special Subjects: Decorative Arts, Photography, Etchings & Engravings, Islamic
Art, Painting-American, Ceramics, Latin American Art, Archaeology, American
Western Art, Asian Art, Furniture, Mexican Art, Oriental Art, Antiquities-Assyrian,
Coins & Medals

ATLANTA

M **ALTERNATE ROOTS, INC,** 1083 Austin Ave NE Rm 7, Little 5 Points
Community Ctr Atlanta, GA 30307-1940. Tel 404-577-1079; Fax 404-577-7991;
Elec Mail info@alternateroots.org; Internet Home Page Address:
www.alternateroots.org; *Exec Dir* Carlton Turner; *Dir Resource Devel* Keryl
McCord; *Mgr Progs & Svcs* Shannon M Turner; *Fin & Office Mgr* Cecille Ericta
Open Mon - Fri 10 AM - 6 PM; Estab 1976 to support the creation & presentation
of original performing art that is rooted in a particular community or place,
tradition or spirit; Mem: 250; dues introductory $20, satellite $50, voting $65;
annual meeting
Income: Financed by grants, mem, private contributions
Activities: Classes for adults

M **THE APEX MUSEUM,** 135 Auburn Ave NE, Atlanta, GA 30303-2567. Tel
404-523-2739; Fax 404-523-3248 (call first); Elec Mail apexmuseum@aol.com;
Internet Home Page Address: www.apexmuseum.org; *Pres, Dir & Founder* Dan
Moore Sr; *Sr Chmn* Mr. Billye Aaron; *Gallery Coordr* Michelle Mitchell
Open June - Aug Sun 1 - 5 PM, Sept - May Tues & Thurs - Sat 10 AM - 5 PM,
Wed 10 AM - 6 PM; Admis adults $4, sr citizens & students $3, members &
children under 5 free; Estab 1978 to preserve & present black history; Average
Annual Attendance: 75,000
Collections: African American art; Sankoya wood & brass artifacts
Publications: The APEX Times; Black Codes in Georgia
Activities: Guided tours; lects; awarded best non-profit in 2008; mus-related items
for sale

M **ATLANTA CONTEMPORARY ART CENTER,** 535 Means St NW, Atlanta,
GA 30318. Tel 404-688-1970; Fax 404-577-5856; Elec Mail
info@thecontemporary.org; Internet Home Page Address:
www.thecontemporary.org; *Mng Dir* Stacie Lindner; *Artistic Dir* Stuart Horodner;
Board Pres Tim Schrager; *Mem & Educ Coordr* Melanie Beal
Open Tues - Sat 11 AM - 5 PM; Thurs 11 AM - 8 PM; Sun 12 PM - 5 PM;
Admis non-mem $5, students & seniors $3, mems free; Estab 1973 as a
non-collecting institution dedicated to the creation, presentation & advancement of
contemporary art by emerging & established artists; Average Annual Attendance:
8,000; Mem: 800; dues $25 - $5,000
Income: $560,000
Library Holdings: Auction Catalogs; Clipping Files; DVDs; Exhibition Catalogs;
Memorabilia; Periodical Subscriptions
Exhibitions: Exhibs quarterly

Publications: Artist books; exhib catalogs; e-news, weekly
Activities: Classes for adults & children; art trips; lects open to pub, gallery talks; concerts; tours; media programs; internship programs; Nexus Award; originate traveling exhibs; sales shop sells Nexus artist books, magazines, prints, contemporary catalogs

M **ATLANTA HISTORICAL SOCIETY INC,** Atlanta History Center, 130 W Paces Ferry Rd, Atlanta, GA 30305. Tel 404-814-4000; Fax 404-814-4186; Internet Home Page Address: www.atlhist.org; *Dir Colls Resources* Pam Meister; *Dir Research & Progs* Andy Ambrose; *Dir Develop* Kinsey Harper; *Dir Operations* Sue Nichols; *Exec Dir* Rick Beard
Open Mon - Sat 10 AM - 5:30 PM, Sun Noon - 5:30 PM, Library/Archives open Tues - Sat 10 AM - 5 PM; Admis $10, discount for seniors, youth, children & groups; $1 additional to tour Tullie Smith Farm; $2 additional to tour Swan House, library/archives free; Estab 1926, dedicated to presenting the stories of Atlanta's past, present & future through exhibits, programs, collections & research; Atlanta History Museum with exhibits, shop, cafe, classrooms, 100 seat theater; two National Historic Register houses: Swan House, a 1928 classically styled mansion with original furnishings & the 1840's Tullie Smith Farm with outbuildings & livestock; 1890s Victorian playhouse; 33 acres of gardens & woodland trails labeled for self-guided tours; McElreath Hall, housing an extensive library/archives; member's room & a 400 seat auditorium; Average Annual Attendance: 175,000; Mem: 6000; dues $30-$1000; annual meeting
Income: $6,000,000 (financed through endowment, county appropriation, donations, admis & shop sales, cafe sales & facility rental)
Purchases: $22,500
Special Subjects: Architecture, Photography, Textiles, Costumes, Decorative Arts, Manuscripts, Dolls, Historical Material, Maps, Dioramas, Period Rooms
Collections: costumes & textiles; general Atlanta history; Burrison Folklife Collection; Thomas S Dickey Civil War Ordnance Collection; DuBose Civil War Collection; Philip Trammell Shutze Collection of Decorative Arts
Exhibitions: Metropolitan Frontiers: Atlanta, 1835-2000; Shaping Traditions: Folk Arts in a Changing South; Turning Point: The American Civil War
Publications: Atlanta History: A Journal of Georgia & the South, quarterly; Atlanta History Center News, quarterly; Atlanta History Programs Calendar, quarterly
Activities: Classes for adults & children; family progs; docent progs; lects open to pub, 15 vis lectrs per yr; symposia; workshops; special events; guided tours; originate traveling exhibs; retail store sells books, prints, magazines, slides, original art, reproductions, folk crafts, educational toys & Atlanta history memorabilia

M **ATLANTA INTERNATIONAL MUSEUM OF ART & DESIGN,** Museum of Design Atlanta, 1315 Peachtree St NE, Atlanta, GA 30309-7515. Tel 404-979-6455; Fax 404-856-5960; Elec Mail info@museumofdesign.org; Internet Home Page Address: www.museumofdesign.org; *Exec Dir* Brenda Gallina; *Educ Dir* Raja Schaar
Open Tues-Sat 11AM-5PM; Admis $10; Estab 1989 to promote the study & impact of design on everyday life; Includes 3 galleries; Average Annual Attendance: 15,000; Mem: 700; dues $50 & up
Income: $1,000,000 (financed by endowment, mem, city & state appropriation & corporate sponsorship)
Special Subjects: Architecture, Metalwork, Graphics, Posters, Jewelry
Exhibitions: The Furniture of Eero Saarinen: Designs for Everyday Living; Marcel Breuer: Design & Architecture; ATLANTA: Beyond Bricks & Sticks; LoveNests: Photographs & Objects
Publications: Exhibit catalogue
Activities: Classes for adults & children; docent training; family workshops; 1st Thursdays Downtown Atlanta Arts Walk; lects open to pub, 3 vis lectrs per yr; originate traveling exhibs 1 per yr to Metro-Atlanta community; sales shop sells books & original art

L **ATLANTA-FULTON PUBLIC LIBRARY,** Central Library Art Gallery, One Margaret Mitchell Sq NW, Atlanta, GA 30303. Tel 404-730-1700; Fax 404-730-1757; Elec Mail anthony.miller@fultoncountyga.gov; Internet Home Page Address: www.afpom/cms; *Acting Dir* Ann Haimes; *Mgr* Anthony Miller; *Gallery Coordr* Chera Baugh
Open Mon-Thurs 9AM-8PM, Fri & Sat 9 AM - 6 PM, Sun 2 - 6 PM; Estab 1950 to provide materials in the fine arts; Some exhibit space maintained; Average Annual Attendance: 2500
Income: Financed by county & state appropriation
Library Holdings: Book Volumes 9,000; Compact Disks 7500; DVDs 100; Video Tapes 200
Exhibitions: exhibitions change monthly
Activities: Lects open to pub; concerts; gallery talks; book traveling exhibs 1-2 per yr

M **CENTER FOR PUPPETRY ARTS,** 1404 Spring St NW at 18th, Atlanta, GA 30309-2820. Tel 404-873-3089; Fax 404-873-9907; Elec Mail info@puppet.org; Internet Home Page Address: www.puppet.org; *Exec Dir* Barbara Wylly; *Exec Dir* Bill Wylly; *Cur Exhibs* Jeremy Underwood; *Educ & Mus Progs Dir* Alan Louis; *Dir Devel* Rainie Jueschke
Open Tues - Fri 9 AM - 3 PM, Sat 9 AM - 5 PM, Sun 11 AM - 5 PM; Admis general $8, mems free, Thurs 1-3 PM free; tour & performance fees apply; Estab 1978 to educate pub of the art of puppetry; Puppetry - National & International Exhibits displayed in 9 rooms with hands-on displays includes 1 special exhibit which changes every 6 months; Mem: dues $25 - $1,000 & up
Income: $1,300,000 (financed by endowment, mem, city & state appropriations)
Special Subjects: Latin American Art, Photography, African Art, Pre-Columbian Art, Costumes, Religious Art, Folk Art, Woodcarvings, Afro-American Art, Posters, Asian Art, Historical Material, Restorations
Collections: Collection of puppets from around the globe; Puppetry
Exhibitions: Permanent Collection: Puppet Power Wonders (800 puppets)
Publications: Articles, brochures, catalogs & reports
Activities: Classes for adults & children; docent training; lects open to pub, 2-3 vis lectrs per yr; gallery talks; tours; schols offered; lending collection contains original objects of art & photographs; book traveling exhibs 3 per yr; originate traveling exhibs 2 per yr; mus shop sells books & puppets

L **Library,** 1404 Spring St, Atlanta, GA 30309-2820. Tel 404-881-5128; Fax 404-873-9907; Internet Home Page Address: www.puppet.org; *Museum Mgr* Susan Kinney; *Exec Dir* Vincent Anthony
Open by appointment; No admis fee; For reference only; Library estab 1978
Library Holdings: Audio Tapes; Book Volumes 1,500; Cassettes; Clipping Files; Exhibition Catalogs; Framed Reproductions; Memorabilia; Original Art Works; Pamphlets; Photographs; Prints; Records; Reproductions; Slides; Video Tapes

A **CITY OF ATLANTA,** Office of Cultural Affairs, 233 Peachtree St, NE, Harris Tower Atlanta, GA 30303-1504. Tel 404-546-6999; Fax 404-546-9473; *Prog Adminr* Eddie Granderson
Estab 1974 to improve the social fabric & quality of life for Atlanta's citizens & visitors by supporting the arts & cultural activities & by nurturing the arts community
Activities: Contracts for art services; music progs; pub art progs; special projects

M **City Gallery East,** 233 Peachtree St NE, Ste 1700 Atlanta, GA 30303-1563. Tel 404-817-6981; Fax 404-817-6827; Elec Mail citygalleryeast@mindspring.com; *Dir* Camille Love
Open Mon - Sat 10AM-5PM; Estab to present contemporary fine art produced by regional, national & international professional artists; focused primarily on Atlanta-based artists; goal: display work that is stimulating & innovative & that presents a new perspective or cross-collaboration with other art disciplines; 8000 sq ft exhibition space; Average Annual Attendance: 30,000
Income: Financed by prog of Bureau of Cultural Affairs
Exhibitions: 5 exhibs per yr
Publications: Catalogs: Larry Walker: Four Decades (2001) & Beverly Buchanan: Habitats & Shotgun Shacks (2000)
Activities: Sponsors lects, forums, demonstrations & performances in collaboration with service agencies; gallery talks; tours

M **Atlanta Cyclorama & Civil War Museum,** 800 Cherokee Dr SE, Atlanta, GA 30315. Tel 404-658-7625; Fax 404-658-7045; Elec Mail info@atlanticyclorama.org; Internet Home Page Address: www.atlantacyclorama.org; *Dir* Keith G Lauer; *Mktg and Pub Rels* Yakingma L Robinson
Open Tues-Sun 9AM-4:30PM, cl Mondays; Admis adults $7 children 6-12 $5, seniors $6, children under 6 free; Estab 1886; Located in Grant Park & listed in the National Historic Register; 184-seat revolving platform; Average Annual Attendance: 100,000
Income: The self-sustaining Cyclorama functions as an enterprise
Special Subjects: Painting-American, Costumes, Historical Material
Collections: Civil War artifacts; lifelike figures in Civil War costume & period props; panoramic painting depicting the Battle of Atlanta; The Locomotive Texas
Activities: Scavenger hunts; Sales shop sells books, videos & Civil War era souvenirs

A **Chastain Arts Center & Gallery,** 135 W Wieuca Rd NW, Atlanta, GA 30342-3221. Tel 404-252-2927; Fax 404-851-1270; Elec Mail chastainarts@atlantaga.gov; Internet Home Page Address: www.ocaatlanta.com; *Dir* Karen Lowe
Open Mon & Fri 9:30 AM - 5 PM, Tues -Thurs 9:30 AM - 9:30 PM, Fri - Sat 9:30 AM - 3 PM, cl Sun; Estab 1968; Located in Chastain Park; oldest City-operated arts facility in Atlanta; Average Annual Attendance: 2,000
Special Subjects: Drawings, Prints, Pottery, Jewelry
Activities: Educ prog; classes for adults & children; workshops; gallery talks; sales shop sells original art

M **The Gallery @ Chastain Arts Center,** 135 W Wieuca Rd NW, Atlanta, GA 30342. Tel 404-257-1804; Fax 404-851-1270; Elec Mail cac135@atlantaga.gov; Internet Home Page Address: www.ocaatlanta.com; *Gallery Dir* Erin Bailey
Open Mon - Sat 1 - 5 PM; No admis fee; Estab c1968. Gallery's mission is to advance the educational prog of the adjacent arts center; Venue for display of art by local, regional & national artists & designers and arts organizations
Exhibitions: Exhibitions demonstrating skill & high level of achievement in arts & crafts and/or exploring history
Activities: Lect; gallery tours; symposiums & workshops in conjunction with exhibitions

M **Gilbert House,** 2238 Perkerson Rd SW, Atlanta, GA 30315-6216. Tel 404-766-9049; Fax 404-765-2806; *Dir* Erin Bailey
Open by appointment; Tues - Fri 10 AM - 5 PM; Estab 1984; Built in 1865 by Jeremiah Gilbert immediately after the Civil War; registered historic landmark located on 12 acres
Activities: Art classes for adults & children; exhibs of art work

L **Arts Clearinghouse,** 233 Peachtree St NE, Ste 1700 Atlanta, GA 30303-1563. Tel 404-817-6815; Fax 404-817-6827; *Dir* Shawn Redding
Estab as a comprehensive arts information & resources referral center; Offers open files on all Hotline presenters: listings of available studio space in Atlanta, health insurance policies for self-employed artists, sets of grant guidelines from National Endowment for the Arts & local arts funding agencies, as well as information on pub art commissions nationwide
Library Holdings: Book Volumes 150; Periodical Subscriptions 30
Activities: Art in educ prog; professional develop workshops; arts hotline; materials for the arts prog

M **EMORY UNIVERSITY,** Michael C Carlos Museum, 571 S Kilgo Circle, Atlanta, GA 30322-1120. Tel 404-727-4282; Fax 404-727-4292; Internet Home Page Address: www.carlos.emory.edu; *Assoc Dir* Catherine Howett Smith; *Dir Exhib & Collections* Joseph Gargasz; *Dir Educ* Elizabeth S Hornor; *Dir* Bonnie Speed
Open Tues - Fri 10 AM - 4 PM, Sat 10 AM - 5 PM, Sun Noon - 5 PM; Admis donation $8; Estab 1919; Mus redesigned in 1985 by Michael Graves, Post-Modernist architect; 15,400 sq ft; permanent exhibition galleries & special exhibition galleries; Average Annual Attendance: 120,000; Mem: 1,400; dues teacher $30, individual $40, Dual $60, Family $75, Doric $150, Ionic $250, Corinthian $500
Income: $2,500,000
Special Subjects: Latin American Art, Mexican Art, Photography, Sculpture, Watercolors, African Art, Archaeology, Pre-Columbian Art, Ceramics, Pottery, Woodcarvings, Etchings & Engravings, Manuscripts, Glass, Jade, Jewelry, Oriental

Art, Asian Art, Antiquities-Egyptian, Antiquities-Greek, Antiquities-Roman, Antiquities-Etruscan
Collections: Art collection from Renaissance to present, African, classical Greek & Egyptian; Old World art & archaeology, including works from Egypt, Mesopotamia, ancient Palestine; Pre-Columbian, American Indian & Far Eastern holdings; Works on Paper, Asian, African
Publications: Exhibition catalogues
Activities: Classes for adults & children; classes for teachers; docent training; lects open to pub; 10 vis lectrs per yr; concerts; gallery talks; tours; schols & fels offered; exten dept; original objects of art lent to other institutions; book traveling exhibs 2-4 per yr; originate traveling exhibs; mus shop sells books, magazines, original art, reproductions, prints, gifts, jewelry, CD ROMs, videos & catalogues

A **GEORGIA COUNCIL FOR THE ARTS,** Georgia's State Art Collection, 260 14th St NW, Ste 401, Atlanta, GA 30318-5360. Tel 404-685-2787; Fax 404-685-2788; Internet Home Page Address: www.gaarts.org; *Exec Dir* Susan S Weimer
Offices open Mon - Fri 8 AM - 5 PM; Gallery by appointment only; No admis fee; Estab 1968 as a state agency providing funding to non-profit, tax-exempt organizations for arts programming & support; Art work of Georgians; Mem: 24 members appointed by governor; meetings four times per yr
Income: $3,900,000 (financed by state appropriation plus federal funding)
Publications: Guide to Programs, annual (one for organizations & one for artists)

L **GEORGIA INSTITUTE OF TECHNOLOGY,** College of Architecture Library, Georgia Institute of Technology, Atlanta, GA 30332-0155. Tel 404-894-4877; Elec Mail kathy.brackney@library.gatech.edu; Internet Home Page Address: www.library.gatech.edu/architect/; *Head Librn* Kathryn S Brackney
Open Mon - Thur 8 AM - 12 AM, Fri 8 AM - 6 PM, Sat 9 AM - 6 PM, Sun Noon - 12 AM
Income: Financed by state appropriation
Library Holdings: Book Volumes 33,800; Periodical Subscriptions 160; Reels

A **GEORGIA LAWYERS FOR THE ARTS,** 887 W Marietta St, NW, Ste J-101 Atlanta, GA 30318-5266. Tel 404-873-3911; Fax 404-873-3911; Elec Mail gla@glarts.org; Internet Home Page Address: www.glarts.org; *Exec Dir* Lisa Moore; *Dir of Vol Services* Elizabeth Wheeler
Open Mon - Fri 9 AM - 5 PM by appointment only; No admis fee; Estab 1975 to provide legal services & educational programming to artists and arts organizations in Georgia; Mem: Dues individual artists $40, nonprofit arts organizations $75
Collections: Copyrights; fundraising; art law related to literature
Publications: An Artists Handbook on Copyright; Handbook on the Georgia Print Law; Art Law in Georgia: A Guide for Artists and Art Organizations
Activities: Educ prog; classes for adults; network of volunteer attorneys who provide free legal services to low income artists; lects open to pub; 50-60 vis lectrs per yr; workshops and seminars on legal issues

L **GEORGIA STATE UNIVERSITY,** School of Art & Design, Visual Resource Center, PO Box 3965, Atlanta, GA 30302-3965. Tel 404-651-2257; Fax 404-651-1779; Internet Home Page Address: www.gsu.edu; *Cur* Ann England
Open Mon - Fri 8:30 AM - 5 PM; No admis fee; Estab 1970 to make visual & literary resource materials available for study, teaching & research; Average Annual Attendance: 20,000
Library Holdings: Book Volumes 300; Exhibition Catalogs; Original Art Works; Pamphlets; Periodical Subscriptions 18; Reproductions; Slides 255,000; Video Tapes 45
Special Subjects: Aesthetics, Afro-American Art
Collections: Rare book collection, original prints emphasis impressionism, 19th - early 20th century artists; extensive Pre-Columbian slide collection, History of textile, Metalsmithing & jewelry making, History of photography
Activities: Lects open to public, 5-10 vis lectrs per year; films; artist's slide presentations; discussions

M **Ernest G Welch Gallery,** 10 Peachtree Center Ave Rm 117, University Plaza Atlanta, GA 30303-3003; PO Box 4107, School of Art & Design Atlanta, GA 30302-4107. Tel 404-413-5230; Fax 404-413-5261; Elec Mail artgallery@gsu.edu; Internet Home Page Address: www.gsu.edu/artgallery; *Dir* Cathy Byrd; *Interim Gallery Dir* Waduda Muhammad
Open Mon - Fri 10 AM - 6 PM & 10 AM - 8 PM during exhibs; No admis fee; Two galleries for student and facility exhibits, national and international traveling shows.
Publications: Catalogues
Activities: Lects open to public; gallery talks; tours

A **GO ANTIQUES, INC,** (Antique Networking, Inc) 3525 Piedmont Rd NE, Bldg 5 Ste 435 Atlanta, GA 30305. Tel 614-923-4250; Fax 614-923-4251; Elec Mail kathy@antiqnet.com; Internet Home Page Address: www.goantiques.com; *Pres* Jim Kamniker; *Sr VPres Bus Develop* Kathy Kamniker; *VPres Opers* Michael Glick
Open 24/7 online, goantiques.com; No admis fee; Estab 1992; Internet provider for antiques dealers

M **HAMMONDS HOUSE MUSEUM,** 503 Peeples St, SW, Atlanta, GA 30313-1815. Tel 404-612-0500; Fax 404-752-8733; Elec Mail info@hammondshouse.org; Internet Home Page Address: hammondshouse.org; *Exec Dir* Myrna Anderson-Fuller; *Interim Cur* Tracy Murrell; *Facilities Mgr & Security* Byron Simmons; *Mem & Vol Coordr* Cheryl Odeleye; *Adm & Communs Mgr* Serena Garcia
Open Tues-Fri 10AM-6PM, Sat-Sun 1PM-5PM; cl Mon & nat holidays; Admis $4, senior citizens, students & children $2, free for mem; guided tours $4 per person; Estab 1988; Original artwork displayed throughout early 19th c. Eastlake Victorian venue; Average Annual Attendance: 10,000; Mem: 400; dues $15 & up
Income: Financed by grants, donations, mem, earned income
Special Subjects: Afro-American Art, Decorative Arts, Folk Art, Historical Material, Collages, Furniture, Photography, Prints, Woodcuts, African Art, Posters
Collections: More than 350 art works from mid-19th century artists; Haitian paintings; African sculptures & masks; Recordings of artist talks
Activities: Educ prog; classes & workshops for adults & children; Art Block Summer Camp for Kids; Spring Break Printmaking; teacher workshop; Wine & Words book series; lects open to pub, 15 vis lectrs per yr; garden concerts; gallery talks; tours; awards & grants; mus shop sells books, magazines, minimal original art, reproductions, prints, jewelry, African masks, small tables

M **HIGH MUSEUM OF ART,** 1280 Peachtree St NE, Atlanta, GA 30309-3502. Tel 404-733-4400; 733-4444; Internet Home Page Address: www.high.org; *Dir* Michael E Shapiro; *Registrar* Frances Francis; *Dir Architectural Planning & Design* Marjorie Harvey; *Dep Dir* Philip Verre; *Dir Finance & Opers* Rhonda Matheison; *Dir Mus Advancement* Sheldon Wolf; *Cur Am Art* Sylvia Yount; *Cur Photography* Tom Southall; *Cur Decorative Arts* Stephen Harrison; *Dir Mus Advan* Sandra K Kidd; *Cur Modern & Contemporary* Carrie Przybilla; *Chief Cur* David Brenneman; *Cur Media Arts* Linda Dubler; *Cur African Art* Carol Thompson; *Cur Folk Arts* Lynne Spriggs; *Pres Mem Guild* Jim Kaltenbach; *Mgr Exhib* Jody Cohen; *Mus Shop Mgr* Adrienne Pierce; *Mgr Publ* Kelly Morris; *Community Rels Mgr* Jacqueline P King
Open Tues - Sat 10 AM - 5 PM, Thurs until 8 PM, Sun Noon - 5 PM, cl Mon & major holidays; Admis adults $18, seniors & students $15, children ages 6-17 $11, children under 6 & mems free, 1st Sat of month free for res w/ID; group rates available; Estab 1926 to make the best in the visual arts available to the Atlanta public in exhibitions & supporting programs; Four floors (46,000 sq ft) exhibition space; top floor for traveling exhibitions; semi-flexible space (moveable walls); ramp & elevator for accessibility; Average Annual Attendance: 500,000; Mem: 39,000; dues $50 & up
Income: $7,500,000 (financed by endowment, mem, Members Guild of the High Museum of Art, city & state appropriations, museum shop sales, grants & foundations, ticket sales & operating income)
Library Holdings: Auction Catalogs; Book Volumes 14,000; Clipping Files; Exhibition Catalogs; Periodical Subscriptions 50; Slides
Special Subjects: Afro-American Art, Decorative Arts, Drawings, Etchings & Engravings, Folk Art, Architecture, Art Education, Art History, Ceramics, Conceptual Art, American Western Art, Photography, Crafts
Collections: American painting & sculpture; European painting & sculpture, 20th Century painting, photography & sculpture; African & Sub-Saharan Art; Works on Paper; 18th & 19th Century decorative art featuring Herter Brothers, William Whitehead & John Henry Belter; contemporary crafts; 20th Century furniture; regional historical decorative arts & English ceramics; 19th Century American landscape paintings; contemporary art since 1970; Western art early Renaissance - present; decorative arts; graphics; sculpture; 19th - 20th century photography; Modern & Contemporary Art
Publications: HighLife, bi-monthly mem magazine; exhibition catalogues
Activities: Workshops for adults, children & families; docent training; teacher resources; lects open to pub; family days; tours; concerts; book signings; performing arts programs; senior citizen programs; gallery talks; speakers bureau; originates traveling exhibs; two mus shops sell books, reproductions, slides, prints, stationery, children's books & toys, crafts, jewelry & gift items

L **SAVANNAH COLLEGE OF ART & DESIGN - ATLANTA,** ACA Library of Atlanta, 1600 Peachtree St NW, Atlanta, GA 30309-2403; PO Box 77300, Atlanta, GA 30357-1300. Tel 404-253-3196; Elec Mail ref_atl@scad.edu; Internet Home Page Address: www.scad.edu/life/libraries/; *Head Librn* Teresa Burk; *Vis Resources Librn* Mary Murphy; *Ref Librn* Caley Cannon; *Cataloging Librn* Jenny Wang
Open Mon - Thurs 8 AM - 5 PM, Fri noon - 5 PM, Sat & Sun noon - 8 PM; No admis fee; Estab 1950 to provide art information & research facility to the Atlanta College of Art community & the southeast art community; Circ 12,000
Library Holdings: Book Volumes 32,000; Clipping Files; DVDs 10; Exhibition Catalogs; Other Holdings Artists' books 1,500; Periodical Subscriptions 185; Slides 98,000; Video Tapes 400
Special Subjects: Art History, Photography, Drawings, Graphic Design, Painting-American, Interior Design
Collections: Artists' Books; rare books; circulating art books
Activities: Classes for adults & children; films; vis artists program; Joane Paschall award for student artists' book competition

A **SOCIETY OF DECORATIVE PAINTERS, INC,** Decorative Arts Collection Museum, PO Box 18028, Atlanta, GA 30316-0028. Tel 404-627-3662; Elec Mail DAC@decorativeartscollection.org; Internet Home Page Address: decorativeartscollection.org/; *Dir* Andy Jones
Open Mon - Fri 8:30 AM - 4:30 PM; Admis $3, tour groups $25; Estab 1982 to preserve & collect items of decorative painting & educate the public about the art form; Average Annual Attendance: 500; Mem: 1,000
Income: Financed by mem & gifts
Library Holdings: Book Volumes; Original Documents; Photographs; Slides
Special Subjects: Porcelain, Watercolors, Painting-American, Decorative Arts, Painting-Dutch, Painting-Japanese, Painting-Canadian, Painting-Russian, Painting-Scandinavian
Collections: Decorative Arts Collection - antique & contemporary decorative art; various media
Publications: Friends, newsletter, twice a year
Activities: Classes for adults and children; industry contribution recognition awards; DAC juried art awards; lending collection; originate traveling exhibs; sales shop sells books, magazines, jewelry & original art

M **SYMMES SYSTEMS,** Photographic Investments Gallery, 3977 Briarcliff Rd NE, Atlanta, GA 30345-2647. Tel 404-320-1012; *Pres* Edwin C Symmes Jr
Open by appointment; No admis fee; Estab 1979 to display & produce traveling exhibits of classical photography
Collections: 19th century photographic images in all media; 20th century black & white & color photos by masters
Exhibitions: 19th Century Albumen Prints of Westminster Cathedral; Netsuke: An Insight into Japan; Color Photography by E C Symmes; 19th & 20th Century Images of China.
Activities: Lects open to pub; original objects of art lent; lending collection contains 1500 19th century Albumen prints; originate traveling exhibs; mus shop sells original art

AUGUSTA

M **GERTRUDE HERBERT INSTITUTE OF ART,** 506 Telfair St, Augusta, GA 30901-2310. Tel 706-722-5495; Fax 706-722-3670; Elec Mail ghia@ghia.org; Internet Home Page Address: www.ghia.org; *Dir* Heather Williams
Open Mon - Fri 10 AM - 5 PM, Sat by appointment, groups by special appointment, cl Sun & all major holidays; No admis fee; donations accepted; Estab 1937 for the advancement & encouragement of art & educ in art; Main gallery located on second fl of historic home; Average Annual Attendance: 5,000; Mem: 400
Special Subjects: Drawings, Photography, Painting-American, Prints, Graphics, Sculpture
Exhibitions: Circulating exhibitions; monthly exhibitions; one-person and group exhibitions; The National Annual Juried Exhibition
Activities: Classes for adults & children; docent training; lect open to public, 4 vis lectrs per year; gallery talks; tours; competitions with awards; scholarships offered; book traveling exhibitions

C **MORRIS COMMUNICATIONS CO. LLC,** Corporate Collection, 725 Broad St, Augusta, GA 30901-1336; PO Box 936, Augusta, GA 30903-0936. Tel 706-724-0851; Fax 706-722-7125; *Chmn & CEO* W S Morris III; *Fine Art Mgr* Louise Keith Claussen
Collections: Alaskan Art; American Paintings; Western Bronzes; Wildlife (birds); European Paintings

M **MORRIS MUSEUM OF ART,** One Tenth St, Augusta, GA 30901-1134. Tel 706-724-7501; Fax 706-724-7612; Internet Home Page Address: www.themorris.org; www.southernsoulandsong.org; *Exec Dir* Kevin Grogan; *Cur Educ* Michelle Schulte; *Registrar* Melinda Gales; *Finance Officer* Louis P Gangarosa Jr; *Dir Retail Svcs* Barbara Morphy; *Dir Mktg & Pub Rels* Nicole McLeod; *Librn & Archivist* Cary Wilkins; *Office Mgr* Brenda Hall; *Exhibition Designer & Preparator* Dwayne Clark; *Spec Events Coordr* Lauren Land; *Dir External Affairs* Phyllis Giddens; *Assoc Cur, Educ & School Programs* Matt Porter; *Creative Dir* Todd Beasley; *Security Officer* Frank Lozito; *Security Officer* Bill Lay; *Security Officer* Al Bostick; *Mus Store* Camila Wopecka; *Educ Progs Mgr* Jessica Stephens; *Store Asst* Margie Van Evera; *Curatorial Asst* Julia Bruton; *Admin Asst* Laura Mason; *Outreach Educ Coordr* Jenna Tankersley
Open Tues - Sat 10 AM - 5 PM, Sun Noon - 5 PM; Admis adults $5, seniors 65+, military & students $3; Estab 1992; 40,000 sq ft facility on 3 floors; 18,000 sq ft of gallery space; 16 galleries; Average Annual Attendance: 40,000; Mem: dues $15-$5000
Income: Financed by endowment, mem, grants, gifts & fundraising activities
Purchases: Southern Art permanent collection
Library Holdings: Auction Catalogs; Audio Tapes; Book Volumes 9,000; CD-ROMs; Cassettes; Clipping Files; Compact Disks; DVDs; Exhibition Catalogs; Filmstrips; Kodachrome Transparencies; Manuscripts; Maps; Memorabilia; Motion Pictures; Original Art Works; Original Documents; Pamphlets; Periodical Subscriptions; Photographs; Records; Reproductions; Slides; Video Tapes
Special Subjects: Afro-American Art, Archaeology, Decorative Arts, Drawings, Historical Material, Illustration, Landscape Architecture, Landscapes, Marine Painting, Architecture, Art Education, Art History, Collages, Conceptual Art, Furniture, Photography, Portraits, Pottery, Painting-American, Prints, Woodcuts, Drawings, Graphics, Painting-American, Sculpture, Watercolors, Textiles, Crafts, Folk Art, Primitive art, Woodcarvings, Etchings & Engravings, Landscapes, Portraits, Glass, Porcelain
Collections: The first museum in the country dedicated to celebrating and exploring the art and artists of the American South. The museum has a permanent collection of some 5,000 works of art. It is a broad-based survey collection, encompassing a history of painting in the South, ranging from the late Colonial Era to the present.; library & archives: 18,000 vols, 20,000 vertical files; 500 films; video; slides; artist papers
Exhibitions: A Southern Collection: Masterworks from a Permanent Collection of Painting in the South
Publications: Exhibition catalogs, books
Activities: Educ dept; classes for adults & children; dramatic progs; Southern circuit tour of independent filmmakers; docent training; film programs; readings; classic film prog; lects open to pub, 12-18 vis lectrs per yr; 18 concerts; gallery talks; tours; competitions with awards; "Combining Voices" Youth Literary competition; Porter Fleming Literary Competition Awards; Smithsonian Affiliations Internship; exten prog serves central Savannah River area; individual paintings lent to mus; book traveling exhibs, 2-3 per yr; originate traveling exhibs circulate principally to Southeastern mus; mus shop sells books, magazines, original art, reproductions, prints, slides, gift items, crafts, food items

BAINBRIDGE

M **FIREHOUSE CENTER & GALLERY,** 119 Water St, Bainbridge, GA 39817-3620; c/o Phyllis Lucas, Pres, 293 Rivervale Dr Bainbridge, GA 39817-7437. Tel 229-243-1010
Open Mon - Fri 12 PM - 4 PM, Sat - Sun 1 PM - 5 PM; groups by appointment
Collections: Paintings; sculpture; photographs

BRUNSWICK

A **GOLDEN ISLES ARTS & HUMANITIES ASSOCIATION,** 1530 Newcastle St, Brunswick, GA 31520-6805. Tel 912-262-6934; Fax 912-262-1029; Elec Mail info@goldenislesarts.org; Internet Home Page Address: www.goldenislesarts.org; *Exec Dir* Heather Heath; *Production Dir* Rob Nixon
Open Thurs - Fri 10 AM - 6 PM, Sat 10 AM - 2 PM; Estab 1989 as a county coordinating arts council & presenter; The Ritz Theatre Lobby; Average Annual Attendance: 10,000; Mem: 700; dues family $50, single $35; annual meeting in July
Income: $285,000 (financed by mem, programs, services & grants)

Activities: Children's classes; dramatic progs; lects open to pub, 4-5 vis lectrs per yr; photographic & visual arts competitions; ribbons & cash awards; concerts; schols offered; book traveling exhibs 1 per yr

CARTERSVILLE

M **BOOTH WESTERN ART MUSEUM,** 501 Museum Dr, Cartersville, GA 30120; PO Box 3070, Cartersville, GA 30120-1702. Tel 770-387-1300; Fax 770-387-1319; Internet Home Page Address: www.boothmuseum.org; *Exec Dir* Seth Hopkins; *Devel* Tom Roberson; *Educ* Lisa Wheeler; *Pub Rels* Tara Currier; *Treas* Cathy Lee Eckert; *Registrar* Nikki Morris; *Cur* Jeff Donaldson; *Librn & Archivist* Liz Gentry; *Mus Shop Mgr* Macra Adair; *Security* Ken Wade
Open Tues - Wed & Fri - Sat 10 AM - 5 PM, Thurs 10 AM - 8 PM, Sun 1 - 5 PM; Admis adults $10, seniors 65 & over & military $8, students $7, discounts to groups of 15 or more, children 12 & under & members no charge; Estab 2000; Western art, Civil War art, presidential photographs; Average Annual Attendance: 48,000; Mem: Dues individual $50, family $95, friend $150, museum package $200, contributor $250, patron $500, curator $1,000, collector's circle $2,500, dir circle $5,000 & up
Library Holdings: Auction Catalogs 200; Book Volumes 12,200; CD-ROMs 300; DVDs 200; Exhibition Catalogs 300; Motion Pictures 200; Periodical Subscriptions 50; Video Tapes 200
Special Subjects: Afro-American Art, Drawings, Historical Material, Landscapes, American Western Art, Photography, Painting-American, Prints, Sculpture, Graphics, Watercolors, Bronzes, Southwestern Art, Pottery, Portraits, Posters, Military Art
Collections: Western American art & culture; Presidential letters & portraits; Western movie posters; contemporary Civil War art
Publications: quarterly newsletter, The Booth Bulletin
Activities: Demonstrations; discussions; docent prog; lects; 25 vis lectrs per yr; concerts; galley talks; guided tours; sponsoring competitions; Lifetime Achievement award; exten prog NW Georgia; book traveling exhibitions 8 per yr; mus shop sells books, magazines, original art, reproductions & prints

M **TELLUS NORTHWEST GEORGIA SCIENCE MUSEUM,** (Weinman Mineral Museum) 100 Tellus Museum Dr Cartersville, GA 30120; PO Box 3663, Cartersville, GA 30120-1712. Tel 770-386-0576; Fax 770-386-0600; Elec Mail info@tellusmuseum.org; Internet Home Page Address: www.tellusmuseum.org; *Dir & Cur* Jose Santamaria; *Educ* Terry Everett; *Asst Dir* Mary Vinson; *Registrar & Archivist* Cherry Johnson; *Guest Svcs* Conilia Dover
Open Tues - Sat 10 AM - 5 PM, Sun 1 - 5 PM; cl Mon & maj holidays; Admis adults $4, seniors $3.50, children $3; Estab 1982; Average Annual Attendance: 21,685; Mem: dues Corporate $250 - $1000, Sponsor $250, Friend $100, Family $50, Indiv $25, Student $20
Library Holdings: Book Volumes 1500; Periodical Subscriptions 3000
Collections: Exhibits related to geological objects: minerals, fossils, rocks, gems & mining artifacts. Emphasis on minerals & fossils from the state of Georgia & its mining heritage.
Exhibitions: Rockfest: Outdoor gem & mineral show with free admis to mus; Holiday Open House: free activities, refreshments & admis
Publications: Weinman Mineral Museum News, Quarterly
Activities: Educ progs for adults & children

COLUMBUS

M **COLUMBUS MUSEUM,** 1251 Wynnton Rd, Columbus, GA 31906-2899. Tel 706-748-2562; Fax 706-748-2570; Elec Mail information@columbusmuseum.com; Internet Home Page Address: www.columbusmuseum.com; *Cur Coll & Exhib* Kristen Miller Zohn; *Assoc Cur History* Mike Bunn; *Dir Develop* Corrin Riley; *Asst to Dir* Patricia Butts; *Art Handler* Chris Land; *Art Handler* Matt Albrecht; *Registrar* Aimee Brooks; *Deputy Dir Opers* Kimberly Beck; *Dir* Charles T Butler; *Youth & Family Programs Coordr* Jessamy South; *Pub Rels Coordr* Frank Etheridge IV; *Asst Cur Exhibs* Deb Weidel; *Asst Registrar* Mellda Alexander; *Exhibit Designer & Production Coordr* Roger Reeves; *Mus Shop Mgr* Jennifer Morgan; *Mem Coordr* Lane Riley; *Spec Events* Wren Gilliam; *Cur Educ* Tim Brown; *Graphic Designer* Marcolm Tatum
Open Tues - Sat 10 AM - 5 PM, Sun 1 - 5 PM, third Thurs every month 10 AM - 8 PM, cl Mon & legal holidays; No admis fee; Estab 1954 to build a permanent collection; encourage work by Georgia & Southern artists; establish loan shows & traveling exhibitions in all fields of American art & history; 11,000 sq ft history gallery, 2,000 sq ft interactive gallery, 25,000 sq ft art gallery. Maintains reference library; Average Annual Attendance: 60-70,000; Mem: 2900; dues $45 - $5,000; annual meeting in May
Library Holdings: Auction Catalogs; Book Volumes; DVDs; Memorabilia; Periodical Subscriptions
Special Subjects: Decorative Arts, Historical Material, Marine Painting, Ceramics, Collages, Glass, Metalwork, Furniture, Portraits, Period Rooms, Sculpture, Tapestries, Architecture, Drawings, Graphics, Painting-American, Photography, Prints, Watercolors, American Indian Art, African Art, Archaeology, Ethnology, Pre-Columbian Art, Textiles, Costumes, Crafts, Folk Art, Pottery, Primitive art, Woodcarvings, Woodcuts, Etchings & Engravings, Landscapes, Afro-American Art, Posters, Eskimo Art, Dolls, Jade, Jewelry, Porcelain, Oriental Art, Asian Art, Silver, Painting-British, Historical Material, Ivory, Maps
Collections: American art from all periods & all media; Artifacts relating to the culture of the Chattahoochee Valley & Southeastern United States; permanent coll includes Landscapes, Paintings & Portraits by Early & Contemporary American Painters, with strong Coll of American drawings & primitive arts; American firearms, quilts & textiles, Southern folk art
Publications: Annual report; gallery guides; newsletter, quarterly; web news
Activities: Classes for adults & children; docent training; workshops; lects open to pub, 5-7 vis lectrs per yr; concerts; gallery talks; tours; scholarships offered; individual paintings & original objects of art lent to qualified institutions which are recognized & meet facilities accreditation standards; book traveling exhibs 6-10 per yr; originate traveling exhibs to other mus; mus shop sells books, original art, reproductions, jewelry & children's toys & gift items; junior mus

M COLUMBUS STATE UNIVERSITY, Norman Shannon and Emmy Lou P Illges Gallery, 4225 University Ave, Dept of Art Columbus, GA 31907-5679. Tel 706-507-8312; Fax 706-571-4353; Elec Mail israel_hannah@columbusstate.edu; Internet Home Page Address: art.columbusstate.edu; *Gallery Dir* Hannah Israel
Open Mon - Fri 9 AM - 5 PM; No admis fee; Average Annual Attendance: 6,000
Income: $11,000 (financed by student activities)
Purchases: Permanent collection
Library Holdings: Auction Catalogs; Audio Tapes; Book Volumes; CD-ROMs; Video Tapes
Exhibitions: Annual art students show; faculty show; regional guest artist & nationally prominent artists
Publications: newsletters
Activities: Classes for adults & col students; workshops for adults & children 12-14; lects open to pub, lects for mems, 1-5 vis lectrs per yr; tours; gallery talks; competitions with awards; fels offered; Artbeat; sculpture walk; mus shop sells slides

DALTON

A CREATIVE ARTS GUILD, 520 W Waugh St, Dalton, GA 30722-3474. Tel 706-278-0168; Fax 706-278-6996; Elec Mail cagarts@creativeartsguild.org; Internet Home Page Address: www.creativeartsguild.org; *Exec Dir* Terry Tomasello; *Visual Arts & Gallery Dir* Bradley Wilson; *Arts in Educ Dir* Renee Rector; *Bookkeeper* Carol Cofield; *Admin Asst & Rental Coordr* Crystal Coker
Open Mon - Thurs 9 AM - 7 PM, Fri 9 AM - 4:30 PM, others by appt; No admis fee; Estab 1963 to build & maintain an environment supportive of the arts in NW Georgia; Average Annual Attendance: 130,000; Mem: 1,000; dues family $35, annual meeting in June
Income: $500,000 (financed by mem, commissions, grants, tuitions & fund raising events)
Library Holdings: Book Volumes
Collections: Permanent collection of regional art
Exhibitions: Changing monthly shows of crafts; graphics; photography; original art; sculpture; fiber
Publications: Bulletins to members, monthly
Activities: Classes for adults & children; dramatic progs; visual & performing arts programs for schools; concerts; gallery talks; competitions with awards; arts & crafts festivals; individual paintings & original objects of art lent to area schools & organizations

DECATUR

M AGNES SCOTT COLLEGE, Dalton Art Gallery, 141 E College Ave, Dana Fine Arts Bldg Decatur, GA 30030-3770. Tel 404-471-5361; Elec Mail daltongallery@agnesscott.edu; Internet Home Page Address: daltongallery.agnesscott.edu; *Chmn Art Dept* Donna Sadler; *Printmaker* Anne Beidler; *Art Historian* Roger Rothman
Open Mon - Fri 10 AM - 9 PM, Sat 9 AM - 5 PM, Sun 2 - 5 PM; No admis fee; Estab 1965 to enhance art program; Gallery consists of four rooms, 300 running ft of wall space, light beige walls & rug; Dana Fine Arts Bldg designed by John Portman
Income: Financed by endowment
Collections: Clifford M Clarke Collection; Harry L Dalton Collection; Steffen Thomas Collection; Ferdinand Warren Collection
Exhibitions: 4 exhibitions per yr
Activities: Lect open to public

DUBLIN

M LAURENS COUNTY HISTORICAL SOCIETY, Dublin-Laurens Museum, 311 Academy Ave, PO Box 1461 Dublin, GA 31040-5219. Tel 478-272-9242; Elec Mail history@nlamerica.com; *Dir* Scott B Thompson Sr
Open Tues - Fri 1 - 4:30 PM; No admis fee; Estab 1967; Average Annual Attendance: 5,000; Mem: 500; dues $15-$200 graduating
Income: $25,000 (financed by mem, city & county appropriation, contributions)
Collections: Indian Artifacts; Art Originals-Lila Moore Keen
Exhibitions: Historical Photographs
Publications: Laurens County Historical Society Newsletter, quarterly

FORT BENNING

M NATIONAL INFANTRY MUSEUM & SOLDIER CENTER, Patriot Park, Fort Benning, GA 31905; 1775 Legacy Way, Columbus, GA 31903-3600. Tel 706-685-5800; 653-9234; Internet Home Page Address: www.nationalinfantrymuseum.com
Open Mon - Sat 9 AM - 5 PM, Sun 11 AM - 5 PM, cl Christmas Day & New Year's Day; No admis fee, donations accepted; 190,000 sq ft facility with galleries & Soldier Center with IMAX, restaurant & mus store; Mem: Dues 1775 society $1000, patron $300, individual/family $50, ret military/ educator $35, active military/ student $25
Collections: Over 30,000 artifacts tracing Infantry history; Era Galleries trace Infantry history from the Revolutionary War to present day
Exhibitions: The Last 100 Yards; The Fort Benning Gallery; The Family Support Gallery; Entering the International Stage; A World Power; The Cold War; The Sole Superpower; Hall of Valor; Officers Candidate School of Honor; Ranger Hall of Honor
Activities: Lects; tours; seminars

FORT VALLEY

L FORT VALLEY STATE COLLEGE, H A Hunt Memorial Library, 1005 State College Dr, Fort Valley, GA 31030-3298. Tel 478-825-6342; Fax 912-825-6916; Elec Mail fvsclib@uscn.cc.uga.edu; Internet Home Page Address: www.fvsu.edu/academics/library; *Dept Head* Frank Mahitas
Open Mon-Thurs 8AM-midnight, Fri 8AM-5PM, Sat 1PM-5PM, and Sun 3PM-10PM; No admis fee; Estab 1939

Income: Financed by state assistance
Special Subjects: Art History, Historical Material, Art Education, Afro-American Art
Collections: Afro - American Art; Graphic Arts
Exhibitions: History of College
Activities: Classes for adults; lending collection contains books

HAWKINSVILLE

M HAWKINSVILLE/PULASKI COUNTY ARTS COUNCIL, 100 Lumpkin St, Hawkinsville, GA 31036; PO Box 266, Hawkinsville, GA 31036-0266. Tel 912-783-1884; Fax 912-783-2333
Open Mon - Fri 10 AM - 4 PM
Collections: Paintings, photographs & sculpture by Georgia artists

JEKYLL ISLAND

M JEKYLL ISLAND MUSEUM, Stable Rd, Jekyll Island, GA 31520; 381 Riverview Dr, Jekyll Island, GA 31527-0874. Tel 912-635-2119; 635-2122; Fax 912-635-4420; Elec Mail jekyllisland@compuserve.com; Internet Home Page Address: www.jekyllisland.com; *Exec Dir Jekyll Island* Bill Donohue; *Dir Mus & Historic Preservation* F Warren Murphey; *Cur Educ* Gretchen Greminger; *Chief Cur* John Hunter
Open Memorial Day - Labor Day Mon - Sun 9:30 AM - 5 PM, Labor Day - Memorial Day Mon - Sun 9:30 AM - 4 PM; Admis adults $10, students 6-18 years $6; Estab 1954; Average Annual Attendance: 51,000
Income: Financed by fees & admis
Special Subjects: Portraits, Furniture, Stained Glass
Collections: 1890 Furniture; Tiffany Stained Glass Windows; portraits
Activities: Programs for adults & children; lects open to pub; tours; mus shop sells books, reproductions, slides & turn-of-the century related items

LAGRANGE

M LAGRANGE ART MUSEUM, (Chattahoochee Valley Art Museum) 112 Lafayette Pkwy, LaGrange, GA 30240. Tel 706-882-3267; Fax 706-882-2878; Elec Mail info@lagrangeartmuseum.org; Internet Home Page Address: www.lagrangeartmuseum.org; *Exec Dir* Karen Briggs; *Bus Mgr* Debbie Howard; *Exhibs Coordr* Melina Clair; *Mem Coordr* Brittony Conner; *Educ Coordr* Sallie Keith
Open Tues - Fri 9 AM - 5 PM, Sat 11 AM - 5 PM, cl Sun & Mon; Admis free to Troup county residents; Estab 1963 to provide visual art experience & educ to people of West Georgia; 100 year old former Troup County Jail refurbished for use as galleries having about 350 running ft of wall space & 7000 sq ft of floor space on two floors; Average Annual Attendance: 22,000; Mem: 300; dues $25 - $5,000; annual meeting in Jan
Income: $350,000 (financed by mem, foundation grant, civic organizations & fundraisers)
Purchases: $10,000, Purchase Awards, LaGrange National Competition
Special Subjects: Drawings, Graphics, Painting-American, Photography, Prints, Watercolors, American Indian Art, Textiles, Ceramics, Folk Art, Pottery, Woodcarvings, Woodcuts, Etchings & Engravings, Afro-American Art, Marine Painting, Carpets & Rugs, Juvenile Art, Stained Glass
Collections: Contemporary American art of all types & media
Exhibitions: Rotating exhibitions, six per yr
Activities: Classes for adults & children; lects open to pub; gallery talks; tours; competitions with awards, Purchase Awards - La Grange Nat Competition; individual paintings & original objects of art lent to bus patrons; originate traveling exhibs; mus shop sells prints, original art & reproductions

M LAGRANGE COLLEGE, Lamar Dodd Art Center Museum, 601 Broad St, LaGrange, GA 30240-2955. Tel 706-882-2911; Fax 706-884-6567; *Dir* John D Lawrence
Open Mon-Fri 8:30AM-4:30PM during school; Estab 1988
Collections: 20th Century Photography; American Indian Collection; Retrospective Collection
Exhibitions: Two shows every six weeks

MACON

M MUSEUM OF ARTS & SCIENCES, INC, 4182 Forsyth Rd, Macon, GA 31210-4869. Tel 478-477-3232; Fax 478-477-3251; Elec Mail info@masmacon.com; Internet Home Page Address: www.masmacon.org; *Exec Dir* Susan Welsh
Open Tues - Sat 10 AM - 5 PM, Sun 1 - 5 PM; Admis adults $10, seniors $8, students $7, children $5, members free; Estab 1956 as a general art & science museum with a planetarium; South Gallery 50 ft x 60 ft; North Gallery 25 ft x 35 ft; Hall Gallery 8 ft x 32 ft; Newberry Hall 1759 sq ft; Average Annual Attendance: 70,000; Mem: 2200; dues $25-$1000
Special Subjects: Ceramics, Drawings, Painting-American, Prints, Sculpture, Archaeology, Painting-European
Collections: American art with emphasis on the Southeast drawings, paintings, prints & sculpture; gems & minerals; doll coll; quilt coll; ethnographic
Publications: Museum Muse, quarterly newsletter; catalogues
Activities: Classes for adults & children; docent training; lects open to pub, 2-6 vis lectrs per yr; concerts; gallery talks; guided tours; movies; special events; summer children's camps; individual paintings & original objects of art lent to other mus; book traveling exhibs; 5 - 10 per yr; originate traveling exhibs to schools or appropriate institutions in Georgia & Southeast; mus shop sells books, magazines, original art, reproductions, prints, small educational toys, t-shirts, gem & minerals, gift items, rocks, shells, science kits

M **TUBMAN AFRICAN AMERICAN MUSEUM,** 340 Walnut St, Macon, GA 31201-0515. Tel 478-743-8544; Fax 478-743-9063; Elec Mail guestservices@tubmanmuseum.com; Internet Home Page Address: www.tubmanmuseum.com; *Dir Educ* Anita Ponder; *Exec Dir* Dr Andy Ambrose; *Dir Exhib* Jeff Bruce
Open Mon - Fri 9AM-5PM, Sat noon-4PM; Admis $6 adults, $5 sr citizens & military, $4 children & students; Estab 1981, to educate people about African American art, history & culture, while promoting racial harmony; Nine galleries, one mural entitled from Africa to America; Average Annual Attendance: 65,000; Mem: 500; dues $10-$1000; annual meeting in Dec
Income: Financed by endowment, mem, city & state appropriation, store
Special Subjects: Drawings, Etchings & Engravings, Historical Material, Ceramics, Collages, Metalwork, Flasks & Bottles, Furniture, Photography, Porcelain, Portraits, Pottery, Painting-American, Prints, Textiles, Woodcuts, Sculpture, African Art, Costumes, Crafts, Folk Art, Primitive art, Woodcarvings, Afro-American Art, Jewelry, Coins & Medals
Collections: African & African-American art & artifacts; 70 foot long mural is signature possession; Medal of Honor, Sgt Rodney Davis; From Africa to America
Exhibitions: Rotating exhibits every 2 1/2 months; Harriet Tubman exhib; African American Inventors exhib
Activities: Classes for adults & children; dramatic progs; docent training; festival last Sun in Apr; black-tie fundraiser All That Jazz in Nov; lects open to pub, 1-7 vis lectrs per yr; gallery talks; tours; Act of Courage Awards (annual), Shelia award (biannual); schols & fels offered; lending of original objects of art; originate traveling exhibs via outreach program sending teachers & exhibs to schools, after-school progs & community ctrs; mus shop sells books, magazines, original art, prints, reproductions, apparel, jewelry & African crafts

L **Keil Resource Center,** 340 Walnut St, Macon, GA 31201-0515. Tel 912-743-8544; Fax 912-743-9063; Internet Home Page Address: www.tubmanmuseum.org;
Open Mon - Fri 9 AM - 5 PM; Estab 1987; For reference only
Income: Financed by endowment, mem, city & state appropriations, store
Library Holdings: Book Volumes 2500; Video Tapes
Special Subjects: Art History, Folk Art, Film, Mixed Media, Photography, Painting-American, Prints, Sculpture, Theatre Arts, Printmaking, Art Education, Afro-American Art, Pottery, Textiles

MADISON

M **MADISON MUSEUM OF FINE ART,** 290 Hancock St, Madison, GA 30650; PO Box 814, Madison, GA 30650-0814. Tel 706-485-4530; Elec Mail mbechtell@prodigy.net; Internet Home Page Address: madisonmuseum.org; *CEO, Pres & Dir* Michele Bechtell; *Chmn* MC Bechtell; *Secy* Sean Gallagher
Open Mon - Sat 1 - 5 PM; Admis by donation; Fine art history museum; Average Annual Attendance: 6,000
Special Subjects: Drawings, Etchings & Engravings, Folk Art, Landscapes, Ceramics, Porcelain, Pottery, Painting-American, Prints, Painting-European, Painting-French, Sculpture, African Art, Religious Art, Painting-Flemish, Antiquities-Oriental, Painting-Italian, Stained Glass
Collections: paintings; sculpture garden
Publications: quarterly newsletter
Activities: Classes for adults & children; docent prog; lects open to the pub; concerts; films; art festivals; gallery talks; tours; lending of original objects of art; mus shop

M **MORGAN COUNTY FOUNDATION, INC,** Madison-Morgan Cultural Center, 434 S Main St, Madison, GA 30650-1640. Tel 706-342-4743; Fax 706-342-1154; Elec Mail cultural@mail.morgan.public.lib.ga.us; Internet Home Page Address: www.madisonmorgancultural.org; *Chmn Bd* Sarah Burbach; *Admin Dir* Rhonda Smith; *Dir Visual Arts* Angela Nichols; *Interim Dir* Tina Lilly
Open Tues - Sat 10 AM - 5 PM, Sun 2 - 5 PM; Admis fee adults $3, seniors $2.50, students $2, members free; Estab 1976 to enhance the educational & cultural life of Georgia & the Southeast; Four galleries for changing exhibits, housed in former classrooms (approx 25 ft x 35 ft) of historic 1895 school facility; heart pine floors, no daylight, tungsten track lighting only, with heat, air conditioning & electronic security; Average Annual Attendance: 30,000; Mem: 1500; dues $15-$1,000; annual meeting second Mon in July
Income: $460,000 (financed by endowment, mem, state grants, admis fees for services & sponsorship contributions)
Exhibitions: Usually two simultaneous exhibits, each 8-12 wks, of work by regional artists &/or collections of museums & private collections from the region or across the nation; Annual Juried Regional Art Exhibit
Publications: Exhibit brochures & catalogs, 4-5 per yr; Madison Georgia - An Architectural Guide
Activities: Performing arts progs; docent training; gallery tours; demonstrations; lects open to pub, 5-10 vis lectrs per yr; concerts; gallery talks; competitions with awards; book traveling exhibs 5-10 per yr; originate traveling exhibs; mus shop sells books, original art & reproductions

MARIETTA

M **MARIETTA-COBB MUSEUM OF ART,** 30 Atlanta St NE, Marietta, GA 30060-1975. Tel 770-528-1444; Fax 770-528-1440; Elec Mail info@mariettacobbartmuseum.org; Internet Home Page Address: www.mariettacobbartmuseum.org; *Exec Dir* Sally Macaulay; *Dir Fin & Opers* Jennifer Fox
Open Tues - Fri 11 AM - 5 PM, Sat 11 AM - 4 PM, Sun 1 - 4 PM; Admis adults $8, seniors & students (6-18 with ID) $5, mems & children (under 6) no charge; Estab 1990 to provide the communities of Cobb County, the city of Marietta & visitors to the area exposure to the visual arts through a diversity of visual art experiences, educational services & outreach activities based upon visiting exhibitions & the acquisition, conservation & exhibition of a permanent collection focused on American Art; Galleries 1-3 on main floor, gallery 4-5 on second level; Average Annual Attendance: 15,000; Mem: 600; dues individual $35 & up

Income: Financed by mem & donations, grants, foundations grants, county grants, city grants
Special Subjects: Painting-American, Prints, Sculpture
Collections: Collection of 400 works of art focusing on 19th & 20 century American Art
Activities: Classes for adults & children; docent training; art camp; lects open to pub; concerts; competitions; individual paintings & original objects of art lent to other mus; mus shop sells original art; junior mus

MOULTRIE

M **COLQUITT COUNTY ARTS CENTER,** 401 7th Ave SW, Moultrie, GA 31768-4633. Tel 229-985-1922; Fax 229-890-6746; Internet Home Page Address: www.colquittcountyarts.com; *Visual Arts Dir* Jane Simpson; *Dir* Jeff Ophime; *Asst Dir* Lin Sheffield; *Cur* Candace Underwood
Open Mon - Fri 10 AM - 5:30 PM Sat 10 AM - 2 PM; No admis fee
Collections: Paintings, photographs & sculpture by national & international artists
Activities: Educ programs; special events; annual events; theater productions

MOUNT BERRY

M **BERRY COLLEGE,** Moon Gallery, PO Box 580, Mount Berry, GA 30149-2289. Tel 706-238-2219; Fax 706-236-7835; Internet Home Page Address: http://www.berry.edu/academics/humanities/finearts/page.aspx?id=2823; *Pres* Stephen R Briggs; *Dept Chair* Dr. Stan Pethel; *Dir* Jere Lykins
Open Mon - Sat 10 AM - 5 PM, Sun 1 - 5 PM; Admis adults $5, children 6-12 $3; Estab 1972; Medium size gallery, carpeted floors & walls, tracking spots; Average Annual Attendance: 3,500
Exhibitions: Guest lecturer & juror for student Honors show
Activities: Classes for adults & children; lects open to pub, 6-8 vis lectrs per yr; gallery talks; competitions with awards; scholarships offered; individual paintings & original objects of art lent; lending collection contains books, cassettes, color reproductions, 20 original prints, paintings, records, photographs & 5000 slides; book traveling exhibs; originate traveling exhibs

L **Memorial Library,** 2277 Martha Berry Hwy NW, Mount Berry, GA 30149. Tel 706-236-2221; Fax 706-236-9596; Elec Mail lfoldes@berry.edu; Internet Home Page Address: berry.edu; *Prof Art* Dr T J Mew III; *Dir* Lance Foldes
Open Mon - Thurs 8 AM - 12 AM, Fri 8 AM - 8 PM, Sat 1 - 6 PM, Sun 1 PM - 12 AM during acad yr, Mon - Thurs 8 AM - 10 PM, Fri 8 AM - 5 PM during summer; Estab 1926 for educational purposes
Library Holdings: Audio Tapes; Book Volumes 350; Cassettes; Clipping Files; Exhibition Catalogs; Filmstrips; Manuscripts; Memorabilia; Motion Pictures; Original Art Works; Pamphlets; Periodical Subscriptions 25; Photographs; Prints; Records; Slides; Video Tapes
Special Subjects: Ceramics

PEACHTREE CITY

M **AMERICAN PRINT ALLIANCE,** 302 Larkspur Turn, Peachtree City, GA 30269-2210. Tel 770-486-6680; Elec Mail director@printalliance.org; Internet Home Page Address: www.printalliance.org; *Dir* Carol Pulin PhD; *Community Coordr* Valerie Dibble
Estab 1992 to provide educ & resource information for the promotion of the print arts; Internet gallery for prints, paperwork, & artists' books; Average Annual Attendance: 18,000 plus 120,000 internet vis per yr; Mem: 15 councils; mem open to non-profit printmakers' councils: dues $100, individual $32-$38, student $19
Income: Financed by mem & journal subscriptions
Exhibitions: Memorial Portfolio: September 11th; Soap Box Prints: For the Environment; Soap Box Prints 2: Prints, Politics & Democracy; On-going traveling exhibs
Publications: Contemporary Impressions, semi-annual; Guide to Print Workshops in Canada & The United States
Activities: Conferences; lect open to pub; originate traveling exhibs 1 per yr to museums, colleges, universities, community & arts centers & other public bldgs; online mus shop sells original prints

POOLER

AMERICAN SOCIETY FOR AESTHETICS
For further information, see National and Regional Organizations

RABUN GAP

M **HAMBIDGE CENTER FOR CREATIVE ARTS & SCIENCES,** 105 Hambidge Ct, Rabun Gap, GA 30568-1525; PO Box 339, Rabun Gap, GA 30568-0339. Tel 706-746-5718; Fax 706-746-9933; Elec Mail center@hambidge.org; Internet Home Page Address: www.hambidge.org; *Exec Dir* Jamie Badoud; *Office Mgr* Debra Sanders
Open Feb - Dec; No admis fee; Estab 1934; residency prog since 1988; Listed on the National Register of Historic Places, 600 acres; Average Annual Attendance: 120; Mem: 775, variable dues
Income: Nonprofit organization
Special Subjects: Crafts, Folk Art
Exhibitions: Fine Craft Exhibs, Annual Georgia Pottery Show
Activities: 2-8 week residencies for professional artists/authors; speakers' forums open to public; guided nature walks; historic mill; anagama pottery firings; lects open to pub; 4 vis lectrs per yr

SAINT SIMONS ISLAND

A **GLYNN ART ASSOCIATION,** 529 Beachview Dr, Saint Simons Island, GA 31522-4705. Tel 912-638-8770; Fax 912-634-2787; Elec Mail glynnart@bellsouth.net; Internet Home Page Address: www.glynnart.org; *Pres* Nancy Muldowney; *Dir* Marcia Marinello; *VPres* Ella Cart; *Treas* Shay Heckle; *Secy* Jeff Lemieox; *Office Mgr* Monica Carter; *Pottery Dir* Debbie Craig
Open Tues-Sat 9 AM - 5 PM; No admis fee; Estab 1953; 1,100 sq ft, largest portion devoted to local art, smaller portion for one man exhibits, traveling shows

& competitions; Average Annual Attendance: 8,000; Mem: 600; dues $250-$400; annual meeting in Apr
Income: $300,000 (financed by mem & commission on sales of art)
Special Subjects: Drawings, Porcelain, Prints, Silver, Pottery, Crafts, Glass, Woodcarvings
Exhibitions: Miniature competition from all over & more than 100 local artists
Publications: Glynn Art News, monthly newsletter
Activities: Classes for adults & children; docent training; lect open to public, 3-4 vis lectrs per year; gallery talks; competitions with prizes; awards, Coastal Nat, Fall Festival; scholarships & fels offered; sales shop sells books, prints & original art

SAVANNAH

M **SHIPS OF THE SEA MARITIME MUSEUM,** 41 Martin Luther King, Jr Blvd Savannah, GA 31401. Tel 912-232-1511; Fax 912-234-7363; Elec Mail contact@shipsofthesea.org; Internet Home Page Address: www.telfair.org; *Exec Dir* Tony Pizzo; *Asst Dir* Karl DeVries; *Gift Shop Mgr* Eileen Lewis
Open Tues - Sun 10 AM - 5 PM; Admis adults $7, seniors & students $5; Estab 1966 to promote Savannah's maritime history & preserve William Scarbrough house; Average Annual Attendance: 50,000
Income: Financed privately
Special Subjects: Painting-American, Marine Painting, Historical Material, Scrimshaw
Collections: Figureheads, maritime antiques, paintings, porcelains, scrimshaw, ship models; Maritime antiques; ship models
Exhibitions: Savannah & Civil War at Sea; Steamship Company (Savannah Line)
Publications: Exhibit catalogues, Flotsam & Jetsam; William Scarbrough's House
Activities: Educ Prog; classes for children; lects open to pub; concerts; tours; mus shop sells books & magazines, gift shop

M **TELFAIR MUSEUMS' JEPSON CENTER FOR THE ARTS LIBRARY,** (Telfair Museum of Art) 121 Barnard St, Savannah, GA 31401-3612; PO Box 10081, Savannah, GA 31412-0281. Tel 912-790-8800; Fax 912-232-6954; Elec Mail hadaways@telfair.org; Internet Home Page Address: www.telfair.org; *Admin* Sandra S Hadaway; *Chief Cur Educ* Harry H DeLorme; *Cur Fine Arts & Exhibs* Holly K McCullough; *Registrar* Jessica Mumford; *Financial Officer* Shelly Cannady; *Cur (Owens-Thomas House)* Tania J Sammons; *Develop Dir* Kristin Boylston; *Dir Diversity & Access* Vaughnette Goode-Walker; *Cur Art* Courtney McNeil
Open Sun & Mon noon - 5 PM; Tues, Wed & Fri 10 AM - 5 PM; Thurs 10 AM - 8 PM; Admis adults $20, seniors & AAA $18, college students $5, children free; Estab 1875 to collect & to preserve, exhibit & interpret; Circ Non-lending 5,000 publications, 18 periodicals; 4 galleries 2400 sq ft, Rotunda gallery 3400 sq ft, Sculpture gallery 2700 sq ft. Maintains reference library, Jepson Center for the Arts, 64,000 sq ft of display & interactive galleries; Telfair Museums' Telfair Academy; Owens-Thomas House; Average Annual Attendance: 188,000; Mem: 3100; dues $45-$10,000; annual meeting in Apr
Income: Financed by endowment, mem, city & state appropriation, banks & corporate foundations & federal government
Library Holdings: Auction Catalogs; Book Volumes; Exhibition Catalogs
Special Subjects: Decorative Arts, Portraits, Painting-French, Period Rooms, Painting-German
Collections: American decorative arts; American & European artists; Late 18th century to present; 19th & 20th century American & European paintings; works on paper
Exhibitions: Special & traveling exhibitions
Publications: The Octagon Room; We Ain't What We Used to Be; Christopher P H Murphy (1869-1939): A Retrospective; Nostrums for Fashionable Entertainments: Dining in Georgia 1800-1850; Classical Savannah: Fine and Decorative Arts 1800-1840; Looking Back: Art in Savannah 1900-1960; Ladies, Landscapes and Loyal Retainers: Japanese Art from a Private Collection; Frederick Carl Frieseke: The Evolution of an American Impressionist; Southern Melodies: A Larry Connatser Retrospective; GA Triennal; Freedom's March; Palliser; Dutch Utopia: American Artists in Holland 1880-1914
Activities: Classes for adults; classes for children; docent training; progs & classes for children; lects open to pub, 6 vis lectrs per year; concerts; gallery talks; tours; Effingham County; Chatham County; parks & playgrounds; individual paintings & original objects of art lent to other mus internationally; lending collection contains over 4000 original art works, over 100 sculptures, 2,186 fine arts and 1,968 decorative; book traveling exhibs 6-10 per yr; originate traveling exhibs to other art mus throughout US; mus shop sells books, reproductions, prints, posters, postcards; original art
   —Telfair Academy of Arts & Sciences Library, 121 Barnard St, Savannah, GA 31401-3612; PO Box 10081, Savannah, GA 31412-0281. Tel 912-790-8800; Fax 912-232-6954; Elec Mail hadaways@telfair.org; Internet Home Page Address: www.telfair.org; *Dir & CEO* Steven High PhD; *CFO* Shelly Cannady; *Dir Mktg & Pub Rels* Kristen Boylston; *Cur Educ* Harry DeLorme; *Cur Fine Arts & Exhibits* Hollis Koons McCullough; *Registrar* Jessica Mumford; *Mus Shop Mgr* Lisa Ocampo; *Admin* Sandra S Hadaway; *Designer & Preparator* Milutin Pavlovic; *VPres & Bd of Trustees* John Kennedy III; *Asst Cur* Elizabeth Moore; *Dir Develop* Barbara Evans; *Asst Cur* Courtney McGowan
Jepson Ctr & Telfair Acad Open Sun noon-5PM, Mon 10AM-5PM, cl Tues, Wed-Sat 10AM-5PM; Owens Thomas House Open Sun 1PM-5PM, Mon noon-5PM, Tues-Sat 10AM-5PM; Admis adults $10, seniors $8, students $5, children 5-12 $4, children under 5 free, members free, group rates; adult tours $7, college group $6, K-12 student groups $4, family with two adults and two kids $25; Estab 1875 to collect, preserve, exhibit, & interpret the objects in its collection of fine & decorative arts & its National Historic Landmark buildings; Circ 4,000; For reference only, for scholars & the public; Average Annual Attendance: 144,500; Mem: 1420; dues grand benefactor $10,000; benefactor $5,000; sponsor $2,500; grand patron $1,500; patron $1,250; sustainer $1,000; friend $600; supporting $300; donor $100; family $60; individual $35; special $25
Income: 2,000,000 (financed by membership, grants, fundraising events & endowments)
Purchases: 40,000

Library Holdings: Book Volumes 3,500; Exhibition Catalogs; Periodical Subscriptions 130
Exhibitions: 4-6 traveling exhibitions per year
Publications: Quarterly newsletter; exhibition brochures & catalogs
Activities: Originate traveling exhibs to local institutions, also to NY & willing to lend nationwide

SUWANEE

A **HANDWEAVERS GUILD OF AMERICA,** 1255 Buford Highway, Ste 211, Suwanee, GA 30024. Tel 678-730-0100; Fax 678-730-0836; Elec Mail hga@weavespindye.org; Internet Home Page Address: www.weavespindye.org; *Exec Dir & Ed* Sandra Bowles; *Asst Ed* Patricia Fowler
Open Mon - Thurs 8 AM - 5 PM; No admis fee; Estab 1969 to promote fiber arts; Mem: 10,000; dues $40; annual meeting in summer; interest in fiber arts req
Income: Financed by mem dues, contributions, advertising & conferences
Library Holdings: Book Volumes; Exhibition Catalogs; Original Documents
Special Subjects: Embroidery, Textiles, Decorative Arts, Crafts, Laces, Leather, Tapestries, Carpets & Rugs
Publications: Shuttle, Spindle & Dyepot, quarterly publication for members
Activities: Fiber progs for adults, classes for children; lects open to mems & pub for fee, 1 vis lectr per yr; gallery talks; tours; Exhib Awards & HGA Award, awards to selected fiber art shows; schols & fels offered; originate traveling exhibs to fiber guilds; e-shop on website sells books

VALDOSTA

M **VALDOSTA STATE UNIVERSITY,** Art Gallery, 1500 N Patterson St, Valdosta, GA 31698-0001. Tel 229-333-5835; Fax 229-259-5121; Elec Mail kgmurray@valdosta.edu; Internet Home Page Address: www.valdosta.edu/art; *Dir Gallery* Karin Murray; *Acting Head Art Dept* A Blake Pearce; *Cur* Dick Bjornseth
Open Mon - Thurs 10 AM - 4 PM, Fri 10 AM - 3 PM; No admis fee; Estab 1970 for educational purposes serving students, faculty, community & region; Gallery is an open rectangular room with approx 122 running ft of exhibition space; Average Annual Attendance: 20,000
Income: Financed by state appropriations
Special Subjects: African Art
Collections: African art; Lamar Dodd
Exhibitions: 8-9 exhibitions per year; national juried Valdosta works on paper exhibition; faculty show
Activities: Classes for adults; dramatic progs; docent training; lects open to pub, 3-5 vis lectrs per yr; Valdosta State Orchestra; concerts; gallery talks; tours; competitions; vis artists; demonstrations; scholarships offered; originate traveling exhibs

WAYCROSS

M **OKEFENOKEE HERITAGE CENTER, INC,** 1460 N Augusta Ave, Waycross, GA 31501-4954. Tel 912-285-4260; Fax 912-283-2858; Elec Mail sbean@wayxcable.com; Internet Home Page Address: www.okefenokeeheritagecenter.org; *Cur & Dir* Steve Bean; *Admin Asst* Nashie Wesley; *Vis Coordr* Betty Callahan
Open Tues - Fri 10 AM - 4:30 PM, Sat 10 AM - 2 PM; Admis $7, children 6-18 $5, children under 5 no charge; Estab 1975 to house displays on arts & history; Four gallery areas; Average Annual Attendance: 10,000; Mem: 350; dues bus $10,000, guardian $5,000, corporate patron $3,000, sponsor & corporate sponsor $1,000, donor & bus donor $500, friend & bus friend $300, heritage club $100, family $50, individual $30
Income: $85,000 (financed by endowment, mem, grants, contributions, admis, special activities, gift shop)
Special Subjects: Afro-American Art, American Indian Art, Historical Material, Painting-American, Prints, African Art, Crafts, Period Rooms
Collections: 1912 Baldwin Steam Locomotive train & caboose; 1940's Homestead; 1870's house exhibit; 1890's printshop; prints, crafts, paintings & photographs
Exhibitions: Annual art show (Sept); Sacred Harp (Permanent); Individual Artists Children Art Show
Publications: Quarterly exhibit catalogues; newsletter
Activities: Classes for adults & children; demonstrations; workshops; lects open to pub; concerts; gallery talks; tours; competitions; purchase awards; book traveling exhibs; mus shop sells books, original art, reproductions, prints gifts & souvenirs

HAWAII

HAWAII VOLCANOES NATIONAL PARK

M **VOLCANO ART CENTER GALLERY,** Crater Rim Drive, Next to Kilauea Visitor Center Hawaii Volcanoes National Park, HI: P.O. Box 129, Volcano, HI 96785-0129. Tel 866-967-7565 (Gallery); Tel 808-967-7565 (Gallery); 967-8222 (Admin Dept); Fax 808-967-7511 (Gallery); 967-8512 (Admin Dept); Elec Mail gallery@volcanoartcenter.org; Internet Home Page Address: www.volcanoartcenter.org; *CEO* Tanya Aynessazian; *Cur & Gallery Mgr* Shelby B Smith; *Chair of Brd* Linda Pratt
Gallery open daily 9 AM - 5 PM; admin open Mon - Fri 8:30 AM - 5 PM; No admis fee; park entrance fees apply; Estab 1974 as a non-profit organization; Mem: 1800, dues range from $42, ann meeting every Oct
Publications: Art Beat
Activities: Classes for adults & children; workshops; progs; docent training; lects open to pub; 1-4 vis lectrs per yr; performances; concerts; gallery talks; tours; sponsoring competitions; mus shop sells books, magazines, original art, reproductions, prints

HILO

M **HILO ART MUSEUM,** 1266 Kamehameha Ave, Hilo, HI 96720; PO Box 636, Kurtistown, HI 96760-0636. Tel 808-982-6006; Elec Mail info@hiloartmuseum.org
Open Mon - Sat 9 AM - 6 PM, Sun 10 AM - 6 PM; No admis fee
Collections: Paintings; drawings; furnishings; sculpture; mixed media

M **WAILOA ARTS & CULTURAL CENTER,** 200 Piopio St, Wailoa State Park Hilo, HI 96720-0416; PO Box 936, Hilo, HI 96720-0936. Tel 808-933-0416; Fax 808-933-0417; Elec Mail wailoa@yahoo.com; *CEO & Dir* Codie King
Open Mon - Tues & Thurs - Fri 8:30 AM - 4:30 PM, Wed Noon - 4:30 PM, cl holidays; No admis fee; Average Annual Attendance: 30,000
Library Holdings: Book Volumes
Collections: works by local artists; Big Island history & culture
Activities: Demonstrations; seminars; workshops; classes; outreach progs; school tours; concerts; live performances

HONOLULU

A **ASSOCIATION OF HAWAII ARTISTS,** PO Box 10202, Honolulu, HI 96816-0202. Tel 808-239-6066; Fax 808-923-1062; Elec Mail ahahawaii@earthlink.net; Internet Home Page Address: associationhawaiiartists.com; *Pres* Anthony Randall; *VPres* Roy O'Kano; *Secy* Philip Riley; *Treas* Charlyn Baillie
Estab 1926 to promote congeniality & stimulate growth by presenting programs; to contribute to the cultural life of the State of Hawaii; Average Annual Attendance: 1,000; Mem: 250; dues $15-$30; monthly meeting every second Tues
Income: Financed by mem
Publications: Paint Rag, monthly
Activities: Lect open to public, 2-3 vis lectrs per year; demonstrations; competitions with cash awards, plaques & rosettes

M **BERNICE PAUAHI BISHOP MUSEUM,** 1525 Bernice St, Honolulu, HI 96817-2704. Tel 808-847-3511; Fax 808-848-4147; Internet Home Page Address: www.bishopmuseum.org; *Pres & CEO* Tim Johns
Open Mon - Sun 9 AM - 5 PM, cl Tues, Christmas Day; Admis adult $17.95, seniors 65 & over & children 4-12 $14.95, children 3 & under no charge; Estab 1889 to preserve & study the culture & natural history of Hawaii; Mem: Dues $35 - $1,000
Exhibitions: Awesome Treasures of Hawaii & the Pacific: A Hands-On Adventure; Treasures; Ocean Planet

L **Library,** 1525 Bernice St, Honolulu, HI 96817-0916. Tel 808-847-3511; Fax 808-847-8241; Elec Mail library@bishopmuseum.org; Internet Home Page Address: www.bishopmuseum.org; *Head Librn* Duane Wenzel; *Archivist* DeSoto Brown; *Reference Librn* Patty Belcher; *Librn* Janet Short; *Archivist* Ron Schaeffer; *Reference Archivist* Judy Kearney
Open Wed - Mon 9 AM - 5 PM, cl Tues & Christmas Day; Admis adults $17.95, youth & seniors (65 & over) $14.95, children (3 & under) no charge; Estab 1889 to stimulate awareness & appreciation of the natural & cultural world of Hawaii & the Pacific; Average Annual Attendance: 200,000; Mem: 10,000; dues $35- $65
Library Holdings: Book Volumes 40,000
Special Subjects: Folk Art, Historical Material, History of Art & Archaeology, Archaeology, Ethnology, Anthropology
Collections: Books; Insect Specimens; Journals; Manuscripts; Pacific & Hawaiian Cultural Objects; Photographics; Plant Specimens; Zoological Specimens; Maps; Fine Art; Moving Images
Activities: Classes for adults & children; docent training; lects open to pub; concerts; gallery talks; tours; competitions with awards; originate traveling exhibs; mus shop sells books; original art & reproductions

L **Archives,** 1525 Bernice St, Honolulu, HI 96817-0916. Tel 808-848-4182; Fax 808-841-8968; *Archivist* DeSoto Brown; *Archivist* Linda Lawrence; *Archivist* Ron Schaeffer
Open Tues - Fri Noon - 3 PM, Sat 9 AM - Noon; Estab 1991
Library Holdings: Manuscripts 3,500; Photographs 1,000,000
Collections: Cylinders, discs & reel to reel tapes; Maps; Moving Images; Oils on Canvas; Works of Art on Paper

M **THE CONTEMPORARY MUSEUM,** 2411 Makiki Heights Dr, Honolulu, HI 96822-2547. Tel 808-526-1322 (General); 237-5230 (Gardens); Fax 808-536-5973; Elec Mail info@tcmhi.org; Internet Home Page Address: www.tcmhi.org; *Exec Dir* Allison Wong; *Deputy Dir Fin & Opers* John Talkington; *Deputy Dir Exhibs & Colls* James F Jensen; *Cur Exhibs* Inger Tully; *Cur Educ* Aaron Padilla
Open Tues - Sat 10 AM - 4 PM, Sun Noon - 4 PM, cl Mon & major holidays; Admis adults $10, children 4-17 $5, children 3 & under & mems free, 1st Wed of month free; Estab 1961 as Contemporary Arts Center to provide a showcase for local, national & international contemporary artists; From 1940 to the present, reorganized & opened in 1988 in present facility situated in 3 1/2 acres of gardens; five galleries comprise 5000 sq ft of exhibition space. Also includes exhibition annex & First Hawaiian Center in downtown Honolulu; maintains lending & reference library; Average Annual Attendance: 45,000; Mem: 2,500; dues partner $500, assoc $250, sponsor $125, dual mems $75, individual $45, out-of-state student $25, res student $20
Income: $1,500,000 (financed by endowment, mem, grants, contributions & earned income)
Collections: Permanent collection of over 1400 works from 1940 to present in all media by local, national & international artists; stage set by David Hockney on permanent view; gardens
Exhibitions: Rotating exhibs presenting works of leading & emerging contemporary artists in 5 galleries: the William Twigg-Smith Gallery, the Samuel N & Mary Castle Gallery, the John Young Gallery, the Laila Twigg-Smith Gallery & the John Hodson Connor Family Gallery; Contemporary Cafe presents changing exhibs
Publications: The C Magazine, 3 times per yr; exhib catalogs
Activities: Classes for adults & children; workshops; docent training; dramatic progs; lects open to pub, 4 vis lectrs per yr; concerts; gallery talks; tours;

artmobile lent to mus; originates traveling exhibs to circulate to other small mus; mus shop sells books, original art, reproductions, prints & unique & fun jewelry by national & local artists

M **First Hawaiian Center,** 999 Bishop St, Honolulu, HI 96813; 2411 Makiki Heights Dr, Honolulu, HI 96822.
Open Mon - Thurs 8:30 AM - 4 PM, Fri 8:30 AM - 6 PM, cl Sat, Sun & banking holidays; No admis fee; Located in main banking hall & on 2nd fl of First Hawaiian Ctr
Exhibitions: Rotating exhibs of art by resident artists, former Hawaii residents, or those who have created a body of work in the Islands; Permanent exhib of glass wall containing 185 prisms
Activities: Docent-guided tours at noon on 3rd Thurs of month; validated parking for mems

L **J Russell & Charlotte McLean Cades Library,** 2411 Makiki Heights Dr, Honolulu, HI 96822. Tel 808-237-5217; Internet Home Page Address: www.tcmhi.org/mi_cades.htm; *Cur Educ* Quala Lynn Young
Open by appt only
Library Holdings: Auction Catalogs; Book Volumes; Clipping Files; Exhibition Catalogs; Other Holdings Surveys; Monographs; Catalogs; Periodical Subscriptions
Collections: Artists Biographical Files

M **THE CONTEMPORARY MUSEUM AT FIRST HAWAIIAN CENTER,** 999 Bishop St, Honolulu, HI 96813; 2411 Makiki Heights Dr, Honolulu, HI 96822-2547. Tel 808-526-1322; Fax 808-536-5973; Elec Mail info@tcmhi.org; Internet Home Page Address: www.tcmhi.org; *Cur* Inger Tully; *Dir* Georgianna Lagoria
Open Mon - Thurs 8:30 AM - 4 PM, Fri 8:30 AM - 6 PM, cl weekends & major holidays; No admis fee; Estab 1996 to provide a place for artists of Hawaii to display their work; Downtown satellite location: ground floor lobby & a second floor gallery that extends along Merchant St behind a glass curtain wall made of over 4000 panels of stone, glass & aluminum; Average Annual Attendance: 26,000; Mem: 2243
Income: underwritten by First Hawaiian Bank
Collections: Contemporary Art (all media) from 1940's to the present
Activities: Educ dept tours; lect

M **HONOLULU MUSEUM OF ART,** 900 S Beretania St, Honolulu, HI 96814-1495. Tel 808-532-8700; Fax 808-532-8787; Internet Home Page Address: www.honolulumuseum.org; Cable HONART; *Dir* Stephan Jost; *Cur Euro & American Art* Theresa Papanikolas; *Mgr Textile Coll* Sara Oka; *Cur Asian Art* Shawn Eichman; *Cur Educ* Betsy Robb; *Cur Art Center* Vince Hazen; *Develop Dir* Karen Sumner; *Librn* Sachiyo Kawaiaea; *Cur Films & Dir Doris Duke Theatre* Gina Caruso; *Chmn* Lynne Johnson; *Mus Shop Mgr* Kathee Hoover; *Dir Vis Svcs* Vicki Reisner; *Dir Communs* Lesa Griffith; *Dir Human Resources* Linda Ferrara
Open Tues - Sat 10 AM - 4:30 PM, Sun 1 - 5 PM, cl Mon & major holidays; Admis adults $10, children 4-17 $5, children 3 & under & mems free; Estab 1927 as the only art museum of a broad general nature in the Pacific; to provide Hawaii's people of many races with works of art representing their composite cultural heritage from both East and West; Circ 45,000; Main building is a Registered National Historic Place; Average Annual Attendance: 255,000; Mem: 7,000; dues $55 & up
Income: $8,261,641
Library Holdings: Auction Catalogs 12,000; Book Volumes 45,000; Clipping Files 56; Exhibition Catalogs 2,000; Periodical Subscriptions 40
Special Subjects: Decorative Arts, Folk Art, Prints, Painting-American, Photography, Prints, American Indian Art, American Western Art, Bronzes, African Art, Pre-Columbian Art, Textiles, Costumes, Religious Art, Ceramics, Etchings & Engravings, Landscapes, Painting-European, Painting-Japanese, Furniture, Jade, Porcelain, Oriental Art, Asian Art, Painting-French, Painting-Flemish, Renaissance Art, Medieval Art, Painting-Italian, Islamic Art
Collections: Kress Collection of Italian Renaissance Painting
Exhibitions: Approx 50 temporary exhibitions annually
Publications: Art Books and Pamphlets; Catalog of the Collection; Catalogs of Spec Exhibs
Activities: Classes for adults & children; docent training; lectr; concerts; sponsoring of competitions; films & videos illustrating contemporary & historic range of the medium; guided tours; gallery talks; arts festivals; workshops; music programs; research in Asian & Western Art; lending collection contains paintings, prints, textiles, reproductions, photographs, slides and ethnographic objects (about 21,000); sales shop sells books, original art, reproductions, prints, jewelry, stationary/note cards & gifts

L **Robert Allerton Art Library,** 900 S Beretania St, Honolulu, HI 96814-1495. Tel 808-532-8754; Fax 808-681-7331; Elec Mail library@honolulumuseum.org; Internet Home Page Address: www.honolulumuseum.org; *Librn* Sachiyo Kawaiaea
Open Wed - Thurs 10 AM - 3:30 PM, Fri - 10 AM - 3 PM, Sat 10 AM - 2 PM; No admis fee; Estab 1927; Circ Non-circulating research library; Reference library for staff & members
Library Holdings: Auction Catalogs; Book Volumes 50,000; Clipping Files; Exhibition Catalogs; Pamphlets; Periodical Subscriptions 42
Special Subjects: Art History, Oriental Art

M **JUDICIARY HISTORY CENTER,** 417 S King St, Honolulu, HI 96813-2943. Tel 808-539-4999; Fax 808-539-4996; Elec Mail info@jhchawaii.net; Internet Home Page Address: www.jhchawaii.net; *Exec Dir* Matt Mattice; *Educ Specialist* Keahe Davis; *Programs Specialist* Toni Han Palermo; *Asst Educ Specialist* David Cypriano
Open Mon - Fri 8 AM - 4 PM; No admis fee; Estab to interpret the history of Hawaii's courts & legal system; Average Annual Attendance: 52,500; Mem: 150; dues $15 - $1,000
Income: Financed by appropriation
Special Subjects: Architecture, Furniture, Manuscripts, Maps
Collections: Art (paintings, prints); Artifacts; Documents (judicial & legal); furniture
Exhibitions: The Monarchy Courts; Martial Law in Hawaii 1941 - 1944; Restored Court Room 1913; Who's Who in the Courtroom

Activities: Educ prog; classes for children; dramatic prog; mus shop sells books, postcards & DVDs

M **UNIVERSITY OF HAWAII AT MANOA,** Art Gallery, 2535 McCarthy Mall, Honolulu, HI 96822-2233. Tel 808-956-6888; Fax 808-956-9659; Elec Mail gallery@hawaii.edu; Internet Home Page Address: www.hawaii.edu/artgallery; *Assoc Dir* Sharon Tasaka; *Design Asst* Wayne Kawamoto; *Dir* Lisa Yoshihara
Open Mon - Fri 10:30 AM - 5PM; Sun Noon - 5PM; cl Sat; No admis fee; Estab 1976 to present a program of regional, national & international exhibitions; Gallery is a teaching tool for all areas of specialization. It is located in the center of the art building & is designed as a versatile space with a flexible installation system that allows all types of art to be displayed; Average Annual Attendance: 50,000
Income: Financed by state govt, grants, pvt contributions
Collections: Japanese, European, American & Polish posters
Publications: Exhibition catalogs
Activities: Classes for adults; lects open to public; gallery talks; competitions; scholarships & fels offered; book traveling exhibs; 1 biennially; originate traveling exhibs to public and university museums; sales shop sells exhibit catalogs

KANEOHE

M **HAWAII PACIFIC UNIVERSITY,** Gallery, 45-045 Kamehameha Hwy, Kaneohe, HI; 1164 Bishop St, Honolulu, HI 96813-2810. Tel 808-544-0287; Fax 808-544-1136; Elec Mail lledward@hpu.edu; Internet Home Page Address: www.hpu.edu; *Admin* Lynne Ledward; *Cur* Sanit Khewhok
Open Mon - Sat 8 AM - 5 PM; No admis fee; Estab 1983 as a cultural & acad resource for students & community; 12,000 sq ft; Average Annual Attendance: 8,500
Income: Financed by college funds & private donations
Exhibitions: 6 exhibitions per year featuring contemporary artists working in Hawaii
Activities: Lect open to public; gallery talks; competitions

LAHAINA

A **LAHAINA ARTS SOCIETY,** Art Organization, 648 Wharf St Ste 103, Lahaina, HI 96761-1272. Tel 808-661-0111, 661-3228; Fax 808-661-9149; Elec Mail info@lahaina-arts.com; Internet Home Page Address: www.lahaina-arts.com; *Pres* Don McCann; *Exec Dir* Amy Fry; *Exec Dir Lahaina Arts Assoc* Priscilla Gonsalves
Open daily 9 AM - 5 PM; No admis fee; Estab 1967 as a nonprofit organization interested in perpetuating culture, art & beauty by providing stimulating art instruction, lectures & art exhibits, exhibiting exclusively local Maui artists; Gallery located in old Lahaina Courthouse; Main Gallery is on ground floor; Old Jail Gallery is in the basement; Average Annual Attendance: 50,000; Mem: 80; dues $100; annual meeting June
Income: financed by mem
Exhibitions: Exhibits once a month
Publications: Newsletter, monthly; exhibition catalogs
Activities: Classes for children; lect for members only; gallery talks; competitions with scholarships; workshops; scholarships offered; gallery sells local original art, prints, cards, ceramics, handcrafted jewelry & sculptures

M **WHALERS VILLAGE MUSEUM,** 2435 Ka'anapali Pkwy, Lahaina, HI 96761. Tel 808-661-4567; Tel 808-661-5992 (Info); Internet Home Page Address: www.whalersvillage.com
Open daily 9:00AM - 10 PM; History-oriented mus brings to life Lahaina's whaling era (1825 - 1860) as told through the eyes of an ordinary sailor & whaleman and illustrates the challenges of daily life on the sea. Nonprofit org
Special Subjects: Anthropology, Archaeology, Decorative Arts, Folk Art, Historical Material, Photography, Sculpture, Scrimshaw
Collections: 19th-century scrimshaw; pictures carved on whale teeth & bone; antique ornaments & utensils made from whale ivory & bone; one of the world's largest scale models of a whaling ship on display; photo murals & interpretive graphics
Activities: Self-guided tours; informational videos shown throughout the day; scrimshaw, jewelry, books & mus related items for sale

LAIE

A **POLYNESIAN CULTURAL CENTER,** 55-370 Kamehameha Hwy, Laie, HI 96762-1113. Tel 808-293-3005; Fax 808-293-3022; Elec Mail culturalexpert@polynesia .com; Internet Home Page Address: www.polynesia.com; *Pres & CEO* Alfred Grace
Open Mon - Sat 12 noon - 9 PM, cl Sun, Thanksgiving, New Year's & Christmas; Admis adults $49.95, children (5-11) $39.95; Estab 1963 by the Church of Jesus Christ of Latter Day Saints as an authentic Polynesian village; Center is a 42 acre living museum with two amphitheaters, it represents villages of Hawaii, Samoa, Tonga, Fiji, Tahiti, New Zealand & the Marquesas; Average Annual Attendance: 700,000
Income: Financed by admis
Collections: Decorative arts, ethnic material, graphics, paintings & sculpture
Publications: Brochures
Activities: Classes for adults & children; workshop training in Polynesian arts & crafts; 2 hr Polynesian Show of Cultures nightly; lect open to public; scholarships offered

LIHUE

M **KAUAI MUSEUM ASSOCIATION, LTD.,** 4428 Rice St, Lihue, HI 96766-1338. Tel 808-245-6931; Fax 808-245-6864; Elec Mail museum@kauaimuseum.org; Internet Home Page Address: www.kauaimuseum.org; *Exec Dir* Jane Gray; *Mem Mgr/Admin* Lyah Kama-Drake; *Cur* Chris Faye; *Shop Mgr* Jan Delavega
Open Mon - Sat 10 AM - 5 PM, cl Sun; Admis adults $10, seniors $8, students $5, children 12 - 6 $2, children 6 & under free; Estab 1960 to provide the history

through the permanent exhibit, the Story of Kauai & through art exhibits; ethnic cultural exhibits in the Wilcox Building to give the community an opportunity to learn more of ethnic backgrounds; Average Annual Attendance: 30,000; Mem: 1,700; dues $25-$1,000; annual meeting in Feb
Income: Financed by mem dues, government grants
Library Holdings: DVDs; Filmstrips; Framed Reproductions; Manuscripts; Maps; Original Art Works; Original Documents; Photographs; Prints; Records; Reproductions; Sculpture; Video Tapes
Collections: Hawaiian coll with emphasis on items dealing with the island of Kauai; school art exhibits, ethnic & heritage displays; 50 year old quilts; Niihau shells; Leis; Necklaces, bracelets, earrings
Exhibitions: Downstairs; Hawaiian History; Quilts; Upstairs
Publications: Hawaiian Quilting on Kauai; Early Kauai Hospitality; Amelia; Moki Goes Fishing; Kauai: The Separate Kingdom; Kauai Museum Quilt Collection
Activities: Classes for adults & children; dramatic progs; docent training; lects open to pub, lects open to mems; 100 vis lectrs per yr; concerts; tours; gallery talks; sponsor competitions; awards: living treasures, children's art contest & May Day contest; educ outreach to schools; lending of original objects of art by request; book traveling exhibs 3 yr; originates traveling exhibs 5 yrs in advance; mus shop sells books, magazines, original art, reproductions, prints, quilts, novelties, Niihau shells, Kauai made products

MAKAWAO MAUI

M **HUI NO'EAU VISUAL ARTS CENTER,** Gallery and Gift Shop, 2841 Baldwin Ave, Makawao Maui, HI 96768-9642. Tel 808-572-6560; Fax 808-572-2750; Elec Mail info@huinoeau.com; Internet Home Page Address: www.huinoeau.com; *Exec Dir* Caroline Killhour
Open Mon - Sat 10 AM - 4 PM; No admis fee; Estab 1934 to encourage & promote the develop of artistic expression & creativity in the individual & to stimulate a broader appreciation & understanding of the visual arts as a vital language in our culture; 1,000 sq ft exhibit space in historic living & dining areas; Average Annual Attendance: 30,000; Mem: 1,050; dues $40
Income: Financed by endowment, mem, state appropriation & earned income
Special Subjects: Drawings, Painting-American, Photography, Prints, Watercolors, Textiles, Ceramics, Pottery, Etchings & Engravings, Landscapes, Jewelry, Porcelain, Marine Painting, Metalwork, Historical Material
Collections: Fiber Art; Woodworking
Publications: Hui News, bi-monthly; Hui brochure
Activities: Classes for adults & children; visitor prog; Hawaiian culture & art; lects open to pub, 12 vis lectrs per yr; competitions with awards; gallery talks; tours; schols offered; book traveling exhibs 1-2 per yr; originate traveling exhibs 1-2 per yr; retail store sells books, original art, reproductions & prints

PAIA

M **MAUI CRAFTS GUILD,** 43 Hana Way, Paia, HI 96779; PO Box 790609, Paia, HI 96779-0609. Tel 808-579-9697; Fax 808-579-8694; Elec Mail info@mauicraftsguild.com; Internet Home Page Address: www.mauicraftsguild.com
Open daily 10 AM - 6 PM
Collections: Works by local artists including ceramics, sculpture, prints, textiles, photographs & baskets

WAILUKU

M **MAUI HISTORICAL SOCIETY,** Bailey House, 2375A Main St, Wailuku, HI 96793-1661. Tel 808-244-3326; 242-5080 (Research); Fax 808-244-3920; Elec Mail baileyhousemuseum@clearwire.net; Internet Home Page Address: www.mauimuseum.org; *Exec Dir* Travis Schnepp; *Admin* Mark Kuaola Raymond; *Archives* Marianne Klaus
Open Mon - Sat 10 AM - 4 PM, cl Sun; Admis Donation requested adults $7, seniors $5, children (7-12) $2, 6 & under free; Estab 1957 to preserve the history of Hawaii, particularly Maui County; housed in former residence of Edward Bailey (1814-1903); Average Annual Attendance: 21,000; Mem: 800; dues $25-$100; annual meeting in Aug
Income: $200,000 (financed by mem, gift shop purchases & admis fees)
Special Subjects: Archaeology, Landscapes, Furniture
Collections: Landscape Paintings (1860-1900); Paintings of Hawaiian Scenes by Edward Bailey; Prehistoric Hawaiian Artifacts
Exhibitions: Exhibits depicting missionary life, throughout the year
Publications: Imi Ike, journal
Activities: Classes for adults & children; docent training; lects open to pub, 4-6 vis lectrs per yr; tours; originate traveling exhibs to schools & other mus; mus shop sells books, reproductions, prints, slides & arts & crafts

WAIPAHU

M **HAWAII OKINAWA CENTER,** 94-587 Ukee St, Waipahu, HI 96797-4214. Tel 808-676-5400; Fax 808-676-7811
Open Mon - Fri 8:30 AM - 5 PM, Sat 9 AM - 3 PM; cl during major holidays
Collections: Local history & culture; Okinawa crafts including pottery, doll making, & fabrics; early plantation & immigration

IDAHO

BOISE

M **BOISE ART MUSEUM,** 670 Julia Davis Dr, Boise, ID 83702. Tel 208-345-8330; Fax 208-345-2247; Elec Mail info@boiseartmuseum.org; Internet Home Page Address: www.boiseartmuseum.org; *Cur Educ* Terra Feast; *Cur Art* Sandy Harthorn; *Exec Dir* Melanie Fales; *Pres Bd Trustees* Nicole Snyder; *Registrar* Kathy Bettis; *Mus Store Mgr* Shauna Van Kleek; *Preparator* Todd Newman; *Fin Mgr* Mary Schaefer; *Coordr Mem* Kate Masterson; *Asst Preparator* Dave Darraugh; *Curatorial Asst* Catherine Rakow; *Develop Specialist* Erin Kennedy; *Special Events Coordr* Mary Corrock; *Mus Resources Coordr* Hana Van Huffel
Open Tues - Sat 10 AM - 5 PM, (1st Thurs 10 AM - 9 PM), Sun Noon - 5 PM, cl

Mon & holidays; Admis general $5, seniors & college students $3, grades K - 12 $1, children under 6 free, discounts to mus professionals, first Thurs of month admis by donation; Estab 1931, inc 1961, mus opened 1937; Art Mus offers exhibs, educational progs & community events; Average Annual Attendance: 55,500; Mem: 2,000; dues student & seniors $35, individual $45, family $60, advocate $125, contributing $250, sustaining $500, patron $1,000, benefactor $2500, grand benefactor $5,000; annual meetings in May
Income: Financed by mem, grants, private & corporate donations, fund raisers
Special Subjects: Porcelain, Portraits, Bronzes, Woodcuts, Painting-American, Photography, Prints, Sculpture, Watercolors, Asian Art
Collections: African Sculpture (masks); American Ceramics; American, European & Asian Collections of Painting, Sculpture; American Realism; Photography; collection of works by Northwest Artists; Contemporary Prints
Publications: Annual report; quarterly bulletin; occasional catalogs & posters of exhibitions
Activities: Classes in art for adults & children; docent training; docent tours; performances; outdoor arts festival; lects for mems only; 5 vis lectrs per yr; gallery talks; tours; originate traveling exhibs statewide & Northwest region 6 per yr; mus shop sells books, original art, reproductions, cards & jewelry

A IDAHO COMMISSION ON THE ARTS, 2410 Old Penitentiary Rd, PO Box 83720 Boise, ID 83720-0008. Tel 208-334-2119; Fax 208-334-2488; Elec Mail info@arts.idaho.gov; Internet Home Page Address: www.arts.idaho.gov; *Exec Dir* Michael Faison; *Dir Community Develop* Michelle Coleman; *Dir Artist Svcs* John McMahon; *Dir Literature* Cort Conley; *Dir Arts Educ* Ruth Piispanen; *Dir Folk & Trade Arts* Steven Hatcher
Open 8 AM - 5 PM; No admis fee; Estab 1966 to promote artistic develop within the state & to make cultural resources available to all Idahoans
Library Holdings: DVDs; Pamphlets; Video Tapes
Publications: Newsletter 3 times a year
Activities: Governors arts awards

M IDAHO HISTORICAL MUSEUM, 2205 Old Penitentiary Rd., Idaho State Historical Society Boise, ID 83712-8250. Tel 208-334-2682; Fax 208-334-2774; Elec Mail jody.ochoa@ishs.idaho.gov; Internet Home Page Address: www.state.id.us/ishs; *Registrar* Jody Ochoa; *Cur* Joe Toluse; *Museum Adminr* Kenneth J Swanson
Open Mon - Sat 9 AM - 5 PM, Sun & holidays 1 - 5 PM; Admis adults $4, seniors $2, children under 6 $1; Estab 1881; Average Annual Attendance: 100,000; Mem: Dues $500 life mem, $100 bus, $25 patron, $15 couple, $10 individual
Income: Financed by donations and mem
Special Subjects: Archaeology, Textiles, Costumes, Decorative Arts, Furniture, Period Rooms
Collections: History artifacts
Exhibitions: Story of Idaho
Activities: Classes for children; dramatic progs; docent training; lects open to pub; tours; competitions; individual paintings & original objects of art lent to agencies & institutions; lending collection contains 7 slide progs; book traveling exhibs; originate traveling exhibs to state schools & libraries; mus shop sells books & gifts

CALDWELL

M THE COLLEGE OF IDAHO, Rosenthal Art Gallery, 2112 Cleveland Blvd, Caldwell, ID 83605-4432; PO Box 60, Caldwell, ID 83606. Tel 208-459-5321; Fax 208-459-5175; Elec Mail gclaassen@collegeofidaho.edu; *Prof Art* Steven M Fisher; *Assoc Prof Art* Lynn Webster; *Dir* Dr Garth Claassen
Open Tues - Thurs 1 PM - 4 PM or by appointment; No admis fee; Estab 1980
Income: Financed by college funds
Special Subjects: Painting-American, Prints
Collections: Luther Douglas, Sand Paintings; Paintings; Prints Collection
Exhibitions: Temporary & traveling exhibitions on an inter-museum loan basis
Publications: Exhibit Brochures
Activities: Lect; gallery talks; guided tours; films

COEUR D ALENE

M THE ART SPIRIT GALLERY, 415 Sherman, Coeur D Alene, ID 83814. Tel 208-765-6006; Elec Mail contactus@theartspiritgallery.com; Internet Home Page Address: www.theartspiritgallery.com; *Owner* Steve Gibbs; *Gallery Asst* Darla Kuhman; *Gallery Asst* Penny Sbicca
Open June - Sept: daily 11 AM - 6 PM; Oct - May: Tues - Sat 11 AM - 6 PM; No admis fee; Estab 1997; Original fine art by regional artists
Collections: Paintings; drawings; sculpture; pottery
Exhibitions: New exhib opens 2nd Friday of every month

EMMETT

M GEM COUNTY HISTORICAL SOCIETY AND MUSEUM, Gem County Historical Village Museum, 501 E 1st St, Emmett, ID 83617-3005. Tel 208-365-9530, 4340; Elec Mail mdavis@gemcountymuseum.org; Internet Home Page Address: www.gemcountymuseum.org; *Dir & Cur* Meg Davis
Open Wed 1-5PM, Thurs & Fri 10:30 AM - 5PM, Sat 1PM - 5 PM; No admis fee, donations accepted; Opened in 1973 with the focus being the interpretation of life in early Gem County beginning with the Native Americans who first inhabited the land to the contributions of the trappers, miners, and settlers. Nonprofit org; Average Annual Attendance: 1,500-2,000; Mem: Dues Gold $1,000; Silver $500; Copper $250; Garnet $100; Opal $50; Benefactor $25; Family $15; Individual $10
Income: Financed by mem, grants, endowments
Library Holdings: Audio Tapes; Book Volumes; Manuscripts; Maps; Memorabilia; Original Documents; Pamphlets; Periodical Subscriptions; Photographs; Prints; Video Tapes
Special Subjects: Archaeology, Historical Material, Flasks & Bottles, Furniture, Photography, Prints, Period Rooms, Painting-American, Photography, Ethnology,

Costumes, Folk Art, Primitive art, Manuscripts, Portraits, Dolls, Furniture, Glass, Period Rooms, Embroidery, Laces, Gold
Collections: Large coll of photographs; full-sized period displays of a general store, a turn-of-the-century parlor, a laundry room, and a combined doctor's and dentist's office; special tribute to the men and women who have served in the armed forces; several pianos, office machines, and other local items; Hunt Memorial House, a turn-of-the-century cottage holding the belongings of former Governor and Mrs Frank W Hunt; Little Red Schoolhouse; Bunkhouse which houses tribute to birds indigenous to the county as well as a tribute to the cattle & sheep industry; blacksmith's shop with variety of tools; reading & research library
Activities: Special events; ladies social, Feb; River Through Time-hands on History, 1st weekend in Oct; cemetery tour to be announced; lects open to the pub; tours; mus shop sells books, reproductions, prints

FORT HALL

M SHOSHONE BANNOCK TRIBES, Shoshone Bannock Tribal Museum, I-15, Exit 80, Fort Hall, ID 83203; PO Box 306, Fort Hall, ID 83203-0306. Tel 208-237-9791; Fax 208-237-4318; Elec Mail rdevinney@shoshonebannocktribes.com; Internet Home Page Address: www.sho-ban.com; *Mgr & Coordr* Rosemary A Devinney
Open June - Aug daily 10 AM - 5 PM; Sept - May Mon - Fri 10 AM - 5 PM; cl on all Tribal Holidays; Admis adults $3.50, children $1, no admis fee for Native Americans with Tribal ID; group rates (5 minimum); Mus was built in 1985 and was cl for several years. It re-opened in 1993 by volunteers with the help of community mems who donated & loaned many photos and precious heirlooms to the mus; Learn all about the Shoshone-Bannock people who live on the Fort Hall Indian Reservation in Southeastern Idaho
Income: By the Shoshone-Bannock tribal government
Special Subjects: American Indian Art, Historical Material, Prints, Photography, Bronzes, Crafts, Jewelry, Dioramas
Collections: photographs, displays & exhibs dating back to 1895; authentic arts & crafts made by tribal mems; reference books on the Shoshone-Bannock people as well as other North American tribes; artifacts from archeological excavations
Exhibitions: Tribal History; Photographs; Beadwork; Paintings; Family History
Activities: Mus shop sells books, prints, music, beadwork & crafts

IDAHO FALLS

M THE ART MUSEUM OF EASTERN IDAHO, 300 S Capital Ave, Idaho Falls, ID 83402-3952. Tel 208-524-7777; Fax 208-529-6666; Elec Mail info@theartmuseum.org; Internet Home Page Address: www.theartmuseum.org; *Pres* Elizabeth Bowhan; *VPres* Debby Myler; *Dir* Miyai Abe Griggs; *Secy* Christine Ott; *Treas* Carla Benson, CPA; *Bus Asst* Myrta Zietz; *Educ Dir* Alexa Stanger; *Admin Asst* Jessica Livesay
Open Tues - Sat 11 AM - 5 PM; Admis family $10, adult $4, Youth $2, 5 & under free; Estab 2002; Mus serves southeastern ID through the coll, preservation & exhibition of works of art by ID artists; Average Annual Attendance: 24,000; Mem: Dues Benefactor $2,500; Dir Club $1,000; Patron $500; Sustaining $250; Supporting $100; Family $50; Contributing $35
Library Holdings: Book Volumes
Special Subjects: Drawings, Mexican Art, American Western Art, Portraits, Painting-American, Woodcuts, Hispanic Art, Watercolors, African Art, Primitive art, Etchings & Engravings
Collections: Original paintings, etchings & lithographs from internationally known and local artists
Activities: Classes for adults & children; children's events; ann events; elementary school art exhib; lects open to public; 10 vis lectrs per yr; concerts; tours; gallery talks; sponsoring of competitions; originates traveling exhibs to Idaho galleries; mus shop sells books, original art & prints

M WILLARD ARTS CENTER, Carr Gallery, Colonial Theater, 450 A St Idaho Falls, ID 83402-3617; 498 A St Idaho Falls, ID 83402-3617. Tel 208-522-0471; Fax 208-522-0413; Elec Mail bnewton@idahofallsarts.org; Internet Home Page Address: www.idahofallsarts.org; *Exec Dir* Brandi Newton; *Technical Dir* Brad Higbee; *Develop Dir* Brandie Leonard; *Office Mgr* Amber Carmichael; *Accnt* Courtney Archibald; *Mktg Dir* Andrea Todd
Open Carr Gallery Mon-Fri 11AM-5PM, Sat 10AM-4PM; No admis fee; Estab to promote visual & performing arts in eastern Idaho; Average Annual Attendance: 10,000; Mem: Dues $50
Collections: Artwork by local, national & international artists; Blake G. Hall Community Gallery
Exhibitions: Rotating exhibs quarterly; 3 day free art festival for families, annually
Publications: Arts Alive! regional art calendar, pub 3 times per yr
Activities: Educ prog; classes for adults & children; workshops; docent training; concerts; gallery talks; tours; support of arts/ achievement in arts awards

MOSCOW

M APPALOOSA MUSEUM AND HERITAGE CENTER, 2720 W Pullman Rd, Moscow, ID 83843-4024. Tel 208-882-5578; Fax 208-882-8150; Elec Mail museum@appaloosa.com; Internet Home Page Address: www.appaloosamuseum.org; *Pres* King Rockhill; *Dir* Jennifer Hamilton
Open Mon - Fri 10 AM - 5 PM, Sat 10 AM - 4 PM; No admis fee donations appreciated; Estab 1974 to collect, preserve, study & exhibit those objects that illustrate the story of the Appaloosa Horse; Average Annual Attendance: 5,000; Mem: 33,000; annual meeting in May
Income: $38,000 (financed by grants from Appaloosa Horse Club, shop sales & fundraising)
Purchases: $1,600
Library Holdings: Audio Tapes 30; Book Volumes 500; Framed Reproductions 10; Maps 10; Original Art Works 40; Original Documents 100; Photographs 15,000; Prints 200; Reproductions; Sculpture 20; Video Tapes 30

Special Subjects: Drawings, Painting-American, Photography, Prints, American Indian Art, American Western Art, Bronzes, Costumes, Crafts, Landscapes, Manuscripts, Maps, Leather, Reproductions
Collections: Bronzes by Shirley Botoham, Less Williver, Don Christian & William Menshew; reproductions of Chinese, European & Persian Art relating to Appaloosas; reproductions of Charles Russell art; original Western by George Phippen, Reynolds; Native American Items, saddle & other tack art work; Trace History of Appoloosa Horses from prehistoric times to present; Early Indian Art
Exhibitions: live horse exhibit
Publications: quarterly newsletter
Activities: Educ programs; programs for children; lects open to pub, 1-2 vis lectrs per yr; gallery talks; tours; trail ride; auction; mus shops sells books, jewelry, cards & games, toys, clothing & Appaloosa Horse reproductions, original art & prints

POCATELLO

M **IDAHO STATE UNIVERSITY,** John B Davis Gallery of Fine Art, PO Box 8004, Pocatello, ID 83209-0001. Tel 208-236-2361; Fax 208-282-4791; Elec Mail kovarudo@isu.edu; Internet Home Page Address: www.isu.edu/departments.art; *Chair* Rudy Kovacs; *Dir Gallery* Amy Jo Johnson
Open Mon - Fri 10 AM - 4 PM; No admis fee; Estab 1956 to exhibit art; Gallery contains 130 running ft of space with 8 ft ceilings; Average Annual Attendance: 2,600
Income: $2600 (financed by city appropriation)
Purchases: $350
Collections: Permanent collection
Exhibitions: Big Sky Biennial Exhibit; Regional Group Graduate Exhibit; exhibitions & national exhibitions; MFA Thesis Exhibits, bi-weekly one-man shows; student exhibits
Activities: Lects talks; tours; competitions with awards; scholarships offered; exten dept serves surrounding communities; individual paintings lent to school offices & community; originate traveling exhibs
M **The Transition Gallery,** 921 S 8th Ave, Earl R Pond Student Union Pocatello, ID 83209. Tel 208-282-3451
M **Mind's Eye Gallery,** 921 S 8th Ave, Rendezvous Complex Pocatello, ID 83209. Tel 208-282-3451

M **POCATELLO ART CENTER,** 444 N Main St, Pocatello, ID 83204-5070. Tel 208-232-0970; Elec Mail pocartctr@da.net; Internet Home Page Address: pocatelloartctr.org

M **THE TRANSITION GALLERY - IDAHO STATE UNIVERSITY,** 921 S 8th Ave, Pocatello, ID 83209. Tel 208-282-3451

TWIN FALLS

M **HERRETT CENTER FOR ARTS & SCIENCES,** (College of Southern Idaho) Jean B King Art Gallery, 315 Falls Ave, Twin Falls, ID 83301; PO Box 1238, Twin Falls, ID 83303-1238. Tel 208-732-6655; Fax 208-736-4712; Elec Mail herrett@csi.edu; Internet Home Page Address: www.csi.edu; *Dir* James Woods; *Colls Mgr* Phyllis Oppenheim; *Art Gallery Mgr* Milica Popovic; *Exhibits Mgr* Joey Heck; *Display Technician* Nick Peterson; *Office Mgr* Wilma Titmus
Open Mon - Fri 9:30 AM - 9 PM, Sat 1 - 9 PM; No admis fee; Estab 1965; Art Gallery, Natural History Gallery, four anthropology galleries (700-2400 sq ft); Average Annual Attendance: 37,000
Special Subjects: American Indian Art, Anthropology, Archaeology, Pre-Columbian Art, Decorative Arts, Eskimo Art
Collections: Pre-Columbian, Prehistoric & Ethnographic Indian Artifacts
Exhibitions: Exhibits change every 5-6 weeks
Activities: Classes for adults & children; lects open to pub, vis lectrs; gallery talks; tours; original objects of art lent to other pub institutions; originate traveling exhibs to schools, libraries & mus; mus shop sells books, original art, prints, mus replicas & novelties

WEISER

M **SNAKE RIVER HERITAGE CENTER,** 2295 Paddock Ave, Weiser, ID 83672-1195; PO Box 307, Weiser, ID 83672-0307. Tel 208-549-0205; Elec Mail info@weisermuseum.com; Internet Home Page Address: www.weisermuseum.com; *Pres* Lynn Isaacson; *VPres* Wesley Higgins; *Treas* Dick Bergquist; *Secy* Jeri Kleppin
Open summer (last weekend in June thru last weekend in Aug): Fri - Sat 10 AM - 1 PM & by appointment, (under construction); Admis by donation; Estab 1962 to preserve the history of Washington County, Idaho; Housed in a 1920 five story, solid concrete building of the Intermountain Institute, founded in 1899; Average Annual Attendance: 750; Mem: 100+; dues $25.00, lifetime $300
Income: $30,000 (financed by mem, county appropriation, gifts & fundraising)
Library Holdings: Audio Tapes; Book Volumes; Cards; Cassettes; DVDs; Framed Reproductions; Manuscripts; Maps; Memorabilia; Original Art Works; Original Documents; Other Holdings; Periodical Subscriptions; Photographs; Prints; Records; Reproductions; Sculpture; Slides
Collections: Washington County memorabilia & artifacts of Snake River Country; Baseball Hall of Famer Walter Johnson's Collection; Arrow Heads; Telephone Pioneers Communication Room; Display of 1925 Seth Thomas Clock weighing 1200 lbs; Historical automobile garages room
Exhibitions: Shoshone Indian Display; Vintage Fashion Collection
Publications: Museum newsletter; annual report
Activities: Classes for adults & children; dramatic progs; historical tours; concerts; gallery talks; tours; mus sales shop sells books, original art, reproductions, prints, reproductions of early pioneer textiles, VCR tapes, DVDs, & clothing reproductions

ILLINOIS

ALTON

M **ALTON MUSEUM OF HISTORY & ART, INC,** Loomis Hall, 2809 College Ave Alton, IL 62002-4743. Tel 618-462-2763; Fax 618-462-2763 (call first); Elec Mail altonmuseum@gmail.com; Internet Home Page Address: www.altonmuseum.com; *Pres Emeritus* Charlene Gill; *Secy* John Langley; *Gift Shop Chmn* Lois Lobbig; *Pres* Norman Showers; *VPres* Brian Combs; *Treas* Lois Mitchell; *Hostess* Patti Culp; *Researcher* Cathy Baghy
Open Wed - Sat 10 AM - 4 PM, Sun 1 - 4 PM; Admis adult $5, children 12 and under $1; Estab 1971 to collect, preserve & exhibit local history; Second location: The Koenig House, 829 E Fourth St, Alton, IL 62002 (by appointment); Average Annual Attendance: 14,000; Mem: 250; dues $15-$100; annual meeting 2nd Wed in Apr
Income: $30,000-40,000 (financed by mem, endowment & tours; admis; grants)
Library Holdings: Clipping Files; Original Art Works; Pamphlets; Photographs; Video Tapes
Special Subjects: Architecture, Drawings, Graphics, Painting-American, Prints, Folk Art, Primitive art, Landscapes, Afro-American Art, Manuscripts, Dolls, Furniture, Glass, Historical Material, Maps, Coins & Medals, Dioramas
Collections: Architecture of Lost Alton; Black Pioneers of River Bend; early glass blowing; Robert Wadlow's life & memorabilia; Mississippi River Pilot House; Shurtleff College; Western Military Academy; Monticello Col
Exhibitions: Early Industry & Education; The History of the Black Pioneers of the River Bend; Ice Cutting on the Mississippi; Lost Alton Architecture; Robert Wadlow - The World's Tallest Recorded Man; Wood River Massacre of 1814; changing art exhibits throughout the year; Elijah P Lovejoy; Underground Railroad; Educational Institutions
Publications: Newsletter
Activities: Classes for adults & children; docent training; lects open to pub, 12 vis lectrs 2nd Fri of every month, 6:30 PM; gallery talks; tours; sponsoring of competitions; mus shop sells books, original art, reproductions & prints

AURORA

M **AURORA REGIONAL FIRE MUSEUM,** New York Ave & Broadway, Aurora, IL 60507; PO Box 1782, Aurora, IL 60507-1782. Tel 630-892-1572; Elec Mail arfminfo@aol.com; Internet Home Page Address: www.auroraregionalfiremuseum.org; *Mus Mgr* Deborah Davis; *Cur* David Lewis
Open Thurs - Sat 1 PM - 4 PM; cl maj holidays; Estab 1990; housed in Central Fire Station built in 1894; preserves & presents the history of firefighting in Aurora & surrounding communities; Average Annual Attendance: 3000 by estimate; Mem: dues Life $500, Inst $100, Patron $50, Family $25, Indiv $15, Student/Senior $10
Collections: 300 various firefighting periodicals; 100 fire service books; 50 local firefighting-related scrapbooks
Publications: Fire Museum News, quarterly newsletter
Activities: Formal educ for adults & children; films; lects; ann event: Fire Engine Muster; mus related items for sale

M **AURORA UNIVERSITY,** Schingoethe Center for Native American Cultures & The Schingoethe Art Gallery, 347 S Gladstone Ave, Dunham Hall, 1400 Marseillaise Aurora, IL 60506-4877. Tel 630-844-5402; Fax 630-844-6529; Internet Home Page Address: www.aurora.edu/museum; *Cur Coll* Elizabeth Easto; *Dir* Meg Bero
Open Wed- Fri 10 AM - 4 PM, Sun 1- 4 PM, cl Sat; No admis fee; Estab 1990 to advance cultural literacy about Native peoples; Two permanent exhibit galleries with rotating displays from the mus collection; total of 3,500 sq ft; Average Annual Attendance: 10,000; Mem: 50; dues donor $50 - $500, individual $20
Income: $150,000 (financed by mem & endowment)
Special Subjects: Latin American Art, Mexican Art, American Indian Art, Archaeology, Ethnology, Pre-Columbian Art, Southwestern Art, Textiles, Folk Art, Eskimo Art
Collections: Ethnographic material from North, Central & South America; Native American Fine Art; Prehistoric & Pre-Columbian material; Inuit Art
Publications: Spreading Wings; quarterly newsletter to membership
Activities: Summer workshops for adults & children; outreach materials for educators; docent progs; lects open to pub; mus shop sells books, original art & reproductions

BISHOP HILL

M **ILLINOIS HISTORIC PRESERVATION AGENCY,** Bishop Hill State Historic Site, PO Box 104, Bishop Hill, IL 61419-0104. Tel 309-927-3345; Fax 309-927-3343; Elec Mail bishophill@mymctc.net; Internet Home Page Address: www.bishophill.com; *Asst Site Mgr* Ed Safiran; *Site Mgr* Martha J Downey
Open Wed - Sun Mar - Oct 9 AM - 5 PM, Nov - Feb 9 AM - 4 PM; Admis suggested donation adults $4, ages 17 & younger $2, family $10; Estab 1946 to preserve & interpret the history of Bishop Hill Colony 1846-1861; Restored Colony Church, 1848 & restored Colony Hotel, 1860, Bishop Hill Mus 1988, Folk paintings of Olof Krans; Average Annual Attendance: 51,000
Income: Financed by state appropriation
Special Subjects: Architecture, Painting-American, Archaeology, Textiles, Crafts, Folk Art, Primitive art, Decorative Arts, Portraits, Furniture, Carpets & Rugs, Historical Material, Restorations
Collections: Bishop Hill Colony artifacts-agricultural items, furniture, household items, textiles & tools; Olaf Krans Collection of Folk Art Paintings

BLOOMINGTON

M **ILLINOIS WESLEYAN UNIVERSITY,** Merwin & Wakeley Galleries, PO Box 2900, Bloomington, IL 61702-2900. Tel 309-556-3822; Fax 309-556-3976; Elec Mail clozar@iwu.edu; Internet Home Page Address: www2.iwu.edu/art/galleries; *Dir* Carmen Lozar
Open Mon - Fri Noon - 4 PM, Tues 7 - 9 PM, Sat & Sun 1 - 4 PM; Estab 1945
Income: Financed by endowment & mem

Special Subjects: Drawings, Painting-American, Prints
Collections: 250 drawings, paintings & prints including works by Baskin, Max Beckmann, Helen Frankenthaler, Philip Guston, John Ihle, Oliviera, Larry Rivers & Whistler
Exhibitions: Rotating exhibits
Publications: Exhibition Posters; Gallery Schedule, monthly;
Activities: Dramatic progs; lects open to pub, 5 vis lectrs per yr; concerts; tours; competitions with awards; original objects of art lent, on campus only; book traveling exhibs; originates traveling exhibs

L   **Sheean Library,** 1312 Park St, Bloomington, IL 61701-1773. Tel 309-556-3003; Fax 309-556-3706; Elec Mail bdelvin@titan.iwu.edu; Internet Home Page Address: www.iwu.edu/library; *Fine Arts Librn* Robert C Delvin
Open Mon - Thurs 7:45 AM - 1:30 AM; Fri 7:45 AM - 10 PM; Sat 10 AM - 10 PM; Sun 11 AM - 1:30 AM
Income: Financed by endowment
Library Holdings: Slides 35,000

A   **MCLEAN COUNTY ART ASSOCIATION,** McLean County Arts Center, 601 N East St, Bloomington, IL 61701-3094. Tel 309-829-0011; Fax 309-829-4928; Elec Mail info@mcac.org; Internet Home Page Address: www.mcac.org; *Exec Dir* Douglas C Johnson; *Cur* Alison Hatcher; *Educ Coordr* Tony Preston-Sohreck; *Preparator* Ben Gardner; *Project Coordr* Kendra Johnson
Open Tues 10 AM - 7 PM, Wed - Fri 10 AM - 5 PM, Sat Noon - 4 PM, Dec only Sun Noon - 4 PM; No admis fee; Estab 1922 to enhance the arts in McLean County. Provides display galleries, sales & rental gallery featuring local professional artists; Brandt Gallery is 2500 sq ft hosting local shows & traveling exhibits; Average Annual Attendance: 10,000; Mem: 600; annual meeting first Fri in May
Income: Financed by mem, art & book sales
Collections: Small permanent collection with concentration on Midwestern artists
Exhibitions: Annual Amateur Competition & Exhibition; Annual Holiday Show & Sale; 10-2 other exhibits, local & traveling
Publications: Quarterly newsletter
Activities: Classes for adults & children; lect open to public; gallery talks; tours; competitions with awards; gift shop sells fine crafts & original art, conservation framing shop

M   **MCLEAN COUNTY HISTORICAL SOCIETY,** McLean County Museum of History, 200 N Main, Bloomington, IL 61701. Tel 309-827-0428; Fax 309-827-0100; Elec Mail marketing@mchistory.org; Internet Home Page Address: www.mchistory.org; *Librn & Archivist* William Kemp; *Cur* Susan Hartzold; *Exec Dir* Greg Koos; *Dir Educ* Candace Summers; *Dir Mktg* Jeff Woodard; *Educ Prog Coordr* Rachael Kramp; *Registrar* Tod Eagleton; *Dir Develop* Beth Whisman; *Develop Asst* Amelia Hill; *Dir Vols* Deb VanAntwerp
Open Mon - Sat 10 AM - 5 PM, Tues 10 AM - 9 PM; Admis adults $5, seniors $4, students & mems free, Tues free; Estab 1892 to promote history of McLean County; Maintain long term exhibits, changing exhibits and traveling exhibits; Average Annual Attendance: 34,000; Mem: 1300
Income: $750,000; Financed by mem, endowment, earned income & government
Purchases: $2,000
Library Holdings: Book Volumes 10,000; CD-ROMs; Clipping Files; Fiche; Kodachrome Transparencies; Lantern Slides; Manuscripts; Maps; Memorabilia; Motion Pictures; Original Art Works; Original Documents; Other Holdings; Pamphlets; Periodical Subscriptions; Photographs; Prints; Records; Reels; Sculpture; Slides; Video Tapes
Special Subjects: Anthropology, Decorative Arts, Drawings, Folk Art, Historical Material, Architecture, Glass, Antiquities-Assyrian, Flasks & Bottles, Porcelain, Pottery, Painting-American, Prints, Textiles, Manuscripts, Maps, Photography, Sculpture, Archaeology, Ethnology, Costumes, Ceramics, Crafts, Portraits, Posters, Dolls, Furniture, Jewelry, Carpets & Rugs, Coins & Medals, Embroidery, Laces
Collections: Civil War; Illinois History; local history; Material Culture; Folk Art; Portraits; Photography; Textiles; personal items; household
Exhibitions: Encounter on the Prairie
Activities: Classes for adults & children; senior citizen progs; dramatic progs; lects open to pub; 12 vis lectrs per yr; galley talks; tours; concerts; exten prog with Central Illinois Elementary Schools & retirement communities; originates traveling exhibs to mus in Midwest; mus shop sells books, reproductions & prints

CARBONDALE

M   **SOUTHERN ILLINOIS UNIVERSITY CARBONDALE,** University Museum, 1000 Faner Dr, MC 4508 SIUC Carbondale, IL 62901-4328. Tel 618-453-5388; Fax 618-453-7409; Elec Mail museum@siu.edu; Internet Home Page Address: www.museum.siu.edu; *Dir* Dona Bachman; *Cur Colls* Lorilee Huffman; *Cur Exhibs* Nate Steinbrink; *Educ Prog Dir* Robert DeHoet; *Registrar* Eric S Jones
Open Tues - Fri 10 - 4 PM, Sat 1 PM - 4 PM; No admis fee; Estab 1874 to reflect the history & cultures of Southern Illinois & promote the understanding of the area; to provide area schools & the University with support through educational outreach programs; to promote the fine arts, humanities & sciences; 12,000 sq ft in 7 gallery spaces, 3 devoted to permanent collections; Average Annual Attendance: 15,000; Mem: Dues $10 - $500
Income: Financed by state appropriated budget, federal, state & private grants, donations & University Mus patrons
Special Subjects: Historical Material, Painting-American, Prints, Sculpture, Bronzes, African Art, Anthropology, Costumes, Ceramics, Etchings & Engravings, Afro-American Art, Dolls, Dioramas
Collections: Decorative Arts; European & American paintings, drawing & prints from 13th-20th century with emphasis on 19th & 20th century; photography, sculpture, blacksmithing & art & crafts; Oceanic Collection; Southern Illinois history; 20th century sculpture, metals, ceramics; Asiatic holdings; archaeology; costumes; textiles; geology; zoology
Exhibitions: A variety of changing exhibitions in all media; ethnographic arts; fine & decorative arts; history & the sciences
Publications: Annual report; seasonal museum newsletter; exhibition catalogs
Activities: Classes for children; gallery talks; lects open to pub; book traveling exhibs; originate traveling exhibs circulated to mus, art centers, libraries & schools; mus shop sells original art, reproductions, jewelry, pottery & crafts

L   **Morris Library,** 605 Agriculture Dr, Mailcode 6632 Carbondale, IL 62901-4310. Tel 618-453-2818; Fax 618-453-8109; Elec Mail lkoch@lib.siu.edu; Internet Home Page Address: www.lib.siu.edu
Primarily lending
Income: Financed by college funds, gifts, pub & private grants
Library Holdings: Book Volumes 35,000; Cards; Cassettes 475; Exhibition Catalogs; Fiche; Periodical Subscriptions 180; Records; Reels

CHAMPAIGN

M   **PARKLAND COLLEGE,** Parkland Art Gallery, 2400 W Bradley Ave, Champaign, IL 61821-1899. Tel 217-351-2485; Fax 217-373-3899; Internet Home Page Address: www.parkland.edu/gallery; *Gallery Dir* Lisa Costello
Open Mon - Thurs 10 AM - 7 PM, Fri 10 AM - 3 PM, Sat noon - 2 PM; No admis fee; Estab 1981 to exhibit contemporary fine art; Average Annual Attendance: 10,000
Income: Nonprofit, supported by Parkland College & in part by Illinois Arts Council, a state agency
Collections: Student, Foundation
Exhibitions: State of the Art - Biennial National Watercolor Invitational; Midwest Ceramics Invitational - Biennial, 2-person shows; solo exhibits
Publications: Bi-annual exhibitional catalogs & brochures
Activities: Local high school art student seminar; art expedition day trips to Chicago, Indianapolis & St Louis; lects open to public; 18 vis lectrs per year; gallery talks; tours; awards given to works of excellence in student exhibits; originate traveling exhibitions

M   **UNIVERSITY OF ILLINOIS AT URBANA-CHAMPAIGN,** Krannert Art Museum and Kinkead Pavilion, 500 E Peabody Dr, Champaign, IL 61820-6913. Tel 217-333-1861; Fax 217-333-0883; Elec Mail kam@illinois.edu; Internet Home Page Address: www.kam.illinois.edu; *Dir* Kathleen Harleman; *Registrar* Christine Saniat; *Dir Mktg & Spec Events* Diane Schumacher; *Dir Educ* Anne Sautman; *Assoc Dir* Claudia Corlett-Stahl; *Cur* Allyson Purpura; *Dir Develop* Brenda Nardi; *Cur* Robert La France
Open Tues - Sat 9 AM - 5 PM, Thurs until 9 PM, Sun 2 - 5 PM; No admis fee; Estab 1961 to house & administer the art collections of University of Illinois, to support teaching & research programs & to serve as an area art mus; Gallery is 48,000 sq ft, with 30,000 devoted to exhibition space; Average Annual Attendance: 145,000; Mem: 500; dues $45 & up
Income: Financed by mem, state appropriation & grants
Library Holdings: Auction Catalogs; Exhibition Catalogs
Special Subjects: American Indian Art, Decorative Arts, Drawings, Etchings & Engravings, Folk Art, Landscapes, Marine Painting, Ceramics, Glass, Mexican Art, American Western Art, Antiquities-Assyrian, Photography, Pottery, Pre-Columbian Art, Painting-American, Prints, Silver, Textiles, Bronzes, Woodcuts, Manuscripts, Painting-British, Painting-European, Sculpture, Graphics, Hispanic Art, Watercolors, African Art, Southwestern Art, Religious Art, Primitive art, Woodcarvings, Afro-American Art, Collages, Painting-Japanese, Portraits, Posters, Furniture, Jade, Jewelry, Porcelain, Oriental Art, Asian Art, Antiquities-Byzantine, Metalwork, Painting-Dutch, Painting-French, Ivory, Tapestries, Baroque Art, Calligraphy, Miniatures, Painting-Flemish, Renaissance Art, Embroidery, Medieval Art, Antiquities-Oriental, Painting-Spanish, Painting-Italian, Islamic Art, Antiquities-Egyptian, Antiquities-Greek, Antiquities-Roman, Gold, Stained Glass, Painting-German, Pewter, Enamels, Painting-New Zealand
Collections: American paintings, sculpture, prints & drawings; Ancient Near Eastern Classical & Medieval Art; European & American Decorative Arts; Trees Collection of European & American Painting; Moore Collection of European & American Decorative Arts; Olsen Collection of Pre-Columbian Art
Publications: Catalogs, 3 or 4 annually
Activities: Classes for adults & students; docent training; Art-to-Go Outreach; lects open to pub; concerts; gallery talks; tours; 15-20 vis lectrs per yr; individual paintings & original objects of art lent to mus & university galleries; book traveling exhibs; originate traveling exhibs; mus cafe

M   **Spurlock Museum,** 600 S Gregory, Urbana, IL 61801. Tel 217-333-2360; Fax 217-244-9419; Elec Mail kflesher@illinois.edu; Internet Home Page Address: www.spurlock.illinois.edu; *Dir* Prof Wayne Pitard; *Dir Educ* Tandy Lacy; *Collections Mgr* Christa Deacy-Quinn; *Registrar* Jennifer White; *Information Technology* Jack Thomas; *Educ Coordr* Beth Watkins; *Asst Educator* Kim Sheahan; *Asst Coll Mgr* John Holton; *Head of Security* Harold Bush; *Asst Registrar* Amy Heggemeyer; *Prog Coordr* Karen Flesher; *Spec Events Coordr & Vol Coordr* Brian Cudianat; *Educ Prog Coordr* Brook Taylor; *Learning Ctr Coordr* Julia Robinson; *Coll Coordr* Melissa Sotelo
Open Tues noon - 5 PM, Wed - Fri 9 AM - 5 PM, Sat 10 AM - 4 PM, Sun noon - 4 PM; No admis fee; Estab 1911; Five permanent galleries covering Africa, ancient Egypt, Mesopotamia, the Americas, the ancient Mediterranean, East & Southeast Asia, Oceania & Europe; Average Annual Attendance: 18,000; Mem: 300
Income: $320,000 (university)
Special Subjects: Archaeology, Historical Material, Ceramics, Glass, African Art, Anthropology, Ethnology, Judaica, Asian Art, Coins & Medals, Antiquities-Egyptian, Antiquities-Greek, Antiquities-Roman
Collections: Original & reproduction artifacts of Greek, Roman, Egyptian, Mesopotamian, African, Asian & European cultures, including sculpture, pottery, glass, implements, coins, seals, clay tablets, inscriptions, manuscripts & items of everyday life
Activities: Classes for adults & children; docent training; lects open to pub; concerts; workshops; gallery talks; tours; accredited with The American Assoc of Mus; original objects of art lent for special shows in established mus; outreach programs within 100 miles of mus; book 1 traveling exhibs per yr

L   **Ricker Library of Architecture & Art,** 608 E Lorado Taft Dr, 208 Architecture Bldg Champaign, IL 61820-6922. Tel 217-333-2290; Fax 217-244-5169; Internet Home Page Address: www.library.uiuc.edu/arx; *Librn* Dr Jane Block; *Asst Librn* Jing Liao
Open Mon - Thurs 8:30 AM - 8 PM, Fri 8:30 AM - 5 PM, Sat 1 AM - 5 PM, Sun 1 - 10 PM; Estab 1878 to serve the study & research needs of the students & faculty of the university & the community; Circ 50,000; Ricker Library lends material through UIUC Interlibrary Loan

Income: (financed by state appropriation, blanket order, gifts & UIUC Library Friends)
Library Holdings: Book Volumes 45,000; CD-ROMs; Clipping Files; Exhibition Catalogs; Fiche; Pamphlets; Periodical Subscriptions 350; Photographs; Reels; Reproductions; Sculpture; Video Tapes
Special Subjects: Art History, Collages, Decorative Arts, Illustration, Drawings, Graphic Design, History of Art & Archaeology, Ceramics, Conceptual Art, Crafts, Interior Design, Art Education, Asian Art, Handicrafts, Architecture
Collections: Architectural Folio; Prairie School Architects; Ricker Papers; Frank Lloyd Wright
Publications: Acquisitions list, 4 per year; annual periodicals list

CHARLESTON

M **EASTERN ILLINOIS UNIVERSITY,** Tarble Arts Center, South 9th St at Cleveland Ave, Charleston, IL 61920-3099; 600 Lincoln Ave, Charleston, IL 61920-3099. Tel 217-581-2787; Fax 217-581-7138; Elec Mail tarble@eiu.edu; Internet Home Page Address: www.eiu.edu/~tarble; *Cur Educ* Kit Morice; *Dir* Michael Watts; *Asst Dir* Michael Schuetz; *Office Admin* Sally Bock
Open Tues - Fri 10 AM - 5 PM, Sat 10 AM - 4 PM, Sun 1 - 4 PM, cl Mon & major holidays; No admis fee; Estab 1982 to encourage the understanding of & participation in the arts; Main Gallery consists of fifteen 20 ft x 20 ft modular units with natural & incandescent lighting; Brainard Gallery, 20 ft x 50 ft; Gallery 40 ft x 20 ft; eGallery 20 ft x 40 ft; Average Annual Attendance: 18,000; Mem: 200; dues $50 - $1,000
Income: Financed by state appropriation, mem contributions, sales & rental commissions, grant & foundation funds
Library Holdings: Audio Tapes; Kodachrome Transparencies; Original Documents; Other Holdings; Photographs; Reels; Slides; Video Tapes
Special Subjects: Drawings, Landscapes, Prints, Sculpture, Painting-American, Watercolors, Folk Art, Woodcuts, Etchings & Engravings
Collections: Contemporary works on paper by Midwest artists; American Scene Works on Paper; Paul Turner Sargent paintings; Contemporary American Art; Indigenous Contemporary Illinois Folk Arts
Exhibitions: Solo exhibitions & group shows.; Annual Exhibitions: Art Faculty Exhibition, All-Student Show (juried, undergraduate), Graduate Art Exhibition (group thesis), Drawing/Watercolor: Illinois (biennial juried competition), Children's Art Exhibition; Folk Arts from the Collection
Publications: Exhibition catalogs
Activities: Classes & workshops for children & adults; dramatic progs; docent training; lects open to pub, 4-6 vis lectrs per yr; concerts; gallery talks; tours; drawing/watercolor: Illinois biennial purchase & merit awards; individual paintings & original objects of art lent to qualified professional galleries, arts centers & mus; book traveling exhibs 2-4 per yr; originate traveling exhibs; sales shop sells books, original art & craft pieces; Sales/Rental Gallery rents & sells original works

CHICAGO

M **ARC GALLERY,** 2156 Damen Ave Ste 1, Chicago, IL 60647-6483. Tel 312-733-2787; Fax 312-733-2787; Elec Mail info@arcgallery.org; Internet Home Page Address: www.arcgallery.org; *Pres* Iris Goldstein; *VPres* Cheri Reif Naselli
Open Wed - Sat noon - 6 PM, Sun noon - 4 PM; No admis fee; Estab 1973 for the exhib of alternative artworks & educ to the pub about contemporary art; Mem: 20; mem open to female professional artists; dues $55/mo
Special Subjects: Painting-American, Sculpture
Collections: Installation-Site Specific
Exhibitions: ARC National Show & Solo Shows, 77 exhibitions annually, seven per month in seven separate galleries, group shows, member shows
Activities: Educ dept; community outreach progs; lects open to pub; gallery talks; juried exhibs & awards; originate traveling exhibs

A **THE ART INSTITUTE OF CHICAGO,** 111 S Michigan Ave, Chicago, IL 60603-6492. Tel 312-443-3600; Fax 312-443-0849; Internet Home Page Address: www.artic.edu; *Chmn Bd Trustees* Thomas Pritzker; *Pres & Dir* James Cuno; *School Pres* Wellington Reiter; *Exec VPres Admin Affairs* Patricia Woodworth; *Exec VPres Develop & Pub Affairs* Edward W Horner Jr; *Cur American Arts* Judith Barter; *Cur European Painting & Prints & Drawings* Douglas W Druick; *Cur European Painting Before 1750* Martha Wolff; *Exec Dir Conservation* Frank Zuccari; *Exec Dir Mus Educ* Robert Eskridge; *Exec Dir Imaging & Technical Serv* Alan B Newman; *Cur Photography* David Travis; *Cur Africa, Oceania & the Americas* Richard F Townsend; *Cur Architecture* John Zukowsky; *Dir Foundation & Corporate Rels* Lisa Key; *Cur Textiles* Christa C Mayer Thurman; *Cur European Decorative Arts, Sculpture & Classical Art* Bruce Boucher; *Exec Dir of Museum Reg* Mary Solt; *Dir Pub Affairs* Erin Hogan; *Exec Dir Publications* Susan F Rossen; *Dir Government Rels* Karin Victoria; *Exec Dir Graphics & Communs Svcs* Lyn Quadri Delli; *Cur Asian Art* Jay Xu; *Exec Dir Libraries* Jack Perry Brown; *Dir Community Rels* Linda Steele; *Cur European Painting* Larry Feinberg; *Cur European Painting* Gloria Groom; *Cur European Decorative Arts & Sculpture* Ghenete Zelleke; *Cur Photography* Colin Westerbeck; *Cur Prints & Drawings* Martha Tedeschi
Open Mon - Wed & Fri - Sun 10:30 AM - 5 PM, Thurs 10:30 AM - 8PM, cl Thanksgiving, Christmas & New Years Days; Admis adults $18, seniors, students & children $12, mems & children under 14 no charge; Estab & incorporated 1879 to found, build, maintain & operate museums of fine arts, schools & libraries of art, to form, preserve & exhibit collections of objects of art of all kinds & to carry on appropriate activities conducive to the artistic develop of the community. Maintains reference library; Average Annual Attendance: 1,300,000; Mem: 145,000; dues life $2,500, family $75, individual $60, national assoc $50 & students $40
Income: $125,000,000 (financed by endowments, gifts, grants, auxiliary activities & others)
Library Holdings: Auction Catalogs; Book Volumes 425,000; CD-ROMs; Clipping Files; Compact Disks; Exhibition Catalogs; Fiche; Original Documents; Pamphlets; Periodical Subscriptions 1500; Slides 450,000
Special Subjects: Architecture, Etchings & Engravings, Prints, Sculpture, Asian Art, Bronzes, Decorative Arts, Folk Art, Pewter, African Art, Afro-American Art, American Indian Art, Ceramics, Collages, Hispanic Art, Latin American Art, Glass, Laces, Baroque Art, Antiquities-Egyptian, Enamels, Gold, Islamic Art, Medieval Art, Oriental Art
Collections: Paintings, sculpture, Asian art, prints & drawings, photographs, decorative arts, architectural fragments, tribal arts & textiles; The painting coll reviews Western art, with a sequence of French Impressionists & Post Impressionists; the print coll illustrates the history of printmaking from the 15th-20th centuries with important examples of all periods. It is particularly rich in French works of the 19th century including Meryon, Redon, Millet, Gauguin & Toulouse-Lautrec; textiles are displayed in the Agnes Allerton Textile Galleries which includes a study room & new conservation facilities; colls also include African, Oceanic & ancient American objects; The Architecture Coll includes 19th & 20th century drawings & architectural fragments in the Institute's permanent coll including the more than 40,000 architectural drawings from the Burnham Library of Architecture; The Columbus Drive Facilities include the reconstructed Trading Room from the Chicago Stock Exchange; Arthur Rubloff Paperweight coll is on view; the America Windows, monumental stained glass windows designed by Marc Chagall are on view in the gallery overlooking McKinlock Ct; decorative arts & sculpture range from medieval to the twentieth century; the Asian coll contains a coll of Ukiyo-e prints
Publications: News & Events every two months; catalogs; Ann Report
Activities: Classes & workshops for adults & children; teacher training; docent training; performances; lects open to pub; concerts; gallery walks & talks; guided lect tours; individual paintings & original objects of art lent to mus around the world; originate traveling exhibs to selected mus; mus shop sells books, reproductions, prints, slides, decorative accessories, crafts, jewelry, greeting cards & postcards; jr mus at Kraft Educ Center

L **Ryerson & Burnham Libraries,** 111 S Michigan Ave, Chicago, IL 60603-6492. Tel 312-443-3666; Fax 312-443-0849; Elec Mail ryerson@artic.edu; Internet Home Page Address: www.artic.edu; *Head Technical Svcs* Anne Champagne; *Head Reader Servs* Melanie Emerson; *Architecture Librn* Mary Woolever; *Archivist* Bart Ryckbosch; *Exec Dir Libraries* Jack Perry Brown
Open Wed & Fri 1 - 5 PM, Thurs 10:30 AM - 8 PM; Mus admis req if non-mem; Estab 1879; Circ 60,000; Open to mus members, staff of mus, students & faculty of the School of Art Institute & vis scholars & cur, for reference only; Average Annual Attendance: 10,000
Income: $1,860,000
Purchases: $600,000
Library Holdings: Auction Catalogs; Audio Tapes; Book Volumes 440,000; CD-ROMs; Cassettes; Clipping Files; Exhibition Catalogs; Fiche; Kodachrome Transparencies; Lantern Slides; Manuscripts; Memorabilia; Pamphlets; Periodical Subscriptions 1,500; Photographs; Reels; Video Tapes
Special Subjects: Art History, Folk Art, Decorative Arts, Drawings, Etchings & Engravings, Graphic Arts, Painting-American, History of Art & Archaeology, Ceramics, Conceptual Art, Crafts, Latin American Art, Bronzes, Asian Art, Furniture, Mexican Art, Ivory, Jade, Glass, Metalwork, Carpets & Rugs, Embroidery, Enamels, Gold, Goldsmithing, Jewelry, Oriental Art, Marine Painting, Laces, Architecture
Collections: Burnham Archive: Chicago Architects, letters, reports; including special Louis Sullivan, Frank Lloyd Wright & D H Burnham Collections; Percier & Fontaine Collection; Chicago Art & Artists Scrapbook: newspaper clippings from Chicago papers from 1880 to 1993; Mary Reynolds Collection: Surrealism; Bruce Goff Archive; Collins Archive of Catalan Art & Architecture
Publications: Architectural Records In Chicago, research guide; Burnham Index to Architectural Literature (1990); Art Through the Pages (2008)
Activities: Classes for adults; docent training; lects for mems only

A **The Woman's Board of the Art Institute of Chicago,** 111 S Michigan Ave, Chicago, IL 60603-6110. Tel 312-443-3629; Fax 312-443-1041; Internet Home Page Address: www.artic.edu; *Pres* Francie Corner
Open Mon - Fri 9 AM - 5 PM; Mus admis fee req for access; Estab 1952 to supplement the Board of Trustees in advancing the growth of the Institute & extending its activities & usefulness as a cultural & educational institution; Used by mem only; Mem: 82; annual meeting May
Income: Financed by contributions

A **Auxiliary Board of the Art Institute of Chicago,** 111 S Michigan Ave, Chicago, IL 60603. Tel 312-443-3674; Fax 312-443-1041; *Pres* Paulita Pike
Open Mon - Fri 9 AM - 5 PM; Estab 1973 to promote interest in programs & activities of the Art Institute among younger men & women; Mem: 60; dues $500; annual meeting in June

A **Antiquarian Society of the Art Institute of Chicago,** 111 S Michigan Ave, Chicago, IL 60603. Tel 312-443-3641; Fax 312-443-1041; Elec Mail theantiquariansociety@artic.edu; *Admin* Dawn Yingst
Open daily 9 AM - 5 PM; Estab 1877; Support American Arts & European Decorative Arts; Mem: 600; by invitation; annual meeting in Nov
Income: Financed by donations, benefits, annual dues
Exhibitions: Preview of Charles Rennie Mackintosh
Publications: Antiquarian Society Catalogue, every 10 years
Activities: Lects & seminars for members; tours; trips

A **Dept of Prints & Drawings,** 111 S Michigan Ave, Chicago, IL 60603-6110. Tel 312-443-3660; Fax 312-443-0085; Elec Mail pdstudy@artic.edu; Internet Home Page Address: www.artic.edu; *Prince Trust Chair & Cur Prints & Drawings* Suzanne Folds McCullagh; *Cur* Mark Pascale; *Coll Mgr* Emily Vokt Ziemba; *Dept Sec* Jason Foumberg; *Paper Conservator* Harriet Stratis; *Conservation Tech* Christine Conniff-O'Shea; *Conservation Tech* Mardy Sears; *Assoc Paper Conservator* Kristi Dahm; *Assoc Paper Conservator* Kim Nichols
call for appt; Estab & incorporated 1922 to study prints & drawings & their purchase for the institute; Mem: 260; dues $75 - $500
Income: Financed by mem contributions
Special Subjects: Cartoons, Drawings, Etchings & Engravings, Graphics, Manuscripts, Posters, Prints, Watercolors, Woodcuts, Collages
Activities: Lects; gallery talks

A **Society for Contemporary Art,** 111 S Michigan Ave, Chicago, IL 60603. Tel 312-443-3630; Fax 312-443-1041; Elec Mail info@scaaic.org; Internet Home Page Address: www.scaaic.org; *Pres* Nancy A Lauter
Estab & incorporated 1940 to assist the Institute in acquisition of contemporary works; Mem: 160; dues $150 - $1,000; annual meeting in May

Income: Financed by mem contributions
Activities: Lects; seminars & biennial exhibs at the Institute; 8 vis lectrs per yr

A **Department of Asian Art,** 111 S Michigan Ave, Chicago, IL 60603. Tel 312-443-3834; Fax 312-443-9281; Elec Mail asianart@artic.edu; *Assoc Cur Chinese Art* Elinor Pearlstein; *Asst Cur Japanese Art* Janice Katz; *Pritzker Chmn Asian Art & Cur Islamic Art* Daniel Walker; *Assoc Cur Indian, SE Asian, Himalayan & Islamic Art* Madhuvanti Ghose
Estab 1925 to promote interest in the Institute's collection of Asian art; Mem: 50; dues $50
Collections: Chinese paintings, furniture; bronze; jade; ceramics; Japanese paintings, ceramics; Clarence Buckingham Collection of Japanese Woodblock Prints; Buddhist art; Indian and southeast Asian paintings and sculpture; Korean ceramics; Islamic arts
Activities: Lects open to pub; symposia on exhibs; lects mems only

A **Department of Textiles, Textile Society,** 111 S Michigan Ave, Chicago, IL 60603. Tel 312-443-3696; Fax 312-214-4304; Internet Home Page Address: www.artic.edu; *Cur Emerita* Christa Thurman; *Cur & Chair* Christopher Monkhouse; *Conservator* Lauren Chang; *Dept Specialist* Isaac Facio; *Asst Cur* Odile Joassin
Open daily 10:30 AM - 4 PM by appointment only; Admis $18 for mus; Estab 1968 to promote appreciation of textiles through lectures, raising of funds, special publications & exhibitions for the Department of Textiles; Changing gallery for permanent coll; Mem: 130, Textile Society; dues $50
Income: Membership fees, funds raised by the soc for periodic purchases
Purchases: Ongoing acquisitions through purchase & gift
Special Subjects: Architecture, Drawings, Embroidery, Etchings & Engravings, Graphics, Landscapes, Manuscripts, Metalwork, Painting-German, Photography, Porcelain, Posters, Prints, Sculpture, Silver, Textiles, Watercolors, Painting-American, Pottery, Stained Glass, Asian Art, Bronzes, Decorative Arts, Folk Art, Pewter, Woodcuts, Ceramics, Hispanic Art, Latin American Art, Miniatures, Portraits, Pre-Columbian Art, Furniture, Glass, Laces, Jewelry, Woodcarvings, Period Rooms, Baroque Art, Enamels, Gold, Medieval Art, Oriental Art, Tapestries, Painting-European, Southwestern Art, Painting-Dutch, Carpets & Rugs, Mexican Art, Painting-British, Painting-Italian, Coins & Medals

M **Kraft Education Center/Museum Education,** 111 S Michigan Ave, Chicago, IL 60603. Tel 312-443-3680; Fax 312-443-0084; Internet Home Page Address: www.artic.edu; *Dir Museum Educ* Robert Eskridge
Open Mon - Wed & Fri 10:30 AM - 4:30 PM, Thur 10:30 AM - 8 PM; Admis adults $12, children, students & sr $7; Estab 1964; The new center includes a main exhibition gallery, family room, classrooms, a Teacher Resource Center, a seminar room, an auditorium, conference room & staff offices
Income: Financed by grants, gifts & endowment; renovation financed by Kraft General Foods & the Woman's Board; exhibitions supported by grants from John D & Catherine T MacArthur Foundation & NEA
Exhibitions: Faces, Places, and Inner Spaces: Interactive Exhibit
Publications: Family Self Guides & teacher packets to permanent collections & spec exhibs; gallery games; yearly publs; Volunteer Directory; Information for Students & Teachers; quarterly brochures on family programs, teachers' services, school & general programs
Activities: Docent training; teacher & family workshops; lects open to the pub; gallery walks & games; tours; performances; artist demonstrations

L **Teacher Resource Center,** 111 S Michigan Ave, Chicago, IL 60603. Tel 312-443-3719; Fax 312-443-3066; Elec Mail erc@artic.edu; Internet Home Page Address: www.artic.edu/aic/education/trc/index.htm; *Coordr* Jocelyn Moralde; *Asst* Elijah Burgher
Open Tues & Wed 1 - 5 PM, Thurs 1 - 8 PM, Sat 10:30 AM - 4:30 PM; Open for reference; Average Annual Attendance: 2,000
Income: Financed by endowment
Library Holdings: Book Volumes 1500; CD-ROMs; Cassettes; Compact Disks; Exhibition Catalogs; Periodical Subscriptions; Slides; Video Tapes
Activities: Classes for adults; gallery games; architectural walks; student self-guides; exten program in Chicagoland, 100 mile radius of mus; sales shop sells prints, slides, videos, postcards

A **THE ARTS CLUB OF CHICAGO,** 201 E Ontario St, Chicago, IL 60611-3204. Tel 312-787-3997; Fax 312-787-8664; Elec Mail information@artsclubchicago.org; Internet Home Page Address: www.artsclubinchicago.org; *Pres* Marilynn B Alsdorf; *Dir* Kathy S Cottong
Open Mon - Fri 11 AM - 6 PM; No admis fee; Estab 1916 to maintain club rooms for members & provide public galleries for changing exhibitions; Gallery has 230 running ft of wall space; Average Annual Attendance: 15,000; Mem: 1,200; annual meeting in Nov
Income: Financed by mem dues
Purchases: Occasional purchases gifts & bequests
Library Holdings: Audio Tapes; Book Volumes; Exhibition Catalogs
Collections: Modern Collection incl Braque, Calder, Noguchi, Picabia, Picasso; Contemporary Coll incl Polke, Katz, Doig
Exhibitions: 3 exhibs per yr
Publications: Exhibition Catalogs
Activities: Lects open to members only; concerts; vis lectrs 100 per yr; gallery talks

L **Reference Library,** 201 E Ontario St, Chicago, IL 60611. Tel 312-787-3997; Fax 312-787-8664; *Dir* Kathy Cottong
Open Mon - Fri 11 AM - 6 PM; No admis fee; Estab 1916; Contemporary art; Average Annual Attendance: 20,000; Mem: 1,200
Library Holdings: Book Volumes 3750; Exhibition Catalogs; Periodical Subscriptions 8
Activities: Lects for members only

M **AVERILL AND BERNARD LEVITON A + D GALLERY,** 619 S Wabash Ave, Chicago, IL 60605. Tel 312-369-8687; Fax 312-369-8009; *Gallery Dir* Jennifer Murray; *Asst Dir* Julianna Cuevas; *Preparator* Megan Ross
Open Tues-Wed & Fri-Sat 11AM-5PM, Thurs 11AM-8PM
Collections: works by emerging & estab artists

M **BALZEKAS MUSEUM OF LITHUANIAN CULTURE,** 6500 S Pulaski Rd, Chicago, IL 60629-5136. Tel 773-582-6500; Fax 773-582-5133; Elec Mail info@balzekasmuseum.org; Internet Home Page Address: www.balzekasmuseum.org; *Exec Dir & Pres* Stanley Balzekas Jr; *Dir Educ & Edit* Karile Vaitkute; *Office Mgr* Rita Striegel; *Cur Folk Art* Frank Zapolis; *Art Dir* Rita Janz; *Dir Genealogy Dept* Robert Balzekas; *Chmn Numismatic* Frank Passic; *Cur Cartography* Edward Pocius; *Dir Periodicals Coll* Irene Norbut; *Librn* Irena Pumputiene; *Chmn Mem, Com Rels & Mus Shop Mgr* Regina Vasiliauskiene; *Dir Intl Prog* Rasa Rudzykte
Open daily 10 AM - 4 PM; Admis adults $5, seniors & students $4, children 12 & under $2, discounts AAM & ICOM mems; mems no charge; Estab 1966 as a repository for collecting and preserving Lithuanian cultural treasures; Main Gallery 40 x 100; two other galleries 20 x20 & 10 x 15; Average Annual Attendance: 44,000; Mem: 2700; dues individual $30, family $40, supporting $50, genealogy $75, patron $100, organizations $250, sponsor $1,000, life $5,000
Income: $10,000 (financed by mem & donations)
Library Holdings: Book Volumes; CD-ROMs; Cards; Cassettes; Clipping Files; Compact Disks; DVDs; Exhibition Catalogs; Filmstrips; Framed Reproductions; Manuscripts; Maps; Motion Pictures; Original Art Works; Original Documents; Pamphlets; Periodical Subscriptions; Photographs; Prints; Records; Reproductions; Sculpture; Slides; Video Tapes
Special Subjects: Decorative Arts, Drawings, Ceramics, Prints, Textiles, Woodcuts, Tapestries, Graphics, Photography, Watercolors, Archaeology, Textiles, Costumes, Religious Art, Crafts, Folk Art, Woodcarvings, Jewelry, Maps, Coins & Medals, Embroidery, Stained Glass
Collections: Amber; archeology; archives; coins; fine art; folk art; graphics; maps; numismatics; paintings; philately; photography; rare books; rare maps; textiles; wooden folk art; Textiles; Wooden folkart; Maps; Paintings; Graphics
Exhibitions: Various exhibits of paintings, graphics & sculpture
Publications: Lithuanian Museum Review, quarterly
Activities: Classes for adults & children; docent progs; demonstrations; folk art workshops; lects open to mem, 20 vis lectrs per yr; gallery talks; tours; man or woman of the year award; original objects of art lent to other museums & galleries; lending collection contains books, nature artifacts, original art works, paintings, photographs & slides; book 5 traveling exhibs per yr; originate traveling exhibs to mem; mus shop sells books, magazines, original art, reproductions, prints, folk art, amber jewelry, souvenirs & t-shirts

L **Research Library,** 6500 S Pulaski Rd, Chicago, IL 60629. Tel 773-582-6500; Fax 773-582-5133; Elec Mail editor@lithuanianmuseum.org; Internet Home Page Address: www.lithaz.org; *Pres* Stanley Balzekas; *Librn* Robert A Balzekas
Open daily 10 AM - 4 PM; Estab 1966 to preserve Lithuanian-American literature & culture; Circ Non-circulating; Open to pub for reference only; Average Annual Attendance: 40,000
Income: Grants
Library Holdings: Audio Tapes; Book Volumes 40,000; Cards; Cassettes; Clipping Files; Exhibition Catalogs; Framed Reproductions; Manuscripts; Maps; Memorabilia; Micro Print; Original Art Works; Original Documents; Pamphlets; Photographs; Prints; Records; Reels; Reproductions; Sculpture; Slides; Video Tapes
Special Subjects: Art History, Folk Art, Decorative Arts, Photography, Graphic Arts, Maps, Prints, Historical Material, History of Art & Archaeology, Archaeology, Ethnology, Anthropology, Furniture, Architecture
Collections: Reproductions of Lithuanian artists; Information on Lithuanian artists & their works; original art work: painting, sculpture & rare maps; folk art
Exhibitions: Exhibs vary
Activities: Classes for adults & children in a variety of Lithuanian crafts; lects for mems only; vis lectrs 20 per yr; gallery talks; tours; originates traveling exhibs 20 per yr; mus sales shop sells books, magazines, original art, reproductions, prints, slides

THE CENTER FOR INTUITIVE AND OUTSIDE ART, 756 N Milwaukee Ave, Chicago, IL 60622-5939. Tel 312-243-9088; Fax 312-243-9089; Elec Mail intuit@art.org; Internet Home Page Address: www.art.org; *Dir* Cleo Wilson
Open Tues - Sat 11 AM - 5 PM, Thurs 11 AM - 7:30 PM; No admis fee; Estab 1991

M **CHICAGO ARCHITECTURE FOUNDATION,** 224 S Michigan Ave, Chicago, IL 60604-2505. Tel 312-922-3432; Fax 312-922-0481; Elec Mail info@architecture.org; Internet Home Page Address: www.architecture.org; *Pres* Lynn J Osmond; *John Hancock Shop* Dave Woollard; *Santa Fe Shop* Maribel Salazar; *Dir Pub Program* Bonita Mall; *Vice Chmn* Jan Grayson; *Dir Finance & Admis* Patrick Furlong
Open Mon-Sat 9AM-7PM ; No admis fee; Estab in 1966; comprehensive program of tours, lectures, exhibitions & special events to enhance pub awareness & appreciation of Chicago architecture; Average Annual Attendance: 200,000; Mem: 7000; dues $40
Income: Financed by mem, shop & tour center, foundation, government & private grants
Special Subjects: Architecture
Exhibitions: City Space
Publications: In Sites Newsletter, quarterly
Activities: Classes for adults; docent training; lect open to public, vis lectrs; tours; competitions; sales shop sells books, magazines, architecturally inspired gift items, stationery & posters

A **CHICAGO ART DEALERS ASSOCIATION,** 730 N Franklin, Ste 4 Chicago, IL 60654. Tel 312-649-0065; Fax 312-649-0255; Elec Mail info@chicagoartdealers.org; Internet Home Page Address: www.chicagoartdealers.org; *Exec Dir* Lynne Remington
Estab 1968; Mem: Membership: 40
Activities: Artist workshops; gallery talks; weekly tours; annual Vision celebration in July

M **CHICAGO ARTISTS' COALITION,** Coalition Gallery, 217 N Carpenter, Chicago, IL 60607-1712. Tel 312-781-0040; Tel 312-491-8888; Elec Mail alyson@chicagoartistscoalition.org; Internet Home Page Address: www.chicagoartistscoalition.org; *Exec Dir* Carolina O Jayaram Esq; *Mem & Mktg Dir* Alyson Koblas; *Exhib Initiatives Dir* Pepper Coate
Open Mon - Fri 10 AM - 5 PM; Estab 1975 to provide services, benefits,

information & support to visual artists. Resource center includes reference books, pamphlets & catalogs; Collaborative/co-operative gallery - artists submit application & a new group is juried in ea yr; Mem: 1800; mem open to all visual artists; dues $75 per yr
Income: $200,000 (financed by mem, city & state appropriation, donations, earned income projects, corporations & foundations)
Exhibitions: Art Loop Open - annual
Activities: Classes for adults; Lect open to public, 10-12 vis lectrs per year; gallery talks; tours; Special Achievement Award for Service to the Visual Arts in Chicago

M **CHICAGO CHILDREN'S MUSEUM,** 700 E Grand Ave, Chicago, IL 60611-3577. Tel 312-527-1000; Fax 312-527-9082; Internet Home Page Address: www.chichildrensmuseum.org; *Chmn Bd* Robert Barnett; *Pres & CEO* Jennifer Farrington; *Immediate Past Chmn* Gigi Pritzker Pucker; *Secy* William Lowry; *Treas* Laura Dunne
Open daily 10 AM - 5 PM, Thurs evenings 5 - 8 PM; Admis adults & children $12. seniors $11, mems & children under 1 no charge; Estab 1982 to inspire discovery & self-expression in children through interactive exhibits & programs; Average Annual Attendance: 500,000; Mem: dues $60 - $500
Income: $6,500,000 (financed by mem, foundation, corporate, government, individual support, earned income)
Exhibitions: Safe 'N' Sound; Under Construction; Water Ways; Inventing Lab; Infotech Arcade; Treehouse Trails; Play Maze
Activities: Classes for adults & children; docent progs; retail store sells books, prints, educational toys & games, music, videotapes, sweatshirts, t-shirts

A **CHICAGO HISTORY MUSEUM,** (Chicago Historical Society) 1601 N Clark St, Chicago, IL 60614-6038. Tel 312-642-4600; Fax 312-266-2077; Elec Mail bunch@chicagohistory.org; Internet Home Page Address: www.chicagohistory.org; *Dir Historical Documentation* Olivia Mahoney; *Dir Exhibs* Tamara Biggs; *Dir Publs* Rosemary Adams; *Deputy Dir Research* Russell Lewis; *VPres Finance* Robert Nauert; *Deputy Dir Interpretation & Educ* Phyllis Rabineau; *Dir Visitor Servs* Ginny Fitzgerald; *Dir Merchandising* Beth Hubbartt; *CEO & Pres* John Rowe; *Dir Human Resources* Bobbie Carter; *Dir History Educ* D Lynn McRainey; *Vice Chmn* Hill Hammock; *Dir Mktg* Karen Brown; *Dir Coll Svcs* Katherine Plourd; *Dir Information Serv* Cheryl Obermeyer; *Dir Properties* Larry Schmitt; *Dir Corporate Event* Kathy Horky; *Dir Accounting* Shari Massey
Open Mon-Sat 9:30AM-4:30PM, Sun Noon-5PM; Admis adults $14, seniors & students 13-22 with ID $12, mems & children under 13 free, Mon free; Estab 1856 to collect, interpret & present the rich, multi-cultural history of Chicago & Ill as well as selected areas of Am history to the public; Maintains galleries & Research Ctr; Average Annual Attendance: 175,000; Mem: 8500; dues family $60, individual $50, seniors & students family $55, seniors & students single $45; annual meeting in Oct
Income: $7,200,000 (financed by endowment, mem, city & state appropriations & public donations)
Library Holdings: Audio Tapes; Book Volumes; Manuscripts; Original Documents; Photographs; Prints; Video Tapes
Special Subjects: Architecture, Costumes, Historical Material, Manuscripts, Photography, Prints, Sculpture, Painting-American, Decorative Arts
Collections: Over 22 million artifacts & documents incl: Architectural Archive; industrial & architectural photographs; Chicago History, Early American History; Chicago Daily News Photo Collection; Oral History, Film & Video Coll; Books & Published Materials Coll
Exhibitions: Chicago History Galleries; We the People; America in the Age of Lincoln; A House Divided
Publications: Books, Calendar of Events & newsletter, quarterly; catalogs; Chicago History, quarterly
Activities: Classes for adults; lect open to public, 15-20 vis lectrs per year; gallery talks; tours; sales shop selling books, magazines, prints, reproductions, slides

L **Research Center,** 1601 N Clark St, Chicago, IL 60614-6038. Tel 312-642-4600; Fax 312-266-2077; Internet Home Page Address: www.chicagohistory.org
Call for hours; Admis general $5 per day, $15 per yr, mems & students gr 1-12 free; children under 6 not admitted; photocopying fees apply
Collections: ARCHIE online catalog; Electronic Encyclopedia of Chicago; Chicago Daily News Database; Online resources for research topics: History Fair, architecture & building history, family history; Online exhibs incl Lincoln at 200: Lincoln & the West: 1809-1860 & The Fiery Trial: Abraham Lincoln & The Civil War; Louis Sullivan at 150; The Great Chicago Fire & The Web of Memory; The Dramas of Haymarket; Wet With Blood; Studs Terkel; History Files website

L **CHICAGO PUBLIC LIBRARY,** Harold Washington Library Center, 400 S State St 8th Fl, Art Information Center, Visual & Performing Arts Chicago, IL 60605-1203. Tel 312-747-4800; Elec Mail art@chipublib.org; Internet Home Page Address: www.chipublib.org; *Commissioner* Brian Bannon; *Head Art Information Center* Robert Sloane; *Picture Coll Librn* Angela Holtzman; *Serials/Architecture* Laura Morgan; *Performing Arts Librn* Wil Sumner; *Fine Arts Librn* Carol LeBras; *Chicago Artists' Archive* Leslie Petterson
Open Mon-Thurs 9AM-9PM, Fri & Sat 9AM-5PM, Sun 1-5PM; No admis fee; Estab 1872 as a free public library & reading room; The original building was built in 1897. New location of central library. The Harold Washington Library Center was opened to the public in 1991
Income: Financed by city & state appropriation
Library Holdings: Book Volumes 175,000; Clipping Files; DVDs 250; Exhibition Catalogs; Fiche 6192; Memorabilia; Original Art Works; Other Holdings Videodiscs; Pamphlets; Periodical Subscriptions 515; Photographs; Records; Reels; Reproductions; Sculpture; Slides; Video Tapes 1500
Special Subjects: Decorative Arts, Bookplates & Bindings, Architecture
Collections: Dance collection: folk dance index, Chicago dance collection, Ann Barzel dance film archive; Fine Arts collection: Chicago Artists' Archive, Picture Collection; Van Damm Collectiion of New York theater photographs 1919-1961; Chicago Stagebills; Chicago Reader motion picture stills
Exhibitions: Various rotating exhibits featuring materials from the collections; (Ongoing) Called to the Challenge: The Legacy of Harold Washington
Activities: Dance & art progs; lect open to pub; concerts; gallery talks; documentary film series; tours; sponsored competitions

M **CHICAGO STATE UNIVERSITY - PRESIDENT'S GALLERY,** 9501 S King Dr, Cook Admin Bldg, 3rd Fl Chicago, IL 60628. Tel 773-995-3905
Open Mon - Fri 8 AM - 6 PM
Collections: Paintings & photographs
Activities: Lectures; demonstrations; workshops; special events

M **COLUMBIA COLLEGE CHICAGO,** Museum of Contemporary Photography, 600 S Michigan Ave, Chicago, IL 60606-1900. Tel 312-663-5554; Fax 312-369-8067; Elec Mail mocp@colum.edu; Internet Home Page Address: www.mocp.org; *Assoc Dir* Natasha Egan; *Mgr Exhib* Stephanie Conaway; *Dir* Rod Slemmons; *Cur* Karen Irvine; *Mgr Col* Kristin Freeman; *Mgr Educ* Corinne Rose; *Mgr Develop Commun* Jeff Arnett
OpenMon - Fri 10 AM -5 PM, Thurs until 8 PM, Sun Noon - 5 PM; No admis fee; Estab 1976 to exhibit, collect & promote contemporary photog; 4000 sq ft on two levels; newly designed 1500 sq ft main exhibition gallery permits a spacious installation of 200 photographs; upper level gallery can accommodate an additional 200-300 prints; Average Annual Attendance: 90,000; Mem: 450; dues $20-2500
Special Subjects: Photography
Collections: Contemporary American photography, including in-depth holdings of works by Harold Allen, Harry Callahan, Barbara Crane, Louise Dahl-Wolfe, Dorothea Lange, Danny Lyon, Barbara Morgan, David Plowden, Anne Naggle & Joel Peter-Witkin
Exhibitions: Rotate exhibitions five times per yr
Publications: Exhibit catalogs
Activities: Educ dept: classes at Chicago Public Schools; lects open to pub, 10 vis lectrs per yr; gallery talks; tours; lending collection contains photographs; book traveling exhibs 2 per yr; originate traveling exhibs; mus shop sells books

L **Library,** 624 S Michigan Ave, Chicago, IL 60605. Tel 312-369-7900; Fax 312-369-8062; Elec Mail askalibrarian@colum.edu; Internet Home Page Address: www.lib.colum.edu; *Dean of Lib* Jo Cates; *Head Technical Serv & Coll Mgr* Dennis McGuire; *Head Access Serv* Roland C Hansen; *Head Ref & Instruction* Arlie Sims; *Head Col Archives & Digital Colls* Heidi Marshall
Open Mon - Thurs 8 AM - 10 PM, Fri 8 AM - 6 PM, Sat 9 AM - 5 PM, Sun Noon - 5 PM; Estab 1893 to provide library & media services & materials in support of the curriculum & to serve the col community as a whole; Circ 101,902; For lending & reference
Library Holdings: Book Volumes 260,000; Compact Disks 8500; DVDs 8000; Exhibition Catalogs; Fiche; Motion Pictures; Other Holdings Sound Recording (CDs) 15,000; Periodical Subscriptions 1400; Video Tapes 12,000
Special Subjects: Film, Photography, Commercial Art, Graphic Arts, Graphic Design, Painting-American, Theatre Arts, Interior Design, Video
Exhibitions: Art in the Library Exhibit ongoing quarterly exhibits; Alumni on Five Biannual Exhibs
Activities: Lectures open to pub; 2 visiting lectrs per year

M **DUSABLE MUSEUM OF AFRICAN AMERICAN HISTORY,** 740 E 56th Pl, Chicago, IL 60637-1495. Tel 773-947-0600; Fax 773-947-0677; Internet Home Page Address: www.dusablemuseum.org; *Founder* Margaret T Burrough; *Registrar* Theresa Christopher; *Chief Cur* Selean Holmes
Open Tues - Sat 10 AM - 5 PM, Sun Noon - 5 PM; Admis adults $3, children 6-13 & students $1, groups by appointment; Estab 1961 as history & art museum on African American history; Mem: Dues corp $1000, family $35, general $25, student & senior citizen $15
Special Subjects: Photography, Prints, Sculpture, Afro-American Art
Collections: Historical archives; paintings; photographs; prints; sculpture
Publications: Books of poems, children's stories, African & African-American history; Heritage Calendar, annual
Activities: Lect; guided tours; book traveling exhibitions; sales shop sells curios, sculpture, prints, books & artifacts

M **FIELD MUSEUM,** 1400 S Lake Shore Dr, Chicago, IL 60605-2496. Tel 312-922-9410; Fax 312-922-0741; Internet Home Page Address: www.fieldmuseum.org; *Pres & CEO* John W McCarter Jr; *VPres Educ & Library Coll* Elizabeth C Babcock; *VPres & Gen Counsel* Joe Brennan; *VPres Institutional Advancement* Sheila Cawley; *Exec VPres* J W Croft; *Sr VPres Colls & Research* Lance Grande; *Sr VPres Mus Enterprises* Laura M Sadler
Open daily 9 AM - 5 PM, cl Christmas; Admis adults $15, sr citizens & students $12, children 3-11 $10, discounts to Chicago residents; Estab 1893 to preserve & disseminate knowledge of natural history; 22 anthropological exhibition halls, including a Hall of Primitive Art are maintained; Average Annual Attendance: 1,400,000; Mem: 25,000; dues $60 & $125
Income: Financed by endowment, mem, city & state appropriations & federal & earned funds
Special Subjects: Primitive art
Collections: Anthropological, botanical, geological & zoological colls totaling over 19,000,000 artifacts & specimens, including 100,000 art objects from North & South America, Oceania, Africa, Asia & prehistoric Europe
Exhibitions: Permanent exhibitions: Ancient Egypt Exhibition; Prehistoric Peoples Exhibition; Dinosaur Hall; The American Indian; Pacific Exhibition
Publications: In the Field, monthly; Fieldiana (serial)
Activities: Classes for adults & children; lects open to pub, 25 vis lectrs per yr; concerts; gallery talks; tours; exten dept serving Chicago area; original objects of art lent to qualified museum or other scholarly institutions; originates traveling exhibs; mus shop selling books, magazines, prints, slides

L **Library,** 1200 S Lake Shore Dr, Chicago, IL 60605-2402. Tel 312-665-7887; Fax 312-427-7269; Elec Mail harlow@fieldmuseum.org; *Librn & Spec Coll Librn* Benjamin Williams
Open Mon - Fri 8:30 AM - 4:30 PM
Library Holdings: Book Volumes 250,000; Periodical Subscriptions 4000
Special Subjects: Archaeology, Asian Art, American Indian Art, Anthropology, Antiquities-Egyptian
Collections: Rare Book Room housing 6500 vols

C **THE FIRST NATIONAL BANK OF CHICAGO,** Art Collection, One Bank One Plaza, Ste IL1-0525 Chicago, IL 60670. Tel 312-732-5935; *Dir Art Prog & Cur* Lisa K Erf; *Registrar* John W Dodge; *Cur Asst* Karen Indeck
Open to public by appointment only; No admis fee; Estab 1968 to assemble works

of art to serve as a permanent extension of daily life; Collection displayed throughout bank building and overseas offices
Special Subjects: African Art, Afro-American Art, Anthropology, Antiquities-Byzantine, Antiquities-Etruscan, Antiquities-Oriental, Antiquities-Roman, Archaeology, Architecture, Asian Art, Bookplates & Bindings, Bronzes, Carpets & Rugs, Cartoons, Ceramics, Drawings, Enamels, Eskimo Art, Etchings & Engravings, Ethnology, Sculpture, Textiles, Watercolors, Woodcarvings, Woodcuts
Collections: Art from Africa, America, Asia, Australia, the Caribbean Basin, Europe, Latin America, Near East & the South Seas ranging from Sixth Century BC to the present
Activities: Individual objects of art lent only to major exhibs in museums; originate traveling exhibs

M **GLESSNER HOUSE MUSEUM,** 1800 S Prairie Ave Chicago, IL 60616-1320. Tel 312-326-1480; Fax 312-326-1397; Elec Mail glessnerhouse@sbcglobal.net; Internet Home Page Address: www.glessnerhouse.org; *Exec Dir& Cur* William Tyre; *Mus Coord* Gwendolyn Carrion; *Asst to Exec Dir* Lynne Mickle Smaczny; *Asst Cur* Rebecca Young LaBarre
Open Wed - Sun 11:30 AM - 4 PM; Admis adults $10/combo $15, students & seniors $12, children $8; Estab. 1966 house saved from demolition; estab 1994 to engage diverse audiences in exploring urban life & design through preservation & interpretation of the historic home of John & Frances Glessner. Glessner House Museum works to increase public awareness, understanding, and appreciation for the history, culture and architecture of Chicago as represented in the lives & home of the of the Glessner household and the surrounding Prairie Ave Historic District; Late 19th c. Arts & Crafts Home designed by H. H. Richardson; Average Annual Attendance: 8,000; Mem: 200; dues $30-50
Income: Non-profit; financed by mem, tours, programs, grants & rentals
Special Subjects: Decorative Arts, Historical Material, Ceramics, Glass, Photography, Porcelain, Prints, Period Rooms, Silver, Textiles, Bronzes, Manuscripts, Architecture, Costumes, Ceramics, Woodcarvings, Etchings & Engravings, Furniture, Metalwork, Carpets & Rugs, Restorations, Calligraphy, Embroidery, Reproductions, Bookplates & Bindings
Collections: William DeMorgan Ceramics; Emil Galle Glass; Morris & Co Textiles; English arts & crafts; Isaac Scott Collection
Exhibitions: Richardson & His Works (permanent)
Publications: The Glessner Journal, quarterly
Activities: Classes for adults & children; docent training; dramatic progs; lects open to pub, 4-8 vis lectrs per yr; gallery talks; forum discussions; symposia; tours; original objects of art lent to galleries which are mounting exhibs on architecture & decorative arts exhibs; lending collection contains architectural ornaments; mus shop sells books, magazines, prints, stationery & small gift items

L **HARRINGTON COLLEGE OF DESIGN,** Design Library, 200 W Madison St 2nd Fl, Chicago, IL 60606-3433. Tel 877-939-4975; Internet Home Page Address: www.interiordesign.edu

M **HENRY B CLARKE HOUSE MUSEUM,** 1827 S Indiana Ave, Chicago, IL 60616-1308. Tel 312-326-1480 (Glessner House Mus); Elec Mail info@clarkehousemuseum.org; Internet Home Page Address: www.clarkehousemuseum.org
Open Wed - Sun Noon & 2 PM; Admis Clarke $10, Glessner & Clarke $15; Estab 1982; Chicago's oldest building & only Greek Revival structure. House was built in 1836 & includes period rooms; Average Annual Attendance: 3,000; Mem: 600; dues $35
Library Holdings: Auction Catalogs 600; Book Volumes
Collections: Early 19th century period furniture & decorative objects
Activities: Docent training; classes for children; lect open to public, 4 vis lectrs per year; concerts; tours; sales shop sells books & magazines

M **HYDE PARK ART CENTER,** 5020 S. Cornell Ave, Chicago, IL 60615-3016. Tel 773-324-5520; Fax 773-324-6641; Elec Mail generalinfo@hydeparkart.org; Internet Home Page Address: www.hydeparkart.org; *Exec Dir* Kate Lorenz; *Chmn* Janis Kanter; *Dir Exhibs* Allison Peters; *Dir Educ* Mike Nourse; *Mktg & Communs Mgr* Brook Rosini
Open Mon - Thurs 10 AM - 8 PM, Fri - Sat 10 AM - 5 PM, Sun noon - 5 PM; No admis fee; Estab 1939 to stimulate an interest in art; Average Annual Attendance: 45,000; Mem: 500; dues family $55
Income: $600,000 (financed by endowment, mem, city & state appropriation, foundations, corporations & private contributions)
Special Subjects: Drawings, Painting-American, Photography, Sculpture, Watercolors, Textiles, Ceramics, Crafts, Folk Art, Etchings & Engravings
Exhibitions: (see website for details)
Publications: Quarterly newsletter, exhibition catalogues
Activities: Classes for adults & children; lect open to public; gallery talks; scholarships offered; exten prog serves South & West sides of Chicago; sales shop sells original art

M **ILLINOIS STATE MUSEUM,** Chicago Gallery, 100 W Randolph, Ste 2-100, Chicago, IL 60601. Tel 312-814-5322; Fax 312-814-3471; Elec Mail jstevens@museum.state.il.us; Internet Home Page Address: www.museum.state.il.us/; *Preparations & Asst Cur* Doug Stapleton; *Dir Art* Jim Zimmer
Open Mon - Fri 9 AM - 5 PM; No admis fee; Estab 1985 for the purpose of promoting an awareness of the variety of art found & produced in Illinois; Three large galleries & three smaller galleries provide a flexible space for a diverse exhibition program. Exhibits are produced by the Illinois State Mus & the State of Illinois Art Gallery; Average Annual Attendance: 47,000
Special Subjects: Painting-American, Photography, Sculpture, American Indian Art, Folk Art, Historical Material
Collections: Illinois Art, Historical & Contemporary
Publications: Exhibit catalogs
Activities: Lects open to pub; 12 vis lectrs per yr; gallery talks; tours; internships offered; book traveling exhibs 4 per yr; originate traveling exhibs traveling to ISM sites; mus shop sells books & original art

M **Illinois Artisans Shop,** 100 W Randolph St, Chicago, IL 60601-3218. Tel 312-814-5321; Fax 312-814-2439; Elec Mail cpatterson@museum.state.il.us; Internet Home Page Address: www.museum.state.us; *Dir IL Artisans Prog* Carolyn Patterson; *Mgr ILL Artisans Shop* Cara Schlorff
Open Mon - Fri 9 AM - 5 PM; No admis fee; Estab 1985; A nonprofit program to showcase the craft work of Illinois artisans accepted in a consignment shop & to educate the pub about the scope of craft art; Mem: 1400 artists in program; qualification for mem: juried art work
Income: Financed by state appropriation & retail sales of art work
Exhibitions: Rotating exhibits
Publications: Craft Events in Illinois, biannual; Illinois Artisan Newsletter, periodic
Activities: Educ dept; public demonstrations; monthly workshops; lects open to pub; sales shop sells original art

M **Illinois Artisans & Visitors Centers,** 14967 Gun Creek Trail, Whittington, IL 62897-1000. Tel 618-629-2220; Fax 618-629-2704; *Dir ILL Artisans Prog* Carolyn Patterson; *Dir SIACM* Mary Lou Galloway; *Mgr IL Artisans Shop* Romaula Coleman; *Dir* Ellen Gantner
Open daily 9 AM - 5 PM; No admis fee; Estab 1990; A nonprofit program to showcase the craft work of Illinois artisans accepted in a consignment shop & to educate the pub about the scope of craft art; Mem: 1500 artists in program; qualification for mem: juried art work
Income: Financed by state appropriation & retail sales of art work
Activities: Demonstrations; classes for adults & children; lects open to pub; gallery talks; sales shop sells books, original art, prints

M **Museum Store,** 502 S Spring St, Springfield, IL 62706-5000. Tel 217-782-7387; Fax 217-782-1254; Elec Mail webmaster@museum.state.il.us; Internet Home Page Address: www.museum.state.il.us; *Mus Dir* Dr Bonnie W Styles; *Bd Chmn Ill State Mus Bd* George Rabb; *Assoc Dir* Karen A Witter; *Chief Fiscal Officer & HR Resources Mgr* Charlotte A Montgomery, CPA; *Dir Art* Kent Smith; *Asst Dir Art* Robert Sill; *Exhibs Design* Joe Hennessy; *Exhibs Prep* Paul Countryman; *Educ Chair* Beth Shea; *Asst Cur Educ* Nina Walthall; *Asst Cur Educ* Jennifer Kuehner; *Anthropology Chmn* Dr Terry Martin; *Cur Anthropology* Dr Robert Warren; *Cur Anthropology* Dr Johnathan Reyman; *Cur Geology* Dr Chris Widga; *Assoc Cur Botany* Dr Hong Qian; *Asst Cur Zoology* Dr Meredith Mahoney; *Asst Cur Zoology* H David Bohlen; *Librn* Pat Burg
Open Mon - Sat 8:30 AM - 5 PM, Sun Noon - 5 PM, cl New Year's Day, Thanksgiving & Christmas; No admis fee; Estab 1990; A not-for-profit program to showcase the craft work of Illinois artisans accepted in a consignment shop & to educate the pub about the scope of craft art; Average Annual Attendance: 230,000; Mem: 1500 artists in program
Income: Financed by state appropriation & retail sales of art work
Activities: Demonstrations; lects open to pub; mus shop sells books, original art, prints, reproductions, educational toys for children

M **INSTITUTE OF PUERTO RICAN ARTS & CULTURE,** 3015 W Division St, Chicago, IL 60622. Tel 773-486-8345; Fax 773-486-8806; Elec Mail info@iprac.org; Internet Home Page Address: www.iprac.org; *CEO & Pres* Billy Ocasio; *Office Mgr* Nereida Aurles
Open Tues - Fri 10 AM - 5 PM, Sat 10 AM - 3 PM; Admis free
Library Holdings: Book Volumes; Pamphlets; Photographs; Sculpture; Video Tapes
Special Subjects: Folk Art, Architecture, Sculpture, Graphics
Activities: Three vis lectrs per yr; concerts; mus shop sells books, magazines, original art & reproductions

M **INTUIT: THE CENTER FOR INTUITIVE & OUTSIDER ART,** 756 N Milwaukee Ave, Chicago, IL 60642-5939. Tel 312-243-9088; Fax 312-243-9089; Elec Mail intuit@art.org; Internet Home Page Address: www.art.org; *Exec Dir* Cleo F Wilson; *Prog Dir, Educ* Amanda Curtis; *Prog Coordr* Heather Holbus; *Mem Coordr* Kevin Mulcahy
Open Tues - Wed & Fri - Sat 11 AM - 5 PM, Thurs 11 AM - 7:30 PM; No admis fee; Estab 1991 to educate the public on outsider art; Maintains reference library & 2 display galleries; Average Annual Attendance: 10,000; Mem: 650; dues $40
Income: $400,000 (financed by mem & grants)
Library Holdings: Auction Catalogs; Audio Tapes; Book Volumes; Cards; Cassettes; Clipping Files; Compact Disks; DVDs; Exhibition Catalogs; Fiche; Kodachrome Transparencies; Lantern Slides; Manuscripts; Memorabilia; Micro Print; Original Documents; Other Holdings; Pamphlets; Periodical Subscriptions; Photographs; Records; Slides; Video Tapes
Special Subjects: Folk Art, Primitive art
Collections: Outsider Art; Henry Darger Room Collection, studio evocation/reproduction
Publications: The Outsider, 2 times per year
Activities: Docent training; lects open to pub; 6 vis lectrs per yr; concerts, gallery talks, tours; films; teacher fellowship prog; lending of original objects of art to Chicago Public Schools; approx once per yr; mus shop sells books, magazines, clothes, CDs, DVDs, jewelry

M **LOYOLA UNIVERSITY CHICAGO,** Loyola University Museum of Art, 820 N Michigan Ave, Chicago, IL 60611. Tel 312-915-7600; Fax 312-915-6388; Elec Mail luma@luc.edu; Internet Home Page Address: www.luc.edu/luma; *Dir Cultural Affairs* Pamela Ambrose; *Cur Martin D'Arcy Col* Jonathan Canning
Open Tues 11 AM - 8 PM, Wed - Sun 11 AM to 6 PM; No admis fee; Estab 1969 to display the permanent university collection of Medieval, Renaissance & Baroque decorative arts & paintings & rotating exhibs; Circ 4,000 titles; Average Annual Attendance: 30,000; Mem: 350; dues $50 - $1,000
Income: Financed by donations, endowment, mem & university support & earned income
Library Holdings: Auction Catalogs; Book Volumes 4,000; CD-ROMs; Cards; DVDs; Exhibition Catalogs
Special Subjects: Anthropology, Decorative Arts, Etchings & Engravings, Architecture, Ceramics, Conceptual Art, Antiquities-Assyrian, Pottery, Textiles, Woodcuts, Sculpture, Tapestries, Latin American Art, Prints, Sculpture, Bronzes, Textiles, Religious Art, Crafts, Painting-European, Silver, Painting-French, Ivory, Baroque Art, Painting-Flemish, Painting-Italian, Islamic Art, Gold, Stained Glass, Painting-German, Pewter, Painting-Russian, Enamels
Collections: Decorative arts, furniture, liturgical objects, paintings, sculptures & textiles

Publications: Exhibition catalogs
Activities: Educ dept, classes for adults & children; docent training; lect open to public, 20 vis lectrs per yr; concerts; gallery talks; tours on request; paintings & original objects of art lent to qualified museums; lending collection contains original art works, paintings & sculpture; organize traveling exhibs to univ mus; mus shop sells books, reproductions & jewelry

M **MUSEUM OF CONTEMPORARY ART,** 220 E Chicago Ave, Chicago, IL 60611-2644. Tel 312-280-2660; Fax 312-397-4095; Internet Home Page Address: www.mcachicago.org; *Dir* Madeleine Grynsztejn; *Educ Dir* Erika Hanner; *Dir of Admin* Helen Dunbeck; *Deputy Dir* Janet Alberti; *Chief Registrar & Exhib Mgr* Jennifer Draffen; *Dir Pub Rels* Karla Loring; *Dir of Performance Prog* Peter Taub; *Dir Spec Events & Rentals* Gina Crowley; *CFO* Peter Walton; *Dir MCA Store* Mark Millmore; *Chief Cur* Michael Darling; *Dir Design* James Goggin
Open Tues 10 AM - 8 PM, Wed - Sun 10 AM - 5 PM, cl Mon, Thanksgiving, Christmas & New Year's Day; No admis fee; suggested donation adults $12, students & seniors $7, members, military & children under 12 free, Tues free for IL residents; Estab 1967 as a forum for contemporary arts in Chicago; Average Annual Attendance: 280,000; Mem: 8500, dues advocate $1000, assoc $500, contributor $250, friend $150, household $75, individual $60, senior $40, student & out-of-town $30
Income: $14,000,000 (financed by endowment, mem, pub & private sources)
Special Subjects: Afro-American Art, Drawings, Collages, Photography, Painting-American, Prints, Sculpture, Oriental Art, Asian Art, Painting-Italian, Painting-German
Collections: Permanent coll: 2,500+ objects of 20th century & contemporary art, constantly growing through gifts & purchases; Examples of visual art from 1945 - present, focusing on surrealism, minimalism, conceptual photography & work by Chicago-based artists
Publications: Bimonthly calendar, exhibition catalogs, membership magazine
Activities: Classes for adults & children; family progs; docent training; teacher workshops; community outreach; lects; gallery talks; tours; performance; films; book traveling exhibs; originate traveling exhibs; mus shop sells books, designer jewelry & other gifts, magazines, original art & reproductions

L **Library,** 220 E Chicago Ave, Chicago, IL 60611. Tel 312-397-3894; Fax 312-397-4099; Elec Mail akaiser@mcachicago.org; *Librn* Dennis McGuire
Library collection, non-circulating; for reference
Income: Financed by endowment, mem, pub & pvt sources
Library Holdings: Book Volumes 15,000; Cassettes 400; Other Holdings Artist Files 125 drawers; Artists' Books 4300; Periodical Subscriptions 125; Slides 45,000; Video Tapes 300
Special Subjects: Art History, Conceptual Art

M **MUSEUM OF SCIENCE & INDUSTRY,** 57th St & Lake Shore Dr, Chicago, IL 60637-2093. Tel 773-684-1414; Fax 773-684-7141; Elec Mail contact@msichicago.org; Internet Home Page Address: www.msichicago.org; *Pres & CEO* David Mosena; *VPres Admin* Candida Miranda; *VPres Prog* Phelan Fretz; *Dir Educ* Jean Franczyk
Open Mon - Sat 9:30 AM - 4 PM, Sun 11 AM - 4 PM, cl Dec 25; see website for extended hours; Admis adults $15, seniors $14, children 3-11 $10, certain days free see website for details; parking fees; Estab 1926 to further pub understanding of science, technology, industry, medicine & related fields; Visitor-participation exhibits depicting scientific principles, technological applications & social implications in fields of art science; Omnimax Theatre; Average Annual Attendance: 2,000,000; Mem: 59,470; dues premier $180, family $115, individual $80, senior & student $55
Income: $16,200,000 (financed by endowment, mem, city & state appropriation, contributions & grants from companies, foundations & individuals)
Publications: AHA quarterly
Activities: Classes for adults & children; dramatic progs; field trips; summer camps; teacher workshops; Snoozeum; lects open to pub; tours; competitions; outreach activities; lending collection contains communications, transportation & textile equipment; book traveling exhibs; originate traveling exhibs; mus shop sells books, magazines, prints, slides, postcards & souvenirs

M **NAB GALLERY,** 1117 W Lake, Chicago, IL 60607. Tel 312-738-1620; Elec Mail contact@nabgallery.org; Internet Home Page Address: www.nabgallery.org; *Dir* Matt Robinson; *Bd Mem* Robert Horn; *Bd Mem* Craig A Anderson
Open Sat Noon - 5 PM; No admis fee; Estab 1974 as an artist-run space to show original artworks; Exhibits of Museum & Contemporary Art; Average Annual Attendance: 3,000; Mem: 10; open to artists with professional portfolio; dues $500; monthly meetings
Income: $15,000 (financed by mem)
Exhibitions: Local Artists Juried Exhibit: Vojta, Sensemann, Robinson, Daniels, Kronquist
Activities: Classes for adults; lect open to public; concerts; competitions; integrated art events; gallery talks

M **NATIONAL MUSEUM OF MEXICAN ART,** 1852 W 19th St, Chicago, IL 60608-2706. Tel 312-738-1503; Fax 312-738-9740; Elec Mail info@nationalmuseumofmexicanart.org; Internet Home Page Address: www.nationalmuseumofmexicanart.org; *Exec Dir* Carlos Tortolero; *Visual Arts Dir* Ceareo Moreno; *Permanent Coll* Rebecca D Meyers; *Assoc Dir* Juana Guzman
Open Tues - Sun 10 AM - 5 PM; No admis fee; Estab 1982; Average Annual Attendance: 110,000; Mem: 1,500; dues $15 & up
Income: $4,000,000 (financed by mem, city, state & federal appropriation, corporations & foundations)
Special Subjects: Latin American Art, Mexican Art, Photography, Prints, Folk Art
Collections: Mexican prints, photography & folk art collection; Latino art collection
Exhibitions: Jose Guadalupe Posada; rotating 4 per year
Activities: Classes for children in docent progs; lects open to pub, 4 vis lectrs per yr; mus shop sells books, original art, folk art & prints

M **NATIONAL VIETNAM VETERANS ART MUSEUM,** 1801 S Indiana Ave, Chicago, IL 60616-1308. Tel 312-326-0270; Fax 312-326-9767; Elec Mail info@nvvam.org; Internet Home Page Address: www.nvvam.org
Open May - Sept Tues - Fri 11 AM - 6 PM, Sat 10 AM - 5 PM, Sun 12 - 5 PM; Labor Day to Memorial Day Tues - Fri 11 AM - 6 PM, Sat 10 AM - 5 PM; Admis adults $10, students $7, members free
Collections: paintings; photographs; sculpture
Publications: newsletter, Artifacts
Activities: Mus shop

L **NEWBERRY LIBRARY,** 60 W Walton St, Chicago, IL 60610-3380. Tel 312-943-9090; Fax 312-255-3513; Internet Home Page Address: www.newberry.org; *Pres & Librn* David Spadafora; *Librn* Mary Wyly; *VPres Finance & Admin* Jim Burke; *VPres Research & Educ* Jim Grossman; *VPres Develop* Michelle Burns
Open Tues - Thurs 10 AM - 6 PM, Fri & Sat 9 AM - 5 PM; No admis fee; Estab 1887 for research in the history & humanities of Western Civilization; Circ Non-circulating; For reference only. Maintains two small galleries for exhibitions; Mem: 1950; dues $35; annual meeting in Oct
Income: $4,500,000 (financed by endowment, mem, gifts, federal, corporate & foundation funds)
Purchases: $400,000
Library Holdings: Audio Tapes; Book Volumes 1,400,000; Cards; Clipping Files; Exhibition Catalogs; Fiche; Manuscripts 5,000,000; Memorabilia; Motion Pictures; Original Art Works; Pamphlets; Periodical Subscriptions 900; Photographs; Records; Reels; Video Tapes
Special Subjects: Art History, Graphic Arts, Manuscripts, Maps, History of Art & Archaeology, Ethnology, American Western Art, American Indian Art, Southwestern Art
Collections: Edward Ayer Collection, Manuscripts & Maps related to European expansion to the Americas & the Pacific; Everett D Graff Collection of Western Americana books & manuscripts; John M Wing Foundation Collection on history of printing & aesthetics of book design; Rudy L Ruggles Collection on American constitutional & legal history
Publications: A Newberry Newsletter, quarterly; Center for Renaissance Studies Newsletter, 3 times per yr; Mapline, quarterly newsletter; Meeting Ground, bi-annual newsletter; Origins, quarterly newsletter
Activities: Classes for adults; dramatic progs; docent training; lects open to pub, some open to members only, 35 vis lectrs per yr; concerts; gallery talks; tours; schols & fels offered; individual paintings & original objects of art lent to mus & libraries on restricted basis; book traveling exhibs 1-2 per yr; sales shop sells books, reproductions, slides

M **NORTH PARK UNIVERSITY,** (North Park College) Carlson Tower Gallery, 3225 W Foster, Chicago, IL 60625. Tel 773-244-6200; Fax 773-244-5230; Internet Home Page Address: www.northpark.edu; *Dir Gallery* Tim Lowly
Open Mon - Fri 9 AM - 4 PM, occasional weekend evenings; No admis fee; Educational develop of aesthetic appreciation
Special Subjects: Religious Art
Collections: Original contemporary Christian, Illinois & Scandinavian art
Activities: Classes for adults; lect open to public, 1-2 vis lectrs per year; concerts; exten dept serves Chicago; book traveling exhibs, 1-2 per year

M **NORTHEASTERN ILLINOIS UNIVERSITY,** Gallery, 5500 N Saint Louis Ave, Art Dept Chicago, IL 60625-4625. Tel 773-442-4944; Fax 773-442-4920; Internet Home Page Address: www.neiu.edu/~avt/gal.html; *Dir* Heather Weber
Open Mon-Fri 10 AM - 6PM & by appt; No admis fee; Estab Feb 1973 for the purpose of providing a link between the University & the local community on a cultural & aesthetic level, to bring the best local & midwest artists to this community; Gallery is located in the Fine Arts building on the University campus; Average Annual Attendance: 8,000
Income: Financed by Department of Art funds and personnel
Exhibitions: Various exhib
Publications: Postcard announcements; brochures; catalogs
Activities: Lects open to pub; 4-6 vis lectrs per yr; gallery talks; tours

M **PALETTE & CHISEL ACADEMY OF FINE ARTS,** 1012 N Dearborn St, Chicago, IL 60610-2804. Tel 312-642-4400; Fax 312-642-4317; Elec Mail fineart1012@sbcglobal.net; Internet Home Page Address: www.paletteandchisel.org; *Pres* Linda Boatman; *Exec Dir* William Ewers
Gallery open Mon - Fri 11AM - 6 PM, Sat 11AM - 4 PM, workshops are open to the pub on a regular basis; No admis fee; Estab & incorporated 1895 to provide a meeting/work place for the visual arts; Building contains galleries, classrooms, studios & library; Mem: 430; dues $360; patron & nonresident mem available
Collections: Permanent Collection: works by James Montgomery Flagg; J Jeffery Grant Permanent Collection; Alphonse Mucha; Richard Schmid Permanent Collection; James Montgomery Flagg Permanent Collection
Exhibitions: Five Members Award Shows; guest artists & organizations frequently exhibited
Publications: The Quick Sketch, monthly
Activities: Educ events; classes for artists; lect open to public; tours; competitions with awards; scholarships offered

M **POLISH MUSEUM OF AMERICA,** 984 N Milwaukee Ave, Chicago, IL 60642-4101. Tel 773-384-3352; Fax 773-384-3799; Elec Mail pma@polishmuseumofamerica.org; monika-nowak@polishmuseumofamerica.org; Internet Home Page Address: www.polishmuseumofamerica.org; *Pres* Maria Ciesla; *Dir* Jan M Lorys; *Archivist* Halina Misterka; *Head Librn* Matgorzata Kot; *Graphic Art Coll Cur* Monika Nowak
Open daily 11 AM - 4 PM; Admis adults $7, seniors & students $6, under 12 $5; Estab 1935 & opened 1937, to preserve the artistic, cultural, historic & literary heritage of Polish Americans and Poles throughout the world; A specialized mus & gallery containing works of Polish artists & Polish-American culture artists is maintained; Average Annual Attendance: 10,000; Mem: 1,500; dues $25
Income: Financed by donations, memberships & grants
Special Subjects: Etchings & Engravings, Prints, Silver, Sculpture, Tapestries, Watercolors, Costumes, Religious Art, Folk Art, Decorative Arts, Historical Material, Maps, Coins & Medals, Miniatures, Painting-Polish, Military Art, Reproductions
Collections: Originals dating to beginning of 20th century, a few older pieces; Pulaski at Savannah (Batowski); works of Polish artists, Polish-American artists & works on Polish subject; Nikifor, Jan Styka, Wojciech Kossak; paintings from the

coll of the Polish Pavilion from 1939 World's Fair in NY; large coll of Paderewski memorabilia, including the last piano he played on; prints & posters coll
Exhibitions: Modern Polish Art; folk art; militaria
Publications: Exhibit Catalogs; Art Collection Catalog
Activities: Classes for children; lects open to pub, 5 vis lectrs per yr; tours; concerts; gallery talks; sponsoring of competitions; mus shop sells books, reproductions, prints, Polish Folk items, amber & crystal, merchandise
L   **Research Library,** 984 N Milwaukee Ave, Chicago, IL 60642-4101. Tel 773-384-3352; Fax 773-384-3799; Elec Mail pma@prcua.org; Internet Home Page Address: www.polishmuseumofamerica.org; *Head Librn* Malgorzata Kot; *Dir* Jan M Lorys; *Treas* Camille Kopielski; *Chmn* Wallace M Ozog; *Secy* Jennifer Crissey; *Archivist* Halina Misterka; *Pres* Maria Ciesla; *Mus Shop Mgr* Mary Jane Robles; *Librn* Krystyna Grell; *Opers Mgr* Richard Kujawa; *Asst Librn* Agnieszka Migiel
Open 11 AM - 4 PM, cl Thurs; No admis fee; suggested donation adults $5, senior or student $4, under 16 $3; Estab 1935; For reference only; interlibrary circulation; Mem : 350
Library Holdings: Audio Tapes; Book Volumes 100,000; Cassettes; Clipping Files; DVDs; Exhibition Catalogs; Fiche; Filmstrips; Framed Reproductions; Manuscripts; Maps; Memorabilia; Motion Pictures; Original Art Works; Other Holdings Newspapers; Pamphlets; Periodical Subscriptions 125; Photographs 20,000; Prints; Records; Reels; Reproductions 1000; Sculpture; Slides 2000; Video Tapes
Special Subjects: Folk Art, Decorative Arts, Film, Photography, Graphic Arts, Manuscripts, Maps, Painting-American, Posters, Historical Material, Judaica, Portraits, Crafts, Theatre Arts, Ethnology, Fashion Arts, Costume Design & Constr, Painting-Polish, Stained Glass, Dolls, Embroidery, Textiles, Woodcarvings, Woodcuts, Coins & Medals, Architecture
Collections: Haiman; Paderewski; Polish Art; Graphical Art; Posters, paintings, sculpture; 1939 New York World's Fair - Polish Pavilion; Music coll: song sheets, records, piano rolls, manuscripts; Genealogy materials
Publications: Art Collection catalog
Activities: Lects

PRINT COUNCIL OF AMERICA
For further information, see National and Regional Organizations

A   **THE RENAISSANCE SOCIETY,** 5811 S Ellis Ave, Cobb Hall - Rm 418 Chicago, IL 60637-1404. Tel 773-702-8670; Fax 773-702-9669; Elec Mail haberman@uchicago.edu; Internet Home Page Address: www.renaissancesociety.org; *Educ Dir & Assoc Cur* Hamza Walker; *Develop Dir* Lori Bartman; *Publications Dir* Karen Reimer; *Mktg Dir* Yuri Stone; *Dir & Chief Cur* Solveig Olvstebo; *Office Mgr* Lise Haberman
Open Tues - Fri 10 AM - 5 PM, Sat & Sun Noon - 5 PM, cl summer; No admis fee; Founded 1915 to advance the understanding & appreciation of the arts in all forms; Average Annual Attendance: 32,000; Mem : 500; dues $50; annual meeting in June
Exhibitions: Four changing exhibitions per yr
Publications: Exhibit catalogs
Activities: Educ dept; lect open to public; concerts; gallery talks; tours; film programs; performances; mus shop sells editions, books

M   **ROY BOYD GALLERY,** 739 N Wells St, Chicago, IL 60654-3520. Tel 312-642-1606; Fax 312-642-2143; Elec Mail info@royboydgallery.com; Internet Home Page Address: royboydgallery.com; *Co-Dir* Ann Boyd; *Dir* Roy Boyd; *Assoc Dir* Marco Pedroso
Open Tues - Sat 10 AM - 5:30 PM; No admis fee; Estab 1972 to exhibit art
Special Subjects: Drawings, Painting-American, Photography, Prints, Sculpture, Watercolors, Bronzes, Collages
Collections: Contemporary American paintings; Russian & Baltic photography; sculpture & works on paper

L   **SAINT XAVIER UNIVERSITY,** Byrne Memorial Library, 3700 W 103rd St, Art Dept Chicago, IL 60655-3105. Tel 773-298-3352, 3364; Fax 773-779-5231; Internet Home Page Address: www.sxu.edu/libr/library; *Dir* Mark Vargas
Open Mon-Thurs 7:45 AM-10 PM, Fri 7:45 AM-7 PM, Sat 8 AM-6 PM, Sun Noon-10 PM; Estab 1847
Income: Financed by college funds & contributions
Library Holdings: Book Volumes 160,600; Cards; Kodachrome Transparencies; Motion Pictures; Original Art Works; Periodical Subscriptions 890; Records; Slides 10,000; Video Tapes
Collections: Permanent art collection

L   **SCHOOL OF ART INSTITUTE OF CHICAGO,** Video Data Bank, 112 S Michigan Ave, Chicago, IL 60603-6105. Tel 312-629-6100; Fax 312-541-8073; Elec Mail info@vdb.org; Internet Home Page Address: www.vdb.org; *Dir* Albina Manning
Open Mon - Fri 9 AM - 5 PM; No admis fee; School estab 1892, library estab 1976 to distribute, preserve & promote videos by & about contemporary artists; Average Annual Attendance: 500,000
Income: $550,000 (finance by grants & earned income)
Library Holdings: Video Tapes 3000
Special Subjects: Art History, Film, Mixed Media, Photography, Painting-American, Painting-British, Painting-German, Sculpture, Video
Collections: Video Tapes: Early Video History, Independent Video/Alternative Media, Latin/South America, Media Literacy, On Art & Artists
Publications: Annual catalog of holdings

L   **SCHOOL OF THE ART INSTITUTE OF CHICAGO,** John M Flaxman Library, 112 S Michigan Ave., Chicago, IL 60603-6105. Tel 312-899-5097; Fax 312-899-1851; Elec Mail ceike@artic.edu; *Reference Librn* Kate Jarboe; *Head Technical Svcs* Fred Hillbruner; *Bibliographer* Henrietta Zielinski; *Artists' Book Coll Specialist* Doro Boehme; *Cataloger* Sylvia Choi; *Dir* Claire Eike
Open Mon - Thurs 8:30 AM - 9:30 PM, Fri 8:30 AM - 6 PM, Sat noon - 6PM, Sun Noon - 6 PM; Estab 1967 to provide a strong working collection for School's programs in the visual & related arts; Circ 54,002; Average Annual Attendance: 80,000

Income: 701,445 (financed by the operational budgets of the school of Art Institute of Chicago)
Purchases: $189,870
Library Holdings: Audio Tapes 1,000; Book Volumes 65,000; CD-ROMs 75; Cassettes 700; Clipping Files; Compact Disks 1,000; DVDs 100; Exhibition Catalogs; Fiche; Filmstrips 750; Motion Pictures 663; Other Holdings 4,000; Periodical Subscriptions 350; Records 100; Video Tapes 1,000
Collections: Joan Flasch Artists Book Collection; Film Study Collection; Tony Zwicker Archives

SOCIETY OF ARCHITECTURAL HISTORIANS
For further information, see National and Regional Organizations

M   **SPERTUS INSTITUTE OF JEWISH STUDIES,** 610 S Michigan Ave, Chicago, IL 60605-1901. Tel 312-322-1700; Fax 312-922-3934; Elec Mail info@spertus.edu; Internet Home Page Address: www.spertus.edu; *Pres & CEO* Hal M Lewis, PhD; *Cur Coll* Ilana Segal; *Coll Mgr* Kathy Bloch; *Coll Asst* Tom Gengler; *Dir Programming* Beth Schenker
Open Sun-Wed 10AM-5PM, Thurs 10AM-6PM, cl Fri & Sat for Jewish Sabbath & Jewish & nat holidays; No admis fee; Estab 1967 for interpreting & preserving the 3500-year-old heritage embodied in Jewish history; Circ 1,000; Changing exhibs of art & artifacts from the Jewish experience; Average Annual Attendance: 35,000; Mem: 1 yr/2 yrs Spertus net $30/55, senior $40/70, basic $50/90, household $65/120, assoc $150, fellow $250, patron $500, benefactor $1,000, angel $5,000
Income: Financed by contributions & subsidy from Spertus Institute
Library Holdings: Auction Catalogs; Audio Tapes; Book Volumes; CD-ROMs; Cassettes; Clipping Files; Compact Disks; DVDs; Exhibition Catalogs; Fiche; Framed Reproductions; Manuscripts; Maps; Motion Pictures; Original Documents; Other Holdings; Pamphlets; Periodical Subscriptions; Photographs; Records; Reels; Slides; Video Tapes
Special Subjects: Decorative Arts, Architecture, Glass, Mixed Media, Painting-American, Textiles, Painting-British, Tapestries, Drawings, Graphics, Painting-American, Photography, Prints, Sculpture, Watercolors, Archaeology, Religious Art, Ceramics, Crafts, Oriental Art, Woodcarvings, Woodcuts, Etchings & Engravings, Decorative Arts, Judaica, Manuscripts, Painting-European, Portraits, Posters, Painting-Canadian, Jewelry, Porcelain, Oriental Art, Silver, Metalwork, Carpets & Rugs, Historical Material, Maps, Coins & Medals, Painting-Polish, Antiquities-Oriental, Antiquities-Greek, Antiquities-Roman, Cartoons, Stained Glass, Painting-German, Pewter, Painting-Russian, Painting-Israeli, Enamels, Bookplates & Bindings
Collections: Permanent collection of sculpture, paintings & graphic art; ethnographic materials spanning centuries of Jewish experience; a permanent Holocaust memorial; Judaica, paintings, ceremonial silver, textiles, archaeology
Publications: Spec pubs with exhibits; Calendar of Events
Activities: Classes for adults; dramatic progs; lects open to pub, 20 vis lectrs per yr; concerts; gallery talks; tours; individual paintings & original objects of art lent to other mus & institutions; originate traveling exhibs to other mus; mus shop sells books, original art, reproductions, prints, objects for Jewish home, children's toys & clothing
L   **Asher Library,** 610 S Michigan Ave, Chicago, IL 60605-1906. Tel 312-322-1712; Fax 312-922-0455; Elec Mail asherlib@spertus.edu; Internet Home Page Address: www.spertus.edu; *Librn* Camille Shotwell
Open Mon - Thurs 1 - 6:30 PM, Sun noon - 4 PM; Library of Jewish studies; Reference library open to public. Includes Badona Spertus Art Library
Library Holdings: Auction Catalogs; Audio Tapes; Book Volumes 100,000; Cassettes; DVDs; Exhibition Catalogs; Fiche; Manuscripts; Pamphlets; Periodical Subscriptions 556; Photographs; Records; Reels; Slides; Video Tapes
Special Subjects: Folk Art, Photography, Calligraphy, Manuscripts, Maps, Posters, Sculpture, Historical Material, Judaica, Portraits, Ceramics, Archaeology, Painting-Israeli, Printmaking, Cartoons, Porcelain, Glass, Stained Glass, Religious Art, Silver, Coins & Medals, Architecture

M   **SWEDISH AMERICAN MUSEUM ASSOCIATION OF CHICAGO,** 5211 N Clark St, Chicago, IL 60640-2101. Tel 773-728-8111; Fax 773-728-8870; Elec Mail museum@samac.org; Internet Home Page Address: www.SwedishAmericanMuseum.org; *Pres* Annika Jaspers; *First VPres* Karen Lindblad; *Treas* Joan Papadopoulos; *Exec Dir* Karin Moen Abercrombie; *Cur* Veronica Robinson
Open Mon - Fri 10 AM - 4 PM, Sat & Sun 11 AM - 4 PM; Admis families $10, adults $4, students children & seniors $3, mems free; Estab 1976 to display Swedish arts, crafts, artists, scientists, and artifacts connected with United States, especially Chicago; Material displayed in the four story museum in Andersonville, once a predominantly Swedish area in Chicago; Average Annual Attendance: 40,000; Mem: 1800; dues $15-$500
Income: $700,000 (financed by mem & donations)
Special Subjects: Photography, Prints, Watercolors, Textiles, Costumes, Religious Art, Ceramics, Crafts, Folk Art, Pottery, Woodcarvings, Etchings & Engravings, Decorative Arts, Manuscripts, Portraits, Furniture, Glass, Jewelry, Porcelain, Carpets & Rugs, Historical Material, Coins & Medals, Embroidery, Stained Glass, Painting-Scandinavian
Collections: Artifacts used or made by Swedes, photographs, oils of or by Swedes in United States
Exhibitions: Dream of America, permanent exhib; Brunk Children's Museum of Immigration, 3rd fl; special art exhibits in the 1st fl gallery - 4/yr
Publications: FLAGGAN quarterly
Activities: Classes for adults & children; docent training; lects open to pub, 3-4 vis lectrs per yr; concerts; gallery talks; tours; awards; individual paintings lent; book traveling exhibs 2-3 per yr; mus shop sells books, magazines, reproductions, prints, gifts, Swedish linen & items; junior mus named Children's Museum of Immigration

M   **TRUMAN COLLEGE ART GALLERY,** 1145 W Wilson Ave, Chicago, IL 60640-5691. Tel 312-989-6059
Call for hours
Collections: Paintings; photographs

M **UKRAINIAN INSTITUTE OF MODERN ART,** 2320 W Chicago Ave, Chicago, IL 60622-4722. Tel 773-227-5522; Elec Mail info@uima-chicago.org; Internet Home Page Address: www.uima-chicago.org; *Pres* Orysia Cardoso; *Adminr* Andriy Hudzan; *Cur* Stanislav Grezdo
Open Wed - Sun Noon - 4 PM; No admis fee; donations accepted; Estab 1971; Two galleries, rotating & permanent exhibs; Average Annual Attendance: 2,700; Mem: 160; dues $50; ex com meets monthly
Library Holdings: CD-ROMs; Exhibition Catalogs; Original Art Works; Original Documents; Other Holdings; Photographs; Prints; Sculpture
Special Subjects: Drawings, Etchings & Engravings, Ceramics, American Western Art, Photography, Painting-American, Textiles, Bronzes, Painting-French, Painting-Japanese, Sculpture, Tapestries, Watercolors, African Art, Woodcarvings, Woodcuts, Painting-Canadian, Calligraphy, Embroidery
Collections: Kowalsky Coll, over 500 artworks; Permanent Colls (1,000 Artworks)
Exhibitions: 5-6 exhibs per year; Temporary & permanent exhibits
Publications: 5-6 yearly catalogs for temporary exhibits; permanent coll catalog
Activities: 4-6 classical music & jazz performances; 4 literary events; poetry & fiction readings; collaborative events; concerts; tours; lects open to pub; lects for mems only; 4-5 vis lectrs per yr; concerts; mus shop sells books, magazines, original art, reproductions, prints, slides

L **UKRAINIAN NATIONAL MUSEUM & LIBRARY,** 2249 W Superior St, Chicago, IL 60612-1327. Tel 312-421-8020; Fax 773-772-2883; Elec Mail theukranianmuseum@sbcglobal.net; *Dir & Pres* Jaroslaw J Hankewych; *Dir* Dr George Hrycelak; *VPres* Lydia Tkaczuk; *Treas* Irene Subota
Open Thurs - Sun 11 AM - 4 PM; Suggested donation $5; Estab 1954, to collect & preserve Ukrainian cultural heritage; Average Annual Attendance: 6,000; Mem: 200; dues $40; annual meeting in Jan-Feb; sales shop sells forms of folk art
Income: Financed through mem & donations
Library Holdings: Book Volumes 18,000; Cards; Clipping Files; Framed Reproductions; Kodachrome Transparencies; Manuscripts; Memorabilia; Original Art Works; Pamphlets; Periodical Subscriptions 100; Photographs; Sculpture; Slides
Special Subjects: Embroidery, Folk Art, Portraits, Pottery, Tapestries, Textiles, Woodcarvings
Collections: Ukrainian Folk Art
Exhibitions: Ukrainian Holodomor - Genecid
Activities: Classes for adults; tours; lending collection contains 18,000 books; originates traveling exhibs; mus shop sells books, magazines, original art

M **UNIVERSITY OF CHICAGO,** Lorado Taft Midway Studios, 6016 S Ingleside Ave, Chicago, IL 60637-2618. Tel 773-753-4821; Fax 773-834-7630; Elec Mail dova@uchicago.edu; Internet Home Page Address: www.dova.uchicago.edu; *Dir* Robert Peters
Open Mon - Fri 8:30 AM - 4:30 PM; cl Sat & Sun; Studios of Lorado Taft and Assoc, a Registered National Historic Landmark; now University of Chicago, Comt on Art & Design
Exhibitions: Graduate MFA & Undergraduate Exhibitions
Activities: Special performances; schols offered

M **Smart Museum of Art,** 5550 S Greenwood Ave, Chicago, IL 60637-1506. Tel 773-702-0200; Fax 773-702-3121; Elec Mail smart-museum@uchicago.edu; Internet Home Page Address: www.smartmuseum.uchicago.edu; *Dir* Anthony Hirschel; *Admin Asst* Cindy Hansen; *Chief Preparator* Rudy Bernal; *Sr Cur* Richard A Born; *Mgr Educ Programs* Lisa Davis; *Asst Security Supv* Paul Bryan; *Assoc Registrar* Sara Hindmarch; *Mgr Family & New Media Interpretation* Melissa Kinkley; *Cur & Mellon Prog Coordr* Anne Leonard; *Pub Rel & Mktg Mgr* C J Lind; *Dir Finance & Admin* Peg Liput; *Asst Cur* Jessica Moss; *Bus Mgr* Joyce Norman; *Dir Edu* Kristy Peterson; *Events & Retail Oper Mgr* Sarah Polachek; *Facilities & Security Supv* Patrick Flanagan; *Deputy Dir & Chief Cur* Stephanie Smith; *Registrar Loans & Exhib* Angela Steinmetz; *Dir Develop & Extrn Affairs* Nora Hennessy; *Consulting Cur* Wu Hung; *Preparator* Ray Klemchuk; *Mgr Develop Communs* Kate Nardin
Open Tues, Wed, Fri 10 AM - 4 PM, Thurs 10 AM - 8 PM, Sat - Sun 11 AM- 5 PM; No admis fee; Estab 1974 to assist the teaching & research programs of the University of Chicago by maintaining a permanent collection & presenting exhibitions & symposia of scholarly & general interest; Gallery designed by E L Barnes; exhibit space covers 9500 sq ft & also contains print & drawing study room, Elden Sculpture Garden; Average Annual Attendance: 60,000; Mem: 650; dues individual $40
Income: Financed by mem, university, special funds, corporations, foundations & government grants
Special Subjects: Etchings & Engravings, Collages, Glass, Furniture, Portraits, Silver, Woodcuts, Painting-British, Painting-French, Drawings, Graphics, Painting-American, Photography, Prints, Sculpture, Watercolors, Religious Art, Decorative Arts, Painting-European, Painting-Japanese, Oriental Art, Asian Art, Painting-Dutch, Baroque Art, Painting-Flemish, Renaissance Art, Painting-Italian, Antiquities-Greek, Antiquities-Roman, Painting-German, Pewter
Collections: American, Ancient, Baroque, decorative arts, drawings, Medieval, Modern European, Oriental & Renaissance paintings, photographs, prints, sculpture; Asian, contemporary
Publications: Looking and Listening in Nineteenth-Century France; Displacement: Three Gorges Dam and Contemporary Chinese Art; Echoes of the Past: The Buddhist Cave Temples of Ziangtangshan; Heartland
Activities: Classes for adults & children; docent training; lects open to pub, 5-6 vis lectrs per yr; concerts; gallery talks; tours; individual paintings & original objects of art lent to professional art mus; book traveling exhibs 1-3 per yr; originate traveling exhibs to professional art mus; sales shop sells books, post cards, posters, jewelry & photographs

M **Oriental Institute,** 1155 E 58th St, Chicago, IL 60637-1540. Tel 773-702-9514; Fax 773-702-9853; Elec Mail oi-museum@uchicago.edu; Internet Home Page Address: www.oi.uchicago.edu; *Registrar* Helen McDonald; *Archivist* John Larson; *Museum Chief Cur* Jack Green; *Head of Conservation* Laura D Alissandro; *Head of Museum Educ* Carole Krucoff; *Dir* Gil Stein
Open Tues 10 AM-6PM, Wed 10 AM-8:30 PM, Thurs-Sat 10 AM-6 PM, Sun Noon-6 PM, cl Mon; No admis fee; Estab 1919 as a research institute & mus of antiquities excavated from Egypt, Mesopotamia, Assyria, Syria, Palestine, Persia,

Anatolia & Nubia, dating from 7000 years ago until the 18th Century AD; 8 permanent galleries & 1 special exhibits gallery; Average Annual Attendance: 62,000; Mem: 2650; dues $50 & up
Income: Financed by parent institution, admis donations, federal, state grants & proceeds from sales
Special Subjects: Architecture, Photography, Sculpture, Watercolors, Bronzes, Archaeology, Textiles, Costumes, Religious Art, Ceramics, Pottery, Manuscripts, Dolls, Furniture, Glass, Jewelry, Historical Material, Ivory, Dioramas, Medieval Art, Antiquities-Persian, Islamic Art, Antiquities-Egyptian, Gold, Leather, Antiquities-Assyrian
Collections: Ancient Near Eastern antiquities from pre-historic times to the beginning of the present era plus some Islamic artifacts; Egypt: colossal statue of King Tut, mummies; Iraq; Assyrian winged human-headed bull (40 tons); Mesopotamia temple & house interior, reconstructions, sculpture, jewelry; Iran: Persepolis bull; column & capital; Palestine: Megiddo ivories & horned alter
Publications: Annual report; News & Notes, monthly; museum guidebook; brochures
Activities: Classes for adults & children; dramatic progs; docent training; family progs; lects open to pub; 10 vis lectrs per yr; gallery talks; tours; competitions with awards; original objects of art lent to mus & institutions; lending collection contains kodachromes, original art works & mini mus boxes; book traveling exhibs; sales shop sells books, magazines, original art, reproductions, prints, slides, items of jewelry, clothing, household furnishings from the Near East

—Oriental Institute Research Archives, 1155 E 58th St, Chicago, IL 60637-1540. Tel 773-702-9537; Fax 773-702-9853; Elec Mail oi-library@uchicago.edu; Internet Home Page Address: www.oi.uchicago.edu; *Librn* Charles E Jones
Open daily 10 AM-4 PM by appointment; Circ Non-circulating; Open to staff, students & members for reference
Library Holdings: Audio Tapes; Book Volumes 38,000; Cards; Cassettes; Clipping Files; Exhibition Catalogs; Fiche; Kodachrome Transparencies; Lantern Slides; Manuscripts; Memorabilia; Motion Pictures; Pamphlets; Periodical Subscriptions 500; Photographs; Reels; Slides
Special Subjects: Antiquities-Greek, Anthropology, Antiquities-Assyrian, Antiquities-Byzantine, Antiquities-Egyptian, Antiquities-Persian, Archaeology, Asian Art, Historical Material, History of Art & Archaeology, Islamic Art, Textiles

L **Visual Resources Collection,** 5540 S Greenwood, Chicago, IL 60637-1506. Tel 773-702-0261; Fax 773-702-5901; Internet Home Page Address: www.humanities.uchicago.eduhumanitiesartslide.htmlartfulprojectslide; *Cur* John L Butler-Ludwig
Open Mon - Fri 9 AM - 5 PM, cl Sat & Sun; Estab 1938; Circ Restricted circulation-faculty & students; For reference only
Library Holdings: Lantern Slides 88,000; Other Holdings 500,000; Photographs 740,000; Slides 386,000

L **Max Epstein Archive,** 1100 E 57th St, Chicago, IL 60637-1502. Tel 773-702-7080; Fax 773-702-5901; *Cur* Meg Klinkow
Open Mon - Fri 9 AM - 5 PM, cl Sat & Sun; Estab 1938; Circ Non-circulating; For reference only
Income: Financed by gifts & donations
Library Holdings: Book Volumes 55,500; Other Holdings Mounted photographs of art; catalogued & mounted photographs added annually 8000; auction sales catalogs, Union Catalog of Art Books in Chicago
Collections: Photographs of architecture, sculpture, painting, drawing & decorative arts illustrating Far Eastern, South Asian & Western art history; illustrated Bartsch Catalogue; DIAL Index; Marburger Index; Papal Medals Collection; Courtauld Institute Illustrated Archive; Courtauld Photo Survey; Armenia Architecture; Dunlap Society Architecture; Willoughby Collection

M **UNIVERSITY OF ILLINOIS AT CHICAGO,** Gallery 400, 400 S Peoria St, Art & Exhibition Hall (MC034) Chicago, IL 60607-7032. Tel 312-996-6114; Fax 312-355-3444; Elec Mail gallery400@uic.edu; Internet Home Page Address: www.gallery400.uic.edu; *Dir* Lorelei Stewart; *Asst Dir* Whitney Moeller
Open Tues - Fri 10 AM - 6 PM, Sat Noon - 6 PM, other times by appointment; No admis fee; Estab 1983; 2,900 sq ft loft exhibition space & additional 1300 square ft hall for lectures, films & video screenings; Average Annual Attendance: 10,000
Income: $250,000 (financed by state & federal grants, college of A&A, private donations & foundations)
Library Holdings: DVDs; Exhibition Catalogs; Periodical Subscriptions; Video Tapes
Special Subjects: Photography, Prints, Sculpture, Posters
Collections: works by local & nat artists
Publications: The Alchemy of Comedy...Stupid by Edgar Arceneaux
Activities: Lects open to pub, 18 vis lectrs per yr; gallery talks; tours; book traveling exhibs average 1 every 2 yr; originates traveling exhibs 1 per yr, Univ galleries, artist organizations

M **WOMAN MADE GALLERY,** 685 N. Milwaukee Ave, Chicago, IL 60642. Tel 312-738-0400; Fax 312-738-0404; Elec Mail gallery@womanmade.org; Internet Home Page Address: www.womanmade.org; *Exec Dir* Beate C Minkovski
Open Wed - Fri 12 PM - 7 PM, Sat - Sun 12 PM - 4 PM; No admis fee; Estab 1992 to provide exhib opportunities for women artists
Collections: Works by women artists
Activities: Rental facilities; special events; museum-related items for sale

DANVILLE

M **VERMILION COUNTY MUSEUM SOCIETY,** 116 N Gilbert St, Danville, IL 61832-8506. Tel 217-442-2922; Fax 217-442-2001; Elec Mail susricht@aol.com; Internet Home Page Address: www.vermilioncountymuseum.org; *Dir* Susan Richter; *Bookkeeper* Wendy Wilder
Open Tues - Sat 10 AM - 5 PM, cl Sun, Mon, Thanksgiving & Christmas; Admis 18 yrs & older $4, children 13-17 $1, under 13 yrs free, school & scout groups free; Estab 1964; in 1855 doctor's residence and courthouse replica building; Average Annual Attendance: 5,500; Mem: 1,001; dues life $450, patron $75, bus $100, organization $15, family $25, individual $20, student & seniors $15

Income: Financed by endowment fund, mem.
Library Holdings: Book Volumes; Clipping Files; Manuscripts; Maps; Original Documents; Pamphlets; Periodical Subscriptions; Photographs; Prints; Records; Slides; Video Tapes
Special Subjects: American Indian Art, Decorative Arts, Manuscripts, Furniture, Historical Material, Maps, Restorations, Period Rooms
Collections: Costumes; decorative arts; graphics; historical material; paintings; sculpture
Publications: Heritage, quarterly magazine
Activities: Classes for children; dramatic progs; lects open to pub, 2 vis lectrs per yr; tours; children competitions; mus shop sells books, magazines, original art, prints & handmade items
L   **Library,** 116 N Gilbert St, Danville, IL 61832. Tel 217-442-2922; Fax 217-442-2001; Internet Home Page Address: www.vermilioncountymuseum.org; *Dir* Susan E Richter; *Pres* Donald Richter
Open Tues-Sat 10AM-5PM, Sun 1-5PM, cl Mon, Thanksgiving, Christmas; Open to the public for reference
Income: Financed by endowment fund
Library Holdings: Book Volumes 400; Clipping Files; Photographs; Slides; Video Tapes
Collections: Medical equipment, furniture, photographs, arrowheads
Publications: The Heritage of Vermilion County, quarterly; bimonthly newsletter

DEKALB

A   **ILLINOIS ALLIANCE FOR ARTS EDUCATION (IAAE),** 315 Dresser Rd, DeKalb, IL 60115. Tel 312-750-0589; Fax 312-750-9113; Elec Mail barbarah@tbc.net; Internet Home Page Address: www.illinoisalliance4artsed.org; *Exec Dir* Barbara Heimerdinger; *Pres* Becky Blaine
Open daily 9 AM - 5 PM; Estab 1972 to safeguard and expand arts educ for all Illinois students; Mem: 150, dues $45 for individuals, $100 for institutions
Income: $200,000 (financed by nat, state and local govt, also pvt foundations, corporate gifts & the Kennedy Center Alliance for Arts Educ Network)
Publications: Finding Dollar$, a Statewide Guide for Artists & Schools to Locate Funds for Arts Educ Progs; Integrated Curriculum Arts Project, lesson plan book
Activities: Arts integration workshops for pub school teachers; conferences & professional develop workshops for teachers & adminrs; ArtSmart prog to raise pub awareness of importance of arts educ; annual service recognition awards

M   **NORTHERN ILLINOIS UNIVERSITY,** NIU Art Museum, NIU Art Museum, Altgeld Hall, Fl 2, 1425 W Lincoln Hwy DeKalb, IL 60115-2828. Tel 815-753-1936; Fax 815-753-7897; *Dir* Jo Burke
Open Tues - Fri 10 AM - 5 PM, Sat Noon - 4 PM; No admis fee; Estab 1970; Main Gallery is 6000 sq ft; Average Annual Attendance: 50,000
Income: Financed by state appropriation & grants from public agencies & private foundations
Special Subjects: Painting-American, Watercolors, American Indian Art, Woodcuts, Etchings & Engravings, Asian Art
Collections: Contemporary & Modern paintings, prints, sculptures, & photographs, Burmese Art; Native American Art
Activities: Lect open to public; gallery talks; tours; original objects of art lent to accredited museums; book traveling exhibitions
L   **The University Libraries,** University Libraries, 1425 W Lincoln Hwy DeKalb, IL 60115-2828. Tel 815-753-0616; *Arts Librn* Charles Larry
Open Mon - Thurs 7:30 AM - 10 PM, Sat 9 AM - 10 PM, Sun 1 PM - 2 AM; Estab 1977 to provide reference service & develop the collection
Library Holdings: Book Volumes 47,000; Cards; Exhibition Catalogs; Fiche; Motion Pictures; Other Holdings Art book titles 975; Rare bks 250; Periodical Subscriptions 164; Reels; Slides; Video Tapes

DECATUR

M   **MILLIKIN UNIVERSITY,** Perkinson Gallery, 1184 W Main St, Kirkland Fine Arts Ctr Decatur, IL 62522-2084. Tel 217-424-6227; Fax 217-424-3993; Elec Mail kfac@millikin.edu; Internet Home Page Address: www.millikin.edu; *Dir* Barry Pearson; *Dir Gall* Jim Schitinger
Open Mon - Fri 9AM - 5 PM; No admis fee; Estab 1970; Gallery has 3200 sq ft & 224 running ft of wall space
Income: Financed by university appropriation
Special Subjects: Drawings, Painting-American. Prints, Sculpture, Watercolors
Collections: Drawings; painting; prints; sculpture; watercolors
Exhibitions: Annual Senior Group Exhibition; Millikin National Works on Paper.
Publications: Monthly show announcements
Activities: Lect; guided tours; gallery talks

EDWARDSVILLE

L   **SOUTHERN ILLINOIS UNIVERSITY,** Lovejoy Library, 30 Hairpin Dr, Edwardsville, IL 62026-1063. Tel 618-650-2000; Fax 618-650-2381; Internet Home Page Address: www.siue.edu; *Friends of Lovejoy Librn* Kyle Moore
Open Mon - Thurs 8 AM - 11:30 PM, Fri 8 AM - 9 PM, Sat 9 AM - 5 PM, Sun 1 - 9 PM; Estab 1957, as a source for general University undergraduate & graduate instruction, & faculty research
Library Holdings: Book Volumes 500,000; Fiche; Motion Pictures; Other Holdings Illustrated sheet music covers; Periodical Subscriptions 6000; Records; Reels; Slides; Video Tapes
Special Subjects: Art History, Calligraphy, Archaeology, American Western Art, Bronzes, Advertising Design, Art Education, Asian Art, American Indian Art, Anthropology, Aesthetics, Afro-American Art, Bookplates & Bindings, Carpets & Rugs, Architecture
Exhibitions: Louis Sullivan Collection of Terra Cotta
Activities: Photography contest; tours; scholarships

ELMHURST

M   **ELMHURST ART MUSEUM,** 150 Cottage Hill Ave, Elmhurst, IL 60126-3329. Tel 630-834-0202; Fax 630-834-0234; Elec Mail info@elmhurstartmuseum.org; Internet Home Page Address: www.elmhurstartmuseum.org; *Asst Cur* Emily Barney; *Controller* Heather Pastore; *Asst Exec Dir* Stephanie Grow; *Visitor Svcs Coordr* Jeff Francik; *Educ Coordr* Amy Janken; *Develop Mktg Coordr* Stuart W Henn
Open Tues, Thurs & Sat 10 AM - 4 PM, Wed 1 - 8 PM, Fri & Sun 1 - 4 PM; Admis adult $7, seniors & students $5, children under 12 free, members & Tues free; Opened 1997 to exhibit contemporary art, Chicago vicinity to national; Three exhibition galleries, 1 artists' guild gallery & entrance gallery; Average Annual Attendance: 35,000; Mem: 1200; dues individual $40 for 1 yr
Income: Financed by endowment, mem, corporate sponsorships, city & state appropriation
Special Subjects: Architecture, Drawings, Painting-American, Prints, Sculpture, Watercolors, American Western Art, Ceramics, Folk Art, Woodcarvings, Woodcuts, Etchings & Engravings, Afro-American Art, Portraits, Asian Art, Painting-Dutch, Painting-French, Historical Material, Ivory, Juvenile Art
Collections: Contemporary Art-American & Chicago vicinity
Exhibitions: Annual competitions; children's exhibits; one person & group shows; permanent collections; traveling exhibits
Activities: Classes for adults & children; docent training; lects open to pub, 10-12 vis lectrs per yr; concerts; gallery talks; tours; competitions with awards; individual paintings & objects of art lent to other mus & the Federal Reserve; book traveling exhibs 2-3 per yr; mus shop sells books, magazines, original art, reproductions, prints & gift items

M   **LIZZADRO MUSEUM OF LAPIDARY ART,** 220 Cottage Hill Ave, Elmhurst, IL 60126-3351. Tel 630-833-1616; Fax 630-833-1225; Elec Mail info@lizzadromuseum.org; Internet Home Page Address: www.lizzadromuseum.org; *Dir* Dorothy Asher; *Exec Dir* John S Lizzadro
Open Tues - Sat 10 AM - 5 PM, Sun 1 - 5 PM, cl Mon; Admis adults $4, sr citizens $3, students $2, ages 7-12 yrs $1, under 7 free, no charge on Fri; Estab 1962 to promote interest in the lapidary arts & the study & collecting of minerals & fossils; Main exhibit area contains hardstone carvings, gemstone materials, minerals; lower level contains earth science exhibits, gift shop; Average Annual Attendance: 30,000; Mem: 350; dues $30 per yr
Income: Financed by endowment
Special Subjects: Jade, Oriental Art, Asian Art, Ivory, Dioramas, Mosaics
Collections: Hardstone Carving Collection
Exhibitions: Educational exhibits, push button exhibits, rotating special exhibits
Publications: Newsletter & calendar of events 4 times per yr
Activities: Classes for adults & children; lects open to pub, 12 vis lectrs per year; educational films; tours; demonstrations; gallery talks; book 3-4 traveling exhibs per yr; originate traveling exhibs to libraries & universities; sales shop sells books, magazines, hardstone & gemstone souvenirs

ELSAH

M   **PRINCIPIA COLLEGE,** School of Nations Museum, 1 Maybeck Pl, Elsah, IL 62028. Tel 618-374-2131, Exten 5236; Fax 618-374-5122; Internet Home Page Address: www.prin.edu/upper/museum; *Cur* Nancy Boyer-Reehlin
Open Tues & Fri by appointment only
Special Subjects: American Indian Art, Textiles, Ceramics, Crafts, Decorative Arts, Dolls, Glass, Asian Art, Metalwork
Collections: American Indian coll including baskets, bead work, blankets, leather, pottery, quill work and silver; Asian art coll includes arts and crafts, ceramics, textiles from China, Japan and Southeast Asia; European colls include glass, metals, snuff boxes, textiles and wood; costumes and dolls from around the world
Exhibitions: Changing exhibits on campus locations; permanent exhibits in School of Nations lower floor
Activities: Special programs offered throughout the year; objects available for individual study

EVANSTON

L   **C G JUNG CENTER,** (CG Jung Institute of Chicago) 817 Dempster St, Evanston, IL 60201-4303. Tel 847-475-4848; Fax 847-475-4970; Internet Home Page Address: www.cgjungcenter.org; *Asst Dir & Ed* Mary Nolan; *Exhibit Coordr* Barbara Zaretsky; *Librn & AV Production Mgr* Mark Swanson; *Exec Dir* Peter Mudd
Open Mon - Thurs 10 AM - 4 PM; No admis fee; Estab 1965; For reference only
Library Holdings: Audio Tapes; Book Volumes 4000; Clipping Files; Exhibition Catalogs; Manuscripts; Motion Pictures; Pamphlets; Reproductions; Slides; Video Tapes
Special Subjects: Folk Art, Film, Islamic Art, Pre-Columbian Art, History of Art & Archaeology, Judaica, Archaeology, Ethnology, Asian Art, American Indian Art, Anthropology, Oriental Art, Religious Art
Collections: Archive for Research in Archetypal Symbolism (ARAS), photographs & slides
Publications: Transformation, quarterly

A   **EVANSTON ART CENTER,** 2603 Sheridan Rd, Evanston, IL 60201-1776. Tel 847-475-5300; Fax 847-475-5330; Internet Home Page Address: www.evanstonartcenter.org; *Exec Dir* Norah Diedrich; *Pres* Linda Kaufman
Open Mon-Sat 10 AM-4 PM, & 7-10 PM, Sun 1-4 PM; No admis fee; Estab 1929 as a community visual arts center with exhibits, instructions & programs; Focuses primarily on changing contemporary arts exhibitions with emphasis on emerging & under-recognized Midwest artists; Average Annual Attendance: 35,000; Mem: 1800; dues $30, annual meeting in Aug
Income: Financed by state & city arts councils & mem
Exhibitions: Primarily artists of the Midwest, all media
Publications: Concentrics, quarterly; exhibition catalogs

Activities: Classes for adults & children, outreach progs, teaching cert renewal; lects

M **EVANSTON HISTORICAL SOCIETY,** Charles Gates Dawes House, 225 Greenwood St, Evanston, IL 60201-4713. Tel 847-475-3410; Fax 847-475-3599; Elec Mail evanstonhs@nwu.edu; Elec Mail evanstonhs@northwestern.edu; Internet Home Page Address: www.evanstonhistorycenter.org; *Cur* Eden Juron Pearlman; *Develop Officer* Kim Olson-Clark; *Educ Officer* Leslie Goddard
Open Thurs - Sun 1 - 5 PM; Admis $5, seniors & children $3; Estab 1898 to collect, preserve, exhibit & interpret Evanston's history; Average Annual Attendance: 4,000; Mem: 1,050; dues $25-$500; annual meeting in June
Income: Financed by mem & private donations
Special Subjects: Architecture, Painting-American, Photography, Sculpture, American Indian Art, Textiles, Costumes, Ceramics, Crafts, Landscapes, Decorative Arts, Manuscripts, Portraits, Posters, Dolls, Furniture, Glass, Jewelry, Porcelain, Silver, Metalwork, Carpets & Rugs, Historical Material, Maps, Dioramas, Period Rooms, Laces, Stained Glass, Military Art
Collections: Collections reflecting the history of Evanston & its people, especially since the mid 1800s, including costumes & archival material
Exhibitions: Charles Gates Dawes House permanent exhibit; other rotating exhibits year round; Evanston Tackles the Woman Question, the Story of Evanston women who influenced the National Women's Movement; The Sick Can't Wait, the story of Evanston Community Hospital; Your Presence Is Requested, the Story of African-American Social Organization
Publications: TimeLines, mem newsletter, quarterly; annual report
Activities: Docent training; school outreach & in-house educational progs; lects open to pub; gallery talks; tours; individual paintings & original objects of art lent to other cultural institutions; lending collection contains 60 paintings & 30 sculptures; originate traveling exhibs; mus shop sells books & mus & Victorian related gifts

M **NORTHWESTERN UNIVERSITY,** Mary & Leigh Block Museum of Art, 40 Arts Cir Dr, Evanston, IL 60208-2410. Tel 847-491-4000; Fax 847-491-2261; Elec Mail block-museum@northwestern.edu; Internet Home Page Address: www.blockmuseum.northwestern.edu; *Dir* David Alan Robertson; *Sr Cur* Debora Wood; *Cur* Corinne Granof; *Dir Develop* Helen Hilken; *Bd Chmn* James Elesh; *Bus Admin* Carole Towns; *Commun Mgr* Burke Patten; *Dir Educ Progs* Sheetal Prajapati; *Grants Mgr* Nicole Druckman; *Registrar* Kristina Bottomley; *Mgr Exhibs & Facilities* Dan Silverstein; *Asst to Dir* Emily Forsgren; *Mgr Security Svcs* James Foster; *Coll & Exhibs Asst* Elizabeth Wolf; *Security Asst* Aaron Chatman; *Dir Block Cinema* Mimi Brody
Open Tues - Fri 10AM - 8PM, Sat-Sun 10AM - 5PM; No admis fee; Estab 1980 as visual arts venue for univ & surrounding communities; 4 galleries for rotating & permanent displays; Average Annual Attendance: 40,000; Mem: 300; dues $10-$1000
Income: Financed by mem, college, grants
Special Subjects: Photography, Prints
Collections: 4,000 works of art from medieval to contemporary, focusing on prints & photographs
Activities: Classes for adults & children; lects open to pub & mems only, 10-15 vis lectrs per yr; gallery talks; tours; fels offered; book traveling exhibs, 3-4 per yr; originate traveling exhibs circulated through other museums & galleries; mus shop sells books, exhib & coll related gifts

L **Art Collection, University Library,** 1970 Campus Dr, Evanston, IL 60208-2300. Tel 847-491-7484, 491-6471; Fax 847-467-7899; Elec Mail r-clement@northwestern.edu; Internet Home Page Address: www.library.northwestern.edu/art; *Head Art Coll* Russell T Clement; *Pub Svcs Librn* Lindsay King
Open Mon - Thurs 8:30 AM - 10 PM, Fri & Sat 8:30 AM - 5 PM, Sun 1 - 10 PM; No admis fee; Estab 1970 as a separate library collection. Serves curriculum & research needs of the Art History and Art Theory & Practice departments
Income: Financed through the university & endowment funds
Library Holdings: Book Volumes 125,000; Exhibition Catalogs
Special Subjects: Art History, Illustration, Photography, Etchings & Engravings, Graphic Arts, Painting-American, Painting-Dutch, Painting-Flemish, Painting-French, Painting-German, Painting-Italian, Prints, Sculpture, Painting-European, History of Art & Archaeology, Architecture

GALENA

M **CHICAGO ATHENAEUM,** Museum of Architecture & Design, 601 S Prospect St, Galena, IL 61036-2519. Tel 847-777-4444; Fax 815-777-2471; Elec Mail info@chicagoathenaeum.org; Internet Home Page Address: www.chi-athenaeum.org; *Dir & Pres* Christian K Narkiewicz-Laine; *Dir of Design* Timothy A Patula; *Dir Exhib Installation & Architect* Alexander Kozionnyi; *Chmn* Neil Kozokoff; *VPres* Ioannis Karalias; *Secy* Belinda Shastal
Open call for new hrs; Admis non mems $3, seniors & students $2, mems are free; Estab 1988; dedicated to all areas in the art of design - architecture, industrial & product design, graphics & urban planning; One floor of temporary exhibits; Average Annual Attendance: 500,000; Mem: 2500; dues $50-$250
Income: Financed by mem, grants & pvt & pub funding
Special Subjects: Architecture, Graphics, Photography, Textiles, Decorative Arts, Posters, Furniture, Glass
Collections: Architectural Drawings & Models, International Collection; Design-Chicago (1910-1960) Collection; Design-International Product & Graphic Collection; Japanese Graphic Design Collection; Industrial Design; Japanese Graphic Design; Contemporary Art Collection; Contemporary Fabric & Textile
Exhibitions: Large Scale Pub Sculpture; Landmark Chicago; American Architectural awards, Good Design
Activities: Seminars; lects open to pub, 15 vis lectrs per yr; competitions; book traveling exhibs 8 per yr; originate traveling exhibs 6 per yr; mus shop sells glass, toys, jewelry, fashion, book & international high design

GALESBURG

A **GALESBURG CIVIC ART CENTER,** 114 E Main St, Galesburg, IL 61401-4601. Tel 309-342-7415; Elec Mail info@galesburgarts.org; Internet Home Page Address: www.galesburgarts.org; *Office Mgr* Lynn Miller; *CEO & Archivist* Heather L Norman; *Pres* Jim Straub
Open Tues - Fri 10:30 AM - 4:30 PM, Sat 10:30 AM - 3 PM, cl all holidays; No admis fee, donations accepted; Estab 1923 as a non-profit organization for the furtherance of art; The main gallery has about 129 feet of wall space for the hanging of exhibits. The sales-rental gallery runs on a commission basis & is open to professional artists as a place to sell their work under a consignment agreement; Average Annual Attendance: 6,000; Mem: 450; dues begin at $20; annual meeting second Wed in June
Income: Financed by members, grants & fundraisers
Collections: Permanent coll of approx 400 pieces
Exhibitions: GALEX - national juried competition all media; Regional/national artists in a variety of media (change monthly); Art-in-the-Park annual fair
Publications: The Artifacts newsletter
Activities: Classes for adults & children; Art Fair; Film Festival; gallery talks; tours; competitions with awards; lending collection contains original art works, paintings, photographs & sculpture; sales shop sells original art, prints, etc

GREENVILLE

M **GREENVILLE COLLEGE,** Richard W Bock Sculpture Collection, Almira College House, 315 E College Ave, Greenville, IL 62246-0159. Tel 618-664-1840, ext 6724; Elec Mail sharon.grimes@greenville.edu; Internet Home Page Address: www.greenville.edu; *Dir & Cur* Sharon Grimes
Open Wed 1-4PM, Fri 1-5PM, Sat 10AM-2PM & by appointment, cl summer & holidays; No admis fee, donations accepted; Estab 1975 to display an extensive collection of the life work of the American sculptor in a restored home of the mid-19th century period; Five large rooms and two floors have approx 1800 sq ft of exhib space; Average Annual Attendance: 2,500
Income: Financed by endowment, college appropriation, gifts and donations
Special Subjects: Drawings, Painting-American, Sculpture, Posters, Furniture, Oriental Art
Collections: Furniture and furnishings of the 1850-1875 era; late 19th and early 20th century drawing, painting and sculpture; Frank Lloyd Wright artifacts, designs and drawings
Publications: Exhibit catalog; general museum brochures
Activities: Lects open to pub, 1-2 vis lectrs per yr; gallery talks; individual paintings and original objects of art lent to mus only; lending collection contains original art works, paintings, photographs, sculpture and drawings; originates traveling exhibs; mus shop sells books, magazines

L **The Richard W Bock Sculpture Collection & Art Library,** 315 E College Ave, Greenville, IL 62246-0159. Tel 618-664-1840, ext 6724; Internet Home Page Address: www.greenville.edu; *Librn* Sharon Davis
Open by appt only; For reference only, students & academia only
Library Holdings: Book Volumes 1000; Exhibition Catalogs; Memorabilia; Records

HIGHLAND PARK

M **THE ART CENTER - TAC,** The Art Center of Highland Park (TAC), 1957 Sheridan Rd, Highland Park, IL 60035. Tel 847-432-1888; Fax 847-432-9106; Elec Mail info@theartcenterhp.org; Internet Home Page Address: www.theartcenterhp.org; *Exec Dir* Gabrielle Rousso
Open Mon - Sat 9 AM - 4:30 PM; Modern/contemporary work by emerging & established regional artists; Mem: 500
Activities: Classes for adults & children; gallery talks; tours; schols

JACKSONVILLE

M **THE ART ASSOCIATION OF JACKSONVILLE,** The David Strawn Art Gallery, 331 W College, Jacksonville, IL 62650-2474; PO Box 1213, Jacksonville, IL 62651-1213. Tel 217-243-9390; Internet Home Page Address: www.strawnartgallery.org; *Dir* Kelly M Gross; *Pres* Adah Coultas
Open Sept - May, Tues - Sat 4 - 6 PM, Sun 1 - 3 PM; No admis fee; Estab 1873, endowed 1915, to serve the community by offering monthly shows of visual arts and weekly classes in a variety of media. The two main rooms house the monthly exhibitions and a third large room houses a collection of Pre-Columbian pottery; The Gallery is in a large building, previously a private home; Average Annual Attendance: 1,800; Mem: 470; dues $15 & up; annual meeting July
Income: Financed by endowment & mem
Special Subjects: Pre-Columbian Art, Pottery
Collections: Pre-Columbian Pottery; pottery discovered in the Mississippi Valley; Miriam Cowger Allen Doll Collection
Exhibitions: Strawn family antique - permanent exhib; year-round permanent exhib
Activities: Classes for adults & children, art educ; lects workshops open to pub, 9 vis lectrs per yr, 9 gallery talks per season, tours on demand, educ schols; edu schols

JOLIET

M **JOLIET JUNIOR COLLEGE,** Laura A Sprague Art Gallery, 1215 Houbolt Rd, J Bldg Joliet, IL 60431-8938. Tel 815-729-9020, Ext 2423, 2223; Fax 815-744-5507; Internet Home Page Address: www.jjc.cc.il.us; *Dir Gallery* Joe B Milosevich
Open Mon - Fri 8 AM - 8 PM; No admis fee; Estab 1978, to present exhibs related to acad progs, the col & the community; Gallery, approx 20 x 25 ft; located on second floor of Spicer-Brown Hall
Income: Financed by college appropriations

Collections: Permanent collection of student work, annual
Activities: Lect open to public, 2-3 vis lectrs per year; gallery talks; tours; sponsor student competitions with awards

LAKE FOREST

L **LAKE FOREST LIBRARY,** Fine Arts Dept, 360 E Deerpath, Lake Forest, IL 60045-2200. Tel 847-234-0636; Fax 847-234-1453; Elec Mail fsoug@lfl.alibrary.com; Internet Home Page Address: lakeforestlibrary.org; *Adult Svcs Coordr* Felicia Song; *Graphic Artist* Patricia Kreischer; *Admin Librn* Kaye Grabbe
Open Mon - Thurs 9 AM - 9 PM, Fri - Sat 9 AM - 5 PM, Sun 1 - 5 PM (Sept - May); No admis fee; Estab 1898 to make accessible to the residents of the city, books & other resources & services for educ, information & recreation; Circ 500,000; Gallery exhibits small local shows
Income: $3,516,425 (financed by city 96% & state 1% appropriations & local library generated income 3%)
Special Subjects: Landscape Architecture, Architecture
Collections: Folk art; painting; landscape architecture
Exhibitions: local artist & student shows - spring
Publications: Lake Forest Library Newsletter, four times per year
Activities: Annual 10-12 $5,000 student art awards

LE ROY

L **J T & E J CRUMBAUGH MEMORIAL PUBLIC LIBRARY,** 405 E Center, PO Box 129 Le Roy, IL 61752-0129. Tel 309-962-3911; Elec Mail crumbaughlibrary@yahoo.com; *Librn* Lois Evans; *Circ* Fae Morris
Open Mon - Sat 10 AM - 5 PM; No admis fee; Estab 1927
Library Holdings: Book Volumes 14,000; Other Holdings Genealogy Files 655; Local History Scrapbooks 72; Periodical Subscriptions 50; Reels 59
Special Subjects: Historical Material
Collections: Books; genealogy, local history
Publications: JT&EJ Crumbaugh Spiritualist Church & Memorial Library - 1998 (updated every 10 years); Tracing Your Roots (updated every 2 years)
Activities: Classes for children; summer reading prog; holiday story times & progs

LOMBARD

L **HELEN M PLUM MEMORIAL LIBRARY,** 110 W Maple St, Lombard, IL 60148-2514. Tel 630-627-0316; Fax 630-627-0336; Internet Home Page Address: www.plum.lib.il.us; *Adult Servs* Donna Slyfield; *Dir* Robert A Harris
Open Mon - Fri 9 AM - 9 PM, Sat 9 AM - 5 PM, Sun 1 -5 PM; No admis fee; Estab as a pub library
Income: $2,243,693 (financed by local government)
Purchases: $434,451
Library Holdings: Audio Tapes; Book Volumes 210,815; CD-ROMs; Cassettes; Compact Disks; DVDs; Fiche; Filmstrips; Micro Print; Pamphlets; Periodical Subscriptions 358; Prints; Records; Sculpture; Slides; Video Tapes
Special Subjects: Art History, Folk Art, Decorative Arts, Painting-American, Crafts, Handicrafts
Publications: Brochure, annual
Activities: Lect open to public; original objects of art lent to public

MACOMB

M **WESTERN ILLINOIS UNIVERSITY,** Western Illinois University Art Gallery, 1 University Circle Macomb, IL 61455. Tel 309-298-1587; Fax 309-298-2400; Elec Mail JR-Graham@wiu.edu; Internet Home Page Address: www.wiu.edu/artgallery; *Pres* Alvin Goldfarb; *Cur Exhib* John R Graham
Open Mon - Fri 9 AM - 4 PM & Tues 6 - 8 PM; No admis fee; Estab 1945 to present art as an aesthetic and teaching aid; Building has three galleries with 500 running ft; Average Annual Attendance: 9,000
Income: Financed through state appropriation
Special Subjects: Painting-American, Prints, Drawings, Graphics, Sculpture, Watercolors, Ceramics, Woodcuts
Collections: WPA & 20th Century: Prints, Drawing, Paintings & Ceramics; Old Masters Prints
Activities: Classes for adults; lects open to pub, 8 vis lectrs per yr; gallery talks; tours; competitions with awards; individual paintings lent; lending collection contains 100 paintings; originates traveling exhibs

MOLINE

C **DEERE & COMPANY,** One John Deere Pl, Moline, IL 61265. Tel 309-765-8000; Fax 309-765-4735; *Coll Cur* Lisa Spurgeon
Estab 1964 to complement the offices designed by Eero Saarinen & Kevin Roche; to provide opportunities for employees & visitors to view & enjoy a wide variety of art pieces from many parts of the world; Collection displayed at Deere & Company Headquarters
Collections: Artifacts, paintings, prints, sculpture & tapestries from over 25 countries
Activities: Concerts; tours

MOUNT VERNON

M **CEDARHURST CENTER FOR THE ARTS,** Mitchell Museum, 2600 Richview Rd, Mount Vernon, IL 62864; PO Box 923, Mount Vernon, IL 62864. Tel 618-242-1236; Fax 618-242-9530; Elec Mail mitchellmuseum@cedarhurst.org; Internet Home Page Address: www.cedarhurst.org; *Exec Dir* Sharon Bradham; *Dir Operations* Greg Hilliard; *Mus Gift Shop Mgr & Historian* Sarah Lou Bicknell; *CFO* Heather Owens; *Staff Coordr* Linda Wheeler; *Dir Commun* Sarah Sledge; *Dir Educ* Jennifer Sarver; *Dir Shrode Art Center* Carrie Gibbs; *Dir Develop* Dr Hillary Settle
Open Tues - Sat 10 AM - 5 PM, Sun 1 - 5 PM, cl Mon & national holidays; Admis fee for non-mems for special events & exhibs; Estab 1973 to present

exhibitions of paintings, sculpture, graphic arts, architecture & design representing contemporary art trends; to provide continued learning & expanded educ; Marble faced structure houses three galleries for exhibition, 3000 sq ft & 1300 sq ft; flexible designs; Shrode Art Center Gallery; Average Annual Attendance: 50,000; Mem: 800; dues individual $35, family $60, patron $125, sponsor $250, benefactor $500, guarantor $1,000; annual meeting in Nov
Income: Financed by endowment & mem
Special Subjects: Graphics, Painting-American, Sculpture, Woodcarvings, Glass, Jade, Silver, Ivory
Collections: Paintings by late 19th & early 20th century American artists; some drawings & small sculptures; silver, small stone, wood & ivory carvings; jade; small bronzes; 85 acre Cedarhurst Sculpture Park
Publications: Form Beyond Function: Recent Sculpture by North American Metalsmiths; quarterly newsletter; Recent Graphics from American Print Shops; Sculpture at Cedarhurst, catalogue; Kathleen Holmes: Bedtime Stories; Harold Gregor's Illinois
Activities: Classes for adults & children; dramatic progs; docent training; workshops; demonstrations; field trips; lects open to pub, 8-10 vis lectrs per yr; concerts; gallery talks; tours; competitions with awards; scholarships offered; book traveling exhibs 1 per yr; originate traveling exhibs to qualified mus & college galleries with adequate staff & facilities; mus shop sells books, original art, regional glass & ceramics & jewelry

L **Cedar Hurst Library,** Richview Rd, Mount Vernon, IL 62864; PO Box 923, Mount Vernon, IL 62864-0019. Tel 618-242-1236; Fax 618-242-9530; Elec Mail mitchell@midwest.net; Internet Home Page Address: www.cedarhurst.org; *Librn* Rhonda Sparks
Open Tues - Sat 10 AM - 5 PM; Open to public for reference only
Library Holdings: Audio Tapes; Book Volumes 1250; Exhibition Catalogs; Kodachrome Transparencies; Pamphlets; Periodical Subscriptions 20; Records; Slides; Video Tapes
Special Subjects: Painting-American

NAPERVILLE

L **NORTH CENTRAL COLLEGE,** Oesterle Library, 320 E School Ave, Naperville, IL 60540. Tel 630-637-5700; Fax 630-637-5716; Internet Home Page Address: www.noctrl.edu; *Technician* Belinda Cheek; *Pub Servs Librn* Ted Schwitzner; *Reference Librn* Carol Murdoch; *Dir* Carolyn A Sheehy
Open Mon - Thurs 8 AM - midnight, Fri 8 AM - 8 PM, Sat 9 AM - 5:30 PM, Sun Noon - 11 PM; Estab 1861 to provide acad support; For lending & reference. Art Gallery houses 4-5 exhibitions per yr
Library Holdings: Audio Tapes; Book Volumes 120,000; Cassettes; Clipping Files; Compact Disks; Fiche; Filmstrips; Manuscripts; Memorabilia; Motion Pictures; Original Art Works; Pamphlets; Periodical Subscriptions 751; Photographs; Records; Reels; Video Tapes
Collections: Sang Collection of Fine Bindings

NILES

M **THE BRADFORD GROUP,** (The Bradford Museum of Collector's Plates) 9333 Milwaukee Ave, Niles, IL 60714. Tel 847-966-2770; Fax 847-581-8639
Open Mon - Fri 8:30 AM - 4:30 PM; No admis fee; Estab 1978 to house and display limited-edition collector's plates for purposes of study, educ and enjoyment
Income: Financed by The Bradford Exchange
Special Subjects: Porcelain
Collections: 800 Limited-Edition Collector's Plates

NORMAL

M **ILLINOIS STATE UNIVERSITY,** University Galleries, 110 Ctr For Visual Arts, Beaufort St Campus Box 5600 Normal, IL 61790-5600. Tel 309-438-5487; Fax 309-438-5161; Elec Mail Gallery@ilstu.edu; Internet Home Page Address: www.cfa.ilstu.edu/galleries; *Dir* Barry Blinderman; *Cur* Bill Conger; *Reg* Tracy Berner; *Cur* Kendra Paitz
Open Tues 9:30 AM - 9 PM, Wed - Fri 9:30 AM - 4:30 PM, Sat - Mon Noon - 4 PM; No admis fee; Estab 1973 to provide changing exhibits of contemporary art for the students & community at large; The main gallery I contains rotating exhibitions; galleries II & III display student & faculty work, graduate exhibitions, studio area shows & works from the permanent collection; Average Annual Attendance: 10,000
Income: Financed by university & Illinois Arts Council
Library Holdings: Exhibition Catalogs; Original Art Works; Prints; Sculpture
Special Subjects: Drawings, Ceramics, Collages, Photography, Painting-American, Prints, Sculpture
Collections: Contemporary art emphasis; prints & drawings
Exhibitions: Oliver Herring, Student Annual, Julia Fish
Publications: Exhibition catalogs
Activities: Lects open to pub, 3-4 vis lectrs per yr; gallery talks; tours; individual paintings & original objects of art lent for other exhibs; lending collection contains original art works, original prints, paintings, photographs & sculpture; originate traveling exhibs; mus shop sells books

L **Museum Library,** 201 N School St, Campus Box 8900 Normal, IL 61790-8900. Tel 309-438-3451; *Cur* Debra Risberg
Museum library open to scholars, students & staff
Library Holdings: Book Volumes 150; Periodical Subscriptions 8
Special Subjects: Decorative Arts, Pre-Columbian Art, American Indian Art

M **Normal Editions Workshop,** 5620 School of Art, Normal, IL 61790-5620. Tel 309-438-7530; Fax 309-438-2215; Elec Mail normaleditionsworkshop@ilstu.edu; Internet Home Page Address: www.cfa.ilstu.edu/normal_editions; *Dir* Richard D Finch
Open Mon-Thurs 9AM-5PM, other times by appointment
Collections: works by emerging & estab artists

OAK BROOK

C MCDONALD'S CORPORATION, Art Collection, 2915 Jorie Blvd, Oak Brook, IL 60523-2126. Tel 630-623-3585; Fax 630-623-6428; Elec Mail cheryl. ogilvie@us.mcd.com; Internet Home Page Address: www.mcdonalds.com; *Cur* Susan Pertl; *Cur* Cheryl Ogilvie
Open to group tours by appointment; No admis fee; Estab 1971; Walking tour through corporate campus
Income: Financed through McDonald's Corporation
Special Subjects: Sculpture, Painting-American, Glass, Landscapes
Collections: Collection of contemporary paintings & sculpture by established & emerging artists; glass sculptures
Activities: Lect; The Spirit of McDonald's Competition; individual paintings & original objects of art lent; lending collection consists of more than 1000 pieces

PALATINE

AMERICAN SOCIETY OF ARTISTS, INC
For further information, see National and Regional Organizations

PARIS

M BICENTENNIAL ART CENTER & MUSEUM, 132 S Central Ave, Paris, IL 61944-1729. Tel 217-466-8130; Fax 217-466-8130; Elec Mail parisartcenter@frontier.com; Internet Home Page Address: www.parisartcenter.com; *Exec Dir* Susan Stafford; *Treas* Ann Staats; *Chmn & Pres (V)* Tom Hebermehl
Open Tues - Fri 10 AM - 4 PM; No admis fee; Estab 1975 to encourage & bring art to area; Five galleries, 234 running ft; Average Annual Attendance: 4,179; Mem: 325; annual meeting in Oct
Income: $30,000 (financed by mem, contributions & fundraising)
Collections: Paintings & sculptures primarily 20th century period, including extensive collection of Alice Baber works
Exhibitions: Annual Fall Art Show; Annual Paint Illinois; changing exhibits each month
Publications: Monthly newsletter
Activities: Classes for adults & children; docent training; gallery talks; tours; judged competitions; scholarships offered; lending library

PARK RIDGE

M BRICKTON ART CENTER, 306 Busse Hwy, Park Ridge, IL 60068. Tel 847-823-6611; Fax 847-823-6622

PEORIA

M BRADLEY UNIVERSITY, Heuser Art Center, 1501 W Bradley Ave, Peoria, IL 61625-0003. Tel 309-677-2967; Fax 309-677-3642; Elec Mail pkrainak@bradley.edu; Internet Home Page Address: www.art.bradley.edu/guy; *Gallery Dir* Erin Buczynski; *Chmn Art Dept* Paul Krainak
Open Mon-Tues 9 AM - 7 PM, Fri 9 AM - 4 PM; No admis fee; Exhibition space 639 sq ft; Average Annual Attendance: 2,000
Income: Financed by University, Illinois Arts Council
Library Holdings: Audio Tapes 100; Book Volumes 10,000; Exhibition Catalogs 300; Video Tapes 100
Collections: 1500 contemporary print & drawings
Exhibitions: Rotating exhibits; Purchase prizes Bradley Nat Print & Drawing Exhib; Central Time Ceramics - Biennial Exhib
Activities: Classes for adults; docent training; lects open to pub; gallery talks; tours; competitions with awards; master print program; individual paintings lent on campus

M CONTEMPORARY ART CENTER, 305 SW Water St, Peoria, IL 61602. Tel 309-674-6822; Elec Mail artcentr@mtco.com; Internet Home Page Address: www.peoriacac.org

M LAKEVIEW MUSEUM OF ARTS & SCIENCES, 222 SW Washington St, Peoria, IL 61602-2500. Tel 309-686-7000; Fax 309-686-0280; Elec Mail info@lakeview-museum.org; Internet Home Page Address: www.lakeview-museum.org; *VPres Exhibs & Coll* Kristan McKinsey; *VPres Educ* Sheldon Schafer; *Pres & CEO* Jim Richerson
Open Tues - Sat 10 AM - 4PM, Sun noon-4PM, cl Mon; Admis adults $6.00, seniors $5, students $4, children 3 & under free; Estab 1965, new building opened 1965, to provide enjoyment & educ by reflecting the historical, cultural & industrial life of the Central Illinois area; Two changing exhibition galleries, Illinois Folk Art Gallery & Children's Discovery Center; Average Annual Attendance: 250,000; Mem: 2600; dues family $75, individual $40; qualification for mem: Smithsonian Affiliate
Income: $500,000
Special Subjects: Folk Art, Tapestries, African Art, Archaeology, Southwestern Art, Textiles, Primitive art, Woodcarvings, Posters
Collections: Archaeological; decorative arts; Regional American Fine & Folk Art; paintings & graphics; fine arts; anthropology, natural sciences
Exhibitions: Changing exhibitions dealing with the arts & sciences
Publications: Mems bulletin; Lakeviews, exhibition catalogues
Activities: Classes for adults & children; concerts; gallery talks; tours; competitions with awards; individual & original objects of art lent to sister institutions; 4 per yr book traveling exhibs; mus store sells books, magazines, original art, reproductions, prints & craft items

A PEORIA ART GUILD, 203 Harrison Peoria, IL 61602. Tel 309-637-2787; Fax 309-637-7334; Elec Mail info@peoriaartguild.org; Internet Home Page Address: www.peoriaartguild.org; *Dir* Jennifer Lee; *Bus Mgr* Kathy Hunt; *Dir Exhib* Michelle Traver; *Dir Educ* Susie Mathews
Open Mon - Thurs 10 AM - 6 PM, Fri & Sat 10 AM - 5 PM, cl Sun; No admis fee, donations appreciated; Estab 1878 to encourage develop & appreciation of the visual arts; 3000 sq ft floor space; Average Annual Attendance: 40,000; Mem: 1000; dues $30
Income: Financed by mem, Illinois Arts Council, sales & rental, private donations
Collections: Framed & unframed 2-D design, ceramics, sculpture, jewelry, weaving & wood designs; winning works from the Bradley National Print & Drawing Exhibition; 150 featured artists from the US and international
Exhibitions: One-person shows; group theme shows, shows annually; Marsha S. Glaten; Anthony Swan, photojournalism
Activities: Classes for adults & children; workshops; lect open to public, 5-6 vis lectrs per year; gallery talks; tours; awards; individual paintings rented to bus & members of the community; lending collection contains original art work, prints, paintings, photographs & sculptures; sales shop sells original art & prints

M PEORIA HISTORICAL SOCIETY, 611 SW Washington St, Peoria, IL 61602-5104. Tel 309-674-1921; Fax 309-674-1882; Internet Home Page Address: peoriahistoricalsociety.org; *Exec Dir* Walter C Ruppman; *Board Pres* Mark Johnson; *Coll Mgr* Robert Killion
Judge John C Flanagan House open for tours by appt & Wed - Sun 1-4 PM (Mar - Dec); Pettengill-Morron House open by appt only; Admis adults $7, children 15 & under $3; Estab 1934 to acquire, preserve & display artifacts & records relating to the history of Peoria & the Central Illinois Valley; to encourage & support historical research & investigation & to promote & sustain pub interest in history of Peoria & the Central Illinois Valley; Two historic house museums: Flanagan House is post-colonial, Pettengill-Morron house is Victorian; Library housed in Special Collections Ctr of Bradley Univ; Average Annual Attendance: 10,000; Mem: 700; dues $25 & up; annual meeting in May
Income: Financed by mem, endowments; private gifts & grants
Library Holdings: Audio Tapes; Book Volumes; CD-ROMs; Cards; Cassettes; Clipping Files; Framed Reproductions; Kodachrome Transparencies; Manuscripts; Maps; Memorabilia; Original Art Works; Original Documents; Other Holdings; Pamphlets; Periodical Subscriptions; Photographs; Prints; Records; Reproductions; Sculpture; Slides; Video Tapes
Special Subjects: Pottery, Period Rooms
Collections: Household items & artifacts from 1840; Peoria Pottery; Lincoln artifacts; Civil War, WW I & II; Peoria bus; French exploration; fur trade
Exhibitions: Rennick Award (art works relating to historic sites), History Fair; Victorian Mourning Rituals; Peoria's Past Rediscovered; English exploration
Publications: Bi-monthly Newsletter to members
Activities: Educ prog; docent training; internship progs; lects open to pub, 7 vis lectrs per yr; competitions with prizes; tours; Historic Preservation award; Regional History Fair winner, Centenarians & Volunteer of Yr awards; exten prog serves mus, cultural & educational institutions; originates traveling exhibs to regional bus & educational institutions; boutique at Pettengill-Morron House (The Butler's Pantry); sells books & gifts

QUINCY

A QUINCY ART CENTER, 1515 Jersey St, Quincy, IL 62301-4250. Tel 217-223-5900; Fax 217-223-6950; Elec Mail lrabe@quincyartcenter.org; Internet Home Page Address: www.quincyartcenter.org; *Exec Dir* Julie D Nelson; *Dir Educ* Jennifer Teter; *Asst Direct Publ Coordr* Lana Rabe; *Exhibs Prep* Libby Tournear; *Graphic Designer* Shannon Larson
Open Mon - Fri 9 AM - 4 PM, Sat & Sun 1 - 4 PM; cl holidays; Admis adults $3, seniors & students $1,mems free, Thurs free; Estab 1923, incorporated 1951 to foster pub awareness & understanding of the visual arts; Mid sized Sinnock 1945 Gallery - Art Modern Style renovated historic carriage house; large contemporary gallery in 1989-1990 wing; Average Annual Attendance: 18,000; Mem: 500; dues $25 & up
Income: Financed by grants, donations, mem fees & Beaux Art Ball, foundations, special events, individual donations
Purchases: Four new pottery wheels for studio
Library Holdings: Book Volumes
Special Subjects: Drawings, Etchings & Engravings, Landscapes, Photography, Posters, Prints, Sculpture, Watercolors, Painting-American, Woodcuts, Crafts, Portraits, Marine Painting, Period Rooms, Painting-European, Mexican Art
Collections: Donenberg Collection; Early 20th century midwestern art; Small coll 20th century African American Art
Publications: Calendar, brochures &/or catalogs for temporary exhibitions
Activities: Classes & workshops for adults & children; art mentor training; art mentor programs; lects open to pub; gallery talks; tours; competitions with awards; artists presented in solo & two-person exhibits; scholarships offered; inter-museum loan

A QUINCY SOCIETY OF FINE ARTS, 300 Civic Ctr Plaza, Ste 244, Quincy, IL 62301-4162. Tel 217-222-3432; Fax 217-228-2787; Elec Mail art@artsqcy.org; Internet Home Page Address: www.artsqcy.org; *Dir* Rob Dwyer
Open Mon - Fri 8 AM - 5 PM; Estab 1947 as a community arts council to coordinate & stimulate the visual & performing arts in Quincy & Adams County; Mem: 48 art organizations; non-profit, arts & humanities
Income: Financed by endowment, mem & contribution, Illinois Arts Council, National Endowment for the Arts
Publications: Cultural Calendars, monthly; pamphlets & catalogs; Arts Quincy, monthly
Activities: Workshops for adults & students in visual & performing arts

M QUINCY UNIVERSITY, The Gray Gallery, 1800 College Ave, Quincy, IL 62301-2699. Tel 217-228-5371; Internet Home Page Address: www.quincy.edu; *Dir Gallery* Robert Lee Mejer
Open Mon - Thur 8 AM - 10 PM, Fri 8 AM - 6 PM, Sat 1 - 5 PM, Sun 1 - 10 PM; No admis fee; Estab 1968 for cultural enrichment & exposure to

contemporary art forms in the community; Exhibitions are held in the Brenner library foyer & The Gray Gallery; Average Annual Attendance: 6,000
Income: Financed through the coll & student activities assoc
Special Subjects: Drawings, Prints
Collections: 19th century Oriental & European prints; permanent coll of student & faculty works; 20th century American prints & drawings
Exhibitions: Watercolors by Bruce Bobick; Waterbase Monotypes Dennis Olsen
Publications: Brochures, 1-2 times annually; gallery calendars, annually
Activities: Lects open to public, 1 vis lectr per year; gallery talks; tours; student show with awards; individual paintings & original objects of art lent; slide reviews of potential artists/shows; book traveling exhibs 1-2 per year

L **Brenner Library,** 1800 College Ave, Quincy, IL 62301-2699. Tel 217-222-8020; Fax 217-228-5354; Elec Mail qulib@darkstar.rsa.lib.il.ms; Internet Home Page Address: www.quincy.edu; *Dean of Library* Pat Tomczak
Open by appointment only; Reference only for pub; lending for faculty & students
Income: $1,600 (financed by college revenues)
Purchases: $1,600 annually for books
Library Holdings: Book Volumes 7890; Cassettes; Exhibition Catalogs; Filmstrips; Lantern Slides; Motion Pictures; Periodical Subscriptions 20; Prints; Records; Slides; Video Tapes

ROCK ISLAND

M **AUGUSTANA COLLEGE,** Augustana College Art Museum, NW Corner Seventh Ave & 38th St, Rock Island, IL 61201; 639 38th St, Rock Island, IL 61201-2296. Tel 309-794-7469; Fax 309-794-7678; Elec Mail dr.prestonthayer@augustana.edu; Internet Home Page Address: www.augustana.edu; *Dir Gallery* Preston Thayer
Open Tues - Sat Noon - 4 PM; No admis fee; Estab 1973 for the display of visual arts exhibits commensurate with a liberal arts col curriculum; Main gallery serves as an entrance to large auditorium; lower gallery is smaller than main gallery; two galleries total 217 ft wall space; Art Collection Gallery, opened in 1999 is located off lower gallery; Average Annual Attendance: 50,000
Income: $53,785
Purchases: $3000
Special Subjects: American Indian Art, Decorative Arts, Etchings & Engravings, Ceramics, Portraits, Painting-American, Prints, Textiles, Sculpture, Tapestries, Watercolors, African Art, Pottery, Woodcarvings, Woodcuts
Collections: Contemporary, Eastern & Western prints; Swedish American Art; Modern Oriental; Native American
Publications: Exhibit catalogs
Activities: Classes for children; lect open to public; 3-4 vis lectrs per year; concerts; gallery talks; tours; competitions with prizes; individual paintings & original objects of art lent upon requests considered on individual basis; book traveling exhibitions, 2-3 per year

A **QUAD CITY ARTS INC,** 1715 2nd Ave, Rock Island, IL 61201. Tel 309-793-1213; Fax 309-793-1265; Elec Mail info@quadcityarts.com; Internet Home Page Address: www.quadcityarts.com; *Exec Dir* Carmen Darland; *Visual Arts Dir* Dawn Wohlford-Metallo; *Performing Arts & Arts in Educ Dir* Susan Wahlmann; *Community Arts Dir* Jessi Black; *Communs Mgr* Rebecca Green
Open Tues - Fri 10 AM - 5 PM, Sat 11 AM - 5 PM, Mon by appt only, cl Sun & major holidays; No admis fee; Estab 1970 in IL & chartered in 1974 in IA to bring visual arts to the people; Maintains Quad City Arts Gallery & Quad City International Airport Gallery; Average Annual Attendance: 12,800; Mem: Dues seniors, students & educators $25, individual $35, household $50, orchestra $100 - $249, cast $250 - $499, choreographer $500 - $999, playwright $1000+
Activities: Classes for youth; public sculpture prog; literary progs; Vanguard events; vis artist series; lect open to public; concerts; gallery talks; tours; sales shop sells original art & prints

ROCKFORD

A **ROCKFORD ART MUSEUM,** 711 N Main St, Rockford, IL 61103-7204. Tel 815-968-2787; Fax 815-316-2179; Elec Mail staff@rockfordmuseum.org; Internet Home Page Address: www.rockfordartmuseum.org; *Financial Officer* Dave Schroepfer; *Educ Coordr & Mus Asst* Stacy Sauer; *Exec Dir* Linda Dennis; *Cur* Patty Rhea; *Communs Coordr* David Dixon; *Pub Rels & Spec Events* Sarah McNamara; *Registrar* Jeremiah Blankenbaker
Open Mon-Sat 10 AM - 5 PM, Sun Noon-5 PM; Admis adults $5, seniors $3, students & children free; Estab 1913 to enrich the quality of life by communicating the pleasure, appreciation & meaning of the visual arts through a prog of exhib, interpretation, educ & coll; 17,000 sq ft exhibition space; Average Annual Attendance: 40,000; Mem: 1000
Income: Financed by mem, grants, state appropriation & private donations
Collections: Permanent collection 19th & 20th century American oil paintings, graphics, sculpture, photography, ceramics, glassware, textiles, watercolors & mixed media
Exhibitions: Annual Greenwich Village Art Fair; Annual Young Artist's Exhibition; numerous one-person and group shows; Rockford-Midwestern Show (biennial)
Publications: Exhibition brochures & catalogs; magazine, quarterly
Activities: Classes for adults & children; docent training; artist-in-residence; mus school prog; lects open to pub, 5 vis lectrs per yr; gallery talks; tours; competitions with cash awards; book traveling exhibs; mus shop sells books, original art, reproductions, prints, jewelry, ceramics & crafts

M **ROCKFORD COLLEGE ART GALLERY,** 5050 E State St, Clark Arts Center Rockford, IL 61108-2311. Tel 815-226-4034; Fax 815-394-5167; *Dir* Maureen Gustafson
Open Tues-Wed 11AM-2PM, Thurs-Fri 3-6PM; Estab 1970
Activities: Gallery & group tours; lects open to pub, 6 vis lectrs per yr; originate traveling exhibs 1 per yr

SKOKIE

L **SKOKIE PUBLIC LIBRARY,** 5215 Oakton, Skokie, IL 60077. Tel 847-673-7774; Fax 847-673-7797; Elec Mail askpr@skokielibrary.info; Internet Home Page Address: www.skokielibrary.info; *Dir* Carolyn Anthony; *Mktg & Progs* Christie Robinson
Open Mon - Fri 9 AM - 9 PM, Sat 9 AM - 6 PM, Sun noon - 6 PM; No admis fee; Estab 1941 as a general pub library serving the residents of Skokie; reciprocal borrowing privileges offered to members of pub libraries in North Suburban Library System; Art gallery is maintained; Average Annual Attendance: 800,000
Income: $11,664,243 (financed by independent tax levy)
Purchases: $1,136,669
Library Holdings: Book Volumes 342,452; Clipping Files; Compact Disks 43,897; Framed Reproductions; Original Art Works 20; Other Holdings 95,279 w/DVDs incl; Pamphlets; Periodical Subscriptions 1807; Reproductions; Sculpture 12; Video Tapes 46,937
Special Subjects: Art History, Painting-American, Sculpture, Painting-European, Watercolors, Crafts, Dolls, Embroidery, Handicrafts, Architecture
Exhibitions: Sendak & Co children's book art; Resistance & Remembrance: The Story of the White Rose; Gute Aussichten: New German Photography 2013
Activities: Classes for adults & children, dramatic progs; lect open to public; 15 vis lects per yr; concerts; gallery talks; tours

SPRINGFIELD

M **ILLINOIS STATE MUSEUM,** ISM Lockport Gallery, Chicago Gallery & Southern Illinois Art Gallery, Spring & Edwards St, Springfield, IL 62706; 502 S Spring St, Springfield, IL 62706-5000. Tel 217-782-1386; Fax 217-782-1254; Elec Mail ksmith@museum.state.il.us; Internet Home Page Address: www.museum.state.il.us; *Dir* Bonnie W Styles; *Dir Art* Jim Zimmer; *Asst Dir* Robert Sill; *Asst Cur Decorative Arts* Angela Goebel Bain; *Registrar Decorative Art* Irene Boyer; *Registrar Art* Carole Peterson; *Exhibs Designer* Philip Kennedy; *Dir ISM Southern IL Art Gallery* Debra Tayes; *Asst Dir Art ISM Chicago Gallery* Jane Stevens; *Asst Cur ISM Lockport* Jennifer Jaskowiak; *Assoc Cur ISM Chicago Gallery* Douglas Stapleton
Open Mon - Sat 8:30 AM - 5 PM, Sun Noon - 5 PM; No admis fee; Estab 1877 as mus of natural history, art added in 1928. Collection, exhibition & publication of art produced by or of interest to Illinois & its citizens. Three major changing exhibitions annually; Circ Research lib; Changing exhibition space: Springfield Art Gallery 3000 sq ft; Arts of Science Gallery (six changing exhibits), 1364 sq ft; permanent collection galleries present fine, decorative & ethnographic arts, 6400 sq ft, permanent exhibit of Illinois Decorative Arts, At Home in The Heartland 3000 sq ft; Average Annual Attendance: 250,000; Mem: 650; dues $25-$500
Income: $966,000. Art Section & four gallery sites financed by state appropriations & private gifts
Purchases: $5000
Library Holdings: Auction Catalogs; Audio Tapes; Book Volumes 36,000; CD-ROMs; Exhibition Catalogs; Manuscripts; Maps; Original Art Works; Original Documents; Periodical Subscriptions 900 (historial holdings only)
Special Subjects: Afro-American Art, Anthropology, Decorative Arts, Etchings & Engravings, History of Art & Archaeology, Landscapes, Art History, Ceramics, Collages, Glass, American Western Art, Flasks & Bottles, Furniture, Porcelain, Pottery, Pre-Columbian Art, Prints, Woodcuts, Drawings, Graphics, Hispanic Art, Painting-American, Photography, Sculpture, Watercolors, American Indian Art, African Art, Archaeology, Ethnology, Southwestern Art, Religious Art, Crafts, Folk Art, Primitive art, Woodcarvings, Portraits, Posters, Eskimo Art, Dolls, Oriental Art, Silver, Ivory, Maps, Scrimshaw, Tapestries, Miniatures, Dioramas, Period Rooms, Embroidery, Laces, Mosaics, Gold, Stained Glass, Pewter, Leather, Enamels
Collections: Fine art including ceramics, metal work, textiles, glass, furniture, quilts, dolls; Decorative art including sculpture, prints, drawings, photography, contemporary crafts, folk art; quilts; dolls
Exhibitions: Exhibitions featuring contemporary & historical paintings, sculpture, photography, graphics, decorative arts & history, with emphasis on Illinois material
Publications: Living Museum (also in Braille), quarterly; exhibit & collection catalogs; Biennial report; Impressions, bimonthly members publication
Activities: Educ prog; classes for adults & children; dramatic progs; docent training; lects & symposia open to pub; 45+ vis lectures per yr; concerts; gallery talks; tours; competitions with awards; film series; internships; individual paintings lent to other mus, historical sites & galleries; book traveling exhibs; sales shop sells books, original art & work of IL artisans

L **Library,** 502 S Spring, Springfield, IL 62706-5000. Tel 217-524-0496; Fax 217-782-1254; Elec Mail pburg@museum.state.il.us; Internet Home Page Address: www.museum.state.il.us; *Librn* Patricia Burg
Open Mon - Fri 8:30 AM - 5 PM; Estab to provide informational materials & services to meet the requirements of the mus staff in fields pertinent to the purpose & work of the mus
Income: Financed by state appropriation
Purchases: varies
Library Holdings: Book Volumes 30,000; Clipping Files; Manuscripts; Pamphlets; Periodical Subscriptions 900 (historical holdings); Video Tapes
Special Subjects: Art History, Decorative Arts, Manuscripts, History of Art & Archaeology, Archaeology, Ethnology, Art Education, Anthropology, Dolls
Collections: Anthropology and Ornithology; Decorative Arts; Fine Art-Illinois; Natural History

A **SPRINGFIELD ART ASSOCIATION OF EDWARDS PLACE,** 700 N Fourth St, Springfield, IL 62702. Tel 217-523-2631, 523-3507; Fax 217-523-3866; Elec Mail director@springfield.org; Internet Home Page Address: www.springfieldart.org; *Exec Dir* Betsy Dollar; *Coll Cur* Erika Holst; *Educ Coordr* Erin Svendson; *Library Dir* Jan Arnold; *Office Mgr* Megan Metzger
Open Daily 9 AM - 5 PM, Sat 10 AM - 3 PM; No admis fee to gallery, library, studios; suggested donation Edwards Place $5; Estab 1913 to foster appreciation of art, to instruct people in art & to expose people to quality art; Circ 400; 9-12

curated exhibits each yr featuring local, regional & nationally juried work in all media; Average Annual Attendance: 4,200; Mem: 800; dues $50-$500; monthly meeting
Income: $200,000 (financed by mem & grants, interest, tuition & benefits)
Library Holdings: Book Volumes; DVDs; Periodical Subscriptions; Video Tapes
Collections: American decorative arts; American paintings; antique toys; prints; sculpture
Exhibitions: 3 to 4 exhibitions are scheduled annually with one juried exhibition; work is borrowed from museum & artist nationwide
Publications: Membership brochures, quarterly; newsletters
Activities: Classes for adults & children; docent training; art outreach prog in school in community; lects open to pub, 6-8 vis lectrs per yr; gallery talks; tours; schols offered; lends original objects upon request to other mus & institutes exhibs; book traveling exhibs

L **Michael Victor II Art Library,** 700 N Fourth, Springfield, IL 62702. Tel 217-523-2631; Fax 217-523-3866; Elec Mail mvlibrary@springfieldart.org; Internet Home Page Address: springfieldart.org; *Library Dir* Jan Dungey
Open weekdays 9AM-5PM, Sat 10 AM - 3PM, cl Sun; Estab 1965 to provide total community with access to art & art related books
Library Holdings: Book Volumes 7000; CD-ROMs; DVDs; Exhibition Catalogs; Pamphlets; Periodical Subscriptions 20; Reproductions; Video Tapes
Special Subjects: Art History, Collages, Calligraphy, Commercial Art, Ceramics, Conceptual Art, American Western Art, Cartoons, Art Education, Asian Art, American Indian Art, Aesthetics, Afro-American Art, Carpets & Rugs, Architecture
Activities: Classes for children; lect series, 8 vis lectrs per yr; film prog

VERNON HILLS

M **CUNEO FOUNDATION,** Museum & Gardens, 1350 N Milwaukee, Vernon Hills, IL 60061. Tel 847-362-3042; Fax 847-362-4130; *Dir* James Bert
Open Tues - Sun 10 AM - 5 PM; Estab 1991
Income: $300,000 (financed by endowment, mem & admis)
Special Subjects: Decorative Arts, Tapestries, Period Rooms, Painting-Italian
Collections: Architecture; decorative arts; furniture; paintings

WATSEKA

M **IROQUOIS COUNTY HISTORICAL SOCIETY MUSEUM,** Old Courthouse Museum, 103 W Cherry, Watseka, IL 60970. Tel 815-432-2215; Fax 815-432-2215; Elec Mail ichs2215@mchsi.com; Internet Home Page Address: www.iroquoiscountyhistoricalsociety.com; *Pres & Chmn Mgmt Comt* Rolland Light; *VPres* Jean Hiles; *Treas* Bob Ficke; *Art Gallery Chmn & Secy* Marilyn Wilken; *Office Mgr* Judy Ficke
Open Mon - Fri 10 AM - 4 PM, Sat by appointment only - call ahead or 1st Sat of Mon 10 AM - 2 PM; Donation adults $2, children $.50; Estab 1967 to further the interest in history, art & genealogy; One room for county artists; Average Annual Attendance: 10,000; Mem: 800; dues annual $15 - $150 life
Income: Financed by donations by visitors, artists, memberships & art comt sells crafts
Library Holdings: Book Volumes; Fiche; Maps; Memorabilia
Special Subjects: Decorative Arts, Historical Material, Glass, Flasks & Bottles, Furniture, Period Rooms, Manuscripts, Maps, Archaeology, Costumes, Crafts, Dolls, Coins & Medals, Dioramas
Collections: Paintings, prints, posters & pictures; Iroquois Co memorabelia & artifacts
Exhibitions: Art work by local artists - display changes every 2 months
Publications: Genealogical Stalker, quarterly; Iroquois County Historical Society newsletter, quarterly; historic reprints
Activities: Lects open to pub; concerts; gallery talks; tours; competitions with awards; mus shop sells books, T-shirts & misc postcards

WHEATON

A **DUPAGE ART LEAGUE SCHOOL & GALLERY,** 218 W Front St, Wheaton, IL 60187-5111. Tel 630-653-7090; Fax 630-681-0975; Elec Mail tanyaberley@yahoo.com; Internet Home Page Address: www.dupageartleague.org; *Treas* Kandi Husarek; *VPres Educ & Pres Emeritus* Kay Wahlgren; *VPres Exhibits* Julie Luedtke; *VPres Mem* Tammy Proctor; *VPres Buildings & Grounds* Jim Karszewski; *VPres Activities* Margaret Bucholz; *Pres* Tanya Berley; *VPres Organization* Bernie Malovany; *VPres Finance* Carol Kincaid; *Secy* Marguerite Paris; *VPres Office Mgmt* Yvonne Thompson
Open Mon - Fri 9 AM - 5 PM, Sat 9 AM - 2 PM, mems must be 17 yrs & up; No admis fee; Estab 1957 primarily as an educational organization founded to encourage artists & promote high artistic standards through instruction, informative programs & exhibits; Three galleries are maintained where members exhibit & sell their work; Mem: 450; dues $40; annual meeting in May
Income: Financed through mem, gifts & donations
Library Holdings: Book Volumes
Exhibitions: Monthly exhibits; nine juried shows per yr; holiday gift gallery; Fine Art Gallery with monthly exhibits of local artists (Gallery I), one-man or one-woman shows (Gallery II), Fine Crafts (Gallery III)
Publications: Monthly newsletter
Activities: Classes for adults & children; progs; demonstrations; lects open to pub, 8 vis lectrs per yr; gallery talks; competitions; awards; schols offered; individual paintings & original objects of art lent to local libraries & bus; sales shop sells original art & fine crafts (jewelry, ceramics, woodworks fiber & glass)

WINNETKA

A **NORTH SHORE ART LEAGUE,** 620 Lincoln Ave, Winnetka, IL 60093-2308. Tel 847-446-2870; Fax 847-446-4306; Elec Mail info@northshoreartleague.org; Internet Home Page Address: www.northshoreartleague.org; *Exec Dir* Linda Nelson; *Bd Pres* Lisa Lucenti; *Arts Educ Mgr* Andra Nyman
Open Mon - Fri 9 AM - 5 PM; No admis fee; Estab 1924, inc 1954, to promote interest in creative art through education, exhibition opportunities, scholarship & art programs; Year-round gallery exhibs; Mem: 500; dues $45; annual meeting in June

Income: Financed by mem dues, shows & tuition from classes, contributions
Exhibitions: Members show (Sept); Art on the Plaza (June); Printworks (March); Inchworks (Nov); Watercolor Show (May)
Publications: Art League News, quarterly
Activities: Classes for adults & children; lect for mems only & lects open to pub; tours; sponsor juried competitions with awards; scholarships offered for children

INDIANA

ANDERSON

A **ANDERSON FINE ARTS CENTER,** The Anderson Center for the Arts, 32 W 10th, Anderson, IN 46016-1409; PO Box 1218, Anderson, IN 46015-1218. Tel 765-649-1248; Fax 765-649-0199; Elec Mail dstapleton.taca@sbcglobal.net; Internet Home Page Address: www.andersonart.org; *Exec Dir* Deborah McBratney-Stapleton; *Exhib Cur* Holly Renneker; *Exhib Cur* Tim Swain; *Bus Mgr* Viki Jones; *Admin Asst* Cheryl Mitchell
Open Tues - Fri Noon - 5 PM, Sat 10 AM - 5 PM, Sun 2 - 5 PM, cl Mon & national holidays; Admis adults $2, sr citizens $1.50, students $1, family rate $5, Tues & 1st Sun of month free; Estab 1967 to serve the community by promoting & encouraging interest in the fine arts through exhibs, progs & educ activities & the develop of a permanent coll; Three galleries contain 1705 sq ft; also a small sales & rental gallery & a studio/theatre; Average Annual Attendance: 30,000; Mem: 700; dues master $1000 or more, benefactor $500-$999, sustaining $250-$499, patron $125-$249, family $60-$124, individual $40-$59; annual meeting in May
Income: Financed by mem, endowments, grants, individual & corporate contributions
Collections: Midwestern & 20th century American prints, paintings & drawings; Contemporary American Art
Exhibitions: Annual Indiana Artists - Local Exhibit; annual photo exhibits; one-man shows - Local Artist, National Artist, International Artists
Publications: Calendar of Events, quarterly; catalogue of the permanent collection; exhibition catalogs
Activities: Classes for adults & children; dramatic progs; docent training; educational outreach; lects open to pub, 4-6 vis lectrs per yr; concerts; gallery talks; tours; competitions with awards; individual paintings & original objects of art lent to bus, educational facilities & other mus; lending collection contains 300 original art works, 150 original prints, 300 paintings, 10 sculpture & 1000 slides, extension progs serving senior explorations - nursing homes in Madison County; book traveling exhibs; mus shop sells books, original art, reproductions, prints, slides, pottery, handcrafted items, glass, fine cards & note papers, frame shop

BLOOMINGTON

L **INDIANA UNIVERSITY,** Fine Arts Library, 1133 E 7th St, Museum 251 Bloomington, IN 47408-7509. Tel 812-855-3314; Fax 812-855-3443; Elec Mail antmwhite@indiana.edu; Internet Home Page Address: www.indiana.edu/~libfinea; *Head Librn* Tony White; *Reference Technical Assoc* Mary Buechley; *Technical Svcs Asst* Edwin Cheek; *Branch Coordr* Nicole Beatty
Hours vary; Estab c1940; Circ 50,000; For lending
Income: Financed by state & student fees
Library Holdings: Auction Catalogs; Book Volumes 150,000; CD-ROMs; Cassettes; Clipping Files 50,000; Compact Disks; Exhibition Catalogs; Fiche 24,000; Periodical Subscriptions 390; Slides 25,000; Video Tapes 200
Special Subjects: Art History, Collages, Folk Art, Landscape Architecture, Decorative Arts, Illustration, Mixed Media, Photography, Calligraphy, Commercial Art, Drawings, Etchings & Engravings, Graphic Arts, Graphic Design, Islamic Art, Manuscripts, Painting-American, Painting-British, Painting-Dutch, Painting-Flemish, Painting-French, Painting-German, Painting-Japanese, Painting-Russian, Painting-Spanish, Posters, Pre-Columbian Art, Prints, Sculpture, Painting-European, Historical Material, History of Art & Archaeology, Watercolors, Ceramics, Conceptual Art, Crafts, Latin American Art, Archaeology, Painting-Israeli, American Western Art, Bronzes, Printmaking, Advertising Design, Cartoons, Fashion Arts, Interior Design, Lettering, Asian Art, Video, American Indian Art, Primitive art, Anthropology, Eskimo Art, Furniture, Mexican Art, Southwestern Art, Jade, Stained Glass, Aesthetics, Afro-American Art, Metalwork, Antiquities-Oriental, Carpets & Rugs, Enamels, Gold, Goldsmithing, Handicrafts, Jewelry, Oriental Art, Pottery, Religious Art, Restoration & Conservation, Silversmithing, Tapestries, Woodcuts, Marine Painting, Antiquities-Byzantine, Antiquities-Etruscan, Antiquities-Greek, Antiquities-Roman, Painting-Scandinavian, Painting-Australian, Painting-Canadian, Painting-New Zealand, Architecture, Portraits, Textiles, Woodcarvings

M **INDIANA UNIVERSITY,** Art Museum, 1133 E Seventh St, Bloomington, IN 47405-7509. Tel 812-855-5445; Fax 812-855-1023; Elec Mail iuam@indiana.edu; Internet Home Page Address: www.artmuseum.iu.edu; Cable ARTMUSEUM INDVERS; *Dir* Adelheid Gealt; *Assoc Dir Develop* Jeremy Hatch; *Assoc Dir Editorial Servs* Linda Baden; *Assoc Dir Curatorial Services & Cur African & Oceanic Pre-Columbian Art* Diane Pelrine; *Cur Ancient Art* Adriana Calinescu; *Registrar* Anita Bracalente; *Cur Educ* Ed Maxedon; *Asst Registrar* Kathy Taylor; *Cur 19th & 20th Century Art* Jenny McComas; *Assoc Dir Admin* David Tanner; *Cur Works on Paper* Nan Brewer; *Cur Asian Art* Judy Stubbs; *Security Mgr* Debbie Scholl
Open Tues - Sat 10 AM - 5 PM, Sun Noon - 5 PM, cl Mon; No admis fee; Estab 1941 to serve as a teaching & cultural resource for the University community & the public at large; Gallery has 3 permanent exhibitions: Western Art, Medieval - present; Africa, Asian, Oceania & Americas; special exhibits (temporary & travelling); Average Annual Attendance: 40,000
Income: Financed by col & grants
Special Subjects: Drawings, Etchings & Engravings, Ceramics, American Western Art, Antiquities-Assyrian, Prints, Bronzes, African Art, Ethnology, Primitive art, Asian Art, Antiquities-Byzantine, Carpets & Rugs, Coins & Medals, Baroque Art,

Calligraphy, Antiquities-Oriental, Antiquities-Persian, Antiquities-Egyptian, Antiquities-Greek, Antiquities-Roman, Antiquities-Etruscan
Collections: African, ancient to modern, Far Eastern, Oceanic, the Americas, prints, drawings, photographs & sculpture
Exhibitions: 5 rotating exhibs per yr
Publications: Guide to the collection, exhibition catalogs, occasional papers, newsletter
Activities: Classes for adults & children; docent training; lects open to pub; gallery talks; tours; concerts series; competition with awards; book traveling exhibs, 1-2 per yr; originates traveling exhibs, mainly other universities & art mus; mus shop sells books, magazines, reproductions, prints, slides

M **The Mathers Museum of World Cultures,** 416 North Indiana Ave, Bloomington, IN 47405; 601 E Eighth St, Bloomington, IN 47408. Tel 812-855-6873; Fax 812-855-0205; Elec Mail mathers@indiana.edu; Internet Home Page Address: www.indiana.edu/~mathers/home; *Conservator* Judith Sylvester; *Asst Dir* Judith Kirk; *Cur Coll* Deeksha Nagar; *Bus Mgr* Sandra Warren; *Dir* Geoffrey W Conrad; *Cur Educ* Ellen Sieber; *Co-Cur Exhibs* Elaine Gaul; *Co-cur of Exhibits* Matthew Sieber; *Registrar* Theresa Harley-Wilson
Open Tues - Fri 9 AM - 4:30 PM, Sat & Sun 1 - 4:30 PM; No admis fee; Estab 1964 as Indiana University Mus, institute renamed in 1983. Mus of World Cultures housing over 30,000 artifacts; Mem: Dues $25-$45
Income: Financed by mem & col
Special Subjects: Anthropology, Folk Art, Historical Material
Collections: Anthropology, folklore & history with colls of American primitives, Latin American primitives & folk art
Exhibitions: Museum features changing exhibitions
Publications: Papers & monograph series
Activities: Docent prog; mus training classes; lects; tours; film series; school loan collection

CARMEL

M **EVAN LURIE FINE ART GALLERY,** 30 W Main St, Carmel, IN 46032. Tel 317-844-8400; Fax 317-844-8460; Elec Mail info@evanluriegallery.com; *Dir* Evan Lurie
Open Mon - Fri 11 AM - 5 PM, Sat - Sun noon - 4 PM
Collections: paintings; sculpture; photographs

CHESTERTON

M **CHESTERTON ART CENTER,** 115 S 4th St, Chesterton, IN 46304-2344. Tel 219-926-4711; Elec Mail gallery@chestertonart.com; Internet Home Page Address: www.chestertonart.com

ELKHART

M **MIDWEST MUSEUM OF AMERICAN ART,** 429 Main St, Elkhart, IN 46515-3210; PO Box 1812, Elkhart, IN 46515-1812. Tel 574-293-6660; Fax 574-293-6660; Elec Mail mdwstmsmam@aol.com; Internet Home Page Address: www.midwestmuseum.us; *Cur Exhib & Educ* Brian D Byrn; *Dir* B Jane Burns; *Admin Asst* Kayleigh Weber-Byer
Open Tues - Fri 10 AM - 4 PM, Sat - Sun 1 - 4 PM; Admis adults $5, students $4, family (3 or more) $10; Estab 1978 to provide high quality exhibitions, educational programs & permanent collection of 19th & 20th century American art for the public; Nine galleries on two floors (approx 9500 sq ft of exhibit space); Average Annual Attendance: 25,000; Mem: 710; dues $10-$250
Income: $100,000 (financed through mem, grants, foundations, contributions)
Library Holdings: Auction Catalogs; Audio Tapes; Book Volumes; CD-ROMs; Cards; Cassettes; Clipping Files; DVDs; Exhibition Catalogs; Original Art Works; Photographs; Prints; Video Tapes
Special Subjects: Decorative Arts, Etchings & Engravings, Folk Art, Collages, Drawings, Graphics, Latin American Art, Painting-American, Photography, Prints, Sculpture, Watercolors, Bronzes, Southwestern Art, Ceramics, Pottery, Primitive art, Woodcuts, Landscapes, Portraits, Glass
Collections: Paintings: Arthur Bowen Davies; Joan Mitchell; Robert Natkin; Grant Wood; Red Grooms; Carl Olaf Seltzer; Norman Rockwell; LeRoy Neiman; Roger Brown; Art Green; George Luks; Glen Cooper Henshaw; Pennerton West; Robert Reid; Sculpture: Felix Eboigbe; Frederick MacMonnies; Fritz Scholder; Overbeck Art Pottery Collection; Jaune Quick-To-See; Norman Rockwell lithograph
Exhibitions: 6 temporary or changing exhibs annually; (10/11/2013-12/08/2013) 35th Elkhart Juried Regional; (12/13/2013-02/23/2014) Anthony Droege: A 30 Year Survey of Figures, Still Life & Landscape
Publications: Midwest Museum Bulletin, quarterly
Activities: Classes for adults and children; docent training; lects open to pub, 52 vis lectrs per yr; concerts; gallery talks; tours; competitions with awards; regional juried competition & national youth art awards; scholarships; individual paintings & original objects of art lent to other mus only; originate traveling exhibs to other mus & university galleries; mus shop sells books, magazines, original art, reproductions, prints & original crafts

L **RUTHMERE MUSEUM,** Robert B. Beardsley Arts Reference Library, 302 E Beardsley Ave, Elkhart, IN 46514-2719. Tel 574-264-0330; Fax 574-266-0474; Elec Mail jjohns@ruthmere.org; Internet Home Page Address: www.ruthmere.org/library.asp; *Cur* Jennifer Johns
Open Library open by appointment only; Museum open Tues - Sat 10 AM - 4 PM, Sun 1 PM - 4 PM; Admis adults $10, students $4; Campus Pass: adult $13; Estab 1980 as a reference library
Income: Financed by mems
Library Holdings: Auction Catalogs; Book Volumes 1800; Periodical Subscriptions 15; Slides
Special Subjects: Art History, Decorative Arts, Painting-American, Sculpture, Porcelain, Furniture, Stained Glass, Pottery, Restoration & Conservation, Landscapes, Architecture

EVANSVILLE

A **ARTS COUNCIL OF SOUTHWESTERN INDIANA,** The Bower-Suhrheinrich Foundation Gallery, 318 Main St Ste 101, Evansville, IN 47708-1451. Tel 812-422-2111; Fax 812-492-4312; Elec Mail mjschenk@artswin.evansville.net; Internet Home Page Address: www.artswin.evansville.net; *Exec Dir* Mary Jane Schenk; *Activities & Communs Dir* Shannon L Hurt; *Pres Bd Dir* Dirck Stahl
Open Mon-Fri 9AM-5PM; No admis fee; Estab 1970 to increase the awareness & accessibility of the arts in Southwestern Indiana through community programs, arts in educ & festivals; serves as an umbrella organization for over 50 cultural organizations, providing technical assistance, marketing & linkage with local, state & national arts organizations; Average Annual Attendance: 5,000; Mem: 550; $20 & up
Income: Financed by endowment, mem, city appropriation & state appropriation, sales
Exhibitions: Business/Arts Month; titles vary: new exhibs every six weeks
Publications: Artist directory; artist registry; Arts Talk Newsletter, quarterly; cultural calendar; cultural directory; media directory
Activities: Classes for general community; arts-in-education prog; artist residencies in elementary schools; art workshops; lects open to pub; concerts; festivals; outreach program provided to six rural counties; Awards include Mayor's Arts award, Young Artist of the Year, Artist of the Year, Arts in Education, Arts Advocate of the Year, Corporate Arts Award, Regional Arts Awards; mus shop sells books, original art, reproductions, prints, ceramics, pottery, jewelry, cards

M **EVANSVILLE MUSEUM OF ARTS, HISTORY & SCIENCE,** 411 SE Riverside Dr, Evansville, IN 47713-1098. Tel 812-425-2406, 421-7506 (TTY); Fax 812-421-7509; Elec Mail mary@emuseum.org; Internet Home Page Address: www.emuseum.org; *Pres Bd Dir* M Susan Hardwick; *Dir Emeritus* Siegfried Weng; *Cur Educ* Stephanie Gerhardt; *Cur Coll* Mary Bower; *Registrar* Elizabeth Fuhrman Bragg; *Dir Science Planetarium* Mitch Luman; *Dir* John W Streetman; *Cur History* Tom Lonnberg
Open Tues - Sat 10 AM - 5 PM, Sun Noon - 5 PM, cl Mon; No admis fee; suggested donation adults $4, child $2; Estab 1926 to maintain & perpetuate a living mus to influence & inspire the taste & cultural growth of the community, to provide facilities for the collection, preservation & exhibition of objects, data & programs related to the arts, history, science & technology; First Level: 19th century village of homes, shops, offices & town hall, America at War Gallery, two science & technology galleries, classrooms; Second Level: furnished Gothic Room with linefold paneling; Sculpture Gallery: galleries for Dutch & Flemish art, 18th century English art, 19th & 20th century American & European art, Anthropology Gallery; two galleries for monthly exhibits; Third Level: Planetarium; Average Annual Attendance: 100,000; Mem: Dues Founders Society $2,500+, President's Circle $1,000-2,499, Dirs Assoc $500-$999, Donor $250-$499, Patron $125-$249, Contributor $70-$124, Friend $35-$69; annual meeting third Tues in May
Income: $1,295,000 (financed by mem, city & state appropriations)
Special Subjects: Painting-American, Sculpture, Watercolors, African Art, Anthropology, Ethnology, Textiles, Folk Art, Woodcuts, Etchings & Engravings, Decorative Arts, Manuscripts, Painting-European, Dolls, Furniture, Glass, Oriental Art, Painting-British, Painting-Dutch, Maps, Tapestries, Painting-Flemish, Period Rooms, Antiquities-Egyptian
Collections: 19th & 20th Century Indiana Art, 20th Century American Still Life
Publications: Bulletin, 5 times yearly; catalogs of exhibitions
Activities: Classes for adults & children; docent training; lects open to pub, 4-5 vis lectrs per yr; concerts; gallery talks; tours; mus shop sells books, magazines, original art

L **Henry R Walker Jr Memorial Art Library,** 411 SE Riverside Dr, Evansville, IN 47713. Tel 812-425-2406; Fax 812-421-7509; Elec Mail mary@emuseum.org; Internet Home Page Address: www.emuseum.org; *Cur* Mary Bower
Open Tues - Fri 11 AM - 5 PM; No admis fee; For reference only
Library Holdings: Book Volumes 4000; Clipping Files; Exhibition Catalogs; Manuscripts; Memorabilia; Original Art Works; Pamphlets; Periodical Subscriptions 30; Photographs; Prints; Reproductions; Sculpture; Slides
Special Subjects: Drawings, Painting-American, Prints, Sculpture, Painting-European, American Indian Art
Activities: Classes for adults & children; docent training; lects open to pub; concerts; mus shop sells books & original art

M **UNIVERSITY OF EVANSVILLE,** Krannert Gallery & Peterson Gallery, 1800 Lincoln Ave, Evansville, IN 47722-0001. Tel 812-488-2043; Fax 812-488-2101; Elec Mail bb32@evansville.edu; *Chmn Art Dept* Stephanie Frusier; *Dean Arts & Sciences* Jean Beckman; *Gallery Dir* William Brown
Open Mon - Sat 10 AM - 4 PM; No admis fee; Krannert Gallery was estab 1969-70 to bring to the University & pub communities exhibitions which reflect the contemporary arts, ranging from crafts through painting & sculpture; Peterson Gallery has larger open space & higher ceilings; Pub access exhibition space 80 x 40 & located in Fine Arts Building; Melvin Peterson Gallery located in Studio Bldg; Average Annual Attendance: 100 per month
Income: Financed by Department of Art funds
Purchases: private collections
Collections: Dicke Collection; Permanent Collections
Exhibitions: Drawing Exhibition; Indiana Ceramics; New Acquisitions; Student Scholarship Exhibition; Undergraduate BFA Exhibition; Faculty Exhibition; Painting Invitational; Sculpture Invitational; Evansville Artists Guild Show; Photography Exhibition; Various invitationals to other univ; Quilting Exhibit
Activities: Lect open to public, 4 vis lectrs per year; gallery talks; tours; competitions with awards; individual paintings & original objects of art lent to university community

L **University Library,** 1800 Lincoln Ave, Evansville, IN 47722. Tel 812-488-2486; Fax 812-488-6987; Elec Mail kb4@evansville.edu; Internet Home Page Address: www.libraries.evansville.edu; *Librn* William F Louden; *Head Reference Librn* Randy Abbott
Open Mon - Thurs 7:45 AM - midnight, Fri 7:45 AM - 6 PM, Sat 10 AM - 6 PM, Sun noon-midnight
Special Subjects: Cartoons
Collections: Knecht Cartoon Collection

L **WILLARD LIBRARY,** Dept of Fine Arts, 21 First Ave, Evansville, IN 47710. Tel 812-425-4309; Fax 812-421-9742, 425-4303; Elec Mail willard@willard.lib.in.us; Internet Home Page Address: www.willard.lib.in.us; *Dir* Greg Hager; *Spec Coll* Lyn Martin; *Children's Librn* Rhonda Mort; *Adult Librn* Eva Sanford
Open Mon - Tues 9 AM - 8 PM, Wed - Fri 9 AM - 5:30 PM, Sat 9 AM - 5 PM, Sun 1 - 5 PM; Estab 1885
Income: $5000 (financed by endowment & city appropriation)
Library Holdings: Book Volumes 7500; Original Art Works; Periodical Subscriptions 16; Photographs; Records

FORT WAYNE

L **ALLEN COUNTY PUBLIC LIBRARY,** Art, Music & Audiovisual Services, 900 Webster St, Fort Wayne, IN 46802-3602. Tel 219-421-1200 Ext 1210; Fax 219-422-9688; Elec Mail ask@acpl.info; Internet Home Page Address: www.acpl.lib.in.us; *Assoc Dir* Steven Fortriede; *Art, Music & Av Mgr* Stacey Huxhold; *Dir* Jeffrey R Krull
Open Mon - Thurs 9 AM - 9 PM, Fri & Sat 9 AM - 6 PM, Sun noon - 5 PM; Estab 1968 to provide a reference coll of the highest quality & completeness for the community & its colleges, a place where local artists & musicians could exhibit their works & perform to provide a circulating collection of slides & musical scores sufficient to meet the demand; The gallery is reserved for painting, sculpture, graphics, photography, ceramics & other art crafts
Income: $253,699 (financed by local property taxes)
Library Holdings: Audio Tapes; Book Volumes 85,000; Cassettes 9000; Compact Disks 17,000; DVDs 2000; Exhibition Catalogs; Memorabilia; Motion Pictures; Periodical Subscriptions 52; Records; Slides 25,000; Video Tapes 11,000
Special Subjects: Art History, Landscape Architecture, Decorative Arts, Photography, Drawings, Graphic Arts, Graphic Design, Painting-American, Prints, Sculpture, Portraits, Watercolors, Ceramics, Crafts, Video
Exhibitions: Exhibits monthly
Activities: Lect open to public, vis lectr; concerts; lending collection contains books, slides, videos, CDs, cassettes & books-on-tape; sales shop sells books, posters, videos, CDs & cassettes

M **ARTLINK, INC,** Auer Center for Arts & Culture, 300 E Main St, Fort Wayne, IN 46802-1919. Tel 260-424-7195; Fax 260-424-8453; Elec Mail info@artlinkfw.com; Internet Home Page Address: www.artlinkfw.com; *Exec Dir* Deb Washler; *Gallery & Educ Coordr* Rebecca Stockert; *Gallery Receptionist* Diane Groenert; *Gallery Asst* Suzanne Galazka
Open Tues - Fri 10 AM - 5 PM, Sat noon - 6 PM, Sun noon - 5 PM; Admis non-mem $2, mem free; Estab 1979 to promote the work of emerging & mid-career artists as well as educational opportunities for the community; 3,000 sq ft main gallery in renovated Auer Center for Arts & Culture, home of four not-for-profit arts organizations.; Average Annual Attendance: 14,000; Mem: 730; dues $10-$200, individual $30; individual artist $25
Income: Financed by mem, Arts United, Indiana Arts Commission, foundations & donations
Publications: Genre newsletter, quarterly; annual print show catalogue
Activities: Educ prog; classes for adults, summer classes for children; docent training; workshops 2-3 per yr; lects open to pub, 2-3 vis lectrs per yr; competitions with awards; sponsoring of competitions; mus shop sells original art, reproductions & prints

A **ARTS UNITED OF GREATER FORT WAYNE,** 300 E Main St, Fort Wayne, IN 46802-1920. Tel 260-424-0646; Fax 260-424-2783; Internet Home Page Address: www.artsunited.org; *Exec Dir* James Sparrow; *Dir Community Develop* Dan Ross; *Dir Resource Develop* Susan Mendenhall
Open Mon - Fri 8 AM - 5 PM; No admis fee; Estab 1955 to raise funds for cultural organizations in Fort Wayne & to foster a positive atmosphere for arts growth
Income: Financed by pub allocations & private donations
Collections: Bicentennial Collection
Publications: Discovery, quarterly newspaper; fine arts calendar
Activities: Own & manage the Performing Arts Center, umbrella organization for 57 arts organizations

M **FORT WAYNE MUSEUM OF ART, INC,** 311 E Main St, Fort Wayne, IN 46802-1997. Tel 260-422-6467; Fax 260-422-1374; Elec Mail mail@fwmoa.org; Internet Home Page Address: www.fwmoa.org; *Dir* Charles A Shephard III; *Cur of Colls* Sachi Yanari-Rizzo; *Bus Mgr* Lon R Braun; *Dir Develop* Marie Eifert; *Registrar* Leah Reeder
Open Tues - Sat 10 AM - 5 PM, Sun Noon - 5 PM; Admis fee adults $5, students (K-college) $3, family $10; Estab 1922 to heighten visual perception of American fine arts & perception of other disciplines; Average Annual Attendance: 65,000; Mem: 1550; dues $35 for an individual & up; annual meeting in June
Income: Financed by endowment, mem, Arts United & grants
Library Holdings: Book Volumes; Periodical Subscriptions
Special Subjects: Painting-American, Prints, Sculpture
Collections: Dorsky & Tannenbaum Collection (contemporary graphics); Fairbanks Collection (paintings & prints); Hamilton Collection (paintings & sculpture); Thieme Collection (paintings); Weatherhead Collection (contemporary paintings & prints); contemporary pieces by living America artists; paintings, sculptures & works on paper from 1850 to present by artists from the US & Europe; works by significant regional artists
Publications: Books; calendar, bi-monthly; catalogs; fact sheets; posters
Activities: Classes for adults & children; docent training; lects open to pub; gallery talks; tours; artmobile for area schools; book traveling exhibs 5-6 per yr; originate traveling exhibs; mus shop sells books, magazines & original art

M **UNIVERSITY OF SAINT FRANCIS, SCHOOL OF CREATIVE ARTS,** John P Weatherhead Gallery & Lupke Gallery, 2701 Spring St, Fort Wayne, IN 46808-3994. Tel 260-399-7700, ext 8001; Fax 260-399-8171; Elec Mail rcartwright@sf.edu; Internet Home Page Address: www.sf.edu/art; *Dean* Rick Cartwright; *Gallery Dir* Justin Johnson; *Coordr* Molly McGowen
Open Mon - Fri 9 AM - 5 PM, Sat 10 AM - 5 PM, Sun 1 - 5 PM; No admis fee; Estab 1965 to provide art programs to students & community; Weatherhead

Gallery, approx 1,000 sq ft, is located in the Rolland Art Center; Lupke Gallery, approx 700 sq ft, is located in the North Campus facilities; Average Annual Attendance: 20,000
Activities: Classes for adults & children, dramatic progs; lects open to pub, 4 vis lectrs per yr, tours, competitions with awards, gallery talks, concerts, schols; originates traveling exhibs

FRANKFORT

M **FRANKFORT COMMUNITY PUBLIC LIBRARY,** Anna & Harlan Hubbard Gallery, 208 W Clinton St, Frankfort, IN 46041-1899. Tel 765-654-8746; Fax 765-654-8747; Elec Mail fcpl@accs.net; Internet Home Page Address: www.fcpl.accs.net; *Dir* Michelle Bradley; *Arts Dir* Flo Caddell
Open Mon - Thurs, 9 AM - 8 PM, Fri & Sat 9 AM - 5 PM; open Sun, Sept - May, 1 - 5 PM
Library Holdings: Audio Tapes; Book Volumes; CD-ROMs; DVDs; Fiche; Original Art Works; Periodical Subscriptions; Photographs; Prints; Sculpture; Video Tapes
Special Subjects: Painting-American, Prints, Bronzes, Folk Art
Collections: Bronzes; folk art; Indiana art; paintings; prints; Works by Harlan Hubbard, Konrad Juestel & Victor Colby
Activities: Classes for adults & children; concerts; gallery talks

HAMMOND

M **PURDUE UNIVERSITY CALUMET,** Library Gallery, 2200 169th St, Hammond, IN 46323-2094. Tel 219-989-2400; Fax 219-989-2070; Elec Mail univrel@calumet.purdue.edu; Internet Home Page Address: www.calumet.purdue.edu/library/current.html; *Interim Libr Dir* Karen M Corey
Open Mon - Thurs 8 AM - 9:30 PM, Fri 8 AM - 5 PM, Sat 10 AM - 4 PM, Sun 1 - 5 PM; No admis fee; Estab 1976 to present varied art media to the university community & general public; Average Annual Attendance: 25,000
Income: $3000
Collections: 19th century Chinese Scroll coll; 1930 art deco bronze sculptured doors from City Hall
Exhibitions: Area Professional Artists & Students Shows; group shows; traveling shows (Smithsonian Institution, French Cultural Services, Austrian Institute)
Activities: Book traveling exhibs

HUNTINGTON

M **HUNTINGTON UNIVERSITY,** Robert E Wilson Art Gallery, 2303 College Ave, Merillat Center for the Arts Huntington, IN 46750-1237. Tel 260-359-4272; Fax 260-359-4249; Elec Mail bmichel@huntington.edu; Internet Home Page Address: www.huntington.edu/mca/gallery/default.htm; *Gallery Dir* Ms Barbara Michel
Open Mon - Fri 9 AM - 5 PM; No admis fee; Estab 1990 to provide community with art exhibits & support col art prog; Gallery is 25 x 44 ft; Average Annual Attendance: 3,000
Income: $5,000 (financed by college & gifts)
Collections: Robert E Wilson Collection of Paintings & Sculpture; Huntington University - Permanent Student Art Collection
Activities: Art in the schools; gallery talks; vis lectrs 300 per yr; student exhib awards; book traveling exhibs three per yr

INDIANAPOLIS

M **THE CHILDREN'S MUSEUM OF INDIANAPOLIS,** 3000 N Meridian St, Indianapolis, IN 46208-4716; PO Box 3000, Indianapolis, IN 46206-3000. Tel 800-820-6214; Fax 317-921-4019; Elec Mail customerservice@childrensmuseum.org; Internet Home Page Address: www.childrensmuseum.org; *Pres & CEO* Dr Jeffrey Patchen; *VP Devel* Brian Williams; *CFO* Andy Bawel; *VP Human Resources & Organizational Devel* Katy Allen; *VP Mktg & External Rels* Lisa Townsend; *VP Opers & Gen Counsel* Brian Statz; *VP Experience Develop & Family Learning* Jennifer Pace-Robinson; *Pub Rels Coordr* Jaclyn Falkenstein
Open 10 AM - 5 PM; Admis fee adults $15.50, senior 60 & over $14.50, children 2-17 $10.50, under 2 free; Estab 1925 to enrich the lives of children; History, physical science, natural science, world cultures, pastimes, center of exploration, trains, dolls, playscape, planetarium, theater; Average Annual Attendance: 1,000,000+; Mem: 27,660 households; dues family $120
Income: $23,040,000 (funded by endowment, mem, fundraising, admissions)
Collections: Toys and artifacts from around the world; Caplan Collection; Max Simon Comic Book Collection
Exhibitions: Permanent Exhibs: Dinosphere: Now You're in Their World; All Aboard!; Chihuly Fireworks of Class; National Geographic Treasures of the Earth; Take Me There: Egypt; Power of Children; Playscape; Carousel of Wishes & Dreams; Story Avenue; ScienceWorks
Publications: Mem newsletter: Extra!
Activities: Children's classes; dramatic progs; docent training; lects open to pub; The Power of Children Awards; exten prog serves state of Indiana; book traveling exhibs, 1 per yr; originates traveling exhibs to other mus & science centers; retail store sells books, original art, reproductions, prints, & educational toys

M **EITELJORG MUSEUM OF AMERICAN INDIANS & WESTERN ART,** 500 W Washington, Indianapolis, IN 46204. Tel 317-636-9378; Fax 317-275-1400; Internet Home Page Address: www.eiteljorg.org; *Dir Museum Collections* Amy McKune; *Registrar* Kelly Rushing; *Pres & CEO* John Vanausdall; *VPres & Chief Curatorial Officer* James H Nottage; *VPres Pub Progs & Vis Experience* Martha L Hill PhD; *VPres Develop* Susie Maxwell; *VPres Communs & Mktg* Tamara Winfrey Harris
Open Mon - Sat 10 AM - 5 PM, Sun Noon - 5 PM; cl New Year's Day, Thanksgiving & Christmas Day; Admis adults $8, seniors (65 & over) $7, children (5-17), & full-time students with ID $5, children under 4, mems, & IUPUI no

charge; Estab 1989; the mus is dedicated to inspiring an appreciation & understanding of the art, history & cultures of the American West & the indigenous peoples of North America. The Eiteljorg Mus collects & preserves Western art & Native American art & cultural objects of the highest quality & serves the pub through exhibs, educational progs, cultural exchanges & entertaining special events; Average Annual Attendance: 101,000; non-circulating; Mem: 3000; dues $50 individual, $60 family
Income: Financed through mem, grants & donations
Library Holdings: Audio Tapes; Book Volumes; DVDs; Exhibition Catalogs; Fiche; Manuscripts; Maps; Other Holdings; Pamphlets; Periodical Subscriptions; Video Tapes
Special Subjects: Drawings, Painting-American, Photography, Prints, Sculpture, Watercolors, American Indian Art, American Western Art, Bronzes, Southwestern Art, Textiles, Pottery, Etchings & Engravings, Landscapes, Decorative Arts, Portraits, Eskimo Art, Jewelry, Scrimshaw
Collections: American art of the West, 19th century to the present, strongest in Taos Society artists & early modernists in the West; Native American cultural arts of North America, from pre-contact to the present; Contemporary Native American fine art coll of particular importance
Exhibitions: Exhibitions rotate four times per yr
Publications: Out of the West: The Gund Collection of Western Art; Art Quantum: The Eiteljorg Fellowship for Native American Fine Art; Diversity & Dialogue: The Eiteljorg Fellowship for Native American Fine Art; Generations: The Helen Cox Kersting Collection of Southwestern Cultural Arts
Activities: Classes for adults & children; dramatic progs; docent training; educ coll; gallery interpreting; lects open to pub; gallery talks; tours; concerts; mus shop sells books, magazines, original art, prints, jewelry; reproductions

A **HOOSIER SALON PATRONS ASSOCIATION, INC,** Art Gallery & Membership Organization, 714 E 65th St Indianapolis, IN 46220. Tel 317-253-5340; Fax 317-253-5468; Elec Mail hoosiersalon@iquest.net; Internet Home Page Address: www.hoosiersalon.org; *Exec Dir* Donnae Dole; *Pres* Jerry Semler; *Asst Dir* Rachel Conour
Main gallery open Tues - Fri 11 AM - 5 PM, Sat 11 AM - 3 PM; No admis fee; Estab 1925 to promote work of Indiana artists; 1,800 sq ft featuring artwork by Indiana artists; Average Annual Attendance: 60,000; Mem: 600 (artists), 450 (patrons); dues patrons $75 & up, artists $40 artists eligible after 1 yr residence in Indiana
Income: Financed by mem, art sales, grants, gifts & patrons
Collections: Paintings, prints, sculpture
Exhibitions: 6-7 special exhib per yr at galleries in Indianapolis & New Harmony, IN
Publications: Annual Salon Exhibition Catalog; History of the Hoosier Salon; Hoosier Salon Newsletter, four times a year
Activities: Educ dept includes CD Rom "Landscape Painting in Indiana; A Modern Art"; gallery talks & tours at annual exhibit; juried competition with awards 40 awards in 2004 total value $28,050; original prints & paintings lent to qualified organizations; originate traveling exhibs circulating to 30 sites around the state of IN, usually 20 works in 6 groups; sales shop sells books, prints, original art & sculpture

M **INDIANA LANDMARKS,** Morris-Butler House, 1201 Central Ave, Indianapolis, IN 46202. Tel 317-639-4534; Fax 317-639-6734; Elec Mail morris-butler@indianalandmarks.org; Internet Home Page Address: www.indianalandmarks.org; *Mus & Heritage Tourism Dir* Gwendolen Raley; *Pres* Marsh Davis; *Dir Heritage Educ & Info* Suzanne Rollins Stanis
Open Feb-mid Dec Thurs - Sat 10 AM-3 PM, cl Mid Dec-Jan, tours given on the hr; Admis adults $5, seniors $4, students & children $3; Home built 1865 & restored by Indiana Landmarks. Estab in 1969 to document age of picturesque eclecticism in architecture & interior decoration. Interpretation, exhibition & preservation of Victorian Indianapolis architecture, culture, history & society (1865-1901); 16 rooms completely furnished. Facilities for receptions & meetings. All paintings by Indiana artists and/or previously owned by Mid-Victorian homeowners (1865-1901); Average Annual Attendance: 4,000; Mem: Annual dues $20 - $100
Income: Financed by private funds & admis fees
Special Subjects: Architecture, Painting-American, Prints, Sculpture, Watercolors, Textiles, Ceramics, Primitive art, Landscapes, Decorative Arts, Portraits, Furniture, Glass, Porcelain, Silver, Carpets & Rugs, Restorations, Period Rooms, Laces, Painting-Italian
Collections: Rococo, Renaissance & Gothic Revival furniture; paintings by early Indiana artists; Victorian ceramics, silver & glass; Victorian textiles
Activities: Classes for children & adults; dramatic progs; docent training; lects open to pub; tours; individual paintings & original objects of art lent to professional mus; lending collection contains original art work & decorative arts; mus shop sells books, tea items, children's toys

L **Information Center Library,** 1201 Central Ave, Indianapolis, IN 46202. Tel 317-639-4534; Fax 317-639-6734; Elec Mail info@indianalandmarks.org; Internet Home Page Address: www.indianalandmarks.org; *Pres* J Marshall Davis; *Educ & Information Dir* Suzanne Stanis
Open Mon-Fri 9 AM - 5 PM, by appointment; For reference only
Income: Financed by pvt funds & admis fees
Library Holdings: Audio Tapes; Book Volumes 3000; Clipping Files; DVDs; Kodachrome Transparencies; Periodical Subscriptions 100; Slides
Special Subjects: Landscape Architecture, Decorative Arts, Historical Material, Interior Design, Restoration & Conservation, Landscapes, Architecture
Activities: Classes for adults & children; docent training; lects open to pub; tours; sponsoring of competitions

M **INDIANA STATE MUSEUM,** 650 W Washington St, Indianapolis, IN 46204-2185. Tel 317-232-1637 & 5599; Fax 317-232-7090; Elec Mail museumcommunication@dnr.state.in.us; Internet Home Page Address: www.indianamuseum.org; *CEO & Pres* Barry Dressel; *Chmn Bd Trustees* Doug Tillman; *VPres Programs* Jim May; *Dir Collections & Interpretation* Rex Garniewicz; *Dir Educ* Colleen Smyth; *Dir Exhibits* Jennifer Spitzer; *Vol Dir & FSM Vols* Jane Darlage; *Chief Cur Cultural History* Dale Ogden; *Chief Cur Nat History* Ron Richards; *Registrar* Lorri Dunwoody; *Cur Historic Archaeology* Bill Wepler; *Cur Geology* Margaret Fisherkeller; *Cur Biology* Damon Lowe; *Cur Fine Arts* Rachel Perry; *Cur Social History* Mary Jane Teeters-Eichacker; *Cur Agriculture, Industry & Technology* Todd Stockwell; *New Media Mgr* Leslie Lorance; *Mgr Security* James Toler; *Facility Mgr* Ron Tolan; *VPres State Historic Sites* Kathleen Mchary; *VPres Human Resources & Finance* Arlene Phillips
Open Mon.-Sat. 9 AM - 5PM, Sun 1 PM - 5PM; cl major holidays; Admis adults $7; members free; Estab 1869 for collections; current mus building opened 1967 to collect, preserve & interpret the natural & cultural history of the state; Numerous galleries; Average Annual Attendance: 35,721; Mem: 1200; dues Individual $39; Individual Premier $49; Family & Grandparent $59; Patron $100.
Income: Financed by state appropriation
Special Subjects: Archaeology, Architecture, Furniture, Painting-American, Silver, Textiles, Sculpture, Photography, Anthropology, Costumes, Ceramics, Decorative Arts, Manuscripts, Dolls, Historical Material
Publications: Brochures for individual historic sites
Activities: Educ prog; classes for children; docent training; in-school progs; lects open to pub, 4 vis lectrs per yr; concerts; gallery talks; tours; exten prog statewide; I-Reach lends to various organizations; 1-2 book traveling exhibs; mus shop selling books, reproductions & prints

M **INDIANA UNIVERSITY - PURDUE UNIVERSITY AT INDIANAPOLIS,** Herron Galleries, 735 W New York St, Indianapolis, IN 46202-5222. Tel 317-278-9419; Fax 317-278-9471; Elec Mail katzp@iupui.edu; Internet Home Page Address: www.herron.iupui.edu/galleries; *Gallery Dir & Cur* Paula Katz
Open Year-round Mon-Fri 10AM-5PM, Wed 10AM-8PM, Sat 10 AM - 5 PM, cl Sun, summer: MON - Fri 10 AM - 5 PM, Sat 1 PM - 5 PM; No admis fee; School & gallery estab 1902 to educate about the visual arts, provide exhibition opportunities to students & faculty, and to present exhibs by regional, national, and international contemporary artists; Eleanor Prest Reese and Robert B. Berkshire Dorit & Gerald Paul Galleries: 3,000 sq ft, 22 ft ceiling, bamboo floors; Marsh Gallery: 1,100 sq ft, 16 ft ceiling, finished concrete floor; Basile Gallery 500 sq ft, 15 ft ceiling, finished concrete floor; Average Annual Attendance: 30,000
Income: Financed by state appropriation, grants & private support
Activities: lects open to pub; 15-20 vis lectrs/films per yr; gallery talks; tours; competitions; awards; exten dept serving Indianapolis & surrounding communities; facilitators of civic art projects; book traveling exhibs 1 per yr; originate traveling exhibs to other univ galleries mall/mid-size mus
—Herron School of Art Library, 735 W New York St, Indianapolis, IN 46202-5222. Tel 317-278-9484; Fax 317-278-9497; Elec Mail herron@iupui.com; Internet Home Page Address: www.ulib.iupui.edu/herron; *Dir* Sonja Staum; *Circ Mgr* Praseth Kong; *Visual Resource Specialist* Danita Davis
Open (during acad yr) Mon - Thurs 8 AM - 6PM, Fri 8 AM - 5 PM; Estab 1970 as a visual resource center for the support of the curriculum of the Herron School of Art
Income: Financed by state appropriation
Library Holdings: Audio Tapes 615; Book Volumes 27,500; Clipping Files; DVDs; Exhibition Catalogs; Lantern Slides; Other Holdings Laser disc; Pamphlets; Periodical Subscriptions 100; Photographs; Prints; Reproductions; Slides 160,000; Video Tapes 1,500
Special Subjects: Art History, Advertising Design, Afro-American Art, American Indian Art, American Western Art, Antiquities-Greek, Architecture, Art Education, Ceramics, Collages, Commercial Art, Conceptual Art, Crafts, Display, Drawings

A **INDIANAPOLIS ART CENTER,** Marilyn K. Glick School of Art, 820 E 67th St, Indianapolis, IN 46220-1139. Tel 317-255-2464; Fax 317-254-0486; Elec Mail info@indplsartcenter.org; Internet Home Page Address: www.indplsartcenter.org; *Dir Exhibs & Artist Srvcs* Patrick Flaherty; *Dir Mktg* Lisa DeHayes; *Office Mgr* Jennifer Collins; *Dir Develop* Kelly Teller; *Dir Outreach* Michelle Gunter; *Educ Assoc* Christina Garmon; *Dir Finance* Doug Halman; *Educ Assoc* Breiana Cecil-Satchwell; *Dir Educ Develop* Anya Aslanova; *Pres & CEO* Carter Wolf; *Dir Opers* Pam Rosenbert
Open Mon - Fri 9 AM - 10 PM, Sat 9 AM - 6 PM, Sun Noon - 6 PM; No admis fee; Estab 1934 to engage, enlighten & enhance community through art educ, participation & observation; Art Center houses 5 galleries: Churchman-Fehsenfeld Gallery, Allen W Clowes Gallery & Sarah M Hurt Gallery; Frank M Basile Exhibition Hall; Ruth Lilly Library; also has a 9.5 acre sculpture garden called Arts Park; Average Annual Attendance: 325,000; Mem: 2200; dues family $60, individual $45, senior and student $30
Income: Financed by endowment, mem, city & state appropriation
Exhibitions: 35-45 exhibs per yr - visit www.indplsartcenter.org or pflaherty@indplsartcenter.org for list
Publications: Paper Canvas, quarterly; quarterly program & class schedule; periodic exhibition catalogues
Activities: Over 90 art classes offered for all ages & skill levels in all medias; summer fine arts camps; workshops; gallery talks; tours; competitions with awards; scholarships offered; sales shop sells books, original art & prints

L **INDIANAPOLIS MARION COUNTY PUBLIC LIBRARY,** Central Library, One Library Sq, 40 E Saint Clair St Indianapolis, IN 46204; PO Box 211, Indianapolis, IN 46206-0211. Tel 317-275-4100; Fax 317-269-5229; Internet Home Page Address: www.imcpl.org; *Mgr* Kathy Diehl
Open Mon & Tues 9 AM - 9 PM, Wed - Fri 9 AM - 6 PM, Sat 9 AM - 5 PM, Sun 1 - 5 PM; No admis fee; Estab 1873
Income: Financed by state appropriation and county property tax
Library Holdings: Book Volumes 25,000; Cassettes; Clipping Files; DVDs; Exhibition Catalogs; Periodical Subscriptions 200; Video Tapes

Collections: Julia Connor Thompson Collection on Finer Arts in Homemaking
Activities: Lect open to public; concerts; tours

M **INDIANAPOLIS MUSEUM OF ART,** (Columbus Museum of Art and Design) 4000 Michigan Rd, Indianapolis, IN 46208-4196. Tel 317-923-1331; Fax 317-931-1978; Elec Mail ima@imamuseum.org; Internet Home Page Address: www.imamuseum.org; *Melvin and Bren Simon Dir & CEO* Maxwell Anderson; *Deputy Dir of Collections & Programs* Sue Ellen Paxton; *Dep Dir Pub Affairs* Katie Zarich; *Dir Exhibs & Pub Programs* David Chalfie; *Conservator in Charge* David Miller; *Chair Dept of Contemporary Art* Lisa Freiman; *Cur of Textile & Fashion Arts* Niloo Imami-Paydar; *Senior Cur Painting & Sculpture Before 1800* Ronda Kasl; *Cur Prints, Drawings, & Photographs* Marty Krause; *Cur, Assoc for Research* Annette Schlagenhauff; *Wood-Pulliam Dist Senior Cur* Ellen Lee; *Senior Cur Design Arts* Craig Miller; *Cur Emeritus, Art of Africa, South Pacific, & the Americas* Ted Celenko; *Jane Weldon Myers Cur Emeritus* Jim Robinson; *Cur, Asian Art* John Teramoto; *Cur Emerita, Am Painting & Sculpture* Harriet Warkel; *Dir Historic Resources* Bradley Brooks; *Ruth Lilly Dir Environmental & Historic Preservation* Mark Zelonis; *Chief Designer* David Russick; *Dir Education* Linda Duke; *CFO* Jennifer Bartenbach; *Dir of Human Resources* Laura McGrew; *Head Librn* Alba Fernandez-Keys; *Dir IT* Yvel Guelce; *Dir New Media* Daniel Incandela; *Chief Information Officer, Dir of MIS* Rob Stein; *Chief Registrar* Kathryn Haigh; *Chief Oper Officer* Nick Cameron; *Dir Security* Martin Whitfield; *Dir Event and Culinary Service* Tracie Kowalczyk
Open Tues, Wed, & Sat 11AM - 5 PM, Thurs & Fri 11 AM - 9 PM, Sun noon- 5 PM, cl Mon, Thanksgiving, Christmas, and New Years Day; Admis free; Estab 1883; IMA serves the creative interests of its communities by fostering exploration of art, design, & the natural environment. The IMA promotes these interests through the coll, presentation, interpretation & conservation of its artistic, historic & environmental assets; Museum's 152 acre campus includes an encyclopedia art museum, the historic Lilly House, and a 26 acre Oldfields Estate; also includes 100 Acres: The Virginia B Fairbanks Art & Nature Park; IMA owns the Miller House & Garden in Columbus, IN; Average Annual Attendance: 380,000; Mem: 10,000
Income: Financed by corporations, foundations, private individuals & endowment
Special Subjects: Drawings, Painting-American, Prints, Watercolors, Bronzes, Textiles, Ceramics, Decorative Arts, Painting-European, Portraits, Furniture, Jade, Porcelain, Oriental Art, Period Rooms
Collections: J M W Turner Collection of prints, watercolors & drawings; W J Holliday Collection of neo-impressionist art & paintings; Clowes Fund Collection of Old Master paintings; Eli Lilly Collection of Chinese art; European & American painting & sculpture, contemporary art, textiles & costumes, decorative arts; Eteljorg Collection of African Art
Publications: Brochures; handbook of permanent collections; quarterly magazine; catalogues for IMA-organized exhibs; Every Way Possible: 125 Years of the Indianapolis Museum of Art; Oldfields
Activities: Classes for adults & children; docent training; lects open to pub, 15-30 vis lectrs per yr; musical performance; gallery talks; tours; films; 2009 National Medal for Mus & Libr Svcs; book traveling exhibs 12-20 per yr; originate traveling exhibs; mus shop sells books, reproductions, prints, jewelry, & gifts

L **Stout Reference Library,** 4000 Michigan Rd, Indianapolis, IN 46208. Tel 317-920-2647; Fax 317-926-8931; Elec Mail library@imamuseum.org; Internet Home Page Address: imamuseum.org; *Head of Lib & Archives* Alba Fernandez-Keys; *Catalog/Reference Librn* Deborah Evans-Cantrell; *Archivist* Jennifer Whitlock
Open Library: Tues, Wed, Fri 2 - 5 PM, Thurs 2 - 8 PM; No admis fee; Estab 1908 to serve needs of Mus staff & public; For reference only
Income: Financed by endowment, mem, city appropriation & federal grants
Library Holdings: Auction Catalogs; Book Volumes 60,000; Clipping Files; DVDs; Exhibition Catalogs; Original Documents; Other Holdings Artists Files 30,000; Pamphlets; Periodical Subscriptions 490; Reels; Video Tapes
Special Subjects: Asian Art, Carpets & Rugs, Textiles
Collections: Indiana Artists
Publications: Exhibition catalogs as needed; Indianapolis Museum of Art Bulletin, irregularly; newsletter, bimonthly; 100 Masterpieces
Activities: Classes for adults

M **INDIANAPOLIS MUSEUM OF CONTEMPORARY ART,** 1043 Virginia Ave, Ste 5, Indianapolis, IN 46203-1761. Tel 317-634-6622; Fax 317-634-1977; Elec Mail info@indymoca.org; Internet Home Page Address: www.indymoca.org; *Dir* Katherine Nagler
Open Thurs - Sat 11 AM - 6PM, cl holidays; No admis fee; Estab 2001; Average Annual Attendance: 25,000; Mem: Individual $30; Dual $50; Family $70; Sustaining $100; Friend $150.
Activities: Formal educ programs; concerts; films; lects

M **MARIAN COLLEGE,** Allison Mansion, 3200 Cold Spring Rd, Indianapolis, IN 46222-1997. Tel 317-955-6120; Fax 317-955-6407; Internet Home Page Address: www.marian.edu; *Event Coordr* Kathi Ashmore
Conference Ctr open by appointment; Admis $3 per person, minimum group of 50; Estab 1970; house in the National Register of Historical Places since 1936; The interior of the mansion is oak, walnut & marble. The grand stairway in the main hall leads to the balcony overlooking the hall, all hand-carved walnut. A private collection of 17th century paintings.
Income: Financed by donations
Collections: 17th century paintings
Activities: Concerts; tours; corporate meeting site; rent to pub

M **NATIONAL ART MUSEUM OF SPORT,** 850 W Michigan St, University Place at IUPUI Indianapolis, IN 46202-2800; PO Box 441155, Indianapolis, IN 46244-1155. Tel 317-274-3627; Fax 317-274-3878; Elec Mail jshort@iupui.edu; Internet Home Page Address: www.namos.iupui.edu; *Bd Chmn* Shaun Healy Clifford; *Bd Pres* John D Short
Open Mon - Fri 8 AM - 5 PM; No admis fee, donations accepted; Estab 1959 to preserve, exhibit & promote understanding of sport-related art; Public areas including four lobbies of University Place Conference Ctr; Average Annual Attendance: 136,000; Mem: 167; dues $25 - $2,000
Income: Donations, grants

Purchases: 2007-purchase prize in Art Students League competition for sculpture "Joe Louis" Barlow. Most acquisitions by donations
Library Holdings: Auction Catalogs; Book Volumes; Exhibition Catalogs; Framed Reproductions; Kodachrome Transparencies; Memorabilia; Photographs; Reproductions; Sculpture; Slides; Video Tapes
Special Subjects: Marine Painting, Photography, Portraits, Painting-American, Prints, Woodcuts, Sculpture, Tapestries, Drawings, Graphics, Painting-American, Photography, Watercolors, Bronzes, African Art, Woodcarvings, Etchings & Engravings, Posters, Eskimo Art, Painting-Canadian, Cartoons, Painting-Australian, Reproductions
Collections: Over 900 paintings, sculptures & works on paper representing over 40 sports; 90 pieces of Inuit art depicting games of Inuit people
Publications: Score Board, quarterly newsletter; catalogs
Activities: Slide/script prog - also on PowerPoint - for schols; tours; video: The Art of Sport; walking tours; lects open to pub; tours; The 2007 Athlete & the Artist competition for Art Students League of NY; awards include Germain G Glidden Best of Show award in Juried Art Competition; cash prizes; medals; individual paintings & original objects of art lent to archive institutions with adequate security & qualified staff; occasional book traveling exhibs (Neiman Exhibits); organize traveling exhibs; mus shop sells objects related to architects work

M **UNIVERSITY OF INDIANAPOLIS,** Christel DeHaan Fine Arts Gallery, 1400 E Hanna Ave, Indianapolis, IN 46227-3697. Tel 317-788-3253; Fax 317-788-6105; Elec Mail dschaad@uindy.edu; Internet Home Page Address: www.uindy.edu; *Chmn* Dee Schaad; *Exhib Coordr* Christine Bentley
Open Mon - Fri 9 AM - 9 PM; No admis fee; Estab 1964 to serve the campus & community; Average Annual Attendance: 6,000
Income: Financed by institution support
Purchases: $15,000
Special Subjects: Drawings, Etchings & Engravings, Folk Art, Historical Material, Landscapes, Ceramics, Metalwork, Photography, Portraits, Painting-American, Prints, Sculpture, Graphics, Watercolors, Woodcarvings, Coins & Medals, Calligraphy
Collections: Art Department Collection; Krannert Memorial Collection
Exhibitions: Student, faculty & local artists exhibits
Publications: Announcements; annual catalog & bulletin
Activities: Classes for adults; lect open to public; concerts; gallery talks; competitions with prizes; scholarships offered

LAFAYETTE

M **ART MUSEUM OF GREATER LAFAYETTE,** (Greater Lafayette Museum of Art) 102 S Tenth St, Lafayette, IN 47905. Tel 765-742-1128; Fax 765-742-1120; Elec Mail info@artlafayette.org; Internet Home Page Address: www.artlafayette.org; *Dir* Kendall Smith; *Cur* Michael Atwell; *Board Pres* Jeff Love
Open Tues - Sun 11 AM - 4 PM, cl Mon & major holidays; No admis fee; Estab 1909 to encourage & stimulate art & to present exhibitions of works of local, regional & national artists & groups as well as representative works of American & foreign artists; 3 galleries with changing exhibs; 1 permanent coll gallery; Average Annual Attendance: 25,000; Mem: 900; dues $35 & up; annual meeting in Oct
Income: Financed by art assoc foundation, endowment, mem, school of art & special events
Special Subjects: Drawings, Graphics, Hispanic Art, Painting-American, Photography, Prints, Sculpture, Watercolors, American Indian Art, Southwestern Art, Textiles, Religious Art, Ceramics, Crafts, Folk Art, Pottery, Woodcarvings, Woodcuts, Etchings & Engravings, Afro-American Art, Decorative Arts, Portraits, Porcelain
Collections: Permanent collection of over 900 works of art obtained through purchase or donation since 1909; American art coll specializing in Hoosier artist's work; Laura Anne Fry American Art Pottery & Art Glass; Akeley Collection of Mexican Modernists
Exhibitions: See website for current exhibitions
Publications: Annual report; bi-monthly calendar; exhibition catalog; quarterly newsletter
Activities: Classes for adults & children; docent training; lects open to pub; tours; competitions with awards; scholarships & fels offered; mus shop sells work of local artists

L **Alameda McCollough Library,** 1001 South St, Lafayette, IN 47901. Tel 765-476-8411; Fax 765-476-8414; Elec Mail library@tippecanoehistory.org; Internet Home Page Address: www.tippecanoehistory.org
Open Thurs & Fri 1 PM - 5 PM, 1st & 3rd Sat of month 10 AM - 2 PM; Admis $4; Estab 1925, local history, genealogical research; Archives by appt; library open to public; Average Annual Attendance: 2,500; Mem: 600
Income: private not for profit; donations, admis fees
Library Holdings: Audio Tapes; Book Volumes 8,200; Clipping Files; Compact Disks; DVDs; Kodachrome Transparencies; Lantern Slides; Manuscripts; Maps; Memorabilia; Original Art Works; Original Documents; Pamphlets; Periodical Subscriptions 3; Photographs; Prints; Records; Reels 575; Slides; Video Tapes
Special Subjects: Maps, Painting-American, Historical Material
Collections: 250 archival collections, photo archives, George Winter Manuscript and art coll
Activities: Classes for adults and children; seminars, history; lects open to pub, 25 vis lectrs per year; tours; gallery talks; mus shop sells books, reporductions & prints

MADISON

M **JEFFERSON COUNTY HISTORICAL SOCIETY MUSEUM,** 615 W First St, Madison, IN 47250. Tel 812-265-2335; Elec Mail info@jchshc.org; Internet Home Page Address: www.jchshc.org; *Pres* Nick Schultz; *Dir* John Nyberg; *Mus Educator* Joanne Spiller
Open Mon - Fri 10 AM - 4:30 PM, Sat, May 1 - Oct 31, 10 AM - 4:30 PM. Nov - Apr 1 - 4 PM; Admis $4; Estab 1900 to preserve & display art & artifacts

worthy of note & pertinent to local area history & culture; Museum has a permanent gallery of Civil War & steamboating, other gallery has rotating exhibits; Average Annual Attendance: 2,000; Mem: 400; family $35, single $25
Collections: William McKendree Snyder Collection, paintings, portraits; Jefferson County artifacts-textiles, primitives; 1895 Madison Railroad Station
Publications: Beloved Madison
Activities: Classes for children; mus shop sells books

METAMORA

M METAMORA MUSEUM OF ETHNOGRAPHIC ART, Main St, 2nd Fl, Odd Fellows Hall Metamora, IN 47030; PO Box 46, Metamora, IN 47030-0046. Tel 765-647-6365; Internet Home Page Address: www.emetamora.com/museum
Open May - Oct Sat - Sun 10 AM - 5 PM; Admis adults $2, children $1
Collections: prehistoric & historic art; cultural artifacts
Activities: Mus shop

MUNCIE

M BALL STATE UNIVERSITY, Museum of Art, Riverside Ave at Warwick Rd, Muncie, IN 47306. Tel 765-285-5242; Fax 765-285-4003; Elec Mail artmuseum@bsu.edu; Internet Home Page Address: www.bsu.edu/artmuseum; *Dir* Peter F Blume; *Assoc Dir* Carl Schafer; *Cur Educ* Tania Said Schuler
Open Mon - Fri 9 AM - 4:30 PM, Sat & Sun 1:30 - 4:30 PM, cl legal holidays; No admis fee; Estab 1936 as a university & community art museum; Ten galleries, sculpture court & mezzanine; Average Annual Attendance: 29,000
Income: Financed by university, community & federal government
Special Subjects: American Indian Art, Decorative Arts, Drawings, Etchings & Engravings, Architecture, Ceramics, Glass, American Western Art, Furniture, Painting-American, Prints, Painting-European, African Art, Ethnology, Asian Art, Coins & Medals, Baroque Art, Renaissance Art, Antiquities-Oriental, Antiquities-Egyptian, Antiquities-Greek, Antiquities-Roman, Antiquities-Etruscan
Collections: 18th, 19th & 20th c European & American Art; David T Owskley Collection of Ethnographic Art
Exhibitions: A Couple of Ways of Doing Something: Photographs by Chuck Close, Poems by Bob Holman
Publications: Exhibition catalogs
Activities: Art for lunch talks; children's activity sheets; docent training; educ prog; lects open to pub, 10 vis lectrs per yr; gallery talks; tours; sponsoring of competitions; individual paintings & original objects of art lent to qualified mus; book traveling exhibs 2 per yr; mus shop sells books, posters, postcards & catalogues

L Architecture Library, McKinley at Neely, College of Architecture & Planning Muncie, IN 47306-0160. Tel 765-285-5857, 285-5858; Fax 765-285-3726; Elec Mail aetrendler@bsu.edu; Internet Home Page Address: www.bsu.edu/library/collections/archlibrary; *Librn* Amy Trendler; *Asst Librn* Helen Ulrich; *Visual Resources Cur* Cindy Turner
Open Mon - Thurs 7:30 AM - 10 PM, Fri 7:30 AM - 6 PM, Sat 9 AM - 5 PM, Sun 1 - 10 PM; hours vary during acad vacations, interims & summer sessions; Estab 1965 to provide materials necessary to support the acad progs of the College of Architecture & Planning; Average Annual Attendance: 45,000
Income: Financed through University
Library Holdings: Book Volumes 24,000; CD-ROMs 100; DVDs 250; Other Holdings Student theses & 70,000 digital images; Periodical Subscriptions 100; Slides 110,000; Video Tapes 34
Special Subjects: Landscape Architecture, Decorative Arts, Drawings, Graphic Design, Industrial Design, Interior Design, Furniture, Drafting, Restoration & Conservation, Architecture

MUNSTER

M SOUTH SHORE ARTS, 1040 Ridge Rd, Munster, IN 46321-1876. Tel 219-836-1839; Fax 219-836-1863; Internet Home Page Address: southshoreartsonline.org; *Exec Dir* John Cain; *Pres* Liz Valavanis; *Dir Finance & Admin* Susan Anderson; *Gallery Mgr* Mary McClelland; *Dir Mktg & Develop* Tricia Hernandez; *Dir Educ* Linda Eyermann; *Educ Coordr* Kimberly McKinley; *Spec Projects Mgr* Jennifer Vinovich; *Mus Shop Mgr* Jackie Wicklund; *Asst Mus Shop Mgr* Andrea Miller
Open Mon - Fri 10 AM - 5 PM, Sat 10 AM - 4 PM, Sun noon - 4 PM; Admis adults $3, students $2, members no charge; Estab 1969; 5,000 sq ft exhib space
Library Holdings: Book Volumes
Special Subjects: Sculpture, Photography, Prints
Collections: regional art
Publications: quarterly newsletter
Activities: Educ progs; docent prog; lects; guided tours; concerts; arts festivals; theater; mus shop

NASHVILLE

A BROWN COUNTY ART GALLERY FOUNDATION, One Artist Dr, Nashville, IN 47448-8010; PO Box 443, Nashville, IN 47448-0443. Tel 812-988-4609; Elec Mail brncagal@aol.com; Internet Home Page Address: www.browncountyartgallery.org; *Pres* Dr Emanuel Klein; *VPres* Sara Hess; *Secy* Richard Hess; *Treas* Kim Cornelius; *Museum Coordr* Richard Halvorson; *Gallery Mgr* Juanita Moberly; *Gallery Mgr* Pam Crawford; *Grants & Fund-raising Adv to Bd* Susanne Gaudin; *Legal Affairs Adv to Bd* Sharon A Wildey
Open Fri, Sat & Sun 10 AM -5 PM; Sun 2 - 5 PM Jan & Feb only; cl Thanksgiving, Christmas & New Years; No admis fee; Estab 1926 to unite artists and laymen in fellowship; to create a greater incentive for develop of art and its presentation to the public; to estab an art gallery for exhibition of work of members of the Assn; 6 gallery rooms; Average Annual Attendance: 35,000; Mem: 30 artists; 200 supporting members; for foundation mem art patron, for assn mem professional artist; dues life $1,000, individual $20; annual meeting in May
Income: Financed by mem & foundation

Library Holdings: Auction Catalogs; Book Volumes; Memorabilia; Original Documents; Photographs; Sculpture; Video Tapes
Special Subjects: Prints, Watercolors, Painting-American
Collections: 81 paintings & pastels by the late Glen Cooper Henshaw; over 200 paintings by early Brown County Artists
Exhibitions: Three exhibits each year by the artist members & paintings from permanent collection
Publications: Annual catalog
Activities: Classes for adults & children; docent training; lect open to public, various vis lectrs per year; gallery talks; tours; sales shop sells books, original art, reproductions, prints & videos

M T C STEELE STATE HISTORIC SITE, 4220 TC Steele Rd, Nashville, IN 47448. Tel 812-988-2785; Fax 812-988-8457; Elec Mail tcsteeleshs@indianamuseum.org; Internet Home Page Address: www.tcsteele.org; *Cur* Andrea Smith de Tarnowsky
Open Tues - Sat 9 AM - 5 PM, Sun 1 - 5 PM, cl Mon & most holidays; Admis adults $5, sr citizens $4, adult group rate $$4.50, children $2, children's group rate $1.50; Estab 1945 to protect, collect & interpret the art & lives of T C & Selma Steele; 2,400 sq ft incl historic home setting, with 80 T C Steele paintings on display at any one time; Average Annual Attendance: 17,000; Mem: Support organization, The Friends of TC Steele
Income: Financed by state appropriation & admissions
Special Subjects: Decorative Arts, Historical Material, Landscapes, Ceramics, Portraits, Painting-American, Sculpture, Textiles, Furniture, Period Rooms
Collections: 347 paintings, historic furnishing, decorative arts, photos, books, restored historic gardens. No purchases, all part of willed estate
Activities: Classes for adults & children; docent training; Artists in Residence prog; lects open to pub; concerts; gallery talks; tours; annual special events; sponsoring of competitions; individual paintings & original objects of art lent to other mus & universities; lending collection contains original art works & paintings; framed reproductions; mus shop sells books, reproductions, prints & gift items relations to site/collections

NEW ALBANY

M CARNEGIE CENTER FOR ART & HISTORY, 201 E Spring St, New Albany, IN 47150-3422. Tel 812-944-7336; Fax 812-981-3544; Elec Mail info@carnegiecenter.org; Internet Home Page Address: www.carnegiecenter.org; *Pres* Sam Ellington; *Dir Mktg and Outreach* Laura Wilkins; *Cur* Karen Gillenwater; *Pub Rels* Delesha Thomas
Open Tues - Sat 10 AM -5:30 PM; No admis fee; Estab 1971, to exhibit regional professional artists' work on a monthly basis & to promote the arts & history of our community; Two galleries are maintained, approx dimensions: 21 x 30 ft & 21 x 30 ft; Average Annual Attendance: 24,000; Mem: 400; dues $30 - $1,000; annual meeting in Jan
Income: Financed through NAFC Public Library
Library Holdings: Memorabilia; Original Art Works
Special Subjects: Folk Art, Painting-American, Sculpture, Textiles, Portraits, Dioramas
Collections: Permanent collection of historical items
Exhibitions: Hand Carved, Animated Folk Art Diorama on permanent display; Ordinary People Extraordinary Courage:The Men and Women of the Underground Railroad; Remembered: The Life of Lucy Higgs Nichols (permanent); Rotating contemporary exhibs
Publications: Bulletins; Exhibit catalog newsletter
Activities: Classes for adults & children; lect open to public; 12 vis lectrs per yr; concerts; gallery talks; tours; competitions with awards; AAM Bronze Muse Award 2007, AASLH Leadership in History 2007; extension prog includes outreach presentations of underground railroad film off-site; book traveling exhibitions annually

NEW HARMONY

M UNIVERSITY OF SOUTHERN INDIANA, New Harmony Gallery of Contemporary Art, 506 Main St, New Harmony, IN 47631; PO Box 627, New Harmony, IN 47631-0627. Tel 812-682-3156; Elec Mail skrhoades@usi.edu; Internet Home Page Address: www.nhgallery.com; *Asst Dir* Sara Rhoades
Open Tues - Sat 10 AM - 5 PM, Sun Noon - 4 PM (Apr-Dec), cl Mon; No admis fee; Estab 1975 for exhibition of contemporary midwest art & artists; Midwestern contemporary art; consignment gallery; Average Annual Attendance: 25,000
Income: Financed by contributions & grants
Collections: Univ Southern Ind Collection
Exhibitions: 8 exhibitions per year
Activities: Classes for adults; lects open to pub, gallery talks; workshops; sales shop sells original art & prints

NOTRE DAME

M SAINT MARY'S COLLEGE, Moreau Galleries, Moreau Center for the Arts, Notre Dame, IN 46556. Tel 574-284-4655; Fax 574-284-4715; Elec Mail khoefle@saintmarys.edu; Internet Home Page Address: www.moreauartgalleries.com; *Gallery Dir* Krista Hoefle
Open Mon - Fri 10 AM - 4 PM, cl weekends; No admis fee; Estab 1956 for educ, community-related exhibits & contemporary art; Gallery presently occupies three spaces; all exhibits rotate; Average Annual Attendance: 6,000
Income: Financed through college
Special Subjects: Prints
Collections: Cotter Collection; Dunbarton Collection of prints; Norman LaLiberte Collection; various media
Exhibitions: Rotating exhibitions
Publications: Catalogs, occasionally

Activities: Lects open to pub; tours; concerts; gallery talks; competitions with awards; individual paintings & original objects of art lent; originate traveling exhibs

M **UNIVERSITY OF NOTRE DAME,** Snite Museum of Art, Moose Krause Circle, Notre Dame, IN 46556; PO Box 368, Notre Dame, IN 46556-0368. Tel 574-631-5466; Fax 574-631-8501; Internet Home Page Address: www.nd.edu/~sniteart/97/main3.html; *Cur* Stephen B Spiro; *Cur* Douglas Bradley; *Registrar* Robert Smogor; *Chief Preparator* Greg Denby; *Sr Staff Asst* Anne Mills; *Exhib Designer* John Phegley; *Admin Asst* Susan Fitzpatrick; *Dir & Cur* Charles R Loving; *Cur Educ* Diana Matthias; *Cur Educ* Jacqueline Welsh; *Assoc Dir* Ann Knoll; *Cur Arts* Linda Canfield; *Cur* Dinali Cooray; *Mktg & Pub Rels* Gina Costa; *Cur Rev* James F Flanigan C.S.C; *Cur* Joanne Mack PhD; *Staff Accountant* Carolyn Niemier; *Asst Preparator* Ramiro Rodriguez; *Coordr* Heidi Williams
Open Tues & Wed 10 AM - 4 PM, Thurs - Sat 10 AM - 5 PM, Sun 1 - 5 PM (when classes are in session); No admis fee; Estab 1842; Wightman Memorial Art Gallery estab 1917; O'Shaughnessy Art Gallery estab 1952; Snite Museum estab 1980 to educate through the visual arts; during a four year period it is the objective to expose students to all areas of art including geographic, period & media, open 1980; Galleries consist of 35,000 sq ft; Average Annual Attendance: 60,000; Mem: 250; dues from $15 - $5,000; annual meeting in May
Special Subjects: American Indian Art, Drawings, Photography, Porcelain, Pre-Columbian Art, Painting-American, Prints, Painting-British, Painting-European, Painting-French, Sculpture, African Art, Oriental Art, Baroque Art, Painting-Italian
Collections: 18th & 19th century American, English, 17th, 18th & 19th Century French paintings & Master drawings; Kress Study Collection; 19th century French oils; Reilly Collection of Old Master Drawings through 19th century; Fedderson Collection of Rembrandt Collections
Exhibitions: Annual Faculty Exhibition: Annual Student Exhibition
Publications: Exhibition catalogs, 3-5 times per yr; Calendar of Events, semi-annually
Activities: Classes for adults & children, dramatic progs, docent training; lects open to pub, 3-5 vis lectrs per yr; concerts; gallery talks; tours; fellowships; individual paintings & original objects of art lent to qualified institutions; book traveling exhibs 10-12 per yr; originate traveling exhibs to national mus

L **Architecture Library,** 117 Bond Hall, Notre Dame, IN 46556-5652. Tel 574-631-6654; Fax 574-631-9662; Elec Mail library.archlib.1@nd.edu; Internet Home Page Address: www.architecture.library.nd.edu; *Library Supv* Deborah Webb; *Architecture Librn* Jennifer Parker
Open Mon - Thurs 8 AM - 10 PM, Fri 8 AM - 6 PM, Sat 10 AM - 5 PM, Sun 1 - 10 PM, intersessions Mon - Fri 8 AM - 5 PM; Estab 1930 as a branch of the university library
Income: Funding by University
Library Holdings: Book Volumes 28,000; CD-ROMs 6; Fiche; Lantern Slides 4,500; Periodical Subscriptions 119; Reels; Video Tapes 100
Special Subjects: Landscape Architecture, Historical Material, Interior Design, Furniture, Restoration & Conservation, Antiquities-Greek, Antiquities-Roman, Architecture
Collections: Furniture book coll; Rare books on architecture

PORTLAND

M **ARTS PLACE, INC.,** (Jay County Arts Council) Hugh N Ronald Memorial Gallery, 131 E Walnut St, Portland, IN 47371-2108; PO Box 804, Portland, IN 47371-0804. Tel 219-726-4809; Fax 219-726-2081; Elec Mail artsland@jayco.net; Internet Home Page Address: www.artsland.org; *Exec Dir* Eric Rogers; *Asst Dir* Tetia Lee; *Dir Admin* Heidi Bouse; *Regional Srvcs Dir* Sue Burk; *Mktg Dir* Jennifer Nixon
Open Mon - Fri 10 AM - 9 PM; No admis fee; Estab 1967; Local, regional, national & international contemporary art in a wide range of media; Average Annual Attendance: 15,000; Mem: 800
Exhibitions: Contemporary regional art
Activities: Classes for adults & children; dramatic progs; awards during juried exhibs; schols offered; originate traveling exhibs 4-8 per yr

RICHMOND

M **EARLHAM COLLEGE,** Leeds Gallery, 801 National Rd W, Richmond, IN 47374-4095. Tel 765-983-1400; Fax 765-983-1304; Internet Home Page Address: www.earlham.edu; *Dir of Events Coordr* Lynn Knight
Open Mon-Fri 9AM-6PM, Sat-Sun 1PM-8PM; No admis fee; Estab 1847 as a liberal arts col; Leeds Gallery estab 1970
Collections: Regional artist: George Baker, Bundy (John Ellwood), Marcus Mote; prints by internationally known artists of 19th & 20th centuries; regional artists; rotating colls from all areas
Activities: Dramatic progs; lects open to pub, 5-6 vis lectrs per yr; concerts; individual paintings & original objects of art lent; originates traveling exhibs; sales shop sells books

M **Ronald Gallery,** 801 National Rd W, Richmond, IN 47374-4095. Tel 765-983-1410; *Cur* Julia May
Open Mon-Thurs 8AM-midnight, Fri 8AM-10PM, Sat 10AM-10PM, Sun noon-midnight
Collections: over 3,000 paintings, prints & sculptures

A **RICHMOND ART MUSEUM,** 350 Hub Etchison Pkwy, Richmond, IN 47375; PO Box 816, Richmond, IN 47375. Tel 765-966-0256, 973-3369; Fax 765-973-3738; Elec Mail shaund@rc.k12.in.us; Internet Home Page Address: www.richmondartmuseum.org; *Exec Dir* Shaun T Dingwerth; *Educ Dir* Lance Crow
Open Jan - Dec Tues - Fri 10 AM - 4 PM, Sun 1 - 4 PM, cl holidays; No admis fee; Estab 1898 to promote creative ability, art appreciation & art in pub schools; Maintains an art gallery with four exhibit rooms: two rooms for permanent collection & two rooms for current exhibs; Average Annual Attendance: 10,000; Mem: 600; dues students $10 - $1,000; annual meeting in Nov
Income: Financed by mem, grants, donations
Special Subjects: Photography, Prints, Painting-American, Ceramics
Collections: Regional & state art; American, European, Oriental art; Overbeck Pottery
Exhibitions: Annual Area Artists Exhibition; Hands-On Exhibition for grade school children High School Art Exhibition
Publications: Art in Richmond - 1898-1978; quarterly newsletter
Activities: Classes for adults & children; docent training; lects open to pub, 4 vis lectrs per yr; gallery talks; tours; competitions with merit & purchase awards; scholarships offered; individual paintings & original objects of art lent to corporations that annually support the museum or to other galleries for exhib; lending collection contains books, original art works, original prints & photographs; originate traveling exhibs; mus shop sells books, original art & prints

L **Library,** 350 Hub Etchison Pkwy, Richmond, IN 47374. Tel 765-966-0256; Fax 765-973-3738; Internet Home Page Address: www.richmondartmuseum.org; *Exec Dir* Shaun T Dingwerth
Open Tues-Fri 10AM-4PM; est 1898; Open to members; library primarily for reference & art research
Library Holdings: Audio Tapes; Book Volumes 800; Exhibition Catalogs
Special Subjects: Art History, Decorative Arts, Photography, Graphic Arts, Painting-American, Painting-British, Painting-Dutch, Painting-Flemish, Sculpture, Painting-European, Ceramics, Printmaking, Pottery, Landscapes, Reproductions
Activities: Classes for children

ROCHESTER

M **FULTON COUNTY HISTORICAL SOCIETY INC,** Fulton County Museum (Tetzlaff Reference Room), 37 E 375 N, Rochester, IN 46975-9718. Tel 574-223-4436; Fax 574-224-4436; Elec Mail fchs@rtcol.com; Internet Home Page Address: www.fultoncountyhistory.org; *Dir Museum* Melinda Clinger; *Pres* Fred Oden Jr; *Treas* Lola Riddle; *Cataloger* Peggy Van Meter; *Cataloger* Annette Wise; *Pres Emerita* Shirley Willard
Open Mon - Sat 9 AM - 5 PM, cl holidays; No admis fee; Estab 1963 to preserve Fulton County & Northern Indiana history; 64 X 184 ft; new exhibit quarterly, 40 ft addition in 2001; 100 ft meeting rm added in 2008; Average Annual Attendance: 45,000; Mem: 400; dues $20; annual meeting third Mon in Nov
Income: $106,000 (financed by mem, sales & festivals, grants & donations)
Library Holdings: Audio Tapes; Book Volumes; CD-ROMs; Cards; Cassettes; Clipping Files; Compact Disks; DVDs; Exhibition Catalogs; Filmstrips; Framed Reproductions; Kodachrome Transparencies; Lantern Slides; Manuscripts; Maps; Memorabilia; Motion Pictures; Original Art Works; Original Documents; Other Holdings; Pamphlets; Periodical Subscriptions; Photographs; Prints; Records; Reels; Reproductions; Sculpture; Slides; Video Tapes
Special Subjects: American Indian Art, Folk Art, Historical Material, Photography, Porcelain, Portraits, Pottery, Painting-American, Textiles, Prints, Costumes, Woodcarvings, Manuscripts, Posters, Dolls, Furniture, Jewelry, Maps, Coins & Medals, Dioramas, Period Rooms
Collections: Antiques; Elmo Lincoln, first Tarzan; old farm equipment; old household furniture; Woodland Indians; Genealogy; Ogle Library; DAR; Chief White Eagle Library; Manitou Chapter DAR; John Tombaugh World War II Collection; Jack Overmyer Civil War Collection; Fulton County, IN authors
Exhibitions: Traditional & Indian Crafts; Round Barn Festival; Trail of Courage; Redbud Trail; Living History Village of 14 Bldgs (Loyal Indiana) portrays 1900-1925
Publications: Fulton County Images, newsletter; Fulton County Folk Finder, newsletter; Potawatomi Trail of Death Assn, newsletter; Fulton County Historical Assn, newsletter; Rochester - a pictorial history
Activities: Classes for adults & children; dramatic progs; docent progs; Indian dances; living history festivals; classes for children in summer; lects open to pub, 3 vis lectrs per yr; gallery talks; tours; competitions with prizes; Vol of Yr; Benefactor of Yr; retail store sells books, prints, magazines, original art & reproductions, Indian crafts, traditional crafts

SOUTH BEND

L **ENVIRONIC FOUNDATION INTERNATIONAL LIBRARY,** 916 Saint Vincent St, South Bend, IN 46617-1443. Tel 574-233-3357; Fax 574-289-6716; Elec Mail environics@aol.com; *Founder* Patrick Horsbrugh; *Pres* William R Godfrey
Estab 1970
Library Holdings: Clipping Files; Original Art Works; Slides; Video Tapes
Special Subjects: Landscape Architecture, Graphic Design, Painting-British, Watercolors, Archaeology, Advertising Design, Interior Design, Lettering, Anthropology, Furniture, Period Rooms, Stained Glass, Aesthetics, Landscapes, Architecture

A **SOUTH BEND REGIONAL MUSEUM OF ART,** 120 S Saint Joseph St, South Bend, IN 46601-1902. Tel 574-235-9102; Fax 574-235-5782; Elec Mail info@southbendart.org; Internet Home Page Address: www.sbrma.org; *Chief Cur* Bill Tourtillotte; *Exec Dir* Susan R Visser
Open Tues - Fri 11 AM - 5 PM, Sat & Sun noon - 5 PM; Admis non-mems $35 mems free; Estab in 1947 for museum exhibitions, lectures, film series, workshops, and studio classes; The Art Center is located in a three-story building designed by Philip Johnson. There are four galleries: the Warner Gallery features traveling shows or larger exhibits organized by the Art Center & the Art League Gallery features one or two-person shows by local or regional artists; also a community & permanent gallery; Average Annual Attendance: 50,000; Mem: 1,000; dues sustaining $100, family $60, active $40, student & senior citizens $30
Income: Financed by mem, corporate support, city & state appropriations
Special Subjects: Drawings, Photography, Prints, Sculpture, Textiles, Painting-American, Pottery, Folk Art, Woodcuts, Afro-American Art, Ceramics, Collages, Crafts, Woodcarvings
Collections: European and American paintings, drawings, prints and objects; 20th century American art with emphasis on regional and local works
Exhibitions: 4 rotating exhibits

Publications: Checklists; exhibition catalogues; quarterly newsletter
Activities: Studio classes for adults & children; docent training & tours; outreach educational prog conducted by Art League; workshops; lects open to pub, 3 vis lectrs per yr; gallery talks; artist studio tours; competitions with prizes; film series; paintings and original works of art lent to accredited mus; lending collection contains prints, paintings, records and sculptures; mus shop sells gift items and original works of art

L   **Library,** 120 S Saint Joseph St, South Bend, IN 46601. Tel 574-235-9102; Fax 574-235-5782; Elec Mail sbrma@sbt.infi.net; *Exec Dir* Susan R Visser
No admis fee for members; non-members $3; Estab 1947 to provide art resource material to members of the Art Center
Library Holdings: Book Volumes 1100; Exhibition Catalogs; Motion Pictures; Periodical Subscriptions 63; Records
Special Subjects: Collages, Photography, Drawings, Painting-American, Prints, Sculpture, Ceramics, Crafts, Afro-American Art, Pottery, Textiles, Woodcarvings, Woodcuts, Folk Art
Activities: Educ prog; classes for adults & children; docent training; lects open to pub, 4 vis lectrs per yr; concerts; gallery talks; tours; sponsoring of competitions; scholarships; mus shop sells books, original art

TERRE HAUTE

M   **INDIANA STATE UNIVERSITY,** University Art Gallery, Ctr Performing & Fine Arts, Terre Haute, IN 47809; 200 N 7th St, Terre Haute, IN 47809-1902. Tel 812-237-3720; Fax 812-237-4369; Elec Mail mvandenberg@isugw.indstate.edu; Internet Home Page Address: www.indstate.edu/artgallery
Open Mon - Wed & Fri, 11 AM - 4 PM, Thurs 11AM- 8 PM, Sat noon-4PM; No admis fee; Contemporary gallery
Collections: Paintings & sculpture
Exhibitions: Changing exhibitions of national & regional contemporary art during school terms; periodic student & faculty exhibitions
Activities: Lect

M   **SWOPE ART MUSEUM,** 25 S Seventh St, Terre Haute, IN 47807-3692. Tel 812-238-1676; Fax 812-238-1677; Elec Mail info@swope.org; Internet Home Page Address: www.swope.org; *Exec Dir* Marianne Richter; *Collections Mgr* Jennifer Lanman; *Cur Coll & Exhib* Elizabeth (Lisa) Petrulis; *Commun Mgr* Kristi Finley; *Develop Asst* Michelle Adler
Open Tues-Fri 10AM - 5PM, Sat noon - 5PM, 1st Fri Sept - May 6PM - 9 PM; Admis free, suggested donation $5, children/students $3; Estab 1942 to present free of charge American art of the 19th & 20th centuries; Average Annual Attendance: 12,000; Mem: 500; dues individual $40; annual meeting third Wed in Sept
Income: $300,000 (financed by mem & trust fund, annual donations & grants)
Purchases: Caprice 4 by Robert Motherwell; Girl With Cat by William Zorzach; Young Man Playing Double Flute by Ben Shahn; Still Life with Fruit by Barton S. Hays
Library Holdings: Book Volumes; Clipping Files
Special Subjects: Painting-American, Prints, Sculpture, American Western Art
Collections: American art of 19th & 20th centuries; James Farrington Cooking Art; Gilbert Wilson Art
Exhibitions: Listed on mus website
Publications: Membership newsletter; catalogs to spec exhibs
Activities: Classes for children; docent training; lects open to pub, 10 vis lectrs per yr; concerts; gallery talks; tours; competitions with awards; individual paintings & original objects of art lent to other museums; originate traveling exhibs; mus shop sells books, original art, reproductions, note cards, gift items & prints

L   **Research Library,** 25 S Seventh St, Terre Haute, IN 47807-3692. Tel 812-238-1676; Fax 812-238-1677; Elec Mail info@swope.org; Internet Home Page Address: www.swope.org; *Cur Colls & Exhibs* Elizabeth (Lisa) Petrulis; *Commun Mgr* Kristi Finley; *Exec Dir* Marianne Richter; *Coll Mgr* Jennifer Lanman; *Develop Asst* Michelle Adler
Library open Tues - Fri 10 AM - 5 PM; No admis fee; Estab 1942; Circ 1,200; Open to pub; Average Annual Attendance: 12,000; Mem: 500; dues $40; ann meeting 4th Mon in Sept
Income: $337,072 (financed by endowments, sales, individuals, corporations, sponsorships, foundations, federal & state support, fund raising, donations, memorial contributions)
Purchases: John Rogers Cox, White Cloud; Mary Fairchild MacMonnies, Garden in Giverny; Frederick Puckstuhl, Evening; William Edouard Scott, Etaples; Carl Woolsey, Rod to the Village; Abraham Walkowitz, Abstraction; Isadore Duncan, Untitled; Ben Shahn, Young Man Playing Double Flute; Barton S. Hayes, Still Life with Fruit
Library Holdings: Book Volumes 1182; Clipping Files; Periodical Subscriptions 3; Video Tapes 9
Special Subjects: Art History, Landscape Architecture, Photography, Drawings, Etchings & Engravings, Graphic Arts, Graphic Design, Painting-American, Prints, Sculpture, Historical Material, History of Art & Archaeology, Watercolors, Ceramics, Printmaking, Industrial Design, Art Education, American Indian Art, Furniture, Glass, Aesthetics, Afro-American Art, Woodcuts, Landscapes, Architecture
Collections: American 19th & 20th century art works; Gilbert Wilson art; James Farrington Cooking Art
Publications: Newsletter 2 times per yr; Laurette E McCarthy - Swope Art Museum: Selected Works from the Collection
Activities: Classes for adults & children; docent training; lects open to pub, 8-16 vis lectrs per yr; gallery talks; tours; merit & purchase awards for Ann Wabash Valley Juried Exhib; exten prog to Vigo County School District; lending of original objects of art to mus; sales gallery shop sells reproductions, T-shirts, sweatshirts, postcards, caps, bags & button

UPLAND

M   **TAYLOR UNIVERSITY,** Metcalf Art Gallery, 236 W Reade Ave, Art Dept Upland, IN 46989-1001. Tel 765-998-2751, Ext 5322; Fax 765-998-4680; Elec Mail visualarts@tayloru.edu; Internet Home Page Address: www.taylor.edu/academics/acaddepts/art; *Chmn* Jonathan Bouw
Open Mon - Fri 8 AM - 5 PM, cl Sun; No admis fee; Estab 2003 as an educational gallery
Income: Financed by educational funding
Exhibitions: Visiting Artists Exhibits
Activities: Gallery talks; schols offered

VALPARAISO

M   **VALPARAISO UNIVERSITY,** Brauer Museum of Art, 1709 Chapel Dr, Valparaiso, IN 46383-4520. Tel 219-464-5365; Fax 219-464-5244; Internet Home Page Address: www.valpo.edu/artmuseum; *Assoc Cur & Registrar* Gloria Ruff; *Dir & Cur* Gregg Hertzlieb
Open Tues, Thurs & Fri 10 AM - 5 PM, Wed 10AM - 8:30 PM, Sat & Sun Noon - 5 PM, cl Mon; No admis fee; Estab 1953 to present significant art to the University community & people of Northwest Indiana; Average Annual Attendance: 10,000
Income: $18,000 (financed by membership)
Purchases: $45,000
Special Subjects: Drawings, Painting-American, Prints, Religious Art
Collections: 19th, 20th & 21st Century American Paintings, Prints & Drawings
Exhibitions: Rotating Exhibits
Activities: Docent training; lects open to pub; gallery talks; tours; individual paintings and original objects of art lent to museums and art centers

VEVAY

M   **SWITZERLAND COUNTY HISTORICAL SOCIETY INC,** Life on the Ohio: River History Museum, 208 E Market St, Vevay, IN 47043-1233. Tel 812-427-3560; Elec Mail swcomuseums@embarqmail.com; Internet Home Page Address: *www.switzcomuseums.org*; *Exec Dir* Martha Bladen; *Pres* Sundra Whitham; *Treas* Anita Danner; *Secy* Joyce Benbow
Open daily - 4PM; No admis fee; Estab 2004 to exhibit & educate the history of Switzerland County as it relates to the historic Ohio River through the steamboat era; River history mus; Average Annual Attendance: 3,000; Mem: 400; dues vary; quarterly meetings
Income: Financed through memberships, donations, grants & volunteer hours
Library Holdings: Book Volumes; Clipping Files; Original Documents; Other Holdings Genealogy Reference Materials; Photographs
Special Subjects: Landscapes, Marine Painting, Painting-American, Woodcuts, Manuscripts, Maps, Watercolors
Collections: Steamboat models; Pilot Wheel; Extensive coll of photos & documents; Historical colls; Distribution & transportation artifacts; Tools & equip for materials; Original paintings & prints with river themes
Exhibitions: Delta Queen, steamboat memorabilia, ongoing
Activities: Tours; mus shop sells books, reproductions, prints

M   **Switzerland County Historical Museum,** 210 E Market St, Vevay, IN 47043-1233. Tel 812-427-3560; Elec Mail swcomuseums@embarqmail.com; Internet Home Page Address: switzcomuseums.org; *Exec Dir* Martha Bladen; *Pres* Sundra Whitham; *Treas* Anita Danner; *Secy* Joyce Benbow
Open noon - 4 PM; No admis fee; Estab 1925 to unite those people interested in the history of Switzerland County, IN & surrounding region for its protection, preservation & promotion; Average Annual Attendance: 3,000; Mem: 400; dues vary by category; quarterly meetings
Income: Financed by memberships, donations, grants, volunteer hours
Library Holdings: Clipping Files; Manuscripts; Maps; Memorabilia; Original Documents; Other Holdings Genealogy & Family History Files; Periodical Subscriptions; Photographs
Special Subjects: American Indian Art, Archaeology, Decorative Arts, Folk Art, Historical Material, Architecture, Ceramics, Glass, Flasks & Bottles, Furniture, Portraits, Pottery, Painting-American, Woodcuts, Manuscripts, Maps, Religious Art, Porcelain, Restorations, Stained Glass
Collections: Early Swiss settlement; Indian artifacts; Tools & primitive farm equipment; Dolls, military, domestic arts
Activities: Classes for children; quilting prog & exhibits; 3 vis lectrs per yr; concerts; tours; lending of original objects of art to pub library & visitor's ctr; originate traveling exhibs, ann trunk show of IN history to public schools; mus shop sells books, reproductions, prints

WEST LAFAYETTE

M   **PURDUE UNIVERSITY GALLERIES,** 1396 Physics Bldg, West Lafayette, IN 47907-2036; 525 Northwestern Ave, Physics Bldg Room 205 Lafayette, IN 47907-2036. Tel 765-494-3061; Fax 765-496-2817; Elec Mail gallery@purdue.edu; Internet Home Page Address: www.purdue.edu/galleries; *Asst Dir* Michael Atwell; *Dir Gallery* Craig Martin; *Admin Asst* Mary Ann Anderson
Open Mon - Sat 10 AM - 5 PM, Thurs 10 AM - 8 PM, Sun 1 - 5 PM; No admis fee; Estab 1978 to provide aesthetic & educational programs for art students, the university & greater Lafayette community; Galleries are located in three different bldgs to provide approx 5000 sq ft of space for temporary exhibitions; Average Annual Attendance: 15,200
Income: Financed through the university & private & corporate contributions
Special Subjects: Drawings, Mexican Art, Photography, Prints, American Indian Art, Pre-Columbian Art, Ceramics, Woodcuts, Etchings & Engravings, Oriental Art
Collections: American Indian baskets; photographs; Contemporary paintings, prints, sculpture; ceramics; Pre-Columbian textiles; Art of the Americas
Exhibitions: By faculty, students, regionally & nationally prominent artists
Publications: Exhibit catalogs

Activities: Classes for adults & children; lects open to public; 3-34 vis lectrs per yr; gallery talks; competitions with awards, tours; exten program serving professional mus and galleries; book traveling exhibs, 1-2 per yr; originates traveling exhibs

IOWA

AMES

M **IOWA STATE UNIVERSITY,** Brunnier Art Museum, 290 Scheman Bldg, University Museums, Iowa State University Ames, IA 50011. Tel 515-294-3342; Fax 515-294-7070; Elec Mail museums@muse.adp.iastate.edu; *Dir* Lynette Pohlman; *Educ Coordr* Matthew DeLay; *Admin Spec* Janet McMathon; *Assoc Cur* Dana Michels; *Develop Secy* Susan Olson; *Cur Historic House* Eleanor Ostedorf; *Educ Asst* Jackie Wilson
Open Tues, Wed & Fri 11 AM - 4 PM, Thurs 11 AM - 4 PM & 5 - 9 PM, Sat & Sun 1 - 4 PM, cl Mon; No admis fee; Estab 1975, to provide a high level of quality, varied & comprehensive exhibits of national & international scope & to develop & expand a permanent decorative arts collection of the western world; Gallery is maintained & comprised of 10,000 sq ft of exhibit space, with flexible space arrangement; Average Annual Attendance: 50,000; Mem: 400 mems; $40 ann dues
Income: $400,000 (financed through state appropriations & grants)
Special Subjects: Prints, American Indian Art, Ceramics, Pottery, Decorative Arts, Posters, Dolls, Furniture, Glass, Jade, Porcelain, Oriental Art, Enamels
Collections: Permanent collection of ceramics, dolls, furniture, glass, ivory, wood, sculpture, fine arts
Publications: Christian Petersen, Sculptor
Activities: Classes for children; docent training; lects open to pub, 10 - 15 vis lectrs per yr; book traveling exhibs, 3-4 per yr; originates traveling exhibs; mus shop sells books, magazines, catalogs, jewelry, dolls, glass & original works

A **OCTAGON CENTER FOR THE ARTS,** 427 Douglas Ave, Ames, IA 50010-6281. Tel 515-232-5331; Fax 515-232-5088; Elec Mail rpayne@octagonarts.org; Internet Home Page Address: www.octagonarts.org; *Pres* Susan Christensen; *VPres* Mark Peterson; *Treas* Nancy Marion; *Educ Dir* Beth Weninger; *Shop Mgr* Ruth Wiedemeyer; *Exec Dir* Kathy Stevens; *Mktg Dir* Amy Streich; *Cur* Heather Straszheim
Open Tues - Sat 10 AM - 5 PM, Sun 2 - 5 PM; Admis suggested donation or contribution, family (up to five people) $3, individual $2; Estab 1966 to provide year-round classes for all ages; exhibitions of the work of outstanding artists local, regional & worldwide & also special programs in the visual & performing arts; Average Annual Attendance: 33,000; Mem: 365, open to anyone interested in supporting or participating in the arts; dues $15-$500 & up; annual meeting in May; individual $35, household $50, supporter $100, founders $300 & up
Income: $375,000 (financed by mem, city and state appropriations, class fees and fund raising)
Collections: Feinberg Collection of Masks from Around the World
Exhibitions: Octagon Arts Festival-art festival of over 125 Midwest artists; clay, fiber, glass, wood exhibition;
Publications: Exhibition catalogs; newsletter, quarterly
Activities: Classes in the arts for adults & children; special classes for senior citizens & physically & emotionally challenged; outreach progs; lects open to pub, 5-8 vis lectrs per yr; gallery talks; tours; competitions with awards; scholarships offered; book traveling exhibs; mus shop sells books, original art, prints & original fine crafts

ANAMOSA

A **PAINT 'N PALETTE CLUB,** Grant Wood Memorial Park & Gallery, 17314 Hwy 64, Anamosa, IA 52205; 673 Bolton Manor Rd, Springville, IA 52336-9733. Tel 319-462-2680; Elec Mail lshaffer@netins.net; *Cur* Wilbur Evarts
Open June 1 - Oct 15; Sun 1 - 4 PM; other times for groups & organizations; No admis fee (donations accepted); Estab 1955 to maintain Antioch School, the school attended by a famous Iowa artist from 1897-1901 Grant Wood; school restored to 1900 vintage; to provide a studio & gallery for local artists & for pub enjoyment. A log cabin art gallery on the grounds of the Grant Wood Memorial Park contains the work of some local & vis artists; Showcases works by local outsider artists. Most subject matter is rural, & this regionalist theme is echoed through natural surroundings; Average Annual Attendance: 3,000; Mem: 32, members must have art experience; dues $15
Income: Financed by dues and donations
Library Holdings: Audio Tapes; Maps; Memorabilia; Original Art Works; Pamphlets; Prints
Special Subjects: Landscapes, Posters, Painting-American, Folk Art
Collections: Prints of Grant Wood, Iowa's most famous artist; original amateur art; arts and crafts; postcards, memorabilia
Exhibitions: Special exhibits throughout the season; Annual Art Show; additional exhib 2nd Sun in Jun, annually; Annual Grant Wood Art Festival 2nd Sun June
Publications: Bulletin, monthly
Activities: Occasional classes for adults; summer instruction by professional painter; lects open to public, 1-2 vis lectrs per year; tours; competitions; films; lending of original objects of art; sales shop sells prints, original art, prints, reproductions, postcards & commemorative coins

ARNOLDS PARK

M **IOWA GREAT LAKES MARITIME MUSEUM,** 243 W Broadway, Arnolds Park, IA 51360; PO Box 609, Arnolds Park, IA 51331-0609. Tel 712-332-5264; Fax 712-332-2186; Elec Mail mary@arnoldspark.com; Internet Home Page Address: www.okobojimuseum.org; *CEO & Dir* Steven R Anderson; *Chmn* Rick Johnson; *Cur* Mary Kennedy
Open daily 9 AM - 9 PM; cl Easter, Thanksgiving & Christmas; No admis fee, donations accepted; Estab 1987; Pvt nonprofit org; 6000 sq ft exhib space; theater capacity 150; wheelchair available; FT paid 2, FT volunteers 1, PT vols 12. Maritime & antique mus that provides a look at the history of the Iowa Great Lakes region. ; Average Annual Attendance: 75,000; Mem: dues Lifetime $1000, Benefactor $100, Captain $50, Gen $25
Library Holdings: Book Volumes (150) local history; Periodical Subscriptions (1500) wooden boat magazines
Collections: Artifacts; recreational artifacts; tools & equip for materials; furnishings; personal artifacts; photographs; Wooden boats from the Iowa Great Lakes area, steamships, sand pales, fishing lures & paddlefish
Publications: Biannual newsletter: The Steam Whistle
Activities: Formal educ for adults; lects; guided tours

BELMOND

M **JENISON-MEACHAM MEMORIAL ART CENTER & MUSEUM,** 1179 Taylor Ave, Belmond, IA 50421-7568. Tel 641-444-3557; 444-4635

BURLINGTON

A **ART GUILD OF BURLINGTON,** Art Center, 301 Jefferson St, Burlington, IA 52601-5333. Tel 319-754-8069; Fax 319-754-4731; Elec Mail arts4living@aol.com; Internet Home Page Address: www.artguildofburlington.org; *Pres* Matt Bessini; *Exec Dir* Jerry Johnson
Open Mon - Fri 1 PM - 5 PM, Sat & Sun 1 PM - 4 PM; No admis fee; Estab 1966 with the mission enhance the arts through educ exhibs & performance progs in the Burlington area; Historic Downtown bldg; Average Annual Attendance: 8,000; Mem: 450; dues benefactor $1,000, down to student $10
Income: Financed by mem & donations
Library Holdings: Book Volumes; Video Tapes
Exhibitions: Exhibitions of regional professional artists
Publications: Monthly newsletter
Activities: Classes for adults & children; dramatic progs; docent training; films; special workshops; lects open to public; concerts; gallery talks; tours; Len Everett Scholarship; Juried Art Show; scholarships offered; book traveling exhibs 2-3 per yr; originates traveling exhibs organized & circulated; sales shop sells books, original art, reproductions, prints

CEDAR FALLS

M **CITY OF CEDAR FALLS, IOWA,** James & Meryl Hearst Center for the Arts & Sculpture Garden, 304 W Seerley Blvd, Cedar Falls, IA 50613-4050. Tel 319-273-8641; Fax 319-273-8659; Elec Mail mary.huber@cedarfalls.com; Internet Home Page Address: www.hearstartscenter.com; *Dir* Mary Huber; *Educ Coordr* Penny Azbill; *Cur, Registrar* Emily Drennan; *Develop Coordr* Vicki Simpson; *Sr Svcs Coordr* Gail LeFlore
Open Tues - Fri 8 AM - 5 PM, Tues & Thurs evenings 5 - 9 PM, Sat & Sun 1 - 4 PM; No admis fee; Estab 1988; Municipal arts center serving the Cedar Valley in Iowa; Average Annual Attendance: 45,000; Mem: 650; dues $25 - $1,000, Friends of the Hearst req; annual meeting in June
Income: $580,000 (financed by city appropriation, individual contributions, program fees & grants)
Library Holdings: Clipping Files; Exhibition Catalogs; Manuscripts; Memorabilia; Original Art Works; Original Documents; Other Holdings; Sculpture
Special Subjects: Etchings & Engravings, Landscapes, Woodcuts, Manuscripts, Drawings, Graphics, Painting-American, Photography, Prints, Sculpture, Ceramics, Pottery, Portraits, Posters, Reproductions
Collections: Book by Creative Education; complete set of illustrations for Legend of Sleepy Hollow; Gary Kelley Illustrations; children's book illustration; A number of Animals illustrations by Chris Wormell; cover of The Nutcracker by the artist Roberto Innocenti; public art in community; Hearst Sculpture Garden, permanent coll; Mid-western coll
Exhibitions: All-Iowa Competitive Exhibit (The AA Show); annual competition exhibition; annual sculpture garden exhibit; 28 exhibitions per year
Publications: Quarterly class brochure; This Month at the Hearst; spec collection & membership brochures, annual
Activities: Classes for adults & children; docent training; lects open to pub, 4-5 vis lectrs per yr; concert; gallery talks; tours; poetry readings; contemporary music series; chamber music series; sponsoring of competitions, including $1,000 Best in Show, $500 Second Pl, $250 Third Pl, $100 Honorable Mention; schols & fellowships offered; exten dept serves 30 mile radius; individual paintings & original objects of art lent to art organizations & mus; book traveling exhibs every 1.5 yrs; originate traveling exhibs to regional art mus; mus shop sells books, original art, reproductions, prints & gen merchandise related to coll

M **UNIVERSITY OF NORTHERN IOWA,** UNI Gallery of Art, 1601 W 27th St, Cedar Falls, IA 50614-0362. Tel 319-273-2077; Fax 319-273-7333; Elec Mail GalleryOfArt@uni.edu; Internet Home Page Address: www.uni.edu/artdept/gallery/home.html; *Dir* Darrell Taylor
Open Mon - Thurs 10 AM - 7 PM, Fri - Sat noon - 5 PM; also by appointment; No admis fee; Estab 1978 to bring to the University & the community at large the finest quality of art from all over the world; The 5,000 sq ft gallery is divided into five separate exhibition rooms; high security mus space with climate control & a highly flexible light system; the Gallery adjoins a pub reception space & a 144 seat auditorium; the facility also has a newly renovated coll storage facility, a work shop, a general storage room & a fully accessible loading dock; Average Annual Attendance: 12,000
Income: Financed by state appropriation
Purchases: 20th century art work
Library Holdings: DVDs; Exhibition Catalogs; Original Art Works; Photographs; Prints; Sculpture
Special Subjects: Painting-American, Painting-European
Collections: 20th century American & European Art
Exhibitions: 8 rotating & 8 mini-exhibs per yr
Publications: Exhibition catalogs

Activities: Volunteer training; lects open to public, 5 vis lectrs per year; performances; gallery talks; tours; competitions; ann juried student art exhib Merit & Purchase Awards; competition with awards; individual paintings & original objects of art lent to comparable orgs & institutions; traveling exhibs

L **Fine & Performing Arts Collection Rod Library,** 1227 W 27th St, Cedar Falls, IA 50613-3675. Tel 319-273-6252; Fax 319-273-2913; Internet Home Page Address: www.library.uni.edu/collections/fine-performing-arts; *Head Colls & Mus* Kate Martin; *Fine & performing Arts* Angela Pratesi; *Fine & Performing Arts* Julie Ann Beddow; *Dean of Library Svcs* Christopher Cox
Open Mon - Thurs 7:30 AM - 10:50 PM, Fri 7:30 AM - 5 PM, Sat noon - 5PM, Sun noon-10:50 PM; No admis fee; Main Library estab 1964, additions 1975 & 1995; to serve art & music patrons; Circ 3,200; For lending & reference; Average Annual Attendance: 9,300; Mem: 12,000 students
Income: Financed by state
Purchases: $18,000
Library Holdings: Audio Tapes; Book Volumes; Cassettes; Clipping Files; Compact Disks; DVDs; Exhibition Catalogs; Framed Reproductions; Original Art Works; Other Holdings; Pamphlets; Periodical Subscriptions; Photographs; Prints; Records; Reproductions; Sculpture; Video Tapes
Special Subjects: Art History, Textiles
Exhibitions: Continual Exhibs
Activities: Educ prog; acad; lects open to pub; number of vis lectrs per yr vary; tours; sponsoring of competitions

CEDAR RAPIDS

M **AFRICAN AMERICAN MUSEUM OF IOWA,** (African American Historical Museum & Cultural Center of Iowa) 55 12th Ave SE, Cedar Rapids, IA 52401. Tel 319-862-2101; Fax 319-862-2105; Elec Mail information@blackiowa.org; Internet Home Page Address: www.blackiowa.org; *Dir* Michael Kates; *Cur* Brianna Wright; *Develop Dir* Grant Stevens; *Educ Dir* Michelle Poe; *Facilities Coordr* Katherine Smith
Open Mon - Sat 10 AM - 4 PM; Admis adults $4, children, youth & students $3; Estab 1994; Mus with permanent & changing exhibits about Iowa's rich African American heritage.; Average Annual Attendance: 54,000; Mem: Platinum $400+, Golden $200-$399, Century $100-$199, Family $50-$99, Indiv $35-$49, Student & Seniors $25-$34
Income: Grants, donations, mems, endowment & rentals
Library Holdings: Book Volumes 1,500; Clipping Files; Compact Disks; DVDs; Manuscripts; Original Documents; Periodical Subscriptions 200; Photographs; Prints
Special Subjects: Afro-American Art, Historical Material, Manuscripts, Maps, African Art, Dioramas
Collections: African-Americans in Iowa; also includes an archive
Exhibitions: Western Africa: Before the Boats (through 3/30/2014); Behind the Beat (4/19, 2014-)
Publications: Griot, quarterly newsletter; annual report
Activities: Formal educ progs for adults & children; docent prog; guided tours; lects; loan exhibs; participatory, temp & traveling exhibs; Ann Events: Juneteenth, Banquet, Kwanzaa Journey to Freedom; History Makers Gala; exten prog for all of Iowa; mus shop sells books, prints & objects

M **CEDAR RAPIDS MUSEUM OF ART,** 410 Third Ave SE, Cedar Rapids, IA 52401. Tel 319-366-7503; Fax 319-366-4111; Elec Mail info@crma.org; Internet Home Page Address: www.crma.org; *Cur* Sean Ulmer; *Dir* Terence Pitts; *Vis Serv & Retail Mgr* Casey Dunagan; *Registrar* Teri Van Dorston; *Develop Dir* Kelly Leusch; *Facilities Mgr* Carlis Faurot; *Spec Events Coordr* Beth Roof; *Educ Dir* Erin Thomas; *Commun Coordr* Kristan Hellige; *Bus Mgr & CFO* Deanna Clemens Pedersen
Open Tues, Wed, Fri, Sun noon - 8 PM, Sat 10 AM - 4 PM; Admis adults $5, sr citizens $4, students under 18 free; Estab 1905; First & second floors maintain changing exhibits & the Permanent Collection; Average Annual Attendance: 35,000; Mem: 1000; dues Turner soc $1000, Cone Wood soc $500, benefactor $250, patron $125, family $60, individual $40, students & senior citizens $30, educator $30
Income: Financed by endowment, mem & revenues
Special Subjects: Decorative Arts, Ceramics, Photography, Drawings, Painting-American, Prints, Sculpture, Watercolors, Landscapes, Portraits, Coins & Medals, Antiquities-Roman
Collections: Coll of artworks by Grant Wood, Marvin Cone & Mauricio Lasansky; print coll; Roman antiquities; Midwestern art
Exhibitions: Midwestern Visions: Grant Wood, Marvin Cone and Beyond (permanent exhib); Art in Roman Life (permanent exhib); Mauricio Lasansky: Master Printmaker (permanent exhib)
Publications: Newsletter, tri-annual
Activities: Classes for adults & children; docent training; lects for members only; concerts; gallery talks; tours; individual paintings & original objects of art lent to other mus; originate traveling exhibs; mus shop sells books, original art, reproductions, prints; Grant Wood Studio & Visitor Ctr

L **Herbert S Stamats Library,** 410 Third Ave SE, Cedar Rapids, IA 52401. Tel 319-366-7503; Fax 319-366-4111; Elec Mail info@crma.org; Internet Home Page Address: www.crma.org
Open Tues, Wed, Fri & Sun noon - 4 PM, Thurs noon - 8 PM, Sat 10 AM - 4 PM; Admis adults $5, seniors & college students $4, children 18 & under & mems free; Estab Art Assn 1905; first and second floors of mus maintain permanent & changing exhib; Average Annual Attendance: 30,000; Mem: 700; dues - family $60, individual $40, senior/student $30, NARM mems free
Income: endowment, grants & memberships
Library Holdings: Book Volumes 3000; Cassettes; Filmstrips
Special Subjects: Art History, Painting-American, Prints, Ceramics, Art Education, Antiquities-Roman
Collections: Grant Wood, Marvin Cone
Exhibitions: (01/18/2014-05/11/2014) Conger Metcalf; (02/15/2014-05/25/2014) Papier Francias: French Works on Paper; (03/05/2014-11/02/2014) Marvin Cone on my Mind: The Ceramics of Dean Schwartz; (05/24/2014-09/07/2014) Carl Van Vechten: Photographer to the Stars; (06/04/2014-09/21/2014) Grant Wood: American Impressionist

Publications: Clary Illian: A Potter's Potter
Activities: Classes for adults & children; docent training; lects open to pub; 18-22 vis lectrs per yr; concerts; gallery talks; tours; mus shop sells books, original art, reproductions, prints

M **COE COLLEGE,** Eaton-Buchan Gallery & Marvin Cone Gallery, 1220 First Ave NE, Cedar Rapids, IA 52402. Tel 319-399-8217; Fax 319-399-8557; Elec Mail dchance@coe.edu; Internet Home Page Address: www.coe.edu; *Chmn Art Dept* John Beckelman; *Gallery Dir* Delores Chance
Open daily 3 - 5 PM; No admis fee; Estab 1942 to exhibit traveling exhibitions & local exhibits; Two galleries, both 60 x 18 ft with 125 running ft of exhibit space & 430 works on permanent exhibition; Average Annual Attendance: 5,000
Income: $7,090 (financed through college)
Collections: Coe Collection of art works; Marvin Cone Collection; Hinkhouse Collection of contemporary art; Grant Wood Collection; Works of nearly 300 artists spanning several centuries & 5 continents; Conger Metcalf Collection of Paintings
Exhibitions: Circulating exhibits; one-person & group shows of regional nature
Publications: Exhibition brochures, 8-10 per year
Activities: Lects open to public, 5-6 vis lectrs per yr; gallery talks; tours; competitions; individual paintings & original objects of art lent to colleges & local galleries; lending collection contains original art work, original prints, paintings, sculpture & slides; originates traveling exhibs

M **Stewart Memorial Library & Gallery,** 1220 First Ave NE, Cedar Rapids, IA 52402-5092. Tel 319-399-8023; 8585; Fax 319-399-8019; Elec Mail jjack@coe.edu; Internet Home Page Address: www.coe.edu; *Dir Library Svcs* Jill Jack
Open Mon - Thurs 8 AM - midnight, Fri 8 AM - 6 PM, Sat 9 AM - 6 PM, Sun 1 PM - 12 AM; June - Aug Mon - Fri 8 AM - 4 PM; Grant Wood, Marvin Cone, Conger Metcalf galleries; various artists
Collections: 200 permanent coll works

M **MOUNT MERCY COLLEGE,** White Gallery, 1330 Elmhurst Dr NE, Cedar Rapids, IA 52402-4797. Tel 319-363-8213; Fax 319-363-5270; Elec Mail vanallen.david@mcleodusa.net; *Dir* David Van Allen
Open Mon - Thurs 7 AM - 9 PM; No admis fee; Estab 1970 to show work by a variety of fine artists. The shows are used by the art department as teaching aids. They provide cultural exposure to the entire community; One room 22 x 30 ft; two walls are glass overlooking a small courtyard; Average Annual Attendance: 1,000
Income: Financed through the college
Purchases: $300
Collections: Small collection of prints & paintings
Exhibitions: Annual High School Art Exhibit; Senior Thesis Exhibit
Publications: Reviews in Fiber Arts; American Craft & Ceramics Monthly
Activities: Classes for adults; dramatic progs; lects open to pub; gallery talks; competitions with awards; 3 vis lectrs per yr; scholarships; lending original objects of art: campus locations; sales shop: original art, prints, Mexican folk art

L **Library,** 1330 Elmhurst Dr NE, Art Dept Cedar Rapids, IA 52402-4797. Tel 319-363-8213, Ext 244; Fax 319-363-9060; Elec Mail library@mtmercy.edu; Internet Home Page Address: www.mtmercy.edu; *Librn* Marilyn Murphy
Open Mon-Thurs 8 AM - midnight, Fri 8 AM - 8 PM, Sat 9:30 AM - 5 PM, Sun 1 PM - midnight; No admis fee; Estab 1928; Circ 35,000; Ref library & circ
Income: By the college
Library Holdings: Audio Tapes; Book Volumes 2000; Cards; Cassettes; Exhibition Catalogs; Fiche; Filmstrips; Framed Reproductions; Kodachrome Transparencies; Lantern Slides; Micro Print; Motion Pictures; Original Art Works; Pamphlets; Periodical Subscriptions 38; Photographs; Prints; Records; Reels; Reproductions; Sculpture; Slides; Video Tapes

CHARLES CITY

M **CHARLES CITY ARTS CENTER,** 301 N Jackson St, Charles City, IA 50616-2006. Tel 641-228-6284

M **CHARLES CITY LIBRARY,** Mooney Art Collection, 106 Milwaukee Mall, Charles City, IA 50616. Tel 641-257-6319; Fax 641-257-6325; Elec Mail vruzicka@charles-city.lib.ia.us

CLEAR LAKE

M **CLEAR LAKE ARTS CENTER,** 17 S 4th St, Clear Lake, IA 50428. Tel 641-357-1998; Elec Mail clac@netins.net

CLINTON

M **CLINTON ART ASSOCIATION,** River Arts Center, 229 Fifth Ave S, Clinton, IA 52733-0132. Tel 563-243-3300, 242-8055; Elec Mail mthayes9@msn.com; Internet Home Page Address: www.clintonarts.com; *Pres* Ronald Blatchley; *VPres & Publicity* Martha Hayes; *Treas* Nancy Bergess
Open Wed - Sun 1 - 4 PM, cl Christmas & New Year; No admis fee; Estab 1968 to bring visual art to the community; Art gallery, classrooms, pottery studio, permanent coll, community theater in downtown location; Average Annual Attendance: 16,000; Mem: 420; dues single membership $30; annual meeting
Income: Financed by mem & through grants from the Iowa Arts Council
Special Subjects: Painting-American, Photography, Prints, Sculpture, Pottery, Woodcarvings, Woodcuts, Etchings & Engravings, Glass
Collections: Painting (watercolor, oil, acrylic, pastel); beaded loin cloth; photographs; lithograph; engraving; sculptures; etching; prints; pottery; fabric; pencil; wood; slate; Ektaflex Color Printmaking System; glass; ink; lucite; rugs; woodcarving
Exhibitions: Rotating exhibits
Publications: Newsletter, quarterly

Activities: Classes for adults & children in watercolor, oil, drawing, photography & pottery making; docent training; dramatic progs & other; lect open to public; 2-3 vis lectrs per yr; gallery talks; tours; schols; lending collection contains books; sales shop sells original art, prints & stationery, reproductions

CORNING

M **CORNING CENTER FOR THE FINE ARTS,** 706 Davis Ave, Corning, IA 50841-1451. Tel 641-322-4549
Open Wed - Fri 10 AM - 5 PM, Sat 10 AM - 4 PM; No admis fee

DAVENPORT

M **FIGGE ART MUSEUM,** 225 W 2nd St, Davenport, IA 52801-1804. Tel 563-326-7804; Fax 563-326-7876; Elec Mail vbenson@figgeartmuseum.org; Internet Home Page Address: figgeart.org; *Dir Mus Svcs* Jennifer Brooke; *Cur Educ* Ann Marie Hayes-Hawkinson; *Dir Develop* Dan McNeil; *Youth & Family Progs Coordr* Lynn Gringras-Taylor; *Mem Coordr* Susan Horan; *Outreach Progs Coordr* Melissa Hueting
Open Tues - Sat 10 AM - 5 PM, Thurs until 9 PM, Sun Noon - 5 PM, cl Mon & holidays; Admis adults $7, seniors & students with ID $6, children ages 3-12 $4, mems free; Estab 1925 as a mus of art & custodian pub collection & an educ center for the visual arts, renamed in 1963, relocated 2003, reopened 2005; Consists of three levels including a spacious main gallery, exhibition area & two additional floors with galleries; six multipurpose art studios & ceramic gallery, studio workshop & an outdoor studio-plaza on the lower level; 114,000 sq ft facility designed by David Chipperfield; Average Annual Attendance: 100,000; Mem: 600; dues household $50, individual $30, senior citizens $20, student $15
Income: $900,000 (financed by private & city appropriation)
Special Subjects: Mexican Art, Painting-American, Painting-European, Oriental Art, Painting-British, Painting-French, Painting-German
Collections: American Coll: 19th & 20th c works; Midwest Regionalist Coll incl Grant Wood, Thomas Hart Benton, John Steuart Curry; European Coll; Mexican Colonial Coll; Haitian Coll
Exhibitions: Beverly Pepper: The Moline Makers; Byron Burford; Mississippi Corridor; Grandma Moses; Selections: The Union League of Chicago Collection; Thomas Eakins (photographs); Joseph Sheppard; Mauricio Lasansky; Sol LeWitt; Stephen Antonakos - Neons; Frederic Carder: Portrait of a Glassmaker; Paul Brach Retrospective; David Hockney (photographs); Rudie (holograms); McMichael Canadian Collection; Kassebaum Medieval & Renaissance Ceramics; Collected Masterworks: The International Collections of the Davenport Museum of Art; Mexico Nueve; A Different War: Vietnam In Art; Judaica: Paintings by Nathan Hilu & Ceramics by Robert Lipnick; Faith Ringgold: 25 Year Survey
Publications: Quarterly newsletter; biennial report; Focus 1: Michael Boyd - Paintings from the 1980s; Focus 2: Photo Image League - Individual Vision/Collective Support; Focus 3: A Sense of Wonder - The Art of Haiti; Focus 4: Artists Who Teach: Building our Future; Haitian Art: The Legend & Legacy of the Naive Tradition; Three Decades of Midwestern Photography, 1960 - 1990
Activities: Classes for adults, teens, children & families; docent training; lects open to pub; concerts; gallery talks; tours; competitions with prizes; scholarships & fels offered; book traveling exhibs organized & circulated; originate traveling exhibs; mus shop sells books, posters, notecards, t-shirts, jewelry, scarves, original art, gifts & other items; Arterarium environmental installation

L **Art Reference Library,** 225 W 2nd St, Davenport, IA 52801-1804. Tel 563-326-7804; Fax 563-326-7876; Internet Home Page Address: www.figgeartmuseum.org; *Dir* Sean O'Harrow; *Cur* Michelle Robinson; *Dir Educ* Ann Marie Hayes
Open Tues - Sat 10 AM - 5 PM, Sun 1 - 5 PM, cl Mon; Admis adults $7, seniors & students $6, children under 12 $4; mus mem free; Estab 1925 as first municipal art mus in Iowa; Circ non-circulating library; Open for reference; Average Annual Attendance: 50,000; Mem: $65 household; $35 individuals; $25 teachers
Library Holdings: Auction Catalogs; Book Volumes 6000; Kodachrome Transparencies; Periodical Subscriptions 20; Video Tapes
Special Subjects: Decorative Arts, Mixed Media, Photography, Drawings, Etchings & Engravings, Painting-American, Painting-Dutch, Painting-Flemish, Painting-French, Painting-German, Painting-Italian, Sculpture, Painting-European, American Western Art, Mexican Art, Stained Glass, Religious Art, Silver, Woodcuts, Landscapes, Portraits
Collections: 3,500 works of art (American, European, Haitian & Mexican-Colonial)
Exhibitions: Treasures of Mexican Colonial Painting, Marcus Burlee; Tracing the Spirit: Ethnographic Essays on Haitian Art, Karen McCarthy Brown; Grant Wood: An American Master Revealed
Activities: Classes for adults & children; docent training; continuing education classes for teachers; lects open to pub; 12 vis lectrs per yr; gallery talks; tours; sponsored competitions with awards; schol offered; originates traveling exhibs to art mus; mus shop sells books, decorative art, furniture, reproductions & gift items related to collections & traveling exhibs

M **PUTNAM MUSEUM OF HISTORY AND NATURAL SCIENCE,** (Putnam Museum of History & Natural Science) 1717 W 12th St, Davenport, IA 52804-3597. Tel 563-324-1933; Fax 563-324-6638; Elec Mail museum@putnam.org; Internet Home Page Address: www.putnam.org; *Pres & CEO* Kimberly Findlay; *Chief Cur* Eunice Schlichting; *IMAX Theater Mgr* Dean K Fich; *Dir Visitor Svcs* Beth Knaack; *Exhibits Mgr* Michael Murphy; *Dir Mktg* Lori Arquello; *Dir Finance* Kim Nickels; *Cur Natural Science* Christine Chandler; *Dir Educ* Donna Murray; *Mus Shop Mgr* Sue Folwell; *Cur Hist & Anthropology* Christina Kastell
Open Mon - Sat 10AM-5PM, Sun noon-5PM; coll by appt; Admis adults $6, sr citizens $5, ages 3-12 $4, members & children 2 & under free; Estab 1867 as Davenport Academy of Natural Sciences; To provide educational & enriching experiences through interpretive exhibits & mus programming; Average Annual Attendance: 170,000
Income: $3,000,000 (financed by contributions, grants, endowments, mem & earned income)
Library Holdings: Book Volumes 25,000; Lantern Slides; Motion Pictures; Original Art Works; Photographs; Prints; Records
Special Subjects: Drawings, Prints, Watercolors, Archaeology, Textiles, Costumes, Ceramics, Decorative Arts, Manuscripts, Dolls, Furniture, Glass, Asian Art, Silver, Carpets & Rugs, Historical Material, Maps, Coins & Medals, Embroidery, Antiquities-Oriental, Antiquities-Persian, Antiquities-Egyptian, Antiquities-Greek, Antiquities-Roman, Antiquities-Etruscan
Collections: Natural history; American Indian, pre-Columbian; anthropology; arts of Asia, Near & Middle East, Africa, Oceanic; botany; ethnology; paleontology; decorative arts; local history
Exhibitions: Permanent & changing exhibition programs
Activities: Formally organized educ progs for children & adults; films; lects; gallery talks; guided tours; IMAX Theatre presentations; individual paintings & original objects of art lent to mus & educational organizations for special exhibs only; book traveling exhibs 6 per yr; originate traveling exhibs; mus store sells books, original art, prints, miscellaneous collections-related merchandise for children & adults

DECORAH

M **LUTHER COLLEGE,** Fine Arts Collection, 700 College Dr, Decorah, IA 52101-1041. Tel 563-387-1300; Fax 563-387-1132; Elec Mail ellika03@luther.edu; *Gallery Coordr* David Kamm; *Cur* Kate Elliott
Open Sept - June 8 AM - 5 PM; No admis fee; Estab 1900; Five galleries on campus; Average Annual Attendance: 10,000
Income: $4000
Special Subjects: Drawings, Landscapes, Photography, Prints, Painting-American, Sculpture, Watercolors, American Western Art, Bronzes, Pre-Columbian Art, Southwestern Art, Religious Art, Ceramics, Pottery, Primitive art, Woodcarvings, Woodcuts, Etchings & Engravings, Portraits, Posters, Eskimo Art, Carpets & Rugs, Antiquities-Greek, Antiquities-Roman, Enamels, Painting-Scandinavian
Collections: Gerhard Marcks Collection (drawings, prints & sculpture); Marguerite Wildenhain Collection (drawings & pottery); Inuit sculpture; pre-Columbian pottery; Scandinavian immigrant painting; contemporary & historical Prints
Publications: Occasional catalogs & brochures
Activities: Lect open to public; gallery talks; lending collection contains individual paintings & original objects of art; book traveling exhibitions 12 per year

M **VESTERHEIM NORWEGIAN-AMERICAN MUSEUM,** 523 W Water St, Decorah, IA 52101; PO Box 379, Decorah, IA 52101-0379. Tel 563-382-9681; Fax 563-382-8828; Elec Mail info@vesterheim.org; Internet Home Page Address: vesterheim.org; *Chief Cur* Lauran Gilbertson; *Exec Dir* Steven Johnson; *Dir Retail Svcs* Ken Koop; *Ed* Charlie Langton; *Registrar & Librn* Jennifer Kovarik; *Dir Admin* Marcia McKelvey; *Develop Dir* Steve Grinna; *Educ Specialist-Folk Art* Darlene Fossum Martin; *Chair* Lindsay Erdman; *Bookkeeper* Kathy Wilbur; *Mem Mgr* Peggy Sersland; *Vol Coordr* Martha Griesheimer
Open May-Oct daily 9 AM- 5 PM, Nov-Apr daily 10 AM to 4 PM; Admis adults $10, seniors $8, youth $5, members free; Estab 1877, Vesterheim embodies the living heritage of Norwegian immigrants to America. Sharing this cultural legacy can inspire people of all backgrounds to celebrate tradition; Main Building with four floors of exhib, plus numerous historic buildings including two from Norway make up the complex of Vesterheim; Average Annual Attendance: 13,000; Mem: 5600; dues basic mem $35
Income: $1,800,000 (financed by endowment, mem, donations, admis, sales)
Library Holdings: Auction Catalogs 10; Audio Tapes 10; Book Volumes; CD-ROMs 5; Cassettes 25; Clipping Files; DVDs 10; Exhibition Catalogs; Filmstrips; Lantern Slides; Manuscripts; Maps; Memorabilia; Original Art Works 2,200; Original Documents; Pamphlets; Periodical Subscriptions 70; Photographs; Prints; Records; Reels; Reproductions; Sculpture; Video Tapes 100
Special Subjects: Drawings, Etchings & Engravings, Folk Art, Historical Material, Marine Painting, Metalwork, Flasks & Bottles, Furniture, Photography, Porcelain, Portraits, Painting-American, Prints, Period Rooms, Silver, Textiles, Woodcuts, Manuscripts, Maps, Sculpture, Tapestries, Architecture, Photography, Watercolors, Costumes, Religious Art, Ceramics, Crafts, Pottery, Woodcarvings, Landscapes, Decorative Arts, Portraits, Dolls, Glass, Jewelry, Porcelain, Carpets & Rugs, Coins & Medals, Miniatures, Period Rooms, Embroidery, Laces, Pewter, Leather, Reproductions, Painting-Scandinavian
Collections: folk art; furnishings; textiles; machinery; tools; historic buildings; reference & special collections libraries; archives
Exhibitions: exhibitions rotate, please check exhibition schedule on museum's website
Publications: Vesterheim Magazine, semi annual; Time Honored Norwegian Recipes; Rosemaling Letter, 3 times per yr; Vesterheim: Samplings from the Collection; Rosemaler's Recipes Cookbook; Ole Goes to War: Men from Norway Who Fought in America's Civil War; Marking Time: The Primstav Murals of Sigmund Aarseth
Activities: Educ prog; classes for adults; children's educ prog; docent training; dramatic progs; lects open to pub; gallery talks; tours; sponsoring of competitions; Vesterheim gold medal award; periodic book traveling exhibs; originate traveling exhibs for cultural institutions; mus shop sells art & craft supplies, books, original art, prints, related gift items, woodenware, artist supplies for rosemaling & woodworking

DES MOINES

M **EDMUNDSON ART FOUNDATION, INC,** Des Moines Art Center, 4700 Grand Ave, Des Moines, IA 50312-2002. Tel 515-277-4405; Fax 515-271-0357; Elec Mail informationdesk@desmoinesartcenter.org; Internet Home Page Address: www.desmoinesartcenter.org; *Pres Board Trustees* Mary Kelly; *Dir* Jeff Fleming
Open Tues, Wed, Fri 11 AM - 4 PM, Thurs 11 AM - 9 PM, Sat 10 AM - 4 PM, Sun Noon - 4 PM, cl Mon; No admis fee; Estab 1948 for the purpose of displaying, conserving & interpreting art; Large sculpture galleries in I M Pei-designed addition; the main gallery covers 36 x 117 ft area. New Meier wing,

opened 1985, increased space for exhibitions 50 percent; Average Annual Attendance: 350,000; Mem: 3000, dues $35 & up
Income: $4,000,000 (financed by endowment, mem, gifts, grants, shop sales, tuition & state appropriation)
Library Holdings: Auction Catalogs; Book Volumes; CD-ROMs; Clipping Files; Exhibition Catalogs; Original Documents; Periodical Subscriptions; Slides
Special Subjects: Graphics, Painting-American, Sculpture, African Art
Collections: African art; graphics; American & European sculpture & painting of the past 200 years
Publications: Bulletin, bimonthly; catalogs of exhibitions
Activities: Classes for adults & children; docent training; lects open to pub, 6 vis lectrs per yr; concerts; gallery talks; tours; competitions; traveling exhibs organized & circulated; mus shop sells books, original art, prints & postcards

L **Des Moines Art Center Library,** 4700 Grand Ave, Des Moines, IA 50312-2099. Tel 515-277-4405; Fax 515-271-0357; Internet Home Page Address: www.desmoinesartcenter.org
Open by appointment only; Estab 1948 for research of permanent collection, acquisitions, exhibition preparation, class preparation & lectures; Open to the public for reference by appointment
Library Holdings: Auction Catalogs; Book Volumes 14,700; CD-ROMs; Clipping Files; Exhibition Catalogs; Original Documents; Periodical Subscriptions 70; Slides

M **POLK COUNTY HERITAGE GALLERY,** Heritage Art Gallery, Polk County Office Bldg, 111 Court Ave Des Moines, IA 50309-2218. Tel 515-286-2242; Fax 515-286-3082; Elec Mail info@heritagegallery.org; Internet Home Page Address: www.heritagegallery.org; *Pres* Tom Green
Open Mon - Fri 11 AM - 4:30 PM; No admis fee; Estab 1980; exhib space for visual art in the Polk County office building built in 1908 & on the register of historic places; Average Annual Attendance: 4,000
Exhibitions: Greater Des Moines Exhibited (annually, winter); Iowa Exhibited (annually, spring)
Activities: Cash awards for two annual competitions

L **PUBLIC LIBRARY OF DES MOINES,** Central Library Information Services, 1000 Grand Ave, Des Moines, IA 50309-2380. Tel 515-283-4152, Ext 3; Fax 515-237-1654; Elec Mail reference@pldminfo.org; Internet Home Page Address: www.desmoineslibrary.com; *Head Librn* Pam Deitrick; *Dir* Saul Amdursky
Open Mon-Thurs 9AM-8PM, Fri 9AM-6PM, Sun 1PM-5PM; No admis fee; Estab 1866, dept estab 1970 to serve art & music patrons; Circ 20,120
Income: Financed by city appropriation
Library Holdings: Book Volumes 4500; Periodical Subscriptions 12; Video Tapes

M **SALISBURY HOUSE FOUNDATION,** Salisbury House and Garden, 4025 Tonawanda Dr, Des Moines, IA 50312-2909. Tel 515-274-1777; Fax 515-274-0184; Elec Mail contactus@salisburyhouse.org; Internet Home Page Address: www.salisburyhouse.org; *Assoc Dir* Marie Louise Kane; *Dir* Scott Brunscheen
Pub tours Tues - Fri 1 PM & 2:30 PM; cl Jan and Feb; Admis adults $7, seniors $6, children 12 years & under $3; Estab 1954 as a historic house museum; Historic Mansion is modeled after the King's House in Salisbury, England & contains Tudor era furniture, classic paintings & sculpture from East & West, tapestries, Oriental rugs; Average Annual Attendance: 30,000
Income: Financed through admis, mem, contributions, cultural programs, private & corporate function facility fees, endowment & grants
Library Holdings: Book Volumes; Cards; Clipping Files; Kodachrome Transparencies; Manuscripts; Memorabilia; Original Art Works; Original Documents; Prints
Special Subjects: Metalwork, Porcelain, Bronzes, Painting-American, Sculpture, American Indian Art, Southwestern Art, Textiles, Costumes, Ceramics, Decorative Arts, Manuscripts, Portraits, Furniture, Oriental Art, Asian Art, Painting-British, Carpets & Rugs, Historical Material, Tapestries, Period Rooms
Collections: Collection of paintings by Genth, Lillian, Joseph Stella, Sir Thomas Lawrence, Van Dyck; Brussels Brabant tapestries; sculpture by Archipenko, Bourdelle; Chinese, Indian & Oriental (Persian) rugs
Exhibitions: Permanent collection
Activities: Docent training, workshops, dramatic progs; lects open to pub, 4 vis lectrs per yr; concerts; tours; individual paintings & original objects of art lent; lending collection contains motion pictures, original art works, paintings; mus shop sells reproductions, brochures, postcards, stationery, books, prints & videos

DUBUQUE

M **DUBUQUE MUSEUM OF ART,** 701 Locust St, Dubuque, IA 52001-6817. Tel 563-557-1851; Fax 563-557-7826; Elec Mail info@dbqart.com; Internet Home Page Address: www.dbqart.com; *Exec Dir* Mark D Whalert; *Deputy Dir* Diane Sass; *Pres* Alan Bird; *Dir Educ* Margaret Buhr; *Mgr Coll & Exhibs* Stacy Gage
Open Tues - Fri 10 AM - 5 PM, Sat & Sun 1 - 4 PM, cl Mon; No admis fee; Estab 1874, to preserve, collect, exhibit, interpret & teach the fine arts to those in the Dubuque area & surrounding communities; Average Annual Attendance: 9,450; Mem: 400; dues $15-$4000; annual meeting in May
Income: Financed by dues & donations
Collections: Permanent collection consists of regional & historic art, drawings, paintings, prints, sculptures & watercolor; Grant Wood; Edward S Curtis; Arthur Geisert
Exhibitions: Ceramics, drawing, paintings, sculptures
Publications: Art News, quarterly
Activities: Classes for adults & children; lects open to pub, 12-14 vis lectrs per yr; concerts; gallery talks; tours; competitions with awards; mus shop sells books, misc. children's gift items & jewelry

EPWORTH

M **DIVINE WORD COLLEGE,** Father Weyland SVD Gallery, 102 Jacoby Dr SW, Epworth, IA 52045-7716. Tel 319-876-3353; Fax 319-876-3353; Elec Mail jrudd@dwci.edu; Internet Home Page Address: www.dwci.edu; *Asst Prof Art* Jeremy Rudd
Open Mon - Sun 9 AM - 5 PM; No admis fee; Estab 1985; Carpeted walls, track lighting

Exhibitions: Art of Africa & Papua New Guinea; 5 exhibits each year

FAIRFIELD

L **FAIRFIELD ART ASSOCIATION,** 200 N Main, Fairfield, IA 52556; PO Box 904, Fairfield, IA 52556-0016. Tel 641-472-5374; Elec Mail suzan1252@aol.com; *Dir* Suzan Kessel; *Pres* Terry M Klein; *VPres* Cindy Travers
Open Mon - Sat 9 AM - 5 PM; No admis fee; Estab 1966; Large gallery in new Arts & Convention Center; Average Annual Attendance: 20,000
Income: Financed by endowment & mem
Library Holdings: Cards; Original Art Works; Periodical Subscriptions 180
Collections: Graphics; paintings
Exhibitions: New exhibits monthly
Activities: Classes for adults & children; dramatic progs; lects open to pub; competitions; gallery talks; tours; schols offered; sales shop sells original art & prints

A **MAHARISHI UNIVERSITY OF MANAGEMENT,** Department of Art, 1000 N 4th St, c/o MUM Dept of Art Fairfield, IA 52557-0001. Tel 641-472-7000 Ext 5035; Elec Mail art@mum.edu; Internet Home Page Address: www.mum.edu; *Dir* Ceyrona Kay; *Office Mgr* Betsy Henry
Open Mon - Sat 10 AM - 4 PM; No admis fee; Estab 1965 as teaching galley & to foster develop of the arts in the region; One gallery 20 ft X 44 ft for exhibition of contemporary & modern art; 20 artist studios; theater for lectures & performances; classrooms for teaching visual arts courses; Average Annual Attendance: 1,000
Income: Financed by Maharishi University of Management
Collections: Contemporary art in all media
Exhibitions: Regional & in-state artists; student shows
Publications: Exhibit catalogues
Activities: University classes; lects open to public, 6 vis lectrs per year; gallery talks

FORT DODGE

M **BLANDEN MEMORIAL ART MUSEUM,** 920 Third Ave S, Fort Dodge, IA 50501. Tel 515-573-2316; Fax 515-573-2317; Internet Home Page Address: www.blanden.org; *Dir* Margaret Skove; *Educ* Linda Flaherty; *Bus Office* Pamela Kay; *Security & Maintenance* Mark Jessen
Open Tues - Sat 11 AM - 5 PM; cl holidays; No admis fee-donations accepted; Estab 1930 as a permanent municipal, non-profit institution, educational & aesthetic in purpose; the mus interprets, exhibits & cares for a permanent collection & traveling exhibitions; Houses works of art in permanent collection; Average Annual Attendance: 17,000; Mem: 600; dues $25-$1,000
Income: $500,000 (financed by city & state appropriation, mem, Blanden Charitable Foundation & private support)
Library Holdings: Book Volumes; Clipping Files; Exhibition Catalogs; Memorabilia; Original Documents; Other Holdings; Pamphlets; Periodical Subscriptions; Photographs; Prints
Special Subjects: Historical Material, Photography, Porcelain, Pre-Columbian Art, Prints, Period Rooms, Textiles, Bronzes, Sculpture, Architecture, Painting-American, Sculpture, Bronzes, African Art, Ceramics, Woodcarvings, Woodcuts, Etchings & Engravings, Painting-European, Portraits, Posters, Oriental Art, Baroque Art, Calligraphy, Renaissance Art, Medieval Art, Painting-Spanish, Antiquities-Egyptian, Antiquities-Greek, Antiquities-Roman, Painting-German
Collections: Arts of China & Japan; 15th - 20th Century Works on Paper; Pre-Columbian & African Art; Regional Art; Twentieth century American & European masters, paintings & sculpture; Beckman, Chagall, Miro/City of Fort Dodge History
Publications: Annual report; exhibition catalogues; handbook of the permanent collection; membership information; quarterly bulletin
Activities: Educ prog; classes for adults & children; docent training; dramatic progs; volunteer training (front desk); lects open to pub, 4-6 vis lectrs per yr; concerts; gallery talks; tours; competitions with awards; scholarships offered; exten outreach art appreciation prog; loans to art mus meeting necessary professional requirements including climate conditions, security & other physical needs specifications of the art collection; lending of original objects of art to State College/Spain; book traveling exhibs; originate traveling exhibs; mus shop sells books; magazines; artist work

GRINNELL

M **GRINNELL COLLEGE,** Faulconer Gallery, 1108 Park St, Grinnell, IA 50112-1643. Tel 641-269-4660; Fax 641-269-4626; Elec Mail wright@grinnell.edu; Internet Home Page Address: www.grinnell.edu/faulconergallery; *Dir* Lesley Wright; *Assoc Dir* Dan Strong; *Cur Acad & Community Outreach* Tilly Woodward; *Exhib Designer* Milton Severe; *Cur Coll* Kay Wilson; *Admin Asst* Conni Gause
Open Tues - Wed, Sat - Sun noon - 5 PM, Thurs - Fri noon - 8 PM; cl holidays; No admis fee, donations accepted; Estab 1999 as a college gallery of distinction. Faulconer Gallery promotes learning through artistic excellence & creative collaboration; 7,400 sq ft gallery designed by Cesar Pelli; print & drawing study room; Average Annual Attendance: $260,000 (financed by endowment)
Income: $75,000 (financed by endowment)
Purchases: $140,000 (from endowed funds)
Special Subjects: Drawings, Graphics, Photography, Prints, Watercolors, African Art, Woodcuts, Etchings & Engravings
Collections: Works of Art on Paper
Exhibitions: Sandy Skoglund: Raining Popcorn; Layers of Brazilian Art; John Wilson: A Retrospective; William Kentridge Prints; Scandinavian Photography 1: Sweden; Scandinavian Photography 2: Denmark; Hin: The Quiet Beauty of Japanese Bamboo Art; Where Are You From: Contemporary Portuguese Art; Works in Progress; Prints from Wildwood Press; Repeat, Reveal, React: Indentities in Flu; Of Fables & Folly: Diane Victor, Recent Work; From the Book Forest:

Commercial Publishing in Late Imperial China; Walter Burley Griffin & Marion Mahony Griffin in Iowa
Publications: Exhibition catalogs
Activities: Classes for children; lects open to pub; gallery talks; tours; book traveling exhibs 1-2 per yr; organize traveling exhibs occasionally to other col mus; mus shop sells original art

INDIANOLA

M **SIMPSON COLLEGE,** Farnham Gallery, 701 N "C" St, Indianola, IA 50125. Tel 515-961-1486; Fax 515-961-1498; Elec Mail richmond@simpson.edu; Internet Home Page Address: www.simpson.edu; *Head Art Dept* David Richmond; *Asst Prof* Justin Nostrala
Open Mon - Fri 8 AM - 4:30 PM; No admis fee; Estab 1982 to educate & inform the public; Two small gallery rooms each 14 ft, 4 in x 29 ft; Average Annual Attendance: 1,200
Income: college fees
Collections: Small permanent collection being started
Activities: Classes for adults; lects open to pub, 4 vis lectrs per yr; gallery talks; scholarships offered; individual paintings lent; originate traveling exhibs

IOWA CITY

M **UNIVERSITY OF IOWA,** University of Iowa Museum of Art, 376 Iowa Memorial Union at Jefferson & Madison Sts, Iowa City, IA 52242; 1375 Highway 1 W, 1840 Studio Arts Bldg Iowa City, IA 52246-4233. Tel 319-335-1727; Fax 319-335-3677; Elec Mail uima@uiowa.edu; Internet Home Page Address: www.uiowa.edu/uima; *Mgr Exhib & Colls* Jeff Martin; *Dir Educ* Dale William Fisher; *Chief Cur* Kathleen Edwards; *Mems Council Coordr* Buffie Tucker; *Dir* Sean O'Harrow; *Mgr Mktg & Commun* Erika Jo Brown; *Secy* Betty Breazeale
Open Tues, Wed & Fri 10 AM - 5 PM, Thurs 10 AM - 9 PM, Sat - Sun noon - 5 PM; cl Mon & univ holidays; No admis fee; Estab 1969 to collect, exhibit & preserve for the future, works of art from different cultures; to make these objects as accessible as possible to people of all ages in the state of Iowa; to assist the pub, through educational programs & publications, in interpreting these works of art & expanding their appreciation of art in general; Temporary UIMA@IMU visual classroom opened after 2008 flood; Average Annual Attendance: 50,000; Mem: Sponsor $5,000; Director's Circle $1,000; Patron $500; Curator's Circle $250; Benefactor $150; Basic $100; Contributors $25-$99
Income: Financed by state appropriation & private donations
Special Subjects: American Indian Art, Decorative Arts, Drawings, Etchings & Engravings, Metalwork, Pre-Columbian Art, Painting-American, Prints, Silver, Textiles, Painting-French, Sculpture, Graphics, Photography, Watercolors, African Art, Religious Art, Ceramics, Pottery, Woodcarvings, Woodcuts, Jade, Oriental Art, Asian Art, Islamic Art, Painting-German, Antiquities-Etruscan
Collections: African & Pre-Columbian art; Chinese & Tibetan bronzes; Oriental jade; 19th & 20th century European & American paintings & sculpture; prints, drawings, photography, silver; Elliott Collection of 20th Century European Art; Mauricio Lasansky Print Collection
Exhibitions: The Elliott Collection of 20th Century European paintings, silver & prints; a major collection of African sculpture; many changing exhibs each yr, both permanent collection, original & traveling exhibitions
Publications: Magazine 2 times per yr; exhibition catalogs
Activities: Classes for adults; docent training; lects open to pub; lects for mems only; 10-20 vis lectrs per yr; concerts; gallery talks; tours; works of art lent to other museums; traveling exhibs; originate traveling exhibs; sales shop sells posters, postcards, catalogs, mugs, tote bags, t-shirts, anniversary book, notecards, magnets

L **Art Library,** W 145 Art Bldg, Iowa City, IA 52242; 1375 Highway 1 W, W 145 Art Bldg Iowa City, IA 52246-4233. Tel 319-335-3089; Elec Mail art-lib@uiowa.edu; Internet Home Page Address: www.lib.uiowa.edu/art/index; *Head Librn* Rijn Templeton
Open Mon - Thurs 8:30 AM - 8:30 PM, Fri 8:30 AM - 5 PM, Sat 1 - 5 PM, SUN 1 - 7 PM; call for seasonal hours; Estab 1937 to support the University programs, community & state needs; Circ 40,000
Income: Financed by state appropriation
Library Holdings: Book Volumes 100,000; CD-ROMs; Clipping Files; Exhibition Catalogs; Fiche; Memorabilia; Pamphlets; Periodical Subscriptions 230; Reels

KEOKUK

A **KEOKUK ART CENTER,** 210 N 5th St, Keokuk, IA 52632-5614. Tel 319-524-8354; Elec Mail tseabold@keokukartcenter.org; Internet Home Page Address: www.keokukartcenter.org; *Dir* Thomas Seabold
Open Tues - Sat 9 AM - 4PM & by appointment; No admis fee; Estab 1954 to promote art in tri-state area; Gallery maintained in Keokuk Public Library, 210 N Fifth St; Average Annual Attendance: 2,000; Mem: dues sustaining $50, patron $25, family $12, individual $6, student $2; annual meeting first Mon in May
Collections: Paintings, sculpture
Exhibitions: Changing exhibits
Publications: Newsletter, quarterly
Activities: Classes for adults & children; docent training; lects open to public; gallery talks; tours; competitions with cash awards; scholarships; book traveling exhibs; originate traveling exhibs

MARSHALLTOWN

A **CENTRAL IOWA ART ASSOCIATION, INC,** 709 S Center St Ste 1, Marshalltown, IA 50158. Tel 641-753-9013; Elec Mail ciaa@iowatelecom.net; Internet Home Page Address: www.uiowa.edu/uima;
Open Mon - Thurs 11 AM - 4 PM; Estab 1942, incorporated 1959; The large auditorium has changing monthly exhibitions of varied art; glass cases in corridor & studio display contemporary ceramics of high quality; Average Annual Attendance: 3,000; Mem: 330; dues $15; annual meeting Dec/Jan
Income: Financed by mem, contributions & United Way
Special Subjects: Etchings & Engravings, Porcelain, Sculpture, Watercolors, Pottery, Bronzes, American Indian Art, Ceramics, Woodcarvings, Primitive art
Collections: Fisher Collection-Utrillo, Cassatt, Sisley, Vuillard, Monet, Degas, Signac, Le Gourge, Vlaminck and Monticelli; sculpture-Christian Petersen, Rominelli, Bourdelle; ceramic study collection-Gilhooly, Arneson, Nagle, Kottler, Babu, Geraedts, Boxem, Leach, Voulkos; traditional Japanese wares
Exhibitions: Monthly art & crafts in Fisher Community Center Auditorium
Publications: Newsletter, monthly; brochures
Activities: Classes for adults & children in ceramics, sculpture, jewelry, painting; lects open to public, 3 vis lectrs per yr; gallery talks; tours; awards; individual paintings & original objects of art lent; book traveling exhibs; originate traveling exhibs; sales shop sells original art, reproductions, prints, pottery, wood, fiber & metal

L **Art Reference Library,** 709 S Center St Ste 1, Marshalltown, IA 50158-2876. Tel 641-753-9013; Fax 641-753-9013; Elec Mail ciaa@iowatelecom.net; Internet Home Page Address: www.cenraliowaartassociation.org; *Bd Pres* Renaie Hutzel; *Dir* Janet L Busch
Open mid Apr - mid Oct 11 Am - 5 PM daily, mid Oct - mid Apr Mon - Fri 11 AM - 5 PM; No admis fee; Estab 1958 for fine art collecting classes; For reference only; Average Annual Attendance: 5,000; Mem: 400
Income: Grants, memberships & donations
Library Holdings: Book Volumes 700; Cassettes; Original Art Works; Photographs; Sculpture; Slides
Special Subjects: Painting-French, Ceramics
Collections: 18 Impressionist & Post-Impressionist works, including Degas, Matisse, Casatt & Pisarro; 119 ceramics pieces, including Levine, Arruson, Voulkos, W M Daley
Exhibitions: Exhibitions change monthly
Activities: Classes for adults & children; docent training; 25 vis lectrs per yr; concerts; tours; gallery talks; schol; sales shop sells original art

M **FISHER ART GALLERY,** 709 S Center St, Marshalltown, IA 50158-2876. Tel 515-753-9013; Elec Mail ciaa@iowatelecom.net; Internet Home Page Address: www.centraliowaartassociation.org; *Dir* Janet Busch
Open 11 AM - 5 PM weekdays, Sat & Sun 1-5 PM or by appointment; cl holidays; 19 French Impressionist & Post Impressionist works; Average Annual Attendance: 500
Special Subjects: Landscapes, Art Education, Art History, Painting-American, Painting-French, Ceramics
Collections: 114 piece ceramic study collection
Activities: Classes for adults & children; docent training; sales shop sells art supplies

MASON CITY

M **CITY OF MASON CITY,** Charles H MacNider Museum, 303 Second St SE, Mason City, IA 50401-3988. Tel 641-421-3666; Fax 641-422-9612; Elec Mail mlinskeydeegan@masoncity.net; Internet Home Page Address: www.macniderart.org; *Dir* Edith M Blanchard; *Educ Coordr* Linda Willeke; *Assoc Cur & Registrar* Mara Linskey-Deegan
Open Tues - Sat 9 AM - 5 PM; Thurs extended evening hrs until 9 PM; cl Sun & Mon; No admis fee; Estab 1964, opened 1966 to provide experience in the arts through develop of a permanent collection, through scheduling of temporary exhibitions, through the offering of classes & art instruction, through special programs in film, music & other areas of the performing arts. The mus was estab in an English-Tudor style of brick & tile, enhanced by modern, design coordinated additions; It is located in a scenic setting, two & a half blocks from the main thoroughfare of Mason City. Gallery lighting & neutral backgrounds provide a good environment for exhibitions; Average Annual Attendance: 19,480; Mem: 435; dues from contributions $25-$1000 or more
Income: $492,550 (financed by mem, city appropriation & grants)
Library Holdings: Book Volumes 1500; Clipping Files; Exhibition Catalogs; Motion Pictures; Periodical Subscriptions 30; Slides; Video Tapes
Special Subjects: Afro-American Art, American Indian Art, Drawings, Marine Painting, Collages, Metalwork, American Western Art, Photography, Portraits, Pottery, Painting-American, Prints, Period Rooms, Textiles, Sculpture, Painting-American, Photography, Prints, Sculpture, Watercolors, Southwestern Art, Ceramics, Pottery, Woodcuts, Etchings & Engravings, Landscapes, Glass, Cartoons, Stained Glass
Collections: Permanent collection with an emphasis on American art, with some representation of Iowa art; contains paintings, prints, sculpture, pottery; artists represented include Baziotes, Birch, Benton, Burchfield, Bricher, Calder, Cropsey, De Staebler, Dove, Flannagan, Francis, Gottlieb, Graves, Guston, Healy, Hurd, Lasansky, Levine, Marin, Maurer, Metcalf, Sloan & Oliveira; Bil Baird: World of Puppets
Publications: Annual report; newsletter, quarterly; occasional exhibit fliers or catalog
Activities: Classes for adults & children; docent training; lects open to pub; 5 vis lectrs per yr; concerts; gallery talks; tours; competitions; individual paintings & original objects of art lent to other mus & art centers; mus shop sells original art, jewelry & cards

L **MASON CITY PUBLIC LIBRARY,** 225 Second St SE, Mason City, IA 50401. Tel 641-421-3668; Fax 641-423-2615; Elec Mail librarian@mcpl.org; Internet Home Page Address: www.mcpl.org; *Dir* Mary Markwalter; *Reference* Barbara Madson; *Art Librn* Kenneth Enabnit; *Reference* Katrina Bowen
Open Mon - Wed 8:30 AM-8:30 PM, Thurs-Sat 9:30 AM-5:30 PM, cl Sun; No admis fee; Estab 1869 to service pub in providing reading material & information; Circ 197,635; Monthly exhibits of local & regional artists located in main lobby of library
Income: Financed by city, county appropriation & Federal Revenue Sharing
Library Holdings: Book Volumes 110,000; Cassettes; Clipping Files; Fiche; Filmstrips 350; Framed Reproductions; Memorabilia; Motion Pictures; Original Art Works; Other Holdings Original documents; Pamphlets; Periodical Subscriptions 325; Prints; Records; Reels

Collections: Permanent collection of regional artists; signed letters of authors
Exhibitions: Rotating exhibitions; Monthly exhibitions
Activities: Exten dept serves general public; gallery holdings consist of art works & reproductions paintings which are lent to public

MOUNT VERNON

M **CORNELL COLLEGE,** Peter Paul Luce Gallery, McWethy Hall, 600 First St SW Mount Vernon, IA 52314-1098. Tel 319-895-4491; Fax 319-895-4519; Elec Mail scoleman@cornell.college.edu; Internet Home Page Address: www.cornell-iowa.edu; *Chmn Dept Art & Lectr in Art* Prof Christina Penn-Goetsch; *Dir Gallery* Susan Coleman; *Prof* Doug Hanson; *Instr* Sandy Dyas; *Prof* Susannah Biondo-Gemmell; *Prof* Ellen Hoobler; *Prof* Anthony Plaut
Open Mon - Fri 9 AM - 4 PM, Sun 2 - 4 PM; No admis fee; Estab in 2002 with a gift from the Henry Luce Foundation Inc to display student works as well as professional artists; Average Annual Attendance: 1,500
Income: Financed by Cornell College with endowment from Henry Luce Foundation Inc
Special Subjects: Drawings, Prints, Painting-American, American Indian Art, Carpets & Rugs, Baroque Art
Collections: Sonnenschein Collection of European Drawings of the 15th - 17th Century; Thomas Nast Collection; Whiting Collection of Early Phoenician Glass 4th to 5th Century; Bertha Jacques Print Collection; Powers Ceramics Collection
Exhibitions: 4 exhibits per year plus 10-20 student thesis shows
Publications: Hugh Lifton, The Cornell Years (2001)
Activities: Lects open to pub, 3-4 vis lectrs per yr; gallery talks; tours

MUSCATINE

M **MUSCATINE ART CENTER,** 1314 Mulberry Ave, Muscatine, IA 52761-3429. Tel 563-263-8282; Fax 563-263-4702; Elec Mail art@muscanet.com; Internet Home Page Address: www.muscatineartcenter.org; *Dir* Barbara C Christensen; *Registrar* Virginia Cooper; *Educ Coordr* Maria Norton; *Office Coordr* Cynthia Carver
Open Tues - Fri 10 AM - 5 PM, Thurs 7 PM - 9 PM, Sat & Sun 1 - 5 PM, cl Mon & legal holidays; No admis fee; Estab 1965 to collect, preserve & interpret work of art & objects of historical & aesthetic importance; Average Annual Attendance: 14,000; Mem: 500; dues benefactor $1000, patron $500, supporting $100, contributing $60, sustaining $25, family $40, individual $25; annual meeting in June
Income: Financed by city appropriation & Muscatine Art Center Support Foundation
Special Subjects: Drawings, Glass, Pottery, Prints, Painting-French, Graphics, Painting-American, Decorative Arts, Oriental Art, Carpets & Rugs, Historical Material
Collections: Muscatine History; Button Collection; Paperweight Collection; American painting prints, especially Mississippi River views
Publications: Newsletter, quarterly
Activities: Classes for children; docent training; lects open to public, 2 - 5 vis lectrs per yr; concerts; gallery talks; tours; individual paintings & original objects of art lent to qualified museums for exhib purposes; book traveling exhibs 5-7 per yr; originate traveling exhibs 1-2 per yr

M **Museum,** 1314 Mulberry Ave, Muscatine, IA 52761. Tel 563-263-8282; Fax 563-263-4702; Elec Mail art@muscatineiowa.gov; Internet Home Page Address: www.muscatineartcenter.org; *Dir* Melanie K Alexander; *Registrar* Virginia Cooper; *Office Coordr* Lynn Bartenhagen
Open Tues - Fri 10 AM - 5 PM, Thurs 10 AM - 7 PM, Sat & Sun 1 PM - 5 PM; No admis fee, donations accepted; Estab 1965; For reference only; Average Annual Attendance: 30,000; Mem: 500; Friends of Muscatine Art Center, ann mtg July; dues individual $30, family $50, contributing $100, patron $250, sustaining $500, benefactor $1,000
Income: (financed by City of Muscatine, Muscatine Art Center Support Foundation)
Library Holdings: Book Volumes 2600; Memorabilia; Pamphlets; Periodical Subscriptions 10
Special Subjects: Decorative Arts, Drawings, Historical Material, Landscapes, Ceramics, Glass, Furniture, Photography, Portraits, Painting-American, Prints, Period Rooms, Textiles, Maps, Sculpture, Watercolors, Costumes, Pottery, Woodcarvings, Painting-French, Carpets & Rugs
Collections: Mississippi River Collection; paperweights, art glass, button history
Activities: Classes for adults & children; lects open to public; 12 vis lectrs per yr; tours; gallery talks; schol offered; book 4 traveling exhibs per yr

OKOBOJI

M **PEARSON LAKES ART CENTER,** 2201 Hwy 71, Okoboji, IA 51355; PO Box 255, Okoboji, IA 51355-0255. Tel 712-332-7013; Fax 712-332-7014; Elec Mail info@lakesart.org; Internet Home Page Address: www.lakesart.org; *Dir Visual Arts* Danielle Clouse
Open June - Aug Mon - Sat 10 AM - 4 PM, Sept - May Tues - Sat 10 AM - 4 PM; No admis fee; Average Annual Attendance: 20,000
Special Subjects: Painting-American, Painting-Russian
Collections: works by international & national artists
Activities: Educ progs for adults & children, dramatic progs, docent training; lects open to public, 3 vis lectrs per yr, musical & theater events; festivals; film series; readings, gallery talks, tours, sponsoring of exhibs; schols avail

ORANGE CITY

M **NORTHWESTERN COLLEGE,** Te Paske Gallery, 101 7th St SW, Dept of Art Orange City, IA 51041-1923. Tel 712-737-7000, 707-7004; Fax 712-737-3777; Elec Mail rein@nwciowa.edu; Internet Home Page Address: www.nwciowa.edu; *Rotation Exhib Coordr* Rein Vanderhill; *Prof Sculpture* Arnold Carlson; *Prof Graphic Design* Phil Scorza
Open Mon - Sat 8 AM - 12 PM; No admis fee; Estab 1968 to promote the visual arts in northwest Iowa and to function as a learning resource for the col and community; 78 linear feet wall, 10' wall height; Average Annual Attendance: 2,000

Income: Financed by school budget
Special Subjects: Etchings & Engravings
Collections: Approx 75 original works of art; etchings, woodcuts, serigraphs, lithographs, mezzotints, paintings, sculpture & ceramics by modern & old masters of Western World & Japan; Fine Art Permanent Collection of Northwestern College (Iowa); Stegeman Collection of Japanese Woodcut Prints (19th & 20th c)
Exhibitions: Contemporary American Artists Series; student shows
Activities: Lects open to public, 2-3 vis lectrs per year; gallery talks; competitions

M **Denler Art Gallery,** 3003 Snelling Ave N, Totino Fine Arts Center, 2nd Fl Saint Paul, MN 55113-1501. Tel 651-631-5110 (main); Internet Home Page Address: art.nwc.edu/denler; *Dir* Luke Aleckson
Call for hours
Special Subjects: Photography, Painting-American, Sculpture

OTTUMWA

L **AIRPOWER MUSEUM LIBRARY,** 22001 Bluegrass Rd, Ottumwa, IA 52501-8569. Tel 641-938-2773; Fax 641-938-2093; Elec Mail antiqueairfield@sirisonline.com; Internet Home Page Address: www.antiqueairfield.com;
Estab 1971
Library Holdings: Filmstrips; Photographs; Video Tapes
Special Subjects: Film, Photography, Drawings, Maps, Video
Collections: Aviation Collection, blueprints, books, brochures, clothing, drawings, films, lithographs, maps, models, paintings, periodicals, photographs, videos
Publications: Airpower Museum bulletin, annual

SIOUX CITY

M **LOREN D. CALLENDAR GALLERY,** 607 4th St, Sioux City, IA 51101-1634. Tel 712-279-6174; Fax 712-252-5615; Elec Mail scpm@sioux-city.org
Open Tues - Sat 10 AM - 5 PM, Sun 1 PM - 5 PM; cl holidays; No admis fee, donations welcomed
Collections: Photographs; Sioux City history

A **SIOUX CITY ART CENTER,** 225 Nebraska St, Sioux City, IA 51101-1712. Tel 712-279-6272; Fax 712-255-2921; Internet Home Page Address: www.siouxcityartcenter.org; *Bd Trustees Pres* Jan Poulson; *Dir* Al Harris-Fernandez, PhD; *Admin Asst & Contact* Jill Collins; *Cur* Michael Betancourt; *Educ Specialist* Nan Wilson
Open Tues, Wed, Fri & Sat 10 AM - 5 PM, Thurs 10 AM - 9PM, Sun 1 - 5 PM, cl Mon & holidays; No admis fee; Estab 1938 to provide art experiences to the general pub; Four exhibition galleries consisting of nationally known artists from the midwest regional area; includes a permanent collection gallery & changing exhibitions; Average Annual Attendance: 65,000; Mem: 725; dues $15-$5000; monthly meetings
Income: Financed by mem, city & state appropriation
Special Subjects: Drawings, Etchings & Engravings, Graphics, Landscapes, Photography, Prints, Sculpture, Watercolors, Painting-American, Woodcuts
Collections: Permanent collection of over 700 works; consists of paintings & prints of nationally known regional artists, contemporary photography & sculpture & crafts
Publications: Annual Report; quarterly newsletter; class brochures, quarterly; exhibition catalogs; exhibition announcements
Activities: Classes for adults & children; docent training; workshops; outreach progs to schools; Artsplash Festival of the Arts Sat & Sun of Labor Day weekend; lects open to pub; gallery talks; tours; concerts; competitions; awards given in conjunction with juried exhibs & YAM; scholarships offered; original objects of art & individual paintings lent to qualified institutions with approved facilities & security; book traveling exhibs 3-4 per yr; originates traveling exhibs; mus shop sells books, magazines, original art, prints, jewelry & property items

L **Library,** 225 Nebraska St, Sioux City, IA 51101. Tel 712-279-6272; Fax 712-255-2921; Elec Mail aharris@sioux-city.org; Internet Home Page Address: www.siouxcityartcenter.com; *Admin Asst* Jill Collins
Open by appointment; No admis fee; Estab 1938; Reference library - non-circulating
Income: Financed by endowment, gifts, contributions, state appropriations
Library Holdings: Book Volumes 1500; Cassettes; Exhibition Catalogs; Periodical Subscriptions 20; Slides

STORM LAKE

M **WITTER GALLERY,** 609 Cayuga St, Storm Lake, IA 50588-2239. Tel 712-732-3400; Elec Mail wittergallery@yahoo.com; Internet Home Page Address: www.thewittergallery.org; *Pres* Judy Ferguson; *VPres* Bruce Ellingson; *Dir* Ron Stevenson
Open Tues - Fri 1- 5 PM, Thurs 1 - 6 PM, Sat 10AM - 2 PM; No admis fee; Estab 1972 to encourage the appreciation of fine arts & to support fine arts educ, exhibits, lectures & workshops; Gallery occupies a wing of the Storm Lake Pub Library building. It has about 1800 sq ft of floor space & 120 linear ft of hanging wall space; Average Annual Attendance: 10,000; Mem: 300; dues sponsor $250, supporting $100, sustaining $50, active $25
Income: $20,000 (financed by endowment, mem, city appropriation, fundraising projects)
Library Holdings: Exhibition Catalogs; Memorabilia; Original Art Works; Original Documents; Photographs; Slides
Special Subjects: Prints
Collections: Paintings & collected artifacts of Miss Ella Witter; prints by Dorothy D Skewis
Exhibitions: Iowa Women in Art: Pioneers of the Past- touring exhibition of work by Ella Witter and Dorothy Skewis
Publications: Witter Gallery News & Events, The Palette Monthly
Activities: Classes for adults & children; art appreciation progs in area schools; lects open to pub, 10 vis lectrs per yr; gallery talks; concerts; tours; biennial juried

competition with cash awards; originate traveling exhibs; gift gallery sells notecards & original art - pottery, jewelry, prints, silk scarves

WATERLOO

M **WATERLOO CENTER OF THE ARTS,** (Waterloo Museum of Art) 225 Commercial St, Waterloo, IA 50701-1313. Tel 319-291-4490; Fax 319-291-4270; Elec Mail museum@waterloo-ia.org; Internet Home Page Address: www.waterloocenterforthearts.org; *Dir* Cammie V Scully; *Educ Dir* Bonnie Winninger; *Dir Mktg* Shannon Farlow; *Cur* Kent Shankle
Open Tues-Sat 10AM-5PM, Sun 1PM-5PM; No admis fee; Estab 1947 to initiate further awareness, appreciation, & support of the arts by a diverse audience; Maintains reference library; Average Annual Attendance: 110,000, plus junior art gallery attendance of 16,000; Mem: 500; dues individual $40 & up
Income: Financed by city funds, mem, grants & donations
Special Subjects: Afro-American Art, Ceramics, Painting-American, Prints, Sculpture, Woodcarvings, Decorative Arts
Collections: American decorative Arts; Contemporary American art; Haitian/Caribbean paintings & sculpture
Exhibitions: Rotating exhibits & an interactive children's museum
Activities: classes for adults & children, docent training, birthday parties; lects open to pub; concerts; gallery talks; tours; schols; serves area with 45 miles of waterloo; lends original objects of art to other museums; mus shop sells prints, books, magazines, original art, children's merchandise, & jewelry; junior museum

WEST BRANCH

L **NATIONAL ARCHIVES & RECORDS ADMINISTRATION,** Herbert Hoover Presidential Library - Museum, 210 Parkside Dr, West Branch, IA 52358-9685; PO Box 488, West Branch, IA 52358-0488. Tel 319-643-5301; Fax 319-643-6045; Elec Mail hoover.library@nara.gov; Internet Home Page Address: www.hoover.archives.gov; *Library Dir* Tom Schwartz; *Reference Archivist* Matt Schaefer; *Cur Mus* Marcus Eckhardt; *Educ Specialist* Elizabeth Dinschel; *Admin Officer* Kathy Grace; *A/V Archivist* Lynn Smith; *Archivist* Craig Wright; *Registrar* Jennifer Pedersen
Open daily 9 AM - 5 PM, cl Thanksgiving, Christmas, New Year's Day; Admis adults $6, over age 62 $3, children 15 & under free; Estab 1962 as a research center to service the papers of Herbert Hoover & other related manuscript collections; a museum to exhibit the life & times of Herbert Hoover from his 90 years of public service & accomplishments; Average Annual Attendance: 50,000
Income: Financed by federal appropriation
Library Holdings: Audio Tapes; Book Volumes 23,041; Clipping Files; Manuscripts; Memorabilia; Motion Pictures; Original Documents; Other Holdings Original documents; Still photographs; Pamphlets; Periodical Subscriptions 30; Photographs; Records; Reels; Slides
Special Subjects: Manuscripts, Historical Material
Collections: 64 Chinese porcelains; oil paintings; 190 Original Editorial Cartoons; 340 posters; 26 World War I Food Administration; 464 World War I Painted and Embroidered Flour Sacks
Exhibitions: Permanent exhibits on Herbert & Lou Henry Hoover; subjects related to Hoover & the times; temporary exhibits cover subjects related to the memorabilia collection, the decades & activities of Hoover's life & state & national interest
Activities: Classes for children; docent training; lects open to pub, 2-3 vis lectrs per yr; tours; sales shop sells books, prints, slides & medals

WINTERSET

M **WINTERSET ART CENTER,** 216 S John Wayne Dr, Winterset, IA 50273; PO Box 325, Winterset, IA 50273-0325. Tel 515-975-5444; Internet Home Page Address: wintersetartcenter.org; *Chmn* Margaret Ripperger; *Pub Rels* Barbara Cook
Open May - Oct Mon 10 AM - 4 PM, Wed 12 - 4 PM, other times by appointment; No admis fee; Average Annual Attendance: 3,000
Collections: works by local & regional artists
Activities: Educ progs; hobby workshops; arts festivals

KANSAS

ABILENE

L **DWIGHT D EISENHOWER PRESIDENTIAL LIBRARY & MUSEUM,** 200 SE Fourth St, Abilene, KS 67410; PO Box 339 Abilene, KS 67410-0339. Tel 785-263-6700; Fax 785-263-6715; Elec Mail eisenhower.library@nara.gov; Internet Home Page Address: www.eisenhower.archives.gov; *Dir* Karl Weissenbach; *Mus Registrar* Nathan Myers; *Mus Tech* Matthew Thompson
Open daily 9 AM - 4:45 PM, cl Thanksgiving, Christmas & New Year's; Admis $8, sr citizens $5, under 16 free; Estab 1961 as library, in 1954 as museum; Average Annual Attendance: 126,000
Income: Financed by Federal Government appropriation
Library Holdings: Audio Tapes; Book Volumes 22,850; Cassettes; Clipping Files; Filmstrips; Manuscripts; Maps; Memorabilia; Micro Print; Motion Pictures; Original Art Works; Original Documents; Photographs; Prints; Records; Reels; Sculpture; Slides; Video Tapes
Special Subjects: Decorative Arts, Calligraphy, Drawings, Manuscripts, Maps, Painting-American, Prints, Sculpture, Historical Material, Portraits, Watercolors, Ceramics, American Western Art, Cartoons, Asian Art, Ivory, Carpets & Rugs, Textiles, Coins & Medals, Reproductions
Collections: Research Library and Museum contains papers of Dwight D Eisenhower and his assoc, together with items of historical interest connected with the Eisenhower Family. Mementos and gifts of General Dwight D Eisenhower both before, during, and after his term as President of the United States

Activities: Educ dept; docent training; lects open to pub, 5 vis lectrs per yr; libr tours; film series open to pub first three wks of Mar every yr; individual paintings & original objects of art lent; lending collection contains original art work & prints, paintings & sculpture; originate traveling exhibs; mus shop sells books, prints, reproductions & slides

ALMA

M **WABAUNSEE COUNTY HISTORICAL MUSEUM,** 227 Missouri Ave, Alma, KS 66401; PO Box 387, Alma, KS 66401-0387. Tel 785-765-2200; Elec Mail wabcomuseum@emarqmail.com; Internet Home Page Address: www.wabaunsee.org; *Cur* Alan Winkler
Open Tues - Sat 10 AM - 4 PM; No admis fee; suggested donation; Estab 1968 for the purpose of preserving art & artifacts in Wabaunsee County; Paintings are hung throughout the museum in available space. Maintains reference library; Average Annual Attendance: 1,800; Mem: 340; yr $25; annual meeting first Sat in June
Income: $25,000 (financed by mem, donations & endowment)
Library Holdings: Audio Tapes; Compact Disks; DVDs; Maps; Memorabilia; Original Art Works; Photographs
Collections: General Louis Walt display, blacksmith shop, clothing, farm tools & equipment; Native American artifacts; Mainstreet USA-historical town; 1923 Reo fire truck; postal display; organization display case, 1918-1965; leather-making display; early day doctor's office; 1880 school room; Paintings by local artist August Ohst (1851-1939); genealogy records; photo panels; local artist Maude Mitchell, 1875-1957; Civil War Display (Wm Meyers Diary, Colt 45 pistol, GAR badges)
Publications: Stories of the Past, Historical Society newsletter, quarterly
Activities: Classes for children; hist tours fall; mus quilters on Tues & Wed; sales shop sells books, postcards

ASHLAND

M **CLARK COUNTY HISTORICAL SOCIETY,** Pioneer - Krier Museum, 430 W 4th St, Ashland, KS 67831; PO Box 862, Ashland, KS 67831-0862. Tel 620-635-2227; Fax 620-635-2227; Elec Mail pioneer@ucom.net; Internet Home Page Address: www.pioneer-krier.com; *CEO* Tony Maphet
Open Tues-Fri 10AM-noon, 1PM-5PM; Admis donations requested; Estab 1967 to collect & preserve Southwest Kansas history; Maintains reference library; Average Annual Attendance: 2,000; Mem: Dues: lifetime $25; annual meeting in Feb
Income: $42,000 financed by mem, county taxes & donations)
Special Subjects: Painting-American, Photography, American Indian Art, Archaeology, Southwestern Art, Textiles, Woodcarvings, Etchings & Engravings, Manuscripts, Portraits, Dolls, Furniture, Glass, Porcelain, Metalwork, Carpets & Rugs, Historical Material, Maps, Coins & Medals, Tapestries, Dioramas, Period Rooms, Laces, Reproductions
Collections: Archeological coll; Barbed Wire Coll; Early Settlers Coll; Elephant Coll; Gun Coll; Implement Seat coll - Memorabilia from five famous people from Clark County, Kansas; Track Stars, Jerome C Berryma 1921-1925, Wes Santee 1950's; Aerobatic Champion Harold Krier, Notre Dame Coach Jesse Harper; World Renown Counter-Tenor Rodney Hardesty; Implement Seat Coll
Publications: Notes on Early Clark County, Kansas, book; Kings & Queens of the Range, book; Cattle Ranching South of Dodge City - The Early Years (1870 - 1920), book
Activities: Demonstrations & group tours; historical tours; book traveling exhibs, 1 - 2 per yr; mus shop sells books, original art, reproductions

ATCHISON

M **MUCHNIC FOUNDATION & ATCHISON ART ASSOCIATION,** Muchnic Gallery, 704 N 4th St, Atchison, KS 66002-1924. Tel 913-367-4278; Fax 913-367-2939; Elec Mail atchart@ponyexpress.net; Internet Home Page Address: www.atchison-art.org; *Cur* Gloria Davis
Open Mar - Dec Wed 10 AM - 5 PM, Sat & Sun 1PM - 5PM; Admis $2; Estab 1970 to bring fine arts to the people of Atchison; 19th century home furnished with original family belongings downstairs; upstairs there are five rooms devoted to the art gallery; Average Annual Attendance: 3,000; Mem: 120; board meeting second Mon of each month
Income: Financed by Muchnic Foundation, Atchison Art Asn art shows
Purchases: $7,000
Special Subjects: Painting-American, Period Rooms
Collections: Paintings by regional artists: Don Andorfer; Thomas Hart Benton; John Stuart Curry; Raymond Eastwood; John Falter; Jim Hamil; Wilbur Niewald; Jack O'Hara; Roger Shimomura; Robert Sudlow; Grant Wood; Jamie Wyeth; Walter Yost
Activities: Classes for adults; docent training; lects open to pub; tours; scholarships & fels offered; individual paintings lent to local museums; book traveling exhibs 3 per yr; originate traveling exhibs; sales shop sells books, original art & prints

BALDWIN CITY

M **BAKER UNIVERSITY,** Old Castle Museum, 515 5th St, Baldwin City, KS 66006; PO Box 65, Baldwin City, KS 66006-0065. Tel 785-594-8380; Fax 785-594-2522; Elec Mail brenda.day@bakeru.edu; *Dir* Brenda Day
Open Mon-Fri 8AM-noon; Admis by donation; Estab 1953 to display items related to life in early Kansas; Average Annual Attendance: 1,500
Income: Financed by endowment, University & donations
Special Subjects: Pottery, Historical Material, Pewter
Collections: Country store; Indian artifacts & pottery; 19th century print shop; quilts; silver & pewter dishes & table service; tools; old quilts; old cameras; Santa Fe Trail Artifacts
Exhibitions: John Brown material; Indian Pottery; Indian artifacts; old guns
Activities: Lect open to public

CHANUTE

M **MARTIN AND OSA JOHNSON SAFARI MUSEUM, INC,** 111 N Lincoln Ave, Chanute, KS 66720-1819. Tel 620-431-2730; Fax 620-431-2730; Elec Mail osajohns@safarimuseum.com; Internet Home Page Address: www.safarimuseum.com; *Dir* Conrad G Froehlich; *Cur* Jacquelyn L Borgeson; *Store Mgr* Shirley Rogers-Naff; *Dir Develop* Diane L Good
Open Mon - Sat 10 AM - 5 PM, Sun 1 - 5 PM; Admis adults $6, students & seniors $4, children 6-12 $3, children under 6 free; Estab 1961 to be the repository of the Johnson Archives; Average Annual Attendance: 6,000; Mem: 850; dues $25
Income: $200,000 (financed by mem, city appropriation, donations & gift shop)
Special Subjects: African Art
Collections: Fine art-natural history subjects; Martin & Osa Johnson-films, photos, manuscripts; Ethnographic-African, Borneo, South Pacific
Exhibitions: Johnson Exhibition, Imperato African Gallery, Selsor Art Gallery (special exhibit space); Traveling exhibits including Married to Adventure
Publications: Empty Masks; Wait-A-Bit News, quarterly newsletter
Activities: Educ dept; classes for adults & children; docent training; lect open to public, vis lectrs; tours; sponsoring of competitions; Barbara Enlow Henshall award for vol serv; mus boxes for school use; individual paintings & original objects of art lent to qualified institutions; mus shop sells books, prints, original art, imported carvings, brass, fabric & ethnic toys

M **Imperato Collection of West African Artifacts,** 111 N Lincoln Ave, Chanute, KS 66720. Tel 620-431-2730; Fax 620-431-2730; Elec Mail osajohns@safarimuseum.com; Internet Home Page Address: www.safarimuseum.com; *Dir* Conrad G Froehlich; *Cur* Jacquelyn Borgeson
Open Mon - Sat 10 AM - 5 PM, Sun 1 - 5 PM; Admis adults $6, seniors & students $4, children 6-12 $3, children under 6 free; Estab 1974; Average Annual Attendance: 6,000; Mem: 850; $35 dues
Income: $200,000 (financed by members, city, donations, gift shop)
Collections: West African sculpture including masks, ancestor figures & ritual objects, household items, musical instruments
Exhibitions: African culture exhibit of East & West African items; ceremonial masks
Publications: Collection catalogs
Activities: Classes for adults & children; docent training; Tours; pub lects & gallery talks; ann mus volunteer award; exhibit & progs at Walt Disney World & other sites; traveling exhibs to mus, zoos, galleries; mus shop sells books, original art, reproductions, prints

M **Johnson Collection of Photographs, Movies & Memorabilia,** 111 N Lincoln Ave, Chanute, KS 66720. Tel 620-431-2730; Fax 620-431-2730; Elec Mail osajohns@safari.museum.com; Internet Home Page Address: www.safarimuseum.com; *Dir* Conrad G Froehlich; *Cur* Jacquelyn Borgeson
Open Mon - Sat 10 AM - 5 PM, Sun 1 - 5 PM; Admis adults $6, seniors & students $4, children 6-12 $3, children under 6 free; Estab 1961; Average Annual Attendance: 6,000; Mem: 850; $25 dues
Income: $200,000 (financed by members, city, donations, gift shop)
Collections: Photographs & movie footage of the South Seas, Borneo & East Africa between 1917-1936; Manuscript material, archival collection, & artifacts collected by the Johnsons; Photos & films licensed for commercial & non-profit uses
Activities: Classes of adults & children; docent training; pub lects, tours & gallery talks; ann mus volunteer award; exhibit & progs at Walt Disney World & other sites; traveling exhibs to mus, zoos, galleries; mus shop sells books, original art, reproductions & prints

M **Selsor Art Gallery,** 111 N Lincoln Ave, Chanute, KS 66720. Tel 620-431-2730; Fax 620-431-2730; Elec Mail osajohns@safarimuseum.com; Internet Home Page Address: www.safarimuseum.com; *Dir* Conrad G Froehlich; *Cur* Jacquelyn Borgeson
Open Mon - Sat 10 AM - 5 PM, Sun 1 - 5 PM; Admis adults $6, seniors & students $4, children 6-12 $3, children under 6 free; Estab 1981; Average Annual Attendance: 6,000; Mem: 850; $35 dues
Income: $200,000 (financed by members, city, donations, gift shop)
Collections: Original paintings; scratch boards & sketches; bronze, ivory & amber sculpture; lithographs
Exhibitions: Rotating exhibits
Activities: Classes for adults & children; docent training; Tours; objects of art lent to qualified institutions; pub lects; ann mus volunteer award; exhibit & progs at Walt Disney World & other sites; traveling exhibs to mus, zoos & galleries; mus shop sells books, reproductions, prints

L **Scott Explorers Library,** 111 N Lincoln Ave, Chanute, KS 66720. Tel 620-431-2730; Fax 620-431-2730; Elec Mail osajohns@safarimuseum.com; Internet Home Page Address: www.safarimuseum.com; *Dir* Conrad G Froehlich; *Cur* Jacquelyn Borgeson; *Librn* Jane Martin; *Librn* Carla White
Open Mon - Sat 10 AM - 5 PM, Sun 1 - 5 PM; Estab 1980 for research and reference
Library Holdings: Book Volumes 14,000

COTTONWOOD FALLS

M **FLINT HILLS GALLERY,** 321 Broadway St, Cottonwood Falls, KS 66845-2884. Tel 620-273-8235; Fax 620-273-8235

EL DORADO

M **COUTTS MUSEUM OF ART, INC,** 110 N Main St, El Dorado, KS 67042-2016. Tel 316-321-1212; Fax 316-321-1215; Elec Mail rseel@couttsmuseum.org; Internet Home Page Address: couttsmuseum.org; *Exec Dir* Rod Seel; *Admin Asst* Teresa S Scott
Open Tues - Fri 9 AM - 5 PM, Sat Noon - 4 PM; No admis fee; Estab 1970 as a Fine Arts museum; Fine art & antiques; Average Annual Attendance: 6,000; Mem: 300, $55 per couple, quarterly 3rd Thurs
Income: Financed by endowment & gifts

Special Subjects: Drawings, Photography, Portraits, Painting-European, Painting-French, Latin American Art, Mexican Art, Painting-American, Prints, Sculpture, Watercolors, American Indian Art, American Western Art, Southwestern Art, Ceramics, Folk Art, Etchings & Engravings, Landscapes, Decorative Arts, Collages, Furniture, Glass, Oriental Art, Asian Art, Painting-British, Carpets & Rugs, Miniatures, Painting-Spanish, Cartoons, Reproductions, Painting-Russian
Collections: Frederic Remington sculpture coll completed in 1992 (recasts); Western & Contemporary Western; Two & Three-Dimensional Designs; William Dickerson, Prairie Printmakers
Exhibitions: Annual All County Student Art Show; rotating 4-6 wks; 10-11 exhibits a year, changing every 4 weeks; Paint the Parks Annual Exhibit (Nat Parks)
Publications: Quarterly newsletter
Activities: Classes for children; dramatic pros; docent training; lects open to pub, 4-6 vis lectrs per yr; concerts; gallery talks; tours; competitions with awards; schols offered; individual paintings & original objects of art lent; book traveling exhibs 1-2 per yr; organize traveling exhibs; other exhib venues; museum shop sells books, original art, reproductions, prints

M **THE ERMAN B. WHITE GALLERY,** 901 S Haverhill Rd El Dorado, KS 67042-3225.

EMPORIA

M **EMPORIA STATE UNIVERSITY,** Norman R Eppink Art Gallery, 1200 Commercial St, Emporia, KS 66801-5057. Tel 620-341-5246 or 341-5689; Fax 620-341-6246; Elec Mail reichenb@emporia.edu; Internet Home Page Address: www.emporia.edu/art/; *Assoc Prof of Art & Galleries Dir* Roberta Eichenberg
Open Mon - Fri 9 AM - 4 PM, cl university holidays; No admis fee; Estab 1939 to bring a variety of exhibitions to the campus; Main Gallery is 25 x 50 ft & has a 50 ft wall for hanging items; adjacent gallery is 16 x 50 ft; display gallery contains eighteen 40 inch x 28 inch panels; Average Annual Attendance: 10,000
Income: Financed by state, grant & endowment funds
Purchases: Annual purchase of contemporary drawings from the Annual National Invitational Drawing Exhibition & varied works from invited exhibiting artists
Library Holdings: Slides
Collections: Artifacts; contemporary drawings and paintings; sculpture
Publications: Exhibition catalogs
Activities: Lects open to pub, 6 vis lectrs per yr; concerts; gallery talks; tours; scholarships offered; individual paintings & original objects of art lent to university offices; book traveling exhibs 4-6 per yr; originate traveling exhibs to schools

HAYS

M **FORT HAYS STATE UNIVERSITY,** Moss-Thorns Gallery of Arts, 600 Park St, Hays, KS 67601-4099. Tel 785-628-4247; Fax 785-628-4087; Elec Mail ctaylor@fhsu.edu; Internet Home Page Address: www.fhsu.edu; *Chmn* Leland Powers; *Secy* Colleen Taylor
Open Mon - Fri 8:30 AM - 4 PM, weekends on special occasions; summer hours: Mon - Thurs 8 AM - 4:30 PM; No admis fee; Estab 1953 to provide constant changing exhibitions for the benefit of students, faculty & other interested people in an educ situation; Rarick Hall has 2200 sq ft with moveable panels that can be used to divide the gallery into four smaller galleries; Average Annual Attendance: 5,000; Mem: 88
Income: Financed by state appropriation
Purchases: $2000
Special Subjects: Drawings, Painting-American, Prints
Collections: Regionalist Collection (1930s); Oriental Scroll Collection; Vyvyan Blackford Collection
Publications: Exhibitions brochures; Art Calendar, annually
Activities: Lects open to public, 4 vis lectrs per yr; gallery talks; tours; competitions with prizes; concerts; exten dept servs western Kansas

L **Forsyth Library,** 600 Park St, Hays, KS 67601. Tel 785-628-4431; Fax 785-628-4096; Elec Mail jgross@fhsu.edu; Internet Home Page Address: www.fhsu.edu; *Reference Librn* Judy Salm; *Dir* John Ross; *Office Asst* Janet Basgall
Open Mon - Thurs 7:30AM - Midnight, Fri 7:30 AM - 7 PM, Sat 10 AM - 5 PM, Sun 1 PM-Midnight; Reference Library
Library Holdings: Book Volumes 6000; Exhibition Catalogs; Filmstrips; Periodical Subscriptions 1100

M **HAYS ARTS CENTER GALLERY,** 112 E 11th St Hays, KS 67601-3604. *Exec Dir* Brenda K. Meder

HUTCHINSON

A **HUTCHINSON ART ASSOCIATION,** Hutchinson Art Center, 405 N Washington, Hutchinson, KS 67501. Tel 620-663-1081; Fax 620-663-6367; Elec Mail hutchart2@hac.kscoxmail.com; Internet Home Page Address: www.hutchartcenter.org; *Pres* Todd Ray; *Dir* Mark L Rassetti
Open Tues - Fri 9 AM - 5 PM, Sat & Sun 1 - 5 PM; No admis fee; Estab 1949 to bring exhibitions to the city of Hutchinson & maintain a permanent collection; Three galleries & educational area; Average Annual Attendance: 10,000; Mem: 500; dues $20-$5,000; monthly meetings
Income: Financed by mem & endowment
Special Subjects: Metalwork, Prints, Watercolors, Ceramics, Glass
Collections: Permanent collection of watercolors, prints, ceramics, glass, wood, oils & metals
Exhibitions: Two all-member shows per yr; one traveling show per month
Activities: Classes for adults & children; docent training; tours; schols offered; book traveling exhibitions; sales shop sells original art & books

INDEPENDENCE

M **INDEPENDENCE HISTORICAL MUSEUM & ART CENTER,** 123 N 8th & Myrtle, Independence, KS 67301-3501; PO Box 294, Independence, KS 67301-0294. Tel 620-331-3515; Elec Mail museum123@cableone.nrt; Internet Home Page Address: www.independencehistoricalmuseum.org; *Mus Coordr* Sylvia Augustine; *Pres* Ray Rothgeb; *1st VPres* Joy Barta; *2nd VPres* Ellie Culp; *Secy* Jana Shaver; *Treas* Randy Hoffman
Open Tues - Sat 10 AM - 4 PM; Admis adults $5, students (13-18) $3, children 12 & under free; Estab 1882 to secure an art collection for the community; The mus has a large gallery which contains original paintings; Indian art & artifacts; military room, Western room; country store, period bedroom, early 1900 kitchen, children's room, historical oil room, & blacksmith shop; Average Annual Attendance: 6,000; Mem: 275; dues $25-$1000; meeting monthly Sept - May
Income: Financed by mem, bequests, gifts, art exhibits, various projects & donations
Library Holdings: Cards; Clipping Files; Compact Disks; Maps; Memorabilia; Original Documents; Photographs; Prints; Sculpture
Special Subjects: Anthropology, Archaeology, Historical Material, Landscapes, Glass, Mexican Art, American Western Art, Furniture, Photography, Pottery, Textiles, Sculpture, Watercolors, American Indian Art, Southwestern Art, Woodcarvings, Posters, Dolls, Porcelain, Metalwork, Maps, Coins & Medals, Miniatures, Period Rooms, Leather
Collections: American Indian Collection; William Inge Memorabilia Collection; Bill Kurtis; Alf Landon
Exhibitions: Annual Art Exhibit: Quilt Affair; various artists & craftsmen exhibits; Photography Show; Baseball exhibit
Publications: Museum Messenger, monthly members newsletter
Activities: Classes for adults & children; docent training; lectrs open to pub, 2 vis lectrs per yr; gallery talks; tours; competitions with awards; mus shop sells books, reproductions, original art, prints, calendars, KS items, T-shirts & caps

JUNCTION CITY

M **JUNCTION CITY ARTS COUNCIL GALLERY,** 107 W 7th St Junction City, KS 66441-2942; PO Box 403 Junction City, KS 66441-0403.

LAWRENCE

M **UNIVERSITY OF KANSAS,** Spencer Museum of Art, 1301 Mississippi St, Univ of Kansas Lawrence, KS 66045-7500. Tel 785-864-4710; Fax 785-864-3112; Elec Mail spencerart@ku.edu; Internet Home Page Address: www.spencerart.ku.edu/; *Assoc Dir* Stephen Goddard; *Registrar* Janet Dreiling; *Pub Info Liaison* Gina Kaufmann; *Dir Educ* Kristina Mitchell-Walker; *Cur European & American Art* Susan Earle; *Graphic Designer* Tristan Telander; *Dir* Saralyn Reece Hardy; *Exhib Designer* Richard Klocke; *Docent Coordr* Amanda Martin Hamon; *Grant Writer* Rebecca Blocksome; *Coll Mgr* Sofia Galarza Liu; *Accounting Specialist* Cherie Tapahonso; *Coll Mgr* Angela Watts; *Dir Internal Opers* Jennifer Neuburger Talbott; *Info Coordr* Robert Hickerson; *Asst Cur* Kate Meyer; *Cur Global Cont & Asian Art* Kris Ercums; *Dir External Affairs* Margaret Perkins-McGuinness; *IT* Edith Bond; *Matter & Frames* Sue Ashline; *Exhibs* Dan Coester; *Exhibs* Doug Bergstrom; *Dir Acad Progs* Celka Straughn; *Web Designer* Bill Kummerow; *External Affairs Asst* Cathy Brashler; *Accounting Specialist* Carla Gardner
Open Tues, Fri & Sat 10 AM - 4 PM, Wed & Thurs 10 AM - 8 PM, Sun Noon - 4 PM, cl Mon; No admis fee; donations accepted; Dedicated in Spooner Hall 1928, Spencer dedicated 1978. The Museum has traditionally served as a laboratory for the visual arts, supporting curricular study in the arts & art history. Primary emphasis is placed on acquisitions & publications, with a regular schedule of changing exhibitions; Museum has a two level Central Ct, seven galleries devoted to the permanent collections & five galleries for temporary exhibitions; altogether affording 29,000 sq ft; Average Annual Attendance: 117,690; Mem: 400; Dues $50
Income: Financed by mem, state appropriation & state & federal grants, contributions & foundations
Library Holdings: Auction Catalogs; Book Volumes
Special Subjects: Drawings, Graphics, Painting-American, Photography, Prints, Sculpture, Watercolors, Bronzes, African Art, Textiles, Woodcuts, Etchings & Engravings, Painting-European, Painting-Japanese, Glass, Asian Art, Silver, Painting-British, Painting-Dutch, Carpets & Rugs, Baroque Art, Calligraphy, Renaissance Art, Embroidery, Medieval Art, Painting-Italian
Collections: American paintings; ancient art; Asian art; graphics; Medieval art; 17th & 18th century art, especially German; 19th century European & American art; 20th century European & American art; Ethnographic coll: African, North American; Japanese Painting & Prints; Chinese Paintings & Sculpture
Publications: Calendar, monthly; Murphy Lectures, annually; The Register of the Spencer Museum of Art, annually; exhibition catalogs, 1-2 per year
Activities: Docent training; international artist in residency prog; lects open to pub, 12 & more vis lectrs per yr; concerts; gallery talks; tours; internships offered; book traveling exhibs; originates traveling exhibs; mus shop sells books, reproductions, prints, slides, posters, postcards, jewelry & gifts
L **Murphy Library of Art & Architecture,** 1425 Jayhawk Blvd, University of Kansas Lawrence, KS 66045-7594. Tel 785-864-3020; Fax 785-864-4608; Elec Mail scraig@ukans.edu; Internet Home Page Address: www.2ku.edu/artlib; *Librn* Susan V Craig
Open during school yr, Mon - Thurs 8 AM - 10 PM, Fri 8 AM - 6 PM, Sat Noon - 5 PM, Sun 1 - 10 PM; Estab 1970 to support acad progs & for research; Circ Open to faculty, students & pub; some restrictions on circulating items
Library Holdings: Book Volumes 110,000; CD-ROMs; Exhibition Catalogs; Fiche; Other Holdings Auction catalogs; Pamphlets; Periodical Subscriptions 700; Reels
Special Subjects: Art History, Decorative Arts, Photography, Graphic Design, Painting-American, Painting-Dutch, Painting-Flemish, Painting-Japanese, Prints, Art Education, Asian Art, Textiles, Architecture
L **Architectural Resource Center,** 1465 Jayhawk Blvd, School of Architecture &

Urban Design Lawrence, KS 66045-7594. Tel 785-864-3244; Fax 785-864-5393; Elec Mail u-stammler@ku.edu; *Dir* Ursula Stammler
Open Mon - Fri 8 AM - 5 PM, Sun 7:30 PM - 9:30 PM; Slide Library, estab 1968, is primarily a teaching tool for faculty, but also accessible to students; Donald E & Mary Bole Hatch Architectural Reading Room, estab 1981, is adjacent to studios in School of Architecture & supports the immediate reference needs of students; For reference only
Income: Financed by endowment & state appropriation
Library Holdings: Book Volumes 3000; Periodical Subscriptions 30; Slides 82,000
Special Subjects: Architecture

LEAVENWORTH

M **CARNEGIE ARTS CENTER,** 121 Cherokee St, Leavenworth, KS 66048-2816. Tel 913-651-0765; *Dir* Carolyn Singleton

LIBERAL

M **BAKER ARTS CENTER,** 624 N Pershing Ave, Liberal, KS 67901-3115. Tel 620-624-2810; Fax 620-624-7726; Elec Mail bakerartcenter@sbcglobal.net; Internet Home Page Address: www.bakerartcenter.org; *Dir* Adriane Hatcher
Open Tues - Fri 9 AM - noon & 1 PM - 5 PM, Sat 2 PM - 5 PM; No admis fee
Library Holdings: Book Volumes 2,000
Activities: Classes & workshops

LINDSBORG

M **BETHANY COLLEGE,** Mingenback Art Center, 335 E Swensson, Lindsborg, KS 67456. Tel 785-227-3380, Ext 8145; Elec Mail kahlerc@bethanylb.edu; Internet Home Page Address: www.bethanylb.edu; *Assoc Prof* Mary Kay; *Prof* Dr Bruce Kahler; *Asst Prof* Frank Shaw; *Assoc Prof* Ed Pogue; *Prof* Caroline Kahler; *Instr* Jim Turner
Open daily 8 AM - 5 PM, cl summer & holidays; No admis fee; Estab 1970 as an educational gallery for student & professional exhibitions; Materials are not for pub display, for educational reference only; Average Annual Attendance: 1,500
Income: Financed by collections
Special Subjects: Ceramics, Sculpture, Watercolors
Collections: Oil paintings, watercolors, prints, etchings, lithographs, wood engravings, ceramics & sculpture
Exhibitions: Autumn Exhibition; Messiah Exhibition; Rotating exhibs; Graduating Sr Exhibits
Activities: Classes for adults; lect open to public, 2 vis lectrs per year; Kaymeyer Visiting Artist Lecture Series; gallery talks; competitions with prizes; portfolio-based performance awards; scholarships offered
L **Wallerstedt Library,** 235 E Swensson, Lindsborg, KS 67456. Tel 785-227-3380, Ext 8165; Fax 785-227-2860; Elec Mail carsond@bethanylb.edu; Internet Home Page Address: www.bethanylb.edu/home; *Dir* Denise Carson; *Inter-Library Loan Librn* Brittney Read; *Librn* Lucy Walline
Open Mon - Thurs 7:30 AM - 10:30 PM, Fri 7:30 AM - 5 PM, Sat 1PM-5PM, Sun 3PM-10:30PM; Estab 1881; For reference only
Library Holdings: Book Volumes 121,000; Exhibition Catalogs

M **BIRGER SANDZEN MEMORIAL GALLERY,** 401 N 1st St, Lindsborg, KS 67456-1813; PO Box 348, Lindsborg, KS 67456-0348. Tel 785-227-2220; Fax 785-227-4170; Elec Mail fineart@sandzen.org; Internet Home Page Address: www.sandzen.org; *Dir* Larry L Griffis; *Cur* Ronald Michael; *Sandzen Foundation Pres & CEO* Tremenda Dillon; *VPres* Dr Bryce Loder; *Secy* Judy Langley; *Treas* John Levin
Open Tues - Sun 1 - 5 PM; No admis fee; Estab 1957 to permanently exhibit the paintings & prints by the late Birger Sandzen, teacher at Bethany College for 52 years along with art exhibitions and special exhibitions by regional and nationally recognized artists; Nine exhibition areas; Average Annual Attendance: 17,200; Mem: 350; dues $30-$5,000; annual meeting May for Board of Dir
Income: Financed by admis fees, sales & mem, invested endowment
Library Holdings: Book Volumes; Cards; Clipping Files; Exhibition Catalogs; Memorabilia; Original Documents; Pamphlets; Periodical Subscriptions; Photographs; Slides; Video Tapes
Special Subjects: Art History, Ceramics, Prints, Woodcuts, Sculpture, Painting-American, Photography, Watercolors, Jade, Oriental Art, Asian Art
Collections: H V Poor, Lester Raymer, Birger Sandzen, John Bashor, Elmer Tomasch, Doel Reed & Carl Milles; Prairie Print Maker Society prints
Exhibitions: (03/11/2014-04/20/2014) 116th Annual Midwest Art Exhibition
Publications: Birger Sandzen: An Illustrated Biography; The Graphic Work of Birger Sandzen; Sandzen & the New Land, catalogue; color reproductions & posters of Sandzen oils
Activities: Classes for children; docent training; lects open to pub, 3 - 7 vis lectrs per yr; concerts; gallery talks open to pub; chamber music concerts; tours; Birger & Alfrida Sandzen Award for Excellence in Music; Aesthetics biannual juried competition; lending of original objects of art to art museums; 1-2 book traveling exhibs per yr; originates traveling exhibs to art museums & cultural organizations; sales shop sells books, reproductions, prints & cards; consignment art sales

LOGAN

M **DANE G HANSEN MEMORIAL MUSEUM,** PO Box 187, Logan, KS 67646-0187. Tel 785-689-4846; Fax 785-689-4892; Elec Mail hansenmuseum@ruraltel.net; Internet Home Page Address: www.hansenmuseum.org; *Dir* Shirley A Henrickson
Open Mon - Fri 9 AM - Noon & 1 - 4 PM, Sat 9 AM - Noon & 1 - 5 PM, Sun & holidays 1 - 5 PM, cl Thanksgiving, Christmas & New Year's; No admis fee; Estab 1973; Traveling exhibitions; Average Annual Attendance: 9,000; Mem: 300; dues sustaining $50, patron $25, benefactor $10

Collections: Coins; guns; paintings; sculptures
Activities: Classes for adults & children; lect open to public; concerts; gallery talks; tours; 6 traveling book exhibitions per year

LUCAS

M GRASSROOTS ART CENTER, 213 S Main St, Lucas, KS 67648; PO Box 304, Lucas, KS 67648-0304. Tel 785-525-6118; Elec Mail grassroots@wtciweb.com; Internet Home Page Address: www.grassrootsart.net; *Exec Dir* Rosslyn Schultz; *Staff Asst* Peg Gilbert; *Staff Asst* Christy Weaver; *Staff Asst* Lynn Merchant
Open May - Sept Mon - Fri 10 AM - 5 PM, Sun 1 PM - 5 PM; Oct & Apr Thurs - Mon 1 PM - 4 PM, Nov - Mar Thurs - Sat 1 PM - 4 PM, cl holidays; Admis adults $6, children 6-12 $2, discounts to groups of 10+; Estab 1991 to preserve, document, educate, exhibit self taught, outsider, recycled art & folk art of the region; Average Annual Attendance: 7,000; Mem: 321; mtgs 2nd Mon; various levels
Library Holdings: Audio Tapes; Book Volumes; CD-ROMs; DVDs; Original Art Works; Photographs; Slides; Video Tapes
Special Subjects: Folk Art, Architecture, Metalwork, Textiles, Woodcarvings, Dolls, Miniatures, Mosaics
Collections: Self taught artists
Exhibitions: (10/10/2013-04/17/2014) Metal Wire Charaters - Joe Malin; (04/24/2014-09/06/2014) Recycled Wonders - Ron Alexander
Publications: Newsletter May & Oct
Activities: Classes for adults & children; docent training; lects open to pub; vis lectrs 2 per yr; gallery talks; tours; 8 Wonders of Kansas Art & KS Governor's Tourism awards; lending original art to galleries by request; mus shop sells books & original art

MANHATTAN

L KANSAS STATE UNIVERSITY, Paul Weigel Library of Architecture Planning & Design, 323 Seaton Hall, College of Architecture Planning & Design Manhattan, KS 66506-2900. Tel 785-532-5968; Internet Home Page Address: www.lib.k-state.edu/branches/arch; *Library Asst* Judy Wyatt; *Ref Librn* Ann Scott; *Librn* Jeff Alger
Open Mon - Thurs 8 AM - 10 PM, Fri 8 AM - 5 PM, Sat 1- 5 PM, Sun 2 - 10 PM; No admis fee; Estab 1917; Circ 29,861
Income: $40,000 (financed by state appropriations & gifts)
Library Holdings: Book Volumes 38,806; Clipping Files; Fiche; Periodical Subscriptions 225; Reels
Special Subjects: Landscape Architecture, Graphic Design, Historical Material, Drafting, Restoration & Conservation, Architecture
Publications: Subject catalog

M RILEY COUNTY HISTORICAL SOCIETY & MUSEUM, (Riley County Historical Society) Riley County Historical Museum, 2309 Claflin Rd, Manhattan, KS 66502-3421. Tel 785-565-6490; Fax 785-565-6491; Elec Mail ccollins@rileycountyks.gov; Internet Home Page Address: www.rileycountyks.gov/index.asp; *Cur Archives & Libr* Linda Glasgow; *Dir & Cur* D Cheryl Collins; *Cur Exhibits* Allana Saenger; *Cur Coll & Registrar* Corina Hugo
Open Tues - Fri 8:30 AM - 5 PM; Sat & Sun 2 - 5 PM; No admis fee. donations accepted; Estab 1916 to exhibit history & current & historical arts & crafts; Maintains reference library & exhibit galleries; Average Annual Attendance: 25,000; Mem: 1000; dues life $300, patron $100+, sustainer $75 - $99, sponsor $50 - $74, friend $10 - $49; dinner meetings in Jan, Apr, July & Oct
Income: Mus financed by Riley County budget; Society a pvt dues org
Special Subjects: Decorative Arts, Folk Art, Flasks & Bottles, Prints, Architecture, Textiles, Costumes, Pottery, Decorative Arts, Manuscripts, Portraits, Posters, Dolls, Furniture, Glass, Porcelain, Carpets & Rugs, Historical Material, Maps, Coins & Medals, Period Rooms, Laces
Collections: Photo Collections; Riley County History Artifacts
Exhibitions: Household Work Week; The Land & the People - standing exhib
Publications: RCHS Newsletter, 10 times per year; Tracing Traditions, a coloring book for children; The Architects & Buildings of Manhattan, Kansas by Dr Patricia J O'Brien; This Land is Our Land by Donald Parrish; Rural Schools of Riley Co, Kansas by Bogart, Brannon, Setterquist, Setterquist & Tippin
Activities: Classes for children: hands on tours using educational coll; Docent progs & training; lects open to pub; tours; originate traveling exhibs to schools & club meetings; mus shop sells books, Kansas crafts, wood cuts & KS themed items

L Seaton Library, 2309 Claflin Rd, Manhattan, KS 66502. Tel 785-565-6490; Fax 785-565-6491; Elec Mail ccollins@rileycountyks.gov; *Library Archivist* Linda Glasgow; *Dir* D Cheryl Collins; *Exhibits* Allana Saenger; *Registrar* Corina Hugo
By appointment only; No admis fee; Estab 1976; research library; Reference, non-circulating collection
Income: Financed by Riley County
Library Holdings: Audio Tapes; Book Volumes 4000; Clipping Files; Lantern Slides; Manuscripts; Maps; Memorabilia; Motion Pictures; Original Documents; Pamphlets; Periodical Subscriptions; Photographs; Slides; Video Tapes
Special Subjects: Manuscripts, Maps, Historical Material, Architecture
Collections: Photo Collection; Family files, maps, club records, school records, bus records, county government & city records
Activities: Mus shop sells books

MCPHERSON

M MCPHERSON COLLEGE GALLERY, 1600 E Euclid, Friendship Hall McPherson, KS 67460-3847. Tel 316-241-0731; Fax 316-241-8443; Internet Home Page Address: www.mcpherson.edu; *Dir* Wayne Conyers
Open Mon - Fri 8 AM - 10 PM; No admis fee; Estab 1960 to present works of art to the col students & to the community; A long gallery which is the entrance to an auditorium, has four showcases & 11 panels 4 x 16 ft; Average Annual Attendance: 2,500
Income: Financed through college
Special Subjects: Painting-American, Prints, Watercolors
Collections: Oils, original prints, watercolors
Exhibitions: change monthly
Activities: Classes for adults; scholarships offered; book traveling exhibitions

M MCPHERSON MUSEUM AND ARTS FOUNDATION, 1111 E Kansas Ave, McPherson, KS 67460. Tel 620-241-8464; Fax 620-241-2676; Elec Mail carla-barber@sbcglobal.net; Internet Home Page Address: www.mcphersonmuseum.com; *Exec Dir* Carla Barber; *Cur* Brett Whitenack; *Registrar* Michael Lindblade
Open Tues - Sat 1PM - 5 PM, cl Sun, Mon & holidays; Admis adults $3, seniors & students $2, children 2-12 $1; Estab 1890; Birger Sandzen prints on display year round; one annual feature art exhibit; Average Annual Attendance: 7,000; Mem: 200, dues $35-$1,000
Income: Financed by city appropriation & pvt donations
Special Subjects: American Indian Art, Anthropology, Decorative Arts, Folk Art, Landscapes, Glass, Pottery, Prints, Textiles, Painting-American, African Art, Archaeology, Costumes, Woodcarvings, Dolls, Furniture, Asian Art, Historical Material, Antiquities-Oriental
Collections: Fossils of mammoths, mastodons, saber tooth tigers & many other fossils; oriental & African coll; Pioneer artifacts & Native American Pottery; Sandzen Prints, folk art collection; Folk art carvings of artist Anna Larkin
Exhibitions: 4 feature exhibits per year, including 1 art exhibit
Publications: McPherson Museum & Art Foundation newsletter, The Diamond
Activities: Sponsor Wordfest, an annual writer's conference; sponsor writers' group; summer music series (6 concerts); educ prog; classes for adults & children; winter lect series (7 lects); lects open to pub, 7 vis lectrs per year; concerts; tours; sponsoring of competitions; mus shop sells books, original art & reproductions

MONTEZUMA

M STAUTH FOUNDATION & MUSEUM, Stauth Memorial Museum, 111 N Aztec St, Montezuma, KS 67867-0396; PO Box 396, Montezuma, KS 67867. Tel 620-846-2527; Fax 620-846-2810; Elec Mail stauthm@ucom.net; Internet Home Page Address: www.stauthmemorialmuseum.org; *Dir & Financial Dir* Kim Legleiter
Open Tues - Sat 9 AM - Noon & 1 - 4:30 PM, Sun 1:30 - 4:30 PM; No admis fee; Estab 1996; Four galleries; Average Annual Attendance: 4,000
Income: $95,000 (financed by endowment & donations)
Library Holdings: Maps National Geo 1945-present; Slides
Special Subjects: Folk Art, Ceramics, Flasks & Bottles, Latin American Art, Photography, Sculpture, Bronzes, African Art, Textiles, Costumes, Woodcarvings, Etchings & Engravings, Decorative Arts, Posters, Eskimo Art, Dolls, Furniture, Glass, Jewelry, Oriental Art, Asian Art, Metalwork, Ivory, Maps, Scrimshaw, Coins & Medals, Embroidery, Enamels
Collections: Coins-foreign; decorative arts; jewelry-foreign; natural history coll; slides-over 10,000; musical instruments; Remington bronze miniatures & other western bronze miniatures; North American Big Game Specimen
Exhibitions: Around The World with Claude & Donald Stauth; The Ralph Fry Wildlife Collection; Wall Western Collection; Special exhibitions gallery
Activities: Classes for children; lects open to pub; 2-3 vis lectrs per yr; tours; book traveling exhibs 7 - 8 per yr

NORTH NEWTON

L BETHEL COLLEGE, Mennonite Library & Archives, 300 E 27th St, North Newton, KS 67117-1716. Tel 316-284-5304; Fax 316-284-5843; Elec Mail mla@bethelks.edu; Internet Home Page Address: www.bethslks.edu/mla/index.php; *Archivist* John D Thiesen; *Librn* Barbara A Thiesen; *Asst Archivist* James Lynch
Open Mon - Thurs 10 AM - 5 PM; No admis fee; Estab 1936 to preserve resources related to Mennonite history for the use of researchers
Income: $70,000 (financed by college & church conference support)
Library Holdings: Audio Tapes; Cassettes; Clipping Files; Exhibition Catalogs; Fiche; Filmstrips; Framed Reproductions; Kodachrome Transparencies; Lantern Slides; Manuscripts; Memorabilia; Motion Pictures; Original Art Works; Pamphlets; Photographs; Prints; Records; Reels; Reproductions; Slides; Video Tapes
Special Subjects: Photography, Manuscripts, Painting-American, Painting-Dutch, Painting-German, Historical Material, Ethnology, Religious Art
Collections: 500 paintings and etchings by Mennonite artists; Photographs of Hopi and Cheyenne Indians
Publications: Mennonite Life, on-line only
Activities: Lects

NORTON

C FIRST STATE BANK, They Also Ran Gallery, 105 W Main St, Norton, KS 67654-1947; PO Box 560, Norton, KS 67654-0560. Tel 785-877-3341; Fax 785-877-5808; Elec Mail firstate@ruraltel.net; Elec Mail theyalsoran@firstatebank.com; Internet Home Page Address: www.firststatebank.com; Internet Home Page Address: www.theyalsoran.com; *Chmn* Norman L Nelson; *Pres* John P Engelbert; *Contact* Lee Ann Shearer
Open Mon - Fri 9 AM - 3 PM, Sat 8:30 AM - 11:30 AM; No admis fee; Estab 1965 as a gallery of those who ran for President of the United States & lost; 60 portraits & biographies; Average Annual Attendance: varies
Income: through the bank
Special Subjects: Historical Material
Collections: Also Ran Gallery; Take Off Elephants
Exhibitions: Permanent
Publications: Take off brochure available
Activities: Tours

OVERLAND PARK

M **KANSAS CITY JEWISH MUSEUM OF CONTEMPORARY ART - EPSTEN GALLERY,** 5500 W 123rd St, Overland Park, KS 66209. Tel 913-266-8414; *Prog & Develop Asst* Abby Rufkahr; *Exec Dir* Eileen Garry; *Cur* Marcus Cain
Open Tues-Fri 11AM-4PM, Sat-Sun 1PM-4PM; No admis fee, donations accepted
Collections: works by contemporary artists

RUSSELL

M **DEINES CULTURAL CENTER,** 820 N Main St, Russell, KS 67665-1932. Tel 785-483-3742; Fax 785-483-4397; Elec Mail info@deinesculturalcenter.org; Internet Home Page Address: www.deinesculturalcenter.org; *Dir* Shannon Trevethan
Open Tues - Fri 12--5PM, Sat-Sun 1PM-5PM; No admis fee; Estab 1990 to promote the arts & humanities; Average Annual Attendance: 2,500; Mem: 175; dues $25
Income: $30,000 (financed by mem & city appropriation)
Special Subjects: Etchings & Engravings, Folk Art, Historical Material, Landscapes, Ceramics, Collages, Painting-American, Photography, Prints, Sculpture, Watercolors, Pottery, Woodcuts, Dolls, Jewelry, Juvenile Art
Collections: E Hubert Deines Wood Engravings; Various regional artists
Exhibitions: Monthly exhibits
Activities: Classes for adults & children; recitals; lects open to pub; book traveling exhibitions 1 per year; mus shop sells original art

SALINA

M **SALINA ART CENTER,** 242 S Santa Fe, Salina, KS 67401-3932; PO Box 743, Salina, KS 67402-0743. Tel 785-827-1431; Fax 785-827-0686; Elec Mail info@salinaartcenter.org; Internet Home Page Address: www.salinaartcenter.org; *Dir Community Develop* Wendy Moshier; *Communs Coordr* Pamela Harris; *Comm Coordr* Libby Shoup; *Gallery Mgr* Joshua Smith
Open Tues, Wed, Fri & Sat noon - 5 PM, Thurs noon - 7 PM, Sun 1- 5 PM, cl Mon; No admis fee; Estab 1979 as an international & national private non-profit, non-collecting contemporary art & educ center; One floor, 50 ft x 150 sq. ft.; Average Annual Attendance: 50,000; Mem: 500; dues $40 basic
Income: $350,000 (financed by mem & private donations)
Exhibitions: Contemporary Art; changing exhibitions; Annual Juried Show
Publications: Brochures; newsletters
Activities: Classes for adults & children; docent progs; lects open to pub, 6-8 vis lectrs per yr; competitions; traveling exten dept serves rural Kansas; book traveling exhibs 4 per yr; originate traveling exhibs 5 per yr

SCOTT CITY

M **KEYSTONE GALLERY,** 401 US 83, Scott City, KS 67871-8013. Tel 620-872-2762; Internet Home Page Address: www.keystonegallery.com; *Artist* Charles Bonner; *Photographer* Barbara Shelton; *Web Designer* Logan Bonner
Call for hours; Admis fee $5; Estab 1991 as an art gallery & fossil mus; displays of fossils & Western Kansas paintings; Average Annual Attendance: 5,000
Special Subjects: Historical Material, American Western Art, Photography, Sculpture, Graphics, Jewelry
Collections: Local history & culture; paintings; fossils; period artifacts; photographs
Activities: Gallery talks; tours; mus shop sells books; original art; reproductions, prints, minerals & fossils

TOPEKA

M **KANSAS STATE HISTORICAL SOCIETY,** Kansas Museum of History, 6425 SW Sixth Ave, Topeka, KS 66615-1099. Tel 785-272-8681; Fax 785-272-8682; Elec Mail KansasMuseum@kshs.org; Internet Home Page Address: www.kshs.org; *Exec Dir* Jennie Chinn; *Cur Fine Art* Larry Fritzsch; *Cur of Decorative Art* Blair Tarr; *Dir Mus* Robert Keckeisen; *Coll Mgr* Rebecca Martin
Open Tue - Sat 9 AM - 5 PM, Sun 1 - 5 PM, cl Mon, state holidays, New Year's & Christmas; Admis adults $6, students $4, mems & children 5 & under free; Estab 1875 to collect, preserve & interpret the historical documents & objects of Kansas history; Average Annual Attendance: 75,000; Mem: 3400; dues life $1000, special $50 - $1000, family $35, individual $25, student $15; meetings in spring & fall
Income: $784,000 (financed by endowment & state)
Special Subjects: Historical Material, Cartoons
Collections: Regional collection for period from middle 19th century to present, especially portraiture, native art, political cartoons & folk art
Exhibitions: Rotating Exhibits
Publications: Kansas History: Journal of the Central Plains, quarterly; exhibit catalogs
Activities: Classes for adults & children; dramatic progs; docent training; craft demonstration prog; lects open to pub, 4 vis lectrs per yr; provided by staff to public organizations on request; tours; slide tape progs; limited schols available for student groups; exten dept serves entire state of Kansas; traveling trunks on Kansas topics; book traveling exhibs 1-2 per yr; sales shop sells books, prints, cards, slides, postcards, folk art, crafts, souvenirs and jewelry; junior mus

M **TOPEKA & SHAWNEE COUNTY PUBLIC LIBRARY,** Alice C Sabatini Gallery, 1515 SW Tenth St, Topeka, KS 66604-1374. Tel 785-580-4515; Fax 785-580-4496; Elec Mail sbest@tscpl.org; Internet Home Page Address: www.tscpl.org; *Gallery Dir* Sherry L Best; *Exec Dir* Gina Millsap; *Gallery Assoc* Zan Popp; *Gallery Assoc* Betsy Knab Roe; *Gallery Assoc* Heather Kearns; *Special Colls/Art Librn* Brea Black
Open Mon - Fri 9 AM - 9 PM, Sat 9 AM - 6 PM, Sun 12 - 9 PM; No admis fee; Estab 1870 to serve the city & the Northeast Kansas Library System residents with public information, both educational & recreational; to be one of the areas cultural centers through services from the Gallery within the library; Circ Public library circulation, over 2 million items; Gallery reopened in 2001 with a 1864 sq ft plus space, professional lighting, security system; gallery furniture; Average Annual Attendance: 20,000+; Mem: 90; dues $30 per yr
Income: Financed by city, county & property taxes
Purchases: Contemporary ceramics & Kansas artists
Library Holdings: Audio Tapes; Book Volumes; CD-ROMs; Cassettes; Clipping Files; Compact Disks; DVDs; Exhibition Catalogs; Fiche; Lantern Slides; Maps; Memorabilia; Micro Print; Original Art Works; Original Documents; Pamphlets; Periodical Subscriptions; Photographs; Prints; Sculpture; Slides; Video Tapes
Special Subjects: Architecture, Drawings, Latin American Art, Mexican Art, Painting-American, Prints, Watercolors, American Indian Art, American Western Art, Bronzes, African Art, Religious Art, Ceramics, Pottery, Primitive art, Woodcarvings, Etchings & Engravings, Landscapes, Glass, Jewelry, Oriental Art, Asian Art, Metalwork, Carpets & Rugs, Enamels
Collections: 19th Century Chinese Decorative Arts; Hirschberg Collection of West African Arts; Johnson Collection of Art; Contemporary American Ceramics; Glass paperweight coll; New Mexican Woodcarving; Rare Book Room; Regional painting, drawing & prints; Wilder Collection of Art Nouveau Glass & Ceramics; Books as art
Exhibitions: Juried national Topeka Competition of 3D contemporary works; Juried National Printmaking competition; Permanent collections, children's & group exhibits
Publications: Creative Expression in Rural West Africa; Rookwood Pottery: One Hundred Year Anniversary
Activities: Docent training; lects open to pub, concerts; gallery; talks; tours by request; special programs for exhibits; competitions with awards; cash & purchase awards for Competitions; Institute for Museum and Library Svcs: Mus assessment program grant; individual paintings & original objects of art lent to other qualified mus; mus shop sells used books

M **WASHBURN UNIVERSITY,** Mulvane Art Museum, 17th & Jewell Sts, Topeka, KS 66621-0001; 1700 SW College Ave, Topeka, KS 66621-0001. Tel 785-670-1124; Fax 785-670-1329; Elec Mail mulvane@washburn.edu; Internet Home Page Address: www.washburn.edu/mulvane; *Dir* Connie Gibbons; *Cur* Carol Emert; *Admin Asst* Delene Van Sickle; *Cur Educ* Kandis Barker; *Preparator* Michael Allen; *Asst Cur Educ* Jane Hanni; *Mus Receptionist* Jan Bychinski
Open Tues 10 AM - 7 PM, Wed, Thurs & Fri 10 AM - 5 PM, Sat & Sun 1 - 4 PM, cl holidays; No admis fee; Estab 1922; Building gift of Joab Mulvane: provides six galleries with 600 running ft of hanging space with temperature & humidity controlled; Average Annual Attendance: 120,000; Mem: 600; dues student or senior $25, individual $35, dual/family $60, director's circle $ 125, silver $250, gold $500, platinum $1000
Income: $450,000 (Financed by Washburn Univ endowed funds & Friends of The Mulvane Art Mus, Inc)
Purchases: $10,000
Special Subjects: Graphics, Painting-American, Prints, Sculpture, Watercolors, Southwestern Art, Ceramics, Woodcuts, Etchings & Engravings, Glass, Asian Art
Collections: 18th-19th Century Japanese Fine & Decorative Art; 19th & 20th Century American Art; 16th-20th Century European Prints
Exhibitions: Contemporary Mountain-Plains regional painting, prints, sculpture, ceramics; changing exhibitions include a Kansas Artist Exhibit & Annual Mountain-Plains Art Fair
Publications: Exhibition brochures
Activities: Classes for adults & children; outreach progs: Art Beginning in Childhood; Art in School, After School; docent training; lects open to pub, 4-6 vis lectrs per yr; gallery talks; tours; scholarships; individuals painting & original objects of art lent to accredited art mus; book traveling exhibs; mus shop sells books, original art, reproductions, jewelry, note cards, toys, unusual gifts for all ages

WAMEGO

M **HISTORIC COLUMBIAN THEATRE FOUNDATION,** Columbian Theatre Museum & Art Center, 521 Lincoln Ave, Wamego, KS 66547. Tel 785-456-2029; Fax 785-456-9498; Elec Mail boxoffice@columbiantheatre.com; Internet Home Page Address: www.columbiantheatre.com; *Exec Dir* Clint Stueve; *Office Coordr* Mary Beth Peterson; *Gift Shop coordr* Brooke Rindt
Open Tues-Fri 10 AM - 5 PM, Sat 10AM-3PM, cl Mon; No admis fee, suggested donation $5; Estab 1994; Average Annual Attendance: 24,000; Mem: 400; dues $50-$1500
Income: $460,000 (financed by endowment, mem, grants, gifts, earned income (ticket sales) & underwriters)
Special Subjects: Architecture, Painting-American, Decorative Arts, Historical Material
Collections: A 20-painting coll from the Columbian Exposition, the 1893 Chicago World's Fair, representing 60 percent of the decorative art from the Government Building. Includes 6 large oil on canvas paintings (restored & on display) by Ernest Theodore Behr
Exhibitions: Swogger gallery houses an average of 6-8 rotating exhibits per year featuring artists & collections from or pertaining to the region &/or the mission of the Columbian
Activities: Dramatic progs; dinners; children's Summer Theatre Academy; gallery/building tours; gift shop sells local items

WICHITA

M **FRIENDS UNIVERSITY,** Riney Fine Arts Center Gallery, Riney Fine Arts Bldg, 2100 University Ave Wichita, KS 67213-3379. Tel 316-295-5537; Elec Mail artgallery@friends.edu; *Gallery Coordr* Adam C Achey
Open daily in the fall 7 AM - 10 PM, daily in the summer 7 AM-6 PM, cl summer weekends; No admis fee; Estab 1963 to bring art-craft exhibits to campus

as an educational learning experience & to supply the local community with first class exhibits; 1224 sq ft of exhibit space; Average Annual Attendance: 20,000
Activities: 4 vis lectrs per yr; gallery talks; tours; monthly art exhibs & receptions; exten dept

L **Edmund Stanley Library,** 2100 University Ave, Wichita, KS 67213. Tel 316-295-5880; Fax 316-295-5080; Internet Home Page Address: www.friends.edu/library/default.aspx; *Asst Library Dir Reference* Kathy Delker; *Library Dir* Max M Burson; *Circulation Mgr* Kathy Edwards; *Interlibrary Loan* Jan Tillotson; *Serials* Jeanette Parker; *Cataloging/Systems Admin* Anne Crane; *Admin Asst* Jane Johnson
Open summer 9 AM-7 PM, fall Mon - Fri 7:45 AM-10 PM, Fri 7:45 AM - 4 PM; Admis free for community card to check out books; Estab 1979; 500 sq ft of exhibition space, ideal for crafts & locked cases
Library Holdings: Audio Tapes; Book Volumes; Cassettes; Compact Disks; DVDs; Fiche; Filmstrips; Maps; Memorabilia; Original Art Works; Original Documents; Pamphlets; Periodical Subscriptions 90; Photographs; Sculpture 10; Slides; Video Tapes

M **GALLERY XII,** 412 E Douglas Ave, Ste A, Wichita, KS 67202. Tel 316-267-5915; Elec Mail wichitagallery12@yahoo.com; Internet Home Page Address: www.wichitagalleryXII.com; *Pres* Vince Micelli; *VPres* Diane Warta; *Website* Justin Bayles
Open Mon - Sat 10 AM - 5 PM, final Fri of month 6 - 10 PM; No admis fee; Estab 1977 as art cooperative; Gallery specializes in original art by Kansas artists; Average Annual Attendance: 10,000; Mem: dues $400; 22 mem; local artists juried by current mems
Income: financed by mem
Library Holdings: Original Art Works; Photographs; Prints; Sculpture; Slides
Exhibitions: monthly featured artists: May - Jun-Mueller, Wong; July - Williford; Aug - Finnell; Sept - Fiorelli; Oct - Dove; Nov - Engquist; Dec - all mems
Publications: Edition of 20 hand-pulled black & white lithographs
Activities: Exten program serves local nonprofit organizations; local source for pub & pvt schools - field trips, tours & lab; originates traveling exhibs to nonprofits in Kansas; gallery sells original art by Kansas artists, photographs

A **KANSAS WATERCOLOR SOCIETY,** The Wichita Center for the Arts, 9112 E Central, Wichita, KS 67206. Tel 316-634-2787; Fax 316-634-0593; Elec Mail areep@wcfta.com; Internet Home Page Address: wcfta.com; *Gallery Asst* Amy Reep
Open Tues-Sun 1PM-5PM; No admis fee; Estab 1970 to promote watercolor in Kansas; Mem: 185; dues $20
Income: Financed by mem, entry fees, patrons & Kansas Arts Commission
Exhibitions: Rotating exhibits
Publications: Newsletter, quarterly
Activities: Demonstrations & workshops; lects open to public; gallery talks; tours; competitions with awards; originates traveling exhibs

M **MID-AMERICA ALL-INDIAN CENTER,** Indian Center Museum, 650 N Seneca, Wichita, KS 67203. Tel 316-262-5221; Fax 316-316-262-4304; Elec Mail maaic@sbcglobal.net; Internet Home Page Address: www.theindiancenter.org; *Exec Dir* John D'Angelo
Open Tues - Sat 10 AM - 4 PM; Admis adults $7, seniors $5, children 6-12 $3, under 6 free; Estab 1976 to preserve the Indian heritage, culture & traditions; Average Annual Attendance: 70,000; Mem: 400; dues benefactor $500 & up, patron $250 - $499, friend $100 - $249, contributor $50 - $99, family $35 - $49, individual $25 - $34
Income: Financed by admis, donations, mem & gift shop sales
Library Holdings: Book Volumes
Special Subjects: American Indian Art
Collections: Native American arts & artifacts; Plains beadwork; Northwest Coast & Eskimo crafts; Southwest pottery, paintings, sculpture, carvings & basketry; Mildred Manty Memorial Collection; Ray Meadows Collection; Lincoln Ellsworth Collection
Exhibitions: Four changing exhibits per yr, prehistory or specialty exhibits; three dimensional traditional art; two & three dimensional contemporary art
Activities: Classes for adults & children; docent training; lects open to pub; gallery talks; tours; mus shop sells books, magazines, original art, reproductions & prints

L **Black Bear Bosin Resource Center,** 650 N Seneca, Wichita, KS 67203. Tel 316-262-5221; Fax 316-262-4216; Elec Mail maaic@earthlink.net; Internet Home Page Address: www.theindiancenter.com/resource.html; *Dir* Shelly Berger
Open Tues - Sat 10 AM - 5 PM by appointment only; Reference only
Income: financed by donations, gifts
Library Holdings: Book Volumes 400; Filmstrips; Motion Pictures; Pamphlets; Slides
Collections: Indian art & history

M **WICHITA ART MUSEUM,** 1400 W Museum Blvd, Wichita, KS 67203-3296. Tel 316-268-4921; Fax 316-268-4980; Elec Mail info@wichitaartmuseum.org; Internet Home Page Address: www.wichitaartmuseum.org; *Dir* Patricia McDonnell; *Registrar* Leslie Servantez
Open Tues-Sat 10 AM - 5 PM, Sun Noon - 5 PM, cl Mon & holidays; Admis adults $7, seniors & adult students $5 youth 5-17 $3, under 5 free & free Sat; Estab 1935 to house & exhibit art works belonging to permanent collection; to present exhibits of loaned art works, to ensure care & maintain the safety of works through security, environmental controls & appropriate curatorial functions & to interpret collections & exhibitions through formal & educational presentations; Facility designed by Clarence S Stein, 1935 with addition in Oct 1977 designed by Edward Larrabee Barnes; expanded & renovated, opened 2003. Maintains reference library; Average Annual Attendance: 50,500; Mem: dues $40 up
Library Holdings: Auction Catalogs; Book Volumes 10,000; Clipping Files; Exhibition Catalogs; Manuscripts; Pamphlets; Periodical Subscriptions
Special Subjects: Drawings, Mexican Art, Painting-American, Sculpture, Watercolors, Pre-Columbian Art, Southwestern Art, Textiles, Woodcarvings, Porcelain
Collections: Roland P Murdock, American Art; M C Naftzger Collection of Charles M Russell (paintings, drawings & sculpture); Kurdian Collection of Pre-Columbian Mexican Art; Virginia & George Ablah Collection of British Watercolors; L S & Ida L Naftzger Collection of Prints & Drawings; Gwen Houston Naftzger Collection of Boehm & Doughty Porcelain Birds; Florence Naftzger Evans Collection of Porcelain & Faience; F. Price Cossman Collection of Steuben Glass; Elizabeth S Navas Papers; Howard E Wooden Papers
Publications: Catalog of Roland P Murdock Collection; bimonthly newsletter; exhibition brochures & catalogues; Toward an American Identity: Selections from the Wichita Art Mus; Wichita Art Museum: 75 Years of American Art
Activities: Classes for children; docent training; tours of collection; lects open to pub; concerts; gallery talks; tours; exten prog to teachers & parents; lending of items from Art Resource Center (books & visual materials); mus shop sells books, original art, reproductions, prints, slides & jewelry

L **Emprise Bank Research Library,** 1400 W Museum Blvd, Wichita, KS 67203. Tel 316-268-4921; Fax 316-268-4980; Elec Mail info@wichitaartmuseum.org; Internet Home Page Address: www.wichitaartmuseum.org; *Librn* Joyce Goering Norris; *Dir* Patricia McDonnell; *Registrar* Leslie Servantez
Library open by appointment, Tues & Thurs 10 AM - 2:30 PM, for reference use only; Admis adult $7, seniors & adult students $5, youth 5-17 $3, children under 5 & Sat no admis fee.; Estab 1963 as research library for mus staff; Reference only
Library Holdings: Auction Catalogs; Book Volumes 10,000; Clipping Files; Exhibition Catalogs; Manuscripts; Other Holdings Auction catalogs; Museum handbooks; Pamphlets; Periodical Subscriptions 15; Video Tapes
Special Subjects: Art History, Folk Art, Decorative Arts, Drawings, Etchings & Engravings, Painting-American, Pre-Columbian Art, Prints, Sculpture, Watercolors, American Western Art, American Indian Art, Landscapes
Collections: Elizabeth S Navas Papers; Howard E Wooden Papers; Chris Paulsen Polk Papers
Exhibitions: (12/14/2013-05/04/2014) Downtown Abbey; (10/05/2013-02/23/2014) Blackbear Bosin; (09/27/2014-01/04/2015) American Moderns 1910-1960: O'Keeffe to Rockwell

A **WICHITA CENTER FOR THE ARTS,** 9112 E Central, Wichita, KS 67206. Tel 316-634-2787; Fax 316-634-0593; Elec Mail arts@wcfta.com; Internet Home Page Address: www.wcfta.com; *Chmn Board* Becky Turner; *Treas* William Tinker Jr; *Exec Dir* Howard W Ellington; *Admin Asst* Randy Brown; *Gallery Adminr* Amy Reep; *Dir Educ* Kathy Sweeney; *Theatre Dir* John Boldenow
Open Tues - Sun 1 - 5 PM, cl national holidays & week of July 4th; No admis fee; Estab 1920, incorporated 1932, as an educational & cultural institution; Gallery contains 1000 running ft of exhibit space; up to five exhibits each six-week period; Average Annual Attendance: 55,000; Mem: 1250; dues $35 & up
Income: Financed by private contributions
Collections: Prints and drawings, paintings, sculpture, American decorative arts & contemporary crafts
Exhibitions: Exhibitions change each six weeks; one man shows; special programs; Biennial National Craft Exhibit
Publications: 6 newsletters per year
Activities: Visual & performing arts classes for adults & children; theatre productions; docent training; lects open to public, up to 6 vis lectrs per yr; gallery talks; classic film series; competitions with awards; scholarships; individual paintings & original objects of art lent to other art museums; book traveling exhibs; originate traveling exhibs; sales shop sells books & original art

L **Maude Schollenberger Memorial Library,** 9112 E Central, Wichita, KS 67206. Tel 316-686-6687; Fax 316-634-2787; *Chmn Board* Carol Wilson; *Exec Dir* Howard W Ellington
Open Mon - Fri 1 PM - 5 PM; Estab 1965; For reference. 57 Reactivated by JRedel 6/98
Income: Financed by private contributions
Library Holdings: Auction Catalogs; Book Volumes 400; Clipping Files; Exhibition Catalogs; Manuscripts; Memorabilia; Original Art Works; Photographs; Sculpture

L **WICHITA PUBLIC LIBRARY,** 223 S Main St, Wichita, KS 67202-3795. Tel 316-261-8500; Elec Mail admin@wichita.lib.ks.us; Internet Home Page Address: www.wichita.lib.ks.us; *Exec Dir* Leah Barnhard
Open Mon - Thurs 10 AM - 9 PM, Fri & Sat 10 AM - 5:30 PM, Sun 1 - 5 PM; No admis fee; research charges apply; Estab 1876 & grown to be informational center & large free public library to improve the community with educational, cultural & recreational benefits through books, recordings, films, art works & other materials; Circ 1,100,000
Income: Financed by local taxes
Library Holdings: Framed Reproductions; Motion Pictures; Records; Reels
Special Subjects: Folk Art, Decorative Arts, Film, Graphic Arts, Crafts, American Western Art, Advertising Design, American Indian Art, Furniture, Glass, Afro-American Art, Coins & Medals, Architecture
Collections: Kansas Book Collection; John F Kennedy Collection; Harry Mueller Philately Book Collection
Exhibitions: Preview of Academy Award Short Subjects; Rotating exhibits
Activities: Progs for adults, teens, children & families; tech training classes; reference & research svcs; lect; tours; book discussions; films; talks; concerts; crafts

M **WICHITA STATE UNIVERSITY,** Ulrich Museum of Art, 1845 Fairmount, Wichita, KS 67260-0046. Tel 316-978-3664; Fax 316-978-3898; Elec Mail ulrich@wichita.edu; Internet Home Page Address: www.ulrich.wichita.edu; *Registrar* Stephanie Teasley; *Dir* Bob Workman; *Asst Dir* Linda Doll; *Cur of Educ* Aimee Geist; *Pub Rels Mgr* Jessy Clonts; *Special Projects Coordr* Carolyn Copple; *Designer/Preparator* James Porter; *Cur Modern & Contempory Art* Jodi Throckmorton
Open Tues - Fri 11 AM - 5 PM, Sat & Sun 1 - 5 PM, cl Mon & national/univ holidays; No admis fee; Estab 1974. Collecting, preserving, exhibiting & interpreting modern & contemporary art; 5 galleries on 2 floors, 18 ft ceiling, 10,000 sq ft exhibition space; Average Annual Attendance: 18,000; Mem: 400
Special Subjects: Afro-American Art, American Indian Art, Etchings & Engravings, Landscapes, Marine Painting, Photography, Painting-American, Bronzes, Drawings, Hispanic Art, Prints, Sculpture, Watercolors, Woodcuts, Portraits, Furniture

Collections: Over 7,000 works of contemporary & modern works of art; Martin H Bush Outdoor Sculpture Coll
Activities: Classes for adults and children; docent training; lects open to pub; 12 vis lecrts per yr; gallery talks; concerts; tours; scholarships; 1-2 book traveling exhibs per yr

WINFIELD

L   **SOUTHWESTERN COLLEGE,** Deets Library - Art Dept, 100 College St, Winfield, KS 67156-2499. Tel 620-229-6225, 866-734-1275; Fax 620-229-6382; Elec Mail gzuck1@swcart.edu; Internet Home Page Address: www.sckans.edu/library; *Lib Dir* Veronica McAsey
Open school year Mon - Thurs 7:45 AM-12AM, Fri 7:45AM-5PM, Sat noon-4PM, Sun 3PM-12AM; Estab 1885 as a four-year liberal arts col; Circ 77,000
Income: Financed by college budget
Library Holdings: Book Volumes 77,000; Exhibition Catalogs; Fiche; Periodical Subscriptions 120; Reels
Collections: Arthur Covey Collection of paintings, mural sketches, etchings, lithographs, drawings and watercolors; Cunningham Asian Arts Collection of books, catalogues & exhibition catalogs
Publications: databases
Activities: Tours

KENTUCKY

ASHLAND

C   **ASHLAND INC,** PO Box 391, Ashland, KY 41114-0001. Tel 606-329-3333; Fax 606-329-3559; *Corporate Art Admin* Tim Heaberlin
Open by appt only; Estab 1972, primary function is decorative art, but also to establish a creative atmosphere; to enhance community cultural life; Collection displayed in public areas of corporate office buildings
Collections: Mainly contemporary printmaking, emphasis on Americans; paintings, sculpture, wall hangings
Activities: Tours; competitions; sponsorship consists of purchase awards for local art group & museum competitions; provides purchase & merit awards for certain museum & university competitions; individual objects of art lent; originate traveling exhibs to museums, colleges, universities & art centers in general marketing areas

BEREA

M   **BEREA COLLEGE,** Ulmann Doris Galleries, CPO 2162, Berea, KY 40404. Tel 859-985-3083; Fax 859-985-3541; Elec Mail meghan_doherty@berea.edu; Internet Home Page Address: www.berea.edu/art/doris-ulman-galleries; *Dir & Cur* Dr Meghan C Doherty
Open Mon, Wed - Fri 8 AM - 5 PM, Tues & Thurs 8 AM - 8 PM, Sat & Sun 1 - 5 PM, cl col holidays, Oct 2, Nov 27, Dec 1, 14, 2013, Jan 7, 20, Feb 25, Mar 1-9, Apr 18-20, 2015; No admis fee; Estab 1936 for educational purposes; Gallery with rotating & permanent colls.; Average Annual Attendance: 1,500; Mem: None; open free to pub & researchers
Income: Financed by college budget
Library Holdings: CD-ROMs; Periodical Subscriptions 25; Prints
Special Subjects: Archaeology, Art History, Photography, Prints, Textiles, African Art, Textiles, Ceramics, Asian Art
Collections: General
Activities: student learning; Lect open to public, 4 vis lectrs per year; gallery talks; tours; competitive exhibs; lending of original objects of art

A   **KENTUCKY GUILD OF ARTISTS & CRAFTSMEN INC,** 210 N Broadway, Ste 3 Berea, KY 40403-1505; PO Box 291, Berea, KY 40403. Tel 859-986-3192; Fax 859-986-0334; Elec Mail info@kyguild.org; Internet Home Page Address: www.kyguild.org; *Dir* Jeannette Rowlett; *Prog Admin Mgr* Glenna Combs; *Prog Asst* Susan England
Open Mon - Fri 9 AM - 5 PM; Admis adults $5, children 12 and under free; Estab 1961 for the pursuit of excellence in the arts & crafts & to encourage the pub appreciation thereof; Average Annual Attendance: 8,000; Mem: 350; must be a Kentucky resident & be juried for exhibiting status; dues exhib mem $50
Income: $80,000 (financed by grants, contributions, corporate donations, admis & mem fees)
Publications: The Guild Record, 4 times per yr; Online Update - electronic newsletter; Art & Craft Insight Network = Art & Craft Learning Opportunities
Activities: Classes for adults & children; docent training; workshops; lect open to public; demonstrations; competitions with awards; 2 ann retail fairs; originates traveling exhibs to KY & surrounding states

BOWLING GREEN

M   **CAPITOL ARTS ALLIANCE,** (Capitol Arts Center) Houchens Gallery, 416 E Main St, Bowling Green, KY 42101; PO Box 748, Bowling Green, KY 42102-0748. Tel 270-782-2787; Fax 270-782-2804; Elec Mail gallery@capitolarts.com; Internet Home Page Address: www.capitolarts.com; *Gallery Dir* Lynn Robertson; *Exec Dir* Karen Hume
Open Mon - Fri 9 AM - 4 PM; No admis fee; Estab 1981 as a community arts center; Main floor Ervin G Houchens & upper level Mezzanine Gallery
Exhibitions: Rotating exhibitions selected annually by a review panel including an All State Juried Exhibition; Youth Art (K-6th grade); Women In the Arts; Scholastic (9th-12th grade); Annual Jack E. Lunt Memorial Exhib

Activities: Classes for children; dramatic progs; summer arts camp, school day performances; concerts, tours; competitions with awards, All KY Juried Exhibition-12 awards, Best of Show $500, Honor $250, merit $100; scholarships given

M   **WESTERN KENTUCKY UNIVERSITY,** Kentucky Library & Museum, 1 Big Red Way, Bowling Green, KY 42101-5730. Tel 270-745-5083; Fax 270-745-6264; Internet Home Page Address: www.wku.edu/library/dlsc/; *Dept Head* Timothy Mullin; *Libr Coordr* Connie Mills; *Librn* Jonathan Jeffery; *Manuscript Librn* Pat Hodges; *Univ Archivist* Sue Lynn McDaniel; *Ky Spec* Nancy Baird; *Exhib Cur* Donna Parker; *Coll Cur* Sandy Staebell
Open Mon-Fri 8:30AM-4:30PM, Sat 9:30AM-4PM; Admis fee $2; Estab 1939 to preserve KY's cultural heritage; Open to the public; Average Annual Attendance: 18,000; Mem: 400, $50
Library Holdings: Audio Tapes; Book Volumes 70,000; Cassettes; Clipping Files; Framed Reproductions; Kodachrome Transparencies; Lantern Slides; Manuscripts; Maps; Memorabilia; Original Art Works; Other Holdings Broadsides; Maps; Postcards; Pamphlets; Periodical Subscriptions 1800; Photographs; Records; Reels; Slides
Special Subjects: Decorative Arts, Folk Art, Costumes
Collections: Ellis Collection of steamboat pictures; Gerard Collection of Bowling Green Photographs; McGregor Collection of rare books; Neal Collection of Utopian materials; Kentucky Genealogy Collection; Collections of and about Shakers and other religious den; Collections about state and national politics and politicians, literary figures, wars, bus, every day life and univ archives; Felts Log House
Activities: Classes for adults & children, dramatic progs; lects open to pub, gallery talks, sponsoring of competitions; sells books, prints, gifts

M   University Gallery, 1906 College Heights Blvd, Ivan Wilson Center for Fine Arts Rm 441 Bowling Green, KY 42101-1000. Tel 270-745-3944, 2592; Fax 270-745-5932; Elec Mail art@wku.edu; Internet Home Page Address: www.wku.edu/dept/academic/ahss/art.html; Internet Home Page Address: www.wku.edu/art/; *Dept Head* Kim Chalmers; *Gallery Dir* Kristina Arnold
Open Mon - Fri 8:30 AM - 4:30 PM; No admis fee; Estab 1973 for art exhibitions relating to university instruction & regional cultural needs; Average Annual Attendance: 12,000
Income: Financed by state appropriation
Exhibitions: Annual student & faculty shows

CRESTVIEW

M   **THOMAS MORE COLLEGE,** Eva G Farris Art Gallery, 333 Thomas More Pkwy, Crestview, KY 41017-3495. Tel 859-344-3420, 344-3419; Fax 859-344-3345; *Dir* Barb Rauf
Open Mon - Thurs 9AM-9PM, Fri 9AM-4:30PM, Sat 10AM-4:30PM, Sun noon-5PM; No admis fee; Estab for cultural & educational enrichment for the institution & area; Average Annual Attendance: 2,000
Special Subjects: Drawings, Graphics, Photography, Sculpture, Ceramics
Exhibitions: Full acad season of exhibitions
Activities: Lects open to public, 4 vis lectrs per year; gallery talks; schols & fels offered; book traveling exhibs

DANVILLE

M   **MCDOWELL HOUSE & APOTHECARY SHOP,** (Ephraim McDowell-Cambus-Kenneth Foundation) 125 S Second St, Danville, KY 40422. Tel 859-236-2903; Fax 859-236-2804; Elec Mail mcdhse@kih.net; Internet Home Page Address: www.mcdowellhouse.com; *Dir* Carol Johnson Senn; *Asst Dir* Alberta Moynahan; *Educ Dir* Lauren Klontz; *Admin Asst* Marlene Hale
Open Mon - Sat 10 AM - Noon & 1 - 4 PM, Sun 2 - 4 PM, cl Mon Nov 1 - Mar 1; Admis adults $7, sr citizens $5, students $1.50, children under 12 $1, group rates by phone; Estab 1935 to preserve the home of the Father of Abdominal Surgery in Danville, 1795 - 1830; Average Annual Attendance: 5,000; Mem: 600; dues $25-$1,000 & up
Income: $60,000 (financed by endowment, mem, private contribution from groups & individuals)
Special Subjects: Decorative Arts, Drawings, Glass, Architecture, Painting-American, Pottery, Portraits, Dolls, Furniture, Jewelry, Porcelain, Silver, Carpets & Rugs, Historical Material, Maps, Coins & Medals, Miniatures, Period Rooms, Embroidery, Pewter
Collections: All furnishings pre-1830; apothecary collection: late 18th & early 19th Century, 320 pieces; portraits & folk art, 1795-1830; Shelby Family: 2 fancy chairs, baby high chair; McDowell Family: cooin & English silver
Publications: Annual newsletter
Activities: Docent training; lects open to pub, 5 vis lectrs per yr; tours; sales shop sells books, prints, slides, pewter mugs, DVDs, videos of tours

DAWSON SPRINGS

M   **DAWSON SPRINGS MUSEUM AND ART CENTER,** 127 S Main St, Dawson Springs, KY 42408; PO Box 107, Dawson Springs, KY 42408-0107. Tel 270-797-3503; *Exec Dir* Sylvia Lynn Thomas; *Chmn* Shirley Menser
Open Feb - Dec Tues - Sat 1 - 4 PM, cl major holidays; No admis fee; 535 sq ft exhibit space; Average Annual Attendance: 2,200
Library Holdings: Book Volumes 70
Collections: Dawson Springs history; Japanese art
Publications: Brochure, The Dawson Springs Museum & Art Center
Activities: Book traveling exhibs

FORT KNOX

M   **CAVALRY-ARMOR FOUNDATION,** Patton Museum of Cavalry & Armor, 4554 Fayette Ave, Fort Knox, KY 40121; PO Box 1304, Fort Knox, KY 40121-1304. Tel 502-624-3812; Fax 502-624-2364; Elec Mail knox.museum@conus.army.mil; Internet Home Page Address: www.knox.army.mil/pattonmuseum; *Cur* Charles R Lemons
Open year round weekdays 9 AM - 4:30 PM, weekends 10 AM - 5:30 PM, cl New Year's Day, Easter, Thanksgiving Day, Christmas Eve & Day; No admis fee;

Estab 1975 to preserve historical materials relating to Cavalry & Armor & to make these properties available for public exhibit & research. The Museum is administered by the US Army Armor Center, Fort Knox & is one of the largest in the US Army Museum System; Galleries feature a variety of armored equipment & vehicles, weapons, art & other memorabilia which chronologically present the develop of the Armor branch from the beginning of mechanization to the present
Income: Financed through state
Collections: Military Equipment Relating to Mech Cavalry & Armor
Exhibitions: Permanent & rotating exhibitions
Activities: Retail store sells books & prints

FRANKFORT

M **KENTUCKY HISTORICAL SOCIETY,** Old State Capitol & Annex, 100 W Broadway, Frankfort, KY 40601-1931. Tel 502-564-1792; Fax 502-564-4701; Internet Home Page Address: www.history.ky.gov; *Exec Dir* Kent Whitworth; *Pub Rels & Mktg* Laura Coleman
Open Tues-Sat 10AM-6PM; Admis adults $4, youth 6-18 $2, children 5 and under free; Estab 1836 as a general history & art mus emphasizing the history, culture & decorative arts of the Commonwealth of Kentucky & its people; The Old Capitol Galleries located in the Old State House consist of two rooms totaling 2740 sq ft which are used by the Mus to display its fine arts exhibitions, painting, silver, furniture & sculpture, one temporary exhibits gallery in Old Capitol Annex; Average Annual Attendance: 250,000; Mem: 5000; dues for life $300 individual $35
Income: $7 million (financed by state appropriation)
Special Subjects: Historical Material, Period Rooms
Collections: Kentucky & American furniture coverlets, furniture, paintings, quilts, silver, textiles
Exhibitions: 3 - 4 exhibitions per year
Publications: The Register, The Bulletin, quarterly
Activities: Lects open to pub, 4 vis lectrs per yr; tours; individual paintings & original objects of art lent to qualified mus; lending collection consists of original art works, original prints; paintings; sculpture & historical artifacts; book traveling exhibs; originates traveling exhibs; mus shop sells books & reproductions
L **Library,** 100 W Broadway, Frankfort, KY 40601-1931. Tel 502-564-1792 ext 4460; Fax 502-696-3846; Elec Mail Refdesk@ky.gov; Internet Home Page Address: http://history.ky.gov
No admis fee; Reference library
Library Holdings: Book Volumes 90,000; Other Holdings Microfilm: 16,000

M **KENTUCKY NEW STATE CAPITOL,** Division of Historic Properties, 700 Louisville Rd, Frankfort, KY 40601-3304. Tel 502-564-3000, Ext 222; Tour Desk: 502-564-3449; Fax 502-564-6505; *Cur* Lou Karibo
Open Mon - Fri 8:30AM-3:30PM, Sat 10AM-2PM, Sun 1-4PM; No admis fee
Income: Funded by state appropriation
Collections: First Lady, Miniature Dolls; Oil Paintings of Chief Justices; Statues of Famous Kentuckians including Abraham Lincoln & Jefferson Davis
Publications: Brochures; exhibition catalogs
Activities: Tours; sales shop sells books, reproductions & prints

M **KENTUCKY STATE UNIVERSITY,** Jackson Hall Gallery, 400 E Main St, Art Dept Frankfort, KY 40601-2334. Tel 502-597-5995, 597-5994; Elec Mail JAlexandra@qwmail.kysu.edu; Internet Home Page Address: www.kysu.edu; *Area Head* John Bater
Open Mon - Fri 8 AM - 4:30 PM; No admis fee; Estab 1886 to present exhibition of African art; Gallery; Average Annual Attendance: 1,000
Income: Financed through small grants & university appropriations
Library Holdings: Book Volumes 500
Collections: A small coll of student & faculty work; African Art
Exhibitions: Rotating exhibits
Activities: Lects open to pub, 2 vis lectrs per yr; competitions; schols offered; book traveling exhibs 2-3 per yr

M **LIBERTY HALL HISTORIC SITE,** Liberty Hall Museum, 202 Wilkinson St, Frankfort, KY 40601-1826. Tel 502-227-2560; Fax 502-227-3348; Elec Mail director@libertyhall.org; Internet Home Page Address: www.libertyhall.org; *Cur* Kate Hesseldenz; *Exec Dir* Karla Nicholson; *Educ* Jennifer Koach; *Tour Admin* Rebecca Shipp; *Office Mgr & Bookkeeper* Judy Isaacs
Open Apr - Dec Tues - Sat 10 AM - 4:30 PM; Admis adults $4, seniors 60 and over $3, students/children 4-18 $1, children 3 & under free; Estab 1937 as an historic museum; A Georgian house built in 1796, named Historic Landmark in 1972; Average Annual Attendance: 5,000; Mem: 250; $50 ann dues
Income: Privately funded non-profit institution
Special Subjects: Decorative Arts, Architecture, Painting-American, Silver, Photography, Watercolors, Textiles, Costumes, Portraits, Furniture, Period Rooms
Collections: 18th century furniture; china; silver; portraits; original Kentucky 19th century art work; 19th century clothing & textiles; archives
Publications: Gazette newsletter
Activities: Classes for adults; dramatic progs; docent training; 6 vis lectrs per yr; concerts; guided tours; ann seminars; gallery talks; mus shop sells books, reproductions & prints
L **Library,** 202 Wilkinson St, Frankfort, KY 40601-1826. Tel 502-227-2560; Fax 502-227-3348; Elec Mail libhall@dcr.net; Internet Home Page Address: www.libertyhall.org; *Exec Dir* Sara Farley Harger; *Treas* Helen Chenery; *Educ Coordr* Megan Canfield; *VPres* Katherine M Davis
Open by appointment only; No admis fee; Estab 1965; Non-circulating library; Average Annual Attendance: 100
Income: Privately funded nonprofit institution
Library Holdings: Book Volumes 2000
Collections: Books belonging to John Brown, Kentucky's first US senator & builder of Liberty Hall
M **Orlando Brown House,** 202 Wilkinson St, Frankfort, KY 40601-1826. Tel 502-875-4952; Fax 502-227-3348; Elec Mail libhall@der.net; Internet Home Page Address: www.libertyhall.org; *Dir* Sara Harger

Open for tours Tues-Sat 10:30 AM, Noon, 1:30 & 3PM, Sun 1:30 & 3 PM; No admis fee; Estab 1956; Built in 1835 by architect Gilbert Shryock; Average Annual Attendance: 2,500
Income: Privately funded non-profit institution
Collections: Paul Sawyier paintings; original furnishings
Activities: Guided tours

GEORGETOWN

M **GEORGETOWN COLLEGE GALLERY,** 400 E. College St., Georgetown, KY 40324. Tel 502-863-8106, 863-8399; Elec Mail galleries@georgetowncollege.edu; Internet Home Page Address: www.georgetowncollege.edu/art; *Chmn* Juilee Decker; *Dir Gallery* Laura Stewart
Open Mon - Fri Noon - 4:30 PM or by appointment; No admis fee; Estab 1959 as educational gallery with various mediums & styles; Gallery has 141 linear ft wall space, portable screens; Average Annual Attendance: 1,200
Income: Financed by college & grants
Special Subjects: Graphics, Sculpture, Crafts
Collections: Contemporary graphics; contemporary painting & sculpture; crafts; artifacts
Exhibitions: Rotating exhibits; student shows
Activities: Classes for children; lects open to public; 1-2 vis lectrs per year; schols & fels offered; exten dept; individual paintings & original objects of art lent to museums

HARRODSBURG

M **OLD FORT HARROD STATE PARK MANSION MUSEUM,** S College St, Harrodsburg, KY 40330; PO Box 156, Harrodsburg, KY 40330-0156. Tel 859-734-3314; Fax 859-734-0794; Elec Mail joan.huffman@ky.gov; Internet Home Page Address: www.parks.kg.gov/findparsk/recparks/fh; *Park Supt* Joan Huffman
Open daily 9 AM - 5:00 PM; Admis $4.50 adults; $2.50 children; winter rates $2 adults, $1 children; seniors $4; Estab 1925; History museum, Union, Confederate & Lincoln memorabilia; music & gun collection; Average Annual Attendance: 30,000
Income: State agency
Special Subjects: Period Rooms
Collections: Antique China; Confederate Room; Daniel Boone & George Rogers Clark Room; furniture; gun collection; Indian artifacts; Lincoln Room; musical instruments; silver
Exhibitions: Permanent collection
Activities: Dramatic progs; concerts; tours; awards for top 10 events; one Smithsonian exhibit; sells books, original art, reproductions & prints

M **SHAKER VILLAGE OF PLEASANT HILL,** 3501 Lexington Rd, Harrodsburg, KY 40330-8846. Tel 859-734-5411, 800-734-5611; Fax 859-734-7278; Elec Mail lcurry@shakervillageky.org; Internet Home Page Address: www.shakervillageky.org; *Pres & CEO* Madge B Adams; *VChmn Bd* G Watts Humphrey
Open Apr-Oct 10AM-5PM, Nov-Mar 10AM-4:30PM; Admis April-Oct adults $14, youth $12-17 $7, child 6-11 $5, Nov-Mar adult $7, youth 12-17 $3.50, child 6-11 $2.50; Estab 1961 to restore, preserve & interpret the architecture, artifacts & culture of Shakers; 2800 acres, 34 historic buildings (1805-1855); Primary exhibition building: 40 room Centre family dwelling (1824-1834); stone, three story dwelling full of artifacts & furniture of Shakers; Shaker Life Exhib with permanent & changing exhib gallery; Average Annual Attendance: 80,000; Mem: 1200; dues family $50, annual meeting in Feb
Income: Financed by mem, endowment, inn & lodging, sales, village-generated income
Special Subjects: Architecture, Archaeology, Textiles, Costumes, Religious Art, Crafts, Folk Art, Decorative Arts, Manuscripts, Furniture, Historical Material
Collections: Shaker culture including furniture, textiles, manuscripts, cultural artifacts, architecture, period rooms & shops
Publications: Pleasant Hill & Its Shakers; The Gift of Pleasant Hill; Keepsake Art Calendar; Two Cookbooks
Activities: Classes for adults & children; dramatic progs; docent training; self-guided village tours; guided tours; lects open to pub, 15-25 vis lectrs per yr; concerts; tours; lending collection contains videos; mus shop sells reproductions, prints & slides

HIGHLAND HEIGHTS

M **NORTHERN KENTUCKY UNIVERSITY,** Galleries, Art Galleries, Northern KY Univ Highland Heights, KY; 100 Nunn Dr, Art Galleries Newport, KY 41099. Tel 859-572-5148; Fax 859-572-6501; Elec Mail knight@nku.edu; Internet Home Page Address: artscience.nku.edu/departments/art/galleries.html; *Dir Exhib & Colls* David Knight
Open Mon - Fri 9 AM - 9 PM or by appt, cl Sat, Sun & major holidays; No admis fee; Estab 1968, new location 1990, to provide an arts center for the University & community area; Main Gallery & 3rd Floor Gallery maintained, the smaller is 15 X 30; Average Annual Attendance: 20,000
Income: Financed by university & state funds
Special Subjects: Photography, Prints, Sculpture, Folk Art
Collections: Permanent collection of Red Grooms Monumental Sculpture in Metal; Donald Judd Monumental Sculpture; earth works, other outdoor sculpture, prints, painting, photographs, folk art
Exhibitions: Annual Juried Student Exhibition; state, regional & natl visiting artists
Publications: Bulletins, 4-5 per year
Activities: Lects open to pub, 3-5 vis lectrs per yr; gallery talks; tours; individual paintings & original objects of art lent to univ mems to be used in their offices only; lending coll contains 379 prints, paintings, photographs & ceramics; traveling exhibs to Univ & Col

LEXINGTON

M **THE ART MUSEUM AT THE UNIVERSITY OF KENTUCKY,** 405 Rose St & Euclid Ave, Singletary Center for the Arts Lexington, KY 40506-0241. Tel 859-257-5716; Fax 859-323-1994; Elec Mail artmuseum@uky.edu; Internet Home Page Address: www.uky.edu/ArtMuseum; *Registrar* Barbara Lovejoy; *Preparator* Michael Witzel; *Dir Educ* Deborah Borrowdale-Cox; *Dir* Kathleen Walsh-Piper; *Pub Rels & Publ Coordr* Dorothy Freeman; *Cur Coll & Exhibs* Janie Welker; *Budget Officer & Gallery Mgr* Rebecca Hudson; *Dir Grants & Community Assets* Amy Nelson Young; *Mus Security* Judith Brin; *Mktg & Mem* Lyndi Van Deursen; *Teacher Outreach Coordr* Sonja Brooks
Open Tues-Sun Noon-5PM, Fri Noon-8PM, cl Mon; No admis fee for permanent collection; fees vary for special exhibs; Estab 1976 to collect, preserve, exhibit & interpret world art for the benefit of the university community & the region; New building completed & opened Nov 1979; 20,000 sq ft of galleries & work space; Average Annual Attendance: 24,000; Mem: 450; dues $45 - $1,000
Income: $325,000 (financed by state appropriation & gifts)
Special Subjects: Afro-American Art, American Indian Art, Decorative Arts, Drawings, Etchings & Engravings, Folk Art, Landscapes, Marine Painting, Ceramics, Collages, Glass, Metalwork, Mexican Art, Flasks & Bottles, Furniture, Photography, Porcelain, Portraits, Pottery, Pre-Columbian Art, Painting-American, Prints, Silver, Textiles, Bronzes, Woodcuts, Painting-British, Painting-European, Painting-Japanese, Sculpture, Tapestries, Graphics, Latin American Art, Watercolors, African Art, Ethnology, Costumes, Religious Art, Crafts, Primitive art, Woodcarvings, Posters, Jade, Jewelry, Oriental Art, Asian Art, Painting-Dutch, Carpets & Rugs, Ivory, Coins & Medals, Baroque Art, Miniatures, Painting-Flemish, Renaissance Art, Embroidery, Medieval Art, Antiquities-Oriental, Painting-Spanish, Painting-Italian, Antiquities-Persian, Islamic Art, Antiquities-Roman, Cartoons, Painting-German, Enamels
Collections: European & American paintings, sculpture & graphics, 15th-20th Century; photographs; Pre-Columbian; African & Asian artifacts; decorative arts
Publications: Museum Newsletter; exhibitions catalogs; posters, family guide
Activities: Classes for adults & children; docent training; lects open to pub, 8 vis lectrs per yr; gallery talks; tours; book traveling exhibs 8 per yr; mus shop sells original art, reproductions, jewelry & exhibit-related merchandise
L **Lucille Little Fine Arts Library,** 160 Patterson Dr, Lexington, KY 40506-0224. Tel 859-257-2800; Fax 859-257-4662; Elec Mail falib@email.ukg.edu; Internet Home Page Address: www.libraries.uky.edu/falib; *Librn* Meg Shaw; *Dir* Gail Kennedy
Open Mon-Thur 7:30 AM-11 PM, Fri 7:30 AM-6 PM, Sat 10 AM-6 PM, Sun 10 AM-11 PM; Open to students, faculty & general public
Library Holdings: Auction Catalogs; Book Volumes 53,000; Clipping Files; DVDs; Fiche 812; Original Art Works; Pamphlets; Periodical Subscriptions 202; Reels 223; Video Tapes 24
Special Subjects: Art History, Photography, Theatre Arts, Art Education
L **Photographic Archives,** Margaret King Library Annex, King Bldg 0039 Lexington, KY 40506-0039. Tel 859-257-8611, 257-9611; Fax 859-257-1563; Elec Mail sclibraryrefdesk@lsv.uky.edu; Internet Home Page Address: www.uky.edu/libraries/scdp; *Dir Spec Coll & Archives* William J Marshall; *Photographic Archivist* Lisa R Carter
Open Mon-Fri 8AM-5PM; Estab for reference & loan purposes for general pub, staff & students; Circ Non-circulating
Library Holdings: Audio Tapes; Book Volumes 100,000; Exhibition Catalogs; Motion Pictures; Other Holdings Manuscript materials; Periodical Subscriptions 60
Collections: Over 350,000 photographs documenting the history of photography as well as Kentucky, Appalachia & surrounding areas

ASSOCIATION OF MEDICAL ILLUSTRATORS
For further information, see National and Regional Organization

M **BODLEY-BULLOCK HOUSE MUSEUM,** 200 Market St, Lexington, KY 40507-1030. Tel 859-259-1266; Elec Mail nr_travel@nps.gov; Internet Home Page Address: www.cr.nps.gov/nr/travel/lexington/bod.htm
Open by appt year-round; cl holidays; Mus housed in historic mansion built in 1814 for Lexington Mayor Thomas Pindell. House was later sold to General Thomas Bodley, a veteran of the War of 1812. House served as headquarters for both Union & Confederate forces during Civil War. House was purchased in 1912 by Dr Waller Bullock, an accomplished sculptor
Special Subjects: Historical Material, Furniture
Activities: Tours by appt

M **HEADLEY-WHITNEY MUSEUM,** 4435 Old Frankfort Pike, Lexington, KY 40510-9657. Tel 859-255-6653; Fax 859-255-8375; Elec Mail hwmuseum@headley-Whitney.org; Internet Home Page Address: www.headley-whitney.org; WATS 800-310-5085; *Dir & Cur* Amy Gundrum Greene; *Cur Educ* Lauren Hunter-Smith
Open Mar - Dec Wed - Fri 10 AM - 5 PM, Sat & Sun Noon - 5 PM, cl Jan, Feb & major holidays; Admis adults $10, senior & students $7, children 5 & under free, discounts for AAM, AAA, KAM & SEMC members & Univ KY employees; Estab 1968 in central Kentucky for the care collection, preservation & interpretation of the decorative & fine arts. Five principal galleries are maintained which include the work of the founder, jewelry designer, George W Headley III & temporary exhibits on the decorative & fine arts; Average Annual Attendance: 17,950; Mem: 600; dues individual $55, family $85, benefactor $400, patron $150, dir circle $2,500
Income: Financed by admis, mem, benefits, grants, contributions, trust, affiliated with Smithsonian
Library Holdings: Auction Catalogs; Original Art Works; Original Documents; Periodical Subscriptions
Special Subjects: Glass, Gold, Portraits, Sculpture, Bronzes, Textiles, Ceramics, Decorative Arts, Jade, Jewelry, Porcelain, Oriental Art, Asian Art, Silver, Ivory, Miniatures
Collections: Bibelots, jewelry, gemstones, Kentucky Silver
Exhibitions: Quarterly exhibitions
Publications: The Jewel newsletters quarterly, for mem
Activities: Classes for adults & children; outreach progs; lects open to pub, concerts; gallery talks; tours; international bibelot contest; book traveling exhibs; mus shop sells books, prints, jewelry, rocks gems, loose jewels

A **LEXINGTON ART LEAGUE, INC,** 209 Castlewood Dr, Loudoun House Lexington, KY 40505-3629. Tel 859-254-7024, 800-914-7990; Fax 859-254-7214; Elec Mail info@lexingtonartleague.org; Internet Home Page Address: www.lexingtonartleague.org; *Exec Dir* Allison Kaiser; *Mktg Dir* Kandace Tatum; *Develop Dir* Stephanie Pevec; *Program Coordr* Julia Curiel
Open Tues - Sun 1 - 4 PM; No admis fee; Estab 1957, to encourage an active interest in the visual arts among its members & community as a whole; Three visual art galleries; Project Space has installation & work in new media; Average Annual Attendance: 200,000; Mem: 700; open to all interested in visual arts; dues $45; annual meeting in May
Income: Financed by mem, art fairs, donations, grants
Library Holdings: Book Volumes; Periodical Subscriptions
Exhibitions: Changing monthly exhibitions; member, group, one person exhibitions
Publications: Annual Membership Book; email newsletter
Activities: Classes for adults; lects open to pub, 4 vis lectrs per yr; gallery talks; competitions; juried awards for most exhibits; scholarships offered; originate traveling exhibs

M **LIVING ARTS & SCIENCE CENTER, INC,** 362 N Martin Luther King Blvd, Lexington, KY 40508-1889. Tel 859-252-5222; Fax 859-255-7448; Elec Mail info@lasclex.org; Internet Home Page Address: www.lasclex.org; *Exec Dir* Heather Lyons; *Educational Outreach Coordr* Katherine Bullock; *Art Educ Coordr* Molly Wilson
Open Jun-Aug Mon-Fri 8AM-5:30PM, Sept-May Mon-Fri 8:30AM-5PM, Sat 10AM-2PM; No admis fee; Estab 1968 to provide enrichment opportunities in the arts & sciences; Gallery features 6-8 exhibits per yr of regional art; Average Annual Attendance: 25,000; Mem: 400; dues $30-500; annual meetings
Income: Financed by grants, fundraising events, memberships, tuition & sponsorships
Exhibitions: Rotating exhibitions; Two science exhib per year
Publications: Exhibition catalogs
Activities: Classes for adults & children; field trips for over 5500 school children; lect open to public; tours; children's art, artist-in-residence; sponsoring of competitions; class scholarships offered; programs for at-risk & underserved; book traveling exhibitions once per year; sales shop sells original art, reproductions, prints & notecards

M **TRANSYLVANIA UNIVERSITY,** Morlan Gallery, 300 N Broadway, Mitchell Fine Arts Ctr Lexington, KY 40508-1797. Tel 859-233-8142; Fax 859-233-8797; Elec Mail afisher@mail.transy.edu; Internet Home Page Address: transy.edu/morlan; *Dir* Andrea Fischer
Open Mon - Fri Noon - 5 PM; No admis fee; Estab 1978 to exhibit contemporary art; Gallery is housed in Mitchell Fine Arts Building on Transylvania University's campus located in Lexington, KY; Average Annual Attendance: 3,000
Income: Financed by endowment
Special Subjects: Portraits, Historical Material
Collections: 19th century natural history works; 19th century portraits; decorative arts
Exhibitions: Temporary exhibitions, primarily contemporary works, various media
Activities: Lects open to pub, 2-4 vis lectrs per yr; concerts; gallery talks; tours; competitions; originate traveling exhibs

L **UNIVERSITY OF KENTUCKY,** Hunter M Adams Architecture Library, 200 Pence Hall, Lexington, KY 40506-0001. Tel 859-257-1533; Fax 859-257-4305; Elec Mail fharders@pop.uky.edu; Internet Home Page Address: www.ukyedu/library; *Library Technician* Lalana Powell; *Librn* Faith Harders
Open Mon - Thurs 8 AM - 10 PM, Fri 8 AM - 6 PM, Sun 5PM-9PM, summer Mon - Fri 8 AM - 4:30 PM; Estab 1963
Library Holdings: Audio Tapes; Book Volumes 34,000; Cassettes; Fiche 1903; Other Holdings Architectural drawing; Periodical Subscriptions 91; Reels 606; Sculpture
Special Subjects: Interior Design, Furniture, Architecture

LOUISVILLE

M **21C MUSEUM,** 700 W Main St, Louisville, KY 40202-2634. Tel 502-217-6300; Fax 502-217-6347; *Dir* William Morrow
Call for hours
Collections: works by regional, national & international artists

M **CONRAD-CALDWELL HOUSE MUSEUM,** 1402 St James Ct, Louisville, KY 40208. Tel 502-636-5023; Fax 502-636-1264; Elec Mail info@conradcaldwell.org; Internet Home Page Address: www.conradcaldwell.org
Open Sun & Wed - Fri 12 - 4 PM, Sat 10 AM - 4 PM; also by appt; Admis adults $5, seniors $4, students $3; Estab as mus in 1987; purchased & operated by St James Ct Historic Foundation; With its woodwork, stained glass, gargoyles & arches, mansion defines Richardsonian-Romanesque architecture. Mansion was built for Theophilus Conrad, who made his fortune in the tanning bus. House was purchased by the Caldwell family in 1905 and it later served as the Rose Anna Hughes Presbyterian Retirement Home
Special Subjects: Historical Material, Furniture, Period Rooms
Activities: Tours; facilities can be rented for special events

A **EMBROIDERERS GUILD OF AMERICA,** Margaret Parshall Gallery, 1355 Bardstown Rd, #157 Louisville, KY 40204-1355. Tel 502-589-6956; Fax 502-584-7900; Elec Mail egahq@egausa.org; Internet Home Page Address: www.egausa.org; *Exec Dir* Anita Streeter; *Mem Coordr* Tonya Parks; *Accnt* Paula Kirk; *Gallery Cur & Educ Dir* Anita Skeeter; *Receptionist* Jennifer Oladipe
Open Mon -Fri 9 AM - 4:30 PM; No admis fee; Estab 1958; Permanent & special exhibs of a wide range of embroidery; Mem: 16,000; dues $40; annual meeting in fall; interest in embroidery & needle arts
Income: Financed by endowment & mem
Library Holdings: Auction Catalogs; Book Volumes; Kodachrome Transparencies; Manuscripts; Memorabilia; Original Art Works; Original Documents; Slides; Video Tapes

Special Subjects: Costumes, Embroidery, Textiles, American Western Art, Decorative Arts, American Indian Art, Crafts, Dolls
Collections: 900 Embroidery Pieces
Exhibitions: Through the Needle's Eye; varied throughout the yr
Publications: Needle Arts Magazine
Activities: Classes for adults & children; lects for mems only; originates traveling exhibs to mus & galleries; mus shop

L **Dorothy Babcock Memorial Library,** 1355 Bardstown Rd, Ste 157 Louisville, KY 40204-1353. Tel 502-589-6956; Fax 502-584-7900; *Office Mgr* Bonnie Key
Lending & reference library for members only
Library Holdings: Slides; Video Tapes
Special Subjects: Embroidery, Tapestries, Textiles

A **THE FILSON HISTORICAL SOCIETY,** (The Filson Club) 1310 S Third St, Louisville, KY 40208. Tel 502-635-5083; Fax 502-635-5086; Elec Mail filson@filsonhistorical.org; Internet Home Page Address: www.filsonhistorical.org; *Dir* Dr Mark V Wetherington; *Assoc Cur Art, Photos & Prints* Robin Wallace; *Cur Spec Coll* Jim Holmberg; *Head Librn* Judith Partington
Open Mon - Fri 9 AM - 5 PM, first Sat of month 9AM-4PM, cl national holidays; Research fee for non-mem $10; Estab 1884 to collect, preserve & publish historical material, especially pertaining to Kentucky & the upper South; Changing exhibits; Average Annual Attendance: 20,000; Mem: 4,500; dues $50 & up
Income: Financed by mem dues & private funds
Purchases: All historical materials, including appropriate paintings
Library Holdings: Book Volumes; Clipping Files; DVDs; Fiche; Manuscripts; Maps; Motion Pictures; Original Art Works; Original Documents; Pamphlets; Periodical Subscriptions; Photographs; Prints; Sculpture; Video Tapes
Collections: Books & manuscripts; collection of portraits of Kentuckians; artifacts, textiles, silver, photographs, maps, prints; artist research colls
Publications: Ohio Valley History; The Filson History Quarterly 75vol, The Filson News Gallery
Activities: Classes for adults & children; dramatic progs; family history; reading & discussion groups; dramatic progs for children; tours of historic sites; lects; public & acad conferences; lects open to pub, 45-50 vis lectrs per yr; gallery talks; concerts; tours; Filson Historical Society High School Artistry Essay Contest; schols & fellowships offered; fellowships & internships on a competitive basis; individual paintings & original objects of art lent to accredited mus & historical societies in KY & OH Valley region; mus shop sells books, magazines, reproductions, prints

L **Reference & Research Library,** 1310 S Third St, Louisville, KY 40208. Tel 502-635-5083; Fax 502-635-5086; Elec Mail filson@filsonclub.org; Internet Home Page Address: www.filsonclub.org; *Librn* Judith Partington
Open Mon - Fri 9 AM - 5 PM, 1st Sat of every month 9AM-4PM; Estab 1884 to collect, preserve & publish Kentucky historical material & assoc material
Income: Financed by endowments, mem & gifts
Library Holdings: Book Volumes 55,000; Clipping Files; Manuscripts; Memorabilia; Original Art Works; Pamphlets; Photographs; Prints; Reels; Sculpture
Collections: Civil War Collection
Exhibitions: Portraits of Kentuckians
Publications: Filson Club History Quarterly; Series & Series 2 publication (40 vols)
Activities: Lects open to pub 6-10 per yr; tours; individual paintings & original objects of art lent to other organizations for special exhibits; mus shop sells books, reproductions & prints

M **KENTUCKY DERBY MUSEUM,** 704 Central Ave Gate 1, Louisville, KY 40201-1212. Tel 502-637-1111; Fax 502-636-5855; Elec Mail info@derbymuseum.org; Internet Home Page Address: www.derbymuseum.org; *Cur Exhib* Brenda Kiefer; *Dir Finance* Dennis Loomer; *Dir Communs* Wendy Treinen; *Exec Dir* Lynn Ashton
Open daily 9AM-5PM, Sun 11AM-5PM; Admis adults $13, sr citizen $11, children 5-11 $5, children under 5 free; Estab 1985 to expand appreciation for Kentucky Derby & Thoroughbred racing; 2 floors of interactive exhibs designed to share the fun of the Kentucky Derby experience; Average Annual Attendance: 200,000; Mem: 1100; dues $25-$2000
Income: $3,500,000 (financed by Earned revenues)
Special Subjects: Glass, Flasks & Bottles, Sculpture, Painting-American, Photography, Bronzes, Costumes, Manuscripts
Collections: Archives from industry; Kentucky Derby memorabilia; 19th & 20th century Equine Art; Thoroughbred Racing Industry Collection (artifacts)
Exhibitions: Permanent exhibits about Derby & Thoroughbred Racing Industry; Barbaro: Heart of a Winner
Publications: Inside Track newsletter, quarterly
Activities: Classes for children; lects for mem only, 4 vis lectrs per yr; gallery talks; competitions with prizes; individual paintings lent to qualified mus; originate traveling exhibs; originate traveling exhibs statewide; mus shop sells books, original art, prints

M **KENTUCKY MUSEUM OF ART AND CRAFT,** (Kentucky Art & Craft Gallery) 715 W Main St, Louisville, KY 40202-2633. Tel 502-589-0102; Fax 502-589-0154; Elec Mail admin@kentuckyarts.org; Internet Home Page Address: www.kmacmuseum.org; *Dir & Chief Cur* Aldy Milliken; *Develop Dir* Angela Hagan; *Assoc Cur* Joey Yates; *Communs Dir* Julie Gross; *Office Coordr* Ann Drury; *Dir Educ* Dane Waters; *Asst Dir Educ* Julie Yoder; *Mem & Commun Assoc* Amanda Horton; *Shop Sales Mgr* Shelley Hulsey
Open Tues - Sat 10 AM - 5 PM, Sun 11 AM - 5 PM; Admis adults $6, seniors & military $5, children (18 & under) free; Estab 1981 to advance & perpetuate Kentucky's art & craft heritage; Works by over 400 Kentucky makers & artisians displayed & sold in restored 19th century building; Average Annual Attendance: 65,000; Mem: 427; dues $500, $200, $75 & $40
Income: Financed by mem dues, state appropriation, corporations, foundations & fund-raising events
Library Holdings: Book Volumes; CD-ROMs; Exhibition Catalogs; Original Art Works; Periodical Subscriptions; Photographs; Slides
Special Subjects: Afro-American Art, Decorative Arts, Drawings, Folk Art, Collages, Glass, Portraits, Pottery, Painting-American, Prints, Textiles, Sculpture, Tapestries, Graphics, Photography, Watercolors, Southwestern Art, Costumes, Ceramics, Crafts, Primitive art, Woodcarvings, Furniture, Jewelry, Oriental Art, Silver, Juvenile Art, Mosaics
Collections: Small collection of contemporary American folk art
Exhibitions: Rotating exhibits
Publications: Matthew Ronay The Third Attention, forward by Aldy Milliken & Ying Kit Chan & John Begley; Essays by Matthew Drutt & John R Hale
Activities: Annual: 8-10 exhibs; avg 100 field trips; 3-4 vis lects; 37 maker workshops; 1 winter plus 9 summer camps; 12 musical performances; 3 special event fundraisers; 13 traveling mobile museum suitcases; 2 artist in residence; community events; group tours; extension prog to surrounding area public schools; 2 book traveling exhibs per yr; kmac shop sells original art & functional objects

A **LOUISVILLE VISUAL ART ASSOCIATION,** 3005 River Rd, Water Tower Louisville, KY 40207-1012. Tel 502-896-2146; Fax 502-896-2148; Elec Mail keith@louisvillevisualart.org; Internet Home Page Address: www.louisvillevisualart.org; *Artistic Dir* Kay Grubola; *Exec Dir* Shannon Westerman
Open Mon - Fri 9 AM - 5 PM, Sat 9 AM - 3 PM, Sun Noon - 4 PM; No admis fee; Estab 1909 to provide programs for local & regional artists, adults & children; slide registry; Located at designated national historic landmark building, the water tower at Louisville's original water pumping station 1; Gallery area: Price Gallery 125-150 running ft, Brown Hall 125-150 running ft, 3500 sq ft total; Average Annual Attendance: 200,000; Mem: 5000; dues $25 and up; monthly meeting of Board of Dir
Income: $750,000 (financed by endowment, mem, state appropriation, Louisville Fund for the Arts, grants, rental of space & annual fundraising events)
Exhibitions: Group Invitational; regional artist emphasis; regional competitions
Publications: Exhibit catalogs
Activities: Classes & workshops for adults & children; docent training; lects open to pub, 50 vis lectrs per yr; concerts; gallery talks; tours; competitions with awards; scholarships offered; exten dept serves Jefferson, Bullitt, Oldham & Shelby Counties in Kentucky & Clark, Floyd & Harrison Counties in Indiana; individual paintings & original objects of art lent to prospective buyers; book traveling exhibs 1-2 per yr; originate traveling exhibs; sales shop sells magazines, original art, prints, jewelry, pottery, glass & hand crafted items

M **RIVERSIDE, THE FARNSLEY-MOREMEN LANDING,** 7410 Moorman Rd, Louisville, KY 40272-4572. Tel 502-935-6809; Fax 502-935-6821; Internet Home Page Address: www.riverside-landing.org; *CEO & Dir* Patti Linn; *Vol Chmn* Reba Doutrick; *Mus Shop Mgr* Heather French
Open Tues - Sat 10 AM - 4:30 PM, Sun 1 - 4:30 PM; cl New Year's Day, Thanksgiving Day & the day after & Christmas Day; Admis family $15, adults $6, seniors $5, students & children 6-12 $3, mems no admis fee; Estab 1993; 300-acre historic farm site with focus on the restored 1837 Farnsley-Moremen House. The museum's mission is to promote, preserve, restore & interpret historic farm life on the Ohio River. 200-capacity auditorium; 3000 sq ft exhib space; 3rd congressional dist; FT Paid 4, PT Paid 3, PT vols 60+; Average Annual Attendance: 25,341; Mem: dues Family $35, Indiv $20
Collections: coll of printed materials on local history, reproduction toys & games, and other site-specific publs; structures; furnishings; archaeological specimens; decorative arts; tools & equipment for materials
Publications: Riverside Review, quarterly newsletter
Activities: Formal educ progs for adults & children; docent prog; concerts; lects; guided tours; Ice Cream Social; Riverside Heritage Festival; Plant & Herb Sale; A Riverside Christmas; research in historic interiors & decorative arts for the 1840s - 1880s in Louisville, KY; mus related items for sale

M **SOUTHERN BAPTIST THEOLOGICAL SEMINARY,** Joseph A Callaway Archaeological Museum, 2825 Lexington Rd, Louisville, KY 40280-0001. Tel 502-897-4011, 4132; Fax 502-897-4880; Elec Mail jdrinkard@sbts.edu; Internet Home Page Address: www.sbts.edu; *Librn* Bruce Keisling
Open Mon - Fri 8 AM - 4:30 PM; No admis fee; Estab 1961
Income: Financed by the seminary & donations
Special Subjects: Sculpture, Archaeology, Textiles, Religious Art, Pottery, Antiquities-Byzantine, Antiquities-Egyptian, Antiquities-Assyrian
Collections: Biblical archeology; coptic religious materials; glass; materials excavated from Jericho, AI & Jerusalem; mummy; numismatics; ostraca; pottery; sculpture; textiles; copy of the Rosetta Stone
Exhibitions: Rotating exhibits
Activities: Guided tours; films

M **THE SPEED ART MUSEUM,** 2035 S Third St, Louisville, KY 40208-1812. Tel 502-634-2700; Fax 502-636-2899; Elec Mail info@speedmuseum.org; Internet Home Page Address: www.speedmuseum.org; *Dir* Chislain d'Humieres; *CFO* David Knopf; *Registrar* Charles Pittenger; *COO* Lisa Betson Resnik; *Dir Coll & Exhibs* Scott Erbes
Museum is currently undergoing a multi-phase expansion & closed to the public until early 2016. Local Speed the museum's satellite space is open Fri noon - 8 AM, Sat 11 AM - 4 PM; Admis fee $10, ticket fee for admis to special progs & exhibs; parking fees apply; Estab 1925, opened 1927 for the collection & exhibition of works of art of all periods & cultures, supported by a full special exhibition program & educational activities; Galleries are arranged to present painting, sculpture & decorative arts of all periods & cultures; special facilities for prints & drawings; Average Annual Attendance: 180,000; Mem: 4,000; dues supporter $250, reciprocal $130, family/ dual $70, individual $50
Income: Financed by endowments, donations, grants, ticket sales & memberships
Special Subjects: Afro-American Art, American Indian Art, Decorative Arts, Drawings, Folk Art, Landscapes, Marine Painting, Ceramics, Collages, Glass, Mexican Art, Flasks & Bottles, Gold, Photography, Painting-American, Silver, Textiles, Woodcuts, Manuscripts, Maps, Painting-British, Painting-European, Painting-French, Sculpture, Tapestries, Architecture, Prints, Watercolors, American Western Art, Bronzes, African Art, Costumes, Religious Art, Crafts, Pottery, Woodcarvings, Etchings & Engravings, Painting-Japanese, Portraits, Posters, Painting-Canadian, Dolls, Furniture, Jade, Jewelry, Porcelain, Asian Art, Metalwork, Painting-Dutch, Carpets & Rugs, Ivory, Coins & Medals, Baroque Art, Miniatures, Painting-Flemish, Painting-Polish, Renaissance Art, Period Rooms,

Embroidery, Laces, Medieval Art, Painting-Spanish, Painting-Italian, Antiquities-Persian, Antiquities-Egyptian, Antiquities-Greek, Antiquities-Roman, Mosaics, Cartoons, Stained Glass, Painting-Australian, Painting-German, Pewter, Leather, Antiquities-Etruscan, Painting-Russian, Painting-Israeli, Enamels, Painting-Scandinavian
Collections: Comprehensive permanent coll; Coll spans 6,000 yrs of human creativity
Publications: The Speed Art Museum: Highlights from the Collection; newsletter, bi-annually; Bulletin, occasional
Activities: Classes for children, ArtSparks; docent training; summer camps; teacher progs; lects open to pub, 12 vis lectrs per yr; concerts; gallery talks; tours; Art Explorer Prog; Youth Apprentice Prog; book traveling exhibs three times per yr; mus shop sells books & museum-related items

L **Art Reference Library,** 2035 S Third St, Louisville, KY 40208. Tel 502-634-2710; Fax 502-636-2899; Elec Mail library@speedmuseum.org; Internet Home Page Address: www.speedmuseum.org; *Librn* Allison Gillette
Open Wed, Thurs, Sat 10 AM - 5 PM, Fri 10 AM - 9 PM, Sun noon - 5 PM; Library (by appointment only), cl Mon & Tues; Admis fee adults $10, seniors (65+) $8, children 3-17 $5, children under 3 free; 1927; Circ Non-circulating library; Collection is extensive, spanning 6000 yrs
Income: Financed by general budget
Library Holdings: Auction Catalogs; Book Volumes 2500; Clipping Files; Exhibition Catalogs; Manuscripts; Other Holdings Vertical files 23; Pamphlets; Periodical Subscriptions 13
Special Subjects: Art History, Constructions, Folk Art, Decorative Arts, Photography, Drawings, Etchings & Engravings, Painting-American, Painting-British, Painting-Dutch, Painting-Flemish, Painting-French, Painting-German, Painting-Italian, Prints, Sculpture, Painting-European, Historical Material, History of Art & Archaeology, Watercolors, Ceramics, Conceptual Art, Crafts, Latin American Art, Bronzes, Asian Art, American Indian Art, Porcelain, Furniture, Costume Design & Constr, Glass, Aesthetics, Afro-American Art, Antiquities-Oriental, Oriental Art, Pottery, Silver, Silversmithing, Tapestries, Textiles, Woodcuts, Landscapes, Antiquities-Egyptian, Antiquities-Greek, Antiquities-Roman, Painting-Canadian, Architecture
Collections: Frederick Weygold's Indian Collection; African Art, Ancient Art, Native American Art, American Art, European Art, Contemporary Art
Publications: Index to J B Speed Art Museum bulletins, index to dealers catalogs; J B Speed Handbook
Activities: Classes for adults & children; docent training; Lects open to pub; lects for members only; concerts; gallery talks; tours; mus shop sells books, prints

M **UNIVERSITY OF LOUISVILLE,** Hite Art Institute, 104 Schneider Hall, Belknap Campus Louisville, KY 40292-0001. Tel 502-852-6794; Fax 502-852-6791; Internet Home Page Address: www.art.louisville.edu; *Chmn* James Grubola; *Gallery Dir* John Begley; *Studio Program Head* Ying Kit Chan; *Art History Program Head* Linda Gigante; *Art Librn* Gail Gilbert
Open Mon - Fri 8:30 AM - 4:30 PM, cl Sat 10 AM - 2 PM, Sun 1 - 6 PM; No admis fee; Estab 1935 for educ & enrichment; There are three galleries: Morris Belknap Gallery, Dario Covi Gallery, Gallery X; Average Annual Attendance: 35,000
Income: Financed by endowment & state appropriation
Special Subjects: Drawings, Prints
Collections: Teaching collection
Publications: Exhibition catalogs
Activities: Lects open to public, 9-12 vis lectrs per yr; gallery talks; tours; Winthrop Allen Memorial Prize for creative art; scholarships offered; original objects of art lent to other departments on campus & to other exhibitions; lending collection includes Kentucky regional art, prints & drawings, alumni; book traveling exhibs

L **Margaret M Bridwell Art Library,** Schneider Hall, Louisville, KY 40292-0001. Tel 502-852-6741; Elec Mail gail.gilbert@louisville.edu; Internet Home Page Address: louisville.edu/library/art; *Dir Art Library* Gail R Gilbert; *Asst to Librn* Kathleen A Moore
Open Mon - Thurs 8 AM - 9 PM, Fri 8 AM - 5 PM, Sat 10 AM - 3 PM, Sun 1 - 8 PM, summer Mon-Fri 8AM-5PM, Sat 10AM-1PM; Estab 1956 to support the programs of the art department; For reference only
Income: Financed by endowment & state appropriation
Purchases: $125,000
Library Holdings: Book Volumes 93,000; CD-ROMs 323; Clipping Files; DVDs 606; Exhibition Catalogs; Fiche 2,500; Manuscripts; Memorabilia; Pamphlets; Periodical Subscriptions 310; Video Tapes 506
Special Subjects: Art History, Decorative Arts, Photography, Drawings, Etchings & Engravings, Graphic Design, Painting-American, Painting-British, Painting-Flemish, Painting-French, Painting-German, Painting-Italian, Painting-Spanish, Posters, Prints, Sculpture, Painting-European, History of Art & Archaeology, Watercolors, Archaeology, Printmaking, Interior Design, Art Education, Glass, Afro-American Art, Pottery, Textiles, Woodcuts, Antiquities-Byzantine, Antiquities-Etruscan, Antiquities-Greek, Antiquities-Roman, Architecture
Collections: Original Christmas cards; Ainslie Hewett bookplate coll; artist's books; Morton Woodblock collection; Brecher Tobacco & chewing gum card collection

L **Ekstrom Library Photographic Archives,** 2301 S 3rd St, Ekstrom Library Louisville, KY 40292-0001. Tel 502-852-6752; Fax 502-852-8734; Elec Mail special.collections@louisville.edu; *Imaging Mgr* Bill Carner
Open Mon - Fri 9 AM - 5 PM; No admis fee; Estab 1967 to collect, preserve, organize photographs & related materials; primary emphasis on documentary photography; Circ Restricted circ; Four exhibits per year
Income: Financed through the University & revenue
Library Holdings: Book Volumes 1000; Clipping Files; Exhibition Catalogs; Photographs 1,200,000; Reels 200
Collections: Antique Media & Equipment; Lou Block Collection; Will Bowers Collection; Bradley Studio--Georgetown; Theodore M Brown--Robert J Doherty Collection; Caldwell Tank Co Collection; Caulfield & Shook, Inc; Lin Caulfield Collection; Cooper Collection; Flexner Slide Collection; Erotic Photography; Fine Print Collection; Arthur Y Ford Albums; Forensic Photographic Collection; Vida Hunt Francis Collection; K & IT Railroad Collections; Mary D Hill Collections; Griswold Collections; Joseph Krementz Collection; Kentucky Mountain Schools

Collection; The Macauley Theater Collection; Manvell Collection of Film Stills; Boyd Martin Collection; Kate Matthews Collection; J C Rieger Collections; Roy Emerson Stryker Collections; A W Terhune Collection; Joseph & Joseph Collection; Andre Jeneut Collection
Publications: Exhibition catalogues; collections brochures; guide to spec collections
Activities: Lects open to public, vis lectrs per yr varies; gallery talks; educational groups; individual prints lent to museums & galleries; book traveling exhibs; originates traveling exhibs; sales shop sells reproductions, prints, slides & postcards, reference and research services

L **Visual Resources Center,** Lutz Hall, Louisville, KY 40292-0001. Tel 502-852-5917; Elec Mail alex@louisville.edu; Internet Home Page Address: www.louisville.edu; *Asst Cur* Theresa Berbet
Open Mon - Fri 8:30 AM - 4:30 PM; Estab 1930s to provide comprehensive collection of slides for use in the university instructional program; 300,000 catalogued slides primarily illustrating history of western art for faculty & students of fine arts; Circ restricted
Library Holdings: Clipping Files; Kodachrome Transparencies; Other Holdings Computer Digital Image Bank; Slides 350,000
Special Subjects: Photography, Painting-American, Pottery, Architecture
Collections: American Studies; Calligraphy; Manuscript of Medieval Life

MAYSVILLE

M **MAYSVILLE,** (Mason County Museum) Kentucky Gateway Museum Center, 215 Sutton St, Maysville, KY 41056-1109. Tel 606-564-5865; Fax 606-564-4372; Elec Mail communications@kygmc.org; Internet Home Page Address: www.kygmc.org; *Pres* Dee Werline; *Dir* Dawn C Browning; *Librn* Myra Hardy; *Bus Mgr* Gayle H McKay; *Dir Pub Rels* Lynn David; *Educ Coordr* Dr James Shires; *Cur Books & Art* Sue Ellen Grannis; *VPres* Kent Kalb; *Accounting* Joyce Weigott; *Libr Asst* Cay Chamness; *Receptionist* Marion Browning; *Reference Tech* Paula Ruble; *Cur Miniatures* Kaye Browning
Open Tues - Fri 10 AM - 5 PM, Sat 10 AM - 4 PM, Sun 1-4PM; Admis adults $10, children $2; Estab 1878 to maintain historical records & artifacts for area; Average Annual Attendance: 3,000; Mem: 450; dues $25-$50
Income: $150,000 (financed by endowment and members)
Special Subjects: Anthropology, Archaeology, Decorative Arts, Drawings, Etchings & Engravings, Folk Art, Architecture, Ceramics, Glass, Flasks & Bottles, Prints, Manuscripts, Painting-American, Photography, Sculpture, Watercolors, Textiles, Costumes, Pottery, Woodcarvings, Landscapes, Portraits, Posters, Dolls, Furniture, Jewelry, Silver, Marine Painting, Historical Material, Maps, Coins & Medals, Miniatures, Dioramas, Embroidery, Laces, Reproductions
Collections: Paintings & maps related to area; genealogical library; KSB Miniatures Collection
Publications: Quarterly Newsletter
Activities: Classes for children; lects open to pub, 5 vis lectrs per yr; gallery talks; tours; individual paintings & original objects of art lent to different museums; book traveling exhibs, 2-4 per yr; mus shop sells books, reproductions, prints, postcards, souvenirs, miniatures, toys, jewelry

MOREHEAD

M **MOREHEAD STATE UNIVERSITY,** Kentucky Folk Art Center, 102 W First St, Morehead, KY 40351. Tel 606-783-2204; Fax 606-783-5034; Elec Mail m.collinswor@morehead-st.edu; Internet Home Page Address: www.kyfolkart.org; *Cur* Adrian Swain; *Dir* Matt Collinsworth
Open Mon - Sat 9 AM - 5 PM, Sun 1 - 5 PM; Admis adults $3, seniors $2; Estab 1985 to promote contemporary folk art; Includes two galleries: Lovena & William Richardson Gallery which houses Collection & the Garland & Minnie Adkins Gallery housing rotating exhibits; Average Annual Attendance: 10,000; Mem: 400; dues $15-$5000; annual meeting in Sept
Income: $335,000 (financed by mem, state appropriations, grants & earnings
Purchases: $5000 (African-American, Kentucky)
Special Subjects: Painting-American, Sculpture, Watercolors, Textiles, Folk Art, Pottery, Primitive art, Woodcarvings, Afro-American Art
Collections: Kentucky Folk Art; Kentucky Self-Taught Art
Exhibitions: Kentucky Folk Art from permanent collection; Kentucky Quilts: Roots & Wings
Publications: KFAC Newsletter, quarterly
Activities: Classes for adults & children; dramatic progs; docent training; lects open to pub; 10 vis lectrs per yr; individual paintings & original objects of art lent; lending collection contains 800 items; book traveling exhibs 2 per yr; originate traveling exhibs; sales shop sells books, magazines, original art, prints

M **MOREHEAD STATE UNIVERSITY,** Claypool-Young Art Gallery, Claypool Young Bldg, 150 University Blvd Morehead, KY 40351-1684. Tel 606-783-5446; Fax 606-783-5048; Elec Mail j.reis@moreheadstate.edu; Internet Home Page Address: www.moreheadstate.edu; *Chmn* Robert Franzini; *Dir* Jennifer Reis
Open Mon - Fri 8 AM - 4 PM, by appointment; No admis fee; Estab 1969 as univ art gallery; An exhibition gallery is maintained for traveling exhibitions, faculty & student work. The Claypool-Young Art Gallery is tri-level with 2344 sq ft of exhibition space; Average Annual Attendance: 8,000
Income: Financed by appropriation
Special Subjects: Prints
Collections: Permanent coll: prints by major contemporary figures; several works added each year through purchase or bequest. Additions to lending coll include: The Maria Rilke Suite of lithographs by Ben Shahn consisting of 23 pieces; the Laus Pictorum Suite by Leonard Baskin, consisting of 14 pieces; & three lithographs by Thomas Hart Benton: Jesse James, Frankie & Johnny, & Huck Finn
Exhibitions: A large number of group & thematic exhibits; 8 exhibits per yr, student shows & regional shows
Activities: Educ dept; classes for adults & children; lects open to public; 6-10 vis lectrs per yr; concert; gallery talks; tours; competitions; Bluegrass Biennial: Kentucky Exhib awards

MORGANFIELD

M   CAMP BRECKINRIDGE MUSEUM & ARTS CENTER, 1116 N Village Rd.
Morganfield, KY 42437; PO Box 60, Morganfield, KY 43437-0060.
Open Tues - Fri 10 AM - 3 PM, Sat 10 AM - 4 PM, Sun 1 PM - 4 PM
Collections: Military history; murals; photographs; paintings

MURRAY

M   MURRAY STATE UNIVERSITY, Art Galleries, 604 Fine Arts Bldg, Corner of
15th & Olive Sts Murray, KY 42071-3342. Tel 270-762-3052; Fax 270-762-3920;
Elec Mail becky.atkinson@murraystate.edu;
Open Mon - Fri 8 AM - 5 PM, Sat & Sun 1 - 4 PM, cl University holidays; No
admis fee; Estab 1971; Gallery houses the permanent art collection of the
University; the Main Gallery is located on the sixth floor & its dimensions are 100
x 40 ft; the Upper Level is divided into three small galleries that may be used as
one or three; the Curris Center Art Gallery is also part of the offerings; Average
Annual Attendance: 12,000
Income: Financed by state appropriation and grants
Special Subjects: Drawings, Painting-American, Photography, Prints, Sculpture,
Textiles, Etchings & Engravings, Portraits, Furniture, Juvenile Art
Collections: Asian Collection (given by Asian Cultural Exchange Foundation);
Collection of Clara M Eagle Gallery; WPA prints, drawings; Magic Silver
Photography Collection; Harry L Jackson Print Collection
Exhibitions: Biennial Magic Silver Show (even years); Annual Student
Exhibition; Biennial Faculty Exhibitions (odd years); Contemporary Regional Arts
Publications: Brochures and posters for individual shows
Activities: Vis artists; workshops; demonstrations; lects open to public, 8 vis lectrs
per yr; gallery talks; tours; competitions with merit & purchase awards; exten dept
serving Jackson Purchase Area of Kentucky; individual paintings & original
objects of art lent; lending collection consists of original prints, paintings,
photographs & sculpture; books traveling exhibs; originates traveling exhibs

OWENSBORO

M   BRESCIA UNIVERSITY, (Brescia College) Anna Eaton Stout Memorial Art
Gallery, 717 Frederica St, Owensboro, KY 42301-3019. Tel 270-685-3131; Elec
Mail maryt@brescia.edu; *Chair, Div Fine Art* Sr Mary Diane Taylor; *Prof of Art &
Gallery Dir* David Stratton; *Asst Prof of Art* Frank Krevens
Open Mon - Fri 8 AM - 4:30 PM, Sat 8 AM - Noon; No admis fee; Estab 1950;
Gallery space is 20 x 30 ft, walls are covered with neutral carpeting; Average
Annual Attendance: 4,000
Activities: Lects open to public, 2-3 vis lectrs per year; competitions with awards;
schols offered; book traveling exhibs; originate traveling exhibs

M   OWENSBORO MUSEUM OF FINE ART, 901 Frederica St, Owensboro, KY
42301. Tel 270-685-3181; Fax 270-685-3181; Elec Mail info@omfa.us; Internet
Home Page Address: www.omfa.us; *Dir* Mary Bryan Hood; *Dir Operations* Jason
Hayden; *Bus Mgr* Jamie Scheffer; *Registrar* Tony Hardesty; *Admin Asst* Sharon
Hagerman; *Preparator* Rocky Cecil
Open Tues - Thurs 10 AM - 4 PM, Fri 10 AM - 7 PM, Sat & Sun 1 PM - 4 PM,
cl Mon & national holidays; No admis fee, donations suggested: Adult $2,
Children under 13 $1; Estab 1977 to showcase regional, national & international
art & to promote the cultural history of Kentucky through acquisition & exhib of
artists with connections to the state through birth, educ & residency; Three Wings:
Decorative Arts in restored pre-Civil War mansion; temporary & permanent
collection exhibition galleries; stained glass gallery; atrium sculpture ct & two
outdoor sculpture parks; Average Annual Attendance: 70,000; Mem: 800; dues
$25-$10,000
Income: Financed by pvt & pub sectors supplemented by foundation grants &
major fundraising events
Library Holdings: Auction Catalogs; Audio Tapes; Book Volumes; Cassettes;
Clipping Files; DVDs; Exhibition Catalogs; Kodachrome Transparencies; Slides;
Video Tapes
Special Subjects: Afro-American Art, Architecture, American Western Art,
Porcelain, Portraits, Painting-American, Silver, Woodcuts, Painting-British,
Painting-French, Drawings, Graphics, Hispanic Art, Photography, Prints, Sculpture,
Watercolors, American Indian Art, Bronzes, African Art, Southwestern Art,
Textiles, Religious Art, Ceramics, Crafts, Folk Art, Pottery, Woodcarvings,
Etchings & Engravings, Landscapes, Decorative Arts, Collages, Furniture, Glass,
Oriental Art, Asian Art, Carpets & Rugs, Juvenile Art, Period Rooms, Stained
Glass, Painting-Australian
Collections: 14th-18th century European drawings, graphics, decorative arts;
19th-20th century American, French & English paintings, sculpture & stained
glass, 20th century studio glass, American folk Art; monumental outdoor sculpture
Publications: Exhibition catalogues; newsletters
Activities: Classes for adults & children; docent training; seminars & critiques led
by major American artists; performing arts events; children's art gallery &
interactive art studio; lects open to pub, 6 vis lectrs per yr; concerts; gallery talks;
tours; competitions with awards; pre-tour visits to the classroom; film series;
individual & original objects of art lent to mus in western Kentucky & So
Indiana; book traveling exhibs 3-5 per yr; sales shop sells books, original art &
decorative arts objects

PADUCAH

M   THE NATIONAL QUILT MUSEUM, (The National Quilt Museum: Museum of
the American Quilter's Society) 215 Jefferson St, PO Box 1540 Paducah, KY
42002-1540. Tel 270-442-8856; Fax 270-442-5116; Elec Mail
info@quiltmuseum.org; Internet Home Page Address: www.quiltmuseum.org; *Exec
Dir* Frank Bennett; *Cur & Registrar* Judy Schwender; *Dir Pub Rels* Amanda Ball;
Cur Educ Becky Glasby; *Bus Mgr* Stacy Canter
Open Mon - Sat 10 AM - 5 PM yr round, Apr 1 - Oct 31 also open Sun 1 PM - 5
PM; Admis adult $11, seniors 60 & over $9, student 13-college $5, group rates

available, children 12 & under & school groups free; Estab 1991; Three climate
controlled galleries - Gallery A (7000 sq ft) displays selection from Mus
Collection. Gallery B (2900 sq ft) and Gallery C (3500 sq ft) display temporary
exhibits of contemporary & antique quilts; Average Annual Attendance: 45,000;
Mem: 2,000 Friends of the Museum; donations of $40 and above
Income: $882,702; financed by private & corporate donations & grants including
Kentucky Arts Council grant
Library Holdings: Book Volumes; Compact Disks; DVDs; Exhibition Catalogs
Special Subjects: Textiles, Crafts, Decorative Arts, Embroidery
Collections: Quilts made in 1980 to present; Education Coll & Paul D Pilgrim
Coll; Miniature Quilt Coll
Exhibitions: 10 - 12 exhibs each yr incl antique, contemporary & special topics &
curated exhibs
Publications: NQM Friends, quarterly newsletter; New Quilts from an Old
Favorite, annual; Coll of Quilts from the National Quilt Museum
Activities: Classes for adults & children; docent training; lects open to pub &
some for mem only; occasional vis lectrs; gallery talks; tours; sponsoring of
competitions; schols offered; exten prog serves the school &community groups in
the region, off-site, lending slide show, & trunk with art samples to quilt guilds &
schools; college credit offered for adult quilt class; book traveling exhibitions 6-8
times per yr; originate traveling exhibs circulate to quilt & art mus; mus shop sells
books, magazines, original art, reproductions, prints & fine crafts in all media

L   PADUCAH MERIKS PORTRAIT LIBRARY, 3240 Lone Oak Rd, #131,
Paducah, KY 42003-0370. *Asst Dir* Rey Horn
Open Mon - Thurs 9 AM - 6 PM, Fri - Sun 11 AM - 3 PM; no admis fee;
Average Annual Attendance: 15,000

M   RIVER HERITAGE MUSEUM, 117 S Water St, Paducah, KY 42001-0787. Tel
270-575-9958; Fax 270-444-9944; Internet Home Page Address:
www.riverheritagemuseum.org; *Exec Dir & Mus Shop Mgr* Julie Harris; *Develop
Mem & Pub Rels* Nate Heider; *Vol Chmn* Ken Wheeler; *Educ* E J Abell
Open Apr - Nov Mon - Sat 9:30 AM - 5 PM, Sun 1 PM - 5 PM; cl at noon on
Christmas Day; cl Easter, Thanksgiving Day & Christmas Day; Admis adults $5,
seniors $4.50, tours & groups $4, children $3, mems no admis fee; Estab 1990;
mus explores the history & significance of the river & the impact it has on
people's lives through its use of state-of-the-art interactive exhibs, music stations,
films, colls & aquariums; Average Annual Attendance: 10,600; Mem: dues Captain
$1000, Pilot $500, Engineer $250, Crew $100, First Mate $50, Deckhand $25
Collections: Riverboat; steamboat; towboat; paddlewheel models; river
memorabilia; nautical memorabilia; Civil War artifacts
Publications: The Anchor, quarterly newsletter
Activities: Events: Marine Industry Day; Sand In the City; River Trek; films;
guided tours; participatory exhibs; rental gallery; school loan svc; mus shop sells
books, clothing, jewelry, educ toys & related items

A   YEISER ART CENTER INC, 200 Broadway, Paducah, KY 42001. Tel
270-442-2453; Fax 270-442-0828; Elec Mail info@theyeiser.org; Internet Home
Page Address: www.theyeiser.org; *Exec Dir* Teri Moore
Open Tues - Sat 10 AM - 4 PM, cl Sun, Mon & major holidays; Admis by
donation; Estab 1957 as a nonprofit cultural and educational institution to provide
the community and the membership with visual art exhibitions, classes and related
activities of the highest quality; Average Annual Attendance: 16,000; Mem: 600;
monthly programs & mem meetings
Income: $150,000 (financed by mem fees, donations, commissions & grants)
Purchases: $100,000
Collections: Primarily regional/contemporary with some 19th century works on
paper & Japanese prints; teaching coll; Collection includes R Haley Lever;
Matisse; Goya; Emil Carlsen; Philip Moulthrop; Ron Isaacs
Exhibitions: Fantastic Fibers, Annual national Fibers Exhibit; National State
Annual Competition; changing exhibitions of historical & contemporary art of
regional, national & international nature
Publications: Fantastic Fibers, annual catalog; exhibit catalog; monthly newsletter
Activities: Classes for adults & children; dramatic progs; docent training; lects
open to pub, 12 vis lectrs per yr; gallery talks; tours; competitions with awards;
sponsoring of competitions; scholarships offered; individual and original objects of
art lent to qualified institutions; lending collection contains original art works,
prints and paintings; originate traveling exhibs; mus shop sells books, original art,
prints, gifts & unique items

PARIS

M   HISTORIC PARIS - BOURBON COUNTY, INC, Hopewell Museum, 800
Pleasant St, Paris, KY 40361-1734. Tel 859-987-7274; Fax 859-987-8107; Elec
Mail hopewellmuseum@yahoo.com; Internet Home Page Address:
www.hopewellmuseum.org; *Exec Dir* Betsy Kephart
Open Wed-Sat Noon-5 PM, Sun 2 PM-4 PM; Admis $2; Estab 1994 to display
Kentucky fine art & Bourbon County history; Six gallery rooms & a hall; building
originally constructed in Beaux Arts Style as a post office; Average Annual
Attendance: 2,500; Mem: 100; dues $35
Income: $95,000; (financed by mem, donations & pledges)
Special Subjects: Costumes, Crafts, Decorative Arts, Furniture, Glass
Collections: Bourbon County History (books, clothing, furniture, photography,
others); Kentucky Fine Art (paintings); Bourbon County History; Kentucky Fine
Art
Exhibitions: Victorian Children's Room; Civil War; Main Street
Views-photography of Doris Ullman; Agricultural Heritage Exhibit
Activities: Classes for children; dramatic progs; docent training; lects open to pub,
3-5 vis lectrs per yr

WHITESBURG

C   APPALSHOP INC, Appalshop, 91 Madison St, Whitesburg, KY 41858. Tel
606-633-0108; Orders: 800-545-7467; Fax 606-633-1009; Elec Mail
info@appalshop.org; Internet Home Page Address: www.appalshop.org; *Mng Dir
& Gallery Dir* Beth Bingman; *Theater Dir* Dudley Cocke; *Commus Dir* Mark
Kidd; *Mktg & Sales* Derek Mullins
Open Mon - Fri 9 AM - 5 PM; Admis fee for special events; Estab 1969 as the
Community Film Workshop of Appalachia, part of a national program to train

poor & minority young people in the skills of film & television production, now an incorporated nonprofit media arts center; In 1982 a renovated 13,000 sq ft warehouse, became the Appalshop Center with offices, video & radio editing suites, a 150 seat theater, an art gallery & educational facilities. A community radio station was added in 1987

Income: financed by grants & contributions

Publications: Newsletter, annual

Activities: Films, plays, music & educational progs to schools, college, mus, libraries, churches, festivals, conferences & community in the region, throughout the US & in Europe, Asia & Africa; classes for children; lect open to pub; concerts; originate traveling exhibs circulating to colleges in eastern Kentucky; sales shop sells music & films

WILMORE

M **ASBURY COLLEGE,** Student Center Gallery, One Macklem Dr, Wilmore, KY 40390-1198. Tel 859-858-3511; Fax 859-858-3921; Elec Mail kbarker@asbury.edu; Internet Home Page Address: www.asbury.edu/art; *Prof Art History* Dr Linda Stratford; *Photography & Graphic Arts, Dept Chair* Prof Keith Barker; *Painting & Drawing* Prof Chris Sigre-Lewis; *Prof Ceramics Sculpture* Margaret Parks Smith
Open 8 AM - 11 PM Mon - Sat; No admis fee; Estab 1976 for the purpose of exhibiting the works of national, local, and student artists; Track lighting in a 20 x 20 ft space; Average Annual Attendance: 2,000; Mem: Christians in the Visual Arts (CIVA)
Income: Financed by college funds
Special Subjects: Drawings, Painting-American, Photography, Prints, Sculpture, Watercolors, Religious Art, Ceramics, Pottery, Woodcuts, Etchings & Engravings, Landscapes, Portraits, Glass, Stained Glass
Collections: Ongoing permanent collection of varied media
Exhibitions: 8-10 per year
Activities: Classes for adults; lects open to public, 4 vis lectrs per year; gallery talks; tours; schols offered

LOUISIANA

ABBEVILLE

M **ALLIANCE CENTER MUSEUM AND ART GALLERY,** 200 N Magdalen Sq, Abbeville, LA 70510-4645. Tel 337-898-4114
Open Tues & Sat 10AM-3PM, Wed-Fri 10AM-5PM; Average Annual Attendance:
Collections: local history & culture; genealogy; photographs; documents; period artifacts; paintings

ALEXANDRIA

M **LOUISIANA STATE UNIVERSITY AT ALEXANDRIA,** University Gallery, 8100 Hwy 71 S, Alexandria, LA 71302-9119. Tel 318-473-6449; Elec Mail rdeville@lsua.edu; Internet Home Page Address: www.lsua.edu; *Dir University Gallery* Roy V de Ville
Open Mon - Fri 10 AM - 3 PM; No admis fee; Estab 1960 as university art department gallery; Gallery located in student union for both students & public. Meets all state & university guidelines for climate control; Average Annual Attendance: 800
Income: Financed by university
Exhibitions: Local & student art shows
Publications: University Gallery Catalogue, quarterly
Activities: Docent training; lects open to pub, 3-4 vis lectrs per yr; concerts; galley talks; competitions; schols; individual paintings & original objects of art lent

BAKER

M **HERITAGE MUSEUM & CULTURAL CENTER,** 1606 Main St, Baker, LA 70704-0707; PO Box 707, Baker, LA 70704-0707. Tel 225-774-1776; Fax 225-775-5635; Elec Mail bakermuseum@bellsouth.net; Internet Home Page Address: www.bakerheritagemuseum.org
Open Mon - Sat 10 AM - 4 PM; No admis fee, donations accepted; Estab 1974 in a restored c.1906 local residence; mus collects, preserves, documents & exhibits items relating to local history. Nonprofit org
Special Subjects: Historical Material, Costumes, Crafts, Coins & Medals, Restorations
Exhibitions: Mus has traveling box exhibits including: The Ballot Box, The Money Box, The Sewing Box, The Music Box, The Letter Box, The Hat Box, The Memory Box & The Way We See It
Publications: Musings, community newsletter
Activities: Guided tours; Educ progs; Christmas displays; speakers; originates traveling exhibs

BATON ROUGE

M **BATON ROUGE GALLERY,** (East Baton Rouge Parks & Recreation Commission) Center For Contemporary Art, 1515 Dalrymple Dr, Baton Rouge, LA 70808-1037. Tel 225-383-1470; Fax 225-336-0943; Elec Mail jandreasen@batonrougegallery.org; Internet Home Page Address: www.batonrougegallery.org; *Exec Dir* Jason Andreasen; *Special Facility Mgr* Jennifer Poulter; *Center Supv* Cynthia Sanders
Open Tues - Sun Noon - 6 PM; No admis fee; Estab 1966 to educate & promote contemporary art; Nonprofit, cooperative, contemporary gallery made up of

general members from community & artist members; Average Annual Attendance: 15,000; Mem: 51 artist mems meet semi-annually
Income: $00,000 (financed by mem & East Baton Rouge Parks & Recreation Commission)
Special Subjects: Hispanic Art, Painting-American, Photography, Sculpture, Watercolors, Ceramics, Etchings & Engravings, Landscapes, Afro-American Art
Collections: Southern regional artists based around Baton Rouge & New Orleans; international artists
Exhibitions: Rotating exhibitions; Surreal Salon (ann juried exhib)
Publications: The Art & Artists of Baton Rouge Gallery (2012)
Activities: Classes for adults & children; docent training; lects open to pub; concerts; gallery talks; tours; competitions with awards; individual paintings & original objects of art lent to State of Louisiana; mus shop sells books & original art

M **LOUISIANA ARTS & SCIENCE MUSEUM,** (Louisiana Arts & Science Center Museum) PO Box 3373, Baton Rouge, LA 70821-3373; 100 River Rd S, Baton Rouge, LA 70802-5730. Tel 225-344-5272; Fax 225-344-9477; Elec Mail info@lasm.org; Internet Home Page Address: www.lasm.org; *Exec Dir* Sam Losavio; *Museum Cur* Elizabeth Weinstein; *Cur Art Educ* Tammy Johnson; *Cur Science Educ* Nita Mitchell; *Pub Rels Coordr* Elizabeth Tadie; *Registrar* Leslie Charleville; *Exec Dir* Carol S Gikas; *Planetarium Dir* Jon Elvert; *Planetarium Producer* Mike Snail; *Develop* Pamela Sills
Open Tues - Fri 10 AM - 3 PM, Sat 10AM-5PM, Sun 1-5PM; Admis adults $7, seniors 65 and over $6, free for members; Estab 1960. General mus - art & science; Housed on the banks of the Mississippi River, the Louisiana Art & Science Mus (LASM) offers educational entertainment for visitors of all ages, including exhibs of internationally renowned artists, innovative programming in the state-of-the-art Pennington Planetarium, interactive art & science galleries for children & an Ancient Egypt Gallery; Average Annual Attendance: 80,000; Mem: 1200; Dues $20-$1000
Income: Financed by mem, city appropriation & donations
Special Subjects: Drawings, Graphics, Painting-American, Prints, Sculpture, Bronzes, African Art, Textiles, Costumes, Ceramics, Folk Art, Landscapes, Painting-European, Eskimo Art, Dolls, Antiquities-Egyptian, Antiquities-Greek, Antiquities-Roman
Collections: 18th & 20th century European & American paintings; contemporary photographs; Clementine Hunter paintings; Ivan Mestrovic; sculpture; Egyptian artifacts; Eskimo graphics & soapstone carvings; North American Indian crafts; Tibetan religious art
Exhibitions: Discovery Depot, a participatory gallery that introduces children to art; Irene W Pennington Planetarium; Ancient Egyptian Gallery
Publications: LASM Calendar, quarterly
Activities: Classes for children; workshops, YouthALIVE; lects open to pub, 7 vis lectrs per yr; gallery talks; tours; individual paintings & original objects of art lent to other mus & galleries; book traveling exhibs 8-10 per yr; originate traveling exhibs; mus shop sells books, magazines, original art, reproductions, slides, educational toys & t-shirts

L **Library,** 100 S River Rd, Baton Rouge, LA 70802; PO Box 3373, Baton Rouge, LA 70821-3373. Tel 225-344-5272; Fax 225-344-9477; Internet Home Page Address: www.lasm.org; *Exec Dir* Carol S Gikas; *Asst Dir* Sam Losavio
Open Tues - Fri 10 AM - 3 PM, Sat 10 - 4 Pm, Sun 1 PM - 4 PM, cl Mon; Estab 1971; Small reference library open to staff only. Two floor gallery for changing exhibitions; Average Annual Attendance: 69,000; Mem: 2000
Library Holdings: Book Volumes 1000; Exhibition Catalogs; Pamphlets; Periodical Subscriptions 32; Slides; Video Tapes
Special Subjects: Photography, Painting-American, Sculpture, Painting-European
Collections: 18th-20th American & European art; 2d largest coll of Ivan Mestrovic in U.S.
Publications: LASM Quarterly membership newsletter; exhibition catalogues
Activities: Classes for adults & children; docent training; lects open to pub, 6 vis lectrs per yr; gallery talks; workshops; school group programs; exten art programs in local schools; 8-10 traveling exhibs

M **LOUISIANA MUD PAINTINGS,** 16950 Strain Rd, Baton Rouge, LA 70816-1823. Tel 225-275-5126
Open Tues-Sat 10AM-5PM
Collections: paintings by Henry Neubig using mud & clay found in Louisiana

M **LOUISIANA STATE UNIVERSITY,** (Louisiana State University) Museum of Art, 100 Lafayette, Baton Rouge, LA 70801. Tel 225-389-7200; Fax 225-389-7219; Elec Mail radam14@lsu.edu; Internet Home Page Address: www.lsumoa.org; *Exec Dir* Jordana Pomeroy, PhD; *Cur* Natalie Mault; *Asst Dir Coll Develop* Fran Huber; *Assoc Dir Develop* Fairleigh Jackson; *Shop Mgr* LeAnn Dusang
Open Tues - Sat 10AM - 5 PM, Thurs 10 AM - 8 PM, Sun 1 PM - 5 PM; Admis adults (12 & older) $5, children (under 12) no admis fee; Estab 1959 to collect, conserve, exhibit & protect the works of art entrusted to its care; 19,500 sq ft; Average Annual Attendance: 55,000; Mem: 1200; dues $25 - $1,000
Income: Financed by LSU, state, fundraising & earned
Purchases: 20th century - 21st century American art
Library Holdings: Auction Catalogs 150; Book Volumes 2,100; Exhibition Catalogs 250; Original Art Works 4,250; Photographs; Prints; Sculpture
Special Subjects: Decorative Arts, Drawings, Ceramics, Glass, Painting-American, Sculpture, Graphics, Photography, Watercolors, Furniture, Jade, Silver, Painting-British
Collections: Hogarth & Caroline Durieux Graphics Collection; Newcomb Crafts; 19th century lighting devices; New Orleans Silver; early Baton Rouge Subjects
Publications: Catalogues; newsletter
Activities: Classes for adults & children; docent training; lects open to pub; gallery talks; tours; originate traveling exhibs; mus shop sells books, magazines, original art, reproductions, prints, slides, jewelry, cards, games

L **Library,** 114 Memorial Tower, Baton Rouge, LA 70803-0001. Tel 225-388-5652; Internet Home Page Address: www.lib.lsu.edu; *Dean LSU Libraries* Jennifer Cargill
Open Mon - Thurs 9:15 AM - noon, Fri & Sat 10 AM - 5 PM, Sun noon - midnight, cl university holidays; No admis fee, guided tours $2 per person; Reference library; Average Annual Attendance: 7,500

Library Holdings: Book Volumes 700; Clipping Files; Exhibition Catalogs; Original Art Works; Photographs; Prints; Sculpture
Special Subjects: Decorative Arts, Drawings, Painting-American, Painting-British
Exhibitions: English period rooms 17th & 19th century; American period rooms 18th & 19th centuries; Collection of Newcomb Crafts; New Orleans made Silver; Hogarth Prints; Works by Caroline Durieux; 18th century lighting devices
Publications: Exhibit catalogs
Activities: Lects for members only, 1-2 per yr; tours; individual paintings & objects of art lent to other museums

M **Student Union Art Gallery,** LSU Box 25123, 210 LSU Student Union Baton Rouge, LA 70803. Tel 225-578-8256; Fax 225-578-4329; Elec Mail unionartgallery@lsu.edu; jstahl1@lsu.edu; Internet Home Page Address: www.lsu.edu; *Gallery Dir* Judith R Stahl
Open Mon - Fri 10 AM - 6 PM, Sun 1 PM - 5 PM; No admis fee; Estab 1964, designed for exhibitions for university & community interests; Gallery is centrally located on the main floor of the LSU Student Union with 3000 sq ft; Average Annual Attendance: 55,000
Income: Financed by fundraising, grants & university support
Purchases: To be determined by Accession Comt
Special Subjects: Photography, Painting-American, Prints, Woodcuts, Graphics, Stained Glass
Collections: Contemporary American Art; European Viennese Realism
Exhibitions: Annual National Art Competition; 8 annual rotating exhibits; state & student competition; curated exhibits & travelling art shows
Publications: Brochures and postcards for exhibits, exhibit catalogs, semester calendars & e-newsletters
Activities: Educ prog; docent training; lects open to public, 4 vis lectrs per yr; concerts; gallery demonstrations; competitions with awards, national $5,000, state $3,000, student $1,800; interactive activities

M **School of Art - Glassell Gallery,** Shaw Center for the Arts, 100 Lafayette St Baton Rouge, LA 70801-1201. Tel 225-389-7180; Fax 225-389-7185; Elec Mail artgallery@lsu.edu; Internet Home Page Address: www.glassellgallery.org; *Dir, School of Art* Rod Parker; *Gallery Coordr* Kristin Malia Krolak; *Asst Dir School of Art* Denyce Celentano
Open Tues - Fri 10 AM - 5 PM, Sat & Sun noon - 5 PM; No admis fee; Mem: Dues patron $1000, benefactor $500, contributor $250, supporter $100, artist $50, student $20
Special Subjects: Drawings, Prints, Graphics
Collections: Department coll
Activities: Lects open to public, 2 vis lectrs per yr; gallery talks; tours; sponsoring of competitions; scholarships & fees offered; lending of original art to local bus; book traveling exhibs, 2 per yr; originate traveling exhibs

L **Middleton Library,** 141 Middleton Library, Baton Rouge, LA 70803. Tel 225-578-6897; Elec Mail cargill@lsu.edu; Internet Home Page Address: www.lib.lsu.edu; *Dean Libraries* Jennifer Cargill; *Dept Head Educ Resources* Peggy Chalaron; *Head Ref & Coll Develop Svcs* Tom Diamond; *Dept Head Cataloging* Linda Smith Griffin; *Cur Manuscripts* Tara Zachary Laver; *Head Special Colls* Elaine Smythe
Hours subject to change; call to confirm; No admis fee; Estab 1958
Library Holdings: Auction Catalogs; Book Volumes 15,000; CD-ROMs; DVDs; Exhibition Catalogs; Maps; Other Holdings Vertical files 8 drawers, blueprints; Periodical Subscriptions 100; Video Tapes
Special Subjects: Art History, Landscape Architecture, Decorative Arts, Graphic Design, Sculpture, Printmaking, Interior Design, Asian Art, Architecture
Activities: Educ prog; library instruction; virtual tour

M **LOUISIANA STATE UNIVERSITY SCHOOL OF ART,** (Alfred C Glassell Jr Exhibition Gallery) Alfred C Glassell Jr Exhibition Gallery, LSU School of Art, Shaw Center for the Arts, 100 Lafayette St Baton Rouge, LA 70801. Tel 225-389-7180; Elec Mail artgallery@lsu.edu; *Dir* K Malia Krolak; *Asst Dir* Renee Smith
Open Tues - Fri 10 AM - 5 PM, Sat - Sun noon - 5 PM; No admis fee
Collections: works by local, national & international contemporary artists

L **SOUTHERN UNIVERSITY,** Architecture Library, Southern University Post Office Branch, Baton Rouge, LA 70813. Tel 225-771-3290; Fax 225-771-4709; Elec Mail lucille@lib.subr.edu; Internet Home Page Address: www.subr.edu; *Librn* Lucille Bowie
Open Mon - Fri 8 AM - 9 PM, Fri 8 AM-5 PM, cl weekends; Estab 1971 to encourage support of fine arts & architecture; Circ 12,000
Income: Financed by state appropriation
Library Holdings: Book Volumes 7500; Cassettes; Fiche; Motion Pictures; Pamphlets; Periodical Subscriptions 87; Reels; Slides; Video Tapes

COLUMBIA

M **THE SCHEPIS, LOUISIANA ARTISTS MUSEUM,** 106 Main St Columbia, LA 71418; PO Box 743 Columbia, LA 71418-0743. *Cur* Jane Meredith

COVINGTON

A **ST TAMMANY ART ASSOCIATION,** 320 N Columbia, Covington, LA 70433-2918. Tel 985-892-8650; Fax 985-898-0976; Elec Mail info@sttammanyartassociation.org; Internet Home Page Address: www.sttammanyartassociation.org; *Art House Coordr* Mary Monk
Open Tues - Fri 10 AM - 4 PM, Sat 11 AM - 4 PM; Estab 1958

CROWLEY

A **CROWLEY ART ASSOCIATION,** The Gallery, 220 N Parkerson Ave, Crowley, LA 70526-5003; PO Box 2003, Crowley, LA 70527-2003. Tel 337-783-3747; Fax 337-783-3747; Elec Mail gallerythe@bellsouth.net; Internet Home Page Address: crowleyartgallery.com; *Pres* Isabella dela Houssaye; *VPres* Virginia Duson; *Treas* Shirley Griffin; *Secy* Hurley Gautreaux
Open daily 10 AM - 4 PM; No admis fee; Estab 1980 to promote art in all forms; 1,100 sq ft; Average Annual Attendance: 3,000; Mem: 250; dues $25; monthly meetings; mem qualifications: interest in & production of art

Income: Financed by mem, fundraisers & grants
Exhibitions: Juried Art Show; International Rice Festival Arts & Crafts Show
Publications: Monthly newsletter
Activities: Classes for adults & children; lects open to pub, 3 vis lectrs per yr; competitions; sales shop sells original art, prints & Cajun crafts

FRANKLIN

M **ST MARY LANDMARKS,** Grevemberg House Museum, 407 Sterling Rd (Hwy 322), Franklin, LA 70538-0400; PO Box 400, Franklin, LA 70538-0400. Tel 337-828-2092; Fax 337-828-2028; Elec Mail info@grevemberghouse.com; Internet Home Page Address: www.grevemberghouse.com; *Vol Pres* Fred Schwitz; *Pub Rels & Treas* Ron Bailey; *Archivist* Margie L Luke; *Lead Interpreter* Craig Landry; *VPres* Katie Siem; *Secy* Ruthie Heard
Open daily 10 AM - 4 PM; cl New Year's Day, Good Friday, Easter Sunday, Thanksgiving Day, Christmas Eve & Day; Admis adults $10 seniors, students & group rates $8, children $5, mems no admis fee; Estab 1972; 1851 Greek-revival townhouse that showcases 19th c life in south Louisiana; listed on National Register of Historic Places; managed by St Mary Landmark's 17-mem vol Bd of Trustees; Average Annual Attendance: 500; Mem: dues Corinthian $1000, Queen Anne $500, Victorian $250; Gothic $100; Conservator $75; Pillar $60; Foundation $35
Income: corporate and personal dues; public and private grants; fundraisers
Special Subjects: Decorative Arts, Historical Material, Furniture, Portraits, Painting-American, Dolls, Period Rooms
Collections: Antique furnishings from the period of 1820 - 1870 based on items listed in the estates of Gabriel and Frances Wikoff Grevemberg, with exceptions allowed for items of local historic significance from other periods
Publications: Landmark Lagniappe, semiannual newsletter
Activities: Research in the translation of Grevemberg family papers from French to English; mid-19th c south Louisiana graveyards; lects open to pub; 1-2 vis lectrs per yr; Victorian Christmas Celebration; guided tours; St Mary Landmarks Historic Preservation Award; mus shop sells books, prints, notecards, tote bags, sugarcane, jewelry

JENNINGS

M **ZIGLER ART MUSEUM,** 411 Clara St, Jennings, LA 70546-5235. Tel 337-824-0114; Fax 337-824-0120; Elec Mail zigler-museum@charter.net; Internet Home Page Address: www.ziglerartmuseum.org; *Cur* Dolores Spears; *Pres Bd Trustees* Gregory Marcantel; *VPres* Wendell Miller; *Treas* Burt Tietje
Open Tues - Sat 10 AM - 4 PM, Sun 1 - 4 PM; Admis fee adults $5, children & students $2; Estab 1963 to place the art of western civilization & the area in a historical context; West Wing has permanent collection of American & European paintings & sculptures. East Wing contains a gallery of wildlife art. Central galleries are reserved for a new art exhibit each month; Average Annual Attendance: 20,000
Income: Income from private foundation
Purchases: 29 paintings by William Tolliver; One painting by Vlaminck; One painting by Whitney Hubbard; One painting by van Dyck; One painting by Herring
Special Subjects: Afro-American Art, Drawings, Glass, Bronzes, Woodcuts, Painting-Japanese, Painting-American, Photography, Prints, Sculpture, American Indian Art, Religious Art, Ceramics, Pottery, Woodcarvings, Woodcuts, Etchings & Engravings, Landscapes, Painting-European, Portraits, Porcelain, Asian Art, Marine Painting, Painting-British, Painting-Dutch, Miniatures, Painting-Flemish, Painting-Polish, Dioramas, Painting-Italian, Painting-German
Collections: Bierstadt; Chierici; Constable; Crane; Gay; Heldner; George Inness Jr; Pearce; Pissarro; Frank Smith; Vergne; Whistler; Gustave Wolff; Robert Wood; J Chester Armstrong Sculpture Collection; Tolliver Collection: 29 pieces
Exhibitions: Rotating exhibits
Publications: Brochure
Activities: Classes for adults & children; docent training; lects open to pub; gallery talks; tours; individual paintings & original objects of art lent; originates traveling exhibs that travel to other museums; mus shop sells books, magazines, original art, reproductions, prints, Indian baskets & hand-painted porcelain

LAFAYETTE

M **LAFAYETTE MUSEUM ASSOCIATION,** Lafayette Museum-Alexandre Mouton House, 1122 Lafayette St, Lafayette, LA 70501-6838. Tel 337-234-2208; *Pres* Jolyn S Cole
Open Tues - Sat 10 AM - 4 PM, cl Sun & Mon; Admis free $2 suggested donation; Estab 1954 as a historical house; Average Annual Attendance: 3,000
Income: $35,000 (financed by endowment, city appropriation)
Purchases: Refurbishing two rooms in mus
Library Holdings: Book Volumes; DVDs; Framed Reproductions; Memorabilia; Original Art Works; Original Documents; Photographs; Records
Special Subjects: Costumes, Historical Material
Collections: Historical Costumes & Dress, Documents, Furnishings, Objects
Activities: Children's tours; French tours; mus shop sells cookbooks & postcards

M **LAFAYETTE SCIENCE MUSEUM & PLANETARIUM,** (Lafayette Natural History Museum & Planetarium) 433 Jefferson St, Lafayette, LA 70501-7013. Tel 337-291-5544; Fax 337-291-5464; Elec Mail kkrantz@lafayettela.gov; Internet Home Page Address: www.lafayettesciencemuseum.org; *Cur Planetarium* David Hostetter; *Admin Asst* Karen Miller; *Museum & Planetarium Tech* Paul McCasland; *Dir* Kevin Krantz; *Cur Educ* Dawn Edelen; *Colls Cur* Deborah Clifton; *Asst Cur* Charlotte Guillot; *Receptionist* Likassina Brown; *Tour Scheduling* Edi Gilbert
Open Mus Tues-Fri 9AM-5PM, Sat 10AM-6PM, Sun 1-6PM, call for planetarium show times; Admis adults $5, seniors 65 & over $3, children 4 - 17 yrs $2, children 3 & under free; Estab 1969 to provide a focus on the physical world in order to benefit the citizens of the community; 5,800 sq ft of exhibition space,

interior walls constructed as needed; Average Annual Attendance: 65,000; Mem: 300; annual meeting in Oct
Income: $650,000 (financed by mem & city & parish appropriation)
Purchases: $4000
Library Holdings: Audio Tapes; Book Volumes; CD-ROMs; Cassettes; Clipping Files; Compact Disks; Exhibition Catalogs; Manuscripts; Maps; Memorabilia; Original Art Works; Original Documents; Pamphlets; Periodical Subscriptions; Photographs; Prints; Records; Reels; Reproductions; Video Tapes
Special Subjects: Painting-American, Textiles, Drawings, Graphics, Photography, Prints, Sculpture, Anthropology, Archaeology, Ethnology, Costumes, Crafts, Folk Art, Primitive art, Woodcarvings, Etchings & Engravings, Landscapes, Afro-American Art, Manuscripts, Posters, Furniture, Historical Material, Maps, Restorations, Tapestries, Dioramas, Embroidery, Bookplates & Bindings
Collections: Acadian artifacts; Audubon prints; Historical Louisiana maps; Louisiana moths & butterflies; Louisiana shells; Louisiana Indian artifacts; Louisiana Landscape Art; Louisiana Related Harper's Weekly Prints; Meteorites
Exhibitions: Titanic; Star Wars; Dinosaurs; Giant Worlds; Mars Quest; Lafayette; Water World; Leaving Earth: Story of Space Travel
Activities: Classes for adults & children; docent training; tours; lending collection contains 20 nature artifacts, original art works, 400 photos, 1000 slides, 200 Louisiana Indian & Acadian artifacts to home schools, scouts; book traveling exhibs

M UNIVERSITY OF LOUISIANA AT LAFAYETTE, Paul and Lulu Hilliard University Art Museum, PO Box 42571, Lafayette, LA 70504-2571; 710 E Saint Mary Blvd Lafayette, LA 70503. Tel 337-482-2278; Fax 337-262-1268; Elec Mail artmuseum@louisiana.edu; Internet Home Page Address: museum.louisiana.edu; *Dir* Lance Harris; *Cur* Lee Gray, PhD; *Registrar* Ramona East; *Visitor Svcs* Cindy Hamilton; *Asst Dir* Debby Mayne
Open Tues - Thurs 9 AM - 5 PM, Fri 9 AM - Noon, Sat 10 AM - 5 PM; Admis adult $5, seniors $4, youth $3; Estab 1968 as an art mus, for educ of the population of the region; Three galleries totaling 8,000 sq ft built in 2003; Average Annual Attendance: 25,000; Mem: 600; dues $25-$5000
Income: $600,000 (financed by mem & state appropriation)
Purchases: Lowe Collection of Outsider Art
Special Subjects: Afro-American Art, Decorative Arts, Drawings, Etchings & Engravings, Folk Art, Landscapes, Architecture, Ceramics, Collages, Glass, Furniture, Portraits, Pottery, Painting-American, Prints, Silver, Woodcuts, Sculpture, Graphics, Photography, Watercolors, Primitive art, Oriental Art, Coins & Medals, Miniatures, Antiquities-Egyptian
Collections: Henry Botkin Collection; Cohn Collection-19th & 20th Century Japanese Prints; Louisiana Collection-19th & 20th Century Art, all media; Lowe Collection-Outsider Art; 19th & 21st Century Art
Publications: exhibition catalogues
Activities: Educ programs; docent training; lects open to pub, 11 vis lectrs per yr; concerts; gallery talks; tours; book traveling exhibs, 4 per yr; originate traveling exhibs one per yr circulating to art mus, univ mus, & others; mus shop sells books, original art, prints

LAKE CHARLES

M ABERCROMBIE GALLERY, McNeese State University, Ryan & Sale Sts Lake Charles, LA 70609. Tel 337-475-5060; Fax 337-475-5927; *Dir* Heather Ryan Kelley
Call for hours
Collections: works by local, regional, & national contemporary artists

M IMPERIAL CALCASIEU MUSEUM, 204 W Sallier St, Lake Charles, LA 70601-5844. Tel 337-439-3797; Fax 337-439-6040; Elec Mail impmuseum@bellsouth.net; Internet Home Page Address: www.imperialcalcasieumuseum.org; *Dir* Susan H Reed
Open Tues-Sat 10AM-5PM; Admis adults $2, students $1; Estab Mar 1963 by the Junior League of Lake Charles & housed in City Hall; After several moves in location, the mus is now housed in a building of Louisiana Colonial architecture which incorporates in its structure old bricks, beams, balustrades & columns taken from demolished old homes. In Dec 1966 admin was assumed by the Fine Arts Center & Mus of Old Imperial Calcasieu Mus, Inc, with a name change in 1971. Site of the building was chosen for its historic value, having been owned by the Charles Sallier family, the first white settler on the lake & the town named for him. The mus depicts the early history of the area; Average Annual Attendance: 12,500; Mem: 350; dues $50-$1500
Income: Financed by mem
Special Subjects: Period Rooms
Collections: Artifacts of the Victorian Period, especially Late Victorian
Exhibitions: American Indian Artifacts in Calcasieu Collections; Antique Quilts & Coverlets; Calcasieu People & Places in 19th Century Photographs; Christmas Around The World; special exhibitions every six weeks, with smaller exhibits by other organizations at times
Activities: Docent training; lects open to members only, 2-3 vis lectrs per yr; gallery talks; book traveling exhibs 1 per yr; originate traveling exhibs; sales shop sells books, original art

M Gibson-Barham Gallery, 204 W Sallier St, Lake Charles, LA 70601. Tel 337-439-3797; Fax 337-439-6040; *Coordr* Mary June Malus
Open Tues - Sat 10 AM - 5 PM, Sun 1 - 5 PM, cl Mon; Admis adults $2, students $1; Estab 1963 to collect & display history & artifacts at five parishes in the original Imperial Land Grant; 1000 running ft; Average Annual Attendance: 10,000; Mem: 300; dues $50
Income: financed by membership, donations
Special Subjects: Drawings, Graphics, Painting-American, Photography, Prints, American Indian Art, Costumes, Ceramics, Crafts, Folk Art, Pottery, Etchings & Engravings, Decorative Arts, Manuscripts, Dolls, Furniture, Jewelry, Carpets & Rugs, Historical Material, Maps, Coins & Medals, Period Rooms, Embroidery, Laces, Pewter
Exhibitions: 6-10 rotating exhibitions per year
Activities: Lects open to public, 2 vis lectrs per yr; gallery talks; tours; individual paintings & original objects of art lent to established museums or collectors; book traveling exhibs 3-4 per yr; originate traveling exhibs; sales shop sells books & original art

L Gibson Library, 204 W Sallier St, Lake Charles, LA 70601. Tel 337-439-3797; Fax 337-439-6040; *Coordr* Mary June Malus
Open Mon - Fri 10 AM - 5 PM, Sat & Sun 1 - 5 PM; No admis fee; Estab 1971, to display early school books & bibles; Circ non-circulating; Reference Library; Mem: Part of museum
Income: Financed by mem, memorials & gifts
Library Holdings: Audio Tapes; Book Volumes 100; Cassettes; Memorabilia; Original Art Works; Pamphlets; Periodical Subscriptions 100; Photographs; Sculpture; Slides; Video Tapes
Special Subjects: Folk Art, Decorative Arts, Photography, Manuscripts, Maps, Painting-American, Prints, Historical Material, Crafts, Porcelain, Furniture, Drafting, Period Rooms, Pottery, Pewter
Collections: Audubon animal paintings; Audubon bird paintings; Calcasieu photographs; Boyd Cruise
Exhibitions: History of Imperial Calcasieu Parish, with settings & objects

LEESVILLE

M MUSEUM OF WEST LOUISIANA, 803 S Third St, Leesville, LA 71446. Tel 337-239-0927; Internet Home Page Address: www.museumofwestla.org
Open Tues - Sun 1 - 5 PM; other times by appt; No admis fee, donations accepted; Opened in 1987 for the purpose of displaying & preserving artifacts illustrative of the history, culture, folk art & resources of Vernon Parish and the West Central area of the Louisiana Territory. Nonprofit org; Mem: different levels of annual mem dues
Special Subjects: Archaeology, Decorative Arts, Folk Art, Furniture, Dolls, Military Art
Collections: Archaeological artifacts; logging implements; railroad memorabilia; quilts; clothing; cooking & household items; furniture & special displays; POW paintings & WWII memorabilia; children's toys & dolls
Activities: Pioneer Park is available for special events; mus related items for sale

MADISONVILLE

LAKE PONTCHARTRAIN BASIN MARITIME MUSEUM, 133 Mabel Dr, Madisonville, LA 70447-9301. Tel 985-845-9200; Fax 985-845-9201; Elec Mail info@lpbmaritimemuseum.org; Internet Home Page Address: www.lpmaritimemuseum.org; *CEO & Dir* Nixon Adams
Open Tues - Sat 10 AM - 4 PM, Sun 12 PM - 4 PM, cl Thanksgiving, Christmas Eve & Day; Admis adults & seniors $2, mems & age 12 & under no admis fee; Unique nautical & cultural heritage of Lake Pontchartrain, research in archeological survey of shipwrecks in the Lake Pontchartrain (pvt nonprofit mus; maintains library; vols available for inter-library loan); Average Annual Attendance: 1000 - 9999; Mem: dues Supporting $500, Friend $100, Family $25
Exhibitions: Madisonville Wooden Boat Festival, ann festival held the third weekend in Oct, 10 AM - 6 PM

MINDEN

L WEBSTER PARISH LIBRARY, 521 East & West Sts, Minden, LA 71055. Tel 318-371-3080; Fax 318-371-3081; *Dir* Beverly Hammett; *Librn* Eddie Hammontree
Open Ferguson Stewart Building Mon-Fri 8AM-5PM, Main Mon, Wed, Thurs 8:15AM-8PM, Tues, Fri, Sat 8:15AM-5PM; Estab 1929 to serve as headquarters & main branch for county; Circ 145,508
Income: $221,353 (financed by parish tax)
Library Holdings: Book Volumes 60,000; Cassettes; Clipping Files; Filmstrips; Framed Reproductions; Original Art Works; Pamphlets; Periodical Subscriptions 800; Photographs; Records; Reels; Slides; Video Tapes
Activities: Exten dept serves the elderly; individual paintings lent to registered borrowers, lending collection contains 54 art prints & 50 b & w photographs depicting parish history

MONROE

M NORTHEAST LOUISIANA CHILDREN'S MUSEUM, 323 Walnut St, Monroe, LA 71201-6711. Tel 318-361-9611; Fax 318-361-9613; Elec Mail nelcm@nelcm.org; Internet Home Page Address: www.nelcm.org
Open Tues - Fri 9 AM - 2 PM, Sat 10 AM - 5 PM; Admis $5 per person; Group Rate: $3 per person for groups of 15 or more
Exhibitions: The Kids' Cafe: sponsored by the Louisiana Restaurant Assoc, exhib recreates a true-to-life restaurant environment where each child can explore the different types of jobs found in a restaurant; Health Hall: children may drive an ambulance to the ER, listen to a patient's heart & check out his x-ray, as well as learn about how the body works; The Think Tank: visitor is challenged to use problem-solving skills to figure out puzzles, utilize creativity in putting on a puppet show, as well as explore The Gravity Wall; Stuffee: 9-ft soft sculptured doll sponsored by the Ouachita Medical Alliance Society, whose internal organs are removable & teach us how our body works; Toddler Town: a picket fence-surrounded area designated for toddlers, features soft blocks & educational toys
Activities: Monthly events; Birthday Parties & events; Summer Drop-Off Days for children ages 4 - 8; traveling & permanent exhibs; educational-related items for sale

M TWIN CITY ART FOUNDATION, Masur Museum of Art, 1400 S Grand St, Monroe, LA 71202-2012. Tel 318-329-2237; Fax 318-329-2847; Elec Mail info@masurmuseum.org; Internet Home Page Address: www.masurmuseum.org; *Dir* Sue Prudhomme; *Pres* Allyson C Young
Open Tues - Thurs 9 AM - 5 PM, Fri - Sun 2 - 5 PM; No admis fee; Estab 1963 to encourage art in all media & to enrich the cultural climate of this area; Gallery has 400 running ft hanging space; Average Annual Attendance: 20,000; Mem: 380; dues $250, $125, $35
Income: $225,000 (financed by mem & appropriations)

Special Subjects: Painting-American, Photography, Prints, Sculpture, Watercolors, Woodcuts
Collections: Contemporary art all media, approx 300 works
Publications: Brochures of shows, monthly
Activities: Classes for adults & children; lects open to pub, 4 vis lectrs per yr; tours; competitions; book traveling exhibs

M **UNIVERSITY OF LOUISIANA AT MONROE,** (Northeast Louisiana University) Bry Gallery, 700 University Ave, Bry Hall Monroe, LA 71203-3708. Tel 318-342-1375; Fax 318-342-1369; Elec Mail tresner@ulm.edu; Internet Home Page Address: www.ulm.edu/art/gallery/welcome.html; *Head* Gary Ratcliff, MFA; *Gallery Dir* Cliff Tresner; *Asst Gallery Dir* Dara Engler
Open Mon-Thurs 8 AM - 4:30 PM, Fri 8AM-noon; No admis fee; Estab 1931; Gallery is 45 x 26 sq ft with 14 ft ceilings; Average Annual Attendance: 8,000
Collections: Kit Gilbert; Pave Brou of New Orleans
Activities: Classes for adults & children; docent training; 6 vis lectrs per yr; gallery talks

NEW IBERIA

M **NATIONAL TRUST FOR HISTORIC PRESERVATION,** Shadows-on-the-Teche, 317 E Main St, New Iberia, LA 70560-3728. Tel 337-369-6446; Fax 337-365-5213; Elec Mail shadows@shadowsontheteche.org; Internet Home Page Address: www.shadowsontheteche.org; *Dir* Patricia Kahle; *Cur Educ* Catherine Schramm
Open Mon - Sat 9 AM - 5 PM, cl major holidays; Admis adults (18-64) $10, seniors (65 & over) $8, students (6-17) $6.50; The Shadows is a property of the National Trust for Historic Preservation. Preserved as a historic house mus: operated as a community preservation center, it is a National Historic Landmark. On the Bayou Teche, it faces the main street of modern New Iberia, but is surrounded by 2 1/2 acres of landscaped gardens shaded by live oaks. Built in 1834, the Shadows represents a Louisiana adaptation of classical revival architecture. The life & culture of a 19th century southern Louisiana sugar plantation are reflected in the possessions of four generations of the Weeks family on display in the house, which was restored during the 1920s by Weeks Hall, great-grandson of the builder; Average Annual Attendance: 16,000; Mem: 450
Income: Financed by mem in Friends of the Shadows, admis fees & special events
Special Subjects: Decorative Arts, Landscapes, Architecture, Textiles, Photography, Portraits, Furniture, Restorations, Period Rooms
Collections: Paintings by Louisiana's itinerant artist Adrien Persac & period room settings (1830s-60s); paintings by Weeks Hall; furnishings typical of those owned by a planter's family between 1830 and 1865
Activities: Docent training; interpretive programs which are related to the Shadows historic preservation program; tours; mus shop sells books, original art and prints

NEW ORLEANS

A **ARTS COUNCIL OF NEW ORLEANS,** 935 Gravier St Ste 850, New Orleans, LA 70113. Tel 504-523-1465; Fax 504-529-2430; Elec Mail dbrown@artscouncilofneworleans.org; Internet Home Page Address: www.artscouncilofneworleans.org; *Interim Dir & CEO* Mary Len Costa; *Pub Art Mgr* Morgana King; *Grants Mgr* Joclyn L Reynolds; *Grants Mgr* Karen Kern; *Fin Mgr* John Vigo; *Dir Devel* Aimee Freeman; *Dir Mktg & Communs* Lindsay Glatz
Estab 1975 to support & expand the opportunities for diverse artistic expression & to bring the community together in celebration of rich multicultural heritage; provides a variety of Cultural Planning, Advocacy, Public Art, Economic Develop, Arts Education, Grants & Service Initiatives focused on its vision of New Orleans as a flourishing cultural center; Average Annual Attendance: 1,000; Mem: Dues organization $154, individuals free with qualifications
Activities: Lect open to public & members; workshops

M **CALLAN CONTEMPORARY,** 518 Julia St, New Orleans, LA 70130. Tel 504-525-0518; Fax 504-525-0516; Elec Mail info@gallerybienvenu.com; *Dir* Borislava Callan; *Owner* Steven Callan
Open Tues-Sat 10AM-5PM, other times by appointment
Collections: works by contemporary artists; paintings; sculpture

M **COLLINS C. DIBOLL ART GALLERY,** 4th Fl Monroe Library, 6363 St Charles Ave New Orleans, LA 70118-6143. Tel 504-864-7248; Elec Mail gallery@loyno.edu; Internet Home Page Address: www.loyno.edu/dibollgallery; *Gallery Dir* Karoline Schleh
Open Mon - Sat 10 AM - 4 PM; No admis fee
Collections: Paintings

A **CONFEDERATE MEMORIAL HALL,** Confederate Museum, 929 Camp St, New Orleans, LA 70130-3907. Tel 504-523-4522; Fax 504-523-8595; Elec Mail Memhall@aol.com; Internet Home Page Address: www.confederatemuseum.com; *Chmn Memorial Hall Comt* Dr Keith Cangelosi; *Cur* Pat Ricci
Open Mon - Sat 10 AM - 4 PM; Admis adults $5, students & sr citizens $4, children $2; Estab 1891 to collect & display articles, memorabilia & records surrounding the Civil War; Gallery is maintained in a one story brick building; one main hall paneled in cypress, one side hall containing paintings of Civil War figures & display cases containing artifacts; Average Annual Attendance: 15,000; Mem: 2000; dues benefactor $500, patron $250, assoc $100, support $50, gen $25, student $10; annual meeting Mar
Income: Financed by mem & admis
Publications: Louisiana Historical Assn Newsletter; Louisiana History, quarterly
Activities: Lect open to public; competitions; sales shop sells books, reproductions & novelties

A **CONTEMPORARY ARTS CENTER,** 900 Camp St, New Orleans, LA 70130-3908. Tel 504-528-3805 (Admin), 3800 (Tickets & Info); Fax 504-528-3828; Elec Mail info@cacno.org; Internet Home Page Address: www.cacno.org; *Exec/Artist Dir* Jay Weigel; *Guest Visual Arts Cur* Dan Cameron; *VPres* Mark Fullmer; *Exhib Mgr* Johnny King; *Performing Arts Mgr & Mem Coordr* Beth Shippert-Meyers; *Educ Cur* Marie Lamb
Open Thurs - Sun 11 AM - 4 PM, hours vary for special events, cl holidays; Admis $5, seniors & students $3, members free; Estab 1976 to support experimentation & innovative products of work in visual arts & performing arts. Interdisciplinary arts center; Average Annual Attendance: 100,000; Mem: 3000; dues $25 & up; annual meeting in June
Special Subjects: Glass
Exhibitions: Art for Arts Sake; White Linen Night; Absolut; Jazz America Series
Activities: Classes for children; lect open to public; concerts; gallery talks; tours; sales shop sells magazines, original art & prints

M **THE HISTORIC NEW ORLEANS COLLECTION,** Williams Research Center, 410 Chartres St, New Orleans, LA 70130-2102. Tel 504-598-7171; Fax 504-598-7168; Elec Mail wrc@hnoc.org; Internet Home Page Address: www.hnoc.org; *Chmn* Mary Louise Christovich; *Dir The Historic New Orleans Collection* Priscilla Lawrence; *Dir Mus Prog* John Lawrence; *Dir Williams Research Ctr* Dr Alfred Lemmon; *Pub Rel Dir* Teresa Devlin; *Dir Publications* Jessica Dormon; *Senior Librn* Pamela D Arceneaux; *Historian & Cur* John Magill; *Manuscripts* Mark Cave
Open Tues - Sat 9:30AM - 4:30PM, Sun 10:30 AM - 4:30PM; No admis fee to Gallery, admis to Williams Residence & Louisiana History Galleries, tour by guide $5; Main bldg constructed in 1792 by Jean Francois Merieult; renovated by Koch & Wilson to accommodate the Louisiana History galleries which house a collection of paintings, prints, documents, books & artifacts relating to the history of Louisiana from the time of its settlement, gathered over a number of years by the late L Kemper Williams & his wife. The foundation was estab in 1966 with private funds to keep original collection intact & to allow for expansion; Research Center for State & Local History/Mus; Average Annual Attendance: 45,000
Library Holdings: Book Volumes 18,000; CD-ROMs; Clipping Files; Compact Disks; Exhibition Catalogs; Fiche; Manuscripts; Maps; Memorabilia; Motion Pictures; Original Art Works; Original Documents; Other Holdings Broadside 200; Pamphlets 10,000; Periodical Subscriptions 30; Photographs; Prints; Records; Slides; Video Tapes
Special Subjects: Historical Material, Photography, Manuscripts
Collections: Charles L Franck, photographs (1900-1955); Dan Leyrer, photographs (1930-1970); Clarence Laughlin, photographs (1935-1965); James Gallier Jr & Sr, architectural drawings (1830-1870); Morries Henry Hobbs, prints (1940); B Lafon, drawings of fortifications (1841); B Simon lithographs of 19th-century bus; Alfred R & William Waud, drawings of Civil War & post-war; maps, paintings, photographs, prints, three-dimensional objects; Civil War Collection
Exhibitions: Various exhibs
Publications: Guide to Research at the Historic New Orleans Collection; exhibition brochures & catalogs; historic publications, monograph series; quarterly newsletter; Guide to The Vieux Carre Survey, a guide to a collection of material on New Orleans
Activities: Docent training; lects open to pub; tours; competitions with awards; gallery talks; concerts; awards Kemper and Leila Williams Prize in Louisiana History; fels; individual paintings & original objects of art lent to mus, institutions, foundations, libraries & research centers; mus shop sells books, original art, magazines, reproductions, prints, slides & ephemera; research collections

M **Royal Street Galleries,** 533 Royal St, New Orleans, LA 70130-2113. Tel 504-523-4662; Fax 504-598-7108; Elec Mail wrc@hnoc.org; Internet Home Page Address: www.hnoc.org; *Exec Dir* Priscilla Lawrence; *CFO* Michael Cohn; *Coll Mgr* Warren J Woods; *Dir Develop & External Affairs* Jack Pruitt Jr; *Dir Mus Progs* John H Lawrence; *Cur Educ* Sue Laudeman; *Sr Cur* Judith H Bonner; *Head Photographer* Keely Merritt; *Head Preparator* Scott Ratterree; *Head Docent* Bunny Hinckley
Open Tues - Sat 9:30 AM - 4:30 PM, Sun 10:30 AM - 4:30 PM, cl holidays; No admis fee to gallery, admis to Williams Residence & Louisiana History Galleries, tour by guide $3; Main bldg constructed in 1792 by Jean Francoise Merieult; renovated by Koch & Wilson to accommodate the Louisiana History Galleries which house a coll of paintings, prints, documents, books & artifacts relating to the history of Louisiana from the time of its settlement, gathered over a number of years by the late L Kemper Williams & his wife; Foundation estab 1966 with pvt funds to keep original coll intact & allow for expansion; Complex comprised of museum & historic French Quarter bldgs: Williams Gallery, Louisiana History Gallery, Williams Residence, Merieult House, Counting House, Maisonette, Townhouse, Louis Adam House & Creole Cottage; Average Annual Attendance: 45,000
Income: Financed by endowment
Special Subjects: Decorative Arts, Drawings, Etchings & Engravings, Folk Art, Architecture, Glass, American Western Art, Furniture, Photography, Portraits, Painting-American, Prints, Silver, Manuscripts, Maps, Watercolors, Embroidery, Bookplates & Bindings
Collections: Charles L Franck, photographs (1900-1955); Dan Leyrer, photographs (1930-1970); Clarence Laughlin, photographs (1935-1965); James Gallier Jr & Sr, architectural drawings (1830-1870); Morries Henry Hobbs, prints (1940); B Lafon, drawings of fortifications (1841); B Simon, lithographs of 19th-c bus; Alfred R & William Waud, drawings of Civil War & post-War; maps, paintings, photographs, prints, 3-D objects; Civil War Collection
Publications: Guide to Research at the Historic New Orleans Collection; exhib brochures & catalogs; historic publications; monograph series; newsletter, quarterly; Guide to The Vieux Carre Survey, a guide to the collection of material on New Orleans
Activities: Docent training; lects open to pub; tours; competitions with awards; gallery talks; concerts; film screenings; awards Kemper & Leila Williams Prize in Louisiana History; fels; individual paintings & original objects of art lent to mus, institutions, foundations, libraries & research ctrs; mus shop sells books, original art, magazines, reproductions, prints, slides & ephemera; research collections

M **LONGUE VUE HOUSE & GARDENS,** 7 Bamboo Rd, New Orleans, LA 70124-1007. Tel 504-488-5488; Fax 504-486-7015; Elec Mail info@longuevue.com; Internet Home Page Address: www.longuevue.com; *Dir* Joe Baker; *Asst Dir* Mary E D'Aquin Fergusson; *Cur* Lenora Costa; *Dir Programs* Jen Gick; *Operations & Sales* Melyne Holmes; *Operations & Sales* Anna Bell Jones; *Head Gardener* Amy Graham; *Dir Finance* Patrick Nedd; *Mktg & Commun* Hillary Strobel; *Community Initiatives* Hilairie Schackai
Open Tues - Sat 10 AM - 4:30 PM, Sun 1 - 5 PM, cl Mon; Admis adults $10, seniors $9, students & children $5; Estab 1968 to preserve & interpret Longue

Vue House & Gardens; Period 1930-40 house & gardens; Average Annual Attendance: 51,000; Mem: 1700; dues family $75, individual $35, biannual meetings in spring & fall
Income: $1,240,000 (financed by endowment, fundraising & admis)
Special Subjects: Decorative Arts, Historical Material, Architecture, Glass, Pottery, Painting-American, Prints, Drawings, Sculpture, Textiles, Costumes, Ceramics, Landscapes, Dolls, Furniture, Silver, Carpets & Rugs, Embroidery, Cartoons, Pewter
Collections: 18th - 19th century English & American furniture; textile coll of 18th - 20th century English, French, & American fabrics, needlework, Karabagh & Aubusson rugs, 19th - 20th century French wallpapers; 18th - 20th century British ceramics; Chinese exports; contemporary & modern art, including Vasarely, Gabo, Picasso, Michel, Agam, Hepworth, & Laurens
Exhibitions: Rotating exhibits
Publications: The Art of the Craftsmen: Ruppert Kohlmaier; The Decorative Arts at Longue Vue; The Queen's Table
Activities: Classes for adults & children; docent training; lects open to pub, 25 vis lectrs per yr; gallery talks; tours; original objects of art lent to other like institutions contingent on facilities; mus shop sells books, original art, reproductions, prints, slides, decorative arts

M **LOUISIANA DEPARTMENT OF CULTURE, RECREATION & TOURISM,** Louisiana State Museum, 751 Chartres St, New Orleans, LA 70116-3205; PO Box 2448, New Orleans, LA 70176-2448. Tel 504-568-6968; Fax 504-568-4995; Internet Home Page Address: www.lsm.crt.state.la.us; *Chmn* Rosemary Ewing; *Dir Cur Serv* Jeff Rubin; *Registrar* Jennae Biddiscombe; *Mus Dir* Sam Rykels; *Dir Coll* Greg Lambousey
Open Tues - Sun 10 AM - 4:30PM; Admis adults $6, seniors & students $5, children 12 & under free, educational groups free by appointment; Estab 1906, to collect, preserve & present original materials illustrating Louisiana's heritage; Gallery is maintained & has eight historic buildings in New Orleans with facilities in Patterson, Natchitoches, Thibodaux & Baton Rouge containing paintings, prints, maps, photographs, decorative arts, furniture, costumes & jazz; Average Annual Attendance: 320,000; Mem: 3000; dues $20-$35; annual meeting in May
Income: $9,000,000 (financed by state appropriation)
Special Subjects: Afro-American Art, Decorative Arts, Drawings, Etchings & Engravings, Folk Art, Marine Painting, Architecture, Glass, Portraits, Pottery, Prints, Period Rooms, Silver, Manuscripts, Sculpture, Graphics, Painting-American, Photography, Watercolors, Bronzes, Ethnology, Textiles, Costumes, Ceramics, Primitive art, Woodcarvings, Decorative Arts, Posters, Dolls, Furniture, Jewelry, Historical Material, Maps, Miniatures, Military Art
Collections: Carnival costumes (2000 items); Colonial documents (500,000 folios); decorative art (8000 items); flat textiles (1000 items); historic costumes (6000 items); jazz & Louisiana music (40,000 objects); Louisiana silver (300); maps & cartography (3000); Newcomb pottery & allied arts (750); paintings (1500 canvases); photography (70,000 images); post Colonial manuscripts (500,000); prints (3000 works); rare Louisiana books (40,000); Sculpture (125 works)
Exhibitions: 8 -12 rotating exhibitions per year
Publications: Louisiana's Black Heritage; Louisiana Portrait Gallery. Vol I; A Social History of the American Alligator; A Medley of Cultures: Louisiana History at the Cabildo; exhibit catalogs
Activities: Classes for adults & children; docent training; dramatic progs; lects open to pub, 6-10 vis lectrs per yr; tours; concerts; gallery talks; individual paintings & original objects of art lent to mus; book traveling exhibs 2-3 per yr; originate traveling exhibs to Louisiana museums, libraries, & community centers; mus shop sells books, original art, reproductions, prints, maps & crafts

L **Louisiana Historical Center Library,** 751 Chartres Ave.; PO Box 2448, New Orleans, LA 70116-2448. Tel 504-568-6968; Fax 504-568-6969; Elec Mail ism@crt.state.la.us; Internet Home Page Address: www.lsm.crt.state.la.us; *Cur Maps & Documents* Kathryn Page; *Dir* James F Sefcik; *Dir Curatorial Svcs* James Carboni; *Dir Mktg & Pub Rels* Lorry Lovell
Open 9 AM - 5 PM Tue - Sun; Admis adults $5, students, seniors, active military $4; Estab 1930, to collect materials related to Louisiana heritage
Library Holdings: Book Volumes 40,000; Clipping Files; Manuscripts; Maps; Original Art Works; Original Documents; Other Holdings Non-circulating Louisiana historical material; Pamphlets; Periodical Subscriptions 5; Records; Reels; Sculpture; Slides
Collections: Costumes, textiles, science & technology, maps & manuscripts, material culture, visual arts, jazz
Activities: Classes for adults & children; docent training; lects open to pub; concerts; gallery talks; tours; sponsoring of competitions; originate traveling exhibs; mus shop sells books, reproductions, prints

M **NEW ORLEANS ACADEMY OF FINE ARTS,** Academy Gallery, 5256 Magazine St, New Orleans, LA 70115-1852. Tel 504-899-8111; Fax 504-897-6811; Elec Mail patsya@noafa.com; Internet Home Page Address: noafa.com; *Pres* Dorothy J Coleman; *Dir Academy* Auseklis Ozolis; *Gallery Dir & Adminr* Patsy Baker Adams
Open Mon - Fri 9 AM - 4 PM, Sat 10 AM - 4 PM; No admis fee; Estab 1978 to provide instruction in the classical approaches to art teaching adjunct to school; Average Annual Attendance: 300
Income: Financed by the academy & endowments
Exhibitions: Rotating exhibits
Activities: Classes for adults; lects open to mems only, 3 vis lectrs per yr; acad awards in painting, drawing, sculpture

M **NEW ORLEANS ARTWORKS AT NEW ORLEANS GLASSWORKS & PRINTMAKING STUDIO,**(New Orleans GlassWorks Gallery & Printmaking Studio at New Orleans ArtWorks Gallery)727 Magazine St, New Orleans, LA 70130-3629. Tel 504-529-7279; Fax 504-539-5417 (call before faxing); Elec Mail neworleansglassworks@gmail.com; Internet Home Page Address: www.neworleansartworks.com; *Pres* Geriod Baronne
Open Mon - Sat 10AM - 5 PM; No admis fee; Estab 1990 to educate visitors about glassworking, printmaking & book binding; 25,000 sq ft front room collectors' gallery with daily demonstrations in the glass, print & book arts studio; Average Annual Attendance: 20,000; Mem: approx 3,500; dues $40, monthly meetings
Income: Financed by mem, sale of art works, national & international corporate funding, tax deductible donations & grants
Library Holdings: Auction Catalogs; Cards; Exhibition Catalogs; Memorabilia; Original Art Works; Other Holdings; Prints; Sculpture
Special Subjects: Prints, Sculpture, Etchings & Engravings, Decorative Arts, Furniture, Metalwork, Enamels
Exhibitions: Gilles Chambrier; Curtiss Brock; Josh Cohen; Fabienne Picaud; Richard Royal; Pino Signoretto; Paul Stankard; Frank Van Denham; Udo Zembok; Dan Schreiber; Terri Walker; Stephen Williams; Jim Mongrain; Jason Christian; Kyle Herr
Activities: Classes for adults & children; classes in torchworking, copper enameling; two-hour short courses; design & wine glasses; hands-on daily glass & print demonstrations in working artist studio; lects open to pub; 4 vis international master artists per year; 6 vis lectrs per yr first Sat of each month; tours; extension prog first Sat of month; dinner receptions while master glassblowers and artists create pieces, tours & demonstrations in their studios; book traveling exhibs at leading museums & universities; sales shop sells original art, books, glasswork & prints made in the glass sculpture & printmaking studio, bookbinding, bronze pours, papermaking, repair of broken glass, commissions available

M **NEW ORLEANS MUSEUM OF ART,** 1 Collins Diboll Cir, City Park New Orleans, LA 70124-4603; PO Box 19123, New Orleans, LA 70179-0123. Tel 504-658-4100; Fax 504-658-4199; Elec Mail palexander@noma.org; Internet Home Page Address: www.noma.org; *Dir* Susan M Taylor; *Cur Decorative Arts* John W Keefe; *Asst Dir Art & Cur Asian Art* Lisa Rotondo-McCord; *Ed Arts Quarterly* Caroline Goyette; *Registrar& Cur Native American & Pre-Columbian Art* Paul Tarver; *Librn* Sheila Cork; *Cur African Art* William A Fagaly; *Asst Registrar* Jennifer Ickes; *Asst to Dir Emer* Emma Haas; *Sculpture Garden Mgr* Pamela Buckman; *Asst Dir for Admin & Fin* Gail Asprodites; *Mus Shop Mgr* Patricia Trautman; *Dir Publications & Design* Aisha Champagne; *Cur Photography* Diego Cortez; *Cur Contemporary & Modern Art* Miranda Lash; *Asst Dir Educ* Alice Yelen; *Facility Mgr* Karl Oelkers; *Dir Develop* Marilyn Dittman
Open Tues - Sun 10 AM - 5 PM, Fri until 9 PM; Admis adults res $10, seniors, active military & students $8, children 7-17 $6, children 6 & under free; Estab 1910; building given to city by Issac Delgado, maintained by municipal funds & private donations to provide a stimulus to a broader cultural life for the entire community. Stern Auditorium, Ella West Freeman wing for changing exhibitions; Wisner Educ wing for learning experiences; Delgado Building for permanent display shop; 135,000 sq ft space, three fl; Average Annual Attendance: 220,000; Mem: 7,000; dues $60-$20,000; annual meeting in Nov
Income: Financed by mem, city appropriation, federal, state & foundation grant, corporate contributions & individual donations
Special Subjects: Afro-American Art, Decorative Arts, Folk Art, Furniture, Porcelain, Portraits, Pre-Columbian Art, Painting-American, Period Rooms, Silver, Bronzes, Painting-European, Painting-French, Painting-Japanese, Sculpture, Graphics, Latin American Art, Photography, American Indian Art, African Art, Glass, Oriental Art, Asian Art, Painting-Dutch, Painting-Flemish
Collections: Kress Collection of Italian Renaissance & Baroque Painting; Chapman H Hyams Collection of Barbizon & Salon Paintings; Edgar Degas works; 20th century English & Continental art, including Surrealism & School of Paris; Melvin P Billups Glass Collection; 19th & 20th century United States & Louisiana painting & sculpture; Latter- Schlesinger Collection of English & Continental Portrait Miniatures; Victor Kiam Collection of African, Oceanic American Indian, & 20th century European & American Painting & Sculpture; The Matilda Geddings Gray Foundation Collection of Works by Peter Carl Faberge; Rosemonde E & Emile Kuntz Federal & Louisiana Period Rooms; 16th - 20th century French art; Bert Piso Collection of 17th century Dutch painting; Imperial Treasures by Peter Carl Faberge from the Matilda Geddings Gray Foundation Collection; Morgan-Whitney Collection of Chinese Jades; Rosemonde E & Emile Kuntz Rooms of Late 18th - Early 19th Century American Furniture; Stern-Davis Collection of Peruvian Painting; Sydney & Walda Besthoff Sculpture Garden
Publications: Arts Quarterly; catalogs of New Orleans Museum of Art organized exhibitions; History of New Orleans Museum of Art
Activities: Classes for adults & children; docent training; teacher workshops; art therapy prog; internships; Taylor Scholars Prog; lects open to pub, 10 vis lectrs per yr; concerts; gallery talks; tours including multi-language; competitions incl Cox Art Contest; Isaac Delgado Memorial Award ann to outstanding art patron; individual paintings & original objects of art lent in metropolitan New Orleans; book traveling exhibs 5 per yr to schools and libraries; originate traveling exhibs to other art mus in USA and Europe; mus shop sells books, original art, reproductions, prints, cards, slides, toys & jewelry

L **Felix J Dreyfous Library,** 1 Collins Diboll Cir, New Orleans, LA 70124-4603; PO Box 19123, New Orleans, LA 70179-0123. Tel 504-658-4100; Fax 504-658-4199; Internet Home Page Address: www.noma.org; *Librn* Sheila Cork
Admis non-LA residents $8, adults $7, seniors 65 & over $4, children 3 & under free; Estab 1971 to provide information for reference to the cur, mus members & art researchers; Open Wed-Sun 10 AM - 4:30 PM; Average Annual Attendance: 100,000
Income: Financed by mem, donations & gifts
Library Holdings: Audio Tapes; Book Volumes 20,500; Cassettes; Clipping Files; Exhibition Catalogs; Fiche; Memorabilia; Pamphlets; Periodical Subscriptions 50; Reels; Slides; Video Tapes
Special Subjects: Photography
Collections: WPA Project - New Orleans Artists
Activities: Mus shop sells collectibles; books; jewelry & art related items

M **THE OGDEN MUSEUM OF SOUTHERN ART, UNIVERSITY OF NEW ORLEANS,** 925 Camp St, New Orleans, LA 70130-3907. Tel 504-539-9600; Fax 504-539-9602; Elec Mail info@ogdenmuseum.org; Internet Home Page Address: www.ogdenmuseum.org; *Dir* William Andrews; *Deputy Dir/Music Cur* Libra LaGrone; *Educ* Ellen Balkin; *Cur* Bradley Sumrall; *Pub Relations* Sue Strachan; *Security* Monica Barre; *Chair* Julia Reed; *Cur Center for So Craft & Design* Elizabeth Bowie; *Develop Dir* Colleen Connor
Open Wed - Mon 10 AM - 5PM & Thurs 6PM - 8PM after hrs; cl New Year's Day, Mardi Gras Day, Memorial Day, July 4th, Labor Day, Thanksgiving & Christmas; Admis adults $10, seniors $8, students $5, discount to groups, free

admis for Louisiana residents on Thurs 10 AM - 5PM; Founded 1994, Grand Opening 2003; Mus showcases the visual art & culture of the American south. Pub nonprofit org; FT paid 16, PT paid 6, interns 6, docents & vols approx 50; Average Annual Attendance: 50,000 - 99,999; Mem: 1,800; dues vary
Special Subjects: Afro-American Art, Decorative Arts, Drawings, Etchings & Engravings, Folk Art, Architecture, Ceramics, Glass, Furniture, Photography, Portraits, Pottery, Painting-American, Prints, Textiles, Woodcuts, Sculpture, Graphics, Watercolors, Costumes, Religious Art, Crafts, Primitive art, Woodcarvings, Landscapes, Posters, Embroidery
Collections: Coll showcases the visual art of the southern states & WA DC from 1733 - present; Center for Southern Craft and Design
Activities: Educ prog; docent training; classes for adults & children; dramatic progs; docent training; live music by Southern musicians every Thurs night: Ogden After Hours; summer camps for children; lects open to pub; lects for mems only; 4 vis lects per yr; guided tours; concerts; gallery talks; sponsoring of competitions; hobby workshops; Sunday afternoon programming; Sundays At the O; schols; fels; organize traveling exhibs to mus; Mus shop sells books, magazines, original art, reproductions, prints, crafts & many other items

M **TULANE UNIVERSITY,** Newcomb Art Gallery, 6823 St Charles Ave, Woldenberg Art Center #81 New Orleans, LA 70118-5665. Tel 504-865-5328; Fax 504-865-5329; Elec Mail gallery@tulane.edu; Internet Home Page Address: www.newcombartgallery.tulane.edu; *Cur* Sally Main, MFA; *Interim Dir* Jeremy Jernegan, MFA; *Mktg Coordr* Teresa Parker Farris, MA; *Registrar Univ Colls* Thomas Strider; *Educ Coordr* Laura Ledot; *Visitor Servs* Beau Box; *Accountant* Melissa Russell
Open Tues - Fri 10 AM - 5 PM, Sat & Sun 11 AM - 4 PM; No admis fee; Gallery estab 1996 to enrich culture & intellectual life of the Gulf South with exhibitions & programming; Four exhibition galleries with one semi-permanent display of Newcomb College decorative objects; Mem: Please refer to website for info
Income: Financed by endowment, membership & university support
Purchases: Newcomb pottery
Special Subjects: Decorative Arts, Metalwork, Photography, Painting-American, Sculpture, Drawings, Latin American Art, Ceramics, Crafts, Pottery, Landscapes, Glass, Asian Art
Collections: Newcomb College Collection: Louisiana arts & crafts; Tulane University Art Collection: 18th-century contemporary paintings, sculpture, works on paper
Exhibitions: (10/2013) Women, Art, & Social Change: The Newcomb Pottery Enterprise
Publications: Newsletter & exhibition catalogs
Activities: Classes for children; lects open to pub, 2-4 vis lectrs per yr; gallery talks; tours; originate traveling exhibs, 1 per yr

M **TULANE UNIVERSITY,** University Art Collection, 7001 Freret St, Tulane University Library New Orleans, LA 70118-5549. Tel 504-865-5685; Fax 504-865-5761; Internet Home Page Address: tulane.edu; *Cur* Joan G Caldwell
Open Mon - Fri 9 AM - 4:45 PM, cl school holidays & Mardi Gras; No admis fee; Estab 1980
Special Subjects: Decorative Arts, Drawings, Historical Material, Photography, Pottery, Prints, Manuscripts, Maps, Graphics, Sculpture, Watercolors, Religious Art
Collections: Linton-Surget Collection; La Artists; Modern British Prints; 19th & 20th Century paintings; photograph coll
Activities: Gallery talks; tours; original objects of art lent to other institutions; book traveling exhibs; originate traveling exhibs

L **Architecture Library,** 7001 Freret St, Howard-Tilton Memorial Library New Orleans, LA 70118-5549. Tel 504-865-5391; Fax 504-862-8966; Internet Home Page Address: www.architecture.tulane.edu/facilities/the-architecture-library; *Unit Supervisor* Alan Velasquez; *Library Technician* Joshua Windham
Open fall & spring Mon - Thurs 8:30 AM - 9:30 PM, Fri 8:30 AM - 4:45 PM, Sat 1 - 6 PM, Sun 2 - 7 PM; summer Mon - Thurs 8:30 AM - 5:30 PM; cl Sat & Sun; Estab 1971; For reference only; Average Annual Attendance: 8415
Income: Donations
Purchases: Architecture trade catalogs
Library Holdings: Book Volumes 26,000; Periodical Subscriptions 249
Special Subjects: Architecture

L **Southeastern Architectural Archive,** 6801 Freret St, New Orleans, LA 70118-5549. Tel 504-865-5699; Elec Mail krylance@tulane.edu; Internet Home Page Address: http:// library.tulane.edu/eaa; *Head* Keli E Rylance PhD; *Archivist* Kevin Williams
Open Mon - Fri 9 AM - noon, 1 - 5 PM; cl Tulane Univ Holidays ; Estab 1980; preservation & conservation of architectural records associated with the southeastern Gulf Region; Average Annual Attendance: 765
Income: Donations
Purchases: Architecture trade catalogs
Library Holdings: Book Volumes; Kodachrome Transparencies; Lantern Slides; Maps; Original Art Works; Original Documents; Other Holdings; Pamphlets; Photographs; Prints; Sculpture; Slides; Video Tapes Drafting/Architectural Office Tools & Supplies
Special Subjects: Landscape Architecture, Drawings, Maps, Architecture
Collections: (over 180 colls)
Exhibitions: (01/10/2013-12/10/2013) The Super Dome; (03/15/2014-12/10/2014) Bungalows & Cottages
Activities: Classes for adults

M **UNIVERSITY OF NEW ORLEANS,** Fine Arts Gallery, 2000 Lakeshore Dr, New Orleans, LA 70122-3520. Tel 504-280-6493; Fax 504-280-7346; Elec Mail finearts@uno.ed; Internet Home Page Address: www.uno.edu; *Gallery Dir* Doyle Gertjejansen
Open Mon - Fri 8:30 AM - 4:30 PM; No admis fee; Estab 1974 to expose the students & community to historic & contemporary visual arts; Gallery consists of 1800 sq ft, 165 lineal ft of wall space, 20 ft ceilings, natural & artificial lighting; Average Annual Attendance: 15,000
Income: Financed by state appropriation
Exhibitions: Rotating exhibits
Activities: Cr & non-cr classes for adults in conjunction with Univ of New Orleans; lects open to public, 20 vis lectrs per year

L **Earl K Long Library,** 2000 Lakeshore Dr, New Orleans, LA 70122-3520. Tel 504-280-6549; Fax 504-280-7277; Internet Home Page Address: www.library.uno.edu; *Chmn Reference Svcs* Robert T Heriard
Open Mon-Thurs 8AM-11AM; Fri 8AM-8PM, Sat 9AM-6PM, Sun Noon-8PM; Estab 1958 for scholarly & professional research; Circ 110,140; For lending & reference
Income: $2,401,104 (financed by state appropriation)
Purchases: $797,407
Library Holdings: Book Volumes 394,729; Cards; Fiche; Other Holdings Art per subs 250; Art vols 12,974; Periodical Subscriptions 4500; Reels

OPELOUSAS

M **OPELOUSAS MUSEUM OF ART, INC (OMA),** 106 N Union St, Opelousas, LA 70570-6267. Tel 337-942-4991; Fax 337-942-4930; Elec Mail omamuseum@aol.com; Internet Home Page Address: http://auction.lpb.org/oma.htm; *Cur* Keith J Guidry
Open Tues - Fri1 - 5 PM, Sat 9 AM - 5 PM, cl Sun & Mon; Admis adults $3, accompanying children & mems free; Estab 1997 to display traveling art exhibitions; Shows exhibitions from major museums, private collections & community & local exhibitions; Average Annual Attendance: 3,500; Mem: 500+
Special Subjects: Historical Material, Architecture, Drawings, Hispanic Art, Latin American Art, Mexican Art, Painting-American, Photography, American Indian Art, American Western Art, Folk Art, Etchings & Engravings, Landscapes, Afro-American Art, Decorative Arts, Collages, Painting-Canadian, Marine Painting, Painting-French, Maps, Juvenile Art, Medieval Art, Painting-Spanish, Painting-Italian, Painting-German, Military Art, Painting-Israeli
Activities: Lects open to pub; lect for members only; 6 vis lectrs per yr; tours; book traveling exhibs 4 per yr; originate traveling exhibs 2 per yr

PATTERSON

M **WEDELL-WILLIAMS MEMORIAL AVIATION MUSEUM,** LA 90 in Kemper Williams Park, 118 Cotton Rd Patterson, LA 70392; P.O. Box 2448, New Orleans, LA 70176. Tel 985-399-1268; Internet Home Page Address: www.lsm.crt.state.la.us/wedellex.htm
Open Tues-Sat 9AM-5PM.; Admis adults $3, students $2, seniors, military, & children 12 and under free; Estab by the Legislature as the state's official aviation mus, mus is named after Jimmie Wedell & Harry Williams, two Louisiana aviators who formed an air service in 1928; Mus is committed to preserving & presenting artifacts & documents reflecting aviation history in Louisiana
Special Subjects: Historical Material
Collections: Airworthy replica of Wedell's "44" racer; 1939 D175 Beechcraft; Presidential Aero-Commander 680 that was used during the Eisenhower administration; race trophies from the 1930s; the state's largest coll of model airplanes; vintage hot air balloon basket
Activities: Model airplane-building classes; astronomy workshop for children

PORT ALLEN

M **WEST BATON ROUGE PARISH,** (West Baton Rouge Historical Association) West Baton Rouge Museum, 845 N Jefferson Ave, Port Allen, LA 70767-2417. Tel 225-336-2422; Fax 225-336-2448; Elec Mail contact_us@wbrmuseum.com; Internet Home Page Address: www.westbatonrougemuseum.com; *Dir* Julia Rose; *Educ Cur* Jeannie Giroir Luckett; *Admin Asst* Alice LeBlanc; *Cur* Lauren Davis
Open Tues - Sat 10 AM - 4:30 PM, Sun 2 - 5 PM; Admis adults $4 seniors & students $2, West Baton Rouge Parish residents free; Estab 1968 to foster interest in history, particularly that of West Baton Rouge Parish; to encourage research, collection & preservation of material illustrating past & present activities of the parish; to operate one or more museums; to receive gifts & donations; to accept exhibits & historical materials on loan; A large room housing a scale model of a sugar mill (one inch to one ft, dated 1904) & parish memorabilia; restored French Creole cottage (c 1830); a room 31 X 40 ft for art exhibits; restored plantation quarters cabin (1850); Average Annual Attendance: 18,000; Mem: 300; dues $10; annual meeting in Jan
Income: $250,000 (financed by mem, gifts & millage levied on parish)
Library Holdings: Original Documents; Pamphlets; Photographs; Prints
Special Subjects: Drawings, Furniture, Photography, Pottery, Painting-American, Prints, Sculpture, Architecture, Costumes, Crafts, Manuscripts, Furniture, Maps, Restorations, Period Rooms
Collections: Art coll of parish artifacts; c1830 French Creole Cottage; contemporary Louisiana (drawings, paintings, prints & sculpture); early 19th century furnishings; historic photographs & family papers; Newcomb Pottery Coll; duck decoys; c1880s Share Cropper Cabins (2); early 20th century shot gun dwelling
Exhibitions: Gallery with six shows yearly
Publications: Ecoutez, 4 times a yr
Activities: Classes for children; docent training; lects open to pub, 1 vis lectr per yr; tours; book traveling exhibs semi-annually; mus shop sells books, magazines, original art, reproductions & prints

SAINT MARTINVILLE

M **LONGFELLOW-EVANGELINE STATE COMMEMORATIVE AREA,** 1200 N Main St, Hwy 31 Saint Martinville, LA 70582-3516. Tel 337-394-4284, 394-3754, 888-677-2900; Fax 337-394-3553; Elec Mail longfellow@crt.state.la.us; Internet Home Page Address: www.crt.state.la.us; *Site & Cur Mus* Suzanna Laviolette; *Mgr* Reinaldo Barnes
Open daily 9 AM - 5 PM, cl Thanksgiving, Christmas & New Year; Admis adults $2, adults over 61 free, children under 13 free, all school groups free; Estab 1934 to display & describe 19th century French lifeways & folk items; Artworks are displayed in a 19th century plantation home, in the interpretive center of the site & in the 18th century cabin; Average Annual Attendance: 26,000
Income: Financed by state appropriations

Special Subjects: Architecture, Painting-American, Photography, Prints, Textiles, Religious Art, Ceramics, Crafts, Folk Art, Pottery, Landscapes, Decorative Arts, Portraits, Dolls, Furniture, Glass, Porcelain, Painting-French, Historical Material, Coins & Medals, Period Rooms, Embroidery, Laces, Pewter, Reproductions
Collections: Early 19th century portraits; 18th, 19th & 20th centuries textile arts; local craft & folk art; Louisiana cypress furniture; 19th century antiques; religious art of the 19th century; wood carvings; Plantation House; Acadian Art
Exhibitions: Attakapas Trade Days (Fall); Creole Holidays (Dec); Plantation Days (Spring)
Activities: Dramatic progs; docent training; lects open to pub, 4 vis lectrs per yr; tours; workshops

SHREVEPORT

M CENTENARY COLLEGE OF LOUISIANA, Meadows Museum of Art, 2911 Centenary Blvd, Shreveport, LA 71104-3335; PO Box 41188, Shreveport, LA 71134-1188. Tel 318-869-5169; 5040; Fax 318-869-5730; Elec Mail ddufilho@centenary.edu; Internet Home Page Address: www.centenary.edu/departme/meadows; *Dir* Diane Dufilho
Open Tues - Fri Noon - 4 PM, Sat & Sun 1 - 4 PM, Thurs open late until 5PM; No admis fee; Estab 1975 to house the Indo-China Collection of Drawings & Paintings by Jean Despujols; Eight galleries; main gallery on first floor 25 x 80 ft; other galleries 25 x 30 ft; linen walls, track lights and no windows; Average Annual Attendance: 18,000
Income: Financed by endowment
Special Subjects: Ethnology, Painting-French
Collections: 360 works in Indo-China Collection, dealing with Angkor Region, The Cordillera, Gulf of Siam, Laos, The Nam-Te, The Thai, Upper Tonkin, Vietnam
Exhibitions: Rotating exhibits
Publications: Partial Catalog of Permanent Collection with 21 color plates
Activities: Docent training; lects open to pub, 4 vis lectrs per yr; gallery talks; tours; individual paintings & original objects of art lent to qualified mus; lending coll includes one motion picture

M LOUISIANA STATE EXHIBIT MUSEUM, 3015 Greenwood Rd, Shreveport, LA 71109; PO Box 38356, Shreveport, LA 71133-8356. Tel 318-632-2020; Fax 318-632-2056; Elec Mail lsem@sos.louisiana.gov; Internet Home Page Address: www.sos.louisiana.gov/museums; *Cur* Nita Cole; *Asst Dir* Rodney Clements; *Pub Info Officer* Cynthia Grogan
Open Mon - Fri 9 AM - 4 PM; No admis fee; Estab 1939 to display permanent & temporary exhibitions demonstrating the state's history, resources & natural beauty; Art Gallery is maintained; Average Annual Attendance: 200,000
Income: Financed by state appropriation
Special Subjects: American Indian Art, Anthropology, American Western Art, Flasks & Bottles, Pottery, Maps, Architecture, Bronzes, Archaeology, Costumes, Crafts, Woodcarvings, Dolls, Historical Material, Miniatures, Dioramas, Military Art
Collections: Archaeology; dioramas; historical artifacts; Indian artifacts; murals; natural history
Publications: brochures
Activities: Classes for children; docent training; pub Archaeology prog; lects open to pub, 4-6 vis lectrs per yr; gallery talks; films; concerts; tours; competitions sponsored; book traveling exhibs, 3 per yr

M THE MULTICULTURAL CENTER OF THE SOUTH, 520 Spring St Shreveport, LA 71101-3257; PO Box 305 Shreveport, LA 71101-0305. Tel 318-424-1380; Fax 318-424-1384; Elec Mail jgatlin-mccs@comcast.net; Internet Home Page Address: www.mccsouth.org; *Dir Progs* Janice Gatlin; *Curriculum Specialist* Priscilla Metoyer
Open to pub Tues - Fri 10 AM - 4 PM; Sat by appointment for large groups; Admis adults $3, students & seniors $2; Estab 1999; 16 cultural exhibs; Average Annual Attendance: 1500

M R W NORTON ART FOUNDATION, R W Norton Art Gallery, 4747 Creswell Ave, Shreveport, LA 71106-1899. Tel 318-865-6201; Fax 318-869-0435; Elec Mail gallery@rwnaf.org; Internet Home Page Address: www.rwnaf.org; *Pres Bd M* Lewis Norton; *Secy-Treas & Dir Pub Rels* Jerry M Bloomer; *Bldg & Grounds Supt* Gerry Ward; *Dir Research & Rare Coll* Everl Adair; *Educ Dir* Emily Boykin; *Tour & Spec Events Coordr* Ashleigh Newberry-Mills
Open Tues - Fri 10 AM - 5 PM, Sat & Sun 1 - 5 PM, cl Mon & holidays; No admis fee; Estab 1946, opened 1966. Founded to present aspects of the develop of American & European art & culture through exhibition & interpretation of fine works of art & literature, both from the Gallery's own collections & from those of other institutions & individuals; American & European art spanning over four centuries spotlighting art of the American West by Frederic Remington and Charles Russell; Average Annual Attendance: 17,000
Income: Financed by endowment
Library Holdings: Auction Catalogs; Audio Tapes 12,000; Book Volumes; Exhibition Catalogs; Original Documents; Pamphlets; Periodical Subscriptions
Special Subjects: Painting-American, Sculpture, American Western Art, Pottery, Painting-European, Portraits, Silver, Tapestries, Miniatures
Collections: American miniatures & colonial silver; contemporary American & European painting & sculpture; painting & sculpture relating to Early American history; Paintings by 19th century American artists of the Hudson River School; Portraits of famous confederate leaders; 16th Century Flemish tapestries; Wedgwood collection; paintings & sculpture by western American artists Frederic Remington & Charles M Russell; Frederic Remington Collection; Charles M Russell Collection
Publications: Announcements of spec exhibs; catalogs (60 through 2007); catalogs of the Charles M Russell Collection & of the Wedgwood Collection; electronic newsletter
Activities: Educ dept; docent training; classes for children; lects open to pub; vis lectrs 3 per yr; gallery talks; tours; serves elderly in nursing homes; book traveling exhibs 2 per yr; mus shop sells exhibition catalogs, catalogs of permanent collection

L Library, 4747 Creswell Ave, Shreveport, LA 71106-1899. Tel 318-865-4201; Fax 318-869-0435; Elec Mail jb@rwnaf.org; Internet Home Page Address: www.rwnaf.org; *Secy-Treas* Jerry Bloomer
Open by appointment only; No admis fee; Estab 1946 to acquire and make available for public use on the premises, important books, exhibition catalogs, etc relating to the visual arts, literature, American history and genealogy, as well as other standard reference and bibliographic works for reference only; Circ Non-circulating; A mus of Am & European art spanning over 4 centuries; Average Annual Attendance: 20,000 - 30,000
Income: Financed by endowment
Library Holdings: Auction Catalogs; Book Volumes 12,000; Clipping Files; Exhibition Catalogs; Manuscripts; Memorabilia; Other Holdings Original documents; Auction catalogs; Pamphlets; Periodical Subscriptions 100; Photographs; Reels; Slides
Special Subjects: Art History, Decorative Arts, Illustration, Photography, Drawings, Etchings & Engravings, Graphic Arts, Manuscripts, Painting-American, Painting-British, Painting-Flemish, Painting-French, Painting-German, Prints, Sculpture, Painting-European, History of Art & Archaeology, Portraits, Watercolors, Ceramics, American Western Art, Bronzes, Printmaking, Porcelain, Southwestern Art, Glass, Stained Glass, Metalwork, Dolls, Goldsmithing, Miniatures, Pottery, Silver, Silversmithing, Marine Painting, Landscapes, Coins & Medals, Pewter, Architecture
Collections: James M Owens Memorial Collection of Early Americana (725 volumes on Colonial history, particularly on Virginia); large coll of books on Frederic Remington & Charles M Russell
Activities: Conduct tours & slide progs; sales of collection & special exhib catalogs

L SOUTHERN UNIVERSITY LIBRARY, 3050 Martin Luther King Jr Dr, Attn Library Shreveport, LA 71107. Tel 318-674-3400; Fax 318-670-6403; Internet Home Page Address: www.susla.edu; *Dir* Orella R Brazile
Open Mon-Thurs 8AM-9PM, Fri 8AM-5PM, Sat 9AM-1PM Summer Mon-Fri 8AM-5PM; Estab 1967 to supplement the curriculum & provide bibliographic as well as reference service to both the acad community & the pub
Library Holdings: Book Volumes 48,789; Cassettes 1121; Clipping Files; Fiche 24,308; Filmstrips 414; Framed Reproductions; Motion Pictures 59; Original Art Works; Pamphlets 750; Periodical Subscriptions 379; Prints; Records 293; Reels; Reproductions 12; Sculpture; Slides 22,874; Video Tapes 240
Collections: Black Collection, pictures, clippings & books; Louisiana Collection; Black Ethnic Archives (local people)
Exhibitions: Show Local Artists Exhibitions

M SOUTHERN UNIVERSITY MUSEUM OF ART IN SHREVEPORT, 3050 Martin Luther King Jr Dr, Attn Art Shreveport, LA 71107.

SORRENTO

M LOUISIANA POTTERY, 6470 Hwy 22, Cajun Village Sorrento, LA 70778. Tel 225-675-5572; Elec Mail lapottery@cox.net; Internet Home Page Address: www.louisianapottery.com; *Owner* Judy L Starrett
Open Tues-Sun 10AM-5PM; No admis fee; Apr, 1999; Fine hand-crafted wares made by Louisiana artisans; Mem: 135+ artists represented
Collections: pottery; etchings; hand-blown glass; pine needle baskets; hand-carved wooden ducks & boats; original art
Exhibitions: Permanent coll - exhib on site Pat Wagner, creating beauty for the World
Activities: Classes for adults & children; 2 vis lectrs per yr; organize traveling exhibs open; sales shop sells books, magazines, original art, pottery & clay sculpture

WEST MONROE

M OUACHITA RIVER ART GALLERY, 308 Trenton St West Monroe, LA 71291-3148.

MAINE

ALNA

M WISCASSET, WATERVILLE & FARMINGTON RAILWAY MUSEUM (WW&F), 97 Cross St, Alna, ME 04535; PO Box 242, Alna, ME 04535-0242. Tel 207-882-4193; Elec Mail info@wwfry.org; Internet Home Page Address: www.wwfry.org; *Pres* Stephen Suppa; *Finance Dir* James Patten; *Publicity* Gordon Davis; *Archivist* Bruce Wilson; *Mem Chmn* Frances Hernandez; *Mus Gift Shop Mgr* Linda Zeller
Open Memorial Day - Columbus Day: Sat & Sun 9 AM - 5 PM; after Columbus Day - before Memorial Day: Sat 9 AM - 5 PM; Admis adults $7, children $4; Estab 1989; Operating restored two-ft gauge railroad with mus & shops (pvt nonprofit org; vol hrs 25,000; 1st Maine Congressional Dist); Average Annual Attendance: 1000 - 9999; Mem: Dues Indiv Life $300, Indiv Annual $30
Income: $200,000 - Financed by donations, gift shop sales, tickets
Library Holdings: Book Volumes; Clipping Files; DVDs; Framed Reproductions; Manuscripts; Maps; Memorabilia; Original Documents; Photographs
Collections: Numerous books, photos, documents, artifacts, and original railroad equip from 2-ft gauge railroad
Publications: WW&F Newsletter, six times per yr; WW&F Musings, 128-pg book
Activities: Docent prog; guided tours; training progs for professionals; films; ann picnic; Christmas trains

AUGUSTA

M **UNIVERSITY OF MAINE AT AUGUSTA,** Jewett Hall Gallery, 46 University Dr Augusta, ME 04330. Tel 207-621-3243; Fax 207-621-3293; Elec Mail peter.precourt@maine.edu; *Dir* Peter Precourt
Open Mon - Thurs 10 AM - 7 PM, Fri 10 AM - 5 PM; No admis fee; Estab 1970 to provide changing exhibitions of the visual arts for the university students and faculty and for the larger Augusta-Kennebec Valley community; the principal exhibition area is a two level combination lounge and gallery; Average Annual Attendance: 9,000
Income: Financed by university budget
Collections: Drawings, paintings, outdoor sculpture
Exhibitions: Five major art exhibits
Activities: Lects open to public, 2-3 vis lectrs per year; gallery talks; tours

BANGOR

M **UNIVERSITY OF MAINE,** Museum of Art, 40 Harlow St, Bangor, ME 04401-5102. Tel 207-561-3350; Fax 207-561-3351; Internet Home Page Address: www.umma.umaine.edu; *Asst Mus Coordr & Mem Mgr* Kathryn Jovanelli; *Dir* George Kinghorn; *Educ Coordr* Eva Wagner; *Registrar/Preparator* Sean Flannigan; *Mus Tech* Aaron Pyle
Open Mon - Sat 10 AM - 5 PM; No admis fee; Estab 1946 to add to the cultural life of the university student; to be a service to Maine artists; to promote good & important art, both historic & modern; The mus is located in downtown Bangor's Historic Norumbega Hall; Average Annual Attendance: 13,000
Income: Financed by state appropriation to university, donations & grants
Special Subjects: Painting-American, Prints, Drawings, Photography, Watercolors, Woodcuts, Etchings & Engravings, Portraits, Posters
Collections: The Mus of Art's permanent coll has grown to a stature which makes it a nucleus in the state for historic & contemporary art. It includes more than 6000 original works of art & is particularly strong in American mid-20th century works
Publications: Biennial catalogs & exhibition notes, newsletter
Activities: Classes for adults and children; lects open to pub & mems only, 1-2 vis lectrs per yr; gallery talks, tours; scholarships & fels offered; museums by mail program; individual paintings & original objects of art lent to qualified museums & campus departments; book traveling exhibs 1-5 per yr; originate traveling exhibs 1-3 yr

BATH

M **MAINE MARITIME MUSEUM,** 243 Washington St, Bath, ME 04530-1638. Tel 207-443-1316; Fax 207-443-1665; Internet Home Page Address: www.bathmaine.com; *Exec Dir* Amy Lent Jr; *Dir Library* Nathan Lipfert; *Cur* Christopher Hall
Open daily 9:30 AM - 5 PM, cl New Year's Day, Thanksgiving, Christmas; Admis adults $9.50, children under 17 $6.50, under 6 free, seniors $8.50, group rates available; Estab 1964 for the preservation of Maine's maritime heritage; Several galleries; Average Annual Attendance: 65,000; Mem: 1800; dues $25 & up; annual meeting in Sept.
Income: Financed by mem, gifts, grants & admis
Special Subjects: Marine Painting
Collections: Marine art; navigational instruments; ship models; shipbuilding tools; shipping papers; traditional watercraft
Exhibitions: Historical Percy & Small Shipyard; Lobstering & the Maine Coast; Maritime History of Maine; small watercraft; other rotating exhibits
Publications: Rhumb Line, quarterly
Activities: Classes for adults & children; docent training; lects open to pub, 20 vis lectrs per yr; group tours; concerts; gallery talks; individual paintings & original objects of art lent to non-profit institutions with proper security & climate control; Mus shop sells books, reproductions, prints & related novelties

L **Archives Library,** 243 Washington St, Bath, ME 04530. Tel 207-443-1316; Fax 207-443-1665; Elec Mail lipfert@maritime.org; Internet Home Page Address: www.mainemaritimemuseum.org; *Senior Cur* Nathan Lipfert; *Registrar* Kelly Page
Open Tues & Thurs 9:30AM-3PM; Admis $12; Estab 1964; Circ Non-circ; Small reference library; Average Annual Attendance: 1,800
Income: Financed by mem, admis, gifts & grants
Library Holdings: Auction Catalogs; Audio Tapes 220; Book Volumes 14,000; Cassettes; Clipping Files; Kodachrome Transparencies; Lantern Slides; Manuscripts 2,000 lin ft; Maps 1,000; Memorabilia; Motion Pictures; Original Art Works; Other Holdings vessel papers-42,000 sheets; Pamphlets; Periodical Subscriptions 50; Photographs 130,000; Reels 620; Slides; Video Tapes 482
Special Subjects: Manuscripts, Maps, Painting-American, Painting-European, Historical Material, Marine Painting, Scrimshaw, Painting-Australian
Collections: Sewall Ship Papers, shipbuilding firms bus papers; vessel plans, nautical charts
Exhibitions: Maritime History of Maine, Lobstering & the Maine Coast
Activities: Classes for adults; docent training; boat building shop; lects open to public; lects for members only; concerts; tours; Mariner's Award; White House "Preserve America Stewards" award (2010); mus shop sells books, magazines, original art, reproductions & prints

BLUE HILL

M **PARSON FISHER HOUSE,** Jonathan Fisher Memorial, Inc, 44 Mines Rd, Rte 15, Blue Hill, ME 04614; PO Box 537, Blue Hill, ME 04614-0537. Tel 207-374-2459; Fax 207-374-5082; Elec Mail info@jonathanfisherhouse.org; Internet Home Page Address: www.jonathanfisherhouse.org; *Pres* Eric Linnell; *Adminr* Sandra Linnell
Open Thurs, Fri, & Sat 1-4PM; Admis $2; Estab 1965 to preserve the home & memorabilia of Jonathan Fisher. The house was designed & built by him in 1814; Average Annual Attendance: 300; Mem: 260; dues endowment $1000, contributing $100, sustaining $25, annual $10; annual meeting in Aug

Income: Financed by admis fees, dues, gifts & endowment funds
Purchases: Original Fisher paintings or books
Collections: Furniture, Manuscripts, Paintings & Articles made by Fisher
Exhibitions: Annual Arts & Crafts Fair
Activities: Lects open to public, 1-2 vis lectrs per year; individual paintings & original objects of art lent to state museum or comparable organizations for exhibit; sales shop sells reproductions

BOOTHBAY HARBOR

A **BOOTHBAY REGION ART FOUNDATION,** One Townsend Ave, Boothbay Harbor, ME; PO Box 124, Boothbay Harbor, ME 04538-0124. Tel 207-633-2703; Elec Mail braf@boothbayartists.org; Internet Home Page Address: www.boothbayartists.org; *Pres* Jennifer Litchfield; *Gallery Mgr* June Rose; *VPres* Donna Denniston
Open Apr 15 - Oct 12 Mon - Sat 11 AM - 5 PM, Sun Noon - 5 PM; No admis fee; Estab 1967, originated to help develop an art curriculum in the local schools, presently functions to bring art of the region's artists to enrich the culture of the community; Store front gallery providing exhibit space in heart of Boothbay Harbor; includes prints, drawings, pastels, oils & watercolors; Average Annual Attendance: 6,000; Mem: 250; dues $25 & up; annual meeting third Tues in Oct
Income: Financed by mem, contributions & commissions
Exhibitions: Seven juried & invitational shows of graphics, paintings & sculpture by artists of the Boothbay Region
Activities: Adult & children workshop, Jan, Feb & Mar (fee); two schols offered ea yr to post graduates attending college for visual art studies

BRUNSWICK

M **BOWDOIN COLLEGE,** Peary-MacMillan Arctic Museum, 9500 College Station, Brunswick, ME 04011-9112. Tel 207-725-3416; Fax 207-725-3499; Elec Mail ahawkes@bowdoin.edu; Internet Home Page Address: www.bowdoin.edu/arctic-museum; *Cur* Genevieve LeMoine; *Exhib Coordr* David Maschino; *Dir* Susan A Kaplan; *Mus Outreach Coordr* Amy Hawkes; *Asst Cur* Anne Witty; *Exhib Technician* Steve Bunn
Open Tues - Sat 10 AM - 5 PM, Sun 2 - 5 PM, cl Mon & national holidays; No admis fee; Estab 1967; Museum consists of 3 galleries containing ivory, fur & soapstone Inuit artifacts, Arctic exploration equipment, natural history specimens, prints & paintings; Average Annual Attendance: 15,437
Special Subjects: Painting-American, Photography, Sculpture, American Indian Art, Anthropology, Ethnology, Primitive art, Eskimo Art, Painting-Canadian, Historical Material, Ivory, Maps, Leather
Collections: Drawing & exploration films
Activities: Docent training; lects open to pub, 3-7 vis lectrs per yr; tours; individual paintings & original objects of art or ethnographic objects lent to other museums; mus shop sells books, cards & original native art

M **Museum of Art,** 9400 College Station, Brunswick, ME 04011-8494. Tel 207-725-3275; Fax 207-725-3762; Elec Mail artmuseum@bowdoin.edu; Internet Home Page Address: www.bowdoin.edu/art-museum; *Asst Dir* Suzanne K Bergeron; *Cur* Joachim Homann; *Registrar* Laura Latman; *Preparator* Jose Ribas; *Co-Dir* Anne Collins Goodyear; *Co-Dir* Frank Goodyear; *Assoc Dir* Martina Duncan
Open Tues - Sat 10 AM - 5 PM, Sun 1 - 5 PM, cl Mon & holidays; No admis fee; Estab 1891-1894; 14 galleries containing paintings, medals, sculpture, decorative arts, works on paper & antiquities; Average Annual Attendance: 35,000
Special Subjects: Painting-European, Sculpture, Drawings, Painting-American, Photography, Prints, Watercolors, Pre-Columbian Art, Textiles, Ceramics, Woodcarvings, Woodcuts, Decorative Arts, Collages, Portraits, Asian Art, Silver, Painting-Dutch, Painting-French, Coins & Medals, Painting-Flemish, Antiquities-Greek, Antiquities-Roman, Painting-German, Pewter, Antiquities-Etruscan, Antiquities-Assyrian
Collections: Kress Study Collection; Molinari Collection of Medals & Plaquettes
Exhibitions: 14 - 20 temporary exhibitions per year; three major exhibitions per year
Activities: Docent training; lects open to pub, 3 vis lectrs per yr; gallery talks; tours; individual paintings & original objects of art lent to accredited mus; book traveling exhibs 3 per yr; originate traveling exhibs to other accredited mus; mus shop sells books, reproductions, slides, jewelry

DAMARISCOTTA

M **RIVER ARTS,** (Round Top Center for the Arts Inc) Arts Gallery, 170 Main St, Damariscotta, ME 04543; PO Box 1316, Damariscotta, ME 04543-1316. Tel 207-563-1507; Elec Mail info@riverartsme.org; Internet Home Page Address: www.riverartsme.org
Open Mon - Sat 10 AM - 4PM, Sun Noon - 4PM; No admis fee; Mem: dues steward $1,000; patron $500; contributor $125; household $75; individual $60; student & senior $25
Special Subjects: Painting-American
Collections: All facets & eras of visual arts history; classical music coll; theatre script coll
Publications: Catalogues, gallery booklets & newsletters
Activities: Classes for adults & children; dramatic progs; lects open to pub, 5-10 vis lectrs per yr; mus shop sells prints, crafts & paintings

DEER ISLE

M **HAYSTACK MOUNTAIN SCHOOL OF CRAFTS,** 89 Haystack School Dr, Deer Isle, ME 04627-0518; PO Box 518, Deer Isle, ME 04627-0518. Tel 207-348-2306; Fax 207-348-2307; Elec Mail haystack@haystack-mtn.org; Internet Home Page Address: www.haystack-mtn.org; *Chmn Bd* Lissa Ann Hunter; *Dir* Stuart J Kestenbaum; *Pres* Claire Sanford; *Treas* Miguel Gomez-Ibanez; *Develop* Ginger Aldrich
Open tours Wed 1PM; Admis adults $5; Estab 1950 to provide craft educ workshops & residency; Average Annual Attendance: 500

Income: pvt funding
Library Holdings: Book Volumes; Exhibition Catalogs; Kodachrome Transparencies; Maps; Memorabilia; Slides; Video Tapes
Special Subjects: Glass, Mixed Media, Furniture, Gold, Textiles, Woodcuts, Graphics, Southwestern Art, Ceramics, Crafts, Woodcarvings, Decorative Arts, Jewelry, Porcelain, Silver, Metalwork, Embroidery
Exhibitions: Seasonal - Spring Summer
Publications: Annual brochure
Activities: One & two week summer sessions in ceramics, graphics, glass, jewelry, weaving, blacksmithing, papermaking, furniture, sculpture & fabrics; lects open to pub, 40 vis lectrs per yr; scholarships offered

L **Center for Community Programs Gallery,** PO Box 518, Deer Isle, ME 04627-0518. Tel 207-348-2306; Fax 207-348-2307; Elec Mail haystack@haystack-mtn.org; Internet Home Page Address: www.haystack-mtn.org; *Dir* Stuart J Kestenbaum; *Asst Dir* Ellen Wieske; *Develop Dir* Ginger Aldrich
Open June-Aug Thurs - Sun noon - 5 PM; Estab 2007 for community programs & exhibs; Contemporary craft; Average Annual Attendance: 1,000
Income: Privately financed
Library Holdings: Book Volumes 1000; Exhibition Catalogs; Kodachrome Transparencies; Maps; Memorabilia; Periodical Subscriptions 10; Slides; Video Tapes
Special Subjects: Decorative Arts, Mixed Media, Graphic Arts, Graphic Design, Ceramics, Crafts, Printmaking, Porcelain, Furniture, Glass, Metalwork, Enamels, Gold, Goldsmithing, Handicrafts, Jewelry, Silver, Silversmithing, Textiles, Woodcuts, Embroidery, Pottery, Woodcarvings
Exhibitions: fall, spring, & summer exhibs
Publications: Monograph series
Activities: Classes for adults & children, community programs; lects open to pub; 40 vis lectrs per yr; AIA 25 year award, ACC Gold Medal award; National Historic Register; schols and fels offered; mus shop sells books

EASTPORT

M **TIDES INSTITUTE & MUSEUM OF ART,** 43 Water St Eastport, ME 04631-1532; PO Box 161 Eastport, ME 04631-0161. *Dir* Hugh French

ELLSWORTH

M **HANCOCK COUNTY TRUSTEES OF PUBLIC RESERVATIONS,** Woodlawn: Museum, Gardens & Park, 19 Black House Dr, Ellsworth, ME 04605; PO Box 1478, Ellsworth, ME 04605-1478. Tel 207-667-8671; Fax 207-667-7950; Elec Mail director@woodlawnmuseum.org; Internet Home Page Address: www.woodlawnmuseum.org; *Pres* Sandra Blake Leonard; *Exec Dir* Joshua C Torrance
Open May & Oct Tues - Sun 1 - 4 PM, June - Sept Tues - Sat 10 AM - 5 PM, Sun 1 - 4 PM; Admis adults $10, children & students $3; Estab 1929; Historical estate operated by the Hancock County Trustees of Pub Reservations; Average Annual Attendance: 10,000; Mem: 450
Income: Financed by private trust fund, donations admis, & special events
Library Holdings: Maps; Original Documents; Pamphlets; Photographs; Prints; Slides
Special Subjects: Landscape Architecture, Landscapes, Painting-American, Painting-British, Painting-European, Tapestries, Painting-American, Photography, Prints, Watercolors, Textiles, Ceramics, Folk Art, Woodcarvings, Etchings & Engravings, Decorative Arts, Manuscripts, Portraits, Furniture, Glass, Jewelry, Silver, Carpets & Rugs, Maps, Miniatures, Period Rooms, Embroidery
Collections: fine examples of American & European fine & decorative arts in original setting; carriages & sleighs
Publications: Colonel John Black of Ellsworth (1781 - 1856); David Cobb an American Patriot; Legacy of the Penobscot Million; Quarterly newsletter
Activities: Classes for adults & children; docent training; dramatic prog; craft workshops; Ellsworth Antiques Show at Woodlawn; lects open to pub; 6 vis lectrs per yr; concerts; gallery talks; tours; fellowships; mus shop sells books, prints & reproductions

M **THE NEW ENGLAND MUSEUM OF TELEPHONY, INC.,** The Telephone Museum, 166 Winkumpaugh Rd, Ellsworth, ME 04605; PO Box 1377, Ellsworth, ME 04605-1377. Tel 207-667-9491; Elec Mail switchboard@downeast.net; Internet Home Page Address: ellsworthme.org/ringring; *Pres & Dir* Charles S Dunne; *Finance Dir* Dave Thompson; *VPres & Dir* Sandra Galley; *Secy & Dir* Stan St Onge
Open Jul - Sept Thurs - Sun 1 PM - 4 PM, open by appt June & Oct, cl Nov - June; Admis adults $10, children $5; Estab 1983; Mus traces the history of telecommunications through hands-on working exhibs of telephone switching systems. By illustrating the technical, social & corporate evolution of the telephone network the mus provides a basis for understanding modern communication systems; Average Annual Attendance: approx 350; Mem: dues The LongLines Club (life members) $1,000, Sustaining $250, Participating $100, Org $75, Family $50, Indiv $30
Special Subjects: Historical Material
Collections: Technical documents; personal & corporate papers; manuals & reference materials; Large-scale electro-mechanical telephone switching systems; switchboards; telephone sets; central office equip; outside plant equip
Publications: The Pole Line, biannual newsletter; Subscriber Directory, annual; The Telephone: A Love/Hate Relationship, Aug 2004; Military Communications, Aug 2004; Telstar and Andover, Maine, Aug 2004
Activities: Lects; guided tours; ann Telephone Fair (Open House); spec exhibs; project days: allows mus mems to work on equip restoration projs; research in early telephone lines in Hancock Co, Maine; children's workshops; mus shop sells books, telephone wire baskets, t-shirts, toys, puzzles, DVDs, projects

FRYEBURG

M **FRYEBURG ACADEMY,** The Palmina F & Stephen S Pace Galleries of Art, 745 Main St, Laura Hill Eastman Performing Arts Ctr Fryeburg, ME 04037. Elec Mail alumni@fryeburgacademy.com; TWX 207-935-9232; *Dir* John Day
Open Mon - Fri 9 AM - 1 PM

HALLOWELL

A **KENNEBEC VALLEY ART ASSOCIATION,** Harlow Gallery, 160 Water St, Hallowell, ME 04347-1315. Tel 207-622-3813; Elec Mail kvaa@harlowgallery.org; Internet Home Page Address: www.harlowgallery.org; *Exec Dir* Nancy Barron; *Treas* Karen Johnson; *Admin Asst* Nancy Bixler; *Bd Mem* Marie Giguere; *Bd Mem* Larry Brown; *Pres* Patricia O'Brien; *Bd Mem* Peggy Siegle; *VPres* Perry McCourtney; *Gallery Sitter* Allison McKeen; *Bd Mem* Billiann Dolby; *Bd Mem* Anne Young
Open Wed - Sat noon - 6 PM; No admis fee; Estab 1959; supports artistic development of member artists, providing workshops, lectrs, demonstrations; space available to artists' groups for mtgs & events; Single gallery on ground level having central entrance & two old storefront windows which provide window display space; Average Annual Attendance: 7,000; Mem: 350; dues $30; meetings see website
Income: Financed by mem, dues, donations, art sales & rent
Exhibitions: Monthly exhibitions include individual, member shows & juried shows
Publications: Newsletter, bimonthly
Activities: Classes for adults & children, poetry readings; weekly figure drawing sessions & other artists groups; lects open to pub, 10 vis lectrs per year; gallery talks; concerts; sponsoring of competitions; scholarships offered

HOULTON

M **AROOSTOOK COUNTY HISTORICAL & ART MUSEUM,** 109 Main St, Houlton, ME 04730-2123. Tel 207-532-2519

KENNEBUNK

M **BRICK STORE MUSEUM,** (Brick Store Museum & Library) 117 Main St, Kennebunk, ME 04043-7088. Tel 207-985-4802; Elec Mail info@brickstoremuseum.org; Internet Home Page Address: www.brickstoremuseum.org; *Registrar* Kathryn Hussey; *Exec Dir* Christopher J Farr; *Archivist* Roz Magnuson; *Assoc Dir & Cur* Cynthia Walker
Open Tues - Fri 10 AM - 4:30 PM, Sat 10 AM - 1 PM; Admis adult $7.50, senior $6, children $3; Estab 1936 to preserve & present history & art of southern Maine; Non-circulating reference library only; Average Annual Attendance: 5,500; Mem: 450; dues vary
Library Holdings: Audio Tapes; Book Volumes 4000; Cards; Clipping Files; Compact Disks; Exhibition Catalogs; Fiche; Filmstrips; Framed Reproductions; Manuscripts; Maps; Memorabilia; Original Art Works; Original Documents; Other Holdings Architectural drawings & plans; Pamphlets; Periodical Subscriptions; Photographs; Prints; Reels; Reproductions; Sculpture; Video Tapes
Special Subjects: Decorative Arts, Historical Material, Landscapes, Marine Painting, Architecture, Glass, Flasks & Bottles, Furniture, Portraits, Painting-American, Textiles, Maps, Sculpture, Costumes, Dolls, Porcelain, Painting-Dutch, Carpets & Rugs, Coins & Medals, Dioramas, Laces, Bookplates & Bindings
Collections: Art Library of Edith Cleaves Barry; Maritime - Kenneth Roberts, Booth Tarkington & Maine authors in general; Papers of Architect William E Barry; 40,000 items: photographs, documents, fine art & decorative arts; Abbott Graves paintings; John Brewster Jr paintings; William Badger paintings
Exhibitions: Marine Art (2013); Civil War (2013); Permanent exhibs of furniture decorative arts
Publications: Chapters in Local History newsletter; Architectural Walking Tour Book
Activities: Docent training; classes for adults & children; history camp, architectural walking tours; field trips; lects open to pub, 4 vis lectrs per yr; concerts; tours; gallery talks; Edith Barry book award for excellence in art; Joyce Butler Book award for excellence in hist; individual paintings & original objects to other nonprofit mus; originate traveling exhibs to schools & senior citizen groups; mus shop sells books, reproductions

M **HEARTWOOD GALLERY,** Heartwood College, 123 York St, Kennebunk, ME 04043. Tel 207-985-0985; Elec Mail hca@heartwoodcollege.org; Internet Home Page Address: heartwoodcollegeofart.org/galleries.html

KINGFIELD

M **STANLEY MUSEUM, INC,** 44 School St, Kingfield, ME 04947; PO Box 77, Kingfield, ME 04947-0077. Tel 207-265-2729; Fax 207-265-4700; Elec Mail maine@stanleymuseum.org; Internet Home Page Address: www.stanleymuseum.org; *Dir* Susan S Davis; *Office Mgr* Marjorie Trenholm
Open Tues - Sun 1 - 4 PM May 1 - Oct 3l, Mon - Fri 1 - 4 PM Nov 1 - Apr 30; Admis adults $2, children $1; Estab 1981; Average Annual Attendance: 3,000; Mem: 700; dues $30-$1,000; annual meeting in July
Income: $100,000 (financed by endowment, mem, donations & grants)
Purchases: $35,000 (steam car)
Special Subjects: Architecture, Drawings, Painting-American
Collections: Chansonetta Stanley Emmons (photography, glass plate negatives); Raymond W Stanley Archives; Collection of Steam cars, photography & violins
Activities: Classes for adults & children in dramatic & docent progs; lects open to pub, 10 vis lectrs per yr; tours; original objects of art lent to other mus & galleries; mus shop sells books, magazines, reproductions, prints & gift items

LEWISTON

M **BATES COLLEGE,** Museum of Art, 75 Russell St, Olin Arts Ctr Lewiston, ME 04240-6044. Tel 207-786-6158; Fax 207-786-8335; Elec Mail museum@bates.edu; Internet Home Page Address: www.bates.edu/museum; *Cur Coll* Bill Low; *Educ Cur* Anthony Shostak; *Dir* Dan Mills; *Educ Fellow* Catherine Jones
Open Mon - Sat 10 AM - 5 PM, Wed until 7 PM during acad yr; cl major holidays; No admis fee; Estab in the Olin Arts Center, Oct 1986 to serve Bates

College & the regional community; Average Annual Attendance: 25,000; Mem: Please see website

Special Subjects: Afro-American Art, Drawings, Etchings & Engravings, Photography, Pre-Columbian Art, Painting-American, Prints, Sculpture, Ceramics, Posters, Oriental Art, Painting-British, Painting-French, Painting-Italian
Collections: Marsden Hartley Memorial Collection; 19th & 20th Century American & European Collection; Modern & contemporary works on paper; photography; contemporary Chinese art, art about Maine by artists of nat & international significance
Exhibitions: Wenda Gu; Cryptozoology; Green Horizons
Publications: Documenting China: Contemporary Photography and Social Change; Cryptozoology; Robert Indiana; Charlie Hewitt; Starstruck: The Fine Art of Astrophotography; Xiaoze Xie: Amplified Moments; Tale Spinning
Activities: School progs; life drawing classes weekly; lects open to pub, 4-6 vis lectrs per yr; gallery talks; tours; loan at to mus; organize traveling exhibs to college mus & acad galleries; mus shop sells books, film series

LIBERTY

M **DAVISTOWN MUSEUM,** Liberty Location, 58 Main St # 4, Liberty, ME 04949; PO Box 346, Liberty, ME 04949-0346. Tel 207-589-4900; Fax 207-589-4900; Elec Mail curator@davistownmuseum.org; Internet Home Page Address: www.davistownmuseum.org; *Cur* HG Skip Brack; *Dir Educ* Judith Brown; *Technical Dir* Sett Balise; *Web & Office Mgr* Beth Sundberg
Open Mar - Dec 11 AM - 5 PM; always by appt; No admis fee, donations accepted; Regional tool, history & art mus located in Liberty Village, Maine; features colonial & 18th - 19th century hand tools; mus is forum for the work of local & regional artists
Library Holdings: Auction Catalogs; Book Volumes; Exhibition Catalogs; Original Art Works; Original Documents; Photographs; Prints; Sculpture
Special Subjects: Historical Material, Furniture, Pottery, Painting-American, Sculpture, Photography, Crafts, Metalwork
Collections: Extensive coll of 18th & 19th century tools; outdoor flower garden; contemporary Maine sculpture; sculpture garden exhibiting the work of over a dozen Maine artists on 2 1/2 acres of field, located at the Hulls Cove site
Publications: Hand Tools in History Series
Activities: Ann art exhib featuring local artists; mus shop sells books, original art, prints

MILLINOCKET

M **NORTH LIGHT GALLERY,** 256 Penobscot St, Millinocket, ME 04462-1510. Tel 207-723-4414; *Founder* Marsha Donahue
Open Mon-Sat 10AM-6PM, other times by appointment
Collections: paintings; drawings; sculpture

MONHEGAN

M **MONHEGAN MUSEUM,** 1 Lighthouse Hill, Monhegan, ME 04852. Tel 207-596-7003; Elec Mail museum@monheganmuseum.org; Internet Home Page Address: www.monheganmuseum.org; *Pres* Edward L Deci; *Cur Annual Exhibs* Emily Grey; *Cur Coll* Jennifer Pye
Open daily 11:30 AM - 3:30 PM (July-Aug), June 24 - 30 & Sept 1 - 30, 1:30 PM - 3:30 PM daily; Suggested donation $4; Estab 1968 to preserve the history of Monhegan Island; Housed in the historic Monhegan Island Light Station; Average Annual Attendance: 6,000; Mem: 300; dues $5-$1,000
Income: $170,000 (financed by endowment, mem, donations, rental, interest & fundraisers)
Special Subjects: Painting-American, Photography, Prints, Landscapes, Marine Painting, Historical Material, Period Rooms
Collections: Art, natural history, social history & fishing industry exhibits all related to Monhegan Island; Natural History; Social History

NEW GLOUCESTER

M **UNITED SOCIETY OF SHAKERS,** Shaker Museum, 707 Shaker Rd, New Gloucester, ME 04260-2652. Tel 207-926-4597; Elec Mail usshakers@aol.com; Internet Home Page Address: www.shaker.lib.me.us; *Dir & Cur* Michael S Graham; *Librn/Archivist* Charles Rand
Open Mon - Sat 10 AM - 4:30 PM Memorial Day - Columbus Day; Admis for tours; adults $10, children 6-12 yrs $2, under 6 free with adult; Estab 1931, incorporated 1971, to preserve for educational & cultural purposes Shaker artifacts, publications, manuscripts & works of art; to provide facilities for educational & cultural activities in connection with the preservation of the Shaker tradition; to provide a place of study & research for students of history & religion; 4 historic bldgs
Library Holdings: Auction Catalogs; Audio Tapes; Book Volumes; Cassettes; Clipping Files; DVDs; Exhibition Catalogs; Kodachrome Transparencies; Lantern Slides; Manuscripts; Maps; Memorabilia; Motion Pictures; Original Art Works; Original Documents; Pamphlets; Photographs; Prints; Records; Slides; Video Tapes
Special Subjects: Historical Material, Flasks & Bottles, Porcelain, Prints, Architecture, Drawings, Photography, Watercolors, Textiles, Costumes, Religious Art, Ceramics, Crafts, Folk Art, Pottery, Landscapes, Decorative Arts, Manuscripts, Portraits, Posters, Dolls, Glass, Historical Material, Maps, Coins & Medals, Miniatures, Period Rooms, Embroidery, Pewter, Leather
Collections: Drawings & paintings by Shaker artists; Shaker textiles; community industries; furniture; manuscripts; metal & wooden ware; Radical Christian; herbal collection
Exhibitions: Creating Chosen Land (architectural history)
Publications: The Shaker Quarterly
Activities: Classes for adults; workshops in summer for herb dyeing, oval box making, cultivating, weaving, spinning, photography, baskets; lects open to pub; concerts; tours; individual paintings & original objects of art lent to institutions

mounting exhibs; originate traveling exhibs; mus shop sells books, magazines, prints, slides, herbs produced in the community, yarn from flock, woven items

L **The Shaker Library,** 707 Shaker Rd, New Gloucester, ME 04260-2652. Tel 207-926-4597; Elec Mail brooksl@shaker.lib.me.us; Internet Home Page Address: www.shaker.lib.me.us; *Dir & Cur* Michael Graham; *Archivist & Librn* Charles E Rand
Open Mon - Thurs 8:30AM-4:30PM, appointments required; Estab 1882; For reference only
Library Holdings: Audio Tapes; Book Volumes 12,000; Cassettes; Clipping Files; Exhibition Catalogs; Filmstrips; Kodachrome Transparencies; Manuscripts; Maps; Micro Print 317; Motion Pictures; Original Art Works; Original Documents; Other Holdings Ephemera; Periodical Subscriptions 57; Photographs; Prints; Records; Reels 353; Slides; Video Tapes
Special Subjects: Folk Art, Mixed Media, Photography, Manuscripts, Maps, Posters, Historical Material, History of Art & Archaeology, Crafts, Archaeology, Video, Furniture, Period Rooms, Textiles, Woodcuts, Architecture
Collections: Shaker; Radical Christian
Publications: The Shaker Quarterly
Activities: Classes for adults & children; lects open to public; concerts

OAKLAND

M **MACARTNEY HOUSE MUSEUM,** 25 Main St, Oakland, ME 04963; Oakland Area Historical Society, PO Box 59 Oakland, ME 04963-0059. Tel 207-465-7549; Elec Mail meporters@myfairpoint.net; Internet Home Page Address: www.rootsweb.ancestry.com; *Pres* Alberta Porter; *Vol Treas* Richard Lord; *Cur* Ruth W Wood
Open Jun - Aug Wed 1:30 - 4:30 PM; No admis fee, donations accepted; Estab 1979; Historical period home specializing in Oakland area history. Pvt nonprofit org; Mem: dues Life $50, Family $7.50, Indiv $5
Activities: Classes for children; tours

OGUNQUIT

M **BARN GALLERY,** Shore Rd & Bourne Ln, Ogunquit, ME 03907; PO Box 529, Ogunquit, ME 03907-0529. Tel 207-646-8400

M **OGUNQUIT MUSEUM OF AMERICAN ART,** 543 Shore Rd, Ogunquit, ME 03907-0815; PO Box 815, Ogunquit, ME 03907-0815. Tel 207-646-4909; Fax 207-646-6903; Elec Mail ogunquitmuseum@aol.com; Internet Home Page Address: www.ogunquitmuseum.org; *Dir & Cur* Michael Culver
Open July - Oct 31, Mon - Sat 10:30 AM - 5 PM, Sun 2 - 5 PM, cl Labor Day; Admis adults $7, sr citizens $5, students $4, children under 12 free; Estab 1953 to exhibit, collect & preserve American art; Museum consists of five interior galleries with 6000 sq ft; central gallery provides an expansive view of the Atlantic Ocean & the rockbound coast; outdoor sculpture garden; Average Annual Attendance: 13,000; Mem: 600; dues benefactor $5000, partner's circle $1000, donor $500, supporting $250, assoc $150, family $85, dual $60, individual $35
Income: Financed by endowment, mem, donations
Purchases: works by Will Barnet, Gertrude Fiske, Robert Henri, Winslow Homer, Edward Hopper, Jack Levine, Fairfield Porter
Library Holdings: Exhibition Catalogs; Original Documents; Photographs; Slides; Video Tapes
Special Subjects: Drawings, Painting-American, Sculpture
Collections: Paintings, drawings & sculpture by 20th Century contemporary Americans, including Marsh, Burchfield, Hartley, Lachaise, Tobey, Kuhn, Strater, Graves, Levine & Marin
Publications: Exhibition catalog, annually; Museum Bulletin
Activities: Educ dept; docent training; lects open to pub, 2 vis lectrs per yr; gallery talks; tours; concerts; individual paintings & original objects of art lent to other mus; lending collection contains 1500 original art works; originate traveling exhibs; mus shop sells books, magazines, original art, reproduction prints, posters, postcards, museum catalogs & art books

L **Reference Library,** 543 Shore Rd, Ogunquit, ME 03907; PO Box 815, Ogunquit, ME 03907-0815. Tel 207-646-4909; Fax 207-646-6903; Elec Mail ogunquitmuseum@aol.com; Internet Home Page Address: ogunquitmuseum.org; *Dir & Cur* Michael Culver; *Bd Pres* Timothy Ellis
Open July - Oct 31, Mon - Sat 10:30 AM - 5 PM, Sun 2 - 5 PM; Admis adults $5, seniors $4, students $3; Estab 1953; For reference only; Average Annual Attendance: 13,000; Mem: 780, dues $30 - $5,000
Income: financed by endowments, memberships, donations
Library Holdings: Book Volumes 400; Clipping Files; Exhibition Catalogs; Manuscripts; Memorabilia; Pamphlets; Photographs; Reproductions
Activities: Docent training; lects open to pub, 6 vis lectrs per yr; concerts; gallery talks; tours; mus shop sells books, reproductions & prints

PEMAQUID POINT

A **PEMAQUID GROUP OF ARTISTS,** Pemaquid Art Gallery, Lighthouse Park, Pemaquid Point, ME; 1311 Bristol Rd, c/o Barbara Applegate Bristol, ME 04539. Tel 207-677-2752; Elec Mail pjsfarrell@gmail.com; Internet Home Page Address: www.pemaquidartgallery.com; *Pres* Sally Loughridge; *Vice Pres* Jan Kilburn; *Secy* Peggy Farrell; *Treas* Barbara Applegate
Open daily 10 AM - 5 PM; No admis fee; $2 to enter Pemaquid Lighthouse Park; Estab 1929 to exhibit & sell paintings, sculpture, carvings by members & to give scholarships & passes to Portland Museum of Art, Maine; Maintains an art gallery, open Jun - Oct; Average Annual Attendance: 10,000; Mem: 26; must be residents of the Bristol Peninsula, Damariscotta or Newcastle & pass jury; dues $80; annual meeting in Oct
Income: Financed by dues, patrons, commissions on paintings & sculpture
Purchases: Office equipment
Exhibitions: Summer members exhibition
Activities: Schols offered; gallery sells original art

PORTLAND

ART GALLERY AT THE UNIVERSITY OF NEW ENGLAND, 716 Stevens Ave, Portland, ME 04103-2693. Tel 207-221-4499; Fax 207-523-1901; Elec Mail azill@une.edu; Internet Home Page Address: www.une.edu; *Dir* Anne B Zill
Open Wed - Sun 1 - 4 PM, Thurs 1-7PM; Estab 1976; Average Annual Attendance: 1,600

L **MAINE COLLEGE OF ART,** Joanne Waxman Library, 522 Congress St, Portland, ME 04101-3378. Tel 207-775-5153; Fax 207-772-5069; Elec Mail library@meca.edu; Internet Home Page Address: http://library.meca.edu; *Libr Dir* Moira Steven; *Circ Mgr* Heather Dawn Driscoll
Open Mon - Fri 10 AM - 12 PM, also by appointment; Estab 1973, to support the curriculum & serve the needs of students & faculty; Circ 340; circulation 12,000; Lending library; Mem: Membership fee for non-MECA $50 per yr; patrons over 65 $25 per yr
Library Holdings: Book Volumes 40,200; CD-ROMs; Compact Disks; DVDs 480; Exhibition Catalogs; Original Art Works 25; Other Holdings Ephemera Files; Pamphlets; Periodical Subscriptions 103
Special Subjects: Art History, Collages, Constructions, Folk Art, Intermedia, Landscape Architecture, Decorative Arts, Film, Illustration, Mixed Media, Photography, Calligraphy, Commercial Art, Drawings, Etchings & Engravings, Graphic Arts, Graphic Design, Islamic Art, Manuscripts, Maps, Painting-American, Painting-British, Painting-Dutch, Painting-Flemish, Painting-French, Painting-German, Painting-Italian, Painting-Japanese, Painting-Russian, Painting-Spanish, Posters, Pre-Columbian Art, Prints, Sculpture, Painting-European, History of Art & Archaeology, Portraits, Watercolors, Ceramics, Conceptual Art, Crafts, Latin American Art, Archaeology, Ethnology, American Western Art, Bronzes, Printmaking, Advertising Design, Cartoons, Fashion Arts, Lettering, Art Education, Asian Art, American Indian Art, Porcelain, Primitive art, Anthropology, Eskimo Art, Furniture, Mexican Art, Southwestern Art, Ivory, Jade, Drafting, Costume Design & Constr, Glass, Mosaics, Painting-Polish, Stained Glass, Aesthetics, Afro-American Art, Bookplates & Bindings, Metalwork, Enamels, Gold, Goldsmithing, Handicrafts, Jewelry, Oriental Art, Religious Art, Silversmithing, Woodcuts, Marine Painting, Landscapes, Painting-Scandinavian, Pewter, Painting-Australian, Painting-Canadian, Display, Architecture, Embroidery, Pottery, Tapestries, Textiles, Woodcarvings
Collections: 40,200 titles; special coll of rare books & artist books

M **The Institute of Contemporary Art,** 522 Congress St, Portland, ME 04101. Tel 207-699-5029; Elec Mail ica@meca.edu; Internet Home Page Address: www.meca.edu/ica; *Dir* Daniel Fuller; *Assoc Cur & Educ Coordr* Linda Lambertson
Open Wed, Fri - Sun 11 AM - 5 PM, Thurs 11 AM - 7 PM; No admis fee; Gallery estab 1983 to present temporary exhibs of contemporary art & design; Newly renovated 3300 sq ft gallery located on first floor of Beaux Arts building; Average Annual Attendance: 20,000
Income: $38,700
Special Subjects: Conceptual Art, Photography, Painting-American, Prints, Sculpture, African Art
Collections: Contemporary Art-National & International; Video
Publications: Exhibition catalogues, 2 yearly
Activities: Tours of exhibitions; classes for children; docent training; lects open to pub; 6 vis lectrs per yr; gallery talks; tours; Originates traveling exhibs

A **MAINE HISTORICAL SOCIETY,** 489 Congress St, Portland, ME 04101-3414. Tel 207-774-1822; Fax 207-775-4301; Elec Mail info@mainehistory.org; Internet Home Page Address: www.mainehistory.org; Internet Home Page Address: www.mainememory.net; *Exec Dir* Stephen Bromage; *Cur* John Mayer; *Head Library Svcs* Nick Noyes; *Dir Maine Memory Network* Kathy Amoroso
Maine Historical Society Museum & Shop, Wadsworth-Longfellow House tours - call ahead for seasonal hours, cl state & federal holidays; Admis charged; Estab 1822 to collect, preserve & teach the history of Maine; the soc owns & operates a historical research library & the Wadsworth - Longfellow House of 1785; Average Annual Attendance: 15,000; Mem: 2,700; dues $15 & up; annual meeting in May or June
Income: Donations, admis, dues
Library Holdings: Manuscripts; Maps; Original Documents; Other Holdings; Pamphlets; Periodical Subscriptions; Photographs; Prints
Special Subjects: Historical Material
Collections: Architecture; books archival; material culture; photographs; special coll-prints
Exhibitions: Changing exhibs on Maine history
Publications: Maine Historical Society, quarterly; tri-annual monograph
Activities: Classes for adults; docent training; lects open to pub, 4 vis lectrs per yr; gallery talks; tours; individual paintings & original objects of art lent; mus shop sells books, reproductions & prints

M **Wadsworth-Longfellow House,** 489 Congress St, Portland, ME 04101. Tel 207-774-1822; Fax 207-775-4301; Elec Mail info@mainehistory.org; Internet Home Page Address: www.mainehistory.org; *Exec Dir* Richard D'Abate
Open Mon - Sat 10:30-4, Sun noon-4; Admis adults $7, children $3, 17 & under, children under 5 free, seniors and students $6; Average Annual Attendance: 19,000; Mem: Part of the society
Income: Financed by donations, admis, dues & endowment income
Library Holdings: Manuscripts; Maps; Original Documents; Periodical Subscriptions; Photographs
Special Subjects: Architecture, Costumes, Ceramics, Landscapes, Decorative Arts, Manuscripts, Furniture, Miniatures, Period Rooms, Embroidery
Collections: Maine furniture; glass; historic artifacts; paintings; photographs; pottery; prints; textiles; Maine artists; Maine portraits, seascapes
Publications: Quarterly, spec publs
Activities: Classes for adults; docent training; lects open to pub; individual paintings & original objects of art lent to mus; mus shop sells books, reproductions, prints

L **Library and Museum,** 489 Congress St, Portland, ME 04101. Tel 207-774-1822; Fax 207-775-4301; Elec Mail info@mainehistory.org; Internet Home Page Address: www.mainehistory.org; *Reference Asst* William D Barry; *Cataloger* Nancy Noble; *Dir Library Svcs* Nicholas Noyes; *Pub Svcs Librn* Jamie K Rice; *Mus Cur* John Mayer

Open Tues - Sat 10 AM - 4 PM; Admis $12; seniors, AAA & students $10; first day free; Estab 1822; Circ Non-circ; For reference only; Average Annual Attendance: 5,500; Mem: 2,500
Income: Part of society
Library Holdings: Auction Catalogs; Audio Tapes; Book Volumes 100,000; CD-ROMs; Cards; Cassettes; Clipping Files; Compact Disks; Exhibition Catalogs; Fiche; Lantern Slides; Manuscripts 2,000,000; Maps 5,000; Memorabilia; Motion Pictures; Original Art Works; Original Documents; Other Holdings; Pamphlets; Periodical Subscriptions; Photographs; Prints; Reels; Sculpture; Slides
Special Subjects: Folk Art, Decorative Arts, Photography, Graphic Arts, Painting-American, Historical Material, Printmaking, Cartoons, Interior Design, American Indian Art, Costume Design & Constr, Goldsmithing, Miniatures, Marine Painting, Architecture
Publications: Maine History Society Newsletter
Activities: Classes for adults & children; docent training; lects open to pub; 3-5 vis lectrs per yr; gallery talks; tours; fellowships; Baxter Award; Ring Award; NW Allen Award; Maine statewide; mus shop sells books, reproductions & prints

M **MHS Museum,** 489 Congress St, Portland, ME 04101. Tel 207-774-1822; Fax 207-775-4301; Elec Mail info@mainehistory.org; Internet Home Page Address: www.mainehistory.org; Internet Home Page Address: www.mainememory.net; Internet Home Page Address: www.vintagemaineimages.com; *Exec Dir* Richard D'Abate
Open May - Oct, daily 10 AM - 5 PM; winter hours Mon-Sat 10 AM - 5 PM, Sun noon - 5 PM; Admis adults $7; students & seniors $6; children 6-17 & under $3; Estab 1822 to preserve & promote the understanding of Maine history; Changing exhibitions; one or two exhibitions at a time; Average Annual Attendance: 17,000; Mem: 2,500; dues $40; annual meeting in the Spring
Income: Mem, donations, grants, admissions
Library Holdings: Book Volumes; Fiche; Manuscripts; Maps; Memorabilia; Original Art Works; Original Documents; Pamphlets; Periodical Subscriptions; Photographs
Special Subjects: Glass, Painting-American, Archaeology, Costumes, Folk Art, Decorative Arts, Historical Material
Collections: Archaeological artifacts; costumes; decorative arts; folk art; history artifacts; paintings; books, manuscripts, maps, photos
Exhibitions: Rotating 1-2 times per yr
Publications: Maine History, qtr
Activities: Classes for adults & children; docent training; lects open to pub, 5 vis lectrs per yr, gallery talks; tours; individual paintings & original objects of art lent to other mus & historical societies; lending collection contains original art works, books, photographs, slides, paintings & sculptures; book traveling exhibs; originate traveling exhibs; mus shop sells books, reproductions & prints

M **PORTLAND MUSEUM OF ART,** 7 Congress Sq, Portland, ME 04101-1119. Tel 207-775-6148; Fax 207-773-7324; Elec Mail info@portlandmuseum.org; Internet Home Page Address: www.portlandmuseum.org; *Chief Cur* Karen Sherry; *Registrar* Lauren Silverson; *Educ Dir* Dana Baldwin; *Dir Pub Rels* Kristen Levesque; *Financial Officer* Elena Murdock; *Dir* Mark Bessire; *Dir Develop* Elizabeth Cartland; *Pres* Ann Wells; *Cur Modern Art* Margaret Burgess; *Mus Shop Mgr* Sally Struever; *Cur Contemporary & Modern Art* Jessica May
Open Tues, Wed, Thurs 10 AM - 5 PM, Fri 10 AM - 9PM, Sat & Sun 10 AM - 5 PM; Memorial Day through Columbus Day: Mon 10 AM - 5 PM; Admis adults $12, sr citizens & students $10, youth 13 -17 yrs $6, children 12 & under & Fri 5 - 9 free; Estab 1882 as a non-profit educational institution based on the visual arts & critical excellence; The Museum includes the McLellan-Sweat House, built in 1800, a Registered National Historic Landmark; the LDM Sweat Memorial Galleries, built in 1911; & the Charles Shipman Payson Building, built in 1983, designed by Henry N Cobb. This building is named for Mr Charles Shipman Payson, whose gift of 17 Winslow Homer paintings spurred expansion; Average Annual Attendance: 150,000; Mem: 9,000; dues $50+
Income: $6,000,000 (financed by endowment, mem, private & corporate donations, grants from national, state & municipal organizations)
Special Subjects: Painting-American, Prints, Sculpture, Decorative Arts, Painting-European, Glass
Collections: 19th & 20th century American & European paintings; neo-classic American sculpture; contemporary prints; State of Maine Collection of artists assoc with Maine including Winslow Homer, Andrew Wyeth & Marsden Hartley; American decorative arts of the Federal period; American glass
Exhibitions: Visit website
Publications: Mem mag, monthly; exhibition catalogs; general information brochure
Activities: Classes for adults & children; docent training; lects open to pub; lects for mems only; tours; gallery talks; concerts; films; competitions; members' openings of exhibs; mus shop sells books, reproductions, prints, posters, cards, jewelry, gifts & items by Maine artists & artisans

L **PORTLAND PUBLIC LIBRARY,** Art - Audiovisual Dept, 5 Monument Sq, Portland, ME 04101-4072. Tel 207-871-1700; Fax 207-871-1703; Elec Mail wilsbach@portland.lib.me.us; Internet Home Page Address: www.portlandlibrary.com; *Dir* Stephen Podgajny; *Art & AV Librn* Tom Wilsbach; *AV Mgr* Patti Delois
Open Mon - Thurs 10 AM - 7 PM, Fri 10 AM - 6 PM, Sat 10 AM - 5 PM; Estab 1867 as the public library for city of Portland; Circ 51,700
Income: Financed by endowment, city & state appropriation
Purchases: $32,000
Library Holdings: Book Volumes 18,000; Compact Disks; DVDs; Exhibition Catalogs; Fiche; Motion Pictures; Original Art Works; Pamphlets; Periodical Subscriptions 35; Records; Sculpture; Video Tapes
Collections: Costume Book Collection; Maine Sheet Music; Press Books - Anthoensen Press, Mosher Press; The Drummond Collection of Opera
Exhibitions: Monthly exhibits concentrating on Portland & Maine artists
Activities: Lects open to pub

M   **VICTORIA MANSION - MORSE LIBBY HOUSE,** (Victoria Mansion, Inc)
109 Danforth St, Portland, ME 04101-4504. Tel 207-772-4841; Fax 207-772-6290;
Elec Mail information@victoriamansion.org; Internet Home Page Address:
www.victoriamansion.org; *Adminr* Timothy Brosnihan; *Museum Shop Mgr* Alice
Ross; *Dir* Robert Wolterstorff; *Asst Dir* Julia Kirby; *Site Mgr/Educ Asst* Katie
Worthing
Open Mon - Sat 10 AM - 4 PM, Sun 1 - 5 PM May - Oct, spec Christmas hours;
Admis adults $15, seniors $13.50, children 6-17 $5, under 6 free; Estab 1941
Italian Villa, Victorian Period architecture built by Henry Austin of New Haven,
Connecticut in 1858-1860; interiors by Gustav Herter; Average Annual Attendance:
20,000; Mem: 360; dues $35; annual meeting in Apr
Income: $480,000 (financed by endowment, mem, grants & contributions
Library Holdings: Manuscripts; Memorabilia; Original Documents; Photographs;
Slides
Special Subjects: Ceramics, Painting-American, Silver, Textiles, Manuscripts,
Sculpture, Architecture, Photography, Decorative Arts, Portraits, Furniture, Glass,
Porcelain, Carpets & Rugs, Historical Material, Restorations, Period Rooms,
Stained Glass
Collections: Mid 19th Century Decorative Arts (luxury) & Architecture; Original
Interior-Exterior & Original Furnishings, Gifts of the Victorian Period; Porcelain
tableware
Exhibitions: Christmas Opening Exhibition
Activities: Docent training; lects open to pub, 2-4 vis lectrs per yr; tours; mus
shop sells books, original art, reproductions, jewelry, textiles, stationary,
&Victorian style gifts

PRESQUE ISLE

M   **NORTHERN MAINE MUSEUM OF SCIENCE,** 181 Main St, University of
Maine at Presque Isle Presque Isle, ME 04769. Tel 207-768-9482; Internet Home
Page Address: www.umpi.maine.edu/info/nmms/museum.htm; *Dir* Kevin
McCartney, PhD; *Cur Chemistry* Michael Knopp, PhD; *Cur Herbarium* Robert J
Pinette, PhD; *Cur Colls* Jeanie McGowan; *Cur Outdoor Areas* Chad Loder; *Cur
Mathematics* Richard Rand, PhD; *Cur Mathematics* Richard Kimball; *Asst Cur
Mathematics* Frank Kitteredge; *Asst Cur Physics* Alan Dearborn; *Asst Cur
Entomology* Beth Taylor; *Cur Colls (Emeritus)* Earl Oman; *Asst Cur Agriculture
(Emeritus)* Alvin Reeves, PhD
Mus mission is to support science educ in northern Maine by means of exhibs &
progs for educators & students
Special Subjects: Anthropology, Archaeology
Collections: The Maine Solar System Model built by the People of Aroostook
County, Maine; whale vertebrae & jawbone; dinosaur & miscellaneous animal &
insect models; meteorology station; Coral Reef exhib & mural; mineral & rock
exhibs
Activities: Tours; Library of Traveling Trunks; Campus Nature Trail

RANGELEY

M   **RANGELEY LAKES REGION LOGGING MUSEUM,** PO Box 154, Rangeley,
ME 04970-0154; 221 Stratton Rd, Rangeley, ME 04970. Tel 207-864-5595; Elec
Mail myocom@gmu.edu; Internet Home Page Address:
http://mason.gmu.edu/~myocom; *Vol Mus Folklorist, Cur & Archivist* Dr Margaret
Yocom; *Vol Pres & Dir* Rodney C Richard Sr; *Festival Coordr* Stephen A
Richard; *Vol Treas* Laura Haley; *Vol Secy* Lucille Richard
Open Jul - Labor Day Sat & Sun 11 AM - 2 PM; No admis fee, donations
accepted; Estab 1979; mus preserves & celebrates the heritage of logging in the
western mountains of Maine; collects & displays artifacts that speak of the history
& folklife of logging; Average Annual Attendance: under 500 by estimate; Mem:
dues Indiv $5
Special Subjects: Folk Art, Historical Material
Collections: Tools & equipment for logging; folk culture; paintings; photographs;
letters; journals; botanicals (nonliving); quilts; knitting; woodcarvings
Publications: Logging in the Maine Woods: The Paintings of Alden Grant, book
by Yocom; Working the Woods, book by Yocom & Mundell
Activities: 2-day logging festival; Craft Show & Sale; Auction; lects; group visits;
mus related items for sale

ROCKLAND

M   **WILLIAM A FARNSWORTH LIBRARY & ART MUSEUM,** Museum, 16
Museum St, Rockland, ME 04841-2867. Tel 207-596-6457; Fax 207-596-0509;
Elec Mail writeus@farnsworthmuseum.org; Internet Home Page Address:
www.farnsworthmuseum.org; *Dir* Christopher B Crosman; *Assoc Dir* Victoria
Woodhull; *Chief Cur* Suzette McAvey; *Coll Cur* Helen Ashton Fisher
Summer: daily, 10AM - 5PM, Wed until 8 PM, Winter: Wed -Sun 10AM - 5PM,
cl Mon & Tues; Admis Rockland Campus: $12, seniors & students 17 & older
$10, Rockland Campus & Olson House: $17, seniors & students 17 & older $15,
Olson House only $10, seniors & students 17 & older $8; Estab 1948 to house,
preserve & exhibit American art; Twelve galleries house permanent & changing
exhibitions; Average Annual Attendance: 79,000; Mem: 2500; dues $50 individual,
$75 dual
Income: Financed by pvt donations, grants, dues
Special Subjects: Painting-American, Decorative Arts, Painting-European
Collections: American Art; two historic houses; emphasis on Maine art; works on
paper; prints; sculpture; photography; decorative artifacts; manuscripts
Publications: Exhibition catalogs & brochures 6-8 per year; quarterly newsletter
for members
Activities: Classes for adults & children; docent training; interactive computer
progs; lects open to pub, 6-10 vis lectrs per yr; concerts; gallery talks; tours; films;
outreach progs; scholarships; individual paintings & original objects of art lent to
other mus & galleries; originate traveling exhibs; mus shop sell books,
reproductions, notecards, educational toys & contemporary design objects; Julia's
Gallery for Young Artists
L   **Library,** 16 Museum St Rockland, ME 04841-2867. Tel 207-596-6457; Fax
207-596-0509; Elec Mail farnsworth@midcoast.com; Internet Home Page Address:

www.farnsworthmuseumart.org; *Dir* Christopher B Crosman; *Assoc Dir* Victoria
Woodhull; *Cur 19th & 20th Century* Pamela Belanger; *Chief Cur* Suzette L
McAvoy; *Coll Cur* Helen Ashton Fisher
Summer: daily, 10-5; Winter: Tues-Sun 10-5; please call for shoulder season
hours; Admis $9 gen, Rockland res, mems, 17 & younger free; Estab 1948; Circ
non-circulating; Art reference only. Archives on American artists, including papers
of Louise Nevelson, Andrew Wyeth, N C Wyeth, George Bellows, Robert Indiana
& Waldo Peirce; Average Annual Attendance: 75,000; Mem: 2,500 - Dues $50
individual, $75 dual
Income: Income from pvt donations, grants, dues
Library Holdings: Auction Catalogs; Audio Tapes; Book Volumes 4000; Clipping
Files; Exhibition Catalogs; Kodachrome Transparencies; Manuscripts; Maps;
Memorabilia; Motion Pictures; Original Art Works; Other Holdings American
artists' file; Pamphlets; Periodical Subscriptions 13; Photographs; Prints;
Sculpture; Slides; Video Tapes
Special Subjects: Art History, Folk Art, Etchings & Engravings,
Painting-American, Prints, Watercolors, Printmaking, Marine Painting
Collections: American art with an emphasis on Maine Art; paintings, works on
paper, prints, sculpture, photography, decorative arts, artifacts & manuscripts;
N.C., Andrew, James Wyeth
Publications: Maine in America: American Art at the Farnsworth Museum
Activities: Classes for adults & children; docent training; interactive computer
progs; lects open to pub; 6-10 vis lectrs per yr; concerts; gallery talks; tours;
scholarships offered; exten progs to Maine schools statewide; originate traveling
exhibs; mus shop sells books, reproductions; Julia's Gallery for Young Artists

ROCKPORT

A   **CMCA-CENTER FOR MAINE CONTEMPORARY ART,** Art Gallery, 162
Russell Ave, Rockport, ME 04856; PO Box 147, Rockport, ME 04856-0147. Tel
207-236-2875; Fax 207-236-2490; Elec Mail info@cmcnow.org; Internet Home
Page Address: www.cmcanow.org; *Dir* Suzette McAvoy; *Operations & Communs
Mgr* Paula Blanchard; *Admin Asst* Jean Thompson
Open Tues - Sat 10 AM - 5 PM, Sun 1 PM - 5 PM May to Dec; Admis free to
mems, suggested donation $5; 1952; to advance contemporary art in Maine
through exhibitions & educational programs; Gallery building was an old livery
stable & fire station overlooking Rockport Harbor; Average Annual Attendance:
15,000; Mem: 500; dues $30-$50; annual meeting in April
Income: Financed by mem, contributions, grants, an art auction, craft sale &
gallery shop
Exhibitions: Seasonal: varied exhibitions of contemporary Maine art; Annual
Juried Craft Fair; Biennial Juried Exhibition
Publications: Email newsletter; exhibition catalogues; brochures
Activities: Art lab classes for adults & children; professional develop for artists;
lects open to pub; 3-6 lects per yr; films; concerts; gallery talks; tours; mus shop
sells books, original art, prints, gift merchandise

A   **MAINE PHOTOGRAPHIC WORKSHOPS/ROCKPORT COLLEGE,** (Maine
Photographic Workshops) PO Box 200, Rockport, ME 04856-0200. Tel
207-236-8519; Fax 207-236-2558; Elec Mail info@theworkshops.com; *Founder &
Dir* David H Lyman
Open Mon - Sun 9 AM - 5 PM & 7 - 9 PM June - Aug; Admis lectures $3; Estab
1973 as photographic center; Contains four separate spaces for the display of
vintage & contemporary photographers; Average Annual Attendance: 10,000;
Mem: 1,400; dues $20; annual meetings Nov
Income: $2,000,000 (financed by mem, tuitions, sales & accommodations)
Special Subjects: Prints
Collections: Eastern Illustrating Archive containing 100,000 vintage glass plates;
The Kosti Ruohomaa Collection, prints of Life photographers; Master Work
Collection; Paul Caponigro Archive
Exhibitions: Forty photographic exhibitions
Publications: The Work Print, bi-monthly newsletter; Catalogues - Programs,
semi-annual
Activities: Classes for adults & children; dramatic progs; lects open to pub, 50 vis
lectrs per yr; competitions with awards; schols offered; lending collection contains
photographs; book traveling exhibs; originate traveling exhibs; sales shop sells
books, magazines, original art, reproductions, prints, photographic equipment &
supplies
L   **Carter-Haas Library,** PO Box 200, Union Hall Rockport, ME 04856-0200. Tel
207-236-8314; Fax 207-236-2558; Elec Mail library@theworkshops.com; *Library
Mgr* Rachel Jones
Open Mon - Wed 1 - 10 PM, Thurs 10 AM - 3 PM; Estab 1975 to support student
studies
Purchases: $5,000
Library Holdings: Audio Tapes; Book Volumes 6,500; Cards; Cassettes; Clipping
Files; Exhibition Catalogs; Filmstrips; Framed Reproductions; Kodachrome
Transparencies; Lantern Slides; Memorabilia; Micro Print; Motion Pictures;
Original Art Works; Pamphlets; Periodical Subscriptions 45; Photographs;
Records; Reproductions; Slides; Video Tapes
Special Subjects: Film, Photography
Activities: Schols offered

SACO

M   **SACO MUSEUM,** (York Institute Museum) 371 Main St, Saco, ME 04072-1520.
Tel 207-283-3861; Fax 207-283-0754; Elec Mail museum@sacomuseum.org;
Internet Home Page Address: www.sacomuseum.org; *Coll Mgr* Marie O'Brien;
Programs & Educ Mgr Camille Smalley
Open Tues, Wed, Thurs noon-4PM, Fri noon-8PM, Sat 10AM-4PM, Sun June-Dec
only noon-4PM; Admis adults $5, seniors $3, students & groups $2; Estab 1866 as
a museum of regional history & culture; Permanent collections feature Maine
furniture, decorative arts & paintings. Special exhibitions on regional art, social
history & student art; Average Annual Attendance: 10,000
Income: Financed by endowment, private & corporate contributions, federal, state
& municipal support

Special Subjects: Architecture, Painting-American, Photography, Sculpture, Watercolors, Archaeology, Textiles, Costumes, Ceramics, Folk Art, Landscapes, Decorative Arts, Manuscripts, Portraits, Dolls, Furniture, Glass, Porcelain, Silver, Metalwork, Maps, Coins & Medals, Miniatures, Period Rooms, Pewter
Collections: Federal period Maine books, ceramics, decorative arts, glass, manuscripts, maps, natural history paintings, pewter, sculpture, silver
Publications: Saco Revisited, Arcadia Publishing, 2010
Activities: Classes for adults & children; art workshops; dramatic progs; docent training; lects open to pub, 1-2 vis lectrs per month; concerts; gallery talks; historic walking tours; house tour; individual paintings & original objects of art lent to other mus; mus shop sells books

SEARSPORT

M **PENOBSCOT MARINE MUSEUM,** 40 E Main St, Searsport, ME 04974-3351; PO Box 498, Searsport, ME 04974-0498. Tel 207-548-2529, store 548-0334; Fax 207-548-2520; Elec Mail museumoffices@pmm-maine.org; Internet Home Page Address: www.penobscotmarinemuseum.org; *Exec Dir* Liz Lodge
Open Memorial Day weekend - mid Oct, Mon - Sat 10 AM - 5 PM, Sun Noon - 5 PM; Admis adults $12, seniors (65+) $10, youth 7-15 $8, 6 & under free; Estab 1936 as a memorial to the maritime record of present & former residents of the State of Maine in shipbuilding, shipping & all maritime affairs; The Museum consists of eight historic buildings, including the Old Town Hall (1845), Nickels-Colcord Duncan House (1880); Fowler True Ross House (1825); Cap Merithew House; Dutch House; two new buildings: Stephen Phillips' Memorial Library (1983) & Douglas & Margaret Carver Memorial Art Gallery (1986) & Educ Center; Average Annual Attendance: 15,000; Mem: 800; dues $45 & up
Income: Financed by endowment, mem, grant, gifts & admis
Special Subjects: Historical Material, Marine Painting, Photography, Porcelain, Scrimshaw, Period Rooms
Collections: Marine Artifacts; China Trade Exports; paintings & prints; Ship Models; small water craft; decorative arts; ceramics; glass; textiles & extensive archives; photography archives
Exhibitions: Permanent exhibit: Marine Painting of Thomas & James Buttersworth; Working the Bay; Gone Fishing: Maine's Sea Fisheries
Publications: Searsport Sea Captains, 1989; Lace & Leaves: The Art of Dolly Smith, 1994 (exhibit catalogue); annual report; newsletter, 3 times per year
Activities: Classes for adults & children; docent training; maritime-based literacy curriculum; lects open to pub; awards: accredited; AAM; scholarships offered; individual paintings & original objects of art lent to other institutions in accordance with museum policies; originate traveling exhibs; sales shop sells Marine books, magazines, original art & reproductions & prints
L **Stephen Phillips Memorial Library,** 11 Church St, PO Box 498 Searsport, ME 04974-0498. Tel 207-548-2529; Fax 207-548-2520; Elec Mail cgood@pmm-maine.org; Internet Home Page Address: www.penobscotmarinemuseum.org; *Colls Mgr* Cipperly Good
Open by appointment; No admis fee; Estab 1936 to support research at Penobscot Marine Museum and to serve the public; Open for reference to researchers; Average Annual Attendance: 1,050; Mem: 1,000; dues $20 and up
Library Holdings: Audio Tapes; Book Volumes 12,000; Cassettes; Clipping Files; Compact Disks; DVDs; Exhibition Catalogs; Fiche; Filmstrips; Manuscripts; Maps 3,000; Memorabilia; Motion Pictures; Original Art Works; Original Documents; Other Holdings Nautical charts; Pamphlets; Periodical Subscriptions 40; Photographs 60,000; Prints; Records; Reels; Slides; Video Tapes
Special Subjects: Photography, Maps, Painting-American, Painting-European, Marine Painting, Scrimshaw
Publications: The Bay Chronicle newsletter
Activities: Classes for adults & children; lects open to pub; 12 vis lects per yr; mus shop sells books & prints

SOUTHPORT

M **HENDRICKS HILL MUSEUM,** 417 Hendricks Hill Rd, Rte 27, Southport, ME 04576; PO Box 3, Southport, ME 04576-0003. Tel 207-633-1102; *Pres* Richard Snyder; *Treas* Joyce Duncan
Open July 1 - Labor Day Tues, Thurs & Sat 11 AM - 3 PM; also open by appt in Sept; No admis fee, donations accepted; Mus is housed on farmhouse built in 1810; 11 rooms of household furnishings, archival material & fishing equipment dating from 1850 - 1960; separate boatshop houses boats, tools & ice harvesting equipment
Special Subjects: Historical Material, Furniture
Collections: Genealogical material, photographs & postcards depicting Southport Island life
Activities: Reference room with Southport Town Reports

SOUTHWEST HARBOR

M **WENDELL GILLEY MUSEUM,** 4 Herrick Rd, Southwest Harbor, ME 04679-4431; PO Box 254, Southwest Harbor, ME 04679-0254. Tel 207-244-7555; Elec Mail info@wendellgilleymuseum.org; Internet Home Page Address: www.wendellgilleymuseum.org; *Pres* Eleanor T M Hoagland; *Exec VPres* Robert L Hinckley; *Exec Dir* Nina Z Gormley; *VPres* Carol L Weg; *Carver-in-Residence* Steven Valleau; *Educator* Jennifer Linforth
Open June, Sept & Oct Tues - Sun 10 AM - 4 PM, July - Aug Tues - Sun 10 AM - 5 PM, May, Nov & Dec Fri - Sun 10 AM - 4 PM; Admis adults $5.00; Estab 1981 to house collection of bird carvings & other wildlife related art; Gallery occupies 3000 sq ft on one floor of a solar heated building; handicapped access; Average Annual Attendance: 21,000; Mem: 2000; dues $35-$1000; annual meeting in Jan
Income: $219,000 (financed by mem, admis, sales & fundraising events)
Special Subjects: Prints, Folk Art, Woodcarvings
Collections: Decorative wood carvings of birds & working decoys by Wendell Gilley; Birds of America, 1972 ed J J Audubon; Birds of Mt Desert Island by Carroll S Tyson (prints); Photos by Eliot Porter

Exhibitions: Bird Carvings by Wendell Gilley (rotating); Audubon prints (rotating); Ann temporary contemporary & historical art exhibits
Publications: The Eider, bi-annual newsletter
Activities: Classes for adults & children; films; lects open to pub, gallery talks; tours; schols offered; original objects of art lent to qualified institutions; book traveling exhibs 1 per yr; mus shop sells books, original art, carving tools, gift items, jewelry, posters & toys

WATERVILLE

M **COLBY COLLEGE,** Museum of Art, 5600 Mayflower Hill, Waterville, ME 04901-4799. Tel 207-859-5600; Fax 207-859-5606; Elec Mail museum@colby.edu; Internet Home Page Address: www.colby.edu/museum; *Asst Dir* Greg Williams; *Dir* Daniel Rosenfeld; *Cur* Sharon Corwin
Open Tues - Sat 10 AM - 4:30 PM, Sun 12 - 4:30 PM, cl major holidays; No admis fee; Estab 1959 to serve as an adjunct to the Colby College Art Program & to be a mus center for Central Maine; Average Annual Attendance: 20,000; Mem: Friends of Art at Colby, 700; dues $25 & up
Income: Financed by college funds, mem & donations
Collections: Bernat Oriental ceramics & bronzes; American Heritage coll; The Helen Warren & Willard Howe Cummings Collection of American Art; American Art of the 18th, 19th & 20th centuries; Jette Collection of American painting in the Impressionist Period; John Marin Collection of 25 works by Marin; Adelaide Pearson Collection; Pre-Columbian Mexico; Etruscan art; Paul J Schupf Wing For the Works of Alex Katz; William J Pollock Collection of American Indian Art
Publications: Exhibition catalogs; periodic newsletter
Activities: Docent training; lects open to pub; gallery talks; tours; individual paintings lent to other museums; originate traveling exhibs; mus shop sells books, note cards, postcards & posters
L **Bixler Art & Music Library,** 5660 Mayflower Hill, Waterville, ME 04901. Tel 207-859-5660; Fax 207-859-5105; Elec Mail mericson@colby.edu; Internet Home Page Address: libguides.colby.edu/bixler; *Librn* Margaret Ericson; *Library Coordr* Robin Duperry
Open acad yr Mon - Thurs 8 AM - 12 AM, Fri 8 AM - 6 PM, Sat 10 AM - 6PM, Sun 10 AM - 12 AM; No admis fee; Estab 1959 as a study space and arts collections, computer lab facilities and seminar rooms; Circ 14,000 vols/yr; For reference & acad lending to college community & Maine residents; Average Annual Attendance: 85,000
Library Holdings: Book Volumes 45,000; CD-ROMs; Compact Disks 10,000; DVDs 1,500; Other Holdings Music; Periodical Subscriptions 90; Records 1,800; Slides 60,000
Special Subjects: Art History, Painting-American, Asian Art, Afro-American Art, Religious Art, Architecture

M **THOMAS COLLEGE,** Art Gallery, 180 W River Rd, Waterville, ME 04901-5097. Tel 207-859-1362; Fax 207-877-0114; *Pub Rels Dir* Mark Tardif; *Admin Asst* Nancy Charette
Open Mon - Fri 8 AM - 4 PM; No admis fee; Estab 1968 for presentation of instructional shows for student & community audiences; Displays various works by local artists; Average Annual Attendance: 1,500
Income: Financed through college funds
Exhibitions: Monthly & bimonthly exhibitions by local artists
L **Mariner Library,** 180 W River Rd, Waterville, ME 04901. Tel 207-859-1319; Fax 207-877-1114; Elec Mail charetten@thomas.edu; Internet Home Page Address: www.thomas.edu/library; *Librn* Steven Larochelle; *Asst Librn* Cynthia Mitchell
Open Mon - Thurs 8 AM - 10 PM, Fri 8 AM - 4:30 PM, Sun 2 - 9 PM, cl Sat; For reference only
Income: state appropriation; funded by college
Library Holdings: Book Volumes 21,500; Periodical Subscriptions 400; Slides

M **WATERVILLE HISTORICAL SOCIETY,** Redington Museum, 62 Silver St, Unit B, Waterville, ME 04901. Tel 207-872-9439; Internet Home Page Address: www.rediingtonmuseum.org; *Resident Custodian* Bryan Finnemore; *Resident Custodian* Bonny Finnemore; *Librn* Diane Johnson; *Pres Historical Society* Frederic P Johnson; *VPres* Stephen R McGraw; *Secy* Nancy Gaunce; *Treas* Allan Rancourt; *Cur* Sarah Sugden
Open Memorial Day - Labor Day Tues - Sat 10 AM - 3 PM; tours 10 & 11 AM, 1 & 2 PM; Admis adults $5, children 12 & under free; Estab 1903; Average Annual Attendance: 500; Mem: 250; dues friend $100, family $40, single $20; annual meeting second Thurs in June
Income: Financed by mem & limited endowment
Special Subjects: Flasks & Bottles, Maps, Costumes, Decorative Arts, Manuscripts, Dolls, Furniture, Glass, Historical Material
Collections: Early Silver & China; 18th & 19th century furniture; 19th century apothecary; portraits of early local residents; Victorian clothing; Indian artifacts; Early photos, tools & toys
Activities: Lect open to public, tours

WISCASSET

A **LINCOLN COUNTY HISTORICAL ASSOCIATION, INC,** Pownalborough Courthouse, 133 Federal St, Wiscasset, ME 04578. Tel 207-882-6817; Elec Mail lcha@wiscasset.net; Internet Home Page Address: www.lincolncountyhistory.org; *Exec Dir* Jay Robbins
Open July & Aug Tues - Sat 10 AM - 4 PM, Sun Noon - 4 PM, June & Sept Sat 10 AM - 4 PM, Sun Noon - 4 PM; Admis adults $4, children 18 & under free; Incorporated 1954, to preserve buildings of historic interest; Average Annual Attendance: 700; Mem: 350; dues $25 & up; ann meeting in July
Income: Financed by dues, fundraisers, admis, bequests & donations
Special Subjects: Architecture, Embroidery, Historical Material, Manuscripts, Porcelain, Reproductions, Textiles, Painting-American, Pottery, American Western Art, Decorative Arts, Folk Art, American Indian Art, Crafts, Archaeology, Furniture, Glass, Woodcarvings, Period Rooms, Maps, Scrimshaw, Flasks & Bottles, Restorations
Collections: Furniture; hand tools; household articles; textiles

Publications: Newsletter; occasional monographs
Activities: School progs & docent training; lects open to pub approx 250 per yr; tours; gallery talks; slide shows; mus shop sells books, original art, reproductions
L **Library,** 133 Federal St, Wiscasset, ME 04578. Tel 207-882-6817; *Dir* Anne R Dolan
Open by appointment for reference & research
Library Holdings: Book Volumes 200
M **1811 Old Lincoln County Jail & Lincoln County Museum,** 133 Federal St, Wiscasset, ME 04578. Tel 207-882-6817; Elec Mail lcha@wiscasset.net; Internet Home Page Address: www.lincolncountyhistory.org; *Exec Dir* Jay Robbins
Open July & Aug Tues - Sat 10 AM - 4 PM, Sun Noon - 4 PM, June & Sept Sat 10 AM - 4 PM, Sun Noon - 4 PM, Oct-May by appointment; Admis adults $4, children 18 & under free; Estab 1954 for historical preservation; Average Annual Attendance: 1,500; Mem: 350; dues $20 & up, annual meeting in Oct
Income: Financed by mem, donations, restricted funds & bequests
Special Subjects: American Indian Art, Archaeology, Decorative Arts, Folk Art, Historical Material, Glass, American Western Art, Furniture, Photography, Porcelain, Portraits, Painting-American, Prints, Period Rooms, Silver, Maps, Architecture, Watercolors, Textiles, Costumes, Ceramics, Crafts, Woodcarvings, Scrimshaw, Restorations, Embroidery, Pewter, Reproductions
Collections: Early American tools; jail artifacts; quilts; prison equipment; samplers; textiles; Scrimshaw; Ephemera; Photographs; Baskets; Fans
Exhibitions: shows once a year
Publications: Lincoln County Chronicle - Newsletter
Activities: Docent training; lects open to pub, over 2 vis lectrs per yr; tours; gallery talks; mus shop sells books; original art; reproductions; cards; postcards
M **Maine Art Gallery,** 15 Warren St, Wiscasset, ME 04578. Tel 207-882-7511; Elec Mail meartgallery@gwi.net; Internet Home Page Address: www.maineartgallery.org; *Bd Pres* Sally Loughridge Bush; *Gallery Mgr* Kay Liss; *Treas* Marcia Mansfield; *Asst Mgr* Michele Roberge
Open early May thru late Nov daily 10 AM - 4 PM, Sun 11 AM - 4 PM, cl Winter; No admis fee, donations appreciated; Estab 1958 as a cooperative, non-profit gallery created by the Artist Members of Lincoln County Cultural & Historical Assoc to exhibit the work of artists living or working in Maine; Gallery occupies a red brick federal two-story building built in 1807 as a free Academy. The building is now on National Historical Register; Average Annual Attendance: 6,000; Mem: 200; dues $35; bd meets 4 times per year
Income: Financed by patrons, art sales & fundraising
Exhibitions: Summer Exhibition: A juried show in parts of 4 weeks featuring approx 100 painters & sculptors living or working in Maine; 6 exhibitions per year, 1 juried show, 1 members show, 4 invitational or from show proposals
Activities: Classes for adults; lects open to pub; gallery talks; school art classes; visits

MARYLAND

ANNAPOLIS

M **HAMMOND-HARWOOD HOUSE ASSOCIATION, INC,** Hammond-Harwood House, 19 Maryland Ave, Annapolis, MD 21401-1626. Tel 410-263-4683; Fax 410-267-6891; Elec Mail clively@hammondharwoodhouse.org; Internet Home Page Address: www.hammondharwoodhouse.org; *Exec Dir* Carter Lively; *Asst Dir & Cur* Allison Titman
Open Tues - Sat noon - 5 PM, Sun Noon - 4 PM; cl Oct - Mar, open for group tours & reservations; Admis adults $6, students between 6 & 18 $3; Estab 1938 to preserve the Hammond-Harwood House (1774), a National Historic Landmark; to educate the pub in the arts & architecture of Maryland in the 18th century; Average Annual Attendance: 15,000; Mem: 350; dues varied; meeting May & Nov
Income: Financed by endowment, mem, attendance & sales
Library Holdings: Audio Tapes; Clipping Files; Manuscripts; Original Art Works; Original Documents; Photographs; Prints; Slides
Special Subjects: Decorative Arts, Drawings, Historical Material, Marine Painting, Ceramics, Glass, Manuscripts, Painting-British, Architecture, Painting-American, Prints, Landscapes, Portraits, Dolls, Furniture, Porcelain, Oriental Art, Silver, Metalwork, Maps, Baroque Art, Miniatures, Period Rooms, Embroidery, Pewter
Collections: Paintings by C W Peale; Chinese export porcelain; English & American furnishings, especially from Maryland; prints; English & American silver; colonial architectural interiors designed by William Buckland
Publications: Maryland's Way (Hammond-Harwood House cookbook); Hammond-Harwood House Guidebook
Activities: Interpretive progs; docent training; classes for adults; classes for children; docent training; lects open to pub; lectrs for mems only; concerts; gallery talks; tours; special architecture tours; individual paintings & original objects of art lent to bona fide mus within reasonable transporting distance; mus shop sells books, magazines, reproductions & prints

M **MARYLAND HALL FOR THE CREATIVE ARTS,** Chaney Gallery, 801 Chase St, Annapolis, MD 21401-3530. Tel 410-263-5544; Fax 410-263-5114; Elec Mail cmanucy@mdhallarts.org; Internet Home Page Address: www.marylandhall.org; *Exec Dir* Linnell R Bowen; *Dir Exhibs* Sigrid Trumpy
Open Mon - Sat 9 AM - 5 PM; No admis fee; Estab 1979 to exhibit work of contemporary regional artists; Two room post modern space with 100 ft of wall space & 1100 sq ft of floor space. Contemporary grid-track lighting. Second gallery 450 sq ft, track lighting, also outdoor sculpture; Average Annual Attendance: 7,000; Mem: 2,000; dues $25 & up
Income: Financed by local, state & special grant funds
Special Subjects: Drawings, Photography, Sculpture, Watercolors, Woodcarvings, Woodcuts, Afro-American Art
Exhibitions: Rotating exhibitions, 12-15 per yr
Publications: Postcards
Activities: Classes for adults & children; dramatic progs; concerts; gallery talks; competitions

M **ST JOHN'S COLLEGE,** Elizabeth Myers Mitchell Art Gallery, 60 College Ave, Annapolis, MD 21404-2800; PO Box 2800, Annapolis, MD 21404-2800. Tel 410-263-2371, Ext 256, (Direct line) 626-2556; Fax 410-263-4828; Elec Mail hydee.schaller@sjca.edu; Internet Home Page Address: www.stjohnscollege.edu; *Exhibit Preparator* Sigrid Trumpy; *Outreach Coordr* Lucinda Edinberg; *Dir* Hydee Schaller
Open Sept - May Tues - Sun Noon - 5 PM, Fri 7 - 8 PM; No admis fee; Estab 1989 to present museum quality exhibits & educational progs for the area; Two adjoining galleries; one gallery of 1300 sq ft, rectangle with corner windows and one gallery of 525 sq ft, rectangular, no windows; Average Annual Attendance: 10,000; Mem: 800 members; 427 memberships; dues $50-$1000
Exhibitions: Please refer to our website: www.stjohnscollege.edu/events/Mitchell Gallery
Publications: Catalogs; exhibition programs; gallery guides
Activities: Educ dept offers studio courses in painting, life drawing; workshops for children; sculpture for adults & children; docent training; lectrs open to pub, 6 vis lectrs per yr; gallery talks; tours; concerts; sponsoring of competitions; book traveling exhibs 2-4 per yr; originate traveling exhibs

M **UNITED STATES NAVAL ACADEMY,** USNA Museum, 118 Maryland Ave, Annapolis, MD 21402-1321. Tel 410-293-2108; Fax 410-293-5220; Internet Home Page Address: www.usna.edu/museum; *Sr Cur* James W Cheevers; *Cur Ship Models* Robert F Sumrall; *Cur Robinson Coll* Sigrid Trumpy; *Exhibit Specialist* Robert Chapel; *Dir* Dr J Scott Harmon; *Registrar* Donald Leonard; *Research Assoc* Grant Walker
Open Mon - Sat 9 AM - 5 PM, Sun 11 AM - 5 PM; No admis fee; Estab 1845 as Naval School Lyceum for the purpose of collecting, preserving & exhibiting objects related to American naval history; Mus contains two large galleries totaling 9000 sq ft, with other exhibits in other areas of the campus; Average Annual Attendance: Approx 250,000
Income: Financed by federal government appropriations & private donations
Purchases: $36,170
Special Subjects: Drawings, Painting-American, Prints, Sculpture, Ceramics, Manuscripts, Silver, Metalwork, Coins & Medals
Publications: Collection catalogs & spec exhib brochures, periodically
Activities: Lects; tours upon request; individual paintings & original objects of art lent to other museums & related institutions for special, temporary exhibs; originate traveling exhibs
L **Naval Academy Museum,** 118 Maryland Ave, Annapolis, MD 21402-5034. Tel 410-293-2108; Fax 410-293-5220; Internet Home Page Address: www.usna.edu/museum; *Dir* J Scott Harmon; *Sr Cur* James W Cheevers; *Cur of Ship Models* Robert F Sumrall; *Cur of Beverley R Robinson Collection* Sigrid Trumpy
Open Mon - Sat 9 AM - 5 PM, Sun 11 AM - 5 PM; No admis fee; Estab 1845; Open to students, scholars & public with notice, reference only; Average Annual Attendance: 160,000
Income: Financed by the academy
Library Holdings: Book Volumes 400; Exhibition Catalogs; Periodical Subscriptions 15
Special Subjects: Historical Material, Marine Painting
Collections: US Navy Trophy Flag Collections; Beverley R Robinson Collection
Exhibitions: 100 Years & Forward, Rogers Collection of Ship Models

BALTIMORE

M **ALBIN O KUHN LIBRARY & GALLERY,** Univ Maryland Baltimore County Campus, 1000 Hilltop Circle Baltimore, MD 21250-0001. Tel 410-455-3827; Elec Mail beck@umbc.edu; Internet Home Page Address: www.umbc.edu/aok/main/index.html; *Dir* Larry Wilt; *Chief Cur* Tom Beck; *Spec Coll Librn* Susan Graham; *Archivist* Lindsey Loeper
Open (gallery) Mon - Fri 12 PM - 4:30 PM, Thurs 12 PM - 8 PM, Sat - Sun 1 - 5 PM; (library) Aug - Dec, Mon - Thurs 8 AM - 12 AM, Fri 8 AM - 6 PM, Sat 10 AM - 6 PM, Sun 12 PM - 12 AM; Estab 1973 to promote scholarly exhibitions of original works of art & historic materials for UMBC & the greater Baltimore & Maryland region; 300 running ft to 4,500 sq ft; Average Annual Attendance: 5,000
Library Holdings: Auction Catalogs; Exhibition Catalogs; Manuscripts; Original Art Works; Original Documents; Photographs
Special Subjects: Photography, Manuscripts
Collections: 2,000,000 photographs
Exhibitions: Three to four exhibitions annually of photographs, rare books, manuscripts & historic artifacts
Publications: Music of the Mind: Jaromir Stephan Photographs & Digital Images
Activities: Classes for adults & children; lects open to public, 1 vis lectrs per yr; gallery talks; tours; symposia

M **BALTIMORE CITY COMMUNITY COLLEGE,** Art Gallery, 2901 Liberty Heights Ave, Fine & Applied Arts Dept Baltimore, MD 21215-7807. Tel 410-462-8000; Fax 410-462-7614; *Coordr Arts* Carlton Leverette
Open Mon - Fri 10 AM - 4 PM; No admis fee; Estab 1965 to bring to the Baltimore & col communities exhibs of note by regional artists & to serve as a showplace for the artistic productions of the col art students & faculty; Consists of one large gallery area, approx 120 running ft, well-lighted through the use of both natural light (sky domes) & cove lighting which provides an even wash to the walls
Income: Financed through the college
Special Subjects: Graphics, Painting-American
Collections: Graphics from the 16th century to the present; paintings by notable American artists & regional ones
Exhibitions: Groups shows & three-man shows representing a broad cross section of work by regional artists; art faculty show; three-man show featuring graphic designs & paintings; exhibition of portraits by 15 artists; annual student show
Publications: Gallery announcements
Activities: Lect open to public; gallery talks

M **THE BALTIMORE MUSEUM OF ART,** 10 Art Museum Dr, Baltimore, MD 21218-3827. Tel 443-573-1700; Fax 443-573-1582; Elec Mail amannix@artbma.org; Internet Home Page Address: www.artbma.org; *Deputy Dir Finance & Admin* Christine Dietze; *Deputy Dir Mktg & Communs* Becca Seitz; *Deputy Dir Operations & Capital Planning* Alan Dirican; *Sr Cur Painting & Sculpture Emeritus* Sona Johnston; *Sr Cur Painting & Sculpture* Katherine Rothkopf; *Cur Textiles* Anita Jones; *Assoc Cur Art of Africa, Asia, the Americas & Pacific Islands* Frances Klapthor; *Dir* Doreen Bolger; *Dir Retail Operations* Deana Karras; *Deputy Dir Develop* Judith Gibbs; *Librn* Linda Tompkins-Baldwin; *Cur Contemporary* Kristen Hileman; *Assoc Cur & Dept Head Art of Africa, Asia, The Americas & Pacific Islands* Kathryn Gunsch; *Dir Communs* Anne Mannix; *Deputy Dir Curatorial Affairs* Jay Fisher; *Assoc Cur Drawings & Photographs* Rena Hoisington; *Sr Cur Dec Arts & American Painting & Sculpture* David Park Curry
Open Wed - Fri 10 AM - 5 PM, Sat - Sun 11 AM - 6 PM, cl Mon, Tues & major holidays; No admis fee; some exhibitions may be ticketed; Estab 1914 to house & preserve art works, to present art exhibitions, art-related activities & offer educational programs & events; The original building was designed by John Russell Pope in 1929; addition in 1982 with cafe, auditorium & traveling exhibition galleries; sculpture gardens opened in 1980 & 1988; wing for Contemporary Art opened in 1994, maintains reference library; Average Annual Attendance: 222,000; Mem: 8000; dues $40 & up
Income: $12,900,000 (financed by city, state, county & Federal appropriation; corporate, individual & foundation gifts; mem, earned revenue & endowment income)
Library Holdings: Auction Catalogs; Book Volumes; CD-ROMs; Cassettes; Clipping Files; Exhibition Catalogs; Fiche; Lantern Slides; Manuscripts; Memorabilia; Micro Print; Motion Pictures; Original Art Works; Original Documents; Other Holdings; Pamphlets; Periodical Subscriptions; Photographs; Prints; Reels; Reproductions
Special Subjects: Silver, Textiles, Architecture, Drawings, Latin American Art, Mexican Art, Painting-American, Photography, Prints, Sculpture, American Indian Art, American Western Art, African Art, Pre-Columbian Art, Ceramics, Afro-American Art, Decorative Arts, Painting-European, Portraits, Furniture, Jewelry, Asian Art, Renaissance Art, Painting-Spanish, Antiquities-Egyptian, Mosaics, Gold, Painting-Israeli
Collections: Cone Collection: featuring works of Matisse & Picasso & other 20th century American & European artists; George A Lucas Collection: drawings, esp19th c French
Publications: Exhibition catalogs; members newsletter; posters & postcards; gallery guides; family guides
Activities: Classes for adults & children; docent training; lects open to pub; concerts; films; gallery talks; tours; individual paintings & original objects of art lent to other art mus regionally to internationally; lending collection contains original art works, original prints, paintings, photographs & sculpture; book traveling exhibs; 1 per yr; originate traveling exhibs; mus shop sells books, reproductions, slides, jewelry & children's gifts

L **E Kirkbride Miller Art Library,** 10 Art Museum Dr, Baltimore, MD 21218-3827. Tel 443-573-1778; Fax 443-573-1781; Elec Mail ltompkins@artbma.org; Internet Home Page Address: www.artbma.org; *Library Dir* Linda Tompkins-Baldwin; *Asst Librn* Emily Connell
Open by appointment
Library Holdings: Book Volumes 55,000; Clipping Files; Exhibition Catalogs; Other Holdings 15,000; Pamphlets; Periodical Subscriptions 302
Special Subjects: Decorative Arts, Photography, Drawings, Etchings & Engravings, Painting-American, Prints, Sculpture, Painting-European, Ceramics, Printmaking, American Indian Art, Porcelain, Primitive art, Eskimo Art, Furniture, Glass, Afro-American Art, Carpets & Rugs, Pottery, Tapestries, Textiles, Woodcuts, Laces, Painting-Australian, Embroidery

M **CENTER FOR ART DESIGN AND VISUAL CULTURE,** 1000 Hilltop Circle, Baltimore, MD 21250-0002. Tel 410-455-3188
Open Tues-Sat 10AM-5PM; cl New Year's Eve & Day; Christmas Eve, Day & week
Collections: paintings; sculpture; drawings; printmaking; graphic design; digital art; video; film; architecture; art history

M **CENTER FOR ART DESIGN AND VISUAL CULTURE,** Fine Arts Bldg 105, 1000 Hilltop Cir Baltimore, MD 21250-0001. Symmes Gardner

L **ENOCH PRATT FREE LIBRARY OF BALTIMORE CITY,** 400 Cathedral St, Fine Arts Dept Baltimore, MD 21201-4401. Tel 410-396-5430 (General); 396-5490 (Fine Arts & Music Dept); Fax 410-396-1409 (Fine Arts & Music Dept); Elec Mail far@prattlibrary.org; Internet Home Page Address: www.prattlibrary.org; *Dir* Carla Hayden; *Chief State Library Resource Center* Wesley Wilson
Open Oct - May, Mon - Wed 10 AM - 7 PM, Thurs - Sat 10 AM - 5 PM, Sun 1 - 5 PM ; No admis fee; Estab 1882 to provide materials, primarily circulating on the visual arts and music; Exhibition space in display windows, interior display cases, corridors and special departments
Income: Financed by city and state appropriation
Library Holdings: Book Volumes 97,000; Filmstrips; Framed Reproductions; Other Holdings Framed prints; Unframed pictures; Records; Reproductions; Slides
Publications: Book lists, periodically
Activities: Lect & film showings

M **EUBIE BLAKE JAZZ MUSEUM & GALLERY,** 847 N Howard St, Ste 323 Baltimore, MD 21201-4605. Tel 410-225-3130; Fax 410-225-3139; Elec Mail eubieblake@erols.com, or eblake847@aol.com; Internet Home Page Address: www.eubieblake.org; *Exec Dir* Camay Murphy; *Exec Dir* Troy Burton; *Program Dir* Ronald Malone
Open Wed-Fri 11AM-6PM, Sat 11AM-3PM, Sun by appointment only; Admis varies, call for more info; Estab 1983; The gallery is for minority & emerging artists; maintains a library; Average Annual Attendance: 10,000; Mem: 100; dues $20; annual meeting in Feb
Income: $2,300,000 (financed by mem, city & state appropriation)
Special Subjects: Afro-American Art
Exhibitions: Monthly exhibits
Publications: Ragtime, quarterly newsletter
Activities: Classes for children; dramatic progs; lects open to pub; 4 vis lectrs per yr; competitions; concerts; tours; mus shop sells books, original art & prints

M **GOUCHER COLLEGE,** Rosenberg Gallery, 1021 Dulaney Valley Rd Baltimore, MD 21204. Tel 410-337-6477; Fax 410-337-6405; Elec Mail laura.amussen@goucher.edu; Internet Home Page Address: www.goucher.edu/rosenberg; *Exhib Dir & Coll Coordr* Laura Amassen
Open Mon - Fri 9 AM - 5 PM during the acad calendar & on evenings & weekends of pub events; No admis fee; Estab 1964 to display temporary & continuously changing exhibitions of contemporary & historically important visual arts; Gallery spaced located in the lobby of the Kraushaar Auditorium; 144 running ft of wall space; Average Annual Attendance: 125,000
Income: Financed privately
Collections: Ceramics; coins; drawings; paintings; prints; sculpture; photography
Publications: Exhibit brochures, 4 per year
Activities: Lect open to public, gallery talks; original objects of art lent to qualified museums & educational institutions; book traveling exhibitions 1 per year

M **JOHNS HOPKINS UNIVERSITY,** Archaeological Collection, 3400 N Charles St, Baltimore, MD 21218-2608. Tel 410-516-7561; Elec Mail emaguire@jhu.edu; *Dir Near Eastern & Egyptian Art* Dr Betsy Bryan; *Cur* Dr Eunice Maguire; *Asst Cur* Violaine Chauvet
Special Subjects: Antiquities-Egyptian, Antiquities-Roman
Collections: Egyptian through Roman material 3500 BC to 500 AD

M **Evergreen Museum & Library,** 4545 N Charles St, Baltimore, MD 21210. Tel 410-516-0341; Fax 410-516-0864; Elec Mail james.abbot@jhu.edu; Internet Home Page Address: www.museums.jhu.edu; *Cur* James Archer Abbot; *Commun and Mktg Mgr* Heather Stalfort; *Tour Coordr and Office Adminr* Nancy Powers
Open Tues - Fri 11 AM - 4 PM, Sat & Sun noon - 4 PM, Last tour daily at 3 PM; Admis fee adults $6, seniors $5, students $3; Estab 1952 for promotion of cultural & educational functions & research; Formerly the residence of Ambassador John W Garrett which he bequeathed to the University; Average Annual Attendance: 10,000; Mem: 200; dues $25 - $250
Income: Evergreen House Found; John Hopkins Univ
Library Holdings: Book Volumes; Other Holdings
Special Subjects: Decorative Arts, Drawings, Etchings & Engravings, History of Art & Archaeology, Interior Design, Landscape Architecture, Landscapes, Art History, Ceramics, Furniture, Portraits, Painting-American, Silver, Painting-French, Architecture, Drawings, Hispanic Art, Mexican Art, Painting-American, American Western Art, Bronzes, Ethnology, Ceramics, Pottery, Etchings & Engravings, Landscapes, Decorative Arts, Manuscripts, Furniture, Glass, Jade, Porcelain, Oriental Art, Asian Art, Metalwork, Painting-French, Carpets & Rugs, Historical Material, Maps, Coins & Medals, Miniatures, Painting-Spanish, Antiquities-Persian, Islamic Art, Antiquities-Egyptian, Antiquities-Greek, Antiquities-Roman, Mosaics, Stained Glass, Painting-German, Painting-Russian, Enamels, Bookplates & Bindings
Collections: Leon Baskt-designed private theatre; American and European Ceramics; American art glass; 19th and 20th century European paintings; American, European, and Middle Eastern Decorative and Applied Arts; Japanese Inro Nesuke and lacquerwares; Chinese porcelains; 30,000 Vol John Work Garret Libr; Laurence Hall Fowler architectural drawing collection
Exhibitions: Changing exhibitions
Publications: Raoul Dufy at Evergreen and the Evolution of Alice Warder Garret as a Patron of Contemp Art, 2007; Leon Basket at the Evergreen House: A Collection Built Around a Friendship, 2004
Activities: Classes for adults; classes for children; docent training; dramatic programs; lects open to pub; 4 vis lectrs per year; concerts; gallery talks; tours; individual paintings & original objects of art lent to other mus, national & international; mus shop sells books, reproductions & prints; original art

L **George Peabody Library,** 17 E Mount Vernon Pl, Baltimore, MD 21202-2308. Tel 410-659-8179; Fax 410-659-8137; *Librn Asst* Erika Cooper; *Librn* Carolyn Smith
Open Mon - Fri 9 AM - 3 PM
Library Holdings: Book Volumes 250,000
Special Subjects: Decorative Arts, Architecture
Collections: British History; art and architecture; decorative arts; religion; travel; geography; maps

M **Homewood Museum,** 3400 N Charles St, Baltimore, MD 21218-2680. Tel 410-516-5589; Fax 410-516-7859; Elec Mail homewoodmuseum@jhu.edu; Internet Home Page Address: www.museums.jhu.edu; *Dir* Winston Tab; *Cur* Catherine Arthur; *Programs Coordr* Judith Proffitt; *Communs Dir* Heather Egan Stalfort; *Develop Coordr* Rosalie Parker
Open Tues -Fri 11 AM - 4 PM, Sat - Sun noon - 4 PM; Admis fee $6, seniors $5, students $3; Estab 1987; a historic house mus; Restored Federal Period country seat of Charles Carroll, Jr, with period furnishings; Average Annual Attendance: 10,000; Mem: 350; annual dues $50
Special Subjects: Glass, Furniture, Architecture, African Art, Archaeology, Textiles, Ceramics, Decorative Arts, Porcelain, Silver, Restorations, Period Rooms, Pewter
Collections: English & American decorative arts of the late 18th & early 19th Century
Activities: Docent Training; Lectures open the public; concerts; internships offered; mus shop sells books, original art, object reproductions, prints, slides, exclusive Homewood items & jewelry

M **MARYLAND ART PLACE,** 8 Market Pl Ste 100, Baltimore, MD 21202-4015. Tel 410-962-8565; Fax 410-244-8017; Elec Mail map@mdartplace.org; Internet Home Page Address: www.mdartplace.org; *Exec Dir* Amy Cavanaugh Royce; *Pres* Barbie Hart; *Prog Mgr & Registry Coordr* Sofia Rutica; *Develop Mgr* Emily Sollenberger
Open Tues - Sat 11 AM - 5 PM; No admis fee; Estab 1981, to provide opportunities for artists to exhibit work, nurture & promote new ideas & forms; Three galleries within one floor; Average Annual Attendance: 30,000; Mem: 4000; dues $35-$1000 and up
Income: $450,000 (financed by mem, federal, state & corporate appropriation)

Special Subjects: Drawings, Graphics, Hispanic Art, Painting-American, Ceramics, Folk Art, Landscapes, Collages
Exhibitions: Varies
Publications: Annual catalogs; exhibition brochures, 4-6 per year; quarterly newsletter
Activities: Annual public forum; professional develop; lects open to pub, 4 vis lectrs per yr; gallery talks; tours; competitions; originate traveling exhibs 1-2 per yr

M **MARYLAND HISTORICAL SOCIETY,** Museum of Maryland History, 201 W Monument St, Baltimore, MD 21201-4601. Tel 410-685-3750; Fax 410-385-2105; Internet Home Page Address: www.mdhs.org; *Deputy Dir & Chief Cur* Jeannine Disviscour; *Dir* Robert W Rogers; *Dir Communs* Anne Garside
Open Wed - Sun 10 AM - 5 PM; Admis adults $4, seniors & students $3; children under 12 free; Estab 1844 to collect, display & interpret the history of the State of Maryland; Average Annual Attendance: 70,000; Mem: dues family $60, individual $50; annual meeting in June
Income: Financed by endowment, mem, city & state appropriations
Library Holdings: Audio Tapes; Book Volumes; Clipping Files; Compact Disks; DVDs; Exhibition Catalogs; Filmstrips; Framed Reproductions; Kodachrome Transparencies; Lantern Slides; Manuscripts; Maps; Memorabilia; Motion Pictures; Original Documents; Other Holdings; Pamphlets; Periodical Subscriptions; Photographs; Records; Reproductions; Slides
Special Subjects: Architecture, Painting-American, Textiles, Pottery, Glass, Porcelain, Silver, Metalwork
Collections: Architectural drawings; crystal & glassware; ethnic artifacts, all of Maryland origin or provenance; metalwork; paintings, both portrait & landscape; porcelain & pottery; silver; textiles & costumes; furniture
Exhibitions: Continually changing exhibitions reflecting the history & culture of the state
Publications: Maryland Historical Society Magazine, quarterly; MDHS/news 3 times per yr
Activities: Classes for adults & children; docent training; lects open to pub; 12 vis lectrs per yr; concerts; gallery talks; tours; competitions with awards; exten dept; individual paintings & original objects of art lent to other organizations in State of Maryland; originate traveling exhibs; mus shop sells books, original art, prints

L **Library,** 201 W Monument St, Baltimore, MD 21201-4601. Tel 410-685-3750; Fax 410-385-2105; Elec Mail webcomments@mdhs.org; Internet Home Page Address: www.mdhs.org/library; *Cur Coll* Nancy Davis; *CEO* Dennis Fiori; *Registrar* Louise Brownell; *COO* John W Eller; *Head Librn* Bea Hardy; *VPres* Barbara P Katz; *Mus Shop Mgr* Barbara Gamse
Open Wed-Sat 10AM-4:30PM; Estab 1844; Library for reference only; Average Annual Attendance: 70,000; Mem: 6,500
Library Holdings: Audio Tapes; Book Volumes 70,000; Cassettes; Clipping Files; Exhibition Catalogs; Fiche; Filmstrips; Kodachrome Transparencies; Lantern Slides; Manuscripts; Memorabilia; Motion Pictures; Pamphlets; Periodical Subscriptions 125; Photographs; Prints; Records; Reels; Reproductions; Slides; Video Tapes

M **MARYLAND INSTITUTE,** College of Art Exhibitions, 1300 Mount Royal Ave, Baltimore, MD 21217. Tel 410-225-2280; Fax 410-225-2396; *Pres* Fred Lazarus IV; *Gallery Dir* Will Hipps; *Asst Dir Exhib* Anthony Cervino
Open Mon - Sat 10 AM - 5 PM, Sun Noon - 5 PM; No admis fee; Estab 1826, including the Decker & Meyerhoff Galleries, the Graduate Thesis Gallery & 2 student galleries; Average Annual Attendance: 10,000
Income: Financed by endowment & student tuition
Exhibitions: Changing exhibitions of contemporary work in Meyerhoff & Decker Galleries
Publications: Several small catalogs; two major publications per year
Activities: Lect open to public; concerts; gallery talks; tours; original objects of art lent

L **Decker Library,** 1401 Mt Royal Ave, Baltimore, MD 21217; 1300 Mt Royal Ave, Baltimore, MD 21217. Tel 410-225-2272; Fax 410-225-2316; Elec Mail awhite03@mica.edu; Internet Home Page Address: mica.edu; *Library Dir* Tony White; *Sr Reference Librn* Kathy Cowan; *Instructional Librn* Marianne Sade; *Reference Librn* Chris Drolsum; *Digital Media Librn* Michael Scott; *Catalog Librn* Kelly Swickard
Open Mon - Thurs 8:30 AM - 9 PM, Fri 8:30 AM - 4:30 PM, Sat - Sun noon - 6 PM; Circ 36,000; Open to the pub for reference only.; Average Annual Attendance: 101,000
Library Holdings: Book Volumes 85,000; Clipping Files; DVDs; Exhibition Catalogs; Motion Pictures; Original Documents; Periodical Subscriptions 275; Video Tapes
Collections: Artists' Books

M **MEREDITH GALLERY,** 805 N Charles St, Baltimore, MD 21201-5307. Tel 410-837-3575; Fax 410-837-3577; Internet Home Page Address: www.meredithgallery.com; *Assoc Dir* Terry Heffner; *Dir* Judith Lippman
Open Tues - Fri 10 AM - 4 PM, Sat 11 AM - 3 PM; No admis fee; Estab 1977 to exhibit a variety of contemporary art by living American artists, including art furniture, ceramics, glass; The building is divided into two floors with regular monthly exhibits & ongoing representation of gallery artists; Average Annual Attendance: 4,000
Activities: Classes for adults & children; educational lect on current exhibitions; lect open to public; gallery talks; tours

M **MORGAN STATE UNIVERSITY,** James E Lewis Museum of Art, 1700 E Cold Spring Lane, Baltimore, MD 21251. Tel 443-885-3030; Fax 410-319-4024; Elec Mail gtenabe@moac.morgan.edu; *Dir & Cur* Gabriel S Tenabe; *Asst Cur* Eric Briscoe; *Dir of Mktg& Develop* Virginia Jenkins; *Mus Registrar* Deborah Nobles-McDaniel; *Secy* Tyvonia Young
Open Mon - Fri 10 AM - 4:30 PM, Sat, Sun, holidays by appointment only, cl Easter, Thanksgiving, Christmas; No admis fee; Estab 1950; Average Annual Attendance: 5,000
Income: $5,500
Collections: 19th & 20th centuries American & European sculpture; graphics; paintings; decorative arts; archaeology; African & New Guinea Sculptures
Publications: Monthly catalogs
Activities: Lects open to pub, vis lectrs; lending collection contains Kodachromes; originate traveling exhibs

L **Library,** 1700 E Cold Spring Lane, Baltimore, MD 21251. Tel 443-885-3488; Internet Home Page Address: www.morgan.edu/library; *Dir* Karen Robertson
Open Mon - Thurs 8 AM - 11 PM, Fri 8 AM - 9 PM, Sat noon- 5PM, Sun 1 - 11 PM
Library Holdings: Book Volumes 8800; DVDs; Photographs

M **NATIONAL MUSEUM OF CERAMIC ART & GLASS,** 2406 Shelleydale Dr, Baltimore, MD 21209-3242. Tel 410-764-1042; Fax 410-764-1042; *Adminr* Shirley B Brown; *Pres* Richard Taylor; *VPres* Bruce T Taylor, MD; *Secy & Treas* Robert B Brown
Estab 1994 to exhibit ceramic art & glass & develop educational progs; Average Annual Attendance: 9,000; Mem: 478; dues $25-$150; meetings in Oct & Apr
Income: Financed by mem, city & state appropriation & grants
Special Subjects: Art Education, Sculpture, Pre-Columbian Art, Ceramics, Crafts, Pottery, Glass, Porcelain, Mosaics, Stained Glass, Enamels
Activities: Classes for adults & children; ceramic programs in 59 middle schools in Baltimore Metropolitan area; original objects of art lent

M **NATIONAL SOCIETY OF COLONIAL DAMES OF AMERICA IN THE STATE OF MARYLAND,** Mount Clare Museum House, 1500 Washington Blvd, Carroll Park Baltimore, MD 21230-1727. Tel 410-837-3262; Fax 410-837-0251; Elec Mail info@mountclare.org; Internet Home Page Address: www.mountclare.org; *Dir* David Shackelford
Open Thurs - Sun 11 AM - 4 PM; Admis adults $6, seniors $5, children (2-12) $4; Estab 1917 to preserve the home of Charles Carroll, Barrister & teach about the colonial period of Maryland history. Maintained by the National Soc of Colonial Dames of America; Rooms of the house are furnished with 18th & early 19th century decorative arts, much of which belonged to the Carroll family who built the house in 1760 & has been designated a National Historic Landmark; Average Annual Attendance: 5,000; Mem: 14,000; dues vary
Income: Financed by admis, gift shop sales & contributions from pub & private sectors
Library Holdings: Book Volumes
Special Subjects: Etchings & Engravings, Folk Art, Historical Material, Landscapes, Architecture, Metalwork, Flasks & Bottles, Gold, Portraits, Pottery, Prints, Manuscripts, Tapestries, Graphics, Painting-American, Watercolors, Textiles, Costumes, Ceramics, Primitive art, Decorative Arts, Dolls, Furniture, Glass, Jewelry, Silver, Ivory, Restorations, Miniatures, Period Rooms, Embroidery, Laces, Pewter, Military Art, Reproductions
Collections: American paintings; 18th & early 19th century English & American furniture; English silver; Irish crystal; Oriental export porcelain; other English & American decorative arts; rare books
Exhibitions: Special exhibs periodically, see website; (2013-2014) Civil War
Publications: Brochure on Mount Clare; Mount Clare: Being an Account of the Seat Built by Charles Carroll, Barrister Upon His Lands at Patapsco; booklet on the house; others pertaining to collection & Maryland
Activities: Classes for adults & children; docent training; school tours; traveling trunk shows; colonial camp; lects open to pub, 4 vis lectrs per yr; gallery talks; tours; original objects of art lent to historical societies by request; mus shop sells books, magazines, original art, reproductions, gift items, souvenirs & historical replicas

L **Library,** 1500 Washington Blvd, Carroll Park Baltimore, MD 21230-1727. Tel 410-837-3262; Fax 410-837-0251; Elec Mail info@mountclare.org; Internet Home Page Address: www.mountclare.org; WATS www.users.errolls/mountclaremuseumhouse.org;
Open Wed - Fri 11 AM - 4 PM; Admis free; Estab 1917; Circ 1,500; Open to members & the pub for reference only; Average Annual Attendance: 5,000; Mem: 14,000; application dues vary
Income: Private finance
Library Holdings: Book Volumes 1000; Clipping Files; Exhibition Catalogs; Framed Reproductions; Kodachrome Transparencies; Lantern Slides; Manuscripts; Maps; Memorabilia; Original Art Works; Original Documents; Other Holdings; Pamphlets; Periodical Subscriptions; Photographs; Prints; Slides
Special Subjects: Art History, Folk Art, Landscape Architecture, Decorative Arts, Drawings, Etchings & Engravings, Painting-American, Prints, Historical Material, History of Art & Archaeology, Portraits, Ceramics, Archaeology, American Western Art, Art Education, Asian Art, Porcelain, Primitive art, Anthropology, Furniture, Ivory, Period Rooms, Costume Design & Constr, Glass, Metalwork, Carpets & Rugs, Dolls, Embroidery, Gold, Goldsmithing, Handicrafts, Jewelry, Miniatures, Pottery, Restoration & Conservation, Silver, Silversmithing, Textiles, Pewter, Flasks & Bottles, Architecture
Collections: 18th century furniture; decorative arts; part of the library of Charles Carroll, Barrister-at-law, builder of the house, 1756; art; photos
Publications: Library of rare book; out of print; MD history; MD genealogy
Activities: Classes for adults & children; docent training; social & material culture progs; lects open to pub; 4 vis lectrs per yr; tours; Congressional schols; history essay award; extension prog to Maryland & mid-Atlantic; traveling trunk to schools; mus shop sells book, magazines

M **NORMAN AND SARAH BROWN ART GALLERY,** Jewish Community Center, 5700 Park Heights Ave Baltimore, MD 21215. Tel 410-542-4900 ext 239; Internet Home Page Address: www.jcc.org/index.php; *Dir Baltimore Jewish Film Festival* Claudine Davison
Open Mon - Tues 11 AM - 5 PM, Wed - Thurs 3 PM - 5 PM, Fri noon - 2:30, Sun noon - 5 PM
Collections: Paintings; prints; sculpture; photographs; documents; drawings; books
Activities: Community center; classrooms; garden; museum-related items for sale

A **SCHOOL 33 ART CENTER,** 1427 Light St, Baltimore, MD 21230-4528. Tel 443-263-4350; Fax 410-837-6947; Elec Mail school33@promotionandarts.com; Internet Home Page Address: www.school33.org; *Dir Cultural Affairs* Randi Vega; *Asst Dir Cultural Affairs* Krista Green; *Exhibs Coordr* Rene Trevino; *Bright Starts Coordr* Cash Hester; *Cultural Affairs Assoc* William Pace
Gallery open Wed - Sat Noon - 6 PM during exhibs; Estab 1979

A STAR-SPANGLED BANNER FLAG HOUSE ASSOCIATION, Flag House & 1812 Museum, 844 E Pratt St, Baltimore, MD 21202-4495. Tel 410-837-1793; Fax 410-837-1812; Elec Mail info@flaghouse.org; Internet Home Page Address: www.flaghouse.org; *Dir* Sally Johnston; *Cur & Grants Mgr* Kathleen Browning
Open Tues - Sat 10 AM - 4 PM, cl Sun; Admis adults $5, students 13-18 & children 12 & under $3, seniors $4, military personnel w/id $2; Estab 1927 for the care & maintenance of 1793 home of Mary Pickersgill, maker of 15 stars, 15 stripes flag used at Fort McHenry during Battle of Baltimore, war of 1812, which inspired Francis Scott Key to pen his famous poem, now our national anthem; also to conduct an educational program for pub & private schools; Mus houses artifacts, portraits & library. 1793 house furnished & decorated in Federal period to look as it did when Mary Pickersgill was in residence; Average Annual Attendance: 10,000; Mem: 500; dues $20; annual meeting in Apr
Income: Financed by mem, admis, special events fund-raisers & sales from mus shop
Collections: Original antiques of Federal period
Publications: The Star (newsletter), quarterly
Activities: Classes for children; dramatic progs; docent training; lects open to pub, 10 vis lectrs per yr; tours; competition with cash awards; original objects of art lent to Pickersgill Retirement Home; mus sales shop sells books, reproductions, prints, slides, Baltimore souvenirs, flags from all nations, maps, country crafts & small antiques
M Museum, 844 E Pratt St, Baltimore, MD 21202-4495. Tel 410-837-1793; Fax 410-837-1812; Internet Home Page Address: www.flaghouse.org; *Dir* Sally S Johnston
Open Tues - Sat 10 AM - 4 PM; Admis $3-$5; Estab 1927; Mem: 500; dues $30; annual meeting in Apr
Income: mem, admis, special events fundraisers, sales from museum shop
Special Subjects: Porcelain
Collections: House furnished in authentic federal period furniture & artifacts; books, photographs & documents
Publications: The Star, quarterly
Activities: Lects open to pub, 5 vis lectrs per yr; mus shop sells books & flags of all descriptions

M UNITED METHODIST HISTORICAL SOCIETY, Lovely Lane Museum, 2200 Saint Paul St, Baltimore, MD 21218-5805. Tel 410-889-4458; Elec Mail director@lovelylanemuseum.com; Internet Home Page Address: www.lovelylanemuseum.com; *Dir of Librn* James Reaves; *Asst Librn* Wanda Hall; *Exec Secy* Edwin Schell
Open Mon & Fri 10 AM - 4 PM, Sun after church; groups by appointment; No admis fee; research fee for non-member genealogists; Estab 1855; a religious collection specializing in Methodism; The main mus room contains permanent exhibits; three other galleries are devoted largely to rotating exhibits; Average Annual Attendance: 4,000; Mem: 417; dues $25-$300; annual meeting in May
Income: $58,000 (financed by mem & religious den)
Purchases: $868
Library Holdings: Clipping Files; Manuscripts; Maps; Memorabilia; Original Documents; Pamphlets; Periodical Subscriptions; Photographs; Prints; Slides
Special Subjects: Archaeology, Historical Material, Portraits, Maps, Photography, Religious Art, Decorative Arts, Manuscripts, Calligraphy, Bookplates & Bindings
Collections: Archaeological items from Evans House; Artifacts with Methodist significance; medallions; Methodist Library & Archives; oil portraits & engraving of United Methodist leader, quilts; Papers of Leading Methodists
Publications: Third Century Methodism, quarterly; annual report
Activities: Docent training; lects open to pub, 1-2 vis lectrs per yr; tours; competitions with awards; individual paintings & original objects of art lent to institutions able to provide proper security upon application & approval by Board of Dir; originate traveling exhibs to United Methodist Churches & Conferences; mus shop sells books, prints, reproductions
L Library, 2200 Saint Paul St, Lovely Lane Museum Baltimore, MD 21218-5805. Tel 410-889-4458; Elec Mail research@lovelylanemuseum.com; *Asst Librn* Betty Ammons; *Librn* Suni Johnson; *Secy* Edwin Schell
Open Thurs & Fri 10 AM - 4 PM & by appointment; No admis fee; Estab 1855 specializing in United Methodist history & heritage; Open to general pub for reference; Average Annual Attendance: 4,000; Mem: 600
Income: $43,000
Purchases: $700
Library Holdings: Audio Tapes; Book Volumes 4000; Cassettes; Clipping Files; Filmstrips; Kodachrome Transparencies; Lantern Slides; Manuscripts; Memorabilia; Micro Print; Motion Pictures; Original Art Works; Other Holdings Archives; Pamphlets; Periodical Subscriptions 17; Photographs; Prints; Records; Reels; Reproductions; Sculpture; Slides; Video Tapes
Special Subjects: Film, Etchings & Engravings, Manuscripts, Maps, Painting-American, Posters, Prints, Historical Material, Portraits, Archaeology, Bookplates & Bindings, Religious Art, Textiles, Architecture
Publications: Third Century Methodism, 3 per year
Activities: Tours

M WALTERS ART MUSEUM, 600 N Charles St, Baltimore, MD 21201-5185. Tel 410-547-9000; Fax 410-783-7969; Elec Mail info@thewalters.org; Internet Home Page Address: www.thewalters.org; *Chair Bd Trustees* Andrea Laporte; *Dir* Dr Gary Vikan; *Assoc Dir* Nancy E Zinn; *Dir Conservation & Technical Research* Terry Drayman Weistr; *Registrar* Joan Elizabeth Reid; *Pres Bd Trustees* Douglas W Hamilton Jr; *Cur Renaissance & Baroque Art* Joaneath Spicer; *Cur Asian Art* Robert Mintz; *Cur Medieval Art* Martina Bagnoli; *Cur Mss & Rare Books* William Noel; *Dir Develop* Joy Heyman; *Dir Develop & Dir Educ* Jackie Copeland; *Sr Dir Admin* Harold Stevens; *Dir Mktg* Matthew Fry; *Chief Technology Officer* James Maza; *Asst Cur 18th-19thc Art* Jo Briggs
Open Wed - Sun 10 AM - 5 PM, cl Mon, Tues & federal holidays except New Year's Day, MLK Jr Day & Easter Sunday; No admis fee for permanent coll; special coll fees apply, discounted rates for adult & college groups of 10+; Estab 1931 by the will of Henry Walters & opened in 1934 as an art mus. Hackerman House Mus of Asian Art opened in 1990; A Renaissance revival mus of 1905 with a contemporary wing of five floors opened in 1974, covering 126,000 sq ft of exhibition space with auditorium, library & conservation laboratory; Average Annual Attendance: 190,000; Mem: 4600; dues $55 & up

Income: $15 (financed by endowment, mem, city & state appropriation, grants & admis
Library Holdings: Auction Catalogs; Book Volumes; CD-ROMs; Compact Disks; Exhibition Catalogs; Kodachrome Transparencies; Maps; Photographs; Prints; Slides
Special Subjects: Porcelain, Painting-American, Sculpture, Religious Art, Decorative Arts, Painting-European, Jewelry, Oriental Art, Asian Art, Antiquities-Byzantine, Painting-British, Painting-French, Ivory, Baroque Art, Renaissance Art, Medieval Art, Antiquities-Oriental, Antiquities-Persian, Islamic Art, Antiquities-Egyptian, Antiquities-Greek, Antiquities-Roman, Antiquities-Etruscan, Antiquities-Assyrian
Collections: The Collection covers the entire history of art from Egyptian times to the beginning of the 20th century. It includes important groups of Roman sculpture, Etruscan, Byzantine & medieval art
Publications: Bulletin, bi-monthly; journal, annually; exhibition catalogues
Activities: Classes for adults & children; dramatic progs; docent training; seminars; lects open to pub; concerts; gallery talks; tours; films; fellowships offered; exten dept serves Baltimore City & nearby counties; book traveling exhibs 3-4 per yr; originate traveling exhibs to mus throughout the world; mus shop sells books, reproductions, slides, Christmas cards, notepaper, gifts
L Library, 600 N Charles St, Baltimore, MD 21201-5185. Tel 410-547-9000; Fax 410-783-7969; Elec Mail chenry@thewalters.org; Internet Home Page Address: www.thewalters.org/research/library.asp; *Head of Library* Chris Henry; *Dir Educ* Jacqueline Tibbs Copeland; *Dir* Gary Vikan; *Cur Renaissance* Joaneath Spicer; *Mus Shop Mgr* Alice McAuliffe; *Chmn* Andrea B Laporte; *Cur Mss* William Noel; *Dir Mktg & Commun* Matt Fry; *Registrar* Joan-Elisabeth Reid; *Pres* Douglas Hamilton Jr; *Dir Finance* Harold Stephens; *Cur Asian Art* Robert Minty; *Dir Conservation* Terry Drayman-Weisser; *Dir Develop* Joy Heyrman; *Assoc Dir Colls & Exhibs* Nancy Ziun
Open Tues - Fri 10 AM - 5 PM; No admis fee - only special exhibs; Estab 1934 serves staff of the mus & open to the pub by appointment; Non-circulating
Income: $154,000
Purchases: $73,000
Library Holdings: Auction Catalogs; Book Volumes 104,000; DVDs; Maps; Photographs; Reproductions
Special Subjects: Decorative Arts, Drawings, Painting-American, Sculpture, History of Art & Archaeology, Ceramics, Archaeology, American Western Art, Stained Glass, Religious Art, Restoration & Conservation, Silver, Silversmithing, Antiquities-Assyrian, Architecture
Activities: Classes for adults & children; docent training; Lects open to pub; 6 vis lectrs per yr; concerts; gallery talks; tours; mus shop sells books, reproductions, prints, cards & jewelry

CHESTERTOWN

A HISTORICAL SOCIETY OF KENT COUNTY, 101 Church Alley, Chestertown, MD 21620; PO Box 665, Chestertown, MD 21620-0665. Tel 410-778-3499; Elec Mail director@kentcountyhistory.org; Internet Home Page Address: www.kentcountyhistory.com; *Exec Dir* Diane Daniels
Open Tues-Fri 10AM-4PM, Sat May-Oct 1 - 4PM; Admis adults $3 children & students free; Estab 1936; dedicated to the collection & presentation of county history; Headquarters are in the early 18th century Geddes-Piper House (c 1784), beautifully restored and furnished; Average Annual Attendance: 2,000; Mem: 700; dues family $50, single $30; annual meeting in Apr
Income: Financed by mem & donations
Special Subjects: Embroidery, Manuscripts, Painting-American, Furniture, Period Rooms, Maps
Collections: Furniture, pictures; Indian artifacts; fans; Chinese porcelain teapots; Maps; Portraits; Archival library (genealogy)
Exhibitions: Permanent house museum
Activities: Lect for members & community; vis lectrs 5 per yr; tours; open house with traditional costuming; sales shop sells books & maps

M WASHINGTON COLLEGE, Kohl Gallery, 300 Washington Ave, Gibson Ctr for the Arts Chestertown, MD 21620. Tel 410-778-2800; Tel 800-422-1782; *Contact* Donald McColl

CHEVY CHASE

C RITZ-CARLTON HOTEL COMPANY, Art Collection, 4445 Willard Ave, Ste 800 Chevy Chase, MD 20815. Tel 301-547-4700; Fax 801-468-4069; Internet Home Page Address: www.ritzcarlton.com; *Design Coordr* Marilyn Bowling; *Pres & CEO* Simon Cooper
Activities: Lect open to public on request; sales shop sells books & reproductions

COLLEGE PARK

M UNIVERSITY OF MARYLAND, COLLEGE PARK, The Art Gallery, 1202 Art-Sociology Bldg, College Park, MD 20742. Tel 301-405-2763; Fax 301-314-7774; Elec Mail ag210@umail.umd.edu; Internet Home Page Address: www.artgallery.umd.edu; *Dir* John Shipman; *Arts Admin Mgr* Jewell Watson
Open during exhibs Mon - Sat 11 AM - 4 PM, cl summer & between exhibs; No admis fee, donations accepted; Estab 1966 to present historic & contemporary exhibitions; Gallery has 4000 sq ft of space, normally divided into one large & one smaller gallery; Average Annual Attendance: 8,000
Income: Financed by university & department funds, grants, catalog sales, traveling exhibitions
Special Subjects: Drawings, Painting-American, Prints, Sculpture, African Art
Collections: 20th century paintings, prints & drawings, including WPA mural studies, paintings by Warhol, Prendergast & Gottlieb; prints by Hundertwasser, Appel, Kitaj, Rivers & Chryssa; 20th century Japanese prints by Hiratsuka, Kosaka, Matsubara, Iwami, Ay-O & others; West African sculpture; Andy Warhol Collection

Exhibitions: Masters of Fine Arts Thesis Exhibitions; Regional Artists & National Artists
Publications: Exhibition catalogs, 1 - 2 per year
Activities: Lects; symposiums & films open to public; 2-3 vis lectrs per yr; gallery talks; tours; individual paintings & original objects of art lent; lending collection contains original art work & print, paintings, photographs & sculpture; one book traveling exhib every other yr; originate traveling exhibs; exhib catalogs sold in gallery

L **Art Library,** Art-Sociology Bldg, College Park, MD 20742. Tel 301-405-9061; Fax 301-314-9725; Internet Home Page Address: www.lib.umd.edu/umcp/art/art.html; *Reference Librn* Louise Green; *Library Asst* Amrita Kaur; *Library Technical Asst* Warren Stephenson; *Head Art Library* Lynne Woodruff; *Library Technical Asst* Bonnie Cawthorne
Open Mon - Thurs 8:30 AM - 10 PM, Fri 8:30 AM - 5 PM, Sat 1 AM - 5 PM, Sun 1 - 10 PM; Estab 1979 in new building to serve the needs of the art & art history departments & campus in various art subjects
Income: Financed by university library system
Library Holdings: Book Volumes 95,000; CD-ROMs 30; Exhibition Catalogs; Fiche; Periodical Subscriptions 234; Reels; Reproductions 33,000
Special Subjects: Photography, Graphic Arts, Advertising Design, American Indian Art, Afro-American Art
Collections: Art & Architecture in France; Index photographic de l'art de France; Index Iconologicus; Decimal Index to art of Low Countries; Marburg index; Index of American Design; Deloynes Collections; Southeast Asia Collection
Publications: Bibliography; Checklist of Useful Tools for the Study of Art; Western Art; Asian Art
Activities: Tours

L **Architecture Library,** College Park, MD 20742-7011. Tel 301-405-6317 (architecture), 405-6320 (Libr Colls); Internet Home Page Address: www.lib.umb.edu/arch/architecture.html; *Head* Anita Carrico
Open Mon - Thurs 8:30 AM - 10 PM, Fri 8:30 AM - 5 PM, Sat 1 - 5 PM, Sun 1 - 10 PM; Estab 1967 for lending & reference; Circ 25,000
Library Holdings: Book Volume 37,000; Clipping Files; Fiche 200; Filmstrips; Other Holdings Bd per 6200; Periodical Subscriptions 180; Reels 600
Special Subjects: Landscape Architecture, Interior Design, Architecture
Collections: World Expositions: books & pamphlets on buildings, art work & machinery
Publications: Architecture Library (brochure), annual; Access to Architectural Literature; Periodical Indexes, annual

L **National Trust for Historic Preservation Library Collection,** Hornbake Library, College Park, MD 20742-0001. Tel 301-405-6320, 405-3300; Fax 301-314-2709; Elec Mail nt_library@umail.umd.edu; Internet Home Page Address: www.lib.umd.edu/ntl/; *Librn* Sally Sims Stokes; *Prog Management Specialist* Kevin Hammett
Open Mon - Fri 10 AM - 5 PM; Circ For reference only; Accessible via Maryland Room in Hornbake Library
Income: Financed by the University of Maryland
Library Holdings: Audio Tapes; Book Volumes 11,000; Cassettes; Clipping Files; Fiche; Manuscripts; Motion Pictures; Pamphlets; Periodical Subscriptions 300; Photographs; Video Tapes
Special Subjects: Historical Material, Period Rooms, Restoration & Conservation, Architecture

M **Stamp Gallery,** 1220 Stamp Student Union, Adele Stamp Memorial Union College Park, MD 20742. Tel 301-314-8493; Elec Mail stampgallery@umd.edu; Internet Home Page Address: www.thestamp.umd.edu/gallery/; *Cur & Coordr* Jackie Milad
Open Fall & Spring: Mon - Thurs 10 AM - 8 PM, Fri 10 AM - 6 PM, Sat 11 AM - 4 PM; Summer: Mon - Thurs 10 AM - 6 PM, Fri -Sat 11 AM - 4 PM
Special Subjects: Photography
Collections: Contemporary Art

COLUMBIA

M **AFRICAN ART MUSEUM OF MARYLAND,** 5430 Vantage Point Rd Ste B, Columbia, MD 21044-2642. Tel 410-730-7106; Fax 410-730-7105; Elec Mail africanartmuseum@aol.com; Internet Home Page Address: www.africanartmuseum.org; *Dir* Doris Hillian Ligon; *Events Coordr* Carole L Oduyoye; *VChmn Bd Trustees* Jean W Toomer
Open Tues - Fri 10 AM - 4 PM, Sun 1 - 4 PM & by appointment; Admis adults $3, seniors 55+ $2, AAA guests $1.50, children 12 & under $1, AAAMM mems free; Estab 1980; better understanding of African art & culture; Exhibits African Art: traditional and contemporary; Average Annual Attendance: 40,000; Mem: 300; dues family $50, individual $25, students & senior citizens $20; dues annually; interest in African Art & Culture req
Income: Financed by memberships, grants, corporate support, endowment
Library Holdings: Auction Catalogs; Book Volumes; DVDs; Motion Pictures; Original Documents; Photographs; Sculpture; Slides; Video Tapes
Special Subjects: Decorative Arts, Art Education, Furniture, Photography, Architecture, Bronzes, African Art, Archaeology, Ethnology, Textiles, Costumes, Ceramics, Crafts, Jewelry, Historical Material, Ivory, Maps, Islamic Art, Antiquities-Egyptian
Collections: African art consisting of household items, jewelry, masks, musical instruments, sculpture & textiles; 202 Gold Weights Harold Courlander Coll
Exhibitions: 2-3 exhibits per yr
Publications: Museum Memos, quarterly; The Quartet jazz quarterly
Activities: Workshops & classes for adults, children & families; docent training; lects open to pub, 5 or more vis lectrs per yr; concerts; gallery talks; ann tours to Africa; Akua'ba & Dir's awards given; Legacy in the Arts-Howie Award; original objects of art lent to other mus, institutions & trustees; originates traveling exhibs; mus shop sells books, magazines, original art, reproductions, prints, jewelry, clothing, textiles & crafts

M **HOWARD COMMUNITY COLLEGE,** The Rouse Company Foundation Gallery, 10901 Little Patuxent Pkwy, Columbia, MD 21044. Tel 443-518-1200; *Asst to Dir* Chaya Shapiro; *Art Dir* Rebecca Bafford
Open Mon - Fri 10 AM - 8 PM, Sat - Sun 12 PM - 5 PM, cl univ holidays
Collections: paintings; sculpture; photographs

CUMBERLAND

M **ALLEGANY ARTS COUNCIL THE SAVILLE GALLERY,** (The Saville Gallery) 9 N Centre St, Cumberland, MD 21502. Tel 301-777-2787; Fax 301-777-7719; Elec Mail arts@allconet.org; Internet Home Page Address: www.alleganyartscouncil.org
Open Mon-Fri 9AM-5PM, Sat 11AM-4PM; May-Nov only Sun 11 AM-4PM; No admis fee
Collections: works by local, regional, & national artists

M **ALLEGANY COUNTY HISTORICAL SOCIETY,** Gordon-Roberts House, 218 Washington St, Cumberland, MD 21502-2827. Tel 301-777-8678; Fax 301-777-8678; Elec Mail info@gordon-robertshouse.com; Internet Home Page Address: www.gordon-robertshouse.com; *Pres* Nadeane Gordon; *VPres* Nancy Cotton; *Treas* Jim Riggleman; *Rec Sec* Mona Lee Taylor; *Exec Dir* Sharon Nealis
Open Wed - Sat 10 AM - 5 PM; Admis $7, seniors $6, children under 12 $5; Estab 1937; 1867 Victorian house, each room furnished with furniture, antiques, pictures, paintings; Average Annual Attendance: 10,000; Mem: 500; dues individual $20, couple $30; meetings in March, Sept & Nov
Library Holdings: Book Volumes; Maps; Original Documents; Photographs; Prints; Slides
Special Subjects: Decorative Arts, Landscapes, Architecture, Ceramics, Photography, Pottery, Manuscripts, Drawings, Painting-American, Prints, Watercolors, Textiles, Costumes, Etchings & Engravings, Portraits, Dolls, Furniture, Glass, Porcelain, Silver, Carpets & Rugs, Historical Material, Maps, Restorations, Tapestries, Period Rooms, Laces, Pewter
Collections: period clothing & furnishings; Paintings, Books, Textiles
Publications: Quarterly newsletter
Activities: Classes for adults & children; docent training; dramatic progs; lects for mem only; tours; competitions; concerts; 2 vis lectrs per yr; educational trunk show for elementary schools; lending of art objects to other museums; originate traveling exhibs to area schools; mus shop sells books, prints, teapots & tea accessories, toys

M **CUMBERLAND THEATRE,** Lobby for the Arts Gallery, corner of Johnson & Fayette Sts, Cumberland, MD 21502; 101 N Johnson St, Cumberland, MD 21502-2918. Tel 301-759-4990; Fax 301-777-7092; Elec Mail boxoffice@cumberlandtheatre.com; Internet Home Page Address: www.cumberlandtheatre.com; *Asst Dir* Bev Walker
Open daily Noon - 8 PM; No admis fee; Estab 1987 to showcase artists & educate audiences; 24 x 30 ft, well-lighted & equipped for work of all sizes; Average Annual Attendance: 24,000; Mem: 29; ann meeting in Nov; meeting monthly
Income: $260,000 (financed by mem, city & state appropriation)
Exhibitions: Juried exhibits accompany the theatrical season
Activities: Dramatic progs; book traveling exhibs 2 per yr; originate traveling exhibs 22 per yr; mus shop sells original art

EASTON

M **ACADEMY ART MUSEUM,** 106 South St, Easton, MD 21601-2949. Tel 410-822-2787; Fax 410-822-5997; Elec Mail academy@academyartmuseum.org; Internet Home Page Address: www.academyartmuseum.org; *Exec Dir* Erik Neil; *Chmn* Richard Bodorff; *Asst to Dir* Maria Bradley; *Develop Dir* Beth Jones; *Facilities Mgr* Edward Robinson; *Cur* Anke Van Wagenberg; *Dir Progs & Design* Janet Hendricks
Open daily 10 AM - 4 PM, cl New Year's Day, Easter, Memorial Day, Independence Day, Labor Day, Thanksgiving & Christmas; Admis fee $3; free to members; Estab 1958 to promote the knowledge, appreciation & practice of all the arts; a private nonprofit art museum; The museum campus includes three 19th-century historical structures connected during two expansion programs. The 35,000 sq. ft. facility includes six galleries, five educational classrooms, performance hall and a 3,000 volume resource library.; Average Annual Attendance: 80,000; Mem: 3000; dues benefactor $5000, patron $1000, sustaining $500, contributing $250, friend $100, dual/family $65, individual $50
Income: Financed by mem, contributions, government, corporate & foundation grants, admis, tuitions, endowment & investments
Library Holdings: Book Volumes; Exhibition Catalogs
Special Subjects: Drawings, Etchings & Engravings, Landscapes, Painting-American, Woodcuts, Sculpture, Prints, Watercolors
Collections: Coll focus includes 19th and 20th century works on paper, painting and sculpture. Sampling of artists represented in the coll include Pierre Bonnard, James McNeill, Whistler, Robert Rauschenberg, Jim Dine, James Rosenquist, Robert Motherwell, Richard Diebenkorn, Gene Davis, Anne Truitt, The Ashcan School & more.
Exhibitions: The Academy mounts 16 exhibits per year featuring local, regional & nationally known artists
Publications: Academy. Printed quarterly; Exhibition catalogues
Activities: Classes in drawing, painting, sculpture, fine crafts plus weekend workshops & open studio sessions; dance & music classes for all ages; children's summer arts prog in all discipined & arts media; lects open to pub, 8 vis lectrs per yr; gallery talks; concerts; tours; dramatic progs; annual members shows with prizes awarded; sponsored competitions; exten dept serving regional schools & Eastern Shore of Maryland; book traveling exhibs 1-2 per yr

ELLICOTT CITY

A **HOWARD COUNTY ARTS COUNCIL,** 8510 High Ridge Rd, Ellicott City, MD 21043-7502. Tel 410-313-2787; Fax 410-313-2790; Elec Mail info@hocorts.com; Internet Home Page Address: www.hocoarts.org; *Exec Dir* Coleen West
Open office: Mon - Fri 9 AM - 5 PM; gallery: Mon - Fri 10 AM -8 PM, Sat 10 AM - 4 PM, Sun noon - 4 PM; No admis fee; Estab 1981 to serve pub fostering arts, artists & art organizations; Two exhibition galleries, 2000 sq ft; 10-12 exhibitions annually, studios, classrooms, black box theater, meeting rm; Average Annual Attendance: 50,000; Mem: Dues $25-$500; annual meeting in Sept

Income: $1,000,000 (financed by pub & pvt funds, spec events & earned income
Exhibitions: Changing exhibs every 6 weeks
Activities: Classes for adults & children; dramatic progs, summer camp; lects open to pub; 3-4 lectrs per yr; concerts; gallery talks; tours; sponsoring of competitions; juror's awards; schols offered; sales shop sells original art

FORT MEADE

M **FORT GEORGE G MEADE MUSEUM,** 4674 Griffin Ave, Fort Meade, MD 20755-7047. Tel 301-677-6966; Fax 301-677-2953; Elec Mail robert.johnson31@conus.army.mil; Internet Home Page Address: www.ftmeade.army.mil/museum.index.htm; *Exhibits Specialist* Barbara Taylor; *Museum Technician* Mark Henry; *Cur* Robert S Johnson
Open Wed - Sat 11 AM - 4 PM, Sun 1 - 4 PM, cl Mon, Tues & holidays; No admis fee; Estab 1963 to collect, preserve, study & display military artifacts relating to the United States Army, Fort Meade & the surrounding region; Average Annual Attendance: 40,000
Income: Financed by federal funds
Special Subjects: Graphics, Photography, Textiles, Costumes, Manuscripts, Posters, Historical Material, Maps, Cartoons, Military Art
Collections: World War I, World War II & Civil War Periods; Military Art Collection
Exhibitions: Development of Armor, 1920-1940; History of Fort George G Meade
Activities: Lects open to pub, 4 vis lectrs per year; gallery talks; tours; living history programs

FREDERICK

M **DELAPLAINE VISUAL ARTS EDUCATION CENTER,** 40 S Carroll St, Frederick, MD 21701. Tel 301-698-0656; Fax 301-663-1080; Elec Mail info@delaplaine.org; Internet Home Page Address: www.delaplaine.org; *Exec Dir & CEO* Catherine Moreland; *Dir Mktg & Develop* Sarah McKee Gemmell; *Dir Opers* Marilyn Orsinger; *Gift Gallery Mgr* Jean Frank; *Asst to Dir* Denise Goulin; *Finance Mgr* Kathleen Hardison; *Staff Asst* Padraig Higgins; *Outreach Mgr & Dir Educ* Virginia Rose Kane; *Vol Coordr* Margie Mott; *Special Projects Mgr* Tim Ryan; *Exhibits Mgr* Diane Sibbison; *Educ Coordr* Kristen Grubbs
Open Mon - Sat 9 AM - 5 PM, Sun 11 AM - 5 PM, cl New Year's Day, Easter, Memorial Day, Independence Day, Labor Day, Thanksgiving, Christmas; No admis fee; Estab 1986 to provide the Frederick region with educational opportunities & experiences in the visual arts through classes, exhibits & progs; Kline Gallery/F&M Gallery: main floor 1,500 sq ft combine, drywall & brick with hanging system; Side Gallery: main floor 240 sq ft; Gardiner Gallery: main Floor, 1,800 sq ft, wall space only; Hall Gallery 2nd floor, 150 sq ft wall space only; New Gallery 2nd floor, 240 sq ft; Average Annual Attendance: 85,000 visitors; Mem: 1,400 mems; dues family $50; individual $30
Library Holdings: Book Volumes 4,000
Collections: photographs; paintings; sculpture
Exhibitions: 50 exhibs ann including:; The National Juried Quilt Exhibit; The National Juried Photography Exhibit; The Annual Juried Exhibit; The Frederick County Art Assoc Members' Exhibit; The Frederick All-County Student Art Exhibit & numerous other exhibs
Publications: Spring, Summer, Fall & Winter catalogs
Activities: Classes for adults & children; variety of art enrichment progs for the community including: Creative Outlet, Art Night, The Community Supported Art Project, Easels in Frederick, Focus at the Delaplaine, Local Color, Art Carnival & Frederick Festival of Arts; Community Outreach Progs; lects open to pub; 5 vis lectrs per yr; schols, M&T Senior Schol in Arts; awards; mus shop sells original art, reproductions, prints

FROSTBURG

M **FROSTBURG STATE UNIVERSITY,** The Stephanie Ann Roper Gallery, 101 Braddock Rd, Fine Arts Bldg Frostburg, MD 21532-2303. Tel 301-687-4797; Fax 301-687-3099; Elec Mail ddavis@frostburg.edu; *Chair* Dustin P Davis; *Admin Asst* Sharon Gray
Open Sun - Wed 1 - 4 PM; No admis fee; Estab 1972 for educational purposes; Average Annual Attendance: 1,000
Income: Financed by state appropriation
Special Subjects: Prints, Folk Art
Collections: Folk art; prints
Activities: Educ dept; lect open to public, 5 vis lectrs per year; gallery talks; competitions with awards; book traveling exhibitions 4 per year

L **Lewis J Ort Library,** 1 Stadium Dr, Frostburg, MD 21532-2342. Tel 301-687-4395; Fax 301-687-7069; Elec Mail mprice@frostburg.edu; *Exhib Librn* Mary Jo Price; *Dir* Dr David M Gillespie
Open Mon - Fri 8 AM - 12 AM, Sat & Sun 1 PM - 12 AM
Library Holdings: Audio Tapes; Book Volumes 500,000; Cassettes; Exhibition Catalogs; Fiche; Filmstrips; Kodachrome Transparencies; Motion Pictures; Periodical Subscriptions 1300; Prints; Reproductions; Slides; Video Tapes
Collections: poster coll Communist USA 1920's to present

GERMANTOWN

M **BLACKROCK CENTER FOR THE ARTS,** 12901 Town Commons Dr, Germantown, MD 20874. Tel 301-528-2260; Fax 301-528-2266; Elec Mail info@blackrockcenter.org; Internet Home Page Address: blackrockcenter.org

GRANTSVILLE

M **SPRUCE FOREST ARTISAN VILLAGE,** 177 Casselman Rd, Grantsville, MD 21536. Tel 301-895-3332; Elec Mail artisans@spruceforest.org; Internet Home Page Address: www.spruceforest.org
Open May-Dec, call for hours; Average Annual Attendance:
Collections: paintings, pottery, sculpture

HAGERSTOWN

M **MANSION HOUSE ART CENTER,** 501 Highland Way, Hagerstown, MD 21740. Tel 301-797-6813
Open Fri-Sat 11AM-4PM, Sun 1PM-5PM; Average Annual Attendance:
Collections: paintings; etchings; silk screen; lithographs; carvings

M **WASHINGTON COUNTY ARTS COUNCIL,** Gallery, 34 S Potomac St, Hagerstown, MD 21740-5513. Tel 301-791-3132; Elec Mail info@washingtoncountyarts.com; *Exec Dir* Mary Ann Burke; *Gallery Mgr* Chris Brewer
Open Tues-Fri 10 AM - 5 PM, Sat 10 AM - 4 PM; Admis free; Exhib gallery & the gallery shop representing local artists
Collections: works by regional artists
Exhibitions: Exhibs change monthly

M **WASHINGTON COUNTY MUSEUM OF FINE ARTS,** 401 Museum Dr, City Park Hagerstown, MD 21740-6271; PO Box 423 Hagerstown, MD 21741-0423. Tel 301-739-5727; Fax 301-745-3741; Elec Mail info@wcmfa.org; Internet Home Page Address: www.wcmfa.org; *Pres* Bradley Pingrey; *Assoc Cur* Jennifer Smith; *Registrar* Linda Dodson; *Educator* Amy Hunt; *Dir* Rebecca Massie Lane
Open Tues - Fri 9 AM - 5 PM, Sat 9 AM - 4 PM, Sun 1 - 5 PM, cl Mon; No admis fee; Estab 1930 to exhibit, interpret & conserve art; The mus consists of eleven galleries; Average Annual Attendance: 70,000; Mem: 980; dues $30 & up
Income: Financed by local government, mem & donations
Special Subjects: Drawings, Painting-American, Prints, Sculpture, Glass, Jade, Oriental Art, Laces
Collections: American pressed glass; sculpture; 19th & early 20th century American art
Exhibitions: Exhibits drawn from the Permanent Collection - 19th & 20th Century American Art
Publications: American Pressed Glass; Old Master drawings; bi-monthly bulletin; catalogs of major exhibitions; catalog of the permanent collection
Activities: Classes for adults & children; dramatic progs; docent training; lects open to pub, 10 vis lectrs per yr; concerts; gallery talks; tours; competitions with awards; original objects of art lent to accredited mus; originate traveling exhibs; sales shop sells books & original art

LAUREL

M **MARYLAND-NATIONAL CAPITAL PARK & PLANNING COMMISSION,** Montpelier Arts Center, 9652 Muirkirk Rd, Laurel, MD 20708-2605. Tel 301-953-1993, 410-792-0664; Fax 301-206-9682; Elec Mail montpelier.arts@pgparks.com; Internet Home Page Address: www.pgparks.com; *Dir* Richard Zandler; *Asst Dir* Ruth Schilling Harwood; *Technical Dir* John Yeh
Open daily 10 AM - 5 PM; No admis fee; Estab 1979 to serve artists regionally & to offer high quality fine arts experiences to pub; Main Gallery houses major invitational exhibitions by artists of regional or national reputation; Library Gallery houses local artists' exhibitions; Resident Artists' Gallery provided to artists who rent studio space; Small library of donated volumes; Average Annual Attendance: 56,000; Mem: 83; 50 individuals; 30 families
Income: $300,000 (financed by county appropriation, grants, classes & studio rentals)
Library Holdings: Book Volumes; Periodical Subscriptions
Publications: Exhibit catalogs; promotional invitations; jazz concerts
Activities: Educ prog; classes for adults & children; workshops in specialized areas; lects open to pub, 3-4 vis lectrs per yr; gallery talks; concerts (14 jazz, 7 blues & folk, 4 classical recitals); tours; competitions with exhibs awards/honorariums; book traveling exhibs, annually; originate traveling exhibs; Jazzmont label produces and sells jazz CD's

LEONARDTOWN

M **NORTH END GALLERY,** 41652 Fenwick St, Leonardtown, MD 20650. Tel 301-475-3130
Open Tues - Sat 11 AM - 6 PM, Sun 12 PM - 4 PM
Collections: Paintings; photographs; drawings; sculpture; jewelry
Activities: Annual Event: Community Show in summer

MARBURY

M **MATTAWOMAN CREEK ART CENTER,** Smallwood State Park, Marbury, MD 20658; PO Box 258, Marbury, MD 20658-0258. Tel 301-743-5159; Elec Mail mattawomanart@aol.com; Internet Home Page Address: www.mattawomanart.org; *Pres* Rolland Hower; *Coordr* Renee Nelson
Gallery open Fri-Sun 11AM-4PM, Office Mon & Wed-Thurs 9AM-1PM; cl Thanksgiving; Christmas; No admis fee, donations appreciated; Non-profit art gallery; a variety of art classes yearly; Mem: Any adult interested in the visual arts
Collections: works by regional, national, & international artists; paintings; sculpture
Exhibitions: 9-10 Exhibs per yr
Activities: Classes for adults; docent training; lects open to pub; gallery talks; sales shop sells books, original art, prints, jewelry & sculpture

MOUNT AIRY

M **SWETCHARNIK ART STUDIO,** 7044 Woodville Rd, Mount Airy, MD 21771-7934. Tel 301-829-0137; Elec Mail sara@swetcharnik.com; Internet Home Page Address: www.swetcharnik.com; *Dir & Artist* William Swetcharnik; *Project Coordr & Artist* Sara Morris Swetcharnik
Open by appointment; No admis fee; donations accepted; Estab1980; Artwork by Sara Morris Swetcharnik & William Swetcharnik; Average Annual Attendance: 5,000

Library Holdings: Book Volumes; Exhibition Catalogs; Reproductions; Sculpture
Special Subjects: Decorative Arts, Drawings, Photography, Sculpture
Collections: Works by Sara & William Swetcharnik
Activities: Formal educ progs; guided tours; lects open to pub; Fulbright grants; alumni award; loan, temporary & traveling exhibs; mus shop sells books, original art & reproductions

ROCKVILLE

M **JEWISH COMMUNITY CENTER OF GREATER WASHINGTON,** Jane L & Robert H Weiner Judaic Museum, 6125 Montrose Rd, Rockville, MD 20852-4857. Tel 301-881-0100; Fax 301-881-5512; Internet Home Page Address: www.jccgw.org; *Pres* Steven Lustig; *Exec Dir* Michael Witkes; *Gallery Dir* Karen Falk; *Art Gallery Mgr* Phyllis Altman; *CEO* Toni Goodman; *Chief Operating Officer* Michael Feinstein; *Prog Dir* Tracey Dorfmann
Open Mon - Thurs Noon - 4 PM & 7:30 - 9:30 PM, Sun 2 - 5 PM; No admis fee; Estab 1925 to preserve, exhibit & promulgate Jewish culture; Center houses mus & Goldman Fine Arts Gallery; Average Annual Attendance: 25,000
Income: Financed by endowment, corporate, private & pub gifts, grants & sales
Exhibitions: Monthly exhibits, Sept-June; Fine art, fine craft, documentary photography; seven to eight temporary exhibitions yearly including Israeli Artists & American & emerging artist
Publications: Exhibition catalogues; brochures
Activities: Classes for adults & children; docent training; lects open to pub; concerts; gallery talks; tours; book traveling exhibs; originate traveling exhibs; mus shop sells books, original art, reproductions & prints

SAINT MICHAELS

M **CHESAPEAKE BAY MARITIME MUSEUM,** 213 N Talbot St, Saint Michaels, MD 21663; PO Box 636, Navy Point Saint Michaels, MD 21663-0636. Tel 410-745-2916; Fax 410-745-6088; Elec Mail comments@cbmm.org; Internet Home Page Address: www.cbmm.org; *Pres* Langley Shook; *Cur* Pete Lesher
Open daily 10 AM - 6 PM (Summer), 10 AM - 5 PM (Fall), 10 AM - 4 PM (Winter); cl New Year's Day, Thanksgiving, Christmas; Admis adults $13, seniors $9, children $5; Estab 1965 as a waterside mus dedicated to preserving the maritime history of the Chesapeake Bay; Consists of twenty buildings on approx 18 acres of waterfront property including Hooper's Strait Lighthouse, 1879; Average Annual Attendance: 63,000; Mem: 7000; dues $55 - $125
Income: Financed by mem, admis & endowment
Library Holdings: Audio Tapes 300; Book Volumes 9800; Clipping Files; Manuscripts; Maps; Original Art Works; Original Documents; Pamphlets; Periodical Subscriptions 17; Photographs 55,000; Prints; Slides; Video Tapes
Special Subjects: Prints, Manuscripts, Photography, Watercolors, Folk Art, Woodcarvings, Marine Painting, Historical Material
Collections: Paintings; ship models; vessels including skipjack, bugeye, log canoes, & many small crafts; waterfowling exhibits; working boat shop
Publications: Beacons of Hooper Strait (2000)
Activities: Classes for adults & children; docent training; lects open to pub, 4 vis lectrs per yr; concerts; tours; individual paintings & original objects of art lent to other mus; 1-2 book traveling exhibs per yr; mus shop sells books, magazines, reproductions, prints
L **Howard I Chapelle Memorial Library,** PO Box 636, Navy Point Saint Michaels, MD 21663-0636. Tel 410-745-2916; Fax 410-745-6088; Internet Home Page Address: www.cbmm.org; *Cur* Pete Lesher; *Coll Mgr* Lynne Phillips
Open by appointment; Estab 1965 for preservation of Chesapeake Bay maritime history & culture; Non-circulating research facility; Average Annual Attendance: 100
Income: Financed by endowment
Library Holdings: Auction Catalogs; Audio Tapes 300; Book Volumes 9800; Cards; Clipping Files; Manuscripts; Pamphlets; Periodical Subscriptions 17; Photographs 55,000
Special Subjects: Folk Art, Maps, Woodcarvings, Marine Painting
Collections: Ships plans, registers, manuscripts; oral histories
Activities: Classes for adults & children; docent training; lects open to pub; 4 vis lectrs per yr; 1-2 book traveling exhibs per yr; mus shop sells books, magazines & prints

SALISBURY

M **SALISBURY UNIVERSITY,** (Ward Foundation) Ward Museum of Wildfowl Art, 909 S Schumaker Dr, Salisbury, MD 21804. Tel 410-742-4988; Fax 410-742-3107; Elec Mail ward@wardmuseum.org; Internet Home Page Address: www.wardmuseum.org; *Exec Dir* Lora Bottinelli; *Accounting Officer* Vermell Dickerson; *Educ Dir* Kim Check; *Educ Coordr* Mark Bushman; *Exhibits/Folklife* Dr Cindy Byrd; *Events Coordr* Eric Turner; *Mem/Mktg Dir* Rose Taylor; *Exec Admin Asst* Sarah Maciarello; *Registrar* Barbara Gehrm; *Vol Dir* Renee Fredericksen
Open Mon - Sat 10 AM - 5 PM, Sun Noon - 5 PM; Admis adults $7, seniors $5, students $3, family $17, mem & SU faculty, staff & students free; Estab 1968 as a non-profit organization dedicated to preservation & conservation of wildfowl carving; Over 30,000 sq ft with 10 galleries includes interactive theatre, walking audio tour, mus store, observation deck & more; Average Annual Attendance: 30,000; Mem: 2000; dues family $60, individual $35
Income: $1,000,000 (financed by mem, city & state appropriations, grants, donations, gift shop sales)
Library Holdings: Auction Catalogs 200; Audio Tapes 200; Book Volumes 300; Cassettes 200; Clipping Files; Exhibition Catalogs 50; Memorabilia; Original Art Works; Pamphlets; Periodical Subscriptions; Photographs; Prints; Reproductions
Special Subjects: Decorative Arts, Folk Art, Sculpture, Woodcarvings
Collections: Decoys & decorative bird carvings, fowling skiffs & firearms
Exhibitions: Ward World Championship Wildfowl Carving Competition & Art Festival (last weekend of April ann); Chesapeake Wildfowl Expo (2nd wk of October ann)
Publications: Wildfowl Art Journal, bi-annual

Activities: Classes for adults & children, docent training; lects open to pub; tours; competition with awards; carving workshops held in Apr, June & Feb; mus shop sells books, magazines, original art, reproductions, prints, decoys & birding items

M **SALISBURY UNIVERSITY,** Salisbury University Art Galleries, 1101 Camden Ave, Salisbury, MD 21801-6860. Tel 410-548-2547; Fax 410-548-3002; Elec Mail eckauffman@salisbury.edu; Internet Home Page Address: www.salisbury.edu/universitygalleries; *Dir of Galleries* Elizabeth Kauffman
See website for hours; No admis fee; Estab 1967 to provide a wide range of art exhibitions to the University & community, with emphasis on educational value of exhibitions; Average Annual Attendance: 8,000
Income: Financed mainly by Salisbury State University with additional support from the Maryland State Arts Council, The Salisbury/Wicomico Arts Council & other agencies
Special Subjects: Prints
Exhibitions: Annual faculty & student shows; wide range of traveling exhibitions from various national & regional arts organizations & galleries; variety of regional & local exhibitions; speakers & special events; sculpture gardens
Publications: Announcements
Activities: Workshops for children, students & gen pub; film series; lects open to pub, 1-2 vis lectrs per yr
L **Blackwell Library,** 1101 Camden Ave, Salisbury, MD 21801. Tel 410-543-6130; Fax 410-543-6203; Internet Home Page Address: www.salisbury.edu/library; *Dean of Libraries & Instructional Resources* Dr Beatriz Hardy
Open Mon - Thurs 8 AM - 2 AM, Fri 8 AM - 10 PM, Sat 10 AM - 8 PM, Sun 11 AM - 2 AM; Estab 1925, to support the curriculum of Salisbury University; Circ 2,500; Library has total space of 66,000 sq ft; Average Annual Attendance: 367,204
Library Holdings: Audio Tapes 340; Book Volumes 287,318; Cards 2,278; Cassettes 495; Clipping Files; Compact Disks 132; DVDs 711; Fiche 738,625; Original Art Works 6; Periodical Subscriptions 942; Reels 15,747; Video Tapes 113

SILVER SPRING

A **PYRAMID ATLANTIC,** 8230 Georgia Ave, Silver Spring, MD 20910-4511. Tel 301-608-9101; Fax 301-608-9102; Elec Mail hello@pyramid-atlantic.org; Internet Home Page Address: www.pyramidatlanticartcenter.org; *Dir* Jose Dominguez; *Artistic Dir* Gretchen Schermerhorn; *Dir Bus Devel* Matthew Sole; *Develop Mgr* Catherine Aselford; *Pres Bd Dir* Amy Kincaid
Open Tues-Thurs 12PM-5PM, Fri 12PM-7PM, Sat 10AM-5PM, Sun 12PM-5PM; No admis fees; Estab 1981; Mem: Dues $40 - $500
Collections: works by nat & international artists

SOLOMONS

M **CALVERT MARINE MUSEUM,** PO Box 97, Solomons, MD 20688-0097. Tel 410-326-2042; Fax 410-326-6691; Elec Mail mccormaaj@co.cal.md.us; Internet Home Page Address: www.calvertmarinemuseum.com; *Registrar* Robert J Hurry; *Exhib Designer* James L Langley; *Master Woodcarver* Skip Edwards; *Cur Maritime History* Richard J Dodds; *Cur Estuarine Biology* David Moyer; *Cur Paleontology* Stephen Godfrey; *Dir* C Douglass Alves Jr; *Deputy Dir* Sherrod A Sturrock; *Bus Mgr* Roxie Welch; *Develop Dir* Vanessa Gill
Open Mon - Sun 10 AM - 5 PM; Admis $9, seniors 55 & over $7, children 5-12 $4; Estab 1970, to provide the public with a marine oriented museum on maritime history, estuarine natural history, marine paleontology and natural & cultural history of the Patuxent River region; 5,500 sq ft gallery is maintained on maritime history of the region, three to four shows per yr; Average Annual Attendance: 78,000; Mem: 3800; dues family $60, individual $40
Income: $4,000,000 (financed by county appropriation & Calvert Marine Museum Society)
Purchases: $1000
Special Subjects: Watercolors, Archaeology, Woodcarvings, Manuscripts, Marine Painting, Historical Material, Maps
Collections: J S Bohannon Folk Art Steamboat Collection; Tufnell Watercolor Collection; A Aubrey Bodine Collection; Louis Feuchter Collection; August H O Rolle Collection; local Chesapeake Bay Ship Portraits
Publications: Bugeye Times, quarterly newsletter; Cradle of Invasion: A History of the US Amphibious Training Base, Solomons, Maryland, 1942-45; The Drum Point Lighthouse, brochure; Early Chesapeake Single-Log Canoes: A Brief History & introduction to Building Techniques; The Last Generation: A History of a Chesapeake Shipbuilding Family; The Othello Affair; The Pursuit of French Pirates on the Patuxent River, Maryland, August 1807; War on the Patuxent, 1814: A Catalog of Artifacts; Watercraft Collection, brochure; Working the Water: The Commercial Fisheries of Maryland's Patuxent River; Solomons Island & Vicinity An Illustrated History & Walking Tour; miscellaneous spec publications on history
Activities: Classes for adults and children; docent training; lects open to pub, 8 lectrs per yr; concerts; gallery talks; tours; individual paintings & original objects of art lent to other appropriately qualified nonprofit organizations; lending collection contains 3000 black & white photographs, lantern slides, art works, original prints, 2800 slides; mus shop sells books, magazines, original art, prints, reproductions, hand crafts
L **Library,** 14150 Solomons Island Rd, Solomons, MD 20688; PO Box 97, Solomons, MD 20688-0097. Tel 410-326-2042 exten 14; Fax 410-326-6691; Elec Mail information@calvertmarinemuseum.com; Internet Home Page Address: www.calvertmarinemuseum.com/library; *Librn* Paul Berry; *Registrar* Robert J Hurry
Open Mon - Fri 9 AM - 4:30 PM, cl weekends; Estab 1970; Library open for research and reference, local maritime history, paleontology; Average Annual Attendance: 100
Income: $2500 (finance by Calvert County government, mem, gift shop, donations & grants)
Purchases: $1000
Library Holdings: Audio Tapes 10; Book Volumes 7,500; CD-ROMs 15; Cassettes 15; Clipping Files; DVDs 12; Exhibition Catalogs; Fiche 10;

Manuscripts; Maps; Memorabilia; Micro Print; Original Art Works; Pamphlets; Periodical Subscriptions 40; Photographs 12,500; Prints; Records; Reproductions; Slides 10,000; Video Tapes 175
Special Subjects: Manuscripts, Maps, Prints, Historical Material, Archaeology, Woodcarvings, Marine Painting
Collections: marine/maritime paintings, ship models
Activities: Classes for children; lects open to pub, 3-4 vis lectrs per yr; concerts; mus shop sells books, prints, ship models & jewelry

ST MARY'S CITY

M **ST MARY'S COLLEGE OF MARYLAND,** The Dwight Frederick Boyden Gallery, SMC, St Mary's City, MD 20686; 18952 E Fisher Rd, Saint Mary's College St Mary's City, MD 20686-3002. Tel 240-895-4246; Fax 240-895-4958; Elec Mail mebraun@smcm.edu; Internet Home Page Address: www.smcm.edu/boydengallery; *Dir* Mary E Braun; *Gallery Asst* Daniel Holden
Open Mon - Fri 11AM-5PM; No admis fee; 1600 sq ft exhibition space for temporary exhibits of art; five bldgs with art hung in public areas; Average Annual Attendance: 2,500
Income: Financed by St Mary's College
Purchases: Collection is from donation
Special Subjects: Afro-American Art, Decorative Arts, Etchings & Engravings, Landscape Architecture, Marine Painting, Painting-American, Prints, Textiles, Painting-French, Painting-Japanese, Sculpture, Drawings, Photography, Watercolors, African Art, Costumes, Ceramics, Crafts, Woodcarvings, Woodcuts, Portraits, Posters, Asian Art, Painting-Dutch, Painting-Flemish, Antiquities-Greek, Antiquities-Roman
Collections: Study; developmental; Long Term Loan; SMC; Permanent
Activities: Lects open to pub; gallery talks; tours; competitions sponsored; individual paintings & original objects of art lent to local, nonprofit organizations; lending collection contains original art works & prints, paintings & sculptures; originates traveling exhibs

TAKOMA PARK

L **MONTGOMERY COLLEGE OF ART & DESIGN LIBRARY,** 7600 Takoma Ave CF 120, Takoma Park, MD 20912. Tel 301-649-4454; Fax 301-649-2940; Elec Mail mcadlibrary@aol.com; Internet Home Page Address: www.mcadmd.org; *Head Librn* Kate Cooper
Open Mon - Fri 9 AM - 5 PM; Estab 1977 to facilitate & encourage learning by the students & to provide aid for the faculty; Circ 8000; College maintains Gudelsky Gallery
Purchases: $7000
Library Holdings: Auction Catalogs; Book Volumes 12,000; Cassettes 50; Clipping Files; Motion Pictures; Periodical Subscriptions 35; Slides 30,000; Video Tapes
Special Subjects: Art History, Decorative Arts, Calligraphy, Drawings, Graphic Arts, Graphic Design, History of Art & Archaeology, Afro-American Art, Antiquities-Assyrian, Antiquities-Byzantine, Antiquities-Egyptian, Antiquities-Etruscan, Antiquities-Greek, Antiquities-Roman, Architecture
Activities: Classes for adults & children

TOWSON

M **TOWSON UNIVERSITY,** Center for the Arts Gallery, Osler Dr, Towson, MD 21204; 8000 York Rd, Towson, MD 21252-0002. Tel 410-704-2808; Fax 410-704-2810; Elec Mail artdepartment@towson.edu; *Dir & Prof* Christopher Bartlett
Open Tues - Sun 11 AM - 4 PM; No admis fee; Estab 1973 to provide a wide variety of art exhibitions, primarily contemporary work, with national importance; The main gallery is situated in the fine arts building directly off the foyer. It is 30 x 60 ft with 15 ft ceiling & 15 x 30 ft storage area; Average Annual Attendance: 10,000
Income: $18,000 (financed by state appropriation, cultural services fees & private gifts)
Special Subjects: Historical Material, Marine Painting, Prints, Maps, Sculpture, African Art, Asian Art
Collections: Asian arts, through Roberts Art Collection; Maryland Artists Collection
Exhibitions: Teresa Barkley: A Life in Quilts; Wunderkammer: A Cabinet of Curiosities, Ann Chahbandour & Rebecca Kamen Installation
Publications: Calendar, each semester; exhibition posters & catalogs
Activities: Lect open to public, 3 vis lectrs per year; concerts; gallery talks; book traveling exhibitions 2-3 per year
M **Asian Arts & Culture Center,** 6000 York Rd, Center for the Arts-Towson University Towson, MD 21252-0001. Tel 410-704-2807; Fax 410-704-4032; Internet Home Page Address: www.towson.edu/asianarts; *Dir* Suewhei T Shieh
Open during acad yr Mon - Fri 11 AM - 4 PM, Sat hours posted for each exhib; No admis fee; Estab 1972 to provide an area to display the Asian art collections of the University & present art & culture programs on Asia through-out school year; The gallery is located on the second floor of the Fine Arts Building; also includes a small reference library; Average Annual Attendance: 10,000; Mem: Dues Dragon Circle $1,000 & up, Phoenix Circle $500-$999, Tiger Soc $250-$499, Crane Club $100-$249, general mem $30-$99
Income: Financed by membership, grants & corporate sponsorship
Special Subjects: Prints, Sculpture, Bronzes, Southwestern Art, Textiles, Costumes, Ceramics, Folk Art, Pottery, Woodcuts, Decorative Arts, Painting-Japanese, Furniture, Porcelain, Oriental Art, Asian Art, Metalwork, Ivory, Antiquities-Oriental
Exhibitions: Permanent collection; special loan exhibitions; exhibitions on contemporary art of Asia
Publications: Asian Arts & Culture Center newsletter, biannual
Activities: Classes for adults & children; lect open to public, 2 vis lectrs per year; gallery talks; tours; workshops; concerts; performances; individual & original

objects of art lent to educational & cultural institutions; 4-5 book traveling exhibitions per year

WESTMINSTER

M **MCDANIEL COLLEGE,** (Western Maryland College) Esther Prangley Rice Gallery, 2 College Hill, Dept of Art & Art History, Preston Hall Westminster, MD 21157-4303. Tel 410-857-2595; Fax 410-386-4657; Elec Mail scorerst@wmdc.edu, mlosch@wmdc.edu; Internet Home Page Address: www.wmdc.edu; *Dir* Michael Losch
Open Mon - Fri 9 AM - 4 PM, call in advance; No admis fee; Estab to expose students to original works by professional artists; Top floor of Peterson Hall/Art Bldg
Income: Financed by college funds
Collections: Permanent collection of international artifacts; Egyptian, African, Native American, Asian, Prints (Picasso, Daumier, Mark Tobey)
Exhibitions: Rotating artist and one student show per yr

MASSACHUSETTS

AMESBURY

M **THE BARTLETT MUSEUM,** 270 Main St, Amesbury, MA 01913; PO Box 692, Amesbury, MA 01913-0016. Tel 978-388-4528; Elec Mail museum@bartlettmuseum.org; Internet Home Page Address: www.bartlettmuseum.org; *Cur* Hazele Kray; *Pres* John McCone; *Treas (V)* Wayne Gove; *Mus Shop Mgr* Gina Moscardini
Open Memorial Day - Labor Day Fri & Sun 1 - 4 PM, Sat 10 AM - 4 PM; Estab 1968; Two-room Victorian-style Ferry School built in 1870. Name later changed to The Bartlett School in honor of Josiah Bartlett, signer of America's Declaration of Independence, near whose home the school was sited; Mem: dues patron $100 & up, contributing $25, family $15, individual $5, student $1
Special Subjects: Architecture, Painting-American, Sculpture, Costumes, Manuscripts, Portraits, Furniture, Silver, Historical Material, Maps, Dioramas, Period Rooms
Collections: Natural science artifacts; Genealogy
Activities: Workshops

AMHERST

M **AMHERST COLLEGE,** Mead Art Museum, Corner of Rte 9 & Rte 116, Amherst, MA 01002; PO Box 5000, Amherst, MA 01002-5000. Tel 413-542-2335; Fax 413-542-2117; Elec Mail mead@amherst.edu; Internet Home Page Address: www.amherst.edu/mead; *Dir* Elizabeth E Barker, PhD; *Senior Cur & Cur Russian Art* Bettina Jungen PhD; *Head Ed Cur AC Progs* Pamela Russell PhD; *Cur Teaching Fellow Japanese Prints* Bradley Bailey; *Media & Marketing Coordr & Exec Asst to Dir* Rachel Rogol; *Head Security & Facility* Heath Cummings; *Preparator* Tim Gilfillan; *Colls Mgr* Stephen Fisher; *Study Room Supv* Mila Waldman; *Accounting Mgr* Karen Summers
Open acad season Tues - Thurs & Sun 9 AM - midnight, Fri - 9 AM - 8 PM, Sat 9 AM - 5 PM, academic recess Tues - Sun 9 AM - 5 PM, first Thurs of month open till 8 PM; No admis fee; Estab 1949; The Mead Art Museum houses the art coll of Amherst college spanning 5,000 yrs & encompassing the achievements of many world cultures; Average Annual Attendance: 21,000; Mem: 500; annual meetings in the spring
Collections: Western European & Oriental Collections; African Art; Oriental Art; American Art; Ancient Art; English; Russian Art
Publications: American Art at Amherst: A Summary Catalogue of the Collection at the Mead Art Gallery; American Watercolors & Drawings from Amherst College; Mead Museum Monographs; catalogues for major exhibitions; Mead Art Museum at Amherst College Collection Guide; Picturing Enlightenment: Tangka in the Mead Art Museum; Reinventing Tokyo
Activities: Classes for adults & children; educ dept; docent training; Mellon faculty seminars; lect open to public, 5-10 vis lectrs per year; gallery talks; tours; concerts; Wise prize for fine art; individual paintings & original objects of art lent for exhibition only to other museums; mus shop sells books, magazines, reproductions, prints, postcards, vintage colls
L **Robert Frost Library,** PO Box 5000, Amherst, MA 01002-5000. Tel 413-542-2677; Fax 413-542-2662; *Reference & Fine Arts Librn* Michael Kasper
Open Mon - Thurs 8 AM - 1 AM, Fri 8 AM - midnight, Sat 9:30 AM - 11 PM, Sun 10 AM - 1 AM; Circulating to Amherst College students & five college faculty
Library Holdings: Book Volumes 40,000; Exhibition Catalogs; Fiche; Periodical Subscriptions 82; Slides

ARTS EXTENSION SERVICE
For further information, see National and Regional Organizations

L **JONES LIBRARY, INC,** 43 Amity St, Amherst, MA 01002-2285. Tel 413-259-3090; Fax 413-256-4096; Elec Mail info@joneslibrary.org; Internet Home Page Address: www.joneslibrary.org; *Asst Dir, Children's Librn* Sondra M Radosh; *Reference Librn* Rosemary Loomis; *Adult Svc Librn* Beth Girshman; *Cur* Tevis Kimball; *Dir* Bonnie Isman
Open Mon & Wed 9 AM 5:30 PM, Tues & Thurs 9 AM - 9:30 PM, Fri & Sat 1 - 5:30 PM, Special Collections has limited hours; No admis fee; Estab 1919 as a public library; Circ 520,000; Burnett Gallery - exhibs by local artists; permanent art coll of oil paintings & sculpture; special coll of prints & photographs; Average Annual Attendance: 400,000; Mem: Open to public, no fee
Income: Financed by endowment & city appropriation
Library Holdings: Audio Tapes; Book Volumes 185,000 (all subjects); Cassettes; Clipping Files; Compact Disks; DVDs; Framed Reproductions; Manuscripts;

Memorabilia; Original Art Works; Pamphlets; Periodical Subscriptions 150; Photographs; Records; Reels; Sculpture; Slides
Collections: Ray Stannard Baker; Emily Dickinson; Robert Frost; Julius Lester; Harlan Fiske Stone; Sidney Waugh Writings; local history & genealogy; Burnett Family; Clifton Johnson
Exhibitions: Permanent collection & rotating exhibits on local history
Publications: Annual Report
Activities: Lect open to public; concerts; tours

M **UNIVERSITY OF MASSACHUSETTS, AMHERST,** University Gallery, 151 Presidents Dr (Ofc 2), Fine Arts Ctr, University of Massachusetts Amherst, MA 01003-9311. Tel 413-545-3670; Fax 413-545-2018; Elec Mail ugallery@acad.umass.edu; Internet Home Page Address: www.umass.edu/fac/universitygallery; *Gallery Mgr* Craig Allaben; *Coll Registrar* Justin Griswold; *Dir* Loretta Yarlow; *Educ Cur* Eva Fierst
Open Tues - Fri 11 AM - 4:30 PM, Sat & Sun 2 - 5 PM during school yr; No admis fee; Estab 1975; Main Gallery 57-1/2 x 47 ft, East Gallery 67-1/2 x 20-1/2 ft, West Gallery 56-1/2 x 23-1/2 ft, North Gallery 46-1/2 x 17-1/2 ft; Average Annual Attendance: 15,000; Mem: 150; dues $25 & up
Income: University
Special Subjects: Drawings, Etchings & Engravings, Pottery, Painting-American, Prints, Photography, Sculpture, Southwestern Art
Collections: 20th century American works on paper including drawings, prints & photographs
Publications: Exhibition catalogs
Activities: Lects open to public, 2-3 vis lectrs per yr; gallery talks; tours; individual art works from the permanent collection loaned to other institutions; originate traveling exhibs; peer institutions/museums

M **Herter Art Gallery,** 125A Herter Hall, Amherst, MA 01003. Tel 413-545-0976; *Contact* Trevor Richardson

L **Dorothy W Perkins Slide Library,** 130 Hicks Way, 221 Barlett Hall Amherst, MA 01003-9269. Tel 413-545-3314; Fax 413-545-3880, 3135; Internet Home Page Address: www.umass.edu; *Cur Visual Coll* Nathalie Bridegam
Open Mon - Fri noon - 4 PM; Graduate student reference slide library; Circ 60,000 (slides); campus only
Library Holdings: Other Holdings Interactive video disks; Magnetic disks 50; Study Plates 7000; Slides 270,000

ANDOVER

A **ANDOVER HISTORICAL SOCIETY,** 97 Main St, Andover, MA 01810-3803. Tel 978-475-2236; Fax 978-470-2741; Elec Mail andover@historical.org; Internet Home Page Address: www.andoverhistorical.org; *Exec Dir* Elaine Clements; *Mus Educ* Sarah Syct
Open Jan 1 - July 31, Tues - Sat 10 AM - 4 PM, cl Mon & Aug; Admis adults $4, student & seniors $2; 1911; 1819 period rm, museum & barn as well as research lib & archives; Average Annual Attendance: 8,335
Library Holdings: Auction Catalogs; Book Volumes; Clipping Files; Manuscripts; Original Art Works; Pamphlets; Photographs; Prints; Sculpture
Special Subjects: Costumes, Historical Material, Manuscripts, Photography, Painting-American, Portraits, Furniture, Jewelry, Period Rooms, Maps
Exhibitions: Amos Blanchard Home, Contemporary Andover Artist Series, quarterly changing exhibits
Activities: Adult, 3rd grade school children & family day progs; lects; walking tours; house & garden tours; originate traveling exhibs; mus shop sells books, original art & prints

A **NORTHEAST DOCUMENT CONSERVATION CENTER, INC,** 100 Brickstone Sq, Andover, MA 01810-1494. Tel 978-470-1010; Fax 978-475-6021; Elec Mail nedcc@nedcc.org; Internet Home Page Address: www.nedcc.org; *Registrar* Jonathan Goodrich; *Develop & Pub Rels Coordr* Julie Martin; *Mgr Financial Servs* Joanne Masse; *Admin Asst* Juanita Singh
Open Mon - Fri 8:30 AM - 5 PM; Estab 1973 to improve preservation programs of libraries, archives, mus & other historical & cultural organizations; to provide services to institutions that cannot afford in-house conservation facilities or that require specialized expertise; & to provide leadership to the preservation field; Headquarters located in a fire-proof 1920's mill building with masonry construction, including concrete floors 8″ thick; 20,000 sq ft; state-of-the-art security systems & environmental controls

M **PHILLIPS ACADEMY,** Addison Gallery of American Art, Chapel Ave, Andover, MA 01810; 180 Main St, Andover, MA 01810-4161. Tel 978-749-4015; Fax 978-749-4025; Elec Mail addison@andover.edu; Internet Home Page Address: www.addisongallery.org; *Dir* Brian T Allen; *Dir Devel* Susannah Abbott; *Registrar* Denise Johnson; *Cur (art before 1950)* Susan Faxon; *Cur (art after 1950)* Allison Kemerer
Open Tues - Sat 10 AM - 5 PM, Sun 1 - 5 PM, cl Aug; No admis fee; Estab 1931 in memory of Mrs Keturah Addison Cobb, to enrich permanently the lives of the students by helping to cultivate & foster in them a love for the beautiful; The gift also includes a number of important paintings, prints & sculpture as a nucleus for the beginning of a permanent collection of American art; Maintains small reference library for mus use only; Average Annual Attendance: 35,000; non-circulating libraries; Mem: 500, dues $50-10,000
Income: Financed by endowment & gifts
Purchases: American art
Library Holdings: Book Volumes; Exhibition Catalogs; Other Holdings Slides
Special Subjects: Decorative Arts, Glass, American Western Art, Furniture, Silver, Woodcuts, Drawings, Graphics, Painting-American, Photography, Prints, Sculpture, Watercolors
Collections: 18th, 19th & 20th centuries drawings, paintings, prints, sculpture; photographs; film; videotapes
Publications: Sheila Hicks! 50 Years; William Wegman; American Vanguards
Activities: Educ Program, classes for children; lect open to public, 8-10 vis lectrs per year; gallery talks; fellowships; book traveling exhib: 2-3; originates traveling exhibs for nat and internat mus; mus shop sells books, original art, reproductions & other gift items

ARLINGTON

M **ARLINGTON CENTER FOR THE ARTS,** 41 Foster St, Gibbs Ctr Arlington, MA 02474-6813. Tel 781-648-6220; Elec Mail info@acarts.org; Internet Home Page Address: www.acarts.org

ATTLEBORO

M **ATTLEBORO ARTS MUSEUM,** (Attleboro Museum, Center for the Arts) 86 Park St, Attleboro, MA 02703-2335. Tel 508-222-2644; Fax 508-226-4401; Elec Mail office@attleboroartsmuseum.org; Internet Home Page Address: www.attleboroartsmuseum.org; *Pres Bd Trustees* Nancy Aleo; *Exec Dir* Mim Brooks Fawcett
Open Tues - Sat 10 AM - 4 PM, cl Sun & Mon; No admis fee, donations accepted; Estab 1927 to exhibit the works of contemporary New England artists, as well as the art works of the museum's own collection. These are pub openings plus several competitive exhibits with awards & an outdoor art festival; Three galleries with changing monthly exhibits of paintings, drawings, sculpture, ceramics, jewelry, glass, metals & prints; Average Annual Attendance: 7,800; Mem: 230; dues life mem & corporate $1000, patron $500, benefactor $250, sponsor & supporting $125, assoc $40, family $ 50, artist mem $35 student & senior citizen $25
Income: Financed by mem, gifts, local & state grants
Library Holdings: Auction Catalogs; Audio Tapes; Cards; Clipping Files; Original Art Works; Original Documents; Pamphlets; Periodical Subscriptions; Photographs; Prints; Records; Sculpture; Slides
Special Subjects: Painting-American, Prints
Collections: Paintings & prints
Exhibitions: Holiday Show; Annual Area Artist Exhibit; Individual & Group Exhibits of Various Media & Subject; Competitive Painting Show; Fall Members Show; Competitive Photography Show; Selections from the Permanent Collection; Hi-art
Publications: Newsletter, every 2 months
Activities: Classes for adults & children; workshops; lects open to pub; vis lectrs; 2 concerts per yr; gallery talks; tours; competitions, schols offered; painting & photography; 1st, 2nd, 3rd place awards & Honorable Mention; original objects of art lent; mus shop sells photograph albums, ceramics & jewelry

BEVERLY

M **BEVERLY HISTORICAL SOCIETY,** Cabot, Hale & Balch House Museums, 117 Cabot St, Beverly, MA 01915-5196. Tel 978-922-1186; Elec Mail info@beverlyhistory.org; Internet Home Page Address: www.beverlyhistory.org; *Dir & Cur* Susan J Goganian; *Pres* Dan Lohnes
Cabot Museum open yearly Tues & Thurs 10 AM - 4 PM, Wed 1 - 9 PM, Balch House open June - Oct; Hale House open June - Oct; Admis adults $5, seniors & students $4, children under 16 free; 1891; The Balch House built in 1636 by John Balch contains period furniture. The Hale House was built in 1694 by the first minister, John Hale. Cabot House built in 1781-82 by prominent merchant & private owner, John Cabot; Average Annual Attendance: 2,000; Mem: 450; dues families $50, single $30; annual meeting in March
Special Subjects: Decorative Arts, Marine Painting, Glass, Porcelain, Painting-American, Photography, Prints, Archaeology, Textiles, Ceramics, Folk Art, Pottery, Portraits, Posters, Furniture, Historical Material, Maps, Embroidery, Pewter
Collections: 120 paintings containing portraits, folk & Revolutionary War scenes; 1000 pieces furniture, toys, doll houses, military & maritime items & pewter, books, manuscripts & photographs
Exhibitions: Beverly and the American Revolution
Publications: Quarterly newsletter
Activities: Docent training; lect open to pub & some for members only; gallery talks by arrangement; tours; individual paintings & original objects of art lent to other museums & libraries; sales shop sells books, reproductions & postcards

L **Library,** 117 Cabot St, Beverly, MA 01915. Tel 978-922-1186; Elec Mail info@beverlyhistory.org; Internet Home Page Address: www.beverlyhistory.org; *Dir* Susan Goganian; *Cur* Darren Brown
Open Tues, Thurs-Sat 10 AM - 4 PM, Wed 1 PM - 9 PM; Admis adults $5, children under 16 free; Estab 1891; Mem: 500/50family
Library Holdings: Audio Tapes; Book Volumes 4100; Clipping Files; Manuscripts; Maps; Memorabilia; Motion Pictures; Original Art Works; Original Documents; Pamphlets; Periodical Subscriptions 8; Photographs; Prints; Sculpture; Slides; Video Tapes
Special Subjects: Folk Art, Decorative Arts, Photography, Drawings, Manuscripts, Maps, Painting-American, Prints, Sculpture, Historical Material, Watercolors, Ceramics, Crafts, Archaeology, Lettering, Furniture, Costume Design & Constr, Glass, Embroidery, Silver, Textiles, Marine Painting, Landscapes, Coins & Medals, Pewter, Architecture, Pottery
Collections: 800,000+ objects & documents connected to Beverly history
Activities: mus shop sells books, reproductions & prints

BOSTON

ARCHAEOLOGICAL INSTITUTE OF AMERICA
For further information, see National and Regional Organizations

A **BOSTON ARCHITECTURAL COLLEGE,** (Boston Architectural Center) McCormick Gallery, 320 Newbury St, Boston, MA 02115-2703. Tel 617-262-5000; Fax 617-585-0110; Internet Home Page Address: www.the-bac.edu; *Pres* Ted Landsmark; *Dir Admin Operations* Patti Vaughn
Open Mon - Thurs 9 AM - 10:30 PM, Fri & Sat 9 AM - 5 PM, Sun Noon - 5 PM; No admis fee; Estab 1889 for educ of architects & designers; Small exhibition space on first floor; Average Annual Attendance: 2,000; Mem: Annual meetings of institutes of higher education in September

Activities: Classes for adults; lects open to pub, 16 vis lectrs per yr; competitions; exten dept servs professional architects; originates traveling exhibs

L **Library,** 320 Newbury St, Boston, MA 02115. Tel 617-585-0155; Fax 617-285-0151; Internet Home Page Address: www.the-bac.edu/library; *Chief Librn* Susan Lewis; *Assoc Dir* Whitney Vitale
Open Mon - Thurs Noon - 10 PM; No admis fee; 1889 to create a place to learn & relax with those in architecture & related fields; Circ 13,500; Open to pub
Income: $168,000
Library Holdings: Book Volumes 2000; CD-ROMs 200; Manuscripts 15; Original Art Works 5; Periodical Subscriptions 125; Sculpture 12; Slides 25,000
Collections: 18th, 19th & early 20th centuries architectural books from the colls of practicing architects; 20th century architecture, interior design & landscape arch
Activities: Classes for adults; 3 vis lectrs per yr; multiple awards

A **THE BOSTON PRINTMAKERS,** 700 Beacon St, Boston, MA 02115-2508. Tel 617-735-9898; Elec Mail info@bostonprintmakers.org; Internet Home Page Address: www.bostonprintmakers.org; *Pres* Marc Cole
Estab 1947 to aid printmakers in exhibiting their work; to bring quality work to the public; Average Annual Attendance: 15,000; Mem: 250; dues $40; mem by jury selection; annual meeting April; North American Printmaker
Income: Financed by mem, entry fees, and commission on sales
Purchases: $20,700
Exhibitions: Prints, artist books, etchings, lithograph, mixed media, monotypes, serigraph & woodcut; biennial open, juried North American print biennial and Arches biennial student exhibition, contemporary Cuban printmakers
Publications: Exhibition catalogs; 60 Years of North American Prints by David Acton
Activities: Lects open to pub; gallery talks; competitions with awards and prizes; purchase & materials awards at biennial; individual paintings and original objects of art lent to local museums, galleries, libraries and schools including Duxbury Art Complex Museum, Boston Public Library, DeCordova Museum; book 5 traveling exhibs per yr; originates traveling exhibs to galleries at libraries, universities and schools

L **BOSTON PUBLIC LIBRARY,** Central Library, 700 Boylston St, Copley Sq Boston, MA 02116-2813. Tel 617-536-5400; Fax 617-236-4306; Elec Mail mfobrien@bpl.org; Internet Home Page Address: www.bpl.org; *Pres* Amy E Ryan; *Chief Pub Servs* Mary Francis O'Brien; *Keeper of Special Colls* Susan Glover; *Cur the Arts* Kimberly Tenney; *Cur Fine Arts* Eve Griffin; *Cur Music* Metro Voloshin
Open Mon - Thurs 9 AM - 9 PM, Fri & Sat 9 AM - 5 PM, Sun (Oct - May) 1 - 5 PM; Print & Rare Books: Mon - Fri 9AM - 5 PM; No admis fee; Estab library 1848; Circ Reference only; Building contains mural decorations by Edwin A Abbey, John Elliott, Pierre Puvis de Chavannes, & John Singer Sargent; bronze doors by Daniel Chester French; sculptures by Frederick MacMonnies, Bela Pratt, Louis Saint Gaudens; paintings by Copley & Duplessis; & bust of John Deferrari by Joseph A Coletti; Average Annual Attendance: 2,500,000
Income: Financed by city & state appropriation
Library Holdings: Book Volumes 6,000,000 (entire library); Clipping Files; Exhibition Catalogs; Fiche; Lantern Slides; Manuscripts; Memorabilia; Original Art Works; Original Documents; Other Holdings Architectural Drawings, 700,000; Pamphlets; Periodical Subscriptions 16,704 (entire library); Photographs; Prints; Reels; Reproductions; Sculpture
Special Subjects: Art History, Landscape Architecture, Decorative Arts, Illustration, Photography, Calligraphy, Drawings, Etchings & Engravings, Graphic Arts, Manuscripts, Maps, Prints, Watercolors, Crafts, Latin American Art, Archaeology, Printmaking, Cartoons, Fashion Arts, Interior Design, Costume Design & Constr, Stained Glass, Aesthetics, Bookplates & Bindings, Handicrafts, Miniatures, Restoration & Conservation, Woodcuts, Dioramas, Architecture
Publications: Exhibition catalogues
Activities: Classes for adults & children; lect open to public; concerts; tours

L **Arts Reference Department,** 700 Boylston St, Boston, MA 02116-2813. Tel 617-859-2275; Fax 617-262-0461; Elec Mail fineartsref@bpl.org; Internet Home Page Address: www.bpl.org; *Cur Arts Dept* Kim Tenney; *Cur Fine Arts* Eve Griffin; *Cur Music* Metro Voloshin; *Sr Fine Arts Reference Librn* Evelyn W Lannon; *Sr Music Reference Librn* Charlotte Kolczynski
Open Mon - Thurs 9 AM - 9 PM, Fri & Sat 9 AM - 5 PM, Sun 1 - 5 PM (Oct-May); Estab for visual, design, decorative arts & music reference collections and services; Circ Non-circ
Library Holdings: Book Volumes 215,000; CD-ROMs; Clipping Files; Exhibition Catalogs; Fiche 125,292; Lantern Slides; Manuscripts; Memorabilia; Original Documents; Other Holdings Architectural drawings; Pamphlets; Periodical Subscriptions 112; Photographs; Reels 9,157; Reproductions
Special Subjects: Art History, Decorative Arts, Etchings & Engravings, Painting-American, Prints, Ceramics, Porcelain, Stained Glass, Pottery, Architecture
Collections: Connick Stained Glass Archives; Cram & Ferguson architectural drawings; Maginnis & Walsh architectural drawings; Peabody & Stearns Architectural Drawings; W G Preston Architectural Drawings; Archives of American Art (unrestricted) Microfilm; Society of Arts & Crafts Archives; Vertical files on local artists, galleries, museums societies; Vertical & image files on Boston's built-environment; Clarence Blackall scrapbooks & sketchbooks; Allen A Brown Music Collection
Activities: Educ prog; Bibliographic instruction; student & public orientations

M **Albert H Wiggin Gallery & Print Department,** Copley Sq, Boston, MA 02117; 700 Boylston St, Boston, MA 02117-2813. Tel 617-859-2280; Fax 617-262-0461; Elec Mail prints@bpl.org; Internet Home Page Address: www.bpl.org; *Asst Keeper of Prints* Karen Smith Shafts; *Librn* Jane Winton
Open Gallery: Mon - Fri 9 AM - 5 PM, Print Study Room: Mon - Fri 9 AM- 5 PM by appointment only, cl Sat & Sun; Admis free
Library Holdings: Book Volumes 3600; Clipping Files; Exhibition Catalogs; Lantern Slides 6,623; Memorabilia; Original Art Works 150,000; Photographs 1.2 mil; Prints
Special Subjects: Drawings, Etchings & Engravings, Historical Material, Portraits, Prints, Woodcuts, Architecture, Photography, Prints, Watercolors, Posters
Collections: Collection of 18th, 19th & 20th century French, English & American prints & drawings, including the Albert H Wiggin Collection; 20th century American prints by Boston artists; 19th century photographs of the American West & India & Middle East; Boston Pictorial Archive; paintings; postcards; Boston Herald Traveler Photo Morgue; ephemera; Chromolithographs of Louis Prang & Co., Historic American Collection
Exhibitions: Eight or nine per year drawn from the print department's permanent collections
Activities: Lect open to public, 1-2 vis lectrs per year; internships offered

L **Rare Book & Manuscripts Dept,** 700 Boylston St, Copley Sq Boston, MA 02116-2813. Tel 617-536-5400, Ext 2225; Internet Home Page Address: www.bpl.org/WWW/rb/rbd; *Librn* Sean Casey; *Adams Libr Cur* Elizabeth Prindle; *Conservator* Christopher Letizia; *Cur Manuscripts* Kimberly Reynolds
Open 9 AM - 5 PM weekdays; Estab 1934; Average Annual Attendance: 1,400
Income: Financed by trust funds
Purchases: Books, manuscripts, maps, prints & photographs relevant to our current subject strengths
Library Holdings: Book Volumes 600,000; Lantern Slides; Manuscripts; Memorabilia; Micro Print; Periodical Subscriptions 4; Photographs; Reels
Special Subjects: Landscape Architecture, Calligraphy, Etchings & Engravings, Manuscripts, Historical Material, Ethnology, Fashion Arts, Costume Design & Constr, Bookplates & Bindings, Antiquities-Greek, Antiquities-Roman, Coins & Medals
Collections: FEER World's Fair Collection; Americana; book arts; Boston theater; history of printing; juvenilia; landscape & gardening; theater costume design; Boston history; Colonial & Revolutionary America; library of John Adams; antislavery; library of John Adams; Medieval Manuscripts, Barton Collection of Shakespeare
Exhibitions: Exhibits change every 3-4 months & feature books, manuscripts, maps & prints that make up department collections
Activities: Seminars; lect open to public, 3 vis lectrs per year; concerts; tours; sales shop sells postcards & pamphlets

M **THE BOSTONIAN SOCIETY,** Old State House Museum, 206 Washington St, Boston, MA 02109-1773. Tel 617-720-1713; Fax 617-720-3289; Internet Home Page Address: www.bostonhistory.org; *Exec Dir* Brian Lemay; *Dir The Old State House Museum* Rainey Tisdale; *Dir Research Center* Anne Vosikas
Open daily 9 AM - 5 PM; Admis adults $5, seniors & students $4, children ages 6-18 $1; Estab 1881 to collect & preserve the history of Boston; Average Annual Attendance: 90,000; Mem: 1250; dues supporter $150, family $80, individuals $50, seniors $40, student/teacher $25
Income: Financed by endowment, mem, admis, grants, state & federal appropriations
Library Holdings: Book Volumes; Lantern Slides; Manuscripts; Maps; Memorabilia; Original Documents; Other Holdings; Pamphlets; Periodical Subscriptions; Photographs; Prints; Reproductions; Slides
Special Subjects: Architecture, Furniture, Manuscripts, Drawings, Painting-American, Prints, Sculpture, Watercolors, Costumes, Ceramics, Folk Art, Decorative Arts, Portraits, Marine Painting, Historical Material, Maps, Scrimshaw, Coins & Medals, Military Art
Collections: Paintings & artifacts relating to Boston history; Maritime art; Revolutionary War artifacts; prints
Exhibitions: Ongoing exhibitions
Publications: Proceedings of The Bostonian Society; The Bostonian Society Newsletter
Activities: Classes for children; lects open to pub; concerts; gallery talks; walking tours; Boston History Award; individual paintings & original objects of art lent to other mus; mus shop sells books, decorative arts, reproductions, prints & toys

L **Library,** 15 State St, 3rd Fl Boston, MA 02109-3502; 206 Washington St, Old State House Boston, MA 02109-1702. Tel 617-720-1713; Fax 617-720-3289; Elec Mail library@bostonhistory.org; Internet Home Page Address: www.bostonhistory.org; *Librn* Nicole DeLaria; *Dir Library & Spec Colls* Anne Vosikas
Open Tues - Thurs 10 AM - 3:30 PM; Admis nonmembers $10; college students $5; Estab 1881 to collect & preserve material related to the history of Boston; For reference only; Mem: Dues benefactor $500, supporter $100, family & individual $50, sr 62 & over $40, student $25
Library Holdings: Book Volumes 7500; Clipping Files; Fiche; Lantern Slides; Manuscripts; Maps; Memorabilia; Original Art Works; Other Holdings Documents; Ephemera; Postcards; Scrapbooks; Pamphlets; Periodical Subscriptions 10; Photographs 30,000; Prints 2000; Reproductions; Slides 3000
Special Subjects: Photography, Manuscripts, Maps, Prints, Historical Material
Publications: Bostonian Society Newsletter, quarterly; monthly e-news
Activities: Educ prog; classes for adults & children; lects open to pub, over 6 vis lectrs per yr for members only; concerts; gallery talks; tours; Boston History Award; mus shop sells books, reproductions & prints

M **BROMFIELD ART GALLERY,** 450 Harrison Ave, Boston, MA 02118. Tel 617-451-3605; Elec Mail gduehr@comcast.net; Internet Home Page Address: www.bromfieldgallery.com; *Pres* Florence Montgomery; *Secy* Arthur Hendigg; *Treas* Barbara Poole; *Media & Exhibitions Coordr* Heidi M Marsten
Open Wed - Sat Noon - 5 PM; No admis fee; Estab 1974 to exhibit art; Two galleries, approx 500 sq ft; Average Annual Attendance: 3,000; Mem: 20; dues $750; monthly meetings
Income: Financed by mem and sales
Activities: Lect open to public, 5 vis lectrs per year; gallery talks; sponsoring of competitions

M **CHASE YOUNG GALLERY,** 450 Harrison Ave No 57, Boston, MA 02118. Tel 617-859-7222; Elec Mail mail@chaseyounggallery.com; Internet Home Page Address: www.chaseyounggallery.com; *Dir & Owner* Jane Young
Open Tues-Sat 11AM-6PM, Sun 11AM-4PM, other times by appointment
Collections: contemporary paintings, sculpture, & photographs

C **FEDERAL RESERVE BANK OF BOSTON,** 600 Atlantic Ave, Boston, MA 02210-2211. Internet Home Page Address: www.bos.frb.org

C **FLEET BOSTON FINANCIAL,** Gallery, 100 Federal St, Boston, MA 02110-1802. Tel 617-434-2200, 434-6314, 434-3921; Fax 617-434-6280; Elec Mail llambrechts@bkb.com; *Dir & Cur* Lillian Lambrechts
Collections: Contemporary paintings; historical documents; non-contemporary paintings & textiles; photography; sculpture

Publications: Exhibition catalogs, 6-10 times per yr
Activities: Originate traveling exhibs

M **FLORENCE & CHAFETZ HILLEL HOUSE AT BOSTON UNIVERSITY,** (Boston University) Boston University Art Gallery at the Stone Gallery, 855 Commonwealth Ave, Boston, MA 02215-1303. Tel 617-353-3329, 4672; Fax 617-353-4509; Elec Mail gallery@bu.edu; Internet Home Page Address: www.bu.edu/art; *Acting Dir* Lynne Conney; *Asst Dir* Joshua Buckno
Open Sep - May Tues - Fri 10 AM - 5 PM, Sat & Sun 1 - 5 PM, cl Boston Univ Holidays & winter & summer intersessions; No admis fee; Estab 1960; One exhibition space, 250 running ft, 2500 sq ft
Collections: Contemporary & New England Art
Exhibitions: Rotating 8 week Exhib
Publications: Annual exhibition catalogs
Activities: Lects open to pub; 2-3 vis lectrs per yr; gallery talks; book traveling exhibs 1 per yr; originate traveling exhibs

M **Rubin-Frankel Gallery,** 213 Bay State Rd, Boston, MA 02215-1499. Tel 617-353-7634; Fax 617-353-7660; Elec Mail rubinfrankelgallery@gmail.com; Internet Home Page Address: www.bu.edu/hillel/gallery; *Dir* Holland Dieringer
Winter: Mon-Fri 9AM-10PM, Sat 8:30AM-9PM, Sun 3PM-9PM; Summer: Mon-Fri 10AM-4PM
Special Subjects: Photography, Painting-American, Prints, Sculpture, Tapestries, Watercolors, Religious Art, Judaica, Painting-Israeli
Collections: paintings; drawings; sculpture; photographs

M **GIBSON SOCIETY, INC,** Gibson House Museum, 137 Beacon St, Boston, MA 02116-1504. Tel 617-267-6338; Fax 617-267-5121; Elec Mail info@thegibsonhouse.org; Internet Home Page Address: www.thegibsonhouse.org; *Dir Educ* Edward Gordon; *Dir* Barbara Thibault; *Exec Dir* J Charles Swift; *Museum Asst* Kyla MacKay-Smith; *Mus Admin* Laura Gresh
Open year round, tours at 1, 2 & 3 PM Wed - Sun; Admis adults $9, seniors & students $6, children $3; Estab 1957 as a Victorian House museum; memorial to Gibson family & Boston's Back Bay; Victorian time capsule, early Back Bay Town House, eight rooms with Victorian & Edwardian era furnishings; Average Annual Attendance: 2,300
Income: Financed by trust fund & admis
Special Subjects: Period Rooms
Collections: Decorative arts; paintings; sculpture; Victorian period furniture; objects assoc with Gibson & related families
Activities: Lect open to public, 6-10 vis lectrs per year; holiday open house; galley talks; guided tours; summer lect series July & Aug, Thurs 5:30 PM; original objects of art lent to museums & galleries; sales shop sells books, prints & postcards

A **THE GUILD OF BOSTON ARTISTS,** 162 Newbury St, Boston, MA 02116-2889. Tel 617-536-7660; Elec Mail gallery@guildofbostonartists.org; Internet Home Page Address: www.guildofbostonartists.org; *Pres* Paul Ingbretson; *Gallery Dir* William Everett; *Asst to Dir* Steven Bloomenthal
Open Tues - Sat 10:30 AM - 5:30 PM, Sun noon - 5 PM; No admis fee; Estab & incorporated 1914, nonprofit art assn; Exhibiting 65 of New England's finest contemporary realist painters; front gallery features continual show of general membership; President's gallery showcases solo or group themed shows; Mem: 65+ artist members - ann dues $250; $100 assoc mems & patron mems $100 ann; student mems $35 ann; artist mems meeting in Apr, must live in New England & work in form of tradition, representational painting or sculpture. No qualifications for assoc or patron mems. Student mems must show proof of full time study under professional artist.
Income: Sales, donations
Exhibitions: Rotating exhibitions; Annual Representational Painting Competition (non-mem)
Publications: American Art Collection
Activities: Artist demonstrations, painting workshops & classes for adults; lect open to public, receptions, gallery talks & tours

A **HISTORIC NEW ENGLAND,** (Society for the Preservation of New England Antiquities) 141 Cambridge St, Harrison Gray Otis House Boston, MA 02114-2702. Tel 617-227-3956; Fax 617-227-9204; Internet Home Page Address: www.historicnewengland.org; *Pres* Carl R Nold; *PR Officer* Susanna Crampton
Open Wed - Sun 11 AM - 4:30 PM; Admis $8, discounts to senior citizens, ICOM, AAA, AAM, WGBH members, members no charge; Estab & incorporated 1910, the Otis House serves as both headquarters & mus for Historic New England. Formerly known as Society for the Preservation of New England Antiquities; owns over 36 historic houses throughout New England; Average Annual Attendance: 179,000; Mem: 7,210; dues individual $45, household $55, garden & landscape $75, contributing $100, historic homeowner $200, supporting $250, national $35
Income: financed by members, grants
Special Subjects: Architecture, Landscapes, Photography, Textiles, Decorative Arts, Furniture, Period Rooms
Collections: American & European decorative arts & antiques with New England history; photographs; houses
Publications: Historic New England Magazine (3xs)
Activities: Classes for adults & school children; lects open to pub, 5-10 vis lectrs per yr; tours; awards book prize, prize for collecting works on paper, Community Preservation Grants; originate traveling exhibs; mus shop sells books/merchandise

L **Library and Archives,** 141 Cambridge St, Harrison Gray Otis House Boston, MA 02114-2702. Tel 617-227-3957; Fax 617-973-9050; Elec Mail lcondon@historicnewengland.org; Internet Home Page Address: www.historicnewengland.org; *Cur Library & Archives* Lorna Condon; *Librn/Archivist* Ann Kardos; *Library & Archives Specialist* Jeanne Gamble; *Systems Librn & Archivist* David Dwiggins
Open Wed - Fri 9:30 AM - 4:30 PM; Admis nonmembers $5, students $3, mems free; Estab 1910 to document New England architecture and material culture from the 17th century to the present with emphasis on 19th & 20th centuries; For reference; Mem: 6500; dues individual $45, household $55
Library Holdings: Auction Catalogs; Audio Tapes; Book Volumes; Cards; Clipping Files; Exhibition Catalogs; Fiche; Filmstrips; Kodachrome Transparencies; Lantern Slides; Manuscripts; Maps; Memorabilia; Original Art Works; Original Documents; Pamphlets; Periodical Subscriptions; Photographs; Prints; Slides; Video Tapes
Special Subjects: Landscape Architecture, Decorative Arts, Photography, Drawings, Etchings & Engravings, Graphic Design, Manuscripts, Historical Material, Advertising Design, Interior Design, Drafting, Period Rooms, Bookplates & Bindings, Architecture
Collections: 450,000 photographs & negatives; 35,000 architectural drawings; 10,000 books including rare; 10,000 newspaper clippings; 25,000 pieces of ephemera; 2,500 prints; 800 maps & atlases; 700 drawings & watercolors; 1,000 linear ft manuscripts
Activities: Internships; lects open to pub; tours; Historic New England book prize & Collector's prize; mus shop sells books & reproductions

A **INQUILINOS BORICUAS EN ACCION,** 405 Shawmut Ave, Boston, MA 02118-2029. Tel 617-927-1707; Fax 617-536-5816; Elec Mail info@iba-etc.org; Internet Home Page Address: www.iba-etc.org; *CEO* Vanessa Calderon-Rosado; *Chief Fin & Admin* Mayra Negron; *Dir Devel* David Kay; *Dir Community Empowerment Progs* Anita Mercado; *Dir Youth Progs* Julio Cesar Roman; *Dir Educ* Matilde Graciano
Open Mon - Fri 9 AM - 5 PM; La Galeria open Thurs - Fri 4 PM - 7 PM, Sat 1 PM - 4 PM; Estab 1968 to support the development & empowerment of the Villa Victoria community in Boston's south end; Maintains La Galeria at Villa Victoria Ctr for the Arts
Activities: Classes for children

M **INSTITUTE OF CONTEMPORARY ART,** 100 Northern Ave, Boston, MA 02210-1870. Tel 617-478-3100; Elec Mail info@icaboston.org; Internet Home Page Address: www.icaboston.org; *Dir* Jill Medvedow; *Chief Cur* Helen Molesworth; *Assoc Cur* Randi Hopkins; *Chief Preparator* Tim Obetz; *Sr Registrar* Janet Moore; *Dir Educ* Monica Garza; *Dir Fin & Opers* Michael Taubenberger; *Dir Progs* David Henry; *Dir Film & Video* Branka Bogdanov; *Dir Mem & Develop Opers* Chris Rosol; *Dir Facilities & Security* Jana Dengler
Open Tues - Wed & Sat - Sun 10 AM - 5 PM, Thurs - Fri 10 AM - 9 PM, cl Thanksgiving, Christmas & New Year's; Admis adults $15, seniors $13, students $10, mems & youth 17 & under free; New England's premier contemporary art museum, the ICA presents provocative exhibitions by national and international artists that explore the ideas, issues and images of our times. For over 65 years the ICA has been the first to show many of the most innovative and inspired artists from around the world; Mem: 1600; dues $40 & up; annual meeting in Sept
Income: Financed by mem, gifts & grants, earned income
Publications: Exhibition catalogs
Activities: Educ dept; classes for adults & children; docent training; lects open to pub, 20 vis lectrs per yr; film series; video; concerts; gallery talks; tours; performances; competitions; ICA Artist prize; book traveling exhibs annually; originate traveling exhibs, circulating to other national & international contemporary art mus; mus shop sells books, magazines, t-shirts, catalogs, cards, posters

M **ISABELLA STEWART GARDNER MUSEUM,** 280 Fenway, Boston, MA 02115; 2 Palace Rd, Boston, MA 02115-5807. Tel 617-566-1401; Fax 617-566-7653; Elec Mail information@isgm.org; Internet Home Page Address: www.gardnermuseum.org; *Dir* Anne Hawley
Open Tues - Sun 11 AM - 5 PM, cl Mon, Independence Day, Thanksgiving & Christmas; Admis adults $12 ($11 on weekends), seniors $10, college students $5, college students on Wed $3, children under 18 free; Estab 1903, the mus houses Isabella Stewart Gardner's various collections; Mus building is styled after a 16th century Venetian villa; all galleries open onto a central, glass-roofed courtyard, filled with flowers that are changed with the seasons of the year; Average Annual Attendance: 175,000; Mem: 3,000; dues $35 & up
Income: Financed by endowment, fundraising, mem donations & door charge
Special Subjects: Painting-American, Oriental Art, Painting-Dutch, Painting-French, Painting-Flemish, Painting-Italian, Antiquities-Greek, Antiquities-Roman
Collections: Gothic & Italian Renaissance, Roman & classical sculpture; Dutch & Flemish 17th century; Japanese screens; Oriental & Islamic ceramics, glass, sculpture; 19th century American and French paintings; major paintings of John Singer Sargent & James McNeill Whistler
Exhibitions: Laura Owens, Community Creations, Isabella Gardner: Her Life & Memories
Publications: Guide to the Collection; Oriental & Islamic Art in the Isabella Stewart Gardner Museum; Drawings - Isabella Stewart Gardner Museum; Mrs Jack; Sculpture in the Isabella Stewart Gardner Museum; Textiles - Isabella Stewart Gardner Museum; children's books - Isabella Stewart Gardner Museum; Fenway Court; History & Companion Guide; Spec Exhibition Catalogs
Activities: Progs for children; lects open to pub, 10 vis lectrs per yr; concerts; gallery talks; tours; symposia; sales shop selling books, reproductions, prints, slides, postcards & annual reports, jewelry, gifts

L **Isabella Stewart Garden Museum Library & Archives,** 2 Palace Rd, Boston, MA 02115. Tel 617-278-5121; Fax 617-278-5177; Elec Mail collection@isgm.org; Internet Home Page Address: www.gardnermuseum.org; *Librn & Asst Cur* Richard Lingner; *Archivist* Kristin Parker; *Cur* Alan Chong
Open by appointment Mon, Wed, Fri & Sat; Estab 1903; Open to scholars who need to work with mus archives; building designed in style of 15th century Venetian palace; Mem: 3000
Income: endowments & mem donations
Library Holdings: Auction Catalogs; Book Volumes 800; Clipping Files; Exhibition Catalogs; Manuscripts; Memorabilia; Periodical Subscriptions 19; Photographs
Special Subjects: Art History
Collections: Objects spanning 30 centuries; 1,000 rare books spanning 6 centuries including papers of museum founder; rich in Italian Renaissance painting
Exhibitions: Rotating exhibits
Activities: Educ prog; lects open to pub, 6-8 vis lectrs per yr; symposia; concerts; gallery talks; tours; sales shop sells books, gifts, reproductions, prints, slides & postcards

M KAJI ASO STUDIO, Gallery Nature & Temptation, 40 Saint Stephen St, Boston, MA 02115-4510. Tel 617-247-1719; Fax 617-247-7564; Elec Mail administrator@kajiasostudio.com; Internet Home Page Address: www.kajiasostudio.com; *Music Dir* Katie Sloss; *Dir & Adminr* Kate Finnegan; *Gallery Dir* Gary Tucker; *Ceramic Dir* Jeanne Gugino
By appointment; No admis fee; Estab 1973 to foster new/emerging artists representational to abstract-positive feeling; Two rooms on 1st floor 10' x 14' in historic brownstone; track lighting; Mem: 40; monthly dues $150
Exhibitions: Watercolor, Oil, Drawing, Ceramic, Japanese Calligraphy & Sumi Painting
Publications: Dasoku Journal of Arts, biannual
Activities: Classes for adults; lects open to pub; concerts; gallery talks; tours

M LESLEY UNIVERSITY, (The Art Institute of Boston at Lesley University) Main Gallery, 700 Beacon St, Boston, MA 02215-2598. Tel 617-585-6600; Internet Home Page Address: www.lesley.edu; *Dir Gallery & Exhib* Bonnell Robinson
Open Mon - Sat 9 AM - 6 PM, Sun Noon - 5 PM; No admis fee; Estab 1969 to present major contemporary & historical exhibitions of the work of established & emerging artists & to show work by students & faculty of the Institute; 3,000 sq ft of gallery; Average Annual Attendance: 4,000
Exhibitions: Works from the Collaboration of Richard Benson & Callaway Editions; Luis Gonzalez Palma (Guatemalan photographer); Contemporary Book Design; Edward Sorel; Pedro Meyer; Edward Gorell; Chuck Close; Magnuw Photographers
Activities: Classes for adults & children; professional progs in fine & applied arts & photography; lects open to pub, 5 vis lectrs per yr; lect series coordinated with exhibitions; gallery talks; competitions, local & regional; exten dept serves Greater Boston area; individual paintings & original objects of art lent to other galleries; curate & mount exhibitions for major public spaces

L College of Art & Design Library, 700 Beacon St, Boston, MA 02215; 29 Everett St, Cambridge, MA 02138. Tel 617-585-6670; Fax 617-585-6720; Elec Mail aib_circ@lesley.edu; Internet Home Page Address: www.lesley.edu; *Head Librn* Carrie L McDade; *Library Asst* Raye Yankavskas
Open Mon - Thurs 8:30 AM - 9:30 PM, Fri 8:30 AM - 5:30 PM, Sat Noon - 6 PM, Sun 2 - 8 PM; Estab 1969 to support school curriculum
Library Holdings: Book Volumes 10,000; CD-ROMs 5; DVDs; Exhibition Catalogs; Other Holdings Vertical File; Periodical Subscriptions; Slides; Video Tapes
Special Subjects: Art History, Collages, Constructions, Intermedia, Illustration, Photography, Commercial Art, Drawings, Etchings & Engravings, Graphic Arts, Graphic Design, Painting-American, Painting-British, Painting-Dutch, Painting-Flemish, Painting-French, Painting-German, Painting-Italian, Painting-Japanese, Painting-Russian, Posters, Pre-Columbian Art, Prints, Sculpture, Painting-European, History of Art & Archaeology, Portraits, Watercolors, Ceramics, Crafts, Latin American Art, Printmaking, Cartoons, Art Education, Asian Art, Video, American Indian Art, Primitive art, Afro-American Art, Metalwork, Pottery, Religious Art, Woodcarvings, Antiquities-Egyptian, Painting-Scandinavian, Architecture
Activities: Classes for adults; lects open to pub; 6 vis lectrs per yr; gallery talks; sponsoring competitions, schols, fellowships

C LIBERTY MUTUAL, Safeco Insurance Co Art Collection, 175 Berkeley St, Liberty Mutual Corporate Real Estate Boston, MA 02116-5066. Tel 617-357-9500 x42958; Elec Mail Joanne.Bragg@LibertyMutual.com; Internet Home Page Address: www.safeco.com/about-us/community-relations/art-collection; *Coll Mgr* Jackie Kosak
Open to employees & invited guests by appt only; Coll estab 1973 to support the work of both established & emerging Northwest artists through purchase and display; Art in offices
Purchases: On hold
Collections: 2-D works
Publications: Checklists & essays for some exhibitions; Frye Art Museum; Washington Art Consortium catalogs; Safeco Field catalog

L LIBRARY OF THE BOSTON ATHENAEUM, 10 1/2 Beacon St, Boston, MA 02108-3703. Tel 617-227-0270; Fax 617-227-5266; Elec Mail matthews@bostonathenaeum.org; Internet Home Page Address: www.bostonathenaeum.org/; *Dir & Librn* Paula Matthews; *Assoc Dir & Cur Maps* John H Lannon; *Susan Morse Hilles Cur Paintings & Sculpture & Head Art Dept* David Dearinger; *Cur Prints & Photos* Catharina Slautterback; *Chief Conservator* Jim Reid-Cunningham
Open Labor Day - Memorial Day, Mon & Wed 8:30 AM - 8 PM, Tues Thurs Fri 8:30 AM - 5:30 PM, Sat 9 AM - 4 PM; cl national holidays; No admis fee
Library Holdings: Auction Catalogs; Book Volumes 550,000; CD-ROMs; Clipping Files; Exhibition Catalogs; Manuscripts; Maps; Memorabilia; Original Art Works; Original Documents; Pamphlets; Periodical Subscriptions 100; Photographs; Prints; Reels; Reproductions; Sculpture
Collections: 19th century Boston prints & photographs; American & European painting & sculpture; World War II posters; George Washington's Library
Exhibitions: 3 art exhibitions per year, open to the public
Activities: Tours for pub & mem only; seminars

L MASSACHUSETTS COLLEGE OF ART, Morton R Godine Library, 621 Huntington Ave, Boston, MA 02115-5801. Tel 617-879-7150; Fax 617-879-7110; Internet Home Page Address: www.massart.edu/library; *Slide Cur* Staci Stull; *Library Dir* Paul Dobbs
Open Mon - Thurs 8 AM - 9 PM, Fri 8 AM - 6 PM, Sat 11 AM - 5 PM, Sun 2 - 8 PM; For lending

Library Holdings: Audio Tapes; Book Volumes 35,000; Cards; Cassettes; Compact Disks; DVDs; Exhibition Catalogs; Fiche 8,000; Filmstrips; Memorabilia; Motion Pictures; Original Art Works; Pamphlets; Periodical Subscriptions 491; Photographs; Prints; Records; Sculpture; Slides
Special Subjects: Art History, Art Education

M Bakalar & Paine Galleries, 621 Huntington Ave, Boston, MA 02115-5801. Tel 617-879-7333; Fax 617-879-7340; Elec Mail galleryinfo@massart.edu; Internet Home Page Address: www.massart.edu/galleries; *Dir* Lisa Tung
Open Mon-Tues & Thurs-Fri 12PM-6PM, Wed 12PM-8PM, Sat 12PM-5PM
Collections: works by contemporary artists

A MASSACHUSETTS HISTORICAL SOCIETY, 1154 Boylston St, Boston, MA 02215-3631. Tel 617-536-1608; Fax 617-859-0074; Elec Mail library@masshist.org; Internet Home Page Address: www.masshist.org; *Pres* Dennis Fiori; *Cur Art* Anne E Bentley
Open Mon - Wed 9 AM - 4:45 PM, Thurs 9 AM - 7:45 PM, Sat 9 AM - 4 PM, cl Sun & holidays; No admis fee; Estab 1791; Art works by appt only; for exhib hours see www.masshist.org/events; Average Annual Attendance: 3,000
Income: Financed by endowment, grants, individual gifts
Special Subjects: Historical Material, Manuscripts
Collections: Archives; historical material; paintings; sculpture
Exhibitions: Temporary exhibitions
Publications: Journal
Activities: Educ prog; teacher progs; lects open to pub; special exhibits for members & their guests

L Library, 1154 Boylston St, Boston, MA 02215-3631. Tel 617-536-1608; Fax 617-859-0074; Elec Mail library@masshist.org; Internet Home Page Address: www.masshist.org; *Librn* Peter Drummey; *Cur Art* Anne E Bentley; *Pres* Dennis A Fiori; *Chair* Charles C Ames
Open Library: Mon & Wed - Fri 9 AM - 4:45 PM, Tues 9 AM - 7:45 PM, Sat 9 am - 4 PM; Gallery: Mon - Sat 10 AM - 4 PM; No admis fee; Estab 1791; Galleries, progs, research library; Average Annual Attendance: 8,000
Income: Endowment, grants & individual gifts
Library Holdings: Book Volumes 250,000; Fiche; Manuscripts 3500; Maps; Original Art Works; Original Documents; Photographs; Prints
Special Subjects: Photography, Manuscripts, Maps, Painting-American, Prints, Historical Material, Portraits, Miniatures, Coins & Medals
Publications: Portraits in the Massachusetts Historical Society, Boston 1988 (one edition)
Activities: Lects open to pub; lects for mems only; gallery talks; tours; exhibs; fels

A MAYORS OFFICE OF ARTS, TOURISM AND SPECIAL EVENTS, City Hall Galleries, Boston City Hall, Rm 802, Boston, MA 02201. Tel 617-635-3911; Fax 617-635-3031 & 4428; Elec Mail arts@ciytofboston.gov; Internet Home Page Address: www.cityofboston.gov/arts; *Gallery Dir* John Crowley
Open Mon - Fri 8:30 AM - 5:30 PM; No admis fee; Estab 1965 to showcase Boston art & its cultural heritage; gallery space throughout bldg, incl Mayor's Gallery & Scollay Square Gallery; Average Annual Attendance: 100,000; Mem: none
Purchases: Artwork available to public for purchase
Special Subjects: Photography, Sculpture, Painting-American, Afro-American Art, Ceramics, Crafts, Juvenile Art, Archaeology
Exhibitions: Jan-Feb Black History Month; March - Women's History; Apr-May Boston Public Schools Ann Art Show; June-Dec Juried Art Show
Publications: Catalog and guide to the art work owned by the City of Boston, in preparation; Passport to Public Art
Activities: Competitions, 12 lects, concerts, gallery talks & tours

M MILLS GALLERY - BOSTON CENTER FOR THE ARTS, 551 Tremont St Boston, MA 02116-6338.

M MUSEUM OF AFRICAN AMERICAN HISTORY, (Museum of Afro-American History) 46 Joy St, Boston, MA 02114-4005; 14 Beacon St Ste 719, Boston, MA 02108-3710. Tel 617-725-0022; Fax 617-720-5225; Elec Mail history@maah.org; Internet Home Page Address: www.maah.org; *Exec Dir* Beverly Morgan Welch; *Dir Educ* L'Merchie Frazier; *Dir Capital Improvements of Facility Opers* Dana Parcon; *Develop Assoc* Nancy Cao
Open Mon - Sat 10 AM - 4 PM; Admis adults $5, student & seniors $3, children under 5 no charge; A nonprofit educ institution founded to study the social history of New England's Afro American communities & to promote an awareness of that history by means of educational programs, publications, exhibits & special events. The African Meeting House, the Abiel Smith School, the African Meeting House on Nantucket, & the Black Heritage Trail are the chief artifacts of the mus of African American History; 2 galleries; Mem: 200; dues Frederick Douglass Society $1000, Maria Stewart society $500, national hist friends $125, family $50, $25, students & seniors $15
Income: Financed by grants, mem & donations
Library Holdings: Auction Catalogs; Book Volumes; Exhibition Catalogs; Maps; Memorabilia; Original Art Works; Pamphlets; Photographs; Prints; Reproductions; Sculpture; Video Tapes
Collections: 18 & 19th Century African American History; Hamilton Sutton Smith Glass Plate Negatives
Exhibitions: Rotating exhibits
Activities: Educ progs; classes for adults & children; lects open to pub; lectrs for mems only; 4 vis lectrs per yr; concerts; gallery talks; tours; individual sculptures & original objects of art lent; book traveling exhibs; mus shop sells books, magazines, original art, reproductions, prints, slides & gifts

M **MUSEUM OF FINE ARTS,** 465 Huntington Ave, Boston, MA 02115-5523. Tel 617-267-9300; Fax 617-247-6880; Elec Mail webmaster@mfa.org; Internet Home Page Address: www.mfa.org; *C&E Vermeule Cur & Keeper of Coins, Greek & Roman Art* Mary Comstock; *Cur Ancient Egyptian, Nubian, & Near Eastern Art* Mary Denise Doxey; *Cur Prints & Drawings* Stephanie Stepanek; *Cur Dec Arts & Sculpture* Marietta Cambareri; *Cur Textiles & Fashion Arts* Lauren Whitley; *Ellyn McColgan Cur Decorative Arts* Kelly L'Ecuyer; *Jean S & Frederic A Sharf Cur Design* Meghan Melvin; *Kristin & Roger Servison Cur Paintings* Karen Quinn; *Leonard A Lauder Cur Visual Culture* Benjamin Weiss; *Lynch Cur Decorative Arts & Sculpture* Dennis Carr; *Monica S Sadler Cur Provenance* Victoria Reed; *Mrs Russel W Baker Cur Paintings* Frederick Ilchman; *Pamela & Peter Voss Cur Prints & Drawings* Helen Burnham; *Rita J Kaplan Cur Jewelry* Yvonne Markowitz; *Ronald & Anita Wornick Cur Contemporary Decorative Arts* Emily Zilber; *Lane Coll Curator Photographs* Karen Haas; *William & Helen Pounds Sr Cur Japanese Art* Anne Morse; *Alfond Cur Educ* Barbara Martin; *Calderwood Sr Cur Egyptian Nubian & Near Eastern Art* Lawrence Berman; *Croll Sr Cur Paintings Art of the Americas* Erica Hirshler; *Dir/Cur NCAAA Art of the Americas* Edmund Gaither; *Estrellita & Yousuf Karsh Sr Cur Photographs* Anne Havinga; *George D & Margo Behrakis Sr Cur Greek & Roman Art* Christine Kondoleon; *Robert, Enid & Bruce Beal Sr Cur Contemporary Art* Jennifer Mergel; *Russel B & Andree Beauchamp Stearns Sr Cur DA&S* Thomas Michie; *Teal Sr Cur African & Oceanic Art* Christraud Geary; *Weems Sr Cur Decorative Arts & Sculpture AOA* Eleanore Gadsden; *William & Ann Elfers Sr Cur Paintings* Rhonda Baer; *Dept Head & Logie Cur Textiles & Fashion Arts* Pamela Parmal; *Pappalardo Cur Musical Instruments* Darcy Kuronen; *Cur Fashion Arts* Michelle Finamore; *Dir Exhib & Design* Patrick McMahon; *Dir MFA Publs* Emiko Usui; *Dir Bus Develop & Strategic Partnerships* Debra LaKind; *Hilles Dir Libraries & Archives* Maureen Melton
Open Mon - Tues & Sat - Sun 10 AM - 4:45 PM, Wed - Fri 10 AM - 9:45 PM, cl New Year's Day, Patriots Day, Independence Day Thanksgiving, Christmas Day; Admis adults $25, seniors (65+) & students (18+) $23, weekdays after 3 PM, weekends & Boston pub school holidays $10, youths (6 & under) no charge; Estab & incorporated in 1870; present building opened 1909; Average Annual Attendance: 1,200,000; Mem: 82,000; dues $75 - $3,000+
Special Subjects: Prints, Sculpture, Decorative Arts, Porcelain, Oriental Art, Silver, Period Rooms, Antiquities-Egyptian, Antiquities-Greek, Antiquities-Roman
Collections: Ancient Nubian & Near Eastern art; Art of Africa, Oceania & Ancient Americas; Chinese, Japanese & Indian art; Egyptian, Greek & Roman art; European & American decorative & minor arts, including period rooms, porcelains, silver, Western & Asian tapestries, costumes & musical instruments; master paintings of Europe & America; print coll from 15th century to present; sculpture
Exhibitions: Specially organized exhibitions are continually on view
Publications: (www.mfa.org/collections/publications)
Activities: Classes for adults & children; lects open to pub; concerts; gallery talks; tours; films; mus shop sells books, magazines, original art, reproductions, prints & slides

L **William Morris Hunt Memorial Library,** 300 Massachusetts Ave, Boston, MA 02115; 465 Huntington Ave, Boston, MA 02115-5523. Tel 617-369-3385; Fax 617-369-4257; Internet Home Page Address: www.mfa.org/library; *Dir Library & Archives* Maureen Melton; *Head Librn* Deborah Barlow Smedstad; *Mgr Technical Svcs* Laila Abdel-Malek; *Librn* Darin Murphy, SMFA
Open Mon-Fri 1 - 5 PM; No admis fee; Estab 1870 to house, preserve, interpret & publish its collections; Circ Non-circulating; For reference only; Average Annual Attendance: 1,000,000; Mem: 59,000
Income: Institution
Library Holdings: Auction Catalogs 50,000; Book Volumes 300,000; CD-ROMs; Clipping Files; Exhibition Catalogs; Fiche; Pamphlets 117,000; Periodical Subscriptions 650; Reels
Special Subjects: Decorative Arts, Drawings, Etchings & Engravings, Painting-American, Prints, Sculpture, Painting-European, Ceramics, Furniture, Mosaics, Carpets & Rugs, Restoration & Conservation, Textiles
Activities: Classes for adults & children; docent training; dramatic progs; lects open to pub; concerts; gallery talks; tours; book traveling exhibs

M **MUSEUM OF THE NATIONAL CENTER OF AFRO-AMERICAN ARTISTS,** 300 Walnut Ave, Boston, MA 02119-1369. Tel 617-442-8014; Fax 617-445-5525; Internet Home Page Address: www.ncaaa.org/museum.html; *Dir & Cur* Edmund B Gaither; *Asst to Dir* Gloretta Baynes; *Artistic Dir* Elma Lewis
Open Tues - Sun 1 - 5 PM; Admis adults $4, seniors & students $3; Estab 1969 to promote visual art heritage of Black people in the Americas and Africa; Suite of three special exhibition galleries; suite of three African Art Galleries; suite of three permanent collection galleries; one local artist gallery; Average Annual Attendance: 10,000; Mem: 250; dues $25
Income: $250,000 (financed by private gifts, contracts, etc)
Special Subjects: Afro-American Art
Collections: Early 19th & 20th Century Afro-American Prints & Drawings; visual fine arts of the black world; Caribbean Collection
Exhibitions: Aspelpa: A Nubian King's Buriel Chamber
Publications: Newsletter, quarterly
Activities: Dramatic progs; lects open to pub, 6 vis lectrs per yr; concerts; gallery talks; tours; competitions with awards (Edward Mitchell Barrister Award); book traveling exhibs; originates traveling exhibs; sales shop sells books, magazines, prints and small sculpture

M **NATIONAL ARCHIVES & RECORDS ADMINISTRATION,** John F Kennedy Presidential Library & Museum, Columbia Point, Boston, MA 02125. Tel 617-514-1600; Fax 617-514-1652; Internet Home Page Address: www.jfklibrary.org; *Dir* Thomas Putnam; *Deputy Dir* James Roth; *Cur* Stacey Bredhoff
Open daily 9 AM - 5 PM, cl holidays; Admis adults $12, seniors & college students $10, youth 13-17 $9, children 12 & under free; Estab 1964 to preserve collections of Kennedy papers & other material pertaining to his career; to educate public about J F Kennedy's career & political system; to make materials available to researchers; Library is a nine-story building overlooking Boston Harbor, has two theaters & an exhibition floor; Average Annual Attendance: 250,000
Income: Financed by federal government & national archives trust fund
Library Holdings: Audio Tapes; Book Volumes; Cards; Cassettes; Fiche; Filmstrips; Lantern Slides; Memorabilia; Micro Print; Motion Pictures; Original Art Works; Pamphlets; Photographs; Prints; Reproductions; Slides; Video Tapes
Special Subjects: Historical Material
Collections: 48,000,000 documents & personal papers of John F Kennedy, Robert Kennedy & many others assoc with life & career of John F Kennedy; 7,550,000 ft of film relating to political career, 200,000 photographs, 1300 oral histories, 22,000 paintings & museum objects (personal); manuscripts of Ernest Hemingway, 10,000 photographs of him with family & friends; 800 glass plates coll of Josiah Johnson Hawes
Activities: Classes for children; docent training; lects open to pub; 24 vis lectrs per yr; tours; Profiles in Courage awards; fels & research grants; mus shop sells books, reproductions, prints and slides

M **NICHOLS HOUSE MUSEUM, INC,** 55 Mount Vernon St, Boston, MA 02108-1330. Tel 617-227-6993; Fax 617-723-8026; Elec Mail info@nicholshousemuseum.org; Internet Home Page Address: www.nicholshousemuseum.org; *Historian* William H Pear; *Exec Dir* Flavia Cigliano; *Asst Dir* Mary Maresca
Open Apr 1 - Oct 31 Tues - Sat 10 AM - 4 PM, Nov 1 - Mar 31 Thurs - Sat 10 AM - 4 PM, cl most major holidays; Admis $7, children 12 & under free; Estab 1961; Historic house museum offers a unique glimpse of late 19th, early 20th century life of Boston's Beacon Hill; original federal design attributed to architect Charles Bulfinch; Average Annual Attendance: 3,000; Mem: 280; dues donor $250, sponsor $100, $35-55; annual meeting in May
Income: $133,000 (financed by endowment, admis sales, donations, grants, mem)
Special Subjects: Tapestries, Prints, Textiles, Decorative Arts, Furniture, Carpets & Rugs, Period Rooms
Collections: Decorative Arts Collection; Portraits; Oriental Rugs; Sculptures by Augustus Saint-Gaudens
Activities: Docent training; lects open to pub; tours; INLS 2002 Conservation Project; NEH 2002 Conservation Project; mus shop sells books

L **PAYETTE ASSOCIATES,** Library, 290 Congress St 5th Fl, Boston, MA 02210-1005. Tel 617-895-1000; Elec Mail info@payette.com; *Librn* Ardys Kozbial
Library Holdings: Book Volumes 1500; Clipping Files; Periodical Subscriptions 120; Slides
Special Subjects: Architecture
Collections: Interiors Sample Library; Manufacturer's Catalogs; Medical & Laboratory Planning

M **PHOTOGRAPHIC RESOURCE CENTER AT BOSTON UNIVERSITY,** 832 Commonwealth Ave, Boston, MA 02215-1205. Tel 617-975-0600; Fax 617-975-0606; Elec Mail info@prcboston.org; Internet Home Page Address: www.prcboston.org; *Exec Dir* Glenn Ruga; *Prog & Exhib Mgr* Evin Nederbrook Yuskaitis; *Mem, Finance & Opers Mgr* Julie Kukharenko; *Commun Mem Assoc* Laura Norris; *Cur & Loupe Ed* Francine Weiss
Open Tues - Fri 10 AM - 5 PM, Sat - noon - 4 PM, cl Sun & Mon; Admis: suggested donation $3, mems & students of mem schools no charge; Estab 1976; gallery added 1985; The PRC is a vital forum for the exploration, interpretation, celebration of new work, ideas & methods in photography; Mem: 1,000; dues $50
Library Holdings: Auction Catalogs; Book Volumes 4000; Clipping Files; Exhibition Catalogs; Periodical Subscriptions
Special Subjects: Photography, Historical Material
Publications: Loupe
Activities: Photography workshops with guest artists; classes for adults; lects open to pub, gallery talks; sponsoring of competitions; Leopold Godowsky Jr Color Photography Awards, every 4 yrs; mus shop sells books, original art & prints

M **ROBERT KLEIN GALLERY,** 38 Newbury St, 4th Fl Boston, MA 02116. Tel 617-267-7997; Fax 617-267-5567; Elec Mail inquiry@robertkleingallery.com; Internet Home Page Address: www.robertkleingallery.com; *Owner* Robert Klein; *Dir* Maja Orsic
Open Tues-Fri 10AM-5:30PM, Sat 11AM-5PM, other times by appointment; No admis fee; Estab 1980; Fine art photography gallery specializing in 19th century, 20th century & contemporary artists
Collections: photographs; photography books

A **THE SOCIETY OF ARTS & CRAFTS,** 175 Newbury St, Boston, MA 02116-2896. Tel 617-266-1810; Fax 617-266-5654; Elec Mail societycraft@earthlink.net; Internet Home Page Address: www.societyof crafts.org; *Exhib Mgr* Fabio J Fornandez; *Retail Gallery Mgr* George Summers; *Exec Dir* Beth Ann Gerstein
Open Mon - Fri 10 AM - 6 PM, Sat 10 AM - 6 PM, Sun Noon - 5 PM, cl Sun in Aug; No admis fee; Estab 1897 to promote high standards of excellence in crafts & to educate the pub in the appreciation of fine craftsmanship; Two galleries, second level exhibitions; Average Annual Attendance: 8,000; Mem: 700; dues family/dual $60, single $35
Income: financed by mem, gallery sales, grants
Exhibitions: Juried exhibitions presented year round;
Publications: Mass Crafts, guide to crafts in central New England, annual
Activities: Lect open to public, vis lectr; gallery talks; awards; sales shop sells fine handmade crafts in ceramics, wood, glass, metal & fiber

L **SUFFOLK UNIVERSITY,** (New England School of Art & Design at Suffolk University) New England School of Art & Design Library, 75 Arlington St, Boston, MA 02116-3936. Tel 617-994-4282; *Librn* Brian Tynemouth, MLS; *Libr Mgr* Ellen Sklaver
Open Mon - Thurs 9 AM - 9:30 PM, Fri 9 AM - 5 PM, Sat - Sun - 9 AM - 5:30 PM; Circ 4300; For lending; Mem: Open to students
Income: Financed by Suffolk Univ
Purchases: $28,000
Library Holdings: Book Volumes 10,000; CD-ROMs 203; Clipping Files; DVDs 173; Exhibition Catalogs; Pamphlets; Periodical Subscriptions 55; Slides 20,000; Video Tapes 147

Special Subjects: Art History, Landscape Architecture, Decorative Arts, Illustration, Commercial Art, Drawings, Graphic Design, Advertising Design, Interior Design, Furniture, Drafting, Architecture

A **URBANARTS INSTITUTE AT MASSACHUSETTS COLLEGE OF ART,** (UrbanArts, Inc) 621 Huntington Ave, Boston, MA 02115-5801. Tel 617-879-7000; Fax 617-879-7969; Elec Mail Christina.Lanzl@massart.edu; Internet Home Page Address: www.urbanartsinstitute.org; *Exec Dir* Ricardo Barreto; *Project Mgr* Christina Lanzl
Estab to provide services which integrate the arts into American Urban environments in the context of Urban design & community building
Income: Financed by pub & pvt foundations, donations, grants & Mass College of Art
Collections: Artist Registry: 2,000+ national & international artists listed
Activities: Educ progs; facilitation of public art projects; conferences & symposia; workshops

M **USS CONSTITUTION MUSEUM,** Bldg 22, Charlestown Navy Yard, Boston, MA 02129; PO Box 291812, Boston, MA 02129-0215. Tel 617-426-1812; Fax 617-242-0496; Elec Mail info@ussconstitutionmuseum.org; Internet Home Page Address: www.ussconstitutionmuseum.org; *Deputy Dir* Anne Gimes Rand; *Dir Educ* Michael Bonanno; *Exec Dir* Burt Logan; *Dir Educ* Celeste Bernardo; *Cir Corp Mems* Marianne Cohen; *Dir Retail Opers* Chris White; *Chmn, VPres* G West Saltonstall; *Cur* Margherita Desy; *Dir Finance & Admin* Adrian Bresler
Open 9 AM - 6 PM, varies by season, Nov 1 - Mid Apr 10 AM -5 PM; No admis fee (subject to change); Estab 1972 to collect, preserve & display items relating to the sailing frigate USS Constitution; Average Annual Attendance: 300,000; Mem: 2800; dues $35-$1000; annual meeting in the fall
Income: $1,850,000 (financed by endowment, mem, admis, gift shop, federal, state & private grants)
Special Subjects: Graphics, Photography, American Western Art, Costumes, Ceramics, Manuscripts, Portraits, Furniture, Marine Painting, Coins & Medals, Military Art
Collections: Documents relating to the sailing frigate USS Constitution; Personal possessions of crew members; Shipbuilding & navigational tools; Souvenirs depicting Old Ironsides; USS Constitution images (paintings, prints & photos); Historic naval uniforms; Naval weapons; USS Constitution models
Exhibitions: Around the World Aboard Old Ironsides; Old Ironsides in War & Peace; Annual Juried Ship Model Show
Publications: Chronicle, quarterly newsletter
Activities: Classes for adults & children; dramatic progs; family progs; docent training; summer teen internship prog; teachers' workshops; lects open to pub, 6-12 vis lectrs per yr; tours; originate traveling exhibs; sales store sells books, prints, magazines, slides, reproductions, clothing, souvenirs & sponsors book signings

M **VILLA VICTORIA CENTER FOR THE ARTS,** 85 W Newton St, Boston, MA 02118-1523. Tel 617-927-1707; Fax 617-236-7375; *Contact* Javier Torres

A **VOLUNTEER LAWYERS FOR THE ARTS OF MASSACHUSETTS INC,** 249 A St, Studio 14 Boston, MA 02210-1615. Tel 617-350-7600; Fax 617-350-7610; Elec Mail mail@vlama.org; Internet Home Page Address: www.vlama.org; *Exec Dir* James F Grace
Open Mon - Fri 9 AM - 5 PM; Estab 1989 to provide arts related legal assistance to artists & arts organizations
Income: Financed in part by the Massachusetts Cultural Council, a state agency & by the Boston Bar Assoc
Activities: Lect open to public; legal referral program

L **WENTWORTH INSTITUTE OF TECHNOLOGY LIBRARY,** 550 Huntington Ave, Boston, MA 02115-5998. Tel 617-989-4040; Fax 617-989-4091; Elec Mail punchw@admin.wit.edu; Internet Home Page Address: www.wit.edu/library; *Dir* Walter Punch; *Reference* Pia Romano; *Architectural Librn* Priscilla Biondi; *Circ Librn* Dan O'Connell; *Access Mgr* Kurt Oliver; *Asst Dir* Marianne Thibodean
Open Mon - Thurs 7:45 AM - 11 PM, Fri 7:45 AM - 5:30 PM, Sat 7:45 AM - 6 PM, Sun 11 AM - 10 PM; No admis fee
Library Holdings: Audio Tapes; Book Volumes 75,000; Clipping Files; DVDs; Memorabilia; Micro Print; Periodical Subscriptions 600; Photographs; Video Tapes
Special Subjects: Art History, Landscape Architecture, Historical Material, Industrial Design, Interior Design, Drafting, Architecture

BROCKTON

L **BROCKTON PUBLIC LIBRARY SYSTEM,** Joseph A Driscoll Art Gallery, 304 Main St, Brockton, MA 02301-5300. Tel 508-580-7890; Fax 508-580-7898; Elec Mail lshannon@ocln.org; Internet Home Page Address: www.brocktonpubliclibrary.org; *Dir* Harry R Williams III; *Head Adult Serv* Lucia M Shannon
Open Mon, Tues noon - 8 PM, Wed & Thurs 9 AM - 5 PM, Fri noon - 5 PM, Sat 9 AM - 5 PM; No admis fee; Estab 1913; Special room for monthly art exhibitions; Average Annual Attendance: 20,000
Library Holdings: Book Volumes 258,768
Collections: W C Bryant Collection of 19th & 20th century American paintings, chiefly by New England artists; gifts of 20th century paintings which includes four paintings by Hendricks Hallett & an oil painting by Mme Elisabeth Weber-Fulop; loan coll of 20th century painters from the Woman's Club of Brockton; mounted photographs of Renaissance art & watercolors by F Mortimer Lamb
Exhibitions: Monthly exhibitions by local & nationally known artists

M **FULLER CRAFT MUSEUM,** 455 Oak St, Brockton, MA 02301-1340. Tel 508-588-6000; Fax 508-587-6191; Elec Mail director@fullercraft.org; Internet Home Page Address: www.fullercraft.org/; *Dir* Wyona Lynch-McWhite; *Asst Cur* Perry Price; *Dir Educ* Noelle Foye; *CFO* Martin Gredinger
Open Tues - Sun 10 AM - 5 PM, Wed 10 AM - 9 PM; Admis adults $8, seniors & students $5, mem & children 12 & under Free, Wed 5 - 9 PM Free; Estab 1969 to provide a variety of craft exhibitions & educ programs of regional & national

interest; The center houses six galleries; Average Annual Attendance: 23,000; Mem: Mem: 2,000
Income: $784,000 (financed by endowment, mem, gifts & government grants)
Special Subjects: Collages, Metalwork, Textiles, Tapestries, Drawings, Graphics, Painting-American, Photography, Prints, Sculpture, Watercolors, African Art, Pre-Columbian Art, Ceramics, Crafts, Pottery, Woodcarvings, Woodcuts, Etchings & Engravings, Decorative Arts, Portraits, Furniture, Glass, Jewelry, Silver, Carpets & Rugs, Miniatures, Embroidery, Laces, Mosaics, Stained Glass, Leather, Enamels, Bookplates & Bindings
Collections: Contemporary American art; Early American & Sandwich glass; contemporary regional crafts; Sandwich Glass Collection
Exhibitions: Avg 12 exhibs organized per yr
Publications: Quarterly newsletter & calendar of events
Activities: Classes for adults & children; dramatic progs; docent training; special progs for children; lects, open to pub & mem only, 4 vis lectrs per yr; gallery talks; tours; concerts; individual paintings & original objects of art lent to accredited mus of the American Assn of Museums; lending collection contains paintings & art; book traveling exhibs 2 per yr; originate traveling exhibs 2 per yr; mus shop sells book, original art, reproductions, prints, contemporary crafts, t-shirts & mugs

L **Library,** 455 Oak St, Brockton, MA 02301-1340. Tel 508-588-6000; Fax 508-587-6191; Internet Home Page Address: www.fullermuseum.org; *Exec Dir* Wyona Lynch-McWhite
Open to members, staff & students
Library Holdings: Book Volumes 500; Exhibition Catalogs; Pamphlets

BROOKLINE

M **GATEWAY ARTS GALLERIES,** 62 Harvard St, Brookline, MA 02445. Tel 617-734-1577; Fax 617-734-3199; Elec Mail gatewayarts@vinfen.org; Internet Home Page Address: www.gatewayarts.org

CAMBRIDGE

A **CAMBRIDGE ART ASSOCIATION,** 25 Lowell St, Cambridge, MA 02138-4725. Tel 617-876-0246; Fax 617-876-1880; Elec Mail info@cambridgeart.org; Internet Home Page Address: www.cambridgeart.org; *Dir* Kathryn Schultz; *Dir Sales & Rental* Susan Vrotsus; *Asst to Dir* Jodi Hays Gresham
Open Mon - Fri 9 AM - 6 PM, Sun 9 - 1 PM, cl Aug; No admis fee; Estab 1944 to exhibit, rent & sell members' work & to encourage an interest in fine arts & crafts in the community; 2 gallery spaces located in & near Harvard Sq; Mem: 575; dues artist $75, friends $40, students $15; jury of artist mems meets 4 times per yr to review work, slides & resumes
Income: Financed by dues, sale of art, annual appeal & endowment
Exhibitions: Invited shows in Rental Gallery & Craft Gallery; foreign exhibition each year; members' juried exhibitions in Main Gallery every month; National Prize Show (June)
Publications: Newsletter, quarterly
Activities: Classes for members; lect & demonstrations; competitions with prizes

M **CAMBRIDGE ARTS COUNCIL,** CAC Gallery, 344 Broadway, 2nd fl, Cambridge, MA 02139. Tel 617-349-4380; Fax 617-349-4669; Elec Mail hsu@mlittman@cambridgema.gov; Internet Home Page Address: www.cambridgeartscouncil.org; *Exec Dir* Jason Weeks; *Dir Pub Art* Lillian Hsu; *Dir Community Arts* Julie Madden; *Dir Mktg & Pub Rels* Mara Littman; *Pub Arts Admin* Jeremy Gaucher
Open Mon & Wed 8:30 AM - 8 PM, Tues & Thurs 8:30 AM - 5 PM, Fri 8:30 AM - Noon; No admis fee; Estab 1974 by city ordinance & inc 1976 as public nonprofit. As the official arts agency for the City of Cambridge, MA, it's mission is to ensure arts remain vital for people living, working & vis Cambridge.; Exhibs are designed to support and present the work of local, national and international artists and explore the relationship between visual art, pub art and civic dialogue; Average Annual Attendance: 2,500
Exhibitions: 6-8 exhibitions annually; Exhibition focus: contemporary public art & community engagement
Activities: Progs for Public Art Youth Council; Lect open to pub; gallery talks; tours; rotating collection to municipal bldgs & offices only

L **CAMBRIDGE HISTORICAL COMMISSION,** (City of Cambridge Historical Commission) Research Library on Architectural Social History of Cambridge, Mass, 831 Massachusetts Ave, 2nd Floor, Cambridge, MA 02139. Tel 617-349-4683; Fax 617-349-3116; Elec Mail histcomm@cambridgema.gov; Internet Home Page Address: www.cambridgema.gov/historic; *Dir* Charles M Sullivan; *Preservation-Planner* Sarah L Burks; *Dir Survey* Susan E Maycock; *Asst Dir* Kathleen L Rawlins; *Archival* Katherine Gyllensvard; *Oral Historian* Sarah Boyer; *Preservation Adminr* Eiliesh Tuffy
Open Mon 8:30 AM - 8 PM, Tues - Thurs 8:30 AM - 5 PM, Fri 8:30 Am - noon, research by appointment; No admis fee; Estab 1963
Income: $490,000 (financed by city appropriation)
Library Holdings: Book Volumes 1000; Clipping Files; Kodachrome Transparencies; Manuscripts; Maps; Memorabilia; Original Art Works; Original Documents; Pamphlets; Periodical Subscriptions; Photographs; Prints; Slides
Special Subjects: Architecture
Collections: Architectural & social history of Cambridge
Publications: Cambridgeport (1971); Northwest Cambridge (1977); Photographic History of Cambridge (1984); East Cambridge (1988); Crossroads: Stories of Central Square, 1912-2000 (2001); All in the Same Boat: 20th century stories of adults of East Cambridge (2005)
Activities: Educ dept; offsite lectrs & tours for children; Cambridge Historical Commission Preservation Recognition Program; historic preservation grants to nonprofit institutions; lects open to pub; tours; mus sells prints, slides

M **HARVARD UNIVERSITY,** Harvard University Art Museums, Cambridge, MA 02138-3845. Tel 617-495-9400; Fax 617-495-9936; Elec Mail huam@fas.harvard.edu; Internet Home Page Address: www.artmuseums.harvard.edu; *Deputy Dir* Richard Benefield; *Registrar* Maureen Donovan; *Mem, Dir Fellows & Spec Prog* Mary Rose Bolton; *Visitor Servs* Margaret Howland; *Dir Straus Center Conservation* Henry Lie; *Pub Rels* Matthew Barone; *Acting Dir* Marjorie B Cohn
Open Tues - Sat 10 AM - 5 PM, Sun 1 - 5 PM, cl national holidays; Admis (applies to all three museums) adults $9, seniors $7, students $6, children under 18 & mems free; Estab 1895; 225,000 vol fine arts library (Fogg Art Mus) & Rubel Asiatic Research Collection (Sackler) available for use by request only; extensive visual collection; reading room; classrooms; Average Annual Attendance: 129,898; Mem: 2,700; dues corporate/institutional $1,000-$10,000, patron $1,000, Forbes fellow $500, contributor $100, junior fellow (ages 21-40) $100, family $50, individual $35, students & seniors $25, admis only $20
Income: Financed by endowment, mem & federal grants
Collections: European and North American painting, prints and photography (Fogg Museum; Ancient, Asian & Islamic and Indian art (Sackler Museum); German Expressionist painting (Busch Reisinger Museum)
Publications: Director's report, quarterly newsletter; exhibit catalogs; gallery guides
Activities: Classes for adults & children; docent training; lects open to pub; gallery talks; tours; seminars; concerts; mus shop sells books, magazines, reproductions & prints

—**Busch-Reisinger Museum,** 32 Quincy St, Cambridge, MA 02138-3836; 485 Broadway, Cambridge, MA 02138. Tel 617-495-9400; Fax 617-495-9936; Elec Mail am_webmaster@harvard.edu; Internet Home Page Address: www.harvardartmuseums.org; *Acting Cur* Linda Muir; *Cur Asst* Joanna Wendel; *Cur Intern* Clelia Pozzi
Open Mon - Sat 10 AM - 5 PM, Sun 1 - 5 PM, cl national holidays; Admis adults $9, seniors $7, students $6, under 18 & Sat AM free; Estab 1901 & opened in 1920, it has one of most important & extensive collections of Central & European art outside of Europe, ranging from the Romanesque to the present day. This coll serves the teaching prog of the Dept of Fine Arts, outside scholars & the gen pub; Werner Otto Hall contains 7 galleries, 6 for German Art (1880-1980), 1 for rotating exhibits; Average Annual Attendance: 83,696; Mem: 2,700; dues individual $35
Special Subjects: Painting-European, Renaissance Art, Sculpture
Collections: 18th Century Painting Coll; Late Medieval, Renaissance & Baroque Sculpture Coll; 16th Century Porcelain Coll; 20th Century German Works Coll; largest coll of Bauhaus material outside Germany; drawings; paintings; prints; sculpture
Publications: Newsletter
Activities: Classes for children; lects open to pub; concerts; gallery talks; tours; symposia; individual paintings & original objects of art lent to other museums, considered on request; book traveling exhibs 1-2 per yr; originate traveling exhibs; Mus shop sells books, reproductions, prints & small gift items

—**William Hayes Fogg Art Museum,** 32 Quincy St, Cambridge, MA 02138-3883. Tel 617-495-9400; Fax 617-495-9936; Elec Mail artmuseums@fas.harvard.edu; *Deputy Dir* Frances A Beane; *Cur Drawings* William W Robinson; *Cur Prints* Marjorie B Cohn; *Cur Painting* Ivan Gaskell; *Dir* James Cuno
Open Mon - Sat 10 AM - 5 PM, Sun 1 - 5 PM, cl national holidays; Admis adults $5, seniors $4, students $3, Sat AM free; University estab 1891; mus estab 1927; serves both as a pub mus & as a laboratory for Harvard's Dept of Fine Arts, which trains art history mus professionals; The Straus Center for Conservation operates a training program for conservators & technical specialists; Average Annual Attendance: 83,696; Mem: 2,700; dues $35 & up
Income: Financed by endowment, mem & federal grants
Special Subjects: Painting-European, Antiquities-Egyptian, Antiquities-Greek, Antiquities-Oriental, Antiquities-Roman, Bronzes, Ceramics, Decorative Arts, Drawings, Jade, Painting-American, Photography, Prints, Sculpture, Silver
Collections: Maurice Wertheim Collection of Impressionist & Post-Impressionist Art; European & American paintings, sculpture, decorative arts, photographs, prints & drawings; English & American silver; Wedgwood
Exhibitions: (Permanent) Circa 1874: The Emergence of Impressionism; France & The Portrait, 1799-1870; Subliminations: Art & Sensuality in the Nineteenth Century.
Publications: Annual report; newsletter, 4 - 5 per year
Activities: Docent training; lects open to pub; concerts; gallery talks; tours; individual paintings & original objects of art lent to other museums, considered on individual basis; book traveling exhibs 1-2 per yr; originate traveling exhibs; Mus shop sells books, reproductions, prints & small gift items

—**Arthur M Sackler Museum,** 485 Broadway, Cambridge, MA 02138-3845. Tel 617-495-9400; Fax 617-495-9936; Elec Mail artmuseums@fas.harvard.edu; *Deputy Dir* Frances A Beane; *Cur Chinese Art* Robert Mowry; *Cur Ancient Art* David Gordon Mitten; *Dir* James Cuno
Open Mon - Sat 10 AM - 5 PM, Sun 1 - 5 PM; Admis adults $9, seniors $7, Students $6; Estab 1985 to serve both as a pub mus & a laboratory for Harvard's Dept of Fine Arts, which trains art historians & mus professionals
Special Subjects: Antiquities-Egyptian, Bronzes, Ceramics, Jade, Prints, Sculpture, Asian Art, Islamic Art, Jewelry, Manuscripts, Metalwork, Textiles
Collections: Ancient coins; Asian bronzes, ceramics, jades, painting, prints & sculpture; Egyptian antiquities; Greek red & black figure vases; Greek & Roman bronze & marble sculpture; Greek, Roman & Near Eastern jewelry & metalwork; Islamic & Indian ceramics, illuminated manuscripts; metalwork, paintings & textiles
Exhibitions: (Permanent) Serveran Silver Coinage
Activities: Mus shop sells books, prints & reproductions

L **Fine Arts Library,** 1805 Cambridge St, Littauer Ctr Harvard University North Yard Cambridge, MA 02138-3001. Tel 617-495-3373; Fax 617-496-4889; Elec Mail altenhof@fas.harvard.edu; Internet Home Page Address: http://hcl.harvard.edu/libraries/finearts/
Open to Harvard Community Mon - Thurs 9 AM - 10 PM, Fri 9 AM - 6 PM, Sat 10 AM - 5 PM, Sun 1-6 PM during school yr

L **Frances Loeb Library,** 48 Quincy St, Graduate School of Design - Gund Hall Cambridge, MA 02138-3000. Tel 617-495-9163; Fax 617-496-5929; Internet Home Page Address: www.gsd.harvard.edu/loeb_library; *Librn* Hugh Wilburn
Open Mon - Thurs 8:30 AM - 10 PM, Fri 8:30 AM - 6 PM, Sat 10 AM - 6 PM, Sun noon - 8 PM; Estab 1900 to serve faculty & students of graduate school of design; Circ 55,000
Income: $1,100,000 (financed by endowment & tuition)
Purchases: $208,381
Library Holdings: Audio Tapes 350; Book Volumes 266,852; Cassettes 326; Clipping Files; Exhibition Catalogs; Fiche; Filmstrips 65; Kodachrome Transparencies; Lantern Slides; Manuscripts; Memorabilia; Motion Pictures; Original Art Works; Other Holdings Drawings; Pamphlets; Periodical Subscriptions 1100; Photographs; Records; Reels; Slides 169,515; Video Tapes
Special Subjects: Architecture
Collections: Cluny Collection; Curutchet Collection (Le Corbusier's built works); Edward Larrabee Barnes Collection; Charles Elliot Collection; Daniel Kiley Collection; John C Olmsted Collection; H H Richardson Collection; Charles Mulford Robinson Collection; Hugh Stubbins Collection; Joseph Luis Sert Collection; Jesse Tarbox Beals Photographic Collection; Richard Marsh Bennett Collection; John S Bolles Collection; Walter Frances Bogner Collection; Grady E Clay Collection; Arthur Coleman Comey Papers; George Roseborough Collins Collection in Linear City Planning; CIAM Collection; Arland Augustus Dirlam Architectural Drawings Collection; Robin Evans Collection; Jorge Ferrari Hardoy Collection
Activities: Tours

M **Semitic Museum,** 6 Divinity Ave, Cambridge, MA 02138-2020. Tel 617-495-4631; Fax 617-496-8904; Elec Mail semiticm@fas.harvard.edu; Internet Home Page Address: www.fas.harvard.edu./~semitic; *Asst Dir* Joseph A Greene; *Asst Cur* Adam Aja; *Cur Cuneiform Coll* Piotr Steinkeller; *Dir* Lawrence Stager; *Dir Publ* Michael Coogan
Open Mon - Fri 10 AM - 4 PM, Sun 1 - 4 PM, cl Sat & holiday weekends; No admis fee, donations accepted; Estab 1889 to promote sound knowledge of Semitic languages & history; an archaeological research mus; Average Annual Attendance: 3,000-5,000; Mem: 250; dues $35 & up
Income: Financed by endowment, mem, private research grants, gifts
Special Subjects: Archaeology, Costumes, Antiquities-Byzantine, Coins & Medals, Antiquities-Persian, Islamic Art, Antiquities-Egyptian, Antiquities-Greek, Antiquities-Roman
Collections: Excavated archaeological & excavation archives materials from Egypt, Mesopotamia, Syria-Palestine, Cyprus, Arabia, North Africa; ethnographic coll (Ottoman period)
Exhibitions: Ancient Cyprus: The Cesnola Collection; Nuzi & The Hurrians: Fragments from a Forgotten Past; The Houses of Ancient Israel: Domestic, Royal, Divine; Ancient Egypt: Magic and the Afterlife
Publications: Harvard Semitic Series; exhibit catalogs; Harvard Semitic Monographs; Semitic Museum Newsletter; Studies in the Archaeology & History of the Levant
Activities: Classes for adults & children; docent training; teacher workshop; lect-film series; tours; lects open to pub, 4-6 vis lectrs per yr; gallery talks; tours; children's vacation prog; scholarships offered; exten dept serves Harvard University; original objects of art lent to universities & museums; Mus shop sells books, reproductions & magazines

M **LONGFELLOW NATIONAL HISTORIC SITE,** Longfellow House - Washington's Headquarters, 105 Brattle St, Cambridge, MA 02138-3407. Tel 617-876-4491; Fax 617-497-8718; Elec Mail FRLA_longfellow@nps.gov; Internet Home Page Address: www.nps.gov/long; *Coll Mgr* David Daly; *Supt* Myra Harrison; *Site Mgr* Beth Wear; *Park Ranger* Rick Jenkins; *Park Ranger* Garrett Cloer
Open daily 10 AM - 4:30 PM; No admis fee; Estab 1972 to acquaint the pub with the life, work & time of the American poet Henry W Longfellow & as a memorial to George Washington; Average Annual Attendance: 40,000
Income: Financed by US Department of the Interior
Library Holdings: Book Volumes; Manuscripts; Memorabilia; Original Art Works; Original Documents; Pamphlets; Photographs; Prints; Sculpture
Special Subjects: Period Rooms
Collections: Paintings, sculpture, prints, letters, furniture & furnishings once belonging to Henry W Longfellow & his daughter Alice; 19th century photographic coll including views of China & Japan; American, European & Asian Colls
Activities: Classes for adults & children; lect open to public; 5 vis lectrs per yr; concerts; tours; gallery talks; fels; individual paintings & original objects of art lent to qualified institutions; mus shop sells books, reproduction & slides

M **MASSACHUSETTS INSTITUTE OF TECHNOLOGY,** List Visual Arts Center, 20 Ames St, Wiesner Bldg E 15 - 109 Cambridge, MA 02142-1308. Tel 617-253-4680; Fax 617-258-7265; Elec Mail hiroco@mit.edu; Internet Home Page Address: www.mit.edu/lvac; *Cur* Bill Arning; *Registrar* John Rexine; *Admin Officer* David Freilach; *Gallery Mgr* Tim Lloyd; *Dir* Jane Farver; *Pub Art Cur* Kathleen Goncharov; *Educ/Outreach Coordr* Hiroko Kikuchi
Open Tues - Sun Noon - 6 PM, Fri Noon - 8 PM; No admis fee; Estab 1963 to organize exhibitions of contemporary art in all media; Contemporary Art gallery; Average Annual Attendance: 15,000
Income: Financed by MIT, pub & private endowments, art councils, corporations & individuals
Special Subjects: Drawings, Painting-American, Photography, Prints, Sculpture
Collections: Major public sculpture, paintings, drawings, prints, photographs & site-specific commissions all publicly sited through the campus. All collections are being enlarged through donations & purchases
Exhibitions: Six - eight exhibitions per year of contemporary art in all mediums
Publications: Exhibition catalogs, artists' books
Activities: Educ Dept; tours; films; lects open to pub, 10 vis lectrs per yr; gallery talks; Vera List Prize for Writing on the Visual Arts; lending collection of original art to student, faculty & admin staff; Student Loan Print Collection of over 300 pieces; book traveling exhibs 2 per yr; originate traveling exhibs to major mus 2 per yr; mus shop sells exhibs catalogues

M **MIT Museum,** 265 Massachusetts Ave, Bldg N51 Cambridge, MA 02139. Tel 617-253-4444, 5927; Fax 617-253-8994; Elec Mail museum@mit.edu; Internet

Home Page Address: web.mit.edu/museum; *Dir* John Durant; *Assoc Dir* Mary Leen; *Cur Hart Nautical Coll* Kurt Hasselbalch; *Cur Science & Technology* Deborah Douglas; *Registrar* Joan Whitlow; *Cur Architecture & Design* Gary Van Zante; *Mgr Exhibs* Donald Stidsen; *Emerging Technologies Coordr* Seth Riskin; *Dir Cambridge Science Festival* PA J'Arbeloff; *Dir Pub Rel & Mktg* Josie Patterson; *Dir Programs* Robin Melsner
Open Daily 10 AM - 5 PM; Admis for people outside MIT community adults $7.50, youth 5-17, students & seniors $3, Sun 10 AM - noon free; Estab 1971 as a mus facility to document, interpret & communicate the activities & achievements of MIT; Main exhibition facility & two campus galleries; Average Annual Attendance: 100,000; Mem: not applicable
Income: Financed by University, outside funding & earned income
Special Subjects: Architecture, Photography, Watercolors, Portraits, Marine Painting, Historical Material, Maps
Collections: Architectural drawings; biographical information; holograms; maritime; objects d'art; paintings; photographs; portraits; scientific instruments & apparatus; Nautical Prints
Publications: Gallery exhibition notes; collection catalogs
Activities: Progs for adults, children & families, after school camps; lects open to pub, 1-2 vis lectrs per yr; gallery talks; tours; individual paintings & original works lent to other mus; originate traveling exhibs; mus shop sells books, prints, MIT - & exhibit-related items, toys, games & gift items
—**Hart Nautical Galleries & Collections,** 55 Massachusetts Ave, Cambridge, MA 02139; 265 Massachusetts Ave, Cambridge, MA 02139. Tel 617-253-5942; Fax 617-258-9107; Elec Mail kurt@mit.edu; Internet Home Page Address: http://web.mit.edu/museum/; *Cur* Kurt Hasselbalch
Gallery open daily 9 AM - 7 PM; reference Mon - Fri 10 AM - 5 PM by appointment only; Estab 1922 to preserve history of naval architecture, shipbuilding & related nautical technology; Galleries include permanent exhibit of ship models & MIT Ocean Engineering exhibit; Average Annual Attendance: 16,000
Income: Financed by University & pvt gifts
Special Subjects: Maps, Marine Painting
Activities: Individual paintings & original objects of art lent to qualified mus; lending collection contains prints, slides & models; mus shop sells books

L **Rotch Library of Architecture & Planning,** 77 Massachusetts Ave, Rm 7-238, Cambridge, MA 02139-4307. Tel 617-258-5592, 258-5599; Fax 617-253-9331; Internet Home Page Address: www.mit.edu; *Head of GIS* Lisa Sweeney; *Librn Urban Studies, Planning & Real Estate* Peter Cohn; *Librn Architecture & Visual Arts* Jolene De Verges; *Librn Architecture & Visual Arts* Jennifer Friedman; *Librn Urban Studies & Planning* Heather McCann; *Librn Aga Khan Prog* Omar Khalidi; *Aga Khan Cataloger* Yahya Melhem
Open Mon - Thurs 8:30 AM - 11 PM, Fri 8:30 AM - 7 PM, Sat 1 - 6 PM, Sun 2 - 10 PM; Mon - Fri 10 AM - 6 PM when school is not in session; Estab 1868 to serve the students & faculty of the School of Architecture & Planning & other members of the MIT community
Library Holdings: Audio Tapes; Book Volumes 236,873; CD-ROMs; Cassettes; Compact Disks; DVDs 619; Exhibition Catalogs; Fiche; Kodachrome Transparencies; Lantern Slides; Maps 3,000; Motion Pictures; Original Documents; Pamphlets 33,000; Periodical Subscriptions 1944; Photographs; Reels; Slides; Video Tapes
Special Subjects: Art History, Landscape Architecture, Film, Illustration, Photography, Drawings, Graphic Arts, Graphic Design, Islamic Art, Maps, Painting-American, Painting-British, Painting-German, Sculpture, Painting-European, Historical Material, History of Art & Archaeology, Conceptual Art, Latin American Art, Printmaking, Industrial Design, Interior Design, Video, Drafting, Glass, Stained Glass, Architecture

A **MOBIUS INC,** 55 Norfolk St, Cambridge, MA 02139-2614. Tel 617-945-9481; Elec Mail info@mobius.org; Internet Home Page Address: www.mobius.org

CHATHAM

M **CHATHAM HISTORICAL SOCIETY,** The Atwood House Museum, 347 Stage Harbor Rd, Chatham, MA 02633; PO Box 709, Chatham, MA 02633-0709. Tel 508-945-2493; Fax 508-945-1205; Elec Mail info@chathamhistorical.org; Internet Home Page Address: www.chathamhistoricalsociety.org; *Chmn* John J King; *Exec Dir* Mark Wilkins; *Admin* Margaret Martin; *Head Archivist* Mary Ann Gray
Open June, Sept & Oct Tues - Sat 1 - 4 PM; July & Aug, Tues - Fri 10 AM - 4 PM, Sat 1 - 4 PM; Admis $6, students 7 - 18 $3, members & children under 7 free; Estab 1923 to preserve local Chatham history; Murals Barn houses Alice Stallknecht murals of Chatham people, Portrait Gallery houses Frederick Wight paintings of local sea captains; Fishing Gallery offers paintings by Harold Brett, Frederick Wight; Atwood House houses Giddings Ballou portraits; Average Annual Attendance: 3,700; Mem: 950; ann meeting in Aug
Income: Financed by mem dues, donations & grants
Purchases: Local historical artifacts & paintings
Library Holdings: Book Volumes; DVDs; Manuscripts; Maps; Original Art Works; Pamphlets; Periodical Subscriptions; Photographs; Video Tapes
Special Subjects: Decorative Arts, Drawings, Folk Art, Landscapes, Architecture, Ceramics, Glass, Photography, Painting-American, Textiles, Manuscripts, Watercolors, Costumes, Religious Art, Pottery, Woodcarvings, Portraits, Dolls, Furniture, Porcelain, Marine Painting, Carpets & Rugs, Historical Material, Ivory, Maps, Scrimshaw, Period Rooms, Embroidery, Stained Glass
Collections: Giddings Ballou portraits, Harold Brett, paintings; Harold Dunbar, Wendell Rogers paintings; Frederick Wight, paintings; Sandwich Glass; 17th & 18th century furnishings; antique tools; china; items brought back by Chatham sea captains; maritime paintings; ship models; Crowell miniature decoys & sea shells from around the world; Parian Ware, Sandwich glass, Transfer ware; map & sea charts; Alice Stallknecht murals; fishing equipment; lantern room with Freshnel lens
Exhibitions: Exhibits change every year
Publications: The Atwood log, quarterly newsletter; Three Centuries in a Cape Cod Village
Activities: Classes for adults & children; Docent training; talks & slideshows; lects open to pub; 9 vis lectrs per yr; tours; gallery talks; Ann Bringing History to Life Award; mus shop sells books, reproductions, prints & gifts

CHESTNUT HILL

M **BOSTON COLLEGE,** McMullen Museum of Art, 140 Commonwealth, Devlin Hall 108 Chestnut Hill, MA 02467-3800. Tel 617-552-8587; Fax 617-552-8577; Elec Mail artmuseum@bc.edu; *Media Specialist* John McCoy; *Dir* Nancy Netzer; *Designer & Collections Mgr* Diana Larsen; *Publications & Exhibs Admin* Margaret Neeley
Open Mon - Fri 11 AM - 4 PM, Sat & Sun noon - 5 PM; No admis fee; Estab 1986 to enhance the teaching mission of the University & extend it to a wider audience; Two floors; flexible galleries; Maintains lending & reference library; Average Annual Attendance: 50,000; Mem: 200; dues $50 & up
Income: Financed through University funds & donations
Collections: Old Master Paintings, Modern, Irish Paintings, American Art
Exhibitions: Rotating exhibitions
Publications: Catalogues
Activities: Classes for adults; docent training; lects open to pub, 10 vis lectrs per yr; concerts; gallery talks; tours; scholarships offered; individual paintings & original objects of art lent to other exhibs; book traveling exhibs 3 per yr; originates traveling exhibs to other museums

COHASSET

M **COHASSET HISTORICAL SOCIETY,** Pratt Building (Society Headquarters), 106 S Main St, Cohasset, MA 02025; PO Box 627, Cohasset, MA 02025-0627. Tel 781-383-1434; Fax 781-383-1190; Elec Mail cohassethistory@yahoo.com; Internet Home Page Address: www.cohassethistoricalsociety.org; *Exec Dir* Lynne DeGiacomo; *Historian* David Wadsworth; *Pres* Kathleen L O'Malley
Headquarters open Mon - Fri 10 AM - 4 PM; Admis by donations; Estab 1928 ; Paintings & artifacts of local significance are displayed in various rooms; Cohasset Historical Society's library & archives, costumes, textile coll located here; Average Annual Attendance: 2,000; Mem: 400; dues sustaining $50, family $35, single $25; annual meetings in Oct & Apr
Library Holdings: Book Volumes 1000; DVDs 100; Lantern Slides 100; Manuscripts 50; Maps 100; Memorabilia 5000; Original Art Works 50; Original Documents 5000; Pamphlets 50; Periodical Subscriptions 5; Photographs 3500; Slides 1000; Video Tapes 25
Special Subjects: Historical Material, Ceramics, Furniture, Painting-American, Manuscripts, Maps, Textiles, Costumes, Decorative Arts, Dolls, Marine Painting, Dioramas, Embroidery
Collections: Works of art; historical artifacts & archives; costumes; textiles; theatre; Maritime Museum located at 4 Elm St., Cohasset; Historic House at 4 Elm St, Cohasset
Exhibitions: Dec Christmas Exhibit; Two additional exhibits per year
Publications: Historical Highlights, newsletter 4 times per yr; Images of America; Cohasset (2004)
Activities: Lect open to public Sept - Jun, 6 vis lectrs per yr; tours; mus shop sells books

M **Cohasset Maritime Museum,** 4 Elm St, Cohasset, MA 02025; 106 S Main St, Cohasset, MA 02025. Tel 781-383-1434; Fax 781-383-1190; Elec Mail cohassethistory@yahoo.com; Internet Home Page Address: www.cohassethistoricalsociety.org; *Historian* David H Wadsworth; *Exec Dir* Lynne DeGiacomo; *Pres* Kathleen L O'Malley
Open - June 20 - Labor Day Wed - Fri 1 PM - 4 PM, Sat 10 AM - 2 PM; Admis by donation; Estab 1957 to display the seafaring history of Cohasset; Average Annual Attendance: 800; Mem: 370
Special Subjects: Portraits, Marine Painting, Historical Material
Collections: Local maritime history, fishing gear of 19th century, ship models, lifesaving, shipwreck memorabilia, pictures & charts

M **Captain John Wilson Historical House,** 4 Elm St, Cohasset, MA 02025. Tel 781-383-1434; Fax 781-383-1190; Elec Mail cohassethistory@yahoo.com; Internet Home Page Address: cohassethistoricalsociety.org; *Pres* Kathleen L O'Malley; *Exec Admin* Lynne DeGiacomo
Open mid-June - Labor Day 1:30 - 4:30 PM, cl Sat, Sun, Mon; No admis fee - Donations welcome; Estab 1928; Historic house mus; Average Annual Attendance: 1,000; Mem: 400; Dues - sustaining $50, family $35, single $25
Income: Financed by dues, donations & grants, in-kind serv & goods
Library Holdings: Auction Catalogs; Book Volumes 200; Clipping Files; Lantern Slides; Manuscripts; Maps; Memorabilia; Original Art Works; Original Documents; Other Holdings; Pamphlets; Periodical Subscriptions; Photographs 2000; Prints; Reels 3; Reproductions; Slides 2000; Video Tapes 25
Special Subjects: Historical Material
Collections: Old household furnishings, toys, kitchenware & artwork from the old homes of Cohasset; Wilson family artifacts
Publications: Qu newsletter; Historical Highlights
Activities: Classes for adults & children; lects open to public; 8 lects per year; gallery talks, tours, schols; mus shop sells books

M **SOUTH SHORE ART CENTER,** 119 Ripley Rd, Cohasset, MA 02025-1744. Tel 781-383-2787; Fax 781-383-2964; Elec Mail info@ssac.org; Internet Home Page Address: www.ssac.org; *Dir* Sarah Hannan
Open Mon-Sat 10AM-4PM, Sun 12PM-4PM
Collections: works by regional & nat contemporary artists; paintings; sculpture

CONCORD

A **CONCORD ART ASSOCIATION,** 37 Lexington Rd, Concord, MA 01742-2570. Tel 978-369-2578; Fax 978-371-2496; Elec Mail gallery@concordart.org; Internet Home Page Address: www.concordart.org; *Cur* Betsy Adams; *Pres* John S Tilney; *Dir* Lili Oh
Open Tues - Sat 10 AM - 4:30 PM, Sun Noon - 4 PM, cl Mon; No admis fee; Estab 1916 for the encouragement of art & artists; Housed in a 1740 house with four galleries, rent out to weddings & meetings; Average Annual Attendance: 10,000; Mem: 1000; dues life member $500, bus & patron $100, family $75, individual $50, artist $40, student $20, sr citizen $25, corporate $1000
Income: Financed by mem

Collections: Bronze sculptures; colonial glass
Exhibitions: Changing exhibition per year
Publications: Exhibition notices
Activities: Classes for adults and children; lect open to public, 4-6 vis lectrs per year; tours; competitions with prizes; original objects of art lent; room for mems use

M **CONCORD MUSEUM,** 200 Lexington Rd, Concord, MA 01742-3711; PO Box 146, Concord, MA 01742-0146. Tel 978-369-9763; Fax 978-369-9660; Elec Mail cm1@concordmuseum.org; Internet Home Page Address: www.concordmuseum.org; *Cur* David Wood; *Bus Mgr* Susan Bates; *Exec Dir* Peggy Burke; *Designer* Adrienne Donohue; *Dir Mktg & PR* Emer McCourt
Open Apr - May & Sept - Dec Mon - Sat 9 AM - 5 PM, Sun Noon - 5 PM, Jun - Aug 9 AM - 5 PM daily; Admis adults $10, seniors & students $8, children $5, members & children under 5 free; Estab 1886 to further public understanding & appreciation of Concord's history & its relationship to the cultural history of the nation by collecting, preserving & interpreting objects used or made in the Concord area. The museum serves as a center of learning and cultural enjoyment for the region & as a gateway to the town of Concord for visitors from around the world; Twenty galleries & period rooms including six Why Concord? history galleries; Average Annual Attendance: 45,000; Mem: 1200; dues $50 & up
Income: $1,300,000 (financed by mem, admis, grants, endowment & giving)
Special Subjects: Archaeology, Decorative Arts, Historical Material, Ceramics, Metalwork, Furniture, Painting-American, Silver, Textiles, Sculpture, Costumes, Portraits, Period Rooms, Pewter
Collections: Coll incl: the lantern that hung in the church steeple on the night of Paul Revere's ride, Thoreau's possessions, including the desk where he penned Walden and Civil Disobedience, and Emerson's Study. The museum's collections contain many 17th-19th-century furniture, clocks, silver, ceramics & needlework.
Publications: Newsletter, quarterly; Concord: Climate for Freedom by Ruth Wheeler; Forms to Sett On: A Social History of Concord Seating Furniture; Musketaquid to Concord: The Native & European Experience; Native American Source Book: A Teacher's Guide to New England Natives; The Concord Museum: Decorative Arts from a New England Collection; An Observant Eye: The Thoreau Collection at the Concord Museum
Activities: Classes for adults & children; docent training; lects open to pub; 8 vis lectrs per yr; concerts; gallery talks; tours; mus shop sells books, reproductions, prints, gift items & crafts which complement the mus collection

A **LOUISA MAY ALCOTT MEMORIAL ASSOCIATION,** Orchard House, 399 Lexington Rd, Concord, MA 01742-3712; PO Box 343, Concord, MA 01742-0343. Tel 508-369-4118; Fax 508-369-1367; Elec Mail info@louisamayalcott.org; *Dir Educ* Cara Shapiro; *Cur* Patty Bruttomesso; *Dir* Lisa A Simpson
Open Apr - Oct Mon - Sat 10 AM - 4:30 PM, Sun noon - 4:30 PM, Nov - Mar Mon - Fri 11 AM - 3 PM, Sat 10 AM - 4:30 PM, Sun 1 - 4:30 PM, cl Easter, Thanksgiving, Christmas & Jan 1 - 15; Admis adults $9, seniors & students $8, children $5, family rate $25; Estab 1911, preservation of house & family effects for educational purposes; Historic House Museum. Maintains reference library; Average Annual Attendance: 45,000; Mem: 500; dues family $40, individual $25
Income: Financed by mem, admis, gift shop sales, donations & grants
Special Subjects: Architecture, Costumes, Drawings, Manuscripts, Photography, Porcelain, Prints, Sculpture, Silver, Textiles, Watercolors, Decorative Arts, Portraits, Dolls, Furniture, Glass, Period Rooms, Dioramas
Collections: Books & photographs of Alcott's; Household furnishings; House where Little Women was written; Louisa May Alcott's paintings & sketches
Publications: Exhibit catalogs
Activities: Classes for adults & children; dramatic progs; living history performances; lects open to pub, 5 vis lectrs per yr; tours; original objects of art lent to other mus; lending collection contains books, original art works, original prints, paintings, photographs & sculpture; sales shop sells books, magazines, prints & exclusive reproductions

COTUIT

M **CAHOON MUSEUM OF AMERICAN ART,** 4676 Falmouth Rd, PO Box 1853 Cotuit, MA 02635-1853. Tel 508-428-7581; Fax 508-420-3709; Elec Mail rwaterhouse@cahoonmuseum.org; Internet Home Page Address: www.cahoonmuseum.org; *Dir & Cur* Richard Waterhouse; *Mus Store Mgr* Susan Quinlan-Brown; *Bus Mgr* Agnes Maloney; *Mem Coordr* Christy Laidlaw
Open Tues - Sat 10 AM - 4 PM, Sun 1 PM - 4 PM, cl Jan & major holidays; No admis fee for members & children under 12; Estab 1984; A stately 1775 Georgian colonial farmhouse maintained with period furnishings stenciled floorboards, numerous fireplaces, a 200-year old beehive oven & wall stenciling; Average Annual Attendance: 10,000; Mem: 500; dues patron $1000, sponsor $500, assoc $250, contributor $100, family/dual $50, individual $30, adults $25, student $15
Income: $350,000 financed by fundraisers, memberships, admissions, annual appeal, mus shop
Special Subjects: Folk Art, Landscapes, Portraits, Marine Painting
Collections: Primitive paintings of Ralph and Martha Cahoon; 19th and early 20th Century American Art including works by James E. Buttersworth, William Matthew Prior, William Bradford & John J. Enneking
Exhibitions: Six - eight yearly exhibitions
Publications: Spyglass Newsletter, quarterly
Activities: Classes for adults; lect open to public; docent tours SmART! field trip program for elementary school classes; gallery talks; mus store sells books, prints, jewelry, gifts

M **COTUIT CENTER FOR THE ARTS,** 4404 Rte 28, Cotuit, MA 02635; PO Box 2042, Cotuit, MA 02635. Tel 508-428-0669; Elec Mail info@cotuitcenterforthearts.org; Internet Home Page Address: www.artsonthecape.org; *Dir* David Kuehn
Open Summer: daily 10 AM - 4 PM; Winter: Mon - Sat 10 AM - 4 PM; cl Sun; Admis ticket prices vary; no charge for gallery; Estab 1995; 2 levels of space; Average Annual Attendance: 50,000; Mem: 850; fees vary by level
Collections: works by contemporary artists

Exhibitions: Exhibs vary changing every 3-7 wks
Activities: Classes for adults & children; Dramatic progs; lects open to pub; 2 vis lectrs per yr; concerts; gallery talks; tours; sales shop sells original art

CUMMINGTON

M **TOWN OF CUMMINGTON HISTORICAL COMMISSION,** Kingman Tavern Historical Museum, 41 Main St, Cummington, MA 01026; PO Box 10, Cummington, MA 01026-0010. Tel 413-634-5527; *Chmn* Stephen Howes; *VChmn* Donald Pearce; *Secy* Stephanie Pasternak; *Archivist* Sondra Huntley
Open 2 - 5 PM, Jul & Aug; Admis donation suggested; Estab 1968 to have & display artifacts of Cummington & locality; 17 rm house with artifacts of Cummington & area including 17 miniature rms, two flr barn, tools, equipment, carriage shed, cider mill; Average Annual Attendance: 300; Mem: 7, appointed by selectmen
Income: $30,000 (financed by endowment & donations)
Library Holdings: Cards; Clipping Files; Memorabilia; Original Documents; Photographs
Collections: Art of WWII Refugees; paintings of local New England artists
Publications: Only One Cummington, history of Cummington; Vital Records, Town of Cummington 1762 - 1900
Activities: Demonstrators; lects open to pub; 2 vis lectrs per yr; mus shop; books

DEERFIELD

M **HISTORIC DEERFIELD, INC,** 80 Old Main St, Deerfield, MA 01342-0321; PO Box 321, Deerfield, MA 01342-0321. Tel 413-774-5581; Fax 413-775-7220; Elec Mail info@historic-deerfield.org; Internet Home Page Address: www.historic-deerfield.org; *Chair* Anne K Groves; *Pres* Philip Zea; *VPres Mus Affairs* Anne Lanning; *Cur Chair* Amanda E Lange; *Cur Furniture* Joshua Lane
Open Daily 9:30 AM - 4:30 PM; Admis adults $12, children 6 - 17 $5, children 5 & under free; Estab 1952 to collect, study & interpret artifacts related to the history of Deerfield, the culture of the Connecticut Valley & the arts in early American life; Maintains 11 historic house museums, Flynt Center of Early New England life; Average Annual Attendance: 30,000; Mem: dues $40 and higher; annual meeting 2nd or 3rd Sun in Sep
Income: $1,923,527 (financed by endowment, mem, rental, royalty & museum store income)
Purchases: $163,694
Special Subjects: Glass, Furniture, Pottery, Period Rooms, Silver, Maps, Painting-American, Textiles, Costumes, Ceramics, Decorative Arts, Furniture, Silver, Embroidery, Pewter
Collections: American & English silver; American & European textiles & costume; American needlework; American pewter; Chinese export porcelain; early American household objects; early American paintings & prints; early New England furniture; English ceramics; American furniture; Powder horns; English creamware
Exhibitions: Into the Woods: Crafting Early American Furniture; Celebrating the Fiber Arts
Publications: Historical Deerfield Magazine; Annual Report
Activities: Classes for adults, children & families; docent training; lects open to pub, 17 vis lectrs per yr; gallery talks; tours; scholarships & fels; mus shop sells books, reproductions, slides & local crafts

L **Henry N Flynt Library,** 84B Old Main St, Deerfield, MA 01342; PO Box 321, Deerfield, MA 01342-0341. Tel 413-775-7125; Fax 413-775-7223; Elec Mail library@historic-deerfield.org; Internet Home Page Address: www.historic-deerfield.org/library; *Librn* David C Bosse; *Asst Librn* Martha Noblick; *Asst Librn* Heather Harrington
Open Mon - Fri 9 AM - 5 PM; No admis fee; Estab 1970 to support research on local history & genealogy & the museum collections; also for staff training; For reference & research on early New England & Connecticut River Valley
Income: Grants & Historic Deerfield budget
Purchases: 500 vols per year
Library Holdings: Auction Catalogs; Audio Tapes; Book Volumes 23,000; Cards; Clipping Files; Compact Disks; DVDs; Exhibition Catalogs; Fiche; Filmstrips; Manuscripts; Maps; Original Documents; Pamphlets; Periodical Subscriptions 110; Reels 550; Video Tapes 25
Special Subjects: Folk Art, Landscape Architecture, Decorative Arts, Manuscripts, Painting-American, Historical Material, Ceramics, Porcelain, Furniture, Glass, Pottery, Silver, Silversmithing, Textiles, Landscapes, Architecture
Collections: Decorative Arts; Works dealing with the Connecticut River Valley
Publications: Research at Deerfield, An Introduction to the Memorial Libraries, irregular
Activities: Mus sales shop sells books, reproductions, prints & slides

A **POCUMTUCK VALLEY MEMORIAL ASSOCIATION,** Memorial Hall Museum, 8 Memorial St, Deerfield, MA 01342; PO Box 428, Deerfield, MA 01342-0428. Tel 413-774-7476, 774-3768; Fax 413-774-5400, 774-7070; Elec Mail info@old-deerfield.org; Internet Home Page Address: www.old-deerfield.org; *Pres* Carol Letson; *Cur* Suzanne Flint; *Dir* Timothy C Neumann
Open May 1 - Oct 31 Tues - Sun 11 AM - 5 PM; Admis adults $6, students $3, children (6-12) $3; Estab 1870 to collect the art & other cultural artifacts of Connecticut River Valley & western Massachusetts; Maintains 15 galleries; Average Annual Attendance: 17,000; Mem: 800; dues $10; annual meeting last Tues in Feb
Income: $1,400,000 (financed by endowment, mem, sales & fundraising)
Special Subjects: Architecture, Costumes, Embroidery, Etchings & Engravings, Historical Material, Landscapes, Manuscripts, Photography, Textiles, Painting-American, Pottery, Decorative Arts, Folk Art, Pewter, American Indian Art, Ceramics, Crafts, Miniatures, Portraits, Furniture, Glass, Period Rooms, Maps, Primitive art
Collections: Folk art; furniture; Indian artifacts; paintings; pewter; textiles; tools; toys; dolls
Activities: Classes for children; dramatic progs; lects open to pub; concerts; tours; individual paintings & original objects of art lent to other mus; lending collection

contains original art works, original prints, paintings & artifacts; mus shop sells books, original art, reproductions & slides; Old Deerfield Children's Museum, Main St, Deerfield, MA 01342

DENNIS

M CAPE COD MUSEUM OF ART INC, (Cape Museum of Fine Arts Inc.) 60 Hope Lane Rt 6A Dennis Village, Dennis, MA 02638; PO Box 2034, Dennis, MA 02638-5034. Tel 508-385-4477; Fax 508-385-7533; Elec Mail info@ccmoa.org; Internet Home Page Address: www.ccmoa.org; *Exec Dir* Elizabeth Ives Hunter; *Mgr Exhib* Michael Giaquinto; *Deputy Dir* Debra Hemeon; *Dir Educ* Linda McNeil-Kemp; *Registrar* Angela Bilsky; *Mem Adminr* Peg Vetorino
Open May - Oct Mon - Sat 10 AM - 5 PM, Sun noon - 5 PM; Oct -May Tues - Sat 10 AM - 5 PM, Thurs eves until 8 PM; Admis adults $8, mem & ages 18 & under free; Estab 1981 for artists associated with Cape Cod, the Islands & southeastern Massachusetts; Six permanent collection galleries, temporary exhibitions; maintains reference library; Average Annual Attendance: 35,000; Mem: 2,000; dues $50-$5000
Income: $1,000,000 (financed by endowment, mem, events to earned income)
Purchases: New England Torso, bronze by Gilbert Franklin
Library Holdings: Book Volumes; Clipping Files; Exhibition Catalogs; Memorabilia; Original Documents; Periodical Subscriptions; Slides
Special Subjects: Graphics, Painting-American, Prints, Sculpture, Watercolors, Bronzes, Ceramics, Woodcarvings, Woodcuts, Etchings & Engravings, Glass
Collections: Artists assoc with Cape Cod
Publications: Art Matters Quarterly; exhibit catalogues
Activities: Classes for adults & children; docent training; lects open to pub; 15 vis lectrs; concerts; gallery talks; tours; individual paintings & original objects of art lent; 1-2 book traveling exhibs per yr; organize traveling exhibs to other mus; mus shop sells books, magazines & prints

DUXBURY

M ART COMPLEX MUSEUM, Carl A. Weyerhaeuser Library, 189 Alden St., Duxbury, MA 02331; PO Box 2814, Duxbury, MA 02331-2814. Tel 781-934-6634; Fax 781-934-5117; Elec Mail info@artcomplex.org; Internet Home Page Address: www.artcomplex.org; *Communs Coordr* Laura Doherty; *Cur Asst & Registrar* Maureen Wengler; *Asst to Dir* Mary Curran; *Dir & CEO* Charles A Weyerhaeuser; *Librn* Cheryl O'Neill; *Contemporary Cur* Craig Bloodgood; *Consulting Cur* Alice R M Hyland; *Community Coordr* Doris Collins; *Grounds & Maint* William Thomas; *Coordr Educ* Sally Dean Mello; *Staff Asst* Elaine Plakias; *Accnt* Mary Wallace
Open Wed - Sun 1 - 4 PM; No admis fee, donations accepted; Estab 1971 as a center for the arts; Circ Non-circulating; Average Annual Attendance: 10,000
Income: Financed by endowment
Library Holdings: Auction Catalogs; Book Volumes 6500; Clipping Files; DVDs; Exhibition Catalogs; Manuscripts; Pamphlets; Periodical Subscriptions 15; Slides; Video Tapes
Special Subjects: Art History, Painting-American, Prints, Painting-European, Painting-Japanese, Ceramics, Asian Art
Collections: American paintings, prints & sculpture; European paintings & prints; Asian art; Native American art; Shaker furniture
Publications: Complexities (newsletters); exhibit catalogues
Activities: Educ dept; workshops for children & adults; docent training; Japanese Tea Ceremony presentations; lects open to pub; concerts; gallery talks; tours of vis groups; Gold Star Award from MA Cultural Council; lending of original objects of art to museums & traveling exhibs
L Library, 189 Alden St, Duxbury, MA 02332-2801; PO Box 2814, Duxbury, MA 02331-2814. Tel 718-934-6634; *Dir* Charles Weyerhaeuser; *Librn* Cheryl O'Neill
Open Wed-Sun 1 PM-4 PM; Estab 1971; Circ Non-circulating; Open to the pub for reference; Average Annual Attendance: 12,000
Income: Financed by endowment
Library Holdings: Book Volumes 5000; Clipping Files; Exhibition Catalogs; Pamphlets; Periodical Subscriptions 20; Slides; Video Tapes
Special Subjects: Prints, Asian Art
Activities: Docent reading group

ESSEX

M ESSEX HISTORICAL SOCIETY AND SHIPBUILDING MUSEUM, 66 Main St, Essex, MA 01929; PO Box 277, Essex, MA 01929-0005. Tel 978-768-7541; Fax 978-768-2541; Elec Mail info@essexshipbuildingmuseum.org; Internet Home Page Address: www.essexshipbuildingmuseum.org; *Pres* Mark Lindsay; *Treas* Tia Schlaikjer; *Operations Mgr* Catherine Ageloff; *Dir Educ* Kerry Schwarz
Open Nov - May, Weekends 10 AM - 5 PM; June - Oct, Wed - Sun 10 AM - 5 PM; Admis adults $7, seniors $6, children $5; Estab 1976 to preserve & interpret Essex history with special emphasis on its shipbuilding industry; Maintains reference library; Average Annual Attendance: 4,500; Mem: 600; dues $35, annual meeting in June
Special Subjects: Drawings, Photography, Prints, Archaeology, Crafts, Woodcarvings, Landscapes, Decorative Arts, Marine Painting, Historical Material, Maps
Collections: Collection of ship building tools, documents, paintings, plans & photographs, models-both scale & builders; fishing schooner hulls; shipyard site 300 years old; Shipbuilding
Exhibitions: Five rigged ship models & 15 builder's models on loan from the Smithsonian Institution's Watercraft Collection; Frame-Up (ongoing); Caulker's Art (ongoing).
Publications: A list of vessels, boats & other craft built in the town of Essex 1860-1980, a complete inventory of the Ancient Burying Ground of Essex 1680-1868; Essex Electrics, 1981; Dubbing, Hooping & Lofting, 1981
Activities: Classes for adults & children; lects open to pub, 5-7 vis lectrs per r; gallery talks; tours; mus shop sells books, prints, original art, reproductions, & audio-video cassettes, t-shirts, models, plans, magazines & notecards

FALL RIVER

M FALL RIVER HISTORICAL SOCIETY, 451 Rock St, Fall River, MA 02720-3398. Tel 508-679-1071; Fax 508-675-5754; Internet Home Page Address: www.lizzieborden.org; *Pres* Elizabeth Denning; *VPres* Andrew Mann Lizak; *Cur* Michael Martins
Open Tues - Fri (Apr - Nov) Tours 10 & 11 AM, 1, 2 & 3 PM, (June - Sept) Tours 1, 2, 3 & 4 PM, open house day after Thanksgiving Day before New Year's Day; Admis adults $5, children 6-14 $3.00, children under 6 free; Estab 1921 to preserve the social & economic history of Fall River; Average Annual Attendance: 6,000; Mem: 659; dues $45 family, $25 individual
Income: Financed by endowment, mem
Special Subjects: Painting-American, Costumes, Decorative Arts
Collections: Fall River School Still Life Paintings & Portraits; Antonio Jacobsen marine paintings; Period costumes, furs, fans; Victorian furnishings & decorative arts; Victorian Decorative Stenciling: A Lost Art Revived
Exhibitions: Still Life painting by 19th Century Artists of the Fall River School
Activities: Small private tours for local schools; lect open to public, 4 vis lectrs per year; individual paintings lent; shop sells books, prints, postcards, paperweights

FITCHBURG

M FITCHBURG ART MUSEUM, 185 Elm St, Fitchburg, MA 01420-7503; 25 Merriam Pkwy, Fitchburg, MA 01420-7523. Tel 978-345-4207; Fax 978-345-2319; Elec Mail info@fitchburgartmuseum.org; Internet Home Page Address: www.fitchburgartmuseum.org; *Pres* Rod Lewin; *Treas* Denise Senecal; *Dir* Peter Timms; *Bus Mgr* Sheryl Demers; *Dir Educ* Laura Howick; *Dir Mem* Janice Goodrow; *Dir Corporate Mem Svcs* Jane Keough; *Dir Docents* Ann Descoteaux; *Dir Mktg* Jerry Beck
Open Wed - Fri noon - 4 PM, Sat - Sun 11 AM - 5 PM; cl Mon & Tues; Admis fee $9, seniors & students $5; Estab 1925; Three building complex, twelve galleries & two entrance halls, offices & admin; Average Annual Attendance: 19,000; Mem: 1156; dues $35 - 1000; annual meeting Dec
Income: Financed by endowment & mem
Purchases: Mary Verplanck McEvers, 1771 by John Sargent Copley; Riverside Village, Normandy by John Henry Twachtman (1853-1902); Drummers by Sokari Douglas-Camp, 1987; Steerage by Alfred Stieglitz (1907)
Special Subjects: Drawings, Painting-American, Prints
Collections: American & European paintings, prints, drawings & decorative arts; African, Egyptian, Greek, Roman, Asian art & antiquities
Exhibitions: Rotating exhibits
Publications: Exhibitions catalogs; event notices
Activities: Classes for adults & children; docent training; lect open to public, 12 vis lectrs per year; gallery talks; tours; competitions with awards; scholarships; individual paintings & original objects of art lent to colleges & museums; sales shop sells reproductions & jewelry

FRAMINGHAM

M DANFORTH MUSEUM OF ART, Danforth Museum of Art, 123 Union Ave, Framingham, MA 01702-8291. Tel 508-620-0050; Fax 508-872-5542; Elec Mail dmadev@conversent.net; Internet Home Page Address: www.danforthmuseum.org; *Dir* Katherine French; *Dir Fin & Opers* Mary Kiely; *Dir Educ* Pat Walker; *Cur Asst* Kristina Wilson
Open Wed, Thurs & Sun Noon - 5 PM, Fri & Sat 10 AM - 5 PM. cl Mon & Tues; Admis adults $11, seniors $9, students $8, mems & children under 17 free; Estab 1975 to provide fine arts & art-related activities to people of all ages in the South Middlesex area; There are seven galleries, including a children's gallery with hands-on activities; Average Annual Attendance: 30,000; Mem: 1500; dues individual $45, family $60, friend $100, supporter $250, sponsor $500, patron $1000, seniors get $10 off any category, annual meeting in Oct
Income: Financed by mem, Framingham State College & Town of Framingham, federal & state grants; foundations & corporate support
Special Subjects: Ceramics, Glass, Photography, Pottery, Painting-American, Drawings, Painting-American, Prints, Watercolors, Crafts
Collections: Old master & contemporary prints, drawings & photography; 19th & 20th c American art by: Gilbert Stuart, James McNeill Whistler, Charles Sprague Pearce, Meta Vaux Warrick Fuller, Albert Bierstadt, Yves Tanguy, Karl Knaths, Thomas Hart Benton & Faith Ringgold; African & Oceanic art
Exhibitions: Varied program of changing exhibitions, traveling shows, selections from the permanent collection, in a variety of periods, styles & media
Publications: Newsletter; exhibition brochures & catalogues, museum school brochure
Activities: Classes for adults & children; docent training; progs for area schools; workshops; teacher development; family progs; lects open to pub; concerts; gallery talks; trips; receptions; competitions; book traveling exhibs 2-3 per yr; originate traveling exhibs to other mus & galleries nationally; mus shop sells original art & reproductions; junior gallery
L Library, 123 Union Ave, Framingham, MA 01701-8291. Tel 508-620-0050; Fax 508-872-5542; Elec Mail kfrench@danforthmuseum.org; Internet Home Page Address: www.danforthmuseum.org; *Dir* Katherine French; *Mus Educ* Pat Walker
Open Wed, Thurs, Sun 12 PM - 5 PM, Fri - Sat 10 AM - 5 PM; Admis adults $8, seniors & students $7; Estab 1975 as an educational resource of art books & catalogues; For reference only; research as requested; Average Annual Attendance: 40,000; Mem: 1,400; dues family $60, individual $45
Library Holdings: Auction Catalogs; Book Volumes 6500; Clipping Files; Exhibition Catalogs; Pamphlets; Video Tapes
Special Subjects: Painting-American, American Indian Art
Collections: Meta Warrick Fuller
Activities: Classes for adults & children; docent training; lects; 15 vis lectrs per yr; concerts; gallery talks; tours; competitions; juried exhib awards; purchase awards; schols & fels offered; mus shop sells books, magazines, original art, reproductions & prints

GARDNER

M **MOUNT WACHUSETT COMMUNITY COLLEGE,** East Wing Gallery, 444 Green St, Gardner, MA 01440-1378. Tel 978-632-6600, Ext 168; Internet Home Page Address: www.mwcc.mass.edu; *Chmn Dept Art* Gene Cauthen; *Painting Prof* John Pacheco; *Ceramics Prof* Joyce Miller; *Adjunct Faculty* Joslin Stevens; *Adjunct Faculty* Susan Montgomery; *Adjunct Faculty* Keith Hollingwood
Open Mon - Thurs 8 AM - 9 PM, Fri 8 AM - 5 PM; No admis fee; Estab 1971 to supply resources for a two-year art curriculum; develop an art collection; Well-lighted gallery with skylights & track lighting, white paneled walls; two open, spacious levels with Welsh tile floors; Average Annual Attendance: 8,000-10,000
Income: Financed by city & state appropriations
Purchases: Pottery by Makato Yabe, print by Bob Roy, 17 student paintings, ten student prints, five student ceramic works, eight student sculpture, two bronze works
Collections: Approx 100 works; framed color art posters & reproductions; prints; ceramic pieces; student coll
Exhibitions: Annual student competition of painting, sculpture, drawing, ceramics, printmaking; local, national & international artists & former students' works
Publications: Annual brochure
Activities: Continuing educ classes for adults & children; lect open to public, 8-10 vis lectrs per year; gallery talks; tours; competitions with awards; exten dept serves Mount Wachussett
L **La Chance Library,** 444 Green St, Gardner, MA 01440. Tel 978-630-9125; Tel 888-884-6922; Fax 978-630-9556; Internet Home Page Address: www.mwcc.mass.edu; *Asst Dean & Library Info Servs* Linda R Oldach; *Coordr, Library Svcs* Jess Mynes
Open Mon - Thurs 7:30 AM - 7:30 PM, Fri 7:30 AM - 4 PM, (when school is in session); Estab 1964; Circ 12,998; Lending library
Income: Financed by state appropriation
Library Holdings: Book Volumes 55,000; CD-ROMs; Cassettes; Compact Disks; DVDs; Memorabilia; Periodical Subscriptions 82; Records
Exhibitions: Periodic exhibitions

GLOUCESTER

M **CAPE ANN HISTORICAL ASSOCIATION,** (Cape Ann Historical Museum) Cape Ann Museum, 27 Pleasant St, Gloucester, MA 01930-5909. Tel 978-283-0455; Fax 978-283-4141; Elec Mail rondafaloon@capeannmuseum.org; Internet Home Page Address: www.capeannmuseum.org; *Dir* Ronda Faloon; *Museum Educator* Courtney Richardson; *Mus Shop Mgr* Jeanette Smith; *Pres* John Cunningham; *Cur* Martha Oaks; *Prog Dir* Linda Marshall; *Librn & Archivist* Stephanie Buck
Open Tues - Sat 10 AM - 5 PM, Sun 1 - 4 PM, cl Feb; Admis adults $8, seniors, students & Cape Ann residents $6, members free; Estab 1873 to foster appreciation of the quality & diversity of life on Cape Ann past & present; Fine arts, decorative arts & American furniture; Fisheries/maritime galleries; granite industry gallery; 1804 furnished house; maintains reference library; Average Annual Attendance: 17,000; Mem: 1500; dues $35-$1000
Income: Financed by memberships, donations, admissions & endowment
Library Holdings: Auction Catalogs; Audio Tapes; Book Volumes; CD-ROMs; Clipping Files; Compact Disks; DVDs; Exhibition Catalogs; Manuscripts; Maps; Memorabilia; Original Documents; Pamphlets; Periodical Subscriptions; Photographs
Special Subjects: Drawings, Historical Material, Art Education, Art History, American Western Art, Painting-American, Prints, Textiles, Bronzes, Manuscripts, Maps, Painting-American, Photography, Sculpture, Watercolors, Pottery, Etchings & Engravings, Landscapes, Decorative Arts, Portraits, Dolls, Furniture, Jade, Porcelain, Silver, Marine Painting, Coins & Medals, Dioramas, Period Rooms, Embroidery, Pewter
Collections: Fitz Henry Lane Collection: paintings; 20th Century: Maurice Prendergast, John Sloan, Stuart Davis, Marsden Hartley, Milton Avery; Granite Industry of Cape Ann, Maritime & Fishing Industry; 20th Century Sculpture-Walker Hancock, Paul Manship; Folly Cove Designs-Textiles
Exhibitions: Charles Hopkinson
Activities: Classes for adults & children; outreach to area schools; on-site progs for students; docent training; lects open to pub; vis lectrs 4 per yr; concerts; gallery talks; tours; individual paintings & original objects of art lent to mus, galleries & local bus; mus shop sells books, magazines, reproductions, original art, prints, slides, jewelry, postcards, note paper & Cape Ann related items
L **Cape Ann Historical Museum,** 27 Pleasant St, Gloucester, MA 01930. Tel 978-283-0455; Fax 978-283-4141; Internet Home Page Address: www.capeannhistoricalmuseum.org; *Dir* Judith McCulloch
Open 10 AM - 5 PM Tues - Sat, cl Feb; Admis adults $6.50, seniors $6, students $4.50; Estab 1876; Reference only
Income: mem, donations, admissions, sales
Library Holdings: Auction Catalogs; Book Volumes 3000; Clipping Files; Exhibition Catalogs; Manuscripts; Memorabilia; Motion Pictures; Original Art Works; Pamphlets; Photographs; Prints; Records; Reproductions; Sculpture
Special Subjects: Art History, Decorative Arts, Photography, Manuscripts, Maps, Painting-American, Sculpture, Historical Material, Portraits, Watercolors, Porcelain, Period Rooms, Silver, Marine Painting
Collections: Fitz Henry Lane Collection; 20th century art, fisheries/maritime, granite quarrying
Exhibitions: Leon Kroll
Activities: Classes for children; 6 lects open to pub per yr; mus shop sells books, reproductions, prints

M **HAMMOND CASTLE MUSEUM,** 80 Hesperus Ave, Gloucester, MA 01930-5299. Tel 978-283-7673, 283-7620; Fax 978-283-1643; Internet Home Page Address: www.hammondcastle.org; *Acting Dir & Cur* John W Pettibone; *VPres* Craig Lentz
Open daily June - Aug 10 AM - 6 PM, weekends Sept - May 10 AM - 3 PM; Admis adults $6.50, seniors & students $5.50, children between 4 & 12 $4.50; Estab 1931 by a famous inventor, John Hays Hammond Jr. Incorporated in 1938

for the pub exhib of authentic works of art, architecture and specimens of antiquarian value and to encourage and promote better educ in the fine arts, with particular reference to purity of design and style; Built in style of a medieval castle with Great Hall, courtyard and period rooms, Dr Hammond combined elements of Roman, Medieval and Renaissance periods in his attempt to recreate an atmosphere of European beauty; Average Annual Attendance: 60,000
Income: Financed by tours, concerts, special events & rentals
Collections: Rare collection of European artifacts; Roman, Medieval and Renaissance Periods
Publications: Exhibition catalogs; Hammond Biography
Activities: Classes for children; docent training; educational & teacher workshops; lect open to public; concerts; self guided & group tours; exten dept servs neighboring schools; sales shop sells books, reproductions, crafts, jewelry, art cards & postcards

A **NORTH SHORE ARTS ASSOCIATION, INC,** 11 Pirate's Lane, Gloucester, MA 01930. Tel 978-283-1857; Elec Mail arts@nsarts.org; Internet Home Page Address: www.nsarts.org; *Pres* George Martin; *VPres* Kathy Moore; *VPres* Dolores Erikson Reid; *Treas* Mary Kathryn Gray; *Gallery Dir* Suzanne Gilbert
Open daily 10 AM - 5 PM, Sun Noon - 5 PM, May 1 - Oct 31; No admis fee; Estab 1922 by the Cape Ann Artists to promote American art by exhibitions; Gallery owned by assn; maintains reference library; Average Annual Attendance: 8,000; Mem: 375; dues artist $75, patron $50, assoc $40; juried membership
Income: Financed by dues, contributions & rentals
Library Holdings: Cards; Exhibition Catalogs; Original Art Works; Original Documents; Pamphlets; Periodical Subscriptions; Prints; Reproductions; Sculpture
Special Subjects: Painting-American
Collections: Member paintings
Exhibitions: 4 summer exhibs in addition to solo exhibs; hosts national shows on even numbered yrs
Publications: Calendar of Events; exhibit catalogs; brochures
Activities: Classes for adults & children; dramatic progs; docent training; art auctions; children's festival; lects open to pub, 4 vis lectrs per yr; concerts; gallery talks; sponsored competitions; schols; lending of original objects of art to other mus; sales shop sells books, original art & members cards

GREAT BARRINGTON

M **BARD COLLEGE AT SIMON'S ROCK,** (Simon's Rock College of Bard) Hillman-Jackson Gallery, 84 Alford Rd, Great Barrington, MA 01230-2499. Tel 413-644-4400; Fax 413-528-7365; Elec Mail mcherin@simons-rock.edu; Internet Home Page Address: www.simons-rock.edu; *Cur* Margaret Cherin
Open daily; No admis fee; Estab 1966 as a liberal arts col; 25 ft x 16 ft gallery
Income: Financed by the college
Exhibitions: A continuing exhibition program of professional faculty & student works in drawing, painting, photography, sculpture & ceramics
Activities: Gallery talks; tours; Juror's prize for annual juried student show; faculty prize
L **Library,** 84 Alford Rd, Great Barrington, MA 01230. Tel 413-528-7274; Tel 413-528-0771; Elec Mail goodkind@simons rock.edu; Internet Home Page Address: www.simons-rock.edu; *Librn* Joan Goodkind
Open Mon - Tues 8:30 AM - 2 AM, Wed - Fri 8:30 AM - Midnight, Sat 11 AM - Midnight, Sun 11 AM - 2 AM; No admis fee; Estab 1964; 20 ft x 30 ft
Income: Financed by the college
Library Holdings: Book Volumes 60,500; Cassettes; Fiche; Periodical Subscriptions 350; Records; Reels
Exhibitions: In the Atrium Gallery, exhibits change monthly

HADLEY

M **PORTER-PHELPS-HUNTINGTON FOUNDATION, INC,** Historic House Museum, 130 River Dr, Hadley, MA 01035-9782. Tel 413-584-4699; Internet Home Page Address: www.pphmuseum.org; *Pres* Thomas N Harris; *VPres* Dan Huntington Fenn; *Exec Dir* Susan J Lisk
Open May 15 - Oct 15 Sat - Wed 1 - 4:30 PM; Admis fee $5, children under 12 $1; Estab 1948; Historic house built in 1752; twelve rooms house the accumulated belongings of ten generations of one family; carriage house; corn barn; historic gardens; sunken garden; Average Annual Attendance: 5,500; Mem: 500; dues $25 - $1,000; annual meeting in Dec
Income: $65,000 (financed by endowment, grants, programs & mem)
Special Subjects: Drawings, Architecture, Glass, Furniture, Silver, Painting-American, Photography, Prints, Watercolors, Textiles, Costumes, Decorative Arts, Manuscripts, Portraits, Jewelry, Porcelain, Historical Material, Maps, Scrimshaw, Miniatures, Pewter
Collections: Porter-Phelps-Huntington family collection of 17th, 18th & 19th century furniture, paintings, papers, decorative arts; clothing collection; Porter-Phelps - Hunting Family Paper on deposit at Amherst College Special Collections & Archives
Activities: Dramatic progs; History Inst for the Teachers; lects open to pub, 1 vis lectr per yr; concerts; tours; individual paintings & objects of art lent to other mus; mus shop sells books, cards & pamphlets

HARVARD

M **FRUITLANDS MUSEUM, INC,** 102 Prospect Hill Rd, Harvard, MA 01451-1348. Tel 978-456-3924; Fax 978-456-8078; Elec Mail education@fruitlands.org; Internet Home Page Address: www.fruitlands.org; *Cur* Michael Volmar, PhD; *Dir Educ* Maggie Green; *Dir Develop* Kerry Castorano; *Exec Dir* Wyona Lynch-McWhite
Open mid-April 1 thru - Oct Daily 10 AM - 4 PM, weekends & holidays 10 AM - 5 PM, cl Tuesdays; Admis adults $12, seniors & college students $10, ages 5 & under no charge; Estab 1914, incorporated 1930 by Clara Endicott Sears. Fruitlands was the scene of Bronson Alcott's Utopian experiment in community living; The Fruitlands Farmhouse contains furniture, household articles, pictures,

handcrafts, books & valuable manuscript collection of Alcott, Lane & Transcendental group. The Shaker House, built in 1794 by the members of the former Harvard Shaker Village, was originally used as an office. Moved to its present location, it now forms the setting for the products of Shaker Handicrafts & Community Industries. Native American Mus contains ethnological exhibs. Art gallery contains portraits by itinerant artists of the first half of the 19th century & landscapes by Hudson River School & rotating exhibits; Average Annual Attendance: 11,000; Mem: 700; dues senior/students $30, individual $55, family $70, Patron $250, Fruitlands Benefactor $500; annual meeting in June
Income: Financed by earned income, Sears Trust, mem fees, gifts & grants
Purchases: Books, paintings & ethnographic materials
Library Holdings: Original Art Works; Original Documents; Photographs; Records; Sculpture
Special Subjects: American Indian Art, Folk Art, Landscapes, Furniture, Painting-American, Manuscripts, Maps, Sculpture, Drawings, Sculpture, Etchings & Engravings, Eskimo Art, Dolls, Dioramas, Period Rooms, Embroidery
Collections: Hudson River Landscapes; Philip Sears Sculpture Collection; Shaker Handcraft Furniture, household articles & pictures
Publications: The View Newsletter, 3 times/yr
Activities: Art classes for adults & children; lects open to pub, 2-4 vis lectrs per yr; concerts; gallery talks; competitions; individual & original objects of art lent to other mus in the area; lending collection includes original art works, prints, paintings; book traveling exhibs; mus shop sells books, reproductions, prints & handcrafted gifts
L **Library,** 102 Prospect Hill Rd, Harvard, MA 01451. Tel 978-456-3924; Fax 978-456-8078; Elec Mail mvolmar@fruitlands.org; Internet Home Page Address: www.fruitlands.org; *Cur* Michael A Volmar PhD
Open yr round by appointment; Estab 1914 for staff resource & scholarly research
Library Holdings: Book Volumes 10,000; Filmstrips; Manuscripts; Memorabilia; Motion Pictures; Original Art Works; Periodical Subscriptions 10; Photographs; Records; Reels; Slides; Video Tapes
Special Subjects: Art History

HAVERHILL

L **HAVERHILL PUBLIC LIBRARY,** Special Collections, 99 Main St, Haverhill, MA 01830-5092. Tel 978-373-1586 ext 642; Fax 978-373-8466; Internet Home Page Address: www.haverhillpl.org; *Cur Spec Coll* Greg Laing
Open Tues & Fri 10 AM - 1 PM, 2 - 5 PM; No admis fee; Estab 1873
Income: Financed by private endowment
Library Holdings: Audio Tapes; Book Volumes 8650; Cassettes; Clipping Files; Kodachrome Transparencies; Lantern Slides; Manuscripts; Motion Pictures; Original Art Works; Periodical Subscriptions 16; Photographs; Prints; Video Tapes
Special Subjects: Photography, Manuscripts, Prints
Collections: Illuminated manuscripts; mid-19th century photographs, work by Beato and Robertson, Bourne, Frith, Gardner, Naya, O'Sullivan, and others; small group of paintings including Joseph A Ames, Henry Bacon, Sidney M Chase, William S Haseltine, Thomas Hill, Harrison Plummer, Winfield Scott Thomas, Robert Wade
Exhibitions: Changing exhibits

HOLYOKE

M **WISTARIAHURST MUSEUM,** 238 Cabot St, Holyoke, MA 01040-3904. Tel 413-322-5660; Fax 413-534-2344; Internet Home Page Address: www.wistariahurst.org; *Dir* Melissa Boisselle; *Event Coordr* Marjorie Latham; *Chmn Historical Comt* Bruce Mitchell; *Cur & City Hist* Penni Martorell
Open year-round Sat, Sun & Mon noon - 4 PM; Admis adults $7, seniors $5, members & children under 12 free; Historic house museum estab to show history of Holyoke 1850-1930; Sponsored by the City of Holyoke under the jurisdiction of the Holyoke Historical Commission; Average Annual Attendance: 1,400; Mem: annual meeting May
Income: Financed by city appropriation
Special Subjects: Decorative Arts, Historical Material, Landscapes, Period Rooms, Textiles, Maps, Architecture, Ethnology, Costumes, Landscapes, Manuscripts, Portraits, Furniture, Glass, Oriental Art, Historical Material, Restorations, Miniatures, Embroidery, Stained Glass
Collections: Late 19th & early 20th centuries furniture, paintings, prints, decorative arts & architectural details; period rooms; History of Holyoke 1850-1930; Native American ethnographic material; Historical Landscape Tour; Textile Collection
Publications: Museum newsletter, quarterly (Spring & Fall)
Activities: Progs for adults & children; docent training; visual arts gallery; dramatic progs; lects open to pub; 25 vis lectrs per yr; concerts; tours; mus shop sells books, prints & other items

IPSWICH

M **THE TRUSTEES OF RESERVATIONS,** The Mission House, 290 Argilla Rd, Castle Hill Ipswich, MA 01938-2647. Tel 978-921-1944; Fax 978-921-1948; Elec Mail history@ttor.org; Internet Home Page Address: www.thetrustees.org; *Chmn (V)* Elliot M Surkin; *Dir Devel* Ann Powell; *Communs* Michael Triff; *Dir Historic Resources* Susan C S Edwards; *Dir Finance & Admin* John McCrane; *Dir Land Conservation* Wesley Ward; *Exec Dir* Andrew Kendall; *Bd Pres (V)* Janice Hunt
Open Memorial Day through Columbus Day Daily 10 AM - 5 PM; Admis adults $5, children 6-12 $2.50; Built 1739, the home of John Sergeant, first missionary to the Stockbridge Indians, it is now an Early American Mus containing an outstanding collection of Colonial furnishings. Mus opened in 1930; Average Annual Attendance: 3,000
Special Subjects: Period Rooms
Publications: Yearly brochure

LAWRENCE

M **ESSEX ART CENTER,** 56 Island St, Lawrence, MA 01840. Tel 978-685-2343; Fax 978-688-0276; Elec Mail info@essexartcenter.com; Internet Home Page Address: essexartcenter.com; *Contact* Leslie Costello

LEXINGTON

M **NATIONAL HERITAGE MUSEUM,** (Museum of Our National Heritage) 33 Marrett Rd, Lexington, MA 02421-5703. Tel 781-861-6559; Fax 781-861-9846; Elec Mail info@monh.org; Internet Home Page Address: www.nationalheritagemuseum.org; *Others TTY:* 781-274-8539; *Dir Exhibits* Hilary Anderson; *Dir Admin & Finance* June Cobb; *Designer* Mike Rizzo; *Dir Coll* Aimee Newell; *Archivist* Catherine Swanson; *Mgr Lib* Jeffrey Croteau
Open Tues - Sat 10 AM - 4:30 PM, Sun Noon - 4:30PM, Library open Tues - Sat 10 AM - 4 PM, cl Sun; No admis fee; Estab 1972 as an American history museum, including art and decorative art; Four modern galleries for changing exhibs, flexible lighting & climate control. Two galleries of 3000 sq ft, two 1500 sq ft; Average Annual Attendance: 58,000; Mem: 225; dues benefactor $500, assoc mem $250, contributing $100, family $60, individual $40, senior and student $30
Income: $2,900,000 (financed by endowment & appeal to Masons)
Library Holdings: Auction Catalogs; Audio Tapes; Book Volumes; Cassettes; Compact Disks; DVDs; Exhibition Catalogs; Kodachrome Transparencies; Manuscripts; Maps; Original Documents; Other Holdings; Pamphlets; Periodical Subscriptions; Photographs; Records; Slides; Video Tapes
Special Subjects: Historical Material, Painting-American, Decorative Arts
Collections: General American & American Paintings; American decorative art; objects decorated with Masonic, patriotic & fraternal symbolism; Masonic Collection
Exhibitions: Images of Women in WWI posters opens; Pets in America opens; The Art of the Needle: Master. Quilts from the Shelburne Mus opens; Raymond Loewy: Designs for a consumer Culture opens; Telephones opens
Publications: Exhibition catalogs
Activities: Docent training; lects open to pub; 12 vis lectrs per yr; concerts; gallery talks; tours for school groups; paintings and art objects lent; originate traveling exhibs; mus shop sells books and a variety of gift items related to exhibit prog; mus courtyard cafe

LINCOLN

M **DECORDOVA MUSEUM & SCULPTURE PARK,** DeCordova Museum, 51 Sandy Pond Rd, Lincoln, MA 01773-2699. Tel 781-259-8355; Fax 781-259-3650; Elec Mail info@decordova.org; Internet Home Page Address: www.decordova.org; *Mus Dir* Dennis Kois; *Dir Fin & Admin* Steve Fabiano; *Dir External Affairs* Laurie J LaMothe; *Develop Coordr* Catalina Rojo; *Head Mem & Community Outreach* Elizabeth P Herring; *Sr Cur* Nick Capasso; *Assoc Cur Contemporary Art* Dina Deitsch; *Koch Cur Fellow* Lexi Lee; *Registrar* Lynn Hermann Traub; *Cur Educ* Emily Silet; *Preparator* Brian McNamara; *Assoc Preparator* Eugene Finney; *Acting Dir Educ* Lynn Thompson; *Dir Visitor Svcs & Events* Jessica Kriley; *Dir Retail Opers* David A Duddy
Open Tues - Sun 10 AM - 5 PM & on select holidays; Admis adults $12, children 6-12, students & seniors $8, mems, res, military & children 5& under free; discounts available; Estab 1948, opened 1950 to exhibit, to interpret, collect & preserve modern & contemporary American art; Maintains multiple galleries with climate control, cafe, library & Sculpture Garden; Average Annual Attendance: 125,000; Mem: 3,500; dues Dir's Cir $2,500, Julian Club $1,000, patron $600, sponsor $300, school & friend $150, household $90, household teacher $80, individual $60
Income: Financed by endowment, individual/corporate mem, foundation & government grants
Library Holdings: Book Volumes 3,000; Exhibition Catalogs; Other Holdings Museum Catalogs; Periodical Subscriptions 10
Special Subjects: Painting-American, Graphics, Painting-American, Photography, Prints, Sculpture, Woodcuts, Etchings & Engravings, Landscapes, Portraits, Glass
Collections: 3,000+ artworks of various media; 20th century American painting, graphics, sculpture & photography; American Art, with emphasis on New England
Publications: Exhib catalogs; newsletter
Activities: Classes for adults & children; Art ExperienCenter; docent training; teacher training, outreach & resources; Sculpture on Site prog; Teen to Screen video prog; lects open to pub, 4 vis lectrs per yr; concerts; gallery talks; guided tours; arts festivals; outreach progs; exten prog serves Boston area; individual paintings & original objects of art lent to corporate program members & schools; book traveling exhibs 2-3 per yr; originate traveling exhibs; mus shop sells books, magazines, original art, art supplies, handcrafted gifts, jewelry, wearable art & contemporary crafts
M **Sculpture Park,** 51 Sandy Pond Rd, Lincoln, MA 01773-2699. Tel 781-259-3626; Fax 781-259-3650; Elec Mail info@decordova.org; Internet Home Page Address: www.decordova.org; *Mus Dir* Dennis Kois; *Cur Dept Asst* Jenn Schmitt
Open daily dawn to dusk; Admis joint with mus admis; Estab 1985, name changed 1989; acts as outdoor sculpture exhibition space & recreation area for Lincoln & the surrounding Boston area metropolitan communities; 35 acres with approx 75 artworks at any given time; Average Annual Attendance: 125,000
Special Subjects: Sculpture
Collections: First Tier: outdoor sculpture from the DeCordova Permanent Collection, incl 20th c sculpture from artists such as George Rickey, Alexander Liberman & Nam June Paik; Second Tier: large-scale outdoor sculptures on loan, currently from artists Ursula von Rydingsvard, William Tucker, Mark diSuvero, Sol LeWitt, Chakaia Booker & Jim Dine; Third Tier: site-specific, temporary, long-term (1-5 yrs) outdoor sculpture & installations designed for specific sites in the park, incl works by Steven Siegel, Ronald Gonzalez, Carlos Dorrien & Rick Brown
Activities: Tours

LOWELL

M AMERICAN TEXTILE HISTORY MUSEUM, 491 Dutton St, Lowell, MA 01854-4289. Tel 978-441-0400; Fax 978-441-1412; Elec Mail lcarpenter@athm.org; Internet Home Page Address: www.athm.org; *Chmn* Kenneth J McAvoy; *Chmn Emeritus* Edward B Stevens; *Pres & CEO* James S Coleman; *Dir Finance & Admin* Steven Jackson; *Dir Advancement* Linda Carpenter; *Cur* Karen Herbaugh; *Dir Exhib* Diane Fagan Affleck; *Librn* Clare Sheridan; *Dir Museum Educ* Sue Bunker; *Mgr Museum Store* Ann Lochhead
Open Wed - Sun 10 AM - 5 PM; Admis adults ages 17+ $8, children ages 6-16 & seniors 62+ $6, mems & children under 6 free; Estab 1960 to preserve artifacts, documents & records of the American textile industry; Textile & social history exhib & special exhib gallery; Average Annual Attendance: 43,478; Mem: 1,082 4-5 events; Student/senior $40; Individual $50; Dual $65; Family $95; Contributing $125; Supporting $250
Income: Financed by endowment & annual fund
Library Holdings: Audio Tapes; Book Volumes; Exhibition Catalogs; Lantern Slides; Manuscripts; Motion Pictures; Original Art Works; Original Documents; Other Holdings Engineering & architectural plans; Pamphlets; Periodical Subscriptions; Photographs; Records; Slides; Video Tapes
Special Subjects: Historical Material, Textiles, Manuscripts, Photography, Prints
Exhibitions: Textile Revolution: An Exploration through Space and Time
Publications: Exhib catalogs; Linen Making in America
Activities: Classes for adults & children; docent training; pub progs; vacation & summer workshops; lects open to pub; gallery talks; special exhibs; sales desk sells textiles, books, prints & postcards; fiber art
L Library, 491 Dutton St, Lowell, MA 01854. Tel 978-441-0400; Fax 978-441-1412; Internet Home Page Address: www.athm.org; *Librn* Clare Sheridan
Open by appointment; For reference only
Income: Financed by endowment
Library Holdings: Book Volumes 30,000; Exhibition Catalogs; Manuscripts; Memorabilia; Motion Pictures; Original Art Works; Other Holdings Ephemera; Original documents; Trade literature; Pamphlets; Periodical Subscriptions 50; Photographs; Prints; Reels; Reproductions; Sculpture
Publications: Checklist of prints and manuscripts

M THE BRUSH ART GALLERY & STUDIOS, 256 Market St, Lowell, MA 01852-1877. Tel 978-459-7819; *Exec Dir* E Linda Poras
Open Tues - Fri 11 AM - 5 PM; Estab 1982; Nonprofit; in national historic park. Gallery with changing exhibitions plus 13 artist studios; Average Annual Attendance: 200,000; Mem: dues $25-$40
Income: Financed by mem, grants, fundraising & sales
Activities: Classes for adults & children; lect open to public; schols offered; sales shop sells original art

M THE LOADING DOCK GALLERY, 122 Western Ave Lowell, MA 01851-1433.

A LOWELL ART ASSOCIATION, INC, Whistler House Museum of Art, 243 Worthen St, Lowell, MA 01852-1874. Tel 978-452-7641; Fax 978-454-2421; Elec Mail mlally@whistlerhouse.org; Internet Home Page Address: www.whistlerhouse.org; *Exec Dir* Michael H Lally; *Exhibits Mgr* James Dyment
Open Wed - Sat 11 AM - 4 PM; Admis Adults $5, Seniors & Children $4; Estab 1878 to preserve the birthplace of James McNeill Whistler; to promote the arts in all its phases & to maintain a center for the cultural benefit of all the citizens of the community; Average Annual Attendance: 5,000; Mem: 500; dues family $45, adults $35, senior citizens $25, students $20
Income: Financed by endowment, mem, admis, grants & earned income
Special Subjects: Prints, Painting-American, Portraits
Collections: Mid 19th through early 20th century American Art: Hibbard, Benson, Noyes, Spear, Paxton, Phelps; Whistler etchings & lithographs; Gorky
Exhibitions: Galleries of works from permanent collection & periodic exhibits by contemporary artists
Publications: Brochures; S P Howes: Portrait Painter, catalog
Activities: Classes for adults & children; docent training; lects open to pub, 3 vis lectrs per yr; concerts; gallery talks; tours; progs of historical interest; book traveling exhibs 1-2 per yr; originate traveling exhibs to small mus & schools; mus shop sells books, original art, reproductions, prints & postcards

M THE REVOLVING MUSEUM, 290 Jackson St, Lowell, MA 01852. Tel 978-937-2787; Elec Mail dcoluntino@revolvingmuseum.org; Internet Home Page Address: www.revolvingmuseum.org; *Artistic Dir* Diana Coluntino
Office open Mon - Fri 10 AM - 6 PM; call for appt; No admis fee; Estab 1984 for pub art projects, educational programs, exhibitions & special events that encourage collaboration & dialogue with artists, youth & community members, to increase pub understanding of the importance of the arts & arts education & to advance cultural awareness; Average Annual Attendance: 15,000
Income: Financed by donations, grants & earned revenue
Activities: Classes for children; public art progs; Vanguardian Arts prog; The Visionary School prog; Wonders of the World summer festival & carnival; mus shop sells books, original art & other museum related items

LYNN

M LYNN ARTS, 25 Exchange St, Lynn, MA 01901-1423. Tel 781-598-5244; Fax 781-599-8926; *Contact* Susan Halter

MAGNOLIA

M CRANE COLLECTION, GALLERY OF AMERICAN PAINTING AND SCULPTURE, (Crane Collection Gallery) 2 Old Salem Path, Magnolia, MA 01930-5275. Tel 978-526-1698; Fax 781-235-4181; Elec Mail bonnie@cranecollection.com; Internet Home Page Address: www.cranecollection.com; *Owner, Dir & Pres* Bonnie L Crane
Open by appointment; No admis fee; Estab 1983 to exhibit 19th & early 20th century American paintings; Art gallery with changing inventory, on Boston's North Shore; Average Annual Attendance: 7,500

Library Holdings: Auction Catalogs; Book Volumes; Exhibition Catalogs; Original Art Works; Sculpture
Special Subjects: Painting-American, Period Rooms
Collections: 19th century & early 20th century American paintings & sculptures, including Hudson River School, Boston School & regional artists; outstanding contemporary artists of region
Exhibitions: Boston School: Then & Now; Summer Scenes II; Bruce Crane; Tonalism; Inspiration of Cape Ann; City Scenes; Little Picture Show; American Barbizon; Interiors; Russian Light I, II & III
Publications: The Gentle Art of Still Life; Russian Light

MALDEN

L MALDEN PUBLIC LIBRARY, Art Dept & Gallery, 36 Salem St, Malden, MA 02148-5291. Tel 781-324-0218, 381-0238; Fax 781-324-4467; Elec Mail maldensup@sbln.lib.ma.us; Elec Mail mbln@lib.ma.us; Internet Home Page Address: www.mbln.lib.ma.us/malden/index.htm; *Dir & Librn* Dina G Malgeri
Gallery has changing hours; please contact for available times; No admis fee; Estab 1879, incorporated 1885 as a public library and art gallery; Circ 239,493; Maintains three galleries, the main gallery being the Ryder Gallery, and the others known as the Upper & Lower Galleries
Income: $421,530 (financed by endowment, city and state appropriations)
Library Holdings: Exhibition Catalogs; Framed Reproductions; Manuscripts; Memorabilia; Original Art Works; Pamphlets; Photographs; Prints; Reproductions; Sculpture
Activities: Lect open to pub, 6-12 vis lectrs per yr; concerts; gallery talks; tours

MARBLEHEAD

A MARBLEHEAD ARTS ASSOCIATION, INC, 8 Hooper St, King Hooper Mansion Marblehead, MA 01945-3213. Tel 781-631-2608; Elec Mail info@marbleheadarts.org; Internet Home Page Address: www.marbleheadarts.org; *Exec Dir* Deborah Greel; *Asst to the Dir* May Britt Wang; *Pres* Jim Regis; *VPres* Claudia Leighton; *Secy* Margie Detkin; *Treas* Barbara Naeser
Open Summer Tues, Wed, & Sun noon-5PM, Thurs-Sat 10AM-5PM, Winter Tues, Wed, & Sun noon-5PM, Thurs-Sat 11AM-5PM; No admis fee; Estab 1922. Owns & occupies the historic King Hooper Mansion, located in historic Marblehead; Located in the historic King Hooper Mansion; contains four galleries of exhibits by association mems & guest artists that change monthly and educ programs. classes, and special events throughout the year.; Average Annual Attendance: 3000; Mem: 500 assoc, artist, & corporate mems; mem upon application (open); jury process for artist mem acceptance; dues assoc $35, family $55, senior over 65 $30, senior family $50, student to age 23 $15, supporter $75, patron $100, benefactor $150, artist $50, artist family $70
Income: Financed by mem & mansion rentals, gallery & shop sales, tuition fees & programs
Special Subjects: Etchings & Engravings, Prints
Collections: Works of: Sam Chamberlain; Claire Leighton; Lester Hornby; Sam Thal; Nason; Grace Albee & Phillip Kappel from the 1940s series: Friends of Contemporary Prints; Paintings by Mary Bradish Titcomb, Orlando Rouland, William Haseltine, Harry Powers, & Frank Flanagan
Exhibitions: Annual Town Show; Annual Member Show; Monthly Exhibits in four galleries of local and regional artists displaying over 1200 pieces of art annually
Publications: Newsletter, monthly
Activities: Classes for adults & children; drama programs; workshops; demonstrations; lects open to pub, 3 vis lectrs per yr; fall lect series; musical performances; Dancing with the Arts Gala; gallery talks; competitions with awards; schols offered; mus sales shop sells books, original art, reproductions, prints, fine crafts, glass, jewelry, greeting cards

M MARBLEHEAD MUSEUM & HISTORICAL SOCIETY, (Marblehead Historical Society) 170 Washington St, Marblehead, MA 01945-3340. Tel 781-631-1768; Fax 781-631-0917; Elec Mail info@marbleheadmuseum.org; Internet Home Page Address: www.marbleheadmuseum.org; *Dir* Pam Peterson; *Cur* Karen MacInnis
Open June 1 - Oct 31 Tues - Sat 10 AM - 4 PM; Nov - May Tues - Fri 10 AM - 4 PM; Average Annual Attendance: 2,500; Mem: 700; dues based on sliding scale
Library Holdings: Audio Tapes; Book Volumes; Kodachrome Transparencies; Lantern Slides; Manuscripts; Maps; Memorabilia; Original Art Works; Original Documents; Other Holdings; Pamphlets; Photographs; Slides
Special Subjects: Folk Art, Historical Material, Marine Painting, Architecture, Ceramics, Furniture, Photography, Porcelain, Portraits, Silver, Textiles, Maps, Watercolors, Costumes, Decorative Arts, Dolls, Jewelry, Carpets & Rugs, Coins & Medals, Period Rooms, Embroidery
Collections: Folk Art Paintings
Exhibitions: 2 or 3 per yr-changing exhibs of a variety of Marblehead subjects & media
Activities: Educ prog; classes for adults & children; lect open to the pub; approx 4 vis lectrs per yr; walking tours
M John Orne Johnson Frost Gallery, 170 Washington St, Marblehead, MA 01945. Tel 781-631-1768; Fax 781-631-0917; Elec Mail info@marbleheadmuseum.org; Internet Home Page Address: www.marbleheadmuseum.org/; *Dir* Pam Peterson; *Cur* Karen MacInnis
Open Tues - Sat 10 AM - 4 PM June - Oct; Open Tues - Fri 10 AM - 4 PM Nov - May; cls Christmas week; No admis fee; 1920s folk art paintings & models by J O J Frost depicting life in Marblehead & fishing at sea in the past; Average Annual Attendance: 2,700; Mem: 700; dues based on sliding scale
Income: Financed by endowment, mem, & admis
Collections: Ceramics, decorate arts, documents, dolls, folk art, furniture, glass, military items, nautical items, period rooms, portraits, ship paintings, textiles
Exhibitions: Permanent exhibit; Rotating exhibit
Publications: Semi-annual newsletter
Activities: Classes for children; docent training; workshops; lect open to public, 4 vis lectrs per year; gallery talks; tours; mus shop sells books, magazines, prints & postcards

M Jeremiah Lee Mansion, 161 Washington St, Marblehead, MA 01945; 170 Washington St, Marblehead, MA 01945. Tel 781-631-1768; Fax 781-631-0917; Elec Mail info@marbleheadmuseum.org; Internet Home Page Address: www.marbleheadmuseum.org; *Dir* Pam Peterson; *Cur* Karen MacInnis
Open June 1 - Oct 31 Tues - Sat 10 AM - 4 PM; Admis adults $5, mems & children under 12 free; Built 1768; mansion purchased 1909; Georgian-style three-story mansion made of woodcut blocks to simulate stone with elegant rococo interior carving & original hand-painted English wallpaper depicting Roman ruins; 18th-century-style-garden; top floor has been converted to a museum of Marblehead history; Average Annual Attendance: 2,500; Mem: 800; dues based on sliding scale
Income: Financed by endowment, mem & admis
Special Subjects: Decorative Arts, Folk Art, Historical Material, Marine Painting, Architecture, Ceramics, Furniture, Porcelain, Portraits, Painting-American, Period Rooms, Silver, Textiles, Maps, Watercolors, Costumes, Dolls, Jewelry, Carpets & Rugs, Coins & Medals, Embroidery
Collections: Ceramics, decorative arts, documents, dolls, folk art, furniture, glass, military items, nautical items, period rooms, portraits, ship paintings & textiles
Activities: Architecture classes for adults; classes for children; docent training; lect open to public, vis lectr; gallery talks; house or mansion tours; walking tours; sales shop sells books

L Archives, 170 Washington St, Marblehead, MA 01945. Tel 781-631-1768; *Cur* Karen MacInnis
Open Tues - Fri 10 AM - 4 PM; Admis non-members $5, members free; Estab 1898 to collect & maintain artifacts of Marblehead history; No galleries. Art & decorative art displayed in historic 1768 mansion; Average Annual Attendance: 4,000; Mem: 700; dues on a sliding scale
Income: Financed by mem fees & donations
Library Holdings: Auction Catalogs; Audio Tapes; Book Volumes; CD-ROMs; Cassettes; Clipping Files; Framed Reproductions; Kodachrome Transparencies; Lantern Slides; Manuscripts; Maps; Memorabilia; Motion Pictures; Original Art Works; Original Documents; Other Holdings; Pamphlets; Periodical Subscriptions; Photographs; Prints; Reproductions; Slides; Video Tapes
Special Subjects: Manuscripts, Historical Material
Collections: Archives
Publications: Members semiannual newsletter
Activities: Classes for adults & children; docent training; lect open to public, 3 vis lectrs per year; tours; sales shop sells books, original art, reproductions, prints & postcards

MARION

A MARION ART CENTER, Cecil Clark Davis Gallery, 80 Pleasant St, Marion, MA 02738; PO Box 602, Marion, MA 02738-0011. Tel 508-748-1266; Fax 508-748-2759; Elec Mail marionartcenter@verizon.net; Internet Home Page Address: www.marionartcenter.org; *Pres* Patricia White; *Dir* Wendy Bidstrup; *VPres* Joy Horstmann; *Secy* Kate Marvel; *Treas* Eric Strand
Open Tues - Fri 1 - 5 PM, Sat 10 AM - 2 PM; No admis fee; Estab 1957 to provide theater, concerts & visual arts exhibitions for the community & to provide studio art, theater arts, music & dance classes for adults & children; Two galleries, 125 ft of wall space, 500 sq ft floor space; indirect lighting; entrance off Main St; Average Annual Attendance: 2,000; Mem: 650; dues angel $1,000, patron $500, donor $250, sponsor $100, family $50, basic $25; annual meeting in Jan
Income: Financed by mem dues, donations & profit from ticket & gallery sales
Collections: Cecil Clark Davis (1877-1955), portrait paintings
Exhibitions: Monthly one person & group shows; Arts in the Park - one day outdoor festival in July
Publications: Annual mem folder; monthly invitations to opening; quarterly newsletter
Activities: Classes for adults & children; dramatic progs, pvt lessons in piano & voice; lects open to pub; concerts; gallery talks; competitions; schols; sales shop sells fine crafts, small paintings, prints, cards, original art and reproductions

MEDFORD

M TUFTS UNIVERSITY, Tufts University Art Gallery, 40 Talbot Ave, Aidekman Arts Center Medford, MA 02155. Tel 617-627-3518; Fax 617-627-3121; Elec Mail art gallery@tufts.edu; Internet Home Page Address: www.artgallery.tufts.edu; *Dir* Amy Ingrid Schlegel PhD; *Preparator* Doug Bell; *Colls Registrar* Laura McCarty; *Publs Coordr* Jeanne Koles; *Colls Assoc Registrar* John Rossetti; *Educ Outreach Coordr* Dorothee Perin; *Exhib Coordr* Lissa Cramer
Open Tues - Wed & Fri - Sun 11 AM - 5 PM, Thurs 11 AM - 8 PM, cl holidays & Aug; No admis fee; suggested donation $3; Estab 1991; 7,000 sq ft of exhibit space over 4 galleries; Average Annual Attendance: 8,000; Mem: Contemporary Arts Circle Friends Group
Special Subjects: Painting-American, Photography, Prints, Antiquities-Egyptian, Antiquities-Greek, Antiquities-Roman
Collections: Primarily 19th & 20th centuries American paintings, prints & drawings; contemporary paintings, photographs & works on paper
Exhibitions: Approx ten shows annually, three of which are thesis exhibits of candidates for the MFA degree offered by Tufts in affiliation with the School of the Boston Museum of Fine Arts; New media wall, sculpture ct; Annual summer exhibition of local artists
Publications: Catalogues & brochures
Activities: Docent training; tours for adults; lects open to pub, 4 vis lectrs per yr; gallery talks; tours; intra-univ art loan prog; originate traveling exhibs

MILTON

M CAPTAIN FORBES HOUSE MUSEUM, 215 Adams St, Milton, MA 02186-4215. Tel 617-696-1815; Fax 617-696-1815; Elec Mail forbeshousemuseum@verizon.net; *Dir* Christine M Sullivan; *Admin* Nadine Leary; *Mktg & Events Coordr* Lauren Pauly; *Develop Coordr* Sara Collard
Open Tues - Thurs & Sun 1 - 4 PM; Admis $5, seniors & students $3, children under 12 free; Estab 1964 as a Historic House museum; for preservation, research,

education: 19th century through Forbes family focus; Average Annual Attendance: 1,000; Mem: 400; dues life member $1,000, benefactor $500, sponsor $250, donor $100, friend $50, family $40,individual $25
Income: $70,000 (financed by endowment, mem & fundraising)
Library Holdings: Book Volumes 2500; Exhibition Catalogs; Manuscripts; Memorabilia; Micro Print; Original Art Works; Pamphlets; Periodical Subscriptions 6; Photographs; Prints
Special Subjects: Decorative Arts, Porcelain, Period Rooms
Collections: Abraham Lincoln Civil War Collections & Archives; Forbes Family Collection of China trade & American furnishings
Exhibitions: Annual Abraham Lincoln essay contest for grades K - 8th grade
Publications: Forbes House Jottings, four times per year
Activities: Classes for adults & children; docent training; lects open to pub, 3 vis lectrs per yr; tours; competitions & awards; lending collection contains decorative arts, Lincoln memorabilia, original art works, original prints & sculpture; mus sells books & cards

NANTUCKET

A ARTISTS ASSOCIATION OF NANTUCKET, 19 Washington St., & 1 Gardner Perry Ln Nantucket, MA 02554; PO Box 1104, Nantucket, MA 02554-1104. Tel 508-228-0722; Fax 508-228-9700; Elec Mail aanoff@verizon.net (office); Elec Mail anngallery@verizon.net (gallery); Internet Home Page Address: www.nantucketarts.org; *Pres (V)* Katie Frinkle Legge; *Gallery Dir* Robert Foster; *Admin* Meghan Valero; *Dir Arts Prog* Liz Hunt O'Brien
Open spring daily Noon - 5 PM, summer daily 10 AM - 6 PM; No admis fee; Estab 1945 to provide a place for Nantucket artists of all levels & styles to show their work & encourage new artists; Maintains one gallery: at 19 Washington St, 2 fls; Average Annual Attendance: 50,000 - 70,000; Mem: 600; dues patron $50 - $500, artist $100; annual meeting Aug
Income: $75,000 - $100,000 (financed by mem, fundraising & commissions, large patron gifts)
Library Holdings: Auction Catalogs; Book Volumes; Clipping Files; Exhibition Catalogs; Original Art Works; Periodical Subscriptions
Collections: 600 pieces, most by Nantucket artists; Wet Paint Auction
Exhibitions: Annual Craft Show; juried shows; changing one-person & group member shows during summer; occasional off-season shows
Publications: Monthly newsletter; annual brochure
Activities: Classes for adults & children; workshops; lect open to public, 5-6 vis lectrs per year; gallery talks, competitions with awards; scholarships; individual paintings & original objects of art lent to local hospital & public offices; sales shop sells original art, prints & lithographs

M EGAN INSTITUTE OF MARITIME STUDIES, 4 Winter St, The Coffin School Nantucket, MA 02554-3638. Tel 508-228-2505; Fax 508-228-7069; Elec Mail egan@eganinstitute.com; Internet Home Page Address: www.eganinstitute.com; *Assoc Dir & Cur* Margaret Moore; *Dir* Nathaniel Philbrick
Open daily 1 - 5 PM, May - Oct; Admis $1; Estab 1996; Historic 1854 Greek Revival building with 1 main gallery & 2 special exhibition galleries; maintains reference library; Average Annual Attendance: 3,000
Income: Financed by the foundation
Special Subjects: Architecture, Painting-American, Photography, Watercolors, Etchings & Engravings, Landscapes, Decorative Arts, Manuscripts, Portraits, Marine Painting, Painting-British, Historical Material, Maps
Collections: Coffin School memorabilia; 19th century American portraits & landscapes; 19th & 20th century marine paintings; ship models
Exhibitions: Nantucket Spirit; The Life and Art of Elizabeth R. Coffin
Publications: Millhill Press-book
Activities: Adult classes; lect open to public, 7-10 vis lectrs per year; lending collection contains paintings & objects of art; sales shop sells books & prints

M NANTUCKET HISTORICAL ASSOCIATION, Historic Nantucket, 15 Broad St, Nantucket, MA 02554-3502; PO Box 1016, Nantucket, MA 02554-1016. Tel 508-228-1894; Fax 508-228-5618; Elec Mail nhainfo@nha.org; Internet Home Page Address: www.nha.org; *Exec Dir* Jean M Weber; *Cur Library & Archives* Georgen Gilliam; *CEO* Frank D Milligan; *Dir Develop* Jean Grimmer; *Museum Shop Mgr* Georgina Winton; *VPres* Arie Kopelman; *Chief Cur* Niles Parker
Open June - Oct 10 AM - 5 PM; Admis a visitor pass to all buildings, adults $10, children 5-14 $5, individual building admis $2-$5; Estab 1894 to preserve Nantucket & maintain history; Historic Nantucket is a collection of 10 historic buildings & 3 museums throughout the town, open to the public & owned by the Nantucket Historical Assoc. Together they portray the way people lived & worked as Nantucket grew from a small farming community to the center of America's whaling industry; maintains reference library; Mem: 3000; dues $30-$1000; annual meeting in July
Income: Financed by endowment, contributions, events, mem & admis
Special Subjects: Painting-American
Collections: Portraits, Oil Paintings, Watercolors, Needlework Pictures, baskets, furniture, photographs, scrimshaw, textiles, whaling tools & all other manner of artifacts related to Nantucket & Maritime History; all objects exhibited in our historic houses & museums which cover the period 1686-1930
Publications: Art on Nantucket; Historic Nantucket, quarterly, magazine for members
Activities: Classes for children; docent training; lects open to pub, 24 vis lectrs per yr; concerts; gallery talks; tours; research fels offered; mus shop sells books, reproductions, prints, slides, period furniture, household items, silver, bone & ivory scrimshaw, candles & children's toys

NEW BEDFORD

M ARTWORKS!, 384 Acushnet Ave New Bedford, MA 02740-6238.

L NEW BEDFORD FREE PUBLIC LIBRARY, (New Bedford Free Public Library Special Collections) Special Collections Dept: Art Collection, 613 Pleasant St, New Bedford, MA 02740-6203. Tel 508-979-1787; Fax 508-979-1614; Elec Mail jhodson@sailsinc.org; Internet Home Page Address: www.ci.new-bedford.ma.us/nbfpl.htm; *Cur Art* Janice Hodson; *Head Spec Colls* Paul Cyr; *Spec Colls Family Historian* Joan Barney
Open Mon - Thurs 9 AM - 9 PM, Fri & Sat 9 AM - 5 PM; Art Room open Tues - Wed 1 PM - 5 PM, Thurs 1 PM - 5 PM & 6 PM - 9 PM, Fri 9 Am - 5 PM, Sat 9 AM - Noon, 1 PM - 5 PM; cl Sun & holidays; No admis fee; Estab 1852; Circ non-circulating; 19th & 20th Century Am & European art; Average Annual Attendance: 4500
Income: Financed by endowment, city, & state appropriation
Library Holdings: Auction Catalogs; Book Volumes; CD-ROMs; Cassettes; DVDs; Exhibition Catalogs; Fiche; Filmstrips; Framed Reproductions; Kodachrome Transparencies; Lantern Slides; Manuscripts; Maps; Memorabilia; Motion Pictures; Original Art Works; Original Documents; Pamphlets; Periodical Subscriptions; Photographs; Prints; Records; Reels; Sculpture; Slides; Video Tapes
Special Subjects: Art History, Decorative Arts, Photography, Etchings & Engravings, Maps, Painting-American, Painting-Dutch, Painting-German, Prints, Historical Material, Portraits, Watercolors, American Western Art, Handicrafts, Miniatures, Silver, Textiles, Woodcarvings, Woodcuts, Marine Painting, Landscapes
Collections: Paintings by Clifford Ashley, Albert Bierstadt, F D Millet, William Wall, Dodge MacKnight, William Bradford, R Swain Gifford, Ralph Fasenella; John James Audubon's Birds of America Folio; maritime art; landscapes; portraiture; auction catalogs; rare books; early study prints; Hudson River School painters
Activities: Art progs for children & adults; lects open to pub; vis lectrs; gallery talks; tours; internships offered; objects of art lent to museums for special exhibits

M OLD DARTMOUTH HISTORICAL SOCIETY, New Bedford Whaling Museum, 18 Johnny Cake Hill, New Bedford, MA 02740. Tel 508-997-0046; Fax 508-997-0018; Internet Home Page Address: www.whalingmuseum.org; *Cur* Michael Jehle; *Dir* Anne Brengle
Open daily 9 AM - 5 PM, Sun 1 - 5 PM; Admis $6 youth & seniors $5, children between 6 & 14 $4, children under 6 free; Estab 1903 to collect, preserve & interpret objects including printed material, pictures & artifacts related to the history of the New Bedford area & American whaling; Average Annual Attendance: 50,000; Mem: 3000; dues $15-$850; annual meeting in May
Income: $713,000 (financed by endowment, mem, private gifts, grants, special events & admis)
Special Subjects: Drawings, Painting-American, Photography, Prints, Sculpture, Ethnology, Costumes, Crafts, Folk Art, Etchings & Engravings, Decorative Arts, Manuscripts, Portraits, Dolls, Furniture, Glass, Marine Painting, Historical Material, Ivory, Maps, Scrimshaw, Restorations, Miniatures, Embroidery, Laces
Collections: Paintings, watercolors, drawings, prints, photographs, whaling equipment, ship models, including 89 foot 1/2 scale model of whaler Lagoda
Exhibitions: 66 Ft Skeleton of Blue Whale; Two Brothers Gowlart; changing exhibits every 6 months
Publications: Bulletin from Johnny Cake Hill, quarterly; exhibition catalogs; calendar, quarterly
Activities: Classes for adults & children; docent training; lects open to pub, 12 vis lectrs per yr; gallery talks; tours; individual paintings & original objects of art lent to other mus; lending collection contains microfilm, nature artifacts, original art works, original prints, paintings, photographs & sculptures; originates traveling exhibs; mus shop sells books, magazines, reproductions, prints, slides & gift items

L Whaling Museum Library, 18 Johnny Cake Hill, New Bedford, MA 02740. Tel 508-997-0046; Fax 508-997-0018; Internet Home Page Address: www.whalingmuseum.org
Open by appointment only Mon - Fri 10 AM - Noon & 1 - 5 PM, first Sat of each month; For reference only
Income: Financed by private gifts & grants
Library Holdings: Book Volumes 15,000; Clipping Files; Exhibition Catalogs; Filmstrips; Manuscripts; Memorabilia; Pamphlets; Periodical Subscriptions 12; Reels

NEWBURYPORT

M HISTORICAL SOCIETY OF OLD NEWBURY, Cushing House Museum, 98 High St, Newburyport, MA 01950-3053. Tel 978-462-2681; Elec Mail hson@newburyhist.org; Internet Home Page Address: www.newburyhist.org; *Cur* Jay S Williamson
Open Office: Tues - Fri yr round 10 AM - 4 PM, Tours: Wed - Fri 10 AM - 4 PM, Sat & Sun noon - 4 PM (June 1 - Oct 31); Admis adults $8, seniors 65+ $7, students $2; Estab 1877 to preserve heritage of Old Newbury, Newbury, Newburyport & West Newbury; Average Annual Attendance: 3,000; Mem: 600; dues patron $500, benefactor & sustaining $250, friend $100, friend $50, family $35, individual $20
Income: $50,000 (financed by dues, tours, endowments, fund-raisers)
Library Holdings: Auction Catalogs; Exhibition Catalogs; Manuscripts; Memorabilia; Original Art Works; Original Documents; Other Holdings; Pamphlets; Periodical Subscriptions; Photographs; Prints; Reproductions; Slides
Special Subjects: Architecture, Painting-American, Textiles, Decorative Arts, Manuscripts, Furniture, Historical Material, Period Rooms, Embroidery
Collections: China; dolls; furniture; glass; miniatures; needlework; paintings; paperweights; sampler coll; silver; military & other historical material representative of over three centuries of Newbury's history
Exhibitions: 150th Anniversary of Newbury
Publications: Old-Town & The Waterside, 200 years of Tradition & Change in Newbury, Newburyport & West Newbury - 1635-1835
Activities: Classes for adults; docent training; lects open to pub, 8 vis lectrs per yr; gallery talks; tours for children; annual auction; scholarships & fels offered;

exten dept serves Merrimack Valley; individual paintings & original objects of art lent to nonprofit cultural institutions; mus shop sells books

M NEWBURYPORT MARITIME SOCIETY, INC, (Newburyport Maritime Society) Custom House Maritime Museum, 25 Water St, Newburyport, MA 01950-2754. Tel 978-462-8681; Elec Mail info@thchmm.org; Internet Home Page Address: www.thechmm.org; *Chmn* Daniel May; *Exec Dir* Michael Mroz
Open Jan - Apr: Sat 10 AM - 4 PM, Sun & holiday Mon noon - 4PM May - Dec: Tues - Sat 10 AM - 4 PM, Sun Noon - 4 PM, holiday Mon noon - 4 PM; Admis adults $7, seniors & students $5, military & children under 6 free; Estab 1975 to exhibit the maritime heritage of Newburyport & the Merrimack Valley; 7 galleries housed in an 1835 Custom House designed by Robert Mills. The structure is on the National Register of Historic Places; Average Annual Attendance: 17,000; Mem: 400; dues $40 & up; annual meeting in Apr
Income: Financed by mem, admis, fundraisers, gifts & grants
Library Holdings: Book Volumes; Manuscripts; Maps; Original Documents; Photographs; Prints
Special Subjects: Historical Material, Portraits, Manuscripts, Maps, Painting-American, Photography, Ethnology, Decorative Arts, Marine Painting
Collections: Coll of portraits, ship models & decorative art objects 1680-1820; original coll of ethnographic items owned by Newburyport Marine Society Members, half hull models of Merrimack River Valley Ships; portraits of sea captains; navigational instruments & models; core exhibits on populations, natural resources, urban seaport, coast guard
Exhibitions: See website for activities & events
Publications: Year round news & event emails
Activities: Classes for adults & children; docent training; lects open to pub, 15-20 vis lectrs per yr; concerts; gallery talks; tours; individual paintings & original objects of art lent to other mus & historical agencies; book traveling exhibs; mus shop sells books, original art, reproductions, prints, nautical & Newburyport related items

NEWTON

M HISTORIC NEWTON, (Jackson Homestead) 527 Washington St, Newton, MA 02458-1433. Tel 617-796-1450; Fax 617-552-7228; Elec Mail cstone@newtonma.gov; Internet Home Page Address: www.historicnewton.org; *Cur Manuscripts* Sara Goldberg; *Dir* Cindy Stone
Open Tues - Sat 11 AM - 5 PM, Sun Noon - 5 PM; Admis adult $5, children & seniors $3; Estab 1950 to encourage inquiry into Newton, MA within the broad context of American history; Permanent & temporary exhibitions highlight Newton's role as one of the country's earliest railroad suburbs & the Homestead as a station on the Underground Railroad; Average Annual Attendance: 7,500
Income: Mem, grants & contributions
Library Holdings: Audio Tapes; Book Volumes; Cards; Cassettes; Clipping Files; Exhibition Catalogs; Lantern Slides; Manuscripts; Maps; Memorabilia; Original Art Works; Original Documents; Photographs; Slides; Video Tapes
Special Subjects: Drawings, Painting-American, Photography, Archaeology, Textiles, Costumes, Ceramics, Landscapes, Manuscripts, Portraits, Dolls, Furniture, Silver, Historical Material, Maps, Embroidery, Pewter
Collections: Costumes, furniture, household & personal items, paintings, textiles, tools, toys, archives of papers, photographs & maps
Activities: Classes for adults & children; special progs & events; docent training; lects open to pub, 8 per yr; gallery talks; tours; awards, Historic Presentation; mus shop sells books, reproductions & prints

NEWTONVILLE

M NEW ART CENTER, 61 Washington Park, Newtonville, MA 02460-1915. Tel 617-964-3424; Fax 617-630-0081

NORTH EASTON

L AMES FREE-EASTON'S PUBLIC LIBRARY, 53 Main St, North Easton, MA 02356-1452. Tel 508-238-2000; Fax 508-238-2980; Elec Mail info@amesfreelibrary.org; Internet Home Page Address: www.amesfreelibrary.org; *Reference Librn & Adult Svcs* Steven Somerdin; *Children's Librn* Catherine Coyne; *Exec Dir* Annalee Bundy; *Asst Dir* Madeline Miele Holt; *Admin Asst* Michelle DuPrey; *Circ & Interlibrary Loan* Joan Roan; *Cataloger* Anne Marie Large; *Computer Instr* Whitney Anderson; *Serials Technician* Lorraine Robinacci; *Circ Asst* Amy Dean
Open Mon & Thurs 10 AM - 8 PM, Tues & Wed 1 - 8 PM, Fri - Sat 10 AM - 5 PM; No admis fee; Estab 1879; Circ 97,000
Income: $684,760 (financed by local endowment) & public funds
Purchases: $90,110
Library Holdings: Audio Tapes 187; Book Volumes 56,000; Cassettes; Clipping Files; Periodical Subscriptions 137; Video Tapes
Special Subjects: Decorative Arts, Architecture
Collections: Architecture (Richardsonian); Decorative Arts
Activities: Classes for adults & children; dramatic prog; story hours; storytellers; booktalks

NORTH GRAFTON

M WILLARD HOUSE & CLOCK MUSEUM, INC, 11 Willard St, North Grafton, MA 01536-2011. Tel 508-839-3500; Fax 508-839-3599; Elec Mail cynthia@willardhouse.org; Internet Home Page Address: www.willardhouse.org; *VPres* Sumner Tilton; *Dir* Patrick Keenan; *Pres* Richard Currier; *Conservator* David Gow
Open Wed - Sat 10 AM - 4 PM, Sun 1 - 4 PM, cl Mon & holidays; Admis adults $7, seniors $6, children $3; Estab 1971 for educ in the fields of history, horology, decorative arts & antiques; Maintains nine rooms open in house mus; Average Annual Attendance: 1,500; Mem: 200; dues $25 individual, $40 family

Income: Financed by endowment, mem, admis, gifts & sales
Library Holdings: Auction Catalogs; Book Volumes; Memorabilia; Original Documents; Pamphlets; Periodical Subscriptions; Photographs; Prints; Slides
Special Subjects: Ceramics, Painting-American, Architecture, Textiles, Costumes, Folk Art, Decorative Arts, Portraits, Dolls, Furniture, Glass, Jewelry, Silver, Carpets & Rugs, Historical Material, Coins & Medals, Restorations, Calligraphy, Period Rooms, Embroidery, Gold, Pewter
Collections: Native American Artifacts Collection; Willard Clockmaking Family Collection, furnishings, memorabilia & portraits; 18th & 19th Century Early Country Antique Furniture Collection; 19th Century Embroidery Collection; 18th & 19th Century Firearms Collection; 19th Century Children's Toy Collection; 19th Century Costume Collection; 19th Century Oriental Rug Collection; Willard Clockmaking Collection
Exhibitions: Annual Clock Collectors Workshop; Annual Christmas Open House
Publications: Mem newsletter, biannual
Activities: Classes for adults & children; docent training; lects open to pub; 1 vis lectr per yr; tours; mus shop sells books, magazines, clocks, antiques, jewelry

NORTHAMPTON

L **FORBES LIBRARY,** 20 West St, Northampton, MA 01060-3798. Tel 413-587-1011, 587-1013; Fax 413-587-1015; Elec Mail art@forbeslibrary.org; Internet Home Page Address: www.forbeslibrary.org; *Arts & Music Librn* Faith Kaufmann
Open Mon 1 - 9 PM, Tues 9 AM - 6 PM, Wed 9 AM - 9 PM, Thurs 1 - 5 PM, Fri - Sat 9 AM - 5 PM, cl Sun & holidays; Estab 1894 to serve the community as a general public library and a research facility; Circ 292,950; Houses Hosmer Gallery and Calvin Coolidge Presidential Library & Museum. Gallery and exhibit cases for regional artists, photographers and craftspeople
Library Holdings: Audio Tapes; Book Volumes 40,000; Cassettes 2000; Compact Disks 4000; DVDs 200; Exhibition Catalogs; Original Art Works; Original Documents; Periodical Subscriptions 52; Photographs; Prints; Reels; Video Tapes 2000
Special Subjects: Photography, Posters
Collections: Bien edition of Audubon Bird Prints; Library of Charles E Forbes; Walter E Corbin Collection of Photographic Prints & Slides; Connecticut Valley History; Genealogical Records; Official White House Portraits of President Calvin Coolidge & Grace Anna Coolidge; World War I & II Poster Collection; Local History Photograph Collection & Print Collection
Exhibitions: Monthly exhibits of works by regional artists, photographers and crafts people; Calvin Coolidge Presidential Library & Mus
Activities: Films; readings; lects open to public; Concerts; Gallery talks; exten dept serves elderly & house bound

M **HISTORIC NORTHAMPTON MUSEUM & EDUCATION CENTER,** 46 Bridge St, Northampton, MA 01060-2428. Tel 413-584-3669, 584-6011; Fax 413-584-7956; Elec Mail hstnhamp@jauanet.com; Internet Home Page Address: www.historic-northampton.org; *Exec Dir* Kerry Buckley
Open Tues - Fri 10 AM - 4 PM, weekends Noon - 4 PM, cl Mon & holidays; Estab 1905 to collect, preserve & exhibit objects of human history in Northhampton & Connecticut Valley; The mus maintains three historic houses from about 1728, 1798 & 1813; a barn from about 1825 with newly added educ center; a non-circulating reference library; Average Annual Attendance: 9,500; Mem: 500; dues bus $100 - $500, individual $20 - $100; annual meeting in Nov
Income: $95,000 (financed by endowment, mem, gifts)
Special Subjects: Photography, Textiles, Costumes, Decorative Arts, Furniture
Collections: Collections focus on material culture of Northampton & the upper Connecticut River Valley, costumes, textiles, ca. 1900 Howes Brothers photographs; archaeological artifacts from on-site excavation, decorative arts; oil paintings of local personalities & scenes; Collection of costumes, textiles, furniture & decorative art
Publications: Newsletter, quarterly; booklets on local subjects; brochures & flyers
Activities: Classes for adults & children; docent progs; workshops; internships; lects open to pub; gallery talks; schols offered; mus shop sells books, merchandise related to mus's collections, reproductions of collection items, maps, period toys & games

M **NORTHAMPTON CENTER FOR THE ARTS,** 17 New South St, Northampton, MA 01060; PO Box 366, Northampton, MA 01061-0366. Tel 413-584-7327; Fax 413-582-9014; Elec Mail ncfa@nohoarts.org; Internet Home Page Address: nohoarts.org

M **SMITH COLLEGE,** Museum of Art, Elm St at Bedford Terrace, Northampton, MA 01063. Tel 413-585-2760; Fax 413-585-2782; Elec Mail artmuseum@ais.smith.edu; Internet Home Page Address: www.smith.edu/artmuseum; *Others* TTY 413-585-2786; *Cur Paintings & Sculpture* Linda Muehlig; *Assoc Dir Museum Svcs* David Dempsey; *Registrar, Coll Mgr* Louise Laplante; *Cur Prints, Drawings & Photographs* Aprile Gallant; *Mem & Mktg Dir* Margi Caplan; *Web & Mktg Coordr* Martha Ebner; *Mus Store Mgr* Nan Fleming; *Asst Mus Shop Mgr* Susan Gelotte; *Exhib Coordr* Kelly Holbert; *Admin Asst* Louise Krieger; *Preparator* William Myers; *Dir* Jessica Nicoll; *Financial & Systems Coordr* Stacey Anasazi; *SIAMS Coordr/Brown Post-Bac Fel Mus Educ* Ashley Brickhouse; *Educ Prog Planner* Taiga Ermansons; *Colls Management Imaging Proj Coordr* Kate Kearns; *Cunningham Center Mgr* Henriette Kets de Vries; *Mem & Gifts Asst* Louise Kohrman; *Assoc Educator Acad Progs* Maggie Lind; *Assoc Educator School & Family Progs* Julie Zappie McLean; *Mgr Security & Guest Servs* Ann Mayo; *Assoc Acad Progs & Pub Educ* Ann Musser; *Installation Asst* Stephanie Sullivan; *Asst Mgr Security & Guest Servs* Rick Turschman; *Freeman/McPherson Post-Doc Fel & Lectr Art* Fan Zhang
Open Tues - Sat 10 AM - 4 PM, Sun Noon - 4 PM, 2nd Fri 10 AM - 8 PM, cl Mon & Holidays; Admis adults $5, seniors (65 & over) $4, students (13 & over w/ID) $3, youth (6-12) $2; free second Friday of mon 4 PM - 8 PM; Collection founded 1879; Hillyer Art Gallery built 1882; Smith College Museum of Art estab 1920; Tryon Art Gallery built 1926; present Smith College Museum of Art in Tryon Hall opened 1973; renovated and expanded 2003; Average Annual Attendance: 34,000; Mem: 1200; dues student $20, educator $35, individual $50, family/household $75, contributor $150, sustainer $500, patron $1,000
Special Subjects: Drawings, Painting-American, Photography, Prints, Decorative Arts, Painting-European
Collections: Examples from most periods and cultures with special emphasis on European and American paintings, sculpture, drawings, prints, photographs and decorative arts of the 17th-20th centuries
Exhibitions: Temporary exhibitions and installations 12-24 annually
Publications: Catalogues
Activities: Lect; gallery talks; guided tours; audio tours; concerts; individual works of art lent to other institutions; mus shop sells publications, post and note cards, posters, art-related merchandise

L **Hillyer Art Library,** Elm St at Bedford Terrace, Northampton, MA 01063. Tel 413-585-2940; Fax 413-585-6975; Elec Mail hillinfo@smith.edu; Internet Home Page Address: www.smith.edu/libraries/libs/hillyer/; *Librn* Barbara Polowy; *Art Library Asst* Lisa DeCarolis
Open Mon - Thurs 9 AM - 11 PM, Fri 9 AM - 9 PM, Sat 10 AM - 9 PM, Sun Noon - Midnight; Estab 1918 to support courses offered by art department of Smith College; Circ 23,500; For reference use only
Income: Financed by endowment
Library Holdings: Auction Catalogs 10,000; Book Volumes 125,000; CD-ROMs 300; Exhibition Catalogs; Periodical Subscriptions 180
Special Subjects: Art History, Drawings, Etchings & Engravings, Painting-American, Painting-British, Painting-Italian, Painting-Spanish, Sculpture, Painting-European, History of Art & Archaeology, Antiquities-Oriental, Antiquities-Etruscan, Antiquities-Greek, Antiquities-Roman, Architecture

NORTON

M **WHEATON COLLEGE,** Beard and Weil Galleries, 26 E Main St, Norton, MA 02766-2311. Tel 508-286-3578; Fax 508-286-3565; Elec Mail amurray@wheatonma.edu; Internet Home Page Address: www.wheatoncollege.edu/acad/art/gallery; *Dir* Ann H Murray; *Prog Coordr for the Arts* Betsy Cronin; *Asst Prof Mus Studies/Art History & Cur Permanent Coll* Leah Niederstadt
Open Mon - Sat 12:30 - 4:30 PM except during col vacations; No admis fee; Estab 1960, gallery program since 1930 to provide a wide range of contemporary one-person & group shows as well as exhibitions from the permanent collection of paintings, graphics & objects; Gallery is of fireproof steel-frame, glass & brick construction; Average Annual Attendance: 5,000
Income: Financed by college budget & occasional grants
Purchases: Marble portrait bust of Roman boy; Etruscan antefix head; Head of Galienus, Roman c 260 AD; Cycladic Figurine, 2500-1100 BC Greek Black Figure Amphora, 6th c BC; DuBourg Book of Hours, 1475-1490
Library Holdings: Auction Catalogs; Book Volumes; Exhibition Catalogs; Original Documents
Special Subjects: American Indian Art, Decorative Arts, Drawings, Etchings & Engravings, Landscapes, Marine Painting, Ceramics, Glass, Flasks & Bottles, Pre-Columbian Art, Painting-American, Prints, Textiles, Painting-British, Painting-French, Sculpture, Graphics, Watercolors, Bronzes, African Art, Woodcarvings, Woodcuts, Manuscripts, Asian Art, Antiquities-Byzantine, Painting-Dutch, Ivory, Coins & Medals, Baroque Art, Embroidery, Laces, Antiquities-Greek, Antiquities-Roman, Mosaics, Stained Glass, Painting-German, Antiquities-Etruscan
Collections: 19th & 20th centuries prints, drawings, paintings & sculpture; Wedgewood, 18th & 19th centuries glass; ancient bronzes, sculptures & ceramics; Cass Wedgewood Collection
Exhibitions: Changing exhibitions
Publications: Exhibition catalogs; Prints of the 19th Century: A Selection from the Wheaton College Collection; The Art of Drawing; The Art of the Print & The Art of Painting and Sculpture: Selections from the Permanent Collection; The Realist Impulse: Paintings & Sculpture from the Wheaton Col Collection, c 1830-1940; Dorothea Rockburne: Astronomy Drawings
Activities: Lects open to pub, 5-8 vis lectrs per yr; concerts; gallery talks; tours; sponsoring of competitions; individual paintings & original objects of art lent to colleges, other museums & galleries; originate traveling exhibs

OAK BLUFFS

A **MARTHA'S VINEYARD CENTER FOR THE VISUAL ARTS,** Firehouse Gallery, 88 Dukes County Ave, Oak Bluffs, MA 02557; PO Box 4377, Vineyard Haven, MA 02568-0934. Tel 508-693-9025; Elec Mail dreyerc@earthlink.net; *Pres* Chris Dreyer
Open from Memorial Day weekend noon - 6 PM, cl Mon; No admis fee; Estab 1991; Old firehouse, semi-cooperative space; Average Annual Attendance: 500; Mem: 100; $40 ann dues; ann meeting Aug
Income: Financed by mem, donations, grant from local cultural council
Exhibitions: July - Aug weekly shows of member art
Publications: Arts Directory, annually
Activities: Classes & workshops; scholarships offered; originate traveling exhibs

PAXTON

M **ANNA MARIA COLLEGE,** Saint Luke's Gallery, 50 Sunset Ln, Moll Art Ctr Paxton, MA 01612-1106. Tel 508-849-3318; Internet Home Page Address: www.annamaria.edu/; *Chmn Art Dept* Alice Lambert
Open Mon - Fri 1 - 5 PM, Sun Noon - 2 PM, Sun 1 - 4 PM; No admis fee; Estab 1968 as an outlet for the art student and professional artist, and to raise the artistic awareness of the general community; Main Gallery is 35 x 15 ft with about 300 sq ft of wall space; Average Annual Attendance: 500
Income: Financed by the college
Special Subjects: Painting-American, Sculpture, Furniture
Collections: Small assortment of furniture, paintings, sculpture
Exhibitions: Annual senior art exhibit; local artists; faculty & students shows
Publications: Exhibit programs

Activities: Educ Dept; lect open to public; individual paintings & original objects of art lent to campus offices

PEMBROKE

NEW ENGLAND WATERCOLOR SOCIETY
For further information, see National and Regional Organizations

PITTSFIELD

L   BERKSHIRE ATHENAEUM, Reference Dept, One Wendell Ave, Pittsfield, MA 01201. Tel 413-499-9480 ext 4; Fax 413-499-9489; Elec Mail pittsref@cwmars.org; Internet Home Page Address: www.berkshire.net/PittsfieldLibrary; *Dir* Ron Latham; *Supv Reference* Madeline Kelly; *Music & Arts Specialist* Mary Ann Knight
Open Mon & Fri 9 AM - 5 PM, Tues - Thurs 9 AM - 9 PM, Sat 10 AM - 5 PM; reduced hours July & Aug; No admis fee; Estab 1872
Income: Financed by city & state appropriations
Library Holdings: Book Volumes; Cassettes 300; Compact Disks; Other Holdings Compact Discs 2,000; Periodical Subscriptions 15-20; Video Tapes
Collections: Mary Rice Morgan Ballet Collection: a reference room of programs, artifacts, prints, original art, rare & current books on dance & costume design
Activities: Lects open to pub, concerts

M   BERKSHIRE MUSEUM, 39 South St, Pittsfield, MA 01201-6169. Tel 413-443-7171, ext 10; Fax 413-443-2135; Elec Mail pr@berkshiremuseum.org; Internet Home Page Address: www.berkshiremuseum.org; *Dir* Stuart A Chase; *Dir Finance & Admin* Jon C Provost; *Dir Develop* Mary Jo Murphy; *Dir Educ & Progs* Maria Mingalone; *Bldg & Security Mgr* Brian Warner; *Mus Shop Mgr* Rebecca Petrie; *Colls Mgr* Leanne Hayden; *Exhib Mgr* Kirsti Scutt Edwards; *Dir Commun* Kimberly Rawson
Open to pub Mon - Sat 10 AM - 5 PM, Sun Noon - 5 PM, cl New Year's Day, Memorial Day, Independence Day, Labor Day, Thanksgiving & Christmas; Admis Adults $10, children 3-18 $5, members & children under 2 free; Estab 1903 as a mus of art, natural science & history; Maintains reference library for staff & teachers; Average Annual Attendance: 82,000; Mem: 2000; dues single $45, dual $60, family $75, special members $100-$500, corporate members $200 & up, Crane Society $1,000 & up
Income: Financed by endowment, mem, fundraising & gifts
Special Subjects: Drawings, Painting-American, American Indian Art, American Western Art, Anthropology, Ethnology, Costumes, Ceramics, Folk Art, Etchings & Engravings, Landscapes, Decorative Arts, Dolls, Furniture, Glass, Jewelry, Painting-British, Painting-Dutch, Coins & Medals, Painting-Flemish, Dioramas, Painting-Italian, Antiquities-Egyptian, Antiquities-Greek, Antiquities-Etruscan
Collections: Paintings of the Hudson River School (Inness, Moran, Blakelock, Martin, Wyant, Moran, Church, Bierstadt & others); early American portraits; Egyptian, Babylonia & Near East arts; grave reliefs from Palmyra; Paul M Hahn Collection of 18th-Century English & American Silver; Old Masters (Pons, de Hooch, Van Dyck & others); contemporary painting & sculpture; three Norman Rockwell paintings
Publications: Schedule of events, quarterly; annual report
Activities: Classes for adults & children; lects open to pub, 20 vis lectrs per yr; concerts; gallery talks; tours; sponsoring of competitions; scholarships; individual paintings & original objects of art lent to corporate & individual members; originate traveling exhibs primarily to New England institutions; mus shop sells gifts, books, original art, reproductions, jewelry, toys & games

M   CITY OF PITTSFIELD, Berkshire Artisans, 28 Renne Ave, Pittsfield, MA 01201-4720. Tel 413-499-9348; Fax 413-442-6803; Elec Mail berkart@taconic.net; Internet Home Page Address: www.berkshireweb.com/artisans; *Commissioner of Cultural Affairs & Artistic Dir* Daniel M O'Connell, MFA
Open Mon - Fri 11 AM - 5 PM, summer Mon - Fri 11 AM - 5 PM, Sat Noon - 5 PM; No admis fee; Estab 1976; Three story 100 yr old brownstone, municipal gallery; Average Annual Attendance: 56,000; Mem: 350; dues $10; annual meeting in Sep
Income: $100,000 (financed by endowment, mem, city, state & federal appropriations)
Special Subjects: Drawings, Hispanic Art, Painting-American, Photography, Prints, Sculpture, Watercolors, Textiles, Crafts, Pottery, Woodcuts, Landscapes, Glass, Tapestries
Exhibitions: Doe, Warner Freidman, Dave Novak, Jay Tobin, Daniel Balvez, John Dilg, Sally Fine, Linda Bernstein, David Merritt
Publications: The Berkshire Review
Activities: Classes for adults & children; dramatic progs; docent training; lects open to pub, 12 vis lectrs per yr; concerts; gallery talks; tours; competitions; schols & fels offered; artmobile; lending collection contains paintings, art objects; book traveling exhibs 12 per yr; originate traveling exhibs 12 per yr; mus shop sells books, prints, magazines, slides, original art, pub murals

M   HANCOCK SHAKER VILLAGE, INC, US Rte 20, Pittsfield, MA 01202; PO Box 927, Pittsfield, MA 01202-0927. Tel 413-443-0188; Fax 413-447-9357; Elec Mail info@hancockshakervillage.org; Internet Home Page Address: www.hancockshakervillage.org; *Cur Coll* Christian Goodwillie; *Interpretation & Educ* Todd Burdick; *Mus Shop Mgr* Barbara Quirino; *Pres* Lawrence J Yerdon; *Dir Mktg* Sally Majewski; *Pres* Ellen Spear; *Dir Visitor Svcs* Laura Marks; *Collections Mgr* Lesley Hertzberg
Open daily late May 10AM-4PM, Memorial Day -late Oct 10AM-5PM; Admis adults $ 16.50, teens $8, under12 free; Estab 1961 for the preservation & restoration of Hancock Shaker Village & the interpretation of Shaker art, architecture & culture. Period rooms throughout the village; Circ no circulation; Exhibition Gallery contains Shaker inspirational drawings & graphic materials; Average Annual Attendance: 55,000; Mem: dues vary, start at $75
Income: Financed by mem, donations

Special Subjects: Anthropology, Historical Material, Furniture, Portraits, Prints, Textiles, Architecture, Drawings, Archaeology, Crafts, Folk Art, Decorative Arts, Manuscripts, Posters, Dolls, Furniture, Maps, Period Rooms
Collections: Shaker architecture, furniture & industrial material; Shaker inspirational drawings; Buildings; furniture; farm & crafts artifacts; inspirational drawings; over 22,000 shaker objects; textiles
Exhibitions: Gather up the Fragments: The Andrews Shaker Collection
Publications: Newsletter, quarterly; specialized publications
Activities: Classes for adults & children; docent training; workshops; seminars; lects open to pub; vis lectrs 6 per yr; gallery talks; tours; individual paintings & original objects of art lent to qualified mus with proper security & environmental conditions; originates traveling exhibs to Portland Mus Art, Stamford Mus & Nature Center, & more; mus shop sells books, magazines, reproductions & prints

PLYMOUTH

M   PILGRIM SOCIETY, Pilgrim Hall Museum, 75 Court St, Plymouth, MA 02360-3823. Tel 508-746-1620; Fax 508-746-3396; Elec Mail director@pilgrimhall.org; Internet Home Page Address: www.pilgrimhall.org; *Pres* Barrie Young; *Dir & Librn* Ann Berry; *Assoc Cur* Stephen O'Neill; *Dir Visitor Servs* Ann Young; *Develop Dir* Robin Nutter
Open daily 9:30 AM - 4:30 PM, cl Jan & Christmas Day; Admis family $25, adults $8, seniors $7, AAA $6, children $5; Estab 1820 to depict the history of the Pilgrim Colonists in Plymouth Colony; Average Annual Attendance: 27,000; Mem: 600; dues $35; annual meetings in Dec
Income: Financed by endowment, mem & admis
Special Subjects: Ceramics, Glass, Furniture, Painting-American, Silver, Manuscripts, Decorative Arts, Portraits, Furniture, Embroidery, Stained Glass, Pewter
Collections: Arms & armor, decorative arts, furniture & paintings relating to the Plymouth Colony settlement (1620-1692) & the later history of Plymouth
Exhibitions: Permanent collections; exhibitions change year round
Activities: Lects open to pub, 6 vis lectrs per yr; tours; mus shop sells books, magazines, reproductions, prints, slides, ceramics, souvenir wares

L   Library, 75 Court St, Plymouth, MA 02360. Tel 508-746-1620; Fax 508-746-3396; *Dir Ann Berry; Dir & Cur* Stephen O'Neill
Open by appointment only; No admis fee; Estab 1820 to collect material relative to the history of Plymouth; For reference only
Library Holdings: Audio Tapes; Book Volumes 10,000; Cassettes; Clipping Files; Exhibition Catalogs; Kodachrome Transparencies; Lantern Slides; Manuscripts; Memorabilia; Motion Pictures; Original Art Works; Pamphlets; Periodical Subscriptions 5; Photographs; Prints; Records; Reels; Reproductions; Sculpture; Slides
Special Subjects: Manuscripts, Historical Material

A   PLYMOUTH ANTIQUARIAN SOCIETY, 126 Water St, Plymouth, MA 02361; PO Box 3773, Plymouth, MA 02361-3773. Tel 508-746-0012; Elec Mail pasm@verizon.net; Internet Home Page Address: www.plymouthantiquariansociety.org; *Pres* Ron Lunderman; *Exec Dir* Donna Curtin
Open June - Aug 2 - 6 PM, days vary, call for more information; Admis adults $5, children (5-14) $2; Estab 1919 to maintain & preserve the three museums: Harlow Old Fort House (1677), Spooner House (1747) & Antiquarian House (1809); Average Annual Attendance: 5,000; Mem: 500; dues Individual $25, family $40; annual meeting in Nov
Income: Financed by mem & donations
Special Subjects: Costumes, Embroidery, Historical Material, Manuscripts, Textiles, Painting-American, Decorative Arts, Portraits, Furniture, Period Rooms
Collections: American furniture & decorative arts, costumes & textiles, toys & dolls
Activities: Classes for adults & children; lect open to pub; concerts; tours; sales shop sells books, reproductions & antiques; open for special events, call for more information

PROVINCETOWN

A   FINE ARTS WORK CENTER, 24 Pearl St, Provincetown, MA 02657-1500. Tel 508-487-9960; Fax 508-487-8873; Elec Mail general@fawc.org; Internet Home Page Address: www.fawc.org; *Exec Dir* Margaret Murphy; *Summer Prog Dir* Dorothy Antczak; *Visual Coordr* Maryalice Johnston
Open Mon - Fri 9 AM - 5 PM; Maintains Hudson D Walker Gallery
Activities: Summer workshop prog; senior writers progs; Returning Res Prog; fels offered

A   PROVINCETOWN ART ASSOCIATION & MUSEUM, 460 Commercial St, Provincetown, MA 02657-2415. Tel 508-487-1750; Fax 508-487-4372; Elec Mail info@paam.org; Internet Home Page Address: www.paam.org; *Exec Dir* Christine McCarthy; *Registrar* Peter Macara; *Archivist & Preparator* Jim Zimmerman; *Develop Assoc* Sheila McGuinness; *Educ Coordr* Lynn Stanley; *Mem Coordr* Annie Longley; *Educ Asst* Grace Ryder-O'Malley
Open daily Mon - Thurs 11 AM - 8 PM, Fri 11 AM - 10 PM, Sat & Sun 11 AM - 5 PM; Admis adults $7, mems free; Estab in 1914 to promote & cultivate the practice & appreciation of all branches of the fine arts, to hold temporary exhibitions, forums & concerts for its members & the pub; Five galleries are maintained; Average Annual Attendance: 50,000; Mem: 2,000; mem open; dues $50 ann
Income: $1,100,000 (financed by mem, private contributions, state agencies, earned income & others)
Library Holdings: Auction Catalogs; Audio Tapes; Book Volumes; CD-ROMs; Compact Disks; DVDs; Exhibition Catalogs; Kodachrome Transparencies; Memorabilia; Original Art Works; Photographs; Prints; Reproductions; Slides; Video Tapes
Special Subjects: Etchings & Engravings, Graphics, Photography, Prints, Sculpture, Watercolors, Painting-American, Woodcuts, Collages, Marine Painting

Collections: Permanent collection consists of artists work who have lived or worked on the Lower Cape; Permanent collection mem, Blanche Lazzell: The Hofmann Drawings; Ross Moffett

Exhibitions: Edna Boies Hopkins; Hars Hofmann & his students; Ciro Cozzi; Paula Kotis' photographs; Zolo Jack Tworkov; Will Barnett; Zoll Robert Motherwell

Publications: Exhibitions catalogues & newsletters

Activities: Classes for adults & children; docent training; lects open to pub, 8 vis lectrs per yr; concerts; gallery talks; tours; film series; competitions; schol; Leed Certification (Silver) US Green Buildings Commission award; AIA Award of Merit; BSA Design Award; Green Good Design Award, AIA Sustainable Design Award, Top Ten Art Green Projects Award; individual paintings & original objects of art lent to other mus; book traveling exhibs; originate traveling exhibs; mus shop sells books, magazines, original art, prints, reproductions

L **Library,** 460 Commercial St, Provincetown, MA 02657. Tel 508-487-1750; Fax 508-487-4352; Elec Mail Info@paam.org; Internet Home Page Address: www.paam.org; *Exec Dir* Christine McCarthy

Open yr round, check for times; Admis non mem $2; Estab 1914; Average Annual Attendance: 35,000; Mem: 1300; dues individual $50

Library Holdings: Auction Catalogs; Book Volumes 500; Clipping Files; Compact Disks; Exhibition Catalogs; Pamphlets; Photographs

Special Subjects: Photography, Drawings, Etchings & Engravings, Painting-American, Sculpture, Landscapes, Portraits

Collections: Memorabilia of WHW Bicknell; Provincetown Artists; Outer Cape American Art from 1900 - Present

Activities: Classes for adults & children; lects open to pub, 8 vis lectrs per yr; concerts; gallery talks; tours; original art objects lent to mus; originate traveling exhibs to other mus; mus shop sells books, magazines, original art, reproductions, prints

M **THE SCHOOLHOUSE GALLERY,** 494 Commercial St, Provincetown, MA 02657-2414. Tel 508-487-4800; Elec Mail mike@schoolhouseprovincetown.com; Internet Home Page Address: schoolhouseprovincetown.com; *Contact* Mike Carroll

QUINCY

M **ADAMS NATIONAL HISTORIC PARK,** 135 Adams St, Quincy, MA 02169-1749. Tel 617-773-1177; Fax 617-471-7562; Elec Mail ADAM_Visitor_Center@nps.gov; Internet Home Page Address: www.nps.gov/adam; *Supt* Marianne Peak; *Cur* Kelly Cobble

Open daily Apr 19 - Nov 10 9 AM - 5 PM; Admis adults $5, children under 16 admitted free if accompanied by an adult; Estab 1946; The site consists of three houses, part of which dates to 1731; a library containing approx 14,000 books, a carriage house, a woodshed & grounds which were once owned & enjoyed by four generations of the Adams family; Average Annual Attendance: 81,000

Income: Financed by Federal Government

Library Holdings: Clipping Files; Maps; Original Art Works; Original Documents; Pamphlets; Photographs; Slides

Special Subjects: Historical Material, Ceramics, Decorative Arts, Portraits, Furniture, Period Rooms, Bookplates & Bindings

Collections: Original furnishings belonging to the four generations of Adams who lived in the house between 1788 and 1937

Activities: Classes for children; dramatic progs; docent training; lect (4per yr); concerts; tours; sales shop sells books, reproductions & prints

ROCKPORT

A **ROCKPORT ART ASSOCIATION,** 12 Main St, Old Tavern Rockport, MA 01966-1513. Tel 978-546-6604; Fax 978-546-9767; Elec Mail rockportart@verizon.net; Internet Home Page Address: www.rockportartassn.org; *Pres* Judi Rotenberg; *Exec Dir* Carol Linskey

Open summer daily 10 AM - 5 PM, Sun Noon - 5 PM, winter daily 10 AM - 4 PM, Sat 10 AM - 5 PM, Sun Noon - 5 PM; No admis fee; Estab 1921 as a non-profit educational organization established for the advancement of art; Four galleries are maintained in the Old Tavern Building; two large summer galleries are adjacent to the main structure; Average Annual Attendance: 75,000; Mem: 1300; mem open to Cape Ann resident artists (minimum of one month), must pass mem jury; contributing mem open to public; photography mem subject of resident/jury restrictions

Income: Financed by endowment, mem, gifts, art programs & sales

Collections: Permanent collection of works by Cape Ann artists of the past, especially those by former members

Exhibitions: Special organized exhibitions are continually on view; fifty exhibitions scheduled per year

Publications: Quarry Cookbook; Rockport Artists Book 1990; Reprints (recent); Rockport Artists Book 1940; Rockport Sketch Book

Activities: Classes & workshops for adults & children; lects open to pub; painting lectr/demonstrations; Tavern Door shop sells books, cards & notes by artist members

A **SANDY BAY HISTORICAL SOCIETY & MUSEUMS,** Sewall Scripture House-14 King St & Castle Lane, Rockport, MA 01966-1460; PO Box 63, Rockport, MA 01966-0063. Tel 978-546-9533; *Cur* Cynthia Peckham

Open mid-June to mid-Sept; Admis $3, mem free; Estab 1925 to preserve Rockport history; Sewall Scripture House built in 1832, Old Castle built c 1700; Average Annual Attendance: 300; Mem: 500; dues $10; annual meeting first Fri in Sep

Income: $15,000 (financed by endowment & mem)

Collections: Extensive Granite Tools & Quarry Materials; 55 local paintings in oil, prints, watercolor; old quilts, samplers, textiles; Genealogical reference libr

Exhibitions: A Town That Was; Some Rockporters Who Were (for the Sesqui-centennial of the town); Deceased Artists

Publications: Mem bulletins, 3-4 annually; brochures

Activities: Docent training, monthly progs; tours

SALEM

M **PEABODY ESSEX MUSEUM,** Corner Essex & New Liberty, Salem, MA 01970; 161 Essex St, East India Sq Salem, MA 01970-3783. Tel 978-745-9500; Fax 978-744-6776; Elec Mail pem@pem.org; Internet Home Page Address: pem.org; *Exec Dir* Dan L Monroe; *Deputy Dir* Josh Basseches; *Chief Cur* Lynda Hartigan; *Dir Mus Coll Svcs* Will Phippen; *CFO* Anne Munsch

Open Tues - Sun 10 AM - 5 PM; cl Mon, Thanksgiving, Christmas, New Year's Day, open select Mon holidays; Admis adults $15, seniors $13, students $11, youth 16 & under & residents of Salem, Mass free; ticket fees for special exhibs, $5 admis to Yin Yi Tang Chinese House; Estab 1799; The recently transformed Peabody Essex Museum presents art and culture from New England and around the world. In addition to its vast collections, the museum offers changing exhibitions and a hands-on education center. The museum campus features numerous parks, period gardens, and 24 historic properties, including Yin Yu Tang, the only example of Chinese vernacular architecture in the United States; Average Annual Attendance: 150,000; Mem: 4200; dues $30-$65; annual meeting in Nov

Income: $6,000,000 (financed by endowment, mem, gifts & admis)

Special Subjects: American Indian Art, Decorative Arts, Drawings, Marine Painting, Architecture, Ceramics, Furniture, Photography, Porcelain, Painting-American, Textiles, Sculpture, African Art, Oriental Art, Asian Art, Ivory, Scrimshaw

Collections: American Art & Architecture; African Art; Asian Export Art; Chinese Art; Indian Art; Japanese Art; Korean Art; Maritime Art & History; Native American Art; Oceanic Art; Photography; Over 1 million works of art, primarily from 16th c - present

Publications: Peabody Essex Museum Collections, quarterly; The American Neptune, quarterly; The Review of Archaeology, semiannually; member's magazine, quarterly; occasional books

Activities: Classes for adults & children; docent training; lects open to public; originates traveling exhibs: Geisha, Beyond the Painted Smile; mus shop sells books, reproductions, prints, furniture, jewelry, ceramics

L **Phillips Library,** 132 Essex St, Salem, MA 01970-3701. Tel 978-745-9500; Fax 978-741-9012; Elec Mail pem@pem.org; Internet Home Page Address: pem.org; *Dir Phillips Libr* Sidney Berber

Open Wed 10 AM - 5 PM, Thurs 1-5 PM; For reference only

Library Holdings: Book Volumes 400,000; Clipping Files; Exhibition Catalogs; Fiche; Kodachrome Transparencies; Lantern Slides; Manuscripts; Memorabilia; Motion Pictures; Original Art Works; Pamphlets; Periodical Subscriptions 200; Slides

Special Subjects: Folk Art, Decorative Arts, Etchings & Engravings, Ceramics, Crafts, Archaeology, Ethnology, Asian Art, American Indian Art, Anthropology, Furniture, Ivory, Glass, Bookplates & Bindings, Architecture

Collections: The library supports the entire range of the collections of this international & multi-disciplinary museum of arts & cultures

Publications: Peabody Essex Museum Collections; Monographic Series, annual; The American Neptune, quarterly journal of maritime art & history

M **Andrew-Safford House,** 13 Washington Sq W, Salem, MA 01970; 161 Essex St, East India Salem, MA 01970. Tel 978-745-9500; Elec Mail pem@pem.org; Internet Home Page Address: pem.org; *Cur* Dean Lahikainen

Open Mon - Sat 10 AM - 5 PM, Sun Noon - 5 PM, cl Mon, Nov - Mar; Admis adults $8.50, seniors & students $7.50, children 6-16 $5, children under 6 free; Built in 1818-1819 & purchased by the Institute in 1947 for the purpose of presenting a vivid image of early 19th century urban life; It is the residence of the Institute's director

M **Peirce-Nichols House,** 80 Federal St, Salem, MA 01970; 161 Essex St, East India Sq Salem, MA 01970-3726. Tel 978-745-9500; Elec Mail pem@pem.org; Internet Home Page Address: pem.org; *Cur* Robert Saarnio

Open Mon - Sat 10 AM - 5 PM, Sun Noon - 5 PM, Nov - Mar cl Mon; Admis adults $8.50, seniors & students $7.50, children 6-16 $5, children under 6 free; Built in 1782 by Samuel McIntire; Maintains some original furnishings & a counting house

M **Cotting-Smith-Assembly House,** 138 Federal St, Salem, MA 01970; 161 Essex St, East India Square Salem, MA 01970-3726. Tel 978-744-2231; Fax 978-744-0036; Elec Mail pem@pem.org; Internet Home Page Address: pem.org; *Exec Dir* Dan L Monroe

Open Mon - Sat 10 AM - 5 PM, Noon - 5 PM, Nov - Mar cl Mon; Admis adults $8.50, seniors & students $7.50, children 6-16 $5, children under 6 free; Built in 1782 as a hall for social assemblies; remodeled in 1796 by Samuel McIntire as a home residence; Not open to pub

SANDWICH

M **HERITAGE MUSEUMS & GARDENS,** 67 Grove St, Sandwich, MA 02563-2110. Tel 508-888-3300; Fax 508-888-9535; Elec Mail info@heritagemuseums.org; Internet Home Page Address: www.heritagemuseumsandgardens.org; *Dir* Stewart Goodwin; *Deputy Dir Mus Prog & Svcs* Sunnee Spencer; *Deputy Dir Admin* Lucy Bukowski; *Asst Dir* Nancy Tyrer; *Cur Military History* James Cervantes; *Cur Botanical Science* Jeanie Gillis; *Dir Exhib & Coll* Jennifer Younginger; *Cur Antique Auto Mus* Robert Rogers; *Dir Devel* Wendy Perry

Open Jan & Feb weekends, Mar, Apr, Nov & Dec Wed - Sun 10 AM - 4 PM, May - Oct Daily 10 AM - 6 PM; Admis adults $12, seniors $10, children $6; Estab 1969 as a mus of Americana. Heritage Museums & Gardens is a Massachusetts charitable corporation; Maintains three galleries which house collections; Average Annual Attendance: 100,000; Mem: $2000; dues $45-$1000

Income: Financed by endowment, mem & admis

Special Subjects: American Indian Art, Folk Art, Primitive art, Scrimshaw

Collections: American Indian artifacts; folk art; primitive paintings; Scrimshaw; Antique Automobiles; Folk Art; Fine Arts; Tools; Weapons; Military Miniatures; Native American Art

Exhibitions: Landscape Paintings; Antique & Classic Automobiles; Hand painted Military Miniatures & Antique Firearms; Restored 1912 Charles I D Looff Carousel; Currier & Ives prints.

Publications: Exhibit catalogues; quarterly newsletter

Activities: Classes for adults & children; dramatic progs; docent training; lects, 7-10 vis lectrs per yr; concerts; gallery talks; tours; exten dept serving Cape Cod area; individual paintings & original objects of art lent; lending coll includes, original prints, paintings & nature artifacts; 1-2 book traveling exhibs; mus shop sells books, magazines, original art, reproductions & prints

M **THE SANDWICH HISTORICAL SOCIETY, INC & SANDWICH GLASS MUSEUM,** Sandwich Glass Museum, 129 Main St, Sandwich, MA 02563; PO Box 103, Sandwich, MA 02563-0103. Tel 508-888-0251; Fax 508-888-4941; Elec Mail elaine.thomas@sandwichglassmuseum.org; Internet Home Page Address: www.sandwichglassmuseum.org; *Dir* Katharine H Campbell; *Pub Relations* Elaine Thomas; *Retail Mgr* Robert Lee Ward; *Cur Colls* Dorothy Hogan-Schofield
Open Apr - Dec daily 9:30 AM - 5 PM, Feb & Mar, Wed - Sun 9:30 AM - 4 PM, cl Thanksgiving, Christmas & Jan; Admis adults $5, children 6-14 $1.25; Estab 1907 to collect, preserve local history; 16 galleries of Sandwich glass; Average Annual Attendance: 54,000; Mem: 605; dues family $35, individual $25; meeting dates: third Thurs in Feb, Apr, June, Aug & Oct
Income: $482,000 (financed by endowment, mem, admis & retails sales)
Library Holdings: Kodachrome Transparencies; Manuscripts; Maps; Photographs; Prints; Reproductions; Slides
Special Subjects: Glass, Flasks & Bottles, Portraits, Period Rooms, Maps, Painting-American, Ceramics, Decorative Arts, Posters, Furniture, Jewelry, Historical Material, Dioramas, Embroidery, Reproductions
Collections: Glass-Sandwich, American, European; Artifacts relating to the history of Sandwich
Exhibitions: Exhibitions vary; call for details
Publications: Acorn, bi-ann; The Cullet, bi-ann
Activities: Classes for adults & children; docent training; lects open to pub; 2 vis lectr per yr; gallery talks; walking tours of Sandwich; book traveling exhibs 1-2 per yr; mus shop sells books, original art, reproductions, contemporary glass art, jewelry, perfumes, paperweights & ornaments

M **THORNTON W BURGESS SOCIETY, INC,** Museum, 4 Water St, Sandwich, MA 02563; PO Box 972, Sandwich, MA 02563-0972. Tel 508-888-4668; Fax 508-888-1919; Elec twbmuseum@capecod.net; Internet Home Page Address: www.thorntonburgess.org; *Exec Dir* Jeanne Johnson; *Pres* Bob King; *Cur* Bethany S Rutledge
Open Mon - Sat 10 AM - 4 PM, Sun 1 - 4 PM (Apr - Oct); Admis by donation; Estab 1976 to inspire reverence for wildlife & concern for the natural environment; 1756 house; Average Annual Attendance: 60,000; Mem: 1800; dues family $30, individual $20; annual meeting in Feb
Income: Financed by mem, gift shop, mail order sales & admis revenue
Special Subjects: Decorative Arts, Dolls, Glass
Collections: Collection of Thornton Burgess' writings; natural history specimens; original Harrison Cady illustrations from the writings of the children's author & naturalist
Publications: Newsletter, 3 times per year; program schedule, 2 times per year
Activities: Classes for adults & children; docent progs; lects open to pub; lending collection contains books, framed reproductions & nature artifacts

SOUTH HADLEY

M **MOUNT HOLYOKE COLLEGE,** Art Museum, Lower Lake Rd, South Hadley, MA 01075-1499. Tel 413-538-2245; Fax 413-538-2144; Elec Mail artmuseum@mtholyoke.edu; Internet Home Page Address: www.mtholyoke.edu/go/artmuseum; *Interim Dir & Cur* Wendy Watson; *Bus & Events Mgr* Debbie Davis; *Coll Mgr* Linda Delone Best; *Educ & Pub Rels Coordr* Jane Gronau; *Mus Technician* Brian Kiernan; *Coordr Acad Affairs* Ellen Alvord; *Curatorial Asst* Rachel Beaupre; *Digitization Specialist* Laura Weston; *Art Adv Bd Fellow* Sadie Shillieto
Open Tues - Fri 11 AM - 5 PM, Sat - Sun 1 - 5 PM, cl Mon & certain Col holidays, same schedule yr-round; No admis fee; Estab 1876, mus now occupies a building dedicated in 1970. In addition to its permanent collections, mus also organizes special exhibitions of international scope; Art mus with 8 galleries houses the permanent collection & special exhibitions; Average Annual Attendance: 15,000; Mem: Dues $25-$1000
Income: Financed by endowment, mem & college funds
Special Subjects: Drawings, Painting-American, Prints, Sculpture, Pre-Columbian Art, Painting-European, Asian Art, Medieval Art, Antiquities-Egyptian, Antiquities-Greek, Antiquities-Roman
Collections: Asian art, European & American paintings, sculpture, photographs, prints & drawings; Egyptian, Greek, Roman, Pre-Columbian; Ancient coins (mostly Greek & Roman)
Exhibitions: 2-4 rotating special exhibitions per yr
Publications: Newsletter, bi-annually; exhibition catalogues; calendar, bi-annual
Activities: Educ dept; docent training; lects open to pub; 5-6 vis lectrs per yr; concerts; gallery talks; tours; "Jane Hammond: Paper Work" catalog awarded prize for design; excellence by the Assn of American Univ Presses; individual paintings lent to qualified mus; book traveling exhibs 1-2 per yr; originate traveling exhibs to qualified mus; mus shop sells reproductions, mugs, tote bags & posters
L **Art Library,** 50 College St, South Hadley, MA 01075-6404. Tel 413-538-2225; Fax 413-538-2370; Elec Mail sperry@mtholyoke.edu; Internet Home Page Address: www.mtholyoke.edu; *Dir* Susan L Perry
Open to college community only
Library Holdings: Book Volumes 15,550; Periodical Subscriptions 64; Slides

SPRINGFIELD

A **SPRINGFIELD CITY LIBRARY,** 220 State St, Springfield, MA 01103-1772. Tel 413-263-6828; Fax 413-263-6825; Internet Home Page Address: www.springfieldlibrary.org; *Dir* Emily Bader; *Asst Dir* Lee Fogerty; *Head Adult Information Svcs* John Clark
Open Mon & Wed 11 AM - 8 PM, Tues 9 AM - 6 PM, Fri & Sat 9 AM - 5 PM, Sun 12 PM - 5 PM; cl holidays; No admis fee; Estab 1857, Department opened 1905; Circ 611,893 (totals for system); In addition to the City Library system, the

Springfield Library & Mus Assn owns & administers, as separate units, the George Walter Vincent Smith Mus, the Springfield Mus of Fine Arts, the Science Mus & the Connecticut Valley Historical Mus; Average Annual Attendance: 1,100,000; Mem: 3,400; $35 & up
Library Holdings: Audio Tapes 36,000; Book Volumes 700,000; Video Tapes 26,500
Exhibitions: Occasional exhibitions from the library's collections & of work by local artists

M **SPRINGFIELD COLLEGE,** William Blizard Gallery, Visual & Performing Arts Dept, 263 Alden St Springfield, MA 01109-3788. Tel 413-747-3000, 748-0204; Fax 413-748-3580; *Chmn* Ronald Maggio; *Dir Gallery* Holly Murray
Open Mon - Fri 9 AM - 4 PM, Fri 8 AM - 8 PM, Sat 9 AM - 8 PM, Sun Noon - 12 AM; Estab 1998 to bring a wide range of quality exhibits in all areas of the visual arts to the Springfield College campus & surrounding community
Income: Financed by William Simpson Fine Arts Comt
Library Holdings: Book Volumes; Cassettes; Filmstrips; Micro Print; Motion Pictures; Original Art Works; Periodical Subscriptions; Prints; Video Tapes
Exhibitions: Rotating exhibits monthly
Activities: Lect open to public; gallery talks

M **SPRINGFIELD MUSEUMS,** (Springfield Library & Museums Association) Michele & Donald D'Amour Museum of Fine Arts, 21 Edwards St, Springfield, MA 01103-1548. Tel 413-263-6800; Fax 413-263-6814; Elec Mail info@springfieldmuseums.org; Internet Home Page Address: www.springfieldmuseums.org; *Pres* Holly Smith-Bove; *Dir* Heather Haskell; *VPres* Kathleen Simpson
Open Tues - Sat 10 AM - 5 PM, Sun 11 AM - 5 PM, cl Mon & major holidays; Admis adults $12.50, seniors & college students $9, children $6.50 (includes admis to four museums); Estab 1934 to collect, preserve & exhibit fine & decorative arts; Average Annual Attendance: 110,000; Mem: 3200; dues $45 & up; annual mtg in Sept
Income: Financed by mem, admis & prog fees; local, state, federal grants, pvt foundations & corporate sponsorships
Special Subjects: Prints, Graphics, Painting-American, Sculpture, Primitive art, Woodcuts, Painting-European, Oriental Art, Painting-British, Painting-Dutch, Painting-French, Renaissance Art, Painting-Italian
Collections: Japanese woodblock prints; Currier & Ives American Print Collection
Exhibitions: Special exhibitions, historic to contemporary are continually on view in addition to permanent collection; changing exhibitions
Publications: Handbook to the American & European Collection, Museum of Fine Arts, Springfield; exhibition catalogs; Selections from the American Collections; Legacy of Currier & Ives: Shaping the American Spirit catalog
Activities: Classes for adults & children; docent progs; outreach progs; lects open to pub; book traveling exhibs 6-8 per yr; mus shop sells books, gift items & scientific objects

M **Connecticut Valley Historical Society,** Tel 413-263-6800; Fax 413-263-6898; Internet Home Page Address: www.quadrangle.org; *Head Library & Archive Coll* Margaret Humbertson; *Pres & Exec Dir* Joseph Carvalho; *VPres Mktg & Develop* Susan Davison; *Vice Pres Finance* Richard Dunbar
Open Wed-Fri Noon - 4 PM, Sat & Sun 11 AM - 4 PM; Admis adults $7, seniors & college students $5, children $3, under 6 free. Includes admis to all four mus at Quadrangle; Estab 1927 to interpret history of Connecticut River Valley; Average Annual Attendance: 463,493; Mem: Mem: 3645; dues $35 & up; annual meeting in Sept
Special Subjects: Decorative Arts, Folk Art, Historical Material, Furniture, Portraits, Painting-American, Silver, Embroidery, Pewter
Collections: Decorative arts of Connecticut Valley, including furniture, paintings & prints, pewter, firearms, glass, silver, early games; Genealogy Library
Exhibitions: Many exhibits pertaining to history & decorative arts of Connecticut River Valley
Publications: Say Goodbye to the Valley
Activities: Classes for adults & children; lects open to pub; lects for mems only; gallery talks; tours; book traveling exhibs 1-2 per yr; mus shop sells books, note cards, genealogy shirts & tote bags
M **Springfield Science Museum,** 21 Edwards St, Springfield, MA 01103-1548. Tel 413-263-6800; Fax 413-263-6884; Elec Mail info@springfieldmuseums.org; Internet Home Page Address: www.springfieldmuseums.org; *Exec Dir & Pres* Joseph Carvalho; *Dir* David Stier; *CFO* Holly Smith-Bove; *Dir Museum Educ & Institutional Advancement* Kathleen Simpson
Open Tues - Sat 10 AM - 5 PM, Sun 11 AM - 5 PM; Admis adults $12.50, seniors & college students $9, child $6.50 (includes admis to four museums); Estab 1899 to collect, preserve & exhibit material related to natural & physical science; Average Annual Attendance: 221,000; Mem: 3200; dues $45 & up; annual meeting in Sept
Income: Financed by mem, admis & prog fees; local, state, federal grants, pvt foundations & corporate sponsorships
Special Subjects: American Indian Art, African Art
Collections: Aquarium; Dinosaur Hall; Exploration Center; habitat groupings of mounted animals; Planetarium; live animal eco-center
Activities: Classes for adults & children; docent progs; outreach progs; lects open to pub; book traveling exhibs 2-3 per yr; mus shop sells books & gift items & scientific objects

STOCKBRIDGE

M **NATIONAL TRUST FOR HISTORIC PRESERVATION,** Chesterwood, 4 Williamsville Rd, Stockbridge, MA 01262; PO Box 827, Stockbridge, MA 01262-0827. Tel 413-298-3579; Fax 413-298-3973; Elec Mail chesterwood@nthp.org; Internet Home Page Address: www.chesterwood.org; *Buildings & Grounds Supt* Gerard J Blache; *Dir* Donna Hassler; *Curatorial Asst* Anne Cathcart; *Office Mgr* Lisa I Reynolds; *Bldgs & Grounds Coordr* Brian McElhiney
Open daily 10 AM - 5 PM, Memorial Day weekend to Columbus Day; Admis (Please visit chesterwood.org); Estab 1955 to preserve the country home & studio of Daniel Chester French; Chesterwood, a National Trust Historic Site, was the

former estate of Daniel Chester French (1850-1931), sculptor of the Lincoln Memorial, Minute Man & leading figure of the American Renaissance. The 122 acre property includes: the sculptor's studio (1898) & residence (1900-1901), both designed by Henry Bacon, architect of the Lincoln Memorial; Barn Gallery, a c1825 barn adapted for use as an exhibition space & a museum gift shop; a 1909 garage adapted as an exhib space & country place garden with woodland walls laid out by French; Average Annual Attendance: 12,000; Mem: Dues & mem levels beginning individual $50
Special Subjects: Architecture, Painting-American, Sculpture, Bronzes, Textiles, Landscapes, Decorative Arts, Painting-European, Portraits, Furniture, Painting-Italian
Collections: American Renaissance; Daniel Chester French Collection: sculpture by or owned by the artist, memorabilia, plaster models, marble & bronze casts of French's work & paintings
Exhibitions: Annual Outdoor Contemporary Sculpture Exhibition; Annual Antique Car Show; Barn Gallery Exhib; special exhibits dealing with aspects of Chesterwood & the Berkshire region, career, social & artistic milieu & summer estate
Activities: Classes for adults & children; docent training; demonstrations open to pub; gallery talks; tours; competitions; landscape tours; sculpture demonstrations; awards, Yankee Magazine's Best Artist's Retreat; original objects of art lent to qualified institutions; mus shop sells books, cards, reproductions, magazines, prints, gift items

L **Chesterwood Museum Archives,** 4 Williamsville Rd, Glendale Section Stockbridge, MA 01262-0827; PO Box 827, Stockbridge, MA 01262-0827. Tel 413-298-3579; Fax 413-298-3973; Elec Mail chesterwood@taconic.net; Internet Home Page Address: www.nationaltrust.org; *Archivist* Wanda Magdeleine Styka
Open by appointment only, staff & spec hours, gen pub; Estab 1969; Library consists of books on sculpture, historic preservation, decorative arts, history of art, architecture, garden & landscape design, including books collected personally by sculptor Daniel Chester French, Mary Adams French (wife) & Margaret French Cresson (daughter) as well as archival material; serves art, social, landscape & architectural historians & historic preservationists
Library Holdings: Audio Tapes; Book Volumes 5000; Cards; Cassettes; Clipping Files; Exhibition Catalogs; Lantern Slides; Manuscripts; Memorabilia; Motion Pictures; Original Art Works; Pamphlets; Periodical Subscriptions 5; Photographs; Prints; Reels; Sculpture; Slides; Video Tapes
Special Subjects: Art History, Landscape Architecture, Decorative Arts, Photography, Painting-American, Sculpture, Historical Material, History of Art & Archaeology, Portraits, Bronzes, Furniture, Period Rooms, Restoration & Conservation, Coins & Medals, Architecture
Collections: Oral histories: Daniel Chester French & his summer estate Chesterwood; blueprints & plans of sculpture commissions & of Chesterwood; period photographs of French & his family, summer estate & sculptures; papers, correspondence, photograph albums & scrapbooks of D C French & Margaret French Cresson, sculptor, writer & preservationist; literary manuscripts of Mary Adams French
Publications: The Chesterwood Pedestal, newsletter; educational brochures; annual exhibit catalogues
Activities: Intern archivist prog; mus shop sells books, reproductions, prints

M **NORMAN ROCKWELL MUSEUM,** 9 Route 183, Stockbridge, MA 01262; PO Box 308, Stockbridge, MA 01262-0308. Tel 413-298-4100; Fax 413-298-4142; Elec Mail questions@nrm.org; Internet Home Page Address: www.nrm.org; *Chmn* Thomas L Pulling; *Assoc Dir External Relations* Judy Shaw; *Dir* Laurie Norton Moffatt; *Dir Mktg & Communs* Margit Hotchkiss; *Assoc Dir Fin* Terry Smith; *Pres Bd* Anne H Morgan; *Deputy Dir & Chief Cur* Stephanie Haboush Plunkett; *Mgr Traveling Exhibs* Mary Melius
Open May - Oct daily 10 AM - 5 PM & Thurs until 7 PM in Jul & Aug, Nov - Apr Mon - Fri 10 AM - 4 PM, Sat & Sun 10 AM - 5 PM, cl Thanksgiving, Christmas, New Year's Day; Admis adults $16, senior discounts; Estab 1967 to collect, manage, preserve, study, interpret & present to the public material pertaining to the life & career of Norman Rockwell while featuring the work of other illustrators; Consists of a main building (1993), situated on 36 acres in a country setting with galleries for permanent & changing exhibitions, classrooms, the Norman Rockwell Reference Center, meeting room & store. Norman Rockwell Studio is located on the museum site. Terrace Cafe open May-Oct; Average Annual Attendance: 130,000; Mem: 1,680; dues $50-$5000; annual meeting in Sept
Income: Financed by admis, mem, donations, sales & grants
Library Holdings: Auction Catalogs; Audio Tapes; Book Volumes; CD-ROMs; Cards; Cassettes; Clipping Files; Compact Disks; DVDs; Exhibition Catalogs; Fiche; Filmstrips; Framed Reproductions; Kodachrome Transparencies; Lantern Slides; Manuscripts; Maps; Memorabilia; Micro Print; Motion Pictures; Original Art Works; Original Documents; Other Holdings; Pamphlets; Periodical Subscriptions; Photographs; Prints; Records; Reels; Reproductions; Sculpture; Slides; Video Tapes
Special Subjects: Drawings, Photography, Portraits, Painting-American
Collections: Largest permanent collection of original Rockwell art (more than 900 original paintings & drawings); artifacts & furnishings of Norman Rockwell's studio; archives including bus letters, memorabilia, negatives & photographs; Norman Rockwell Collection; American Illustration - William Steig, George Bridgman, Edmund Ward
Exhibitions: Norman Rockwell Highlights from the Permanent Collection
Publications: Norman Rockwell: A Definitive Catalogue; The Portfolio, quarterly newsletter; Programs & Events, quarterly calendar, Pictures for the American People, American Chronicles, Peter Rockwell: A Sculptors Retrospective
Activities: Classes for adults & children; docent training; lects open to pub; tours; educator's seminars, art workshops for adults & children; school programs; family days; special performances & events; free admis days; schols & internships offered; individual paintings & original objects of art lent to qualifying not for profit educational institutions; originate traveling exhibs; mus shop sells books, prints, reproductions & gift items

L **Library,** 9 Route 183, Stockbridge, MA 01262; PO Box 308, Stockbridge, MA 01262. Tel 413-298-4100; 931-2251; Fax 413-298-4145; Elec Mail inforequest@nrm.org; Internet Home Page Address: www.nrm.org; *Archivist* Venus Van Ness
Open Tues, Thurs & Sat 1 - 5 PM, in winter 1-4 PM, or by appt; Admis to libr incl in mus admis; 1993
Library Holdings: Auction Catalogs; Audio Tapes; Book Volumes 300; Cassettes; Clipping Files; DVDs; Exhibition Catalogs; Kodachrome Transparencies; Lantern Slides; Manuscripts; Memorabilia; Motion Pictures; Original Documents; Periodical Subscriptions 10; Photographs; Prints; Records; Reproductions; Slides; Video Tapes
Special Subjects: Art History, Illustration, Commercial Art, Graphic Arts, Painting-American, Advertising Design, Art Education
Collections: Norman Rockwell Archives; Al Parker Archives; Tom Lovell Archives; Illustration Ephemera
Activities: Educ prog; classes for adults & children; lects open to pub; gallery talks; schols offered; originates traveling exhibs; mus shop sells books, magazines, reproductions, & prints

SUDBURY

M **LONGFELLOW'S WAYSIDE INN MUSEUM,** 72 Wayside Inn Rd, Sudbury, MA 01776-3206. Tel 978-443-1716; Tel 800-339-1776; Fax 978-443-8041; Elec Mail innkeeper@wayside.org; Internet Home Page Address: www.wayside.org; *Chmn Trustees* Richard Davidson; *Innkeeper* Robert H Purrington
Open daily 9 AM - 8 PM cl Christmas Day & July 4th; No admis fee, donations accepted; Estab 1716 as one of the oldest operating Inns in America. The ancient hostelry continues to provide hospitality to wayfarers from all over the world; 18th century period rooms including Old Barroom, Longfellow Parlor, Longfellow Bed Chamber, Old Kitchen, Drivers and Drovers Chamber. Historic buildings on the estate include Redstone School of Mary's Little Lamb fame, grist mill, and Martha Mary Chapel; Average Annual Attendance: 170,000
Income: Nonprofit organization
Special Subjects: Painting-American, Prints, Decorative Arts, Furniture, Period Rooms
Collections: Early American furniture and decorative arts; Howe family memorabilia; paintings; photographs of the Inn; prints; historic papers
Exhibitions: Various exhibits
Activities: Classes for adults; colonial crafts demonstrations and workshops; lect open to public, 5 vis lectrs per year; tours; sales shop selling books, original art, reproductions & prints

TAUNTON

M **OLD COLONY HISTORICAL SOCIETY,** Museum, 66 Church Green, Taunton, MA 02780. Tel 508-822-1622; Elec Mail oldcolony@oldcolonyhistoricalsociety.org; Internet Home Page Address: www.oldcolonyhistoricalsociety.org; *VPres* David F Gouveia, MD; *Cur* Jane Emack-Cambra; *Dir, CEO* Katheryn P Viens; *Asst to Dir* Elizabeth Bernier
Open Tues - Sat 10 AM - 4 PM, mus tours 10:30 AM, 1:30 PM & 2:30 PM; Admis adults $2, seniors & children 12-18 $1, children under 12 free; Estab 1853 to preserve & perpetuate the history of the Old Colony in Massachusetts; Four exhibition halls; Average Annual Attendance: 7,000; Mem: 700; dues $10-$250; annual meeting third Thurs in Apr
Income: $120,000 (financed by endowment, mem, service fees, grants)
Special Subjects: Textiles, Furniture, Silver
Collections: Fire fighting equipment; furniture, household utensils, Indian artifacts, military items; portraits, silver, stoves
Publications: Booklets; pamphlets
Activities: Classes for adults & children; docent training; workshops; lects open to pub, 8-10 vis lectrs per yr; fels offered; mus shop sells books & souvenirs

L **Library,** 66 Church Green, Taunton, MA 02780. Tel 508-822-1622; *Library Asst* Greta Smith; *Cur* Jane Emack-Cambra; *Dir* Katheryn P Viens
Open Tues - Sat 10 AM - 4 PM; Admis genealogy $5, other research $2; Estab 1853; For reference only; research services available for a fee
Library Holdings: Audio Tapes; Exhibition Catalogs; Manuscripts; Memorabilia; Pamphlets; Periodical Subscriptions 10; Photographs; Prints; Reels; Slides
Special Subjects: Art History, Folk Art, Decorative Arts, Manuscripts, Maps, Painting-American, Ceramics, Furniture, Glass, Metalwork, Dolls, Coins & Medals, Pewter, Flasks & Bottles, Architecture

TYRINGHAM

M **SANTARELLA MUSEUM & GARDENS,** 75 Main Rd, Tyringham, MA 01264; PO Box 466, Tyringham, MA 01264-0466. Tel 413-243-3260; Fax 413-243-9178; *Dir* Hope C Talbert
Open 10 AM - 5 PM (May - Oct), cl Tues & Wed; Admis $4, children under 6 free; Estab 1996 to exhibit & sell paintings, prints & sculptures by recognized artists, including world masters; The building was designed as a sculpture studio by the late Sir Henry Kitson; Average Annual Attendance: 15,000
Income: Financed privately
Special Subjects: Architecture, Sculpture, Bronzes, Decorative Arts
Collections: Santarella Sculpture Gardens; Henry Hudson-Kitson Studios
Exhibitions: One-person shows by established artists; Outdoor sculpture exhibitions (various artists)
Activities: Lects open to pub; 2 vis lectrs per yr; gallery talks; tours; mus shop sells books, original art, reproductions & prints

WALTHAM

M **BRANDEIS UNIVERSITY,** Rose Art Museum, 415 South St Stop 069, Waltham, MA 02453-2728. Tel 781-736-3434; Fax 781-736-3439; Elec Mail rosemail@couries.brandeis.edu; Internet Home Page Address: www.brandeis.edu/rose; *Dir Mus Operations* Roy Dawes; *Colls Mgr* Kristin Parker; *Educator* Dabney Hailey
Open Tues - Sun Noon - 5 PM; Admis adults $3; Estab 1961 to exhibit and collect modern and contemporary art; Sept - July revolving displays of Brandeis Art; Average Annual Attendance: 10,000; Mem: 250; $125 basic mem

Purchases: William Kentridge; Barry McGee; Robin Rhode
Special Subjects: American Indian Art, Pre-Columbian Art, Prints, Asian Art
Collections: The permanent collections consist of African art; contemporary art (post World War II); modern art (1800 to World War II), including the Riverside Museum Collections & the Teresa Jackson Weill Collection; pre-modern art (before 1800); Mr & Mrs Edward Rose Collection of early ceramics; Helen S Slosberg Collection of Oceanic art; Teresa Jackson Weill Collection
Publications: Exhibition catalogs
Activities: Classes for children; docent training; lect open to public; gallery talks; concerts; tours; individual paintings & original objects of art lent to students & individuals within the university; lending collection contains original art works, original prints, paintings; book traveling exhibitions 1 per year

L **Leonard L Farber Library,** 415 South St, Norman & Rosita Creative Arts Ctr Waltham, MA 02453-2728; PO Box 9110, Waltham, MA 02254-9110. Tel 781-736-4681; Fax 781-736-4675; *Librn* Darwin Scott
Open Mon - Thurs 8:30 AM - Noon, Fri 8:30 AM-8 PM, Sat 11 AM -8 PM, Sun 11 AM-Midnight; Estab 1948 to provide materials & services for the teaching, research & pub interest in the arts of the Brandeis community; For lending & reference
Library Holdings: Book Volumes 40,000; Cards; Cassettes; Exhibition Catalogs; Fiche; Micro Print; Periodical Subscriptions 130; Photographs; Records; Reels
Special Subjects: Art History
Collections: collection of books on Daumier; Dr Bern Dibner Collection of Leonardo da Vinci - Books; Benjamin A & Julia M Trustman Collection of Honore Daumier Prints (4,0000)
Exhibitions: Rotating exhibition of Daumier Prints

WELLESLEY

M **WELLESLEY COLLEGE,** Davis Museum & Cultural Center, 106 Central St, Wellesley, MA 02181-8203. Tel 781-283-2051; Fax 781-283-2064; Internet Home Page Address: www.davismuseum.wellesly.edu; *Dir* David Mickenberg; *Dir Museum Develop & Mem* Nancy Gunn; *Assoc Dir* Dennis McFadden; *Registrar* Bo Mompho; *Cur* Anja Chavez; *Cur* Elizabeth Wyckoff; *Cur* Dabney Hailey; *Cur* Elaine Mehalakes
Open Tues & Fri - Sat 11 AM - 5 PM, Wed 11 AM - 8 PM, Sun 1 - 5 PM; cl New Year's Day, Thanksgiving and Dec 24 - Jan 2; No admis fee; Estab 1889, dedicated to acquiring a collection of high quality art objects for the primary purpose of teaching art history from original works; Main gallery houses major exhibitions; Corridor Gallery, works on paper; Sculpture Ct, permanent installation, sculpture, reliefs, works on wood panel; Average Annual Attendance: 18,000; Mem: 650; dues donor $100, contributor $50, regular $25
Income: Financed by mem, through college & gifts
Special Subjects: Drawings, Etchings & Engravings, Landscapes, Photography, Portraits, Pre-Columbian Art, Painting-American, Prints, Woodcuts, Painting-British, Painting-European, Sculpture, Hispanic Art, Latin American Art, Watercolors, African Art, Religious Art, Baroque Art, Painting-Flemish, Renaissance Art, Medieval Art, Painting-Spanish, Painting-Italian, Antiquities-Greek, Antiquities-Roman
Collections: Paintings; sculpture; graphic & decorative arts; Asian, African, ancient, medieval, Renaissance, Baroque, 19th & 20th century European & American art; photography; prints; drawings
Publications: Exhibition catalogs; Wellesley College Friends of Art Newsletter, annually
Activities: Docent training; lects open to pub & members only; gallery talks; tours; VTS viewing sessions for students; lending collection contains original prints; book traveling exhibs; originate traveling exhibs; sales shop sells catalogs, postcards & notecards

L **Art Library,** 106 Central St, Wellesley, MA 02481-8203. Tel 781-283-3258; Fax 781-283-3647; Elec Mail artlib@wellesley.edu; Internet Home Page Address: www.wellesley.edu; *Art Librn* Brooke Henderson
Circ 18,000
Income: Financed by College appropriation
Library Holdings: Book Volumes 67,000; CD-ROMs 61; Exhibition Catalogs; Fiche 1700; Pamphlets; Periodical Subscriptions 158
Special Subjects: Art History, Decorative Arts, Photography, Painting-American, Painting-Italian, Painting-European, History of Art & Archaeology, Archaeology, Asian Art, Oriental Art, Antiquities-Roman, Architecture

WELLFLEET

M **WELLFLEET HISTORICAL SOCIETY & MUSEUM, INC,** (Wellfleet Historical Society Museum) 266 Main St, Wellfleet, MA 02667; PO Box 58, Wellfleet, MA 02667-0058. Tel 508-349-2954; Elec Mail info@wellfleethistoricalsociety.org; Internet Home Page Address: www.wellfleethistoricalsociety.org; *Pres* Brad Williams; *Cur* Joan Hopkins Coughlin; *Treas* Dawn Rockman; *VPres* Deidre Portnoy; *Secy* William Carlson
Open late June - early Oct, Wed, Thurs & Sat - 2 - 5 PM, Tues & Fri 10 AM - Noon; No admis fee; Estab 1951; Average Annual Attendance: 1,200; Mem: 350; dues $20; 12 general meetings per yr
Income: $25,000 (financed by mem); grants & awards
Purchases: $5,000
Special Subjects: Dolls
Collections: Books; china & glass; documents; Indian artifacts; paintings & photographs; personal memorabilia of Wellfleet; pewter; shellfish & finfish exhibit; shop models; shipwreck & marine items
Publications: Beacon, annual
Activities: Classes for children; lects open to public, 5 vis lectrs per year; walking tours during summer; mus shop sells books & prints

WENHAM

A **WENHAM MUSEUM,** 132 Main St, Wenham, MA 01984-1520. Tel 978-468-2377; Fax 978-468-1763; Internet Home Page Address: www.wenhammuseum.org; *Business Affairs* Elizabeth Stone; *Office Admin* Felicia Connolly; *Doll Cur* Diane Hamblin; *Cur* Bar Browdo; *Dir* Emily Stearns
Open Tues - Sun 10 AM - 4 PM, cl Mon & major holidays; Admis adults $5, seniors $4, children $2 & up $3, mem free; Estab 1921 as Historical Soc,

incorporated 1953, to acquire, preserve, interpret & exhibit collections of literary & historical interest; to provide an educational & cultural service & facilities; Maintains three permanent galleries & one gallery for changing exhibits; Average Annual Attendance: 10,000; Mem: 650; dues family $55, individual $30; annual meeting Apr
Income: Financed by endowment, mem, earned income
Collections: Dolls; doll houses; figurines; costumes & accessories 1800-1960; embroideries; fans; needlework; quilts; toys
Exhibitions: Ice Cutting Tool Exhibit; 19th Century Shoe Shops; Still Lifes; Quilts Old & New; Samplers; Tin & Woodenware; Weavers; Wedding Dresses
Publications: Annual report; newsletter
Activities: Classes for children; lects open to pub; gallery talks; tours; mus shop sells books, miniatures, original needlework, dolls & small toys

L **Timothy Pickering Library,** 132 Main St, Wenham, MA 01984. Tel 978-468-2377; Fax 978-468-1763; Elec Mail info@wenhammuseum.org; Internet Home Page Address: www.wenhammuseum.org; *Exec Dir* Lindsay Diehl; *Mus Shop Mgr* Diane McMahon
Research by appointment; Open to members & the pub for reference
Income: Endowments, earned income, mem
Library Holdings: Book Volumes 2200; Manuscripts; Memorabilia; Pamphlets; Photographs

WEST NEWTON

M **BOSTON SCULPTORS AT CHAPEL GALLERY,** The Second Church in Newton, 60 Highland St West Newton, MA 02465-2405. Tel 617-244-4039; Internet Home Page Address: www.bostonsculptors.com; *Dir* Julie Scaramella
Open Wed - Sun 1 - 5:30 PM; No admis fee; Estab 1992 as an alternate venue for contemporary sculpture; Collaborative gallery operated by 20 sculptors; Mid-career sculptors by invitation; Average Annual Attendance: 5,000 - 7,000; Mem: 20
Income: Dues & sales
Exhibitions: Group & solo invitations - Sept - June
Activities: Lect open to public, gallery talks: Best of Boston Award; mus shop sells original art & postcards

WESTFIELD

M **WESTFIELD ATHENAEUM,** Jasper Rand Art Museum, 6 Elm St, Westfield, MA 01085-2997. Tel 413-568-7833; Fax 413-568-1558; Elec Mail pcramer@exit3.com; Internet Home Page Address: www.ci.westfield.ma.us/athen.html; *Pres* James Rogers; *Treas* Mark Morin; *Dir* Patricia T Cramer; *Asst Dir* Donald G Buckley
Open Mon - Thurs 8:30 AM - 8 PM, Fri & Sat 8:30 AM - 5 PM, cl Sat in July & Aug; No admis fee; Estab 1927 to provide exhibitions of art works by area artists & other prominent artists; Gallery measures 25 x 30 x 17 feet, with a domed ceiling & free-standing glass cases & wall cases; Average Annual Attendance: 13,500; Mem: Annual meeting fourth Mon in Nov
Income: Financed by endowment
Exhibitions: Changing exhibits on a monthly basis

WESTON

M **REGIS COLLEGE FINE ARTS CENTER,** Carney Gallery, 235 Wellesley St, Weston, MA 02493-1545. Tel 781-768-7034 (Dir); Fax 781-768-7030; Elec Mail fac@regiscollege.edu; Internet Home Page Address: www.regiscollege.edu; *Dir* Steven B Hall; *Assoc Dir* Nancy Rosata; *Technical Dir* Andre Schiff
Open Mon - Fri 10 AM - 4 PM; No admis fee; Estab 1993 and houses the music, art and theater depts as well as the Casey Theatre & Carney Gallery; Carney Gallery is one room, 26 x 40 ft; Average Annual Attendance: 1,500
Income: Financed by college
Exhibitions: Rotate every 6 wks, focus on works of contemporary women artists
Activities: Classes for adults; lects open to pub; 1-4 vis lectrs per year, gallery talks

WILLIAMSTOWN

M **STERLING & FRANCINE CLARK ART INSTITUTE,** 225 South St, Williamstown, MA 01267-2878; PO Box 8, Williamstown, MA 01267-0008. Tel 413-458-2303; Fax 413-458-2324; Elec Mail info@clarkart.edu; Internet Home Page Address: www.clarkart.edu/; *Dir* Michael Conforti; *Sr Cur of Paintings & Sculpture* Richard Rand; *Registrar* Mattie Kelley; *Deputy Dir* Anthony King; *Dir Research & Acad Progs* Darby English; *Contact Person* Sally Morse Majewski
Open daily July & Aug 10 AM - 5 PM; Tues - Sun rest of year 10 AM - 5 PM, cl Mon, New Year's Day, Thanksgiving & Christmas; Admis (July - Oct); no admis fee (Nov - May); Estab 1955 as a mus of fine arts with galleries, art research library & pub events in auditorium; Intimately scattered galleries in a rural setting; Average Annual Attendance: 175,000; Mem: 4,000; dues $60 & up
Library Holdings: Auction Catalogs; Book Volumes; CD-ROMs; Exhibition Catalogs; Periodical Subscriptions; Slides
Special Subjects: Decorative Arts, Etchings & Engravings, Landscapes, Ceramics, Flasks & Bottles, Furniture, Photography, Portraits, Painting-American, Prints, Woodcuts, Painting-British, Painting-European, Drawings, Sculpture, Watercolors, Religious Art, Posters, Glass, Porcelain, Silver, Painting-Dutch, Painting-French, Painting-Flemish, Painting-Italian
Collections: English and American silver; Dutch, Flemish, French, Italian Old Master paintings from the 14th-18th centuries; French 19th century paintings, especially the Impressionists; 19th century sculpture; Old Master prints & drawings; selected 19th century American artists (Homer & Sargent); Early photography; American furniture; British Art
Exhibitions: The Permanent Collection & Traveling Exhibitions
Publications: Calendar of Events, quarterly; Journal, annually; miscellaneous exhib catalogues; Research Academic Program Volumes

Activities: Classes for adults & children; docent training; lects open to pub & mem only, 12+ vis lectrs per yr; concerts; gallery talks; tours for school children; Awards, Clark Prize for Excellence in Arts Writing; fels available; individual paintings & original objects of art lent to other mus whose facilities meet criteria, for exhibs of acad importance; book traveling exhibs 1-2 per yr; organize traveling exhibs circulating to global selected partners; mus shop sells books, reproductions, prints, slides, jewelry, glass, games, puzzles, gifts

L **Library,** 225 South St, Williamstown, MA 01267-2878; PO Box 8, Williamstown, MA 01267-0008. Tel 413-458-2303 ext 350; Fax 413-458-9542; Elec Mail library@clarkart.edu; Internet Home Page Address: www.clarkart.edu/library; *Librn* Susan Roeper
Open Mon - Fri 9 AM - 5 PM, cl holidays; Estab 1962; For reference only; Average Annual Attendance: 14,000
Purchases: $260,000
Library Holdings: Auction Catalogs; Book Volumes 200,000; Exhibition Catalogs; Fiche; Other Holdings Auction sale catalogues 40,000; Periodical Subscriptions 640; Photographs; Reels; Reproductions; Slides
Collections: Mary Ann Beinecke Decorative Art Collection; Duveen Library & Archive; Juynboll Collection

M **WILLIAMS COLLEGE,** Museum of Art, 15 Lawrence Hall Dr, Ste 2 Williamstown, MA 01267-2584. Tel 413-597-2429; Fax 413-458-9017; Elec Mail wcma@williams.edu; Internet Home Page Address: www.wcma.org; *Dir & Art Lect* Lisa C Corrin; *Deputy Dir, Chief Cur & Lect Art* John Stomberg; *Budget Admin & Asst to Deputy Dir* Dorothy H (Dee Dee) Lewis; *Asst to Dir* Amy M Tatro; *Dir Communs & Strategy* Suzanne Silitch; *Pub Rels Asst* Aimee C Hirz; *Cur 19th & 20th Century Art & Art Lect* Nancy Mowll Mathews; *Cur Coll* Vivian Patterson; *Cur Special Projects* Kathryn Price; *Dir Educ & Visitor Experience* Cynthia Way; *Coordr Mellon Acad Programs* Elizabeth Gallerani; *Coordr Educ Programs* Joann Harnden; *Dir Mus Donor Relations* Christine Naughton; *Mem & Spec Events Mgr* Raymond Torrenti; *Mus Shop Mgr* Michele Migdal; *Mus Shop Asst* Christine F Maher; *Mgr Exhibs Design & Planning* Hideyo Okamura; *Prep* Gregory Jay Smith; *Preparator* Richard Miller; *Dir Mus Reg* Diane M Hart; *Assoc Registrar* Rachel U Tassone; *Supv Mus Security & Facility* Terence A White; *Mus Security Officer* Michele S Alice; *Mus Security Officer* Joseph Congello; *Mus Security Officer* Jason Wandrei
Open Tues - Sat 10 AM - 5 PM, Sun 1 - 5 PM; No admis fee; Estab 1926 for the presentation of the permanent collection & temporary loan exhibitions for the benefit of the Williams College community & the general pub; Original 1846 Greek Revival building designed by Thomas Tefft; 1983 & 1986 additions & renovations designed by Charles Moore & Robert Harper of Centerbrook Architects & Planners. Building also houses Art Department of Williams College; Average Annual Attendance: 50,000; Mem: 370; individual $30, family/dual $50, patron $100, benefactor $250, donor $500
Special Subjects: Latin American Art, African Art, Pre-Columbian Art, Religious Art, Folk Art, Afro-American Art, Decorative Arts, Oriental Art, Asian Art, Historical Material, Baroque Art, Renaissance Art, Medieval Art, Islamic Art
Collections: Ancient & medieval art; Asian & African art; modern & contemporary art; 18th-20th century American art; 20th century American photography
Publications: Brochures; exhibition catalogs, 3-4 per year
Activities: After school progs for children, teachers workshops; docent training; lects open to pub, 10 vis lectrs per yr; concerts; gallery talks; tours; individual paintings & original objects of art are lent to other mus; book traveling exhibs 1 per yr; originate traveling exhibs to mus; mus shop sells books, jewelry, magazines, posters & postcards

L **Sawyer Library,** 55 Sawyer Library Dr, Williamstown, MA 01267-2562. Tel 413-597-2501; Fax 413-597-4106; Elec Mail david.pilachowski@williams.edu; Internet Home Page Address: www.williams.edu/library/sawyer; *Librn* David Pilachowski; *Asst Librn* Betty Milanesi
Open Mon - Thurs 8 AM - 10 PM, Sat 9 AM - 10 PM, Sun 9 AM - 2 AM; No admis fee
Income: Financed by endowments, gifts, Williams College
Library Holdings: Book Volumes 697,023; Periodical Subscriptions 3024; Slides 22,800

L **Chapin Library,** Southworth Schoolhouse, 96 School St Williamstown, MA 01267-0426; PO Box 426, Williamstown, MA 01267-0426. Tel 413-597-2462; Fax 413-597-2929; Elec Mail chapin.library@williams.edu; Internet Home Page Address: www.chapin.williams.edu; *Custodian* Robert L Volz; *Asst Librn* Wayne G Hammond; *Admin Asst* Elaine Yanow
Open Mon - Fri 10 AM - 5 PM; summer: Mon - Fri 1 - 4:30 PM; No admis fee; Library estab 1923; For reference only; Average Annual Attendance: 1,000
Income: Financed by Williams College, endowments & gifts
Library Holdings: Auction Catalogs; Audio Tapes; Book Volumes 52,000; Cassettes; Clipping Files; Compact Disks; DVDs; Exhibition Catalogs; Kodachrome Transparencies; Manuscripts; Maps; Memorabilia; Motion Pictures; Original Art Works; Original Documents; Pamphlets; Periodical Subscriptions 20; Photographs; Prints; Records; Sculpture; Slides; Video Tapes
Special Subjects: Art History, Landscape Architecture, Decorative Arts, Film, Illustration, Photography, Calligraphy, Commercial Art, Drawings, Etchings & Engravings, Graphic Arts, Graphic Design, Manuscripts, Maps, Posters, Prints, Sculpture, Historical Material, History of Art & Archaeology, Judaica, Portraits, Stage Design, Theatre Arts, Ethnology, Printmaking, Advertising Design, Cartoons, Fashion Arts, Industrial Design, Lettering, Furniture, Costume Design & Constr, Bookplates & Bindings, Restoration & Conservation, Woodcuts, Coins & Medals, Architecture
Collections: Pauline Baynes; Samuel "Erewhon" Butler; John DePol; CB Falls; Julio Granda; Herman & Helena Rosse; Frank Lloyd Wright; Leo Wyatt; Chesterwood Archives (Daniel Chester French Etal); Artist's Books; Illustrated Books; Posters; Historic Prints, Photographs & medallions

A **WILLIAMSTOWN ART CONSERVATION CENTER,** 227 South St, Williamstown, MA 01267-2891. Tel 413-458-5741; Fax 413-458-2314; Elec Mail wacc@williamstownart.org; Internet Home Page Address: www.williamstownart.org; *Dir* Thomas J Branchick; *Objects Conservator & Dept Head* Helene Gillette-Woodard; *Furniture Conservator & Dept Head* Hugh Glover; *Paper Conservator* Rebecca Johnston; *Paintings Conservator* Montserrat Le Mense; *Paintings Conservator* Sandra Webber; *Paper Conservator & Dept Head* Leslie Paisley; *Paintings Conservator & Internatl Projs Specialist* Cynthia Luk
Open Mon - Fri 9 AM - 5 PM; Estab 1977
Income: $1,000,000 (financed by state appropriation & earned income)
Activities: Progs for undergrad, grad & post grad; internships; fellowships; apprentice training; lect open to public, 2-4 vis lectrs per year; IIC Keck Award 1996

WINCHESTER

M **ARTHUR GRIFFIN CENTER FOR PHOTOGRAPHIC ART,** Griffin Museum of Photography, 67 Shore Rd, Winchester, MA 01890-2821. Tel 781-729-1158; Fax 781-721-2765; Elec Mail agcfpa@gis.net; Internet Home Page Address: www.griffincenter.org; www.griffinmuseum.org; *Exec Dir* Paula Tognarelli; *Assoc Dir* Frances Jakubek; *Gallery Monitor* Martha Stone
Open Tues - Thurs 11 AM - 5 PM, Fri 11 AM - 4 PM, Sat & Sun noon - 4 PM; Admis $7, seniors $3; Estab 1992 to promote historic & contemporary photography through photographic exhibitions; 1,500 sq ft modern gallery for photography; 4 satellite galleries, 58 shows per year; Average Annual Attendance: 5,000; Mem: 4,000
Income: Mem, entrance fee & photo sales
Special Subjects: Photography
Collections: Photographic works of Arthur Griffin
Exhibitions: Annual Juried Photography Show; over 58 shows per year
Activities: Classes for adults & children; lects open to pub, 12-20 vis lectrs per yr; gallery talks; juried competitions; original objects of art lent; book traveling exhibs; originate traveling exhibs to mus & galleries; mus shop sells books, original art & prints, magazines

WORCESTER

AMERICAN ANTIQUARIAN SOCIETY
For further information, see National and Regional Organizations

L **BECKER COLLEGE,** William F Ruska Library, 61 Sever St, Worcester, MA 01615-2195. Tel 508-791-9241, Ext 211; Fax 508-849-5131; Elec Mail plummer@go.becker.edu; *Asst Dir* Sharon Krauss; *Catalog & Reference Librn* Alice Baron; *Dean Library* Bruce Plummer
Open Mon - Thur 8 AM - 9 PM, Fri 8 AM - 5 PM, Sat 11 AM - 3 PM, Sun 2 PM - 10 PM; Estab 1887
Library Holdings: Slides; Video Tapes
Special Subjects: Graphic Design, Interior Design
Collections: Graphic Design; Interior Design
Publications: Acquisition List; Faculty Handbook, annual

M **CLARK UNIVERSITY,** The Schiltkamp Gallery/Traina Center for the Arts, 950 Main St, Worcester, MA 01610-1477. Tel 508-793-7113; Fax 508-793-8844; Internet Home Page Address: www.clarku.edu; *Dir* Sarah Buie
Open Mon - Fri 9 AM - 5 PM; Sat Noon - 5 PM; Sun Noon - 10 PM; No admis fee; Estab 1976 to provide the Clark community & greater Worcester community the opportunity to view quality exhibitions of art, primarily, but not exclusively, contemporary; First floor foyer of the Traina Center for the Arts; Average Annual Attendance: 2,000
Income: Financed through the University
Exhibitions: Six to eight exhibitions per year of, primarily emerging artists & well-known artists
Publications: Announcements of exhibitions
Activities: Exhibitions; art events; gallery talks; lects open to pub; 4-6 lectrs per year

L **COLLEGE OF THE HOLY CROSS,** Dinand Library, One College St, Worcester, MA 01610-2349. Tel 508-793-3372; Fax 508-793-2372; Elec Mail kreilly@holycross.edu; Internet Home Page Address: www.holycross.edu; Internet Home Page Address: academics.holycross.edu/libraries; *Assoc Dir* Karen Reilly; *Dir* Kathleen Carney
Open Sun - Thurs 8:30 AM - 1 AM, Fri & Sat 8:30 AM - 11 PM; mid-May - Sept summer hours Mon - Fri 8:30 AM - 4:30 PM; Estab 1843 to support the acad study & research needs of a liberal visual arts department
Library Holdings: Book Volumes 637,000 for all campus, 17,100 in N clas; Compact Disks; DVDs; Exhibition Catalogs; Original Art Works; Periodical Subscriptions 900; Sculpture; Slides 94,000
Special Subjects: Art History, Decorative Arts, Film, Commercial Art, Graphic Arts, Painting-American, Theatre Arts, Fashion Arts, Industrial Design, Art Education, Antiquities-Byzantine, Antiquities-Greek, Architecture
Exhibitions: Various exhibitions
Publications: Art reference bibliographies, semi-annual

M **HIGGINS ARMORY MUSEUM,** 100 Barber Ave, Worcester, MA 01606-2444. Tel 508-853-6015; Fax 508-852-7697; Elec Mail higgins@higgins.org; Internet Home Page Address: www.higgins.org; *Exec Dir* Suzanne Maas; *CFO* Lenore Tracey; *Paul S Morgan Cur* Dr Jeffrey Forgeng; *Conservator* William MacMillan; *Info & Pub Rels* Libbie Armstrong
Open Tues - Sat 10 AM - 4 PM, Sun Noon - 4 PM, cl Mon & major holidays; Admis adults $10, seniors $8 children 4-16 $7, mems & children 3 & under free, senior discount on Tues; Estab 1929 to collect & maintain arms, armor & related artifacts; Museum has a Gothic Hall with high vaulted ceilings; Average Annual Attendance: 60,000; Mem: 400; dues students & seniors $25, individual $50, dual

$60, family $70, family plus $90, Crusader $100 - $249, Squire $250 - $499, Knight $500 - $999, Renaissance Society $1,000+
Income: Financed by admis, mem, grants, gift shop & endowment
Special Subjects: Drawings, Graphics, Photography, Sculpture, African Art, Archaeology, Ethnology, Religious Art, Ceramics, Primitive art, Woodcarvings, Decorative Arts, Manuscripts, Painting-European, Glass, Asian Art, Carpets & Rugs, Historical Material, Juvenile Art, Tapestries, Miniatures, Mosaics, Gold, Stained Glass, Reproductions
Collections: Arms & armor from antiquity through the 1800s: 3,000+ armors & components, 1,000+ weapons & accessories, 500 swords & daggers, 100 firearms; art from related periods: paintings; tapestries; stained glass; woodcarvings; Evolution of European Armor; Arms & Courtly Life; Great Hall: Ancient Arms & Armor, Combat Wing, Arms & Armor Around the World, The Armorer's Craft, Tournament Wing
Publications: Quarterly calendar; teacher materials; gallery study-guide series; annual report
Activities: Classes for adults & children; dramatic progs; docent training; Academy of the Sword; lects open to pub, gallery talks; tours; competitions; schols offered; individual paintings & original objects of art lent to other mus; lending collection contains paintings, sculptures & several thousand objects of armor; book traveling exhibs; originate traveling exhibs; mus shop sells books, magazines, original art, reproductions, prints, slides, gifts, children's books & toys

L **Olive Higgins Prouty Library & Research Center,** 100 Barber Ave, Worcester, MA 01606-2444. Tel 508-853-6015; Fax 508-852-7697; Elec Mail higgins@higgins.org; Internet Home Page Address: www.higgins.org; *Vol Librn* Alan Catalano; *Cur* Jeffrey Forgeng
Open Wed 2 - 4 PM & by appt; No admis fee for mems; Estab 1968; Circ 6000; Average Annual Attendance: 250
Library Holdings: Book Volumes 3000; Clipping Files; Exhibition Catalogs; Manuscripts; Memorabilia; Photographs
Special Subjects: Art History, Metalwork
Activities: Classes for adults & children; docent training; lects open to pub, 6-12 vis lectrs per yr; concerts; gallery talks; tours; exten dept servs New England & Middle Atlantic States; individual paintings & original objects of art lent to other museums; lending collection contains 3000 original art works, 40 paintings & 6 sculptures; mus shop sells books, magazines, reproductions & souvenirs

M **WORCESTER ART MUSEUM,** 55 Salisbury St, Worcester, MA 01609-3196. Tel 508-799-4406; Fax 508-798-5646; Elec Mail information@worcesterart.org; Internet Home Page Address: www.worcesterart.org; *Deputy Dir Admin* David Sjosten; *Dir Educ* Honee A Hess; *Cur Prints, Drawings & Photography* David L Acton; *Registrar* Deborah Diemente; *Chief Preparator & Exhib Designer* Patrick Brown; *Dir Operations* Francis Pedone; *Mgr Facility Usage* Janet Rosetti; *Cafe Mgr* Laurie Krohn-Andros; *Cur Asian Art* Louise Virgin; *Librn* Deborah Aframe; *Mus Shop Mgr* Susan Giordano; *Cur Contemporary Art* Susan Stoops; *Pres* Sarah Berry; *Dir Develop* Martin Richman; *Dir* James A Welu; *Chief Conservator* Rita Albertson
Open Wed - Fri & Sun 11 AM - 5 PM, Sat 10 AM - 5 PM, until 8 PM on 3rd Thurs of month, cl Mon, Tues & holidays; Admis adults $14, seniors & college students with ID $12, mems, military & children under 18 free, 1st Sat of month 10 AM - noon free to all; Estab Museum 1896, School 1898. The Mus and School were founded for the promotion of art and art educ in Worcester; for the preservation and exhib of works and objects of art and for instruction in the industrial, liberal and fine arts. There are 42 galleries housed in a neoclassical bldg. The Higgins Educ Wing, built in 1970, houses studios and classrooms and contains exhib space for shows sponsored by the Educ Dept; Average Annual Attendance: 130,000; Mem: 4400, dues $45 - $65; annual meeting in Nov
Income: $6.5 million (financed by endowment, mem, private corporate contributions & government grants)
Library Holdings: Auction Catalogs; Book Volumes; Exhibition Catalogs; Pamphlets; Periodical Subscriptions; Slides
Special Subjects: Decorative Arts, Drawings, Etchings & Engravings, Landscapes, Ceramics, Sculpture, Painting-American, Prints, Watercolors, Pre-Columbian Art, Religious Art, Woodcuts, Jade, Asian Art, Silver, Painting-British, Painting-Dutch, Painting-French, Coins & Medals, Baroque Art, Painting-Flemish, Renaissance Art, Medieval Art, Antiquities-Oriental, Antiquities-Egyptian, Antiquities-Roman, Mosaics
Collections: John Chandler Bancroft Collection of Japanese Prints; American Paintings of 17th - 20th Centuries; British Paintings of 18th and 19th Centuries; Dutch 17th & 19th Century Paintings; Egyptian, Classical, Oriental & Medieval Sculpture; French Paintings of 16th - 19th Centuries; Flemish 16th - 17th Century Paintings; Italian Paintings of the 13th - 18th Centuries; Mosaics from Antioch; Pre-Columbian Collection; 12th Century French Chap House; Paul Revere Silver & Engravings
Publications: American Portrait Miniatures: The Worcester Art Museum Collection; In Battle's Light: Woodblock Prints of Japan's Early Modern Wars; Calendar of Events, quarterly; The Second Wave: American Abstractions of the 1930s & 1940s; A Spectrum of Innovation: American Color Prints, 1890 - 1960; Paths to Impressionism: French & American Landscape Paintings; Photography at the Worcester Art Museum: Keeping Shadows
Activities: Classes for adults & children; docent training; lects open to pub, 10-15 vis lectrs per yr; symposia; concerts; gallery talks; tours; scholarships offered; originates traveling exhibs; mus shop sells books, reproductions, jewelry & exhib related merchandise

L **Library,** 55 Salisbury St, Worcester, MA 01609-3196. Tel 508-799-4406, Ext 3070; Fax 508-798-5646; Elec Mail library@worcesterart.org; Internet Home Page Address: www.worcesterart.org; *Librn* Debby Aframe; *Asst Librn* Christine Clayton
Open Wed - Fri 11 AM - 5 PM, Sat 10 AM - 5 PM Sept - May & by appointment during acad yr; Estab 1909 to provide resource material for the Mus Depts; Maintains non-circulating collection only
Library Holdings: Auction Catalogs; Book Volumes 50,000; Exhibition Catalogs; Other Holdings Auction & sale catalogues; Pamphlets; Periodical Subscriptions 100; Slides
Special Subjects: Art History, Collages, Constructions, Intermedia, Landscape Architecture, Decorative Arts, Film, Illustration, Mixed Media, Calligraphy, Commercial Art, Drawings, Etchings & Engravings, Graphic Arts, Graphic Design, Islamic Art, Manuscripts, Maps, Painting-American, Painting-Flemish,

Painting-European, Historical Material, History of Art & Archaeology, Judaica, Conceptual Art, Crafts, Latin American Art, Archaeology, Ethnology, American Western Art, Bronzes, Advertising Design, Fashion Arts, Industrial Design, Interior Design, Lettering, Art Education, Asian Art, American Indian Art, Anthropology, Eskimo Art, Furniture, Mexican Art, Ivory, Jade, Drafting, Glass, Mosaics, Aesthetics, Afro-American Art, Bookplates & Bindings, Metalwork, Antiquities-Oriental, Antiquities-Persian, Carpets & Rugs, Dolls, Embroidery, Enamels, Goldsmithing, Handicrafts, Jewelry, Leather, Miniatures, Oriental Art, Marine Painting, Landscapes, Antiquities-Assyrian, Antiquities-Byzantine, Antiquities-Egyptian, Antiquities-Etruscan, Antiquities-Greek, Antiquities-Roman, Dioramas, Coins & Medals, Flasks & Bottles, Laces, Display, Folk Art
Exhibitions: Periodic book displays related to museum exhibitions and special library collections
Activities: Tours

M **WORCESTER CENTER FOR CRAFTS,** Krikorian Gallery, 25 Sagamore Rd, Worcester, MA 01605-3914. Tel 508-753-8183; Fax 508-797-5626; Elec Mail wcc@worcestercraftcenter.org; Internet Home Page Address: www.worcestercraftcenter.org; *Exec Dir* Barbara Walzer; *Pub Rels & Mktg* Amy Black; *Develop* David Leach
Open Mon, Wed, Fri 10AM - 5:30 PM, Tues & Thurs 10AM-7:30PM, Sat 10 AM - 5 PM, cl Sun; No admis fee; Estab 1856 for educational exhibits of historic & contemporary crafts; Professionally lighted & installed 40 x 60 gallery with six major shows per yr in main gallery; Average Annual Attendance: 20,000; Mem: 1000; dues $40 & up
Income: Financed by mem, grants, contributions & endowment
Special Subjects: Crafts
Collections: Collection contains 200 books, 2000 Kodachromes, 300 photographs
Exhibitions: 10 exhibits per yr; major exhibit focus on 3-D art, reflects work from studio-visual art
Publications: On-Center, newsletter; school for professional crafts brochures; 3 course catalogs, yearly
Activities: Classes for adults & children; weekend professional workshops; 2 yr full-time progs in professional crafts; lects open to pub, 4 vis lectrs per yr; gallery talks; tours; schols & fels offered; City Outreach Prog brings crafts to pub schools; book traveling exhibs 2 per yr; originates traveling exhibs anywhere in Massachusetts; supply shop & gift shop sell books, original craft objects

MICHIGAN

ADRIAN

M **SIENA HEIGHTS COLLEGE,** Klemm Gallery, Studio Angelico, 1247 E Siena Heights Dr, Adrian, MI 49221-1755. Tel 517-264-7860; Fax 517-264-7739; Elec Mail creising@sienahts.edu; Internet Home Page Address: www.sienaheights.edu/~art; *Dir* Dr Peter Barr
Open Tues- Fri 9 AM - 4 PM, Sun Noon - 4 PM, cl major holidays & summers; No admis fee; Estab 1970's to offer cultural programs to Lenawee County & others; Average Annual Attendance: 6,000
Income: Funded by college
Exhibitions: Invitational Artists Shows; major national culturally-based exhibitions; professional artists & student shows; fall semester 3 month-long solo or group exhibitions
Activities: Classes for adults; lects open to public, gallery talks; tours; performances; scholarships offered

L **Art Library,** 1247 E Siena Heights Dr, Adrian, MI 49221-1755. Tel 517-264-7152; Fax 517-264-7711; Elec Mail sbeck@sienahts.edu; Internet Home Page Address: www.sienahts.edu/~libr/library.htm; *Pub Servs Librn* Melissa M Sissen; *Cataloging* Mark Dombrowski
Open Mon - Fri 8:30 AM - 11 PM, Sat Noon - 5 PM, Sun 1 - 11 PM
Income: Funded by college
Library Holdings: Audio Tapes; Book Volumes 10,000; Cards; Cassettes; Clipping Files; Fiche; Filmstrips; Pamphlets; Periodical Subscriptions 35; Photographs; Records; Reels; Slides; Video Tapes

ALBION

M **ALBION COLLEGE,** Bobbitt Visual Arts Center, 611 E Porter, Albion, MI 49224. Tel 517-629-0246; Fax 517-629-0752; Elec Mail art@albion.edu; Internet Home Page Address: www.albion.edu; *Prof* Lynne Chytilo, MFA; *Prof Emer* Frank Machek, MFA; *Prof Emeritus* Douglas Goering, MFA; *Assoc Prof* Dr Bille Wickre, PhD; *Assoc Prof & Dept Chair* Anne McCauley, MFA; *Vis Asst Prof* Gary Wahl; *Asst Prof* Michael Dixon; *Asst Prof* Anne Barber
Open Mon - Thurs 9 AM - 9 PM, Fri 9 AM - 5 PM, Sat 10 AM - 2 PM; No admis fee; Estab 1835 to offer art educ at col level & gen art exhib prog for campus community & pub; Maintains one large gallery & one print gallery; Average Annual Attendance: 500
Income: Privately funded
Library Holdings: Lantern Slides; Manuscripts; Original Art Works; Prints; Sculpture
Special Subjects: Etchings & Engravings, Folk Art, Furniture, Painting-American, Textiles, Woodcuts, Prints, African Art, Southwestern Art, Ceramics, Decorative Arts, Glass, Asian Art, Carpets & Rugs
Collections: African Art; ceramics; glass; prints
Exhibitions: From the Print Collection; Pieces from the Permanent Collection; various one-person & group exhibitions, contemporary artists
Activities: Lects open to pub, 4-8 vis lectrs per yr; gallery talks; competitions with awards; scholarships offered; individual paintings & original objects of art lent to acad institutions, museums & galleries; lending collection contains 2350 original prints; originate traveling exhibs

ALPENA

M **BESSER MUSEUM FOR NORTHEAST MICHIGAN,** (Jesse Besser Museum) 491 Johnson St, Alpena, MI 49707-1496. Tel 989-356-2202; Fax 989-356-3133; Elec Mail sanderson@bessermuseum.org; Internet Home Page Address: www.bessermuseum.org; *Dir* Janet Smoak, PhD
Open Mon - Sat 10 AM - 5 PM, Sun Noon - 4 PM; Admis adults $5, seniors, students & children $3; Estab assoc 1962, building open to pub 1966, an accredited mus of history, science & art serving northern Michigan; Mus has a research library, a planetarium, a Foucault Pendulum, Indian artifact collection, Ave of shops, lumbering exhibits & preserved furnished historical buildings on grounds. Also on grounds, sculptured fountain by artist Glen Michaels. Three galleries are utilized for shows, traveling exhibits, & changing exhibitions of the Museum's collection of modern art & art prints, decorative arts & furniture. There are 260 running ft of wall space on lower level, 1250 sq ft & 16 45 sq ft on upper level galleries; Average Annual Attendance: 25,000
Income: Financed by Besser Foundation, federal & state grants, private gifts & donations, Museums Founders Soc, Operation Support Grant from Michigan Council for the Arts, & other sources
Special Subjects: Drawings, Graphics, Painting-American, Photography, Prints, American Indian Art, Anthropology, Archaeology, Textiles, Costumes, Ceramics, Crafts, Folk Art, Pottery, Etchings & Engravings, Landscapes, Decorative Arts, Manuscripts, Posters, Dolls, Furniture, Glass, Porcelain, Marine Painting, Maps, Dioramas, Laces
Collections: Art prints; Clewell pottery; contemporary Native American art; maps of the Great Lakes; modern art; photography
Exhibitions: Changing exhibitions of all major collecting areas & touring exhibits; Northeast Michigan Juried Art
Activities: Classes for adults & children; art workshops; seminars; docent training; lects open to pub, 5 vis lectrs per yr; gallery talks; tours; competitions with awards; book traveling exhibs 8 per yr; originate traveling exhibs; mus shop sells books, magazines, original art, handicrafts

L **Philip M Park Library,** 491 Johnson St, Alpena, MI 49707-1496. Tel 517-356-2202; Fax 517-356-2202; Elec Mail cwitulski@bessermuseum.org; Internet Home Page Address: www.bessermuseum.org; *Dir* Christine Witulski; *Exhibs Dir* Randy Shultz
Library open Tues - Sat 10 AM - 5 PM; Admis adults $5, children 5 - 7 & seniors $3; Museum estab 1966; Art, history & science exhibits; Average Annual Attendance: 25,000
Library Holdings: Book Volumes 4200; Cassettes; Clipping Files; Exhibition Catalogs; Fiche; Manuscripts; Maps; Original Documents; Pamphlets; Periodical Subscriptions 46; Photographs; Prints; Reels; Slides; Video Tapes
Special Subjects: Art History, Folk Art, Decorative Arts, Painting-American, Prints, Ceramics, Printmaking, American Indian Art, Glass, Dolls, Pottery, Restoration & Conservation, Flasks & Bottles, Architecture
Collections: History, art, & science
Activities: Educ prog; classes for adults & children; docent training; gallery talks, tours, competitions

ANN ARBOR

A **ANN ARBOR ART CENTER,** Art Center, 117 W Liberty, Ann Arbor, MI 48104. Tel 734-994-8004, ext 110; Fax 734-994-3610; Elec Mail a2artcen@aol.com; Internet Home Page Address: www.annarborartcenter.org; Telex 101; *CEO & Pres* Marsha Chamberlin; *Gallery Dir* Terry Browning; *Dir Operations* Eric Wolff
Open Mon - Fri 10 AM - 6 PM, Sat 10 AM - 6 PM, Sun Noon - 5:30 PM; Estab 1909 to provide for the well-being of the visual arts through programs that encourage participation in & support for the visual arts, as well as foster artistic development; Maintains 750 sq ft of exhibit gallery space with monthly shows; & 1300 sq ft sales - rental gallery next to exhibit areas; classes in studio art & art appreciation; special events; Average Annual Attendance: 52,000; Mem: 1300; dues vary; annual meeting in Feb
Income: Financed by mem, Michigan Council for the Arts grant, rental of studios & retail sales
Exhibitions: 8 juried & nonjuried shows throughout yr
Publications: Class catalog, quarterly; gallery announcements, monthly; lecture listings, quarterly; newsletter, quarterly
Activities: Classes for adults & children; artist workshops on professional development; lect open to public, 4-6 vis lectrs per year; gallery talks; tours; competitions with prizes; scholarships offered; exten dept lends individual paintings & original objects of art to organizations & community facilities; sales shop sells original art & fine contemporary crafts

A **ARTRAIN, INC,** 1100 N Main St Ste 106, Ann Arbor, MI 48104-1059. Tel 734-747-8300; Fax 734-747-8530; Elec Mail info@artrainusa.org; Internet Home Page Address: www.artrainUSA.org; *Chmn* Burt Althaver; *Exec Dir* Debra Polich
No admis fee; Estab 1971 to tour major art exhibits throughout the nation & provide catalyst for community arts development; Traveling art museum in a train; consists of converted railroad cars with large walls & cases; Average Annual Attendance: 122,000
Income: Financed by endowment, state appropriation, individual foundation & corporation campaigns
Publications: Exhibition catalogs; newsletter
Activities: Classes for children; docent training; lects open to pub; competitions; book traveling exhibs; mus shop sells exhibs related items

A **MICHIGAN GUILD OF ARTISTS & ARTISANS,** Michigan Guild Gallery, 118 N Fourth Ave, Ann Arbor, MI 48104. Tel 734-662-3382; Fax 734-662-0339; Elec Mail info@theguild.org; Internet Home Page Address: www.michiganguild.org; *Gallery Coordr* Esther Kirshenbaum; *Gallery Coordr* Pamela Stoddard; *Exec Dir* Debra Clayton; *Receptionist* Audrey Libke
Open Mon - Fri 9 AM - 5 PM; No admis fee; Estab with no percentage, small artist fee for artists who have never had an exhib locally & artists with new, unshown work; Small, street level; highly thought of locally; Average Annual Attendance: 2,000; Mem: 1100; dues $45-$75; annual meeting in July
Income: Financed by mem fees & art fair fees
Publications: Mem newsletter, bi-monthly
Activities: Educ dept provides workshops; lect open to public; concerts; member art shown in pub places

M **UNIVERSITY OF MICHIGAN,** Museum of Art, 525 S State St, Ann Arbor, MI 48109-1354. Tel 734-764-0395; Fax 734-764-3731; Elec Mail umma.info@umich.edu; Internet Home Page Address: www.umma.umich.edu; *Chief Admin Officer* Kathryn Huss; *Dir Educ* Ruth Slavin; *Dir Develop* Todd Ahrens; *Dir* Joseph Rosa; *External Rels Mgr & Sr Writer* Stephanie Rieke Miller
Open year round Tues, Wed, Sat 10 AM - 5 PM, Thurs & Fri 10 AM - 5 PM, Sun noon - 5 PM; No admis fee, $5 suggested donation; Estab 1946, as a university art mus & mus for the Ann Arbor community; Average Annual Attendance: 225,000; Mem: 1400; dues individual $50
Income: Financed by state appropriation other federal and state agencies, and private donations
Special Subjects: Afro-American Art, Etchings & Engravings, Landscapes, American Western Art, Photography, Porcelain, Portraits, Painting-American, Prints, Painting-European, Sculpture, Tapestries, Watercolors, African Art, Religious Art, Painting-Japanese, Asian Art, Restorations, Baroque Art, Painting-Flemish, Renaissance Art, Medieval Art, Painting-Italian, Stained Glass
Collections: Arts of the Western World from the Sixth Century AD to the Present; Asian, Near Eastern, African & Oceanic, including ceramics, contemporary art, decorative art, graphic arts, manuscripts, painting, sculpture; James McNeill Whistler Collection
Publications: Bulletin of the Museum of Art & Archaeology, irregular; bimonthly Insight, Catalogues & Gallery Brochures, irregular
Activities: Classes for adults & children, dramatic programs, visiting writers series, film series, Educ dept; docent training; community days; lects open to pub, vis lectrs; gallery talks; tours; concerts; individual paintings & original objects of art lent to other mus; originate traveling exhibs to national & international mus; mus shop sells publications, posters, postcards & gifts, original art, prints

M **Kelsey Museum of Archaeology,** 434 State St, Ann Arbor, MI 48109-1390. Tel 734-764-9304; Fax 734-763-8976; Internet Home Page Address: www.lsa.umich.edu/kelsey; *Dir* Sharon C Herbert; *Cur* Elaine K Gazda; *Assoc Cur* Janet Richards; *Assoc Cur* Terry Wilfong; *Assoc Dir & Assoc Cur Educ* Lauren E Talalay; *Conservator* Suzanne Davis; *Exhibit Preparator* Scott Meier; *Coordr of Mus Visitor Programs* Todd Gerring; *Cur* Margaret Root; *Conservator* Claudia Chemello; *Communs Ed* Margaret Lourse; *Mus Coll Mgr* Michelle Fortenot; *Mus Coll Mgr* Sebastian Encina; *Adminr* Helen Baker; *Assoc Prof* Nicholas Terrenato; *Assoc Prof* Christopher Ratte
Open Tues - Fri 9 AM - 4 PM, Sat - Sun 1-4 PM, cl Mon & univ holidays; No admis fee; Estab 1928; Seven galleries are maintained; Average Annual Attendance: 37,000
Income: State, Grants, Tuition
Special Subjects: Sculpture, Bronzes, Textiles, Pottery, Ivory, Antiquities-Egyptian, Antiquities-Greek, Antiquities-Roman
Collections: Objects of the Graeco-Roman period from excavations conducted by the University of Michigan in Egypt & Iraq; Greece, Etruria, Rome & provinces: sculpture, inscriptions, pottery, bronzes, terracottas; Egyptian antiquities dynastic through Roman; Roman & Islamic glass, bone & ivory objects, textiles, coins; 19th century photographs
Publications: Biannual newsletter; Bulletin of the Museums of Art & Archaeology, irregular; Kelsey Museum Studies Series, irregular
Activities: Educ dept; classes for children; lects open to pub, 4 vis lectrs per yr; tours, gallery talks; original objects of art lent to other mus upon request; book traveling exhibs; originate traveling exhibs to mus with similar collections; Mus shop sells books, reproductions

M **Jean Paul Slusser Gallery,** 2000 Bonisteel Dr, School of Art & Design Ann Arbor, MI 48109-2069. Tel 734-936-2082; Fax 734-615-6761; Elec Mail slussergallery@umich.edu; Internet Home Page Address: www.umich.edu/~webteam/SOAD/; *Dir* Mark Nielsen
Open Tues & Thurs Noon - 8 PM, Wed, Fri, Sat & Sun 11 AM - 4 PM; No admis fee; Estab 1974; Gallery is located on the main floor of the Art & Architecture Building. Comprised of 3600 sq ft of exhibition space; Average Annual Attendance: 11,000
Income: Financed by School of Art general fund
Collections: Artifacts of the School's history; works by faculty & alumni of the University of Michigan School of Art
Exhibitions: Emese Benczur; Olafur Eliasson; Annika Eriksson; Anna Gaskell; Liam Gillick; Carsten Holler; Pierre Huyghe; Koo Jeong-a; Aernout Mik; Manfred Pernice; Stephanie Rowden; Superflex; Apolonija Sustersic; Elin Wikstrom; Andrea Zittel
Publications: catalogues
Activities: Lects open to pub, 11 vis lectrs per yr; gallery talks; books 2 traveling exhibs per yr; sales shop sells books

L **Asian Art Archives,** 525 S State St, Ann Arbor, MI 48109-1354. Tel 734-764-5555; Fax 734-647-4121; Elec Mail wholden@umich.edu; *Sr Assoc Cur* Wendy Holden
Open Mon - Fri 9 AM - 5 PM; Estab 1962 for study & research. Contains 180,000 black & white photographs of Asian art objects or monuments. Library also houses the Asian Art Photographic Distribution, a nonprofit bus selling visual resource materials dealing with Chinese & Japanese art. Houses Southeast Asia Art Foundation Collection of 100,000 slides & photographs of Southeast Asian art; For research only
Income: $5000 (financed by endowment, federal funds)
Purchases: $4000 - $5000
Library Holdings: Book Volumes 50; Clipping Files; Exhibition Catalogs; Fiche 10,000; Other Holdings Black/white negatives 26,000; Photographs 80,000; Reels; Reproductions 3000; Slides
Special Subjects: Art History, Decorative Arts, Calligraphy, Graphic Arts, Islamic Art, Ceramics, Bronzes, Asian Art, Ivory, Jade, Glass, Gold, Landscapes, Coins & Medals, Architecture
Collections: National Palace Museum, Taiwan, photographic archive; Chinese art, painting, decorative arts; Southeast Asian Art Archive, sculpture, architecture; Islamic Art Archive; Asian Art Archive, Chinese & Japanese arts, painting
Publications: Newsletter, East Asian Art & Archaeology (three issues per year)

L **Fine Arts Library,** 855 S University Ave, 260 Tappan Hall Ann Arbor, MI 48109-1357. Tel 734-764-5405; Fax 734-764-5408; Elec Mail finearts@umich.edu;

Internet Home Page Address: www.lib.umich.edu/finearts; *Head Fine Arts Library, Head Librn* Deirdre Spencer; *Information Resources Specialist* Jessica DuVerneay; *Information Resources Asst* Myrtle Hudson; *Information Resources Supv* Nancy Damm

Open Mon - Thurs 8 AM - 10 PM, Fri 8 AM - 5 PM, Sat 1 PM - 6 PM, Sun 1 - 10 PM, summer hours Mon - Thurs 8 AM - 8 PM, Fri 8 AM - 5 PM, Sun 1 - 5 PM, cl Sat; Estab 1949, to support the acad programs of the History of the Art Department, including research of faculty & graduate students; Circ 17,200

Income: Financed by state appropriation

Library Holdings: Book Volumes 100,000; CD-ROMs; Compact Disks; Exhibition Catalogs; Fiche; Filmstrips; Other Holdings Marburger index of photographic documentation of art in Germany; Pamphlets; Periodical Subscriptions 232; Reels

Special Subjects: Art History, Folk Art, Decorative Arts, Film, Mixed Media, Photography, Calligraphy, Islamic Art, Painting-American, Painting-British, Painting-Dutch, Painting-Flemish, Painting-French, Painting-German, Painting-Italian, Painting-Japanese, Painting-Russian, Painting-Spanish, Prints, Sculpture, Painting-European, History of Art & Archaeology, Judaica, Portraits, Watercolors, Ceramics, Conceptual Art, Latin American Art, Painting-Israeli, American Western Art, Bronzes, Cartoons, Asian Art, American Indian Art, Porcelain, Primitive art, Furniture, Mexican Art, Ivory, Jade, Mosaics, Stained Glass, Afro-American Art, Antiquities-Oriental, Antiquities-Persian, Carpets & Rugs, Embroidery, Jewelry, Miniatures, Oriental Art, Pottery, Religious Art, Silver, Tapestries, Textiles, Antiquities-Assyrian, Antiquities-Byzantine, Antiquities-Egyptian, Antiquities-Etruscan, Antiquities-Greek, Antiquities-Roman

Activities: Educ prog; library instruction

L **Department of the History of Art, Visual Resources Collection,** 855 S University Ave, 110 Tappan Hall Ann Arbor, MI 48109-1357. Tel 734-764-5400; Fax 734-647-4121

By appt only for Asian Art archives; Estab 1911, as a library for teaching & research collection of slides & photos of art objects; limited commercial distribution; nonprofit slide distribution projects; (Asian Art Photographic Distribution; Univ of Mich Slide Distribution); For in-house research only

Income: Financed by state appropriation

Library Holdings: Lantern Slides; Photographs 200,000; Reproductions; Slides 290,000

Special Subjects: History of Art & Archaeology

Collections: Islamic Archives; Palace Museum Archive (Chinese painting); Romanesque Archive (sculpture & some architecture concentrating on Burgundy, Southwestern France, Spain & southern Italy); Southeast Asian & Indian Archives

Activities: Materials lent only to University of Michigan faculty & students; archive materials may not be circulated, restrictions apply

L **Media Union Library,** 2281 Bonisteel Blvd, Ann Arbor, MI 48109-2094. Tel 734-647-5735; Fax 734-764-4487; Elec Mail mu.ref@umich.edu; Internet Home Page Address: www.lib.umich.edu/ummu/; *Visual Resources Librn & Selector Art & Design, Architecture & Urban Planning Librn* Rebecca Price; *Head Librn & Dir Arts & Engineering Librs* Michael D Miller; *Art & Design Field Librn* Annette Haines

Open 24 hours daily for students, 8 AM - 10 PM for non-students; Estab to support the teaching & research activities of the School of Art & the College of Architecture & Urban Planning

Library Holdings: Audio Tapes; Book Volumes 75,000; CD-ROMs 120; Cards; Cassettes 100; Clipping Files; DVDs 10; Exhibition Catalogs; Fiche; Filmstrips; Kodachrome Transparencies; Lantern Slides 17,000; Manuscripts; Maps 100; Micro Print; Original Art Works; Other Holdings Digital Images 20,000; Pamphlets; Periodical Subscriptions 400; Photographs 30,000; Reels; Sculpture; Slides 105,000; Video Tapes 1350

Special Subjects: Tapestries

Activities: 1500 computer workstations with various software

BATTLE CREEK

M **ART CENTER OF BATTLE CREEK,** 265 E Emmett St, Battle Creek, MI 49017-4601. Tel 269-962-9511; Fax 269-969-3838; Elec Mail artcenterofbc@yahoo.com; Internet Home Page Address: www.artcenterofbattlecreek.org; *Exec Dir* Linda Holderbaum; *Pres* Sharyn Austin; *Educ Coordr* Kay Doyle; *Admin Asst* Keri Steele

Open Tues- Fri 10 AM - 5 PM, Sat 11AM-3PM, cl Aug & legal holidays; Admis adults $3, seniors & students $2; Estab 1948 to offer classes for children & adults & to present monthly exhibitions of professional work; Four galleries of varying sizes with central vaulted ceiling gallery, track lighting & security; Average Annual Attendance: 30,000; Mem: 750; dues $15; annual meeting in Sept

Income: Financed by mem, endowment fund, grants, UAC, special projects, tuition, sales of artwork

Special Subjects: Decorative Arts, Drawings, Prints, Textiles, Graphics, Photography, Sculpture, Costumes, Calligraphy

Collections: Michigan Art Collection featuring 20th century Michigan artists

Exhibitions: Group & Solo Shows: Paintings; Photography; Prints; Sculpture; Crafts; American Art 40s & 50s; Artist's competitions

Publications: Newsletter, bi-monthly

Activities: Classes for adults & children; docent training; workshops & progs; lects open to pub, 5 vis lectrs per yr; gallery talks; tours; competitions with prizes; scholarships offered; individual paintings & original objects of art lent to qualified institutions; book traveling exhibs 1-2 per yr; originate traveling exhibs to mus & art centers; mus shop sells original art by Michigan artists; KidSpace hands-on gallery

L **Michigan Art & Artist Archives,** 265 E Emmett St, Battle Creek, MI 49017-4601. Tel 616-962-9511; Fax 616-969-3838; Elec Mail artcenterofbc@yahoo.com; Internet Home Page Address: www.artcenterofbc.org; *Exec Dir* Linda Holderbaum; *Educ Coordr* Kay Doyle; *Office Mgr* Keri Steele

Open Tues - Fri - 10 AM - 5 PM, Sat 11 AM - 3 PM; Admis adults $3, seniors & students $2, free Thurs; Estab 1946; 3 exhib galleries; Average Annual Attendance: 10,000; Mem: 300

Library Holdings: Book Volumes 550; Clipping Files; Exhibition Catalogs; Original Art Works; Periodical Subscriptions 12; Photographs; Sculpture; Slides

Special Subjects: Art History, American Indian Art, Afro-American Art, Antiquities-Egyptian

Collections: MI-Art, Michigan Art Coll - 200 pieces of 2-D + 3-D work by Michigan Arts

Exhibitions: Exhibs change monthly

Activities: Classes for adults & children; docent training; lects open to pub; gallery talks; tours; sponsoring of competitions; sales shop; original art

BAY CITY

M **BAY COUNTY HISTORICAL SOCIETY,** Historical Museum of Bay County, 321 Washington Ave, Bay City, MI 48708-5837. Tel 989-893-5733; Fax 989-893-5741; Internet Home Page Address: www.bchsmuseum.org; *Exec Dir* Gay McInerney

Open Mon - Fri 10 AM - 5 PM, Sat Noon - 4 PM; No admis fee; Estab 1919 to preserve, collect, & interpret the historical materials of Bay County; 2 new permanent galleries; 1 features 7 period rooms; the other interactive displays - Selling Mrs. Consumer & Bay City: Seaport to the World; Average Annual Attendance: 60,000; Mem: 500; dues corporate $500, patron $100, small bus $50, sustaining $25; annual meeting in Apr

Income: Financed by mem, gift shop, county funds

Special Subjects: Photography, American Indian Art, Anthropology, Archaeology, Textiles, Crafts, Landscapes, Decorative Arts, Historical Material, Period Rooms

Collections: Hand crafts, photographs, portraits, quilts; Patrol Craft Sailor Assn National Collections: mid-1800 - post WW II historical material; native American materials & paintings; sugar beet history (memorabilia & materials)

Publications: Anishinabe - People of Saginaw; Ghost Towns & Place Names; Historic Architecture of Bay City, Michigan; Vanished Industries; Women of Bay County

Activities: Classes for adults & children; home tours; historical encampment; living history progs; traveling displays & educational kits; lects open to pub, 2-3 vis lectrs per yr; gallery talks; tours; mus shop sells books, reproductions, hand crafts, historical gifts

BIRMINGHAM

A **BIRMINGHAM BLOOMFIELD ART CENTER,** Art Center, 1516 S Cranbrook Rd, Birmingham, MI 48009-1855. Tel 248-644-0866; Fax 248-644-7904; Internet Home Page Address: www.bbartcenter.org; *Pres & CEO* Annie Van Gelderen; *VP Progs* Cynthia K Mills; *VP Finance* Gwenn Rosseau; *Educ* Debra Callahan; *Exhib* Amy Kantgias

Open Mon - Thurs 9 AM - 6 PM, Fri & Sat 9 AM - 5 PM; No admis fee; Estab 1957 to provide a community-wide, integrated studio-gallery art center; to enhance life within our region by promoting the appreciation and understanding of the arts; 4 gallery spaces; Average Annual Attendance: 30,000; Mem: 2000; dues $50 & up; annual meeting in May

Income: $1,500,000 (financed by mem, tuitions, special events funding & donations)

Collections: Sol LeWitt Wall Drawing

Exhibitions: Annual Michigan Fine Arts Competition; juried exhibits & competitions; local high school exhibit; local and regional artist groups; traveling exhibition

Publications: Class brochure; bi-annual newsletter

Activities: Classes for adults & children; competitions with prizes; holiday shop; children's art camps and interdisciplinary art camps; annual festival; scholarships offered; gallery shop sells original art

XOCHIPILLI ART GALLERY, 568 N Woodward Ave, Birmingham, MI 48009. Tel 313-645-1905; *Dir* Mary C Wright
Open Tues - Sat 11 AM - 5 PM

BLOOMFIELD HILLS

M **CRANBROOK ART MUSEUM,** (Cranbrook Academy of Art) 39221 Woodward Ave, Bloomfield Hills, MI 48303; Box 801, Bloomfield Hills, MI 48303-0801. Tel 248-645-3323; Fax 248-645-3324; Elec Mail artmuseum@cranbrook.edu; Internet Home Page Address: www.cranbrook.edu; *Admin Mgr* Denise Collier; *Preparator* Abby Newbold; *Dir* Greg Wittkopp; *Registrar* Roberta Frey Gilboe; *Asst Cur* Emily Zilber

See website for hours; Estab 1930; Modern and contemporary art, crafts, architectural and design museum; Average Annual Attendance: 37,000; Mem: 900; dues family $65, individual $45

Special Subjects: Architecture, Drawings, Graphics, Painting-American, Photography, Prints, Sculpture, Textiles, Ceramics, Crafts, Pottery, Etchings & Engravings, Decorative Arts, Furniture, Porcelain, Silver, Metalwork, Tapestries

Collections: Artists associated with Cranbrook Academy of Art: ceramics by Maija Grotell; architectural drawings & decorative arts by Eliel Saarinen; porcelains by Adelaide Robineau; sculpture by Carl Milles; contemporary paintings; 19th century prints; study coll of textiles; Shuey Collection: paintings and sculptures by Albers, Dubuffet, Judd, de Kooning, Lichtenstein, Martin, Motherwell, Rauschenberg, Riley, Stella, Warhol and more

Exhibitions: 13 exhibitions annually of contemporary art, architecture & design

Activities: Docent training; dramatic progs; lects open to pub, 18 vis lectrs per yr; gallery talks; tours; concerts; individual paintings & original objects of art lent to other institutions; book traveling exhibs 1-2 per yr; originate traveling exhibs & circulate to other mus national & international; mus shop sells books, magazines, original art, reproductions, gift items & cards

L **Library,** 39221 Woodward Ave, Bloomfield Hills, MI 48303-0801; PO Box 801, Bloomfield Hills, MI 48303-0801. Tel 248-645-3355; Fax 248-645-3464; Internet Home Page Address: www.cranbrookart.edu/library; *Dir Library* Judy Dyki; *Librn* Mary Beth Kreiner; *Library Asst* Elizabeth Dizik

Open Mon & Thurs 9 AM - 8 PM, Fri 9 AM - 5 PM, Sat & Sun 1 PM - 5 PM; Estab 1928 to support research needs of Art Academy & Mus; Library is for Academy students, faculty & staff; open to pub for reference only

Income: Financed by academy

Library Holdings: Audio Tapes; Book Volumes 28,000; Cassettes 800; Clipping Files; DVDs 1,500; Exhibition Catalogs; Other Holdings Masters theses; Periodical Subscriptions 190; Video Tapes 1,400
Special Subjects: Art History, Photography, Graphic Arts, Sculpture, Ceramics, Printmaking, Metalwork, Architecture

BYRON CENTER

M **VAN INGEL FINE ARTS CENTER,** Gainey Gallery, 8500 Burlingame SW, Byron Center, MI 49315. Tel 616-678-6801; *Contact* Cindi Ford

CHARLEVOIX

M **KOUCKY GALLERY,** 325 Bridge St, Charlevoix, MI 49720-1414. Tel 231-547-2228; Fax 231-547-2455; *Dir* Charles J Koucky Jr
Open Winter: Wed - Sat 10 AM - 5 PM, Sun 10 AM - 4 PM, Summer: Mon - Sat 10 AM - 9 PM, Sun 10 AM - 4 PM

DAVISON

M **THE ART CAFE,** 217 Shoppers Alley, Davison, MI 48423-1424. Tel 248-210-0862; Elec Mail staff@artcafeonline.org; Internet Home Page Address: www.artcafeonline.org; *Exec Dir* Cora Smilkovich; *Treas* Kurt C Kohl; *Secy* Andrew Sumner
Admis. donations accepted; Estab. 12/03 to provide a space for artists to create & exhibit art with an outreach component to promote emerging & established art & native art awareness; Exhibit space onsite & outreach exhibits
Activities: Classes for adults; concerts; gallery talks tours; sponsoring of competitions; awards

DEARBORN

M **ARAB AMERICAN NATIONAL MUSEUM,** 13624 Michigan Ave, Dearborn, MI 48126-3519. Tel 313-582-AANM; Fax 313-582-1086; Elec Mail aanm@accesscommunity.org; Internet Home Page Address: www.arabamericanmuseum.org; *Dir* Dr Anan Ameri
Open Wed, Fri & Sat 10 AM - 6 PM, Thurs 10 AM - 8 PM, Sun 12 - 5 PM, cl Mon & Tues, New Year's Day, Thanksgiving Day & Christmas Day; Admis adults $6, seniors 62 & up, students w/ID & children 6 - 12 $3, children 5 & under no admis fee; 2005. Mus maintains library & resource center; Average Annual Attendance: 35,000; Mem: 3,000; $65 family, twice yr
Library Holdings: Audio Tapes; CD-ROMs; Compact Disks; DVDs; Manuscripts; Maps; Motion Pictures; Original Documents; Pamphlets; Periodical Subscriptions; Photographs
Special Subjects: Drawings, Historical Material, Ceramics, Glass, Metalwork, Photography, Textiles, Manuscripts, Maps, Sculpture, Graphics, Ethnology, Costumes, Religious Art, Pottery, Woodcarvings, Decorative Arts, Posters, Furniture, Jewelry, Oriental Art, Calligraphy, Islamic Art, Mosaics, Reproductions
Collections: Art; three-dimensional artifacts; documents; personal papers; photographs
Exhibitions: "Coming to America" is an exhibit that examines the history of Arab American immigration from 1500 to the present, with spec emphasis on waves of immigration since the 1800s; "Living in America" focuses on the life of Arab Americans in the US at different time periods, and examines such topics as family life, religion, activism and political involvement, institution-building, work, and leisure.; "Making an Impact " highlights the contributions of individuals and community organizations
Activities: Adult & children classes; lects open to pub; tours avail by appt; awards: Arab American National Museum Book Award; mus shop sells books, original art & reproductions

C **FORD MOTOR COMPANY,** Henry Ford Museum & Greenfield Village, 20900 Oakwood Blvd, Dearborn, MI 48124-4088. Tel 313-982-6001; Internet Home Page Address: www.hfmgv.org; *Dir Media & Film Relations* Wendy Metrou; *Mgr* Kate Storey; *Mgr* Carrie Nolan
Open daily 9:30 AM - 5 PM, cl Christmas & Thanksgiving; Admis adult $15, seniors (62+ & active military) $14, youth (5-12) $11, child 4 & under free; Estab 1929

M **PADZIESKI ART GALLERY,** 15801 Michigan Ave, Dearborn, MI 48126-2904. Tel 313-943-3095

DETROIT

L **CENTER FOR CREATIVE STUDIES,** College of Art & Design Library, 201 E Kirby, Detroit, MI 48202-4034. Tel 313-664-7425; Fax 313-872-8377; Elec Mail admission@ccscad.edu; Internet Home Page Address: www.ccscad.edu; *Slide Librn* Donna Rundels; *Librn* Jean Peyrat; *Visual Cur* Lisa Morrow; *Dir* Lynell Morr; *Reference Librn* Beth Walker
Open Mon - Fri 8:30 AM - 4:30 PM, Sat 1 - 4 PM; Estab 1966 to serve students & faculty of an undergraduate art school. Primarily a how-to, illustrative collection
Income: Financed by private school
Library Holdings: Book Volumes 23,000; Exhibition Catalogs; Periodical Subscriptions 72; Slides 70,000
Special Subjects: Photography, Graphic Design, Crafts, Advertising Design, Industrial Design

M **CENTRAL UNITED METHODIST CHURCH,** Swords Into Plowshares Peace Center & Gallery, 33 E Adams, Detroit, MI 48226. Tel 313-963-7575; Fax 313-963-2569; Elec Mail swordsintoplowshares@prodigy.net; *Dir* Wendy Hamilton
Open Tues, Thurs & Sat 11 AM - 3 PM; No admis fee; Estab 1985 to use the arts for peace in the world; Main gallery 1,475 sq ft, height 13 ft 7 inches;

multipurpose gallery 1,043 sq ft, height 7 ft 8 inches; second floor balcony gallery 357 sq ft, height 7 ft 3 inches. Maintains reference library; Average Annual Attendance: 7,000; Mem: 1800 supporters
Income: Financed by endowment, individuals, city & state appropriation, grants, sales, local churches
Library Holdings: Audio Tapes; Book Volumes; CD-ROMs; Cassettes; Clipping Files; Compact Disks; Exhibition Catalogs; Kodachrome Transparencies; Lantern Slides; Memorabilia; Original Art Works; Photographs; Reproductions; Sculpture; Slides; Video Tapes
Special Subjects: Architecture, Graphics, Painting-American, Prints, American Indian Art, Religious Art, Ceramics, Folk Art, Pottery, Woodcarvings, Etchings & Engravings, Landscapes, Afro-American Art, Painting-Japanese, Posters, Painting-Canadian, Painting-French, Maps, Calligraphy, Embroidery, Cartoons, Painting-Australian, Painting-German, Reproductions, Painting-Israeli
Collections: Peace Art Collection (permanent)
Publications: Harbinger Newsletter, 3-4 times per year; periodic exhibit catalogs
Activities: Classes for adults & children; docent training; 4 -6 concerts per yr; lects open to pub; concerts; gallery talks; tours; individual paintings & original objects of art lent to groups, events; book traveling exhibs, 4-5 exhibits per yr; traveling exhibs to churches, other galleries & events; mus shop sells books, original art, reproductions, prints, cards, t-shirts, posters & buttons

M **DETROIT ARTISTS MARKET,** 4719 Woodward Ave, Detroit, MI 48201-1307. Tel 313-832-8540; Fax 313-832-8543; Elec Mail info@detroitartistsmarket.org; Internet Home Page Address: www.detroitartistsmarket.org; *Chmn Bd Dir* Dante Stella; *Exec Dir* Nancy Sizer; *Gallery Mgr* Sarah Balmer; *Gallery Asst* Matthew Hanna
Open Tues - Sat 11 AM - 6 PM; No admis fee, donations accepted; Estab 1932 to educate pub & promote, exhibit & sell artwork by local Michigan artists; Average Annual Attendance: 10,000; Mem: 500; dues $20 - $2500
Income: $340,000 (financed by endowment, mem, state appropriation, mini-grants, MCA, contributions, percent of art work sales)
Exhibitions: Small Group Exhibition; All Media Juried Exhibition; The Garden Sale.; Art For The Holidays; Scholarship Show
Publications: catalogs for targeted exhibs; artists' statements & show information for exhibs
Activities: Educ prog; lects open to pub; tours; gallery talks; competitions with awards; schols offered; exten prog lends original objects of art to movie productions & local businesses; sales shop sells magazines, original art, prints & unique gift items

M **DETROIT INSTITUTE OF ARTS,** 5200 Woodward Ave, Detroit, MI 48202-4094. Tel 313-833-7900; Fax 313-833-3756; Internet Home Page Address: www.dia.org; *COO* Nettie Seabrooks; *Cur African, Oceanic & New World Cultures Art* Nii Quarcoopome; *Cur European Painting* George Keyes; *Dir Educ* Nancy Jones; *Cur Prints, Drawings & Photographs* Nancy Sojka; *Cur Modern Art* MaryAnn Wilkinson; *Head Conservator* Barbara Heller; *Cur European Sculpture & Decorative Arts* Alan Darr; *Dir* Graham WJ Beal; *Cur Native American Art* David Penney; *Cur Film* Elliot Wilhelm; *Cur African American Art* Valerie Mercer; *Cur American Art* Kenneth Meyers; *CFO* Loren Lau; *Adjunct Cur Contemp Art* Mark Rosenthal; *Cur Islamic Art* Heather Ecker
Open Wed - Thurs 10 AM - 4 PM, Fri 10 AM - 10 PM, Sat - Sun 10 AM - 5 PM, cl Mon, Tues & holidays; Admis adults $8, seniors $6, college students (w/ school ID) $5, youth 6-17 $4, children 5 & under & mems free; Detroit residence free on Fri; Estab & incorporated 1885 as Detroit Mus of Art; chartered as municipal department 1919 & name changed; original organization continued as Founders Soc Detroit Institute of Arts; present building opened 1927; Ford Wing addition completed 1966; Cavanagh Wing addition opened 1971. In 1998 the Founders Soc signed a 20 yr operating agreement with City of Detroit to run the DIA as a 501(c)(3) org; Average Annual Attendance: 500,000; Mem: 32,000 households; dues Chair Assoc $10,000, Dirs Assoc $5,000, Sustaining Assoc $3,000, Assoc $2,000, Conservator $1,000, Contributor $600, Patron $300, Affiliate $180, Family Plus $110, Individual $65, Senior Citizen (age 62 & over) $60
Library Holdings: Auction Catalogs; Audio Tapes; Book Volumes; Exhibition Catalogs; Manuscripts
Special Subjects: Marine Painting, Architecture, Ceramics, Glass, Metalwork, Mexican Art, Antiquities-Assyrian, Flasks & Bottles, Furniture, Gold, Porcelain, Portraits, Prints, Period Rooms, Silver, Textiles, Bronzes, Woodcuts, Manuscripts, Maps, Sculpture, Tapestries, Drawings, Graphics, Hispanic Art, Latin American Art, Painting-American, Photography, Watercolors, African Art, Archaeology, Pre-Columbian Art, Costumes, Religious Art, Crafts, Pottery, Woodcarvings, Etchings & Engravings, Landscapes, Afro-American Art, Decorative Arts, Judaica, Collages, Painting-European, Painting-Japanese, Posters, Eskimo Art, Jade, Jewelry, Oriental Art, Asian Art, Antiquities-Byzantine, Painting-British, Painting-Dutch, Carpets & Rugs, Ivory, Scrimshaw, Coins & Medals, Restorations, Baroque Art, Calligraphy, Miniatures, Painting-Flemish, Painting-Polish, Renaissance Art, Embroidery, Laces, Medieval Art, Antiquities-Oriental, Painting-Spanish, Painting-Italian, Antiquities-Persian, Islamic Art, Antiquities-Egyptian, Antiquities-Greek, Antiquities-Roman, Mosaics, Stained Glass, Painting-Australian, Painting-German, Pewter, Leather, Military Art, Antiquities-Etruscan, Painting-Russian, Painting-Israeli, Enamels, Painting-Scandinavian, Painting-New Zealand
Collections: Robert H Tannahill Collection of Impressionist & Post Impressionist paintings; German Expressionist Art; African, Oceanic & New World Cultures; Elizabeth Parke Firestone Collection of 18th Century Silver; William Randolph Hearst Collection of Arms & Armor & Flemish Tapestries; Grace Whitney-Hoff Collection of Fine Bindings; Paul McPharlin Collection of Theatre & Graphic Arts
Publications: Exhibition catalogues; bulletin; annual report; collection catalogues
Activities: Classes for adults & children; dramatic progs; docent training; lects open to pub; gallery talks; tours; concerts, Detroit film theatre; scholarships & fels offered; book traveling exhibs; originate traveling exhibs; mus shop sells books, calendars, games, jewelry, prints, slides & t-shirts

L **Research Library & Archives,** 5200 Woodward Ave, Detroit, MI 48202. Tel 313-833-3460; Fax 313-833-6405; Elec Mail mketcham@dia.org; Internet Home Page Address: www.dia.org; *Dept Head* Maria Ketcham
Open by written request only; Estab 1905 to provide material for research, interpretation & documentation of mus collection; For reference only

Income: Financed by city & memberships
Library Holdings: Auction Catalogs; Book Volumes 185,000; Exhibition Catalogs; Other Holdings; Pamphlets; Periodical Subscriptions 150
Special Subjects: Art History, Folk Art, Decorative Arts, Film, Photography, Drawings, Etchings & Engravings, Graphic Arts, Islamic Art, Manuscripts, Painting-American, Painting-British, Painting-Dutch, Painting-Flemish, Painting-French, Painting-German, Painting-Italian, Painting-Japanese, Painting-Russian, Painting-Spanish, Pre-Columbian Art, Sculpture, Painting-European, History of Art & Archaeology, Ceramics, Conceptual Art, Latin American Art, Theatre Arts, Archaeology, Painting-Israeli, Bronzes, Printmaking, Asian Art, American Indian Art, Porcelain, Furniture, Mexican Art, Ivory, Glass, Painting-Polish, Afro-American Art, Bookplates & Bindings, Antiquities-Oriental, Antiquities-Persian, Carpets & Rugs, Silver, Woodcuts, Marine Painting, Antiquities-Assyrian, Antiquities-Byzantine, Antiquities-Egyptian, Antiquities-Etruscan, Antiquities-Greek, Antiquities-Roman, Coins & Medals, Painting-Scandinavian, Pewter, Painting-Australian, Painting-Canadian, Painting-New Zealand, Architecture, Portraits, Pottery
Collections: Albert Kahn Architecture Library; Paul McPharlin Collection of Puppetry; Grace Whitney-Hoff Collection of Fine Bindings

L   DETROIT PUBLIC LIBRARY, Art & Literature Dept, 5201 Woodward Ave, Detroit, MI 48202-4093. Tel 313-833-1470; Fax 313-833-1474; Elec Mail esimmons@detroit.lib.mi.us; Internet Home Page Address: www.detroitpubliclibrary.org; *Library Dir* Nancy Skowronski; *Mgr Art & Literature Dept* Ellen Simmons; *Asst Dir Main Library* Margaret Bruni; *Asst Mgr* Julie Fornell; *Librn* Pati Bolourchi; *Librn* Peggy Hart
Open Tues & Wed Noon-8 PM, Thurs, Fri, Sat 10 AM-6PM; Estab 1865. Serves residents of Michigan with circulating and reference materials; Ann fee for library card for non- Detroit res $100
Income: Financed by city and state appropriation
Library Holdings: Book Volumes 81,000; Clipping Files; Exhibition Catalogs; Pamphlets; Periodical Subscriptions 550; Photographs
Special Subjects: Art History, Landscape Architecture, Decorative Arts, Photography, Calligraphy, Etchings & Engravings, Painting-American, Sculpture, Ceramics, American Western Art, Industrial Design, Furniture, Afro-American Art, Architecture
Activities: Tours

M   DETROIT REPERTORY THEATRE GALLERY, 13103 Woodrow Wilson, Detroit, MI 48238. Tel 313-868-1347; Fax 313-259-8242; Elec Mail detrepth@aol.com; Elec Mail gsnow19543@aol.com; Internet Home Page Address: www.detroitreptheatre.com; *Gallery Dir* Gilda Snowden
Open Thurs-Sat 8:30PM-11:30PM, Sun 2PM-4PM & 7:30PM-10:30PM; Estab 1957 to show Detroit Art; 1 fl in lobby of theater; Average Annual Attendance: 30,000
Income: Financed by endowment & state appropriation
Special Subjects: Drawings, Photography, Prints, Watercolors, Textiles, Folk Art, Woodcarvings, Woodcuts, Etchings & Engravings, Afro-American Art, Decorative Arts, Collages, Portraits, Reproductions
Collections: works by Detroit-area artists; 2-D works
Exhibitions: One person shows for emerging Detroit Area Artists; Amy Kelly, Robert Hyde, Jay Jurma, Kris Essen, Kathy Arkley, Renee Dooley, Albert Nassar, Sabrina Nelson; New exhibit for every show
Publications: Exhibition catalogs
Activities: Adult classes; dramatic progs

M   NATIONAL CONFERENCE OF ARTISTS, Michigan Chapter Gallery, 18100 Meyers Rd, NW Activities Center Ste 395 Detroit, MI 48235-1497. Tel 313-875-0923; Fax 313-875-7537; Elec Mail info@ncamich.org; Internet Home Page Address: www.ncamich.org; *Gallery Dir* Shirley Woodson; *Proj Dir* Raymond Wells; *Museum Liaison* Bamidele Demerson
Open Mon - Fri 11 AM - 5 PM, Sat 11 AM - 4 PM; Estab 1959 to promote cultural support for artists & community through visual arts; Average Annual Attendance: 4,500; Mem: 300; dues $50; monthly meetings & forums
Income: $50,000 (financed by mem, city & state appropriation, corporate, National Endowment for the Arts & private donations)
Special Subjects: African Art, Afro-American Art
Collections: Documentation of African American Artists: Books, Journals, Slides, Photographs, Periodicals, Audio Tapes, Video Tapes
Publications: NCA Newsletter, quarterly
Activities: Classes for adults & children; docent progs; lects open to pub, gallery talks, tours, 15 vis lectrs per yr; originate traveling exhibs 3 per yr; sales shop sells art videos, books, original art & prints

M   PEWABIC SOCIETY INC, Pewabic Pottery, 10125 E Jefferson, Detroit, MI 48214. Tel 313-626-2000; Fax 313-626-2100; Elec Mail info@pewabic.org; Internet Home Page Address: www.Pewabic.org; *Exec Dir* Barb Sido; *Bd Chair* Mary Wisgerhof; *VChair* Ann Marie Erickson
Open Mon - Sat 10 AM - 6 PM, Sun noon-4PM; No admis fee; Estab 1903 to continue its tradition of leadership in the areas of ceramic production & education; Average Annual Attendance: 40,000; Mem: 1200; dues $60 family, $40 individual
Income: Financed by mem, donations & grants
Special Subjects: Ceramics
Collections: The work of the founder (Mary Chase Stratton)
Exhibitions: 8 annually - vary each year
Activities: Classes for adults & children; residencies & internships; lects open to pub; tours; competitions; original objects of art lent; originate traveling exhibs to libraries & mus; sales shop sells original art

M   WAYNE STATE UNIVERSITY, Community Arts Gallery, 150 Community Arts Bldg, Detroit, MI 48202. Tel 313-577-2980; Fax 313-577-3491; Elec Mail art@wayne.edu; Internet Home Page Address: http://art.wayne.edu/

ESCANABA

M   WILLIAM BONIFAS FINE ART CENTER GALLERY, Alice Powers Art Gallery, 700 First Ave S, Escanaba, MI 49829. Tel 906-786-3833; Fax 906-786-3840; Internet Home Page Address: www.bonifasarts.org; *Adminr* Samantha Gibb-Roff; *Gallery Dir* Pasgua Warstler
Open Tues - Fri 10 AM - 5:30 PM, Sat 10 AM - 3 PM; No admis fee; Estab 1974

to advance the arts in the area; 40 x 80, lower gallery inside Center; additional upper gallery; Mem: Dues patron $50 & up, family $35, individual $25
Collections: Local artists working shows & regional artwork
Exhibitions: Northern Exposure; Smithsonian Matthew Brady Photographs; Michigan Watercolor Society; Regional & Touring Exhibits
Publications: Arts News quarterly
Activities: Classes for adults & children; dramatic progs; docent training; lects open to pub, 6-12 vis lectrs per yr; tours; concerts; gallery talks; sponsor competitions; awards in connection with annual regional competition; scholarships offered; individual paintings & original objects of art lent to arts organizations & bus in return for promotional assistance; book traveling exhibs to 6-8 area schools per yr

FLINT

M   BUCKHAM FINE ARTS PROJECT, Gallery, 134-1/2 W Second St, Flint, MI 48502. Tel 810-239-6334; Tel 810-239-6233; Elec Mail assistant@buckhamgallery.org; Internet Home Page Address: www.buckhamgallery.org; *VPres* Sally Kagerer; *Pres* Paul Hauth; *Treas* Margo Lakin; *Exec Dir* Sam Huff; *Gallery Asst* Monica Snyder; *Secy* Traci Currie
Open Wed-Fri noon - 5:00 PM, Sat 10 AM - 3 PM; No admis fee; Estab 1984 to present contemporary arts; 40 x 60 ft gallery with 14 ft arched ceiling, no permanent interior walls; Average Annual Attendance: 5,000; Mem: 250; dues $15-$200; annual meeting in first week of Mar
Income: $35,000 (financed by mem, state appropriation, grants, gifts, commissions from sales)
Exhibitions: New exhibitions on rotating monthly basis, eleven each year
Activities: Exhibitions; performances; readings; lects open to pub; competitions with prizes; gallery talks; book traveling exhibs 1 per yr; mus shop sells original art

M   FLINT INSTITUTE OF ARTS, 1120 E Kearsley St, Flint, MI 48503-1915. Tel 810-234-1695; Fax 810-234-1692; Elec Mail info@flintarts.org; Internet Home Page Address: www.flintarts.org; *Dir* John B Henry III; *Develop Dir* Kathryn Sharbaugh; *Cur Educ* Monique Desormeau; *Dir Finance & Admin* Michael Melenbrink; *Coordr Colls & Exhibs* Michael Martin; *Art School Dir* Jeff Garrett; *Assoc Cur Exhibs* Tracee Glab
Open Mon-Fri noon-5PM, Thurs noon-9PM, Sat 10AM-5PM, Sun 1-5PM; No admis fee to perm coll galleries; Temporary Exhibits: adults $7, students & seniors $5, discounts to AAM & ICOM members, children under 12 & members no charge; Estab 1928 with a mission to advance the understanding & appreciation of art for all through colls, exhibs & educ progs; 1 large temporary & 9 rotating permanent collection; Average Annual Attendance: 146,725; Mem: 4,745
Income: 4.4 million; financed by endowments, grants, contributions & earned income, including memberships
Library Holdings: Book Volumes 8,750
Special Subjects: Afro-American Art, American Indian Art, Decorative Arts, Drawings, Etchings & Engravings, Folk Art, Landscapes, Ceramics, Collages, Glass, Metalwork, Mexican Art, Flasks & Bottles, Portraits, Pottery, Painting-American, Prints, Textiles, Bronzes, Painting-British, Graphics, Photography, Sculpture, Watercolors, African Art, Pre-Columbian Art, Religious Art, Woodcarvings, Woodcuts, Painting-European, Eskimo Art, Furniture, Jade, Porcelain, Oriental Art, Asian Art, Silver, Painting-Dutch, Painting-French, Ivory, Tapestries, Baroque Art, Painting-Flemish, Renaissance Art, Embroidery, Laces, Painting-Spanish, Painting-Italian, Mosaics, Painting-German, Leather
Collections: American & European Fine Arts; Native American, African, Chinese, Japanese, & Pre-Columbian Art
Exhibitions: (10/12/2013-12/30/2013) Toulouse-Lautrec & His World
Publications: Exhibition catalogs; bimonthly magazine for members & public
Activities: Classes for adults & children; docent training; lects open to the public; lects for mems only; gallery talks; tours; schols awarded; exten program serves ArtReach, Art on the Go (senior centers & nursing homes); books traveling exhibs 3-4 per yr; originates traveling exhibs to mus & galleries; mus shop sells books, original art, reproductions, prints, gift items

L   Library, 1120 E Kearsley St, Flint, MI 48503-1915. Tel 810-234-1695; Fax 810-234-1692; Internet Home Page Address: www.flintarts.org; *Exhib Coordr* Kristie Everett Zamora; *Dir* John B Henry III; *Develop Dir* Deborah Gossel; *Cur Educ* Monique Desormeau; *Bus Mgr* Michael Melenbrink
Open Tues - Sat 10 AM - 5 PM, Sun 1 - 5 PM; No admis fee, donations accepted; Estab 1928; Average Annual Attendance: 85,000
Library Holdings: Book Volumes 4500; Exhibition Catalogs; Periodical Subscriptions 19
Special Subjects: Folk Art, Decorative Arts, Photography, Drawings, Etchings & Engravings, Painting-American, Painting-European, Ceramics, Crafts, Asian Art, American Indian Art, Furniture, Oriental Art, Pottery, Architecture
Collections: American & European Fine Arts; Native American, African, Chinese & Japanese
Publications: Bimonthly magazine; exhibit catalogs
Activities: Classes for adults & children; docent training; film series; museum art school; annual art fair; lects open to pub, 8 vis lectrs per yr; concerts; gallery talks; tours; exten program lends original objects of art to other mus; 1 book traveling exhib per yr; mus shop sells books

GRAND RAPIDS

M   CALVIN COLLEGE, Center Art Gallery, 3201 Burton St SE, Grand Rapids, MI 49546-4388; Covenant Fine Arts Center, 1795 Knollcrest Cir SE Grand Rapids, MI 49546-4388. Tel 616-526-6271; Fax 616-526-8551; Internet Home Page Address: www.calvin.edu/centerartgallery; *Dir Exhibs* Joel Zwart
Open Sept - May Mon - Thurs 9 AM - 9 PM, Fri 9 AM - 5 PM, Sat Noon - 4 PM; summer by appointment; No admis fee; Estab 1974 & relocated 2010, to provide the art students, & the col community & the pub at large with challenging visual monthly exhibs; Gallery is spread over 3 exhib spaces totalling 3,800 sq ft, with HVAC control & proper lighting; Average Annual Attendance: 10,000
Income: Financed through private budget

Special Subjects: Etchings & Engravings, Historical Material, Landscapes, Porcelain, Portraits, Pottery, Painting-American, Prints, Woodcuts, Sculpture, Drawings, Graphics, Hispanic Art, Photography, Prints, Sculpture, Watercolors, Textiles, Religious Art, Ceramics, Posters, Asian Art, Painting-Dutch, Islamic Art
Collections: Dutch 17th & 19th centuries paintings & prints; Japanese prints; contemporary American paintings, prints, drawings, sculpture, weaving & ceramics
Exhibitions: Invitational exhibits by various artists, exhibits of public & private collections & faculty & student exhibits
Publications: Various exhibition brochures & catalogs
Activities: Classes for adults; lect open to public; concerts; gallery talks; competitions; scholarships offered; book traveling exhibitions, 1-2 per year

M **GRAND RAPIDS ART MUSEUM,** 101 Monroe Center St NW, Grand Rapids, MI 49503-2801. Tel 616-831-1000; Fax 616-831-1001; Elec Mail pr@artmuseumgr.org; Internet Home Page Address: www.gramonline.org; *Interim Dir* Randy Van Antwerp; *Dir Devel* Mary Panek; *Dir Mktg & Pub Rels* Kerri VanderHoff; *Sr Cur Prints & Photographs* Richard H Axsom; *Registrar* Kathleen Ferres
Open Tues-Thurs & Sat 10Am - 5 PM, Fri 10AM - 9 PM, Sun noon - 5 PM, cl Mon & major holidays; Admis adults $8, students (w/ID) & seniors $7, youth 6-17 $5, children under 6 & GRAM members free, Fri 5 PM - 9 PM mems free, non-mems $5; Museum allocated a 1910 Beaux Arts former post office & courthouse, renovated & opened in Sept 1981; Average Annual Attendance: 94,500; Mem: 2500; dues corporate benefactor $2500, corporate patron $1000, corporate donor $600, corporate $300, benefactor $2500, grand patron $500-$1000, Masters $1000, Beaux Arts $500, collections patron $300, sponsor $350, donor $150, Arts Alive/Friends of Art $100, patron $74, family $50, individual $35, full-time student $15; annual meeting in Sept
Income: $919,000 (financed by endowment, mem, state appropriation & federal grants)
Purchases: $30,000
Special Subjects: Graphics, Painting-American, American Indian Art, American Western Art, African Art, Costumes, Ceramics, Crafts, Folk Art, Etchings & Engravings, Afro-American Art, Collages, Painting-Japanese, Furniture, Glass, Oriental Art, Metalwork, Painting-Dutch, Coins & Medals, Miniatures, Painting-Polish, Painting-Spanish, Antiquities-Egyptian, Painting-Russian, Painting-Scandinavian
Collections: American & European 19th & 20th Centuries paintings; prints & photographs; Renaissance to Contemporary drawings; 20th Century design & decorative arts; German expressionist paintings; master prints of all eras; Renaissance paintings; sculpture
Publications: Catalogs of major exhibitions; quarterly newsletter
Activities: Classes for adults & children; dramatic progs; docent training; lects open to pub, 7-10 vis lectrs per yr; concerts; gallery talks; tours; competitions with awards; exten dept serves elementary schools; individual paintings & original objects of art lent to mus; lending collection contains books, original art works, original prints, paintings, photographs, sculpture & slides; book traveling exhibs; originate traveling exhibs; mus & sales shops sells books, magazines, original art, reproductions, gift items & prints; Gram for Kids

L **Reference Library,** 101 Monroe Center St NW, Grand Rapids, MI 49503. Tel 616-242-5030; Fax 616-831-1001; Elec Mail cbuckner@artmuseumgr.org; Internet Home Page Address: www.artmuseumgr.org; *Assoc Cur* Cindy Buckner
Open Tues - Sat 1 PM - 4 PM; Estab 1969; Reference only lib
Income: Financed by mem, gifts, museum general budget allowance
Purchases: $2000
Library Holdings: Auction Catalogs; Book Volumes 8,000; Clipping Files; DVDs; Exhibition Catalogs 10,000; Pamphlets; Periodical Subscriptions 5; Video Tapes
Special Subjects: Art History, Photography, Drawings, Etchings & Engravings, Painting-American, Prints, Painting-European, Watercolors, Ceramics, American Western Art, Bronzes, Art Education, Furniture, Aesthetics, Afro-American Art, Woodcuts, Architecture
Activities: Docent Training

L **GRAND RAPIDS PUBLIC LIBRARY,** 111 Library St NE, Grand Rapids, MI 49503-3268. Tel 616-988-5400; Fax 616-988-5419; Elec Mail kcorrado@grpl.org; Internet Home Page Address: www.grpl.org; *Library Dir* Marcia Warner; *Asst Library Dir* Marla Ehlers; *Mktg & Communs Mgr* Kristen Krueger-Corrado; *Reference & Adult Svcs Coordr* Asante Cain; *Tech Svcs & Circ Coordr* Michele Montague; *Youth Svcs Coordr* Sarah McCarville; *Info Sys Mgr* William Ott
Open Mon - Thurs 9 AM - 9 PM, Fri & Sat 9 AM - 6 PM & Sun (Labor Day - Memorial Day) 1 - 5 PM; No admis fee; Estab 1871 to provide information & library materials for people in Grand Rapids, expansion in 1967, renovation 1997-2003; Circ 1,523,566; Average Annual Attendance: 950,000
Income: Financed by city & state appropriations
Library Holdings: Book Volumes; CD-ROMs; Cassettes; Clipping Files; Compact Disks; DVDs; Fiche; Filmstrips; Lantern Slides; Manuscripts; Maps; Memorabilia; Micro Print; Original Art Works; Original Documents; Pamphlets; Periodical Subscriptions; Photographs; Prints; Records; Reels; Reproductions; Video Tapes
Special Subjects: Furniture
Collections: The Furniture Design Collection
Activities: Classes for adults & children; lects open to pub; tours; sales shop sells books & magazines

M **GRAND RAPIDS PUBLIC MUSEUM,** (Public Museum of Grand Rapids) Public Museum of Grand Rapids, 272 Pearl NW, Grand Rapids, MI 49504-5371. Tel 616-456-3977; Elec Mail info@grmuseum.org; Internet Home Page Address: www.grmuseum.org; *Pres & CEO* Dale Robertson; *Dir Educ & Interpretation* Christian Carron; *Dir Exhibits & Facilities* Thomas Bantle; *Dir Colls & Preservation* Marilyn Merdzinski; *Dir Communs, Mktg & Customer Serv* Rebecca Westphal; *Dir Develop* Beth Banta; *Dir Finance & Bus Serv* Karen Wilburn
Open Mon - Sat 9 AM - 5 PM, Sun Noon - 5 PM; Admis adults $8, seniors $7, children $3; Estab 1854 for the interpretation of environment, history & culture of West Michigan & Grand Rapids; Maintains non-circulating reference library; 150,000 sq ft museum (Van Andel Museum Center) with 9600 sq ft temporary gallery; 140,000 sq ft research center, historic house museum; Average Annual Attendance: 400,000; Mem: 4000; dues $35-500; annual meeting in May
Income: $6,500,000 (financed by endowment, mem, city & state appropriations, grants, contributions & foundations)
Library Holdings: Audio Tapes; Book Volumes; Clipping Files; Exhibition Catalogs; Filmstrips; Lantern Slides; Manuscripts; Maps; Memorabilia; Motion Pictures; Original Art Works; Original Documents; Other Holdings; Pamphlets; Photographs; Prints; Records; Slides
Special Subjects: Flasks & Bottles, Photography, Portraits, Pottery, Pre-Columbian Art, Painting-American, Prints, Textiles, Manuscripts, Maps, Drawings, Graphics, American Indian Art, Anthropology, Archaeology, Ethnology, Costumes, Ceramics, Etchings & Engravings, Decorative Arts, Dolls, Furniture, Glass, Porcelain, Oriental Art, Asian Art, Carpets & Rugs, Historical Material, Ivory, Coins & Medals, Dioramas, Period Rooms, Laces, Antiquities-Egyptian, Pewter
Collections: Costumes & household textiles; Decorative arts; Ethnology; Furniture of the 19th & 20th centuries; Industrial & agricultural artifacts; Anthropology; Paleontology
Exhibitions: Permanent exhibitions: Furniture City; Habitats; Streets of Old Grand Rapids; Anishinabek: People of this Place
Publications: Museum, quarterly; Discoveries, monthly; exhibition catalogs
Activities: Classes for adults & children; dramatic progs; docent training; classes in film, music & dance; lects open to pub; 20 vis lectrs per yr; concerts; gallery talks; tours; individual paintings, objects of art & historical & anthropological artifacts lent to nonprofit educational institutions; book traveling exhibs 2 per yr; originate traveling exhibs; mus shop sells books, magazines, original art, reproductions, prints, publications & catalogs

L **KENDALL COLLEGE OF ART & DESIGN,** Kendall Gallery, 17 Fountain St NW, Grand Rapids, MI 49503-3194. Tel 616-451-2787; Fax 616-451-9867; Elec Mail kcadgallery@ferris.edu; Internet Home Page Address: www.kcad.edu; *Dir Exhibitions* Sarah Joseph
Open Mon - Sat 10 AM - 5 PM; No admis fee; Estab to serve Kendall students & faculty, as well as surrounding community; Focus on contemporary art by nat and international artists; Average Annual Attendance: 8,506
Income: Financed by tuition
Special Subjects: Art History, Folk Art, Photography, Commercial Art, Graphic Arts, Painting-American, Pre-Columbian Art, Prints, Sculpture, History of Art & Archaeology, Ceramics, Interior Design, Asian Art, Drafting, Landscapes
Activities: Lects open to public; 7-12 vis lectrs per year; gallery talks; sponsoring competitions

M **URBAN INSTITUTE FOR CONTEMPORARY ARTS,** 2 W Fulton, Grand Rapids, MI 49503. Tel 616-454-7000; Fax 616-454-9395; Elec Mail info@uica.org; Internet Home Page Address: www.uica.org; *Exec Dir* Jeffrey Meeuwsen; *Managing Dir* Janet Teunis; *Film Program Mgr* Ryan Dittmer; *Clay Program Dir* Israel Davis; *Dir Develop* Jill May; *Bus Mgr* Stacy Carrizzi; *Mgr Youth Programs* Becca Schaub; *Mgr Educ* Elizabeth Goddard
Open Tues - Sat 11 AM - 9 PM, Sun noon - 7 PM, cl Mon; No admis fee; Estab 1976, dedicated to the development of a vital cultural community; Visual arts gallery-multi disciplinary arts center; Average Annual Attendance: 15,000; Mem: 650; dues families $75, individuals $40, students $25
Income: Financed by grants, donations, mem, ticket sales, studio rental & fundraising events
Publications: Quarterly newsletter
Activities: Film prog & literature readings, music, performance arts, visual arts, classes for adults & children; lects open to pub, 3 vis lectrs per yr; dance events

GROSSE POINTE SHORES

M **EDSEL & ELEANOR FORD HOUSE,** 1100 Lake Shore Rd, Grosse Pointe Shores, MI 48236-4106. Tel 313-884-4222; Fax 313-884-5977; Elec Mail info@fordhouse.org; Internet Home Page Address: www.fordhouse.org; *Pres* Kathleen Stiso Mullins; *VPres Communs* Ann Fitzpatrick; *VPres Finance & Admin* Robert Seestadt; *Dir Interpretation & Progs* Christopher Shires; *Group Tour Sales Dir* Donna Buchanan; *Dir Develop* Bernadette Banko; *Cur* Josephine Shea; *Colls Mgr* Megan Callewaert
Open Tues - Sat 10 AM - 4 PM Sun noon - 4 PM (Apr - Dec); Jan - Mar: please call for tour schedule; Admis adults $12, seniors $11, children $8; Estab 1978 to help educate public on local history, fine & decorative arts; The Edsel & Eleanor Ford House experience is an authentic witness to the past that inspires, educates & engages visitors through exploration of its unique connections to art, design, history & environment while celebrating family traditions & community relationships; Average Annual Attendance: 50,000
Income: Financed by endowment, admissions, sponsors & grants
Special Subjects: Ceramics, Architecture, Drawings, Mexican Art, Painting-American, Sculpture, Costumes, Decorative Arts, Furniture, Glass, Porcelain, Asian Art, Metalwork, Painting-French, Carpets & Rugs, Period Rooms, Painting-Italian, Antiquities-Persian
Collections: Fine art, decorative arts including French & English antique furniture, ceramics, textiles; interior modern rooms by Walter Dorwin Teague; Jens Jensen landscape
Exhibitions: Rotating exhibits
Publications: Edsel & Eleanor Ford House Book
Activities: Classes for adults & children; seasonal children's programs; docent training; lects open to pub, house & grounds tours; concerts; books traveling exhibs occasionally; mus shop sells books, gifts; Cotswold Cafe

HARTLAND

A **HARTLAND ART COUNCIL,** PO Box 126, Hartland, MI 48353-0126. Tel 810-632-6022; *Pres* Nadine Cloutier
No admis fee; Estab 1973 to promote arts in Hartland community; Mem: 35; dues $10 - $100; annual meeting in May
Income: Financed by mem, admissions & grants
Collections: Paintings, photographs, sculptures, fibers, works of Michigan artists exhibited in local public buildings

Publications: Recollections, exhibit catalog

HOLLAND

M **HOPE COLLEGE,** DePree Art Center & Gallery, 160 E 12th St, Holland, MI 49422-3609. Tel 616-395-7500; Fax 616-395-7499; Elec Mail art@hope.edu; Internet Home Page Address: www.hope.edu/academic/art; *Dir* Dr Heidi Kraus; *Mgr* Steve Nelson; *Admin* Kristin Underhill
Open Mon - Sat 10 AM - 5 PM, Sun 1 - 5 PM; No admis fee; Estab as a place for the col & community to enjoy art; Acad gallery featuring historical and contemporary exhibs; Average Annual Attendance: 5,000
Collections: 625 items of Western & Non-Western art
Publications: Exhibition catalogs, e.g. Going Dutch: Contemporary Artists and the Dutch Tradition
Activities: Lect open to public; gallery talks

INTERLOCHEN

L **INTERLOCHEN CENTER FOR THE ARTS,** PO Box 199, Interlochen, MI 49643-0199. Tel 231-276-7420; *Head Librn* Sandra Besselsen
Open daily 8 AM - 5 PM & 6:30 - 9:30 PM; Estab 1963; Circ 9000; Special music library with over 50,000 titles
Library Holdings: Book Volumes 23,000; Periodical Subscriptions 140
Publications: Interlochen Review, annual
Activities: Dramatic progs; lects open to pub; concerts; tours; competitions; awards; schols & fels offered; originate traveling exhibs

JACKSON

M **ELLA SHARP MUSEUM,** 3225 Fourth St, Jackson, MI 49203. Tel 517-787-2320; Fax 517-787-2933; Elec Mail info@ellasharp.org; Internet Home Page Address: www.ellasharp.org; *Exec Dir* Amy Reimann
Open Tues - Wed & Fri - Sat 10 AM - 5 PM, Thurs 10 AM - 7 PM, cl Sun, Mon & holidays; Admis adults $5, children 5-12 $3, children under 5 free; Estab 1965 to promote the understanding & appreciation of art & history through exceptional exhibs, interpretation of historical bldgs & engaging educ progs.; 3 permanent galleries: Jackson History Gallery, Andrews Gallery of Wildlife Art, Never Enough Time Clock Gallery; 3 rotating exhibs ; Average Annual Attendance: 18,000; Mem: 1,165; dues $40, $50, $125; annual meeting in June
Income: Financed by endowment & mem along with grants & sponsorships
Special Subjects: Decorative Arts, Ceramics, Photography, Maps, Sculpture, Costumes, Woodcarvings
Collections: China; coverlets & quilts; furniture from Victorian period; items related to Jackson history; wildlife art; (contact mus for further information)
Exhibitions: Rotating exhibits; outdoor sculptures
Publications: Online & print newsletter
Activities: Classes for adults & children; docent training; four seasonal festivals; lects open to pub, 10+ vis lectrs per yr; gallery talks; tours; competitions; awards; schols offered; art objects lent to schools; lending collection contains photographs; gift shop, Granary Restaurant; original art, reproductions, gifts, archives

KALAMAZOO

M **KALAMAZOO INSTITUTE OF ARTS,** 314 S Park St, Kalamazoo, MI 49007-5102. Tel 269-349-7775, ext 3001; Fax 269-349-9313; Elec Mail museum@kiarts.org; Internet Home Page Address: www.kiarts.org; *Exec Dir* James A Bridenstine; *Dir Finance & Personnel* George Baltmanis; *Registrar* Robin Goodman; *Dir Mus Educ* Susan Eckhardt; *Dir Develop* Joe Bower; *School Dir* Denise Lisiecki; *Dir Facilities* Ron Boothby; *Coordr Mktg* Farrell Howe; *Mem Coordr* Darlene Pontenello; *Librn* Dennis Kreps; *Gallery Shop Mgr* Karyn Juergens; *Vol Coordr* Sandy Linabury; *Events Coordr* Caroline DeNooyer
Open Tues -Sat 10 AM - 5 PM, Sun noon - 5 PM, cl Mon & major holidays; No admis fee; Incorporated 1924 to further interest in the arts, especially in the visual arts; new building opened in 1998; Four permanent collection galleries & four temporary exhibition galleries devoted to pieces from the permanent collection; Average Annual Attendance: 109,000; Mem: 2500; dues individual $40; family $70; sustaining $100; donor $130; patron $250; benefactor $500; dir circle: founder $1,000-$2,499; leader $2,500-$4,999; visionary $5,000 & up
Income: $800,000 (financed by endowment, private donations, corporate & foundation grants, state & federal grants & mem)
Special Subjects: Drawings, Hispanic Art, Latin American Art, Painting-American, Photography, Prints, Watercolors, Bronzes, African Art, Pre-Columbian Art, Ceramics, Woodcarvings, Woodcuts, Etchings & Engravings, Landscapes, Portraits
Collections: 19th & 20th-century American art; 20th-century European art; 15th to 20th-century graphics; ceramics; small sculpture; photography; works on paper
Exhibitions: Various rotating exhib call for information
Publications: Exhibition catalogs, issued irregularly; newsletters, monthly
Activities: Classes for adults & children; docent training; mus educ dept; lects open to pub; tours; 12 vis lectrs per yr; gallery talks; competitions with awards; art & antique auction; scholarships; exten dept serves Southwest Michigan; individual paintings lent for selected mus exhibs; Lending collection contains photographs, paintings, prints & ceramics; originate traveling exhibs; gallery shop sells books, magazines, original art, reproductions, prints, slides, craft items, jewelry & cards

L **The Mary & Edwin Meader Fine Arts Library,** 314 S Park St, Kalamazoo, MI 49007-5102. Tel 269-349-7775; Fax 269-349-9313; Elec Mail museum@kiarts.org; Internet Home Page Address: www.kiarts.org; *Exec Dir* James A Bridenstine; *Head Librn* Malcolm McBryde; *Dir of School* Denise Lisiecki; *Dir Museum Educ* Susan Eckhardt; *Registrar* Robin Goodman; *Dir Develop* Joe Bower; *Dir Colls & Exhibs* Vicki Wright; *Dir Finance & Personnel* George Baltmanis
Open Tues - Sat 10 AM - 5 PM; Estab 1924 to stimulate the creation & appreciation of visual arts; Library estab 1961 as a reference for curatorial staff & school faculty; Circ 2100; 10 galleries for temporary exhibitions & permanent

collection; library for public reference only, open to members for circulation (2,000 items annually); Average Annual Attendance: 130,000; Mem: 2700; dues $25 & up; annual meeting in Sept
Income: Privately financed through donation & membership sales
Library Holdings: Auction Catalogs; Book Volumes 10,500; Clipping Files 1000; Compact Disks; DVDs; Exhibition Catalogs; Pamphlets; Periodical Subscriptions 52; Slides 10,000; Video Tapes 200
Special Subjects: Art History, Folk Art, Photography, Etchings & Engravings, Painting-American, Painting-British, Painting-European, Watercolors, Ceramics, Printmaking, Lettering, Jewelry, Pottery, Woodcuts
Collections: Art on paper; ceramics; watercolors; sculpture; 20th century American art; German Expressionist prints
Publications: Exhibit catalogues; biennial reports
Activities: Classes for adults & children; docent training; pub progs; lects; tours; concerts; gallery talks; sponsors competitions; scholarships; sales shop sells books, original art, stationery, children's items & jewelry

M **WESTERN MICHIGAN UNIVERSITY RICHMOND CENTER FOR VISUAL ARTS,** (Western Michigan University-Art Dept) Gwen Frostic School of Art, 1903 W. Michigan Ave, Department of Art Kalamazoo, MI 49008-5200. Tel 269-387-2455; Fax 269-387-2477; Elec Mail donald.desmett@wmich.edu; Internet Home Page Address: www.wmich.edu/art/exhibitions/exhibitions/index.html; *Exhib Dir* Don Desmett; *Registrar* Mindi Bagnall; *Sculture Tour Coordr* John Remning-Johnson
Open Mon - Thurs 10AM-6PM, Fri10AM-9PM, Sat Noon -6PM; No admis fee; Estab 1965 to provide visual enrichment to the university & Kalamazoo community. The School of Art Galleries are located in the Richmond Center for Visual Arts; Sculpture Tour is a rotating outdoor exhibit of traveling sculpture for which a catalog is available. 10,000 sq ft of exhib space with special features for lightening, data, and projection capabilities; Average Annual Attendance: 12,000; Mem: 350; annual member fees
Income: Financed by state appropriation, 1 program support 1, corporate foundations
Special Subjects: Prints
Collections: Contemporary print coll; 19th & 20th century American & European Art
Exhibitions: Rotating exhibition on contemporary arts
Publications: Sculpture Tour 92-93, 93-94, 94-95, 96-97, 98-99, 00-01, 01-06, 08-09; Sculptural Concepts Exhib Catalog 2008; Charismatii Abstraction 2008; Heroes Like Us 2010
Activities: Classes for adults; lect open to public, 12 vis lectrs per year; gallery talks; tours; awards; scholarships offered; collection contains 2000 original art works, 750 original prints; exhibitions 7 per yr; Univ galleries & museums

LAKESIDE

M **LAKESIDE STUDIO,** 15486 Red Arrow Hwy, Lakeside, MI 49116; PO Box 3, Three Oaks, MI 49128-0003. Tel 269-469-3022; Fax 269-469-1011; Elec Mail lakesidegal@triton.net; Internet Home Page Address: www.lakesidegalleries.com; *Exec Dir* John Wilson
Open daily 10 AM - 5 PM; No admis fee; Estab 1968, international; Represents international artists, American, Soviet, Chinese, Dutch work done by Artists-in-Residence
Income: Financed by pvt ownership
Exhibitions: Rotating exhibits
Activities: Award placement in Artist-in-Residence Prog through selection process; mus shop sells original art

LANSING

M **LANSING ART GALLERY,** 113 S Washington Sq, Lansing, MI 48933-1703; 119 N Washington Sq, Lansing, MI 48933. Tel 517-374-6400; Fax 517-374-6385; Elec Mail lansingartgallery@ygmail.com; Internet Home Page Address: www.lansingartgallery.org; *Pres* Mary Cusack; *Dir* Catherine Babcock; *Prog Mgr* Jane Kramer; *Gallery Coordr* Sara Pulver
Open Tues - Fri 10 AM - 4 PM, Sat & 1st Sun of the month 1 - 4 PM; No admis fee; Estab 1965 as a nonprofit gallery to promote the visual arts in their many forms to citizens of the greater Lansing area; Maintains large exhibit area, gallery shop & rental gallery; Average Annual Attendance: 25,000; Mem: 500; dues $25-$2500; annual meeting in June
Income: $250,000 (financed by mem, sales, grants, contributions & fees)
Publications: Image, quarterly
Activities: Classes for adults; classes for children; docent training; lect open to public, 5 vis lectrs per year; gallery talks; tours; competitions with awards; scholarships; individual paintings & original objects of art available for lease or purchase, including original art works, original prints, paintings, photographs & sculpture; book traveling exhibitions, 1-2 per year; sales shop sells books, original art, sculpture

LELAND

M **LEELANAU HISTORICAL MUSEUM,** 203 E Cedar St, Leland, MI 49654-5015; PO Box 246, Leland, MI 49654-0246. Tel 231-256-7475; Fax 231-256-7650; Elec Mail leemuse@traverse.com; Internet Home Page Address: www.leelanauhistory.org; *Cur* Laura Quackenbush
Call for hours; Admis adults $2, student $1; Estab 1959 for the preservation & exhibition of local history; One gallery for temporary exhibits of traditional & folk arts, 40 ft x 20 ft; Average Annual Attendance: 5,000; Mem: 550; dues $25; annual meeting in Aug
Income: $160,000 (financed by endowment, mem, fundraising & activities & grants)
Special Subjects: American Indian Art, Ethnology, Crafts, Folk Art, Manuscripts, Historical Material, Laces

Collections: Collections of local paintings, both folk & fine art; Leelanau County Native American baskets, birch bark crafts
Publications: Lee Muse newsletter, quarterly
Activities: Educ dept; sales shop sells books, reproductions, local crafts & original needlework kits

MARQUETTE

M **NORTHERN MICHIGAN UNIVERSITY,** De Vos Art Museum, 1401 Preque Isle Ave, Marquette, MI 49855. Tel 906-227-1481, 227-2194; Fax 906-227-2276; Elec Mail mmatusca@nmu.edu; Internet Home Page Address: www.art.nmu.edu/devosartmuseum; *Mus Dir & Cur* Melissa Matuscak
Open Mon - Fri 10 AM - 5 PM, Sun 1 - 4 PM; No admis fee; Estab 1975 to bring exhibits the visual arts to the University, community & the upper peninsula of Michigan; Museum covers approx 5000 sq ft of space, built in 2005 by HGA Architects; Average Annual Attendance: 10,000; Mem: 130; dues & mtgs vary
Income: $6500 (financed by University funds)
Collections: Contemporary printing & sculpture; student coll; Japanese & American illustration; Japanese prints & artifacts; permanent coll
Exhibitions: Average of 4-5 major exhibits each yr of regional, nat & internat contemporary art in all media.
Publications: Exhibit Announcement, monthly
Activities: Educ dept; lects open to pub, 5 vis lectrs per yr; gallery talks; tours; competitions; individual paintings & original objects of art lent; originates traveling exhibs

MIDLAND

M **ARTS MIDLAND GALLERIES & SCHOOL,** (Midland Center for the Arts, Inc) Alden B. Dow Museum of Science & Art, 1801 W Saint Andrews Rd, Midland, MI 48640-2656. Tel 989-631-5930; Fax 989-631-7890; Internet Home Page Address: www.mcfta.org; *Dir* Bruce Winslow; *Pres* Bill Henninger; *Bus & Opers Mgr* Emmy Mills; *Cur Educ* Deb Anderson; *Museum School Mgr* Armin Mersmann
Seasonal hours; Admis adults $8, children $5; Estab 1971; Average Annual Attendance: 179,000; Mem: 1,800; dues family $60
Income: varies according to exhibs(financed by endowment & mem)
Special Subjects: Art Education
Collections: Collection of local history photographs; Collection of local books
Publications: Salt of the Earth; Midland Log
Activities: Educ outreach prog to schools in the area; classes for children; docent progs; lects open to pub, 3 vis lectrs per yr; mus shop sells books, original art & reproductions

A **ARTS MIDLAND GALLERIES & SCHOOL,** 1801 W St Andrews, Midland, MI 48640. Tel 989-631-5930; Fax 989-631-7890; Elec Mail info@mcfsta.org; Internet Home Page Address: www.mcfta.org; *Dir* B B Winslow; *Prog Coordr* Cheryl Gordon; *Admin Asst* Emmy Mills; *Studio School Coordr & Registrar* Armin Mersmann
Open Mon - Sun 10 AM - 6 PM; No admis fee; Estab 1956 to generate interest in & foster understanding & enjoyment of the visual arts; Exhibition space consists of three galleries, one 40 x 80 ft & two smaller 20 x 40 ft space; spot tracking lighting; Average Annual Attendance: 20,000; Mem: 550; dues family $45, senior citizen $30; annual meeting in fall; monthly board meetings
Income: $200,000 (financed by endowment, mem, grants, fees for services, fundraising events)
Exhibitions: Great Lakes Regional Art Exhibition; Annual All Media Juried Competition & Exhibition (open to all Michigan artists age 18 & over); Annual Juried Summer Art Fair; Juried Holiday Art Fair
Publications: Calendar of events; quarterly newsletter for members; yearly report
Activities: Classes for adults & children; docent training; workshops; Picture Parent; lects open to public, 4 vis lectrs per yr; gallery talks; self-guiding tours; tours; juried art fairs; competitions with awards; scholarships offered; book traveling exhibs 5-10 per yr; originate traveling exhibs

L **GRACE A DOW MEMORIAL LIBRARY,** Fine Arts Dept, 1710 W Saint Andrews, Midland, MI 48640. Tel 989-837-3430; Fax 989-837-3468; Internet Home Page Address: www.gracedowlibrary.org/; *Dir* Melissa Barnard; *Chair* Cherie Hutter
Open Mon - Fri 9 AM - 9 PM, Sat 10 AM - 5 PM; during school year, Sun 1 - 5 PM; No admis fee; Estab 1955 as a pub library; Maintains art gallery
Income: Financed by city appropriation & gifts
Library Holdings: Audio Tapes; Book Volumes 12,000; Cassettes; Clipping Files; Framed Reproductions; Motion Pictures; Original Art Works; Other Holdings Compact Discs; Pamphlets; Periodical Subscriptions 80; Prints; Records; Reproductions; Video Tapes
Collections: Alden P Dow Fine Arts Collection
Exhibitions: Exhibits from local artists, art groups & schools
Activities: Films

MONROE

A **MONROE COUNTY COMMUNITY COLLEGE,** Fine Arts Council, 1555 S Raisinville Rd, Monroe, MI 48161-9746. Tel 734-384-4153; Fax 734-457-6023; Elec Mail vmaltese@monroeccc.edu; Internet Home Page Address: www.monroeccc.edu; *Dean* Vinnie Maltese; *Assoc Prof Art* Gary Wilson; *Asst Prof Art* Theodore Vassar; *Adjunct Instr Art* Daniel Stuart
Open Mon & Tues 8:30 AM - 7 PM, Wed - Fri 8:30 AM - 4:30 PM; No admis fee; Estab 1967 to promote the arts; Average Annual Attendance: 120
Income: $3000 (financed by endowment, mem & county appropriation)
Activities: Classes for children; gallery talks; competitions with awards; schols

MONTAGUE

M **NUVEEN COMMUNITY CENTER FOR THE ARTS,** 8697 Ferry St, Montague, MI 49437-1395. Tel 231-894-2787; Elec Mail nuveen@artscouncilofwhitelake.org; Internet Home Page Address: www.artscouncilofwhitelake.org

MOUNT CLEMENS

A **ANTON ART CENTER,** 125 Macomb Pl, Mount Clemens, MI 48043-5650. Tel 586-469-8666; Fax 586-469-4529; Internet Home Page Address: www.theartcenter.org; *Exec Dir* Jennifer Callans
Open Tues - Sat 10 AM - 5 PM, Sun 10AM-4PM; No admis fee; Estab 1969 to foster art appreciation and participation for people of Macomb County; The only public facility of its kind in the northeast Detroit metro area; The Center has two rooms, 17 x 27 ft, connected by lobby area in the former Carnegie Library Bldg, a Historical State Registered building; Average Annual Attendance: 10,000; Mem: 500; dues individual $25; annual meeting in June
Income: Financed by mem, city & state appropriation, commissions from sales, class fees & special fundraising events
Exhibitions: Annual season of exhibitions both regional & statewide by established & emerging Michigan artists
Publications: Newsletter, quarterly
Activities: Classes for adults and children; docent training; tours; competitions; gallery & gift shops sell original art

MOUNT PLEASANT

M **CENTRAL MICHIGAN UNIVERSITY,** University Art Gallery, 132 Wightman Hall, CMU Mount Pleasant, MI 48859. Tel 989-774-3800, 774-7457; Fax 989-774-2278; Elec Mail goche1as@cmich.edu; Internet Home Page Address: www.uag.cmich.edu; *Gallery Dir* Anne Gochenour
Open Tues - Fri 11 AM - 6 PM, Sat 11 AM - 3 PM, cl school holidays; No admis fee; Estab 1970 to serve Mount Pleasant & university community; offer nat and international artists exhibs of contemporary art; Corner of Franklin & Preston Streets. 154 linear ft of wall space & 2100 sq ft of unobstructed floor space; Average Annual Attendance: 10,000
Income: Financed by art dept & grant
Library Holdings: Book Volumes; CD-ROMs; Cards; Clipping Files; DVDs; Exhibition Catalogs; Kodachrome Transparencies; Manuscripts; Maps; Original Art Works; Prints
Collections: Twentieth Century Anishinabe Art - The Olga Denison Collection; modern & contemporary prints
Publications: Subverting the Market: Artwork on the Web Exhib Catalogue; Twentieth Century Anishinabe Art
Activities: Educ prog; docent training; mus studies prog instruction; collaborate with pub schools; part of art dept curriculum; lects open to pub, 5 vis lectrs per yr; gallery talks; tours; competitions; annual award for juried student exhib; originates traveling exhibs to colleges & universities

MUSKEGON

M **MUSKEGON MUSEUM OF ART,** 296 W Webster Ave, Muskegon, MI 49440-1282. Tel 231-720-2570; Fax 231-720-2585; Elec Mail mgawron@mpsk12.net; Internet Home Page Address: www.muskegonartmuseum.org; *Exec Dir* Judith Hayner; *Sr Cur & Dir Colls & Exhib* E Jane Connell; *Cur Educ* Cathy Mott; *Communs, Pub Rels & Vol Coordr* Marguerite Curran-Gawron; *Assoc Cur & Mgr Coll* Art Martin; *Develop Officer* Kirk Hallman
Open Wed, Fri & Sat 10 AM - 4:30 PM, Thurs 10 AM - 6 PM, Sun noon - 4:30, cl Mon & Tues; Admis adults 18 & over $7, students 18 & over (w/ID) $5, children 17 & under & mems free; Estab 1912; Permanent coll & changing exhib galleries; Average Annual Attendance: 29,000; Mem: 995; chmn's Society $10,000, coll's cir $5,000, Hackley Guild $2,500, ambassador $1,000, benefactor $500, patron $300, friend $150, mem+guest & household $70, artist or educ $50, student $30
Income: Privately funded
Special Subjects: Decorative Arts, Drawings, Etchings & Engravings, Landscapes, Marine Painting, Ceramics, Collages, Glass, Photography, Portraits, Painting-American, Prints, Textiles, Woodcuts, Painting-British, Painting-European, Painting-French, Graphics, Photography, Sculpture, Watercolors, Bronzes, Crafts, Woodcarvings, Woodcuts, Painting-European, Posters, Asian Art, Marine Painting, Painting-Dutch, Miniatures, Painting-Flemish, Painting-Italian, Cartoons, Painting-German
Collections: Significant holdings of American and European Art
Publications: Pictures of the Best Kind: The First Century of the Muskegon Museum of Art; exhib catalogues
Activities: Classes for adults & children; docent training; lects open to pub, 8 vis lectrs per yr; concerts; gallery talks; tours; sponsoring of competitions; individual & original objects of art lent to qualified museums; originate traveling exhibs to US art mus; mus shop sells books, original art, jewelry, gifts, handcrafts & reproductions

OLIVET

M **OLIVET COLLEGE,** Armstrong Collection, 320 S Main St, Olivet, MI 49076-9406. Tel 269-749-7000 Ext 7661; Fax 269-749-7178; Internet Home Page Address: www.olivetcollege.edu; *Dir* Donald Rowe; *Chmn Arts & Comm Depts* Gary Wortheimer
Call for hours; Estab 1960 to collect artifacts & display for educational purposes; Average Annual Attendance: 1,200
Special Subjects: Prints, Sculpture, Primitive art

Collections: American Indian, Mesopotamian, Philippine & Thai Artifacts; Modern American Prints; Primitive Art; Sculpture
Exhibitions: Invitational shows; one-man shows; student shows; traveling shows

L   **Library,** Corner of Main & College Sts, Olivet, MI 49076; 320 S Main St, Olivet, MI 49076-9406. Tel 616-749-7608; Fax 616-749-7178; Internet Home Page Address: www.olivet.edu; *Library Dir* Mary Jo Blackport
Open during school yr Mon - Thurs 8 AM - Noon, Fri 8 AM - 5 PM, Sat 11 AM - 5 PM, Sun 2 - 11 PM
Library Holdings: Book Volumes 78,000; Micro Print

ORCHARD LAKE

M   **ST MARY'S GALERIA,** 3535 Indian Trail, Orchard Lake, MI 48324. Tel 248-683-0345; *Dir* Marian Owczarski
Open Mon - Fri upon request, first Sun of the month Noon - 5 PM & anytime upon request; No admis fee; Estab to house major Polish & Polish-American art; Average Annual Attendance: 6,700
Special Subjects: Painting-Polish
Collections: Contemporary Polish Painting; Sculpture by Marian Owczarski; History of Polish Printing: Rare Books & Documents; Polish Folk Art; Polish Tapestry; Paintings of A Wierusz Kowalski; Watercolors by J Falat; Watercolors by Wojciech Gierson; Louvre by Night, a sketch by Aleksander Gierymski; oil paintings by Jacek Malczewski; lithographs by Irene Snarski & Barbara Rosiak
Exhibitions: Various exhib
Activities: Lect open to public; concerts; gallery talks; tours; competitions for youngsters & artists

OWOSSO

M   **SHIAWASSEE ARTS CENTER,** 206 Curwood Castle Dr, Owosso, MI 48867-2723. Tel 989-723-8354; Fax 989-729-9134; Elec Mail sac@shiawasseearts.org; Internet Home Page Address: www.shiawasseearts.org; *Contact* Piper Brewer

PETOSKEY

M   **CROOKED TREE ARTS COUNCIL,** Virginia M McCune Community Arts Center, 461 E Mitchell St, Petoskey, MI 49770-2623. Tel 231-347-4337; Fax 231-347-5414; Internet Home Page Address: www.crookedtree.org; *Dir* Liz Ahrens
Open Mon - Sat 10 AM - 5 PM; No admis fee; Estab 1981 as a non-profit arts council & arts center; 40 ft x 25 ft exhibition gallery featuring monthly shows, modern lighting & security systems; 85 x 45 ft gallery featuring work of Michigan artists on consignment; Average Annual Attendance: 50,000; Mem: 1600; dues family $50, individual $30; annual meeting in Sept
Income: $300,000 (financed by endowment, city & state appropriation, ticket sales, tuition income, fundraisers)
Exhibitions: Monthly exhibits
Publications: Art news, bimonthly
Activities: Classes for adults & children; dramatic progs; docent progs; music & dance classes; 3 competitions per yr (crafts, fine arts, photography); cash prizes; book traveling exhibs 7 per yr; sales shop sells original art, reproductions, prints, art postcards

PONTIAC

A   **CREATIVE ARTS CENTER,** 47 Williams St, Pontiac, MI 48341-1759. Tel 248-333-7849; Fax 248-333-7841; Elec Mail cpaster@aol.com; Internet Home Page Address: www.pontiac.mi.us/cac; *Exec Dir* Carol Paster; *Chmn (V)* John Manfredi
Open Wed - Sat 10 AM - 5 PM, cl holidays; No admis fee; Estab 1965 to present the best in exhibitions, educational activities, & community art outreach; Main gallery is a two story central space with carpeted walls; Clerestory Gallery is the second floor balcony overlooking the main gallery; Average Annual Attendance: 3,000; Mem: 160; dues organizational $50, general $35, artists & citizens $20, annual meeting in Mar
Income: Financed by endowment, mem, city & state appropriation, trust funds, United Way, Michigan Council for the Arts
Exhibitions: Temporary exhibits of historic, contemporary & culturally diverse works
Publications: Biannual newsletter, Creative Arts Center
Activities: Classes for adults & children; dramatic progs, music, dance, visual arts progs; lects open to pub, 30 vis lectrs per yr; gallery talks; concerts; tours; competitions with awards; schols offered; book traveling exhibs semi-annually; originate traveling exhibs; sales shop sells books & original art work

M   **MUSEUM OF NEW ART,** 7 N Saginaw St, Pontiac, MI 48342; 327 W 2nd St, Rochester, MI 48307. Tel 248-210-7560; Elec Mail detroitmona@aol.com; Internet Home Page Address: www.detroitmona.com; *Contact* Jef Bourgeau

PORT HURON

M   **PORT HURON MUSEUM,** 1115 Sixth St, Port Huron, MI 48060. Tel 810-982-0891; Fax 810-982-0053; Elec Mail info@phmuseum.org; Internet Home Page Address: www.phmuseum.org; *Exec Dir* Susan Bennett; *Dir Bus Oper* Sheila Lindsey; *Dir Educ, Coll & Exhibs* Katherine Bancroft; *Vol & Tour Mgr* Anita Varty
Open daily 11AM - 4PM, cl Mon & Tues; Admis adults $7, seniors & students $5, 4 & under free; Estab 1968 to preserve area historical & marine artifacts; exhibit living regional artists; exhibit significant shows of national & international interest. Maintains reference library; Two galleries are maintained for loaned exhibitions & the permanent collection; also a decorative arts gallery & a sales

gallery; Average Annual Attendance: 40,000; Mem: 900; dues family $45, individual $35, seniors $25, students $15
Income: $200,000 (financed by endowment, mem, city appropriation, state & federal grants & earned income through program fees)
Special Subjects: Painting-American, Photography, Prints, Watercolors, American Indian Art, Anthropology, Archaeology, Textiles, Costumes, Folk Art, Landscapes, Decorative Arts, Painting-European, Portraits, Painting-Canadian, Dolls, Furniture, Glass, Jewelry, Silver, Marine Painting, Carpets & Rugs, Maps, Embroidery, Cartoons
Collections: Civil War Collection; Thomas Edison Collection
Exhibitions: Blue Water Art
Publications: Quarterly newsletter
Activities: Classes for adults & children; docent training; lects open to pub; tours; festivals; book traveling exhibs, 2 per yr; sales shop sells books, magazines, original art; prints

M   **SAINT CLAIR COUNTY COMMUNITY COLLEGE,** Jack R Hennesey Art Galleries, 323 Erie St, Port Huron, MI 48060; PO Box 5015, Port Huron, MI 48061-5015. Tel 810-989-5709; Fax 810-984-2852; Elec Mail dkorff@stclair.cc.mi.us; Internet Home Page Address: www.sc4.edu; *Coordr Galleries & Exhibits* David Korff
Open Mon - Fri 8 AM - 4:30 PM; No admis fee; Estab 1975 to serve the community as an exhib site & to serve the faculty & students of the col as a teaching tool; Maintains three galleries connected by common hall with approx 2,000 sq ft; Average Annual Attendance: 3,000
Special Subjects: Painting-American, Prints, Sculpture, Woodcarvings, Metalwork
Collections: Paintings, print, and sculpture (wood and metal)
Activities: Educ dept; lect open to public; concerts; competitions with awards; scholarships offered; book traveling exhibitions, one per year or as funds permit

ROCHESTER

M   **OAKLAND UNIVERSITY,** Oakland University Art Gallery, 2200 N Squirrel Rd, 208 Wilson Hall Rochester, MI 48309-4401. Tel 248-370-3005; Fax 248-370-4368; Elec Mail goody@oakland.edu; Internet Home Page Address: www.oakland.edu; Internet Home Page Address: www.ouartgallery.com; www.oakland.edu/ouag; *Dir* Dick Goody
Open Tues - Sun Noon - 5 PM, evenings in conjunction with Meadow Brook Theater Performances through the intermission; No admis fee; Estab to provide exhib schedule that emphasizes excellence in fine arts, provide exhib opportunities for emerging & mid career Mich artists & raise awareness & enthusiasm about contemporary art in South Eastern Mich; 2400 sq ft space across hallway from theatre; Average Annual Attendance: 16,000; Mem: Various levels; $15-1,000; AAM required
Income: Financed by university budget, mem, contributions & outside grant funding
Special Subjects: Photography, African Art, Collages, Asian Art
Collections: Art of Africa, Oceania and Pre-Columbian America; contemporary art and Sculpture Park; Oriental art; numerous fine prints
Exhibitions: Minimum of 6 exhibs annually
Publications: Exhibition catalogs
Activities: Lect open to public; symposiums; gallery talks; slide presentations in conjunction with exhibitions; paintings & original art objects lent within university; on loan exhibs

M   **PAINT CREE CENTER FOR THE ARTS,** 407 Pine St, Rochester, MI 48307-1933. Tel 248-651-4110; Fax 248-651-4110; Elec Mail comments@pccart.org; Internet Home Page Address: www.pccart.org; *Contact* Suzanne Wiggins

ROYAL OAK

M   **DETROIT FOCUS,** PO Box 843, Royal Oak, MI 48068-0843. Tel 248-541-2210; Elec Mail director@detroitfocus.org; Internet Home Page Address: http://www.detroitfocus.org/; *Dir* Michael Sarnacki; *Co-Dir* Gene Baskin
Open by appointment; No admis fee; Estab 1978 as an exhibition space for Michigan visual artists; Foundation
Income: $21,000 (financed by mem, city & state appropriation, fundraising)
Exhibitions: Juried exhibitions, visual & performance art
Publications: Detroit Focus Quarterly; exhibition catalogues
Activities: Lects open to pub, 5 vis lectrs per yr; competitions with awards; originate traveling exhibs

M   **DETROIT ZOOLOGICAL INSTITUTE,** Wildlife Interpretive Gallery, 8450 W 10 Mile, PO Box 39 Royal Oak, MI 48068-0039. Tel 248-398-0903; Fax 248-398-0504; *Cur Educ* Gerry Craig
Open daily 10 AM - 5 PM (Summer), 10 AM - 4 PM (Winter); No admis fee with zoo admis; Estab 1995 to celebrate & interpret humans' relationship with animals; The permanent art collection of the Wildlife Interpretive Gallery is displayed on the mezzanine level of the main rotunda, under the glass dome. Commissioned works are on display throughout the building. A temporary art gallery has 4 shows annually focusing on fine arts or educ exhibits; Average Annual Attendance: 1,200,000; Mem: 55,000; dues $50-$500
Special Subjects: Painting-American, Photography, Prints, Sculpture, African Art, Pre-Columbian Art, Textiles, Ceramics, Eskimo Art, Asian Art, Metalwork, Tapestries, Embroidery, Antiquities-Persian, Antiquities-Egyptian
Activities: Classes for adults & children; dramatic progs; lects open to pub, 4-6 vis lectrs per yr; exten services to schools with performing arts prog; book traveling exhibs 4 per yr; originate traveling exhibs 1-2 per yr

SAGINAW

M   **SAGINAW ART MUSEUM,** 1126 N Michigan Ave, Saginaw, MI 48602-4795. Tel 989-754-2491; Fax 989-754-9387; Elec Mail info@saginawartmuseum.org; Internet Home Page Address: www.saginawartmuseum.org; *Exec Dir* Stacey Gannon; *Deputy Dir & Asst Cur* Ryan Kattenbach; *Mktg & Outreach Coordr* Shelby Riggle; *Accounting Clerk* Roxanne Lone; *Gardner & Asst Facilities* Raul Servantes
Open Tues - Sat 10 AM - 5 PM, Thurs 10 AM - 7 PM, Sun 1 - 5 PM; Admis $5, seniors 65 & students with ID $3, children under 16 free; Estab 1947; Circ 1100

non-lending; 4,000 sq ft gallery with 550 running feet; 6 additional small galleries; Average Annual Attendance: 10,000; Mem: 250; dues $40-$1,000; meetings 2nd Thurs

Income: Grants, local business

Library Holdings: Auction Catalogs; Book Volumes; Exhibition Catalogs; Memorabilia; Original Documents; Other Holdings Archives of Michigan artists; Pamphlets; Periodical Subscriptions; Video Tapes

Special Subjects: Folk Art, Landscapes, Architecture, Collages, Glass, American Western Art, Photography, Portraits, Pottery, Prints, Bronzes, Woodcuts, Painting-British, Painting-Japanese, Tapestries, Drawings, Graphics, Hispanic Art, Painting-American, Sculpture, Watercolors, American Indian Art, Southwestern Art, Textiles, Costumes, Religious Art, Ceramics, Crafts, Woodcarvings, Etchings & Engravings, Decorative Arts, Painting-European, Posters, Porcelain, Oriental Art, Asian Art, Marine Painting, Painting-Dutch, Painting-French, Carpets & Rugs, Historical Material, Painting-Polish, Embroidery, Laces, Medieval Art, Antiquities-Oriental, Painting-German, Military Art, Antiquities-Etruscan, Painting-Russian

Collections: African, Asian & Etruscan, painting, sculpture 7 decorative areas; 18th-21st Century American/European/Asian painting, sculpture & decorative art; Eanger Irving Couse, Corot, Inness, Cropsey, Minor, Arneson, Held, Blakelock

Exhibitions: Art 4 All Exhibs: Featuring Great Lakes Bay Region & Michigan artists (all year)

Publications: Annual report; Quarterly newsletter

Activities: Classes for adults & children; docent training; progs: Art Goes to School, Art Across the Curriculum & Art Across the Valley; lects open to pub; 6-12 vis lectrs per yr; concerts; gallery talks; tours, awards: 2004 American Architecture Award from Chicago Athenaeum, 2005 NY AIA Merit Award, 2005 Michigan AIA Honor Award; exten dept serves mid-Michigan region; lending of original objects of art to AAM accredited institutions; originates traveling exhibs; mus shop sells books, original art, reproductions & decorative art

SAINT JOHNS

M DEPOT CENTER FOR THE ARTS, 107 E Railroad St, Saint Johns, MI 48879-1525. Tel 989-224-2429; Elec Mail ccarts@voyager.net

SAINT JOSEPH

M KRASL ART CENTER, 707 Lake Blvd, Saint Joseph, MI 49085-1398. Tel 269-983-0271; Fax 269-983-0275; Elec Mail info@krasl.org; Internet Home Page Address: www.krasl.org; *Exec Dir* Julia Gourley; *Dir Exhibs & Colls* Tami Miller; *Dir Community Rels* Joshua Nowicki; *Dir Admin & Gift Shop Mgr* Patrice Rose; *Dir Krasl Art Fair on the Bluff & Special Events* Sara Shambarger; *Educ Progs Coordr* Rebecca Hunt

Open Mon - Wed & Fri - Sat 10 AM - 4 PM, Thurs 10 AM - 9 PM, Sun 1 - 4 PM; No admis fee; Estab 1980 with the mission to bring people & art together; 3 galleries; 200 running ft; Average Annual Attendance: 29,000; Mem: 1015; dues $25 & up; annual meeting 1st wk in Nov

Income: $1,000,000 (financed by earned income, endowment, membership, state appropriations & foundations)

Library Holdings: Book Volumes; DVDs; Exhibition Catalogs; Periodical Subscriptions; Slides; Video Tapes

Special Subjects: Sculpture

Collections: Krasl Art Center Sculpture Collection

Publications: Krasl Newsletter, bimonthly; exhibit catalogs; collection catalogs

Activities: Classes for adults & children; docent training; lect open to pub; 10-12 vis lectrs per yr; concerts; gallery talks; tours; scholarships offered; 1-3 book traveling exhibs; mus shop sells books, original art & prints

TRAVERSE CITY

M NORTHWESTERN MICHIGAN COLLEGE, Dennos Museum Center, 1401 College Dr., Traverse City, MI 49686-3016; 1201 E Front St, Traverse City, MI 49686-3016. Tel 231-995-1055; Fax 231-995-1597; Elec Mail dmc@nmc.edu; Internet Home Page Address: www.dennosmuseum.org; *Dir Mus* Eugene A Jenneman; *Registrar* Kim Hanninen; *Museum Shop Mgr* Terry Tarnow; *Opers Mgr* Gale Cook; *Educ Cur* Jason Dake

Open Mon - Sat 10 AM - 5 PM, Sun 1 - 5 PM, Thurs until 8PM; Admis adults $6, children $4, family $20 (subject to change with exhib); Estab 1991; 40,000 sq ft complex features three changing exhibit galleries & a sculpture ct; a hands on Discovery Gallery; & a Gallery of Inuit Art, the museum's major permanent collection. The 367 seat Milliken Auditorium offers theater & musical performances throughout the year; Average Annual Attendance: 60,000; Mem: 1200; dues $40 individual, $60 family, and up; Scholarships

Income: $900,000 (financed by earned income/endowment)

Collections: Canadian Inuit sculpture & prints

Activities: Classes for adults & children, docent training; lect open to public, 12-15 vis lectrs per year; concerts; Governor's Award for Arts & Culture; gallery talks; tours; individual paintings & original objects of art lent to mus; lending coll contains original art works & original prints; originate traveling exhibs to mus; mus shop sells books, magazines, original art, reproductions & prints

WILLIAMSBURG

M ARTCENTER TRAVERSE CITY, 5152 US Hwy 31N, Williamsburg, MI 49690-9316. Tel 231-941-9488; Tel 866-242-0120; Fax 231-941-0886; Elec Mail patt@artcentertraversecity.com; Internet Home Page Address: artcentertraversecity.com

YPSILANTI

M EASTERN MICHIGAN UNIVERSITY, Ford Gallery, 114 Ford Hall, Bldg 114 Ypsilanti, MI 48197-2251. Tel 734-487-0465, 1077; Fax 734-487-2324; Elec Mail gtom@emich.edu; Internet Home Page Address: art.emich.edu; *Dept Head* Colin Blackely; *Dir Gallery* Gregory Tom

Open Mon & Thurs 10 AM - 5 PM, Tues & Wed 10 AM - 7 PM, Fri & Sat 10 AM - 2 PM; No admis fee; Estab 1925, in present building since 1982, for

educational purposes; Art Dept gallery is maintained displaying staff & student exhibitions from a wide variety of sources; also on large, well-lighted gallery with lobby & a satellite student-operated gallery are maintained

Income: Financed by state appropriation

Purchases: $500

Exhibitions: Seven changing exhibitions annually; Annual Faculty Exhibition; Annual Juried Student Exhibition; Biannual Michigan Drawing Exhibition

Publications: Exhibition catalogs

Activities: Classes for adults; lects open to pub; gallery talks; competitions

L Art Dept Slide Collection, 214 Ford Hall, Ypsilanti, MI 48197-2251. Tel 734-487-1268; Fax 734-487-2324; Elec Mail cpawloski@emich.edu; Internet Home Page Address: webstage.emich.edu/art; *Visual Resource Librn* Carole Pawloski

Open 8 AM - 5 PM; Estab 1978 to foster slide circulation for art faculty

Library Holdings: Lantern Slides; Slides 100,000; Video Tapes

Special Subjects: Painting-American, Pre-Columbian Art, History of Art & Archaeology, American Western Art, American Indian Art, Furniture, Mexican Art, Afro-American Art, Oriental Art, Restoration & Conservation

Collections: 100,000 art slides; 4,000 digital images

Activities: Classes for adults; lectrs open to pub & lectrs for mems only; gallery talks; exten prog serves entire univ

MINNESOTA

AITKIN

M THE JAQUES ART CENTER, 121 Second St NW, Aitkin, MN 56431. Tel 218-927-2363; Elec Mail info@jaquesart.com; Internet Home Page Address: jaquesart.com

Open Tues-Sat 11AM-4PM; No admis fee

Collections: paintings, sculptures, photographs

BLOOMINGTON

M BLOOMINGTON THEATRE & ART CENTER, (Bloomington Art Center) Inez Greenberg Gallery, 1800 W Old Shakopee Rd, Bloomington, MN 55431-3071. Tel 952-563-8575; Fax 952-563-8576; Elec Mail info@btacmn.org; Internet Home Page Address: www.bloomingtonartcenter.com; *Visual Arts Dir* Rachel D Flentje; *Exec Dir* Andrea Specht

Open Mon - Fri 8 AM - 10 PM, Sat 9 AM - 5 PM, Sun 1 - 10 PM; No admis fee; Estab 1976 to serve emerging & established local artists; Circ 13,000; Inez Greenberg Gallery, 1800 sq ft; Atrium Gallery, single artist shows; Average Annual Attendance: 65,000; Mem: 500; dues individual $35, household $50

Income: (financed by mem, programming, city appropriation); 1.5 million

Exhibitions: Ongoing

Activities: Classes for adults & children in visual, literary & dramatic progs; lects open to pub, 1-2 vis lectrs per yr; gallery talks; competitions with prizes; annual members' juried exhib; sales shop sells books, original art & prints

M MHIRIPIRI GALLERY, 9001 Penn Ave S, Bloomington, MN 55431-2225. Tel 952-285-9684; Fax 952-848-0306; Elec Mail rexandjulie@shonasculpturemhiripir.com; Internet Home Page Address: www.shonasculpturemhiripir.com; *Co-Owner* Julie Mhiripiri; *Co-Owner* Rex Mhiripiri

Open 10 AM - 6 PM & by appt; Estab 1986; commercial art gallery 5,200 sq ft

BRAINERD

M CROW WING COUNTY HISTORICAL SOCIETY, PO Box 722, Brainerd, MN 56401-0722. Tel 218-829-3268; Fax 218-828-4434; Elec Mail history@co.crow-wing.mn.us; Internet Home Page Address: www.crowwinghistory.org; *Exec Dir* Mary Lou Moudry

Open Tues-Sat 10AM-3PM, cl holidays; Admis adults $3; Estab 1927 to preserve & interpret county history; Average Annual Attendance: 6,000; Mem: 350; dues $15-$250; annual meeting in Apr

Income: $60,000 (financed by mem, county, state grants, private donations)

Special Subjects: Architecture, Drawings, Painting-American, Photography, Archaeology, Costumes, Etchings & Engravings, Manuscripts, Portraits, Dolls, Furniture, Glass, Jewelry, Carpets & Rugs, Maps, Embroidery

Exhibitions: N.P. Railroad; Sarah Thorp Heald & Freeman Thorp Paintings; Home & Community: Rotating Artifacts Reflecting Country Life; American Indian Tools & Beadwork; When Lumber Was King; Mining; 19th & Early 20th Century Furnishings

Publications: The Crow Wing County Historian, quarterly newsletter

Activities: Docent training; lects open to pub; tours; competitions with awards; mus shop sells books, Victorian items, American Indian items, notecards & stationery, archival supplies

BROOKLYN PARK

M NORTH HENNEPIN COMMUNITY COLLEGE, Joseph Gazzuolo Fine Arts Gallery, 7411 85th Ave N, Brooklyn Park, MN 55445-2231. Tel 763-424-0779, 424-0775; Fax 763-424-0929; Elec Mail will.agar@nhcc.mnscu.edu; Internet Home Page Address: www.nhcc.edu; *Dir* Will Agar

Open Mon, Thurs & Fri 8 AM - 4:30 PM, Tues & Wed 8 AM - 7 PM; No admis fee; Estab 1966 to make art available to students & community; Two gallery spaces: smaller gallery is for one person exhibs & installation; larger gallery is for group exhibitions; Average Annual Attendance: 8,000

Income: Financed by state appropriation & foundation grants

Purchases: Yearly student & local artist purchases

Collections: Student works & local artists in Minnesota

Exhibitions: Mid-West Artist on regular basis
Activities: Lects open to pub; concerts; gallery talks; tours; student show with prizes; individual paintings & original objects of art lent to faculty members on campus; book traveling exhibs 1-2 per year; sales shop sells books

COLLEGEVILLE

M **ST. JOHNS UNIVERSITY,** Alice R Rogers/Target Galleries, SJU Art Center, Collegeville, MN 56321; BAC, 37 S College Ave, Saint Joseph, MN 56374-2001. Tel 320-363-2701; Tel 320-363-5792 (office); Fax 320-363-6097; Elec Mail tdietzel@csbsju.edu; Internet Home Page Address: www.csbsju.edu/fine-arts; *Dir Exhibs* Tracy Doreen Dietzel, MFA
Open Thurs noon - 9 PM, Fri - Wed noon - 6 PM; No admis fee; Univ estab 1857, gallery estab 1991; 2 secured fully equipped galleries
Income: Financed by college
Exhibitions: contemporary artworks from established & emerging regional, national & international artists. Solo & group shows change every 6-8 weeks
Activities: Lects open to pub; 10-16 vis lectrs per yr

COMFREY

M **JEFFERS PETROGLYPHS HISTORIC SITE,** 27160 County Rd 2, Comfrey, MN 56019. Tel 507-628-5591; Fax 507-628-5593; Elec Mail jefferspetroglyphs@mnhs.org; Internet Home Page Address: www.mnhs.org/places/sites/jp; *Site Mgr* Tom Sanders; *Site Supervisor* Pam Jensen
Open Memorial weekend to Labor Day Mon & Thurs - Sat 10 AM - 5 PM, Sun noon - 5 PM; Admis adults $7, seniors $6, children 6 - 17 $5, group of 10 or more with advanced reservation $4, children under 6 & MHS members free; Estab 1966; Historical site; sacred site to the American Indians; mus concentrates on American Indian history & spirituality which dates back to the plain's Archaic Period (7000 BC - 600 AD); mus situated on over 160 acres of prairie. 1300 sq ft exhib space; theater capacity 50; nonprofit, governed by state; Average Annual Attendance: 7,000; Mem: Dues North Star Circle $1000, Sustaining $500, Contributing $250, Assoc $145, Household plus $95, Household $75, Sr Household of two adults 65 & over plus Indiv $65, Indiv $50, Sr Indiv $45
Collections: Over 2000 carvings on quartzite rock ranging from 5000 - 10,000 yrs old that are symbols of thunderbirds, bison, turtles, lightning strikes, humans & other figures; book vols on Native American history & culture; book vols on prairie flowers & grasses
Publications: The Jeffers Petroglyphs, book
Activities: Research in archaeology, geology, petroglyphs, and prairie grasses & flowers; training progs for professional mus workers; educ progs for children, college students & adults; guided tours; Native American books, jewelry, soap, dreamcatchers & other mus related items for sale

DULUTH

M **SAINT LOUIS COUNTY HISTORICAL SOCIETY,** St. Louis County Historical Society, 506 W Michigan St, Duluth, MN 55802-1517. Tel 218-733-7580; Fax 218-733-7585; Elec Mail history@thehistorypeople.org; Internet Home Page Address: www.thehistorypeople.org; *Exec Dir* JoAnne Coombe
Open Winter, Mon - Sat 10 AM - 5 PM, Sun 1 PM - 5 PM; Summer 9:30AM-6PM Daily; Admis adults 13 yrs & older $12, children 3-13 $6, 2 and under free; Estab in 1922. Housed in the Saint Louis County Heritage & Arts Center along with Minnesota Ballet, Duluth Playhouse, Duluth Art Institute, & Lake Superior Railroad Mus; Soc exhibit areas consist of three galleries interspersed in viewing areas & Veterans Memorial Hall Mus; Average Annual Attendance: 120,000; Mem: 900; dues $30 & up
Income: $660,338 (financed by pub support, dues, earned profit, & volunteer service)
Purchases: $689,009
Library Holdings: Audio Tapes; Book Volumes; Cards; Cassettes; Clipping Files; Filmstrips; Manuscripts; Maps; Memorabilia; Original Art Works (in artifact coll); Original Documents; Other Holdings Military; Pamphlets; Periodical Subscriptions; Photographs; Records; Reels; Reproductions; Slides; Video Tapes
Special Subjects: Folk Art, Historical Material, Ceramics, Glass, Flasks & Bottles, Painting-American, Textiles, Watercolors, American Indian Art, Costumes, Pottery, Woodcarvings, Dolls, Furniture, Coins & Medals, Miniatures, Embroidery, Laces, Stained Glass, Reproductions
Collections: E Johnson Collection; drawings; paintings; Ojibwe & Sioux beadwork, quill work, basketry; Logging Exhibit; Herman Melheim hand-carved furniture; Priley Collection (carved figures)
Exhibitions: Changing exhibits on topics related to the history of northeastern Minnesota & Lake Superior region
Publications: Books & pamphlets on topics related to the history of northeastern Minn; semi-annual newsletter
Activities: Workshops; lect; 12-15 vis lectrs per yr; annual dinners; veterans' march; antique appraisals; various fundraising events; exhib openings/receptions; schols; sales shop sells books, prints & gift items

M **UNIVERSITY OF MINNESOTA DULUTH,** Tweed Museum of Art, 1201 Ordean Ct, Duluth, MN 55812-2496. Tel 218-726-7823; Fax 218-726-8503; Elec Mail tma@d.umn.edu; Internet Home Page Address: www.d.umn.edu/tma/; *Mus Educ Mgr* Susan Hudec; *Dir* Ken Bloom; *Registrar* Camille Doran; *Preparator* Eric Dubnicka; *Head of Security* Scott Stevens; *Commus Mgr* Christine Strom
Open Tues 9 AM - 8 PM, Wed - Fri 9 AM - 4:30 PM, Sat & Sun 1 - 5 PM, cl Mon & univ holidays; No admis fee; donations family $5, individual $2, seniors & students free; Estab 1950 to serve both the univ & community as a center for exhib of works of art & related activities; Nine galleries within the mus; Average Annual Attendance: 35,000; Mem: 500; dues $10-$1000
Income: Financed by mem, state appropriation & foundation
Purchases: 50% (state; 20% income & endowments) 15% private foundations; 15% members

Library Holdings: Auction Catalogs 300; Audio Tapes 50; Book Volumes 2,000; CD-ROMs 50; Clipping Files 500; Exhibition Catalogs; Periodical Subscriptions 5; Slides 1000; Video Tapes 300
Special Subjects: American Indian Art, Drawings, Etchings & Engravings, Photography, Pottery, Painting-American, Prints, Textiles, Woodcuts, Painting-European, Painting-French, Sculpture, Watercolors, Painting-Canadian, Renaissance Art
Collections: Jonathan Sax Collections of 20th Century American Prints; George P Tweed Memorial Art Collections: 5,000 paintings with emphasis on Barbizon School & 19th Century American; Glenn C Nelson international ceramics; George Morrison Collection; Potlatch Collection of Royal Canadian Mounted Police Illustrations; Richard E & Dorothy Rawlings Nelson Collection of American Indian Art; Wiiken Contemporary Glass Collection
Exhibitions: 8-10 major exhibs annually
Publications: European Paintings in the Tweed Museum of Art by David Stark; American Painting in the Tweed Museum of Art by J Gray Sweeney; Luis Gonzalez Palma; Frank Big Bear
Activities: Classes for adults & children; docent training; lects open to pub, 5-8 vis lectrs per yr; gallery talks; tours; individual paintings & original objects of art lent to qualifying mus & institutions; one-two book traveling exhibs per yr; originates traveling exhibs to national & international mus & galleries; mus shop sells books, magazines, original art, reproductions, prints, gift items

EDINA

M **EDINA ART CENTER,** Margaret Foss Gallery, 4701 W 64th St, Edina, MN 55435-1501. Tel 952-903-5780; Fax 952-903-5781; Elec Mail artcenter@edinamn.gov; Internet Home Page Address: www.edinaartcenter.com; *Contact* Michael Frey

ELYSIAN

M **LESUEUR COUNTY HISTORICAL SOCIETY,** Chapter One, PO Box 240, Elysian, MN 56028-0240. Tel 507-267-4620, 362-8350; Fax 507-267-4750; Elec Mail museum@lchs.mus.mn.us; Internet Home Page Address: www.lesueurcountyhistory.org; *VPres* Patricia Nusbaum; *Genealogist* Shirley Zimprich; *Pres* Audrey Knutson; *Treas* Michael La France
Open May - Sept Sat & Sun 1 - 5 PM, June - Aug Wed - Sun 1 - 5 PM; No admis fee; Estab 1966 to show the works of Adolf Dehn, Roger Preuss, David Maass; Lloyd Herfindahl & Albert Christ-Janer to preserve early heritage & artifacts of the pioneers of LeSueur County; Mus is depository of Dehn, Preuss, Maass & Lloyd Herfindahl; examples of originals, prints & publications of the artists are on display; Average Annual Attendance: 1,000; Mem: 700; dues annual $15; annual meeting
Income: $17,000 (financed by mem, county appropriation, county government & grants)
Purchases: $51,000
Special Subjects: Painting-American, Architecture, Drawings, Painting-American, Photography, Costumes, Ceramics, Folk Art, Pottery, Etchings & Engravings, Landscapes, Manuscripts, Portraits, Posters, Dolls, Furniture, Glass, Metalwork, Carpets & Rugs, Historical Material, Maps, Juvenile Art, Miniatures, Period Rooms, Leather, Enamels
Collections: Adolf Dehn; David Maass; Roger Preuss; Lloyd Herfindahl; Albert Christ-Janer
Exhibitions: Exhibitions of works by Adolf Dehn, David Maass, Roger Preuss, Lloyd Herfindahl, Albert Christ-Janer
Publications: Newsletters, quarterly
Activities: Slide carousel to show the sites & early history of the County & works of the Artists; classes for children; lects open to pub; gallery talks; tours; lending collection contains books, cassettes, color reproductions, lantern slides, original prints, paintings, motion pictures & 1000 photographs; mus shop sells books, original art

L **Collections Library,** PO Box 240, Elysian, MN 56028-0240. Tel 507-267-4620, 362-8683; *Dir* Shirley Zimprich
Open by appointment only; Estab 1970 to collect locally & state-wide for purposes of genealogy; history of the artists
Library Holdings: Audio Tapes; Book Volumes 300; Cassettes; Clipping Files; Framed Reproductions; Lantern Slides; Original Art Works; Periodical Subscriptions 3; Prints; Reels 120; Reproductions; Slides
Collections: Original Adolf Dehn Watercolors & Lithographs; Duck Stamp Prints of Roger Preuss & David Maass; Lloyd Herfindahl; All Media
Exhibitions: Lloyd Herfindahl
Publications: Newsletters, 4 per yr

FARIBAULT

M **PARADISE CENTER FOR THE ARTS,** 321 Central Ave, Faribault, MN 55021. Tel 507-332-7372; Internet Home Page Address: www.paradisecenterforthearts.org; *Exec Dir* Ryan Heinritz
Open Tues - Sat noon - 5 PM, Thurs until 8 PM; Admis free except for ticketed events; Estab 2007; multidisciplinary center for the arts, theatre, music, gallery, education; 3 galleries; Carlander Family Gallery, Lois Varnesh Boardroom Gallery & Cory Lynn Creger Memorial Gallery; Mem: 500; dues: family $60, individual $45
Income: Financed by donations, mem, ticketed events, fundraisers & grants
Exhibitions: View all exhibs at www.paradisecenterforthearts.org
Activities: Classes for adults & children; dramatic progs; concerts; gallery talks; tours; sales shop sells original art

FOUNTAIN

A **FILLMORE COUNTY HISTORICAL SOCIETY,** Fillmore County History Center, 202 County Rd, Fountain, MN 55935. Tel 507-268-4449; Elec Mail fchc@frontier.com; Internet Home Page Address: fillmorecountyhistory.wordpress.com; *Exec Dir* Debra Richardson
Open Tues - Sat 9 AM - 4 PM; No admis fee, donations accepted, library fees; Estab 1934 to preserve & illustrate the written & photographic history; Average Annual Attendance: 8,000; Mem: 350; dues $5-$150; annual meeting second Sat in Oct

Income: $50,000 (financed by mem, county appropriations, donations)
Purchases: An Original Bernard Pietenpol Airplane
Library Holdings: Memorabilia; Original Documents; Photographs; Records
Collections: Bue Photography; Antique Agricultural Equipment; Hand Made Wooden Tools; Vintage Clothing & Tractors
Exhibitions: Rotation exhibitions
Publications: Rural Roots, quarterly
Activities: Lects open to pub; 4 vis lectrs per yr; gift shop sells books

FRANCONIA

M   **FRANCONIA SCULPTURE PARK,** 29836 St Croix Trail, Franconia, MN 55074. Tel 651-257-6668; Elec Mail info@franconia.org; Internet Home Page Address: www.franconia.org

FRIDLEY

M   **BANFILL-LOCKE CENTER FOR THE ARTS,** 6666 E River Rd, Fridley, MN 55432-4229. Tel 763-574-1850; Fax 763-502-6946; Elec Mail info@banfill-locke.org; Internet Home Page Address: banfill-locke.org

GLENWOOD

M   **POPE COUNTY HISTORICAL SOCIETY,** Pope County Museum, S Hwy 104, Glenwood, MN 56334; 809 S Lakeshore Dr, Glenwood, MN 56334. Tel 320-634-3293; Elec Mail pcmmuseum@wisper-wireless.com; Internet Home Page Address: www.popecountymuseum.wordpress.com; *Cur* Merlin Peterson; *Archivist* Jackie Gartner; *Collections Mgr* Ann Grady
Open Tues - Sat 10 AM - 5 PM; Admis adults $3, students $1.50, children $.50; Estab 1932 to display & preserve artifacts & genealogy files; 8,000 sq ft & seven historic buildings; Average Annual Attendance: 4,500; Mem: 400; dues $10; annual meeting
Income: $70,000 (financed by county appropriation, admis & gifts)
Special Subjects: Architecture, Drawings, Painting-American, Photography, American Indian Art, Southwestern Art, Textiles, Costumes, Religious Art, Crafts, Woodcarvings, Landscapes, Decorative Arts, Manuscripts, Portraits, Eskimo Art, Dolls, Furniture, Glass, Metalwork, Historical Material, Period Rooms, Embroidery, Painting-Scandinavian
Publications: Semi-annual newsletter
Activities: Educ dept; classes for children; guided tours for students; gallery talks; sales shop sell books & prints

INTERNATIONAL FALLS

M   **KOOCHICHING MUSEUMS,** (Koochiching County Historical Society Museum) 214 Sixth Ave, International Falls, MN 56649. Tel 218-283-4316; Fax 218-283-8243; *Exec Dir* Edgar Oerichbauer
Open Mon - Fri 9 AM - 5 PM; Admis adults $2, students $1; Estab 1958 to collect, preserve & exhibit the material & social cultures of Koochiching County, North Central Minnesota & the southern border portions of southern Ontario; 2 mus; The Koochiching Historical Society & The Bronco Mus; Mem: 500; dues $15-$1000
Income: Financed by county, mem, admis funds & grants
Special Subjects: Painting-American, Photography, Textiles, Crafts, Pottery, Landscapes, Manuscripts, Portraits, Dolls, Furniture, Glass, Jewelry, Porcelain, Maps, Coins & Medals, Period Rooms, Embroidery, Laces
Collections: 100 paintings relating to the history of the region, including many by local artists & six of which were commissioned for the museum, various small collectors, football memorabilia
Exhibitions: Permanent coll
Publications: Koochiching Chronicle, quarterly
Activities: Classes for adults & children; dramatic progs; lects open to pub; tours; originate traveling exhibs; sales shop sells books, Indian craft items, post cards, unique gifts

LANESBORO

M   **LANESBORO ARTS CENTER,** 103 Parkway Ave N, Lanesboro, MN 55949-0152; PO Box 152, Lanesboro, MN 55949-0152. Tel 507-467-2446; Elec Mail info@lanesboroarts.org; Internet Home Page Address: lanesboroarts.org

LE SUEUR

M   **LESUEUR MUSEUM,** 709 N 2nd St, Le Sueur, MN 56058. Tel 507-665-2050; Internet Home Page Address: www.lesueurchamber.org/visiting_lesueur/
Open year round by appt; No admis fee, donations accepted
Special Subjects: Historical Material
Exhibitions: Green Giant & Canning; Agriculture; Genealogy; Veterinary Medicine; War in the Valley

LITTLE FALLS

M   **CHARLES A LINDBERGH HISTORIC SITE,** 1620 Lindbergh Dr S, Little Falls, MN 56345; 345 W Kellog Blvd, Minnesota Historic Society Saint Paul, MN 55102-1906. Tel 320-616-5421; Fax 320-616-5423; Elec Mail lindbergh@mnhs.org; Internet Home Page Address: www.mnhs.org; *Historic Site Mgr* Charles D Pautler
Open Memorial Day - Labor Day: Thurs - Sat 10 AM - 5 PM, Sun 12 - 5 PM; cl Mon -Wed except holidays; open by appt year-round; Admis adults $7, seniors $6, students $5, children $4; spec rates for grps; mems no admis fee; Estab 1969; Childhood home of Charles A Lindbergh where he lived from 1902-1920; also

contains visitor ctr which has state-of-the-art exhibs on Lindbergh's life & that of his wife, Anne Morrow Lindbergh; visitors can take guided tour of the 1906 home, tour three levels of mus exhibs & galleries in the visitor ctr & see films containing footage from Lindbergh's life. 2500 sq ft exhib space; 50-capacity theater with large screen; one classroom; nonprofit org governed both privately and by state govt; Average Annual Attendance: 14,000
Collections: 200 books vols on politics 1870 - 1920; 100 book vols of children's books; 50 vols on secondary reference resources; over 100 folders & research on Lindbergh & aviation
Exhibitions: Comprehensive exhibs on Lindbergh & his family, as well as the WPA
Activities: Lects; research in Lindbergh's aviation 1924 - 1927, Lindbergh's involvement in the anti-war effort 1939 - 1940; gen aviation history 1903 - 1940; Lindbergh's Pacific War experience 1944; guided tours; films; hobby workshops; participatory & traveling exhibs; spec events: Children's Day, Family Fun Day, Air Show, Film Festival; Lindbergh & aviator books, souvenirs, children's items & other mus related items for sale

MANKATO

M   **MANKATO AREA ARTS COUNCIL,** Carnegie Art Center, 120 S Broad St, Mankato, MN 56001-3611. Tel 507-625-2730; Elec Mail artctr@hickorytech.net; Internet Home Page Address: www.thecarnegiemonkato.com; *Gallery Coordr* Hope Cook; *Gift Shop Coordr* Janet Husar
Open Thurs 1 - 7 PM, Fri 1 - 4 PM, Sat 11 AM - 5 PM; No admis fee; Estab 1980 to provide exhibition space for regional artists; Three galleries (Rotunda Gallery, Cook Gallery & Fireplace Gallery) housed in historic Carnegie Library; library of author Maud Hart Lovelace; Average Annual Attendance: 5,000; Mem: 200; dues $25 individual & up; annual meeting in Nov
Exhibitions: Monthly regional shows by visual artists
Activities: Gallery exhibs; tours of Art Center & historic Carnegie Library on request; studio rental; studio art classes for adults; annual CAC juried exhib; gift shop sells handmade work by local & regional artists

M   **MINNESOTA STATE UNIVERSITY, MANKATO,** 228 Wiecking Ctr, Mankato, MN 56001-6062. Tel 507-389-6412; Elec Mail harlan.bloomer@mnsu.edu; Internet Home Page Address: www.mnsu.edu; *Dir* Harlan Bloomer
Open Mon - Fri 9AM-4PM; No admis fee; Estab 1979 to provide cultural enrichment in the visual arts to the campus & community through a prog of exhibs from local, regional & national sources & student exhibs; Gallery has 150 running ft of carpeted display area, track lighting & climate controlled
Income: Financed by univ
Special Subjects: Drawings, Painting-American, Prints, Crafts, Bookplates & Bindings
Collections: American bookplates; contemporary prints, drawings, paintings, photographs, sculpture & crafts; student works in all media

MAPLEWOOD

C   **3M,** Art Collection, 2501 Hudson Rd, 3M Center Maplewood, MN 55144-1000. Tel 651-733-1110; Fax 651-737-4555; *Cur, Art Coll* Charles Thames
Estab 1902, dept estab 1974; Concourse Gallery provides changing exhibitions drawn from the collection
Collections: Collection of paintings, drawings, sculpture, watercolors, original prints, photographs & textiles
Publications: Exhibition brochures
Activities: Tours by appointment only & must be scheduled two weeks in advance; individual paintings & original objects of art lent to scholarly exhibitions

MINNEAPOLIS

AMERICAN CRAFT COUNCIL
For further information see National and Regional Organizations

M   **AMERICAN SWEDISH INSTITUTE,** 2600 Park Ave, Minneapolis, MN 55407-1090. Tel 612-871-4907; Fax 612-871-8682; Elec Mail info@americanswedishinst.org; Internet Home Page Address: www.americanswedishinst.org; *Dir* Bruce Karstadt; *Cur* Curt Pederson; *Dir Colls & Exhibs* Nina Clark
Open Tues, Thurs, Fri & Sat Noon - 4 PM, Wed Noon - 8 PM, Sun 1 - 5 PM, cl Mon & national holidays; Admis adults $6, seniors $5, students under 12 $4 & children under 6 free; Estab & incorporated 1929 to preserve, collect, procure & exhibit objects related to Swedish-Americans in the Midwest from 1845; Building donated by Swan J Turnblad & contains, in a home setting, a coll of Swedish artifacts, plus many items of gen cultural interest pertaining to Scandinavia. The Grand Hall is paneled in African mahogany. Throughout the mansion there are eleven porcelain tile fireplaces; Average Annual Attendance: 50,000; Mem: 5000; dues, life $3000, patron $150, sustaining $100, family (husband, wife & all children under age 18, living at home) $50, regular (single) $35, non-resident single, or husband & wife outside of fifty mile radius of Twin Cities $35, students attending school, below the age of 18 $20, other mem levels available
Library Holdings: Book Volumes; Clipping Files; Fiche; Lantern Slides; Manuscripts; Maps; Memorabilia; Motion Pictures; Original Documents; Other Holdings; Photographs; Video Tapes
Special Subjects: Period Rooms, Textiles, Architecture, Sculpture, Ceramics, Crafts, Folk Art, Woodcarvings, Glass, Porcelain, Tapestries, Painting-Scandinavian
Collections: Paintings, sculpture, tapestries, ceramics, china, glass, pioneer items & textiles, immigration related objects
Publications: ASI Posten (newsletter), bimonthly
Activities: Classes for adults & children; dramatic progs; docent training; lect open to public; concerts; gallery talks; tours; scholarships offered; individual paintings lent to other museums; book traveling exhibs 1-2 per year; bookstore sells books, magazines, original art, reproductions & prints

A ARTS MIDWEST, 2908 Hennepin Ave Ste 200, Minneapolis, MN 55408-1954. Tel 612-341-0755; Fax 612-341-0902; Elec Mail midwestartsconference@artsmidwest.org; Internet Home Page Address: www.artsmidwest.org; *Others* TDD 612-341-0901; *Exec Dir* David J Fraher; *Asst Dir* Susan T Chandler; *Develop Dir* Colleen McLaughlin; *Midwest Arts Conference Dir* Angela Urbanz; *Sr Prog Dir* Adam Perry; *Prog Dir* Christine M Taylor
Estab 1985, provides funding programs, conferences & publications to individuals & organizations in Illinois, Indiana, Iowa, Michigan, Minnesota, North Dakota, Ohio, South Dakota & Wisconsin. Works in collaboration with corporations, foundations, state government arts agencies, the National Endowment for the Arts & art enthusiasts to connect the arts to audiences, enabling individuals & families to share in & enjoy the arts & cultures of the region & the world
Publications: Inform, bimonthly newsletter; Insights on Jazz, booklets; Midwest Jazz, quarterly newsmagazine
Activities: Conferences

C FEDERAL RESERVE BANK OF MINNEAPOLIS, 90 Hennepin Ave, Minneapolis, MN 55401-2171. Tel 612-204-6065; Fax 612-204-6070; Elec Mail keithjablonski@mpls.frb.org; *Cur* Keith Jablonski
Open by appointment with Cur; Estab 1973 to enhance the working environment of bank; to support the creative efforts of ninth district artists; Circ ; Collection displayed throughout the bank in offices, lounges, public areas & work areas
Collections: Regional collection consists of works by artists living & working in the Ninth Federal Reserve District

M HIGHPOINT CENTER FOR PRINTMAKING, 912 W Lake St, Minneapolis, MN 55408. Tel 612-871-1326; Elec Mail info@highpointprintmaking.org; Internet Home Page Address: www.highpointprintmaking.org; *Contact* Kristin Makholm

M INTERACT STUDIO, Inside Out Gallery, 212 3rd Ave N #140, Minneapolis, MN 55401. Tel 612-339-5145; Elec Mail sandy@interactcenter.com; Internet Home Page Address: interactcenter.com

M INTERMEDIA ARTS MINNESOTA, 2822 Lyndale Ave S, Minneapolis, MN 55408-2108. Tel 612-871-4444; Fax 612-871-6927; Elec Mail info@intermediaarts.org; Internet Home Page Address: www.intermediaarts.org; *Exec & Artistic Dir* Theresa Sweetland; *Office & Vol Coordr* Kim Arleth; *Assoc Dir* Julie Bates
Open Mon - Fri 10 AM - 6 PM, Sat noon - 5 PM, cl Jan 1 - 4, Martin Luther King Day, Memorial Day, Independence Day, Labor Day, Thanksgiving, Dec 24 & 25; Suggested donation $2; Estab 1973; 2,000 sq ft space used for installations, screenings & performances; Average Annual Attendance: 5,000; Mem: 250; dues $40 & up
Income: Financed by donations, grants
Library Holdings: Book Volumes; Cassettes; DVDs; Other Holdings Caroline Holbrook Poetry Library; Video Tapes
Exhibitions: Exhibition supporting New Works in Media & interdisciplinary Arts
Publications: Annual report; calendar of events
Activities: Professional develop for teaching artists; classes for children; lects open to pub, 3 vis lectrs per yr; gallery talks; tours; schols & fels offered; community-based progs to promote understanding among people through art; mus shop sells t-shirts

M JUXTAPOSITION ARTS, 2007 Emerson Ave N, Minneapolis, MN 55411-2507. Tel 612-588-1148; *Contact* DeAnna Cummings

A MIDWEST ART CONSERVATION CENTER, (Upper Midwest Conservation Association) 2400 3rd Ave S, Minneapolis, MN 55404. Tel 612-870-3120; Fax 612-870-3118; Elec Mail info@preserveart.org; Internet Home Page Address: www.preserveart.org; *Sr Paper Conservator* Elizabeth Buschor; *Dir Preservation Svcs* Neil Cockerline; *Sr Paintings Conservator* Joan Gorman; *Sr Objects Conservator* Donna Haberman; *Sr Paintings Conservator* David Marquis; *Contract Textile Conservator* Beth McLaughlin; *Asst Dir Preservation Svcs* Elisa Redman; *Exec Dir* Colin D Turner
Open Mon - Fri 8:30 AM - 5:00 PM; Estab 1977 for art conservation & education; Non-profit org; Mem: 170; dues $50-600; annual meeting in the Fall
Income: $1,000,000 (financed by mem, earned income & grants)

L MINNEAPOLIS COLLEGE OF ART & DESIGN, Library, 2501 Stevens Ave S, Minneapolis, MN 55404. Tel 612-874-3791; Fax 612-874-3704; Elec Mail library@mcad.edu; Internet Home Page Address: www.library.mcad.edu; *Technical Svcs Librn* Kay Streng; *Slide Librn* Allan Kohl; *Dir* Suzanne Degler; *Pub Svcs Librn* Amy Naughton
Open Mon - Thurs 8:30AM-10PM, Fri 8:30AM-7PM, Sat noon-7PM, Sun noon-10PM; No admis fee (students only); Estab to provide library & materials in support of the curriculum of the College; includes a library & slide library; Circ 21,000, circulation limited to students, staff, alumni & faculty; Average Annual Attendance: 90,000
Income: Financed by student tuition, grants & gifts
Library Holdings: Book Volumes 55,000; CD-ROMs; Clipping Files; Compact Disks; DVDs; Exhibition Catalogs; Pamphlets; Periodical Subscriptions 175; Records; Slides 145,000; Video Tapes
Special Subjects: Art History, Film, Illustration, Photography, Graphic Design

M MINNEAPOLIS INSTITUTE OF ARTS, 2400 Third Ave S, Minneapolis, MN 55404. Tel 888-642-2787; Fax 612-870-3004; Internet Home Page Address: www.artsmia.org; *Deputy Dir* Patricia J Grazzini; *Dir & Pres* Kaywin Feldman; *Dir Curatorial Affairs & Cur Japanese & Korean Art* Matthew Welch; *Dir Ctr for Alt Mus Practice & Cur Contemporary Art* Elizabeth Armstrong; *Dir External Affairs* Leann Standish; *Cur Prints & Drawings* Thomas Rassieur; *Cur Photography & New Media* David Little; *Head Reg* Brian Kraft; *Cur Paintings* Patrick Noon; *Cur Decorative Arts, Textiles & Sculpture* Eike Schmidt; *Cur Arts of Africa & Americas* Jan Lodewijk Grootaers; *Dir Admin Affairs* Michele Callahan
Open Tues - Wed & Fri - Sat 10 AM - 5 PM, Thurs 10 AM - 9 PM, Sun 11 AM-5 PM, cl Mon, Thanksgiving, Christmas Eve, Christmas Day & July 4; Admis to museum's permanent coll free; Estab 1883 to foster the knowledge, understanding & practice of the arts; The first gallery was opened in 1889 & the original bldg was constructed in 1911-15. The south wing was added in 1926 & the entire structure features the classical elements of the day. The mus was expanded to twice the original size in 1972-74 & has incorporated modern themes designed by Kenzo, Tange & URTEC of Tokyo; Average Annual Attendance: 570,000; Mem: 21,000; dues family $65, individual $50; annual meeting in Oct
Income: Financed by endowment, mem, county & state appropriations & admis
Special Subjects: Drawings, Painting-American, Photography, Prints, Sculpture, American Indian Art, African Art, Decorative Arts, Painting-European, Oriental Art, Period Rooms, Antiquities-Greek, Antiquities-Roman
Collections: Nearly 100,000 works of art representing more than 5,000 years of world history; European masterworks by Rembrandt, Poussin, van Gogh; modern & contemporary paintings & sculpture by Picasso, Matisse, Mondrian, Stella & Close; Decorative arts, Modernist design, photographs, prints, drawings; Asian, African & Native American art; Chinese and Japanese coll
Exhibitions: Rotating exhibitions
Publications: Bulletin, biannually; exhibitions catalogs; member's magazine, monthly
Activities: Classes for adults & children; docent training; workshops; lects open to pub, 15 vis lectrs per yr; concerts; gallery talks; tours; paintings & original art objects lent to other professional arts organizations; originate traveling exhibs; mus shop sells books, magazines, original art, reproductions, prints, slides & jewelry

L Art Research & Reference Library, 2400 Third Ave S, Minneapolis, MN 55404. Tel 612-870-3117; Fax 612-870-3004; Internet Home Page Address: www.artsmia.org; *Visual Resource Librn* Heidi Raatz; *Head Librn* Janice Lea Lurie; *Asst Librn* Jessica McIntyre
Open Tues - Fri 11:30 AM - 4:30 PM, hours vary around holidays; Estab 1915 to provide a reference collection based around the museum's collection of works of art; Has exhibitions of books & prints. For reference only
Library Holdings: Auction Catalogs; Book Volumes 50,000; Exhibition Catalogs; Pamphlets; Periodical Subscriptions 125
Collections: Leslie Collection: History of Books & Printing; Minnick Collection: Botanical, Floral & Fashion Books
Exhibitions: Jean Cocteau
Publications: Imperial Silks by Robert Jacobsen; Chaining the Sun: Portraits by Jeremiah Gurney, by Christian Peterson; Classical Chinese Furniture in the Minneapolis Institute of Arts by Robert Jacobsen; Progressive Design in the Midwest by Jennifer Komar Olivarez

A Friends of the Institute, 2400 Third Ave S, Minneapolis, MN 55404. Tel 612-870-3045; Fax 612-870-3004; Internet Home Page Address: www.artsmia.org; *Pres* Suzanne Payne
Open Mon - Fri 8:30 AM - 4:30 PM; Estab 1922 to broaden the influence of the Institute in the community & to provide volunteer support within the mus; Mem: 1900; annual meeting in May
Activities: Coordinates docent prog, mus shop, sales & rental gallery, speaker's bureau, information desk, special lect, exhibs & fundraising projects

M MUSEUM OF RUSSIAN ART, 5500 Stevens Ave S, Minneapolis, MN 55419. Tel 612-821-9045; *Chmn* Raymond Johnson; *Pres* Bradford Shinkle IV; *Spec Events Mgr* Lynda Holker
Open Mon - Fri 10 AM - 5 PM, Sat 10 AM - 4 PM; Admis adults $5, students & seniors 60 & over voluntary donation, discount to AAM members, members free; Average Annual Attendance: 40,000
Library Holdings: Book Volumes 500
Collections: Russian art
Publications: semiannual newsletter
Activities: Seminars; children's educational events; lects; rental facilities; mus shop

M SOAP FACTORY, PO Box 581696, Minneapolis, MN 55458-1696; 514 2nd St SE, Minneapolis, MN 55414-2105. Tel 612-623-9176; Elec Mail info@soapfactory.org; Internet Home Page Address: www.soapfactory.org; *Contact* Ben Heywood

M SOO VISUAL ARTS CENTER, 2638 Lyndale Ave S, Minneapolis, MN 55408. Tel 612-871-2263; Elec Mail info@soovac.org; Internet Home Page Address: www.soovac.org; *Contact* Suzy Greenberg

M THRIVENT FINANCIAL FOR LUTHERANS, (Lutheran Brotherhood Gallery) Gallery of Religious Art, 625 Fourth Ave S, Minneapolis, MN 55415. Tel 612-340-7000, 800-847-4836; Fax 612-340-8447; Elec Mail mail@thrivent.com; Internet Home Page Address: www.thrivent.com/heritage/art; *Consultant & Cur* Richard L Hillstrom; *Cur* Joanna Reiling Lindell
Open Mon - Fri 10 AM - 4 PM; No Admis fee; Estab 1982 as a cultural & educational gallery; Art is exhibited in a modest sized gallery & in the corporate library
Income: Financed by mem, gifts, donations
Collections: Bing & Grondahl Plate Collection; Martin Luther Commemorative Medals 16th-20th centuries; collection restricted to religious prints & drawings (15th-20th centuries)
Exhibitions: 8-10 Exhibitions per year
Activities: Originate traveling exhibs

M TRAFFIC ZONE CENTER FOR VISUAL ARTS, 250 3rd Ave N, Minneapolis, MN 55401. Tel 612-204-0012; Elec Mail trafficzoneart@gmail.com; Internet Home Page Address: www.trafficzoneart.com

M UNIVERSITY OF MINNESOTA, Katherine E Nash Gallery, 405 21st Ave S Minneapolis, MN 55455. Tel 612-624-7530; Fax 612-625-7881; Elec Mail shank001@unm.edu; Internet Home Page Address: nash.umn.edu; *Dir* Nick Shank
Open Fall& Spring Tues-Sat 11AM-7PM, Summer Tues-Sat 11AM-7PM; No admis fee; Provides educational exhibition space; Student exhibits
Special Subjects: Ceramics, Painting-American, Prints, Photography, Sculpture, Metalwork
Exhibitions: Rotating exhibitions every 3-4 weeks

Activities: Lect open to public, 5-8 vis lectrs per year; gallery talks; purchase awards; McKnight Fel

M **UNIVERSITY OF MINNESOTA,** Frederick R Weisman Art Museum, 333 E River Rd, Minneapolis, MN 55455. Tel 612-625-9494; Fax 612-625-9630; Elec Mail wampr@unm.edu; Internet Home Page Address: www.weisman.umn.edu; *Dir* Lyndel King; *Educ Dir* Colleen Sheehy; *Registrar* Karen Duncan; *Cur* Diane Mullin; *Technical Dir* John Allen; *Mus Shop Mgr* Kay McGuire; *Accounts Supvr* Carol Stafford; *Develop Dir* Matt Nielsen
Open Tues, Wed & Fri 10 AM - 5 PM, Thurs 10 AM - 8 PM, Sat & Sun 11 AM - 5 PM, cl Mon; No admis fee; Estab 1934; the progs of the Weisman Art Museum are geared to meet broad objectives of an all-Univ mus, as well as the specific teaching & research needs of various University of Minnesota depts; Average Annual Attendance: 130,000; Mem: 1,200
Income: Financed by state appropriation, grants & gifts
Special Subjects: Drawings, Painting-American, Prints, Sculpture
Collections: Paintings, drawings & prints by American artists working in the first half of the 20th century, & contains notable works by Avery, Biederman, Dove, Feininger, Hartley, MacDonald-Wright, Marin, Maurer, Nordfeldt & O'Keeffe; print coll includes works by artists of all schools & periods; Ceramic colls include ancient American Indian Pottery; ancient Chinese & Korean objects; ancient Greek vases, German, French & English 18th & 19th century porcelain, international 20th century ceramics
Exhibitions: The Weisman Art Museum stresses a program of major loan exhibitions, held concurrently with smaller exhibitions organized for specific teaching purposes or from the permanent collection
Activities: Docent training; concerts; tours; lending prog to Univ, staff & students of Minnesota faculty of framed two-dimensional material; mus shop sells books, magazines, reproductions, cards

M **The Studio/Larson Gallery,** 2017 Buford Ave, St Paul Student Center Saint Paul, MN 55108-6180. Tel 612-625-0214, 624-3742; Fax 612-624-9124; Elec Mail larsonart@umn.edu; Internet Home Page Address: www.sua.umn.edu/arts/events; *Coordr* Tricia Schweitzer; *Visual Arts Comt Chair* Jackie Beutell; *Visual Arts Comt Chair* Ruby Brayman
Open Mon-Wed 10AM-3PM, Thurs noon-8PM, Fri 10AM-3PM; No admis fee; Estab 1976 to make art accessible to univ community & gen pub; Average Annual Attendance: 30,000
Income: Financed by student fees
Exhibitions: 7-10 Exhibitions, annually
Activities: Educ dept; lects; gallery talks

L **Arts & Architecture Collections,** 309 19th Ave S, Minneapolis, MN 55455-0438. Tel 612-624-1638, 624-0303; Elec Mail ultan004@umn.edu; Internet Home Page Address: lib.umn.edu; *Arts, Architecture & Landscape Architecture Librn* Deborah K Ultan
Open Mon - Fri 7 AM - 9 PM, Sat 9 AM - 5 PM, Sun Noon - 9 PM; Estab 1950 to serve undergraduate & graduate teaching programs in Art History, Fine Arts, Architecture, Landscape Architecture & Humanities to PhD level & in Studio Art to MA level; to provide art related books to other departments & to the entire acad community
Library Holdings: Book Volumes 150,000; Cassettes 52; Exhibition Catalogs 5000; Fiche 7000; Pamphlets; Periodical Subscriptions 339
Special Subjects: Art History, Intermedia, Landscape Architecture, Mixed Media, Theatre Arts, Architecture
Exhibitions: Annual book exhibs of rare art materials & special collections
Activities: Lects; tours

L **Architecture & Landscape Library,** 89 Church St SE, East Bank Minneapolis, MN 55455-0148. Tel 612-624-6383, 624-1638; Fax 612-625-5597; Elec Mail j-morn@tc.umn.edu; Internet Home Page Address: arch.lib.umn.edu/; *Library Head* Joon Mornes
Open Mon - Fri 9 AM - 9 PM, Sat & Sun 1 - 6 PM; Circ 20,641; Used as a reference lending library
Income: Financed by University
Library Holdings: Book Volumes 38,000; Periodical Subscriptions 165; Reels 244; Video Tapes
Special Subjects: Landscape Architecture, Interior Design, Architecture

L **Children's Literature Research Collections,** 222 21st Ave S, 113 Andersen Library Minneapolis, MN 05545-4403. Tel 612-624-4576; Fax 612-625-5525; Elec Mail clrc@umn.edu; Internet Home Page Address: special.lib.umn.edu/clrc/; *Cur* Karen Nelson Hoyle
Open Mon - Fri 8:30 AM - 4:30 PM; refer to website for extended hrs; No admis fee; Estab 1949 to collect children's books, manuscripts & illustrations for use by researchers & for exhibits; For reference & research only
Income: Financed by endowment, University of Minnesota libraries
Library Holdings: Audio Tapes; Book Volumes 140,000; Cassettes; Clipping Files; Exhibition Catalogs; Fiche; Filmstrips; Manuscripts; Original Art Works; Original Documents; Other Holdings Toys; Pamphlets; Periodical Subscriptions 37; Photographs; Records; Slides; Video Tapes
Special Subjects: Illustration, Photography, Drawings, Manuscripts, Painting-American, Posters, Watercolors, Lettering
Collections: Figurine Coll
Publications: Kerlan Newsletter, 4 times per yr
Activities: Classes for adults; lects open to pub, 2 vis lectrs per yr; competitions with awards; fels; annual Kerlan Award; schols offered; individual paintings lent to art galleries; traveling exhibits; lending coll contains books, original art work, manuscript material; book traveling exhibs 6 per yr; originate traveling exhibs in Sweden, Spain & US; sales shop sells notecards, posters, books, keepsakes & catalogs, publs

M **The Bell Museum of Natural History,** 10 Church St SE, Minneapolis, MN 55455-0145. Tel 612-624-7083; Fax 612-626-7704; Elec Mail slanyon@biosci.cbs.umn.edu; Internet Home Page Address: www.1.umn.edu/bellmuse/; *Touring Exhib Coordr* Ian Dudley; *Cur Exhib* Donald T Luce; *Dir* Scott M Lanyon
Open Tues - Fri 9 AM - 5 PM, Sat 10 AM - 5 PM, Sun Noon - 5 PM; Admis adults $3, seniors & students $2, children under 3 & members free, free admis Sun; Estab 1872 to explore the diversity of life in the natural world; Dioramas, Discovery Room, temporary exhibits gallery; Average Annual Attendance: 60,000; Mem: 600; dues $20-$35

Special Subjects: Drawings, Painting-American, Prints, Watercolors, Etchings & Engravings, Dioramas
Collections: Owen T Gromme Collection; Francis Lee Jaques Collection; three separate Audubon colls; works by other artist-naturalists; natural history art (wildlife)
Exhibitions: Exotic Aquatics; Francis Lee Jaques-Images of the North Country; The Peregrine Falcon-Return of an Endangered; The Photography of Jim Brandenburg; 18 touring exhibits
Publications: Imprint & Calendar, quarterly
Activities: Classes for adults & children; docent training; lects open to public, 2 vis lectrs per year; gallery talks; tours; competitions; lends to other non-profit art museums; lending coll contains original art works, original prints, paintings & sculpture; originate traveling exhibs to libraries, art mus, nature centers, environmental learning centers & schools

M **WALKER ART CENTER,** 1750 Hennepin Ave, Minneapolis, MN 55403. Tel 612-375-7600; Fax 612-375-7618; Elec Mail info@walkerart.org; Internet Home Page Address: www.walkerart.org; *Pres* Ralph W Burnet; *Chmn Bd* H Brewster Atwater; *Admin Dir* Ann Bitter; *Chief Cur* Richard Flood; *Publ & Design Mgr* Lisa Middag; *Registrar* Gwen Bitz; *Dir Develop* Christopher Stevens; *Design Dir* Andrew Blauvelt; *Dir Film & Video* Cis Bierinckx; *Pub Information* Margaret Patridge; *Dir* Kathy Halbreich
Galleries & Box Office open Tues - Sun 11 AM - 5 PM, Thurs until 9 PM, cl Mon & major holidays; Sculpture Garden open daily 6 AM - Midnight; Admis adults $10, seniors $8, students & teens $6, mems & children 12 & under free, 1st Sat of month free, admis to Sculpture Garden free; Estab 1879 by T B Walker, reorganized 1939 as Walker Art Center, Inc; building erected 1927; new museum building opened 1971; expanded in 2005; The Center consists of nine galleries, three sculpture terraces, the Center Bookshop 11 acre Sculpture Garden, Conservatory & the Gallery 8 Restaurant; Average Annual Attendance: 906,605; Mem: 8000; dues household $45, individual & special $25; annual meeting in Sept
Income: Financed by corporate & individual contributions, endowment, mem, state & federal appropriation, grants, book shop, museum admis & prog ticket sales
Special Subjects: Drawings, Painting-American, Photography, Prints, Sculpture
Collections: Joseph Beuys Collection; Jasper Johns Collection; Sigmar Polke Collection; Complete Archive of Tyler Graphics; Contemporary Print Collection; Edmond R Ruben Film Study Collection; Visual Arts Study Coll; Minneapolis Sculpture Garden
Exhibitions: Selections from Permanent Collection
Publications: Brochures; calendar of events; exhibition catalogs
Activities: Classes for adults & children; docent training; internships; lects open to pub, 25 vis lectrs per yr; concerts; gallery talks; school & adults tours; films; individual paintings & original objects of art lent to mus; book traveling exhibs; originates traveling exhibs; mus shop selling books, magazines, posters, jewelry & gift items

L **Staff Reference Library,** 1750 Hennepin Ave, Minneapolis, MN 55403-1169. Tel 612-375-7680; Fax 612-375-7590; Elec Mail rosemary.furtak@walkerart.org; Internet Home Page Address: www.walkerart.org; *Librn* Rosemary Furtak; *Archivist* Jill Vuchetich; *Visual Resources Librn* Barbara Economon
Open by appointment to outside researchers; Open to museum personnel & scholars by appointment. For reference only; Average Annual Attendance: 500 outside researchers
Library Holdings: Auction Catalogs; Audio Tapes 2000; Book Volumes 35,000; Cassettes; Clipping Files; Compact Disks; Exhibition Catalogs; Lantern Slides; Motion Pictures; Original Documents; Other Holdings Artists' Books 1500; Periodical Subscriptions 110; Photographs; Slides; Video Tapes
Special Subjects: Art History, Intermedia, Decorative Arts, Film, Photography, Drawings, Graphic Arts, Graphic Design, Painting-American, Painting-British, Painting-Dutch, Painting-Flemish, Painting-French, Painting-German, Painting-Japanese, Painting-Russian, Painting-Spanish, Prints, Sculpture, Painting-European, Painting-Israeli, Industrial Design, Painting-Polish, Painting-Scandinavian, Painting-Australian, Painting-New Zealand
Collections: Catalogs dating back to 1940

MOORHEAD

M **HISTORICAL AND CULTURAL SOCIETY OF CLAY COUNTY,** (Heritage Hjemkomst Interpretive Center) Hjemkomst Center, 202 First Ave N, Moorhead, MN 56560; PO Box 157, Moorhead, MN 56561-0157. Tel 218-299-5511; Fax 218-299-5510; Internet Home Page Address: www.hjemkomst-center.com; *Exec Dir* Maureen Kelly Jonason; *Dir Visitor Svcs* Markus Kraeger; *Events Coordr* Tim Jorgenson; *Commun Coordr* Michelle Kittleson; *Cur* Lisa Vedaa; *Archivist* Mark Peihl
Open Mon - Sat 9 AM - 5 PM, a Tues 9 AM - 8 PM, Sun Noon - 5 PM; Admis adults $7, sr citizens $6, youths 5-17 $5; Estab 1986 to interpret River Valley heritage & Clay county history through interdisciplinary exhibits & programs; 7000 sq ft exhibition area for traveling exhibits; Average Annual Attendance: 40,000; Mem: Dues $30; annual meeting in May
Income: $410,000 (financed by mem & attendance & Clay County appropriations)
Special Subjects: Anthropology, Folk Art
Collections: Clay County Artifacts and Archives; Tom Arp Collection
Exhibitions: Focus on humanities, but are supplemented by art and/or science exhibits
Publications: Hourglass quarterly
Activities: Docent progs; lects open to pub, concerts, gallery talks, tours; Clay County library exhibits; book traveling exhibs 3 per yr; sales shop sells books, prints, Scandinavian items, reproductions, original art

NORTHFIELD

M **CARLETON COLLEGE,** Art Gallery, One N College St, Northfield, MN 55057. Tel 507-222-4469, 4342; Fax 507-646-7042; Elec Mail lbradley@carleton.edu; Internet Home Page Address: apps.carleton.edu/campus/gallery/info; *Dir & Cur* Laurel Bradley PhD; *Registrar* James F Smith
Open during exhibs Mon-Wed noon-6PM, Thurs & Fri noon-10PM, Sat & Sun noon-4PM; No admis fee; Estab 1971 for art exhibitions & programs emphasizing

quality & interdisciplinary ideas; One gallery 30 x 40 ft, secure; Average Annual Attendance: 5,000
Income: $100,000 (financed by parent organization)
Special Subjects: Painting-American, Photography, Prints, Woodcuts, Asian Art, Antiquities-Greek, Antiquities-Roman
Collections: American Paintings; Asian Objects; Photographs (1945-Present); Prints European & American (19th-20th century)
Activities: Lects open to pub, 10 vis lectrs per yr; book traveling exhibs 1-2 per yr; originates traveling exhibs

A **NORTHFIELD ARTS GUILD,** 304 Division St. Northfield, MN 55057. Tel 507-645-8877; Fax 507-645-6201; Elec Mail nfldarts@rconnect.com; Internet Home Page Address: www.northfieldartsguild.org; *Visual Arts Specialist* Toni Bennett Easterson; *Theater Specialist* Ann Etter; *Literary Arts Specialist* Paula Granquist; *Pres & Dance Specialist* Mary Hahn; *Music Specialist* David Wolff
Open Office Mon-Fri 10AM-1PM & 2PM-5PM, Gallery & Gift Shop Mon-Sat 10AM-5PM, Thurs until 8PM; Estab 1958 as a non-profit organization which offers classes & programming in visual arts, theater, music, dance & literary art; Mem: 570 households
Publications: NAG Notes, quarterly
Activities: Classes for adults & children; dramatic progs; dance school; lects open to pub; concerts; gallery talks; schols offered; mus shop sells books, original art

M **SAINT OLAF COLLEGE,** Flaten Art Museum, 1520 St Olaf Ave, Dittmann Center Northfield, MN 55057-1574. Tel 507-786-3556; Fax 507-786-3776; Elec Mail ewaldj@stolaf.edu; Internet Home Page Address: www.stolaf.edu/collections/flaten/; *Dir* Jill Ewald; *Registrar* Mona Weselmann
Open Mon, Tues, Wed & Fri 10 AM - 5 PM, Thurs 10 AM - 8 PM, Sat & Sun 2 - 5 PM; cl during col breaks; No Admis fee; Estab 1976; 2500 flexible sq ft, shows regional, national, international work, no unsolicited shows; Average Annual Attendance: 10,000
Library Holdings: Exhibition Catalogs; Original Art Works; Photographs; Prints; Sculpture
Special Subjects: Drawings, Pottery, Pre-Columbian Art, Painting-European, Sculpture, Tapestries, Painting-American, Photography, Prints, Watercolors, Bronzes, African Art, Textiles, Religious Art, Ceramics, Woodcuts, Etchings & Engravings, Landscapes, Painting-Japanese, Portraits, Oriental Art, Asian Art, Painting-British, Carpets & Rugs, Miniatures, Painting-Spanish, Painting-Italian, Painting-Russian, Painting-Scandinavian
Collections: Chris Janer prints & paintings; Nygaard sculpture; Contemporary and traditional paintings; sculpture, prints, work by Norwegian artists; Japanese Prints; Southwestern Native American Pottery; Richard N. Tetlie European & American paintings, drawings, prints, sculpture & photography; Andy Warhol Polaroids & b/w photographs
Publications: Exhibit announcements every 5-6 weeks; Occasional catalogs
Activities: Supports acad progs & classes; lects open to pub, 4-6 vis lectrs per yr; concerts; gallery talks; tours; lend original objects of art to nearby educational institutions; book traveling exhibs 1 per yr

OWATONNA

A **OWATONNA ARTS CENTER,** 435 Garden View Lane, Owatonna, MN 55060; PO Box 134, Owatonna, MN 55060-0134. Tel 507-451-0533; Fax 507-446-0198; Elec Mail info@oacarts.org; Internet Home Page Address: oacarts.org; *Dir & Cur* Silvan A Durben; *Pres* Ray Lacina; *VPres* Doug Parr; *Develop & Bus Dir* Megan Proft; *Educ Coordr* Christina Spencer
Open Tues - Sun 1 - 5 PM; No admis fee except for specials; Estab 1974 to preserve local professional artists' work & promote the arts in the community; The West Gallery (32 x 26 x 12 ft) & the North Gallery (29 x 20 x 12 ft) provide an interesting walk through space & a versatile space in which to display two & three dimensional work; the two galleries can be combined by use of moveable panels & the Sculpture Garden which was completed in 1979 of multi-level construction; Average Annual Attendance: 17,000; Mem: 400; dues basic $50 & up, sustaining $300 & up
Income: $102,000 (financed by mem & fund raising activities plus sustaining fund from industries & bus)
Collections: Marianne Young World Costume Collection of garments & jewelry from 27 countries; painting, prints, sculpture by local professional artists; 2 Bronzes by John Rood, Paul Grandland; steel sculpture by Hammel; print coll of Adolph Den
Exhibitions: Annual Christmas Theme Display; Annual Outdoor Arts Festival; Annual Steele County Show; Festival of the Arts - July
Publications: Newsletter to members & other arts organizations
Activities: Classes for adults & children; 2 vis lectrs per year; festivals; concerts; gallery talks; tours; schols offered; original objects of art & Costume Collection lent to other arts organizations

L **Library,** 435 Dunnell Dr, Owatonna, MN 55060; PO Box 134, Owatonna, MN 55060-0134. Tel 507-451-0533; Fax 612-224-8854; *Dir* Silvan Berben; *Admin Asst* Julie Enzenaurer
Open Tues - Sat 1 PM - 5 PM by appointment; Open to members only; for reference
Library Holdings: Book Volumes 255

PARK RAPIDS

M **NORTH COUNTRY MUSEUM OF ARTS,** Third & Court St, Park Rapids, MN 56470-0328; PO Box 328, Park Rapids, MN 56470-0328. Tel 218-237-5900; Elec Mail ncma77@gmail.com; *Newsletter Ed* Joan Brandach; *Treas* Bill Steen; *Cur & CEO* Ryan Loomis; *V Chmn* William Weeks; *Chmn Bd* Louie Falk; *Secy* Jean Ruzicka
Open May -Sept Tues-Thurs Sat 11AM-5PM; Admis $1; Estab 1977 to provide a cultural and educational center to house a permanent study collection of old school European paintings & to house traveling exhibitions for the benefit of persons of all ages through contact & work with art in its many forms; Maintains

Great Gallery, Members Gallery, four Revolving Galleries & studio; Average Annual Attendance: 6,000; Mem: 120; dues family $25, individual $15
Income: $25,000 (financed by mem, individual & corporate grants & gifts)
Special Subjects: African Art, Painting-European, Period Rooms
Collections: 160 Nigerian arts, crafts & artifacts; 45 Old School European paintings; 18 Contemporary Prints; 10 Contemporary paintings & artwork; 19 Drawings of Native American Children
Exhibitions: Annual Juried High School Fine Arts Exhibition
Activities: Classes for adults & children; docent training; lects open to pub, 2-3 lectrs per yr; concerts; gallery talks; tours; competitions; book traveling exhibs 5-6 per yr; originate traveling exhibs; mus shop selling original art, books, reproductions, prints and other memorabilia

RICHFIELD

M **NEW MERIKS SKETCH GALLERY,** 2200 W 66th St, #190 Richfield, MN 55423-2196. Tel 717-555-1212; Fax 717-555-1213; Elec Mail info@northeasternpenngallery.com; *CEO* Shawna Condon
Open Tues - Sat Noon - 9 PM, Sun Noon - 5 PM; Admis fee adult $2, student free; Estab as a sketch gallery in 1972. Displays various art works by local artists; Average Annual Attendance: 800
Income: $350,000
Library Holdings: CD-ROMs 100; Exhibition Catalogs; Photographs; Prints
Collections: Over 2,000 works by local artists in the Scranton area
Exhibitions: Various exhib by local & nationally renowned artists
Activities: Classes for adults & children; docent training; lects open to the public; 4 vis lectrs per year; gallery talks; tours; museum shop sells paintings & books

ROCHESTER

A **ROCHESTER ART CENTER,** 40 Civic Center Dr SE, Rochester, MN 55904-3773. Tel 507-282-8629; Fax 507-282-7737; Elec Mail info@rochesterartcenter.org; Internet Home Page Address: www.rochesterartcenter.org; *Exec Dir* Shannon Fitzgerald; *Facility Dir/Exhib Preparator* Phillip Ahnen; *Pub Programs Dir* Naura Anderson; *Chief Cur* Kris Douglas; *Event Mgr* Emily Tweten; *Develop Dir* Sandy Thompson; *Educ Coordr* Jason Pearson; *Admin Opers Dir* Joan Lovelace
Open Wed - Sat 10 AM - 5 PM, Thurs 10 AM - 9 PM, Sun Noon - 5 PM, cl Mon & Tues; Admis adults $5, seniors $3, students, children, res of Olmstead Co, mems & families in military free; Estab 1946, today the Rochester Art Center presents significant contemporary art exhibs; community-oriented pub progs; arts educ progs for pre-K, K-12, col & univ, & Life-Long Learning; & is a premier gathering place for community events; Maintains 4 galleries: Judy & Burton Onofrio Main Gallery, 3rd Floor Emerging Artists Gallery, Accent Gallery & ArtSpeak; Average Annual Attendance: 20,000; Mem: 750; dues $30 - $2,500
Income: city & state appropriations, fund raising & class tuition, private donations, corporate & foundation grants
Exhibitions: Varied exhibits in Contemporary Fine Arts & Crafts
Publications: Quarterly newsletter
Activities: Classes for adults & children; docent training; lects open to public; concerts, gallery talks; tours; scholarships; originate traveling exhibs; sales shop sell books, jewelry & gift items

SAINT CLOUD

M **SAINT CLOUD STATE UNIVERSITY,** Atwood Memorial Center Gallery, 720 4th Ave S, 118 Atwood Memorial Center Saint Cloud, MN 56301-4498. Tel 320-308-2205; Fax 320-308-1669; Elec Mail upbvisualarts@stcloudstate.edu; Internet Home Page Address: www.stcloudstate.edu/atwood; *Arts Advisor & Asst Dir* Janice Courtney; *Prog Dir* Jessica Ostman
Open Mon - Fri 8 AM - 7 PM, Sat & Sun 9 AM - 5 PM; No admis fee; Estab 1967 as a university student union facility; Gallery curated by the UPB Visual Arts Committee, designed for maximum exposure of art by local, regional, national & international artists
Income: Financed by student enrollment fee assessment
Collections: Collections of artists work from Minnesota & some national
Exhibitions: Monthly exhibits in various media
Activities: Artists' residencies, lect & workshops that coincide with exhibs; gallery talks

M **Kiehle Gallery,** 720 4th Ave S, 102 Kiehle Visual Arts Center Saint Cloud, MN 56301-4442. Tel 320-308-4283; Fax 320-308-2232; Elec Mail art@stcloudstate.edu; Internet Home Page Address: www.stcloudstate.edu/art; *Gallery Dir* Bill Gorcica
Open Mon - Fri 8 AM - 4 PM; No admis fee; Estab 1974 to expose col community to ideas & attitudes in the field of visual arts; The gallery has 1600 sq ft of enclosed multi use gallery floor space & 2500 sq ft outside sculpture ct; Average Annual Attendance: 15,000
Income: Financed by student fund appropriation
Activities: Lects open to public, 5 vis lectrs per yr; gallery talks; competitions; individual paintings & original objects of art lent to other departments on campus; lending collection contains original prints, paintings, photographs & sculpture; originates traveling exhibs

A **VISUAL ARTS MINNESOTA,** (Saint Cloud Community Arts Council) 913 W St Germain Saint Cloud, MN 56301; PO Box 972, Saint Cloud, MN 56302-0972. Tel 320-257-3108; Fax 320-257-3111; Elec Mail vam@visualartsminnesota.org; Internet Home Page Address: www.visualartsminnesota.org; *Exec Dir* Kerry K Osberg
Estab 1973 to serve as an advocate & a resource for visual artists, art groups, educators & the community; Mem: 100; dues $20-$250
Income: Grants, pvt support (nonprofit)
Collections: Works donated by artists or friends/family of artists popular at various times in the community; collection can be loaned for a small fee

Exhibitions: Essential Art Show with awards; High School Art Competition; Children's Art Exhibit, Art ala Carte with awards
Publications: Ann newsletter
Activities: Artists critiques; scholarships offered; individual painting & original objects of art lent for public display; lending collection contains original artwork, original prints, sculptures & slides; sales shop sells books & original art

SAINT JOSEPH

M COLLEGE OF SAINT BENEDICT, Gorecki Gallery & Gallery Lounge, 37 S College Ave, Benedict Arts Center Saint Joseph, MN 56374-2001. Tel 320-363-5792; Fax 320-363-6097; Elec Mail jdubbeldeekuhn@csbsju.edu; Internet Home Page Address: www.csbsju.edu/finearts
Open Mon - Sat 10 AM -9PM; Sun noon-9PM; No admis fee; Estab 1963; contemporary artworks from established & emerging regional, national, & international artists; Average Annual Attendance: 15,000
Income: Financed by college
Special Subjects: Mixed Media, Photography, Sculpture, Drawings, Prints, Ceramics
Collections: Contemporary coll of crafts, drawings, paintings, prints and sculpture; East Asian Coll of ceramics, crafts, drawings, fibers and prints; Miscellaneous African, New Guinea, Indian and European
Exhibitions: Ongoing exhibitions every 6-8 weeks; contemporary artworks in all media, bookarts
Activities: Lects open to pub, gallery talks; tours; concerts; competitions with awards; individual paintings & original objects of art lent to dept faculty & staff members of the college

SAINT PAUL

M ARCHIVES OF THE ARCHDIOCESE OF ST PAUL & MINNEAPOLIS, 226 Summit Ave, Saint Paul, MN 55102-2121. Tel 651-291-4485; Fax 651-290-1629; Elec Mail archives@archspm.org; *Archivist* Steven T Granger
Estab 1987 to collect & preserve materials of archival value relating to the Catholic Church of the Archdiocese of Saint Paul & Minneapolis
Income: Financed by Diocesan funds
Special Subjects: Religious Art
Collections: Artifacts; documents; letters; painting; papers & photographs
Activities: Lects, 2 vis lectrs per yr

M HAMLINE UNIVERSITY STUDIO ARTS & ART HISTORY DEPTS, Gallery, 1536 Hewitt Ave, Drew Fine Arts Center Saint Paul, MN 55104-1205. Tel 651-523-2396; Fax 651-523-3066; Elec Mail jschlink01@hamline.edu; Internet Home Page Address: www.hamline.edu/cla/acad/depts_programs/art_art_history/index.html; *Dir Exhibs* John-Mark T Schlink; *Registrar* Kimberly Arleth
Open Mon - Fri 10 AM - 4 PM, cl holidays; Display of original modern works from BC to 21st century; extensive color slide library of paintings, architecture, sculpture, minor arts & graphics, prints, ceramics
Publications: Icons of Perfection: Figurative Sculpture from Africa

M IFP MN CENTER FOR MEDIA ARTS, 2446 University Ave W, Ste 100 Saint Paul, MN 55114. Tel 651-644-1912; Fax 651-644-5708; Elec Mail word@ifpmn.org; Internet Home Page Address: www.ifpmn.org; *Contact* Jane Minton

M MACALESTER COLLEGE, Macalester College Art Gallery, 1600 Grand Ave, Saint Paul, MN 55105-1899. Tel 651-696-6416; Fax 651-696-6266; Elec Mail gallery@macalester.edu; Internet Home Page Address: www.macalester.edu; *Gallery Cur* Gregory Fitz
Open Mon - Fri 10 AM - 4 PM, Thurs until 8PM, Sat & Sun Noon-4 PM, cl June -Aug, national holidays & school vacations; No admis fee; Estab 1964 as a col facility to bring contemporary art exhibs to the students, faculty & community; Average Annual Attendance: 18,000
Special Subjects: Painting-American, Photography, Prints, Sculpture, African Art, Textiles, Ceramics, Pottery, Painting-European, Porcelain, Asian Art, Tapestries, Painting-German
Collections: African Art; Asian & British Ceramics; Oriental Art; contemporary & historical prints, paintings, sculpture & crafts
Exhibitions: Temporary, traveling & student exhibitions with special emphasis on international & multi-cultural
Activities: Lects open to pub; concerts; gallery talks; tours; competitions with awards; individual paintings & original objects of art lent; lending collections contains original paintings, paintings & sculpture; book traveling exhibs; originates traveling exhibs; sales shop sells art books & supplies
L DeWitt Wallace Library, 1600 Grand Ave, Saint Paul, MN 55105. Tel 651-696-6345; Internet Home Page Address: www.macalester.edu; *Dir Library* Teresa Fishel
Open Sep-May daily 8AM-Noon; No admis fee; Estab 1964; Circ 66,531
Library Holdings: Book Volumes 273,668; Cards; Cassettes; Fiche; Framed Reproductions; Pamphlets; Periodical Subscriptions 1311; Reels
Special Subjects: Art History
Activities: Individual paintings & original objects of art lent to faculty & staff of the college

A MINNESOTA HISTORICAL SOCIETY, 345 Kellogg Blvd W, Saint Paul, MN 55102-1903. Tel 651-259-3000; Tel 800-657-3773; Fax 651-296-3343; Internet Home Page Address: www.mnhs.org; *Media Relations Mgr* Marjorie Nugent; *CEO & Dir* Nina M Archabal; *Dir Historic Sites* William Keyes; *Pub Rels* Lory Sutton; *Develop Officer* Mark Haidet; *MHS Pres* Pamela McClanahan; *Head Exhib* Dan Spock; *Dir Finance* William Irrgang; *Mus Shop Mgr* Meta DeVine; *Deputy Dir* Michael Fox; *Deputy Dir External Relations* Andrea Kajer
Open Tues 10 AM - 8 PM, Wed - Fri noon - 5 PM, Sat 9 AM - 4 PM, Sun noon - 4 PM; Admis $10 adults, $8 seniors & college students, $5 children 6-17, MHS members & children 5 & under no charge; Estab 1849 to collect, preserve & make

available to the pub the history of Minnesota; 40,000 sq ft of exhibition space; Average Annual Attendance: 500,000; Mem: 20,000; dues household $75, individual $50, senior citizens $45
Income: Financed by endowment, mem & state appropriation
Library Holdings: Audio Tapes; Book Volumes; CD-ROMs; Cards; Cassettes; Clipping Files; Compact Disks; Memorabilia; Original Documents; Other Holdings; Pamphlets; Periodical Subscriptions; Photographs; Prints; Slides; Video Tapes
Special Subjects: Historical Material
Collections: Archives; art works; books; maps; manuscripts; museum artifacts relating to the history of Minnesota; newspapers; photographs
Exhibitions: Minnesota A to Z; Exhibits on families, communities; Minnesota Music, Minnesota Territory
Publications: Minnesota History, quarterly; History Matters, 6 issues per year; books & exhibit catalogs
Activities: Classes for adults & children; lects open to pub; tours; concerts; gallery talks; 2-3 book traveling exhibs per yr; originate traveling exhibs; mus shop sells books, magazines, prints, reproductions, original art, slides & other merchandise
L Library, 345 Kellogg Blvd W, Saint Paul, MN 55102-1903. Tel 651-296-2143; Fax 651-297-7436; Elec Mail reference@mnhs.org; *Asst Dir Library* Michael Fox; *Dir* Richard Morphy
Open Tues, Wed, Fri & Sat 10 AM - 5 PM; No admis fee; For reference
Library Holdings: Audio Tapes; Book Volumes 500,000; Cassettes; Clipping Files; Exhibition Catalogs; Fiche; Filmstrips; Kodachrome Transparencies; Manuscripts; Memorabilia; Motion Pictures; Pamphlets; Prints; Records; Reels; Sculpture; Slides; Video Tapes
Collections: 19th & 20th centuries art relating to Minnesota

M North West Company Fur Post, 12551 Voyager Ln, Pine City, MN 55063; PO Box 51, Pine City, MN 55063-0051. Tel 320-629-6356; Fax 320-629-4667; Elec Mail nwcfurpost@mnhs.org; Internet Home Page Address: www.mnhs.org/nwcfurpost; *Site Mgr* Patrick Schifferdecker
Open May 1 - Labor Day Mon - Sat 10 AM - 5 PM, Sun 12 noon - 5 PM; Sept - Oct Fri - Sat 10 AM - 5 PM, Sun 12 noon - 5 PM; Admis adults $8, seniors $6, tours, groups & children $5, mems free; Estab 1965; mus is reconstruction of an 1804 Northwest company wintering post & Ojibwe encampment; 2700 sq ft exhib space; handicapped-accessible; historical site; Average Annual Attendance: 13,500; Mem: Pvt nonprofit org; FT paid 1, PT paid 18; 8th congressional dist. See Minn Historical Society for mem details
Collections: Recreated 1804 Ojibwe encampment
Activities: Classes for adults; formal educ progs for children; dramatic progs; concerts; guided tours; hobby workshops & hands-on activities; lects open to pub; 2-3 per yr; mus shop sells books, original art, reproductions, prints & misc gift items

M MINNESOTA MUSEUM OF AMERICAN ART, 408 Saint Peter St, Ste 419, Saint Paul, MN 55102-1111. Tel 651-797-2571; Fax 651-797-4748; Elec Mail info@mmaa.org; Internet Home Page Address: www.mmaa.org; *Exec Dir* Kristin Makholm
Open Thurs 11 AM - 6 PM, Sat & Sun 10 AM - 4 PM, (while under construction call 651-222-6080 during open hrs to make accessibility arrangements); No admis fee; Estab 1927 as the Saint Paul Gallery & School of Art; Average Annual Attendance: 50,000; Mem: 800; dues household $50, individual $35
Income: $350,000 (financed by endowment, individual contributions, mem, foundation & government grants)
Library Holdings: Audio Tapes; Book Volumes; CD-ROMs; Cassettes; Clipping Files; Compact Disks; Exhibition Catalogs; Pamphlets; Periodical Subscriptions; Slides
Special Subjects: Drawings, Painting-American, Photography, Prints, Sculpture, Watercolors, Bronzes, Ceramics, Crafts, Pottery, Etchings & Engravings, Collages, Portraits, Posters, Glass
Collections: American Art; contemporary art of the Upper Midwest; Paul Manship; Late 19th & 20th Century Art, Native American; George Morrison
Publications: Annual report
Activities: lects open to public; gallery talks; tours; originated traveling exhibs to midsized art museums

L SAINT PAUL PUBLIC LIBRARY, Central Adult Public Services, 90 W Fourth St, Saint Paul, MN 55102. Tel 651-266-7000; Elec Mail charlenm@library.stpaul.libmn.us; Internet Home Page Address: www.stpaul.lib.mn.us; *Fine Arts Coll Develop* Charlene McKenzie; *Library Dir* Melanie Huggins; *Media Rels* Sheree Savage
Open Mon 11:30 AM - 8 PM, Tues, Wed & Fri 9 AM - 5:30 PM, Thurs 9 AM - 8 PM, Sat 11 AM - 4 PM; Estab 1882; Circ 92,642
Income: Financed by city appropriation
Purchases: $42,700
Library Holdings: Book Volumes 16,000; Clipping Files; Exhibition Catalogs; Other Holdings Compact discs 4000; Periodical Subscriptions 95; Video Tapes 4500
Collections: Field coll of popular sheet music

M SAINT PAUL WESTERN SCULPTURE PARK, c/o Public Art Saint Paul, 351 Kellogg Blvd E Saint Paul, MN 55101. Tel 651-290-0921; Fax 651-292-0345; Elec Mail johnhock@franconia.org; Internet Home Page Address: www.publicartstpaul.org; *Dir* John Hock
Open daily from dawn to dusk
Collections: contemporary sculpture

M UNIVERSITY OF MINNESOTA, Paul Whitney Larson Gallery, 2017 Buford, Saint Paul, MN 55108. Tel 612-625-0214; Fax 612-624-8749; Internet Home Page Address: www.spsc.umn.eduvacprespective.html; *Gallery Mgr* Tricia Schweitzer
Open Mon - Wed 10 AM - 5 PM, Thurs 10 AM - 8 PM, Fri 10 - 5 PM; No admis fee; Estab 1979 to bring art of great variety into the daily lives of students & university community; Intimate gallery featuring traditional & contemporary visual arts
Income: Financed by student fees
Publications: Annual report & activity summary

Activities: Mus shop sells jewelry

M **Goldstein Museum of Design,** 241 McNeal Hall, 1985 Buford Ave Saint Paul, MN 55108-6134; 364 McNeal Hall, Saint Paul, MN 55108. Tel 612-624-7434; Fax 612-625-5762; Elec Mail gmd@umn.edu; Internet Home Page Address: www.goldstein.design.umn.edu; *Dir* Lin Nelson-Mayson; *Asst Cur* Jean McElvain; *Registrar* Eunice Haugen; *Admin Asst* Barbara Lutz; *Grant Writer* Kathleen Campbell
Open Tues - Fri 10 AM - 5 PM, Thurs 10 AM - 5 PM, Sat & Sun 1:30 - 4:30 PM; No admis fee; donations welcome; Estab 1976, collects, exhibits & researches design; Average Annual Attendance: 14,000; Mem: 315; mem $20 & up
Income: Financed by private gifts, mem & grants
Library Holdings: Book Volumes; Clipping Files; Exhibition Catalogs; Periodical Subscriptions
Special Subjects: Folk Art, Interior Design, Architecture, Textiles, Graphics, Textiles, Costumes, Ceramics, Crafts, Pottery, Decorative Arts, Furniture, Glass, Porcelain, Silver, Metalwork, Carpets & Rugs, Tapestries, Embroidery, Laces, Pewter, Leather
Collections: Historic apparel & accessories; 20th century designer apparel & accessories; historic & contemporary decorative arts; furniture; textiles; graphic commun
Publications: Exhibition catalogs
Activities: Educ dept classes for adults; lects open to pub, 3-5 vis lectrs per yr; gallery talks; tours; College of Design Senior award; collection objects lent to other institutions; book traveling exhibs to general mus, 1 per yr; originate traveling exhibs to academic museums & galleries; mus shop sells books & notecards

A **WOMEN'S ART REGISTRY OF MINNESOTA GALLERY,** 550 Rice St, Saint Paul, MN 55103-2116. Tel 651-292-1188; Elec Mail info@thewarm.org; Internet Home Page Address: www.thewarm.org; *Board Pres* Bethany Whitehead; *Treas* Phyllis Burdette
Estab 1975; Office only; Mem: 170; dues $60; women artists
Income: Financed by mem, grants for projects & operating expenses
Collections: Members work on display in one area
Exhibitions: Local & national exhibitions; Annual Juried Members Exhibit
Publications: e-warm-ups, biweekly online publication
Activities: Educ dept; Fresh Art; Mentor Prog; lects open to pub; 1 vis lectrs per yr; gallery talks; competitions with awards; juror awards for juried mem exhibs; individual paintings lent & original objects of art lent to non-profit groups for fee

SPRING GROVE

M **BLUFF COUNTRY ARTISTS GALLERY,** 111 W Main St, Spring Grove, MN 55974. Tel 507-498-2787; Elec Mail bcagallery@springgrove.coop; Internet Home Page Address: bluffcountryartistsgallery.org

ST PAUL

M **MINNESOTA HISTORICAL SOCIETY,** Minnesota State Capitol Historic Site, 75 Rev Dr Martin Luther King Jr Blvd, St Paul, MN 55155-1605. Tel 651-296-2881; Fax 651-297-1502; Internet Home Page Address: www.mnhs.org/statecapitol; *Historic Site Mgr* Brian Pease; *Prog Mgr* Linda Cameron; *Tour Registrar* Candice Christensen; *Site Supv* Jaymie Korman
Open Mon - Fri 9 AM - 5 PM, with the last tour at 3 PM; Sat 10 AM - 3 PM with the last tour at 2 PM; Sun 1 - 4 PM, last tour at 3 PM; cl all holidays except President's Day; No admis fee to mus; Special Event fees: adults $8, seniors $7, children 6 - 12 $5, educ grps $2 - $5, mems $2 discount; Estab 1969; Minn State Capitol bldg designed by renowned 19th-century architect Cass Gilbert; 377,000 sq ft exhib space. Nonprofit org; Average Annual Attendance: 205,508; Mem: North Star Circle $1000, Sustaining $500, Contributing $250, Assoc $125, Household $65, Sr Household & Indiv $55, Sr Indiv $45
Special Subjects: Decorative Arts, Architecture, Furniture, Portraits, Painting-American, Sculpture, Restorations, Military Art
Collections: Over 800 pieces of orig 1905 furniture; works of art throughout the capitol that includes 33 canvas murals, 16 paintings, 15 plaques, 30 statues/busts, 37 governor's portraits and 21 historic battle flags; over 200 vols on historical info on the state capitol
Publications: Minnesota History, quarterly magazine
Activities: Year-round progs on four themes of the capitol: Art, Architecture, Minn History & State Govt; formal educ for adults, students & children; guided tours; temporary exhibs; books, postcards, small gifts & other mus related items for sale; cafe on-site (legislative session only)

WAYZATA

M **MINNETONKA CENTER FOR THE ARTS,** 2240 N Shore Dr, Wayzata, MN 55391-9347. Tel 952-473-7361x16; Fax 952-473-7363; Elec Mail information@minnetonkaarts.org; Internet Home Page Address: www.minnetonkaarts.org

WHITE BEAR LAKE

M **WHITE BEAR CENTER FOR THE ARTS,** Gallery, 1280 N Brich Lake Blvd, White Bear Lake, MN 55110. Tel 651-407-0597; Fax 651-429-1569; Elec Mail wbca@whitebeararts.org; Internet Home Page Address: whitebeararts.org

WORTHINGTON

A **NOBLES COUNTY ART CENTER,** 407 12th St, Worthington, MN 56187; PO Box 343, Worthington, MN 56187-0343. Tel 507-372-8245; Elec Mail noblearts@knology.net; *Co-Dir* Martin Bunge; *Co-Dir* Jean Bunge; *Pres* Tricia Mikle
Open Mon - Fri 2 - 4:30 PM, cl Sat, Sun & holidays; No admis fee; Estab 1960 to nourish the arts & to bring arts & cultures of other communities & nations, civilizations to Nobles County & the surrounding area so residents become more universal in their thinking; Circ 300; Located on the ground floor; handicapped accessible; Average Annual Attendance: 3,000; Mem: 100; dues $10-$500; annual meeting in Jan
Income: Financed by mem dues, donations, memorial gifts, county appropriation bequest & grants
Collections: International art
Exhibitions: Two juried fine art shows per year; annual student exhibition; the work of area artists; new exhibit every month
Publications: Gallery, monthly newsletter; monthly press releases
Activities: Classes for adults & children; lects open to public; concerts; gallery talks; tours; competitions with awards; originate traveling exhibs

MISSISSIPPI

BAY SAINT LOUIS

M **ALICE MOSELEY FOLK ART AND ANTIQUE MUSEUM,** 511 Spanish Acres Dr, Bay Saint Louis, MS 39520-3217. Tel 228-467-9223; Tel 717-725-6851; Elec Mail alicemoseley@gmail.com; Internet Home Page Address: www.alicemoseley.com; *Cur* W L Tim Moseley
Open Tues - Fri Noon - 5 PM, Sat 10 AM - 5 PM, Sun 1 - 4 PM, other times by chance or appointment; No admis fee

BELZONI

M **CATFISH CAPITAL VISITORS CENTER AND MUSEUM,** 111 Magnolia St, Belzoni, MS 39038; PO Box 385, Belzoni, MS 39038-0385. Tel 800-408-4838; 662-247-4838; Fax 662-247-4805; Elec Mail catfish@belzonicable.com; Internet Home Page Address: www.belzonims.com; *Exec Dir* Steve Anderson
Open Mon-Fri 9AM-5PM; No admis fee
Collections: local history & culture; photographs; paintings; personal artifacts; sculpture

M **THE ETHEL WRIGHT MOHAMED STITCHERY MUSEUM,** 307 Central St, Belzoni, MS 39038-3603; PO Box 254, Belzoni, MS 39038-0254. Tel 662-247-3633; Fax 662-247-1433; Elec Mail hwilson493@aol.com; Internet Home Page Address: www.mamasdreamworld.com; *Cur* Carol Mohamed Ivy; *Asst Cur* Amy Harris Hawkins; *Asst Cur & Webmaster* Hazel Mohamed Wilson
Open by appt only; Admis adults $2, children & bus driver no admis fee; Mus is former home of Ethel Wright Mohamed, award-winning artist who lived from 1906-1992 and was also known as "Mississippi's Grandma Moses of Stitchery"; mus contains stitchery created by the artist that centered on her family & life
Special Subjects: Decorative Arts, Folk Art, Tapestries
Collections: Coll of stitchery & sketches
Publications: My Life in Pictures, by Ethel Wright Mohamed
Activities: Guided tours; mus shop sells reproductions, prints & cards

CLARKSDALE

M **DELTA BLUES MUSEUM,** (Carnegie Public Library) 1 Blues Alley, Clarksdale, MS 38614-4336; PO Box 459, Clarksdale, MS 38614-0459. Tel 662-627-6820; Fax 662-627-7263; Elec Mail info@deltabluesmuseum.org; Internet Home Page Address: www.deltabluesmuseum.org; *Group Tour Mgr* Maie Smith; *Gift Shop Mgr* Christopher Coleman; *Dir* Shelley Ritter
Open Nov-Feb Mon-Sat 10AM-5PM, Mar-Oct Mon-Sat 9AM-5PM; Admis $7 adults; $5 student and seniors; group rates available; Estab 1979 to preserve & promote understanding of MS Delta blues music & heritage; 5,000 sq ft of exhibits; Average Annual Attendance: 20,000
Income: $283,000 (financed by gift shop, federal & state grants, mem & corporate donors)
Special Subjects: Afro-American Art, Photography, Portraits, Pottery, Maps, Architecture, Painting-American, Sculpture, Costumes, Crafts, Folk Art, Primitive art, Posters
Collections: Books & tapes; Interpretative exhibits; memorabilia; photography & art (sculpture, paintings); recordings; stage & music; videos
Exhibitions: All Shook Up; Bancas to Blues: West African Stringed Instrument traditions & the origin of pre-civil War American Music; MS Roots of American Music; Vintage American Guitar Collection; Blues Booze & BBQ; Give My Poor Heart Ease
Publications: Delta Blues Museum Brochure
Activities: Monthly Blues performances; classes for adults; classes for children; music lessons; Traveling Trunk; lects open to pub, 10 vis lectrs per yr; lending of original objects of art to schools- traveling trunk; books traveling exhibs 1-2 per yr; mus shop sells books, magazines, original art, reproductions, prints

CLEVELAND

M **DELTA STATE UNIVERSITY,** Fielding L Wright Art Center, 1003 W Sunflower Rd, Cleveland, MS 38733-0001. Tel 662-846-4729; Fax 662-846-4726; Internet Home Page Address: www.deltastate.edu; *Exhib Chmn* Patricia Brown; *Chmn Dept* Ronald G Koehler
Open Mon - Thurs 8 AM - 8:30 PM, Fri 8 AM - 4 PM, cl weekends & school holidays; No admis fee; Estab 1968 as an educational gallery for the benefit of the students, but serves the entire area for changing art shows; it is the only facility of this nature in the Mississippi Delta Region; Three gallery areas; Average Annual Attendance: 3,600
Income: Financed by state appropriation
Collections: Delta State University permanent coll; Photography Study Coll; Ruth Atkinson Holmes Collection; Marie Hull Collection; Smith-Patterson Memorial

Collection; Whittington Memorial Collection; Joe & Lucy Howorth Collection; John Miller Photography Collection; James Townes Medal Collection
Publications: Announcements of exhibitions, monthly during fall, winter & spring; exhibit catalogs
Activities: Lects open to public, 10 vis lectrs per yr; gallery talks; tours; competitions; exten dept serving the Mississippi Delta Region; individual paintings & original objects of art lent to offices of campus; lending collection contains color reproductions, film strips, motion pictures, original art works, 30,000 slides; originates traveling exhibs

L **Roberts LaForge Library,** Le Flore Cir, Cleveland, MS 38733-0001. Tel 662-846-4440; Fax 662-846-4443; Elec Mail refdesk@deltastate.edu; Internet Home Page Address: www.library.deltastate.edu; *Dir Library Svcs* Terry S Latour; *Asst Dir* Jeff H Slagell
Open Mon-Thurs 7:30 AM-10 PM, Fri 7:30 AM-4 PM, Sat 10 AM-5 PM, Sun 2 PM-10 PM; No admis fee; Estab as gen acad library covering all topics for students & staff; Mabelle Smith and William Mountjoy Garrad Collection of Art
Income: col funding
Library Holdings: Audio Tapes; Book Volumes 7500; CD-ROMs; Cards; Cassettes; Clipping Files; Compact Disks; DVDs; Exhibition Catalogs; Fiche; Filmstrips; Framed Reproductions; Kodachrome Transparencies; Micro Print; Original Art Works; Periodical Subscriptions 31; Photographs; Prints; Records; Reels; Sculpture; Slides 381; Video Tapes 78
Special Subjects: Art History, Film, Illustration, Photography, Drawings, Etchings & Engravings, Graphic Design, Painting-European, Historical Material, History of Art & Archaeology, Portraits, Printmaking, Interior Design, Art Education, Pottery
Collections: Sculptures & paintings for variety of Mississippi Delta artists

KAPPA PI INTERNATIONAL HONORARY ART FRATERNITY
For further information, see National and Regional Organizations

COLUMBUS

M **COLUMBUS HISTORIC FOUNDATION,** (Columbus & Lowndes County Historical Society) Blewett-Harrison-Lee Museum, 316 7th St, Columbus, MS 39710-1300. Tel 662-329-3533, 800-327-2686; Fax 662-329-1027; Internet Home Page Address: www.historic-columbus.org; *Cur* Carolyn Neault; *CAS Gen* Steph D Lee
Open Fri 10 AM - 4 PM or by appointment; Admis $5, students free; Estab 1960 for a memorabilia 1832-1907 pertaining to Lowndes County preserved & exhibited; Average Annual Attendance: 2,000; Mem: 210; dues $5; annual meeting third Thurs in Sept
Income: $600 (financed by mem, bequests, donations, memorials, sale of souvenirs)
Special Subjects: Historical Material
Collections: 100 years of artifacts, books, china, crystal, clothes, flags, furniture, jewelry, pictures, portraits, swords, wedding gowns
Activities: Docent training; tours for school children; awards; mus shop sells books & souvenirs

M **MISSISSIPPI UNIVERSITY FOR WOMEN,** Fine Arts Gallery, 1100 College St, MuW-70, Columbus, MS 39701-5800. Tel 662-329-7341; Tel 662-241-6976; Fax 662-241-7815; Elec Mail aswills@muw.edu; *Recorder* Shawn Dickey; *Cur* Alex Stelioeswills
Open Mon - Fri 2 AM - Noon, 1 -4PM every day the univ is open; No admis fee; Estab 1948, new bldg 1960, renovated 1998; 3 galleries with 350 running ft wall space, the main gallery with 173 ft wall space covered with fabric; Average Annual Attendance: 1,200
Income: Financed by state appropriation & private funds
Special Subjects: Drawings, Painting-American, Prints
Collections: American Art; paintings, sculpture, photographs, drawings, ceramics, prints; Permanent collection of Mississippi artists
Exhibitions: Frequent special and circulating exhibitions; Selections from permanent collection, periodically
Activities: Visiting artists prog; workshops; lects open to pub, 4 vis lectrs per yr; gallery talks; tours; scholarships; individual paintings & original objects of art lent to offices & pub student areas on the campus; lending collection contains 400 original prints, 300 paintings, 100 records; book traveling exhibs; originate traveling exhibs

GREENWOOD

M **COTTONLANDIA MUSEUM,** 1608 Hwy 82 W, Greenwood, MS 38930-2725. Tel 662-453-0925; Fax 662-455-7556; Elec Mail cottonlandia@bellsouth.net; Internet Home Page Address: www.cottonlandia.org/museum.asp; *Exec Dir* Robin Seage Person; *Mus Shop Mgr* Lyllian Tubbs; *Pres* Tommy Ellett; *Pres (V)* Jean Codney; *Interim Dir* Dave Freeman; *Educ & Art Coordr* Jennifer Whites
Open Mon - Fri 9 AM - 5 PM, Sat - Sun 2 - 5 PM; Admis adults $5, seniors 65 & over $3.50, students $3, children 3-18 $2; Estab 1969 as a mus for tourism & learning facility for schools; Two well lighted rooms plus available space in mus for temporary & competition, permanent hangings in some corridors; Average Annual Attendance: 7,500; Mem: 270; dues vary; annual meeting early Nov
Income: Financed by mem, county appropriation, donation & admis
Library Holdings: Book Volumes; Clipping Files; Original Documents; Periodical Subscriptions; Photographs
Collections: Permanent collection of works of past Cottonlandia Collection; competition winners; other accessions by Mississippi Artists
Exhibitions: Temporary exhibs change every two months
Activities: Classes for adults; lects open to pub; gallery talks; tours; competitions with awards; individual paintings lent; lending collection contains nature artifacts; mus shop sells books, original art, reproductions, prints & natural stone jewelry

HATTIESBURG

M **UNIVERSITY OF SOUTHERN MISSISSIPPI,** Museum of Art, Dept of Art & Design, 118 College Dr, #5033 Hattiesburg, MS 39406-0001. Tel 601-266-5200; Elec Mail artmuseum@usm.edu; Internet Home Page Address: www.usm.edu/visualarts/museum.php; *Dir* Dr. Jan Siesling; *Asst Dir* Mark Rigsby
Open Jan - May & Sept - Dec: Tues - Fri 10 AM - 5 PM, Sat 10 AM - 4 PM; June - Aug: Tues - Fri noon - 5 PM; No admis fee
Collections: Regional, international, historical & contemporary artwork

L **UNIVERSITY OF SOUTHERN MISSISSIPPI,** McCain Library & Archives, 118 College Dr #5148, Hattiesburg, MS 39406-0002. Tel 601-266-4345; Internet Home Page Address: www.lib.usm.edu/mccain.html; *Dir* Kay L Wall, MLS; *Cur* Ellen Ruffin; *Archivist* Diane Ross; *Librn* Peggy Price
Open Mon - Fri 8 AM - 5 PM; No admis fee; University estab 1912, library estab 1976; For reference only
Collections: Cleanth Brooks Collection; de Grummond Children's Literature Research Collection (historical children's literature & illustrations); Earnest A Walen Collection; Genealogy Collection
Publications: Juvenile Miscellany, 2 times per year

JACKSON

M **MISSISSIPPI MUSEUM OF ART,** 380 S Lamar St, Jackson, MS 39201-4007. Tel 601-960-1515; Fax 601-960-1505; Elec Mail mmart@netdoor.com; Internet Home Page Address: www.msmuseumart.org; *Exec Dir* Betsy Bradley; *Deputy Dir Progs* Daniel Piersol; *Cur Educ, Docents & Vols* Ivy Alley; *Registrar* Joanna Biglane
Open Tues-Sat 10AM-5PM, Sun noon-5PM, cl Mon; Admis adults $5, seniors $4, students age 6 - college $3, mems & children 5 & under free; group rates available; Chartered in 1911; Mus opened 1978; East Exhibition Galleries 6500 sq ft; West Exhibition Galleries 2600 sq ft; Graphics Study Center 800 sq ft, houses exhibitions area, study & storage rooms; Open Gallery 2000 sq ft, includes special power, lighting & water requirements for technological media; Upper & Lower Atrium Galleries 4500 sq ft & outdoor Sculpture Garden; Nonprofit Corporation; Average Annual Attendance: 40,000; Mem: 1800; dues Rembrandt Soc $1000, benefactor $500, donor $250, patron $100, family $50, individual $35, senior $25
Income: $130,000 (financed by endowment, mem, contributions, pub sector grants & appropriations, earned income)
Purchases: A Bierstadt, Edward Potthast, Eugene Auffrey, Birney Imes III (45 color photographs) Thomas Salley Croprey, A B Davies
Library Holdings: Book Volumes; Clipping Files; Exhibition Catalogs; Memorabilia; Original Art Works; Pamphlets; Periodical Subscriptions; Photographs; Prints
Special Subjects: Photography, Pre-Columbian Art, Prints, Asian Art
Collections: American art by artists incl: Albert Bierstadt, Arthur B Davies, Robert Henri, George Inness, Georgia O'Keefe, Reginald Marsh, Thomas Sully & James McNeill Whistler; Mississippi Coll incl works by 19th c painter G Ruder Donoho, photographer & writer Eudora Welty, & outsider artists Theora Hamblett, Elizabeth Wright Mohammed & Sultan Rogers in addition to contemporary & historical works by Mississippi artists & quilt coll; 19th c British paintings by Thomas Lawrence & Thomas Sully; European Coll incl impressions by Picasso, Joan Miro, Marc Chagall & Rembrandt
Publications: Bi-monthly newsletter; selected exhibition catalogs; (book) Andrew Wyeth: Close Friends
Activities: Classes for adults & children; docent training; weekend activities for children; community progs; lects open to pub, some for members only, 3 vis lectrs per yr, 10 vis artists per yr; tours; competitions; music series; concerts; receptions; Scholastic Art Awards; scholarships offered; individual paintings & original objects of art lent to qualifying mus & other institutions & educational/cultural centers; lending collection contains 3500 original art works, 700 original prints, 300 paintings, 150 photographs & 50 sculptures; book traveling exhibs; originate traveling exhibs to other mus, art, educational & cultural institutions, Mississippi, Affiliate Network; mus shop sells books, magazines, reproductions, prints, posters, slides, paper goods, designer items, Mississippi crafts, jewelry, pottery

L **Howorth Library,** 201 E Pascagoula St, Jackson, MS 39201. Tel 601-960-1515; Fax 601-960-1505; Elec Mail mmart@netdoor.com; Internet Home Page Address: www.msmuseumart.org; *Cur Educ* J Marshall Adams; *Asst Cur Educ* Lianne Takemori; *VChmn* Chuck Dunn; *Auxiliary VPres* Margo Heath; *Dir Finance* Sheryl Trim; *Registrar* Tobin Fortenberry; *Dir* Betsy Bradley; *Office Mgr* Sonya Croins; *Chief Preparator* LC Tucker; *Dir Develop* Shari Veazey; *Asst to Dir* Nina Moss; *Visitor Info Center* Annette French; *Asst Preparator* Melvin Johnson; *Deputy Dir Prog* Rene Paul Barilleaux; *Mus Shop Mgr* Erdell Hart
Open Mon - Fri 10 AM - 5 PM by appointment; For reference only, open to the general pub
Income: Museum funded
Library Holdings: Book Volumes 10,000; Clipping Files; Exhibition Catalogs; Pamphlets; Periodical Subscriptions 12; Slides; Video Tapes
Collections: Walter Anderson Collection on Slides; Marie Hull Collection of Art Reference Books; Metropolitan Miniature Album; E Benezit Vol 1 - 14, 1999
Activities: Classes for children; docent training; lects open to pub; concerts; gallery talks; tours; sponsoring of competitions; 5 vis lectrs per yr

LAUREL

M **LAUREN ROGERS MUSEUM OF ART,** 565 N 5th Ave, Laurel, MS 39440; PO Box 1108, Laurel, MS 39441-1108. Tel 601-649-6374; Fax 601-649-6379; Elec Mail info@lrma.org; Internet Home Page Address: www.lrma.org; *Registrar* Tommie Rodgers; *Mktg Dir* Holly Green; *Dir* George Bassi; *Bus Mgr* Jo-Lyn Helton; *Develop Dir* Allyn Boone; *Cur* Jill Chancey; *Cur Educ* Mandy Buchanan; *Outreach Educ Coordr* Angie King; *Visitor Svcs Coordr* Lizabeth Brumley
Open Tues - Sat 10 AM -4:45 PM, Sun 1 - 4 PM, cl Mon; No admis fee; Estab 1923 as a reference & research library & mus of art for pub use & employment; Six smaller galleries open off large American Gallery; these include European Gallery, Catherine Marshall Gardiner Basket collection, Gibbons Silver Gallery plus 2 temporary exhibit galleries; Average Annual Attendance: 20,000; Mem: Dues $15-$2500
Income: Financed by endowment (Eastman Memorial Foundation), mem, donations, fundraising, events government appropriations, grants
Library Holdings: Auction Catalogs; Book Volumes; Cards; DVDs; Exhibition Catalogs; Original Documents; Periodical Subscriptions; Video Tapes
Special Subjects: Painting-American, Prints, Painting-European, Silver, Period Rooms, Bookplates & Bindings

Collections: European Artists of the 19th century; 18th-century English Georgian Silver; 19th- & 20th-century American Paintings; Native American; Native American Baskets

Exhibitions: Annual schedule of exhibitions by regional & nationally recognized artists; collections exhibits

Publications: Gibbons Silver Catalog; Jean Leon Gerome Ferris, 1863-1930: American Painter Historian; Handbook of The Collections; Mississippi Portraiture; By Native Hands: Woven Treasures from the Lauren Rogers Mus Art; The Floating World: Ukiyo-e Prints from the Wallace B Rogers Collection

Activities: Workshop for adults & children; musical concerts; docent training; lects open to pub; concerts; gallery talks; tours; individual art objects lent to AAM accredited mus or galleries; mus shop sells books, prints, Choctaw baskets, silver, jewelry, toys, Mississippi arts & crafts & t-shirts

L **Library,** PO Box 1108, Laurel, MS 39441-1108. Tel 601-649-6374; Fax 601-649-6379; Elec Mail lrmalibrary@c-gate.net; Internet Home Page Address: www.lrma.org; *Head Librn* Donnelle Conklin

Open Tues - Sat 10 AM - 4:45 PM, Sun 1 - 4 PM, cl Mon; Estab 1923; Circ Non-circ; For reference only; Mem: Membership: part of museum

Income: Financed by endowment (Eastman Memorial Foundation), mem, donations

Library Holdings: Auction Catalogs; Book Volumes 11,000; Cassettes; Clipping Files; Exhibition Catalogs; Manuscripts; Memorabilia; Pamphlets; Periodical Subscriptions 60; Photographs; Reproductions; Slides 500; Video Tapes

Special Subjects: Painting-American, Prints, Painting-European, Silver

Collections: Museum archives

Publications: by Native Hands: Woven treasures from the Lauren Rogers Mus of Art

MERIDIAN

M **MERIDIAN MUSEUM OF ART,** Seventh St at Twenty-Fifth Ave, PO Box 5773 Meridian, MS 39301; PO Box 5773, Meridian, MS 39302-5773. Tel 601-693-1501; Elec Mail meridianmuseum@bellsouth.net; Internet Home Page Address: meridianmuseum.org; *Dir* Kate Cherry; *Educ Dir* Marsha Iverson

Open Wed - Sat 11 AM - 5 PM, cl Sun, Mon & Tues; No admis fee; Estab 1970 to provide exhibition space for local, state & nationally known artists. Mus has four galleries; Housed in a national landmark building, the mus offers over twenty exhibitions annually in four galleries; Average Annual Attendance: 10,500; Mem: 500; dues $45-$5000; annual meeting mid-Jan

Income: Financed by mem & appropriation

Library Holdings: Original Art Works; Sculpture

Special Subjects: Landscapes, Portraits, Drawings, Painting-American, Photography, Prints, Sculpture, Watercolors, Pottery, Decorative Arts

Collections: 20th century Southern fine arts & photography; 18th century European portraits; contemporary & traditional crafts & decorative arts

Exhibitions: Annual Bi-State; People's Choice Art Competition; Mem Invitational Exhibits

Activities: Classes for adults & children; youth art classes held each summer & after school; symposia lects open to pub; gallery talks; tours; competitions with awards; original objects of art lent to mus, traveling shows & offices in the city; book traveling exhibs 2 per yr; originate traveling exhibs for circulation to mus & galleries; muse & crafts

OCEAN SPRINGS

M **WALTER ANDERSON MUSEUM OF ART,** 510 Washington Ave, Ocean Springs, MS 39564-4632. Tel 228-872-3164; Fax 228-875-4494; Elec Mail wama@walterandersonmuseum.org; Internet Home Page Address: www.walterandersonmuseum.org; *Exec Dir* Rosemary Roosa; *Dir Colls & Exhibs* Doug Myatt; *Registrar* Ligla Romer; *Opers Mgr* Julie Franc; *Finance Mgr* Donna Andrus; *Gift Shop Mgr* Andrea Singhoff; *Educ Dir* Melissa Johnson; *Week-End Mgr* Genie Martz; *Vis Servs* Kyla Grace

Open Mon - Sat 9:30 AM - 4:30 PM, Sun 12:30 PM - 4:30 PM; Admis $10 adults, $8 seniors, $5 students (4 & under free); Estab 1991 to exhibit the works of Walter Anderson & other artists; The museum includes a main galleria & 4 galleries; Average Annual Attendance: 30,000; Mem: 800; dues $20-$1,000

Income: Financed by mem, attendance, grants, fundraisers, shop proceeds & donations

Library Holdings: Audio Tapes; Book Volumes; Clipping Files; DVDs; Exhibition Catalogs; Motion Pictures; Original Documents; Pamphlets; Periodical Subscriptions; Photographs; Prints; Video Tapes

Special Subjects: Art Education, Art History, Photography, Pottery, Woodcuts, Sculpture, Drawings, Painting-American, Watercolors, Woodcarvings, Reproductions

Collections: Work of Walter Inglis Anderson; ceramics; textiles; wood carving; works of art on paper; linoleum blocks & prints; Peter & Mac Anderson (brothers of Walter) Collection, furniture, oil paintings; education collection; adjunct collection

Exhibitions: Brent Funderburk Watercolors (Spring 2014); The Voyage of the Beagle-Illustrations (2013-14)

Publications: Motif, quarterly newsletter

Activities: Classes for adults & children; docent progs; lects open to mems & to pub, 5-15 vis lectrs per yr; concerts; gallery talks; tours; schols; Governor's award for excellence in art; 3 state educational outreach progs; organize traveling exhibs for mus & other cultural institutions; mus shop sells books, prints, reproductions, games & educational materials

OXFORD

M **UNIVERSITY OF MISSISSIPPI,** Rowan Oak, Home of William Faulkner, 916 Old Taylor Ave, Oxford, MS 38655; PO Box 1848, Univ of Miss University, MS 38677-1848. Tel 662-234-3284; Fax 662-915-7035; Elec Mail wgriffit@olemiss.edu; Internet Home Page Address: www.olemiss.edu; *Cur* William Griffith

Open Aug 2 - May 31 Tues - Sat 10 AM - 4 PM, Sun 1 - 4 PM; Jun 1 - Aug 1, open Mon - Sat 10 AM - 6 PM, Sun 1 - 6 PM; cl New Years Day, Jul 4,

Thanksgiving, Christmas Eve & Day; Admis adults, seniors & students $5, free to children & college & univ students; Estab 1977; Rowan Oak was home of William Faulkner from 1930 - 1962; house & grounds have been recently restored & are a National Historic Landmark as well as Literary Landmark owned & maintained by the Univ of MS. Nonprofit org; Average Annual Attendance: 23,000 by accurate count

Collections: Furnishings; personal artifacts

M **UNIVERSITY OF MISSISSIPPI,** University Museum & Historic Houses, University Ave & Fifth St, Oxford, MS 38655; PO Box 1848, University, MS 38677-1848. Tel 662-915-7073; Fax 662-915-7035; Elec Mail museums@olemiss.edu; Internet Home Page Address: www.olemiss.edu; *Dir* Robert Saarnio; *Rowan Oak Cur & Colls Mgr* William Griffith; *Preparator* Robert J Pekala; *Admin Asst* Michelle Perry; *Security* Tracy Stricklin; *Educ Cur* Emily Dean; *Coll Mgr/Registrar* Marti Funke; *Mem, Publicity & Events Coordr* Alyssa Yuen; *Spec Projects Mgr* Melanie Munns

Open Tues - Sat 10 AM - 6 PM, Sun 1 - 4:30 PM, cl Mon & univ holidays; No admis fee for permanent exhibs; special exhibs require admis fee; Estab 1977 to collect, conserve & exhibit objects related to history of the University of Mississippi & to the cultural & scientific heritage of the people of the state & region; Main gallery contains 3000 sq ft with 12 ft ceilings for permanent collections & 800 sq ft with 18 ft ceilings for temporary exhibs; each of the four galleries of the Mary Buie Mus contains 400 sq ft for permanent collection; Lawrence & Fortune Galleries; Walton Young Historic House; Average Annual Attendance: 14,000; Mem: 150

Income: $190,000 (financed by state appropriation)

Special Subjects: Prints, Drawings, Painting-American, Photography, Sculpture, Watercolors, African Art, Anthropology, Textiles, Folk Art, Woodcarvings, Etchings & Engravings, Afro-American Art, Decorative Arts, Portraits, Dolls, Furniture, Glass, Jewelry, Porcelain, Asian Art, Silver, Historical Material, Antiquities-Greek, Antiquities-Roman

Collections: Theora Hamblett Collection (paintings, glass, drawings); Fulton-Meyer Collection of African Art; Millington-Barnard Collection of 19th Century Scientific Instruments; David Robinson Collection of Greek & Roman antiquities

Publications: Department essays; exhibit catalogs

Activities: Classes for adults & children; children's hands-on gallery; lects open to pub, 15 vis lectrs per yr; gallery talks; tours; school outreach program; mus shop sells books, magazines, original art, reproductions, prints, souvenirs related to collections

M **University Gallery,** 85 Cross St, 116 Meek Hall University, MS 38677; PO Box 1848, University, MS 38677-1848. Tel 662-915-7193; Fax 662-915-5013; Elec Mail art@olemiss.edu; Internet Home Page Address: www.olemiss.edu/; *Chair & Prof* Dr Nancy L Wicker

Open daily 8:30 AM - 4:30 PM; No admis fee; Estab 1954 as a teaching gallery; Average Annual Attendance: 1,000

Income: Financed by state appropriation & tuition

Collections: Faculty & student work; some work purchased from traveling exhibitions

Exhibitions: Faculty, students, alumni & visiting artists

Activities: Lects open to pub, 6-8 vis lectrs per yr; gallery talks; individual paintings & original objects of art lent to departments within the University; lending collection contains original art works, original prints, paintings & sculpture

RAYMOND

M **HINDS COMMUNITY COLLEGE DISTRICT,** Marie Hull Gallery, 501 E Main St, PO Box 1100 Raymond, MS 39154-1100. Tel 601-857-3276; Internet Home Page Address: www.hindscc.edu; Internet Home Page Address: www.hindscc.edu/Departments/art/gallery.aspx; *Dept Chmn, Painting & Drawing* Melanie Atkinson; *Gallery Dir* Paula L Duren

Open Sept - May Mon - Thurs 8 AM - 3 PM, Fri 8 AM - Noon, cl school holidays; No admis fee; Estab 1971 as a community service & cultural agent for the visual arts; Main gallery measures 60 x 60 ft; an adjacent gallery 8 x 45 ft; reception area 15 x 25 ft; Average Annual Attendance: 2,500

Income: $2,900 (financed by Art Department budget)

Collections: Permanent collection of state artist, with 400 pieces in prints, sculptures & paintings

Exhibitions: Sponsors 6 exhibits during college session

Activities: Lects open to public, 3 vis lectrs per yr; gallery talks; tours; sponsor competitions; schols & fels offered

RIDGELAND

M **CRAFTSMEN'S GUILD OF MISSISSIPPI, INC,** Agriculture & Forestry Museum, 950 Rice Rd, Ridgeland, MS 39157-3040. Tel 601-856-7546; Fax 601-856-7531; Elec Mail info@mscrafts.org; Internet Home Page Address: www.mscrafts.org; *Exec Dir* Julia Daily

Open Mon - Sat 9 AM - 5 PM; No admis fee; Estab 1973 to preserve, promote, educate, market & encourage excellence in regional crafts; Two galleries: Mississippi Crafts Center, Natchez Trace milepost marker 102.6, Ridgeland 39158, sales demonstrations, festival of regional crafts; Chimneyville Craft Gallery; Average Annual Attendance: 100,000; Mem: 400; dues $75; annual meeting in Jan

Income: $360,000 (financed by mem, state arts commission grant, corporate & private contributions & earned income)

Special Subjects: Afro-American Art, American Indian Art, Glass, Metalwork, Furniture, Crafts, Folk Art, Jewelry, Mosaics, Leather

Exhibitions: Weekend exhibitions, Apr - Oct

Activities: Classes for adults & children; suitcase museum for schools & civic groups; gallery talks; 2006 Governor's Award for Excellence in the Arts; original objects of art lent to Mississippi schools & civic groups, could arrange in Southeastern region; lending collection contains original art works, video tapes, script & lesson plan; originate traveling exhibs; sales shop sells original craft

M CRAFTSMEN'S GUILD OF MISSISSIPPI, INC, Mississippi Crafts Center, 950 Rice Rd, Ridgeland, MS 39157-3040. Tel 601-856-7546; Fax 601-856-7531; Elec Mail info@mscrafts.org; Internet Home Page Address: www.mscrafts.org; *Event Coordr* Sheri Cox; *Exec Dir* Julia Daily; *Co-Gallery Mgr* Stephen Nettles; *Co-Gallery Mgr* Carmen Castilla; *Bus Mgr* Tomella Hall-Cheathan
Open Mon - Sun 9 AM - 5 PM; No admis fee; Estab 1973 to provide access to & educ in fine crafts to the pub & to provide a marketing venue for juried mem artists; A new contemporary bldg just off the Natchez Trace Pkwy nat Park; Average Annual Attendance: 100,000; Mem: 400; mem by Standards Comt evaluation; dues $75; annual meeting in Dec
Income: Financed by sales & grants
Special Subjects: Afro-American Art, American Indian Art, Folk Art, Metalwork, Pottery, Textiles, Sculpture, Crafts, Woodcarvings, Jewelry, Scrimshaw, Stained Glass, Pewter, Leather
Collections: Choctaw Indian crafts created by members; crafts created by members; Choctaw Indian Crafts
Activities: Classes for adults & children; craft demonstration, lect & festivals; docent training; lects open to pub, 1-2 vis lectrs per yr; gallery talks; Gov's Leadership in Arts Award 2006; MS Travel Attraction of the Year by MS Tourism Assn 2009; Best Place to Buy Unique Gifts by Best of Jackson 2010; artmobile; original objects of art lent by negotiation in response to requests; lending collection contains original art works, photographs & slides; originate traveling exhibs; sales shop sells books, magazines, prints & original art, primarily original craft objects (Native American to contemporary)

STONEVILLE

A MISSISSIPPI ART COLONY, PO Box 387, Stoneville, MS 38756-0387. Tel 888-452-5332; Internet Home Page Address: www.msartcolony.com; *Dir* Mrs Jamie Tate; *Pres* Bryon Myrick; *VPres* Keith Alford; *Treas* Evelyn Breland; *Secy* Patty Pilic
Estab 1948 to hold workshops at least twice yearly, for painting & drawing instruction and occasionally other areas; to organize juried show, with prizes awarded, that travels state of Mississippi between workshops; Average Annual Attendance: 50; Mem: $200; annual dues $20
Income: Financed by mem
Exhibitions: Two travel exhibitions each year; Painting workshops
Publications: Bulletin, newsletter
Activities: Annual fall workshop last week in Sept, $300; competitions judged; awards; scholarships; traveling exhibs in Mississippi museums

TOUGALOO

M TOUGALOO COLLEGE, Art Collection, 500 W County Line Rd, Tougaloo, MS 39174-9799. Tel 601-977-7743; Fax 601-977-7714; *Pres* Joe A Lee; *VPres Acad Affairs* Dr Lewis L Jones; *Photographer* John Wright; *Dir* Ron Schnell; *Chair* Johnnie Mae Gilbert
Open by appointment; No admis fee; Estab 1963 to service the community & the metropolitan Jackson area; Located in Student Union Building & Library; Average Annual Attendance: 2,500
Income: Financed by endowment & department budget
Collections: Afro-American; African; International Print Collection with emphasis on European art; New York School (abstract, expressionism, minimal art, surrealism)
Exhibitions: African Collection; Afro-American Collection; Faculty & Student Show; Local artists
Publications: Mississippi Museum of Art, African Tribal Art; Calder-Hayter-Miro; G M Designs of the 1960s; Hans Hofmann, Light Prints; brochure; catalog; newspaper of spec events
Activities: Classes for adults; dramatic progs; lects open to pub, 2-3 vis lectrs per yr; concerts; gallery talks; tours by appointment; schols offered; exten dept; individual paintings & original objects of art lent to libraries, universities & mus; lending collection contains 8000 lantern slides, 700 original art works, 350 original prints, 140 paintings, 150 sculpture; originate traveling exhibs; mus shop sells original art
L Coleman Library, 500 W Count Line Rd, Tougaloo, MS 39174-9700. Tel 601-977-7706; Fax 601-977-7714; Internet Home Page Address: www.tougaloo.edu/library/index.htm; *Dir Library Svcs* Charlene Cole
Open Mon - Fri 8 AM - 4PM, Sat noon - 4 PM, Sun 5 -11 PM; No admis fee; Estab 1963; Open to students & faculty
Income: Financed by rental fees
Library Holdings: Audio Tapes; Book Volumes 135,000; Cards; Cassettes; Clipping Files; Exhibition Catalogs; Fiche; Filmstrips; Framed Reproductions; Kodachrome Transparencies; Manuscripts; Memorabilia; Motion Pictures; Original Art Works; Pamphlets; Periodical Subscriptions 432; Photographs; Prints; Records; Reels; Reproductions; Sculpture; Slides
Special Subjects: Folk Art, Graphic Arts, Archaeology, American Western Art, Advertising Design, American Indian Art, Anthropology, Glass, Aesthetics, Afro-American Art, Antiquities-Oriental, Antiquities-Persian, Antiquities-Egyptian, Antiquities-Greek, Antiquities-Roman
Collections: Tracy Sugerman (wash drawings, civil rights studies 1964); African masks & sculpture
Exhibitions: Four major exhibits per year
Publications: Tougaloo College Art Collections
Activities: Lects open to pub, 2 vis lectrs per yr; symposium; gallery talks; tours

TUPELO

C BANCORP SOUTH, (Bank of Mississippi) Art Collection, 1 Mississippi Plaza, Tupelo, MS 38802-4926; PO Box 789, Tupelo, MS 38802-0789. Tel 662-680-2000; *Pres* Aubrey B Patterson Jr; *Chief Financial Officer* Nash Allen
Estab to encourage local artists & provide cultural enrichment for customers & friends; Works displayed throughout building
Purchases: $500
Collections: Oils, prints, watercolors

M GUMTREE MUSEUM OF ART, 211 W Main St, Tupelo, MS 38804; PO Box 786, Tupelo, MS 38802-0786. Tel 662-844-2787; Fax 662-844-9751; Elec Mail tina@gumtreemuseum.com; Internet Home Page Address: www.gumtreemuseum.com; *Exec Dir & Pub Rels* Tina Lutz; *Chmn* Nancy Difee; *Asst* George Maynard
Open Tues - Fri 10 AM - 4 PM, Sat 10 AM - 2 PM, cl New Year's Day, Independence Day, Thanksgiving, Christmas; No admis fee, donations accepted; Average Annual Attendance: 13,200
Collections: paintings; drawings
Activities: Educ prog; study clubs; lect; guided tours

L LEE COUNTY LIBRARY, 219 N Madison, Tupelo, MS 38804. Tel 662-841-9029; Fax 662-840-7615; Elec Mail lils@li.lib.ms.us; Internet Home Page Address: www.li.lib.ms.us; *Technical Servs Librn* Barbara Anglin; *Dir* Jan Willis; *Reference Librn* Brian Hargett; *Bookmobile Librn* Ann Grimes
Open Mon - Thurs 9:30 AM - 8:30 PM, Fri & Sat 9 AM - 5 PM, cl Sun; Estab 1941 to provide books & other sources of information to serve the intellectual, recreational & cultural needs of its users; Maintains art gallery; The Mezzanine Gallery & Helen Foster Auditorium are used as exhibit space for works by University Art students, local professional artists & traveling exhibitions
Income: Financed by city, state & county appropriations
Library Holdings: Book Volumes 200,000; Cassettes; Fiche; Framed Reproductions; Photographs; Prints; Records; Sculpture; Video Tapes
Collections: The Tupelo Gum Tree Festival purchase prizes, these include paintings and pottery
Activities: Children's summer reading series: Children's series Thurs at 10am; Helen Foster lect series every Apr with renowned authors

MISSOURI

ARROW ROCK

M ARROW ROCK STATE HISTORIC SITE, 4th and Van Bruen St, Arrow Rock, MO 65320; PO Box 1, Arrow Rock, MO 65320-0001. Tel 660-837-3330; Fax 660-837-3300; Elec Mail dspasso@4mail.dns.state.mo.ks; Internet Home Page Address: www.mostateparks.com/arrowrock; *Adminr* Mike Dickey
Open daily 7 AM-10 PM, Dec-Feb: Fri-Sun from 10 AM - 4 PM, Visitor Ctr open 10 AM - 4 PM.; No admis fee; Estab 1923 to preserve, exhibit & interpret the cultural resources of Missouri, especially those assoc with George Caleb Bingham & his era in central Missouri; The 1837 home of G C Bingham serves as a mus house & the 1834 Tavern; Average Annual Attendance: 80,000
Income: Financed by state appropriation
Collections: Bingham Collection; Central Missouri Collection (textiles, furnishing & glass of the 19th century)
Exhibitions: Annual Art Fair; Annual Summer Workshop Exhibit; Annual Craft Festival
Publications: Friends of Arrow Rock Letter, quarterly
Activities: Classes for children; tours

BOLIVAR

M THE ELLA CAROTHERS DUNNEGAN GALLERY OF ART, 511 N Pike, Bolivar, MO 65613; PO Box 468, Bolivar, MO 65613. Tel 417-326-3438; Elec Mail dunnegan@windstream.net; Internet Home Page Address: www.dunnegangallery.com; *Dir* Jo Roberts
Open Mon, Wed & Fri 1 - 4 PM; special hours for special shows; No admis fee; Fine arts mus
Collections: Paintings, sculpture
Activities: Book 2 traveling exhibs per yr

CAPE GIRARDEAU

L SOUTHEAST MISSOURI STATE UNIVERSITY, Kent Library, 1 University Plz, MS 4600 Cape Girardeau, MO 63701-4710. Tel 573-651-2235; Fax 573-651-2666; Elec Mail scron@semoum.semo.edu; Internet Home Page Address: www.library.semo.edu; *Lib Dir* Ed Buis
Open Mon - Thurs 7:30AM-11:30PM, Fri 7:30AM-6PM, Sat 11AM-5PM; No admis fee; Exhibition areas on second & third levels; Artium Gallery on fourth level. The Jake K Wells Mural, 800 sq ft covers the west wall of the library foyer, depicting the nature & the development of the southeast region of the state
Income: Financed by the univ & grants
Library Holdings: Book Volumes 400,000
Collections: Charles Harrison Collection (rare books including some of the finest examples of the book arts); books & manuscripts from the 13th to the 20th centuries
Exhibitions: Exhibits by local artists
Activities: Tours

CLINTON

M HENRY COUNTY MUSEUM & CULTURAL ARTS CENTER, 203 W Franklin St, Clinton, MO 64735-2008. Tel 660-885-8414; Fax 660-890-2228; Elec Mail hcmus1@centurylink.net; Internet Home Page Address: www.henrycountymuseum.org; *Dir* Brenda Dehn; *Asst Dir* Betty Maxwell
Open Mon - Sat, 10 AM - 4 PM; Admis adults $5, students under 12 free; Estab 1976; Turn of the 20th-century museum; Average Annual Attendance: 4,500; Mem: 600; dues $15 individual, $25 family; semi-annual meetings
Income: Financed by members
Library Holdings: Clipping Files; Maps; Memorabilia; Original Art Works; Original Documents; Photographs; Records; Slides

Special Subjects: American Indian Art, Historical Material, Metalwork, Prints, Bronzes, Woodcuts, Maps, Painting-French, Painting-Japanese, Sculpture, Architecture, Drawings, Painting-American, Photography, Watercolors, Archaeology, Ethnology, Pre-Columbian Art, Textiles, Costumes, Religious Art, Pottery, Woodcarvings, Decorative Arts, Portraits, Posters, Eskimo Art, Dolls, Furniture, Glass, Jewelry, Porcelain, Oriental Art, Asian Art, Carpets & Rugs, Miniatures, Period Rooms, Embroidery, Antiquities-Oriental, Antiquities-Persian, Antiquities-Greek, Mosaics, Stained Glass, Pewter, Leather, Military Art
Collections: Paintings of Mr & Mrs Louis Freund; Ike Parker Collection: Callie Hart; over 250 pieces of Thomas Clark sculptures
Exhibitions: Louis Freund WPA Work at all Times
Activities: Classes for adults & children; docent training; 3 vis lectrs per yr; tours; sponsoring of competitions; Heritage Award; schols available; book traveling exhibs, 1-2007, Between Fences, from MO Humanities; mus shop sells books, magazines, original art, reproductions & prints

COLUMBIA

A **STATE HISTORICAL SOCIETY OF MISSOURI,** 1020 Lowry, Columbia, MO 65201-7298. Tel 573-882-7083; Fax 573-884-4950; Elec Mail shsofmo@umsystem.edu; Internet Home Page Address: shs.umsystem.edu; *Exec Dir* Dr Gary R Kremer; *Vol Pres* Stephen N Limbaugh Jr; *Art Cur* Dr Joan Stack; *Mus Preparator Chief* Greig Thompson
Open Tues-Fri 8 AM - 4:45 PM, Sat 8 AM - 3:30 PM; No admis fee; Estab 1898 to collect, preserve, make accessible & publish materials pertaining to the history of Missouri & the Middle West; Circ Non-circulating; Major art gallery 54 ft x 36 ft; corridor galleries; Average Annual Attendance: 5,233; Mem: 4,864; dues $30 individual, $50 household; annual meeting in fall
Income: Financed by state appropriation, membership dues & private giving
Library Holdings: Book Volumes; Clipping Files; Lantern Slides; Manuscripts; Maps; Original Art Works; Original Documents; Pamphlets; Periodical Subscriptions; Photographs; Prints; Records; Reels; Slides; Video Tapes
Special Subjects: Cartoons, Drawings, Historical Material, Manuscripts, Photography, Prints, Watercolors, Painting-American, Portraits, Maps
Collections: Works by Thomas Hart Benton, George C Bingham, Karl Bodmer, Fred Geary, Carl Gentry, William Knox, Roscoe Misselhorn, Frank B Nuderscher, Charles Schwartz, Fred Shane, Frederick Sylvester; contemporary artists coll containing work of over fifty outstanding Missouri related artists; original cartoon coll of works by Tom Engelhardt, Daniel Fitzpatrick, Don Hesse, Bill Mauldin, S J Ray and others
Publications: Missouri Historical Review, quarterly; R Douglas Hurt & Mary K Dains, eds; Thomas Hart Benton: Artist, Writer & Intellectual (1989); Lynn Wolf Gentzler, ed., "But I Forget That I am a Painter and not a Politician": The Letters of George Caleb Bingham (2011)
Activities: Lects open to public; tours; 8-10 vis lectrs per yr; gallery talks; individual paintings lent, loans based on submitted requests; sales shop sells books & prints

L **Gallery and Library,** 1020 Lowry St, Columbia, MO 65201-7207. Tel 573-882-7083; Fax 573-884-4950; Elec Mail shsofmo@umsystem.edu; Internet Home Page Address: www.shs.umsystem.edu; *Exec Dir* Dr Gary R Kremer; *VPres* Dick Franklin; *Art Cur* Dr Joan Stock
Open Library: Mon, Wed - Fri 8 AM - 4:30 PM, Tues 8 AM - 9 PM, Sat 9 AM - 4:30 PM; Gallery: Mon, Wed - Sat 9 AM - 4 PM, Tues 5 PM - 8 PM; No admis fee, donations accepted; Estab 1898; Open to public; Mem: 5,167; $20 individual, $30 family
Income: Financed by state appropriation
Library Holdings: Audio Tapes; Book Volumes 460,000; Cassettes; Clipping Files; Exhibition Catalogs; Fiche; Kodachrome Transparencies; Manuscripts; Maps 4,405; Original Art Works; Original Documents; Pamphlets; Periodical Subscriptions 984; Photographs; Prints; Records; Reels; Slides; Video Tapes
Special Subjects: Photography, Manuscripts, Maps, Historical Material
Collections: George Caleb Bingham Collection; Thomas Hart Benton Collection; Karl Bodmer: 90 colored engravings; Bay Collection of Middle Western America
Activities: Lects open to public; gallery talks; tours; sales shop sells books, prints, notecards & t-shirts

M **STEPHENS COLLEGE,** Lewis James & Nellie Stratton Davis Art Gallery, 1200 Broadway, Columbia, MO 65215-0001. Tel 573-876-7627; Fax 573-876-7248; Elec Mail irene@stephens.edu; *Dir* Robert Friedman; *Cur* Irene Alexander
Open Mon - Fri 10 AM - 4 PM, cl school holidays & summer; No admis fee; Estab 1964 to provide exhibs of art for the gen interest of the local community & for the educ of the student body in gen; Average Annual Attendance: 500
Income: $2000 (financed by endowment)
Special Subjects: Graphics, Painting-American, Sculpture, Primitive art
Collections: Modern graphics; modern paintings; primitive sculpture
Exhibitions: Elizabeth Layton's Drawing on Life; Ron Meyers: Ceramics; Margaret Peterson Paintings; Burger Sandzen exhibit
Activities: Lects open to public, 6 vis lectrs per year; gallery talks; exhibs; competitions with awards

M **UNIVERSITY OF MISSOURI,** Museum of Art & Archaeology, 1 Pickard Hall, Columbia, MO 65211-1420. Tel 573-882-3591; Fax 573-884-4039; Elec Mail museumuser@missouri.edu; Internet Home Page Address: maa.missouri.edu; *Cur European & American Art* Mary Pixley; *Cur Ancient Art* J Benton Kidd; *Registrar* Jeffrey Wilcox; *Cur Educ* Cathy Callaway; *Preparator* Barb Smith; *Fiscal Officer & Admin Assoc* Carol Geisler; *Dir* Alex Barker; *Asst Dir* Bruce Cox; *Academic Coordr* Arthur Mehrhoff; *Graphic Designer* Kristie Lee
Open Tues - Fri 9 AM - 4PM, Sat & Sun Noon - 4 PM, Thurs open til 8 PM, cl Mon & holidays; No admis fee; Estab 1957 to exhibit a study collection for students in Art History & Archaeology; a comprehensive collection for the enjoyment of the general area of Missouri; Housed in renovated 1890's building. Ten galleries for permanent collection & special exhibitions; Average Annual Attendance: 35,000; Mem: 600
Income: $1,088,667 (financed by mem, grants & state appropriation)
Special Subjects: Afro-American Art, Archaeology, Drawings, Etchings & Engravings, Landscapes, Ceramics, Collages, Glass, Antiquities-Assyrian, Portraits, Pottery, Pre-Columbian Art, Painting-American, Prints, Textiles, Woodcuts, Manuscripts, Painting-French, Painting-Japanese, Sculpture, Photography, Watercolors, Bronzes, African Art, Religious Art, Ceramics, Folk Art, Primitive art, Landscapes, Painting-European, Jade, Jewelry, Oriental Art, Asian Art, Antiquities-Byzantine, Painting-British, Painting-Dutch, Ivory, Baroque Art, Painting-Flemish, Medieval Art, Antiquities-Oriental, Antiquities-Persian, Islamic Art, Antiquities-Egyptian, Antiquities-Greek, Antiquities-Roman, Mosaics, Gold, Antiquities-Etruscan, Enamels
Collections: Ancient Art-Egypt, Western Asia, Greek & Roman; European & American painting & sculpture; Early Christian-Byzantine & Coptic; Modern paintings & sculpture; Prints & drawings; African, Pre-Columbian; Oriental-Chinese & Japanese; South Asian-Indian, Thai, Tibetan, Nepalese
Exhibitions: Weinberg Gallery of Ancient Art, ongoing; European and American Gallery of Art, ongoing; Barton Gallery of Modern and Contemporary Art, ongoing; Collecting for a New Century: Recent Acquisitions, Black Women in Art and the Stories They Tell, Ran In-Ting's Watercolors: East and West Mix in Images of Rural Taiwan, A Midwestern View: The artists of the Ste. Genevieve Art Colony, Love, Life, Death and Mourning: Remembrance in Portraits by George Caleb Bingham, The Mediterranean Melting Pot: Commerce and Cultural Exchange in Antiquity, The Sacred Feminine: Prehistory to Postmodernity, Narratives of Process and Time in the Prints of Jorg Schmeisser
Publications: Muse, annually; exhibition catalogues; Museum Magazine, 2 per yr; calendars, 12 per yr; Glen Lukens: Innovations in Clay, Testament of Time; Antiquities from the Holy Land; Golden Treasures by Akelo: The Voyage of a Contemporary Italian Goldsmith in the Classical World
Activities: Classes for adults & children; docent training; workshops on conservation; lects open to pub, 5-10 vis lectrs per yr; tours; gallery talks, concerts; original objects of art lent to institutions; book traveling exhibs 2-3 per yr; originate traveling exhibs; mus shop sells books, prints, reproductions, slides, gifts & jewelry

L **Art, Archaeology & Music Collection,** MU Libraries, University of Missouri, Room 104, Ellis Library Columbia, MO 65201; 1020 Lowry St Stop 1, Ellis Library Columbia, MO 65201-5149. Tel 573-882-4581; Fax 573-882-8044; *Librn* Michael Muchow; *Music* Anne Barker; *Reference Desk Coordr* Cynthia Cotner
Open Mon-Thurs 8AM-11PM, Fri 8AM-6PM, Sat 9 AM-6PM, Sun Noon-11PM; Estab 1841 to house material for the faculty & students of the University
Income: Financed by state appropriation
Library Holdings: Book Volumes 81,000; CD-ROMs; Exhibition Catalogs; Fiche; Periodical Subscriptions 300; Records; Reels; Video Tapes

FAYETTE

M **CENTRAL METHODIST UNIVERSITY,** Ashby-Hodge Gallery of American Art, 411 Central Methodist Sq, Fayette, MO 65248-1104. Tel 660-248-6324 or 6304; Fax 660-248-2622; Elec Mail jegeist@centralmethodist.edu; Internet Home Page Address: www.centralmethodist.edu; *Cur* Denise Gebhardt; *Supv Coll* Dr Doe Geist
Open Tues - Thurs & Sun 1:30-4:30 PM, other times by appointment; No admis fee; Estab 1993; focus on American art; Average Annual Attendance: 5,000; Mem: 750
Purchases: Lithographs: Coney Island-Paul Cadnus; Color Prints: River at Asot Neg-Maxfield Parrish; Wooden Sculpture: Scene From Pittsburgh-Joseph Falsetti; Barrel & Sack Corn - Alfred Montgomery; Still Life with Strawberries - August Laux; in 2012: etching by Stephen Maxwell Pamuk, etching by Joseph Meers, lithograph by Donald Roberts & Morea Soyer, The Hunt by Leroy Neiman
Special Subjects: Photography, Painting-American, Sculpture, Watercolors
Collections: Ashby Collection of American Art
Activities: Docent training; 2 vis lectrs per yr; tours

FENTON

L **MARITZ, INC,** Library, 1400 S Highway Dr, Fenton, MO 63099-0001. Tel 636-827-1501; Fax 636-827-3006; *Mgr* Jan Meier
Estab 1968; Circ 12,000; For reference & lending
Library Holdings: Book Volumes 7500; Periodical Subscriptions 250
Special Subjects: Illustration, Graphic Arts

FLORIDA

M **MARK TWAIN BIRTHPLACE,** State Historic Site Museum, 37352 Shrine Rd, Florida, MO 65283-2127. Tel 573-565-3449; Fax 573-565-3718; Elec Mail mark.twain.birthplaced.state.historic.site@dnr.mo.gov; Internet Home Page Address: mostatesports.com/twainsite.htm; *Site Adminr* John Huffman; *Interpretive Resource Technician* Connie Ritter
Open every day 10 AM - 4:30 PM, daylight savings 10 AM - 5 PM, cl Thanksgiving Day, Christmas and New Years; Admis adults $2.50, children between 6 & 12 $1.50, children under 6 free; Estab 1960 to preserve the birth cabin of Samuel L Clemens, interpret his life and inform visitors of local history; Foyer and two large exhibit areas, research library; Average Annual Attendance: 24,000
Income: Financed by state appropriation
Special Subjects: Historical Material, Sculpture, Painting-American, Photography, Manuscripts, Portraits, Furniture
Collections: Samuel Clemens memorabilia; manuscripts; period furnishings and paintings
Exhibitions: Permanent exhibits depicting the life of Samuel Clemens
Activities: Lects; tours; craft demonstrations; sales of books

FULTON

M **WESTMINSTER COLLEGE,** Winston Churchill Memorial & Library in the United States, 501 Westminster Ave, Fulton, MO 65251-1299. Tel 573-592-5369; *Dir* Dr Gordon Davis; *Asst Dir* Sara Winingear; *Exec Dir* Dr Robert Havers
Open daily 10AM-4:30PM, cl Thanksgiving, Christmas & New Year's; Admis adults $6, seniors $4, college students $4, children 6-11 $3, children 5 and under

free; Estab 1969 to commemorate life & times of Winston Churchill & attest to ideals of Anglo-American relations; Special exhibits gallery changes quarterly; ecclesiastical gallery contains historic robes & communion vessels; connecting gallery houses historic map collection; Average Annual Attendance: 22,000; Mem: 900

Income: Financed by endowment, mem, admis, friends fundraising, gift shop sales
Special Subjects: Historical Material, Maps
Collections: Churchill & family memorabilia, including documents, manuscripts & photographs; Churchill oil paintings; rare maps
Exhibitions: Iron Curtain speech memorabilia
Publications: MEMO, quarterly newsletter
Activities: Churchill classes for WC students; docent training; lects open to pub; concerts; tours; schols & fels offered; individual paintings & original objects of art lent to other mus & libraries; book traveling exhibs 2-4 per yr; originate traveling exhibs; mus shop sells books, original art, reproductions, prints, slides, Churchill busts & memorabilia, English china, posters, collectible English toy soldiers

M **WILLIAM WOODS UNIVERSITY,** Cox Gallery, 1 University Ave, Fulton, MO 65251-2388. Tel 573-592-4245; Fax 573-592-1623; Elec Mail jennifer.sain@williamwoods.edu; Internet Home Page Address: www.williamwoods.edu; *Dir* Jennifer George Sain; *Chmn Arts & Humanities* Dr Aimee Sapp
Open Mon - Fri 9 AM - 6 PM while in session, cl Univ Holidays; No admis fee; Estab 1967 to be used as a teaching aid for the Art Center; Maintains 3200 sq ft sky-lighted gallery with a mezzanine
Income: Financed by endowment
Activities: Classes for children; lects open to pub, 2 vis lectrs per yr; tours; gallery talks; schols

HOLLISTER

L **WORLD ARCHAEOLOGICAL SOCIETY,** Information Center, Library, & Timbertop Studio, 120 Lakewood Dr, Hollister, MO 65672-5176. Tel 417-334-2377; Elec Mail ronwriterartist@aol.com; Internet Home Page Address: www.worldarchaeologicalsociety.com; *Dir* Ron Miller
Not open to public; Estab 1971 to study related areas of archaeology, anthropology & art history & to help with worldwide mail & telephone queries; Lending & reference by special arrangement; Mem: dues $16, outside US $20; must sign good archaeology requirements on member card
Income: Financed by endowment, contributions, print & newsletter sales
Purchases: serials & books
Library Holdings: Book Volumes 7,000; Clipping Files; Original Art Works; Periodical Subscriptions 32; Photographs; Prints; Slides
Special Subjects: Art History, Intermedia, Landscape Architecture, Film, Illustration, Mixed Media, Calligraphy, Commercial Art, Drawings, Etchings & Engravings, Graphic Arts, Graphic Design, Islamic Art, Manuscripts, Maps, Painting-American, Painting-British, Painting-Dutch, Painting-Flemish, Painting-French, Painting-German, Painting-Italian, Painting-Japanese, Painting-Russian, Painting-Spanish, Pre-Columbian Art, Prints, Sculpture, Painting-European, Historical Material, History of Art & Archaeology, Judaica, Ceramics, Crafts, Latin American Art, Archaeology, Ethnology, Painting-Israeli, American Western Art, Bronzes, Cartoons, Interior Design, Lettering, Art Education, Asian Art, American Indian Art, Primitive art, Anthropology, Eskimo Art, Mexican Art, Ivory, Jade, Drafting, Mosaics, Painting-Polish, Bookplates & Bindings, Metalwork, Antiquities-Oriental, Carpets & Rugs, Goldsmithing, Handicrafts, Jewelry, Leather, Miniatures, Marine Painting, Landscapes, Antiquities-Egyptian, Antiquities-Greek, Antiquities-Roman, Dioramas, Coins & Medals, Painting-Scandinavian, Laces, Painting-Australian, Painting-Canadian, Painting-New Zealand, Display, Architecture, Folk Art
Collections: Steve Miller Library of Archaeology; Rose O'Neil Art
Publications: WAS Newsletter, occasional; spec publs, occasional
Activities: WAS award for best book, illustration & photo; individual paintings & original objects of art lent; query for print costs & titles

INDEPENDENCE

M **CHURCH OF JESUS CHRIST OF LATTER-DAY SAINTS,** Mormon Visitors' Center, 937 W Walnut, Independence, MO 64050. Tel 816-836-3466; Fax 816-252-6256; Internet Home Page Address: www.LDS.org; *Dir* Barrie G McKay
Open daily 9 AM - 9 PM; No admis fee; Estab 1971 as a center of Church of Jesus Christ of Latter Day Saints beliefs & history for residents of Missouri, Ohio & Illinois; Average Annual Attendance: 50,000
Income: Financed by The Church of Jesus Christ of Latter Day Saints
Special Subjects: Portraits, Woodcuts, Religious Art
Collections: Large 30 ft mural of Christ; painting; computer reproductions; Short movies about history & life experiences of Jesus Christ
Exhibitions: Paintings; movies; audio-visual shows; historical maps exhibits; special flag display; log cabin 1800s (original)
Publications: Brochures
Activities: Lect open to public; free guided tours

M **JACKSON COUNTY HISTORICAL SOCIETY,** The 1859 Jail, Marshal's Home & Museum, 114 S Main St, Ste 103, Independence, MO 64050-3703; PO Box 4241, Independence, MO 64051-4241. Tel 816-252-1892; Fax 816-461-1897; Internet Home Page Address: www.jchs.org; *Exec Dir* Steve Noll
Open Mon - Sat 10 AM - 5 PM, Sun 1 - 4 PM, Mar, Nov & Dec Mon 10 AM - 4 PM, cl Jan & Feb; Admis adults $4.00, sr citizens $3.50, children 6-16 $1, under 5 free, group rates available; Estab 1958 for interpretation of Jackson County history; 1859 Federal town house of county marshal, attached limestone jail which served as federal headquarters during the Civil War. Restored historical interior c 1860s. Restored cell of Frank James c 1882; Average Annual Attendance: 12,000; Mem: 1,000; dues $20-$1,000
Income: Financed by mem, tours, fundraising events
Special Subjects: Historical Material, Period Rooms

Collections: Jackson County history, 1800-present; home furnishings of mid-19th century in restored areas
Exhibitions: Permanent exhibits on Jackson County history; changing exhibits
Publications: Jackson County Historical Society Journal, bi-annual
Activities: Classes for children; docent training; lects open to pub; tours; mus shop sells books

L **Research Library & Archives,** 112 W Lexington Ave Ste 103, Independence, MO 64050-2843; PO Box 4241, Independence, MO 64051-4241. Tel 816-252-7454; Fax 816-461-1510; Internet Home Page Address: www.jchs.org; *Dir Archives* David Jackson; *Exec Dir* Steve Noll
Open Tues - Fri 10 AM - 4 PM, Sat 10 AM - 1 PM; No admis fee; Estab 1966; Gallery collects, preserves, & makes available for research exhibition & education materials that relate to Jackson County history; Mem: $20-1,000
Income: Financed by mem, fees, donations, sales
Library Holdings: Audio Tapes; Book Volumes 2000; Clipping Files; Filmstrips; Kodachrome Transparencies; Lantern Slides; Motion Pictures; Periodical Subscriptions 15; Photographs; Reels; Slides; Video Tapes
Collections: Photograph collection for reference; extensive manuscript collection

M **John Wornall House Museum,** 6115 Warnall Rd, Kansas City, MO 64113. Tel 816-444-1858; Fax 816-361-8165; Elec Mail jwornall@crn.org; Internet Home Page Address: www.wornallhouse.org; *Dir* Rebecca Fye; *Asst Dir* Karla Horkman
Open Tues - Sat 10 AM - 4 PM, Sun 1 - 4 PM; Admis adults $3, sr citizens $2.50, children 5-12 $2, children 4 & under free, group rates available; Estab 1972 restored to interpret the daily lives of prosperous frontier farm families between 1830-1875 in early Kansas City; House was used as field hospital by both armies during the Civil War. Built in 1858; opened to pub in 1972; Average Annual Attendance: 7,000; Mem: 200: dues $25-500
Income: Financed by mem, tours & fund raisings
Special Subjects: Decorative Arts, Architecture, Furniture, Maps
Collections: Home furnishings of prosperous farm families; Civil War Period Collection
Exhibitions: Special exhibitions on subjects dealing with interpretation of home & Civil War period
Activities: Classes for adults & children; docent training; tours; lects open to pub; 2-3 vis lectrs per yr; mus shop sells books, holiday & gift items

L **NATIONAL ARCHIVES & RECORDS ADMINISTRATION,** Harry S Truman Museum and Library, 500 West Hwy 24, Independence, MO 64050-1798. Tel 816-833-1400; Fax 816-833-4368; Elec Mail truman.library@nara.gov; Internet Home Page Address: www.trumanlibrary.org; *Acting Dir* Michael Devine; *Mus Cur* Clay Bauske
Open Mon - Sat 9 AM - 5 PM, Thurs 9 AM - 9 PM, Sun Noon - 5 PM; Admis adults $8, seniors $7, children 6-15 $3, under 6 free; Estab 1957 to preserve & make available for study & exhibition the papers, objects & other materials relating to President Harry S Truman & to the history of the Truman admin; Gravesite of President & Mrs Truman in the courtyard. Admin by the National Archives & Records Administration of the Federal Government; Average Annual Attendance: 150,000
Income: Financed by federal appropriation, federal trust fund & private donations
Library Holdings: Audio Tapes; Book Volumes 40,000; Clipping Files; Framed Reproductions; Manuscripts; Memorabilia; Motion Pictures; Original Art Works; Other Holdings Documents; Pamphlets; Periodical Subscriptions 23; Photographs; Prints; Records; Reels; Sculpture; Slides
Collections: Papers of Harry S Truman, his assoc, and of officials in the Truman administration; Portraits of President Truman; paintings, prints, sculptures & artifacts presented to President Truman during the Presidential & Post-Presidential periods; original political cartoons; mural by Thomas Hart Benton
Exhibitions: Permanent & temporary exhibits relating to the life & times of Harry S Truman; the history of the Truman administration; the history & nature of office of the Presidency
Publications: Historical materials in the Truman Library
Activities: Educ dept; lect; conferences & commemorative events; tours to tour groups; film series; research grants; sales shop sells books, reproductions, slides & postcards

JEFFERSON CITY

M **MISSOURI DEPARTMENT OF NATURAL RESOURCES,** Missouri State Museum, Jefferson Landing SHS, Jefferson City, MO 65101; PO Box 176, Division of State Parks Jefferson City, MO 65102-0176. Tel 573-751-2854; Fax 573-526-2927; Internet Home Page Address: www.mostateparks.com; *Mus Dir* Kurt Senn; *Asst Dir* Linda Endersby; *Interpretive Progs & Tours* Chris Sterman; *Cur Exhibs* Julie Kemper; *Cur Collections* Kate Keil
Open daily 8 AM - 5 PM, cl New Years, Easter, Thanksgiving, Christmas; No admis fee; Estab 1920; History art & natural history of Missouri; Average Annual Attendance: 250,000
Income: Financed by state sales tax, affiliated with Missouri Department of Natural Resources
Special Subjects: Painting-American, Anthropology, Costumes, Historical Material
Collections: Art murals by T H Benton, Berninghaus, Frank Brangwyn, N C Wyeth; historical material and natural specimens representing Missouri's natural and cultural resources; Indian artifacts; History hall
Exhibitions: Permanent & temporary exhibits
Publications: Pamphlets
Activities: Guided tours of Capitol; audio-visual presentations; gallery tours; state parks & historic sites; books

M **Elizabeth Rozier Gallery,** 101 Jefferson St, Union Hotel Jefferson City, MO 65101-3054; PO Box 176, Division of State Parks Jefferson City, MO 65102-0176. Tel 573-751-2854; Fax 573-526-2927; *Dir* Kurt Senn; *Asst Dir* Linda Endersby; *Cur* Julie Kemper
Open 10 AM - 4 PM, Tues - Sat; No admis fee; Estab 1981 to provide art, crafts & history educational exhibits; Located in mid-nineteenth century building with a large & small gallery; Average Annual Attendance: 6,000
Income: Financed by state sales tax affiliated with Missouri Dept of Natural Resources
Special Subjects: Historical Material

Exhibitions: New exhibit every month
Activities: Lects open to pub; 2 vis lectrs per yr; gallery talks; tours

JOPLIN

A GEORGE A SPIVA CENTER FOR THE ARTS, 222 W Third St, Joplin, MO 64801. Tel 417-623-0183; Fax 417-623-3805; Elec Mail spiva@spivaarts.org; Internet Home Page Address: www.spivaarts.org; *Exec Dir* Jo Mueller; *Bd Pres* Ann Leach; *2nd Bd VPres* Kerstin Landner; *Exhibs Coordr* Shaun Conroy; *Educ* Karalee McDonald; *Bookkeeper* Rhea Cooper; *Develop. Coordr* Marta Churchwell; *Office Mgr* Linda Kyger; *PR Coordr* Lori Marble
Open Tues - Sat 10 AM - 5 PM, Sun 1 - 5 PM, cl Mon & national holidays; No admis fee - donations are appreciated; Estab 1948, incorporated 1959, as a non-profit, to provide cultural, educational & artistic exhibits & progs to increase public's appreciation of art; 3 galleries for Nat/International & local artist exhibits; Average Annual Attendance: 15,000; Mem: 800; dues $20-$1000; annual meeting in Nov
Library Holdings: Book Volumes; Clipping Files; Exhibition Catalogs; Periodical Subscriptions
Collections: Permanent collection
Exhibitions: PhotoSpiva; Annual Membership Show
Publications: Calendar; newsletter
Activities: Classes for adults & children; vol training; dramatic progs; lects open to public, 3 vis lectrs per year; tours; competitions with awards; mus shop sells original art

L WINFRED L & ELIZABETH C POST FOUNDATION, Post Memorial Art Reference Library, 300 S Main St, Joplin, MO 64801-2384. Tel 417-782-7678; Elec Mail lsimpson@postlibrary.org; Internet Home Page Address: www.postlibrary.org; *Dir* Leslie T Simpson
Open Mon & Thurs 9:30 AM - 7:30 PM, Tues, Wed, Fri & Sat 9:30 AM - 5:30 PM, Sun 1 - 5 PM; No admis fee; Estab 1981 to provide information on the fine & decorative arts to members of the community; Circ non-circulating; Located in a wing of the Joplin Public Library. Replica of English hall, furnished with European antiques; Average Annual Attendance: 6,500
Income: Financed by private endowment
Library Holdings: Book Volumes 3500; Clipping Files; Exhibition Catalogs; Original Art Works; Pamphlets; Periodical Subscriptions 25; Photographs; Reproductions; Sculpture
Special Subjects: Art History, Decorative Arts, Photography, Historical Material, Furniture, Architecture
Collections: 16th-17th Century Antiques & Artworks; Joplin, Missouri historic architecture coll; fine arts books colls; mounted reproductions
Exhibitions: Monthly exhibits of works by area artists
Publications: From Lincoln Logs to Lego Blocks: How Joplin Was Built by Leslie Simpson; Now and Then and Again: Joplin Historic Architecture by Leslie Simpson; Joplin: Post Card History by Leslie Simpson
Activities: Educ dept; film & slide progs; lects open to pub; concerts; tours; lects to civic groups offsite; mus shop sells books, notecards, t-shirts, posters & local history items

KANSAS CITY

M AVILA UNIVERSITY, Thornhill Art Gallery, 11901 Wornall Rd, Dallavis Ctr Kansas City, MO 64145-1007. Tel 816-501-3659; Fax 816-501-2459; Elec Mail aylwardme@avila.edu; Internet Home Page Address: www.avila.edu; *Acad Dean* Sr Marie Joan Harris, PhD; *Visual Commun Chair* Dr Dotty Hamilton; *Pres* Ron Slepitza; *Gallery Dir* Marci Aylward; *Office Mgr* Janine Urness
Open Tues - Fri 10 AM - 5 PM & by appointment; No admis fee; Estab 1978; Gallery space 60 x 35 ft is maintained with carpeted floor and walls and track lighting; Average Annual Attendance: 2,000
Income: Financed through school budget
Collections: Avila University Art Collection
Exhibitions: Japanese Woodblock Prints, Faculty Biennial
Activities: Lect open to public; gallery talks; sponsoring of competitions; originate traveling exhibits with the Mid-America Arts Alliance

M BELGER ARTS CENTER, 2100 Walnut St, Kansas City, MO 64108. Tel 816-474-3250; Fax 816-221-1621; Elec Mail tbembnister@belgerartscenter.org; Internet Home Page Address: www.belgerartscenter.org; *Dir* Evelyn Craft
Open Wed-Fri 10AM-4PM, Sat 12PM-4PM, other times by appointment
Collections: works by contemporary artists

C COMMERCE BANCSHARES, INC, Fine Art Collection, 922 Walnut St, Commerce Bank Art Dept Kansas City, MO 64106-1871. Tel 816-760-7885; Fax 816-234-2356; Elec Mail robin.trafton@commercebank.com; *CEO & Pres* David W Kemper; *Cur* Robin Trafton; *Dir Art Coll* Laura Kemper Fields
Open Mon - Sat 8 AM - 5 PM; No admis fee; Estab 1964; 125 ft barrel vaulted gallery with 13 ft ceiling to exhibit mus quality paintings
Activities: Individual paintings lent on restricted basis

C HALLMARK CARDS, INC, Hallmark Art Collection, 2501 McGee, Kansas City, MO 64141. Tel 816-545-6993; Elec Mail jhovst5@hallmark.com; Internet Home Page Address: www.hallmarkartcollection.com; *Cur* Joe Houston
Estab 1949; Corporate art collection
Special Subjects: Ceramics, Drawings, Prints, Photography
Collections: Hallmark Art Collection; illustration art
Publications: Exhibition catalogs
Activities: Lects; individual objects of art lent to reputable institutions for temporary exhibs; originate traveling exhibs

L Creative Library, 2501 McGee, No 146, Kemo, MO 64108. Tel 816-274-5525; Fax 816-274-7245;
Open to Hallmark personnel only; Estab to provide pictorial research
Income: Financed by corp funds
Library Holdings: Book Volumes 22,000; Periodical Subscriptions 150

Special Subjects: Illustration
Collections: Old & rare collection

M KANSAS CITY ARTISTS COALITION, 201 Wyandotte, Kansas City, MO 64105. Tel 816-421-5222; Fax 816-421-0656; Internet Home Page Address: www.kansascityartistscoalition.org; *Exec Dir* Janet F Simpson; *Asst Dir* Marissa Flyhn
Open Wed - Sat 11 AM - 5 PM; No admis fee; Estab 1975 to promote contemporary art & artists from Kansas City & the Midwest; nonprofit organization; Average Annual Attendance: 19,000; Mem: 800; dues $45
Collections: Contemporary Art
Exhibitions: Exhibs of high-quality, innovative work by emerging & mid-career artists; exhib series features a diverse combination of local, regional & national artists
Publications: Forum, online
Activities: Res prog; exhibs & lects open to pub; gallery talks; competitions with awards; workshops; schols & grants available; Money for Artists Promotion (MAP) Grant; Lighton International Artists Exchange Prog (LIAEP)

A KANSAS CITY MUNICIPAL ART COMMISSION, 414 E 12th St, City Hall, 17th Fl Kansas City, MO 64106-2702. Tel 816-513-2529; Fax 816-513-2523; Elec Mail porter_arneill@kcmo.org; Internet Home Page Address: www.kcmo.oorg/cimo.nsf/web/art; *Dir* Porter Arneill
Estab 1926. Administers the One-Percent-for-Art Program in Kansas City, setting aside one percent of all construction costs for new building & renovation projects for artwork
Exhibitions: Shown at various pub locations, such as libraries, col campuses & museums on a rotating basis
Activities: Originate traveling exhibs

L KANSAS CITY PUBLIC LIBRARY, 14 W 10th St, Kansas City, MO 64105-1702. Tel 816-701-3400; Fax 816-701-3401; Internet Home Page Address: www.kclibrary.org; *Exec Dir* R Crosby Kemper III; *Dep Exec Dir* Cheptoo Kositany-Buckner; *Dir Central Libr* Lillie Brack
Open Mon - Wed 9 AM - 9 PM, Thurs 9 AM - 6 PM, Fri 9 AM - 5 PM, Sat 10 AM - 5 PM, Sun 1 - 5 PM; No admis fee

M LEEDY-VOULKOS ART CENTER, 2010 Baltimore Ave, Kansas City, MO 64108-1914. Tel 816-474-1919; Fax 816-221-8474; Internet Home Page Address: www.leed-voulkos.com; *Exec Dir* James Leedy; *Managing Dir* Holly Swangstu
Open Wed - Sat 11 AM - 5 PM or by appointment; Estab 1985 to showcase contemporary arts & crafts; 10,000 sq ft of exhib space; Average Annual Attendance: 50,000
Exhibitions: Showcase contemporary art in all media-changing exhibits every six weeks
Activities: Classes for adults & children; 4 vis lectrs per yr; gallery talks; mus shop sells books & original art

M LIBERTY MEMORIAL MUSEUM & ARCHIVES, The National Museum of World War I, 100 W 26th St, Kansas City, MO 64108-4616. Tel 816-784-1918; Fax 816-784-1929; Elec Mail info@nwwone.org; Internet Home Page Address: www.libertymemorialmuseum.org; *Archivist* Jonathan Casey; *Cur* Doran L Cart; *Dir* Eli Paul
Open Tues - Sun 10 AM - 5 PM; Admis prices vary per exhibit; Estab 1919 to exhibit World War I memorabilia; Two rectangular spaces 45 x 90 ft; permanent & temporary exhibits; expanded mus space of 32,000 sq ft open Nov 2006; Average Annual Attendance: 62,000; Mem: 1000+; ann meeting Nov
Income: Financed by city appropriation & pvt donations
Purchases: 1917 Harley Davidson Army Motorcycle
Library Holdings: Kodachrome Transparencies; Lantern Slides; Manuscripts; Maps; Memorabilia; Motion Pictures; Original Art Works; Original Documents; Other Holdings; Periodical Subscriptions; Photographs; Prints; Records; Reels; Sculpture; Slides; Video Tapes
Special Subjects: Etchings & Engravings, Historical Material, Painting-American, Prints, Painting-French, Drawings, Photography, Costumes, Manuscripts, Posters, Maps, Coins & Medals, Painting-German, Military Art
Collections: WWI: books, documents, militaria, original sketches & paintings, photos, posters, sheet music; Soldiers' Art & Crafts; Sheet Music Covers; World War I Covers
Exhibitions: Trench Warfare; Aviation; Artillery; Medical Care; Uniforms; Women at War
Publications: Quarterly newsletter
Activities: Children's progs; lect open to pub; 2-4 vis lectrs per yr; mus shop sells books, reproductions, postcards & posters

MID AMERICA ARTS ALLIANCE & EXHIBITS USA
For further information, see National and Regional Organizations

M THE NELSON-ATKINS MUSEUM OF ART, 4525 Oak St, Kansas City, MO 64111-1873. Tel 816-751-1278; Internet Home Page Address: www.nelson-atkins.org; *Dir & CEO* Julian Zugazagoitia
Open Wed 10 AM - 4 PM, Thurs & Fri 10AM-9PM, Sat 10 AM - 5 PM, Sun Noon - 5 PM, cl Mon, Tues, New Years Day, July 4, Thanksgiving, Christmas Eve & Day; No admis fee; Estab 1933 as a gen mus serving the greater Kansas City region; Circ 135,000; Maintains reference library; Average Annual Attendance: 400,000; Mem: 11,000; dues $50 - $10,000
Income: Financed by endowment, mem & contributions
Library Holdings: Auction Catalogs; Book Volumes; Other Holdings; Periodical Subscriptions
Special Subjects: Furniture, Pottery, Painting-American, Bronzes, Sculpture, Drawings, Hispanic Art, Photography, Prints, American Indian Art, American Western Art, African Art, Costumes, Ceramics, Woodcuts, Etchings & Engravings, Landscapes, Afro-American Art, Decorative Arts, Glass, Jewelry, Asian Art, Carpets & Rugs, Ivory, Restorations, Baroque Art, Calligraphy, Period Rooms, Medieval Art, Antiquities-Egyptian, Antiquities-Greek, Antiquities-Roman, Antiquities-Assyrian

Collections: Burnap Collection: English pottery, Oriental ceramics, paintings, sculpture, bronze, Egyptian tomb sculpture, American painting, period rooms & furniture; Hallmark Photographic Collection; Kansas City Sculpture Park

Publications: Explore art calendar, 6 times per yr; Member magazine, 2 times per yr

Activities: Classes for adults & children; dramatic progs; docent training; lects open to pub, 50 vis lectr per yr; gallery talks; tours; concerts; individual paintings and original objects of art lent to qualified organizations & exhibs; organize various traveling exhibs; mus shop sells books, magazines, original art, reproductions & slides

L **Spencer Art Reference Library,** 4525 Oak St, Kansas City, MO 64111-1873. Tel 816-751-1216; Fax 816-751-0498; Internet Home Page Address: www.nelson-atkins.org; *Head Lib Svcs* Marilyn Carbonell; *Sr Acquisitions Librn* Jessica Zhang; *Sr Catalogue Librn* Katharine Reed; *Sr Librn Pub Svcs & Coll Develop* Dr. Jeffrey Weidman; *Visual Resource Librn* Noriko Ebersole; *Archives Asst* Holly Wright; *Asian Catalogue Asst* Lihui Xiong
Open Tues by appointment, Wed 10 AM - 4 PM, Thurs - Fri 10 AM - 6 PM, Sat - Sun 1 - 4 PM; No admis fee; For reference only; library instruction for college & univ classes in art & art hist; topical book displays and readings
Library Holdings: Auction Catalogs 42,254; Audio Tapes; Book Volumes 127,277; Cassettes; Clipping Files 8,379; DVDs 286; Exhibition Catalogs; Fiche; Manuscripts; Original Documents; Other Holdings Archives: 96 coll; Per titles 1,200; 48,198 vols; Pamphlets; Periodical Subscriptions 650; Photographs; Slides 119,738; Video Tapes
Special Subjects: Art History, Landscape Architecture, Decorative Arts, Illustration, Mixed Media, Photography, Etchings & Engravings, Painting-American, Painting-British, Painting-Dutch, Painting-Flemish, Painting-French, Painting-German, Painting-Italian, Painting-Japanese, Posters, Prints, Sculpture, Painting-European, Historical Material, History of Art & Archaeology, Portraits, Ceramics, Archaeology, American Western Art, Printmaking, Art Education, Asian Art, Video, American Indian Art, Porcelain, Primitive art, Furniture, Southwestern Art, Jade, Metalwork, Antiquities-Oriental, Oriental Art, Pottery, Religious Art, Restoration & Conservation, Silver, Woodcuts, Antiquities-Egyptian, Antiquities-Etruscan, Antiquities-Greek, Antiquities-Roman, Pewter
Collections: Chinese Art; Auction Catalogs

M **Creative Arts Center,** 4525 Oak St, Kansas City, MO 64111-1873. Tel 816-751-1236; Fax 816-561-7154; Internet Home Page Address: www.nelson-atkins.org; *CEO & Cur* Julian Zugazagoitia
Open Wed 10 AM - 4 PM, Thurs & Fri 10 AM - 9 PM, Sat 10 AM - 5 PM, Sun noon - 5 PM; cl Mon & Tues, New Year's Day, Independence Day, Thanksgiving, Christmas Eve & Day; No admis fee
Activities: Art classes for children ages 3-18 & adults; workshops for schools; family workshops & events; tours

M **PRINT CONSORTIUM,** 6121 NW 77th St, Kansas City, MO 64151-1587. Tel 816-587-1986; Elec Mail eickhors@missouri western.edu; Internet Home Page Address: www.printexhibits.com; *Exec Dir* Dr William S Eickhorst
Estab 1983 to promote printmaking as a fine art; Mem: 300; mem open to professional printmaking artists; dues $25
Income: Financed by mem & exhib rental
Collections: Prints by estab professional artists from the US & 9 foreign countries
Publications: Artist's Proof, quarterly newsletter
Activities: Book traveling exhibs 4-6 per yr; originate traveling exhibs to museums, art centers, cols & universities

M **SOCIETY FOR CONTEMPORARY PHOTOGRAPHY,** 2016 Baltimore Ave, Kansas City, MO 64108. Tel 816-471-2115; Fax 816-471-2462; *Exec Dir* Kathy Aron
Open Wed - Sat 11 AM - 5 PM; No admis fee; Estab 1984 to bring fine art photography to Kansas City; Dedicated to teaching & learning about photography from local, national & international photographers. The society is committed to bring gallery shows to the Midwest as well as supporting emerging local artists; Mem: 425; dues $35, students $20; ann meeting in Dec
Income: Financed by mem & grants
Exhibitions: Exhibitions vary; call for details
Publications: Update, bimonthly; exhibit catalogs
Activities: Classes for adults & children; lects open to pub, 8 vis lectrs per yr; competition with awards

C **UMB FINANCIAL CORPORATION,** PO Box 419226, Kansas City, MO 64141-6226. Tel 816-860-7000; Fax 816-860-7610; Elec Mail carol.sturn@umb.com; Internet Home Page Address: www.umb.com; *Chmn* R Crosby Kemper
Estab 1947 to display classic & contemporary art for viewing by patrons & employees; Collection is displayed in lobbies & customer access areas in various UMB Banks in Oklahoma, Colorado, Kansas, Missouri & Illinois
Collections: Americana Collection, including American portraits (George Caleb Bingham, Benjamin Blythe, Gilbert Stuart, Charles Wilson Peale), regional coll (William Commerford, Peter Hurd, J H Sharp, Gordon Snidow), modern art (Fran Bull, Olive Rush, Wayne Thiebaud, Ellsworth Kelly)
Activities: Objects of art lent to galleries for spec exhibits

M **UNIVERSITY OF MISSOURI-KANSAS CITY,** Gallery of Art, 5100 Rockhill Rd, 205C Fine Arts Bldg Kansas City, MO 64110-2446. Tel 816-235-1502; Fax 816-235-6528; Elec Mail csubler@cctr.umkc.edu; Internet Home Page Address: cas.umkc.edu/art/gallery.cfm; *Dir* Craig Subler
Open Mon, Wed, Fri, & Sat 11AM-4PM; No admis fee; Estab 1977 to bring a broad range of art to both students and the community; 1,725 sq ft; Average Annual Attendance: 5,000; Mem: 100; dues $50
Income: Financed by endowment, city & state appropriation, contribution
Publications: Exhib catalogues
Activities: Adult classes; lect open to pub; book traveling exhibs; originate traveling exhibs that circulate to museums & galleries in US & abroad

MARYVILLE

M **NORTHWEST MISSOURI STATE UNIVERSITY,** DeLuce Art Gallery, 800 University Dr, Dept of Art Maryville, MO 64468-6015. Tel 660-562-1326; Fax 660-562-1346; Elec Mail plaber@mail.nwmissouri.edu; Internet Home Page Address: wwwnwmissouri.edu/dept/art/index.htm; *Chmn Dept Art* Philip Laber; *Olive DeLuce Art Gallery Coll Cur* Laura Kukee
Open Mon 6 - 9 PM, Tues - Sat 1 - 5 PM, Sun 1:30 - 5 PM; No admis fee; Estab 1965 to provide exhibitions of contemporary works in all media as part of the learning experiences in the visual arts; Gallery is maintained with 150 running ft exhib space with high security, humidity-controlled air conditioning & flexible lighting; Average Annual Attendance: 6,000
Income: Financed by state appropriation & external grants
Collections: Percival DeLuce Memorial Collection consisting of American paintings, drawings, prints and decorative arts; some European furniture and prints
Exhibitions: Rotating exhibs
Activities: Classes for adults; lects open to pub, 6 vis lectrs per yr; gallery talks; tours; schols offered; individual & original objects of art lent within the institution; lending coll contains original art works, original prints, paintings & drawings; book traveling exhibs 3 per yr

MEXICO

M **AUDRAIN COUNTY HISTORICAL SOCIETY,** Graceland Museum & American Saddlehorse Museum, 501 S Muldrow Ave, Mexico, MO 65265-2082; PO Box 398, Mexico, MO 65265-0398. Tel 573-581-3910; Elec Mail info@audrain.org; Internet Home Page Address: www.audrain.org; *Exec Dir* Kathryn Adams
Open Tues - Sat 10 AM - 4 PM, Sun 1-4 PM, cl Mon, Jan & holidays; Admis $3, children 12 & under $1; Estab 1959; Average Annual Attendance: 2,500; Mem: 600; dues $15 & up
Income: $25,000 (financed by endowment & mem)
Collections: Currier & Ives; Photographs; Lusterware; Dolls; Tom Bass Artifacts

L **MEXICO-AUDRAIN COUNTY LIBRARY,** 305 W Jackson, Mexico, MO 65265. Tel 573-581-4939; Fax 573-581-7510; Elec Mail mexicoaudrain@netscape.net; Internet Home Page Address: mexico-audrain.lib.mno.us/mexico-audrain; *Children's Librn* Aletha Taylor; *Acquisitions Librn* Ruth Taylor; *Dir* Ray Hall; *Head Librn* Christal Brunner
Open winter hours, Mon - Thurs 9 AM -8PM, Fri 9 AM - 5:30 PM, Sat 9AM-1PM; summer hours Mon, Tues, Thurs, & Fri 9AM-5:30PM, Wed 9AM-8PM, Sat 9AM-1PM; No admis fee; Estab 1912 to provide library services to the residents of Audrain County, Missouri; Exhibit room with different exhibits each month; children's dept has a continuously changing exhibit
Income: Financed by donations
Library Holdings: Book Volumes 112,529; Filmstrips; Kodachrome Transparencies; Motion Pictures; Other Holdings Art print reproductions; Newspapers; Periodical Subscriptions 127; Records
Collections: Audrain County history; paintings by Audrain County artists
Exhibitions: Local Federated Womens Club sponsored a different exhibit each month during the fall, winter & spring, these included local artists, both adult & young people, & recognized artists of the area; The Missouri Council of the Arts also provide traveling exhibits that we display
Activities: Classes for children; story hour (one hour, four days a wk); individual paintings & original objects of art lent

OSAGE BEACH

NATIONAL OIL & ACRYLIC PAINTERS SOCIETY
For further information, see National and Regional Organizations

RAYTOWN

THE STAINED GLASS ASSOCIATION OF AMERICA
For further information, see National and Regional Organizations

SAINT CHARLES

M **FOUNDRY ART CENTRE,** 520 N Main Center, Saint Charles, MO 63301-2181. Tel 636-255-0270; Fax 636-925-0345; Elec Mail director@foundryartcentre.org; Internet Home Page Address: foundryartcentre.org

M **LINDENWOOD UNIVERSITY,** Harry D Hendren Gallery, 209 Southkings Hwy, School of Fine and Performing Arts Saint Charles, MO 63301-1693. Tel 636-949-4862; Fax 636-949-4610; Elec Mail etillinger@lindenwood.edu; Internet Home Page Address: www.lindenwood.edu; *Chmn* Dr Elaine Tillinger; *Dean Fine Arts & Performing Arts* Dean Marsha H Parker
Open Mon - Fri 9 AM - 5 PM, Sat & Sun 1 - 4 PM; No admis fee; Estab 1969 as a col exhib gallery; Gallery is approx 3,600 sq ft with skylight & one wall of side light; 2 additional galleries; Lindenwood Univ Cultural Ctr off campus; Studio East on campus; Average Annual Attendance: 4,000
Income: Financed by endowment
Special Subjects: Prints
Collections: Contemporary American & European prints in various media including Works by Paul Jenkins, William Hayter, Will Barnet, Mauricio Lazansky, Werner Drewes, William Sett
Exhibitions: Rotating Exhibits
Activities: Lects open to pub, 5-6 vis lectrs per yr; gallery talks; tours; original objects of art lent; lending coll contains photographs; originates traveling exhibs through the Missouri State Council on the Arts; artist workshops at Daniel Boone Village (owned by Univ)

SAINT JOSEPH

M **THE ALBRECHT-KEMPER MUSEUM OF ART,** 2818 Frederick Ave, Saint Joseph, MO 64506-2903. Tel 816-233-7003; Fax 816-233-3413; Elec Mail frontdesk@albrecht-kemper.org; Internet Home Page Address: www.albrecht-kemper.org; *Registrar* Ann Tootle; *Dir Pub Events* Robyn Enright; *Dir* Terry Oldham
Open Tues - Fri 10 AM - 4 PM, Sat & Sun 1 - 4 PM, cl Mon; Admis adults $5, seniors 65 & over $2, students $1, children 5 & under free, group rates available; Estab 1913 to increase pub knowledge & appreciation of the arts; Repository of 18th, 19th, 20th Century American art, serving as a cultural arts center for Northwest Missouri; Average Annual Attendance: 17,000; Mem: 550; dues $35 & up, students $15; ann meeting in Apr
Income: Financed by mem & fundraising events
Special Subjects: Drawings, Painting-American, Prints, Watercolors, American Indian Art, American Western Art, Woodcuts, Etchings & Engravings, Landscapes, Marine Painting
Collections: Collections of American Art consisting of paintings by George Bellows, Thomas Hart Benton, Albert Bierstadt, Alfred Bricher, William Merritt Chase, Francis Edmonds, George Hall, Robert Henri, Edward Hopper, George Inness, Eastman Johnson, Fitz Hugh Lane, Ernest Lawson, William Paxton, Rembrandt Peale, John Sloan, Gilbert Stuart, Andrew Wyeth; drawings by Leonard Baskin, Isabel Bishop, Paul Cadmus, Kenneth Callahan, William Gropper, Gabor Peterdi, Robert Vickrey & John Wilde; prints by John Taylor Arms, George Catlin, Thomas Nason; sculpture by Deborah Butterfield, L E Gus Shafer & Ernest Trova
Publications: Annual report including catalog of year's acquisitions, exhibition catalogs & brochures; Art Matters Quarterly
Activities: Classes for adults; docent training; lect open to pub; performances & progs in fine arts theater; concerts; gallery talks, tours, competitions; individual paintings & original objects of art lent to other museums; originate traveling exhibs to other museums; mus shop sells books, magazines & misc items

L **Bradley Art Library,** 2818 Frederick Ave, Saint Joseph, MO 64506. Tel 816-233-7003; Fax 816-233-3413; Internet Home Page Address: www.albrecht-kemper.org; *Dir* Terry Oldham
Open museum hrs; Non-circulating art reference library open to the pub
Library Holdings: Book Volumes 2,500; Periodical Subscriptions

A **ALLIED ARTS COUNCIL OF ST JOSEPH,** 118 S Eighth St, Saint Joseph, MO 64501. Tel 816-233-0231; Fax 816-233-6704; Elec Mail artstaff@stjoearts.org; Internet Home Page Address: www.stjoearts.org; *Exec Dir* Teresa Fankhauser; *Opers Mgr* Cathy Ketter; *Prog Coordr* Tammy Santos
Open Mon - Fri 8 AM - 5 PM; No admis fee; Estab 1963 to bring the Arts & people together; Remote at Heartland Hospital; Mem: 1800
Income: Financed by state appropriation
Activities: Classes for children; Biennial Artist awards

M **MISSOURI WESTERN STATE UNIVERSITY,** (Missouri Western State College) Gallery 206 Foyer Gallery, 4525 Downs Dr, Thompson E Potter FA Bldg Saint Joseph, MO 64507-2246. Tel 816-271-4282; Fax 816-271-4181; Elec Mail sauls@griffon.mwsc.edu; Internet Home Page Address: www.missouriwestern.edu; *Pres* Dr James Scanlon; *VPres* Dr James Roever; *Chmn Dept Art* Allison Sauls PhD
Open Mon - Fri 8:30 AM - 4 PM; No admis fee; Estab 1971 to bring an awareness of contemporary directions in art to students & to the community; Foyer gallery is in front of building, next to theater; 120 ft long, 30 ft wide, with 25 ft high ceiling; rug paneling on walls; modern decor, gallery 206 is on second fl; 25 sq ft, 10 ft ceiling; rug paneling on walls, carpeted; Average Annual Attendance: 10,000
Income: Financed by state appropriation
Exhibitions: Invitational of juried art exhibs
Activities: Classes for adults; lects open to pub, 3-4 vis lectrs per yr; gallery talks; tours; book traveling exhibs

M **SAINT JOSEPH MUSEUM,** 3406 Frederick Ave, Saint Joseph, MO 64508-2913; PO Box 8096, Saint Joseph, MO 64508-8096. Tel 816-232-8471; Fax 816-232-8482; Elec Mail sjm@stjosephmuseum.org; Internet Home Page Address: www.stjosephmuseum.org; *Registrar* Carol Wills; *Cur Ethnology* Marilyn S Taylor; *Cur Collections* Sarah M Elder; *Dir Mktg & Pub Rels* Kathy Reno; *Cur History* Jackie Lewin
Open Mon - Sat 9 AM - 5 PM, Sun & holidays 1 - 5 PM; Admis adults $3.50, students $1.50, children under 6 free; free on Sun & holidays; Estab 1927 to increase & diffuse knowledge & appreciation of history, art & the sciences & to aid the educational work that is being done by the schools of Saint Joseph & other educ organizations; Mini-gallery, usually for small, low security traveling exhibits; Average Annual Attendance: 30,000; Mem: 400 dues $30 & up; ann meeting in Jan
Income: $550,000 (financed by mem & city appropriation)
Special Subjects: American Indian Art, Anthropology, Archaeology, Ethnology, Costumes, Manuscripts, Eskimo Art, Dolls, Furniture, Glass, Scrimshaw, Dioramas
Collections: Harry L George Collection of Native American Art
Exhibitions: Lewis & Clark; Native American material
Publications: The Happenings (newsletter), bimonthly
Activities: Classes for children; craft prog; lect open to pub; mus shop sells books, magazines, prints, slides & gift items

L **Library,** 3406 Frederick Ave, PO Box 8096 Saint Joseph, MO 64508-2913. Tel 816-232-8471; Fax 816-232-8482; Elec Mail sjm@stjosephmuseum.org; *Cur Educ* Sarah Elder; *Dir* Richard A Nolf
Open Mon - Sat 9 AM - 5 PM, Sun 1 - 5 PM, Library open Mon - Fri 9 AM - Noon & 1 - 4 PM by appointment only; No admis fee; Estab 1926 to hold mus colls; Circ For research only; Mini gallery for traveling exhibits. Maintained as a reference library only
Purchases: $1200
Library Holdings: Book Volumes 5000; Clipping Files; Framed Reproductions; Manuscripts; Memorabilia; Original Art Works; Periodical Subscriptions 40; Photographs; Prints; Sculpture
Publications: The Happenings, bimonthly newsletter

Activities: Classes for children; tours; originate traveling exhibs to schools

SAINT LOUIS

M **AMERICAN KENNEL CLUB,** Museum of the Dog, 1721 S Mason Rd, Saint Louis, MO 63131-1518. Tel 314-821-3647; Fax 314-821-7381; Elec Mail info@museumofthedog.com; Internet Home Page Address: www.museumofthedog.org; *Cur & Mgr* Barbara Jedda McNab
Open Tues - Sat 10 AM - 4PM, Sun 1 - 5PM; Admis adults $5, seniors $2.50, children 5-14 $1; Estab 1984; Average Annual Attendance: 12,000; Mem: 650; dues $25 minimum; ann meeting in Oct
Purchases: Kathy Jacobson - Dog Walking in Central Park
Special Subjects: Drawings, Painting-American, Prints, Sculpture, Watercolors, Ceramics, Folk Art, Pottery, Primitive art, Woodcarvings, Woodcuts, Etchings & Engravings, Painting-European, Portraits, Posters, Porcelain, Silver, Painting-British, Historical Material, Period Rooms, Cartoons, Reproductions
Collections: Fine Art: art, artifacts & literature dedicated to the dog
Exhibitions: Artists' Registry Exhibition
Publications: SIRIUS, quarterly newsletter
Activities: Classes for adults; docent progs; lect open to pub; book traveling exhibs 2 per yr; mus shop sells books & prints

L **Reference Library,** 1721 S Mason Rd, Saint Louis, MO 63131-1518. Tel 314-821-3647; Fax 314-821-7381; Elec Mail dogarts@aol.com; Internet Home Page Address: www.akc.org;
Open Tues - Sat 9 AM - 5 PM, Sun Noon - 5 PM; Admis adults $3, sr citizens $1.50, children $1; Estab 1982; For reference only; Average Annual Attendance: 10,000; Mem: 800; dues from patron $1,000 to individual $35
Income: $400,000 (financed by endowment, mem & gift shop sales)
Library Holdings: Book Volumes 2000; Cassettes; Exhibition Catalogs; Framed Reproductions; Memorabilia; Motion Pictures; Original Art Works; Periodical Subscriptions 10; Photographs; Prints; Sculpture; Slides; Video Tapes
Collections: Fine Arts Collection; paintings, drawings & sculptures; decorative arts
Publications: Newsletter, SIRIUS (3 times per yr)
Activities: Fun Day activities for children; Guest Dog of the Week events; gallery talks; tours; sales shop sells books, magazines, jewelry, wearables & luggage

M **ART SAINT LOUIS,** 555 Washington Ave, Ste 150 Saint Louis, MO 63101-1249. Tel 314-241-4810; Fax 314-241-6933; Elec Mail info@artstlouis.org; Internet Home Page Address: www.artstlouis.org; *Dir Mktg & Develop* Christine Malinee; *Assoc Dir* Robin Hirsch
Open Mon & Sat 10AM-4PM, Tues-Fri 10AM-5PM. Cl holidays; No charge
Collections: paintings; sculpture

A **ARTS & EDUCATION COUNCIL OF GREATER SAINT LOUIS,** 3526 Washington Ave, Saint Louis, MO 63103-1019. Tel 314-535-3600; Fax 314-535-3606; Internet Home Page Address: artsstl.tripod.com; *Pres* James F Weidman; *Chmn* Peter F Mackie
Estab 1963 to coordinate, promote & assist in the development of cultural & educ activities in the Greater St. Louis area; to offer planning, coordinating, promotional & fundraising service to eligible organizations & groups, thereby creating a valuable community-wide assoc; Mem: 150
Income: Financed by funds from pvt sector
Exhibitions: Saint Louis Arts Awards
Publications: Ann report; calendar of cultural events, quarterly; quarterly newsletter

M **ATRIUM GALLERY,** 4814 Washington Blvd, Ste 110 Saint Louis, MO 63108-1833. Tel 314-367-1076; Fax 314-367-7676; Elec Mail atrium@earthlink.net; Internet Home Page Address: www.atriumgallery.net; *Dir* Carolyn Miles
Open Wed - Sat 10 AM - 6 PM, Sun noon-4PM; Tues by appointment; No admis fee; Estab 1986; Commercial gallery featuring contemporary artists who are active regionally & nationally featuring one-person shows
Income: Financed by donations
Activities: Buffet luncheon/lects art series; 8 vis lectrs per yr; salon progs featuring talks by exhibiting artists, 6 progs per yr

M **BELAS ARTES MULTICULTURAL CENTER,** Art Gallery, 1854 Russell Blvd, Saint Louis, MO 63104. Tel 314-772-2787; *Contact* Cileia Miranda Yuen

M **CENTER OF CREATIVE ARTS (COCA),** Millstone Gallery, 524 Trinity Ave, Saint Louis, MO 63130. Tel 314-725-6555

M **CHATILLON-DEMENIL HOUSE FOUNDATION,** Chatillon-DeMenil House, 3352 DeMenil Pl, Saint Louis, MO 63118. Tel 314-771-5828; Fax 314-771-3475; Elec Mail demenil@sbcglobal.net; demenil@demenil.org; *Dir* Kevin O'Neill
Open Wed - Sat 10 AM - 3 PM; Admis $5, children $2; Estab 1965 to educate & inform the community on 19th century life & culture; Average Annual Attendance: 8,000; Mem: 500; dues $15 - $1,000; ann meeting in May
Income: Financed by mem, grants & donations
Special Subjects: Architecture, Painting-American, Decorative Arts, Portraits, Furniture, Porcelain, Silver, Historical Material, Period Rooms
Collections: Decorative art from c1770 through 19th century; period rooms with furnishings; paintings; 1904 St. Louis World's Fair
Exhibitions: Historic Photos-French & Indian Families in American West; Victoria Mourning Event last Sunday of October; Victorian Home Crafts
Publications: Newsletter, quarterly
Activities: Educ progs; docent training; lects open to pub; tours; retail store sells books, reproductions, eclectic merchandise

M **CONCORDIA HISTORICAL INSTITUTE,** 804 Seminary Pl, Saint Louis, MO 63105-3014. Tel 314-505-7900; Fax 314-505-7901; Elec Mail chi@lutheranhistory.org; Internet Home Page Address: www.lutheranhistory.org; *Assoc Dir Archives* Marvin A Huggins; *Museum Mgr* Patrice Russo; *Exec Dir* Laurence L Lumpe
Open Mon-Fri 8:30 PM - 4 PM, cl international holidays; No admis fee; Estab 1847, to collect & preserve resources on the history of Lutheranism in America.

Affiliated with The Lutheran Church, Missouri Synod; Average Annual Attendance: 13,000; Mem: 700; dues life $5,000, patron $100, organization, active & subscription $50
Special Subjects: Hispanic Art, Painting-American, African Art, Costumes, Crafts, Etchings & Engravings, Manuscripts, Furniture, Asian Art, Coins & Medals
Collections: Church archives & vast historical materials; crafts; handcrafts; Reformation & Lutheran coins & medals; Works by Lutheran artists & paintings & artifacts for Lutheran worship; Native artwork from Foreign Mission Fields, especially China, India, Africa & New Guinea
Exhibitions: Temporary exhibitions
Publications: Concordia Historical Institute Quarterly; Historical Footnotes
Activities: Lect open to pub; competitions with awards; Distinguished Service Award & awards of commendation for contributions to Lutheran History & archives; sales shop sells books, slides & craft items

A **CONTEMPORARY ART MUSEUM ST LOUIS,** 3750 Washington Blvd, Saint Louis, MO 63108-3612. Tel 314-535-4660; Fax 314-535-1226; Elec Mail info@camstl.org; Internet Home Page Address: www.camstl.org; *Exec Dir* Paul Ha; *Cur* Dominic Molon; *Asst Cur* Kelly Shindler; *Exhib Mgr* David Smith; *Deputy Dir* Lisa Grove
Open Wed - Sat 10 AM - 5 PM, Sun 11 AM - 4 PM, cl Mon & Tues; Admis $5, free for children, senior citizens & students; Estab 1980 to promote & advocate contemporary arts; Multi-disciplinary visual arts center, maintains cafe; Average Annual Attendance: 35,000; Mem: 600; dues $45 & up
Income: $500,000 (financed by mem, corporation & foundation funds)
Publications: Exhibit catalogs; newsletter, quarterly; ann magazine
Activities: Educ outreach; workshops; Artreach; family, teen & student progs; lects open to public, 12 - 15 vis lectrs per year; concerts; gallery talks; tours; Great Rivers Biennial award; book traveling exhibs to mus & not for profits w/contemporary art progs; mus shop sells books, magazines, prints & branded items

M **CRAFT ALLIANCE,** 6640 Delmar Blvd, Saint Louis, MO 63130-4503. Tel 314-725-1177; Fax 314-725-2068; Elec Mail gallery@craftalliance.org; Internet Home Page Address: www.craftalliance.org; *Educ Dir* Luanne Rimel; *Exec Dir* Boo McLoughlin; *Dir Exhibs* Stefanie Kirkland; *Develop Dir* Saskya Bryon
Open Tues-Thurs 10AM-5PM, Fri & Sat 10 AM - 6 PM, Sun 11AM-5PM; No admis fee; Estab 1964 for exhib & sales of craft objects; 1500 sq ft; Average Annual Attendance: 60,000; Mem: 750; $50 minimum dues per yr; Scholarships
Income: Financed by mem, Missouri Arts Council, St Louis Arts & Educ Council, Regional Arts Commission
Exhibitions: Monthly exhibits by nat & international artists
Publications: Mem newsletter; Winter-Spring, Summer & Fall catalogs
Activities: Classes for adults & children; vis artists prog; outreach; lects open to pub; gallery talks; tours; sales shop sells original art

M **The Kranzberg Arts Center,** 501 N Grand, Saint Louis, MO 63103.

M **LAUMEIER SCULPTURE PARK,** 12580 Rott Rd, Saint Louis, MO 63127-1212. Tel 314-615-5278; Fax 314-615-5288; Elec Mail info@laumeier.org; Internet Home Page Address: www.laumeier.org; *Chmn Bd Trustees* David Schlafly; *Accounting Dir* Mary Ruskin; *Cur Educ* Karen Mullen; *Cur Educ Interpretation* Clara Collins Coleman; *Mgr Mem & Mus Servs* Jennie Swanson; *Special Events Mgr* Marie Oberkirsch; *Chief Preparator* Nick Lang; *Admin Asst* Julia Norton; *Dir* Marilu Knode; *Lib & Archivist* Joy Wright; *Cur Exhib* Dana Turkovic; *Collec Mgr & Registrar* Ashley Wenzel; *Opers Mgr* Don Gerling; *Mktg/Commun Mgr* Emily Rodenbeck; *Develop Officer* Jacqueline Chambers
Park open daily 8 AM - half hour past sunset; Museum open Tues - Sat 10 AM - 5 PM & Sun Noon - 5 PM, cl Christmas day & Art Fair weekend; No admis fee except special events; Estab 1976 to exhibit contemporary sculpture by internationally acclaimed artists; Circ non-circulating research lib & archives; 5 indoor galleries feature changing exhib 2 per yr; Average Annual Attendance: 350,000; Mem: 1,000; dues Visionary $5000 & up, Laumeier Society $2,500 & up, Collector's Circle $1,000 - $2,499, Dir Circle $500, Sculptor's Forum $250, Casting Circle $125, Family $65, Friends $45, ArtLink $20
Income: Financed by mem, corporate gifts & grants
Library Holdings: Audio Tapes; Book Volumes; Clipping Files; Compact Disks; DVDs; Exhibition Catalogs; Original Documents; Periodical Subscriptions; Video Tapes
Special Subjects: Landscape Architecture, Art History, Sculpture, Restorations
Collections: Contemporary Art; monumental & site specific sculpture & related works; representative examples of Vito Acconci, Mark di Suvero, Jackie Ferrara, Charles Ginnever, Michael Heizer, Alexander Liberman, Beverly Pepper & Ursula Von Rydingsvard; Ernest Trova sculptures; Tony Tasset; Joseph Havel; Mary Miss
Publications: Objectivity, quarterly newsletter
Activities: Classes for adults & children; docent training; lects open to pub; concerts; guided tours; lects; temp indoor & outdoor art exhib; perm installations; art fair; special events; mus shop sells books, original art, jewelry, toys, souvenirs

M **MARYVILLE UNIVERSITY SAINT LOUIS,** Morton J May Foundation Gallery, 650 Maryville University Dr, Saint Louis, MO 63141-7299. Tel 314-529-9381; Fax 314-529-9940; Internet Home Page Address: www.maryville.edu; *Gallery Dir* John Baltrushunas
Open during Univ Library hrs (check website for times or call 314-529-9595); No admis fee; Estab to show work of regional, national artists & designers; Average Annual Attendance: 3,000
Income: $4,500 (university)
Library Holdings: Book Volumes; Exhibition Catalogs; Kodachrome Transparencies; Periodical Subscriptions; Records; Slides; Video Tapes
Special Subjects: Painting-American
Activities: Curating experience for advanced students; lects open to pub, 3-4 vis lectrs per yr; gallery talks; sponsoring of competitions; individual paintings & original objects of art lent to organizations, art guilds & schools

A **MISSOURI ARTS COUNCIL,** 815 Olive St Ste 16, Saint Louis, MO 63101-1503. Tel 314-340-6845; Fax 314-340-7215; Elec Mail moarts@ded.mo.gov; Internet Home Page Address: www.missouriartscouncil.org; *Exec Dir* Beverly Strohmeyer; *Asst Dir* Michael Donovan
Open Mon - Fri 8 AM - 5 PM; Estab 1965 to promote & develop cultural resources on the arts & as sets in Missouri
Income: Financed by state appropriation
Activities: Poetry Out Loud; Missouri Arts Awards

M **MISSOURI HISTORICAL SOCIETY,** Missouri History Museum, Lindel & De Baliviere in Forest Park, 5700 Lindell Blvd Saint Louis, MO 63112-0040. Tel 314-746-4599; Fax 314-454-3162; Elec Mail info@mohistory.org; Internet Home Page Address: www.mohistory.org; *Pres* Robert Archibald; *Mng Dir Opers* Karen M Goering; *Mus Shop Mgr* Susan Ponciroli; *Dir Exhib* Becki Hartke; *CFO* Harry Rich; *Mng Dir Institutional Advancement* Vicki Kaffenberger; *Mng Dir Educ* Melanie Adams; *Mng Dir Mus Svcs* Katherine Van Allen
Open daily 10 AM - 5 PM, Tues until 8 PM; Summer hrs daily 10 AM - 6 PM, Tues until 8 PM; No admis fee; fees apply to special exhibs; Estab 1866 to col & preserve objects & information relating to the history of St Louis, Missouri & the Louisiana Purchase Territory; Circ 6000; dues from $45 & up; Average Annual Attendance: 200,000; Mem: 5500; dues from $55; ann meeting Sept; Scholarships, Fellowships
Income: Financed by pvt endowment, mem, special events, city & county taxes
Special Subjects: Historical Material
Collections: 19th & 20th century art of St Louis and the American West; paintings; photographs; prints
Exhibitions: Lindbergh Memorabilia; St Louis Memory & History: 1904 Worlds Fair; 5 rotating exhibs per yr
Publications: MHS magazine, bimonthly, mems only pub; Voices, online; Gateway, ann journal
Activities: Classes for adults & children; dramatic progs; docent training; outreach prog festivals; lects open to pub; concerts; gallery talks; tours; individual paintings & original objects of art lent to qualified mus & galleries that meet AAM standards; book traveling exhibs; originate traveling exhibs; Sales shop sells books, prints, slides, souvenirs, china

M **PHILIP SLEIN GALLERY,** 4735 McPherson Ave, Saint Louis, MO 63108-1918. Tel 314-621-4634; *Dir.* Bridget Melloy; *Owner* Philip Slein; *Owner* Tom Bussmann
Open Tues-Sat 10AM-5PM, other times by appointment
Collections: works by regional & nat artists; painting; drawings; printmaking; photographs; sculpture

M **SAINT LOUIS ART MUSEUM,** 1 Fine Arts Dr, Forest Park Saint Louis, MO 63110-1331. Tel 314-721-0072; Fax 314-721-6172; Elec Mail public relations@slam.org; Internet Home Page Address: www.slam.org; *Dir* Brent Benjamin; *Deputy Dir* Carolyn Schmidt; *Asst Dir Curatorial Affairs* Andrew Walker; *Asst Dir Exhib & Coll* Linda Thomas; *Acting Asst Dir Develop* Shelia Manion; *Acting Asst Dir External Affairs* Jennifer Stoffel; *Asst Dir Pub Prog & Educ* Bill Appleton
Open Tues - Sun 10 AM - 5 PM, Fri until 9 PM, cl Mon, Thanksgiving & Christmas Day; No admis fee except for featured exhibitions; admis fee for featured exhibs free on Fridays; Estab 1879, originally called St Louis School & Mus of Fine Arts, an independent entity within Washington Univ; Mus contains over 30,000 works of art. Collections include works from virtually every culture & time period; Average Annual Attendance: 450,000; Mem: 15,000; dues $55 - $25,000
Income: Property tax provides 60% of operating income & balance from grants & pvt donations
Library Holdings: Auction Catalogs; Audio Tapes; Book Volumes 109,000; CD-ROMs; Cassettes; Clipping Files; Compact Disks; DVDs; Exhibition Catalogs; Fiche; Lantern Slides; Memorabilia; Original Documents; Pamphlets; Periodical Subscriptions 220; Slides 75,000; Video Tapes 300
Collections: African; American; Ancient & Islamic; Asian; Contemporary; Decorative Arts & Design; European Art to 1800; Modern; Oceanic; Pre-Columbian & American Indian; Prints, Drawings & Photographs; ancient Chinese bronzes; 20th century German painting; Henri Matisse's Bathers with a Turtle; George Caleb Bingham's Election Series; Hans Holbein the Younger's Mary; Lady Guilford; Vincent van Gogh's Stairway at Auvers; Bartolomeo Manfredi's Appollo and Marsyas
Publications: Biennial report, quarterly magazine and program guide, exhibition catalogs
Activities: Classes for adults & children; docent training; lects open to pub, 30 vis lectrs per yr; lects for members only; concerts; gallery talks; tours; competitions with prizes; exten dept serves state of Missouri; individual paintings & original objects of art lent to other museums; book traveling exhibs; originates traveling exhibs; mus shop sells books, magazines, prints & reproductions

L **Richardson Memorial Library,** 1 Fine Arts Dr, Forest Park Saint Louis, MO 63110-1331. Tel 314-655-5252; Fax 314-721-4911; Elec Mail library@slam.org; Internet Home Page Address: www.slam.org; *Head Librn* Marianne L Cavanaugh; *Archivist* Norma Sindelar; *Pub Serv Librn* Clare Vasquez; *Technical Servs Librn* Christopher Handy
Open Thurs by appt only; No admis fee; Estab 1915 to provide reference & bibliographical service to the mus staff & the adult pub; to bibliographically support the colls owned by the mus; For research only; Average Annual Attendance: Non-circulating
Income: Financed by endowment & city appropriation
Library Holdings: Auction Catalogs; Book Volumes 109,000; CD-ROMs; Clipping Files; DVDs; Exhibition Catalogs; Fiche; Manuscripts; Original Documents; Pamphlets; Periodical Subscriptions 167; Photographs; Reels
Special Subjects: Art History, Decorative Arts, Photography, Etchings & Engravings, Painting-American, Ethnology, Asian Art, American Indian Art, Furniture, Glass, Afro-American Art, Antiquities-Oriental, Carpets & Rugs, Antiquities-Greek, Antiquities-Roman
Collections: Museum Archives, includes records of Louisiana Purchase Expo (1904) & papers of Morton D May

L **SAINT LOUIS PUBLIC LIBRARY,** 1301 Olive St, Saint Louis, MO 63103. Tel 314-241-2288; Fax 314-241-3840; Elec Mail webmaster@slpl.org; Internet Home Page Address: www.slpl.org; *Mgr Fine Arts Dept* Suzy Enns Frechette
Open Mon - Thurs 10 AM - 9 PM, Fri & Sat 10 AM - 6 PM, Sun 1 - 5 PM (1st fl only); Estab Art Dept in 1912

Library Holdings: Book Volumes 115,000; CD-ROMs; Clipping Files 500; Compact Disks 12,000; Exhibition Catalogs; Original Art Works 4; Pamphlets; Periodical Subscriptions 45; Reproductions 300; Sculpture 5; Slides 17,500
Special Subjects: Art History, Decorative Arts, Illustration, Photography, Graphic Arts, Interior Design, Afro-American Art, Architecture
Collections: Steedman Architectural Library; Local Architects & Buildings Files; Local Artists Files

M **SHELDON ART GALLERIES,** 3648 Washington Blvd, Saint Louis, MO 63108-3610. Tel 314-533-9900; Fax 314-533-2958; *Dir* Olivia Lahs-Gonzales
Open Tues 12 PM - 8 PM, Wed - Fri 12 PM - 5 PM, Sat 10 AM - 2 PM, cl New Years Eve & Day, Independence Day, Thanksgiving Day, Christmas Eve & Day
Special Subjects: Photography, Painting-American, Sculpture

A **ST. LOUIS ARTISTS' GUILD,** Two Oak Knoll, Saint Louis, MO 63105. Tel 314-727-6266; Fax 314-727-9190; Elec Mail guild-info@stlouisartistsguild.org; Internet Home Page Address: www.stlouisartistsguild.org; *Pres* Joanne Stremsterfer; *Office Mgr* Robyn Conroy; *Mus Shop Mgr* Karen Roodman; *Gallery Dir* Gina Alvarez; *Exec Dir* David Weaver; *Educ Dir* Hannah Montford
Open Tues - Sun Noon - 4 PM, cl Mon; No admis fee; Estab 1886 for the purpose of promoting excellence in the arts; Maintains reference library; Average Annual Attendance: 30,000; Mem: 900+, dues $55
Income: Financed by mem
Special Subjects: Cartoons, Drawings, Photography, Prints, Sculpture, Silver, Watercolors, Painting-American, Pottery, Bronzes, Woodcuts, Afro-American Art, Ceramics, Crafts, Portraits, Furniture, Glass, Woodcarvings
Exhibitions: 15-20 exhibits per yr
Publications: Quarterly newsletter
Activities: Classes for adults & children; lects open to pub, 5 vis lectrs per yr; gallery talks; tours; competitions with awards; workshops; sales shop sells original art

M **TROVA FOUNDATION,** Philip Samuels Fine Art, 1011 E Park Industrial, Saint Louis, MO 63130. Tel 314-727-2444; Fax 314-727-6084; Elec Mail rgiancola@universalsewing.com; *Dir* Clifford Samuels; *Pres* Philip Samuels
Open Mon - Fri by appointment only; Estab 1988; Contemporary painting, collage, drawing & sculpture

M **UNIVERSITY OF MISSOURI, SAINT LOUIS,** Gallery 210, 1 University Blvd, 210 Lucas Hall, Art Dept Saint Louis, MO 63121-4400. Tel 314-516-5000; Fax 314-516-5816; Elec Mail gallery@umsl.edu; Internet Home Page Address: www.umsl.edu; *Dir* Terry Suhre; *Chmn* Jack Rushing
Open Tues-Sat 11AM-5PM; Estab 1972 to exhibit contemporary art of national importance & to provide visual enrichment to campus & community; Average Annual Attendance: 5,000
Income: Financed by state appropriation & grants
Publications: Exhibition catalogs: Color Photography; Light Abstractions
Activities: Educ dept on art history; lect open to pub; originate traveling exhibs

M **WASHINGTON UNIVERSITY,** Mildred Lane Kemper Art Museum, 1 Brookings Dr, Campus Box 1214 Saint Louis, MO 63130-4862. Tel 314-935-4523; Fax 314-935-7282; Elec Mail kemperartmuseum@wustl.edu; Internet Home Page Address: www.kemperartmuseum.wush.edu; *Dir & Chief Cur* Sabine Eckmann; *Assoc Cur* Meredith Malone; *Asst Cur* Karen K Butler; *Facilities Mgr & Art Preparator* Jan Hessel; *Dir Develop* Lynn Giardina; *Registrar* Rachel Keith; *Asst Registrar* Kim Broker; *Asst Registrar* Bryan Stusse; *Publications* Jane Neidhardt; *Mktg* Kimberly Singer; *Admin* John Foughty
Open Mon, Wed, & Thurs 11AM-6PM, Fri 11AM-8PM, Sat & Sun 11AM-6PM; No admis fee; Estab 1881, present building opened 1960, for the students of Washington University & the community at large to share resources, enrich environment, preserve exhibits, acquire & research art; A modern building containing two fls of gallery space for exhibit of the permanent coll & special exhibs. Also houses a library of art, archaeology, architecture & design; Average Annual Attendance: 40,215
Income: Financed by univ & pvt support
Special Subjects: Drawings, Etchings & Engravings, Landscapes, Ceramics, American Western Art, Photography, Portraits, Painting-American, Prints, Woodcuts, Painting-British, Painting-European, Painting-French, Painting-Japanese, Sculpture, American Indian Art, Religious Art, Woodcarvings, Posters, Asian Art, Painting-Dutch, Coins & Medals, Baroque Art, Renaissance Art, Painting-Spanish, Painting-Italian, Antiquities-Egyptian, Antiquities-Greek, Painting-German
Collections: Emphasis on modern artists, including Miro, Ernst, Picasso, Leger, Beckman; many Old Masters, 19th & 20th, 21st century European & American paintings, sculpture, drawings & prints
Publications: Exhibition catalogs
Activities: Educ prog; docent training; lects open to pub, 15-20 vis lectrs per yr by artists, art historians & architects; symposia; music concerts; gallery talks; tours; films; individual paintings & original objects of art lent to other museums; originate traveling exhibs to other museums; primarily American & European venues (i.e. McNay Museum/San Antonio, TX & Opelvillen, Russelsheim, Germany; sales shop sells books, exhib catalogs, postcards, gifts

L **Art & Architecture Library,** 1 Brookings Dr, Saint Louis, MO 63130-4862; PO Box 1061, Saint Louis, MO 63130. Tel 314-935-5268; Fax 314-935-4362; Elec Mail artarch@wumail.wustl.edu; Internet Home Page Address: library.wustl.edu/units/artarch/; *Art Libm* Kasia Leousis; *Art & Architecture Libm* Rina Vecchiola
Open Mon - Thurs 8:30 AM - 11 PM, Fri 8:30 AM - 5 PM, Sat 11 AM - 5 PM, Sun 1 PM - 9 PM, cl nights & weekends during vacations & intercessions; Supports the acad progs of the School of Art, the School of Architecture & the Department of Art History & Archaeology
Income: Financed through the university
Library Holdings: Book Volumes 101,000; DVDs 50; Exhibition Catalogs; Periodical Subscriptions 310; Reproductions; Video Tapes 550

SAINTE GENEVIEVE

M **STE GENEVIEVE MUSEUM,** Merchant & DuBourgh St, Sainte Genevieve, MO 63670. Tel 573-883-3461; *Treas* Delores Koetting; *Pres* Jim Baker
Open Mon - Sat 10 AM - 4 PM, Sun noon - 4 PM, Nov - Mar noon - 4 PM;

Admis adults $2, students (hs & below) $.50; Estab 1935; Average Annual Attendance: 8,000; Mem: Dues bus $50, family $25, individual $10
Income: Financed by mem, admis
Special Subjects: American Indian Art, Archaeology, Historical Material, Maps, Dolls, Jewelry, Coins & Medals, Embroidery, Laces
Collections: Indian artifacts; salt spring kettles, hair jewelry, guns, quilts, cookware
Activities: Mus shop sells books

SEDALIA

M **DAUM MUSEUM OF CONTEMPORARY ART,** 3201 W 16th St, State Fair Community College Sedalia, MO 65301-2188. Tel 660-530-5888; Fax 660-530-5890; Elec Mail info@daummuseum.org; Internet Home Page Address: www.daummuseum.org; *Dir* Thomas Piche Jr; *Pres* Dr Joanna Anderson; *Mus Coordr* Marcia Teter; *Cur Educ* Victoria Weaver; *Registrar* Matthew Clause
Open Tues - Fri 11 AM - 5 PM, Sat - Sun 1 - 5 PM; No admis fee; Average Annual Attendance: 26,000
Special Subjects: Drawings, Etchings & Engravings, Collages, Porcelain, Painting-American, Prints, Textiles, Woodcuts, Sculpture, Photography, Watercolors, Ceramics, Landscapes
Collections: Contemporary art spanning the last 60 yrs
Activities: Docent training; art & lect series; lects open to pub; 3 vis lectrs per yr; gallery talks; tours

SPRINGFIELD

A **SOUTHWEST MISSOURI MUSEUM ASSOCIATES INC,** Springfield Art Museum, 1111 E Brookside Dr, Springfield, MO 65807-1829. Tel 417-837-5700; Fax 417-837-5704; Elec Mail artmuseum@springfieldmo.gov; printsusa@ci.springfield.mo.us; Internet Home Page Address: www.ci.springfield.mo.us/egov/art/index.html; *Dir* Jerry Berger
Open Tues, Wed, Fri, Sat 9 AM - 5 PM, Thurs 9 AM - 8 PM, Sun 1PM-5PM, cl Mon; Admis donation; Estab 1928 to inform & interest citizens in appreciation of art & to maintain an art mus as an essential pub institution; Mem: 1300; dues sustaining life $1000, life $500, supporting $50, family $40, at large $30, art group: resident $20, exten groups $10
Income: $14,000 (financed by mem)
Publications: Bimonthly newsletter, in cooperation with the Museum
Activities: Gift shop sells books, original art, prints, reproductions, stationery & gift items; maintain a sales gallery

M **SPRINGFIELD ART MUSEUM,** 1111 E Brookside Dr, Springfield, MO 65807-1899. Tel 417-837-5700; Fax 417-837-5704; Elec Mail artmuseum@springfieldmo.gov; Internet Home Page Address: www.springfieldmo.gov/art/index.html; *Cur Coll* Chalen Phillips; *Dir* Jerry A Berger; *Mus Educ* Dan Carver; *Libm* Susan Potter; *Exec Secy* Tyra Knox; *Cur Exhibs* Sarah Buhr
Open Tues - Sat 9 AM - 5 PM, Thurs until 8 PM, Sun 1 - 5 PM, cl Mon & city & national holidays; No admis fee, donations accepted; Estab 1928 to encourage appreciation & foster educ of the visual arts; Mus has four temporary exhib galleries for traveling & spec exhibs totaling approx 7500 sq ft; wing opened in 1994 with 13,400 sq ft including four galleries for the permanent coll; 400-seat auditorium & sales gallery; new wing w/ 10,000 sq ft including 4 new galleries and new lib opened in 2008; Average Annual Attendance: 50,000; Mem: 1,300; dues $15-$1000; ann meeting second Wed in May
Income: $1,000,000 (financed by mem, city & state appropriations)
Purchases: $70,000
Library Holdings: Auction Catalogs; Book Volumes; Exhibition Catalogs; Periodical Subscriptions; Video Tapes
Special Subjects: Afro-American Art, American Indian Art, Art History, Mixed Media, American Western Art, Prints, Bronzes, Silversmithing, Painting-Japanese, Drawings, Painting-American, Photography, Sculpture, Watercolors, Southwestern Art, Ceramics, Folk Art, Pottery, Woodcarvings, Woodcuts, Etchings & Engravings, Landscapes, Decorative Arts, Collages, Portraits, Furniture, Glass, Asian Art, Painting-British, Painting-Dutch, Painting-Spanish
Collections: American & European decorative arts; American drawing & photography; American painting & sculpture of all periods; American prints of all periods with emphasis on the 20th Century; European prints, drawings & paintings from the 17th-20th Centuries
Activities: Classes for adults & children; lects open to pub; concerts; gallery talks; tours; competitions with awards; originate traveling exhibs; mus shop sells books, original art, reproductions, pottery, jewelry, cards, stationery & t-shirts

L **Library,** 1111 E Brookside Dr, Springfield, MO 65807-1899. Tel 417-837-5700; Fax 417-837-5704; Internet Home Page Address: www.springfieldmo.gov/art/; *Libm* Susan Potter
Open Tues - Sat 9 AM - Noon & 1 - 5 PM; No admis fee; Estab 1928 to assist those persons interested in securing information regarding art & artists, craftsmen from ancient times to the present; Circ 971; Lending & reference library; Average Annual Attendance: 2,060
Income: Financed by city
Purchases: $6,000 (library acquisitions), $60,000 (artwork acquisitions)
Library Holdings: Auction Catalogs; Audio Tapes; Book Volumes 5615; Cassettes; Clipping Files; Exhibition Catalogs; Filmstrips; Manuscripts; Other Holdings Art access kits; Exhibition cards; slide kits; Pamphlets; Periodical Subscriptions 53; Slides; Video Tapes
Special Subjects: Art History, Folk Art, Decorative Arts, Watercolors, Ceramics, Archaeology, American Western Art, Bronzes, Art Education, American Indian Art, Afro-American Art, Architecture
Collections: American & European paintings, prints & sculpture-primarily 19th & 20th century
Exhibitions: Prints USA - a biennial print juried exhib
Publications: Exhib catalogs; bimonthly newsletter; watercolor USA Catalog, annually

Activities: Classes for adults & children; docent training; lects open to pub, 2 vis lectrs per yr; gallery talks; tours; competitions with prizes; lending coll contains 6000 books, 446 slide sets; sales of books, original art

WARRENSBURG

M **UNIVERSITY OF CENTRAL MISSOURI,** Art Center Gallery, 217 Clark St, Warrensburg, MO 64093-2606. Tel 660-543-4498; Fax 660-543-8006; Elec Mail crane@ucmo.edu; Internet Home Page Address: www.cmsu.edu; *Gallery Dir* Michael Crane
Open Mon - Fri 9 AM - 5 PM; No admis fee; Estab 1984 for the purpose of educ through exhib; Small outer gallery & large main gallery located in the University Art Center; Average Annual Attendance: 8,000
Income: Financed by state appropriation & univ funding
Collections: University permanent coll
Activities: Classes for adults; Lects open to public; 2-3 vis lectrs per yr; concerts; gallery talks; tours; competitions with awards; Book 1-2 traveling exhibs per yr

WEBSTER GROVES

M **WEBSTER UNIVERSITY,** Cecille R Hunt Gallery, 8342 Big Bend Blvd, Webster Groves, MO 63119. Tel 314-968-7171; Elec Mail langtk@websteruniv.edu; Internet Home Page Address: www.webster.edu/depts/finearts/art/; *Dept Chair* Tom Lang
Open Mon - Fri 10 AM - 4 PM, Sat 10 AM - 2 PM, cl Christmas; No admis fee; Estab 1950; Average Annual Attendance: 4,000
Income: Financed by col funds, donations & contributions
Exhibitions: Exhibs of local, national & international artists in all media; rotating exhibits
Publications: Monthly news releases; exhibition catalogs; books
Activities: Lects open to pub, 6 vis lectrs per yr; competitions with awards; Hunt Awards for student shows; individual paintings & original objects of art lent

L **Emerson Library,** 101 Edgar Rd, St Louis, MO 63119; 470 E Lockwood Ave, Saint Louis, MO 63119. Tel 800-985-4279; Fax 314-968-7113; Elec Mail emilyscharf99@webster.edu; Internet Home Page Address: www.library.webster.edu; *Instruction & Liaison ServLibrn* Emily Scharf
Open Mon - Sun 8 AM - Midnight; For reference & lending
Income: Financed by col funds
Library Holdings: Book Volumes 300,000; Cassettes; DVDs; Exhibition Catalogs; Motion Pictures; Periodical Subscriptions 1235; Photographs; Prints; Records; Slides; Video Tapes

WEST PLAINS

M **HARLIN MUSEUM,** 505 Worcester Ave, West Plains, MO 65775-2709; PO Box 444, West Plains, MO 65775-0444. Tel 417-256-7801; Elec Mail staff@harlinmuseum.com; Internet Home Page Address: harlinmuseum.com
Collections: Lennis L Broadfoot
Publications: Pioneers of the Ozarks, book on Broadfoot art & personal papers, auth Lennis L Broadfoot

WESTON

M **NATIONAL SILK ART MUSEUM,** 423 Main St, Weston, MO 64098. Tel 816-640-9902; Elec Mail info@nationalsilkart museum.com; Internet Home Page Address: www.nationalsilkartmuseum.com; *Cur* John Pottie; *Cur* Venessa Pottie
Call for hours; No admis fee; Average Annual Attendance: 4,500
Special Subjects: Decorative Arts, Historical Material, Tapestries, Religious Art, Portraits, Embroidery
Collections: over 200 French silk tapestries by artists from the 19th & 20th century
Activities: Lects open to pub

MONTANA

ANACONDA

A **COPPER VILLAGE MUSEUM & ARTS CENTER,** 401 E Commercial, Anaconda, MT 59711. Tel 406-563-2422; Fax 406-563-2422; Elec Mail copper_village@hotmail.com; Internet Home Page Address: coppervillageartcenter.com; *Dir* Mary Lynn McKenna; *Grant Writer* Susan Lanes; *Pres* Brian Tesson
Open Mon - Fri 10 AM - 4 PM, open Sat by appointment; No admis fee; Estab 1971 as Community Arts Center, gallery & regional historical mus; Average Annual Attendance: 15,000; Mem: 150; dues $10 - $100
Income: Financed by endowment, mem, fundraising events & individual donations
Library Holdings: Auction Catalogs; Exhibition Catalogs; Memorabilia; Original Art Works; Original Documents
Collections: Permanent coll holds paintings & prints
Exhibitions: Monthly exhibits of local, national & international art work
Publications: Quarterly newsletters, brochures
Activities: Classes for adults & children; dramatic progs; docent training; lects open to pub, 4 vis lectrs per yr; concerts; gallery talks; tours; awards; schols; book traveling exhibs 4-8 per yr; originate traveling exhibs which circulate to Montana Galleries; sales shop sells books, original art, prints, pottery, glass & jewelry

L **Library,** 401 E Commercial, Anaconda, MT 59711. Tel 406-563-2422; *Dir* Carol Jette
Open Tues - Sat 10 AM - 4 PM, cl Mon & holidays; Library open to the pub for reference

Library Holdings: Book Volumes 45; Clipping Files; Memorabilia; Motion Pictures; Pamphlets; Periodical Subscriptions 11; Reproductions; Sculpture; Slides
Publications: Newsletters, quarterly; brochures
Activities: Book traveling exhibs

BILLINGS

M **MONTANA STATE UNIVERSITY AT BILLINGS,** Northcutt Steele Gallery, 1500 University Dr, Billings, MT 59101-0245. Tel 406-657-2011; Fax 406-657-2187; Elec Mail leanne.gilbertson@msu-billings.edu; Internet Home Page Address: www.msubillings.edu/cas/art; *Pub Rels* Patricia Vettel-Becker; *Prof of Art* Neil Jussila; *Gallery Dir* Leanne Gilbertson
Open Mon - Fri 8 AM - 4:00 PM during the acad yr; No admis fee; Located on the 1st fl of the library bldg
Income: Financed by univ
Collections: MSU-Billings permanent collection; Opal Leonard Coll of Chinese & Japanese Art; Helen & Paul Covert Collection
Exhibitions: Ann faculty & student exhib; visiting artists; Independent Student Exhibition with awards
Activities: Vis artist prog; lects open to pub; 4 vis lectrs per yr; awards for ann juried student exhib

M **PETER YEGEN JR YELLOWSTONE COUNTY MUSEUM,** Logan Field, PO Box 959 Billings, MT 59103; 1950 Terminal Cir, Billings, MT 59105-1988. Tel 406-256-6811; Fax 406-254-6031; Elec Mail ycm@pyjrycm.net; Internet Home Page Address: www.pyjrycm.org; *Dir & Educ Coordr* Suzanne MM Warner
Open Mon - Fri 10:30 AM - 5 PM, Sat 10:30 AM - 3 PM, cl Sun; No admis fee; Estab 1953; 5,000 sq ft, 2 fls, 25,000 artifacts; Average Annual Attendance: 15,000; Mem: dues lifetime $1000, corporate $100, family $25, individual $20, senior $15; ann Open House in Sept/Oct
Income: $32,000 (financed by county, mem, memorials, donations & grants)
Special Subjects: Photography
Collections: Dinosaur bones; Montana Pioneers; Native American; Northern Pacific Steam Switch Engine; Yellowstone Valley; Photographs; Ranching Artifacts; Roundup Wagon; Sheep Wagon
Exhibitions: Dinosaur bones; Leory Greene (local artist) paintings of Crow Indians, 1930-1968; Indian artifacts; military items; Western memorabilia; Lewis & Clark fur trading post exhibit
Publications: Cabin Chat, quarterly newsletter
Activities: Lect for mems only; tours; originate traveling exhibs; mus shop sells books, reproductions, original art (beadwork)

A **YELLOWSTONE ART MUSEUM,** 401 N 27th St, Billings, MT 59101-1290. Tel 406-256-6804; Fax 406-256-6817; Elec Mail artinfo@artmuseum.org; Internet Home Page Address: www.yellowstone.artmuseum.org; *Exec Dir* Robyn G Peterson; *Educ Dir* Linda Ewert; *Senior Cur* Bob Durden; *Fin Dir* Lisa Berke; *Registrar* Nancy Clark; *Assoc Cur* Liz Harding
Open Tues - Sat 10 AM - 5 PM, Sun 11 AM - 4 PM, Thurs & Fri 10 AM - 8 PM; Admis adults $6, seniors, students & children $4, mems free; Estab 1964 to offer a broad prog of art exhibs, both historical & contemporary, of the highest quality, to provide related educ progs; two large galleries & five smaller ones in a large brick structure, plus pub accessible storage vault; Average Annual Attendance: 40,000; Mem: 1,000; dues $40 & up; ann meeting in July
Income: $1,200,000 (financed by mem, contributions, county appropriations, grants, mus shop & fundraising events)
Purchases: Current work by regional artists
Library Holdings: Auction Catalogs; Book Volumes; CD-ROMs; Cards; Cassettes; Memorabilia; Original Art Works; Original Documents; Periodical Subscriptions; Photographs; Prints; Sculpture; Slides
Special Subjects: Drawings, Landscapes, Manuscripts, Metalwork, Photography, Sculpture, Watercolors, Painting-American, American Western Art, Bronzes, American Indian Art, Ceramics, Archaeology, Furniture, Glass, Painting-European
Collections: Poindexter Collection of Abstract Expressionism; Contemporary Regional Artists; Will James; Montana Modernism
Exhibitions: 10 - 12 changing exhibitions per yr
Publications: Newsletter; exhib catalogues, 4-6 per yr
Activities: Classes for adults & children; docent training; lects open to pub, 6-10 vis lectrs per yr; concerts; gallery talks; tours; sponsoring of competitions; individual paintings & original art objects lent to museums & art centers; Art Suitcase prog goes out to all 4th & 5th grade students including rural areas; President's award for service to the arts; 2-3 book traveling exhibs; originate traveling exhibs circulate to other museums; 1-6 book traveling exhibs per yr; mus shop sells books, magazines, original art, reproductions, prints, handmade jewelry, textiles, clothing, home furnishings, gifts & consignment art gallery; junior mus on site, Young Artists' Gallery

BOZEMAN

M **MONTANA STATE UNIVERSITY,** Museum of the Rockies, 600 W Kagy, Bozeman, MT 59717-2730. Tel 406-994-3466; Fax 406-994-2682; Elec Mail wwwmor@montana.edu; Internet Home Page Address: www.museumoftherockies.org; *Dean & Dir* Sheldon McKamey; *Assoc Cur Art & Photog* Steve Jackson; *Dir Develop* Candace Strauss; *Dir Finance & Admin* Jeff Krauss; *Cur History* Michael Fox
Call for hours; Admis varies call for schedule; Estab in 1958 to interpret the physical & cultural heritages of the Northern Rockies region; Average Annual Attendance: 160,000; Mem: 4200; dues dir circle $500, sustaining $250, contribution $100, family $50, non-resident family $40, individual $25, MSU student $15
Income: Financed by MSU, fundraising, grants & revenue
Special Subjects: American Indian Art, Anthropology, Archaeology, Decorative Arts, Drawings, Etchings & Engravings, Folk Art, Ceramics, Collages, American Western Art, Furniture, Bronzes, Ethnology, Dolls, Carpets & Rugs, Embroidery, Cartoons

Collections: Art Works by R E DeCamp; Edgar Paxton; C M Russell; O C Seltzer; William Standing; geology; paleontology; astronomy, archaeological artifacts; history & western art; regional native Americans
Exhibitions: Rotation Gallery features changing exhibs
Publications: Quarterly newsletter; papers
Activities: Classes for adults & children; docent training; progs in science, history & art; lect open to pub, 20 vis lectrs per yr; planetarium shows; field trips; field schools; gallery talks; tours; traveling portable planetarium; book traveling exhibs; originate traveling exhibs; mus shop sells books, magazines, original art, reproductions, prints, slides, crafts, toys, hats, t-shirts, stationery

M **Helen E Copeland Gallery,** 213 Haynes Hall, Bozeman, MT 59717; PO Box 173680, Bozeman, MT 59717-3680. Tel 406-994-4501; Fax 406-994-4099; Elec Mail art@montana.edu; Internet Home Page Address: www.montana.edu/wwwart; *Gallery Dir* Kate Jo; *Dir School of Art* Vaughan Judge
Open Mon - Fri 8 AM - 5 PM; No admis fee; Estab 1974 to present exhibitions of national interest & educate students; Gallery space adjacent to offices & studio classrooms on 2nd fl; Average Annual Attendance: 10,000
Income: Financed by univ appropriation
Collections: Japanese Patterns; Native American Ceramics; WPA Prints
Exhibitions: 7-8 exhibs ann including graduate & undergraduate exhibs
Activities: Lect open to pub, 8-12 vis lectrs per yr; gallery talks; competitions; individual paintings lent to univ offices; book traveling exhibs; originate traveling exhibs to Montana Galleries

L **Creative Arts Library,** 207 Cheever Hall, Creative Arts Complex Bozeman, MT 59717; PO Box 173320, Bozeman, MT 59717-3320. Tel 406-994-4091; Fax 406-994-2851; Elec Mail jjthull@montana.edu; Internet Home Page Address: www.lib.montana.edu/collections/cal.php; *Ref Librn* Jim Thull
Open Mon - Thurs 8 AM - 10 PM, Fri 8 AM - 5 PM, Sat 10AM-5PM, Sun 10AM-10PM; Estab 1974 to support the Schools of Architecture & Art
Income: Financed by state appropriation
Library Holdings: Book Volumes 30,000; Other Holdings Matted reproductions; Periodical Subscriptions 150

BROWNING

M **MUSEUM OF THE PLAINS INDIAN & CRAFTS CENTER,** Junction of 2 & 89 W, Browning, MT 59417; PO Box 410, Browning, MT 59417-0410. Tel 406-338-2230; Fax 406-338-7404; Elec Mail mpi@3rivers.com; Internet Home Page Address: www.iacb.doi.gov; *Cur* David Dragonfly
Open June - Sept, daily 9 AM - 5 PM, Oct - May Mon - Fri 10 AM - 4:30 PM, cl New Year's Day, Thanksgiving Day and Christmas; Admis Jun - Sept adults $4, groups of 10 or more $3 per person, children (6-12) $1; Estab 1941 to promote the development of contemporary Native American arts & crafts, administered and operated by the Indian Arts and Crafts Board, US Dept of the Interior; New exhib every 4 months; Average Annual Attendance: 80,000; Mem: Friends of the Museum $25 fee
Income: Financed by federal appropriation
Special Subjects: American Indian Art, Drawings, Photography, Prints, Woodcuts, Sculpture, Sculpture, American Indian Art, Bronzes, Textiles, Ceramics, Crafts, Woodcarvings, Etchings & Engravings, Eskimo Art, Dolls, Dioramas, Stained Glass
Collections: Contemporary Native American arts & crafts; historic works by Plains Indian craftsmen & artists
Exhibitions: Historic arts created by the tribal peoples of the Northern Plains; Traditional costumes of Northern Plains men, women & children; Art forms related to the social & ceremonial aspects of the regional tribal cultures; One-Person exhibs of Native American artists & craftsmen; Architectural decorations, including carved wood panels by sculptor John Clarke & a series of murals by Victor Pepion
Publications: Continuing series of brochures for one-person shows, exhib catalogues
Activities: Gallery talks; tours; demonstrations of Native American arts & crafts; originates traveling exhibs; Pikuni gift shop sells books, original art, prints

BUTTE

M **BUTTE SILVER BOW ARTS CHATEAU,** 321 W Broadway, Butte, MT 59701. Tel 406-723-7600; Fax 406-723-5083; Elec Mail bsbaf@hotmail.com; Internet Home Page Address: www.bsbarts.org; *Dir* Glenn Bodish; *Educ Dir* Shawn Crowe; *MoFAB Mgr* Jana Faught
Open Sept - May Mon - Sat Noon - 5 PM, June - Aug Tues - Sat 10:30 AM - 5:30 PM, Sun 1 - 4 PM, cl major holidays; Admis family $6, single $3, seniors & children $2; Estab 1977 to further all forms of art; 1898 French Chateau converted to galleries & museum; Mem: 350; dues Bus: benefactor $1000, patron $750, sustaining $500, contributing $100, active $10; Individual: benefactor $1000, patron $500, sustaining $100, contributing $50, family $25, active $10; ann meeting Jan
Collections: Contemporary regional art; Elizabeth Lochrie Coll of Native American Portraits
Exhibitions: Exhibs change every 3 months
Publications: Newsletter
Activities: Classes for adults & children, dramatic progs; lect open to pub, 10 vis lectrs per yr; gallery talks; tours; book traveling exhibs 4 per yr; art supply store sells original art, reproductions, prints & recitals

CHESTER

M **LIBERTY VILLAGE ARTS CENTER & GALLERY,** 410 Main St, Chester, MT 59522; PO Box 269, Chester, MT 59522-0269. Tel 406-759-5652; Fax 406-759-5652; Elec Mail lvac@mtintouch.net; Internet Home Page Address: www.libertyvillagearts.org; *Treas* Laurie S Lyders; *Dir* Patricia Aaberg
Open Tues, Wed & Fri 12:30 PM - 4:30 PM, other times by request; cl New Years, Easter, Thanksgiving & Christmas; No admis fee; Estab 1976 to provide community with traveling exhibs & educ center; Renovated Catholic Church c

1910; Average Annual Attendance: 1,500-2,000; Mem: 70; dues patron $100 & up, Friend of the Arts $50-$99, family $25, individual $20; ann meeting in Oct
Collections: Works by local artists, paintings & quilts
Exhibitions: Traveling exhibs
Activities: Classes for adults & children; workshops; film series; lect open to pub, 3 vis lectrs per year; gallery talks; competitions with awards; book traveling exhibs; originate traveling exhibs; mus shop sells books, original art & prints

COLSTRIP

SCHOOLHOUSE HISTORY & ART CENTER, 400 Woodrose St, Colstrip, MT 59323; PO Box 430, Colstrip, MT 59323-0430. Tel 406-748-4822; Elec Mail shac@bhwi.net; Internet Home Page Address: www.schoolhouseartcenter.com; *Exec Dir* Lu Shomale
Open Memorial Day to Labor Day Tues - Sat 11 AM - 5 PM, Fall & Spring Mon - Fri 11 AM - 5 PM; No admis fee
Collections: photographs; period artifacts
Activities: Educ progs; art classes; children's activities; mus shop

DILLON

M **THE UNIVERSITY OF MONTANA - WESTERN,** Art Gallery Museum, 710 S Atlantic, Dillon, MT 59725-3958. Tel 406-683-7232; WATS 800-WMC-MONT; *Dir* Randy Horst
Open Tues - Fri Noon - 4:30 PM; No admis fee; Estab 1970 to display art works of various kinds, used as an educ facility; Located in the south end of Old Main Hall houses the Seidensticker Wildlife Coll of taxidermy; Average Annual Attendance: 7,000
Income: Financed through col funds
Collections: Seidensticker Wildlife Trophy Collection
Activities: Educ dept

L **Lucy Carson Memorial Library,** 710 S Atlantic St, Dillon, MT 59725-3511. Tel 406-683-7541; Fax 406-683-7493; Elec Mail m.shultz@wmc.edu; Internet Home Page Address: www.wmc.edu/academics/library; *Library Dir* Mike Shultz
Open Mon - Thurs 7:30 AM - 11 PM, Fri 7:30 AM - 5 PM, Sat 11 AM - 5 PM, Sun 3 - 10PM; Library open to the pub
Income: Financed by col & state
Library Holdings: Book Volumes 4500; Cassettes; Compact Disks; DVDs; Fiche; Filmstrips; Framed Reproductions; Lantern Slides; Maps; Memorabilia; Micro Print; Motion Pictures; Original Art Works; Original Documents; Periodical Subscriptions 12; Photographs; Prints; Reels; Reproductions; Sculpture; Slides; Video Tapes 140
Collections: Emerick Arts Collection

DRUMMOND

M **OHRMANN MUSEUM AND GALLERY,** 6155 Hwy 1, Ohrmann Designs Drummond, MT 59832. Tel 406-288-3319; Elec Mail ohrmann@blackfoot.net; Internet Home Page Address: www.ohrmannmuseum.com; *Artist & Owner* Bill Ohrmann
Open daily 10 AM - 5 PM; Located 2 1/2 miles S of Drummond on Hwy 1, mus houses the paintings, woodcarvings, bronzes & steel sculptures of Bill Ohrmann
Special Subjects: Painting-American, Bronzes, Woodcarvings
Activities: Artist's works available for sale

EAST GLACIER PARK

M **THE JOHN L. CLARKE WESTERN ART GALLERY & MEMORIAL MUSEUM,** 900 Montana Hwy 49, East Glacier Park, MT 59434; PO Box 141, East Glacier Park, MT 59434-0141. Tel 406-226-9238; Internet Home Page Address: www.eastglacierpark.info; *Owner & Mgr* Joyce Clarke Turvey
Open May - Sept: Mon - Sat 10 AM - 7 PM, Sun 10 AM - 5 PM; No admis fee; Estab 1977
Special Subjects: American Indian Art, American Western Art, Painting-American, Prints, Bronzes, Photography, Sculpture, Watercolors, Woodcarvings, Woodcuts
Collections: Wood carvings & paintings by John L. Clarke; 28 Montana Artists represented

GLENDIVE

M **FRONTIER GATEWAY MUSEUM,** I-94, Exit 215 (201 State St), Glendive, MT 59330; PO Box 1181, Glendive, MT 59330-1181. Tel 406-377-8168; Elec Mail frontiermuseum@ymail.com; Internet Home Page Address: www.frontiergatewaymuseum.org; *Cur* Fayette Miller; *Treas* Patty Atwell; *1st VPres* Audre Avilla; *2nd VPres* Rosanne Bos; *Pres* Mark Geiger; *Asst Cur* Trena Kuehn
Open Mon - Sat 9 AM - noon & 1 - 5 PM, Sun & holidays 1 - 5 PM; cl mid-Sept to mid-May; No admis fee, donations accepted; Founded 1963; Gen historical mus of Glendive & Dawson Counties in MT; 10,080 sq ft exhib space situated on 7 bldgs on one acre; Average Annual Attendance: 1785; Mem: dues Life $50, ann $5
Income: $10,000 (financed by memberships, memorials, county allotted)
Library Holdings: Book Volumes 650; Clipping Files 33 drawers; Maps 263; Photographs 7 file drawers
Special Subjects: Historical Material, Photography, Period Rooms
Collections: Prehistoric to contemporary coll consists of fossils, mammoth, mastodon, buffalo, Indians, cattlemen, homesteads, small towns, fashions; personal artifacts; tools & equipment for materials; paleontological items; structures; folk culture; technology; furnishings
Publications: Report to the Membership, ann newsletter
Activities: Open house; tours; demonstrations; lects; hobby workshops; mus related souvenirs for sale & books

GREAT FALLS

M **C M RUSSELL MUSEUM,** 400 13th St N, Great Falls, MT 59401-1498. Tel 406-727-8787; Fax 406-727-2402; Elec Mail info@cmrussell.org; Internet Home Page Address: www.cmrussell.org; *Cur* Anne Morand; *Dir* Darrell Beauchamp; *Pub Rels* Kate Swartz
Open Memorial Day-Labor Day daily 9AM-6PM, Winter Tues-Sat 10AM-5PM; Admis adults $9, students $4, seniors $7, children under 5 free; Estab 1953 to preserve art of Charles M Russell, western painter; Mus includes Russell's home & original studio; has seven galleries of Western art & photographs & Indian artifacts. Maintains reference library; Average Annual Attendance: 50,000; Mem: 1,750; dues $25 - $3,000 & up
Income: Financed by operating budget
Library Holdings: Auction Catalogs; Clipping Files; Memorabilia; Micro Print; Original Documents; Other Holdings; Pamphlets; Periodical Subscriptions; Photographs; Records
Special Subjects: Drawings, Latin American Art, Mexican Art, Painting-American, Photography, Prints, Sculpture, American Indian Art, American Western Art, Bronzes, Anthropology, Archaeology, Ethnology, Pre-Columbian Art, Southwestern Art, Folk Art, Pottery, Etchings & Engravings, Decorative Arts, Manuscripts, Portraits, Historical Material, Period Rooms, Cartoons, Reproductions
Collections: Works by Charles M Russell & other Western works including Seltzer, Couse, Wieghorst, Sharp, Heikka, Reiss, Farny; Historical & contemporary; Contemporary & western art; Native American art
Exhibitions: Traveling exhibs of western art; permanent exhibs; The Bison: American Icon, Heart of Plains Indian Culture
Publications: Quarterly magazine; monthly e-newsletter
Activities: Classes for adults & children; docent training; lects for mems only & lects open to pub; 0-6 vis lectrs per yr; gallery talks; tours; individual paintings & original objects of art lent to qualified museums; book traveling exhibs 1 per yr; mus store sells books, magazines, reproductions, prints, jewelry, pottery

L **Frederic G Renner Memorial Library,** 400 13th St N, Great Falls, MT 59401. Tel 406-727-8787; Fax 406-727-2402; Elec Mail smcgowan@cmrussell.org; Internet Home Page Address: www.cmrussell.org/library; *Registrar* Brenda Kornick; *Cur* Sarah Burt; *Mus Shop Dir* Donna Camp; *Educ & Tours* Kim Kapalka; *Librn* Sharon McGowan; *Exec Dir* Dr Darrell Beauchamp; *Dir Opers* Susan Johnson
Open Mon, Wed, & Thurs 9AM-noon & 1PM-3PM by appointment; Admis Adults $9, seniors $7, children & students $4, under 5 free; Library estab 1965 to provide research material on Western art & artists, primarily C M Russell & The History of Montana & The West; Museum estab 1953 to showcase CM Russell's work; Circ 3,700; For reference only; Average Annual Attendance: 56,000; Mem: 2,000, $35 - $2,500
Income: (financed by pvt contributions)
Library Holdings: Auction Catalogs; Audio Tapes; Book Volumes 3,500; CD-ROMs; Clipping Files; DVDs; Exhibition Catalogs; Kodachrome Transparencies; Manuscripts; Memorabilia; Micro Print; Motion Pictures; Original Documents; Pamphlets; Periodical Subscriptions 4; Photographs; Prints; Reproductions; Slides; Video Tapes
Special Subjects: Art History, Photography, Etchings & Engravings, Painting-American, Prints, Sculpture, Historical Material, Watercolors, Ceramics, Ethnology, American Western Art, Bronzes, American Indian Art, Southwestern Art, Carpets & Rugs, Landscapes, Woodcarvings
Collections: Yost Archival Collection; Flood Archival Collection; Taliaferro Reference Notes; Joseph Henry Sharp Collection of Indian Photographs; Fred Renner Collection
Publications: Russell's West Quarterly, quarterly; Studio Talk, monthly
Activities: Classes for adults & children; dramatic prog; docent training; Native American classes; summer day camps; lects open to pub & members; 6 vis lectrs per year; concerts; gallery talks; tours; fel; sponsoring of competitions; Trigg award; mus shop sells books, magazines, original art, reproductions, prints, slides, clothing, souvenirs & children's items; Discovery Gallery: Hands-on Experience for Children & Families

M **CASCADE COUNTY HISTORICAL SOCIETY,** The History Museum, 422 2nd St S, Great Falls, MT 59405-1816. Tel 406-452-3462; Fax 406-461-3805; Elec Mail info@thehistorymuseum.org; Internet Home Page Address: www.thehistorymuseum.org; *Interim Exec Dir* Marcia Clary; *Archivist* Judy Ellinghausen
Open year-round, Tues- Fri 10AM-5PM; Admis $5 per person, mems & students $3, under 5 free; Estab 1976 to preserve & interpret the history of the Central Montana area & the diverse area heritage; The historical mus is housed in the Internal Harvester building built in 1929. We have the regional archival research center for North Central Montana and a large collection that supports regional history exhibits; Average Annual Attendance: 82,000; Mem: Dues benefactor $500; patron $250; sponsor $125; sustainer $75; family $40; individual $25. Bd dirs meeting held monthly on 4th Thurs
Income: $200,000 (financed by mem dues, donations, memorials, & grants)
Purchases: 1925 chickering 9 foot piano for historical events
Library Holdings: Auction Catalogs; Audio Tapes; Book Volumes; Cards; Cassettes; Clipping Files; Exhibition Catalogs; Framed Reproductions; Kodachrome Transparencies; Lantern Slides; Manuscripts; Maps; Memorabilia; Motion Pictures; Original Art Works; Original Documents; Pamphlets; Periodical Subscriptions; Photographs; Prints; Records; Reproductions; Sculpture; Slides; Video Tapes
Collections: Art, documents, manuscripts, photographs, objects reflecting the history of the local area; clothing, furniture & memorabilia from Great Falls & Cascade County
Exhibitions: Exhibits from the permanent colls, changed quarterly; Celebrate Central Montana; Handcrafted: An Expression of American Tradition
Activities: Classes for adults & children; docent training; lect open to public, 10-15 vis lectrs per yr; gallery talks; tours; sponsoring of competitions; Community Heritage Preservation Award; individual paintings & original objects of art lent to other museums in central Montana; lending of original objects of art to fellow museums; book traveling exhibs 1 per yr; originate traveling exhibs to schools & smaller area town bus in Montana; mus shop sells books, magazines, original arts, reproductions

M **PARIS GIBSON SQUARE,** Museum of Art, 1400 First Ave N, Great Falls, MT 59401. Tel 406-727-8255; Fax 406-727-8256; Elec Mail info@the-square.org; Internet Home Page Address: www.the-square.org; *Interim Exec Dir* Michelle Klundt; *Cur Art* Laura Cotton; *Cur Educ* Jeff Kuratnick
Open Mon - Fri 10 AM - 5 PM, Tues evening 7 PM - 9 PM, Sat & Sun Noon - 5 PM; No admis fee; Estab 1976 to exhibit contemporary art; Maintains 7 galleries of assorted sizes and dimensions; Average Annual Attendance: 25,000; Mem: 550-650; mem open to pub; dues $30 & up; ann meetings in June
Income: $670,000 (financed by mem, grants, contributions & county mill)
Special Subjects: Decorative Arts, Drawings, Etchings & Engravings, Collages, Porcelain, Portraits, Painting-American, Photography, Prints, Sculpture, Watercolors, American Indian Art, Ceramics, Folk Art, Pottery, Primitive art, Woodcarvings, Woodcuts
Collections: Contemporary regional & national artists; Montana folk-art sculptures (polychromed wood), Lee Steen
Exhibitions: Various exhibs
Publications: Artist postcards, catalogs; quarterly newsletter
Activities: Classes for adults, children & disabled; docent training; Native American Contemporary Art Suitcase Museum; lect open to pub, 6-12 vis lectrs per yr; gallery talks; tours; schols & fels offered; individual paintings & original objects of art lent to other museums; lending coll contains original art works, original prints, paintings & photographs; book traveling exhibs 1-2 per yr; originate traveling exhibs to regional art institutions

HAMILTON

M **RAVALLI COUNTY MUSEUM,** 205 Bedford St, Old Court House Hamilton, MT 59840-2853. Tel 406-363-3338; Elec Mail rcmuseum@qwestoffice.net; Internet Home Page Address: www.brvhsmuseum.org; *Dir* Tamar Stanley; *Hist* Bill Whitfield; *Cur* Bev Adams
Open Tues - Fri 10 AM - 4 PM, Sat 9 AM - 1 PM, cl Sun & Mon; Admis adults $3, couple $5, students $1; Estab 1979 to preserve the history of the Bitterroot Valley; Museum contains Flathead Indian exhibit, Discovery room encompasses Native Am lifestyles in the Bitterroot Valley, Lewis & Clark travelling through the Bitterroot, The Salish Indians; Rocky Mt Spotted Fever display, pioneer rooms, tack & trophy room, veterans room, rotating exhibits in old ct room; extensive archives; Average Annual Attendance: 10,000; Mem: 350; dues corporate $100, family $25, regular $15; meetings third Mon each month
Income: gifts from Bitterroot Valley Historical Society
Purchases: $5000
Library Holdings: Audio Tapes; Fiche; Filmstrips; Framed Reproductions; Manuscripts; Maps
Collections: Home furnishings reflecting early life of the Bitterroot Valley; Indian, Railroad; Bertie Lord Collection; Ernst Peterson Collection
Exhibitions: Special Exhibits of historical Interest; Special Local Collection Exhibit; Veterans Exhibit; Lewis & Clark Exhibit
Publications: Bitter Root Trails One, Two, Three, Bitter Root Historical Society; McIntosh Apple Cookbook; Historic Survey of Hamilton Buildings 1890-1940; The Yellow Pine; Newsletter; The Bitterrooter, George Hayes, Rocky Mountain Spotted Fever in Western Montana; Anatomy of a Pestilence-Dr Robert Philip; Bitter Root Trails IV
Activities: Educ dept; classes for adults & children; art classes; docent training, cultural progs; concerts; tours; gallery talks; competitions with awards; mus shop sells books, original art, reproductions, prints, porcelain, jewelry & gifts featuring Lewis & Clark

HARDIN

M **BIG HORN COUNTY HISTORICAL MUSEUM,** RR 1 Box 1206A, Hardin, MT 59034-9720. Tel 406-665-1671; Fax 406-665-3068; Elec Mail di@bhwi.net; Internet Home Page Address: bighorncountymuseum.org; *Dir* Diana Scheidt; *Pres* Beth Mehling; *Treas* Merna Kincaid; *Mus Shop Mgr & Mus Asst* Joan Miller; *Asst Dir* Bonnie Stark
Open May - Sept: daily 8 AM - 6 PM, Oct - Apr: Mon - Fri 9 AM - 5 PM; historic bldgs cl Oct - Apr; mus cl New Year's Day, Thanksgiving Day, Christmas Day; Adult $5, seniors (62 & over) $4, student (12 & over with valid ID) $3; bus tours $1, children (11 & under), school groups, & mems no admis fee; donations accepted; Estab 1979; mus is located on 23-acre former vegetable farm that was donated to Big Horn County in 1979 & features orig farmhouse & barn; authentic historic structures have been restored & placed on site; Average Annual Attendance: 10,000 - 49,999 by estimate; Mem: dues Lifetime $500, Bus $50, Family $25, Indiv $15
Special Subjects: Historical Material
Collections: Includes items of historical significance related to the development of Big Horn County, MT from 1900 to modern times with emphasis on the cultures of people who have settled in the area, including The Crow Indians, Northern Cheyenne Indians, Japanese, German, Russian, Korean & Norwegian cultures; historic structures; horse-drawn equipment; restored tractor; farm equipment; furnishings; photographs & personal artifacts; hundreds of book vols on the Plains Indians; hundreds of local publs; Kenneth F Roahen - Photographs - Will James Studio
Publications: On the Bighorn, quarterly newsletter
Activities: Tractor Show; Auction; Hands on For Students; classes for children; guided tours; mus shop sells books

HELENA

M **HOLTER MUSEUM OF ART,** 12 E Lawrence St, Helena, MT 59601-4019. Tel 406-422-6400; Fax 406-442-2404; Elec Mail holter@holtermuseum.org; Internet Home Page Address: www.holtermuseum.org; *Cur Educ* Sondra Hines; *Exec Dir* Karen Bohlinger; *Cur Art* Yvonne Seng
Open Tues - Sat 10 AM - 5:30 PM, Sun noon - 4 PM; Admis by donation; Estab 1987 to educate & enhance the quality of life of constituents; Average Annual Attendance: 32,000; Mem: 1,000; dues individual $50, guardian $50-$1,000; ann meeting in fall

Income: $700,000 (financed by endowment, mem & state appropriation)
Library Holdings: Audio Tapes; Book Volumes; Exhibition Catalogs; Pamphlets; Photographs; Slides; Video Tapes
Special Subjects: Painting-American, Photography, Sculpture, Watercolors, American Indian Art, Textiles, Ceramics, Folk Art, Pottery, Woodcarvings, Landscapes, Glass, Jewelry, Porcelain, Metalwork
Collections: Contemporary Northwest Regional Art in all mediums
Exhibitions: ANA
Publications: Monthly newsletter
Activities: Classes for adults & children; docent training; lect open to pub, 8 vis lectrs per yr; gallery talks; tours; youth electrum $750 awards; national Juried exhib; schols offered; book traveling exhibs 4 per yr; originate traveling exhibs 2 per yr; mus shop sells books, original art, prints, ceramics, jewelry, mixed media arts

A **MONTANA HISTORICAL SOCIETY,** 225 N Roberts, Helena, MT 59601-4514; PO Box 201201, Helena, MT 59620-1201. Tel 406-444-2694; Fax 406-444-2696; Internet Home Page Address: www.montanahistoricalsociety.org; *Dir* Richard Sims; *Cur* Kirby Lambert; *Dir Mus Svcs* Susan R Near; *Archivist* Jodie Foley; *Mus Shop Mgr* Sherry Jonckheere; *Registrar* Jennifer Bottomly-O'Looney; *Preservation Officer* Mark Baumler; *Publ Mgr* Molly Holz; *Pub Rels* Tom Cook; *Educ* Deb Mitchell
Open Mon - Fri 8 AM - 5 PM, Sat 9 AM - 5 PM, cl Sun & holidays; Admis general $5; Estab 1865 to collect, preserve & present articles relevant to history & heritage of Montana & the Northwest; Mackay Gallery of C M Russell Art; temporary exhibits gallery; Montana Homeland; Average Annual Attendance: 93,000; Mem: 4000; dues $60
Income: $545,000 (financed by State of Montana General Fund, pvt gifts & grants, federal grants, earned revenue)
Library Holdings: Auction Catalogs; Clipping Files; Exhibition Catalogs; Manuscripts; Maps; Memorabilia; Original Documents; Photographs
Special Subjects: Architecture, Costumes, Historical Material, Photography, Posters, Sculpture, Textiles, Watercolors, Painting-American, American Western Art, Bronzes, Decorative Arts, American Indian Art, Portraits, Archaeology, Furniture, Ethnology, Leather
Collections: Haynes Collection of Art, Photographs & Artifacts; Mackay Collection of C M Russell Art; Poindexter Collection of Abstract Art; Montana artists; late 19th & 20th century Western art; Bob Scriver - the artist's coll
Exhibitions: Montana Homeland; changing temporary exhibits
Publications: Montana, Magazine of Western History, quarterly; Montana Post (newsletter), quarterly
Activities: Educ progs for adults & children; docent training; lect open to pub, 30 vis lectrs per yr; gallery talks, tours; individual paintings & original objects of art lent to museums, galleries, historical societies; lending coll includes 300 color transparencies, 200 original art works, 500,000 photographs, 40 sculptures, 1000 slides; originates traveling exhibs; sales shop selling books, magazines, prints, reproductions, slides

L **Library,** 225 N Roberts, Helena, MT 59620; PO Box 201201, Helena, MT 59620-1201. Tel 406-444-1799; Fax 406-444-2696; Elec Mail gashmore@state.mt.us; Internet Home Page Address: www.montanahistoricalsociety.org; *Head Librn & Archivist* Charlene Porsild; *Photograph Cur* Delores Morrow; *Cur Coll* Kirby Lambert
Open Mon - Fri 8 AM - 5 PM by appointment; For reference and research only
Income: Financed by State of Montana
Library Holdings: Book Volumes 4000; Clipping Files; Exhibition Catalogs; Manuscripts; Pamphlets; Periodical Subscriptions 100; Photographs
Special Subjects: Photography, Manuscripts, Painting-American, Historical Material, Archaeology, Ethnology, American Western Art, American Indian Art, Anthropology
Collections: Late 19th & 20th century art
Publications: Montana: The Magazine of Western History, quarterly

KALISPELL

A **HOCKADAY MUSEUM OF ART,** 302 2d Ave E, Kalispell, MT 59901-4942. Tel 406-755-5268; Fax 406-755-2023; Elec Mail information@hockadaymuseum.org; Internet Home Page Address: www.hockadaymuseum.org; *Exec Dir* Elizabeth Moss; *Dir Educ* Kathy Martin; *Develop Dir* Lucy Smith; *Commun & Mktg Dir* Brian Eklund; *Adminstr Asst* Leanne Starett; *Mem & Events Coordr* Holly Ridgway; *Advising Cur* Mark Norley; *Coll Admin* James Udick; *Bookkeeper* Rae Ellen Zeits
Open Tues - Sat 10 AM - 5 PM; Admis adults $5, seniors $4, students $2, mems & children K-12 free; Estab 1968 to enrich the cultural life of the community and region and preserve the artistic legacy of Montana and Glacier National Park; Mus is housed in the former Carnegie Library in downtown Kalispell; has six spacious exhib galleries & a gift gallery; classroom; Average Annual Attendance: 20,000; Mem: 750; dues $25 & up; annual meeting in March
Income: Financed by mem, contributions, grants, exhib sponsors, corporate donations & city funds
Special Subjects: Drawings, Etchings & Engravings, Landscapes, Photography, Posters, Painting-American, Pottery, American Western Art, Bronzes, American Indian Art, Ceramics, Glass, Islamic Art
Collections: Focus on the art and culture of Montana and the artists of Glacier National Park
Exhibitions: (Permanent) Crown of the Continent
Publications: Exhib catalogs; Sketch Pad Newsletters; annual reports
Activities: Classes for adults & children; docent training; lect open to pub, 3 per yr; gallery talks; tours; sponsoring of competitions; schols offered; ext prog serving Flathead, Lake, Lincoln & Glacier Counties; originate traveling exhibs to Museum and Art Gallery Directors Assn of Montana (MAGDA); mus shop sells books, original art, reproductions, prints

LEWISTOWN

A **LEWISTOWN ART CENTER,** 323 W Main St, Lewistown, MT 59457; PO Box 1018, Lewistown, MT 59457-1018. Tel 406-535-8278; Fax 406-535-6024; Elec Mail lewistownartcenter@gmail.com; Internet Home Page Address: www.lewistownartcenter.org; *Exec Dir* Linda Tullis; *Educ Dir* Carol Poppenga; *Gift Shop Coordr* Peter Hingle
Open Tues - Fri 11:30 AM - 5:30 PM, Sat 10 AM -4 PM; No admis fee; Estab 1971 for advancement & educ in the arts. The gallery exhibs change monthly showing a variety of local, state artwork; A sales gallery features Montana artists & local artists; Average Annual Attendance: 5,000; Mem: 250; dues $15 & up; ann meeting in Aug
Income: $100,000 (financed entirely by mem, donations, sponsorships by local bus, art grants, sales from gift shop, auction & market room)
Special Subjects: Photography, Porcelain, Posters, Prints, Reproductions, Sculpture, Silver, Textiles, Watercolors, Painting-American, Pottery, Stained Glass
Collections: Collection of art work from artists from Central Montana, bronze & all other mediums
Exhibitions: In-state shows
Publications: Newsletter, quarterly
Activities: Arts classes & workshops for adults & children; lects open to pub, concerts, 1-2 vis lectrs per yr; gallery talks; schols; competitions with awards; art educ offered; sales shop sells books, magazines, original art, reproductions, prints, sculpture, pottery, wall hangings, jewelry, fiber arts, Montana made consignment

LIVINGSTON

M **LIVINGSTON CENTER FOR ART & CULTURE,** 119 S Main St, Livingston, MT 59047-2668. Tel 406-222-5222; Elec Mail admin@livingstoncenter.org

MILES CITY

A **CUSTER COUNTY ART & HERITAGE CENTER,** 85 Waterplant Rd, Miles City, MT 59301-4032; PO Box 1284, Miles City, MT 59301-1284. Tel 406-234-0635; Fax 406-234-0637; Elec Mail ccartc@midrivers.com; Internet Home Page Address: www.ccac.milescity.org; *Exec Dir* Kevin D Layton; *Educ Dir* Jordan Pehler; *Admin Asst* Sandra Brunetti
Open Tues - Sun 1 - 5 PM, cl holidays; Summer hours 9 AM - 5 PM; No admis fee; Estab 1977 to provide an arts prog of exhibits and educ activities to residents of Southeastern Montana; Maintains The WaterWorks Gallery, located in the former holding tanks of the old Miles City Treatment Plant; Average Annual Attendance: 20,000; Mem: 500; dues benefactor $500, patron $300, sponsor $100, sustaining $75, bus $60, contributing $50, family $40, individual $25, student & sr citizens $15
Income: Financed by mem, fundraising events & grants
Library Holdings: Original Art Works; Photographs; Prints
Special Subjects: Historical Material, Photography, Prints, Sculpture, Watercolors, Painting-American, Pottery, Stained Glass, Woodcuts, Woodcarvings, Southwestern Art
Collections: Vintage photographic coll, includes ES Curtis, LA Huffman, E Cameron; Historical & Contemporary Montana Artists
Exhibitions: Changing exhibs every 4-8 wks
Publications: Biannual exhibit catalogs; quarterly newsletter
Activities: Classes for adults, children & disabled srs; lect open to pub, 10 vis lectrs per yr; gallery talks (speakers bureau); artmobile, serving art classes through artist-in-schools & communities program; 100 mile radius (30,000 sq miles) in 9 counties of SE Montana; 2 book traveling exhibs; mus store sells books & original art

MISSOULA

M **HISTORICAL MUSEUM AT FORT MISSOULA,** Bldg 322, Fort Missoula, Missoula, MT 59804-7251; 3400 Captain Rawn Way, Missoula, MT 59804. Tel 406-728-3476; Fax 406-543-6277; Elec Mail ftmslamuseum@montana.com; Internet Home Page Address: www.fortmissoulamuseum.org; *Dir Educ* Kristjana Eyjolfsson; *Dir* Robert Brown; *Grants Admin* Kristina Swanson; *Mus Aide* Sharon Garner; *Educ Asst* Carolyn Thompson; *Cur Colls* Nicole Webb; *Maintenance* Mark Gessner
Open Memorial Day to Labor Day Mon - Sat 10 AM - 5 PM, Sun Noon - 5 PM, Labor Day to Memorial Day Tues - Sun Noon - 5 pm; Admis adults $3, seniors $2, students $1, children under 6 free; Estab July 4, 1976 to collect and exhibit artifacts related to the history of western Montana; Changing gallery, 900 sq ft used for temporary exhibits; Meeting room gallery, 200 sq ft; Permanent gallery, 1200 sq ft; Average Annual Attendance: 45,000; Mem: 300; dues $25; quarterly meetings; Scholarships, Fellowships
Income: $450,000 (financed by mem, county appropriation & fundraising events)
Special Subjects: Architecture, American Western Art, Archaeology
Collections: Forest industry artifacts from Western Montana; Fort Missoula & the military presence in Western Montana; Missoula history
Exhibitions: The Road to Today: 250 Years of Missoula County History, changing exhibs, building exhib
Publications: The Military History of Fort Missoula; Missoula: The Way It Was; Purple & Gold: Missoula County High School, 1905-1965
Activities: Classes for adults & children; docent training; Forestry Day; 4th of July Celebration; lect open to pub; 3-5 vis lectrs per yr; gallery talks; tours; Dale & Coby Johnson Volunteer Award; fels offered; book traveling exhibs; originates traveling exhibs to mus & art galleries; sales shop sells books, magazines, original art & post cards

M **MISSOULA ART MUSEUM,** 335 N Pattee, Missoula, MT 59802. Tel 406-728-0447; Fax 406-543-8691; Elec Mail museum@missoulaartmuseum.org; Internet Home Page Address: www.missoulaartmuseum.org; *Cur Exhibit* Stephen Glueckert; *CEO & Dir* Laura J Millin; *Chmn (V)* J Martin Burke; *Cur Educ* Ranee Taaffe; *Registrar* Jennifer Reifsneider; *Pres (V)* Cynthia Shott; *Admin Officer* Eva Dunn-Froebig; *Visitor Servs Coordr* Nici Holt
Open Tues-Sat 11AM-5PM; No admis fee; Estab 1975 to collect, preserve & exhibit international art; to educate through exhibits, art school, special progs &

forums; Housed in renovated Carnegie Library (1903) featuring soft-panel covered walls; moveable track lighting; approx 3500 sq ft of exhibit space on two floors; fire and security alarm systems; meeting rooms; Average Annual Attendance: 25,000; Mem: 1000

Income: $500,000 (financed by mem, grants, fundraising events & ann permissive mill levy by Missoula County)

Purchases: Contemporary Art of Western United States

Library Holdings: Auction Catalogs; Audio Tapes; Book Volumes; CD-ROMs; Cards; Cassettes; Clipping Files; Exhibition Catalogs

Special Subjects: Architecture, Painting-American, Photography, American Indian Art, American Western Art, Bronzes, African Art, Ethnology, Ceramics, Crafts, Etchings & Engravings, Landscapes, Afro-American Art, Decorative Arts, Collages, Eskimo Art, Jewelry, Metalwork, Calligraphy, Embroidery

Collections: Contemporary Art of Western United States with an emphasis on Montana; Contemporary Art of Western Montana

Exhibitions: Paintings, Prose, Poems & Prints: Missouri River Interpretations; 23rd Annual Art Auction Exhib; Jacob Lawrence: Thirty Years of Prints (1963-1993); Beth Lo: Sabbatical Exhib.; Narrative Painting; Talking Quilts: Possibilities in Response; Jim Todd: Portraits of Printmakers; David Regan: WESTAF Fellowship Winner; Art Museum of Missoula Permanent Coll; Lucy Capehart: Interiors

Publications: Exhibit catalogs; membership newsletter; mailers & posters advertising shows

Activities: Classes for adults & children; dramatic progs; docent training; lect open to pub & for mems only; concerts; gallery talks; tours; artmobile; lending of original objects of art; book traveling exhibs; originate traveling exhibs to museums in region; mus shop sells books, prints, artist-made jewelry & other objects of design emphasis

M ROCKY MOUNTAIN MUSEUM OF MILITARY HISTORY, Fort Missoula, Bldg T-310, Missoula, MT 59807; PO Box 7263, Missoula, MT 59807-7263. Tel 406-549-5346; Elec Mail info@fortmissoula.org; Internet Home Page Address: www.fortmissoula.org; *Pres* Gary R Lancaster; *Exec Dir* Tate Jones; *Vice-Pres* Stan Cohen

Open June 1 - Labor Day: daily noon - 5 PM; day after Labor Day - end of May Sun noon - 5 PM; Admis no charge, donations accepted; Mus bldgs constructed in 1936 by the US Fourth Infantry Regiment & the Civilian Conservation Corps. Pvt nonprofit org; Mus promotes the commemoration & study of the US armed svcs, from the Frontier Period to the War on Terrorism; strives to impart a greater understanding of the roles played by America's service men & women through this period of dramatic social change; Mem: dues $25

Collections: Wide coll of documents & artifacts, ranging from Civil War artillery to Vietnam-era anti-tank missiles; home of Montana Civilian Conservation Corps aka "The Tree Army"

M UNIVERSITY OF MONTANA, Gallery of Visual Arts, Social Sciences Bldg, 1st Fl, University of Montana Missoula, MT 59812; 32 Campus Dr, School of Art Missoula, MT 59812-0003. Tel 406-243-2813; Fax 406-243-4968; Elec Mail gallery.visarts@umontana.edu; Internet Home Page Address: www.umt.edu/art/galleries/gva;

Open Mon by appt, Tues - Fri 11AM - 5PM; No admis fee; Estab 1981 to present faculty, student & outside exhibs of contemporary emphasis for community interest; Gallery has 220 linear ft, 2,200 sq ft; adjustable lighting; Average Annual Attendance: 15,000

Exhibitions: Various rotating exhibits call for details

Activities: Internships for gallery management; lects open to pub, 4-8 vis lectrs per yr; gallery talks; tours; competitions; campus art awards

M Montana Museum of Art & Culture, Main Hall, Room 006, University of Montana Missoula, MT 59812. Tel 406-243-2019; Fax 406-243-2797; Elec Mail museum@umontana.edu; Internet Home Page Address: www.umt.edu/montanamuseum; *Dir* Barbara Koostra; *Cur* Brandon Reintjes; *Reg* Lucy Capehart; *Asst Cur* Bill Queen; *Program & Publ Coordr* Rebecca Garner; *Admin Assoc* Kelly Hart

Open Wed, Thurs & Sat noon - 3 PM, Fri noon - 6 PM; June - Aug: cl Sun - Tues; Sep - May: Tues, Wed, Sat noon - 3 PM, Thurs, Fri noon - 6 PM, cl Sun, Mon; Admis general $5; Mus acquires & preserves art that expresses the spirit of the American West & its relationship to the broader world. As a univ & state mus, MMAC presents exhibs & educational programs that explore local, regional & global themes; The coll of the Montana mus of Art & Culture has been in existence since 1894. Currently with more than 10,000 works in its permanent coll, MMAC is home to one of the oldest & most prominent colls in the Rocky Mountain northwest; Average Annual Attendance: 50,000-60,000

Income: State, grants

Library Holdings: Auction Catalogs; Book Volumes; Kodachrome Transparencies; Pamphlets; Slides; Video Tapes

Special Subjects: Painting-American, Ceramics, Furniture

Collections: The Rudy Autio Contemporary Ceramic Collection; The Fra Dana Collection of American Impressionists; Pop Art & Contemporary Prints; Contemporary Native American Art; Bill & Polly Nordeen Collection of Western Art; New Deal Prints; Stella Duncan Collection of European Paintings; Cappadocia Collection of Southeast Asian Textiles; Henry Meloy Collection; Edgar S Paxton Collection; University of Montana Public Art Works

Publications: Contemporary Native American Art: Reflections after Lewis & Clark; The Original Man: The Life & Work of Montana Architect A J Gibson

Activities: Classes for adults & children; docent training; internships for coll & gallery management; lect open to pub; gallery talks; tours; Campus Art Award; original objects of art lent to Montana Art Gallery Dir Assn mems & to Wildling Art Mus, Los Olivos, CA; loans of historical objects to Montana museums; lending coll contains original prints, paintings & photographs; book traveling exhibs 1-3 per yr; originate traveling exhibs to Oregon Historical Society, National Cowboy and Western Heritage Mus, CM Russell Mus, Booth Mus of Western Art, Yellowstone Art Mus, Plains Art Mus, Three Affiliated Tribes Mus, Washington State Capitol Mus; mus shop sells books, reproductions & prints

PRYOR

M CHIEF PLENTY COUPS MUSEUM STATE PARK, (Chief Plenty Coups Museum) PO Box 100, Pryor, MT 59066-0100. Tel 406-252-1289; Fax 406-252-6668; Elec Mail plentycoups@plentycoups.org; Internet Home Page Address: www.plentycoups.org; *Dir* Rich Furber

Open May 1 - Sept 30 daily 10 AM - 5 PM; Admis $1 per person (park entrance fee includes mus); Estab 1972; Average Annual Attendance: 10,000

Income: Financed by state appropriation; affiliated with Montana Fish, Wildlife & Parks

Special Subjects: American Indian Art, Ethnology, Historical Material

Collections: Ethnographic materials of the Crow Indians; paintings; drawings; prehistoric artifacts

Exhibitions: Crow clothing and adornment; Pro Life Ways

Publications: Newsletter, annually

Activities: Fishing day for children; lect open to pub; 8 vis lectrs per yr; tours; sales shop sells books, magazines, original art, reproductions, prints, stationery notes, Crow crafts & beadwork

SIDNEY

M MONDAK HERITAGE CENTER, History Library, 120 Third Ave SE, Sidney, MT 59270. Tel 406-433-3500; Fax 406-433-3503; Elec Mail mdhc@richland.org; Internet Home Page Address: www.mondakheritagecenter.org; *Exec Dir* Benjamin L Clark; *Admin Asst* Leann Pelvit

Open year round Tues-Fr 10AM-4PM, Sat 1-4PM, cl Jan; No admis fee; Estab 1972 to preserve history of area & further interest in fine arts; For reference only; Average Annual Attendance: 7,000; Mem: Annual meeting Sep

Income: Financed by county appropriations, mem dues, grants & donations

Library Holdings: Audio Tapes; Book Volumes 2,000; Cassettes; Clipping Files; Fiche; Lantern Slides; Manuscripts; Maps; Memorabilia; Original Documents; Pamphlets; Periodical Subscriptions; Photographs; Records; Video Tapes

Special Subjects: Painting-American, American Western Art, Woodcuts, Dolls, Historical Material, Period Rooms

Publications: MonDak Historical & Arts Society Newsletter, quarterly

Activities: Classes for adults & children; lects open to pub & mem only, 10 vis lectrs per yr; concerts; gallery talks; tours; competitions; schols; book traveling exhibs, 8 per yr

M Museum, 120 3rd Ave SE, Sidney, MT 59270-4324. Tel 406-433-3500; Fax 406-433-3503; Elec Mail mdhc@richland.org; Internet Home Page Address: www.mondakheritagecenter.org; *Exec Dir* Benjamin L Clark

Open Tues - Fri 10 AM - 4 PM, Sat 1 - 4 PM; cl Jan; No admis fee; Estab 1967 as mus, for cultural events & shows; Average Annual Attendance: 10,000; Mem: Annual meeting Sep

Income: Financed by County Mill levy, memberships, & donations

Library Holdings: Audio Tapes; Book Volumes 1500; Cards; Clipping Files; Exhibition Catalogs; Fiche; Manuscripts; Maps; Memorabilia; Original Art Works; Original Documents; Other Holdings; Pamphlets; Photographs; Reels

Collections: Local history & art

Exhibitions: Regularly changing exhibs

Publications: newsletter, quarterly

Activities: Classes for adults & children; docent training; traveling trunks for children; lects open to pub & mem only, 6 vis lectrs per yr; concerts; gallery talks; tours; competitions; schols; book travelling exhibs, 4 per yr; mus shop sells books, original art, prints, regional arts & crafts

THREE FORKS

M THREE FORKS AREA HISTORICAL SOCIETY, Headwaters Heritage Museum, 202 S Main, Three Forks, MT 59752; PO Box 116, Three Forks, MT 59752-0116. Tel 406-285-4778; Elec Mail museumthreeforks@aol.com; Internet Home Page Address: www.tfhistory.org; *Vol Dir, Cur & Mus Shop Mgr* Robin Cadby-Sorensen; *Vol Pres* Pat O'Brien Townsend; *Vol Treas* Patrick Finnegan; *Vol Secy* Richard Townsend; *Mem Chairperson* Joan Burwell

Open Jun 1 - Sept 30 Mon-Sat 9 AM - 5 PM, Sun11AM-3PM; other times by appt; No admis fee, donations accepted; Estab 1979 (Historical Society); Mus: 1982; Mus was constructed in 1910 and originally housed one of the first banks in Three Forks and contains thousands of artifacts & memorabilia depicting the local history of the Headwaters of the Missouri area; upstairs rooms depict a turn-of-the-century kitchen, schoolroom, blacksmith shop, railroad room, beauty shop & more. pvt nonprofit org; Average Annual Attendance: 2,500; Mem: dues Gen Mem $25, Gallatin Patron $125, Madison Patron $250, Jefferson Patron $500, Missouri Patron $1,000, Headwaters Patron $5,000

Special Subjects: Flasks & Bottles, Furniture, Photography, Period Rooms, Bronzes, Portraits, Dolls, Historical Material

Collections: Colls are from the local families of the Missouri Headwaters area; largest brown trout caught in Montana; fur trapp; anvil, barbed wire coll; misc artifacts from 1900s - 1950s; fossils; rocks; arrowheads; maps; agricultural tools; photographs; costumes; furnishings; papers & more; railroad press & hat shop

Publications: Headwaters History, 1983; Selected Papers of the 2010 Fur Trade Symposium at the Three Forks

Activities: Lects; guided tours; loan exhibs; traveling exhibs; docent prog; Ann Events: Journey of Discovery; Christmas Stroll; children's tours; mus shop sells books, postcards, souvenirs, prints & mus related items for sale

VICTOR

M VICTOR HERITAGE MUSEUM, Blake & Main St, Victor, MT 59875; PO Box 610, Victor, MT 59875-0610. Tel 406-642-3997; *Pres* Mark K Hafer

Open Memorial Day - End of Aug: Tues - Sat 1 - 4 PM, cl holidays; No admis fee, donations accepted; Estab 1989 on land that was donated by Alvin & Ruth Cote; mus focuses on history of the town of Victor from the early 1900s, including mining, railroad & Native American history. Pvt nonprofit org ; Average Annual Attendance: 500 by estimate; Mem: dues Family $10

Collections: Permanent displays of items & artifacts that relate to Victor's history that are supplemented by thematic displays that change each yr; structures; personal artifacts; folk culture; distribution & transportation artifacts; tools & equip for commun; tools & equip for materials
Activities: Research on the Victor area & its residents prior to the 1930s; Ann event: Chocolate-Tasting Party, a fundraiser taking place on the first Mon in Dec

WHITEFISH

M **STUMPTOWN ART STUDIO,** Whitefish Gallery, 145 Central Ave, Whitefish, MT 59937. Tel 406-862-5929; Fax 406-862-5029; Elec Mail info@stumptownartstudio.org; Internet Home Page Address: www.whitefishgallerynights.org

NEBRASKA

ALLIANCE

M **CARNEGIE ARTS CENTER,** 204 W 4th St, Alliance, NE 69301-3332. Tel 308-762-4571; Fax 308-762-4571; Elec Mail carnegieartscenter@bbc.net; Internet Home Page Address: www.carnegieartscenter.com; *Gallery Dir* Lynne C Messersmith
Open Tues - Sat 10 AM - 4 PM, Sun 1 PM - 4 PM
Collections: Paintings; various art exhibits

ASHLAND

M **GENE RONCKA WILLOW POINT GALLERY/MUSEUM,** (Willow Point Gallery & Museum) 1431 Silver St Ashland, NE 68003-1845. Tel 402-944-3613; Fax 402-944-3613; Elec Mail gr35419@windstream.net; Internet Home Page Address: www.generoncka.com; *Artist* Gene Roncka; *Gallery Dir* Mary Roncka; *Sales Assoc* Marge Anderson; *Sales Assoc* Melissa Poulter; *Sales* Frank Demeter
Open Mon - Sat 10 AM - 5:30 PM, Sun 1 PM - 4 PM; No admis fee; Estab1994 - art sales; Gene Roncka art sales, framing, big game collection; Average Annual Attendance: 8,000
Activities: Tours; mus shop sells original art, reproductions & prints

AURORA

M **PLAINSMAN MUSEUM,** 210 16th, Aurora, NE 68818. Tel 402-694-6531; Elec Mail plainsman@hamilton.net; Internet Home Page Address: www.plainsmanmuseum.org; *Dir* Megan Sharp; *Asst Dir* Gary Gustafson
Open Apr 1 - Oct 31 Mon - Sat 9 AM - 5 PM, Sun 1 - 5 PM, Nov 1 - Mar 31 Mon - Sun 1 - 5 PM; Admis adults $6, seniors $4, students $2, AAA discounts available; Estab 1976 to tell the story of Hamilton County, Nebraska, focusing on the time from 1860 -1950; Free-standing panels in area of Historical Mus (5 large folding panels). Maintains reference library; Average Annual Attendance: 7,000; Mem: 350; dues family $25, singles $15; ann meeting Dirs meet 2nd Thurs of every month
Income: $60,000 (financed by mem, county allowance & individual donations)
Library Holdings: Book Volumes; Clipping Files; Lantern Slides; Manuscripts; Maps; Original Documents; Periodical Subscriptions; Photographs; Prints
Special Subjects: Painting-American, Photography, Textiles, Folk Art, Woodcarvings, Portraits, Dolls, Furniture, Glass, Jewelry, Historical Material, Maps, Coins & Medals, Period Rooms, Embroidery, Laces, Mosaics, Leather
Collections: One large pen & ink mural (20 ft x 8 ft) by Larry Guyton; 13 Wesley Huenefeld murals; Sidney E King Collection of murals; two large murals by Ernest Ochsner; Six Pioneer Scene Mosaic floor murals; Ted Bergren woodcarvings; Early Terrance Duren drawings
Publications: Events Past & Upcoming, Plainsman newsletter, 4 times yearly
Activities: Lect open to pub; concerts; gallery talks; tours; mus shop sells books, original art

CAMBRIDGE

M **CAMBRIDGE MUSEUM,** 612 Penn St Cambridge, NE 69022; Box 129, Cambridge, NE 69022. Tel 308-697-4385; *Cur* Betty Kruger; *Pres* Marilyn Kester; *Sec* Mae Groshong; *Board Mem* Arla Mae Pearson; *Board Mem* Loyd Thompson; *Board Mem* Roy Patterson
Open Apr - Sep Tues - Sun 1 - 5 PM, Oct - Mar Sat - Sun 1 PM - 5 PM; No admis fee, donations accepted; Estab 1938 to give local people & tourists a place to learn about history; Average Annual Attendance: 1,074; Mem: 6
Income: Financed by donations
Purchases: $75 (Norris House painting)
Special Subjects: American Indian Art, Historical Material, Landscapes, American Western Art, Painting-American, Archaeology, Costumes, Pottery, Dolls, Furniture, Maps, Coins & Medals, Period Rooms, Embroidery
Collections: Painting by Musi Muse; Paintings by Leonna Cowels & Gale Kasson; Clare Heumphreus Bettridge, Gary Hobbs, Henriette Johnson, Dorothy Lendall, Donna Flammang; Tea pot coll (159); bell coll (98); glass dog coll (130)
Exhibitions: Rotating exhibits
Activities: Classes for children; scavenger hunts; lect open to pub - 1 per yr; schols ($500); originate traveling exhibs 1 per yr

CHADRON

M **CHADRON STATE COLLEGE,** Memorial Hall Main Gallery & Memorial Hall Gallery 239, 1000 Main St, Chadron, NE 69337-2690. Tel 308-432-6380; Fax 308-432-7784; Elec Mail sjohns@csc.edu; Internet Home Page Address: www.csc.edu; *Coordr Conf* Shellie Johns; *Chair Performing & Visual Arts* Richard Bird
Open Mon - Fri 8 AM - 4 PM; No admis fee; Estab 1967 to offer opportunities for national recognized artists, students, faculty & local artists to present their

works; to bring in shows to upgrade the cultural opportunities of students & the general pub; Main gallery has space for traveling & larger shows; Gallery 239 suffices for small shows; Average Annual Attendance: 5,000
Income: Financed by college budget, fine art student fee & state appropriation
Library Holdings: Book Volumes; CD-ROMs; Compact Disks; DVDs; Manuscripts; Maps; Memorabilia; Motion Pictures; Original Art Works; Pamphlets; Photographs; Prints; Records; Sculpture; Slides; Video Tapes
Collections: Chadron Foundation Art Collection
Activities: Docent training; lects open to pub, 3 vis lectrs per yr; gallery talks; tours; concerts; individual objects of art lent to campus bldgs; 4 book traveling exhibs per yr; circulate to regn bus & libraries; mus shop sells books, original art & prints

CHAPPELL

L **CHAPPELL MEMORIAL LIBRARY AND ART GALLERY,** 289 Babcock Ave, Chappell, NE 69124-0248; PO Box 248, Chappell, NE 69124-0248. Tel 308-874-2626; *Head Librn* Dixie Riley; *Asst Librn* Doris McFee
Open Tues - Thurs 1 - 5 PM, Tues & Thurs evening 7 - 9 PM, Sat 2 - 5 PM; No admis fee; Estab 1935 by gift of Mrs Charles H Chappell
Income: Financed by city of Chappell
Library Holdings: Book Volumes 10,398; Periodical Subscriptions 31
Collections: Aaron Pyle Collection; permanent personal coll of art works from many countries, a gift from Mrs Charles H Chappell
Exhibitions: Rotating Exhibits
Activities: Gallery talks; library tours

DAVID CITY

M **BONE CREEK MUSEUM OF AGRARIAN ART,** 575 "E" St, David City, NE 68632. Tel 402-367-4488; Elec Mail artinfo@bonecreek.org; Internet Home Page Address: www.bonecreek.org
Open Wed - Sat 10 AM - 4 PM, Sun 1 PM - 4 PM; cl major holidays; No admis fee; Estab 2007; Nat center for preserving, viewing, learning about exceptional Agrarian art
Income: pvt & limited pub
Library Holdings: Exhibition Catalogs; Framed Reproductions; Manuscripts; Memorabilia; Original Art Works; Original Documents; Other Holdings; Photographs; Prints; Records; Sculpture
Special Subjects: American Indian Art, Drawings, Etchings & Engravings, Landscapes, American Western Art, Photography, Pottery, Prints, Woodcuts, Manuscripts, Graphics, Latin American Art, Painting-American, Sculpture, Watercolors, Southwestern Art, Ceramics, Folk Art, Primitive art, Posters, Military Art
Collections: Agrarian art; Dale Nichols, Thomas Hart Benton, Robert Bateman; Birger Sandzen, Robert Gwathmey, Thomas Mangelsan, Wigi Lucioni
Publications: "Dale Nichols: Transcending Regionalism," exhib catalog; Robert Lougheed: "Beyond Cowboys, Fields of the Heart", exhib catalog
Activities: Educ prog, tour & field trips for adults & children; lects open to pub, 4-5 vis lectrs per yr; gallery talks; tours; sales shop sells prints, t-shirts & books

FREMONT

M **GALLERY 92 WEST,** 92 W 6th St Fremont, NE 68025-4956; PO Box 335 Fremont, NE 68025-0009.

GERING

M **OREGON TRAIL MUSEUM ASSOCIATION,** Scotts Bluff National Monument, Hwy 92 W, Gering, NE 69341; PO Box 27, Gering, NE 69341-0027. Tel 308-436-4340, 9700; Fax 308-436-7611; Internet Home Page Address: www.NPS.gov/scbl; *Admin Mgr* John Kussack; *Bus Mgr* Jolene Kaufman; *Historian* Dean Knudsen; *Supt* Valerie J Naylor
Open June - Sept 8 AM - 8 PM, Oct - May 8 AM - 5 PM, cl Christmas & New Year's Day; Admis $5 per vehicle; Estab 1919 to preserve & display Oregon Trail landmark, artifacts, art & natural resources; 3 exhibit rooms; Average Annual Attendance: 120,000; Mem: 75; dues $10, renewal $5
Income: Financed by sales of Oregon Trail Museum Assn
Collections: Watercolors, drawings, & photographs by William H Jackson; surface finds from the Oregon Trail vicinity; paleontological specimens from within Monument boundaries
Exhibitions: 6 exhibits depicting geological, prehistoric, archaeological, ethnological history of the area; 15 exhibits depicting history of western migration from 1840-1870s; photos, drawings & paintings by W H Jackson; 2 dioramas depicting interaction between white men & buffalo
Publications: The Overland Migration; brochures & handbooks
Activities: Slide presentation of history of Oregon Trail & Scotts Bluff; Living History presentation of life on the trail; lect open to pub; mus shop sells books, prints, slides, postcards

HASTINGS

M **HASTINGS MUSEUM OF NATURAL & CULTURAL HISTORY,** (Hastings Museum) 1330 N Burlington Ave, Hastings, NE 68901; PO Box 1286, Hastings, NE 68902-1286. Tel 402-461-4629; Fax 402-461-2379; Elec Mail hastingsmuseum@alltel.net; Internet Home Page Address: www.hastingsmuseum.org; *Educ* Russanne Erickson; *Cur & Coll* Teresa Kreutzer-Hodson; *Vol Coord* Lynn Zeleski
Open Tues - Thurs 9 AM - 5 PM, Fri - Sat 9 AM - 5 PM, Sun noon - 6 PM; Winter Mon - Fri 9 AM -5 PM, Sat & Sun 1 AM - 5 PM, cl Thanksgiving & Christmas; Admis adults $6, seniors (60+) $5.50, children (3-12) $4, tots free, large format films additional; Estab 1927 for a program of service & exhibits to augment & stimulate the total educative prog of schools & the gen pub; Animal

displays in natural habitat settings; IMAX Theater open daily; Average Annual Attendance: 83,000; Mem: 5,900; premier $100, $250, $500, family $40, individual $28

Income: Financed by city appropriation & pvt donations

Special Subjects: Furniture, Glass, Coins & Medals, Dioramas

Collections: Discover the Dream: Kool-Aid; Richards Coin Collection; George W Cole Smith & Wesson Gun Collection; Irma Kruse Collection

Exhibitions: Groundwater Discovery Adventure - open year round; World's Largest Display of Whooping Cranes

Publications: Museum Highlights, quarterly

Activities: Classes for adults & children; lects open to pub, vis lectrs varies per yr; exten prog serving pre-k; traveling exhibs one per Summer; mus shop sells books & selected gift items

HOLDREGE

M **PHELPS COUNTY HISTORICAL SOCIETY,** Nebraska Prairie Museum, N Hwy 183, Holdrege, NE 68949-0164; PO Box 164, Holdrege, NE 68949-0164. Tel 308-995-5015; Fax 308-995-2241; Elec Mail prairie995@gmail.com; Internet Home Page Address: www.nebraskaprairie.org; *Pres* Dr Bob Butz; *VPres* Eileen Schrock; *Treas & Exec Dir* Dan Christensen; *Secy* Warner Carlson; *Genealogy Librn* Sandra Slater

Open Mon - Sat 9 AM - 5 PM, Sun 1 - 5 PM, cl Jan 1, July 4, Thanksgiving, Easter, Christmas Eve & Christmas; Admis (suggested) adults $5, children $2; Estab 1966 for preservation of County history & artifacts; Thomas F. Naegele Gallery, over 60 works depicting live in German POW camps in the US; Average Annual Attendance: 9,500; Mem: 450; dues life $1,000, family ann $30, ann $20; ann meeting in May

Income: Financed by mem, county mill levy, state contributions & estate gifts

Library Holdings: Book Volumes; Clipping Files; Fiche; Maps; Original Documents; Other Holdings genealogy information; Photographs; Records

Special Subjects: Architecture, Sculpture, Bronzes, Anthropology, Costumes, Ceramics, Crafts, Pottery, Woodcarvings, Dolls, Carpets & Rugs, Historical Material, Coins & Medals, Period Rooms, Embroidery

Collections: Agriculture equipment, china, furniture, historical items, photos, POW, military, Native American

Publications: Centennial History of Holdrege, 1883; History of Phelps County, 1873-1980; Holdrege Centennial Coloring Book; Prisoners On The Plains; Stereoscope, quarterly

Activities: Classes for children; docent training; pow film; lect open to pub, 4 vis lectrs per yr; tours; book traveling exhibs; mus shop sells books, magazines, labels, souvenir plates, original art & reproductions

L **Donald O. Lindgren Library,** 2701 Burlington, Holdrege, NE 68949-0164; PO Box 164, Holdrege, NE 68949-0164. Tel 308-995-5015; Fax 308-995-2241; Internet Home Page Address: www.nebraskaprairie.org; *Genealogy Librn* Sandra Slater; *Office Mgr* Cheryl Mill; *Pres* Dr Robert Butz; *Exec Dir* Dan R Van Dyke

Open Tues - Oct Mon - Fri, 9 AM - 5 PM; Nov - Apr Mon - Fri, 9 AM - 4 PM, Sat - Sun 1 PM - 5 PM; Admis donations only; Estab 1966 for historic preservation & educ; Average Annual Attendance: 10,000; Mem: 400; dues $30; ann meeting in May

Income: $100,000 (financed by taxes, investment earnings & contributions

Library Holdings: Audio Tapes; Book Volumes 1000; Cassettes; Clipping Files; Fiche; Kodachrome Transparencies; Lantern Slides; Manuscripts; Motion Pictures; Original Documents; Pamphlets; Periodical Subscriptions; Photographs; Prints; Video Tapes

Special Subjects: Posters, Historical Material, Crafts, Porcelain, Period Rooms, Dolls, Embroidery, Dioramas, Coins & Medals, Pottery

Collections: The Thomas F. Naegele Gallery contains 60 paintings depicting life in the POW camps at Atlanta & Indianola, Nebraska

Publications: The Stereoscope, quarterly

Activities: Classes for adults & children; docent training; lect open to public, 4 vis lectrs per year; tours; ext prog to schools; sales shop sells books, magazines, original art, reproductions, prints, toys, jewelry & ceramics

LEXINGTON

M **DAWSON COUNTY HISTORICAL SOCIETY,** Museum, PO Box 369, Lexington, NE 68850-0369. Tel 308-324-5340; Fax 308-324-5340; Elec Mail dcmuseum@atcjet.net; Internet Home Page Address: www.dchsmuseum.com/index.html; *Pres* Gail Hall; *Treas* Jan Wightman; *Sec* Barb Knapple; *Dir* Barbara Vondras; *Staff Asst* Carol Nelson

Open Mon - Sat 9 AM - 5 PM, Sun by appt only; No admis fee; Estab 1958 to preserve Dawson County's heritage; Art gallery features exhibits by local artists; exhibits change monthly; Average Annual Attendance: 6,000; Mem: 450; dues life $150, family $20, individual $12.50

Income: Financed by endowment, mem, grants, county appropriation

Special Subjects: Textiles, Furniture

Collections: Agricultural Equipment; Furniture; Glassware; Household Implements; Quilts; Tools; Agricultural Equipment; Glassware

Exhibitions: 1919 McCave Aeroplane; Restored Country Schoolhouse; Restored Train Engine & Depot; Log Cabin Gallery Show monthly exhibit

Publications: Dawson County Banner newsletter, quarterly

Activities: Docent progs; lect open to pub, 3 vis lectrs per yr; book traveling exhibs 2 per yr; retail store sells books, original art

LINCOLN

A **LINCOLN ARTS COUNCIL,** 1701 S 17th St, Ste 1A Lincoln, NE 68502-2641. Tel 402-434-2787; Fax 402-434-2788; Elec Mail info@artscene.org; Internet Home Page Address: www.artscene.org; *Pres* David Erickson; *Pres* Jack Olivia; *Office & Prog Mgr* Trisha Spanbauer; *VP Prog* Diane Gonzolas; *Exec Dir* Deborah Weber

Open Mon-Fri 8AM-4PM; Estab 1966 to promote & encourage arts in Lincoln & serves as central information & advocacy source for the arts in the capital city; Mem: 60 arts

Income: Financed by pvt contributions, grants, city of Lincoln contract & Nebraska Arts Council

Publications: Artscene arts calendar, bimonthly; pub art guide, gallery guide

M **NEBRASKA STATE CAPITOL,** 1445 K St, Lincoln, NE 68509-4924; PO Box 94696, Lincoln, NE 68509-4696. Tel 402-471-0448; Fax 402-471-6952; Elec Mail hello@capitol.org; Internet Home Page Address: www.capitol.org; *Capitol Adminr* Robert C Ripley; *Preservation Architect* Thomas L Kaspar; *Tourism Supvr* Roxanne E Smith; *Archivist* Karen Wagner; *Preservation Architect* Matt Hansen

Open Mon - Fri 8 AM - 5 PM, Sat & holidays 10 AM - 5 PM, Sun 1 - 5 PM; Stone carvings at BAS reliefs; mosaic tile vaulting & fl panels; painted & mosaic murals; vernacular architectural ornamentation; Average Annual Attendance: 100,000

Income: Financed by state appropriation & pvt donations

Purchases: Eight murals commissioned to complete Capitol Thematic Prog

Special Subjects: Architecture, Painting-American, Sculpture, Woodcarvings, Decorative Arts, Posters, Furniture, Historical Material, Restorations, Tapestries, Leather

Collections: Lee Lawrie, building sculptor; Hildreth Meiere, mosaicist; muralists - Augustus V Tack, Kenneth Evett, James Penny, Elizabeth Dolan, Jean Reynal, Reinhold Marxhausen, F John Miller, Charles Clement, Stephen C Roberts

Publications: A Harmony of the Arts - The Nebraska State Capitol

Activities: Univ of Nebraska lect & service organization lect; guided tours; sales shop sells books, reproductions, prints, original art & Nebraska related items

M **NEBRASKA WESLEYAN UNIVERSITY,** Elder Gallery, 5000 Saint Paul Ave, Department of Art Lincoln, NE 68504-2760. Tel 402-466-2371, 465-2230; Fax 402-465-2179; Internet Home Page Address: www.nebrwesleyan.edu; *Dir* Dr Donald Paoletta; *Gallery Preparator* Regina O'Reere

Open Tues - Fri 10 AM - 4 PM, Sat & Sun 1 - 4 PM; No admis fee; Estab 1966 as a cultural addition to col & community; Average Annual Attendance: 10,000

Special Subjects: Painting-American, Prints, Sculpture

Collections: Campus coll; permanent coll of prints, paintings & sculpture

Exhibitions: Annual Fred Wells National Juried Exhib; Nebraska Art Educators; faculty show; students shows; other changing monthly shows

Activities: Classes for adults

M **NOYES ART GALLERY,** 119 S Ninth St, Lincoln, NE 68508. Tel 402-475-1061; Elec Mail julianoyes@aol.com; Internet Home Page Address: www.noyesartgallery.com; *Dir* Julia Noyes; *Asst* Tom Marshall; *Cur* Janna Harsch; *IT* Lisa Gustafson

Open Mon - Sat 10 AM - 5 PM, Nov - Dec 24 Mon - Sun 10 AM -5 PM, first Fri 10 AM - 9 PM; No admis fee; Estab 1993 as a commercial, cooperative profit organization to exhibit, promote & sell works by 60 regional artists; Located in a 100 yr old building near downtown Lincoln; main fl includes over 1200 sq ft exhibit area, office, storage & kitchen; second floor contains rented artist studios & classrooms; Mem: Guest artists & co-op artists apply

Income: 20,000; Financed by mem, commissions on sales

Special Subjects: Decorative Arts, Drawings, Landscapes, Collages, Furniture, Pottery, Textiles, Bronzes, Painting-Japanese, Graphics, Painting-American, Photography, Sculpture, Watercolors, Ceramics, Crafts, Folk Art, Woodcarvings, Portraits, Glass, Asian Art, Silver, Metalwork, Miniatures, Mosaics, Stained Glass, Painting-Russian, Enamels

Exhibitions: Monthly exhibits of gallery & visiting artists' work; Special monthly & private openings

Publications: Exhibit announcements, monthly

Activities: Classes for adults & children; docent training; music & poetry readings; lect open to pub; 4 competitions with awards; gallery talks; tours; 4 book traveling exhibs per yr; originates traveling exhibs of various venues to 5 locations across Nebr; sales shop sells books, original art

M **UNIVERSITY OF NEBRASKA, LINCOLN,** Sheldon Memorial Art Gallery & Sculpture Garden, PO Box 880300, Lincoln, NE 68588-0300. Tel 402-472-2461; Fax 402-472-4258; Internet Home Page Address: www.sheldonartgallery.org; *Dir* Jorge Daniel Veneciano; *Coll Cur* Sharon Kennedy; *Coll Mgr* Stacey Walsh; *Develop Dir* Laura Reznicek; *Dir Educ* Karen Janovy; *Programs Coordr* Laurie Sipple

Open Tues - Thurs 10AM-5PM, Fri 10AM-8PM, Sat 10AM-5PM, Sun noon-5PM; No admis fee; Estab 1888 to exhibit the permanent colls owned by the Univ & to present temporary exhibs on an ann basis; These activities are accompanied by appropriate interpretive progs; The Sheldon Gallery, a gift of Mary Frances & Bromley Sheldon, was opened in 1963 & is the work of Philip Johnson. Facilities in addition to 15,000 sq ft of exhib galleries, include an auditorium, a print study, mems room a 25-acre outdoor sculpture garden; Average Annual Attendance: 125,000

Income: Financed by endowment, state appropriation & Nebraska Art Assoc

Purchases: $200,000

Special Subjects: Decorative Arts, Drawings, Folk Art, Ceramics, Photography, Portraits, Painting-American, Prints, Bronzes, Sculpture, Graphics, Watercolors

Collections: Frank M Hall Collection of contemporary paintings, sculpture, prints, drawings, photographs & ceramics; Nebraska Art Assn Collection of American paintings & drawings; University Collections; Permanent collection includes more than 12,000 objects in various media

Publications: Exhib catalogs & brochures; sculpture coll catalogue

Activities: Educ dept; docent training; lect open to pub, 3-5 vis lectrs per yr; tours; exten dept serves State of Nebraska; individual paintings & original objects of art lent to campus offices & other institutions in US & abroad; originate traveling exhibs; gift shop sells reproductions of works of original art within the permanent coll, prints, jewelry, ceramics & unique gifts

L **Architecture Library,** PO Box 880300, Lincoln, NE 68588-0300. Tel 402-472-1208, 1193; Fax 402-472-0665; Elec Mail archmail@unlnotes.unl.edu; Internet Home Page Address: www.unl.edu/libr/libs/arch; *Prof* Kay Logan-Peters; *Slide Cur* Judith Winkler

Open Mon - Thurs 8 AM - 9PM, Fri 8AM-5PM, Sat 1-5PM, Sun 1-9PM, Slides open Mon-Fri 8AM-5PM; Estab to provide acad support for students & faculty in architectural concentration; Circ 21,000

Purchases: $25,000

Library Holdings: Audio Tapes; Book Volumes 65,000; Cassettes; Clipping Files; Exhibition Catalogs; Fiche; Filmstrips; Periodical Subscriptions 203; Photographs; Records; Reels; Slides 100,000; Video Tapes
Special Subjects: Architecture
Collections: American Architectural Books (microfilm); Architecture: Urban Documents (microfiche); Fowler Collection of Early Architectural Books (microfilm); National Register of Historic Places (microfiche); Historic American Building Survey Measure & Drawings; Slide coll

M **Eisentrager Howard Gallery,** Stadium Dr and T St (1st fl), Richards Hall 120 Lincoln, NE 68588-0114. Tel 402-472-5025; Fax 402-472-9746; Internet Home Page Address: www.unl.edu/art/facilities_eisentrager-howard.shtml; *Chmn & Dir* Joseph M Ruffo
Open Mon - Thurs noon-4PM Call to confirm hours; No admis fee; Estab 1985 to exhibit contemporary art by national artists; student & faculty exhibs; 2,300 sq ft with 238 running ft of exhib space in two spacious rooms; track lights; Average Annual Attendance: 8,000
Collections: Coll of UNL Student Work from BFA & MFA degree prog
Exhibitions: Undergrad, grad & faculty exhibs
Publications: Exhib catalogs

M **UNIVERSITY OF NEBRASKA-LINCOLN,** Great Plains Art Museum, Hewit Place, 1155 Q St Lincoln, NE 68588-0250; PO Box 880250, Lincoln, NE 68588-0250. Tel 402-472-6220; Fax 402-472-0463; Elec Mail gpac2@unl.edu; Internet Home Page Address: www.unl.edu/plains; *Cur* Amber Mohr; *Coll Mgr* Susan Curtis
Open Tues - Sat 10 AM - 5 PM, Sun 1:30 - 5 PM; No admis fee; Estab 1980 to promote educ & gen awareness of Western art with an emphasis on Great Plains; Circ non-circulating, on-site research only; Three galleries rotating 8-12 exhibits per year & maintaining a research space and lib of Western Americana with approx 7,000 vols; Average Annual Attendance: 10,000; Mem: 150; dues $25 - $1000
Income: Financed by endowment, mem & state appropriation
Library Holdings: Book Volumes; Exhibition Catalogs; Manuscripts; Original Documents
Special Subjects: American Indian Art, Landscapes, American Western Art, Photography, Portraits, Prints, Bronzes, Sculpture, Drawings, Painting-American, Watercolors, Woodcuts, Posters
Collections: Broder Collection of 20th century American Indian paintings; Christlieb Collection of bronze sculpture, paintings & works on paper including drawings, prints & photographs depicting western subjects; Dwight and John Kirch Collection; Charles W Guildman Collection
Publications: Exhib catalogs & brochures
Activities: Lect open to pub, 6 vis lectrs per yr; tours; gallery talks; individual paintings & original objects of art lent; lending coll contains 1600 items; lends original objects of art to mus of schools with common region of interest; traveling exhibs to schools throughout Nebr; sales shop sells books, original art & reproductions

MCCOOK

M **HIGH PLAINS MUSEUM,** 423 Norris Ave, McCook, NE 69001-2003. Tel 308-345-3661; *Chmn Bd* Russell Dowling
Open Tues - Sat 1 - 5 PM, Sun 2 PM - 4 PM, cl Mon & holidays; No admis fee, donations accepted; Estab 1963 to preserve the items pertaining to local history & to interpret them for the pub; Mus is located in new building. New additions include complete pioneer kitchen; railroad section (inside & out); complete Old Time Pharmacy; 1942 Airbase; George W Norris Room; Governors From Nebraska; Average Annual Attendance: 5,000; Mem: 210; mem qualification is art display by local art club; dues $5 - $200; ann meeting in Apr
Income: Financed by mem & donations
Library Holdings: Memorabilia; Original Art Works; Pamphlets; Photographs; Records 33 1/2 phonograph records; Sculpture; Video Tapes
Collections: Paintings made on the barracks walls of prisoner of war camp near McCook; paintings donated by local artists; model railroad; displays pertaining to life of Southwest Nebraska
Exhibitions: Art Exhibit
Publications: Flyer, 3-page pamphlet describing hours & show displays
Activities: Lect open to pub, 8 vis lectrs per yr; competitions; lending coll contains books, framed reproductions & motion pictures; mus shop sells books, postcards, rings for children, petrified wood, arrowheads, medallions

MINDEN

M **HAROLD WARP PIONEER VILLAGE FOUNDATION,** 138 E Hwy 6, Minden, NE 68959-0068. Tel 308-832-2750; Fax 308-832-1181; Elec Mail manager@pioneervillage.com; Internet Home Page Address: www.pioneervillage.org; WATS 800-445-4447; *Pres* Harold Warp; *Gen Mgr* Marshall Nelson
Open Winter daily 9AM-4:30PM, Summer daily 8AM-6PM; Admis adults $10, children 6-12 $5, children under 6 free; spec group rates; Estab 1953 to preserve man's progress from 1830 to present day; Foundation includes a 90-unit motel, 350-seat restaurant & 135-site campground; Elm Creek Fort; The People's Store; Bloomington Land Office; fire house; Lowell Depot; country school; sod house; China house; church; merry-go-round; horse barn; homes & shops building; antique farm machinery building; antique tractor & 350 autos & trucks; livery stable; agricultural building, blacksmith shop; Pony Express barn; Pony Express station; home appliance building; hobby house; John Roger statuary; William Jackson paintings; Albert Tilburne paintings; Average Annual Attendance: 80,000
Special Subjects: Historical Material
Collections: Airplanes; automobiles; bath tubs; bicycles; boats; clocks; fire wagons; guns; harvesters; horse drawn rigs; kitchens; lighting; locomotives; musical instruments; numismatics; paintings; plows; rare china; sculpture; street cars; telephones; threshers; toys; tractors; trucks
Publications: 500 Fascinating Facts; History of Man's Progress (1830-present); Pioneer Cookbook; Sister Clara's Letters (Over Our Hill-Past Our Place)

Activities: Classes for adults; elder hostel; docent training; children's progs, Holiday & Pioneer life in the Midwest; lect for mems only; tours; mus shop sells books, reproductions, prints & slides

NEBRASKA CITY

M **KIMMEL-HARDING-NELSON CENTER FOR THE ARTS,** 801 Third Corso, Nebraska City, NE 68410-2819. Tel 402-874-9600; Elec Mail info@khncenterforthearts.org; Internet Home Page Address: www.khncenterforthearts.org

M **NEBRASKA GAME AND PARKS COMMISSION,** Arbor Lodge State Historical Park & Morton Mansion, 2600 Arbor Ave, Nebraska City, NE 68410-1072; PO Box 15, Nebraska City, NE 68410-0015. Tel 402-873-7222; Fax 402-874-9885; Elec Mail ngpc.arbor.lodge @nebraska.gov; Internet Home Page Address: outdoornebraska.org; *Asst Supt* Mark Kemper; *Supt* Randall Fox
Open mid Apr - End of Oct Mon - Sun 11AM - 5 PM; Admis adults $5, children 3-12 $2, children 2 & under free; Estab 1923; Art coll of mems of the J S Morton family & outdoor scenes spread through a 52-room mansion; Average Annual Attendance: 90,000
Income: Financed by state appropriation
Special Subjects: Afro-American Art, Historical Material, Landscapes, American Western Art, Furniture, Photography, Portraits, Painting-American, Period Rooms, Bronzes, Sculpture, Architecture, Costumes, Woodcarvings, Dolls, Furniture, Jewelry, Carpets & Rugs, Historical Material, Stained Glass, Leather
Activities: Lect open to pub; tours; awards; Arbor Day Tree plantings on last weekend in Apr; Apple Jack Fine Art show & sale 3rd Sat & Sun in Sept; living history demonstrations 4th & 5th Sun in Sept, 1st & 2nd Sun in Oct; mus shop sells books, magazines, prints, Arbor Day tree pins, postcards, nature crds, DVD's & t-shirts

NORFOLK

M **NORFOLK ARTS CENTER,** 305 N 5th St Norfolk, NE 68701-4092. Tel 402-371-7199; Fax 402-371-1971; Elec Mail info@norfolkartscenter.org; Internet Home Page Address: www.norfolkartscenter.org; *Exec Dir* Kara Weander-Gaster; *Prog Coordr* Melinda Wriedt Kozel
Open Tues - Fri 10 AM - 8 PM, Sat 10 AM - 4 PM; No admis fee; Estab 1978
Exhibitions: Midwest Regional Artist exhibs
Activities: Classes for adults & children; dramatic progs; teacher resources; concerts; gallery talks; tours; competitions; sales shop sells original art, jewelry, crafts

OMAHA

M **ARTISTS' COOPERATIVE GALLERY,** 405 S 11th St, Omaha, NE 68102-2805. Tel 402-342-9617; Internet Home Page Address: www.artistsco-opgallery.com; *Pres* Robert Dewaele; *VPres* Peter Wrobewski; *Bd Dir* Pam King; *Asst Secy* Dyane Adams; *Bd Secy* Nicki Byram Luth; *Bd Mem* Marcia Jeff-Bouska
Open Tues - Thurs 11 AM - 5 PM, Fri & Sat 11 AM - 10 PM, Sun Noon - 6 PM; No admis fee; Estab 1975 to be gathering place for those interested in visual art; to display quality local, contemporary art; to offer progs, panels & discussions on related issues to the pub; Gallery contains 4000 sq ft consisting of large open area with 1 small, self-contained gallery; Average Annual Attendance: 30,000; Mem: 35; dues $400 yearly; monthly meetings, work at gallery
Income: $30,000
Special Subjects: Painting-American
Exhibitions: Each month a different show features 2 - 4 mems of the gallery with a major show. Dec features an all-mem show; exchange exhibits & special exhibits are featured by arrangement
Activities: Metro area senior high art exhibits; lect open to pub, 2 vis lectrs per yr; concerts; gallery talks; tours; originate traveling exhibs to other cooperative galleries

M **BEMIS CENTER FOR CONTEMPORARY ARTS,** 724 S 12th St, Omaha, NE 68102-3202. Tel 402-341-7130; Fax 402-341-9791; Elec Mail info@bemiscenter.org; Internet Home Page Address: www.bemiscenter.org; *Exec Dir & Chief Cur* Mark Masuoka; *Media Dir* Andrew Hershey; *Residency Program Mgr* Heather Johnson; *Cur* Hesse McGraw; *Community Arts Prog Mgr* Holly McAdams; *Technical Svcs Mgr* Matt Lowe
Open Tues - Sat 11 AM - 5 PM; No admis fee; Estab 1981; Maintains reference library, 3 galleries & 8 live/work studios; Average Annual Attendance: 20,000; Mem: Dues student $20, individual $35, dual $65, family $100, donor 250, patron $500, contributor $1,000, benefactor $2,500+
Library Holdings: Auction Catalogs; Book Volumes; DVDs; Exhibition Catalogs; Periodical Subscriptions; Video Tapes
Special Subjects: Decorative Arts, Photography, Sculpture, Ceramics
Collections: Aesthetics; Art History; Film; Bemis Collection
Publications: Monthly e-news
Activities: Lect open to pub, 25-30 vis lectrs per yr; concerts; gallery talks; tours; awards; educ progs; schols offered; individual paintings & original objects of art lent to museums & galleries; sales shop sells original art, books, & prints

M **CREIGHTON UNIVERSITY,** Lied Art Gallery, 2500 California Plaza, Omaha, NE 68178-0303. Tel 402-280-2261; Fax 402-280-2320; Elec Mail liedartgallery@creighton.edu; Internet Home Page Address: www.creighton.edu/liedgallery; *Chmn Fine & Performing Arts Dept* Dr Fred Hanna; *Gallery Dir* Dr Erin Walcek Averett
Open daily 1- 4 PM; No admis fee; Mus estab 1973; Gallery handles 5-8 exhibitions per acad yr; space provided for student thesis exhibits; 149 running ft; Average Annual Attendance: 2,000
Income: $8,000 (financed by school's gen funding)

Special Subjects: Drawings, Graphics, Painting-American, Photography, Prints, Sculpture, Ceramics, Pottery
Collections: Ceramics; drawings; graphics; paintings; photography; pottery & sculpture; printmaking
Exhibitions: Senior Thesis Exhibits; Creighton University Faculty Exhibit
Activities: Lect open to pub, 1-5 vis lectrs per yr; gallery talks; book traveling exhibs

M **EL MUSEO LATINO,** 4701 S 25th St, Omaha, NE 68107-2728. Tel 402-731-1137; Fax 402-733-7012; Elec Mail mgarcia@elmuseolatino.org; Internet Home Page Address: elmuseolatino.org; *Exec Dir* Magdalena Garcia; *Pres* Jim Mammel; *VPres* Jeffrey Keating
Open Mon, Wed & Fri 10 AM - 5 PM, Tues & Thurs 1 - 5 PM, Sat 10 AM - 2 PM, cl New Year's Eve & Day, Independence Day, Thanksgiving, Christmas; Admis adults $5, college students $4, senior citizens & students K-12 $3.50, children under 5 & members free; Estab May 5, 1993; Average Annual Attendance: 50,000
Library Holdings: Book Volumes 500
Collections: Latin American art & history
Activities: Workshops for adults & children; docent prog; bilingual prog; lect; concerts; guided tours; gallery talks

M **HOT SHOPS ART CENTER,** 1301 Nichols St, Omaha, NE 68102-4212. Tel 402-342-6452; Elec Mail manager@hotshopsartcenter.com; Internet Home Page Address: www.hotshopsartcenter.com; *Contact* Tim Barry

M **JOSLYN ART MUSEUM,** 2200 Dodge St, Omaha, NE 68102-1292. Tel 402-342-3300; Fax 402-342-2376; Internet Home Page Address: www.joslyn.org; *Exec Dir & CEO* Jack F Becker; *Chief Cur* Toby Jurovics
Open Tues, Wed, Fri & Sat 10 AM - 4 PM, Thurs 10 AM - 8 PM, Sun noon - 4 PM; Admis adults $8, seniors & college students $6, youth 5-17 $5, free to all Sat 10 AM - Noon; Estab in 1931; Nebraska's largest general art mus. Emphasis on 19th-C European & American art; Average Annual Attendance: 150,000; Mem: 5,000+ mem households
Special Subjects: Decorative Arts, Architecture, Glass, Furniture, Textiles, Painting-French, Drawings, Graphics, Painting-American, Photography, Prints, Sculpture, Watercolors, American Indian Art, American Western Art, Bronzes, African Art, Pottery, Woodcuts, Etchings & Engravings, Landscapes, Painting-European, Portraits, Jade, Asian Art, Painting-British, Painting-Dutch, Historical Material, Ivory, Coins & Medals, Painting-Flemish, Renaissance Art, Medieval Art, Antiquities-Oriental, Painting-Spanish, Painting-Italian, Antiquities-Egyptian, Antiquities-Greek, Antiquities-Roman, Painting-Russian
Collections: 11,000+ works comprising ancient through modern art with emphasis on 18th & 19th c American & European art, incl Greek pottery, Renaissance & Baroque masterworks by Titian, El Greco, Veronese, Jacob Van Ruisdael & Claude Lorrain; portraits by James Peale, Mary Cassatt & Thomas Eakins; genre paintings by Severin Roesen, Eastman Johnson & William M Harnett; 20th c paintings by Grant Wood, Thomas Hart Benton, George Ault, Jackson Pollock, Kenneth Noland & Helen Frankenthaler; contemporary works by Robert Irwin, Donald Judd, George Segal & Martin Puryear; American West holdings by Alfred Jacob Miller & 400 watercolors & drawings by Swiss artist Karl Bodmer; paintings of Plains chiefs by Charles Bird King & Henry Inman
Publications: Members calendar, bimonthly; exhib catalogs; art books
Activities: Classes for adults & children; docent training; special events; reading & art progs; lects open to pub; lects for mems only; 15-20 vis lectrs per yr; concerts; gallery talks; tours; awards fully-accredited by American Assoc of Mus; teacher resource prog serves State of Nebraska & Southwest Iowa; remote classroom to serve worldwide; lend original objects of art to other major mus; 8-10 book travel exhibs per yr; travel exhibs to mus worldwide; mus shop sells books, original art, reproductions & prints

M **OMAHA CHILDREN'S MUSEUM,** (Omaha Children's Museum, Inc) 500 S 20th St, Omaha, NE 68102-2505. Tel 402-342-6164; Fax 402-342-6165; Internet Home Page Address: www.ocm.org; *Exec Dir* Lindy Hoyer; *Mgr* Gayla Houck; *Chief Mus Officer* Jeff Barnhart
Open Tues - Sat 10 AM - 5 PM, Sun 1 - 5 PM, Thurs open until 8PM, cl Mon; Admis adults & children $9, seniors $8, mem & children under 2 free; Purpose, to engage the imagination & create excitement about learning; Average Annual Attendance: 253,000; Mem: 2500 families; dues $45
Income: Financed by mem, admis, grants, donations from individuals, foundations & corporations
Exhibitions: Hands-on exhibits which promote learning in the arts, science & humanities; traveling exhibits; workshops by local professional educators & artists
Publications: Bimonthly calendar; mus newsletter, quarterly
Activities: Classes for children; summer camp; exten dept serves local metro area; book traveling exhibs 2-3 per yr; mus shop sells books, educational games & toys

M **UNIVERSITY OF NEBRASKA AT OMAHA,** UNO Art Gallery, 6001 Dodge St, Dept Art & Art History, WFA Rm 129 Omaha, NE 68182-0012. Tel 402-554-2796; Fax 402-554-3435; Elec Mail unoartgallery@unomaha.edu; Internet Home Page Address: www.unoartgallery.org; *Coordr* Denise Brady
Open Mon - Thurs 10 AM - 3 PM by appointment (call ahead); No admis fee; Estab 1967 to heighten cultural & aesthetic awareness in the metropolitan & midlands area; 2 galleries - 1500 sq ft & 675 sq ft hexagon; Average Annual Attendance 5000
Income: Financed by state appropriation
Special Subjects: Prints
Collections: University Visiting Printmaker's Coll
Exhibitions: Six exhibs during academic yr, including student, faculty & regional/national contemporary artists; see website
Activities: Lect open to pub, 4 vis lectrs per yr; gallery talks; tours; competitions; schols

SCOTTSBLUFF

M **WEST NEBRASKA ART CENTER,** Gallery, 106 E 18th St, Scottsbluff, NE 69361-2423. Tel 308-632-2226

SEWARD

M **CONCORDIA UNIVERSITY,** (Concordia College) Marxhausen Art Gallery, 800 N Columbia Ave, Seward, NE 68434-1500. Tel 402-643-3651, Ext 7435; Internet Home Page Address: www.cune.edu/finearts/art; *Dir* James Bockelman
Open Mon - Fri 11 AM - 4 PM, Sat & Sun 1 PM - 4 PM; No admis fee; Estab 1959 to provide the col & community with a wide variety of original art; both monthly exhibs & permanent coll serve primarily an educational need; spacious gallery has additional showcases
Income: Financed by col funds
Special Subjects: Prints, Ceramics
Collections: Ceramics; Contemporary Original Prints
Exhibitions: One & two artists exhibs; shows drawn from Permanent Coll & Annual Student Exhibs; The Art of Cartoons; Animal Show; The Computer & its Influence on Art & Design; Part II; Rotating exhibits
Activities: Gallery talks; original objects of art lent; lending coll of framed reproductions, original prints & paintings; book traveling exhibs, 6 per yr

WAYNE

M **WAYNE STATE COLLEGE,** Nordstrand Visual Arts Gallery, Peterson Fine Arts Bldg, Room 203, Anderson Dr, Wayne State Campus Wayne, NE 68787; 1111 Main St, Art Dept Wayne, NE 68787-1172. Tel 402-375-7000; Fax 402-375-7204; *Chmn Art* Prof Pearl Hansen; *Prof* Marlene Mueller; *Prof* Wayne Anderson
Open Mon - Fri 8AM-4PM; No admis fee; Estab Jan 1977 to provide art students with a space to display work; to enhance student's educ by viewing incoming regional professional work; to enrich cultural atmosphere of col & community; Small gallery, carpeted floors & walls, ceiling spotlights on tracts; Average Annual Attendance: 800
Income: Financed by city & state appropriation, as well as Wayne State Foundation
Library Holdings: Audio Tapes; Book Volumes; Slides
Special Subjects: Prints
Collections: Wayne State Foundation Print Collection
Activities: Lects open to pub, 1-2 vis lectrs per yr; competitions; tours

NEVADA

ELKO

M **NORTHEASTERN NEVADA MUSEUM,** (Northeastern Nevada Historical Society Museum) 1515 Idaho St, Elko, NV 89801-4021. Tel 775-738-3418; Fax 775-778-9318; Elec Mail info@museumelko.org; Internet Home Page Address: www.museumelko.org; *Dir* Claudia Wines; *Archivist* Toni Mendive; *Archives Asst* Nancy Clausen; *Registrar* Stephanie Youngquist; *Exhibs Coordr* Tracy Beatty
Open Tues-Sat 9AM-5PM, Sun 1 - 5PM; Admis adults $5, seniors 65 and over $3, students $3, children 3-12 $1, children under 3 free; Estab 1968; gen mus concentrating on Northeastern Nevada; also area cultural center; Gallery is 4000 sq ft, 12 exhibits per yr local, state, regional & national artists; Average Annual Attendance: 20,000; Mem: 1300; dues $25 - $1000; ann meeting date varies
Income: Financed by grants, contributions, dues, sales shop & memorials
Special Subjects: American Western Art, Photography, Painting-American, Watercolors, Historical Material
Collections: History; Pre-History; Natural History; Art; Wildlife Exhibit
Exhibitions: Ann statewide touring photography exhibs; sound slide show - Nevada subjects; Will James art & books (permanent); Ansel Adams photos (permanent)
Publications: Historical, quarterly; Northeastern Nevada Historical Society Quarterly
Activities: Classes for adults & children; lect open to pub; concerts; gallery talks; tours; exten dept serving Nevada; lending coll of 5,000 photographs; 1,700 books & 12 cassettes; mus shop sales books, magazines, reproductions, prints & local craft items

ELY

M **NEVADA NORTHERN RAILWAY MUSEUM,** 1100 Ave A, Ely, NV 89301; PO Box 150040, Easy Ely, NV 89315-0040. Tel 775-289-2085, 866-407-8326; Fax 775-289-6284; Elec Mail info@nnry.com; Internet Home Page Address: www.nevadnorthernrailway.net; *CEO & Exec Dir* Mark S Bassett; *Finance Dir* Maggie O'Brien; *Mus Shop Mgr* Sharon Tilley; *Cur* Joan Bassett
Open daily June - Aug 8 AM - 6:30 PM, Sept - May 8 AM - 5 PM, cl Tues; cl Thanksgiving, Christmas Eve & Day, New Year's Eve & Day; Admis adults $4, children 4-12 $2; Estab 1985; site of the orig railroad serving the mining district; consists of a rail yard with 48 structures, 3 steam locomotives, 13 diesel locomotives & many other rail cars; Average Annual Attendance: 10,000 - 49,999 by estimate; Mem: 2,300; dues Leader $10,000, Benefactor $5,000, Supporter $2,500, Friend $1,000, Sustaining $250, Centennial $100, Family $50, Active $30
Special Subjects: Historical Material, Period Rooms, Restorations
Collections: Railroad equipment; buildings & artifacts related to NV Northern Railroad; mining rail equipment from the White Pine County mines
Publications: Ghost Tracks; quarterly newsletter
Activities: Railroad Camp; Memorial Day Members weekend; Polar Express; docent prog; formal educ for adults; guided tours; temp exhibs; mus related items for sale

LAS VEGAS

M BELLAGIO RESORT & CASINO, Bellagio Gallery of Fine Art, 3600 Las Vegas Blvd S, Las Vegas, NV 89109-4339. Tel 702-693-7871; Tel 877-957-9777; Fax 702-693-7872; Elec Mail fineartgallery@bellagioresort.com; Internet Home Page Address: www.bellagio.com/bgfa
Open Sun - Thurs 10 AM - 6 PM, Fri & Sat 10 AM - 7 PM; Admis adults $16, NV residents, seniors 65 and over $13, students, teachers & military $11; children under 12 free; estab 1998; temporary exhib space; Mem: Dues student, teacher & senior $30, individual $50, dual $75, family $100, modern council individual $250, MC Dual $400
Special Subjects: Photography, Sculpture
Activities: Intern prog; school group tours; school & lib outreach; book traveling exhibs, 2 per yr; mus shop sells books, exhib merchandise (postcards, magnets etc)

M CENTAUR ART GALLERIES, 3200 S Las Vegas Blvd Ste 1040, Fashion Show Mall Las Vegas, NV 89109-1234. Tel 702-737-1234
Open Mon-Sat 10AM-9PM, Sun 11AM-7PM; No admis fee
Collections: works of art from the 16th century to modern times; paintings; sculptures

M LAS VEGAS ART MUSEUM, 3065 S Jones Blvd Ste 100, Las Vegas, NV 89146-6780. Tel 702-360-8000; Fax 702-360-8080; Elec Mail info@lasvegasartmuseum.com; Internet Home Page Address: www.lasvegasartmuseum.org; *Dir* Libby Lumpkin, Ph.D; *Exec Asst to Dir* Alex Codlin; *Dir Develop* Stephanie Salamah; *Educ Programs Dir* Ellen Alvord; *Registrar* Melissa de Bie
Open Tues - Sat 10 AM - 5 PM, Sun 1 - 5 PM; Admis adults $6, seniors $5, children & students $3, children under 12 & mems free; Estab 1950 to bring national & international art to the community of Las Vegas; to offer artists a place to show, work & study; to offer good educ in fine arts to adults & children of the community; Three galleries that change bimonthly; Average Annual Attendance: 30,000; Mem: 3,000; dues family $50, individual $40, student & srs $25
Income: $600,000 (financed by mem, admis fees, donations & grants)
Collections: Contemporary artists
Exhibitions: Local & international exhibits; Art History Revisited; Dale Chihuly: The Stroemple Foundation
Publications: The Art Beat Newsletter, monthly; Monthly bulletin
Activities: Sculpture classes for adults; mus sponsors outreach prog for school; docent training; competitions; mus shop

M LAS VEGAS NATURAL HISTORY MUSEUM, 900 Las Vegas Blvd N, Las Vegas, NV 89101-1112. Tel 702-384-3466; Fax 702-384-5343; Elec Mail dunis@lvnhm.org; Internet Home Page Address: www.lvnhm.org; *Exec Dir* Marilyn Gillepsie; *Office Mgr* Linda Beirdneau; *Mktg Coordr* Jennifer Fox
Open daily 9 AM - 4 PM; Admis adults $8, seniors $7, children $4, children under 2 & mems free; Estab 1989; Gallery has a classroom & a children's hands-on room; Average Annual Attendance: 60,000; Mem: 930, dues $35
Income: $400,000 (financed by mem & admis)
Purchases: $25,000 (Exhibit in Dinosaur Room)
Special Subjects: African Art
Collections: Art (prints), fossils, live animals, mounted animals, teaching coll; Murals of Wildlife & Habitats; Wildlife Art
Publications: Newsletter, quarterly
Activities: Classes for adults & children; docent training; lect open to pub; book traveling exhibs annually; sales shop sells books & educ toys

L LAS VEGAS-CLARK COUNTY LIBRARY DISTRICT, 1401 E Flamingo Rd, Las Vegas, NV 89119-5256. Tel 702-734-7323; Fax 702-732-7271; Internet Home Page Address: www.lvccld.org; *Dir* Daniel Walters; *Asst Dir* Gene Nelson; *Exten Svcs* Ann Langevin; *Branch Adminr* Beryl Andrus; *Branch Adminr* Sally Feldman; *Branch Adminr* Jane Lorance; *Bus Serv* Irene Voit; *Library Develop* Stan Colton; *District Gallery Dir* Denise Shapiro
Open Mon - Thurs 9 AM - 9 PM, Fri-Sun 10AM-6PM; No admis fee; Estab 1965 to provide information in all its varieties of form to people of all ages; nine branch libraries, including three art galleries; Circ 1,770,951; Galleries provide regularly rotating art exhibs of regional & national repute as well as ten solo shows per yr, & a regional mixed media competition every spring
Income: $5,500,000 (financed by state & county appropriation)
Purchases: $700,000
Library Holdings: Audio Tapes; Cassettes; Clipping Files; Fiche; Filmstrips; Framed Reproductions; Motion Pictures; Original Art Works; Pamphlets; Periodical Subscriptions 586; Photographs; Prints; Records; Reels; Reproductions; Sculpture
Collections: Model ship collection; Nevada materials
Exhibitions: Art-a-Fair; Nevada Watercolor Society; All Aboard: Railroads, Memorabilia; Neon: Smithsonian Exhibition; Expressions in Fiber; Graham & Breedlove; Sand & Water; Dottie Burton; Woodworks: Christian Brisepierre & Jack Daseler; KNPR Craftworks; It's a Small, Small World: Dollhouses, Kimberly House
Publications: Exhib brochures, monthly; library prog, bimonthly
Activities: Lect open to pub; concerts; tours; competitions with awards; exten dept & regional servs dept serving the area; individual paintings & original objects of art lent; book traveling exhibs; originate traveling exhibs; used book store sells books, magazines, original art & handcrafts
M Flamingo Gallery, 833 Las Vegas Blvd North, Las Vegas, NV 89101. Tel 702-733-7810; Fax 702-732-7271; Internet Home Page Address: www.lvccld.org; *District Gallery Mgr* Denise Shapiro
Open Mon - Thurs 9 AM - 9 PM, Fri - Sat 9 AM - 5 PM, Sun 1 - 5 PM; No admis fee; Estab 1970; Gallery is located in Clark County Library, main gallery has 80 running ft of exhibit space, upstairs gallery is used for photographic displays; Average Annual Attendance: 36,000 - 40,000; Mem: 500; dues $15, ann meeting in summer
Income: Financed by tax support, federal & state grants

Exhibitions: Art-A-Fair (judged and juried); Spirit Impressions; The Potter & the Weaver; Nevada Watercolor Society Annual exhibit
Publications: Bimonthly library calendar of events
Activities: Classes for adults & children; dramatic progs; string quartet; feature films; lect open to pub, 10 vis lectrs per yr; concerts; Art-A-Fair competition; monetary awards

M UNIVERSITY OF NEVADA, LAS VEGAS, Donna Beam Fine Art Gallery, 4505 Maryland Pky, Las Vegas, NV 89154-5002. Tel 702-895-3893; Fax 702-895-3751; Elec Mail jerry.schefcik@unlv.edu; Internet Home Page Address: donnabeamgallery.unlv.edu; *Dir* Jerry Schefcik
Open Mon - Fri 9 AM - 5 PM, Sat noon - 5 PM, cl Sun & holidays; No admis fee; Estab 1962 to exhibit contemporary art; Gallery measures 1400 sq ft, 175 linear ft with track lighting; Average Annual Attendance: 10,000
Income: Financed by mem & appropriation
Special Subjects: Painting-American, Photography, Prints
Collections: General coll of about 300 objects of all media. Works are from the United States & the 2nd half of the 20th century; Dorothy & Herbert Vogel Collection: Fifty Works for Fifty States, Nevada
Activities: Classes for adults & children; docent training; lect open to pub, 3 vis lectrs per yr; gallery talks; juried competitions with cash awards; individual painting & original objects of art lent; lending coll includes 150 original art works; book traveling exhibs 1 per yr; originate traveling exhibs to other universities & galleries

M THE WALKER AFRICAN AMERICAN MUSEUM & RESEARCH CENTER, 705 W Van Buren Ave, Las Vegas, NV 89106; 2105 Travis St, North Las Vegas, NV 89030-4051. Tel 702-752-6043 (call for appt); Tel 702-752-6043 (call for appt); Elec Mail walkeraamuseum1@yahoo.com; Internet Home Page Address: www.walkerafricanamericanmuseum.com; *Founder & Cur* Gwendolyn Walker; *Develop Mem* Belinda Strong; *Educ* Margaret Crawford; *Pub Rels* Lillian McMorris; *Treas* Juanita Walker; *Mus Shop Mgr* Nika Sewell; *Financial Secy* Shalonda Jones
Open by appointment; Admis adults $2, children $1 under 12 yrs; Estab 1993; Mus is designed to promote & preserve the history of people of African descent (locally, nat & internat) with a concentration on the history of Black & African Americans in Nevada; Mem: Dues Supporting $100; Mem $25
Income: Financed by mem dues & donations
Library Holdings: Book Volumes 600; Memorabilia; Original Documents; Other Holdings; Pamphlets; Photographs; Prints; Records; Reproductions; Video Tapes
Special Subjects: Decorative Arts, Drawings, Historical Material, Ceramics, Collages, Photography, Portraits, Pottery, Pre-Columbian Art, Prints, Graphics, Photography, African Art, Costumes, Crafts, Folk Art, Afro-American Art, Manuscripts, Collages, Posters, Dolls, Jewelry, Porcelain, Ivory, Maps, Juvenile Art, Coins & Medals, Miniatures, Dioramas, Reproductions
Collections: Books, documents, artifacts, news articles, photographs, dolls, stamps & ann publs of local & state history; Interchangeable, Moulin Rouge, Dr M L King, Pres Barack Obama, local political
Publications: Black Pioneers of Nevada, ann booklet; From the Kitchen to the Boardroom: Nevada's Black Women, book; Courage, Strength & Faith: Nevada's Black Men, booklet publishes every other yr
Activities: Classes for adults & children; African-American Cultural Arts Festival; films; research in early bus owned by African-Americans in NV; tours; sponsoring of competitions; mus shop sells books, magazines, reproductions, prints, stamps, Kwanzaa supplies, dolls, figurines & related items

MESQUITE

M MESQUITE FINE ARTS CENTER & GALLERY, 15 W Mesquite Blvd, Mesquite, NV 89027-4754. Tel 702-346-1338; Fax 702-346-1339; Elec Mail warts@gmail.com; Internet Home Page Address: www.mesquitefineartscenter.com; *Pres* Barbara Withelder; *VPres* Gayle Pfeiffer
Open Mon - Sat 10 AM - 4 PM, cl holidays; Estab 2003; Fine art by local artists; Mem: 180; dues $35 yr; 3rd Mon of every month
Income: Dues, sale commission, donation, grants, city of Mesquite NV art council
Purchases: Gallery operation & improvement for bldg & landscaping
Exhibitions: Lucky 13, Nov - Dec
Publications: Mem application brochure
Activities: Educ progs; classes for adults & children; brown bag lects (1st Tues each month); monthly art reception; docent training; ann student art exhib; lects open to pub; gallery talks; schols; awards, Outside Venue-display art at local bus; mus shop sells books, original art, reproductions

NORTH LAS VEGAS

M LEFT OF CENTER ART GALLERY & STUDIO, 2207 W Gowan, North Las Vegas, NV 89032-7961. Tel 702-647-7378; Fax 702-647-7340; *Dir* Vicki Richardson
Call for hours
Collections: works by national and local artists

RENO

M NEVADA MUSEUM OF ART, 160 W Liberty St, Reno, NV 89501-1916. Tel 775-329-3333; Fax 775-329-1541; Elec Mail art@nevadaart.org; Internet Home Page Address: www.nevadaart.org; *Exec Dir & CEO* David B Walker; *Dir Communs* Rachel Milon; *Cur & Deputy Dir* Ann M Wolfe; *Pres* Nancy Fennell; *Cur of Educ* Colin Robertson; *Dir Center for Art & Environ* William L Fox; *Cur Asst* Pamela Paterson; *Deputy Dir & COO* Amy Oppio; *Managing Dir Mus Advancement* Heidi Loeb
Open Wed - Sun 10 AM - 5 PM, Thurs 10 AM - 8 PM; Admis adults $10, students & seniors $8, children 6 - 12 $1, under 5 & members free; Estab 1931 to collect, conserve & exhibit 19th & 20th century American art with an emphasis on artwork which articulates our interaction with the land & environment. The colls

are divided into 5 focus areas including The Altered Landscape Coll; The facility is a 60,000 sq ft state of the art building built in 2003 which holds 12 exhibs simultaneously; Average Annual Attendance: 80,000; Mem: 6,700; dues corporation $1,000, family $50; ann meeting in June; AAM mem req; Scholarships
Income: Financed by endowment, mem, federal & pvt foundation grants, individual grants & earned income
Library Holdings: Auction Catalogs; Audio Tapes; Book Volumes; CD-ROMs; Cassettes; Compact Disks; DVDs; Exhibition Catalogs; Maps; Memorabilia; Original Art Works; Pamphlets; Periodical Subscriptions; Photographs; Prints; Video Tapes
Special Subjects: Decorative Arts, Landscape Architecture, Art Education, Art History, Architecture, Drawings, Painting-American, Photography, Prints, Sculpture, Watercolors, American Indian Art, American Western Art, Bronzes, Textiles, Ceramics, Woodcarvings, Woodcuts, Etchings & Engravings, Landscapes, Manuscripts, Painting-European, Portraits, Glass, Marine Painting, Leather
Collections: E L Wiegand Art Collection (emphasis on the American work ethic); Altered Landscape Collection (photography); Contemporary Collection; Historical Collection; Sierra Nevada Great Basin Collection; CA&E Archive Collection
Exhibitions: Rotating exhibs every 3 wks; Edward Burtynsky; Picasso; Titian; Leo Villareal; Ansel Adams; Touloose Lautrec; Richard Misrach
Publications: Annual Report; brochures; calendar; event calendar; newsletter, bimonthly; postcards for events
Activities: Educ programs; classes for adults & children; hands-on exhibs; docent training; lects open to pub; 3-5 vis lectrs per yr; gallery talks; tours; concerts; competitions; schols offered; outreach services to schools, sr citizens & other community groups in Greater Reno-Carson-Tahoe area; exchange prog with other mus; originate traveling exhibs; mus shop sells books, original art, prints, stationery, jewelry & other items

L **Art Library,** 160 W Liberty St, Donald W. Reynolds Center for the Visual Arts, E.L. Wiegand Gallery Reno, NV 89501-1916. Tel 775-329-3333; Fax 775-329-1541; Elec Mail art@nevadaart.org; Internet Home Page Address: www.nevadaart.org; *Exec Dir & CEO* David B Walker; *Deputy Dir* Amy Oppio; *Cur Exhibs & Coll* Ann M Wolfe; *Dir Operations* Russell Simonov
Open Tues - Sun 10 AM - 5 PM, Thurs 10 AM - 8 PM, cl Mon; Admis adults $10, $8 students & seniors, $1 children 6-12, children five and under free; Estab 1931; New 55,000 sq ft facility designed by Will Bruder opened in 2003
Library Holdings: Book Volumes 1400; Clipping Files; Exhibition Catalogs; Manuscripts; Memorabilia; Pamphlets; Periodical Subscriptions 6; Photographs; Reproductions
Special Subjects: Archaeology, American Western Art, Advertising Design, Art Education, American Indian Art, Anthropology, Aesthetics, Afro-American Art, Antiquities-Oriental, Antiquities-Byzantine, Antiquities-Egyptian, Antiquities-Etruscan, Antiquities-Greek, Antiquities-Roman, Architecture
Collections: Focus on art and environment; Altered landscape photography; Sierra Nevada/Great Basin; Contemporary; Historical
Activities: Classes for adults & children; docent training; mus school on site; lects open to pub; concerts; gallery talks, tours; mus shop

A **SIERRA ARTS FOUNDATION,** Sierra Arts Gallery, 17 S Virginia St, Ste 120, Reno, NV 89501. Tel 775-329-2787; Fax 775-329-1328; Elec Mail jill@sierra-arts.org; Internet Home Page Address: www.sierra-arts.org; *Exec Dir* Jill Berryman; *Opers Mgr* Allison Sertic; *Prog Mgr* Stacey Spain; *Creative Resources Dir* Nicole Martin; *Communs Dir* Andy Guzman
Open Mon - Fri 8:30 AM - 5 PM; No admis fee; Estab 1971 as a nonprofit, pvt community arts agency, advocates for & supports the arts; Contemporary works by emerging artists; Average Annual Attendance: 5,000; Mem: 500; dues $35 - $10,000 & up; ann meeting in June; Fellowships
Income: Financed by endowment, corporate & individual mem, grants & fundraising activities
Exhibitions: 6-wk exhibs of contemporary artworks throughout the yr
Publications: Art Resource Guide; Artist Registry, current list of culture organizations, facilities list & media list; Encore, monthly community arts magazine; Master Calendar; Services Booklet
Activities: Classes for children in elementary school; classes for at-risk youths in local detention facility shelter for runaway kids & alternative high school; dramatic prog; lects open to pub; concerts; gallery talks; tours; sponsoring of competitions; grants offered; fels & schols available; exten dept; Endowment Income Grants Program for local individual artists; sales shop sells original art on consignment

M **STREMMEL GALLERY,** 1400 S Virginia St, Reno, NV 89502-2806. Tel 775-786-0558; Fax 775-786-0311; Elec Mail info@stremmelgallery.com; *Mgr* Sara Gray
Open Mon-Fri 9AM-5:30PM, Sat 10AM-3PM; cl holidays
Collections: works by contemporary artists

M **UNIVERSITY OF NEVADA, RENO,** (University of Nevada) Sheppard Contemporary & University Galleries, Church Fine Arts Complex, Art Dept, Mail Stop 224 Reno, NV 89557. Tel 775-784-6658; Fax 775-784-6655; Elec Mail bakerprindle@unr.edu; Internet Home Page Address: www.unr.edu/art; *Art Dept Chmn* Peter Goin; *Dir, Cur* Paul Baker Prindle; *Dept Secy* Wendy Ricco; *Preparator* Richard Jackson
Open Tues & Wed 11 AM - 5 PM, Thurs 11 AM - 8 PM, Fri & Sat 10 AM - 8 PM, Sun noon - 3 PM, cl Mon; No admis fee; Estab 1960; Sheppard Contemporary has 1800 sq ft finished exhib space & additional galleries including student exhib spaces; Average Annual Attendance: 15,000 - 24,000; Scholarships
Income: $20,000
Special Subjects: Etchings & Engravings, Folk Art, Illustration, Landscapes, Ceramics, Photography, Pottery, Painting-American, Prints, Sculpture, Drawings, Latin American Art, Watercolors, Southwestern Art, Textiles, Costumes, Woodcarvings, Woodcuts, Portraits, Furniture, Glass, Asian Art, Baroque Art
Collections: Local & regional Nevada artists, works on paper from16th century; Valentine's Day Benefit
Exhibitions: Annual Student Exhibition
Publications: Exhibit catalogs
Activities: Lect open to pub, 6-10 vis lectrs per yr; gallery talks; tours; competitions with awards; poetry readings; curators conversations; studio arts; Sheppard Contemporary on the road studio visits across Nevada

SEARCHLIGHT

M **SEARCHLIGHT HISTORIC MUSEUM & MINING PARK,** 300 Michael Wendell Way, Searchlight, NV 89046; PO Box 36, Searchlight Museum Guild Searchlight, NV 89046-0036. Tel 702-297-1642; *Founder* Jane Bunker Overy; *Pres* Joyce Nowlin; *VPres* Jon Palmer; *Secy* Pat Hattersley; *Treas* Lori McCoy
Open Mon - Fri 9 AM - 5 PM, Sat 9 AM - 1 PM, cl Sun & Holidays; available upon notice for pvt tour groups; No admis charge, donations accepted; Estab 1989; Through the use of photos & exhibs, the Searchlight Historic Mus tells the story of early mining days of Searchlight & it's former residents. Names include Clara Bow, Rex Bell, Edith Head, Louis Meyer, John MacReady, Lt William Nellis & U S Senator Harry Reid; Average Annual Attendance: 1000 - 9999; Mem: Dues Lifetime Accessor $5000 & up; Lifetime Recorder $1000 - $4999; Grubstaker $100; Miner $75; Surveyor $50; Prospector $25; Promoter $15; Founder $5
Collections: Gold Mining memorabilia; historic photos & maps; early mining town piano; Clara Bow's clothing trunk & several of her hats as well as some of Rex Bell's clothing, both available on a rotating basis
Activities: Searchlight town founding celebration held on even-numbered yrs during the 1st Sat of Oct

NEW HAMPSHIRE

CENTER SANDWICH

M **SANDWICH HISTORICAL SOCIETY,** 4 Maple St, Center Sandwich, NH 03227; PO Box 244, Center Sandwich, NH 03227-0244. Tel 603-284-6269; Fax 603-284-6269; Elec Mail sandwichhistory@gmail.com; Internet Home Page Address: sandwichhistorical.org; *Pres* Geoff Burrows; *CEO* Craig Evans; *Mus Shop Mgr* Sue Bowden; *Admin Asst & Shop Mgr* Jenny Vierus
Open late June - late Sept Wed - Sat 10 AM - 4 PM, otherwise by appointment only; Admis donations accepted; Estab 1917; Four bldgs, including period house & school house, transportation mus & mus of home occup & trade equipment; Average Annual Attendance: 1,500; Mem: 400
Income: Mems, donations & grants
Library Holdings: Audio Tapes; Book Volumes; CD-ROMs; Fiche; Filmstrips; Manuscripts; Maps; Memorabilia; Original Documents; Other Holdings Sandwich NH History & Family Genealogies; Pamphlets; Periodical Subscriptions; Photographs; Prints; Slides; Video Tapes
Collections: Paintings by Albert Gallatin Hoit (oil & water); Paintings by E Wood Perry (oil); Furniture; Horse-drawn vehicles; Yearly seasonal featured exhibits
Publications: Annual Excursion Bulletin; newsletter, 3 per yr
Activities: Excursions, tours; school outreach; jr historian progs; lects open to pub; 1-3 vis lectrs per yr; gallery talks; mus shop sells books, reproductions, prints & postcards

CONCORD

M **KIMBALL JENKINS ESTATE,** 266 N Main St, Concord, NH 03301-5053. Tel 603-225-3932; Internet Home Page Address: www.kimballjenkins.com
Open Mon-Thurs 10AM-4PM, other times by appointment
Collections: paintings; sculpture; photographs

M **LEAGUE OF NEW HAMPSHIRE CRAFTSMEN,** Grodin Permanent Collection Museum, 49 S Main St (Suite 100), Concord, NH 03301-5080. Tel 603-224-3375; Fax 603-225-8452; Elec Mail nhleague@nhcrafts.org; Internet Home Page Address: www.nhcrafts.org; *Dir* Susie Lowe-Stockwell; *Finance Dir* Prudence Gagne; *Opers Mgr* Terri Wiltse
Open Mon - Fri 8:30 AM - 4:30 PM, Sat 10 AM - 4 PM during exhibs; Admis free; Estab 1932 to encourage the economic development & educ of the crafts; gallery displaying exhibits of mems' works; Over 1500 volumes on a variety of fine craft technique & history; Average Annual Attendance: 5,000; Mem: 800 juried mems; must be res of New Hampshire or within 10 miles of Ntl border& make work by hand; Scholarships
Income: Financed by grants, memberships, fundraising
Special Subjects: Decorative Arts, Etchings & Engravings, Folk Art, Historical Material, Ceramics, Collages, Glass, Metalwork, Furniture, Gold, Bronzes, Crafts, Dolls, Jewelry, Carpets & Rugs, Calligraphy, Miniatures, Embroidery, Mosaics, Leather, Enamels
Collections: Permanent coll museum over 300 lots fine craft 1930-present
Exhibitions: Annual Craftsmen's Fair; Living with Crafts; Annual Juried Exhibit
Publications: Newsletter, quarterly
Activities: Classes for adults; exhibs; competitions with awards; lending collection of books; traveling exhibs & various exhibs throughout the yr

L **Kira Fournier Resource Library Center,** 49 S Main St (Suite 100), Concord, NH 03301. Tel 603-224-3375; Fax 603-225-8452; Internet Home Page Address: www.nhcrafts.org; *Dir* Susie Lowe-Stockwell
Open to members
Income: Financed by league operating funds
Library Holdings: Book Volumes 1100; Cassettes; Periodical Subscriptions 30
Special Subjects: Art History, Folk Art, Mixed Media, Calligraphy, Ceramics, Crafts, Bronzes, Art Education, Furniture, Glass, Mosaics, Metalwork, Carpets & Rugs, Dolls, Embroidery, Enamels, Goldsmithing, Handicrafts, Jewelry, Leather

L **Library of History & Genealogy,** 30 Park St, Concord, NH 03301-6384. Tel 603-228-6688, 856-0641; Fax 603-224-0463; Elec Mail shays@nhhistory.org; Internet Home Page Address: www.nhhistory.org; *Library Dir* Sarah Hays
Open Tues - Fri 9:30 AM - 5 PM; Research fee for non-members, $7 per day; Estab 1823; Reference library only; Average Annual Attendance: 2,000; Mem: 4,500; dues $40
Library Holdings: Auction Catalogs; Audio Tapes; Book Volumes 50,000; Cassettes; Exhibition Catalogs; Manuscripts; Maps; Memorabilia; Motion Pictures;

Original Documents; Other Holdings Newspapers; Pamphlets; Periodical Subscriptions 100; Photographs; Records; Reels; Slides; Video Tapes
Special Subjects: Art History, Decorative Arts, Illustration, Photography, Manuscripts, Maps, Painting-American, Prints, Sculpture, Ceramics, Crafts, Porcelain, Furniture, Glass, Bookplates & Bindings, Handicrafts, Pottery, Silver, Textiles, Pewter, Architecture, Portraits
Collections: History & genealogy of New Hampshire & New England; American art
Activities: Classes for adults & children; docent training; lects open to pub; 4 vis lectrs per yr; concerts; tours; book traveling exhibs; originates traveling exhibs; mus shop sells books, reproductions & New Hampshire products, gift items, music CDs

M **SAINT PAUL'S SCHOOL,** Art Center in Hargate, 325 Pleasant St, Concord, NH 03301-2591. Tel 603-229-4643; Fax 603-229-5696; Elec Mail ccallahan@sps.edu; Internet Home Page Address: www.sps.edu; *Gallery Asst* Mary Gaudette; *Dir Art Center* Colin J Callahan
Open Tues - Sat 9 AM - 4 PM, during school yr; No admis fee; Estab 1967 to house the Art Dept of St Paul's School, to provide a cultural center for the school community as well as central New Hampshire; Secure gallery, 50 X 40 ft; Average Annual Attendance: 5,000
Income: Financed by endowment
Collections: Collection represents varied periods & nationalities, chiefly gifts to the school, drawings, graphics, painting & sculpture
Activities: Lect & classes for students & school community only; gallery receptions & lects open to pub; tours; original objects of art lent to qualifying institutions
L **Ohrstrom Library,** 325 Pleasant St, Concord, NH 03301-2591. Tel 603-229-4862; Fax 603-229-4888; Elec Mail brettew@sps.edu; Internet Home Page Address: www.sps.edu/library; *Librn* Robert H Rettew
Open Mon - Fri 7:30 AM - 10 PM, Sat 8 AM - 10 PM, Sun 10 AM - 10 PM; Estab 1967 for art reference only; Circ 600
Income: $1000 (financed by endowment)
Purchases: Approx $1000
Library Holdings: Book Volumes 50,000; Exhibition Catalogs; Periodical Subscriptions 150; Reproductions; Slides

CORNISH

M **SAINT-GAUDENS NATIONAL HISTORIC SITE,** 139 Saint-Gauden Rd, Cornish, NH 03745-4232. Tel 603-675-2175; Fax 603-675-2701; Elec Mail saga@valley.net; Internet Home Page Address: www.sgnhs.org; *Supt & Cur* John H Dryfhout; *Cur* Henry Duffy; *Chief Ranger* Gregory Schwarz
Open May 22- Oct 31 daily 9 AM - 4:30 PM; Admis ages 17+ $6; Estab 1926, transferred to Federal Government (National Park Service) in 1965 to commemorate the home, studios & works of Augustus Saint-Gaudens (1848-1907), one of America's foremost sculptors. The site has historically (1907) furnished rooms, studios & gardens displaying approx half of the work of Augustus Saint-Gaudens; Average Annual Attendance: 40,000; Mem: Friends of Saint-Gaudens Memorial
Income: Financed by federal appropriation (National Park Service)
Purchases: Works by Augustus Saint Gaudens; original furnishings of the Cornish Property
Library Holdings: Auction Catalogs; Book Volumes; CD-ROMs; Cassettes; Clipping Files
Special Subjects: Furniture, Sculpture, Period Rooms
Collections: Historic furnishings & sculpture; plaster, bronze & marble works by Augustus Saint-Gaudens
Publications: Catalogs & books, exhib checklists, postcards, pamphlets, handbooks
Activities: Gallery talks; tours; original objects of art lent to museums; book traveling exhibs; originate traveling exhibs; mus shop sells books & slides
L **Library,** 139 Saint-Gaudens Rd, Cornish, NH 03745-4232. Tel 603-675-2175; Fax 603-675-2701; Internet Home Page Address: www.sgnhs.org; *Supt* B J Dunn; *Supv Interpretation* Gregory C Schwarz; *Cur & Div Chief* Henry J Duffy; *Mus Spec* Martha Knapp
Library open by appointment only; Museum open Memorial Day weekend - Oct 31 9:00 AM - 4:30 PM; Admis ages 16+ $5; Circ Non-circulating; Sculpture by Augustus Saint-Gaudens
Income: Financed by federal appropriations
Library Holdings: Audio Tapes; Book Volumes 1400; Clipping Files; Exhibition Catalogs; Manuscripts; Memorabilia; Pamphlets; Photographs; Slides; Video Tapes
Special Subjects: Art History, Landscape Architecture, Decorative Arts, Painting-American, Historical Material, History of Art & Archaeology, Ceramics, American Western Art, Bronzes, Art Education, Period Rooms, Jewelry, Landscapes, Coins & Medals, Architecture
Collections: Sculpture; Antique furnishings relating to Augustus Saint-Gaudens
Activities: Classes for adults & children; lects open to pub; concerts; gallery talks; tours; lend original objects of art to other mus; mus shop sells books

DURHAM

M **UNIVERSITY OF NEW HAMPSHIRE,** Museum of Art, 30 Academic Way, Paul Creative Arts Ctr Durham, NH 03824-2617. Tel 603-862-3712, 3713 (outreach); Fax 603-862-2191; Elec Mail museum.of.art@unh.edu; Internet Home Page Address: www.unh.edu/moa; *Dir* Kristina Durocher; *Educ & Publicity Coordr* Catherine Mazur; *Admin Asst* Cynthia Farrell; *Exhibs & Colls Mgr* Jacqueline Finnegan
Open Mon - Wed 10 AM - 4 PM, Thurs 10 AM - 8 PM, Sat & Sun 1 - 5 PM, Sept-May only; No admis fee; Estab 1960 renovated 1973, teaching coll for univ faculty & students outreach & pub service functions for the non-univ community; Circ 40,000 students per yr; Upper mezzanine & lower level galleries with a total of 3800 ft of exhib space; 900 ft storage room to house permanent coll & temporary loans; additional storage & office space; Average Annual Attendance: 8,500; Mem: 243

Income: $220,000 (financed by state, mem, sales, interest & private support)
Special Subjects: Drawings, Painting-American, Photography, Prints, Etchings & Engravings, Landscapes
Collections: 19th century American landscapes, 19th century Japanese prints & 20th century works on paper
Exhibitions: Temporary exhibs; The Museum of Art features exhibs ranging from historical to contemporary from Sept through May each yr
Publications: Exhib catalogs
Activities: Educ prog for area schools; workshops; docent training; children's art camp; lect open to pub, 6-8 vis lectrs per yr; concerts; gallery talks; tours; fellowships; lending of original objects of art to other museums; book traveling exhibs 1-3 per yr; originate traveling exhibs; mus shop sells books, posters, notecards & postcards
L **Dept of the Arts Slide Library,** 30 Academic Way, Paul Creative Arts Ctr Durham, NH 03824-2617. Tel 603-862-1366; Fax 603-862-2191; Internet Home Page Address: www.unh.edu; *Slide Librn* Barbara Steinberg
Open daily 8 AM - 4:30 PM; Estab as a teaching coll for the univ; Slides do not circulate off-campus
Library Holdings: Slides 132,000

EXETER

M **PHILLIPS EXETER ACADEMY, FREDERICK R. MAYER ART CENTER,** Lamont Gallery, 11 Tan Lane, Exeter, NH 03833; 20 Main St, Exeter, NH 03833-2460. Tel 603-777-3461; Fax 603-777-4371; Elec Mail gallery@exeter.edu; Internet Home Page Address: www.exeter.edu/arts/9140.aspx; *Prin* Thomas E Hassan; *Interim Dir* Sara B Zela
Open Mon 1 - 5 PM, Tues - Sat 9 AM - 5 PM; No admis fee; Estab 1953 to provide an Art Center & studios for art instruction dedicated to the memory of Thomas William Lamont II, lost in action in 1945. The Lamont gallery forms an exhib & teaching space which through exhibs & progs seek to create an appreciation to the visual arts & to integrate the arts into the curriculum of Phillips Exeter Academy.; Four bays with moveable walls to alter number & size of bays, sky lit with sol-r-veil screen; Average Annual Attendance: 3500
Exhibitions: Exhibits change every 4-6 weeks
Activities: Classes for Academy students; dramatic progs; lects open to pub, 5 vis lectrs per yr; gallery talks; one book traveling exhibs per yr

HANOVER

M **DARTMOUTH COLLEGE,** Hood Museum of Art, Hineman Box 6034, Hanover, NH 03755-4008. Tel 603-646-2808, 2900; Fax 603-646-1400; Elec Mail hood.museum@dartmouth.edu; Internet Home Page Address: www.hoodmuseum.dartmouth.edu; *Assoc Dir & Cur Acad Programming & Registrar & Colls Mgr* Katherine Hart; *Asst Dir* Juliette Bianco; *Security & Bldg Mgr* Gary Alafat; *Cur European Art* T Barton Thurber; *Asst Dir & Cur Educ* Lesley Wellman; *Cur American Art* Barbara J MacAdam; *Assoc Registrar* Kathleen O'Malley; *Asst Registrar* Cynthia Gilliland; *Adjunct Cur Costumes* Margaret E Spicer; *Lead Preparator* John Reynolds; *Bus Mgr* Nancy A McLain; *Gift Shop Mgr* Mary Ellen Rigby; *Bus Asst* Christine Macdonald; *Exec Asst* Roberta Shin; *Data Mgr* Deborah Haynes; *Coordr Pub Rels* Alison Sharp; *Publications & Web Mgr* Nils Nadeau; *Exhibitions Designer* Patrick Dunfey; *School & Family Programs Coordr* Neely McNulty; *Preparator* Matthew Zayatz; *Exhibitions & Events Coordr* Karen Miller; *Asst Cur Educ* Amy Driscoll; *Tour Coordr* Adrienne Kermond
Open Tues - Sat 10 AM - 5 PM, Wed 10 AM - 9 PM, Sun Noon - 5 PM, cl Mon; No admis fee; Estab 1772 to serve the Dartmouth community & Upper Valley region; New building, designed by Charles Moore & Chad Floyd of Centerbrook, completed in 1985, houses ten galleries; Average Annual Attendance: 40,000; Mem: 2100; dues $45 - $1000; ann meeting in July
Income: Financed through Dartmouth College, endowment income, contributions & grants
Special Subjects: Afro-American Art, Decorative Arts, Glass, American Western Art, Pre-Columbian Art, Painting-French, Drawings, Latin American Art, Mexican Art, Painting-American, Photography, Prints, Sculpture, Watercolors, American Indian Art, Bronzes, African Art, Anthropology, Costumes, Religious Art, Ceramics, Woodcuts, Etchings & Engravings, Landscapes, Painting-European, Portraits, Posters, Eskimo Art, Furniture, Asian Art, Silver, Painting-British, Painting-Dutch, Coins & Medals, Tapestries, Baroque Art, Painting-Flemish, Renaissance Art, Painting-Italian, Antiquities-Egyptian, Antiquities-Greek, Mosaics, Painting-Australian, Pewter, Antiquities-Etruscan, Antiquities-Assyrian
Collections: 65,000 fine art objects; Native American, African, Asian & Pre-Columbian art; Oceanic Collection
Exhibitions: Approx fifteen temporary exhibs per yr on a wide range of subjects. Exhibs include those organized by the mus, traveling exhibs & exhibs drawn from permanent colls
Publications: Hood Quarterly; exhib catalogues; ann gen brochure; gallery brochures; ann report; school programs brochure; teacher manuals; family guide brochures, A Space for Dialogue
Activities: Classes for adults & children; family days; art discovery bags; docent training; teacher training; teacher workshops; Dartmouth student workshops & panels; classes for Dartmouth students & for medical students; lects open to pub, 24 vis lectrs per yr (mix of vis & faculty); symposia; films; concerts; gallery talks; tours; awards: Volunteer of the Yr (Natl arts/humanities month), Friendship Fund Award (teacher who demonstrated exemplary use of visual arts in curriculum); individual paintings & original objects of art lent to other museums & campus depts; book traveling exhibs 1-2 per yr; originate traveling exhibs for mus in US & Internationally; mus shop sells books, cards, posters, original art, reproductions & jewelry
L **Sherman Art Library,** Hinman Box 6025, Carpenter Hall Hanover, NH 03755-4008. Tel 603-646-2305; Fax 603-646-1218; Elec Mail sherman.library.reference@dartmouth.edu; Internet Home Page Address: www.dartmouth.edu/~library/sherman; *Librn* Barbara E Reed
Open Mon - Thurs 8 AM - midnight, Fri 8 AM - 6 PM, Sat 9 AM - 6 PM, Sun 1 PM - midnight, during school terms (reduced hours in summer & during intersessions); Estab 1928

Library Holdings: Book Volumes 110,000; CD-ROMs; Exhibition Catalogs; Fiche 100,000; Other Holdings Videodiscs; Pamphlets; Periodical Subscriptions 530; Reels 111
Special Subjects: Photography, Architecture
M **Hopkins Center for the Arts,** 2 E Wheelock St, Hanover, NH 03755. Tel 603-646-2422

HOOKSETT

M **SOUTHERN NEW HAMPSHIRE UNIVERSITY,** McIninch Art Gallery, 2500 N River Rd, Robert Frost Hall Hooksett, NH 03106. Tel 800-668-1249

HOPKINTON

M **NEW HAMPSHIRE ANTIQUARIAN SOCIETY,** Hopkinton Historical Society, 300 Main St, Long Memorial Bldg Hopkinton, NH 03229-2627. Tel 603-746-3825; Elec Mail nhas@tds.net; Internet Home Page Address: www.hopkintonhistory.org; *Exec Dir* Heather Mitchell
Open Thurs & Fri 9AM - 4PM, Sat 9AM-1PM; No admis fee; Estab 1859 to preserve local & state historical genealogical records & colls & to provide the community with cultural & historical progs of local significance; Gallery houses artifacts pertaining to local history; maintains a reference library; Average Annual Attendance: 2,000; Mem: 425; dues $25 - $500; ann meeting in Jan
Library Holdings: Audio Tapes; CD-ROMs; Cassettes; Clipping Files; Compact Disks; Lantern Slides; Manuscripts; Maps; Memorabilia; Original Art Works; Original Documents; Other Holdings; Pamphlets; Photographs; Prints; Records
Special Subjects: Archaeology, Decorative Arts, Drawings, Etchings & Engravings, Folk Art, Landscapes, Ceramics, Glass, Painting-American, Silver, Textiles, Manuscripts, Maps, Architecture, Photography, Watercolors, Costumes, Crafts, Pottery, Portraits, Posters, Dolls, Furniture, Historical Material, Coins & Medals, Restorations, Embroidery, Military Art
Collections: Early American furniture, clothing, china, portraits; local historical material
Exhibitions: Annual history exhibit; annual art show featuring works of regional artists; rotate 2 per yr
Activities: Educ prog; classes for adults & children; pub progs; lect open to pub, 6 vis lectrs per yr; concerts; gallery talks; tours; competitions; individual paintings & original objects of art lent; mus shop sells books, artisan wares, gifts, cards, magnets & T-shirts

KEENE

M **HISTORICAL SOCIETY OF CHESHIRE COUNTY,** 246 Main St, Keene, NH 03431-4143; PO Box 803, Keene, NH 03431-0803. Tel 603-352-1895; Fax 603-352-9226; Elec Mail hscc@hscocnh.org; Internet Home Page Address: www.hsccnh.org; *Exec Dir* Alan Rumrill, MLS; *Educ Dir* Thomas Haynes; *Admin Asst* Katharine Schillemat; *Develop Coordr* Gail Currier; *Develop Dir* Richard Swanson
Open Tues, Thurs - Fri 9 AM - 4 PM, Wed 9 AM - 9 PM, Sat 9 AM - Noon (1st & 3rd Sat only); No admis fee; Estab 1927 to collect, preserve & share history of southwest New Hampshire; Average Annual Attendance: 12,000; Mem: 900; dues $25- $200; ann meeting fourth Mon in Apr
Income: $295,000 (dues, donations, grants, fees for programs)
Purchases: $1,000
Library Holdings: Book Volumes; CD-ROMs; Compact Disks; DVDs; Manuscripts; Maps; Memorabilia; Original Documents; Periodical Subscriptions; Photographs; Slides; Video Tapes
Special Subjects: Landscapes, Flasks & Bottles, Photography, Sculpture, Architecture, Painting-American, Watercolors, Textiles, Ceramics, Pottery, Manuscripts, Portraits, Furniture, Glass, Silver, Historical Material, Maps, Coins & Medals, Period Rooms, Pewter
Collections: Archival colls, books, furniture, glass, maps, photos, pottery, silver, toys; paintings
Publications: Newsletter, 5 times annually
Activities: Classes for adults & children; lects open to pub, 6 vis lectrs per yr; gallery talks; tours; book traveling exhibs 1-2 per yr; mus shop sells books, reproductions, original art, colonial toys & DVDs

M **KEENE STATE COLLEGE,** Thorne-Sagendorph Art Gallery, Wyman Way, Keene, NH 03435-3501; 229 Main St, Keene, NH 03435. Tel 603-358-2720; Fax 603-358-2238; Elec Mail thorne@keene.edu; Internet Home Page Address: www.keene.edu/tsag; *Dir* Maureen Ahearn; *Admin Asst* Colleen Johnson; *Tech* Paul Knowlton
Open Sept - May Sun - Wed Noon - 5 PM, Thurs - Sat Noon - 8 PM, June - July Wed, Thurs, Sat, Sun Noon - 5 PM, Fri 3 PM - 8 PM; No admis fee; Estab 1965 to provide a year-round calendar of continuing exhibs; to sponsor related progs of artistic & educ interest & to maintain small permanent coll displayed on campus; Two adjacent galleries occupy space in new facility opened in 1993 on campus; Average Annual Attendance: 9,000; Mem: 575; dues $20, students & sr $15
Income: Financed by endowment, state appropriation & college budget
Special Subjects: Painting-American, Prints, African Art
Collections: Paintings & Prints of Historical Interest included: Pierre Alechinsky; Milton Avery; Chuck Close; Robert Mapplethorpe; Paul Pollero; Gregorio Prestopino; George Rickey; Sidney Twardowicz; Artists of National Prominence including Jules Olitski; Paintings by Dublin Art Colony Artists; Dublin Art Colony
Publications: Small catalogs or brochures to accompany exhibits
Activities: Classes for children; docent training; lects open to pub, 1-2 vis lectrs per yr; gallery talks; competitions & awards; originates book traveling exhibs; originates traveling exhibs regionally

MANCHESTER

M **THE CURRIER MUSEUM OF ART,** 150 Ash St, Manchester, NH 03104-4380. Tel 603-669-6144; Fax 603-669-7194; Elec Mail visitor@currier.org; Internet Home Page Address: www.currier.org; *Pres* David Jensen; *Mktg & Pub Rels* Vicky Jaffe; *Librn* Meghan Petersen; *Cur P* Andrew Spahr; *Asst Cur* Nina Bozicnik; *Dir* Susan Strickler; *Dir Finance* Sherry Collins; *Registrar* Karen Papineau; *Shop Mgr* Heidi Norton; *Preparator* Jeff Allen; *Cur Dr* K Sundstrom; *Dir Art Center* Bruce McColl; *Asst Registrar* Cindy Mackey
Open Sun, Mon, Wed, Thurs & Fri 11 AM - 5 PM, 1st Thurs of each month 11 AM - 8 PM, Sat 10 AM - 5 PM, cl Tues; Admis adults $10, students 18 & older $8, seniors $9, under 18 free; Estab & incorporated 1915 by will of Mrs Hannah M & Governor Moody Currier, which included endowment, building opened in 1929; Circ Non-circulating; Building contains nine galleries, library & auditorium, two pavilions. Currier Art Center offers after-school & Sat classes for adults & children; Average Annual Attendance: 60,000; Mem: 3800; dues $30 & up
Income: Financed by endowment
Library Holdings: Auction Catalogs; Book Volumes 15,000; CD-ROMs; Clipping Files; Exhibition Catalogs; Lantern Slides; Manuscripts; Pamphlets; Periodical Subscriptions; Photographs; Records; Slides; Video Tapes
Special Subjects: Historical Material, Landscapes, Ceramics, Glass, American Western Art, Prints, Painting-French, Sculpture, Architecture, Drawings, Painting-American, Photography, Watercolors, American Indian Art, African Art, Textiles, Folk Art, Woodcarvings, Etchings & Engravings, Manuscripts, Portraits, Porcelain, Oriental Art, Asian Art, Silver, Painting-British, Painting-Dutch, Tapestries, Baroque Art, Painting-Flemish, Renaissance Art, Embroidery, Medieval Art, Painting-Spanish, Painting-Italian, Painting-German, Pewter, Painting-Russian, Enamels, Bookplates & Bindings
Collections: American Furniture, glass & textiles 18th - 20th century; American Paintings & Sculpture 18th century to present; European Paintings, prints & sculpture, 13th - 20th century; European Masters 13th - 20th century; Fine American Decorative Art 17th - 19th century including furniture, glass textiles & silver; Frank Lloyd Wright designed residence, Zimmerman House, opened seasonally for tours
Publications: Bulletin, semiannually; calendar, quarterly; exhib catalogs, occasionally; Ann Report
Activities: Classes for adults & children; docent training; lect open to pub, 10 vis lectrs per yr; concerts; gallery talks; tours; school progs & outreach presentations for 4th & 5th graders; individual paintings & original objects of art lent to art institutions worldwide; lending coll contains original art works, original prints, paintings, photographs & sculpture; book traveling exhibs 2 per yr; originate traveling exhibs to art museums; mus shop sells books, jewelry, prints & reproductions
L **Library,** 201 Myrtle Way, Manchester, NH 03104. Tel 603-669-6144 x 127; Internet Home Page Address: www.currier.org; *Librn* Michele Turner
Open Wed - Fri 1 - 4:30 PM
Library Holdings: Auction Catalogs; Book Volumes 15,000; Clipping Files; Exhibition Catalogs; Periodical Subscriptions 26
Special Subjects: Folk Art, Decorative Arts, Photography, Architecture
Collections: Frank Lloyd Wright, general photography coll

M **FRANCO-AMERICAN CENTRE,** 100 St Anselm Dr, Manchester, NH 03102-1308. Tel 603-669-4045; Fax 603-669-0644;
Open Mon-Fri 10AM-4PM
Income:
Collections: French heritage & culture; paintings; photographs; personal artifacts; period furnishings; sculpture

L **MANCHESTER CITY LIBRARY,** 405 Pine St, Manchester, NH 03104-6199. Tel 603-624-6550, ext 334; Fax 603-624-6559; Internet Home Page Address: www.manchester.lib.nh.us; *Lib Dir* Denise Van Zanten; *Branch Mgr* Sarah Basbas; *Head of Info Svcs* Lichen Rancourt; *Deputy Dir* Dee Santoso
Open Mon, Tues & Thurs 8:30 AM - 8:30 PM, Wed, Fri & Sat 8:30 AM - 5:30 PM
Income: Financed by city appropriations, endowment & fines
Purchases: $8,000
Library Holdings: Book Volumes 15,373; Cassettes; Compact Disks 3,197; Framed Reproductions 104; Records; Video Tapes
Exhibitions: Patron's art works, crafts, collectibles

A **MANCHESTER HISTORIC ASSOCIATION,** Millyard Museum, 255 Commercial St, Manchester, NH 03101; 129 Amherst St, Manchester, NH 03101-1809. Tel 603-622-7531; Elec Mail history@manchesterhistoric.org; Internet Home Page Address: www.manchesterhistoric.org; *Exec Dir* Aurore Eaton; *Mus Educator* Jennifer Yakunovich; *Asst Exec Dir* Jeffrey Barraclough
Open Tues - Sat 10 AM - 4 PM, cl national & state holidays; Admis adults $8, students & seniors $6, children $4, under 12 free; Estab 1896 to collect, preserve & make known Manchester's historical heritage; Permanent exhibit on Manchester history; 12,000 sq ft changing exhibit gallery; Average Annual Attendance: 10,000; Mem: 700; dues $30, individual & up
Library Holdings: Book Volumes; Clipping Files; Fiche; Manuscripts; Maps; Memorabilia; Micro Print; Original Documents; Periodical Subscriptions; Photographs; Video Tapes
Special Subjects: Historical Material
Collections: Amoskeag Manufacturing Company records; artifacts, books, documents, maps & photographs on Manchester History; paintings, sculpture, decorative arts relating to Manchester
Exhibitions: Permanent & changing exhibs reflecting all aspects of Manchester history; 2 -3 changing exhibits per yr
Publications: Annual report; newsletter, calendar of events, books, videos
Activities: Educ prog; classes for adults & children; walking tours; family progs; lects open to pub; concerts; gallery talks; tours; pub & school progs linked to permanent & changing exhibits; outreach progs, research library; ann Historic Preservation awards prog; mus shop sells books, original art, reproductions, gift items
L **Library,** 129 Amherst St, Manchester, NH 03101. Tel 603-622-7531; Elec Mail library@manchesterhistoric.org; Internet Home Page Address:

www.manchesterhistoric.org; *Exec Dir* Aurore Eaton; *Asst Exec Dir* Jeffrey Barraclough; *Mus Educator* Jennifer Yakunovich
Open Sat 10 AM - 4 PM & by appointment; Admis adults $8, students & seniors $6, 6 - 18 yrs $4; Estab as research library open to pub
Library Holdings: Book Volumes 5000; Cassettes; Clipping Files; Manuscripts; Memorabilia; Other Holdings Maps 500; Pamphlets; Periodical Subscriptions 14; Photographs 20,000; Prints; Reproductions
Collections: Amoskeag Manufacturing Company Archives; art; architecture; cloth samples; decorative arts; documents; early textile mill records; manuscripts; 19th century music; photos; publications of local history

M **NEW HAMPSHIRE INSTITUTE OF ART,** (Manchester Institute of Arts & Sciences Gallery) 148 Concord St, Manchester, NH 03104-4858. Tel 603-623-0313; Fax 603-641-1832; Internet Home Page Address: www.nhia.edu; *VPres Acad Affairs* Karen Burgess Smith; *Acad Affairs Asst* Christine Fales; *Dir Communs* Linda Seabury; *VPres Operations* Sandra Barry; *Interim Pres* Daniel Lyman; *VPres Finance* Erik Gross
Open Mon - Sat 9:30 AM - 5 PM; No admis fee; Estab 1898, as a pvt nonprofit educational institution in order to promote, encourage & stimulate educ in the arts & sciences; Gallery has limited space which is devoted to a variety of exhibs including historical as well as contemporary themes; Mem: 670; dues family $35, individual $25; ann meeting in June
Income: Financed by endowment, mem, tui & grants
Publications: Exhib catalogs; schedule of courses, exhibs & progs, 2 - 3 times per yr
Activities: Classes for adults & children; competitions with prizes; schols & fels offered; sales shop sells handcrafted items, books & art supplies

M **SAINT ANSELM COLLEGE,** Alva de Mars Megan Chapel Art Center, 100 Saint Anselm Dr #1718, Saint Anselm College Manchester, NH 03102-1308. Tel 603-641-7470; Fax 603-641-7116; Elec Mail chapelartcenter@anselm.edu; Internet Home Page Address: www.anselm.edu/chapelart; *Dir* Iain MacLellan, OSB; *Asst Cur* Julia Welch
Open Tues - Sat 10 AM - 4 PM, Thurs until 7 PM; No admis fee; Estab 1967; Large gallery, formerly college chapel with painted, barrel-vaulted ceiling, stained glass windows; Average Annual Attendance: 5,000
Income: Financed through col
Special Subjects: Drawings, Painting-American, Prints, Sculpture, Crafts, Decorative Arts
Collections: New Hampshire artists & craftsmen; Prints; Paintings; Sculpture
Publications: Exhib catalogues, occasional
Activities: Lect open to pub; 2-4 vis lectrs per yr; gallery talks; concerts; EW Poore Award, King Award & Premiere Award for student works; individual paintings lent to faculty & staff of Saint Anselm College; lending coll contains paintings; book traveling exhibs 1-2 per yr; originate traveling exhibs

M **SEE SCIENCE CENTER,** 200 Bedford St, Manchester, NH 03101-1132. Tel 603-669-0400; Fax 603-669-0400; Elec Mail info@see-sciencecenter.org; Internet Home Page Address: www.see-sciencecenter.org; *Dir* Douglas Heuser; *Educ & Mem* Rebecca Mayhew; *Opers & Design* Adele Maurier; *Develop Coord* Peter Gustafson
Open Mon-Fri 10AM-4PM, Sat & Sun 10AM-5PM; Admis $5, mems & children under 1 no admis fee; Estab 1986; A hands-on science ctr estab to promote the understanding & excitement of science for all ages. Pvt nonprofit org; FT paid 4, PT paid 6, PT vols 20; 1st congressional district; Average Annual Attendance: 50,000 - 99,999; Mem: dues Family $60
Publications: SEE News, quarterly newsletter
Activities: Guided tours; traveling exhibs

MERIDEN

M **AIDRON DUCKWORTH ART PRESERVATION TRUST,** Aidron Duckworth Art Museum, 21 Bean Rd, Meriden, NH 03770; PO Box 61, Meriden, NH 03770-0061. Tel 603-469-3444; Elec Mail info@aidronduckworthmuseum.org; Internet Home Page Address: www.aidronduckworthmuseum.org; *Trustee & Dir* Grace Harde; *Contact Registrar* Kathleen P O'Malley
Open Fri - Sun 10 AM - 5 PM; other times by appointment; No admis fee; donations accepted; Estab May 2002 to preserve & present works by the late Aidron Duckworth; Former school bldg; modern galleries built in 2002; Average Annual Attendance: 750
Income: Rental studio income & donations; grants
Library Holdings: Book Volumes
Special Subjects: Painting-American
Collections: Artwork by Aidron Duckworth
Exhibitions: Exhibs of works by regional artists in guest gallery & on grounds
Publications: Aidron Duckworth-Paintings & Drawings (2007)
Activities: Lects open to pub; gallery talks; tours

PETERBOROUGH

M **SHARON ARTS CENTER,** Sharon Arts Center Exhibition Gallery, 30 Grove St, Peterborough, NH 03458-1453. Tel 603-924-7676; Fax 603-924-6795; Elec Mail sharonarts@sharonarts.org; Internet Home Page Address: www.sharonarts.org; *School Dir* Deb DeCicco; *Exec Dir* Elizabeth Smith; *CEO, Pres* Beth Rank-Beauchamp; *Dir Communs* Lajla LeBlanc; *Asst Gallery Mgr* Laurie Rebac; *Admin Asst* Barbara Nay; *Asst Gallery Mgr* Susan Schaefer; *Financial Admin* Diane Hayden
Open Summer Mon-Thurs 10AM-6PM, Fri & Sat 10AM-8PM, Sun noon-5PM, Winter Mon-Thurs 11AM-6PM, Fri 11AM-7PM, Sat 10AM-6PM, Sun noon-5PM; No admis fee; Estab 1947 to promote the educ, sales & enjoyment of the arts; Center consists of three galleries, store & classroom facility; maintains lending library to mems only; Average Annual Attendance: 32,000; Mem: 1100; dues family $50, individual $35; ann meeting in Sept
Income: Financed by endowment, mem & state appropriation, tuition & sales
Library Holdings: Book Volumes; Exhibition Catalogs

Collections: Bird carvings of Virginia & Robert Warfield; Nora S Unwin Collection of Wood Engravings, Drawings, Watercolors
Exhibitions: Annual members exhib of paintings, drawings & sculpture; 16 exhibits per yr featuring fine artists & craftsmen throughout New England
Publications: Exhibit catalogs
Activities: Classes for adults & children; lect open to pub, 3 vis lectrs per yr; concerts; gallery talks; tours; schols offered; exten dept serves area elementary schools; individual paintings & original objects of art lent to area pvt schools, banks, Town Hall, resorts; lending coll contains 20 original prints, 50 paintings, & assorted crafts (weaving & pottery); originate traveling exhibs; sales shop sells original art, reproductions & fine crafts

PLYMOUTH

M **PLYMOUTH STATE UNIVERSITY,** Karl Drerup Art Gallery, Main St, Fl 1 Draper & Maynard Bldg MSC 21B Plymouth, NH 03264; 17 High St, D & M Bldg, MSC 21 B Plymouth, NH 03264-1595. Tel 603-535-2614; Fax 603-535-2938; Internet Home Page Address: www.plymouth.edu/gallery; *Dir* Catherine Amidon; *Asst* Greg Finley
Open Mon -Sat 10AM-4PM, Wed until 8PM; Estab 1871 to serve the acad and personal needs of the col's students & faculty; Maintains exhib space of 1960 sq ft; Average Annual Attendance: 6,000
Income: 40,000
Purchases: $250,000
Library Holdings: Pamphlets
Activities: Lect open to pub; library tours; bibliographic instruction; gallery talks

PORTSMOUTH

A **LA NAPOULE ART FOUNDATION,** Chateau de la Napoule, 799 South St, Portsmouth, NH 03801-5420. Tel 603-436-3040; Fax 603-430-0025; Elec Mail LNAF@clews.org; Internet Home Page Address: www.LNAF.org; *Pres* Christopher S Clews; *Exec Dir* Noele M Clews; *Chair Residency Comt* Natasha Gallaway; *Chair Pub Rels Comt* Christina Clews
Open Feb 7 - Nov 7 daily 10 AM - 6 PM, Nov 8 - Feb 10 Mo n - Fri 2 PM - 5 PM, Sat & Sun 10 AM - 5 PM; Admis $5; Estab 1950 as an American organization to build Franco-American relations through a wide range of educational & artistic programs; Foundation's programs & artists' residencies take place year-round at the architecturally significant Chateau de la Napoule, located West of Cannes on the shores of the Mediterranean. The Chateau houses the permanent collection of 20th century sculptor, Henry Clews & changing contemporary exhibitions fill the Strawbridge Gallery; Average Annual Attendance: 40,000
Income: Financed by private & pub funds, governmental agencies, private foundations & individuals
Library Holdings: Book Volumes; Clipping Files; Exhibition Catalogs; Framed Reproductions; Lantern Slides; Manuscripts; Maps; Memorabilia; Original Art Works; Original Documents; Other Holdings; Photographs; Prints; Reproductions; Sculpture; Slides
Special Subjects: Architecture, Drawings, Etchings & Engravings, Historical Material, Landscapes, Manuscripts, Porcelain, Posters, Sculpture, Watercolors, Painting-American, Pottery, Stained Glass, Antiquities-Oriental, Bronzes, Decorative Arts, Ceramics, Portraits, Furniture, Woodcarvings, Period Rooms, Maps, Painting-European, Painting-Italian
Collections: Henry Clews Collection: paintings and sculpture of the 20th-century artist; Staffordshire Pottery of James & Ralph Clews
Exhibitions: on-going exhibitions: architecture of the chateau, extensive gardens; 3 exhibits per year of contemporary art & sculpture; exhibits of resident artists; garden sculpture
Activities: Classes for children & adults; artist residencies in France, summer cultural events including concerts & opera; awards, tours & 3 vis lectrs per year; books, reproductions, prints & Chateau-related items

A **THE NATIONAL SOCIETY OF THE COLONIAL DAMES OF AMERICA IN THE STATE OF NEW HAMPSHIRE,** Moffatt-Ladd House & Garden, 154 Market St, Portsmouth, NH 03801-3730. Tel 603-436-8221, 430-7968; Fax 603-431-9063; Elec Mail moffatt-ladd@juno.com; Internet Home Page Address: www.moffattladd.org/; *Dir & Cur* Barbara McLean Ward, Ph.D.; *Asst to Dir* Brielly Allen; *Mus Properties Chmn* Cheryl E Cullimore; *Archivist Cur Asst & Event Coordr* Stephanie Rohwer
Open Mon - Sat 11 AM - 5PM, Sun 1 - 5 PM; Admis adults $6, children $2.50; Soc estab 1892, mus estab 1912; Moffatt-Ladd House was completed in 1763; Average Annual Attendance: 6,000; Mem: 140; annual meeting in June; NSCDA-NH mem based on lineage; Friends of Moffatt-Ladd House open to all
Income: $150,000 variable (financed by memberships, rents, donations, grants & investments)
Library Holdings: Manuscripts; Memorabilia; Original Art Works; Original Documents; Photographs; Prints; Slides; Video Tapes
Special Subjects: Architecture, Costumes, Embroidery, Historical Material, Manuscripts, Porcelain, Prints, Sculpture, Silver, Textiles, Painting-American, Pottery, Decorative Arts, Pewter, Ceramics, Portraits, Dolls, Furniture, Glass, Jewelry, Marine Painting, Leather, Period Rooms, Maps, Carpets & Rugs
Collections: Original china & porcelain, furniture, documents, letters & papers, portraits, wallpaper & documented wallpaper, prints, floor cloths (all documented to house), textiles, costumes
Publications: The Moffatt-Ladd House: From Mansion to Museum, The Garden Book of Alexander H Ladd
Activities: Educ progs; school tours; lects open to members only, 4 vis lectrs per year; guided tours open to the public; competitions with awards; concerts; gallery talks; tours; scholarships offered; individual paintings lent to Currier Gallery of Art; mus shop sells books, prints & historic related items

M **NEW HAMPSHIRE ART ASSOCIATION,** 136 State St, Portsmouth, NH 03801-3826. Tel 603-431-4230; Fax 603-431-4230; Elec Mail nhartassociation@comcast.net; Internet Home Page Address: nhartassociation.org; *Exec Dir* Billie Tooley
Open Wed-Sat 10AM-5PM, Sun noon-4PM; No admis fee; Estab 1940, statewide art assn; Mem: Mem: 425; dues $80; juried mem

Collections: paintings; photographs; sculpture; drawings; graphic arts
Exhibitions: Monthly exhibs with special exhibs; 3-4 juried (open) offsite around state exhibs per yr
Activities: Workshops, lect, demos open to pub; gallery talks

A **NEW HAMPSHIRE ART ASSOCIATION, INC,** 136 State St, Portsmouth, NH 03802. Tel 603-431-4230; Elec Mail nhartassociation@gmail.com; Internet Home Page Address: www.nhartassociation.org; *Admin* Angus Locke
Open Mon - Sat 10 AM - 5 PM, Sun noon-4PM; Estab 1940, incorporated 1962, as a nonprofit organization, to promote the public's understanding & appreciation of the arts; to provide artists with a forum for their work & ideas. Offers a year-round exhib & sales gallery at its headquarters in Boscawen & Portsmith; an Aug exhib at Sunapee State Park; Mem: 400; dues $60; ann meeting in June
Income: Financed by grants, dues, patrons, rental art & sales
Exhibitions: Annuals at Currier Gallery of Art; Summer Annual combined with New Hampshire League of Arts & Crafts at Mount Sunapee State Park; Summer Annual Juried Exhibition at Prescott Park; Year-Round exhibits at N E Center; Durham NH; various one-person & group shows
Activities: Educ prog for schools; patron prog; lect demonstrations by mem artists; awards; originate traveling exhibs

M **PORTSMOUTH ATHENAEUM,** Joseph Copley Research Library, Peter Randall Gallery, 9 Market Sq, Portsmouth, NH 03801. Tel 603-431-2538; Fax 603-431-7180; Elec Mail info@portsmouthathenaeum.org; Internet Home Page Address: www.portsmouthathenaeum.org; *Pres* Michael Chubrich; *Treas* Michael Kinslea; *Keeper* Tom Hardiman; *Cataloger* Robin Silva; *Librn* Lynn Aber; *Research Libr* Ursula Wright; *Archival Project* Susan S Kindstedt
Open Tues & Thurs 1-4PM, Sat 10AM-4PM and by special apt; No admis fee; Estab 1817 to house mus of historical objects of local, statewide & national interest & is listed on National Register of Historical Sites; Maintains local history research library; Average Annual Attendance: 8,500; Mem: 375; dues $175; annual meeting 2nd Wed in Jan
Income: Financed by endowment & mem
Special Subjects: Historical Material, Marine Painting, Architecture, Furniture, Manuscripts, Painting-American
Collections: American paintings; Colonial & later portraits; ship models & half-models; New England history; maritime history
Exhibitions: Rotating exhibits 3 - 4 times per year
Activities: Lect; gallery talks; concerts; tours

M **PORTSMOUTH HISTORICAL SOCIETY,** John Paul Jones House & Discover Portsmouth, 43 Middle & State St, Portsmouth, NH 03802-0728; PO Box 728, Portsmouth, NH 03801-0728. Tel 603-436-8433; Elec Mail info@portsmouthhistory.org; Internet Home Page Address: www.portsmouthhistory.org; *Pres* Richard Candee; *VPres* Martha Fuller Clark; *Secy* Karen Carpenter; *Treas* Fred Englebach; *Exec Dir* Maryellen Burke; *Prog Dir* Laura Calhoun; *Cur* Sandra Rux
Open year round 10 AM - 5 PM; Admis John Paul Jones House: adults $6, AAA & special discounts $5, Portsmouth residents $5, children 14 & under free; Discover Portsmouth: no charge; Estab 1920 to identify & retain local history. The House was built in 1758 by Gregory Purcell, a merchant sea-captain. Purchased & restored in 1920 by the Portsmouth Historical Society; Free changing exhibits; Average Annual Attendance: 15,000; Mem: 450; dues $15; ann meeting Apr
Income: Financed by mem, investment & admis fees
Special Subjects: Afro-American Art, Decorative Arts, Marine Painting, Painting-American, Costumes, Ceramics, Furniture, Glass, Historical Material, Maps, Period Rooms, Embroidery, Military Art
Collections: Guns, books, china, costumes, documents, furniture, glass, portraits and silver pertaining to the early history of Portsmouth
Activities: Lect, 3-4 vis lectrs per year; daily tours; original objects of art lent to other museums; lending coll contains looking glass & furniture; mus shop sells books, prints, slides, cards & jewelry

M **PORTSMOUTH MUSEUM OF FINE ART,** 909 Islington St, Portsmouth, NH 03801. Tel 603-436-0332
Open Mon - Fri 11 AM - 5 PM, Sat - Sun Noon - 6 PM, other times by appt
Collections: paintings; photographs; sculpture

M **THREE GRACES GALLERY,** 105 Market St, Portsmouth, NH 03801-3703. Tel 603-436-1988
Open Sun noon-5PM, Mon-Tues & Thurs-Sat 10AM-6PM, Wed by appt
Income:
Collections: paintings; sculpture; pottery; mixed-media

M **WARNER HOUSE ASSOCIATION,** MacPheadris-Warner House, 150 Daniel St, Portsmouth, NH 03801-3831; PO Box 895, Portsmouth, NH 03264-0895. Tel 603-436-5909; Elec Mail info@warnerhouse.org; Internet Home Page Address: www.warnerhouse.org; *Chmn* Philip Wright; *Cur* Carolyn Roy; *Cur* Louise Richardson
Open 2nd week in June - 2nd week in Oct Mon - Tues & Thurs - Sat 10 AM - 4 PM, Sun 1 - 4 PM; cl Wed; Admis adults $5, seniors $4, children 7-12 $2.50, children under 7 free; Estab 1931; Period rooms from 1717-1930; Average Annual Attendance: 1500; Mem: 200; dues $25 and up; annual meeting in Nov; Scholarships
Income: $50,000 (financed by endowment, mem, admis, grants & fundraising)
Special Subjects: Historical Material, Architecture, Portraits, Pottery, Painting-American, Period Rooms, Ceramics, Decorative Arts, Portraits, Furniture
Collections: Joseph Blackburn Collection: portraits; Portsmouth Furniture; Stair murals (1720); complete set of English Copperplate bed hangings made in America (1780-85); Family Memorabilia
Exhibitions: Joseph Blackburn: Portraits (1761); Archaeological Exhibits
Activities: Lect open to pub, 1-2 vis lectrs per yr; gallery talks; tours; original objects of art lent to museums & other historic houses; Mus shop sells books

WATERVILLE VALLEY

M **THE MARGARET & H A REY CENTER AND CURIOUS GEORGE COTTAGE,** 35 Village Rd (Bldg C), Waterville Valley, NH 03215; PO Box 286, Waterville Valley, NH 03215-0286. Tel 603-236-3308; Elec Mail info@thereycenter.org; Internet Home Page Address: www.thereycenter.org/welcome.html
Open July - Sept 5: Wed - Sat 10 AM - 5 PM, Sept 6 - June: Sat 10 AM - 5 PM; No admis fee, donations accepted
Activities: Educ progs

NEW JERSEY

ATLANTIC CITY

M **ATLANTIC CITY ART CENTER,** New Jersey Ave & Boardwalk, Atlantic City, NJ 08401. Tel 609-347-5837 & 5838; Fax 609-347-5844
Open summer: daily 9 AM - 4 PM; Fall: Tues - Sun 10 AM - 4 PM, cl national holidays; No admis fee
Activities: Educ progs

L **PRINCETON ANTIQUES BOOKSERVICE,** Art Marketing Reference Library, 2915-17 Atlantic Ave, Atlantic City, NJ 08401. Tel 609-344-1943; Fax 609-344-1944; Elec Mail princetn@earthlink.net; Internet Home Page Address: www.princetonantiques.com; *Pres* Robert E Ruffolo Jr
Open Mon-Fri 8:30AM-5PM, Sat 8AM-1PM; No admis fee; Estab 1974 for pricing documentation of books and antiques; Open by appointment only; maintains art gallery; Average Annual Attendance: 1,000
Library Holdings: Book Volumes 250,000; Framed Reproductions; Memorabilia; Other Holdings Exhibition catalogs; Original art works & prints; Periodical Subscriptions 20
Collections: 19th century art; Postcard Photo Library Information Bank, 1900 - 1950, consisting 12,500 postcards
Activities: Mus shop sells books, original art, reproductions, prints & Atlantic City photographs & memorabilia; Sales shop sells books & original art

BAYONNE

L **BAYONNE FREE PUBLIC LIBRARY,** Cultural Center, 697 Ave C, Bayonne, NJ 07002. Tel 201-858-6971; Fax 201-437-6928; Elec Mail library@bayonnelibrary.org; Internet Home Page Address: www.bayonnelibrary.org; *Library Dir* Sneh Bains
Open Mon & Thurs 9 AM - 9 PM, Fri - Sat 9 AM - 5PM; Estab 1894; Art Gallery has 194 running ft exhib space
Income: Financed by city appropriation & state aid
Library Holdings: Book Volumes 222,000; Clipping Files; Filmstrips; Periodical Subscriptions 517; Slides 736
Activities: Adult & children film progs weekly; concerts

BELMAR

M **OCEANSIDE GALLERY,** 1010 Main St, Belmar, NJ 07719-2726. Tel 732-280-2167; Fax 732-280-2167; Elec Mail gallery@oceansidegallery.com; Internet Home Page Address: www.oceansidegallery.com
Open Tues & Sat 10 AM - 5 PM, Wed 10 AM - 8:30 PM, Thurs 10 AM - 6 PM, Fri 10 AM - 8 PM

BERKELEY HEIGHTS

L **BERKELEY HEIGHTS FREE PUBLIC LIBRARY,** 290 Plainfield Ave, Berkeley Heights, NJ 07922-1494. Tel 908-464-9333; Fax 908-464-7098; Internet Home Page Address: library.bhpl.nj.org; *Dir* Stephanie Bakos; *Asst Dir* Laura Fuhro; *Reference Head* Anne deFurio
Open Mon - Thurs 9 AM - 9 PM, Fri & Sat 9 AM - 5 PM, Sun 2 - 5 PM, Summer Mon-Tues & Thurs 9AM-9PM, Wed & Fri 9AM-5PM, Sat 9AM-1PM; Estab 1953
Income: $570,000 (financed by city appropriation)
Library Holdings: Audio Tapes; Book Volumes 71,890; Cassettes; Clipping Files; Fiche; Pamphlets; Periodical Subscriptions 32; Reels; Video Tapes
Special Subjects: Art History, Folk Art, Landscape Architecture, Decorative Arts, Photography, Painting-American, Painting-British, Painting-Japanese, Painting-European, Crafts, Asian Art, American Indian Art, Glass, Afro-American Art, Architecture
Collections: Art & art history prints

BLOOMFIELD

M **HISTORICAL SOCIETY OF BLOOMFIELD,** 90 Broad St, Bloomfield, NJ 07003-2585. Tel 973-743-8844; Fax 201-429-0170; Elec Mail bloomhist@aol.com; Internet Home Page Address: www.firstbaptistbloomfield.org/hist-society.htm; *Pres* Ina Campbell; *2nd VPres* Alan Slaughter; *Treas* Dorothy Greenfield; *Cur* Lucy Sant Ambrogio
Open Wed 2 - 4PM, Sept-May Sat 10AM-12:30PM, also by appointment; No admis fee; Estab 1966 to collect, preserve & exhibit items which may help to establish or illustrate the history of the area; Mus located in the gallery of the Bloomfield Pub Library; Average Annual Attendance: 1,436; Mem: 115; dues, commercial organization $25, nonprofit organization $10, couple $10, individual $7, student under 18 $3; meeting Sept, Nov, May - 4th Mon of the month
Income: Financed by mem, Ways & Means Comt & bequests

Special Subjects: Costumes, Ceramics, Furniture, Glass, Dioramas
Collections: Miscellaneous items of books, clothing & accessories, deeds & other documents, dioramas, early maps & newspapers, furniture, household articles, letters, memorabilia, paintings, postcards, posters, tools, toys
Exhibitions: Revolving Charles Warren Eaton (items donated by people of Bloomfield and/or heirs)
Activities: Lect open to pub, 3 vis lectrs per yr; tours; sales shop sells books, prints, postcards, mugs, notepaper, medallions

BORDENTOWN CITY

M   **THE ARTFUL DEPOSIT, INC.,** The Artful Deposit Gallery, 201 Farnsworth Ave, Bordentown City, NJ 08505-1807. Tel 609-298-6970; Fax 609-609-298-6975; Elec Mail artfuldeposit@gmail.com; Elec Mail artfullivingwithcj@gmail.com; Internet Home Page Address: www.artfuldeposit.com; *Owner* C J Mugavero
Open Wed thru Sat 1PM-6PM, Fri1PM-8PM, Sun 1PM-5PM, Mon & Tues by appointment; No admis fee; Estab in 1986 for display & sale of original fine art; Representation in gallery stable for approx 20 artists with local, national & international acclaim. Primary location in Bordentown, NJ. Tel: 609-298-6970
Collections: Representative of original works by Thomas Kelly (Painter); Joseph Dawley (Impressionist); Hanneke de Neve (Expressionist); Ken McIndoe (Naturalist); Gennady Spirin (Illustrator); Michael Budden (pleinair and studio oil painter); Richard McKinley (Pastel Society of America); Eleinne Basa (plein air award winner); Sarah J. Webber (AZ & WY)
Exhibitions: Works by Patrick Antonelle, Joseph Dawley, Hanneke de Neve, Ken McIndoe, Gennady Spirin, Thomas Kelly, Michael Budden
Activities: Educ prog; artist run workshops; gallery talks; lect open to pub; sponsor competitions

BRANCHBURG

A   **PRINTMAKING COUNCIL OF NEW JERSEY,** 440 River Rd, Branchburg, NJ 08876-3565. Tel 908-725-2110; Fax 908-725-2484; Elec Mail director@printnj.org; Internet Home Page Address: www.printnj.org; *Dir* Elise Fuscarino
Open Tue - Fri 10 AM - 4 PM, Sat 1 - 4 PM, cl Sun; No admis fee; Estab 1973 to promote & educate the fine art of printmaking, photography & papermaking; Average Annual Attendance: 50,000; Mem: 450; dues $35 & up; ann meeting in June
Income: Financed by mem & individual, foundation & corporate gifts including NJ State Council on the Arts & Somerset County Parks Commission
Exhibitions: 4 exhibs per yr; national juried exhibits
Activities: Classes for adults & children; lect open to pub; competitions with awards; lending coll contains art objects, lent to corporate mems & libraries; Roving Press (traveling print mentoring prog for pub schools); book traveling exhibs 9 per yr; originate traveling exhibs 9 per yr; sales shop sells original art

BURLINGTON

A   **BURLINGTON COUNTY HISTORICAL SOCIETY,** 457 High St, Burlington, NJ 08016-4514. Tel 609-386-4773; Fax 609-386-4828; Elec Mail burlcohistsoc@verizon.net; Internet Home Page Address: www.burlingtoncountyhistoricalsociety.org; *VPres* Herman O Benninghoff; *CEO* Douglas E Winterick; *Pres* Louis A Colaguori; *Librn* Annie Brogan; *Exec Asst* Patricia Stip; *Exec Dir* Lisa Fox-Pfeiffer; *Educ Dir* Jeffrey Macechak
Open Tues-Sat 1PM-5PM; Admis $3 for library & mus gallery, $3 guided tour of 3 period houses, $5 combination; Estab 1915 to preserve & interpret Burlington County history; Average Annual Attendance: 5,000; Mem: 1,000; dues $15 & up; ann meeting fourth Thurs in May
Income: Financed by endowment & donations
Special Subjects: Decorative Arts
Collections: Clocks; Decorative Arts; Delaware River Decoys; Quilts; Samplers
Exhibitions: Ingenuity & Craftsmanship
Publications: Quarterly newsletter
Activities: Tours for children; docent training; lect open to pub, several vis lectrs per yr; tours; mus shop sells books, magazines & reproductions

CALDWELL

M   **CALDWELL COLLEGE,** The Visceglia Art Gallery, 120 Bloomfield Ave, Caldwell, NJ 07006-5310. Tel 973-618-3457; Internet Home Page Address: www.caldwell.edu; *Dir* Kendall Baker
Open Mon - Fri 9 AM - 5 PM, Sat & Sun 10 AM - 5 PM; No admis fee; Estab 1970 to provide students & area community with exposure to professional contemporary talent, to afford opportunities for qualified artists to have one-person shows; Scholarships
Income: Financed by col budget
Exhibitions: 3-4 exhibits per yr; Alumni Show
Activities: Educ dept in connection with the col art dept; lect open to pub, 3 vis lectrs per yr; lending coll contains 12,000 Kodachromes, motion pictures

CAMDEN

M   **RUTGERS UNIVERSITY,** Stedman Art Gallery, 326 Penn St, Camden, NJ 08102-1410. Tel 856-225-6245, 225-6350; Fax 609-225-6597; Elec Mail arts@camden.rutgers.edu; Internet Home Page Address: seca.camden.rutgers.edu; *Others* TTY 609-225-6648; *Dir & Cur* Virginia Oberlin Steel; *Cur Educ* Noreen Scott Garrity
Open Mon - Sat 10 AM - 4 PM, Thurs 10AM-8PM; No admis fee; Estab 1975 to serve educ needs of the campus & to serve community of southern New Jersey; Average Annual Attendance: 14,000
Income: Financed by endowment, state appropriation & gifts from pvt sources

Special Subjects: Painting-American, Photography, Prints, Sculpture, Watercolors, Etchings & Engravings
Collections: Modern & contemporary art; works on paper
Exhibitions: Changing exhibs of visual arts & interdisciplinary exhibs
Publications: Catalog for a major exhibition, yearly
Activities: Vis lectr; symposia; concerts & gallery talks open to pub

A   **WALT WHITMAN CULTURAL ARTS CENTER, INC,** 101 Cooper St, Camden, NJ 08102-1617. Tel 856-964-1534; Tel 609-757-7276 (alternate phone); *Prog Dir* Patrick Rinehart
Open Mon - Fri 10 AM - 4 PM; Estab 1975; Average Annual Attendance: 13,000; Mem: 100; dues $20
Activities: Classes for children; dramatic progs; lect open to pub, 6 vis lectrs per yr; concerts; gallery talks; tours

CLINTON

A   **HUNTERDON ART MUSEUM,** (Hunterdon Museum of Art) 7 Lower Center St, Clinton, NJ 08809-1303. Tel 908-735-8415; Fax 908-735-8416; Elec Mail info@hunterdonartmuseum.org; Internet Home Page Address: www.hunterdonartmuseum.org; *Bd Pres* Aram Papazian; *Dir Exhibitions* Kristin Accola; *Dir Educ* Betsy Zalaznick; *Exec Dir* Marjorie Frankel Nathanson; *Dir Develop* Brook Polley; *Financial Adminr* Linda Dunsuir; *Pres Bd Trustees* Hildreth York; *Dir Develop* Eleanor Porter Trubert; *Mus Shop Mgr* Nancy Friedman; *Dir Exhib* Donna Gustafson
Open Tues - Sun 11 AM - 5 PM; Admis by requested donation ; Estab 1952 as a nonprofit organization to provide arts enrichment through fine & performing arts; The first, second & third fls provide gallery space. The old stone mill has been remodeled retaining the original atmosphere with open broad wooden beams, white walls & plank flooring; Average Annual Attendance: 22,000; Mem: 600; dues patron $500, sponsor $250, contributor $100, family $50, individual $35, senior $25; ann meeting in Apr; Scholarships
Income: Financed by mem, city, state & county appropriations, donations, tuitions
Purchases: $100
Special Subjects: Prints
Collections: Print collection
Exhibitions: National Print Exhibition
Activities: Classes for adults & children; lect open to pub, 3 vis lectrs per yr; gallery talks; competitions with cash awards; ann juried mems show; works from print coll lent to nearby corporations; lending coll contains 200 original prints; originate traveling exhibs to Newark Museum and corp mem; sales shop sells books, original art, reproductions & crafts

M   **REDMILL MUSEUM VILLAGE,** (Hunterdon Historical Museum) 56 Main St, Clinton, NJ 08809-1328. Tel 908-735-4101; Fax 908-735-0914; Elec Mail hhmredmill@yahoo.com; Internet Home Page Address: www.theredmill.org; *Cur Educ* Elizabeth Cole; *Dir* Amy Hollander
Open 9:30AM-4PM, Sat 10AM-4PM, Sun noon-5PM; Admis adults $8, seniors $6, children 6-12 $5, pre-schoolers free; Estab 1960 for the preservation & display of artifacts from the 18th & 19th century for educational & cultural purposes; Four-floor grist mill, blacksmith shop, gen store, schoolhouse, log cabin, herb garden & quarry buildings; Average Annual Attendance: 26,000; Mem: 400; dues $25 - $2500; ann meeting in May
Income: $150,000 (financed by mem & donations)
Special Subjects: Historical Material
Collections: Artifacts pertaining to 18th, 19th & early 20th centuries
Exhibitions: Variety of special events
Activities: Classes for children; docent training; re-enactments; lect; concerts; tours; sales shop sells books & gift items

CLOSTER

M   **BELSKIE MUSEUM,** 280 High St, Closter, NJ 07624. Tel 201-768-0286; Fax 201-768-4220; Elec Mail belskiemuseum@hotmail.com; Internet Home Page Address: www.belskiemuseum.com; *Pres* Kurt Haiman; *VPres* Walter Hubbard; *VPres* John Murphy; *VPres Legal* Ed Rogan; *Treas* Donald M Farrell; *Secy* Anita Duquette
Open Sat & Sun 1 - 5 PM, special hours by appt; No admis fee, donations accepted; Founded 1993 by the Closter Lions Club; The goal of the mus is to preserve & display the work of Abram Belskie & to promote his reputation as a major sculpture, medallic artist & medical instructor of the 20th century; mus also displays works of other local & internat artists with new exhibits monthly. Nonprofit org; Average Annual Attendance: 3,000; Mem: 300; Mem Patron $100 (ann); Supporting $25 (ann)
Special Subjects: Art History, Metalwork, Photography, Pottery, Painting-American, Painting-European, Sculpture
Collections: Drawings, sculpture, medical models, medallic molds & completed medallic pieces created by Abram Belskie (1907-1988); Numerous donated original paintings
Exhibitions: Rotating exhibs of international artists & artists within the tri-state area in all mediums; ann exhibition & sale of paintings from students & teachers from the Art Students League, NY & Vytlacil School of Art; art exhibs by students from Northern Valley Regional High School, Demarest, NJ
Activities: Artist receptions; tours; mus shop sells note cards

CRANFORD

M   **CRANFORD HISTORICAL SOCIETY,** The Hanson House, 38 Springfield Ave, Cranford, NJ 07016. Tel 908-276-0489; Elec Mail iambillsenior@hotmail.com; Internet Home Page Address: www.bobdevlin.com/crhis.html; *Dir* Bob Fridlington
Open Sept - June Sun; No admis fee, donations accepted; Founded 1927 and dedicated to the perpetuation of Cranford's history. Nonprofit org
Special Subjects: Historical Material, Photography, Textiles, Costumes, Restorations

Collections: Crane-Phillips Living Museum, a Victorian cottage built in 1845 that served as honeymoon house for Josiah Crane Jr, great-grandson of the original miller. House depicts life in Cranford in the latter part of the 19th Century; photographs; scrapbooks; glass negatives; books; letters; Indian artifacts; costumes & textiles

Publications: Cranford Home Journal; Image of America: Cranford, by Robert Fridlington & Lawrence Fuhro

Activities: Walking tours; research assistance; educ tours; school & scout progs; Autumn Harvest Festival; Christmas Open House; Victorian Garden Tour; ongoing restoration of the Crane-Phillips House

DENVILLE

A BLACKWELL STREET CENTER FOR THE ARTS, PO Box 808, Denville, NJ 07834-0808. Tel 201-337-2143; Fax 201-337-2143; Elec Mail eprovost17@earthlink.net; Internet Home Page Address: www.blackwell-st-artists.org; *VPres* Annette Adrian Hanna; *Pres* David Gruol; *Treas* Elaine Provost
Open - varies according to exhibit; No admis fee; Estab 1983; professional gallery for NJ & NY artists to exhibit variety of art work; Initiated in 1998 as a cyber gallery; Average Annual Attendance: 2,100; Mem: 11 artists; qualifications for mem; artists mems juried by credentials commission; dues $50 once a yr; monthly meeting
Income: $2,200 (financed by mem, grants & donations)
Collections: Member artists' works in many pvt colls
Exhibitions: Six or more exhibs scheduled per yr at different sites; Morris County High School Student Art Show with awards
Activities: Educ dept; lect open to pub; gallery talks; competitions & awards; yearly high school juried exhibit with awards

EAST BRUNSWICK

QUIETUDE GARDEN GALLERY, 24 Fern Rd, East Brunswick, NJ 08816-3213. Tel 908-257-4340; Fax 908-257-1378; *Dir* Sheila Thau; *Dir* Amy Medford
Open Wed - Thurs & Sat - Sun 11 AM - 5 PM

ELIZABETH

L FREE PUBLIC LIBRARY OF ELIZABETH, Fine Arts Dept, 11 S Broad St, Elizabeth, NJ 07202-3486. Tel 908-354-6060; Fax 908-354-5845; Internet Home Page Address: www.ngpublib.org/eliz; *Dir* Joseph Keenan
Open Mon - Fri 9 AM - 9 PM, Sat 9 AM - 5 PM, cl Sun; No admis fee; Estab 1913, the art dept functions within the Linx library system; it offers free service to patrons of Elizabeth & Union County; Special exhibit area displays paintings & miscellaneous objects d'art
Income: Financed by city and state appropriation
Library Holdings: Book Volumes 15,000; Other Holdings Photographs & Illustrations 200,000; Reproductions 800
Collections: Japanese prints by various artists
Exhibitions: Works by artists & photographers; other special exhibs from time to time
Activities: Dramatic progs; lects open to pub, 15 vis lectrs per yr; concerts; material available to patrons of Union County; lending coll contains film strips, projection equipment & motion pictures; printed catalogues of film strips & films available to the pub - 4500 VHS videotapes (circulating)

ENGLEWOOD

L ENGLEWOOD LIBRARY, Fine Arts Dept, 31 Engle St, Englewood, NJ 07631-2903. Tel 201-568-2215; Fax 201-568-6895; Elec Mail englref@bccls.org; Internet Home Page Address: www.englewoodlibrary.org; *Dir Library* Don Jacobsen
Open Mon - Thurs 9 AM - 9 PM, Fri & Sat 9 AM - 5 PM, Sun 1 - 5 PM (Oct-May); No admis fee; Estab 1901 to estab a free pub library for citizens
Income: $510,000 (financed by endowment, city & state appropriation)
Library Holdings: Cassettes; Clipping Files; Filmstrips; Framed Reproductions; Motion Pictures; Original Art Works; Pamphlets; Records; Reels; Slides
Exhibitions: Members of Salute to Women In the Arts; Quilts; Rare Books & Manuscripts; World of Renaissance; rotating exhibits
Activities: Lect open to pub; concerts

EWING

M COLLEGE OF NEW JERSEY, Art Gallery, 2000 Pennington Rd, Ewing, NJ 08618-1104; PO Box 7718, Holman Hall CN 4700 Trenton, NJ 08628-0718. Tel 609-771-2615, 771-2633, 771-2198; Elec Mail masterjp@tcnj.edu; Internet Home Page Address: www.tcnj.edu/~tcag/; *Chmn & Prof* Dr Lois Fichner-Rathus; *Gallery Coordr* Judith P Masterson; *Pres* R Barbara Gittenstein
Open Mon - Fri Noon - 3 PM, Thurs 7 - 9 PM, Sun 1 - 3 PM; No admis fee; Estab to present students & community with the opportunity to study a wide range of artistic expressions & to exhibit their work; Average Annual Attendance: 2,500
Income: Financed by art dept budget & grants including NJ State Council on the Arts, Mercer County Cultural & Heritage Commission
Special Subjects: Drawings, Prints
Collections: Purchases from National Print & Drawing Show
Exhibitions: Craft Show; Faculty Show; Mercer County Competitive Art; Mercer County Competitive Photography; National Drawing Exhib; National Print Exhib; Selections from the State Mus; Sculpture Shows; Student Show; Contemporary Issues; African Arts
Publications: Catalog for African Arts; Catalog for Contemporary Issues; Catalog for National Drawing Exhibition; Catalog for National Print Exhibition

Activities: Classes for adults & children; lect open to pub, 5 vis lectrs per yr; gallery talks; tours; competitions with awards; individual paintings & original objects of art lent to other offices & depts on campus; lending coll contains original art works; original prints; paintings; originates traveling exhibs to other state cols & art schools

FRANKLIN LAKES

M THE GALLERY AT THE PRESBYTERIAN CHURCH AT FRANKLIN LAKES, 730 Old Franklin Lake Rd, The Presbyterian Church at Franklin Lakes, Franklin Lakes, NJ 07417-2200. Tel 201-891-0511; Fax 201-891-0517; Elec Mail pcflmgr@yahoo.com; Internet Home Page Address: pcfl.org
Call for hours; No admis fee
Income: artist donations
Collections: Paintings; photographs; sculpture

GLASSBORO

M HERITAGE GLASS MUSEUM, (Glassboro Heritage Glass Museum) 25 East High St, Glassboro, NJ 08028. Tel 856-881-7468; Elec Mail comments@boroughofglassboro.org; Internet Home Page Address: www.fieldtrip.com; *Pres Bd Trustees* Rick Grenda; *Corresp Secy* June Armstrong
Open Wed noon - 3 PM, Sat 11 AM - 2 PM, 4th Sun 1 - 4 PM, call before visiting; No admis fee, donations accepted; Estab 1979; Historical mus with the purpose to preserve & perpetuate the heritage of the glass industries of the region. Mus situated in the former Whitney Brothers Glass Works land; Average Annual Attendance: 1,200; Mem: 150; $25
Library Holdings: Book Volumes; Clipping Files; Maps; Original Documents; Photographs; Slides
Special Subjects: Historical Material, Flasks & Bottles, Manuscripts, Maps, Costumes, Glass, Coins & Medals
Collections: Display of bottles & jars from the Whitney Glass Company; Glass from other Gloucester County glass factories
Publications: Glassboro Briefs, newsletter
Activities: Educ & historic talks; volunteer progs; docent training; tours; originates traveling exhibs; sales shop sells books, glass articles, postcards, note paper, paperweights

HACKENSACK

M FAIRLEIGH DICKINSON UNIVERSITY, Edward Williams Gallery, 150 Kotte Pl, Hackensack, NJ 07601-6112. Tel 201-692-2449; Fax 201-692-2503; Elec Mail geraghty@fdu.edu; *Dir* Diana Soorikian
Open Mon-Fri 8:30AM-2:30PM, Sat 9:30AM-2:30PM
Collections: works by contemporary artists

HAMILTON

M GROUNDS FOR SCULPTURE, 18 Fairgrounds Rd, Hamilton, NJ 08619-3447. Tel 609-586-0616; Fax 609-586-0968; Elec Mail info@groundsforsculpture.org; Internet Home Page Address: www.groundsforsculpture.org; *Cur Educ* Christine E Finkelstein; *Mus Shop Mgr* Betsy Bowen; *Admin Asst* Yoriko Franklin; *Dir & Cur* Brooke Barrie; *Mem Mgr* Bonnie Brown; *Coordr (V)* Aylin Green; *Registrar* Jacqueline ter Kuile
Open Tues - Sun 10 AM - 6 PM, cl Mon; Admis adults $10, students 13 and over & seniors $8, children 6-12 $6, members and children under 6 free; Estab 1992 to promote greater understanding & appreciation for contemporary sculpture; Two 10,000 sq ft mus buildings with interior gallery spaces sited in a 22-acre landscaped sculpture park; Average Annual Attendance: 50,000
Income: Financed by pub charitable foundation
Special Subjects: Sculpture
Collections: Includes contemporary sculpture
Exhibitions: 3 yearly; spring, summer & fall/winter
Publications: Exhibition catalogues
Activities: Docent progs, yr round activities include art, poetry, music & dance; lect open to pub, 10 vis lectrs per yr, concerts; sales shop sells books, magazines, posters, postcards & children's art kits; full service restaurant

M INTERNATIONAL SCULPTURE CENTER, 19 Fairgrounds Rd Ste B, Hamilton, NJ 08619-3450. Tel 609-689-1051; Fax 609-689-1061; Elec Mail ics@sculpture.org; Internet Home Page Address: www.sculpture.org; *Chmn Bd* Joshua S Kanter; *Exec Dir* Johannah Hutchison
Open Mon - Fri 9 AM - 5 PM; No admis fee; Estab 1960, dedicated to expand the base of understanding & support of contemporary sculpture through its progs & services. The ISC serves the needs & interests of sculptors, educators, arts supporters & the gen pub; Mem: 8,000; dues $95
Income: Financed by mem dues, pvt donations & grants
Publications: A Sculpture Reader: Contemporary Sculpture Since 1980
Activities: Conferences & lectrs; lifetime achievement award; patron award; outstanding student in contemporary sculpture award; educator award

HOPEWELL

M HOPEWELL MUSEUM, 28 E Broad St, Hopewell, NJ 08525-1828. Tel 609-466-0103; *Cur* Beverly Weidl; *Pres* David Mackey
Open Mon, Wed & Sat 2 - 5 PM, cl national holidays; groups by appointment only; No admis fee, donations suggested; Estab 1922 as a mus of local history from early 1700 to the present day; Research on Mon & Wed only; Average Annual Attendance: 2,000
Income: Financed by endowment, mem & donations
Special Subjects: Period Rooms

Collections: Antique china, glass, silver & pewter; colonial furniture; colonial parlor; early needlework; Indian handicrafts; photograph coll; Victorian parlor
Publications: Hopewell Valley Heritage; Pioneers of Old Hopewell; maps

JERSEY CITY

M **CURIOUS MATTER,** 272 5th St, Jersey City, NJ 07302-2304. Tel 201-659-5771; Elec Mail gallery@curiousmatter.org; Internet Home Page Address: www.curiousmatter.org; *Dir* Arthur Bruso; *Dir* Raymond E Mingst
Open Sun 12PM-3PM, & by appointment; No admis fee; Exhibs & publs; Contemporary art
Purchases: Ryan Browning, Suzanne Norris
Collections: works by regional & national artists
Activities: Gallery talks; tours

M **JERSEY CITY MUSEUM,** 350 Montgomery St, Jersey City, NJ 07302-4041. Tel 201-413-0303; Fax 201-413-9922; Elec Mail info@jerseycitymuseum.org; Internet Home Page Address: www.jerseycitymuseum.org; *Dir Fin & External Affairs* Diane Parisien; *Chmn of Brd* Benjamin Dineen; *Registrar* Michelle Larson; *Brd Trustees-Treas* Mark Rodrick
Open Wed-Fri 11 AM - 5 PM, Sat Noon-5PM; Suggested $10 donation; Estab 1901 for the purpose of preserving & interpreting its permanent coll of art & historical objects; Maintains seven gallery spaces for contemporary & historical exhibs; Average Annual Attendance: 30,000; Mem: 500; seniors $30 individuals; $40 dual family; $25 artist
Income: Financed by state
Purchases: $50 friend, $100 patron, $250 cur guild, $500 dir guild
Library Holdings: Exhibition Catalogs; Original Art Works; Prints; Sculpture; Slides
Special Subjects: Painting-American, Prints, Architecture, Drawings, Watercolors, Costumes, Ceramics, Crafts, Folk Art, Etchings & Engravings, Decorative Arts, Dolls, Coins & Medals
Collections: Paintings, drawings & watercolors by 19th century artist August Will; 19th & 20th century paintings & prints; Jersey City & New Jersey related artifacts, documents, decorative & historical objects
Exhibitions: Permanent exhibs: 19th Century Coll, 20th Century Coll; changing exhibs
Publications: Exhibition catalogs
Activities: Lect open to public; gallery talks; tours; slide & panel talks; historical tours; video & performance arts; traveling exhibs; mus sells books

M **NEW JERSEY CITY UNIVERSITY,** Courtney Art Gallery & Lemmerman Gallery, 2039 John F Kennedy Blvd, Dept of Art Grossnickel Hall, 1st Flr Jersey City, NJ 07305-1596. Tel 201-200-3214; Fax 201-200-3224; Elec Mail hbastidas@njcu.edu; *Dir* Hugo Xavier Bastidas; *Dept Chair* Winifred McNiell
Open Mon - Fri 11 AM - 5 PM, or by appointment; No admis fee; Estab 1969 to bring examples of professional work to the campus in each of the areas in which students are involved: Painting, sculpture, film, photog, textiles, weaving, ceramics, graphic design; Gallery is operated by students & with the Jersey City Mus for a student internship training prog; Average Annual Attendance: 3,000
Income: Financed by city, state appropriation & Art Department
Collections: Small coll of prints & paintings
Exhibitions: Robert Blackburn, Robert Indiana, Jose Morales
Activities: Lect open to pub, 5 vis lectrs per yr; concerts; gallery talks; tours; exten dept serving community organizations; individual paintings & original objects of art lent; lending collection contains color reproductions, film strips, Kodachromes, motion pictures, photographs; originates traveling exhibs
M **Lemmerman Art Gallery,** 2039 John F Kennedy Blvd, Hepburn Hall, 3rd Flr Jersey City, NJ 07305-1596. Tel 201-200-3214; Fax 201-200-3224; Elec Mail hbastidas@njcu.edu; *Dir* Hugo Xavier Bastidas
Open Mon - Fri 11 AM - 5PM, or by appointment; Estab 1961 to bridge community (col) to Art of all levels; Gothic structure; Average Annual Attendance: 3,000
Income: Financed by art department, state, city
Activities: Educ dept; lect open to pub; gallery talks; tours; individual paintings lent to galleries & other institutions that have pub access; lending coll contains 31 original art works

M **SAINT PETER'S COLLEGE,** Art Gallery, 2641 Kennedy Blvd, Jersey City, NJ 07306. Tel 201-915-9238; Fax 201-413-1669; Elec Mail oscarmagnan@yahoo.com; *Dir* Oscar Magnan; *Sec* Elga Taki
Open Mon, Tues, Fri & Sat 11 AM - 4 PM, Wed & Thurs 11 AM - 9 PM; No admis fee; Estab 1971 to present the different art trends; Gallery is maintained with good space, lighting and alarm systems; Average Annual Attendance: 2,000
Income: Financed by the col
Special Subjects: Afro-American Art, American Indian Art, Anthropology, Decorative Arts, Drawings, Folk Art, History of Art & Archaeology, Interior Design, Landscape Architecture, Landscapes, Architecture, Art Education, Art History, Ceramics, Collages, Glass, Metalwork, Mexican Art, Antiquities-Assyrian, Flasks & Bottles, Furniture, Photography, Portraits, Pre-Columbian Art, Painting-American, Prints, Textiles, Bronzes, Manuscripts, Painting-British, Painting-European, Painting-French, Painting-Japanese, Sculpture, Graphics, Latin American Art, American Western Art, Bronzes, African Art, Anthropology, Archaeology, Religious Art, Primitive art, Collages, Posters, Painting-Canadian, Dolls, Jewelry, Porcelain, Oriental Art, Asian Art, Antiquities-Byzantine, Metalwork, Painting-Dutch, Carpets & Rugs, Coins & Medals, Restorations, Baroque Art, Calligraphy, Miniatures, Painting-Flemish, Painting-Polish, Embroidery, Antiquities-Oriental, Painting-Spanish, Painting-Italian, Antiquities-Persian, Antiquities-Egyptian, Antiquities-Greek, Antiquities-Roman, Mosaics, Stained Glass, Painting-Australian, Painting-German, Reproductions, Antiquities-Etruscan, Painting-Russian, Painting-Israeli, Enamels, Painting-Scandinavian, Bookplates & Bindings, Painting-New Zealand
Activities: Classes for adults; docent training; lects open to pub, 20 vis lectrs per yr; concerts; gallery talks; tours; extension dept serving students

LAKEWOOD

M **GEORGIAN COURT UNIVERSITY,** (Georgian Court College) M Christina Geis Gallery, 900 Lakewood Ave, Lakewood, NJ 08701-2697. Tel 732-987-2437; Fax 732-987-2010; Elec Mail breimayer@georgian.edu; *Dir* Dr M Phyllis Breimayer
Open Mon - Thurs 9 AM - 8 PM, Fri 9AM-5PM; No admis fee; Estab 1964 to offer art students the opportunity to view the works of professional artists & also to exhibit student work; Gallery is one large room with 100 running ft of wall area for flat work; the center area for sculpture; Average Annual Attendance: 1,000
Income: Financed through the col
Special Subjects: Architecture, Drawings, Photography, Sculpture, Ceramics, Calligraphy
Collections: Advertising Design; Art History; Commercial Art; Drafting; Fashion Arts; Graphic Design; Illustration; Lettering; Painting; Printmaking; Teacher Training; Textile Design; Weaving
Exhibitions: Monthly exhibs
Activities: Schols offered

LAWRENCEVILLE

M **RIDER UNIVERSITY,** Art Gallery, 2083 Lawrenceville Rd, Lawrenceville, NJ 08648-3009; PO Box 6400, Lawrenceville, NJ 08648. Tel 609-895-5588; Fax 609-896-5232; Elec Mail hnaar@rider.edu; Internet Home Page Address: www.rider.edu/artgallery; *Prof Art & Dir* Harry I Naar
Open Tues - Thurs 11 AM - 7 PM, Sun 12 - 4 PM (subject to change); No admis fee; Estab 1970 to afford mems of the community & univ the opportunity to expand their knowledge & exposure to art; Gallery has 1,513 sq ft of space divided into two rooms of different height. Collections displayed throughout campus; main collections displayed in Moore Library; Average Annual Attendance: 5,000
Income: $8,000 (univ funded)
Library Holdings: Exhibition Catalogs; Reproductions
Special Subjects: Drawings, Painting-American, Prints, Textiles, Sculpture, Watercolors
Collections: African Art, statues & masks; contemporary art; drawings; paintings; prints; sculpture
Publications: Exhibit catalogs
Activities: Classes for adults; dramatic progs; docent training; internships; gallery management class; lect open to pub, 4 vis lectrs per yr; concerts; gallery talks; tours; individual paintings & original objects of art lent to museums, group shows, one-person shows, major exhibs; book traveling exhibs; exhib catalogues are available for sale

LAYTON

L **PETERS VALLEY CRAFT CENTER,** 19 Kuhn Rd, Layton, NJ 07851-2004. Tel 973-948-5200; Tel 973-948-5202; Fax 973-948-0011; Elec Mail info@petersvalley.org; Internet Home Page Address: www.pvcrafts.org; *Exec Dir* Kristin Muller; *Office Mgr* Jennifer Brooks; *Gallery Mgr* Brienne Rosner
Call for hours; Estab 1970 as a nonprofit craft educ center to promote & encourage traditional & contemporary crafts through exhibs, demonstrations, workshops & educational programs; Over 300 artists work exhibited in store, gallery has changing exhibs; Average Annual Attendance: 10,000; Mem: 350; dues $50; ann meeting in Oct
Income: Financed in part by a grant from NJ State Council on the Arts/Department of State, the Geraldine R Dodge Foundation & mems, friends, corporations & local companies
Library Holdings: Book Volumes 500; Exhibition Catalogs; Original Art Works; Pamphlets; Photographs; Slides
Special Subjects: Decorative Arts, Photography, Ceramics, Crafts, Metalwork, Handicrafts, Silversmithing, Textiles, Woodcarvings
Collections: Teaching coll of craft works, art & photographs
Exhibitions: Theme Shows & changing Exhibs
Publications: Summer Workshop Catalog, ann
Activities: Educ dept; classes for adults and children; lect open to pub; schols & residencies; exten dept serves North Jersey; sales shop sells original art

LINCROFT

M **MONMOUTH MUSEUM & CULTURAL CENTER,** PO Box 359, Lincroft, NJ 07738-0359. Tel 732-747-2266; Fax 732-747-8592; Elec Mail monmuseum@netlabs.net; Internet Home Page Address: www.monmouthmuseum.org; *Pres & CEO* Dorothy V Morehouse; *First VPres* Jane McCosker; *Second VPres* Barbara Goldfarb; *Asst to Dir* Catherine Jahos; *Exec Dir* Avis Henderson; *Pub Rels Coordr* Julia Fiormo
Open Tues - Sat 10 AM - 4:30 PM, Sun 1 - 5 PM; Admis $7, free to Museum mems, children one and under, & Brookdale Community College students; Estab 1963 to advance interest in art, science, nature & cultural history; Mus houses one large gallery, the Becker Children's Wing, & The Wonder Wing for children age 6 & under. Exhibs are changed eight times per yr; also an educ area & a conference area; Average Annual Attendance: 50,000; Mem: 1600; dues family $60, individual $30, seniors $20; ann meeting in Jan
Income: Financed by mem, donations, county funds & benefits
Exhibitions: Annual Monmouth County Arts Council Juried Exhibition; Biannual NJ Watercolor Society Exhibition; All Aboard at the Monmouth Museum
Publications: Calendar of events; catalogues of exhibitions; newsletter
Activities: Classes for adults & children; docent training; lects open to pub; originate traveling trunks for use in schools; mus shop sells books & gift items

LONG BRANCH

M **LONG BRANCH HISTORICAL MUSEUM,** 1260 Ocean Ave, Long Branch, NJ 07740-4550. Tel 732-223-0874; *Pres* Thomas Cameron; *VPres* Robert Weston
Open by appointment only; No admis fee; Estab 1953 as post Civil War historical mus; Average Annual Attendance: 10,000; Mem: Dues $1

Special Subjects: Historical Material
Collections: Period furniture

LOVELADIES

M **LONG BEACH ISLAND FOUNDATION OF THE ARTS & SCIENCES,** 120
Long Beach Blvd, Loveladies, NJ 08008-6131. Tel 609-494-1241; Fax
609-494-0662; Elec Mail office@lbifoundation.org; Internet Home Page Address:
www.lbifoundation.org; *Exec Dir* Patricia Chamberlin; *Exec Dir* Christopher Seiz
Open Thurs-Mon 9AM-4PM; Estab 1948 to promote understanding of
participation in the arts; Average Annual Attendance: 18,000; Mem: 700 families;
dues $165 per yr; all persons welcome; mem provides discounts on classes &
purchases
Collections: Works by local & national artists
Exhibitions: 17 Exhibs yearly in various media by local, regional, national, and
internationally known artists
Activities: classes for adults & children; Special events; performances; lectrs;
workshops; youth progs; films; lects open to pub; concerts; gallery talks;
competitions with awards; schols awarded; books traveling exhibs 2 per yr

MADISON

M **ARCHIVES & HISTORY CENTER OF THE UNITED METHODIST
CHURCH,** Methodist Archive Bldg, 36 Madison Ave Madison, NJ 07940; PO
Box 127, Madison, NJ 07940-0127. Tel 973-408-3189; Fax 973-408-3909; Elec
Mail rwilliams@gcah.org; *Archivist* L Dale Patterson; *Librn* Christopher Anderson
Open Mon - Fri 9 AM - 5 PM; No admis fee; Estab 1885 as a religious history
mus; The Archives & History Center is located on Drew University Campus & it
contains a mus, a library & a spacious 180,000 cubic ft archival vault. Maintains
reference library
Income: Financed by gen church funds
Special Subjects: Religious Art, Historical Material
Collections: Letters; Photographs
Exhibitions: Chinese Missionaries
Publications: Methodist History, quarterly
Activities: Lects open to pub, 1 vis lectrs per yr; tours; sales shop sells books &
prints
L **Library,** Drew U Campus, 36 Madison Ave Madison, NJ 07940; PO Box 127,
Madison, NJ 07940. Tel 973-408-3590; Fax 973-408-3836; Internet Home Page
Address: www.depts.drew.edu/lib/uma.html; *Head Librn* Christopher J Anderson
Open Mon - Fri 9 AM - 5 PM; No admis fee; Estab 1983; For reference only;
Average Annual Attendance: 580
Library Holdings: Audio Tapes; Book Volumes 70,000; CD-ROMs; Cassettes;
Clipping Files; Compact Disks; DVDs; Exhibition Catalogs; Fiche; Filmstrips;
Lantern Slides; Manuscripts; Maps; Memorabilia; Motion Pictures; Original Art
Works; Original Documents; Pamphlets; Periodical Subscriptions 600;
Photographs; Prints; Records; Reels; Slides; Video Tapes
Special Subjects: Drawings, Manuscripts, Painting-American, Painting-British,
Historical Material, Portraits, Ceramics, Video, Porcelain, Furniture, Religious Art
Collections: Methodist materials; pamphlets & manuscripts of John Wesley & his
assoc; materials pertaining to women & ethnic minorities
Activities: Gallery talks & tours

M **DREW UNIVERSITY,** Elizabeth P Korn Gallery, 36 Madison Ave, Madison, NJ
07940-1493. Tel 973-408-3758; Fax 973-408-3098; Elec Mail ghiltlco@drew.edu;
Internet Home Page Address: www.drew.edu/korngallery; *Dean* John Muccigrosso;
Chmn Art Dept Lee Arnold; *Gallery Coordr* Gabriele Hiltl-Cohen
Open Tues - Fri 12:30 - 4 PM & by appointment, selected weekends; No admis
fee; Estab 1968 to provide exhibs each school year to augment prog of courses &
to serve the community
Income: Financed by Univ instructional budget
Collections: Ancient Near-East archaeological coll; Colonial America;
Contemporary abstraction; Native American artifacts; 19th century acad; Oriental
art
Activities: Lect open to pub, 3-4 vis lectrs per yr; gallery talks
L **Art Dept Library,** 36 Madison Ave, Madison, NJ 07940-1434. Tel 973-408-3000;
Fax 973-408-3770
Library maintained for art history courses
Purchases: $7400 annually (for purchases to support art history courses at the col
level)
Library Holdings: Audio Tapes; Book Volumes 350,000; Exhibition Catalogs;
Fiche; Filmstrips; Manuscripts; Original Art Works; Pamphlets; Periodical
Subscriptions 1900; Photographs; Records; Slides; Video Tapes

MAHWAH

M **THE ART GALLERIES OF RAMAPO COLLEGE,** 505 Ramapo Valley Rd,
Mahwah, NJ 07430-1623. Tel 201-684-7587; *Dir* Shalom Gorewitz
Open Mon - Fri 11 AM - 2 PM, Wed 5 - 7 PM, cl Sat & Sun; No admis fee;
Estab 1979 as outreach for community, faculty, staff & students to support
undergrad curriculum; Three galleries: thematic changing exhibs gallery;
permanent coll gallery; alternate space gallery; Average Annual Attendance: 5,000;
Mem: 300 (friends); dues $15
Income: Financed by state appropriation & grants
Special Subjects: Prints
Collections: Rodman Collection of Popular Art, Art by Haitians; Study Collection
of Prints; fine art printmaking from 15th century to present
Publications: Exhibit catalogs
Activities: Classes for adults & children; dramatic progs; docent training; lect
open to pub, 10 vis lectrs per yr; competitions; schols & fels offered; individual
paintings lent to institutions, cols & museums; book traveling exhibs; originate
traveling exhibs

MERCERVILLE

L **JOHNSON ATELIER TECHNICAL INSTITUTE OF SCULPTURE,** Johnson
Atelier Library, 60 Sculptors Way, Mercerville, NJ 08619-3428. Tel 609-890-7777;
Fax 609-890-1816; Elec Mail Info@ atelier.org; Internet Home Page Address:
www.atelier.org; *Librn* Eden R Bentley; *Dir Gallery* Gyuri Hollosy
Not open to pub; Estab 1977 to provide an information center for apprentices,
instructors & staff on sculpture, art appreciation & art history; Library provides
space for lects, movies, slides & critique sessions; gallery adjacent to library
Income: Financed by appropriation from the Johnson Atelier Technical Institute of
Sculpture
Library Holdings: Book Volumes 2670; Clipping Files; Exhibition Catalogs;
Periodical Subscriptions 23; Slides
Special Subjects: Sculpture, Bronzes
Collections: Exhibition catalogues on sculptors & group shows; slides of about 50
sculptor's work

MILLVILLE

M **RIVERFRONT RENAISSANCE CENTER FOR THE ARTS,** 22 N High St,
Millville, NJ 08332-3830. Tel 856-327-4500
Open Sun - Thurs 11 AM - 5 PM, Fri 11 AM - 8 PM, Sat 11 AM - 7 PM

M **WHEATON ARTS & CULTURAL CENTER,** (Wheaton Cultural Alliance Inc)
Museum of American Glass, 1501 Glasstown Rd, Millville, NJ 08332-1568. Tel
800-998-4552; Fax 856-825-2410; Elec Mail mail@wheatonarts.org; Internet
Home Page Address: www.wheatonarts.org; *Cur Asst* Diane Wood; *Exec Dir*
Susan Gogan; *Registrar* Elizabeth Wilk
Open Jan - Mar Sat & Sun 10 AM - 5 PM; Apr - Dec Tues - Sun 10 AM - 5 PM;
Admis adults $10, seniors (62+) $9, students $7, children 5 & under free; Estab
1970, a cultural center dedicated to American craft; Average Annual Attendance:
60,000
Library Holdings: Auction Catalogs; Book Volumes; Clipping Files; Exhibition
Catalogs; Maps; Original Documents; Photographs; Slides; Video Tapes
Special Subjects: Glass
Collections: American glass
Activities: Educ prog; docent training; tours; mus shop sells books, magazines,
original art

MONTCLAIR

M **MONTCLAIR ART MUSEUM,** 3 S Mountain Ave, Montclair, NJ 07042-1747.
Tel 973-746-5555; Fax 973-746-9118; Internet Home Page Address:
www.montclairartmuseum.org; *Dir* Lora Urbanelli; *Chief Cur* Gail Stavitsky; *Dir
Finance* Michael Frasco; *Deputy Dir* Gary Schneider; *Dir Mktg & Commun*
Michael Gillespie; *Cur Contemporary Art* Alexandra Schwartz; *Interim Dir
Develop* Susan Wall
Open Wed - Sun Noon - 5 PM, cl Mon, Tues & major holidays; Admis adults
$12, seniors & students $10, children under 12 & mems free; 1st Thurs of mon
Oct-June 5 PM - 9 PM free; 1st Fri of mon free; Estab 1914; Two galleries of
changing exhibs; five galleries of permanent exhibs; student gallery; Average
Annual Attendance: 66,000; Mem: 2700; college student $35; individual $50; dual
& family $70; friend $165; curator's circle $325; sustaining $750; benefactor
$1,500; director's circle $3,000; inness $5,500
Income: Financed by endowment & mems
Special Subjects: Anthropology, Archaeology, Landscapes, Ceramics,
Photography, Pottery, Sculpture, Drawings, Painting-American, Prints, American
Indian Art, Ethnology, Costumes, Afro-American Art, Portraits, Silver
Collections: Rand Collection of American Indian Art; George Inness Collection;
Morgan Russell Archive
Exhibitions: (09/22/2013-12/15/2013) Robert Barry: One Billian Colored Dots;
(09/22/2013-01/15/2014) Looking Forward: Gifts of Contemporary Art from the
Patricia A Bell Coll; (01/15/2014-07/31/2014) 100 Works for 100 Years: A
Centennial Celebration; (02/16/2014-06/15/2014) Robert Smithson: New Jersey
Earthworks; (01/21/2014-01/11/2015) Come As You Are: Art of the 1990s
Publications: Bulletin, 3 times per yr; exhib catalogs; pub progs brochure; Art
School Brochure; ann report
Activities: Classes for adults & children; docent training; workshops coordinated
progs with school groups; dramatic progs; family progs; lect open to pub; 10 vis
lectrs per yr; concerts; gallery talks every Sunday; tours; sponsoring of
competitions; schols; mus shop sells books, notecards, reproductions, slides,
Native American jewelry & crafts, jewelry, games/toys for children & diverse
art-related items

MOORESTOWN

M **PERKINS CENTER FOR THE ARTS,** 395 Kings Hwy, Moorestown, NJ
08057-2725. Tel 856-235-6488; Fax 856-235-6624; Elec Mail
create@perkinscenter.org; Internet Home Page Address: www.perkinscenter.org;
Asst Dir Denise Creedon; *Dir* Alan Willoughby; *Dir Educ* Anissa Lewis; *Cur of
Exhibs* Hope Proper; *Asst Dir* Lise Ragbir; *Dir Educ* Melissa Walker
Open Thurs - Sun; No admis fee; Estab 1977 as a multi-disciplinary art center; A
Tudor mansion built in 1910 on 5-1/2 acre lot. The building is listed on the
National Register of Historic Places; Average Annual Attendance: 25,000; Mem:
1200; dues family $50, adult $30, student $20
Income: $1,200,000 (financed by mem, state appropriation, corporate, foundation
& earned income)
Exhibitions: Annual Photography Exhib; Annual Pottery Show & Sale; Annual
Works on Paper Exhib; Annual Watercolor Exhib; Director's Choice; Mems &
Faculty Show
Publications: Perkinsight, quarterly newsletter & class catalog
Activities: Classes for adults & children; docent progs; lect open to pub, 5 vis
lectrs per yr; awards given; schols & fels offered

MORRISTOWN

L COLLEGE OF SAINT ELIZABETH, Mahoney Library, 2 Convent Rd, Morristown, NJ 07960-6989. Tel 973-290-4237; Fax 973-290-4226; Elec Mail pchervenie@liza.st-elizabeth.edu; *Dir Library* Amira Unvir
Open Mon -Thurs 9AM-9PM, Fri 9AM-5PM, Sat 10:30AM-5:30PM, Sun 2AM-6PM; Estab 1899 for acad purposes
Income: Financed by pvt funds
Library Holdings: Book Volumes 140,200; Cassettes; Exhibition Catalogs; Fiche 65,664; Filmstrips 200; Original Art Works; Periodical Subscriptions 848; Photographs; Prints; Records 1800; Reels 4690; Reproductions; Sculpture
Exhibitions: Sculpture, paintings, prints by the Art Dept faculty

M MORRIS MUSEUM, 6 Normandy Heights Rd, Morristown, NJ 07960-4627. Tel 973-971-3700; Fax 973-538-0154; Internet Home Page Address: www.morrismuseum.org; *Coll Mgr* Jacqueline Fletcher; *Chair* Paul Laud; *Cur, Murtogh D Guinness Coll* Ellen Snyder-Grenier; *COO* Linda Moore Esq
Open Wed - Sat 11 AM - 5 PM, Thurs until 8 PM, Sun 1 - 5 PM, cl major holidays; Admis adults $10, seniors & children $7; mems free; Estab 1913 to educate diverse pub on topics in art, humanities & the sciences; 12 galleries of changing & permanent exhibs; Average Annual Attendance: 200,000; Mem: 2500; dues $40 - $65; ann meeting in Sept
Income: Mem dues, funds, grants
Special Subjects: Painting-American, Sculpture, Watercolors, American Indian Art, Bronzes, African Art, Anthropology, Archaeology, Costumes, Ceramics, Crafts, Pottery, Primitive art, Etchings & Engravings, Decorative Arts, Collages, Glass, Asian Art, Carpets & Rugs, Period Rooms
Collections: Antique dolls & toys; fine & decorative arts; geology; mineralogy; paleontology; textiles; zoology; mechanical musical instruments; automata
Exhibitions: North American Indian & Woodland Indian Galleries; Rock & Mineral Gallery; Gallery; Dinosaur Gallery; Children's Room; Mammal Gallery; Model Train Gallery; juried art exhibitions; Mechanical musical instruments & automata
Publications: Sassona Norton Sculpture; Murtough D Guinness Collection of Mechanical Musical Instruments and Automata
Activities: Classes for adults & children; dramatic progs; docent training; lect open to pub, 6-10 vis lectrs per yr; concerts; gallery talks for schools; tours; competitions with prizes; Citation of Excellence from NJ State Council on the Arts; exten dept serves schools, sr centers & hospitals; artmobile; individual paintings & original objects of art lent to other local organizations & museums; book traveling exhibs; originate traveling exhibs; mus shop sells books, reproductions, prints, exhibs-related gifts & toys

M SCHUYLER-HAMILTON HOUSE, 5 Olyphant Pl, Morristown, NJ 07960-4231. Tel 973-267-4039; Fax 908-852-1361; Elec Mail aben85271@aol.com; *Cur* Phyllis Sanftner; *Cur* JoAnn Bownan; *Co-2nd Vice Regent* Mariane Browne; *Co-1st Vice Regent* Patricia Sanftner; *CEO* Anita Brennan
Open Sun 2 - 4 PM, other times by appointment; Admis adults $4, children under 12 free; Estab 1923 for preservation of historical landmark; House is furnished with 18th Century antiques; five large portraits of General & Mrs Philip Schuyler, their daughter, Betsey Schuyler Hamilton, Alexander Hamilton & Dr Jabez Campfield; old lithographs, silhouette of George Washington, needle & petit point; Average Annual Attendance: 1,500; Mem: 90; dues $30; ann meeting 1st Thurs in May, Chap meets Oct - May
Income: Financed by mem, Friends of Schuyler-Hamilton, foundations & matching gifts
Special Subjects: Decorative Arts, Period Rooms
Collections: China - Canton, blue willow, Staffordshire; doll china; pewter; brass candlesticks; rugs; tunebooks
Activities: Docent training; lect for mems; tours; competitions with awards; sales shop sells stationery, cards & reproductions

NEW BRUNSWICK

A MIDDLESEX COUNTY CULTURAL & HERITAGE COMMISSION, 703 Jersey Ave, New Brunswick, NJ 08901-3651. Tel 732-745-4489; Fax 732-745-4524; Elec Mail info@cultureheritage.com; Internet Home Page Address: www.co.middlesex.nj.us/culturalheritage; *Treas* Edmund Spiro; *Exec Dir* Anna M Aschkenes
Open Tues-Friday 8:30AM-4:15PM, Sun 1PM-4PM; No admis fee; Estab 1979 to provide exhib opportunities & information services for mems & educ & cultural opportunities for the gen pub; Slide file of mems' art work is maintained; Mem: 177; dues family or friend $25, mem $15, students & srs $10; monthly board meetings
Income: Financed by mem, state grants, fundraising
Exhibitions: New Brunswick Tomorrow; Annual Statewide Show
Publications: ALCNJ Newsletter, monthly
Activities: Demonstrations open to pub; competitions with awards

M RUTGERS, THE STATE UNIVERSITY OF NEW JERSEY, Zimmerli Art Museum, Rutgers University, 71 Hamilton St, New Brunswick, NJ 08901-1248. Tel 848-932-7237; Fax 732-932-8201; Elec Mail press@zimmerli.rutgers.edu; Internet Home Page Address: www.zimmerlimuseum.rutgers.edu; *Dir* Suzanne Delehanty; *Develop Dir* Whitney Prendergast; *Assoc Cur European Art* Christine Giviskos; *Liaison Acad Progs & Cur* Donna Gustafson, Ph.D.; *Cur Prints and Drawings* Marilyn Symmes; *Assoc Cur Russian & Soviet Art* Julia Tulovsky, Ph.D.; *Registrar* Leslie Kriff
Open Tues - Fri 10 AM - 4:30 PM, Sat & Sun Noon - 5 PM; cl Mon & month of Aug, Memorial Day, Independence Day, Thanksgiving & Fri, Dec 24 & 25, Jan 1; Admis adults $6; mems, Rutgers Univ students & staff (with ID), children under 18 & to pub first Sun of every month free; Estab 1966; 70,000 sq ft facility; Average Annual Attendance: 45,000 (est); Mem: 665 households; dues student $25, individual $50, dual $85, family $100, assoc $250, patron $500, Cur's Circle $1,000, Dir's Gallery $2,500, Hamilton Society $5,000

Income: Ann support from Rutgers, income from the Avenir Foundation & Andrew W Mellon Foundation endowments, ann contributions from individuals, foundations & corps.
Special Subjects: Etchings & Engravings, Landscapes, Portraits, Prints, Painting-French, Sculpture, Painting-American, Antiquities-Greek, Antiquities-Roman, Painting-Russian
Collections: Permanent Collection: 60,000+ works in a wide range of media, incl survey of Western art from 15th c. - present; Russian & Soviet Nonconformist art from the Dodge Collection; American art, with concentrations on prints & original illustrations for children's books; focused presentations of Ancient Greek & Roman art & Pre-Columbian art, always on view at the Zimmerli
Publications: Exhib catalogs; Zimmerli Journal; Annual Prog Guide; Gallery Notes; books
Activities: Tours for K-12 students; teacher training in collaboration with the Grad School of Educ at Rutgers; drawing classes for children, teens, & adults; symposia for the acad community; access to the museum's coll of drawings, prints, & photographs at the Zimmerli's Morse Center; lects open to pub, 4-6 vis lectrs per year; concerts; gallery talks; tours; fels available; Dodge Fellows; Dodge Lawrence Fellows; original objects of art lent to art museums nationally & internationally; book traveling exhibs: one every two or three yrs; organize traveling exhibs to other art museums

L Art Library, 71 Hamilton St, Voorhees Hall New Brunswick, NJ 08901-1248. Tel 732-932-7739; Fax 732-932-6743; Internet Home Page Address: www.libraries.rutgers.edu/rul/libs/art_lib/art_lib.shtml; *Asst Librn* Sara Harrington; *Art Librn* Joseph Consoli
Open Mon - Thurs 9 AM - 10 PM, Fri & Sat 9 AM - 5 PM, Sun 1 - 10 PM; Estab 1966 for acad research; Circ Non-circulating; For reference only
Library Holdings: Book Volumes 65,000; Clipping Files; Exhibition Catalogs; Fiche; Pamphlets; Periodical Subscriptions 240
Collections: Mary Barlett Cowdrey Collection of American Art; Howard Hibbard Collection; George Raibov Collection of Russian Art; Louis E Stern Collection of Contemporary Art
Activities: Bibliographic instruction; lect; tours

M Mary H Dana Women Artists Series, a Partnership of the Institute for Women & Art and the Rutgers University Libraries, 191 College Ave, (2nd Floor) New Brunswick, NJ 08901-8546. Tel 732-932-3726; Fax 732-932-1207; Elec Mail olin@rci.rutgers.edu; Internet Home Page Address: www.libraries.rutgers.edu/rul/exhibits/dana_womens.shtm; *Cur* Ferris Olin, Dr; *Cur & Prof* Judith K Brodsky; *Proj Mgr* Nicole Ianuzzeli
Open Mon - Fri 9 AM - 4:30 PM, weekends by appointment; No admis fee; Estab 1971 to exhibit the work of emerging & established contemporary women artists; Located in galleries of Mabel Smith Douglass Library on the Douglass college campus of Rutgers University
Income: Financed from gifts from endowment, student groups & departmental funds
Exhibitions: Rotating exhibits each acad yr
Publications: Exhib catalogues
Activities: Lect open to pub; vis lectr; artists selected by jury

L Mabel Smith Douglass Library, 8 Chapel Dr, New Brunswick, NJ 08901-8527. Tel 732-932-9407 ext 26; Fax 732-932-6777; Elec Mail olin@rci.rutger
Open Mon - Thurs 8 AM - 1 AM, Fri 8 AM - 9 PM, Sat 10 AM - 6 PM, Sun Noon - 1 AM; Estab 1918
Special Subjects: Photography, Graphic Arts, Graphic Design, Theatre Arts

NEW PROVIDENCE

M CAMBRIA HISTORICAL SOCIETY, 121 Chanlon Rd, New Providence, NJ 07974-1541. Tel 908-665-2846; *Cur* Donald Bruce; *Dir* Tamika Borden
Open Mon - Thurs & Sat 10 AM - 4 PM; Admis adult $3; Estab 1950 as a historic house mus; Average Annual Attendance: 10,000; Mem: 1600; dues $70; ann meeting in Oct
Income: $160,000 (financed by mem)
Special Subjects: Dolls, Furniture, Glass
Collections: China; dolls; furniture; glass; paintings

NEWARK

A ALJIRA CENTER FOR CONTEMPORARY ART, 591 Broad St, Newark, NJ 07102-4403. Tel 973-622-1600; Fax 973-622-6526; Elec Mail info@aljira.org; Internet Home Page Address: www.aljira.org; *Exec Dir* Victor Davson; *Dir Exhibs & Progs* Edwin Ramoran; *Mgr Exhibs & Progs* Christine Walia
Open Wed - Fri Noon - 6 PM, Sat 11 AM - 4 PM; call for information; Admis $5 suggested donation, children under 12 no charge; Estab 1983 as a multi-cultural visual art organization
Exhibitions: Various exhibs; call for information

M NEW JERSEY HISTORICAL SOCIETY, 52 Park Pl, Newark, NJ 07102-4302. Tel 973-596-8500; Fax 973-596-6957; Internet Home Page Address: www.jerseyhistory.org; *Dir Spec Projects* Ellen Snyder-Grenier; *Coll Mgr* Timothy Decker; *Library Dir* Chad Leinaweaver; *Pres* Linda Epps; *Prog & Colls Dir* Janet Rassweiler
Open Tues - Sat 10 AM - 5 PM; No admis fee; Estab 1845 to col, preserve, exhibit & make available to study the materials pertaining to the history of New Jersey & its people; The mus has three changing exhib spaces & special colls library; Average Annual Attendance: 20,000; Mem: 1700; dues adults $30 & up; ann meeting third Wed in Apr
Income: Financed by endowment, mem, gifts, grants & benefits
Special Subjects: Drawings, Glass, Flasks & Bottles, Furniture, Photography, Painting-American, Archaeology, Costumes, Landscapes, Portraits, Posters, Dolls, Historical Material, Coins & Medals, Miniatures, Embroidery
Collections: Ceramics; glassware; furniture; important technical drawings from 1790-1815; New Jersey portraits, landscapes, prints & photographs; sculpture; silhouettes & miniatures; silver; toys; manuscripts; maps; New Jersey history artifacts

Publications: Exhib catalogs; Jersey Journeys; New Jersey History, biannual; New Jersey News, monthly newsletter
Activities: Classes for adults & children; gallery talks; individual paintings & original objects of art lent to established institutions; variable book traveling exhibs; originates traveling exhibs; mus shop sells books, original art, toys

L **Library,** 52 Park Pl, Newark, NJ 07102. Tel 973-596-8500; Fax 973-596-6957; Elec Mail library@jerseyhistory.org; Internet Home Page Address: www.jerseyhistory.org; *Pres & CEO* Sally Yerkovich; *Cur Educ* Claudia Ocello; *Dir Library* Chad Leinaweaver
Open Wed-Thurs & Sat Noon - 5 PM or by appt; No admis fee; Estab 1845 to preserve the history of NJ; Time changing galleries on historical NJ topics; Mem: 1000; $25, ann Apr meetings
Library Holdings: Audio Tapes 100; Book Volumes 65,000; Cassettes; Clipping Files; Exhibition Catalogs; Fiche 7800; Lantern Slides; Manuscripts; Maps 2000; Memorabilia; Original Art Works; Original Documents; Other Holdings Manuscript Material 2000 linear feet; Pamphlets 12,000; Periodical Subscriptions 300; Photographs 100,000; Prints; Reels 3500 reels of microfilm; Video Tapes 200
Special Subjects: Folk Art, Landscape Architecture, Decorative Arts, Illustration, Drawings, Etchings & Engravings, Historical Material, History of Art & Archaeology, Archaeology, Interior Design, American Indian Art, Anthropology, Afro-American Art, Marine Painting, Landscapes
Collections: Manuscript, Book and Special Collections
Publications: New Jersey History; No Easy Walk Summer-Fall 2004; Resourceful New Jersey 2004-2005
Activities: Classes for children; docent training; teacher workshops; teen parent prog; lect open to pub; gallery talks; tours; mus shop sells books & reproductions

L **NEW JERSEY INSTITUTE OF TECHNOLOGY,** Littman Architecture & Design Library, 323 Martin Luther King Blvd, Newark, NJ 07102-1982. Tel 973-642-4390 (reference); Fax 973-643-5601; Internet Home Page Address: archlib.njit.edu; *Dir* Maya Gervits; *Archit Librn* Susan O'Connor
Open Mon - Thurs 8 AM - 8:15 PM, Fri 8AM-5:45PM, Sat noon-5:45PM, Sun 1PM-6:45PM; No admis fee; Estab 1975 to serve the needs of the school of architecture; For lending & reference; Average Annual Attendance: 80,000
Income: Financed by univ
Purchases: $50,000
Library Holdings: Audio Tapes; Book Volumes 20,000; Cassettes; Clipping Files; Compact Disks; DVDs; Exhibition Catalogs; Filmstrips; Maps; Pamphlets; Periodical Subscriptions 80; Slides; Video Tapes
Special Subjects: Art History, Constructions, Landscape Architecture, Decorative Arts, Photography, Drawings, Graphic Design, Maps, History of Art & Archaeology, Industrial Design, Interior Design, Furniture, Drafting, Period Rooms, Restoration & Conservation, Architecture

M **NEWARK MUSEUM ASSOCIATION,** The Newark Museum, 49 Washington St, Newark, NJ 07102-3176. Tel 973-596-6550; Fax 973-642-0459; Internet Home Page Address: www.newarkmuseum.org; *Chmn Board of Trustees* Arlene Lieberman; *Dir* Mary Sue Sweeney Price; *Chief Oper Officer* Meme Omogbai; *Cur Decorative Arts* Ulysses G Dietz; *Cur Africa, Americas* Christa Clark; *Cur American Art* Mary Kate O'Hare; *Merchandise Mgr* Lorelei Rowars; *Dir Exhib* Tim Wintemberg; *Deputy Dir Develop* Peggy Dougherty; *Librn* William Peniston; *Deputy Dir Mktg* Mark Albin; *Dir Science* Ismael Calderon; *Cur Natural Science* Sule Oygur; *Deputy Dir Coll* Rebecca Buck; *Archivist* Jeffrey V Moy; *Cur Asian Arts* Katherine Anne Paul; *Cur American Art* Holly Connor
Open Wed - Sun Noon - 5 PM, cl Mon (except Dr Martin Luther King Jr Day & Presidents Day) & Tues, Christmas, New Year's Day, July 4 & Thanksgiving; Suggested: adults $10, children, seniors & students $6, mems free; Estab 1909 to exhibit articles of art, science & industry & for the study of the arts & sciences; Founded in 1909 in the Newark Pub Library, the bldg was a gift of Louis Bamber, opened in 1926, held in trust by the Newark Museum Assn for the City of Newark. The North and South Wings were acquired in 1937 and 1982. The renovation of the museum was designed by Michael Graves, reopened in 1989, and won the 1992 American Institute of Architects Honor Award. It contains 60,000 sq ft of gallery space, as well as educ facilities and a 300-seat auditorium. The Ballantine House, a 1885 historical mansion, designated a National Historical Landmark in 1985, showcases the decorative arts coll in 8 period rms and 6 thematic galleries; Average Annual Attendance: 500,000; Mem: 4750; dues $50 & up; ann meeting in Feb
Income: $12,000,000 (financed by city & state appropriations, county funds & pvt donations)
Collections: Africa, the Americas (including Pre-Columbian art), and the Pacific; American paintings and sculpture; Asian art, including Japanese, Korean, Chinese, Indian, and Tibetan; the decorative arts; the Classical cultures of Egypt, Greece and Rome, including the Eugene Schaefer Collection of ancient glass; numismatics; as well as the Alice and Leonard Dreyfus Planetarium, and the Natural Science Collection
Publications: Magazine, quarterly; catalogs on major exhibs; New Jersey Arts Annual
Activities: Extensive educ progs including classes for adults & children; docent training; lects open to pub; films; concerts; gallery talks; tours; competitions; exten dept serves community neighborhoods; individual paintings & original objects of art lent to other museums; mus shop sells catalogues, reproductions, prints, original craft items from around the world

M **Junior Museum,** 49 Washington St, Newark, NJ 07102-3176. Tel 973-596-6605; Fax 973-642-0459; Elec Mail juniormuseum@newarkmuseum.org; Internet Home Page Address: www.newarkmuseum.org/juniormuseum/; *Mgr Family Events* Rob Craig; *Jr Mus Supv* Lynette Diaz
Open Wed - Sun Noon - 5 PM; No admis fee; Estab 1926 to provide art & science progs designed to stimulate the individual child in self-discovery & exploration of the world & to teach effective use of the Mus as a whole, which may lead to valuable lifetime interests; Average Annual Attendance: 17,000; Mem: 3500 active; dues $10 lifetime mem; ann meeting in May
Income: Financed through the Newark Mus
Exhibitions: Changing exhibs of children's artwork; ann spring & summer exhibs in Junior Gallery
Activities: Weekday pre-school & after school; Saturday morning & summer workshops for ages 3-16; parents' workshops; community outreach & school enrichment progs; special events workshops & holiday festivals & hospital outreach; Junior Gallery offering a self-guided gallery game & art activity sessions, weekend Sept-June & weekdays in summer

L **NEWARK PUBLIC LIBRARY,** Reference, 5 Washington St, Newark, NJ 07102-3105; PO Box 630, Newark, NJ 07101-0630. Tel 973-733-7779, 733-7820, 733-7745; Fax 973-733-5648; Elec Mail reference@npl.org; Internet Home Page Address: www.npl.org; *Supvr* Leslie Kahn; *Supvr* James Capuano; *Prin Librn* Jane Seiden; *Prin Librn* Curt Idrogo; *Sr Librn* Monica Malinowski; *Librn* Elaine Kiernan Gold; *Librn* Nadine Sergejeff; *Dir* Wilma Grey
Open Sept - June Tues - Thurs 9 AM - 8:30 PM, Mon, Fri & Sat 9 AM - 5:30 PM, July - Aug Mon, Tues, Thurs & Fri 9 AM - 5:30 PM, Wed 9 AM - 8:30 PM, Sat 9:30 AM - 1:30 PM; Estab 1888, provides information on all of the visual arts to the NJ Library Network & pub; Maintains an art gallery: a total of 300 running ft
Income: Financed by city & state appropriations, endowment & gift funds
Library Holdings: Auction Catalogs; Book Volumes 75,000; CD-ROMs; Clipping Files; Exhibition Catalogs; Manuscripts 200; Original Art Works 23,000; Other Holdings Picture Collection; Periodical Subscriptions 40; Prints 20,000
Special Subjects: Art History, Decorative Arts, Illustration, Calligraphy, Drawings, Etchings & Engravings, Graphic Arts, Manuscripts, Ceramics, Crafts, Latin American Art, Cartoons, Fashion Arts, Interior Design, Lettering, Furniture, Glass, Afro-American Art, Bookplates & Bindings, Architecture
Collections: Original Prints (22,000); Historic Posters (5,000); The Richard C Jenkinson Coll of Printing History (2,300); The Wilbur Macy Stone Coll of Historic Books for Children (1,200); Illustrated Book Coll (2,800); Autographs (1,000); The McEwen Christmas Coll (900); Artists Book Coll (600); Pop-Up Book Coll (600); The Rabin & Kreuger Archives (250 folders); Shopping Bags (1,100); Historic Greeting Cards (800)
Exhibitions: Movable Books: A Paradise of Pop-Ups, A Feast of Fold Outs & a Mix of Mechanicals; Prints by Joseph Pennell; Posters & Prints from Puerto Rico, 1950-1990; 20th Century American Illustrations; A Potpourri of Pop (Pop art prints & pop-up books); Over There...1917-1918, A Victory Salute to the USA in World War I; The Essential Calendar: The Art & Design of Calendars; Prints & Posters of the Circus and Vintage Greeting Cards; Travel Posters & Memorable Works on Paper from Africa, China, India & Taiwan; Where, When and Who Took That Photograph?; Nostalgic and Unforgettable Travel Posters from the 20th Century; Robert Sabuda: Travels in Time & Space via Pop-Up Books; Original Prints by African-American Artists; John Cotton Dana: Innovative Librn, Civic Leader, Mus Founder; A Salute to Two Great 20th Century Artists: Picasso & Lichtenstein in prints, posters and rare books; A Contemporary & Historic Survey of Shopping Bags
Activities: Tours; gallery talks; originate traveling exhibs to art institutions

C **PRUDENTIAL ART PROGRAM,** 100 Mulberry St, Gateway Center 2-17th Flr Newark, NJ 07102-4056. Tel 973-367-7151; *Mgr* Carol Skuratofsky
Estab 1969 to enhance the surroundings & living up to social responsibility in supporting art as a genuinely important part of life
Collections: Approx 12,000 holdings of paintings, sculptures & unique works on paper; 2558 signed graphics; 1182 posters; 241 billboards; 200 photographs

NORTH PLAINFIELD

M **FLEETWOOD MUSEUM,** 614 Greenbrook Rd, North Plainfield, NJ 07063-1621; 135 Sandford Ave, North Plainfield, NJ 07060. Tel 908-756-7810; Elec Mail naciampa@aol.com; Internet Home Page Address: www.fleetwoodmuseum.org; *Head Cur* Ms Sara Parmigiani; *Cur Emeritus* Mr George E. Helmke
Open Sat 10AM-4PM; cl major holidays; No admis fee; Estb 1985 ro promote interest in art, science & techniques of photo imaging; Average Annual Attendance: 1800
Income: $3,500; financed by Fleetwood Fond of Plainfield Foundation
Library Holdings: Book Volumes 800; Original Art Works 20; Photographs 500
Collections: over 800 cameras; oil paintings; art & science of photography
Activities: Concerts

OCEAN CITY

A **OCEAN CITY ART CENTER,** 1735 Simpson Ave, Ocean City, NJ 08226-3070. Tel 609-399-7628; Fax 609-399-7089; Elec Mail info@oceancityartscenter.org; Internet Home Page Address: www.pceamcityartcenter.org; *Bd Pres* Jack Devine; *Exec Dir* Lorraine Hansen
Open Mon - Fri 9 AM - 9 PM, Sat 9 AM - 4 PM, Sun by appointment only; Estab 1967 to promote the arts; Teaching studios & a gallery for monthly changing exhibs throughout the yr; Average Annual Attendance: 10,000; Mem: 1200; dues individual $15, family $30; ann meeting in Feb; Scholarships
Income: $70,000 (financed by mem, city appropriation, New Jersey State Council on the Arts Grant 1981)
Collections: Paintings
Exhibitions: Annual Membership Show, Juried Show, Boardwalk Art Show Winners Exhib, Christmas Crafts Fair, Juried Photog Show, Craft Show
Publications: Newsletters, quarterly
Activities: Classes for adults & children; lects open to pub, 12 vis lectrs per yr; concerts; competitions with awards; mus shop sells books, original art & crafts

OCEANVILLE

M **THE NOYES MUSEUM OF ART,** 733 Lily Lake Rd, Oceanville, NJ 08231. Tel 609-652-8848; Fax 609-652-6166; Elec Mail info@noyesmuseum.org; Internet Home Page Address: www.noyesmuseum.org; *Exec Dir* Michael Cagno
Open Tues - Sat 10 AM - 4:30 PM, Sun Noon - 5 PM; Admis adults $4, seniors 65 and over & students $3, children 6 & under free; Estab 1983; Average Annual Attendance: 17,000; Mem: 500+; 8 different member levels
Special Subjects: Painting-American, Sculpture, Crafts, Folk Art

Collections: Contemporary American Art; crafts, folk art
Exhibitions: 12 to 14 rotating exhibitions each yr by national, regional and local artists
Publications: Exhibition catalogues, quarterly newsletter
Activities: Classes for adults & children; docent training; concerts; gallery talks; tours; sponsoring of competitions; scholarships; student photography awards annually; lend original objects of art; mus shop sells books, original art, reproductions, prints & jewelry

ORADELL

M **BLAUVELT DEMAREST FOUNDATION,** Hiram Blauvelt Art Museum, 705 Kinderkamack Rd, Oradell, NJ 07649-1504. Tel 201-261-0012; Fax 201-391-6418; Elec Mail maja218@verizon.net; Internet Home Page Address: www.blauveltartmuseum.com; *Dir* Marijane Singer, PhD; *Dir Educ* Rosa Lara; *Mus Asst* Diane Rivera
Open Wed - Fri 10 AM - 4 PM, Sat & Sun 2 - 5 PM; No admis fee; Estab 1950; 1893 shingle & turret-style Queen Anne carriage house; Average Annual Attendance: 13,224; Mem: ann meeting in June
Library Holdings: Book Volumes; Compact Disks; Exhibition Catalogs; Original Art Works; Prints; Sculpture; Video Tapes
Special Subjects: Drawings, Painting-American, Photography, Prints, Sculpture, Watercolors, American Western Art, Bronzes, African Art, Southwestern Art, Woodcarvings, Painting-European, Portraits, Eskimo Art, Painting-Canadian, Painting-British, Ivory, Scrimshaw, Dioramas, Painting-Scandinavian
Collections: Audubon folio; Big Game Species; Extinct Birds; Ivory Collection; Master & Contemporary Wildlife & Animal Art Paintings & Sculptures; Animal Art & Wildlife Art
Exhibitions: Art works by Guy Coheleach, Charles Allmond, Mary Taylor, Dwayne Harty, Charles Livingston Bull; The Art of Conservation
Publications: Charles Livingston Bull Catalog; Art & the Animal I; Art & the Animal II
Activities: Classes for adults & children; docent training; lect open to pub; gallery talks; tours; ann Purchase Award - Soc Animal Artists; Artists for Conservation - Blauvelt Purchase Award, Ann Mem of society or animal artist; mus shop sells books, magazines, original art, reproductions, prints & videos

PALISADES PARK

L **PALISADES PARK PUBLIC LIBRARY,** 257 Second St, Palisades Park, NJ 07650. Tel 201-585-4150; Fax 201-585-2151; Elec Mail kumar@bccls.org; Internet Home Page Address: www.bccls.org/palisadespark; *Children's Librn* Steven Cavallo; *Dir* Terrie L McColl
Open Mon - Thurs 10:30 AM - 9 PM, Fri 10:30 AM - 5 PM; Estab 1909; Maintains a community room used for exhibits
Library Holdings: Book Volumes 40,000; Cassettes; Periodical Subscriptions 75; Video Tapes

PARAMUS

M **BUEHLER CHALLENGER & SCIENCE CENTER,** 305 N State Rte 17, Paramus, NJ 07653; PO Box 647, Paramus, NJ 07653-0647. Tel 201-262-0984; Fax 201-251-9049; Elec Mail missionservices@bcsc.org (Coordr); Internet Home Page Address: www.bcsc.org; *Mission Coordr* Peggy Silverman
Call for hours & further information; Created in 1994 by the Emil Buehler Trust as the 21st center in the Challenger Learning Center network; Dedicated to inspiring students, educators and the community in the pursuit of scientific educ. Mus is child org of the Challenger Center for Space Science Educ, founded in 1986 by the families of the Challenger 51-L astronauts
Activities: Progs & Outreach progs; tours; Mission Simulations; Space Camp; Astro Camp; Family Science Morning

PARSIPPANY

A **NEW JERSEY WATERCOLOR SOCIETY,** 55 Richard St, Parsippany, NJ 07054; 83 Clifford Dr, Wayne, NJ 07470-3501. Tel 873-887-5860; Internet Home Page Address: www.njwcs.org; *Pres* Ken Hamilton; *Treas* Jack O'Reilly
Estab 1938 to bring to the pub the best in NJ watercolorists - teachers; Mem: 135; dues $25; open to exhibitors in the Annual Open Exhib whose work conforms to standards of the Soc & are legal residents of the State of NJ
Exhibitions: Annual Mems Show in spring; Annual Open Statewide Juried Exhib in fall - alternating between the Ridgewood Art Institute & the Monmouth Museum, Lincroft, NJ
Publications: Illustrated catalogue; newsletter, 3 per yr
Activities: Classes for adults & children; workshops; lect open to pub, 2-4 vis lectrs per yr; competitions with awards; ann dinner; reception for Open & Mems Shows

PATERSON

M **PASSAIC COUNTY COMMUNITY COLLEGE,** Broadway, LRC, and Hamilton Club Galleries, One College Blvd, Paterson, NJ 07505-1179. Tel 973-684-6555; Fax 973-523-6085; Elec Mail jhaw@pccc.edu; Internet Home Page Address: www.pccc.edu/culturalaffairs; *Young People's Theatre Coordr* Susan Amsterdam; *Exec Dir Cultural Affairs* Maria Mazziotti Gillan; *Gallery Cur* Jane Haw; *Outreach Coordr* Ashley Kesling; *Sec* Smita Desai
Open Mon - Fri 9 AM - 9 PM, Sat 9 AM - 5 PM; No admis fee; Changing exhibits of contemporary art & permanent colls of 19th & early 20th century paintings & sculpture & contemporary art
Special Subjects: Painting-American, Prints, Period Rooms, Painting-British, Painting-European, Painting-French, Watercolors, Painting-Flemish, Painting-German, Painting-Scandinavian

Collections: Hamilton Club Art Collections; Federici Studio Collection: sculpture; Contemporary Art Collection
Exhibitions: Monthly & bimonthly exhibits of local & tri-state artists. Works are mostly 2-D; paintings, drawings, mixed media, silkscreens, woodblock prints, photography, textile & some ceramics
Publications: The Hamilton Art Collection; Passaic County Community College Contemporary Art Collections
Activities: Workshops; lects open to pub; gallery talks; tours

M **PASSAIC COUNTY HISTORICAL SOCIETY,** Lambert Castle Museum & Library, 3 Valley Rd, Lambert Castle Paterson, NJ 07503-2932. Tel 973-247-0085; Fax 973-881-9434; Elec Mail lambertcastle@verizon.net; Internet Home Page Address: www.lambertcastle.org; *Pres* Lorraine Yurchak; *VPres* Geraldine Mola; *VPres* Philip Jaeger; *Dir* Alison Faubert
Open Wed - Sun 1 - 4 PM, July-Aug Sat-Sun noon-4PM; Admis adults $5, seniors $4, children 5-17 $3, under 5 free; group tours of 10 or more call for reservation; Estab 1926; Located in Lambert Castle built in 1892; Average Annual Attendance: 25,000; Mem: Dues sustaining $50, family $35, individual $25, seniors $20, student $10, benefactor $100, Patron $2500, organization-bus $75
Income: Financed by donations, gifts, grants, mem dues
Library Holdings: Book Volumes; CD-ROMs; Micro Print; Original Documents; Photographs
Special Subjects: Photography, Textiles, Painting-American, Prints, Watercolors, Costumes, Folk Art, Landscapes, Decorative Arts, Manuscripts, Portraits, Furniture, Historical Material, Maps, Period Rooms, Painting-Italian
Collections: Koempel Spoon Collection; local historical material; paintings
Publications: Historic Passaic County, bimonthly newsletter; pamphlets; exhib catalogues
Activities: Classes for children; lect open to pub, 4-6 vis lectrs per yr; gallery talks; tours; individual paintings & original objects of art lent to qualified museums by written request; mus shop sells books, reproductions, prints, publs, postcards, souvenirs & gifts

PLAINFIELD

L **PLAINFIELD PUBLIC LIBRARY,** 800 Park Ave, Plainfield, NJ 07060-2517. Tel 908-757-1111; Fax 908-754-0063; Internet Home Page Address: www.plainfieldlibrary.info; *Dir* Joseph H Da Rold
Open Mon - Thurs 9 AM - 9 PM, Fri & Sat 9 AM - 5 PM, cl Sun; No admis fee; Estab 1881; Maintains an art gallery with original artworks on permanent display, group shows as scheduled; Average Annual Attendance: 200,000
Income: Financed by endowment & city appropriation
Library Holdings: DVDs 2000; Maps; Original Art Works; Other Holdings Blueprints; Photographs 110000
Special Subjects: Photography, Painting-American, Historical Material, Ceramics, Porcelain
Collections: Winslow Homer Collection; John Carlson; Alonzo Adams; Riva Helfond; Cloisonne Collection; Selections from permanent collection may be viewed at www.plfdpl.info
Activities: Gallery talks

PRINCETON

M **MORVEN MUSEUM & GARDEN,** 55 Stockton St, Princeton, NJ 08540-6812. Tel 609-924-8144; Fax 609-924-8331; Elec Mail info@morven.org; Internet Home Page Address: www.morven.org; *Dir* Clare M Smith; *Cur Colls & Exhibits* Elizabeth Allan
Open Wed, Thurs, Fri 11 AM - 3 PM, Sat & Sun Noon - 4 PM; Admis adults $5, seniors & students $4; Built c1758 by Richard Stockton, a signer of the Declaration of Independence & later the residence of NJ Governors; tours & exhibs highlight Stockton Family & architectural preservation
Income: Program of the NJ State Mus; financed by gifts, grants & benefits
Special Subjects: Decorative Arts, Historical Material, Painting-American, Period Rooms
Collections: Material culture relating to the house

M **PRINCETON UNIVERSITY,** Princeton University Art Museum, Princeton, NJ 08544-1018. Tel 609-258-3788; Fax 609-258-3610; Elec Mail artmuseum@princeton.edu; Internet Home Page Address: artmuseum.princeton.edu; *Dir* James Steward; *Assoc Dir Educ* Caroline Harris; *Assoc Dir Finance & Opers* Karen Ohland; *Assoc Dir Information & Technology* Janet Strohl-Morgan; *Assoc Dir Institutional Advancement* Nancy Stout; *Assoc Dir Publishing & Communs* Curtis Scott; *Research Cur European Painting & Sculpture* Betsy J Rosasco; *Cur American Art* Karl Kusserow; *Cur & Lectr Art of Ancient Americas* Bryan Just; *Cur Ancient Art* J Michael Padgett; *Cur Asian Art* Cary Liu; *Haskell Cur Modern & Contemporary Art* Kelly Baum; *Cur Prints & Drawings* Laura Giles; *Assoc Cur Prints & Drawings* Calvin Brown; *Assoc Dir Colls & Exhibs* Bart Thurber; *Peter C. Bumell Cur Photog* Kate Bussard; *Asst Cur Asian Art* Zoe Kwok
Open Tues, Wed, Fri, Sat 10 AM - 5 PM, Thurs 10 AM - 10 PM, Sun 1 - 5 PM; No admis fee; Estab 1882; one of the nation's leading art mus, with coll of some 72,000 works ranging from ancient to contemporary, concentrating on Europe, the Mediterranean, Asia & the Americas. Works to advance Princeton's teaching mission while serving the local, national & international communities through coll, exhib, educ & social activities; About 65,600 sq ft of gallery space for permanent, semi-permanent & changing installations; Average Annual Attendance: 120,000; Mem: 1,000; dues $75 & up
Income: Financed by endowment, univ & by government, corporate & pvt sources
Special Subjects: American Indian Art, Archaeology, Decorative Arts, Drawings, Etchings & Engravings, Folk Art, Landscapes, Marine Painting, Ceramics, Collages, Glass, Metalwork, American Western Art, Antiquities-Assyrian, Furniture, Gold, Photography, Porcelain, Portraits, Pottery, Pre-Columbian Art, Painting-American, Prints, Silver, Painting-British, Painting-European, Painting-French, Painting-Japanese, Graphics, Hispanic Art, Latin American Art,

Sculpture, Watercolors, African Art, Religious Art, Primitive art, Woodcarvings, Posters, Jade, Jewelry, Oriental Art, Asian Art, Antiquities-Byzantine, Painting-Dutch, Ivory, Scrimshaw, Baroque Art, Calligraphy, Miniatures, Painting-Flemish, Renaissance Art, Medieval Art, Antiquities-Oriental, Painting-Spanish, Painting-Italian, Antiquities-Persian, Islamic Art, Antiquities-Egyptian, Antiquities-Greek, Mosaics, Stained Glass, Painting-German, Antiquities-Etruscan, Painting-Russian, Painting-Scandinavian
Collections: Art of the Ancient Americas; African Art; American Art; Ancient & Islamic Art; Asian Art; Campus Coll; Contemporary Art; European Art; Modern Art; Prints & Drawings; Photography
Publications: Catalogs, occasionally; Record of the Art Museum, annually; magazine, quarterly
Activities: Classes for adults & children; docent training; lects open to pub; concerts; gallery talks; tours; exten prog serves Trenton, NJ schools & mus around the globe; book traveling exhibs, 2-4 per yr; originates traveling exhibs to interested & selected museums; mus store sells books, reproductions, prints, cards, jewelry, apparel, unique works of art, home decor

L **Index of Christian Art,** A Level McCormick Hall, Dept of Art & Archaeology Princeton, NJ 08544-1018. Tel 609-258-3773; Fax 609-258-0103; Elec Mail cph@princeton.edu; Internet Home Page Address: www.ica.princeton.edu; *Dir* Colum Hourihane
Open Mon - Fri 9 AM - 5 PM, cl holidays; No admis fee; Estab 1917 as a division of the Department of Art & Archaeology. It is a research & reference coll of cards & photographs designed to facilitate the study of Christian iconography in works of art before 1400. Duplicate copies exist in Washington, DC in the Dumbarton Oaks Research Center & in Los Angeles in the Getty Research Institute. European copies are in Rome in the Vatican Library & in Utrecht in the Univ; electronic access to files now available on a subscription basis
Library Holdings: Book Volumes; Cards; Exhibition Catalogs; Manuscripts; Photographs; Slides
Special Subjects: Art History
Publications: Studies in Iconography
Activities: Educ prog; lect open to pub, 3-4 vis lectrs per yr; sponsoring of competitions; schols offered

L **Marquand Library of Art & Archaeology,** McCormick Hall, Princeton, NJ 08544-0001; One Washington Rd, Princeton, NJ 08544. Tel 609-258-3783; Fax 609-258-7650; Elec Mail marquand@princeton.edu; Internet Home Page Address: marquand.princeton.edu/; *Asst Librn* Rebecca K Friedman; *Librn* Sandra Ludig Brooke; *Western Bibliographer* Nicola Shilliam; *Chinese Art Specialist* Kimberly Wishart; *Japanese Art Specialist* Nicole Fabricand-Person
open to pub for a fee; access for researchers; see: library.princeton.edu/services/privileges; Estab 1908 to serve study & research needs of the students & faculty of Princeton Univ in the History of Art, Architecture & Archaeology; Circ 24,000 (internal only); Adjacent to the art museum; Average Annual Attendance: 150,000
Income: Financed by endowments & gen univ funds
Library Holdings: Auction Catalogs; Book Volumes 450,000; CD-ROMs; DVDs; Exhibition Catalogs; Fiche; Manuscripts; Periodical Subscriptions 600; Reels
Special Subjects: Art History, Folk Art, Landscape Architecture, Decorative Arts, Photography, Calligraphy, Etchings & Engravings, Islamic Art, Manuscripts, Painting-American, Painting-British, Painting-Dutch, Painting-Flemish, Painting-French, Painting-German, Painting-Italian, Painting-Japanese, Painting-Russian, Painting-Spanish, Posters, Pre-Columbian Art, Sculpture, Painting-European, Historical Material, History of Art & Archaeology, Portraits, Ceramics, Latin American Art, Archaeology, American Western Art, Bronzes, Printmaking, Fashion Arts, Asian Art, Video, American Indian Art, Primitive art, Furniture, Mexican Art, Glass, Painting-Polish, Aesthetics, Afro-American Art, Antiquities-Oriental, Antiquities-Persian, Carpets & Rugs, Oriental Art, Pottery, Religious Art, Restoration & Conservation, Silver, Tapestries, Textiles, Woodcuts, Antiquities-Assyrian, Antiquities-Byzantine, Antiquities-Egyptian, Antiquities-Etruscan, Antiquities-Greek, Antiquities-Roman, Painting-Scandinavian, Painting-Australian, Painting-Canadian, Painting-New Zealand, Architecture

RINGWOOD

M **RINGWOOD MANOR HOUSE MUSEUM,** 1304 Sloatsburg Rd, Ringwood, NJ 07456-1706. Tel 973-962-2240; Fax 973-962-2247; Elec Mail rspris@verizon.net; Internet Home Page Address: www.ringwoodmanor.com/index.html; *Historic Site Admin* Sue Shutte; *Supt* Eric Pain
Open Wed-Sun 10-AM-3PM, cl all holidays except, Memorial Day, Independence Day & Labor Day; Adults $3, children 6-12 $1, children under 6 no charge; Estab 1935; Average Annual Attendance: 35,000
Income: Financed by state appropriation & funds raised by pvt organization-sponsored spec events
Special Subjects: Decorative Arts, Historical Material, Restorations
Collections: Decorative arts; firearms; furniture; graphics; historical material; New Jersey iron making history; paintings
Activities: Docent training; guided tours; spec events; sales shop sells books, magazines, reproductions & prints

RIVER EDGE

M **BERGEN COUNTY HISTORICAL SOCIETY,** Steuben House Museum, 1209 Main St, River Edge, NJ 07661-2026; PO Box 55, River Edge, NJ 07661-0055. Tel 201-343-9492, 487-1739 (museum); Fax 201-498-1696; *Cur* Matt Gebhardt; *Mus Shop Mgr* Marie Ruggerio; *VPres* John Herrernan; *VPres* Todd Braisted; *Secy* Janet Odence
Buildings open for special events; Grounds open daily, dawn - dusk; No admis fee; Estab 1902 to collect & preserve historical items of Bergen County; Maintains reference library; Average Annual Attendance: 10,000; Mem: 300; dues $15; ann meeting in June
Income: Financed by mem, grants & corporate support
Collections: Collection of artifacts of the Bergen Dutch 1680-1914; Campbell Christie House (restored 18th century tavern)
Publications: In Bergen's Attic, quarterly newsletter

Activities: Classes for children; docent progs; lect open to pub, 8 vis lectrs per yr; concerts; gallery talks; mus shop sells books & reproductions

SOUTH ORANGE

M **SETON HALL UNIVERSITY,** 400 S Orange Ave, South Orange, NJ 07079-2697. Tel 973-761-9459; Fax 973-275-2368; Internet Home Page Address: www.shu.edu; *Dir* Charlotte Nichols
Open Mon - Fri 10 AM - 5 PM; No admis fee; Estab 1963. Troast Memorial Gallery, estab 1974, houses permanent coll of contemporary American art; Wang Fang-Yu Collection of Oriental art was estab in 1977; Average Annual Attendance: 35,000
Collections: Archaeology Colls
Activities: Lect open to pub; gallery talks

M **Walsh Gallery & Library,** 400 S Orange Ave, South Orange, NJ 07079. Tel 973-275-2033; Fax 973-761-9550; Elec Mail brasilje@shu.edu; Internet Home Page Address: library.shu.edu/gallery; *Assoc Dean* Paul Chao; *Art Librn* Beth Bloom; *Dean* Dr Howard McGinn; *Gallery Dir* Jeanne Brasile
Open Mon - Fri 10:30 AM - 4:30 PM; call to confirm; Estab 1994; 2100 sq ft gallery offers interdisciplinary exhibitions, 6-8 exhibs per yr
Library Holdings: Book Volumes 500,000; Clipping Files; Exhibition Catalogs; Original Art Works; Slides 12,000
Special Subjects: Painting-American, Prints, Textiles, Sculpture, Watercolors, Religious Art, Reproductions
Collections: Paintings; photographs; sculpture
Activities: Classes for adults & children; poetry readings; film screenings; lects open to pub; 1-5 vis lets per yr; gallery talks; tours; symposia; panel discussions; lending of original art to qualified lenders

SPRINGFIELD

L **SPRINGFIELD FREE PUBLIC LIBRARY,** Donald B Palmer Museum, 66 Mountain Ave, Springfield, NJ 07081-1786. Tel 973-376-4930; Fax 973-376-1334; Elec Mail questions@sfplnj.org; Internet Home Page Address: www.sfplnj.org/joomla; *Head Technical Servs* Jenna Weiss; *Head Reference Dept* Susan Tegge; *Head Circulation Dept* Karen Gallini; *Dir* Susan Permahos
Open Mon, Wed, Thurs 10 AM - 9 PM, Tues, Fri, & Sat 10 AM - 5 PM, Sun 1 - 4 PM; open Sat July & Aug 10 AM - 1 PM; cl Sun June 1 - Sept 30; No admis fee; Estab 1975 as a mus addition to a pub library established to preserve local history; The library, including a meeting room, serves as a cultural center for exhibits, concerts & lectures; Average Annual Attendance: 113,000; Mem: 11,500
Collections: Permanent coll colonial historical artifacts & other ephemera; Changing art exhibits incl painting, photography, sculpture, etc. Artists submit application to display
Activities: Dramatic progs; 20 vis lectrs; concerts; gallery talks; films; puppet shows; lending coll contains books, photographs, slides, periodicals, videos, DVDs & compact disks; mus shop sells original art by exhibiting artists

STOCKHOLM

A **OIL PASTEL ASSOCIATION,** PO Box 374, Stockholm, NJ 07460-0374. Tel 845-353-2483; Fax 845-358-3821; *Pres* John Elliott; *Exec Dir* Dorothy Coleman
Estab 1983 exhib forum for new & traditional types of pastel paintings; Average Annual Attendance: 2,000; Mem: 350; dues $25 per yr
Income: $4,000 (financed by donations & mem)
Exhibitions: Oil pastels; soft pastels; water-soluble pastels
Publications: Art & Artists, USA
Activities: Classes for adults; workshops; schols offered

SUMMIT

A **VISUAL ARTS CENTER OF NEW JERSEY,** 68 Elm St, Summit, NJ 07901-3472. Tel 908-273-9121; Fax 908-273-1457; Elec Mail info@artcenternj.org; Internet Home Page Address: www.artcenternj.org; *Exec Dir* Marion Grzesiak; *Dir Opers* Ernie Palatucci; *Dir Progs & Communs* Mari D'Alessandro; *Dir Devel* Nancy Shannon; *Cur* Mary Birmingham
Gallery Open Mon - Fri 10 AM - 5 PM (includes hours for exhibs & for classes), Sat - Sun 9 AM - 4 PM; Estab 1933 to educate through gallery exhib & classroom instruction for diverse audience in contemporary arts; Three gallery spaces, containing 5000 ft of exhib space, specializing in contemporary art. Outdoor sculpture park.; Average Annual Attendance: 60,000; Mem: 1300; Individual $50, Dual/Family $75, Friend $125, Contributor $250, Supporter $500, Benefactor $1,000
Income: Membership grant tui (classes), fundraising
Exhibitions: Nine annual exhibs of contemporary visual art
Publications: Exhibition catalogs
Activities: Classes for adults & children; docent training; summer camp for children & teens; lects open to pub & mems; 10 vis lectrs per yr; gallery talks; tours; members show; dept serves outreach progs

TRENTON

A **ARTWORKS, THE VISUAL ART SCHOOL OF TRENTON,** 19 Everett Alley, Trenton, NJ 08611. Tel 609-394-9436; Fax 609-394-9551; Elec Mail mccc@artworksnj.org; Internet Home Page Address: www.artsworksnj.org; *Pres* Robert Rose; *Dir* Tricia Fagan
Open Mon, Tues, Wed 5:30 PM - 9:30 PM, Sat 9 AM - 11 PM; No admis fee; Estab 1964 to establish & maintain educ & cultural progs devoted to visual arts; Skylit gallery, 2,000 sq ft, in downtown Trenton; Average Annual Attendance: 7,500; Mem: 1,000; dues $40 - $100; ann meeting in May
Income: Financed by friends, class fees, workshops & demonstration fees, trip fees, entry fees, grants, corporate & pvt contributions

Exhibitions: Exhibitions are held at the Trenton Gallery & at various locations throughout the community
Publications: The Artworks Reader, quarterly
Activities: Classes for adults & children; lect open to pub, 3-10 vis lectrs per yr; tours; competitions with awards; schols offered
L   **Library,** 19 Everett Alley, Trenton, NJ 08611. Tel 609-394-9436; Fax 609-394-9551; Elec Mail mccc@artworksnj.org; Internet Home Page Address: www.artworksnj.org; *Pres* Robert Rose; *Dir* Tricia Fagan
Open Mon, Tues, Wed 5:30 PM - 9:30 PM, Sat 9 AM - 1 PM; Estab 1964, to serve local artists and children and adults in the community; Reference library
Library Holdings: Book Volumes 200; Slides

M   **NEW JERSEY STATE MUSEUM,** Fine Art Bureau, 205 W State St, Trenton, NJ 08608-1001; PO Box 530, Trenton, NJ 08625-0530. Tel 609-292-5420; Fax 609-292-7636; Elec Mail margaret.oreilly@sos.state.nj.us; Internet Home Page Address: www.statemuseum.nj.gov; *Cur Fine Art* Margaret M O'Reilly; *Exec Dir* Anthony Gardner; *Fine Art & Cultural History Registrar* Jenny Martin-Wicoff
Open Tues 9 AM - 4:45 PM, cl Mon & all state holidays; Admis $5 suggested admis, children 12 & under & mems free; Estab 1895 by legislation to collect, exhibit & interpret fine arts, cultural history, archaeology-ethnography & natural history; changing exhibit galleries, fine art & NJ history galleries; planetarium; Average Annual Attendance: 120,000; Mem: 1,000; dues $40 & up; ann meeting in June
Income: $2,000,000 (financed by state appropriation)
Library Holdings: Book Volumes 3000+; Exhibition Catalogs
Special Subjects: Afro-American Art, Anthropology, Drawings, Etchings & Engravings, Folk Art, Historical Material, Landscapes, Ceramics, Collages, Glass, Metalwork, Flasks & Bottles, Furniture, Photography, Porcelain, Painting-American, Prints, Woodcuts, Maps, Sculpture, Graphics, Watercolors, Archaeology, Ethnology, Textiles, Costumes, Crafts, Pottery, Woodcarvings, Decorative Arts, Portraits, Posters, Silver, Ivory, Scrimshaw, Dioramas, Embroidery, Mosaics, Stained Glass, Pewter, Leather
Collections: American fine & decorative arts of the 19th, 20th & 21st centuries; American painting with spec emphasis on the Stieglitz Circle, Regionalist, Abstract Artists; NJ fine & decorative arts; Ben Shahn's graphic work; art by African-Americans; NJ History; Archaeology & Ethnography, Natural History
Exhibitions: Changing exhibs focus on American artists, NJ material culture, science, archaeology; long-term exhib galleries on the fine art, NJ history & archaeology
Publications: Annual report (on line); catalogs & irregular serials
Activities: Classes for adults & children; dramatic progs; docent training; lect open to pub; lect for mems; vis lectrs per yr varies; concerts; gallery talks; tours; individual objects, artifacts & specimens lent to other qualified institutions; book traveling exhibs; mus shop sells books

M   **OLD BARRACKS MUSEUM,** Barrack St, Trenton, NJ 08608. Tel 609-396-1776; Fax 609-777-4000; Elec Mail barracks@voicenet.com; Internet Home Page Address: www.barracks.org; *Chief Historical Interpreter* Gloria Bell; *Dir* Richard Patterson; *Cur* Vivian Lea Stevens; *Office Mgr* Carolyn Cudnik; *Tour Coordr* Linda Mathies; *Develop Coordr* Cathleen Crown
Open daily 10 AM - 5 PM; Admis adults $8, seniors & students $6, children under 6 free; Built 1758, estab 1902 as mus of history & decorative arts; Located in English barracks that housed Hessian Soldiers Dec 1776 & served as American Military hospital during Revolutionary War; Average Annual Attendance: 30,000; Mem: 460; dues $30, $40, $60 $125 & $200; ann meeting Sep
Income: Financed by mem, state appropriation & donations
Special Subjects: Decorative Arts, Historical Material, Period Rooms
Collections: American decorative arts 1750-1820; archaeological materials; early American tools & household equipment; military artifacts; 19th century New Jersey portraits; patriotic paintings & prints
Publications: The Barracks Parade, quarterly newsletter; The Barracks of Trenton & Princeton, book
Activities: Classes for children; dramatic progs; docent training; lects open to pub, 3 vis lectrs per yr; tours; exten dept serves elementary schools; individual paintings & original objects of art lent to mus; lending collection contains slides & reproduction military objects/costumes; book traveling exhibs; mus shop sells books, reproductions, prints, slides, historical toys & ceramics

M   **TRENTON CITY MUSEUM,** 319 E State St, Trenton, NJ 08608-1809. Tel 609-989-3632; Fax 609-989-3624; Elec Mail bhill@ellarslie.org; Internet Home Page Address: www.ellarslie.org; *Dir & Cur* Brian O Hill; *Mus Shop Mgr* Mary Kay Girmschied; *Pres* Stephanie Morgano
Open Tues - Sat 11 AM - 3 PM, Sun 1 - 4 PM; No admis fee; Estab 1973 to provide a cultural window into the ongoing life of the city & its people; Mus is a historical site, an Italian Revival mansion; only remaining example of John Notman architecture in Trenton & is located in historic Cadwalader Park, designed by Frederick Law Olmstead; Average Annual Attendance: 13,000; Mem: Dues $25 - $1,000
Income: Financed by mem & city appropriation
Special Subjects: Ceramics, Porcelain
Collections: Trenton-made Ceramics; objects made in or pertaining to Trenton; full set of Trenton directories
Exhibitions: Ellarslie Open XXIII
Publications: Biannual newsletter
Activities: Classes for adults & children accompany changing exhibits; lect open to pub, 10 vis lectrs per yr; sales shop sells books, prints, original art, jewelry & toys for children

UNION

M   **KEAN UNIVERSITY,** James Howe Gallery, 1000 Morris Ave, Kean University Art Galleries Center for Academic Success Union, NJ 07083-7131. Tel 908-527-2307, 527-2347; Internet Home Page Address: www.library.kean.edu; *Pres* Ronald Applebaun; *Dir Gallery* Alec Nicolescu; *Dir Gallery* Neil Tetkowski
Open Mon - Thurs 11 AM - 3 PM, 5 - 7 PM, Fri 11 AM -2PM, by appointment at other times; No admis fee; Estab 1971 as a forum to present all art forms to

students & the community through original exhibitions, catalogues, fine art, by guest cur, art history & mus training students; One gallery 22 x 34 ft plus an alcove 8 x 18 ft on first floor of arts & humanities building; Average Annual Attendance: 3,000
Income: Financed by state appropriation & private grants
Special Subjects: Painting-American
Collections: American painting, prints sculpture by Audobon, L Baskin, Robert Cooke, Max Ernst, Lamar Dodd, W Homer, P Jenkins, J Stella, Tony Smith, Walter Darbby Bannard, Werner Drewes, B J O Norfeldt, James Rosenquist, Robert Rauschenberg, Odilon Redon; photographs, rare books & 1935-50 design & furniture; Ben Yamimoto Art Work
Exhibitions: Rotating exhibits
Publications: Catalogues for exhibitions
Activities: Dramatic progs; lects open to pub; individual paintings lent to colleges, institutions, corporations & departments on the campus
L   **Nancy Thompson Library,** 1000 Morris Ave, Union, NJ 07083-7133. Tel 908-737-4618; Fax 908-527-2365; Elec Mail library@turbo.kean.edu; Internet Home Page Address: www.library.kean.edu; *Dir Library Svcs* Barbara Simpson; *Univ Librn* Luis Rodriguez
Open Mon - Thurs 8 AM - 12 AM, Fri 8 AM - 5 PM, Sat 9 AM - 4 PM, Sun 1 - 10 PM; Estab 1855 to support instruction
Income: State appropriation & private grants
Purchases: $6,000
Library Holdings: Audio Tapes 150; Book Volumes 265,000; Exhibition Catalogs; Filmstrips; Pamphlets; Periodical Subscriptions 1350; Slides

UPPER MONTCLAIR

M   **MONTCLAIR STATE UNIVERSITY,** Art Galleries, 1 Normal Ave, Life Hall Upper Montclair, NJ 07043-1699. Tel 973-655-3382; Fax 973-655-7665; Elec Mail artgalleries@mail.montclair.edu; Internet Home Page Address: www.montclair.edu/arts/galleries; *Pres* Dr Susan A Cole; *VPres* Richard Lynde; *Dean* Geoffrey Newman; *Dir* M Teresa Lapid Rodriguez; *Chmn Art Dept* Daryl Moore
Open Mon, Wed & Fri 9:30 AM - 4 PM, Tues & Thurs 10 AM - 6 PM; No admis fee; Estab 1973; Circ 100,000; Three galleries with 1,200 sq ft, 600 sq ft & 600 sq ft; Average Annual Attendance: 5,000
Income: Financed by the college
Collections: Cosla Collection of Renaissance Art; Lida Hilton Print Collection; Wingert Collection of African & Oceanic Art; Lucy Lewis Collection of Native American Pottery
Exhibitions: Contemporary East Indian Artists; Japanese Expressions in Paper
Activities: Classes for adults; lect open to public; concerts; gallery talks; scholarships offered
L   **Calcia Art and Design Image Library,** 1 Normal Ave, Calcia Art and Design Bldg Rm 214 Montclair, NJ 07043-1699. Tel 973-655-4445; Fax 973-655-7833
Open by appt only
Income: Financed by state funding
Library Holdings: Slides; Video Tapes
Collections: 100,000 35mm art slides

WAYNE

M   **WILLIAM PATERSON UNIVERSITY,** Ben Shahn Art Galleries, 300 Pompton Rd, Wayne, NJ 07470-2152. Tel 973-720-2654; Fax 973-720-3290; Elec Mail evangelistak@wpunj.edu; Internet Home Page Address: www.wpunj.edu; *Dir* Kristen Evangelista; *Prog Asst* Emily Johnsen
Open Mon - Fri 10 AM - 5 PM, cl Fri (May - June); Estab 1969 to educate students & visitors through exhibits & programs; 5000 sq ft space divided into three gallery rooms specializing in the exhibition of contemporary art; Average Annual Attendance: 10,000
Income: Financed by Univ
Special Subjects: Painting-American, Prints, African Art
Collections: Permanent collection of WPC 19th century landscapes; paintings & sculptures from 1950's to present; Tobias Collection of African and Oceanic Art and Artifacts; prints & artists books
Exhibitions: Three gallery rooms of rotating exhibits of contemporary art that change twice during each semester
Publications: Exhibition catalogs
Activities: Art at Lunch prog; docent progs; lects open to pub, 15 vis lectrs per yr

WEST LONG BRANCH

M   **800 GALLERY & ROTARY ICE HOUSE GALLERY,** Monmouth University, 400 Cedar Ave West Long Branch, NJ 07764-1804. Tel 732-571-3400
Call for hours
Collections: Paintings; photographs; sculpture; drawing; ceramics
Activities: Special events; receptions; temporary exhibits

WEST WINDSOR

M   **MERCER COUNTY COMMUNITY COLLEGE,** The Gallery, 1200 Old Trenton Rd, West Windsor, NJ 08550-3407. Tel 609-586-4800, Ext 3589; Elec Mail gallery@mccc.edu; Internet Home Page Address: www.mccc.edu/community_gallery; *Gallery Dir* Tricia Fagan
Open Tues 6PM-8PM, Wed 7PM-9PM, Thurs 11AM-3PM; check for additional hours; No admis fee; Estab 1971 as an educational resource for students & the community; Gallery of 2,000 sq ft primarily for exhibiting work by New Jersey and other regional artists; Average Annual Attendance: 3,600
Income: Financed by college support, pub funding, M C Cultural & Heritage Commission grant & sales commissions
Purchases: Annual purchases from Mercer county artists and student exhibitions
Special Subjects: Ceramics, Folk Art

Collections: Painting by Wolf Kahn; Sculptures by Salvadore Dali & Isaac Whitkin; Paintings by Reginald Neal; Darby Bannard; B J Nordfeldt; NJ artist collection; Art Work by Frank Rivera; Paintings by Mel Leipzig; Cybis Collection
Exhibitions: Rotating exhibs every 6-8 weeks
Publications: Mailing lists for exhibition post cards; occasional catalogue (ex: "Glimpses of America" catalogue)
Activities: Classes for adults & children; dramatic progs; lects open to pub, 12 vis lectrs per yr; concerts; gallery talks; tours; competitions with purchase awards; Mercer County Artist Purchase Award; scholarships offered; individual paintings & original objects of art lent to other galleries & museums; lending collection contains original prints; MCCC at Artworks located in Trenton, NJ; fine arts classes for adults & children in the central NJ/Bucks County, PA region. Warehouse gallery offers 5-7 annual exhibits by local & regional artists
L **Library,** 1200 Old Trenton Rd, West Windsor, NJ 08550-3407. Tel 609-586-4800; Internet Home Page Address: www.mccc.edu/students/library; *Library Dir* Pam Price
Open Mon - Thurs 8 AM - 10 PM, Fri 8 AM - 5 PM, Sat 9 AM - 4 PM, cl Sun; Estab 1891 to provide library services for the col; portion of the main floor is devoted to permanent display cabinets. In addition display panels are used for faculty exhibits, community exhibits & traveling exhibits
Library Holdings: Audio Tapes 1460; Book Volumes 64,518; CD-ROMs 200; Filmstrips; Pamphlets 644; Periodical Subscriptions 718; Records 3107; Slides 17; Video Tapes 2878
Publications: Library handbook, annually; Videocassette catalog, annually

WOODBRIDGE

M **WOODBRIDGE TOWNSHIP CULTURAL ARTS COMMISSION,** Barron Arts Center, 582 Rahway Ave, Woodbridge, NJ 07095-3419. Tel 732-634-0413; Fax 732-634-8633; Elec Mail barronarts@twp.woodbridge.nj.us; Internet Home Page Address: www.woodbridge.nj.us (link then to Barron Arts Center); *Chmn* Dr Dolores Gioffre; *Program Coordr* Brandon Powell; *Dir* Cynthia Knight
Open Mon - Fri 11 AM - 4 PM, Sat & Sun 2 - 4 PM, cl holidays; No admis fee, $5 suggested donation for concerts & lects; Estab 1977 to provide exhibits of nationally recognized artists, craftsmen & photographers, & of outstanding NJ talent; Gallery is housed in an 1877 Richardsonian Romanesque Revival building on the National Register of Historic Places; Average Annual Attendance: 10,000
Income: $71,000 (city appropriation)
Library Holdings: Cards; DVDs; Pamphlets
Exhibitions: Varied exhibits in art, juried shows, historical exhibits, monthly poetry readings
Activities: Classes for adults & children; dramatic progs; docent training; photography; children's summer camp; lects open to pub, 15 vis lectrs per yr; awards; concerts; tours; poetry readings; gallery talks; awards, Best of the Best Readers Choice Winner; sales shop sells original art, postcards, Tshirts, etc.

NEW MEXICO

ALBUQUERQUE

M **516 ARTS,** 516 Central Ave SW, Albuquerque, NM 87102. Tel 505-242-1445; Fax 505-244-4101; Elec Mail info@516arts.org; Internet Home Page Address: www.516arts.org; *Exec Dir* Suzanne Sbarge
Open Tues - Sat noon - 5 PM; Admis free; 2006; nonprofit exhib space; Independent nonprofit arts & educ organization with a museum-style gallery in downtown Albuquerque; Average Annual Attendance: 35,000; Mem: 300
Income: Financed by grants, business sponsors, membership, art & gift shop sales
Publications: Land/Art New Mexico, art exhib catalogs
Activities: Docent training; tours for students of all ages; lects open to pub; gallery talks; tours; sales shop sells books, magazines, original art, reproductions, prints & t-shirts

M **ALBUQUERQUE MUSEUM OF ART & HISTORY,** 2000 Mountain Rd NW Albuquerque, NM 87104. Tel 505-243-7255; Fax 505-764-6546; Elec Mail albuquerquemuseum@cabq.gov; Internet Home Page Address: www.cabq.gov/museum; *Dir* Cathy Wright; *Asst Dir* Cynthia Garcia; *Cur Art* Andrew Connors; *Cur History* Deborah Slaney; *Cur Exhib* Tom Antreasian; *Cur Coll* Steve Pettit; *Cur Educ* Elizabeth Becker
Open Tues - Sun 9 AM - 5 PM; Admis fee adults $4, seniors $2, children ages 4 - 12 $1, children under 4 free; Estab 1967 as a municipal mus. Maintains photo archive & research library. Owns & operates Casa San Ysidro, the Gutierrez/Minge House, a historic site & Heritage Farm in the village of Corrales; Average Annual Attendance: 120,000; Mem: Benefactor $500, supporter $250, friend $100, general $60, senior $40
Income: Financed by city appropriation & Albuquerque Museum Foundation
Library Holdings: Auction Catalogs; Book Volumes; Exhibition Catalogs; Original Art Works; Original Documents; Photographs; Prints; Sculpture
Special Subjects: Folk Art, Ceramics, Glass, Metalwork, Flasks & Bottles, Prints, Manuscripts, Drawings, Graphics, Hispanic Art, Latin American Art, Painting-American, Photography, Sculpture, Watercolors, American Western Art, Bronzes, Southwestern Art, Textiles, Costumes, Crafts, Pottery, Woodcarvings, Woodcuts, Etchings & Engravings, Landscapes, Decorative Arts, Collages, Portraits, Furniture, Jewelry, Silver, Historical Material, Maps, Coins & Medals, Embroidery, Painting-Spanish, Stained Glass, Leather
Collections: Decorative arts; costumes; fine arts and crafts; objects and artifacts relevant to our cultural history from 20,000 BC to present; photography; permanent coll of Southwest American, Hispanic & Native American art
Exhibitions: Sensory crossovers: Synesthesia in American Art
Publications: Abqmuseum, monthly; Sensory crossovers: Synesthesia in American Art, 2010
Activities: Classes for children; dramatic progs; docent training; lects open to public, 12 vis lectrs per yr; concerts; gallery talks; tour; schols avail; original objects of art lent to qualified museums; organizes exhibs of nat & internatl art;

hosts nat & internat traveling exhibs; originate traveling exhibs with select museums; mus shop sells books, original art & prints, Indian jewelry, local crafts & pottery

A **INDIAN ARTS & CRAFTS ASSOCIATION,** 4010 Carlisle NE, Ste C Albuquerque, NM 87107-4532. Tel 505-265-9149; Fax 505-265-8251; Elec Mail info@iaca.com; Internet Home Page Address: www.iaca.com; *Exec Dir* Gail Chehak; *Mem Coordr* Brian Lush; *Admin Asst* Dottie Tiger
Open 9 AM - 5 PM; Admis varies; Estab 1974 to promote, preserve, protect & enhance the understanding of authentic handmade American Indian arts & crafts; Mem: 882; quarterly meetings in Jan, Apr, July & Oct
Income: Financed by mem dues, markets
Library Holdings: Book Volumes
Special Subjects: American Indian Art
Exhibitions: Annual Indian IACA Artists of the Year; IACA Spring Wholesale Market; IACA Fall Wholesale Market
Publications: Annual directory; brochures on various Indian arts & crafts; newsletter, 6 times per year
Activities: Marketing seminars for Indian artists & crafts persons; lects open to public & mem only, 4-5 vis lectrs per yr; competitions; Artist of the Year Awards

M **INDIAN PUEBLO CULTURAL CENTER,** 2401 12th St NW, Albuquerque, NM 87104-2397. Tel 505-843-7270; Fax 505-842-6959; Elec Mail info@indianpueblo.org; Internet Home Page Address: www.indianpueblo.org; *Pres & CEO* Ron Solimon; *COO* Dwayne Virgint; *Acting Mus Dir* Melanie Labonuit
Open 9 AM - 5 PM; Admis adults $6, seniors $5.50, children & students $1; Estab 1976 to advance understanding & ensure perpetuation of Pueblo culture; Permanent exhibit on Pueblo culture & history & changing gallery on Native artists & issues; Average Annual Attendance: 125,000; Mem: 400; dues family $50, individual $30, students $10, senior citizens $20
Library Holdings: Audio Tapes; Book Volumes; Cassettes; Clipping Files; Fiche; Kodachrome Transparencies; Maps; Original Documents; Pamphlets; Periodical Subscriptions; Photographs; Slides; Video Tapes
Special Subjects: Anthropology, Archaeology, Art History, American Indian Art, Southwestern Art
Collections: Jewelry, paintings, photos, pottery, rugs, sculptures, textiles; Archives & library
Publications: Pueblo Horizons, quarterly membership publ
Activities: Educ progs for adults & children; docent training; lects open to pub; lects members only; 10 vis lectrs per yr; summer camp for children in June; quarterly arts markets; weekend Native dances; art demonstrations; mus shop sells books, original art, reproductions, prints, jewelry, pottery, clothing

M **NATIONAL HISPANIC CULTURAL CENTER, ART MUSEUM,** 1701 4th St SW, Albuquerque, NM 87102-4508. Tel 505-246-2261; Fax 505-246-2613; Internet Home Page Address: www.nhccnm.org; *CEO & Dir* Eduardo Diaz; *Chmn* Matt Martinez; *Museum Shop Mgr* Mary Pena Moskin
Open Tues - Sun 10 AM - 5 PM, cl New Year's Day, Easter, Thanksgiving, Christmas; Admis adults $3, senior citizens $2, school groups, children 16 & under, members & Sun free
Library Holdings: Book Volumes 11,000
Collections: contemporary & historic art; period photographs
Publications: quarterly newsletter, Que Pasa
Activities: Educ prog for children & Univ of New Mexico students; docent prog; computer training prog; lects; guided tours; arts festivals; concerts; dance recitals; films; theater; mus shop

A **NEW MEXICO ART LEAGUE,** Gallery & School, PO Box 16554, Albuquerque, NM 87191-6554. Tel 505-293-5034; *Pres* Charles Carroll; *1st Vice Pres* Cynthia Rowland; *Sec* Dori Rardin; *Treas* Susan Smith
Open Tues - Sat 10 AM - 4 PM, Sun 1 - 4 PM, cl Mon; No admis fee; Estab 1929 to promote artists of New Mexico; art gallery; Members' works exhibited in space 1400 sq ft; Average Annual Attendance: 5,000; Mem: 325; dues $35; monthly mem meetings
Income: Financed by mem, sales, classes & gallery room rentals
Collections: National Small Paintings Exhibit
Exhibitions: 24th Annual Small Painting Exhibit (national competition)
Publications: Newsletter, monthly
Activities: Classes for adults & children; lects & workshops open to pub; 6 vis lectrs per year; gallery talks; tours; competitions with awards; individual paintings lent to schools & museums; lending collection contains original art works & prints, paintings, sculptures & slides; sales shop sells original art

M **NORTH FOURTH ART CENTER & GALLERY,** 4904 4th St NW, Albuquerque, NM 87107. Tel 505-344-4542; Fax 505-345-2896; Elec Mail info@vsartsnm.org; Internet Home Page Address: vsartsnm.org/gallery

A **THE SOCIETY OF LAYERISTS IN MULTI-MEDIA (SLMM),** 1408 Georgia NE, Albuquerque, NM 87110; PO Box 897, Guthrie, OK 73044-0897. Tel 405-260-3455; Fax 405-293-6699; Elec Mail info@slmm.org; Internet Home Page Address: www.slmm.org; *Founder* Mary Carroll Nelson; *Pres* Nina Mihm; *VPres* Catherine Keebler; *Dir* Beverley McInnes; *Exec Adminr* Karen Van Hooser; *Dir* Lana L Grow; *Dir* Jean Nevin; *Dir* Mehri Rae Dollard; *Dir* Lynn C Mikami; *Historian* Dawn McIntyre
Estab 1982; Network for artists; Mem: 400; assoc dues $40; annual meeting
Income: $4000 (financed by mem)
Collections: Mixed Media
Exhibitions: Exhibitions around the country; Calendar of Events on website "slmm.org"
Publications: Bridging Time & Space; newsletter, 2 times per year on web for members; The Art of Layering: Making Connections; Visual Journies
Activities: Art Educ; 3 lectrs per yr open to mems only; gallery talks; national & regional exhibs; ann conferences; mus shop sells books

M **UNIVERSITY OF NEW MEXICO,** University of New Mexico Art Museum, 1 University of New Mexico, MSC04 2570 Albuquerque, NM 87131-0001. Tel 505-277-4001; Fax 505-277-7315; Elec Mail artmuse@unm.edu; Internet Home Page Address: www.unm.edu/~artmusel; *Dir* E Luanne McKinnon; *Cur Photographs & Prints* Michele M Penhall; *Cur Jonson Gallery* Robert Ware; *Cur, Acad Initiatives* Sara Otto-Diniz; *Coll Mgr & Reg* Bonnie Verardo; *Preparator* Steven Hurley; *Office Mgr* Angelina Skonieczka; *Asst Cur, Photographs, & Prints* Sherri Sorenson-Clem; *Cur Asst* Leilani Ringkvist
Open Tues - Fri 10 AM - 4 PM, Sat & Sun 1 - 4 PM; No admis fee; Estab 1963; Maintains five galleries; a print & photograph room which is open to the pub at certain hours; Average Annual Attendance: 49,000; Mem: 200; dues $10-$500; annual meeting in May
Income: Financed by university appropriations, grants & donations
Special Subjects: Drawings, Etchings & Engravings, Historical Material, Collages, Painting-American, Prints, Textiles, Sculpture, Graphics, Southwestern Art
Collections: Spanish Colonial art; Tamarind Archive of lithographs; 19th & 20th century American painting & sculpture, drawings; prints by American & European masters; 19th & 20th century lithographs & photography
Publications: Bulletin; exhibition catalogs
Activities: Educ dept; lects open to pub; vis lectrs 6-8 per yr; gallery talks; tours; individual paintings & original objects of art lent to other comparable institutions; originates traveling exhibs

M **Raymond Jonson Collection & Archive,** MSC04 2570, 1 University of New Mexico, Albuquerque, NM 87131-0001. Tel 505-277-6773; Fax 505-277-7315; Elec Mail cware@unm.edu; Internet Home Page Address: www.unm.edu/~artmuse; *Cur* Chip Ware
Open by appt; No admis fee; Estab 1950 for the assemblage & preservation of a comprehensive collection of the works of Raymond Jonson; a depository for works of art by other artists & their preservation, with emphasis on the Transcendental Painting Group (1938-42); the exhibition of contemporary works of art; Average Annual Attendance: 4,000-6,000
Income: Financed through University & art museum trust & donations
Library Holdings: Audio Tapes; Book Volumes; CD-ROMs; Cards; Cassettes; Compact Disks; Exhibition Catalogs; Kodachrome Transparencies; Manuscripts; Memorabilia; Original Documents; Pamphlets; Photographs; Prints; Records; Slides; Video Tapes
Collections: Raymond Jonson Reserved Retrospective Collection of Paintings; other artists' works; Jonson Estate
Publications: The Art of Raymond Jonson; The Transcendental Painting Group, New Mexico 1938-1941; To Form From Air: Music & the Art of Raymond Jonson (2010)
Activities: individual paintings & original works of art lent to mus; lending collection contains color reproductions, original prints, slides, sculpture, 1000 books, 2000 original art & 2000 paintings; originate traveling exhibs; books sold by order

L **Fine Arts Library,** Fine Arts Ctr, Albuquerque, NM 87131-0001. Tel 505-277-2357; Fax 505-277-7134; Elec Mail falref@unm.edu; Internet Home Page Address: www.unm.edu; *Dir* David Baldwin; *Head Reference Librn* Carroll Botts; *Head Cataloging* Pat Fairchild; *Mgr Library Operations* David Hertzel; *Circ Supv* Kyle Nelson
Open Mon - Thurs 8 AM - 10 PM, Fri 8 AM - 6 PM, Sat 10 AM - 6 PM, Sun Noon - 8 PM fall semester hours; Estab 1963 to provide library assistance, literature, microforms & sound recording materials to support the programs of the university in the areas of art, architecture, music & photography
Library Holdings: Audio Tapes; Book Volumes 120,000; CD-ROMs; Cards; Cassettes; Compact Disks; DVDs; Exhibition Catalogs; Fiche; Other Holdings; Pamphlets; Periodical Subscriptions 237; Records; Reels; Video Tapes
Special Subjects: Art History, Decorative Arts, Drawings, Graphic Arts, Islamic Art, Ceramics, Conceptual Art, American Western Art, Art Education, American Indian Art, Furniture, Drafting, Goldsmithing, Jewelry, Architecture
Collections: Dean Neuforth Landscape 1954; Untitled 1954 Oil on Masonite

M **VSA ARTS OF NEW MEXICO,** (Very Special Arts New Mexico) Very Special Arts Gallery, 4904 4th St NW Albuquerque, NM 87107. Tel 505-345-2872; Fax 505-345-2896; Elec Mail info@vsartsnm.org; Internet Home Page Address: www.vsartsnm.org; *Exec Dir* Marjorie Neset; *Deputy Dir* Brynne Badeaux; *Gallery Dir* Linda Jabra
Open Mon - Fri 9 AM - 5 PM by appointment & theater presentations; No admis fee; Estab 1994 to provide art access to individuals with disabilities; Lobby gallery focusing on the art of individuals with disabilities, outsider, visionary & intuitive art. Exhibits the work of emerging & established artists; Average Annual Attendance: 1,000
Income: Financed by grants, private & corporate donations
Special Subjects: Drawings, Painting-American, Watercolors, Ceramics, Crafts, Folk Art
Exhibitions: 15th Anniversary Exhibit; Holiday Exhibition; Those That Can: Teach II
Publications: Arts Access, quarterly
Activities: Classes for adults & children; concerts; gallery talks; tours; awards; scholarships offered; exten dept serves New Mexico; individual paintings & original objects of art lent; sales shop sells books, original art, cards, jewelry & gift items made by artists at the center

ARTESIA

M **ARTESIA HISTORICAL MUSEUM & ART CENTER,** 505 W Richardson Ave, Artesia, NM 88210-2062. Tel 575-748-2390; Fax 575-748-7345; Elec Mail artesiamuseum@artesianm.gov; Internet Home Page Address: artesianm.gov/index.php/visitors-main/museum-vis; *Mus Mgr* Nancy Dunn; *Registrar* Carissa Baize; *Custodian* Yvette Duarte
Open Tues - Fri 9 AM - Noon & 1 - 5 PM, Sat 1 - 5 PM; No admis fee; Estab 1970 to preserve & make available local history; maintains reference & research library; Gallery showcases local & regional artists, exhibits drawn from permanent art collection, traveling exhibits; Average Annual Attendance: 5,000
Income: Financed by city appropriation

Special Subjects: Architecture, Drawings, Painting-American, Photography, Watercolors, American Western Art, Southwestern Art, Textiles, Pottery, Primitive art, Landscapes, Manuscripts, Furniture, Historical Material, Maps, Period Rooms, Embroidery, Laces, Leather
Collections: Art; Early Area History; Farm; Kitchen; Ranch; Native American Artifacts; Oil & Mineral; WWI & WWII; Genealogy; Native American Artifacts
Exhibitions: Honoring Artesia's Veterans, annual show; Artesia Quilters Guild, annual show; Russell Floore Memorial Student Art Show, annual show
Activities: School & civic club progs; lects open to pub, 1-3 vis lectrs per yr; gallery talks; tours; competitions with awards, Living Treasures (annual); individual paintings & objects of art lent to other mus & organizations; book traveling exhibs 1-2 per yr

CARLSBAD

M **CARLSBAD MUSEUM & ART CENTER,** 418 W Fox St, Carlsbad, NM 88220-5743. Tel 575-887-0276; Fax 575-887-7191; Elec Mail museumstaff@cityofcarlsbadnm.com; Internet Home Page Address: www.cityofcarlsbadnm.com; *Mus Dir* Dave W Morgan; *Asst Dir* Shaun Althouse
Open Mon - Sat 10 AM - 5 PM, cl New Year's Day, Martin Luther King Jr Day, Memorial Day, Independence Day, Labor Day, Veterans Day, Thanksgiving & day after, Christmas Eve & Day; No admis fee; 1931; interpret & preserve history & art of American Southwest, especially New Mexico; Art history; Average Annual Attendance: 10,000
Income: Financed by municipality
Special Subjects: American Indian Art, Historical Material, History of Art & Archaeology, Ceramics, American Western Art, Photography, Pre-Columbian Art, Painting-American, Bronzes, Sculpture, Anthropology, Archaeology, Southwestern Art
Collections: New Mexico art; Pueblo pottery; Taos Society of Artists
Publications: newsletter, Amigos; exhibition brochures
Activities: Classes for adults & children; mus shop sells books, original art

CHURCH ROCK

M **RED ROCK PARK,** Red Rock Museum, PO Box 10, Church Rock, NM 87311-0010. Tel 505-722-3829; Fax 505-726-1277; Elec Mail redrockpark@ci.gallup.nm.us; Internet Home Page Address: www.ci.gallup.nm.us/rrsp; *Parks Exec Dir* Ben Welch; *Parks Supv* Pete Becenti; *Parks Specialist* Beverly Lovett
Open Mon - Fri 8 AM - 5 PM, Memorial Day - Labor Day daily 8 AM - 5 PM; Admis adults $3, children $1.50; Estab 1951 to acquaint visitors with the arts & crafts of the Navajo, Zuni & Hopi Indians & other tribes of the Four Corners area; A small mus manned by Red Rock Park; displaying Indian arts & crafts & exhibitions on natural history; Average Annual Attendance: 20,000
Income: Financed by city of Gallup, private contributions & admis fees
Special Subjects: Painting-American, American Indian Art, American Western Art, Anthropology, Archaeology, Ethnology, Southwestern Art, Costumes, Crafts, Historical Material
Collections: Kachina Carving Doll Collection; Anasazi relics; arts & crafts of Navajo, Zuni, Hopi & other Pueblos; specimens of geological, herbarium, archaeological & cultural materials of the Four Corners area
Exhibitions: Permanent exhibits: Navajo Hogan; Pueblo Culture; Elizabeth Andron Houser Collection of Native American Arts; Gallup Intertribal Indian Ceremonial Posters, Jewelry, Basketry, Navajo Rugs; temporary exhibits vary
Publications: Exhibitions catalog; quarterly newsletter
Activities: Lects open to pub; gallery talks; tours; concerts; rodeos; individual paintings & original objects of art lent to other museums; book traveling exhibs 1-4 per yr; originates traveling exhibs to museums & arts & educational organizations; sales shop sells books, reproductions, magazines, prints, sandpaintings, pottery, jewelry & other Native American crafts, cassettes & compact discs of Native American music

L **Library,** PO Box 10, Church Rock, NM 87311. Tel 505-722-3829; Fax 505-863-1297; Elec Mail rrsp@ci.gallup.nm.us; *Museum Clerk* Theresa Warner; *Museum Specialist* Maxine Armstrong Touchine; *Park Supt* Lisa Lucere
Open Mon - Fri 8 AM - 4:30 PM, Memorial Day - Labor Day daily 8 AM - 6 PM; Admis suggested donation adults $3, children $1.50
Income: Municipally sponsored
Library Holdings: Book Volumes 350; Cards; Clipping Files; Exhibition Catalogs; Manuscripts; Pamphlets; Photographs; Prints
Special Subjects: Anthropology

CIMARRON

M **PHILMONT SCOUT RANCH,** Philmont Museum - Seton Memorial Library, 17 Deer Run Rd, Cimarron, NM 87714-9638. Tel 575-376-2281; Elec Mail philmont.museums@scouting.org; *Dir* David Werhane; *Librn* Robin Taylor; *Cur Villa Philmont* Nancy Klein
Open Mon - Sat 8 AM - 5 PM; No admis fee; Estab 1967 to exhibit art & history of Southwestern United States; 3 galleries (new exhibs ea yr; tours of historic Estate of White Phillips; Average Annual Attendance: 30,000
Income: Financed by endowment & sales desk revenue
Collections: Art by Ernest Thompson Seton; American Indian Art; History of Boy Scouts of America; History of New Mexico
Exhibitions: Ernest Thompson Seton's Collection of Plains Indian Art
Activities: Docent progs; lects open to pub; gallery talks; tours; lending collection contains over 6000 items; BBC, Smithsonian, Seton Centre, The Academy for the Love of Learning; mus shop sells books, original art, reproductions, prints & native American jewelry

CLOVIS

M **EULA MAE EDWARDS MUSEUM & GALLERY,** Clovis Community College, 417 Schepps Blvd Clovis, NM 88101-8345. Tel 505-769-4956; Fax 575-769-4190; Elec Mail stephanie.spencer@clouis.edu; Internet Home Page Address: www.clouis.edu; *Div Chair Fine Art & Commun* Jan Lloyd
Open upon request

Special Subjects: American Indian Art, Mixed Media, Photography, Silversmithing, Sculpture, Watercolors, Woodcarvings, Woodcuts
Collections: Artwork from local artists; Paintings & photographs
Activities: Lects open to pub, vis lectrs 3-4 per yr; gallery talks

DEMING

M **DEMING-LUNA MIMBRES MUSEUM,** 301 S Silver St, Deming, NM 88030. Tel 505-546-2382; Elec Mail dlm-museum@zlanet.com; Internet Home Page Address: www.deminglunamimbremuseum.com; *Coordr* Katy Hofacket; *Archives* Art Ramon; *Dir* Sharon Lein
Open Mon - Sat 9 AM - 4 PM, Sun 1:30 - 4 PM, cl Thanksgiving & Christmas Day, open by appointment during evenings for special interest groups; No admis fee with donations; Estab 1955, moved into Old Armory 1978, to preserve Luna County history, historical items & records for reference; Art gallery is in a passageway 50 ft x 10 ft, one full block, no windows; open to local artists for displays; Average Annual Attendance: 20,000; Mem: 200; dues $3; annual meeting in Jan
Income: Financed by donations & endowment earnings
Special Subjects: American Indian Art, Anthropology, Folk Art, Pottery, Decorative Arts, Eskimo Art, Dolls, Furniture, Glass, Historical Material, Leather
Collections: Chuck wagon, vintage clothing, dolls, frontier life objects & other items on the local history; Mimbres Indian artifacts; mine equipment; minerals; paintings & saddles; camera display; phone equipment; quilt room; old lace display; National Guard display; Bataan-Corregidor display & monument; facsimile of front of Harvey House; bell collection; bottle collection, china, ceramics & silver displays; antiques; Military Room
Publications: History of Luna County & Supplement One
Activities: Dramatic progs; docent training; tours; service awards; mus shop sells Indian jewelry, postcards & pottery

LAS CRUCES

M **BRANIGAN CULTURAL CENTER,** 500 N Water St, Las Cruces, NM 88001-1224. Tel 505-541-2155; Fax 505-525-3645; Internet Home Page Address: www.las-cruces.org/public-services/museums; *Mgr* Garland Courts; *Cur Educ* Mary Kay Shannon; *Cur Educ* Carol Blue; *Asst Mgr* Rebecca Slaughter
Open Mon - Fri 10 AM - 5 PM, Sat 9 AM - 1 PM, cl New Year's Day, Martin Luther King Jr Day, Presidents' Day, Memorial Day, Independence Day, Labor Day, Thanksgiving & day after, Christmas; No admis fee; Average Annual Attendance: 79,000
Collections: Las Cruces history; 20th century art; Victorian artifacts

M **NEW MEXICO STATE UNIVERSITY,** Art Gallery, PO Box 30001, MSC 3572, Las Cruces, NM 88001. Tel 575-646-2545; Fax 575-646-8036; Elec Mail artglry@nmsu.edu; *Interim Dir Gallery* Dr Stephanie Taylor; *Gallery Adminr* Emilia Casillas; *Conservator* Silvia Marinas
Open Tues - Sat 12 PM - 4 PM, Wed evenings 6 - 8 PM; No admis fee; Gallery estab in 1974 as an educational resource for the University & southern New Mexico; 5000 sq ft exhibition space; Average Annual Attendance: 25,000; Mem: 200; dues $10 & up; annual meeting in June
Purchases: Eric Avery, Luis Jimenez, Frances Whitehead, Garo Antreasian, Hollis Sigler & Gregory Amenoff
Special Subjects: Drawings, Hispanic Art, Painting-American, Prints, Pre-Columbian Art, Southwestern Art, Religious Art, Ceramics, Crafts, Folk Art, Woodcuts, Etchings & Engravings, Landscapes
Collections: 19th Century Retablos from Mexico; 20th century prints, photographs, works on paper, graphics & paintings
Exhibitions: El Favor De Los Santos; The Retablo Collection of New Mexico State University; Close to the Border VIII
Publications: Visiones, biannual arts newsletter; semiannual exhibit catalogs
Activities: Docent training; school tours & outreach; family day; lects open to public, 12 vis lectrs per year; gallery talks; tours; competitions with awards; individual paintings & original objects of art lent to museums with appropriate security & climate control conditions; lending collection contains original art works, original prints, paintings & photographs; book traveling exhibs up to 5 per year; originates traveling exhibs circulating to art museums

LAS VEGAS

M **NEW MEXICO HIGHLANDS UNIVERSITY,** The Ray Drew Gallery, PO Box 9000, Las Vegas, NM 87701-9000. Tel 505-425-7511, 454-3338; Fax 505-454-0026; Elec Mail gallery@nmhu.edu; *Art Dir* Bob Read
Open Mon - Fri 8 AM - 5 PM, Sat & Sun 1 - 5 PM; No admis fee; Estab 1956 to acquaint University & townspeople with art of the past & present; Gallery dimensions approx 20 x 40 ft; Average Annual Attendance: 4,000-5,000
Income: Financed by state appropriation
Library Holdings: Original Art Works; Prints
Collections: Permanent coll; Fine art print coll 1500s to present
Exhibitions: Twelve individual & group shows
Publications: University general catalog, annually
Activities: Classes for adults & children; lects open to pub, 1 vis lectr per yr; concerts; gallery talks; tours; competitions; book traveling exhibs, 1-2 per yr; originate traveling exhibs

LORDSBURG

M **SHAKESPEARE GHOST TOWN,** 2 1/2 Mile S of Main St, Lordsburg, NM 88045; PO Box 253, Lordsburg, NM 88045-0253. Tel 505-542-9034; Internet Home Page Address: www.shakespeareghosttown.com; *Dir & Pres* Emanuel D Hough; *Develop Mem* Jeane La Marca; *Pub Rels* Steve Hill
Open during regularly-scheduled tours or by appt; Admis adults & seniors $4, children 6 - 12 $3, mems & children under 6 no admis fee; Estab 1970; A

National Historic Site; pub nonprofit org; FT volunteers 4, PT volunteers 20; handicapped-accessible ramps. Shakespeare Ghost Town is the remains of a pioneer, southwestern town. Walk the streets trod by Billy the Kid, John Ringo, Curley Bill, Russian Bill, The Clantons, Jim Hughes and Sandy King. Emphasis on American SW History 1856 - 1935; Average Annual Attendance: 3000; Mem: dues Life $500, Patron $100, Sponsor or Bus $50, Family $25, Individual $10
Collections: 300-vol library on Southwest History; Blacksmith shop & items; Seven historic buildings including The Grant House, Stratford Hotel, Old Mail Station, among others
Publications: Shakespeare Quarterly, newsletter
Activities: Re-enactments & living history 4 times per yr; guided tours

LOS ALAMOS

M **FULLER LODGE ART CENTER,** 2132 Central Ave Frnt, Los Alamos, NM 87544-4013; PO Box 1295, Espanola, NM 87303-1295. Tel 505-662-1635; Elec Mail info@fullerlodgeartcenter.com; Internet Home Page Address: www.fullerlodgeartcenter.com; *Dir* Ken Nebel; *Communs Coordr* Nancy Coombs; *Gallery Shop Mgr* Amy Bjarke; *Bookkeeper* Pam Erickson
Open Mon - Sat 10 AM - 4 PM; No admis fee; Estab 1977 to provide an art center to the regional area; to foster the interests of the artists & art interested pub of the Community; Circ 100 books monthly; Located on first floor of historic Fuller Lodge; Average Annual Attendance: 20,000
Income: Financed by county, gallery, gallery shop sales, annual arts & crafts fairs
Library Holdings: Book Volumes; Exhibition Catalogs; Original Art Works
Exhibitions: Rotating exhibits every 6 weeks
Activities: Classes for adults & children; seminars for artists; docent training; lects open to pub; competitions with awards; gallery talks; book traveling exhibs; sales shop sells original art, jewelry, cards & prints, small community art library

M **MESA PUBLIC LIBRARY ART GALLERY,** 2400 Central Ave, Los Alamos, NM 87544-4014. Tel 505-662-8240; Fax 505-662-8245; Internet Home Page Address: www.losalamosnm.us; *Dir* Carol Meine; *Dir* Charles Kalogeros-Chattan
Open Mon-Thurs 10AM-9PM, Fri 10AM-6PM, Sat 10AM-5PM, Sun 12PM-5PM
Collections: works by local, regional & nat artists; paintings; prints; drawings; photographs; sculpture; architectural models; digital art; decorative arts

MESILLA

M **GADSDEN MUSEUM,** 1875 Boutz Rd, Mesilla, NM 88046; PO Box 147, Mesilla, NM 88046-0147. Tel 575-526-6293; Internet Home Page Address: www.gadsdenmuseum.org; *Owner & Cur* Mary F Bird; *Co-Owner* R Eileen Betzen
Open Summer Mon - Sat 9 - 11 AM & 1 - 5 PM, Winter Mon - Sat, Sun by appt, cl Easter, Thanksgiving, Christmas; Admis $5 per person; Estab 1931 to preserve the history of Mesilla Valley & ancestor Col. Albert Jennings Fountain history of family to the present generation; 1860 structure; Average Annual Attendance: 3,000
Income: $2,000 (financed by donations)
Special Subjects: Glass, Portraits, Painting-American, Textiles, Southwestern Art, Religious Art, Pottery, Woodcarvings, Dolls, Military Art
Collections: Civil War coll; clothing; gun coll; Indian artifacts, including pottery; paintings; Santo coll
Activities: Tours

PORTALES

M **EASTERN NEW MEXICO UNIVERSITY,** Runnels Gallery, Golden Library, 1500 S Ave K, ENMU Station 54 Portales, NM 88130-7400. Tel 575-562-2778; Fax 575-562-2388; Internet Home Page Address: www.enmu.edu; *Chair Art, Asst Prof Art & Graphic Design* Brad Hamann; *Gallery Mgr* Bryan Hahn; *Prof Art & Animation* Greg Erf; *Prof Art* Greg Senn; *Prof Art* Mic Muhlbauer; *Asst Prof Art & Graphic Design* David Deal
Open 7 AM - 9 PM; No admis fee; Estab 1935 for exhibiting student & professional artists' artwork; gallery is room converted for revolving shows
Income: Financed by University funds
Collections: Student works in Art Department Collection
Activities: Individual paintings & original objects of art lent to the university

L **Golden Library/Runnels Gallery,** 1500 S Ave K, Station 32, Portales, NM 88130-7400. Tel 575-562-2607; Fax 575-562-2388; Elec Mail enmuart@enmu.edu; Internet Home Page Address: www.enmu.edu; *Library Dir* Melveta Walker; *Gallery Mgr* Christopher Calderon
Open Mon - Thurs 7 AM - 12 AM, Fri 7 AM - 8 PM, Sat 10 AM - 7 PM, Sun Noon - 12 AM; No admis fee; Estab 1934; Public exhibits & artist presentations
Income: $3000 (financed by University & grants)
Purchases: Some student art is purchased
Library Holdings: Audio Tapes; Book Volumes 10,000; Cards; Cassettes; Exhibition Catalogs; Fiche; Filmstrips; Framed Reproductions; Kodachrome Transparencies; Micro Print; Motion Pictures; Original Art Works; Pamphlets; Periodical Subscriptions 35; Photographs; Prints; Records; Reels; Sculpture; Slides; Video Tapes
Activities: Gallery talks; sponsoring of competitions; 6 vis lectrs per yr

ROSWELL

M **ROSWELL ARTIST-IN-RESIDENCE FOUNDATION,** (Anderson Museum of Contemporary Art) Anderson Museum of Contemporary Art, 409 E College Blvd Roswell, NM 88201-7524. Tel 575-623-5600; Fax 575-623-5603; Elec Mail email@roswellamoca.org; Internet Home Page Address: www.roswellamoca.org; *CEO & Pres* Donald B Anderson; *Exec Dir* Phelps Anderson; *Graphic Design* Nancy Fleming; *Foundation Admin* Lanice White
Open Mon - Fri 9 AM - 4 PM, Sat & Sun 1 - 5 PM, cl New Year's Day, Independence Day, Thanksgiving, Christmas; No admis fee; Estab 1994; 22,000 sq ft; 9 galleries; Average Annual Attendance: 10,000+; Mem: Supporter levels begin at $20

Income: 501c3 non-profit
Library Holdings: CD-ROMs; DVDs; Exhibition Catalogs; Memorabilia; Pamphlets; Slides
Special Subjects: Landscapes, Metalwork, Photography, Woodcuts, Sculpture, Drawings, Watercolors, Textiles, Ceramics, Woodcarvings, Collages, Dioramas, Mosaics
Collections: Collection of works by 200+ former fellows of the Roswell Artist-in-Residence prog
Publications: brochure; newsletter
Activities: Concerts

M **ROSWELL MUSEUM & ART CENTER,** 100 W 11th St, Roswell, NM 88201-4998. Tel 575-624-6744; Fax 575-624-6765; Elec Mail rufe@roswellmuseum.org; Internet Home Page Address: www.roswellmuseum.org; *Pres Board Trustees* Robert Phillips; *VPres* Jimi Gadzia; *Treas/Secy* Elly Mulkey; *Asst Dir* Caroline Brooks; *Cur Coll* Andrew John Cecil; *Registrar* Stacie Petersen; *Dir* Laurie Rufe; *Cur Educ* Ellen Moore
Open Mon - Sat 9 AM - 5 PM, Sun & holidays 1 - 5 PM, cl Thanksgiving, Christmas Eve, Christmas & New Year's Day; No admis fee; Estab 1937 to promote & cultivate the fine arts. Purpose: To increase public enjoyment of art, history, and cultural change with particular focus in the Southwest; 16 galleries are maintained for art & historical collections; plus Robert H Goddard rocket collection; 24,000 sq ft of exhibition space. Maintains reference library; Average Annual Attendance: 65,000; Mem: 700; dues $15 & up
Income: $1,036,344 (financed by mem, city & county appropriation)
Library Holdings: Auction Catalogs; Audio Tapes; Book Volumes; CD-ROMs; Cassettes; DVDs; Exhibition Catalogs; Manuscripts; Pamphlets; Periodical Subscriptions; Photographs; Video Tapes
Special Subjects: Afro-American Art, Anthropology, Archaeology, Decorative Arts, Landscapes, Collages, American Western Art, Portraits, Pottery, Pre-Columbian Art, Prints, Textiles, Bronzes, Sculpture, Drawings, Graphics, Hispanic Art, Latin American Art, Mexican Art, Painting-American, Prints, Sculpture, Watercolors, American Indian Art, Ethnology, Southwestern Art, Costumes, Ceramics, Crafts, Folk Art, Woodcarvings, Woodcuts, Etchings & Engravings, Dolls, Historical Material, Leather
Collections: Regional & Native American fine arts & crafts & Western historical artifacts; international graphics coll; 20th century Southwestern paintings & sculpture, drawings; Hispanic art
Exhibitions: Permanent collection plus 10-14 temporary exhibitions annually
Publications: Bulletin, quarterly; Exhibition Catalogs
Activities: Classes for adults & children; docent training; school outreach prog; lects open to pub, 8-10 vis lectrs per yr; concerts; gallery talks; tours; schols for children's classes offered; individual paintings & original art objects lent to qualified mus; book traveling exhibs 3-4 per yr; mus shop sells books, magazines, original art, reproductions & prints

L **Library,** 100 W 11th St, Roswell, NM 88201. Tel 505-624-6744; Fax 505-624-6765; Elec Mail jordan@roswellmuseum.org; Internet Home Page Address: www.roswellmuseum.org; *Librn & Mus Library Cataloger* Candace Jordan; *Exec Dir* Jeanie Weiffenbach; *Asst Dir* Caroline Knebelsberger
Open Mon - Fri 1 PM - 4:45 PM, cl holidays & vacation; Estab 1937 as a study for reading, research in art, anthropology and later regional history; Circ 1,000 items ann; Reference only; Average Annual Attendance: 500
Income: Endowments, gifts, grants, City of Roswell pays much of operating expense, portion of museum's budget, whether from City of Roswell or Grant is allocated for library purchases
Library Holdings: Audio Tapes 232; Book Volumes 5812; CD-ROMs 7; Cassettes; Clipping Files 1670; Exhibition Catalogs 1500; Filmstrips; Manuscripts 30; Maps 44; Memorabilia 20; Motion Pictures 33; Original Documents 300; Pamphlets 1500; Periodical Subscriptions 33; Photographs 2000; Slides 7000; Video Tapes 425
Special Subjects: Photography, Painting-American, Pre-Columbian Art, Sculpture, Historical Material, Ceramics, Ethnology, Printmaking, American Indian Art, Southwestern Art, Religious Art, Landscapes, Pottery
Collections: Rogers Aston Library Collection; Robert H Goddard Collection & Archives; New Mexico Artists' Files; Artist-in-Residence Files

SANDIA PARK

M **TINKERTOWN MUSEUM,** 121 Sandia Crest Rd, Sandia Park, NM 87047; PO Box 303, Sandia Park, NM 87047-0303. Tel 505-281-5233; Elec Mail tinker4u@tinkertown.com; Internet Home Page Address: www.tinkertown.com; *Dir & Owner* Carla Ward
Open daily Apr 1 - Nov 1 9 AM - 6 PM, cl Nov - Mar; Admis adults $3.50, seniors $3, children $1, spec rates for groups; Estab 1983; Folk art mus created over the course of 40 yrs by the late Ross Ward (1940 - 2002); what was once a four-room summer cabin has been transformed into a 22-rm legacy showcasing one man's work of carvings & colls; Average Annual Attendance: 23,000
Income: $125,000 admissions & gift shop sales
Special Subjects: Drawings, Folk Art, Painting-American, Sculpture, Woodcarvings, Dolls, Miniatures, Dioramas
Collections: Over 40 yrs worth of woodcarvings including a 1880s miniature animated western town, three-ring circus, and many handmade dolls & toys; colls assembled by Ross Ward & his wife including a wedding cake couple coll made up of 140 couples; modern day & antique swords; circus banners & memorabilia including a side show giant's shoes & pants; 7 antique mechanical coin-operated arcade machines; several hundred dolls & toys; handmade antique western livery & mining memorabilia
Publications: I Did All This While You Were Watching TV-The Tinkertown Story; Emily Finds a Dog-A Tinkertown Tale
Activities: Festival of Tinkering, in conjunction with local school art classes; mus related items for sale

SANTA FE

A **THE CENTER FOR CONTEMPORARY ARTS OF SANTA FE,** 1050 Old Pecos Trail, Santa Fe, NM 87505-2688. Tel 505-982-1338; Fax 505-982-9854; Elec Mail contact@ccasantafe.org; Internet Home Page Address: www.ccasantafe.org; *Dir Media Arts* Jerry Barron; *Cur & Dir Installation & Performance Arts* Chris Jonus; *Educ Dir* Molly Sturges; *Programming Coordr* Adrian Parra
Gallery open Mon - Sat Noon - 5 PM; open evenings for performances or cinema screenings; No admis fee for gallery; performances $2-$15; films: mems $5, non mem $7; Estab 1979, as a multidisciplinary contemporary arts organization. Hosts performance art: dance, poetry, musical, mixed media, films; Exhibition space, gallery, performance space, cinema.; Average Annual Attendance: 84,000 (all events); Mem: 535
Exhibitions: Visual arts exhibitions
Activities: Classes for adults & children; performing, visual, mixed media, & drawing workshops; lects open to public, 12 vis lectrs per year; concerts, film, theatre; gallery talks; tours

M **GEORGIA O'KEEFFE MUSEUM,** 217 Johnson St, Santa Fe, NM 87501-1826. Tel 505-946-1000; Fax 505-946-1091; Internet Home Page Address: www.okeeffemuseum.org; *Dir* Robert A Kret; *Assoc Cur* Carolyn Kastner; *Colls Mgr* Judith Chiba Smith; *Head Conservation* Dale Kronkite; *Mktg Mgr* Shannon Hanson; *Develop Dir* Nina Callanan; *Dir Educ* Jackie M; *Dir Fin* Carl Brown; *Dir Opers* Amy Green
Open Mon - Thurs & Sat - Sun 10 AM - 5 PM, Fri 10 AM - 7 PM (1st Fri of month no charge from 5 - 7 PM); cl Easter Sunday, Thanksgiving Day, Christmas Day; Admis adults $10, seniors & students 18+ w/ID $8, NM residents $5, youth & students under 18 free, 1st Fri of month 5-8 PM free; Estab 1997; Average Annual Attendance: 210,000; Mem: 1000+; dues student $35, senior $45, individual $55, sr household $65, family $75
Income: Financed by endowment
Library Holdings: Original Art Works; Photographs 1,770; Sculpture
Special Subjects: Drawings, Painting-American, Photography, Sculpture, Watercolors
Collections: 2,989 works: 1,149 by Georgia O'Keeffe & 1,840 by other artists; The Georgia O'Keeffe Foundation Collection, acquired 2006; Georgia O'Keeffe Ghost Ranch home; Abiquou House & Studio
Activities: Classes for adults & children; docent training; teacher development; school outreach; Art & Leadership Prog; internships; lects open to pub; 10 vis lectrs per yr; concerts; gallery talks; tours; schols; O'Keefe Mus Prize to Emerging Artist; originates traveling exhibs; sales shop sells books, prints, reproductions & home merchandise

L **Research Center,** 135 Grant St, Santa Fe, NM 87501; 217 Johnson St, Santa Fe, NM 87501. Tel 505-946-1011; Elec Mail center@okeeffemuseum.org; Elec Mail library@okeeffemuseum.org; Internet Home Page Address: www.okeeffemuseum.org; *Emily Fisher Landau Dir, Librn & Asst Dir Research Ctr* Eumie Imm-Stroukoff; *Archives & Digital Colls Librn* Elizabeth Ehrnst
Library open Mon - Fri 9 AM - noon by appointment
Library Holdings: Book Volumes; Clipping Files; DVDs; Exhibition Catalogs; Original Documents; Periodical Subscriptions; Photographs; Video Tapes
Collections: Georgia O'Keeffe's art materials, clothes, & colls of found objects; William Innes Homer Archive; Marie Chabot Archive; Georgia O'Keeffe Foundation Archive; correspondence

M **GUADALUPE HISTORIC FOUNDATION,** Santuario de Guadalupe, 100 S Guadalupe St, Santa Fe, NM 87501-5503. Tel 505-988-2027; *Pres* Leo Kahn; *Treas* Waldo Anton; *VPres* Edward Gonzales
Open Mon - Sat 9 AM - 4 PM, cl weekends Nov - Apr; Admis - donation; Estab 1790, became an international mus 1975 to preserve & extend the community's awareness through educ & in culture areas; Gallery space is used for exhibits of local artists, with emphasis on Hispanic art; Average Annual Attendance: 37,000; Mem: 435; dues life $1000 & up, benefactor $500, bus patron $200, patron $100, sponsor $50, bus & family $25, individual $15; annual meeting in Apr
Income: $41,000 (financed by mem, grants, corporate & private donations)
Special Subjects: Mexican Art, Religious Art, Renaissance Art
Collections: Mexican Baroque paintings; Our Lady of Guadalupe mural by Jose de Alzibar; Renaissance Venetian painting; Archdiocese Santa Fe Art Collection
Publications: Flyers; noticias; newsletter
Activities: Dramatic progs; docent training; performing arts; visual arts; poetry readings; lects open to pub, 1-2 vis lectrs per yr; concerts; tours

M **INSTITUTE OF AMERICAN INDIAN ARTS,** Museum of Contemporary Native Arts, 108 Cathedral Pl, Santa Fe, NM 87501-2027. Tel 505-983-8900; Fax 505-983-1222; Elec Mail museum@iaia.edu; Internet Home Page Address: www.mocnasantafe.org; *Dir* Patsy Phillips; *Chief Cur* Ryan Rice; *Facilities & Security Mgr* Thomas Atencio; *Deputy Security Supv* Maria Favela; *Comm Rel/Spec Proj Officer* Larry Phillips Sr; *Cur Colls* Tatiana Lomahaftewa-Singer; *Graphic Designer* Sallie Wesaw Sloan; *Educ* Hayes Locklear; *Mus Store Mgr* Laura Ellerby
Open Mon - Sat 10 AM - 5 PM, Sun Noon - 5 PM; cl Tues Nov - May; Admis adults $10, students & seniors $5, children under 16, veterans & mems free, native people & NM residents free on Sun; Estab as the only Mus in the world solely dedicated to advancing the scholarship, discourse & understanding of contemporary Native arts; 2100 sq ft of exhibition galleries, 15,000 sq ft outdoor Art Park Performance Gallery; Average Annual Attendance: 100,000; Mem: Dues $25 - $2,500
Income: $928,000 (financed by Congressional appropriation)
Purchases: $50,000
Library Holdings: Book Volumes; Exhibition Catalogs; Manuscripts; Maps; Original Art Works; Original Documents; Pamphlets; Periodical Subscriptions; Photographs; Prints; Reproductions; Slides; Video Tapes
Special Subjects: Painting-American, Photography, Prints, Sculpture, Watercolors, American Indian Art, Textiles, Ceramics, Pottery, Jewelry, Silver, Metalwork, Carpets & Rugs
Collections: National collection of contemporary Native American; includes paintings, graphics, textiles, ceramics, sculpture, jewelry, photographs, printed textiles, costumes

Exhibitions: 2-3 major exhibs & annual student exhib
Publications: Exhib catalogs; gallery guides; coll catalogs
Activities: Docent training; lectrs open to the public; 6 vis lectrs per yr; gallery talks; tours; schols offered; individual paintings & original objects of art lent to mus, state capital & colleges; originate traveling exhibs; mus shop sells books, magazines, original art, reproductions, prints & jewelry

L **College of Contemporary Native Arts Library and Archives,** 83 Avan Nu Po Rd, Santa Fe, NM 87508-1300. Tel 505-424-5715; Internet Home Page Address: www.iaia.edu/academics/library; *Library Specialist* Grace Nuvayestewa; *Library Dir* Valerie Nye; *Librn/Cataloger* Pamela Donegan; *Archivist* Ryan Flahive
Open school yr: Mon - Thurs 8 AM - 9 PM, Fri 8 AM - 5 PM, Sun 1 - 9 PM, cl Sat; summer: Mon - Fri 8 AM - 5 PM; Estab 1962 to support col curriculum; Circ 5,500
Income: Financed by congressional appropriation & pvt fund raising
Library Holdings: Book Volumes 37,000; Clipping Files 500; Compact Disks 150; DVDs 1,100; Exhibition Catalogs 2100; Original Art Works; Original Documents; Other Holdings Artists Files, Oral Histories, IAIA History; Periodical Subscriptions 225; Photographs 25,000; Records 300; Slides; Video Tapes 1,000

LANNAN FOUNDATION
For further information, see National and Regional Organizations

M **MILL FINE ART,** 530 Canyon Rd, Santa Fe, NM 87501. Tel 505-982-9212; Fax 505-982-9215; Elec Mail millfineart@gmail.com; Internet Home Page Address: www.millfineart.com; *Dir* Mary Mill; *Dir* Verne Stanford
Open daily 10AM-5PM
Collections: works by nat & international contemporary artists; paintings; drawings; sculpture

M **MUNOZ WAXMAN GALLERY - CENTER FOR CONTEMPORARY ARTS,** 1050 Old Pecos Trail, Santa Fe, NM 87505. Tel 505-982-1338; *Exec Dir* Craig Anderson
Call for hours
Collections: works by contemporary artists; paintings; sculptures

M **MUSEUM OF NEW MEXICO,** Office of Cultural Affairs of New Mexico, The Governor's Gallery, PO Box 2087, State Capitol Santa Fe, NM 87504-2087. Tel 505-827-3089; Fax 505-827-3026; Internet Home Page Address: www.Gov.State.NM.US; *Cur* Terry Bumpass
Open Mon - Fri 8 AM - 5 PM; No admis fee; Estab 1977 to promote New Mexico artists; Gallery located in Governor's reception area in the State Capitol; Average Annual Attendance: 50,000
Income: Financed by state appropriation & the Mus of New Mexico
Exhibitions: Exhibits of New Mexico Art (all media); New Mexican Governor's Awards Show
Activities: Educ dept; docent training; lects open to pub, 200 vis lectrs per yr; gallery talks; tours; A Governor's Award for Excellence in the Arts; individual paintings & original objects of art lent to other mus; book traveling exhibs 1 per yr; originate traveling exhibs to other pub galleries; mus shop sells books, original art & prints

M **MUSEUM OF NEW MEXICO,** New Mexico Museum of Art, 710 Camino Lejo, Santa Fe, NM 87504-7511; PO Box 2087, Santa Fe, NM 87504-2087. Tel 505-476-1250; Elec Mail rebecca.potance@state.nm.us; Internet Home Page Address: www.nmartmuseum.org; *Dir* Shelby Tisdale
Open Tues - Sun 10 AM - 5 PM; Admis 2 mus/1 Day $15, 4 mus/4-Day pass $20, adults single visit $9, children under 16 free; Estab 1909. Mus is a state institution & operates in 4 major fields of interest: Anthropology, Archaeology, Native American Art & Culture; 1 permanent & 4 temporary galleries; Southwestern Indian art, anthropology & archaeology; Average Annual Attendance: 65,000
Income: Financed by state appropriation, federal grants & private funds
Collections: Over 10 million objects, artifacts & works of art in the fields of Native American art, archaeology & history
Publications: Exhib catalogs; guides; magazines; monographs; pamphlets
Activities: Classes for adults & children; docent training; lects open to pub; concerts; gallery talks; tours; original objects of art lent to other cultural institutions; mus shop sells books, magazines, prints & original art

L **Fray Angelico Chavez History Library,** 120 Washington Ave, Santa Fe, NM 87501; PO Box 2087, Santa Fe, NM 87504-2087. Tel 505-476-5090; Internet Home Page Address: www.state.nm.us/moifa; *Head Librn* Tomas Jaehn
Open Mon - Fri 10 AM - 5 PM; Mus houses four separate research libraries on folk art, fine arts, history & anthropology
Income: Financed by endowments, grants & state
Library Holdings: Book Volumes 15,000; Other Holdings Journals 40

M **New Mexico Museum of Art, Unit of NM Dept of Cultural Affairs,** 107 W Palace, Santa Fe, NM 87501; PO Box 2087 Santa Fe, NM 87504-2087. Tel 505-476-5072; Fax 505-476-5076; Elec Mail mary.jebsen@state.nm.us; Internet Home Page Address: www.nmartmuseum.org; *Cur 20th Century Painting* Joseph Traugott; *Cur Contemporary* Laura Addison; *Asst Dir* Mary Jebsen; *Mus Shop Mgr* John Stafford; *Dir* Mary Kershaw; *Librn & Archivist* Devon Skeele; *Cur Photog* Kate Ware; *Chief Registrar* Michelle Roberts; *Registrar* Dan Goodman; *Admin* Laura Kohl
Open Tues - Sun 10 AM - 5 PM, cl Mon; Admis adults $9, 4-day & annual passes available for $20, children free; Estab 1917 to serve as an exhibitions hall, chiefly for New Mexican & Southwestern art; Building is of classic Southwestern design (adobe); attached auditorium used for performing arts presentations; Average Annual Attendance: 290,000; Mem: 7,000
Income: Financed by state appropriation
Library Holdings: Book Volumes; Clipping Files; Compact Disks; Exhibition Catalogs; Periodical Subscriptions; Photographs; Slides; Video Tapes
Special Subjects: Mexican Art, Photography, Sculpture, American Indian Art, American Western Art, Ceramics
Collections: Drawings, paintings, photographs, prints & sculpture with emphasis on New Mexican & regional art, including Native American artists
Publications: Exhibition catalogs; gallery brochures
Activities: Classes for adults & children; dramatic progs; docent training; lects open to pub, 30 vis lectrs per yr; concerts; gallery talks; tours; competitions;

individual paintings & original objects of art lent to art mus; lending collection contains original prints, paintings, photographs & sculpture; originate traveling exhibs; mus shop sells books, magazines, original art, reproductions & prints

L **New Mexico Museum of Art,** 107 W Palace, Santa Fe, NM 87501-2014; PO Box 2087, Santa Fe, NM 87504-2087. Tel 505-476-5061; Fax 505-827-5076; Elec Mail rebecca.pontance@state.nm.us; Internet Home Page Address: www.nmartmuseum.org; *Librn* Rebecca Pontance; *Dir* Mary Kershaw
Open daily 10 AM - 5 PM; Admis non-residents $9, state residents $6; Estab 1917 to provide fine arts research materials to mus staff, artists, writers & community; Circ 4,000; Average Annual Attendance: 80,000
Library Holdings: Audio Tapes; Book Volumes 7500; Clipping Files; DVDs; Exhibition Catalogs; Manuscripts; Original Documents; Other Holdings; Pamphlets; Periodical Subscriptions 45; Photographs; Slides
Special Subjects: Art History, Illustration, Photography, Drawings, Etchings & Engravings, Graphic Arts, Painting-American, Prints, Sculpture, History of Art & Archaeology, Watercolors, Ceramics, American Western Art, Printmaking, American Indian Art, Mexican Art, Southwestern Art, Glass, Woodcarvings, Woodcuts, Landscapes, Architecture, Portraits
Collections: Biography files of artists; Archives of artists & galleries assoc with New Mexico; Exhibition catalogs
Activities: Tours for children; docent training; lects open to pub; concerts; gallery talks; tours; mus shop sells books, reproductions & prints, slides, jewelry

M **Museum of International Folk Art,** 706 Camino Lejo, Santa Fe, NM 87505; PO Box 2087, Santa Fe, NM 87504-2087. Tel 505-476-1200; Fax 505-476-1300; Elec Mail info@moifa.org; Internet Home Page Address: www.internationalfolkart.org; *Asst Dir* Elena Sweeney; *Cur Latin American Folk Art* Barbara Mauldin; *Cur Textiles & Costumes* Bobbie Sumberg, PhD; *Dir Educ* Aurelia Gomez; *Unit Registrar* Cathy Notarnicola; *Coll Mgr* Paul Smutko; *Outreach Educator* Patricia Sigala; *Dir Dr* Marsha Bol, PhD; *Cur Asian & Mid East* Felicia Katz-Harris; *Cur Catino/Hispano & Spanish Colonial Colls* Nicolasa Chavez
Open daily 10 AM - 5 PM, cl Mon, Labor Day to Memorial Day; Mon open during summer (Memorial Day to Labor Day); Admis adults to 4 museums multiple (4 days) visits $18 res, $20 non-res, single visit $6 res, $9 non-res, children under 17 free, NMex residents free on Sun; Estab 1953 to collect, exhibit & preserve worldwide folk art; Average Annual Attendance: 100,000
Income: Financed by endowment, grants & state appropriation
Special Subjects: Hispanic Art, Textiles, Costumes, Folk Art
Collections: Arts of Traditional Peoples, with emphasis on Spanish Colonial & Hispanic-related cultures; costumes & textiles
Exhibitions: (Permanent) Familia y Fe/Family & Faith; Multi-Visions: A Common Bond.
Publications: American Folk Masters, 1992; the Spirit of Folk Art, 1989, Mud, Mirror & Thread: Folk Traditions of Rural India, 1993; Traditional Arts of Spanish New Mexico, 1994; Rio Grande Textiles, 1994; Recycled, Re-Seen: Folk Art from the Global Scrap Heap, 1996, The Extraordinary in the Ordinary, 1998; Masks in Mexico, fall 1999; Maiolica Ole; Village of Painters, Carnaval, Visionaries, Cermicay Cultura, Folk art Journey, Sin Nombre
Activities: Classes for adults & children; docent training; lects open to pub; concerts; gallery talks; tours; original objects of art lent to responsible mus nationwide; originate traveling exhibs; mus shop sells books, original art, reproductions & prints

L **Bartlett Library,** 706 Camino Lejo, Santa Fe, NM 87505-7511; PO Box 2087, Santa Fe, NM 87504-2087. Tel 505-476-1210; Fax 505-476-1300; Elec Mail ree.mobley@state.nm.us; Internet Home Page Address: www.state.nm.us/moifa; *Librn* Ree Mobley
Open Tues - Fri 10 AM - Noon & 1:30 - 4:30 PM; No admis fee; Estab 1953 to support museum's research needs; Reference library
Income: Financed by private & state support
Purchases: $5500
Library Holdings: Audio Tapes; Book Volumes 12,500; Cassettes; Clipping Files; Exhibition Catalogs; Manuscripts; Original Art Works; Pamphlets; Periodical Subscriptions 180; Photographs; Records; Slides; Video Tapes
Special Subjects: Folk Art, Decorative Arts, Calligraphy, Islamic Art, Crafts, Latin American Art, Ethnology, Asian Art, Anthropology, Mexican Art, Afro-American Art, Carpets & Rugs, Dolls, Embroidery, Handicrafts, Jewelry
Collections: Folk literature & music of the Spanish Colonist in New Mexico c 1800-1971; International folk arts & crafts
Activities: Mus shop sells books, original art & folk art

M **Palace of Governors,** PO Box 2087, Santa Fe, NM 87504-2087. Tel 505-476-5100 (Palace of Governors); Tel 505-476-5200 (NM History Museum); Internet Home Page Address: www.palaceofthegovernors.org; Internet Home Page Address: www.nmhistorymuseum.org; *Cur* Josef Diaz; *Opers Mgr* Norman Edwards; *Registrar* Wanda Edwards; *Colls & Educ Progs Mgr* Rene Harris; *Library* Tomas Jaehn; *Photo Archives* Daniel Kosharek; *Palace Press* Tom Leech; *Dir* Francis Levine; *Admin Asst* Carla Ortiz; *Photo Archives* Mary Anne Redding; *Events Coordr* Inessa Williams
Open Tues - Sun 10 AM - 5 PM; Memorial Day - Labor Day open daily; Admis $9 out-of-state visitors, $6 NM residents; no admis fee: Sun to NM residents, Wed NM senior citizens, mus mems & children under 17; free Fri eves 5 - 8 PM; Built in 1610 (Palace of the Governors) built in 2009 (NM History Mus); History mus; Average Annual Attendance: 120,000
Income: Financed by state appropriations & donations
Special Subjects: Period Rooms, Hispanic Art, Photography, Southwestern Art, Historical Material, Painting-Spanish
Exhibitions: Society Defined; Another Mexico; Long Term Exhibs: Segesser Hide Paintings, Palace of the Governors, West Wing; Telling NM - Stories from then & now, NM History Mus; Treasures of Devotion/Tesoros de Devocion, Palace of the Governors; Santa Fe Found: Fragments of Time, Palace of the Governors; Telling NM, Sant Fe Found
Activities: Awards: Edward L Hewett Award, 2009; 2 first-place honors from the American Assoc of Mus; 2 first-place honors from the Mountain Plains Assoc of Mus, 2009, 2010; Nonprofit Prog Award, 2009 & numerous other awards

M **Laboratory of Anthropology Library,** 708 Camino Lejo, Santa Fe, NM 87505-7511; PO Box 2087, Santa Fe, NM 87504-2087. Tel 505-476-1264; Fax 505-476-1330; Elec Mail Allison.Colborne@state.nm.us; Internet Home Page Address: indianartsandculture.org; *Librn* Allison Colborne
Open Mon - Fri 10 AM - 5 PM; Estab 1929 as a research laboratory in archaeology & ethnology of the Southwest; Circ 25,000+

Library Holdings: Auction Catalogs; Book Volumes; Exhibition Catalogs; Manuscripts; Maps; Periodical Subscriptions
Special Subjects: American Indian Art, Anthropology, Archaeology, History of Art & Archaeology, Pre-Columbian Art, Textiles, Silversmithing, Maps, Ethnology
Collections: Reference materials on various Indian cultures of the Southwest: jewelry, pottery & textiles

A   **PUEBLO OF POJOAQUE,** Poeh Museum, 78 Cities of Gold Rd, Santa Fe, NM 87501-0918. Tel 505-455-5041; 455-1110 (Dir); Fax 505-455-3684; Internet Home Page Address: www.poehmuseum.com; *Dir* Vernon Lujan; *Cur* Nadine Ulibarri; *Colls Mgr* Reuben Martinez; *Admin Asst* Lynda Romero; *Gift Shop Mgr* Frances Quintana
Open 9 AM - 5 PM; No admis fee; Estab 1988 & opened 1991 to house & exhibit contemporary arts & crafts by artists of the Northern Pueblos, to facilitate the educ of Native American people & the pub-at-large & to preserve Pueblo culture; Average Annual Attendance: 1,200
Library Holdings: Photographs 10,000
Collections: Drawings, paintings, photography, prints, sculptures & other works on baskets, beadwork, ceramics, costumes, jewelry, paper, pottery & textiles; Photo Archives
Exhibitions: Poeh Arts Program, semi-annual exhibit; Nah Poeh Meng (Permanent); 3 rotating exhibs per yr
Activities: Classes for Native American adults; original objects of art lent to museums

M   **PUEBLO OF SAN ILDEFONSO,** Maria Martinez Museum, 02 Tunyo PO, Santa Fe, NM 87506. Tel 505-455-2273 (business office), 455-3549 (visitors' center); Fax 505-455-7351; Internet Home Page Address: www.indianpueblo.org; Internet Home Page Address: www.sanipueblo.org; *Tourism Dir* Denise Moquino; *Tourism Asst* Harold Torres
Open Mon - Fri 8 AM - 4 PM; Admis to mus incl in $10 entrance fee to the Pueblo; Estab to display pottery: history, artists & methods of pottery making
Collections: Arts & crafts; clothing; painting; pottery

M   **SCHOOL FOR ADVANCED RESEARCH (SAR),** (School of American Research) Indian Arts Research Center, 660 Garcia St, Santa Fe, NM 87505; PO Box 2188, Santa Fe, NM 87504-2188. Tel 505-954-7205; Fax 505-954-7207; Elec Mail iarc@sarsf.org; Internet Home Page Address: http://sarweb.org; *Pres & CEO* James Brooks; *Dir* Cynthia Chavez Lamar; *Registrar* Jennifer Day; *Admin Asst* Daniel Kurnit; *Prog Coordr* Elysia Poon; *Colls Asst* Sylvanus Paul
Open with appointment public tours Fri at 2 PM; Admis by tour $15, members free, reservations req; Estab 1907, collection initially formed in 1922 as the Indian Arts Fund. Dedicated to advance studies in anthropology, support advanced seminars for post-doctoral scholars, archaeological research, anthropological publication & a pub educ program; Southwest Indian Arts Building houses collections for research; open storage facility; Average Annual Attendance: 1,400; Mem: 1,100; dues begin at $40; Scholarships
Income: Financed by endowment, mem, special grants & individuals
Special Subjects: Pottery, Textiles, American Indian Art, Jewelry
Collections: 12,000+ items
Publications: Publications of Advanced Seminar Series
Activities: Lects open to public; tours; paid & unpaid internships; fels offered; individual paintings & original objects of art lent to other museums; sales shop sells books, note cards, video tapes, posters

M   **SITE SANTA FE,** 1606 Paseo de Peralta, Santa Fe, NM 87501. Tel 505-989-1199; Fax 505-989-1188; Elec Mail sitesantafe@sitesantafe.org; Internet Home Page Address: www.sitesantafe.org; *Phillips Dir* Laura Steward Heon
Open Wed - Sun, 10 AM - 5 PM, Fri 10 AM - 7 PM; Admis $10, seniors & students $5; Estab 1995; 19,000 sq ft exhibition space available. Interior configurations vary according to exhibition demands; Average Annual Attendance: 25-30,000; Mem: 800; dues $35 & up
Income: Financed by mem & private funds
Library Holdings: Audio Tapes; DVDs; Exhibition Catalogs; Kodachrome Transparencies; Periodical Subscriptions; Photographs; Slides; Video Tapes
Exhibitions: Rotating exhibitions; International Biennial exhibition
Publications: Exhibit catalogs
Activities: Classes for adults & children; Docent progs; vol progs; outreach to schools; lects open to public; concerts; gallery talks; tours; book traveling exhibitions 2-3 per year; originate traveling exhibs to all museums; sales shop sells books, original art, prints, t-shirts & hats

M   **WHEELWRIGHT MUSEUM OF THE AMERICAN INDIAN,** PO Box 5153, Santa Fe, NM 87502-5153. Tel 505-982-4636; Fax 505-989-7386; Elec Mail asstdir@wheelwright.org; Internet Home Page Address: www.wheelwright.org; *Cur* Cheri Falkenstien-Doyle; *Dir* Jonathan Batkin; *Asst to Dir* Leatrice A Armstrong
Open Mon - Sat 10 AM - 5 PM, Sun 1 - 5 PM; Admis by donation; Estab 1937 to record & present creative expressions of Native American people; Main gallery is shaped like inside of Navajo Hogan or house. Friends, Slater & info ctr Galleries are smaller exhibit space; Average Annual Attendance: 54,000; Mem: 1500; dues $30-$500
Income: Financed by endowment & mem
Special Subjects: Textiles, Drawings, Photography, Prints, Sculpture, American Indian Art, Anthropology, Ethnology, Costumes, Religious Art, Ceramics, Crafts, Folk Art, Pottery, Primitive art, Manuscripts, Dolls, Jewelry, Silver, Metalwork, Historical Material, Miniatures, Embroidery, Leather
Collections: American Indian art & ethnographic material of Southwestern US, Navajo, Apache & Pueblo people
Exhibitions: Two exhibitions per yr; please call museum for info
Publications: Bulletins & books on Navajo culture; exhibition catalogs
Activities: Classes for adults & children; docent training; tours; lect; slide-lect; lects open to pub, 10 vis lectrs per yr; gallery talks; tours; individual paintings & original objects of art lent to mus; lending collection contains books, color reproductions, framed reproductions, Kodachromes, nature artifacts, original art works, original prints, paintings & phono records; mus shop sells books, magazines, original art, reproductions, prints, pottery, jewelry, textiles & beadwork (all original)

L   **Mary Cabot Wheelwright Research Library,** 704 Camino Lejo, Santa Fe, NM 87505-7511; PO Box 5153, Santa Fe, NM 87502-5153. Tel 505-982-4636; Fax 505-989-7386; Elec Mail wheelwright@wheelwright.org; Internet Home Page Address: www.wheelwright.org; *Dir* Jonathan Batkin; *Cur* Cheri Falkenstien-Doyle
Open to researchers for reference
Income: Financed by mem
Library Holdings: Book Volumes 4000; Other Holdings Per Issues 3000; Periodical Subscriptions 3000
Special Subjects: Art History, Folk Art, Painting-American, Historical Material, Ceramics, Crafts, Archaeology, Ethnology, American Indian Art, Anthropology, Eskimo Art, Costume Design & Constr, Carpets & Rugs, Jewelry, Architecture

TAOS

M   **BENT MUSEUM & GALLERY,** 117 Bent St, Taos, NM 87571-6075; PO Box 153, Taos, NM 87571-0153. Tel 575-758-2376; Fax 575-758-2376; Elec Mail gnideon@laplaza.org; *Owner* Thomas Noeding
Open daily 10 AM - 4 PM; Admis adults $2, children 8 - 15 $1, under 8 free; Estab 1959; Home of the first territorial governor of New Mexico - Site of his death in 1847; Average Annual Attendance: 5,000
Income: Financed from admissions & gift shop
Special Subjects: American Indian Art
Collections: American Indian Art; old Americana; old Taos art
Activities: Mus shop sells books, original art, reproductions, prints, Indian jewelry, pottery & dolls

M   **MILLICENT ROGERS MUSEUM,** 1504 Millicent Rogers Rd, Taos, NM 87571; PO Box 1210, Taos, NM 87571-1210. Tel 505-758-2462; Fax 505-758-5751; Elec Mail mrm@millicentrogers.org; Internet Home Page Address: www.millicentrogers.org; *Ed* Peter Serbert; *Cur* Carmela Quinto; *Office Mgr* Kathleen Michaels; *CFO* Faith Hensley
Open Apr-Oct daily 10 AM - 5 PM; Nov-Mar Tues - Sun 10 AM - 5 PM; cl New Year's Day; Easter; San Geronimo Day (Sep 30, Taos Pueblo feast day); Thanksgiving; Christmas; Admis family $12, adults $10, seniors $8, students $6, New Mexican residents $5, children under 16 $2; members free; Estab 1956 the MRM is dedicated to sharing & celebrating the art & culture of the southwest; The museum's permanent home is a traditional adobe building, once the private residence of Claude J K Anderson; Average Annual Attendance: 25,000; Mem: 400
Income: Financed by endowment, mem, donations, admis, grants & revenue from mus store
Special Subjects: Architecture, Drawings, Hispanic Art, Photography, Sculpture, Watercolors, American Indian Art, American Western Art, Pre-Columbian Art, Southwestern Art, Textiles, Costumes, Religious Art, Ceramics, Crafts, Folk Art, Pottery, Decorative Arts, Furniture, Jewelry, Silver, Metalwork, Historical Material, Embroidery
Collections: American Indian Art of Western United States, emphasis on Southwestern groups; paintings by contemporary Native American artists; religious arts and non-religious artifacts of Hispanic cultures; nucleus of coll formed by Millicent Rogers
Exhibitions: Rotating exhibits & from permanent collection
Activities: Classes for adults & children; lects open to pub, 2-3 vis lectrs per yr; gallery talks; docent tours; field trips; seminars; accredited by the American Assn of Mus; original works of art lent to similar institutions; mus store sells books, jewelry, original art, prints, art & craft work by contemporary Southwest artisans & artists

M   **TAOS ART MUSEUM,** 277 Paseo del Pueblo Norte, Taos, NM 87571-7316; PO Box 1848, Taos, NM 87571-1848. Tel 575-758-2690; Fax 575-758-7320; Elec Mail museum@taosartmuseum.org; Internet Home Page Address: www.taosartmuseum.org; *Exec Dir* Erion Simpson
Open Tues-Sun 10AM-5PM; Admis $8; Taos County Residents free on Sun
Collections: art exhibits dedicated to the art of early 20th century Taos; paintings by the Taos Society of Artists

A   **TAOS CENTER FOR THE ARTS,** Stables Gallery, 133 Paseo de Pueblo Norte, Taos, NM 87571. Tel 575-758-2052; Fax 575-751-3305; Elec Mail info@tcataos.org; Internet Home Page Address: www.tcataos.org; *Pres* Alford Johnson; *Exec Dir* Ron Usherwood
Open Mon - Fri 10 AM - 5 PM, cl Sat & Sun; No admis fee; Estab Oct 1952 as a nonprofit community art center to promote the arts in Taos for the benefit of the entire community; Average Annual Attendance: 30,000; Mem: 300; annual meeting Jan
Income: Financed by mem, contributions, grants, sales of art works & admissions
Activities: Children's program in music & theater; dramatic progs; concerts; classes for adults & children; concerts

L   **TAOS PUBLIC LIBRARY,** Fine Art Collection, 402 Camino De La Placita, Taos, NM 87571-6071. Tel 575-758-3063; Fax 575-737-2586; Elec Mail librarian@taosgov.com; Internet Home Page Address: www.taoslibrary.org; *Librn* Laurie Macrae
Open Tues - Thurs 10 AM - 6PM, Mon Noon - 6 PM, Fri 10 AM - 6 PM, Sat 10 AM - 5 PM; No admis fee; Estab 1936; Circ 60,000
Library Holdings: Book Volumes 55,000; CD-ROMs; Clipping Files; Compact Disks; DVDs; Exhibition Catalogs; Original Art Works; Pamphlets; Periodical Subscriptions 60; Photographs; Prints; Reproductions; Video Tapes
Special Subjects: Art History, Archaeology, American Western Art, American Indian Art, Southwestern Art
Activities: Children's summer prog includes arts & crafts; bilingual reading discussion prog; lects

M   **TAOS HISTORIC MUSEUMS,** (Kit Carson Historic Museums) 222 Ledoux St, Taos, NM 87571-5944. Tel 505-758-0505; Fax 505-758-0330; Elec Mail thm@taoshistoricmuseums.com; Internet Home Page Address: www.taoshistoricmuseums.com; *Dir* Karen S Young
Estab 1949. In 1962 the home of Ernest L Blumenschein was given to the Foundation by Miss Helen C Blumenschein; it is now classified as a Registered

National Landmark. In 1967 Mrs Rebecca S James gave the Foundation the Ferdinand Maxwell House & Property. In 1972, acquired the Hacienda de Don Antonio Serverino Martinez, prominent Taos merchant & official during the Spanish Colonial Period; designated a Registered National Historic Landmark; Average Annual Attendance: 60,000; Mem: 280; dues patron $1000, sponsor $500, benefactor $250, sustaining $150, contributing $75, partners $50, individual $25
Income: $300,000 (financed by admis, museum shops, rentals, donations & grants)
Special Subjects: Furniture, Period Rooms
Collections: Historical & Archaeological Collection; Western Americana
Publications: Director's annual report; Taos Lightning Newsletter, quarterly; publications on the historic sites; technical reports
Activities: Classes for adults & children; docent training; lect; gallery talks; mus shop

L **E.L. Blumenschein Home & Museum & La Hacienda de los Martinez,** 222 Ledoux St, Taos, NM 87571-5944. Tel 575-758-0505; Fax 505-758-0330; Elec Mail director@taoshistoricmuseum.org; Internet Home Page Address: taoshistoricmuseums.org; *Dir* Carmen Zaccerras; *Colls Mgr* Anita McDaniel
Open Mon - Sat 10 AM - 5 PM, Sun noon - 5 PM; Admis adults $8; Museum welcomes visitors
Income: Donations
Library Holdings: Audio Tapes; Book Volumes 5000; Cassettes; Clipping Files; Exhibition Catalogs; Kodachrome Transparencies; Lantern Slides; Manuscripts; Maps; Memorabilia; Original Documents; Other Holdings Maps; Pamphlets; Periodical Subscriptions; Photographs; Reproductions; Slides
Special Subjects: Maps, Historical Material, Archaeology, American Western Art, Anthropology, Southwestern Art
Collections: Photograph archives; Textiles, primary source materials & paintings
Activities: Classes for adults; docent training; gallery talks; tours; museum shop sells books, original art, reproductions, prints & other merchandise

M **Ernest Blumenschein Home & Studio,** 222 Ledoux St, Taos, NM 87571-5944. Tel 505-758-0505; Fax 505-758-0330; Elec Mail thm@taohistoricmuseums.com; Internet Home Page Address: www.taoshistoricmuseums.com; *Dir* Karen S Young; *Educator* Morris Whitten; *Registrar* Joan A Phillips; *Librn* Nita Murphy
Open daily 9 AM - 5 PM, cl Christmas, Thanksgiving & New Year's Day; Admis family rate $10, adults $6, children $3, children under 6 years free with parents, group tour rates available; Home of world renowned artist & co-founder of famous Taos Soc of Artists; Restored original mud plaster adobe dating to 1797 with traditional furnishings of New Mexico & European furnishings; Average Annual Attendance: 17,000; Mem: 280; dues $15-$500
Income: Donations & admissions, shop sales
Special Subjects: Architecture, Drawings, Painting-American, American Western Art, Southwestern Art, Textiles, Ceramics, Pottery, Portraits, Furniture, Carpets & Rugs, Historical Material, Tapestries, Period Rooms
Collections: Taos Society of Artists Collection; fine art paintings; Ernest L Blumenschein & Family Collection
Exhibitions: Temporary exhibits of arts and crafts of the Taos area and of New Mexico
Activities: Classes for adults & children; docent training; lect open to public, 2 vis lectrs per year; tours; annual founder art show; book traveling exhibitions; mus shop sells books, original art, reproductions & prints

M **La Hacienda de Los Martinez,** 222 Ledoux St, Taos, NM 87571-5944. Tel 505-758-1000; Fax 505-758-0330; Elec Mail thm@thoshistoricmuseums.com; Internet Home Page Address: www.taohistoricmuseums.com; *Dir* Karen S Young; *Educator* Morris Witten; *Registrar* Joan A Phillips; *Librn* Nita Murphy
Open daily 9 AM - 5 PM, cl Thanksgiving, Christmas, New Yrs Day; Admis family rate $10, adults $6, children $3, children under 6 free with parents, group tour rates; Estab 1972, built & occupied by Don Antonio Severino Martinez 1804-1827. Last remaining hacienda open to pub in northern New Mexico. Martinez, an important trader with Mexico, also served as Alcalde of Northern New Mexico; Spanish Colonial fortress hacienda having 21 rooms & two large patios. Living mus program; Average Annual Attendance: 30,000
Income: Financed by admis, donations, & shop sales
Special Subjects: Hispanic Art, Mexican Art, Textiles, Religious Art, Woodcarvings, Furniture, Metalwork, Historical Material, Period Rooms, Embroidery
Collections: Furniture, tools & articles of Spanish Colonial period & personal family articles; Blacksmithing; Weaving
Exhibitions: Various art & craft exhibits, irregular schedule
Activities: Classes for adults & children; docent training; lect open to public, 6 vis lectrs per year; tours; The Annual Taos Trade Fair; mus shop sells books, original art, reproductions & prints

M **UNIVERSITY OF NEW MEXICO,** The Harwood Museum of Art, 238 Ledoux St, Taos, NM 87571-7009. Tel 575-758-9826; Fax 575-758-1475; Elec Mail info@harwoodmuseum.org; Internet Home Page Address: www.harwoodmuseum.org; *Cur* Jina Brenneman; *Dir* Susan Longhenry; *Cur of Educ* Rebeca Aubin; *Develop Officer* Juniper Manley
Open Tues - Sat 10 AM - 5 PM, Sun Noon - 5 PM; summer hours Mon 10 AM - 5 PM; Admis adults $10, students & seniors $8, children under 18 free; Estab 1923, Buildings & contents given to the University by Elizabeth Case Harwood, 1936, to be maintained as an art, educational & cultural center; maintained by the University with all activities open to the pub; Building was added to the National Register of Historic Places in 1976; major renovation expansion completed in 1997, another completed in 2010; Average Annual Attendance: 24,000; Mem: 700; dues $35 - $1000 per year
Income: Financed by University of New Mexico, private contributions & grants, government grants, endowment income
Special Subjects: Pottery, Sculpture, Architecture, Drawings, Hispanic Art, Painting-American, Photography, Prints, Watercolors, American Western Art, Southwestern Art, Textiles, Religious Art, Ceramics, Woodcarvings, Etchings & Engravings, Landscapes, Decorative Arts, Portraits, Furniture, Historical Material
Collections: Permanent collection of works by Taos artists; Hispanic traditions, bultos & retables of NMex
Exhibitions: Changing exhibits each year
Publications: Exhibit catalogs; e-newsletter, monthly
Activities: Classes for children; docent training; lects open to pub, 10 vis lectrs per yr; concerts; gallery talks; tours; competitions; individual paintings & original objects of art lent to museums; lending collection contains original prints, paintings, photographs & sculpture; 1-2 exhibs per yr; organize traveling exhibs to Albright-Knox Art Gallery & Tacoma Art Mus; 1 nat exhib circulated every 3 yrs; mus shop sells books, original art, crafts, jewelry & postcards

NEW YORK

ALBANY

M **ALBANY INSTITUTE OF HISTORY & ART,** 125 Washington Ave, Albany, NY 12210-2296. Tel 518-463-4478; Fax 518-462-1522; Elec Mail information@albanyinstitute.org; Internet Home Page Address: www.albanyinstitute.org; *Dir* Christine M Miles; *Deputy Dir Coll & Exhibs* Tammis K Groft; *Dir Educ* Erika Sanger; *Chair Bd Trustees* George R Hearst III; *Dir Facilities* Robert Nilson; *Mus Shop Mgr* Elizabeth Bechand; *Pub Rels & Mktg Mgr* Steve Ricci; *Dir Finance & Admin* Lori Veshia
Open Wed - Sat 10 AM - 5 PM, Sun 12 PM - 5 PM, Tues groups only, cl Mon; Admis adults $10, seniors & students $8, children 6-12 $6, children under 6 & members free; Estab 1791, inc 1793 as the Society for the Promotion of Agriculture, Arts & Manufactures; 1829 as Albany Institute; 1900 as Albany Institute & Historical & Art Soc. Present name adopted 1926; Average Annual Attendance: 100,000; Mem: 2000; dues $35 & up; annual meeting in May
Income: Financed by endowment, mem, sales, foundation, city, county, state & federal grants & special gifts
Special Subjects: Folk Art, Historical Material, Metalwork, Flasks & Bottles, Furniture, Porcelain, Woodcuts, Tapestries, Drawings, Painting-American, Prints, Sculpture, American Indian Art, Textiles, Ceramics, Crafts, Pottery, Woodcarvings, Landscapes, Decorative Arts, Manuscripts, Portraits, Furniture, Glass, Jewelry, Silver, Ivory, Coins & Medals, Miniatures, Embroidery, Antiquities-Egyptian, Pewter
Collections: Art, decorative arts & historical artifacts related to the art, history & culture of Upper Hudson Valley Region from the 17th century to present; 18th & 19th century paintings; Hudson River School; Ceramics; New York (especially Albany) costumes, furniture, glass, pewter, silver & other regional decorative arts; textiles
Exhibitions: Hudson River School paintings from the Institute's collection; Ancient Egypt; 18th & 19th Century Sculpture & Paintings Colonial Albany
Publications: Catalogues; several books about the history of New York State; Remembrance of Patria: Dutch Arts & Culture in Colonial America; Thomas Cole: Drawn to nature members' newsletter & calendar
Activities: Classes for adults & children; dramatic progs; docent training; lects open to pub, 20 vis lectrs per yr; concerts; gallery talks; tours; individual paintings & original objects of art lent to other mus; book traveling exhibs 4 per yr; mus shop sells books, reproductions, prints, handcrafted items

L **Library,** 125 Washington Ave, Albany, NY 12210. Tel 518-463-4478; Fax 518-463-5506; Elec Mail library@albanyinstitute.org; Internet Home Page Address: www.albanyinstitute.org; *Chief Librn & Archivist* Rebecca Rich-Wulfmeyer
Open Thurs 1:30 PM - 4:30 PM & by appointment; Admis $8; Estab 1791 to collect historical material concerning Albany & the Upper Hudson region, as well as books on fine & decorative art related to the Institute's holdings; For reference only; Average Annual Attendance: 600
Library Holdings: Auction Catalogs; Book Volumes 25,000; Clipping Files; Compact Disks; DVDs; Exhibition Catalogs 50; Kodachrome Transparencies; Lantern Slides; Manuscripts; Maps 350; Memorabilia; Original Documents; Other Holdings Architectural Plans; Deeds; Ephemeral; Posters; Pamphlets; Periodical Subscriptions 60; Photographs; Reels; Slides; Video Tapes
Special Subjects: Art History, Folk Art, Photography, Manuscripts, Painting-American, Prints, Sculpture, Ceramics, Art Education, Porcelain, Furniture, Silver, Silversmithing, Antiquities-Egyptian, Pewter, Architecture, Portraits

M **COLLEGE OF SAINT ROSE,** Art Gallery, 324 State St, Albany, NY 12210-2002. Tel 518-485-3902; Fax 518-485-3920; Elec Mail flanagaj@strose.edu; Internet Home Page Address: www.strose.edu; *Dir* Jeanne Flanagan
Open Mon - Fri 10 AM - 4:30 PM, Mon - Thurs 6 - 8 PM, Sun Noon - 4 PM, cl Sat; No admis fee; Estab 1969 exhibiting contemporary art not previously seen in Capital Region; Average Annual Attendance: 2,700
Income: Financed by college funds
Special Subjects: Painting-American, Prints, Sculpture
Collections: Paintings, prints
Exhibitions: Rotating exhibits & student shows
Activities: Classes for adults; lect open to public, 6-8 vis lectrs per year; gallery talks; tours; scholarships offered

M **HISTORIC CHERRY HILL,** 523-1/2 S Pearl St, Albany, NY 12202-1111. Tel 518-434-4791; Fax 518-434-4806; Elec Mail housemus@knick.net; Internet Home Page Address: www.historiccherryhill.org; *Cur* Deborah Emmons; *Educ Dir* Rebecca Watrous; *CEO & Dir* Liselle LaFrance; *VPres* Michael Beiter; *Mus Shop Mgr* Lauren Mastin
Open Apr - June & Oct - Dec Tues - Fri Noon - 3 PM, Sat 10 AM - 3 PM, Sun 1 - 3 PM; July - Sept Tues - Sat 10 AM - 3PM, Sun 1 - 3 PM; Admis adults $5, seniors & students $4, children $2; Estab 1964 to preserve & research the house & contents of Cherry Hill, built for Philip Van Rensselaer in 1787 & lived in by him & four generations of his descendents until 1963; Georgian mansion having 14 rooms of original furniture, ceramics, paintings and other decorative arts spanning all five generations & garden; Average Annual Attendance: 5,000; Mem: 250; dues $15 & up
Income: Financed by endowment fund, admis, mem, program grants, sales shop revenue
Special Subjects: Painting-American, Textiles, Costumes, Ceramics, Pottery, Landscapes, Decorative Arts, Manuscripts, Portraits, Dolls, Furniture, Porcelain, Oriental Art, Silver, Period Rooms

Collections: Catherine Van Rensselaer Bonney Collection of Oriental decorative arts; New York State furniture; textiles and paintings dating from the early 18th thru 20th centuries; Manuscript Collection; Seasonal exhibitions in the period room
Publications: New Gleanings, quarterly newsletter
Activities: Educ dept; docent training; classroom materials; lects open to pub; tours; paintings and art objects are lent to other mus and exhibs; mus shop sells books, postcards & reproductions

A **NEW YORK OFFICE OF PARKS, RECREATION & HISTORIC PRESERVATION,** Natural Heritage Trust, Empire State Plaza, Agency Building 1 Albany, NY 12238. Tel 518-474-0456, 486-1899 (TDD); Internet Home Page Address: www.nyparks.state.ny.us; *Chair & NHT Commissioner* Carol Ash; *Commissioner Dept Environmental Conservation* Pete Grannis; *Chair State Council Parks, Recreation & Historic Preservation* Lucy R Waletzky
See website for admis fees; Estab to administer individual gifts & funds; funding appropriated by state legislatures for various purposes
Exhibitions: Letchworth Art & Crafts Show

L **NEW YORK STATE LIBRARY,** Manuscripts & Special Collections, Cultural Educ Center, 222 Madison Ave Albany, NY 12230. Tel 518-474-6282; Fax 518-474-5786; Elec Mail mscolls@mail.nysed.gov; Internet Home Page Address: www.nysl.nysed.gov; *Assoc Librn* Kathi Stanley; *Research Lib Dir* Loretta Ebert
Open Mon - Fri 9 AM - 5 PM
Income: Financed by State
Library Holdings: Book Volumes; Manuscripts; Maps; Original Documents
Special Subjects: Art History, Manuscripts, Historical Material
Collections: Over 50,000 items: black & white original photographs, glass negatives, daguerreotypes, engravings, lithographs, bookplates, postcards, original sketches & drawings, cartoons, stereograms & extra illustrated books depicting view of New York State & Portraits of its citizens past & present
Exhibitions: Exhibit program involves printed & manuscript materials

M **NEW YORK STATE MUSEUM,** Cultural Education Ctr Rm 3023, Empire State Plaza Albany, NY 12230-0001. Tel 518-474-5877; Fax 518-486-3696; Elec Mail cryan@mail.nysed.gov; Internet Home Page Address: www.nysd.nysed.gov; *Dir & Asst Commissioner* Clifford Siegfried; *Dir Research & Coll* John Hart; *Supvr Exhibit Production* Dave LaPlante; *Dir Exhibits* Mark Schaming; *Chief Geological Survey* Robert Fakundiny; *Dir Commun* Joanne Guilmette; *Head Educ* Jeanine Grinage
Open Mon - Sun 9:30 AM - 5 PM; Admis by donation; Estab 1836 to research, collect, exhibit & educate about the natural & human history of New York State for the people of New York; to function as a cultural center in the Capital District of the Empire State; Museum has 1 1/2 acres of exhibit space; three permanent exhibit halls devoted to people & nature (history & science) themes of Adirondack Wilderness, Metropolitan New York, Upstate New York; three temporary exhibit galleries of art, historical & technological artifacts; Average Annual Attendance: 900,000
Income: $5,700,000 (financed by state appropriation, government & foundation grants & private donations)
Special Subjects: Ethnology, Decorative Arts
Collections: Ethnological artifacts of Iroquois-Algonquian (New York area) Indians; circus posters, costumes, decorative arts, paintings, photographs, postcards, prints, toys, weapons
Activities: Classes for adults & children; lects open to pub; concerts; individual paintings & original objects of art lent to mus; lending collection contains nature artifacts, original art works, original prints, paintings, photographs & slides; book traveling exhibs, 6 per yr; originate traveling exhibs; mus shop sells books, magazines, original art, reproductions, prints, slides, toys, baskets, pottery by local artists, jewelry, stationery & posters

A **PRINT CLUB OF ALBANY,** PO Box 6578, Ft Orange Sta Albany, NY 12206-0578. Tel 518-399-7231; Tel 518-449-4756; Elec Mail semowich@gmail.com; Internet Home Page Address: pcaprint.org; *Pres Print Selection Comt Chmn* Thomas Andress; *VPres & Cur* Dr Charles Semowich; *Treas* Donald Bolon
Open by appointment; No admis fee; Estab 1933 for those interested in all aspects of prints & printmaking; Maintains reference library; permanent collection; temporary exhibs; Average Annual Attendance: 2,000; Mem: 200; dues $90, active mems receive an original print; mem open to artists who have national recognition, non-artists need interest in prints; annual meeting in May; mem application on website
Income: Financed by mem, city & state appropriation, sales, commissions & auction
Purchases: Prints & printmakers' archives
Library Holdings: Auction Catalogs; Book Volumes 150; DVDs; Kodachrome Transparencies; Manuscripts; Original Art Works; Slides; Video Tapes
Special Subjects: Drawings, Etchings & Engravings, Graphics, Prints, Watercolors, Woodcuts
Collections: Drawings; Plates; Prints from all periods & countries concentrating on 20th century America; 18,000 items
Exhibitions: mem exhibs; Nat Open; historical shows
Publications: Exhib catalogues
Activities: Educ dept; workshops; lects open to pub, 1 vis lectrs per yr; talks; competition with prizes; awards, Cogswell, Distinguished Mem; objects of art lent to state capital & county offices; originate traveling exhibs; sales shop sells original art

M **SAGE COLLEGE OF ALBANY,** Opalka Gallery, 140 New Scotland Ave, Albany, NY 12208-3491. Tel 518-292-7742; Fax 518-292-1903; Elec Mail opalka@sage.edu; Internet Home Page Address: www.sage.edu/opalka; *Dir* Jim Richard Wilson; *Exhib Coordr* Fabienne Powell
Open Mon - Fri 10 AM - 8 PM, Sun 12 PM - 4 PM; Summer: Mon - Fri 10 AM - 4 PM; other times by appointment; Estab 2002
Collections: Paintings; photographs; sculpture
Activities: Poetry readings; recitals; symposia; documentary film screenings; lects open to pub; gallery talks

M **The Little Gallery,** 140 New Scotland Ave, Rathbone Hall Albany, NY 12208-3491. Tel 518-292-8625
Open Wed - Thurs 3 PM - 5 PM; other times by appointment
Collections: Works by faculty & student artists

M **SCHUYLER MANSION STATE HISTORIC SITE,** 32 Catherine St, Albany, NY 12202-1605. Tel 518-434-0834; Fax 518-434-3821; Elec Mail marcy.shaffer@oprhp.stat; Internet Home Page Address: www.nysparks.com; *Historic Site Mgr* Marcy Schaffer; *Interpreter* Deborah Emmons-Andarawl; *Interpreter* Umber Gold; *Interpretive Program Dir* Darlene Rogers
Open Wed - Sat 10 AM - 5 PM, Sun 1 - 5 PM, Nov - mid Apr; call for winter hours; Admis adults $3, New York seniors $2, children 5-12 $1; Estab 1917 for the preservation and interpretation of the 18th century home of Philip Schuyler, one of the finest examples of Georgian architecture in the country; The house boasts a substantial collection of Schuyler family pieces & fine examples of Chinese export porcelain, delftware & English glassware; Average Annual Attendance: 15,000
Income: Financed by state appropriation
Special Subjects: Historical Material
Collections: American furnishings of the Colonial & Federal Periods, predominantly of New York & New England origins
Publications: Schuyler Genealogy: A Compendium of Sources Pertaining to the Schuyler Families in America Prior to 1800; vol 2 prior to 1900
Activities: Educ dept; lect; tours; special events

M **UNIVERSITY AT ALBANY, STATE UNIVERSITY OF NEW YORK,** University Art Museum, 1400 Washington Ave, Albany, NY 12222-1000. Tel 518-442-4035; Fax 518-442-5075; Elec Mail museum@albany.edu; Internet Home Page Address: www.albany.edu/museum; *Exhib Designer* Zheng Hu; *Admin Asst* Joanne Lue; *Dir* Janet Riker; *Assoc Dir* Corinna Schaming; *Outreach Coordr* Naomi Lewis; *Colls Asst* Ryan Parr; *Registrar* Darcie Abbatiello
Open Tues 10 AM - 8 PM, Wed - Fri 10 AM - 5 PM, Sat Noon - 4 PM; No admis fee; Estab 1968 to advance knowledge & foster understanding in contemporary visual arts, & to provide a forum for art, artists & audiences through collections, progs & publications; Average Annual Attendance: 25,000
Income: Financed by state appropriation
Special Subjects: Drawings, Painting-American, Prints, Sculpture
Collections: Paintings, prints, drawings & sculpture of 20th century contemporary art; photographs
Exhibitions: Rotating exhibition
Publications: Exhibition catalogs
Activities: Lects open to public, 6-10 vis lectrs per yr; gallery talks; tours; competitions with awards; book traveling exhibs; originate traveling exhibs
Courses: 100 paintings, 25 photographs, 75 sculpture, individual paintings & original objects of art lent to on campus admin offices; lending collection contains 800 original prints

L **Visual Resources Library,** Fine Arts Bldg, Rm 121, Albany, NY 12222-0001. Tel 518-442-4018; Elec Mail cdlewis@albany.edu; Internet Home Page Address: www.albany.edu/val; *Visual Resources Cur* Caitlain Devereaux Lewis
Open Tues - Thurs 9 AM - 4:30 PM; Estab 1967 to provide instruction & reference for the university & community; Circ more than 7,000 slides per year
Income: financed by the college
Library Holdings: Book Volumes; CD-ROMs; Kodachrome Transparencies; Pamphlets; Photographs; Slides 90,000
Collections: Approx 90,000 slides of ancient art, medieval art, pre-modern & modern art, architecture & classics; art periodicals and MFA thesis work

ALFRED

L **NEW YORK STATE COLLEGE OF CERAMICS AT ALFRED UNIVERSITY,** Scholes Library of Ceramics, 2 Pine St, Alfred, NY 14802-1214. Tel 607-871-2494; Fax 607-871-2349; Elec Mail ccjohnson@alfred.edu; Internet Home Page Address: scholes.alfred.edu; *Visual Resources Cur* John Hosford; *Dir* Carla C Johnson
Open acad yr Mon - Thurs 8 AM - 12 AM, Fri 8 AM - 8 PM, Sat 10 AM - 6 PM, Sun noon-midnight, other periods Mon - Fri 8 AM - 4:30 PM; Estab 1947 to service art educ to the Master's level in fine art & the PhD level in engineering & science related to ceramics; Circ Artbooks 5,808; slides 42,859; The College has a 2500 sq ft Art Gallery which is managed by the Art & Design Division; Average Annual Attendance: 80,497
Income: $671,884 (financed by endowment & state appropriation)
Purchases: $55,000
Library Holdings: Audio Tapes 51; Book Volumes 64,495; CD-ROMs 33; Cassettes 643; Clipping Files; Exhibition Catalogs; Fiche; Filmstrips; Lantern Slides 200; Motion Pictures; Original Art Works; Other Holdings Art books 26,188; Audio cassettes 171; College arc; Pamphlets 1408; Periodical Subscriptions 707; Reels; Slides 158,890; Video Tapes 15
Special Subjects: Art History, Folk Art, Decorative Arts, Photography, Commercial Art, Graphic Design, Painting-American, Painting-European, History of Art & Archaeology, Ceramics, Crafts, Bronzes, Printmaking, Asian Art, Glass
Publications: Scholes Library Bulletin, biannual
Activities: Tours

ALMOND

M **ALMOND HISTORICAL SOCIETY, INC,** Hagadorn House, The 1800-37 Museum, 7 Main St, Almond, NY 14804; PO Box 209, Almond, NY 14804-0209. Tel 607-276-6781; Elec Mail almondhistoricalsociety@gmail.com; Internet Home Page Address: www.usgennet.org/usa/ny/tour/almond; *Pres* Lee A Ryan; *VPres* Helen Spencer; *Treas* Teresa Johnson; *Newsletter Ed/Sec* Donna B Ryan; *Archivist* Doris Montgomery
Open Fri 2 - 4 PM & by appointment; Admis free - donations accepted; Estab 1965 to preserve local history, genealogy & artifacts; The Little Gallery 4 ft x 12 ft, burlap covered walls, 4 display cases, 8-track lighting system; Average Annual Attendance: 2,000; Mem: 395; mem open to those interested in local history; life

member single $125, couple $200; bus or professional $12, family $15, couple $12, individual $8; annual meeting in Nov

Income: $25,908 (financed by endowment, mem, city appropriations)

Collections: 1513 genealogies of local families; town & village records; slide coll of local houses; 1500 costumes & hats; 50 quilts; toys; school books; maps; cemetery lists; photographs, scrapbooks

Exhibitions: Local architecture: drawings & photographs; history of the local post office

Publications: The Cooking Fireplace in the Hagadorn House; Forgotten Cemeteries of Almond; My Father's Old Fashioned Drug Store; Recollections of Horace Stillman; School Days; 12 page quarterly newsletter mailed to mems & posted on website

Activities: Classes for children; lect open to public, 3 vis lectrs per yr; tours

AMENIA

A AGES OF MAN FOUNDATION, (Ages of Man Fellowship) 57 Sheffield Rd, Box 5 Amenia, NY 12501-5629. Tel 845-373-9380; *VPres* Andrew Rauhauser; *Pres* Dr Nathan Cabot Hale; *Sub Dir* Dr Niels Berg
Open 10 AM - 5 PM; No admis fee, suggested donation; Estab 1968 for the building & design of a sculpture chapel based on the thematic concepts of the Cycle of Life; Average Annual Attendance: 35; Mem: 20; dues $100; meetings May & Nov

Income: Financed by mem & contributions

Collections: Sculpture & architectural models of the chapel; biological references; forms of nature

Exhibitions: varied sculpture concepts to document historical background & concept of the human form

Publications: Project report, yearly; Abstraction in Art & Nature; Perception of Human Form in Sculpture: A History of Figurative Understanding by NC Hale, PhD

Activities: Art history; apprenticeship & journeyman instruction in Cycle of Life design; lects open to public, 20 vis lectrs per yr; gallery talks; original objects of art lent to museums, art assns, educational institutions; originate traveling exhibs

AMHERST

M AMHERST MUSEUM, 3755 Tonawanda Creek Rd, Amherst, NY 14228-1599. Tel 716-689-1440; Fax 716-689-1409; Elec Mail amhmuseum@adelphia.net; Internet Home Page Address: www.amherstmuseum.org; *Cur Educ* Jean W Neff; *Exec Dir* Joseph G Weickart; *Cur* Jessica A Norton; *Textile Cur* Kristie Rhoback
Open Nov - Mar Tues - Fri 9:30 AM - 4:30 PM, Apr - Oct Tues - Fri 9:30 AM - 4:30 PM, Sat & Sun 12:30 - 4:30 PM, cl Mon & Municipal Holidays; Admis adults $5, children between 5 & 12 $1.50, mems & children under 4 free; Estab 1972 to preserve town of Amherst history; Maintains reference library, local history exhibits & temporary art exhibits; Average Annual Attendance: 40,000; Mem: 825; dues family $35, individual $20

Income: $550,000 (financed by mem, town appropriation, earned income)

Library Holdings: Audio Tapes; Book Volumes; Clipping Files; Fiche; Filmstrips; Lantern Slides; Manuscripts; Maps; Memorabilia; Original Documents

Special Subjects: Costumes, Folk Art, Decorative Arts, Furniture, Glass, Carpets & Rugs, Historical Material, Maps, Dioramas, Period Rooms, Embroidery

Collections: American Material Culture; 19th Century Historic Buildings; textiles & costumes

Exhibitions: The Erie Canal; Pioneer Kitchen; Niagara Frontier Wireless Radio Gallery; How They Moved Here; What's Cooking: Women in the Kitchen; Wedding Belles: The Fashionable Bride 1840-1990; Street of Shops

Publications: Ephemera, quarterly newsletter; researching Amherst House Histories, booklet; Glancing Back: A Pictorial History of Amherst NY

Activities: Classes for adults & children; docent training; special events; lects open to pub, 2-5 vis lectrs per yr; mus shop sells books, prints, reproductions, folk art & unique gift items

L Niederlander Research Library, 3755 Tonawanda Creek Rd, Amherst, NY 14228-1599. Tel 716-689-1440; Fax 716-689-1409; Elec Mail amhmuseum@roadrunner.com; Internet Home Page Address: www.amherstmuseum.org; *Exec Dir* Lynn S Beman; *Librn* Toniann Scime
Open Tues-Fri 9:30 AM-4:30 PM, Sat & Sun by appointment; Admis adults $5, students $1.50; For reference only

Library Holdings: Book Volumes 3000; Clipping Files; Fiche; Kodachrome Transparencies; Lantern Slides; Manuscripts; Memorabilia; Pamphlets; Photographs; Prints; Reels; Slides; Video Tapes

Collections: 19th-20th century photographs & archival materials related to Town of Amherst, NY & Village of Williamsville, NY

Publications: Genealogical Society newsletter

Activities: Lects open to pub

M DAEMEN COLLEGE, Fanette Goldman & Carolyn Greenfield Gallery, 4380 Main St, Duns Scotus Hall Amherst, NY 14226-3544. Tel 716-839-8241; Fax 716-839-8516; Internet Home Page Address: www.daemen.edu; *Dir* Kevin Kegler
Open Mon - Fri 9 AM - 4 PM; No admis fee; Estab to add dimension to the art program & afford liberal arts students opportunity to view art made by established artists as well as art students; Gallery area is part of main building (Duns Scotus Hall), recently renovated exterior & entrance; Average Annual Attendance: 1,500

Income: Financed by College Art Department

Activities: Lect open to public, 4 - 5 vis lectrs per year

L Marian Library, 4380 Main St, Amherst, NY 14226-3592. Tel 716-839-8243; Fax 716-839-8475; Internet Home Page Address: www.daemen.edu; *Reference Librn* Andrea Sullivan; *Ref Librn* Randolph Chojecki; *Asst Head Librn* Frank Carey; *Head Librn* Glenn V Woike; *Circ & ILL Librn* Kara McGuire

Library Holdings: Book Volumes 140,000; DVDs 500; Periodical Subscriptions 940; Slides 4911; Video Tapes 1536

Special Subjects: Art History, Calligraphy, Graphic Arts, Graphic Design, Painting-American, Art Education, Textiles

AMSTERDAM

M MOHAWK VALLEY HERITAGE ASSOCIATION, INC, Walter Elwood Museum, 366 W Main St, Amsterdam, NY 12010-2236. Tel 518-843-5151; Fax 518-843-6098; Elec Mail director@walterelwoodmuseum.org; Internet Home Page Address: www.walterelwoodmuseum.org; *Exec Dir* Ann M Peonie; *Brd Treas* Guy Cappuccio; *Brd Pres* Susan Wollman
Open Sept - June Mon - Fri 8:30 AM - 4 PM & weekend by appointment; July 1 - Labor Day Mon - Thurs 8:30 AM - 3:30 PM, Fri 8:30 AM - 1 PM; Admis fee adults $3, seniors $2, children free; Estab 1939 to preserve local heritage & natural history; Gallery displays changing exhibits, local & professional collections & museum's works of art; Average Annual Attendance: 5,000; Mem: 500; dues family $30, individual $20, seniors $15

Income: $70,000 (financed by grants, donations & mem)

Special Subjects: Historical Material, Painting-American, Bronzes, Etchings & Engravings, Carpets & Rugs, Military Art

Collections: Oil paintings by turn of the century local artists; photographs of early Amsterdam & vicinity; steel engravings by turn of the century artists; Victorian; Native American; military

Exhibitions: Paintings by the Monday Art Group (local area artists); Rotating exhibitions

Publications: Annual newsletter in Fall

Activities: Classes for adults & children; tours; mus shop sells books, original art

ANNANDALE-ON-HUDSON

M BARD COLLEGE, Center for Curatorial Studies and the Hessel Museum of Art, 33 Garden Rd, Annandale-on-Hudson, NY 12504-5000; PO Box 5000, Annandale-on-Hudson, NY 12504-5000. Tel 845-758-7598; Fax 845-758-2442; Elec Mail ccs@bard.edu; Internet Home Page Address: www.bard.edu/ccs; *Asst Dir* Marcia Acita; *Librn* Ann Butler; *Exec Dir* Tom Eccles; *Dir Grad Prog* Johanna Burton; *Asst Dir Admin & Develop* Jaime Baird; *Registrar* Rachel von Wettberg; *Communs Coordr* Ramona Rosenberg; *Grad Program Admin* Letitia Smith; *Prep* Mark DeLura; *Security Mgr* Peter Amentas; *Admin Asst* Christine Delfino
Open Wed - Sun 1 - 5 PM; No admis fee; Estab 1992 for the presentation of contemporary art; Circ Non-circulating, research; 25,000 sq ft of exhibition space, changing exhibitions (temp & coll); Average Annual Attendance: 12,000

Library Holdings: Audio Tapes; Book Volumes; CD-ROMs; Cards; Cassettes; Clipping Files; Compact Disks; DVDs; Exhibition Catalogs; Memorabilia; Original Documents; Other Holdings; Pamphlets; Periodical Subscriptions; Photographs; Slides; Video Tapes

Special Subjects: Drawings, Painting-American, Photography, Painting-European, Painting-British, Restorations, Painting-German

Collections: contemporary art from 1960s to the present in all media, including installations & video; Contemporary Art; International Art; Marieluise Hessel Collection

Activities: Educ progs; artist's talks; grad prog in curatorial studies; AS-AP or archive project; lects open to pub; concerts; gallery talks; tours; schols; fels; annual award for curatorial excellence; book traveling exhibs 1 per yr; originate traveling exhibs; mus shop sells books

M BARD COLLEGE, Fisher Art Center, PO Box 5000, Annandale-on-Hudson, NY 12504-5000. Tel 845-758-7674; Fax 845-758-7683; Elec Mail fishercenter@bard.edu; Internet Home Page Address: www.fishercenter.bard.edu; *Dir* Tambra Dillon; *Chair* Jeanne Donovan Fisher
Open daily 10 AM - 5 PM; No admis fee; Estab 1964 as an educational center; Art center has a gallery, slide library and uses the college library for its teaching

Exhibitions: Four guest-curated exhibitions of contemporary art & two student exhibitions per year; End of Yr Sr Thesis Exhibit

Publications: Catalogs

Activities: Lects open to public; 10 vis lectrs per yr; gallery talks; tours

L Center For Curatorial Studies Library, Tel 914-758-7567; Fax 914-758-2442; Elec Mail ccs@bard.edu; *Librn* Susan Leonard
Estab 1990; For reference only; non-circulating research collection supporting the graduate program in Curatorial Studies

Library Holdings: Book Volumes 11,000; Clipping Files 1000; Exhibition Catalogs; Memorabilia; Pamphlets; Periodical Subscriptions 52; Slides 10,000; Video Tapes

Special Subjects: Art History, Mixed Media, Photography, Painting-American, Painting-British, Painting-German, Painting-Italian, Sculpture, Painting-European, Conceptual Art, Video, Aesthetics, Restoration & Conservation

ASTORIA

M AMERICAN MUSEUM OF THE MOVING IMAGE, 36-01 35th Ave, Astoria, NY 11106-1226. Tel 718-777-6888 Admin Offices, 6820; Fax 718-784-4681; Elec Mail education@movingimage.us; Internet Home Page Address: www.movingimage.us/; *Dir* Rochelle Slovin, MA; *Chmn Bd Trustees* Herbert S Schlosser
Open Tues - Thurs 10:30 AM - 5 PM, Fri 10:30 AM - 8 PM (free admis 4 - 8 PM), Sat & Sun 10:30 AM - 7 PM; Admis adults $12, seniors & col students with valid ID $9, children 3-18 yrs $6, mems & children under 3 yrs no charge; Estab 1988, devoted to art, history, technique & technology of moving image media; Temporary gallery on first floor, 1800 sq ft; 2nd & 3rd floors 5500 sq ft of permanent exhibition space; Average Annual Attendance: 90,000; Mem: 1500; dues $65-$1000

Special Subjects: Costumes, Cartoons

Collections: The museum has a collection of over 70,000 artifacts relating to the material art form of movies & television, magazines, dolls, costumes, clothing; Cinema Arts; Material Culture; Television

Exhibitions: Behind the Screen; Computer Space; Television Set Design: Late Show with David Letterman

Publications: Behind the Screen; Who Does What in Motion Pictures & Television

Activities: Classes for children; ESL progs; docent training; adult tours; lects open to pub, 50 vis lectrs per yr; gallery talks; tours; originate traveling exhibs; mus shop sells books, magazines, & reproductions

AUBURN

M CAYUGA MUSEUM OF HISTORY & ART, 203 Genesee St, Auburn, NY 13021-3380. Tel 315-253-8051; Fax 315-253-9829; Elec Mail cayugamuseum@roadrunner.com; Internet Home Page Address: www.cayuganet.org/cayugamuseum; *Dir* Eileen McHugh; *Cur* Lauren Chyle; *Bus Mgr* Lynn Palmieri
Open Tues - Sun Noon - 5 PM, cl Mon & holidays; No admis fee; $3 suggested donation; Estab 1936 for research & Cayuga County history; Average Annual Attendance: 10,000; Mem: 250; dues $25-$250; annual meeting in May
Income: Financed by endowment, mem & county
Special Subjects: American Indian Art
Collections: Fine & Decorative Arts; Native American Collection; Soundfilm
Exhibitions: Ongoing series of changing exhibits; Auburn Prison; TimeClocks; Case Research Lab
Activities: Classes for adults & children; docent training; lects open to pub; 2-6 vis lectrs per yr; tours; lending collection contains motion pictures & slides; mus shop sells books, reproductions, postcards & small gifts

M SCHWEINFURTH ART CENTER, (Schweinfurth Memorial Art Center) 205 Genesee St, Auburn, NY 13021-3304. Tel 315-255-1553; Fax 315-255-0871; Elec Mail mail@schweinfurthartcenter.org; Internet Home Page Address: www.myartcenter.org; *Dir* Donna Lamb; *Prog Dir* Miranda Traudt; *Prog Coord* Stephanie Lange; *Admin Coord* Monica Hastedt
Open Tues - Fri 10 AM - 5 PM, Sat 10 AM - 5 PM, Sun 1 - 5 PM; Admis $6; Estab 1981; community art center focusing on fine art, architecture & design; 4000 sq ft contemporary gallery; Average Annual Attendance: 20,000; Mem: 550; dues $30-$1000
Income: $240,000 (financed by endowment, mem, city & state, federal, public & private)
Special Subjects: Pottery, Painting-American, Prints, Sculpture, Photography, Watercolors, Textiles, Crafts, Woodcarvings, Woodcuts, Landscapes, Decorative Arts, Collages, Metalwork, Carpets & Rugs, Coins & Medals, Embroidery, Enamels
Exhibitions: Regional artists, traveling & annual childrens exhibit (Feb); annual quilt exhibit (Nov -Jan)
Publications: Monthly calendar
Activities: Classes for adults & children; docent training; lects open to pub; 12 vis lectrs per yr; concerts; gallery talks; tours; scholarships offered; originate traveling exhibs; sales shop sells books, original art & gifts; special events

BALDWIN

M BALDWIN HISTORICAL SOCIETY MUSEUM, 1980 Grand Ave, Baldwin, NY 11510; P.O. Box 762, Baldwin, NY 11510. Tel 516-223-6900, 223-8080 (Chamber of Commerce); *Cur* Gerry Griffin; *Pres* Jack Bryck; *VPres* Connie Grando; *Treas* Robert Grando
Open to the pub Mon, Wed, Fri 9 AM - 11:30 AM - Sun 1 - 4 PM or by appointment; No admis fee; Estab 1971, mus estab 1976 to preserve Baldwin history memorabilia including historical photographs; Average Annual Attendance: 500; Mem: 225; dues family $10, individual $5; monthly meetings except Jan, Feb, July & Aug
Income: $5000 (financed by mem, fundraising)
Special Subjects: Painting-American, Photography, Costumes, Ceramics, Etchings & Engravings, Manuscripts, Furniture, Glass, Jewelry, Maps
Collections: Collection of local history photographs, postal cards, advertising objects, decorative art objects, manuscripts
Exhibitions: Selection of Baldwin's memorabilia
Publications: Newsletter
Activities: Classes for adults & children in local history progs; lects open to pub, 4 vis lectrs per yr; annual American History award given to a senior in History

BALLSTON SPA

A SARATOGA COUNTY HISTORICAL SOCIETY, Brookside Museum, Six Charlton St, Ballston Spa, NY 12020. Tel 518-885-4000; Fax 518-885-4055; Elec Mail info@brooksidemuseum.org; Internet Home Page Address: www.brooksidemuseum.org; *Exec Dir* Joy Houle; *Cur* Kathleen Coleman; *Dir Educ* Anne Clothier; *Admin Asst* Samantha Strevy
Open Tues - Fri 10 AM - 4 PM, Sat 10 AM - 2 PM, cl Sun & Mon; Admis family $5, adults $2, seniors, $1.50, children $1; Estab 1965 to inform pub on the history of Saratoga County; 4 small galleries; Average Annual Attendance: 12,000; Mem: 500; dues individual $25
Income: $160, 000 (financed by endowment, mem, city appropriation & grants)
Library Holdings: Audio Tapes; Book Volumes; Clipping Files; Lantern Slides; Manuscripts; Maps; Original Documents; Other Holdings; Photographs
Special Subjects: Historical Material
Collections: History of Saratoga County, books, manuscripts, objects, photographs
Exhibitions: Saratoga County: The Story of Brookside changing exhibitions; Go to the Head of the Class; Taking the Waters
Publications: Gristmill, 1 per year; columns, 6 per year
Activities: Classes for adult & children; lects open to pub; concerts; sponsor competitions; mus shop sells books, original art, reproducts & prints

BAYSIDE

M QUEENSBOROUGH COMMUNITY COLLEGE, Art Gallery, 222-05 56th Ave, Bayside, NY 11364-1497. Tel 718-631-6396, 281-5095; Fax 718-631-6620; Elec Mail qccartgallery@qcc.cuny.edu; Internet Home Page Address: www.qccartgallery.org; *Dir* Faustino Quintanilla; *Asst Dir* Deanne DeNyse; *Admin Asst* Lisa Scandaliato
Open Tues & Fri 10AM-5PM, Wed & Thurs 10AM-7PM, Sat & Sun noon-5PM; No admis fee; Estab 1981 to provide the col & Queens Community with up to

date documentation outline on the visual arts; Average Annual Attendance: 12,000; Mem: 500; dues $25
Income: $214,793 (financed by endowment & mem)
Purchases: Ruth Rothschild & Hampton Blake
Library Holdings: Book Volumes; CD-ROMs; Exhibition Catalogs; Original Documents; Slides
Special Subjects: Manuscripts, Painting-British, Painting-French, Painting-Japanese, Architecture, Drawings, Graphics, Painting-American, Photography, Prints, African Art, Archaeology, Ceramics, Etchings & Engravings, Painting-European, Painting-Canadian, Painting-Dutch, Painting-Flemish, Painting-Polish, Painting-Spanish, Painting-Italian, Painting-Australian, Painting-German, Painting-Russian, Painting-Israeli, Painting-Scandinavian, Painting-New Zealand
Collections: Contemporary Art; works on paper; Richard Art Schwager; Roger Indiana; Paul Jenkins; R Dichtenstein; Larry Rives; Frank Stella; Judy Ritka; Alfonso Ossorio; Jules Allen; Jimmy Ernst; Josef Albers; Sirena; Pre-Columbian artifacts
Exhibitions: Siri Berg-Suzane Winkler; The Priva B Gross International Works On/Of Paper; Permanent Collection: Larry Rives
Publications: Signal: Politics & Gender; Romanticism & Classicism; Power of Popular Imagery; Art & Politics
Activities: Lects open to pub, 4-8 vis lectrs per yr; gallery talks; tours; competitions with awards; schols offered; individual paintings & original objects of art lent for exhibit purposes to organizations that follow loan criteria; lending collection contains original art works, photographs, sculptures & videos (art-New York & others); art lent to Seoul Art Gallery Korea; originate traveling exhibs annually; mus & accredited galleries; mus shop sells reproductions, books, prints, jewelry; junior mus

BEACON

A DIA ART FOUNDATION DIA: BEACON, RIGGIO GALLERIES, (Dia Center for the Arts) 3 Beekman St, Beacon, NY 12508; 535 W 22nd St, 4th Fl, New York, NY 10011. Tel 845-440-0100; Fax 845-440-0092; Elec Mail info@diacenter.org; Internet Home Page Address: www.diaart.org; *Cur* Yasmil Raymond; *Dir* Susan Batton
Open Oct Thurs - Mon 11 AM - 6 PM, cl Tues & Wed; Nov - Dec Thurs - Mon 11 AM - 4 PM, cl Tues & Wed; Admis general $10, students & seniors (65+) $7, mems & children under 12 free; Estab 1974 for planning, realization & presentation of important works of contemporary art. Commitment to artist's participation in display of works in long term, carefully maintained installations; Galleries: Dan Flavin Art Institute, Bridgehampton, NY; The Lightning Field, Quemado, NM. In 2003 Dia Art Foundation opened a museum to house its permanent collection comprising major works of art from the 1960's to the present.; Mem: Dues special mem $30, individual $50, family $100, friend $500
Income: Financed by grants
Publications: The Foundation has published collections of poetry & translations of poetry
Activities: Educ dept, classes for children; lects open to pub, 3 vis lectrs per yr; concerts, gallery talks, tours; exhibit catalogues; Series of discussions on contemporary cultural issues; mus shop sells books & original art

BINGHAMTON

M ROBERSON MUSEUM & SCIENCE CENTER, 30 Front St, Binghamton, NY 13905-4779. Tel 607-772-0660; Fax 607-771-8905; Elec Mail info@roberson.org; Internet Home Page Address: www.roberson.org; *Cur & Registrar* Eve Daniels; *Exec Dir* Terry McDonald; *Dir Exhibits* Peter Klosky; *Dir Educ* Katherine Howorth-Bouman
Open Wed, Thurs & Sat - Sun noon - 5 PM, Fri noon - 9 PM, cl Mon & Tues; Admis adults $8, seniors & students $5, children under 4 free; Estab 1954 as a regional museum of art, history & science educ; The Roberson Mus & Science Center, built in 1905-06 contains eight galleries; the Martin Building, built in 1968, designed by Richard Neutra, contains five galleries; the A Ward Ford Wing, completed in 1983 contains the Irma M Ahearn Gallery; Average Annual Attendance: 20,000; Mem: 1600; dues $30-$85
Income: $1,500,000 (financed by endowment, mem, city, county & state appropriations, federal funds & foundations)
Special Subjects: Archaeology, Historical Material, Drawings, Painting-American, Photography, Prints, Ethnology, Crafts, Decorative Arts, Furniture
Collections: Loomis Wildlife Collection: Northeastern Birds & Mammals; natural history specimens; historical archives & photographic collections; Hands-on science displays & interactive arts; Link Planetarium
Exhibitions: Voices & Visions; Edwin Link: The Air Age; Local History Gallery; Decker Life Science Learning Center (DNA Lab); Audubon, Masks; Confluence
Activities: Educ prog; classes for adults & children; school progs; pub progs & workshops; dramatic progs; docent training; lects open to pub, 5 vis lectrs per yr; gallery talks; tours; sponsoring of competitions; scholarships offered; progs sent to schools in eleven counties; individual paintings & original objects of art lent; lending collection contains slide tape progs with hands-on-activities for groups; book traveling exhibs 2-3 per yr; originate traveling exhibs to other mus; mus shops sell books, original art, reproductions, prints, contemporary crafts, unique & unusual gifts

M STATE UNIVERSITY OF NEW YORK AT BINGHAMTON, Binghamton University Art Museum, PO Box 6000, University Art Museum Binghamton, NY 13902-6000. Tel 607-777-2634; Fax 607-777-2613; Elec Mail hogan@bighampton.edu; *Cur Educ* Silvia Ivanova; *Asst Dir* Jacqueline Hogan; *Technical Dir* Ronald Polesnak; *Dir* Lynn Gamwell Dr.; *Dir of Develop* Jack Braunstein
Open Tues - Sat Noon - 4 pm, Thurs Noon - 7 PM, cl all holidays; No admis fee; Estab 1967; Eight areas of art; Average Annual Attendance: 4,000
Income: $30,000 (financed by state appropriations)
Library Holdings: CD-ROMs

Special Subjects: Afro-American Art, Decorative Arts, Landscapes, Photography, Porcelain, Pre-Columbian Art, Painting-American, Textiles, Maps, Painting-European, Sculpture, Tapestries, Drawings, Graphics, Photography, Watercolors, African Art, Anthropology, Religious Art, Ceramics, Woodcuts, Etchings & Engravings, Manuscripts, Posters, Furniture, Glass, Jade, Jewelry, Oriental Art, Asian Art, Painting-British, Painting-Dutch, Painting-French, Carpets & Rugs, Ivory, Scrimshaw, Restorations, Baroque Art, Painting-Flemish, Renaissance Art, Embroidery, Medieval Art, Painting-Spanish, Painting-Italian
Collections: Asian coll; Teaching coll from Egyptian to contemporary art; African; Wedgewood
Publications: Exhibit catalogs; books
Activities: Educ prog; classes for adults & children; tours; lects open to pub; 6 vis lectrs per yr; gallery talks; seminars; tours; internships offered; mus shop sells jewelry

BLUE MOUNTAIN LAKE

M **THE ADIRONDACK HISTORICAL ASSOCIATION,** The Adirondack Museum, 9097 State Rte 30, Blue Mountain Lake, NY 12812; PO Box 99, Blue Mountain Lake, NY 12812-0099. Tel 518-352-7311; Fax 518-352-7653; Elec Mail info@adirondackmuseum.org; Internet Home Page Address: www.adirondackmuseum.org; *Pres* Kevin J Arquit; *Cur* Hallie Bond; *Librn* Jerold L Pepper; *Dir Fin* Michael Lombardi; *Dir Mktg & Communs* Kate Moore; *Dir Develop* Sarah Lewin; *Dir* David Kahn; *Human Resources Mgr* Colleen Sage; *Mgr Retail Operations* Vickie Sandiford; *Chief Cur* Laura Rice; *Conservatory Coll Mgr* Doreen Alessi; *Registrar/Cur* Laura Cotton
Open Memorial Day - mid Oct daily 10 AM - 5 PM; Admis Adults 17 & over $18, 13-17 $12, 6-12 $6, 5 & under no charge; Estab 1957 to interpret the history & culture of the Adirondack Park; Museum contains two large galleries for paintings; Average Annual Attendance: 73,000; Mem: 4,000; Individual $40, Family $95
Library Holdings: Audio Tapes 244; Book Volumes 8,809; Manuscripts 650; Maps 1,397; Memorabilia 16,813; Original Art Works; Original Documents; Pamphlets; Periodical Subscriptions; Photographs; Reproductions; Slides; Video Tapes
Special Subjects: Photography, Prints
Collections: Drawings, Paintings, Prints, Photographs
Publications: Newsletters, books
Activities: Classes for adults & children; lects open to pub, 8 vis lectrs per yr; concerts; gallery talks; tours; individual paintings & original objects of art loaned to museums & galleries; mus shop sells books, magazines, reproductions, prints, slides, postcards, clothing, jewelry & toys

L **Library,** PO Box 99, Blue Mountain Lake, NY 12812-0099. Tel 518-352-7311; Fax 518-352-7603; *Librn* Jerold L Pepper
Open by appointment; Estab to provide research materials for mus staff (exhibit documentation) & researchers interested in the Adirondack & to preserve written materials relating to the Adirondack; For research only
Library Holdings: Audio Tapes 25; Book Volumes 8000; Cassettes; Clipping Files; Exhibition Catalogs; Fiche; Kodachrome Transparencies; Lantern Slides; Manuscripts; Other Holdings Maps; Periodical Subscriptions 13; Reels; Slides

A **ADIRONDACK LAKES CENTER FOR THE ARTS,** PO Box 205, Blue Mountain Lake, NY 12812-0205. Tel 518-352-7715; Fax 518-352-7333; Elec Mail info@adirondackarts.org; Internet Home Page Address: www.adirondackarts.org; *Exec Dir* Stephen Svoboda; *Prog Dir* Susan Sessions
Open Mon - Fri 10 AM - 4 PM, Sat 11 AM - 3 PM; Admis concerts $20 for 10 mems; Estab 1967; this Community Art Center offers both amateur & artist - craftsmen the opportunity for creative exchange; 7000 sq ft facility with 4 studios & 130 seat theatre & 3 separate galleries; Average Annual Attendance: 30,000; Mem: 600; annual meeting in July
Income: $180,000 (financed by private contributions, county, state & federal assistance, foundations, local bus, government, mem & fundraising events)
Exhibitions: Exhibits change every month
Publications: Newsletter - Program, quarterly
Activities: Classes for adults & children; dramatic programs; lect open to public, 2 vis lectrs per year; concerts; competitions; gallery talks; tours; scholarships offered; exten dept serves Adirondack Park

BOLTON LANDING

A **MARCELLA SEMBRICH MEMORIAL ASSOCIATION INC,** Marcella Sembrich Opera Museum, 4800 Lake Shore Dr, Bolton Landing, NY 12814; PO Box 417, Bolton Landing, NY 12814-0417. Tel 518-644-9839, 644-2431; Fax 518-644-9531; Elec Mail sembrich@verizon.net; Elec Mail office@thesembrich.org; Internet Home Page Address: www.thesembrich.org; *Assoc Pres* William Post Hubert; *Artistic Dir* Richard Wargo; *Dir* Elizabeth Barton-Navitsky; *VPres* Lisa H Hall; *Secy* Rebecca Smith; *Treas* Elizabeth Spinelli
Open June 15 - Sept 15 10 AM - 12:30 PM & 2 - 5 PM; Admis free, suggested donation $5; Estab 1937 to exhibit memorabilia of Marcella Sembrich & the Golden Age of Opera; Exhibits in Sembrich's former teaching studio on the shore of Lake George; Average Annual Attendance: 2,500; Mem: 300; dues $35 & $50; annual meeting in June
Income: $70,000 (financed by mem & gifts)
Collections: Memorabilia of the life & career of Marcella Sembrich, opera star of international acclaim (1858 - 1935); paintings, sculpture, furnishings, photographs, costumes, art works, gifts & trophies from colleagues & admirers
Publications: Newsletter, biennial; Recollection of Marcella Sembrich, Biography
Activities: Lect open to pub; vis lectrs; concerts; gallery talks; tours; mus shop sells books, postcards, recordings, cassettes & Sembrich CD's

BROCKPORT

M **STATE UNIVERSITY OF NEW YORK, COLLEGE AT BROCKPORT,** Tower Fine Arts Gallery, 350 New Campus Dr, Brockport, NY 14420-2997. Tel 585-395-2805; Fax 585-395-2588; *Dir* Elizabeth McDade
Open Mon-Thurs 10AM-7PM, Fri 10AM-5PM, Sun 1PM-4PM; Estab to present quality exhibitions for purpose of educ; 160 running ft, 1,900 sq ft; Average Annual Attendance: 9,000

Income: Financed by state appropriation & student government
Collections: EE Cummings Collection of Paintings & Drawings
Exhibitions: Alumni Invitational III; The Faculty Selects; Rock, Scissors, Paper; Social Work: Photographs by Vincent Cianni & Jim Tynan
Activities: Lects open to public, 6 vis lectrs per yr; book traveling exhibs 1-2 per yr; originate traveling exhibs

BRONX

M **BARTOW-PELL MANSION MUSEUM & GARDENS,** 895 Shore Rd, Pelham Bay Park Bronx, NY 10464-1030. Tel 718-885-1461; Fax 718-885-9164; Elec Mail info@bpmm.org; Internet Home Page Address: bpmm.org; *Exec Dir* Ellen Bruzelius; *Educ Dir & Cur* Margaret Highland; *Site Adminr* Mary Ellen Williamson; *Gardens Dir* Frazier Holloway; *Educ Asst* Amanda Kraemer
Open Wed, Sat & Sun 12 - 4 PM; Admis adults $5, seniors & students $3, children under 6 free; Estab 1914; Average Annual Attendance: 12,000
Library Holdings: Book Volumes
Special Subjects: Period Rooms
Collections: Greek Revival; period furnishings; paintings; sunken gardens
Activities: Tours for adults & children; lects open to pub; concerts; mus shop sells books

M **BRONX COMMUNITY COLLEGE (CUNY),** Hall of Fame for Great Americans, 2155 University Blvd, Bronx, NY 10453-5100. Tel 718-289-5161; Fax 718-289-6496; Internet Home Page Address: www.bcc.cuny.edu/halloffame; *Dir & Historian* Susan Zuckerman
Open daily 10 AM - 5 PM; Group tour donation suggested; Estab 1900; Nat landmark; Average Annual Attendance: 30,000
Library Holdings: Clipping Files; Exhibition Catalogs; Pamphlets; Sculpture
Special Subjects: Archaeology, Historical Material, Architecture, Bronzes, Sculpture, Coins & Medals, Miniatures, Stained Glass
Activities: Classes for children; dramatic progs; films; puppet shows; musical events; docent training; lect open to public; concerts; tours; NY Conservancy & Municipal Arts Society

M **BRONX COUNCIL ON THE ARTS,** Longwood Arts Gallery @ Hostos, 450 Grand Concourse, C-190, Art Gallery Bronx, NY 10451. Tel 718-518-6728; Fax 718-518-6690; Elec Mail longwood@bronxarts.org; Internet Home Page Address: www.bronxarts.org; *Exec Dir* Deirdre Scott; *Develop* Ellen Pollan; *Dir & Cur* Juanita Lanzo; *Gallery Coordr & Technology Adminr* Kimberly Vaquedano; *Gallery Asst* Vanessa Gonzalez
Open Mon - Sat 10 AM - 6 PM (Oct 2011-May 2012); Summer Hours: Mon - Thurs 10 AM - 5 PM; No admis fee; Estab 1985 for exhibits & programming of interest to artists & pub of all ages. Mission is to support the presentation & creation of work from emerging & underrepresented artists, specially women & artists of color.; Gallery organizes 4-6 exhibs per yr that present group & solo exhibs centering on contemporary themes of interest to artists & our audiences. Recent exhibs included collaborative projects between artists & communities & artists working on issues about migration, environment, social justice & national & cultural identity.; Average Annual Attendance: 300
Income: Financed by city, state & federal grants, foundation & corporate support
Exhibitions: Vietnamese Artists; Post-Colonialism; Feminism & the Body; Puerto Rican Taino Imagery in Contemporary Art; Real Life Comics; Like Butter; Maze-phantasm; Mini-Murals; Sovereign State; Here & Now, Now & Then
Activities: Lects open to pub, 3 vis lectrs per yr; fel; originate traveling exhibs 2 per yr

M **BRONX MUSEUM OF THE ARTS,** 1040 Grand Concourse, at 165th St Bronx, NY 10456-3999. Tel 718-681-6000; Fax 718-681-6181; Elec Mail info@bronxmuseum.org; Internet Home Page Address: www.bronxmuseum.org; *Exec Dir* Holly Block; *Dir Progs* Antonio Sergio Bessa; *Dir Develop* Allison Chernow; *Dir Fin* Alan Highet; *Dir Security* Francisco Rosario
Open Thurs Sun 11 AM - 6 PM, Fri until 8 PM, cl Mon - Wed, Thanksgiving, Christmas & New Year's Day; No admis fee; Estab 1971 as a 20th century & contemporary arts museum; serves the culturally diverse populations of the Bronx and the greater New York metropolitan area; the Museum has a long-standing commitment to increasing & stimulating audience participation in the visual arts through its Permanent Collection, special exhibitions & educational programs; Mem: 125; sponsor $1000, patron $500, assoc $250, sustaining $100, family/dual $75, individual $50, student, artist & senior $25
Income: Financed by mem, city, state & federal appropriations, foundations & corporations
Collections: Collection of 20th & 21st c works by artists s of Latin American, African & Southeast Asian ancestry; File on Bronx artists
Exhibitions: Rotating Exhibits
Publications: Exhibition catalogs; educational workbooks; walking tours of the Bronx
Activities: Classes for adults, children & seniors; lects open to pub; concerts; gallery talks; tours; films; annual arts & crafts festival; originate traveling exhibs; mus shop sells books, posters, catalogs, original art, prints, jewelry, children's & mus gift items

M **BRONX RIVER ART CENTER INC,** Gallery, 1087 E Tremont Ave, Bronx, NY 10460-2328; PO Box 5002, West Farms Station Bronx, NY 10460-0251. Tel 718-589-5819, 589-6379; Fax 718-860-8303; Elec Mail info@bronxriverart.org; Internet Home Page Address: www.bronxriverart.org; *Gallery Dir* Chad Stayrook; *Exec Dir* Gail Nathan; *Educ Mgr* Maria Nigro
Open Mon - Fri 10 AM - 6 PM & Sat 10 AM - 5 PM; No admis fee, nominal fee for classes; Estab 1980 as a professional, multi-cultural art center; 2,000 sq ft, handicapped accessible, ground floor gallery. Two main gallery rooms, natural light; Average Annual Attendance: 5,000
Income: $500,000 (Financed by government, foundations, corporations)
Exhibitions: Exhibitions of contemporary artists focusing on innovative multi-cultural, multi-media work; exhib of interdisciplinary art & environmental justice

Activities: Fee-based classes for adults & children; lects open to pub, 16 vis lectrs per yr; gallery talks; tours; schols available; exten prog BRAC on the Block serves the Bronx; originate traveling exhibs 1 per yr; sales shop sells original art, herbal sachets, eye pillows

M **EN FOCO, INC,** 1738 Hone Ave, Bronx, NY 10461-1403. Tel 718-731-9311; Fax 718-409-6445; Elec Mail info@enfoco.org; Internet Home Page Address: www.enfoco.org; *Exec Dir* Miriam Romais; *Progs Assoc* Hilary Thorsen; *Progs Asst* Dee Campos; *Co-Ed* Daniel Schmeichler
Open Mon - Thurs 10 AM - 5 PM, other hours by appt, cl Fri & all major holidays; No admis fee; Estab 1974 to support photographers of Latino, African, Asian, & Native American heritage via exhibits, publications, & workshops; Circ 36,000; Five exhibits per yr in different NY venues; Average Annual Attendance: 40,000; Mem: dues basic $50
Special Subjects: Afro-American Art, Mexican Art, Photography, Hispanic Art, Latin American Art, American Indian Art, African Art, Asian Art
Collections: Photographs by leading photographers of color
Exhibitions: New Works Exhibitions; Touring Gallery Exhibitions
Publications: Nueva Luz, bilingual photography journal
Activities: lects open to the public; gallery talks; fels; competitions with awards, New Works Photography Awards Fel; honorarium; originates traveling exhibs; sales shop sells magazines

A **HOSTOS CENTER FOR THE ARTS & CULTURE,** 450 Grand Concourse & 149th St, Bronx, NY 10451-5323. Tel 718-518-4444; Internet Home Page Address: www.hostos.cuny.edu; *Dir* Wallace I Edgecombe; *Production Mgr* Jack Jacobs; *Pres* Dolores Fernandez; *Coll Asst* Annie Pena
Open gallery: Mon - Fri 10 AM - 6 PM, Sat 10 AM - 2 PM ; Estab 1993 to present artists of national & international renown; presents emerging & estab local artists; offers workshops in drama, folk arts & dance to community residents; serves as a forge for new art, & thus has estab an individual artists' program consisting of commissions & residencies; Center consists of a museum-grade art gallery, 367-seat theater & 907-seat concert hall; Average Annual Attendance: 33,000
Income: Financed by mem, city appropriation, state appropriation, government sources, corporations
Activities: Dramatic progs; originate traveling exhibs

M **LEHMAN COLLEGE ART GALLERY,** 250 Bedford Park Blvd W, Bronx, NY 10468-1589. Tel 718-960-8731; Fax 718-960-6991; Elec Mail susan@lehman.cuny.edu; Internet Home Page Address: www.lehman.edu/gallery; Internet Home Page Address: www.lehman.edu/publicart; Internet Home Page Address: www.lehman.edu/architecture; *Grants Officer* Mary Ann Siano; *Dir* Susan Hoeltzel; *Asst Cur* Yuneikys Villalonga
Open Tues - Sat 10 AM - 4 PM; No admis fee; Estab 1984 to exhibit work of contemporary artists; Two galleries housed in Fine Arts building on Lehman College campus, City University NY, designed by Marcel Breuer; Average Annual Attendance: 32,000; Mem: 200; dues $30-$1000
Income: Financed by endowment, mem, city & state appropriation, federal grants, & private foundations
Special Subjects: Afro-American Art, Latin American Art
Exhibitions: Changing Contemporary Exhibs
Publications: Online exhib catalogs
Activities: Classes for children & adults; docent training; lects open to pub, 6 vis lectrs per yr; gallery talks; tours; book traveling exhibs; originate traveling exhibs; other mus

M **VAN CORTLANDT HOUSE MUSEUM,** W 246th & Broadway, Bronx, NY 10471-3431. Tel 718-543-3344; Fax 718-543-3315; Elec Mail queries@vancortlandthouse.org; Internet Home Page Address: www.vancortlandthouse.org; *Dir* Laura Correa; *Pres* Ana Duff; *Mus Shop Mgr* Ruragna Sloane
Open Tues - Fri 10 AM - 3 PM, Sat & Sun 11 AM - 4 PM, cl Mon; Admis adults$5, seniors & students $3, children 12 and under free, free to all on Wed; Estab 1898; Average Annual Attendance: 30,000
Special Subjects: Furniture, Historical Material
Collections: Furniture & objects of the 18th century
Activities: Classes for children; slide progs for visitors

M **WAVE HILL,** W 249th St & Independence Ave, Bronx, NY 10471; 675 W 252 St, Bronx, NY 10471-2840. Tel 718-549-3200, 549-2055; Fax 718-884-8952; Elec Mail information@wavehill.org; Internet Home Page Address: www.wavehill.org; *Pub Rels Dir* Marty Weitzman; *Pres* Kate Pearson French; *VChmn* David O Beim; *Dir Visitor Svcs* Michael Wiertz; *Dir Horticulture* Scott Canning; *Dir Educ* Margot Perron; *Dir Exec/Pres* Claudia Bonn
Open Tues - Sun 10 AM - 4:30 PM; No admis fee Tues & Sat AM, adults $4, sr citizens & students $2, children under 6 free, no admis fee Nov 15-Mar 14; Estab 1960 as a pub garden & cultural center; Wave Hill House Gallery; Glyndor Gallery; Outdoor Sculpture Garden; Average Annual Attendance: 100,000; Mem: 8000; dues $35
Income: Financed by mem, city & state appropriation, private funding
Exhibitions: 28 Acres of Gardens; Visual exhibitions
Publications: Calendar, 4 per yr; exhibit catalogues, annually
Activities: Classes for adults & children; dramatic progs; natural history/environmental workshops; lects open to pub, 3 vis lectrs per yr; concerts; originate traveling exhibs; sales shop sells books, magazines, reproductions

BRONXVILLE

L **BRONXVILLE PUBLIC LIBRARY,** 201 Pondfield Rd, Bronxville, NY 10708-4828. Tel 914-337-7680; Fax 914-337-0332; Elec Mail brolibrary@westchesterlibraries.org; Internet Home Page Address: www.bronxvillelibrary.org; *Dir Library* Laura Eckley; *Head of Reference* Patricia Root; *Head of Circ* Marianne Wingertzahn
Open winter Mon, Wed & Fri 9:30 AM - 5:30 PM, Tues 9:30 AM - 9 PM, Thurs 1 - 9 PM, Sat 9:30 AM - 5 PM, Sun 1 - 5 PM, summer Mon, Wed, Thurs & Fri 1

- 5:30 PM, Sat 9:30 AM - 1 PM; No admis fee; Estab as public library in 1906; Average Annual Attendance: 150,000
Income: Financed by city & state appropriations
Special Subjects: Painting-American, Prints
Collections: American painters: Bruce Crane, Childe Hassam, Winslow Homer, William Henry Howe, Frederick Waugh; Japanese Art Prints; 25 Original Currier and Ives Prints
Exhibitions: Current artists, changed monthly; original paintings and prints
Publications: newsletter, quarterly

L **SARAH LAWRENCE COLLEGE LIBRARY,** Esther Raushenbush Library, 1 Meadway, Bronxville, NY 10708-5999. Tel 914-395-2474; Fax 914-395-2473; Elec Mail library@mail@slc.edu; Internet Home Page Address: www.slc.edu/library; *Dir Lib & Acad Computing* Sha Fagan; *Asst Dir* Janet Alexander
Open Mon-Thurs 8:30AM-1AM, Fri 8:30AM-midnight, Sat 11AM-midnight, Sun 11AM-1AM; Estab to provide library facilities for students & members of the community with an emphasis on art history; Slide collection cl to the pub; non-circulating reference materials available to the pub; Mem: $45 per year
Library Holdings: Book Volumes 225,000; Periodical Subscriptions 1073; Slides 88,000; Video Tapes
Exhibitions: Changing exhibits
Activities: Lect in connection with exhibits; tours on request

BROOKLYN

M **A.I.R. GALLERY,** 111 Front St, #228 Brooklyn, NY 11201-1007. Tel 212-255-6651; Fax 212-255-6653; Elec Mail info@airgallery.org; Internet Home Page Address: www.airgallery.org; *Dir* JoAnne McFarland
Open Wed - Sat 11 AM - 6 PM; No admis fee; Estab 1972 as a not-for-profit, artist run gallery; also provides programs & services to women artists; runs fellowship program for emerging women artists; Average Annual Attendance: 10,000; Mem: $500 initiation fee; $200 monthly mem dues; monthly meetings
Income: Financed by mem & grants
Library Holdings: Audio Tapes; CD-ROMs; Clipping Files; DVDs; Exhibition Catalogs; Manuscripts; Memorabilia; Original Art Works; Original Documents; Pamphlets; Photographs; Prints; Slides; Video Tapes
Special Subjects: Painting-American, Photography, Sculpture, Woodcarvings, Woodcuts
Collections: Contemporary Women Artists
Exhibitions: One-woman exhibitions; invitational which can be international, regional and performance or theme shows
Publications: Invitational exhibition catalogues, bi-annually
Activities: Lect open to public; concerts; gallery talks; competitions with awards; sponsored fellowship award; original prints, paintings, photographs, sculpture, slides & videos; organize traveling exhibitions

AMERICAN ABSTRACT ARTISTS
For further information, see National and Regional Organizations

M **AMOS ENO GALLERY,** 111 Front St Ste 202, Brooklyn, NY 11201-1007. Tel 718-237-3001; Elec Mail AmosEnoGallery@gmail.com; Internet Home Page Address: www.amoseno.org; *Dir* Hilary R Whitham
Open Wed - Sat Noon - 6 PM

M **BOSE PACIA,** 163 Plymouth St, Brooklyn, NY 11201. Tel 212-989-7074; Fax 212-989-6982; Elec Mail mail@bosepacia.com; Internet Home Page Address: www.bosepacia.com; *Dir* Rebecca Davis
Open Tues-Sat 11AM-6PM
Collections: works by contemporary S Asian artists; paintings; drawings

M **BRIC - BROOKLYN INFORMATION & CULTURE,** Rotunda Gallery, 33 Clinton St, Brooklyn, NY 11201-2706. Tel 718-875-4047; Fax 718-488-0609; Elec Mail rotunda@bricartsmedia.org; Internet Home Page Address: bricartsmedia.org; *Dir* Elizabeth Ferrer; *Gallery Mgr* Baseera Khan; *Dir Educ* Hawley Hussy
Open Tues-Sat noon-6PM; No admis fee; Estab 1981 to exhibit the works of professional Brooklyn affiliated artists; Average Annual Attendance: 17,500
Income: $250,000 (financed by federal, state & municipal sources, private foundations, corporations & individuals)
Exhibitions: Various exhib
Activities: Classes for adults & children; lects open to public, 6-10 vis lectrs per year; gallery talks; tours; fels; computerized slide registry

A **BROOKLYN ARTS COUNCIL,** BAC Gallery, 111 Front St, Ste 218, Brooklyn, NY 11201; 55 Washington St, Ste 218, Brooklyn, NY 11201. Tel 718-625-0080; Fax 718-625-3294; Elec Mail gallery@brooklynartscouncil.org; Internet Home Page Address: www.brooklynartscouncil.org; *Visual Arts Dir* Courtney J Wendroff; *Pres* Ella J Weiss
Gallery open Mon - Fri 10 AM - 5:30 PM; No admis fee; Estab 1966 to promote education, excellence & exchange in the visual & performing arts; Average Annual Attendance: 600,000; Mem: Artist Registry 6059 artists, free to artists of all disciplines who live or work in Brooklyn, NY
Income: (financed by government, corporate & foundation support, earned income & educational services)
Exhibitions: Solo exhibitions by Brooklyn-based artists; Artist & Guest-curated group & thematic exhibitions
Activities: Dumbo 1st Thurs Gallery Walks; artist & curatorial talks; screenings; installations; receptions

M **BROOKLYN BOTANIC GARDEN,** Steinhardt Conservatory Gallery, 1000 Washington Ave, Brooklyn, NY 11225-1099. Tel 718-623-7200; Fax 718-622-7839; Elec Mail anitajacobs@bbg.org; Internet Home Page Address: www.bbg.org; *Dir Pub Progs* Anita Jacobs
Open Tues - Fri 8 AM - 4:30 PM, Sat & Sun 10 AM - 4:30 PM; Admis adult $8, children 15 & under free, free on Tues & Sat AM; Estab 1988 to display works of botanical, floral & landscape art; Multi-use space serves as an art gallery,

entryway to conservatory pavilions & seasonal eating area; Average Annual Attendance: 800,000
Special Subjects: Landscapes
Collections: Living plants; Botanical Art; Floral Art
Activities: Classes for adults

A **BROOKLYN HISTORICAL SOCIETY,** 128 Pierrepont St at Clinton St, Brooklyn, NY 11201-2711. Tel 718-222-4111; Fax 718-222-3794; Elec Mail jmonger@brooklynhistory.org; Internet Home Page Address: www.brooklynhistory.org; *Pres* Deborah Schwartz; *Mgr Admin & Vis Svcs* Janice Monger; *VP Exhibs & Educ* Kate Fermoile; *Dir Fin & Opers* Jason Pietrangeli; *Dir Devel* Sally Marshall; *Dir Educ* Andrea Del Valle
Open Wed-Fri & Sun Noon-5PM, Sat 10AM-5PM, cl Mon & Tues, July 4, Thanksgiving Day, Christmas Day & New Years Day; Admis adults $6, seniors, teachers & students age 12+ $4, mems, military & children under 12 free; Estab in 1863 to collect, preserve & interpret documentary & other materials relating to the history of Brooklyn & the adjoining geographical areas; Gallery used for exhibits on Brooklyn history; Average Annual Attendance: 15,000; Mem: 1,750; dues $35 - $1,250; annual meeting May
Income: $650,000 (financed by grants, endowment & mem)
Collections: Paintings, drawings, watercolors, prints, sculpture, decorative arts, archeological artifacts relating to Brooklyn's history & key citizens
Publications: Bimonthly newsletter; Neighborhood History Guides
Activities: Educ dept; docent training; lects open to pub, 15 vis lectrs per yr; gallery talks; individual paintings & original objects of art lent to other institutions; lending collection contains 3000 original prints, 275 paintings, sculptures

L **Othmer Library,** 128 Pierrepont St, 2nd Fl Brooklyn, NY 11201-2711. Tel 718-222-4111; Fax 718-222-3794; Elec Mail reference@brooklynhistory.org; Internet Home Page Address: www.brooklynhistory.org; *Dir Library & Archives* Chela Scot Weber; *Special Coll Librn* Elizabeth Call
Open Wed - Fri 1 PM - 5 PM, contact before visiting, appt req for Archive & Manuscript Collections; Mus admis req for libr access; Estab 1863 for the purpose of collecting, preserving & interpreting the history of Brooklyn & its varied cultures-housed in registered landmark building in Brooklyn Heights; Open to general pub; Mem: dues $50 & up
Library Holdings: Book Volumes 100,000; Clipping Files; Fiche; Kodachrome Transparencies; Lantern Slides; Manuscripts 2,000; Maps 2,000; Original Art Works; Original Documents; Pamphlets; Periodical Subscriptions; Photographs 90,000; Prints
Special Subjects: Decorative Arts, Photography, Drawings, Graphic Arts, Manuscripts, Maps, Painting-American, Historical Material, Portraits, Watercolors, Landscapes, Folk Art
Collections: Reference Books
Publications: Neighborhood History Guides; books
Activities: Tours; docent training; concerts; dramatic progs; varied school-oriented progs; book traveling exhibs; originate traveling exhibs circulating to local Brooklyn sites

M **BROOKLYN MUSEUM,** 200 Eastern Pkwy, Brooklyn, NY 11238-6052. Tel 718-638-5000; Fax 718-638-5931; Elec Mail bklynmus@echonyc.com; Internet Home Page Address: www.brooklynart.org; Telex 12-5378; Cable BRKLYN-MUSUNYK; *Dir* Arnold L Lehman; *Hagop Kevorkian Assoc Cur Islamic Art* Ladan Akbarnia; *Assoc Cur Photography* Patrick Amsellem; *Cur European Art* Richard Aste; *Mng Cur Exhibs* Sharon Matt Atkins; *Asst Cur Egyptian Art* Yekaterina Barbash; *Cur Egyptian, Classical & Ancient Near Eastern Art; Mng Cur, Ancient Egyptian, African & Asian Art* Edward Bleiberg; *Andrew W Mellon Cur American Art; Mng Cur, Arts of the Americas & Europe* Teresa A Carbone; *Lisa & Bernard Selz Cur, Asian Art* Joan Cummins; *Asst Cur, Arts of Africa & the Pacific Islands* Kevin D Dumouchelle; *Asst Cur, Elizabeth A Sackler Center for Feminist Art* Saisha M Gayson; *Cur, Decorative Arts* Barry R Harwood; *Cur, Elizabeth A Sackler Center for Feminist Art* Catherine J Morris; *Andrew W Mellon Cur of the Arts of the Americas* Nancy Rosoff; *Cur, Egyptian, Classical & Ancient Near Eastern Art* Ann Russmann; *Asst Cur, American ARt* Karen Sherry; *Cur, Exhibs* Lisa Small; *Chief Cur* Kevin Stayton; *John & Barbara Vogelstein Cur, Contemporary Art* Eugenie Tsai; *Assoc Cur, Native American Art* Susan Kennedy Zeller
Open Wed, Fri - Sun 11 AM - 6 PM, Thurs 11 AM - 10 PM, cl Mon & Tues; No admis fee suggested donation adults $10, seniors & students with valid ID $6, mems & children under 12 accompanied by an adult no charge; Estab 1823 as the Apprentices Library Assoc; Five floors of galleries maintained; Average Annual Attendance: 350,000; Mem: dues benefactor's circle $5,000, curator's circle $2,500, fellow $1,000, donor $600, patron $350, contributor $150, family & friends $85, individual $55, 1stfans $20
Income: $14,374,000 (financed by endowment, mem, city & state appropriation, gifts)
Library Holdings: Audio Tapes; Book Volumes; CD-ROMs; Cards; Clipping Files; Compact Disks; Exhibition Catalogs; Fiche; Manuscripts; Other Holdings; Periodical Subscriptions; Photographs
Collections: Art from the Americas & South Pacific; American period rooms; European & American paintings, sculpture, prints, drawings, costumes, textiles & decorative arts; major colls of Egyptian & Classical; Asian, Middle Eastern & African art; Americas & the Pacific; sculpture garden of ornaments from demolished New York buildings
Exhibitions: (Permanent) The Arts of China; The Arts of the Pacific; European Paintings Reinstallation.
Publications: Newsletter, bimonthly; catalogues of major exhibitions; handbooks
Activities: Classes for adults & children; film; docent training; lects open to pub; gallery talks; tours; concerts; sponsoring of competitions; Augustus Graham medal; schols for student progs; individual paintings & original objects of art lent to other mus; originate traveling exhibs; mus shops sell books, original objects, reproductions, prints, magazines, slides, T-shirts, clothes & bags

L **Libraries Archives,** 200 Eastern Pkwy, Brooklyn, NY 11238-6052. Tel 718-501-6307; Fax 718-501-6125; Elec Mail library@brooklynmuseum.org; Internet Home Page Address: brooklynmuseum.org; *Prin Librn Libraries & Archives* Deirdre E Lawrence
Open Wed - Fri 11 AM - 4:30 PM, first Sat of month 1 - 4PM except July - Sept; Estab 1823 to serve the staff of the mus & pub for reference
Income: Financed by city, state & private appropriation
Purchases: $50,000
Library Holdings: Auction Catalogs; Audio Tapes; Book Volumes 200,000; CD-ROMs; Clipping Files; Exhibition Catalogs; Fiche; Lantern Slides; Original Documents; Pamphlets; Periodical Subscriptions 400; Photographs; Video Tapes
Special Subjects: Art History, Decorative Arts, Photography, Drawings, Etchings & Engravings, Islamic Art, Painting-American, Pre-Columbian Art, Sculpture, History of Art & Archaeology, Ceramics, Crafts, Latin American Art, Archaeology, Fashion Arts, Interior Design, Asian Art, American Indian Art, Primitive art, Anthropology, Eskimo Art, Mexican Art, Southwestern Art, Period Rooms, Costume Design & Constr, Afro-American Art, Antiquities-Oriental, Antiquities-Persian, Oriental Art, Restoration & Conservation, Silversmithing, Antiquities-Assyrian, Antiquities-Egyptian, Antiquities-Greek, Antiquities-Roman, Folk Art
Collections: Fashion plates; original fashion sketches 1900-1950; 19th century documentary photographs
Publications: Newsletter, bi-monthly
Activities: Classes for children; docent training; progs relating to current exhibs; lects open to pub, 30 vis lectrs per yr; gallery talks; tours; originate traveling exhibs to other mus

L **Wilbour Library of Egyptology,** 200 Eastern Pkwy, Brooklyn, NY 11238-6052. Tel 718-501-6219; Fax 718-501-6125; Elec Mail library@brooklynmuseum.org; Internet Home Page Address: brooklynmuseum.com
Open Wed - Fri 10 AM - noon & 1 PM - 4:30 PM, first Sat of month 1PM-4PM except July-Sep; Estab 1934 for the purpose of the study of Ancient Egypt
Income: Financed by endowment & city, state & private appropriation
Purchases: $30,000 annually
Library Holdings: Auction Catalogs; Book Volumes 37,000; Exhibition Catalogs; Fiche; Other Holdings Original documents; Pamphlets; Periodical Subscriptions 150
Collections: Seyffarth papers
Publications: Wilbour Monographs; general introductory bibliographies on Egyptian art available to visitors

L **BROOKLYN PUBLIC LIBRARY,** Art & Music Division, 10 Grand Army Plaza, Brooklyn, NY 11238-5619. Tel 718-230-2183/4; Fax 718-230-2063; Elec Mail k.badalamenti@brooklynpubliclibrary.org; Internet Home Page Address: www.brooklynpubliclibrary.org; *Acting Chief* Kay Badalamenti; *Exec Dir* Dionne Mack-Harvin
Open Mon & Fri 9AM-6PM, Tues-Thurs 9AM-9PM, Sat 10AM-6PM, Sun 1PM-6PM; No admis fee; Estab 1892; Lobby Gallery on 1st fl; Average Annual Attendance: 12,000
Income: Financed by city & state appropriation
Library Holdings: Audio Tapes; Book Volumes 260,000; Cards; Cassettes; Exhibition Catalogs; Filmstrips; Micro Print; Motion Pictures; Other Holdings Mounted pictures; Pamphlets; Periodical Subscriptions 420; Records; Reels; Slides; Video Tapes
Collections: Checkers Collection; Chess Collection; Costume Collection; Picture & Art Reproduction File; Song Finding Collection
Exhibitions: lect of writing on arts by Bookforum
Publications: Monthly calendar
Activities: Classes for children; progs; lects open to pub; 1-2 vis lectrs per yr; gallery talks; films; book traveling exhibs Pop Up Books (2000); sales shop sells books, magazines, original art

L **FRANKLIN FURNACE ARCHIVE, INC,** 80 Hanson Place #301, 80 Arts - The James E Davis Art Bldg Brooklyn, NY 11217-1506. Tel 718-398-7255; Fax 718-398-7256; Elec Mail mail@franklinfurnace.org; Internet Home Page Address: www.franklinfurnace.org; *Admin* Harley Spiller; *Sr Archivist* Michael Katchen; *Founding Dir* Martha Wilson; *Fin Mgr* Judith L Woodward; *Prog Coordr* Eben Shapiro; *Proj Cataloguer* Mary Haberle
Estab 1976 to champion ephemeral art forms neglected by mainstream art institutions; current mission to present, preserve, interpret, proselytize & advocate on behalf of avant-garde art; Virtual institution, accessible to public by web site only; Mem: 1,000 members; dues $33, $66, $99, $333, $999, & $33,000; benefits increase with dues
Library Holdings: Clipping Files; Exhibition Catalogs; Manuscripts; Memorabilia; Motion Pictures; Original Art Works; Original Documents; Pamphlets; Photographs; Prints; Slides; Video Tapes
Publications: Goings On, weekly e-newsletter
Activities: Classes for children; Sequential Art for Kids; awards, Franklin Furnace Furd; mus shop sells books, magazines, & original art

M **HOLLAND TUNNEL ART PROJECTS,** 61 S Third St, Brooklyn, NY 11211; 63 S 3rd St, Brooklyn, NY 11211-5128. Tel 718-384-5738; Fax 718-384-5738; Elec Mail hollandtunnelart@yahoo.com; Internet Home Page Address: www.hollandtunnelgallery.com; *Graphic Designer* Roy Lethen; *Pub Rels* Fran Kornfeld; *Dir* Paulien Lethen; *Asst* Sarah Dalton
Open Sat & Sun 1 - 5 PM & by appt; No admis fee; Estab 1997 connecting people with art; A prefab shed converted into a small gallery featuring local & international artistic talent; Average Annual Attendance: 2,000
Income: Dir assumes costs with artists
Exhibitions: Holland Tunnel in Paros, Greece; "5"; Bound; More Than I Would Say About Most People (Nina Levy)
Publications: Catalogue for "5" (5th anniversary show)
Activities: Concerts; tours; poetry reading & artist talks; films & videos; Holland Tunnel in Paros, Greece, "Inside Harry's House" Holland Tunnel Project in the Netherlands; originate traveling exhibs 3 per yr; mus shop sells original art, flat file in gallery

A **HUDSON VALLEY ART ASSOCIATION,** 8 Everit St, Brooklyn, NY 11201-1321. Elec Mail president@hvaaonline.org; Internet Home Page Address: www.hvaaonline.org; *Pres* John Belardo; *Sec* Winnie O'Dougherty; *Chair Sculpture* Michael Keropian; *Chair Oils* Cesar Jerez; *Chair Graphics* Roseanne Reiff; *Chair Watercolors* Charles Ross
Estab 1928, incorporated 1934 to perpetuate the artistic traditions of American artists such as made famous the Hudson River School of painting through

exhibitions of painting & sculpture with pub support; Mem: By invitation; dues sustaining lay $35, patrons $50, underwriters $50+
Exhibitions: Annual spring exhibition of oils, aqua media, pastels, graphics & sculpture, open to mem & non-mem
Publications: Exhib catalogs
Activities: Awards totaling $100,000

INTERNATIONAL SOCIETY OF COPIER ARTISTS (ISCA)
For further information, see National and Regional Organizations

M **KINGSBOROUGH COMMUNITY COLLEGE, CUNY,** Art Gallery, 2001 Oriental Blvd, Brooklyn, NY 11235-2333. Tel 718-368-5449; Fax 718-368-4872; Elec Mail kccgallery@gmail.com; Internet Home Page Address: www.kingsborough.edu/artgallery; *Dir* Peter Malone
Open Mon - Fri 10 AM - 3 PM; No admis fee; Estab 1975 for exhibition of visual art; 42 ft x 42 ft gallery, 42 x 50 ft outdoor sculpture courtyard; Average Annual Attendance: 5,000
Income: Financed by Kingsborough Community College Assn
Activities: Lect open to public, 2 vis lectrs per yr; competitions with awards; gallery talks

M **MOCADA - THE MUSEUM OF CONTEMPORARY AFRICAN DIASPORAN ARTS,** James E Davis Art Bldg, 80 Hanson Place Brooklyn, NY 11217-1506. Tel 718-230-0492; Fax 718-230-0246; *Exec Dir* Laurie Cumbo
Open Wed - Fri 11 AM - 4 PM
Collections: African American history & culture; paintings; sculpture; photographs
Activities: Educ programs; special events; internships; museum-related items for sale

M **MOMENTA ART,** 56 Bogart St, Brooklyn, NY 11206-3817. Tel 718-218-8058; Fax 718-347-448-8268; Elec Mail momenta@momentaart.org; Internet Home Page Address: www.momentaart.org; *Bd Dir* Laura Parnes; *Dir* Eric Heist; *Resource Dir* Michael Waugh
Open Mon-Thurs Noon- 6PM; No admis fee; Estab 1986 as a not-for-profit exhibition organization promoting the work of under-represented & emerging artists; 1,200 sq ft in Williamsburg, Brooklyn; Average Annual Attendance: 5,000; Mem: 200; dues $30-$500
Income: $105,000 (financed by endowment, mem, city & state appropriation)
Activities: Lects open to pub, 6 vis lectrs per yr; sales shop sells catalogs & artist multiples

L **NEW YORK CITY TECHNICAL COLLEGE,** Ursula C Schwerin Library, 300 Jay St, Brooklyn, NY 11201-1909. Tel 718-260-5470; Fax 718-260-5631; Internet Home Page Address: www.library.citytech.cuny.edu; *Admin Svcs Librn* Prof Paul T Sherman; *Chief Cataloguer* Morris Hownion; *Reference Coordr* Joan Grissano; *Dir Technical Servs* Sharon Swacker; *Chief Librn* Darrow Wood
Open Mon - Thurs 9 AM - 10 PM, Fri 9 AM-7 PM, Sat 10AM-4PM; Estab 1947
Library Holdings: Reproductions
Special Subjects: Graphic Arts, Advertising Design
Publications: Library Alert & Library Notes, occasional publications
Activities: Tours; Library Instruction; BRS Data Base Searching

L **NEW YORK FOUNDATION FOR THE ARTS,** 20 Jay St Ste 740, Brooklyn, NY 11201-8352. Tel 212-366-6900; Fax 212-366-1778; Elec Mail deleget@nyfa.org; Internet Home Page Address: www.nyfa.org; *Exec Dir* Theodore Berger; *Prog Dir* Penny Dannenberg
Open Mon - Fri 9:30 AM - 5:30 PM, or by appointment; Estab to make more available research in art hazards; For reference only
Library Holdings: Book Volumes 500
Activities: Adult classes; lects

A **ORGANIZATION OF INDEPENDENT ARTISTS, INC,** 117 Sterling Pl #8, Brooklyn, NY 11217. Tel 347-405-2422; Elec Mail oiaonline@yahoo.com; Internet Home Page Address: www.oia-ny.org; *Dir* Geraldine Cosentino; *Design & Treas* Remo Cosentino; *Installation Asst* Greg Stowell; *Sec* Robert Cook
Open by appt only; No admis fee at all art spaces used for exhibits; Estab 1976 to facilitate artist-curated group exhibitions in public spaces; Alternative spaces; Average Annual Attendance: 500; Mem: 50+ mems, qualifications practicing artist; dues $60
Income: under $25,000 (financed by mem, private donors)
Activities: Group exhibs in 3 venues

L **PRATT INSTITUTE,** Art & Architecture Dept, 200 Willoughby Ave, Brooklyn, NY 11205-3899. Tel 718-636-3714, 636-3685; Internet Home Page Address: www.lib.pratt.edu/plice; *Art & Architecture Librn* Joy Kestenbaum; *Dean* F William Chickering; *Dir Reader Svcs* Cynthia A Johnson
Open Mon - Thurs 9 AM - 11 PM, Fri 9 AM - 7 PM, Sat & Sun Noon - 6 PM for students, faculty & staff, others by appointment or with METRO or ALB card; Estab 1887 for students, faculty, staff & alumni of Pratt Institute; The school has several galleries, the library has exhibitions in display cases
Library Holdings: Book Volumes 85,000; Clipping Files; Exhibition Catalogs; Fiche; Maps; Motion Pictures; Periodical Subscriptions 150; Prints; Reels; Reproductions; Slides; Video Tapes
Special Subjects: Art History, Photography, Architecture
M **The Rubelle & Norman Schafler Gallery,** 200 Willoughby Ave, Brooklyn, NY 11205. Tel 718-636-3517; Elec Mail exhibits@pratt.edu; Internet Home Page Address: www.pratt.edu/exhibitions; *Dir* Nick Battis; *Asst Dir* Olivia Good
Open Mon - Fri 9 AM - 5 PM, Sat noon - 5 PM; No admis fee; Estab 1960; Contemporary art & design in all media & disciplines; Average Annual Attendance: 4,000
Collections: Permanent collection of fiber art, paintings, pottery, prints, photographs & sculpture

A **PROMOTE ART WORKS INC (PAWI),** Laziza Electrique Dance Co, 123 Smith St, Brooklyn, NY. Tel 718-797-3116; Fax 718-855-4746; Elec Mail executive@micromuseum.com; Internet Home Page Address: www.micromuseum.com; *Technical Dir* William Laziza; *Assoc Producer* Samantha Twyford; *Chmn* Nancy Stern Bain; *Technician* Kevin McCormack; *Technician* Mike MacIvor; *Exec Dir* Kathleen Laziza
Open by appointment; Admis 0-$25; Estab 1980; Gallery includes interactive kinetic sculpture & media installation; Average Annual Attendance: 1,200; Mem: 501(C)3

Income: $65,000 (financed by contributions & earned income)
Library Holdings: CD-ROMs; DVDs; Original Art Works; Photographs; Records; Sculpture; Slides; Video Tapes
Special Subjects: Costumes, Drawings, Photography, Folk Art, Glass
Collections: Electronic & video art
Exhibitions: Micro Museum Dec - June
Activities: Classes for adults & children; internships; archival prog for pub television; lects open to pub, 5 vis lectrs per yr; Art of the Future NY Times selected for new millennium; video traveling exhibs 1 per yr; originate traveling exhibs of videotapes to schools

A **The MicroMuseum,** 123 Smith St, Brooklyn, NY 11201. Tel 718-797-3116; Fax 718-855-1208; Elec Mail tech@micromuseum.com; Internet Home Page Address: www.micromuseum.com; www.pawi.org; *Tech Dir* William Laziza
Open Sun-Fri by appointment 9 AM - 9 PM & Sat noon-7PM; Admis fee 0 - $25; Estab 1993 as art lab for interdisciplinary work; Gallery features media kinetic installation; Mem: National Artists Assoc Org
Income: 63,000 (financed by contributions & earned income)
Library Holdings: Audio Tapes; Cassettes; Kodachrome Transparencies; Lantern Slides; Manuscripts; Memorabilia; Original Art Works; Photographs; Prints; Records; Reproductions; Sculpture; Slides
Collections: 78 RPM record coll from Metropolitan Museum of Art; Spontaneous Combustion
Activities: Originates traveling exhibs of videotapes to schools

SCULPTORS GUILD, INC
For further information, see National and Regional Organizations

A **URBANGLASS,** (Urban Glass) Robert Lehman Gallery, 126 13th St, Brooklyn, NY 11215-4632. Tel 718-625-3685; Fax 718-625-3889; Elec Mail info@urbanglass.org; Internet Home Page Address: www.urbanglass.org; *Exec Dir* Dawn Bennett; *Develop Officer* Jill Smith; *Dir Operations* Brian Kibler; *Interim Dir Educ* Alan Iwamura
Open Mon, Wed - Fri 10 AM - 6 PM, Tues 2 - 5 PM, Sat - Sun 10 AM - 5 PM; No admis fee; Estab 1977 to provide facility for artists who work in glass; 1400 Sq Ft; Average Annual Attendance: 8,000; Scholarships, Fellowships
Income: nonprofit, fund raising
Exhibitions: Rotating-3 per yr
Publications: Glass: The Urban Glass Art Quarterly
Activities: Classes for adults; lects open to pub, 7 vis lectrs per yr; gallery talks; tours; competitions; fels; shop sells magazines & original art

M **WATERFRONT MUSEUM,** 290 Conover St, Brooklyn, NY 11231-1020. Tel 718-624-4719; Elec Mail dsharps@waterfrontmuseum.org; Internet Home Page Address: www.waterfrontmuseum.org; *Pres & CEO* David Sharps; *Vol* Alison Tocci
Open Thurs 4 PM - 8 PM & Sat 1 PM - 5 PM; also by appt; Admis $7, group tours by appt; Estab 1986; The Waterfront Mus & Showboat Barge is housed aboard the 1914 Lehigh Valley Railroad Barge #79 listed on the National Register of Historic Places; mus provides pub access to the NY Harbor's waterfront & progs in maritime & environmental educ. Nonprofit org; congressional district 8; FT paid 1, PT paid 4, PT volunteers 35; floating classroom; ramps to barge; Average Annual Attendance: 10,000 by estimate
Special Subjects: Woodcarvings
Collections: Coll of artifacts from The Lighterage Era (1860 - 1960), a period in which goods traded & consumed in NYC were transferred from port docks to railroad terminals by tug & barge; 1914 LV Barge #79; maritime artifacts
Publications: Transfer Magazine; pub by Railroad Marine Info Group
Activities: Educ progs for adults & children; cultural progs; community meetings; spec events; concerts & various showboat performances; mus shop sells books, prints, juggling balls

M **WILLIAMSBURG ART & HISTORICAL CENTER,** 135 Broadway, Brooklyn, NY 11211-6129. Tel 718-486-6012; Elec Mail lindall@amnumsoc.org; Elec Mail wahcenter@earthlink.net; Internet Home Page Address: www.wahcenter.net; *Pres & Exec Dir* Terrance Lindall; *Founder & Artistic Dir* Yuko Nii
Open Sat & Sun Noon - 6 PM; No admis fee; Estab 1996; First floor is the grand Reception Hall with mahogany interior, information center, gift shop & coffee nook. Gallery on second floor presenting shows of emerging & established artists. Basement facility provides space for artists working in the areas of photography, film, video & computer arts; Average Annual Attendance: 10,000; Mem: dues $35
Income: $150,000 (financed by mem, city & state appropriation & contributions)
Purchases: $5000
Library Holdings: Auction Catalogs; Audio Tapes; Book Volumes; Cassettes; Exhibition Catalogs; Manuscripts; Maps; Original Art Works; Original Documents; Photographs; Prints; Sculpture
Collections: Contemporary art, theater, film, video, music (experimental & other), poetry, any art-related event, symposiums, etc
Exhibitions: The Calculus of Transfiguration: Meaning Form & Process in Late 20th Century Art
Publications: The Williamsburg Papers
Activities: Dramatic progs; lects open to pub, 5 vis lectrs per yr; tours, concerts, gallery talks; sponsoring of competitions; mus shop sells books, mags, original art, prints, reproductions
L **Library,** 135 Broadway, Brooklyn, NY 11211.
Open Sat & Sun Noon to 6 PM, Mon by appointment; 40 ft x 60 ft, 20 ft ceiling in main gallery; for reference use
Income: $150,000 (financed by mem, city & state appropriation)
Purchases: $20,000
Library Holdings: Auction Catalogs; Audio Tapes; Book Volumes 2000; Cassettes; Clipping Files; Compact Disks; Kodachrome Transparencies; Manuscripts; Maps; Memorabilia; Original Art Works; Original Documents; Pamphlets; Photographs; Prints; Records; Reproductions; Sculpture; Slides; Video Tapes

BROOKVILLE

M **C W POST CAMPUS OF LONG ISLAND UNIVERSITY,** Hillwood Art Museum, 720 Northern Blvd, Brookville, NY 11548-1300. Tel 516-299-4073; Fax 516-299-2787; Elec Mail museum@cwpost.liu.edu; Internet Home Page Address: www.liu.edu/museum; *Asst Dir* Ms Barbara Applegate; *Mus Educator* Tonito Valderrama; *Dir* Barry Stern; *Cur of Coll* Elizabeth Fleming; *Pub Rels* Rita Langdon
Open Mon - Fri 9:30 AM - 4:30 PM, Thurs 9:30 AM - 8 PM, Sat 11 AM - 3 PM; No admis fee; Estab 1973; Mus is located in the student complex and occupies a space of approx 5000 sq ft; Average Annual Attendance: 25,000
Income: Financed by university budget, grants & donations
Special Subjects: American Indian Art, Prints, Textiles, Drawings, Painting-American, Photography, African Art, Pre-Columbian Art, Posters, Asian Art, Antiquities-Persian, Antiquities-Egyptian, Antiquities-Greek, Antiquities-Roman, Bookplates & Bindings
Collections: Near Eastern antiquities, American abstract painting, contemporary photography; Pre-Columbian & African Art; Chinese paintings 10th - 19th century
Exhibitions: Chinese Silk: Symbols of Rank & Privilege (Garments from the Ch'ing Dynasty); Esphyr Slobodkina Retrospective (Works from the Permanent Collection); Kuba Kingdom Dress: Textiles from the Congo; Obsessive Compulsive Order (Contemporary sculpture including works by Amanda Guest, Jeanne Jaffe, Lesly Dill & Gail Deery); Dennis Oppenheim: Realized/Unrealized (Works from the Permanent Collection); Theodore Roosevelt: Icon of the American Century (Artists include John Singer Sargent, Edward Curtis & Frederic Remington); Threads of Time: African Textiles
Publications: Exhibition catalogs; newsletter; study guides
Activities: Educ dept; classes for children; lects open to pub; 6-8 vis lectrs per yr; concerts; gallery talks; tours; concerts; AAM Publication Award; individual paintings & original objects of art lent; lending collection contains books, cassettes, 3000 prints; originates 1-2 traveling exhibs; mus shop sells books, original art, prints & catalogues

BUFFALO

L **BUFFALO & ERIE COUNTY PUBLIC LIBRARY,** 1 Lafayette Sq, Buffalo, NY 14203-1887. Tel 716-858-8900; Fax 716-858-6211; Internet Home Page Address: www.buffalolib.org; *Dir* Bridget Quinn-Cary; *Asst Deputy Dir Pub Svcs* Ruth Collins; *Deputy Dir Finance* Kenneth H Stone
Open Mon - Wed, Fri & Sat 8:30 AM - 6 PM, Thurs 8:30 AM - 8 PM; Estab 1954 through a merger of the Buffalo Pub, Grosvenor & Erie County Pub Libraries
Income: $25,000,000 (financed by county appropriation & state aid)
Library Holdings: Book Volumes 3,000,000; Exhibition Catalogs; Manuscripts 4178; Original Art Works; Periodical Subscriptions 3200; Photographs; Prints; Video Tapes
Special Subjects: Drawings, Etchings & Engravings, Prints, Woodcuts
Collections: J J Lankes Collection; William J Schwanekamp Collection; Niagara Falls Collection; Rare book room with emphasis on fine printing
Publications: Bimonthly library bulletin
Activities: Dramatic progs; consumer progs; gallery talks; tours; concerts; book talks; architectural progs

M **BUFFALO ARTS STUDIO,** Art Gallery, 2495 Main St, Ste 500, Buffalo, NY 14214. Tel 716-833-4450 ext 10; Elec Mail cori@buffaloartsstudio.org; Internet Home Page Address: www.buffaloartsstudio.org; *Exec /Artistic Dir* Cori Wolff; *Educ Coordr* Jayne Hughes; *Develop Officer* Catherine Willett; *Accounting Asst* Anne Simon
Open Tues - Fri 11 AM - 5 PM, Sat 11 AM - 3 PM; No admis fee; A not-for-profit arts organization which provides regular pub exposure for regional, national & international artists through exhibs. BAS enriches the community with art classes, mural programs & pub art projects & provides studio space for emerging artists; Three galleries, two classrooms, 36 artist studios; Average Annual Attendance: 350,000
Income: Corporations, foundations & individuals
Exhibitions: Regional, national & international artists; annual resident artists exhibit
Publications: Evolution/Revolution: The 20th Anniversary
Activities: Classes for adults & children; lects open to pub; exhibits; gallery talks; tours; pub art projects; city wide mural programs; scholarships; gift shop sells books, original art & prints

M **THE BUFFALO FINE ARTS ACADEMY,** Albright-Knox Art Gallery, 1285 Elmwood Ave, Buffalo, NY 14222-1096. Tel 716-882-8700; Fax 716-882-1958; Elec Mail info@albrightknox.org; Internet Home Page Address: www.albrightknox.org; *Dir* Louis Grachos; *Chief Cur* Douglas Dreishpoon; *Cur Educ* Mariann Smith; *Cur* Heather Pesanti; *Sr Registrar* Laura Fleischmann; *Deputy Dir* Karen Lee Spaulding; *Interim Head Develop* Jennifer Bayles; *Events Coordr* Caterine Gatewood; *Interim Head Opers* Bryan Gawronski; *Sr Art Preparator* Jody Hanson; *HR Mgr* Andrea Griffa Harden; *Head Publs* Pam Hatley; *COO* Mark Hoffman; *Coll Cur* Holly E Hughes; *Opers Mgr Gallery Shop* Tracey Levy; *Interim Head Mktg, Corp & Pub Rels* Maria Scully-Morreale; *Head Research Resources* Susana Tejada; *Head Bldgs & Grounds* Kenneth D Walker
Open Tues - Sun 10 AM - 5 PM, cl Mon, Independence, Thanksgiving, Christmas & New Year's Day; Admis adults $12, seniors & students 13 & up $8, children 6-12 $5, children 5 & under & mems free; Estab 1862 as The Buffalo Fine Arts Academy. Gallery dedicated in 1905, with a new wing added in 1962; Center of modern and contemporary art, the collection offers a panorama of art through the centuries, dating from 3000 BC; Average Annual Attendance: 150,000; Mem: 9500; dues individual $50; ann meeting in Oct
Income: $4,700,000 (financed by contributions, mem, endowment, county appropriations, individual & corporate grants, earned income & special projects)
Special Subjects: Graphics, Mexican Art, Painting-American, Photography, African Art, Religious Art, Etchings & Engravings, Painting-European, Posters, Glass, Oriental Art, Asian Art, Antiquities-Byzantine, Painting-British, Painting-French, Baroque Art, Antiquities-Oriental, Painting-Italian, Antiquities-Persian, Antiquities-Egyptian, Antiquities-Greek, Antiquities-Roman, Painting-German, Antiquities-Etruscan, Painting-Israeli
Collections: Painting & drawings; prints & sculpture ranging from 3000 BC to the present with special emphasis on American & European contemporary art; sculpture & constructions
Publications: Annual report; calendar (bi-monthly); exhibition catalogs
Activities: Classes for adults & children; docent training; family workshops & progs; progs for the handicapped; outreach progs for inner-city schools; lects open to pub, 12 vis lectrs per yr; concerts; gallery talks; tours; National Award for Museum Service 2000; individual paintings & original objects of art lent to major mus worldwide; lending colls contain paintings, photographs & sculptures; book traveling exhibs; originate traveling exhibs; mus shop sells books, reproductions, slides, jewelry, gift items & toys

L **G Robert Strauss Jr Memorial Library,** 1285 Elmwood Ave, Buffalo, NY 14222. Tel 716-270-8225, 270-8240; Fax 716-882-6213; Elec Mail artref@albrightknox.org; Internet Home Page Address: www.albrightknox.net/library.html; *Asst Librn* Tara Riese
Open Tues - Sat 1 - 5 PM & Fri 3PM-5PM by appt; Estab 1933 to support the staff research & to document the Gallery collection, also to serve the fine art & art history people doing research in the western New York area; Exhibits are prepared in a small vestibule, rare items in the library collection & print collection are displayed
Library Holdings: Audio Tapes; Book Volumes 31,000; Cassettes; Clipping Files; Exhibition Catalogs; Fiche; Manuscripts; Memorabilia; Original Art Works; Other Holdings Original documents; Pamphlets; Periodical Subscriptions 100; Photographs; Prints; Reproductions; Video Tapes
Special Subjects: Photography, Painting-American, Pre-Columbian Art, Prints, Sculpture, History of Art & Archaeology, Printmaking
Collections: Artists books; Graphic Ephemera; Illustrated books
Exhibitions: Books and Prints of Maillol; Photography in Books; Rare Art Periodicals; Woodcuts from the Library Collection; Artists' Books; Illustrated Books; Derriere Le Mirroir; From the Gallery Archives; General Ide; Books with a Difference Circle Press Publications

L **BUFFALO MUSEUM OF SCIENCE,** Research Library, 1020 Humboldt Pkwy, Buffalo, NY 14211-1293. Tel 716-896-5200, Ext 321; Fax 716-897-6723; Elec Mail library@sciencebuff.org; Internet Home Page Address: www.buffalomuseumofscience.org; *Dir Science* Dr John Grehan; *Cur Coll* Kathryn Leacock; *Coll Mgr* Jean Whipking; *Cur Geology* Richard S Laub; *Sch Progs Coordr* Jodi Valenti-Protas; *Pres & CEO* Mark Mortenson; *Dir Opers* Albert Parker; *Mktg & Develop* Michelle Rudnicki; *Chmn, Buffalo Soc Natural Sci Bd Dirs* Randall E Burkard
Open Tues - Fri 10 AM - 5 PM (by appointment only); Estab 1861 to further the study of natural history among the people of Buffalo; Museum has exhibition space for permanent & temporary exhibitions; Average Annual Attendance: 200,000
Income: Financed by endowment, mem, county & state appropriation, grants, gifts
Purchases: $10,000
Library Holdings: Audio Tapes; Book Volumes 40,000; Clipping Files; Exhibition Catalogs; Fiche; Filmstrips; Manuscripts; Pamphlets; Periodical Subscriptions 500; Photographs; Reels; Video Tapes
Special Subjects: History of Art & Archaeology, Archaeology, Ethnology, Bronzes, Asian Art, American Indian Art, Anthropology, Eskimo Art, Mexican Art, Southwestern Art, Jade, Afro-American Art, Oriental Art, Dioramas, Coins & Medals
Collections: African, Asian, American, European, Oceanic & Oriental Art; E W Hamlin Oriental Library of Art & Archaeology
Publications: Bulletin of the Buffalo Society of Natural Sciences, irregular; Collections, quarterly
Activities: Classes for adults & children; docent training; travel talks; lects open to pub & for mems only, 5 vis lectrs per yr; tours; sponsor Camera Club Photo Contests; book traveling exhibs 2-3 per yr; mus shop sells books & reproductions

M **CENTER FOR EXPLORATORY & PERCEPTUAL ART,** CEPA Gallery, 617 Main St, Rm 201, Buffalo, NY 14203-1400. Tel 716-856-2717; Fax 716-270-0184; *interim Exec & Artistic Dir* Sean Donaher; *Educ Dir* Lauren Tent; *Exec Asst* Lynda Kaszubski
Open Mon - Fri 10 AM - 5 PM, Sat Noon - 4 PM; No admis fee; Estab 1974 as a non-profit art center for the advancement of contemporary ideas & issues expressed through photographically related work; Five gallery rooms, 225 running ft of wall space, track light, hardwood floors; Average Annual Attendance: 50,000; Mem: 200; dues $25- $500
Income: $100,000 (financed by mem, city & state appropriation, NY State Council on the arts, National Endowment for the Arts)
Exhibitions: A View from Within; Keepers of the Western Door/Works by Native American Artists; Ritual Social Identity
Publications: CEPA Quarterly; Artist Project Publications, 2 artist books per year
Activities: Adult classes; lect open to public, vis lectr; competitions with awards; book traveling exhibitions 1 per year; shop sells books, original art

L **CEPA Library,** 617 Main St, Rm 201, Buffalo, NY 14203. Tel 716-856-2717; Fax 716-856-2720; Elec Mail cepa@aol.com; Elec Mail info@cepagallery.com; Internet Home Page Address: www.cepagallery.com; *Exec Dir* Lawrence F Brose; *Assoc Dir* Kathleen Kearnan; *Artistic Dir* Sean Donaher; *Educ Coordr* Lauren Tent; *Commun Educ* Crystal Tinch; *Designer & Digital Facility* Kim Meyerer; *Admin Asst* Timothy J Hobin
Open Mon - Fri 10 - 5, Sat Noon - 4; pub galleries daily 9 AM - 9 PM; Estab May 1974; Reference library only
Library Holdings: Clipping Files; Exhibition Catalogs; Lantern Slides; Pamphlets; Records; Slides; Video Tapes
Special Subjects: Photography

M **HALLWALLS CONTEMPORARY ARTS CENTER,** 341 Delaware Ave, Buffalo, NY 14202-1871. Tel 716-854-1694; Fax 716-854-1696; Elec Mail john@hallwalls.org; Internet Home Page Address: www.hallwalls.org; *Dir* Edmund Cardoni; *Visual Arts Cur* John Massier; *Dir Develop* Polly Little; *Music Dir* Steve Baczkowski; *Tech Dir* Bill Sack; *Media Cur* Carolyn Tennant
Open Tues - Fri 11 AM - 6 PM, Sat 11 AM - 2 PM, cl Sun & Mon; No admis fee; Estab 1974 to provide exhibition space for emerging artists; besides

exhibitions, programming includes film, literature, music, performance art & video; The gallery is comprised of 1 large 1400 sq ft room; Average Annual Attendance: 25,000; Mem: 1600; dues $20-$300; annual meeting in Jan
Income: Funded by the National Endowment for the Arts, city, county & state appropriations, New York State Council on the Arts, contributions from private corporations, foundations & individuals
Collections: 400 tape video library
Publications: Consider the Alternatives: 20 Years of Contemporary Art at Hallwalls
Activities: Concerts; gallery talks; tours

M **STATE UNIVERSITY OF NEW YORK COLLEGE AT BUFFALO,** (Burchfield-Penney Art Center) Buffalo State College, 1300 Elmwood Ave Buffalo, NY 14222-1004. Tel 716-878-6011; Fax 716-878-6003; Elec Mail burchfld@buffalostate.edu; Internet Home Page Address: www.burchfieldpenney.org; *Head Colls & Charles Cary Rumsey Cur* Nancy Weekly; *Coll & Traveling Exhibs Mgr* Scott Propeack; *Assoc Dir* Don Metz; *Head Mktg & Pub Rels* Kathleen Hayworth; *Preparator* Patrick Robideau; *COO* Carolyn Morris-Hunt; *Registrar* Mary Helen Miskuly; *Archives & Info Resource Mgr* Tullis Johnson
Open Tues - Sat 10 AM - 5 PM, Sun 1 - 5 PM; Thurs until 9PM; No admis fee; Estab 1966 to honor American artist Charles E Burchfield. In 1969 it began to develop into a regional arts center for the exhibition, collection & interpretation of artistic expression in the Western New York area. Collections include works by Charles Burchfield & both historic & contemporary artists who have lived or worked in the area; Museum has thirteen exhibition galleries, archives, collection study area, Useum (TM), auditorium, cafe & store; Average Annual Attendance: 100,000; Mem: 3358; dues Friend $125, Family/Dual $60, Individual $45, Cur Circle $275, Dir Circle $500, Burchfield's Circle $1,000
Income: Financed by grants, endowment, mem, SUNY & other sources
Library Holdings: Auction Catalogs; Audio Tapes; Book Volumes; CD-ROMs; Cassettes; Clipping Files; Compact Disks; DVDs; Exhibition Catalogs; Kodachrome Transparencies; Lantern Slides; Manuscripts; Memorabilia; Motion Pictures; Original Art Works; Original Documents; Pamphlets; Photographs; Prints; Records; Slides; Video Tapes
Special Subjects: Afro-American Art, Decorative Arts, Drawings, Historical Material, Ceramics, Collages, Glass, Metalwork, Furniture, Photography, Prints, Period Rooms, Bronzes, Woodcuts, Sculpture, Architecture, Painting-American, Watercolors, Crafts, Jewelry, Cartoons
Collections: Charles E Burchfield Collection; Works by contemporary & historical artists of Western New York; Roycroft Objects; American art contextualizing Burchfield; Art Institute of Buffalo; Buffalo Society of Artists; Patteran Society; Paul Sharits Archives; Birge Wallpaper Co; Philip C Elliot Archives; Virginia Cuthbert Archives; Martha Visser't Hooft Archives; Charles Cary Rumsey Archives; Milton Rogorin Archives
Publications: Exhibition catalogues
Activities: Classes for adults & children; docent training; dramatic programs; lects open to pub; concerts; symposia; tours; poetry readings; competitions; gallery talks; Sylvia L Rosen Endowment Purchase Award; Langley H Kenzie Award; educ dept serves area schools & community organizations; originates traveling exhibs nationally; mus shop sells books, magazines, catalogues, craft art, reproductions & wallpapers designed by Charles Burchfield, original art, prints

L **Burchfield Penney Art Center,** 1300 Elmwood Ave, Buffalo State College Buffalo, NY 14222-1004. Tel 716-878-6011; Fax 716-878-6003; Elec Mail burchfld@buffalostate.edu; Internet Home Page Address: www.burchfieldpenney.org; *Dir* Anthony Bannon; *Assoc Dir & Chief Cur* Scott Propeack; *COO* Carolyn Morris-Hunt
Open Tues - Wed & Fri - Sat 10 AM -5 PM, Thurs 10 AM - 9 PM, Sun 1 - 5 PM; Admis adults $10, seniors $8. students $5; Estab 1967; Dedicated to the vision of Charles E Burchfield & artists of western New York
Library Holdings: Audio Tapes; Book Volumes 2500; Cassettes; Clipping Files; Exhibition Catalogs; Kodachrome Transparencies; Manuscripts; Memorabilia; Motion Pictures; Other Holdings Monographs; Periodicals; Pamphlets; Photographs; Records; Reels; Slides; Video Tapes
Special Subjects: Art History, Decorative Arts, Photography, Drawings, Etchings & Engravings, Manuscripts, Painting-American, Posters, Prints, Sculpture, Historical Material, Portraits, Watercolors, Crafts, American Western Art, Printmaking, Art Education, Furniture, Bookplates & Bindings, Pottery, Textiles, Woodcuts, Architecture, Folk Art, Woodcarvings
Collections: Charles Rand Penney colls; Archives relating to Charles E Burchfield, Charles Cary Rumsey, Frank K M Rehn Gallery, J J Lankes, Martha Visser't Hooft, Buffalo Society of Artists, Patteran Society; Artpark; Artist Gallery; Paul Sharits Archives; Milton Rogovin Collection & Archives
Exhibitions: See website for past & present exhibs
Activities: Classes for adults & children; docent training; lects open to pub; concerts; gallery talks; tours; schols; fels; organize traveling exhibs; mus shop sells books, original art, reproductions & prints

CANAJOHARIE

M **CANAJOHARIE LIBRARY & ART GALLERY,** Arkell Museum of Canajoharie, 2 Erie Blvd, Canajoharie, NY 13317-1198. Tel 518-673-2314; Fax 518-673-5243; Elec Mail etrahan@sals.edu; Internet Home Page Address: www.arkellmuseum.org; *Pres of Board* Oliver Simonsen; *Dir* Eric Trahan; *Chief Cur* Diane Forsberg; *Registrar* Emily Spallina; *Head Librn* Kari Munger
Open Mon - Fri 10AM-5PM, Sat-Sun 12:30PM-5PM; Admis adults $7, seniors & students $5; Estab 1914 as a memorial to Senator James Arkell; Two galleries total area 1500 sq ft exhibit works from permanent collection including major collection of paintings by Winslow Homer; Average Annual Attendance: 50,000; Mem: Annual meeting in Jan
Income: Financed by endowment, grants & fundraising
Library Holdings: Book Volumes; CD-ROMs; Compact Disks; Exhibition Catalogs; Framed Reproductions; Original Art Works; Original Documents; Periodical Subscriptions; Photographs; Prints; Slides; Video Tapes
Special Subjects: Painting-American, Photography, Prints, Sculpture, Watercolors, American Western Art, Bronzes, Portraits, Historical Material
Collections: Archival Materials & Artifacts on Regional History; Paintings by American artists, colonial period-present
Exhibitions: Permanent collection
Publications: Catalog of Permanent Art Collection varies
Activities: Lects provided, 5 vis lectrs per yr; concerts; gallery talks; tours; individual paintings & original objects of art lent to other mus & galleries; lending collection contains 28,617 books, 831 cassettes, color reproductions, paintings, 682 phono records, 376 slides, 523 video cassettes; mus shop sells books, original art, prints & reproductions

L **Library,** 2 Erie Blvd, Canajoharie, NY 13317. Tel 518-673-2314; Fax 518-673-5243; *Pres of Board* Oliver Simonsen; *Cur* James Crawford; *Dir Library* Eric Trahan
Open Mon-Thurs 10AM-7PM, Fri 10AM-5PM, Sat-Sun 12:30PM-5PM; No Admis fee; Estab 1914 to represent American Art
Library Holdings: Audio Tapes; Book Volumes 28,617; Cassettes; Clipping Files; Exhibition Catalogs; Framed Reproductions; Pamphlets; Periodical Subscriptions 146; Photographs; Records; Reels; Slides; Video Tapes
Activities: Lects open to pub, 5 vis lectrs per yr; concerts; gallery talks; tours; lending collection contains 29,022 books, cassettes, framed reproductions & 788 phono records; mus shop sells books, magazines, original art, reproductions, prints, slides, notecards & postcards

CAZENOVIA

M **CAZENOVIA COLLEGE,** Chapman Art Center Gallery, 22 Sullivan St, Cazenovia, NY 13035-1085. Tel 315-655-7162; 655-7138; Fax 315-655-2190; Elec Mail jrandall@cazenovia.edu; *Dir* John Aistars
Open Mon - Thurs 1 - 4 PM & 7 - 9 PM, Fri 1 - 4 PM, Sat & Sun 2 - 6 PM; No admis fee; Estab 1977 as a col gallery for students & community; Gallery is 1,084 sq ft with track lighting; Average Annual Attendance: 1,000
Income: Financed by College
Collections: A small permanent coll of work donated to college
Exhibitions: Annual shows of faculty, students & invitational work; Cazenovia Watercolor Society
Activities: Schols offered

M **STONE QUARRY HILL ART PARK,** John & Virginia Winner Memorial Art Gallery, 3883 Stone Quarry Rd, Cazenovia, NY 13035; P.O. Box 251, Cazenovia, NY 13035. Tel 315-655-3196; Fax 315-655-5742; Elec Mail office@stonequarryhillartpark.org; Internet Home Page Address: www.stonequarryartpark.org; *Mgr* Lesley Owens-Pelton, JD
Open daily sunset-sunrise; gallery Thurs - Sun noon - 5 PM during exhibitions; No admis fee ($5 donation requested); Estab 1991; 4 1/2 miles of maintained walking trails; Average Annual Attendance: 25,000; Mem: 400; dues $35-75; annual meeting Jan
Income: $125,000 (financed by memberships, donations, grants & sponsors)
Collections: Environmental land; outside sculpture; permanent coll of Dorothy Riester; 100 installations of environmental art & sculpture
Activities: Classes for adults & children; docent training; lects open to pub; concerts; gallery talks; tours; ann pottery fair; Finding Nature in Art & Kite Festival; artists in residence prog

M **Winner Gallery,** 3883 Stone Quarry Rd, Cazenovia, NY 13035; PO Box 251, Cazenovia, NY 13035-0251. Tel 315-655-3196; Fax 315-655-5742; Elec Mail office@stonequarryhillartpark.org; Internet Home Page Address: www.stonequarryartpark.org; *Site Mgr* Dylan Otts; *Art Adminr* Amber Blanding
Open daily 10AM-5PM; Admis suggested donation for non-mem $5; Estab 1991 to address issues of art & environmental preservation; Average Annual Attendance: 47,000; Mem: 250; dues $35-$5000; annual meeting in Jan
Income: $207,000 (financed by endowment, mem & NYSCA)
Library Holdings: Book Volumes; Exhibition Catalogs; Original Art Works; Original Documents; Sculpture; Slides; Video Tapes
Special Subjects: Afro-American Art, Archaeology, Decorative Arts, Drawings, Etchings & Engravings, Historical Material, History of Art & Archaeology, Interior Design, Landscape Architecture, Landscapes, Art Education, Art History, Ceramics, Conceptual Art, Glass, Intermedia, Mexican Art, Mixed Media, Furniture, Porcelain, Portraits, Pottery, Pre-Columbian Art, Textiles, Woodcuts, Manuscripts, Maps, Sculpture, Architecture, Latin American Art, Sculpture, American Western Art, Bronzes, Ethnology, Southwestern Art, Religious Art, Folk Art, Primitive art, Woodcarvings, Afro-American Art, Posters, Oriental Art, Asian Art, Islamic Art
Collections: Tree houses; Dorothy Riester Sculpture; Emilie Brzezinski
Activities: Classes for adults & children; lects open to pub, 2-3 vis lectrs per yr; concerts; gallery talks; tours; fels offered; sales shop sells books, original art, reproductions, magazines, prints

L **Jenny Library,** 3883 Stone Quarry Rd, No 251, Cazenovia, NY 13035; PO Box 251, Cazenovia, NY 13035. Tel 315-655-3196; Fax 315-655-5742; Elec Mail Office@stonequarryhillartpark.org; Internet Home Page Address: www.stonequarryhillartpark.org; *Arts Admin* Amber Blanding; *Exec Dir* Joseph A Scala; *Site Mgr* Dylan Otts
Open daily sunrise-sunset; Admis free; $5 suggested donation per car; Estab 1991; Circ 3500; 1200 sq ft indoor gallery; Average Annual Attendance: 25,000; Mem: 900; dues $35-$70
Income: financed by mem & endowment
Library Holdings: Book Volumes 3500; Exhibition Catalogs; Original Art Works; Sculpture; Slides
Special Subjects: Art History, Landscape Architecture, Mixed Media, Photography, Painting-American, Sculpture, Watercolors, Crafts, Theatre Arts, Printmaking, Asian Art, Porcelain, Metalwork, Oriental Art, Pottery
Collections: Emily Brzezinski; Steven Siegal
Exhibitions: Bestia Faber, Making Animal: A Celebration of Beavers, Termites, Woodpeckers, & Humans
Publications: Art & the Land-A Narrative History of Stone Quarry Hill Art Park by Dorothy Riester
Activities: classes for children; workshops for adults; active artist in residence prog; lects open to pub; concerts; gallery talks; tours; sponsoring of competitions; mus sales shop sells original art & prints

CHAUTAUQUA

M CHAUTAUQUA CENTER FOR THE VISUAL ARTS, PO Box 28, Chautauqua, NY 14722-0028. Tel 716-357-2771; Elec Mail ccva@mainalley.com; Internet Home Page Address: www.clweb.org/arts.html; *Pres* Thomas Becker; *Exec & Artistic Dir* Cynnie Gaasch; *Asst Dir* Alissa Shields
Open daily 10 AM - 6 PM July - Sept; No admis fee; Estab 1952 to promote quality art, culture & appreciation of the arts; Main gallery with 3 smaller galleries; Average Annual Attendance: 10,000; Mem: 300; dues $25; one annual meeting
Income: Financed by mem, grants, donations & fundraising activities
Collections: 75 two dimensional purchase prizes
Exhibitions: 15 exhibitions per year including prints, paintings, glass, metals & sculpture; Annual Chautauqua National Exhibition of American Art (entering 44th year)
Publications: Chautauqua National, annual catalog; Calendar of Events, annual; Chautauqua National Prospectus, annual; annual report; promotional materials; exhibition brochures; membership brochures
Activities: Lects open to pub, 17 vis lectrs per yr; concerts; gallery talks; docent tours; competitions with awards; annual juried National Exhibition of American Art award $2500; individual paintings & original objects of art lent to Chautauqua institution, area libraries, exhibition sites, area galleries & theatres; book traveling exhibs annually; originate traveling exhibs; sales shop sells books, original art, reproductions, prints, original jewelry, small gifts & handicraft from around the world

CLINTON

M HAMILTON COLLEGE, Emerson Gallery, 198 College Hill Rd, Clinton, NY 13323-1295. Tel 315-859-4396; Fax 315-859-4060; Elec Mail emerson@hamilton.edu; Internet Home Page Address: www.hamilton.edu/gallery; *Assoc Dir & Cur* Susanna White; *Registrar* Dana Krueger; *Office Asst* Megan Austin; *Consulting Dir* Ian Berry
Open Mon - Fri 10AM - 5 PM, Sat & Sun 1 - 5 PM; No admis fee; Estab 1982; Housed in 1914 building; Average Annual Attendance: 20,000
Income: Financed by Hamilton College appropriations
Purchases: Martin Lewis, Rainy Day on Murray Hill, etching; George Bellows Between Rounds 1916, lithograph; Jefferson David Chalfant Working Sketch for the Chess Players, pencil; Roman, c 2nd Century AD; Two Sarcophagi Fragments, marble
Special Subjects: Photography, Drawings, Painting-American, Prints, Watercolors, American Indian Art, Etchings & Engravings, Antiquities-Egyptian, Antiquities-Greek
Collections: Greek vases, Roman glass; Native American artifacts; 16th-20th century prints, 19th-20th century paintings; Pre-Columbian Art
Publications: Exhibition catalogues
Activities: Lects open to pub, 2-3 various vis lectrs per yr; concerts; gallery talks; tours; individual paintings & original objects of art lent

A KIRKLAND ART CENTER, 9-1/2 E Park Row, Clinton, NY 13323-1544; PO Box 213, Clinton, NY 13323-0213. Tel 315-853-8871; Fax 315-853-2076; Elec Mail info@kacny.org; Internet Home Page Address: www.kacny.org; *Operations Mgr* Jennifer Walker
Open Tues - Fri 9:30 AM - 4:30 PM; No admis fee; Estab 1960 to promote the arts in the town of Kirkland & surrounding area; The center has a large main gallery, dance studio & studio space for classes; Average Annual Attendance: 15,000 - 17,000; Mem: 700; dues adults $35; annual meeting June
Income: Financed by endowment, mem, state, county & town appropriation, fund raising events, United Way & United Arts Funds
Exhibitions: Works by contemporary artists
Activities: Classes for adults & children; performances for children; bluegrass & folk music series; film series; dramatic progs; lect open to public; competitions; concerts; tours

COBLESKILL

A TRI-COUNTY ARTS COUNCIL, INC, 108 Union St, 3rd Fl Cobleskill, NY 12043-3830. Tel 518-234-7521 Ext 209; *Exec Dir* Renee Nied
Open Mon - Fri 10 AM - 5:30 PM, Sat 10 AM - 3 PM, cl Sun; No admis fee; Estab 1977; Average Annual Attendance: 5,000; Mem: 450; mem open to individual artists & bus donations of $20 or more; annual meeting 1st Tues in May
Income: $180,000 (financed by mem, government, corporate & foundation support)
Exhibitions: Annual National Small Works Exhibition
Activities: Classes for children; dramatic progs; benefit concerts; acoustic jams; walk-in workshops; technical assistance; NYSCA Decentralization Re-grant site; gallery talks; sales shop sells books, original art, reproductions, prints & pottery

COLD SPRING

M PUTNAM COUNTY HISTORICAL SOCIETY, Foundry School Museum, 63 Chestnut St, Cold Spring, NY 10516-2613. Tel 845-265-4010; Fax 845-265-2884; Elec Mail office@pchs-fsm.org; Internet Home Page Address: www.pchs-fsm.org; *Exec Dir* Mindy Krazmien; *Dir Admin* Kara Shier
Open Wed-Sun 11AM-5PM; Admis free; Estab 1906 to present local history & West Point Foundry artifacts; Three exhib galleries; Average Annual Attendance: 1,000; Mem: 1,000; dues family $100 individual $50, seniors & students $30, annual meeting in Mar
Income: financed by endowment, mem & fundraising events
Library Holdings: Auction Catalogs; Book Volumes; Clipping Files; Fiche; Kodachrome Transparencies; Manuscripts; Maps; Memorabilia; Original Documents; Pamphlets; Photographs; Reproductions; Slides; Video Tapes

Special Subjects: Decorative Arts, Historical Material, Landscapes, Graphics, Painting-American, Photography, Prints, Watercolors, Costumes, Portraits, Furniture, Historical Material, Maps, Period Rooms
Collections: 19th Century Country Kitchen, West Point Foundry; 19th Century Prints and Photographs; 19th and Early 20th Century Costumes
Publications: George Pope Morris: Defining American Culture; This Perfect River-View: The Hudson River School & Contemporaries in Pvt Colls in the Highlands; A Ramble Through the Hudson Highlands: A History in Pictures & the Writings of Donald H MacDonald; The Gilded Age: High Fashion & Society in the Hudson Highlands 1865 - 1914; America the Beautiful: Women & the Flag
Activities: School progs; docent training; lects open to pub, 2 vis lectrs per yr; competitions with awards; gallery tours; individual paintings & original objects of art lent; originates traveling exhibitions to museums and libraries; mus shop sells books, reproductions, prints, postcards, pamphlets, children's toys & books

COOPERSTOWN

A COOPERSTOWN ART ASSOCIATION, 22 Main St, Cooperstown, NY 13326-1170. Tel 607-547-9777; Fax 607-547-1187; Elec Mail gallery@cooperstownart.com; Internet Home Page Address: www.cooperstownart.com; *Dir* Janet Erway; *Asst Dir* Cory Sharer
Open Mon - Sat 11 AM - 4 PM, Sun 1 - 4 PM, cl Tues from Labor Day to Memorial Day; Estab 1928 to provide a cultural program for the central part of New York State; An art gallery is maintained; 3 gallery spaces; Average Annual Attendance: 14,000; Mem: 400; dues $5 & up
Income: Financed by mem
Special Subjects: Etchings & Engravings, Photography, Textiles, Watercolors, Pottery, Bronzes, Woodcuts, Ceramics, Collages, Crafts, Portraits, Furniture, Glass, Jewelry, Woodcarvings
Collections: Crafts; paintings; sculpture
Exhibitions: Annual Regional & National Juried Exhibitions; Solo & Group Shows; Ann NY Craft Invitational
Publications: Annual newsletter
Activities: Classes & workshops for adults & children; monthly exhibits; special events; ann schols; awards; lending collection contains paintings, sculpture, crafts

M NATIONAL BASEBALL HALL OF FAME & MUSEUM, INC, Art Collection, 25 Main St, Cooperstown, NY 13326-1300. Tel 607-547-7200; Fax 607-547-2044; Internet Home Page Address: www.baseballhalloffame.org; *Pres* Jeffrey L Idelson; *VPres* William Haase; *Cur Coll* Peter P Clark; *Librn* James L Gates Jr; *VPres* William T Spencer; *VPres* Sean Gahagan
Open Memorial Day - Labor Day daily 9 AM - 9 PM, Oct - Apr daily 9 AM - 5 PM; Admis adults $16.50, seniors $11.00, children ages 7-12 $6; Estab 1936 to collect, preserve & display memorabilia pertaining to the national game of baseball and honoring those who have made outstanding contributions to our national pastimes; Maintains reference library; Average Annual Attendance: 351,000; Mem: 12,500
Income: $1,500,000 (financed by admis & gift shop sales, Hall of Fame Game & contributions)
Library Holdings: Audio Tapes; CD-ROMs; Cassettes; Clipping Files; Compact Disks; DVDs; Fiche; Manuscripts; Memorabilia; Motion Pictures; Original Art Works; Original Documents; Pamphlets; Photographs; Records; Reels; Slides; Video Tapes
Special Subjects: Decorative Arts, Drawings, Folk Art, Historical Material, Illustration, Ceramics, Collages, Glass, Photography, Portraits, Painting-American, Prints, Silver, Textiles, Bronzes, Manuscripts, Painting-Japanese, Sculpture, Graphics, Watercolors, Costumes, Pottery, Posters, Jewelry, Coins & Medals, Miniatures, Cartoons, Leather
Collections: Baseball & sport-related art & memorabilia; Library collections
Publications: National Baseball Hall of Fame & Museum Yearbook, annually; quarterly newsletter
Activities: Classes for children; educ prog; gallery talks; lects open to public; lending of original art to AAM accredited museums; book traveling exhib on a case by case basis; originate traveling exhib to museums, baseball clubs; bookstore sells books, reproductions, prints, t-shirts, caps, glassware, postcards, mugs & jackets

M NEW YORK STATE HISTORICAL ASSOCIATION, Fenimore Art Museum, Rte 80, Lake Rd, Cooperstown, NY 13326; PO Box 800, Cooperstown, NY 13326-0800. Tel 607-547-1400; Fax 607-547-1404; Elec Mail info@nysha.org; Internet Home Page Address: www.fenimoreartmuseum.org, www.nysha.org; *Pres & CEO* D Stephen Elliott; *Chief Cur* Dr Paul S D'Ambrosio; *VPres Develop & Mktg* John Carnahan; *Library Dir* Melissa McAfee
Open Apr - May & Oct, Tues - Sun 10 AM - 4 PM, May - Oct daily, 10 AM - 5 PM; Admis adults $11, senior $9.50, students & children 7-12 $5, children 6 & under free; Estab 1899 as a historical soc whose purpose is to promote the study of New York State through a state wide educational program, the operation of two museums & graduate programs offering master's degree in conjunction with the State University of New York at Oneonta; Fenimore Art Museum is an art & history museum with an extensive collection of folk, acad, decorative art & North American Indian Art. Opened a new American Indian Art wing in 1995 to house the Eugene & Clare Thaw Collection of American Indian Art; Mem: 2800; dues $25 & up; annual meeting in July
Special Subjects: Decorative Arts, Folk Art, Painting-American
Collections: American folk art; American Indian Art; Browere life masks of famous Americans; James Fenimore Cooper (memorabilia); genre paintings of New York State; landscapes; portraits; Hudson River historic & contemporary school paintings
Publications: Annual Report; New York History, quarterly journal; Heritage, yearly membership magazine, occasional manuscripts, exhibit catalogues
Activities: Classes for adults & children; docent training; seminars on American culture; junior prog; conferences; lects open to pub; gallery talks; tours; individual paintings & original objects of art lent to selected mus; book traveling exhibs; originate traveling exhibs; mus shop sells books, magazines, original art, reproductions, prints & slides
L Research Library, 5798 St Hwy 80, Cooperstown, NY 13326; PO Box 800,

Cooperstown, NY 13326-0800. Tel 607-547-1470; Fax 607-547-1405; Elec Mail library@nysha.org; Internet Home Page Address: www.nysha.org; *Assoc Dir Technical Serv* Susan Deer; *Head Librn* Wayne W Wright; *Pres* Paul D'Ambrosio
Open summer Mon-Fri 10 AM - 5 PM, spring & fall Mon - Fri 10 AM - 5 PM, Sat 1 - 5 PM; Admis $5 daily use free for non-mems; free for NYSHA mems, NYSHA vols & students; Estab 1968 as non-circulating research library; Open to public for reference only
Library Holdings: Auction Catalogs; Audio Tapes; Book Volumes 82,000; Cassettes; Exhibition Catalogs; Manuscripts; Maps; Periodical Subscriptions 160; Records; Reels
Special Subjects: Folk Art, Manuscripts, Maps, Painting-American, American Indian Art, Architecture

CORNING

A **ARTS OF THE SOUTHERN FINGER LAKES,** 32 W Market St, Corning, NY 14830-2617. Tel 607-962-5871; Fax 607-962-4128; Elec Mail infoarts@earts.org; Internet Home Page Address: www.earts.org; *Comm Arts Develop Dir* Lynn Rhoda; *Exec Dir* Ginnie Lupi; *Folk Arts* Lynn Dates; *Office Asst* Laura Illig; *Office Asst* Kristen Stewart
Open Mon - Fri 9 AM - 5 PM; No admis fee; Estab to increase resident participation in the arts; Mem: 34; annual meeting in June
Exhibitions: Artsfest; The Westend Gallery (Local Artists); Easter eggs & paper cuttings (Felicia Dvornicky)
Publications: Artscope, 6 times per year; See, Hear, Do, 12 times per year
Activities: Educ dept; infuses art into education in area schools; lect open to public; partnership awards given; grants to local schools & nonprofit organizations

M **CORNING MUSEUM OF GLASS,** Museum, One Museum Way, Corning, NY 14830-2253. Tel 800-732-9156; Fax 607-974-8470; Elec Mail info@cmog.org; Internet Home Page Address: www.cmog.org; *Exec Dir & Cur Ancient & Islamic Glass* David Whitehouse; *Pres* Marie McKee; *Cur European Glass* Florian Knothe; *Cur Modern Glass* Tina Oldknow; *Cur American Glass* Jane Shadel Spillman
Open daily 9 AM - 5 PM, cl New Years Day, Thanksgiving Day, Dec 24 & 25; Admis adults $14, students $12.60, sr citizens $11.90, local res with ID $6, children under 20 free; Estab 1951 to collect & exhibit the finest glass from 1500 BC to the present; Art, history, science of glass; Average Annual Attendance: 300,000; Mem: 2500; dues $25 & up
Income: $3,000,000 (financed by gifts, interest & sales)
Purchases: Glass & books
Library Holdings: Auction Catalogs; Audio Tapes; Book Volumes; Cards; Cassettes; Exhibition Catalogs; Fiche; Kodachrome Transparencies; Manuscripts; Memorabilia; Original Art Works; Original Documents; Pamphlets; Periodical Subscriptions; Photographs; Prints; Slides; Video Tapes
Special Subjects: Glass
Collections: over 45,000 objects representing 3,500 yrs of glass history; Origins of Glassmaking Gallery; Glass of the Romans; Glass in the Islamic World; Early European Glass Gallery; Later European Glass Gallery; Asian Glass; Glass in America; Crystal City; Paperweights in the World; Modern Glass Gallery; Glass after 1960; Study Gallery
Exhibitions: 3 exhibitions annually
Publications: Annual catalog for spec exhibs; Journal of Glass Studies, ann; New Glass Review, ann
Activities: Classes for adults & children; docent training; annual seminar on glass; lects open to pub, 30 vis lectrs per yr; film series; gallery talks; tours; competitions; Rakow Award; Rakow Commission; annual student art show awards; schols & fels offered; original art objects lent to the other mus; lending collection contains 50,000 books, 350 lantern slides; originate traveling exhibs; mus shop sells books, postcards, prints, reproductions & slides, glass, hands-on glass activities, story hour for youth, jr cur program, glassworking classes

L **Juliette K and Leonard S Rakow Research Library,** 5 Museum Way, Corning, NY 14830-2200. Tel 607-438-5300; Fax 607-438-5392; Elec Mail rakow@cmog.org; Internet Home Page Address: www.cmog.org; *Chief Librn* James Galbraith; *Cataloger* Kelly Bliss; *Bibliographer* Peter Bambo-Kocze; *Reference Librn* Gail Bardhan; *Assoc Librn Pub Svcs* Aprille Nace; *Assoc Librn Coll Mgmt* Lori Fuller; *Reference & Emerging Tech Librn* Regan Brumagen; *Reference & Educ Librn* Beth Hylen; *Rights & Reproductions Mgr* Jill Thomas-Clark
Open Mon - Fri 9 AM - 5 PM; No admis fee; Estab 1951 for the purpose of providing comprehensive coverage of the art, history, & early technology of glass; Circ Non-circulating; The library is a pub facility that welcomes both museum visitors & glass researchers; Average Annual Attendance: 5,000
Library Holdings: Auction Catalogs 27,000; Audio Tapes; Book Volumes 75,000; Cassettes; Clipping Files; Compact Disks; DVDs; Exhibition Catalogs; Fiche 19,000; Framed Reproductions; Manuscripts; Micro Print 21,000; Motion Pictures; Original Art Works; Original Documents 7,500; Other Holdings Monographs: 55,000; Ephemera: 3,000+; Pamphlets; Periodical Subscriptions 850; Photographs; Prints 550; Reels 800; Slides 230,000; Video Tapes 2,600
Collections: Chambon (Raymond) Collection; Digital Files: 100,000+, incl 100+ virtual books; Miscellaneous: incl postage stamps, calendars & glass-related resources; 3,500 linear ft of archival colls (130+ archival collections total)
Exhibitions: (05/24/2012-01/03/2014) The Flood of '72: Community, Collections and Conservation; (05/17/2014-01/04/2015) Designing for a New Century: Works on Paper by Lalique & his Contemporaries
Activities: Docent training, classes for teachers; gallery talks, tours; schols & fels offered; mus shop sells books

M **The Studio,** 1 Museum Way, Corning, NY 14830-2253. Tel 607-974-6467; Elec Mail thestudio@cmog.org; Internet Home Page Address: www.cmog.org; *Dir Devel, Educ & The Studio* Amy Schwartz; *Educ Progs Mgr* Mary Cheek Mills; *RA* William Gudenrath
Activities: Glassmaking classes held yr-round; Schols available

M **THE ROCKWELL MUSEUM OF WESTERN ART,** 111 Cedar St, Corning, NY 14830-2632. Tel 607-937-5386; Fax 607-974-4536; Elec Mail info@rockwellmuseum.org; Internet Home Page Address: www.rockwellmuseum.org; *Cur* Sheila Hoffman; *Supvr Pub Progs* Cindy Weakland; *Controller* Andrew Braman; *Dir* Kristin A Swain; *Mktg Specialist* Beth Harvey; *Dir Educ* Gigi Alvare
Open Mon - Sun 9 AM - 5 PM, Sun 9 AM - 8 PM; Admis adults $6.50, sr citizens $5.50, students $2.50, children 19 & under free; Estab 1976 to house & exhibit the collection of the Robert F Rockwell family & to collect & exhibit American Western art; Average Annual Attendance: 35,000; Mem: 300; dues $40 - $2500; meetings in June & Dec
Income: $$400,000 (financed by a grant from Corning Incorporated)
Purchases: $50,000
Special Subjects: Glass, Pottery, Painting-American, Prints, American Indian Art, American Western Art, Bronzes, Etchings & Engravings, Carpets & Rugs
Collections: Carder Steuben glass (1903-1933); 19th & 20th century American Western paintings & illustrations; Robert F Rockwell Foundation Collection; Carder Steuben Glass Collection
Exhibitions: Celebration of Geniuses: Ansel Adams; Fields & Streams: Hunting & Wildlife
Publications: Exhibition catalog; Newsletter, 3 times per yr
Activities: Classes for adults & children; docent training; lects open to public; gallery talks; tours; concerts; AAM Accredited; paintings, original objects of art lent to established museums; lending collection contains reproductions, original art works, original prints, Carder Steuben Glass; originate traveling exhibs; mus shop sells books, magazines, reproductions, prints, Indian jewelry, postcards, crafts from the Southwest, T-shirts, Pueblo pottery, Hopi Kachinas, toys, glass

L **Library,** 111 Cedar St, Corning, NY 14830. Tel 607-937-5386; Fax 607-974-4536; Elec Mail rmuseum@stny.lrun.com; *Dir* Richard B Bessey
For reference only
Income: Financed by mem, bequests, grants, corporate donations from Corning Glass Works
Library Holdings: Book Volumes 3000; Cards; Cassettes; Clipping Files; Exhibition Catalogs; Filmstrips; Manuscripts; Original Art Works; Pamphlets; Periodical Subscriptions 40; Photographs; Slides; Video Tapes

CORNWALL ON HUDSON

M **MUSEUM OF THE HUDSON HIGHLANDS,** The Boulevard, Cornwall On Hudson, NY 12520; PO Box 337, Cornwall on Hudson, NY 12520-0337. Tel 845-534-5506; *Dir* Jacqueline Grant; *Admin Dir* Susan Brander; *Pres* Edward Hoyt
Call for hours; Admis $2 suggested donation; Estab 1962; primarily a children's natural history & art mus; A large octagonal gallery & a small gallery; Average Annual Attendance: 33,000; Mem: 450; artists qualify by approval of slides; dues $30 and up
Income: $140,000 (financed by mem, city appropriation & grants)
Special Subjects: Drawings
Collections: Richard McDaniels: Hudson River Drawings
Exhibitions: Rotating exhibitions, six per yr
Activities: Classes for adults & children; lects open to pub, 2 vis lectrs per yr; competitions with awards; lending collection contains nature & history kits; book traveling exhibs, annually; mus shop sells books, magazines, original art, reproductions, prints, toys, pottery, jewelry, batik scarves

CORTLAND

M **1890 HOUSE-MUSEUM & CENTER FOR THE ARTS,** 37 Tompkins St, Cortland, NY 13045-2555. Tel 607-756-7551; Fax 607-756-7551; Elec Mail the1890house@verizon.net; Internet Home Page Address: www.1890house.org; *Dir* Deanna L Pace; *Mus Aide* Colin Albro; *Caretaker* Robert W Smith Jr; *Pres* Marieanne Bertini; *1st VPres* Louis Larson; *2nd VPres* Mardis Kelsen
Open Tues - Sun 1 - 4 PM; call to arrange tours; Admis adults $4, seniors & students $3; Estab 1978
Collections: Decorative arts; Oriental Furnishings; Paintings; 1890 - 1900 Documentary Photographs; Victorian Furniture; Victorian Silver
Exhibitions: Late Victorian Cast Iron Lawn Ornaments; Victorian Lighting; Documentary Photographs of Restoration
Publications: Whispers Near the Inglenook

L **Kellogg Library & Reading Room,** 37 Tompkins St, Cortland, NY 13045-2555. Tel 607-756-7551; Fax 607-756-7551; *Admin Asst* Grace Nicholas
Open Tues - Sun 1 - 4 PM; For lending & reference
Library Holdings: Book Volumes 1800; Periodical Subscriptions 12

M **CORTLAND COUNTY HISTORICAL SOCIETY,** Suggett House Museum, 25 Homer Ave, Cortland, NY 13045. Tel 607-756-6071; Elec Mail cchs@clarityconnect.com; *Pres* Robert Ferris; *Treas* Christine Buck; *Dir* Mary Ann Kane; *Coll Mgr* Anita Wright
Open Tues - Sat 1 - 4 PM, mornings by appointment; Admis adults (16 & up) $2; Estab 1925 to collect, store & interpret the history of Cortland County through programs, exhibits & records in our 1882 Suggett House; Some art displayed in period settings, 1825-1900; Average Annual Attendance: 2,000; Mem: 800; dues vary; meetings several times during the year
Income: $75,000 (financed by endowment, mem, county appropriations, grants, sales & fundraisers)
Special Subjects: Folk Art, Furniture
Collections: Antique furniture, children's toys, china, folk art, glass, military memorabilia, paintings, textiles & clothing
Publications: 15 books on local history; bulletin, 1-3 times per yr; newsletter, 1-3 times per yr
Activities: Classes for adults & children; docent training; lects open to pub; individual paintings & original objects of art lent to other mus & college galleries; mus shop sells books

L **Kellogg Memorial Research Library,** 25 Homer Ave, Cortland, NY 13045. Tel 607-756-6071; *Dir* Mary Ann Kane

Open Tues - Sat 1 - 5 PM, mornings by appointment; Estab 1976 to collect, preserve & interpret information about the history of Cortland County; For reference only
Purchases: $500
Library Holdings: Book Volumes 5000; Cassettes; Clipping Files; Exhibition Catalogs; Lantern Slides; Manuscripts; Memorabilia; Original Art Works; Other Holdings Microfilm; Pamphlets; Photographs; Prints; Records; Reels; Reproductions; Sculpture; Slides; Video Tapes
Collections: Cortland County & regional genealogical records

L **CORTLAND FREE LIBRARY,** 32 Church St, Cortland, NY 13045-2798. Tel 607-753-1042; Fax 607-758-7329; Internet Home Page Address: www.flls.org/cortlandlib; *Dir* Kay Zaharis
Open Mon-Thurs 9:30AM-8PM, Fri 9:30AM-5:30PM, Sat 9:30AM-4:30PM; No admis fee; Estab 1938; Circ 1122; Average Annual Attendance: 1,600
Income: financed by dept of assn library
Purchases: $2100
Library Holdings: Book Volumes 1700; Original Art Works; Periodical Subscriptions 14; Reels
Exhibitions: Occasional monthly exhibitions held

M **STATE UNIVERSITY OF NEW YORK COLLEGE AT CORTLAND,** Dowd Fine Arts Gallery, PO Box 2000, Cortland, NY 13045-0900. Tel 607-753-4216; Fax 607-753-5728; Elec Mail mounta@cortland.edu; Internet Home Page Address: www.cortland.edu; *Dir* Allison Mount
Open Tues-Sat 10AM-4PM & also by appt; No admis fee; Estab 1967; Three separate spaces, total 2200 sq ft completely secure, full environmental control. Maintains a lending & reference library; wheelchair accessible; Average Annual Attendance: 15,000
Income: $25,000 (financed by state appropriation)
Purchases: $4500
Special Subjects: Drawings, Graphics, Latin American Art, Painting-American, Photography, Prints, Sculpture, Textiles, Ceramics, Woodcuts, Etchings & Engravings, Landscapes, Manuscripts, Collages, Portraits, Historical Material
Collections: Cortland College Permanent Collection
Publications: Exhibit catalogs, 2-3 per year
Activities: Docent training; lects open to pub, 10-12 vis lectrs per yr

L **STATE UNIVERSITY OF NEW YORK COLLEGE AT CORTLAND,** Visual Resources Collection, PO Box 2000, 87 Dowd Bldg Cortland, NY 13045-0900. Tel 607-753-5519; Elec Mail joycel@cortland.edu; *Visual Resources Cur* Lisa Joyce
Open Mon - Fri 8:30 AM - 5 PM & by appointment; No admis fee; Estab 1967 to provide visual resources to faculty, students & community
Income: Financed by state appropriation
Library Holdings: Book Volumes 1000; Exhibition Catalogs; Fiche; Filmstrips; Kodachrome Transparencies; Lantern Slides 5000; Periodical Subscriptions 10; Photographs 10,000; Slides 125,000; Video Tapes 100
Special Subjects: Art History

COXSACKIE

M **GREENE COUNTY HISTORICAL SOCIETY,** Bronck Museum, 90 County Rte 42, Coxsackie, NY 12051-3022; PO Box 44, Coxsackie, NY 12051-0044. Tel 518-731-6490; Internet Home Page Address: www.gchistory.org; *Pres* Robert Hallock, PhD; *Librn* Steve Pec; *Mus Mgr* Shelby Mattice
Open Memorial Day-Labor Day Wed-Fri noon-4PM, Sat & Mon holidays 10AM-4PM, Sun 1-4PM; Admis adults $5, youth 12-15 $3, children 5-11 $2, children under 5 & members free; Estab 1929 to preserve the history of Greene County & promote the awareness of that history; 20 ft x 20 ft gallery located in the Bronck Mus Visitor Center; maintains also The Vedder Memorial Library, & Bronck Museum, A Historic House Museum; Average Annual Attendance: 1,700; Mem: 900; dues $10 & up; annual meeting in June
Income: $75,000 (financed by endowment, mem, admissions, shop sales)
Special Subjects: Drawings, Painting-American, Textiles, Costumes, Folk Art, Pottery, Landscapes, Portraits, Furniture, Glass, Carpets & Rugs, Historical Material, Period Rooms
Collections: American Art; Ceramics; Costumes; Furniture; Glass; 19th century Agricultural & Handcrafts; Silver; Textiles; Tools
Exhibitions: Local History
Publications: Greene County Historical Journal, quarterly
Activities: Lects open to pub, 3-5 vis lectrs per yr; concerts; tours; individual paintings lent to other mus & occasionally to university galleries; lending collection contains over 50 original prints & over 300 paintings; mus shop sells books, antiques, collectables, memorabilia & old postcards

DOUGLASTON

A **THE NATIONAL ART LEAGUE,** 44-21 Douglaston Pkwy, Douglaston, NY 11363. Tel 718-229-9495, 718-224-3957; Elec Mail info@nationalartleague.org; Internet Home Page Address: www.nationalartleague.org; *VPres* Nat Bukar; *Pres* Robert Stefani; *Correspondence Secy* Mary Anne Klein
Open Mon - Thurs & Sat 1:30PM-4PM; No admis fee; Estab 1930 to unite for common interest in the study & practice of art; Mem: 300; dues $25; monthly meetings 1st Fri every month 8 PM; Scholarships
Income: Financed by mem dues & contributions
Exhibitions: Six annual major shows, one national; gallery exhibitions
Publications: Brochures; bulletins; catalogs; Artworks newsletter, monthly
Activities: Art classes for adults & children; demonstrations; monthly lects & short courses; lects open to pub, 10 vis lectrs per yr; gallery talks; competitions with awards

EAST HAMPTON

L **EAST HAMPTON LIBRARY,** Long Island Collection, 159 Main St, East Hampton, NY 11937-2794. Tel 631-324-0222, Ext. 4; Fax 631-329-7184; Elec Mail lic@easthamptonlibrary.org; Internet Home Page Address: www.easthamptonlibrary.org; *Dir* Dennis Fabiszak; *Dept Head* Gina Piastuck; *Librn & Archivist* Steve Boerner; *Librn* Suzanne Setter
Open Mon -Sat 1PM-4:30PM, cl Wed, mornings by appt; No admis fee; Estab 1930 by Morton Pennypacker; Average Annual Attendance: 400
Income: Financed by donations & fund raisers
Library Holdings: Auction Catalogs; Audio Tapes; Book Volumes; CD-ROMs; Cassettes; Clipping Files; Compact Disks; DVDs; Exhibition Catalogs; Manuscripts; Maps; Original Art Works; Original Documents; Pamphlets; Periodical Subscriptions; Photographs; Prints; Sculpture; Slides; Video Tapes
Special Subjects: Drawings, Etchings & Engravings, Manuscripts, Maps, Painting-American, Prints, Historical Material, Watercolors, American Western Art, Landscapes, Scrimshaw, Architecture, Portraits
Collections: The Long Island Collection contains material relating to the history & people of Long Island; Thomas Moran Biographical Art Collection contains original pen & ink & pencil sketches by Thomas Moran, lithographs, etchings & engravings by Moran & other members of the family, biographical material, exhibit catalogues, books & pamphlets; photographs & postcards
Exhibitions: The Gardiner Family; rotating
Activities: Lect open to public; tours; sales shop sells books, maps, posters

M **GUILD HALL OF EAST HAMPTON, INC,** Guild Hall Museum, 158 Main St, East Hampton, NY 11937-2795. Tel 631-324-0806; Fax 631-329-5043; 324-2722; Elec Mail museum@guildhall.org; Internet Home Page Address: www.guildhall.org; *Chmn* Melville Straus; *1st VChmn* Mike Clifford; *2nd VChmn* Michael Lynne; *Treas* Muriel Siebert; *Mus Dir & Chief Cur* Christina Mossaides Strassfield; *Asst Cur & Registrar* Michelle Klein; *Exec Dir* Ruth Appelhof; *Institutional Advancement Assoc* Genevieve Linnehan
Open Winter - Spring Fri-Sat 11 AM - 5 PM, Sun Noon - 5 PM, Summer open Mon, Wed-Sat 11 AM - 5 PM, Sun noon-5PM; No admis fee for members, non-members $7; Estab 1931 as a cultural center for the visual & performing arts with a State Board of Regents Educational Charter. Emphasis in art collection & exhibitions is chiefly on the many artists who live or have lived in the area; Mus has four galleries and sculpture garden; Average Annual Attendance: 80,000; Mem: 4000; dues $45-$2500; annual meeting in May
Income: $1,400,000 (financed by mem, federal, state, county & town appropriations, corporate, foundation, individual contributions, benefits, fund drives & mus shop)
Special Subjects: Painting-American, Photography, Prints, Sculpture
Collections: Focuses on American artists assoc with the region of Eastern Long Island, including James Brooks, Jimmy Ernst, Adolf Gottlieb, Childe Hassam, William de Kooning, Roy Lichtenstein, Thomas Moran, Jackson Pollock, Larry Rivers, as well as contemporary artists such as Eric Fischl, Donald Sultan & Lynda Benglis, paintings; works on paper, prints, photographs, sculpture
Publications: Newsletter, exhibition catalogues, annual report, monthly calendar
Activities: Classes for adults & children; dramatic programs; docent training; cooperative projects with area schools; lects open to pub, 25 vis lectrs per yr; concerts; gallery talks; tours; competitions; Academy of the Arts; original art objects lent to mus, libraries, schools, public building; lending collection contains cassettes, original art works & prints, paintings, photographs, sculpture, slides; book traveling exhibs; originate traveling exhibs to museums & galleries; mus sales shop sells mainly posters created for Guild Hall by artists of region; also gift items and local crafts, books, reproductions & prints

EAST ISLIP

M **ISLIP ART MUSEUM,** 50 Irish Ln, East Islip, NY 11730-2003. Tel 631-224-5402; Fax 631-224-5009; Elec Mail info@islipartmuseum.org; Internet Home Page Address: www.islipartmuseum.org; *Exec Dir* Lynda A Moran; *Mus Exhibs Dir* Beth Gacummo; *Mus Adminr* Rosa Ramos
Open Thurs - Fri 10 AM - 4 PM, Sat & Sun Noon - 4 PM; cl New Year's Day; Easter; Memorial Day; Independence Day; Labor Day; Thanksgiving; Christmas; Admis suggested donation $5; Estab 1973 for group showings of contemporary art from local & city based artists; 3000 sq ft of exhibition space divided among 4 rooms & a hallway on the Brookwood Hall estate; Average Annual Attendance: 12,000; Mem: 500; dues mem $25; patron $75; sponsor $125; benefactor $250; special benefactor $500; founder $1,000
Income: $150,000 (financed by mem, city & state appropriation, & National Endowment for the Arts)
Collections: Contemporary & avant-garde art
Exhibitions: Satellite Gallery & a Project Space
Publications: Exhibition brochures; Newsletter
Activities: Classes for adults & children; docent training; lects open to pub, 15 vis lectrs per yr; gallery talks; tours; arts festivals; competitions with awards; mus shop sells books, handmade gifts, jewelry, original art, postcards, posters, reproductions

EAST OTTO

A **ASHFORD HOLLOW FOUNDATION FOR VISUAL & PERFORMING ARTS,** Griffis Sculpture Park, 6902 Mill Valley Rd East Otto, NY 14729-9735; 28 Essex St, Buffalo, NY 14213. Tel 716-667-2808; Elec Mail griffispark@aol.com; Internet Home Page Address: www.griffispark.org; *Exec Dir* Nila Griffis Lampman; *Educ Dir* Zack Boehler; *Sculpture Park Dir* Damian Griffis; *Essex Arts Center Dir* Mark Griffis
Open May 1 - Nov 31 8 AM - 8 PM; Admis $5 adults, students & seniors $3, children under 12 no admis fee; Estab 1966 to promote the visual & performing arts by sponsoring exhibitions & performances; Funds for the 400 acre sculpture park donated by Ruth Griffis in memory of her husband, L W Griffis Sr. The original park accommodates the work of Larry Griffis Jr. The expanded areas now include works of numerous other sculptors. Materials include welded steel, wood,

aluminum & bronze, most of which has been cast at the Essex St Foundry. Sculpture park festival stage is an open-air platform for regional artist's performance of dance, music, poetry & drama; Average Annual Attendance: 30,000; Mem: 200
Income: $108,000 (financed by admis fees, donations, mem, grants, programs & pub funds
Exhibitions: Twelve distinctly different groups of work by Larry Griffis Jr are displayed
Publications: Brochure; postcards
Activities: Classes for adults & children; concerts; tours; book 4 traveling exhibitions per year; sales shop sells prints, original art, reproductions, metal sculptures; junior mus, Big Orbit, 30 Essex St, Buffalo, NY

ELMIRA

M **ARNOT ART MUSEUM,** 235 Lake St, Elmira, NY 14901-3118. Tel 607-734-3697, ext 120; Fax 607-734-5687; Elec Mail mmanly@arnotartmuseum.org; Internet Home Page Address: www.arnotartmuseum.org; *Exec Dir* Rick Pirozzolo; *Cur Collections* Laura Wetmore; *Bus Mgr* Lynda Williams; *Cur Educ* Meghan O'Loughlin
Open Tues - Fri 10 AM - 5 PM, Sat 12 noon - 5 PM, cl Sun, Mon & national holidays; Admis Tues - Fri $7 adults, $4 seniors; Estab 1913 with the permanent collection of Matthias H Arnot consisting of 17th to 19th century European art & housed in his 1890's Picture Gallery the collection now includes 19th & 20th century American art & a growing collection of contemporary representational art; Average Annual Attendance: 18,000; Mem: 550; dues $75 & up
Library Holdings: Auction Catalogs; Audio Tapes; Book Volumes; CD-ROMs; Cassettes; Clipping Files; Compact Disks; DVDs; Exhibition Catalogs; Filmstrips; Kodachrome Transparencies; Lantern Slides; Manuscripts; Maps; Memorabilia; Original Documents; Other Holdings; Pamphlets; Periodical Subscriptions; Prints; Records
Special Subjects: American Indian Art, Decorative Arts, Drawings, Etchings & Engravings, Historical Material, Landscapes, Marine Painting, Architecture, Collages, Glass, American Western Art, Photography, Porcelain, Portraits, Pottery, Pre-Columbian Art, Painting-American, Prints, Textiles, Woodcuts, Maps, Painting-British, Painting-European, Painting-Japanese, Sculpture, Tapestries, Graphics, Latin American Art, Painting-American, Bronzes, Southwestern Art, Religious Art, Ceramics, Woodcarvings, Etchings & Engravings, Judaica, Eskimo Art, Painting-Canadian, Furniture, Oriental Art, Asian Art, Silver, Metalwork, Painting-British, Painting-Dutch, Painting-French, Restorations, Baroque Art, Calligraphy, Painting-Flemish, Renaissance Art, Period Rooms, Medieval Art, Antiquities-Oriental, Painting-Spanish, Painting-Italian, Antiquities-Egyptian, Antiquities-Greek, Painting-German, Military Art, Antiquities-Etruscan, Enamels, Painting-Scandinavian
Collections: Matthias H Arnot Collection; Contemporary Realism Collection; Hudson River School Collection
Exhibitions: Annual Regional Art Exhibition with prizes; Representing Representation 8; Art Now group show; Gallery Gala Invitational
Publications: Books; catalogs
Activities: Classes for adults & children, two wk summer adult painting school, docent training, outreach dramatic progs for community groups through educ center; lects & gallery talks open to pub; lects members only; 6 vis lectrs per yr; concerts; tours; gallery talks; competitions; individual paintings lent; one to two book traveling exhibs per yr; originate traveling exhibs to US mus; mus shop sells books, catalogues, original art & craft work, reproductions, slides, prints

M **ELMIRA COLLEGE,** George Waters Gallery, One Park Pl, Elmira, NY 14901. Tel 607-735-1800; Fax 607-735-1723; Internet Home Page Address: www.elmira.edu; *Dir* Leslie Kramer
Open Tues - Sat 1 - 5 PM, cl Mon & Sun (varies); No admis fee; The Gallery is located in the Elmira Campus Center; Average Annual Attendance: 1,000
Income: Financed by school budget
Exhibitions: Annual Student Exhibition

FISHKILL

M **FISHKILL HISTORICAL SOCIETY,** Van Wyck Homestead Museum, 504 Route 9, Fishkill, NY 12524-0133; PO Box 133, Fishkill, NY 12524-0133. Tel 845-896-9560; Elec Mail vanwyckhomestead@aol.com; Internet Home Page Address: www.pojonews.com; *Librn* Roy Jorgensen; *Pres* Steve Lynch; *1st VPres* Jack Hale
Open weekdays by appointment, Weekends 1 - 5 PM (May 30 - Oct 30); No admis fee; Estab 1962; Hudson Valley Portraits, AMMI Phillips Portraits; Average Annual Attendance: 2,000; Mem: 500; dues $10 - $500; meetings yr round
Library Holdings: Book Volumes 800; CD-ROMs; Cassettes 12; Clipping Files; Compact Disks; Maps; Original Documents; Other Holdings; Pamphlets; Photographs; Prints
Special Subjects: Drawings, Textiles, Architecture, Painting-American, Photography, Archaeology, Costumes, Folk Art, Decorative Arts, Portraits, Dolls, Furniture, Jewelry, Porcelain, Silver, Historical Material, Miniatures, Embroidery, Laces
Collections: Hudson Valley Portraits; decorative arts; quilts; Decorative Arts, Local Silver, Forms; Annie Phillips Paintings
Activities: Classes for children; docent training; lect open to public; 3 vis lectrs per year; tours; concerts; sales shop sells books, prints, reproductions

FLUSHING

A **BOWNE HOUSE HISTORICAL SOCIETY,** 37-01 Bowne St, Flushing, NY 11354. Tel 718-359-0528; Elec Mail office@bownehouse.org; Internet Home Page Address: www.bownehouse.org; *Pres* Rosemary Vieter; *VPres* Barly Grodenchik; *Treas* George Farn III; *Dir* Yvonne Engglezos
Open Tues, Sat & Sun 2:30 - 4:30 PM; Admis adults $2, sr citizens, students & children $1; Estab 1945 for historic preservation, educ, collection of 17th, 18th & 19th century furnishing & decorative & fine art. Examples of colonial life; Average Annual Attendance: 5,000; Mem: 620; dues $250, $100, $50, $25, $10; annual meeting third Tues in May
Income: Financed by mem, private & pub contributions
Collections: Furnishings from the 17th, 18th & early 19th centuries; Furniture, pewter, fabrics, china, portraits, prints & documents
Exhibitions: Photo Documentation of ongoing Restoration
Publications: Booklets regarding John Bowne & the House; quarterly newsletter
Activities: Classes for adults & children; docent training; lects open to pub; mus shop sells books, reproductions, prints, slides, products of herb garden, plates & tiles

M **QUEENS COLLEGE, CITY UNIVERSITY OF NEW YORK,** Godwin-Ternbach Museum, 65-30 Kissena Blvd, 405 Klapper Hall Flushing, NY 11367-1575. Tel 718-997-4747; Fax 718-997-4734; Elec Mail amy-winter@qc.edu; Internet Home Page Address: www.qc.cuny.edu/godwin_ternbach; *Dir & Cur* Amy Winter; *Research Asst* Brita Helgesen; *Colls Mgr* Allyson Mellone
Open Mon - Thurs 11 AM - 7 PM, Sat 11 AM - 5 PM; No admis fee; Estab 1957 for a study collection for Queens College students & in 1981 independently chartered; Collection located in one large exhibition gallery on Queens College Campus; Average Annual Attendance: 10,000; Mem: 60, dues $25
Income: Financed by state appropriation, Friends of the Mus, federal state & local grants
Special Subjects: Portraits, Drawings, Graphics, Hispanic Art, Latin American Art, Mexican Art, Painting-American, Photography, Prints, Sculpture, Watercolors, American Indian Art, Bronzes, African Art, Pre-Columbian Art, Textiles, Religious Art, Ceramics, Folk Art, Pottery, Primitive art, Woodcarvings, Woodcuts, Etchings & Engravings, Landscapes, Decorative Arts, Manuscripts, Painting-European, Posters, Eskimo Art, Furniture, Glass, Jade, Jewelry, Porcelain, Oriental Art, Asian Art, Antiquities-Byzantine, Marine Painting, Metalwork, Painting-British, Painting-Dutch, Carpets & Rugs, Historical Material, Ivory, Coins & Medals, Restorations, Baroque Art, Painting-Flemish, Renaissance Art, Embroidery, Medieval Art, Antiquities-Oriental, Painting-Spanish, Painting-Italian, Islamic Art, Antiquities-Egyptian, Antiquities-Greek, Antiquities-Roman, Mosaics, Cartoons, Stained Glass, Painting-German, Leather, Reproductions, Antiquities-Etruscan, Painting-Russian
Collections: Ancient & antique glass; Egyptian, Greek, Luristan antiquities, Old Master & WPA prints; Renaissance & later bronzes; 16th - 20th century paintings
Publications: Brochures, exhibition catalogs; newsletter; posters
Activities: Classes for adults & children; docent training; high school creative arts prog; lects open to pub, 20 lectrs per yr; gallery talks; tours; concerts; individual paintings & original objects of art lent to qualified art organizations & mus

M **Queens College Art Center,** 65-30 Kissena Blvd, Flushing, NY 11367. Tel 718-997-3770; Fax 718-997-3753; Elec Mail artcenter@qc.cuny.edu; Internet Home Page Address: www.qcpages.qc.cuny.edu/art_library; *Cur* Alexandra de Luise; *Dir* Dr Suzanna Simor; *Admin Asst* Mollie Moskowitz; *Asst Cur* Tara Mathison
Open Mon - Thurs 9 AM - 9 PM, Fri Noon - 5 PM (when school is in session); No admis fee; Estab 1937; Gallery presents a variety of exhibitions of modern & contemporary art in diverse media; Average Annual Attendance: 30,000
Income: financed by donations, grants
Collections: modern contemporary art
Publications: exhibition catalogues
Activities: Lects open to pub, 5-10 vis lectrs per yr; gallery talks; tours

L **Art Library,** 65-30 Kissena Blvd, Flushing, NY 11367. Tel 718-997-3770; Fax 718-997-3753; Elec Mail artlibrary@qc.cuny.edu; Internet Home Page Address: qcpages.qc.cuny.edu/art_library; *Head* Dr Suzanna Simor; *Admin Asst* Frances Chan; *Asst Librn* Paul Remeczki; *Admin Asst* Donna Schultz
Open Mon - Thurs 9 AM - 10 PM, Fri 9 AM - 5 PM, Sat-Sun 11AM-5PM, when school is in session, Mon - Fri 9 AM - 5 PM other times; No admis fee; Estab 1937 to support instruction; Circ 80,000
Library Holdings: Book Volumes 80,000; CD-ROMs; Clipping Files; Compact Disks; DVDs; Exhibition Catalogs 20,000; Fiche 2000; Lantern Slides; Micro Print; Original Art Works CA 100; Original Documents; Other Holdings Exhibition catalogs & pamphlets 50,000; Pamphlets; Periodical Subscriptions 200; Photographs; Reels; Reproductions 60,000; Slides 15,000
Collections: Books, periodicals, pictures, pamphlets, reference, special colls
Activities: Lending coll contains 80,000 books, 60,000 color reproductions, 50,000 exhib catalogs & pamphlets & 15,000 slides

A **QUEENS HISTORICAL SOCIETY,** Kingsland Homestead, 143-35 37th Ave Flushing, NY 11354-5729. Tel 718-939-0647 ext 17; Fax 718-539-9885; Elec Mail info@queenshistoricalsociety.org; Internet Home Page Address: www.queenshistoricalsociety.org; *Exec Dir* Ellissa Fazio; *Coll Mgr* Richard Hourahan; *Outreach Coordr* Danielle Hilkin; *Educ Coordr* Karyn Mooney
Open Mon - Fri 9 AM - 5 PM (research appts) Museum: Tues, Sat - Sun 2:30 PM - 4:30 PM; Admis adults $5, seniors & students $3; Estab 1968 as a historical society to collect Queens history materials; First floor for changing exhibits; second floor permanent Victorian parlor room; Maintains reference library/archives; Average Annual Attendance: 5,000; Mem: 600; dues bus $100-$750, family $45, individual $20, students & seniors $15; annual meeting varies
Income: $75,000 (financed by mem, city & state appropriation)
Library Holdings: Audio Tapes; Book Volumes; CD-ROMs; Cards; Cassettes; Clipping Files; Compact Disks; DVDs; Exhibition Catalogs; Filmstrips; Framed Reproductions; Lantern Slides; Manuscripts; Maps; Memorabilia; Motion Pictures; Original Art Works; Original Documents; Pamphlets; Periodical Subscriptions; Photographs; Prints; Reels; Sculpture; Slides; Video Tapes
Special Subjects: Costumes, Drawings, Embroidery, Etchings & Engravings, Historical Material, Manuscripts, Photography, Porcelain, Sculpture, Textiles, Painting-American, Decorative Arts, Folk Art, Ceramics, Portraits, Archaeology, Dolls, Furniture, Jewelry, Period Rooms, Maps, Carpets & Rugs, Flasks & Bottles, Coins & Medals
Collections: photographs, postcards, maps & atlases, personal papers of Margaret Carman, King and Murray families, Doughty; textiles, furniture, decorative arts, ephemera
Exhibitions: Kingsland: From Homestead to House Museum

Publications: Quarterly newsletter; Angels of Deliverance, The Underground Railroad in Queens, Long Island, and Beyond; So this is Flushing, Flushing Freedom Mile; Friends of Freedom: The Underground Railroad in Queens and on Long Island

Activities: Educ prog; classes for adults & children; docent training; lects open to pub; 200 vis lectrs per yr; concerts; gallery talks; tours; sponsoring for competitions; 4th-6th grade art & history contest/Queensmark prog; 1-2 book traveling exhibs per yr; originate traveling exhibs; mus shop sells books, postcards & prints

M **THE QUEENS MUSEUM OF ART,** Flushing Meadows Corona Park, New York City Bldg Flushing, NY 11368-3398. Tel 718-592-9700; Fax 718-592-5778; Elec Mail info@queensmuseum.org; Internet Home Page Address: www.queensmuseum.org; *Exec Dir* Tom Finkelpearl; *Dir Educ* Lauren Schloss; *Dir External Affairs* David Strauss; *Dir Fin* Julie Lou; *Dir Devel* Jodi Hanel
Open Wed - Sun Noon - 6 PM, Fri until 8 PM in Jul & Aug, cl New Year's Day, Thanksgiving, Christmas Day; Admis by suggested donation, adults $5, seniors & children $2.50, children under 5 & members free; Estab 1972 to provide a vital cultural center for the more than 2.5 million residents of Queens County; it provides changing, high-quality, fine art exhibitions & a wide-range of educational & public programs; Museum has approx 25,000 sq ft gallery space, The Panorama of New York City (9,335 sq ft architectural scale model of New York City), theatre, workshops, offices; Average Annual Attendance: 200,000; Mem: 1000; dues family $55, individual $35, seniors & students $25
Income: $3,500,000 (financed by mem, city & state appropriation, corporate & foundation grants, earned income)
Collections: The Panorama of New York City (world's largest architectural scale model); Small collection of paintings, photographs & prints; Collection of materials from 1939 - 1940 & 1964 - 1965 New York World's Fairs
Exhibitions: Tiffany Art from the Egon & Hildegard Neustadt Museum of Tiffany Art (permanent display); A Watershed Moment: Celebrating the Homecoming of the Relief Map of the NYC Water Supply System; The Partnership Gallery
Publications: Catalogs; quarterly newsletter
Activities: Guided tours for adults & children; docent training; projects involving elementary school children; films; drop-in arts & crafts workshops on Sun during school year & certain weekdays in summer; lects open to pub, 10 vis lectrs per yr; concerts; gallery talks; tours; competitions; satellite gallery at Bulova Corporate Center in Jackson Heights, NY; mus shop sells books, reproductions, prints, exhibition catalogs, children's items & 1939-40 & 1964-65 World's Fair memorabilia

L **QUEENSBOROUGH COMMUNITY COLLEGE LIBRARY,** Kurt R Schmeller Library, 22205 56th Ave, Flushing, NY 11364-1432. Tel 718-631-6226; Fax 718-281-5118; Internet Home Page Address: www.web.acc.qcc.cuny.edu/library; *Coordr Technical Svcs* Devin Feldman; *Chief Librn* Kyu Hugh Kim
Open Mon - Thurs 8:30 AM - 9 PM, Fri 8:30 AM - 5 PM, Sat 10 AM - 4 PM; No admis fee; Estab 1961 to serve the students and faculty of the col
Income: Financed by city and state appropriation, state and local grants, through the University, Friends of Library and pvt donations
Purchases: $80,000
Collections: Book & periodical coll includes material on painting, sculpture & architecture; print coll; reproductions of famous paintings; reproductions of artifacts & sculpture; vertical file coll
Publications: Library Letter, biannual

FREDONIA

M **STATE UNIVERSITY OF NEW YORK COLLEGE AT FREDONIA,** Cathy and Jesse Marion Art Gallery, 280 Central Ave, Fredonia, NY 14063-1127. Tel 716-673-4897; Fax 716-673-4990; Elec Mail hastings@fredonia.edu; Internet Home Page Address: www.fredonia.edu; *Dir* Tina Hastings
Open Tues - Thurs & Sun 2 - 6 PM, Fri - Sat 2 - 8 PM; No admis fee; Estab 1963 and relocated in 1969 to new quarters designed by I M Pei and Partners; The gallery serves as a focal point of the campus, uniting the college with the community; Average Annual Attendance: 5,000
Income: Financed by state appropriation and student groups, private endowments
Special Subjects: Architecture, Prints, Sculpture
Collections: Primarily 20th-century American art and architectural archival material, with an emphasis on prints and sculpture
Exhibitions: Graduating Seniors I; Graduating Seniors II; Graduating Seniors III; curated & traveling shows
Activities: Lects open to pub; 2-3 vis lectrs per yr; gallery talks; individual paintings and original objects of art lent to offices and public lobbies on campus

FULTONVILLE

M **THE NATIONAL SHRINE OF THE NORTH AMERICAN MARTYRS,** 136 Shrine Rd, Fultonville, NY 12072. Tel 518-853-3033; Fax 518-853-3051; Elec Mail office@martyrshrine.org; Internet Home Page Address: www.martyrshrine.org; *Dir* Fr Peter J Murray S.J.; *Dir Opers* Thomas F Ralph; *Dir Mktg* Fran Ralph; *Graphics Design & Editor* Dorothy Domkowski; *Martyrs Mus Mgr* Beth Lynch; *Kateria Media Center Mgr* Lily Fiorenza; *Information Systems* Joanne Freeman; *Music Dir* Jenna Poling
Open late Apr-Oct Sun & Weekdays 10AM-5PM, Sat 10AM-5:30PM; No admis fee; Estab 1885 as a religious & historic shrine; Average Annual Attendance: 60,000
Income: Financed by donations
Special Subjects: American Indian Art, Decorative Arts, Painting-American, Tapestries, Textiles, Religious Art, Folk Art, Woodcarvings, Manuscripts, Posters, Historical Material, Maps
Publications: The Pilgrim, quarterly

GARDEN CITY

M **NASSAU COMMUNITY COLLEGE,** Firehouse Art Gallery, 1 Education Dr Garden City, NY 11530. Tel 516-572-7165; Fax 516-572-7302; Elec Mail lynn.rozzi@ncc.edu; Internet Home Page Address: www.art.sunynassau.edu irehouse; *Dir & Cur* Lynn Rozzi Casey; *Cur* Meg Oliveri
Estab 1964 to exhibit fine art & varied media; Two exhibition spaces, carpeted with track lighting
Income: Financed by state, college & county appropriation
Special Subjects: Prints, Sculpture
Collections: Painting; sculpture; prints; photography
Exhibitions: Invitational exhibits, national or regional competition; faculty & student exhibits per year
Activities: Lect open to public; competitions with awards

GARNERVILLE

M **GAGA ARTS CENTER,** Garnerville Arts & Industrial Ctr, 55 W Railroad Ave Garnerville, NY 10923. Tel 845-947-7108; Elec Mail gaga@garnervillearts.com; Internet Home Page Address: gagaartscenter.org; *Dir* James Tyler
Call for hours
Collections: works by estab & emerging artists; paintings; sculpture; photographs; ceramics.

GARRISON

L **ALICE CURTIS DESMOND & HAMILTON FISH LIBRARY,** Hudson River Reference Collection, Routes 9D & 403, Garrison, NY 10524; PO Box 265, Garrison, NY 10524-0265. Tel 845-424-3020; Fax 845-424-4061; Elec Mail donick@highlands.com; Internet Home Page Address: desmondfishlibrary.org; *Library Dir* Carol Donick
Open Mon, Wed, Fri 10 AM - 5 PM, Tues & Thurs 2 - 9 PM, Sat 10 AM - 4 PM, Sun 1 - 5 PM; No admis fee; Estab 1983; Circ 83,000; Average Annual Attendance: 70,000
Library Holdings: Audio Tapes; Book Volumes 30,000; Compact Disks; DVDs; Kodachrome Transparencies 1,000; Periodical Subscriptions 100
Special Subjects: Art History, Landscape Architecture, Painting-American, Art Education, Landscapes
Collections: Slide Archive: Hudson River views in 19th century painting
Exhibitions: Shows annually: Contemporary artists as well as Hudson River School Works
Activities: Lects open to pub; 4 vis lectrs per yr

M **GARRISON ART CENTER,** 23 Garrison's Landing, Garrison, NY 10524; PO Box 4, Garrison, NY 10524-0004. Tel 845-424-3960; Internet Home Page Address: www.garrisonartcenter.org; *Pres* Jaynie Crimmins; *VPres* Bill Burback; *Exec Dir* Elizabeth Turnock
Open daily 12 - 5 PM
Collections: works by local artists

GENESEO

M **BERTHA V B LEDERER FINE ARTS GALLERY-SUNY GENESEO,** Bertha V B Lederer Fine Arts Gallery, 1 College Circle, Brodie Hall 232, Geneseo, NY 14454-1401. Tel 585-245-5814; Fax 585-245-5815; Elec Mail hawkins@geneseo.edu; Internet Home Page Address: www.llbgalleries.geneseo.edu; *Dir Galleries* Cynthia Hawkins; *Secy* Tammy Farral
Open Tues - Thurs 12:30 PM - 3:30 PM, Fri - Sat 1 - 5 PM; No admis fee; Estab 1966 (Fine Arts Bldg); 2,000 sq feet; 2 movable walls
Income: State financed
Special Subjects: Drawings, Etchings & Engravings, Collages, Portraits, Painting-American, Prints, Painting-French, Graphics, Watercolors, Pottery, Woodcuts, Furniture, Stained Glass
Collections: Paintings; sculpture; photographs; prints; drawings; furniture
Activities: Lects open to the pub; concerts; gallery talks

M **LIVINGSTON COUNTY HISTORICAL SOCIETY,** Museum, 30 Center St, Geneseo, NY 14454-1204. Tel 716-243-9147; Elec Mail lchistory@frontier.com; Internet Home Page Address: www.livingstoncountyhistoricalsociety.com; *Mus Admin* Anna Kowalchuk; *Pres* Bill Brummett; *VPres* Liz Porter; *Treas* Jon Perkins; *Research Secy* Sandy Brennan; *Research Sec* Jeanne Galbraith
Open May - Oct Sun & Thurs 2 - 5 PM; No admis fee; Estab 1876 to procure, protect & preserve Livingston County history; Average Annual Attendance: 1,500; Mem: 380; dues $10; meetings first Sun in Nov & May plus monthly programs
Income: Financed by mems, grants, donations
Library Holdings: Book Volumes; Clipping Files; Filmstrips; Framed Reproductions; Manuscripts; Original Documents; Photographs; Records; Video Tapes
Special Subjects: Archaeology, Folk Art, Historical Material, Landscapes, Architecture, Ceramics, Glass, Furniture, Painting-American, Painting-American, Textiles, Crafts, Pottery, Portraits, Posters, Dolls, Furniture, Glass, Silver, Embroidery, Pewter
Collections: China & Silver; Indian Artifacts; primitive tools; Shaker items; toy coll; war items; paintings of local landmarks & personalities; 10-15 paintings of Genesee Valley subjects; Wadsworth coach
Exhibitions: Cobblestone Schoolhouse
Publications: Newsletter, quarterly
Activities: Educ prog for adults & children; work with col students at SUNY Geneseo; docent training; lects open to pub, 6 vis lectrs per yr; concert; sales shop sells books, maps, notepaper, coverlets, big tree pieces, historical society pins & magnets

M **STATE UNIVERSITY OF NEW YORK AT GENESEO,** Bertha V B Lederer
Gallery, 1 College Cir, Brodie Hall Geneseo, NY 14454-1492. Tel 585-245-5814;
Fax 585-245-5815; Elec Mail hawkins@geneseo.edu; Internet Home Page
Address: www.geneseo.edu; *Dir of Galleries* Cynthia Hawkins
Open Mon-Thurs 12:30PM-3:30PM; Fri & Sat 12:30PM-5:30PM; No admis fee;
Estab 1967; the gallery serves the col and community; 2,000 sq ft environmentally
controlled, lighting system; Average Annual Attendance: 6,000
Income: Financed by state appropriation
Special Subjects: Afro-American Art, Drawings, Landscapes, Collages, Pottery,
Prints, Graphics, Latin American Art, Painting-American, Sculpture, Watercolors,
American Indian Art, Ceramics, Woodcuts, Etchings & Engravings, Glass
Collections: Ceramics, furniture, graphics, paintings, sculpture
Exhibitions: Annual Student Art Exhibition; changing exhibitions
Activities: Lect open to public; lending collection contains 400-600 books

M **Lockhart Gallery,** 26 Main St, McClellan House Geneseo, NY 14454-1214; Suny
Geneseo, 1 College Circle, Brodie Hall 232 Geneseo, NY 14454-1401. Tel
585-245-5813; Fax 585-245-5815; Elec Mail hawkins@geneseo.edu; Internet
Home Page Address: www.llbgalleriesgeneseo.edu; *Dir Galleries* Cynthia
Hawkins; *Sec* Tommy Farral
Open Tues-Thurs 12:30PM-3:30PM, Fri & Sat 1PM - 5PM; Estab 2001; 750 sq ft
gallery with environmentally controlled lighting; Average Annual Attendance:
1,000
Income: Private & public funding
Special Subjects: American Indian Art, Drawings, Etchings & Engravings,
Landscapes, American Western Art, Painting-American, Prints, Painting-French,
Watercolors, Woodcuts, Afro-American Art
Collections: Permanent coll & prints (primary)
Activities: Lects open to pub; concerts; gallery talks

GHENT

M **THE FIELDS SCULPTURE PARK AT OMI INTERNATIONAL ARTS
CENTER,** 1405 Cty Rte 22, Ghent, NY 12075-3809. Tel 518-392-4747; Fax
518-392-4748; Elec Mail bmaynes@artomi.org; Internet Home Page Address:
www.artomi.org; *Dir* Bill Maynes
Open daily dawn to dusk
Collections: paintings; photographs; contemporary sculpture

GLENS FALLS

M **HYDE COLLECTION TRUST,** 161 Warren St, Glens Falls, NY 12801-4562.
Tel 518-792-1761; Fax 518-792-9197; Elec Mail info@hydecollection.org; Internet
Home Page Address: www.hydecollection.org; *Dir* David Setford
Open Tues - Sat 10 AM - 5 PM, Sun Noon - 5 PM; No admis fee, call for guided
tour information & cost; Estab 1952 to promote & cultivate the study &
improvement of the fine arts; Historic house and modern wing with 4 temporary
gallery spaces; Average Annual Attendance: 40,000; Mem: 1022; dues $15 - $5000
Income: Financed by endowment, mem, contributions, municipal support & grants
Special Subjects: Prints, Sculpture, Painting-European, Furniture, Tapestries,
Painting-Italian
Collections: Works by Botticelli, da Vinci, Degas, Eakins, El Greco, Hassam,
Homer, Matisse, Picasso, Raphael, Rembrandt, Renoir, Rubens, Ryder, Tintoretto
& others; furniture, sculpture, tapestries
Exhibitions: Nine temporary exhibitions throughout the year
Publications: Exhibit catalogs
Activities: Classes for adults & children; docent training; lects open to pub;
concerts; gallery talks upon request; tours; scholarships offered; original objects of
art lent to accredited museums; originate traveling exhibs; mus shop sells books,
magazines, original art & reproductions

L **Library,** 161 Warren St, Glens Falls, NY 12801. Tel 518-792-1761; Fax
518-792-9197; Internet Home Page Address: www.hydeart.museum.org; *Dir*
Randall Suffolk
Open Tues - Fri 10 AM - 5 PM; For reference only
Income: Financed by the Hyde Collection Trust
Library Holdings: Book Volumes 1000; Clipping Files; Exhibition Catalogs;
Filmstrips; Memorabilia; Other Holdings Original documents 3000; Periodical
Subscriptions 8; Photographs
Collections: Hyde Family Archives

GOSHEN

M **HARNESS RACING MUSEUM & HALL OF FAME,** 240 Main St, Goshen,
NY 10924-2157. Tel 845-294-6330; Fax 845-294-3463; Elec Mail
Library@harnessmuseum.com; Internet Home Page Address:
www.harnessmuseum.com; *Dir* Gail Cunard
Open 7 days a week, 10 AM - 6 PM, holidays 10 AM - 6 PM, cl Christmas &
New Years; No admis fee; Estab 1951 to preserve the artifacts of harness racing;
There are two galleries, three theaters and a 3-D harness racing simulation; Mem:
Dues benefactor $5000, fellow $1000 - $4999, corporate $1000+, family $100 -
$999, associate $50, friend $35
Income: Financed by endowment & mem
Collections: Historic Coll incl: 1,500+ works of fine art; 5,000 pieces of
ephemera; 13,000 photographs; 400 jackets, caps & helmets; 90 sulkies &
harnesses; 800 trophies
Publications: Catalogs
Activities: Educ prog; workshops; tours; mus store sells related items & catalogs

HAMILTON

M **COLGATE UNIVERSITY,** Picker Art Gallery, Charles A Dana Arts Ctr,
Hamilton, NY 13346-1398; 13 Oak Drive, Hamilton, NY 13346. Tel
315-228-7634; Fax 315-228-7932; Elec Mail pickerart@colgate.edu; Internet
Home Page Address: www.pickerartgallery.org; *Dir* Anja Chavex; *Registrar*
Sarisha Guarneiri; *Educ* Melissa Davies; *Technology Coordr* Jesse Henderson;
Admin Asst Tammy Larson
Open Tues-Sat 10AM-5PM, Sun 1PM-5PM during acad session; Fri-Sat 10AM -
5PM, Sun 1PM-5PM when univ is not in session; No admis fee; Estab 1966, as

an educative adjunct to study in the fine arts & liberal arts curriculum; Building
designed by architect Paul Rudolph; Average Annual Attendance: 3,000; Mem: 25;
benefactor, patron, sponsor $150, contributor $75, family $40, individual $25
Income: Financed by the University & Friends of the Picker Art Gallery
Library Holdings: Exhibition Catalogs; Pamphlets; Photographs; Sculpture;
Slides; Video Tapes
Special Subjects: Afro-American Art, American Indian Art, Etchings &
Engravings, Landscapes, Ceramics, Photography, Portraits, Pre-Columbian Art,
Painting-American, Prints, Bronzes, Woodcuts, Painting-European, Sculpture,
Drawings, Watercolors, Religious Art, Primitive art, Manuscripts, Posters, Asian
Art, Painting-British, Painting-French, Renaissance Art, Medieval Art,
Painting-Italian, Cartoons, Painting-Scandinavian
Collections: Herman Collection of Modern Chinese Woodcuts; Gary M Hoffer '74
Memorial Photography Collection; Luis de Hoyos Collection of pre-Columbian
Art; Luther W. Brady: 20th-Century Painting & Sculpture; Harry Neigher
Collection of Political Cartoons, 1928-1975; photographs by Yergeny Khaldei;
Herbert A Mayer: Collection of Artwork
Publications: Exhib catalogs
Activities: Classes for adults & children; high school teaching seminars; lects
open to pub; tours; gallery talks; individual paintings & original objects of art
lent; book traveling exhibs; originate traveling exhibs

A **THE EXHIBITION ALLIANCE,** (Gallery Association of New York State) PO
Box 345, Hamilton, NY 13346-0345. Tel 315-824-2510; Fax 315-824-1683; Elec
Mail mail@exhibitionalliance.org; Internet Home Page Address:
www.exhibitionalliance.org; *Exec Dir* Donna Anderson; *Design Dir* Ted Anderson;
Exhibs Asst Jessie Schmitt
Estab 1972 to facilitate cooperation among exhibiting institution in state/region;
Mem: 200; mem open to exhibiting organization; dues $100-$500

HEMPSTEAD

M **HOFSTRA UNIVERSITY,** Hofstra University Museum, 112 Hofstra University,
Hempstead, NY 11549-1120. Tel 516-463-5672; Fax 516-463-4743; Elec Mail
elgbel@hofstra.edu; Internet Home Page Address: www.hofstra.edu/museum;
Assoc Dir Exhibs & Coll Karen Albert; *Exec Dir* Beth E Levinthal; *Develop &
Mem Coordr* Tiffany Jordan; *Mus Educ Dir* Nancy Richner; *Mus Educ Outreach
Coordr* Marjorie Pillar
Open Tues - Fri, 10 AM - 5 PM, Sat & Sun 1 PM - 5 PM; No admis fee; Estab
1963; a university mus that serves the needs of its student body & the New York
Metropolitan region; Mus includes exhibition facilities; Average Annual
Attendance: 25,000; Mem: 100; dues $35
Income: Financed by university, mem & grants
Library Holdings: Exhibition Catalogs
Special Subjects: Drawings, Etchings & Engravings, Landscapes, Ceramics,
Collages, Photography, Painting-American, Prints, Bronzes, Sculpture, Graphics,
Hispanic Art, Watercolors, African Art, Pre-Columbian Art, Woodcarvings,
Woodcuts, Painting-European, Painting-Japanese, Posters, Oriental Art, Asian Art,
Painting-French, Antiquities-Oriental, Antiquities-Persian, Islamic Art,
Painting-German, Painting-Russian
Collections: American paintings & prints; African, Pre-Columbian, Melanesian;
19th & 20th century European painting; contemporary prints, painting &
photographs; outdoor sculpture; Asian art
Exhibitions: Mother & Child: the Art of Henry Moore; Shapes of the Mind:
African Art from L I Collections; People at Work: 17th Century Dutch Art;
Seymour Lipton; 1979 - 1989: American, Italian, Mexican Art for the Collection
of Francesco Pellizzi; The Coming of Age of America: The First Decades of the
Sculptors Guild; The Transparent Thread: Asian Philosophy in Recent American
Art.; Street Scenes: 1930's - '50's; Leonard Bramer's Drawing of the 17th
Century Dutch Life; T.V. Sculpture; R.B. Kitaj (Art and Literature); Indian
Miniatures; Maelstrom; Preserving Our Heritage: The Realm of the Coin; Money
in Contemporary Art; Appeasing the Spirits: Sui and Early Tang Tomb Sculpture
from the Schloss Collection; The Butcher, The Baker, The Candlestick Maker; Jan
Luyken's Mirrors of 17th Century Dutch Daily Life; Poster: The Art of 10
Masters; Rodin's Gates to Hell; Breaking the Wall of Bias: Art from Survivors;
Paul Jenkins: The Early Years in Paris & New York; Moby Dick Art; Euclid to
E-Books: Ideal Books Moving Ideas; Voiceless in the Presence of Realities:
9/11/01 Remembrances from the Long Island Studies Institute; Baile y Musica;
Am Perspectives: 1907 to 1992; Lawrence Parks Bearden: Artists of Influence;
African American Highlights from the Reader's Digest Assn Collection;
Twardowicz-Dudson: Artists in Parallel; Photographing Suburbia: Crewdson,
Owen, and Weiner; The Greatest of All Time Muhammad Ali; Sacred to the
Memory: The Photography of Robert Reinhardt; Ancient Echoes in Contemporary
Printmaking; Tranquil Power: The Art of Perle Fine; Out of Africa: Works from
the Hofstra University Museum Collection; Burton Morns: Pop!; Indian Art After
Independence: Selected works from the colls of Virginia & Ravi Akhoury &
Shelley & Donald Rubin; Andy Warhol; The Photographic Legacy Program;
Children's Pleasures; American Celebrations of Childhood; Settling into Nature:
Photography of Mikael Levin; America's Irreplaceable Dance Treasures: the First
100; Something's Afoot; Small works from the Hofstra Univ Mus Coll; The
Humanist Spirit: Burton Silverman; Barbara Roux: Environments; Yonia Fain:
Remembrance; The Disappearing Landscape; Opportunity & Impact: Works by
Emigre Artists
Publications: Exhibition catalogs; catalogs available for all of the above listings
Activities: Classes for children; school program K-12; poetry workshops; lects
open to public, 3 vis lectrs per yr; concerts; gallery talks; tours for school groups
& community organizations; exhibitions related to scholarly conferences; lending
of original objects of art; originates small traveling exhibs to other museums &
universities; mus shop sells reproductions & digital jpegs

HEWLETT

L **HEWLETT-WOODMERE PUBLIC LIBRARY,** 1125 Broadway, Hewlett, NY
11557-2336. Tel 516-374-1967; Fax 516-569-1229; Internet Home Page Address:
www.hwpl.org; *Art Librn* Richard Fox; *Dir* Susan de Sciora
Open Mon - Thurs 9 AM - 9 PM, Fri 9 AM - 6 PM, Sat 9 AM - 5 PM, Sun 12:30
- 5 PM (except summer); No admis fee; Estab 1947 as a library for art & music;
Gallery maintained

Income: Financed by state appropriation & school district
Library Holdings: Auction Catalogs; Book Volumes 200,000; CD-ROMs; Cassettes; Compact Disks; DVDs; Exhibition Catalogs; Motion Pictures; Pamphlets; Periodical Subscriptions 520; Photographs; Slides; Video Tapes
Special Subjects: Film, Photography, Crafts, Architecture
Collections: Art Slides/Vintage Posters
Exhibitions: Hold local exhibits
Publications: Index to Art Reproductions in Books (Scarecrow Press)
Activities: Classes for adults & children; dramatic progs; lects open to pub; 10 vis lectrs per yr; concerts; gallery talks; tours

HOWES CAVE

M **IROQUOIS INDIAN MUSEUM,** 324 Caverns Rd, Howes Cave, NY 12092; PO Box 7, Howes Cave, NY 12092-0007. Tel 518-296-8949; Fax 518-296-8955; Elec Mail info@iroquoismuseum.org; Internet Home Page Address: www.iroquoismuseum.org; *CEO & Dir* Erynne Ansel; *Chmn & Pres* Larry Joyce; *Mus Shop Mgr* Steph Shultes
Open May - Nov Tues - Sun 10 AM - 5 PM; cl Easter; Thanksgiving; Christmas Eve & Day; Admis adults $8, sr citizens & students 13 -17 $6.50, children 5 -12 $5; Estab 1980 to teach about Iroquois culture today & in the past; Exhibits follow a time line from the earliest times to present day. Archaeology exhibits trace the development of native culture from the time of Paleo-Indians (8000 BC) through the 1700s, when the Iroquois & colonists lived side-by-side in the Schoharie Valley; Average Annual Attendance: 11,000; Mem: 900; dues students (full-time) & single seniors $20; individuals & senior couples $25; family $35; friend $50; donor $100; sponsor $250; patron $500; benefactor $1,000
Income: $300,000 (financed by mem, admis, sales shop, fundraising & grants)
Library Holdings: Book Volumes; Clipping Files
Special Subjects: American Indian Art, Decorative Arts, Folk Art, Historical Material, Landscapes, Photography, Pottery, Painting-American, Textiles, Maps, Drawings, Sculpture, Anthropology, Archaeology, Ethnology, Costumes, Ceramics, Crafts, Pottery, Woodcarvings, Portraits, Posters, Dolls, Furniture, Jewelry, Silver, Scrimshaw, Juvenile Art, Coins & Medals, Embroidery, Leather
Collections: Contemporary art & craft work of the Iroquois; prehistoric materials of the Iroquois & their immediate antecedents relating to Schoharie County; color slides; black & white prints; photographic collection of Iroquois arts
Exhibitions: Indian Stereotypes as External Avatars.; Art on the Longhouse Wall; Excellence in Iroquois Arts Award
Publications: Exhibition catalogs; Museum Notes, quarterly
Activities: Classes for adults & children; school progs; lects open to pub, 5 vis lectrs per yr; awards; concerts; gallery talks; tours; internships offered; exten dept includes lending collection; mus shop sells books, prints, magazines, prints, slides, reproductions & original art; Iroquois Indian Children's Museum

HUDSON

M **OLANA STATE HISTORIC SITE,** 5720 State Route 9-G, Hudson, NY 12534. Tel 518-828-0135; Fax 518-828-6742; Elec Mail linda.mclean@oprhp.state; Internet Home Page Address: www.olana.org; *Historic Site Mgr* Linda McLean; *Head Educ* Carri Manchester; *Chief Cur* Evelyn Trebilcock; *Assoc Cur* Valerie Balint; *Archivist & Librn* Ida Brier; *Mus Shop Mgr* Rachel Patton; *Pres The Olana* Sara Griffen
Call for hours; main fl studio & 2nd fl open Thurs - Sun; Admis adults $9, sr citizens $8, children 12 & under free; main fl studio admis adults $12, sr citizens 10, children 12 & under free; Opened as historic house museum 1966 to promote interest in & disseminate information of life, works & times of Frederic Edwin Church, landscape painter of the Hudson River School; The building is a Persian-style artists residence & studio overlooking the Hudson River; Average Annual Attendance: House 27,000; Grounds 200,000; Mem: 700; dues $25 - $5000; annual meeting June
Income: Financed by NY State appropriation & The Olana Partnership
Special Subjects: Decorative Arts, Photography, Architecture, Drawings, Painting-American, Prints, Sculpture, Textiles, Ceramics, Pottery, Woodcarvings, Painting-European, Furniture, Oriental Art, Silver, Metalwork
Collections: Frederic Edwin Church Collection: oil sketches, drawings, paintings
Exhibitions: Rotating exhibs Maurice & Evelyn Sharp Gallery
Publications: The Crayon, quarterly (journal produced by the Olana Partnership); Catalogs: Glories of the Hudson, Fern Hunting with the artist FEC in Jamaica, Treasures of Olana
Activities: Classes for adults & children; docent training; lects open to pub, 3-4 vis lectrs per yr; concerts; gallery talks; tours; slide programs; summer arts camp; exten dept with outreach programs, individual paintings & original objects of art lent to other museums & galleries; mus shop sells books & reproductions

L **Library,** 5720 State Route 9-G, Hudson, NY 12534. Tel 518-828-0135; Fax 518-828-6742; Internet Home Page Address: www.olana.org; *Historic Site Mgr* Kimberly Flook; *Cur* Evelyn Trebilcock; *Pres Olana Partnership* Sara Griffen; *Librn & Archivist* Ida Brier; *Cur* Valerie Balint
Open Apr - Oct 10 AM - 5 PM, Nov - Mar Fri - Sun 11 AM - 3 PM, Dec holiday prog; Admis adults $9, seniors & students $8, children 12 & under free; $5 vehicle fee Apr -Oct weekends; Estab in 1968 as historic house museum; Historic House open to the pub; Average Annual Attendance: 24,611; Mem: 400
Library Holdings: Book Volumes; Clipping Files; Exhibition Catalogs 10; Manuscripts; Memorabilia 200; Original Art Works; Original Documents; Photographs; Prints
Special Subjects: Decorative Arts, Painting-American, Pre-Columbian Art, Sculpture, Painting-European, Furniture, Mexican Art, Period Rooms, Antiquities-Persian, Textiles, Landscapes, Antiquities-Greek, Woodcarvings
Collections: Family papers, photographs, books, correspondence diaries, receipts; Decorative arts, coll of Frederic Edwin Church paintings, American & European Art on Canvas, furnishings
Exhibitions: Ann summer exhibs
Publications: Crayon, twice a year; exhib catalogs
Activities: Classes for adults & children; docent training; lects open to pub; historic house & landscape tours; organize traveling exhibs to mus; mus shops sells books, reproductions, prints, gift items

HUNTINGTON

M **THE HECKSCHER MUSEUM OF ART,** 2 Prime Ave, Huntington, NY 11743-7702. Tel 631-351-3250; Fax 631-423-2145; Elec Mail info@heckscher.org; Internet Home Page Address: www.heckscher.org; *Exec Dir & CEO* Michael W Schantz, PhD; *Deputy Exec Dir* H E (Skip) Show Jr; *Cur* Lisa Chalif; *Dir Educ & Pub Progs* Joy L Weiner; *Dir External Affairs* Nina Muller
Open Wed - Fri 10 AM - 4 PM, Sat & Sun 11 AM - 5 PM, cl Mon & Tues, extended viewing 1st Fri of each month 4 PM - 8:30 PM; Admis res: adults $6, seniors (62+) & students (10 & over) $4, mus mems free, town of Huntington residents, Wed after 2PM & Sat before 1PM (proof of residency); non-res: adults $8, seniors (62+) $6, students (10 & over) $5, children under 10 & museums free, active military personnel free; Estab 1957; Five galleries, approx 4,800 sq ft
Income: $1,263,463 (financed by endowment, mem, town appropriations & grants)
Special Subjects: Landscapes, Portraits, Drawings, Graphics, Painting-American, Photography, Prints, Watercolors, Painting-European, Marine Painting, Painting-British, Painting-Dutch, Painting-French, Painting-Flemish, Painting-German
Collections: Permanent Coll: 2,200+ works incl paintings, sculpture, works on paper & photography from early 16th c to present; European holdings; Moran family; George Grosz; Lucas Cranach the Elder; R A Blakelock; Arthur Dove; Helen Torr; Thomas Eakins; James M & William Hart; Asher B Durand; Esphyr Slobodkina
Publications: The Guide, quarterly programming guide; Family Gallery Guide; educator resource packets; exhib catalogs
Activities: Jr docent training; workshops; lects for mems only, 3-6 vis lectrs per yr; gallery talks; panel discussions; musical performances; book groups; Longs Island's Best: Young Artists at the Heckscher Museum - Renzo S Bianchi Memorial Schol; exten progs: School Discovery serves gr K - 12, Adult Discovery serves nursing homes & adult communities

L **Library,** 2 Prime Ave, Huntington, NY 11743-7702. Tel 631-351-3250; Fax 631-423-2145; Elec Mail info@heckscher.org; Internet Home Page Address: www.heckscher.org; *Exec Dir* Beth E Levinthal
Libr open by appointment only; Estab to provide range of research materials & unique resources; Open to researchers & pub. For reference only
Income: $979,735 (financed by endowment, mem, town appropriation & grants)
Library Holdings: Auction Catalogs; Book Volumes 3803; Cards; Clipping Files; Exhibition Catalogs; Memorabilia; Pamphlets; Periodical Subscriptions 2; Reproductions; Slides
Special Subjects: Photography, Painting-American, Painting-British, Painting-Dutch, Painting-Flemish, Painting-French, Painting-German, Prints, Painting-European
Collections: Major works by the Moran family, George Grosz, Lucas Cranach the Elder, R A Blakelock, Arthur Dove, Helen Torr, Thomas Eakins, James M & William Hart, Asher B Durand, Esphyr Slobodkina Research & Study Center, paintings, sculptures, drawings & preparatory sketches
Exhibitions: The Art of Thomas Anshutz; Baudelaire's Voyages: The Poet & His Painters; The Collector's Eye: American Art from Long Island Collections; Coney Island to Caumsett: 50 years of Photography by N Jay Jaffee; Garden of Earthly Delights; Huntington Township Art League Island Artists Exhibition; INSIGHTS Ron Schwerin: Paintings & Studies; Millennium Messages (time capsules by leading artists, architects & designers); Shaping a Generation: The Art & Artists of Betty Parsons; regional artists are featured in contemporary exhibitions
Publications: Bi-monthly newsletter; On Vie, bi-monthly calendar of events; Family Gallery Guides; Educator Resource Packets; Catalog of the collection; exhibition catalogs

HYDE PARK

M **NATIONAL ARCHIVES & RECORDS ADMINISTRATION,** Franklin D Roosevelt Museum, 4079 Albany Post Rd, Hyde Park, NY 12538. Tel 845-229-8114; Fax 845-486-1147; Elec Mail library@roosevelt.nara.gov; Internet Home Page Address: www.fdrlibrary.marist.edu; *Dir* Cynthia Koch, PhD; *Cur* Herman Eberhardt; *Registrar* Michelle Frauenberger; *Chief Archivist* Bob Clark
Open daily 9 AM - 6 PM, (Nov - Apr), 9 AM - 5 PM (Apr - Oct); Admis adults $14 for combination ticket to the Roosevelt Home & Museum, children under 15 free; Estab 1939; contains displays on President & Mrs Roosevelt's lives, careers & special interests, including personal items, gifts & items collected by President Roosevelt; Average Annual Attendance: 120,000
Income: Financed by congressional appropriation, trust fund
Special Subjects: Historical Material
Collections: Papers of President & Mrs Roosevelt & of various members of his administration; prints, paintings & documents on the Hudson Valley; paintings, prints, ship models, documents & relics of the history of the United States Navy as well as other marine items; early juvenile books
Publications: The Museum of The Franklin D Roosevelt Library; Historical Materials in the Franklin D Roosevelt Library; The Era of Franklin D Roosevelt
Activities: Classes for adults & children; docent training; lects open to pub; gallery talks; tours to school groups competitions with prizes; scholarships & fels offered; individual paintings & original objects of art lent to mus; lending collection contains 23,000 artifacts; originate traveling exhibs to libraries & museums; mus shop sells books & reproductions

L **Franklin D Roosevelt Library,** 4079 Albany Post Rd, Hyde Park, NY 12538. Tel 845-486-7760; Fax 845-486-1147; Elec Mail roosevelt.library@nara.gov; Internet Home Page Address: www.fdrlibrary.marist.edu; *Dir* Cynthia M Koch, PhD; *Deputy Dir* Lynn Bassanese; *Cur* Herman Eberhardt; *Coll Mgr* Michelle Frauenberger; *Supervisory Archivist* Robert Clark
Open May - Oct 9 AM - 6 PM, Nov - Apr 9 AM - 5 PM, Research room Mon-Fri 8:45AM-5PM, cl Thanksgiving, Christmas & New Year's Day; Combination ticket for FDR Museum and home $14, children under 15 free; Estab 1939 to preserve, interpret & make available for research archives & memorabilia relating to Franklin & Eleanor Roosevelt, their families & assoc; Average Annual Attendance: 120,000
Income: Financed by Federal government & trust fund

Library Holdings: Audio Tapes; Book Volumes; Cassettes; Clipping Files 500; Exhibition Catalogs; Fiche; Filmstrips; Manuscripts; Maps; Memorabilia 300; Motion Pictures; Original Art Works; Original Documents; Other Holdings Broadsides; Newspapers; Maps; Pamphlets; Photographs 200; Prints; Records; Reels; Sculpture; Slides; Video Tapes
Special Subjects: Posters, Pre-Columbian Art, Prints, Sculpture, Portraits, Silver, Textiles, Scrimshaw
Collections: Naval history; Hudson River Valley history; early juvenile books; illustrated ornithology; Eleanor and Franklin Roosevelt; US History: 20th Century
Exhibitions: Permanent exhibitions on lives & times of Franklin & Eleanor Roosevelt; changing exhibitions gallery
Publications: The Era of Franklin D Roosevelt: A Selected Bibliography of Periodicals, Essays & Dissertation Literature, 1945-1971; Franklin D Roosevelt and Foreign Affairs
Activities: Educ prog; lects open to pub; gallery talks; tours; originate traveling exhibitions; mus shop sells books, reproductions, prints, slides, souvenir items

M **ROOSEVELT-VANDERBILT NATIONAL HISTORIC SITES,** 4097 Albany Post Rd, Hyde Park, NY 12538-1997. Tel 845-229-9115; Fax 845-229-0739; Internet Home Page Address: www.nps.gov/hofr/home.htm; *Supt* Sarah Olson
Open daily 9 AM - 5 PM Apr - Oct, cl Tues & Wed Nov - Mar, cl Thanksgiving, Christmas & New Year's Day, Eleanor Roosevelt NHS open daily Nov, Dec, Mar & Apr, by appt only Thurs - Sun, Jan - Mar, Groups of 10 or more require reservations; Admis $1.50, under 16, over 62 & school groups free ; Vanderbilt Mansion NHS estab 1940; home of Franklin D Roosevelt NHS 1944; Eleanor Roosevelt NHS, 1977; Average Annual Attendance: 330,000
Income: Financed by Federal Government
Special Subjects: Decorative Arts
Collections: Vanderbilt & Home of FDR colls consist of original furnishings; Eleanor Roosevelt site colls are combination of originals, reproductions & like items
Exhibitions: Annual Christmas Exhibition; Antique Car Show
Publications: Vanderbilt Mansion, book; Art in the Home of Franklin D Roosevelt, brochure
Activities: Tours; sales shop sells books, postcards & slides

ITHACA

M **CORNELL UNIVERSITY,** Herbert F Johnson Museum of Art, Central & University Aves, Ithaca, NY 14853-4001. Tel 607-255-6464; Fax 607-255-9940; Elec Mail museum@cornell.edu; Internet Home Page Address: www.museum.cornell.edu; *Dir* Franklin W Robinson; *Sr Cur Prints, Drawings & Photographs* Nancy E Green; *Chief Cur & Cur Asian Art* Ellen Avril; *Registrar* Matthew Conway; *Dir for Develop* Marie Neumer; *Publicity & Publications Coordr* Andrea Potochniak; *Deputy Dir Fin & Admin* Peter Gould; *Assoc Dir Progs & Cur Educ* Cathy Klimaszewski; *Cur Modern & Contemporary Art* Andrea Inselmann; *Assoc Cur & Master Teacher* Andrew Weislogel; *Dir's Admin Asst* Nancy Dickinson; *Registrar Asst* Meghan Reiff; *Cur Asst Rights & Repros* Liz Emrich; *Chief Preparator & Bldg Coordr* Wil Millard; *Preparator* David Ryan; *Digital Photog* David O Brown; *Develop Admin Asst & Mem Coordr* Jennifer Ryan
Open Tues - Sun 10 AM - 5 PM, cl Mon; No admis fee; Estab 1973, replacing the Andrew Dickson White Mus of Art, originally founded in 1953 as Cornell University's Art Mus to serve students, the Tompkins County community & the Finger Lakes region; The collection & galleries are housed in an I M Pei designed building on Cornell University campus overlooking downtown Ithaca & Cayuga Lake; Average Annual Attendance: Approx 90,000; Mem: 650; dues $20 - $5000
Income: Financed by endowment, mem, grants & university funds
Special Subjects: Drawings, Painting-American, Photography, Prints, Sculpture, Watercolors, African Art, Ethnology, Pre-Columbian Art, Primitive art, Woodcuts, Painting-European, Asian Art, Coins & Medals, Painting-German
Collections: Asian art; arts of ethnographic societies; European & American paintings, drawings, sculpture, graphic arts, photographs, video; Ethnographic Arts
Publications: Collections handbook; exhibition catalogs; seasonal newsletter; annual report; gallery brochure
Activities: Workshops for adults & children; residency progs for artists; lects open to pub, 5-10 vis lectrs per yr; gallery talks; tours; individual paintings & original objects of art lent to other institutions for exhibit; originate traveling exhibs; mus shop sells exhib catalogs, postcards & notecards

L **Fine Arts Library,** 235 Sibley Hall, Ithaca, NY 14853-6701. Tel 607-255-3710; Fax 607-255-6718; Elec Mail fineartsarc@cornell.edu; Internet Home Page Address: www.library.cornell.edu/finearts/; *Fine Arts Librn* Martha Walker
Open Sat 10 AM - 5 PM, Sun 1 - 11 PM, Mon - Thurs 8AM - 11 PM, Fri 8AM - 6 PM, hours change for University vacation & summer session; No admis fee; Estab 1871 to serve Cornell students; Circ 68,006
Income: Financed through University funds
Purchases: $195,000
Library Holdings: Auction Catalogs; Book Volumes 207,000; CD-ROMs; Clipping Files; DVDs; Exhibition Catalogs; Fiche 5928; Periodical Subscriptions 1400; Reels 424; Video Tapes
Special Subjects: Art History, Landscape Architecture, Architecture

M **THE HISTORY CENTER IN TOMPKINS COUNTY,** (DeWitt Historical Society of Tompkins County) 401 E State St, Ithaca, NY 14850. Tel 607-273-8284; Fax 607-273-6107; Elec Mail community@thehistorycenter.net; Internet Home Page Address: www.thehistorycenter.net; *Exec Dir* Scott Callan
Open Tues, Thurs, & Sat 11 AM - 5 PM; No admis fee; Estab 1935 to collect, preserve & interpret the history of Tompkins County, New York; 10,000 sq ft; Average Annual Attendance: 8,000; Mem: 750; gifts $35 and up; annual meeting in last quarter
Income: $280,000 (financed by endowment, mem, county appropriation, state & federal grants, earned income & foundations)
Library Holdings: Original Documents; Pamphlets; Photographs; Prints; Records; Reproductions
Special Subjects: Drawings, Folk Art, Glass, Flasks & Bottles, Furniture, Maps, Architecture, Painting-American, Photography, Watercolors, American Indian Art,

Anthropology, Archaeology, Ethnology, Textiles, Costumes, Crafts, Landscapes, Decorative Arts, Portraits, Posters, Furniture, Glass, Carpets & Rugs, Stained Glass, Reproductions
Collections: Decorative arts; local historical objects; painting & sketches by local artists; portraits; photographers - Louise Boyle, Joseph Burritt, Curt Foerster, Charles Howes, Charles Jones, Henry Head, Robert Head, Verne Morton, Sheldon Smith, John Spires, Trevor Teele, Marion Wesp
Exhibitions: Five to six rotating exhibitions per yr
Publications: History Happenings, monthly e-newsletter
Activities: Classes for adults & children; lects open to pub, 12 vis lectrs per yr; gallery talks; tours; mus shop sells books, reproductions of photographs; gift items, postcards & exhib- related items

M **ITHACA COLLEGE,** Handwerker Gallery of Art, 1170 Gannett Ctr, Ithaca, NY 14850-7276. Tel 607-274-3548; Fax 607-274-1774; Elec Mail handwerker@ithaca.edu; Internet Home Page Address: www.ithaca.edu/handwerker; *Dir* Jelena Stojanovic; *Chmn Art History* Steven Clancy; *Gallery Dir* Cheryl Kramer
Open Mon - Wed & Fri 10 AM - 6 PM, Thurs 10 AM - 9 PM, Sat-Sun 10AM-5PM; No admis fee; Estab 1978 for display of contemporary art & critical interpretation of image; Average Annual Attendance: 7,500
Collections: African Art, Photographs, Pre-Columbian Art, 20th Century Graphic Art
Publications: Quarterly newsletter
Activities: Critical forum; lects open to pub; 4 vis lectrs per yr

JAMAICA

M **JAMAICA CENTER FOR ARTS & LEARNING (JCAL),** 161-04 Jamaica Ave, Jamaica, NY 11432-6112. Tel 718-658-7400; Fax 718-658-7222; Elec Mail info@jcal.org; Internet Home Page Address: www.jcal.org; *Interim Exec Dir* Carl Fields Jr; *Dir Finance & Admin* Jennifer Chiang; *Sr Prog & Develop Dir* Akua-Ak Loh Anokye; *Educ Dir* Juan Carlos Salinas; *Gen Mgr, JPAC* Courtney Ffrench
Open Mon - Fri 8:30 AM - 9 PM, Sat 9 AM - 6 PM ; No admis fee; Estab 1972 to provide educational opportunity in the visual & performing arts, exhibitions & performances; Five story landmark building; workshop studios for painting, drawing, mask making, ceramics, silkscreen & photography; 3 dance studios; 1650 sq ft art gallery; 99 seat state-of-the-art theatre; 1 multi-purpose space; 1 computer lab; 1 toddler studio; 1 multi-media studio; Average Annual Attendance: 25,000
Income: $1,600,000 (financed by New York City Department of Cultural Affairs, New York State Council on the Arts, Honorable Claire Shulman, Queens Borough President, foundations, corporations & workshop tuitions)
Exhibitions: Up to 12 changing exhibitions annually in three museum quality galleries
Publications: Exhibition catalogs & posters
Activities: Classes for adults & children; dramatic progs; concerts; gallery talks; tours; competitions; schols offered; exten dept serves New York City; photographs & blow ups of original photographs lent; book traveling exhibs annually

L **QUEENS BOROUGH PUBLIC LIBRARY,** Fine Arts & Recreation Division, 89-11 Merrick Blvd, Jamaica, NY 11432. Tel 718-990-0755; Fax 718-658-8342; Elec Mail username@queens.lib.ny.us; Internet Home Page Address: www.queenslibrary.org; *Div Mgr* Esther Lee; *Asst Mgr* Rebecca Wilkins; *Lib Dir* Thomas Galante
Open Mon - Fri 10 AM - 9 PM, Sat 10 AM - 5:30 PM, Sun, Sept - May, Noon - 5 PM; No admis fee; Estab 1933 to serve the general public in Queens, New York
Income: Financed by city & state appropriations
Library Holdings: Audio Tapes; Book Volumes 150,000; CD-ROMs 270; Cassettes 10,500; Compact Disks 23,000; Pamphlets; Periodical Subscriptions 398; Photographs; Prints; Records 2000; Reels 4100; Reproductions 30,000; Video Tapes 20,000
Collections: The WPA Print Collection
Activities: Concerts

JAMESTOWN

L **JAMES PRENDERGAST LIBRARY ASSOCIATION,** 509 Cherry St, Jamestown, NY 14701-5098. Tel 716-484-7135; Fax 716-483-6880; Elec Mail cway@cclslib.org; Internet Home Page Address: www.prendergastlibrary.org; *Gallery Coordr* Anne Plyler; *Dir* Catherine A Way
Open Mon - Tues & Thurs - Fri 10 AM - 8:30 PM, Wed 10 AM - 5 PM, Sat 10 AM - 4 PM; No admis fee; Estab 1891 as part of library; Circ 657,000; Maintains art gallery; Average Annual Attendance: 259,000; Mem: 43,375
Income: Financed by state & local funds
Library Holdings: Book Volumes 375,816; Cassettes 4,002; Compact Disks 3,203; DVDs 1,221; Maps 652; Original Art Works 60; Pamphlets 12,097; Periodical Subscriptions 359; Reproductions 37
Special Subjects: Prints
Collections: Prendergast paintings, 19th & 20th century paintings; Roger Tory Peterson, limited edition print collection; Alexander Calder mats
Exhibitions: Traveling Exhibitions; local one-person and group shows
Publications: Mirror Up To Nature, collection catalog
Activities: Classes for adults & children; lects open to pub; concerts; competitions; lending collection contains books, cassettes, framed reproductions; books traveling exhibitions

M **JAMESTOWN COMMUNITY COLLEGE,** The Weeks, 525 Falconer St, Jamestown, NY 14701-1999. Tel 716-665-9188; *Dir* James Colby
Open Mon-Wed 11AM-4PM, Fri 11AM-3PM; No admis fee; Estab 1969 to show significant regional, national & international contemporary art; Facility includes 2000 sq ft exhibition area
Income: $93,000 (financed through Faculty Student Assn & private foundation funds)
Exhibitions: PhotoNominal

Publications: Exhibition catalogs, semiannual
Activities: Lects open to pub, 200 vis lectrs per yr

KATONAH

M **CARAMOOR CENTER FOR MUSIC & THE ARTS, INC,** Rosen House at Caramoor, 149 Girdle Ridge Rd Katonah, NY 10536; PO Box 816, Katonah, NY 10536-0816. Tel 914-232-5035, 232-1252 (Box office phone); Fax 914-232-5521; Elec Mail info@caramoor.org; Internet Home Page Address: www.caramoor.org; *Chmn Bd Trustees* Judy Evnin; *Mng Dir* Paul Rosenblum; *Develop Dir* Gary Himes; *CEO & Gen Dir* Michael Barrett; *Dir Finance* Tammy Belanger-Turner; *Archivist* Hilton Bailey; *Dir Spec Events & Facility Rental* Christine Bosco; *Mgr Annual Giving* Alithia Dutschke; *Mktg Mgr* Sal Vaccaro
Open May - Oct Wed - Sun 1 PM - 4 PM, with last tour at 3 PM; Nov - Apr Mon - Fri by appt; Admis adults $10, children 16 & under free; Estab 1970 to preserve the house & its collections, the legacy of Walter T Rosen & to provide interpretive & educ programs; Period rooms from European palaces are showcase for art collection from Europe & the Orient, spanning 6 centuries; Average Annual Attendance: 60,000
Income: $365,000
Special Subjects: Photography, Sculpture, Bronzes, Textiles, Costumes, Religious Art, Ceramics, Decorative Arts, Manuscripts, Portraits, Furniture, Jade, Porcelain, Asian Art, Carpets & Rugs, Ivory, Tapestries, Renaissance Art, Period Rooms, Embroidery, Medieval Art, Painting-Italian, Stained Glass, Painting-German, Enamels
Collections: Period rooms - Fine & decorative arts from Europe & Asia (1400-1950); Tapestries; paintings; sculpture; Urbino Maiolica; jade & cloisonné
Publications: Guidebook to collection; New book Caramoor
Activities: Classes for children; docent training; concerts; lects open to pub, 4 vis lectrs per yr; tours; mus shop sells books & original art, jewelry & other gift items

M **KATONAH MUSEUM OF ART,** 134 Jay St, Katonah, NY 10536-3737. Tel 914-232-9555; Fax 914-232-3128; Elec Mail info@katonahmuseum.org; Internet Home Page Address: www.katonahmuseum.org; *Exec Dir* Neil Watson; *Dir Devel* Allison Chernow; *Dir Fin* Patricia Keane; *Dir Curatorial Affairs* Nancy Wallach
Open Tues - Sat 10 AM - 5 PM, Sun noon - 5 PM, cl Mon; Admis Tues - Fri & Sun Noon - 5PM adults $5, seniors & students $3, Sat 10 AM - 5 PM adults $5, seniors & students $3, mems & children under 12 free; Estab 1953 to present exhibitions created with loaned works of art, programs for schools, films, lectures, demonstrations & workshops; The Katonah Museum consists of 3000 sq ft of exhibition space with a sculpture garden and children's learning center; Average Annual Attendance: 50,000; Mem: 1400; dues $50 & up
Income: financed by mem, contributions & grants
Library Holdings: Exhibition Catalogs
Publications: Exhibition catalogues: Dress Codes: Clothing as Metaphor, 2009; Lichtenstein in Process, 2009; Conversations in Clay, 2008; Here's The Thing: Single Object Still Lifes, 2008; Shattering Glass, 2007; Children Should Be Seen: The Image of the Child in American Picture Book Art, 2006; Ancient Art of the Cyclades, 2006; Andromeda Hotel: The Art of Joseph Cornell, 2006
Activities: For adults: guided tours; lects; symposia; films; workshops; concerts; trips; For children: gallery games; book readings; workshops; community festivals; hands-on activities in Learning Ctr; teacher training workshop; lects open to public; concerts; tours; awards given for best local mus (Westchester Magazine); member school: on-site & out-reach progs & servs; originate traveling exhibs for selected institutions

M **NEW YORK STATE OFFICE OF PARKS RECREATION & HISTORIC PRESERVATION,** John Jay Homestead State Historic Site, 400 Rte 22, Katonah, NY 10536; PO Box 832, Katonah, NY 10536-0832. Tel 914-232-5651; Fax 914-232-8085; Internet Home Page Address: www.johnjayhomestead.org; *Interpretive Progs Asst* Allan M Weinreb; *Historic Site Mgr* Heather Iannucci; *Mus Educator* Bethany White
Open Tues-Sat 10AM-3PM, Sun 11AM-3PM, Nov-Mar; Tues-Sat 10AM-4M, Sun 11AM-4PM Apr-Oct; Admis adults $7, seniors (62 & older) $5, children up to 12 yrs free; Estab 1958 to inform public on John Jay and his contributions to national, state & local history; Ten restored period rooms reflecting occupancy of the Jay family in the 1820s; art distributed throughout; also on exhibit is the art studio of John Jay's great-great-great granddaughter, Eleanor Iselin Wade; Average Annual Attendance: 30,000; Mem: 1000; Friends of John Jay Homestead, Inc; dues $25 & up; annual meeting in spring
Income: Financed by state appropriation
Library Holdings: Original Documents; Other Holdings; Photographs
Special Subjects: Ceramics, Portraits, Sculpture, Painting-American, Photography, Textiles, Etchings & Engravings, Decorative Arts, Manuscripts, Portraits, Furniture, Porcelain, Silver, Metalwork, Historical Material, Maps, Restorations, Period Rooms, Reproductions
Collections: American art and American decorative arts; John Jay memorabilia and archives; Westchester mansion with estate & out-buildings; artworks & art-making tools of equestrian artist, Eleanor Iselin Mason Wade
Exhibitions: Federal Period Decorations; Period Home, Federal decor including art, decorative arts furnishings & memorabilia; Changing exhibitions in Back Parlor Gallery
Publications: John Jay and the Constitution, a Teacher's Guide; John Jay 1745-1829; The Jays of Bedford
Activities: Classes for adults & children; docent training; call for information; lect open to public; concerts; group tours by advance reservation; school on site and outreach; craft demonstrations; special exhibits; sale of books & prints

KINDERHOOK

M **COLUMBIA COUNTY HISTORICAL SOCIETY,** Columbia County Museum and Library, 5 Albany Ave, Kinderhook, NY 12106; PO Box 311, Kinderhook, NY 12106-0311. Tel 518-758-9265; Fax 518-758-2499; Elec Mail cchs@cchsny.org; Internet Home Page Address: www.cchsny.org; *Exec Dir* Ann-Eliza Lewis; *Cur* Diane Shewchuk; *Educator* Ashley Hopkins-Benton
Open Mon, Wed, Fri & Sat 10 AM - 4 PM, Sun noon - 4 PM; Admis adults $5, mems, seniors (65+) & children 12 & under free; Estab 1926; County Historical Society Museum Gallery with changing exhibits; 2 historic houses: 1737 Van Alen House & c1820 Vanderpoel House; In large hall, wall space 40 ft x 38 ft used for 3 exhibitions of paintings per yr; Average Annual Attendance: 12,000; Mem: 1,000; dues $30-1000; annual meeting Oct
Income: $125,000 (financed by mem, endowment, activities, projects, events, private donations, admis, government & corporate grants)
Special Subjects: Architecture, Manuscripts, Maps, Painting-American, Sculpture, Costumes, Ceramics, Decorative Arts, Furniture, Historical Material
Collections: Historical objects pertaining to history of county; New York regional decorative arts; furniture & costumes; paintings of 18th through 20th centuries
Exhibitions: Local history & cultural exhibits
Publications: Brochures; exhibit catalogs; quarterly newsletter
Activities: Classes for children; docent training; lects open to pub; vis lectrs 5 per yr; concerts; gallery talks; tours; schols; originate traveling exhibs; mus shop sells books, reproductions

M **Luykas Van Alen House,** Rte 9 H, Kinderhook, NY 12106; PO Box 311, Kinderhook, NY 12106-0311. Tel 518-758-9265; Fax 518-758-2499; Elec Mail cchs@cchsny.org; Internet Home Page Address: www.cchsny.org; *Exec Dir* Ann-Eliza Lewis; *Educator* Ashley Hopkins-Benton; *Cur* Diane Shewchuk
Open Memorial Day weekend - Labor Day weekend, Fri & Sat 10 AM - 4 PM, Sun noon - 4 PM; Admis adults $5, members, seniors & children 12 & under free; Estab 1737; Mem: 700; dues $25-$1,000; annual meeting 3rd Sat of Oct
Special Subjects: Architecture, Furniture, Decorative Arts
Activities: Classes for children; field trips; tours; sells books & reproductions

M **1820 James Vanderpoel House,** Rte 9, Kinderhook, NY 12106; PO Box 311, Kinderhook, NY 12106-0311. Tel 518-758-9265; *Cur* Helen M McLallen; *Exec Dir* Sharon S Palmer
Open Memorial Day weekend - Labor Day weekend Thurs - Sat 11 AM - 5 PM, Sun 1 PM - 5 PM; tours by appt only; Admis adults $3, senior citizens & students $2, children 12 & under free; Federal Period house museum with furnishings of the period; Mem: 700; dues $25-$1000, annual meeting 3rd Sat in Oct

KINGSTON

M **FRIENDS OF HISTORIC KINGSTON,** Fred J Johnston House Museum, Corner of Main & Wall Sts, Kingston, NY 12401; PO Box 3763, Kingston, NY 12402-3763. Tel 845-339-0720; Elec Mail twothings@hvc.rr.com; Internet Home Page Address: www.fohk.org; *Dir* Jane Kellar; *Pres Bd* Avery Leete Smith; *Pub Rels* Patricia Murphy
Open May - Oct Sat & Sun 1 - 4 PM & by appt; Admis adult $5, children $2; Estab 1965; Gallery of changing exhibs related to the city of Kingston's local history; house mus with period rooms; Average Annual Attendance: 5000 by estimate; Mem: dues Patron $500, Household $50, Student/Senior $10
Library Holdings: Book Volumes; Clipping Files; Kodachrome Transparencies; Manuscripts; Maps; Memorabilia; Original Art Works; Original Documents; Pamphlets; Photographs; Prints
Special Subjects: Drawings, Painting-American, Textiles, Ceramics, Decorative Arts, Painting-European, Period Rooms
Collections: 200 book vols on local history; items of local history for the city of Kingston, NY; 1,400 objects of American decorative arts
Publications: Friends of Historic Kingston, newsletter; Stockade District, walking tour brochure; Kingston New York: The Architectural Guide
Activities: Lects; 1 vis lectr per year; gallery talks; guided tours; temporary exhibs; mus shops sells books, prints

M **NEW YORK STATE OFFICE OF PARKS: RECREATION AND HISTORIC PRESERVATION,** (Palisades Interstate Park Commission) Senate House State Historic Site, 296 Fair St, Kingston, NY; 312 Fair St, Kingston, NY 12401-3836. Tel 914-338-2786; *Historic Site Mgr* Rich Goring
Open Apr - Oct Wed - Sat 10 AM - 5 PM, Sun 1 - 5 PM, Jan - Mar Sat 10 AM - 5 PM, Sun 1 - 5 PM; No admis fee; Estab 1887 as an educational community resource which tells the story of the growth of state government as well as the stories of the lives & works of local 19th century artists; Average Annual Attendance: 20,000
Special Subjects: Decorative Arts
Collections: 18th & 19th century decorative arts; 18th & 19th century paintings & other works of art, particularly those by James Bard, Jervis McEntee, Ammi Phillips, Joseph Tubb & John Vanderlyn
Publications: Exhibition catalogs
Activities: Classes for adults & children; docent training; lects open to pub, 2 vis lectrs per yr; individual paintings & original objects of art lent to well-established institutions; lending coll contains color reproductions, original art works, original prints, paintings & sculptures; book traveling exhibs

L **Reference Library,** 312 Fair St, Kingston, NY 12401. Tel 845-338-2786; *Historic Site Mgr* Rich Goring
Open Mon, Wed, & Sat 10AM-5PM, Sun 11AM-5PM; Admis adults $4, seniors $3, children 11 and under free; Estab 1887; Open by appointment to scholars, students & researchers for reference only
Library Holdings: Book Volumes 10,000; Exhibition Catalogs; Manuscripts; Memorabilia; Pamphlets; Periodical Subscriptions 10
Collections: Collection of letters relating to the artist John Vanderlyn
Publications: Exhibit catalogs

LAKE GEORGE

M **LAKE GEORGE ARTS PROJECT,** Courthouse Gallery, Canada St, Lake George, NY 12845; 1 Amherst St, Lake George, NY 12845. Tel 518-668-2616; Fax 518-668-2616; Elec Mail mail@lakegeorgearts.org; Internet Home Page Address: www.lakegeorgearts.org; *Gallery Dir* Laura Von Rosk; *Dir* John Strong
Open Tues - Fri Noon - 5 PM, Sat Noon - 4 pm (during exhibitions); no admis fee; Estab 1977, gallery estab 1985 to provide income & exposure for national & regional artists; 26 ft by 30 ft; Average Annual Attendance: 1,000; Mem: 500; dues $20-$100; annual meeting in Dec
Income: $150,000 (financed by mem & by city & state appropriation)
Activities: Lects open to the pub, gallery talks

LEROY

A LEROY HISTORICAL SOCIETY, The Jell-O Gallery, 23 E Main St, LeRoy, NY 14482-1209. Tel 585-768-7433; Fax 716-768-7579; Elec Mail info@jellogallery.org; Internet Home Page Address: www.jellogallery.org; *Dir* Lynne Belluscio
Open Apr-Dec Mon-Sat 10AM-4PM, Sun 1-4PM, Jan-Mar Sat-Sun 10AM-4PM; Admis adults $24 children 6-11 $1.50, children 5 & under free; Estab 1940; Mem: 400; dues $18-$30; annual meeting in May
Income: financed by endowment, mem, city & state appropriations
Special Subjects: Drawings, Embroidery, Etchings & Engravings, Historical Material, Metalwork, Photography, Posters, Prints, Silver, Textiles, Watercolors, Painting-American, Pottery, Decorative Arts, Ceramics, Portraits, Dolls, Furniture, Glass, Laces, Jewelry, Period Rooms, Maps, Carpets & Rugs, Flasks & Bottles
Collections: Decorative Arts; Jell-O Museum; LeRoy related; 19th Century Art; Textiles; Tools; Western NY Redware
Publications: Quarterly newsletter
Activities: Classes for adults & children; docent training; lects open to pub; tours; individual paintings & original objects of art lent to other mus; mus shop sells books & reproductions

LITTLE FALLS

M MOHAWK VALLEY CENTER FOR THE ARTS INC, 401 Canal Pl, Little Falls, NY 13365. Tel 315-823-0808; Fax 315-823-0805; Elec Mail director@mohawkvalleyarts.org; Internet Home Page Address: ww.mohawkvalleyarts.org; *Dir* Barbara Boucher
Open Tues-Sat 11AM-4PM
Collections: works by local artists; paintings

LONG BEACH

L LONG BEACH ART LEAGUE, Long Beach Library, PO Box 862, Long Beach, NY 11561-0862. Tel 516-432-0195; Elec Mail mjmlido@aol.com; Internet Home Page Address: www.longbeachartleague.com; *Treas* Mary Mendoza; *VPres* Scott Evans; *Program Dir* Selma Stern; *Pres* Betty Barto; *VPres* Jaclyn Feldman
Open Mon - Sat 9 AM - 6 PM, Sun 1 PM - 5 PM; No admis fee; Estab in 1952 by a group of interested resident artists determined to form an organization to promote art activity & appreciation with emphasis on quality & exhibitions, demonstrations; Public galleries in Long Beach Library, Long Beach Community Center, & Long Beach Medical Ctr; Average Annual Attendance: 500 per week; Mem: 160; dues $25; meetings 1st Wed each month
Income: Member dues, donations, foundation recipient
Purchases: Established gallery at Long Beach Medical Ctr
Exhibitions: 10 monthly exhibits at library; 4 quarterly exhibits at satellite gallery; 6 bimonthly exhibits at community center
Publications: Exhibitions brochures; Monthly newsletter; Art calendar with members art; Publicity flyer monthly
Activities: Classes for adults & children; workshops; demonstrations; lect; 7 vis lectrs/demos per year; gallery talks; sponsoring of competitions; 8 cash awards at 4 open exhibits; senior community ctr exhibits & classes

L LONG BEACH PUBLIC LIBRARY, 111 W Park Ave, Long Beach, NY 11561-3300. Tel 516-432-7201; Fax 516-889-4641; Elec Mail lblibrary@hotmail.com; *Asst Dir* Laura Weir; *Bus & Vocations Librn* Theresa Cahill; *Dir* George Trepp
Open Oct - May Mon, Wed, Thurs 9 AM - 9 PM, Tues & Fri 9 AM - 6 PM, Sat 9 AM - 5 PM, Sun 1 - 5 PM; Estab 1928 to serve the community with information & services, including recreational, cultural & informational materials; The Long Beach Art Assn in cooperation with the library presents monthly exhibits of all types of media
Library Holdings: Book Volumes 100,000; Cassettes; Fiche; Filmstrips; Memorabilia; Pamphlets; Periodical Subscriptions 300; Photographs; Records; Reels; Video Tapes
Collections: Local history; 300 photographs of Long Beach
Exhibitions: Local talent; membership shows; juried exhibitions
Publications: Monthly newsletter
Activities: Dramatic progs; lects open to pub, 18-20 vis lectrs per yr; concerts; gallery talks; films; tours

LONG ISLAND CITY

M DORSKY GALLERY, Dorsky Gallery Curatorial Programs, 11-03 45th Ave, at the corner of 11th St Long Island City, NY 11101-5109. Tel 718-937-6317; Elec Mail info@dorsky.org; Internet Home Page Address: www.dorsky.org; *Dir* David Dorsky
Open Thurs-Mon 11AM-6PM; other times by appointment; Free admis; Contemporary art
Collections: works by contemporary artists
Activities: Lects open to pub; gallery talks; tours

M FISHER LANDAU CENTER FOR ART, 38-27 30th St, Long Island City, NY 11101-2716. Tel 718-937-0727
Open Thurs-Mon noon-5PM; No admis fee
Collections: works of contemporary art

M ISAMU NOGUCHI FOUNDATION, Isamu Noguchi Garden Museum, 32-37 Vernon Blvd, Long Island City, NY 11106. Tel 718-204-7088; Fax 718-278-2348; Elec Mail info@noguchi.org; *Admin Dir* Amy Hau; *Cur* Bonnie Rychlak; *Head Educ* Rebecca Herz; *Exec Dir* Jenny Dixon
Open all yr Wed, Thurs & Fri 10 AM - 5 PM, Sat & Sun 11 AM - 6 PM; Admis suggested contribution $10, sr citizens & students $5, children 11 and under free; Estab 1985 to preserve, protect & exhibit important sculptural, environmental & design work of Isamu Noguchi; 13 galleries & a garden exhibiting over 350 sculptures, models, drawings & photos; 24,000 sq ft factory converted by the artist; Average Annual Attendance: 25,000
Income: $400,000 (financed by Noguchi Foundation, New York City Department of Cultural Affairs & private donations)
Library Holdings: Auction Catalogs; Exhibition Catalogs; Original Documents
Special Subjects: Sculpture
Collections: Sculptures in stone, wood, metal, paper, clay; models and drawings; photos of Noguchi's gardens and plazas; stage sets
Exhibitions: Permanent exhib; temp exhibs that contextualize Noguchi
Publications: Exhib catalogs
Activities: Classes for adults & children; tours; docent training; artist in residence prog; workshops; lects open to pub; gallery talks; tours; concerts; originates traveling exhibs to other mus; mus shop sells books & Noguchis Akari light sculptures

M NEUSTADT COLLECTION OF TIFFANY GLASS, 5-26 46th Ave, Administrative Office Long Island City, NY 11101-5229. Tel 718-361-8489; Fax 718-392-1420; Elec Mail info@neustadtcollection.org; Internet Home Page Address: www.neustadtcollection.org; *Sec* Elizabeth De Rosa; *Dir & Cur* Lindsy R Parrott; *Conservator* Susan Greenbaum; *Bd Pres* David Specter; *Treas* Patricia Specter
Neustadt Gallery at Queens Museum of Art, NYC-call for hours; Admis suggested donation adults $5; Estab 1969; 1,000 sq ft present rotating shows from permanent coll; Average Annual Attendance: 250,000
Special Subjects: Decorative Arts, Historical Material, Furniture, Metalwork, Stained Glass
Collections: Tiffany lamps & windows; Tiffany flat and pressed glass archive; Tiffany metalwork
Exhibitions: (09/2013-09/2015) Shade Garden: Floral Lamps from the Tiffany Studios; Tiffany Glass: Painting with color & light. Traveling Exhib through 12/2015
Publications: The Lamps of Tiffany; Tiffany by Design: An In-Depth Look at Tiffany Lamps
Activities: Educ progs for children & adults; oral history prog; lect; lending of original objects of art to art museums across the USA & Europe & Corning Museum of Glass, New York Historical Soc; organize traveling exhibs to museums (small & mid-size); originate traveling exhibitions to small & mid-size museums across USA; Mus shop sells reproductions & products developed from perm colls & sold at Queens mus shop

M PS1 CONTEMPORARY ART CENTER, (PS1 Institute for Contemporary Art) 22-25 Jackson Ave, Long Island City, NY 11101. Tel 718-784-2084; Fax 718-482-9454; Elec Mail mail@ps1.org; Internet Home Page Address: www.ps1.org; *Exec Dir* Alanna Heiss; *Dir Operations* Tony Guerrero; *Assoc Dir Press & Mktg* Rachael Dorsey
Open Thurs - Mon Noon - 6 PM; Admis Gen $5, students & seniors $2; Estab 1972 as artist studios & exhibition contemporary & experimental art; Located in a vast renovated 19th century Romanesque schoolhouse, the gallery contains 46,000 sq ft of exhibition space; Average Annual Attendance: 60,000; Mem: 100,000+; Dues leadership council $5,000, patrons council $1,000
Income: Financed by city & state appropriations, corporate & private donations, National Endowment for the Arts
Library Holdings: CD-ROMs; Cards; Compact Disks; Fiche; Kodachrome Transparencies; Pamphlets
Special Subjects: Architecture, Drawings, Painting-American, Photography, Sculpture, Collages, Painting-Japanese, Painting-Canadian, Painting-Dutch, Painting-French, Painting-Polish, Painting-Spanish, Painting-Italian, Painting-Australian, Painting-German, Painting-Russian, Painting-Israeli, Painting-Scandinavian, Painting-New Zealand
Collections: Architecture; fashion; film; painting; photography; sculpture; video
Exhibitions: International Studio Exhibition; Alternating 1-100 & Vice Versa by Alighiero e Boetti; Gilles Peress Farewell to Bosnia; Stalin's Choice Soviet Socialistic Realism; The Winter of Love
Publications: Loop; Short Century; Mexico City; Video Acts
Activities: Classes for adults & children; dance; film; video; photography; fashion; architectural presentations; lects open to pub; concerts; gallery talks; tours; competitions for studio program with awards of studio residency; scholarships offered; original works of art lent to nonprofit institutions with appropriate facilities; book traveling exhibs; originate traveling exhibs; sales shop sells books, catalogues, posters, postcards, clothing

M SCULPTURE CENTER, 44-19 Purves St, Long Island City, NY 11101. Tel 718-361-1750; Fax 718-786-9336
Open Thurs - Mon 11 AM - 6 PM ; No admis fee; suggested donation $5
Collections: Contemporary sculpture
Activities: Educ programs

M SOCRATES SCULPTURE PARK, 32-01 Vernon Blvd, Long Island City, NY 11106; P.O. Box 6259, Long Island City, NY 11106. Tel 718-956-1819; Fax 718-626-1533; Elec Mail info@socratessculpturepark.org; Internet Home Page Address: www.socratessculpturepark.org; *Exec Dir* John Hatfield; *Dir of Pub Progs & Community Rels* Shaun Leonardo; *Dir Develop & Communs* Katie Denny; *Studio Mgr* Lars Fisk; *Events Mgr* Leonrd White; *Exhibs Prog Mgr* Elissa Goldstone
Open everyday 10 AM - sunset; No admis fee; Estab 1986; Outdoor sculpture park & artist residency program; Average Annual Attendance: 80,000
Special Subjects: Sculpture
Collections: Changing exhibitions of large scale sculpture & multi media installations
Exhibitions: Annual spring exhibition; Collaborative projects; billboard
Publications: Catalogs
Activities: Classes for adults & children; summer workshops for children; school outreach; fitness progs; family events; internships; concerts; tours; fels

MEDINA

M MEDINA RAILROAD MUSEUM, 530A West Ave, Medina, NY 14103-1554. Tel 585-798-6106; Fax 585-798-1086; Elec Mail office@railroadmuseum.net; Internet Home Page Address: www.railroadmuseum.net; *CEO & Dir* Martin C Phelps; *Vol Pres* James L Dickinson; *VPres, Dir & Pub Rels & Mus Shop Mgr* Hugh F James
Open Tues - Sun 11 AM - 5 PM, cl most major holidays; Admis adults $7, seniors $6, children $4, mem adults no admis fee; Estab 1997; Railroad & firefighting mus with displays; largest coll of railroad artifacts & memorabilia known to exist under one roof; Average Annual Attendance: 35,000 by estimate; Mem: dues Corporate $100, Bus $50, Family $35, Individual $20
Purchases: Pair of 1948 railroad passenger table cars
Library Holdings: Book Volumes; Maps; Original Documents; Pamphlets; Photographs; Prints; Slides
Special Subjects: Historical Material, Flasks & Bottles, Furniture, Photography, Maps, Posters, Coins & Medals, Miniatures, Dioramas, Reproductions
Collections: Over 6000 items including railroad artifacts & memorabilia; HO-scale model train layout (204 ft x 14 ft); photos; models; toy coll & large firefighting artifact
Activities: Excursion train rides; guided tours; loan exhibs; slide presentations; mus shop sells souvenirs & toys

MOUNT VERNON

L MOUNT VERNON PUBLIC LIBRARY, Fine Art Dept, 28 S First Ave, Mount Vernon, NY 10550. Tel 914-668-1840; Fax 914-668-1018; *Dir* Rodney Lee; *Acting Dir* Opal Lindsay
Open Mon - Thurs 10 AM - 9 PM, Fri & Sat 9 AM - 5 PM, Sun 1 - 5 PM, cl Sat & Sun during July and Aug; No admis fee; Estab 1854; Library contains Doric Hall with murals by Edward Gay, NA; Exhibition Room with frescoes by Louise Brann Soverns; & Norman Wells Print Alcove, estab 1941
Income: $2,200,000 (financed by city & other funds)
Library Holdings: Audio Tapes 1,293; Book Volumes 450,000; Cassettes 1,293; Other Holdings Art books 17,000; Periodical Subscriptions 800; Photographs 11,700; Records 12,500
Special Subjects: Decorative Arts, Photography, Painting-American, Prints, Ceramics, Costume Design & Constr, Architecture
Exhibitions: Costume dolls; fans; metalwork; one-man shows of painting, sculpture & photographs; porcelains; silver; woodcarving; jewelry; other exhibits changing monthly cover a wide range of subjects from miniatures to origami
Activities: Lect open to public, 6 vis lectrs per year; concerts; gallery talks; tours; individual paintings & original objects of art lent to library members

MOUNTAINVILLE

M STORM KING ART CENTER, Old Pleasant Hill Rd, Mountainville, NY 10953; PO Box 280, Mountainville, NY 10953-0280. Tel 845-534-3115; Fax 845-534-4457; Elec Mail info@stormkingartcenter.org; Internet Home Page Address: www.stormking.org; *Dir & Cur* David R Collens; *Pres* John P Stern; *Dir Finance* Dwayne Jarvis; *Visitor Ctr Mgr* Colleen Zlock; *Assoc Cur* Nora Lawrence; *Dir Develop* Rachel Coker; *Preparator & Facilities Mgr* Michael Seaman; *Dir Edu & Pub Progs* Victoria Lichtendorf
Open Apr 2 - Nov 30 10 AM - 5:30 PM Wed - Sun (hours vary); Admis adults $12, seniors $10, col students with valid ID & students K-12 $8, children 5 & under & mems free; Estab 1960; Average Annual Attendance: 75,000; Mem: Dues $1,000 patron, $500 sponsor, $250 donor, $150 contributor, $75 household, $50 individual, $40 student & senior (with proper ID)
Special Subjects: Sculpture
Collections: 500 acre sculpture park with over 100 large scale 20th century sculptures, including works by Abakanowicz, Aycock, Armajani, Bourgeois, Calder, Caro, di Suvero, Goldsworthy, Grosvenor, Hepworth, Zang Huan, LeWitt, Liberman, Maya Lin, Moore, Nevelson, Noguchi, Paik, Rickey, Serra, David Smith, Snelson, von Rydingsvard
Publications: Earth, Sky, and Sculpture, Storm King Art Center; Louise Bourgeois; Maya Lin
Activities: Educ dept; lects open to pub; lects for mems only; 4-6 vis lectrs per yr; concerts; guided tours of sculpture park; hikes; outdoor concerts; mus shop sells books, postcards & maps

MUMFORD

M GENESEE COUNTRY VILLAGE & MUSEUM, (Genesee Country Museum) John L Wehle Art Gallery, 1410 Flint Hill Rd, Mumford, NY 14511-0310; PO Box 310, Mumford, NY 14511-0310. Tel 585-538-6822; Fax 585-538-2887 & 6927; Elec Mail email@gcv.org; Internet Home Page Address: www.gvc.org; *Chair, Bd Trustees* A Thomas Hildebrandt; *Pres & CEO* Peter Arnold; *CFO* Samantha Nickerson; *Sr Dir Develop* Laura Scala; *Sr Dir Facilities & Grounds* Roger Magrin; *Sr Dir Human Resources* Cheryl Barney; *Sr Dir Progs & Colls* Chuck LeCount; *Sr Dir Guest Relations & Admin* Christine Rovet; *Cur Colls* Peter Wisbey; *Cur John L Wehle Art Gallery* Patricia Tice; *Dir Retail & Vis Servs* Robin Lott; *Dir Interpretation* Brian Nagel; *Dir Educ Servs* Maria Neale
Call for hours; Gallery is currently cl for renovation until May 2012; Admis adults $15, seniors & students $12, children (4-16) years $9; Estab 1976; Gallery has over 600 paintings & sculptures dealing with wildlife, sporting art & western art.; Average Annual Attendance: 130,000; Mem: 2001 John Hamilton Society $5,000+, MICAH Brooks Society $2,500, Julia Hyde Society $1,000; Sylvester Hosmer Society $500, Premier $175, Family & Grandparent $99, Individual + 1 $$80, Individual $60
Income: Financed by admissions, mem, corporate sponsorship, local, state, federal funding, & foundations
Library Holdings: Book Volumes; Periodical Subscriptions

Special Subjects: Decorative Arts, Folk Art, Architecture, Art Education, Art History, Furniture, Pottery, Painting-American, Period Rooms, Textiles, Sculpture, Watercolors, Costumes, Ceramics, Crafts, Historical Material, Restorations
Collections: Decorative arts, restored 19th Century buildings, paintings & sculpture; Sporting Art; Wildlife Art (North American & European); 19th century textiles & clothing
Publications: Booklets; Four Centuries of Sporting Art; Genesee Country Museum; Scenes of Town & Country in the 19th Century; Bi-monthly newsletter; asst brochures
Activities: Classes for adults & children; docent training; lects open to pub; concerts; gallery talks; tours; movable mus serves schools, nursing homes, etc.; mus shop sells books, magazines & gifts

NEW CITY

M HISTORICAL SOCIETY OF ROCKLAND COUNTY, 20 Zukor Rd, New City, NY 10956-4302. Tel 845-634-9629; Fax 845-634-8690; Elec Mail info@rocklandhistory.org; Internet Home Page Address: www.rocklandhistory.org; *Cur* Kimberly Kennedy; *Cur Educ* Christopher Kenney; *Publications* Marjorie Bauer; *Exec Dir* Sarah E Henrich; *CEO* Erin L Martin; *VPres* Lawrence Codispot
Open Tues - Fri 9:30 AM - 4 PM, Sat & Sun 1 - 5 PM; Admis adults $5, children $3; Estab 1965 to preserve & interpret history of Rockland County; Average Annual Attendance: 15,000; Mem: 2000; dues $30
Income: $250,000 (financed by endowment, mem & state appropriation)
Special Subjects: Archaeology, Historical Material
Collections: Archaeological Collection; Educational Materials Collection/Reproductions; General Collections; Historical Structures; Special Archival Collections
Exhibitions: Dollhouse Exhibition; Miniatures Exhibition
Publications: South of the Mountains, quarterly journal; 28 books on local history
Activities: Classes for adults & children; docent training; lects open to pub, 8 vis lectrs per yr; concerts; gallery talks; tours; competitions; History Awards Program for high school seniors; History Preservation Merit Awards; Student History Awards; individual paintings, original objects of art & artifacts lent to other mus; originate traveling exhibs in Rockland County; mus shop sells books & educational gifts

NEW PALTZ

M HUGUENOT HISTORICAL SOCIETY OF NEW PALTZ GALLERIES, 18 Broadhead Ave, New Paltz, NY 12561-1403. Tel 845-255-1660; Fax 845-255-0376; Elec Mail info@huguenotstreet.org; Internet Home Page Address: www.huguenotstreet.org; *Dir* Eric Roth; *Patron Svcs Coordr* Laura Lucas; *Communs Specialist* Richard Heyl de Ortiz
Open May 1- Oct 31; Tues - Sun 10 AM - 4 PM, cl Mon; Admis standard tour adults $10, seniors & students 12 & up $9, children (5-11) $5, under 5 no admis fee; Estab 1894 to preserve memory & material culture of Huguenot settlers; Includes three galleries: Huguenot Street National Historic Landmark District; Locust Lawn & Terwilliger House. Primarily ancestral portraits - Vanderlyn, Waldo & Dewett. Maintains reference library; Average Annual Attendance: 13,000; Mem: 5,000; dues $35; annual meeting in June
Income: Financed by mem, endowment
Special Subjects: Architecture, Drawings, Painting-American, Photography, Archaeology, Costumes, Ceramics, Folk Art, Pottery, Decorative Arts, Manuscripts, Portraits, Dolls, Furniture, Glass, Porcelain, Painting-Dutch, Carpets & Rugs, Historical Material, Maps, Coins & Medals, Restorations, Period Rooms, Embroidery, Pewter
Collections: American primitive paintings; early 19th century furnishings, paintings, decorative arts & documents
Exhibitions: Revolving in-house displays
Publications: genealogies & histories
Activities: Classes for adults & children; lects open to pub, 3 vis lectrs per yr; concerts; tours; schols offered; individual paintings are lent to institutions & galleries; mus shop sells books, magazines, original art, reproductions, prints & slides

M STATE UNIVERSITY OF NEW YORK AT NEW PALTZ, Samuel Dorsky Museum of Art, 1 Hawk Dr, New Paltz, NY 12561-2447. Tel 845-257-3844; Fax 845-257-3854; Elec Mail sdma@newpaltz.edu; Internet Home Page Address: www.newpaltz.edu/museum; *Coll Mgr* Wayne Lempka; *Dir* Neil C Trager; *Preparator* Bob Wagner; *Visitor Svcs* Amy Pickering; *Educ Coordr* Judi Esmond; *Assoc Cur of Coll* Dr Jaimee Uhlenbrock; *Cur* Brian Wallace; *Interim Dir* Sara Pasti
Open Tues - Fri 11 AM - 5 PM, Sat-Sun 1 - 5 PM, cl school holidays, cl Mon during legal holidays & intersessions; No admis fee; 2001; With an exhib schedule of 10 exhibitions per year, the Samuel Dorsky Mus of Art provides support for the various art curricula & serves as a major cultural resource for the col & surrounding community; There are two wings comprising 6 galleries, 9,000 sq ft; Average Annual Attendance: 16,000; Mem: 100; $15 - $2,500
Income: Financed by university, grants, endowment & membership
Special Subjects: Metalwork, Graphics, Painting-American, Photography, Prints, African Art, Pre-Columbian Art, Ceramics, Pottery, Etchings & Engravings, Landscapes, Painting-Japanese, Posters, Asian Art, Silver, Antiquities-Byzantine, Calligraphy, Islamic Art, Antiquities-Egyptian, Painting-German
Collections: Artifacts, Folk Art, Asian Prints; Painting, principally 20th century America; Photographs; Posters; Pre-Columbian Art; Prints, African & New Guinea; Sculpture; Hudson Valley Art
Exhibitions: Rotating exhibits every 8 weeks
Publications: Exhibition catalogs, Robert Morris, Lesley Dill, George Bellows, Raoul Hague, Rimer Cardillo, Don Nice, Bolton Coit Brown, Judy Pfaff
Activities: Docent training; lects open to public, 8 per yr; concerts; gallery talks; competitions; tours; individual paintings & original objects of art lent to museums & galleries; lending collection contains artifacts, original prints, paintings, photographs, sculpture, folk art, textiles, drawings & posters

L Sojourner Truth Library, 300 Hawk Dr, New Paltz, NY 12561-2452. Tel

845-257-3719; Fax 845-257-3718; Elec Mail leec@newpaltz.edu; Internet Home Page Address: www.lib.newpaltz.edu; *Information Access* Valerie Mittenberg; *Coll Access* Nancy Nielson; *Team Leader Bibliographic Access* Marjorie Young; *Coll Develop* Gerlinde Barley; *Dir* Chui-Chun Lee
Open Mon - Thurs 8:30 AM -11:30 PM, Fri 8:30 AM - 9 PM, Sat 10 AM - 9PM, Sun 1-11:30 PM; Circ 158,000; For lending & reference; Average Annual Attendance: 343,964
Income: Financed by state appropriation
Library Holdings: Book Volumes 476,000; CD-ROMs; Cassettes; Exhibition Catalogs; Fiche; Micro Print; Pamphlets; Periodical Subscriptions 1,029; Video Tapes
Special Subjects: Art History, Photography, Drawings, Painting-American, Painting-Japanese, Painting-European, Watercolors, Theatre Arts, Art Education, Anthropology, Oriental Art, Silversmithing
Publications: Newsletter, biannual

NEW ROCHELLE

M **COLLEGE OF NEW ROCHELLE,** Castle Gallery, 29 Castle Pl, New Rochelle, NY 10805. Tel 914-654-5423; Fax 914-654-5014; Elec Mail krhein@cnr.edu; Internet Home Page Address: www.cnr.edu/arts/artsmain; *Dir* Katrina Rhein; *Mgr* Michelle Jammes
Open Tues & Thurs-Fri 10AM-5PM, Wed 10AM-8PM, Sat-Sun noon-4PM; No admis fee; Estab 1979 as a professional art gallery to serve the col, city of New Rochelle & lower Westchester & provide exhib & interpretation of fine arts & material culture; Located in Leland Castle, a gothic revival building, listed in National Register of Historic Places; gallery is modern facility, with flexible space
Publications: Newsletter
Activities: Docent training; lects open to pub, 6 vis lectrs per yr; originate traveling exhibs

L **NEW ROCHELLE PUBLIC LIBRARY,** Art Section, One Library Plaza, New Rochelle, NY 10801. Tel 914-632-7878; Fax 914-632-0262; Internet Home Page Address: www.nrpl.org; *Head Reference* Beth Mills; *Dir* Tom Geoffino
Open Mon, Tues & Thurs 9 AM -8 PM, Wed 10 AM - 6 PM, Fri & Sat 9 AM - 5 PM, Sun 1-5PM, July & Aug cl Sat & Sun; Estab 1894
Library Holdings: Book Volumes 8,000; Cassettes; Clipping Files; Exhibition Catalogs; Fiche; Original Art Works; Pamphlets; Photographs; Records; Reels; Slides; Video Tapes
Exhibitions: All shows, displays & exhibits are reviewed & scheduled by professional adv panel
Activities: Lect; demonstrations; lending collection contains framed prints & art slides

A **New Rochelle Art Association,** One Library Plaza, New Rochelle, NY 10801. Tel 914-632-7878; Elec Mail info@nraaonline.org; Internet Home Page Address: www.nraaonline.org; *Pres* Jesse Sanchez
Open Mon, Tues, Thurs 9AM-8PM, Wed 10AM-6PM, Fri & Sat 9AM-5PM, Sun 1-5PM; Estab 1912 to encourage art in the area; Lumen Winter Gallery 84' x 18' space in lib lobby of New Rochelle Public Lib; Mem: 200; dues $20; monthly meeting
Income: Financed by mem
Exhibitions: Four exhibitions per yr
Activities: Classes for adults; lects open to public, 4 vis lectrs per year; competitions with awards

NEW YORK

M **55 MERCER GALLERY,** 138 W 120th St, New York, NY 10027-6401. Tel 212-226-8513
Open Tues - Sat 10 AM - 6 PM; No admis fee; Estab 1970 to give unaffiliated artists a space to show their work; Gallery is a cooperative gallery; Average Annual Attendance: 8,000; Mem: 22; dues $1,350; meeting every 2 months
Income: Financed by mem dues
Exhibitions: One Person & Group shows including John Bradford, David Woodell, Joe Sandman, Michael Tice, Kye Carbone, Bob Meltzmuff, Sydney Drum, Barry Malloy, Milt Connors, Megan Lipke, Catherine Hall, Joe Smith, Joy Walker, Diane Whitcomb, Ethlin Honig, Cris Blyth, Courtney Cavalieri, Masako Honjo, Annette Morris, Esme Thompson, Steve Ridell, Daniel Heyman, Virginia Vogel, Jonathan Lev, Robert Jessel, Michael Amato, Alexis Kuhr, Bobbi Goldman, Josh Dorman
Activities: Apprenticeship prog; competitions; individual paintings & original objects of art lent to college shows

A **AESTHETIC REALISM FOUNDATION,** 141 Greene St, New York, NY 10012-3201. Tel 212-777-4490; Fax 212-777-4426; Internet Home Page Address: www.aestheticrealism.org; *Chmn Educ* Ellen Reiss; *Exec Dir* Margot Carpenter
Open Mon - Fri 10 AM - 7:30 PM, Sat 10 AM - 5 PM; Estab 1973 as a nonprofit educational foundation to teach Aesthetic Realism, the philosophy founded in 1941 by the great American poet & critic Eli Siegel (1902-1978), based on his historic principle - "The world, art, & self explain each other; each is the aesthetic oneness of opposites"
Publications: The Right of Aesthetic Realism to Be Known, bi-weekly periodical
Activities: Monthly public seminars & dramatic presentations; classes in the visual arts, drama, poetry, music, educ, marriage; class for children; individual consultations in person & by telephone worldwide

M **Terrain Gallery,** 141 Greene St, New York, NY 10012. Tel 212-777-4490; Fax 212-777-4426; Internet Home Page Address: www.terraingallery.org; *Coordr* Marcia Rackow
Open Wed - Fri Noon - 5 PM, Sat Noon - 4 PM; Estab 1955 with a basis in this principle stated by Eli Siegel: "All beauty is a making one of opposites, and the making one of opposites is what we are going after in ourselves"
Collections: Permanent collection of paintings, prints, drawings & photographs with commentary

L **Eli Siegel Collection,** 141 Greene St, New York, NY 10012-3201. Tel

212-777-4490; Fax 212-777-4426; Internet Home Page Address: www.aestheticrealism.org; *Librn* Richita Anderson; *Librn* Leila Rosen; *Librn* Meryl Simon
Open to faculty, students & qualified researchers by appointment; Estab 1982; The Collection houses the books & manuscripts of Eli Siegel
Library Holdings: Audio Tapes; Book Volumes 25,000; Manuscripts
Special Subjects: Art History, Film, Photography, Sculpture, Theatre Arts, Anthropology, Aesthetics

L **Aesthetic Realism Foundation Library,** 141 Greene St, New York, NY 10012-3201. Tel 212-777-4490; Fax 212-777-4426; Internet Home Page Address: www.terrainGallery.org; *Librn* Richita Anderson
Open to faculty, students & qualified researchers by appointment; Estab 1973
Special Subjects: Art History, Photography, Theatre Arts, Art Education, Anthropology, Aesthetics, Architecture
Collections: Published poems & essays by Eli Siegel; published & unpublished lectures by Eli Siegel

THE ALLIED ARTISTS OF AMERICA, INC
For further information, see National and Regional Organizations

AMERICAN ACADEMY OF ARTS & LETTERS
For further information, see National and Regional Organizations

AMERICAN ARTISTS PROFESSIONAL LEAGUE, INC
For further information, see National and Regional Organizations

THE AMERICAN FEDERATION OF ARTS
For further information, see National and Regional Organizations

M **AMERICAN FOLK ART MUSEUM,** 1865 Broadway Fl 11, New York, NY 10023-7503. Tel 212-265-1040; Fax 212-265-2350; Elec Mail info@folkartmuseum.org; Internet Home Page Address: www.folkartmuseum.org; *Dir* Maria Ann Conelli; *Chief Admin Officer* Linda Dunne; *CFO* Robin Schlinger; *Pres* Laura Parsons; *Mgr Individual Giving* Christine Corcoran; *Dir Exhibs & Sr Cur* Stacy Hollander; *Dir Publications* Tanya Heinrich; *Registrar* Ann-Marie Reilly; *Receptionist* Katya Ullmann; *Mus Shop Mgr* Marie DiManno; *Dir Pub Rels* Susan Flamm; *Dir Develop* Blair Hartley
Open Tues - Sun 10:30 AM - 5:30 PM, Fri 10:30 AM - 7:30 PM cl Mon; Guided tours by appointment, adults $12, mems free, discounts to AAM & ICOM mems; Estab 1961 for the collection & exhibition of American folk art in all media, including painting, sculpture, textiles & painted & decorated furniture; Single floor, cruciform shape gallery approx 3,000 sq ft; Average Annual Attendance: 165,000; Mem: 5,000; dues $35 & up
Income: Financed by mem, state appropriation & personal donations
Special Subjects: Afro-American Art, Decorative Arts, Textiles, Painting-American, American Indian Art, Crafts, Folk Art, Portraits, Furniture, Scrimshaw, Embroidery, Pewter
Collections: American folk paintings & watercolors; folk sculpture including shop & carousel figures, shiphead figures, decoys, weathervanes, whirligigs, wood carvings & chalkware; painted & decorated furniture; tradesmen's signs; textiles including quilts, coverlets, stenciled fabrics, hooked rugs & samplers; works from 18th, 19th & 20th centuries
Publications: Folk Art Magazine, annual
Activities: Educ dept; classes for adults; docent training; lects open to pub; gallery talks; tours; Visionary Award; outreach programs; book traveling exhibs; originate traveling exhibs to qualifying art & educational institutions; mus shop sells books, reproductions & prints

L **Shirley K. Schlafer Library,** 1865 Broadway Fl 11, New York, NY 10023-7503. Tel 212-265-1040; Fax 212-265-2350; Elec Mail library@folkartmuseum.org; Internet Home Page Address: www.folkartmuseum.org; *Cur Spec Projects* Lee Kogn; *Dir* Maria Conelli
Open by appointment Wed - Thurs, 10 AM - 12:30 PM & 1:30 PM - 4 PM; No admis fee; Estab 1961; Library open to pub by appointment Wed & Thurs 10 AM - 12:30 PM & 1:30 PM - 4 PM
Library Holdings: Auction Catalogs 2000; Audio Tapes 200; Book Volumes 10,000; Clipping Files; Exhibition Catalogs; Manuscripts; Memorabilia; Pamphlets; Periodical Subscriptions 200; Photographs; Reproductions; Slides; Video Tapes 250
Collections: Archives and manuscripts of American self-taught artist Henry Darger; Archives of Historical Society of Early American Decoration; Library & archives of quilt scholar Cuesta Benberry
Activities: Classes for adults & children; lects; concerts; gallery talks; talks; book traveling exhib annually; originates traveling exhibs; mus shop sells books & mus-related items

AMERICAN INSTITUTE OF GRAPHIC ARTS
For further information, see National and Regional Organizations

A **AMERICAN JEWISH HISTORICAL SOCIETY,** The Center for Jewish History, 15 W 16th St, New York, NY 10011-6301. Tel 212-294-6160; Fax 212-294-6161; Elec Mail info@ajhs.org; Internet Home Page Address: www.AJHS.org; *Exec Dir* Dr Jonathan Karp; *Dir Library & Archives* Susan Malbin; *Dir Develop* Rachel Lobovsky; *Sr Archivist* Tanya Elder; *Asst Archivist* Marvin Rusinek; *Controller* Jeffrey Kornstein
Open Mon - Thurs 9 AM - 5 PM, Fri 9 AM - 2 PM, Sun 11 AM - 5 PM; Admis varies, call for specific rates; Estab 1892 to collect, preserve, catalog & disseminate information relating to the American Jewish experience; Average Annual Attendance: 5,000; Mem: 3,000; dues $50; annual meeting in May
Income: $500,000 (financed by endowment, mem, Jewish Federation allocations, grants & donations)
Special Subjects: Manuscripts, Portraits
Exhibitions: Gustatory Delights in the New World; German Jews in America; Emma Lazarus, Joseph Pulitzer & The Statue of Liberty; Yiddish Theatre in America; American Jewish Colonial Portraits; Sephardim in America; Machal: American Veterans of Israel's War of Independence
Publications: American Jewish History, quarterly; Heritage; Local Jewish Historical Society News; books; newsletters

Activities: Lects open to public, 10 vis lectrs per yr; tours; individual paintings & original objects of art lent to museums & historical societies; lending collection contains motion pictures, paintings, books, original art works, original prints & photographs

L **Lee M Friedman Memorial Library,** 101 Newbury St, Boston, MA 02116-3062. Tel 617-226-1245; Fax 617-226-1248; Elec Mail info@ajhs.org; *Dir* Judy Garner
Open Mon - Thurs 9:30 AM - 4:30 PM, Fri researcher hours only; No admis fee; Estab 1892 to collect, preserve & catalog material relating to Colonial American Jewish history; Open for reference
Income: $514,000 (financed by endowment, mem, contributions, grants, allocations from Jewish welfare funds)
Library Holdings: Book Volumes 95,000; Cassettes; Manuscripts; Memorabilia; Motion Pictures; Other Holdings Archives; Pamphlets; Periodical Subscriptions 120; Photographs; Prints; Records; Slides
Collections: Stephen S Wise Manuscripts Collection; Archives of Major Jewish Organizations
Exhibitions: Colonial American Jewry; 19th Century Jewish Families; On Common Ground: The Boston Jewish Experience, 1649-1980; Statue of Liberty; German American Jewry; Moses Michael Hays & Post- Revolutionary Boston
Publications: American Jewish History, quarterly; Heritage, bi-annually
Activities: Lects open to public, 2-3 vis lectrs per yr; tours; originate traveling exhibs to libraries, museum societies, synagogues

M **AMERICAN MUSEUM OF NATURAL HISTORY,** Central Park W at 79th St, New York, NY 10024-5192; 15 W 77th St, New York, NY 10024-5193. Tel 212-769-5100; Fax 212-496-3500; Elec Mail postmaster@amnh.org; Internet Home Page Address: www.amnh.org; *Sr VPres Com* Gary Zarr; *Pres* Ellen V Futter; *VPres Government* Lisa J Gugenheim; *Chmn & Cur Divisio* Enid Schildkrout; *Sr Adv* Linda F Cahill; *Chmn Bd Trustees* Lewis Bernard; *Chmn & Cur Divisio* Mark A Norell; *Dir Retail* Paul Murawski; *Sr VPres & Pro* Michael J Novacek; *VPres Develop* Lynn DeBow; *Chmn Div Physical* James D Webster; *Sr VPres* Craig Morris; *Assoc Dean Science* Darrel R Frost; *Sr VPres Fin* Sigmund G Ginsburg; *Gen Counsel* Gerald R Singer; *Chm & Cur Divisio* Randall T Schuh; *Sr VPres Oper* Barbara D Gunn; *Frederick P Rose D* Neil Degrasse Tyson; *VPres Educ* Myles Gordon; *VPres Exhibition* David Harvey
Open daily 10 AM - 5:45 PM, cl Thanksgiving & Christmas; Admis suggested donation adults $19, seniors & students with ID $14.50, children ages 2-12 $10.50, mems no charge; Estab 1869 as a museum for the study & exhibition of all aspects of natural history; Average Annual Attendance: 3,000,000; Mem: 500,000
Income: Financed by special presentations, contributions
Collections: Fossil Halls; Hall of Saurischian Dinosaurs; Hall of Ornithiscian Dinosaurs; Hall of Primitive Mammals; Milstein Hall of Advanced Mammals; Hall of Vertebrate Origins; Hall of Northwest Coast Indians; Hall of Eastern Woodlands & Plains Indians; Hall of African Peoples; Stout Hall of Asian Peoples; Hall of Mexico & Central America; Hall of South American Peoples; Mead Hall of Pacific Peoples; Hall of Asian Mammals; Hall of North American Mammals; Akeley Hall of African Mammals; Hall of Biodiversity; Hall of North American Birds; Hall of Ocean Life; Hall of North American Forests; Hall of Primates; Hall of Reptiles & Amphibians; Spitzer Hall of Human Origins; Akeley Gallery; Theodore Roosevelt Rotunda & Memorial Hall; New York State Environment; Ross Hall of Meteorites; Guggenheim Hall of Minerals; Morgan Memorial Hall of Gems
Publications: Natural History, magazine; Curator; Bulletin of the American Museum of Natural History; Anthropological Papers of the American Museum of Natural History; American Museum of Natural History Novitiates; annual report
Activities: Classes for adults & children; dance & music progs; lects open to pub; tours; schols; mus shop sells books, original art, reproductions & prints; jr mus

L **Library,** 15 W 77th St, New York, NY 10024-5193. Tel 212-769-5400; Fax 212-769-5009; Elec Mail libref@amnh.org; Internet Home Page Address: http://library.amnh.org; *Dir Library Servs* Tom Moritz
Open daily 10 AM - 5 PM, cl Thanksgiving & Christmas
Library Holdings: Audio Tapes; Book Volumes 450,000; Clipping Files; Filmstrips; Kodachrome Transparencies; Lantern Slides; Manuscripts; Memorabilia; Motion Pictures; Original Art Works; Pamphlets; Photographs; Prints; Records; Sculpture; Slides; Video Tapes
Special Subjects: Etchings & Engravings, Historical Material, Ceramics, Archaeology, Ethnology, Bronzes, American Indian Art, Anthropology, Eskimo Art, Mexican Art, Afro-American Art, Carpets & Rugs, Gold, Goldsmithing, Architecture

M **Rose Center for Earth & Space,** Central Park W at W 81st St, New York, NY 10024; 15 W 77th St, New York, NY 10024-5193. Tel 212-769-5100; Internet Home Page Address: www.amnh.org/rose/; *Chair Dept Physical Sciences* Mordecai-Mark Mac Low
Open daily 10 AM - 5:45 PM, cl Thanksgiving & Christmas; Space Shows Mon - Fri every half hour from 10:30 AM - 4:30 PM, Wed begin at 11 AM, Sat & Sun every half hour from 10:30 AM - 5 PM; Admis incl in gen mus admis; admis to Hayden Planetarium Space Shows separate, purchase tickets online or call for more info
Collections: Hayden Planetarium; Hall of Planet Earth; Hall of the Universe; Cosmic Pathway; Scales of the Universe
Exhibitions: Big Bang; See website for planetarium shows
Activities: Progs for students

AMERICAN NUMISMATIC SOCIETY
For further information, see National and Regional Organizations

L **AMERICAN UNIVERSITY,** Jack I & Dorothy G Bender Library & Learning Resources Center, 520 W 43rd St, Apt 21E New York, NY 10036-4352. Tel 202-885-3232; Fax 202-885-3226; Elec Mail librarymail@american.edu; Internet Home Page Address: www.library.american.edu; *University Librn* William A Mayer; *Assoc University Librn* Diana Vogelsong; *Acting Asst University Librn* Janice Flug; *Coll Develop Librn* Martin Shapiro; *Reference Team Leader* Melissa Becher; *Media Librn* Chris Lewis; *Archives & Spec Coll* Susan McElrath
Open 24 hrs starting 9 AM Sun - 9 PM Fri, Sat 9 AM - 9 PM during school yr, see website for hrs during univ holidays; Estab 1893; Circ 315,041 for all disciplines; Mem: Friends of American University Libr, 800 members qualified by donation

Library Holdings: Audio Tapes; Book Volumes 1,112,500; CD-ROMs; Cassettes; Compact Disks; DVDs; Fiche; Filmstrips; Manuscripts; Maps; Memorabilia; Motion Pictures; Original Documents; Other Holdings playbills; Periodical Subscriptions 36,353 electronic, 1,960 print; Photographs; Records; Reels; Video Tapes
Special Subjects: Art History, Film, Mixed Media, Photography, Commercial Art, Graphic Arts, Graphic Design, Painting-American, Painting-British, Painting-French, Painting-German, Painting-Italian, Painting-Russian, Painting-Spanish, Pre-Columbian Art, Prints, Sculpture, Painting-European, Historical Material, History of Art & Archaeology, Judaica, Stage Design, Watercolors, Conceptual Art, Latin American Art, Theatre Arts, Archaeology, Ethnology, Printmaking, Advertising Design, Video, Anthropology, Costume Design & Constr, Aesthetics
Collections: General Academic Collection supporting all Art Fields; archives of the Frederick Law Olmsted Documentary editing project; Charles Nelson Spinks Collection of Japanese prints; Watkins Collection of artist's books
Activities: Lect open to pub

M **AMERICAN UNIVERSITY,** Katzen Art Center Gallery, 520 W 43rd St, Apt 21E New York, NY 10036-4352. Tel 202-885-1300; Fax 202-885-1140; Elec Mail kac@american.edu; Internet Home Page Address: www.american.edu/academic.depts/cas/katzen/index.cfm; *Dir & Cur* Jack Rasmussen, PhD; *Asst Dir* Stephanie Fedor; *Chief Preparator* Bruce Wick
Open Tues - Thurs 11 AM - 4 PM, Fri - Sat 11 AM - 7 PM, Sun Noon - 4 PM; Programming will focus on Contemporary Art; 3-floor, 30,000 sq/ft gallery space
Special Subjects: Drawings, Painting-American, Prints, Sculpture, Watercolors, Woodcuts, Etchings & Engravings, Painting-European, Posters
Collections: Katzen Collection of 19th & 20th century American & European paintings
Activities: Lects open to pub; individual paintings & original objects of art lent to museums & university galleries; originates traveling exhibs

AMERICAN WATERCOLOR SOCIETY
For further information, see National and Regional Organizations

A **THE AMERICAN-SCANDINAVIAN FOUNDATION,** Scandinavia House: The Nordic Center in America, 58 Park Ave, New York, NY 10016-3007. Tel 212-779-3587; Fax 212-686-1157; Elec Mail info@amscan.org; Internet Home Page Address: www.scandinaviahouse.org; *VPres* Lynn Carter; *Pres* Edward Gallagher
Open Tues - Sat 12 - 6 PM; Admis varies by exhib; Foundation estab 1910 to promote cultural exchange Scandinavia House opened in 2000 presents best of Nordic culture incl art & design exhibs from Denmark, Finland, Iceland, Norway & Sweden; Exhibs of Scandinavian art & design; Average Annual Attendance: 110,000; Mem: 7,000; dues $50
Library Holdings: Book Volumes; Exhibition Catalogs; Manuscripts; Pamphlets; Periodical Subscriptions
Special Subjects: Architecture, Drawings, Historical Material, Metalwork, Photography, Prints, Sculpture, Silver, Textiles, Decorative Arts, Folk Art, Crafts, Furniture, Glass, Maps, Painting-Scandinavian
Exhibitions: Scandinavian painting, sculpture, design and crafts; artwork is selected for exhibition by a comt of professional art adv
Publications: Scandinavian Review, 3 times a year; SCAN, newsletter 4 times a year
Activities: Classes for children; language classes in conjunction with NYU School of Continuing & Professional Studies; lect open to public; lects for mems only; 5 vis lectrs per yr; concerts; gallery talks; ASF Cultural Award; schols & fels offered; sales shop sells books, design objects, tableware, jewelry, toys, watches, music, Nordic foods & holiday items

AMERICANS FOR THE ARTS
For further information, see National and Regional Organizations

M **AMERICAS SOCIETY ART GALLERY,** 680 Park Ave, New York, NY 10021-5072. Tel 212-249-8950; Fax 212-249-5668; Elec Mail arts@americas-society.org; Internet Home Page Address: www.americas-society.org; Telex 42-9169; *Dir Visual Arts* Gabriela Rangel; *Coordr Exhibs & Pub Progs* Mariela Hardy; *Asst Cur Visual Arts* Isabela Villanueva
Open Wed - Sat Noon - 6 PM, cl Columbus Day, Veterans Day, Thanksgiving, Dec 24 - Jan 1; No admis fee; Estab 1967 to broaden understanding & appreciation in the United States of the art & cultural heritage of other countries in the Western Hemisphere; One large gallery with 3-4 exhibitions a year of Latin American, Caribbean & Canadian art; Average Annual Attendance: 25,000; Mem: 900; dues $75
Income: $120,500
Library Holdings: Exhibition Catalogs
Special Subjects: Decorative Arts, Photography, Prints, Silver, Textiles, Sculpture, Latin American Art, Mexican Art, Pre-Columbian Art, Painting-Canadian, Furniture, Historical Material
Publications: Exhibition catalogs
Activities: Classes for adults & children in conjunction with exhibitions; docent training; lects open to public, 12 vis lectrs per yr; gallery talks; concerts; tours; book traveling exhibs 1-2 per yr; originate traveling exhibs & circulate to other galleries within; exhibition catalogues available for purchase at front desk

A **ANDY WARHOL FOUNDATION FOR THE VISUAL ARTS,** 65 Bleecker St, Fl 7 New York, NY 10012-2420. Tel 212-387-7555; Fax 212-387-7560; Elec Mail info@warholfoundation.org; Internet Home Page Address: www.warholfoundation.org; *Pres* Joel Wachs; *VP & Liaison to Andy Warhol Mus* John Warhola; *CFO & Treas* KC Maurer; *Chief Cur* Claudia Defendi; *Cur Drawings & Photography* Sally King-Nero; *Proj Cur Photo Legacy Prog* Jenny Moore; *Asst Cur* Bibi Kahn; *Colls Coordr* Beth Savage; *Colls Mgmt* Lambert Corcoran; *Colls Mgmt* Scott Ferguson
Estab 1987 for the advancement of the visual arts
Activities: Grants & fels offered

M **ANTHOLOGY FILM ARCHIVES,** 32 Second Ave, New York, NY 10003. Tel 212-505-5181; Fax 212-477-2714; Elec Mail robert@anthologyfilmarchives.org; Internet Home Page Address: www.anthologyfilmarchives.org; *Dir & Vol Pres* Jonas Mekas; *Publs & Mem* Wendy Dorsett; *Chmn Bd* Barney Oldfield; *Develop Dir* Stephanie Grey; *Admin Dir & Exhibs Coordr* John Mhiripiri; *Archivist* Andrew Lampert; *Dir Colls & Spec Projs* Robert A Haller
Open for film screenings Mon - Fri evenings, Sat & Sun afternoon -evenings, check schedule for time; Admis adults $9, seniors & students $5, spec rates for groups, mems no admis fee; Estab 1970; mus of the cinema with progs in film & video preservation; Average Annual Attendance: 50,000; Mem: dues Preservation Donor $1500, Donor $250, Dual Adult $75, Individual Adult $50, Senior or Student $30
Library Holdings: Book Volumes 8000; Clipping Files 12,000; Other Holdings; Periodical Subscriptions 42,000; Photographs 1200; Prints
Special Subjects: Photography
Collections: Library coll of over 12,000 films & tapes on avant-garde, classic & documentary cinema; mail-order publ svc; approx 1 million books, photos, documents in a closed-stack facility that services scores of scholars every yr
Publications: quarterly film exhibition schedule; Annual Film Preservation Honors Dinner Journal; catalogs; books
Activities: Research projs on Jim Davis, Storm DeHirsch, Marie Menken; films; Film Preservation Honors Dinner

A **ARCHITECTURAL LEAGUE OF NEW YORK,** 457 Madison Ave, New York, NY 10022-6843; 594 Broadway, Ste 3607 New York, NY 10012-3233. Tel 212-753-1722; Fax 212-486-9173; Elec Mail info@archleague.org; Internet Home Page Address: www.archleague.org; *Exec Dir* Rosalie Genevro; *Pres* Calvin Tsao
Office open Mon - Fri 9 AM - 5 PM; Admis seminars $10, mems free; Estab 1881 to promote art & architecture; serves as a forum for new & experimental ideas in the arts; Average Annual Attendance: 7500; Mem: 1,600; dues over 35 years $100, under 35 years $60, students $35; ann meeting in June
Exhibitions: Annual Juried Exhibition of Young Architects Competition; New New York; Toward the Sentient City
Publications: Exhibition catalogs; posters
Activities: Lect; slide lect; gallery talks; tours; competitions; awards for young architects, emerging voices, Deborah J. Norden Fund; urbanomnibus.net; schols offered

ART DEALERS ASSOCIATION OF AMERICA, INC
For further information, see National and Regional Organizations

ART DIRECTORS CLUB
For further information, see National and Regional Organizations

A **ART IN GENERAL,** 79 Walker St, New York, NY 10013-3523. Tel 212-219-0473; Fax 212-219-0511; Elec Mail info@artingeneral.org; Internet Home Page Address: www.artingeneral.org; *Exec Dir* Anne Barlow; *Cur* Andria Hickey; *Develop Dir* Anna Starling
Open Tues - Sat Noon - 6 PM; No admis fee; Estab 1981 as a nonprofit arts organization, which relies on private & public support to meet its expenses; Assists artists with the production & presentation of new work; Average Annual Attendance: 10,000; Mem: 90; dues vary
Income: Financed by state & private funds (foundations, corporations)
Exhibitions: Salon Show
Publications: Manual of exhibitions & programs, annual
Activities: Interactive discussions & art workshops; lects open to pub; lects mems only; 5 vis lectrs per yr; gallery talks; tours; originate traveling exhibs; sales shop sells books & limited editions

A **ART INFORMATION CENTER, INC,** 100 Cabrini Blvd Apt 31, New York, NY 10033-3413. Tel 212-966-3443; *Pres & Dir* Dan Concholar
Open 10 AM - 6 PM or by appointment; No admis fee; Organized 1959, inc 1963, presently a consulting service for artists; The Center helps to channel the many artists in New York, & those coming to New York, seeking New York outlets for their work. Advise artist seeking galleries in New York City
Income: $15,000 (financed by donations & small grants)

A **ART STUDENTS LEAGUE OF NEW YORK,** 215 W 57th St, New York, NY 10019-2193. Tel 212-247-4510; Fax 212-541-7024; Elec Mail info@artstudentsleague.org; Internet Home Page Address: www.theartstudentsleague.org; *Exec Dir* Ira Goldberg; *Cur* Pam Koob; *Archivist* Stephanie Cassidy
Gallery open Mon - Fri 9 AM - 8:30 PM, Sat 9 AM - 3 PM; No admis fee; Estab 1875 to maintain art school & mem activities; Maintains an art gallery open to pub for league exhibits; Average Annual Attendance: 8,000 - 9,000; Mem: 6,000; dues $25; annual meeting in Dec; 3 months full-time study required for mem
Income: Financed by tuitions & investments
Library Holdings: Book Volumes; Clipping Files; Periodical Subscriptions
Collections: Permanent collection of paintings, sculpture & works on paper by former league students & instructors
Exhibitions: Exhibitions by members, students & instructors
Publications: Linea, quarterly newsletter
Activities: Classes for adults & children; lect open to public, 3 vis lectrs per year; sponsoring of competitions; McDowell Travel Grant, Edwards-Gonzalez Travel Grant & Neosa Cohen award; scholarships offered; individual paintings & original objects of art lent to museums

L **Library,** 215 W 57th St, New York, NY 10019. Tel 212-247-4510; Fax 212-541-7024; Elec Mail Stephanie@artstudentsleague.org
Reference library for students & members & archive of instructors, prominent students & members, past & current
Income: Financed by tuition & endowments
Library Holdings: Auction Catalogs; Audio Tapes; Book Volumes 6,000; Cassettes; Clipping Files; Exhibition Catalogs; Filmstrips; Manuscripts; Pamphlets; Photographs; Reproductions; Slides; Video Tapes
Collections: Paintings, Sculpture & works on paper by instructors & students, past & current
Exhibitions: Exhibitions by instructors & students
Publications: Linea, newsletter of the Art Students League of New York, 3-4 issues per yr
Activities: Classes for adults & children; gallery talks; scholarships offered; sales shop sells art supplies

M **ART WITHOUT WALLS INC,** PO Box 2066, New York, NY 10150-1902; PO Box 341, Sayville, NY 11782-0341. Tel 631-567-9418; Fax 631-567-9418; Elec Mail artwithoutwalls@msn.com; Internet Home Page Address: www.artwithoutwalls.net; *Exec Dir* Sharon Lippman; *Representative* Paula Lippman
Open daily 9 AM - 9 PM, weekends by appointment; No admis fee; Estab 1985 to foster non-traditional public art & the historical, social & aesthetic elements of fine art as well as art therapy programs to exhibit to the public innovative & original public art, non-traditional, Holocaust art, contemporary art & art of the handicapped & terminally ill emerging artists, outsider art, national & international artists - thematic exhibs; Circ 2,000; Average Annual Attendance: 2,000; Mem: 450; dues $75; open membership; for artists resume & annual dues $375 with slides of work; representative & show fee $375; estb professional artists must have exhib resume unless outsider or emerging artist
Income: Grants/donations
Library Holdings: Auction Catalogs; Book Volumes; CD-ROMs; Cards; Clipping Files; DVDs; Exhibition Catalogs; Filmstrips; Framed Reproductions; Kodachrome Transparencies; Manuscripts; Motion Pictures; Original Art Works; Original Documents; Pamphlets; Periodical Subscriptions; Photographs; Prints; Reproductions; Sculpture; Slides; Video Tapes
Special Subjects: Marine Painting, Metalwork, Pre-Columbian Art, Painting-American, Prints, Period Rooms, Silver, Textiles, Woodcuts, Maps, Painting-British, Painting-European, Painting-French, Sculpture, Tapestries, Architecture, Drawings, Graphics, Hispanic Art, Latin American Art, Mexican Art, Photography, Watercolors, American Indian Art, American Western Art, Anthropology, Archaeology, Ethnology, Southwestern Art, Costumes, Folk Art, Pottery, Woodcarvings, Landscapes, Afro-American Art, Judaica, Manuscripts, Collages, Painting-Japanese, Portraits, Posters, Eskimo Art, Painting-Canadian, Dolls, Jade, Jewelry, Porcelain, Oriental Art, Asian Art, Painting-Dutch, Historical Material, Ivory, Juvenile Art, Restorations, Baroque Art, Painting-Flemish, Painting-Polish, Renaissance Art, Laces, Medieval Art, Antiquities-Oriental, Painting-Spanish, Painting-Italian, Islamic Art, Antiquities-Egyptian, Antiquities-Greek, Antiquities-Roman, Mosaics, Cartoons, Stained Glass, Painting-Australian, Painting-German, Leather, Reproductions, Painting-Russian, Painting-Israeli, Painting-Scandinavian, Painting-New Zealand
Collections: American Contemporary Art; Art Therapy; International Art; Non-Traditional Art; Public Art; American Contemporary Art; Art Therapy; International Art; Holocaust Art; Outsider Art-Emerging Artists; Southwestern Art/Film/Photography/Fashion Illustration; Design - Architecture
Exhibitions: South Street Seaport-Museum Without Walls; Central Park-Museum Without Walls; Battery Park NYC-Museum Without Walls; Bryant Park-Museum Without Walls; Ellis Island Immigrant Museum, Fort Wadsworth, NY (National Parks Serv; Central Park Zoo, NYC
Activities: Educ prog; classes for adults & children; dramatic progs; art therapy; tours; lects open to pub, 10 vis lectrs per yr; gallery talks; American Artist Award, Newsday; National Women's History Award, National Poetry Press; Suffolk County Legislature Award, Ll Hall of Fame, Suffolk County News Inspiration Award; Honorary Bench: "Art Without Walls, Inc., Sharon Lippman-Founder", Bethpage State Park LI, NY for cultural arts; Brooklyn Borough President Proclamation; schols; individual paintings & original objects of art lent; terminally ill & disabled individuals; book traveling exhibs 2 per yr; originate traveling exhibs 5 per yr; 2 murals donated to National Monument at Fort Wadsworth, NY on NY Waterways and Baymen Homage; mus shop sells original art, reproductions & prints

A **ARTISTS SPACE,** 38 Greene St, 3rd Flr, New York, NY 10013. Tel 212-226-3970; Fax 212-966-1434; Elec Mail info@artistsspace.org; Internet Home Page Address: www.artistsspace.org; *Dir* Stefan Kalmar; *Mgr Communs* Elizabeth Hirsch; *Cur* Richard Birkett; *Dir Finance* Stephanie Jauch
Open Wed - Sun noon - 6 PM; Estab 1972; Artists Space has successfully contributed to changing the institutional & economic landscape for contemporary art in NYC lending support to emerging ideas & emerging artists alike
Activities: Classes for children; presents 4-5 exhibs per yr; pub progs (screenings, talks, etc); sales shop sells books, prints, limited edition artworks

M **Artists Space Gallery,** 38 Greene St, 3rd Flr, New York, NY 10013. Tel 212-226-3970; Fax 212-966-1434; Elec Mail info@artistspace.org; Internet Home Page Address: www.artistsspace.org; *Asst Dir* Greg Hendren; *Dir* Barbara Hunt
Open Tues - Sat noon - 6 PM, Thurs noon - 8 PM; No admis fee for exhibitions, films & events $4; Estab 1973 to assist emerging & unaffiliated artists; Five exhibition rooms & hall gallery; Average Annual Attendance: 20,000
Income: Financed by National Endowment for the Arts, New York State Council, corporate & foundation funds & private contributions
Exhibitions: Five exhibitions of local emerging artists
Activities: Gallery talks by appointment; financial aid to artists for public presentation; book traveling exhibs; originate traveling exhibs; junior mus

L **Irving Sandler Artists File,** 38 Greene St, 3rd Fl, New York, NY 10013. Tel 212-226-3970; Elec Mail artspace@artistsspace.org; Internet Home Page Address: www.artistsspace.org; *Cur* Jenelle Porter; *Artists File Coordr* Letha Wilson; *Dir* Barbara Hunt
Open Fri - Sat 10 AM - 6 PM; Slide file of over 2,500 New York state artists; Available to dealers, critics, cur & artists for reference only

A **ARTISTS TALK ON ART,** 10 Waterside Plaza #33 D, New York, NY 10010-2608; PO Box 1384, Old Chelsea Sta New York, NY 10113-1384. Tel 212-779-9250; Elec Mail dougsheer@gmail.com; Internet Home Page Address: www.atoa.org; *Chmn Bd of Dir* Doug Sheer; *Programming Dir* Peter Duhan; *Pres* Lynne Mayocole; *IT Dir* Flash Light; *Office Mgr* Margarida Guilarte
Open Fri 7 AM - 10 PM, call for updates; Admis $7, students & seniors $3; Estab 1974 to promote dialogue in the arts; Average Annual Attendance: 5,000; Mem: dues season pass $60
Income: $30,000 (financed by mem, state appropriation, admis, contributions & corporate funding)

Library Holdings: Audio Tapes; CD-ROMs; Cassettes; DVDs; Manuscripts; Photographs; Prints; Video Tapes
Publications: Artists Talk on Art Calendar, semi-annually
Activities: Lects open to pub, 24 vis lectrs per season; gallery talks; competitions with awards; annual: Curator's Choice contest; book traveling exhibs 1-3 per yr; originate traveling exhibs 1-3 per yr

ARTISTS' FELLOWSHIP, INC
For further information, see National and Regional Organizations

A **ARTS, CRAFT & THEATER SAFETY,** 181 Thompson St #23, New York, NY 10012. Tel 212-777-0062; Elec Mail actsnyc@cs.com; Internet Home Page Address: www.artscraftstheatersafety.org; *Pres* Monona Rossol
Not open to off-street traffic, but 6 days/wk e-mails, letters & phone calls are answered or returned. ACTS answers an average of 35 inquiries/day; Estab 1986 to provide health & safety services to artists & theatrical professionals. ACTS provides lectures; US & Canadian reg compliance training & inspections; technical assist for bldg planning, renovations & ventilation projects; research & editing of safety publications; books & articles; & newsletter; Mem: Not a membership organization
Income: Nonprofit
Publications: Newsletter
Activities: Outreach activities; safety services on artists procedures, ventilation, OSHA compliance

A **ARTSCONNECTION INC,** 520 8th Ave, Ste 321 New York, NY 10018. Tel 212-302-7433; Fax 212-302-1132; Elec Mail coveneyc@arts connectin.org; Internet Home Page Address: www.artsconnection.org; *Exec Dir* Steve Tennen; *Deputy Dir Education* Carol Morgan; *Deputy Dir Fin* Tavia Huggins; *Dir Progs* Carol Rice; *Communs Mgr* Claire Coveney
Estab 1979 to make the arts an essential part of educ & connect artists with children, families & schools in creative partnerships for teaching & learning
Activities: Educ progs; activities & after-school classes for children; family events; High 5 teen ticket discounts to arts performances, mus & events; teacher & artist professional devel; in-school artist res; school outreach publications; artist grants available

M **THE ASIA SOCIETY MUSEUM,** (The Asia Society Galleries) 725 Park Ave, New York, NY 10021-5088. Tel 212-288-6400; Fax 212-517-8315; Internet Home Page Address: www.asiasociety.org; Telex 22-4953 ASIA UR; Cable ASIAHOUSE NEW YORK; *Museum Dir* Melissa Chiu
Open Tues - Sun 11 AM - 6 PM, Fri 11 AM - 9 PM; cl Mon & major holidays. Summer hours change; Admis fee $10, seniors $7, students w/id $5, mems & children under 16 free; Estab 1956 as a nonprofit organization to further greater understanding & mutual appreciation between the US & peoples of Asia. The Asia House Gallery was inaugurated in 1960 to acquaint Americans with the historic art of Asia; In 1981 the Asia Society came into possession of its permanent collection, the Mr & Mrs John D Rockefeller 3D Collection of Asian Art, which is shown in conjunction with temporary exhibitions of traditional & contemporary Asian art; Average Annual Attendance: 95,000; Mem: 4,400; dues $50 & up; annual meeting in May
Income: Financed by endowment, mem, & grants from foundation, individual, federal & state government
Special Subjects: Asian Art
Collections: Mr & Mrs John D Rockefeller 3D Collection of Asian Art; loans obtained from the US & foreign colls for special exhibs
Exhibitions: Rotating exhibits
Publications: Archives of Asian Art, annually
Activities: Lect by guest specialists in connection with each exhibition & recorded lect by the gallery educ staff available to visitors, 40 vis lectrs per year; concerts; gallery talks; tours; loan exhibitions originated; book traveling exhibitions 2 per year; sales shop sells books, magazines, prints & slides

A **ASIAN AMERICAN ARTS CENTRE,** 111 Norfolk St, Fl 1 New York, NY 10002. Tel 212-233-2154; Elec Mail aaacinfo@artspiral.org; Internet Home Page Address: www.artspiral.org; *Exec Dir* Robert Lee; *Prog & Web Mgr* Adliana Bahrin; *Archivist & Develop Assoc* Talice Lee
Open weekdays 1 - 6:30 PM; No admis fee; Estab 1974 to promote the cultural presence of Asian-American contemporary art in the US; Circ Packet historical materials available; Maintains research library & artist archive; Average Annual Attendance: 12,000
Library Holdings: Audio Tapes; Book Volumes; Cards; Cassettes; Exhibition Catalogs; Kodachrome Transparencies; Memorabilia; Original Art Works; Original Documents; Pamphlets; Photographs; Slides; Video Tapes
Special Subjects: Asian Art, Folk Art
Collections: Permanent collection of works commemorating Tiananmen Square; China June 4; collection of works by contemporary Asian-American artists (400+); folk arts collection (predominantly Chinese - 150+); Asian American Art; Asian American artist archive, 1,700+ items; Digital Artist Archive, at www.artasiamerica.org
Publications: Out of the Archive catalog
Activities: Lects open to pub, 5 vis lectrs per yr; competitions with awards; originate traveling exhibs

ASSOCIATION OF ART MUSEUM DIRECTORS
For further information, see National and Regional Organizations

M **ATLANTIC GALLERY,** 547 W 27th St or 548 W 28th St, Ste 540 New York, NY 10001. Tel 212-219-3183; Elec Mail info@atlanticgallery.org; Internet Home Page Address: atlanticgallery.org
Open Tues - Sat Noon - 6 PM; No admis fee; Estab 1971 as an artist-run gallery presenting the work of member & guest artists in solo exhibitions & group shows; 1 large gallery; Average Annual Attendance: 10,000; Mem: Upon request
Income: Financed by mem & artists of the gallery
Exhibitions: Solo and group show every three weeks
Publications: Periodic flyers

Activities: Lect open to public; life-drawing sessions; concerts; gallery talks; tours; poetry readings; individual paintings & original objects of art lent; sales shop sells original art

M **AUSTRIAN CULTURAL FORUM GALLERY,** (Austrian Cultural Institute Gallery) 11 E 52nd St, New York, NY 10022-5301. Tel 212-319-5300; Fax 212-644-8660; Elec Mail desk@acfny.org; Internet Home Page Address: www.acfny.org; Telex 17-7142; Cable AUSTRO-CULT; *Dir* Andreas Stadler; *Deputy Dir* Martin Rauchbauer; *Admin Mgr* Johannes Korherr
Open Mon - Sat 10 AM - 6 PM; No admis fee; Estab 1962 for presentation of Austrian Art & culture in America; 4 - 10 exhibs per yr, focus on contemporary Austrian art & architecture
Publications: Austria Kultur, bimonthly
Activities: Lect open to public; gallery talks

M **BARUCH COLLEGE OF THE CITY UNIVERSITY OF NEW YORK,** Sidney Mishkin Gallery, 135 E 22nd St, Box D-0100 New York, NY 10010-5505. Tel 646-660-6652; Internet Home Page Address: www.baruch.cuny.edu/mishkin; *Dir* Dr Sandra Kraskin, PhD
Open Mon - Fri Noon - 5 PM, Thurs Noon - 7 PM; No admis fee; Estab 1983; 2,400 sq ft; Average Annual Attendance: 10,000
Income: Financed by the Baruch College Fund & federal, state & private grants
Special Subjects: Afro-American Art, Painting-American, Prints, Sculpture, Drawings, Hispanic Art, Etchings & Engravings
Collections: American & European drawings, paintings, photographs, prints & sculptures
Publications: Exhibition catalogues
Activities: Lect open to public, 3-7 vis lectrs per year; gallery talks; tours; book traveling exhibitions 1-2 per year

M **BLUE MOUNTAIN GALLERY,** 530 W 25th St 4th Fl, New York, NY 10001-5516. Tel 646-486-4730; Elec Mail bluemountaingallery@verizon.net; Internet Home Page Address: www.bluemountaingallery.org; *Treas* Gulgan Aliriza; *Dir* Marcia Clark; *Secy* Janet Sawyer
Open Tues - Sat 11 AM - 6 PM; No admis fee; Estab 1980, an artist supported co-op gallery exhibiting works of gallery members & guests; 30 ft x 30 ft, white walls, wood floors; Mem: 32; members must be artists willing to exhibit & sell own work & must be chosen by existing members; dues $1500; 8 meetings a yr
Income: Financed through membership
Exhibitions: (12/03/2013-12/21/2013) Juried Show, Juror: Andrea Wells; (12/26/2013-01/25/2014) West 9th Views by Sharyn Finnegan
Publications: Evolution of a Gallery, 1968-2010
Activities: Lect open to public; 5-8 vis lectrs per yr; concerts; gallery talks; sponsoring competitions, juried show; organize traveling exhibs to universities

A **CARIBBEAN CULTURAL CENTER,** Cultural Arts Organization & Resource Center, 1825 Park Ave Rm 602, New York, NY 10035-1636. Tel 212-307-7420; Fax 212-315-1086; Internet Home Page Address: www.caribbeancenter.org; *Dir Archives/Media Resource Center* Manuel Jaimes; *Dir* Melody Capote; *Founder & Bd Pres* Dr Marta Moreno Vega; *Dir Progs* Monthina Williams; *Dir Educ* Manuela Arciniegas; *Dir Internal Affairs* Monica Cortes
Open Mon - Fri 11 AM - 6 PM; Admis $2; Estab 1976; Resource center for reference only; Average Annual Attendance: 100,000; Mem: dues $25
Income: Financed by federal, state & city appropriations, mem, foundation & corporate support
Publications: Caribe Magazine, irregular; occasional papers
Activities: Adult & children classes; concerts; conferences; curriculum development; cultural arts progs; lects open to pub, 5-10 vis lectrs per yr; original objects of art lent to nonprofit organizations, universities & colleges; originate traveling exhibs; retail store sells books, reproductions, artifacts from the Caribbean, Latin America & Africa

A **CATHARINE LORILLARD WOLFE ART CLUB, INC,** 802 Broadway, New York, NY 10003-4804. Elec Mail info@clwac.org; Internet Home Page Address: www.clwac.org; *Pres* Joyce Zeller; *VPres Historian* Frank DeBevoise; *VPres Painting* Naomi Campbell; *VPres Sculpture* Gloria Spevacek; *VPres Catalog* Gaile Snow Gibbs; *Treas* Kathy Krantz Fieramosea; *Sec* Jeanette Koumijian
Estab 1896, incorporated in as a nonprofit club to further fine, representational American Art; A club of professional women painters, graphic artists & sculptors; Mem: 325; dues $45 assoc mem $25; monthly meetings; acceptance in 3 annual exhibs in a 10-year period
Income: Financed by mems
Exhibitions: Members Exhibition (spring); Open Annual Exhibition (fall); Occasional mems & assoc shows
Activities: Lects for mems only, 2 vis lectrs per yr; Metropolitan Museum Benefit, annually; lect; demonstration progs; 8 awards approx $10,000 in 2-3 shows per yr

M **CATHEDRAL OF SAINT JOHN THE DIVINE,** 1047 Amsterdam Ave, New York, NY 10025-1798. Tel 212-316-7490 (General), 316-7540 (visitors center); Tel 212-932-7347 (Tours); Elec Mail info@stjohndivine.org; Internet Home Page Address: www.stjohndivine.org/; *Reverend Canon* Jay D Wegman
Open Mon - Sat 7 AM - 6 PM, Sun 7 AM - 7 PM; No individual admis fee, donations accepted; groups $1 per person; Estab 1974; The museum building was erected in the 1820's & forms part of the complex of the Cathedral of Saint John the Divine; Average Annual Attendance: 500,000
Income: Financed by federal government appropriations & Cathedral assistance
Special Subjects: Religious Art
Collections: Old Master Paintings; decorative arts; sculptures; silver; tapestries; vestments
Exhibitions: Monthly Photography Exhibitions; annual exhibitions planned to spotlight specific areas of the Cathedral's permanent art collection
Activities: Lect open to public, 10 vis lectrs per year; concerts; gallery talks; tours
L **Library,** 1047 Amsterdam Ave, New York, NY 10025. Tel 212-316-7495; *Vol Librn* Madeleine L'Engle
No admis fee; For reference only
Income: $3,000

M **CENTER FOR BOOK ARTS,** 28 W 27th St 3rd Fl, New York, NY 10001-0000. Tel 212-481-0295; Fax 866-708-8994; Elec Mail info@centerforbookarts.org; Internet Home Page Address: www.centerforbookarts.org; *Exec Dir* Alexander Campos; *External Affairs Mgr* Louise Barry; *Admin* Kendra Sullivan; *Coll Specialist* Jen Larson; *Progs Mgr* Sarah Nicholls
Open Mon - Fri 10 AM - 4 PM, Sat 10 AM - 4 PM, cl Sun; No admis fee; Estab 1974, dedicated to contemporary bookmaking; 1 large gallery; Average Annual Attendance: 21,000; Mem: 800; dues $50 to $5,000
Income: Financed by earned and re-earned income
Library Holdings: Exhibition Catalogs; Original Art Works; Prints
Special Subjects: Prints, Etchings & Engravings
Collections: Book Arts Collection; Reference Library
Exhibitions: Annual Chapbook Poetry Competition, 3-4 changing exhibitions annually; Featured Artist Projects, 6 annually
Publications: Exhibition catalogues
Activities: Educ prog; classes for adults & children; lects open to pub, 15 vis lectrs per yr; gallery talks; tours; competitions with prizes; book travelling exhibs, 2 per yr; sales shop sells books, prints & exhib catalogs

M **CHELSEA ART MUSEUM,** 556 W 22nd St, New York, NY 10011-1108; PO Box 20157, New York, NY 10011-0002. Tel 212-255-0719; Fax 212-255-2368; Elec Mail contact@chelseaartmuseum.org; Internet Home Page Address: www.chelseaartmuseum.org

A **CHILDREN'S ART CARNIVAL,** 62 Hamilton Terrace, New York, NY 10031. Tel 212-234-4093; Fax 212-234-4011; Elec Mail info@childrensartcarnival.org; Internet Home Page Address: www.childrensartcarnival.org; *Exec Dir* Pamela Babb; *Prog Dir* Misha McGlown
Open Mon - Thurs 9 AM - 6 PM, Sat 9 AM - 1 PM; No admis fee; Estab 1969 as a center for children; Maintains reference library; Average Annual Attendance: 10,000
Activities: Classes for adults & children; awards; scholarships offered; book traveling exhibitions 3 per year

M **CHILDREN'S MUSEUM OF MANHATTAN,** 212 W 83rd St, The Tisch Bldg New York, NY 10024-4901. Tel 212-721-1223; Fax 212-721-1127; Elec Mail info@cmom.org; Internet Home Page Address: www.cmom.org; *Exec Dir* Andrew Ackerman; *Deputy Dir Exhibits* Karen Snider; *Deputy Dir Educ & Guest Svcs* Leslie Bushara; *Dir Fin & Admin* Candice Carnage
Open Tues - Sun 10 AM - 5 PM; Admis $10; Estab 1973 as a children's museum & art center featuring participatory art, science & nature exhibits; Average Annual Attendance: 350,000; Mem: 4,000; dues $20 - $395, corp mem $5,000 - 25,000
Income: $4,100,000 (financed by city, state, federal, corporate & foundation support, admis, mem, donations, program fees, tuition & sales shop)
Publications: Monthly calendars; program brochures
Activities: Educ dept with parent/child workshops, toddler progs, summer day camp, outreach, performing artists, volunteer/intern training, teacher training prog; classes for families; originates traveling exhibs to other children's mus; mus sales shop sells books, games, prints & toys

M **CHINA INSTITUTE IN AMERICA,** China Institute Gallery, 125 E 65th St, New York, NY 10065-7088. Tel 212-744-8181; Fax 212-628-4159; Elec Mail wchang@chinainstitute.org; Elec Mail gallery@chinainstitute.org; Internet Home Page Address: www.chinainstitute.org; *Dir Galleries* Willow Hai Chang; *Pres* Sara Judge McCalpin; *Dir Arts & Culture Progs* Agnes Hsin-Mei Hsu; *Gallery Registrar & Mgr* Jennifer Lima; *Gallery Coordr* Eva Wen; *Mgr AA Educ Prog (DCTA)* Yue Ma
Open Mon - Sun 10 AM - 5 PM, Tues & Thurs 10 AM - 8 PM; Admis adult $7, students & seniors $5, free Tues & Thurs 6 -8 PM; Estab 1966 to promote a knowledge of Chinese culture & art; Two-room gallery; Average Annual Attendance: 12,000; Mem: 950; dues gen $65, dual family $115, student/sr/faculty/out-of-metro area resident $50, dual student/senior $90
Publications: Exhibition catalogs
Activities: Classes for adults & children; docent training; hands on workshops; lects open to public; concerts; gallery talks; tours; one traveling exhib per yr; originate traveling exhibs; sales shop sells books

A **CHINESE-AMERICAN ARTS COUNCIL,** 456 Broadway, Fl 3 New York, NY 10013. Tel 212-431-9740; Fax 212-431-9789; Elec Mail info@caacarts.org; Internet Home Page Address: www.caacarts.org; *Exec Dir* Alan Chow; *Gallery Cur* Vivian Huang
Open Mon - Fri Noon - 5 PM; No admis fee; Estab 1975 to provide exhibition space to Chinese-American artists; Gallery 456 opened 1989; 700 sq ft with track lighting; Average Annual Attendance: 600 - 800; Mem: 300; dues $10 - $100
Income: Financed by endowment, city & state appropriation & private funds
Special Subjects: Asian Art
Collections: Slide Registry: biographies of Chinese American artists
Exhibitions: 10 - 12 exhibs annually
Activities: Classes for children; performances; concerts

L **CITY COLLEGE OF THE CITY UNIVERSITY OF NEW YORK,** Morris Raphael Cohen Library, 160 Convent Ave, New York, NY 10031-9198. Tel 212-650-7611; Fax 212-650-7604; Elec Mail reference@ccny.cuny.edu; Internet Home Page Address: www1.ccny.cuny.edu/library/; *Head Reference Div* Shea Taylor; *Chief Librn* Pamela Gillespie; *Archivist* Sydney Van Nort; *Architecture Librn* Judy Connorton; *Art/Architecture Visual Resources Librn* Ching-Jung Chen; *Chief of User Services* Robert Laurich
Open Mon - Thurs 8 AM - 11 PM, Fri 8 AM - 9 PM, Sat 9 AM -6 PM, Sun Noon - 6 PM, Dec 1 - 23 Sat - Sun 9 AM - 9 PM; No admis fee; Estab 1847 to support the educ at the City College; Atrium ca 7,000 sf; archives gallery 1300 sf; Average Annual Attendance: 500,000
Library Holdings: Book Volumes 27,000; Clipping Files; Compact Disks; DVDs; Exhibition Catalogs; Fiche; Memorabilia; Original Art Works 1,300; Other Holdings 1,290,000 Digital Images; Pamphlets; Periodical Subscriptions 60; Photographs 45,000; Prints 500; Sculpture; Slides 135,000
Special Subjects: Art History, Folk Art, Landscape Architecture, Decorative Arts, Film, Illustration, Photography, Drawings, Etchings & Engravings, Graphic Arts,

Graphic Design, Islamic Art, Manuscripts, Painting-American, Painting-British, Painting-French, Painting-Italian, Sculpture, Painting-European, Historical Material, Judaica, Portraits, Watercolors, Ceramics, Conceptual Art, Theatre Arts, Ethnology, Interior Design, Art Education, Video, American Indian Art, Anthropology, Costume Design & Constr, Mosaics, Afro-American Art, Jewelry, Oriental Art, Textiles, Landscapes, Antiquities-Greek, Architecture
Collections: History of Costume; Artistic Properties Collection
Exhibitions: 6-10 exhibitions per yr
Publications: CircumSpice newsletter
Activities: Lects open to public; 2-8 vis lectrs per yr; concerts; gallery talks; lending of original objects of art to recognized museums; books traveling exhibs 1 per yr; originates traveling exhibs to institutions in NYC metro area & also upon request; sales shop sells posters from exhibs

L **Architecture Library,** 160 Convent Ave, New York, NY 10031-9101. Tel 212-650-8766; *Librn* Judy Connorton
Reference use for public; circulation for patrons with CUNY ID's
Library Holdings: Audio Tapes; Book Volumes 20,500; Clipping Files; Fiche; Periodical Subscriptions 48; Reels
Special Subjects: Landscape Architecture, Architecture

M **CITY OF NEW YORK PARKS & RECREATION,** Arsenal Gallery, 64th St at Fifth Ave, Arsenal Bldg 3rd Fl New York, NY 10021; The Arsenal Central Park, 830 Fifth Ave New York, NY 10065-7095. Tel 212-360-8163; Fax 212-360-1329; Elec Mail jennifer.lantzas@parks.nyc.gov; Internet Home Page Address: www.nyc.gov/parks; *Cur* Jennifer Lantzas
Open Mon - Fri 9 AM - 5 PM; No admis fee; The purpose is to show art based on natural & urban themes; Large open space in third floor of Arsenal building. Working busy space - work must be hung from monofilament line & molding hooks
Collections: Mixed Media-Park & Nature themes
Exhibitions: Six week shows
Activities: Lects open to pub, 8 vis lectrs per yr

COLLEGE ART ASSOCIATION
For further information, see National and Regional Organization

COLOR ASSOCIATION OF THE US
For further information, see National and Regional Organizations

L **COLUMBIA UNIVERSITY,** Avery Architectural & Fine Arts Library, 1172 Amsterdam Ave, MC-0301, New York, NY 10027. Tel 212-854-3501; Elec Mail avery@libraries.cul.columbia.edu; Internet Home Page Address: www.columbia.edu/cu/web/indiv/avery/index.html; *Dir* Carole Ann Fabian; *Cur Drawings & Archives* Janet Parks; *Ed, Avery Index* Ted Goodman; *Sr Bibliographer* Paula Gabbard; *Assoc Dir* Kitty Chibnik; *Cur Avery Classics* Carolyn Yerkes
Open during Fall & Spring school terms Mon - Thurs 9 AM - 11 PM, Fri & Sat 9 AM - 9 PM, Sun 10 AM - 7 PM; Estab 1890; Circ non-circulating; Primarily for reference; Average Annual Attendance: 177,000
Library Holdings: Book Volumes 450,000; CD-ROMs; DVDs; Fiche; Manuscripts; Maps; Memorabilia; Other Holdings Original documents; Periodical Subscriptions 1,000; Prints; Reels
Special Subjects: Art History, Architecture
Collections: Over 1.5 million original architectural drawings & manuscripts, mainly American
Publications: Catalog of Avery Memorial Architectural Library; Avery Index to Architectural Periodicals (available as a data base)

L **Dept of Art History & Archaeology,** 826 Schermerhorn Hall, 1190 Amersterdam Ave New York, NY 10027-6900. Tel 212-854-2118; Fax 212-854-7329; Internet Home Page Address: www.columbia.edu/cu/arthistory/; *Dept Chair* Holger A Klein
Library Holdings: Lantern Slides 70,000; Other Holdings Gallery announcements 15,000; Photographs 250,000; Slides 500,000
Collections: Berenson I-Tatti Archive; Dial Iconographic Index; Haseloff Archive; Bartsch Collection; Gaigleres Collection; Arthur Kingsley Porter Collection; Ware Collection; Courtauld Collection; Marburger Index; Windsor Castle; Chatsworth Collection; Millard Meiss Collection

M **Miriam & Ira D Wallach Art Gallery,** Schermerhorn Hall, 8th Fl, New York, NY 10027; 1190 Amsterdam Ave, 826 Schermerhorn Hall New York, NY 10027-7054. Tel 212-854-7288; Fax 212-854-7800; Internet Home Page Address: www.columbia.edu/cu/wallach; *Dir* Sarah Elliston Weiner; *Asst Dir* Jeanette Silverthorne
Open Fall: Wed - Sat 1 - 5 PM, cl Sun - Tues, cl June 15 thru Sept 6; No admis fee; Estab 1987 to complement the educational goals of Columbia University & to embody the research interests of faculty & graduate students; 5 rooms, 2,300 sq ft, 310 running ft; Average Annual Attendance: 4,000
Income: $60,000 (financed by endowment & university)
Exhibitions: Temporary exhibitions only; 4 exhibitions annually during acad yr
Publications: Exhibition catalogs
Activities: Lects open to public; 3 - 6 vis lectrs per yr; gallery talks; tours; originate traveling exhibs to public art institutions

M **CONGREGATION EMANU-EL,** Bernard Judaica Museum, One E 65th St, New York, NY 10021-6596. Tel 212-744-1400; Fax 212-570-0826; *Sr Cur* Elka Deitsch; *Senior Rabbi* Dr David M Posner; *Pres* Marcia Waxman; *VPres* Neil B Cooper; *VPres* Kenneth A Cowin; *VPres* Karen Greenberg
Open daily 10 AM - 4:30 PM; No admis fee; Estab 1928 as a Judaica museum; Building is a landmark & is open for touring
Income: Financed by subvention from congregation
Collections: Congregational Memorabilia; Paintings; Borders & Boundaries: Maps of the Holy Land, 15th - 19th Centuries; Kabbalah: Mysticism in Jewish Life
Exhibitions: Seasonal exhibits; Congregational History; Photographic exhibit of stained glass; A Temple Treasury, The Judaica Collection of Congregation Emanu-El of the City of New York
Activities: Docent training; lects open to public, 2 -4 vis lectrs per year; gallery talks & tours

M **COOPER-HEWITT NATIONAL DESIGN MUSEUM,** Smithsonian Institution, 2 E 91st St, New York, NY 10128-8330. Tel 212-849-8400; Fax 212-849-8401; Elec Mail cheducation@si.edu; Internet Home Page Address: www.cooperhewitt.org; *Cur Drawings & Prints* Gail Davidson; *Cur Textiles* Matilda McQuaid; *Cur Contemporary Design* Ellen Lupton; *Cur Wallcoverings* Gregory Herringshaw; *Cur Dir* Cara McCarty; *Cur, Product Design & Dec Arts* Sarah Coffin; *Cur* Cynthia Smith; *Educ Dir* Caroline Payson; *Assoc Dir* Caroline Baumann; *Communs & Mktg Dir* Jennifer Northrop; *Develop Dir* Sophia Amaro; *Dir* Bill Moggridge; *Registrar* Steve Langehough; *Textile Conservator* Lucy Commoner

Open Mon - Sat 10 AM - 5 PM, Sun noon - 6 PM, cl Thanksgiving, Christmas & New Year's Day; galleries cl for renovation & will reopen fall of 2013; free access to the shop & Arthur Ross Terrace & Garden; Admis adults $15, seniors & students with ID $10, mems & children under 12 free; Founded 1897 as the Cooper Union Museum, to serve the needs of scholars, artisans, students, designers & everyone who deals with the built environment; Museum is based on large & varied collections of historic & contemporary design & a library strong in those fields; changing exhibitions are based on the museum's vast collections or loan shows illustrative of how design affects everyone's daily life; its emphasis on educ is expanded by special courses & seminars related to design in all forms & of all periods; the galleries occupy the first & second floors; exhibitions relate to the collections & other aspects of design. Maintains library (Bureau of the Smithsonian Institution); Average Annual Attendance: 200,000; Mem: 10,000; dues $75-$2500

Income: Financed by private contributions, mem & partly Smithsonian Institution

Special Subjects: Silver, Architecture, Drawings, Latin American Art, Prints, Watercolors, Textiles, Ceramics, Crafts, Pottery, Etchings & Engravings, Afro-American Art, Decorative Arts, Manuscripts, Posters, Furniture, Glass, Jewelry, Porcelain, Metalwork, Carpets & Rugs, Historical Material, Calligraphy, Embroidery, Gold, Cartoons, Pewter, Leather, Bookplates & Bindings

Collections: Drawings including works by Frederic Church, Winslow Homer, Thomas Moran & other 19th century American artists; ceramics, furniture & woodwork, glass, original drawings & designs for architecture & the decorative arts; 15th-20th century prints; textiles, lace, wallpaper; 200,000 works representing a span of 24 centuries; wall coverings; Contemporary Design; Industrial Design

Publications: Books on decorative arts; collection handbooks; exhibition catalogues; National Design Journal

Activities: Classes for adults & children; performances; docent training; Master's Degree prog in Decorative Arts through Parsons; lects open to pub, 50-100 vis lectrs per yr; concerts; gallery talks; tours; National Design awards; fellowships offered; paintings & original objects of art lent to other mus; lending collection contains original art works, original prints & 40,000 books; book traveling exhibs; originate traveling exhibs; mus shop sells books & objects related to historical & contemporary design

L **Doris & Henry Dreyfuss Memorial Study Center Library & Archive,** 2 E 91st St, Fl 3 New York, NY 10128-8330. Tel 212-849-8330; Fax 212-849-8339; Elec Mail libmail@si.edu; Internet Home Page Address: www.cooperhewitt.org/collections/library.asp; www.sil.si.edu/libraries/CHM/; *Librn* Stephen H Van Dyk; *Ref Librn* Elizabeth Broman; *Librn* Jennifer Cohlman

Open Mon - Fri 9:30 AM - 5:30 PM to researchers by appt only; cl Federal holidays; No admis fee; Estab to serve staff of museum & students from Parsons School of Design; Interlibrary lending only (branch of Smithsonian Institution Libraries)

Income: Financed through SIL budgets

Library Holdings: Book Volumes 55,000; Cards; Clipping Files; Exhibition Catalogs; Fiche; Kodachrome Transparencies; Lantern Slides; Manuscripts; Memorabilia; Micro Print; Original Art Works; Other Holdings Original documents; Pictures & photographs 1,500,900; Pamphlets; Periodical Subscriptions 300; Photographs; Prints; Reels; Reproductions; Slides; Video Tapes

Special Subjects: Decorative Arts, Graphic Design, Advertising Design, Industrial Design, Interior Design

Collections: Spec Coll of Industrial & Graphic Designers; Donald Deskey Archive; Henry Dreyfuss Archive; Ladislav Sutnar Archive

A **CREATIVE TIME,** 59 E 4th St, Fl 6 New York, NY 10003-8963. Tel 212-206-6674; Fax 212-255-8467; Elec Mail info@creativetime.org; Internet Home Page Address: www.creativetime.org; *Pres & Artistic Dir* Anne Pasternak; *Deputy Dir* Katie Hollander; *Chief Cur* Nato Thompson; *Dir Opers* Cynthia Pringle; *Dir Events* Damewe Schmidt; *Mktg Dir* Anna Dinces; *Mktg Assoc* Jessica Shaefer

Open Mon - Fri 10 AM - 5 PM, exhibition hours vary depending on site; Admis performances $8, exhibitions usually free; Estab 1974; Venues include a variety of public locations; Average Annual Attendance: 50,000; Mem: 200; members give tax-deductible contributions

Income: $3,000,000 (financed by National Endowment for the Arts, NY State Council of the Arts, NYC Dept of Cultural Affairs, private corporations & foundations)

Library Holdings: Book Volumes; Exhibition Catalogs; Original Art Works; Prints

Exhibitions: Art in the Anchorage

Publications: Creative Time; biannual program/project catalogs

Activities: Multidisciplinary; lctrs open to pub; Annenberg prize; sales shop sells books

A **DESIGN COMMISSION OF THE CITY OF NEW YORK,** 1 City Hall, Fl 3 New York, NY 10007-1298. Tel 212-788-3071; Fax 212-788-3086; *Exec Dir* Jackie Snyder; *Pres* James P Stuckey

Open by appointment only; No admis fee; Estab 1898 to review designs for city buildings, landscape architecture & works of art proposed for city owned property. Portraits are installed in Governors Room and other areas in City Hall; Mem: 11

Income: Financed by city appropriation

Collections: 100 portraits of historic figures, state, city and national

Publications: The Art Commission & Municipal Art Society Guide to Outdoor Sculpture by Margot Gayle & Michele Cohen; Imaginary Cities, European Views from the Collection of the Art Commission; National Directory of Design Review Agencies (1991); New York Re-Viewed, Exhibition Catalogue of 19th & 20th Century Photographs from the Collection of the Art Commission

A **Associates of the Art Commission, Inc,** 1 City Hall, Fl 3 New York, NY 10007-1298. Tel 212-788-3071; Fax 212-788-3086; Internet Home Page Address: www.nyc-gov/artcommission; *Exec Dir* Deborah Bershad

Estab 1913 to advise and counsel Art Commission as requested; Mem: 35; dues $35; annual meeting in Jan

Income: Financed by mem

M **DIEU DONNE PAPERMILL, INC,** Gallery, 315 W 36th St, New York, NY 10018-6404. Tel 212-226-0573; Fax 212-226-6088; Internet Home Page Address: www.dieudonne.org; *Exec Dir* Kathleen Flynn; *Artistic Dir* Paul Wong; *Prog Mgr* Jessica Svenson; *Studio Mgr & Collaborator* Amy Jacobs; *Registrar & Gallery Asst* Molly Nutt

Open Tues - Fri 10 - 6 PM, Sat Noon - 6 PM & by appt; No admis fee; Estab 1976 to promote the art of hand papermaking; Editions gallery for recent works at Dieu Donne, main gallery works in hand paper; maintains archive & reference library; Mem: Dues artist & friend $50, contributor $125, editions club $500, collectors series $800, publishers support $1500, papermaking patron $3500, corp sponsor $10,000

Collections: Chase Manhattan Banks; Johnson & Johnson; Rutgers University; Zimmerli Art Museum; Metropolitan Museum of Art

Exhibitions: Melvin Edwards Aqua y Acero en Papel

Publications: Pulp, quarterly newsletter; exhib catalogs

Activities: Classes for adults & children; lects open to pub, 5 vis lectrs per yr; gallery talks; tours; competitions; scholarships offered; original objects of art lent to members & institutions; lending collection contains books, slides & works in handmade paper; originate traveling exhibs; sales shop sells books, original art & products in handmade paper, Dieu Donne paper

A **THE DRAWING CENTER,** 35 Wooster St, New York, NY 10013-5300. Tel 212-219-2166; Fax 212-966-2976; Elec Mail info@drawingcenter.org; Internet Home Page Address: www.drawingcenter.org; *Exec Dir* Brett Littman; *Co Chmn* Frances Beatty Adler; *Co Chmn* Eric Rudin; *Exec Ed* Jonathan T.D. Neil; *Educ Dir* Aimee Good; *Cur* Claire Gilman; *Cur Viewing Prog* Nina Katchadourian; *Coordr Opers* Dan Gillespie; *Reg* Anna Martin; *Asst Cur* Joanna Kleinberg; *Asst Cur* Rachel Liebowitz; *Mng Ed* Joanna Ahlberg; *Pub Rels & Mktg Officer* Emily Gaynor

Open Sept - July Wed & Fri - Sun noon - 6 PM, Thurs noon - 8 PM; cl Mon, Tues, New Year's Day, Thanksgiving, Christmas; Admis $3 suggested; Estab 1977 to express the quality & diversity of drawing through exhib & educ; 3,630 sq ft gallery; Average Annual Attendance: 55,000; Mem: 200; dues artist $35, individual $50, dual $85, contributor $150, supporter $300, assoc $500, donor $1,000, friend $2,500, corporate $5,000

Income: Pvt & pub support

Special Subjects: Drawings

Publications: Exhib catalogs; Drawing Papers publ series

Activities: Classes for children; lects open to pub & for mems only, 20 vis lectrs per yr; concerts; gallery talks; tours; internship program offered; originate traveling exhibs to major national & international museums; mus shop sells books & limited edition prints

M **EARTHFIRE,** Art from Detritus: Recycling with Imagination, PO Box 1149, New York, NY 10013-0866. Tel 212-925-4419; Elec Mail ncognita@earthfire.org; Internet Home Page Address: www.ncognita.com; www.artfromdetritus.com; *Founder & Exec Dir* Vernita Nemec

Open by appointment & during exhibit hours; No admis fee; Estab 1993 to raise environmental awareness by organizing exhibits of art made primarily from recycling trash, found objects, throwaways & discarded material that would have otherwise polluted the planet; Circ 4 catalogs available; Exhibition available for travel and adaptable to site; Average Annual Attendance: 5,000

Income: Financed by grants, pub & private contributions incl Puffin Found & Kauffmann Found, nat recycling coalition

Exhibitions: Art From Detritus: Recycling with Imagination

Publications: Exhibit catalogues (1-4)

Activities: Classes for adults & children; lects open to pub, gallery talks, tours; exhib grant from Kaufmann Found for exhibit in Kansas City; Puffin Grant, 2007; sponsorship (NRC) Nat Recycling Coalition, 1994-96; originates traveling exhibs annually, to universities, conferences, corporate galleries & municipal organizations; mus shop sells catalogs of past exhibitions by mail, original art

M **EL MUSEO DEL BARRIO,** 1230 5th Ave, New York, NY 10029-4401. Tel 212-831-7272; Fax 212-831-7927; Elec Mail info@elmuseo.org; Internet Home Page Address: www.elmuseo.org; *Exec Asst Dir* Georgina Nichols; *Dir Cur Progs* Deborah Cullen; *Cur* Elvis Fuentes; *Registrar* Melisa Lujan; *Permanent Coll Mgr* Noel Valentin; *Exhib Mgr & Asst Cur* Trinidad Fombella; *Assoc Cur, Special Projects* Rocio Aranda-Alvarado; *Curatorial Asst* Stephanie Spahr

Open Tues - Sat 11 AM 6 - PM, Wed 11 AM - 9 PM, cl Mon; Admis adults $9 seniors & students with ID $5, children under 12 when accompanied by adult & mems no charge, seniors no charge on Wed, 3rd Sat of month no charge; Estab 1969 to conserve & display works by Puerto Rican artists & other Hispanic artists; Located on Museum Mile. Gallery space divided into 4 wings: Northwest Wing houses Santos de Palo, East Gallery will house Pre-Columbian installation, F-Stop Gallery devoted to photography & Children's Wing opened fall of 1982; Average Annual Attendance: 21,000; Mem: Mems $50 - $2,500+

Collections: 16mm Films on History, Culture and Art; 300 Paintings and 5000 Works on Paper, by Puerto Rican and other Latin American Artists; Pre-Columbian Caribbean Artifacts; Santos (Folk Religious Carvings)

Activities: Classes for adults & children; dramatic progs; children's workshops; lects open to pub, 25 vis lectrs per yr; concerts; gallery talks; tours; awards; schols; individual & original objects of art lent to other mus & galleries; originate traveling exhibs; Junior Museum; 510 seat theatre

A **ELECTRONIC ARTS INTERMIX (EAI),** 535 W 22nd St 5th Fl, New York, NY 10011-1119. Tel 212-337-0680; Fax 212-337-0679; Elec Mail info@eai.org; Internet Home Page Address: www.eai.org; *Exec Dir* Lori Zippay; *Distribution Dir* Rebecca Cleman; *Distribution Mgr* Nick Lesley; *Media Art Coll Mgr* Desiree Leary

Open Mon - Fri 10 AM - 6 PM; Viewing Room open by appt Mon - Fri 11 AM - 5 PM; No admis fee for individuals; group fee negotiable; Estab 1971 as a

nonprofit corporation to assist artists seeking to explore the potentials of the electronic media, particularly television, as a means of personal expression; Viewing Room provides access to EAI coll
Income: Financed by videotape & editing fees & in part by federal & state funds & contributions
Library Holdings: DVDs; Video Tapes
Collections: Over 3,500 works from 200+ artists of video art & digital art projects from mid 1960's-present; A Kinetic History: The EAI Archives Online
Exhibitions: Periodic exhibs
Publications: Electronic Arts Intermix Videocassette Catalog, annual; Online Resource Guide for Exhibiting, Collecting & Preserving Media Art
Activities: Lects open to pub; film screenings; artist talks; panels; performances; internships available; sales shop sells copies of all media in coll in various formats

M **EMEDIALOFT.ORG,** 55 Bethune St Ste A-629, New York, NY 10014-1791. Tel 212-924-4893; Mobile 646-541-4772; Elec Mail xyz@eMediaLoft.org; Internet Home Page Address: eMediaLoft.org; *Co-Dir* Bill Creston; *Co-Dir, Cur & Grants Officer* Barbara Rosenthal; *Pres* C T Rhodes
Open Tues - Sun 11 AM - 4 PM & by appointment; No admis fee; Estab 1982 for artists in video production, artists' books, photography, performance text art, ideas; Conceptual photography, video, post production area, photo studio, darkroom, performance and avant-garde art & documentation; display walls, book shelves, 950 sq ft; maintains reference library; currently houses 7,000 vols & 1,000 papers Barbara Rosenthal authors archives; Average Annual Attendance: 300
Income: $40,000 (financed by private funds & facility fees)
Purchases: Video & audio equipment, filing & office equipment, computer equipment
Library Holdings: Audio Tapes; Book Volumes; Cards; Cassettes; DVDs; Exhibition Catalogs; Manuscripts; Memorabilia; Motion Pictures; Original Art Works; Original Documents; Periodical Subscriptions; Photographs; Slides; Video Tapes
Special Subjects: Conceptual Art, Drawings, Photography
Collections: Artists books, art books, classic literature
Exhibitions: Artists books & photos, videotapes, super 8 film, video, Performance
Publications: Exhibit catalogs
Activities: Educ prog; one-on-one workshops; digital video & photog workshops; individual training in media performance; writing; photog; screenings open to pub; creative projects grant offered; original objects of art lent to exhibitors; lending collection contains artists' books, videos, photos to galleries & museums; originate traveling exhibs to film & video artists; sales shop sells books, original art, photos, videos

M **FASHION INSTITUTE OF TECHNOLOGY,** The Museum at FIT, 7th Ave at 27th St, New York, NY 10001-5992. Tel 212-217-4536; Fax 212-217-4531; Elec Mail museuminfo@fitnyc.edu; tanya_melendez@fitynyc.edu; Internet Home Page Address: www.fitnyc.edu/museum; *Dir* Dr Valerie Steele; *Deputy Dir* Patricia Mears; *Educ Cur* Tanya Melendez; *Sr Conservator* Ann Coppinger; *Registrar* Sonia Dingilian; *Exhib Mgr* Michael Goitia; *Senior Cur* Fred Dennis
Open Tues - Fri Noon - 8 PM, Sat 10 AM - 5 PM, cl Sun, Mon & holidays; No admis fee; Estab 1967; 6,000 sq ft of space divided into three galleries; Average Annual Attendance: 100,000; Mem: 70; dues $1,000
Income: Financed by city, state, endowment & grants
Purchases: fashion, accessories & textile collections
Special Subjects: Textiles, Costumes
Publications: Exhibit catalogs
Activities: Lect open to public, 14 vis lectrs per yr; gallery talks; tours, lects & annual fashion symposium

L **Gladys Marcus Library - SUNY,** 7th Ave at 27th St, New York, NY 10001-5992. Tel 212-217-4370; Fax 212-217-4371; Internet Home Page Address: www.fitnyc.edu/library; *FIT Spec Coll & Archives* Karen T. Cannell; *Dir* N J Wolfe; *Assoc Dir* Greta K Earnest; *Evening Access Servs & ILL* Paul Lajoie; *Elec Resources & Serials* Lana Bittman; *Head Acquisitions & Metadata servs* Leslie Preston; *Head Research Instr Servs* Helen T. Lane; *Daytime Access Servs Mgr* Jennifer Mak; *Library Tech Servs* Jana Duda; *Graphics Lab* Jasper Lin
Open Mon - Thurs 8 AM - 12 midnight, Fri 8 AM - 6:30 PM, Sat 10 - 5 PM, Sun noon - 9 PM; Estab 1944 to meet the acad needs of the students & faculty & to serve as a resource for the fashion & related industries; Circ 59,500; For reference only; Average Annual Attendance: 78,000; Mem: SUNY, METRO, NYLINK, NYLA
Income: $2,467,531, SUNY
Purchases: $349,336
Library Holdings: Audio Tapes; Book Volumes 168,897; CD-ROMs; Cards; Cassettes; Clipping Files; Compact Disks; DVDs; Exhibition Catalogs; Fiche 4712; Filmstrips 357; Memorabilia; Micro Print; Motion Pictures; Original Art Works 184; Original Documents; Other Holdings Artist Books, Online Database; Pamphlets; Periodical Subscriptions 350; Photographs; Prints; Reels; Reproductions; Slides; Video Tapes
Special Subjects: Art History, Decorative Arts, Graphic Design, Advertising Design, Fashion Arts, Interior Design, Furniture, Costume Design & Constr, Jewelry
Collections: Oral History Project on the Fashion Industry; several sketchbook colls; Fashion Illustration

FEDERATION OF MODERN PAINTERS & SCULPTORS
For further information, see National and Regional Organizations

M **FIRST STREET GALLERY,** 526 W 26th St, Rm 209, New York, NY 10001-5518. Tel 646-336-8053; Fax 646-336-8054; Elec Mail firststreetgallery@earthlink.net; Internet Home Page Address: www.firststreetgallery.net; *Mem Dir* Michele Liebler; *Pres* Suz Evaleuko; *Sec* Kathi Parker
Open Tues - Sat 11 AM - 6 PM; No admis fee; Estab 1969 to promote figurative art as well as selected non-objective art & artists; Artist-run 501(c)(3) organization; Average Annual Attendance: 5,600; Mem: 23; dues $195 non-local artists, $135 local artists; monthly meetings, see website for more information
Income: Financed by dues, contributions, grants, juried exhib entry fees, etc.
Exhibitions: 2013-2014 season: 7 solo shows; 1 group members show; (01/2014) 3 Pop Ups; (06/2014-07/2014) 2 competition shows (Natiional Juried Exhibs); (07/2014-08/2014) MFA National Juried Exhib for non-mems
Publications: 40th Anniversary Exhib Catalog, Dec 2009
Activities: Gallery talks; competitions; outreach exhibs for non-mem artists to engage the pub; originate traveling exhibs

C **FORBES MAGAZINE, INC,** Forbes Collection, 60 5th Ave, New York, NY 10011-8868. Tel 212-206-5549; Elec Mail mkellytrombly@forbes.com; *Dir* Margaret Kelly Trombly
Open Tues - Sat 10 AM - 4 PM, Thurs group tours; No admis fee; Estab 1985
Collections: Antique Toys; Faberge Imperial Eggs Collection; French Military Paintings; Presidential Papers; Toy Soldiers
Activities: Gallery talks; individual paintings & original objects of art lent to museums & galleries

M **FRAUNCES TAVERN MUSEUM,** 54 Pearl St, New York, NY 10004-4300. Tel 212-425-1778; Fax 212-509-3467; Elec Mail publicity@frauncestavernmuseum.org; Elec Mail 2director@frauncestavern; Internet Home Page Address: www.frauncestavernmuseum.org; *Develop Officer* Linda Goldberg; *Pub Rels Officer* Andrea Homan; *Cur & Dir* Marion Grzesiak; *Registrar* Stephen Fenney; *Accounting* Cecelia Mahnken; *Bldg Mgr* Bruce Barraclough; *Admin* Margaret O'Shaughnessy; *Dir* Andrew Batten; *Mktg Coordr* Jennifer Eaton; *VChmn* Laurence Simpson
Open Mon - Sat 10 AM - 5 PM; Admis adults $3, students, children & seniors $2; Estab 1907 for focus on early American history, culture, historic preservation & New York City history; Museum is housed in the site of eighteenth-century Fraunces Tavern and four adjacent nineteenth-century buildings. The museum houses two fully furnished period rooms: the Long Room, site of George Washington's farewell to his officers at the end of the Revolutionary War, and the Clinton Room, a nineteenth-century dining room; Mem: 500; dues $20 - $1000
Collections: 17th, 18th, 19th & 20th century prints, paintings, artifacts & decorative arts relating to early American history, culture & historic preservation; New York City history; George Washington & other historic figures in American history
Exhibitions: Various exhib
Publications: Exhibit catalogs
Activities: Educ dept; docent training; lects open to pub; tours; demonstrations; films; off-site programs; individual paintings lent to qualified mus & historical organizations, lending collection contains 750 original works of art, 150 original prints, & 1,300 decorative art & artifacts; book traveling exhibs; mus shop sells books, reproductions, prints & slides

L **FRENCH INSTITUTE-ALLIANCE FRANCAISE,** Library, 22 E 60th St 2nd Fl, New York, NY 10022-1077. Tel 212-355-6100 (Alliance); Tel 646-388-6655 (Library); Fax 212-935-4119 (Alliance & Library); Internet Home Page Address: www.fiaf.org; *Library Technical Asst* Ronda Murdock; *Librn* Katherine Branning; *Dir* David S Black
Open Mon - Thurs 11:30 AM - 8 PM, Sat 9:30 AM - 3 PM, cl Fri & Sun; No admis fee; Estab 1911 to encourage the study of the French language & culture; Library lends to members, reference only for non-members; maintains art gallery
Income: Financed by endowment & mem, tax deductible contributions & foundation grants
Library Holdings: Audio Tapes; Book Volumes 30,000; CD-ROMs; Cassettes 900; Exhibition Catalogs; Periodical Subscriptions 100; Video Tapes
Special Subjects: Film
Collections: Architecture, costume, decorative arts, paintings; French literature & culture
Exhibitions: Changes monthly; concentrates on up & coming artists
Activities: Classes given; lect open to public

L **THE FRICK COLLECTION,** Frick Art Reference Library, 10 E 71st St, New York, NY 10021-4967. Tel 212-547-0641; Fax 212-879-2091; Elec Mail library@frick.org; Internet Home Page Address: www.frick.org/library; *Dir Center for the History of Collecting* Inge Reist; *Chief, Coll Mgmt & Access* Deborah Kempe; *Chief, Coll Preservation* Don Swanson; *Chief Pub Servs* Suzannah Massen; *Chief Archives & Records Mgmt* Sally Brazil; *Andrew W Mellon Chief Librn* Stephen Bury
Open Mon - Fri 10 AM - 5 PM (Sept - May), Sat 9:30 AM - 1 PM (cl Sun, holidays, Sat in June & July, & Mon, Thurs, Fri in Aug; No admis fee; Estab 1920 as a reference library to serve adults & graduate students interested in the history of European & American painting, drawing, sculpture, illuminated manuscripts; For reference only; Average Annual Attendance: 6,000
Library Holdings: Auction Catalogs 75,000; Book Volumes 300,000; CD-ROMs 87; Compact Disks 100; DVDs 20; Exhibition Catalogs 95,400; Fiche 52,000; Other Holdings Mircofiche titles; Negatives 56,000; Architect Plans 5000-10,000 items; Periodical Subscriptions 700; Photographs 900,000; Reels 233; Video Tapes 13
Special Subjects: Art History, Decorative Arts, Painting-American, Painting-British, Painting-Dutch, Painting-Flemish, Painting-French, Painting-German, Painting-Italian, Painting-Russian, Painting-Spanish, Prints, Sculpture, Painting-European, Portraits, Watercolors, Ceramics, Bronzes, Porcelain, Furniture, Period Rooms, Painting-Polish, Enamels, Miniatures, Religious Art, Restoration & Conservation, Tapestries, Marine Painting, Landscapes, Painting-Scandinavian, Painting-Australian, Painting-Canadian, Painting-New Zealand
Collections: Archives (unrecorded); Helen Clay Frick Family Papers
Publications: Frick Art Reference Library Original Index to Art Periodicals; Frick Art Reference Library Sales Catalogue Index (microform); Spanish Artists from the Fourth to the Twentieth Century (4 vols); The Story of the Frick Art Reference Library: The Early Years, by Katharine McCook Knox; Archives Directory for the History of Collecting in America
Activities: Internships; fellowships; tours; awards, Sotheby's prize for a Distinguished Publication in the History of Collecting in America

M **FRICK COLLECTION,** 1 E 70th St, New York, NY 10021-4981. Tel 212-288-0700; Fax 212-628-4417; Elec Mail info@frick.org; Internet Home Page Address: www.frick.org; *Dir* Ian Wardropper; *Cur* Susan Grace Galassi; *Deputy Dir* Robert B Goldsmith; *Mgr Sales & Info* Kate Gerlough; *Registrar* Diane Farynyk; *Mgr Bldgs & Secy* Dennis F Sweeney; *Deputy Dir Extern Affairs* Tia Chapman
Open Tues - Sat 10 AM - 6 PM, Sun 11 AM - 5 PM; cl Mon, Jan 1, July 4, Thanksgiving, Dec 25; Admis adults $20, seniors (65+) $15, students w/ID $10,

children under 10 not admitted; Estab 1920; opened to public 1935 as a gallery of art; The Frick Collection is housed in the former residence of Henry Clay Frick (1849-1919), built in 1913-14 & alterations & additions were made 1931-1935 & further extension & garden were completed in 1977. The rooms are in the style of English & French interiors of the 18th century. Maintains art reference library; Average Annual Attendance: 325,300; Mem: 500 Fellows; dues $1,200 minimum contribution; 4,200 friends; dues $75 minimum contribution
Income: $23,300,000 (financed by endowment, mem, bookshop & admis)
Library Holdings: Auction Catalogs; Book Volumes; Exhibition Catalogs; Fiche; Pamphlets; Periodical Subscriptions; Photographs
Special Subjects: Drawings, Prints, Sculpture, Bronzes, Painting-European, Furniture, Porcelain, Renaissance Art, Painting-Italian
Collections: 15th-18th century sculpture, of which Renaissance bronzes are most numerous; 14th-19th century paintings, with fine examples of Western European masters & suites of Boucher & Fragonard decorations; Renaissance & French 18th century furniture; 17th-18th century Chinese & French porcelains; 16th century Limoges enamels; 16th-19th century drawings & prints
Exhibitions: (09/2013-12/2013) David d'Angers: Making the Modern Monument; (10/2013-01/2014) Vermeer, Rembrandt & Hals; (01/2014-06/2014) The Hill Collection
Publications: Art in the Frick Collection (paintings, sculpture & decorative arts); exhibition catalogs; The Frick Collection, illustrated catalog; guide to the galleries; handbook of paintings; Ingres & the Comtesse d'Haussonville; paintings from the Frick Collection; Building The Frick Collection
Activities: Docent training; Lects open to pub; concerts; gallery talks; originates traveling exhibs; mus shop sells books, prints, postcards & greeting cards

C **FRIED, FRANK, HARRIS, SHRIVER & JACOBSON,** Art Collection, One New York Plaza, New York, NY 10004. Tel 212-859-8000; Telex 747-1526; *Chmn* Arthur Fleischer Jr; *Preparator* Macyn Bolt
Open by appointment; Estab 1979 intended as a survey
Purchases: Over 1,000 pieces in all offices (NY, DC, LA & London)
Collections: Fried, Frank, Harris, Shriver & Jacobson Art Collection; Contemporary Art; Photography
Exhibitions: Permanent exhibition
Activities: Tours

M **GALLERY OF PREHISTORIC PAINTINGS,** 1202 Lexington Ave, Ste 314 New York, NY 10028. Tel 212-861-5152; *Dir* Douglas Mazonowicz
Open by appointment; No admis fee; Estab 1975 to make available to the pub the art works of prehistoric peoples, particularly the cave paintings of France, Spain & the Sahara Desert; Large display area; Average Annual Attendance: 10,000
Income: Financed by private funds
Special Subjects: Primitive art
Collections: Early American Indian Rock Art; Rock Art of Eastern Spain; Rock Art of the Sahara; serigraph reproduction editions of Cave Art of France and Spain
Publications: Newsletter, quarterly
Activities: Classes for adults & children; Cave Art-in-Schools Program; lects open to pub; gallery talks; tours; lending collection contains books, cassettes, framed reproductions, 1,000 Kodachromes, motion pictures, original prints, 1,000 photographs, 2,000 slides; originates traveling exhibs organized & circulated; sales shop selling books, magazines

L **Library,** 1202 Lexington Ave, Ste 314 New York, NY 10028. Tel 212-861-5152; *Dir* Douglas Mazonowicz
Open Mon - Fri 9 AM - 5 PM, Sat 9 AM - Noon; Estab 1975 to make information available to the general public concerning the art works of prehistoric peoples; For reference only
Library Holdings: Book Volumes 250; Cassettes; Clipping Files; Exhibition Catalogs; Framed Reproductions; Kodachrome Transparencies; Manuscripts; Motion Pictures; Pamphlets; Periodical Subscriptions 9; Photographs; Prints; Reproductions; Sculpture; Slides

M **GOETHE-INSTITUT NEW YORK,** Mini/Goethe-Institut Curatorial Residencies Ludlow St, 38 Ludlow St, New York, NY 10002-5425. Tel 212-228-6848; Elec Mail info@ludlow38.org; Internet Home Page Address: www.lvdluw38.org; Internet Home Page Address: www.goethe.de/newyork; *Dir* Dr Christoph Bartmann; *Head Prog Dept* Dr Wenzel Bilger; *Curatorial Res (2012)* Clara Meister; *Curatorial Res (2013)* Jakob Schillinger; *Prog Cur* Sara Stevenson
Open Thurs - Sun 1 PM - 6 PM; No admis fee; 2008; Downtown space for contemporary art of the Goethe-Institut New York with residency prog for young curators from Germany; Average Annual Attendance: 1500
Income: Financed by German government & BMW/Mini
Activities: Lect open to public; gallery talks; tours; exhibs; performances; publications; book sale at library once per yr

A **GRAPHIC ARTISTS GUILD,** 32 Broadway, Ste 1114, New York, NY 10004-1612. Tel 212-791-3400; Elec Mail execdir@gag.org; Internet Home Page Address: www.gag.org; *Exec Dir* Patricia McKiernan; *Pres* John Schmelzer; *Treas* Susan Mathews; *Sec* Lara Kisielewska
Open 10 AM - 6 PM; Estab 1967 to improve the economic & social condition of graphic artists; to provide legal & cr services to members; to increase pub appreciation of graphic art (including illustration, cartooning & design) as an art form; Mem: 1,300
Income: Financed by mem & publication sales
Publications: Cartooning books; GAG Directory of Illustration, annual; GAG Handbook, Pricing & Ethical Guidelines, biennial; monthly newsletter
Activities: Walter Hortens Memorial Awards for Distinguished Service & Outstanding Client

M **GREENWICH HOUSE POTTERY,** First Floor Gallery, 224 W 30th St, Ste 302 New York, NY 10001-4936. Tel 212-242-4106; Fax 212-645-5486; Elec Mail pottery@greenwichhouse.org; Internet Home Page Address: www.gharts.org; *Asst Dir* Lynne Lerner; *Prog Coordr* Jenine Repice; *Dir* Elizabeth Zawada
Open Mon 4 PM - 10 PM, Tues - Fri 9:30 AM - 10 PM, Sat 9:30 AM - 6 PM; No admis fee; First Floor Gallery displays works of its members

Activities: Classes for adults & children; lects open to pub, 10 vis lectrs per yr; competitions; schols & fellowships offered; mus shop sells original art

M **Jane Hartsook Gallery,** 16 Jones St, New York, NY 10014. Tel 212-242-4106; Fax 212-645-5486; Elec Mail pottery@greenwichhouse.org; Internet Home Page Address: www.gharts.org; *Dir* Sarah Archer; *Asst Dir* Adam Welch; *Mgr Educ & Studio Opers* Albert Pfarr; *Educ Coord* Lisa Chicoyne
Open Tues - Sat noon - 6 PM, or by appointment; No admis fee; Estab 1969 as a nonprofit venue for ceramic arts
Exhibitions: Artists on Their Own, annual juried exhibit
Activities: Classes for adults & children; lects open to pub, 10 vis lectrs per yr; competitions; schols offered; mus shop sells original art

L **Library,** 16 Jones St, New York, NY 10014. Tel 212-242-4106; Fax 212-645-5486; Internet Home Page Address: www.gharts.org; *Dir* Sarah Archer; *Asst Dir* Adam Welch
Hours vary, call for information; Estab 1909; For reference only
Library Holdings: Audio Tapes; Book Volumes 700; Exhibition Catalogs; Pamphlets; Periodical Subscriptions 10; Slides; Video Tapes
Special Subjects: Ceramics

L **GROLIER CLUB LIBRARY,** 47 E 60th St, New York, NY 10022-1098. Tel 212-838-6690; Fax 212-838-2445; Elec Mail ejh@grolierclub.org; Elec Mail mconstantinou@grolierclub.org; Internet Home Page Address: www.grolierclub.org; *Dir* Eric Holzenberg; *Pres* Eugene S Flamm; *Librn* Meghan R Constantinou; *Exhibs Coordr* Megan Smith
Open Mon - Fri 10 AM - 5 PM, cl Aug, New Year's Eve, New Year's Day, Presidents' Day, Martin Luther King Day, Memorial Day, Independence Day, Labor Day, Columbus Day, Thanksgiving Day & Fri following, Christmas Eve & Christmas Day; No admis fee; Estab 1884, devoted to the arts of the book; Mem: 800; annual meetings fourth Thurs of Jan
Purchases: $15,000
Library Holdings: Book Volumes 100,000; Periodical Subscriptions 35; Prints
Collections: Bookseller & auction catalogs from 17th century
Activities: Lect for members only

M **GUGGENHEIM MUSEUM SOHO,** 1071 5th Ave. at 89th St., New York, NY 10128-0112. Tel 212-423-3500; Fax 212-423-3787; Elec Mail publicaffairs@guggenheim.org; Internet Home Page Address: www.guggenheim.org; *Deputy Dir & Sr Cur* Lisa Dennison; *Deputy Dir Finance & Adminr* Roy Eddey; *Conservator* Paul Schwartzbaum; *Photographer* David Heald; *Asst to Dir* Desiree Baber; *Dir Pub Affairs* Betsy Ennis; *Dir* Thomas Krens; *Deputy Dir for Spec Projects* Laurie Beckelman; *Dir Mktg* Laura Miller; *Dir Develop* Melanie Forman
Open Thurs - Mon 11 AM - 6 PM, cl Tues, Wed & Christmas, open Christmas Eve & New Years Eve 11 AM - 5 PM; No admis fee; Estab 1992; Housed in a nineteenth century landmark building in SOHO's historic cast-iron district, which was designed by renowned architect Arata Isozaki
Special Subjects: Drawings, Painting-American, Photography, Sculpture, Watercolors, Painting-French, Painting-Spanish, Painting-Italian, Painting-German, Painting-Russian
Collections: Constantin Brancusi Sculpture Collection; Vasily Kandinsky Collection; Paul Klee Collection; Justin K Thannhauser Collection of Impressionist & Post-Impressionist Paintings
Exhibitions: Special exhibitions that complement those at Solomon R Guggenheim Museum with emphasis on multi-media & interactive art; ongoing virtual reality & CD-ROM installations related to art & architecture
Activities: Dramatic progs; docent training; symposia; family activities; teacher training; lects open to pub, 6 vis lectrs per yr; concerts; gallery talks; tours; competitions with prizes; mus shop sells books, original art & reproductions

GUILD OF BOOK WORKERS
For further information, see National and Regional Organizations

L **HAMPDEN-BOOTH THEATRE LIBRARY,** 16 Gramercy Park S, New York, NY 10003-1705. Tel 212-228-1861; Internet Home Page Address: www.hampden-booth.org; *Cur & Librn* Raymond Wemmlinger
Open Mon - Fri 10 AM - 5 PM & by appointment; Estab 1957 to provide scholarly & professional research on American & English theater with emphasis on 19th century
Purchases: $10,000
Library Holdings: Audio Tapes; Book Volumes 10,000; Cassettes; Clipping Files; Exhibition Catalogs; Framed Reproductions; Manuscripts; Memorabilia; Original Art Works; Pamphlets; Photographs; Prints; Records; Reels; Reproductions; Sculpture
Special Subjects: Photography, Etchings & Engravings, Painting-American, Painting-British, Prints, Sculpture, Portraits, Stage Design, Theatre Arts, Costume Design & Constr, Coins & Medals, Reproductions
Collections: Documents, letters, photos, paintings, memorabilia, prompt books of Walter Hampden, Edwin Booth, Union Square Theater; English playbill (18th & 19th century)

A **HARVESTWORKS, INC,** 596 Broadway, Ste 602, New York, NY 10012. Tel 212-431-1130; Fax 212-431-8473; Internet Home Page Address: www.harvestworks.org/; *Dir* Carol Parkinson; *Dep Dir* Hans Tammen
Open Mon - Fri 10 AM - 5PM; Estab 1977 to provide support & facilities for audio art & experimental music; Maintains reference library; Average Annual Attendance: 2,000; Mem: 250; dues $75
Income: $150,000 (financed by endowment, mem, city & state appropriations, recording studio)
Purchases: Pro-tools by Digi Design, Digital Audio Editing
Library Holdings: Audio Tapes
Exhibitions: The New York Electronic Art Festival
Publications: TELLUS, the Audio Series, biannual
Activities: Adult classes; artist in residence prog; computer art; lects open to pub, 20 vis lectrs per yr; concerts; gallery talks; competitions with awards; Van Lier Residency Prog; schols offered; lending collections contains 26 cassettes; retail store sells audio art & music cassettes & CDs

A   **HATCH-BILLOPS COLLECTION, INC,** 491 Broadway 7th Fl, New York, NY 10012. Tel 212-966-3231; Fax 212-966-3231; Elec Mail hatchbillops@yahoo.com; Internet Home Page Address: www.hatch-billopsarchive.org; *Pres* Camille Billops; *Mem Bd Dir* James V Hatch; *Mem Bd Dir* John A Williams; *Mem Bd Dir* Cora Myers Mendoza; *Mem Bd Dir* Noriko Sengoku; *Mem Bd Dir* Gordon Davis
Open by appt; No admis fee; Estab 1975 to collect & preserve primary & secondary resource materials in the Black Cultural Arts, to provide tools & access to these materials for artist, scholars & general pub, to develop programs in arts which use resources of Collection; Maintains Oral History Library & Reference Library
Income: Grants and public donations
Library Holdings: Audio Tapes; Book Volumes; CD-ROMs; Clipping Files; Exhibition Catalogs; Kodachrome Transparencies; Lantern Slides; Manuscripts; Memorabilia; Original Art Works; Original Documents; Other Holdings; Pamphlets; Photographs 4,000; Records; Slides 13,200; Video Tapes
Special Subjects: Historical Material, Photography, Prints, Sculpture, Painting-American, Afro-American Art
Collections: Owen & Edith Dodson Memorial Collection; Theodore Ward Collection: play scripts, interviews & letters; Charles & Elease Griffin Collection: lobby cards, interviews & still photos; Arthur Smith Collection: drawings of his jewelry, patterns, photos, interviews & letters; Harlem Renaissance Theatre Bibliography: photocopies of all theatre articles published in major black periodicals, 1917 - 1930; Dorothy & Reuben Silver Collection: plays & programs from early days at Karamu House, Cleveland OH; Bio-Data Archives
Publications: Artist & Influence, annual journal
Activities: Classes for adults & children; dramatic progs; lects open to pub; book traveling exhibs; originate traveling exhibs

M   **HEBREW UNION COLLEGE MUSEUM,** (Universal Technical Institute) Jewish Institute of Religion Museum, One W Fourth St, New York, NY 10012-1186. Tel 212-824-2218; Fax 212-388-1720; Elec Mail nymuseum@huc.edu; Elec Mail lkruger@huc.edu; Elec Mail emueller@huc.edu; Internet Home Page Address: www.huc.edu/museums/ny; *Cur* Laura Kruger; *Dir* Jean Bloch Rosensaft; *Curatorial Asst* Nancy Mantell; *Curatorial Asst* Phyllis Freedman; *Registrar* Susan Orr
Open Mon - Thurs 9 AM - 6 PM, Fri 9 AM - 3 PM & selected Sun 10 AM - 2 PM; No admis fee; Estab 1984 to present 4000 years of Jewish art with stress on contemporary art expressing Jewish identity & themes; 5000 sq ft of space; Average Annual Attendance: 30,000
Income: Financed by annual budget & fundraising
Library Holdings: Original Art Works; Photographs; Prints; Sculpture
Special Subjects: Architecture, Graphics, Painting-American, Photography, Prints, Sculpture, Bronzes, Archaeology, Religious Art, Ceramics, Crafts, Folk Art, Etchings & Engravings, Judaica, Manuscripts, Collages, Historical Material, Maps, Juvenile Art, Calligraphy, Miniatures, Medieval Art, Painting-Russian, Painting-Israeli, Bookplates & Bindings
Collections: Biblical archaeology; contemporary art expressing Jewish identity & themes; Jewish ritual art; Biblical Archaeology Collection; Jewish Ritual Art Collection
Exhibitions: Living in the Moment: Contemporary Artists Celebrate Jewish Time
Publications: Exhibition catalogs & brochures
Activities: Classes for adults & children; dramatic progs; docent training; lects open to pub, 15 vis lectrs per yr; concerts; gallery talks; tours; lending of original objects of art to other mus; book traveling exhibs 3 per yr; originate traveling exhibs 6 per yr; mus shop sells original art

M   **HENRY STREET SETTLEMENT,** Abrons Art Center, 265 Henry St, New York, NY 10002-4808. Tel 212-766-9200; Fax 212-505-8329; Elec Mail senarts@aol.com; Internet Home Page Address: www.henrystreet.org; *Dir* Jay Wegman; *Performing Arts Training Dir* Daniel Catanach; *Performing Arts Training Assoc* Anna Courter; *Performing Arts Training Assoc* Kim Cox; *Visual Arts Dir* Jonathan Durham
Open second Tues of month group tours of agency 10:30 - 11:30 AM ; No admis fee; Estab 1975 as a multi discipline community arts center for the performing & visual arts programs; Thematic group exhib of the work of contemporary artists, photo gallery for solo shows; Average Annual Attendance: 100,000
Income: government, foundations, individual support
Exhibitions: Contemporary art by emerging artists, women artists & artists of color, changing thematic exhibitions; rotating
Activities: Classes for adults & children in all arts disciplines; drama, dance and music prog; docent training; gallery educ prog for school and community groups; lects open to pub; 5 vis lectrs per yr; concerts; gallery talks; tours; schol and fels offered

M   **THE HISPANIC SOCIETY OF AMERICA,** Museum & Library, Audubon Terrace, Broadway between 155th & 156th Sts New York, NY 10032; 613 W 155th, New York, NY 10032. Tel 212-926-2234; Fax 212-690-0743; Elec Mail info@hispanicsociety.org; Internet Home Page Address: www.hispanicsociety.org; *Dir* Mitchell A Codding; *Asst Dir & Cur Decorative Arts* Margaret Connors McQuade; *Cur Archaeology & Sculpture* Constancio del Alamo; *Cur Prints & Photographs* Patrick Lenaghan; *Cur Emeritus* Priscilla E Muller; *Cur Rare Books* John O'Neill; *Asst Cur Rare Books & US* Vanessa Pintado; *Asst Cur Used Books* Edwin Rolon; *Sr Cur Paintings & Metalwork* Marcus Burke; *Coordr Develop & Pub Relations* Mencia Figueroa
Open Tues - Sat 10 AM - 4:30 PM, Sun 1 - 4 PM, cl Mon & major holidays; No admis fee; Estab 1904 by Archer Milton Huntington as a free public museum and library devoted to the art & culture of the Hispanic world; Average Annual Attendance: 25,000; Mem: Open to the public, basic dues $50; additional group of scholarly members, 400 in 2 categories, by election only
Income: Financed by endowment
Purchases: Hispanic objects in various media
Library Holdings: Auction Catalogs; Audio Tapes; Book Volumes; CD-ROMs; Clipping Files; Exhibition Catalogs; Fiche; Filmstrips; Manuscripts; Maps; Memorabilia; Micro Print; Original Documents; Prints; Records
Special Subjects: Etchings & Engravings, Historical Material, Ceramics, Furniture, Photography, Portraits, Pottery, Prints, Silver, Textiles, Woodcuts, Painting-European, Drawings, Graphics, Hispanic Art, Latin American Art, Mexican Art, Painting-American, Sculpture, Watercolors, Archaeology, Ethnology, Costumes, Religious Art, Ceramics, Crafts, Folk Art, Primitive art, Landscapes, Decorative Arts, Judaica, Manuscripts, Posters, Jewelry, Porcelain, Metalwork, Carpets & Rugs, Ivory, Maps, Coins & Medals, Baroque Art, Calligraphy, Renaissance Art, Embroidery, Laces, Medieval Art, Painting-Spanish, Islamic Art, Antiquities-Greek, Enamels, Bookplates & Bindings
Collections: Hispanic Collection; rare books; photographic reference files
Exhibitions: Permanent gallery exhibits are representative of the arts and cultures of Iberian Peninsula from prehistory to the present; Viceregal Latin America
Publications: Works by members of the staff and society on Spanish art, history, literature & bibliography, with spec emphasis on the collections of the society
Activities: Educational progs for adults & children; docent training; lects open to public, 6 vis lectrs per year; concerts; gallery talks; tours; exten prog serves New York area schools; Mus shop sells books, reproductions, prints, jewelry & accessories

M   **HUDSON GUILD,** Hudson Guild Gallery, 441 W 26th St, New York, NY 10001-5699. Tel 212-760-9800; *Gallery Dir* Jim Furlong
Open Tues - Fri 10 AM - 7 PM; No admis fee; Estab 1948 for exhibition of contemporary art; A modern facility within the Hudson Guild Building. The Art Gallery is also open for all performances of the Hudson Guild Theatre; Average Annual Attendance: 2,000
Income: Financed by the New York City Department of Cultural Affairs, Avery Foundation, Jolie Stahl
Activities: Educ prog; classes for adults & children; lects open to pub; 10 vis lectrs per year; gallery talks; tours for youth & seniors

M   **ILLUSTRATION HOUSE INC,** Gallery Auction House, 135 W 29th St, Rm 1201 New York, NY 10001-5152. Tel 212-966-9444; Fax 212-966-9425; Elec Mail info@illustrationhouse.com; Internet Home Page Address: www.illustration-house.com; *Pres* Roger Reed; *Founder* Walt A Reed; *Advertising Catalog Production & Photog* Emmanuel Montalvo; *Photog* Matthew Walker; *Account Subscriptions* Jenny Pham; *Registrar, Sales* Zaddick Longenbach
Open 10:30 AM - 5:30 PM; No admis fee; Estab 1974 devoted to exhibition & selling original paintings & drawings of America's great illustrators (1880-1990); 1,000 sq ft
Income: Pvt income
Library Holdings: Auction Catalogs; Audio Tapes; Cards; Exhibition Catalogs; Original Art Works; Original Documents; Other Holdings Tearsheets; Periodical Subscriptions
Collections: Illustration Art Reference
Exhibitions: Art Pertaining to Illustration (1880-1980); An Eye for Character: The Illustrations of E F Ward; 100 Years of Comic Art; Pulps & Paperbacks: Sensational Art from the Twenties to the Fifties; semi-annual action of original illustration art of full range of media & genre; Exhibitions rotate for auctions four times per yr
Publications: The Illustration Collector, subscription
Activities: Sales shop sells books & original art

A   **INDEPENDENT CURATORS INTERNATIONAL,** 401 Boradway, Ste 1620, New York, NY 10013-3020. Tel 212-254-8200; Fax 212-477-4781; Elec Mail info@ici-exhibitions.org; Internet Home Page Address: www.ici-exhibitions.org; *Exhib Dir* Susan Hapgood; *Registrar* Kathryn Martini; *Exec Dir* Kate Fowle; *Press Liaison* Mary Derr; *Dir Develop* Jeff Nadler
Open 10 AM - 6 PM; Estab 1975 as a nonprofit traveling exhib service specializing in contemporary art
Income: $750,000
Exhibitions: Everything Can Be Different; My Reality: Contemporary Art and Culture of Japanese Animation; The Gift; Thin Skin; Walkways; Beyond Preconceptions; Pictures, Patents and Monkeys; On Collecting; Telematic Connections; Mark Lombard: Global Networks; Beyond Green: Toward a Sustainable Art; High Times, Hard Times: New York Paintings 1967-1975; Jess: To and From the Printed Page; Phantasmagoria: Specters of Absence
Publications: Exhibition catalogs
Activities: Originate traveling contemporary art exhibs; ICI independents; museums; university galleries & art centers; ICI independents

M   **INTAR GALLERY,** P.O. Box 756, New York, NY 10108-0025. Tel 212-695-6135; *Dir* John McCormack
Open Mon - Fri 11 AM - 6 PM; No admis fee; Estab 1978. Assists & exhibits artists of diverse racial backgrounds. Devoted to artists who inhabit a dimension of their own in which the tension between singularity & universality has been acknowledged successfully; Only Hispanic gallery in area; Average Annual Attendance: 7,000
Income: Financed by endowment
Special Subjects: Latin American Art, Mexican Art, Photography, Sculpture, American Indian Art, Southwestern Art, Afro-American Art
Exhibitions: Rotating exhib
Publications: Exhibition catalogues
Activities: Lect open to public; gallery talks; originates traveling exhibs

M   **THE INTERCHURCH CENTER,** Galleries at the Interchurch Center, 475 Riverside Dr Ste 240, New York, NY 10115-0003. Tel 212-870-2200; Fax 212-870-2440; Elec Mail info@interchurch-center.org; Internet Home Page Address: www.interchurch-center.org; *Dir & Cur* Dorothy Cochran; *Interim CEO* Gleniss Schonholtz
Open daily 9 AM - 5 PM; No admis fee; Estab 1969; Two exhibit spaces Treasure Room Gallery 2,000 sq ft, Corridor Gallery 20 self-lite cases which line North & South Corridor each approx 36 x 50 ft; Average Annual Attendance: 10,000
Income: Financed by the bldg corporation
Purchases: Substantial sales throughout the yr
Special Subjects: Drawings, Graphics, Hispanic Art, Latin American Art, Mexican Art, American Indian Art, African Art, Ceramics, Crafts, Etchings & Engravings, Landscapes, Afro-American Art, Decorative Arts, Collages, Eskimo Art, Dolls, Jewelry, Oriental Art, Asian Art, Marine Painting, Calligraphy, Embroidery, Mosaics, Enamels, Bookplates & Bindings
Collections: Lenore Tawney tapestry (permanent installation)

Exhibitions: Rotating exhibits, 10 per year
Publications: website newsletter
Activities: Educ Prog; lects open to pub, 2 vis lectrs per yr; concerts; gallery talks

L **Library,** 475 Riverside Dr, New York, NY 10115-0003. Tel 212-870-2933; Fax 212-870-2440; Elec Mail icelib1@metgate.metro.org; *Dir & Cur Galleries* Dorothy Cochran; *Pres & Exec Dir* Mary McNamara
Open Mon - Fri 9 AM - 5 PM; Estab 1959 to enhance the employee environment & be a New York City neighborhood art resources; 2,000 sq ft (Treasure Room Gallery) & twenty (46ft x 36 ft) built in, self-light wall display cases; Average Annual Attendance: 4,000
Income: $6,000,000
Purchases: $6,000
Library Holdings: Book Volumes 14,000; Periodical Subscriptions 95
Exhibitions: Changing exhibitions on a 10 month schedule
Publications: 475 Newsletter, monthly
Activities: Noon time music & arts programming; lects open to pub, 5 vis lectrs per yr; concerts; gallery talks; tours

A **INTERNATIONAL CENTER OF MEDIEVAL ART,** 799 Fort Washington Ave, The Cloisters New York, NY 10040-1198. Tel 212-928-1146; Fax 212-928-1146; Elec Mail icma@medievalart.org; Internet Home Page Address: www.medievalart.org; *Treas* Rebecca Corrie; *Pres* Dorothy F Glass; *VPres* Annemarie Weyl Carr; *Adminr* Susan C Katz Karp; *Chair Nom Comt* Nancy Wicker
Estab 1956 as The International Center of Romanesque Art, Inc. The International Center of Medieval Art was founded to promote greater knowledge of the arts of the Middle Ages & to contribute to & make available the results of new research; Sponsor sessions at the annual conferences of the Medieval Institute of Western Michigan University, Kalamazoo the College Art Assn Annual Conference & the International Medieval Congress at Leeds, England; keeps its members informed as to events of interest to medievalists; sponsors the Limestone Sculpture Provenance Project; Mem: 1,300; dues benefactor $1000, supporting $500, patron $250, contributing $125, joint $70, institutional $65, active foreign countries $50, active US $45, independent scholar $35, student $18; annual meeting in Feb, in conjunction with College Art Assn of America
Publications: Gesta (illustrated journal), two issues per year; ICMA Newsletter, 3 issues per year; Romanesque Sculpture in American Collections I, II, III, New England Museums; Gothic Sculpture in American Collections I & II

M **INTERNATIONAL CENTER OF PHOTOGRAPHY,** Museum, 1133 Ave of the Americas at 43rd St, New York, NY 10036-6710. Tel 212-857-0000; 857-9725 (Store); Fax 212-857-0090; Elec Mail visit@icp.org; Internet Home Page Address: www.icp.org; *Deputy Dir for Prog* Philip Block; *Deputy Dir External Affairs* Evan Kingsley; *Deputy Dir for Adminr* Steve Rooney; *Dir Communs* Phyllis Levine; *Dir Exhib & Chief Cur* Brian Wallace; *Traveling Exhibits Coordr* Maren Ullrich; *Dir* Willis Hartshorn; *Cur Coll* Edward Earle
Open Tues - Thurs 10 AM - 6 PM, Fri 10 AM - 8 PM, Sat & Sun 10 AM - 6 PM, cl Mon, July 4th, Thanksgiving, Christmas & New Years Days; Admis adults $12, students & seniors $8, mems & children under 12 free, volunteer contributions Fri 5 - 8 PM; Estab 1974 to encourage & assist photographers of all ages & nationalities who are vitally concerned with their world & times, to find & help new talents, to uncover & preserve forgotten archives & to present such work to the pub; Maintains five exhibition galleries showing a changing exhibition program of photographic expression & experimentation by over 2,500 photographers; Average Annual Attendance: 160,500; Mem: 4,600; dues $55 & up
Income: Financed by public & private grants, NYC Dept of Cultural Affairs
Library Holdings: Audio Tapes; Book Volumes 15,000; Cassettes; Clipping Files; Exhibition Catalogs; Filmstrips; Kodachrome Transparencies; Original Documents; Pamphlets; Periodical Subscriptions 75; Photographs; Slides; Video Tapes
Special Subjects: Photography
Collections: The core of the collection is 20th century documentary photography, with a companion collection of examples of master photographs of the 20th century. Major holdings incl works from the documentary tradition as well as fashion & other aesthetic genres
Publications: Annual report; monographs; exhibition catalogs; programs guide
Activities: Classes for adults & children; docent training; cert & MFA prog; scholarships; lects open to pub; lects for members only; gallery talks; tours; awards; scholarships; book traveling exhibs; originate traveling exhibs; mus shop sells books, magazines, slides

L **Research Center,** 1114 Ave of the Americas at 43rd St, New York, NY 10036-7703. Tel 212-857-0004 (Library); 857-9733 (Archives); Fax 212-857-0091; 768-4688 (Print Study Rm); Elec Mail library@icp.org; collections @ icp.org; Internet Home Page Address: www.icp.org; *Librn* Deirdre Donahue
Open Mon - Thurs 10 AM - 7 PM, Fri 10 AM - 6 PM to students, staff & faculty; open to pub by appt only; Comprised of Mus coll, library, archives, reference materials & digital assets; maintains Print Study Room; available to students & scholars; Average Annual Attendance: 5,000
Income: Financed by pub & private grants
Library Holdings: Auction Catalogs; Audio Tapes; Book Volumes 8,000; Cassettes; Clipping Files; DVDs; Exhibition Catalogs; Filmstrips; Kodachrome Transparencies; Pamphlets; Periodical Subscriptions 100; Slides; Video Tapes
Special Subjects: Photography
Collections: Archives contains films, video tapes & audio recordings of programs related to photographs in the colls as well as programs about the subject & history of photography; Work by: Henri Cartier-Bresson, Martin Munkasci, W Eugene Smith, Gerda Taro; Impact Visuals Coll; September 11 Coll; Time-Life Coll; AIDs Graphics Coll; Artists Poster Committee Coll; Photographic Album Coll; African American History Coll; Hiroshima Coll; Cornell Cappa Archives; Robert Cappa Archives; David Seidner Archives; Roman Vishniac Archives; Weegee Archives; Lecture Series Archive; Photomuse online resource; eMuseum database
Publications: ICP/Steidl books

M **Rita K Hillman Education Gallery,** 1114 Ave of the Americas, at 43rd St New York, NY 10036-7703. Tel 212-857-0001; Fax 212-857-0091; Elec Mail education@icp.org; Internet Home Page Address: www.icp.org; *Facilities Supv* Per Gylfe
Open daily 10 AM - 6 PM; Exhibs the work of students, faculty & staff of the ICP School. See separate listing under US Schools in New York, NY for ICP School

Special Subjects: Photography
Activities: Classes for adults & children; lects open to pub, tours

INTERNATIONAL FOUNDATION FOR ART RESEARCH, INC
For further information, see National and Regional Organizations

M **JAPAN SOCIETY, INC,** Japan Society Gallery, 333 E 47th St, New York, NY 10017-2399. Tel 212-832-1155, 755-6752; Tel 212-715-1258; Fax 212-715-1262; Internet Home Page Address: www.japansociety.org; *Pres Japan Society* Motoatsu Sakurai; *Vice Pres & Gallery Dir* Joe Earle; *Gallery Officer* Haruko Hoyle; *Gallery Asst* Miho Fang
Open Tues - Thurs 11 AM - 6 PM, Fri 11 AM - 9 PM, Sat & Sun 11 AM - 5 PM, cl Mon Summer-Tues-Fri 11AM-6PM, Sat & Sun 11AM-5PM cl Mon; Admis non-members $5, seniors & students $3, mems free for summer exhibitions; Estab 1907, bi-cultural membership organizations to deepen understanding and friendship between Japan and the United States; Asian/Japanese Art; Average Annual Attendance: 30,000 gallery exhibitions/80,000 includ other programs; Mem: 2,500 individual; dues $10,000, $5,000, $2,000, $1,000, $500, $250, $150, $100, $60; Friends of Gallery $2000; Qualifications for mem AAM, ICOM, Mus Council NY
Income: Financed by mem, grants & donations
Special Subjects: Decorative Arts, Textiles, Painting-Japanese, Sculpture, Graphics, Asian Art
Collections: Japan Society permanent coll: ceramics, paintings, prints, sculpture & woodblocks
Publications: Japan Society Newsletter, monthly; exhibition catalogs accompanying each exhibition
Activities: Educ dept; classes for adults & children; docent training; lects open to public; concerts, gallery talks; tours; sponsor competitions; fellowships & Japan Society Award; 1-2 per yr; originate traveling exhibs to museums worldwide

L **C.V. Starr Library,** 333 E 47th St, New York, NY 10017. Tel 212-832-1155, Ext 256; Fax 212-715-6752; Elec Mail gen@japansociety.org; Internet Home Page Address: www.japansociety.org/contentcfn/library; *Dir* Reiko Sassa; *Asst Librn* Rebecca Leonard
Open Mon - Fri Noon - 5 PM; Admis only for members & Toyota language students; Estab 1971; Mem: 3,000; dues $55 - $1500
Income: Financed by mem
Library Holdings: Book Volumes 14,000; Clipping Files; Pamphlets; Periodical Subscriptions 35
Publications: What Shall I Read on Japan

M **THE JEWISH MUSEUM,** 1109 Fifth Ave, New York, NY 10128-0118. Tel 212-423-3200; Fax 212-423-3232; Elec Mail info@thejm.org; Internet Home Page Address: www.jewishmuseum.org; *Dir* Claudia Gould; *Dir Human Resources* Karen Granby; *Cur Archaeology* Susan L Braunstein; *Deputy Dir Fin & Admin* Joseph Rorech; *Dir Communs* Anne J Scher; *Chief Cur* Norman Kleeblatt; *Dir Mktg* Colin Weil; *Dir Coll & Exhib* Jane Rubin; *Chm (V)* Robert Porzan; *Curatorial Mgr* Karen Levitov; *Dir School Family* Nelly Silagy Benedek; *Deputy Dir External* Ellen Salpeter; *Deputy Dir Prog Admin* Ruth Beesch; *Deputy Dir Exhibs & Pub progs* Jens Hoffman
Open Sun - Tues, 11AM - 5:45PM, Thurs 11 AM - 8 PM, Fri & Sat 11 AM - 5:45 PM, cl Wed; Admis adults $15, seniors $12, students with ID cards $7.50, members, children 18 & under & Sat free; Estab 1904 to preserve & present the Jewish cultural tradition. Three exhibition floors devoted to the display of ceremonial objects & fine art in the permanent collection, special exhibitions from the permanent collections & photographs & contemporary art on loan; Maintains reference library; Average Annual Attendance: 180,000; Mem: 13,000; dues $75 & up
Income: Financed by mem, grants, individual contributions & organizations
Special Subjects: Textiles, Architecture, Drawings, Graphics, Archaeology, Ceramics, Etchings & Engravings, Decorative Arts, Judaica, Carpets & Rugs, Coins & Medals, Embroidery, Cartoons
Collections: Broadcast media material; Jewish ceremonial objects; comprehensive collection of Jewish ceremonial art; Harry G Friedman Collection of Ceremonial Objects; Samuel Friedenberg Collection of Plaques & Medals; Rose & Benjamin Mintz Collection of Eastern European Art; Harry J Stein-Samuel Friedenberg Collection of Coins from the Holy Land
Exhibitions: Culture & Continuity: The Jewish Journey, Pickles & Pomegranates; Modigliani: Beyond the Myth; Eva Hesse: Sculpture; Action/Abstraction; Pollock, de Kooning & American Art, 1940-1976; Man Ray: The Art of Reinvention; Edouard Vuillard: A Painter and His Muses, 1890-1940; Chagall: Love, War & Exile, other Primary Structures
Publications: Annual report; exhibition catalogs; newsletter, quarterly; poster & graphics; program brochures
Activities: Classes for adults & children; docent training; dramatic programs; lects open to pub; 20 vis lectrs per yr; concerts; gallery talks; tours; individual paintings lent to other museums; book traveling exhibs 1-2 per yr; originate traveling exhibs circulating to other museums; mus shop sells books, magazines, original art, reproductions, prints, slides, needlecrafts, posters, catalogs & postcards

L **Library,** 1109 Fifth Ave, New York, NY 10128. Tel 212-423-3200; Fax 212-423-3232; *Dir* Joan H Rosenbaum
Open Sun - Mon & Wed - Thurs 11 AM - 5:45 PM, Tues 11 AM - 9 PM, Fri 11 AM - 3 PM; Reference library open to the public by appointment only
Income: Financed by Jewish Museum budget & private sources
Library Holdings: Audio Tapes; Book Volumes 8,000; Cassettes; Clipping Files; Exhibition Catalogs; Other Holdings Vertical Files 2,500; Pamphlets; Photographs; Slides; Video Tapes
Special Subjects: Folk Art, Photography, Painting-American, Painting-Russian, Posters, Painting-European, Judaica, Archaeology, Ethnology, Religious Art
Collections: Esther M Rosen Slide Library (contains slides of objects in the museum's coll)

A **JOHN SIMON GUGGENHEIM MEMORIAL FOUNDATION,** 90 Park Ave, New York, NY 10016-1301. Tel 212-687-4470; Fax 212-697-3248; Elec Mail fellowships@jsgmf.org; Internet Home Page Address: www.gf.org; *Chmn* Joseph A Rice; *Pres* Edward Hirsch; *VPres & Sec* Andre Bernard; *VPres, Chief Finance, & Treas* Coleen Higgins-Jacob; *Dir Develop & Pub Rels* Richard Hatter; *Dir Technology* Joseph Gurvets
Office hours 9 AM - 4:30 PM; Estab & incorporated 1925; offers fellowships to

further the development of scholars & artists by assisting them to engage in research in any field of knowledge & creation in any of the arts, under the freest possible conditions & irrespective of race, color or creed; For additional information see section devoted to Scholarships and Fellowships
Activities: Fels offered

C   **THE JPMORGAN CHASE,** (The Chase Manhattan Bank) Art Collection, 270 Park Ave, New York, NY 10017-2014. Tel 212-270-6000.; Internet Home Page Address: www.jpmorganchase.com; *Dir Art Prog* Lisa K Erf
Open during bank hours; artwork displayed during exhibitions offsite, hours vary by location; Estab 1959 to support young & emerging artists & enhance bank offices world-wide; Collection displayed in branches, offices in New York City, state & world-wide
Collections: Largely contemporary American, 30,000 works in all media
Exhibitions: Various exhibitions
Publications: Exhibit catalogs
Activities: Lects for employees; individual objects of art lent to museum & gallery exhibs; originate traveling exhibs

A   **KENKELEBA HOUSE, INC,** Kenkeleba Gallery, 214 E Second St, New York, NY 10009-8031. Tel 212-674-3939; Fax 212-505-5080; *Art Dir* Joe Overstreet; *Dir* Corrine Jennings
Open Tues - Sat 11 AM - 6 PM; No admis fee; Estab 1975, Committed to the goals of presenting, preserving & encouraging the development of art excluded from the cultural mainstream. Supports experimental & interdisciplinary approaches. Features exhibitions of contemporary & modern painting, sculpture, experimental media, performance, poetry readings & literary forums
Collections: 20th Century African American Artists
Exhibitions: Eleanor Magid & Tom Kendall; Frank Stewart & Adal (photography)

M   **KENNEDY GALLERIES,** Kennedy Galleries, Inc, PO Box 5298, New York, NY 10185-5298. Tel 212-541-9600; Elec Mail inquiry@kgny.com; Internet Home Page Address: www.kgny.com; *Pres* Martha Fleischman
No admis fee; 18th, 19th & 20th Century American Art (Private dealer)
Collections: 18th, 19th & 20th Century American paintings, drawings, prints
Publications: American Art Journal

M   **THE KITCHEN,** 512 W 19th St, New York, NY 10011-2899. Tel 212-255-5793; Fax 212-645-4258; Elec Mail mail@thekitchen.org; Internet Home Page Address: www.thekitchen.org; *Exec Dir* Tim Griffin
Open Tues - Fri noon - 6 PM, Sat 11 AM - 6 PM; No admis fee; Estab 1971 as artists' laboratory for individual ideas & collaborative processes
Income: Financed by endowments, mem, contributions & gifts
Collections: Video Collection: over 600 titles by almost 300 artists
Exhibitions: Exhibitions held in the gallery, often incorporating video, audio & experimental performing arts; Rotating Exhibits
Activities: Concerts

M   **LAMAMA LA GALLERIA,** 6 E First St, New York, NY 10003-9228. Tel 212-505-2476; Internet Home Page Address: www.lamama.org; *Dir & Cur* Barbara Merry Geng
Open Wed - Sun 1 - 6 PM; No admis fee; Estab 1983 for exhibition of emerging artists; 2,500 sq ft, bi-level; Average Annual Attendance: 8,000
Income: Financed through grants & donations
Exhibitions: Rotating exhibitions, 14 per yr
Activities: Classes for adults & children; lects open to pub, 6 vis lectrs per yr; concerts; gallery talks

A   **LEO BAECK INSTITUTE,** 15 W 16th St, New York, NY 10011-6301. Tel 212-744-6400; Fax 212-988-1305; Elec Mail lbi1@lbi.com; Internet Home Page Address: www.lbi.org; *Pres* Bernard Blum; *Art Cur* Renata Stein; *Chief Archivist* Dr Frank Mecklenburg; *Exec Dir* Carol Kahn Strauss
Open Mon - Thurs 9:30 AM - 4:30 PM, Fri 9:30 AM - 2:30 PM; No admis fee; Estab 1955 to document history of German-Speaking Jews; Center includes library & archives; about 180 running ft, various display cases for books & documents; Average Annual Attendance: 2,000; Mem: 800; dues $200
Library Holdings: Book Volumes; Clipping Files; DVDs; Original Art Works; Original Documents; Photographs; Prints; Video Tapes
Special Subjects: Architecture, Cartoons, Costumes, Drawings, Embroidery, Etchings & Engravings, Graphics, Historical Material, Judaica, Landscapes, Manuscripts, Metalwork, Mosaics, Painting-German, Painting-Israeli, Photography, Porcelain, Posters, Prints, Religious Art, Reproductions, Sculpture, Silver, Textiles, Watercolors
Collections: Drawings, paintings, prints, sculpture, ritual objects, textiles from 15th - 20th centuries; 19th - 20th Century German-Jewish Artists, including Max Liebermann, Lesser Ury, Ludwig Meidner, Hugo Steiner-Prag
Exhibitions: Portraits of German Jews; Special thematic exhibits e.g.: Publishing in Exile (German); Publishers in U.S.; Radical Departure - avant garde Expressionist art 1900-1950 (German)
Publications: Year Book; LBI News, semi-annually
Activities: Lect open to public, 7-8 vis lectrs per year; concerts; gallery talks; tours; annual Leo Baeck Medal; scholarships & fellowships offered; individual paintings & original objects of art lent to cultural art institutions; lending collection contains paintings, sculptures, 50,000 books, 5,000 original art works, 2,500 original prints, 40,000 photographs; sells books
L **Library,** 15 W 16th St, New York, NY 10011-6301. Tel 212-744-6400; Fax 212-988-1305; Elec Mail lbaeck@lbi.cjh.org; Internet Home Page Address: www.lbi.org/; *Archivist* Frank Mecklenburg PhD; *Cur* Renata Stein; *Dir* Carol Kahn Strauss; *Librn* Renate Evers
Open Mon - 9:30 AM - 7:30 PM, Tues - Thurs 9:30 AM - 5:30 PM, Fri - 9:30 AM - 1:30 PM, Sun 11 AM - 4 PM (Sun requests must be rec'd on preceding Thurs by 4:30PM); Estab 1955 to collect & preserve materials by & about history of German-speaking Jews; For reference only; Mem: $200 general, $500 institutional
Income: Financed by endowment & mem

Library Holdings: Book Volumes 80,000; Fiche; Original Art Works 6,300; Original Documents; Pamphlets; Periodical Subscriptions 150; Photographs 30,000; Prints 5,000; Sculpture 30
Special Subjects: Folk Art, Drawings, Painting-German, Prints, Historical Material, History of Art & Archaeology, Judaica, Portraits, Stage Design, Watercolors
Collections: Archival library and art colls relating to German-Jewish life & history
Exhibitions: 3-4 exhibs per year
Publications: LBI yearbook; LBI memorial lect
Activities: Lects open to public; concerts; gallery talks; Fels

C   **LOIS WAGNER FINE ARTS,** (Lois Wagner Fine Arts Inc) 15 E 71st St Ste 2A, New York, NY 10021-4171. Tel 212-396-1407; Fax 212-396-1408; Elec Mail wagnerfa2@verizon.net; Internet Home Page Address: www.artnet.com/loiswagner.html; *Pres* Lois Wagner
Open by appointment only; No admis fee; Estab 1993; 19th & 20th Century American art
Collections: American Impressionism & Realism Collection (1880-1930); Contemporary Realism Collection; figurative, landscape & still-life paintings; American Impressionism & Realism Collection; Contemporary Photography

L   **M KNOEDLER & CO, INC,** Library, 444 W 55th St, New York, NY 10019-4403. Tel 212-794-0550; Fax 212-772-6932; *Pres & Dir* Ann Freedman; *Sr VPres & Assoc Dir* Frank Del Deo; *VPres* Per Haubro Jensen
Open Tues - Fri 9:30 AM - 5:30 PM, Sat 10 AM - 5:30 PM; No admis fee; Research by appointment on a fee basis, for scholars, museum cur & students use
Income: Financed by usage fees
Library Holdings: Book Volumes 55,000; Clipping Files; Exhibition Catalogs; Fiche; Other Holdings Auction catalogs; Pamphlets; Periodical Subscriptions 27; Photographs
Special Subjects: Painting-American, Painting-European

M   **THE MARBELLA GALLERY INC,** 28 E 72nd St, New York, NY 10021-4234. Tel 212-288-7809; Fax 212-288-7810; Elec Mail marbellagallery@aol.com; *Dir* Mildred Thaler Cohen
Open Tues - Fri 11 AM - 5:30 PM; No admis fee; Estab 1971 to buy & sell American art of the 19th century & early 20th century; 1,000 sq ft
Income: Pvt income
Collections: Extensive collection of 19th & early 20th C American paintings
Exhibitions: Season rotating exhibitions every 6 - 7 weeks
Activities: Lect open to public; book traveling exhibitions 2 per year

M   **MARYMOUNT MANHATTAN COLLEGE HEWITT GALLERY,** 221 E 71 St, New York, NY 10021. Tel 212-517-0692; Fax 212-517-0413; Elec Mail gallery@mmm.edu; Internet Home Page Address: marymount.mmm.edu; *Dir* Millie Burns
Open daily 9 AM - 9 PM; No admis fee; Estab 1982 as a showcase for unaffiliated artists; Gallery is 30 x 40 ft; Average Annual Attendance: 2,500
Exhibitions: Various exhibitions
Activities: Classes for adults; lect by artist; gallery talks

M   **THE METROPOLITAN MUSEUM OF ART,** 1000 5th Ave, Main Bldg New York, NY 10028-0113. Tel 212-535-7710 (General Information), 879-5500 (Museum Offices); Fax 212-570-3879; Elec Mail communications@metmuseum.org; Internet Home Page Address: www.metmuseum.org; *Anthony W & Lulu Alice Cooney; Sr VPres Exter* Emily K Rafferty; *John Pope Henness Chmn* Everett Fahy; *Drue Heinz Chmn Dr* George R Goldner; *Alice Pratt Brown Chm* H Barbara Weinberg; *VPres Communs* Harold Holzer; *Cur In Charge Cost* Harold Koda; *Jacques & Natasha* William S Lieberman; *Chief Registrar* Herb Moskowitz; *Cur In Charge Robert Lehman Coll* Laurence B Kanter; *Assoc Dir Exhibition* Mahrukh Tarapor; *Cur In Charge Photog* Maria Morris Hambourg; *Museum Shop Mgr* Will Sullivan; *Lila Acheson Wallace* Dorothea Arnold; *Cur Henry R Kravis* James David Draper; *Conservator In Charge* James H Frantz; *Assoc Dir Educ* Kent Lydecker; *Sherman Fairchild Chmn* Hubert Von Sonnenburg; *Arthur K Watson C* Kenneth Soehner; *Mgr Visitor Servs* Kathleen Arffmann; *Cur in Charge Arts* Julie Jones; *VPres Merchandise* Sally Pearson; *Lawrence A Fleisch* Morrison H Heckscher; *Conservator In charge* Nobuko Kajitani; *Ed In Chief* John P O'Neill; *VPres Facilities* Philip T Venturino; *VPres & Secy* Sharon H Cott; *Cur In Charge* Carlos Picon; *Dir & CEO* Philippe de Montebello; *Sr VPres & CF* Deborah Winshel; *Distinguished Research* Dietrich Von Bothmer
Open Tues - Thurs & Sun 9:30 AM - 5:15 PM, Fri & Sat 9:30 AM - 9 PM, cl Thanksgiving, Christmas & New Years Days, cl all Mon except select holiday Mon; Admis suggested for adults $25, seniors $17, students $12, members & children under 12 with adult free; incl admis to Cloisters; Estab 1870 to encourage & develop the study of the fine arts & the application of arts to life; of advancing the general knowledge of kindred subjects & to that end of furnishing popular instruction & recreation; Average Annual Attendance: 5,000,000; Mem: 97,245; dues patron $4000, sponsor $2000, donor $900, contributing $600, sustaining $300, dual $125, individual $70, student $30, national assoc $35
Income: $78,146,461 (financed by endowment, mem, city & state appropriations & other)
Special Subjects: Drawings, Painting-American, Photography, Sculpture, Costumes, Primitive art, Decorative Arts, Painting-European, Oriental Art, Asian Art, Antiquities-Byzantine, Medieval Art, Antiquities-Persian, Antiquities-Egyptian, Antiquities-Greek, Antiquities-Roman, Painting-German, Antiquities-Etruscan, Antiquities-Assyrian
Collections: Acquisitions-Departments: Africana, Oceanic; American decorative arts, paintings & sculpture; Ancient Near Eastern art; arms & armor; Costume Institute; Egyptian art; European paintings, sculpture & decorative arts; Greek & Roman art; Islamic art; Lehman Collection, medieval art & The Cloisters; musical instruments; prints; photographs; Twentieth Century Art Exhibitions; Charles A Greenfield Collection; Sackler Collection; Leon Spilliaert Collection; Photograph Study Collection
Publications: Bulletin, quarterly; Calendar, bi-monthly; The Journal, annually; exhibition catalogs, scholarly books

Activities: Classes for adults & children; docent training; films; progs for the disabled touch collection; lects open to pub; concerts; gallery talks; tours; outreach; exten dept serves community progs for greater New York City area; color reproductions, individual paintings & original objects of art lent to other institutions; book traveling exhibs; originate traveling exhibs to US mus; mus shop sells books, magazines, original art, reproductions, prints, slides, children's activities, records, postcards & posters

L **Museum Libraries,** 1000 5th Ave, New York, NY 10028-0113. Tel 212-650-2225; Fax 212-570-3847; Elec Mail watson.library@metmuseum.org; Internet Home Page Address: library.metmuseum.org; *Chief Librn* Kenneth Soehner; *Assoc Chief Librn* Daniel Starr; *Reader Servs Librn* Linda Seckelson; *Acquisitions Coordr* Ross Day; *Conservation Librn* Mindell Dubansky; *Interlibrary Servs Librn* Robyn Fleming; *Electronic Resource Librn* Deborah Vincelli; *Systems Librn* Oleg Kreymer
Open to visiting researchers Tues - Thurs 9:30 AM - 5:15 AM, Fri 9:30 AM - 6 PM, Sat 10 AM - 2 PM, cl holidays & weekends; No admis fee; Estab 1880; primary mission is to serve museum staff; researchers col age & older may apply for Reader's Card w/ photo ID & are welcome; see library website for details; Circ Collections circulate to Mus research staff, non-circulating for visitors; Incl the Thomas J Watson Library, Irene Lewisohn Costume Library, Joyce F Menschel Photography Library, Onassis Library for Hellenic & Roman Art, Robert Goldwater Library, Robert Lehman Collection Library, & other departmental libraries; Average Annual Attendance: 30,000
Income: Financed by endowment
Library Holdings: Auction Catalogs; Book Volumes 700,000; Clipping Files; Exhibition Catalogs; Fiche; Micro Print; Other Holdings Ephemera; Monographs; Periodical Subscriptions 2,250
Special Subjects: Art History, Decorative Arts, Drawings, Islamic Art, Painting-American, Prints, Sculpture, Painting-European, Asian Art

L **Dept of Drawings & Prints,** 1000 5th Ave, New York, NY 10028-0113. Tel 212-570-3920 (Print Study Rm); 570-3912 (Drawing Study Rm); Fax 212-570-3921; Internet Home Page Address: www.metmuseum.org; *Chmn* Dr George R Goldner
Open Tues - Fri 10 AM - 12:30 PM & 2 - 4:30 PM by appointment; No admis fee; Estab 1917 to collect & preserve prints, illustrated books & drawings for ornament & architecture; dept created 1993; Has 3 exhibition galleries; Average Annual Attendance: 2,600
Income: financed by museum
Library Holdings: Original Art Works; Prints
Special Subjects: Art History, Landscape Architecture, Decorative Arts, Illustration, Drawings, Etchings & Engravings, Prints, Portraits, Printmaking, Woodcuts, Architecture

L **Image Library,** 1000 5th Ave, New York, NY 10028. Tel 212-650-2368; 650-2562; Fax 212-396-5050; Elec Mail image.licensing@metmuseum.org; Internet Home Page Address: www.metmuseum.org/education/er_photo_lib.asp; *Mus Librn* Julie Zeftel; *Assoc Mus Librn* Eileen Sullivan; *Assoc Mus Librn* Claire Dienes; *Chief Librn* Andrew P Gessner; *Assoc Mus Librn* Billy Kwan; *Asst Mus Librn* Stephanie Post; *Assoc Mus Librn* Roberto Ferrari
Cl to pub except by appointment; Estab 1907; provides digital images, color transparencies & photographs of the coll of the Metropolitan Mus of Art for study & publication purposes
Library Holdings: Kodachrome Transparencies; Lantern Slides; Original Documents; Other Holdings Color transparencies; Periodical Subscriptions; Photographs; Reproductions; Slides 800,000
Special Subjects: Art History
Collections: Art & architecture coll; William Keighley slide coll

L **The Nolen Library in the Ruth and Harold D. Uris Center for Education,** 1000 5th Ave, New York, NY 10028. Tel 212-570-3788; Elec Mail nolen.library@metmuseum.org; Internet Home Page Address: library.metmuseum.org; *Librn* Naomi Niles
Open to Mus visitors of all ages: Sept - May, Tues - Thurs 9:30 AM - 5 PM, Fri 9:30 AM - 8 PM, Sat 10 AM - 8 PM, Sun 11 AM - 5 PM; Jun - Jul, Tues - Fri 9:30 AM - 5 PM, Sat 10 AM - 5 PM, Sun 11 AM - 5 PM; Aug same as Jun - Jul but cl Sun; cl holidays & weekends; Circ Non-circulating; curriculum-related materials can circulate to teachers, registration req
Library Holdings: Book Volumes; DVDs; Other Holdings Teacher materials; Video Tapes
Collections: 8,000+ items on art & art history geared to gen pub, incl books, MMA publications, picture books, books for young adults, DVDs & videos

M **The Cloisters Museum & Gardens,** 99 Margaret Corbin Dr, Fort Tryon Park New York, NY 10040. Tel 212-923-3700; Fax 212-795-3640; Elec Mail cloisters@metmuseum.org; Internet Home Page Address: www.metmuseum.org/cloisters/; Cable CLOMUSE; *Chmn & Cur* Peter Barnet; *Cur* Timothy Husband; *Mgr Admin* Jose Ortiz; *Mgr Admin* Christina Alphonso; *Cur* Julien Chapuis
Open Mar - Oct, Tues - Sun - 9:30 AM - 5:15 PM; Nov - Feb, Tues - Sun - 9:30 AM - 4:45 PM, cl New Year's Day, Thanksgiving & Christmas; Admis suggested for adults $20, seniors $15, students $10, mems & children under 12 with adult free; incl admis to main bldg; Estab 1938 to display in an appropriate setting works of art & architecture of the Middle Ages; Medieval French cloisters incorporated into the building, as well as the chap house, a chapel & Romanesque apse; also Medieval herb garden. Branch of Metropolitan Museum of Art, New York, NY; Mem: Part of Met Museum
Collections: Frescoes, ivories, precious metalwork, paintings, polychromed statues, stained glass, tapestries, and other French and Spanish architectural elements; gardens
Publications: A Walk Through The Cloisters; exhib catalogs; Medieval Gardens Enclosed, blog
Activities: Dramatic progs; workshops; lects open to pub; concerts; gallery talks; tours; original objects of art lent to other mus; mus shop sells books, reproductions, prints and slides

L **The Cloisters Library & Archives,** 99 Margaret Corbin Dr, Fort Tryon Park New York, NY 10040. Tel 212-396-5319; Fax 212-795-3640; Elec Mail cloisters.library@metmuseum.org; Internet Home Page Address: www.metmuseum.org/education/; http://libmma.org;
Open Tues - Fri 10 AM - 4:30 PM; No admis fee; Estab 1938 to be used as a small highly specialized reference library for the curatorial staff at The Cloisters; scholars & accredited graduate students are welcome & qualified researchers by appointment only
Income: Financed by endowment
Library Holdings: Book Volumes 12,000; Fiche 9,000; Other Holdings Original documents; Periodical Subscriptions 58; Photographs 22,000; Reels; Slides 20,000
Special Subjects: Art History, Sculpture, Stained Glass, Enamels, Tapestries, Architecture
Collections: George Grey Barnard Papers; Harry Bober Papers; Joseph & Ernest Brummer Papers; Summer McKnight Crosby Papers; Demotte Photograph Archive; Archives of the Cloisters

L **MIDMARCH ASSOCIATES/MIDMARCH ARTS PRESS,** Midmarch Arts Press and Library, 300 Riverside Dr, Apt 8A, New York, NY 10025. Tel 212-666-6990; Fax 212-865-5510; *Exec Dir* Cynthia Navaretta; *Educ* Judy Seigel; *Educ* Sylvia Moore
Open by appointment; Estab 1975 to maintain archival material on women artists world wide & to publish books on 20th century art & artists; 20th C paintings & sculpture; pre-Columbian shards & sculpture
Income: Financed by public funding, contributions & book sales
Library Holdings: Book Volumes; Clipping Files; Exhibition Catalogs; Manuscripts; Memorabilia; Original Art Works; Original Documents; Pamphlets; Photographs; Sculpture; Video Tapes
Special Subjects: Art History, Constructions, Film, Mixed Media, Photography, Drawings, Painting-American, Painting-British, Painting-Japanese, Pre-Columbian Art, Sculpture, Painting-European, Watercolors, Ceramics, Conceptual Art, Crafts, Latin American Art, Theatre Arts, Mexican Art, Afro-American Art, Flasks & Bottles, Architecture, Embroidery
Collections: In-house collection of 20thC art
Publications: Please visit website www.midmarchartspress.org for list of publications or midmarchartsbooks.org
Activities: Educ dept; lect provided

M **THE MORGAN LIBRARY & MUSEUM,** Museum, 225 Madison Ave at 36th St, New York, NY 10016-3405. Tel 212-685-0008; Fax 212-481-3484; Elec Mail visitorservices@themorgan.org; Internet Home Page Address: www.themorgan.org; *Cur Mary Hagler Cary Music Manuscripts & Dept Head* Frances Barulich; *Astor Cur & Dept Head Printed Books & Bindings* John Bidwell; *Cur & Dept Head Medieval & Renaissance Manuscripts* William M Voelkle; *Cur Drawings & Prints* Jennifer Tonkovich; *Cur & Dept Head Seals & Tablets* Sidney Babcock; *Dir Coll Info Systems* Elizabeth O'Keefe; *Robert H Taylor Cur & Dept Head* Declan Kiely
Open Tues - Thurs 10:30 AM - 5 PM, Fri 10:30 AM - 9 PM, Sat 10 AM - 6 PM, Sun 11 AM - 6 PM, cl Mon, Thanksgiving Day, Christmas Day & New Years Day; Admis adults $15, children under 16, seniors 65+ & students with ID $10, mems & children 12 & under free, Fri 7 - 9 PM free; Estab 1924 for research & exhibition purposes; The Gallery has changing exhibition with Old Master drawings, Medieval & Renaissance illuminated manuscripts, rare printed books & literary, historical, & music manuscripts; Average Annual Attendance: 156,000; Mem: 1,100; dues conservator $1,000, sustainer $500, contributor $250, dual/family $150, individual $100, intro individual $75
Income: $4,000,000 (financed by endowment & mem)
Purchases: $1,000,000
Special Subjects: Drawings, Etchings & Engravings, Historical Material, Architecture, Prints, Manuscripts, Painting-European, Photography, Religious Art, Portraits, Miniatures, Renaissance Art, Period Rooms, Medieval Art, Painting-Spanish, Painting-Italian, Islamic Art, Bookplates & Bindings
Collections: Ancient written records including seals, cuneiform tablets and papyri; art objects; autograph manuscripts; book bindings; early children's books; Medieval & Renaissance illuminated manuscripts; later printed books; letters and documents; mezzotints; modern calligraphy; music manuscripts; original drawing from 14th-19th centuries; printed books before 1500; Rembrandt prints
Publications: Report to the Fellows, annual; books; catalogs; facsimiles
Activities: Lects open to pub; tours; concerts; readings; video presentations; sales shop sells books, reproductions, prints, slides, cards, calendars, address books and posters

L **Library,** 225 Madison Ave at 36th St, New York, NY 10016-3405. Tel 212-590-0315 (Reading Room); 590-0386 (Photography & Rights); Elec Mail readingroom@themorgan.org; Internet Home Page Address: www.themorgan.org; *Dir Library & Mus Svcs* Robert Parks; *Head Reader Svcs* Inge Dupont; *Head Reference Coll* V Heidi Haas
Open by appt only; Tues - Thurs 10:30 AM - 5 PM, Fri 10:30 AM - 9 PM, Sat 10 AM - 6 PM, Sun 11 AM - 6 PM, cl Mon, Thanksgiving Day, Christmas Day & New Year's Day; Admis adults $12, children under 16, seniors 65+ & students with ID $8, mems & children 12 & under free, Fri 7-9 PM free; Circ Non-circulating; Maintains Reading Room & Drawing Study Ctr
Library Holdings: Auction Catalogs; Book Volumes 160,000; Exhibition Catalogs; Kodachrome Transparencies; Manuscripts 70,000; Original Art Works 8,000; Original Documents; Photographs; Prints 13,000; Slides

M **MORRIS-JUMEL MANSION, INC,** 65 Jumel Terr, New York, NY 10032. Tel 212-923-8008; Fax 212-923-8947; Elec Mail mjm1765@aol.com; Internet Home Page Address: www.morrisjumel.org; *Dir* Kenneth Moss; *Pres* James Kerr Esq; *Gift Shop Coordr* Barbara Mitchell; *Dir Educ* Loren Silber; *Cur* Sheena Brown; *Sec* Kathleen Parker; *Treas* Steven J Taylor
Open Wed - Sun 10 AM - 4 PM, Mon - Tues by appt; Admis adults $3, students & seniors $2, children under 12 free; Estab 1904 as a Historic House Museum; Morris-Jumel Mansion consists of 11 period rooms which are restored to represent the colonial, revolutionary & nineteenth-century history of the mansion, highlighting its owners & inhabitants (the Morris family, George Washington, Eliza Jumel & Aaron Burr); Average Annual Attendance: 30,000; Mem: 200; contributors 500; dues $35-$2500
Income: Financed by mem, contributions, private sources, state & city funds
Special Subjects: Architecture, Painting-American, Textiles, Costumes, Ceramics, Etchings & Engravings, Decorative Arts, Portraits, Furniture, Glass, Historical Material, Period Rooms, Laces, Painting-Italian
Collections: Architecture; decorative art; furniture of the 18th & 19th centuries
Publications: Morris-Jumel News, biannual
Activities: Classes for adults; classes for 4th - 11th grade students, focus on study of historical artifacts, documents & architecture; dramatic progs; docent training;

lects open to pub; concerts; tours; originate traveling exhibs; mus shop sells books, reproductions, postcards & CDs

M **MOUNT VERNON HOTEL MUSEUM & GARDEN,** 421 E 61st St, New York, NY 10065-8736. Tel 212-838-6878; Fax 212-838-7390; Elec Mail info@mvhm.org; Internet Home Page Address: www.mvhm.org; *Dir* Mary Anne Caton; *Cur* Charlotte Trautman; *Educ* Dana Settles; *Pub Rels* Terri Daly
Open Tues - Sun 11 AM - 4 PM, cl Mon; Admis adults $8, seniors (65 & up) & students with ID $7, children under 12 free; Estab 1939, historic site representing early 19th century New York City hotel; Eight period rooms in original 1826 interiors; 1799 Landmark building; Average Annual Attendance: 10,000; Mem: 450; dues $30-$500
Special Subjects: Decorative Arts, Painting-American, Prints, Silver, Textiles, Architecture, Archaeology, Ceramics, Pottery, Landscapes, Afro-American Art, Manuscripts, Portraits, Furniture, Glass, Porcelain, Silver, Painting-British, Carpets & Rugs, Historical Material, Maps, Restorations, Period Rooms, Pewter, Reproductions
Collections: Decorative arts-furniture, ceramics, silver, textiles; documents & manuscripts; Fine Art: paintings/prints; Landscapes, portraits, pewter
Exhibitions: Period rooms in original 1820s interiors; American Decorative Arts
Publications: Newsletter & brochure, quarterly
Activities: Classes for adults & children; dramatic progs; docent progs; musical performances; craft demonstrations; workshops ie (knitting; talking, terrariums); lects open to pub; 10 vis lectrs per yr; awards; concerts; gallery talks; tours; schols & fels offered; mus shop sells books, original art, prints, reproductions, slides, toys, jewellry, garden related items & craft items

A **MUNICIPAL ART SOCIETY OF NEW YORK,** 111 W 57th St, New York, NY 10019-2202. Tel 212-935-3960; Fax 212-753-1816; Elec Mail info@mas.org; Internet Home Page Address: www.mas.org; *Pres* Vin Cipolla; *Sr VP* Frank E Sanchis III; *Exec VP Devel* Jean Tatge; *Sr VP Policy & Advocacy* Rona Wist; *Dir Special Projs* Vanessa Gruen; *Sr Dir Preservation & Sustainability* Lisa Kersavage; *Sr Dir Pub Progs* Christine Tripoli Krische; *VP Fin & Admin* James S J Liao; *Dir Adopt-A-Monument/ Mural Progs* Phyllis Samitz Cohen; *Dir Progs & Tours* Tamara Coombs; *Dir Communs* Karen Crowe
Open Mon - Fri 9 AM - 5 PM; No admis fee; Estab 1892, incorporated 1898; The Society is the one organization in New York where the layman, professional & bus firm can work together to encourage high standards for pub art, architecture, planning, landscaping & preservation in the five boroughs; Mem: 4,500; dues $25 & up; annual meeting in June
Income: Financed by members & grants
Collections: Photographs
Exhibitions: Rotating exhibits; Tribute in Light, annual 9/11 commemoration
Publications: The Livable City, quarterly
Activities: Pub progs incl Livable Neighborhoods; lects; architectural walking tours; competitions

L **Greenacre Reference Library,** 111 W 57th St, New York, NY 10019-2202. Tel 212-935-3960 x 1274; Fax 212-753-1816; Elec Mail ebutler@mas.org; Internet Home Page Address: mas.org; *Project Mgr* Erin Butler
Open Mon - Fri 10 AM - 5 PM by appointment; No admis fee; Estab 1978; Reference Library; Mem: Parent inst has a membership program
Income: Supported by Greenacre Foundation
Library Holdings: Book Volumes 2,000; Clipping Files 5,000; Manuscripts 2,000 printed archival pubs & materials; Periodical Subscriptions 50
Special Subjects: Landscape Architecture, Decorative Arts, Illustration, Photography, Maps, Painting-American, Sculpture, Historical Material, History of Art & Archaeology, Watercolors, Theatre Arts, Industrial Design, Interior Design, Aesthetics, Architecture

M **MUSEUM FOR AFRICAN ART,** 1280 5th Ave, Apt 20A New York, NY 11129-7815. Tel 718-784-7700; Fax 718-784-7718; Elec Mail admin@africanart.org; Internet Home Page Address: www.africanart.org; *Cur* Lisa Binder; *Publs Mgr* Carol Braide; *Acct* Idalia Cajigas; *Traveling Exhibit Coordr* Ryan Dennis; *Sr Develop Mgr* Margo Donaldson; *Community Outreach Liaison* Lawrence Ekechi; *Assoc Producer Theater Progs* Dana Elmquist; *Mgr Opers & Admin* Bridget Foley; *Assoc Dir Institutional Giving* Nicolet Gatewood; *Dir Educ & Pub Progs* Erika Gee; *Assoc Dir Curatorial Affairs* Donna Ghelerter; *Individual Giving Assoc* Clair Hoffman; *Youth Progs Coordr* Dan'etta Jimenez; *CFO* Raji Kalra; *Deputy Dir & COO* Kenita Lloyd; *Pres* Elise McCabe Thompson; *Project Mgr Nelson Mandela Ctr* Zeheda Mohamed; *Asst Registrar* Asst Registrar Eve Perry; *Dir Merchandising & Traveling Progs* Michelle Pinedo; *Develop Assoc* Virginia Reinhart; *Facilities Mgr* Winston Rodney; *Asst to Pres* Raina Sutton; *Registrar* Amanda Thompson; *Dir Develop & Dir Theater Progs* Marietta Ulacia; *Sr Acct* Velky Valentin; *Special Adv to Pres* Jerry Vogel; *Dir Communs* Dexter Wimberly
Open varies with exhib (see website for details); Admis varies with exhib (see website for details); Estab 1984 to increase public understanding & appreciation of African art & culture. Devoted exclusively to traditional & contemporary African art; Admin offices; Average Annual Attendance: 40,000; Mem: 125; dues vary
Library Holdings: Book Volumes
Special Subjects: African Art
Exhibitions: Rotating exhibitions; Hair in African Art and Culture;
Publications: Over 40 scholarly catalogues (see website for a full list of publs)
Activities: Educ prog; docent training; lects open to pub; 15 vis lectrs per yr; originate traveling exhibs to circulate to other mus; mus shop sells catalogues, books, original art, reproductions, magazines, handcrafts, jewelry, musical recordings, clothes, furniture, musical instruments

M **MUSEUM OF ARTS & DESIGN,** 2 Columbus Circle, New York, NY 10019. Tel 212-299-7777; Fax 212-299-7701; Elec Mail info@madmuseum.org; Internet Home Page Address: www.madmuseum.org; *Registrar* Ellen Holdorf; *Pub Progs* Jake Yuzha; *Mgr Pub Affairs* Claire Laporte; *VPres Educ* Cathleen Lewis; *CFO* Robert Salerno; *Chief Cur* David McFadden; *VPres External Affairs* Sophie Henderson
Open Tues - Wed & Sun 10 AM - 6 PM, Thurs - Fri 10 AM - 9 PM, cl Mon & major holidays; Admis adults $16, seniors $14, students $12, 18 & under free; Estab 1956 by the American Craft Council (see National Organizations); Gallery displays contemporary art, design, craft & jewelry; Average Annual Attendance: 500,000; Mem: 7,500; dues $75, student & out-of-town $50, dual $100, family $125, contributing $250, supporting $500
Income: Financed by mem, government grants, private & corporate donations
Special Subjects: Decorative Arts, Ceramics, Glass, Metalwork, Furniture, Porcelain, Pottery, Silver, Textiles, Sculpture, Tapestries, Sculpture, Crafts, Woodcarvings, Jewelry, Embroidery, Laces, Stained Glass
Collections: 2,000 objects that document the history of craft, art & design from the mid 20th century to present; 500 pieces of contemporary art jewelry
Exhibitions: 6-10 exhibitions per year
Publications: MAD Views, biannual newsletter; exhib catalogs
Activities: Classes for adults & children; docent training; lects open to public; tours; Visionaries award; museum shop sells artists' jewelry, decorative objects & fashion accessories

M **MUSEUM OF BIBLICAL ART,** 1865 Broadway, New York, NY 10023-7503. Tel 212-408-1500; Fax 212-408-1292; Elec Mail info@mobia.org; Internet Home Page Address: www.mobia.org; *Exec Dir* Dr Ena Heller; *Chmn* Brian O'Neil; *Gen Mgr* Ute Keyes; *Museum Asst* Michelle Oing; *Dir Develop & Finance* Clay Dean
Open Tues - Wed & Fri - Sun 10 AM - 6 PM, Thurs 10 AM - 8 PM; Admis adults $7, senior citizens & students $4, members & children under 12 free; Average Annual Attendance: 17,977
Collections: art in the Jewish & Christian traditions
Publications: exhibition catalogs; newsletter; educational brochures & booklets
Activities: Educ prog; classes for children; workshops; lect open to pub; lect series; concerts; guided tours; gallery talks; mus shop sells books

M **MUSEUM OF CHINESE IN AMERICA,** 211-215 Centre St, New York, NY 10013-3601; 215 Centre St, New York, NY 10013. Tel 212-619-4785; Fax 212-619-4720; Elec Mail info@mocanyc.org; Internet Home Page Address: www.mocanyc.org; *Exec Dir* Helen Koh; *Cur & Dir Exhib* Herb Tam; *Assoc Dir Coll* Yue Ma; *Dir Tech* Frank Liu; *Assoc Dir External Affairs* Emily Chovanec; *Exec Asst* Michelle Lee Oltvero; *Deputy Dir External Affairs* Carolyn Antonio; *Dir Educ* Karen Lew
Open Tues, Wed, Fri, Sat & Sun 11 AM - 6 PM, Thurs 11 AM - 9 PM, cl Mon; Admis general $7, seniors & students $4, mems & children under 12 in groups less than 8 free, Target Free Thursday Prog; Estab 1980 dedicated to preserving 160 years of Chinese American history; Located in a stunning new site designed by Maya Lin with over 6,000 sq ft of exhib space, a mixed-use classroom, gallery & tech spaces; Average Annual Attendance: 30,000; Mem: 335; dues $25 - $5000
Income: Financed by mem, pub & private funds
Library Holdings: Audio Tapes; Book Volumes; CD-ROMs; Cards; Cassettes; Clipping Files; Compact Disks; DVDs; Exhibition Catalogs; Framed Reproductions; Manuscripts; Memorabilia; Motion Pictures; Original Art Works; Original Documents; Other Holdings; Pamphlets; Periodical Subscriptions; Photographs; Records; Reels; Reproductions; Sculpture; Slides; Video Tapes
Special Subjects: Anthropology, Decorative Arts, Drawings, Folk Art, Architecture, Photography, Period Rooms, Textiles, Maps, Ethnology, Costumes, Crafts, Manuscripts, Asian Art, Historical Material, Restorations, Cartoons, Reproductions
Collections: Archives: Chinese American history & culture, including oral histories, photographs, documents, personal & organizational records, sound recordings, textiles, artifacts & a library of over 2,000 volumes covering Asian American topics
Exhibitions: With a Single Step: Stories in the Making of America (core exhib)
Activities: Classes for adults & children; docent training; workshops; lects open to pub & mems only, 12-24 vis lectrs per yr; concerts; gallery talks; walking tours; competitions; family events; legacy awards; mus shop sells books, magazines, original art, souvenirs, apparel, gift items

M **MUSEUM OF COMIC AND CARTOON ART,** 666 Greenwich St, Apt 554 New York, NY 10014-6333. Tel 212-254-3511; Fax 212-254-3590; Elec Mail info@moccany.org; Internet Home Page Address: moccany.org
Open Tues-Sun noon-5PM; Admis adults $5, discounts to groups, children 12 & under free
Collections: comic & cartoon art; sketches

M **MUSEUM OF MODERN ART,** 11 W 53rd St, New York, NY 10019-5497. Tel 212-708-9400, (Exhibit & Film Info) 708-9480; Fax 212-708-9889; Elec Mail info@moma.org; Internet Home Page Address: www.moma.org; Telex 6-2370; Cable MODERNART; *Hon Chmn* Ronald Lauder; *Chmn Emeritus* Robert B Menschel; *Asst Treas* James Gara
Open Sun-Mon, Wed-Thurs & Sat 10:30 AM - 5:30 PM, Fri 10:30 AM - 8 PM, cl Tues, Thanksgiving day & Christmas day; Admis adults $25, seniors $18, students with ID $14, guests of mem $5, mem & children under 16 free, Fri 4-8:30 PM free; Estab 1929, the Museum offers an unparalleled overview of modern art; maintains exhibitions of wide range of subject matter, mediums & time periods; Designed in 1939 by Phillip Goodwin & Edward Durell Stone, the building is one of the first examples of the International Style in the US. Subsequent expansions took place in the 1950s & 1960s under the architect Philip Johnson, who also designed the Abby Aldrich Rockefeller Sculpture Garden. A major renovation, completed in 1984, doubled the Museum's gallery space & enhanced visitor facilities; Average Annual Attendance: 1,500,000; Mem: 52,000; dues student $25, others $45 & up
Income: Financed by admis, mem, sales of publications, other services & contributions
Special Subjects: Architecture, Drawings, Graphics, Painting-American, Photography, Prints, Sculpture, Posters
Collections: Painting, sculptures, drawings, prints, photographs, films, videos & other media works, architectural models & Plans, & design objects 175,000; artist books & periodicals 300,000; museum archives hold historical documentation & photographs
Publications: Annual report; books on exhibitions & artists; Members Quarterly; Members Calendar; monographs; catalogs; exhibitions catalogs
Activities: Classes for adults & children; prof develop for teachers & admins; lects open to pub; concerts; gallery talks; tours; film showings, international in scope; virtual visits & audio progs; courses at MoMA; weekend family programs;

sales shop sells publications, postcards, note & seasonal cards, posters, slides, calendars, design objects & furniture

L **Library and Museum Archives,** 4 W 54th St, midtown Manhattan New York, NY 10022-4203; 4520 33rd St, Long Island City, NY 11101-2406; 11 W 53rd St, New York, NY 10019-5498. Tel 212-708-9433 (library), 708-9617 (archives); Fax 212-333-1122; Elec Mail library@moma.org; archives@moma.org; Internet Home Page Address: www.moma.org/research/library; *Librn, Collection Develop* Jennifer Tobias; *Chief Library & Mus Archives* Milan Hughston; *Archivist* Michelle Elligott
Open Manhattan Wed - Fri - 11 AM - 5 PM by appointment, cl Aug; Queens Mon - Tues - 11 AM - 5 PM by appointment, cl Aug; No admis fee; Estab 1929 as a research library; For museum staff, art researchers & the public
Library Holdings: Auction Catalogs; Audio Tapes; Book Volumes 260,000; CD-ROMs; Cassettes; Clipping Files; Exhibition Catalogs; Fiche; Original Documents; Other Holdings Artists files 53,000; Pamphlets; Periodical Subscriptions 300; Records; Reels; Video Tapes
Special Subjects: Art History, Collages, Film, Mixed Media, Photography, Drawings, Graphic Design, Posters, Prints, Sculpture, Conceptual Art, Latin American Art, Industrial Design, Architecture
Collections: Archives of artists' groups; artists' books; avant-garde art; Dada & Surrealism; archive of museum publications; Latin American art; personal papers of artists, writers, dealers; political art documentation archives
Exhibitions: Fluxus: Selections from the Gilbert & Lila Silverman Collection, 1988-89 (catalog)
Publications: Annual Bibliography of Modern Art; Bibliography of Modern Art on Disc; catalog of the Library of the Museum of Modern Art
Activities: Internship prog

M **MUSEUM OF THE CITY OF NEW YORK,** Museum, 1220 5th Ave at 103rd St, New York, NY 10029-9958. Tel 212-534-1672; Fax 212-423-0758; Elec Mail info@mcny.org; Internet Home Page Address: www.mcny.org; *Dir* Susan Henshaw Jones
Open daily 10 AM - 6 PM, cl New Years Day, Thanksgiving Day, Christmas Day; Admis adults $10, seniors & students $6, mems & children 12 & under free, family & group rates available; Estab 1923 to preserve the cultural accomplishments of New York City & to meet the needs & interests of the community of today; Permanent & temporary exhibition galleries on subjects related to mission; Average Annual Attendance: 350,000; Mem: 2,500; dues $35 & up
Income: $5,000,000 (financed by private & nonprofit institutions, individual contributions, city, state & federal funds)
Special Subjects: Photography, Painting-American, Prints, Sculpture, Architecture, Drawings, Graphics, Anthropology, Archaeology, Costumes, Ceramics, Crafts, Folk Art, Etchings & Engravings, Landscapes, Decorative Arts, Manuscripts, Dolls, Furniture, Glass, Jewelry, Marine Painting, Metalwork, Historical Material, Maps, Coins & Medals, Dioramas, Embroidery, Cartoons
Collections: NY Fashions, Costumes & Textiles Coll; Decorative Arts Coll; marine colls; NYC Photography, Prints & Drawings; NYC Theatre & Broadway Coll; NY Toy Coll; NY Paintings & Sculpture
Publications: Annual report; exhibit catalogs; quarterly newsletter; quarterly programs brochure for members
Activities: Classes for adults & children; docent training; History Day for high school & younger students; lects open to pub; gallery talks; concerts; city walking tours; competitions with awards; original objects of art lent to affiliated institutions; lending collection contains sculptures, 40,000 books, 5,000 original art works, 15,000 original prints, 2,000 paintings & 300,000 photographs; book traveling exhibs 1-2 per yr; originate traveling exhibs to other mus; mus shop sells books, reproductions, prints & slides

L **Research Room,** 1220 5th Ave at 104th St, New York, NY 10029-9958. Tel 212-534-1672; Fax 212-534-5974; Elec Mail research@mcny.org; Internet Home Page Address: www.mcny.org; *Pres & Dir* Susan Henshaw Jones; *Deputy Dir* Dr Sarah Henry; *VPres Fin & Admin & CFO* Carl Dreyer; *VPres Develop* Susan Madden; *Dir Colls* James W Tottis; *VPres Communs* Barbara Livenstein
Open Tues - Sun 10 AM - 6 PM; Suggested admis families (max 2 adults) $20, adults $10, seniors & students $6, mems & children under 12 no admis fee; Museum founded 1923, devoted to the history of New York City; Museum exhib focus on history of NYC and its people; Average Annual Attendance: 150,000; Mem: Various categories of membership
Income: public & private partnership
Library Holdings: Book Volumes 8,000; Clipping Files; Manuscripts; Maps; Memorabilia; Original Art Works; Original Documents; Periodical Subscriptions 25; Photographs; Prints; Reproductions; Sculpture
Special Subjects: Decorative Arts, Photography, Drawings, Etchings & Engravings, Graphic Arts, Manuscripts, Maps, Painting-American, Posters, Prints, Sculpture, Historical Material, Watercolors, Ceramics, Cartoons, Porcelain, Furniture, Period Rooms, Costume Design & Constr, Glass, Metalwork, Dolls, Jewelry, Leather, Miniatures, Silver, Marine Painting, Landscapes, Dioramas, Coins & Medals, Pewter, Architecture, Portraits, Textiles
Collections: Paintings, sculpture, prints, photography, costumes, decorative arts, toys, theater memorabilia; manuscripts & ephemera
Exhibitions: see website www.mcny.org for current schedule
Publications: various
Activities: Classes for children; docent training; lects open to pub; concerts; gallery talks; tours; museum shop sells books, magazines, original art, reproductions & prints

NATIONAL ANTIQUE & ART DEALERS ASSOCIATION OF AMERICA, INC
For further information, see National and Regional Organizations

NATIONAL ASSOCIATION OF WOMEN ARTISTS, INC
For further information, see National and Regional Organizations

M **NATIONAL MUSEUM OF THE AMERICAN INDIAN,** George Gustav Heye Center, One Bowling Green, New York, NY 10004. Tel 212-514-3700; Elec Mail nmaicollections@si.edu; Internet Home Page Address: www.AmericanIndian.si.edu; *Dir* Kevin Grover; *Dir Heye Ctr* John Hanworth
Open daily 10 AM - 5 PM, Thurs until 8 PM, cl Christmas; No admis fee; Estab 1989 to recognize & affirm the historical & contemporary cultures & cultural achievements of the Native peoples of the Western Hemisphere; 20,000 sq ft exhibition galleries. Bureau of the Smithsonian Institution; Average Annual Attendance: 300,000; Mem: dues $25
Income: Financed by trust, endowments & revenues, gifts, grants, contributions, mem & funds appropriated by Congress
Special Subjects: Latin American Art, Painting-American, Photography, Sculpture, American Indian Art, Anthropology, Archaeology, Ethnology, Pre-Columbian Art, Textiles, Costumes, Ceramics, Pottery, Decorative Arts, Manuscripts, Eskimo Art, Historical Material, Coins & Medals
Collections: Native American art & objects
Exhibitions: Rotating exhibits
Publications: Books, occasionally; brochures; catalogs; recordings
Activities: Classes for adults & children; lects open to pub, 3-5 vis lectrs per yr; concerts; gallery talks; tours; guided tours for children; scholarships offered; individual paintings & original objects of art lent to museums, including tribal mus & cultural ctrs, nonprofit institutions & other appropriate sites; originate traveling exhibs; mus shop sells Indian crafts, jewelry, masks, pottery, beadwork, basketry, weavings, carvings, paintings, prints, books, magazines, original art, reproductions, slides, postcards & notepaper

NATIONAL SCULPTURE SOCIETY
For further information, see National and Regional Organizations

NATIONAL SOCIETY OF MURAL PAINTERS, INC
For further information, see National and Regional Organizations

M **NEUE GALERIE NEW YORK,** 1048 5th (at 86th St), New York, NY 10028-0111. Tel 201-994-9494; WATS www.neueglaerie.org
Open Thurs - Mon 11AM - 6PM; Admis adult $20, students & seniors 65 & up $10
Collections: paintings; sculpture; works on paper; decorative arts; photographs

M **NEW MUSEUM OF CONTEMPORARY ART,** 235 Bowery, New York, NY 10002. Tel 212-219-1222; Elec Mail info@newmuseum.org; Internet Home Page Address: www.newmuseum.org
Open Wed - Sun 11 AM - 6 PM & Thurs until 9 PM; cl Mon, Tues, Thanksgiving, Christmas & New Year's Days; Admis general $12, seniors $10, students $8, mem & under 18 free, free Thurs 7-9 PM
Publications: Exhib catalogs
Activities: Family, school & youth progs; tours; mus shop sells limited editions

L **The Soho Center Library,** 235 Bowery, New York, NY 10002-1218. Tel 212-219-1222; Fax 212-431-5328; Elec Mail newmu@newmuseum.org; Internet Home Page Address: www.newmuseum.org; *Dir* Lisa Phillips
Open by appointment; Estab 1985; Reference library, cl to pub for renovations
Income: Financed by mem & city appropriation
Library Holdings: Book Volumes 200; Periodical Subscriptions 150
Special Subjects: Art History, Film, Painting-American, Painting-British, Painting-Dutch, Painting-French, Painting-German, Painting-Italian, Painting-Japanese, Painting-European, Conceptual Art, Painting-Australian, Painting-Canadian, Painting-New Zealand, Architecture
Activities: Mus shop sells books, clothing, cd-rom, dvd, video

M **NEW WORLD ART CENTER,** T F Chen Cultural Center, 250 Lafayette St (SoHo), New York, NY 10012. Tel 212-966-4363; Tel 212-941-9296; Fax 212-966-5285; Elec Mail chen@tfchen.org; Internet Home Page Address: www.tfchen.org; *Dir* Julie Chen; *Pres* Lucia Hou; *Exec Asst* Louise Chen; *VPres* Ted Chen
Open Tues - Sat 1 - 6 PM, appt preferred; No admis fee; Estab 1996 to advance new artistic & cultural ideas & further global harmony; A strikingly redesigned six-story art center that aims to be the hub of a New Renaissance & act as a unifying force to bring together a world family of artists, thinkers, art lovers & visionaries focus on art educ & a global cultural of peace; Average Annual Attendance: 5,000; Mem: Dues $30 & up
Income: Financed by mem & private donations
Library Holdings: Book Volumes; Cards; Clipping Files; Exhibition Catalogs; Framed Reproductions; Original Documents; Pamphlets; Photographs; Records; Reproductions; Slides; Video Tapes
Special Subjects: Drawings, Graphics, Hispanic Art, Latin American Art, Painting-American, Photography, American Indian Art, American Western Art, African Art, Ethnology, Ceramics, Folk Art, Etchings & Engravings, Afro-American Art, Decorative Arts, Painting-European, Painting-Japanese, Portraits, Posters, Furniture, Oriental Art, Asian Art, Calligraphy, Antiquities-Oriental, Painting-Italian
Collections: African Art; T F Chen, Neo-Iconography paintings; Emerging Artists, all media; Italian Art; Master Artists (Picasso, Miro, Chagall & others); Vietnamese Art & Art Objects
Exhibitions: Post-Van Gogh Retrospective (1954-1998); Art from the Mediterranean; Japanese Art; group shows
Publications: Art Books, 12 & up
Activities: Classes for adults & children; Lects open to pub; gallery talks; concerts; tours; awards: art competitions, essay on Neo-Iconography; lending of original objects of art to Taiwan mus of art; book traveling exhibs, 2 per yr; originates traveling exhibs; mus shop sells books, original art, reproductions & prints

A **NEW YORK ARTISTS EQUITY ASSOCIATION, INC,** 498 Broome St, New York, NY 10013-2213; PO Box 1258, New York, NY 10116-1258. Tel 212-941-0130; Fax 212-941-0138; Elec Mail reginas@anny.org; Internet Home Page Address: www.anny.org; *Exec Dir* Regina Stewart
Open Tues - Fri 11 AM - 6 PM; No admis fee; Estab 1947 as a politically non-partisan group to advance the cultural, legislative, economic and professional interest of painters, sculptors, printmakers, and others in the field of visual arts. Various committees concerned with aims. Administrators of the Artists Welfare Fund, Inc; Broome Street Gallery; Mem: Over 3000; dues $35
Income: Financed by dues
Collections: Artbank; NYAEA Collection
Publications: The Artists Proof newsletter, quarterly

Activities: Lect open to public; trips to cultural institutions; advocacy; information services; artists benefits

L **THE NEW YORK PUBLIC LIBRARY,** Humanities Department, 476 5th Ave, Rm 313 New York, NY 10018-2788. Tel 212-930-0830; Elec Mail grdref@nypl.org; Internet Home Page Address: www.nypl.org; *Chief, Art Info Resources* Clayton Kirking
Open Mon, Thurs, Fri & -Sat 10 AM - 6 PM, Tues & Wed 11 AM - 7:30 PM; Estab 1895; Entire library contains over 30,000,000 items

L **Print Room,** Fifth Ave & 42nd St, Rm 308 New York, NY 10018. Tel 212-930-0817; Fax 212-930-0530; Elec Mail prnref@nypl.org; Internet Home Page Address: www.nypl.org; *Cur Prints* Alvaro Gonzalez-Lazo
Open Tues - Sat 1 PM - 5:45 PM; Estab 1899
Library Holdings: Book Volumes 25,000; Other Holdings Stereographs 72,000; Photographs 15,000; Prints 175,000
Collections: Samuel Putnam Avery Collection (primarily 19th century prints); Radin Collection of Western European bookplates; British & American caricatures; Beverly Chew bequest of Milton & Pope portraits; Eno Collection of New York City Views; McAlpin Collection of George Washington Portraits; Smith Collection of Japanese Prints; Phelps Stokes Collection of American Views; Lewis Wickes Hine Collection; Robert Dennis Collection of Stereoscopic Views; Pageant of America Collection; Romana Javitz Collection; Portrait File; Artists Book Collection
Exhibitions: 2 rotating exhibits per year
Activities: Classes for adults; tours; fels available

L **Spencer Collection,** 5th Ave & 42nd St, Third Fl, Rm 308 New York, NY 10018. Tel 212-275-6975; 930-0817; Fax 212-930-0530; Elec Mail prnref@nypl.org; Internet Home Page Address: www.nypl.org
Open Tues - Sat 1-6 PM by appt only; Available through Prints & Photographs Study Room
Library Holdings: Book Volumes 9000

L **Art & Architecture Collection,** 476 5th Ave, Rm 300, Stephen A Schwarzman Bldg New York, NY 10018-2788. Tel 212-930-0722; Fax 212-930-0530; Elec Mail artrof@nypl.org; Internet Home Page Address: www.nypi.org; *Chief Art Information Resources* Clayton C Kirking; Vincenzo Rutigliano; *Librn* Caroline Gifford; *Librn* Ryan M Helay
Open Mon - Fri 10AM - 6 PM, Tues & Wed 10 AM - 7:30 PM, Sun 1 PM - 5 PM (Sept-May); Estab 1995; Circ 104,000
Income: pub/private
Library Holdings: Auction Catalogs; Book Volumes 556,000; Clipping Files; Exhibition Catalogs; Fiche; Other Holdings; Pamphlets; Periodical Subscriptions
Special Subjects: Art History, Collages, Constructions, Folk Art, Decorative Arts, Illustration, Mixed Media, Photography, Drawings, Graphic Arts, Graphic Design, Islamic Art, Painting-American, Painting-British, Painting-Dutch, Painting-Flemish, Painting-French, Painting-German, Painting-Italian, Painting-Japanese, Painting-Russian, Painting-Spanish, Sculpture, Painting-European, Portraits, Watercolors, Ceramics, Conceptual Art, Crafts, Latin American Art, Painting-Israeli, American Western Art, Bronzes, Cartoons, Fashion Arts, Interior Design, Asian Art, Video, Porcelain, Eskimo Art, Furniture, Mexican Art, Southwestern Art, Ivory, Jade, Costume Design & Constr, Glass, Mosaics, Painting-Polish, Stained Glass, Aesthetics, Metalwork, Carpets & Rugs, Enamels, Gold, Goldsmithing, Handicrafts, Jewelry, Miniatures, Oriental Art, Pottery, Silver, Silversmithing, Tapestries, Textiles, Marine Painting, Landscapes, Painting-Scandinavian, Pewter, Laces, Painting-Australian, Painting-Canadian, Painting-New Zealand, Architecture, Embroidery, Woodcarvings
Activities: Classes for adults; lectrs open to pub

L **Schomburg Center for Research in Black Culture,** 515 Malcolm X Blvd, New York, NY 10037-1801. Tel 212-491-2200; Elec Mail scgenref@nypl.org; Internet Home Page Address: www.nypl.org; *Dir* Howard Dodson
Open Mon - Wed Noon - 8 PM, Thurs & Fri 11 AM - 6 PM, Sat 10 AM - 5 PM, cl Sun; Circ 4,817; A reference library devoted to black people throughout the world; two galleries in lobby for rotating exhibition program; comprised of Schomburg Bldg, Langston Hughes Bldg & Landmark Bldg; Average Annual Attendance: 84,055
Library Holdings: Book Volumes 130,000; Clipping Files; Filmstrips; Other Holdings Broadsides; Maps; Playbills; Programs; Photographs; Prints; Records; Reels
Collections: Books on Black Culture & Art; a research collection containing African Art, American Art by Black artists, Afro-Caribbean art & artifacts; Art & Artifacts Division; Manuscripts, Archives & Rare Books Division; Moving Image & Recorded Sound Division; Photographs & Prints Division
Exhibitions: Rotating exhibits
Activities: Lects open to pub; gallery talks; tours; fellowships offered; originate traveling exhibs; sales shop sells books, reproductions, exhib catalogs & cards

L **Mid-Manhattan Library, Art Collection,** 455 Fifth Ave at 40th St, Fl 3 New York, NY 10016-0119. Tel 970-275-6975 (General); Tel 212-340-0871 (Coll); Elec Mail mmart@nypl.org; Internet Home Page Address: www.nypl.org; *Supvr Libr Art & Picture Coll* Susan Chute
Open Mon - Thurs 8 AM - 11 PM, Fri 8 AM - 8 PM, Sat - Sun 10 AM - 6 PM; No admis fee
Library Holdings: Book Volumes 40,000; Clipping Files; Exhibition Catalogs; Fiche; Other Holdings; Periodical Subscriptions 200; Photographs; Prints; Reels; Video Tapes
Collections: Vertical Files on Artists with brochures & exhib catalogs
Exhibitions: Art Wall on Third Exhib Series; Art in the Window Exhib Series
Activities: Lects open to pub
—Mid-Manhattan Library, Picture Collection, 455 Fifth Ave at 40th St, Fl 3 New York, NY 10016-0119. Tel 917-275-6975 (General); Tel 212-340-0878 (Coll); Elec Mail mmpic@nypl.org; Internet Home Page Address: www.nypl.org; *Supervising Librn* Constance Novak
Open Mon - Thurs 8 AM - 9 PM, Fri 8 AM - 8 PM, Sat - Sun 10 AM - 6 PM; No admis fee; Estab 1915
Library Holdings: Other Holdings; Photographs; Prints
Collections: Approx 5,000,000 classified images; Original prints, photographs, poster, postcards & illustrations from books, magazines & newspapers classified into 12,000 subject headings; Digital Picture Coll: 38,000+ images in NYPL Digital Gallery

M **The New York Public Library for the Performing Arts,** 40 Lincoln Ctr Plaza, New York, NY 10023-7498. Tel 212-870-1630; Fax 212-870-1860; Internet Home Page Address: www.nypl.org; *Dir* Jacqueline Z Davis; *Cur Exhib* Barbara Cohen-Stratyner; *Cur Dance* Jan Schmidt; *Theatre Cur* Karen Nickeson; *Cur Recordings* Sarah Ziebell; *Chief Librn Circ Coll Mgr* David Callahan
Open Mon & Thurs noon - 8 PM, Tues Wed & Fri 11 AM - 6 PM, Sat 10 AM - 6 PM, cl Sun ; No admis fee; Estab 1965 to present exhibitions of high quality pertaining directly with the performing arts; Vincent Astor Gallery is 38 x 36 x 16 ft; Oenslager Gallery is 116 x 20-36 x 10 ft + 20 x 40 x 24 ft section. Both galleries have full media playback capability; Average Annual Attendance: 300,000
Income: Financed by endowment & city appropriation
Library Holdings: Audio Tapes; Book Volumes; CD-ROMs; Cassettes; Clipping Files; Compact Disks; DVDs; Exhibition Catalogs; Fiche; Lantern Slides; Manuscripts; Memorabilia; Motion Pictures; Original Art Works; Original Documents; Pamphlets; Periodical Subscriptions; Photographs; Prints; Records; Reels; Slides; Video Tapes
Collections: Prints; letters; documents; photographs; posters, films; video tapes; memorabilia; dance music; recordings
Activities: Docent training; symposia; lects open to pub, 20 vis lectrs per yr; concerts; gallery talks; tours; awards; lending collection contains books, cassettes, motion picture videos & phono records; book traveling exhibs 1 per yr; originate traveling exhibs 3 per yr; mus shop sells books, magazines, original art, reproductions & prints

L **NEW YORK SCHOOL OF INTERIOR DESIGN,** New York School of Interior Design Library, 170 E 70th St, New York, NY 10021-5167. Tel 212-472-1500, Ext 214; Fax 212-472-8175; Elec Mail paul@nysid.edu; Internet Home Page Address: www.nysid.edu; Internet Home Page Address: www.nysid.net/library; *Dir of Libr* Eric Wolf; *Library Assoc* Christopher Spinelli; *Library Assoc* Mary Lynch; *Asst Librn* Rebecca Uranz
Open Mon - Thurs 9 AM - 9 PM, Fri 9 AM - 5 PM, Sat 10 AM - 5 PM (reduced hours between sems); Pub admitted with METRO referral card; Estab 1924 to supplement the courses given by the school & to assist students & faculty in their research & information needs; Circ 7000; Average Annual Attendance: 40,000
Income: $195,490 (financed by New York State grant & general operating fund)
Purchases: $44,000
Library Holdings: Auction Catalogs 250; Audio Tapes 35; Book Volumes 15,000; CD-ROMs 100; DVDs; Exhibition Catalogs; Lantern Slides; Other Holdings Product Literature; Samples; Periodical Subscriptions 102; Slides 3,500; Video Tapes 125
Special Subjects: Decorative Arts, Interior Design, Architecture

A **NEW YORK SOCIETY OF ARCHITECTS,** 299 Broadway, Ste 206, New York, NY 10007. Tel 212-385-8950; Fax 212-385-8961; Elec Mail office@nysarch.com; Internet Home Page Address: www.nysarch.com; *Pres* Jorge Bosch; *VPres* Elliott Vilkas; *Treas* Mitchell J Goldberg; *Exec Sec* Nereida Sanchez
Open 9:30 AM - 4:30 PM; Incorporated 1906; Mem: 450; dues $275
Income: $100,000 (financed by dues & sales)
Publications: Bulletin, bi-monthly; New York City Building Code Manual; New York City Fire Prevention Code
Activities: Educ progs; educ seminars; Honorary Membership Certificate to affiliated professions other than architect, Distinguished Service Award to members, Sidney L Strauss Memorial Award to architect or layman, Fred L Liebmann Book Award

M **NEW YORK STUDIO SCHOOL OF DRAWING, PAINTING & SCULPTURE,** Gallery, 8 W Eighth St, New York, NY 10011. Tel 212-673-6466; Fax 212-777-0996; Elec Mail gallery@nyss.org; Internet Home Page Address: www.nyss.org; *Dean* Graham Nickson; *Assoc Dean* Jeffrey Hoffeld
Open daily 10 AM - 10 PM; No admis fee; Estab 1964, a nonprofit organization; Gallery is located on ground floor of the Studio School, site of the original Whitney Mus of Art; 2 large rooms on courtyard; Average Annual Attendance: 1,000
Income: Financed by private funding
Library Holdings: Auction Catalogs; Book Volumes; Exhibition Catalogs; Periodical Subscriptions
Special Subjects: Drawings, Painting-American, Sculpture, Watercolors, Etchings & Engravings, Painting-European, Painting-British, Painting-French, Painting-Australian
Exhibitions: See website for archive of past exhibs
Publications: Evening lecture schedule, exhibition series
Activities: Classes for adults; drawing instruction; lect open to public, 50-60 vis lectrs per year; gallery talks; tours; scholarship & fels offered; exten dept

L **Library,** 8 W Eighth St, New York, NY 10011. Tel 212-673-6466 (Ext 118); Elec Mail library@nyss.org; *Dean* Graham Nickson
Open appointments required; No admis fee; Estab 1964 for pedagogical purposes; Open to pub
Library Holdings: Audio Tapes; Book Volumes 4700; Cassettes; Clipping Files; Exhibition Catalogs; Periodical Subscriptions; Reproductions; Slides; Video Tapes
Special Subjects: Drawings, Sculpture
Activities: Lectures open to public

M **NEW YORK UNIVERSITY,** Grey Art Gallery, 100 Washington Sq E, New York, NY 10003-6688. Tel 212-998-6780; Fax 212-995-4024; Elec Mail greyartgallery@nyu.edu; Internet Home Page Address: www.nyu.edu/greyart; *Registrar & Gallery Mgr* Michele Wong; *Deputy Dir* Frank Poueymirou; *Dir* Lynn Gumpert
Open Tues, Thurs & Fri 11 AM - 6 PM, Wed 11 AM - 8 PM, Sat 11 AM - 5 PM; Admis suggested contribution $3; Estab 1975 as university art mus to serve pub as well as university community. The New York University Art Collection of approx 5000 works is now under the Grey Art Gallery; Gallery space of approx 4000 sq ft used for changing exhibitions; Average Annual Attendance: 50,000
Special Subjects: Painting-American, Prints, Painting-European, Watercolors, Asian Art
Collections: New York University Art Collection; Ben & Abby Grey Foundation Collection of Asian & Middle Eastern Art
Publications: Exhibition catalogs

Activities: Lects open to public, 2-3 vis lectrs per yr; individual paintings & original objects of art lent to other cultural institutions & sister organizations for exhibs; originate traveling exhibs; sales shop sells exhibition catalogs

M **Washington Square East Galleries,** 80 Washington Sq E, New York, NY 10003-6697. Tel 212-998-5747; Fax 212-998-5752; Elec Mail 80wse@nyu.edu; Internet Home Page Address: www.nyu.edupagesgalleries; *Dir* Ruth D Newman; *Faculty Dir* Dr Marilynn Karp
Open Tues 10 AM - 7 PM, Wed & Thurs 10 AM - 6 PM, Fri & Sat 10 AM - 5 PM; No admis fee; Estab 1975 for exhibitions of works by graduate student artists; Eight gallery rooms containing solo shows; Average Annual Attendance: 10,000
Exhibitions: 70 group shows annually; Annual Small Works Competition; Thesis Exhibitions
Publications: Press releases
Activities: Annual International Art Competition, Small Works

L **Stephen Chan Library of Fine Arts,** One E 78th St (Duke House), New York, NY 10075. Tel 212-992-5825; Fax 212-992-5807; Elec Mail ifa.library@nyu.edu; Internet Home Page Address: www.nyu.edu/gsas/dept/fineart; *Head Librn* Amy Lucker; *Libr Serv Supv* Michael Hughes; *Libr Asst* Kimberly Hannah; *Libr Asst* Shlrin Khaki
Open Mon & Fri 9 AM - 5 PM, Tues - Thurs 9 AM - 7 PM; Estab to provide scholarly materials for graduate studies in art history, archaeology & conservation of works of art; Circ Non-circulating; Research Library
Library Holdings: Book Volumes 140,000; CD-ROMs; Exhibition Catalogs; Periodical Subscriptions 460
Special Subjects: Art History, Painting-European, Archaeology, Asian Art, Antiquities-Oriental, Antiquities-Persian, Antiquities-Assyrian, Antiquities-Byzantine, Antiquities-Egyptian, Antiquities-Etruscan, Antiquities-Greek, Antiquities-Roman

L **Institute of Fine Arts Visual Resources Collection,** One E 78th St (Duke House), B Level, New York, NY 10075. Tel 212-992-5810; Fax 212-992-5807; Elec Mail jenni.rodda@nyu.edu; Internet Home Page Address: www.ifa.nyu.edu; *Photographer* Nita Roberts; *Cur* Jenni Rodda; *Information Svc Asst* Michael Konrad; *Circ & Reference Asst* Fatima Tanglao; *Info Serv* Jason Varone
Open Mon - Fri 9 AM - 6 PM by appointment; Circ Non-circulating; Library open to qualified researchers & academia
Library Holdings: Lantern Slides 150,000; Other Holdings B&W photographs, mounted & unmounted 750,000; 35mm slides 350,000
Special Subjects: Art History, Archaeology
Collections: Biblioteca Berenson; Frank Caro Archives (b&w, Oriental); Census; Gertrude Achenbach Coor Archives; D.I.A.L.; Walter Friedlaender Archives; Corpus Gernsheim (85,000 pieces; drawings); Henry Russell Hitchcock Archives (b&w, architecture); Richard Offner Archives (b&w, Italian painting); James Stubblebine Archives (b&w, Italian painting); Emile Wolf Archives (b&w, Spanish art); photographs are used for teaching & research purposes only

A **NEW-YORK HISTORICAL SOCIETY,** Museum, 170 Central Park W, New York, NY 10024-5194. Tel 212-873-3400; Fax 212-874-8706; Elec Mail webmaster@nyhistory.org; Internet Home Page Address: www.nyhistory.org; *Pres & CEO* Louise Mirrer; *VPres & Sr Art Historian* Linda S Ferber; *VPres Communs* Laura Washington; *VPres Educ* Sharon Dunn; *VPres Opers* Andrew Buonpastore; *VPres Pub Prog* Dale Gregory; *CFO* Rich Shein; *Dir Exhib* Gerhard Schlanzky; *Dir Visitor Svcs* Chris Catanese; *Chief Cur Mus Div* Stephen Edidin; *VPres History Exhibs* Marco Reaven; *Sr Dir Resources & Progs* Jean Ashton; *Historian & VPres Scholarly Progs* Valerie Paley
Open Tues -Sat 10 AM - 6 PM, Fri 10 AM - 8 PM, Sun 11 AM - 5 PM, cl Mon; Hours subject to change due to construction, call ahead to confirm; Admis adults $15, seniors & educators$12, students w/ID $10, children 5-13 $5, children under 5 free; Estab 1804 to collect & preserve material relating to the history of the US through the eyes of New York; Maintains 1st & 2nd Floor Galleries, W 77th St Rotunda Gallery, Henry Luce III Center for the Study of American Culture; Average Annual Attendance: 175,000; Mem: 4200; dues individual $55, student/senior/educator $40, dual senior $70, dual family $00, young friend $125, friend $250, Patron $500, benefactor $1,000, Gotham Fellow $2,500, chmn council $5,000-25,000
Income: $16,000,000 (financed by endowment, grants, contributions, federal, state & local government, mem, admis)
Library Holdings: Book Volumes; Clipping Files; Exhibition Catalogs; Fiche; Manuscripts; Maps; Memorabilia; Original Art Works; Original Documents; Other Holdings ephemera; Pamphlets; Periodical Subscriptions; Photographs
Special Subjects: Architecture, Drawings, Historical Material, Landscapes, Manuscripts, Photography, Prints, Sculpture, Silver, Watercolors, Painting-American, Decorative Arts, Ceramics, Portraits, Maps
Collections: The Birds of America: Audubon's 433 original watercolors; American paintings from the Colonial period to 20th century, including genre scenes, portraits & landscapes by major artists of this period; 60,000+ objects & works of art relating to the founding of America, history of art in the US, & history of NY & its people; Tiffany Lamp Collection; World Trade Center artifacts; Hudson River landscapes; Gilder Lehrman Collection
Exhibitions: Slavery in New York Panel Exhib (permanent); A Portrait of the City (permanent)
Publications: catalogs & compendia of permanent collections; portraits, drawings, Tiffany lamps, Slaver, Grant/Lee
Activities: Classes for adults & children; docent talks; teacher resources; outreach progs; Saturday Academy; lects open to pub, 75 vis lectrs per yr; Bernard & Irene Schwartz Distinguished Speakers Series; concerts; gallery talks; tours; symposia; fellowships; individual paintings & original objects of art lent to mus; lending collection contains 2700 paintings, 5000 drawings, 675 sculptures, 800 miniatures; Touch Collection, Web-based training; book traveling exhibs 4 per yr; originate traveling exhibs to other mus; mus shop sells books, original art, prints, reproductions, cards, magazines, slides, history and themed decorative objects

L **Library,** 2 W 77th St, New York, NY 10024; 170 Central Park West, New York, NY 10024. Tel 212-485-9226; Fax 212-875-1591; Internet Home Page Address: www.nyhistory.org; *Dir Libr Div* Jean Ashton; *Dir Libr Opers* Nina Nazionale
Printed & Manuscript Collections open Tues - Sat 10 AM - 5 PM, Summer: Tues - Fri 10 AM - 5 PM; Graphic Collections open Tues - Fri 10 AM - 5 PM by appt only; No admis fee; photocopying fees apply
Library Holdings: Book Volumes 500,000; Cards 10,000; Clipping Files; Exhibition Catalogs; Fiche; Manuscripts; Maps; Memorabilia; Micro Print; Original Art Works; Original Documents; Other Holdings AV maps 15,000, Micro film 50,000, Vertical files 10,000 (including menus); Pamphlets; Periodical Subscriptions 150; Photographs; Prints; Reels; Sculpture
Special Subjects: Art History, Photography, Manuscripts, Maps, Posters, Prints, Historical Material, Woodcuts, Architecture
Collections: American Almanacs; American Art Patronage; American Genealogy; American Indian (accounts of & captivities; Early American Imprints; Early Travels in America; Early American Trials; Civil War Regimental Histories & Muster Rolls; Jenny Lind (Leonidas Westervelt) Maps; Military History (Military Order of the Loyal Legion of the United States, Commander of the State of New York) Military History & Science (Seventh Regiment Military Library); Naval & Marine History (Naval History Society); 18th & 19 Century New York City & New York State Newspapers; Slavery & the Civil War; Spanish American War (Harper); Among the Manuscript Collections; Horatio Gates, Alexander McDougall, Rufus King, American Fur Company, Livingston Family, American Art Union, American Academy of Fine Arts; Broadside Collection; Hotel Files; Arnold Shircliffe Menu Collection; Newspapers Collection; Online Catalog; Manuscript Collections Relating to Slavery (online); Children's Aid Society Images (online); Marion Mahoney Griffin's The Magic of America, typescript & illustrations; Examination Days: The NY African Free School Collection; Alexander Hamilton Digital Project; Witness to the Early American Experience
Exhibitions: Civil War Treasures from the NY Historical Society; Brooklyn Revealed

M **NICHOLAS ROERICH MUSEUM,** 319 W 107th St, New York, NY 10025-2799. Tel 212-864-7752; Fax 212-864-7704; Elec Mail director@roerich.org; Internet Home Page Address: www.roerich.org; *Pres* Edgar Lansbury; *Exec Dir* Daniel Entin
Open daily 2 - 5 PM; cl Mon & holidays; No admis fee; donations accepted; Estab 1958 to show a permanent collection of paintings by Nicholas Roerich, internationally known artist, to promote his ideals as a great thinker, writer, humanitarian, scientist, and explorer, and to promote his Pact and Banner of Peace; New York brownstone with three exhibit floors; Average Annual Attendance: 20,000; Mem: 800; dues patron $100, contributing $50, assoc $25
Income: Financed by mem & donations
Collections: Permanent collection of paintings by Nicholas Roerich
Publications: Altai-Himalaya, A Travel Diary; Flowers of Morya, The Theme of Spiritual Pilgrimage in the Poetry of Nicholas Roerich; The Invincible; Nicholas Roerich, An Annotated Bibliography; Nicholas Roerich, A Short Biography; Nicholas Roerich 1874-1974 Centenary Monograph; Roerich Pact & Banner of Peace; Shambhala; two books by Nicholas Roerich: On Eastern Crossroads, and Foundations of Buddhism
Activities: Lects open to pub; concerts; tours; mus shop selling books, reproductions and postcards

M **THE NIPPON GALLERY AT THE NIPPON CLUB,** (The Nippon Club) 145 W 57th St, New York, NY 10019-2220. Tel 212-581-2223; Fax 212-581-3332; Elec Mail info@nipponclub.org; Internet Home Page Address: www.nipponclub.org; *Dir* Yasuko Honda
Open Mon - Sat 10 AM - 6 PM, cl Sun & holidays; No admis fee; Estab 1981 for the purpose of international cultural exchange of arts & crafts from Japan & US; Located in the main lobby of a 7 story club house; gallery space is 1000 sq ft; Mem: 1200; dues $420
Income: Financed by mem
Special Subjects: Crafts
Publications: The Nippon Club Directory, annual; The Nippon Club News, monthly
Activities: Classes for adults; lects for members and the public, various sports activities & cultural events, concerts, gallery talks & tours

A **THE ONE CLUB,** 260 5th Ave, 2nd Fl New York, NY 10001. Tel 212-979-1900; Fax 212-979-5006; Internet Home Page Address: www.oneclub.com; *CEO* Mary Warlick; *Pres* Kevin Swanepoel; *Mng Dir* Emily Isovitsch; *Ed-in-Chief* Yash Egami
Check website for hrs; Estab 1975 to support the craft of advertising, informal interchange among creative people, develop advertising excellence through advertising students who are tomorrow's professionals; Exhibits feature different advertising agencies; Mem: dues individual & faculty $200, junior $150, student $95
Publications: The One Show Annual, Advertising's Best Print, Radio & TV, annually
Activities: Educ dept; lect open to public & some for members only; gallery talks; competitions with awards; scholarships offered; sales shop sells books & DVDs

M **PAINTING SPACE 122 ASSOCIATION INC,** 150 First Ave, New York, NY 10009. Tel 212-228-4249; Fax 212-505-6854; Elec Mail ps122gallery@verizon.net;
Open Thurs - Sun Noon - 6 PM; Estab 1979 to show work by emerging artists; 600 sq ft ground floor space; Average Annual Attendance: 20,000
Income: Financed by NYSCA & private funds
Activities: Competitions

L **PARSONS SCHOOL OF DESIGN,** Adam & Sophie Gimbel Design Library, 2 W 13th St 2d Fl, New York, NY 10011. Tel 212-229-8914; Fax 212-229-2806; Internet Home Page Address: http://:library.newschool.edu/gimbel; *Dir* Joy Kestenbaum; *Circ Mgr* Hanna Bachrach; *Supv* Christine Butler
Open Mon - Thurs 8 AM - 9 PM, Fri 8 AM - 6 PM, Sat noon - 6 PM, Sun noon - 8 PM, summer hours vary; Estab as a school in 1896, The Gimbel Library moved to its present location in 1974; collections & services support the curriculum of the school as well as general design research; Circ 165,000; Lending to Parsons students & library consortium members; limited reference to general public; Average Annual Attendance: 103,000
Income: Pvt
Library Holdings: Book Volumes 50,000; CD-ROMs 400; Exhibition Catalogs; Memorabilia; Micro Print; Original Art Works; Other Holdings Pictures 60,000; Periodical Subscriptions 201; Prints; Slides 80,000; Video Tapes 450

Special Subjects: Art History, Illustration, Photography, Graphic Design, Historical Material, Crafts, Fashion Arts, Industrial Design, Interior Design, Furniture, Metalwork, Jewelry, Oriental Art, Textiles, Architecture
Collections: Claire McCardell Fashion Sketchbooks

PASTEL SOCIETY OF AMERICA
For further information, see National and Regional Organizations

A **PEN & BRUSH, INC,** 29 E 22nd St, New York, NY 10010. Tel 212-475-3669; Fax 212-475-6018; Elec Mail info@penandbrush.org; Internet Home Page Address: www.penandbrush.org; *Exec Dir* Janice Sands; *Assoc Dir* Dawn Delikat; *Pres* Eleanor Campulli
Open Tues - Sun 4 - 6 PM; No Admis fee; Estab 1894, incorporated 1912 for encouragement in the arts; The Clubhouse was purchased in 1923, and contains artists studios, meeting room and 3 exhibition galleries; Average Annual Attendance: 1,000; Mem: 270; dues $250 professional women writers, artists, sculptors, craftsmen, musicians; annual meeting in Apr
Library Holdings: Other Holdings Members' Books
Collections: Collages; crafts; graphics; mixed media; oil; paintings; pastels; sculpture; watercolor
Exhibitions: Ten annual exhibitions of members' work; one man shows; solo winner shows
Publications: Pen & Brush bulletin, monthly
Activities: Dramatic progs; lects open to pub; concerts; scholarships; scholarships offered; sales shop sells original art, paintings, sculpture & craft items
L **Library,** 29 E 22nd St, New York, NY 10010. Tel 212-475-3669; Fax 212-475-6018; *Dir* Janice Sands
For members only
Library Holdings: Book Volumes 1000; Periodical Subscriptions 5
Publications: Bulletin, monthly

M **PHOENIX GALLERY,** 210 11th Ave, (at 25th St) Ste 902 New York, NY 10001-1224. Tel 212-226-8711; Fax 212-343-7307; Elec Mail info@phoenix-gallery.com; Internet Home Page Address: www.phoenix-gallery.com; *Dir* Linda Handler
Open Tues - Sat 11:30 AM - 6 PM; No admis fee; Estab 1958; 190 linear ft of exhibition walls. Not for profit artist-member gallery; Average Annual Attendance: 10,000; Mem: 33; dues non-active $2700, active $2160; meetings one per month
Income: $64,000 (financed by mem)
Collections: Contemporary Art - 33 members from all over the United States, Paris & Korea; Contemporary Art
Activities: Dramatic progs; poetry & dance progs; lects open to pub, 5 vis lectrs per yr; sponsoring of competitions

M **PRINCE STREET GALLERY,** 530 W 25th St, New York, NY 10001-5516. Tel 646-230-0246; Internet Home Page Address: www.princestreetgallery.com; *Co-Dir* Daniel Abrams; *Co-Dir* Arthur Kvarnstrom; *Sec* Ellen Piccolo; *Treas* Arthur Elias
Open Tues - Sat 11 AM - 6 PM; No admis fee; Estab 1970 to provide a showing place for members, mainly figurative art; cooperative artist run gallery; Gallery has about 30 members who have shown in New York as well as throughout the country & internationally; Average Annual Attendance: 8,000; Mem: 30; mem enrollment fees $500, mem $100 per month for 12 months (local), $130 (non-local); 6 meetings per yr
Income: Financed by mem
Exhibitions: Gallery Artists: Barbara Kulicke, Elizabeth Higgins, Marion Lerner-Levine, Gerald Marcus, Mary Salstrom, Gina Werfel, Rani Carson, Arthur Elias, Barbara Tipping Fitzpatrick, Nancy Grilikhes, Arthur Kvarnstrom, Paul Warren; Summer: invitational shows
Publications: Annual catalog
Activities: Lects open to public; gallery talks

C **PRINTED MATTER, INC,** 195 10th Ave Frnt, New York, NY 10011-4739. Tel 212-925-0325; Fax 212-925-0464; Elec Mail aabronson@printedmatter.org; Internet Home Page Address: www.printedmatter.org; *Pres* AA Bronson; *Dir* Catherine Krudy; *Assoc Dir* Max Schumann; *Bibliographer & Inventory Asst* Andrea Moreau; *Admin Asst* Carolyn Lockhart; *Distribution Asst* Shannon Michael Cane
Open Tues - Wed 11 AM - 6 PM, Thurs - Sat 11 AM - 7 PM; Estab 1976 to foster appreciation, dissemination & understanding of artists' publications; Small gallery; Average Annual Attendance: 100,000
Special Subjects: Maps
Exhibitions: Conceptual artists books from the 70's & early 80's
Publications: On-line
Activities: Lect open to pub; concerts; gallery talks; tours; Mus shop sells books, magazines, original art, prints, audio, video

A **PUBLIC ART FUND, INC,** One E 53rd St, New York, NY 10022. Tel 212-980-4575; Fax 212-980-3610; Elec Mail info@publicartfund.org; Internet Home Page Address: www.publicartfund.org; *Pres* Susan K Freedman; *Dir & Chief Cur* Nicholas Baume; *Finance & HR Mgr* Ciara Besson; *Proj Mgr* Elizabeth Linden; *Archivist* Tara Hart; *Project Mgr* Jesse Hamerman; *Communs Dir* Gabrielle Fisher
Open Mon - Fri 9:30 AM - 5:30 PM; No admis fee; Estab 1977 to present artists projects, new commissions, installations & exhibitions in public space
Publications: Catalogues; manuals on public art; newsletter; postcards
Activities: Temporary exhibition program; artist talks; In the Public Realm
L **Visual Archive,** One E 53rd St 11th Floor, New York, NY 10022. Tel 212-980-4575; Fax 212-980-3610; Elec Mail info@publicartfund.org; Internet Home Page Address: www.publicartfund.org; *Pres* Susan K Freedman; *Dir & Chief Cur* Nicholas Baume; *Project Mgr* Elizabeth Linden; *Project Mgr* Jesse Hamerman; *Admin Asst* Abigail Clark; *Pres & Mktg Mgr* Anita Iannacchione; *Finance & Human Resource* Ciara Besson; *Archivist* Tara Hart; *Communs Dir* Gabrielle Fisher
Open by appointment only, other project specific hours; No admis fee; Estab 1977; NYC's leading presenter of artists' projects, new commissions & exhibs in public spaces

Library Holdings: Audio Tapes; Cassettes; Clipping Files; Compact Disks; DVDs; Exhibition Catalogs; Kodachrome Transparencies; Lantern Slides; Manuscripts; Original Art Works; Original Documents; Other Holdings Documentation of public art projects; Pamphlets Brochures on all PAF projects; Photographs; Slides 4000; Video Tapes
Collections: Murals; outdoor sculpture; sponsors temporary installations throughout New York City
Publications: PAFlet; various books; semi-annual magazine
Activities: Lects open to pub; 6 vis lectrs per yr; sales shop sells books

A **QUEEN SOFIA SPANISH INSTITUTE,** (Queen Sofia Spanish Institute, Inc) 684 Park Ave, New York, NY 10065-5043. Tel 212-628-0420; Fax 212-734-4177; Elec Mail info@qssi.org; Internet Home Page Address: www.qssi.org; *Pres & CEO* Inmaculada de Habsburgo; *Chmn* Oscar de la Renta; *VChmn* Beatrice Santo Domingo; *Treas* David L Askren
Open Mon - Thurs 10 AM - 6 PM, Fri 10 AM - 8 PM, Sat 10 AM - 5 PM; Estab 1954 to promote understanding of Spanish culture, past & present, & current Spanish pub affairs & economic issues in the United States; enhance an understanding of the influence of Spanish culture in Americas; Housed in a McKim, Mead & White landmark building donated by Margaret Rockefeller Strong de Larrin, Marquesa de Cuevas; Mem: Dues individual $60, friend $500, patron $1000+, sponsor $5000+, benefactor $15,000+, golden benefactor $25,000+
Income: Financed by individual & corporate mem fees, donations, foundation grants & endowment
Special Subjects: Latin American Art
Exhibitions: Exhibits of rich & varied traditions of the visual arts of Spain & Latin America
Activities: Spanish language classes; lect open to public; symposia; Queen Sofia Spanish Institute Translation Prize

C **THE READER'S DIGEST ASSOCIATION INC,** 750 Third Ave, New York, NY 10007-2703. Tel 646-293-6000; *Cur* Marianne Brunson Frisch
Art collection located throughout corporate headquarters
Collections: Over 8000 works of art, 19th century American & contemporary American artists & International artists; graphics; decorative arts; sculpture; painting; mixed media; works on paper; Photography; Bloomsbury Group

M **THE RENEE & CHAIM GROSS FOUNDATION,** Chaim Gross Studio, 526 LaGuardia Pl, New York, NY 10012. Tel 212-529-4906; Fax 212-529-1966; Elec Mail info@rcgrossfoundation.org; Internet Home Page Address: www.rcgrossfoundation.org; *Pres* Mimi Gross; *Dir* Susan Fisher
Open Thurs 1- 5 PM; No admis fee; Estab 1989 to demonstrate the continuity of Gross's personal vision in sculpture over 70 years of work; Sculpture studio where Gross worked for over 30 years
Library Holdings: Auction Catalogs; Clipping Files; Exhibition Catalogs; Lantern Slides; Memorabilia; Original Documents; Pamphlets; Photographs; Prints; Records; Reels; Reproductions; Sculpture; Slides; Video Tapes
Collections: Permanent collection consists of 70 years of Chaim Gross's (1904-91) sculpture in wood, stone & bronze, drawings, prints & watercolors
Exhibitions: Exhibs, biannual
Activities: Tours for groups; gallery talks; lect open to public

M **RUBIN MUSEUM OF ART,** 150 W 17th St, New York, NY 10011-5402. Tel 212-620-5000; Elec Mail info@rmanyc.org; Internet Home Page Address: www.rmanyc.org; *Exec Dir* Patrick Sears; *Dir Finance & Admin* Marilena Christodoulou; *Dir External Affairs* Cynthia Guyer; *Dir Exhibs, Colls & Research* Jan Van Alphen; *Dir Educ & Visitor Experience* Marcos Stafne; *Dir Pub Progs & Performances* Tim McHenry
Open Mon & Thurs 11 AM - 5 PM, Wed 11 AM - 7 PM, Fri 11 AM - 10 PM, Sat - Sun 11 AM - 6 PM; Admis adults $10, seniors, students & artists with ID $7, college students with ID $2, children under 12, mems & seniors 1st Mon of month & Fri 6 PM - 10 PM free; Estab 2004; One of the world's most important colls of Himalayan Art; Average Annual Attendance: 170,000; Mem: 4,000
Special Subjects: Sculpture, Religious Art, Asian Art, Metalwork, Carpets & Rugs, Embroidery
Collections: Paintings, sculptures & textiles relating to the Himalayas
Activities: Classes for adults & children; docent training; lectrs open to the public, 30-40 vis lectrs per year; concerts; gallery talks; tours; organize traveling exhibs; mus shop sells books, magazines

C **RUDER FINN ARTS & COMMUNICATIONS, INC,** (Ruder Finn Inc) 301 E 57th St, New York, NY 10022-2905. Tel 212-593-6400; Fax 212-715-1507; Internet Home Page Address: www.ruderfinn.com; *Pres* Philippa Polskin
Estab to link corporations which support the arts with museum exhibitions and performing arts events, to develop major corporate sponsored exhibitions and special projects created for public spaces. Assistance given for marketing and publicity assignments for cultural institutions and the selection, installation and documentation of corporate art collections
Activities: Originate traveling exhibs to museums nationwide

SALMAGUNDI CLUB
For further information, see National and Regional Organizations

M **SCHOOL OF VISUAL ARTS,** Visual Arts Museum, 209 E 23rd St, New York, NY 10010-3994. Tel 212-592-2144; Fax 212-592-2095; Elec Mail galleriesandmuseum@adm.schoolofvisualarts.edu; Internet Home Page Address: www.schoolofvisualarts.edu/MuseumGalleries; *Dir* Francis DiTommaso; *Asst Dir* Richard Brooks
Open Mon - Wed & Fri 9 AM - 6:30 PM, Thurs 9 AM - 8 PM, Sat 10 AM - 5 PM; No admis fee; Estab 1961; College gallery; Average Annual Attendance: 8,000
Special Subjects: Photography, Drawings, Graphics, Painting-American, Prints, Watercolors, Etchings & Engravings, Collages, Posters, Juvenile Art, Cartoons
Exhibitions: New York Digital Salon; The Master's Series; Sculptors Drawings; Ann international traveling exhibition of art made with computers; Ann award exhibition honoring the great visual communicators of our time
Publications: Exhibition catalogs & posters

A **SEGUE FOUNDATION,** Reading Room-Archive, 300 Bowery, Apt. 2, New York, NY 10012-2802. Tel 212-674-0199; Fax 212-254-4145; Elec Mail sequefoundation@verizon.net; Internet Home Page Address: www.seguefoundation.com; WATS 800-869-7553; *Pres* James Sherry; *Exec Dir* Daniel Machlin
Open by appointment; Estab 1977; For reference only
Library Holdings: Audio Tapes; Cassettes; Manuscripts; Memorabilia; Other Holdings Vols & per subs 2000; Reproductions; Video Tapes
Collections: Language poetry books; periodicals; rare archival materials manuscripts; reading series footage
Publications: Poetry, literary criticism, film & performance texts

SOCIETY OF AMERICAN GRAPHIC ARTISTS
For further information, see National and Regional Organizations

M **SOCIETY OF ILLUSTRATORS,** Museum of American Illustration, 128 E 63rd St, New York, NY 10065-7303. Tel 212-838-2560; Fax 212-838-2561; Elec Mail info@societyillustrators.org; Internet Home Page Address: www.societyillustrators.org; *Pres* Dennis Dittrich; *Dir* Anelle Miller; *Dir Opers* Tom Stavrinos
Open Tues 10 AM - 8 PM, Wed - Fri 10 AM - 5 PM, Sat Noon - 4 PM, cl Mon, Aug & legal holidays; Suggested donation $5; members & students free; Estab 1901; Average Annual Attendance: 30,000
Collections: Original illustrations from 1838 to present, all media
Exhibitions: Student Scholarship competition - May; Children's book illustration exhibit - Oct; Members open - July
Activities: Classes for Adults; Lects open to pub, 18 vis lectrs; sponsor competitions for professional illustrators; awards; individual paintings & original objects of art lent to muse & universities; lending collection contains 1200 art works; originate traveling exhibs to schools; mus shop sells books, prints, t-shirts & gift items

SOCIETY OF ILLUSTRATORS
For further information, see National and Regional Organizations

SOCIETY OF PHOTOGRAPHERS & ARTISTS REPRESENTATIVES
For further information, see National and Regional Organizations

A **SOCIETY OF SCRIBES, LTD,** PO Box 933 New York, NY 10150-0933. Tel 212-452-0139; Tel 516-707-9926; Elec Mail info@societyofscribes.org; Internet Home Page Address: www.societyofscribes.org; *Pres* Eva J Kokoris; *Treas* Rebecca Kennedy Lakhani; *Recording Sec* Pamela Williams; *VPres* Chi Nguyen; *Registrar* Jerise Fogel; *Corresp Secy* Patricia Whitman; *Advertising & Publicity* Susan Steele
Open Mon - Fri 10 AM - 7 PM; Calligraphic exhibitions throughout New York City; Estab 1974; Mem: Dues overseas $45, Canada & Mexico $45, USA $40; annual meeting in Feb, annual Fair in Dec; memberships open to all interested in the calligraphic arts.
Exhibitions: Donnell Library
Publications: NewSOS Newsletter publ twice a year; Our journal Letters from New York
Activities: Adult classes in calligraphy & lettering arts & calligraphy in the graphic arts; lects & demonstrations open to public; 4-6 vis lectrs per year; gallery talks; competitions; lects at the Morgan Library, Grolier Club & the Donnell

M **SOHO 20 GALLERY,** 547 W 27th St, Ste 301, New York, NY 10001. Tel 212-367-8994; Fax 212-367-8984; Elec Mail soho20@verizon.net; Internet Home Page Address: www.soho20gallery.com; *Gallery Dir* Jenn Dierdorf
Open Tues - Sat Noon - 6 PM; No admis fee; Estab 1973 as a women's nonprofit, artist-run gallery; 1400 sq ft for exhibition. Main gallery 1000 sq ft invitational space; Average Annual Attendance: 50 per day; Mem: 27; dues $1320; meetings first Tues each month
Income: Financed by funding programs, sponsored exhibitions
Activities: Lects open to pub, 52 vis lectrs per yr; gallery talks; tours; individual paintings & original objects of art lent to corporations, universities & other galleries; originate traveling exhibs to other museums

M **SOLOMON R GUGGENHEIM MUSEUM,** 1071 Fifth Ave, New York, NY 10128-0173. Tel 212-423-3500; Elec Mail visitorinfo@guggenheim.org; Internet Home Page Address: www.guggenheim.org; *Dir Mus & Foundation* Richard Armstrong; *Deputy Dir & Chief Cur* Nancy Spector; *Sr Deputy Dir COO* Marc Steglitz; *Deputy Dir & Chief Officer Global Strategies* Juan Ignacio Vidarte; *Deputy Dir & Gen Counsel* Sarah Austrian; *Deputy Dir & Chief Global Commun* Eleanor Goldhar; *Deputy Dir & Dir Educ* Kim Katani; *Deputy Dir & Chief Conservator* Carol Stringari; *Deputy Dir Foundation* Ari Weisman; *Sr Cur Colls & Exhibs* Susan Davidson; *Cur Asian Art* Alexandra Munroe; *Cur Photography* Jennifer Blessing; *Cur 19th & Early 20th c Art* Vivian Greene; *Cur Colls & Exhibs* Tracy Bashkoff; *Assoc Cur Contemporary Art & Mgr Cur Affairs* Joan Young; *Assoc Cur Colls & Exhibs, Abu Dhabi Proj* Valerie Hillings; *Assoc Cur* Nat Trotman; *Asst Cur* Karole Vail; *Asst Cur* Katherine Brinson; *Asst Cur Asian Art* Sandhini Poddar; *Asst Cur Architecture & Design* David Van Der Leer; *Asst Cur* Maria Nicanor; *Asst Cur Colls* Lauren Hinkson; *Asst Cur* Megan Fontanella; *Conservator Colls & Exhibs* Julie Barten; *Sr Conservator Colls* Gillian McMillan; *Conservator, Sculpture* Nathan Otterson; *Assoc Conservator Paper* Jeffrey Warda; *Assoc Conservator Contemporary Art* Joanna Phillips; *Asst Dir Educ School & Family Progs* Sharon Vatsky; *Assoc Dir Educ Pub Progs* Christina Yang
Open Sun - Wed & Fri 10 AM - 5:45 PM, Sat 10 AM - 7:45 PM, cl Thurs, Thanksgiving, Christmas Eve & Day; Admis general $18, students with valid ID cards & seniors over 65 $15, children under 12 free, Sat 5:45 - 7:45 PM Pay What You Wish; Estab 1937 as a nonprofit organization which is maintained by the Solomon R Guggenheim Foundation; founded for the promotion, encouragement & educ in art; to foster an appreciation of art by acquainting mus visitors with significant paintings & sculpture of our time; The gallery was designed by architect Frank Lloyd Wright; Average Annual Attendance: 700,000; Mem: 7,000; dues $30-$5,000
Income: Financed by endowment, mem & state & federal appropriations
Special Subjects: Drawings, Painting-American, Photography, Sculpture, Watercolors, Painting-French, Painting-Spanish, Painting-Italian, Painting-German, Painting-Russian
Collections: Reflects the creative accomplishments in modern art from the time of the Impressionists to the constantly changing experimental art of today. The coll of nearly four thousand works, augmented by the Justin K Thannhauser Collection of 75 Impressionists & Post-Impressionist masterpieces, including the largest group of paintings by Vasily Kandinsky; one of the largest & most comprehensive coll of paintings by Paul Klee; largest number of sculptures by Constantin Brancusi in any New York museum; paintings by Chagall, Delaunay, Lager, Marc, Picasso, Bacon, Bonnard, Braque, Cezanne, Malevitch, Modigliani, Moore, Reusseau & Seurat, with concentration of works by Dubuffet, Miro & Mondrian among the Europeans; Americans such as Davis, deKooning, Diebenkorn, Gottlieb, Guston, Johns, Lichtenstein, Agnes Martin, Motherwell, Nevelson, Noguchi, Pollack, younger artists include Andre, Flavin, Judd, Christenson, Hamilton, Hesse, Mangold, Nauman, Stella & Serra; paintings, drawings & sculpture colls are being enlarged; Constantin Brancusi Sculpture Collection; Vasily Kandinsky Collection; Paul Klee Collection; Justin K Thannhauser Collection of Impressionist & Post-Impressionist Paintings
Publications: Exhibition catalogs, Guggenheim Museum Magazine (2 times per year)
Activities: Classes & workshops for children, youth, teens & adults; teacher resources & school collaboration progs; professional development progs; Works & Process performances & receptions, artist interaction; lects open to pub; concerts; gallery talks; acoustiguide & docent-led tours; individual paintings & original objects of art lent to other mus & galleries; lending collection contains original art works, original prints, painting, sculpture; originates traveling exhibs; mus shop sells books, jewelry & t-shirts

L **Library & Archives,** 345 Hudson St, Fl12 New York, NY 10014. Tel 212-360-4230; Elec Mail library@guggenheim.org; archives @ guggenheim.org; Internet Home Page Address: www.guggenheim.org
Open to qualified scholars by appt only on Mon, Tues & Fri 10:30 AM - 5:30 PM; Library estab 1952 to document the Museum's coll of 20th century art; Archives estab 1973 to trace develop of Guggenheim's coll & the Foundation, as well as actively collecting materials on the Museum's history since its inception as the Museum of Non-Objective Painting in 1939; For reference only
Library Holdings: Book Volumes; Cards; Exhibition Catalogs; Kodachrome Transparencies; Other Holdings Artist Files; Early Avant-Garde Periodicals; Pamphlets; Periodical Subscriptions 50; Slides

M **Sackler Education Center,** 1071 5th Ave, New York, NY 10128-0173. Tel 212-423-3500; Elec Mail visitorinfo@guggenheim.org; Internet Home Page Address: www.guggenheim.org
Estab 2001 as an educ hub & learning laboratory offering pub progs in visual, performing & literary arts; Located below the rotunda of the Guggenheim Museum; Maintains Peter B Lewis Theater, News Corporation New Media Theater, JP Morgan Chase Foundation Exhib Gallery, studio art lab, multimedia lab, computer lab, resource center
Activities: Classes for adults & children; variety of pub progs; film screenings; tours; gallery progs; competitions; awards; internships; fellowships

M **SOUTH STREET SEAPORT MUSEUM,** 12 Fulton St, New York, NY 10038-2109. Tel 212-748-8600; Fax 212-748-8610; Internet Home Page Address: www.southstreetseaportmuseum.org; *Historian & Librn* Norman Brouwer; *Pres* Peter Neill; *VPres* Yvonne Simons; *Chmn* Frank J Sciame Jr
Open Jan - Mar: Fri - Sun 10 AM - 5 PM all galleries, Mon 10 AM - 5 PM (Schermerhorn Row Galleries only), ships open noon - 4 PM (weather permitting); Apr - Dec: Tues - Sun 10 AM - 6 PM all galleries & ships, cl Mon; Admis gen $10, seniors & students with valid ID $8, children ages 5-12 $5, children under 5 & mems free; Estab 1967 to preserve the maritime history & traditions of the Port of New York; Several gallery spaces: The Seaport Gallery for art exhibits; the printing press gallery at Bowne & Co Stationers; the mus children's center; Average Annual Attendance: 325,000; Mem: 9000; dues family $60, individual $40, seniors & students $30; annual meeting May
Income: Financed by mem & corporate grants
Special Subjects: Architecture, Drawings, Photography, Prints, Archaeology, Folk Art, Woodcarvings, Manuscripts, Posters, Marine Painting, Historical Material, Maps, Scrimshaw
Collections: Restored historic buildings; fleet of historic ships; permanent coll of marine art & artifacts; colls of ship models; archive of ship plans, photos & negatives
Exhibitions: Traveling In Style, ongoing; My Hammer Hand; Mens Lives; New York Trades Transformed; Peking At Sea; Recent Archeology in Lower Manhattan; Titanic; Waterfront Photography
Publications: Seaport Magazine, quarterly
Activities: Educ dept; docent training; lects open to pub; gallery talks; tours; individual paintings and original objects of art lent to institutions; mus shop sells books & prints; junior mus

L **Melville Library,** 213 Water St, New York, NY 10038. Tel 212-748-8648; Fax 212-748-8610; *Historian & Librn* Norman Brouwer
Open Mon - Frid 10:15 AM - 6 PM; For reference
Income: Mem and corporate grants
Library Holdings: Audio Tapes; Book Volumes 20,000; Clipping Files; Exhibition Catalogs; Kodachrome Transparencies; Manuscripts; Memorabilia; Motion Pictures; Original Art Works; Other Holdings Negatives; Pamphlets; Periodical Subscriptions 30; Photographs; Prints; Reels; Reproductions; Slides
Special Subjects: Folk Art, Maps, Painting-American, Painting-British, Historical Material, Archaeology, Industrial Design, Woodcarvings, Marine Painting, Scrimshaw

M **STOREFRONT FOR ART & ARCHITECTURE,** 97 Kenmare St, New York, NY 10012-4506. Tel 212-431-5795; Fax 212-431-5755; Elec Mail info@storefrontnews.org; Internet Home Page Address: www.storefrontnews.org; *Founder* Kyong Park; *Dir* Eva French; *Opers Mgr* Erica Freyberger; *Producer* Gjergji Shkurti; *Pres* Charles Renfro; *Dir External Relations* Kara Meyer
Open Tues - Sat 11 AM - 6 PM, cl Sun & Mon; No admis fee; Estab 1982 to show interdisciplinary & experimental works of art & architecture, often never

previously shown in New York. Organizes large events or competitions of an experimental nature; 15 ft x 100 ft x 2 ft, triangle; Average Annual Attendance: 80,000
Income: Financed by grants and contributions
Exhibitions: Ecotec Forum, held in Corsica, France; Future Systems; Gunther Domeney (Austrian architect); Mark West (Canadian artist); Big Soft Orange, Dutch architectural exhibit
Publications: Exhibition catalogs; monthly bulletin; quarterly reports
Activities: Lects open to pub; 20 vis lectrs per yr; mus shop sells books

M   **THE STUDIO MUSEUM IN HARLEM,** 144 W 125th St, New York, NY 10027-4423. Tel 212-864-4500; Fax 212-864-4800; Elec Mail director@studiomuseum.org; Internet Home Page Address: www.studiomuseum.org; *Adjunct Cur* Lowery Stokes Sims; *Dir & Chief Cur* Thelma Golden; *Chmn* Raymond J McGuire; *Museum Shop Mgr* Jamie Glover; *Deputy Dir, Finance & Admin* Sheila McDaniel; *Cur & Dir Educ & Pub Prog* Romi Crawford; *Pub Rels Mgr* Ali Evans; *Assoc Cur* Christine Y Kim
Open Thurs, Fri & Sun Noon - 6 PM, Sat 10 AM - 6 PM, cl Mon - Wed, Jul 4, Thanksgiving, Christmas & New Years Days; Admis adults $7, students & seniors $3, mems & children under 12 free & Target Free Sundays; Estab 1967 to exhibit the works of contemporary Black American artists, mount historical & informative exhibitions & provide culturally educational programs & activities for the general pub; 10,000 sq ft of exhib & educ space, new exhib space & cafe (spring 2005); Average Annual Attendance: 100,000; Mem: 50,000; dues $15 - $1000
Income: Financed by mem, city & state appropriation, corporate & foundation funding, federal funding, rental income, gift shop sales & individual contributions
Special Subjects: Photography, Sculpture, Afro-American Art
Collections: James VanDerZee Collection of Photography; over 1500 works of art by African-American artists including sculpture, painting & works on paper
Publications: Freestyle; Challenge of the Modern; Black Belt; Photographs; Africa Comics; Frequency
Activities: Classes for adults & children; docent training; workshops; panel discussions; demonstrations; cooperative school prog; internship prog; lects open to pub, 10 vis lectrs per yr; concerts; gallery talks; tours; schols offered; book traveling exhibs; originate traveling exhibs; mus shop sells books, magazines, original art, reproductions, prints, jewelry, baskets, crafts, pottery & catalogues

M   **SWISS INSTITUTE,** 18 Wooster St, New York, NY 10013-2227. Tel 212-925-2035; Fax 212-925-2040; Elec Mail info@swissinstitute.net; *Dir* Gianni Jetzer; *Head Develop* Leonie Kruizenga; *Asst Cur* Piper Marshall
Open Tues - Sat 11 AM - 6 PM, cl Sun & Mon; No admis fee; Estab 1986 to promote artistic dialogue between Switzerland & the United States; 2000 sq ft; Average Annual Attendance: 10,000; Mem: 300; dues $25-$1000; annual meeting in Fall
Income: Financed by mem, corporate contributions, sponsors & foundations
Special Subjects: Painting-European
Collections: Swiss affairs
Exhibitions: Rotating
Publications: Exhibition catalogs, 3 per year
Activities: Educ dept; lects open to pub, 4 vis lectrs per yr; concerts; gallery talks; tours; originate traveling exhibs

L   **TAIPEI ECONOMIC & CULTURAL OFFICE,** Chinese Information & Culture Center Library, 1 E 42nd St, 4th Fl, New York, NY 10017-6904. Tel 212-557-5122 (Press); Tel 212-317-7342 (Library); Fax 212-557-3043 (Press); Fax 212-557-7342 (Library); Elec Mail roctaiwan@taipei.org; Internet Home Page Address: www.taipei.org; *Dir* Jack Lee
Open Mon - Fri 10 AM - noon, 2 - 4 PM by appointment only; Estab 1991
Library Holdings: Book Volumes 42,000; Clipping Files; Motion Pictures; Pamphlets; Periodical Subscriptions 155; Prints; Reels; Reproductions; Video Tapes
Special Subjects: Oriental Art
Publications: CICC Currents, bimonthly

M   **U GALLERY,** 221 E Second St, New York, NY 10009. Tel 212-995-0395; Elec Mail saccodik@gmail.com; Internet Home Page Address: www.ugallery.org; *Artist* Robert Walter; *Dir* Darius Gubala; *Artist* Amy Banker; *Artist* Richard Ahntholz; *Artist* Walker Fee; *Artist* Phoebe Legere; *Artist* Hanne Lauridsen; *Artist* Taylor Mead; *Artist* Barnaby Ruhe
by Appointment; Estab 1991 to support culture in America; Multi-Media; Average Annual Attendance: 600; Mem: 205
Income: privately financed
Special Subjects: Furniture, Painting-American, Restorations, Painting-Polish
Collections: Cyber Culture, Local Community, Psychotic
Exhibitions: Florescent Light; Saccadis Art; East Village Artist NYC
Activities: Lectrs for members only, 8 vis lectr per yr; concerts; mus shop sells original art & art objects

A   **UKRAINIAN INSTITUTE OF AMERICA, INC,** 2 E 79th St, New York, NY 10021-0106. Tel 212-288-8660; Fax 212-288-2918; Elec Mail mail@ukrainianinstitute.org; Internet Home Page Address: www.ukrainianinstitute.org; *Dir Prog* Dr Walter Hoydysh
Open Tues - Sat 11 AM - 6 PM, Sun by appointment; Admis $5; Estab 1948 to develop, sponsor & promote educational activities which will acquaint the general public with history, culture & art of Ukrainian people; Ukrainian & East European art; Average Annual Attendance: 8,500; Mem: 480
Income: Financed by endowment, mem & contributions
Purchases: $2,500
Library Holdings: Original Art Works; Sculpture
Collections: Church & religious relics; folk art, ceramic & woodwork; patents of Ukrainian-American engineers; Gritchenko Foundation Collection; sculptures by Archipenko, Kruk, Mol & others; Ukrainian paintings
Publications: UIA Newsletter, irregular; Anniversary of UIA
Activities: Dramatic progs; seminars; symposiums; workshop seminars; literary evenings; lects open to pub, concerts; gallery talks; Awards: Person of the Year; Chicago Ukrainian Museum of Modern Art; mus shop sells books, magazines, original art, reproductions & prints

M   **THE UKRAINIAN MUSEUM,** 222 E 6th St below 2nd & 3rd Aves, New York, NY 10003. Tel 212-228-0110; Fax 212-228-1947; Elec Mail info@ukrainianmuseum.org; Internet Home Page Address: www.ukrainianmuseum.org; *Admin Dir* Daria Bajko; *Mus Shop Mgr* Chrystyna Pevny; *Dir* Maria Shust; *Pres (V)* Olha Hnateyko
Open Wed - Sun 11:30 AM - 5 PM; Admis adults $3, seniors, students & children $2; Since 1976, The Ukrainian Museum preserves the cultural heritage of Ukrainian Americans through exhibitions, educational/community oriented programs for adults and children, scholarly research and publications. The museum maintains folk art, fine arts and photographic/documentary collections. Current major projects include building a new museum facility and computerization of collections data; Average Annual Attendance: 25,000; Mem: 1700; dues family $60, adults $35, seniors & students $10
Income: $295,000 (financed by mem, donations & grants)
Special Subjects: Drawings, Graphics, Photography, Sculpture, Watercolors, Ethnology, Textiles, Costumes, Ceramics, Crafts, Folk Art, Primitive art, Woodcarvings, Woodcuts, Etchings & Engravings, Landscapes, Decorative Arts, Jewelry, Metalwork, Historical Material, Coins & Medals, Embroidery
Collections: Major crafts in Ukrainian folk art: woven & embroidered textiles (including costumes & kilns), woodwork, ceramics, metalwork, Ukrainian Easter Eggs; fine arts; photographic/documentary archival coll on Ukrainian cultural heritage, among them photographs of individuals in their native dress, architectural landmarks as well as photographic records of historic events; Ukrainian paintings
Exhibitions: Rotating exhibits 3 times yr
Publications: Annual report; bulletins; bilingual exhibition catalogs or brochures
Activities: Classes for adults & children; lects open to pub, 2-3 vis lectrs per yr; gallery talks; tours; individual paintings & original objects of art lent; lending collection contains 3000 Ukrainian Folk Art, including costumes & textiles, 1000 original prints, 500 paintings, 200 works on paper; originate traveling exhibs; mus shop sells books, magazines, original art & reproductions

L   **Library,** 222 E 6th St, New York, NY 10003-8201. Tel 212-228-0110; Fax 212-228-1947; Elec Mail info@ukrainianmuseum.org; Internet Home Page Address: ukrainianmuseum.org; *Dir* Maria Shust
Open Wed - Sun 11:30 AM - 5 PM; Library for internal use only. For reference by appointment
Library Holdings: Book Volumes 4000; Exhibition Catalogs; Pamphlets; Photographs; Slides 600; Video Tapes
Special Subjects: Art History, Folk Art, Drawings, Etchings & Engravings, Sculpture, Portraits, Crafts, Archaeology, Jewelry, Leather, Pottery, Religious Art, Woodcarvings, Landscapes, Architecture
Collections: Historical photographic documentary archives; Folk Art; Ukrainian Fire
Publications: Extensive catalogues with major exhibitions; Annual reports

L   **UNION FOR REFORMED JUDAISM,** Synagogue Art & Architectural Library, 633 Third Ave, 7th Fl, New York, NY 10017. Tel 212-249-0100; Tel 212-650-4000; Fax 212-650-4109; Internet Home Page Address: urj.org; *Dir, Synagogue Mgr* Dale Glasser; *Dir Library* John Crotty
Open Mon - Fri 9 AM - 5 PM; cl Sat & Sun & Jewish holidays; Estab 1957; Books for use on premises only
Income: Financed by budgetary allocation plus rental fees for slides
Library Holdings: Book Volumes 350; Slides 3400
Publications: An American Synagogue for Today & Tomorrow (book); Contemporary Synagogue Art (book)
Activities: Slide rental service

L   **UNIVERSITY CLUB LIBRARY,** One W 54th St, New York, NY 10019. Tel 212-572-3418; Fax 212-572-3452; *Assoc Dir & Cur* Scott Overall; *Librn* Maureen Manning; *Conservation Librn* Laurie Bolger; *Dir & Cur Collections* Andrew Berner
Open to members & qualified scholars (inquire by letter or telephone first) Mon - Fri 9 AM - 6 PM; No admis fee; Estab 1865 for the promotion of the arts & culture in post-university graduates; Art is displayed in all areas of the building; Average Annual Attendance: 7,000; Mem: 4,250
Income: Financed by endowments & mem
Library Holdings: Book Volumes 90,000; CD-ROMs; Compact Disks; Manuscripts; Original Art Works
Collections: Art; architecture, fine printing, book illustration, works by George Cruikshank
Publications: The Illuminator, occasional

M   **VIRIDIAN ARTISTS INC,** 548 W 28th St, Ste 632 New York, NY 10001-5673. Tel 212-414-4040; Fax 212-414-4040; Elec Mail viridianartists@gmail.com; Internet Home Page Address: www.viridianartists.com; *Dir* Vernita Nemec; *Pres* Susan Sills; *VPres* Arthur Dworin; *Asst to Dir* Lauren Purje
Open Tues - Sat noon - 6 PM; Estab 1968 to exhibit work by emerging & established artists; Gallery shows contemporary work by emerging & established artists; Average Annual Attendance: 10,000; Mem: 30; dues $235 per mo; application to current mems see website
Income: Mem; sales; competitions
Special Subjects: Drawings, Painting-American, Photography, Prints, Sculpture, Landscapes, Afro-American Art, Collages, Painting-Japanese, Portraits
Exhibitions: Juried exhibitions every spring, cur from a contemporary museum; Member's exhib changing every 3 weeks; Guest shows; curated shows; theme shows; Director's choice shows
Publications: Gallery Artists; Gallery Catalogue; individual artist books & catalogues
Activities: Docent training; lects open to pub; gallery talks; national juried show annually with cash or exhibs prize; sponsoring of competitions; exten dept lends paintings, sculpture & photographs; book traveling exhibs 1 per yr; originate traveling exhibs 2 per yr

VISUAL ARTISTS & GALLERIES ASSOCIATION (VAGA)
For further information, see National and Regional Organizations

L **VISUAL ARTS LIBRARY,** 380 Second Ave, New York, NY 10010; 209 E 23rd St, New York, NY 10010-3901. Tel 212-592-2660; Fax 212-592-2655; Internet Home Page Address: www.sva.edu/library; *Visual Resources Cur* Lorraine Gerety; *Dir Library* Robert Lobe; *Tech Serv/Systems Librn* Zimra Panitz; *Assoc Dir Library* Caitlin Kilgallen
Open to students & faculty Mon - Thurs 8:30 AM - 10 PM, Fri 8:30 AM - 7:30 PM, Sat noon - 5 PM, Sun Noon - 8 PM; No admis fee; Estab 1962 to serve needs of School of Visual Arts students and faculty; Circ 50,000; Exclusively for student & faculty use, lending to students
Income: Financed by tuition
Purchases: $80,000
Library Holdings: Audio Tapes; Book Volumes 70,000; CD-ROMs; Cassettes; Clipping Files; Compact Disks; Exhibition Catalogs; Filmstrips; Other Holdings Comic books; Periodical Subscriptions 260; Slides; Video Tapes
Special Subjects: Art History, Film, Illustration, Photography, Commercial Art, Graphic Design, Advertising Design
Publications: Library Handbook; accessions lists

M **WARD-NASSE GALLERY,** 178 Prince St, New York, NY 10012-2905. Tel 212-925-6951; Fax 212-334-2095; Elec Mail markherd@wardnasse.org; Internet Home Page Address: www.wardnasse.org; *Dir & Chmn Bd* Harry Nasse; *Dir Sales* Jeanette Sherrard; *Gallery Mgr* Beste Atvur; *Outreach* Leda Nasse
Open Tues - Sat 11 AM - 6 PM, Sun 1 - 6 PM; No admis fee; Estab 1969 to provide an artist-run gallery; also serves as resource center for artists & pub; to provide internships for students; First floor, 2,000 sq ft space; Average Annual Attendance: 7,000; Mem: 300; dues $40
Income: Financed by mem
Exhibitions: Seventeen exhibitions per year ranging from 3 person shows, up to large salon shows with 100 artists
Publications: Brochure; gallery catalog, every two years; quarterly newsletter
Activities: Work study progs; lects open to pub; concerts; poetry readings; multi-arts events; sales shop sells original art

M **WHITE COLUMNS,** White Columns Curated Artist Registry, 320 W 13th St, New York, NY 10014-1200. Tel 212-924-4212; Fax 212-645-4764; Elec Mail info@whitecolumns.org; Internet Home Page Address: www.whitecolumns.org; *Dir & Chief Cur* Matthew Higgs; *Deputy Dir & Cur* Amie Scally; *Pres* Gregory Miller; *Curatorial Assoc* Jeff Eaton; *Dir Finance* Carolyn Lockhart
Open Tues - Sat Noon - 6 PM; No admis fee; Estab 1970 to showcase the works of emerging artists; Exhibs, progs, & servs for emerging artists; Average Annual Attendance: 12,000; Mem: 500; dues $35-$1,000
Exhibitions: Annual benefit auction

M **WHITNEY MUSEUM OF AMERICAN ART,** 945 Madison Ave, New York, NY 10021-2790. Tel 212-570-3600; Elec Mail info@whitney.org; Internet Home Page Address: www.whitney.org; *Dir* Adam Weinberg; *Chief of Staff* Marella Consolini; *Chief Financial Officer* Bridget Elias; *Dir Human Resources* Hillary Blass; *Dir Communs* Jeffrey Levine; *Dir Educ* David Little; *Exhib Mgr* Lauren DiLoreto; *Cur Prewar Art* Barbara Haskell; *Cur Postwar Art* Dana Miller; *Chief Cur* Donna DeSalvo; *Librn & Assoc Cur Spec Coll* Carol Rusk; *Independent Study Prog Dir* Ron Clark; *Branch Dir & Cur Altria* Shamim Momin; *Cur Film & Video* Chrissie Iles; *Dir Retail & Wholesale* Robert Tofolo; *Pub Prog Coordr* Marjorie Weinstein; *Librn* Lindsay Turley; *Dir Publs* Rachel Wixom; *Cur Prints* David Kiehl; *Cur Drawings* Carter Foster; *Assoc Dir Exhibs* Christy Putnam; *Head Registrar* Barbi Spieler; *Cur Photography* Elisabeth Sussman; *Chmn* Leonard A Lauder; *Legal Officer* Nicholas Holmes
Open Wed - Thurs & Sat -Sun 11 AM - 6 PM, Fri 1-9 PM, cl Mon, Tues & national holidays; Admis general $18, seniors 62+, adults ages 19-25 & students with ID $12, mems & children 18 & under free, Fri 6-9 PM pay what you wish; Estab 1930, inc 1931 by Gertrude Vanderbilt Whitney for the advancement of contemporary American art; Museum opened 1931 on Eighth Street & moved to 54th Street in 1954; new building opened in 1966; Average Annual Attendance: 500,000; Mem: 5,000; dues $75 & up
Income: Financed by endowment, admis, grants, mem
Purchases: Numerous annual acquisitions
Library Holdings: Auction Catalogs; Audio Tapes; Book Volumes; Clipping Files; Compact Disks; DVDs; Exhibition Catalogs; Manuscripts; Original Documents; Pamphlets; Periodical Subscriptions; Photographs
Special Subjects: Drawings, Painting-American, Prints, Sculpture
Collections: Drawings, paintings, prints, sculpture of mainly 20th & 21st century American artists
Exhibitions: Rotating exhibits every 3-4 months
Publications: Annual report; brochures, cards, posters; calendars; exhibition catalogues; gallery brochures
Activities: Classes for adults, teens, children, students & families; progs for seniors; docent training; symposia & panel discussions; teachers' workshops; school partnerships; Regent Family Residence art progs; access for the disabled; lects open to pub; concerts; gallery talks; tours; independent study; Artreach provides introductory art education to elementary & high school students; individual paintings & original objects of art lent; originate traveling exhibs for mus here & abroad; sales shop sells books, magazines, reproductions, slides, cards & posters

L **Frances Mulhall Achilles Library,** 945 Madison Ave, New York, NY 10021. Tel 212-570-3648; Elec Mail library@whitney.org; Internet Home Page Address: www.whitney.org; *Benjamin & Irma Weiss Librn* Carol Rusk; *Asst Librn & Cataloger* Ivy Blackman; *Asst Archivist* Kristen Leipert; *Library Asst* Lindsey Reynolds
Open by appointment for advanced research; No admis fee; Estab 1931 for encouragement & advancement of American art & art scholarship; Circ Non-Circulating
Library Holdings: Auction Catalogs; Audio Tapes; Book Volumes 50,000; CD-ROMs; Cassettes; Clipping Files; Compact Disks; DVDs; Exhibition Catalogs; Fiche; Manuscripts; Memorabilia; Original Documents; Other Holdings Vertical Files: 450+ linear ft; Pamphlets; Periodical Subscriptions 500; Photographs; Records; Reels; Reproductions; Slides; Video Tapes
Special Subjects: Art History, Film, Photography, Drawings, Painting-American, Prints, Sculpture, American Western Art, Printmaking, Video
Collections: 20th - 21st century & contemporary American art; Special Collections: artists' books, portfolios, photographs, titles in the White Fellows Artist & Writers Series (1982-2001), posters & valuable ephemera related to Museum's permanent coll; Museum Archives: 2,500+ linear ft of historical records documenting the evolution of the Whitney Museum from inception of the Whitney Studio (1914) to present, incl: Whitney Studio Club & Galleries: Administrative & Exhib Records, 1916-1930; Whitney Mus of American Art: Admin Records, 1930 - 1960; Exhib Records 1931-2000 (Ongoing); Curatorial Records, 1935-2000 (Ongoing); Film & Video Artist Files, 1970 - 1998; Film & Video Image Files; Performance Series, 1968-1997; Property Records, 1949-1993; Photograph Coll; Special Coll Artist Files; Arshile Gorky Research Coll 1920s-1990s; Edward Hopper Research Coll 1894-2000; Resources for Rebels on 8th St: Juliana Force & The Whitney Museum of American Art by Avis Berman; Lloyd Goodrich Artists Correspondence, 1917-1978; John Depol Coll, 1953-2004; Francis M Naumann Research Coll for How, When & Why Modern Art Came to New York by Marius de Zayas, 1910-1936; Florence Rubenfeld Coll of Archival Material for Clement Greenberg: A Life, 1988-1998

WOMEN'S CAUCUS FOR ART
For further information, see National and Regional Organizations

M **WOMEN'S INTERART CENTER, INC,** Interart Gallery, 549 W 52 St, New York, NY 10019. Tel 212-246-1050; *VPres* Bill Perlman; *Artistic Dir* Margot Lewitin; *Dir Programming* Ronnie Geist
Open Mon - Fri 1 - 6 PM; No admis fee; Estab 1970 to present to the pub the work of significant, emerging women artists; Average Annual Attendance: 9,000; Mem: Dues $35
Income: Financed by state appropriation, National Endowment for the Arts, private foundations, corporations & individuals
Exhibitions: Community as Planner
Publications: Women's Interart Center Newsletter, quarterly
Activities: Classes for adults; lects open to pub, 2 vis lectrs per yr; originate traveling exhibs

M **YESHIVA UNIVERSITY MUSEUM,** 15 W 16th St, Center for Jewish History New York, NY 10011-6301. Tel 212-294-8330; Fax 212-294-8335; Elec Mail info@yum.cjh.org; Internet Home Page Address: www.yumuseum.org; *Cur & Registrar* Bonni-Dara Michaels; *Assoc Dir Museum Admin* Jody Heher; *Asst Cur* Zachary Levine; *Dir* Jacob Wisse, PhD; *Educator* Ilana Benson
Open Mon 5 PM - 8 PM, Tues, Thurs & Sun 11 AM - 5 PM, Wed 11 AM - 8 PM, Fri 11 AM - 2:30 PM; Admis adults $8, students & seniors $6; Mon & Fri free; Estab 1973 to collect, preserve & interpret Jewish art & objects of material culture in the light of Jewish history; 6000 sq ft of galleries; maintains reference library; Average Annual Attendance: 40,000; Mem: 550; dues $50-$1000
Special Subjects: Photography, Sculpture, Textiles, Religious Art, Decorative Arts, Judaica, Manuscripts
Collections: Architectural models, ceremonial objects, documents, ethnographic material, fine & decorative art, manuscripts, photographs, sculpture, textiles; Art history; History of Art & Archaeology; Contemporary art
Exhibitions: Changing exhibs of Contemporary & Historical Fine Arts; Multi-disciplinary exhibs of Jewish history & culture
Publications: Catalogs
Activities: Classes for children; dramatic progs; docent training; craft workshops; lects open to pub; concerts; gallery talks; tours; individual paintings & original objects of art lent for purposes of exhibs to institutions which provide specified levels of care; book traveling exhibs 1 per yr; originate traveling exhibs; sells books

NIAGARA

M **NIAGARA UNIVERSITY,** Castellani Art Museum, 5795 Lewiston Rd, Niagara, NY 14109; PO Box 1938, Niagara University, NY 14109-1938. Tel 716-286-8200; Fax 716-286-8289; Elec Mail cam@niagara.edu; Internet Home Page Address: www.niagara.edu/cam; *Registrar* Kathleen Fraas; *Gallery Mgr* Kurt VonVoetcsch; *Museum Shop Mgr* Anne LaBarbera; *Asst Mus Shop Mgr* Carla Castellani; *Dir* Kate Koperski; *Cur Colls & Exhibs* Michael J Beam
Open Tues - Sat 11 AM - 5 PM, Sun 1 - 5 PM, cl Mon; No admis fee; Estab 1978; The gallery is a 10,000 sq ft museum that displays the permanent collection of over 3000 works of art encompassing 19th century to present with a concentration on contemporary art; Mem: 300
Income: $120,000
Special Subjects: Graphics, Painting-American, Photography, Prints, Sculpture, Watercolors, Pre-Columbian Art, Woodcuts, Afro-American Art, Collages, Painting-Canadian, Painting-British, Painting-French, Painting-German
Collections: Modern paintings, sculpture & works on paper (19th -20th centuries); Pre-Columbian Pottery
Exhibitions: Glass art: Arnold Mesches; John Moore; Michael Kessler; Arcadia Revisted: Niagara River & Falls from Lake Erie to Lake Ontario, Photographs by John Pfahl
Publications: Exhibition catalogs, 4 per yr
Activities: Classes for adults & children; Public Art Project on Underground Railroad; docent training; learning disabled prog; senior citizen outreach prog; lects open to pub, 1-6 vis lectrs per year; concerts; gallery talks; tours; competitions; awards; scholarships & fels offered; individual paintings & original objects of art lent to qualified museums; originate traveling exhibitions

NORTH SALEM

M **HAMMOND MUSEUM & JAPANESE STROLL GARDEN,** Cross-Cultural Center, 28 Deveau Rd, North Salem, NY 10560; PO Box 326, North Salem, NY 10560-0326. Tel 914-669-5033; Fax 914-669-8221; Elec Mail gardenprogram@yahoo.com; Internet Home Page Address: www.hammondmuseum.org; *Dir* Lorraine Laken; *Bus Mgr* Judy Schurmacher; *Receptionist* Ellen Mancini
Open Apr - Nov, Wed - Sat Noon - 4 PM; Admis to Museum & Garden, adults $5, seniors $4, mems & children under 12 free; Estab 1957; Exhib provide an

East-West cultural experience supplemented by programs of related special events such as the Asian Arts Festival and Moonviewing Concert. The 3.5 acre Japanese Stroll Garden includes a pond, waterfall, Zen garden, bamboo grove, Maple Terrace, etc; Average Annual Attendance: 5,000; Mem: 250; dues $35-$1000
Income: Financed by mem, matching funds, private foundations & corporations
Special Subjects: Decorative Arts, Photography, Portraits, Photography, Ethnology, Costumes, Asian Art
Collections: Fans; Carl Van Vechten Collection of Photographs
Activities: Classes for adults & children; lect open to public, 5 vis lectrs per year; concerts; gallery talks; tours; individual paintings & original objects of art lent to other museums; lending collection contains photographs & slides; mus shop sells books, original art, prints, jewelry, giftware

NORTH TONAWANDA

M   **NORTH TONAWANDA HISTORY MUSEUM,** 54 Webster St, North Tonawanda, NY 14120-5814. Tel 716-213-0554; Elec Mail nthistorymuseum@aol.com; Internet Home Page Address: www.nthistorymuseum.org; *Dir* Donna Zellner Neal; *Archival Records Coordr & Cur* Jane Garis; *Admin & Colls Asst* Carol Kopczynski; *Research Coordr* Faith Jaskulski; *Events Coord* Danielle Oney
Open Mon & Tues 9 AM - 9 PM, Wed - Fri 9 AM - 5 PM, cl Independence Day, Thanksgiving Day, Christmas Eve & Day, New Year's Eve & Day; Donations accepted; school tours $2 per student, Seaway Trail walks: adults $8, children $4; other history walks: adults $4, children $2; Estab 2004; History mus with emphasis on rich ethnic heritage, Erie Canal/Niagara River Influence as role of lumber & industrial ctr in 19th & 20th centuries. Pvt nonprofit org; FT vols 1, PT vols 4, interns 3; 26th Congressional Dist; Mem: dues Life $250, Contributing $100, Bus/Civic $50, Family of 2 or more $25, Individual $15, Senior $10
Collections: Artifacts, oral histories, photographs, directories & archival materials; 50 vols of city directories & other local history books, 10 high school yearbooks
Publications: Quarterly newsletter; Annual Report
Activities: Formal educ progs for adults & children; research in ethnic, industrial, lumber & Erie Canal heritage; ethnic heritage festivals; historic home tours & tours of other historic venues; garden walks; concerts; virtual mus online

NORTHPORT

L   **NORTHPORT-EAST NORTHPORT PUBLIC LIBRARY,** 151 Laurel Ave, Art Dept Northport, NY 11768-3161. Tel 631-261-6930; Fax 631-261-6718; Elec Mail nenpl@suffolk.lib.ny.us; Internet Home Page Address: www.nenpl.org; *Asst Dir* Eileen Minogue; *Dir* Stephanie Heineman; *Chairperson* Michael L Glennon
Open Mon - Fri 9 AM - 9 PM, Sat 9 AM - 5 PM, Sun 1 - 5 PM (Sep - June only); No admis fee; Estab 1914; Circ 968,285
Library Holdings: Audio Tapes; Book Volumes 215,000; Cassettes; Clipping Files; Exhibition Catalogs; Fiche; Filmstrips; Manuscripts; Other Holdings Compact discs 2250; Pamphlets; Periodical Subscriptions 720; Prints; Records; Reproductions; Sculpture; Video Tapes 7890
Publications: Library, monthly
Activities: Lect open to public, 5 vis lectrs per year; concerts; competitions

NYACK

M   **EDWARD HOPPER HOUSE ART CENTER,** 82 N Broadway, Nyack, NY 10960-2628. Tel 845-358-0774; Elec Mail info@hopperhouse.org; Internet Home Page Address: www.hopperhouse.org; *Exec Dir* Carole Perry; *Prog Coord* Danee Gilmarten; *Pres* Ginger Stoltze; *VPres House & Grounds* Lynn Saaby; *VPres Mktg* Sheila Elliot
Open Thurs - Sun 1 PM - 5 PM; Admis $1; Estab 1971 to memorialize Edward Hopper & exhibit current regional artists; Four galleries on first floor of historical house. Interior of house intact; Average Annual Attendance: 2,200; Mem: 400; dues $15-$75
Income: Financed by mem
Special Subjects: Painting-American, Photography, Posters, Reproductions
Exhibitions: Exhibits by local & national American artists
Activities: Adult classes; lects open to public, 3 vis lectrs per year; juried art competitions; concerts; book fairs; sales shop sells books & prints

OGDENSBURG

M   **FREDERIC REMINGTON ART MUSEUM,** 303 Washington St, Ogdensburg, NY 13669-1517. Tel 315-393-2425; Fax 315-393-4464; Elec Mail info@fredericremington.org; Internet Home Page Address: www.fredericremington.org; *Dir & Cur* Laura Foster; *Admin Aid* Shannon Ghize; *Project Coordr* Shirley McDonald; *Accnt Mgr* Debbie Ormasen; *Mus Shop Mgr* Stephanie Billington; *Educ Specialist* Lauren Woodcock
Open May 15 - Oct 15 Mon - Sat 10 AM - 5 PM, Sun 1 - 5 PM, Oct 16 - May 14 Wed - Sat 11 AM - 5 PM, Sun 1 - 5 PM, cl legal holidays; Admis adults $9, seniors & youth $8, mems & 16 & under free; organized tour groups $7 per person; Estab 1923 to house & exhibit works of art of Frederic Remington (1861-1909), a native of northern New York; The mus is in the converted Parish Mansion, built 1809-1810 & the recently constructed Newell Wing.; Average Annual Attendance: 15,000; Mem: 1200; dues family $50
Income: Financed by endowment & city appropriation
Library Holdings: Framed Reproductions; Manuscripts; Original Art Works; Original Documents; Pamphlets; Sculpture
Special Subjects: Prints, Painting-American, Sculpture, Watercolors, American Western Art, Bronzes, Painting-European, Furniture, Glass, Porcelain, Silver, Stained Glass
Collections: Remington paintings, bronzes, watercolors, drawings, photographs, letters & personal art collection; studies in plaster by Edwin Willard Deming; sculpture by Sally James Farnham; Parish Collection of Furniture; Haskell Collection of 19th century American & European paintings; Sharp Collection of Period Glass, China, Silver & Cameos

Exhibitions: The Children's Exhibit; The Frederic Remington Exhibit
Activities: Classes for adults & children; docent training; lects open to pub; gallery talks; tours; for anyone; mus shop sells books, reproductions, prints

OLD CHATHAM

M   **SHAKER MUSEUM & LIBRARY,** 88 Shaker Museum Rd, Old Chatham, NY 12136-2601. Tel 518-794-9100, ext 218; Fax 518-794-8621; Elec Mail contact@shakermuseumandlibrary.org; Internet Home Page Address: www.shakermuseumandlibrary.org; *Finance Mgr* Ann Montag; *Dir* Lili Ott; *Cur* Starlyn D'Angelo
Open May - Oct daily 10 AM - 5 PM, cl Tues; Admis adults $8, reduced rates for seniors, children & groups; Estab 1950 to promote interest in & understanding of the Shaker cultural heritage; The exhibits are housed in a complex of eight buildings; Average Annual Attendance: 16,000; Mem: 475; dues $35 - $1000
Income: $700,000 (financed by earned revenue, endowment, contributions, private & public grants)
Purchases: $3000
Library Holdings: Auction Catalogs; Book Volumes; Clipping Files; Manuscripts; Maps; Memorabilia; Slides
Special Subjects: Drawings, Watercolors, Textiles, Costumes, Decorative Arts, Dolls, Furniture, Glass, Historical Material, Embroidery
Collections: 35,000 artifacts & archival material representing 200 years of Shaker history & culture including, baskets, furniture, metal work, personal artifacts, stoves, textiles, tools & equipment, transportation
Exhibitions: Orientation to Shaker History; Shakers in the 20th Century; Shaker Cabinetmakers and Their Tools; study storage related to individual collections
Publications: Members update; The Shaker Adventure; Shaker Seed Industry; pamphlets; booklets; gallery guide; catalogs; postcards, reprints, and broadsides
Activities: Classes for adults & children; docent training; seminars; lects open to pub; concerts; adult tours; symposia; family events; originate traveling exhibs; mus shop sells Shaker reproduction furniture, craft items & publications

L   **Emma B King Library,** 88 Shaker Museum Rd, Old Chatham, NY 12136. Tel 518-794-9100, Ext 111; Fax 518-794-8621; Elec Mail jgrant@shakermuseumandlibrary.org; Internet Home Page Address: www.shakermuseumandlibrary.org; *Librn* Jerry Grant
Open by appointment Mon - Fri, cl holidays; Admis research use fee; Circ non-circulating; For reference only; Mem: Part of museum
Income: financed by museum
Library Holdings: Audio Tapes; Book Volumes 2000; Cassettes; Clipping Files; Filmstrips; Kodachrome Transparencies; Manuscripts; Memorabilia; Motion Pictures; Original Art Works 100; Pamphlets; Photographs 3500; Prints; Records; Reels 189; Slides; Video Tapes
Collections: Manuscripts and records; Photographic and map archive

OLD WESTBURY

M   **NEW YORK INSTITUTE OF TECHNOLOGY,** Gallery, PO Box 8000, Old Westbury, NY 11568-8000. Tel 516-686-7542; *Chmn* Peter Voci
Open Mon - Fri 9 AM - 5 PM; Estab 1964; Gallery maintained for the many exhibits held during the year; Average Annual Attendance: 5,000
Exhibitions: Annual faculty & student shows; some traveling exhibitions
Publications: Graphic Guild Newsletter, quarterly
Activities: Classes in custom silk-screen printmaking; gallery talks; awards; scholarships offered; exten Dept serves all areas

L   **Art & Architectural Library,** PO Box 8000, Education Hall Old Westbury, NY 11568-8000. Tel 516-686-7579; Fax 516-686-7921; Elec Mail lheslin@nyit.edu; Internet Home Page Address: www.nyit.edu; *Librn* Karen Cognato; *Branch Dir* Linda Heslin; *Lib Asst* Kim Renskers
Open Mon - Thurs 9 AM - 9 PM, Fri 9 AM - 5 PM, Sat 10 AM - 5 PM; No admis fee; Estab 1976
Library Holdings: Book Volumes 1808; DVDs; Exhibition Catalogs; Motion Pictures 23; Other Holdings CD's; Periodical Subscriptions 258; Video Tapes 80
Special Subjects: Art History, Folk Art, Decorative Arts, Drawings, Etchings & Engravings, Graphic Arts, Graphic Design, Islamic Art, Painting-American, Painting-British, Painting-Dutch, Painting-Flemish, Painting-French, Painting-German, Painting-Italian, Painting-European, History of Art & Archaeology, American Western Art, Art Education, Asian Art, Furniture, Mexican Art, Southwestern Art, Afro-American Art, Antiquities-Egyptian, Architecture
Exhibitions: Architecture dept student projects
Activities: Tours

M   **STATE UNIVERSITY OF NEW YORK COLLEGE AT OLD WESTBURY,** Amelie A Wallace Gallery, Rte 107 (Broadway), Old Westbury, NY 11568; PO Box 210, Old Westbury, NY 11568-0210. Tel 516-876-3056; Fax 516-876-4984; Elec Mail yih@oldwestbury.edu; Elec Mail amelieawallacegallery@gmail.com; Internet Home Page Address: www.owestbury.edu; *Gallery Dir* Hyewon Yi; *Chmn Art Dept* Patricia McLaughlin
Open Mon - Thurs; No admis fee; Estab 1976 to serve as a teaching aid & for community enlightenment; 2,000 sq ft on three levels; Average Annual Attendance: 3,000
Income: $4,500 (financed by endowment & HYS)
Collections: none
Exhibitions: 4 annual exhibitions by contemporary artists + 2 student shows
Publications: Exhibit brochures
Activities: Lect open to public, 4 vis lectrs per year; gallery talks

ONEIDA

M   **MADISON COUNTY HISTORICAL SOCIETY,** Cottage Lawn, 435 Main St, Oneida, NY 13421-2440. Tel 315-363-4136, 361-9735; Elec Mail history@mchs1900.org; Internet Home Page Address: www.mchs1900.org; *Exec Dir* Sydney Loftus; *Pres* Mishell Magnusson; *VPres* Barbara Chamberlain; *Treas* Julie Stokes
Open Mon - Fri 10 AM - 4 PM by appointment; Admis adults $5, discounts for school groups, children 12 & under & members free; Estab 1898 to collect,

preserve & interpret artifacts indigenous to the history of Madison County; 1849 A J Davis gothic dwelling with period rooms, library & craft archive; Average Annual Attendance: 9,000; Mem: 500; dues $15-$100; annual meeting last Wed in Oct

Income: $100,000 (financed by endowment, mem, county, city & state appropriation, Annual Craft Fair)
Library Holdings: Clipping Files; Fiche; Maps
Special Subjects: Decorative Arts
Collections: Locally produced & or used furnishings, paintings, silver, textiles & ceramics
Exhibitions: Permanent exhibit in the barn; Bittersweet: Hop Culture in Central New York
Publications: Quarterly Newsletter; Madison County Heritage, published annually; Country Roads Revisited
Activities: Educ outreach progs for nursing homes & schools; lects open to pub, 10 vis lectrs per yr; slides, tapes & movies documenting traditional craftsmen at work; individual paintings & original objects of art lent to qualified mus & galleries for special exhibits; sales shop sells books, magazines, prints & slides, reproductions

ONEONTA

M **HARTWICK COLLEGE,** Foreman Gallery, PO Box 4020, Oneonta, NY 13820-4020. Tel 607-431-4575; Fax 607-431-4191; Elec Mail goldenn@hartwick.edu; Internet Home Page Address: www.hartwick.edu; *Cur* Nancy Golden
Open Tues - Fri Noon - 8 PM, Sat noon - 4 PM or by appointment, cl last half of Dec & summers; No admis fee; Estab 1968, contemporary exhibitions for benefit of faculty, students & community; Open space housed within the Campus Arts Center; Average Annual Attendance: 1,000
Library Holdings: Clipping Files; DVDs; Exhibition Catalogs; Kodachrome Transparencies; Slides
Special Subjects: Drawings, Painting-American, Prints, Sculpture, Baroque Art, Renaissance Art, Cartoons
Exhibitions: Changing exhibitions; student & faculty exhibitions; 3 professional artist exhibs per yr
Activities: Lects open to pub, vis lectrs 3 per yr; gallery talks; books traveling exhibs 1-2 per yr

M **The Yager Museum,** 1 Hartwick Dr, Oneonta, NY 13820-4000. Tel 607-431-4480; Fax 607-431-4457; Elec Mail dejardinf@hartwick.edu; Elec Mail museum@hartwick.edu; Internet Home Page Address: www.hartwick.edu/museum.xml; *Dir & Cur Fine Arts* Dr Fiona M Dejardin; *Cur of Foreman Gallery* Gloria Escobar; *Bus Mgr* Nancy Martin-Mathewson; *Cur Anthropology* Dr David Anthony; *Coll Mgr* Gary Norman; *Exhibit Mgr* Andrew Pastore; *Secy* Denise Wagner
Open Tues - Sat noon - 4:30 PM, cl acad holidays; No admis fee; Estab 1928; Seven galleries feature traveling exhibits, anthropology, fine art & Yager collections; Average Annual Attendance: 8,500; Mem: 200
Income: Income from college budget & endowment
Special Subjects: Anthropology, Archaeology, Landscapes, Mexican Art, Painting-European, Sculpture, Drawings, Graphics, Hispanic Art, Painting-American, Prints, Watercolors, American Indian Art, Ethnology, Woodcuts, Etchings & Engravings, Renaissance Art, Cartoons
Collections: Coll of North American, Mexican & South American Indian art & artifacts & mask coll; fine arts featuring European and American works from 15th - 20th centuries; Micronesia
Exhibitions: Changing exhibitions.
Publications: The Rüdisühli: A Family of Painters; Oneonta's Native Son: Carleton E. Watkins, photographer
Activities: Classes in museum studies; lect; tours; films; 6 vis lectrs per yr; gift shop sells cards, jewelry, pottery, books, crafts & handmade objects

M **STATE UNIVERSITY OF NEW YORK COLLEGE AT ONEONTA,** Martin - Mullen Art Gallery, 108 Ravine Pkwy, 222 Fine Arts Ctr Oneonta, NY 13820-3717. Tel 607-436-3456; Fax 607-436-3466; Elec Mail timothy.sheesley@oneonta.edu; Internet Home Page Address: www.oneonta.edu/academics/art/gallery.html; *Gallery Dir* Timothy Sheesley
Open Mon - Fri 11 AM - 5 PM; No admis fee; Contemporary fine art/teaching; Art Gallery is a major feature of the Art Wing, separate fine arts & student galleries; Average Annual Attendance: 3,000
Income: Financed by state appropriation
Exhibitions: Annual student art exhibition; 2 exhibs per semester
Activities: Prog for interns; gallery talks; 6 vis lectrs per yr; James Mullen annual student exhib awards

ORIENT

M **OYSTERPONDS HISTORICAL SOCIETY,** Museum, 1555 Village Ln, Orient, NY 11957; PO Box 70, Orient, NY 11957-0070. Tel 631-323-2480; Fax 631-323-3719; Elec Mail ohsorieut@optonline.net; Internet Home Page Address: www.oysterpondshistoricalsociety.org; *Exec Dir* Ellen M Cone Busch; *Colls Mgr* Amy Folk
Open June - Sept Thurs, Sat & Sun 2 - 5 PM, other times by appointment; Admis adults $5, children under 12 & mems free; Estab 1944 to discover, procure, & preserve material related to the civil & military history of Long Island, particularly the East Marion & Orient Hamlets; Average Annual Attendance: 6,000; Mem: 700; dues family $50, individual $30; annual meeting in Sept
Income: $160,000 (financed by endowment, mem, grants & fundraising)
Library Holdings: Audio Tapes; Cassettes; DVDs; Lantern Slides; Manuscripts; Maps; Memorabilia; Motion Pictures; Original Documents; Photographs
Special Subjects: Historical Material, American Indian Art, Decorative Arts, Furniture, Marine Painting, Maps
Collections: Early Indian artifacts, including arrowheads, baskets & clay vessels; 18th century furniture & decorative arts; late 19th century Victorian furniture; marine & portrait paintings; photographs; textile coll, including quilts, scarves,

fans; tools, & equipment related to the agricultural & sea-related occupations of this area; manuscript colls relating to local history
Exhibitions: Toys & Dolls; Indian Artifacts; 19th Century Boarding House; 18th Century Period Rooms; Rotating exhibs
Publications: Griffin's Journal, book; Historical Orient Village, book; She Went A'Whaling, book; quarterly newsletter; Captain's Daughter, book; Coasterman's Wife, book; In the Wake of Whales, book.
Activities: Classes for adults & children; docent training; lects open to pub; 4 - 5 vis lectrs per yr; mus shop sells books, magazines, original art, reproductions & prints

OSSINING

M **MUSEUM OF OSSINING HISTORICAL SOCIETY,** 196 Croton Ave, Ossining, NY 10562-4504. Tel 914-941-0001; Elec Mail info@ossininghistorical.org; Internet Home Page Address: www.ossininghistorical.org; *Dir* Roberta Y Arminio; *Pres* Norman D McDonald
Open Sun - Thurs 1 - 4 PM & by appointment; No admis fee; Estab 1931 to educate the pub in the history & traditions of the vicinity; East Gallery contains changing exhibitions & a portion of the permanent collection; West Gallery contains permanent collection; Average Annual Attendance: 2,500; Mem: 497; dues patron $100, civic, commercial & contributing $25, family $15, individual $10, senior citizens & students $5
Income: Financed by mem & town appropriation
Library Holdings: Video Tapes 32
Special Subjects: Costumes
Collections: Costumes; textiles & quilts; slides & films of old Ossining; old photographs & daguerreotypes; Victorian dollhouse complete in minute detail, contains antique dolls, toys, miniatures, old school books & photographs; oil portraits; fine arts; Italian Art & Architecture
Publications: Monthly brochure
Activities: Educ dept; class visits; special assignment guidance; lect open to public, 4 vis lectrs per year; gallery talks; tours; competitions with awards; individual paintings & original objects of art lent to schools, banks & industry; sales shop sells books, magazines

L **Library,** 196 Croton Ave, Ossining, NY 10562. Tel 914-941-0001; *Librn* Vidal Abreu
Library Holdings: Audio Tapes; Book Volumes 1000; Cassettes; Clipping Files; Exhibition Catalogs; Framed Reproductions; Lantern Slides; Memorabilia; Original Art Works; Photographs; Prints; Reels; Reproductions; Slides; Video Tapes 32

OSWEGO

M **STATE UNIVERSITY OF NEW YORK AT OSWEGO,** Tyler Art Gallery, 126 Tyler Hall, SUNY Oswego Oswego, NY 13126. Tel 315-312-2113; Fax 315-312-5642; Elec Mail lbuckley@oswego.edu; *Asst Dir* Laurene Buckley; *Admin Aide* Lisa M Shortslef; *Asst Dir* Michael Flanagan
Open Mon - Fri 10 AM - 4 PM, Sat & Sun 12:30 PM - 4:30 PM, Sept - May; summer hours as posted; No admis fee; Estab 1969 to provide cultural stimulation & enrichment of art to the col community & to the residents of Oswego County; Two gallery spaces in Tyler Hall, the North Gallery is approx 2400 sq ft & the South Gallery is approx 1300 sq ft; Average Annual Attendance: 20,000
Income: Financed by University funds
Special Subjects: Painting-American, Sculpture, African Art, Pottery, Posters, Painting-British
Collections: Grant Arnold Collection of Fine Prints; Contemporary American Prints & Paintings
Exhibitions: Two galleries show a combined total of 14 exhibitions per school year
Publications: Brochures; occasional catalogs for exhibitions; posters
Activities: Lects open to public, 8-10 vis lectrs per yr; concerts, gallery talks; lending collection contains individual & original objects of art; originates traveling exhibs

L **Penfield Library,** 7060 State Rte 104, Oswego, NY 13126-3501. Tel 315-312-4267; Fax 315-312-3194; Elec Mail refdesk@oswego.edu; Internet Home Page Address: www.oswego.edu/library; *Dir* Marybeth Bell; *Art Subject Librn* Nedra Peterson
Open Mon - Thurs 8 AM - 11 PM, Fri 8 AM - 9 PM, Sat 10 AM - 9 PM, Sun 11:30 AM - 11 PM; For lending & reference
Income: Financed by univ
Library Holdings: Audio Tapes; Book Volumes 437,000; Cassettes; Fiche; Filmstrips; Framed Reproductions; Motion Pictures; Original Art Works; Pamphlets; Periodical Subscriptions 1469; Records; Reels; Sculpture; Slides; Video Tapes
Special Subjects: Art History, Graphic Arts, Advertising Design, Art Education, Costume Design & Constr, Aesthetics

OYSTER BAY

L **PLANTING FIELDS FOUNDATION,** Coe Hall at Planting Fields Arboretum, 1395 Planting Fields Rd, Oyster Bay, NY 11771-1302; PO Box 660, Oyster Bay, NY 11771-0660. Tel 516-922-9210; Fax 516-922-9226; Elec Mail coehall@plantingfields.org; Internet Home Page Address: www.plantingfields.org; *Dir* Ellen Cone Busch; *Dir Develop* Cindy Krezel; *Coll Mgr* Marianne Della Croce
Open Apr - Sept Mon - Fri noon - 3:30 PM; Admis adults $6.50, seniors $5, children 7-12 $2; Archives estab 1979 for Coe family papers, architectural drawings, photos, Planting Fields Foundation documents; For reference only. Coe Hall, a Tudor revival mansion being restored to its 1920's appearance, contains 17th-20th century paintings; Mem: $40 & up individual
Income: Financed by endowment
Library Holdings: Audio Tapes; Book Volumes 6000; Cassettes; Clipping Files; Filmstrips; Lantern Slides; Manuscripts; Memorabilia; Motion Pictures; Original Art Works; Pamphlets; Photographs; Prints; Slides; Video Tapes

Special Subjects: Landscape Architecture, Decorative Arts, Photography, Painting-British, Painting-Dutch, Painting-Italian, Painting-European, Historical Material, Portraits, American Western Art, Porcelain, Period Rooms, Stained Glass, Restoration & Conservation, Architecture
Activities: Classes for adults & children; docent training; outdoor science programs grades Pre K - 6; lect open to public, 5 vis lectrs per year; concerts; guided tours of historic house; sales shop sells books & garden related items

SOCIETY OF AMERICAN HISTORICAL ARTISTS
For further information, see National and Regional Organizations

PELHAM

M **PELHAM ART CENTER,** 155 Fifth Ave, Pelham, NY 10803-1503. Tel 914-738-2525; Fax 914-738-2686; Elec Mail info@pelhamartcenter.org; Internet Home Page Address: www.pelhamartcenter.org; *Exec Dir* Lisa Robb; *Prog Mgr* Jessica Cioffoletti; *Finance Mgr* Bridget Beltke; *Educ & Outreach Mgr* Filomena Iolascon
Open Tues - Fri 10 AM - 5 PM; Sat 10 AM - 4 PM; Sun ((in Dec only) 12 - 4 PM; No admis fee; Estab 1972 as a community art center to give area residents & visitors a place, the opportunity & the resources to see, study & experience the arts in a community setting; Multipurpose space; Gallery A 1120 sq ft; Gallery B 670 sq ft; Average Annual Attendance: 20,000; Mem: 500; dues $25-$1000
Income: $280,000 (financed by mem, tuition, earned income & gift shop sales)
Activities: Classes for adults & children; studio classes; workshops, docent progs; lects open to pub, 7 exhibs annually, 2-3 vis lectrs per yr; gallery talks; schols offered; retail store sells unique gift items

PENN YAN

M **THE AGRICULTURAL MEMORIES MUSEUM,** 1110 Townline Rd, Penn Yan, NY 14527-9002. Tel 315-536-1206; Elec Mail jr.jensen@usadatanet.net; Internet Home Page Address: www.agriculturalmemoriesmuseum.com; *Owner & Operator* Jennifer R Jensen; *Mus Asst* Hilbert J Jensen
Open June - Oct Sun 1 PM - 4 PM, Mon - Sat by appt, cl Nov - May; Admis adults $4, students & children 2 - 12 $1, children under 5 no admis fee; Estab 1997, dedicated in 1998; Pvt, family-owned org; 6500 sq ft exhib space; over 40-yr coll of horse-drawn carriages/sleighs, antique tractors, gasoline engines, toys, signs & misc. Mus preserves & restores items independently
Library Holdings: Book Volumes; Filmstrips
Collections: Over 45 carriages/sleighs, 50 gasoline engines, 50 antique tractors, pedal tractors & cars, signs & misc toys
Activities: Lects; guided tours & films

PLATTSBURGH

M **CLINTON COUNTY HISTORICAL ASSOCIATION,** Clinton County Historical Museum, 98 Ohio Ave, Plattsburgh, NY 12903-4401. Tel 518-561-0340; Elec Mail director@clintoncountyhistorical.org; Internet Home Page Address: http://clintoncountyhistorical.org; *Dir & Cur* Carol Blakeslee-Collin; *Pres* Roger Harwood
Open Wed - Sat 10 AM - 3 PM & by appt; Admis adults $4, seniors $3, children ages 12 & under $2, mems & organized school & youth groups free
Special Subjects: Glass, Photography, Porcelain, Portraits, Textiles, Painting-American, Decorative Arts, Furniture, Maps
Exhibitions: Area history from 1600's to present
Activities: mus shop sells books

M **STATE UNIVERSITY OF NEW YORK AT PLATTSBURGH,** Art Museum, 101 Broad St, Plattsburgh, NY 12901-2637. Tel 518-564-2813 Kent, 564-2288 Burke, 564-2474 Main Office; Fax 518-564-2473; Internet Home Page Address: www.plattsburgh.edu/museum; *Dir* Cecilia Esposito; *Coll Mgr* David Driver; *Coll Specialist* Eric Ruckler; *Docent Coordr* Marguerite Eisinger
Open daily Noon - 4 PM, cl university holidays; No admis fee; Estab 1978; Kent Gallery & Burke Gallery; Average Annual Attendance: 17,000
Special Subjects: Etchings & Engravings, Porcelain, Painting-American, Bronzes, African Art, Eskimo Art, Painting-Canadian, Asian Art
Collections: Rockwell Kent Collection, paintings, prints, drawings, sketches, proofs & designs, books; Nina Winkle Sculpture Garden; Slathin Collection; Louise Norton Classic Design Collection; Outlook Sculpture Park; Myers Lobby Gallery
Exhibitions: Twelve exhibitions each year; antique & contemporary, all media
Publications: Exhibition catalogs; monthly exhibition announcements; semi-annual calendar of events
Activities: Progs for undergrad students, elementary & secondary schools & community groups in area; docent progs; lects open to pub, 6 vis lectrs per yr; tours; gallery talks; competitions with awards; individual paintings lent

PLEASANTVILLE

M **PACE UNIVERSITY GALLERY,** Art Gallery in Choate House, 861 Bedford Rd, Pleasantville, NY 10570-2799. Tel 914-773-3694; Fax 914-773-3676; Elec Mail tromer@pace.edu; Internet Home Page Address: www.pace.edu; *Dept Chair* Dr John Mulgrew; *Admin Asst* Teresa Romer
Open Mon - Wed Noon - 4PM, Thurs noon - 6 PM, cl Sat; No admis fee; Estab 1978 to exhibit the works of nationally known professional artists & groups, & to serve as a focal point for artistic activities within the university & surrounding communities; The gallery has a commanding view of the center of campus; it is both spacious & modern
Income: Financed by the university
Activities: Lect open to public, 8-10 vis lectrs per year; gallery talks; tours

POCANTICO HILLS

M **HISTORIC HUDSON VALLEY,** 639 Bedford, Pocantico Hills, NY 10591. Tel 914-631-8200; Fax 914-631-0089; Elec Mail info@hudsonvalley.org; Internet Home Page Address: www.hudsonvalley.org; *Pres* Waddell Stillman; *Librn* Catalina Hannan; *Dir Finance* David Parsons; *Dir Devel* Peter Pockriss; *Dir Human Resources* Lynda Jones; *Dir Pub Rels* Rob Schweitzer; *Colls Mgr* Jessa J Krick; *Archivist* Karen W Morse
See website for current hours & rates; Chartered 1951 as a nonprofit educational foundation; Owns & operates six historic properties which are Sunnyside in Tarrytown, the home of author Washington Irving; Philipsburg Manor in Sleepy Hollow, A Dutch-American gristmill-farm site of the early 1700s; Van Cortlandt Manor in Croton-on-Hudson, a manorial estate of the Revolutionary War period; Montgomery Place in Annandale-on-Hudson- a 380 acre estate overlooking the Hudson River, Catskill Mountains, and the Union Church of Pocantico Hills, with windows by Matisse & Chagall. Historic Hudson Valley also operates the visitation program of Kykuit, the Rockefeller estate in Sleepy Hollow, NY; Average Annual Attendance: 200,000
Library Holdings: Auction Catalogs; Book Volumes; Clipping Files; Exhibition Catalogs; Lantern Slides; Manuscripts; Maps; Memorabilia; Original Art Works; Original Documents; Pamphlets; Periodical Subscriptions; Photographs; Prints; Reels; Reproductions
Special Subjects: Folk Art, Architecture, Ceramics, Metalwork, Portraits, Pottery, Painting-American, Textiles, Maps, Costumes, Decorative Arts, Furniture, Porcelain, Marine Painting, Coins & Medals, Restorations, Stained Glass, Pewter
Collections: Memorabilia of Washington Irving, Van Cortlandt and Philipse families; 17th, 18th and 19th century decorative arts
Exhibitions: Beauty and the Brick (online)
Publications: American Industrialization, Economic Expansion, & the Law; America's Wooden Age; Aspects of Early New York Society & Politics; Bracebridge Hall; Business Enterprise in Early New York; Diedrich Knickerbocker's A History of New York; An Emerging Independent American Economy: 1815-1875; The Family Collections at Van Cortlandt Manor; The Howe Map; The Hudson River 1850-1918, A Photographic Portrait; Life Along the Hudson; Life of George Washington; The Loyalist Americans; Material Culture of the Wooden Age; The Mill at Philipsburg Manor, Upper Mills, & a Brief History of Milling; Old Christmas; Party & Political Guidebook; A Portfolio of Sleepy Hollow Prints; Rip Van Winkle & the Legend of Sleepy Hollow; Six Publications related to Washington Irving; An American Treasure: The Hudson River Valley; Cross Roads and Cross Rivers: Diversity in New York; Beauty and the Brick; The Great Estates regions of the Hudson Valley; Great Houses of the Hudson River
Activities: Classes for adults and children; docent training; school progs; demonstrations of 17th and 18th century arts and crafts; lectrs open to pub; guided tours by interpreters in period clothing; candlelight tours; gallery talks; John D Rockefeller Founder's Award (annual); Hudson Valley Hero (annual); mus shop sells books, original art, reproductions, prints & Hudson Valley memorabilia

L **Library,** 639 Bedford Rd, Pocantico Hills, NY 10591. Tel 914-366-6901; Fax 914-631-0089; Elec Mail librarian@hudsonvalley.org; Internet Home Page Address: www.hudsonvalley.org; *Librn* Catalina Hannan; *Mgr Library & Archival Servs* Karen Walton Morse
Open Tues-Thurs 9-5 by appointment; Specialized reference library with particular emphasis on 17th, 18th and 19th century living in the Hudson River Valley and Washington Irving
Income: financed by donations, gifts, grants
Library Holdings: Auction Catalogs; Book Volumes 5000; Exhibition Catalogs; Manuscripts; Original Documents; Periodical Subscriptions 123; Records; Reels
Special Subjects: Art History, Folk Art, Decorative Arts, Maps, Painting-American, Sculpture, Historical Material, History of Art & Archaeology, Portraits, Ceramics, Art Education, Porcelain, Furniture, Stained Glass, Handicrafts, Pottery, Silver, Tapestries, Textiles, Pewter

PORT CHESTER

L **PORT CHESTER-RYE BROOK PUBLIC LIBRARY,** One Haseco Ave, Port Chester, NY 10573. Tel 914-939-6710; Fax 914-939-4735; Internet Home Page Address: www.portchesterlibrary.org; *Dir* Robin Lettieri
Open Mon 9 AM - 9 PM, Tues 9 AM - 8 PM, Wed - Fri 9 AM - 5 PM, Sep - June: Sat 9 AM - 5 PM, July - Aug: 9 AM - noon; No admis fee; Estab 1876 to circulate books, records, magazines, to the general public to provide reference services; Circ 103,598; Maintains a small art gallery, with mostly local artists; Average Annual Attendance: 32,493
Income: $494,600 (financed by endowment, villages & state appropriations)
Purchases: $50,500
Library Holdings: Book Volumes 85,000; Filmstrips; Framed Reproductions; Pamphlets; Periodical Subscriptions 2000; Prints; Records; Reels; Slides
Exhibitions: Water colors, oils, acrylics, photographs
Activities: Educ dept; lect & films open to public; films; career seminars & workshops; individual paintings lent

PORT WASHINGTON

M **THE GRAPHIC EYE GALLERY,** (Long Island Graphic Eye Gallery) 402 Main St Port Washington, NY 11710. Tel 516-883-9668; Elec Mail gallery@graphiceyegallery.com; Internet Home Page Address: www.graphiceyegallery.com
Open Thurs - Sun 12 PM - 5 PM; No admis fee; Estab 1974; Works in all mediums
Income: Financed by mem & individual project grants
Special Subjects: Prints
Collections: Slide collection; Private collections
Exhibitions: Annual Winter Show: Journeys-Group Show; Group, individual & juried shows throughout the year
Activities: Educ dept; lect & demonstrations in print & other media open to public, 3-4 vis lectrs per year; Salmagundi Award; Bell Award; competitions with awards; scholarships offered; sales shop sells reproductions, prints, handmade gifts

L **PORT WASHINGTON PUBLIC LIBRARY,** One Library Dr, Port Washington, NY 11050-2794. Tel 516-883-4400; Fax 516-944-6855; Internet Home Page Address: www.pwpl.org; *Dir* Nancy Curtin
Open Mon, Tues, Thurs & Fri 9 AM - 9 PM, Wed 11 AM - 9 PM, Sep - June: Sat 9 AM - 5 PM, Sun 1 - 5 PM, July - Aug: 9 AM - 1 PM; No admis fee; Estab 1892; Circ 303,500
Income: Financed by state appropriation & school district
Library Holdings: Audio Tapes; Book Volumes 128,000; Cards; Cassettes; Clipping Files; Filmstrips; Manuscripts; Pamphlets; Periodical Subscriptions 750; Photographs; Prints; Records; Reels; Video Tapes
Special Subjects: Illustration, Photography, Drawings, Manuscripts
Collections: Ernie Simon Collection of Photographs & Newspaper Articles on the History of Port Washington; Sinclair Lewis Collection of books, manuscripts, photographs & ephemera; Mason Photograph Archive of photographic negatives spanning over 75 years of Port Washington social history; P W Play Troupe Archive of memorabilia covering the 60 year history of the oldest theatre group on Long Island; Collection of drawings by children's illustrator Peter Spier
Exhibitions: Lita Kelmenson (drawings & wood sculpture); Hajime Okubo (box constructions); Paul Wood (oil painting & watercolors); Photographers: Dency Ann Kane, Mariou Fuller, Christine Osinski
Publications: Monthly guide catalog

POTSDAM

M **THE STATE UNIVERSITY OF NEW YORK AT POTSDAM,** (Potsdam College of the State University of New York) Roland Gibson Gallery, 44 Pierrepont Ave, Potsdam, NY 13676-2200. Tel 315-267-3290, 267-2481; Fax 315-267-4884; Elec Mail vasherak@potsdam.edu; Internet Home Page Address: www.potsdam.edu/gibson; *Colls Mgr* Romi Sebald; *Secy* Claudette Fefee; *Dir* April Vasher-Dean
Open Mon & Fri Noon - 5 PM, Tues - Thurs Noon - 7 PM, Sat Noon - 4 PM, Summer hours: Tues - Fri 1 - 4 PM; No admis fee; Estab 1967 to serve col & community as a teaching gallery; Gallery has 4800 square feet of exhibition space on three levels with security & environmental controls; Average Annual Attendance: 18,000
Library Holdings: Compact Disks; DVDs; Exhibition Catalogs; Video Tapes
Special Subjects: Drawings, Painting-American, Prints, Sculpture, Painting-Japanese, Painting-Italian
Collections: Contemporary Japanese, Italian & American art (painting, sculpture & prints); Modern & contemporary drawing collection; Andy Warhol Polaroids & gelatin silver prints; available for travel: Max Klinger, The Intermezzi Print Cycle; Resounding Spirit: Japanese Contemporary Art of the 1960's; Warhol!
Publications: Exhibition catalogs & posters
Activities: lects open to public, gallery talks; tours; competitions; original objects of art lent to public institutions, art museums; book traveling exhibs 1-3 times per yr; originates traveling exhibs to other mus

M **VILLAGE OF POTSDAM,** (Potsdam Public Museum) Potsdam Public Museum, 2 Park St, Civic Center Potsdam, NY 13676-2099; PO Box 5168, Potsdam, NY 13676-5168. Tel 315-265-6910; Elec Mail museum@vl.potsdam.ny.us; Internet Home Page Address: www.potsdampublicmuseum.org; *Dir & Cur* Mimi Van Deusen; *Mus Aide* Mickey Champagne; *Mus Aide* Fred Rollins; *Mus Aide* Tom Dashnaw
Open Tues - Sat 10 AM - 4 PM; Admis $1 suggested donation; Estab 1940; educational, cultural & historical center for the Village of Potsdam & surrounding area with pub research & archives available to the pub; History of Potsdam & rotating exhibits; Average Annual Attendance: 12,000
Income: Village financed by town, state & federal appropriation
Library Holdings: Clipping Files; Maps; Memorabilia; Original Documents; Pamphlets; Periodical Subscriptions
Special Subjects: Historical Material, Flasks & Bottles, Furniture, Painting-American, Textiles, Maps, Costumes, Pottery, Dolls, Asian Art, Carpets & Rugs, Tapestries, Antiquities-Roman, Stained Glass
Collections: Burnap Collection of English Pottery; costumes of the 19th & 20th centuries; Mandarin Chinese hangings, china & costumes; photograph coll, artifacts & material on local history; pressed glass & art glass of the 19th & early 20th century
Exhibitions: Changing exhibitions
Publications: Newsletter, ann; news website
Activities: Progs for schools; lects open to pub; concerts; architectural tours; gallery talks; mus shop sells books, prints

POUGHKEEPSIE

M **DUTCHESS COUNTY ARTS COUNCIL,** 9 Vassar St, Garden Level Ste Poughkeepsie, NY 12601. Tel 845-454-3222; Fax 845-454-6902; Elec Mail info@artsmidhudson.org; Internet Home Page Address: www.artsmidhudson.org; *Pres* Benjamin Krevolin; *Dir Progs & Arts Svcs* Nico Lang; *Bus Mgr* Lisa Fiorese; *Folklorist* Polly Adema

M **VASSAR COLLEGE,** The Frances Lehman Loeb Art Center, 124 Raymond Ave, Poughkeepsie, NY 12604; PO Box 703, Poughkeepsie, NY 12604-0001. Tel 845-437-5235, 437-5237; Fax 845-437-5955; Internet Home Page Address: www.fllac.vassar.edu; *Cur* Patricia Phagan; *Registrar* Joann Potter; *Preparator* Bruce Bundock; *Dir* James Mundy; *Cur* Mary-Kay Lombino; *Asst Registrar* Karen Hines; *Office Specialist* Francine Brown; *Coordr Educ Pub Prog* Margaret Vetare
Open Tues - Wed & Fri - Sat 10 AM - 5 PM, Thurs 10 AM - 9 PM, Sun 1 - 5 PM; cl Mon, Easter, Thanksgiving & the week between Christmas & New Year's; No admis fee; Estab 1864; collects Eastern & Western art of all periods; New mus opened in Nov 1993 in addition designed by Cesar Pelli; Average Annual Attendance: 37,000; Mem: 1100; dues $35 & up; bi-annual meeting fall & spring
Income: Financed by Vassar College, endowment & mem
Special Subjects: Glass, Photography, Portraits, Architecture, Drawings, Graphics, Painting-American, Sculpture, Watercolors, Archaeology, Ceramics, Etchings &

Engravings, Painting-European, Jade, Jewelry, Oriental Art, Asian Art, Renaissance Art, Medieval Art, Painting-Italian, Antiquities-Egyptian, Antiquities-Greek, Antiquities-Roman, Antiquities-Etruscan
Collections: Matthew Vassar collection of 19th century American paintings of Hudson River School & 19th century English watercolors; Felix M Warburg Collection of medieval sculpture & graphics including Duerer & Rembrandt; 20th century art of all media including photography; European paintings, sculpture & drawings ranging from the Renaissance to the 20th century, including Bacchiacca, Cezanne, Salvator Rosa, Claesz, Tiepolo, Robert, Corot, Cezanne, Delacroix, Gifford, Van Gogh, Tanner, Munch, Klee, Bourdelle, Laurent, Davidson, Gabo, Calder, Moore; 20th Century American & European paintings including Henri, Hartley, O'Keeffe, Bacon, Nicholson, Rothko, de Kooning, Hartigan, Weber; graphics ranging from Barocci to Rembrandt to Goya to Picasso, Matisse, Braque, Kelly, Grooms & Graves; photography from Anna Atkins, Cameron, Gilpin, Steichen, Abbott, Lange, Lynes & Linda Conner; The Classical Collection includes Greek vases, Egyptian, Etruscan & Mycenaean objects, Roman glass, portrait busts, jewelry; other archaeological finds; Dexter M Ferry Collection; Olga Hasbrouck Collection of Chinese Ceramics; Charles Pratt Collection of Chinese Jades
Publications: Occasional exhibition catalogues & biannual newsletter
Activities: Docent training; lects open to public; gallery talks; tours; exten prog lends original objects of art to other museums; book traveling exhibitions vary; originate traveling exhibs to other museums; sales shop sells books, prints, postcards, notecards, posters & exhib catalogues

L **Art Library,** 124 Raymond Ave, Poughkeepsie, NY 12604-6198; PO Box 512, Poughkeepsie, NY 12604-0001. Tel 914-437-5790; Internet Home Page Address: iberia/vassar.edu/art; Internet Home Page Address: www.artlibrary.vassar.edu; *Librn* Thomas Hill
Open Mon - Thurs 8:30 AM - 11:30 PM, Fri 8:30 AM - 10 PM, Sat 9 AM - 10 PM, Sun 10 AM - 1:30 AM, cl summer; Estab 1937; Circulation to students & faculty only
Library Holdings: Book Volumes 45,000; Exhibition Catalogs; Fiche; Other Holdings CD-ROMS; Periodical Subscriptions 250; Reels

PURCHASE

M **ARTHUR M. BERGER ART GALLERY - MANHATTANVILLE COLLEGE,** 2900 Purchase St Purchase, NY 10577-2131. *Dir* Charles McGill

M **MANHATTANVILLE COLLEGE,** Brownson Gallery, 2900 Purchase St, Brownson Bldg Purchase, NY 10577-2131. Tel 914-323-5331; Fax 914-323-3131; Elec Mail mcgillc@mville.edu; Internet Home Page Address: www.mville.edu; www1.mville.edu/gallery/index.htm; *Gallery Dir* Charles McGill; *Faculty Cur* Christine Dehne; *Student Employee* Saul Botier
Open 9:30 AM - 5 PM and by appointment; No admis fee; Estab 1950s to bring artists to col & community; Average Annual Attendance: 6,400
Income: Financed by endowment & tuition
Collections: Sculpture; Photography Collection
Publications: Magazine, bimonthly; catalogs
Activities: Lects open to public, 2 vis lectrs per yr; concerts; gallery talks; scholarships; original objects of art lent; originate traveling exhibs

L **Library,** 2900 Purchase St, Purchase, NY 10577-2132. Tel 914-694-2200, Ext 274, 323-5282; Fax 914-694-6234; Elec Mail goodman@mvill.edu; Internet Home Page Address: www.mville.edu/library; *Dir* Rhonna Goodman; *Asst Library Dir* Jeff Rosedale; *Archivist, Spec Colls Librn* Lauren Georger
Open Mon - Thurs 8 AM - 8PM, Fri 8 AM - 8 PM, Sat 10 AM - 6 PM, Sun 10 AM - 8 PM
Income: financed by endowment & tuition
Library Holdings: Book Volumes 250,000; Periodical Subscriptions 1100

M **Arthur M Berger Gallery,** 2900 Purchase St, Purchase, NY 10577-2131. Tel 914-323-3190; Elec Mail mcgillc@mville.edu; Internet Home Page Address: www1.mville.edu/gallery/index.htm; *Gallery Dir* Charles McGill; *Faculty Cur* Christine Dehne; *Student Employee* Saul Botier
Open Mon - Fri 11 AM - 6 PM, Thurs until 7 PM, Sat Noon - 4 PM, cl Sun; Estab 2008

C **PEPSICO INC,** Donald M Kendall Sculpture Garden, 700 Anderson Hill Rd, Purchase, NY 10577-1444. Tel 914-253-2900; Fax 914-253-3553; *Former Chmn & CEO* Donald M Kendall; *Dir Art Prog* Jacqueline R Millan
Open Mon - Sun 9 AM - 5 PM; Estab 1970 to present sculpture of mus quality; Average Annual Attendance: 10,000
Collections: Forty-two large outdoor sculptures, works by Alexander Calder, Henry Moore, Louise Nevelson, David Smith, Arnaldo Pomodoro, Jacques Lipchitz,; Henry Laurens, Auguste Rodin, Miro, Giacometti, Max Ernst, Jean DuBuffet, Tony Smith, George Segal, Claes Oldenburg, George Rickey, Richard Erdman & Barbara Hepworth

M **PURCHASE COLLEGE STATE UNIVERSITY OF NEW YORK,** Neuberger Museum of Art, 735 Anderson Hill Rd, Purchase, NY 10577-1400. Tel 914-251-6100; Fax 914-251-6101; Elec Mail neuberger@purchase.edu; Internet Home Page Address: www.neuberger.org; *Acting Dir* Lea Emery; *Chief Cur & Deputy Dir Cur Affairs* Helaine Posner; *Chief Preparator* David Bogosian; *Asst Cur* Avis Larson; *Assoc Cur New Media & Digital Mus* Jacqueline Shilkoff; *Cur Art of the Americas* Patrice Giasson; *Cur & Asst Prof Art History* Tracy Fitzpatrick; *Registrar* Patricia Magnani; *Cur Educ* Emily Mello; *Head Mus Educ* Eleanor Brackbill; *Dir Mktg* Kristi McKee
Open Tues - Sun 12 PM - 5 PM; cl Mon & major holidays; Admis adults $5, seniors 62 & over & students $3, mems, college students, faculty, staff & children under 12 free, 1st Sat of month free; Estab 1968, opened May 1974 to serve university & residents of New York State & Connecticut; 78,000 sq ft facility designed by Philip Johnson with nine total galleries, five outside sculpture courts; Average Annual Attendance: 75,000; Mem: Dues dir circle $2500, sustaining $1000, patron $500, donor $250, contributing $100, family-dual $50, individual $35
Income: Financed by State University of New York, endowment fund, government grants, private foundations, donors & mem

Special Subjects: Drawings, Painting-American, Photography, Prints, Sculpture, African Art, Painting-European
Collections: Six thousand objects featuring 20th century European & American paintings, sculpture, drawings, prints, photographs & audio works, African & ancient art
Publications: Exhibition catalogues; brochures; quarterly calendars
Activities: Docent training; internships for Purchase College students; tours for children, adults & citizens with special needs; progs for families & children; lects open to public, vis lectrs; concerts; gallery talks; performances; films; tours; internships offered; original objects of art lent to other museums; book traveling exhibs; originate traveling exhibs to other museums; sales shop sells books, magazines, prints, small gift items & cards

L **Library,** 735 Anderson Hill Rd, Purchase, NY 10577-1402. Tel 914-251-6400; Fax 914-251-6437; Internet Home Page Address: www.purchase.edu/departments/library; *Dir* Patrick Callahan; *Art Librn* Heather Kirkwood
School year open Mon - Thurs 8 AM - 2 AM, Fri 8 AM - 10 PM, Sat 11 AM - 8 PM, Sun 12 PM - 2 AM
Income: Financed by univ
Library Holdings: Audio Tapes; Book Volumes 255,000; Cards; Cassettes; Compact Disks; DVDs; Fiche; Motion Pictures; Periodical Subscriptions 1000; Records; Reels; Reproductions; Slides; Video Tapes
Special Subjects: Art History, Film, Photography, Drawings, Graphic Arts, Graphic Design, Painting-American, Painting-British, Painting-Dutch, Painting-Flemish, Painting-French, Painting-German, Painting-Italian, Prints, Sculpture, Painting-European, History of Art & Archaeology, Stage Design, Conceptual Art, Theatre Arts, Printmaking, Video, Furniture, Costume Design & Constr, Afro-American Art

QUEENS

M **SAINT JOHN'S UNIVERSITY,** Dr. M.T. Geoffrey Yeh Art Gallery, 8000 Utopia Pkwy, Sun Yat Sen Hall Queens, NY 11439-9000. Tel 718-990-7476; Fax 718-990-1881; *Dir Gallery* Parvez Mohsin; *Gallery Asst* Aliza Moorji
Open Mon-Fri10 AM - 5 PM, Sat 12 PM- 5 PM; summer hours: Mon - Thurs 10 AM - 5 PM, Sat noon - 5 PM, cl Fri & Sun; No admis fee; Estab 1977 to make available Oriental art objects to the pub & to expose the metropolitan area to the Oriental culture through various exhibits & activities; Gallery displays contemporary as well as ancient objects, mainly Oriental with a few western subjects & newer exhibits; national contemporary American artists; recently hosted Images from the Atomic Front; Average Annual Attendance: 50,000
Income: Financed by the University, endowments & private contributions
Special Subjects: Painting-Japanese, Jade, Porcelain, Oriental Art, Ivory, Calligraphy
Collections: Harry C Goebel Collection: 595 pieces of rare & beautiful art objects dating from the 7th-19th century, incl jades; permanent coll contains 700 pieces of Chinese porcelain, paintings, textiles, calligraphy & paper cuttings dating from 7th-20th century; rare book coll from China
Exhibitions: Two Great Textiles of Modern Chinese Paintings; The Chinese Ancient Coin Exhibit; Images from the Atomic Front; Power Animals: Artwork of Marshall Arisman; From the Inside Art: Feminist Art Then & Now
Publications: Exhibition catalogues
Activities: Lects open to public, 6-10 vis lectrs per yr; concerts; gallery talks; tours; competitions with awards; individual paintings & original objects of art lent; lending collection contains 200 original art works; original prints; 200 paintings; originates traveling exhibs

—Asian Collection, 8000 Utopia Pkwy, Sun Yat Sen Hall Queens, NY 11439-9000. Tel 718-990-1526; Fax 718-990-1881; *Librn* Kenji Niki
Open to the pub for reference only
Library Holdings: Book Volumes 50,500; Cards; Exhibition Catalogs; Fiche; Manuscripts; Micro Print; Periodical Subscriptions 90; Reels
Collections: Collected Works of Chinese & Japanese Calligraphy; Japan Foundation Coll includes 200 volumes on various Japanese art subjects; Series of Chinese Arts

RIVERHEAD

A **EAST END ARTS & HUMANITIES COUNCIL,** 133 E Main St, Riverhead, NY 11901-2494. Tel 631-727-0900; Fax 631-727-0966; Internet Home Page Address: www.eastendarts.org; *Exec Dir* Patricia Snyder; *Gallery Dir* Jane Kirkwood
Open Mon - Sat 10 AM - 4 PM; No admis fee; Estab 1972; Average Annual Attendance: 11,000; Mem: 500; dues $20-$65
Income: Financed by public & private sector
Exhibitions: Various group shows
Activities: Classes for children; music & art pre-school-adult; summer camp ages 5-8 & 8-12; wine press concert series; lect open to public; competitions with awards; gallery talks; tours; sales shop sells books, original art & crafts, hand crafted items

ROCHESTER

M **GEORGE EASTMAN HOUSE-INTERNATIONAL MUSEUM OF PHOTOGRAPHY & FILM,** 900 East Ave, Rochester, NY 14607-2298. Tel 585-271-3361; Fax 585-271-3970; Elec Mail info@geh.org; Internet Home Page Address: www.eastmanhouse.org; *Chmn* Thomas Jackson; *Controller* Paul J Piazza; *Cur Technology Coll* Todd Gustavson; *Dir Develop* Pamela Reed Sanchez; *Operations & Finance* Thomas Combs; *Mgr Publications* Amy Schelemanow; *Dir Communs & Visitor Engagement* Eliza Benington-Kozlowski; *Cur Landscape* Amy Kinsey; *House Cur* Kathy Connor; *Cur Motion Picture Coll* Paolo Cherchi Usai; *Pub Rel Mgr* Kellie Fraver; *Dir* Dr Bruce Barnes
Open Tues - Sat 10 AM - 5 PM, Thurs 10 AM - 8 PM, Sun 11 AM - 5 PM; Admis adults $10, students $6, seniors 60 & over $8, children 5-12 $4, children under 4 & mems free; Estab 1949 for photography exhibitions, research & educ; Restored landmark, gardens, photography & film mus; Average Annual Attendance: 150,000; Mem: 4200; dues family/dual $70, individual $50, senior citizens $45
Income: Financed by corp & individual gifts, foundation & government grants, earned income
Library Holdings: Book Volumes; Exhibition Catalogs; Kodachrome Transparencies; Lantern Slides; Manuscripts; Maps; Memorabilia; Micro Print; Motion Pictures; Original Art Works; Original Documents; Other Holdings; Pamphlets; Periodical Subscriptions; Photographs; Prints; Records; Reels; Reproductions; Sculpture; Slides; Video Tapes
Special Subjects: Landscapes, Photography
Collections: Equipment (photographic); film; 19th, 20th & 21st century photography; George Eastman Legacy Collection
Publications: Image, bi-annual books & catalogs
Activities: Classes for children; docent training; teacher workshops; school exhibs prog; lects open to pub; concerts; gallery talks; tours; fellowships; awards, George Eastman Award, Eastman Honorary Scholar Award; exten dept; lending collection contains photographs & original objects of art; book traveling exhibs; originates traveling exhibs; mus shop sells books, magazines & reproductions

L **Museum,** 900 East Ave, Rochester, NY 14607. Tel 585-271-3361; Fax 585-271-3970; Elec Mail info@geh.org; Internet Home Page Address: www.eastmanhouse.org; *Archivist* Joe Struble; *Librn* Rachel Stuhlman; *Dir* Bruce Barnes; *Cur Technology* Todd Gustavson; *Cur* Paab Cherchi Usai; *Cur Legacy Coll* Kathy Connor; *Cur Landscape* Amy Kinsey; *Develop* Pamela Reed Sanchez
Open Tues - Sat 10 AM - 5 PM, Thurs 10 AM - 5 PM, Sun 11 AM - 5 PM; Admis $12, seniors $10, students $5, children 12 & under free; Estab 1947; Circ 53,000; International museum of photography & film; Average Annual Attendance: 149,000; Mem: 4,200; dues beginning at $55
Library Holdings: Audio Tapes; Book Volumes 40,000; Clipping Files; Exhibition Catalogs; Fiche; Manuscripts; Pamphlets; Periodical Subscriptions 375; Records; Reels 75; Reproductions; Slides
Special Subjects: Photography, Historical Material, Furniture, Landscapes
Collections: Camera technology & Library dealing with the history & aesthetics of photography: 400,000 photographs including major colls of Edward Steichen, Alvin Langdon Coburn, Southworth & Hawes, Louis Walton Sipley, Lewis Hine, Edward Muybridge & Nickolas Muray; Motion picture stills & titles
Publications: Image
Activities: Classes for adults & children; Discovery Room for children; lects open to pub; concerts; gallery talks; tours; George Eastman Award; schols & fels offered; originate traveling exhibs to mus and univs worldwide; mus shop sells books, reproductions, prints, gen merchandise

M **LANDMARK SOCIETY OF WESTERN NEW YORK, INC,** The Campbell-Whittlesey House Museum, 133 S Fitzhugh St, Rochester, NY 14608-2204. Tel 585-546-7029 (Ext 10); Fax 585-546-4788; Elec Mail mail@landmarksociety.org; Internet Home Page Address: www.landmarksociety.org; *Exec Dir* Joanne Arony; *Dir Mus* Cindy Boyer
Open Mon - Fri 9 AM - 3 PM, other times by appointment; Admis adults $3, children under 14 $1; Estab 1937; Mem: dues keystone $500, cornerstone $250, pillar $125, patron $75, family $35, active $25
Library Holdings: Book Volumes; Kodachrome Transparencies; Manuscripts; Maps; Memorabilia; Original Art Works; Original Documents; Periodical Subscriptions; Photographs; Prints; Reproductions; Slides; Video Tapes
Special Subjects: Architecture, Landscapes, Decorative Arts, Furniture, Historical Material, Restorations, Period Rooms
Collections: Art, furnishings & decorative arts of the 1830s; furnishings & decorative arts of early 19th century
Publications: Bi-monthly newsletter; booklets; brochures; guides; postcards
Activities: Dramatic progs; docent training; tours

L **Wenrich Memorial Library,** 133 S Fitzhugh St, Rochester, NY 14608-2204. Tel 716-546-7029; Fax 716-546-4788; Elec Mail chowk@landmarksociety.org; Internet Home Page Address: www.landmarksociety.org; *Res Coordr* Cynthia Howk
Open Tues - Fri 9 AM - 4 PM only by appointment; No admis fee for mem of the Landmark Soc; $10 per hr for all other patrons; Estab 1937 to preserve historic resources & neighborhoods in Western New York; information center containing drawings, photographs, slides, books & periodicals, as well as archives of local architecture & information on preservation & restoration techniques; Mem: 3200
Income: Financed by mem & special grants
Purchases: $1000
Library Holdings: Book Volumes 5000; Clipping Files; Exhibition Catalogs; Kodachrome Transparencies; Manuscripts; Original Art Works; Pamphlets; Periodical Subscriptions 15; Photographs; Prints; Slides; Video Tapes
Special Subjects: Landscape Architecture, Decorative Arts, Historical Material, Interior Design, Furniture, Architecture
Collections: Claude Bragdon Collection of Architectural Drawings; Historic American Buildings: Survey Drawings of Local Architecture; John Wenrich & Walter Cassebeer Collection of Prints & Watercolors; Cobblestone Buildings; Covered Bridges; Erie Canal Photo Surveys
Exhibitions: Adaptive Use: New Uses for Old Buildings; The Architecture of Ward Wellington Ward; Rochester Prints, from the drawings of Walter Cassebeer
Publications: Newsletter, bi-monthly
Activities: Classes for adults & children; docent training; lects open to pub; tours; originate traveling exhibs to area schools, colleges, banks, community centers; mus shop sells books, original art, reproductions, prints, apparel, jewelry & gifts

M **ROCHESTER CONTEMPORARY,** (Pyramid Arts Center) Art Center, 137 East Ave, Rochester, NY 14604-2572. Tel 585-461-2222; Fax 585-461-2223; Elec Mail info@rochestercontemporary.org; Internet Home Page Address: www.rochestercontemporary.org; *Exec Dir & Cur* Bleu Cease; *Pres* Stewart D Davis; *VPres* Colleen Buzzard
Open Mon - Fri 10 AM - 5 PM; Admis non-mems $1; Estab 1977 to hold exhibitions & performances, nonprofit organization; a venue for the exchange of ideas providing unique encounters for audiences & opportunities for emerging artists; Average Annual Attendance: 16,902; Mem: 500; dues $20-$250
Income: Financed by mems, gifts & donations
Activities: Educ dept; workshops with guest artists; docent training; lect open to public, 10 vis lectrs per year; concerts; gallery talks; new history & bicycle tours; competitions; Best in Show award for members exhib; sales shop sells screenings

A **ROCHESTER HISTORICAL SOCIETY,** 115 South Ave, Rochester, NY 14604-1817. Tel 585-428-8470; Internet Home Page Address: www.rochesterhistory.org; *Exec Dir* Meredith Keller; *Librn* William Keeler; *Coll Mgr* Dan Cody; *Mem & Admin* Christy Zuhlke
Open Tues - Thurs 10 AM - 3 PM; Admis adults $5, children $3, children under 12 & mems free; Estab 1860, refounded 1888, to obtain & preserve relics & documents & publish material relating to Rochester's history; Headquarters at Rundel Library, 2nd floor; Average Annual Attendance: 2,000; Mem: 450; annual meeting in Spring
Income: Financed by mem
Special Subjects: Costumes, Drawings, Embroidery, Etchings & Engravings, Graphics, Historical Material, Landscapes, Photography, Posters, Prints, Sculpture, Textiles, Watercolors, Painting-American, Pottery, Decorative Arts, Pewter, Ceramics, Portraits, Furniture, Glass, Maps
Collections: Rochester costumes, furnishings & portraits; Over 200,000 books, archives & objects
Exhibitions: 3-4 exhibs each yr
Publications: Observer Magazine
Activities: Lects open to public

L **ROCHESTER INSTITUTE OF TECHNOLOGY,** Corporate Education & Training, 67 Lomb Memorial Dr, Rochester, NY 14623-5602. Tel 716-475-2411, Ext 7090; Fax 716-475-7000; Internet Home Page Address: www.rit.edu/cims/cet; WATS 800-724-2536; *Dir* Kitren Van Strander
Center has been a leading provider of professional training for the graphic arts & imaging industries for more than 40 years. The T & E Center provides seminars & hands on workshops in traditional & leading edge technologies for graphic design & publishing software, image editing & compositing, digital photography & electronic prepress & publishing. In addition, introductory & advanced programs are also offered in printing production & technologies, business & production management, & Total Quality. T & E Center programs draw upon resources from RIT's School of Printing Management & Sciences, School of Photographic Arts & Sciences & the Center for Imaging Science as well as from industry to deliver practical training to today's graphic arts professional
Publications: T & E Update, monthly
Activities: Seminars for the graphic arts & imaging industries

M **UNIVERSITY OF ROCHESTER,** Memorial Art Gallery, 500 University Ave, Rochester, NY 14607-1414. Tel 585-276-8900; Fax 585-473-6266; Elec Mail maginfo@mag.rochester.edu; Internet Home Page Address: mag.rochester.edu; *Others TDD* 716-473-6152; *Dir* Grant Holcomb; *Dir Develop* Joseph T Carney; *Dir Admin* Kim Hallatt; *Dir Educ* Susan Dodge-Peters Daiss; *Pub Rels Mgr* Patti Giordano; *Mem Mgr* Lourdes Douglas; *Cur* Marjorie B Searl; *Cur Exhib* Marie Via
Open Wed-Sun 11AM- 5PM and Thurs until 9PM; cl Mon & Tues; Admis adults $10, seniors & students $6, children 6-18 $4, 5 & under, mems & University of Rochester students free; $6 admis fee Thurs 5 - 9 PM; Estab 1913 as a university art mus & pub art mus for the Rochester area; The original building is in an Italian Renaissance style; Average Annual Attendance: 325,000; Mem: 10,000; dues $50 & up
Income: Financed by endowment, mem, grants, earned income & University support
Special Subjects: Afro-American Art, American Indian Art, Decorative Arts, Drawings, Folk Art, Landscapes, Marine Painting, Ceramics, Antiquities-Assyrian, Furniture, Porcelain, Portraits, Pottery, Prints, Painting-French, Sculpture, Hispanic Art, Watercolors, African Art, Crafts, Primitive art, Oriental Art, Renaissance Art, Medieval Art, Antiquities-Egyptian
Collections: Covers all major periods & cultural areas from Assyria & predynastic Egypt to the present, paintings, sculpture, prints, drawings, decorative arts; special strengths are medieval, 17th century Dutch painting, English Portraiture, 19th & early 20th century French painting, American art & American folk art
Publications: Mem magazine, Articulate; calendar
Activities: Studio art classes for adults & children; docent training; lects open to public; gallery talks; tours; concerts; exten dept serving Rochester area & surrounding nine counties; lending collection contains slides; book traveling exhibs 4-6 per yr; originate traveling exhibs 10-12 per yr; gallery store sells original art, fine crafts, prints, books & paper products, reproductions, prints

L **Charlotte W Allen Library-Memorial Art Gallery,** 500 University Ave, Rochester, NY 14607-1414. Tel 585-276-8999; Fax 585-473-6266; Elec Mail lharper@mag.rochester.edu; Internet Home Page Address: mag.rochester.edu/library; *Librn* Lucy Bjorklund Harper; *Libr Asst* Kathleen Nicastro
Open Wed - Fri 1 - 5 PM; No admis fee; Estab 1913 as a research library; Circ 3,900
Income: Financed by endowment, mem & grants
Library Holdings: Auction Catalogs; Book Volumes 45,860; CD-ROMs; Clipping Files; Compact Disks; DVDs; Exhibition Catalogs; Manuscripts; Memorabilia; Pamphlets; Periodical Subscriptions 60; Photographs; Reels; Reproductions; Slides; Video Tapes
Special Subjects: Art History, Folk Art, Decorative Arts, Drawings, Etchings & Engravings, Graphic Arts, Painting-American, Painting-British, Painting-European, History of Art & Archaeology, Art Education, Landscapes, Laces, Architecture
Collections: Memorial Art Gallery Archives
Activities: Teacher resource ctr

L **Art/Music Library,** 755 Library Rd, PO Box 270055 Rochester, NY 14627-0055. Tel 585-275-4476; Fax 585-273-1032; Elec Mail artlib@lib.rochester.edu; *Visual Resources Cur* Kim Kopatz; *Librn* Stephanie J Frontz; *Library Asst* Marc Bollmann; *Library Asst* Katie Kinsky
Open Mon - Thurs 9 AM - midnight, Fri 9 AM - 10 PM, Sat noon - 5 PM, Sun noon - midnight; Estab to support acad progs of Dept of Art & Art History, Music Dept & other acad depts within the University; Small gallery is maintained by Art & Art History Dept & Library
Library Holdings: Auction Catalogs; Audio Tapes 100; Book Volumes 90,000; Compact Disks 3,000; Exhibition Catalogs; Lantern Slides; Periodical Subscriptions 425; Records 850; Slides 125,000

ROME

A **ROME ART & COMMUNITY CENTER,** 308 W Bloomfield St, Rome, NY 13440-4197. Tel 315-336-1040; Fax 315-336-1090; Elec Mail executivedirector@romeart.org; Internet Home Page Address: www.romeart.org; *Dir* Lauren Marie Getek; *Office Mgr* Dale A Kaier
Open Tues-Thurs 10AM-6PM, Fri & Sat 10AM-2PM; No admis fee; Estab 1967 for art exhibits & classes, community events, educ; Four galleries; Average Annual Attendance: 20,000; Mem: 1000; dues from $5-40
Income: Financed by city appropriation, New York State Council on the Arts, mem, donations & private foundations
Exhibitions: Various art exhibitions every month
Publications: Newsletter, bimonthly; community calendar, quarterly; class brochures, quarterly
Activities: Classes for adults & children; dramatic progs; docent training; lect open to public, 20 vis lectrs per yr; readings; concerts; gallery talks; tours; weekly films; scholarships to gifted children; monetary awards art exhibs

M **ROME HISTORICAL SOCIETY,** Museum & Archives, 200 Church St, Rome, NY 13440-5872. Tel 315-336-5870; Fax 315-336-5912; Elec Mail robert@romehistorical.com; *Bd Pres* Virginia Batchelder; *First VPres* Richard Calidonna; *Exec Dir* Robert Avery; *Coll Mgr* Ann Swanson; *Library Asst* Michael Huchko; *Admin Asst* Mary Centro
Open Tues - Fri 10 AM - 5 PM & during special events, cl holidays; No admis fee; library & archives $15 per day for non-mem; Estab 1936 as a historical mus & soc; 2 galleries for temporary exhibitions on specific topics of local interest; Average Annual Attendance: 15,000; Mem: 695; dues $20-$100; annual meeting in Aug
Income: Financed by mem, city appropriation, private foundations, federal & state grants
Library Holdings: Book Volumes; Filmstrips; Manuscripts; Maps; Memorabilia; Original Art Works; Original Documents; Other Holdings; Pamphlets; Periodical Subscriptions; Prints; Slides; Video Tapes
Special Subjects: Archaeology, Costumes, Crafts, Decorative Arts, Furniture, Glass
Collections: E Buyck; P F Hugunine; Forest Moses; Ann Marriot; Will Moses; Revolutionary War period paintings; Rome Turney Radiator; Griffiss Air Force Base; Joan Evans Doll House Village
Exhibitions: Our Goodly Heritage - movie on Rome NY
Publications: RHS News quarterly; quarterly newsletter
Activities: Classes for children; lects open to pub; 24 vis lectrs per yr; concerts; gallery talks; tours; medal of 1777 yearly award; outreach program to schools, sr citizens' homes & community organizations; sales shop sells books

L **William E Scripture Memorial Library,** 200 Church St, Rome, NY 13440. Tel 315-336-5870; Fax 315-336-5912; Elec Mail robert@romehistorical.com; *Dir* Robert Avery; *Coll Mgr* Ann Swanson; *Library Asst* Michael Huchko
Open Mon - Fri 10 AM - 5 PM; Admis $15 per day for non-mem; Estab 1936 for historical research of Rome & the Mohawk Valley; Circ Non-circulating; Reference library; Average Annual Attendance: 1,000
Income: Financed by mem, city appropriation grants
Library Holdings: Book Volumes 3500; Clipping Files; Manuscripts; Pamphlets; Photographs; Prints; Reels
Special Subjects: Folk Art, Decorative Arts, Manuscripts, Maps, Historical Material, Crafts, Archaeology, Furniture, Architecture
Collections: Area paintings from the Revolutionary War period to the present; Frederick Hodges Journals; The Hathaway Papers; Local Militia Records 1830-1840; Griffiss Air Force Base articles & pictures; La Vita: Local newspaper printed in Rome New York 1918-1950
Exhibitions: History of Rome; History of Griffiss Air Force Base
Activities: Lects open to the public; tours; museum shop sells books

ROSENDALE

A **WOMEN'S STUDIO WORKSHOP, INC,** 722 Binnewater Ln, Rosendale, NY 12472; PO Box 489, Rosendale, NY 12472-0489. Tel 845-658-9133; Fax 845-658-9031, 658-9133; Elec Mail info@wsworkshop.org; Internet Home Page Address: www.wsworkshop.org; *Artistic Dir* Tana Kellner; *Exec Dir* Ann Kalmbach; *Develop Dir* Anita Wetzel; *Dir Mktg* Sarah Burt; *Studio Mgr* Chris Petrone; *Office Mgr* Sandra Brown; *Technician* Robert Woodruff; *Clay Prog Coordr* Ruth McKinney Burket
Open Tues - Fri 10 AM - 5 PM; Estab 1974; Mem: 400; dues $35
Income: $625,000 (financed by sales, tuition & grants)
Library Holdings: Book Volumes; Kodachrome Transparencies; Original Art Works; Original Documents; Photographs; Prints; Slides
Collections: Artists' books; Prints (contemporary)
Exhibitions: 12 exhibitions yearly of work by grant recipients; Traveling Exhibs: Hand, Voice, Vision: Artists' Books from Women's Studio Workshops
Publications: Artists' books, 5-7 per yr
Activities: Classes for adults & children; lect open to public, 45 vis lectrs per year; tours; grants offered; exten dept; original objects of art lent; book traveling exhibitions, annually; sales shop sells workshop products, books & handmade paper

ROSLYN

L **BRYANT LIBRARY,** 2 Paper Mill Rd, Roslyn, NY 11576-2193. Tel 516-621-2240; Fax 516-621-7211, 621-5905, 621-2542; Elec Mail rnlinfo@lilrc.org; Internet Home Page Address: www.nassaulibrary.org/bryant; *Coordr Progs & Pub Rels* Victor Caputo; *Dir* Cathleen Mealing
Open Mon, Tues, Thurs, Fri 9 AM - 9 PM, Wed 10 AM - 9 PM, Sat 9 AM - 5 PM, Sun (Oct - May) 1 - 5 PM; No admis fee; Estab 1878 as a public library; Circ 288,865; Gallery houses monthly exhibits, mostly paintings. Has been renamed the Heckscher Museum of Art at Bryant Library
Income: $3,200,000 (financed by property tax)

Library Holdings: Book Volumes 230,320; Cassettes 25,964; Clipping Files; Fiche; Filmstrips; Manuscripts 11,933; Pamphlets 1866; Periodical Subscriptions 299; Photographs 7697; Reels; Video Tapes 5493
Special Subjects: Historical Material, Architecture
Collections: William Cullen Bryant; Christopher Morley; local history of Roslyn, Long Island, New York
Publications: Bryant Library Calendar of Events, monthly; Bryant Library Newsletter, bi-monthly; The Bryant Library: 100 Years, 1878-1978, exhibit catalogue; W C Bryant in Roslyn, book; exhibit catalog
Activities: Lect open to public, 30-40 vis lectrs per year; concerts

ROSLYN HARBOR

M **NASSAU COUNTY MUSEUM OF ART,** One Museum Dr, Roslyn Harbor, NY 11576. Tel 516-484-9337; Fax 516-484-0710; Elec Mail kwillers@nassaumuseum.org; Internet Home Page Address: nassaumuseum.org; *Dir* Karl Emil Willers Ph.D.; *Registrar* Fernanda Bennett; *Dir Educ* Laura Lynch; *Office Mgr* Rita Mack; *Dir Develop* Monica Reischmann; *Asst Cur* Rhianna Ellis
Open Tues - Sun 11 AM - 4:45 PM; Admis adults $10, sr citizens $8, children $4; Estab 1989 to exhibit major exhibitions; Art mus housed in c 1900, three story Neo-Georgian brick mansion, former estate of Childs Frick, 9 galleries & 145 acres for sculpture park, formal gardens; hiking trails, pinetum; Average Annual Attendance: 250,000; Mem: 3000; dues $40-$5,000; annual meeting in Jan
Income: $900,000 (financed by mem, county appropriation, corporate & foundation grants, admis & special events)
Library Holdings: Exhibition Catalogs; Sculpture Outdoor
Special Subjects: Period Rooms, Drawings, Hispanic Art, Latin American Art, Painting-American, Prints, Sculpture, Watercolors, Collages, Painting-European, Painting-French, Renaissance Art, Painting-German, Painting-Russian
Collections: 20th century American prints; drawings; outdoor sculpture; architectural blueprints & drawings relating to the museum building & property; major Latin contemporary coll; Pop & Minimalist Prints
Exhibitions: 3 major exhibs per yr
Publications: Catalogs for exhibitions
Activities: Educ prog; classes for adults & children; docent training; lects open to pub; vis lectrs 8 per yr; gallery talks; tours; competition; originates traveling exhibs to the Gallery Assn of New York State; mus shop sells art books, related gifts of mus exhibs; jewelry

SAINT BONAVENTURE

M **SAINT BONAVENTURE UNIVERSITY,** Regina A Quick Center for the Arts, Rte 417 at Constitution Ave, Saint Bonaventure, NY 14778; Drawer BH, Saint Bonaventure, NY 14778. Tel 716-375-2494; Fax 716-375-2690; Elec Mail quick@sbu.edu; Internet Home Page Address: www.sbu.edu; *Exec Dir* Joseph A LoSchiavo; *Cur* Evelyn Penman; *Asst Dir* Ludwig Brunner
Open Mon - Fri 10 AM - 5 PM, Sat - Sun 12 PM - 4 PM; No admis fee; Estab 1995 to house the University's art coll; 18,000 sq ft of exhib space; Average Annual Attendance: 30,000
Income: Financed by university budget
Special Subjects: Decorative Arts, Drawings, Etchings & Engravings, Landscapes, Ceramics, Photography, Porcelain, Pottery, Pre-Columbian Art, Prints, Woodcuts, Painting-European, Painting-French, Painting-American, Sculpture, Watercolors, Religious Art, Jade, Painting-Dutch, Ivory, Painting-Flemish, Renaissance Art, Antiquities-Greek
Collections: Paintings; sculpture; drawings; prints; decorative arts
Publications: Art Catalog of Collection
Activities: Educ progs for K - 12 children; dramatic progs; lects open to pub; 10 vis lectrs per yr; concerts; gallery talks; tours; sponsoring of competitions & fellowships; artist residencies in schools; lending of original objects of 'art to other art organizations with appropriate facility report to 6 counties of Southern Tier NY: Allegany, Cattaraugus, Chautauqua & PA: McKean, Potter & Warren; artmobile; originates traveling exhibs to university & art mus; mus shop sells prints & local artisan items

SALAMANCA

M **SENECA-IROQUOIS NATIONAL MUSEUM,** 814 Broad St, Salamanca, NY 14779-1378. Tel 716-945-1760; Fax 716-945-1624; Elec Mail sue.grey@sni.org; Internet Home Page Address: www.senecamuseum.org; *Dir* Jaré Cardinal; *Mus Educator* Kari Kennedy; *Shop Mgr* Nadine Jimerson
Open Mon - Fri 9 AM - 5 PM (Nov-Apr), Mon - Sat 9 AM - 5 PM, Sun 12 - 5 PM (May - Oct); Admis adult $5, college students & seniors $3.50, children 7-13 & Military $3, Children 6 & under free, bus group discount rates available; Estab 1977 to present historical & contemporary Iroquois arts & culture & ancestral materials; Six exhibit areas, dedicated to various cultural periods up to contemporary & central seating space for video; Average Annual Attendance: 20,000
Income: Seneca Nation of Indians
Special Subjects: Drawings, Painting-American, Photography, Sculpture, Watercolors, American Indian Art, Archaeology, Ethnology, Costumes, Religious Art, Ceramics, Crafts, Pottery, Woodcarvings, Decorative Arts, Dolls, Furniture, Jewelry, Silver, Metalwork, Historical Material, Maps, Dioramas, Leather, Reproductions
Collections: Archeological, anthropological & archival colls, including photography, audio; traditional & contemporary works
Publications: SINM - Collection
Activities: Games demos; interactive children's area; tours; mus shop sells books, original art, prints, hand-made Iroquois art, calendars, videos, CDs, games

SANBORN

M **NIAGARA COUNTY COMMUNITY COLLEGE,** Art Gallery, 3111 Saunders Settlement Rd, Sanborn, NY 14132-9460. Tel 716-614-5775; Fax 716-614-6826; Internet Home Page Address: www.sunyniagara.cc.ny.us; *Dir Gallery* Kathleen Sherin
Open Mon - Tues 10 AM - 5 PM, Wed - Thurs 10 AM - 8 PM, Fri 10 AM - 2 PM; No admis fee; Estab 1973 for varied exhibits that will be of interest to

students & the community; Gallery has 270 sq ft of area & approx 250 running ft; Average Annual Attendance: 9,000
Income: Financed by the college
Exhibitions: African Treasures; Faculty Exhibit; Spring Student Exhibit; Student Art Exhibit; Student Illustration Exhibit/SUNY Buffalo; NCCC Student Exhibition; Runca-NCC Alumni Exhibition (paintings, mixed media)
Publications: Catalogs
Activities: Classes for adults; dramatic progs; lects; 2-3 vis lectrs per yr; gallery talks

SARATOGA SPRINGS

M **NATIONAL MUSEUM OF RACING,** National Museum of Racing & Hall of Fame, 191 Union Ave, Saratoga Springs, NY 12866-3556. Tel 518-584-0400; Fax 518-584-4574; Elec Mail nmrinfo@racingmuseum.net; Internet Home Page Address: www.racingmuseum.org; *Dir* Joe Aulisi; *Cur Hall of Fame* Kate Cravens; *Cur Coll* Beth Sheffera
Open Jan - Mar: Tues - Sat 10 AM - 4 PM, Sun noon - 4 PM, cl Mon & Tues; Apr - Oct: Mon - Sat 10 AM - 4 PM, Sun Noon - 4 PM; Nov - Dec: Tues - Sat 10 AM - 4 PM, Sun noon - 4 PM cl Mon; Admis adults $7, seniors & students $5, mems & children under 5 free, children under 12 must be accompanied by parents; Estab 1950 as a mus for the collection, preservation & exhibition of all kinds of articles assoc with the origin, history & development of horse racing; There are 10 galleries of sporting art. The handsome Georgian-Colonial design brick structure houses one of the world's greatest collections of equine art along with trophies, sculptures & memorabilia of the sport from its earliest days; Average Annual Attendance: 60,000; Mem: 1950; dues $35-2500
Income: Financed through annual appeal, individual contributions, grants, shop sales & endowment
Library Holdings: Book Volumes; Clipping Files; Manuscripts; Motion Pictures; Original Documents; Periodical Subscriptions; Photographs
Special Subjects: Prints, Bronzes
Collections: Oil paintings of thoroughbred horses, trophies, racing silks, bronzes, prints, racing memorabilia
Activities: Classes for children; gallery talks; tours; art & photography competitions; mus shop sells books, magazines, original art, reproductions, prints, clothing & toys

L **Reference Library,** 191 Union Ave, Saratoga Springs, NY 12866. Tel 518-584-0400; Fax 518-584-4574; Elec Mail nmrinfo@racingmuseum.net; Internet Home Page Address: www.nationalmuseumofracing.org; *Acting Dir* Joseph E Aulisi; *Cur Coll* Beth Sheffer; *Asst Dir* Catherine Maguire
Library open by appointment; Estab 1970 as a reference library on Thoroughbred racing; Open to researchers, students & authors by appointment; Average Annual Attendance: 50; Mem: 2300; dues varies
Library Holdings: Book Volumes 3000; Clipping Files; Exhibition Catalogs; Manuscripts; Memorabilia; Original Art Works; Pamphlets; Photographs
Special Subjects: Painting-American, Painting-British

M **NEW YORK STATE MILITARY MUSEUM AND VETERANS RESEARCH CENTER,** 61 Lake Ave, Saratoga Springs, NY 12866-2315. Tel 518-581-5100; Fax 518-581-5111; Elec Mail historians@ny.ngb.army.mil; Internet Home Page Address: www.nysmm.org; *CEO & Dir* Michael Aikey; *Registrar* Christopher Morton; *Chief Cur* Courtney Burns; *Archivist* Jim Gandy; *Mus Shop Mgr* Lucille Millarson
Open Tues - Sat 10 - 4, Sun noon - 4; cl all NY state holidays; no admis fee; Estab 1863; 9000 sq ft exhib space; auditorium capacity 70; handicapped-accessible in mus only; FT Paid 10, PT Paid 1, PT Volunteers 50, Interns 3; NY Congressional Dist 20. New York State's military history coll that ranges from colonial times to the present; Average Annual Attendance: 13,000
Library Holdings: Book Volumes; Lantern Slides; Manuscripts; Maps; Memorabilia; Motion Pictures; Original Art Works; Original Documents; Photographs; Prints; Sculpture
Special Subjects: Drawings, Photography, Portraits, Painting-American, Prints, Silver, Textiles, Sculpture, Graphics, Watercolors, Costumes, Furniture, Leather, Military Art
Collections: Coll includes NY state's battle flag coll & the state's Veterans Oral History coll; 3000 vols of books on military history; Military art; military uniforms
Activities: Educ prog for adults & children; ann events: Civil War Weekends; lects open to pub; 5-10 vis lectrs per yr; guided tours; docent prog; mus shop sells books, original art, prints

M **SKIDMORE COLLEGE,** Schick Art Gallery, 815 N Broadway, Saratoga Springs, NY 12866-1632. Tel 518-580-5049; Fax 518-580-5029; Elec Mail mjablons@skidmore.edu; Internet Home Page Address: www.skidmore.edu/schick; *Asst Dir* Mary Kathryn Jablonski
Open Sept - May Mon - Fri 9 AM - 5 PM, Sat & Sun 1 - 4:30 PM; summer hours variable according to summer class schedules, cl Aug; No admis fee; Estab 1978 for educational enrichment of the col & community. Exhibs are intended to bring awareness of both contemporary & historical trends in art; Average Annual Attendance: 20,080
Income: Financed through College
Exhibitions: Rotating exhibits monthly
Publications: Exhibition catalogs, occasionally
Activities: Lect open to public, vis lectr; gallery talks; originates traveling exhibitions

L **Lucy Scribner Library,** 815 N Broadway, Art Reading Area Saratoga Springs, NY 12866-1632. Tel 518-580-5002; Internet Home Page Address: www.skidmore.edu/library; *Visual Resource Assoc* Theresa Somaio; *Supv* Nancy Rudick
Open Mon - Thurs 8 AM - 1 AM, Fri 8 AM - 10 PM, Sat 9 AM - 10 PM, Sun 11 AM - 1 AM; Estab 1925
Income: Financed by col
Library Holdings: Book Volumes 392,014; Cards; Exhibition Catalogs; Filmstrips; Kodachrome Transparencies; Lantern Slides; Memorabilia; Motion

Pictures; Original Art Works; Periodical Subscriptions 1653; Photographs; Prints 600; Records; Reproductions; Sculpture; Slides 53,000
Collections: Anita Pohndorff Yates Collection of Saratoga History

SCHENECTADY

A **SCHENECTADY COUNTY HISTORICAL SOCIETY,** Museum of Schenectady History, 32 Washington Ave, Schenectady, NY 12305-1600. Tel 518-374-0263; Fax 518-688-2825; Elec Mail librarian@schist.org; curator@schist.org; office@schist.org; Internet Home Page Address: www.schist.org; *Pres* Edwin D Reilly Sr; *VPres* Kim A Mabee; *Treas* Richard Clowe; *Site Mgr Mabee Farm* Patricia Barrot; *Librn* Virginia Bolen; *Office Mgr* Jennifer Hanson; *Secy Bd Trustees* Cynthia Seacord; *Cur* Kate Weller
Open Mon - Fri 9 AM - 5 PM, Sat 10 AM - 4 PM; Admis adults $4, seniors $3, children $2; Estab 1905, for the preservation of local historical materials; Three-story Victorian house has antique furniture & oil paintings from 18th century; Average Annual Attendance: 7,500; Mem: 850; dues sponsor $100, donor $50, family $40, individual $25; annual meeting 2nd Sat of Apr
Income: Financed by mem, grants, donations
Library Holdings: Book Volumes; CD-ROMs; Clipping Files
Special Subjects: Historical Material
Collections: Decorative arts; gun room; historical material; Indian artifacts; paintings; photographs; Schenectady artifacts from 18th century
Publications: Bi-monthly newsletter
Activities: Lects open to public, 20 vis lectrs per year; concerts; tours; exten dept serves elementary schools; sales shop sells books & gifts

L **Library,** 32 Washington Ave, Schenectady, NY 12305. Tel 518-374-0263; Elec Mail librarian@schist.org; Internet Home Page Address: www.schenectadyhistory.net; *Librn/Archivist* Melissa Tacks; *Cur* Ryan Mahoney
Open Mon - Fri 9 AM - 5 PM, Sat 10 AM - 2 PM; Admis research $5, mus tour $5, mems free; Estab 1905 to promote history & genealogy of the county & nearby counties; Circ Non-circulating; For reference only; Mem: 700; dues $25 & up; annual meeting in Apr
Income: Financed by mem, grants, donations
Library Holdings: Audio Tapes; Book Volumes 4000; Cassettes; Clipping Files; Fiche; Filmstrips; Manuscripts 16,000; Memorabilia; Motion Pictures; Pamphlets; Photographs; Reels; Reproductions; Slides
Activities: Educ dept; some lect open to public & some to members only; tours; sales shop sells books, reproductions & gifts

SEA CLIFF

M **SEA CLIFF VILLAGE MUSEUM,** 95 Tenth Ave, Sea Cliff, NY 11579; PO Box 72, Sea Cliff, NY 11579-0072. Tel 516-671-0090; Fax 516-671-2530; Elec Mail seacliffmuseum@aol.com; *Dir, Treas & Cur* Sara Reres; *Vol Chmn* Patricia F Smith; *Mus Shop Mgr* Kathleen Diresta
Open Sun 2 - 5 PM; cl Jun - Aug; No admis fee, donations accepted; Estab 1979; Housed in former Sea Cliff Methodist Church built in 1913, the mus is made of brick & stucco and is of Tudor style; mus focuses on Sea Cliff history from 1870 - mid 20th c; Average Annual Attendance: 1,000; Mem: dues Family $25, Indiv $10, Senior $10
Income: municipal govt
Library Holdings: Audio Tapes; Book Volumes; Motion Pictures; Original Art Works; Original Documents; Photographs; Prints; Reels; Slides
Special Subjects: Historical Material, Maps, Costumes, Dolls
Collections: Over 3,000 photos, artifacts, documents & costumes that span this time period
Publications: Friends, annual newsletter
Activities: Friends Exhib Opening Reception; two lects per yr; shop sells books, original art, reproductions, prints, posters & postcards

SENECA FALLS

M **SENECA FALLS HISTORICAL SOCIETY MUSEUM,** 55 Cayuga St, Seneca Falls, NY 13148-1222. Tel 315-568-8412; Fax 315-568-8426; Elec Mail sfhs@rochester.rr.com; Internet Home Page Address: www.sfhistoricalsociety.org; *Exec Dir* Philomena M Cammuso; *Educ Dir* Frances J Barbieri; *Colls Mgr* Kathleen Jans-Duffy
Open Mon - Fri 9 AM - 4 PM; Admis adults $5, children & students $2, AARP & AAA $4; Estab 1896 as an educational institution dedicated to the preservation & interpretation of Seneca County; Victorian 23 room house with decorative arts collection; Average Annual Attendance: 15,000; Mem: 600; dues family $50, single $30; annual meeting in May
Income: $100,000 (financed by endowment, mem, city, state & federal appropriation, United Way)
Library Holdings: Book Volumes; Original Documents
Special Subjects: Furniture, Photography, Manuscripts, Maps, Architecture, Costumes, Historical Material, Period Rooms
Collections: Victoriana; Women's Rights Memorabilia; history of industry, canal, geneology research
Exhibitions: Civil War
Publications: Reprints of archival material
Activities: Classes for adults & children; docent training; school group progs; lects open to pub, 3-4 vis lectrs per yr; concerts; gallery talks; tours; original objects of art lent to other institutions; mus shop sells books, prints, reproductions & articles published by members

SETAUKET

M **GALLERY NORTH,** 90 N Country Rd, Setauket, NY 11733-1352. Tel 631-751-2676; Fax 631-751-0180; Elec Mail gallerynorth@aol.com; Internet Home Page Address: www.gallerynorth.org; *Pres & Chmn* Paul Lamb; *Asst* Carolyn Fell; *Dir & Cur* Colleen W Hanson
Open Tues - Sat 10 AM - 5 PM, Sun 12 - 5 PM, cl Easter, Thanksgiving, Christmas; No admis fee; Estab 1965 to exhibit the work of contemporary Long

Island artists & crafts people; Gallery is housed in Victorian building with 3 main exhibition rooms; Average Annual Attendance: 10,000; Mem: 185; dues $50 - $1,000; quarterly meetings
Income: $210,000 (financed by mem, sales & fundraisers)
Library Holdings: Book Volumes; Memorabilia; Periodical Subscriptions
Collections: Long Island Landscapes
Exhibitions: Eight changing exhibitions per yr; annual outdoor art show open to artists & crafts people
Activities: Lect open to public; tours; artist workshops; competitions with awards; 6 vis lectrs per yr; gallery talks; art scholarship - graduating HS Senior; sales shop sells crafts from local artists & imported crafts, original art & reproductions

SKANEATELES

M **JOHN D BARROW ART GALLERY,** 49 E Genesee St, Skaneateles, NY 13152-1341. Tel 315-685-5135; Elec Mail jdbag1900@aol.com; Internet Home Page Address: www.barrowgallery.org; *Dir* Margaret M Whitehouse; *Treas* Elizabeth K Dreyfuss; *Sec* Elizabeth M Sio
Open Memorial Day-Labor Day Mon-Sat 1-4PM, Sept-May Thurs & Fri 10 AM - 3 PM, tours by appt; No admis fee; Estab in 1900 to exhibit paintings of John D Barrow; Single artist mus, second generation Hudson River Sch; Average Annual Attendance: 4,000; Mem: AAM
Income: Financed by donations
Special Subjects: Painting-American
Collections: Paintings of John D Barrow 1824 - 1906
Activities: Classes & hands-on activities for children; docent training; pvt & school children tours; lects open to public, 3 vis lectrs per yr; gallery talks; tours; competitions; John D Barros Scholastic Art Award for young artists; schols; lending of original objects of art to individuals, area bus, Skaneateles & surrounding communities; sales shop sells postcards, ornaments, reproductions, prints, notecards, tote bags

A **SKANEATELES LIBRARY ASSOCIATION,** 49 E Genesee St, Skaneateles, NY 13152-1396. Tel 315-685-5135; Internet Home Page Address: www.skaneateleslibrary.com; *Pres* Meg O'Connell
Open Mon, Wed, Fri 10 AM - 5 PM, Tues & Thurs 10 AM - 8:30 PM, Sat 10 AM - 4 PM and by request; Summer hours: Memorial Day - Labor Day Mon & Wed 9 AM - 5 PM, Tues & Thurs 9 AM - 8 PM, Fri - Sat 9 AM - 4 PM; Library estab 1890; Gallery estab 1900 to display paintings of John D Barrow; Annex of Library, 2 rooms, one with single & one with triple wainscoting of paintings; Mem: Ann meeting
Income: Financed by annual fundraising drive & endowments
Collections: 300 paintings by John D Barrow; 19th century landscapes & portraits
Exhibitions: Occasional special exhibitions
Activities: Annual guided tours for 4th graders; docent training; occasional open lect; tours; paintings lent for one year on the condition that borrower pays for restoration

SOUTH SALEM

A **TEXTILE CONSERVATION WORKSHOP INC,** 3 Main St, South Salem, NY 10590-1413. Tel 914-763-5805; Fax 914-763-5549; Elec Mail textile@bestweb.net; Internet Home Page Address: www.textileconservationworkshop.org; *Exec Dir* Patsy Orlofsky; *Sr Conservator* Karen Clark; *Sr Conservator* Mary Kaldany; *Conservator* Rebecca Johnson-Dibb; *Field Svcs Dir* Katherine Barker; *Conservator* Barbara Lehrecke
Open Mon - Fri 9:30 AM - 5 PM, visits by appt
Activities: Workshops; lects

SOUTHAMPTON

M **BLACK & WHITE GALLERY,** 55 Island Creek Rd, Southampton, NY 11968-2253. Tel 718-599-8775; Fax 718-599-8798; Elec Mail info@blackandwhiteartgallery.com; Internet Home Page Address: www.blackandwhiteartgallery.com; *Dir* Tatyana Okshteyn
Collections: works by contemporary artists; paintings; sculpture; drawings

STAATSBURG

M **NEW YORK STATE OFFICE OF PARKS, RECREATION & HISTORIC PRESERVATION,** Staatsburgh State Historic Site, 95 Mills Mansion Dr, Staatsburg, NY 12580; PO Box 308, Staatsburg, NY 12580-0308. Tel 845-889-8851; Fax 845-889-8843; Elec Mail pam.malcolm@parks.ny.gov; Internet Home Page Address: www.nysparks.com; *Historic Site Mgr* Pamela Malcolm
Open Apr - Oct 31, Thurs - Sun 11 AM - 5 PM, last tour 4 PM, special holiday hrs, Jan-Mar weekends only; Admis adults $8, seniors, students & groups $6, children under 12 free; Estab 1938 to interpret lifestyle of the very affluent segment of American society during the period 1890-1929; Original furnishings & art left by the Mills family after their gift of the mansion to the state of NY; Average Annual Attendance: 20,000; Mem: Friends of Mills Mansion
Special Subjects: Period Rooms
Collections: Original furnishings, paintings, prints, decorative art objects and tapestries from Mr and Mrs Mills
Activities: Classes for children; docent training; workshops; lects open to pub; concerts; gallery tours; house tours; landscape tours; loans of paintings or original art objects have to be approved by New York State Office of Parks and Recreation, Division of Historic Preservation; mus shop sells books, reproductions, jewelery, scarves, cards, etc

STATEN ISLAND

M **JACQUES MARCHAIS MUSEUM OF TIBETAN ART,** 338 Lighthouse Ave, Staten Island, NY 10306-1217. Tel 718-987-3500 (main office); Fax 718-351-0402; Elec Mail mventrudo@tibetanmuseum.org; Internet Home Page Address: www.tibetanmuseum.org; *Exec Dir* Meg Ventrudo; *Bookkeeper* Jayne Catalfo
Open Wed - Sun 1 - 5 PM; Admis adults $6, seniors & students $4; Estab 1945
The mission of the Jacques Marchais Museum of Tibetan Art is to foster interest,

research, & appreciation of the art and culture of Tibet & other Asian countries through collections, preserving & interpreting art objects & photographs & making them available to the public through exhibitions, programs & publications; The Jacques Marchais Museum of Tibetan Art displays its collection of Tibetan art in two Himalayan-style fieldstone buildings set in a terraced hillside in Staten Island; Average Annual Attendance: 7,000

Income: Financed by membership dues & contributions, city, state & federal appropriations, foundation & corporate grants

Purchases: Art, artifacts & photographs related to Tibet & other Asian countries

Library Holdings: Auction Catalogs; Audio Tapes; Book Volumes; Cassettes; Clipping Files; Compact Disks; DVDs; Exhibition Catalogs; Lantern Slides; Manuscripts; Maps; Memorabilia; Motion Pictures; Original Art Works

Special Subjects: Decorative Arts, Historical Material, Furniture, Photography, Silver, Maps, Sculpture, Bronzes, Anthropology, Ethnology, Textiles, Religious Art, Portraits, Oriental Art, Asian Art, Metalwork, Carpets & Rugs, Calligraphy, Miniatures, Period Rooms, Reproductions

Collections: Tibetan, Mongolian, Nepalese & Chinese art including sculpture, paintings, textiles, furniture, as well as the archive & library of Jacques Marchais

Publications: Treasures of Tibetan Art: The Collections of the Jacques Marchais Museum of Tibetan Art

Activities: The mus features a diverse range of programming - rotating exhibs, musical concerts, lectures, films, children's workshops, yoga, tai chi, & meditation courses; classes for adults; 10-15 lects per yr open to pub; concerts, gallery talks, tours; exten servs New York City; individual paintings & original objects of art lent to mus for special exhibs; originate traveling exhibs - 1-2 annually; mus shop sells books, crafts, jewelry, CDs & music tapes, posters, prints, textiles, gift ware & unique items from Tibet & Nepal

M **THE NOBLE MARITIME COLLECTION,** 1000 Richmond Terrace, Staten Island, NY 10301. Tel 718-447-6490; Fax 718-447-6056; Elec Mail erinurban@noblemaritime.org; Internet Home Page Address: www.noblemaritime.org; *Dir* Erin Urban; *Asst Dir* Ciro Galeno Jr; *Prog Dir* DB Lampman
Open Thurs - Sun 1 - 5 PM; Donations accepted; Estab 1986 to present art & maritime history; Permanent installation of John A Noble's Houseboat Studio; art; gallery for changing exhibitions of prints & maritime history; exhibs about sailors' snug harbor; Average Annual Attendance: 15,000; Mem: 500; dues $25; annual meeting in Apr
Income: $300,000 (financed by mem, state & city appropriation)
Library Holdings: Auction Catalogs; Exhibition Catalogs; Kodachrome Transparencies; Manuscripts; Maps; Motion Pictures; Original Art Works; Original Documents; Periodical Subscriptions; Photographs; Prints; Reproductions; Slides
Special Subjects: Decorative Arts, Etchings & Engravings, Folk Art, Landscapes, Glass, Painting-American, Manuscripts, Maps, Drawings, Graphics, Prints, Watercolors, Manuscripts, Furniture, Marine Painting, Historical Material, Restorations
Collections: Archives; Art; Maritime Artifacts; Coll of the trustees of sailer's Snug Harbor
Exhibitions: Lifespan of the Bayonne Bridge in Transition; Tugboats Night & Day
Publications: Hold Fast, quarterly newsletter
Activities: Classes for adults & children; dramatic progs; lects open to public, vis lectrs 2 per yr; concerts; tours; schols; lending collection contains 80 paintings & art objects; mus sales shop sells books, original art, reproductions, prints, crafts, & toys

M **ORDER SONS OF ITALY IN AMERICA,** Garibaldi & Meucci Museum, 420 Tompkins Ave, Staten Island, NY 10305-1704. Tel 718-442-1608; Fax 718-442-8635; Elec Mail info@garibaldimeuccimuseum.org; Internet Home Page Address: www.garibaldimeuccimuseum.org; *Dir* Michela Traetto; *Publicity Coordr* Bonnie McCourt; *Admin Asst* Stephanie Lundegard; *Educ Dir* Janet Grillo
Open Tues - Sun 1 - 5 PM; Admis $5, children 10 & under free; Estab 1919 to collect, preserve & interpret material pertaining to Italian culture; Circ 12,000; Average Annual Attendance: 70,000; Mem: 400; dues household $50; individual $40; seniors/students $25
Income: $140,000 (financed by endowment, mem, city & state appropriation, Order Sons of Italy in America)
Special Subjects: Prints, Bronzes, Decorative Arts, Coins & Medals, Painting-Italian
Collections: Books; Bronzes; Coins; Decorative Arts; Medals; Paintings; Paper; Photographs; Prints; Stamps; Weapons; Giuseppe Garibaldi's "Red Shirt"
Exhibitions: Historical exhibitions; Antonio Meucci "The True Inventor of the Telephone"
Activities: Italian language classes for adults & children; school programs for children; lect open to pub, many progs per yr; 12 vis lectrs per yr; concerts; gallery talks; tours; schols offered; mus shop sells books & souvenirs

M **SNUG HARBOR CULTURAL CENTER,** Newhouse Center for Contemporary Art, 1000 Richmond Terrace, Staten Island, NY 10301-1114. Tel 718-448-2500; Fax 718-815-0198; Elec Mail fverpoorten@snug-harbor.org; Elec Mail info@snugharbor.org; Internet Home Page Address: www.snug-harbor.org; *Acting Pres & CEO* JoAnn Mardikos; *Chief Financial Officer* Gerard Kelly; *Dir Performing Arts & Pub Progs* Larry Anderson
Open mid-Mar - Nov 6 Tues - Fri 8 AM - 6 PM; Admis adults $5, seniors (65 & over), students (6-17 with valid IDs) $4, children (under 5) & mems no charge; Estab 1977 to provide a forum for regionally & nationally significant visual art; Average Annual Attendance: 50,000; Mem: Dues $35 - $150
Income: Financed by mem, city & state appropriation, corporate funds
Library Holdings: Exhibition Catalogs; Original Documents; Photographs; Prints; Records; Slides; Video Tapes
Publications: Exhibition catalogs
Activities: Classes for adults & children; children's progs; docent progs; lects open to pub; gallery talks; tours; mus shop sells books & reproductions

M **STATEN ISLAND MUSEUM,** 75 Stuyvesant Pl, Staten Island, NY 10301-1998. Tel 718-727-1135; Fax 718-273-5683; Elec Mail info@statenislandmuseum.org; Internet Home Page Address: www.statenislandmuseum.org; *Chmn Board* Henry A Salmon; *Cur History* Patricia Salmon; *Dir Science* Edward Johnson; *Dir Exhib & Programs* Diane Matyas; *Dir Mktg & External Affairs* Henry Behnke; *Communs Coordr* Rachel Somma; *Conservator of Art* Lenora Paglia; *COO* Cheryl Adolph; *Facilities Mgr* Frank Perkins; *Mgr Exhibs* Donna Pagano; *Arts in Educ Mgr* Jeanine Otis; *Visitor Svcs Mgr* Renee Bushelle; *Dir Fin* Dorothy Pinkston
Open Mon - Fri & Sun noon - 5 PM, Sat 10 AM - 5 PM; Admis adults $3, seniors & students $2; Estab 1881, inc 1906; Average Annual Attendance: 79,000; Mem: 500; dues $25 & up
Library Holdings: Book Volumes; Clipping Files; Kodachrome Transparencies; Manuscripts; Maps; Memorabilia; Original Documents; Photographs; Prints; Records; Reproductions
Special Subjects: Decorative Arts, Etchings & Engravings, Historical Material, Landscapes, Marine Painting, Ceramics, Glass, Flasks & Bottles, Furniture, Photography, Pre-Columbian Art, Painting-American, Textiles, Bronzes, Woodcuts, Manuscripts, Maps, Sculpture, Tapestries, Graphics, Painting-American, Prints, African Art, Ethnology, Costumes, Religious Art, Crafts, Pottery, Primitive art, Painting-European, Portraits, Posters, Jade, Jewelry, Porcelain, Oriental Art, Silver, Painting-Dutch, Ivory, Scrimshaw, Coins & Medals, Baroque Art, Miniatures, Renaissance Art, Embroidery, Laces, Medieval Art, Antiquities-Oriental, Antiquities-Greek, Antiquities-Roman, Reproductions
Collections: American paintings of the 19th & 20th centuries; Oriental, Greek, Roman & primitive art objects; prints & small sculptures; science & history publs; history, archives, postcards; Natural Science Coll, Entomology, Botany
Exhibitions: Decorative arts; design exhibitions in various media; major loan shows of paintings & prints; special exhibitions of graphic arts & of photography; permanent: Staten Island Ferry, The Lenape: The First Staten Islanders, Hall of Natural Science; changing art exhibits
Publications: Annual Reports; catalog; Proceedings (scholarly book), The Cemeteries of Staten Island; The Staten Island Ferry: A History
Activities: Fall & spring terms for adults & children classes; teacher training; lects on art & science open to pub; complete prog of lectr, art & natural history for school children with annual registration of 30,000; concerts; gallery talks; tours; competitions with awards; mus shop sells books, original art, reproductions, prints, ferry mugs & magnets

L **Archives Library,** 75 Stuyvesant PL, Staten Island, NY 10301. Tel 718-727-1135 (Ext 122); Fax 718-273-5683; Elec Mail info@statenislandmuseum.org; Internet Home Page Address: www.statenislandmuseum.org; *Archivist* Cara Dellatte; *Dir Exhibs & Programs* Diane Matyas; *CEO & Pres* Elizabeth Egbert; *Mgr Exhibs* Donna Pagano; *Chief Operating Officer* Cheryl Adolph
Open Mon - Fri & Sun 11 AM - 5 PM, Sat 10 AM - 5 PM, Tues, Thurs, Fri 10 AM - 4 PM by appointment only; History Center: Tues - Sat 1 - 4 PM; Admis adults $5, seniors $3, under 12 free; Estab Nov 1881 for research and reference only; History, Arts & Sciences exhibitions; Average Annual Attendance: 80,000; Mem: Dues family $50, indiv $35, others $25
Income: state, city, pvt foundations, pvt citizens & memberships
Library Holdings: Audio Tapes; Book Volumes 30,000; Clipping Files; Exhibition Catalogs; Lantern Slides; Manuscripts; Maps; Memorabilia; Micro Print; Original Art Works; Original Documents; Other Holdings; Pamphlets; Periodical Subscriptions 10; Photographs; Prints; Reproductions; Sculpture; Slides; Video Tapes
Special Subjects: Folk Art, Photography, Manuscripts, Maps, Painting-American, Prints, Portraits, Watercolors, Archaeology, Asian Art, Furniture, Glass, Landscapes, Flasks & Bottles, Architecture
Collections: 30,000 volumes on science, art and history; Staten Island newspapers on microfilm 1834-1934, various letters, documents, journals, clippings and other ephemera relating to the history of Staten Island and the metropolitan region; architecture, environmental and genealogy documents; George W Curtiss collection of books, manuscript & memorabilia, the Staten Island Ferry coll
Publications: The Realms of History: Cemeteries of Staten Island; The Staten Island Ferry: A History
Activities: Classes for adults & children; dramatic progs; summer earth camp; lects open to pub; concerts; gallery talks; tours; sponsoring of competitions; lending of original art objects; book 1-2 traveling exhibs per yr; mus shop sells books, prints & toys

A **WOMEN IN THE ARTS FOUNDATION, INC,** 100 Stuyvesant Pl. #T2, c/o Estelle Levy Staten Island, NY 10301; c/o M Schepis, 149 Marine Ave #6J Brooklyn, NY 11209. Tel 212-749-5492; Elec Mail wiafoundationorg@aol.com; Internet Home Page Address: www.anny.org/organizations; Internet Home Page Address: www.wiaf.org; *Newsletter Ed & Bd Mem* Erin Butler; *Financial Coordr* Diane Waller; *Coordr Bd Mem* Helaine Soller; *Coordr Bd Mem* Pamela Hawkins; *Coordr Bd Mem* Betsy Gross; *Coordr Bd Mem* Marcia Ostwind
Open 3rd Wed 7 - 9 PM for monthly progs & meetings; Admis fee free; Estab 1971 for the purpose of overcoming discrimination against women artists both in government & the private sector; Circ Newsletter circ 150 mem; Sponsors discussions, workshops, panels and exhibits the work of women artists, both established & unknown; Average Annual Attendance: 250; Mem: 75; mems pay dues & be involved in the arts; dues $65; meeting 3rd Wed Sept thru June
Income: $12,000 (financed by endowment & mem)
Library Holdings: CD-ROMs; Cards; Cassettes; Clipping Files; Exhibition Catalogs; Memorabilia; Original Documents; Pamphlets; Periodical Subscriptions; Photographs; Reproductions
Publications: WIA Newsletter, three times a yr (Women in the Arts)
Activities: Public educ as to the problems & discrimination faced by women artists; lects open to public; individual paintings & original objects of art lent to museum & university art galleries for special exhibitions; original art works for exhibitions are obtained from member artists; career edu & encouragement for women artists

STONE RIDGE

M STATE UNIVERSITY OF NEW YORK AT ULSTER, (Ulster County Community College) Muroff-Kotler Visual Arts Gallery, 491 Cottekill Rd, Stone Ridge, NY 12484. Tel 845-687-5113; Internet Home Page Address: www.sunyulster.edu; *Gallery Coordr* Susan Jeffers
Open Mon - Fri 11 AM - 3 PM, fall & spring semesters, cl summer; No admis fee; Estab 1963 as a center for creative activity; Gallery is maintained as an adjunct to the college's cultural & acad prog; John Vanderlyn Hall has 40 x 28 ft enclosed space & is located on the campus; Average Annual Attendance: 3,000
Income: Financed by college funds
Special Subjects: Drawings, Painting-American, Photography, Prints, Sculpture
Collections: Contemporary drawings, paintings, photographs, prints, sculpture, historical works
Exhibitions: 6 exhibitions per year annual student show
Publications: Flyers announcing each exhibit, every four to six weeks
Activities: Lect open to public, 2-3 vis lectrs per year; concerts

STONY BROOK

M THE LONG ISLAND MUSEUM OF AMERICAN ART, HISTORY & CARRIAGES, 1200 Rte 25A, Stony Brook, NY 11790. Tel 631-751-0066; Fax 631-751-0353; Elec Mail mail@longislandmuseum.org; Internet Home Page Address: www.longislandmuseum.org; *Exec Dir* Neil Watson; *Dir Develop* Deirdre Doherty; *Develop Assoc* Lorraine Whiffen; *Dir Pub Rels* Julie Diamond; *Dir Coll & Interpretation* Joshua Ruff; *Coll Mgr* Christa Zaros; *Designer & Preparator* Joe Esser; *Dir Educ* Lisa Unander
Open Thurs - Sat 10 AM - 5 PM, Sun Noon - 5 PM; Admis adults $9, seniors 62 & over $7, children 6-17 $4, students $3, under 6 & mems free; Estab 1942 to make Long Island history & American Art available to pub; The Museums' 22 buildings, 13.5 acre complex include a History Mus, Art Mus, Carriage Mus, various period buildings, a mus store & the Hawkins-Mount House (currently not open to the pub); Average Annual Attendance: 50,000; Mem: 1,000; dues $25-$5,000
Library Holdings: Auction Catalogs; Book Volumes; CD-ROMs; Clipping Files; Compact Disks; DVDs; Exhibition Catalogs; Kodachrome Transparencies; Manuscripts; Maps; Original Art Works; Original Documents; Pamphlets; Periodical Subscriptions; Photographs; Prints; Records; Sculpture; Slides; Video Tapes
Special Subjects: Etchings & Engravings, Landscapes, Marine Painting, Flasks & Bottles, Gold, Photography, Portraits, Pottery, Prints, Silver, Textiles, Manuscripts, Maps, Sculpture, Tapestries, Drawings, Graphics, Painting-American, Prints, Watercolors, Costumes, Ceramics, Crafts, Folk Art, Woodcarvings, Woodcuts, Decorative Arts, Collages, Posters, Dolls, Furniture, Glass, Jewelry, Porcelain, Metalwork, Carpets & Rugs, Historical Material, Juvenile Art, Coins & Medals, Miniatures, Embroidery, Laces, Leather
Collections: Paintings & drawings by William Sidney Mount & other American Artists including Shepard Alonzo Mount, Henry S Mount, William M Davis, Edward Lange, Charles H Miller
Publications: Annual Report; Quarterly Newsletter; exhibition catalogs; brochures
Activities: Classes for adults & children; lects open to pub; 12 vis lectrs per yr; concerts; gallery talks; tours sponsoring competitions; 1-2 book traveling exhibs per yr; mus shop sells books, original art, reproductions, prints & gift items

L Library, 1200 Rte 25A, Stony Brook, NY 11790. Tel 631-751-0066; Fax 631-751-0353; Elec Mail mail@longislandmuseum.org; Internet Home Page Address: www.longislandmuseum.org; *Exec Dir* Neil Watson; *Dir Colls & Interpretation* Joshua Ruff; *Colls Mgr* Christa Zaros; *Curatorial Asst* Matthew Schery; *Exhib Designer* Joseph Esser
Open Thurs - Sat 10 AM - 5 PM, Sun Noon - 5 PM; Admis adults $9, seniors 60 & up $7, students 6-17 & college with id $4, children free; Estab 1942; 3 galleries: art, history & carriage; Average Annual Attendance: 70,000
Library Holdings: Auction Catalogs; Book Volumes 2194; Cards; Clipping Files; Exhibition Catalogs; Framed Reproductions; Lantern Slides; Manuscripts; Memorabilia; Motion Pictures; Original Art Works; Other Holdings Trade catalogs; Pamphlets; Periodical Subscriptions 62; Photographs; Prints; Reproductions; Sculpture; Slides; Video Tapes
Special Subjects: Art History, Folk Art, Decorative Arts, Drawings, Graphic Arts, History of Art & Archaeology, American Western Art, Advertising Design, Fashion Arts, Art Education, Anthropology, Embroidery, Jewelry, Marine Painting, Flasks & Bottles
Collections: William Cooper, shipbuilder, 19th century, Sag Harbor; Israel Green Hawkins, Edward P Buffet, Hal B Fullerton; Daniel Williamson & John Williamson, Stony Brook, Etta Sherry; 19th through 21st century art, history & carriage artifacts; Artworks & papers of William Sidney Mount, Long Island; Carriage & horse drawn vehicles, clothing, furniture, decoys
Activities: Educ program; classes for adults & children; dramatic progs; docent training; lects open to pub, 20 vis lectrs per yr; concerts; gallery talks; tours; average four; originates traveling exhibs; mus shop sells books, reproductions, prints, slides, various jewelry & decorative items

M STATE UNIVERSITY OF NEW YORK AT STONY BROOK, University Art Gallery, Stony Brook University, Staller Center for the Arts Stony Brook, NY 11794-5425. Tel 631-632-7240; Internet Home Page Address: www.stallercenter.com/gallery; *Dir* Rhonda Cooper
Open Tues - Fri Noon - 4 PM, Sat 7 - 9 PM; No admis fee; Estab 1967 to serve both the campus and the community by exhibiting student and professional artists; One gallery 41 x 73 with 22 ft ceiling; second space 22 x 73 ft with 12 ft ceilings; Average Annual Attendance: 10,000 students & members of the community per yr
Income: Financed by donations
Publications: Catalogues, four times a year

SYRACUSE

M EVERSON MUSEUM OF ART, 401 Harrison St, Syracuse, NY 13202-3091. Tel 315-474-6064; Fax 315-474-6943; Elec Mail everson@everson.org; Internet Home Page Address: www.everson.org; *Exec Dir* Steve Kern; *Sr Cur* Debora Ryan; *Cur Educ & Pub Progs* Pam McLaughlin; *Pres Bd Trustees* Laurence Bousquet; *Catalogs* Joyce Bird; *Dir Pub Rels* Sarah Massett
Open Sun, Tues - Fri Noon - 5 PM, Sat 10 AM - 5 PM, cl Mon; Admis by suggested donation, general $5; Estab 1896 to present free exhibitions by lending artists, chiefly American to serve as an educational element for the cultural & general community; The Syracuse China Center of the Study of American Ceramics provides 4022 sq ft of open storage for the museum's collection of 2000 pieces of American ceramics, ranging from Native American pots, c AD 1000, to contemporary ceramic sculpture & vessel forms, also includes study collections of world ceramics, numbering 2000 objects; Average Annual Attendance: 72,000; Mem: 2000; dues Founders Cir $10,000, Dir Cir $5,000, Everson Cir Gold $2,500, Everson Cir $1,000, patron $500, fellow$100, household $75, sr household $60, individual $50, sr citizen, student, military, educator $40
Income: Financed by mem, county & state appropriation, New York Council on the Arts, gifts & grants
Library Holdings: Auction Catalogs; Book Volumes; Clipping Files; Exhibition Catalogs; Periodical Subscriptions
Special Subjects: Decorative Arts, Photography, Painting-American, Sculpture, African Art, Ceramics, Portraits, Porcelain, Oriental Art
Collections: African Coll; contemporary American ceramics; contemporary American painting & sculpture; 17th, 18th & 19th century English porcelain; traditional American painting & portraiture; video-tape coll; Cloud Wampler Collection of Oriental Art; photographs
Publications: Art books; Quarterly bulletin; Educational materials; exhibition catalogs
Activities: Docent training; classes for adults, teens & children; family progs; educ dept services public schools of Syracuse; lects open to pub; 4-6 vis lectrs per yr; gallery talks; films; tours; competitions; originate traveling exhibs to nat mus; mus shop sells books, magazines, original art

M LE MOYNE COLLEGE, Wilson Art Gallery, 1419 Salt Springs Rd. Syracuse, NY 13214-1301. Tel 315-445-4331; Internet Home Page Address: www.lemoyne.edu; *Library Dir* Robert C Johnston
Open Mon - Thurs 9 AM - 11 PM, Fri 9 AM - 9 PM, Sat & Sun 9 AM - 5 PM; No admis fee; Estab 1966; Average Annual Attendance: 1,500
Collections: Paintings, etchings, prints & watercolors
Exhibitions: Student, Faculty & outside exhibitions
Activities: Individual painting & original objects of art lent

A LIGHT WORK, Robert B Menschel Photography Gallery, 316 Waverly Ave, Syracuse, NY 13244-0001. Tel 315-443-1300, 443-2450; Fax 315-443-9516; Elec Mail info@lightwork.org; Internet Home Page Address: www.lightwork.org; *Prog Mgr* Mary Lee Hodgens; *Exec Dir* Jeffrey Hoone; *Customer Svcs Mgr* Vernon Burnett; *Digital Lab Mgr* John Mannion; *Dir* Hannah Frieser; *Promotions Coordr* Jessica Reed; *Technical Producer* Anneka Herre
Galleries open Sun - Fri 10 AM - 6 PM, darkrooms Sun & Mon 10AM-10PM, Tues-Fri 10AM-6PM, cl Sat; No admis fee to galleries, darkrooms carry semester lab fee; Estab 1973 to support artists working in the photographic arts; Circ 5,000; Maintains small reference library
Income: Financed by NEA, NYSCA, Institute of Museum & Library Services & private contributions
Library Holdings: Original Art Works
Special Subjects: Photography
Collections: Light Work Collection, photographic prints; Computer Imaging; Permanent collection of over 3,500 photographs
Exhibitions: Temporary exhibs held throughout the yr
Publications: Contact Sheet, 5 per year
Activities: Classes for adults & children; lects open to pub, 4 vis lectrs per yr; gallery talks; competitions with awards; tours; artist residence grants offered; schols & fels; book traveling exhibs occasionally; sales shop sells books & prints

M SYRACUSE UNIVERSITY, SUArt Galleries, Shaffer Art Bldg, Sims Hall Syracuse, NY 13244-1230. Tel 315-443-4097; Fax 315-443-9225; Elec Mail suart@syr.edu; Internet Home Page Address: suart.syr.edu/; *Dir* Domenic J Iacono; *Assoc Dir* David Prince; *Registrar* Laura Wellner; *Designer & Preparator* Andrew Saluti; *Budget Analyst* Joan Recuparo; *Coll & Exhib Coordr* Emily Dittman; *Secy & Office Coordr* Alex Hahn; *Cur Contemporary Art* Anja Chavez
Open Tues - Sun 11 AM - 4:30 PM; Thurs until 8PM; No admis fee; Average Annual Attendance: 20,000
Income: Financed through University with additional outside grants
Special Subjects: Decorative Arts, Drawings, Etchings & Engravings, Folk Art, Ceramics, Glass, Metalwork, Photography, Painting-American, Prints, Textiles, Bronzes, Woodcuts, Painting-French, Sculpture, Watercolors, African Art, Pre-Columbian Art, Religious Art, Coins & Medals, Laces, Cartoons
Collections: Encyclopedic from pre-history to contemporary strength in 20th century American art & prints
Exhibitions: Various exhibitions, call for details
Activities: Classes for adults & children; lects open to pub; gallery tours; private tours on request; originate traveling exhibs to small & medium mus & galleries
M Art Collection, Sims Hall, Syracuse, NY 13244-1230. Tel 315-443-4097; Fax 315-443-9225; Internet Home Page Address: sumweb.syr.edu/suart/; *Assoc Dir* Domenic J Iacono; *Cur* David Prince; *Preparator* William Kramer; *Registrar* Laura Wellner; *Dir* Alfred T Collette
Open Mon - Fri 9 AM - 5 PM; No admis fee; The Art Collection is housed in a temperature & humidity-controlled area of Sims Hall, adjacent to the Art Gallery. Used primarily for exhibition, storage & care of the 35,000 object collection, this facility also includes a teaching display area to accommodate classes & individuals involved in research; Average Annual Attendance: 15,000
Income: Financed by university funds & endowments
Purchases: WPA Federal Art Projects Prints, Contemporary American Prints, 20th Century American Art

Special Subjects: Drawings, Graphics, Painting-American, Bronzes, African Art, Ceramics, Etchings & Engravings, Landscapes, Decorative Arts, Glass, Oriental Art, Painting-French, Laces, Cartoons, Painting-German
Collections: West African tribal art; Korean, Japanese & American ceramics; Indian folk art; Pre-Columbian & contemporary Peruvian ceramics; Scandinavian designs in metal, wood, clay & textiles; 20th century American works with an emphasis on the Depression & War years (prints & paintings); 19th century European Salon paintings; history of printmaking (emphasis on American artists); decorative arts; Mary Petty-Alan Dunn Center for Social Cartooning
Exhibitions: Rembrandt: The Consummate Etcher (subject to change); Thematic Interpretation in Western Art, John R Fox Collection of Korean Ceramics, American Woodblock Prints 1900-1995
Activities: Originate traveling exhibs to small museums, university museums, galleries & libraries

L **Syracuse University Library,** 222 Waverly Ave, ES Bird Library Syracuse, NY 13210-2412. Tel 315-443-2440, 443-2093; Fax 315-443-9510; Elec Mail artdesk1@library.syr.edu; Internet Home Page Address: libwww.syr.edu; *Fine Arts Librn* Randall Bond; *Architecture Librn* Barbara A Opar; *Music Librn* Carole Vidali; *Slide Coll Supv* Susan Miller; *Dir Spec Colls* Sean Quimby; *Librn & Dean Libraries* Suzanne Thorn
Open Mon - Thurs 8 AM - 10 PM, Fri 8 AM - 6 PM, Sat 10 AM - 6 PM, Sun Noon - 10 PM; Estab 1870 for reference & research in the history of art
Library Holdings: Audio Tapes; Book Volumes 82,420; Cards; Cassettes 1500; DVDs; Exhibition Catalogs 15,000; Fiche; Filmstrips; Manuscripts; Micro Print; Motion Pictures; Other Holdings Compact discs 4000; Picture file 27,000; Periodical Subscriptions 335; Photographs; Records 20,000; Reels; Slides 370,000; Video Tapes
Collections: Manuscript Collections of many American artists

TARRYTOWN

M **THE NATIONAL TRUST FOR HISTORIC PRESERVATION,** (The Lyndhurst Museum) Lyndhurst, 635 S Broadway, Tarrytown, NY 10591-6401. Tel 914-631-4481; Fax 914-631-5634; Elec Mail info@lyndhurst.org; Internet Home Page Address: www.lyndhurst.org;
Open mid Apr - Dec Fri - Sun 10 AM- 5 PM; Admis adults $14, seniors & students $13, children 6-16 $10, group rates by arrangement, National Trust mems $7; National Trust Historic site & a National Historic Landmark. Lyndhurst is a Gothic revival mansion designed in 1838 for General William Paulding by Alexander Jackson Davis, one of America's most influential 19th century architects. Commissioned in 1865 by second owner George Merritt to enlarge the house, Davis continued the Gothic revival style in the additions. It was purchased in 1880 by Jay Gould & willed to his daughter, Helen. Later acquired by another daughter, Anna, Duchess of Talleyrand-Perigord, Lyndhurst was left to the National Trust in 1961; Period rooms with original furnishings owned by Lyndhurst families; Average Annual Attendance: 65,000; Mem: 1100; dues $50-$1000
Income: Financed by admis fees, mem, private contributions & special events
Special Subjects: Glass, Furniture
Collections: Collection of Gothic furniture designed by architect A J Davis in the 1830s & 1860s; Herter Brothers furniture; 19th century furnishings & paintings; Tiffany glass; Jay Gould's Collection of 19th century paintings by Daubigny, Bouguereau, Gerome & others
Publications: Lyndhurst (guide book)
Activities: Classes for adults & children; dramatic progs; lects open to pub; 8 vis lects per yr; concerts; tours; mus shop sells books & magazines

TICONDEROGA

M **FORT TICONDEROGA ASSOCIATION,** PO Box 390, Ticonderoga, NY 12883-0390. Tel 518-585-2821; Fax 518-585-2210; Elec Mail fort@fort-ticonderoga.org; Internet Home Page Address: www.fort-ticonderoga.org; *Pres* Peter S Paine Jr; *Cur* Christopher D Fox; *Cur Landscape* Heidi teRiele-Karkoski; *Exec Dir* Beth Hill
Open daily early May - late Oct 9:30 AM - 5 PM; Admis adults $17.50, seniors 62 & over $14, children 5-12 $8, children 4 & under no charge; Estab 1909 to preserve & present the Colonial & Revolutionary history of Fort Ticonderoga; The Mus is in the restored barracks of the Colonial fort; Average Annual Attendance: 100,000; Mem: 1000; dues $50 & up
Income: Financed by admis fees, mus shop sales & donations
Library Holdings: Auction Catalogs; Book Volumes 13,000; CD-ROMs; Exhibition Catalogs; Fiche; Manuscripts; Maps; Motion Pictures; Pamphlets; Periodical Subscriptions; Photographs; Prints; Slides; Video Tapes
Special Subjects: Decorative Arts, Etchings & Engravings, Painting-American, Photography, Prints, Archaeology, Costumes, Woodcuts, Landscapes, Manuscripts, Portraits, Historical Material, Maps, Military Art, Bookplates & Bindings
Collections: Artifacts; manuscripts; paintings; prints; rare books
Exhibitions: Held in mid-May - mid-Oct
Activities: Classes for adults & children; dramatic progs; lects open to pub, concerts; tours; original objects of art lent to qualified mus; mus shop sells books, magazines, reproductions & prints

TROY

A **THE ARTS CENTER OF THE CAPITAL REGION,** (Rensselaer County Council for the Arts) 265 River St, Troy, NY 12180-3215. Tel 518-273-0552; Fax 518-273-4591; Elec Mail lauren@artscenteronline.org; Internet Home Page Address: www.artscenteronline.org; *Pres* Christopher Marblo; *Dir Performing Arts & Outreach* Jill Rafferty-Weinisch; *Educ & Exhibs Mgr* Caroline Corrigan; *Dir Devel* Beth Schroeder; *Mktg & Develop Mgr* Lauren Hittinger
Open Mon - Thurs 11 AM - 7 PM, Fri - Sat 9 AM - 5 PM, Sun Noon - 4 PM; No admis fee; Estab 1961, a regional center for the advancement of the arts in daily life. Through education, presentation, outreach, service advocacy; The Arts Center promotes a richer community through broad participation in the making & personal experience of art
Activities: Classes for adults, teens & children; family Sundays; dramatic progs; dance; lectures open to pub; films; concerts; performances; grants; gallery talks; sponsoring of competitions; schols

M **RENSSELAER COUNTY HISTORICAL SOCIETY,** Hart-Cluett Mansion, 1827, 59 Second St, Troy, NY 12180. Tel 518-272-7232; Fax 518-273-1264; Elec Mail info@rchsonline.org; Internet Home Page Address: www.rchsonline.org; *Dir* Donna Hassler; *Cur* Stacy F Pomeroy Draper; *Registrar* Kathryn Sheehan; *Pres* David Brown; *VPres* John Roy; *Admin* Cynthia Silkworth; *Dir Develop* Alane Hohenberg; *Librn* James Corsaro; *Mus Shop Mgr* Sandie Reizen; *Pub Program Mgr* Ilene Frank
Open Feb - Dec Tues - Sat 10 AM - 4 PM, call for varying hours; Admis donation for adults $3; Estab 1927 to promote historical research & to collect & exhibit materials of all kinds related to the history of the Rensselaer County area including books, papers, fine & decorative arts. The Hart-Cluett Mansion is an historic house mus with 11 furnished rooms; Average Annual Attendance: 15,000; Mem: 600; dues individual $35, family $50; annual meeting 2nd Mon in Sep
Income: $327,000 (financed by endowment, mem, grants, foundations & other contributions)
Special Subjects: Portraits, Drawings, Graphics, Prints, Sculpture, Textiles, Costumes, Ceramics, Crafts, Folk Art, Pottery, Etchings & Engravings, Landscapes, Decorative Arts, Manuscripts, Dolls, Furniture, Glass, Jewelry, Silver, Carpets & Rugs, Historical Material, Ivory, Maps, Embroidery, Laces
Collections: Three centuries of fine & decorative arts, including ceramics; Elijah Galusha 19th century furniture; paintings by local artists including C G Beauregard, Joseph Hidley & Abel Buel Moore; quilts & coverlets
Publications: Annual report; quarterly newsletter
Activities: Classes for adults & children; docent training; lects open to pub, 3 vis lectrs per yr; concerts; gallery talks; tours; competitions; book traveling exhibs; originates traveling exhibs; mus shop sells books, prints, original art & reproductions

L **Museum & Library,** 57 Second St, Troy, NY 12180. Tel 518-272-7232; Fax 518-273-1264; Elec Mail info@rchsonline.org; Internet Home Page Address: www.rchsonline.org; *Cur* Stacy Pomeroy Draper; *Registrar* Kathryn Sheehan; *Dir Educ* Mari Shopsis
Open Tues - Sat Noon - 5 PM, cl Dec 24 - Jan 31 & major holidays; Admis adults $5, seniors $4, youth $4, children under 12 free, group rates available; Estab 1927; Circ Non-circulating; Two historic townhouse buildings; Hart-Cluett House(1827); Carr Building; Average Annual Attendance: 10,000; Mem: 550; individual dues $35 & up, family $50; annual meeting in Sep
Income: Financed by endowment, mem, grants & events
Library Holdings: Audio Tapes; Book Volumes 2000; Clipping Files; Filmstrips; Framed Reproductions; Lantern Slides; Manuscripts; Maps; Memorabilia; Motion Pictures; Original Documents; Pamphlets; Periodical Subscriptions 4; Photographs; Prints; Slides
Special Subjects: Folk Art, Decorative Arts, Photography, Etchings & Engravings, Manuscripts, Maps, Painting-American, Historical Material, Watercolors, Ceramics, Crafts, Porcelain, Furniture, Period Rooms, Costume Design & Constr, Glass, Embroidery, Pottery, Silver, Textiles, Landscapes, Architecture, Portraits
Collections: Library & museum collections relating to Rensselaer County history
Publications: Call for information
Activities: Classes for adults & children; docent training; lects open to public; gallery talks; tours; traveling exhibs; museum shop sells books, reproductions & prints

M **RENSSELAER NEWMAN FOUNDATION CHAPEL + CULTURAL CENTER,** The Gallery at the Chapel & Cultural Center, 2125 Burdett Ave, Troy, NY 12180; 10 Tom Phelan Pl, Troy, NY 12180. Tel 518-274-7793; Fax 518-274-5945; Elec Mail rnf@rpi.edu; Internet Home Page Address: www.rpi.edu/web/C+CC; *Pres* Sharon Valiquette; *VPres* Megan Fannon; *Treas* Father Ed Kacerguis; *Secy* Brett Hutton; *C+CC Dir* Tom Mattern
Open 8:30AM - 10PM; Estab 1968 to provide religion and culture for members of the Rensselaer Polytechnic Institute and Troy area, a broadly ecumenical service; Gallery maintained; Average Annual Attendance: 60,000
Income: $150,000 (financed by contributions)
Library Holdings: Audio Tapes; Book Volumes; Cassettes; Compact Disks; Filmstrips; Framed Reproductions; Original Art Works; Photographs; Sculpture; Slides; Video Tapes
Special Subjects: Sculpture, Religious Art, Medieval Art
Collections: Contemporary paintings, sculpture and needlework; liturgical vestments & artifacts; medieval sculpture
Exhibitions: New York State Council on the Arts; local one man shows
Publications: Sun & Balance, three times a year
Activities: Classes for adults & children; dramatic progs; lects open to pub, 10 vis lectrs per yr; concerts; gallery talks; Poetry Series; Peace Fair; Festival of Religion & the Arts; Sun and Balance medal

UTICA

M **MUNSON-WILLIAMS-PROCTOR ARTS INSTITUTE,** (Munson-Williams-Proctor Institute) Museum of Art, 310 Genesee St, Utica, NY 13502-4799. Tel 315-797-0000; Fax 315-797-5608; Elec Mail info@mwpai.org; Internet Home Page Address: www.mwpai.org/museum/; *Dir Emeritus* Paul D Schweizer PhD; *Dir & Chief Cur* Anna T D'Ambrosio; *Librn* Kathryn Corcoran; *Cur Modern & Contemporary Art* Mary E Murray; *Educ Dir* April Oswald; *Registrar & Exhib Mgr* Michael Somple
Open Tues - Sat 10 AM - 5 PM, Sun 1 - 5 PM, cl Mon & holidays; No admis fee, donations accepted (admis fees for some special exhibs); Estab 1919 to collect, preserve & exhibit art, artifacts & articles of importance; Circ 17,000; The institute became active in 1953 with the purpose of establishing & maintaining a gallery & collection of art to give instruction & to have an auxiliary library. It consists of a School of Art estab 1941; a Mus of Art opened in 1960; Fountain Elms, a house-mus was restored in 1960; a Meetinghouse opened in 1963 & a Performing Arts Division. Maintains reference library; Average Annual Attendance: 182,000; Mem: 3,823; dues individual $50, student $25

Income: Financed by endowment, tuition & private contributions, voluntary donations at entrances

Purchases: 19th - 21st century American, European paintings, sculpture, graphic & 19th century decorative arts

Library Holdings: Auction Catalogs; Audio Tapes; Book Volumes; CD-ROMs; Cassettes; Clipping Files; Compact Disks; DVDs; Exhibition Catalogs; Fiche; Other Holdings; Periodical Subscriptions; Slides; Video Tapes

Special Subjects: Decorative Arts, Drawings, Landscapes, Marine Painting, Furniture, Photography, Painting-American, Prints, Sculpture, Watercolors, Pottery, Portraits, Silver, Carpets & Rugs, Miniatures, Period Rooms

Collections: Arts of Central New York; 19th & 20th century European paintings & sculpture; 18th - 21st century American paintings, sculpture, 19th century decorative arts

Exhibitions: Rotating exhibits from permanent collection

Publications: Bulletin, monthly; exhibition catalogues

Activities: Classes for adults & children; docent training; workshops, dramatic progs; lects open to pub, lects for mems. only, 5 vis lectrs per yr; gallery talks; tours. N.Y. Upstate Organization award for Advancing Cultural Development, 2002; fellowships; individual paintings & original objects of art lent to members from the Art Lending Library; lending collection contains original prints, paintings, sculpture; book traveling exhibs 2-3 per yr; originate traveling exhibs to mus in other areas including international mus; mus shop sells books, magazines, original art, prints, handmade jewelry, catalogs, children's items, pottery, note cards, greeting cards & crafts, textiles

L **Art Reference Library,** 310 Genesee St, Utica, NY 13502-4799. Tel 315-797-0000, Ext 2123; Fax 315-797-5608; Elec Mail library@mwpai.org; *Dir Library Svcs* Kathryn L Corcoran; *Library Asst* Kathleen Salsbury
Open Mon - Fri 10 Am - 5 PM, Sat Noon - 4 PM, cl Sun; No admis fee; Estab 1940 to support School of Art, Mus of Art staff, Institute Mem & general pub; circulation only to members & staff of the Institute & Pratt MWP students; Circ 5,000

Library Holdings: Auction Catalogs; Book Volumes 29,000; CD-ROMs; Clipping Files; Compact Disks 2,980; DVDs 1,324; Exhibition Catalogs; Manuscripts; Pamphlets; Periodical Subscriptions 60; Slides 20,000; Video Tapes 754

Special Subjects: Art History, Collages, Constructions, Folk Art, Decorative Arts, Illustration, Mixed Media, Photography, Commercial Art, Drawings, Etchings & Engravings, Graphic Arts, Graphic Design, Painting-American, Painting-British, Painting-Dutch, Painting-Flemish, Painting-French, Painting-German, Painting-Italian, Painting-Japanese, Painting-Spanish, Posters, Prints, Sculpture, Painting-European, History of Art & Archaeology, Portraits, Watercolors, Ceramics, Conceptual Art, Crafts, Latin American Art, Printmaking, Art Education, Asian Art, Video, Porcelain, Furniture, Aesthetics, Afro-American Art, Bookplates & Bindings, Metalwork, Carpets & Rugs, Jewelry, Pottery, Silver, Silversmithing, Marine Painting, Landscapes, Pewter, Architecture, Woodcarvings

Collections: Fountain Elms Collection; autographs, rare books & manuscripts, book plates; artists' files; archives

Publications: Bibliographies related to museum exhibitions; bibliographic instructional materials

M **SCULPTURE SPACE, INC,** 12 Gates St, Utica, NY 13502-3414. Tel 315-724-8381; Fax 315-797-6639; Elec Mail info@sculpturespace.org; Internet Home Page Address: www.sculpturespace.org; *Exec Dir* Sydney Waller; *Office Mgr* Holly Flitcroft
Open by appointment only; Admis $10; Estab 1976 to provide professional artists with studio space; 5,500 sq ft open studio plus two private studios (800 sq ft); Average Annual Attendance: 1,000

Income: $200,000 (grants, special events, ann appeal)

Library Holdings: Compact Disks; DVDs; Exhibition Catalogs; Original Art Works; Original Documents; Photographs; Slides; Video Tapes

Special Subjects: Sculpture

Publications: Sculpture Space News, semi-annual

Activities: Lect open to public; gallery talks; Awards (20 funded residences); fellowships offered; organization also manages commissioned works, sells books, prints, original art & limited edition sculptures

VALLEY COTTAGE

L **VALLEY COTTAGE LIBRARY,** Gallery, 110 Rte 303, Valley Cottage, NY 10989. Tel 914-268-7700; *Library Dir* Amelia Kalin; *Dir Exhib* Joanne McNally
Open Mon - Thurs 10 AM - 9 PM, Fri & Sat 10 AM - 5 PM; Sep - June Sun noon - 4 PM ; Estab 1959; 27 x 7, artificial & natural light

Publications: Focus, quarterly

WATER MILL

M **PARRISH ART MUSEUM,** 279 Montauk Hwy, Water Mill, NY 11976-2639. Tel 631-283-2118; Fax 631-283-7006; Elec Mail info@parrishart.org; Internet Home Page Address: www.parrishart.org; *Dir* Terrie Sultan; *Asst Dir* Anke Jackson; *Lewis B & Dorothy Cullman Chief Cur Art & Educ* Alicia Longwell; *Registrar* Chris McNamara; *Dir Special Events* Nina Madison; *Dir Educ* Cara Conklin-Wingfield; *Cur, Robert Lehman* Klaus Ottmann
Open Mon, Thurs, Fri, Sat 11 AM - 5 PM, Sun 1 - 5 PM; open every day June - mid-Sep, cl Tues & Wed; Admis suggested donation $5, seniors & students $3, children under 18 & mems free; Estab 1898 to exhibit, care for & research permanent collections & loan works of art with emphasis on American 19th, 20th & 21st century art and the art of Eastern Long Island; Three main galleries are maintained; total dimensions 4288 sq ft, 355 running feet; Average Annual Attendance: 40,000; Mem: 1,800; dues $25-$1,000 & up

Income: Financed by contributions & grants

Library Holdings: Book Volumes; Clipping Files; Exhibition Catalogs; Original Documents; Periodical Subscriptions; Photographs; Prints; Slides

Special Subjects: Drawings, Photography, Sculpture, Painting-American, Etchings & Engravings, Oriental Art, Reproductions

Collections: William Merritt Chase Collection; Dunnigan Collection of 19th-century etchings; Samuel Parrish Collection of Italian Renaissance panel;

Fairfield Porter Collection; American paintings, 19th, 20th & 21st century; Japanese woodblock prints & stencils

Publications: Fairfield Porter: Raw - The Creative Process of an American Master by Klaus Ottmann; American Landscapes: Treasures from the Parrish Art Museum by Alicia Longwell; First Impressions: 19th C. American Master Prints by Alicia Longwell; Rackstraw Downes: Onsite Paintings, 1972-2008 by Klaus Ottmann; Underground Pop by David Pagel

Activities: Classes for adults & children; dramatic progs; docent training; lects open to pub, special lectrs; concerts; gallery talks; films; tours; individual paintings & original objects of art lent; originates traveling exhibs; mus shops sells books, original art, jewelry, note cards, prints, educational toys; gifts, posters & stationery

WATERFORD

A **NEW YORK STATE OFFICE OF PARKS, RECREATION AND HISTORIC PRESERVATION,** Bureau of Historic Sites, Peebles Island, PO Box 189 Waterford, NY 12188-0219. Tel 518-237-8643; Fax 518-235-4248; Internet Home Page Address: www.nysparks.com; *Dir* Mark Peckham; *Assoc Cur* Susan B Walker; *Coll Mgr* Ronna Dixson; *Asst Cur* Amanda Massie; *Interpretation Supv* Audrey Nieson; *Chief Conservator* Deborah Trupin
Open by appointment only; No admis fee; Estab 1974 as a resource center providing technical services to state historic sites & parks in the areas of research, interpretation, collections management, curatorial & conservation services, restoration of historic structures, exhibit design, fabrication & historic archeology; All exhibits are housed at the state historic sites

Income: A branch of state government

Special Subjects: Costumes, Drawings, Embroidery, Etchings & Engravings, Historical Material, Landscapes, Manuscripts, Porcelain, Reproductions, Sculpture, Textiles, Painting-American, Decorative Arts, Folk Art, Ceramics, Portraits, Archaeology, Dolls, Furniture, Glass, Period Rooms, Maps, Islamic Art, Tapestries, Painting-European, Carpets & Rugs, Restorations, Coins & Medals

Collections: Painting collections exist at several sites most notably Olana & Senate House. Artists include Church, Cole, Vanderlyn, Stuart, Pissaro.; furniture, decorative arts & textiles at most of the sites includ furniture designed by Frank Lloyd Wright at the Darwin Martin House

Activities: Internships offered

WATERTOWN

M **JEFFERSON COUNTY HISTORICAL SOCIETY,** 228 Washington St, Watertown, NY 13601. Tel 315-782-3491; Fax 315-782-2913; Elec Mail curator@jeffersoncountyhistory.org; Internet Home Page Address: www.jeffersoncountyhistory.org; *Cur Educ* Melissa Widrick; *Dir* Timothy J Abel; *Pres* Roxanne M Burns; *Progs & Chmn* Judith N George; *Exec Sec* Elaine Bock; *Cur Coll* Elise Chan
Open May-Dec Tues - Fri 10 AM - 5 PM, Sat 10 AM - 4 PM, Jan - Apr Tues - Fri 10 AM - 5 PM; Admis $2 donation; Estab 1886; Average Annual Attendance: 12,000; Mem: 924; annual meeting in May

Income: $142,000 (financed by endowment, mem, county appropriation, grants, private foundations & gifts)

Special Subjects: Textiles, Costumes, Furniture, Glass, Historical Material

Collections: Tyler Coverlet Collection; Costume Collection; Kinne Water Turbine Collection; 19th century Furniture; Prehistoric Indian Arts, Jefferson County

Exhibitions: Fort Drum: A Historical Perspective

Publications: Bulletin, 1-2 times per yr; Museum Musings; 6 times per yr; Abraham Tuthill (catalogue)

Activities: Classes for adults & children; in-school local history progs; docent training; lects open to pub, 2-6 vis lectrs per yr; tours; artmobile; lending collection includes; artifacts, 155 items; book traveling exhibs 1-2 per yr; originate traveling exhibs; mus shop sells books, toys & other souvenir items

L **Library,** 228 Washington St, Watertown, NY 13601. Tel 315-782-3491; Fax 315-782-2913; Internet Home Page Address: www.jeffersoncountyhistory.org; *Exec Dir* William G Wood; *Coll Mgr* Lenka Walldroff; *Office Mgr* Lisa C Earp; *Caretaker* David Coleman
Open Tues - Fri 10 AM - 5 PM, Sat 10 AM - 4 PM; Admis adult $6, military & seniors $5, students $4; Estab 1886; Mem: 650

Income: Endowment, county appropriation, grants, pvt foundations

Library Holdings: Book Volumes 2211; Clipping Files; Exhibition Catalogs; Framed Reproductions; Manuscripts; Memorabilia; Original Art Works; Pamphlets; Prints

Special Subjects: Art History, Decorative Arts, Historical Material, American Indian Art, Furniture, Glass, Architecture

Publications: Museum Musings Newsletter, quarterly; Bulletin, annually

Activities: Mus shop sells books, original art, reproductions, prints

M **ROSWELL P FLOWER MEMORIAL LIBRARY,** 229 Washington St, Watertown, NY 13601-3324. Tel 315-788-2352; Fax 315-788-2584; Elec Mail ueblertm@northnet.org; Elec Mail watlib@nnyln.net; Internet Home Page Address: www.flowermemoriallibrary.org; *Dir* Barbara Wheeler; *Reference Librn* Yvonne Reff; *Children's Librn* Ginger Tebo
Open Labor Day - Memorial Day Mon, Tues & Thurs 9 AM - 9 PM, Wed, Fri & Sat 9 AM - 5 PM, cl Sun; No admis fee; Estab 1904; The library contains murals, paintings & sculptures throughout the building

Income: $900,000 (financed by NY State and City of Watertown)

Library Holdings: Audio Tapes; Book Volumes; CD-ROMs; Cassettes; Clipping Files; Compact Disks; DVDs; Fiche; Filmstrips; Maps; Micro Print; Original Art Works; Other Holdings; Pamphlets; Periodical Subscriptions; Prints; Sculpture; Slides; Video Tapes

Collections: New York State material & genealogy; United States military history

Activities: Lects open to pub; tours

WELLSVILLE

M **THE MATHER HOMESTEAD MUSEUM, LIBRARY & MEMORIAL PARK,** 343 N Main St, Wellsville, NY 14895-1016. Tel 585-593-1636; *Dir & Owner* Barbara Williams
Open by appt; No admis fee; Estab 1981; Pvt nonprofit mus; home of Mather family & descendants. House & grounds share a look at lifestyles of different

decades and in different parts of the world. Emphasis on pleasures for those who are blind or poorly sighted; Average Annual Attendance: 500 - 999
Income: private
Library Holdings: Audio Tapes; Book Volumes; Cards; Cassettes; Exhibition Catalogs; Kodachrome Transparencies; Memorabilia; Original Art Works; Pamphlets; Periodical Subscriptions; Prints; Sculpture; Video Tapes
Collections: Barn holds coll of artifacts, music, books, games, catalogues & toys of the 1930s; visiting 1937 automobile returned to working condition; antiques; art; arts & crafts; children's mus; historic house/site; library; musical instruments; typography mus; wildlife refuge/bird sanctuary; info sharing about cultural lifestyles; works of area artists; aids for poorly-sighted; coll on British Arts Council's Festival (1951); coll of printed materials; samplers, tools
Publications: The Homestead Hoot, newsletter; An in-house publishing program: Sound Adventures, music and papers
Activities: Lects; concerts; guided tours; ann events: Easter Egg Hunt for ages 6 & under; Halloween Paint-Out; reading of Declaration of Independence

WEST NYACK

M   **ROCKLAND CENTER FOR THE ARTS,** 27 S Greenbush Rd, West Nyack, NY 10994-2700. Tel 845-358-0877; Fax 845-358-0971; Elec Mail info@rocklandartcenter.org; Internet Home Page Address: www.rocklandartcenter.org; *Exec Dir* Julianne Ramos, MFA; *School Dir* Daly Flanagan, MS; *Artistic Dir* Lynn Stein
Open Mon - Fri 9 AM - 5 PM, Sat - Sun 9 AM - 4 PM; No admis fee; Estab 1947 to present excellence in the arts, educ & servs; 40 ft x 70 ft gallery space, 2 acre sculpture park; 4 exhibit areas, Emerson Gallery, Gallery One, Project Media Space & Catherine Konner Sculpture Park; Average Annual Attendance: 25,000; Mem: 1500; dues family $45, singles $25; annual meeting in Oct
Income: $850,000 (financed by mem, state appropriations, corporations, foundations & earned income)
Exhibitions: Sculpture in the Park; 8 curated exhibs annually
Publications: Art school catalogues; exhibition catalogue, Sculpture Park catalogue
Activities: Classes for adults & children in visual, literary & performing arts; lects open to pub; performances in classical, jazz, folk music; exten prog for Rockland Cty NY schools

WEST POINT

M   **UNITED STATES MILITARY ACADEMY,** West Point Museum, Olmsted Hall at Pershing Center, West Point, NY 10996-5000; 2110 S Post Rd, West Point, NY 10996. Tel 845-938-3590; Fax 845-938-7478; Internet Home Page Address: www.usma.edu/museum/; *Dir* David M Reel; *Cur History* Michael Mcafee; *Cur Weapons* Leslie D Jensen; *Registrar* Marlana L Cook; *Mus Specialist* Paul Ackermann; *Security Chief* Gloria J Johnson; *Mus Technician* Brian Rayca; *Exhib Designer* Jose Cartagena
Open daily 10:30 AM - 4:15 PM; No admis fee; Estab 1854, supplementing the acad, cultural & military instruction of cadets; also disseminates the history of the US Army, the US Military Academy & the West Point area; Collections open to the pub; Average Annual Attendance: 130,000
Income: Federal Institution
Purchases: $5000
Library Holdings: Book Volumes; Manuscripts; Maps; Memorabilia; Original Art Works; Original Documents; Pamphlets; Periodical Subscriptions; Photographs; Records
Special Subjects: Portraits, Painting-American, Prints, Painting-European, Drawings, Graphics, Watercolors, American Indian Art, American Western Art, Bronzes, Folk Art, Etchings & Engravings, Posters, Coins & Medals, Dioramas, Cartoons, Military Art
Collections: Alexander M Craighead Collection of European & American Military Art; Jonas Lie Collection of Panama Canal Oils; Liedesdorf Collection of European Armor; Peter Rindisbacher Watercolors; Thomas Sully Portrait Collection; cadet drawings from 1820-1940; European & American war posters; extensive holdings from World War I & World War II, military & homefront subjects; military artifacts including weapons, flags, uniforms, medals, etc; military paintings & prints; paintings & prints of West Point; Hudson River School artists
Exhibitions: Cadet Drawings from the 19th Century to World War I; Jonas Lie & the Building of the Panama Canal; The Land of Counterpane: Toy Soldiers; Art of the Panama Canal; Come Join Us Brothers, African Americans in the US Army; Timeless Treasures: 200 Years of West Point Memories (A bicentennial exhibition); Tabletops and Tradition: The Officer's Mess and Cadet Mess at West Point; The West Point Museum: A Museum for the Army (1854-2004); Age of Exploration - Hudson's 400th Anniversary; The Mexican War; Remember Fort Sumter (1861-1865); Dark Blue is the National Color
Publications: The West Point Museum: A Guide to the Collections; Exhibition brochures; West Point Museum Treasure Hunt
Activities: 20th century re-enactment progs and military memorabilia displays from volunteer's collections; lects open to pub; 2 vix lects per yr; gallery talks; tours; individual paintings & original objects of art lent to accredited mus; mus shop sells books, original art, reproductions, prints & West Point memorabilia

WESTFIELD

L   **PATTERSON LIBRARY & ART GALLERY,** 40 S Portage St, Westfield, NY 14787-1496. Tel 716-326-2154; Fax 716-326-2554; Elec Mail pattersondirector@gmail.com; Internet Home Page Address: www.pattersonlibrary.info/index.html; *Dir* Eli Guinnee; *Arts Specialist* Nancy H Nixon
Open Mon - Tues & Thurs 9 AM - 8 PM, Wed & Fri - Sat 9 AM - 5 PM, cl Sun; No admis fee; Estab 1896 (Octagon Gallery estab 1971) to provide opportunity for educ & recreation through the use of literature, music, films, paintings & other art forms; Circ 72,000; Octagon Gallery is 1115 sq ft with 11 ft ceilings & 100 ft running space, maintains lending/reference library; Average Annual Attendance: 14,000

Income: Financed by endowment & private sources
Library Holdings: Audio Tapes; Book Volumes 34,000; Cassettes 125; Clipping Files; Compact Disks; DVDs; Filmstrips; Framed Reproductions; Manuscripts; Memorabilia; Motion Pictures; Original Art Works; Original Documents; Pamphlets; Periodical Subscriptions 120; Photographs 10,000; Records; Reels; Sculpture; Slides; Video Tapes
Collections: Glass plates of local history, mounted birds, Seashells, WWI posters, photographs, postcards
Exhibitions: Annual Westfield Revisited Exhibition; Patterson Library Biennial Juried Show for regional artists
Activities: Classes for adults & children; docent training; lects open to pub, 2 vis lectrs per yr; concerts; gallery talks; tours; competitions with awards; individual paintings & original objects of art lent to local institutions; book traveling exhibs infrequently; originates traveling exhibs

WOODSTOCK

A   **CENTER FOR PHOTOGRAPHY AT WOODSTOCK INC,** 59 Tinker St, Woodstock, NY 12498-1236. Tel 845-679-9957; Fax 845-679-6337; Elec Mail info@cpw.org; Internet Home Page Address: www.cpw.org; *Exec Dir* Ariel Shanberg; *Educ Coordr* Lindsay A Stern; *Opers Mgr* Lawrence R Lewis; *Prog Assoc* Akemi Hiatt; *Digital Lab Mgr* Phil Mansfield
Open gallery Wed - Sun noon - 5 PM, office Mon - Fri 10 AM - 6 PM; No admis fee; Estab 1977, a nonprofit organization, an art & educ center, an artist-centered space; 2 large galleries showcase contemporary photography, hosting workshops, lect & artist residencies; Average Annual Attendance: 50,000; Mem: Open mem
Income: Financed by pub funding, foundations, individuals
Library Holdings: Exhibition Catalogs
Collections: Permanent collection contains 1750 photographic prints & art work which incorporates photography; Maverick Festival Archive
Exhibitions: Ten shows per year
Publications: Photography magazine, quarterly (featuring best of contemporary photography)
Activities: Classes for adults, children, professionals & amateurs; workshops; lects open to pub, 30 vis lectrs per yr; gallery talks; tours; sponsoring of competitions; scholarships; fels; originates traveling exhibs; mus shop sells books, notecards, postcards

A   **WOODSTOCK ARTISTS ASSOCIATION & MUSEUM,** (Woodstock Artists Association) 28 Tinker St, Woodstock, NY 12498-1233. Tel 845-679-2940; Fax 845-679-2198; Elec Mail info@woodstockart.org; Internet Home Page Address: www.woodstockart.org; *Exec Dir & Cur Permanent Coll* Josephine Bloodgood; *Gallery Dir* Carl Van Brunt; *Preparator & Bldg Mgr* Ben Caswell; *Educ Cur* Beth Humphrey; *Archivist* Emily Jones; *Gallery Assoc* Patricia Seminara
Open Sun, Mon & Thurs noon - 5 PM, Fri & Sat noon - 6 PM, cl Tues & Wed; Suggested donation $5; Estab 1919 to exhibit the work of artists of the region; Upstairs Gallery, Members Group Exhibitions; Downstairs Gallery-Solo exhibitions; Phoebe & Belmont Towbin Wing; Exhibitions from the Permanent Collection; exhibiting members must live within 50 miles of Woodstock; Average Annual Attendance: 24,000; Mem: 400; dues (check website for current info)
Income: $90,000 (financed by endowment, mem, city appropriation, donations, earned income)
Special Subjects: Drawings, Historical Material, Landscapes, Photography, Prints, Sculpture, Watercolors, Painting-American, Pottery, Decorative Arts, Woodcuts, Portraits, Jewelry
Collections: Permanent Collection incl oils, prints & sculpture; graphic arts; intermedia; prints; Historic Woodstock Artists
Exhibitions: Rotating juried exhibits for members; solo shows for members
Publications: Woodstock Art Heritage: The Permanent Collection of the Woodstock Artists Assn (1987)
Activities: Classes for adults & children; Lects open to pub, concerts; gallery talks; tours; competitions with multiple monthly & year-end awards; lending collection contains books, color reproductions, original art works, original prints, paintings, sculpture, slides & videos; mus shop sells books, gift items, original art, prints & reproductions

YONKERS

M   **THE HUDSON RIVER MUSEUM,** 511 Warburton Ave, Yonkers, NY 10701-1899. Tel 914-963-4550; Fax 914-963-8558; Elec Mail visitorserv@hrm.org; Internet Home Page Address: www.hrm.org; *Dir* Michael Botwinick; *Dir Pub Rels* Linda Locke; *Dir Community Devel* Richard Halevy; *Chief Cur Collections* Laura Vookles; *Cur Exhibs* Bartholomew Bland; *Planetarium Coordr* Marc Taylor
Open Wed - Sun noon - 5 PM, cl Mon & Tues; Planetarium shows Sat & Sun 12:30 PM, 2 PM & 3:30 PM; Admis museum adults $5, seniors & children $3, mems free; planetarium admis adults $2 + mus admis, seniors & children $1 + mus admis, mems free; Estab 1924 as a general mus of art, history & science; Maintains Planetarium; Average Annual Attendance: 70,000; Mem: 800
Income: $700,000 (financed by mem, city & county appropriation, state arts council, federal grants & donations)
Special Subjects: Architecture, Painting-American, Photography, Sculpture, Decorative Arts
Collections: 19th & 20th century American art, decorative arts, furniture, toys, dolls, costumes, accoutrement, silver, china, paintings, sculpture, photography; Red Grooms: The Bookstore; Nybelwyck Hall
Publications: Tri-annual calendar of events; spec exhibs flyers; ann report
Activities: Classes for children; docent training; teacher resources; family workshops; progs for seniors; community progs & celebrations; holiday progs; lects & special events open to pub; concerts; gallery talks; tours; performances; art lent to other mus for exhib purposes; lending collection contains original art works, paintings, photographs, sculpture; originates traveling exhibs organized and circulated to mus, college galleries - regional & national; mus disciplines, art history & science

M **PHILIPSE MANOR HALL STATE HISTORIC SITE,** 29 Warburton Ave, Yonkers, NY 10701-2721. Tel 914-965-4027; Fax 914-965-6485; Internet Home Page Address: www.nystateparks.com; *Mus Educ* Lucille Sciacca; *Historic Site Mgr* Heather Iannucci; *Res Prog Coordr* Joanna Pessa; *Historic Site Asst* Charles Casimiro
Open Apr - Oct Tues - Fri noon - 5 PM, Sat - Sun 11 AM - 5 PM, Nov - Mar Sat - Sun noon - 4 PM, cl holidays; Admis $4, seniors & students $3, children under 12 $1, children under 5 free; Estab 1908 to preserve Georgian manor house owned by the Frederick Philipse family; to interpret Philipse Manor Hall's architecture, its significance as the home of an American Loyalist & its importance as an example of 17th & 18th century Anglo-Dutch patterns in landholding & development; The State Historic Site is part of the New York State Office of Parks & Recreation; the Hall houses contemporary style exhibits of history, art & architecture hung against a backdrop of fine 18th & 19th century architectural carvings; Average Annual Attendance: 29,000
Income: Financed by state appropriation
Library Holdings: Book Volumes; Clipping Files; Kodachrome Transparencies; Maps; Memorabilia; Photographs; Prints; Slides
Special Subjects: Portraits, Historical Material
Collections: Cochran Portrait of Famous Americans; Cochran Collection of Windsor Chairs
Exhibitions: Historic Trail; People's Choice: Presidential Portraits from Washington to FDR
Activities: Docent training; lect open to public, 4 vis lectrs per yr; concerts; tours; demonstrations; films

L **YONKERS PUBLIC LIBRARY,** Fine Arts Dept, 1500 Central Park Ave, Yonkers, NY 10710-6007. Tel 914-337-1500, Ext 311; *Librn* Joanne Roche; *Librn* John Connell
Open Mon - Thurs 10 AM - 9 PM, Fri & Sat 10 AM - 5 PM, Sun Noon - 5 PM, cl Sat & Sun during summer; Estab 1962 to serve the general pub with a special interest in the arts, especially the fine arts, performing arts & the decorative & applied arts; Circ printed material approx 22,000; recorded material approx 66,000
Income: $65,000 (financed by city appropriation & gifts)
Purchases: $65,000
Library Holdings: Audio Tapes 3100; Book Volumes 14,000; Cassettes 1000; Clipping Files; Fiche; Other Holdings Scores 3000; Pamphlets 7000; Periodical Subscriptions 82; Records 15,000; Reels; Video Tapes 200
L **Will Library,** 1500 Central Park Ave, Yonkers, NY 10710. Tel 914-337-1500; *Librn* John Connell; *Librn* Joanne Roche
Library Holdings: Book Volumes 126,000; Periodical Subscriptions 75
Exhibitions: Exhibits work by local artists & craftsmen

YORKTOWN

AMERICAN SOCIETY OF CONTEMPORARY ARTISTS (ASCA)
For further information, see National and Regional Organizations

NORTH CAROLINA

ASHEVILLE

M **ASHEVILLE ART MUSEUM,** 2 S Pack Sq, Asheville, NC 28801-3521; PO Box 1717, Asheville, NC 28802-1717. Tel 828-253-3227; Fax 828-257-4503; Elec Mail mailbox@ashevilleart.org; Internet Home Page Address: www.ashevilleart.org; *Cur* Frank Thomson; *Exec Dir* Pamela L Myers; *Capital Campaign Coordr* Rebecca Lynch-Maas; *Communications Mgr* Kathleen Glass; *Educ Progs Mgr* Sharon McRorie; *Events & Mus Shop Coordr* Laila Alamiri; *Vis Servs & Mus Shop Mgr* Cornelia Katchen; *Grant Mgr* Melisa Holman; *Mem Coordr & Financial Officer* Lindsay G Rosson; *Curatorial Asst* Lauren Bellard; *Curatorial Asst* Luiza deCamargo; *Mus Registrar & Preparator* Jake Ehrlund
Open year round Tues-Sat 10AM - 5 PM, Sun 1 - 5 PM.; Admis adults $8, students & seniors $7, special exhibition fees may apply, free to mems; Estab 1948 to provide art experiences to the Southeast & Western North Carolina area through exhibitions of American 20th & 21st century art; Eight galleries maintained, 4 with changing exhibits; maintains reference library; Average Annual Attendance: 100,000; Mem: 1200; dues family $70, single $50; annual meeting in Oct
Income: Financed by mem, earned income, grants & pvt contributions
Purchases: Romare Bearden, James Chapin, Joseph Fiore, William Wegman, Whitfield Lovell, Willie Cole, Karen Karnes
Library Holdings: Auction Catalogs; Audio Tapes; Book Volumes; CD-ROMs; Clipping Files; DVDs; Exhibition Catalogs; Kodachrome Transparencies; Periodical Subscriptions; Slides
Special Subjects: Etchings & Engravings, Architecture, Painting-American, Photography, Prints, Watercolors, American Indian Art, Ceramics, Crafts, Folk Art, Pottery, Afro-American Art, Portraits, Posters, Furniture, Glass, Metalwork
Collections: southeast regional; 20th & 21st Century American Art; Studio craft; Black Mountain College Collections
Exhibitions: Experiments in Animation - 6/4/2013 - ongoing; (07/27/2013-01/19/2014) Lasting Gifts; Selections from the Permanent Collection: 140 Years of American Art - 9/14/2013 - ongoing; (09/14/2013-01/12/2014) Esteban Vicente: The Art of Interruption; (09/28/2013-01/26/2014) Rebels With a Cause; (10/12/2013-03/16/2014) Experiments in Color: Selections from Josef Alber's Portfolios; (11/02/2013-03/09/2014) Cityscapes by Ben Aronson; (01/25/2014-03/09/2014) Western North Carolina Regional Scholastic Art Award Exhibition; (05/13/2014-09/28/2014) Farm to Table: American Silver
Publications: Quarterly membership; newsletter, catalogues
Activities: Classes for adults & children; docent training; art camp; lects open to pub, 6-10 vis lectrs per yr; concerts; gallery talks; tours; competitions with awards; WNC Regional Scholastic Art Awards; schols offered; individual paintings & original objects of art lent to other mus; books traveling exhibs 1-3 per yr;

originates traveling exhibs to other mus venues; mus shop sells books, magazines, original art, reproductions, prints, cards, art supplies, toys & other gift items

A **SOUTHERN HIGHLAND CRAFT GUILD,** Folk Art Center, 382 Blue Ridge Pkwy, Asheville, NC 28805; PO Box 9545, Asheville, NC 28815-0545. Tel 828-298-7928; Fax 828-298-7962; Elec Mail shcg@buncombe.main.nc.us; Internet Home Page Address: www.Southernhighlandguild.org; *Dir* Ruth Summers; *Archivist* Ginny Daley; *Librn* Deb Schillo; *Mem Adminr* Rebecca Orr
Open Mon - Sun 9 AM - 5 PM, cl Thanksgiving, Christmas & New Year's; No admis fee; Estab 1930 to encourage wider appreciation of mountain crafts; raise & maintain standards of design & craftsmanship & encourage individual expression; Main exhib gallery, a focus gallery & interpretive gallery; Average Annual Attendance: 300,000; Mem: 700; open to eligible craftsmen from Southern Appalachian Mountain Region upon approval of applicant's work by Standards Comt & Board of Trustees; dues group $40, single $20; annual meeting in Apr
Income: Financed by mem & merchandising
Library Holdings: Audio Tapes; Book Volumes; Clipping Files; Exhibition Catalogs; Kodachrome Transparencies; Manuscripts; Maps; Memorabilia; Motion Pictures; Original Documents; Pamphlets; Periodical Subscriptions; Photographs; Records; Reels; Slides; Video Tapes
Special Subjects: Embroidery, Textiles, Decorative Arts, American Indian Art, Ceramics, Crafts, Dolls, Enamels, Calligraphy
Collections: Object coll focused on regional contemporary crafts & historical folk arts; Library & Archives
Publications: Highland Highlights; monthly newsletter
Activities: Workshops for adults & children; lects open to pub & some for mems only; gallery talks; tours; competitions; lending collection contains 2500 objects/American crafts; originate traveling exhibs to museums & nonprofit galleries

M **YMI CULTURAL CENTER,** 39 S Market St, Asheville, NC 28801-3725; PO Box 7301, Asheville, NC 28802. Tel 848-252-4614; 257-4541; Fax 828-257-4539; Elec Mail ymicc1@aol.com; Internet Home Page Address: www.ymicc.org

BLOWING ROCK

M **BLOWING ROCK ART AND HISTORY MUSEUM,** 7738 US 321 Bus, Blowing Rock, NC 28605. Tel 828-295-9099; Fax 828-295-9029; Internet Home Page Address: www.blowingrockmuseum.org; *Exec Dir* Joann Mitchell
Open Tues-Wed & Fri-Sat 10AM-5PM, Thurs 10AM-7PM, Sun 1PM-5PM; Adults $8, children, students & active military $5; children 4 & under and mem no charge
Collections: local visual arts, history & heritage; paintings; period artifacts

BOONE

M **APPALACHIAN STATE UNIVERSITY,** (Turchin Center for the Visual Arts) Turchin Center for the Visual Arts, 423 W King St, Boone, NC 28608-2139; ASU Box 32139, Boone, NC 28608-2139. Tel 828-262-3017; Fax 828-262-7546; Elec Mail turchincenter@appstate.edu; Internet Home Page Address: www.tcva.org; *Dir & Chief Cur* Hank T Foreman; *Asst Cur* Brook Bower; *Visitor & Mem Serv* Cassie McDowell; *Dir Admin* Sandra Black
Open Tues-Thurs & Sat 10AM-6PM, Fri noon-8PM; No admis fee; Estab 2003; Contemporary art gallery & mus; Average Annual Attendance: 20,000; Mem: 150; dues variable levels
Income: Private & state funding
Collections: Works by regional, national, & international artists
Exhibitions: 20-26 exhibs per yr
Activities: Docent training; community art school; lects open to pub; 30 vis lectrs per yr; gallery talks; tours; sponsoring of competitions; 2 competitions (Nat) per yr; lending of original objects of art (Intra Campus Art Loan Prog); 1-2 book traveling exhibs per yr; traveling exhibs; 1 per year (varies); sales shop sells books & other small items

BREVARD

M **BREVARD COLLEGE,** Spiers Gallery, 1 Brevard College Dr, Brevard, NC 28712-4283. Tel 828-883-8292, ext 2245; Tel 828-884-8188; Fax 828-884-3790; Elec Mail bbyers@brevard.edu; Internet Home Page Address: http://www.brevard.edu/library; *Dir* Bill Byers; *Library Dir* Dr Michael M McCabe
Open Mon - Fri 8 AM - 3 PM; No admis fee; Estab 1969 as art dept with gallery; Center has three areas, 160 ft running space, & 1500 sq ft floor space
Income: Financed by departmental appropriation
Library Holdings: Book Volumes 4500; Exhibition Catalogs; Manuscripts; Original Art Works; Original Documents; Periodical Subscriptions 25; Records; Video Tapes 400
Special Subjects: Prints, Watercolors, Pottery
Collections: Contemporary art; 1940-1970 paintings & watercolors; print & pottery coll
Exhibitions: Student & visiting artist exhibitions
Activities: Classes for adults; dramatic progs; college classes & continuing education; lects open to pub, 4 vis lectrs per yr; 4 gallery talks; competitions with cash awards; schols offered; lending collection contains books, cassettes, color reproductions, film strips, photographs, slides
L **James A Jones Library,** One Brevard College Dr, Brevard, NC 28712-4283. Tel 828-884-8268; Elec Mail library@brevard.edu; Internet Home Page Address: www.brevard.edu/library; *Library Dir* Michael M McCabe; *Chmn Art* Anne Chapin
Open Mon - Fri 8:30 AM - 5 PM; Estab 1934; For reference & circulation for students & faculty
Income: Financed by parent institution
Library Holdings: Book Volumes 4,725; DVDs 85; Exhibition Catalogs; Periodical Subscriptions 20; Records

Special Subjects: Art History, Photography, Graphic Arts, Graphic Design, Painting-American, Painting-British, Sculpture, History of Art & Archaeology, Ceramics
Publications: New book list, bi-monthly

CARRBORO

M   **THE ARTSCENTER,** The Nicholson Gallery at the Arts Center, 300-G Main St, Carrboro, NC 27510. Tel 919-929-2787 ext 201; Fax 919-969-8574; Elec Mail info@artscenterlive.org; Internet Home Page Address: www.artscenterlive.org; *Exec Dir* Art Menius; *Gallery Coordr* Heather Germi
Ctr Gallery: Mon - Sat 10 AM - 9 PM; No admis fee except for special events; 1974; Atrium Gallery with new exhibit each month; Average Annual Attendance: 89,000; Mem: 640; $75/yr
Collections: Paintings; photographs; sculpture
Exhibitions: Exhibs change ea month
Activities: Classes for adults & children; dramatic progs; lects open to pub; 6 visiting lectrs per yr; concerts; schols; ArtsCenter honors award; extension prog serves rural Orange County; sales shop sells original art & prints

CARY

M   **PAGE-WALKER ARTS & HISTORY CENTER,** 119 Ambassador Loop, Cary, NC 27511; PO Box 8005, Cary, NC 27512-8005. Tel 919-460-4963; Fax 919-388-1141; Elec Mail kris.carmichael@townofcary.org; *Supv* Kris Carmichael
Open 10AM - 9PM Mon- Thurs, 10AM-5PM Fri, 10AM-1PM Sat; No admis fee; Estab 1992; Galleries housed in renovated historic hotel (c 1868); Average Annual Attendance: 30,000; Mem: 300
Special Subjects: Architecture, Latin American Art, Painting-American, Photography, Sculpture, American Indian Art, American Western Art, African Art, Textiles, Religious Art, Folk Art, Etchings & Engravings, Afro-American Art, Manuscripts, Furniture, Glass, Jewelry, Historical Material, Maps, Restorations
Exhibitions: Monthly changing exhibs
Activities: Classes for adults & children; dramatic progs; docent training; lects open to pub; 30 vis lectrs per yr; concerts; gallery talks; tours; sponsoring competitions; Books 1-2 traveling exhibs per yr; originate traveling exhibs

CHAPEL HILL

M   **UNIVERSITY OF NORTH CAROLINA AT CHAPEL HILL,** Ackland Art Museum, Campus Box 3400, Chapel Hill, NC 27599-3400; 101 S Columbia St, Chapel Hill, NC 27514. Tel 919-966-5736; Fax 919-966-1400; Elec Mail ackland@email.unc.edu; Internet Home Page Address: www.ackland.org; *Others* TTY 919-962-0837; *Dir* Emily Kass; *Chief Cur* Peter Nisbet; *Cur Colls* Timothy Riggs; *Dir Acad Progs* Carolyn Allmendinger; *Dir External Affairs* Amanda Hughes
Open Wed, Fri, & Sat 10 AM - 5 PM, Thurs 10 AM - 8 PM, Sun 1 - 5 PM, cl Mon, Tues & most major holidays; No admis fee; Estab 1958 as an art mus which serves the members of the university community as well as the pub; The mus houses a permanent collection & presents a program of changing exhibitions; Average Annual Attendance: 60,000; Mem: 1300; dues $500, $100, $50 & $30
Income: Financed by endowment, mem, donations & state appropriation
Special Subjects: Drawings, Etchings & Engravings, Folk Art, Landscapes, Ceramics, Glass, Painting-American, Bronzes, Manuscripts, Painting-British, Painting-European, Painting-French, African Art, Asian Art, Antiquities-Byzantine, Painting-Dutch, Baroque Art, Painting-Flemish, Antiquities-Oriental, Islamic Art, Antiquities-Greek
Publications: Newsletter, fall, winter, spring & summer
Activities: Classes for adults & children; free family days; docent training; lects open to pub; concerts; gallery talks; tours; musical performances; individual paintings & original objects of art lent to other mus; organize travelling exhibs vary; mus shop sells books, magazines, original art, reproductions, exhib catalogs, household goods, jewelry & accessories

L   **Joseph Curtis Sloane Art Library,** 102 Hanes Art Ctr CB# 3405, Univ of North Carolina at Chapel Hill Chapel Hill, NC 27599-3405. Tel 919-962-2397; Fax 919-962-0722; Elec Mail hockensm@email.unc.edu; Elec Mail hgendron@email.unc.edu; Internet Home Page Address: www.lib.unc.edu/art/index.html; *Art Librn* Heather Gendron; *Libr Technical Asst* Josh Hockensmith
Open Mon - Thurs 8 AM - 9 PM, Fri 8 AM - 5 PM, Sat Noon - 5 PM, Sun 3 - 9 PM; 1985; Circ 19,000
Income: Financed by state appropriation
Library Holdings: Auction Catalogs; Book Volumes 105,000; CD-ROMs 64; Clipping Files; DVDs 60; Exhibition Catalogs; Fiche 15,174; Pamphlets; Periodical Subscriptions; Reels 401; Video Tapes 302
Activities: Bibliographic instruction

CHARLOTTE

A   **ARTS & SCIENCE COUNCIL,** 227 W Trade St Ste 250, Charlotte, NC 28202. Tel 704-333-2272; Fax 704-332-2720; Elec Mail asc@artsandscience.org; Internet Home Page Address: www.artsandscience.org; *Pres* Scott Provancher; *Sr VP & CFO* Laura Belcher; *Sr Develop Officer* Chase Law; *VP Pub Rels & Communs* Krista Terrell; *Sr VP Cultural & Community Investment* Robert Bush
Estab 1958 to provide planning, oversight & funding required to ensure & support a vibrant, culturally diverse arts & science community in Mecklenburg County
Income: Financed by government appropriations & private fund drive
Activities: Grants offered

M   **BECHTLER MUSEUM OF MODERN ART,** 420 S Tryon St Charlotte, NC 28202-1937. Pam Davis

M   **CLAYWORKS GALLERY,** 4506 Monroe Rd, Charlotte, NC 28205. Tel 704-344-0795; Fax 704-344-0795; Elec Mail adellinger@clayworksinc.org; *Exec Dir* Adrienne Dellinger; *Studio Mgr* Kimberly Tyrrell

M   **DISCOVERY PLACE INC,** Nature Museum, 301 N Tryon St, Charlotte, NC 28202-2138. Tel 704-372-6261 ext 605; Fax 704-333-8948; Internet Home Page Address: www.discoveryplace.org; *CEO* John L Mackay; *VPres Mktg* Carl McIntosh
Open Mon - Wed 9 AM - 5 PM, Thurs - Sat 9 AM - 6 PM, Sun noon - 6 PM; Admis adults $6.50, youth & seniors $5, children 3-5 with parent $2.75, mems and children under 2 yrs free; Estab 1981 as a science museum with hands on concept of learning by doing; A small staff reference library is maintained; Average Annual Attendance: 600,000; Mem: 7000; dues family $70, senior $35, student $30
Income: $7,500,000 (financed by city & county appropriations, fees, sales shop & pvt donations)
Special Subjects: Pre-Columbian Art, Primitive art, Eskimo Art
Collections: Arthropods; gems & minerals; Lepidoptera; Pre-Columbian: Mayan, North American, Peruvian; primitive art: African, Alaskan Eskimo, Oceania, South America; reptilia
Publications: Science Magazine, quarterly; activities bulletin, quarterly
Activities: Classes for adults & children; volunteer training prog for demonstrators & guides; major programming for school lects; tours; acceptable for internship from UNCC & Queens College; book traveling exhibs 4 per yr; originate traveling exhibs that circulate to science mus collaborations; mus shop sells books, prints, shells, jewelry, school supplies & souvenirs; junior mus is primarily geared to pre-school and early elementary age children

M   **ELDER GALLERY,** 1520 S Tryon St, Charlotte, NC 28203. Tel 704-370-6337; Elec Mail lelder@elderart.com; Internet Home Page Address: www.elderart.com

M   **JERALD MELBERG GALLERY,** 625 S Sharon Amity Rd, Charlotte, NC 28211-2811. Tel 704-365-3000; Elec Mail gallery@jeraldmelberg.com; Internet Home Page Address: www.jeraldmelberg.com; *Dir* Jerald Melberg
Open Mon - Sat 10 AM - 6 PM; Estab 1983; Classic contemporary art on two parallel tracks: mid-career & well established living artists, incl Wolf Kahn & Robert Kushner. Also exhib important 20th cen estates, incl Robert Motherwell & Romare Bearden
Activities: Lects open to pub; 6 vis lectrs per yr; gallery talks y artists & Jerald Melberg; Lend art to museums & Art In Embassies; organize traveling exhibs to mus & galleries & other non-profit arts institutions

M   **THE LIGHT FACTORY CONTEMPORARY MUSEUM OF PHOTOGRAPHY AND FILM,** (Light Factory) 345 N College St, Charlotte, NC 28202-2113. Tel 704-333-9755; Fax 704-333-5910; Elec Mail info@lightfactory.org; Internet Home Page Address: www.lightfactory.org; *Exec Dir* Marcie Kelso; *Dir Educ* Jen Crickenberger; *Develop Coordr* Kara Marentette; *Dir Film/Video* Linnea Beyer; *Chief Cur* Dennis Kiel; *Outreach Coordr* Laurie Schorr; *Mktg Dir* Dee Grano
Open Mon - Sat 9 AM - 6 PM, Sun 1 - 6 PM; No admis fee, donations accepted; Estab 1972, non-collecting mus presenting the latest in photography, video & the internet. Year-round educ programs, community outreach & special events complement its changing exhibitions; Average Annual Attendance: 30,000; Mem: 400; dues $25-$75
Income: Financed by grants, NEA, memberships, Arts & Sci Council
Exhibitions: Rotating
Publications: Exhibit catalogs
Activities: Classes for adults & children; lects open to pub, 3 vis lectrs per yr; gallery talks; tours; scholarships offered; originate traveling exhibs to museums & galleries nationally

M   **MCCOLL FINE ART GALLERY,** 126 Cottage Pl, Charlotte, NC 28201-2210. Tel 704-333-5983; Fax 704-333-5816; Elec Mail info@mccollfineart.com; Internet Home Page Address: www.mccollfineart.com

M   **THE MINT MUSEUM,** 2730 Randolph Rd, Charlotte, NC 28207-2012. Tel 704-337-2000, 337-2020; Fax 704-337-2101; Elec Mail elizabeth.isenhour@mintmuseum.org; Internet Home Page Address: www.mintmuseum.org; *Exec Dir* Phil Kline; *Dir Finance & Admin* Michael Smith; *Dir Fine Arts* Charles Mo; *Dir Craft & Design* Annie Carlano; *Head Design & Installation* Kurt Warnke; *Dir Educ* Cheryl Palmer; *Dir Develop* Stacy Sumner Jesso; *Cur Decorative Arts* Brian Gallagher; *Librn* Joyce Weaver; *Registrar* Martha T Mayberry
Open Tues 10 AM - 10 PM, Wed - Sat 10 AM - 5 PM, Sun Noon - 5 PM, cl Mon & holidays; Admis adults $6, college students & seniors $5, students 6-17 $3, children 5 & under & members free; free Tues 5 PM-10 PM; Estab 1936 as an art mus in what was the first branch of the US mint erected in 1837; Mus houses seven changing galleries, 16 permanent galleries, Delhom Decorative Arts Gallery; Average Annual Attendance: 135,000; Mem: 5,350; dues Mint Master $1000, benefactor $500, sustainer $250, patron $125, family $45, individual $30, senior citizen or student discounted
Income: Financed by endowment, mem & city appropriation, foundation & corporate giving
Special Subjects: Architecture, Drawings, Photography, American Indian Art, African Art, Costumes, Ceramics, Crafts, Etchings & Engravings, Afro-American Art, Decorative Arts, Collages, Painting-Japanese, Portraits, Porcelain, Asian Art, Antiquities-Byzantine, Painting-French, Baroque Art, Calligraphy, Period Rooms, Antiquities-Oriental, Painting-Spanish, Painting-Italian, Antiquities-Persian, Painting-German, Painting-Russian, Enamels, Antiquities-Roman, Painting-Russian, Enamels, Antiquities-Assyrian
Collections: African art; decorative arts; historic pottery; 19th & 20th century European & American paintings; porcelain; pre-Columbian art; sculpture; Spanish Colonial art
Exhibitions: Rotating exhibits

Publications: Mint Museum Newsletter and calendar of events, six times a year

Activities: Classes for adults; docent training; lects open to pub, 25 vis lectrs per yr; concerts; gallery talks; tours; competitions; schols & fels offered; original objects of art lent to other mus; mus shop selling books, original art, prints, gifts, museum replicas, jewelry, cards

L **Art Organization & Library,** 2730 Randolph Rd, Charlotte, NC 28207-2012. Tel 704-337-2000; Fax 704-337-2101; Elec Mail info@mintmuseum.org; Internet Home Page Address: www.mintmuseum.org; *Exec Dir* Kathleen V Jameson; *CFO* Michael Smith; *Chief Cur Fine Arts* Charles Mo; *Dir Craft Design* Annie Carlano Open Tues 10 AM - 9 PM, Wed - Sat 10 AM - 6 PM, Sun 1-5PM, cl Mon; Admis members free, adults $10, seniors (65+) $8, college students $8, students (5-17) $5, 4 yr & under free, & free Tues 5 PM - 9 PM; Estab 1936; Mem: dues: teachers & students $45, individuals $60, dual $80, family $100, supporting mems available from $250-$10,000

Library Holdings: Auction Catalogs; Book Volumes 18,000; CD-ROMs; Clipping Files; Exhibition Catalogs; Original Documents; Other Holdings; Periodical Subscriptions 100

Special Subjects: Art History, Decorative Arts, Photography, Painting-American, Pre-Columbian Art, Prints, Ceramics, Crafts, Fashion Arts, Art Education, American Indian Art, Glass, Aesthetics, Afro-American Art, Metalwork, Jewelry, Coins & Medals

Collections: American Art; Contemporary Art; Decorative Arts; Historic Costumes; Ancient American Art; Craft & Design

Activities: Classes for adults & children; dramatic progs; docent training; lects open to pub; concerts; gallery talks; tours; Spirit awards; fels; outreach progs for schools & community; lend original objects of art to other mus; mus shop sells books, magazines, original art, reproductions, prints, jewelry, cards & gifts

M **Mint Museum of Craft & Design,** 2730 Randolph Rd, Charlotte, NC 28202-2137. Tel 704-337-2000; Fax 704-337-2101; Elec Mail info@mintmuseum.org; Internet Home Page Address: www.mintmuseum.org; *Dir* Annie Carlano; *Asst Cur* Allie Farlowe; *Cur Asst* Michelle Mickey Open Tues, Wed, Thurs, Fri & Sat 10 AM - 5 PM, cl Sun & Mon; Admis adults $10, seniors & students $8, children 5-17 $5, members & children 4 & under free; Estab 1999; 82,000 sq ft total with 16,000 sq ft of gallery space, 26,000 sq ft of commercial rental space & 40,000 sq ft for offices, storage, workshop & museum shop; Average Annual Attendance: 150,000

Purchases: Works by Stanislav Libinsky & Jarsolava Brychtova

Library Holdings: Auction Catalogs; Book Volumes; CD-ROMs; Exhibition Catalogs; Kodachrome Transparencies; Original Documents; Other Holdings; Periodical Subscriptions; Photographs; Records; Slides; Video Tapes

Special Subjects: Decorative Arts, Historical Material, Ceramics, Furniture, Painting-American, Sculpture, African Art, Costumes, Crafts, Pottery, Woodcarvings, Glass, Jewelry, Porcelain, Metalwork

Collections: Bresler Collection of Historic Am Quilts; Allan Chasanoff Ceramic Collection; Jane & Arthur Mason Collection; Founders' Circle Collection; Grice Native American Ceramic Collection

Exhibitions: Turning Wood into Art: The Jane and Arthur Mason Collection; Selections from the Allan Chasanoff Ceramic Collection

Activities: Classes for adults & children; docent training; lects open to pub; lects open to members only; gallery talks; tours; Purchase awards; fels offered; lending of original objects of art to mus; originates traveling exhibs; mus shop sells books, crafts, jewelry, original art, reproductions, prints & posters, clothing items

M **Uptown,** 500 S Tryon St, Charlotte, NC 28202-1811.

M **PROVIDENCE GALLERY,** 601 A Providence Rd, Charlotte, NC 28207. Tel 704-334-4535; Fax 704-333-3726; Elec Mail providenceframes@bellsouth.net; Internet Home Page Address: www.providencegallery.net; *Senior Design Consultant* Rod Wimer; *Sales Assoc* Tonya Jay Open Mon - Fri 9 AM - 6 PM; No admis fee; Estab 1978; Representing 30 local & regional artists

Activities: Four vis lectrs per yr

L **PUBLIC LIBRARY OF CHARLOTTE & MECKLENBURG COUNTY,** 310 N Tryon St, Charlotte, NC 28202-2139. Tel 704-416-0100; Fax 704-336-2677; Elec Mail infoserv@plcmc.lib.nc.us; Internet Home Page Address: www.plcmc.org; *Deputy Dir* Judith Sutton; *Dir* Robert Cannon Open Mon - Thurs 9 AM - 9 PM, Fri & Sat 9 AM - 6 PM, Sun 1 - 6 PM, cl Sun June - Aug; No admis fee; Estab 1903 to provide free public library service to citizens of Mecklenburg County; Gallery contains 90 linear feet of wall space, often dedicated to children's art; "L" Gallery with quarterly changing exhibits

Income: $10.9 million (financed by state & county appropriations)

Library Holdings: Audio Tapes; Book Volumes 1,615,682; CD-ROMs; Cassettes; Compact Disks; DVDs; Filmstrips; Motion Pictures 2772; Other Holdings Maps 6865; Prints 424; Records 27,869; Sculpture; Slides 9261; Video Tapes

Exhibitions: Theme exhibitions changing quarterly dedicated to children's art

Activities: Computer learning center accessible to people with physical & mental disabilities

M **SHAIN GALLERY,** 2823 Selwyn Ave, Charlotte, NC 28209. Tel 703-334-7744; Fax 704-334-7754; Elec Mail shainart@earthlink.net; Internet Home Page Address: www.shaingallery.com; *Owner* Gabrielle Shain-Bryson; *Dir* Joy Mills Widener Open Tues - Sat 10 AM - 5 PM or by appointment; No admis fee; Original fine art

A **SPIRIT SQUARE CENTER FOR ARTS & EDUCATION,** 345 N College St, Charlotte, NC 28202-2113. Tel 704-372-9664; Fax 704-377-9808; *Pres* Judith Allen Open Mon - Fri, 8 AM - 5 PM; Estab 1983; 5000 sq ft for six art galleries; Average Annual Attendance: 20,000

Income: $3,000,000 (financed by mem, city & state appropriation & local arts drive)

Activities: Classes for adults & children; dramatic progs; docent training; lects open to pub, 18 vis lectrs per yr; concerts; gallery talks; tours; schols; artmobile; mus shop sells books & original art

CONCORD

M **SAM BASS GALLERY,** 6104 Performance Dr, Concord, NC 28207-3435. Tel 800-556-5464; Fax 704-455-6916; Elec Mail info@sambass.com; Internet Home Page Address: www.sambass.com Open Tues - Fri 10 AM - 12:30 & 1:30 PM - 5 PM

CORNELIUS

M **THE COMMUNITY ARTS PROJECT GALLERY,** 19725 Oak St, Unit 1 Cornelius, NC 28031-5705. Tel 704-896-8823

DALLAS

M **GASTON COUNTY MUSEUM OF ART & HISTORY,** 131 W Main St, Dallas, NC 28034-2021; PO Box 429, Dallas, NC 28034-2021. Tel 704-922-7681; Fax 704-922-7683; Elec Mail museum@co-gaston.nc.us; Internet Home Page Address: www.gastoncountymuseum.org; *Dir* Elizabeth Dampier; *Progs Coordr* Jeff Pruett; *Registrar* Regan Brooks Open Tues - Fri 10 AM - 5 PM, Sat 1 - 5 PM, every 4th Sun 2 - 5 PM; No admis fee; Estab 1975, opened 1976 to promote the fine arts & local history in Gaston County, through classes, workshops & exhibitions; to preserve Historic Dallas Square; promote the history of the textile industry; The mus is located in an 1852 Hoffman Hotel; the Hands-On Gallery includes sculpture & weaving which may be touched; the two small galleries are on local history, with three galleries for changing & traveling exhibitions; Average Annual Attendance: 53,000; Mem: 300 households; dues $15-0$1000; annual meeting in Oct, with 6 meetings per year

Income: $345,000 (financed by mem & county appropriation)

Purchases: $1000 per yr for regional art

Special Subjects: Painting-American, Sculpture, Textiles

Collections: Period furniture; documents; 19th - 20th century American art; objects of local history; paintings by regional artists, 450,000 documented photographs; textile history

Publications: Patchworks quarterly

Activities: Classes for adults & children; docent training; lect open to public, 2 vis lectrs per year; gallery talks, tours; Getaway Sunday, Blues Outback summer concert series, summer drop in day camp; book traveling exhibitions 2 per year; sales shop sells books, magazines, original art, reproductions, prints, stationery, postcards, gifts & jewelry

DAVIDSON

M **DAVIDSON COLLEGE,** William H Van Every Jr & Edward M Smith Galleries, 315 N Main St, Davidson, NC 28036-9404; PO Box 7117, Davidson, NC 28035-7117. Tel 704-894-2519; Fax 704-894-2691; Elec Mail linewman@davidson.edu; Internet Home Page Address: www.davidson.edu; *Dir* Lia Newman Open Mon - Fri 10 AM - 5 PM, Sat & Sun Noon - 4 PM, cl holidays; No admis fee; Estab 1993 to provide exhibitions of educational importance; William H Van Every Jr Gallery-1400 sq ft; Edward M Smith Gallery-400 sq ft; Average Annual Attendance: 10,000

Income: $32,000

Special Subjects: Architecture, Drawings, Hispanic Art, Latin American Art, Mexican Art, Painting-American, Prints, Sculpture, Watercolors, Ethnology, Textiles, Ceramics, Folk Art, Primitive art, Woodcarvings, Woodcuts, Etchings & Engravings, Afro-American Art, Collages, Asian Art, Historical Material, Embroidery

Collections: Over 3,200 works, mainly graphics, from all periods; Contemporary Art; campus sculpture prog

Exhibitions: (10/24/2013-12/13/2013) Paula Gaetano Adi, Desiring Machine; (10/24/2013-12/13/2013) Parodic Machines

Publications: Exhibition brochures & catalogs, 3-5 per year

Activities: Intern training; lect open to public, 5-7 vis lectrs per year; gallery talks; tours; scholarships offered; individual paintings & original objects of art lent

L **Katherine & Tom Belk Visual Arts Center,** PO Box 7117, Visual Resources Collection Davidson, NC 28035-7117. Tel 704-894-2590; Elec Mail jeerickson@davidson.edu; Internet Home Page Address: www.davidson.edu/personal/jeerickson/jeerick1.htm; *Visual Resources Cur* Jeffrey Erickson Estab 1993; Open to students, faculty & staff of the college

Library Holdings: Slides 65,000

Collections: Slide & digital images

DURHAM

M **DUKE UNIVERSITY,** Nasher Museum of Art at Duke University, 2001 Campus Dr, Durham, NC 27705; PO Box 90732, Durham, NC 27708-0732. Tel 919-684-5135; Fax 919-681-8624; Elec Mail nasherinfo@duke.edu; Internet Home Page Address: www.nasher.duke.edu; *Dir* Kimberly Rorschach; *Cur Contemporary Art* Trevor Schoonmaker; *Registrar* Myra Scott; *Pub Affairs* Wendy Hower Livingston Open Tues, Wed, Fri, Sat 10 AM - 5 PM, Thurs 10 AM -10 PM, Sun noon - 5 PM, cl Mon, New Year's Day, Independence Day, Thanksgiving, Christmas Eve, Christmas Day; Admis gen $5, seniors, mems Duke Alumni Assn with mem card $4, non-Duke students with ID $3, children 16 & younger, Duke Univ students, faculty & staff with ID & Durham city residents free; Estab 1969 as a study mus with the collections being used & studied by various university departments, as well as the pub school system & surrounding communities; The museum is located on the East Campus in a renovated two-story neo-Georgian building; gallery space includes part of the first floor & entire second floor with the space divided into eight major gallery areas; Average Annual Attendance: 30,000; Mem: 850; dues $35 - $1000

Income: Financed by University

Special Subjects: African Art, Pre-Columbian Art, Etchings & Engravings, Decorative Arts, Painting-European, Renaissance Art, Medieval Art, Painting-Russian
Collections: African; Contemporary Russian; Greek & Roman; Medieval decorative art & sculpture; paintings; Pre-Columbian, ceramics & textiles; American paintings; Old Masters
Exhibitions: 3-4 temporary exhibitions per year
Publications: Exhibition catalogs 1-2 per year
Activities: Educ dept; docent training; tours; competitions with awards; lects open to pub, 6-8 vis lectrs per yr; concerts; gallery talks; tours; scholarships offered; individual paintings & original objects of art lent to other mus & galleries; lending collection contains paintings & sculpture; book traveling exhibs 1-3 per yr; originate traveling exhibs to other mus 1-2 per yr; mus shop sells books

L **Lilly Art Library,** PO Box 90727, Durham, NC 27708-0727. Tel 919-660-5995; Fax 919-660-5999; Elec Mail lilly-requests@duke.edu; Internet Home Page Address: www.lib.duke.edu/lilly/artsearch/home.htm; *Art Librn* Lee Sorensen
Open 8 AM - 2 AM; No admis fee; Estab 1930 to support the study of art at Duke University
Income: Financed by budget & endowment
Purchases: $85,000 excluding approval plan expenditure
Library Holdings: Book Volumes 155,000; CD-ROMs; Cards; Clipping Files; Compact Disks; DVDs; Exhibition Catalogs; Fiche; Motion Pictures; Pamphlets 5125; Periodical Subscriptions 416; Reels; Video Tapes
Special Subjects: Art History, Graphic Arts, Painting-American, Painting-British, Painting-Dutch, Painting-Flemish, Painting-French, Painting-German, Painting-Italian, Painting-European, History of Art & Archaeology, Judaica, American Western Art, Afro-American Art, Architecture
Collections: Emphasis on European & American Art; Germanic-Language Historiography
Publications: Duke University Libraries, quarterly

L **DUKE UNIVERSITY LIBRARY,** Hartman Center for Sales, Advertising & Marketing History, Box 90185, Durham, NC 27708-0185. Tel 919-660-5827; Fax 919-660-5934; Elec Mail hartman-center@duke.edu; Internet Home Page Address: library.duke.edu/specialcollections/hartman; *Reference Archivist* Lynn Eaton; *Dir* Jacqueline Reid
Open Mon - Fri 9 AM - 5 PM, Sat 1 - 5 PM; No admis fee; Estab 1992; Open to acad, bus, general pub, for on-premises use. Fees charged for extended research by staff
Library Holdings: Audio Tapes; Book Volumes 3000; Cassettes; Clipping Files; Filmstrips; Kodachrome Transparencies; Manuscripts; Memorabilia; Motion Pictures; Original Art Works; Original Documents; Other Holdings Advertising Proofs & Tearsheets; Pamphlets; Photographs; Records; Reels; Slides; Video Tapes
Special Subjects: Illustration, Commercial Art, Graphic Arts, Graphic Design, Manuscripts, Historical Material, Advertising Design
Collections: DMB&B Archives; Outdoor Advertising Assn of America (OAAA) Archives; J Walter Thompson Co Archives; billboards; print advertising; TV commercials
Publications: Front & Center, semiannual newsletter

M **DUKE UNIVERSITY UNION,** Louise Jones Brown Gallery, 101 Bryan Center, Durham, NC 27708; PO Box 90834, Durham, NC 27708-0834. Tel 919-684-2911; Tel 919-684-2323; Fax 919-684-8395; Elec Mail lisa.gao@duke.edu; Internet Home Page Address: www.union.duke.edu; Internet Home Page Address: student.groups.duke.edu/visual_arts; *Visual Arts Comt Chair* Lisa Geo; *Program Coordr & Visual Arts Comt Advisor* Janicanne Shane
Open Mon - Fri 9 AM - 4 PM, Sat - Sun 10 AM - 6 PM; No admis fee; Founded in 1968 under the name Graphic Arts, the DUU Visual Arts Comt is dedicated to promoting the presence of the visual arts on the Duke Univ campus; Two 15X15 sq rooms with 7'2" high walls; these two rooms are connected by two bridges. The gallery is situated in the student union of Duke Univ; Mem: 30; bi-weekly meetings
Income: Financed by endowment, commission on exhibit works sold & student fees
Exhibitions: Professional & local artists, approx 3 monthly (1 in each gallery); plus Duke student artists in 1 gallery monthly
Activities: Classes for adults; lects open to pub, 1 vis lectr per yr; competitions; gallery talks

M **DURHAM ART GUILD,** (Durham Art Guild Inc) 120 Morris St, Durham, NC 27701-3230. Tel 919-560-2713; Fax 919-560-2704; Elec Mail director@durhamartguild.org; Internet Home Page Address: www.durhamartguild.org; *Dir* Taj Forer
Open Mon - Sat 9 AM - 9 PM, Sun 1 - 6 PM; No admis fee; Estab 1948 to exhibit work of NC artists; 3600 sq ft gallery located in Arts Council Building; Average Annual Attendance: 15,000; Mem: 400; dues $25; annual member show in June
Income: $72,000 (financed by mem, city & state appropriations)
Special Subjects: Photography, Prints, Sculpture, Textiles, Crafts, Etchings & Engravings, Landscapes, Portraits, Furniture, Metalwork
Exhibitions: Exhibitions of work by regional artists, 20+ per year; annual juried art show
Publications: Juried Show Catalogue, annual
Activities: 1 vis lectr per yr; receptions; competitions with awards, special proposals accepted

M **THE HAYTI HERITAGE CENTER,** Lyda Moore Merrick Gallery, 804 Old Fayetteville St, Durham, NC 27701-3958. Tel 919-683-1709; Fax 919-682-5869; Elec Mail info@hayti.org; Internet Home Page Address: www.hayti.org

M **NORTH CAROLINA CENTRAL UNIVERSITY,** NCCU Art Museum, 1801 Fayetteville St, Durham, NC 27707; PO Box 19555, Durham, NC 27707-0021. Tel 919-530-6211; Fax 919-560-5649; Internet Home Page Address: web.nccu.edu/artmuseum/; *Dir* Kenneth G Rodgers
Open winter Tues - Fri 8 AM - 5 PM, Sun 2 - 5 PM, summer Mon - Fri 8:30 AM - 4:30 PM; No admis fee; Estab 1971 in a former black teaching institution with a collection of contemporary art, many Afro-American artists, reflecting diversity in

style, technique, medium & subject; Three galleries are maintained: one houses the permanent collection & two are for changing shows; Average Annual Attendance: 10,500
Income: Financed by state appropriation
Special Subjects: Painting-American, Sculpture, African Art
Collections: African & Oceanic; Contemporary American with a focus on minority artists
Exhibitions: Rotating exhibits
Publications: Artis, Bearden & Burke: A Bibliography & Illustrations List; exhibition catalogs
Activities: Lect open to public; gallery talks; tours

FAYETTEVILLE

M **ARTS COUNCIL OF FAYETTEVILLE-CUMBERLAND COUNTY,** The Arts Center, 301 Hay St, Fayetteville, NC 28301-5535; PO Box 318, Fayetteville, NC 28302-0318. Tel 910-323-1776; Fax 910-323-1727; Elec Mail admin@theartscouncil.com; Internet Home Page Address: www.TheArtsCouncil.com; *Exec Dir* Deborah Mintz; *Exhibits Coordr* Kelvin Culbreth; *Gen Mgr* Nancy Silver
Open Mon - Thurs 8:30 AM - 5 PM, Fri 8:30 AM - Noon, Sat Noon - 4 PM; No admis fee; Estab 1973 to nurture, celebrate & advocate all of the arts in Cumberland County; Main gallery & featured artist gallery; Average Annual Attendance: 60,000; Mem: 575
Income: Financed by contributions, grants & taxes
Special Subjects: Architecture, Drawings, Hispanic Art, Mexican Art, Painting-American, Photography, Sculpture, American Indian Art, African Art, Crafts, Pottery, Landscapes, Afro-American Art, Decorative Arts, Judaica, Manuscripts, Collages, Portraits, Posters, Dolls, Glass, Oriental Art, Juvenile Art, Leather, Military Art
Exhibitions: exhibitions for local and area residents
Publications: monthly newsletter
Activities: Arts educ prog; artists in schools progs; Duke nonprofit management courses; awards for annual juried competitions; local grants offered, grants for artists, workshops, assemblies & residencies; school tours of exhibits; book traveling exhibs

GREENSBORO

M **AFRICAN AMERICAN ATELIER,** 200 N Davis St, Box 14 Greensboro, NC 27401. Tel 336-333-6885; Fax 336-373-4826; Elec Mail info@africanamericanatelier.org; Internet Home Page Address: www.africanamericanatelier.org; *Asst Gallery Mgr* Angela Fitzgerald; *Asst Gallery Mgr* Lou Mecia Koonce; *Youth Dir* Leshari Clemmons
Open Tues - Sat 10AM - 5PM, Sun 2PM - 5PM; No admis fee; Estab 1991 to promote awareness, appreciation & sensitivity to the visual arts & culture of African Americans & work in harmony with other ethnic groups
Special Subjects: Afro-American Art, African Art
Collections: African American history & culture; paintings; photographs
Activities: Classes for adults & children; lects open to pub; gallery talks; tours; mus shop sells books, original art, reproductions & prints

A **THE CENTER FOR VISUAL ARTISTS - GREENSBORO,** (Greensboro Artists' League) 200 N Davie St, Box 13, Greensboro, NC 27401. Tel 336-333-7475 (Office); 333-7485 (Gallery); Fax 336-333-7477; Elec Mail info@greensboroart.org; Internet Home Page Address: www.greensboroart.org; *Gallery Cur* Kristy Thomas; *Educ Dir* Katie Lank; *Educ Asst* Christie Gulley
Open Tues, Thurs Fri, Sat 10 AM - 5 PM, Wed 10 AM - 7 PM, Sun 2 - 5 PM, cl Mon; No admis fee; Estab 1956 to encourage local artists to show & sell their works; Exhibitions gallery located in the Greensboro Cultural Center, a nonprofit contemporary art gallery featuring emerging local artists; Average Annual Attendance: 100,000; Mem: 500
Income: $110,000
Exhibitions: All mem exhibs; student art & design exhib; solo exhib; invitational exhib; holiday show; Dirty Fingernails; Trash exhib; photography exhibition; skate art show; typography exhib
Publications: Monthly newsletter
Activities: Classes & workshops for adults & children; summer camps for children ages 3 - 15; afterschool & outreach progs; gallery tours; schols offered; exten dept; originate traveling exhibs 1 per yr

M **GREEN HILL CENTER FOR NORTH CAROLINA ART,** 200 N Davie St, Greensboro, NC 27401-2819. Tel 336-333-7460; Fax 336-333-2612; Elec Mail info@greenhillcenter.org; Internet Home Page Address: www.greenhillcenter.org; *Exec Dir* Bill Baites; *ArtQuest & Educ Dir* Mary Young; *ArtQuest Educ Cur* Mario Gallucci; *Mktg Mgr* Liz Busch; *Sales Gallery Coordr* Lu Dickson; *Educ Outreach Coordr* Jaymie Meyer; *Group Coordr* Verna Fricke; *Cur* Edie Carpenter; *Curatorial Asst* Sarah Collins; *Bus Mgr* Evelyn Nadler
Open Tues - Sat 10 AM - 5 PM, Wed 10 AM - 7 PM, Sun 2 - 5 PM, cl Mon & legal holidays; No admis fee, $2 donation suggested; Art Quest $5 per person, members no charge; Estab & incorporated 1974 as a nonprofit institution offering exhibition & educational programming featuring the visual arts of North Carolina; Nonprofit visual arts ctr exhibiting works by NC artists & promoting educ with programs on site and through outreach; Average Annual Attendance: 83,000; Mem: 700; dues $50-$2500
Income: Financed by mem, United Arts Council of Greensboro, Institute of Museum Services, North Carolina Arts Council
Publications: Catalogues; quarterly newsletter
Activities: Classes for adults & children; docent training; artists-in-the-schools prog; lects open to pub; lect for members only; tours; exten prog serves primarily Guilford County, NC; originate traveling exhibs internationally; mus shop sells books & original art

M **GREENSBORO COLLEGE,** Irene Cullis Gallery, 815 W Market St, Greensboro, NC 27401-1875. Tel 336-272-7102; Fax 336-271-6634; Elec Mail bkowski@gborocollege.edu; Internet Home Page Address: www.art.gborocollege.edu/gallery.html; *Instr Art* Janet Gaddy; *Prof Art* Ray Martin; *Asst Prof Art* James V Langer; *Instr Art* Ginger Williamson
Open Mon - Fri 10 AM - 4 PM, Sun 2 - 5 PM, cl col holidays; Estab to exhibit

visual art by visiting professional artists, Greensboro College art students & faculty; College art gallery
Exhibitions: Scholastic High School Competition, February

M **GUILFORD COLLEGE,** Art Gallery, 5800 W Friendly Ave, Greensboro, NC 27410-4173. Tel 336-316-2438; Tel 336-316-2251; Fax 336-316-2950; Elec Mail thammond@guilford.edu; Internet Home Page Address: www.guilford.edu/artgallery; *Dir & Cur* Theresa Hammond; *Pres* Kent Chabotar
Open Mon - Fri 9 AM - 5 PM, Sun 2 - 5 PM during acad yr, cl holidays; Atrium areas open Mon - Fri 8 AM - 8 PM, Sat & Sun 10 AM - 8 PM; No admis fee; Estab 1990; 5000 sq ft of exhibition space located in Hege Library
Special Subjects: Ceramics, Drawings, Graphics, Painting-American, Photography, Prints, Sculpture, Watercolors, African Art, Religious Art, Woodcuts, Etchings & Engravings, Landscapes, Glass, Coins & Medals, Baroque Art, Calligraphy, Renaissance Art, Painting-Italian
Collections: Contemporary American Crafts; Contemporary Polish etching & engraving; Renaissance & Baroque Period Collection; 20th Century American Art; 19th & 20th Century African; Maness Collection of West and Central African Art
Activities: Lect open to public; gallery talks; tours; book traveling exhibitions 1-2 per year

M **UNIVERSITY OF NORTH CAROLINA AT GREENSBORO,** Weatherspoon Art Museum, Spring Garden & Tate St, Greensboro, NC 27402; PO Box 26170, Greensboro, NC 27402-6170. Tel 336-334-5770; Fax 336-334-5907; Elec Mail weatherspoon@uncg.edu; Internet Home Page Address: weatherspoon.uncg.edu; *Cur Coll* Elaine D Gustafson; *Cur Educ* Ann Grimaldi; *Pub & Community Relations* Loring Mortensen; *Dir* Nancy Doll; *Cur of Exhib* Xandra Eden; *Registrar* Heather Moore; *Asst Registrar* Myra Scott; *Preparator* Susan Taaffe; *Preparator* Joel VanderKamp; *Accnt* Cathy Rogers; *Chief of Security* Brad Young; *Assoc Cur of Educ* Terri Dowell-Dennis; *Security Officer* Kenneth Crane; *Exec Asst* Elizabeth L'Eplattenier
Open Tues, Wed & Fri 10 AM - 5 PM, Thurs 10 AM - 9 PM, Sat & Sun 1 - 5 PM, cl mon, university holidays; No admis fee; Estab 1941; Circ Ca 400; The museum collects & presents modern & contemporary art; 6 galleries, 46,271 sq ft; Average Annual Attendance: 36,000; Mem: 600; dues $35 & up; annual meeting in May
Income: State of NC, UNCG, individuals, foundations, government grants & endowment
Purchases: Acquisition endowments
Library Holdings: Auction Catalogs; Exhibition Catalogs; Pamphlets
Special Subjects: Afro-American Art, Drawings, Photography, Sculpture, Latin American Art, Painting-American, Prints, Asian Art
Collections: Modern & Contemporary American paintings, drawings, prints & sculpture; Dillard Collection: Works on Paper; Cone Collection: Matisse prints & bronzes; Lenoir C. Wright Collection of Japanese Woodblock Prints
Publications: Art on Paper Catalogue, biannually; exhibition catalogues, gallery handouts; Matisse brochure; 3 per yr member newsletter; Weatherspoon Art Museum bulletin, biannually
Activities: Classes for adults; docent training; member progs; trips to national art centers; lects open to pub, 50 vis lectrs per yr; concerts; gallery talks; tours; children's programs; exhib related film & video; opening receptions & special events; volunteer opportunities; lend original objects of art nationally & internationally; originate traveling exhibs to mus across the country; mus shop sells books, prints, gifts, exhib related items & jewelry

GREENVILLE

M **EAST CAROLINA UNIVERSITY,** Wellington B Gray Gallery, 1000 E 5th St, Leo Jenkins Fine Arts Center (Rm 200) Greenville, NC 27858-4353. Tel 252-328-6336; Fax 252-328-6441; Elec Mail braswellg@ecu.edu; Internet Home Page Address: www.ecu.edu/graygallery; *Dir* Tom Braswell; *Admin Asst* Susan Nicholls
Open Mon - Fri 10 AM - 4 PM, Sat 10 AM - 2 PM yr round, cl university holidays; No admis fee; Estab 1977, the Gallery presents 10 exhibitions annually of contemporary art in various media. Understanding of exhibitions is strengthened by educational programs including lectures, workshops, symposia & guided tours; The gallery is a 6000 sq ft facility; Average Annual Attendance: 23,000; Mem: Art Enthusiasts Group $25
Income: Financed by state appropriation, Art Enthusiasts of Eastern Carolina, state & federal grants, corporate & foundation donations
Special Subjects: Hispanic Art, Latin American Art, Mexican Art, Painting-American, American Indian Art, American Western Art, African Art, Anthropology, Folk Art, Afro-American Art
Collections: African art 1000 works; Larry Rivers: The Boston Massacre - Color Lithographs; Baltic States Ceramic Collection
Publications: Anders Knuttson: Light Paintings; The Dream World of Minnie Evans; Jacob Lawrence: An American Master; exhibition catalogs
Activities: Classes for adults & children; lects open to public, 20 vis lectrs per yr; workshops & symposia; gallery talks; sponsoring of competitions; 5 $1,000 awards; photog image exhib; scholarships offered; individual paintings & original objects of art lent; originate traveling exhibs

L **Media Center,** Jenkins Fine Arts Ctr, Rm 2000 Mail Stop 502 Greenville, NC 27858-4353. Tel 252-328-6785; Fax 252-328-6441; Elec Mail adamsk@mail.ecu.edu; Internet Home Page Address: www.ecu.edu; *Dir* Kelly Adams
Open daily 8 AM - 5 PM; Estab 1977 for Art School study of current & selected periodicals & selected reference books & slides; For lending & reference
Library Holdings: Audio Tapes; Book Volumes 3500; Cards; Cassettes; Exhibition Catalogs; Filmstrips; Manuscripts; Micro Print 30; Motion Pictures; Periodical Subscriptions 62; Prints; Slides 80,000; Video Tapes

A **GREENVILLE MUSEUM OF ART, INC,** 802 S Evans St, Greenville, NC 27834. Tel 252-758-1946; Fax 252-758-1946; Elec Mail info@gmoa.org; Internet Home Page Address: www.gmoa.org; *Exhib Design* Christopher Daniels; *Exhib Preparator* Kristen McGlauflin; *Educ Dir* Charlotte Fitz; *Exec Dir* Meredith Harrington
Open Tues - Fri 10 AM - 4:30 PM, cl Mon; No admis fee; Estab 1939, incorporated in 1956, to foster pub interest in art & to form a permanent

collection; Six galleries 2000 sq ft including a children's gallery; Average Annual Attendance: 28,000; Mem: 600; dues $45 & higher; annual meeting in Spring
Income: $100,000 (financed by plus Foundation income for acquisition of art, contributions, mem, appropriations & grants)
Collections: 20th century contemporary paintings; drawings; graphics; regional & national; North Carolina artists featured
Exhibitions: Exhibitions featuring work of regional artists; National traveling exhibits; Collection exhibits
Publications: Annual Report; A Visit to GMA, brochure; monthly exhibit announcements; quarterly members' newsletter
Activities: Classes for adults & children; demonstrations; docent training; workshops; lects open to pub, 8 vis lectrs per yr; gallery talks; tours; individual paintings & original objects of art lent to mus & educational institutions; lending collection contains prints, paintings, sculpture & drawings; book traveling exhibs 3-5 per yr; mus shop sells books, catalogues & notecards

L **Reference Library,** 802 S Evans St, Greenville, NC 27834. Tel 252-758-1946; Fax 252-758-1946; *Exec Dir* Barbour Strickland
Open Tues - Fri 10 AM - 4:30 PM, Sat & Sun 1 - 4 PM; No admis fee; Estab as a reference source for staff
Library Holdings: Book Volumes 300; Periodical Subscriptions 150

HICKORY

M **HICKORY MUSEUM OF ART, INC,** 243 Third Ave NE, Hickory, NC 28601; PO Box 2572, Hickory, NC 28603-2572. Tel 828-327-8576; Fax 828-327-7281; Elec Mail info@hickorymuseumofart.org; Internet Home Page Address: www.hickorymuseumofart.org; *Exec Dir* Lise C Swensson; *Youth Educator* Ginny Zellmer; *Develop Mgr* Chrissy Schramm; *Galleria & Visitor Serv Mgr* Ronni Smith; *Exhibs Communs Mgr* Kristina Anthony; *Bookkeeper* Mary Johnson
Open Tues - Sat 10 AM - 4 PM, Sun 1 - 4 PM, cl Mon; No admis fee; Estab 1944 to collect, exhibit & foster American art; Located in a renovated 1926 high school building; 10,000 sq ft gallery space for exhibition of permanent collection & traveling shows; Average Annual Attendance: 38,000; Mem: 700; dues $25-$5000
Income: Financed by mem, donations, local United Arts Fund grants
Library Holdings: Book Volumes; Exhibition Catalogs
Special Subjects: Drawings, Graphics, Painting-American, Photography, Prints, Sculpture, Watercolors, Religious Art, Folk Art, Pottery, Primitive art, Woodcuts, Etchings & Engravings, Landscapes, Collages, Portraits, Glass, Marine Painting
Collections: collection of 19th & 20th century American paintings; NC glass, American art pottery, NC pottery; Southern Contemporary Folk Art
Publications: Quarterly newsletter; calendar; exhibition catalogs
Activities: Classes for adults & children; dramatic progs; docent training; periodic art classes; films; lects open to pub; concerts; gallery talks; tours; competitions with awards; exten dept serves Catawba County & surrounding area; individual paintings & original objects of art lent to other mus & galleries; traveling exhibs; originate traveling exhibs which circulate to qualifying mus & galleries; mus shop sells books, magazines, reproductions, gift items & original artworks

L **Library,** 243 3rd Ave NE, Hickory, NC 28601; PO Box 2572, Hickory, NC 28603-2572. Tel 828-327-8576; Fax 828-327-7281
Open Tues - Sat 10 AM - 4 PM; Estab as reference library open to staff & pub; Circ Non-circulating
Library Holdings: Book Volumes 2000; Cassettes 50; Clipping Files; Exhibition Catalogs; Manuscripts; Memorabilia; Motion Pictures; Pamphlets; Periodical Subscriptions 8; Photographs; Reproductions; Slides 500; Video Tapes

HIGH POINT

M **CITY OF HIGH POINT,** High Point Museum, 1859 E Lexington Ave, High Point, NC 27262-3499. Tel 336-885-1859; Fax 336-883-3284; Elec Mail hpmuseum@highpointnc.gov; Internet Home Page Address: www.highpointmuseum.org; *Exec Dir* Edith Brady; *Community Rels* Teresa Loflin; *Mus Store Mgr* Mary Barnett; *Registrar* Corinne Midgett; *Cur Colls* Marian Inabinett
Open Wed - Sat 10 AM - 4:30 PM; No admis fee; Estab 1971 to preserve the history of High Point; History of High Point, mus displays variety of exhibits interpreting local history; Average Annual Attendance: 15,000; Mem: 300; dues $20 - $2,000; annual meeting 4th Tues in May
Library Holdings: Book Volumes; Clipping Files; Maps; Original Documents
Special Subjects: Decorative Arts, Photography, Pottery, Textiles, Maps, Costumes, Folk Art, Dolls, Furniture, Historical Material, Coins & Medals, Miniatures, Reproductions
Collections: Over 35,000 objects including artifacts, photos & historic documents relating to High Point & inhabitants
Exhibitions: High Point's Furniture Heritage; Meredith's Miniatures
Publications: Quarterly newsletter
Activities: Adult classes; docent training; lects open to pub, 14 vis lectrs per yr; concerts; guided tours; mus store sells books, magazines, original art, jewelry, toys, CDs

HIGHLANDS

M **THE BASCOMB,** 323 Franklin Rd, Highlands, NC 28741; PO Box 766, Highlands, NC 28741-0766. Tel 828-526-4949; Fax 828-526-0277; Elec Mail info@thebascom.org; *Dir* Jane Jery
Open Mon - Sat 10 AM - 5 PM, Sun noon - 5 PM; No admis fee; Estab 1983, Center of Visual Arts
Activities: Classes for adults & children; lects open to the pub; 4 vis lectrs per yr; gallery talks; tours; fells; mus shop sells books, original art

KINSTON

A **COMMUNITY COUNCIL FOR THE ARTS,** 400 N Queen St, Kinston, NC 28501-4328. Tel 252-527-2517; Fax 252-527-8280; Internet Home Page Address: www.kinstoncca.com; *Pres* Vickie Robinson; *Exec Dir* Sandy Landis; *Dir Educ & Exhibs* Niki Litts; *Fin Mgr* Elaine Carmon
Open Tues - Fri 10 AM - 6 PM, Sat 10 AM - 2 PM; No admis fee; Estab 1965 to promote the arts in the Kinston-Lenoir County area; Six exhibition galleries & one

sales gallery; Average Annual Attendance: 50,000; Mem: 750; dues renaissance $5000, sustainer $1000, patron $500, donor $150, sponsor $250, family $100, individual $50
Income: Financed by local govt appropriations, mem, grants & rentals
Library Holdings: Book Volumes; Cassettes; Clipping Files; Compact Disks; DVDs; Framed Reproductions; Memorabilia; Original Art Works; Original Documents; Other Holdings; Pamphlets; Photographs; Prints; Sculpture; Video Tapes
Special Subjects: Drawings, Graphics, Photography, Prints, Sculpture, Painting-American, Decorative Arts
Collections: Louis Orr engravings-history of North Carolina; Henry Pearson Collection-donations of works by Henry Pearson & other leading modern artists; permanent coll of over 250 works; Public Art Program
Publications: Kaleidoscope, monthly newsletter
Activities: Classes for adults & children; docent training; dramatic progs; concerts; tours; gallery talks; competitions with awards; sponsorships; individual paintings & original objects of art lent to adjoining counties; lending collection contains original art works, original prints, paintings & sculpture; book traveling exhibs; originates traveling exhibs; sales shop sells books, original art, reproductions, prints & gift items; Art Center Children's Gallery

LEXINGTON

M **ARTS UNITED FOR DAVIDSON COUNTY,** (Davidson County Museum of Art) The Arts Center, 220 S Main St, Lexington, NC 27292. Tel 336-249-2742; Fax 336-249-6302; Internet Home Page Address: www.co.davidson.nc.us/arts; *Exec Dir* Doris Brown
Open Mon - Fri 10 AM - 4:30 PM, Sat 10 AM - 2 PM; No admis fee; Estab 1968 to expose & to educate the public in different art forms; 2 main galleries in a Greek revival-style building built in 1911; 1986 building was renovated into an arts center; Average Annual Attendance: 20,000; Mem: 575; due $35 - $99 friend, $100 - $249 patron, $250 - $499 sponsor, $500 - $999 producer, $1000 - $1999 dir circle, $2000 - $4999 president's circle, $5000 benefactor
Income: $130,000 (financed by foundations, contributions, sponsorships, local and state appropriation, sales)
Exhibitions: Ann Juried Photography Exhib; Ann Mems Open; Juried Spotlight Exhib
Publications: Ann Guide to the Arts, quarterly
Activities: Adult & children's classes; workshops; demonstrations; museum trips; lect open to public, gallery talks; tours; competitions with awards; celebration series; artist residency in 3 sch systems; sales shop sells books, original art, reproductions, prints, pottery, jewelry & glass

LOUISBURG

M **LOUISBURG COLLEGE,** Art Gallery, 501 N Main St, Louisburg, NC 27549-2399. Tel 919-496-2521; Tel 919-497-3238; Elec Mail whinton@louisburg.edu; Internet Home Page Address: www.louisburg.edu; *Dir & Cur* William Hinton
Open Jan - Apr, Aug - Dec Mon - Fri 9 AM - 4 PM, cl holidays; No admis fee; Estab 1957
Collections: American Impressionist Art; Primitive Art
Activities: Arts festivals; lect; gallery talks; tours

MONROE

M **UNION COUNTY PUBLIC LIBRARY UNION ROOM,** 316 E Windsor St, Monroe, NC 28112-4842. Tel 704-283-8184; Fax 704-282-0657; Elec Mail deasley@union.lib.nc.us; Internet Home Page Address: www.union.lib.nc.us; *Others* TDD 704-225-8554; *Dir* Martie Smith; *Asst Dir* Dana Eure; *Outreach Mgr* Debbie Easley
Open Mon & Tues 9 AM - 8 PM, Wed & Thurs 9 AM - 7 PM, Fri 9 AM - 6 PM, Sat 9 AM - 5 PM, Sun 2 - 6 PM; Gallery accommodates 25 large paintings & monthly exhibits of local work or traveling exhibitions
Exhibitions: Various local artists exhibitions

MOREHEAD CITY

M **CARTERET COUNTY HISTORICAL SOCIETY,** The History Place, 1008 Arendell St, Morehead City, NC 28557. Tel 252-247-7533; Fax 252-247-2756; Elec Mail historyplace@starfishnet.com; Internet Home Page Address: www.thehistoryplace.org; *Pres* Janet Eshleman; *VPres* Carol Smith; *Exec Dir* Cindi Hamilton; *Bd Secy* Emily Holtz; *Treas* Pam Janoskey; *Library Dir* Kelly Fiori
Open Tues - Sat 10 AM - 4 PM; No admis fee; Estab 1985 to promote the heritage of Carteret County; org began 1971; Research library, exhibs & artifacts from 1700, 1800 & art gallery, mus shop & tea room; Average Annual Attendance: 45,000; Mem: 1,000; dues $25 per month
Income: financed by fundraisers, grants, donations & membership
Library Holdings: Book Volumes; Clipping Files; Compact Disks; DVDs; Manuscripts; Maps; Micro Print; Original Documents; Periodical Subscriptions; Photographs; Video Tapes
Special Subjects: Drawings, Etchings & Engravings, Folk Art, Marine Painting, Glass, Flasks & Bottles, Furniture, Archaeology, Ethnology, Costumes, Afro-American Art, Decorative Arts, Dolls, Jewelry, Historical Material, Military Art
Collections: Artifacts from early American Indians (8000 BC) to Tuscarora (1400's-1700's) to Civil War, World War I & II; Art; Aviation; Dolls Toys; Genealogy; Medicine; Native American Studies; Victoriana; Women's Studies
Activities: Educ prog; classes for children-preschool, 4th & 5th grades; docent training; history camps; traveling trunks; lects open to pub, 20 vis lectrs per yr; tours; concerts family programs; Albert Ray Newsome Award, Claude Hunter Moore Journal Award, DT Smithwick Newspaper Award, Willie Parker Peace History Book Award, the Garland P Stout Publishers Award, Robert Bruce Cook

Family History Book Award, Malcolm Fowler Society Award, Paul Green Multimedia Award, Joe M McLaurin Newsletter Award, Paul Jehu Barringer Award, Evelina Davis Miller Museum Award & the National Certificate of Commendation; mus shop sells books, magazines, original art, reproductions, prints & merchandise

MORGANTON

M **BURKE ARTS COUNCIL,** Jailhouse Galleries, 115 E Meeting St, Morganton, NC 28655-3548. Tel 828-433-7282; Fax 828-433-7282; Elec Mail director@burkearts.org; Internet Home Page Address: www.burkearts.org; *Exec Dir* Nikki Brant
Open Tues - Fri 9 AM - 5 PM; No admis fee, gifts accepted; Estab 1977 to provide high quality art shows in all media; Circ 200; One large gallery in an old jail; Average Annual Attendance: 2,500; Mem: 500; dues from $35; annual meeting in May
Income: $55,000 (financed by mem, city & state appropriations, foundations & grants)
Library Holdings: Book Volumes; Original Art Works; Records; Sculpture; Slides
Special Subjects: Drawings, Art Education, Ceramics, Conceptual Art, Pottery, Textiles, Painting-American, Prints, Sculpture, Watercolors, Religious Art, Pottery
Collections: Wachovia Permanent Collection
Exhibitions: First frost juried sculpture exhibit & sale (Nov - Dec); Tour d'Art (1st weekend Jun)
Publications: Burke County Artists & Craftsmen, every 3-4 years
Activities: Classes for adults & children; tours; competitions with awards, including Top 20 events of SE - Tour d'Art; fundraisers; concerts; tours; schols; scholarships offered; individual paintings & original objects of art lent to local bus & corporations; lending collection contains books, original art works, original prints, paintings, phono records, photographs & sculpture; sales shop sells original art, prints, local & regional crafts, books

NEW BERN

M **TRYON PALACE HISTORIC SITES & GARDENS,** 610 Pollock St, New Bern, NC 28562; PO Box 1007, New Bern, NC 28563-1007. Tel 252-514-4900; Tel 800-767-1560; Fax 252-514-4876; Elec Mail kwilliams@tryonpalace.org; Elec Mail info@tryonpalace.org; Internet Home Page Address: www.tryonpalace.org; *Dir* Kay P Williams; *Commus Specialist* Nancy Hawley; *Cur Interpretation* Katherine Brightman; *Cur Coll* Nancy Richards; *Horticulturist* Lisa Wimpfheimer; *Registrar* Dean Knight; *Deputy Dir* Philippe Lafargue; *Dir Develop* Cheryl Kite; *Exhibits Coordr* Nancy Gray
Open Mon - Sat 9 AM - 5 PM, Sun 1 - 5 PM; Admis adults $15, children $6; Estab 1945; accredited by American Assn of Museums in 1989, 1998 & 2008; Maintained are the historic house museums & galleries (Tryon Palace, Dixon-George House, Robert Hay House, John Wright Stanly House & New Bern Academy) with 18th & 19th century English & American furniture, paintings, prints, silver, ceramic objects & textiles; Average Annual Attendance: 100,000; Mem: Tryon Palace Council of Friends, 1200 mem, annual meeting in Apr
Income: Financed by state & private bequests, endowment, furniture, paintings, historic artifacts
Library Holdings: Auction Catalogs; Audio Tapes; Book Volumes; Compact Disks; DVDs; Fiche; Manuscripts; Maps; Memorabilia; Original Documents; Periodical Subscriptions; Reels
Special Subjects: Architecture, Prints, Archaeology, Costumes, Ceramics, Manuscripts, Portraits, Furniture, Glass, Porcelain, Carpets & Rugs, Historical Material, Maps, Period Rooms, Pewter
Collections: Paintings by William Carl Brown; Nathaniel Dance; Gaspard Dughet; Thomas Gainsborough; Daniel Huntington; School of Sir Godfrey Kneller; Claude Lorrain; Paul LaCroix; David Martin; Richard Paton; Matthew William Peters; Charles Willson Peale; Charles Phillips; Alan Ramsay; Jan Siberechts; Edward B Smith; E Van Stuven; Simon Preter Verelst; Richard Wilson; John Wollaston; Graphics
Exhibitions: Temporary exhibitions on history & decorative arts, 3 per yr
Activities: Crafts demonstrations for adults & children; audio-visual orientation prog; annual symposium on 18th & 19th century decorative arts; interpretive drama prog; docent training; educ prog; Fife & Drum Corp, 1st person interpretation; lects open to pub, 25 vis lectrs per yr; concerts; tours; scholarships offered; lending of original objects of art to museum organizations that meet requirements; mus shop sells books, magazines, reproductions, prints, slides & ceramics
L **Library,** 610 Pollock St, New Bern, NC 28562-5614; PO Box 1007, New Bern, NC 28563-1007. Tel 252-514-4900; Fax 252-514-4876; Internet Home Page Address: www.tryonpalace.org; *Librn* Dean Knight
For reference; open for use with permission
Income: Financed by state
Library Holdings: Book Volumes 8500; Clipping Files; Pamphlets; Periodical Subscriptions 45; Photographs; Slides; Video Tapes
Special Subjects: Art History, Landscape Architecture, Decorative Arts, Painting-American, Painting-British, Prints, Historical Material, Portraits, Archaeology, Interior Design, Porcelain, Period Rooms, Costume Design & Constr, Restoration & Conservation, Architecture
Collections: 18th & early 19th century decorative arts

NORTH WILKESBORO

M **WILKES ART GALLERY,** 913 C St, North Wilkesboro, NC 28659-4119. Tel 336-667-2841; Fax 336-667-9264; Elec Mail info@wilkesartgallery.org; Internet Home Page Address: www.wilkesartgallery.org; *Exec Dir* Kara Milton-Elmore; *Bd Pres* Paul Coggins; *Vol Coordr* Vonnie Williams; *Office Mgr* Chelsy Miller
Open Tues 10 AM - 8 PM, Wed -Fri 10 AM - 5 PM, Sat 10 AM - 2 PM, evenings for special events, cl New Year's Day, Easter, Easter Mon, Independence Day, Thanksgiving, Labor Day, Memorial Day & Christmas; No admis fee; Estab 1962 to take art to as many areas as possible; Recently completed renovation of 10,000 sq ft facility in downtown North Wilkesboro. The WAG offers 12 annual exhibits,

classes & workshops for all ages; Average Annual Attendance: 10,400; Mem: 400; dues patron & corp $500, donor $250, sponsor $125, family $75; annual meeting in May
Income: Financed by mem, local governments, state arts council & corporations
Special Subjects: Graphics, Painting-American, Sculpture
Collections: Contemporary paintings, graphics, sculpture, primarily of NC artists
Exhibitions: Artist League Juried Competition; Blue Ridge Overview (amateur photography); temporary exhibitions; Fall Harvest Competition; Northwest Artist League Competition; Youth Art Month in March
Publications: Title of Exhibition, monthly brochures & catalogues; Wilkes Art Gallery Newsletter, monthly
Activities: Classes for adults & children; docent training; arts festivals; films; art & craft classes; lects open to pub, 3 vis lectrs per yr; gallery talks; tours; competitions with awards; concerts; individual paintings lent to medical center; originate traveling exhibs; sales shop sells, books, crafts, original art, pottery, prints & reproductions

RALEIGH

A **ARTSPACE INC,** 201 E Davie St, Raleigh, NC 27601-1869. Tel 919-821-2787; Fax 919-821-0383; Elec Mail info@artspacenc.org; Internet Home Page Address: www.artspacenc.org; *Exec Dir* Mary Poole
Open Tues - Sat 10 AM - 6 PM, first Fri 10 AM - 10 PM, office Mon - Fri 9 AM - 5 PM; No admis fee; Estab 1986; Two fls; Average Annual Attendance: 100,000; Mem: Annual meeting in Apr
Income: $400,000 (financed by mem, city & state appropriation, rental income)
Exhibitions: Exhibits rotate every 4 - 8 weeks
Activities: Classes for adults & children; lects open to pub; tours; gallery talks; scholarships; residencies for emerging artists (2 six month residencies per yr) & established artists (summer); book traveling exhibs 2 per yr; originate traveling exhibs annually; sales shop sells original art, prints

M **CAM CONTEMPORARY ART MUSEUM,** (Contemporary Art Museum) 409 W Martin St, Raleigh, NC 27603-1819. Tel 919-513-0946; Fax 919-836-2239; Internet Home Page Address: www.camraleigh.org; *Exec Dir* Elysia Borowy-Reeder; *Cur Educ* Nicole Welsh; *Camps & Workshops Coordr* Sarah Blackmon; *Mem, Grants & Vis Svcs Coordr* Sarah Mason
Open Mon, Wed- Fri 11 AM - 6:30 PM, Sat - Sun noon - 5 PM, cl Tues; $5; Estab 1983 to support new & innovative works by regional, national & international artists & designers; presents & interprets contemporary art & design through a schedule of diverse exhibitions that explore aesthetic, cultural & ideological issues; Renovated 20,000 sq ft historic warehouse-turned-museum; Average Annual Attendance: 50,000; Mem: 700; dues small bus $150, student $15; annual meeting in June
Income: Financed by mem, city & state appropriation, contributions & foundations
Publications: Exhibition catalogues
Activities: Teacher workshops; mentoring prog for adolescents; lects; performances; film series; gallery talks; tours; video programs; internships for college & graduate students; book traveling exhibs; originate traveling exhibs; sales area sells catalogs, posters, postcards, T-shirts, caps, mugs & novelty items

A **CITY OF RALEIGH ARTS COMMISSION,** Miriam Preston Block Gallery, 222 W Hargett St, Raleigh, NC 27601-1479; PO Box 590, Raleigh, NC 27602-0590. Tel 919-996-3610; Fax 919-831-6351; Internet Home Page Address: www.raleighnc.gov/arts; *Admin Asst* Carol S Mallette; *Arts Prog Coordr* Belua Parker; *Pub Art Coordr* Kim Curry-Evans
Open Mon - Fri 8:30 AM - 5:15 PM; No admis fee; Estab 1984 to showcase Raleigh-based artists/art collections in the local area; First & second floor lobbies of the Raleigh Municipal Building; Average Annual Attendance: 10-20,000
Income: $4340 (financed by city & state appropriation)

M **MEREDITH COLLEGE,** Frankie G Weems Gallery & Rotunda Gallery, Gaddy-Hamrick Art Ctr, 3800 Hillsborough St Raleigh, NC 27607-5298. Tel 919-760-8239; Fax 919-760-2347; Elec Mail rotha@meredith.edu; Internet Home Page Address: www.meredith.edu/art; *Dir* Ann Roth
Open Mon - Fri 9 AM - 5 PM, Sat & Sun 2 - 5 PM; No admis fee; Rotunda Gallery estab 1970, Weems Gallery 1986; Weems Gallery; 30 ft x 43 ft & dividers, skylights; Rotunda Gallery: 3 story, domed space, located in admin building; Average Annual Attendance: 2,000
Special Subjects: Architecture, Drawings, Painting-American, Photography, Sculpture, American Indian Art, African Art, Costumes, Ceramics, Crafts, Woodcarvings, Etchings & Engravings, Afro-American Art, Collages, Painting-European, Posters, Dolls, Furniture, Jewelry, Carpets & Rugs, Historical Material, Juvenile Art, Painting-Italian, Painting-Russian, Enamels
Exhibitions: Weems Gallery: North Carolina Photographer's Annual Exhibition; Raleigh Fine Arts Society Annual Exhibition; Meredith College Art Faculty Exhibition; Rotunda Gallery: Annual Juried Student Exhibition
Activities: Lect open to public, 3 vis lectrs per year, competitions with awards; lending collection contains paintings & original objects of art; book traveling exhibitions annually

M **NORTH CAROLINA MUSEUM OF ART,** 2110 Blue Ridge Rd, Raleigh, NC 27607-6494; 4630 Mail Services Ctr, Raleigh, NC 27699-4630. Tel 919-839-6262; Fax 919-733-8034; Elec Mail kmolesky@ncmamail.dcr.state.nc.us; Internet Home Page Address: www.ncartmuseum.org; *Chief Cur* Linda Dougherty; *Chief Conservator* William Brown; *Registrar* Maggie Gregory; *Librn* Natalia Lonchyna; *Dir, Develop & Mem* Ellen Stone; *Dir* Lawrence J Wheeler; *Dep Dir Art Coll* John Coffey; *Dir Planning & Design* Dan Gottlieb; *Dir Educ* Susan Glasser; *Dir Performing Arts* George Holt; *Dir Mktg* Melanie Davis-Jones; *Exhibs Mgr* Tiara L Paris; *CFO* Caterri Woodrum; *Dir Opers* John Knox
Open Tues - Sun 10 AM - 5 PM, Fri until 9 PM, cl Mon, Thanksgiving, & Christmas Eve & Day; Park open daily dawn - dusk; No admis fee to Museum or Park; fees apply for special exhibs & progs; Estab 1947, open to pub 1956, to acquire, preserve, & exhibit international works of art for the educ & enjoyment of the people of the state & to conduct programs of educ, research & publications designed to encourage interest in & an appreciation of art; European Galleries with Dutch, Flemish, French, Italian, British, Spanish & N European Galleries, Classical, Ancient Egyptian, Jewish Ceremonial, Ancient American, African, American, 20th Century Galleries; Expansion opened 2010 adds 127,000 sq ft of exhib space & transformed East Bldg into ctr for temp exhibs; Average Annual Attendance: 265,000; Mem: 63,000; dues $40 & up
Income: Financed by state appropriations, contributions & grants administered by the NCMA Foundation
Special Subjects: American Indian Art, Decorative Arts, Painting-American, Sculpture, African Art, Pre-Columbian Art, Textiles, Afro-American Art, Painting-European, Painting-British, Painting-Dutch, Painting-French, Baroque Art, Painting-Flemish, Renaissance Art, Painting-Spanish, Painting-Italian, Antiquities-Egyptian, Antiquities-Greek, Antiquities-Roman, Painting-German, Painting-Israeli
Collections: Jewish Ceremonial; 20th century art coll; Samuel H Kress Collection
Exhibitions: North Carolina Artists Exhibitions; wide range of temporary exhibitions
Publications: Preview, bimonthly; exhibition & permanent collection catalogs
Activities: Classes for adults & children; dramatic progs; docent training; lects open to pub; concerts; gallery talks; tours; competitions; outreach dept serving North Carolina; individual paintings & original objects of art lent to state institutions & offices, mus, & national & international exhibits; book traveling exhibs; originate traveling exhibs; mus shop sells books, reproductions, prints, slides, educational gifts for children & adults, jewelry, & other gifts

L **Art Reference Library,** 2110 Blue Ridge Rd, Raleigh, NC 27607; 4630 Mail Service Center, Raleigh, NC 27699-4630. Tel 919-664-6770; Fax 919-733-8034; Elec Mail natalia.lonchyna@ncdcr.gov; Internet Home Page Address: www.ncartmuseum.org/collection/library; *Librn* Natalia Lonchyna
Open Tues - Fri 10 AM - 4 PM; Estab 1957 to serve research needs of museum staff, citizens of NC and anyone interested in NCMA; Circ non-circulating; Open to pub for reference
Income: Financed by State and NCMA Foundation
Purchases: $40,000
Library Holdings: Auction Catalogs; Book Volumes 43,000; Clipping Files; Exhibition Catalogs; Pamphlets; Periodical Subscriptions 90
Special Subjects: Art History, Folk Art, Photography, Painting-American, Painting-British, Painting-Dutch, Painting-Flemish, Painting-French, Painting-German, Painting-Italian, Painting-Spanish, Pre-Columbian Art, Painting-European, History of Art & Archaeology, Judaica, Conceptual Art, Painting-Israeli, Art Education, Mosaics, Afro-American Art, Pottery, Marine Painting, Antiquities-Byzantine, Antiquities-Egyptian, Antiquities-Greek, Antiquities-Roman, Painting-Scandinavian

A **NORTH CAROLINA MUSEUMS COUNCIL,** PO Box 2603, Raleigh, NC 27602-2603. Tel 919-832-3775; Fax 919-832-3085; Internet Home Page Address: www.ncmuseum.org; *Pres* Troy Burton; *Treas* Julie Bledsoe Thomas; *VPres* Richard Sceiford
Estab 1963 to stimulate interest, support & understanding of museums; all-vol organization; Mem: 300; dues individual $20; annual meeting in the fall
Income: Financed by mem
Publications: NCMC Newsletter, quarterly; North Carolina Museums Guide
Activities: Awards given

L **NORTH CAROLINA STATE UNIVERSITY,** Harrye Lyons Design Library, Design Library 209 Brooks Hall, Campus Box 7701 Raleigh, NC 27695-7701. Tel 919-515-2207; Fax 919-515-7330; *Head Design Library* Karen DeWitt; *Visual Resources Librn* Barbara Brenny; *Library Asst* Sharon Silcox; *Library Technical Asst* Stephanie Statham
Open Mon - Thurs 7:30 AM - 11 PM, Fri 7:30 AM - 10 PM, Sat 9 AM - 10 PM, Sun 1 - 11 PM; Estab 1942 to serve the reading, study, reference & research needs of the faculty, students & staff of the School of Design & the University campus, as well as off-campus borrowers; Circ 56,058; Primarily for lending
Income: Financed by state appropriation, private funds & mem
Purchases: $41,450
Library Holdings: Audio Tapes; Book Volumes 40,747; Motion Pictures; Other Holdings Trade literature, Vertical files; Pamphlets; Periodical Subscriptions 210; Slides; Video Tapes
Special Subjects: Art History, Landscape Architecture, Illustration, Graphic Arts, Graphic Design, Advertising Design, Industrial Design, Asian Art, Furniture, Aesthetics, Afro-American Art, Landscapes, Architecture
Collections: File on measured Drawings of North Carolina Historic Sites; 458 maps & plans; 300 bibliographies compiled by the Design Library staff
Publications: Index to the School of Design, student publication book Vols 1-25

M **Gregg Museum of Art & Design,** Campus Box 7306, Raleigh, NC 27695-7306. Tel 919-515-3503; Fax 919-515-6163; Elec Mail gregg@ncsu.edu; Internet Home Page Address: www.ncsu.edu/gregg; *Dir* Roger Manley; *Registrar* Mary Hauser; *Cur Educ* Zoe Starling
In transition period, exhibits being held at other venues; No admis fee; Estab 1979 to collect, exhibit & provide changing exhibitions in the art & design; Average Annual Attendance: 20,000; Mem: 200; dues $25-$1500; annual meeting in June
Income: (financed by student fees)
Purchases: $3,000 - $5,000
Library Holdings: Book Volumes; Exhibition Catalogs
Special Subjects: Afro-American Art, Drawings, Architecture, Metalwork, Photography, Porcelain, Pottery, Pre-Columbian Art, Painting-American, Prints, Sculpture, Tapestries, Latin American Art, Photography, African Art, Pre-Columbian Art, Southwestern Art, Textiles, Costumes, Religious Art, Ceramics, Crafts, Folk Art, Pottery, Woodcarvings, Woodcuts, Decorative Arts, Portraits, Dolls, Furniture, Glass, Jewelry, Porcelain, Carpets & Rugs, Tapestries, Miniatures, Embroidery, Laces, Reproductions
Collections: American, Indian, Asian & pre-Columbian textiles; ceramics (fine, ironstone, porcelain, traditional); furniture; product design; photographs, contemp glass
Publications: Exhibition catalogs
Activities: Docent & self-guided tours; lects open to public; gallery talks; tours; competitions; scholarships offered; individual paintings & original objects of art lent to other museums; exten prog serves NC, SC, VA; originate traveling exhibs

A **PORTRAITS SOUTH,** 105 S Bloodworth St, Raleigh, NC 27601-1503. Tel 919-833-1630; Fax 919-833-3391; Elec Mail info@portraitsouth.com; Internet Home Page Address: www.portraitsouth.com; *Owner & CEO* Stephen W ReVille; *Operations Mgr* Beverly Graves; *Accounting Mgr* Karen O'Connell
Open by appointment, Mon - Fri 9 AM - noon ; No admis fee; Estab 1980, agent for professional portrait artists; 3,500 sq ft; Mem: 100 represented artists
Income: Pvt income
Publications: Newsletters for artists, twice a year
Activities: Book traveling exhibs 100 per yr; originate traveling exhibs 100 per yr

A **VISUAL ART EXCHANGE,** 309 W Martin St, Raleigh, NC 27601-1352. Tel 919-828-7834; Fax 919-828-7833; Elec Mail info@visualartexchange.org; Internet Home Page Address: www.visualartexchange.org; *Exec Dir* Sarah Powers; *Finance & Mem Dir* Erika Corey; *Prog & Mktg Dir* Rachel Herrick; *Exhib Coordr* Rachel Berry
Open Tues - Sat 11 AM - 4 PM, 1st Fri of month 6 PM - 9 PM; No admis fee; Estab 1980 to serve emerging & professional artists; Mem: 300; dues $55
Income: Financed by grants & corporate sponsors
Exhibitions: Holiday Show; New Show; Young Artist Show; International Show; Lay of the Land; Salonde Refuses
Publications: Expressions, 10 per year
Activities: Classes for adults & children; lects open to pub, 10 vis lectrs per yr; gallery talks; competitions with prizes; workshops; book traveling exhibs 1 per yr; originate traveling exhibs; sales shop sells original art

ROCKY MOUNT

A **ROCKY MOUNT ARTS CENTER,** 270 Gay St, Rocky Mount, NC 27804-5442. Tel 252-972-1163; Tel 252-972-1266 (Box Office); Fax 252-972-1563; Elec Mail maureen.daly@rockymountnc.gov; Elec Mail info@rockymountnc.gov; Internet Home Page Address: www.imperialcentre.org; *Admin Cultural Arts* Maureen Daly; *Theatre Dir* David Nields; *Prog Coordr* Catherine Coulter; *Educ Coordr* Jennifer Rankin; *Admin Secy* Felicia Murphy; *Registrar* Marion Weathers; *Preparator* Tripp Jarvis; *Prog Asst* Andre Jenkins
Open Tues - Sat 10 AM - 5 PM, Sun 2 - 5 PM; No admis fee; Estab 1957 to promote the development of the creative arts in the community through educ, participation & appreciation of music, dance, painting, drama, etc; to provide facilities & guidance for developing talents & enriching lives through artistic expression & appreciation; Maintains the Permanent Collection Gallery, Student Gallery, 4 Exhibition Galleries; Average Annual Attendance: 25,000; Mem: 600; dues $25 & up; annual meeting in May
Income: Financed by City Recreation Department with supplemental support by mem
Library Holdings: Book Volumes; Clipping Files; Kodachrome Transparencies; Periodical Subscriptions; Slides; Video Tapes
Collections: Regional works
Exhibitions: Permanent collection & traveling shows change every 3 1/2 months; The Young at Art Annual Student Exhibition; Sculpture Salmagundi (indoor & outdoor); Handcrafted; National Juried Art Show
Publications: Arty Facts for Friends
Activities: Conduct art classes; year-round theatre prog; classes for adults & children; after school progs; concerts; gallery talks; tours; sponsoring of competitions; gallery shop sells books, original art, prints, pottery, jewelry, stationery, art supplies

SALISBURY

M **HORIZONS UNLIMITED SUPPLEMENTARY EDUCATIONAL CENTER,** Science Museum, 1636 Parkview Circle, Salisbury, NC 28144. Tel 704-639-3004; Fax 704-639-3015; Internet Home Page Address: www.rss.k12.nc.us; *Dir* Lisa Wear
Office Hours Mon - Fri 7:30 AM - 4 PM; Open to public by appointment; No admis fee; Estab 1968 to exhibit art work of pub schools, supplemented by exhibits of local artists from time to time during the school year; primary purpose is to supplement science educ activities in the pub schools; The center is comprised of two areas, one approx 24 x 65 ft, the other 15 x 70 ft with an adjoining classroom for instruction & demonstrations; Average Annual Attendance: 19,000
Income: Financed by mem, state & county appropriation & from local foundations
Collections: Planetarium; touch tank Rain Forest
Activities: Classes for adults & children; lect open to public, 5 vis lectrs per year; gallery talks; tours; individual & original objects of art lent; summer camps

M **WATERWORKS VISUAL ARTS CENTER,** 123 E Liberty St, Salisbury, NC 28144-5038. Tel 704-636-1882; Fax 704-636-1895; Elec Mail info@waterworks.org; Internet Home Page Address: www.waterworks.org; *Exec Dir* Anne Scott Clement; *Educ Coordr* Ingrid Erickson; *Admin Dir* Cathi Brandt
Open Mon - Fri 9 AM - 5 PM, Tues & Thurs 9 AM - 7 PM, Sat 11 AM - 3 PM; No admis fee; Estab 1977 for exhibition & instruction of visual arts; Four galleries with changing exhibitions. Accredited by the American Alliance of Museums; Average Annual Attendance: 22,200; Mem: 400; dues $75 & up; annual meeting in the spring
Income: $315,605 (financed by mem, city, county, grants & foundations, United Arts Fund, exhibition & educational corporate sponsors)
Library Holdings: Book Volumes 750+
Special Subjects: Decorative Arts, Etchings & Engravings, Glass, Portraits, Pottery, Silver, Woodcuts, Painting-European, Drawings, Graphics, Painting-American, Photography, Prints, Sculpture, Watercolors, Bronzes, Textiles, Costumes, Religious Art, Ceramics, Crafts, Folk Art, Woodcarvings, Landscapes, Afro-American Art, Judaica, Posters, Jewelry, Painting-British, Historical Material, Juvenile Art, Mosaics, Stained Glass
Exhibitions: Rotating exhibs throughout the yr; approx 15 professional exhibs per yr; 5 galley changes per yr; 6 young people's exhibs per yr
Publications: Annual exhibition catalogue

Activities: Classes for adults & children; classes for special populations; classes for children in pub housing; in-school progs; outreach progs; docent training; lects open to pub; 4 vis lectrs per year; gallery talks; tours; competitions & cash awards; annual Dare to Imagine Award given to one talented high school senior in the Rowan-Salisbury school system each yr; scholarships offered; book traveling exhibs; museum shop books, sells original art

SEAGROVE

M **MUSEUM OF NC TRADITIONAL POTTERY,** 122 Main St Seagrove, NC 27341-8246; PO Box 500 Seagrove, NC 27341-0500.

STATESVILLE

M **IREDELL MUSEUMS,** (Iredell Museum of Arts & Heritage) 134 Court St, Statesville, NC 28677; P O Box 223, Statesville, NC 28687. Tel 704-873-4734; Fax 704-873-4407; Elec Mail tgolas@iredellmuseums.org; Internet Home Page Address: www.iredellmuseums.org; *Exec Dir* Theresa Golas; *Program Dir* Debbie Overcash
Open Mon - Fri 10 AM - 5 PM; No admis fee; Merged with children's museum 12/2004 to preserve, promote & provide learning experiences in culture, heritage, science & the arts; Rotating exhibits approx every 5-6 wks with artists from NC and surrounding region; Average Annual Attendance: 20,000; Mem: 300; dues based on categories of giving; yearly meetings
Income: Financed by mem, grants & sponsorships
Special Subjects: Afro-American Art, Anthropology, Etchings & Engravings, Ceramics, Metalwork, Flasks & Bottles, Photography, Portraits, Pottery, Pre-Columbian Art, Painting-American, Prints, Textiles, Woodcuts, Manuscripts, Maps, Painting-British, Sculpture, Tapestries, Drawings, Watercolors, Costumes, Folk Art, Primitive art, Woodcarvings, Landscapes, Decorative Arts, Dolls, Furniture, Glass, Oriental Art, Carpets & Rugs, Historical Material, Miniatures, Embroidery, Antiquities-Egyptian, Antiquities-Roman, Stained Glass, Painting-Australian
Collections: Collections entail Ancient Arts, Decorative Arts, Fine Arts, Natural History, Historic Cabins, Mummy (Egyptian), Glassware, Textiles, Military
Activities: Tours

TARBORO

M **EDGECOMBE COUNTY CULTURAL ARTS COUNCIL, INC,** Blount-Bridgers House, Hobson Pittman Memorial Gallery, 130 Bridgers St, Tarboro, NC 27886-3868. Tel 252-823-4159; Fax 252-823-6190; Elec Mail edgecombearts@embarqmail.com; Internet Home Page Address: www.edgecombearts.org; *Mgr* Carol Banks; *Dir* Mr Ellis (Buddy) Hooks
Open Wed-Sat 10AM-4PM, Sun 2 - 4 PM; Admis $5; Estab 1982, to present local culture as it relates to state & nation; Located in a restored 1810 plantation house, 5 rooms in period interpretation, 3 used as gallery space for 20th century art permanent & traveling exhibits; Average Annual Attendance: 5,000; Mem: 350; dues $25; monthly meeting 2nd Thurs
Income: $175,000 (fin by state, local, fed & pvt)
Library Holdings: Book Volumes; Cassettes; Clipping Files; DVDs; Manuscripts; Maps; Original Art Works; Pamphlets; Periodical Subscriptions; Photographs; Prints; Records
Special Subjects: Historical Material, Furniture, Textiles, Manuscripts, Maps, Architecture, Archaeology, Ceramics, Decorative Arts, Period Rooms
Collections: Pittman Collection of Oil, Watercolors & Drawings; American Collection of oils, watercolor & drawings; Decorative arts 19th century Southern
Exhibitions: Hobson Pittman retrospect; period rooms, 1810-1870
Publications: quarterly newsletter
Activities: Classes for adults & children, docent progs; lects open to pub, 5 vis lectrs per yr; concerts; gallery talks; tours; exten dept lends out paintings; 1 - 2 book traveling exhibs; originate traveling exhibs, once per yr to accredited mus; mus shop sells original art, reproductions, prints

TRYON

M **TOY MAKERS HOUSE MUSEUM,** 43 E Howard St, Tryon, NC 28782-2400. Tel 828-290-6600

WADESBORO

M **ANSON COUNTY HISTORICAL SOCIETY, INC,** 209 E Wade St, Wadesboro, NC 28170-2228. Tel 704-694-6694; Fax 704-694-3763; Elec Mail ansonhistorical@windstream.net; Internet Home Page Address: www.ansonhistoricalsociety.org; *Pres* Don Scarborough
Open Mon - Fri 10 AM - 4 PM, other times by appointment; No admis fee; Estab 1960 as a mus of 18th & 19th century furniture; Average Annual Attendance: 1,000; Mem: 240; dues family $15, single $10; annual meeting in Nov
Income: $12,000 (financed by mem)
Special Subjects: Furniture
Collections: Collection of 18th & 19th century furniture
Publications: Cemeteries of Anson County, Volume 1; History of Anson County, 1750 - 1976

WASHINGTON

A **BEAUFORT COUNTY ARTS COUNCIL,** 108 Gladden St, Washington, NC 27889-4910; PO Box 634, Washington, NC 27889-0634. Tel 252-946-2504; *Admin Asst* Eleanor Rollins; *Dir* Wanda Johnson; *Prog Dir* Joey Toler; *Visual Arts Coordr* Sally Hofmann
Open Tues - Fri 9 AM - 4 PM; No admis fee; Estab 1972
Collections: Aslando Suite by Jim Moon; Johannes Oertel Collection

Exhibitions: Rotating multi-media exhibits
Activities: Book traveling exhibs

WILMINGTON

M CAMERON ART MUSEUM, (Louise Wells Cameron Art Museum) 3201 S 17th St, Wilmington, NC 28412-6554. Tel 910-395-5999; Fax 910-395-5030; Internet Home Page Address: www.cameronartmuseum.com; *Dir* Deborah Velders; *Cur Pub Programs* Daphne Holmes; *Develop Officer* Heather Wilson; *Registrar* Holly Tripman; *Exhib Mgr* Robert Unchester; *Cur Educ* Georgia Mastroeini; *Chmn Bd* Frances Goodman; *Asst Dir* Anne Brennan
Open Tues - Fri 11 AM - 5 PM, Thurs 11 AM - 9 PM, Sat - Sun 11 AM - 5 PM; Admis non-mems $8, mems & children $5, discounts to NARM members; Estab 1962 to promote the visual arts in southeastern North Carolina; 42,000 sq ft designed by Gwathmey Siegel & Assoc Architects (NYC); Average Annual Attendance: 40,000
Library Holdings: Auction Catalogs; Audio Tapes; Book Volumes; CD-ROMs; Cassettes; Clipping Files; DVDs; Exhibition Catalogs; Original Documents; Pamphlets; Slides; Video Tapes
Special Subjects: Decorative Arts, Drawings, Etchings & Engravings, Folk Art, Landscapes, Ceramics, Glass, Photography, Pottery, Prints, Textiles, Painting-European, Sculpture, Tapestries, Painting-American, Watercolors, Crafts, Collages, Portraits, Furniture, Asian Art, Mosaics, Stained Glass, Pewter, Bookplates & Bindings
Collections: Mary Cassatt's color prints including The Ten, Minnie Evans, Utagawa Hiroshige, Claude Howell; Jugtown Pottery; 17th century - present American, European, Asian Fine Art, crafts, design
Publications: Robert Delford Brown; William Ivey Long; Maud Gatewood & Gwathmey Siegel exhib catalogs
Activities: Classes for adults & children; docent training; lects open to pub; 3+ vis lectrs per yr; concerts; gallery talks; tours; originates traveling exhibs to museums, Montgomery Mus of Fine Arts, Yale Univ Art & Architecture; mus shop sells books, reproductions, prints, crafts & jewelry

M STATE OF NORTH CAROLINA, Battleship North Carolina, Battleship Rd #1, Wilmington, NC 28401; PO Box 480, Wilmington, NC 28402-0480. Tel 910-251-5797; Fax 910-251-5807; Elec Mail museum@battleshipnc.com; Internet Home Page Address: www.battleshipnc.com; *Asst Dir* Chris Vargo; *Mktg Dir* Heather Loftin; *Mus Services Dir* Kim Robinson Sincox; *Dir Sales* Leesa McFarlane; *Exec Dir* Terry A Bragg; *Cur Colls* Mary Ames Booker; *Controller* Elizabeth Rollinson; *Prog Dir* Danielle Wallace
Open daily Labor Day - Memorial Day 8AM - 5PM, Memorial Day weekend - Labor Day 8AM - 8PM; Admis adults $12, children between 6 & 11 $6, under 6 free; 65 & over, active & retired military $10; Estab 1961 as a historic ship museum to memorialize the North Carolinians of all the services that gave their lives in WWII; Average Annual Attendance: 200,000; Mem: 182; $15-$1,000 memberships; bimonthly meetings
Income: Financed by admis, sales in gift shop & snack bar, rental functions & donations
Special Subjects: Folk Art, Photography, Period Rooms, Maps, Painting-American, Watercolors, Textiles, Costumes, Manuscripts, Silver, Marine Painting, Historical Material, Military Art
Collections: Artifacts, photos & archival materials associated with or appropriate to the ships bearing the name North Carolina: BB-55 (1936-1947); CA-12 (1905-1930) & Ship-of-the-line (1818-1867); SSN777 attack submarine North Carolina (2008); also artifacts assoc with the memorial itself
Publications: Battleship North Carolina; Ship's Data 1; Battleship North Carolina, Capt Ben Blee, USN (Retired)
Activities: Educ progs for schools; progs open to pub; lifelong learning progs; special event progs; sales shop sells books, reproduction prints, slides, souvenirs & post cards

WILSON

M BARTON COLLEGE, Barton Museum - Virginia Graves Gallery - Lula E Rackley Gallery, 704A College St, Wilson, NC 27893; PO Box 5000, Wilson, NC 27893-7000. Tel 252-399-6477; Fax 252-399-6571; Elec Mail sfecho@barton.edu; Internet Home Page Address: www.barton.edu/departmentofart/bartonmus;
Open Mon - Fri 10 AM - 3 PM; No admis fee; Estab 1960 to provide art exposure for our students & community; Gallery has 200 linear feet wall space; Average Annual Attendance: 2,000
Income: Financed by endowment income
Library Holdings: Audio Tapes; Book Volumes; DVDs; Original Art Works; Original Documents; Photographs; Prints; Reproductions; Sculpture; Slides
Collections: African masks; various objects of fine and decorative arts; watercolors by Paula W Patterson
Exhibitions: National Scholastic Art Award Competition for Eastern North Carolina; Annual graduating artists exhibitions
Activities: Educ prog; classes for adults; lects open to pub; gallery talks; tours; gallery tours for children; 4 lects per yr open to pub; 2 lects per yr for mems; schols

L Library, Whitehead & Gold Sts, College Station Wilson, NC 27893; PO Box 5000, Wilson, NC 27893-7000. Tel 252-399-6500; Fax 252-237-4957; *Dir* Shirley Gregory
For reference only
Library Holdings: Book Volumes 2500; Exhibition Catalogs; Kodachrome Transparencies; Original Art Works; Pamphlets; Periodical Subscriptions 94; Sculpture; Video Tapes 50
Special Subjects: Art History

WINSTON SALEM

A THE ARTS COUNCIL OF WINSTON-SALEM & FORSYTH COUNTY, 305 W Fourth St, Winston Salem, NC 27101. Tel 336-722-2585; Fax 336-761-8286; Elec Mail info@IntoTheArts.org; Internet Home Page Address: www.IntoTheArts.org; *Pres & CEO* Milton Rhodes; *Admin Mgr* Mona Campbell
Open Mon - Fri 8:30 AM - 5 PM; Estab 1949, The Arts Council of Winston-Salem and Forsyth County enriches the quality of life for people in Winston-Salem and neighboring communities by strengthening cultural resources, promoting the arts and united arts fundraising. Each year we award more than $1 million in grant support to arts and cultural organizations, arts educ progs and individual artists throughout the community; Facilities include Hanes Community Center: theatre, classroom, & rehearsal rooms; Mem: Annual meeting in the fall
Income: Financed by fund drives, pub & private grants & endowments
Activities: R Philip Hanes Jr Young Leader Recognition award given

A ASSOCIATED ARTISTS OF WINSTON-SALEM, 251 N Spruce St, Winston Salem, NC 27101-2735. Tel 336-722-0340; Fax 336-722-0446; Elec Mail staff@associatedartists.org; Internet Home Page Address: www.associatedartists.org; *Exec Dir* Sharon Nelson; *Communs Dir* Terri Goff; *Gallery Coordr* Ginger Wiggins
Open Mon - Fri 9 AM - 5 PM, Sat Sept - Thanksgiving 10 AM - 2 PM; No admis fee; Estab 1956 to promote & conduct activities that support the awareness, educ, enjoyment & appreciation of visual fine art; The assn rents the walls of the gallery from the Arts Council; Average Annual Attendance: 75,000; Mem: 500; dues $15-$40; regular programs
Income: $100,000 (financed by mem & Arts Council funds)
Exhibitions: One Southeastern regional show; two national art competitions; professional & assoc invitational shows; various member exhibitions
Publications: Exhibit catalogs; newsletter, quarterly
Activities: Membership progs; workshops; lect; demonstrations; lects open to pub, 8 vis lectrs per yr; gallery talks; tours; opening receptions; competitions with awards; gallery sells original art

M OLD SALEM MUSEUMS & GARDENS, (Old Salem Inc.) Museum of Early Southern Decorative Arts, 924 S Main St, Winston Salem, NC 27101-5335. Tel 336-721-7360; Fax 336-721-7367; Elec Mail mashley@oldsalem.org; Internet Home Page Address: www.oldsalem.org; *VPres Publs* Gary J Alpert; *Dir Educ & Spec Progs* Sally Gant; *Librn & Cur Research Coll* June Lucas; *Dir Research Center* Martha Rowe
Open Jan - Feb Tues - Sat 9:30 AM - 4:30 PM, Sun 1 - 5 PM, Mar - Dec Mon - Sat 9:30 AM - 4:30 PM, Sun 1 - 5 PM; Admis adults $14, children ages 5-16 $10; Estab 1965 to bring to light the arts & antiquities produced in Maryland, Virginia, Kentucky, Tennessee, North & South Carolina & Georgia through the first two decades of the 19th century; Three galleries are furnished with Southern decorative arts or imported objects used in the South & fifteen period settings from Southern houses dating from 1690 to 1821; Average Annual Attendance: 25,000; Mem: 1250; dues $25 & up; annual meeting in spring
Income: $225,000 (financed by endowment, mem, state appropriation & other funds)
Purchases: $50,000
Special Subjects: Ceramics, Folk Art, Landscapes, Decorative Arts, Furniture, Glass, Metalwork, Historical Material, Maps, Gold
Collections: Southern decorative arts in general, & specifically furniture, paintings, silver, ceramics, metalwares, & woodwork of southern origin
Exhibitions: Ongoing Research in Southern Decorative Arts
Publications: Journal of Early Southern Decorative Arts, semiannually; catalog of the collection 1991, Museum of Early Southern Decorative Arts; The Luminary, newsletter, semiannually
Activities: Classes for adults & children; graduate Summer Institute; lects open to public, 15 vis lectrs per yr; gallery talks; scholarships offered; exten dept serves eight Southern States; individual paintings & original objects of art lent to museums & cultural institutions & with special permission from staff are available for special exhibs; lending collection contains 2000 original art works, 100 paintings, 18,000 photographs & 30,000 slides; originate traveling exhibs; sales shop sells books, slides

L Library and Research Center, 924 S Main St, Winston Salem, NC 27101-5335. Tel 336-721-7372; Elec Mail library@oldsalem.org; *Dir Research* June Lucas; *Librn* Michele Doyle; *Admin Research Assoc* Martha Rowe
Open Thurs - Fri 9:30 AM - 4:30 PM, except holidays; Estab 1965 to display & research early southern decorative arts through 1860
Library Holdings: Auction Catalogs; Audio Tapes; Book Volumes 20,000; CD-ROMs; Cards; Cassettes; Clipping Files; Compact Disks; DVDs; Exhibition Catalogs; Fiche; Manuscripts; Micro Print; Other Holdings Craftsman Database & Object Database; Periodical Subscriptions 125; Photographs; Reels; Slides; Video Tapes
Special Subjects: Art History, Ceramics, Archaeology, Furniture, Architecture
Publications: Journal of Early Southern Decorative Arts, bi-annual magazine for friends & supporters
Activities: Docent training; Lects open to public; concerts; gallery talks; tours; fels offered; furniture & needlework seminars; Mus shop sells books, reproductions & prints

M SOUTHEASTERN CENTER FOR CONTEMPORARY ART, 750 Marguerite Dr, Winston Salem, NC 27106-5861. Tel 336-725-1904; Fax 336-722-9142; Elec Mail seccainfo@secca.org; Internet Home Page Address: www.secca.org; *Exec Dir* Mark R Leach; *Cur Contemporary Art* Steven Matijcio; *Dir Fin & Opers* Karin Burnette; *Mktg & Pub Rels Mgr* Ellen Wallace; *Cur Educ* Deborah Randolph
Open Tues - Sat 10 AM - 5 PM, Thurs until 8 PM, Sun 1-5 PM, cl Mon & major holidays; No admis fee; Estab 1956 to identify & exhibit the world's major contemporary artists of exceptional talent; to present educational programs for children & adults; to bring the viewing public in direct contact with artists & their art. SECCA fosters creative excellence through temporary exhibs; Maintained are three indoor & outdoor exhibition areas; Average Annual Attendance: 34,000
Income: Financed by mem, local & state arts councils, grants, sales commissions & contributions
Library Holdings: Exhibition Catalogs; Periodical Subscriptions
Special Subjects: Drawings, Hispanic Art, Latin American Art, Painting-American, Photography, Prints, Sculpture, Ceramics, Crafts, Folk Art, Landscapes, Afro-American Art, Collages, Glass, Metalwork, Juvenile Art
Collections: Contemporary Art
Publications: Catalogs, 3-4 per yr; newsletter, quarterly
Activities: Classes for adults & children; dramatic progs; docent training; teacher resources; lects open to pub; 10 vis lectrs per yr; concerts; gallery talks; tours; sponsoring of competitions; scholarships; book 2 traveling exhibs per yr; originate traveling exhibs; mus shop sells original art

L **WAKE FOREST UNIVERSITY,** A Lewis Aycock Visual Resource Library, 1834 Reynolda Rd, Winston Salem, NC 27106-5193; PO Box 7232, 110 Scales Fine Art Ctr Winston Salem, NC 27109-7232. Tel 336-758-5078; Fax 336-758-6014; Elec Mail martine@wfu.edu; Internet Home Page Address: www.wfu.edu/art; *Visual Resources Librn* Martine Sherrill; *Visual Libr Tech* Kendra Battle
Open Mon - Fri 9 AM - 5 PM; Estab 1968; Reference and research for students and faculty only
Income: Financed by University
Library Holdings: CD-ROMs; Clipping Files; Compact Disks; DVDs; Exhibition Catalogs; Kodachrome Transparencies; Lantern Slides; Original Art Works; Other Holdings Laserdisks; Pamphlets; Periodical Subscriptions 19; Photographs; Prints; Records 128,088; Slides 136,000; Video Tapes
Special Subjects: Art History, Folk Art, Etchings & Engravings, Islamic Art, Pre-Columbian Art, Prints, History of Art & Archaeology, Printmaking, American Indian Art, Mexican Art, Period Rooms, Afro-American Art, Oriental Art, Religious Art, Restoration & Conservation, Woodcuts, Architecture
Collections: Art Department Slide Collection; University Print Collection

M **Charlotte & Philip Hanes Art Gallery,** PO Box 7232, Reynolda Sta, Scales Fine Arts Ctr Winston-Salem, NC 27109-7232. Tel 336-758-5585; Elec Mail faccinto@wfu.edu; Internet Home Page Address: www.wfu.edu/art; *Asst Dir* Paul Bright; *Dir* Victor Faccinto
Open Mon - Fri 10 AM - 5 PM, Sat & Sun 1 - 5 PM; No admis fee; Estab 1976 for international contemporary & historical exhibitions; 3,500 sq ft of exhibition space in two separate galleries; Average Annual Attendance: 9,000
Income: Financed by university
Collections: R J Reynolds Collection; Simmons Collection; General Collection; Portrait Collection; Print Collection; Student Union Collection of Contemporary Art
Publications: Exhibit catalog
Activities: Lects open to pub, 6 vis lectrs per yr

M **Museum of Anthropology,** Wingate Dr, Winston-Salem, NC 27109-7267; PO Box 7267, Winston-Salem, NC 27109-7267. Tel 336-758-5282; Fax 336-758-5116; Elec Mail moa@wfu.edu; Internet Home Page Address: http://moa.wfu.edu; *Museum Educ* Tina Smith; *Pub Rels, Mem & Mktg Coordr* Sara Cromwell; *Dir* Stephen Whittington; *Registrar & Colls Mgr* Kyle Bryner
Open Tues - Sat 10 AM - 4:30 PM; No admis fee; Estab 1963; Average Annual Attendance: 20,000; Mem: 100; dues $25 - $1,000
Income: $44,000 (financed by University, educ programs & mem)
Special Subjects: American Indian Art, Anthropology, Archaeology, Folk Art, Mexican Art, Pottery, Pre-Columbian Art, Textiles, Latin American Art, Mexican Art, African Art, Ethnology, Pre-Columbian Art, Costumes, Ceramics, Pottery, Primitive art, Eskimo Art, Dolls, Jewelry, Oriental Art, Asian Art, Carpets & Rugs
Collections: Archaeological & ethnographic objects from the Americas, Africa, Asia & Oceania
Publications: MOA News
Activities: Classes for adults & children; lects open to pub, 6 vis lectrs per yr; gallery talks; tours; awards for AAM Publication Design, SEMC Publication Design, SEMC Exhibition; exten prog: Forsyth County K-12 schools; traveling exhibs 1-2 per yr

M **WINSTON-SALEM STATE UNIVERSITY,** Diggs Gallery, 601 Martin Luther King Jr Dr, Winston Salem, NC 27110-0003. Tel 336-750-2458; Fax 336-750-2463; Elec Mail diggsinfo@wssu.edu; Internet Home Page Address: www.wssu.edu; *Gallery Asst* Leon Woods; *Dir, Cur, Develop & Registrar* Belinda Tate
Open Tues - Sat 11 AM - 5 PM; No admis fee; Estab 1990 as a university exhibition space highlighting African & African-American Art; 7000 sq ft, state of the art gallery, flexible space; Average Annual Attendance: 15,000
Income: $150,000-$200,000 (financed by endowment, state appropriation, grants & donations)
Library Holdings: CD-ROMs; DVDs; Exhibition Catalogs
Special Subjects: Painting-American, Photography, Prints, Sculpture, Watercolors, African Art, Textiles, Religious Art, Pottery, Primitive art, Woodcarvings, Woodcuts, Afro-American Art
Collections: African-American Art Collection
Exhibitions: African-American Quilts; Romare Bearden, John Biggers; Memory Juggs; Jacob Lawrence; Juan Logan; Alison Saar; Richmond Barthe; Lloyd Toone
Publications: Ashe Improvisation & Recycling In African-American Art Through African Eyes; Forget-Me-Not: The Art & Mystery of Memory Jugs; Model In The Mind
Activities: Classes for adults & children; lect open to public, 10-15 vis lectrs per year; individual paintings & original objects of art lent; book traveling exhibitions 5 per year

WINSTON-SALEM

M **REYNOLDA HOUSE MUSEUM OF AMERICAN ART,** 2250 Reynolda Rd, Winston-Salem, NC 27106-5117; PO Box 7287, Winston Salem, NC 27109-7287. Tel 336-758-5150; Fax 336-758-5670; Elec Mail reynolda@reynoldahouse.org; Internet Home Page Address: reynoldahouse.org; *Exec Dir* Allison C Perkins; *Dir Educ* Kathleen Hutton; *Dir Mktg & Communs* Sarah Smith; *Dir Pub Prog* Phil Archer; *Dir Cur & Educ* Dr Elizabeth Chew; *Dir Colls Management* Rebecca Eddins
Open Tues - Sat 9:30 AM - 4:30 PM, Sun 1:30 - 4:30 PM, cl Mon; Admis adults $14, students, mems & children free; Estab 1964 to offer a learning experience through a correlation of art, music & literature using the house & the collection of American Art as resources; 2,869 sq ft for changine exhibs; Average Annual Attendance: 36,000; Mem: 1200; board meeting in Sep, Nov, Mar, June
Income: Financed by endowment, annual fund, government & foundation grants, admis & earned income, Wake Forest Univ, donations
Special Subjects: Sculpture, Architecture, Painting-American, Prints, Costumes, Decorative Arts, Furniture
Collections: Doughty Bird Collection
Exhibitions: changing exhibs featured twice a year; exhibs from the museum's permanent collection offered throughout the year; (02/07/2014-05/04/2014) American Moderns, 1910-1960; (08/23/2014-12/31/2014) The Art of Seating; (02/12/2015-05/03/2015) George Catlin's American Buffalo

Publications: Annual Report; Calendar of Events, 2 per year; Reynolda House: An American Country Home becomes a Home for American Art
Activities: Classes for adults and children; dramatic progs; docent training; lects open to pub, concerts; gallery talks; tours; Best Gallery by Winston-Salem Journal; individual paintings and original objects of art lent to specific mus with reciprocity agreement; lending collection contains original prints, paintings; sales shop sells books, reproductions, gifts for adults & children

L **Library,** PO Box 7287, Winston Salem, NC 27109-7287. Tel 336-758-3139; Fax 336-758-5704; *Dir Archives & Libr* F Todd Crumby
Open 9:30 AM - 4:30 PM; Circ 2,500; Open to public
Library Holdings: Audio Tapes; Book Volumes 2,500; Clipping Files; Compact Disks; Original Art Works 300; Periodical Subscriptions 30; Records; Video Tapes
Special Subjects: Art History, Painting-American, Art Education, Costume Design & Constr, Afro-American Art
Activities: Classes for adults & children; docent training; concerts; gallery talks; original objects of art lent to mus

YADKINVILLE

M **CHARLES BRUCE DAVIS MUSEUM OF ART, HISTORY & SCIENCE,** 127 Hemlock St, Yadkinville, NC 27055; PO Box 356, Yadkinville, NC 27055-0356. Tel 910-679-2941
Call for hours
Collections: Local history; paintings; photographs; sculpture

NORTH DAKOTA

BELCOURT

M **TURTLE MOUNTAIN CHIPPEWA HISTORICAL SOCIETY,** Turtle Mountain Heritage Center, PO Box 257, Belcourt, ND 58316-0257. Tel 701-477-2639; *Exec Dir* Sheldon Williams; *Chm Bd* Jeremy Laducer
Open summer hours Mon - Fri 8 AM - 4:30 PM, Sat & Sun 1 - 5 PM, winter hours Mon - Fri 8 AM - 4:50 PM; No admis fee; Estab 1985 to promote & preserve culture; Small gallery consisting of historical photos, memorabilia, artifacts, art works, beadwork, all pertaining to the Turtle Mountain Chippewa; Mem: 200; dues $10-$500; annual meeting in Aug
Income: $98,496 (financed by mem, sales, bazaars & promotions)
Special Subjects: Architecture, Archaeology, Manuscripts, Historical Material, Maps
Collections: Ancient tools & implements; basketry; beaded artifacts; contemporary Indian crafts; costumes; memorabilia; paintings; pottery; sculpture; stones
Publications: Newsletter, twice a year
Activities: Lects open to pub; competitions with prizes; originate traveling exhibs to high school juried art shows & tri-state museums; sales shop sells books, prints, original art & reproductions

BISMARCK

A **BISMARCK ART & GALLERIES ASSOCIATION,** 422 E Front Ave, Bismarck, ND 58504-5641. Tel 701-223-5986; Fax 701-223-8960; Elec Mail baga@midconetwork.com; Internet Home Page Address: bismarck-art.org; *Exec Dir* Linda Christman; *Program Dir* Sherry Niesar; *Admin Asst* Kathy Fetig
Open Tues - Fri 10 AM - 5 PM, Sat 1 PM - 3 PM; Mem: Student & Senior $20; Artist $25; Individual $40; Family $50; Contributor $100-$499; Donor $500-$999; Supporter $1,000-$4,499; Sustainer $2,500-$4,999; Benefactor $5,000-$9,999; Patron $10,000 & up.
Collections: Local history & culture; art exhibits

CANDO

M **CANDO ARTS CENTER,** 1115 4th Ave, Cando, ND 58324-6161. Tel 701-968-4501; Elec Mail sblordtwo@gondtc.com; *Dir* Shelley Lord
Open Tues - Sun 1 PM - 4 PM
Collections: Paintings; student artwork

DICKINSON

M **DICKINSON STATE UNIVERSITY,** Art Gallery, 291 Campus Dr, Dickinson, ND 58601-4896. Tel 701-483-2312; Fax 701-483-2006; Elec Mail carol.eacret-simmons@dickinsonstate.edu; *Assoc Dir* Rhonda Walter-Frojen; *Dir* Carol Eacret-Simmons
Open Mon - Fri 8 AM - 8 PM; No admis fee; Estab 1972 as a visual arts gallery presenting monthly exhibits representing the work of local, national & international artists; Gallery is a secure, large room approx 40 x 30 ft, with a 10 ft ceiling & approx 120 running ft of sheetrock display space; Average Annual Attendance: 6,000; Mem: 38
Income: Financed by North Dakota Council on the Arts, grants, students activities fees & mem
Special Subjects: American Indian Art, Ceramics, Graphics, Painting-American
Collections: Zoe Beiler Paintings Collection
Exhibitions: Student Exhibition; Senior Exhibition; Faculty Show; Jari Chevalier collages; Yellowstone: Then and Now; Brad Bachmeier Raku; Rhonda Walter Frojen: Willoway Tales; Carol Eacret-Simmons: Anonymous is Another Name for Woman
Publications: Exhibit announcements
Activities: Classes for adults & children; ongoing artist-in-residence prog; lects open to pub, 4 vis lectrs per yr; gallery talks; student competitions; concerts; tours; merit awards; scholarships offered; individual paintings & original objects

of art lent to faculty members; lending collection contains 70 original art works, 20 original prints & 10 photographs; book traveling exhibs 4 per yr; originate traveling exhibs

L Stoxen Library, 291 Campus Dr, Dickinson, ND 58601-4896. Tel 701-483-2135; Fax 701-483-2006; Elec Mail eileen.kopren@dsu.nodak.edu; Internet Home Page Address: www.dsu.nodak.edu/library.asp; *Dir Acquisition & Cataloging* Rita Ennen; *Dir Pub Svcs* Eileen Kopren; *Librn Dir* Lillian Crook
Open Mon - Thurs 8 AM -11 PM, Fri 8 AM - 4 PM, Sat 1 - 4 PM, Sun 6 - 11 PM; Open to college students & general pub
Library Holdings: Book Volumes 97,000; Periodical Subscriptions 650

FARGO

M GALLERY 4, LTD, 114 Broadway, Fargo, ND 58102-4942. Tel 701-237-6867; Internet Home Page Address: www.gallery4fargo.com
Open Tues-Wed & Fri-Sat 11AM-5PM, Thurs 11AM-7PM; Circ
Collections: works by local artists including paintings, drawings, & sculpture

M NORTH DAKOTA STATE UNIVERSITY, Memorial Union Gallery, PO Box 6050, Dept 5340, Fargo, ND 58105-6050. Tel 701-231-8239, 231-7900; Fax 701-231-7866; Elec Mail esther.hockett@ndsu.edu; Internet Home Page Address: mu.ndsu.edu/programs/gallery; *Dir* Esther Hocket
Open Tues-Sat 11AM-5PM, Thurs 11AM-8PM; Estab 1975 to educate through exposure to wide variety of visual artwork; 2,000 sq ft of track lighting, glass doors, temperature & in-line humidity control, attendant & security system; Average Annual Attendance: 12,000
Income: $17,000 (financed by student activity fee allocation)
Purchases: Master printmakers, original prints, original oils
Library Holdings: Book Volumes; Exhibition Catalogs; Framed Reproductions; Original Art Works
Special Subjects: Drawings, Graphics, Photography, Prints, Sculpture, Watercolors, Southwestern Art, Textiles, Ceramics, Pottery, Woodcarvings, Woodcuts, Etchings & Engravings, Landscapes, Collages, Painting-European, Painting-Japanese, Portraits, Posters
Collections: Permanent collection of contemporary work by American artists; Contemporary Art; Native America
Exhibitions: Contemporary works by American artists; Betty Laduke, Children of the World
Publications: Roseanne Olson Photography
Activities: Educ dept; lect open to public, 4 vis lectrs per year; concerts; gallery talks; tours; competitions & awards; book traveling exhibitions 4-6 per year to museums & galleries in North Dakota & Minnesota; sales shop sells prints, reproductions & original art

M PLAINS ART MUSEUM, 704 First Ave N, Fargo, ND 58102-4904; PO Box 2338, Fargo, ND 58108-2338. Tel 701-232-3821; Fax 701-293-1082; Elec Mail museum@plainsart.org; Internet Home Page Address: www.plainsart.org; *VP Cur* Rusty Freeman; *VPres Develop & Mktg* Joni Janz; *VPres & CFO* Mark Henze; *Pub Rels Mgr* Sue Petry; *Bd Dir Chmn* Michael Olsen; *VP Coll* Mark Ryan; *Bd Dir Treas* Stacie Heiden; *Bd Dir VChmn* Sally McCravey; *Bd Dir Secy* Carole Kline; *Grants & Corporate Support* Camille Weber; *Mem Mgr* Renae Streifel; *Vis Svcs Mgr* Amanda Sayre; *Digital Svcs Mgr* Jesse Andersen; *Cur Educ* Sandra Ben-Haim; *Cur Pub Programming* Andy Maus; *Cur Outreach* Pam Jacobson; *Graphic Designer* Cody Jacobson
Open Tues, Wed, Fri & Sat 10 AM - 5 PM, Thurs 10 AM - 8 PM, Sun 1 PM - 5 PM; cl Mon; Admis adults $5, seniors & educators w/ID $4, mems, students w/ID & youth free; every 2nd & 4th Thurs each month no admis fee; tours call for reservation & pricing; Estab 1975 to bring people & art together.; Former International Harvester Building (1908); 3 galleries for permanent collection & traveling exhibs. Maintains reference library; Average Annual Attendance: 60,000; Mem: 1000; annual meeting in May
Income: Financed by mem, NEH, NEA & foundations grants & charitable gaming, special events, state & bus grants
Library Holdings: Exhibition Catalogs; Periodical Subscriptions
Special Subjects: American Indian Art, Folk Art, Landscapes, Glass, Portraits, Pottery, Painting-American, Drawings, Graphics, Photography, Prints, Sculpture, Watercolors, American Western Art, African Art, Ceramics, Woodcarvings, Woodcuts, Posters, Painting-Canadian
Collections: Contemporary American, American Indian & West African Art; regional, national, international, fine arts, Woodland & Plain Indian Art; Contemporary Painting, Native American, West African Art
Publications: Plains Art Museum, quarterly; exhibition checklist & catalogs with each exhibition
Activities: Classes for adults & children; docent training; lects open to pub; 6 vis lectrs per yr; concerts; gallery talks; tours; competitions with prizes; family art workshops; exten dept serves North Dakota, Minnesota, Montana, South Dakota & Manitoba; book traveling exhibs; originate traveling exhibs circulated to galleries and mus in a 6 state area: ND, SD, MN, MT, Manitoba, Saskatchewan; mus shop sells books, magazines, original art, posters and prints, reproductions, t-shirts, jewelry, postcards and local craft items

FORT RANSOM

M SVACA - SHEYENNE VALLEY ARTS & CRAFTS ASSOCIATION, Bjarne Ness Gallery at Bear Creek Hall, PO Box 21, Fort Ransom, ND 58033-0021. Tel 701-973-4461, 973-4491; *Prog Coordr* Georgia Rusfvold
Open Sat, Sun & holidays 1 - 6 PM, June 1 - Sept 30; No admis fee, donations accepted; Estab 1966 to promote & encourage the arts in a rural setting; The Gallery is the former studio of the late Bjarne Ness; Average Annual Attendance: 2,400; Mem: 180; dues couple $8; annual meeting in Oct
Income: Financed by mem, grants & Annual Festival
Special Subjects: Painting-American, Woodcarvings
Collections: Bjarne Ness Paintings Collection; paintings & wood carvings by area artists in SVACA's Bear Creek Hall
Activities: Classes for adults & children

A Organization, Box 21, Fort Ransom, ND 58033. Tel 701-973-4461; Elec Mail svaca@drtel.net; Internet Home Page Address: www.svaca.org;
Open last weekend in Sept 10 AM - 5 PM; Admis $2; Open to members for reference; Average Annual Attendance: 5,000; Mem: dues individual $5, family $10
Library Holdings: Book Volumes 100; Periodical Subscriptions 3

FORT TOTTEN

A FORT TOTTEN STATE HISTORIC SITE, Pioneer Daughters Museum, PO Box 224, Fort Totten, ND 58335-0224. Tel 701-766-4441; Elec Mail shstotten@nd.gov; *Co-Site Supv* Rhonda Greene; *Co-Site Supv* John Mattson
May 16 - Sept 15 8 AM - 5 PM, Sept 16-May 15 weekdays by appointment; Admis adults $5, children 6-15 $2, children 5 & under free; Estab 1867 to preserve & display local & state history; Average Annual Attendance: 14,000; Mem: 150; dues $40
Income: Financed by state appropriation, donations
Collections: Buildings of historic site, outdoor museum; Pioneer Artifacts
Activities: Classes for adults & children; guided group tours; lects open to pub; tours; competitions; originate traveling exhibs; mus shop sells books & magazines; junior mus

GRAND FORKS

M BROWNING ARTS, 23 S Fourth St, Grand Forks, ND 58201-4733. Tel 701-746-5090
Open Jan- late Nov Mon-Fri 9AM-5:30PM, Thanksgiving-Christmas Mon-Sat 9AM-5:30PM
Collections: ceramics; painting; drawings; photography; computer art; sculpture; jewelry

M NORTH DAKOTA MUSEUM OF ART, 261 Centennial Dr, Stop 7305 Grand Forks, ND 58202-6003. Tel 701-777-4195; Fax 701-777-4425; Elec Mail ndmoa@ndmoa.com; Internet Home Page Address: www.ndmoa.com; *Dir & Chief Cur* Laurel J Reuter; *Exhib Coordr* Greg Vettel; *Dir Educ* Sue Fink; *Bus Mgr* Amy Hovde; *Dir Develop* Bonnie Sobolik; *Asst to Dir* Brian Lofthus; *Asst Dir Educ* Matt Wallace; *Office Mgr* Connie Hulst; *Tech Asst* Justin Dalzell; *Mem Coordr* Stacy Warcup
Open Mon - Fri 9 AM - 5 PM, Sat & Sun 1PM- 5 PM, cl major holidays; No admis fee; Estab 1971 as a contemporary art museum; In 1989 the museum moved into a renovated 1907 campus building/gymnasium after 3 yrs of renovations; Average Annual Attendance: 50,000; Mem: 500; dues individual $35; annual meeting in June
Income: Financed by private endowments, gifts, grants, mem & earned income
Collections: American, Contemporary & International art in all media from 1970s to present; Contemporary Native American Art
Publications: Exhibition catalog with some exhibits
Activities: Dramatic progs; docent training; workshops; annual concert series; readers series; summer art camp; lects open to pub, 25 vis lectrs per yr; gallery talks; tours; originate traveling exhibs for circulation to US mus & abroad; mus shop sells books, magazines, folk & ethnic art

M UNIVERSITY OF NORTH DAKOTA, Hughes Fine Arts Center-Col Eugene Myers Art Gallery, Dept of Visual Arts, Rm 127, UND Art Department Grand Forks, ND 58202-7099; 3350 Campus Rd Stop 7099, Grand Forks, ND 58202-7099. Tel 701-777-2257; Fax 701-777-2903; Elec Mail art.jones@und.edu; Internet Home Page Address: www.und.edu;
Open 11:30 AM - 4 PM; No admis fee; Estab 1979 to augment teaching & offer another location to display art; 96 running ft of wall space; Average Annual Attendance: 1,200
Income: Financed through university
Purchases: CE Myers Trust Fund
Special Subjects: Drawings, Sculpture, Textiles, Ceramics, Jewelry, Calligraphy
Collections: Collection chosen from Annual Print & Drawing Juried Exhibit; Myers Foundations
Exhibitions: Rotating exhibitions

MAYVILLE

M MAYVILLE STATE UNIVERSITY, Northern Lights Art Gallery, 330 NE 3rd St, Mayville, ND 58257. Elec Mail director@northernlightsart.org; Internet Home Page Address: www.northernlightsart.org; *Dir* Cynthia Kaldor; *Dir Comm Sch Arts* Mike Bakken
Open Mon - Fri 11 AM - 3 PM; No admis fee; Estab 1999; Gallery in student center bldg 40 'x 40'; Average Annual Attendance: 900; Mem: over 100 mem, $25 fee
Income: mem fees, ann auction
Exhibitions: Contemporary American & North Dakota artists; student exhibitions; visiting collections
Activities: Classes for adults; docent training; January auction; vis artists; gallery tours; sponsoring of competitions

MINOT

M LILLIAN & COLEMAN TAUBE MUSEUM OF ART, 2 N Main St, Minot, ND 58703. Tel 701-838-4445; Fax 701-838-6471; Elec Mail taube@srt.com; Internet Home Page Address: www.taubemuseum.org; *Exec Dir & Cur* Nancy F Brown; *Educ Coordr* Margaret Lee
Open Jan 1 - Dec 31, Tues - Fri 10:30 AM - 5:30 PM, Sat 11 AM -4 PM; Admis is by suggested contribution; Estab 1970 to promote means & opportunities for the educ of the pub with respect to the study & culture of the fine arts; Renovated bank; Average Annual Attendance: 20,000; Mem: Membership 500; dues $25 - $1000, board meeting 3rd Thurs of month

Income: Financed by endowment, mem, contributions, sales, grants & mem fees
Library Holdings: Compact Disks; Framed Reproductions; Memorabilia; Original Art Works; Pamphlets; Photographs; Prints; Sculpture
Special Subjects: Afro-American Art, Landscapes, Ceramics, Glass, Metalwork, Mexican Art, American Western Art, Photography, Porcelain, Portraits, Pottery, Painting-American, Prints, Textiles, Sculpture, Hispanic Art, Latin American Art, Watercolors, American Indian Art, African Art, Woodcarvings, Jewelry, Oriental Art, Asian Art, Juvenile Art, Stained Glass
Collections: Original art works; paintings; pottery; printmaking; sculpture; all done by local & national artists
Exhibitions: Art competitions; art fests; one-person exhibits; traveling art exhibits; exhibitions change monthly
Publications: Calendar of Exhibits; quarterly newsletter
Activities: Classes for adults & children; dramatic progs; educ prog; gallery talks; concerts; tour; competitions; North Dakota juried student art awards; book traveling exhibs 2-3 per yr; originates traveling exhibs to North Dakota galleries; mus shop sells books, original art, reproductions, prints, cards, & children's art supplies

M **MINOT STATE UNIVERSITY,** Northwest Art Center, 500 University Ave W, Minot, ND 58707-0002. Tel 701-858-3264; Fax 701-858-3894; Elec Mail nac@minotstateu.edu; Internet Home Page Address: www.minotstateu.edu/nac; *Dir* Avis Veikley
Open Mon - Fri 8 AM - 4:30 PM, cl holidays; No admis fee; Estab 1975 as a supplementary teaching aid, resource for Minot State University, Northwest & Central North Dakota; Two galleries: Hartnett Hall Gallery & Gordon B Olson Library Gallery; 600 sq ft; Average Annual Attendance: 6,000
Income: $25,000 (financed by grants, university, juried show entry fees)
Purchases: $2,500
Library Holdings: Exhibition Catalogs; Original Art Works; Photographs; Prints; Slides
Special Subjects: Etchings & Engravings, Landscapes, American Western Art, Photography, Pottery, Painting-American, Prints, Woodcuts, Drawings, Graphics, Watercolors, Ceramics, Portraits, Posters
Collections: Over 400 works in collection; focus is contemporary 2-D works on paper in all media (printmaking, drawing, painting)
Exhibitions: America's 2000: All Media (Aug-Sept); America's 2000: Paperworks Exhibition (Jan-Feb); 20 exhibitions annually
Publications: Calendar of exhibits, annual; posters
Activities: Classes for adults; artist in residence; lects open to pub, 10-12 vis lectrs per yr; gallery talks; tours; competitions with awards, merit, best of show & purchase; book traveling exhibs 6-10 per yr; originate traveling exhibs to regional venues, galleries in ND

MOTT

M **MOTT GALLERY OF HISTORY & ART,** PO Box 116, Mott, ND 58646. Tel 701-824-2163

OHIO

AKRON

M **AKRON ART MUSEUM,** One South High, Akron, OH 44308-2084. Tel 330-376-9185; Fax 330-376-1180; Elec Mail mail@akronartmuseum.org; Internet Home Page Address: www.akronartmuseum.org; *Dir & CEO* Dr Mitchell Kahan; *Dir Curatorial Affairs* Dr Barbara Tannenbaum; *Colls Mgr* Arnold Tunstall; *COO* Gail Wild; *Dir Develop* Jon Trainor; *Dir Educ* Melissa Higgins; *Sr Educator* Alison Caplan; *Pres (V)* Myrian Altieri Haslinger; *Mus Shop Mgr* Laura Firestone; *Librn* Ellie Ward; *Assoc Educator* Gina Thomas-McGee; *Mem Mgr* Jen Shipman; *Dir Mktg* Betty Wilson
Open Wed - Sun 11 AM - 5 PM, Thurs 11 AM - 9 PM, cl Mon & Tues, New Year's Day, Memorial Day, Independence Day, Labor Day, Thanksgiving, Christmas Eve & Day; Admis adults $7, students $5, seniors 65 & over $5, children 12 & under & members free; Estab 1922 as a mus to exhibit & collect art; In 1981 opened new Akron Art Mus in restored & reconstructed 1899 National Register Historic Building; Coop Himmelblau's 64,000 sq ft bldg opened in 2007 connected to existing bldg; Mem: 2,300; dues general $45; annual meeting in Sept
Income: $3,250,000 (financed by mem, endowment, corporate, foundation & government grants)
Purchases: John McLaughlin, Yinka Shonibare, Mickalene Thomas
Library Holdings: Auction Catalogs; Audio Tapes; Book Volumes 12,000; Clipping Files; DVDs; Exhibition Catalogs; Kodachrome Transparencies; Pamphlets; Periodical Subscriptions; Slides; Video Tapes
Special Subjects: Art History, Painting-American, Sculpture, Latin American Art, Photography, Folk Art, Decorative Arts, Painting-European
Collections: 20th Century American & European painting, photography & sculpture; Late 19th Century American painting; Harry Callahan; Chuck Close; Richard Deacon; Minnie Evans; Walker Evans; Robert Frank; Philip Guston; Donald Judd; Philip Pearlstein; Elijah Pierce; Cindy Sherman; Nancy Spero; Thomas Struth; Mark Di Suvero; Andy Warhol; Carrie Mae Weems
Publications: Biennial report, quarterly magazine, gallery guides & exhib catalogues
Activities: Educ dept; classes for adults & children; docent training; lects open to pub, 8+ vis lectrs per yr; concerts; gallery talks; tours; Knight Purchase Award for Photographic Media; book traveling exhibs 4 per yr; originates traveling exhibs; mus shop sells books, magazines, original art, reproductions & prints, gift items
L **Martha Stecher Reed Art Library,** One South High, Akron, OH 44308. Tel 330-376-9185; Fax 330-376-1180; Elec Mail eward@akronartmuseum.org; Internet Home Page Address: www.akronartmuseum.org; *Librn* Ellie Ward; *Dir Cur Affairs* Dr Barbara Tannenbaum

Open Wed - Fri 11 AM - 4 PM; no admis fee; Circ 12,000; Open to pub for reference, non-circulating
Library Holdings: Auction Catalogs; Audio Tapes; Book Volumes 12,000; Clipping Files; DVDs; Exhibition Catalogs; Kodachrome Transparencies; Pamphlets; Periodical Subscriptions 45; Slides; Video Tapes 50
Special Subjects: Photography, Painting-American, Sculpture, Conceptual Art, Latin American Art, Folk Art
Collections: Edwin Shaw Volumes, to accompany coll of American Impressionist Art
Activities: Classes for children; docent training; lects open to pub; gallery talks

L **AKRON-SUMMIT COUNTY PUBLIC LIBRARY,** Fine Arts Division, 60 S High St, Akron, OH 44326-1000. Tel 330-643-9040; Fax 330-643-9033; Elec Mail esdiv@akronlibrary.org; Internet Home Page Address: www.akronlibrary.org; *Mgr History & Humanities Div* Bob Ethington; *Dir* David Jennings; *Asst Dir* Pam Hickson-Stevenson; *Main Library Gen Mgr* Rick Ewing; *Mktg Dir* Carla Davis
Open Mon - Thurs 9 AM - 9 PM, Fri 9 AM - 6 PM, Sat 9 AM - 5 PM, Sun 1 - 5 PM; Estab 1904 to serve the educational & recreational needs of the general public of Summit & contiguous counties
Income: $75,000 (financed by state and local taxes)
Library Holdings: Book Volumes 55,000; Clipping Files; Exhibition Catalogs; Fiche; Pamphlets; Periodical Subscriptions 150
Special Subjects: Art History, Folk Art, Decorative Arts, Illustration, Photography, Drawings, Graphic Arts, Ceramics, Crafts, Costume Design & Constr, Glass, Embroidery, Jewelry, Architecture
Activities: Book traveling exhibs 1-3 per year

M **STAN HYWET HALL & GARDENS,** 714 N Portage Path, Akron, OH 44303-1399. Tel 330-836-5533; Fax 330-836-2680; Elec Mail info@stanhywet.org; Internet Home Page Address: www.stanhywet.org; *Pres & CEO* Harry P Lynch; *VPres Mus Svcs & Cur* Mark Heppner; *Dir Horticulture* Tom Hrivnak
Open Feb - Mar Tues - Sat 10 AM - 4 PM, Sun 1 - 4 PM, Apr - Dec 10 AM - 4:30 PM; Admis adults $12, children 6 - 12 $6, children under 6 free; Incorporated 1957, Stan Hywet Hall is a house mus & garden, serving as a civic & cultural center. All restoration & preservation work is carefully researched to retain the original concept of the property, which represents a way of life that is gone forever; The mansion, the focal point of the estate, is a 65-room Tudor Revival manor house, furnished with priceless antiques & works of art dating from the 14th century. The property is the former home of Frank A Seiberling, (Akron rubber industrialist & co-founder of Goodyear Tire & Rubber) & was completed in 1915. There are 70 acres of formal gardens, meadow, woods & lagoons; Average Annual Attendance: 200,000; Mem: 3700; dues $55 & up; annual meeting in May
Income: $1,000,000 (financed by endowment, mem, admis, gifts, grants, rentals & special events)
Library Holdings: Audio Tapes; Book Volumes; CD-ROMs; Clipping Files; Compact Disks; DVDs; Framed Reproductions; Manuscripts; Maps; Memorabilia; Motion Pictures; Original Art Works; Original Documents; Pamphlets; Periodical Subscriptions; Photographs; Prints; Records; Reels; Reproductions; Sculpture; Slides; Video Tapes
Special Subjects: Period Rooms
Collections: Antique furniture; china; crystal; paintings; porcelain; rugs; sculpture; silver; tapestries; architectural drawings, manuscripts & photographs
Exhibitions: Permanent & temporary exhibitions through the year
Publications: Stan Hywet Hall and Gardens Annual Report, yearly; Stan Hywet Hall Newsletter, quarterly
Activities: Children's progs; dramatic progs; docent training; classes for adults & children; lects open to pub, open to mems only; 6 vis lectrs per yr; yr round special events; concerts; tours; exten dept serves libraries; original objects of art lent to historical societies & mus; lending collection includes 5000 books & 250 slides; mus shop sells books, original art, reproductions, slides & wide variety of gift items

M **THE SUMMIT COUNTY HISTORICAL SOCIETY OF AKRON, OH,** (Summit County Historical Society) 550 Copley Rd, Akron, OH 44320-2398. Tel 330-535-1120; Fax 330-535-0250; Elec Mail schs@summithistory.org; Internet Home Page Address: www.summithistory.org/blog; *Dir* Leianne Neff Heppner; *Pres* Richard Comstock; *Bus Mgr* Sandy Pecimon; *Educ Coordr* Alison First; *Admin* Mary Conley; *Vol Coordr* Melinda Sedelmeyer
Office open Tues - Fri 8 AM - 4 PM, Tours Wed - Fri 1 PM - 3 PM; Admis adults $6, seniors $4, children $2; Estab 1924 for the collection, preservation & display of items of an historical nature from Summit County; mission to preserve, interpret & educate others on the history of Akron; 1837 Perkins Stone Mansion - Greek revival home with period rooms; Average Annual Attendance: 5,000; Mem: 500; dues $40 - $500; annual meeting in spring
Income: $150,000 (financed by endowment, mem & foundations)
Library Holdings: Audio Tapes; Book Volumes; Lantern Slides; Manuscripts; Maps; Memorabilia; Motion Pictures; Original Art Works; Pamphlets; Photographs; Prints; Records; Reels; Slides; Video Tapes
Special Subjects: Decorative Arts, Etchings & Engravings, Folk Art, Architecture, Ceramics, Photography, Painting-American, Prints, Period Rooms, Textiles, Maps, Tapestries, Costumes, Pottery, Manuscripts, Portraits, Dolls, Furniture, Glass, Silver, Carpets & Rugs, Historical Material, Embroidery, Military Art
Collections: 19th & 20th century costumes & accessories; 1810-1900 era furniture; 19th century chinaware, glassware, silverware & pottery; 19th century portraits; 19th & 20th century tools, household items & toys; Native Am material; The John Brown House; Numerous works of art on paper & canvas; Works of art on paper are stored at Akron-Summit County Pub Libr
Exhibitions: Perkins Stone Mansion; Framework of Fashion; Photography: An Invention Without Future; 10 intern-led exhibitions due to grant from the Ohio Humanities Council, a state affiliate of the National Endowment for the Humanities and the Ohio Assn of Historical Societies & Museums; Securing the Shadow: Portrait Photography in Akron, 1850-1900; A Garden Wedding; (2011-2015) Current exhibs focus on Civil War 150 commemorative
Publications: Old Portage Trail Review, quarterly
Activities: Educ dept; classes for adults & children; docent training; outreach focused; gallery talks; tours; Stuart B Steiner award for Volunteerism; The Summit

Awards to Akron & Summit County residents who have made a national impact; scholarships; lending of original objects of art to city, county, regional & some out-of-state exhib; SCHS books available for purchase about the local history

M **UNIVERSITY OF AKRON,** University Art Galleries, 150 E Exchange St, Akron, OH 44325-7801. Tel 330-972-5950; Fax 330-972-5960; Elec Mail bengsto@uakron.edu; Internet Home Page Address: art.uakron.edu/university-galleries/; *Gallery Dir* Rod Bengston
Open Mon, Tues & Fri 10 AM - 5 PM, Wed & Thurs 10 AM - 9 PM; No admis fee; Estab 1974 to exhibit the work of important contemporary artists working in all regions of the United States, as well as to provide a showcase for the work of artists working within the university community; Two galleries: Emily H Davis Art Gallery, 2000 sq ft of floor space; 200 running ft of wall space; Guzzetta Hall Atrium Gallery, 120 running ft of wall space; Average Annual Attendance: 12,000-15,000
Income: Financed by university funds & grants
Collections: Contemporary Art
Exhibitions: Rotating exhibits, call for details
Publications: Catalogs & artists books in conjunction with exhibitions
Activities: Lects open to pub, 5-10 per yr; gallery talks; tours; competitions; awards for Student Show; scholarships & fels offered; book traveling exhibs; originate traveling exhibs, circulation to other university galleries & small museums with contemporary program

ASHLAND

M **ASHLAND COLLEGE ARTS & HUMANITIES GALLERY,** The Coburn Gallery, 401 College Ave, Ashland, OH 44805-3799. Tel 419-289-4142; Tel 419-289-5652; Fax 419-289-5999; *Dir* Larry Schiemann
Open Mon-Fri 10 AM-5PM; No admis fee; Estab 1969; Gallery maintained for continuous exhibitions
Collections: Mostly contemporary works, some historical
Exhibitions: Invitational Printmaking; annual student exhibition; rotating exhibitions
Activities: Classes for children; dramatic progs; lects open to pub; 2-3 gallery talks; tours & regular tours to leading art mus; concerts; schols; original objects of art lent to Akron Art Institute and Cleveland Museum of Art

ASHTABULA

A **ASHTABULA ARTS CENTER,** 2928 W 13th St, Ashtabula, OH 44004-2498. Tel 440-964-3396; Fax 440-964-3396; Elec Mail aac@suite224.net; Internet Home Page Address: www.artscenternews.com; *Pres* Judy Robson; *Exec Dir* Elizabeth Koski; *Bus Mgr* Cindy Rimpela; *Dance Dept Coordr* Shelagh Dubsky; *Art Coordr* Meeghan Humphery
Open Mon - Thurs 9 AM - 9 PM, Fri - Sat 9 AM - 5 PM, cl holidays; No admis fee; Estab 1953 as a nonprofit, tax exempt art organization, to provide high quality instruction; One major gallery area with smaller annex-fixed panels on all walls; Average Annual Attendance: 15,000; Mem: 1000; dues family $50, individual $25; annual meeting in Oct
Income: Financed by mem, NEA, OAC, WSL, JTPA
Collections: Local & regional contemporary work, small international contemporary print collection, regional wood sculpture (major portion of collection represents local & regional talent)
Publications: Ashtabula Arts Center News, bimonthly; monthly exhibit information
Activities: Classes for adults & children; dramatic prog; lects open to pub, 5-10 vis lectrs per yr; concerts; gallery talks; tours; competitions; cash awards; schols & fels offered; exten dept serves Ashtabula County hospitals & pub buildings; individual paintings & original objects of art lent to schools & pub buildings; lending collection contains books, cassettes, color reproductions, framed reproductions, original art works, original prints, paintings, phonorecords, photographs, sculpture & slides; book traveling exhibs; originate traveling exhibs

ATHENS

A **THE DAIRY BARN ARTS CENTER,** 8000 Dairy Ln, Athens, OH 45701-9393. Tel 740-592-4981; Fax 740-592-5090; Elec Mail artsinfo@dairybarn.org; Internet Home Page Address: www.dairybarn.org; *Exec Dir* Andrea Lewis; *Dir Educ* Lyn Smith; *Quilt Natl Dir* Kathleen Dawson; *Facilities Mgr* Reid Secoy; *Gallery Shop Mgr* Claire White; *Dir Exhibs* Deanna Schwartz
Open Tues - Sat Noon - 5 PM, Thurs until 8 PM, Sun 1-5 PM; Admis varies; Estab 1977 to promote art & culture; 7000 sq ft gallery located in historic dairy barn; Average Annual Attendance: 15,000; Mem: 650; dues $50-$100; annual meeting in Jan
Income: Financed by admis, mem, corp sponsorships, grants, exhib tours & art sales
Special Subjects: Landscapes, Sculpture, Watercolors, Decorative Arts, Folk Art, Ceramics, Collages, Crafts, Juvenile Art, Furniture, Glass
Exhibitions: Athens Voices, Quilt National (summer-odd years); OH+5 (winter)
Activities: Educ prog; classes for adults & children; dramatic progs; docent training; summer art camp; lects open to pub; concerts; gallery talks; tours; competitions with awards; exten dept serves area schools; book traveling exhibs nationally; originate traveling exhibs; open to galleries, museums, universities; mus shop sells books, magazines, original art, reproductions & prints

M **OHIO UNIVERSITY,** Kennedy Museum of Art, Ohio University, Lin Hall Athens, OH 45701-2979. Tel 740-593-1304; Fax 740-593-1305; Elec Mail kennedymuseum@ohio.edu; Internet Home Page Address: www.ohiou.edu/museum; *Registrar* Jeffrey Carr; *Cur Educ* Sally Delgado; *Dir* Edward E Pauley; *Cur* Petra Kralickova
Open Tues, Wed, Fri Noon - 5 PM, Thurs Noon - 8 PM, Sat - Sun 1 - 5 PM; No admis fee; 1993; Average Annual Attendance: 10,000; Mem: 220; dues vary; annual meeting in spring

Special Subjects: Historical Material, Landscapes, Ceramics, Painting-American, Silver, Drawings, Graphics, Painting-American, Photography, Prints, Sculpture, Watercolors, American Indian Art, Bronzes, African Art, Southwestern Art, Textiles, Woodcuts, Etchings & Engravings, Jewelry, Metalwork, Carpets & Rugs
Collections: Contemporary prints, paintings, photographs & sculpture; Edwin L & Ruth E Kennedy Southwest Native American Collection; African masks; Southwest Native American jewelry & weavings
Exhibitions: Four rotating exhibits per yr; Permanent exhibit - rotates every 2 yrs
Publications: Exhibition catalogs; Member Newsletter
Activities: Classes for children; lec for members; gallery talks; tours; individual paintings & original objects of art lent for southeastern Ohio; artmobile for K-12 schools; book traveling exhibitions 1 per year

M **Seigfred Gallery,** 528 Seigfred Hall, School of Art Athens, OH 45701-2978. Tel 740-593-1994; Fax 740-593-0457; *Dir* Jenita Landrum-Bittle
Open Mon- Fri 10 AM - 4 PM; No admis fee; Gallery is used for faculty exhibitions, student exhibitions & vis artist shows
Exhibitions: Rotating exhibits by students & faculty

L **Fine Arts Library,** Alden Library, 30 Park Place Athens, OH 45701-2978. Tel 740-593-2663; Fax 740-593-0138; Elec Mail ginther@ohio.edu; Internet Home Page Address: library.ohio.edu/finearts/index.html; *Art Librn* Gary Ginther; *Sr Libr Assoc* Elizabeth Story
Open Mon - Thurs 8 AM - 12 AM, Fri 8 AM - 9 PM, Sat 10 AM - 9 PM, Sun Noon - 12 AM; Selective exhibition of student & faculty work
Income: Financed by state appropriation
Library Holdings: Book Volumes 75,000; CD-ROMs; DVDs; Exhibition Catalogs; Fiche; Periodical Subscriptions 300
Special Subjects: Photography
Collections: Research coll in history of photography; small coll of original photographs for study purposes; Yao Research Collection of Vietnamese cultural objects

BAY VILLAGE

A **BAY ARTS, INC.,** (Baycrafters, Inc.) 28795 Lake Rd, Huntington Metropark Bay Village, OH 44140-1364. Tel 440-871-6543; Fax 440-871-0452; Elec Mail info@bayarts.net; Internet Home Page Address: www.bayarts.net; *Dir* Nancy Heaton
Open Mon - Sat 12 - 5 PM; No admis fee; Estab 1948 for advancement & enjoyment of arts & crafts in the region; Average Annual Attendance: 30,000; Mem: 1800, dues individuals $25, family $40, students $10, bus people $50
Exhibitions: Christmas Show; Emerald Necklace Juried Art Show; Juried Art Show; Renaissance Fayre; student competition; individual gallery shows; floral juried art show; Victoria Garden Party; Heritage Days
Publications: Bulletins & competition notices
Activities: Classes for adults & children; lect open to public, 9-12 vis lectrs per year; gallery talks; tours; tea room for children's birthday parties; monetary prizes awarded; scholarships offered; sales shop sells original art, reproductions, prints, pottery & other crafts work from local & out-of-town artists

BEACHWOOD

M **THE TEMPLE-TIFERETH ISRAEL,** The Temple Museum of Religious Art, 26000 Shaker Blvd, Beachwood, OH 44122-7199. Tel 216-831-3233, ext 108; Elec Mail skoletsky@ttti.org; Internet Home Page Address: www.ttti.org; *Dir Mus* Susan Koletsky
Open daily 9 AM - 3 PM by appointment only; No admis fee; Estab 1950 for the display & teaching of Judaica; Two galleries, each housed in a national landmark temple; Average Annual Attendance: 10,000; Mem: 15,000; annual meeting
Special Subjects: Graphics, Watercolors, Archaeology, Ethnology, Textiles, Costumes, Religious Art, Pottery, Etchings & Engravings, Landscapes, Decorative Arts, Judaica, Manuscripts, Portraits, Glass, Silver, Metalwork, Historical Material, Maps, Embroidery, Stained Glass, Leather, Painting-Israeli
Collections: Antique Torah hangings; Holy Land pottery; Israel stamps; paintings; sculpture; stained glass; Torah ornaments
Exhibitions: 50 Years of Israel Stamps from the Miriam Leikind Collection & Albert Friedberg Collection
Activities: Classes for adults & children; lects open to pub, 12 vis lectrs per yr; gallery talks; tours; original objects of art lent to other professional institutions; mus shop sells Judaic ritual objects

L **Lee & Dolores Hartzmark Library,** 26000 Shaker Blvd, Beachwood, OH 44122. Tel 216-831-3233, ext 120; Fax 216-831-4216; Internet Home Page Address: www.ttti.org; *Dir & Librn* Andrea Davidson; *Asst Librn* Wendy Wasman
Two buildings
Library Holdings: Audio Tapes; Book Volumes 10,000; Cassettes; Exhibition Catalogs; Filmstrips; Framed Reproductions; Manuscripts; Memorabilia; Original Art Works; Other Holdings Audio Books; Computer Software; Pamphlets; Periodical Subscriptions 50; Photographs; Prints; Records; Reproductions; Sculpture; Video Tapes
Special Subjects: Art History, Folk Art, Calligraphy, Drawings, Painting-European, Historical Material, Judaica, Archaeology, Ethnology, Painting-Israeli, Bookplates & Bindings, Embroidery, Handicrafts, Religious Art, Architecture
Collections: Permanent collection of silver, manuscripts & fabrics of Judaica over the last 200 years; pottery from antiquity
Exhibitions: 50 years of Israel Stamps from the Miriam Leikind Collection & Albert Friedberg Collection
Publications: The Loom and the Cloth: an exhibition of the fabrics of Jewish life

BEREA

M **BALDWIN-WALLACE COLLEGE,** Fawick Art Gallery, 275 Eastland Rd, Berea, OH 44017-2088. Tel 440-826-2152; Fax 440-826-3380; Elec Mail info@bw.edu; Internet Home Page Address: www.bw.edu/academics/art/gallery; *Dir* Prof Paul Jacklitch
Open Mon - Fri 2 - 5 PM; No admis fee; The Art Gallery is considered to be a part of the art prog & the dept of art; its purpose is that of a teaching mus for the students of the col & the general public; Average Annual Attendance: 2,500

Income: Financed through budgetary support of the college
Special Subjects: Drawings, Painting-American, Prints, Sculpture
Collections: Approx 200 paintings and sculptures by Midwest artists of the 20th century; approx 1900 drawings and prints from 16th - 20th century, with a concentration in 19th & 20th century examples
Exhibitions: Annual Spring Student Show & Senior Exhibition
Activities: Lect open to public; gallery talks; tours; competitions; individual paintings lent to schools; book traveling exhibitions

BOWLING GREEN

M **BOWLING GREEN STATE UNIVERSITY,** Fine Arts Center Galleries, Fine Arts Bldg, Bowling Green, OH 43403-0211. Tel 419-372-8525; Fax 419-372-2544; Internet Home Page Address: www.digitalarts.bgsu.edu/art/galleries; *Dir Galleries* Jacqueline S Nathan
Open Tues - Sat 11 AM - 4 PM, Thurs 6PM-9PM, Sun 1 - 4 PM, cl holidays; No admis fee; Estab 1964 to contribute to the enrichment of the broader area community while supporting the acad mission of the university; 12-14 exhibits are produced each yr with goals of stimulating and educating artists & art audiences, communicating ideas, and promoting the vitality & significance of the arts; Three galleries located in the Fine Arts bldg have a combined total of approx 8000 sq ft of exhib space; Average Annual Attendance: 9,500
Income: Financed by the University, state grants & donations
Collections: Contemporary prints; Student work
Activities: Lects open to public, 6-8 lectrs per yr; book traveling exhibs; originate traveling exhibs

BROOKLYN

M **BROOKLYN HISTORICAL SOCIETY,** 4442 Ridge Rd, Brooklyn, OH 44144-0422; PO Box 44422, Brooklyn, OH 44144-0422. Tel 216-749-2804; Elec Mail groundhogsgarden@wowway.com; *VPres* Elaine Schmidt; *Trustee* John Geralds; *Pres* Barbara Stepic; *Treas* Thomas Hites; *Secy* Jeanne Hartman; *Trustee* Barbara Paulitzky; *Trustee* Carole Thomson
Open Tues 10 AM - 2 PM, tours by appointment; No admis fee; Estab 1970 to preserve history of area; Wheelchair accessible to 1st floor. Maintains reference library; Average Annual Attendance: 1,500; Mem: 150; dues life $100, couple $7, single $5; meetings last Wed of month, except Jan, Feb, July, Aug & Nov
Income: $10,000 (financed by fundraisers)
Purchases: New routed wooden sign
Library Holdings: Audio Tapes; Clipping Files; Maps; Memorabilia; Original Documents; Other Holdings; Pamphlets; Periodical Subscriptions; Photographs; Records
Special Subjects: Textiles, Dolls, Furniture, Glass, Historical Material, Maps, Period Rooms, Laces
Collections: China, dolls; pre-1900 & 1920's furniture; glass; herb garden; kitchenware; old tools; quilts & linens
Exhibitions: World War I & Brooklyn Airport; Early schools in Brooklyn
Publications: Early Schools in Brooklyn, 2003
Activities: Classes for children; docent training; quilting & rug loom weaving demonstrations; lect open to public, 4 vis lectrs per year; 3rd grade tours every May; sales shop sells handicrafts, rag rugs, quilted items, dried herb products, handmade crafts

CANTON

M **CANTON MUSEUM OF ART,** 1001 Market Ave N, Canton, OH 44702-1075. Tel 330-453-7666; Fax 330-453-1034; Elec Mail al@cantonart.org; Internet Home Page Address: www.cantonart.org; *Treas* Lee DeGraaf; *Exec Dir* Manuel J Albacete; *Bus, Admin & Mus Shop Mgr* Kay McAllister; *Pres* David Baker; *Coordr Educ* Lauren Kuntzman; *Cur Coll & Registrar* Lynnda Arrasmith; *Asst Cur & Mus Guild Coordr* Kathy Fleeher
Open Mon-Sat 10 AM-5 PM, Tues, Wed, and Thurs 7PM-9PM, Sun 1PM-5PM; Admis adults $4, seniors & students $2.50, mems & children under 10 free; Estab 1935, incorporated 1941; Nine modern gallery areas of various sizes; Average Annual Attendance: 50,000; Mem: 1200; dues $15 and higher; annual meeting Fall
Special Subjects: Ceramics, Graphics, Painting-American, Sculpture, Watercolors, Costumes, Decorative Arts, Portraits, Painting-Spanish, Painting-Italian
Collections: Collection focus is 19th & 20th century American watercolors and works on paper, also contemporary ceramics
Exhibitions: Approx 25-40 traveling or collected exhibs of commercial & industrial arts; painting; sculpture annually; French Music Hall Posters from 1890 to 1940's
Activities: Formally organized education progs for adults & children; docent training; lects open to pub, 10 vis lectrs per yr; films; gallery talks; art festivals; competitions with awards; guided tours; scholarships offered; individual and original objects of art lent; book traveling exhibs; originate traveling exhibs; mus shop sells books, original art, prints

L **Art Library,** 1001 Market Ave N, Canton, OH 44702. Tel 330-453-7666; Fax 330-453-1034; Elec Mail max@cantonart.org; Internet Home Page Address: www.cantonart.org; *Exec Dir* M J Albacete; *Mktg Dir* Max Barton; *Develop Dir* Christine Shearer; *Cur & Registrar* Lynnda Arrasmith
Open Tues & Wed 10 AM - 8 PM, Thurs & Fri 10 AM - 5 PM, Sat 10 AM - 3 PM, Sun 1 PM - 5 PM; Admis adults $6, seniors $4; Estab 1935; National Touring & CMA produced exhibs; Average Annual Attendance: 40,000; Mem: Go to: www.cantonart.org/membership
Income: Local, state & National Grant supported; pub & private donors
Library Holdings: Audio Tapes; Book Volumes 2500; Clipping Files; Exhibition Catalogs; Pamphlets; Periodical Subscriptions 25; Prints; Slides; Video Tapes 120
Special Subjects: Art History, Ceramics
Collections: CMA permanent collection: 19th, 20th & 21st century American Works on Paper; American ceramics
Exhibitions: (12/05/2013-03/02/2014) The Saint John's Bible; (09/02/2013-10/26/2014) Intent to Deceive: Fakes & Forgeries in the Art World; (05/01/2014-07/20/2014) 1950's - Present Wayland & Gregory Ceramics

Activities: Classes for adults & children; docent training; in-school & in-museum educ outreach; lects open to pub; gallery talks; tours; sponsor competitions; schols; mus shop sells books, original art, reproductions, jewelry & local art

CHILLICOTHE

M **PUMP HOUSE CENTER FOR THE ARTS,** PO Box 1613, Chillicothe, OH 45601-5613. Tel 740-772-5783; Fax 740-772-5783; Elec Mail info@pumphouseartgallery.com; Internet Home Page Address: www.pumphouseartgallery.com; *Dir* Charles Wallace
Open Tues - Fri 11 AM - 4 PM, Sat & Sun 1 - 4 PM, Cl. Mon; No admis fee; Estab 1986; Historic Pump House restored for art center, gift shop & gallery. Arts Festival held the last weekend in June; Average Annual Attendance: 20,000; Mem: 350; dues 15-375
Income: $110,000 (financed by mem, sales of artwork & Rio Grande Univ Partnership)
Library Holdings: Book Volumes; Periodical Subscriptions
Special Subjects: Painting-American, Photography, Prints, Sculpture, Watercolors, American Indian Art, Pottery, Woodcarvings, Woodcuts, Afro-American Art, Portraits, Posters, Porcelain, Silver, Painting-Dutch, Scrimshaw, Stained Glass, Pewter, Reproductions
Collections: Baskets, fine art, fine designer crafts, glass, prints, quilts, woodcarving, woodworking; All media
Activities: Classes for adults & children; dramatic progs; docent training; lects open to pub, 4 vis lectrs per yr; gallery talks; tours; competitions

CINCINNATI

A **CINCINNATI ART CLUB,** 1021 Parkside Pl, Cincinnati, OH 45202-1550. Tel 513-241-4591; Elec Mail info@cincinnatiartclub.com; Internet Home Page Address: www.cincinnatiartclub.com; *Pres* Tom Bluemlein; *Vice Pres* George Hageman; *Secy* Clark Stevens; *Treas* Donnita Geary; *Historian* Dave Klocke; *Cur* Roger Heuck
See website for show schedule; No admis fee; Estab 1890, incorporated 1923 for purpose of advancing love & knowledge of fine art; Gallery contains a small collection of paintings by American artists; modern building 100 ft x 50 ft; Average Annual Attendance: 3,500; Mem: 340; open to all who show interest & appreciation of art; signature members must be judged by proficiency of works; dues signature $120, assoc $105
Income: Financed by dues, rental of gallery, sales commissions, bequests
Library Holdings: Compact Disks; Exhibition Catalogs; Original Art Works
Collections: Small collection of works by former members; Henry Farney; Frank Duveneck; John Rettig; Herman Wessel; Bessie Wessel
Exhibitions: Exhibition of members' work changed monthly. Annual Club Shows Sept, Feb, Spring (March-Apr) & Christmas Art Bazaar; juried annual national competition in Nov
Publications: Dragonfly Members Newsletter, monthly
Activities: Classes for adults; weekend workshops, monthly; lects open for mems only, 8 vis lectrs demonstrations per year; competitions with awards; schols offered to Cincinnati Art Academy

M **CINCINNATI ART MUSEUM,** Cincinnati Art Museum, 953 Eden Park Dr, Cincinnati, OH 45202-1596. Tel 513-639-2995; Fax 513-721-0129; Elec Mail information@cincyart.org; Internet Home Page Address: www.cincinnatiartmuseum.org; *Dir* Aaron Betsky; *Dir Develop* David Linnenberg; *Deputy Dir Opers* Debbie Bowman; *Chief Cur & Cur Photography* James Crump; *Cur Ed* Emily Holtrup; *Cur Prints & Drawings* Kristin L Spangenberg; *Cur Classical, Near Eastern Art* Glenn E Markoe; *Cur Am Painting & Sculpture* Julie Aronson; *Dir Mktg* Scott Hisey; *Head Exhibits & Reg* Matthew Leininger; *Cur European Painting & Sculpture* Benedict Leca; *Deputy Dir Cur Affairs* Anita Ellis; *Head Library & Archives* Galina Lewandowicz; *Cur Asian Art* Hou-mei Sung; *Assoc Cur Contemporary* Jessica Flores; *Assoc Cur Decorative Arts* Amy Dehan; *Cur Fashion & Textile* Cynthia Amneus
Open Tues - Sun 11AM - 5 PM, cl Mon, Thanksgiving, Christmas, New Year's Day, Martin Luther King Jr Day, Presidents Day, Memorial Day, Fourth of July & Labor Day; No admis fee; Estab 1881 to collect, exhibit, conserve & interpret works of art from all periods & civilizations (range of 5000 years of major cultures of the world); Circ 12,000; Exhibition galleries cover an area of approx 4 acres, occupying three floors, assembly areas & social center on ground level; altogether some 80 galleries given over to permanent collections, with additional galleries set aside for temporary exhibitions; Average Annual Attendance: 300,000; Mem: 6,293; dues $1,500 founder - $35 student
Income: $11,374,000 (financed by endowment, mem, city appropriation, private donations, admis & Cincinnati Fine Arts Fund, mus shop earnings, federal, state, city & private grants)
Library Holdings: Auction Catalogs; Book Volumes; Cards; Clipping Files; DVDs; Exhibition Catalogs; Fiche; Framed Reproductions; Manuscripts; Maps; Memorabilia; Micro Print; Original Documents; Pamphlets; Periodical Subscriptions; Photographs; Prints; Video Tapes
Special Subjects: Decorative Arts, Ceramics, Silver, Textiles, Prints, Sculpture, Watercolors, American Indian Art, Bronzes, African Art, Pre-Columbian Art, Southwestern Art, Costumes, Religious Art, Woodcarvings, Woodcuts, Landscapes, Oriental Art, Asian Art, Antiquities-Byzantine, Painting-French, Carpets & Rugs, Coins & Medals, Baroque Art, Calligraphy, Miniatures, Painting-Flemish, Renaissance Art, Medieval Art, Antiquities-Oriental, Painting-Spanish, Painting-Italian, Antiquities-Persian, Islamic Art, Antiquities-Egyptian, Antiquities-Greek, Antiquities-Roman, Painting-German, Antiquities-Etruscan, Antiquities-Assyrian
Collections: Artists; art in Cincinnati; Egyptian, Greek, Roman, Near and Far Eastern arts; musical instruments; paintings (European & American); world costumes, textiles; arts of Africa & the Americas; world prints, drawings & photographs; world sculpture; world decorative arts & period rooms; portrait miniatures; Cincinnati wing; contemporary
Publications: Catalogues for exhibitions & collections

Activities: Classes for adults & children; dramatic progs; docent training; lects open to pub & mem only, 4-8 vis lectrs per yr; gallery talks; tours; concerts; Cincinnati Art Award; artmobile; book traveling exhibs 4-6 per yr; originate traveling exhibs to other mus, 2 per yr; mus shop sells books, magazines, reproductions, prints, slides, original art & .JPGs

L **Mary R Schiff Library & Archives,** 953 Eden Park Dr, Cincinnati, OH 45202-1596. Tel 513-639-2978; Fax 513-721-0129; Elec Mail library@cincyart.org; Internet Home Page Address: www.cincinnatiartmuseum.org; *Head Librn* Galina Lewandowicz; *Libr Archives Tech* Jennifer Pettigrew; *Asst Librn* Jennifer Hardin
Open Tues - Fri 11 AM - 5 PM; 2nd Sat (Sep - June); No admis fee; Estab in 1881 to satisfy research needs of museums staff, art academy faculty & students; Circ 5,200; 5,000 vols per yr; Reference library
Income: Financed by endowment
Library Holdings: Auction Catalogs 20,000; Book Volumes 85,000; Clipping Files; Exhibition Catalogs; Fiche; Manuscripts; Memorabilia; Original Documents; Other Holdings; Pamphlets; Periodical Subscriptions 150; Photographs; Prints; Reproductions; Video Tapes 600
Special Subjects: Art History, Folk Art, Decorative Arts, Commercial Art, Drawings, History of Art & Archaeology, American Western Art, American Indian Art, Furniture, Costume Design & Constr, Afro-American Art, Oriental Art, Antiquities-Assyrian, Architecture
Collections: Files on Cincinnati Artists, Art in Cincinnati; Archives of the Cincinnati Art Museum & the Art Academy of Cincinnati; Reference collection covering 6000 yrs of art & art history; rare books

A **CINCINNATI INSTITUTE OF FINE ARTS,** 20 E Central Pkwy, Cincinnati, OH 45202-7239. Tel 513-871-2787; Fax 513-871-2706; Elec Mail info@fineartsfund.org; Internet Home Page Address: www.fineartsfund.org; *Chmn Bd & Pres* Raymond R Clark; *VChmn* Dudley S Taft; *Exec Dir* Mary McCullough-Hudson
Open Mon - Fri 8 AM - 5 PM, cl Sat & Sun; Estab & incorporated in 1927 to provide for the continuance & growth of educ & culture in the various fields of fine arts in the metropolitan community of Cincinnati; Mem: Annual meeting Oct
Income: Financed through endowments by Cincinnati Symphony Orchestra, Cincinnati Art Museum, Cincinnati Opera, Taft Museum, May Festival, Cincinnati Ballet, Contemporary Arts Center, Playhouse in the Park, Special Projects Pool & Annual Community Wide fine Arts Fund Drive
Publications: Quarterly calendar

M **COLLEGE OF MOUNT SAINT JOSEPH,** Studio San Giuseppe, 5701 Delhi Rd, Art Dept Cincinnati, OH 45233-1669. Tel 513-244-4314; Fax 513-244-4222; Elec Mail jerry-bellas@mail.msj.edu; Internet Home Page Address: www.msj.edu; *Dir* Gerald Bellas
Open Mon - Fri 10 AM - 5 PM, Sat & Sun 1:30 - 4:30 PM, cl holidays; No admis fee; Estab 1962 to exhibit a variety of art forms by professional artists, faculty & students; Average Annual Attendance: 5,000
Activities: Lect open to public; concerts; gallery talks; tours

L **Archbishop Alter Library,** 5701 Delhi Rd, Cincinnati, OH 45233-1670. Tel 513-244-4216; Tel 513-244-4307; Fax 513-244-4355; Elec Mail library@mail.msj.edu; Internet Home Page Address: www.inside.msj.edu/departments/library; *Dir* Paul Jenkins; *Head Pub Svcs* Susan M Falgner
Open acad yr Mon - Thurs 8 AM - 10:30 PM, Fri 8 AM - 7 PM, Sat 10:30 AM - 5:30 PM, Sun Noon - 10:30 PM; Estab 1920 to serve students of art department; Circ 1,200
Library Holdings: Audio Tapes; Book Volumes 97,863; Cassettes; Compact Disks; DVDs; Exhibition Catalogs; Filmstrips; Periodical Subscriptions 706; Prints; Slides; Video Tapes
Collections: Salv Dali Prints
Exhibitions: Student art exhibit
Activities: Competition with award

M **CONTEMPORARY ARTS CENTER,** 44 E Sixth St, Cincinnati, OH 45202-2518. Tel 513-345-8400; Fax 513-721-7418; Elec Mail rplatow@contemporaryartscenter.org; Internet Home Page Address: www.contemporary arts center.org; *Dir & Chief Cur* Raphaela Platow; *Chief Preparator* Joel Armor; *Acting Develop Dir* Susan Berliant; *Exhib Dir* Carissa Barnard; *Develop Officer Grant Funding* Michelle Devine; *Exhib Coordr* David Dillon; *Finance Dir* Jane Fisher; *Facility Dir* Dave Gearding; *Pub Progs Mgr* Janelle Hopper; *Asst Cur Educ* Antwan Jones; *Visitor Svcs Team Leader* Lindsey Jones; *IT Mgr* Mark Kamphuis; *Asst Cur* Justin Ludwig; *Dir Commun & Community Engagement* Molly O'Toole; *Cur Educ* Jaime Thompson
Open Mon 10 AM - 9 PM, Wed - Fri 10 AM - 6 PM, Sat & Sun 11 AM - 6 PM, cl Tues, Thanksgiving, Christmas & New Year's Day; Admis adults $7.50, seniors $6.50, students w/ID $5.50, children ages 3-13 $4.50, mems & children under 3 free, Mon 5 PM - 9 PM free; Estab 1939. The Center is a mus for the presentation of current developments in the visual & related arts. It does not maintain a permanent collection but offers changing exhibitions of international, national & regional focus; Average Annual Attendance: 150,000; Mem: 2200; dues from $45-$5000
Income: $2,595,000 (financed by endowment, fine arts fund drive, city state art council & federal groups, corporate sponsorship)
Exhibitions: Selections from Cincinnati: The Shore Coll
Publications: Catalogues of exhibitions, 1-2 per year
Activities: Classes for adults & children; docent training; performance progrs; family progs; lects open to pub & mems only, 8-10 vis lectrs per yr; concerts; gallery talks; progs for adults & children; tours; book traveling exhibs 2-5 per yr; originates traveling exhibs; mus shop sells books, cards, reproductions & prints

L **Library,** 44 E 6th St, Cincinnati, OH 45202-2518. Tel 513-345-8400 (admin office); Fax 513-721-7418

M **HEBREW UNION COLLEGE - JEWISH INSTITUTE OF RELIGION,** Skirball Museum Cincinnati, 3101 Clifton Ave, Cincinnati, OH 45220-2488. Tel 513-487-3053; Fax 513-221-0316; Elec Mail hucinu@gmail.com; Internet Home Page Address: www.huc.edu; *Coordr Outreach Educ* Jen Ladu
Open to groups of 5+ for tours Mon - Thurs 8:30 AM - 3:30 PM, by appointment; No admis fee, donations welcome; Estab 1913 to interpret Judaism to the gel pub

through Jewish art & artifacts; also the archaeological work of the col in Israel; 2,450 sq ft of exhibition space; traveling exhibition gallery; Average Annual Attendance: 5,000; Mem: 300; dues $35-$500
Income: Financed by endowment, donations & grants
Special Subjects: Archaeology, Folk Art, Furniture, Photography, Painting-American, Prints, Textiles, Bronzes, Woodcuts, Drawings, Painting-American, Archaeology, Textiles, Religious Art, Folk Art, Judaica, Manuscripts, Carpets & Rugs, Historical Material, Calligraphy, Antiquities-Egyptian, Antiquities-Roman, Stained Glass, Painting-Israeli
Collections: Jewish ceremonial art; archaeology artifacts; paintings, drawings & sculpture by Jewish artists; photography; textiles
Exhibitions: An Eternal People: The Jewish Experience (permanent)
Activities: Docent training; lect open to public, tours

M **HILLEL FOUNDATION,** Hillel Jewish Student Center Gallery, 2615 Clifton Ave, Cincinnati, OH 45220-2822. Tel 513-221-6728; Fax 513-221-7134; Elec Mail email@hillelcincinnati.org; Internet Home Page Address: hillelcincinnati.org; *Rabbi Emeritus* Rabbi Abie Ingber; *Interim Exec Dir* Lizzy Harold; *Program Dir* Heather Zucker; *Outreach Coordr* Bobby Covitz; *Cur* Sandy Spinner
Open Mon - Thurs 9 AM - 5 PM, Fri 9 AM - 3 PM; No admis fee; Estab 1982 to promote Jewish artists & educate students; Jewish artists in various media (exhibit & sale) & collection of antique Judaica from around the world. Listed in AAA guide
Income: Financed by contributions, fundraisers, & The Jewish Federation of Cincinnati
Special Subjects: Architecture, Judaica
Collections: Antique architectural Judaica from synagogues throughout the US; Art in various media by living Jewish artists

L **PUBLIC LIBRARY OF CINCINNATI & HAMILTON COUNTY,** Info & Reference Dept, 800 Vine St, Cincinnati, OH 45202-2009. Tel 513-369-6955; Tel 513-369-6900; Fax 513-665-3388; Elec Mail information.and.reference@cincinnatilibrary.org; Elec Mail ereference@cincinnatilibrary.org; Internet Home Page Address: www.cincinnatilibrary.org; *Dir* Kimber L Fender; *Art & Music Dept* Judy Inwood; *Head Info & Reference* Angela Farmar
Open Thurs, Fri & Sat 9 AM - 6 PM, Sun 1 - 5 PM; Estab 1872 to provide the community with both scholarly & recreational materials in area of fine arts; Circ 112,400; Display cases in the department to exhibit collections
Income: $85,000 (financed by taxes, state & county appropriations)
Library Holdings: Audio Tapes; Book Volumes 207,337; Cards; Cassettes; Clipping Files 825,560; Exhibition Catalogs 6,440; Fiche 9375; Filmstrips; Lantern Slides; Memorabilia; Micro Print; Motion Pictures; Original Art Works; Other Holdings Vertical file; Pamphlets; Periodical Subscriptions 60; Photographs; Prints 5,340; Records; Reels 505; Reproductions; Slides; Video Tapes
Special Subjects: Art History, Folk Art, Landscape Architecture, Mixed Media, Photography, Calligraphy, Drawings, Painting-American, Pre-Columbian Art, History of Art & Archaeology, Archaeology, American Western Art, Advertising Design, American Indian Art, Mexican Art, Southwestern Art, Aesthetics, Afro-American Art, Religious Art, Antiquities-Assyrian
Collections: Langstroth Collection of Chromolithographs of the 19th Century; Plaut Collection, 20th century artist's books, slides, audio tapes & DVDs; Valerio Collection of Italian art; Film & recording center coll of videos, slides & audio tapes; Contemporary Artists' Book Coll
Activities: Tours; sales shop sells books, reproductions, prints, tote bags, toys & stationery items

M **TAFT MUSEUM OF ART,** 316 Pike St, Cincinnati, OH 45202-4293. Tel 513-241-0343; Fax 513-241-7762; Elec Mail taftmuseum@taftmuseum.org; Internet Home Page Address: www.taftmuseum.org; *Dir* Deborah Emont Scott; *Chief Cur* Lynne Ambrosini, PhD; *Cur Educ* Nancy Huth; *Chmn Bd Overseers* Paul W Chellgren; *Finance Dir* Patricia Hassel, CPA; *Dir Institutional Advancement* Natalie Mathis; *Asst Cur* Tamera Muente
Open Wed -Fri 11 AM - 4 PM, Sat & Sun 11 AM - 5 PM, cl New Year's Day, Thanksgiving & Christmas; Admis adults $10, seniors & students $8, children 18 or younger free; Estab 1927, a gift of Mr and Mrs Charles P Taft's art collection to the Cincinnati Institute of Fine Arts including the house and an endowment fund for maintenance. Active control was taken in 1931; museum opened in 1932; Built in 1820, a National Historic Landmark. The federal period building is home to nearly 730 works of art, including European & American paintings by masters such as Rembrandt, Sargent, Turner, Hals & Whistler; Chinese Porcelains; and European Decorative Arts. Taft Museum reopened in May 2004 after a 2.5 yr renovation and expansion. Renovated museum houses new amenities including parking garage, spec exhib gallery, performance & lecture facility, cafe, expanded museum shop, redesigned garden; Average Annual Attendance: 60,000; Mem: dues $45-$1000
Income: Financed by endowment & annual fine arts fund drive
Library Holdings: Book Volumes; Exhibition Catalogs; Original Documents; Photographs; Prints; Slides
Special Subjects: Architecture, Drawings, Painting-American, Religious Art, Ceramics, Afro-American Art, Decorative Arts, Painting-European, Portraits, Furniture, Jade, Jewelry, Porcelain, Oriental Art, Asian Art, Painting-British, Painting-Dutch, Painting-French, Ivory, Miniatures, Painting-Flemish, Renaissance Art, Medieval Art, Painting-Spanish, Gold, Enamels
Collections: Furnishings include antique toiles, satins & a notable coll of Duncan Phyfe furniture; paintings including works by Rembrandt, Hals, Turner, Corot, Gainsborough, Raeburn; Whistler & other Old Masters; 200 notable Chinese Porcelains Kangxi, Yongzheng & Qianlong; 97 French Renaissance enamels; Renaissance jewelry & 16th-18th century watches from Europe
Exhibitions: three to four exhibitions scheduled per year
Publications: The Portico, quarterly
Activities: Educ prog; classes for adults & children; dramatic progs; docent training; lects open to pub, 10-15 vis lectrs per yr; chamber music; concerts; gallery talks; tours; individual paintings & objects of art lent to accredited mus; lending collection contains paintings, sculptures, Chinese ceramics, European decorative arts; book traveling exhibs 2-3 per yr; originate traveling exhibs to accredited mus; mus shop sells books, reproductions, prints, slides, gifts, jewelry, porcelains & art kits

M **UNIVERSITY OF CINCINNATI,** DAAP Galleries-College of Design Architecture, Art & Planning, 5470 Aronoff Bldg, Cincinnati, OH 45221; PO Box 210016, Cincinnati, OH 45221-0016. Tel 513-556-2839; Fax 513-556-3288; Elec Mail daapgalleries@uc.edu; Internet Home Page Address: www.uc.edu/galleries; *Dir* Aaron J Cowan
Open Sun - Thurs 10 AM - 5 PM; No admis fee; Estab 1967 to preserve & maintain the University's art collection & to present quality contemporary & historical exhibitions of works by artists of local, regional & national reputation. Operates three exhibition facilities: Reed Gallery, Meyers Gallery; Gallery is maintained & presents quality contemporary & historical exhibitions of works by artists of local, regional & national reputation; Average Annual Attendance: 10,000
Income: Financed through university, grants & co-sponsorships
Special Subjects: Drawings, Etchings & Engravings, Landscapes, Photography, Portraits, Pre-Columbian Art, Painting-American, Prints, Bronzes, Sculpture, Graphics, Watercolors, Posters, Asian Art, Antiquities-Greek, Painting-German, Painting-Russian, Painting-Scandinavian
Collections: Art of the United States, Europe, Asia & the Americas; Julius Fleischman Collection
Publications: Fragments, catalogue
Activities: Lects open to public; performances; film & dance; gallery talks; tours; originate small traveling exhibs

L **Robert A. Deshon and Karl J. Schlachter Library for Design, Architecture, Art, and Planning,** 5480 Aronoff Center for Design and Art, Cincinnati, OH 45221-0033. Tel 513-556-1335; Fax 513-556-3006; Elec Mail jennifer.pollock@uc.edu; Internet Home Page Address: www.libraries.uc.edu/libraries/daap; *Visual Resources Librn* Elizabeth Meyer; *Circ & Student Supvr* Sara Mihaly
Open Mon - Thurs 8 AM - 10 PM, Fri 8 AM - 5 PM, Sat 1 - 5 PM, Sun 1 - 10 PM, summer hours vary; No admis fee; Estab 1925 to support the programs of the College of Design, Architecture, Art & Planning; Circ 42,000; Rotating exhibits; Average Annual Attendance: 78,000
Library Holdings: Book Volumes 90,000; DVDs; Exhibition Catalogs; Fiche; Filmstrips; Kodachrome Transparencies; Manuscripts; Memorabilia; Motion Pictures; Original Art Works Artist's Books; Pamphlets; Periodical Subscriptions 400; Photographs; Reels 1000; Slides; Video Tapes
Special Subjects: Art History, Graphic Design, Industrial Design, Interior Design, Art Education, Architecture
Collections: architecture, art educ, art history, fashion arts, graphic design, design (interior, landscape), urban planning, industrial
Activities: Classes for adults; docent training; lects open to pub; tours; sponsoring of competitions

L **Visual Resource Center,** PO Box 0016, Aronoff Design & Art, 5480 Cincinnati, OH 45221-0016. Tel 513-556-0279; Fax 513-556-3006; Internet Home Page Address: www.libraries.uc.edu; *Vis Reference Librn* Elizabeth Meyer
Open Mon - Thurs 8 AM - 10 PM, Fri 8 AM - 5 PM, Sat 1 - 5 PM, Sun 1 - 10 PM; Library contains 210,000 slides
Library Holdings: Memorabilia; Slides
Special Subjects: Drafting, Architecture

M **XAVIER UNIVERSITY,** Art Gallery, 1658 Herald Ave, Cincinnati, OH 45207-7311; 3800 Victory Pkwy, Cincinnati, OH 45207. Tel 513-745-3811; Fax 513-745-1098; Elec Mail uetz@xavier.edu; Internet Home Page Address: www.xavier.edu/art; *Dir* M Katherine Uetz; *Publicist* Terri Yontz
Open Mon - Fri 10 AM - 4 PM; No admis fee; Estab 1987 as acad facility for students, faculty & community; Spacious galleries with white walls & hardwood floors; main gallery 21 x 50 ft, adjacent gallery 20 x 20 ft
Income: Privately financed
Special Subjects: Drawings, Graphics, Anthropology, Ceramics, Crafts, Etchings & Engravings, Embroidery
Exhibitions: Professional artists; qualified students of Xavier University; temporary exhibitions only
Activities: Classes for adults; lect open to public, 4-6 vis lectrs per year; gallery talks; give awards; scholarships offered

CLEVELAND

L **CLEVELAND BOTANICAL GARDEN,** Eleanor Squire Library, 11030 East Blvd, Cleveland, OH 44106-1706. Tel 216-721-1600; Fax 216-721-2056; Elec Mail info@cbgarden.org; Internet Home Page Address: www.cbgarden.org; *Mus Shop Mgr* Kate Fox; *Exec Dir* Natalie Ronayne; *Dir Develop* Sara Stone; *Dir Educ* Geri Unger; *Librn* Gary Esmonde; *CFO* Kenneth Sinchak
Open Mem Day - Labor Day: Tues -Sat 10 AM - 5 PM, Sun Noon - 5PM, Wed until 9 PM; Admis adult $8.50; Estab 1930; Circulation to members only
Income: Financed by endowment
Library Holdings: Audio Tapes; Book Volumes 16,000; Cassettes; Clipping Files; DVDs; Exhibition Catalogs; Original Art Works; Pamphlets; Periodical Subscriptions 120; Photographs; Prints; Sculpture; Slides
Special Subjects: Landscape Architecture, Landscapes
Collections: Rare book coll: 2,000 vols
Publications: The Bulletin, monthly
Activities: Educ prog; classes for adults & children; docent training; lects open to pu, 1 - 3 vis lectrs per yr; mus shop sells books

M **CLEVELAND INSTITUTE OF ART,** Reinberger Galleries, 11141 East Blvd, University Circle Cleveland, OH 44106-1710. Tel 216-421-7407; Fax 216-754-3631; Elec Mail reinbergergallery@cia.edu; Internet Home Page Address: www.cia.edu; *Pres* Grafton Nunes; *Gallery Dir* Bruce Checefsky
Open Tues-Sat 10 AM - 5 PM, Fri 10 AM - 9 PM, Sun 10 AM - 5 PM; No admis fee; Estab 1882 as a 4 yr, fully accredited professional col of art; Gallery is maintained with extensive exhibitions
Income: Financed by federal, state, local grants & private foundations
Publications: Link (alumni magazine), quarterly; posters to accompany each exhibit
Activities: Classes for adults & children; lects open to pub, 5-10 vis lectrs per yr; gallery talks; tours; book traveling exhibs; originate traveling exhibs

L **Jessica Gund Memorial Library,** 11141 East Blvd, Cleveland, OH 44106-1710. Tel 216-421-7440; Fax 216-421-7439; Elec Mail referencehelp@gate.cia.edu; Internet Home Page Address: www.cia.edu; *Technical Svcs Librn* Dana Bjorklund; *Image & Instruc Srvcs Librn* Laura Ponikvar; *Library Dir* Cristine Rom; *Patron Svcs Librn* Beth Owens
Acad Term: open Mon - Thurs 8 AM - 9 PM, Fri 8 AM - 5 PM, Sat & Sun noon - 6 PM, Otherwise: Mon - Fri 10 AM - 4 PM; Estab to select, house & distribute library material in all media that will support the Institute's studio & acad areas of instruction; Circ 20,000; Average Annual Attendance: 30,000
Income: Financed by tuition, gift, endowments
Library Holdings: Book Volumes 47,000; CD-ROMs; Clipping Files; Compact Disks; DVDs; Exhibition Catalogs; Fiche; Memorabilia; Micro Print; Original Art Works; Original Documents; Other Holdings Artists' books 1,500; Periodical Subscriptions 130; Video Tapes
Special Subjects: Intermedia, Decorative Arts, Illustration, Mixed Media, Photography, Commercial Art, Drawings, Graphic Arts, Graphic Design, Sculpture, Ceramics, Conceptual Art, Crafts, Printmaking, Advertising Design, Industrial Design, Interior Design, Video, Glass, Metalwork, Enamels, Goldsmithing, Jewelry, Silversmithing, Textiles
Activities: Library tours & library instruction

A **Cleveland Art Association,** 11141 East Blvd, Develop Office-University Circle Cleveland, OH 44106-1710. Tel 216-421-7359; Fax 216-421-7438; Elec Mail clevelandartassociatiion@gmail.com; Internet Home Page Address: www.clevelandartassociation.org; *Pres* Janer Danforth Belson
Open during gallery hours-varies; Estab & inc 1916, re-incorporated 1950 as a non-profit organization, to unite artists & art lovers of Cleveland into a working body whose purpose it shall be to advance, in the broadest possible way, the art interest of the city; Gallery utilizes space periodically at Reinberger Gallery; Mem: 200; dues $100, active mem
Income: $30,000 (financed through endowment, sales & dues)
Purchases: $12,000
Collections: Collection of art by Cleveland artists which includes ceramics, drawings, glass, paintings, prints & small sculpture
Exhibitions: Lending collection exhibited annually; art auction
Activities: Competitions; awards; scholarships offered; works of art lent to members for one yr period

M **THE CLEVELAND MUSEUM OF ART,** 11150 East Blvd, Cleveland, OH 44106-1796. Tel 216-421-7340; Tel 877-262-4748; Fax 216-421-0411; Elec Mail info@clevelandart.org; Internet Home Page Address: www.clevelandart.org; *Dir, Pres & CEO* Dr David Franklin; *Chmn of Brd* R Steven Kestner; *Deputy Dir & Chief Advancement Officer* August A Napoli Jr; *Dir Information Management & Tech Servs* Jane Alexander; *Treas & Controller* Edward W Bauer; *Chief Conservator* Per Knutas; *Dir Educ & Interpretation* Dr Caroline Goeser; *Dir Protection Servs* Jaime Juarez; *Dir Facilities* Paul Krenisky; *Dir Library & Archives* Elizabeth Lantz; *Dir Human Resources* Sharon C Reaves; *Cur Performing Arts, Music & Film* Massound Saidpour; *Dir Exhibs & Publs* Heidi Strean; *Dir Design & Architecture* Jeffrey Strean; *Dir Auxiliary Serv* Catherine Surratt; *Dir Colls Management* Mary Suzor; *Cur Greek & Roman Art* Dr Michael Bennett; *Cur Chinese Art* Dr Anita Chung; *Cur American Painting & Sculpture* Dr Mark Cole; *Cur Medieval Art* Stephen Fliegel; *Cur Prints* Dr Jane Glaubinger; *Cur Decorative Art & Design* Stephen Harrison; *Cur Drawings* Dr Heather Lemonedes; *Cur Textiles & Islamic Art* Louise Mackie; *Cur African Art* Dr Constantine Petridis; *Cur Indian & Southeast Asian Art Dir* Sonya Rhie Quintanilla; *Cur Modern European Art* Dr William Robinson; *Cur Euorpean Painting & Sculpture* Dr Jon Seydl; *Cur Photog* Dr Barbara Tannenbaum; *Cur Contemporary Art* Reto Thuring
Open Tues, Thurs, Sat & Sun 10 AM - 5 PM, Wed & Fri 10 AM - 9 PM, cl Mon; No admis fee; Estab & incorporated 1913; building opened 1916; Circ 12,803; Educ Wing in 1971; East Wing addition 2009; West & North addition 2013; Average Annual Attendance: 300,000; Mem: 19,842; dues $55 & up
Income: $38,000,000 (financed by trust & endowment income, earned revenue, mem, gifts, grants, retail, parking & cafe)
Purchases: $7,500,000
Library Holdings: Auction Catalogs; Book Volumes; CD-ROMs; Clipping Files; Compact Disks; DVDs; Exhibition Catalogs; Fiche; Lantern Slides; Manuscripts; Maps; Memorabilia; Original Documents; Pamphlets; Periodical Subscriptions; Photographs; Prints; Reproductions; Slides; Video Tapes
Special Subjects: Painting-American, Sculpture, Textiles, Ceramics, Decorative Arts, Painting-European, Painting-Japanese, Oriental Art, Antiquities-Egyptian, Antiquities-Greek, Antiquities-Roman
Collections: Ancient Near Eastern, Egyptian, Greek, & Roman art; drawings & prints; European & American paintings, sculpture & decorative arts of all periods, with notable colls of medieval art, 18th-century French decorative arts & 17th-century European painting & 19th-century European & American painting; Islamic art; North American Indian, African & Oceanic art; Oriental art, including important colls of Chinese & Japanese painting & ceramics & Indian sculpture; photographs; Pre-Columbian American art; textiles, especially from Egypt & medieval Persia
Exhibitions: (09/29/2013-01/05/2014) Sicily: Art and Invention Between Greece and Rome; (09/30/2013-01/05/2014) Focus: Apollo; (10/27/2013-02/09/2014) Fragments of the Invisible: Delenne Collection of Congo Sculpture
Publications: Members magazine, 6 per yr; collection catalogs; exhibition catalogs
Activities: Classes for adults, students & children, studio workshops; teacher resource center; disability access dramatic progs; docent training; lects open to pub, lects for mems; 14 vis lectrs per yr; concerts; gallery talks; tours; originate traveling exhibs; mus shop sells books, reproductions, prints & slides

L **Ingalls Library,** 11150 East Blvd, Cleveland, OH 44106-1797. Tel 216-707-2530; Fax 216-421-0921; Elec Mail circulation@clevelandart.org; Internet Home Page Address: library.clevelandart.org; *Dir Libr & Archives* Elizabeth A Lantz; *Senior Librn* Louis Adrean; *Reference Librn* Chris Edmonson; *Assoc Librn Technical Servs* Carissa Hernandez; *Head Cataloger* Margaret Castellani; *Access Servs Librn* Matthew Gengler; *Systems Librn* Will Hannah; *Serials Librn* Jane Kirkland; *Archivist & Records Mgr* Leslie Cade; *Electronic Records Archivist* Susan Miller
Open Tues - Fri 10 AM - 5 PM, Wed 10 AM - 7:30 PM; Estab 1916; Circ 12,803; Open to mus members, vis graduate students, faculty, cur, pub; Average Annual Attendance: 6,209

Library Holdings: Auction Catalogs 93,000; Book Volumes 468,000; CD-ROMs; Clipping Files 18,000; Compact Disks; DVDs; Exhibition Catalogs; Fiche; Lantern Slides; Original Documents Digital Images, 285,000; Other Holdings; Pamphlets; Periodical Subscriptions 1300; Photographs 388,000; Prints; Reels; Video Tapes 400
Special Subjects: Art History, Decorative Arts, Mixed Media, Etchings & Engravings, Islamic Art, Painting-American, Painting-British, Painting-Dutch, Painting-Flemish, Painting-French, Painting-German, Painting-Italian, Painting-Japanese, Painting-Spanish, Pre-Columbian Art, Sculpture, Painting-European, History of Art & Archaeology, Watercolors, American Western Art, Printmaking, Asian Art, American Indian Art, Porcelain, Ivory, Jade, Afro-American Art, Metalwork, Antiquities-Oriental, Antiquities-Persian, Jewelry, Miniatures, Oriental Art, Religious Art, Restoration & Conservation, Silver, Silversmithing, Textiles, Woodcuts, Antiquities-Egyptian, Antiquities-Greek, Antiquities-Roman, Pewter, Laces, Portraits, Pottery, Tapestries, Woodcarvings
Activities: Classes for adults & children; docent training; lects open to pub

A **Print Club of Cleveland,** 11150 East Blvd, Cleveland, OH 44106-1797. Tel 216-707-2579; Elec Mail printclub@clevelandart.org; info@printclubcleveland.org; Internet Home Page Address: www.printclubcleveland.org; *Cur Prints & Mem* Dr Jane Glaubinger
Estab 1919 to stimulate interest in prints & drawings through educ, collecting & commissioning of new works & enhancement of the museum's collection by gifts & purchases; Mem: 250; dues $200 & up; annual meeting in Jan
Income: Financed by endowment, dues, sells prints from club inventory & sponsors annual fine print fair
Publications: The Print Club of Cleveland 1969-1994, Available at Museum Sales Desk, $19.94 plus postage
Activities: Lects open to pub & members, 1 vis lectr per yr; gallery talks; tours; awards; Ralph E King Award

L **CLEVELAND PUBLIC LIBRARY,** Fine Arts & Special Collections Dept, 325 Superior Ave NE, Fl 3 Cleveland, OH 44114-1271. Tel 216-623-2800; 623-2848; Fax 216-623-7015; Elec Mail information@cpl.org; Internet Home Page Address: www.cpl.org; *Head Spec Colls* Stephen Zietz; *Head Main Library* Joan Clark; *Interim Dir* Holly Carroll; *Library Admin* Cindy Lombardo; *Mgr* Pamela J Eyerdam
Open Mon - Sat 10 AM - 6 PM, cl Sun; No admis fee; Estab 1869; Circ 5,624,099
Income: $34,577,461
Library Holdings: Book Volumes 190,092; Clipping Files; Compact Disks 40,000; Fiche 31,196; Manuscripts; Micro Print; Other Holdings Folklore & Chess Archives; Original Documents; Special Collections-Rare Book vols 178,906 & per sub 425; Pamphlets; Periodical Subscriptions 217; Photographs; Prints; Reels 2008
Special Subjects: Art History, Decorative Arts, Primitive art, Oriental Art, Architecture
Collections: Cleveland Artist Original Graphics; Architecture: plans, blueprints, drawings, monographs, general & professional books, career materials, histories, treatises; Sheet Music: 20,000+ song titles; Music Educ: theory, instruction, history, composition, techniques, educ & info about the industry; Antiques & Collectibles: price guides for items incl furniture, ceramics, glass, jewelry, clocks & toys; Art: instruction guides, dictionaries, biographical listings, international art encyclopedias, monographs, catalogues raisonnes, museum catalogs & handbooks, annual indexes, Lockwood Thompson bequest; Arts Educ: materials to assist teachers; Magazines: circ copies of current & popular magazines on art, architecture, decoration & music
Publications: Descriptive pamphlets of holdings
Activities: Lect & collections open to public; tours available for groups; sales shop sells books, reproductions, prints & gift items

M **Art Gallery,** 2121 Euclid Ave AB 108, Cleveland, OH 44115-2214. Tel 216-687-2103; Fax 216-687-9340; Elec Mail artgallery@csuohio.edu; Internet Home Page Address: www.csuohio.edu/artgallery; *Asst Dir* Tim Knapp; *Dir* Robert Thurmer
Open Mon - Fri 10 AM - 5 PM, Sat Noon - 4 PM, summer hours vary; No admis fee; Estab 1965 to present important art to University & Northeast Ohio community; 4,500 sq ft hardwood floor space, 260 running ft wall space, 14 ft high track lighting, air conditioned, humidity controlled, motion detectors & cl circuit 24 hr surveillance by university police; Average Annual Attendance: 19,000
Income: $140,000 (financed by student fees & grants)
Special Subjects: Religious Art
Exhibitions: People's Art Show (biennial, fall, even years); Cleveland Biennial Juried Show (fall, odd years); Solo faculty exhibitions, fall semester, thematic curated exhibitions, spring semester
Publications: Exhibition Catalog, 2-3 times per year
Activities: Educ dept; docent training; on-time studio workshops on request for adults & children; lects open to pub, 4 vis lectrs per yr; concerts; gallery talks; tours; competitions with awards; extension progs for seniors in nursing homes; book traveling exhibs; originate traveling exhibs

C **FEDERAL RESERVE BANK OF CLEVELAND,** 1455 E 6th St, Cleveland, OH 44114; PO Box 6387, Cleveland, OH 44101-1387. Tel 216-579-2461; Elec Mail anne.s.ujczo@clev.frb.org; Internet Home Page Address: www.clevelandfed.org; *Consulting Cur* Jane B Tesso; *Facilities Planner* Anne Ujczo
Limited open access; No admis fee; Collection represents fine art and artists who have lived or worked in the 4th District of the Federal Reserve since its institution in 1914
Collections: High quality regional art made after 1910 including painting, sculpture, drawing, prints & photographs

INTERMUSEUM CONSERVATION ASSOCIATION
For further information, see National and Regional Organizations

M **MUSEUM OF CONTEMPORARY ART CLEVELAND,** (Cleveland Center for Contemporary Art) 11400 Euclid Ave, Ste 100, Cleveland, OH 44106-5923. Tel 216-421-8671; Fax 216-421-0737; Internet Home Page Address: www.mocacleveland.org; *Exec Dir* Jill Snyder; *Sr Adjunct Cur* Margo Crutchfield; *Deputy Dir Finance* Grace Garver
Open Tues-Sun 11AM-5PM, Offices Mon-Fri 9AM-5PM; Admis $4 non-members, $3 students & seniors, children under 12 free; Estab 1968 to enrich the cultural life of the community; Five galleries 20,000 sq ft, which change exhibits every 6-8 wks. Located in a renovated building which is part of the Cleveland Playhouse complex. Maintains reference library; Mem: 600; dues center circle $500; sustaining $129; contributing $50; family $35; single $25; student or artist $15
Income: $175,000 (financed by mem, state appropriation, federal & state agencies & local foundations)
Publications: Exhibition catalogues
Activities: Educ dept; docent training; lects open to pub; 20 vis lectrs per yr; gallery talks; tours; individual & original objects of art lent to corporate members; originate traveling exhibs; mus shop sells original art works, books, prints & reproductions

L **Library,** 11400 Euclid Ave, Ste 100, Cleveland, OH 44106-5923. Tel 216-421-8671; Fax 216-421-0737; *Dir* Jill Snyder
Reference Library; Mem: 900; dues $35
Library Holdings: Book Volumes 2000; Clipping Files; Exhibition Catalogs; Periodical Subscriptions 10; Photographs; Slides

L **NORTHEAST OHIO AREAWIDE COORDINATING AGENCY (NOACA),** Information Resource Center, 1299 Superior Ave, Cleveland, OH 44114-3204. Tel 216-241-2414, Ext 240; Fax 216-621-3024; Elec Mail kgoldberg@mpo.noaca.org; Internet Home Page Address: www.noaca.org; *Librn* Kenneth P Goldberg
Open Mon - Fri 8 AM - 4:30 PM; Estab 1965, staff checkout only, public phone inquiries or browsing welcome; calling for appointment advisable; Transportation, environment-related & archival displays scattered around Agency
Library Holdings: Auction Catalogs; Audio Tapes; Book Volumes 5850; CD-ROMs; Cassettes; Clipping Files; Compact Disks; DVDs; Exhibition Catalogs; Fiche; Filmstrips; Manuscripts; Maps; Memorabilia; Micro Print; Original Art Works; Original Documents; Pamphlets; Periodical Subscriptions 205; Photographs; Prints; Reels; Reproductions; Sculpture; Slides; Video Tapes
Special Subjects: Photography, Graphic Arts, Graphic Design, Maps, Historical Material, History of Art & Archaeology, Judaica, Ceramics, Advertising Design, Industrial Design, Interior Design, Porcelain, Furniture, Metalwork, Miniatures, Religious Art, Restoration & Conservation, Display
Collections: Relative to the arts & art history: Architectural Preservation & Restoration; Land use & sprawl-related issues; Urban Planning & Urban Design; Ohio architecture; Ohio history
Publications: Decision Maker; NOACA News; various reports related to planning, transportation & environmental issues; Seeking Grants in Times of Uncertainty
Activities: Tours; Northeast Ohio, 5 counties+

M **SAINT MARY'S ROMANIAN ORTHODOX CATHEDRAL,** Romanian Ethnic Museum, 3256 Warren Rd, Cleveland, OH 44111-1144. Tel 216-941-5550; Fax 216-941-3368; Internet Home Page Address: www.smroc.org; *Dir* George Dobrea
Open Mon - Fri 8:30 AM - 4:30 PM, & on request; No admis fee; Estab 1960; Average Annual Attendance: 5,000
Income: Financed by parish appropriation
Special Subjects: Folk Art
Collections: Anisoara Stan Collection; O K Cosla Collection; Gunther Collection; Romanian art, artifacts, costumes, ceramics, painters, rugs, silver & woodwork; icons on glass & wood; books
Activities: Lect open to public; tours; individual paintings & original objects of art lent to other ethnic museums & faiths for exhibits; lending collection contains 100 original art works, 250 original prints, 50 paintings, sculpture, 2000 costumes, rugs & artifacts

A **SOCIETY FOR PHOTOGRAPHIC EDUCATION (SPE),** SPE Gallery, 2530 Superior Ave #403, Cleveland, OH 44114-4239. Tel 216-622-2733; Fax 216-622-2712; Elec Mail membership@spenational.org; Internet Home Page Address: www.spenational.org; *Exec Dir* Virginia Morrison; *Exposure Ed* Stacey McCarroll Cutshaw; *Registrar* Meghan Borato; *Office & Accts Mgr* Carla Kurtz; *Events & Publs Coordr* Ginenne Clark; *Advertising, Exhibs & Design* Nina Barcellona; *Exposure Designer* Amy Schelemanow; *Exposure Copyeditor* Ann Stevens
Open Mon - Fri 9 AM - 5 PM; Estab 1963 to provide a forum for discussion of photog; Circ 2,000; Open to all with an interest in photog; Average Annual Attendance: 1,500; Mem: 2,000; dues $55 - $125; national conference in March
Income: $250,000 (financed by mem & conference registrations)
Publications: Exposure, biannual; SPE Newsletter, triannually; ann mem directory & resource guide; Conference Prog Guide, ann
Activities: Classes for adults; Lect open to pub, 75 vis lectrs per yr; lects for mems; gallery talks; tours; SPE Student Awards; Freestyle Crystal Apple Award; schols offered

M **SPACES,** 2220 Superior Viaduct, Cleveland, OH 44113-2367. Tel 216-621-2314; Fax 216-621-2314; Elec Mail contact@spacesgallery.org; Internet Home Page Address: wwwspacesgallery.org; *Gallery Mgr* Marilyn Ladd-Simmons; *Develop Dir* Martha Loughridge; *Office Admin* Michelle Epps
Open Tues - Sun noon - 5 PM, thurs open until 8 PM, cl Mon; No admis fee; Estab 1978 to show innovative work by living artists; Single room, 6000 sq ft & 12 ft ceiling. Exhibitions, curated & group exhibitions change monthly; Average Annual Attendance: 15,000; Mem: 400
Income: $420,000 (financed by mem, state appropriation & foundations)
Exhibitions: 6 exhibitions annually
Publications: Exhibition catalogs, 3 annually
Activities: Docent training; educator outreach; Lects open to pub, gallery talks, tours

M **WESTERN RESERVE HISTORICAL SOCIETY,** 10825 East Blvd, Cleveland, OH 44106-1788. Tel 216-721-5722; Fax 216-721-8934; Internet Home Page Address: www.wrhs.org; *Pres & CEO* Gainor B Davis PhD; *COO* Kermit J Pike; *Vice Pres* Kelly Falcone-Hall
Open Tues 10AM - 4PM, Wed 10AM - 9PM, Fri & Sat 10AM - 4PM, Sun Noon - 4PM, cl Mon; Admis adults $8, seniors $7.50, youth $5, group rates available; Estab 1867 to discover, collect & preserve whatever relates to the history, biography, genealogy & antiquities of Ohio; Average Annual Attendance: 210,000; Mem: 5300; dues from $40 - $500
Income: Operating budget $7.3 million

Special Subjects: Decorative Arts, Costumes, Historical Material, Period Rooms
Exhibitions: People at the Crossroads-Settling the Western Reserve, 1796- 1870; Chisholm Halle Custom Wing; Crawford Auto-Aviation collection
Publications: Books on Regional History; Western Reserve Historical Society News, bi-monthly
Activities: Classes for adults & children; docent training; lects open to public, 25 vis lectrs per yr; tours; gallery talks; awards; individual paintings & objects of art lent to qualified institutions; originate traveling exhibs to children's museums and history museums; sales shop sells books, magazines, reproductions & prints

L **Library,** 10825 East Blvd, Cleveland, OH 44106-1788. Tel 216-721-5722; Fax 216-721-0891; Internet Home Page Address: www.wrhs.org; *COO* Kermit J Pike; *Dir Mus Servs* Ed Pershey; *VPres* Patrick H Reymann; *Dir Research* John Grabowski; *Dir Educ* Janice Ziegler; *CFO* John Holtzhauser; *Dir Mktg & Communs* Rita Kueber
Open Mon - Sat 10 AM - 5 PM, Sun Noon - 5 PM; Admis adults $8, seniors $7.50, children ages 3-12 $5; Estab 1867; For reference only
Library Holdings: Audio Tapes; Book Volumes 250,000; Cards 200; Exhibition Catalogs; Fiche 2000; Lantern Slides; Manuscripts 5,000,000; Other Holdings Microfilm 40,000; Pamphlets; Periodical Subscriptions 100; Photographs; Prints; Records; Reels 25,000; Slides
Special Subjects: Folk Art, Decorative Arts, Photography, Manuscripts, Maps, Prints, Furniture, Period Rooms, Glass, Architecture
Collections: Crawford Auto Aviation Mus; Halle Costume Wing; Library Archives; History Museum
Activities: Lects open to pub; mus shop sells books, reproductions, prints & gifts

COLUMBUS

M **CAPITAL UNIVERSITY,** Schumacher Gallery, 1 College & Main, Columbus, OH 43209-2394. Tel 614-236-6319; Fax 614-236-6490; Internet Home Page Address: www.schumachergallery.org; *Dir* Dr Cassandra Lee Tellier; *Asst Dir* David Gentilini
Open Mon - Sat 1 - 5 PM; No admis fee; Estab 1964 to provide the best available visual arts to the students; to serve the entire community with monthly traveling shows, community programming & permanent colls; Gallery is 16,000 sq ft, that includes six display galleries of permanent holdings, gallery area for temporary monthly exhibits, galleries, fabrication room, lect area seating 25; Average Annual Attendance: 9,000
Income: Financed by foundation grants & individual gifts
Special Subjects: Graphics, Painting-American, Sculpture, Watercolors, American Indian Art, African Art, Pre-Columbian Art, Primitive art, Painting-European, Eskimo Art, Asian Art, Painting-British
Collections: Ethnic Arts (including American Indian, African, Inuit, Oceanic); American paintings, sculpture & graphics of 20th century; Period works from 16th - 19th century; Major Ohio Artists; Graphics; Asian Art; Inuit Art
Exhibitions: Seven individual & group visiting shows per yr; individual exhibits include contemporary artists & loans from individuals & other museums
Activities: Lect open to public; gallery talks; competitions; individual paintings & original art objects lent by special request only

L **Art Library,** 1 College & Main, Columbus, OH 43209; 2199 E Main St, Columbus, OH 43209. Tel 614-236-6615; Fax 614-236-6490; *Dir* Dr Albert Maag
Open to students, faculty, staff & for reference only to the pub
Library Holdings: Book Volumes 5300; Periodical Subscriptions 15

L **COLUMBUS COLLEGE OF ART & DESIGN,** Packard Library, 60 Cleveland Ave Columbus, OH 43215-1758. Tel 614-222-3273; Elec Mail library@ccad.edu; Internet Home Page Address: www.ccad.edu; *Library Dir* Gail Storer; *Visual Resources Librn* Tara Haas; *Tech Svcs Librn* Leslie Jankowski; *Pub Svcs Librn* Christine Mannix
Open Mon - Thurs 7:30 AM - 9:30 PM, Sat 1 PM - 5 PM during acad yr; Estab 1879 to support the programs of the Columbus Col of Art & Design; Circ 15,400
Income: tuition, grants & gifts
Library Holdings: Book Volumes 82,323; CD-ROMs; Clipping Files 35,000; Compact Disks 353; DVDs 3,186; Exhibition Catalogs; Fiche; Periodical Subscriptions 300; Slides 76,150; Video Tapes
Special Subjects: Art History, Intermedia, Landscape Architecture, Film, Illustration, Mixed Media, Photography, Commercial Art, Drawings, Graphic Arts, Graphic Design, Painting-American, Sculpture, Painting-European, Portraits, Ceramics, Printmaking, Advertising Design, Fashion Arts, Industrial Design, Interior Design, Lettering, Asian Art, Video, Costume Design & Constr, Glass, Textiles

M **COLUMBUS CULTURAL ARTS CENTER,** 139 W Main St, Columbus, OH 43215-5064. Tel 614-645-7047; Fax 614-645-5862; Elec Mail jljohnson@columbus.gov; Internet Home Page Address: www.culturalartscenteronline.org; *Arts Adminr* Jennifer Johnson
Open Mon - Fri 8:30 AM - 4:30 PM, Mon - Thurs 6:30 PM - 9:30 PM, Sat & Sun 1 - 4:30 PM; No admis fee; Estab 1978, visual arts facilities & gallery; Maintains small reference library; Average Annual Attendance: 50,000
Income: Financed by city of Columbus gen funds
Library Holdings: Book Volumes
Exhibitions: local, regional, & national artists monthly exhibitions
Publications: Quarterly catalog
Activities: Classes for adults & youth outreach. Studio classes for adults offered in 8-wk terms include painting, drawing, relief printing, sculpture, jewelry, weaving, copper enameling, ceramics, surface design, stone carving & bronze casting; lect open to pub, 58 vis lectrs per yr; gallery talks; tours; festivals

L **COLUMBUS METROPOLITAN LIBRARY,** Arts & Media Division Carnegie Gallery, 96 S Grant Ave, Columbus, OH 43215-4781. Tel 614-645-2ask; Fax 614-645-2883; Elec Mail artsnmedia@columbuslibrary.org; Internet Home Page Address: www.columbuslibrary.org; *CEO* Patrick Losinski; *Div Mgr* Chuck Cody; *Asst Mgr* Tonia M Derring
Open Mon - Thurs 9 AM - 9 PM, Fri & Sat 9 AM - 6 PM, Sun 1 - 5 PM; No admis fee; Main library estab 1873 ; Supported by Friends of the Library, the gallery creates unique cultural experiences for library visits by presenting quality art exhibits, featuring emerging & established artists; Average Annual Attendance: 1,000
Income: Financed by state & county appropriation
Library Holdings: Book Volumes 100,000; Compact Disks; DVDs; Exhibition Catalogs; Maps; Original Art Works; Other Holdings Catalogs; Periodical Subscriptions 2181
Special Subjects: Art History, Decorative Arts, Film, Photography, Theatre Arts, Architecture
Exhibitions: OOVAR, Annual
Activities: Classes for adults & children; summer reading for all ages; lects open to pub; 3 vis lectrs per yr; tours; concerts; Celebration of Learning Award; exten prog serves Columbus Metropolitan Area; sales shop sells books & original art

M **COLUMBUS MUSEUM OF ART,** 480 E Broad St, Columbus, OH 43215-3823. Tel 614-221-6801; Fax 614-221-0226; Elec Mail info@cmaohio.org; Internet Home Page Address: www.columbusmuseum.org; *Exec Dir* Nannette V Maciejunes; *Deputy Dir Oper* Rod Bouc; *Assoc Cur Contemp Art* Tyler Cann; *Cur American Art* Melissa Wolfe; *Dir Educ* Cynthia Meyers Foley; *Chief Registrar & Exhib Mgr* Melinda Knapp; *Dir Mktg & Communs* Melissa Ferguson; *Dir Vis Svcs & Vols* Pam Edwards; *Pres* Jay Vorys; *Exhib Designer* Greg Jones; *Dir Devel* Norma Sexton; *Dir Curatorial Admin & Cur European Art* Dominique Vasseur; *Cur Photography* Catherine Evans; *1st VPres* Steve English; *2nd VPres* Joy Gonsiorowski; *Dir Publs* Chris Duckworth; *Deputy Dir Institutional Develop* Sarah J Rogers; *Dir Community Relations* Nancy Turner; *Adjunct Cur Folk Art* Michael Hall; *Adjunct Cur* Carole Genshaft
Open Tues - Wed & Fri - Sun 10 AM - 5:30 PM, Thurs until 8:30 PM, cl Mon & holidays; Suggested admis, adults $12, students 6-17 $5, seniors 60+ & students 18+ with valid ID $8, Sun & children under 5 free; Estab 1931; Present main building constructed in 1931 in a Renaissance Revival style; addition built in 1974; Russell Page Sculpture Garden added in 1979. Interactive children's area. Maintains reference library. Euro & American Modernism; Contemporary Art; expansion planned for completion 2014; Average Annual Attendance: 175,000; Mem: 5700; dues $75 household
Income: Financed by ann contributions, endowment, mem & pub support
Special Subjects: Folk Art, American Western Art, Textiles, Painting-European, Sculpture, Drawings, Painting-American, Photography, Prints, Pre-Columbian Art, Religious Art, Pottery, Etchings & Engravings, Landscapes, Decorative Arts, Painting-Japanese, Portraits, Eskimo Art, Glass, Porcelain, Oriental Art, Painting-British, Painting-French, Carpets & Rugs, Painting-Flemish, Renaissance Art, Painting-Italian, Painting-German
Collections: 16th - 18th century European paintings; Late 19th & early 20th century European and American paintings, sculpture & works on paper; 20th century Folk Art; 19th century American textiles; Schiller Collection of Social Commentary Art 1930-1970
Publications: Exhib & permanent coll catalogs; interpretive materials; bimonthly mems' magazine & calendar of events; six-month guide to progs & events; gallery handouts
Activities: Classes for adults & children; docent training; summer arts camp; lect open to pub, 15 vis lectrs per yr; concerts; gallery talks; tours; competitions; schols offered; exten dept serves Speaker Bureau & Docents-in-the-Schools; individual paintings & original objects of art lent to other museums & government buildings; lending coll contains 30 color reproductions, 5000 slides & videos; originate traveling exhibs; mus shop sells books, reproductions & prints

M **OHIO HISTORICAL SOCIETY,** National Road-Zane Grey Museum, 800 E 17th Ave, Columbus, OH 43211-2474. Tel 614-297-2300; Fax 614-297-2318; Internet Home Page Address: www.ohiohistory.org; WATS 800-752-2602; *Mgr* Alan King; *Chief Educ* Sharon Antle; *Cur History* William Gates; *Mus Shop Mgr* Susan Brouillette; *CEO* Gary C Ness; *Cur Natural History* Robert Glotzhober; *Actg Chief Coll* Michael Harsh
Open daily Mar - Nov 9:30 AM - 5 PM; Admis $5; Estab 1973; American art pottery; Average Annual Attendance: 15,000; Mem: 40,000; dues $50; ann meeting in Sept
Income: Financed by endowment, mem & state appropriation
Special Subjects: Ceramics, Pottery, American Indian Art, American Western Art, Southwestern Art, Dioramas
Collections: Zanesville Art Pottery & Tile
Exhibitions: Zanesville Art Pottery & Tile
Activities: Lects open to pub, 6 per yr; tours; sales shop sells books, original art, reproductions, prints, souvenirs

A **OHIO HISTORICAL SOCIETY,** 800 E 17 Ave, Columbus, OH 43211-2474. Tel 614-297-2300; Fax 614-297-2411; *Chief Educ Div* Sharon Antle; *Head Archaeology* Martha Otto; *Head Natural History* Carl Albrecht; *Head Historic Preservation* Amos Loveday; *Dir* Gary Ness
Open Mon - Sat 9 AM - 5 PM, Sun 10 AM - 5 PM; No admis fee; Estab 1885, Ohio Historical Soc was chartered on this date, to promote a knowledge of history, natural history & archaeology, especially of Ohio; to collect & maintain artifacts, books & archives relating to Ohio's history; Main gallery covers over one acre of fl space & includes exhibits on history, natural history, archaeology; also houses a natural history demonstration laboratory & av theatre; Average Annual Attendance: 500,000; Mem: 12,000; dues individual $32; ann meeting in Sept
Income: Financed by endowment, mem, state appropriation & contributions
Collections: Archaeology; artifacts; ceramics; clothing; furniture; glassware; paintings
Publications: Museum Echoes, newsletter, monthly; Ohio History, scholarly journal, quarterly; Timeline, popular journal, bimonthly
Activities: Classes for adults & children; docent training; lect open to pub; photographic competitions with awards; individual paintings & original art objects lent; lending coll to mus & art galleries; books traveling exhibs; originate traveling exhibs; sales shop sells books, magazines, reproductions, prints, slides and other souvenir items, postcards, jewelry

L **Archives-Library Division,** 800 E 17th Ave, Columbus, OH 43211-2474. Tel 614-297-2510; Fax 614-297-2546; *Div Chief & State Archivist* George Parkinson; *Head Collections* Michael Harsh; *Head Conservation* Vernon Will
Open Tues - Sat 9 AM - 5 PM; Estab 1885, to collect, preserve & interpret evidences of the past; For reference only; Average Annual Attendance: 13,000

Income: $1,100,000 (financed by state appropriation & pvt revenue)
Purchases: $80,000
Library Holdings: Audio Tapes; Book Volumes 148,600; Cassettes 2500; Exhibition Catalogs; Filmstrips; Kodachrome Transparencies; Lantern Slides; Manuscripts 1000; Memorabilia; Motion Pictures; Other Holdings Maps 5000; Pamphlets; Periodical Subscriptions 300; Photographs 50,000; Prints; Records; Reels 47,500; Reproductions; Slides; Video Tapes
Collections: Broadsides; Ohio government documents; Ohio newspapers; Temperance coll; maps; papers of early Ohio political leaders; posters; rare books; trade catalogs; photographs; manuscripts
Publications: Ohio History (biannual); Timeline (bimonthly)
Activities: Classes for adults & children; docent training

M **OHIO STATE UNIVERSITY,** Wexner Center for the Arts, 1871 N High St, Columbus, OH 43210-1393. Tel 614-292-0330; Fax 614-292-3369; Internet Home Page Address: www.wexarts.org; *Cur Media Arts* William Horrigan; *Exhib Designer* Jim Scott; *Dir Performing Arts* Charles R Helm; *Dir Communs* Darnell Lautt; *Dir Educ* Patricia Trumps; *Dir* Sherri Geldin; *Dir Develop* Jeffrey Byars
Open Tues - Fri 11 AM - 6 PM, Thurs until 9 PM, Sat - Sun Noon - 6 PM, cl Mon; No admis fee for gallery, performances and screenings vary; Estab 1989 the Wexner Center for the arts is Ohio State University's multidisciplinary, international laboratory for exploration and advancement of contemporary art.; Administers the permanent coll & exhibs in 4 professionally-equipped galleries & is the center for long-range planning in visual arts; Average Annual Attendance: 273,000; Mem: 1,835
Income: $7,623,260 (financed by operating funds from the univ, prog support from the Wexner Center Foundation & government foundation & corporate grants, earned income)
Special Subjects: Painting-American
Collections: Contemporary Collection; Study Collection of graphic arts & manuscripts; Wiant Collection of Chinese art
Exhibitions: Various exhibits
Publications: Exhib catalogs
Activities: Docent training; lect open to pub, 12 vis lectrs per yr; concerts; gallery talks; tours; invitational juried exhibs; Wexner Prize, presented ann; rent traveling exhibs 1-5 per yr; originate traveling exhibs

L **Fine Arts Library,** 1871 N High St, Columbus, OH 43210-1105. Tel 614-292-6184; Fax 614-292-4573; Elec Mail wyngaard.1@osu.edu; *Head Librn* Susan E Wyngaard; *Asst* Maria van Boekel; *Asst* Gretchen Donelson
Open Mon - Thurs 8 AM - 10 PM, Fri 8 AM - 5 PM, Sat Noon - 6 PM, Sun 2 - 10 PM, while classes are in session; vacation, 10 AM - 5 PM daily; No admis fee; Estab during 1930's to support teaching & research in art, art educ, design, history of art & photography; Average Annual Attendance: 200,000
Purchases: $120,000
Library Holdings: Book Volumes 130,000; Cards; Exhibition Catalogs; Fiche; Original Art Works; Periodical Subscriptions 350; Reels; Slides; Video Tapes 250
Special Subjects: Art History, Collages, Constructions, Folk Art, Intermedia, Decorative Arts, Illustration, Mixed Media, Photography, Calligraphy, Commercial Art, Drawings, Etchings & Engravings, Graphic Arts, Graphic Design, Manuscripts, Maps, Painting-American, Painting-British, Painting-Dutch, Painting-Flemish, Painting-French, Painting-German, Painting-Italian, Painting-Japanese, Painting-Russian, Painting-Spanish, Posters, Prints, Sculpture, Painting-European, History of Art & Archaeology, Judaica, Portraits, Watercolors, Ceramics, Conceptual Art, Crafts, Latin American Art, Archaeology, Ethnology, Painting-Israeli, Bronzes, Printmaking, Advertising Design, Industrial Design, Interior Design, Art Education, Asian Art, Video, Porcelain, Primitive art, Eskimo Art, Furniture, Mexican Art, Ivory, Jade, Drafting, Glass, Mosaics, Painting-Polish, Stained Glass, Afro-American Art, Metalwork, Antiquities-Oriental, Antiquities-Persian, Carpets & Rugs, Embroidery, Enamels, Gold, Goldsmithing, Handicrafts, Jewelry, Miniatures, Oriental Art, Pottery, Religious Art, Silver, Silversmithing, Tapestries, Woodcarvings, Woodcuts, Marine Painting, Landscapes, Antiquities-Assyrian, Antiquities-Greek, Antiquities-Roman, Dioramas, Painting-Scandinavian, Painting-Australian, Painting-Canadian, Painting-New Zealand, Display, Architecture

L **Visual Resources Library,** 204 Hayes Hall, Columbus, OH 43210; 108 N Oval Mall, Columbus, OH 43210-1318. Tel 614-292-0520; Fax 614-292-4401; Internet Home Page Address: www.history-of-art.ohio-state.edu; *Asst* Nora Kilbane; *Cur* Stephanie Janquith
Open Mon - Fri 9 AM - 5 PM, summer hours vary; Estab 1925 to provide visual resources for instruction & research in history of art; Teaching - Reference Coll, restricted circulation, staff & students
Income: Financed by state funds through State Univ System
Library Holdings: Audio Tapes 30; Book Volumes 150; Exhibition Catalogs; Framed Reproductions; Original Art Works; Photographs 230,000; Prints; Reproductions; Slides 270,000; Video Tapes 150
Special Subjects: Islamic Art, Asian Art, Architecture
Collections: history of Western art & architecture

L **Billy Ireland Cartoon Library & Museum,** 27 W 17th Ave Mall, Columbus, OH 43210-1343. Tel 614-292-0538; Fax 614-292-9101; Elec Mail cartoons@osu.edu; Internet Home Page Address: www.cartoons.osu.edu; *Cur* Jenny E Robb
Open Mon - Fri 9 AM - 5 PM, hours vary between terms; Estab 1977, renamed 2009
Income: Financed by state appropriation
Library Holdings: Book Volumes 50,000; serial & comic book titles: 61,000; Cassettes; Clipping Files 2,500,000; DVDs; Exhibition Catalogs; Manuscripts 3,000 ft; Memorabilia; Original Art Works cartoons: 450,000; Other Holdings; Photographs; Records
Special Subjects: Illustration, Manuscripts, Cartoons
Collections: Cartoonist Collection, clippings, proofs & scrapbooks (hundreds of artists represented); editorial cartoons; comic strips; comic books; graphic novels; manga; sports cartoons; magazine cartoons; Nick Anderson Collection; Jim Borgman Collection; Milton Caniff Collection; Eldon Dedini Collection; Edwina Dumm Collection; Will Eisner Collection; Woody Gelman Collection of Winsor McCay cartoons; Walt Kelly Collection; Toni Mendez Collection; Bill Watterson Deposit Collection; International Museum of Cartoon Art Collection: 200,000+ original cartoons; San Francisco Academy of Comic Art Collection; Jay Kennedy Collection: 9,500+ underground comic books; Robert Roy Metz Collection; Archives of professional organizations including: Assoc of American Editorial Cartoonists, National Cartoonists Society, Newspaper Features Council & Cartoonists Guild; biographical registry of cartoonists

L **The Education, Human Ecology, Psychology and Social Work Library,** 1813 N High St, Columbus, OH 43210-1307. Tel 614-292-2075; Internet Home Page Address: www.osu.edu; *Librn* Leta Hendricks
Open Mon - Thurs 8 AM - 12 AM, Fri 8 AM - 10 PM, Sat 10 AM - 2 PM, Sun 11 AM - 12 AM, summers vary
Library Holdings: Audio Tapes; Book Volumes 23,000; Cassettes; Exhibition Catalogs; Fiche; Filmstrips; Motion Pictures; Pamphlets; Periodical Subscriptions 200; Slides; Video Tapes
Special Subjects: Folk Art, Decorative Arts, Crafts, Fashion Arts, Furniture, Carpets & Rugs, Embroidery, Jewelry, Textiles

A **WORTHINGTON ARTS COUNCIL,** 777 Evening St, Columbus, OH 43085-3048. Tel 614-431-0329; Fax 614-431-2491; Elec Mail arts@worthingtonarts.org; Internet Home Page Address: www.worthingtonarts.org; *Exec Dir* Elizabeth A Jewell; *Arts Coordr* Anne E Raynor
Estab 1977 to encourage & stimulate the practice & appreciation of the arts by providing opportunities in the community to participate in, experience & enjoy the arts so as to enrich the quality of daily life & further cultural growth of Worthington & to help the art & cultural organizations of the city grow & flourish
Activities: Visual arts series & sculpture on village green; classes for children; lect open to pub; performance series; schols offered; teacher in-service workshops

COSHOCTON

M **JOHNSON-HUMRICKHOUSE MUSEUM,** 300 N Whitewoman St, Roscoe Village Coshocton, OH 43812-1061. Tel 740-622-8710; Fax 740-622-8710, Ext 51; Elec Mail jhmuseum@clover.net; Internet Home Page Address: www.jhm.lib.oh.us; *Dir* Patti Malenke; *Registrar* Sharon Buxton
Open daily Noon - 5 PM May through Oct, 1 - 4:30 PM Nov through Apr, cl Mon, Thanksgiving, Christmas Eve, Christmas, New Year's Day & Easter Sun; Admis family $5, adults $2, seniors $1.50, children 5-12 $1; Estab 1931, as a gift of two pioneer residents; Five galleries: American Indian, Decorative Arts, Historical Ohio & Special Exhibits; Average Annual Attendance: 16,000; Mem: Dues, indiv $20, family $30, contributing $50, supporting $100, sustaining $200, benefactor $350 & founder $500
Special Subjects: Prints, American Indian Art, Pottery, Decorative Arts, Oriental Art
Collections: American Indian baskets and bead work; Aztec, Toltec and Mayan pottery heads; Chinese and Japanese cloisonne, embroideries, ivory, jade, lacquers, metals, porcelains, prints, samurai armor & swords, wood carvings; European glass, laces, pewter, porcelains, prints; Eskimo artifacts; material from Coshocton County Mound Builders; 19th century furnishings and implements used by Coshocton County pioneer families; Early Americana; Newark holy stones
Exhibitions: Permanent collection exhibitions changed periodically; traveling exhibitions.
Publications: American Indian Barketry; Newark Holy Stones Symposium; Pop-Gosser China; quarterly newsletter
Activities: Educ dept; classes for adults & children; lect open to pub; 4 vis lectrs per yr; tours; mus shop sells books, collection-oriented items & original art

M **POMERENE CENTER FOR THE ARTS,** 317 Mulberry St, Coshocton, OH 43812-2037. Tel 740-622-0326; Internet Home Page Address: www.pomerenearts.org; *Dir* Jenifer Eubanks
Open call for hours
Collections: works by local, regional & national artists

CUYAHOGA FALLS

M **JACK RICHARD GALLERY, ALMOND TEA MUSEUM & JANE WILLIAMS GALLERIES,** Divisions of Studios of Jack Richard, 2250 Front St, Cuyahoga Falls, OH 44221-2510. Tel 330-929-1575; Elec Mail jackrichard@att.net; Internet Home Page Address: jackrichard.com; *Agent* Jane Williams; *Dir* Jack Richard; *Chief of Staff* Maric Giangaspero
Open Tues - Fri 11:30 AM - 5 PM, Tues Eve 7 - 10 PM, cl Sun, Mon, & Sat other hours by appointment; No admis fee; Estab 1961, for exhib of local, regional & national works of art; Circ 2,000; 14,400 sq ft; Average Annual Attendance: 12,000
Income: Financed privately
Library Holdings: Auction Catalogs; Audio Tapes 30; Book Volumes 2,000; CD-ROMs 40; Cassettes 60; Clipping Files 1/2 million; DVDs 30+; Framed Reproductions; Kodachrome Transparencies; Original Art Works 400; Pamphlets 30; Photographs; Prints; Reproductions; Sculpture; Slides; Video Tapes
Special Subjects: American Indian Art, Drawings, History of Art & Archaeology, Illustration, Marine Painting, Art Education, Art History, Conceptual Art, Mixed Media, American Western Art, Photography, Painting-American, Woodcuts, Painting-European, Sculpture, Prints, Watercolors, Costumes, Religious Art, Landscapes, Painting-Japanese, Portraits, Posters, Oriental Art, Asian Art, Maps, Restorations, Painting-Flemish, Renaissance Art, Antiquities-Oriental, Painting-Spanish, Painting-Italian, Cartoons, Painting-Australian, Painting-German, Reproductions, Painting-Russian
Collections: Ball; Brackman; Cornwell; Grell; Gleitsmann; Loomis; Oriental; Over 260 additional pieces; Native American: 50 pieces
Exhibitions: 50 Women Plus; student exhibits; Japanese Prints; mems exhibits; 30 one-person exhibits; Pastel Exhibit; Age Old Masters; Brackman Masterpieces; Flowers, Flowers, Flowers; Great American Nude; Progress & Change in Paintings; over 500 exhibs
Publications: Asahi Press, Japan; over 20 other publications
Activities: Classes for adults & children; lect open to pub, lects for mems only, 5 vis lectrs per yr; gallery talks; tours; competitions with awards; over 30 regional, local, & national awards, sponsoring of competitions; schols offered; individual paintings & original objects of art lent; lending coll contains paintings, prints & cassettes; book traveling exhibs; originate traveling exhibs; sales shop sells books, magazines, original art, reproductions, prints & slides; frame shop, sculpture

L **Library,** 2250 Front St, Cuyahoga Falls, OH 44221. Tel 330-929-1575; Mobile 330-929-2285; Elec Mail jackrichard@att.net; Internet Home Page Address: www.jackrichard.com; *Owner* Jack Richard; *Chief of Staff* Mark Giangaspero
Open Tues, Thurs, Fri 11:30 AM - 5 PM, Tues evening 7 - 10 PM; Sat - Mon by appointment; No admis fee; 1961; For reference & limited lending only; Average Annual Attendance: 16,000
Income: Art sales, restoration, tuition
Library Holdings: Auction Catalogs; Audio Tapes; Book Volumes 2,000+; Cards; Cassettes; Clipping Files Half million; DVDs; Exhibition Catalogs; Framed Reproductions; Kodachrome Transparencies; Motion Pictures; Original Art Works 800+; Other Holdings; Pamphlets 40; Photographs 20,000; Prints 2,000; Records 300; Reproductions; Sculpture 8; Slides 208,000; Video Tapes 400
Special Subjects: Decorative Arts, Mixed Media, Photography, Commercial Art, Etchings & Engravings, Painting-American, Painting-Japanese, Painting-Russian, Prints, Sculpture, Portraits, Watercolors, Advertising Design, Cartoons, Art Education, Video, American Indian Art, Costume Design & Constr, Antiquities-Oriental, Oriental Art, Religious Art, Restoration & Conservation, Marine Painting, Landscapes
Exhibitions: Various year-round exhibs
Publications: Over 30 (various subjects)
Activities: Art classes for adults & children; over 50 special art progs for various groups; lectrs open to the public; gallery talks; tours; sponsoring of competitions; over 100 local & national awards; schols available; mus shop sells books, magazines, original art, reproductions, prints, slides, photographs, sculptures, & art supplies

DAYTON

M **DAYTON ART INSTITUTE,** 456 Belmonte Park N, Dayton, OH 45405-4700. Tel 937-223-5277; Fax 937-223-3140; Elec Mail info@daytonart.org; Internet Home Page Address: www.daytonartinstitute.org; *Dir* Janice Driesbach; *Dir Educ Resources & Svcs* Susan Anable; *Mus Shop Mgr* Diane Haskel; *Dir Planned Gifts & Mem Coordr* Laura Letton; *Chmn* Michael Gretizer; *Dir Pub Rels & Mktg* Dona Vella; *Chief Cur* Will South
Open Wed, Fri & Sat 10 AM - 5 PM, Thurs 10 AM - 8 PM, Sun noon - 5 PM, cl Mon, Tues & major holidays; No admis fee; some spec exhibs may carry an admis fee; Estab 1919 for the pub benefit; Some of the galleries include: African Gallery, Glass Gallery, Contemporary Gallery, European 16th-18th Century Galleries, Experiencenter Gallery, Regional Artists Gallery, Special Exhibs Gallery & an Asian Wing & an American Wing; Average Annual Attendance: 569,155; Mem: 12,000; dues $35 - $5000+; ann meeting Jan
Income: $1,300,000 (financed by federal, state & local funds, mem dues, endowment & corporate grants)
Special Subjects: Painting-American, Painting-European, Oriental Art
Collections: American Coll; European Art From Medieval Period to Present; Oriental Coll
Publications: Annual report; bulletin; Calendar of Events, monthly; gallery guides & catalogs, periodically
Activities: Classes for adults & children; docent training; lect open to pub, 3-6 per yr; gallery talks; tours; concerts; ann Oktoberfest; Leonardo League Volunteer Organization; schols offered; mus shop sells books, reproductions, original art, toys & jewelry
L 456 Belmonte Park N, Dayton, OH 45405-4700. Tel 937-223-5277; Fax 937-223-3140; Elec Mail library@daytonartinstitute.org; Internet Home Page Address: www.daytonartinstitute.org; *Ref Librn* Alice Saidel; *Librn* Ellen Rohmiller; *Archivist* Kristina Klepacz
By appointment; Estab 1922; Open to the pub for art reference only
Income: Financed by Dayton Art Institute budget
Library Holdings: Book Volumes 25,000; Clipping Files; Exhibition Catalogs; Other Holdings Auction catalogs - from 1975-2007; Periodical Subscriptions 30; Slides
Special Subjects: Carpets & Rugs
Collections: Louis J P Lott & Walter G Schaeffer, architectural libraries; Guy Elbert Alloh & Gwen Jones Allott Collection of Oriental Carpets
Activities: Fiction, Fine Art, and Fun Book Club

M **DAYTON VISUAL ARTS CENTER,** 118 N Jefferson St, Dayton, OH 45402-1708. Tel 937-224-3822; Elec Mail dvac@daytonvisualarts.org; Internet Home Page Address: www.daytonvisualarts.org; *Exec Dir* Eva Buttacavoli; *Gallery Mgr* Patrick Mauk
Open Tues 11 AM - 6 PM; No admis fee; Estab 1991 to showcase important regional contemporary art; New gallery space located in downtown Dayton; Average Annual Attendance: 15,000; Mem: 700; dues $45 - $1,000
Income: Financed by mem, county appropriation & grants
Collections: Contemporary Art
Publications: Sketches, quarterly newsletter; exhibit catalogues
Activities: Classes for adults; 6-8 exhibs annually in gallery; professional develop workshops & critiques for artists; lect, forums & field trips; gallery talks open to pub; 12 vis lectrs per yr; schols offered; sales gallery of original art during Nov-Dec & at off-site locations during the yr; ann art auction in Apr

M **WRIGHT STATE UNIVERSITY,** Art Galleries, 3640 Colonel Glenn Hwy, Dayton, OH 45435-0001. Tel 937-775-2978; Fax 937-775-4082; Internet Home Page Address: www.wright.eduartgalleries;
Open Tues - Fri 10 AM - 4 PM, Sat & Sun Noon - 5 PM, cl Mon & holidays; No admis fee; Estab 1974, devoted to exhibs of & research in contemporary art; Four galleries; multi-level contemporary building with over 5000 sq ft & over 500 running ft of wall space. Available also are areas outside on the campus; Average Annual Attendance: 25,000
Income: Financed through the univ & grants
Collections: Collection of Contemporary Art
Publications: Artist's books & exhib catalogs, 2 per yr
Activities: Lect open to pub; individual paintings & art objects lent to faculty & admin areas; lending coll contains original art works, original prints, paintings, drawings, photographs & sculpture; originate traveling exhibs; sales desk sells catalogs

L **Visual Resources Center, Department of Art & Art History,** 3640 Colonel Glenn Hwy, Dayton, OH 45435-0001. Tel 937-775-2896; Elec Mail shannon.michalak@wright.edu; Internet Home Page Address: www.wright.edu/cola/dept/art/resourcecenter.html; *Visual Resource Cur* Shannon Michalak
Open Mon - Thurs 9 AM - 2 PM; Estab 1970 to serve instruction at Wright State Univ ; Circ Approx 475 slides per wk
Library Holdings: Book Volumes 750; Exhibition Catalogs; Other Holdings Art school catalogs; Periodical Subscriptions 12; Slides 100,000
Special Subjects: Art History, Drawings, Etchings & Engravings, Painting-American, Painting-British, Painting-Dutch, Painting-Flemish, Painting-French, Painting-German, Painting-Italian, Painting-Russian, Painting-European, History of Art & Archaeology, Painting-Polish, Architecture

DELAWARE

M **RICHARD M ROSS ART MUSEUM AT WESLEYAN UNIVERSITY,** 61 S Sandusky St, Delaware, OH 43015-2333; 60 S Sandusky St, Delaware, OH 43015-2333. Tel 740-368-3606; Fax 740-368-3515; Elec Mail ramuseum@owu.edu; *Dir* Justin Kronewetter; *Sr Asst* Tammy Wallace; *Gallery Asst* Stephen Perakis
Open Tues - Fri 10 AM - 5 PM, Thurs until 9 PM, Sun 1 PM - 5 PM, cl Mon & Sat; Admis free; Estab 2002 to house permanent art coll, 4 galleries, 1 dedicated to display of objects from mus coll, 3 dedicated to display of temporary exhibs; Average Annual Attendance: 10,000
Income: Income from endowed accounts and donations
Purchases: Purchases made with funds from endowed accounts
Collections: Primarily works on paper; minimal non-paper based works
Exhibitions: 10-12 solo & group shows per school yr; solo & group shows in the 2 off-site galleries
Activities: Artist lectrs open to pub; 15 vis lectrs per yr; gallery talks; tours; venue for various univ & community related events; lend original object of are to other mus; periodic book traveling exhibs

DOVER

M **WARTHER MUSEUM INC,** 331 Karl Ave, Dover, OH 44622-2767. Tel 330-343-7513; Elec Mail info@warthers.com; Internet Home Page Address: www.warthers.com; *Pres & Gen Mgr* Mark Warther
Open daily 9 AM - 5 PM; Admis $13 adults, students 6 - 17 yrs old $5; Estab 1936 to display carvings; Average Annual Attendance: 100,000
Income: $250,000 (financed by admis)
Special Subjects: Woodcarvings, Ivory
Collections: Carvings of American Railroad History; Carvings of ivory, ebony & walnut depicting the evolution of the steam engine
Exhibitions: Carvings of American Railroads by Ernest Warther
Activities: Tours; retail store sells books, souvenirs, gen gifts, handcrafted cutlery

DUBLIN

M **BUNTE GALLERY,** Dublin Arts Council, 7125 Riverside Dr, Dublin, OH 43016-9586. Tel 614-889-7444; Internet Home Page Address: www.dublinarts.org; *Mktg Dir* Janet Cooper; *Exec Dir* David S Guin, Ph.D
Open tues 10 AM - 7 PM, Wed-Fri 10 AM - 5 PM, Sat 11 AM - 2 PM; Estab 1983
Collections: Artwork of local & regional artists; Dublin Art in Public Places Collection (commissioned, on-loan & gifted)
Activities: Educational workshops; classes; camps; visual arts series; DAC Sundays at Suoto summer concert series; Dublin Art in Public Places prog

ELYRIA

M **SOUTHERN LORAIN COUNTY HISTORICAL SOCIETY,** Spirit of '76 Museum, 509 Washington Ave, Elyria, OH 44035-5128. Tel 216-647-4367; *VPres* Phyllis Perkins; *Cur* Diane Stanley; *Pres* Dick Landis
Open Apr - Oct Sat & Sun 2:30 - 5 PM, groups of ten or more any time by reservation; No admis fee; Estab 1970 to memorialize Archibald M Willard who created the Spirit of '76, nation's most inspirational painting; Average Annual Attendance: 2,000; Mem: 259; dues couple $10, individual $5; ann meeting in Apr
Income: $10,000 (financed by mem, gifts & gift shop)
Purchases: $10,000
Special Subjects: Painting-American, Costumes, Portraits, Furniture, Historical Material
Collections: Archibald M Willard Paintings; artifacts of local interest; memorabilia of Myron T Herrick
Publications: Quarterly newsletters
Activities: Sales shop sells books, reproductions, prints & miscellaneous items

FINDLAY

M **MAZZA MUSEUM,** The University of Findlay, Gardner Arts Pavilion, Findlay, OH 45840-3653; 1000 N Main St, Findlay, OH 45840-3653. Tel 800-472-9502; Fax 419-434-6480; Elec Mail sapp@findlay.edu; Internet Home Page Address: www.mazzamuseum.org
Open Wed-Fri noon-5PM, Sun1PM-4PM, other times by appointment; cl major holidays; No admis fee; donations accepted; Mus of original art from picture books; Average Annual Attendance: 10,000
Collections: over 3000 works of art; children's picture book art; literacy
Activities: Classes for adults & children; docent training; lects open to pub, 20 vis lectrs per yr; gallery talks, tours; lending coll contains original objects of art; mus shop sells books, autographed books, & other literature related items

M **UNIVERSITY OF FINDLAY,** Dudley & Mary Marks Lea Gallery, 1000 N Main St, Findlay, OH 45840-3653. Tel 419-434-4534; Fax 419-434-4531; *Dir* Ed Corle
Open Mon - Fri 9 AM - 4:30 PM; Estab in 1962 as an auxiliary to the col art department; Gallery is maintained
Income: Financed by endowment & tui
Special Subjects: Prints
Exhibitions: Annual Student Exhibition; Contemporary Art & Crafts; Regional & Nat Faculty & Student Exhibits
Publications: Individual exhib catalogs
Activities: Classes for adults & children; dramatic progs; lect open to pub, 2-3 vis lectrs per yr; gallery talks; tours; competitions with awards; schols; fels; individual paintings & original objects of art lent, primarily to College offices

FOSTORIA

M **FOSTORIA OHIO GLASS ASSOCIATION,** Glass Heritage Gallery, 109 N Main St, Fostoria, OH 44830-2215. Tel 419-435-5077; Elec Mail museum@fostoriaglass.com; Internet Home Page Address: fostoriaglass.com
Open Mar Thurs-Sat 10AM-4PM, Apr - Dec Tues-Sat 10AM-4PM; No admis fee, donations accepted; Estab 1992 to show glass made in Fostoria, OH 1887-1920; Over 1,200 pieces on display; Mem: annual dues $20
Income: Corporate sponsors & donations, dues
Collections: glassmaking history & industries; local industry glass, 1887-1920; vases; lamps; pitchers; records & glass works
Publications: "Victoria Views" quarterly newsletter
Activities: Shop sells glass on consignment from mems

GALLIPOLIS

A **FRENCH ART COLONY,** 530 1st Ave, Gallipolis, OH 45631-1245; PO Box 472, Gallipolis, OH 45631-0472. Tel 740-446-3834; Fax 740-446-3834; Elec Mail info@frenchartcolony.org; Internet Home Page Address: www.frenchartcolony.org; *Bd Mem* Janice M Thaler; *Bd Mem* Peggy Evans; *Exec Dir* Joseph Wright
Galleries open Tues - Fri 10 AM - 5 PM, Sun 1 - 5 PM, Sat 10 AM - 3 PM; No admis fee; Estab 1964 to promote the arts throughout the region; Monthly regional artists & traveling exhibs; Average Annual Attendance: 7,000; Mem: 325; dues $15 & up
Income: Financed by mem & donations
Special Subjects: Costumes, Drawings, Metalwork, Photography, Prints, Sculpture, Watercolors, Painting-American, Pottery, Folk Art, Ceramics, Collages, Crafts, Miniatures, Portraits, Glass, Woodcarvings
Collections: 2D Art coll of various artists & media
Exhibitions: Exhibits change monthly & include: International, Juried Festival, Ceramics, Watercolors, Oils & Mixed-Media; 3D sculpture
Publications: Newsletter, bimonthly "Currens"
Activities: Classes & progs for adults & children in visual & performing art; community progs; creative writing; volunteer progs; juried competitions; historic tours; facility rental; fundraising events; lects open to pub; concerts; book traveling exhibs; mus shop sells prints

L **Library,** 530 First Ave, PO Box 472 Gallipolis, OH 45631. Tel 740-446-3834; Elec Mail facart@zoomnet.net; *Dir* Mary Bea McCalla
Open Tues - Fri 10 AM - 3 PM, Sat & Sun 1 - 5 PM; Estab 1972 as small reference library dealing primarily with visual arts
Library Holdings: Book Volumes 2000; Cassettes; Clipping Files; Exhibition Catalogs; Lantern Slides; Memorabilia; Pamphlets; Periodical Subscriptions 5; Photographs; Prints; Reproductions; Slides

GAMBIER

M **KENYON COLLEGE,** Olin Art Gallery, 106 College Park Dr, Olin Library Gambier, OH 43022-5020. Tel 740-427-5000; Fax 740-427-5272; Internet Home Page Address: www.kenyon.edu; *Coordr* Ellen Sheffield; *VPres Library* Daniel Temple
Open daily 8:30 AM - 8:30 PM, through school yr only; No admis fee; Estab 1973 as teaching arm of the Art Dept of Kenyon Col
Income: Financed by col
Collections: Art coll and items of some historical importance
Activities: Lect open to pub; gallery talks; tours; Honors Day cash awards

GRANVILLE

M **DENISON UNIVERSITY,** Art Gallery, Burke Hall of Music & Art, Granville, OH 43023; PO Box 810, Granville, OH 43023-0810. Tel 740-587-6255; Fax 740-587-5701; Elec Mail harlacher@denison.edu; Internet Home Page Address: www.denisonmuseum.org; *Dir* Sherry Harlacher; *Cur Colls* Anna Cannizzo; *Cur Asst* Sarah Baker
Open Mon - Sat noon - 5 PM; extended hrs Thurs 5 - 7 PM; No admis fee; Estab 1943 for educ & exhib purposes; 2 galleries, conservation lab, storage; Average Annual Attendance: 2,000
Income: Financed through Univ
Special Subjects: Archaeology, Porcelain, Textiles, Bronzes, Manuscripts, Painting-French, Painting-American, Photography, Prints, Sculpture, Watercolors, American Indian Art, Ethnology, Textiles, Costumes, Religious Art, Ceramics, Folk Art, Woodcarvings, Woodcuts, Etchings & Engravings, Decorative Arts, Painting-European, Furniture, Asian Art, Silver, Baroque Art, Painting-Italian, Cartoons, Reproductions
Collections: American and European paintings, prints, drawings and sculpture; Burmese textiles, lacquerware and Buddhist sculpture; Chinese bronzes, robes and porcelains; Cuna Indian Molas, Uchus and ceremonial objects; American Indian pottery, baskets and rugs; African sculpture and basketry
Exhibitions: Faculty show; senior student shows; special exhibs from permanent coll; visiting artists exhibs; traveling exhibs

Activities: Book Club; film screenings; family day; lects open to pub, 4-6 vis lectrs per yr; gallery talks; tours; fels offered; exten dept; individual paintings & original objects of art lent to other museums

L **Slide Library,** 400 West Loop, Rm 503 Granville, OH 43023. Tel 740-587-6480; Fax 740-587-5701; Elec Mail hout@denison.edu; Internet Home Page Address: www.denison.edu; *Art Image Cur & Developer* Jacqueline Pelasky Hout
Open Mon - Fri 9 AM - 4 PM; Open to faculty & to students for reference only
Library Holdings: Slides 200,000

HAMILTON

M **FITTON CENTER FOR CREATIVE ARTS,** 101 S Monument Ave, Hamilton, OH 45011-2833. Tel 513-863-8873 ext 110; Fax 513-863-8865; Elec Mail cathy@fittoncenter.org; Internet Home Page Address: www.fittoncenter.org; *Exec Dir* Rick H Jones; *Arts in Common Dir* Henry Cepluch; *Exhib* Cathy Mayhugh; *Dir Pub Rel and Mktg* Jodi Fritsch; *Dir Develop* Elaine Hemmelgarn; *Educ Coordr* Jenn Acus-Smith
open office: Mon - Thurs 8:30 AM - 8PM, Fri 8:30 AM - 5 PM, Sat 9 AM - Noon, cl Sun; gallery: Mon - Thurs 9 AM - 8 PM, Fri 10 AM - 5 PM, Sat 9 AM - noon, cl Sun (except for special events); No admis fee; Estab 1992 to build community excellence through the arts & culture; Two large galleries with foyer on second floor. Large lobby display area on ground fl. Student gallery on ground fl; Average Annual Attendance: 100,000; Mem: 300; dues $30 & up
Income: Financed by Ohio Arts Council, corporations, Hamilton Community Foundation & mem, sponsorship & special gifts, ticket sales, & classifieds
Special Subjects: Graphics, Hispanic Art, Latin American Art, Painting-American, Photography, Prints, Sculpture, African Art, Pre-Columbian Art, Textiles, Pottery, Primitive art, Landscapes, Afro-American Art, Decorative Arts, Manuscripts, Painting-Japanese, Portraits, Posters, Jewelry, Asian Art, Silver, Historical Material, Leather, Reproductions
Publications: The Schooled Mind: Spectra+; quarterly newsletter; ann report
Activities: Classes for adults & children; dramatic progs; performing arts series; teacher workshops; lect open to pub; concerts; gallery talks; tours; competitions with prizes; schols offered

M **PYRAMID HILL SCULPTURE PARK & MUSEUM,** 1763 Hamilton-Cleves Rd, Hamilton, OH 45013-9601. Tel 513-868-8336 (office), 887-9514 (park); Fax 513-868-3585; Elec Mail pyramid@pyramidhill.org; Internet Home Page Address: www.pyramidhill.org; *Trustee* Harry T Wilks; *Dir* Nanci Lanni
Open daily Mon - Sun 8 AM - 5 PM; Admis adults $8, children 5-12 $2; Estab 1995; 265 acres, 7 lakes with fountains, pavilion, amphitheater & tea room, 65+ sculptures; Average Annual Attendance: 120,000; Mem: 1183; dues founder's society $5000, ambassador $2500, benefactor $1000, sponsor $500, patron $250, contributor $125, family $45, individual $40
Income: Non-profit
Special Subjects: Architecture, Sculpture, Antiquities-Byzantine, Antiquities-Egyptian, Antiquities-Greek, Antiquities-Roman, Antiquities-Etruscan
Collections: Monumental Sculpture, 65 pieces; Museum of Ancient Sculpture new indoor museum
Publications: Quarterly newsletter
Activities: Classes for adults & children; dramatic progs; music; bus trips (art excursions); summer series for children; docent training; lects for members only; concerts; gallery talks; tours; sponsoring of competitions; 2 vis lectrs per yr; sales shop sells books & original art

KENT

M **KENT STATE UNIVERSITY,** School of Art Galleries, Terrace Dr, Kent, OH 44242-0001; PO Box 5190 Kent, OH 44242-0001. Tel 330-672-7853, 672-2192 (Art Dept); Fax 330-672-4729; Elec Mail haturner@kent.edu; Internet Home Page Address: www.galleries.kent.edu; *Galleries Dir* Anderson Turner; *School of Art Dir* Christine Havice, PhD
School of Art Gallery: Tues - Fri 11 AM - 5 PM; Downtown Gallery: Wed - Fri noon - 5 PM, Sat 10 AM - 4 PM, cl school holidays; No admis fee; Estab 1950 as part of the instructional prog at Kent State; One main gallery 2200 sq ft; two student galleries; Eells Gallery; Blossom Music Center; Downtown Gallery 1200 sq ft; Michener Gallery 1,000 sq ft; Average Annual Attendance: 22,000; Mem: 76; dues $20; ann meeting in June
Income: Financed by Univ, grants & fundraising
Special Subjects: Painting-American, Prints, Sculpture
Collections: Michener Coll, contemporary prints & paintings; permanent coll sculpture, paintings, prints, crafts & photog, textiles
Exhibitions: Annual Invitational; faculty & student one-man & group exhibitions; traveling exhibitions from museums
Publications: Brochures; catalogs, 2-3 per yr
Activities: Classes for students in mus preparation; lect open to pub, 6 vis lectrs per yr; gallery talks; tours; competitions; individual paintings & original objects of art lent to offices on campus; book traveling exhibs 3 per yr; organize 1-2 traveling exhibs to circulate nationally

LAKEWOOD

A **BECK CENTER FOR THE ARTS,** 17801 Detroit Ave, Lakewood, OH 44107-3499. Tel 216-521-2540; Fax 216-228-6050; Elec Mail yvette@beckcenter.org; Internet Home Page Address: www.lkwdpl.org/beck; *Pres Bd Trustees* Fred Unger; *Dir Develop* John Farina; *Educ & Outreach* Rachel Spence; *Dir Educ* Edward Gallagher; *Exec Dir* Jim Walton; *Dir Mktg* Yvette A Hanzel; *Artistic Dir* Scott Spence
Open Mon - Fri 9 AM - 8 PM, Sat Noon - 6 PM, performance evenings Thurs & Fri 6 - 9 PM, 8 - 10 PM, Sun 2 - 4 PM; No admis fee; Estab 1976 to present a wide variety of the fine & graphic arts; A cooperative art gallery, home to 73 artists, juried art shows & visual art progs; Average Annual Attendance: 50,000
Income: Financed by individual, corporate & foundation donations, box office & class registration revenue

Collections: Contemporary pieces including acrylics, collages, etchings, oils, sculpture & watercolors
Exhibitions: Kwo, Miller, Thurmer (paintings & sculpture); Touching Stories, from Cleveland Mus of Art; Hungarian Art; Krabill (paintings)
Publications: Bulletins; Programs, every five weeks
Activities: Classes for adults & children; dramatic progs; music; dance; visual arts; creative arts therapy; docent training; lects open to pub; 5 vis lectrs per yr; concerts; gallery talks; competitions with awards; exten dept serves youth in schools; sales shop sells original art, prints, jewelry & all art media

LIMA

M　**ARTSPACE/LIMA,** 65 Town Sq, Lima, OH 45801-4950. Tel 419-222-1721; Fax 419-222-8439; Elec Mail artspacelima@woh.rr.com; Internet Home Page Address: www.artspacelima.com; *Mgr Opers* William J Sullivan; *Assoc Mgr* Kay Van Meter
Open Tues - Fri 10 AM - 5 PM, Sat 10 AM - 2 PM, cl Sun & Mon; No admis fee; Estab 1953 for the promotion of visual arts through educ & exhib; Maintains resource center; Average Annual Attendance: 5,000; Mem: 300; dues family $65, individual $40, student & senior $25; ann meeting in Aug
Income: $25,000 (financed by mem, grants & fundraising events)
Library Holdings: Book Volumes; Compact Disks; DVDs; Kodachrome Transparencies; Memorabilia; Original Art Works; Photographs; Prints; Slides; Video Tapes
Special Subjects: Architecture, Drawings, American Indian Art, American Western Art, Bronzes, Anthropology, Archaeology, Ethnology, Costumes, Ceramics, Crafts, Folk Art, Woodcuts, Etchings & Engravings, Afro-American Art, Decorative Arts, Collages, Dolls, Furniture, Glass, Asian Art, Coins & Medals, Calligraphy, Cartoons, Enamels
Exhibitions: 18 exhibits annually; Permanent gallery space at St Rita's hospital with 4 new exhibs annually
Publications: Newsletter
Activities: Classes for adults & children; docent progs; lect open to pub, 6 vis lectrs per yr; gallery talks; tours; competitions with awards; schols offered; individual paintings & original objects of art lent to local bus, pub school classrooms & art teachers; mus shop sells books, original art, reproductions, prints & children's art kits

MANSFIELD

A　**MANSFIELD FINE ARTS GUILD,** Mansfield Art Center, 700 Marion Ave, Mansfield, OH 44906-5007. Tel 419-756-1700; Fax 419-756-0860; Internet Home Page Address: www.mansfieldartcenter.com; *Dir* H Daniel Butts III
Open Tues - Sat 11 AM - 5 PM, Sun Noon - 5 PM, cl Mon & national holidays; No admis fee; Estab 1945, incorporated 1956 to maintain an art center in which exhibs, lects, gallery talks, spec progs, symposia & series of classes for adults & children are provided for the North Central Ohio area; maintained by mem, commission on sales & classes; Gallery dimensions 5000 sq ft with flexible lighting, movable walls, props, etc to facilitate monthly exhib changes; Average Annual Attendance: 25,000; Mem: 1050; dues $2 5- $1000; ann meeting in Apr
Income: Financed by mem, grants, donations
Exhibitions: Changing exhibs of member artists' work; traveling shows & locally organized one-man, group & theme exhibs changing monthly throughout the yr
Publications: Catalogs; class schedules; monthly newsletter
Activities: Classes for adults & children; lect open to pub, 6 vis lectrs per yr; gallery talks mainly for school groups; competitions; schols offered
L　Library, 700 Marion Ave, Mansfield, OH 44906-5007. Tel 419-756-1700; Internet Home Page Address: www.mansfieldartcenter.com; *Art Dir* H Daniel Butts III
Open by appointment only; Estab 1971; The library is basically a collection of monographs & studies of styles & periods for teacher & student reference
Income: financed by arts center
Library Holdings: Book Volumes 500

MARIETTA

M　**MARIETTA COLLEGE,** Grover M Hermann Fine Arts Center, 215 Fifth St, Marietta, OH 45750. Tel 740-376-4696; Fax 740-376-4529; Internet Home Page Address: www.marietta.edu; *Chmn* Valdis Garoza
Open Mon - Fri 8 AM - 10:30 PM, Sat & Sun 1 - 10:30 PM; No admis fee; Estab 1965; Gallery maintained; Average Annual Attendance: 20,000
Special Subjects: Painting-American, Sculpture, American Western Art, African Art, Crafts
Collections: Permanent coll of contemporary American paintings, sculpture & crafts; significant coll of African & pre-Columbian art
Activities: Lect open to pub; competitions

M　**THE OHIO HISTORICAL SOCIETY, INC,** Campus Martius Museum & Ohio River Museum, 601 Second St, Marietta, OH 45750-2122. Tel 740-373-3750; Tel 800-860-0145; Fax 740-373-3680; Elec Mail cmmoriv@ohiohistory.org; Internet Home Page Address: www.ohiohistory.org; *Mgr* Andrew J Verhoff; *Secy* Leann Hendershot; *Educational Specialist* Sherry Potochnik
Campus Martius Mus: Mar - Oct Wed - Sat 9:30 AM - 5 PM, Sun noon - 5 PM, Memorial Day, July 4, Labor Day noon - 5 PM; Ohio River Mus: Memorial Day Oct Sat 9:30 AM - 5 PM, Sun 1 2 - 5 PM, Memorial Day, July 4, Labor Day 12 - 5 PM; Admis fee adults $7, student $3, mem & children under 6 free; Estab 1929 the Campus Martius Mus is the Ohio Historical Soc's gateway to the settlement of Ohio & the movement of people into & within the state; buildings, artifacts, audio and video exhibits tell the story; estab 1941 the Ohio River Mus is the Ohio Historical Soc's interpretive ctr for river history, especially steamboats; exhibits include a steam towboat, river diorama, small craft, steamboat artifacts, models, paintings & a video history of steamboats; Campus Martius Mus has 12,500 sq ft of exhib space on three floors plus a two-story home, a portion of the original fort of 1790-95 enclosed within the building. The Ohio River Mus has approx 4500 sq ft of exhib space in three separate bldgs connected by walkway; Average Annual Attendance: 18,000

Income: Financed by state appropriation, mem, grants, fundraising, admis & sales
Special Subjects: Drawings, Painting-American, Photography, American Indian Art, Archaeology, Textiles, Costumes, Crafts, Folk Art, Pottery, Landscapes, Decorative Arts, Portraits, Dolls, Furniture, Glass, Jewelry, Porcelain, Silver, Marine Painting, Historical Material, Restorations, Period Rooms, Pewter
Collections: Steamer W P Snyder Jr; Tell City Pilothouse, a replica of the 18th century flatboat; decorative arts from 19th century Ohio; early Ohio paintings, prints, & photographs; items from early Putnam, Blennerhassett & other families; Ohio Company & Marietta materials; Ohio River landscapes
Activities: Classes for adults & children; tours; mus shop sells books & souvenir items

MASSILLON

M　**MASSILLON MUSEUM,** 121 Lincoln Way E, Massillon, OH 44646-6633. Tel 330-833-4061; Fax 330-833-2925; Internet Home Page Address: www.massillonmuseum.org; *Exec* Alexandra Nicholis Coon; *Archivist* Mandy Pond; *Registra* Cristina Savu
Open Tues - Sat 9:30 AM - 5 PM, Sun 2 - 5 PM; No admis fee; Estab 1933 as a mus of art & history; The mus places emphasis on the Ohio area by representing the fine arts & crafts & the Massillon area with an historical collections; Average Annual Attendance: 20,000; Mem: 750, dues $25 & higher
Income: Financed by local property tax
Library Holdings: Audio Tapes; CD-ROMs; Cards; Cassettes; Clipping Files; Exhibition Catalogs; Lantern Slides; Manuscripts; Memorabilia; Motion Pictures; Original Art Works; Original Documents; Photographs; Prints; Records; Reels; Sculpture; Video Tapes
Special Subjects: American Indian Art, Decorative Arts, Drawings, Landscapes, Ceramics, Glass, Furniture, Photography, Portraits, Pottery, Painting-American, Textiles, Photography, Watercolors, Archaeology, Ethnology, Costumes, Dolls, Carpets & Rugs, Renaissance Art, Antiquities-Roman, Military Art
Collections: Ceramics, china, costumes, drawings, furniture, glass, jewelry, paintings, prints, photography
Exhibitions: Monthly exhibs; Immel miniature circus diorama; Massillon Tiger Football gallery; (06/2014-09/2014) Fragile Waters: Photographs by Dorothy Kerper Monnelly, Ernest Brooks, Ansel Adams
Publications: Pamphlet of activities & exhibs, quarterly
Activities: Classes for adults & children; docent training; lect open to pub, 3 vis lectrs per yr; gallery talks; tours; concerts; sponsoring of competitions; exten dept serves pub schools; individual paintings & original objects of art lent to area museums; organize traveling exhibs to accredited mus & galleries; mus shop sells books, original art, reproductions, prints & jewelry

MAYFIELD VILLAGE

L　**MAYFIELD REGIONAL LIBRARY,** Cuyahoga County Public Library, 6080 Wilson Mills Rd, Mayfield Village, OH 44143-2179. Tel 440-473-0350; Fax 440-473-0774; Elec Mail kneal@cuyahogalibrary.org; Internet Home Page Address: www.cuyahogalibrary.org; *Art Librn* Kenneth Neal
Open Mon - Thurs 9 AM - 9 PM, Fri & Sat 9 AM - 5:30 PM, Sun 1 - 5 PM (during school months); No admis fee; Estab 1972; Circ 100,000
Income: Financed by county-CCPL
Library Holdings: Auction Catalogs; DVDs; Exhibition Catalogs; Original Art Works; Periodical Subscriptions; Video Tapes
Exhibitions: Original art works by local artists; Exhibs on a monthly basis
Activities: Classes for adults; lectr open to pub, concerts, sponsor competitions

MEDINA

M　**PORTHOLES INTO THE PAST,** 4450 Poe Rd, Medina, OH 44256; 2027 Lyndway, Lyndhurst, OH 44121. Tel 330-725-0402; Fax 330-722-2439; *Pres & Dir* Merle Mishne
Open by appointment, cl New Year's Day, Christmas; No admis fee
Collections: over 2,000 images of car art, blue prints & cutaway drawings; over 200 images of Bugatti cars; over 60 c.1910 Montaut-Gamy lithographs; over 500 images of airplanes; impressionist art; models; American Indian artifacts; World War II posters; paintings; drawings; photographs; advertising art
Publications: biannual brochure, Portholes
Activities: Lect, guided tours, films, rental gallery

MIDDLETOWN

A　**MIDDLETOWN ARTS CENTER,** (Middletown Fine Arts Center) 130 N Verity Pkwy, Middletown, OH 45042-1916; PO Box 441, Middletown, OH 45042-0441. Tel 513-424-2417; Fax 513-424-1682; Elec Mail contact@middletownartscenter.com; Internet Home Page Address: www.middletownartscenter.com; *Dir* Patt Belisle; *Pres* David E Beck
Open Mon 9 AM - 4 PM, Tues - Thurs 9 AM - 9 PM, Sat 9 AM - noon, cl Sun; No admis fee; Estab 1957 to offer exhibits & classes to the pub; Auditorium for large exhibits; gallery for small exhibits; Average Annual Attendance: 2500; Mem: 596; dues minimum $15; ann meeting in July
Income: Funds generated through mem & donations
Exhibitions: 10-12 exhibitions per year including Annual Area Art Show; Annual Student Show; plus one & two-man invitational shows of regional artists; American Watercolor Society & Ohio Watercolor Society
Publications: Brochures publicizing exhibs; e-newsletters; schedule of classes
Activities: Classes for adults, children & the handicapped; workshops with nat artists; lects open to pub, 1-3 vis lectrs per yr; tours; competitions with awards; schols offered; individual paintings & original objects of art lent usually to bus for display; lending coll contains books, original art works & paintings; book traveling exhibs; sales shop sells pottery, jewelry & paintings produced at Center
L　Library, 130 N Verity Pkwy, Middletown, OH 45042-1916; PO Box 441, Middletown, OH 45042-0441. Tel 513-424-2417; Fax 513-424--1682; Elec Mail

mfac@siscom.net; Internet Home Page Address: www.middletownfinearts.com; *Adminr* Peggy Davish

Open Mon 9 AM - 4 PM, Tues - Thurs 9 AM - 9 PM, Sat 9 AM - noon, cl Sun; Estab 1963, to provide information and enjoyment for students and instructors; Circ 30; Library open for lending or reference

Income: Financed through ann budget & donations

Purchases: $150

Library Holdings: Book Volumes 1500; Periodical Subscriptions 6; Slides

Special Subjects: Art History, Folk Art, Decorative Arts, Illustration, Photography, Drawings, Sculpture, Historical Material, Portraits, Watercolors, Ceramics, Conceptual Art, Crafts, Art Education, Southwestern Art

Collections: All books pertain only to art subjects: Art history; ceramics; crafts; illustrations; references; techniques; theory

Activities: Classes for adults & children; one vis lectr per yr; sponsoring of competitions; schols

NEWARK

M LICKING COUNTY ARTS, Art Gallery, 38 S 3rd St, Newark, OH 43055-5528; PO Box 15, Newark, OH 43058-0015. Tel 740-349-8031; Elec Mail lca@lcagallery.com; Internet Home Page Address: www.lickingcountyarts.org; *Pres* Tony Reynolds

Open Tues - Sat 11 AM - 4 PM

NORTH CANTON

L NORTH CANTON PUBLIC LIBRARY, The Little Art Gallery, 185 N Main St, North Canton, OH 44720-2595. Tel 330-499-4712, Ext 12; Fax 330-499-7356; Elec Mail harberla@oplin.lib.oh.us; Internet Home Page Address: www.northcantonlibrary.org/lag; *Chmn Art Comt* David Smetana; *Cur* Laurie G Fife Harbert; *Library Dir* Karen Sonderman; *Asst* Debbie Hansel

Open Mon - Thurs 9 AM - 9 PM, Fri 9 AM - 6 PM, Sat 9 AM - 5 PM, Sun 1 - 5 PM (Labor Day - Memorial Day); No admis fee; Estab 1936 to encourage & promote appreciation & educ of fine art & other related subjects; also recognizes & encourages local artists by promoting exhibs of their work; 600 sq ft; approx 30-50 works on view at a time; Average Annual Attendance: 7,000; Mem: 175; dues $15; meetings in Sept, Nov, Feb, Apr & Jun

Income: Financed by city & state appropriation

Purchases: $500

Library Holdings: Book Volumes 54,014; Original Art Works; Periodical Subscriptions 180; Photographs; Sculpture

Special Subjects: Photography, Drawings, Etchings & Engravings, Painting-American, Prints, Sculpture, Watercolors, Ceramics, Glass, Stained Glass, Embroidery, Jewelry, Pottery, Religious Art, Textiles, Landscapes

Collections: Original works by contemporary artists; religious reproductions; reproductions for juvenile

Exhibitions: Monthly exhibits; Stark County Competitive Artists Show

Activities: Classes for adults & children; classes for home schooled students; gallery talks; tours; competitions with awards; lending of original objects of art to estab art organizations

OBERLIN

A FIRELANDS ASSOCIATION FOR THE VISUAL ARTS, 39 S Main St, Oberlin, OH 44074-1662. Tel 440-774-7158; Fax 440-775-1107; Elec Mail favagallery@oberlin.net; Internet Home Page Address: www.favagallery.org; *Exec Dir* Elizabeth Manderen; *Dir Gallery* Kyle Michalak; *Educ Coordr* James Peake

Gallery open Tues - Sat 11 AM - 5 PM, Sun 1 - 5 PM; No admis fee; Estab 1979 as a nonprofit community art organization with exhib, educ & outreach programs; Average Annual Attendance: 10,000; Mem: 350; dues basic $25 - $50, contributors up to $1000; ann meeting in May

Income: $205,000 (financed by grants, mem, fees, tui, commissions, contributions fundraisers & the Ohio Arts Council)

Exhibitions: Monthly changing exhibits by contemp regional artists; Annual Juried Six-State Photography; Annual FAVA Members' Holiday Show; Biennial national juried Artist as Quiltmaker Exhibition

Activities: Classes for adults, teens & children; family workshops; lect open to pub; gallery talks; tours; competitions with awards; schols for low income children; sales shop sells original art

M OBERLIN COLLEGE, Allen Memorial Art Museum, 87 N Main St, Oberlin, OH 44074-1151. Tel 440-775-8665; Fax 440-775-8799; Elec Mail sally.moffitt@oberlin.edu; Internet Home Page Address: www.oberlin.edu/amam; *Dir* Andria Derstine; *Registrar* Lucille Stiger; *Cur Educ* Jason Trimmer; *Mus Preparator* Kendall Christian; *Asst Preparation* Mike Reynolds; *Cur American & European Art* Andaleeb Barta; *Asst Registrar* Selina Bartlett; *Admin Asst* Sally Moffitt; *Publications & Media* Megan Harding; *Cur Acad Progs* Liliana Milkova; *Asst Cur Modern & Contemporary Art* Denise Birkhofer

Open Mon - Sat 10 AM - 5 PM, Sun 1 - 5 PM, cl Mon; No admis fee; Estab 1917 to serve teaching needs of Oberlin Col & provide cultural enrichment for Northern Ohio region; Original building was designed by Cass Gilbert, a new addition opened in 1977 & was designed by Venturi, Rauch & Assoc; Average Annual Attendance: 40,000; Mem: 525; dues Dir Circle $1000, supporting $500, contributing $100, family $50, individual $40, student & senior $20, Oberlin College student $15

Income: Financed by endowment, mem & Oberlin College gen fund

Library Holdings: Auction Catalogs; Book Volumes; CD-ROMs; Compact Disks; Exhibition Catalogs; Fiche; Lantern Slides; Manuscripts; Maps; Micro Print; Original Documents; Periodical Subscriptions; Slides; Video Tapes

Special Subjects: Painting-American, Sculpture, Asian Art, Painting-Dutch, Painting-Flemish

Collections: The collection which ranges over the entire history of art is particularly strong in the areas of Dutch & Flemish paintings of the 17th century,

European Art of the late 19th & early 20th centuries, contemporary American art, old masters & Japanese prints

Exhibitions: 4 -6 exhibs per yr drawn from permanent colls & loan exhibs

Publications: AMAM Newsletter, 2 times per yr; exhib catalogues

Activities: Classes for adults & children; docent training; lect open to pub, 16 vis lectrs per yr; gallery talks; concerts; tours; original objects of art lent to other institutions for spec exhib; art rental coll contains 400 original art works for lending to students on a semester basis; books; cards

L Clarence Ward Art Library, 83 N Main St, Allen Art Bldg Oberlin, OH 44074-1151. Tel 440-775-8635; Fax 440-775-5145; Elec Mail art.help@oberlin.edu; Internet Home Page Address: www.oberlin.edu/library/art; *Art Librn* Barbara Q Prior; *Art Library Asst* Paula Baymiller

Open Mon - Thurs 8:30 AM - 5:30 PM & 7 - 11 PM, Fri 8:30 AM - 5:30 PM, Sat 12:30 - 5:30 PM, Sun 12:30 - 5:30 PM & 7 - 11 PM; No admis fee; Estab 1917 to serve the library needs of the art dept, the Allen Memorial Art Mus & the Oberlin Col community in the visual arts; Circ 22,000; Average Annual Attendance: 35,000

Income: Financed by appropriations from Oberlin Col Libraries

Library Holdings: Auction Catalogs; Book Volumes 100,000; CD-ROMs; Clipping Files; Compact Disks; DVDs; Exhibition Catalogs; Motion Pictures; Other Holdings Auction sales catalogs 10,000; Periodical Subscriptions 250; Video Tapes

Special Subjects: Art History, Landscape Architecture, Illustration, Photography, Islamic Art, Painting-American, Painting-British, Painting-Dutch, Painting-Flemish, Painting-French, Painting-German, Painting-Italian, Painting-Japanese, Painting-Russian, Painting-Spanish, Posters, Prints, Sculpture, Painting-European, History of Art & Archaeology, Judaica, Watercolors, Conceptual Art, Archaeology, Bronzes, Printmaking, Asian Art, Video, Aesthetics, Afro-American Art, Antiquities-Oriental, Oriental Art, Religious Art, Restoration & Conservation, Woodcarvings, Woodcuts, Landscapes, Antiquities-Etruscan, Antiquities-Greek, Portraits

Collections: Thomas Jefferson Collection of American architectural books

Publications: Bibliographies & library guides

Activities: Classes for students; tours

OXFORD

M HIESTAND GALLERIES, 124 Art Bldg, Oxford, OH 45056. Elec Mail art@muohio.edu; Internet Home Page Address: arts.muohio.edu/art/facilities/hiestand-galleries; Telex 513-529-2900; *Dir* Ann Taulbee

Open Mon-Fri 9AM-4:30PM, other times by appointment

Collections: paintings; sculpture; drawings

M MIAMI UNIVERSITY, Art Museum, 801 Patterson Ave, Oxford, OH 45056-3404. Tel 513-529-2232; Fax 513-529-6555; Internet Home Page Address: www.muohio.edu/artmuseum/; *Cur Coll* Edna Carter Southard; *Cur Educ* Bonnie C Mason; *Museum Registrar* Beverly Bach; *Preparator* Mark DeGennaro; *Dir* Richard Wicks, PhD

Open Tues - Fri 10 AM - 5 PM, Sat & Sun Noon - 5 PM, cl Mon & university holidays; No admis fee; Estab 1978, Art Mus facility opened Fall 1978, to care for & exhibit Univ art colls, to arrange for a variety of traveling exhibitions & for the educational & cultural enrichment of the University & the region; Mus is maintained with exhib space of 9000 sq ft, consisting of 5 galleries in contemporary building designed by Walter A Netsch, Skidmore, Owing & Merrill, Chicago; operates the McGuffey Mus, home of William Holmes McGuffey, a national historic landmark; accredited by the American Assoc of Museums; Average Annual Attendance: 35,000; Mem: 1000; dues $25 & up

Income: Financed by gift & state appropriation

Special Subjects: Painting-American, Photography, Prints, Sculpture, Textiles, Folk Art, Decorative Arts

Collections: Charles M Messer Leica Camera Collection; Ancient Art; Decorative Arts; International Folk Art, largely Middle European, Middle Eastern, Mexican, Central & South America; European & American paintings, prints & sculpture; African art; Chinese Art; Gandharan art; Native American Art; Oceanic Art; photography; textiles

Exhibitions: Twelve per yr; Looking Back: 20th Century American Art; From Puri to Bombay: Art of India

Publications: Brochures; catalogs, approx 6-8 per year; quarterly newsletter

Activities: Progs for adults & children; docent training; lect open to pub, 5-6 vis lectrs per yr; concerts; gallery talks; tours; individual paintings & original objects of art lent to qualified museums in US; book traveling exhibs 2-3 per yr; originate traveling exhibs; mus shop sells books, magazines, original art, prints, note cards, jewelry & collectibles

L Wertz Art & Architecture Library, 501 E High St, Oxford, OH 45056-1846. Tel 513-529-6638; Internet Home Page Address: www.lib.muohio.edu; *Librn* Stacy Brinkman; *Library Assoc* Jessica Wray

Open Mon - Thurs 8 AM - 10 PM, Fri 8 AM - 5 PM, Sat 1 - 5 PM, Sun 1 - 10 PM during acad yr; No admis fee; Estab to support the progs of the Schools of Art & Architecture & related disciplines

Income: Part of univ

Library Holdings: Book Volumes 65,000; Exhibition Catalogs; Other Holdings Per & serial subs 400

Special Subjects: Art History, Folk Art, Landscape Architecture, Decorative Arts, Photography, Islamic Art, Painting-American, History of Art & Archaeology, Latin American Art, American Western Art, Art Education, Asian Art, American Indian Art, Mexican Art, Southwestern Art, Afro-American Art, Jewelry, Oriental Art, Marine Painting, Architecture

PORTSMOUTH

M SOUTHERN OHIO MUSEUM CORPORATION, Southern Ohio Museum, 825 Gallia St, Portsmouth, OH 45662-4137; PO Box 990, Portsmouth, OH 45662-0990. Tel 740-354-5629; Fax 740-354-4090; Elec Mail tricia@somacc.com; Internet Home Page Address: www.somacc.com; *Dir* Pegi Wilkes; *Chief Cur* Sara Johnson; *Galleries & Coll Mgr* Darren Baker

Open Tues - Fri 10 AM - 5 PM, Sat 1 - 5 PM; No admis fee; Estab 1977 to provide exhibs & performances; Mus facility is a renovated & refurbished

neoclassical building, 21,000 sq ft, constructed in 1918 as a bank. Facility has three temporary exhibit galleries & a theatre; maintain reference library; permanent colls; Average Annual Attendance: 19,000; Mem: 1000; dues family $35
Income: $300,000 (financed by endowment, mem & city appropriation, fundraisers & grants)
Library Holdings: Book Volumes; Exhibition Catalogs; Photographs
Special Subjects: Historical Material, Landscapes, Ceramics, Collages, Glass, Furniture, Porcelain, Painting-American, Prints, Painting-European, Sculpture, Photography, Watercolors, Folk Art, Woodcarvings, Woodcuts, Dolls, Baroque Art, Dioramas
Collections: Clarence Carter Paintings; Historic photograph coll, Native American artifacts - Hopewell & Adena cultures of Ohio River Valley; Carl Ackerman Collection of Historic Photographs; Ann Louise Stanton Antique Dollhead Collection
Exhibitions: Contemporary & traditional arts, history, or humanities
Publications: Annual report; exhib catalogs
Activities: Classes for adults & children; dramatic progs; docent training; lect open to pub, 6-10 vis lectrs per yr, concerts, gallery talks, tours, sponsor competitions; exten dept serves county; 1 or 2 book traveling exhibs; originates traveling exhibs periodically to Ohio museums & galleries; mus shop sells books, original art, gift items, jewelry & prints

SPRINGFIELD

M **CLARK COUNTY HISTORICAL SOCIETY,** Heritage Center of Clark County, 117 S Fountain Ave, Springfield, OH 45502. Tel 937-324-0657; Fax 937-324-1992; Internet Home Page Address: www.heritagecenter.us; *Dir Coll* Virginia Weygandt; *CEO* Roger Sherrock; *Cur* Kasey Eichensehr; *Asst Cur* Natalie Fritz; *Dir Educ & Progs* Ardath Dellapina
Open Tues - Sat 9 AM - 5 PM, cl Mon; No admis fee; suggested donation, $5 person, $10 family; Estab 1897 for coll & preservation of Clark County history & historical artifacts; Average Annual Attendance: 32,000; Mem: 600; dues individual $35, family $50, friend $100, patron $250, student $5; ann meeting Nov
Income: $650,000 (financed by memberships, rentals, grants)
Library Holdings: Manuscripts; Maps; Memorabilia; Original Documents; Other Holdings; Periodical Subscriptions; Photographs; Prints
Special Subjects: Archaeology, Drawings, Etchings & Engravings, Landscapes, Glass, Flasks & Bottles, Furniture, Painting-American, Manuscripts, Maps, Costumes, Crafts, Decorative Arts, Dolls, Historical Material, Embroidery
Collections: Oil Paintings, mostly mid-late 19th century, of prominent Springfielders; artifacts
Publications: Newsletter, quarterly
Activities: Docent training; classes for children; tours; individual paintings & original objects of art lent to museums; lending coll contains 150 original artworks, 50 original prints, 75 paintings & 2000 photographs; sales shop sells books

L **Library,** 117 S Fountain Ave, Springfield, OH 45504-1207. Tel 937-324-0657; Fax 937-324-1992; *Cur* Virginia Weygandt; *Dir* Robert Fuhrman; *Dir Opers & Personnel* Roger Sherrock; *Develop Secy* Barbara Brown; *Pub Historian* Tamara Wait
Open Wed - Sat 10 AM - 5 PM; No admis fee; Estab 1897; For reference only
Library Holdings: Book Volumes 4000; Clipping Files; Manuscripts; Maps; Memorabilia; Original Art Works; Original Documents; Periodical Subscriptions; Photographs; Reels; Slides
Collections: Photograph Collection; Local History Collection
Publications: Chronicles of Clark County
Activities: Classes for adults & children; docent training; Benjamin F Prince Award; mus shop sells books, reproductions & gen merchandise

M **SPRINGFIELD MUSEUM OF ART,** 107 Cliff Park Rd, Springfield, OH 45501-2501. Tel 937-325-4673; Fax 937-325-4674; Elec Mail smoa@main-net.com; Internet Home Page Address: spfld-museum-of-art.org; *Pres* Andy Irick; *Dir* Mark J Chepp; *Mus Educ* Lynda Collins; *Progs & Mem* Patricia Funk; *Deputy Dir* Dominique Vasseur; *VPres* Samuel Petroff; *Facilities Mgr* Rusty Davis; *Dir* Angus M.C. Randolph; *Mus Educ* Deena Pinales; *Cur* Charlotte Gordon; *Facilities Mgr* Marty Brewer
Open Tues, Thurs, Fri 9 AM - 5 PM; Thurs 9 AM - 9 PM; Sat 9 AM - 5 PM; Sun 12:30 - 4:30 PM; cl Mon; Admis general $5, Sun free; Estab 1951 for educ & cultural purposes, particularly the encouragement of the appreciation, study of, participation in & enjoyment of the fine arts; American Collection; Average Annual Attendance: 30,000; Mem: 1000; dues benefactor $100, sustaining $55, family $35, individual $25; meetings third Tues in June
Income: $250,000 (financed by endowment, mem & tui fees)
Collections: 19th & 20th Century Artists (mostly American, some French)
Exhibitions: Rotating exhibits every 2-3 months
Publications: Newsletter, bimonthly
Activities: Classes for adults & children; docent training; lects open to pub, vis lectrs; tours; gallery talks; competitions; schols offered; individual paintings & original objects of art lent; sales shop selling original art

L **Library,** 107 Cliff Park Rd, Springfield, OH 45501. Tel 937-325-4673; Fax 937-325-4674; Elec Mail smoa@main-net.com; Internet Home Page Address: www.springfieldart.museum; *Dir* Mark Chepp; *Mus Cur* Thomas Skwerski; *Mus Educ* Deena Pinales; *Develop Dir* Rosemary Navlty
Open Tues, Thurs, Fri 9 AM - 5 PM, Wed 9 AM - 9 PM, Sat 9 AM - 3 PM, Sun 2 - 4 PM; No admis fee; Estab 1973 for art study; For reference only; Average Annual Attendance: 35,000
Income: Financed by endowment & mem
Library Holdings: Book Volumes 4500; Clipping Files; Exhibition Catalogs; Pamphlets; Slides 400
Special Subjects: Art History, Photography, American Western Art, Art Education, American Indian Art, Afro-American Art
Collections: American Art
Activities: Classes for adults & children; docent training; lects open to pub; concerts; gallery talks; tours; sponsoring of competitions; scholarships; schols; book traveling exhibs, 8-10 per yr; mus shop

SYLVANIA

L **LOURDES COLLEGE,** Duns Scotus Library, 6832 Convent Blvd, Sylvania, OH 43560-4805. Tel 419-824-3761; Fax 419-824-3511; Internet Home Page Address: www.lourdes.edu/library/; *Dir Libr Svcs* Sr Sandra Rutkowski; *Asst Librn* Sr Karen Mohar
Open to students & guests Mon - Thurs 8:30 AM - 9 PM, Fri - Sat 8:30 AM - 4 PM, Sat 9 AM - 4 PM, cl Sun; Estab 1949; Art pieces exhibited on walls of three acad bldgs; classroom & library; Average Annual Attendance: 600
Income: Financed through col
Library Holdings: Audio Tapes; Book Volumes 67,000; Cassettes; Fiche 13,599; Manuscripts; Memorabilia; Original Art Works; Periodical Subscriptions 420; Prints; Reproductions; Sculpture; Slides; Video Tapes
Special Subjects: Art History, Decorative Arts, Calligraphy, Commercial Art, Drawings, Etchings & Engravings, Graphic Arts, Ceramics, Crafts, American Western Art, Art Education, Asian Art, American Indian Art, Afro-American Art, Enamels
Collections: 350 art pieces in library cataloged
Activities: Lect open to pub; tours; schols & fels offered

TOLEDO

A **SPECTRUM GALLERY,** 5403 Elmer Dr, Toledo Botanical Garden Toledo, OH 43615-2803. Tel 419-531-7769; *Gallery Coordr* Mandi Gorbelt; *Pres* Buzz Meyers; *1st VPres* Mary Jane Erard; *Treas* Millard Stone; *VPres* Marge Cadaret
Open Wed - Sun Noon - 4 PM; No admis fee; Estab 1975 to encourage & support pub appreciation of fine art & to organize & promote related activities; promote mutual understanding & cooperation among artists, artist groups & the pub promote beautification of Toledo through use of art work; Clubhouse (3 galleries, sales room office & working studio) part of Artist Village in Toledo Botanical Garden; large adjacent Art Educ Center; Average Annual Attendance: 15,000-20,000; Mem: 200
Income: $20,000 (financed by mem & fundraising events, sales of art, donations & art classes)
Exhibitions: Juried Membership Show; Crosby Festival of the Arts; Toledo Festival; spot exhibitions
Publications: Spectrum (newsletter), monthly
Activities: Classes for adults & children; lect open to pub, 4-5 vis lectrs per yr; competitions; originates traveling exhibs; sales shop sells original art

A **TOLEDO ARTISTS' CLUB,** Toledo Artists' Club & Gallery, 5403 Elmer Dr, Toledo Botanical Garden Toledo, OH 43615-2803. Tel 419-531-4079; Fax 419-531-4079; Elec Mail toledoartist@sbcglobal.net; Internet Home Page Address: toledoartistclub.com; *Pres* Thomas Sorrell; *Office Mgr* Claudia Gast; *First VPres* Elaine Scarvelis; *Secy* Sharon Larrow; *Treas* James Larrow
Open Tues - Fri 1 - 5 PM, Sat 1 - 4 PM; No admis fee; Estab 1943 to promote art in the area; Clubhouse-Gallery opened at Crosby Gardens, Toledo in Aug 1979; new gallery dedicated Oct 1994; classroom enlarged 2000; Mem: 400; dues $58 active couples under 65, $48 under 65, $43 sr couples over 65, $38 srs over 65 (variable); monthly board meetings
Income: Financed by mem & exhibs, sales of paintings, ann art auction, workshop classes
Special Subjects: Drawings, Embroidery, Graphics, Landscapes, Photography, Sculpture, Textiles, Watercolors, Pottery, Miniatures, Portraits, Glass, Jewelry
Exhibitions: Approx 40 pieces of artwork exhibited each month in main gallery; includes paintings, pottery, sculpture, stained glass
Publications: Newsletter, monthly
Activities: Classes for adults & children; workshops; demonstrations; lects open to pub; competitions with awards; jointly present Crosby Gardens Art Festival in June with Toledo Botanical Gardens, Toledo Forestry Division & the Arts Commission of Greater Toledo; Arts in the Garden in Aug; Heralding the Holidays in Dec; sales shop selling original art

M **TOLEDO MUSEUM OF ART,** 2445 Monroe St at Scottwood Ave, Toledo, OH 43620-1517; PO Box 1013, Toledo, OH 43697-1013. Tel 419-255-8000; Fax 419-255-5638; Elec Mail information@toledomuseum.org; Internet Home Page Address: www.toledomuseum.org; Cable TOLMUSART; *Bd Chmn* David Welles Jr; *Reg* Andrea Mall; *Cur European Painting & Sculpture Before 1900* Lawrence Nichols; *Chief Cur & Cur of Asian Art* Carolyn M Putney; *Dir Develop* Susan Palmer; *Communs Dir* Kelly Fritz Garrow; *Dir Educ* Kathy Danko-McGhee; *Pres, Dir & CEO* Brian P Kennedy; *Assoc Cur Modern & Contemporary Art, Asst Dir Coll Exhib* Amy Gilman; *Cur Glass & Decorative Arts* Jutta Annette Page; *Asst Cur Works on Paper* Tom Loeffler; *Asst Cur Visual Resources Coll* Julia Hayes; *CFO* Tim Szymanski; *Dir Info Tech* Sandra Moore; *COO* Carol Bintz; *Dir HR* Lynn Miller; *Interim Head Visitor Engagement* Adam Levine
Open Tues & Wed 10 AM - 4 PM, Thurs & Fri 10 AM - 9 PM, Sat 10 AM - 5 PM, Sun noon - 5 PM, cl Mon & major holidays; No admis fee; Estab & incorporated 1901; building erected 1912, additions 1926, 1933 & 2006 (Glass Pavilion). Mus contains Canaday Gallery, Print Galleries, School Gallery, Collector's Corner & a museum store; jewelry gallery; glass pavilion erected 2006; Average Annual Attendance: 427,000; Mem: 7500; dues $50 & up
Income: Financed by contributed funds & memberships
Library Holdings: Auction Catalogs; Book Volumes; Clipping Files; Exhibition Catalogs
Special Subjects: Painting-American, Prints, Sculpture, Ceramics, Decorative Arts, Painting-European, Glass, Medieval Art, Antiquities-Oriental, Antiquities-Egyptian, Antiquities-Greek, Antiquities-Roman, Antiquities-Assyrian
Collections: Ancient to modern glass; European paintings, sculpture & decorative arts; American paintings, sculpture & decorative arts; books & manuscripts; Egyptian, Greek, Roman, Near & Far East art, African art; Modern & Contemporary Art, Jewelry
Publications: American Paintings; Ancient Glass; Art in Glass; Corpus Vasorum Antiquorum I & II; European Paintings; Guide to the Colls
Activities: Educ prog; classes for adults & children; docent training; community outreach; lects open to pub; 12 vis lectrs per yr; concerts; tours; awards, Institutional Excellence-Ohio Museums Assn, 2005, 2006 & 2008, 2012 Visual

Communications Gold Award & Best Exhib; book traveling exhibs; originate traveling exhibs; mus shop sells books, original art, reproductions, prints, gifts, jewelry

L **Art Reference Library,** 2445 Monroe St, Toledo, OH 43620; PO Box 1013, Toledo, OH 43697-1013. Tel 419-254-5770; Fax 419-255-5638; Elec Mail library@toledomuseum.org; Internet Home Page Address: www.toledomuseum.org/learn/reference-library; *Head Librn* Alison L Huftalen; *Asst Librn* Teressa Conlan
Open Mon - Thurs 10 AM - 9 PM, Fri 10 AM - 5 PM, Sat & Sun Noon - 4 PM during university sessions; Summer: Mon - Fri 10 AM - 5 PM, Sat noon - 4 PM; Estab 1901 to provide resources for the museum's staff; Circ 4,700; Primarily for reference but does lend to certain groups of users; Average Annual Attendance: 10,000; Mem: 90; dues $10 - $100
Income: Financed by mus & mem
Library Holdings: Auction Catalogs; Book Volumes 90,000; Clipping Files 21,000; Exhibition Catalogs 18,000; Fiche; Periodical Subscriptions 300; Reels 75
Special Subjects: Art History, Decorative Arts, Photography, Graphic Arts, Painting-American, Painting-European, Art Education, Glass

VAN WERT

M **WASSENBERG ART CENTER,** 643 S Washington St, Van Wert, OH 45891-2307. Tel 419-238-6837; Fax 419-238-6828; Elec Mail artcentr@bright.net; Internet Home Page Address: www.vanwert.com/wassenberg; *Admin Asst* Kay R Sluterbeck; *Exec Dir* Michele L Smith
Open Tues-Sun 1 - 5 PM, cl Mon; No admis fee; Estab 1954 to encourage the arts in the Van Wert area; Two large gallery areas, basement classroom; maximum exhibit 150 pieces; Average Annual Attendance: 1,500; Mem: 350; dues individual $20, various other
Income: $20,000 (financed by endowment, mem, fundraisers)
Library Holdings: Audio Tapes; Book Volumes 250; Cassettes; Filmstrips; Original Art Works; Periodical Subscriptions 6; Prints; Reproductions; Sculpture; Slides; Video Tapes
Collections: Wassenberg Collection; Prints & Original Art; All subjects & media
Exhibitions: Annual June Art Exhibit; Annual Oct Photography Exhibit; 8 different free exhibits per year
Publications: Gallery Review, quarterly
Activities: Classes for adults & children; docent progs; lects open to pub, some only to mems; competitions; book traveling exhibs 6-8 per yr

VERMILION

M **GREAT LAKES HISTORICAL SOCIETY,** Inland Seas Maritime Museum, 480 Main St, Vermilion, OH 44089-1015; PO Box 435, Vermilion, OH 44089-0435. Tel 440-260-0230; Elec Mail glhsl@inlandseas.org; Internet Home Page Address: www.inlandseas.org; WATS 800-893-1485; *Exec Dir* Christopher Gillcrist
Open daily 10 AM - 5 PM, cl major holidays; Admis adults $5, seniors $4, youth $3, children under 6 free; Estab 1944 to promote interest in discovering and preserving material about the Great Lakes and surrounding areas; Maintains an art gallery as part of the Maritime History Mus; Average Annual Attendance: 20,000+; Mem: 2500; dues family $49; ann meetings in May
Income: $500,000 (financed by endowment, mem, sales from mus store & fundraising)
Special Subjects: Drawings, Photography, Prints, Marine Painting, Historical Material, Maps, Dioramas, Reproductions
Collections: Collection of Ship Models; Marine Relics; Paintings & Photographs dealing with the history of the Great Lakes; paintings by Sprague, Shogren, LaMarre, Nickerson, Forsythe & Huntington
Exhibitions: Annual Antique Boat Show Exhibition
Publications: Chadburn (newsletter), quarterly; Inland Seas, quarterly journal
Activities: Classes for adults & children; dramatic progs; docent training; boat building & lofting classes; lect open to pub, 16 vis lectrs per yr; gallery talks; tours; competitions with prizes; individual painting lent to other museums; book traveling exhibs 1 per yr; originate traveling exhibs; mus shop sells books, reproductions, prints, slides & videotapes

WEST LIBERTY

M **PIATT CASTLES,** 10051 Township Rd, West Liberty, OH 43357; PO Box 497, West Liberty, OH 43357-0497. Tel 937-465-2821; Fax 937-465-7774; Elec Mail macochee@logan.net; Internet Home Page Address: www.piattcastles.org; *Pres & CEO* Margaret Piatt; *VPres* James White; *Prog Asst* Beverly Lee
Open Apr - May & Sept - Oct Sat-Sun 11 AM - 4 PM, Memorial Day - Labor Day 11 AM - 5 PM; Admis adults $8, students $6, children 5-12 $5; sr & AAA discount; Estab 1912; Paintings & sculptures displayed throughout both homes - room like settings; Average Annual Attendance: 40,000
Special Subjects: Decorative Arts, Architecture, American Indian Art, Furniture, Restorations, Period Rooms
Collections: Early American family furnishings; Native American artifacts; Rare Art; Weapons; European & Asian Furnishings
Publications: Brochures; Don Piatt of Mac-O-Chee, Wit and Wisdom of Donn Piatt
Activities: Dramatic progs; docent training; ann vintage baseball game; storytelling; Christmas prog; musical events; tours; gallery talks; concerts; art festival; mus shop sells books & original art

WESTERVILLE

AMERICAN CERAMIC SOCIETY
For further information, see National and Regional Organizations

WILBERFORCE

M **OHIO HISTORICAL SOCIETY,** National Afro-American Museum & Cultural Center, 1350 Brush Row Rd, Wilberforce, OH 45384-0578; PO Box 578, Wilberforce, OH 45384-0578. Tel 937-376-4944; Fax 937-376-2007; Elec Mail lbuckwalter@ohiohistory.org; Internet Home Page Address: www.ohiohistory.org; *Acting Dir* Floyd Thomas Jr, Ph.D; *Coordr Traveling Exhibs & Registrar* Wendy Felder; *Educ Specialist* Dianne Turner-Ingham; *Archivist* Dr Charles Wash
Open Wed - Sat; Admis adults $4, seniors $3.60, children $1.50; Estab 1987; Maintains staff reference library, archives & 5 exhib spaces totaling 6000 sq ft; Average Annual Attendance: 45,000
Library Holdings: Book Volumes; Clipping Files; Exhibition Catalogs; Records; Sculpture; Slides
Special Subjects: Painting-American, Photography, Sculpture, Ethnology, Crafts, Folk Art, Afro-American Art, Manuscripts, Dolls, Historical Material, Coins & Medals
Collections: African American Art, noted for Black Nationalist/Black Protest art of the 1960s & 70s; African Coll (ethnographic material); Craft
Exhibitions: Dolls; Photography; The Legend of John Brown: prints by Jacob Lawrence; When the Spirit Moves: African American Dance in History & Art; Uncommon Beauty in Common Objects: The Legacy of African American Craft Art; Quilting African American Woman's History
Activities: docent training; Lects open to pub; galley talks; tours; Individual paintings & original objects of art lent to qualified museums; lending coll contains original art works & paintings; book traveling exhibs; originate traveling exhibs from small institutions to the Smithsonian; mus shop sells books, original art, reproductions & prints

WILLOUGHBY

M **ARCHAEOLOGICAL SOCIETY OF OHIO,** Indian Museum of Lake County, Ohio, Technical Center Bldg B, Willoughby, OH 44094; PO Box 883, Willoughby, OH 44096-0883. Tel 440-951-3813; Internet Home Page Address: indianmuseumoflakecounty.org; *Dir* Ann Dewald; *Dir Emeritus* Gwen G King
Open Mon - Fri 10 AM - 4 PM, Sat & Sun 1 - 4 PM, cl major holiday weekends; Admis adults $2, students (K-12) $1, seniors $1.50, preschool children free; Estab 1980 to educate & preserve arts & crafts of all cultures of Native Americans; Average Annual Attendance: 5,000; Mem: 250; dues $20 - $1,000
Income: Financed by mem
Library Holdings: Book Volumes; Clipping Files
Special Subjects: American Indian Art, Archaeology, Eskimo Art
Collections: Crafts & art of all cultures of Native Americans of North America; Prehistoric artifacts from 10,000 BC to 1650 AD of early Ohio & Reeve Village Site, Lake County, Ohio
Activities: Classes for adults & children; docent training; lect open to pub; tours; competitions with awards; mus shop sells books, Native American crafts

L **Indian Museum of Lake County Library,** WE Tech Ctr - Bldg B, 25 Public Sq Willoughby, OH 44094; 25 Public Sq, PO Box 883 Willoughby, OH 44096-0883. Tel 440-951-3813; Internet Home Page Address: indianmuseumoflakecounty.org; *Dir* Ann Dewald
Open Mon-Fri 10AM-4PM, June-Aug 10AM-4PM, Sat-Sun 1PM-4PM, cl holidays & winter & spring break; Admis adults $2, seniors $1.50, children grades K-12 $1; Estab 1980; For reference
Income: Financed by mem
Library Holdings: Book Volumes; Periodical Subscriptions 4
Special Subjects: Archaeology, American Indian Art, Eskimo Art
Activities: Classes for adults & children, docent training; mus sales shop sells Native American items

A **FINE ARTS ASSOCIATION,** School of Fine Arts, 38660 Mentor Ave, Willoughby, OH 44094-7797. Tel 440-951-7500; Fax 440-975-4592; Elec Mail faa@bbs2.rmrc.net; Internet Home Page Address: www.fineartsassociation.org; *Pres* Richard T Spote Jr; *Exec Dir* Charles D Lawrence
Open Mon - Fri 9 AM - 8 PM, Sat 9 AM - 5 PM; No admis fee; Estab 1957 to bring arts educ to all people regardless of their ability to pay, race or social standing; Main floor gallery houses theme, one-man & group monthly exhibs; 2nd floor gallery houses monthly school exhibits; Average Annual Attendance: 70,000; Mem: 500; dues $25 & up; ann meeting in Sept
Income: Financed by class fees and donations
Exhibitions: Monthly exhibs, theme, one man & group; ann juried exhibit for area artists
Activities: Classes for adults & children; dramatic progs; lect open to pub, 10 vis lectrs per yr; gallery talks; tours; concerts; competitions with awards; schols; mus shop sells original art

WOOSTER

M **THE COLLEGE OF WOOSTER,** The College of Wooster Art Museum, 1220 Beall Ave, Ebert Art Center Wooster, OH 44691-2393. Tel 330-263-2388; Tel 330-263-2495; Fax 330-263-2633; Elec Mail kzurko@wooster.edu; Internet Home Page Address: www.wooster.edu/cwam; *Dir* Kitty McManus Zurko; *Preparator* Douglas McGlumphy; *Art Mus Admin Coordr* Rose Seling
Open Tues - Fri 10:30 AM - 4:30 PM, Sat & Sun 1 - 5 PM, cl Mon & during col breaks; No admis fee; College art mus; Average Annual Attendance: 9,000
Income: Financed by col gen fund & grants
Special Subjects: Decorative Arts, Pottery, Graphics, Painting-American, Prints, American Indian Art, Bronzes, African Art, Ethnology, Pre-Columbian Art, Textiles, Ceramics, Woodcuts, Collages, Portraits, Furniture, Glass, Porcelain, Oriental Art, Asian Art, Painting-French, Carpets & Rugs, Historical Material, Coins & Medals, Tapestries, Antiquities-Oriental, Antiquities-Egyptian, Antiquities-Greek
Collections: John Taylor Arms Print Collection; William C Mithoefer Collection of African Art; ancient & contemporary ceramics; Chinese snuff bottles & bronzes; Cypriote pottery; ethnographic materials; WWII posters; Middle Eastern pottery

Exhibitions: Traveling exhibs & special in-house exhibs. Average six yearly exhibs drawn either from the colls or focusing on the work of contemporary artists
Publications: Exhibition catalogs, brochures
Activities: Lect & receptions open to pub, 4-6 vis lectrs per year; gallery talks; tours; sponsoring of competitions; concerts; originates traveling exhibs to other museums, col & univ galleries

M **WAYNE CENTER FOR THE ARTS,** 237 S Walnut St, Wooster, OH 44691-4753. Tel 330-264-2787; Fax 330-264-9314; Elec Mail WayneCtr@wayneartscenter.org; *Exec Dir* Robb Hyde; *Educ Coordr* Lisa Zemancik
Open Mon noon - 9 PM, Tues - Thurs 9 AM - 9 PM, Fri 9 AM - 7 PM, Sat 9 AM - 2 PM, cl Sun; No admis fee for exhibs; performances vary; Estab 1973 to strengthen our community by enriching peoples' lives through the arts; The Ctr for the Arts is housed in a former school bldg, offering large & open galleries & studios; Average Annual Attendance: 12,000; Mem: 400+
Income: donations; memberships; ticket fees; grants; sponsorships
Special Subjects: Painting-American, Prints, Bronzes, African Art, Ceramics, Porcelain, Oriental Art, Tapestries
Exhibitions: Monthly showing of local, regional and nationally renowned artists
Publications: Artalk newsletter, quarterly
Activities: Classes for adults & children; community outreach progs; lect open to pub, 10-15 vis lectrs per yr; gallery talks; concerts; book traveling exhibs

XENIA

A **GREENE COUNTY HISTORICAL SOCIETY,** 74 W Church St, Xenia, OH 45385-2902. Tel 937-372-4606; Fax 937-376-5660; Elec Mail GCHSXO@yahoo.com; Internet Home Page Address: www.gchsxo.org; *Exec Dir* Catherine Wilson
Open Tues, Thurs, Fri 9 AM - Noon & 1 - 3:30 PM; Admis adult $3, under 18 $2; Estab 1929 to preserve the history of Greene County, OH; Average Annual Attendance: 2,000; Mem: 450; dues individual $20, seniors $10; monthly meeting 2nd Mon
Income: Financed by mem, county appropriation & various fund raising activities
Library Holdings: Clipping Files; Manuscripts; Memorabilia; Original Documents; Photographs
Collections: Clothing; Medical; Military; Railroad (historic model)
Exhibitions: Conestoga Wagon; Log House & furnishings; Railroad; Victorian House & furnishings
Publications: Historic Greene County
Activities: Lect open to pub, 12 vis lectrs per yr; sales shop sells books, notepaper, materials relating to county

YELLOW SPRINGS

M **ANTIOCH COLLEGE,** Noyes & Read Gallery/Herndon Gallery, 150 ES South College St, Yellow Springs, OH 45387-1635. Tel 937-769-1149; *Dir* Nevin Mercede
Open Mon - Sat 1 - 5 PM; No admis fee; Estab 1972. Noyes Gallery to offer works to students & the community that both challenge & broaden their definitions of Art; Read Gallery is primarily a student gallery; Herndon Gallery offers works in many medias, including painting, photography & video
Exhibitions: World Community of Ceramists

YOUNGSTOWN

M **THE BUTLER INSTITUTE OF AMERICAN ART,** Art Museum, 524 Wick Ave, Youngstown, OH 44502-1286. Tel 330-743-1107; Fax 330-743-9567; Elec Mail info@butlerart.com; Internet Home Page Address: www.butlerart.com; *Dir & Chief Cur* Dr Louis A Zona; *Registrar* Rebecca Davis; *Bus Mgr* Marty Menk; *Pub Rels* Kathy Earnhart; *Mem* Georgiana Carfano; *Mus Shop Mgr* Renee Sheakoski; *Preparator* Ed Hallahan; *Preparator* Ray Johnson
Open Tues - Sat 11 AM - 4 PM, Sun Noon - 4 PM, cl Mon & major holidays; No admis fee; Estab 1919 & is the first mus building to be devoted entirely to American Art; Eighteen galleries containing 11,000 works of American artists; Average Annual Attendance: 120,000; Mem: 2,500; dues individual $35, household (couple) $45, sustainer $60, sponsor $300, patron $500, collector $1,000, connoisseur $3,000, corporate $5,000; meetings in Sept
Income: Financed by endowment, grants & gifts
Library Holdings: Auction Catalogs; Clipping Files; Exhibition Catalogs; Kodachrome Transparencies; Photographs; Slides
Special Subjects: Drawings, Painting-American, Prints, Sculpture, Watercolors, American Indian Art, Ceramics, Marine Painting
Collections: Comprehensive coll of American art covering three centuries; American Impressionism; The American West & Marine & Sports Art colls; Principle artists: Winslow Homer, Albert Bierstadt, Martin Johnson Heade, Georgia O'Keeffe, Charles Sheeler, Helen Frankenthaler, John S Sargent, J M Whistler, Mary Cassatt, Thomas Cole, Edward Hopper, Romare Bearden, Andy Warhol & Robert Motherwell; American Glass Bells, Miniatures of all the Presidents of the United States (watercolor); Robert Rauschenberg
Publications: Exhib catalogues; bimonthly newsletter; biennial report
Activities: Classes for adults & children; docent training; lects open to pub; concerts; gallery talks; tours; competitions with awards; objects of art lent to Trumball & Columbiana Counties; book traveling exhibs 10 per yr; originates traveling exhibs; mus shop sells books, original art, prints & reproductions; Trumball Branch, Salem Branch

L **Hopper Resource Library,** 524 Wick Ave, Youngstown, OH 44502. Tel 330-743-1107, 743-1711
Open Tues & Thurs - Sat 11 AM - 4 PM, Wed 11 AM - 8 PM, Sun Noon - 4 PM; No admis fee; For reference only; Average Annual Attendance: 122,000; Mem: 3090
Income: Financed by endowment, grants & gifts

Library Holdings: Book Volumes 1500; Clipping Files; Exhibition Catalogs; Framed Reproductions; Kodachrome Transparencies; Memorabilia; Pamphlets; Periodical Subscriptions 10; Photographs; Slides

M **YOUNGSTOWN STATE UNIVERSITY,** The John J McDonough Museum of Art, One University Plaza, Youngstown, OH 44555. Tel 330-742-1400; Fax 330-742-1492; Elec Mail sbkreism@cc.ysu.edu; Internet Home Page Address: www.ysu.edu; *Interim Dir* Angela DeLucia
Open Thurs - Sat 11 AM - 4 PM, Sun Noon - 4 PM; cl Tues; No admis fee; Estab 1991 to serve as a professional exhib facility for all art students & studio art faculty, to present visual arts progs of educ & artistic significance to the community, to exhibit works of established & emerging regional artists & present works from other university & larger mus colls; The purely post-modern structure has 18,000 sq ft & includes two outdoor sculpture terraces. The mus offers a 50-seat seminar auditorium, a two-story raw space installation gallery & two traditional galleries. Maintains lending library; Average Annual Attendance: 20,000
Collections: Contemporary Art
Exhibitions: Exhibs vary; call for details
Publications: Exhib catalogs; gallery guides
Activities: In-service workshops, art workshops; tours; competitions; lending coll contains slides; Contemporary Latino Voices; Aspects of Photography: Work on Loan from Mother Jones Magazine; GNATLAND: An Installation by Kay Willens; Governor's Institute for Gifted & Talented Students; Scholastic Art Awards Exhib

ZANESVILLE

A **ZANESVILLE MUSEUM OF ART,** 620 Military Rd, Zanesville, OH 43701-1533. Tel 740-452-0741; Fax 740-452-0797; Elec Mail vanessa@zanesvilleart.org; Internet Home Page Address: www.zanesvilleart.org; *Pres Bd Trustees* Richard Duncan; *VPres* Alice Graham; *Secy* Vanessa Brosie; *Opers Tech* Fred Orr; *Temp Opers Mgr* Andrew Near
Open Wed & Fri 10 AM - 5 PM, Thurs 10 AM - 7:30 PM, Sat 10 AM - 5 PM, cl Sun, Mon, Tues & holidays; Admis adults $6, seniors 60 & over & children 10-18 $4, children under 10 & mems free; Estab 1936 to provide a pub center for the arts, permanent colls & temporary exhibs, classes in arts, library of art volumes & a meeting place for art & civic groups; There are 10 galleries for permanent collection & temporary exhibitions; handicapped facilities; Average Annual Attendance: 25,000; Mem: 250; dues $30 & up
Income: Financed by endowment & mem
Collections: American, European & Oriental paintings, sculptures, ceramics, prints, drawings & crafts; children's art; Midwest & Zanesville ceramics & glass
Exhibitions: Rotating exhibits
Publications: Bulletin, trimonthly
Activities: Classes for adults & children; docent training; lect open to pub; gallery talks; tours; competitions with awards; book 2 traveling exhibs per yr; originate traveling exhibs to Ohio museums; mus shop sells books

OKLAHOMA

ANADARKO

M **NATIONAL HALL OF FAME FOR FAMOUS AMERICAN INDIANS,** PO Box 548, Anadarko, OK 73005-0548. Tel 405-247-5555; *Dir & Exec VPres* Joe McBride; *Treas* George F Moran; *Secy* Carolyn N McBride
Open Mon - Sat 9 AM - 5 PM, Sun 1 - 5 PM; No admis fee; Estab 1952 to honor famous American Indians who have contributed to the culture of America, including statesmen, innovators, sportsmen, warriors; to teach the youth of our country that there is a reward for greatness; An outdoor mus in a landscaped area containing bronze sculptured portraits of honorees; Average Annual Attendance: 23,000; Mem: 250; dues life $100, Individual or Family $25; ann meeting Aug
Income: Finance by mem, city & state appropriation & donation
Purchases: $2500 - $20,000
Special Subjects: American Indian Art, Bronzes
Collections: Bronze sculptured portraits & bronze statues of two animals important to Indian culture
Publications: Brochure
Activities: Dedication ceremonies for honorees in Aug; sales shop sells books & postcards

M **SOUTHERN PLAINS INDIAN MUSEUM,** 715 E Central, Anadarko, OK 73005-4437; PO Box 749, Anadarko, OK 73005-0749. Tel 405-247-6221; Fax 405-247-7593; *Chief Cur* Rosemary Ellison
Open June - Sept Mon - Sat 9 AM - 5 PM, Sun 1 - 5 PM; Oct - May Tues - Sat 9 AM - 5 PM, Sun 1 - 5 PM; cl New Year's Day, Thanksgiving & Christmas; Admis adults $3, groups of 10 or more & children ages 6-12 $1, children under 6 free, Sun no admis fee; Estab 1947-48 to promote the development of contemporary Native American arts & crafts of the United States. Administered & operated by the Indian Arts & Crafts Board, US Department of the Interior; Average Annual Attendance: 40,000
Income: Financed by federal appropriation
Purchases: Primarily dependent upon gifts
Special Subjects: American Indian Art, Crafts
Collections: Contemporary Native American arts & crafts of the United States; Historic Works by Southern Plains Indian Craftsmen; Historic Southern Plains Indian arts
Exhibitions: Historic Southern Plains Indian Arts; changing exhibs by contemporary native American artists & craftsmen; continuing series of one-person exhibs
Publications: One-person exhib brochure series, quarterly
Activities: Gallery talks

ARDMORE

A CHARLES B GODDARD CENTER FOR THE VISUAL & PERFORMING ARTS, 401 First Ave SW, Ardmore, OK 73402; PO Box 1624, Ardmore, OK 73402-1624. Tel 580-490-6556; Fax 580-226-8891; Elec Mail Leila@goddardcenter.org; Internet Home Page Address: www.goddardcenter.org; *Treas* Charles Williams; *Exec Dir* Leila Lenore; *Admin Asst* Marjorie Dolman; *Chmn* Millard Ingram; *Cur* Rudy Ellis; *Asst Cur* Natalie Garrison; *Art Studios Mgr* Liz Waltz
Open Tues - Fri 9 AM - 5 PM, Sat 1 - 4 PM, cl Sun, Mon & major holidays; No admis fee to art galleries; Estab Mar 1970 to bring fine art progs in the related fields of music, art & theater to local community at minimum cost, gallery to bring traveling exhibs to Ardmore; Four exhibit galleries; maintains lending & reference art library; Average Annual Attendance: 50,000; Mem: 600; dues $25 - $1000
Income: Supported by memberships, sponsorships & grant funding
Collections: Western & Contemporary Art, paintings, sculpture, prints; Small coll of Western Art & bronzes; American Graphic Art; photography; lifetime works of watercolor artist Dorothy Bertine
Exhibitions: Ardmore Art Exhibition; exhibits bi-monthly
Publications: Annual season review guide
Activities: Classes for adults & children in art & theatre; docent training; dramatic progs; art studio classes for adults & children; granite carving workshops; concerts; gallery talks; competitions with awards; tours; individual paintings & original objects of art lent to qualified institutions & museums

BARTLESVILLE

M THE FRANK PHILLIPS FOUNDATION INC, Woolaroc Museum, 1925 Woolaroc Ranch Rd, Bartlesville, OK 74003; PO Box 1647, Bartlesville, OK 74005-1647. Tel 918-336-0307; Fax 918-336-0084; Elec Mail lstone@woolaroc.org; Internet Home Page Address: www.woolaroc.org; *Dir* Ken Meek; *Cur Art* Linda Stone; *CEO* Bob Fraser
Open Summer: Memorial Day - Labor Day Tues - Sun 10 AM - 5 PM, Winter: Wed - Sun - 10 AM - 5 PM, cl Mon, Thanksgiving & Christmas; Admis 12 & older $10, 65 & older $8, under 12 free; Estab 1929 to house art & artifacts of the Southwest. Mus dedicated by Frank Phillips; Gallery has two levels, 8 rooms upstairs & 4 rooms downstairs; Average Annual Attendance: 125,000; Mem: 500
Income: Financed by endowment & revenues generated by admis fees & sales
Special Subjects: Archaeology, Drawings, Etchings & Engravings, American Western Art, Pottery, Painting-American, Prints, Textiles, Graphics, Watercolors, American Indian Art, Bronzes, Anthropology, Archaeology, Ethnology, Southwestern Art, Dolls, Historical Material, Mosaics
Collections: American Indian artifacts; prehistoric artifacts; paintings, drawings, graphics, minerals, sculpture, weapons
Exhibitions: various exhibits call for details
Publications: Woolaroc Story; Woolaroc, mus guidebook
Activities: Educ prog; docent training; gallery talks; tours; lending coll contains transparencies to be used to illustrate educ publs; book traveling exhibs; mus & sales shops sell books, magazines, original art, reproductions, prints, slides, Indian-made jewelry and pottery, postcards
L Library, State Hwy 123, Route 3 Box 2100 Bartlesville, OK 74003; PO Box 1647, Bartlesville, OK 74003-1647. Tel 918-336-0307; Fax 918-336-0084; Elec Mail lstone@woolaroc.com; *Dir* Robert R Lansdown
Open to employees only; Circ Reference library open to employees only; private facility
Library Holdings: Book Volumes 1000; Clipping Files; Exhibition Catalogs; Kodachrome Transparencies; Pamphlets; Photographs; Slides

CLAREMORE

M WILL ROGERS MEMORIAL MUSEUM & BIRTHPLACE RANCH, (Will Rogers Memorial & Museum) 1720 W Will Rogers Blvd, Claremore, OK 74018-3208; PO Box 157, Claremore, OK 74018-0157. Tel 918-341-0719; Fax 918-343-8119; Elec Mail wrinfo@willrogers.com; Internet Home Page Address: willrogers.com; *Cur* Gregory Malak; *Library & Colls* Steven Gragert; *Ranch Mgr* Jim Williams
Open daily 8 AM - 5 PM; No admis fee, donations accepted; Estab 1938 to perpetuate the name, works & spirit of Will Rogers; There are nine main galleries, diorama room, foyer & gardens. The large Jo Davidson statue of Will Rogers dominates the foyer; the north gallery includes photographs & paintings of Will Rogers & his ancestors (including a family tree, explaining his Indian heritage) & many other personal items; east gallery has saddle collection & other Western items; Jo Mora dioramas; additional gallery, research library & theatre; children's mus in basement. Maintains reference library; Average Annual Attendance: 202,000
Income: $750,000 (financed by state appropriation & pvt donations)
Library Holdings: Audio Tapes; Book Volumes; CD-ROMs; Clipping Files; Framed Reproductions; Manuscripts; Memorabilia; Motion Pictures; Original Art Works; Original Documents; Photographs; Prints; Records; Sculpture; Slides; Video Tapes
Collections: Colls of Paintings by various artists commissioned by a calendar company with originals donated to Memorial; Count Tamburini Oil of Will Rogers; Jo Mora Dioramas (13); Large Equestrian Statue by Electra Wagoner Biggs; Mural by Ray Piercey; Original of Will Rogers by Leyendecker; Paintings of Will & his parents by local artists; Original of Will Rogers by Charles Banks Wilson; 7-foot oil on canvas by Wayne Cooper of Will Rogers on horseback; Gordon Kuntz Coll (81 original movie poster coll of Will Rogers' movies)
Publications: Brochures and materials for students
Activities: Lect open to pub; tours; assist with publishing project: The Papers of Will Rogers; originate traveling exhibs; sales shop sells VHS tapes, Will Rogers & Oklahoma items; Will Rogers Youth Museum
L Media Center Library, 1720 W Will Rogers Blvd, Claremore, OK 74017-3208; PO Box 157, Claremore, OK 74018-3208. Tel 918-341-0719; Fax 918-341-8246; WATS 800-324-9455; *Librn* Patricia Lowe; *Cur* Gregory Malak; *Dir* Joseph Carter

Reference library for research by appointment only
Library Holdings: Audio Tapes; Book Volumes 2500; CD-ROMs; Cassettes; Clipping Files; Exhibition Catalogs; Filmstrips; Framed Reproductions; Kodachrome Transparencies; Manuscripts; Memorabilia; Motion Pictures; Original Art Works; Original Documents; Other Holdings Original writings on CD Rom; Pamphlets; Periodical Subscriptions 15; Photographs 1500; Prints; Records; Reproductions; Sculpture; Slides; Video Tapes
Collections: Will Rogers Collection

CUSHING

L LACHENMEYER ARTS CENTER, Art Resource Library, 700 S Little, Cushing, OK 74023; PO Box 586, Cushing, OK 74023-0586. Tel 918-225-7525; Elec Mail roblarts@sbcglobal.net; *Dir* Rob Smith
Open Mon, Wed & Fri 9 AM - 5 PM, Tues & Thurs 6 - 9 PM ; No admis fee; Estab 1984 to provide art classes & art exhibits to the pub
Income: Financed by endowment
Library Holdings: Book Volumes 125; Periodical Subscriptions; Video Tapes
Exhibitions: Youth Arts Exhibit (March annually); Community Art Show (every other Sept); Tour de Quartz (Dec annually)
Activities: Classes for adults & children

GOODWELL

M NO MAN'S LAND HISTORICAL SOCIETY, (No Man's Land Historical Society Museum) No Man's Land Museum, 207 W Sewell St, Goodwell, OK 73939-0278; PO Box 278, Goodwell, OK 73939-0278. Tel 580-349-2670; Fax 580-349-2670; *Pres* Romald Kincannon; *VPres* V. Pauline Hodges; *Mgr* Sue Weissinger
Open Tues - Sat 10 AM - 3 PM, cl Sun, Mon & holidays; No admis fee; Estab 1934 to procure appropriate mus material with spec regard to portraying the history of No Man's Land (Oklahoma Panhandle) & the immediate adjacent regions; The gallery is 14 ft x 40 ft (560 sq ft); Average Annual Attendance: 4,000; Mem: 307; dues life $200, organization $100, individual $15
Income: Financed by state appropriation & donations
Special Subjects: Sculpture, Painting-American, Watercolors, American Indian Art, American Western Art, Anthropology, Archaeology, Ethnology, Southwestern Art, Textiles, Folk Art, Dolls, Historical Material, Embroidery
Collections: Duckett Alabaster Carvings; Oils by Pearl Robison Burrows Burns
Exhibitions: Nine exhibits each yr by regional artists
Activities: Sales shop sells books & prints

LANGSTON

M LANGSTON UNIVERSITY, Melvin B Tolson Black Heritage Center, PO Box 1600, Langston, OK 73050-1600. Tel 405-466-3346; Fax 405-466-2979; Elec Mail egrady@lunet.edu; *Dir Library* Bettye Black; *Cur Tolson Ctr* Jovani Williams; *Asst Cur Tolson Ctr* Edward Grady
Open Mon, Wed & Fri 8 AM - 5 PM, Tues - Thurs 8 AM - 8 PM; No admis fee; Estab 1959 to exhibit pertinent works of art, both contemporary & traditional; to serve as a teaching tool for students; Library reading room; Average Annual Attendance: 6,000
Income: Financed by state appropriation
Library Holdings: Book Volumes; Cassettes; Clipping Files; Compact Disks; DVDs; Fiche; Filmstrips; Framed Reproductions; Memorabilia; Original Art Works; Original Documents; Periodical Subscriptions; Records; Reels; Sculpture; Slides
Special Subjects: Afro-American Art, Painting-American, Sculpture, African Art
Collections: African American Art & Artifacts; Paintings & Photographs; Books, tapes, video colls
Activities: Classes for adults; lects open to pub, 6-10 vis lectrs per yr; gallery talks; tours

LAWTON

M CAMERON UNIVERSITY ART GALLERY, 2800 Gore Blvd, Lawton, OK 73502-6377. Tel 580-581-2211
No admis fee
Collections: Paintings; photographs; sculpture

M TRUST AUTHORITY, Museum of the Great Plains, 601 NW Ferris, Lawton, OK 73507-5443. Tel 580-581-3460; Fax 580-581-3458; Elec Mail develop@museumgreatplains.org; Internet Home Page Address: www.museumgreatplains.org; *Photo Lab Technician* Brian Smith; *Head Cur* Deborah Baroff; *Exec Dir* John Hernandez; *Dir Develop* Bart McClenny; *Educator Cur* Jana Brown; *Exec Asst* Mary Owensby
Open Mon - Sat 10 AM - 5 PM, Sun 1 - 5 PM; Admis adults 12 & over $6, seniors $5, children between 7 & 11 $2.50, children under 6 free; Estab 1960 to collect, preserve, interpret & exhibit items of the cultural history of man in the Great Plains of North America. Galleries of the Mus of the Great Plains express a regional concept of interpreting the relationship of man to a semi-arid plains environment; 27,000 sq ft; Average Annual Attendance: 25,000; Mem: 700; dues $30 - $200
Income: Financed by endowment, city appropriations & contributions
Library Holdings: Original Documents; Periodical Subscriptions; Photographs
Special Subjects: Architecture, Photography, American Indian Art, American Western Art, Anthropology, Archaeology, Ethnology, Southwestern Art, Costumes, Crafts, Manuscripts, Historical Material, Maps, Restorations, Period Rooms
Collections: Archaeological, ethnological, historical & natural science colls relating to man's inhabitance of the Great Plains; photographs relating to Plains Indians, agriculture, settlement, ranching
Exhibitions: Changing History, archaeology & ethnological exhibits
Publications: Great Plains Journal, ann; Museum Newsletter, quarterly

Activities: Classes for adults & children; dramatic progs; docent training; lects open to pub, 6 vis lectrs per yr; gallery talks; tours; AAM accredited; lending colls contains framed reproductions, kodachromes, photographs & slides; originate traveling exhibs; mus store sells books, magazines, original art, reproductions, prints, slides, clothing & souvenir items

L   **Research Library,** 601 NW Ferris, Lawton, OK 73507-5443. Tel 580-581-3460; Elec Mail mgp@sirinet.net; *Cur Spec Coll* Deborah Baroff
Open Tues - Fri 8 AM - 5 PM; Estab 1961 to provide research materials for the 10-state Great Plains region; Lending to staff only
Income: Financed by endowment, city & state appropriations
Library Holdings: Book Volumes 30,000; Clipping Files; Exhibition Catalogs; Filmstrips; Kodachrome Transparencies; Manuscripts; Memorabilia; Motion Pictures; Original Art Works; Other Holdings Documents 300,000; Pamphlets; Periodical Subscriptions 150; Photographs 22,000; Prints; Reels; Slides
Special Subjects: Photography, Painting-American, Historical Material, Archaeology, Ethnology, American Western Art, American Indian Art, Anthropology, Southwestern Art, Period Rooms, Coins & Medals
Collections: Archives; photographic colls
Publications: Great Plains Journal, annual; Museum of the Great Plains Newsletter, irregularly

MUSKOGEE

M   **ATALOA LODGE MUSEUM,** 2299 Old Bacone Rd, Muskogee, OK 74403-1568. Tel 918-781-7283; Fax 918-683-4588; Elec Mail jtimothy@bacone.edu; Internet Home Page Address: www.bacone.edu/ataloa; *Dir* John Timothy
Open Mon - Sat 8 AM - 5 PM, cl noon - 1 PM, Sun 1 - 5 PM; No admis fee, donations accepted; Estab to enhance Indian culture by having a coll of artifacts from various Indian tribes; Three large rooms; Average Annual Attendance: 3,000
Income: Financed through Bacone Col
Special Subjects: American Indian Art
Collections: Indian art; Indian crafts & artifacts; silverwork, weapons, blankets, dolls, beadwork, pottery, weaving & basketry, items of daily use
Exhibitions: Rotating exhibits
Activities: Tours; sales shop sells books, magazines, original art, reproductions, prints, ceramics, beadwork, silversmithing work, baskets & handcrafted items

M   **FIVE CIVILIZED TRIBES MUSEUM,** 1101 Honor Heights Dr, Agency Hill Muskogee, OK 74401-1321. Tel 918-683-1701; Fax 918-683-3070; Elec Mail 5tribesdirector@sbcglobal.net; Internet Home Page Address: www.fivetribes.org; *Pres Bd Dirs* Richard Bradley; *Dir* Clara Reekie; *Admin Asst* Michael Parks; *Store Mgr* Deena Wood
Open Mon - Sat 10 AM - 5 PM, Sun 1 - 5 PM; Admis adults $2, seniors $1.75, students $1, children under 6 free; Estab 1966 to exhibit artifacts, relics, history, and traditional Indian art of the Cherokee, Chickasaw, Choctaw, Creek, and Seminole Indian Tribes; Average Annual Attendance: 30,000; Mem: 1000; dues vary; ann meeting in Mar
Income: $48,000 (financed by mem & admis)
Special Subjects: Photography, Sculpture, American Indian Art, Bronzes, Pottery, Woodcarvings, Maps
Collections: Traditional Indian art by known artists of Five Tribes heritage, including original paintings & sculpture; large coll of Jerome Tiger originals
Exhibitions: Four Annual Judged Exhibitions: Competitive Art Show; Students Competitive Show; Craft Competition; Masters' Exhibition
Publications: Quarterly newsletter
Activities: Docent training; lect open to pub; gallery talks; tours; competitions with awards; individual paintings & original objects of art lent to other museums & spec exhibits with board approval; lending coll contains original art works; mus shop selling books, original art, reproductions, prints, beadwork, pottery, basketry & other handmade items

L   **Library,** 1101 Honor Heights Dr, Agency Hill Muskogee, OK 74401-1321. Tel 918-683-1701; Fax 918-683-3070; Internet Home Page Address: www.fivetribes.com; *Dir* Mary Robinson
Open Mon - Sat 10 AM - 2 PM, cl Sun; Admis adult $3, senior $2, student $1.50; Estab 1966 to preserve history, culture, traditions, legends, etc of Five Civilized Tribes (Cherokee, Creek, Choctaw, Chickasaw, and Seminole tribes); Maintains an art gallery
Income: 501(c)(3)
Library Holdings: Book Volumes 3500; Cassettes; Clipping Files; Exhibition Catalogs; Framed Reproductions; Lantern Slides; Manuscripts; Memorabilia; Original Art Works; Other Holdings Original documents; Pamphlets; Periodical Subscriptions 5; Photographs; Prints; Reproductions; Sculpture
Special Subjects: Manuscripts, Maps, Historical Material, American Indian Art
Exhibitions: Mar - Student Art Show; Apr - Art under the Oaks; July - Competitive Art Show; Nov - Master Art Show
Publications: Newsletter, every three months

NORMAN

M   **FIREHOUSE ART CENTER,** 444 S Flood, Norman, OK 73069. Tel 405-329-4523; Fax 405-292-9763; Elec Mail firehouse@info.com; Internet Home Page Address: www.normanfirehouse.com; *Exec Dir* Douglas Shaw Elder
Open Mon - Fri 9:30 AM - 5:30 PM, Sat 10 AM - 4 PM; Estab 1971; 6 exhibits per year of contemporary work by local, state, regional & national artists; Average Annual Attendance: 10,000; Mem: 300; dues family $70
Income: $485,000 (financed by mem, city & state appropriation, grants, donations, fundraising)

Exhibitions: Annual Holiday Gallery; February Competitions in Chocolate Art; changing monthly exhibits
Activities: Classes for adults & children; workshops; lect open to pub, 2 vis lectrs per yr; gallery talks; competitions; awards, 2012 Governor's Award for Art Educ; schols offered; sales store sells original art, prints, pottery, jewelry, wood works & metal works

M   **UNIVERSITY OF OKLAHOMA,** Fred Jones Jr Museum of Art, 555 Elm Ave, Norman, OK 73019-3003. Tel 405-325-3272; Fax 405-325-7696; Internet Home Page Address: www.ou.edu/fjjma; *Dir & Chief Cur* Eric M Lee, PhD; *Cur Educ* Susan Baley; *Mus Preparator* Ross Cotts; *Mgr Admin & Operations* Becky Zurcher; *Supv Security & Registrar* Joyce Cummins; *Community Rels Officer* Mary Jane Rutherford; *Asst Dir & Cur of Coll* Gail Kana Anderson; *Cur of Ceramics* Jane Aerbersold; *Secy I* Jan Ragon; *Pub Rels* Stephanie Royse; *Cur of Native American Art* Mary Jo Watson, PhD
Open Tues - Thurs & Sat 10 AM - 5 PM, Fri 10 AM - 9 PM, Sun 1 - 5 PM, cl Mon; Admis adults $5, seniors 65 & over $4, children 6-17 $3, OU faculty & staff $2, children under 6, mems & OU students with valid ID free; Estab 1936 to provide cultural enrichment for the people of Oklahoma; to collect, preserve, exhibit & research art of various periods; Approx 15,000 sq ft for permanent & temporary exhibs on two indoor levels; 34,000 sq ft expansion added to existing bldg which totals 29,000 sq ft; Average Annual Attendance: 50,000; Mem: 495; dues $15 - $1000; meetings in Sept & Jan
Income: Financed by state, univ allocation, foundation endowment, Board of Visitors & grants
Purchases: Focus upon French Impressionism, American art, Native American art, contemporary art & photography
Special Subjects: Photography, Painting-European, African Art
Collections: French Impressionism; American art; Native American art; contemporary art; photography; icons
Publications: Calendar of activities; posters; announcements; exhib catalogues
Activities: Docent training; classes for children; dramatic progs; 5-10 lectrs per yr open to pub; concerts; gallery talks; tours; family days; student exhibs with awards; 3 per yr; sales shop sells books, magazines, reproductions, prints, jewelry, notecards, children's toys & other gifts

L   **Architecture Library,** 830 Van Vleet Oval, Gould Hall Rm 105 Norman, OK 73019. Tel 405-325-5521; Fax 405-325-6637; Internet Home Page Address: libraries.ou.edu/depts/architecture; *Library Technician* Tracy Chapman; *Fine & Applied Arts Librn* Matthew Stock
Open fall Tues - Fri 8 AM - 7 PM, Sun 1 - 5 PM, summer Tues - Fri 8 AM - 7 PM, cl weekends
Library Holdings: Book Volumes 17,000; Periodical Subscriptions 42
Special Subjects: Landscape Architecture, Interior Design, Architecture

L   **Fine Arts Library,** 500 W Boyd St, Catlett Music Ctr Norman, OK 73019-3130. Tel 405-325-4243; Fax 405-325-4243; Elec Mail drmosser@ou.edu; Internet Home Page Address: libraries.ou.edu; *Library Technician III* Dennis Mosser; *Fine & Applied Arts Librn* Matthew Stock
Open fall sem Mon - Thurs 8 AM - 9 PM, Fri 8 AM - 5 PM, Sat 11 AM - 4 PM, Sun 2 - 9 PM; Estab to provide instructional support to the acad community of the univ & gen service to the people of the state; Circ 6900
Income: Financed by state appropriation
Library Holdings: Book Volumes 27,000; CD-ROMs; Fiche; Periodical Subscriptions 50; Reels; Video Tapes

OKLAHOMA CITY

C   **AMERICAN HOMING PIGEON INSTITUTE,** 2300 Northeast 63rd St, Oklahoma City, OK 73111-8208. Tel 405-478-5155; Fax 405-478-4552; Elec Mail pigeoncenter@aol.com; Internet Home Page Address: www.pigeoncenter.org; *Admin Asst* Linda Oughton; *Facilities Mgr & Gen Mgr* Randy Good Pasture
Estab 1973 to preserve & display the rich heritage of domestic pigeons & doves & to foster the keeping of registered pigeons as a unique & rewarding hobby; Mem: 1000; dues $20
Income: Financed by mem
Purchases: Several pigeon art book colls
Activities: Classes for children; exten dept

M   **CITY ARTS CENTER AT FAIR PARK,** 3000 General Pershing Blvd, Oklahoma City, OK 73107-6202. Tel 405-951-0000; Fax 405-951-0003; Elec Mail info@cityartscenter.org; Internet Home Page Address: www.cityartscenter.org; *Admin Dir* Sherry Fair; *Artistic Dir* Clint Stone; *Develop Dir* Annah Chakola-Ramsey; *Accounting Mgr* Gloria Dale; *Pub Rels Mgr* Kristen Richter; *Educ Dir* Josh Buss
Open Mon-Thurs 9AM-10PM, Fri-Sat 9AM-5PM; cl Sun & major holidays; No admis fee; donations accepted
Collections: contemporary works

M   **INDIVIDUAL ARTISTS OF OKLAHOMA,** 811 N Broadway, Oklahoma City, OK 73102-6008; PO Box 60824, Oklahoma City, OK 73146-0824. Tel 405-232-6060; Fax 405-232-6061; Elec Mail iaogallery@coxinnet.net; Internet Home Page Address: www.iaogallery.org; *Dir* Jeff Stokes
Open Thurs & Sat noon - 5:30 PM, Fri noon - 8 PM; No admis fee; Estab 1979 to promote Oklahoma artists of all disciplines; Average Annual Attendance: 7,000; Mem: 400; dues $35; ann meeting in summer
Income: Financed by mem, fundraising & art sales
Exhibitions: Monthly exhibits of 3 visual artists, including spec photog gallery
Publications: Artzone, monthly newsletter

Activities: Lect open to pub, 1-2 vis lectrs per yr; competitions; concerts, gallery talks; film & video; traveling exhibs 1 per yr; originate traveling exhibs 1 per yr statewide

M **OKLAHOMA CITY MUSEUM OF ART,** 415 Couch Dr, Oklahoma City, OK 73102-2214. Tel 405-236-3100; Fax 405-236-3122; Elec Mail info@okcmoa.com; Internet Home Page Address: www.okcmoa.com; *Pres & CEO* Glen Gentele; *Exec Asst to Dir* Desiree Baber; *IT & Network Admin* Garrett Cullum; *Finance Asst* Diane Glenn; *Finance Dir* Rodney Lee; *Human Resources Mgr & Mus Store Coordr* Marcee Smith; *Mus Store Assoc* Heather King; *Mus Cafe Asst Mgr* Lauren Cates; *Mus Cafe Mgr* Ahmad Farnia; *Cur Colls* Alison Amick; *Consulting Cur* Hardy George, PhD; *Film Cur* Brian Hearn; *Assoc Cur & Dept Coordr* Jennifer Klos; *Senior Assoc Cur Educ & Mus School Admin* Chandra Boyd; *Asst Educ Cur* Bryon Chambers; *Registrar* Jim Meeks; *Head, Exhibit Design & Reg* Ernesto Sanchez Villarreal; *Facility Opers Dir* Jack Madden; *Projectionist & Film Asst* John Dudley Marshall; *Ed & Publications Coordr* Nicole Emmons; *Communs Mgr* Leslie Spears; *Chief Preparator* Freddy Harth; *Sr Develop Officer* Jim Eastep; *Assoc Develop Officer* Whitney Cross; *Security Chief* Adam Edwards; *Educ Asst* Brittany Kelly
Open Mon - Sun 10 AM - 7 PM, Thurs 10 AM - 9 PM (May - Oct), cl New Year's Day, Independence Day, Thanksgiving & Christmas Day; Admis adults $12, college students, seniors & children 6-18 $10, military w/ID $5, children under 5 & mems free; Estab 1945; Circ Library; 15 galleries, theatre, library, classrooms, store & full service cafe; Average Annual Attendance: 130,000; Mem: 4000; dues $50 - $1000; ann meeting in June
Income: Pvt funded by earned income, corp, foundations & indiv contributions & interest earned on endowments
Library Holdings: Auction Catalogs; Audio Tapes; Book Volumes; DVDs; Exhibition Catalogs; Kodachrome Transparencies; Motion Pictures; Original Art Works; Periodical Subscriptions; Photographs; Prints; Reels; Sculpture; Slides; Video Tapes
Special Subjects: Painting-British, Drawings, Latin American Art, Painting-American, Photography, Prints, Sculpture, Watercolors, Woodcuts, Etchings & Engravings, Landscapes, Painting-European, Portraits, Glass, Oriental Art, Painting-French, Maps, Painting-Italian, Painting-German
Collections: 19th-20th century American paintings including works by Bellows, Tiffany, Chase, Cropsey, Benton, Moran, Hassam; 20th century American paintings & graphics, including Henri, Marin, Kelly, Indiana, Francis, Davis, Warhol; Sculpture by Bertoia, Bontecou, Calder, Henry Moore; Most comprehensive collection of Chihuly glass in world; Washington Gallery of Modern Art collection; RA Young Collection; Westheimer Family Collection
Exhibitions: Dale Chihuly: The Collection
Publications: Coll catalogues; spec exhib catalogs
Activities: Classes for adults & children; docent training; lects open to pub; gallery talks; tours; schol; individual paintings & original objects of art lent to other accredited mus; lending collection contains original art works, original prints, paintings & photographs; book traveling exhibs 1-3 per yr; originate traveling exhibs to other mus nationally; mus shop sells books, magazines & prints

M **OKLAHOMA CITY UNIVERSITY,** Hulsey Gallery-Norick Art Center, 2501 N Blackwelder, Oklahoma City, OK 73106. Tel 405-208-5226; Tel 405-208-5230; Fax 405-557-6029; Internet Home Page Address: www.okcu.edu; *Admin Asst* Maria Amos; *Gallery Dir* Burt Harbison
Open Mon - Fri 10 AM - 4 PM, Sun 2 - 5 PM; No admis fee; Estab 1985 to educ in the arts; Gallery is 2,200 sq ft with fabric covered walls & moveable display forms; Average Annual Attendance: 2,000
Income: Financed by endowment & the Univ
Collections: Oklahoma City University Art Coll; Art donated by individuals & organizations from Oklahoma
Exhibitions: Oklahoma City University Student Exhibit; Oklahoma High School Print & Drawing Exhibit; exhibits change monthly
Activities: Classes for adults; lect open to pub, 2-3 vis lectrs per yr; individual paintings & original works of art lent to various departments of the Oklahoma City Univ campus

L **Scheme Shop,** 2501 N Blackwelder, Oklahoma City, OK 73106. Tel 405-521-5082; Fax 405-521-5493; Elec Mail dhall@okcu.edu; *Dir* Dale Hall
Open Mon - Fri 9 AM - 5 PM, hours vary on weekends, call for appointment; For lending & reference
Income: Financed by endowment, donation & University
Library Holdings: Book Volumes 207; Exhibition Catalogs; Original Art Works; Photographs; Prints; Reproductions; Sculpture; Video Tapes

M **OKLAHOMA HISTORICAL SOCIETY,** State Museum of History, 2401 N Laird Ave, Oklahoma City, OK 73105-7914. Tel 405-522-5248; Tel 405-521-2491; Fax 405-522-5402; Elec Mail statemuseum@ok-history.mus.ok.us; Internet Home Page Address: www.okhistory.org; *Dir* Dan Provo; *Asst Dir Coll* Jeff Briley; *Admin Asst* Trish Liscomb
Open Mon - Sat 9 AM - 5 PM, Sun noon - 5 PM, cl State holidays; Admis adults $5, seniors 62 & over $4, students $3, children 5 & under & mems free; Estab 1893 to provide an historical overview of the State of OK, from prehistory to the present, through interpretive exhibits, 3-D artifacts, original art & photographs; Average Annual Attendance: 150,000; Mem: 3500; dues $15; ann meeting Apr
Income: Financed by state appropriations & mem; soc depends on donations for additions to its colls
Special Subjects: Painting-American, American Indian Art, American Western Art, Anthropology, Archaeology, Ethnology, Decorative Arts, Historical Material, Period Rooms, Military Art
Collections: Anthropology; archaeology; historical artifacts; documents; American Indian art; Oklahoma art; Western art
Exhibitions: Permanent exhibits depicting pre-history, Oklahoma Indian Tribes' history, the Five Civilized Tribes' occupancy of Indian Territory, the land openings of the late 19th and early 20th centuries, statehood, and progress since statehood; spec exhibits 2-3 times per yr
Publications: Mistletoe Leaves, monthly newsletter; The Chronicles of Oklahoma, Society quarterly; various brochures and reprints
Activities: Special presentations & films for children & adults; interpretive progs; self-guided tours; individual paintings & original objects of art lent to qualified museums; lending coll contains paintings, 19th century beadwork & Indian artifacts; originate traveling exhibs; sales shop sells books, magazines

L **Library Resources Division,** 2401 N Laird Ave, Oklahoma City, OK 73105-7914. Tel 405-521-2491; Tel 405-522-5225; Fax 405-521-2492; Elec Mail libohs@ok-history.mus.ok.us; Internet Home Page Address: www.okhistory.org/research/index.html; *Dir Library Resources Div* Edward C Shoemaker; *Deputy Dir* Robert Thomas; *Dir Educ* Whit Edward; *Mus Shop Mgr* Mike Tippit; *Manuscripts & Archives* William Welge; *Okla Mus* Dan Provo; *Exec Dir* Bob Blackburn; *VChmn* Denzil Garrison
Open Mon - Sat 9 AM - 4:45 PM, first Mon of month 9 AM - 7:45 PM, cl Sun & legal holidays; Estab 1893 to collect & preserve historical materials & publications on Oklahoma history; For reference only
Income: financed by state appropriations & members
Library Holdings: Book Volumes 65,000; Clipping Files; Fiche; Pamphlets; Periodical Subscriptions 80; Photographs; Reels 12,493
Publications: Chronicles of Oklahoma, quarterly; Mistletoe Leaves, monthly newsletter

M **OMNIPLEX SCIENCE MUSEUM,** (Omniplex) 2100 NE 52nd, Oklahoma City, OK 73111. Tel 405-602-6664 (Omniplex), 427-5461; Fax 405-424-5106; Elec Mail omnipr@omniplex.org; Internet Home Page Address: www.omniplex.org; *Exec Dir* Chuck Schillings
Open Mon - Fri 9 AM - 5 PM, Sat 9 AM - 6 PM, Sun 11 AM - 6 PM; Admis adults $13.95, children & seniors $10.75, one price for entire center; Estab 1958 to focus on the inter-relationships between science, arts & the humanities & to supplement educ facilities offered in the pub schools in the areas of arts & sciences; The Kirkpatrick Center houses Omniplex, a hands-on science mus; mus shop; George Sutton bird paintings; Oklahoma Aviation & Space Hall of Fame & Mus; Center of American Indian Gallery; Sanamu African Gallery; Oriental Art Gallery; International Photography Hall of Fame; Oklahoma Zoological Society Offices; Kirkpatrick Planetarium; miniature Victorian house; antique clocks; US Navy Gallery; retired senior volunteer program; Oklahoma City Zoo offices; Average Annual Attendance: 350,000
Income: Financed by mem, pvt donations, Allied Arts Foundation, admis fees, & class tui
Special Subjects: Painting-American, Prints, African Art, Pre-Columbian Art, Oriental Art, Ivory
Collections: European & Oriental Ivory Sculpture; Japanese Woodblock Prints; Oceanic art; Pre-Columbian & American Indian art; Sutton paintings; Traditional & Contemporary African art; 1,000 photographs in Photography Hall of Fame
Exhibitions: Changing exhibs every 6-10 weeks; Dinosaurs
Publications: Insights, quarterly; Omniplex Newsletter, monthly
Activities: Classes for adults & children; docent training; lect open to pub; tours; book traveling exhibs; mus shop sells books, prints, science-related material, cards & jewelry

OKMULGEE

M **CREEK COUNCIL HOUSE MUSEUM,** 106 W 6th St, Okmulgee, OK 74447-5014; PO Box 918, Okmulgee, OK 74447-0918. Tel 918-756-2324; Fax 918-756-3671; Elec Mail creekmuseum@prodigy.n; *Dir* David Anderson; *VPres* Terry Bernis; *Mus Shop Mgr* Becka Hutchinson
Open Tues - Sat 10 AM - 4:30 PM; No admis fee; Estab 1867, first Council House built, present Council House erected in 1878 to collect & preserve artifacts from Creek history; Five rooms downstairs containing artifacts; four rooms upstairs showing art work, early time of Okmulgee; rooms of House of Warriors & House of Kings; Average Annual Attendance: 10,000-12,000
Income: Financed by mem & city appropriation
Special Subjects: Period Rooms
Collections: Creek Artifacts
Exhibitions: Annual Oklahoma Indian Art Market (juried competitions)
Activities: Seminars on Creek Culture & history; Ann Wild Onion Feast (traditional tribal foods); lect open to pub, 5-10 vis lectrs per yr; gallery talks; artmobile; book traveling exhibs; mus shop sells books, original art, reproductions, prints & Native American art & craft items

L **Library,** 106 W 6th St, Okmulgee, OK 74447-5014; PO Box 918, Okmulgee, OK 74447-0918. Tel 918-756-2324; Fax 918-756-3671; *Dir* David Anderson
Open Tues - Sat 10 AM - 4:30 PM & by appointment; Estab 1923 to collect & educate all Native American Tribes with emphasis on Muscogee Creek; For reference only, staff & academia
Library Holdings: Audio Tapes; Book Volumes 250; Clipping Files; Exhibition Catalogs; Framed Reproductions; Manuscripts; Memorabilia; Motion Pictures; Original Art Works; Pamphlets; Periodical Subscriptions 10; Photographs; Prints; Reels; Sculpture; Video Tapes

PARK HILL

A **CHEROKEE HERITAGE CENTER,** 21192 S Keeler Dr, Park Hill, OK 74451; PO Box 515, Tahlequah, OK 74465-0515. Tel 918-456-6007, 888-999-6007; Fax 918-456-6165; Elec Mail membership@cherokeeheritage.org; Internet Home Page Address: www.CherokeeHeritage.org; *Exec Dir* Carey Tilley; *Cur* Mickel Vantz; *Mktg Dir* Judy Pierce
Open Feb - Dec Mon - Sat 10 AM - 5 PM, Sun 1 - 5 PM, cl Jan; Admis adults $8.50, seniors 55 & over & students with ID $7.50, children $5, 6 & under free; rates vary with each show; Estab 1963 to commemorate & portray the history, traditions & lore of a great Indian tribe & to assist in improving local economic conditions; Maintains an art gallery, primarily Indian art; Average Annual Attendance: 150,000; Mem: 1500; dues $25 & up
Income: Financed by mem, admis & grants
Special Subjects: Historical Material, Manuscripts, Photography, Textiles, Pottery, Archaeology
Collections: Indian artists interpretations of Trails of Tears
Exhibitions: Trail of Tears Art Show, annually; various shows, lectures & classes
Publications: The Columns, quarterly

Activities: Classes for adults; lect open to pub; mus shop sells books, reproductions, prints & slides

L **Library & Archives,** PO Box 515, Tahlequah, OK 74465. Tel 918-456-6007, 888-999-6007; Fax 918-456-6165; Elec Mail archives@cherokeeheritage.org; Internet Home Page Address: www.CherokeeHeritage.org; *Archivist & Cur* Tom Mooney
Open Mon - Sat 10 AM - 5 PM, Sun 1 - 5 PM; Admis fees vary, call for details; Estab 1976 to preserve remnants of Cherokee history & to educate the general pub about that cultural heritage; a repository of Indian art & documents; Maintains an art gallery with work by artists of several different tribes; heavy emphasis given to the Cherokee experience
Income: Financed by mem, admis & grants
Library Holdings: Audio Tapes; Book Volumes 3000; Cassettes; Clipping Files; Filmstrips; Framed Reproductions; Kodachrome Transparencies; Manuscripts; Memorabilia; Original Art Works; Other Holdings Archival materials in excess of 500 cu ft; Manuscripts; Pamphlets; Periodical Subscriptions 10; Photographs; Prints; Reels 127; Sculpture; Slides
Exhibitions: Annual Trail of Tears Art Show (Indian artists' interpretation of the Trail of Tears theme); Cherokee Artists Exhibition; rotating exhibitions; special exhibitions, periodically (primarily Indian artists)
Publications: Quarterly columns
Activities: Classes for adult; tours

PONCA CITY

A **PONCA CITY ART ASSOCIATION,** 819 E Central Ave, Ponca City, OK 74601-5506; PO Box 1394, Ponca City, OK 74602-1394. Tel 580-765-9746; Elec Mail poncacityartcenter@gmail.com; Internet Home Page Address: poncacityartcenter.com; *Dir* Jerry Cathey
Open Wed - Sun 1 - 5 PM; No admis fee; Estab 1947 to encourage creative arts, to furnish place & sponsor art classes, art exhibits & workshops; Historical mansion; Average Annual Attendance: 3,000; Mem: 250; dues $20 family; ann meeting third Tues in Apr
Income: $40,000 (financed by mem, flea market, corporate & pvt)
Collections: Permanent fine arts coll; additions by purchases & donations
Exhibitions: Eight per year
Publications: Assn Bulletin, 6 per yr
Activities: Classes for adults & children; lect open to pub; tours; competitions for mems only with awards; schols offered; individual paintings lent to city-owned buildings; sales shop sells original art, reproductions & prints

M **PONCA CITY CULTURAL CENTER & MUSEUM,** 1000 E Grand Ave, Ponca City, OK 74601-5607. Tel 405-767-0427; *Exec Dir* Kathy Adams
Open Mon, Wed - Sat 10 AM - 5 PM, Sun & holidays 1 - 5 PM; cl Tues, Thanksgiving, Christmas Eve & Christmas Day, New Year's Eve & New Year's Day; Admis adults $1; The Cultural Center & Mus, a National Historic House since 1976, houses the Indian Mus, the Bryant Baker Studio, the 101 Ranch Room, & the DAR Memorial Mus; The Indian Mus, estab in 1936, places an emphasis on materials from the five neighboring tribes (Ponca, Kaw, Otoe, Osage, and Tonkawa) whose artistic use of beading, finger weaving & ribbon-work are displayed throughout the Mus. The Bryant Baker Studio is a replica of the New York Studio of Bryant Baker, sculptor of the Pioneer Woman Statue, a local landmark, & the studio contains original bronze & plaster sculpture. The 101 Ranch Room exhibits memorabilia from the world renowned Miller Brothers' 101 Ranch, located south of Ponca City in the early 1900s. The mus is the former home of Ernest Whitworth Marland, oilman & philanthropist & the tenth governor of Oklahoma; Average Annual Attendance: 35,000; Mem: Dues $10 - $1000
Income: Financed by the City of Ponca City & donations
Special Subjects: Sculpture, American Indian Art, Archaeology
Collections: Bryant Baker Collection: original sculpture; 101 Ranch memorabilia; Indian ethnography & archeology of Indian tribes throughout the United States
Exhibitions: Smithsonian Indian Images; Indian costumes, jewelry, pottery, baskets, musical instruments & tools
Publications: Brochure
Activities: Tours; sales shop sells books, arrowheads, Indian arts & crafts
L **Library,** 1000 E Grand Ave, Ponca City, OK 74601. Tel 405-767-0427; *Exec Dir* Kathy Adams
Open Mon, Wed - Sat 10 AM - 5 PM, Sun 1 - 5 PM, cl Tues; Primarily research library
Income: Financed by Ponca City
Library Holdings: Book Volumes 230; Periodical Subscriptions 13
Special Subjects: Archaeology, Anthropology

L **PONCA CITY LIBRARY,** Art Dept, 515 E Grand, Ponca City, OK 74601. Tel 580-767-0345; Fax 580-767-0377; *Head Technical Svcs* Paula Cain; *Dir* Holly LaBossiere
Open Mon - Thurs 9 AM - 9 PM, Fri 9 AM - 6 PM, Sat 9 AM - 5 PM, Sun 2 - 5 PM, cl Sun in June, July & Aug; Estab 1904 to serve the citizens of Ponca City; Circ 150,000; Gallery maintained
Library Holdings: Book Volumes 75,000; Cassettes; Framed Reproductions; Original Art Works; Pamphlets; Periodical Subscriptions 250; Photographs; Sculpture
Collections: Oriental Art Collection; Sandzen Collection; paintings

SHAWNEE

M **MABEE-GERRER MUSEUM OF ART,** 1900 W MacArthur Dr, Shawnee, OK 74804-2403. Tel 405-878-5300; Fax 405-878-5133; Elec Mail info@mgmoa.org; Internet Home Page Address: www.mgmoa.org; *Dir and Chief Cur* Dane Pollei; *Cur Collections* Delaynna Trim; *Cur Educ* Donna Merkt; *Preparator* Daniel Lay
Open daily Tues - Sat 10 AM - 4 PM, Sun 1 - 4 PM, cl Mon & holidays; Admis $5; Estab 1915 to contribute to the cultural growth & appreciation of the gen pub of Oklahoma as well as of the student body of Saint Gregory's Univ; A new 16,000 sq ft gallery was completed in 1979. In 1990, 1500 sq ft was added which includes a new gallery, a multi-purpose room & theater. Collections are being enlarged by purchases & by gifts; Average Annual Attendance: 40,000
Income: Financed by endowment, mem & foundation funds & grants
Special Subjects: American Indian Art, Decorative Arts, Drawings, Landscapes, Ceramics, Photography, Sculpture, Hispanic Art, Mexican Art, Painting-American, Prints, African Art, Ethnology, Pre-Columbian Art, Southwestern Art, Religious Art, Primitive art, Etchings & Engravings, Painting-European, Asian Art, Ivory, Renaissance Art, Medieval Art, Antiquities-Oriental, Painting-Italian, Antiquities-Persian, Antiquities-Egyptian, Antiquities-Greek, Antiquities-Roman, Military Art
Collections: Artifacts from ancient civilization; African, Egyptian, Roman, Grecian, Babylonian, Pre-Columbian North, South and Central American Indian, and South Pacific; etchings, engravings, serigraphs and lithographs; oil paintings by American and European artists; Native American; Icons: Greek, Russian & Balkan; Retablos from Mexico & New Mexico
Activities: Classes for adults & children; dramatic programs; docent training, teacher in service; arts integration teacher training; lects open to pub, 5 vis lectrs per yr; gallery talks; tours; individual paintings & original objects of art lent to other museums; books 1-2 traveling exhibs per yr; originates traveling exhibs; mus shop sells books, original art, reproductions

STILLWATER

M **OKLAHOMA STATE UNIVERSITY,** Gardiner Art Gallery, 108 Bartlett Ctr, Dept of Art, Bartlett Ctr for Studio Arts Stillwater, OK 74078-4084. Tel 405-744-9086; Tel 405-744-6016; Fax 405-744-5767; Elec Mail nwilkin@okway.okstate.edu; *Dir* B J Smith
Open Mon - Fri 8 AM - 4 PM, Sun 1 - 5 PM; No admis fee; Estab 1970 as a visual & educ exten of the department's classes & as a cultural service to the community & area; One gallery located on the ground fl, Bartlett Center for the Studio Arts; 250 running ft of wall space, 12 ft ceiling; Average Annual Attendance: 5,500
Income: Financed by col
Collections: 7250 drawings, prints, paintings, sculptures & ceramics, mostly mid-late 20th century
Exhibitions: Exhibitions change every 3-4 weeks year round; faculty, student, invitational & traveling shows
Publications: Exhib brochures; exhib schedules
Activities: Book traveling exhibs
L **Architecture Library,** 201A Architecture Bldg, Stillwater, OK 74078-0185. Tel 405-744-6047; Elec Mail bobos@okstate.edu; Internet Home Page Address: www.library.okstate.edu; *Architecture Librn* Susan Bobo
Open fall & spring semesters Mon - Thurs 9 AM - 9 PM Fri 9 AM - 5:30 PM, Sun 5 - 9 PM, hours may vary; Estab 1976 to meet the needs of the faculty & students of the School of Architecture
Income: financed by college
Purchases: $14,000
Library Holdings: Book Volumes 13,000; Other Holdings Compact discs; Periodical Subscriptions 40; Photographs; Slides; Video Tapes

TULSA

C **BANK OF OKLAHOMA NA,** Art Collection, 1 William Ctr, Tulsa, OK 74172-0172; PO Box 2300, Tulsa, OK 74102-2300. Tel 918-588-6000; Fax 918-588-8692; *VPres Exec Comt* Scott Ellison
Open 8 AM - 5 PM; Estab 1968 to enhance work environment; Coll displayed on 7 floors of the Bank of Oklahoma Tower
Purchases: $15,000
Collections: Modern Art
Activities: Lect; tours; schols offered to University of Tulsa

M **PHILBROOK MUSEUM OF ART,** 2727 S Rockford Rd, Tulsa, OK 74114-4104; PO Box 52510, Tulsa, OK 74152-0510. Tel 918-749-7941; Fax 918-743-4230; Elec Mail information@philbrook.org; Internet Home Page Address: www.philbrook.org; *Dir Exhib & Coll* Christine Kallenberger; *Deputy Dir* David Singleton; *Mus Shop Mgr* Susan Shrewder; *Preparator* George Brooks; *Dir Develop* Janis Updike Walker; *Facility Coordr* Charisse Cooper; *Cur Native American & Non-Western Art* Christina Burke; *Dir Educ & Pub Prog* Sarah Jesse; *Mgr Gardens* Melinda McMillan; *Dir & Pres* Randall Suffolk; *Cur European Art* Tanya Paul; *Chief Cur* Catherine Whitney; *Cur Modern & Contemp Art* Lauren Ross
Open Tues, Wed, Fri & Sat 10 AM - 5 PM, Thurs 10 AM - 8 PM, Sun 10 AM - 5 PM; free 2nd Sat of the month; Admis adults $9, students, groups of 10 or more & seniors $7, children 18 & under free; Estab 1939 as a gen art mus in an Italian Renaissance Revival Villa, the former home of philanthropist & oil baron Waite Phillips; Twenty-three acres of formal & natural gardens. Also contains a special exhib gallery; Average Annual Attendance: 148,452; Mem: 5000; dues $50 & up; ann meeting in June
Income: Financed by endowment, mem, earned income, corporate & pvt gifts & pub grants
Library Holdings: Auction Catalogs; Audio Tapes; Book Volumes; CD-ROMs; Clipping Files; Exhibition Catalogs; Pamphlets; Periodical Subscriptions; Photographs; Slides; Video Tapes
Special Subjects: Historical Material, American Western Art, Painting-American, Prints, Sculpture, Watercolors, American Indian Art, African Art, Ceramics, Painting-European, Furniture, Glass, Oriental Art, Asian Art, Painting-Italian
Collections: Laura A Clubb Collection of American & European Paintings; Clark Field Collection of American Indian Baskets & Pottery; Gillert Collection of Southeast Asian Ceramics; Samuel H Kress Collection of Italian Renaissance Paintings & Sculpture; Roberta Campbell Lawson Collection of Indian Artifacts; Tabor Collection of Oriental Art; Gussman Collection of African Sculpture; Eugene B Adkins Collection of Native American & Western Art; George R Kraus II Collection of Modern & Contemporary Design; Tabor Collection of Oriental Art
Publications: Quarterly magazine; exhibition catalogs

Activities: Dramatic progs; classes for adults & children; docent training; lect open to pub, 27 vis lectrs per yr; concerts; gallery talks; tours; scholarships; awards: 2010 Oklahoma Mus Assoc Educ program & conservation project, 2010 Oklahoma Magazine Best Museum; individual & original objects of art lent to museums, schools, corporations & city government; book traveling exhibs 2 - 4 per yr; originate traveling exhibs; mus shop sells books, magazines, original art, reproductions, prints, slides, jewelry, children's toys, garden items & gift items

L H.A. & Mary K Chapman Library, 2727 S Rockford Rd, Tulsa, OK 74114-4104; PO Box 52510, Tulsa, OK 74152-0510. Tel 918-748-5306; Fax 918-743-4230; Elec Mail tyoung@philbrook.org; Internet Home Page Address: www.philbrook.org; *Librn* Thomas E Young
Open Tues 10 AM - Noon, 1 - 5 PM, Wed - Fri 10 AM - noon, Mon by appointment; No admis fee; Estab 1940; Circ 24,000 vol library; Reference-resource center for the curatorial staff, teaching faculty, volunteers & mem
Library Holdings: Book Volumes 24,000; Clipping Files; DVDs; Exhibition Catalogs; Pamphlets; Periodical Subscriptions 135; Reproductions; Slides; Video Tapes
Special Subjects: Art History, Folk Art, Landscape Architecture, Decorative Arts, Photography, Painting-American, Painting-Italian, Pre-Columbian Art, Painting-European, History of Art & Archaeology, American Western Art, Asian Art, Primitive art, Pottery
Collections: Oklahoma art & artists

L Eugene B Adkins Study Center, 116 E Brady St, Tulsa, OK 74107-2014; PO Box 52510, Tulsa, OK 74152-0510. Tel 918-748-5306; Fax 918-743-4239; Elec Mail tyoung@philbrook.org; Internet Home Page Address: www.philbrook.org; *Librn* Thomas E Young
Open Wed - Fri 1 - 5 PM (or by appointment); No admis fee; Estab 2013; Circ 5,000 vols; Reference & Special Colls with focus on Native Amrican Art
Library Holdings: Auction Catalogs; Book Volumes 5,000; Clipping Files; DVDs; Exhibition Catalogs; Manuscripts; Original Documents; Pamphlets 20; Periodical Subscriptions; Photographs 1,000; Slides; Video Tapes
Special Subjects: American Indian Art
Collections: Native American Art; Eugene B Adkins Library & Archives; Roberta Campbell Library & Archives; Nettie Wheeler Collection; Native American artists files, photograph coll of Native Americans

M SHERWIN MILLER MUSEUM OF JEWISH ART, (Gershon & Rebecca Fenster Museum of Jewish Art) 2021 E 71st St, Tulsa, OK 74136-5408. Tel 918-492-1818; Fax 918-492-1888; Elec Mail info@jewishmuseum.net; Internet Home Page Address: www.jewishmuseum.net; *Cur* Karen York; *Exec Dir* Arthur M Feldman; *Develop Dir* Melissa Schnur
Open Mon - Fri 10 AM - 5 PM, Sun 1 - 5 PM; Admis adults $6.50, seniors & groups $5.50, students $3.50, groups of 10+ $3; Estab 1966 to collect, preserve & interpret cultural, historical & aesthetic materials attesting to Jewish cultural history, Jewish history of Oklahoma & the Holocaust; Average Annual Attendance: 8,000; Mem: 300; dues $35 - $2,500, ann meeting in Dec
Income: $450,000 (financed by endowment, mem & special events)
Library Holdings: Audio Tapes; Cassettes; Compact Disks; DVDs; Exhibition Catalogs; Memorabilia; Original Documents; Photographs; Prints; Records; Reels; Reproductions; Sculpture; Slides; Video Tapes
Special Subjects: Judaica
Collections: Anti-semitica; archeology of old world; ethnographic materials; fine art by Jewish artists & on Jewish themes; ritual & ceremonial Judaica; Holocaust, Oklahoma Jewish Archive
Exhibitions: Permanent Jewish History & Practice exhibit; Permanent Holocaust exhibit
Publications: newsletter, monthly by email
Activities: Classes for adults & children, docent training; lect open to pub; gallery talks; tours; awards; individual paintings & original objects of art lent to other museums & religious institutions; mus shop sells books & Judaica

M UNIVERSITY OF TULSA, Alexandre Hogue Gallery, 600 S College Ave, Art Dept Tulsa, OK 74104-9700. Tel 918-631-2202; Fax 918-631-3423; *Dir* Ron Predel
Open Mon - Fri 8:30 - 4:30 PM; No admis fee; Estab 1966 to display the works of regionally & nationally known artists; 176 running ft; Average Annual Attendance: 1,000
Income: Financed by Univ
Exhibitions: Annual Student Art Competition; National Scholastic Art Awards Scholarships & Competition; various regional & local artists on a rotating basis
Activities: Lect open to pub, 6 vis lectrs per yr; competition with awards; schols offered; individual paintings & original objects of art lent

M UNIVERSITY OF TULSA, Gilcrease Museum, 1400 Gilcrease Museum Rd, Tulsa, OK 74127-2100. Tel 918-596-2700, 2787 (Automated Gen Information), 888-655-2278 (Toll free); Fax 918-596-2770; Internet Home Page Address: www.gilcrease.org; *Exec Dir* Duane King; *Exec Asst* Sandi Freeman; *Dir Exhibs & Publs* Randy Ramer; *Sr Cur* Robert B Pickering; *Assoc Cur* Carol Klein
Open Tues - Sun 10 AM - 5 PM, cl Mon, Christmas Day; Admis adults $8, seniors (62 & older), active US military, groups of 10 or more $6, college students with ID $5, children 18 & under & mems no charge; Estab by the late Thomas Gilcrease as a pvt institution; acquired by the City of Tulsa 1954 (governed by a Board of Dir & City Park Board); building addition completed 1963 & 1987; partner with the University of Tulsa in 2008; Average Annual Attendance: 100,000; Mem: 4500; dues $25 & up
Income: Financed by city funds & the University of Tulsa
Special Subjects: Drawings, Hispanic Art, Latin American Art, Mexican Art, Painting-American, Photography, Sculpture, American Indian Art, American Western Art, Bronzes, Anthropology, Ethnology, Pre-Columbian Art, Southwestern Art, Folk Art, Pottery, Etchings & Engravings, Landscapes, Manuscripts, Portraits, Eskimo Art, Historical Material, Maps, Gold, Leather
Collections: American art from Colonial period to 20th century with emphasis on art of historical significance, sculpture, painting, graphics. Much of the work shown is of documentary nature, with emphasis on the Native American material & the opening of the Trans-Mississippi West. Art Collections include 100,000 books; 10,000 paintings by 400 American artists; artifact collections include

300,000 objects including both prehistoric & historic materials from most of the Native American cultures in Middle & North America
Exhibitions: Special exhibitions periodically; rotating exhibits during fall, winter, spring seasons; Gilcrease Rendezvous; 8000 sq ft permanent exhibit of Art from Mexico
Publications: The Journal, biannual
Activities: Classes for adults & children; docent training; lect open to pub; gallery talks; tours; individual paintings & original objects of art lent to comparable art institutions; book traveling exhibs 3-4 per yr; originate traveling exhibs to other museums; mus shop sells books, magazines, original art, reproductions, prints, slides, pottery & jewelry

L Library, 1400 Gilcrease Museum Rd, Tulsa, OK 74127-2100. Tel 918-596-2700; Fax 918-596-2770; *Cur Archival Coll* Sarah Erwin
Open Tues - Sat 9 AM - 5 PM, Sun 11 AM - 5 PM, cl Christmas; No admis fee; donations $3 per person, $5 per family; Library open for research by appointment, contains 90,000 books & documents, many rare books & manuscripts of the American frontier period, as well as materials concerning the Five Civilized Tribes
Income: Financed by city appropriation
Library Holdings: Book Volumes 40,000; Exhibition Catalogs; Manuscripts; Memorabilia; Pamphlets; Periodical Subscriptions 10; Photographs
Special Subjects: Manuscripts, Historical Material, American Western Art, American Indian Art

WOODWARD

M PLAINS INDIANS & PIONEERS HISTORICAL FOUNDATION, Museum & Art Center, 2009 Williams Ave, Woodward, OK 73801-5717. Tel 580-256-6136; Fax 580-256-2577; Elec Mail pipm@swbell.net; *Dir & Cur* Louise James; *Dir Asst* Robert Roberson
Open Tues - Sat 10 AM - 5 PM, cl Sun & Mon; No admis fee; Estab 1966 to preserve local history & to support visual arts; Average Annual Attendance: 15,000; Mem: 450; dues $25 - $500; ann meeting in Nov
Income: Financed by mem & trust fund
Special Subjects: American Indian Art
Collections: Early day artifacts as well as Indian material
Exhibitions: Juried contests for high school students & photographers; Fine Arts, Creative Crafts (guest artist featured each month in the gallery)
Publications: Below Devil's Gap (historical book); brochures; quarterly newsletter; Oklahoma's Northwest Territory Map; Woodward County Pioneer Families, 1907-57 (2 volumes)
Activities: Classes for adults & children; docent training; lect open to pub; tours; competitions with prizes; book traveling exhibs 3 per yr; mus shop sells books, magazines, original art & prints & Northwest Oklahoma artisans crafts

OREGON

ASHLAND

M SOUTHERN OREGON UNIVERSITY, Stevenson Union Gallery, 1250 Siskiyou Blvd, Ashland, OR 97520-5001. Tel 541-552-6465; Fax 541-552-6440; Internet Home Page Address: www.sou.edu
Open Mon - Fri 8 AM - 9 PM, Sat 9:30 AM - 2 PM; No admis fee; Estab 1972 to offer col & community high quality arts; Located on the third floor of Stevenson Union, the gallery is about 1200 sq ft; Average Annual Attendance: 20,000
Income: Financed by student fees
Collections: Permanent collection: prints, paintings by local artists & a sculpture by Bruce West
Exhibitions: Ceramics, paintings, photography, prints, sculpture, faculty & student work.; Annual Student Art Show; Installations, Alternative Works
Activities: 3 vis lectrs per yr; competitions

M Schneider Museum of Art, 1250 Siskiyou Blvd, Ashland, OR 97520-5001. Tel 541-552-6245; Fax 541-552-8241; Elec Mail cranem@sou.edu; Internet Home Page Address: www.sou.edu/sma; *Preparator & Registrar* Stephen Fraizer; *Dir* Michael Crane; *Office Coordr* Kim Hearon; *Cur* Josine Ianco Starrels
Open Mon - Sat 10 AM - 4 PM; Admis: $5 donation suggested; Estab 1986; Univ Art Mus - Contemporary Art Focus; Average Annual Attendance: 20,000; Mem: 350; dues $30 - $250+; ann meeting in Oct
Income: Financed by endowment, mem, state appropriations & federal grants
Special Subjects: Drawings, Landscapes, Painting-American, Latin American Art, Prints, African Art, Oriental Art
Collections: Waldo Peirce-oils, watercolors & lithographs & a diverse collection of contemporary American art; Pre-Columbian work; W Zundel Collection: Oriental Materials
Activities: Classes for adults & children; docent training; lect open to public, lects for mem only, 2 lect per yr; concerts; gallery talks; tours; lending original objects of art to other mus; book traveling exhibitions 1 per year; exhibs change every 7-8 wks

ASTORIA

M COLUMBIA RIVER MARITIME MUSEUM, 1792 Marine Dr, Astoria, OR 97103-3525. Tel 503-325-2323; Fax 503-325-2331; Elec Mail information@crmm.org; Internet Home Page Address: www.crmm.org; *CEO & Dir* Sam Johnson; *Cur* Jeff Smith; *Mus Shop Mgr* Blue Anderson; *Educ Dir* Betsey Ellerbroek; *VPres* Roger Qualman; *Deputy Dir* David Pearson
Open daily 9:30 AM - 5 PM, cl on Thanksgiving & Christmas; Admis adults $10, seniors $8, children $5, children under 6 free; Estab 1962 as a maritime mus, to collect, preserve & interpret maritime history of Pacific Northwest; Maintains seven galleries of nautical history including works of art; Average Annual Attendance: 97,000; Mem: 2000; dues 30; ann meeting in Nov
Income: $500,000 (financed by admis, sales, mem & individual & corporate donations

Special Subjects: Marine Painting
Collections: Maritime Paintings, Prints & Photography; Ship Models & nautical artifacts; Lightship Columbia
Exhibitions: Rotating & temporary exhibit space in Great Hall; visiting vessels as available
Publications: The Quarterdeck, quarterly
Activities: Classes for adults; volunteer opportunities; docent training; lect open to pub, 6 vis lectrs per yr; tours; competitions; outreach program to schools; individual paintings & original objects of art lent to accredited museums; mus shop sells books, limited edition prints, posters, reproductions, contemporary scrimshaw & jewelry
L **Library,** 1792 Marine Dr, Astoria, OR 97103-3525. Tel 503-325-2323; Fax 503-325-2331; Internet Home Page Address: www.crmm.org; *Mem Records Coordr* Lee Clinton; *Cur* Jeff Smith
Open by appointment only; Estab as reference library for maritime activities relevant to the Northwest; Circ Non-circulating; Library for use on the premises; majority of contents are not relevant to art; Mem: 2000
Income: Financed by admis, trusts, mem dues & donations
Library Holdings: Book Volumes 6000; Cassettes; Clipping Files; Exhibition Catalogs; Manuscripts; Motion Pictures; Original Art Works; Pamphlets; Periodical Subscriptions 196; Photographs; Prints; Reproductions
Special Subjects: Maps, Historical Material, Drafting, Marine Painting, Scrimshaw
Publications: The Quarterdeck, quarterly

BEND

M **HIGH DESERT MUSEUM,** 59800 S Hwy 97, Bend, OR 97702-7962. Tel 541-382-4754; Fax 541-382-5256; Internet Home Page Address: www.Highdesert.org; *VPres Opers* Forrest Rodgers; *Dir Communs* Denise Costa; *VPres Progs & Exhibs Dir* Kevin Britz
Open daily 9 AM - 5 PM, cl Jan 1, Thanksgiving Day & Christmas; Admis adults $7.75, seniors $6.75, youth 13-18 $6.75, children between 5-12 $3.75; Estab 1974 to bring to life natural & cultural history of region; Brooks Gallery, Spirit of the West Gallery & Nancy R Chandler Memorial Gallery; Average Annual Attendance: 185,000; Mem: 5000; dues $35 & up; ann meeting in Sept
Income: Financed by mem, donations, grants, admis & sales
Special Subjects: Photography, Sculpture, Architecture, Drawings, Mexican Art, Painting-American, Prints, Watercolors, American Indian Art, American Western Art, Anthropology, Archaeology, Southwestern Art, Textiles, Primitive art, Woodcarvings, Manuscripts, Furniture, Historical Material, Maps, Painting-Spanish
Collections: Sherry Sander Sculpture Collection; Rod Frederick Collection of Prints; Georgia Gerber Sculpture Collection; Joe Halco Sculpture Collection; Philip Hyde Photography Collection
Exhibitions: Spirit of the West; The Plato of the Indians; Raptors of the Desert Sky
Publications: High Desert Quarterly; biannual exhibit catalogues
Activities: Classes for adults & children; docent progs; teacher in-service training; lect open to publ, 5-8 vis lectrs per yr; gallery talks; awards given; book traveling exhibs 1 per yr; mus shop sells books, magazines, original art, reproductions, prints, slides, folk art, jewelry, educ games & toys, nature items

COOS BAY

M **COOS ART MUSEUM,** 235 Anderson Ave, Coos Bay, OR 97420-1610. Tel 541-267-3901, 267-4877; Fax 541-267-4877; Elec Mail adavenport@coosart.org; Internet Home Page Address: www.coosart.org; *Bd Pres* William Delimont; *Admin* A J Davenport; *Exec Dir* Steven Broocks; *Finance Mgr* Deryl Beebe; *Dir Art Educ* Karen Hammer
Open Tues - Fri 10 AM - 4 PM, Sat 1 - 4 PM, cl Sun & Mon; Admis adults $5, seniors & students $2, members no charge; Estab 1950 (relocated to an historic former Post Office Building in downtown district) to bring contemporary art to Northwestern Oregon through colls, exhibs & educ programming; Six galleries; Average Annual Attendance: 20,255; Mem: 400; dues family $70, individual $45, student $15; annual meeting first quarter of yr
Special Subjects: Painting-American, Prints, Sculpture, Woodcuts
Collections: Contemporary American Printmakers; paintings, photographs, sculpture
Exhibitions: Changing exhibits of painting, print, sculpture
Publications: Annual Museum Newsletter; exhibit announcements, every 6 wks
Activities: Classes & workshops for adults & children; Artists-in-Educ Program for pub schools; lect open to pub; concerts; gallery talks; tours; schols; lend original objects of art to CAM Business Members; rental & sales

COQUILLE

A **COQUILLE VALLEY ART ASSOCIATION,** 10144 Hwy 42, Coquille, OR 97423. Tel 541-396-3294; *Pres* Kathy Phillips; *VPres* Pat Haley; *Treas* Jean Waggoner; *Sec* Nancy Shinn; *Bd Mem (Past Pres)* Anna Crosby; *Bd Mem* Patsy Weaver; *Bd Mem* Leland Simpson; *Bd Mem* Robin Hurston; *Bd Mem* DeAnn Shaw; *Bd Mem* Shirley Lee
Open Mon - Fri 10 AM - 3 PM, cl Sun & holidays; No admis fee; Estab 1950 to teach art & art appreciation; Gallery maintained on main floor of Art Assoc owned old refurbished schoolhouse; Average Annual Attendance: 2,900 including classes, workshops & events; Mem: 140; dues $50, seniors $45; ann meetings first Wed in Apr
Income: Financed by mem, auctions, plant & rummage sales, donations, grants, comm on classes, sales & workshops
Library Holdings: Book Volumes; Clipping Files; Periodical Subscriptions
Collections: Permanent coll of paintings 1950 - 2010; largest coll of J Pajares-Barret Paintings
Exhibitions: Exhibits by local members; monthly shows
Publications: Monthly newsletter

Activities: Classes for adults & children; competitions; Youth Show; awards for Youth Art Show, Best of Show for Youth at the Coos Co Fair; individual paintings lent to banks & lobbies; sells original art, miniatures & handicraft
L **Library,** 10144 Hwy 42, Coquille, OR 97423. Tel 541-396-3294; *Pres* Diana Amling
Open to mems only

CORVALLIS

M **CORVALLIS ART CENTER,** 700 SW Madison Ave, Corvallis, OR 97333-4514. Tel 541-754-1551

M **OREGON STATE UNIVERSITY,** Fairbanks Gallery, 220 SW 26th St, Corvallis, OR 97331. Tel 541-737-5009; Fax 541-737-8686; Elec Mail drussell@oregonstate.edu; *Gallery Dir* Douglas Russell
Open Mon - Fri 8 AM - 5 PM, weekends during special events; No admis fee; Estab 1933 to display work of contemporary artists; 120 linear ft; Average Annual Attendance: 5,000
Income: Financed by state appropriation & grants
Collections: Fine art print coll includes: Goya to Rauschenberg; Japanese Print Coll; German Expressionism; Wendel Black Print Coll
Activities: Lect open to public; gallery talks
M **Memorial Union Art Gallery,** 1500 SW Jefferson Ave, Corvallis, OR 97331-8655. Tel 541-737-8511; Fax 541-737-1565; Elec Mail ksumner@orst.edu; Internet Home Page Address: osumu.org/mu/events_coucourse1.htm; *Dir* Kent Sumner
Open daily 8 AM - 11 PM; Estab 1928; Average Annual Attendance: 50,000
Income: $70,000
Collections: William Henry Price Memorial Collection of Oil Paintings
Exhibitions: Various exhibs, call for details
Publications: Calendar & exhib pamphlets
Activities: Educ prog; lect; exten dept serving the State; individual paintings lent to schools; material available to responsible galleries for fees
M **Giustina Gallery,** 875 SW 26th St, 100 LaSells Stewart Ctr Corvallis, OR 97331-3301. Tel 541-737-2402; Internet Home Page Address: oregonstate.edu/lasells/gallery; *Gallery Cur* Tina Green-Price
Open Mon - Fri 8 AM - 5 PM, additional hrs during special events at LaSells Stewart Ctr; No admis fee; Estab 1981 to display work of contemporary artists in northwest; Gallery is 4,800 sq ft
Income: Financed by grants & state appropriation
Exhibitions: Exhibs changing monthly

DALLAS

A **NORTHWEST PASTEL SOCIETY (NPS),** 1785 SW Woodbridge Ct, Dallas, OR 97338. Internet Home Page Address: www.nwps.org;
Open by appointment; Estab 1988 to promote, encourage & foster creative painting with pastels, encourage pastel artists in their artistic growth & success, promote a fellowship of pastel artists & to promote public awareness about pastel; Mem: dues $30
Income: Financed by mem, gifts & donations
Exhibitions: Open juried international exhibitions & member exhibitions
Publications: Bimonthly newsletter

EUGENE

M **LANE ARTS COUNCIL,** Jacobs Gallery, 1590 Willamette St #200, Eugene, OR 97401. Tel 541-684-5635; Fax 541-485-2478; *Gallery Dir* Tina Rinaldi
Open Tues - Sat 11 AM - 3 PM and during Hult Ctr performances; No admis fee; Estab 1982 for art appreciation & educ; Gallery in lower level of Hult Center for the Performing Arts. Functions as a meeting & reception area, as well as a gallery; Average Annual Attendance: 10,000
Income: $70,000 (financed by gallery sales commissions & cost reimbursements from artists, fundraising & community donations)
Exhibitions: Exhibits selected rotating jury (3 mems) & scheduled by Jacobs Gallery Exhibition Comt

M **LANE COMMUNITY COLLEGE,** Art Dept Gallery, 4000 E 30th Ave, Eugene, OR 97405-0640. Tel 541-463-3034; Fax 541-744-4185; Internet Home Page Address: www.lanecc.edu/artgallery
Open Mon - Fri 8 AM - 5 PM; No admis fee; Estab 1970 as an educational gallery exhibiting works by National & Northwest artists; 1 fl; Average Annual Attendance: 15,000
Income: Financed through county funds & state funds; donations & grants
Collections: Contemporary Art
Exhibitions: Rotating exhibs every three weeks
Activities: Lect open to pub, 9 vis lectrs per yr; gallery talks; competitions; schols offered

M **MAUDE KERNS ART CENTER,** (Maude I Kerns Art Center Galleries) 1910 E 15th Ave, Eugene, OR 97403-2094. Tel 541-345-1571; Fax 541-345-6248; Elec Mail mkart@pond.net; Internet Home Page Address: www.premierelink.com/clients/mkac; Internet Home Page Address: www.mkartcenter.org; *Pres* Bryce Krehbiel; *Exec Dir* Hilary Moster
Open Mon - Fri 10 AM - 5:30 PM, Sat Noon - 4 PM; Admis suggested $2 donation; Estab 1950, the Center is a nonprofit educational organization dedicated to promoting quality in the arts & crafts through classes, exhibs, workshops, community projects & special events; The center houses 3 galleries: Henry Korn Gallery, Brockelbank Gallery & Maude I Kerns Salon Gallery. Features monthly shows of contemporary artists, the work of Maude Kerns, Ceramics Co-op; Average Annual Attendance: 12,000; Mem: 500; dues family $55, individual $35; annual meeting in Jan/Feb
Income: $300,000 (financed by mem, class tui, art sales, contributions, grants, proceeds from ann outdoor fundraising festival)

Special Subjects: Drawings, Graphics, Ceramics, Crafts, Etchings & Engravings, Furniture, Glass, Jewelry
Collections: Maude I Kerns Collection
Exhibitions: Every 6 weeks exhibits featuring individual theme & group shows by Pacific Northwest artists; satellite gallery temporarily at 68 W Broadway downtown Eugene
Publications: Quarterly newsletter
Activities: Classes for adults & children; dramatic progs; volunteer prog; workshops; seminars; lects open to pub; concerts; gallery talks; tours; competitions; schols offered; exten dept

M **NEW ZONE VIRTUAL GALLERY,** 164 W Broadway, Eugene, OR 97401-3004. Tel 541-343-5651; Fax 541-313-5651; Elec Mail ross@newzone.org; Internet Home Page Address: www.newzone.org; *Dir* Jerry Ross
Open Tues, Fri & Sat, 7 PM - 1 AM; Admis $3; Estab 1978 as a modern experimental gallery; A cyberspace gallery featuring experimental 2-D & 3-D art; Average Annual Attendance: 1,500; Mem: 20; dues $50; monthly meetings
Income: $10,000 (financed by federal & local arts grants)
Collections: Mike Randells Collection (abstract figurative); Jerry Ross Collection (oils, landscape, figurative, portraits); Experimental Art; Modern Art; Eric Peterson Collection (etchings); Steve Lariccia; Stephen Livingstone; Bob Devine Collection
Exhibitions: Exhibits by members; invitationals
Publications: Exhibit brochures
Activities: Lect open to pub; competitions; sales shop sells prints

SOCIETY OF NORTH AMERICAN GOLDSMITHS
For further information, see National and Regional Organizations

M **UNIVERSITY OF OREGON,** Jordan Schnitzer Museum of Art, 1223 University of Oregon, Eugene, OR 97403-1205. Tel 541-346-3027; Fax 541-346-0976; Internet Home Page Address: jsma.uoregon.edu; *Educ Dir* Lisa Abia-Smith; *Assoc Dir* Kurt Neugebauer; *Exec Dir* Jill Hartz; *Chief Cur* Anne Rose Kitagawa; *Communs Mgr* Debbie Williamson Smith; *Collections Mgr* Chris White
Open Thurs - Sun 11 AM - 5 PM, Wed 11 AM - 8 PM, cl Mon & university holidays; Admis adults $5, seniors $3, K-12 students, university students & museum members free; Estab 1933 to promote among university students & faculty & the general pub an active & continuing interest in the cultures around the world; Average Annual Attendance: 50,000; Mem: 1,100; dues $45-$10,000; annual party in summer
Income: $1,000,000 (financed by state appropriation, endowment income & private donations)
Special Subjects: Painting-American, Textiles, Oriental Art, Asian Art
Collections: Greater Pacific Basin Collection; Asian Art representing the cultures of China, Japan, Cambodia, Korea, Mongolia, Tibet, Russia, American & British works executed in the traditional Oriental manner; Northwest Art; Contemporary Northwest Collection; Cuban, South America
Exhibitions: Various exhibits
Publications: Exhibition catalog
Activities: Classes for adults & children; docent training; school tours; outreach to k-12; lects open to pub; 20+ vis lectrs per yr; gallery talks; concerts; tours; individual paintings & original objects of art lent to other museums that can provide suitable security & climate control; book traveling exhibs1-2 per yr; originate traveling exhibs to other art museums; mus shop sells books, slides, cards, gifts

M **Aperture Photo Gallery - EMU Art Gallery,** 1228 University of Oregon, L110 Erb Memorial Union Eugene, OR 97403. Tel 541-346-4373; Fax 541-346-4400; Internet Home Page Address: www.darkwing.uoregon.edu/cultural; *Office Mgr* Rafael Arroyo; *Prog Coordr* Laura Morris
Open daily 7:30 AM - midnight; No admis fee; Estab 1981 to provide space for the display of art & exhibs; Average Annual Attendance: 5,000
Income: Financed by student fees
Collections: EMU Permanent Art Collection
Exhibitions: Periodic art exhibs on display in the Adell McMillan Gallery, Apeture Gallery & Buz Gallery
Activities: Classes for adults; lects open to pub; 1 vis lectr per yr

L **Architecture & Allied Arts Library,** 200 Lawrence Hall, Eugene, OR 97403; 1299 University of Oregon, Eugene, OR 97403-1299. Tel 541-346-3637; Internet Home Page Address: www.uoregon.edu/.aaa/home; *Reference Librn* Kara List; *Visual Resources Cur* Christine L Sundt; *Head Librn* Ed Peague
Open Mon - Thurs 8 AM - 11 PM, Fri 8 AM - 7 PM, Sat 11 AM - 7 PM, Sun 11 AM - 11 PM; Estab 1915 to provide resources for the courses, degree programs & research of the departments in the School of Architecture & Allied Arts; Primarily for lending
Income: Financed by state appropriation
Library Holdings: Book Volumes 71,000; Exhibition Catalogs; Fiche; Periodical Subscriptions 400; Photographs 30,000; Slides 275,000
Special Subjects: Art History, Landscape Architecture, Interior Design, Aesthetics, Architecture

FOREST GROVE

M **VALLEY ART GALLERY,** 2202 Main St, Forest Grove, OR 97116; Valley Art Assoc, PO Box 333 Forest Grove, OR 97116. Tel 503-357-3703; Elec Mail office@valleyart.org; Internet Home Page Address: www.valleyart.org
Open Mon - Sat 11 AM - 5:30 PM; Estab 1966

GRANTS PASS

M **GRANTS PASS MUSEUM OF ART,** 229 SW G St, Grants Pass, OR 97526; PO Box 966, Grants Pass, OR 97528-0081. Tel 541-479-3290; Fax 541-479-1218; Elec Mail museum@gpmuseum.com; Internet Home Page Address: www.gpmuseum.com; *Exec Dir* Chris Pondelick; *Pres* Susan E Burnes; *VPres* Barbara Burnett
Open Tues - Sat noon - 4 PM, cl Easter, Independence Day, Memorial Day, Labor Day, Thanksgiving weekend, Christmas week; No admis fee; Estab 1979 - Art

Mus & Educ Center; Circ Circ (art libraries) 2,000 vols; Average Annual Attendance: 15,000; Mem: Student & teacher $20-$29, individual $30-$59, family $60-$99, guild $100-$249, patron $250-$499, benefactor $500 & up
Income: Mems & donations
Library Holdings: Audio Tapes; Book Volumes 1,000; CD-ROMs; DVDs; Exhibition Catalogs
Collections: contemporary regional art
Activities: Watercolor slide prog; educ prog for children; docent training; workshops; lects; 6 vis lectrs per yr; guided tours; gallery talks; schols; originates traveling exhibs to schools & retirement communities; book traveling exhibitions; sales shop sells original art, prints

M **ROGUE COMMUNITY COLLEGE,** Wiseman Gallery - FireHouse Gallery, 3345 Redwood Hwy, Grants Pass, OR 97527-9298. Tel 541-956-7339; Fax 541-471-3588; Elec Mail hgreen@roguecc.edu; Internet Home Page Address: www.roguecc.edu/galleries; *Dir* Karl Brake; *Gallery Coordr* Heather Green
Call for hours; No admis fee; Estab 1985 to present exhibits of high artistic content in a range of aesthetics which contribute to the educational environment & serve to inspire the community & to serve our community & students with an additional venue for fine art that will inspire, create & promote understanding of the arts & the part they play in our lives
Special Subjects: Painting-American, Prints, Sculpture
Collections: African tools; Japanese woodblock prints; varied paintings
Publications: Exhibit brochures; quarterly catalogues; monthly postals
Activities: Classes for adults & children; docent training; artist talks; workshops; lect open to pub, 10 vis lectrs per yr; gallery talks; competitions

KLAMATH FALLS

M **FAVELL MUSEUM OF WESTERN ART & INDIAN ARTIFACTS,** 125 W Main St, Klamath Falls, OR 97601-4287. Tel 541-882-9996; Fax 541-850-0125; Elec Mail favellmusem@favellmuseum.org; Internet Home Page Address: www.favellmuseum.org
Open Tues - Sat 10 AM - 5PM, cl Sun, Mon & all major holidays; Admis adults $7, youth 6 - 16 years $4, children under 6 free; Estab 1972 to preserve Western heritage as represented by Indian artifacts & contemporary Western art; Gallery features contemporary western artists combined with art & artifacts displays; Average Annual Attendance: 20,000; Mem: Patron mem $100 per yr
Income: $250,000 (financed by admis, sales & non-profit)
Purchases: Paintings by: Charles Russell, McCarthy, Arlene Hooker Fay & James Bama; 800 works of art by 300 artists
Library Holdings: Book Volumes; Periodical Subscriptions
Special Subjects: Historical Material, Bronzes, American Indian Art, American Western Art, Pottery, Jewelry, Coins & Medals, Miniatures, Dioramas
Collections: Contemporary western art; Western Indian artifacts: pottery, stonework, baskets, bead and quiltwork; miniature firearms; archeological excavation site displays
Publications: A Treasury of Our Western Heritage (book on cross section of museum collection)
Activities: Tours for groups & children; featured artist each month; lects open to pub, 3 vis lectrs per yr; gallery talks; fels offered; mus shop sells books, original art, prints, jewelry, consigned items, & unique gifts

A **KLAMATH ART ASSOCIATION,** 120 Riverside Dr, Klamath Falls, OR 97601-4250; PO Box 955, Klamath Falls, OR 97601-0051. Tel 541-883-1833; *Pres* Will Dawson; *Co-Pres* Ken Barkee
Open Thurs - Sun Noon - 4 PM; No admis fee; Estab 1948 to provide art training for local residents; Gallery estab 1948 to provide display & teaching space for the Assn's activities; Average Annual Attendance: 5,000; Mem: 150; dues $15 - $20; meetings 7 PM third Wed of month
Income: Financed by mem, gallery sales, tuition
Collections: Ceramics; paintings; weaving (owned by members)
Exhibitions: Twelve annually; one mem show, remainder varies
Activities: Classes in painting, drawing, weaving; children's summer art classes; workshops; lect, vis lectr

M **KLAMATH COUNTY MUSEUM,** 1451 Main St, Klamath Falls, OR 97601-5915. Tel 541-883-4208; Fax 541-884-0666; *Dir* Kim Bellabia
Open all year daily 9 AM - 5 PM Tues - Sat, cl Sun & Mon; Admis 12 & up $12, 62 & up, 5-12 $1, under 5 free; Estab 1957 to tell the story of the Klamath County & to preserve & exhibit related material; Average Annual Attendance: 20,000
Income: Financed by county appropriation
Special Subjects: Historical Material
Collections: Indian & pioneer artifacts; four original Rembrandt etchings; Healey paintings; photograph document files
Exhibitions: Rotating exhibitions
Publications: Museum Research Papers
Activities: Mus shop sells books, reproductions of photos & area souvenirs

L **Research Library,** 1451 Main St, Klamath Falls, OR 97601-5915. Tel 541-883-4208; Fax 541-884-0666; Elec Mail tourklco@cdsnet.net; *Dir* Kim Bellabia
Open to the pub for reference Tues - Sat 9 AM - 4:30 PM by appointment; Admis research fee; Estab 1955 to collect, preserve, document & interpret the local history
Income: Financed by County General Fund
Library Holdings: Book Volumes 10,000; Clipping Files; Manuscripts; Motion Pictures; Original Art Works; Pamphlets; Photographs 5000; Reels; Slides
Collections: Modoc Indian Books, Documents & Manuscripts
Activities: Guided tours for 4th grade students; school kits lent to area schools; sales shop sells books, prints, paintings, ceramic & other miscellaneous items

M **Baldwin Hotel Museum Annex,** 31 Main St, Klamath Falls, OR 97601-3174. Tel 503-883-4208; Fax 541-884-0666; *Dir* Kim Bellabia
Open Tues - Sat 10 AM - 4 PM, June - Sept; Admis family $6, adults $3, students & seniors $2, under 3 free; A State & national historic landmark purchased by Klamath County in Jan 1978. Restoration of building began in Feb 1978 & it was

dedicated as a mus by Oregon's Governor Robert Straub June 3, 1978. Opened to the pub Aug 19, 1978; May be viewed by tour only; Average Annual Attendance: 20,000
Income: Financed by county appropriations
Activities: Guided tours for 5th grade students; Mus shop sells books & original art

MARYLHURST

M **MARYLHURST UNIVERSITY,** The Art Gym, 17600 Pacific Hwy, Marylhurst, OR 97036-7036. Tel 503-636-8141; Fax 503-636-9526; Elec Mail artgym@marylhurst.edu; Internet Home Page Address: www.marylhurst.edu; *Dir* Terri M Hopkins
Open Tues - Sun Noon - 4 PM; No admis fee; Estab 1980; 3,000 sq ft; Average Annual Attendance: 5,000; Mem: 150; dues $15 - $500
Income: $100,000 (financed by mem, grants & college budget)
Special Subjects: Drawings, Graphics, Painting-American, Photography, Prints, Sculpture, Ceramics, Folk Art, Etchings & Engravings, Landscapes, Collages, Portraits, Furniture, Cartoons
Collections: Contemporary Northwest Art; Installation Art
Publications: Exhibition catalogs
Activities: Lect open to pub, 5 vis lectrs per yr; gallery talks; tours; schols offered; book traveling exhibs; originate traveling exhibs circulate to col galleries & museums; sales shop sells art gym catalogs & books

MEDFORD

A **ROGUE VALLEY ART ASSOCIATION,** Rogue Gallery & Art Center, 40 S Bartlett, Medford, OR 97501. Tel 541-772-8118; Fax 541-772-0294; Elec Mail info@roguegallery.org; Internet Home Page Address: www.roguegallery.org
Open Tues - Fri 10 AM - 5 PM, Sat 11 AM - 3 PM, cl Sun & Mon; No admis fee, donations accepted; Estab 1960 to provide a full range of programs, exhibits & classes to the region; Gallery 6000 sq ft, 2200 sq ft, sales & rental space, 2000 sq ft & 200 running ft of sliding panels; Average Annual Attendance: 20,000; Mem: 671; dues $20-$500; annual meeting in Oct
Income: Financed by mem dues, grants, fund raising events
Collections: Contemporary Northwest prints
Publications: Newsletter, 6 per yr
Activities: Classes for adults & children; lect open to pub, 2 vis lectrs per yr; gallery talks; tours; schols & fels offered; individual paintings lent through a rental prog to mems; lending coll contains art works, paintings, photographs & sculpture; book traveling exhibs 2-3 per yr; sales shop sells original art, crafts, books, prints, reproductions, prints, sculpture, pottery, jewelry, greeting cards

L **Library,** 106 N Central Ave, Medford, OR 97501. Tel 541-773-6536; Fax 541-776-7994; *Library Mgr* Pat Harper; *Cur Special Projects* Amy Drake; *Mem Asst* Brenda Conway
Open Tues - Fri noon - 4 PM; Admis Adults $5, students $2, mems no charge; Open to public for reference only
Income: Financed by mem, sales & county tax
Library Holdings: Book Volumes 4900; Cassettes; Clipping Files; Exhibition Catalogs; Fiche; Filmstrips; Manuscripts; Maps; Memorabilia; Original Art Works; Other Holdings Ephemera, art on paper; Pamphlets; Periodical Subscriptions 30; Photographs; Prints; Reels; Video Tapes
Special Subjects: Photography, Maps, Painting-American, Historical Material, Portraits, Watercolors, Archaeology, American Western Art, Anthropology, Furniture, Gold, Restoration & Conservation, Textiles, Architecture
Publications: Southern Oregon History, quarterly

MONMOUTH

M **WESTERN OREGON UNIVERSITY,** Dan & Gail Cannon Gallery of Art, 345 N Monmouth Ave, Monmouth, OR 97361. Tel 503-838-8340; Fax 503-838-8128; Elec Mail boothp@wou.edu; Internet Home Page Address: www.wou.edu; *Head Art Dept* Jodie Garrison; *Dir Gallery* Paula Booth
Open Thurs & Fri 8 AM - 5 PM during scheduled exhibits, Mon - Wed 8 AM - 6 PM; No admis fee; Estab to bring contemporary art work to the community & the col for study & visual understanding; Library located in Art Department, Campbell Hall; Average Annual Attendance: 3,000-4,000
Income: $6,000 (financed by state appropriation & student fees)
Exhibitions: Contemporary Northwest Visual Art; rotating faculty & student exhibits
Activities: Educ prog; lects open to pub, 6 vis lectrs per year; gallery talks; tours; competitions with awards; scholarships offered

NEWPORT

M **NEWPORT VISUAL ARTS CENTER,** 777 NW Beach Dr, Newport, OR 97365-3565. Tel 541-265-6540; Elec Mail shouck@coastarts.org; Internet Home Page Address: www.coastarts.org

NORTH BEND

M **COOS COUNTY HISTORICAL SOCIETY MUSEUM,** 1220 Sherman Ave, North Bend, OR 97459-3666. Tel 541-756-6320; Fax 541-756-6320; Elec Mail museum@ucii.com; Internet Home Page Address: www.coohistory.org; *Dir* Ann Koppy; *Pres* Reg Pullen; *VPres* Steve Grief
Open Tues - Sat 10 AM - 4 PM; Admis $2, children 12 & under $1; Estab 1891 to collect, preserve & interpret history of Coos County; Average Annual Attendance: 7,255; Mem: 450; dues $10-$250; annual meeting in June
Income: $60,000 (financed by endowment, mem, admis, sales & donations)
Collections: Maritime objects; Native American artifacts; photographs; tools/implements of pioneer lifeways; Native American Artifacts
Exhibitions: Pioneer Kitchen; Formal Parlor (c1900); rotating Exhibits; Maritime

Publications: Coos Historical Journal, annual; trimonthly newsletter
Activities: Lect open to pub, vis lectr; lending coll contains 100 items

PENDLETON

M **PENDLETON CENTER FOR THE ARTS,** 214 N Main St, Pendleton, OR 97801-1644. Tel 541-278-9201; Elec Mail info@pendletonarts.org; Internet Home Page Address: www.pendletonarts.org; *Contact* Roberta Lavadour

PORTLAND

M **3D CENTER OF ART & PHOTOGRAPHY,** 1928 NW Lovejoy St, Portland, OR 97209; PO Box 700, Gladstone, OR 97027-0700. Tel 503-227-6667

L **ART INSTITUTES INTERNATIONAL AT PORTLAND,** 1122 NW Davis St, Portland, OR 97209-2911. Tel 503-228-6528; Fax 503-228-4227; Elec Mail aipdadm@aii.edu; Internet Home Page Address: www.aii.edu; *Pres* Dr Steven Goldman; *Dean Educ* Eric Lindstrom; *Librn* Nancy Thurston
Open daily 7:30 AM - 6 PM, open some evenings, Sat 10 AM - 4:30 PM; No admis fee; Estab 1964 to provide practical instruction in retail merchandising, interior design, display, fashion design, advertising & promotion, fashion history & textiles, industrial design; Average Annual Attendance: 200
Library Holdings: Book Volumes 14,000; Clipping Files; Periodical Subscriptions 120; Slides; Video Tapes 300
Special Subjects: Art History, Fashion Arts, Industrial Design, Interior Design, Furniture, Costume Design & Constr, Textiles
Collections: Collection of Fashion & Costume History Books; Collection in Furniture & Interior Decoration Fields; Collection of Graphic Design & Muffimedia
Exhibitions: Rotating exhib
Activities: Schols offered

M **BLUE SKY GALLERY,** Oregon Center for the Photographic Arts, 122 NW 8th Ave, Portland, OR 97209-3502. Tel 503-225-0210; Fax 503-225-2990; Elec Mail bluesky@blueskygallery.org; Internet Home Page Address: www.blueskygallery.org; *Exec Dir* Todd J Tubutis; *Mem & Gallery Mgr* Amanda Clem; *Exhibs Mgr* Zemie Barr
Open Tues - Sun Noon - 5 PM, 1st Thurs 6 - 9 PM, New Year's Eve & Christmas Eve noon - 3 PM, cl New Year's Day, Independence Day, Thanksgiving Day, Christmas Day; No admis fee; Estab 1975; Average Annual Attendance: 12,000; Mem: Dues $25-500
Income: 501(c)3 - mems, grants, sales
Library Holdings: Book Volumes
Special Subjects: Photography
Exhibitions: Monthly rotating exhibits
Activities: Lect open to pub; 12 vis lectrs per yr

L **MULTNOMAH COUNTY LIBRARY,** Henry Failing Art & Music Dept, 801 SW 10th Ave, Portland, OR 97205-2597. Tel 503-988-5234 (reference line); Internet Home Page Address: www.multcolib.org; *Multnomah County Libr Dir* Vailey Oehlke
Open Mon & Thurs - Sat 10 AM - 6 PM, Tues & Wed 10 AM - 8 PM, Sun noon - 5 PM; No admis fee; Estab 1864 as a pub library service to Multnomah County; Collins Gallery - rotating exhibs of fine & decorative arts, book arts
Library Holdings: Book Volumes over 60,000; Clipping Files 800,000
Special Subjects: Art History, Decorative Arts, Photography, Painting-American, Painting-French, Painting-Italian, Prints, Sculpture, Painting-European, History of Art & Archaeology, Watercolors, Ceramics, Crafts, Latin American Art, Asian Art, Oriental Art, Pottery, Architecture
Exhibitions: Rotating exhibits in the Collins Gallery
Activities: Concerts; gallery talks; tours

M **MUSEUM OF CONTEMPORARY CRAFT,** (Contemporary Crafts Gallery) 724 NW Davis St, Portland, OR 97209-3663. Tel 503-223-2654; Fax 503-223-0190; Elec Mail info@museumof contemporarycraft.org; Internet Home Page Address: www.museumofcontemporarycraft.org; *Cur* Namita Gupta Wiggers; *Sr Div Develop* Deniz H Conger; *Gallery Mgr* Dylan Morgan
Open Tues - Sat 11 AM - 6 PM; No admis fee; Estab 1937 to promote, exhibit & preserve the art of craft; Gallery is maintained also as a consignment outlet & holds exhibits monthly; Average Annual Attendance: 75,000; Mem: 1,500; dues $40
Income: $2,200,000 (financed by mem)
Library Holdings: Book Volumes; Cassettes; Clipping Files; Exhibition Catalogs; Lantern Slides; Manuscripts; Original Documents; Other Holdings; Periodical Subscriptions 260; Photographs; Slides; Video Tapes
Special Subjects: Ceramics, Glass, Furniture, Watercolors, Crafts, Jewelry, Embroidery
Collections: Craft objects in ceramic, glass, metal, wood & fiber
Exhibitions: Several changing curated exhibs ann, permanent coll, retail gallery & broad spectrum educ prog for all ages & abilities
Publications: 3934 Corbett, Soul of a Bowl; Unpacking the Collection; Selection from The Museum of Contemporary Craft
Activities: lects open to pub, gallery talks; tours; sales shop sells original art & fine crafts on consignment

M **NEWSPACE CENTER FOR PHOTOGRAPHY,** 1632 SE 10th Ave, Portland, OR 97214-3107. Tel 503-963-1935; Elec Mail info@newspacephoto.org; Internet Home Page Address: www.newspacephoto.org

L **OREGON COLLEGE OF ART & CRAFT,** (Oregon College of Art Craft) Hoffman Gallery, 8245 SW Barnes Rd, Portland, OR 97225-6349. Tel 503-297-5544; Fax 503-297-9651; Elec Mail adebow@ocac.edu; Internet Home Page Address: www.ocac.edu; *Pres* Bonnie Laing-Malcolmson; *Develop Officer* Barb Audiss; *Exhibs Dir* Arthur DeBow; *Dir Communs* Jody Creasman; *Exten Prog Dir* Sara Black
Open daily 10 AM - 5 PM, cl holidays; No admis fee, except for special events & classes; Estab 1907 to teach seven disciplines in the arts & crafts; Hoffman

Exhibition Gallery features national & international craftspeople. Maintains library; Average Annual Attendance: 30,000; Mem: 600; dues $35 - $1000; annual meeting in June
Income: Financed by tui, endowment, mem, state appropriation & National Endowments of the Arts, Washington, DC
Library Holdings: Book Volumes; Exhibition Catalogs; Periodical Subscriptions; Slides
Special Subjects: Art History, Collages, Folk Art, Decorative Arts, Calligraphy, Etchings & Engravings, Ceramics, Crafts, Asian Art, Furniture, Costume Design & Constr, Glass, Bookplates & Bindings, Carpets & Rugs, Embroidery, Enamels
Collections: Permanent collection of historic, traditional craftwork
Exhibitions: Annual Juried Student Show; Thesis Show; Craft Biennial; Biennial faculty show
Publications: Course schedules, quarterly; gallery announcements, 12 per yr; newsletter to mems, 2 per yr; 2 yr catalog; 2 yr viewbook
Activities: Classes & workshops for adults; classes for children; BFA & cert prog in crafts; lects open to pub; 10-12 vis lectrs per yr; concerts; gallery talks; tours; schols offered; exten prog serves fine craft: book arts, ceramics, drawing, fibers, metals, photography, wood; mus shop sells books, magazines, original art, prints & crafts

L **Library,** 8245 SW Barnes Rd, Portland, OR 97225-6349. Tel 503-297-5544; Fax 503-297-9651; *Librn* Elsa Loftis
Open Mon - Fri 9 AM - 5 PM (during acad terms); Estab 1979; Craft reference library for students & faculty & others interested in crafts
Library Holdings: Book Volumes 5500; DVDs; Exhibition Catalogs; Original Art Works; Pamphlets; Periodical Subscriptions 90; Photographs; Prints; Slides; Video Tapes
Special Subjects: Photography, Drawings, Painting-American, Ceramics, Printmaking, Glass, Metalwork, Textiles, Architecture
Activities: Interlibrary loan services available

A **OREGON HISTORICAL SOCIETY,** Oregon History Museum, 1200 SW Park Ave, Portland, OR 97205-2483. Tel 503-222-1741; Fax 503-221-2035; Elec Mail orhist@ohs.org; Internet Home Page Address: www.ohs.org; *Exec Dir* Kerry Tymchuk; *Dir Develop & Mktg* Sue Metzler; *Dir Pub Servs* Marsha Matthews; *Facilities Mgr* Brian Cooley; *Dir Finance* Sheri Neal; *Dir Information Technology* Dwight Peterson; *Library Mgr* Geoff Wexler; *Ed* Eliza Canty-Jones
Open Tues, Wed, Fri & Sat 10 AM - 5 PM, Thurs 10 AM - 5 PM, Sun Noon - 5 PM; Admis adults $11, students seniors $9, $5 children 6 - 18, under 5 yrs free; Estab 1873, incorporated 1898, to collect, preserve, exhibit & publish materials pertaining to the Oregon country; Average Annual Attendance: 200,000; Mem: 5,000; dues individual & family $60 - $80, student $25; 10% senior & teacher mem discount; annual meeting Apr
Income: $4,000,000 biennially (financed by state appropriation, mem, grants, gifts & donations)
Library Holdings: Book Volumes; Manuscripts; Maps; Motion Pictures; Original Documents; Photographs; Video Tapes
Special Subjects: Historical Material
Collections: Artifacts, Manuscripts, paintings, photographs, coll by Oregon Country & Oregon State artists
Publications: Oregon Historical Quarterly
Activities: Programming for adults & children; docent training; lects open to the pub; gallery talks; Fellowships; ALA Cleo Award AAM; book traveling exhibs; organize traveling exhibs; mus shop sells books, reproductions & prints

L **Research Library,** 1200 SW Park Ave, Portland, OR 97205. Tel 503-306-5240; Fax 503-219-2040; Elec Mail orhist@ohs.org; Internet Home Page Address: www.ohs.org; *Libr Dir* Maryann Campbell
Open Wed 1 - 5 PM; Admis Fee $10 non-mems; Estab 1898; For reference only; Average Annual Attendance: 4,000
Income: Dept within Oregon Hist Soc
Library Holdings: Audio Tapes; Book Volumes 100,000; Cards; Cassettes; Clipping Files; Exhibition Catalogs; Fiche; Filmstrips; Framed Reproductions; Kodachrome Transparencies; Lantern Slides; Manuscripts; Maps; Memorabilia; Micro Print; Motion Pictures; Original Art Works; Original Documents; Pamphlets; Periodical Subscriptions 620; Photographs; Prints; Records; Reels; Reproductions; Sculpture; Slides; Video Tapes
Special Subjects: Film, Manuscripts, Maps, Painting-American, Historical Material, Architecture
Collections: 4500 separate manuscript colls containing 18,000,000 pieces; 2,500,000 historic photographs & negatives; 15,000 maps; Oral history; Microfilm; Film
Activities: Geneology & archives workshops

M **PORTLAND ART MUSEUM,** 1219 SW Park Ave, Portland, OR 97205-2430. Tel 503-226-2811; Fax 503-226-4842; Elec Mail info@pam.org; Internet Home Page Address: portlandartmuseum.org; *Dir* Brian J Ferriso; *Arlene & Harold Schnitzer Cur Asian Art* Maribeth Graybill; *Cur Native American Art* Deana Dartt; *Minor White Cur Photog* Julia Dolan; *Cur Graphic Arts* Mary Weaver Chapin; *Dir Educ & Pub Rels* Michael Muirawski; *Registrar* Ann Eichelberg; *Chief Cur & The Robert & Mercedes Eichholz Cur of Modern & Contemporary Art* Bruce Guenther
Open Tues - Sat 10 AM - 5 PM, Thurs & Fri until 8 PM, Sun Noon - 5 PM, cl most holidays; Admis adults $15, adult groups $8, seniors & students 18+ $12, mems, school groups & children under 18 free, 4th Fri of month 5-8 PM free. Special exhib fees & extended hours may apply; Estab 1892 to serve the pub by providing access to art of enduring quality, by educating a diverse audience about art & by collecting & preserving a wide range of art for the enrichment of present & future generations; The mus campus consists of two buildings. The main building, designed by Pietro Belluschi, was built in three stages. The Ayer (1932) & Hirsch (1939) wings comprise the museum's current 19 galleries (26,942 sq ft). The Hoffman wing (1968) is undergoing renovation. Maintains reference library, Jubitz Ctr for Modern & Contemporary Art, Gilkey Ctr fror Graphic Arts & Northwest Film Ctr; Average Annual Attendance: 350,000; Mem: 23,000 households; dues $35 & up; ann meeting in Sept
Income: Financed by admis, endowment, grants, contributions & mem
Library Holdings: Auction Catalogs; Audio Tapes; Book Volumes; Clipping Files; DVDs; Exhibition Catalogs; Other Holdings; Periodical Subscriptions
Special Subjects: Bronzes, Drawings, Graphics, Painting-American, Photography, Prints, Sculpture, American Indian Art, African Art, Pre-Columbian Art, Ceramics, Etchings & Engravings, Decorative Arts, Painting-European, Eskimo Art, Oriental Art, Asian Art, Silver, Carpets & Rugs, Coins & Medals, Calligraphy, Miniatures, Renaissance Art, Laces, Antiquities-Oriental, Antiquities-Greek
Collections: Alice B Nunn Collection of English Silver; Rasmussen Collection of Northwest Coast Indian & Eskimo Arts; Evan H Roberts Memorial 19th & 20th Century Sculpture Collection; Elizabeth Cole Butler Collection of Native American Art; Gebauer Collection of Cameroon Art; Vivian & Gordon Gilkey Graphics Art Collection; Samuel H Kress Collection of Renaissance Painting & Sculpture; Mary Andrews Ladd Collection of Japanese Prints; Lewis Collection of Classical Antiquities; Hirsh Collection of Oriental Rugs; Lawther Collection of Ethiopian Crosses; William S Ladd Collection of Pre-Columbian Art; Clement Greenberg Collection
Exhibitions: Contemporary Northwest Art Awards
Publications: Annual report; exhibition catalogs; collection catalogs
Activities: Educ dept; workshops for students & adults; docent training; lects open to pub, 20-25 vis lectrs per yr; concerts; gallery talks; tours; competition; individual paintings & original objects of art lent to mus & art galleries; book traveling exhibs 4-5 per yr; originate traveling exhibs; mus shop sells books, reproductions, cards, unique items, handbags, jewelry

L **Crumpacker Family Library,** 1219 SW Park Ave, Portland, OR 97205-2430. Tel 503-276-4215; Fax 503-226-4842; Elec Mail library@pam.org; Internet Home Page Address: www.pam.org; *Library Dir* Debra Royer
Open Sun - Wed noon - 5 PM, cl Thurs - Sat; Estab 1892 to provide reference for pub & Portland Art Assn members, mus staff; Circ Non-circulating; Located on 2nd Fl of Mark Bldg, maintains reading room
Library Holdings: Auction Catalogs; Audio Tapes; Book Volumes 35,000; CD-ROMs; Cassettes; Clipping Files; DVDs; Exhibition Catalogs; Lantern Slides; Motion Pictures; Original Documents Portland Art Assn Archive; Other Holdings Northwest artist archive; Pamphlets; Periodical Subscriptions 75; Photographs; Records; Slides 5000; Video Tapes 300
Special Subjects: Art History, Folk Art, Islamic Art, Painting-American, Pre-Columbian Art, American Western Art, Asian Art, American Indian Art, Mexican Art, Afro-American Art, Oriental Art
Collections: Portland Art Museum Archive; The Portland Center for the Visual Arts (PCVA) Archive; NW Artists Archive; Art Museum Collection Artists File; Contemporary Artists & Photographers Files; Art Subject Files; 300+ videos & DVDs about art
Activities: Educ prog; docent training; lects open to pub; gallery talks; tours; mus shop sells books, gift items; Rental Sales Gallery sells original art

A **Northwest Film Center,** 934 SW Salmon St, Portland, OR 97205-2431; 1219 SW Park Ave, Portland, OR 97205-2430. Tel 503-221-1156x10; Fax 503-294-0874; Elec Mail info@nwfilm.org; Internet Home Page Address: www.nwfilm.org; *Dir* Bill Foster; *Opers & Event Develop Mgr* Russ Gage; *Mem & Pub Progs Coordr* Kristy Conrad; *Pub Rels & Mktg Mgr* Jessica Lyness; *Regional Svcs Coordr* Thomas Phillipson; *Exhib Asst* Ted Hurliman
Open Tues - Sat 10 AM - 5 PM; Estab 1972 as a regional media arts center; Maintains film archive, circ film library, film & video exhib prog & classes; Average Annual Attendance: 60,000
Income: financed by admissions, grants, contributions, mems, endowments
Library Holdings: Filmstrips; Other Holdings
Exhibitions: Portland International Film Festival; Northwest Film & Video Festival; Jewish Film Festival; Reel Music; Young People's Film & Video Festival; Northwest Tracking
Activities: Film screening prog; courses in film and video; video/filmmaker-in-schools prog; lects open to pub, 24 vis lectrs per yr; competitions with awards; scholarships & fels offered; exten dept; originate traveling exhibs

M **PORTLAND CHILDREN'S MUSEUM,** 4015 SW Canyon Rd Portland, OR 97221. Tel 503-233-6500; Fax 503-223-6600; Internet Home Page Address: www.portlandcm.org; *Exec Dir* Sarah Orleans; *Dir Progs & Outreach* Ingrid Anderson; *Dir Educ & Research* Judy Graves; *Dir Develop & External Affairs* Betzy Fry; *Dir Opers & Exhibs* Dennis Spidal; *Dir Communs & Mktg* Shannon Grosswiler
Open Mar - Labor Day 9 AM - 5 PM daily, Labor Day - Apr Tues - Sun 9 AM - 5 PM; cl July 4, Thanksgiving, Christmas Eve & Day, wk following Labor Day; closes at 4 PM Dec 31; Admis general $8, ages 55+ & military $7, mems & infants under 1 free; Estab 1946; mission is to inspire imagination, creativity & the wonder of learning in children & adults by inviting moments of shared discovery. Mus includes Opal School & Mus School as resources for early childhood development & research; Mus has 3 art studios, 3 party rooms, cafe & mus store; Average Annual Attendance: 300,000; Mem: 6,500; dues premier plus $250, premier $135, family plus $100, family & grandparent $85, 1 + 1 $65
Income: Financed 85% by earned income & 15% contribution
Collections: Children's art; natural history, toys, dollhouses, miniatures; multicultural artifacts relating to children's culture; teaching coll
Exhibitions: Water Works; Vroom Room; Baby's Garden; The Pet Hospital; Grasshopper Grocery & Butterfly Bistro; The Clay Studio; The Garage; Dig Pit; Play It Again Theatre; Wonder Corner; Treehouse Adventure; Building Bridgetown; Twilight Trail & more
Activities: Classes for adults & children; hands-on art activity for children; mus shop sells educ books & toys for children, creative teaching material for teachers, parents & caregivers

M **PORTLAND COMMUNITY COLLEGE,** North View Gallery, 12000 SW 49th Ave, Portland, OR 97219-7199. Tel 503-977-4269; Fax 503-977-4874; *Dir* Hugh Webb
Open Mon - Fri 8 AM - 4 PM; No admis fee; Estab 1970; Gallery's primary focus on contemporary Northwest artists, through solo shows, group invitations, installations & new genres; Average Annual Attendance: Over 20,000 in the Portland Metro area
Income: Financed by the college
Exhibitions: Contemporary art of the Northwest
Activities: Lect open to pub; 4-6 vis lectrs per yr; schols & fels offered

M **PORTLAND STATE UNIVERSITY,** Littman Gallery, 1825 SW Broadway, Rm 250 Portland, OR 97201-3256; PO Box 751, Portland, OR 97207-0751. Tel 503-725-5656; Fax 503-725-5680; Elec Mail artcom@pdx.edu; Internet Home Page Address: littmanandwhitegalleries.blogspot.com; *Gallery Dir, Coordr* Laura White
Open Mon - Fri Noon - 4 PM; No admis fee; Estab 1969, seeks to cultivate artistic experience and educ on campus and in community; Gallery space has 1500 sq ft
Income: Financed by PSU; non-profit
Exhibitions: 7-10 exhibs annually
Activities: Lect open to pub; 5 vis lectrs per yr; gallery talks

M **White Gallery,** 1825 SW Broadway, Smith Ctr Fl 2 Portland, OR 97201-3256; PO Box 751, Smith Ctr Portland, OR 97207-1751. Tel 503-725-5656; Fax 503-725-5080; Elec Mail artcom@pdx.edu; *Gallery Dir, Coordr* Emilie Gerber
Open Mon - Fri 8 AM - 10 PM, Sat 9 AM - 7 PM; No admis fee; Estab 1970 as a student operated gallery exhibiting works by professional artists representing primarily photog
Income: Financed by PSU
Collections: Permanent collection contains work by local professional artists with a few nationally recognized artists
Exhibitions: 11 exhibitions annually
Activities: Lect open to pub; gallery talks; individual paintings & original objects of art lent to other schools or museums; lending coll contains original prints, paintings & sculpture

M **QUARTERSAW GALLERY,** 528 NW 12th Ave, Portland, OR 97209-3001. Tel 503-223-2264; Fax 503-227-8748; *Dir* Victoria Frey
Open Tues - Fri 10 AM - 6 PM, Sat Noon - 5 PM

M **REED COLLEGE,** Douglas F Cooley Memorial Art Gallery, 3203 SE Woodstock Blvd Portland, OR 97202-8199. Tel 503-777-7251, 777-7790; Fax 503-788-6691; Internet Home Page Address: www.reed.edu; *Dir* Stephanie Snyder
Open Tues - Sun Noon - 5 PM, Drawings Room open by appointment for study of works on paper; No admis fee; Estab 1989 to enhance the teaching of art, art history & the humanities. The prog brings to the col & the community exhibs of art from a variety of periods & traditions as well as significant contemporary art not otherwise available in the Northwest
Special Subjects: Prints
Collections: Pre-20th century prints; 20th century prints, drawings, paintings, photographs & sculptures
Publications: Brochures; catalogues
Activities: Pub openings; lects; gallery talks

A **REGIONAL ARTS & CULTURE COUNCIL,** Metropolitan Center for Public Arts, 1120 SW 5th Ave, Portland, OR 97209; 411 NW Park, Ste 101, Portland, OR 97209-3318. Tel 503-823-5111; Fax 503-823-5432; Elec Mail info@racc.org; Internet Home Page Address: www.racc.org; *Others* 503-823-6868; *Exec Dir* Eloise Damrosch; *Dir Opers* Cindy Knapp; *Dir Commun Affairs* Jeff Hawthorne; *Chmn* Lina Garcia Seabold
Open Mon - Fri 8:30 AM - 5:30 PM; No admis fee; Estab 1973, to promote and encourage progs to further the development and pub awareness of and interest in the visual and performing arts
Income: Financed by city & county appropriation
Purchases: Visual Chronicle of Portland, 2 percent for Public Art projects, Portable Works Coll
Collections: Works by local artists
Publications: Newsletter, bimonthly
Activities: Artist in Residence Program for elementary schools; competitions with awards; schols offered; individual paintings & original objects of art lent

M **RONNA AND ERIC HOFFMAN GALLERY OF CONTEMPORARY ART,** 0615 SW Palatine Hill Rd, MSC 95 Portland, OR 97219. Tel 503-768-7687; Elec Mail gallery@lclark.edu; Internet Home Page Address: www.lclark.edu/hoffman_gallery; *Dir* Linda Tesner
Open Tues-Sun 11AM-4PM; Circ No admis fees
Collections: works by contemporary artists; paintings; sculpture; drawings

M **UNIVERSITY OF PORTLAND,** Buckley Center Gallery, 5000 N Willamette Blvd, Portland, OR 97203-5798. Tel 503-943-7792; Fax 503-943-7805; Elec Mail bognar@up.edu; *Dir* Pat Bognar
Open Mon - Fri 8:30 AM - 8 PM, Sat 8:30 AM - 4 PM; Estab 1977
Exhibitions: Noel Thomas; Terry Waldron; Martha Wehrle

L **UNIVERSITY OF PORTLAND,** Wilson W Clark Memorial Library, 5000 N Willamette Blvd, Portland, OR 97203-5743. Tel 503-943-7111; Elec Mail library@up.edu; *Dir* Rich Hines; *Reference Librn* Heidi Senior; *Technical Svcs Librn* Susan Hinken
Open Mon - Thurs 7:30 AM - midnight, Fri 7:30 AM - 10 PM, Sat 10 AM - 6 PM, Sun Noon - 12 AM; Estab 1901 to support the university curriculum; Circ 50,000; Maintains an art gallery with a rotating exhibit
Income: Financed through the univ
Library Holdings: Book Volumes over 121,000; Compact Disks; Fiche; Filmstrips; Manuscripts; Maps; Original Art Works; Original Documents; Periodical Subscriptions; Records; Sculpture; Slides; Video Tapes over 4000
Exhibitions: Rotating exhibs

A **WEST HILLS UNITARIAN FELLOWSHIP,** Doll Gardner Art Gallery, 8470 SW Oleson Rd, Portland, OR 97223-6977. Tel 503-246-3351 ext 4; Elec Mail dollgardnergallery@yahoo.com; Internet Home Page Address: www.whuuf.net; *Dir* Karen Van Hoy
Open Tues & Thurs 9 AM - Noon, Wed & Fri 12:30 - 3 PM; No admis fee; Estab 1970 gallery has exhibited work of a wide range of artists& organizations from the celebrated to the emerging; The entire sanctuary wall space is like a large gallery & the building is light, airy with a woodsy backdrop
Income: $30,000 (financed by mem)
Collections: Paintings, wall sculptures by local artists
Publications: Bulletin, weekly; newsletter, monthly

Activities: Classes for adults & children; dramatic progs; lect open to pub, 8 vis lectrs per yr; concerts

ZADO GALLERY, 319 SW Pine St, Portland, OR 97204-2725. Tel 503-222-9236; Elec Mail zadogallery@yahoo.com
Open daily 10 AM - 5 PM

ROSEBURG

PASTEL SOCIETY OF OREGON
For further information, see National and Regional Organizations

SAINT BENEDICT

L **MOUNT ANGEL ABBEY LIBRARY,** 1 Abbey Rd, Saint Benedict, OR 97373-9700. Tel 503-845-3317; Fax 503-845-3500; Elec Mail paulah@mtangel.edu; *Head Librn* Paula Hamilton
Open 8:30 AM - 5 PM & 6:30 - 9:30 PM, weekends 10:30 AM - 4:30 PM; No admis fee; Estab 1882; The library serves Mount Angel Abbey, Mount Angel Seminary & the pub. It sponsors art exhibits in the foyer designed for this purpose & makes the auditorium available for concerts
Library Holdings: Book Volumes 275,000; Fiche 10; Framed Reproductions 30; Manuscripts; Original Art Works 100; Periodical Subscriptions 1000; Prints 30
Exhibitions: Local artists; changes monthly
Publications: Angelus, quarterly
Activities: Classes for adults

SALEM

A **SALEM ART ASSOCIATION,** 600 Mission St SE, Salem, OR 97302-6203. Tel 503-581-2228; Internet Home Page Address: www.salemart.org; *Exec Dir* Debby Leahy
Open Tues - Fri 10 AM - 5 PM, Sat & Sun Noon - 5 PM; No admis fee; Estab 1919 to collect, preserve & interpret history & art; Sales gallery & exhib galleries featuring contemporary art; Average Annual Attendance: 125,000; Mem: 1500; dues $25; ann meeting in Sept
Income: $900,000 (financed by sales, Salem Art Fair & Festival special fundraisers, admis, mem & donations)
Exhibitions: 10 exhibits yearly in 2 galleries
Publications: Art Matters newsletter, 3 per year; class schedule, 5 per year
Activities: Classes for adults & children; lect open to pub; gallery talks; sales shop sells original art

M **Bush Barn Art Center,** 600 Mission St SE, Salem, OR 97302-6203. Tel 503-581-2228; Internet Home Page Address: www.salemart.org; *Exec Dir* Sandra Burnett; *Gallery Dir* Catherine Alexander
Open Tues - Fri 10 AM - 5 PM, Sat & Sun Noon - 5 PM; No admis fee; Estab 1965 to exhibit & interpret works of 20th & 21st century fine art & crafts; Houses the A N Bush Gallery, Focus Gallery & Camas Gallery which features 24 exhibs ea yr & a goft gallery of Northwest art & crafts; Average Annual Attendance: 31,000
Activities: Docent training; lects open to pub; concerts; gallery talks; awards; individual paintings rented to mems only (2-D work only); sales shop sells original art, reproductions & prints

M **Bush House Museum,** 600 Mission St SE, Salem, OR 97302-6203. Tel 503-363-4714; Elec Mail bushhouse@salemart.org; Internet Home Page Address: www.salemart.org; *Bush House Mus Dir* Ross Sutherland
Open visit website; Admis visit website; Estab 1953, illuminating Oregon history & culture associated with the lives & legacy of Salem's Bush family; 100 acre gentleman farm now furnished house mus (1878); art center & city park; cultural heritage & bus history of Salem; Average Annual Attendance: 5,000
Collections: Original furnishings, decorative arts, fine arts & wallpapers
Activities: Educ progs; special events & contemporary exhibs; guided tours

L **Archives,** 600 Mission St SE, Salem, OR 97302-6203. Tel 503-363-4714; Internet Home Page Address: www.salemart.org; *Bush House Coordr* Patricia Narcum-Perez
Open Tues - Sun Noon - 4 PM by appointment only; No admis fee; Estab 1953; Circ Non-circulating; For reference only
Library Holdings: Audio Tapes; Book Volumes 150; Cassettes; Clipping Files; Manuscripts; Memorabilia; Motion Pictures; Photographs; Video Tapes
Collections: Bush family papers 1840-1950
Exhibitions: Victorian Historic House with furniture

M **WILLAMETTE UNIVERSITY,** Hallie Ford Museum of Art, 700 State St, Salem, OR 97301; 900 State St, Salem, OR 97301-3931. Tel 503-370-6855; Fax 503-375-5458; Elec Mail museum-art@willamette.edu; Internet Home Page Address: www.willamette.edu/arts/hfma; *Dir* John Olbrantz; *Asst to Dir* Carolyn Harcourt; *Coll Cur* Jonathan Bucci; *Educ Cur* Elizabeth Garrison; *Designer/Preparator* David Andersen; *Mem/Pub Rels Mgr* Andrea Foust
Open Tues - Sat 10 AM - 5 PM; Sun 1 PM - 5PM; Admis adults $3, students & seniors $2, children under 12 free; Estab 1998 to support the liberal arts curriculum of Willamette Univ & to serve as an intellectual & cultural resource for the campus, the City of Salem & surrounding area; The Hallie Ford Mus of Art maintains a 27,000 sq ft facility which includes permanent galleries devoted to colls of regional art, Native American Art, & Asian, European & American Art; Average Annual Attendance: 30,000; Mem: 375 mem; Dues $25 - $1,000
Income: Financed by endowment, mem, admissions, grants, sales
Collections: Regional art; Native American art; American, European, Asian art; American, European, Asian works on paper
Exhibitions: Temporary exhibs devoted to historic & contemporary art
Publications: Newsletter - Brushstrokes; Collection Guides; Exhibition Catalogues
Activities: Docent training; lect; gallery talks; films; workshops; artist demonstrations; symposia; poetry readings; concerts; originates traveling exhibs to regional & nat museums; mus shop sells books

SPRINGFIELD

A EMERALD EMPIRE ART ASSOCIATION, Emerald Art Center, 500 Main St, Springfield, OR 97477-5469. Tel 541-726-8595; Fax 541-726-2954; Elec Mail admin@emeraldartcenter.org; Internet Home Page Address: www.emeraldartcenter.org; *Pres (2013)* Chris Mackay; *Gallery Dir* Paula Goodbar
Open Tues - Sat 11 AM - 4 PM; No admis fee; Estab 1957 to promote cultural arts in Springfield & surrounding areas; Downtown area is 12,000 sq ft; Average Annual Attendance: 10,800; Mem: 220; dues assoc mem $175, contributing mems $75; monthly meetings 3rd Tues every other month
Income: Financed by mem dues, commission on sales, fundraisers, revenue from workshops
Library Holdings: Book Volumes; Exhibition Catalogs; Periodical Subscriptions
Special Subjects: Drawings, Graphics, Landscapes, Metalwork, Photography, Porcelain, Prints, Sculpture, Textiles, Watercolors, Pottery, Stained Glass, American Western Art, Asian Art, Bronzes, Decorative Arts, Folk Art, African Art, Afro-American Art, American Indian Art, Ceramics, Collages, Crafts, Hispanic Art, Latin American Art, Miniatures, Glass, Woodcarvings, Oriental Art, Calligraphy, Southwestern Art, Mexican Art
Collections: Paintings donated by workshop teachers & guest artists
Exhibitions: Exhibs bimonthly at local shopping malls & convention centers; Host to Springfield Mayor Annual Art Show; Emerald Spring Exhibition (nat juried show); Photo Zone Annual Juried Show; Photography at Oregon Photographic Auction
Publications: Monthly newsletter
Activities: Classes for adults & children, material available to anyone; lect open to pub, 2 vis lectrs per year; gallery talks; tours; picture of the month award; competitions; awards; schols offered; individual paintings & original objects of art lent; originates traveling exhibs; gift shop sells original art, reproductions, prints, jewelry

THE DALLES

A THE DALLES ART ASSOCIATION, The Dalles Art Center, 220 E 4th St, The Dalles Art Ctr & Gallery The Dalles, OR 97058-2206. Tel 541-296-4759; Elec Mail thedallesart@embarqmail.com; Internet Home Page Address: www.thedallesartcenter.org; *Exec Dir* Carmen Toll
Open Tues - Sat 11 AM - 5 PM; No admis fee; Estab 1959 for presentation of community arts activities; Gallery maintained; Average Annual Attendance: 5,000+; Mem: 250; dues corporate $250, sponsor $100, bus $75, family $45, individual $35, senior $25; meeting held second Tues of each month
Income: Financed by dues, fundraising events, grants, sponsorships & sales
Exhibitions: Member & guest exhibits; state services exhibits
Publications: Bimonthly newsletter
Activities: Art classes for adults & children; docent training; lect open to pub; competitions; cash for awards; 2 open judged & juried shows per yr; gallery shop sells original art, jewelry, pottery, basketry, glass

TOLEDO

M YAQUINA RIVER MUSEUM OF ART, 151 NE Alder St, Toledo, OR 97391-1521. Tel 541-336-1907; Fax 541-336-1907; Elec Mail yrartmuseum@charter.net; Internet Home Page Address: www.michaelgibbons.net/museum.htm; *Cur* Michael Gibbons
Open Fri-Sun 11AM-6PM
Collections: artwork by Michael Gibbons & other local artists

WOODBURN

M WOODBURN ART CENTER, Glatt House Gallery, 2251 N Boones Ferry Rd, Woodburn, OR 97071-9669. Tel 503-982-6450
Special Subjects: Sculpture

PENNSYLVANIA

ALLENTOWN

M ALLENTOWN ART MUSEUM, 31 N 5th St, Allentown, PA 18101-1605. Tel 610-432-4333; Fax 610-434-7409; Elec Mail membership@allentownartmuseum.org; Internet Home Page Address: www.allentownartmuseum.org; *Pres & CEO* J Brooks Joyner; *Dir Admin* Don Gunn; *Mus Shop Mgr* Sharon Yurkanin; *Colls Mgr* Nathan Marzan; *Bldg Operations Mgr* Douglas Bowerman; *Chmn* Dolores A Laputka Esq; *Interim Dir Educ* Jane Kintzer; *Chief Cur* Diane P Fischer, PhD; *Dir Develp & Mktg* Elizabeth G Haymon
See website for hours; Admis see website; Estab 1939 to acquire, protect, display & interpret the visual arts from the past & present, world wide; Building & land cover a 17,000 sq ft gallery space; Mem: 2,550; see website for dues info
Income: $850,000 (financed by endowment, mem, city, county & state appropriation & contributions)
Special Subjects: Porcelain, Prints, Silver, Sculpture, Architecture, Drawings, Painting-American, Photography, Bronzes, Ceramics, Folk Art, Etchings & Engravings, Landscapes, Decorative Arts, Painting-European, Furniture, Jade, Jewelry, Oriental Art, Painting-Dutch, Historical Material, Baroque Art, Painting-Flemish, Period Rooms, Embroidery, Laces, Painting-Italian, Painting-German, Pewter
Collections: Samuel H Kress Collection of European paintings & sculpture, c 1350-1750 (Bugiardini, Lotto, de Heem, Rembrandt, Ruisdael, Steen & others); Textile study room; Frank Lloyd Wright period room, 1912; American paintings & sculpture

Publications: Calendar of events, quarterly; catalogs of major exhibitions; descriptive gallery handouts
Activities: Classes for adults & children; docent training; 3 family events each yr; lects open to pub; gallery talks; tours; competitions; concerts; mus shop sells books, jewelry & other art related games & stationery; Art Ways, interactive children's gallery

M LEHIGH VALLEY HERITAGE CENTER, (Lehigh County Historical Society) 432 W Walnut St, Allentown, PA 18102-5428. Tel 610-435-1074; Fax 610-435-9812; Elec Mail lchs@voicenet.com; Internet Home Page Address: www.lchs.museum; *Exec Dir* Joseph Garrera; *Cur Coll* Andree Mey; *Coll Mgr* Morgan McMillan; *Archivist* Jan Ballard; *Cur Educ* Sarah Nelson; *Dir Develop* David Voellinger; *Mem Coordr* Linda Buesgen; *Research Librn* Carol Herrity; *Bookkeeper* Elaine Johaneman; *Educ Asst* Lorinda Macaulay; *Properties Mgr* Beverly Renaldi; *Office Mgr* Pat Arnold; *VPres* Raymond Holland; *VChmn* Robert M McGovern
George Taylor House open by appointment only; Trout Hall June-Oct Tues-Sun 1 - 4 PM, Apr-May & Sept-Nov Sat & Sun 1 - 4 PM; Troxell-Stickel House June-Oct Sat & Sun 1 - 4 PM; Lehigh County Mus Mon - Fri 9 AM - 4 PM, Sat & Sun 1 - 4 PM; Claussville School, Lock Ridge Furnace, Saylor Cement Kilns, Haines Mill & Frank Buchman House May - Sept Sat & Sun 1 - 4 PM; Admis $2 for non-mems at Taylor House, Trout Hall, Troxell-Steckel House, Claussville School; others free; Estab 1904 for coll, preservation & exhib of Lehigh County history; Lock Ridge Furnace Mus 1868, Frank Buchman House 1894, Haines Mill Mus 1760 & 1909, Lehigh County Mus 1814-1914, Trout Hall 1770, George Taylor House 1768, Saylor Cementy Industry Mus 1868, Troxell-Steckel House 1756, Claussville One-Room Schoolhouse 1893; Average Annual Attendance: 36,000; Mem: 1,300; dues $15 - $1,000; ann meeting 3rd Wed in Apr
Income: $900,000 (financed by endowment, mem, tax-based support, foundations, corporate & bus support)
Special Subjects: Architecture, Drawings, Painting-American, Photography, Watercolors, Anthropology, Archaeology, Ethnology, Textiles, Costumes, Crafts, Folk Art, Decorative Arts, Manuscripts, Portraits, Furniture, Glass, Porcelain, Historical Material, Maps, Dioramas, Period Rooms, Embroidery, Pewter, Leather
Collections: Extensive regional history archives, 10,000 books, 65,000 photographs & negatives, 1600 linear feet of pamphlets, documents, newspapers, maps, microfilm; 32,000 objects related to social history, daily life, agriculture & industry, textiles, fine & folk art, architectural elements, bus, American Indians, decorative arts, furniture; historic structures & elements of historic structures
Publications: Proceedings, biennial; Town Crier, quarterly newsletter; occasional books & monographs
Activities: Workshops; lects open to pub, 15 vis lectrs per yr; concerts; tours; mus shop sells books, pamphlets & local souvenirs

L Scott Andrew Trexler II Library, Old Court House, Hamilton at Fifth, Allentown, PA; 432 W Walnut St, Allentown, PA 18102. Tel 610-435-1074; Fax 610-435-9812; Internet Home Page Address: www.voicenet.com/~lchs; *Librn & Archivist* Jan Ballard; *Reference Librn* Carol M Herrity
Open Mon - Sat 10 AM - 4 PM; No admis fee for mems, $5 for non-mems; Estab 1974; For reference only; Average Annual Attendance: 2,000
Income: $45,000
Purchases: $14,000
Library Holdings: Audio Tapes 10; Book Volumes 10,000; Cassettes 200; Framed Reproductions; Lantern Slides 1000; Manuscripts 1000; Memorabilia 1000; Original Art Works; Pamphlets 200; Periodical Subscriptions 20; Photographs 50,000; Prints; Reels 400
Collections: Allentown imprints; broadsides; Civil War; early German newspapers; fraktur; Native American materials; photographs
Publications: Proceedings, semi-annual; Town Crier

M MUHLENBERG COLLEGE, Martin Art Gallery, 2400 Chew St, Allentown, PA 18104-5586. Tel 484-664-3467; Fax 484-664-3113; Elec Mail kburke@muhlenberg.edu; Internet Home Page Address: www.muhlenberg.edu; *Exhib & Colls Mgr* Kathryn Burke
Open Tues - Sat 12 PM - 8PM; No admis fee; Estab 1976; The building was designed by architect Philip Johnson; the focal point of its design & function is a 220 ft glass-covered galleria which bisects the structure; Average Annual Attendance: 7,000
Income: Financed by the col
Special Subjects: Etchings & Engravings, American Western Art, Painting-American, Woodcuts, Drawings, Photography, Prints, Sculpture, Religious Art
Collections: Master prints; Rembrandt, Durer, Whistler, Goya; 20th century American & contemporary art; Edward S Curtis Photogravures of the North American Indian
Exhibitions: Year round schedule of 6 to 8 exhibitions
Publications: Exhibition catalogs
Activities: Lect open to pub; films; gallery talks

AUDUBON

M NATIONAL AUDUBON SOCIETY, (Mill Grove Audubon Wildlife Sanctuary) John James Audubon Center at Mill Grove, 1201 Pawlings Rd Audubon, PA 19403. Tel 610-666-5593; Fax 484-831-5305; Elec Mail millgrove@audubon.org; Internet Home Page Address: pa.audubon.org/centers-mill-grove.html; *Dir* Jean Bochnowski; *Senior Cur* Nancy Powell; *Facilities Coordr* Susannah Conard; *Admin Coordr* Linda Ridgway; *Educ Coordr* Carrie Ashley
Open Tues - Sat 10 AM - 4 PM, Sun 1 - 4 PM & major holidays; Admis adults $4, seniors (60 & over) $3, children $2; Estab 1951 to display the major artwork of John James Audubon, artist-naturalist, who made Mill Grove his first home in America 1803-06; This is a National Historic Landmark & features original artworks by Audubon, plus examples of all his major publs; Average Annual Attendance: 20,000
Library Holdings: Auction Catalogs; Book Volumes; Manuscripts; Original Art Works
Special Subjects: Prints, Painting-American, Period Rooms

Collections: Birds of America (double elephant folio, 4 vols, Audubon & Havell); Birds of America (first ed Octavo, 7 vols, Audubon, Lithos by Bowen); Quadrupeds of North America (Imperial size, 2 vols, Audubon & Bachmann); Quadrupeds of North America (Octavo, 3 vols, Audubon, Lithos by Bowen); Birds of America; Art, work, and life of artist John James Audubon; 19th Century American Art; Ornithological Art of the 20th Century
Exhibitions: Annual Juried Art Show in April
Activities: Classes for adults & children; docent training; lects open to pub; gallery talks, tours; ann award Friends of A Feather: for art in serv of nature/wildlife conservation; mus shop sells books, prints, original art, reproductions, bird related items, work by local artists & artisans

BETHLEHEM

M ARTS QUEST, (Banana Factory) Banana Factory, 25 W Third St Bethlehem, PA 18015-1238; Art Center at SteelStacks, 101 Founders Way Bethlehem, PA 18015. Tel 610-332-1300; Internet Home Page Address: www.artsquest.org; *Dir Visual Art & Educ* Janice Lipzin; *Mgr* Debra Miller
Open Gallery 11AM-4PM, Building Mon-Fri 8AM-9:30PM, Sat-Sun 8:30AM-5PM Call to verify; Making the arts accessible to the community; Two gallery spaces: Banana Factory & SteelStacks; Average Annual Attendance: 12,000
Special Subjects: Glass, Jewelry
Collections: paintings; photographs; sculpture
Exhibitions: 22 exhibs per yr
Activities: Classes for adults & children; Invision Photo Festival; gallery talks; tours; sponsoring of competitions; schols

M LEHIGH UNIVERSITY ART GALLERIES, Museum Operation, 420 E Packer Ave, Zoellner Arts Ctr Bethlehem, PA 18015-3010. Tel 610-758-3615; Fax 610-758-4580; Elec Mail rv02@lehigh.edu; Internet Home Page Address: www.luag.org; *Dir Exhib & Coll* Ricardo Viera; *Asst to Dir* Denise Stangl; *Ed* Patricia Kandianis; *Coll Mgr* Mark Wonsidler; *Coll Asst* Vasti DeEsch; *Preparator* Jeffrey Ludwig; *Asst Preparator* Khalil Allaik
Open Mon - Fri 9 AM - 10 PM, Sat 9 AM - Noon, cl Sun (DuBois Gallery), Wed - Sat 11 AM - 5 PM, Sun 1 - 5 PM (Zoellner Gallery); Mon - Thurs 9 AM - 10 PM, Fri 9 AM - 5 PM (Siegel Gallery Iacocca Hall); No admis fee; Estab to bring diverse media & understanding to the Lehigh students & general pub of the Lehigh Valley area; Collection is maintained in three galleries; DuBois Gallery has four floors of approx 250 running ft of wall hanging space per floor; Zoellner Gallery has two floors of exhibition space; Average Annual Attendance: 25,000 (per all galleries)
Income: Financed by endowment & gifts
Special Subjects: Afro-American Art, Etchings & Engravings, Landscapes, Architecture, Photography, Portraits, Pre-Columbian Art, Prints, Woodcuts, Graphics, Hispanic Art, Latin American Art, Painting-American, Photography, Prints, Sculpture, Watercolors, Bronzes, African Art, Pre-Columbian Art, Textiles, Folk Art, Primitive art, Painting-European, Painting-Japanese, Portraits, Posters, Porcelain, Antiquities-Byzantine, Painting-British, Painting-French, Coins & Medals, Antiquities-Oriental, Painting-Spanish, Antiquities-Roman, Antiquities-Etruscan
Collections: Baker Collection of Chinese Porcelain; Phillip & Muriel Berman Collection of Japanese prints, Paintings & Outdoor Sculpture; Dreyfus Collection of French Paintings. Folk & Outsider Art; Grace Collection of Paintings; Ralph Wilson Collection of American Paintings & Graphics; Prasse Collection of Prints; Fearnside Collection of European Old Master Prints & Drawings; Langermann Collection of Pre-Columbian & Ethnographic Sculpture; Mr & Mrs Franklin H Williams Collection of African Art; Photography Collection; Latin American Collection; Contemporary Prints & Drawings Collection
Publications: Calendar, twice per year; exhibition catalogs
Activities: University classes & workshops for children; docent training; lects open to pub, 4 vis lectrs per yr; gallery talks; tours; individual paintings & original objects of art lent to other schools & galleries; originate traveling exhibs; gallery shop sells books, original art, prints, handcrafted ceramics & jewelry

M MORAVIAN COLLEGE, Payne Gallery, Main & Church Sts, Bethlehem, PA 18018; 1200 Main St, Bethlehem, PA 18018-6650. Tel 610-861-1675, 861-1680 (office); Fax 610-861-1682; Elec Mail medjr01@moravian.edu; dradycki@moravian.edu; Internet Home Page Address: www.moravian.edu; *Dir Dr* Diane Radycki; *Asst to Dir* David Leidich; *Chmn Art Dept* Anne Dutlinger
Open Tues - Sun 11 AM - 4 PM; No admis fee; Estab 1982 to present historic & contemporary art to a diverse audience; Main floor & mezzanine have a combined total of 200 running ft; Average Annual Attendance: 15,000
Income: Financed by endowment & through the col
Purchases: Coll of paintings by W Elmer Schofield, Susan Eakins, John Marin, Albert Bierstadt, Cecilia Beaux, Reginald Marsh & Gustavus Grunewald acquired
Special Subjects: Drawings, Painting-American, Photography, Prints, Watercolors, Woodcuts
Collections: American Impressionists of the New Hope Circle; Collection of 19th & 20th century landscape paintings of Eastern Pennsylvania; Previously Underrecognized Women of the Philadelphia School; Collection of contemporary paintings & prints; Nineteenth & Twentieth Century American Landscape Art; Paintings - Susan Eakins, Gustavus Grunewald, Antonio Martino, Elmer Schofield; Twentieth Century Paintings; Edward S Curtis's The North American Indian, 20 volumes (1928)
Publications: Exhib catalogues
Activities: Lects open to pub; 6 vis lectrs per yr; concerts; gallery talks; schols offered; lending of original objects of art to other museums & galleries; book 1-2 traveling exhibs per yr; originate traveling exhibitions to other museums & galleries

BLOOMSBURG

M BLOOMSBURG UNIVERSITY OF PENNSYLVANIA, Haas Gallery of Art, 400 E Second St, Dept of Art & Art History Bloomsburg, PA 17815-1301. Tel 570-389-4708; Fax 570-389-4459; Elec Mail lmillard@bloomu.edu; Internet Home Page Address: departments.bloomu.edu/haasgallery; *Chmn Dept of Art Dr* Christine Sperling; *Gallery Assoc* Lee S Millard
Open Mon - Fri 9 AM - 4 PM; No admis fee; Estab 1966 as an educational &

cultural exten of the College's Dept of Art; Gallery covers 875 sq ft with approx 90 ft of running wall space & track lighting ; Average Annual Attendance: 16,000
Income: Financed by community activities & grants
Collections: Permanent Collection
Exhibitions: 8 - 10 spring exhibs annually in a variety of media by established, emerging & student artists
Activities: Lect open to public, 5 vis lectrs per yr; gallery talks

BOALSBURG

M COLUMBUS CHAPEL & BOAL MANSION MUSEUM, 163 Boal Estate Dr, Boalsburg, PA 16827; PO Box 116, Boalsburg, PA 16827-0116. Tel 814-466-6210; Elec Mail office@boalmuseum.com; Internet Home Page Address: www.boalmuseum.com; *CEO* Christopher Lee
Open June - Labor Day daily (except Mon) 10 AM - 5 PM, May, Sept & Oct 1:30 - 5 PM; Admis adults $10, children $6; Estab 1952 as a nonprofit educational organization devoted to preservation of this unique American & international heritage & collection; Christopher Columbus relics imported from Spain in 1909 to the 1789 Boal Family Mansion; Average Annual Attendance: 25,000
Income: Financed by admis
Library Holdings: Book Volumes; Manuscripts; Memorabilia; Original Art Works; Original Documents; Photographs; Prints; Sculpture
Special Subjects: Painting-American, Furniture, Glass, Painting-Flemish, Painting-Spanish, Painting-Italian, Painting-German
Collections: Chapel contains 16th & 17th century Spanish, Italian & Flemish art; furniture, china & glassware; mansion contains 18th & 19th century French, Spanish, Italian, Flemish & American art; weapons: American, French & German (1780-1920)
Activities: Classes for adults & children, docent training, experimental action learning for grade 5; lects open to public, 2 lects per year; concerts; gallery talks; tours; three ann awards for educ, preservation & community svcs; mus shop or sales shop sells books, prints

BRYN ATHYN

M ACADEMY OF THE NEW CHURCH, Glencairn Museum, 1001 Cathedral Rd, Bryn Athyn, PA 19009; PO Box 757, Bryn Athyn, PA 19009-0757. Tel 267-502-2600; Fax 267-502-2686; Elec Mail info@glencairnmuseum.org; Internet Home Page Address: www.glencairnmuseum.org; *Dir* Brian Henderson; *Educ Coordr* Diane Fehon; *Tour Coordr* Leah Smith; *Cur* C Edward Gyllenhaal; *Colls Mgr* Bret Bostock; *Outreach & Pub Rels Coordr* Joralyn Echols; *Concert Coordr* Peter Childs; *Operations Mgr* Doreen Carey; *Mng Dir Academy of the New Church* Jim Adams; *Special Asst to Dir* Stephen Morley
Open Mon - Fri 9 AM - 5 PM by appointment, Sat 1 PM - 4:30 PM; Tours Mon-Fri 2:30 PM, Sat 1 PM, 1:30 PM, 2:30 PM & 3 PM; Admis adults $8, seniors & students $6, children under 4 free, discounts for mems; Estab 1878 to display, study & teach about works of art & artifacts which illustrate the history of world religions; Museum housed in family crafted Romanesque style building (1939), former home of Raymond & Mildred Pitcairn; Average Annual Attendance: 19,500; Mem: 582; dues Individual $30; Family $60; Gold Individual $100; Gold Family & Friends $200
Income: Financed by endowment
Library Holdings: Book Volumes; Exhibition Catalogs
Special Subjects: Decorative Arts, Historical Material, Glass, Textiles, Maps, Tapestries, Architecture, Drawings, Painting-American, Photography, Sculpture, Watercolors, American Indian Art, African Art, Archaeology, Costumes, Religious Art, Ceramics, Pottery, Primitive art, Woodcarvings, Landscapes, Manuscripts, Portraits, Furniture, Jewelry, Oriental Art, Asian Art, Metalwork, Carpets & Rugs, Ivory, Scrimshaw, Coins & Medals, Calligraphy, Dioramas, Period Rooms, Embroidery, Medieval Art, Antiquities-Oriental, Islamic Art, Antiquities-Egyptian, Antiquities-Greek, Antiquities-Roman, Mosaics, Stained Glass, Antiquities-Etruscan, Enamels, Antiquities-Assyrian
Collections: American Indian; Ancient Near East; Egypt; Greece & Rome; Medieval sculpture, stained glass & treasury objects; 19th & 20th Century art by Swedenborgian artists; oriental rugs; Asian; African Beads
Exhibitions: (11/29/2013-01/04/2014) Follow the Star: World Nativities
Publications: Monthly e-newsletter
Activities: Progs for school groups; college internship prog; lects open to publ; lects for mems only; concerts; gallery talks; tours; individual paintings & original art objects are lent to mus & institutions which provide satisfactory evidence of adequate security, insurance, fire protection; mus shop sells books, original art, prints, jewelry, postcards, CDs, DVDs, hand blown glass decorations & souvenirs

BRYN MAWR

L BRYN MAWR COLLEGE, Rhys Carpenter Library for Art, Archaeology, Classics & Cities, 101 N Merion Ave, Bryn Mawr, PA 19010-2899. Tel 610-526-5271; Fax 610-526-7911; Elec Mail cmackay@brynmawr.edu or jblatchl@brynmawr.edu; Internet Home Page Address: www.brynmawr.edu/Library; *Head Librn* Camilla MacKay; *Reference Librn* Jeremy Blatchley; *Library Asst* Christine Purkiss
Open during acad yr Mon - Thurs 8 AM - midnight, Fri 8 AM - 8 PM, Sat 10 AM - 7 PM, Sun noon - midnight, summer Mon - Fri 9 AM - 9 PM (hours vary); No admis fee; Estab 1931 to serve the needs of the general col prog, the undergraduate majors & graduate students through the PhD degree in History of Art; Classical & Near Eastern archaeology, classics & the undergraduate prog in Growth & Structure of Cities
Income: Financed by college funds
Library Holdings: Auction Catalogs; Book Volumes 100,000; Compact Disks; Exhibition Catalogs; Fiche; Framed Reproductions; Kodachrome Transparencies; Lantern Slides; Original Art Works; Pamphlets; Periodical Subscriptions 400; Photographs; Prints; Reels; Reproductions; Sculpture; Slides; Video Tapes
Special Subjects: Art History, Landscape Architecture, Islamic Art, Manuscripts, Painting-American, Painting-British, Painting-Dutch, Painting-Flemish, Painting-French, Painting-German, Painting-Italian, Painting-Japanese,

Painting-Russian, Painting-Spanish, Painting-European, Latin American Art, Archaeology, Asian Art, Furniture, Antiquities-Persian, Carpets & Rugs, Antiquities-Assyrian, Antiquities-Byzantine, Antiquities-Egyptian, Antiquities-Greek, Coins & Medals, Architecture
Exhibitions: Changing exhibitions curated by college collections

CARLISLE

M **DICKINSON COLLEGE,** The Trout Gallery, 240 W High St, Carlisle, PA 17013; PO Box 1773, Carlisle, PA 17013-2896. Tel 717-245-1344; Fax 717-254-8929; Elec Mail trout@dickinson.edu; Internet Home Page Address: www.dickinson.edu/trout; *Registrar & Exhib Preparator* James Bowman; *Cur Educ* Wendy Pires; *Dir* Phillip Earenfight; *Admin Asst* Stephanie Keifer
Open Tues - Sat 10 AM - 4 PM; No admis fee; Estab 1983 as display & care facilities for col's art coll, serves col & community; Two floors with exhib & permanent coll space; Average Annual Attendance: 9,000
Income: $325,000 (financed by endowment, college & special grants)
Purchases: Auguste Rodin's St John the Baptist; Joseph Stella's Bold Flowers; African Art; Baselitz's Madchen mit Harmonika IV; Thomas Sully's Portrait of Benjamin Rush; Fabio Mauroner's etchings
Library Holdings: Auction Catalogs; Book Volumes; Exhibition Catalogs
Special Subjects: Drawings, Graphics, Painting-American, Photography, Prints, American Indian Art, African Art, Pre-Columbian Art, Southwestern Art, Religious Art, Ceramics, Pottery, Primitive art, Woodcuts, Etchings & Engravings, Landscapes, Decorative Arts, Portraits, Posters, Oriental Art, Asian Art, Painting-French, Historical Material, Baroque Art, Calligraphy, Renaissance Art, Painting-Spanish, Islamic Art, Antiquities-Egyptian, Antiquities-Roman
Collections: Carnegie Collection of Prints; Old Master & modern prints; photographs; Cole Collection of Oriental & Decorative Arts; Gerofsky Collection of African Art; Potamkin Collection of 19th & 20th Century Work
Exhibitions: (11/8/2013-2/8/2014) Sue Coe Exhibition
Publications: Exhibition catalogues, 3 - 5 per year
Activities: Classes for adults & children by appointment only; lects open to pub, 1 - 2 vis lectrs per yr, awards given; book traveling exhibs 2 - 4 per yr; originate traveling exhibs

CHADDS FORD

M **BRANDYWINE CONSERVANCY,** Brandywine River Museum, 1 Hoffman's Mill Rd Chadds Ford, PA 19317; PO Box 141, Chadds Ford, PA 19317-0141. Tel 610-388-2700; Fax 610-388-1197; Elec Mail inquiries@brandywine.org; Internet Home Page Address: www.brandywinemuseum.org; *Dir Fin & Admin* Joel E. Necowitz; *Cur Collections* Virginia O'Hara; *Dir Pub Rels* Hillary Holland; *Registrar* Jean A Gilmore; *Supv Educ* Mary W Cronin; *Brandywine Conservancy Exec Dir* Virginia A Logan; *Vol Coordr* Donna M Gormel; *Chmn (V)* George A Weymouth; *Chief Security* Robert Booker; *VPres* Wendell Fenton; *Assoc Cur NC Wyeth Collections* Christine B Podmaniczky; *Mus Shop Mgr* Erika G Bucino; *Dir Develop* Suzanne M Regnier; *Asst Educ* Jane V Flitner; *Assoc Cur* Audrey Lewis; *Brandywine River Mus Dir* Thomas Padon
Open daily 9:30 AM - 4:30 PM; cl Christmas; Admis adults $10, seniors & students (6 - 12) $6, mems and children under 6 free; Estab 1971, devoted to the preservation, documentation & interpretation of art history in the Brandywine Valley, the history of American illustration, American still-life paintings & the relationship of regional art to the natural environment; Six galleries of permanent colls & special exhibs, changing approx 5 times per yr; Average Annual Attendance: 115,655; Mem: 4600; dues vary
Library Holdings: Book Volumes; Clipping Files; Exhibition Catalogs; Manuscripts; Maps; Memorabilia; Original Documents
Special Subjects: Drawings, Painting-American, Prints, Sculpture, Watercolors, Etchings & Engravings, Landscapes
Collections: American illustration; American still-life painting, drawing & sculpture, including a major Wyeth Family Collection; art of the Brandywine Valley from early 19th century; regional artists of the 20th century; Nineteenth Century Landscapes
Publications: The Catalyst, quarterly; Catalogue of the Collection; exhibition catalogs
Activities: Classes for adults & children; docent training; family progs; school progs; lects for mems & open to pub; 1 vis lectr per yr; guided tours; volunteer activities; individual paintings & original objects of art lent to other mus for exhib purposes; book traveling exhibs; originates traveling exhibs to other mus; mus shop sells books, magazines, reproductions, prints, gifts, jewelry, children's items & cards

L **Library,** PO Box 141, Chadds Ford, PA 19317. Tel 610-388-2700; Fax 610-388-1197; *Librn* Ruth Bassett; *Coll Librn* Gail Stanislow
Open daily 9:30 AM - 4:30 PM; For reference to staff & volunteers; by appointment to the pub
Purchases: $4000
Library Holdings: Book Volumes 6500; Clipping Files; Exhibition Catalogs; Manuscripts; Other Holdings Artist memorabilia; Posters; Pamphlets; Periodical Subscriptions 20; Photographs; Reproductions; Video Tapes 25
Special Subjects: Art History, Illustration, Painting-American
Collections: Howard Pyle's published work; Other collections related to American illustration & American art history; Wyeth family memorabilia

CHESTER

M **WIDENER UNIVERSITY,** Art Collection & Gallery, 1 University Center, Fl 1 Chester, PA 19013-5700. Tel 610-499-1189, 499-4000; Fax 610-499-4425; Elec Mail rmwarda@widener.edu; Internet Home Page Address: www.widener.edu; *Coll Mgr* Rebecca Warda
Open Tues 10 AM - 7 PM, Wed - Sat 10 AM - 4:30 PM; call for summer hours; Estab 1970
Income: Financed by endowment & univ funding
Special Subjects: Painting-American, Sculpture, Pre-Columbian Art, Painting-European, Oriental Art

Collections: 18th & 19th century Oriental art objects; 19th century European landscape & genre pictures; 20th century American paintings & sculpture
Exhibitions: Contemporary exhibs, 6-7per yr
Publications: Exhib catalog
Activities: Lect; guided tours

CLARION

M **CLARION UNIVERSITY,** Hazel Sandford Gallery, Merick-Boyd Bldg, Clarion, PA 16214; 840 Word St, Clarion, PA 16214. Tel 814-226-2412, 393-2000, 393-2412 (gallery); Fax 814-226-2723; Internet Home Page Address: www.clarion.edu; WATS 800-669-2000; *Chmn* Joe Thomas; *Dir* Diane Malley
Open Mon - Fri 11 AM - 4:30 PM; No admis fee; Estab 1970 for aesthetic enjoyment & artistic educ of students; Gallery is 66 ft long, 17ft 3 inches wide; lit by some 50 adjustable spotlights; one side of gallery is glassed in; other side is fabric-covered panels & a dozen free-standing panels, available for hanging; Average Annual Attendance: 4,000; Mem: 95
Income: Financed by univ & mem
Collections: Original paintings, drawings & prints, purchased from selected artists who have shown at gallery; sculpture & ceramics; photographs
Exhibitions: Rotating Exhibits
Publications: Monthly announcements of shows
Activities: Lect open to pub, 2-3 vis lectrs per yr; concerts; gallery talks; tours; competitions; individual paintings & original objects of art lent to departments on campus & other state colleges; lending collection contains original art works, original prints, paintings, photographs & sculpture; book traveling exhibs

COLLEGEVILLE

M **URSINUS COLLEGE,** Philip & Muriel Berman Museum of Art, 601 E Main St, Collegeville, PA 19426; PO Box 1000, Collegeville, PA 19426-1000. Tel 610-409-3500; Fax 610-409-3664; Elec Mail lhanover@ursinus.edu; Internet Home Page Address: www.ursinus.edu/berman; *Assoc Dir Educ* Susan Shifrin; *Admin Asst* Suzanne Calvin; *Coll Mgr* Julie Choma
Open Tues - Fri 10 AM - 4 PM, Sat & Sun Noon - 4:30 PM; No admis fee; Estab 1987 to support the educational goals of Ursinus College & to contribute to the cultural life of the campus & regional community; Main gallery: 3200 sq ft; sculpture ct; upper gallery 800 sq ft; Average Annual Attendance: 32,000; Mem: 250; dues minimum $50; ann meeting in June
Income: $150,000 (financed by endowment, mem, Ursinus College, government, foundation & corporate grants)
Purchases: $25,000
Special Subjects: Drawings, Latin American Art, Painting-American, Prints, Sculpture, Watercolors, Textiles, Religious Art, Folk Art, Pottery, Woodcuts, Etchings & Engravings, Landscapes, Painting-European, Painting-Japanese, Portraits, Posters, Furniture, Marine Painting, Painting-British, Painting-Dutch, Painting-French, Tapestries, Painting-Flemish, Painting-Spanish, Painting-Italian, Painting-German, Painting-Russian, Painting-Israeli
Collections: Philip & Muriel Berman Collection; Lynn Chadwick Sculpture Collection; 18th, 19th & 20th century European & American Art (drawings, paintings, prints & sculpture); Japanese Prints & Scrolls
Exhibitions: Temporary exhibitions, 10 per year; selections from permanent collections on continuous view
Publications: Quarterly exhib calendar; exhibs catalogues; museum newsletter, 3 times per year
Activities: Lect open to pub, 6 vis lectrs per yr; concerts; gallery talks; tours; individual paintings & original objects of art lent to museums & galleries for exhib; book traveling exhibs 4-6 per yr; originate traveling exhibs; sales shop sells books & prints

CONSHOHOCKEN

M **MONTGOMERY COUNTY GUILD OF PROFESSIONAL ARTISTS,** Philadelphia Inquirer Bldg, Rte 23 Conshohocken, PA 19428. Tel 610-803-3248; Tel 610-292-6084; Elec Mail mcgopa@comcast.net; *Dir* Maria Lourdes Solomon
Call for hours
Collections: paintings; sculpture; drawings

DOYLESTOWN

M **BUCKS COUNTY HISTORICAL SOCIETY,** Mercer Museum, 84 S Pine, Doylestown, PA 18901. Tel 215-345-0210; Fax 215-230-0823; Elec Mail info@mercermuseum.org; Internet Home Page Address: www.mercermuseum.org; *Exec Dir* Douglas Dolan; *Cur Coll* Cory Amsler; *Chmn* William Maeglin
Open Mon-Sat 10AM-5PM, Sun noon-5PM; Admis adults $12, seniors $10, children 5-17 $6, mems and children under 5 free; Estab 1880; Inside this poured, reinforced concrete castle, four galleries wrap around a towering central court where early American hand crafts are exhibited inside small cubicles. Additional artifacts hang from ceilings, walls and railings. Changing exhibitions & an audio tour complete a visit.; Average Annual Attendance: 55,000; Mem: 2400; dues $40 & up
Income: Contributions, grants, earned incom-admis & mem
Special Subjects: Crafts, Folk Art
Collections: Over 50,000 artifacts representing more than 60 early American crafts, their tools and finished products; large American folk art coll; the history and growth of our country as seen through the work of the human hand
Exhibitions: Continuous changing exhibits.
Publications: Newsletter, twice annually
Activities: Classes for adults & children; lect open to pub; individual paintings & original objects of art lent to other mus; 3-5 per yr; mus shop sells books & hand crafts

L **Mercer Museum Library,** 84 S Pine, Doylestown, PA 18901. Tel 215-345-0210; Fax 215-230-0823; Elec Mail mmlib@mercermuseum.org; Internet Home Page Address: www.mercermuseum.org; *Colls Mgr* Sara C Good

Open Tues - Thurs 1 PM - 5 PM, Fri & Sat 10 AM - 5 PM, cl July 4th, Thanksgiving, Christmas & New Year's Day; No admis fee for BCHS members only; fee for museum; Circ Non-circulating; Open to the pub for reference only; Bucks County history, Delaware Valley
Library Holdings: Book Volumes 20,000; Clipping Files; Manuscripts; Other Holdings Archives; Pamphlets; Periodical Subscriptions 100; Photographs; Reels
Collections: Life of Henry Mercer, papers
Activities: Classes held through historical society

M **JAMES A MICHENER ART MUSEUM,** 138 S Pine St, Doylestown, PA 18901-4931. Tel 215-340-9800; Fax 215-340-9807; Internet Home Page Address: www.michenerartmuseum.org; *Registrar* Sara Beuhler; *Mem Coordr* Louise Beder; *Cur Exhib & Sr Cur* Brian Peterson; *Cur Pub Progs* Zorianne Siokalo; *Dir* Lisa Tremper Hanover; *Dir Mktg* Ilene Dube; *Comm Coord* Keri Smotrich; *Dir Advanc* Laurie McGahey; *Deputy Dir* Candace Clarke; *Exec Asst* Kip Malloy; *Information Mgmt Specialist* Alyson Avery
Open Tues-Sun 11AM-5PM, Sat 11AM-6PM; Admis $15, seniors $13, children 6-18 $7.50, children under 6 & mems free; Estab 1987; Circ Reference only; Average Annual Attendance: 300,000; Mem: 5000; dues $40 - $1000
Library Holdings: Audio Tapes; Book Volumes 1400; CD-ROMs; Cassettes; Clipping Files 1500; Compact Disks; DVDs; Exhibition Catalogs; Lantern Slides; Manuscripts; Memorabilia; Original Documents; Pamphlets; Periodical Subscriptions; Photographs; Slides; Video Tapes
Special Subjects: Drawings, Painting-American, Photography, Prints, Sculpture, Watercolors
Collections: American Art Collection, special focus on the arts in Bucks County, Pennsylvania; 20th Century American Sculpture Collection; American Art Collection
Activities: Classes for adults & children; docent training; mus trips; walking tours; lects open to pub, 15-20 vis lectrs per yr; concerts; gallery talks; tours; schols offered; individual paintings & original objects of art lent to mus & cultural institutions; originate traveling exhibs; mus shop sells books, magazines, original art, reproductions, prints, pottery, crafts, toys, stationery, tiles & jewelry

DUBOIS

M **WINKLER GALLERY OF FINE ART,** 36 N Brady St, DuBois, PA 15801-2256. Tel 814-375-5834
Open Tues-Thurs 11AM-5PM, Fri-Sat 11AM-8PM
Collections: paintings; photography; mosaics; blown glass; sculpture

EASTON

M **LAFAYETTE COLLEGE,** Lafayette College Art Galleries, 317 Hamilton St, Williams Center for the Arts Easton, PA 18042-1768; 111 Quad Dr, Easton, PA 18042-1768. Tel 610-330-5361, 330-5010; Fax 610-330-5642; Elec Mail artgallery@lafayette.edu; Internet Home Page Address: artgalleries.lafayette.edu; *Dir Gallery* Michiko Okaya; *Registrar* Steve Gamler
Open Mon - Fri 11 AM -5 PM, Sat & Sun noon - 5 PM, performance nights 7:30 PM - 9:30 PM; No admis fee; Estab 1983 to present a variety of exhibs for enrichment of campus & community's exposure to visual arts; Versatile space with movable panels & 160 running ft of wall space, climate control & track lighting; Average Annual Attendance: 6,000
Income: Financed by endowment, prog subsidy, government grants
Special Subjects: Decorative Arts, Drawings, Etchings & Engravings, Landscapes, Ceramics, Pottery, Textiles, Woodcuts, Painting-British, Painting-European, Painting-French, Sculpture, Graphics, Painting-American, Photography, Prints, Watercolors, Portraits, Cartoons
Collections: 19th & 20th century American painting, prints, photographs & sculpture; Nineteenth & Twentieth Century American Painting, Prints & Photographs Collection
Exhibitions: OnIce: Art Science Poetry
Publications: Annual exhibit catalogue; brochures; exhibit handouts
Activities: Lects open to pub, 4-8 vis lectrs per yr; gallery talks; lending of original art varies; book traveling exhibitions; organize traveling exhibitions varies; mus shop sells slides, catalogues, license art collection images

EPHRATA

A **HISTORICAL SOCIETY OF THE COCALICO VALLEY,** 249 W Main St, Ephrata, PA 17522-2016; PO Box 193, Ephrata, PA 17522-0193. Tel 717-733-1616; Internet Home Page Address: www.cocalicovalleyhs.org; *Librn* Cynthia Marquet
Open Mon, Wed & Thurs 9:30 AM - 6 PM, Sat 8:30 AM - 5 PM; No admis fee; Estab 1957; Average Annual Attendance: 1,200; Mem: 585; dues family $25, individual $18
Income: Endowment, mem, publs
Special Subjects: Historical Material, Folk Art, Furniture
Collections: Pennsylvania German Folk Art
Publications: Journal of the Historical Society of the Cocalico Valley, annual
Activities: Classes for children; lect open to pub, 10 vis lectrs per yr

ERIE

M **ERIE ART MUSEUM,** 411 State St, Erie, PA 16501-1106. Tel 814-459-5477; Fax 814-452-1744; Internet Home Page Address: www.erieartmuseum.org; *Pres* Barbara Haggerty; *Dir* John Vanco; *Treas* Art Laneve; *Publ Coordr* Andrea Krivak; *Registrar* Vance Lupher; *Educ Coordr* Ally Thomas; *Asst Cur* Amanda Steadman; *Frame Shop Mgr* Lin-Lang Su; *Vol Coordr* Karen Dodson; *Dir Educ & Folk Art* Kelly Armor; *Dir Mktg & Pub Rels* Carolyn Eller; *Dir Develop* Jennifer Dobbs
Open Tues - Fri 11 AM - 5 PM, Sun 1 - 5 PM; Admis adults $7; seniors & students $5; children $3 free Wed & 2nd Sun ea month; Estab 1898 for the

advancement of visual arts; Galleries are located in historic buildings connected with a new (2010) structure that also houses galleries & other pub facilities; Average Annual Attendance: 40,000; Mem: Dues family $75, individual $45
Income: $1,100,000 (financed through pvt donations, fundraising, mem & grants)
Library Holdings: Auction Catalogs 13; Book Volumes 2,023
Special Subjects: Drawings, Folk Art, Photography, Pottery, Painting-American, Textiles, Graphics, Painting-American, Photography, Prints, Sculpture, Bronzes, Pre-Columbian Art, Southwestern Art, Textiles, Ceramics, Crafts, Pottery, Etchings & Engravings, Landscapes, Decorative Arts, Collages, Dolls, Jade, Porcelain, Oriental Art, Asian Art, Silver, Juvenile Art, Embroidery, Antiquities-Oriental, Cartoons
Collections: Indian Bronze & Stone Sculpture; Chinese Porcelains, Jades, Textiles; American Ceramics (historical & contemporary); Graphics (European, American & Oriental); Photography; Paintings & Drawings (predominately 20th century); Contemporary Baskets
Exhibitions: Annual Spring Show; Art of China & Japan; Art of India; Chicago Works - Art from the Windy City; Early Color Photography; Paperthick: Forms & Images in Cast Paper; A Peculiar Vision: The Work of George Ohr, the Mad Potter of Biloxi; Frederick Hurten Rhead: An English Potter in America; The Tactile Vessel - New Basket Forms; TECO - Art Pottery of the Prairie School; Looking at Lincoln: Images Our 16th President, Main Gallery
Publications: Four exhibition catalogues
Activities: Classes for adults & children; docent training; lect open to pub, 3-5 vis lectrs per yr; concerts; gallery talks; tours; competitions; individual paintings & original objects of art lent to pub buildings, colleges & universities, galleries & museums; originates traveling exhibs; mus shop sells books, postcards, pencils, t-shirts & mugs. Frame shop offers retail framing

M **ERIE COUNTY HISTORICAL SOCIETY,** (Erie Historical Museum) 419 State St, Erie, PA 16501. Tel 814-454-1813 x26; Fax 814-454-6890; Elec Mail aandrick@eriecountyhistory.org; Internet Home Page Address: www.eriecountyhistory.org; *Dir Library & Archives* Annita Andrick; *Dir Visitor & Mem Svcs* Melanie Kuebel-Stanky; *Educ & Events Dir* Andrew Adams; *Exec Dir* Alyson Amendola Cummings
Watson-Curtze Mansion & Erie Co History Ctr open Sept - May Wed - Sat 11 AM - 4 PM, June - Aug Tues - Sat 11 AM - 4 PM, hours subject to change; Libr in HQ History Ctr open yr round Tues - Sat, 11 AM - 4 PM; Admis adults $5, students with ID & seniors $4, children $3; Research Library: day pass or mem $7; Estab 1903 to collect & preserve Erie County history; Mus has exhibits on all 3 properties it owns. Maintains Victorian Watson - Curtze Mansion & Planetarium, built in 1891-1892 & designed by Green & Wicks of Buffalo, NY; Cashier's House; Erie Co History Ctr features formal galleries, exhibs and research libr & archives; Battles Mus of Rural Life with 2 c. 1860 historic houses; Average Annual Attendance: 24,500; Mem: 600; dues corporate $500, couple $45, individual $45, student $15, family $60, grandparent $60, patron $75, sustaining $100, sponsor $250
Income: Financed by soc, grants
Library Holdings: Book Volumes; CD-ROMs; Cassettes; Manuscripts; Maps; Memorabilia; Original Art Works; Original Documents; Photographs; Prints; Reels; Video Tapes
Special Subjects: American Indian Art, Decorative Arts, Drawings, Folk Art, Historical Material, Marine Painting, Ceramics, Furniture, Photography, Portraits, Pottery, Prints, Period Rooms, Silver, Textiles, Bronzes, Manuscripts, Maps, Watercolors, Costumes, Crafts, Posters, Dolls, Jewelry, Asian Art, Carpets & Rugs, Embroidery, Stained Glass
Collections: Moses Billings (paintings); George Ericson-Eugene Iverd (paintings); genre paintings; Native American pottery; Southwest & Northwest Coast baskets; Victorian decorative arts; Local history & maritime; Robert J MacDonald Great Lakes Maritime Coll; Erie Art Mus Archives; Erie Art Center Archives; Erie Art Club Archives; Battles Family coll; FJ Bassett coll; CB Hall coll; Ottomar Jarecki coll; Ossowski coll; Sanford-Spencer coll
Activities: Classes for adults & children; docent tours; lesson tours for students; concerts; lects open to pub; local history & preservation awards prog; lending coll serves Erie Maritime Mus; mus shop sells books, magazines, original art, reproductions, prints, photographs

FARMINGTON

A **TOUCHSTONE CENTER FOR CRAFTS,** Hart Moore Museum, 1049 Wharton Furnace Rd, Farmington, PA 15437-1195. Tel 724-329-1370; Fax 724-329-1371; Elec Mail info@touchstonecrafts.org; Internet Home Page Address: www.touchstonecrafts.org; *Admin Asst* Meghan Feather; *Exec Dir* Scott Hilliard; *Opers Dir* Stephanie Glover; *External Relations & Events Coordr* Kari Garber; *Campus Mgr* Matt DiNardo; *Accnt* Sue Cromwell
Open Mon - Fri 9 AM - 5 PM; Tuition & materials fees; Estab 1972 to promote excellence in art & craft educ; Average Annual Attendance: 1200; Mem: 400
Income: $690,000 (financed by opers, grants & donations)
Special Subjects: Sculpture, Ceramics, Glass, Jewelry
Exhibitions: 3 to 5 per yr
Activities: Classes for adults, children, college credit & continuing educ reqs; lect & demos open to pub; concerts; tours; schols offered; outreach programs; field trips; artist-in-residency projects; sales shop sells books, magazines, original art, reproductions, prints, ceramics, jewelry, t-shirts, sweatshirts, hats, iron works & glass art

GETTYSBURG

M **ADAMS COUNTY HISTORICAL SOCIETY,** 111 Seminary Ridge, Gettysburg, PA 17325; PO Box 4325, Gettysburg, PA 17325-4325. Tel 717-334-4723; Fax 717-334-0722; Elec Mail info@achs-pa.org; Internet Home Page Address: www.achs-pa.org; *Exec Dir* Wayne E Motts; *Coll Mgr* Benjamin F Nelly; *Admin Asst* Sheryl Snyder; *Research Asst* Timothy H Smith
Research lib open Wed - Sat 9 AM - noon & 1 PM - 4 PM, Thurs 6 PM - 9 PM, mus by appt only; Admis $3 museum, non-member researcher $5; Historical Soc estab 1939, mus estab 1987; Museum of local history; Average Annual

Attendance: 5,750; Mem: 1,100; dues family $50, supporting $35; meetings Jan - June & Sept - Dec

Income: $200,000 (financed by mem, appeal, grants, sale of publs)

Special Subjects: American Indian Art, Folk Art, Historical Material, Glass, Flasks & Bottles, Furniture, Portraits, Silver, Textiles, Manuscripts, Maps, Costumes, Religious Art, Dolls, Historical Material, Coins & Medals, Period Rooms, Stained Glass, Military Art

Collections: Blacksmith Shop/Earth Science; Barber Shop Equipment; 1940's Doll House; Uniforms; Spanish & American/WW I & WW II; 1930 Conoco Gas Station; Agriculture; Art History

Publications: Annual journal; 6 newsletters per year

Activities: Classes for adults; lect open to pub; tours; lending coll consists of lantern slides; originate traveling exhibs; mus shop sells books & maps

GLENSIDE

M **ARCADIA UNIVERSITY ART GALLERY,** (Beaver College Art Gallery) Spruance Fine Arts Center, 450 S Easton Rd, Glenside, PA 19038-3215. Tel 215-572-2131; Fax 215-881-8774; Elec Mail gallery@arcadia.edu; Internet Home Page Address: www.arcadia.edu/gallery; *Gallery Dir* Richard Torchia; *Cur Asst* Jamar Nicholas
Open Tues-Wed & Fri 10AM-5PM, Thurs 10AM-8PM; No admis fee; Estab 1974 to show contemporary art generally; Gallery dimensions 20 x 50 ft; Average Annual Attendance: 6,500; Mem: 150; dues $35
Income: College & board funding
Collections: Benton Spruance Print Collection
Exhibitions: Contemporary artist solo & thematic exhibitions
Publications: Brochures for major exhibitions
Activities: Lect open to pub, 4 vis lectrs per yr; gallery talks; competitions with awards

GREENSBURG

L **SETON HILL COLLEGE,** Reeves Memorial Library, 1 Seton Hill Dr, Reeves Memorial Library, Seton Hill University Greensburg, PA 15601-1548. Tel 724-838-4291; Fax 724-834-4611; *Reference & Pub Servs Librn* Denise Sticha
Open Mon-Thurs 8AM-10:50PM, Fri 8AM-4:50PM, Sat, 9AM-4:50PM, Sun 1PM-10:50PM; For lending & reference; Circ 40,000
Library Holdings: Audio Tapes; Book Volumes 101,000; Cards; Cassettes; Filmstrips; Motion Pictures; Original Art Works; Pamphlets; Periodical Subscriptions 500; Records; Sculpture; Slides; Video Tapes

M **WESTMORELAND MUSEUM OF AMERICAN ART,** 221 N Main St, Greensburg, PA 15601-1898. Tel 724-837-1500; Fax 724-837-2921; Elec Mail info@wmuseumaa.org; Internet Home Page Address: www.wmuseumaa.org; *Dir & CEO* Judith H O'Toole; *Cur* Barbara L Jones; *Dir Develop & Finance* Amy B Baldonieri; *Preparator* PJ Zimmerlink; *Colls Mgr* Douglas W Evans; *Dir Mktg & Vis Svcs* Judith Linsz Ross; *Cur Educ* Joan McGarry; *Mus Shop Mgr* Virginia Leiner; *Dir Facilities* Chuck Ballein
Open Wed - Sun 11 AM - 5 PM, cl Mon & Tues & major holidays; suggested donation: adults $5, children under 12 free; Estab 1949 to operate & maintain a free pub art mus; The mus houses three galleries for changing exhibs; eight galleries for permanent coll; Average Annual Attendance: 23,300; Mem: 675; dues $25 - $2000
Income: Financed by endowment, grants & gifts
Special Subjects: Drawings, Painting-American, Photography, Sculpture, Watercolors, Textiles, Folk Art, Pottery, Etchings & Engravings, Decorative Arts, Portraits, Dolls, Furniture, Glass, Silver
Collections: Extensive toy coll; Furniture, paintings, sculpture & works on paper; 19th & early 20th century Southwestern Pennsylvania paintings; American Art, 1750-1950
Publications: quarterly newsletter; exhibition catalogs
Activities: Educ prog; classes for children; docent training; lects open to pub, 20-24 vis lectrs per yr; gallery talks; tours; Westmoreland Society Gold Medal (annually); individual paintings & original objects of art lent to other mus & institutions accredited by AAM; lending collection contains original art works & paintings; book traveling exhibs 1-2 per yr; originate traveling exhibs to other museums; mus shop sells books, reproductions, postcards & notepaper, jewelry, and giftware

L **Art Reference Library,** 221 N Main St, Greensburg, PA 15601-1898. Tel 724-837-1500; Fax 724-837-2921; Elec Mail info@wmuseumaa.org; Internet Home Page Address: www.wmuseumaa.org; *Dir & CEO* Judith H O'Toole; *Preparator* PJ Zimmerlink; *Cur Educ* Katie Barnard; *Dir Mktg & Pub Rels* Judy Linz Ross; *Cur* Barbara L Jones; *Asst Pub & Finance* Pat Erdelsky; *Registrar* Douglas R Evans; *VPres* Jack Smith; *Asst to Dir* Janet Carns; *Mus Shop Mgr* Virginia Leiner; *Dir Develop & Finance* Amy Baldonieri
Open Tues - Sat 10 AM - 5 PM, Sun 1 - 5 PM, cl Mon & holidays; Estab 1949 for art reference; For reference only; Average Annual Attendance: 20,000
Income: Financed by endowment, grants & gifts
Purchases: $1200
Library Holdings: Book Volumes 8000; Clipping Files; Exhibition Catalogs; Pamphlets; Periodical Subscriptions 15

GREENVILLE

M **THIEL COLLEGE,** Weyers-Sampson Art Gallery, 75 College Ave, Greenville, PA 16125-2181. Tel 724-589-2095; Fax 724-589-2021; *Dir Spec Events* Marianne Colenda; *Dir Permanent Coll* Sean McConnor
No admis fee; Estab 1971 to provide students, faculty, col staff & the community with a gallery featuring a variety of exhibs & give students an opportunity to show their work; Two galleries 20' x 38' & 20' x 31', grey carpeted walls & track lighting; Average Annual Attendance: 1,000
Income: $1,000 (financed by college budget)
Collections: 18th & 19th century paintings & prints

Exhibitions: Monthly exhibs by students & faculty
Activities: Lect open to pub; gallery talks

HARRISBURG

M **ART ASSOCIATION OF HARRISBURG,** School & Galleries, 21 N Front St, Harrisburg, PA 17101-1625. Tel 717-236-1432; Fax 717-236-6631; Elec Mail carrie@artassocofhbg.com; Internet Home Page Address: www.artassocofhbg.com; *Cur* Terrie Hosey; *Admin Asst* Kelly McGee; *Pres* Carrie Wissler-Thomas; *Webmaster* Randall Miller III; *Gallery Asst* Bryan Molloy; *Gallery Asst* Mark Bradshaw
Open Mon - Thurs 9:30 AM - 9 PM, Fri 9:30 AM - 4 PM, Sat 10 AM - 4 PM, Sun 2 - 5 PM; No admis fee; Estab 1926 to act as showcase for mem artists and other professionals; community services offered; Building is historic Brownstone Building, former Governor's mansion (1817) & holds 4 floors of galleries, classrooms & a garden; Average Annual Attendance: 20,000; Mem: 800, dues $40 - $1000; ann meeting in May
Income: Financed by mem, tuitions, contributions, grants
Collections: Old area masters; member's work; Lavery & Lebret
Exhibitions: Annual International Juried Exhibition; Art School Annual; invitational shows; mem shows, 2 times per yr; community shows in 10 locations - 90 total per yr
Publications: Monthly exhibition announcements; newsletter, quarterly newsletter with class schedule
Activities: Classes for adults and children; lect open to pub; competitions open to all states; monetary awards; concerts; gallery talks; tours; schols offered; sales shop sells original art & prints by mem artists

A **CITIZENS FOR THE ARTS IN PENNSYLVANIA,** (Pennsylvania Arts Alliance) 100 N Cameron St, Ste 108A Harrisburg, PA 17101-2424. Tel 717-234-0959; Fax 717-234-1501; Elec Mail info@citizensfortheartsinpa.org; Internet Home Page Address: www.citizensfortheartsinpa.org; *Mng Dir* Jenny Hershour; *Chair* Robert Lettieri
Estab 1986 to develop & strengthen Pennsylvania arts at the local, state & federal levels by networking arts admin, arts organizations, artists & volunteers & by providing technical assistance & professional training programs & services
Publications: eNewsletter
Activities: Conferences & educational workshops

A **PENNSYLVANIA DEPARTMENT OF EDUCATION,** Arts in Education Program, 333 Market St, Fl 8 Harrisburg, PA 17126-0333. Tel 717-525-5058; Fax 717-783-3946; Elec Mail jakasper@state.pa.us; Internet Home Page Address: www.pde.state.pa.us; *State Advisor* Jamie Kasper; *Exhibs Coordr* Wendy Sweigart
The Arts in Educ Prog provides leadership & consultative & evaluative servs to all Pennsylvania schools & arts educ agencies in arts prog develop & instructional practices. Infusion of arts processes into differentiated curriculums for all students is a particular thrust. The prog offers assistance in designing aesthetic learning environments & consultation in identifying & employing regional & community resources for arts educ
Exhibitions: rotating exhibs and permanent collections of student work
Activities: Arts educ program

A **PENNSYLVANIA HISTORICAL & MUSEUM COMMISSION,** The State Museum of Pennsylvania, 300 North St, Harrisburg, PA 17120-0024. Tel 717-787-4980; Fax 717-783-4558; Internet Home Page Address: www.statemuseumpa.org; *Cur Adminr* Bradley K Smith; *Mus Dir* David W Dunn; *PHMC Exec Dir* James M Vaughan; *Colls Mgr* Mary Jane Miller; *Dir External Affairs* Howard Pollman; *PHMC Chmn* Andrew Masich
Open Wed - Sat 9 AM - 5 PM, Sun Noon - 5 PM, cl Mon & Tues to pub; Admis adult $5, children 12 & under $4; Estab 1945 to interpret the history & heritage of Pennsylvania; Mem: 3000; dues vary; ann meeting second Wed in Apr
Income: $18,000,000 for entire commission
Exhibitions: Art of the State, ann spring-summer juried statewide exhib; Contemporary Artists Series; changing history exhibits
Publications: Pennsylvania Heritage, quarterly
Activities: Classes for adults; docent training; lects open to pub; concerts; tours; exhibits; special events

M **The State Museum of Pennsylvania,** 300 North St, Harrisburg, PA 17120-0024. Tel 717-783-9911; Fax 717-783-4558; Elec Mail hpollman@state.pa.us; Internet Home Page Address: www.statemuseumpa.org; *Sr Cur Art* N Lee Stevens; *Acting Cur* Dr Curt Miner; *Acting Registrar* Mary Jane Miller; *Mus Dir* David Dunn
Open Wed - Sat 9 AM - 5 PM, Sun Noon - 5 PM; offices Mon - Fri 8:30 AM - 5 PM; Admis adults $5, seniors, children, & groups $4, free every third Sat; Mus estab 1905; Three floors of permanent & changing exhibs, including art; Average Annual Attendance: 350,000
Income: Financed by state & pvt funds minimal, rely on donations
Special Subjects: Anthropology, Archaeology, Decorative Arts, Historical Material
Collections: Anthropology; archaeology; art photography; ceramics; decorative arts; folk art; glass; Indian artifacts; paintings & sculpture; paleontology & geology; silver; textiles; works on paper; 2 million objects in all disciplines relating to Pennsylvania
Publications: Books, brochures, quarterly calendar, quarterly newsletter
Activities: Classes for adults & children; docent training; dramatic progs; lects open to pub; concerts; gallery talks; tours; awards; individual paintings & original objects of art lent to accredited mus, history orgs; book traveling exhibs 1-2 per yr; originate traveling exhibs; mus shop sells books, reproductions, prints & gift items

—**Brandywine Battlefield Park,** Box 202, Chadds Ford, PA 19317-0202. Tel 610-459-3342; Fax 610-459-9586; *Mus Educ* Helen Mahnke; *Educ Coordr* Richard Wolfe; *Adminr* Toni Collins
Open 9 AM - 5 PM; Estab 1947 to commemorate Battle of the Brandywine, Sept 11, 1777; 2 historic Quaker farmhouses; Average Annual Attendance: 90,000; Mem: 95; dues $35; ann meeting in summer
Income: $295,000 (financed by endowment, mem & state appropriation)
Activities: Classes for children

L **State Archives Div,** 350 North St, Harrisburg, PA 17120-0150. Tel 717-783-3281;

Elec Mail ra-statearchives@state.pa.us; Internet Home Page Address:
www.portal.state.pa.us/portal/server.pt/community/state_archives/2887; *Educ*
Robert McFadden
Open Wed - Fri 9 AM - 4 PM, Sat for microfilm only 9 AM - Noon & 1-4 PM; cl
Mon, Tues & major holidays

M **Railroad Museum of Pennsylvania,** 300 Gap Rd, Strasburg, PA 17579; PO Box
15, Strasburg, PA 17579-0015. Tel 717-687-8628; Fax 717-687-0876; Elec Mail
info@rrmuseumpa.org; Internet Home Page Address: www.rrmuseumpa.org; *Cur*
Bradley Smith; *Office Mgr* Cindy Adair; *Librn & Archivist* Kurt Bell; *Asst Educ*
Troy Grubb; *Dir* David W Dunn; *Restoration Mgr* Allan Martin; *Educ* Patrick
Morrison; *Dir Mus Advancement* Deborah Reddig
Open Mon - Sat 9 AM - 5 PM, Sun Noon - 5 PM, cl Mon Nov - Apr; Admis
adults $8, seniors $7, children 6-17 $6; Estab 1975 for preservation of significant
artifacts appropriate to railroading; Maintains reference library & railroad art
gallery; Average Annual Attendance: 150,000; Mem: 1,900; dues $35; ann meeting
in the fall
Income: $1,800,000 (financed by state appropriation & pvt fundraising)
Library Holdings: Auction Catalogs; Book Volumes; Cards; Filmstrips;
Kodachrome Transparencies; Lantern Slides; Manuscripts; Maps; Memorabilia;
Motion Pictures; Original Art Works; Original Documents; Pamphlets; Periodical
Subscriptions; Photographs; Prints; Records; Reels; Slides; Video Tapes
Special Subjects: Portraits, Painting-American, Textiles, Painting-American,
Photography, Prints, Sculpture, Watercolors, Manuscripts, Posters, Historical
Material, Maps, Restorations, Dioramas
Collections: Railroad Rolling Stock; locomotives & related artifacts including
tools, maps, manuals, timetables, passes, uniforms, silverware & lanterns;
Transportation History (Railroad Locomotives & Train Cars); Railroad art &
photographs
Publications: Milepost, 5 times annually
Activities: Children progs; docent progs; lects open to pub, 5-10 vis lectrs per yr;
concerts; gallery talks; tours; schols offered; individual paintings & original
objects of art lent; lending coll includes paintings & art objects; mus shop sells
books, magazines, original art, reproductions, prints & slides

M **ROSE LEHRMAN ART GALLERY,** Harrisburg Area Community College, One
HACC Dr Harrisburg, PA 17110-2903. Elec Mail kebanist@hacc.edu; Internet
Home Page Address: www.hacc.edu; *Cur* Kim Banister
Open Summer: Mon & Wed 11 AM - 3 PM, Tues & Thurs 11 AM - 3 PM and 5
PM - 7 PM; small gallery, 10 exhibs per yr, contemporary art; Average Annual
Attendance: 10,000
Special Subjects: Drawings, Etchings & Engravings, Ceramics, Glass, Graphics,
Crafts, Landscapes
Collections: Painting & photographs; art exhibitions

A **SUSQUEHANNA ART MUSEUM,** 15 N 3rd St, Harrisburg, PA 17101; PO Box
11818, Harrisburg, PA 17108-1818. Tel 717-233-8668; Fax 717-233-8155; Elec
Mail info@sqart.org; Internet Home Page Address: www.sqart.org; *Pres* Stephen A
Moore; *Exhibs Mgr* Amy Hammond; *Dir Outreach Educ* Wendy Sweigart; *Mus
Opers Coordr* Susan Bennett
Offices open Mon - Fri 9 AM - 5 PM; Mus Shop Wed - Fri 11 AM - 2 PM; Estab
1989 as a nonprofit; During transition to new facility, SAM will hold various
off-site exhibs; Average Annual Attendance: 7,000; Mem: 300
Exhibitions: 3 exhibs per yr
Activities: Classes for adults & children; student internships; lect open to pub;
gallery talks; tours; exten prog serves PA, schools & communities; artmobile; mus
shop sells books, prints & jewelry

HAVERFORD

A **MAIN LINE ART CENTER,** 746 Panmure Rd, Haverford, PA 19041-1218. Tel
610-525-0272; Fax 610-525-5036; Elec Mail jherman@mainlineart.org;
info@mainlineart.org; Internet Home Page Address: www.mainlineart.org; *Exec
Dir* Judy Herman
Open Mon - Thurs 9 AM - 9 PM, Fri 9 AM - 5 PM, Sat & Sun 9 AM - 5 PM; No
admis fee; Estab 1937 to develop and encourage the fine arts; Three large, well-lit
galleries, completely modernized to accommodate exhibits including sculptures,
ceramics, paintings, crafts; Average Annual Attendance: 1,200; Mem: 800; dues
family $75; individual $50; children $35
Income: Financed by mem, tui, fundraising, & sponsors
Exhibitions: Ann mem exhib
Publications: Brochures, five times per yr
Activities: Classes for adults, teens & children; lect open to pub; gallery talks;
trips; tours; member exhibitions juried; competitions with awards; curated
exhibitions

HERSHEY

M **HERSHEY MUSEUM,** 111 W Chocolate Ave, Hershey, PA 17033-1558. Tel
717-520-5722; Fax 717-534-8940; Elec Mail info@hersheymuseum.org; Internet
Home Page Address: www.hersheystory.org; *Exec Dir* Marta Howell; *Interim Dir*
Don Papson; *Dir Educ* Mariella Trosko; *Pub Programs Mgr* Lois Miklas; *Coll
Mgr* Valerie Seiber
Open Memorial Day - Labor Day daily 10 AM - 8 PM, Sept - May daily 10 AM -
5 PM, cl New Year's Day, Thanksgiving, Christmas Eve & Day; Admis adults
$10, seniors $9 children 3-12 $7.50, 2 & under free; Estab 1933 to preserve &
collect history of Hershey, Central Pennsylvania heritage (Pennsylvania Germans);
Average Annual Attendance: 90,215; Mem: 2600; dues individual $35, household
$60, inventor $150, industrialist $250, entrepreneur $500, philanthropist $1,000
Special Subjects: American Indian Art, Folk Art, Historical Material, Ceramics,
Glass, Painting-American, Textiles, Crafts, Pottery, Woodcarvings, Decorative Arts,
Furniture, Porcelain
Collections: History of Hershey (the town, the bus, & M S Hershey); 19th
century Pennsylvania German Life American Indian
Publications: Quarterly newsletter

Activities: Classes for adults & children; docent training; family progs; progs in
schools; lect open to pub; concerts; gallery talks; tours; mus shop sells books &
craft items relating to mus colls; childrens' discovery room

HONESDALE

M **WAYNE COUNTY HISTORICAL SOCIETY,** Museum, 810 Main St,
Honesdale, PA 18431-1847; PO Box 446, Honesdale, PA 18431-0446. Tel
570-253-3240; Fax 570-253-5204; Elec Mail wchs@ptd.net; Internet Home Page
Address: www.waynehistorypa.org; *Pres* Elaine Herzog; *Dir* Sally Talaga; *Librn*
Gloria McCullough; *Shop Mgr* Kay Stephenson; *VPres* Lars Hanson; *Treas* Tom
Colbert
Open Wed - Sat 10 AM - 4 PM (Apr - Dec), cl Jan - mid-Apr; Admis adults $5,
children 6-18 $3, children under 5 free; Estab 1924 as a repository of artifacts,
publs, archival & other items relating to Wayne County; Historic building;
Average Annual Attendance: 19,750; Mem: 750; dues $35 - $50; 12 meetings per
yr
Income: $82,000 (financed by dues, donations, sales & grants)
Special Subjects: Painting-American, Photography, American Indian Art,
Archaeology, Manuscripts, Portraits, Furniture, Glass, Historical Material, Maps
Collections: Artifacts of Wayne County History; Jennie Brownscombe (paintings),
Native American Archaeology Coll, Costume Coll, Cut Glass Coll, Early Glass
Coll; Stourbridge Lion (first locomotive to run in America)
Exhibitions: Wayne County Glass, Window Pane to White House Crystal; Datt
Canal Company permanent exhibit
Publications: Quarterly newsletter
Activities: School group tours; docent training; lect open to public, 4 vis lectrs per
year; tours; ann historic preservation awards; sales shop sells books, maps, t-shirts,
train memorabilia & art reproductions

HUNTINGDON

M **JUNIATA COLLEGE MUSEUM OF ART,** 1700 Moore St, Huntingdon, PA
16652-2119. Tel 814-641-3505; Fax 814-641-3607; Elec Mail
maloney@juniata.edu; Internet Home Page Address: www.juniata.edu/museum;
Dir Judy Maloney
Open May - Aug Wed - Fri noon - 4 PM; Sept - Apr Mon - Fri 10 AM - 4 PM,
Sat noon-4PM; cl major holidays & col holidays; No admis fee; Estab 1998 to
serve the Pennsylvania & mid-Atlantic arts community; 2 galleries, 1,000 sq ft
each, 1 permanent coll & 1 temporary exhib; Average Annual Attendance: 2,000;
Mem: 35; dues student & sr citizen $15; family $35; contributor $100; supporter
$250; parton $500
Income: Financed by parent institution (Juniata College) & endowments
Purchases: W B Stottlemyer Coll of Art
Special Subjects: Decorative Arts, Drawings, Etchings & Engravings,
Photography, Woodcuts, Painting-British, Painting-French, Graphics,
Painting-American, Prints, Watercolors, American Indian Art, Landscapes, Posters,
Painting-Dutch, Painting-Italian, Painting-German
Collections: American Portrait miniatures; Contemporary works on paper; Hudson
River School paintings; Navajo weavings; Old Master prints & paintings; 19th
century Japanese prints
Publications: Exhib publs
Activities: Mus studies prog; lect open to pub; book traveling exhibs 4 per yr

HUNTINGDON VALLEY

AMERICAN COLOR PRINT SOCIETY
For further information, see National and Regional Organizations

INDIANA

M **INDIANA UNIVERSITY OF PENNSYLVANIA,** Kipp Gallery, 470 Sprowls
Hall, 11th St Indiana, PA 15705-0001. Tel 724-357-6495; Fax 724-357-7778; Elec
Mail field27@hotmail.com; Internet Home Page Address: www.iup.edu; *Dir
Gallery* Dr Richard Field
Open Tues - Wed & Fri-Sat noon-5PM, Thurs noon-9PM; No admis fee; Estab
1970 to make available a professional gallery prog to Western Pennsylvania & to
the university community; Versatile space with portable wall system, track
lighting, secure, humidity controlled; Average Annual Attendance: 12,000
Income: Financed by Student Coop Assoc
Exhibitions: Student Honors Show; National Metal & Clay Invitational; rotating
exhibits
Activities: Lect open to pub, 3-5 vis lectrs per yr; gallery talks; tours; book
traveling exhibs; originates traveling exhibs

JENKINTOWN

M **ABINGTON ART CENTER,** 515 Meetinghouse Rd, Jenkintown, PA 19046-2964.
Tel 215-887-4882; Fax 215-887-5789; Elec Mail info@abingtonartcenter.org;
Internet Home Page Address: abingtonartcenter.org; *Exec Dir* Laura E Burnham;
Chmn Eric Weckel; *Educ Dir* Marge Horner; *Develop Dir* Betsy Weand-Kilkenny
Open Wed - Fri 10 AM - 5 PM, Thurs 10 AM - 7 PM, Sat - Sun 10 AM - 3 PM,
cl New Year's Eve & Day, Presidents Day, Passover, Good Friday, Memorial Day,
Independence Day, Labor Day, Rosh Hashanah, Yom Kippur, Thanksgiving &
Christmas week; No admis fee; Estab 1939; Average Annual
Attendance: 34,500; Mem: 649; dues individual $50, dual/family $65, mem plus
$75, patron plus $125 & up
Income: Financed by mem, donations, earned income
Special Subjects: Decorative Arts, Photography, Painting-American, Prints,
Textiles, Sculpture, Drawings, Graphics, Costumes
Exhibitions: Sculpture park; semi-permanent installations; Exhibs feature work by
regional contemporary artists
Publications: Exhibit catalogs

Activities: Classes for adults & children; lect open to the pub; 2-6 vis lectrs per yr; concerts; gallery talks; tours; sponsoring of competitions; schols; ann juried show awards for best of show & other outstanding work; sales shop sells original art, eco-themed merchandise

KUTZTOWN

M **KUTZTOWN UNIVERSITY,** The Martin & Regina Miller Gallery, College Blvd & Main St, Kutztown, PA 19530-0730; PO Box 730, Kutztown, PA 19530-0730. Tel 646-484-5803; Tel 610-683-1575; Fax 610-683-4547; Elec Mail stanford@kutztown.edu; Internet Home Page Address: www.kutztown.edu/acad/artgallery; *Acting Dir* Karen Stanford
Open Tues - Fri 10 AM - 4 PM; Sat Noon - 4 PM, Sun 2 - 4 PM; No admis fee; Estab 1956 to make high quality contemporary art available to the college, community & region; 2400 sq ft facility that presents contemporary art, design & crafts; Average Annual Attendance: 6,000
Income: Financed by state & pvt appropriations
Collections: Approx 1,000 works in prints, drawings & paintings
Exhibitions: 7 temporary exhibs per year
Publications: Brochure listing gallery shows; ann catalog
Activities: Artist-in-residence series; lectr progs; lects open to pub

L **Rohrbach Library,** 15200 Kutztown Rd, Bldg 5 Kutztown, PA 19530-9335. Tel 610-683-4480; Fax 610-683-4747; Internet Home Page Address: www.kutztown.edu/library; *Reference Librn* Janet Bond; *Dean Library Serv* Barbara Simpson Darden
Open Mon - Thurs 7:45 AM - 12 AM, Fri 7:45 AM - 5 PM, Sat 9 AM - 5 PM, Sun 2 PM - 12 AM during school; Estab 1866; Circ 118,592
Library Holdings: Audio Tapes; Book Volumes 414,000; Cards 17,331; Cassettes; Exhibition Catalogs; Fiche 1,201,000; Filmstrips; Micro Print 212,908; Motion Pictures; Pamphlets; Periodical Subscriptions 1926; Records; Reels 35,000; Slides
Special Subjects: Art History, Art Education
Collections: Curriculum Materials; maps; Russian Culture

M **NEW ARTS PROGRAM, INC,** NAP Museum, Gallery, Resource Library, 173 W Main St, Kutztown, PA 19530-1742; PO Box 82, Kutztown, PA 19530-0082. Tel 610-683-6440; Fax 610-683-6440; Elec Mail info@napconnection.com; Elec Mail napconn@aol.com; Internet Home Page Address: www.napconnection.com; *Dir* James F L Carroll; *Admin Asst* Joanne Carroll; *Vice Pres* Ted Ormai
Open Fri - Sun 11 AM - 3 PM or by appointment; No admis fee; min fee for performances & concerts; Estab 1974 for artists to have pub one to one consultation residencies, exhibs, performance & presentations; Circ For reference libraries 150; 325 sq ft, 65 linear ft; Average Annual Attendance: 3,500; Mem: 250 mem, dues $30 supporting members
Income: $55,000 (financed by mem, state appropriation, foundations, sales, supporting individuals & bus)
Library Holdings: Audio Tapes 100; Book Volumes 2,500; CD-ROMs 400; Cassettes 100; DVDs 1,500; Exhibition Catalogs 1,800; Kodachrome Transparencies 40,000 (slides); Original Art Works 350; Original Documents; Other Holdings 400; Pamphlets 100; Periodical Subscriptions 35; Photographs 200; Prints 1200; Records 200; Reels 100; Slides 40,000; Video Tapes 2,000
Collections: Prints, paintings, drawings, 40,000 slides; Booklets, 1,500 DVDs, 400 CDs
Exhibitions: International Salon Invitational (small works) exhib; one juried solo and residency exhibition & 3 invitation solo exhibits
Publications: In & Out of Kutztown; NAP Text(s), International video festival booklets; NAP Preview and annual fan fold cards, DVDs CDs
Activities: Two one hour TV progs monthly; Fanfold Cards for yearly activities; preview for yearly activities; Dance on Paper; ideas from individual impressions & marks; Prints of non-printmakers; In & Out of New York; First 10 Composers & Musicians through 1974; Keith Haring DVD; individual consultations (one-to-one) 2 day residency for each artist; presentations open to pub; 4 vis presentations per yr; concerts; gallery talks & presentations; sponsoring of competitions; exhibition residency and consultation; lects open to pub; solo exhibition competition; residency and consultation; sales shop sells original art, prints, and NAP publications, CDs, DVDs, VHS, catalogues, posters, T-shirts

L **PENNSYLVANIA GERMAN CULTURAL HERITAGE CENTER AT KUTZTOWN UNIVERSITY,** (Pennsylvania Dutch Folk Culture Society Inc) 22 Luckenbill Rd, Kutztown, PA 19530-9203. Tel 610-683-1589; Elec Mail heritage@kutztown.edu; Internet Home Page Address: www.kutztown.edu/community/pgchc
Open Mon - Fri 10 AM - Noon and 1 - 4 PM, cl holidays; tours by appt; Admis non-mems $5, mems free; Estab 1992 to preserve the Pennsylvania German Culture; Reference library for genealogy, history & folk art, mus tours & pub events; Mem: Dues $25
Income: Financed by donations & mems
Library Holdings: Audio Tapes; Book Volumes 1500; CD-ROMs; Cassettes; Clipping Files; Filmstrips; Manuscripts; Maps; Memorabilia; Pamphlets; Periodical Subscriptions 4; Photographs; Prints; Records; Reels 27; Slides; Video Tapes
Special Subjects: Folk Art, Decorative Arts, Maps, Historical Material, Crafts, Ethnology, Carpets & Rugs, Handicrafts, Textiles, Architecture
Collections: Approx 10,000 items relating to 18th & 19th century homelife, farmlife & schooling
Publications: Review
Activities: Classes for adults & children; Easter on the Farm; Children's Cultural Camp; Christmas on the Farm; lects open to pub; school tours

LANCASTER

M **HERITAGE CENTER OF LANCASTER COUNTY MUSEUM,** PO Box 417, Lancaster, PA 17608-0417. Tel 717-299-6440; Fax 717-299-6916; Elec Mail info@lancasterheritage.com; Internet Home Page Address: www.lancasterheritage.com; *Cur Educ* Kim Fortney; *Cur* Wendel Zercher; *Exec Dir* Peter S Seibert
Open Mon-Sat 9AM-5PM, 1st Fri 5PM-9PM; No admis fee; Estab 1976 to preserve & exhibit Lancaster County decorative arts; Five major galleries; Average Annual Attendance: 30,000; Mem: 800; dues vary; ann meeting third Wed in May

Income: Financed by endowment, mem, city appropriation, grants & fundraising efforts
Special Subjects: Painting-American, Sculpture, Folk Art, Portraits, Furniture, Silver, Metalwork, Calligraphy, Pewter
Collections: Lancaster County Decorative Arts & Crafts; furniture, silver, regional painting; folk art; architectural
Exhibitions: Rotating exhibs
Activities: Classes for adults & children; lect open to pub; tours; individual paintings & original objects of art lent to other museums; mus shop sells books & reproductions

M **LANCASTER MUSEUM OF ART,** 135 N Lime St, Lancaster, PA 17602-2952. Tel 717-394-3497; Fax 717-394-0101; Elec Mail info@lmapa.org; Internet Home Page Address: www.lmapa.org; *Dir* Stanley I Grand PhD
Open Tues - Sat 10 AM - 4 PM, Sun Noon - 4 PM; Admis by donation; Estab 1965 to present contemporary art exhibits; 4,000 sq ft facility in historic 1845; Grubb mansion; Average Annual Attendance: 35,000; Mem: 1,000; dues, various categories
Income: $750,000 (financed by mem, local foundations, corporations)
Collections: Permanent collection focusing on works by regional artists
Exhibitions: Exhibition schedule includes 15 exhibits per year
Publications: Quarterly newsletter
Activities: Classes for adults & children; lect open to pub, vis lectrs; gallery talks; tours; competition with awards; mus shop sells original art & prints

M **LANCASTER QUILT & TEXTILE MUSEUM,** 37 N Market St, Lancaster, PA 17603. Tel 717-397-2970; 299-6440; Fax 717-299-6916; Elec Mail inco@lancasterheritage.com; Internet Home Page Address: www.quiltandtextilemuseum.com
Open first fri Apr - Dec 5 - 9 PM, also open by reservation for groups & special events booked through Dec; Admis $6

M **LANDIS VALLEY VILLAGE AND FARM MUSEUM, PA HISTORICAL & MUSEUM COMMISSION,** 2451 Kissel Hill Rd, Lancaster, PA 17601-4809. Tel 717-569-0401; Fax 717-560-2147; Elec Mail bbomberger@pa.gov; Internet Home Page Address: www.landisvalleymuseum.org; *Dir* Stephen S Miller; *Cur* Bruce Bomberger; *Cur Community Life* Susan Messimer; *Events Coordr* Susan Kelleher; *Mus Shop Mgr* Shelby Chunko; *Farm & Garden Mgr* Joseph Meyer; *Heirloom Seed Project* Joseph Schott; *Bus Mgr* Judy Weese; *Board Pres* Peter Barber; *Interpretation Supvr* April Frantz; *Mktg & Develop* Marilyn Monath
Open Mon - Sat 9 AM - 5 PM, Sun Noon - 5 PM, cl some holidays; Admis adults $10, seniors $8, children 6-17 $7, children under 6 free, group rates available; Estab 1925 to collect, preserve & interpret Pennsylvania rural life & Pennsylvania German culture, c 1750 to 1940; farm implements, crafts, tools, domestic furnishings & folk art; The outdoor mus has 25 exhibit buildings, including restored 18th & 19th century structures & historical garden landscapes, as well as historical animal breeds; Average Annual Attendance: 57,000; Mem: 480; dues information upon request
Income: Financed by state appropriation & local support group
Special Subjects: Architecture, Crafts, Folk Art, Decorative Arts, Furniture, Glass, Calligraphy
Collections: Baskets, books, ceramics & glass, farm equipment, Fraktur; ironware, musical instruments, Pennsylvania German furniture, textiles, toys & weapons; tools, vehicles
Exhibitions: Dreamers and Visionaries: Focusing on the Landis Valley Legacy
Publications: Newsletter, 4 times per yr; Valley Gazette; spec exhibit catalogs
Activities: Classes for children; tours; research coll contains ceramics & glass, textiles, tools & equipment; mus shop sells books, original art, prints, craft items and period reproductions

L **Landis Collections Gallery,** 2451 Kissel Hill Rd, Lancaster, PA 17601-4809. Tel 717-569-0401; Fax 717-560-2147; Elec Mail bbomberger@pa.gov; Internet Home Page Address: www.landisvalleymuseum.org; *Dir* James Lewars; *Cur* Dr Bruce D Bomberger; *Cur* Mrs Jennifer Royer
Open Mon - Sat 9 AM - 5 PM, Sun noon - 5 PM; Admis adults $12; estab 1925; Open to staff, scholars by appointment for reference only; Average Annual Attendance: 65,000; Mem: 2,500
Income: Financed by state appropriations & Landis Valley Assoc support group
Library Holdings: Book Volumes 12,000; Exhibition Catalogs; Manuscripts; Maps; Original Art Works; Original Documents; Periodical Subscriptions 25; Photographs
Special Subjects: Folk Art, Decorative Arts, Historical Material, Furniture, Tapestries
Collections: Approx 100,000 objects, most representing PA German & rural PA heritage
Exhibitions: Changing annually
Activities: Classes for adults & children; Lects open to pub; gallery talks; tours; mus shop sells books, original art, reproductions & prints

M **ROCK FORD FOUNDATION, INC,** Rock Ford Plantation, 881 Rock Ford Rd, Lancaster, PA 17602-1225. Tel 717-392-7223; Fax 717-392-7283; Elec Mail rockforddirector@comcast.net; Internet Home Page Address: www.rockfordplantation.org; *Pres Bd* Ray Bradley; *Exec Dir* Samuel C Slaymaker
Open Apr - Oct Wed - Sun 11 AM - 3 PM, cl Mon - Tues; Admis adult $7, senior $6, children 6 -12 $5; Estab 1958 for preservation of General Edward Hand Mansion; Late 18th century & American furnishing & decor; Average Annual Attendance: 4,500; Mem: 600; dues $25 - $100; ann meeting first Fri in Dec
Income: $220,000 (financed by mem, endowment, shop sales & special events)
Library Holdings: Book Volumes; CD-ROMs; Compact Disks; Exhibition Catalogs; Memorabilia; Original Art Works; Photographs; Reproductions
Special Subjects: Folk Art, Decorative Arts, Furniture, Period Rooms
Collections: American furniture & decorative arts 1780 - 1802; Pennsylvania Folk Arts 1780 - 1850; Portraits of General Hand & Family Members
Publications: Newsletter
Activities: Classes for children & adults; docent progs; Revolutionary War encampment; Colonial Tavern Nights Yuletide tours; Haunted History Prog; lects open to pub; tours; serves Lancaster PA region; mus shop sells books, prints & reproductions

M **WOLF MUSEUM OF MUSIC AND ART,** 423 W Chestnut Ave, Lancaster, PA 17603; PO Box 701, Lancaster, PA 17608-0701. Tel 717-392-6382
Open by appointment & for public recitals
Collections: Family history; period furnishings; personal artifacts; two 1915 Knabe concert grand pianos; paintings
Activities: Public recitals

LEWISBURG

M **BUCKNELL UNIVERSITY,** Edward & Marthann Samek Art Gallery, 701 Moore Ave, Elaine Langone Ctr Fl 3 Lewisburg, PA 17837-2010. Tel 570-577-3792; Fax 570-577-3215; Elec Mail peltier@bucknell.edu; Internet Home Page Address: www.departments.bucknell.edu/samek; *Operations Mgr* Cynthia Peltier; *Asst Registrar* Tracy Graham
Open Mon - Wed & Fri 11 AM - 5 PM, Thurs 11 AM - 8 PM, Sat & Sun 1 - 5 PM; No admis fee; Estab 1983; Gallery contains a permanent display of 20 Baroque & Renaissance paintings and 1 sculpture of the Renaissance given by the Samuel H Kress Foundation; Average Annual Attendance: 24,853
Income: Financed by endowment, tui, gifts, & grants
Library Holdings: DVDs; Exhibition Catalogs; Original Art Works; Photographs; Prints; Sculpture; Video Tapes
Special Subjects: Decorative Arts, Drawings, Etchings & Engravings, Historical Material, Landscapes, Ceramics, Collages, Mexican Art, Photography, Portraits, Painting-American, Bronzes, Manuscripts, Painting-British, Painting-European, Painting-French, Painting-Japanese, Sculpture, Tapestries, Graphics, Hispanic Art, Latin American Art, Prints, Watercolors, African Art, Religious Art, Woodcarvings, Woodcuts, Posters, Painting-Canadian, Oriental Art, Asian Art, Painting-Dutch, Carpets & Rugs, Baroque Art, Calligraphy, Painting-Flemish, Painting-Polish, Renaissance Art, Antiquities-Oriental, Painting-Spanish, Painting-Italian, Antiquities-Persian, Antiquities-Egyptian, Antiquities-Greek, Antiquities-Roman, Painting-German, Antiquities-Etruscan, Painting-Russian, Painting-Scandinavian
Collections: The permanent coll contains over 5,000 objects from many cultures & all over the globe
Exhibitions: Rotating exhibits 5 times per yr
Publications: see catalogue & brochure section on website-www.bucknell.edu/samek
Activities: Lect open to pub, 1-5 vis lectrs per yr; concert; gallery talks; tours; competitions; individual paintings & original objects of art lent to mus & acad inst; occasionally 1-2 book traveling exhibs per yr; originate traveling exhibs to Univ galleries & museums; mus shop sells books

M **FETHERSTON FOUNDATION,** Packwood House Museum, 15 N Water St, Lewisburg, PA 17837-1531. Tel 570-524-0323; Fax 570-524-0548; Elec Mail info@packwoodhousemuseum.com; Internet Home Page Address: www.Packwoodhousemuseum.com; *Admin* Jennifer Snyder
Open Tues - Sat 10 AM - 5 PM, tours at 11AM, 1PM & 3:30 PM daily; Admis adults $10, seniors $7, students $7, under 12 free; Estab 1976 to serve the community as an educational institution; Historic house with decorative arts, 18th-20th century & changing exhibits galleries; Average Annual Attendance: 4,500; Mem: 300; dues life-time $2,500, benefactor $500, patron $250, sponsor $125, family $45, individual $30, student $5
Income: Financed by endowment, admis, mem, mus shop & grants
Library Holdings: Auction Catalogs; Book Volumes; Exhibition Catalogs; Lantern Slides; Manuscripts; Maps; Original Documents; Pamphlets; Photographs; Slides
Special Subjects: American Indian Art, Archaeology, Etchings & Engravings, Folk Art, History of Art & Archaeology, Landscapes, Art History, Ceramics, Antiquities-Assyrian, Flasks & Bottles, Pre-Columbian Art, Manuscripts, Maps, Painting-American, Photography, Sculpture, Watercolors, Bronzes, Ethnology, Textiles, Costumes, Crafts, Pottery, Woodcarvings, Decorative Arts, Portraits, Dolls, Furniture, Glass, Jade, Jewelry, Porcelain, Oriental Art, Asian Art, Silver, Antiquities-Byzantine, Metalwork, Carpets & Rugs, Historical Material, Ivory, Coins & Medals, Dioramas, Embroidery, Antiquities-Oriental, Antiquities-Persian, Islamic Art, Antiquities-Egyptian, Antiquities-Greek, Antiquities-Roman, Stained Glass, Antiquities-Etruscan
Collections: American Fine Arts; Central Pennsylvania artifacts; Fine Period Clothing ranging from 1890s to 1960s; 1780-1940 decorative arts: ceramics, furniture, glass, metalwork, textiles; Fetherston Family Archives; Edith H K Fetherston Collection
Exhibitions: Packwood House; annual summer exhibit (June-Sept); annual scholastic Art Exhibit (Apr-May); one-person art exhibits
Publications: Chanticleer, three times yearly, newsletter for members
Activities: Classes for adults & children; docent training; lect open to pub; 3 vis lectrs per year; tours; gallery talks; Scholastic Arts Exhibit; mus shop sells books, original art, prints, slides, reproductions & local handcrafted items

LORETTO

M **SOUTHERN ALLEGHENIES MUSEUM OF ART,** Loretto Facility, St Francis University Mall, Loretto, PA 15940; PO Box 9, Loretto, PA 15940-0009. Tel 814-472-3920; Fax 814-472-4131; Elec Mail loretto@sama-art.org; Internet Home Page Address: www.sama-art.org; *Exec Dir* G Gary Moyer; *Cur Visual Arts* Dr V Scott Dimond; *Educ Coordr* Jessica Campbell; *Coll Mgr* Bobby J Moore; *Facilities Mgr* Lee Rummel; *Bookkeeper* Sandra Hampton
Open Tues - Fri 10 AM - 5 PM, Sat 1 - 5 PM, cl Sun, Mon & holidays; No admis fee; fees for special exhibs & progs apply; Estab & dedicated June 1976 to facilitate interest, understanding & the appreciation of the visual arts of the past, present & future through the exhibition of our permanent as well as temporary colls; Large open main gallery with flexible space, second floor graphics gallery; Average Annual Attendance: 10,000; Mem: 1000
Income: Financed by mem, bus, corporate & foundation grants
Purchases: Contemporary American Art especially by living Pennsylvania artists are purchased for the permanent collection
Special Subjects: Drawings, Graphics, Painting-American, Prints, Sculpture, Ceramics, Crafts

Collections: Frank & Margaret Sullivan Collection; Nicholas Unkovic Collection; Charles M Schwab Collection; Mark Del Costello Collection; Rezk Collection
Publications: Online catalogs; newsletters; exhib & events brochures
Activities: Classes for adults & children; intern prog in cooperation with area colleges; school progs; workshops; family activities; artist-in-res progs; lects open to pub, 8 vis lectrs per yr; gallery talks; film series; exten dept serves Altoona, Johnstown & Ligonier; individual paintings & original objects of art lent to other institutions on request for special exhibs; lending collection contains 2000 lantern slides; book traveling exhibs 1-3 per yr; originate traveling exhibs to art galleries

M **Johnstown Gallery,** 450 Schoolhouse Rd, Pasquerilla Performing Arts Center at University of Pittsburgh Johnstown, PA 15904-2912; PO Box 9, Loretto, PA 15940. Tel 814-269-7234; Fax 814-269-7240; Elec Mail loretto@sama-art.org; Internet Home Page Address: www.sama-art.org; *Exec Dir* G Gary Moyer; *Johnstown Coordr* Tina Lehman
Open Mon - Fri 9:30 AM - 4:30 PM, before & during all performing arts events, cl holidays; No admis fee; fees for special exhibs & progs apply; Estab 1982 to bring regional art to a wider audience & provide educational opportunities; Gallery 135 running ft; Average Annual Attendance: 38,500
Income: Financed by mem, city appropriation, private & foundation support, state & federal art agency funding
Special Subjects: Drawings, Painting-American, Photography, Prints, Sculpture, Watercolors, Textiles, Ceramics, Folk Art, Woodcuts, Etchings & Engravings, Landscapes, Collages, Portraits, Posters, Asian Art
Publications: Online catalogs; newsletters; exhib & events brochures
Activities: Classes for adults & children; docent progs; film series; workshops; family progs; artist-in-res progs; lects open to pub, 8 vis lectrs per yr; gallery talks; tours; book traveling exhibs 1 per yr; originate traveling exhibs nationally to other mus

M **Altoona Facility,** 1210 11th Ave, Altoona, PA 16601; PO Box 9, Loretto, PA 15940-0009. Tel 814-946-4464; Fax 814-946-3131; Elec Mail loretto@sama-art.org; Internet Home Page Address: www.sama-art.org; *Exec Dir* G Gary Moyer; *Altoona Coordr* Barbara J Hollander
Open Tues - Fri 10 AM - 5 PM, Sat 1-5 PM, cl Sun, Mon & holidays; No admis fee; special progs & exhib fees apply; State of the art exhib space, storage space
Special Subjects: Photography
Collections: Shirley & Fred A Pechter Gallery; Wolf Gallery; William H Rau Collection: albumen photographic prints c1900
Exhibitions: Quarterly exhibs
Publications: Online catalogs; newsletters; exhib & events brochures
Activities: Classes for adults & children; family progs; workshops; artist-in-res progs; lects open to pub; film series; tours

M **Ligonier Valley Facility,** 1 Boucher Ln, Rte 711 Ligonier, PA 15658; PO Box 9, Loretto, PA 15940-0009. Tel 724-238-6015; Fax 724-238-6281; Elec Mail loretto@sama-art.org; Internet Home Page Address: www.sama-art.org; *Exec Dir* G Gary Moyer; *Ligonier Valley Coordr* Sommer Toffle; *Pub Rels Coordr* Travis Mearns
Open Tues - Fri 10 AM - 5 PM, Sat & Sun 1-5 PM, cl Mon & holidays; No admis fee; fees for special exhibs & progs apply; Modeled on an authentic log cabin design that reflects the historic community, & surrounded by gardens
Special Subjects: Glass
Collections: Walter Carlyle Shaw Paperweight Collection
Publications: Online catalogs; newsletters; exhib & event brochures
Activities: Classes for adults & children; family progs; workshops; artist-in-res progs; lects open to pub; film series; tours

MEADVILLE

M **ALLEGHENY COLLEGE,** Bowman, Megahan & Penelec Galleries, 520 N Main St, Campus Box 23 Meadville, PA 16335-3903. Tel 814-332-4365; Fax 814-332-6238; Elec Mail damiller@allegheny.edu; Internet Home Page Address: www.allegheny.edu/artgalleries; *Gallery Dir* Darren Lee Miller; *Dept Secy* Rhonda Hershelman
Open Tues - Fri 12:30 - 5 PM, Sat 1:30 - 5 PM, Sun 2 - 4 PM, cl Mon; No admis fee; Estab 1971 as one of the major exhibition spaces in northwest Pennsylvania; the galleries present exhibits ranging from works of contemporary artists to displays relevant to other fields of study; Galleries are housed in three spacious rooms, white walls, terrazzo floor, 10 ft ceilings; Average Annual Attendance: 5,000
Income: Financed by college funds & grants
Collections: Allegheny College Permanent Collection
Activities: Lects open to pub, 8-10 vis lectrs per yr; gallery talks; tours; student awards; individual paintings & original objects of art lent to art galleries & museums; book traveling exhibitions, 1 every 1-2 yrs

M **CRAWFORD COUNTY HISTORICAL SOCIETY,** Baldwin-Reynolds House Museum, 411 Chestnut St, Meadville, PA 16335-2902. Tel 814-333-9882 (Mus, seasonal); 724-6080 (Historical Society, yr round); Elec Mail museum@baldwinreynolds.org; crawfordhistorical@zoominternet.net; Internet Home Page Address: www.baldwinreynolds.org; www.crawfordhistorical.org
Open mid-May - Aug Wed - Sun Noon - 4 PM; tours at Noon, 1, 2 & 3 PM; Admis adults $5, children ages 6 - 18 $3, children under 6 with adult free; group rates available

A **MEADVILLE COUNCIL ON THE ARTS,** PO Box 337, Meadville, PA 16335-0337. Tel 814-336-5051; Fax 814-336-5051; Elec Mail artscouncil@zoominternet.net; Internet Home Page Address: www.meadvillecouncilonthearts.com
Open Wed & Fri Noon - 4 PM; Sat 10 AM - 2 PM; No admis fee; Estab 1975 for local arts information & programming; to create community arts center; Gallery has 50 ft of wall space; Average Annual Attendance: 8,000; Mem: benefactor $500, partner $200-499, sustaining $100-199, family $70, individual $40, student/senior $20
Income: $60,000 (financed by mem & state appropriation)
Purchases: Yearly piece for permanent collection

Exhibitions: Annual October Evenings Exhibition; annual county wide exhibits; monthly gallery shows for local artists and crafters exhibits; Annual juried member exhib; annual photo juried exhib
Publications: Quarterly newsletter
Activities: Classes for adults & children; dramatic progs; special populations; lects open to pub; concerts; $1100 visual arts awards, annual juried show; gallery talks; plays & shows in theatre; schols offered; exten prog serving Meadville & surrounding area; Taste of Arts Prog for nursing homes & senior ctrs; collaborate with Meadville Housing Authority - art related progs for children

MERION

M **BARNES FOUNDATION,** 300 N Latch's Ln, Merion, PA 19066-1729; 2025 Benjamin Franklin Pkwy, Philadelphia, PA 19130. Tel 215-278-7000; Fax 215-278-7017; Elec Mail info@barnesfoundation.org; Internet Home Page Address: www.barnesfoundation.org; *Pres Board Trustees* Dr Bernard Watson; *Exec Dir* Kimberly Camp; *Dir Educ* Robin Muse-Mclea; *Dir Develop* Daniel Dupont; *Dir of Arboretum* Dr Jacob Thomas; *Dir Licensing & Repr* Andrew Stewart
Open Sun, Mon & Wed, Thurs, Sat 10 AM - 6 PM; Fri 10 AM - 10 PM; cl Tues; Admis general $15, mems & children under 3 free; Estab 1922 to promote the advancement of educ & the appreciation of fine art & horticulture; Maintains Gallery & Arboretum, & owns Ker-Feal farmhouse; Average Annual Attendance: 65,000; Mem: 600; dues $75
Income: Grants, individual contributions & earned income
Library Holdings: Auction Catalogs; Book Volumes 5,000; Exhibition Catalogs; Lantern Slides; Manuscripts; Maps; Original Documents; Other Holdings Correspondence; Publications; Photographs; Video Tapes
Special Subjects: Drawings, Painting-American, Watercolors, African Art, Southwestern Art, Textiles, Ceramics, Pottery, Decorative Arts, Painting-European, Furniture, Asian Art, Painting-Dutch, Painting-French, Carpets & Rugs, Tapestries, Painting-Flemish, Antiquities-Oriental, Antiquities-Egyptian, Painting-German
Collections: Permanent coll of post-impressionism & early French modern art. Includes works by Cezanne, Matisse & Renoir; 18th century American decorative art; Native American decorative art; African Art; Greek, Roman & Egyptian antiquities; Botanical coll featuring magnolias, fern, stewartia
Activities: Classes for adults; docent training, K-12 teacher training & ACE evaluation for undergraduate cr; lects for mems only, 3-4 vis lectrs per yr, tours; mus shop sells books, reproductions & prints

MILL RUN

M **WESTERN PENNSYLVANIA CONSERVANCY,** Fallingwater, PO Box R, Mill Run, PA 15464-0167. Tel 724-329-8501; Fax 724-329-0881; Elec Mail fallingwater@paconserve.org; Internet Home Page Address: www.fallingwater.org; *Mus Prog Asst* Clinton Piper; *Dir* Lynda Waggoner; *VPres Institutional Advancement* Genny McIntyre; *Dir Communs* Allison Schlesinger; *Cur Educ* Roy Young; *Dir Preservation* Scott Perkins
Open daily 10 AM - 4 PM, Mid-Mar - Nov, cl Wed; Admis $20 advance, $23 purchase on site; Estab 1963 to preserve, maintain & make available for public educ & appreciation Frank Lloyd Wright's Fallingwater; 1935 Frank Lloyd Wright weekend house for Edgar J Kaufmann family of Pittsburgh built between 1936-1939; Average Annual Attendance: 160,602; Mem: 300: dues $20-$40
Income: $2,800,000 (financed by mem, grants, admis, sales & royalties)
Library Holdings: Audio Tapes; Original Art Works
Special Subjects: Architecture
Collections: Ceramics; Decorative Arts, including furniture by Frank Lloyd Wright; Glass; Paintings & Graphic Works by Picasso, Diego Rivera; 19th century Japanese Prints; Sculptures by Lipschitz, Arp & Voulkos; Textiles
Activities: Educ prog; classes for adults & children; docent training; lect open to pub; tours; mus shop sells books, reproductions, prints, original art & slides

NARBERTH

M **SWEET MABEL FOLK ARTS & FINE CRAFT GALLERY,** 41 N Narberth Ave, Narberth, PA 19072-2347. Tel 610-667-3041
Open Tues-Sat 11AM-6PM, Sun noon-5PM
Collections: works by regional & national artists; carving; paintings; photographs

NAZARETH

M **MORAVIAN HISTORICAL SOCIETY,** Whitefield House Museum, 214 E Center St, Nazareth, PA 18064-2209. Tel 610-759-5070; Fax 610-759-2461; Elec Mail info@moravianhistoricalsociety.org; Internet Home Page Address: www.moravianhistoricalsociety.org; *Exec Dir* Wendy S Weida
Open 1PM-4PM, other times by appointment; Admis adults $5, students & sr citizens $3; Built in 1740 by George Whitefield, famous preacher, bought by the Moravians in 1741 & continued in use by various segments of the church. Now the seat of the Moravian Historical Soc (organized on Apr 13, 1857 to elucidate the history of the Moravian Church in America; not however, to the exclusion of the general history of the Moravian Church); used as a mus, which houses many unique & distinctive items pertaining to early Moraviana & colonial life; Average Annual Attendance: 5,500; Mem: 500; dues $50 & up; ann meeting in Oct
Income: Financed by endowment, mem & donation
Library Holdings: Audio Tapes; Book Volumes; Clipping Files; Compact Disks; DVDs; Framed Reproductions; Lantern Slides; Manuscripts; Maps; Original Art Works; Original Documents; Pamphlets; Periodical Subscriptions; Photographs; Prints; Records; Reels; Reproductions; Slides; Video Tapes
Special Subjects: Etchings & Engravings, Glass, Pottery, Textiles, Manuscripts, Painting-American, Watercolors, Religious Art, Folk Art, Decorative Arts, Portraits, Eskimo Art, Furniture, Historical Material, Maps
Collections: John Valentine Haidt Collection of Religious Paintings
Publications: Transactions, biennial

Activities: Classes for adults & children; docent training; internship opportunities; lects open to pub, 13 vis lectrs per yr; concerts; gallery talks; library tours; original objects or art lent to recognized & approved museums & historical societies; lending coll contains individual & original objects of art; originate travel exhibs mostly to Moravian organizations, mus, historical societies, churches & schools; mus shop sells books, original art, reproductions, prints

NEW BRIGHTON

M **MERRICK ART GALLERY,** 1100 5th Ave, New Brighton, PA 15066; PO Box 312, New Brighton, PA 15066-0312. Tel 724-846-1130; Elec Mail merrickartgallery@verizon.net; *Dir & Educ Dir* Cynthia A Kundar; *Trustee* Karen Capper
Open Tues - Sat 10 AM - 4 PM; Sun 1 - 4 PM, Summer Wed-Sat 10AM-4PM cl Mon & holidays; No admis fee; charge for docent tour; Estab 1880 to preserve & interpret the collection of paintings & other objects owned by Edward Dempster Merrick, the founder. Also to foster local art through classes & one-man shows; All galleries are on the second floors of two parallel buildings with a connecting bridge; there are three small rooms & one large one. Three rooms have skylight monitors overhead; Average Annual Attendance: 6,000; Mem: 350; dues $25, $15 & $10; ann meeting Jan or Feb
Income: Financed by endowment & mem
Library Holdings: Memorabilia; Original Art Works; Original Documents; Photographs; Records; Sculpture; Slides
Special Subjects: Painting-American, Painting-European
Collections: Most paintings date from the 18th & 19th century. American artists Emil Bott; Birge Harrison; Thomas Hill; A F King; Edward and Thomas Moran; E Poole; F K M Rehn; W T Richards; W L Sonntag; Thomas Sully; Charles Curran; John F Kensett; Andrew Melrose; Ralph A Blackelock; Asher B Durand; Worthington Whittredge. European artists Gustave Courbet; Hans Makart; Pierre Paul Prud'hon; Richard Westall; Franz Xavier; Winterhalter; Peter Baumgartner; Leon Herbo; Jaques Bertrand; Rocks & minerals; Zoological
Publications: Newsletter, bimonthly
Activities: Classes for adults & children; docent training; dramatic progs; lects open to public; 2 vis lectrs per yr; concerts; gallery talks; tours; sponsoring of competitions; scholarships; mus shop sells books

NEW CASTLE

M **HOYT CENTER FOR THE ARTS,** (Hoyt Institute of Fine Arts) 124 E Leasure Ave, New Castle, PA 16101-2398. Tel 724-652-2882; Fax 724-657-8786; Elec Mail hoyt@hoytartcenter.org; Internet Home Page Address: www.hoytartcenter.org; *Pres* Richard Flannery Esq; *Exec Dir* Kimberly Koller Jones; *Prog Dir* Robert Presnar; *Exhib Coordr* Patricia McLatchy
Open Tues & Thurs 11AM - 8 PM, Wed, Fri & Sat 11AM-4PM; No admis fee; Estab 1965 to encourage the development of the arts within the community; Maintains reference library; Average Annual Attendance: 22,000; Mem: 530; dues $30 - $2,500
Income: Classes, commissions, events, rentals, competitions, sponsorship, grants
Library Holdings: Auction Catalogs; Book Volumes; Exhibition Catalogs; Maps; Memorabilia; Original Art Works; Original Documents; Periodical Subscriptions; Reproductions; Sculpture; Video Tapes
Special Subjects: Etchings & Engravings, Historical Material, Architecture, Glass, Furniture, Portraits, Prints, Silver, Textiles, Woodcuts, Maps, Drawings, Graphics, Painting-American, Photography, Sculpture, Watercolors, American Western Art, Textiles, Costumes, Ceramics, Crafts, Folk Art, Pottery, Landscapes, Decorative Arts, Collages, Posters, Dolls, Jewelry, Porcelain, Metalwork, Carpets & Rugs, Period Rooms, Embroidery, Stained Glass, Pewter, Enamels
Collections: Historic & contemporary works of national & regional artists; 19th Century Antiquities & Decorative Arts
Exhibitions: Hoyt Regional Art Show; Hoyt MidAtlantic Show; Juried Art Shows
Publications: Quarterly newsletter
Activities: Classes for adults & children; dramatic progs; 21 vis lects per yr; concerts; gallery talks; tours; sponsoring of competitions; lect open to pub, lects year-round; concerts; gallery talks; tours; competitions; festivals; schols awarded; multiple venues; 1-2 traveling exhibs per yr; mus shop sells original art; prints; jewelry & other items

NEW WILMINGTON

M **WESTMINSTER COLLEGE,** Art Gallery, Market St, New Wilmington, PA 16172-0001. Tel 724-946-7266; Fax 724-946-7256; Internet Home Page Address: www.westminster.edu; *Dir* Kathy Koop
Open Mon & Fri 9 AM - 9 PM, Sun 1 - 9 PM; No admis fee; Estab 1854 to organize & present 7 exhibs per season, to organize traveling exhibs, publish art catalogs of national interest & to conduct visiting artists program; Average Annual Attendance: 15,000
Income: Financed by endowment, state & local grants
Special Subjects: Drawings, Painting-American, Prints
Collections: 19th & 20th century paintings; 20th century drawings & prints
Exhibitions: Seven exhibs annually by regional & national artists
Publications: Catalogs; Westminster College Art Gallery, annually
Activities: Lect open to pub, 4 vis lectrs per yr; gallery talks; originates traveling exhibs

NEWTOWN

M **BUCKS COUNTY COMMUNITY COLLEGE,** Hicks Art Center, 275 Swamp Rd, Fine Arts Dept Newtown, PA 18940-1524. Tel 215-968-8425; Fax 215-504-8530; *Dir Exhib* Fran Orlando; *Chmn* Frank Dominguez
Open Mon & Fri 9 AM - 4 PM, Tues - Thurs 8 AM - 8 PM, Sat 9 AM - Noon; No admis fee; Estab 1970 to bring outside artists to the community; Gallery covers 960 sq ft; Average Annual Attendance: 5,000

Income: Financed by county and state appropriation
Exhibitions: Six exhibits each acad yr, ending with student ann exhibit
Activities: Lect open to pub, 4 vis lectrs per yr; competitions; gallery talks; artmobile; 1 book traveling exhib per yr

PAOLI

M **WHARTON ESHERICK MUSEUM,** PO Box 595, Paoli, PA 19301-0595. Tel 610-644-5822; Fax 610-644-2244; Elec Mail information@whartonesherickmuseum.org; Internet Home Page Address: www.whartonesherickmuseum.org; *Cur* Paul Eisenhauer; *Pres* Laurence A Liss
Open Sat 10 AM - 5 PM, Sun 1 - 5 PM, weekdays groups only Mon - Fri 10 AM - 4 PM, cl Jan - Feb & major holidays; Admis adults $10, children under 12 $5; Estab 1971 for the preservation and exhib of the Studio and coll of sculptor Wharton Esherick (1887-1970), one of America's foremost artist/craftsmen. Esherick worked mostly in wood and is best known for his sculptural furniture; Studio is set high on hillside overlooking the Great Valley & is one of Wharton Esherick's monumental achievements. He worked forty years building, enlarging & altering it. A National Historic Landmark; Average Annual Attendance: 5,000; Mem: 450; dues family $75, individual $40
Income: $220,600 (financed by mem, endowment, admis, sales & grants)
Library Holdings: Audio Tapes; Clipping Files; Compact Disks; DVDs; Exhibition Catalogs; Original Documents; Photographs; Prints; Records
Special Subjects: Furniture, Painting-American, Sculpture, Watercolors, Ceramics, Crafts, Woodcarvings, Woodcuts, Decorative Arts, Furniture
Collections: 200 pieces of the artist's work, including furniture, paintings, prints, sculpture in wood, stone and ceramic, utensils and woodcuts
Exhibitions: Annual Thematic Woodworking Competition/Exhibition; Annual Woodworking Competition
Publications: Brochures; coll & exhibit catalogues
Activities: Lects open to pub; 6 vis lectrs per yr; tours; competitions with awards: PMA Craft Show - Excellence in Wood, Woodcut Award - Pennsylvania Academy of the Fine Arts; individual paintings & original objects of art lent to mus or exhibs; lending coll contains original art works & sculptures; originate traveling exhibs to colleges, galleries & mus; mus shop sells books, magazines, reproductions; slides, videos, posters, notecards, postcards & T-shirts

PHILADELPHIA

M **AFRICAN AMERICAN MUSEUM IN PHILADELPHIA,** 701 Arch St, Philadelphia, PA 19106-1504. Tel 215-574-0380; Fax 215-574-3110; Elec Mail gadams@aampmuseum.org; Internet Home Page Address: www.aampmuseum.org; *Pres & CEO* Romona Riscoe Benson; *Exhib Dir* Richard Watson; *Educ Dir* Ivan Henderson; *Bookings Mgr* Gladys Adams; *Mem Mgr* Cassandra Murrary; *Cur Colls* Leslie Guy; *Exec Asst* Liz Kent; *VPres Opers* Patricia Wilson Aden
Open Tues - Sat 10 AM - 5 PM, Sun Noon - 5 PM, cl New Years, Memorial Day, July 4, Labor Day, Thanksgiving & Christmas; Admis adults $10 seniors, children & students $8; group rates adults, children & students $6; Estab 1976; Gallery has 2 changing exhibits & 1 perm exhibit; Average Annual Attendance: 67,000; Mem: 1,000; dues benefactor $1,000, fellow $500, bus $400, patron $250, assoc $150, family $75, individual $50, students & seniors $30
Special Subjects: Archaeology, Etchings & Engravings, Collages, Woodcuts, Drawings, Graphics, Painting-American, Photography, Prints, Sculpture, Watercolors, Textiles, Costumes, Religious Art, Crafts, Woodcarvings, Afro-American Art, Portraits, Posters, Dolls, Furniture, Historical Material, Coins & Medals, Military Art
Collections: Negro Baseball Leagues Collection of photographs & documents; Chief Justice Robert N C Nix Sr Collection, legal writings & memorabilia; Afro-American; artifacts relating to African American contributions to political, religions & family life, Civil Rights Movement, arts & entertainment, sports, medicine, law & technology; paintings, prints & sculpture by African American artist; archival documents; Joseph E Coleman Collection; Jack T Franklin Photographic Collection; Dr Ruth Wright Hayre Collection; Anna Russell Jones Collection
Exhibitions: Audacious Freedom-Permanent
Publications: Annual report; brochure; exhib catalog
Activities: Classes for adults & children; docent training; lect open to pub; concerts; gallery talks; tours; awards; fels; individual paintings & original objects of art lent to other museums & institutions which conform to our security & climatic specifications; book traveling exhibs 2 per yr; originate traveling exhibs; mus sales shop sells books, magazines, original art, reproductions, prints & novelties

M **ALLENS LANE ART CENTER,** Carolyn-Fielder-Alber Gallery, 601 W Allens Ln, Philadelphia, PA 19119. Tel 215-248-0546; Fax 215-248-0559

M **AMERICAN SWEDISH HISTORICAL FOUNDATION & MUSEUM,** American Swedish Historical Museum, 1900 Pattison Ave, Philadelphia, PA 19145-5999. Tel 215-389-1776; Fax 215-389-7701; Elec Mail info@americanswedish.org; Internet Home Page Address: www.americanswedish.org; *Assoc Dir* Birgitta W Davis; *Exec Dir* Tracey Beck; *Cur* Carrie Hogan; *Mem & Mktg* Caroline Rossy; *Maintenance* Frank Sanders; *Educ Mgr* Lauren Zalut; *Board Chmn* Leonard Busby
Open Tues - Fri 10 AM - 4 PM, Sat & Sun Noon - 4 PM, cl Mon & holidays; Admis adults $6, seniors & students $5, children under 12 free; Estab 1926 to create an awareness & understanding of the contributions of Swedish-American people & of Sweden; 14 galleries containing materials interpreting over 300 years of Swedish influence on American life; Average Annual Attendance: 12,000; Mem: 750; dues family $65, individual $50; ann meeting in Sept
Library Holdings: Book Volumes
Special Subjects: Architecture, Drawings, Costumes, Crafts, Folk Art, Etchings & Engravings, Decorative Arts, Furniture, Glass, Coins & Medals, Embroidery, Painting-Scandinavian
Collections: History and culture of Americans of Swedish descent
Exhibitions: Scandinavian history & culture; temporary exhibitions of paintings, arts & crafts by Scandinavian & Swedish-American artists
Publications: Newsletter, quarterly
Activities: Classes for adults & children; lects open to pub, 1-3 vis lectrs per yr; concerts; gallery talks; tours; Spirit of Raoul Wallenberg Humanitarian Award; individual paintings & original objects of art lent to other mus & cultural attractions; book traveling exhibs 1 per yr; exten dept serves history & Swedish museums & historical societies; mus shop sells books & prints

L **Nord Library,** 1900 Pattison Ave, Philadelphia, PA 19145-5999. Tel 215-389-1776; Fax 215-389-7701; Elec Mail info@americanswedish.org; Internet Home Page Address: www.americanswedish.org; *Exec Dir* Tracey Beck; *Cur Exhib* Carrie Hogan; *Assoc Dir* Birgitta W Davis; *Educ & Vis Servs* Tricia Davies
Open Tues - Fri 10 AM - 4 PM, Sat & Sun Noon - 4 PM; Admis adults $8, seniors & students $6, children 5-12 $4, children under 5 free; Estab 1926 to create an awareness of Swedish & Swedish-American contribution to the US; Library is for research & reference only; Average Annual Attendance: 20,000; Mem: 750; dues $35 to $75; ann meeting in Sept
Library Holdings: Book Volumes 15,000; Clipping Files; Exhibition Catalogs; Memorabilia; Periodical Subscriptions 5; Records; Reels; Slides
Special Subjects: Painting-Scandinavian
Collections: Patent models & papers of John Ericsson
Exhibitions: (03/2013) The Works of Sigeele Oldenberg
Publications: Elin's America by Marguerite DeAngeli
Activities: Classes for adults & children; lects open to pub; 1-3 vis lectrs per yr; concerts; gallery talks; tours; Outstanding Achievement Award (given annually to notable Swedes & Swedish Americans); The Spirir of Raoul Wallenberg Award; traveling exhibs to other Scandinavian mus & organizations; mus shop sells books & prints

L **ART INSTITUTE OF PHILADELPHIA LIBRARY,** 1622 Chestnut St, Philadelphia, PA 19103-5198. Tel 215-405-6402; Fax 215-405-6378; Internet Home Page Address: www.artinstitute.edu; *Libr Dir* Ruth Schachter
Open Mon - Thurs 7:50AM-10PM, Fri 7:50AM-9PM, Sat 11AM-5PM; Estab 1966; Reference library for students & staff only
Library Holdings: Book Volumes 21,500; Exhibition Catalogs; Periodical Subscriptions 200; Video Tapes
Special Subjects: Art History, Decorative Arts, Film, Illustration, Commercial Art, Graphic Arts, Graphic Design, Painting-American, Advertising Design, Cartoons, Fashion Arts, Industrial Design, Interior Design, Lettering, Architecture

M **ATHENAEUM OF PHILADELPHIA,** 219 S Sixth St, Philadelphia, PA 19106-3794. Tel 215-925-2688; Fax 215-925-3755; Elec Mail athena@philaathenaeum.org; Internet Home Page Address: www.philaathenaeum.org; *Asst Dir Progs* Eileen Magee; *Architectural Archivist* Bruce Laverty; *Circ Librn* Jill L Lee; *Dir* Sandra L Tatman; *Mem Coordr* Brittany Koch
Open Mon - Fri 9 AM - 5 PM, 1st, 2nd & 3rd Sat of month 11 AM - 3 PM; No admis fee; Estab 1814 to collect, preserve & make available original sources on American cultural history, 1814-1914; Haas gallery: 4 exhibs ann; Average Annual Attendance: 25,000; Mem: 1375; ann meeting in Apr; dues $200 per yr
Income: $1,000,000 (financed by endowments, dues & fees)
Library Holdings: Audio Tapes; Book Volumes; CD-ROMs; DVDs; Manuscripts; Memorabilia; Original Art Works; Original Documents; Pamphlets; Periodical Subscriptions; Photographs; Prints
Special Subjects: Historical Material, Furniture, Painting-American, Architecture, Decorative Arts, Bookplates & Bindings
Collections: Permanent study collection of American decorative arts, 1810-1850; 19th & 20th century architectural books; architectural drawings; trade catalogues; rare books - 19th century
Publications: Monthly e-newsletter; Archive; Annual Report; Bookshelf, 6 per yr
Activities: Classes for adults & children; lect open to pub, 10 vis lectrs per yr; concerts; gallery talks; tours; competitions with awards, Annual Literary Award; Charles E Peterson Research Fellowships; Literary Award; architectural research; originate traveling exhibs to small historic site museums; sells books, prints & slides

L **Library,** 219 S Sixth St, Philadelphia, PA 19106. Tel 215-925-2688; Fax 215-925-3755; Elec Mail laverty@philaathenaeum.org; Internet Home Page Address: www.philaathenaeum.org; *Cur Architecture* Bruce Laverty; *Circ Librn* Ellen Rose
Open Mon - Fri 9 AM - 5 PM by appointment for reference only; No admis fee; Estab 1814; Haas Gallery; Mem: 1300
Library Holdings: Book Volumes 75,000; Cards; Cassettes; Fiche; Manuscripts; Original Art Works; Other Holdings Architectural drawings & related materials; Periodical Subscriptions 50; Reels
Special Subjects: Decorative Arts, Architecture
Collections: Nineteenth century fiction and literary periodicals; trade materials relating to the building arts; architectural drawings; manuscripts; photographs
Publications: Biographical dictionary of Philadelphia Architects, monograph
Activities: Tours of National Historic Landmark library building; symposia; lects open to pub, lects for mems only; gallery talks; tours; fels offered; sales shop sells books

A **BRANDYWINE WORKSHOP,** Center for the Visual Arts, 730 S Broad St, Philadelphia, PA 19146-2203. Tel 215-546-3675; Fax 215-546-2825; Elec Mail prints@brandywineworkshop.com; Internet Home Page Address: www.brandywindworkshop.com; *Pres & Exec Dir* Allan L Edmunds; *Admin Coordr* Lisa Sok; *Dir Develop* Stan Isaacson
Open Mon - Fri 10 AM - 5 PM, Sat & Sun by appointment only; No admis fee; Estab 1972 to develop interest & talent in printmaking & other fine visual arts; Over 39,000 sq ft with 2 buildings in downtown Philadelphia. Facilities include offset lithography presses, screen printing & computer/video technology lab & classrooms. Printed Image Gallery for professional exhibits of works on paper by contemporary artists; Average Annual Attendance: 2,600 - 10,000; Mem: 220; dues $30 & up
Income: Financed by mem, city & state appropriations, pvt corporations & foundations
Special Subjects: Prints, Afro-American Art, American Indian Art

Collections: Contemporary fine art prints, including etchings, woodblocks, offset lithographs, silkscreens

Exhibitions: USA Artworks; Contemporary Print Images; Rotating exhibits

Activities: Classes for adults & teenagers; docent training; teacher in-service training; free computer/video classes for high school students; lect open to pub, 6 vis lectrs per yr; gallery talks; tours; fels offered; original objects of art donated to historically black colleges, major mus collections, centers for research & Library of Congress; lending coll contains original prints; book traveling exhibs 1 per yr; originate traveling exhibs; mus shop sells books, original art, prints, note cards, calendars, t-shirts, caps, tote bags & mugs

M CLAY STUDIO, 139 N Second St, Philadelphia, PA 19106. Tel 215-925-3453; Fax 215-925-7774; Elec Mail info@theclaystudio.org; Internet Home Page Address: www.theclaystudio.org; *Pres* Christopher Taylor; *Artistic Dir* Jeff Guido; *Dir Educ & Opers* Jennifer Martin; *Outreach Prog Dir* Annette Monnier; *Gallery Coordr* Naomi Cleary
Open Tues - Sat 11AM - 6PM, Sun Noon - 6 PM; No admis fee; Estab 1974; Two galleries with exhibits changing monthly of various ceramic artwork of solo, group & historical shows; Average Annual Attendance: 33,000; Mem: Dues $50 & up
Income: Financed through mem, donations & grants, tui, host fees
Special Subjects: Ceramics
Collections: Ceramic Arts
Exhibitions: Annual Fellowship Artist Solo Show; Annual Resident Artist Group Show; Clay Studio Assoc Artists Exhibition; Inner City Students from the Claymobile Show
Activities: Classes for adults & children; lect open to pub, 4 - 6 vis lectrs per yr; gallery talks; tours; spring jurying for group & solo exhibition & one year residency program; schols; exten dept serves Philadelphia & suburbs; sales shop sells books, magazines, original art

M CLIVEDEN, 6401 Germantown Ave, Philadelphia, PA 19144-1925. Tel 215-848-1777; Fax 215-438-2892; Elec Mail info@cliveden.org; Internet Home Page Address: www.cliveden.org; *Cur History* Phillip Sietz; *Deputy Dir Develop* Robert A MacDonnell; *Pub Rels Coordr* Anne Roller; *Exec Dir* David Young
Open May - Dec Thurs - Sun Noon - 4 PM, cl Easter, July 4th, Thanksgiving & Christmas; Admis adults $8, students $6, two for one admis for AAA mems; Estab 1971 in celebration of American Revolutionary War History; 18th Century house mus; Average Annual Attendance: 14,000; Mem: 250,000
Special Subjects: Historical Material, Period Rooms
Collections: 18th Century house museum with decorative arts, furniture, paintings, colls site related only, no acquisitions
Activities: Classes for children; docent training; guided tours for individuals & groups; mus shop sells books, reproductions, prints, gift items

A THE COMMUNITY EDUCATION CENTER, 3500 Lancaster Ave, Philadelphia, PA 19104-4916. Tel 215-387-1911; Fax 215-387-3701; Elec Mail cec@cecarts.org; Internet Home Page Address: www.cecarts.org; *Exec Dir* Teresa Shockley
Open Mon - Fri 9 AM - 5 PM; No admis fee; Estab 1973 to support emerging talent; 35 ft x 60 ft room, 14 ft ceilings; Average Annual Attendance: 1,500
Income: $180,000 (financed by mem, city & state appropriation, foundation, corporate & pvt donors)
Activities: Classes for adults & children; lect open to pub, 4 vis lectrs per yr

A CONSERVATION CENTER FOR ART & HISTORIC ARTIFACTS, 264 S 23rd St, Philadelphia, PA 19103-5530. Tel 215-545-0613; Fax 215-735-9313; Elec Mail ccaha@ccaha.org; Internet Home Page Address: www.ccaha.org; *Exec Dir* Ingrid E Bogel
Open Mon - Fri 9 AM - 5 PM; Estab 1977 as a nonprofit regional conservation laboratory serving cultural, educational & research institutions as well as private individuals & organizations throughout the United States; Maintains small reference library; Mem: Dues $250
Income: $3,000,000 (financed by earned income & grants)
Activities: Workshops & conferences; Fels offered

M DREXEL UNIVERSITY, (The Museum at Drexel University) Drexel Collection, 3141 Chestnut St, Rm 304 Philadelphia, PA 19104-2816. Tel 215-895-0480; Fax 215-895-6157; Elec Mail degraff@drexel.edu; Internet Home Page Address: www.drexel.edu; *Cur* Jacqueline M DeGroff
Open Mon - Fri 3:30 PM - 5:30 PM, cl Sat, Sun & holidays; No admis fee; Estab 1891; Anthony J Drexel Picture Gallery 1902; Main Gallery contains the John D Lankenau & the Anthony J Drexel Collections of German & French paintings, sculpture & decorative arts of the 19th century & a changing exhib gallery; Average Annual Attendance: 10,000
Income: Financed by Drexel University
Special Subjects: Sculpture, Textiles, Ceramics, Decorative Arts, Oriental Art, Asian Art, Painting-French, Painting-German
Collections: 19th century sculpture, acad European painting, decorative arts & costumes; ceramics; Anthony J Drexel Collection of 19th Century Paintings & Sculptures; John D Lankenau Collection of 19th Century Paintings & Sculptures
Exhibitions: Annual Student Art Show; Regional Artists
Activities: Lect open to pub, 5 vis lectrs per yr; book traveling exhibs

M THE FABRIC WORKSHOP & MUSEUM, 1214 Arch St, Philadelphia, PA 19107-2800. Tel 215-561-8888; Fax 215-561-8887; Elec Mail info@fabricworkshopandmuseum.org; Internet Home Page Address: www.fabricworkshopandmuseum.org; *Dir* Marion Boulton Stroud
Open Mon - Fri 10AM - 6 PM, Sat & Sun Noon - 5PM; Admis adults $3, children under 12 & FWM mems no charge; Estab 1977 devoted to experimental fabric design & silkscreen printing by nationally recognized & emerging artists representing all mediums, incl painting, sculpture, ceramics, architecture & theater. Invites artists to collaboratively explore new directions for their work, while furthering the use of fabric as an integral medium for contemporary art
Collections: Extensive permanent coll of unique contemporary art (over 2300 artworks)
Exhibitions: Ongoing series of exhibs including print multiples, monoprints, sculptural objects, installation pieces, performance costumes, furniture &

functional objects, along with preliminary objects & paintings for artists projects & related sculptures & ceramics
Publications: An Industrious Art; exhibit catalogs; New Materials as New Media
Activities: Classes for adults & children; high school & college apprentice training progs; workshops; lect open to pub, study tours; print demonstrations; gallery talks; tours; mus sales shop sells unique, artist-designed functional objects & workshop publs, books, original art, artist multiples

A FAIRMOUNT PARK ART ASSOCIATION, 1528 Walnut St, Ste 1000, Philadelphia, PA 19102-3627. Tel 215-546-7550; Fax 215-546-2363; Elec Mail postmaster@fpaa.org; Internet Home Page Address: www.fpaa.org; *Pres* Charles E Mather III; *VPres* Gregory M Harvey; *Exec Dir* Penny Balkin Bach; *Asst Dir* Laura S Griffith; *Treas* William McCall; *Office Mgr* Ginger Osbourne; *Prog Mgr* Susan Myers; *Develop & Communs Mgr* Jennifer Richards
Open by appointment only (not open to pub); Estab 1872 to promote integration of art & urban planning & to promote appreciation of pub art through progs & advocacy efforts; Mem: 350; dues $25 - $100; ann meeting May
Income: Financed by mem, grants & endowment
Special Subjects: Sculpture
Exhibitions: New-Land-Marks: Public Art, Community & the Meaning of Place
Publications: New Land Marks
Activities: Children's progs; lects open to pub, lects for mems only; 1 vis lectr per yr, tours

L FREE LIBRARY OF PHILADELPHIA, Art Dept, 1901 Vine St, Philadelphia, PA 19003-1189. Tel 215-686-5403; Elec Mail erefart@freelibrary.org; Internet Home Page Address: www.freelibrary.org; *Library Pres & Dir* Siobhan A Reardon; *Head Librn Art, Dept* Karen Lightner
Open Mon-Thurs 9AM-9PM, Fri 9AM-6PM, Sat 9AM-5PM, Sun 1-5PM; Estab 1891, art department estab 1896, to serve the citizens of the City of Philadelphia; Circ 16,000; Reference & research coll
Income: Financed by endowment, city & state appropriations
Purchases: $15,000
Library Holdings: Book Volumes 60,000; Clipping Files; Exhibition Catalogs; Fiche; Other Holdings Vertical files 40,000; Pamphlets; Periodical Subscriptions 150
Collections: 18th & 19th century architectural pattern books; John Frederick Lewis Collection of books on fine prints & printmaking; 368 original measured drawings of colonial Philadelphia buildings, Philadelphia Chap, American Institute of Architects
Exhibitions: Rotating exhibs

L Print & Picture Collection, 1901 Vine St, Philadelphia, PA 19103-1189. Tel 215-686-5405; Fax 215-563-3628; Elec Mail erefpix@freelibrary.org; Internet Home Page Address: www.freelibrary.org; *Head* Karen Lightner
Open Mon - Fri 9 AM - 5 PM; Estab 1954 by combining the Print Department (estab 1927) & the Picture Coll
Income: Financed by endowment & city appropriations
Purchases: $8,000
Library Holdings: Original Art Works; Photographs; Prints
Special Subjects: Photography, Drawings, Etchings & Engravings, Portraits, Printmaking
Collections: (non-circulating) Americana (1200); Hampton L Carson Collection of Napoleonic prints (3400); Fine Art Prints (8000); Fine Art Photographs (3000); graphic arts (2000); greeting & tradesmen cards (27,000); John Frederick Lewis Collection of portrait prints (211,000); Philadelphiana (15,000); Rosenthal Collection of American Drawings (900); Benton Spruance lithographs (450); (circulating) coll of pictures in all media and universal in subject coverage (1,000,000); Artists books (200)
Activities: Friends of the Print & Picture Collection, meets 4 times per yr; lects open to pub, 1 vis lectr per yr; lending collection of original objects of art extended to mus

L Rare Book Dept, 1901 Vine St, Philadelphia, PA 19103-1189. Tel 215-686-5416; Fax 215-563-3628; Elec Mail refrbd@library_phila.gov; *Head* James D DeWalt; *Asst Head* Janine Pollock
Open Mon - Fri 9 AM - 5 PM; No admis fee; Estab 1949; Average Annual Attendance: 3,000
Special Subjects: Illustration, Manuscripts
Collections: American Sunday-School Union; Early American children's books including Rosenbach Collection of Early American Children's books (1682-1836); Elisabeth Ball Collection of Horn books; Borneman & Yoder Collection of Pennsylvania German Fraktur; Hampton L Carson Collection of legal prints; Frederick R Gardner Collection of Robert Lawson original drawings; Kate Greenaway; Grace Clark Haskell Collection of Arthur Rackham; John Frederick Lewis Collection of cuneiform tablets & seals, Medieval & Renaissance manuscripts & miniatures, Oriental manuscripts & miniatures (mostly Mughal, Rajput & Persian); Thornton Oakley Collection of Howard Pyle & His School, books & original drawings; Beatrix Potter, including H Bacon Collamore Collection of original art; Evan Randolph Collection consisting of angling prints from the 17th to the 20th century & prints of Philadelphia from 1800-1950; original drawings, paintings, prints & other illustrative material relating to the works of Dickens, Goldsmith, Poe & Thackeray
Activities: Individual paintings & original objects of art lent to other institutions for exhib not to exceed 3 months; lending coll contains books, original artworks & paintings

M GERMANTOWN HISTORICAL SOCIETY, 5501 Germantown Ave, Philadelphia, PA 19144-2225. Tel 215-844-1683; Fax 215-844-2831; Elec Mail info@germantownhistory.org; Internet Home Page Address: www.germantownhistory.org; *Exec Dir* Laura E Bradley; *Librn* Alex Bartlett; *Ed* Andrea Niepold
Open Tues 9AM-1PM, Thurs1PM-5PM; Admis Museum $3, children under 12 $2; libr $7.50, students with ID $5; Estab 1900 as an historical society; Maintains reference library & mus galleries; Average Annual Attendance: 1,000; Mem: 250; dues $30
Income: $200,000 (financed by endowment, mem, city & state appropriations, foundations & corporations)
Library Holdings: Audio Tapes; Book Volumes; Clipping Files; Lantern Slides; Manuscripts; Maps; Memorabilia; Micro Print; Motion Pictures; Original Documents; Pamphlets; Photographs; Prints; Slides; Video Tapes

Special Subjects: Decorative Arts, Historical Material, Photography, Painting-American, Prints, Manuscripts, Drawings, Costumes, Dolls, Furniture
Collections: African-American history; costume; family papers; furniture; genealogy; German immigration; glass negatives; industrial heritage; local bus archives; local history; photographs; textiles; toys & dolls; Wissahickon natural area
Publications: The Germantown Crier, semiannual
Activities: Classes for adults & children; lects open to pub & mems only, 2 vis lectrs per yr; individual paintings & original objects of art lent to institutions meeting professional standards; shop sells books, magazines & original art

M **GIRARD COLLEGE,** Stephen Girard Collection, 2101 S College Ave, #116, Philadelphia, PA 19121-4857. Tel 215-787-4434; Fax 215-787-4404; Elec Mail e_laurent@girardcollege.edu; Internet Home Page Address: www.girardcollege.edu; *Dir Historical Resources* Elizabeth Laurent; *Pres* Clay Armbrister; *Vol Archivist* Gil Bunker
Open Thurs 9AM-3PM; Admis free Thurs; reserved group tours other days of wk fee charged; Estab 1848; The art and historical colls of Girard Col are housed on the second fl of Founder's Hall. Of white marble and monumental scale, the bldg is generally regarded the finest example of Greek Revival architecture in America. Designed by Thomas U Walter in 1832 and constructed 1833-1848, Founder's Hall was the school's original classroom bldg; Average Annual Attendance: 1,800
Income: Financed by endowment, grant support & donations
Library Holdings: Manuscripts; Maps; Memorabilia; Original Art Works; Original Documents; Pamphlets; Photographs; Prints; Sculpture
Special Subjects: Historical Material, Architecture, Graphics, Painting-American, Sculpture, Watercolors, Decorative Arts, Furniture, Glass, Porcelain, Silver, Period Rooms
Collections: Furniture, silver, porcelain, paintings, marble busts & statues which belonged to Stephen Girard (1750 - 1831) founder of Girard College; Philadelphia's finest single-owner coll from the early national period
Exhibitions: Continuous display in room settings
Publications: Monument to Philanthropy: The Design and Construction of Girard College 1833-47; Girard College a Living History; The Stephen Girard Collection
Activities: Classes for children

M **HIGH WIRE GALLERY,** 2040 Frankford Ave, Philadelphia, PA 19125-1921. Tel 215-829-1255; Elec Mail waring4@comcast.net; Internet Home Page Address: http://www.kenbmiller.com/highwire/; *Asst Dir* Jeff Waring; *Treas* Barbara Spadaro; *Pres* Ted Mosher; *Secy* Lisa Spera
Open Thurs noon-4PM, Fri 3PM-7PM, Sat & Sun noon-5PM; No admis fee; Estab 1985 as an independent cooperative arts & performance space; Exhibs of plastic arts & poetry, dance, music & performance in the heart of Philadelphia's Old City arts district; Average Annual Attendance: 30,000; Mem: 24; mem qualification-juried review; dues $540; meetings 1st Mon each month
Income: $13,000 (financed by mem & donation)
Exhibitions: Members Solo Exhibitions; Poets & Prophets (poetry series); This Not That (open art forum); musical & dance performances
Activities: Lect open to pub; weekly public art forums; lending coll contains individual paintings & original objects of art

L **HISTORICAL SOCIETY OF PENNSYLVANIA,** 1300 Locust St, Philadelphia, PA 19107-5699. Tel 215-732-6200; Fax 215-732-2680; Elec Mail hsppr@hsp.org; Internet Home Page Address: www.hsp.org; *Interim Pres* Page Talbott; *Dir Library* Lee Arnold; *Mem Coordr* Keith Lyons; *Ed* Tammy Miller; *Dir Archives* Matthew Lyons; *Grants Coordr* Jon-Chris Hatalski; *Dir Finance* Michael Hairston; *Communs Coordr* Lauri Cielo; *Dir Progs* Beth Twiss-Houting; *Dir Research* David Haugaard; *Dir Conservation* Tara O'Brion
Open Tues & Thurs 12:30 - 5:30 PM, Wed 12:30 - 8:30 PM, Fri 10 AM - 5:30 PM; Admis $8, students $5 to library $8 & $5; Estab 1824, the library collects & preserves documentary records relating primarily to 18th century national US history, 19th century regional Pennsylvania & 20th century Delaware Valley history, ethnic, immigration & family history; Average Annual Attendance: 11,000; Mem: 1200; dues $75; meetings once per yr
Income: (financed by endowment, mem dues & contributions)
Purchases: $49,204
Library Holdings: Auction Catalogs; Book Volumes; Clipping Files; Exhibition Catalogs; Manuscripts; Maps; Memorabilia; Original Art Works; Original Documents; Pamphlets; Periodical Subscriptions; Photographs; Prints
Special Subjects: Landscape Architecture, Photography, Drawings, Etchings & Engravings, Graphic Arts, Manuscripts, Maps, Posters, Prints, Historical Material, Portraits, Watercolors, Cartoons, Miniatures, Woodcuts, Landscapes, Reproductions, Architecture
Collections: Collection of 19 million+ manuscripts, archives, graphics from pre-Revolution through the present; Balch Institute holdings document ethnic & immigrant experience in the USA since 1877
Publications: Guide to the Manuscript Collections of the Historical Society of Pennsylvania; Pennsylvania Magazine of History & Biography, quarterly; The Historical Society of Pennsylvania in the Twentieth Century; Index to the Pennsylvania Magazine of History and Biography (vols 76-123, 1952-99); Pennsylvania Legacies, semi-annually
Activities: Lects open to the public; lects for mems; 1,000 vis lectrs per year; workshops for adults; conferences on history & historical research; orientations to documentary colls; 2 exhibits per yr; Founder's Award; sales shop sells books & magazines

M **INDEPENDENCE NATIONAL HISTORICAL PARK,** 143 S 3rd St, Philadelphia, PA 19106-2818. Tel 215-965-2305; Fax 215-861-4950; Internet Home Page Address: www.nps.gov/inde; *Chief Mus Branch* Karie Diethorn
Open daily 9 AM - 5 PM; No admis fee; Estab 1948 to preserve & protect for the American people, historical structures, properties & other resources of outstanding national significance & assoc with the Revolution & growth of the Nation; Seventeen pub buildings with 54 period rooms & 38 on-site exhibits. Maintains reference library; Average Annual Attendance: 4,500,000
Income: Financed by federal agency
Library Holdings: Auction Catalogs; Manuscripts; Original Art Works; Periodical Subscriptions
Special Subjects: Painting-American, Archaeology, Decorative Arts, Portraits, Period Rooms
Collections: 18th century American period furnishings; decorative arts; American portraits from 1740-1840
Exhibitions: Rotating exhibs
Activities: Classes for adults & children; docent training; lect open to pub, 6 vis lectrs per yr; tours; individual paintings & original objects of art lent to qualified professional institutions; mus shop sells books, magazines, reproductions, prints & slides

L **Library,** 313 Walnut St, Philadelphia, PA 19106-2705. Tel 215-597-8787; Fax 215-597-5556; Elec Mail andrea_ashley@nps.gov; Internet Home Page Address: www.nps.gov/inde; *Archivist* Karen Stevens; *Librn Technician* Andrea Ashby; *Chief Cur* Karie Diethorn; *Chief Architect* Charles Tonetti; *Pub Affairs Officer* Phil Sheridan; *Chief Historian* James Meuleer; *Chief Cultural Resources* Doris Fanelli; *Supt* Martha B Aikens; *Chief Interpretation* Chris Schillizzi
Open to pub Mon - Fri 9:30 AM - 4:30 PM by appointment only; No admis fee; Circ 300
Income: financed by federal funds
Library Holdings: Audio Tapes; Book Volumes 9500; Cassettes; Clipping Files; Exhibition Catalogs; Fiche; Kodachrome Transparencies; Manuscripts; Motion Pictures; Other Holdings Research notecard file; Pamphlets; Periodical Subscriptions 12; Photographs; Records; Reels; Slides; Video Tapes
Collections: Decorative arts of Philadelphia & Pennsylvania from the 18th century

M **INDEPENDENCE SEAPORT MUSEUM,** 211 S Columbus Blvd, Penn's Landing Philadelphia, PA 19106-3100. Tel 215-925-5439; Fax 215-925-6713; Elec Mail seaport@phillyseaport.org; Internet Home Page Address: phillyseaport.org; *Educator* William Ward; *CEO & Pres* Lori Dillard Rech; *Cur* Craig Bruns; *Colls Mgr* Sue Levy; *Controller* Rose Marine; *Dir Communs* Michele DiGirolamo; *Dir Institutional Advancement* Claire M Allamby; *Chmn* Peter McCausland
Open Mon - Sun 10 AM - 5 PM; Admis adults $12, seniors $10, children 3-12 $7, military free; Estab 1960 to preserve & interpret the maritime heritage of the Bay & River Delaware & the Ports of Philadelphia; Gallery 1, The Sea Around Us, general maritime history; Gallery 3, changing exhibits; Gallery 4 changing exhibits; Average Annual Attendance: 80,000; Mem: 700; dues $35 minimum
Income: Financed by endowment, mem & federal, pvt & corporate gifts
Library Holdings: Audio Tapes; Book Volumes; CD-ROMs; Cassettes; Clipping Files; DVDs; Exhibition Catalogs; Fiche; Filmstrips; Kodachrome Transparencies; Lantern Slides; Manuscripts; Maps; Memorabilia; Micro Print; Motion Pictures; Original Art Works; Original Documents; Other Holdings; Pamphlets; Periodical Subscriptions; Photographs; Prints; Records; Reels; Reproductions; Slides; Video Tapes
Special Subjects: Decorative Arts, Drawings, Etchings & Engravings, Folk Art, Landscapes, Ceramics, Glass, Furniture, Photography, Porcelain, Prints, Silver, Textiles, Maps, Graphics, Painting-American, Watercolors, Archaeology, Costumes, Crafts, Woodcarvings, Woodcuts, Manuscripts, Posters, Marine Painting, Historical Material, Scrimshaw, Coins & Medals, Dioramas, Embroidery, Bookplates & Bindings
Collections: Paintings by major American marine artists; Philadelphia Views; 19th-20th century maritime prints
Publications: Annual Report; books & catalogs, intermittently; Masthead, quarterly newsletter
Activities: Classes for adults & children; docent training; lects open to pub, lects for mems only; concerts; gallery talks; tours; competitions; individual paintings & original objects of art lent to recognized nonprofit museums with adequate facilities & pertinent need, six months only; mus shop sells books, reproductions & maritime related gifts

L **Library,** 211 S Columbus Blvd, ISM Archives and Library Philadelphia, PA 19106-3100. Tel 215-925-5439; Fax 215-925-6713; Elec Mail library@phillyseaport.org; Internet Home Page Address: www.phillyseaport.org; *Library Dir* Megan Good; *Colls Mgr* Josh Fox
Open by appointment only; Mus admis required; Estab 1960; Open to members & scholars, for reference only
Income: Financed by federal funding, donations
Library Holdings: Auction Catalogs; Book Volumes 15,000; Cassettes 150; Clipping Files; Exhibition Catalogs; Fiche; Kodachrome Transparencies; Lantern Slides; Manuscripts; Memorabilia; Motion Pictures; Original Art Works; Original Documents; Other Holdings Boat plans 9000, Rare books & maps; Pamphlets; Periodical Subscriptions 100; Photographs 25,000; Prints; Reels; Slides 2000
Special Subjects: Constructions, Film, Photography, Commercial Art, Drawings, Etchings & Engravings, Manuscripts, Maps, Painting-American, Posters, Prints, Historical Material, Watercolors, Archaeology, Industrial Design, Asian Art, Drafting, Silver, Marine Painting, Scrimshaw, Portraits, Textiles, Woodcarvings
Collections: Photographic file of Birch prints; photographic file of ships built by New York Shipbuilding Corp; art reference books on marine artists
Activities: Mus shop sells books, original art, reproductions, prints

M **LA SALLE UNIVERSITY ART MUSEUM,** 20th & Olney Ave, Philadelphia, PA 19141; 1900 W Olney Ave, Philadelphia, PA 19141-1199. Tel 215-951-1221; Fax 215-951-5096; Elec Mail artmuseum@lasalle.edu; Internet Home Page Address: www.lasalle.edu/museum; *Cur* Carmen Vendelin; *Cur Educ* Miranda Clark-Binder; *Dir* Klare Scarborough; *Mus Asst* Rebecca Oviedo
Open Mon - Fri 10 AM - 4 PM; cl Sat & Sun; No admis fee; Estab 1975 for educ purposes and to house the coll begun in 1965, also as support for the art history prog and as a service to the community; a collection of European & American art from the Renaissance to the present, plus special coll of non-west; Average Annual Attendance: 7,000; Mem: 150; dues $25 - $5000
Income: Financed by endowment, univ budget, grants, pub & pvt donations
Special Subjects: Etchings & Engravings, Landscapes, Ceramics, Collages, Photography, Portraits, Pre-Columbian Art, Prints, Period Rooms, Woodcuts, Painting-British, Painting-European, Painting-French, Sculpture, Drawings, Graphics, Painting-American, Watercolors, African Art, Religious Art, Pottery, Asian Art, Painting-Dutch, Baroque Art, Painting-Flemish, Renaissance Art, Painting-Italian, Antiquities-Greek, Painting-German
Collections: 15th - 21st century paintings, drawings & prints; Western, European & American art, with a few pieces of sculpture & decorative art; Japanese prints, Indian miniatures, African art, Pre-Colombian artifacts; Chinese ceramics

Exhibitions: Five special exhibs are held each year; Additional exhibitions of art produced by students & the community are held in the community gallery
Publications: La Salle Art Museum Guide to the Collection
Activities: Educ prog; classes for children; internships; lects open to pub, 3 vis lectrs per yr; gallery talks; tours; individual paintings & original objects of art lent to museums; mus shop sells reproductions

L **LIBRARY COMPANY OF PHILADELPHIA,** 1314 Locust St, Philadelphia, PA 19107-5679. Tel 215-546-3181; Fax 215-546-5167; Elec Mail cking@librarycompany.org; Internet Home Page Address: www.librarycompany.org; *Librn* James N Green; *Cur Prints* Sarah Weatherwax; *Cur African American History* Krystal Appiah; *Chief Conservation* Jennifer Woods Rosner; *Dir & CEO* John C Van Horne; *Chief Cataloguer* Holly Phelps; *Chief of Ref* Cornelia S King; *Cur Printed Books* Rachel D'Agostino
Open Mon - Fri 9 AM - 4:45 PM; No admis fee; Estab 1731 for the purpose of scholarly research; Revolving exhibits that highlight colls; Average Annual Attendance: 6,000; Mem: 750; dues $100; ann meeting in May
Income: Financed by endowment, mem, city appropriation, state & federal grants
Library Holdings: Auction Catalogs; Book Volumes 500,000; Cards; Exhibition Catalogs; Filmstrips; Framed Reproductions; Maps; Memorabilia; Original Art Works; Pamphlets; Periodical Subscriptions 60; Photographs; Prints; Sculpture
Special Subjects: Art History, Landscape Architecture, Drawings, Etchings & Engravings, Manuscripts, Historical Material, History of Art & Archaeology, Judaica, Cartoons, Fashion Arts, Afro-American Art, Bookplates & Bindings, Landscapes, Coins & Medals, Architecture
Collections: American Printing; Philadelphia prints, watercolors, drawings and photography; collection of Americana; paintings, sculpture, decorative arts
Publications: Annual Report; Occasional Miscellany, 2 times per year; exhibition catalogs
Activities: Lect open to pub; 10 vis lects per yr; gallery talks; tours; fel; individual & original objects of art lent to museums, libraries & cultural institutions; sale of books & publs

L **LUTHERAN THEOLOGICAL SEMINARY,** Krauth Memorial Library, 7301 Germantown Ave, Philadelphia, PA 19119-1794. Tel 215-248-4616; Fax 215-248-4577; Elec Mail lutthelib@ltsp.edu; Internet Home Page Address: www.ltsp.edu/krauth; *Head Pub Serv* Darren Poley; *Head Technical Servs* Lois Reibach; *Cur Archives* John E Peterson; *Dir Library* Karl Krueger
Open Mon-Fri 9AM-5PM, during acad sessions, Mon-Thurs 5PM-10PM, summer Mon-Fri 8:30AM-5PM, June intensive Tues & Thurs 6:30PM-9:30PM; Estab 1906
Library Holdings: Audio Tapes; Book Volumes 185,000; Cassettes; Filmstrips; Kodachrome Transparencies; Lantern Slides; Manuscripts; Memorabilia; Original Art Works; Periodical Subscriptions 570; Records; Reproductions; Slides; Video Tapes
Special Subjects: Religious Art, Architecture
Collections: Liturgical arts; Modern Prints; Rentschler Collection of Last Supper Art; Schreiber Collection of Numismatic Art on Martin Luther & the Reformation
Exhibitions: 20 Religious Artists

M **MOORE COLLEGE OF ART & DESIGN,** The Galleries at Moore, 20th & The Parkway, Philadelphia, PA 19103. Tel 215-965-4027; Fax 215-568-5921; Elec Mail galleries@moore.edu; Internet Home Page Address: thegalleriesatmoore.org; *Dir & Chief Cur* Kaytie Johnson; *Gallery Mgr* Gabrielle Lavin; *Outreach & Pub Progs Coordr* Elizabeth Gilly
Open Mon - Thurs 11 AM - 5 PM, Fri 11 AM - 8 PM, Sat 11 AM - 5 PM, cl Sun, acad & legal holidays; No admis fee; Estab 1984 to display contemporary art, photog, design & works by Moore's faculty & students; Gallery is housed in moderate exhib space with flexible panels to accommodate current exhibit; Average Annual Attendance: 35,000
Income: Financed by endowment, government & foundation grants, individual & corporate donation
Special Subjects: Architecture, Drawings, Photography, Sculpture, Watercolors, Textiles, Ceramics, Crafts, Folk Art, Portraits
Exhibitions: William Daley; Hanne Darboven; Marlene Dumas, Terry Fox; Valie Export; Dan Graham; Benedetta Cappa Marmetti; Jean-Frederic Schnyder; Pat Ward Williams; Rosamond Purcell; Mary Cassatt; Alice Neel; Karen Kilimnik; Faith Ringgold; Lisa Kereszi; Anthony Campuzano; Artur Barrio; Andrea Baldeck; Mary McFadden; Sarah McEneaney; Deb Sokolow
Publications: Catalogs for major exhibitions; exhibition brochures & gallery notes
Activities: lect open to pub, 6 vis lectrs per yr; gallery talks; tours; book signings; films; performances; symposia; originate traveling exhibs to other univ galleries & small exhib spaces in large museums throughout US & Canada

L **Library,** 20th & The Parkway, Philadelphia, PA 19103. Tel 215-965-4054; Fax 215-965-8544; Elec Mail amacrina@moore.edu; Internet Home Page Address: library.moore.edu; *Slide Cur* Helen F McGinnis; *AV Specialist* Chuck Duguense; *Archivist* Annabelle Curran; *Cataloging Librn* Elisa Graydon; *Lib Dir* Sharon Watson-Mauro
Open Mon - Thurs 8 AM - 10 PM, Fri 8 AM - 5 PM, Sat 8:30 AM - 5 PM, for student use; pub use Mon - Fri 8:30 - 10 PM & by appointment; Circ privileges $15/yr, alumni only; Estab to serve Moore staff & students; Circ 17,752; For lending & reference; Average Annual Attendance: 30,000
Purchases: $37,000
Library Holdings: Audio Tapes; Book Volumes 40,000; Cassettes; Clipping Files; DVDs; Exhibition Catalogs; Filmstrips; Lantern Slides; Manuscripts; Memorabilia; Motion Pictures; Original Art Works In archives; Original Documents In archives; Other Holdings Picture files; Periodical Subscriptions 230; Photographs; Prints; Records; Reproductions; Slides 117,000; Video Tapes
Collections: Sartain Family Collection; Bookworks Artists Books Collection
Activities: Classes for adults and children; lect open to pub; gallery talks; tours

M **MUSE ART GALLERY,** 52 N Second St, Philadelphia, PA 19106. Tel 215-627-5310; Elec Mail muse1arts@musegalleryphiladelphia.com; Internet Home Page Address: www.musegalleryphiladelphia.com; *Dir* Dr Nancy Halbert
Open Wed - Sun noon- 5 PM; Estab 1970 as an art cooperative exhibiting members works; Gallery is a co-op; Average Annual Attendance: 2,500; Mem: 15; qualifications: professional exhibiting or emerging artist; dues $600; monthly meetings
Income: Financed by mem, sales commissions, Pennsylvania State Council of the Arts & pvt contributions
Exhibitions: Mems & community-oriented exhibs
Publications: Catalogues; MUSE Gallery and Her Own Space
Activities: Art consultant prog; lects open to pub, 2 vis lectrs per yr; poetry readings; competitions; originate international traveling exhibs; original art for sale

M **PAINTED BRIDE ART CENTER GALLERY,** 230 Vine St, Philadelphia, PA 19106-1293. Tel 215-925-9914; Fax 215-925-7402; Elec Mail info@paintedbride.org; Internet Home Page Address: www.paintedbride.org; *Exec Dir* Laurel Raczka; *Assoc Dir* Lisa Nelson-Haynes; *Audience Serv Mgr* Rai Nelson; *Music Cur* Lenny Seidman; *Dir Develop* Cheryl Carson; *Mktg Coordr* LaNeshe Miller White
Open Tues - Sat noon - 6 PM; No admis fee; Estab 1968, forum for work outside traditional channels to present interdisciplinary work; Average Annual Attendance: 27,000; Mem: 350
Collections: Contemporary Art & Theater; Contemporary Art; Theater
Activities: Educ workshops for all ages; lects open to pub; concerts; gallery talks; tours; exten prog serves Philadelphia & suburbs; sales shop sells books & original art

M **PENNSYLVANIA ACADEMY OF THE FINE ARTS,** 118 N Broad St, Philadelphia, PA 19102. Tel 215-972-7600; Fax 215-569-0153; Elec Mail pafa@pafa.org; Internet Home Page Address: www.pafa.org; *Chmn Bd* Kevin Donohoe; *Pres* David Brigham; *Exec VPres* Melissa DeRuiter; *Sr Cur* Robert Cozzolino; *Mus Registrar* Gale Rawson; *Dir Retail Sales* Mark DeLelys; *Chief Conservator* Aella Diamantopoulos; *Dir Mktg & Communs* Marsha Braverman; *Mus Dir* Harry Philbrick
Open Tues - Sat 10 AM - 5 PM, Sun 11 AM - 5 PM; Admis adults $10, seniors & students $8, youth 13-18 $6, child 12 & under no admis fee; Estab 1805 by Charles Willson Peale to cultivate collecting, training & development of the fine arts in America; The Academy Building, opened in 1876, was restored for the American Bicentennial. Considered the masterpiece of its architect, Philadelphian Frank Furness, its style is called, alternatively, polychrome picturesque & High or Gothic Victorian. It was designated a Registered National Historic Landmark in 1975. The School Gallery features faculty & student exhibs; Average Annual Attendance: 75,000; Mem: 3000; dues $40 - 10,000
Income: Financed by endowment, mem, city & state appropriations, contributions & federal grants
Special Subjects: Architecture, Graphics, Painting-American, Prints, Sculpture, Bronzes, Woodcarvings, Woodcuts, Etchings & Engravings, Landscapes, Afro-American Art, Collages, Portraits, Posters, Marine Painting, Historical Material, Coins & Medals, Tapestries
Collections: American contemporary works; 18th, 19th & early 20th century American paintings, sculpture, drawings & prints, including Allston, West, the Peale Family, Stuart, Sully, Rush, Neagle, Mount, Eakins, Cassatt, Homer, Hopper, Hassam, Carles, Bellows, Henri, Beaux, Pippin
Publications: Annual report; Calendar of Events; exhibition & school catalogues; quarterly newsletter
Activities: Classes for adults & children; docent training; lect open to pub, 50 vis lectrs per yr; concerts; gallery talks; tours; competitions with awards; schols offered; exten dept serves senior citizens; original objects of art lent to other institutions, the White House, the Governor of Pennsylvania & embassies abroad; book traveling exhibs 2-3 per yr; originate traveling exhibs; mus shop sells books, magazines, reproductions, prints, slides, ceramics, games, stationery, jewelry, toys & pottery

L **Library,** 1301 Cherry St, Philadelphia, PA 19107; 118 North Broad St, Philadelphia, PA 19107. Tel 215-972-7600, Ext 2030; Fax 215-569-0153; Elec Mail library@pafa.org; Internet Home Page Address: www.library.pafa.org; *Librn* Aurora Deshauteurs
Open Mon - Fri 8:30AM-7PM, Sat 10AM-4PM; Admis by appointment; Estab 1805, the library serves students of painting, sculpture, printmaking & research in American Art; Open to pub for reference
Income: Financed by school funds
Library Holdings: Book Volumes 13,500; Clipping Files; Exhibition Catalogs; Periodical Subscriptions 82; Slides; Video Tapes

L **Archives,** 118 N Broad St, Philadelphia, PA 19102-1598. Tel 215-972-7600, ext 2066; Fax 215-567-2429; Elec Mail archives@pafa.org; Internet Home Page Address: www.pafa.org; *Archivist* Cheryl Leibold
Open weekdays 9:30AM-4:30PM by appointment only for researchers; No admis fee
Library Holdings: Audio Tapes; Clipping Files; Exhibition Catalogs; Filmstrips; Kodachrome Transparencies; Lantern Slides; Manuscripts; Memorabilia; Other Holdings Artifacts; Pamphlets; Photographs; Slides; Video Tapes
Collections: Charles Bregler's Thomas Eakins Collection, consisting of more than 1000 art objects & documents
Publications: Brochure about the archives; Index to Annual Exhibitions, 3 vols

A **Fellowship of the Pennsylvania Academy of the Fine Arts,** 321 Greenbank Rd, Bryn Mawr, PA 19010. Tel 610-520-9286; Internet Home Page Address: www.pafafellowship.org; *Pres* Hilarie V Hawley
Estab 1897 to provide opportunities for creative incentive & sharing in responsibilities for the development of facilities & activities in the field of art for its members & to maintain relations with the students of the Pennsylvania Academy of the Fine Arts; Mem: 200; dues $35
Income: $20,000 (financed by mem & investments)
Purchases: $1000 (art collection & operating expenses)
Special Subjects: Sculpture
Exhibitions: Annual Fellowship Show; Juried Members Exhibition
Publications: Perspective magazine, 3 times yr
Activities: lect; awards; juried student exhibs; individual paintings & original objects of art lent to schools, library & other pub institutions; lending coll contains original art works, original prints, paintings, photographs, sculpture

A **PHILADELPHIA ART ALLIANCE,** 251 S 18th St, Philadelphia, PA 19103-6168. Tel 215-545-4305; Fax 215-545-0767; Elec Mail info@philartalliance.org; Internet Home Page Address: www.philartalliance.org; *Pres* Carole Price Shanis; *Dir Exhibs* Melissa Caldwell; *Exec Dir* Molly Dougherty
Galleries open Tues - Sun 11 AM - 5 PM, cl Mon; Suggested donation $5 adults,

$3 seniors; Contemporary craft design; 3 fls of exhib space; Average Annual Attendance: 20,000; Mem: 300; both artist & non-artist categories are available; dues $75-$5000

Income: Financed by mem, board & corporate, foundation & pvt contributions

Library Holdings: Auction Catalogs; Cards; Exhibition Catalogs

Special Subjects: Metalwork, Porcelain, Textiles, Pottery, Ceramics, Crafts, Glass, Jewelry

Collections: Collection of archives to 1980 are located at Univ of Pa Library

Exhibitions: 3 exhibs annually

Publications: Quarterly newsletter & exhib catalogs

Activities: Lects open to pub; concerts; gallery talks; 10 vis lectrs per yr

A   PHILADELPHIA ART COMMISSION, 1515 Arch St, 13th Floor Philadelphia, PA 19102. Tel 215-683-2095; Fax 215-683-2105; *Exec Dir* William J Burke; *Pres* William L Wilson

Open 8:30 AM - 5 PM; No admis fee; Estab 1911 under Philadelphia Home Rule Charter as the Art Jury, later retitled Art Commission. An Art Ordinance passed in 1959 provides for art work in city buildings and on city owned property; The Art Commission reviews architectural designs and art work covering all media for municipal locations or other locations in which municipal funds are expended. The Art Commission's files are open to inspection by anyone since the information contained therein qualifies as public information. As indicated, the material deals solely with art proposals and architectural designs. Designs cover all buildings, major highways, and bridges; Mem: 9; between 20 and 24 meetings annually

Income: Financed by city appropriation

M   PHILADELPHIA HISTORY MUSEUM, (Atwater Kent Museum of Philadelphia) 15 S Seventh St, Philadelphia, PA 19106. Tel 215-685-4830; Fax 215-685-4837; Elec Mail info@philadelphiahistory.org; Internet Home Page Address: www.philadelphiahistory.org; *Sr Cur* Jeffrey Ray; *Acting Exec Dir* Christine Davis; *Dir of Coll* Kristen Froehlich; *Historian, Dir Interpretive Programming* Cynthia Little

See website for hours; Admis varies, see website; Estab 1938. The mus is dedicated to the history of Philadelphia; Renovations in 2009 - 2010 made room for additional gallery space for exhibition of 100,000+ item coll; Mem: dues $40 - $1000

Income: $1.2 million (financed by grants, contributions, earned revenue & city support

Special Subjects: Decorative Arts, Drawings, Etchings & Engravings, Historical Material, Metalwork, Flasks & Bottles, Photography, Porcelain, Painting-American, Silver, Graphics, Sculpture, Watercolors, Textiles, Costumes, Ceramics, Folk Art, Portraits, Dolls, Furniture, Glass, Maps, Coins & Medals, Embroidery

Collections: Artifacts of the colonial city; costumes; print & painting coll; manufactured & trade goods; maritime artifacts; toys & dolls; ceramics & glassware; urban archaeology; Art & Artifact Coll of the Historical Society of PA

Exhibitions: Traveling Neighborhood Exhibits; Experience Philadelphia; How Philly Works

Publications: Historically Speaking

Activities: Classes for children; dramatic progs; after-school prog; lect open to pub; 4-6 vis lectrs per yr; gallery talks; media events; tours; 1500 original art works, 2500 original prints, 100 paintings available on loan to museums with adequate security systems; originates traveling exhibs to community organizations & schools; mus shop sells books, prints & Philadelphia products

M   PHILADELPHIA MUSEUM OF ART, Main Building, 26th & Benjamin Franklin Pkwy, Philadelphia, PA 19130; PO Box 7646, Philadelphia, PA 19101-7646. Tel 215-763-8100; Fax 215-236-4465; Elec Mail visitorservices@philamuseum.org; Internet Home Page Address: www.philamuseum.org; *The George D Widener Dir & CEO* Anne d'Harnoncourt; *COO* Gail Harrity; *Dir* Cheryl McClenney-Brooker; *McNeil Cur American Art* Kathy Fostor; *Sr Cur Prints, Drawings & Photographs* Innis Shoemaker; *Cur Drawings* Ann B Percy; *Cur Educ* Marla Shoemaker; *Registrar* Irene Taurins; *Spec Exhibs Coordr* Suzanne Wells; *Dir Develop* Betty Marmon; *Assoc Dir Colls & Project Support* Alice Beamesdofer; *Cur American Decorative Arts* David Barquist

Open Tues -Sun 10 AM - 5 PM, Fri until 8:45 PM for select galleries, cl Mon, July 4, Thanksgiving Day & Christmas Day; Admis adults $16, seniors $14, students & children 13-18 $12, mems & children 12 & under free; special exhib fees apply; Estab 1876 as an art mus & for art educ; known as Pennsylvania Mus of Art until the present name was adopted in 1938; Museum founded in 1876; buildings owned by the City, opened 1928; wings 1931 & 1940; fashion galleries 1949, 1951 & 1953; Gallatin & Arensberg Collections 1954; Far Eastern Wing 1957; decorative arts galleries 1958; Charles Patterson Van Pelt Auditorium 1959; Nepalese-Tibetan Gallery 1960; new galleries of Italian & French Renaissance Art 1960; American Wing, galleries of contemporary painting, sculpture & decorative arts & special exhibs galleries 1976; Alfred Stieglitz Center of Photography 1978; print & drawing gallery 1979; 19th century decorative arts galleries 1980 & 1981. Mus contains 200 galleries; Average Annual Attendance: 800,000; Mem: 50,000; dues $25 - $50,000

Income: $46,000,000 (financed by endowment, mem, city & state appropriations, grants, bequests & auxiliary activities)

Special Subjects: Architecture, Painting-American, Folk Art, Painting-European, Furniture, Glass, Porcelain, Oriental Art, Asian Art, Period Rooms

Collections: Indian sculpture & miniature painting & the installation of 16th century South Indian temple; Chinese & Southwest Asian sculpture, ceramics & decorative arts from the Crozier, Crofts, Williams, McIlhenny, Thompson & other colls, with installations of a Ming period Chinese palace hall & temple & a Ch'ing scholar's study; Japanese scroll paintings, prints & decorative arts, with installations of a tea house & a 14th century temple; Himalayan sculpture & painting; Middle Eastern tile, miniatures & decorative arts from the White & other colls; Oriental carpets from the McIlhenny, Williams & other colls; Pre-Columbian sculpture & artifacts from the Arensberg Colls; Medieval & Renaissance sculpture, painting & decorative arts from the Foulc, Barnard & other colls; installations of a Gothic chapel, Romanesque cloister, French Renaissance choir screen & period rooms; Kienbusch Collection of Arms & Armor; French, Dutch, English & Italian painting & decorative arts of the 14th-19th centuries, from the Wilstach, Elkins,

McFadden, Tyson, John G Johnson, McIlhenny, Coxe-Wright & other colls; Italian, Dutch & French drawings from the Clark & other colls; French & English 17th & 18th century decorative arts from the Rice, Bloomfield-Moore & other colls, with period rooms; French & English art-nouveau decorative arts; costume & textiles from all periods of western & eastern art, including the Whitman sampler coll; American colls include painting, sculpture & decorative arts from the colonial era to the present, with period rooms, Philadelphia furniture & silver, Tucker porcelain, Lorimer Glass Collection & the Geesey Collection of Pennsylvania German folk art; 20th century painting, sculpture & works on paper from the Gallatin, Arensberg, Tyson, White, Stern, Stieglitz, Zigrosser, Greenfield, Woodward & other colls; Ars Medica Collection of prints on the subject of sickness & healing from all periods of western art; Alfred Stieglitz Center Collection of Photography; 20th century decorative arts; Stiegal Glass

Publications: Bulletin, quarterly; exhibs catalogs; members' magazine, semi-annually; monthly calendar

Activities: Classes for adults, children & families; guide & docent training; symposia; concerts; lect open to pub; concerts; gallery talks, films; tours; originates traveling exhibs; mus shops sells books, magazines, reproductions, prints, slides, jewelry, needlework & postcards; art sales & rental gallery

M   Rodin Museum of Philadelphia, 2600 Benjamin Franklin Pkwy at 22nd St, Philadelphia, PA 19130-2302; PO Box 7646, Philadelphia, PA 19101-7646. Tel 215-568-6026; Fax 215-763-8955; Elec Mail jvanim@philamuseum.org; Internet Home Page Address: www.rodinmuseum.org; *Cur of Pre-1900 European Painting & Sculpture* Joseph Rishel; *Assoc Cur* Jennifer Thompson

Open Tues - Sun 10 AM - 5 PM, cl Mon & holidays; No admis fee, suggested donation $3; Estab 1926; Rodin Mus of Philadelphia houses one of the largest colls outside of Paris of works by the major late 19th Century French sculptor, Auguste Rodin; Average Annual Attendance: 60,000

Special Subjects: Sculpture

Collections: Coll includes many of the most famous sculptures created by Rodin, as well as drawings, prints, letters, books & a variety of documentary material; The Thinker; The Gates of Hell; The Burghers of Calais; Eternal Springtime; Apotheosis of Victor Hugo

Exhibitions: Rotating exhibits

Activities: Classes for adults & children; docent training; concerts; gallery talks; tours; lending of original objects of art to other museums for exhibs; mus shop sells books, reproductions, slides, cards & memorabilia; audio tour, prints

M   Mount Pleasant, Fairmount Park, Philadelphia, PA 19101; PO Box 7646, Philadelphia, PA 19101-7646. Tel 215-763-8100; Elec Mail visitorservices@philamuseum.org; Internet Home Page Address: www.philamuseum.org; *Cur American Decorative Arts* Jack Lindsey; *Mgr Vol Servs* Caroline T Gladstone; *Admin Asst* Deborah W Troemner

Open Tues-Sun 10AM-5PM, cl major holidays; Admis adults $5, seniors $3, children 6-12 $2, mems & children under 6 free; Historic house built in 1761; an outstanding example of the Georgian style in 18th century building & woodcarving; installed with period furnishings

Collections: Period furnishings from the mus represent the elegant way of life in Philadelphia in the 1760s

Activities: Tours

M   Cedar Grove, Cedar Grove Mansion Fairmount Park, Lansdowne Dr Philadelphia, PA 19101; PO Box 7646, Philadelphia, PA 19101-7646. Tel 215-763-8100; Elec Mail visitorservices@philamuseum.org; Internet Home Page Address: www.philamuseum.org;

Open Tues - Sun 10 AM - 5 PM, cl Mon; Admis adults $5, seniors $3, children ages 6-12 $2, mems & children under 6 free; This Quaker farmhouse built as a country retreat in 1748 was moved stone by stone to Fairmount Park in 1928 & restored with the furnishings of the five generations of Quakers who lived in it

Collections: The furniture was given with the house & reflects changes in styles through the 17th, 18th & 19th centuries

Activities: Tours

M   John G Johnson Collection, Parkway & 26th, Philadelphia, PA 18101; PO Box 7646, Philadelphia, PA 19101-7646. Tel 215-684-7615, 7610; Fax 215-763-8955; Elec Mail jvanim@philamuseum.org; Internet Home Page Address: www.philamuseum.org; *Adjunct Cur* Carl B Strehlke; *Cur* Joseph Rishel; *Assoc Cur* Lloyd DeWitt

Open Tues - Sun 10 AM - 5 PM; Admis to Philadelphia Mus of Art $16, senior $14, students with ID $12; Upon his death in 1917, prominent Philadelphia lawyer, John Graver Johnson left his extensive coll intact to the city of Philadelphia; since 1933 the coll has been housed in the Philadelphia Mus of Art; admin & trusteeship of the coll is maintained separately from the other colls in the mus

Income: Financed by trust, contributions city of Philadelphia & Philadelphia Mus of Art

Special Subjects: Portraits, Painting-British, Painting-European, Painting-French, Religious Art, Painting-Dutch, Painting-Flemish, Renaissance Art, Painting-Italian, Painting-German

Collections: Early & later Italian Renaissance paintings; French 19th century paintings; northern European schools of Flanders, Holland & Germany in the 15th, 16th & 17th centuries

Exhibitions: In house exhibs featuring works from permanent coll

Publications: Several catalogs for various parts of the collection including Catalog of Italian Paintings & Catalog of Flemish & Dutch Paintings

Activities: Special lect & related activities; occasional lending of collection to significant exhibitions; lending of original objects of art to other museums; mus shop sells books, reproductions

M   Samuel S Fleisher Art Memorial, 719 Catharine St, Philadelphia, PA 19147-2811. Tel 215-922-3456; Fax 215-922-5327; Elec Mail info@fleisher.org; Internet Home Page Address: www.fleisher.org; *Exec Dir* Matthew Braun; *Dir Educ & Community Engagement* Magda Martinez; *Dir Develop & Fin* Meg Wise; *Exhib Coordr* Jong Kyu Kim; *Mgr Adult Progs* Kathleen Ogilvie Greene; *Mgr Children & Youth Progs* Anne Harrison; *Mgr Vis Svcs & Rentals Coordr* Nicole Krom; *Mktg Communs Coordr* Eileen Owens

Open during exhibs Mon - Fri 11 AM - 5 PM, Mon - Thurs 6:30 - 9:30 PM, Sat 10AM - 3 PM; No admis fee; Estab 1898 as a free art school & sanctuary (Mus of Religious Art); Comprised of 4 bldgs: the Sanctuary, the St Martin's College bldg, & 2 three-story row houses. Permanent colls are housed in the Sanctuary, an Italian Romanesque Revival building designed by Louis C Baker & E James Dallett of Furness & Evans; Maintains Dene M Louchheim Galleries & Suzanne

Leisher & Ralph Joel Roberts Gallery. Administered by Philadelphia Museum of Art; Average Annual Attendance: 8,000; Mem: 2,800; mem contribution $25 per term
Income: $650,000 (financed by estate income, mem, materials fees, grants & gifts)
Collections: Medieval & Renaissance religious paintings & sculpture; 18th-19th century Portuguese liturgical objects; 17th-20th century Russian icons; some sculpture
Exhibitions: Challenge Series, ann schedule of four exhibs featuring work by Philadelphia area artists; annual student, faculty, adult & childrens' exhibs; occasional special subject exhibs
Activities: Classes for adults & children; workshops; lect open to pub, 4 vis lectrs per yr; concerts; gallery talks; tours; competitions; sales shop sells art materials & books

L **Library & Archives,** 2525 Pennsylvania Ave, Perelman Bldg Philadelphia, PA 19130; PO Box 7646, Philadelphia, PA 19101-7646. Tel 215-684-7650; Fax 215-236-0534; Elec Mail library@philamuseum.org; Internet Home Page Address: www.philamuseum.org/library; *Arcadia Dir Libr & Archives* Danial Elliott; *Librn Collection Develop* Mary S Wassermann; *Archivist* Susan K Anderson; *Librn Reader Svcs* Evan Towle; *Asst Reader Svc Librn* Richard Sieber; *Project Archivist* Bertha Adams; *Asst Cataloger* Ryan McNally; *Asst Library Dir* Billy Chi Hing Kwan
Open Tues - Fri 10 AM - 4 PM, Sat mid Sept- mid May 10AM-4PM; Estab 1876 as research library for mus staff, members & scholars (appointments recommended); Circ 10,282; For reference only
Library Holdings: Auction Catalogs; Book Volumes 220,000; Clipping Files; Exhibition Catalogs; Fiche; Manuscripts; Original Documents; Other Holdings Digital Images; Pamphlets; Periodical Subscriptions 450; Photographs; Reels; Slides
Special Subjects: Art History, Decorative Arts, Photography, Drawings, Etchings & Engravings, Painting-American, Prints, Painting-European, Ceramics, Conceptual Art, Latin American Art, Fashion Arts, Asian Art, Period Rooms, Costume Design & Constr, Glass, Enamels, Gold, Jewelry, Miniatures, Silver, Textiles
Collections: Albert M Greenfield Visual & Digital Resources Ctr: 200,000+ digital images & slides
Activities: Lect open to pub; one vis lectr per yr

A **Women's Committee,** PO Box 7646, Philadelphia, PA 19101-7646. Tel 215-684-7931; Fax 215-236-8320; Elec Mail info@twcpma.org; twcpma@philamuseum.org; Internet Home Page Address: twcpma.org; *Exec Dir* Nancy G O'Meara; *Pres* Judy Pote
Open Mon - Fri 9 AM - 5 PM; Estab 1883, inc 1915; takes an active interest in the mus; Organization sponsors Art Sales & Rental Gallery, park houses & mus guides, The Philadelphia Mus of Art Craft Show, classes for blind artists & tours for the deaf; Mem: 45
Income: Financed by fund raising events

M **Ruth & Raymond G Perelman Building,** Fairmount & Pennsylvania Aves, Philadelphia, PA 19130; PO Box 7646, Philadelphia, PA 19101-7646. Tel 215-763-8100; Elec Mail visitorservices@philamuseum.org; Internet Home Page Address: www.philamuseum.org
Open Tues - Sun 10 AM - 5 PM; Admis adults $8, seniors $7, students & children 13-18 $6, mems & children 12 & under free; special exhib fees apply; Newly renovated & expanded, bldg is the first phase of enhancement & modernization of Philadelphia Mus of Art

A **PHILADELPHIA SKETCH CLUB,** 235 S Camac St, Philadelphia, PA 19107-5609. Tel 215-545-9298; Elec Mail info@sketchclub.org; Internet Home Page Address: www.sketchclub.org; *Pres* William C Patterson; *VPres* Richard A Harrington; *Treas* Frank Foster; *Secy* Elizabeth Azzolina; *Exec Dir* Barbara Murray
Open Mon & Wed and Fri-Sun 1PM-5PM; No admis fee; Estab 1860 to promote the creation & appreciation of the visual arts; 30 ft X 40 ft with skylight & spotlights; Average Annual Attendance: 19,000; Mem: 225; applicants must be proposed by two mems & show portfolio of their artwork to Board of Dir; dues $150; monthly meetings 2nd Fri of each month
Income: Financed by mem, grants & fundraising activities
Special Subjects: Cartoons, Drawings, Etchings & Engravings, Graphics, Landscapes, Metalwork, Photography, Posters, Prints, Sculpture, Watercolors, Painting-American, Stained Glass, Bronzes, Woodcuts, Portraits, Woodcarvings, Marine Painting, Coins & Medals
Collections: Permanent collection is from past & present members, oils, watercolors, etchings; forty-four Thomas Anshutz Portraits; J Pennell Lithographs
Exhibitions: Approximately 15 exhibs per yr
Publications: The Portfolio, (bulletin), monthly
Activities: Classes for adults; life classes; 5 art workshops per wk; lect open to pub, 9 vis lectrs per yr; gallery talks; tours; competitions with cash awards; individual paintings & original objects of art lent to art museums who have exhibs of PSC past mems; lending coll contains original prints, paintings & sculptures

M **PHILADELPHIA UNIVERSITY,** (Philadelphia College of Textiles & Science) Paley Design Center, 4201 Henry Ave, Philadelphia, PA 19144-5497. Tel 215-951-2860; Fax 215-951-2662; Internet Home Page Address: www.philadelphia.edu
Open Tues - Fri 10 AM - 4 PM; No admis fee; free guided tour by reservation; Estab 1978 to promote knowledge & appreciation of textiles & their design; Three galleries; small library of textile & costume subjects available to scholars & mems
Income: Financed by PU&S & grants from the PCA, pvt & individual foundations
Special Subjects: Textiles, Costumes
Collections: Costumes - 18th to 20th centuries; historic & contemporary textiles 1st - 20th centuries, International; Manufacturers' fabric swatches 19th & 20th centuries, American & Western European; manuscripts, records, textile fibers, tools & related materials
Publications: The Art of the Textile Blockmaker; Floribunda: The Evolution of Floral Design on Fabrics; Flowers of the Yayla, Yoruk Weaving of the Toros Mountains; The Philadelphia System of Textile Manufacture 1884 - 1984
Activities: Mus shop sells unique works by craft artists in jewelry, pottery, glass, wood, paper & textiles; ann holiday crafts market

A **PLASTIC CLUB,** Art Club, 247 S Camac St, Philadelphia, PA 19107-5609. Tel 215-545-9324; Elec Mail plasticclub@att.net; Internet Home Page Address: plasticclub.org; *Pres* Cynthia Arkin; *1st VPres* Bob Jackson; *Treas* Jane J Wilkie; *Corresp Secy* Eileen Eckstein; *Recording Secy* Janice Moore; *2nd VPres* Alan J Klawans; *Exhib Chair* Susan Stromquist; *3rd VPres* Michael Guinn
Open Tues 9:30 AM - 12:30 PM, Wed - Thurs 10 AM - 1 PM, Thurs evening 6:30 PM - 9:30 PM, Fri evening 6:30 PM - 9:30 PM, Sat 1 PM - 4 PM & by appointment; No admis fee; Estab 1897 to promote wider knowledge of art and to advance its interest among artists; Two historic homes provide space for exhibits & a studio; Average Annual Attendance: 3,000; Mem: 180; must qualify for mem by submitting three framed paintings or other works of art to be juried; dues $60; assn mems (non-exhibiting) $40; ann meeting in May; work juried by board of dir for active membership; no jurying for assoc
Income: Financed by mem, donations, gifts & money-making projects
Library Holdings: Book Volumes; Exhibition Catalogs; Manuscripts; Memorabilia; Original Art Works; Original Documents; Pamphlets; Photographs; Records
Special Subjects: Drawings, Historical Material, Landscapes, Posters, Watercolors, Painting-American, Portraits
Collections: American Women artists; Art History; Printmaking; paintings & posters
Exhibitions: Monthly exhibs of paintings by mems & invited artists; Open Works on Paper; Open Show All Media; workshop & various theme exhibs
Publications: Calendar of Events, 3 times a year; newsletter, 4 times per yr
Activities: Classes for adults; workshops open to mems & pub; lects open to pub; 4-5 vis lects per yr; competitions with awards; exhib prizes; ann Plastic Club Gold & Silver medals; contains original art works, original prints, paintings

M **PLEASE TOUCH MUSEUM,** 4231 Ave of the Republic, Memorial Hall & Fairmount Park Philadelphia, PA 19103-3719. Tel 215-581-3181; Fax 215-581-3182; Elec Mail info@pleasetouchmuseum.org; Internet Home Page Address: www.pleasetouchmuseum.org; *Pres & CEO* Laura Foster; *Exec VPres* Lynn McMaster; *VPres Develop* Stephanie Capello; *VPres Opers* John McDevitt; *VPres Educ & Family Learning* Trapeta Mason; *VPres Finance* Michael Armento; *VPres External Affairs* Joe Costello; *VPres Community Progs* Leslie Walker
Open Mon-Sat 9 AM - 5PM, Sun 11AM-5PM, cl Thanksgiving, Christmas & New Year's Day; Admis $16; Estab 1976 & accredited by American Assoc of Museums (1986) to provide a developmentally appropriate mus for young children, their parents & teachers; Gallery spaces are small-scaled, objects are accessible; two-tiered interpretation for adults coming with children (arts, crafts, ethnic materials & childlife exhibits); Average Annual Attendance: 600,000; Mem: 14,000; family of 4 $150, family of 6 $180, family of 6 with extra benefits $220
Income: $1,600,000 (financed by earned income: admis, store receipts, program fees; contributions, mem, governmental appropriations, foundations, corporate support & individuals)
Special Subjects: Maps, Costumes, Crafts, Dolls, Restorations
Collections: Contemporary American toys, artifacts & archives documenting American childhood; art works by contemporary artists, sculpture, environmental, paintings & crafts; cultural artifacts from around the world: costumes, playthings, musical instruments, objects from daily life: Materials from the natural sciences
Exhibitions: Wonderland; City Capers; Flight Fantasy; Roadside Attractions; Centennial Exploration; Liberty Arm & Torch; River Adventures; Woodside Park: Dentzel Carousel
Publications: Annual report; The Please Touch Museum Cookbook; quarterly newsletter; thematic exhib catalog, biannual
Activities: Workshops for adults & children; theater progs; docent training; work with area colleges, universities & art schools; coop progs; lect open to pub, 3 vis lectrs per yr; concerts; tours; competitions with awards; original objects of art lent; lending coll contains art works, sculpture & artifacts concerning childhood; originate traveling exhibs; mus shop sells books, toys, arts & crafts kits, souvenirs

THE PRINT CENTER
For further information, see National and Regional Organizations

M **THE ROSENBACH MUSEUM & LIBRARY,** 2008-2010 DeLancey Pl, Rosenbach Foundation Philadelphia, PA 19103-6510. Tel 215-732-1600; Fax 215-545-7529; Elec Mail info@rosenbach.org; Internet Home Page Address: www.rosenbach.org; *Dir* Derick Dreher; *Librn* Elizabeth E Fuller; *Mgr External Relations* Alice Emerson
Open Tues & Fri 12 PM - 5 PM, Wed& Thurs 12 PM - 8 PM, Sat & Sun 12 PM - 6PM; Open for research: Wed & Thurs 10:30 AM - 6 PM, Fri 10:30 AM - 4:30 PM; Admis adults $10, seniors $8, students & children $5, children 5 and under no charge; Estab 1953 as a nonprofit corporation; Changing exhibitions based on collections; Average Annual Attendance: 80,000; Mem: approx. 600 members
Library Holdings: Book Volumes; Exhibition Catalogs; Manuscripts; Maps; Memorabilia; Original Art Works; Photographs; Prints; Sculpture
Special Subjects: Photography, Drawings, Prints, Judaica, Manuscripts, Porcelain, Silver, Painting-British, Carpets & Rugs, Miniatures, Antiquities-Egyptian
Collections: 18th & 19th century English & American antiques & silver, paintings, prints & drawings, porcelain, rugs & objets d'art; rare books & manuscripts, consisting of British & American literature, Americana, & book illustrations; 300,000 manuscripts; 30,000 books, Marianne Moore Archive; Maurice Sendak Archive
Publications: A Selection from Our Shelves; Fantasy Sketches; The Rosenbach Newsletter; exhib catalogs
Activities: Classes for adults & children; dramatic progs; docent training; lect open to pub, 3 vis lectrs per yr; gallery talks; tours; individual paintings & original objects of art lent to mus & libraries with proper environmental & security systems; originate traveling exhibs; mus shop sells books, prints & reproductions

M **RYERSS VICTORIAN MUSEUM & LIBRARY,** 7370 Central Ave, Philadelphia, PA 19111-3059. Tel 215-685-0544, 685-0599; Elec Mail ryerssmuseum@hotmail.com; Internet Home Page Address: ryerssmuseum.org; *Librn* Peter Lurowist; *Site Supvr* Theresa Stuhlman; *Site Supvr* Martha Moffat
Open Mus & Library Fri - Sun 10 AM - 4 PM; No admis fee; Estab 1910; House (Historic Register) left to City complete with contents in 1905; three period

rooms; three other mus rooms with art objects - eclectic coll from around the world; fine Asian gallery; Average Annual Attendance: 20,000; Mem: 75; dues $5; meeting first Mon every month

Income: Financed by endowment, city appropriation, volunteer fundraising & trust fund

Library Holdings: Book Volumes; Manuscripts; Original Documents; Photographs

Special Subjects: American Indian Art, Landscapes, Ceramics, Glass, Porcelain, Painting-American, Painting-French, Sculpture, Architecture, Painting-American, Prints, Sculpture, Religious Art, Decorative Arts, Portraits, Furniture, Jewelry, Porcelain, Asian Art, Ivory, Period Rooms

Collections: Static collection; export china, ivory, paintings, period rooms, prints, sculpture, weapons, natural history Asian artifacts

Activities: Educ prog; children's craft activities; Lects open to public; 1 vis lectr per yr; tours; lending coll contains 12,000 books; Mus shop sells T-shirts; greeting cards; local history publs

A TALLER PUERTORRIQUENO INC, Lorenzo Homar Gallery, 2721 N 5th St, Philadelphia, PA 19133. Tel 215-426-3311; Fax 215-426-5682; Elec Mail cfebo@tallerpr.org; Internet Home Page Address: www.tallerpr.org; *Exec Dir* Carmen Febo San Miguel; *Visual Arts Prog Mgr* Daniel de Jesus
Open Mon - Fri 10 AM - 5 PM, Sat 11 AM - 5 PM, cl Sun; No admis fee; Estab 1974 to develop, educate & promote Puerto Rican arts & cultural traditions while exploring common Latin American roots; Contemporary Latin American art with social relevance to Latino culture; Average Annual Attendance: 5,000; Mem: 450; dues $15 & up

Income: Financed by gov, federal, corp & pvt foundations

Purchases: Permanent coll of prints & works on paper

Library Holdings: Audio Tapes; Book Volumes; Exhibition Catalogs; Maps; Original Art Works; Original Documents; Other Holdings; Pamphlets; Periodical Subscriptions; Photographs; Prints; Records; Slides; Video Tapes

Special Subjects: Prints, Religious Art, Latin American Art, Pre-Columbian Art

Collections: Permanent coll includes silk prints, lithographs & woodcuts

Exhibitions: Five exhibs annually

Publications: 25 Years - 25 Prints: catalogue documenting permanent collection & history of the organization

Activities: Classes for adults & children; summer arts prog; lect open to pub, 2-3 vis lectrs per yr; concerts; gallery talks; tours; schols or fels offered; originate traveling exhibs; galleries, pvt & pub orgs; mus shop sells books, crafts, reproductions & prints

M TEMPLE UNIVERSITY, Tyler School of Art-Galleries, 2001 N 13th St, Philadelphia, PA 19122-6016. Tel 215-777-9144; Fax 215-777-9143; Elec Mail exhibitions@temple.edu; Internet Home Page Address: www.temple.edu/tyler/exhibitions; *Interim Dean* Robert Stroker; *Interim Dir* Shayna V McConville; *Interim Preparator* Adam Blumberg
Open Wed - Sat 10 AM - 5 PM; No admis fee; Track lighting; Average Annual Attendance: 12,000

Income: Financed by state appropriation & grants

Exhibitions: Peter Eiseman: Tow Projects; Martin Poryear: The Cave Project

Publications: Brochures, posters, announcements or exhibitions catalogs for major shows

Activities: Lect open to pub, 8 vis lectrs per yr; gallery talks; special events; concerts

L Tyler School of Art Library, 2001 N 13th St., Philadelphia, PA 19122-6016. Tel 215-782-2849; Fax 215-782-2799; Internet Home Page Address: www.library.temple.edu/tyler; *Librn* Andrea Goldstein
Open Mon - Thurs 8:30 AM - 9 PM, Fri 8:30 AM - 4:30 PM, Sat 9 AM - 5 PM, Sun 1 - 9 PM; Estab 1935 to provide library services to students & faculty; Circ 27,254

Income: $118,368 (financed by appropriation from Central University Library)

Purchases: $32,600

Library Holdings: Book Volumes 38,000; Cassettes; Exhibition Catalogs; Fiche; Other Holdings Auction sale catalogs; Pamphlets; Periodical Subscriptions 100; Prints; Reels; Video Tapes

—Slide Library, Beech & Penrose Aves, Elkins, PA 19027; 2001 N 13th St., Philadelphia, PA 19122-6016. Tel 215-782-2848; Fax 215-782-2848; Elec Mail sliderm@vm.temple.edu; Elec Mail slidelib@unix.temple.edu; *Asst Cur* Beth Peckman; *Slide Cur* Kathleen Szpila

Library Holdings: Slides 390,000

Special Subjects: Art History, Decorative Arts, Ceramics, Graphic Design, Photography

M TEMPLE UNIVERSITY, TYLER SCHOOL OF ART, Temple Gallery, 2001 N 13th St, Philadelphia, PA 19122-6016. Tel 215-777-9144; Fax 215-777-9143; Elec Mail exhibitions@temple.edu; Internet Home Page Address: www.temple.edu/tyler/exhibitions; *Interim Dean* Robert Stroker; *Dir* Robert Blackson
Open Wed - Sat 11 AM - 6 PM; no admis fee; Estab 1985; Contemporary art; Average Annual Attendance: 20,000

Income: $160,000 (financed by the univ)

Exhibitions: Exhibits by Paula Suter, Mike Glier, Lorna Simpson, Louise Fishman, Pepon Osorio

Activities: Classes for children; docent training; lect open to pub; originate traveling exhibs 1 per yr

M THOMAS JEFFERSON UNIVERSITY, Eakins Gallery, 1020 Locust St, Jefferson Alumni Hall Philadelphia, PA 19107. Tel 215-503-7743; Internet Home Page Address: www.jefferson.edu/eakins/access.cfm
Open Mon - Sat 10 AM - 4 PM, Sun Noon - 4 PM, cl major holidays & special functions

M UNIVERSITY OF PENNSYLVANIA, Arthur Ross Gallery, 220 S 34th St, Philadelphia, PA 19104-3808; Box 5 College Hall, University of Pennsylvania Philadelphia, PA 19104-6303. Tel 215-898-2083; Fax 215-573-2045; Elec Mail arg@pobox.upenn.edu; Internet Home Page Address: www.upenn.edu/ARG; *Dir & Univ Cur* Lynn Marsden-Atlass; *Assoc Dir* Dejay B Duckett; *Gallery Coordr* Sara Stewart
Open Tues - Fri 10 AM - 5 PM, Sat & Sun Noon - 5 PM; No Admis fee; Estab 1983 to make art accessible to campus community & the general pub; One large

high-ceilinged room & an entrance room with approx 1700 sq ft of exhibition space; Average Annual Attendance: 12,000; Mem: 54; dues $100; ann meeting

Income: $400,000 (financed by endowment, grants, gifts, in-kind contributions)

Special Subjects: Drawings, Painting-American, Photography, Prints, Sculpture, African Art, Etchings & Engravings, Afro-American Art, Painting-French, Carpets & Rugs, Stained Glass

Collections: University art collection of paintings, prints, photographs, books, manuscripts, textiles & sculpture; Irish paintings

Exhibitions: Four - six rotating per yr

Publications: Exhibition catalogues

Activities: Classes for children; lects open to pub, 2-3 vis lectrs per yr; concerts; gallery talks; tours; book traveling exhibs 1 per yr; originate traveling exhibs to other univ galleries & museums

L UNIVERSITY OF PENNSYLVANIA, Fisher Fine Arts Library, 220 S 34th St, Philadelphia, PA 19104-6308. Tel 215-898-8325; Fax 215-573-2066; Elec Mail finearts@pobox.upenn.edu; Internet Home Page Address: www.library.upenn.edu/finearts; *Librn* William B Keller; *Asst Librn* Heather M Glaser
Open Mon-Fri 8:30 AM-5PM; Research library

Library Holdings: Book Volumes 150,000; CD-ROMs; Cassettes; Exhibition Catalogs; Fiche; Kodachrome Transparencies; Lantern Slides; Maps; Pamphlets; Periodical Subscriptions 800; Photographs; Reels; Slides; Video Tapes

Special Subjects: Art History, Religious Art, Landscapes, Architecture

A UNIVERSITY OF PENNSYLVANIA, Institute of Contemporary Art, 118 S 36th St, Philadelphia, PA 19104-3211. Tel 215-898-7108; Fax 215-898-5050; Elec Mail info@icaphila.org; Internet Home Page Address: www.icaphila.org; *Dir* Claudia Gould; *Dir Devel* Marilyn Pollick; *Sr Cur* Ingrid Schaffner; *Cur* Jenelle Porter; *Asst Cur* Kate Kraczon; *Dir Mktg & Communs* Jill Katz; *Visitor Svcs & Educ Asst* William Hidalgo; *Staff Writer* Rachel Pastan; *Bus & Bldg Adminr* Nikyia Rogers; *Asst to Dir* Eliza Coviello; *Registrar* Darcey Sawicz; *Dir Cur Affairs* Robert Chaney; *Develop Admin Asst* Jeffrey Bussmann
Open Wed 11 AM - 8 PM, Thurs & Fri 11 AM - 6 PM, Sat & Sun 11 AM - 5 PM, cl Mon. & Tues; No admis fee; Estab 1963 to provide a continuing forum for the active presentation of advanced development in the visual arts; Gallery space devoted to exhibiting contemporary art in all media; Average Annual Attendance: 25,000; Mem: 218; dues $40, $100, $250, $500 & up

Income: financed by endowment, mem & grants

Library Holdings: Audio Tapes; Cards; Cassettes; Clipping Files; DVDs; Exhibition Catalogs; Fiche; Kodachrome Transparencies; Original Art Works; Original Documents; Pamphlets; Periodical Subscriptions; Photographs; Prints; Records; Slides; Video Tapes

Special Subjects: Architecture, Drawings, Photography, Prints, Sculpture

Publications: Annual newsletter; calendar of events; exhibition catalogs

Activities: School groups; teacher training; lect open to pub, vis lectrs; concerts; gallery talks; tours; fellowships; originates 1-2 traveling exhibs; sales shop sells original art, catalogs & Cereal Art

M Museum of Archaeology & Anthropology, 3260 South St, Philadelphia, PA 19104-6324. Tel 215-898-4000; Fax 215-898-7961; Elec Mail websiters@museum.upenn.edu; Internet Home Page Address: www.museum.penn.edu; *Deputy Dir* Dr Gerald Margolis; *Historical Arch Assoc Cur* Dr Robert L Schuyler; *American Sections Cur* Dr Robert Sharer; *Near East Section Assoc Cur* Dr Richard Zettler; *Egyptian Section Cur* Dr David Silverman; *Mediterranean Section Cur* Dr Brian Rose; *Physical Anthropology Cur* Dr Janet Minge; *Dir* Dr. Richard Hodges
Open Tues-Sat 10 AM - 4:30 PM, Sun 1 - 5 PM, cl Mon, holidays, summer Suns & Memorial Day thru Labor Day; Admis adults $8, students & seniors $5, children under 6, members, University of Pennsylvania faculty, staff & students with Penn card free; Estab 1887 to investigate the origins & varied developments of human cultural achievements in all times & places; to preserve & maintain colls to document these achievements & to present to the pub the results of these investigations by means of permanent exhibits, temporary exhibs & special events; Average Annual Attendance: 150,000; Mem: 2000; dues individual $35, Loren Eiseley Assoc $1000

Income: $5,000,000 (financed by endowment, mem, state appropriation & univ)

Special Subjects: American Indian Art, Folk Art, Historical Material, Ceramics, Glass, Flasks & Bottles, Gold, Pottery, Textiles, Tapestries, Hispanic Art, Latin American Art, Mexican Art, Photography, Sculpture, Bronzes, African Art, Anthropology, Archaeology, Ethnology, Pre-Columbian Art, Southwestern Art, Costumes, Crafts, Woodcarvings, Eskimo Art, Jade, Jewelry, Oriental Art, Asian Art, Metalwork, Ivory, Coins & Medals, Antiquities-Oriental, Islamic Art, Antiquities-Egyptian, Antiquities-Greek, Antiquities-Roman, Mosaics, Antiquities-Etruscan

Collections: Archaeological & ethnographic artifacts relating to the Old & New World; the classical civilization of the Mediterranean, Egypt, Mesopotamia, Iran & the Far East, North & Middle America, Oceania; Africa

Exhibitions: Ancient Greek World. Living in Balance: The Universe of The Hopi, Zuni, Navajo & Apache

Publications: Expedition Magazine, quarterly; Museum Applied Science Center for Archaeology Journal; Museum Monographs; exhib catalogues

Activities: Classes for adults & children; docent training; family day; lect open to pub, 20 vis lectrs per yr; concerts; gallery talks; tours; 5 or more book traveling exhib; exten dept servs Pennsylvania Commonwealth; objects of art lent to libraries & instructional centers in the state; lending coll contains motion pictures, original art works & slides; originates traveling exhibs; mus shop sells books, magazines, reproductions, slides, jewelry & craft items

L Museum Library, 3260 South St, Philadelphia, PA 19104-6324. Tel 215-898-7840; Fax 215-573-2008; Internet Home Page Address: www.library.upenn.edu/museum; *Dir* Dr John Weeks
Open Mon & Fri-Sat 9AM-5PM, Tues & Thurs 9AM-9PM, Sun 1PM-5PM; For reference & research only

Library Holdings: Book Volumes 110,000; Fiche; Filmstrips; Other Holdings Microforms 70,000; Pamphlets; Periodical Subscriptions 800; Reels

Special Subjects: Archaeology, Anthropology

Collections: Univ Anthropology Collection

M   **THE UNIVERSITY OF THE ARTS,** Rosenwald-Wolf Gallery, 333 South Broad St, Philadelphia, PA 19107-5839; 320 South Broad St., Philadelphia, PA 19102. Tel 215-717-6480; Fax 215-717-6468; Elec Mail ssachs@uarts.edu; Internet Home Page Address: www.uarts.edu; *Provost* Kirk Pillow; *Pres* Sean Buffington; *Dir Exhibs* Sid Sachs
Open Mon - Fri 10 AM - 5 PM, Sat 12 noon - 5 PM; No admis fee; College contains two galleries; Rosenwald-Wolf Gallery & Hamilton Hall Building Galleries; Temporary exhibs which relate to the University's diverse instruction. The galleries present high quality contemporary exhibs which attract national & international artists to the campus. Major exhibs are accompanied by catalogs, symposia & lects; Average Annual Attendance: 4,000
Income: Financed by city, state & federal appropriations, pvt & corporate support
Exhibitions: Contemporary & 20th century work in visual arts & design
Publications: Catalogs & brochures accompany major gallery exhibs
Activities: Lect open to pub; gallery talks; 2-4 vis lectrs per yr; originates traveling exhibs for museums, univ galleries

L   **University Libraries,** 333 South Broad St Philadelphia, PA 19102; 320 South Broad St, Philadelphia, PA 19102-4901. Tel 215-717-6280; Fax 215-717-6287; Internet Home Page Address: library.uarts.edu; *Visual Resources & Special Colls Librn* Laura Grutzeck; *Pub Services Librn* Sara MacDonald; *Music Librn* Dr Mark Germer; *Library Dir* Carol H Graney; *Reference Librn* Mary Louise Castaldi; *Technical Svcs* Kathryn Coyle; *Digital Initiatives & Systems Librn* Joshua Roberts; *Access Servs Librn* Kimberly Lesley
Open Mon - Fri 9 AM - 5 PM by appointment; Estab 1876 to support the acad progs of the School; Circ 30,000; Lending to univ patrons only & mem holders; Average Annual Attendance: 102,000; Mem: Dues general pub $50
Library Holdings: Audio Tapes 565; Book Volumes 127,600; CD-ROMs 350; Cassettes 567; Clipping Files; Compact Disks 10,058; DVDs 2,276; Exhibition Catalogs; Fiche; Kodachrome Transparencies; Micro Print; Other Holdings Picture files 114,830; Laserdiscs 6; Textiles; Periodical Subscriptions 322; Photographs; Prints; Records 9,653; Reels 450; Reproductions; Slides 176,994; Video Tapes 1,175
Special Subjects: Decorative Arts, Film, Illustration, Mixed Media, Photography, Graphic Arts, Graphic Design, Sculpture, History of Art & Archaeology, Stage Design, Ceramics, Crafts, Theatre Arts, Printmaking, Industrial Design, Art Education, Jewelry, Textiles

L   **WILLET HAUSER ARCHITECTURAL GLASS INC,** (Willet Stained Glass Studios) 811 E Cayuga St, Philadelphia, PA 19124-3815. Tel 215-247-5721; Fax 215-247-2951; Elec Mail ecwillet@earthlink.net; Internet Home Page Address: www.willethauser.com; *Pres* E Crosby Willet; *Gen Mgr* Richard Prigg; *Librn* Jessica Crowley
Open by appointment; No admis fee; Estab 1898 as the largest stained glass studio in the United States; For reference only
Special Subjects: Art History, Illustration, Photography, Calligraphy, History of Art & Archaeology, Printmaking, Costume Design & Constr, Mosaics, Stained Glass, Antiquities-Oriental, Antiquities-Persian, Restoration & Conservation, Antiquities-Assyrian, Antiquities-Byzantine, Antiquities-Egyptian, Antiquities-Etruscan, Antiquities-Greek, Antiquities-Roman, Architecture
Collections: Lumiere Watercolor Collection
Publications: Black & White Photos of works in progress, Design & slides of installations
Activities: Lect open to pub; gallery talks; tours; internships offered; individual paintings & original objects of art lent; lending coll contains photographs, Kodachromes & motion pictures; originates traveling exhibs

M   **WOODMERE ART MUSEUM INC,** (Woodmere Art Museum) 9201 Germantown Ave, Philadelphia, PA 19118-2618. Tel 215-247-0476; Fax 215-247-2387; Elec Mail dpastella@woodmereartmuseum.org; Internet Home Page Address: www.woodmereartmuseum.org; *Dir* Dr Michael W Schantz; *Registrar* Sally Larson; *Dir Develop* Mary Agnes Williams; *Cur Coll* Nicholas Yzzi; *Cur Edn* Pamela Birmingham
Open Tues - Sat 10 AM - 5 PM, Sun 1 - 5 PM; No admis fee; suggested donation; Estab 1940; founded by Charles Knox Smith, in trust for benefit of the pub; A large addition in 1965 provides additional gallery & studio space; Average Annual Attendance: 48,000; Mem: 2500; dues $35 & higher; annual meeting in Dec
Income: Financed by endowments, gifts, grants & mem fees
Purchases: Philadelphia art, past & present
Library Holdings: Cards; Clipping Files; Exhibition Catalogs
Special Subjects: Architecture, Drawings, Graphics, Painting-American, Photography, Prints, Sculpture, Ceramics, Folk Art, Etchings & Engravings, Landscapes, Decorative Arts, Painting-European, Portraits, Furniture, Porcelain, Oriental Art, Asian Art, Carpets & Rugs, Juvenile Art, Renaissance Art, Period Rooms, Embroidery, Laces, Antiquities-Oriental, Antiquities-Persian
Collections: Contemporary Philadelphia paintings, sculpture & graphics; European porcelains & furniture; European & American sculpture; Oriental rugs, furniture, porcelains; Smith Collection of European & American paintings
Exhibitions: 12 changing exhibitions annually; prizes awarded in winter Juried Annual & Special Exhibitions
Publications: Selections from the permanent coll of the Woodmere Art Museum
Activities: Classes for adults & children; docent training; lect open to pub; concerts; gallery talks; tours; competitions with prizes; individual paintings & original objects of art lent to other museums & galleries; mus shop sells books, gifts, jewelry & original art

L   **Library,** 9201 Germantown Ave, Philadelphia, PA 19118. Tel 215-247-0948; Fax 215-247-2387; Elec Mail pdhoffman@woodmereartmuseum.com; Internet Home Page Address: www.woodmereartmuseum.org; *Cur Educ* Pamela Birmingham; *CEO, Dir & Cur* Michael W Schantz; *Mus Shop Mgr* Betty R Stein; *Registrar* Sally Larson; *Dir Develop* Mary Agnes Williams; *Cur Coll* W Douglass Paschall; *VPres* Joseph Nicholson
Open Tues-Fri 10AM-4PM; Reference only
Library Holdings: Cards; Clipping Files; Exhibition Catalogs; Slides

PITTSBURGH

M   **THE ANDY WARHOL MUSEUM,** Museum, 117 Sandusky St, Pittsburgh, PA 15212-5890. Tel 412-237-8300; Fax 412-237-8340; Elec Mail information@warhol.org; Internet Home Page Address: www.warhol.org; *Dir* Thomas Sokolowski; *Deputy Dir* Bethany Tucke; *Cur Film & Video* Geralyn Huxley; *Dir Exhibs* Jesse Kowalski; *Dir Devel* Betsy Magley; *Cur Educ & Interpretation* Tresa Varner
Open Tues - Sun 10 AM - 5 PM, cl Mon & major holidays; Admis adults $15, seniors $9, students with ID & children ages 3 - 18 $8, Carnegie Mus of Pittsburgh mem free, Fri 5-10 PM half price, group rates available; Estab 1994; Mem: Carnegie Mus of Pittsburgh; maintains cafe
Special Subjects: Photography, Portraits, Painting-American, Manuscripts, Graphics, Costumes, Posters
Collections: Film & Video (permanent); Over 4,000 art works in all media; sketchbook drawings; hand-painted images; self-portraits
Exhibitions: Rotating exhibs featuring 500 items from permanent collection; special exhibs on specific areas of Worhols work & work of related artists; (3/28/2010-3/26/2017) I Just Want to Watch: Warhols Film, Video & Television
Activities: Weekend Factory hands-on art prog; lects open to pub; concerts; film screenings; parties; exhib openings; mus shop sells accessories, books, calendars, magnets, posters, prints, stationery, videos

L   **Archives,** 117 Sandusky St, Pittsburgh, PA 15212-5890.
Open to researchers by appt, cl to gen pub
Library Holdings: Audio Tapes 4,000; Book Volumes; Clipping Files; Filmstrips 273; Other Holdings Source Material; Periodical Subscriptions; Photographs; Records; Sculpture; Video Tapes
Special Subjects: Decorative Arts, Film, Photography, Graphic Arts, Manuscripts, Posters, Sculpture
Collections: Over 8,000 cubic ft of material; Time Capsules; scrapbooks; art supplies & material; run of Interview magazine

M   **ART INSTITUTE OF PITTSBURGH,** John P. Barclay Memorial Gallery, 420 Blvd of the Allies, Pittsburgh, PA 15219-1328. Tel 412-263-6600; Fax 412-263-6667; Internet Home Page Address: www.artinstitutes.edu/pittsburgh; *Dir Resource Center* Susan Moran; *Dir* Nancy Ruttner
Open Mon, Tues & Thurs 9 AM - 8 PM, Wed & Fri 9 AM - 5 PM, Sat 9 AM - 4 PM; No admis fee; Estab 1921 as an art school & proprietary trade school
Exhibitions: Local art group shows; local artists; loan exhibs; student and faculty mems; technical art exhibits
Publications: Brochures; Catalog; School Newspaper
Activities: Classes for adults & teens; lect open to pub, 2-4 vis lectrs per yr; schols offered

L   **Resource Center,** 420 Blvd of the Allies, Pittsburgh, PA 15219-1328. Tel 412-291-6357; Elec Mail aiplibrary@aii.edu; Internet Home Page Address: www.aiplib.aiiresources.com; www.artinstitutes.edu/pittsburgh; *Dir Libr Svcs* Kathy Ober
Open Mon - Thurs 7:30 AM - 9:30 PM, Fri 7:30 AM - 5 PM, Sat 9 AM - 4 PM
Library Holdings: Book Volumes 5674; Cassettes; Clipping Files; Exhibition Catalogs; Fiche; Filmstrips; Framed Reproductions; Memorabilia; Pamphlets; Periodical Subscriptions 208; Records; Slides

A   **ASSOCIATED ARTISTS OF PITTSBURGH,** 6300 Fifth Ave, Pittsburgh, PA 15232. Tel 412-361-1370; Fax 412-471-1765; Elec Mail aapgh1@verizon.net; Internet Home Page Address: www.aapgh.org; *Exec Dir* Frances A Frederick; *Bd Pres* Patti Beachley
Open Tues - Fri 11 AM - 4 PM, Sat 11 AM - 3 PM; No admis fee; Estab 1910 to give exposure to mem artists & for educ of the area in the field of art; 2 fls of galleries with changing exhibits; Average Annual Attendance: 15,000; Mem: 500 (must be juried into the group) & live within 150 miles of Pittsburgh; dues $80
Income: Financed by mem; donations from foundations, corporations & individuals
Exhibitions: Annual Exhibition at Carnegie Museum of art open to all regional artists; Changing exhibs, 10 per yr
Publications: The First 75 Years
Activities: Special progs linking students & artists; classes for adults & children; workshops for professional artists; lect open to pub; competitions with awards; individual paintings & original objects of art lent to interested individuals & bus; sells mems artwork

C   **BANK OF NY MELLON CORPORATION,** (Mellon Financial Corporation) 500 Grant St, One Mellon Financial Ctr Pittsburgh, PA 15219-2502. Tel 412-234-4775; Fax 412-234-0831; *Art Dir* Brian J Lang
Collections: 18th & 19th century British drawings & paintings; American historical prints; 19th century American & Pennsylvanian paintings; contemporary American & British paintings; contemporary works on paper; textiles; contemporary photography

M   **CARNEGIE MELLON UNIVERSITY,** The Frame, 5200 Forbes Ave, Pittsburgh, PA 15213-3890. Tel 412-268-2000 (main), 268-2409 (art dept); Internet Home Page Address: www.cmu.edu, www.art.cfa.cmu.edu; *Co-Dir* Jamie Walters
Open Wed 3 - 6 & 7 - 9 PM, Thurs & Fri Noon - 6 PM & Thurs evening 7 - 9 PM, Sat Noon - 6 PM, Sun Noon - 3 PM; Estab 1969 to offer exhib space to students, & an opportunity to learn about gallery management through practice; Gallery is approx 20 x 40 ft plus small back room space; Average Annual Attendance: 750
Income: $5000 (financed by univ fundings)
Exhibitions: Weekly senior art student exhibs

L   **Hunt Library,** 4909 Frew St, 5th Fl Pittsburgh, PA 15213-3890. Tel 412-268-7272; Fax 412-268-7148; Elec Mail artsref@andrew.cmu.edu; Internet Home Page Address: www.library.cmu.edu; *Head of Access Services* Joan Stein; *Head of Hunt Reference* Jean Alexander
Open Mon-Thurs 8AM-Midnight, Fri 8AM-0PM, Sat 10AM-9PM, Sun noon-Midnight; Estab 1912; The Arts Library is on the 4th fl of the Hunt Library, supports College of Fine Arts prog & is open to the pub
Income: Financed by Univ Libraries operating funds & endowments

Library Holdings: Audio Tapes; Book Volumes 80,000; CD-ROMs; Cassettes; Clipping Files; Compact Disks; DVDs; Exhibition Catalogs; Fiche; Manuscripts; Memorabilia; Original Art Works; Original Documents; Other Holdings Architectural drawings; electronic data files; Pamphlets; Periodical Subscriptions 350; Photographs; Prints; Records; Reels; Reproductions; Sculpture; Slides 120,700; Video Tapes
Special Subjects: Architecture
Collections: Architecture Archives, Swiss Poster Coll, Thomas Gonda design coll, artists books

M **Hunt Institute for Botanical Documentation,** Frew St, Pittsburgh, PA 15213-3890; 5000 Forbes Ave, Pittsburgh, PA 15213-3890. Tel 412-268-2434; Fax 412-268-5677; Elec Mail huntinst@andrew.cmu.edu; Internet Home Page Address: huntbot.andrew.cmu.edu; *Asst Dir* Terry D Jacobsen; *Cur Art* Lugene Bruno; *Librn* Charlotte Tancin; *Archivist* J Dustin Williams; *Dir* Robert W Kiger; *Bibliographer* Donald W Brown; *Ast Librn* Jeannette McDevitt
Open Mon - Fri 9 AM - Noon & 1 - 5 PM, Sun 1 - 4 PM during exhibs; No admis fee; Estab 1961 for the study of botany, history of botany, botanical art & illustration; Two exhibs per yr
Special Subjects: Prints, Woodcuts, Drawings, Watercolors, Etchings & Engravings
Collections: Botanical Art Collection; Archives
Publications: Huntia, irregular; Bulletin, semi-annually; exhib catalogues, reference works, monographs
Activities: Gallery talks; tours; traveling exhibs to mus, galleries, botanical gardens; Retail store sells books, posters & cards

M **CARNEGIE MUSEUMS OF PITTSBURGH,** (Carnegie Institute) Carnegie Museum of Art, 4400 Forbes Ave, Pittsburgh, PA 15213-4080. Tel 412-622-3131; Fax 412-622-3112; Elec Mail cma-general@carnegiemuseums.org; Internet Home Page Address: www.cmoa.org; *Deputy Dir* Maureen Rolla; *Chmn Mus Art Board* Martin McGuinn; *Cur Architecture* Tracy Myers; *Cur Decorative Arts* Jason Busch; *Cur Educ* Marilyn M Russell; *Cur Fine Art* Louise W Lippincott; *Chief Conservator* Ellen Baxter; *Head Publ* Katie Reilly; *Registrar* Monika Tomko; *Dir of Exhib* Sarah Minnaert; *Asst Dir Mktg & Communs* Jonathan Gaugler; *Dir* Lynn Zelevansky; *Cur Architecture* Raymund Ryan
Open Tues - Sat 10 AM - 5 PM, Thurs 10 AM - 8 PM, Sun noon - 5 PM, cl Mon (except July & Aug) & major holidays; Admis adults $17.95, seniors (65+) $14.95, children (3-18) & students with ID $11.95, mems free; Estab 1895, incorporated 1926. Original building 1896-1907; Scaife Wing 1974; Most coll & special exhibs are on view in 50,000 sq ft Scaife Wing designed by Edward Larrabee Barnes in 1974; Average Annual Attendance: 700,000; Mem: 27,400; dues $50 & up
Income: Financed by endowment, mem, city, county & state appropriation & other funds
Library Holdings: Auction Catalogs; Fiche
Special Subjects: Drawings, Painting-American, Photography, Prints, Sculpture, Woodcuts, Decorative Arts, Painting-European, Dolls, Furniture, Oriental Art
Collections: American & European paintings & sculpture, especially Impressionist & Post-Impressionist; Contemporary International Art; Japanese woodblock prints; American & European decorative arts; Antiquities; Asian Art; African Art; Films; Video tapes; Photographs, Prints & Drawings
Exhibitions: Carnegie International
Publications: Carnegie Magazine, four times per yr; catalogue of permanent coll; exhib catalogs; quarterly newsletter, email newsletters to members & non-members
Activities: Classes for adults & children; docent training; lect open to pub; concerts; gallery talks; tours incl free audio guide; Carnegie award; inter-museum loans; originate traveling exhibs; mus shop sells books, periodicals, original art, posters, reproductions, textiles, jewelry, ceramics, postcards, designer household objects: furniture, lighting, tableware

L **Carnegie Library of Pittsburgh,** 4400 Forbes Ave, Pittsburgh, PA 15213. Tel 412-622-3131; Fax 412-578-2561; Elec Mail info@carnegielibrary.org; Internet Home Page Address: www.clpgh.org; *Pres & Dir* Barbara K Mistick
Open Mon-Thurs 10AM-8PM, Fri & Sat 9AM-5:30 PM, Sun noon-5PM; Open to staff & mus docents for reference only
Library Holdings: Book Volumes 2,000,000; CD-ROMs; Cassettes; Fiche; Filmstrips; Memorabilia; Periodical Subscriptions; Photographs; Prints; Video Tapes

M **CHATHAM COLLEGE,** Art Gallery, Woodland Rd, Art & Design Center Pittsburgh, PA 15232. Tel 412-365-1100; Fax 412-365-1505; Internet Home Page Address: www.chatham.edu; *Dir* Michael Pestel; *Dir Fine & Performing Arts* William Lenz
Open Mon - Fri 11 AM - 5 PM; No admis fee; Estab 1960 as an art gallery in a small liberal arts col, serving both the col & community by mounting exhibs of high quality; Gallery is 100 running ft, is located in Jennie King Mellon Library & is fitted with track lighting; Average Annual Attendance: 1,500
Income: Financed by col
Exhibitions: Linda Benglis; Don Reitz; Idelle Weber; Jerry L Caplan
Activities: Lect open to pub, 2 vis lectrs per yr; gallery talks; schols offered; individual paintings & original objects of art lent

M **THE FRICK ART & HISTORICAL CENTER, INC,** (The Frick Art & Historical Center) Frick Art Museum, 7227 Reynolds St, Pittsburgh, PA 15208-2923. Tel 412-371-0600; Fax 412-241-5393; Elec Mail info@thefrickpittsburgh.org; Internet Home Page Address: www.thefrickpittsburgh.org; *Dir* William Bodine Jr; *Dir Cur Affairs* Sarah Hall; *Dir Fin & Admin* Christine D Chambers; *Dir Educ* Pam St. John; *Dir External Affairs* Susan Neszpaul; *Dir Opers & Vis Servs* Bill Nichols
Open Tues - Sun 10AM-5PM; Admis to Clayton Mansion $12 non-mem; $10 seniors & students; mem free; art mus free; Estab 1970 as an art mus for pub enjoyment & educ; Average Annual Attendance: 132,000; Mem: 3,200
Income: Financed by endowment
Special Subjects: Glass, Furniture, Painting-American, Painting-British, Tapestries, Drawings, Sculpture, Watercolors, Bronzes, Religious Art, Ceramics, Decorative Arts, Portraits, Furniture, Porcelain, Silver, Painting-Dutch, Painting-French, Tapestries, Painting-Flemish, Renaissance Art, Period Rooms, Medieval Art, Painting-Italian

Collections: Italian, French Renaissance; bronzes, Chinese porcelains, furniture, sculpture, tapestries; antique cars
Publications: Exhibit catalogs
Activities: Classes for adults & children; dramatic progs; docent training; studio workshops; family progs; elderhostel; lect open to pub, 10 vis lectrs per yr; concerts; gallery talks; tours; competitions with awards; schols & fels offered; original objects of art lent to museums; book traveling exhibs 3 per yr; originate traveling exhibs to museums; mus shop sells books, catalogues, color reproductions, photographs, posters, post cards & gifts, clothing

M **MANCHESTER BIDWELL CORPORATION,** Manchester Craftsmen's Guild Youth & Arts Program, 1815 Metropolitan St, Pittsburgh, PA 15233-2233. Tel 412-322-1773; Fax 412-321-2120; Elec Mail rmgubser@mcg-btc.org; Internet Home Page Address: http://mcgyouthandarts.org; *Exec Asst* Rose Mary Gubser; *Dir MCG Youth & Arts* Dave Deily; *Teaching Artist Coordr* Justin Mazzei
Open Mon-Fri 9AM-5:30PM; Estab 1968 to present photog & ceramic art of regional & nationally recognized artists; Connie Kerr Gallery; Average Annual Attendance: 2,500-5,000
Special Subjects: Afro-American Art, Landscapes, Ceramics, Metalwork, Photography, Textiles, Drawings, Sculpture, Watercolors, African Art, Crafts, Jewelry, Juvenile Art, Mosaics, Cartoons, Leather
Collections: Martin Luther King permanent exhib of photographs
Activities: Art classes for adults & children; lect open to pub, 6-8 vis lectrs per yr; gallery talks; tours; scholarships; gift shop sells original art

M **THE MATTRESS FACTORY,** (Mattress Factory) 500 Sampsonia Way, Pittsburgh, PA 15212-4444. Tel 412-231-3169; Fax 412-322-2231; Elec Mail info@mattress.org; Internet Home Page Address: www.mattress.org; *Bd Mem, Co-Dir* Michael Olijnyk; *Bd Mem, Co-Dir* Barbara Luderowski; *Bd Mem* Scott Bergstein; *Bd Chmn* Michael White
Open Tues - Sat 10 AM - 5 PM, Sun 1 - 5 PM, cl Mon, New Year's Day, Easter, Memorial Day, Independence Day, Thanksgiving & Christmas; Admis fee Adults $10, students $7, seniors $8, children under 6 & mems free; Estab 1977 as a research & development residency program featuring site-specific installations; Average Annual Attendance: 55,000
Collections: Permanent collection of William Anastasi, Jene Highstein, Rolf Julius, Yayoi Kusama, Winifred Lutz, James Turrell, Allan Wexler & Bill Woodrow
Activities: Classes for adults, children & teachers; lectures open to the public; concerts, gallery talks & tours; mus shop sells books, magazines, original art & prints

A **PITTSBURGH CENTER FOR THE ARTS,** 6300 5th Ave, Pittsburgh, PA 15232-2922. Tel 412-361-0873; Fax 412-361-8338; Elec Mail info@pittsburgharts.org; Internet Home Page Address: www.pittsburgharts.org/index.php; *Exec Dir* Charlie Humphrey; *Dir* Laura Domencic; *Cur* Adam Welch
Open Tues- Wed & Mon in Dec, 10 AM - 5 PM, Thurs 10 AM - 9 PM, Fri - Sat 10 AM 7 PM, Sun Noon - 5 PM, cl Mon, New Year's Day, Thanksgiving, Christmas; No admis fee, suggested donation $5, mems no charg; Estab 1945 by artists; Non-profit community arts ctr that offers arts educ programs & contemporary art exhibits & provides services & resources for artists throughout western PA; Average Annual Attendance: 150,000; Mem: 6500; dues vary; patron mems
Income: Financed by school tui, mem, commission on art sales & contributions
Publications: Artists directory; class schedule; exhib catalogs; monthly calendar
Activities: Arts & crafts classes for adults and children; workshops; summer art camps; lect open to pub; concerts; gallery talks; tours; ann holiday art sales; awards: Artist of the Year, Emerging Artist of the Year, Service to the Arts Award & Lifetime Achievement Award; schols & fels offered; exten dept serves western Pennsylvania; originate traveling exhibs; sales shop sells books & original art

L **PITTSBURGH HISTORY & LANDMARKS FOUNDATION,** James D Van Trump Library, 100 W Station Sq Dr, Ste 450, Pittsburgh, PA 15219-1134. Tel 412-471-5808; Fax 412-471-1633; Elec Mail info@phlf.org; Internet Home Page Address: www.phlf.org; *Pres* Arthur P Ziegler Jr; *Exec Dir* Louise Sturgess
Open Mon - Fri 9 AM - 5 PM; Estab 1964 to preserve the architectural legacy & historic neighborhoods of Allegheny County; Reference for mems only; Mem: 2200; dues $5
Library Holdings: Book Volumes 4700; Clipping Files; Original Art Works; Other Holdings Architectural & engineering drawings; Periodical Subscriptions 17; Photographs; Prints
Special Subjects: Landscape Architecture, Drawings, Architecture
Collections: Paintings: Aaron Gorson, Otto Kuhler, Edward B Lee, William C Wall
Activities: Classes for adults & children; dramatic progs; docent training; lect open to pub, 2 vis lectrs per yr; tours; competitions with prizes; mus shop sells books, reproductions, prints & slides

A **SILVER EYE CENTER FOR PHOTOGRAPHY,** 1015 E Carson St, Pittsburgh, PA 15203-1109. Tel 412-431-1810; Fax 412-431-5777; Elec Mail info@silvereye.org; Internet Home Page Address: www.silvereye.org; *Exec Dir* Ellen Fleurov
Open Tues - Sat Noon-6PM; No admis fee; Mem: dues $35 - $750
Income: Financed by government, corporations, foundations & individuals
Special Subjects: Photography
Exhibitions: Rotating exhibits of national & international photography, 2 national photo competitions per yr
Activities: Classes for children; outreach pub school prog; lects open to pub, 1-5 vis lectrs per yr; gallery talks; fels available

M **SOCIETY FOR CONTEMPORARY CRAFT,** 2100 Smallman St, Pittsburgh, PA 15222-4440. Tel 412-261-7003; Fax 412-261-1941; Elec Mail info@contemporarycraft.org; Internet Home Page Address: www.contemporarycraft.org; *Dir Exhibs* Kate Lydon; *Exec Dir* Janet McCall; *Sales Mgr* Megan Crowell; *Dir Develop* Pam Quatchak; *Exec Asst* Yu-San Cheng; *Studio Prog Coordr* Rachel Saul; *Dir Finance* Robert Musca; *Marketing Mgr* Norah Guigmon; *Develop Asst & Office Mgr.* Erin McKevilt
Open Mon - Fri 10 AM - 5 PM, Sat 10 AM - 5 PM; No admis fee; Estab 1971 to engage pub in the creative experience through contemporary craft; Gallery features

contemporary crafts by nationally & internationally recognized artists in thematic shows; educ & outreach progs; retail store; Average Annual Attendance: 30,000; Mem: No mem prog

Income: Financed by mem, donations & grants

Library Holdings: Exhibition Catalogs; Original Art Works; Periodical Subscriptions

Special Subjects: Mixed Media, Silversmithing, Textiles, Ceramics, Crafts, Pottery, Furniture, Glass, Jewelry, Metalwork, Mosaics, Pewter, Enamels

Collections: Ceramics; contemporary crafts; fiber; furniture; glass; jewelry; metals; mixed media

Exhibitions: (9/27/2013-3/22/2014) Enough Violence: Artists Speak Out

Publications: Exhibit catalogs

Activities: Classes for adults & children; docent training; lect open to pub, 4 vis lectrs per yr; competitions with cash awards, Leap Award, Raphael Founder's Prize; gallery talks; tours; biennial Raphael Prize; schols; lends original objects of art to educational insts; originate traveling exhibs 4 per yr to museums and university art galleries; museum shop sells books, magazines, original art, crafts

M UNIVERSITY OF PITTSBURGH, University Art Gallery, 650 Schenley Dr, Frick Fine Arts Bldg Pittsburgh, PA 15260. Tel 412-648-2423; Fax 412-648-2792; Elec Mail uag@pitt.edu; Internet Home Page Address: www.haa.pitt.edu; *Cur* Isabelle Chartier

Open Mon - Fri 10 AM - 4 PM; No admis fee; Estab 1970 to provide exhibs for the univ community & the community at large & to provide students with gallery experience; Gallery comprised of 350 running ft in five areas; Average Annual Attendance: 4,000

Income: Financed through the univ

Special Subjects: Drawings, Etchings & Engravings, Historical Material, Landscapes, Architecture, Ceramics, Glass, Flasks & Bottles, Photography, Pottery, Painting-American, Prints, Bronzes, Painting-British, Painting-European, Painting-Japanese, Sculpture, Tapestries, Sculpture, Watercolors, Archaeology, Woodcuts, Portraits, Eskimo Art, Oriental Art, Asian Art, Painting-French, Baroque Art, Calligraphy, Antiquities-Oriental, Painting-Italian, Antiquities-Roman, Stained Glass, Reproductions

Collections: Drawings, paintings, prints & sculpture; European, Western Pennsylvania, Asian, Inuit

Exhibitions: Mus studies exhib, studio arts faculty & student show

Activities: Educ prog; guided tours; lects open to pub; gallery talks; tours; Original objects of art lent; lending to nearby art institutions; coll contains original art works, original prints, paintings, photographs, sculptures & drawings; originate traveling exhibs

L Henry Clay Frick Fine Arts Library, 6509 Schenley Dr, Frick Fine Arts Bldg, first fl Pittsburgh, PA 15260. Tel 412-648-2410; Fax 412-648-7568; Elec Mail uls-fineartslibrary@mail.pitt.edu; Internet Home Page Address: www.library.pitt.edu/libraries/frick/fine_arts; *Head Librn* James P Cassaro; *Bibliographer & Pub Svcs Librn* Ray Anne Lockard

Open Mon - Thurs 9 AM - 9 PM, Fri 9 AM - 5 PM, Sat & Sun noon-5PM; Estab 1928 to support the teaching activities of the Departments of History Art & Architecture & Studio Arts; For reference only

Library Holdings: Book Volumes 82,000; CD-ROMs 20; Exhibition Catalogs; Fiche 20,000; Pamphlets; Periodical Subscriptions 250; Reels

Special Subjects: Landscape Architecture, Decorative Arts, Graphic Arts, Islamic Art, Sculpture, History of Art & Archaeology, Archaeology, Oriental Art, Religious Art, Tapestries, Landscapes, Architecture

Collections: Facsimile mss; small coll of rare books & artists book

READING

M ALBRIGHT COLLEGE, Freedman Gallery, 13th & Bern Sts, Reading, PA 19612-5234; PO Box 15234, Reading, PA 19612-5234. Tel 610-921-7541; Fax 610-921-7768; Internet Home Page Address: www.albright.edu/freedman; *Dir* Michael Howell

Open Tues, Noon - 8 PM, Wed - Fri Noon - 6 PM, Sat & Sun Noon - 4 PM, also by appointment; No admis fee; Estab 1976 to present primarily contemporary art in a context of teaching; Large Gallery: 40 ft x 50 ft; Small Gallery: 20 ft x 24 ft; Average Annual Attendance: 18,000; Mem: 220; dues Dir Circle $1000, supporter $500, contributor $100, family $50, individual $25

Income: $150,000 (financed by endowment, college, mem & grants)

Special Subjects: Painting-American, Photography, Prints, Sculpture

Collections: Contemporary Painting, Prints, Sculpture, Photography

Publications: Exhibit catalogues & brochures available

Activities: Classes for children; workshops & tours; ann student juried exhibs; lect open to pub, 4 vis lectrs per yr; gallery talks; tours; Freedman Gallery Student Award; produce video-tapes on exhibs, these include interviews with artists & commentary, tapes are available for rent; film series; individual paintings & original objects of art lent to galleries & museums; originate traveling exhibs; sales shop sells catalogues, prints, t-shirts

A BERKS ART ALLIANCE, 1100 Belmont Ave, Institute of the Arts Reading, PA 19610-2004. Tel 610-376-1576, 775-9444; *Pres* Fred Gurman; *VPres Prog* Barbara T Post; *Mem* Katherine Bradley; *Rec Secy* Deb Gurman; *Treas* Ted Thomas; *Corresp Secy* Vicki Rhodier; *Publicity* Maria Ruoff; *Newsletter Ed* Amanda Condict

Estab 1941 to maintain active art center in Reading & Berks county; Mem: 305; dues $25; ann meetings 2nd Tues of odd months: Sept, Nov, Jan, Mar, May; mems must be 18 or older interested in the purpose of the Alliance

Income: Financed by dues; commissions from mems shows, including ann juried show at Reading Public Museum, Jul & Aug

Library Holdings: Book Volumes 250; Video Tapes 50

Exhibitions: Two annual membership shows, plus solo or two-persons shows of a two week period each; juried show at Reading Public Museum or Goggle Works, Jul & Aug

Publications: Palette, every other month Aug - Apr

Activities: Life or costume drawing workshop Thurs morning, Sept - May; open painting workshop Thurs afternoon; life drawing workshop Thurs evening; three day seminars by professional artists; 5 vis lectrs per yr; sponsors ann trip to American Watercolor Society Show in New York and other bus trips to Baltimore & Washington, DC

M READING PUBLIC MUSEUM, 500 Museum Rd, Reading, PA 19611-1425. Tel 610-371-5850; Fax 610-371-5632; Elec Mail museum@readingpublicmuseum.org; Internet Home Page Address: www.readingpublicmuseum.org; *Chmn* Kathleen Kleppinger; *1st VChmn* Richard Zuidema; *Sec* Leigh Rye; *Treas* Socrates J Georgeadis Esq; *Cur Arts & Civilization* Scott A Schweigert; *Dir Educ* Anne Corso; *CFO* Jennifer Wilson; *Asst Secy* Judith Phelps; *Immediate Past Chair* Rolf D Schmidt; *Dir & CEO* John Graydon Smith

Open Tues - Sat 11 AM - 5 PM, Sun Noon - 5PM; Admis adults $8, children $6, students, seniors; Estab 1904; Gen-art to nat history; Average Annual Attendance: 60,000; Mem: 2,800; $60, AAM accredited

Income: donations, admis, grant

Library Holdings: Auction Catalogs; Book Volumes; Exhibition Catalogs

Special Subjects: Landscapes, Marine Painting, Glass, Flasks & Bottles, Photography, Portraits, Pottery, Silver, Textiles, Manuscripts, Painting-British, Painting-Japanese, Sculpture, Tapestries, Drawings, Latin American Art, Mexican Art, Painting-American, Watercolors, American Indian Art, Bronzes, African Art, Anthropology, Religious Art, Ceramics, Folk Art, Woodcarvings, Woodcuts, Etchings & Engravings, Decorative Arts, Judaica, Painting-European, Eskimo Art, Dolls, Furniture, Jade, Jewelry, Oriental Art, Asian Art, Metalwork, Painting-French, Ivory, Scrimshaw, Coins & Medals, Baroque Art, Painting-Flemish, Painting-Polish, Renaissance Art, Dioramas, Medieval Art, Antiquities-Oriental, Painting-Spanish, Painting-Italian, Antiquities-Persian, Islamic Art, Antiquities-Egyptian, Antiquities-Greek, Antiquities-Roman, Stained Glass, Painting-German, Antiquities-Etruscan, Painting-Russian, Enamels, Painting-Scandinavian

Collections: American & European paintings; Natural Science; 19th Century Paintings; Old Masters Gallery; Pennsylvania-German Gallery; Ancient Civilizations; North American Indian Arms & Armor; Pre-Colombian Latin American

Exhibitions: Rotating & permanent exhibs

Publications: Catalog of selections from Permanent Collection & Exhibits

Activities: Classes for adults & children; lects open to pub, 6 vis lectrs per yr; concerts, gallery talks, tours; lending of original objects of art to international mus; books traveling exhibs 1 per yr; mus shop sells books, original art, reproductions & novelties

SCRANTON

M EVERHART MUSEUM, 1901 Mulberry St, Scranton, PA 18510-2390. Tel 570-346-7186; Fax 570-346-0652; Elec Mail general.information@everhart-museum.org; Internet Home Page Address: www.everhart-museum.org; *Cur* Nezka Pfeifer; *Exec Dir* Cara A Sutherland; *Dir Progs* Stefanie Colarusso

Open Mon, Thurs - Fri Noon - 4 PM, Sat 10 AM - 5 PM, Sun Noon - 5 PM cl Tues, Wed, Thanksgiving, Christmas, Easter, anuary & July 4; Admis adults $7, seniors & students $5, children 6 - 12 $3, under 6 no charge; Estab & incorporated 1908, a gift to the city by Dr Isaiah F Everhart; building enlarged 1928-29; Average Annual Attendance: 20,000; Mem: 1400; dues $25 & up

Income: Financed by endowment, city, state & county appropriations & mem

Library Holdings: Book Volumes; Exhibition Catalogs; Memorabilia; Pamphlets; Periodical Subscriptions; Reels

Special Subjects: Anthropology, Archaeology, Decorative Arts, Drawings, Glass, Photography, Porcelain, Portraits, Painting-American, Prints, Sculpture, Watercolors, African Art, Ethnology, Pre-Columbian Art, Ceramics, Folk Art, Woodcuts, Dolls, Oriental Art, Asian Art, Coins & Medals, Tapestries, Miniatures, Dioramas, Antiquities-Egyptian, Antiquities-Greek, Antiquities-Roman

Collections: Dorflinger Glass Collection; local environment dioramas; birds, fossils, rocks; American fine & folk art; ethnographic collections: Africa, Papua New Guinea, Native American

Exhibitions: 9 exhibs per year & permanent colls

Publications: Newsletter, once per yr; brochures; rack cards; e-news, weekly

Activities: Classes for adults & children; docent training; gallery talks; tours; educ progs for schools & other groups by appointment; book traveling exhibs; sales shop sells books, gifts & crafts

SELINSGROVE

M SUSQUEHANNA UNIVERSITY, Lore Degenstein Gallery, 514 University Ave, Selinsgrove, PA 17870-1164. Tel 570-372-4385; Fax 570-372-2729; Elec Mail gallery@susqu.edu; Internet Home Page Address: www.susqu.edu/art_gallery/; *Dir* Dr Daniel Olivette; *Registrar* Judy Marvin; *Coll Mgr* Sara Herlinger

Open daily noon-4PM; No admis fee; Estab 1993 to exhibit, interpret, collect & preserve objects of art & material culture through a rich & diverse exhibition program of inquiry supporting acad investigations & contributing to the cultural life of central Pennsylvania; Gallery offers a schedule of changing exhibs focusing its program on historic, contemporary, regional, national & decorative art. Sponsors lects & opening receptions; Average Annual Attendance: 4,000

Special Subjects: Drawings, Painting-American, Etchings & Engravings, Landscapes, Decorative Arts, Manuscripts, Furniture, Glass, Historical Material

Collections: American Painting

Activities: Docent training; lect open to pub, gallery talks, 3-4 vis lectrs per yr; book traveling exhibs 2-3 per yr; traveling exhibs

SHIPPENSBURG

M SHIPPENSBURG UNIVERSITY, Kauffman Gallery, 1871 Old Main Dr, Shippensburg, PA 17257-2299. Tel 717-477-1530; Fax 717-477-4049; Elec Mail clgrah@ship.edu; Internet Home Page Address: www.ship.edu; *Secy* Cathy Graham; *Dir* Steve Dolbin

Open Mon - Thurs 9 AM - 4 PM, Wed 7 PM - 9 PM, Fri 9 AM - noon; No admis fee; Estab 1972 to bring art to the col community; Average Annual Attendance: 1,500

Income: Financed by Student Assn funds & univ
Exhibitions: Scholastic Art Awards - Area 6; Faculty Exhibits; Student Art Exhibits; changing exhibs every month; Senior Art Exhibits
Activities: Lects open to pub, 4 vis lectrs per yr; gallery talks

SOMERSET

M **LAUREL ARTS,** 214 S Harrison Ave, Somerset, PA 15501; PO Box 414, Somerset, PA 15501-0414. Tel 814-443-2433; Fax 814-443-3870; Internet Home Page Address: www.laurelarts.org; *Dir* Michael S Knecht
Open Mon - Thurs 10 AM - 8 PM, Fri 10 AM - 4 PM, Sat Noon - 4 PM; No admis fee; Estab 1975; Average Annual Attendance: 51,015

STRASBURG

A **LANCASTER COUNTY ART ASSOCIATION, INC,** 149 Precision Ave, Strasburg, PA 17579-9608. Tel 717-687-7061; Elec Mail imajgin@aol.org; Internet Home Page Address: www.lcaaonline.org; *VPres* Anne Fisher; *Treas* Harry McCandless; *Pres* Jill Weidman
Open Wed - Sun 1 - 5 PM; No admis fee; Estab 1936, inc 1950, to increase appreciation of & participation in the fine arts; Average Annual Attendance: 10,000; Mem: 300; dues $35; general mem meeting the second Sun of the month, Sept - May
Income: Financed by dues, classes, contributions & volunteer service
Exhibitions: Monthly exhibs for professional & non-professional mems
Publications: Monthly newsletter; annual mem brochure
Activities: Classes for adults & children; lect open to pub, 7-10 vis lectrs per yr; competitions with awards; schols offered

STROUDSBURG

M **MONROE COUNTY HISTORICAL ASSOCIATION,** Elizabeth D Walters Library, 900 Main St, Stroudsburg, PA 18360-1604. Tel 570-421-7703; Fax 570-421-9199; Elec Mail mcha@ptd.net; Internet Home Page Address: www.monroe.historical.org; *Exec Dir* Amy Leiser
Open Tues - Fri 9 AM - 4 PM, Sat 10 AM - 4 PM, cl Sun & Mon; Admis adults $8, seniors $6, children $4; Estab 1921 for research; Average Annual Attendance: 5,000; Mem: 550; dues $20; ann meeting 4th Sun in Feb
Income: $116,000 (financed by endowment, mem, state appropriation & county)
Special Subjects: Painting-American, Textiles, Decorative Arts, Collages, Furniture, Historical Material, Period Rooms, Embroidery
Collections: Decorative Arts; Furniture; Indian Artifacts; Textiles
Exhibitions: Period Room; Toy Room; Rotate 4 per yr
Publications: Fanlight Newsletter, six times per year
Activities: Lect open to pub, 5 vis lectrs per yr; Historic Preservation Awards; mus shop sells books

SWARTHMORE

L **SWARTHMORE COLLEGE,** Friends Historical Library of Swarthmore College, 500 College Ave, Swarthmore, PA 19081-1306. Tel 610-328-8496; Fax 610-690-5728; Elec Mail friends@swarthmore.edu; Internet Home Page Address: www.swarthmore.edu/library/friends; *Cur* Christopher Densmore; *Cur Peace Coll* Wendy Chmielewski
Open Mon - Fri 8:30 AM - 4:30 PM, Sat 10 AM - 1 PM; cl Sat when col not in session; No admis fee; Estab 1871 to preserve & make available to the pub material by & about Quakers & their concerns, records of non-sectarian peace organizations & papers of peace movement leaders; Gallery housed in McCabe Library
Income: financed by endowment & col
Library Holdings: Audio Tapes; Book Volumes 55,000; Cassettes; Clipping Files; Kodachrome Transparencies; Lantern Slides; Manuscripts; Memorabilia; Motion Pictures; Original Art Works; Original Documents; Other Holdings charts; Maps; Posters; Pamphlets; Periodical Subscriptions 584; Photographs; Prints; Records; Reels; Sculpture; Slides; Video Tapes
Special Subjects: Photography, Painting-American, Painting-British, Posters, Historical Material, Portraits, Religious Art
Collections: Quaker paintings; Quakers as subject in art; Meeting House Picture Collection; portraits, group pictures, residence pictures, silhouettes & sketches of individual Friends; Swarthmore College pictures; Swarthmore College Peace Collection: primarily archival material, records of non-sectarian peace organizations in the United States and 59 foreign countries, papers of peace leaders including Jean Addams, Emily Greene Balch, Elihu Burritt, A J Muste,Wilhelm Sollmann and others; 6000 peace posters and war posters; Benjamin West sketches; Edward Hicks journals

UNION DALE

A **SUSQUEHANNA STUDIO,** (Art Exchange) Susquehanna Studio, 16 Lewis Lake Rd, Union Dale, PA 18470-0021. Tel 570-972-2662; Elec Mail susquehannastudio@gmail.com; Internet Home Page Address: susquehannastudio.blogspot.com; *Dir* Robert Stark
Open by appointment Sat - Sun; No admis fee; Estab 1970 to provide opportunities for community participation in the creative voices & forms of expression within the region, to bring to the community the art forms of other cultures & people, to support local & regional artists in the documentation & exhib of their work; & to be a vigorous advocate for the development of the visual, verbal, performing, & craft arts within the community & region; Maintains reference library; Average Annual Attendance: 500
Activities: Sales shop sells original art, reproductions & prints

UNIVERSITY PARK

M **THE PENNSYLVANIA STATE UNIVERSITY,** Palmer Museum of Art, Curtin Rd, University Park, PA 16802-2507. Tel 814-865-7672; Fax 814-863-8608; Elec Mail jkm11@psu.edu; Internet Home Page Address: www.palmermuseum.psu.edu; *Cur* Dr Joyce Henri Robinson; *Registrar* Beverly Sutley; *Cur* Dr Patrick J McGrady; *Sr Preparator* Richard Hall; *Cur Educ* Dana Carlisle Kletchka; *Coordr Mem & Pub Rels* Jennifer Cozad Feehan; *Mus Store Mgr* Lynne McCormack; *Mus Security & Facility Mgr* Jeremy Warner; *Preparator* Craig Witter; *Asst Security & Facility Mgr* Dan Esposito
Open Tues - Sat 10 AM - 4:30 PM, Sun Noon - 4 PM, cl Mon & major holidays; No admis fee; Estab 1972 to promote a program of changing exhibs; a window to the world for the university & surrounding communities; The mus expanded in 1993 and again in 2002, has eleven galleries which accommodate continuous display of the permanent coll as well as changing exhibs that are national & international in scope; Average Annual Attendance: 42,000; Mem: 434; students $10 - $34, individual $35 - $59, family/household $60 - $99, sustaining $100 - $299, benefactor $300 - $599, sponsor $600 - $999, dir's cir $1000 & more
Income: Financed by state appropriation & donations
Purchases: American & European paintings, prints, drawings, & photographs
Library Holdings: Auction Catalogs; Book Volumes; Clipping Files; Exhibition Catalogs; Periodical Subscriptions; Slides
Special Subjects: Afro-American Art, Decorative Arts, Drawings, Etchings & Engravings, Historical Material, Landscapes, Marine Painting, Collages, Glass, Metalwork, Furniture, Photography, Portraits, Pre-Columbian Art, Painting-American, Prints, Bronzes, Woodcuts, Manuscripts, Painting-European, Painting-French, Sculpture, Graphics, Watercolors, African Art, Ceramics, Judaica, Painting-Japanese, Posters, Jade, Porcelain, Oriental Art, Asian Art, Coins & Medals, Baroque Art, Miniatures, Painting-Flemish, Renaissance Art, Medieval Art, Painting-Spanish, Painting-Italian, Painting-German, Painting-Scandinavian
Collections: American & European paintings, drawings, sculpture, prints & photographs, 19th & 20th Centuries; Asian paintings, sculpture, prints & decorative art (ceramics, jade & cloisonne); British, Japanese, Scandinavian & American Contemporary ceramics; Pennsylvania Prints from the late 18th to the early 20th Century; Tonkin Collection of Chinese export porcelain, Chinese jade carvings, paintings & watercolors related to the Oriental Trade; Baroque paintings; Japanese prints; ancient coins & ancient Peruvian ceramics; Adolf Austrian Academic Painting Collection; Markley Ancient Peruvian Ceramic Collection
Publications: Brochures; exhibition catalogs; newsletter, triannual
Activities: Educ prog; classes for adults with Osher Lifelong Learning Institute; summer workshops; docent training; print study club; lects open to pub; concerts; gallery talks; tours; symposia; book & originate traveling exhibits to other art mus; mus store sells books, original art & reproductions, paper products

L **Arts & Humanities Library,** 510 Paterno Library, University Park, PA 16802-1812. Tel 814-865-6481; Fax 814-863-7502; Elec Mail henryp@psu.edu; Internet Home Page Address: www.libraries.psu.edu; *Head Arts & Humanities Library* Eric Novotny; *Arts & Architecture Librn* Henry Pisciotta
Open Mon - Thurs 7:45 AM - 11 AM, Fri 7:45 AM - 11 PM, Sat 9 AM - 7PM, Sun Noon - 11 PM; Estab 1957 to support the acad progs of the College of Arts & Architecture & the Division of Art & Music Educ; to provide information on the arts to members of the univ & community; reestablished in 1998 to support arts & humanities programs at Penn State and its community
Income: Financed through University Library, operating expenses & endowments
Library Holdings: Book Volumes 1,000,000; CD-ROMs 50; Compact Disks 22,000; DVDs 3,500; Exhibition Catalogs; Other Holdings Electronic texts; Image databases; Periodical Subscriptions 2300; Prints 250; Records 20,000; Video Tapes 2,600
Special Subjects: Prints, Art Education, Antiquities-Byzantine
Collections: Prints Collection (original prints); Faculty works on paper

M **HUB Robeson Galleries,** 241 HUB Robeson Ctr, University Park, PA 16802-6601. Tel 814-865-2563; Fax 814-865-6034; Elec Mail studentaffairs@pennstate/hub-robesongalleries; Internet Home Page Address: www.sa.psu.edu/usa/galleries; *Dir* Ann Shields
Open Tues-Thurs noon-6PM, Fri & Sat noon-4PM; No admis fee; Estab 1976 to provide life-enriching visual arts experiences to the University & community; HUB Gallery; Robeson Gallery; Art Alley Exhibit Areas & Cases; Average Annual Attendance: 55,000
Income: financed by Pennsylvania State University
Collections: John Biggers and murals
Exhibitions: Central Penn Arts Exhibit; variety of contemporary exhibits
Publications: art brochure
Activities: Educ program; classes for college students; book traveling exhibs 7 per yr; sales shop

L **Architecture & Landscape Architecture Library,** 111 Stuckeman Family Bldg, University Park, PA 16802-1901. Tel 814-865-3614; Fax 814-865-5073; Elec Mail arch@psulias.psu.edu; Internet Home Page Address: www.libraries.psu.edu; *Library Supv* Stephanie Movahedi-Lankarani; *Arts & Architecture Librn* Henry Pisciotta
Open Mon - Thurs 7:45 AM - 11 PM, Fri 7:45 AM - 7 PM, Sat Noon - 5 PM, Sun Noon - 11 PM; Estab 1978 to support the acad progs of the Dept of Architecture & Dept of Landscape Architecture to provide information on architecture & landscape architecture to members of the university & community
Income: Financed through university libraries, operating expenses & endowments
Library Holdings: Book Volumes 29,500; CD-ROMs; DVDs; Exhibition Catalogs; Other Holdings; Periodical Subscriptions 150; Video Tapes Digital Images
Special Subjects: Landscape Architecture, Architecture

VILLANOVA

M **VILLANOVA UNIVERSITY ART GALLERY,** The Art Gallery, Connelly Ctr, 800 Lancaster Ave Villanova, PA 19085. Tel 610-519-4612; Fax 610-519-6046; Elec Mail annetta.stowman@villanova.edu; Internet Home Page Address: www.artgallery.villanova.edu; *Asst Dir* Annetta T Stowman; *Workshop Coordr* Vladimir Pearce-Adashkevich; *Dir* Richard Cannuli O.S.A.
Open Mon - Fri 9 AM - 5 PM, call for weekend hours; No admis fee; Estab 1979 to enrich the learning experience of Villanova University Students & the

surrounding community through its programs of study & presentations of works of art in the gallery & throughout the campus; Average Annual Attendance: 2,500
Income: Financed by gifts & university budget
Collections: Abstract Art 20th century, African & Oceanic Art, Philadelphia Artists 19th & 20th century, Southeast Asian Antiquities
Activities: Classes for children; lect open to pub; lending coll contains over 4000 items

WARREN

M **CRARY ART GALLERY INC,** Grary Art Gallery, 511 Market St, Warren, PA 16365-1765. Tel 814-723-4523; Elec Mail crarygallery@gmail.com; Internet Home Page Address: www.crarygallery.org; *Pres* Barbara Kersey; *VPres* Thomas Paquette
Open Thurs - Sun during special exhibs; No fee; Estab 1977 for art appreciation & educ & to exhibit the work of Clare J Crary, Gene Alden Walker & guest artists; The gallery was constructed in 1962 as a private dwelling on the general plan of a Roman Villa. There are 6 gallery rooms, one housing a permanent exhibit of Crary photographs. The others accommodate other permanent-collection art & traveling shows.; Average Annual Attendance: 1500; Mem: 150 mems; $50 annual dues
Income: financed by endowment
Special Subjects: Photography, Painting-American, Prints, Woodcuts, Watercolors
Collections: Photographs by Clare J Crary; Oils by Gene Alden Walker; drawings, etchings, oils, acrylics by various artists; 19th Century Japanese wood-block prints, Edward Curtis
Exhibitions: (2014-2014) Brigham Dimick
Activities: Lects open to pub; 6 vis lects per yr; gallery talks; tours; book traveling exhibs

WASHINGTON

M **WASHINGTON & JEFFERSON COLLEGE,** Olin Fine Arts Center Gallery, 60 S Lincoln St, Washington &Jefferson College Art Dept Washington, PA 15301-4812. Tel 724-503-1001 ext 6043; Fax 724-250-3319; Elec Mail dmcglumphy@washjeff.edu; Internet Home Page Address: www.washjeff.edu/olin.uspx; *Gallery Mgr* Doug McGlumphy
Open daily noon-7PM; No admis fee; Estab 1980 to provide col & community with art shows; Flexible lighting, air conditioned gallery; Average Annual Attendance: 6,000
Income: Financed by college
Purchases: Over $3,000 annually during National Painting Show
Collections: Art dept coll; college historical coll; National Painting Show coll
Exhibitions: Monthly exhibits
Publications: Exhibition catalogs
Activities: Lects open to pub; 2-3 vis lectrs per yr; concerts; gallery talks; tours; competitions with awards; individual paintings & original objects of art lent to students, faculty & staff; lending coll contains 200 original art works, 100 original prints, 300 paintings, 200 photographs & 4 sculpture; book traveling exhibs 1 - 2 per yr

WAYNE

A **WAYNE ART CENTER,** 413 Maplewood Ave, Wayne, PA 19087-4792. Tel 610-688-3553; Fax 610-995-0478; Elec Mail info@wayneart.org; Internet Home Page Address: www.wayneart.com; *Dir* Nancy Campbell
Open Mon - Fri 9 AM - 5 PM, Sat 10 AM - 4 PM; No admis fee; Estab 1930 as a community art center; Two galleries offer rotating exhibits of work by local artists; Average Annual Attendance: 2,000; Mem: 400; dues $20; annual meeting May
Income: $60,000 (financed by mem, grants, corporations & Pennsylvania Council on the Arts)
Exhibitions: 10-12 changing exhibs per yr
Publications: promotional catalogs
Activities: Classes for adults & children; workshops; gallery talks; competitions

WEST CHESTER

A **CHESTER COUNTY HISTORICAL SOCIETY,** 225 N High St, West Chester, PA 19380-2658. Tel 610-692-4800; Fax 610-692-4357; Elec Mail cchs@chestercohistorical.org; Internet Home Page Address: www.chestercohistorical.org; *Exec Dir* Roland H Woodward; *Educator Group Tours* Barbara Jobe; *Dir Pub Prog* William C Kashatus; *Dir Coll & Cur* Ellen Endslow
Open Tues - Sat 10 AM - 5 PM; Admis adults $5, seniors 65 & over $4, children 6-17 & students with ID $2.50, children under 6 free; Estab 1893 for the acquisition & preservation of art and information historically significant to Chester County; A historical center encompassing a reference library, historical archives, photo archives, a collection of Chester County materials covering 300 years and the County archives; Average Annual Attendance: 45,000; Mem: 2500; dues family $50, individual $35
Income: Financed by membership, sponsorship, grants and endowment
Library Holdings: Book Volumes; Clipping Files; Exhibition Catalogs; Fiche; Manuscripts; Maps; Original Art Works; Original Documents; Pamphlets; Periodical Subscriptions; Prints; Records; Reproductions; Slides; Video Tapes
Special Subjects: Costumes, Photography, Porcelain, Silver, Textiles, Painting-American, Pottery, Decorative Arts, Folk Art, Pewter, Ceramics, Portraits, Dolls, Furniture, Glass, Period Rooms
Collections: Museum houses regional collections of furniture, from 1690 to early 20th century through Victorian; ceramics, needlework, glassware, pewter, textiles, clocks, iron, dolls & costumes
Exhibitions: The Underground Railroad; Meeting for Equality: The 1852 Pennsylvania Woman's Rights Convention
Publications: Chester County History, occasionally; Newsletter, 3 times per yr for mems

Activities: Docent training, educational progs for children, Nat History Day for middle & HS students; monthly lect series & conferences, tours, concerts, gallery talks & sponsoring competitions; individual paintings and original objects of art lent to other museums; mus shop sells books, reproductions, prints, ceramics, toys & other gifts with historical significance to Chester County and the surrounding region

WHITEHALL

NATIONAL SOCIETY OF PAINTERS IN CASEIN & ACRYLIC, INC
For further information, see National and Regional Organizations

WILKES-BARRE

M **WILKES UNIVERSITY,** Sordoni Art Gallery, 150 S River St, Wilkes-Barre, PA 18766-0001. Tel 507-408-4325; Fax 507-408-7733; Elec Mail brittany.kramer@wilkes.edu; Internet Home Page Address: www.wilkes.edu/sordoniartgallery; *Interim Dir* Brittany Kramer DeBalko
Open Tues - Sun noon - 4:30 PM; No admis fee; Estab 1973 to encourage the fine arts in the Wilkes-Barre & the northeastern Pennsylvania areas; The Gallery has one exhib space, 1,500 sq ft; Average Annual Attendance: 5,000; Mem: 600; dues $30-$1000
Income: Financed by mem, foundation endowment & Wilkes University
Library Holdings: Exhibition Catalogs; Original Documents; Periodical Subscriptions
Special Subjects: Painting-American, Sculpture, Painting-European
Collections: 20th century American paintings & prints; European prints
Exhibitions: Consists of loan exhibs from other col galleries, independent galleries, major museums & loan services; group & one-person exhibs feature estab modern masters & contemporary artists; curriculum-based exhibs
Publications: Calendar of Events, bimonthly; scholarly catalogs; illustrated brochures; posters
Activities: Lects open to pub; 2 vis lectrs per yr; gallery talks; tours; loans to other universities & museums; book traveling exhibs 1 per yr; originate traveling exhibs to schools & museums

WILLIAMSPORT

M **LYCOMING COLLEGE GALLERY,** 700 College Pl, Lycoming College Art Dept Williamsport, PA 17701-5157. Tel 570-321-4002; Fax 570-321-4090; *Dir* Rose Dirocco
Open Mon - Thurs 8 AM - 11 PM, Fri 8 AM - 4:30 PM, Sat 10 AM - 5 PM, Sun 1 - 11 PM; No admis fee; Estab 1980 to bring quality art work to the students & faculty as well as to the interested community; The new gallery, 30 x 60 ft, is located in the College Library; Average Annual Attendance: 5,000
Income: Financed by school budget & local & state grants
Special Subjects: Painting-American, Prints
Collections: Paintings & prints of 19th & 20th century artists
Exhibitions: One-man shows of regional artists & alumni of the Department
Activities: Gallery talks; tours; individual paintings lent; book traveling exhibs; originate traveling exhibs

YORK

L **MARTIN MEMORIAL LIBRARY,** 159 E Market St, York, PA 17401-1269. Tel 717-846-5300; Fax 717-848-1496 (ref dept); Internet Home Page Address: www.yorklibraries.org; *Dir* William H Schell; *Dir Operations* Paula Gilbert
Open Mon - Thurs 9 AM - 8 PM, Fri & Sat 9 AM - 5:30 PM, Sun 1 PM - 5 PM ; No admis fee; Estab 1935
Library Holdings: Book Volumes 100,000; Cassettes; Motion Pictures; Other Holdings Mounted pictures; Pamphlets; Periodical Subscriptions 200; Records
Publications: Ann Reports; Bulletin, monthly; Martin Memorial Library Historical Series; occasional bibliographies of spec colls
Activities: Programs for adults and children; lect; concerts

M **YORK COLLEGE GALLERIES,** MAC, Wolf Hall, 1 Country Club Rd York, PA 17405-3643. Tel 717-815-1354 & 1528
Open Mon - Tues & Thurs - Fri 10 AM - 5 PM, Wed 10 AM - 9 PM, Sat - Sun 12 PM - 5 PM; No admis fee
Collections: Works by local & national artists
Activities: Lectures & workshops

A **THE YORK COUNTY HERITAGE TRUST,** (Historical Society of York County) 250 E Market St, York, PA 17403-2013. Tel 717-848-1587; Fax 717-812-1204; Elec Mail info@yorkheritage.org; Internet Home Page Address: www.yorkheritage.org; *Pres & CEO* Joan J Mummert; *Dir Libr & Archives* Lila Fourhman-Shaull; *Dir Educ* Daniel Roe; *Colls Mgr* Cindy Brown
Open Tues - Sat 10 AM - 4 PM; Historic Houses call for times, cl Sun, Mon & all major holidays; Admis adults $10, students with ID $7, children 8-18 $5; Estab 1895 to record, preserve, collect & interpret the history of York County & Pennsylvania; Colonial Courthouse: General Gates House (1751); Golden Plough Tavern (1741) & Bobb Log House (1812), 157 W Market; Bonham House (1875), 152 E Market. Maintains reference library, Historical Society Museum, Fire Museum and Agricultural & Industrial Museum; Average Annual Attendance: 30,000; Mem: 1539; dues $40 & up; annual meeting in Sept
Income: $1,200,000 (financed by endowment, gifts & mem)
Library Holdings: Audio Tapes; Book Volumes 32,000; Clipping Files; Exhibition Catalogs; Manuscripts; Memorabilia; Motion Pictures; Pamphlets; Periodical Subscriptions 30; Photographs; Reels; Slides
Special Subjects: Cartoons, Costumes, Drawings, Embroidery, Etchings & Engravings, Porcelain, Prints, Silver, Textiles, Watercolors, Painting-American, Pottery, Decorative Arts, Folk Art, Woodcuts, Ceramics, Crafts, Portraits, Dolls, Furniture, Woodcarvings, Period Rooms, Flasks & Bottles, Coins & Medals

Collections: Fraktur & other Pennsylvania decorative arts & furnishings; Works by Lewis Miller & other local artists; James Shettel Collection of theater & circus material; Horace Bonham artworks

Exhibitions: Six galleries at the Historical Society Museums featuring various subjects of regional interest; historic houses; numerous galleries at the Agricultural and Industrial Museum & Fire Museum

Publications: The Kentucky Rifle; Lewis Miller Sketches & Chronicles; monthly newsletter; The Philadelphia Chair, 1685-1785; William Wagner-Views of York in 1830; J W Gitt & His Legendary Newspaper; York Co Journal

Activities: Educ prog; classes for adults & children; docent training; lects open to pub; concerts; gallery talks; tours; mus shop sells books, reproductions & prints

L **Library,** 250 E Market St, York, PA 17403. Tel 717-848-1587; Fax 717-812-1204; Elec Mail library@yorkheritage.org; Internet Home Page Address: www.yorkheritage.org; *Librn* Lila Fourhman-Shaull; *Asst Librn* Victoria Miller

Open to the public 9 AM - 5 PM, cl Sun & Mon; Admis $6; For reference only

Library Holdings: Audio Tapes; Book Volumes 25,000; Cassettes; Clipping Files; Manuscripts; Memorabilia; Other Holdings Maps; Vertical files 156; Pamphlets; Periodical Subscriptions 50; Photographs; Reels; Slides; Video Tapes

Special Subjects: Art History, Folk Art, Photography, Commercial Art, Drawings, Etchings & Engravings, Manuscripts, Maps, Painting-American, Prints, Sculpture, Historical Material, History of Art & Archaeology, Crafts, Theatre Arts, Archaeology, Ethnology, Printmaking, Industrial Design, Porcelain, Furniture, Drafting, Costume Design & Constr, Glass, Metalwork, Dolls, Embroidery, Gold, Goldsmithing, Jewelry, Restoration & Conservation, Silver, Silversmithing, Tapestries, Textiles, Woodcarvings, Woodcuts, Landscapes, Reproductions, Pewter, Flasks & Bottles, Architecture, Portraits, Pottery

PUERTO RICO

OLD SAN JUAN

L **CENTRO DE ESTUDIOS AVANZADOS,** Art Library, Calle Cristo # 52, Old San Juan, PR 00902; Apartado 9023970, San Juan, PR 00902-3970. Tel 787-723-4481 (Gen); Tel 787-723-4481 x 24 (Library); Fax 787-723-4810; Elec Mail centro@ceaprc.org; Internet Home Page Address: www.ceaprc.edu; *Dir* Prof Francis J Mojica

Open Mon, Wed, Thurs 9 AM - 10 PM, Tues 9 AM - 5:30 PM, Sat 7 AM - 4 PM, cl Fri & Sun; No admis fee; small photocopying fees apply

Library Holdings: Book Volumes 15,000; Compact Disks; Other Holdings; Slides; Video Tapes

Special Subjects: Archaeology, Anthropology

PONCE

M **MUSEO DE ARTE DE PONCE,** The Luis A Ferre Foundation Inc, 2325 Blvd Luis A Ferre-Aguayo, Ponce, PR 00717-0776; PO Box 9027, Ponce, PR 00732. Tel 787-840-1510; Fax 787-841-7309; Elec Mail info@museoarteponce.org; Internet Home Page Address: www.museoarteponce.org; *Deputy Dir* Alejandra Pena; *Conservator of Paintings* Lidia Aravena; *Assoc Cur* Arlette de la Serna; *Chief Educ* Ana M Hernandez; *Dir Finance & Admin* Miriam B Quintero CPA; *Librn* Aida Baez; *Develop Dir* Rafael Irizarry; *Hr Dir* Wanda Ramos; *European Art Asst Cur* Pablo Perez

Open Wed - Mon 10 AM - 6 PM, cl Tues; Admis adults $6, children under 12 & students with ID $3; Estab 1959 to exhibit a representative collection of European paintings & sculpture; Puerto Rican & Latin American art; temporarily cl for renovation and expansion project and will reopen in Nov 2010; Fourteen galleries on two floors, present works from permanent collection & a wide variety of temporary exhibitions; Average Annual Attendance: 80,000; Mem: 1000; dues family $50, individual $30

Income: Financed by endowment, mem & government

Library Holdings: Auction Catalogs; Book Volumes; CD-ROMs; Cassettes; DVDs; Exhibition Catalogs; Manuscripts; Original Documents; Periodical Subscriptions; Photographs; Records; Video Tapes

Special Subjects: Archaeology, Decorative Arts, Drawings, Photography, Painting-American, Prints, Painting-British, Painting-French, Sculpture, Graphics, Painting-Dutch, Painting-Flemish, Painting-Spanish, Painting-Italian

Collections: Pre-Raphaelite painting & drawings, Art Noveau Glass; African, Latin American, Pre-Columbian & Puerto Rican Santos Art; 19th century art, contemporary art, 14th-18th century paintings & sculpture

Exhibitions: Rotating exhibs

Publications: Coincide with large exhibs

Activities: Educ dept, classes for adults and children; docent training, family days, teacher training, student programs; Lects open to pub; 3 vis lectrs per year; concerts, gallery talks, tours; individual paintings & original objects of art lent to other mus & government offices; traveling exhibs 1-2 per yr to museums world wide; originate & organize traveling exhibs worldwide; mus shops sells books, prints, reproductions & various gift items

L **Library,** 2325 Blvd Luis A Ferre, Ponce, PR 00717-0776; PO Box 9027, Ponce, PR 00732-9027. Tel 787-840-1510; Fax 787-841-7309; Elec Mail info@museoarteponce.org; Internet Home Page Address: www.museoarteponce.org; *Deputy Dir* Alejandra Pena; *Chief Librn* Aida E Baez

Open daily 10 AM - 5 PM; Cl for reference with the exception of special permission

Library Holdings: Auction Catalogs 1000; Audio Tapes 40; Book Volumes 5000; DVDs 10; Exhibition Catalogs; Periodical Subscriptions 6

Special Subjects: Art History, Photography, Maps, Painting-American, Painting-British, Painting-Dutch, Painting-Flemish, Painting-French, Painting-Italian, Painting-Spanish, Conceptual Art, Latin American Art, American Western Art, Art Education, Afro-American Art, Religious Art, Restoration & Conservation, Antiquities-Greek, Antiquities-Roman

RIO PIEDRAS

M **UNIVERSITY OF PUERTO RICO,** Museum of Anthropology, History & Art, Ponce de Leon Ave, Rio Piedras, PR 00931; PO Box 21908, San Juan, PR 00931-1908. Tel 787-764-0000; Fax 787-763-4799; *Cur Archaeology* Ivan Mendez; *Cur Art* Flavia Marichal; *Archaeologist* Luis A Chanlatte; *Dir* Petra Barreras

Open Mon 9 AM-1 PM, Tues 9 AM-4:30 PM, Wed & Thurs 9 AM-8:45 PM, Fri 9 AM-4:30 PM, Sat 9 AM-4:30 PM, Sun 1 PM-4:30 PM, cl national holidays; No admis fee; Estab 1940; Maintains reference library; Average Annual Attendance: 30,000

Income: Financed by government grants & pub institutions

Purchases: Puerto Rican prints & drawings; paintings of past & contemporary Puerto Rican artists

Special Subjects: Hispanic Art, Archaeology, Antiquities-Egyptian

Collections: Archaeology; Puerto Rican paintings of the past & present; sculpture & folk art; prints & drawings

Exhibitions: Temporary exhibitions from the collection & from museum loans; Contemporary Puerto Rican art

Activities: Provide concerts; gallery talks; tours; individual paintings & original objects of art lent to organizations & mus; originate traveling exhibs; mus shop sells slides & exhib catalogues

SAN JUAN

M **ATENEO PUERTORRIQUENO,** Ateneo Gallery, PO Box 1180, San Juan, PR 00902-1180. Tel 809-722-4839; Tel 787-202-7425; Fax 809-725-3873; Fax 787-432-8209; Elec Mail info@ateneopuertorriquenosanjan.com; Internet Home Page Address: www.ateneopr.com; *Pres* Eduardo Morales-Coll

Open Mon - Fri 9 AM - 5 PM, cl Sun & holidays; No admis fee; Estab 1876 & is the oldest cultural institution in Puerto Rico; Puerto Rican Art Collection; Mem: dues $25; annual meeting in June

Library Holdings: Audio Tapes; Book Volumes; CD-ROMs; Exhibition Catalogs; Maps; Memorabilia; Motion Pictures; Original Art Works; Photographs; Sculpture; Video Tapes

Special Subjects: Historical Material

Collections: Decorative arts; drawings; historical material; prints; Puerto Rican paintings; sculpture

Exhibitions: Temporary exhibitions, monthly

Publications: Cuadernos (publications on general topics); Revista Ateneo, every 4 months

Activities: Classes for adults; dramatic progs; lects open to pub; gallery talks; guided tours; films; concerts; recitals; competitions with prizes; dramas; Ateneo Medal; individual paintings & original objects of art lent to other cultural institutions; book traveling exhibs 1 per yr; sales shop sells books & reproductions

L **Library,** Avenido Ponce de Leon, Parada 2 San Juan, PR 00902; PO Box 9021180, San Juan, PR 00902-1180. Tel 787-722-4839; Fax 787-725-3873; *Pres* Eduardo Morales-Coll

Library Holdings: Book Volumes 15,000

M **INSTITUTE OF PUERTO RICAN CULTURE,** Instituto de Cultura Puertorriquena, PO Box 9024184, San Juan, PR 00902-4184. Tel 787-724-0700; Fax 787-724-8993; *Dir* Mercedes Gomez

Open Mon - Fri 8 AM - 12 noon, 1 PM - 4:30 PM; No admis fee; Estab 1955 to stimulate, promote, divulge & enrich Puerto Rico's cultural & historical heritage; The institute has created 19 museums around the island, including museums of historical collections, art museums & archaeological museums

Income: Financed by endowment & state appropriation

Collections: Puerto Rican art, archaeology & historical collections

Publications: Revista del Instituto de Cultura Puertorriquena, quarterly

Activities: Educ dept; lects open to pub, gallery talks; concerts; tours; competitions; exten dept serves cultural centers around the island; artmobile; individual paintings & original objects of art lent to government agencies, universities & cultural centers; lending collection contains motion pictures, original art works; original prints, paintings, photographs; originates traveling exhibs; sales shop sells books, records & craft items; junior mus

A **National Gallery,** Apartado 9024184, San Juan, PR 00902-4184. Tel 787-725-2670; Fax 787-723-7837; Elec Mail galerianacional@icp.gobierno.pr; Internet Home Page Address: www.ipc.gobierno.pr; *Exec Dir Institute of Culture* Mercedes Gomez Marrero; *Dir Visual Arts & National Gallery* Marilu Purcell

Open Tues - Sat 9:30 AM - Noon & 1 - 5 PM; No admis fee; Estab 2007 to exhibit iconic artworks from the Institute of Puerto Rican Culture's collection that reflect diverse aspects of a vibrant culture; The institute has created 16 museums around the island & has five more in preparation, including museums of historical collections, art museums & archaeological museums; Average Annual Attendance: 24,000

Income: Financed by endowment & state appropriation

Collections: Puerto Rican art

Exhibitions: Exhibs vary

Publications: Revista del Institute de Cultura Puertorriquena, quarterly

Activities: Educ dept; classes for adults & children; lects open to pub, 10 vis lectrs per yr; gallery talks; concerts; tours; competitions sponsored; exten dept serves cultural centers around the Island; artmobile; individual paintings & original objects of art lent to government agencies, universities, museums & cultural centers; lending collection contains motion pictures, original art works, original prints, paintings, photographs; originates traveling exhibs; sales shop sells books, magazines, original art, reproductions, records & craft items; junior mus

M **Dr Jose C Barbosa Museum,** 35 Barbosa St, Bayamon, PR 00961-6351; PO Box 9024184, San Juan, PR 00902-4184. Tel 787-786-8670; Tel 787-977-2702; Fax 787-723-7837; Elec Mail museosyparques@icp.gobierno.pr; Internet Home Page Address: www.icp.golairno.pr; *Dir* Samuel Febo; *Exec Dir* Liliane Ramos

Open Mon - Fri 8 AM - 12 noon, 1 PM - 4 PM; No admis fee; The house where patriot Jose Celso Barbosa was born & raised, restored to its original status as representative of a typical Puerto Rican family home of the 19th century; Average Annual Attendance: 1,200

Income: Financed by state appropriations

Special Subjects: Historical Material
Collections: Furniture, personal objects & documents belonging to Dr Barbosa, including medical instruments, manuscripts & books
M **Parque Ceremonial Indigena de Caguana,** Rt 111 Km 12 4, Utuado, PR 00641; Apartado 9024184, San Juan, PR 00902-4184. Tel 787-894-7325; Fax 787-894-7310; *Dir* Milagros Castro
Open daily 8:00 AM - 4:30 PM; Admis adults $2, minors $1; Caguana Indian Ceremonial Park & Mus includes the ceremonial center of the Taino Indians in Caguana, Utuado, a small town in the center of the Island, constituting the archeological find of the Caribbean & exposition of Indian primitive engineering. The plazas & walks where the Indians held their ceremonies, celebrations & games were restored & excavated to form an archeological park. Numerous petroglyphs are exhibited in the monoliths bordering the plazas & a mus exhibits Indian objects found during the excavations at the site
Income: Financed by state appropriations
M **Museo de Arte Religioso Porta Coeli,** Plaza Porta Coeli, San German, PR 00683. Tel 787-892-5845; Fax 787-725-5608; Elec Mail www.@icp.gobierno.pr; *Dir* Aida T Rodriguez
Open Wed -Sun 8:30 AM - noon, 1 - 4:30 PM; Admis adults $3, children (under 11) & seniors (over 65) $2 ; Estab 1960 to preserve & expose religious art to our culture; 17th century restored chapel built by Dominican monks in the town of San German; Mem: 15,000
Income: Financed by state appropriations
Special Subjects: Religious Art
Collections: Paintings & sculptures from between the 11th & 19th century obtained from different churches in the island; wood & metal religious artifacts
Activities: Conferences; cultural & craft workshops; 4 vis lectrs per yr; concerts; tours; mus shop sells books, magazines & original art
M **Museo del Grabado Latinoamericano,** Calle San Sebastian, Plaza San Jose Viejo San Juan, PR 00901. Tel 809-724-1844, 724-0700;
Open 8:30 AM - 4:30 PM; No admis fee; Houses representative samples of graphic art of past & contemporary Puerto Rican artists along with outstanding works of Latin American graphic engravers. Collection of prized works from the San Juan Biennial of Latin American Graphics
Income: Financed by state appropriations
Collections: Grafics; works from Orozco, Matta, Tamayo, Martorell, Alicea, Cardillo, Nevarez, Hernandez Acevedo
M **Museo y Parque Historico Ruinas de Caparra,** Carretera 2, PR-2 Km .6.4 Guaynabo, PR 00968; Instituto de Cultura Puertorriquena, Apartado 9024184 San Juan, PR 00902-4184. Tel 787-781-4795; 977-2702; Fax 787-724-8393; Elec Mail museosyparques@icp.gobierno.pr; Internet Home Page Address: www.icp.gobierno.pr/myp; *Dir* Samuel D Febo-Cotto; *Exec Dir* Ora Ramos
Open Mon - Fri 8 AM - 12 noon, 1 PM - 4:30 PM; No admis fee; Contains ruins of Caparra, first nucleus of colonization in Puerto Rico, founded by Ponce de Leon in 1508 & 1509, now excavated & transformed into a park with memorial plaques indicating the historic significance. While the restoration & excavation was being conducted, numerous objects related to the period were discovered, which are now on exhibit; Average Annual Attendance: 1,500
Income: Financed by state appropriations
Special Subjects: Historical Material, Archaeology
Collections: Cannons, flags, pistols, ceramics
L **Library,** Avenida Ponce de Leon 500, Puerta de Tierra San Juan, PR 00901. Tel 787-725-7405; Fax 787-722-9097
Open for reference to pub, investigators & students
Library Holdings: Audio Tapes; Book Volumes 120,000; Cassettes; Clipping Files; Exhibition Catalogs; Filmstrips; Framed Reproductions; Kodachrome Transparencies; Lantern Slides; Manuscripts; Memorabilia; Motion Pictures; Original Art Works; Pamphlets; Photographs; Prints; Reproductions; Sculpture; Slides; Video Tapes
Collections: Pre-Columbian Archaeological Collection

M **LA CASA DEL LIBRO MUSEUM,** 255 Calle Cristo, San Juan, PR 00901. Tel 787-723-0354; Fax 787-723-0354; Elec Mail lcdl@prw.net; Internet Home Page Address: www.lacasadellibro.org; *Pres* Ingrid M Jiminez; *VPres* Gloria A Vega
Open Tues - Sat 11 AM - 4:30 PM; No admis fee; Estab 1955 as a mus-library devoted to the history & arts of the book & related graphic arts; Maintains reference library; Average Annual Attendance: 14,000; Mem: 350; dues $35 & up
Income: Financed by donations & state appropriation
Special Subjects: Manuscripts, Posters, Maps, Bookplates & Bindings
Collections: Bibliography of graphic arts; binding; book illustration; calligraphy; early printing, especially 15th & 16th Century Spanish; modern fine printing; papermaking; Incunabula; Sixteenth-Twentieth Century Books
Exhibitions: Gallery has displays on the first floor relating to printing and other arts of the book, such as: Editions of the Quixote, Spanish Incunables, Sevilla y El Libro Sevillano, Espana 1492, Homenajea Nebrija, Conversosy Sefarditas
Publications: La Imprenta Sevillana; Libros Espanoles; Libros Venecianos
Activities: Classes for adults & children; visits from school groups; students of library science & workers in graphic arts; material available, no fees; book arts workshops; lect open to pub; gallery talks; tours; original objects of printing arts, material must be used on premises; originate traveling exhibs; mus shop sells books, posters & cards

M **MUSEO DE ARTE DE PUERTO RICO,** 299 De Diego Ave, Stop 22, Santurce San Juan, PR 00909; PO Box 41209, Santurce San Juan, PR 00940-1209. Tel 787-977-6277; Fax 787-977-4446; Elec Mail info@mapr.org; Internet Home Page Address: www.mapr.org; *Dir* Lourdes Ramos-Rivas, PhD; *Develop Mem* Myrna Z Perez; *Educ Doreen* Colon; *Vol Pres Bd Trustees* Arturo Garcia-Sola Esq; *Pub Rels Mgr* Yetzenia Alvarez; *Exhibs Mgr* Jacquelina Rodriguez-Mont PhD; *Treas* Sonia Dominguez, CPA; *Cur* Juan C Lopez
Open Tues & Thurs - Sat 10 AM - 5 PM, Wed 10 AM - 8 PM, Sun 11 AM - 6 PM; cl New Year's Day, Good Friday, Election Day, Thanksgiving Day, Christmas Day; Admis adults $6.42, students & children $3.21, seniors $2.68, mems no admis fee; Incorporated in 1996 & open to pub in 2000 with the mission to enrich the lives of its diverse audiences by making accessible & promoting the knowledge, appreciation & enjoyment of visual arts from Puerto Rico & the world. Pvt nonprofit org; 41,962 sq ft exhib space; 400-seat theater; sculpture

botanical garden; conservation lab; 2 classrooms; 4 workshops; computer lab; seminar rm; mus equipped with elevators & ramps; restaurant & cafe on-site; Average Annual Attendance: 140,000; Mem: dues Exec $1000, Friend $250, Family $100, Indiv $50, Students, Teachers, Physically-Impaired & Srs $25
Library Holdings: Auction Catalogs; Audio Tapes; Book Volumes; CD-ROMs; Exhibition Catalogs; Other Holdings; Pamphlets; Periodical Subscriptions; Video Tapes
Special Subjects: Latin American Art
Collections: 17th - 21st c Puerto Rican paintings, sculpture, prints & drawings, photos, installations, conceptual art & multi-media art; Master painters Jose Campeche, Francisco Oller, Rafael Tufino, Augusto Marin, Myrna Baez, Rafael Ferrer, Franciso Rodon, etc; sculpture garden; silkscreens from 1940 to the present
Publications: MAPR, quarterly newsletter; Report, annually; exhib catalogs & brochures
Activities: Docent prog; formal educ progs for adults & children; mus training for professional mus workers; lects open to pub; guided tours; arts festivals; concerts; films; loan exhibs, temporary exhibs & traveling exhibs; ann events: MAPR Ann Gala; mus shop sells books, magazines, prints & miscellaneous merchandise

VIEJO SAN JUAN

M **MUSEO DE LAS AMERICAS,** Cuartel de Ballajá, 2nd piso, Viejo San Juan, PR 00902; Apartado 9023634, San Juan, PR 00902-3634. Tel 787-724-5052; Fax 787-722-2848; Internet Home Page Address: www.museolasamerias.org; *Exhib Designer* Marlene Hernandez Casillas; *Exec Dir* Maria Angela Lopez Vilella; *Reg* Ileamarie Vazquez Contreras; *Educ Coordr* Shirley Padilla Virola; *Coll Supvr* Maria del Carmen Rodriguez; *Supvr Educ Guides* Pavlova Mezguida
Open Tues-Sat 9 AM - 12 PM & 1 PM - 4 PM, Sun 12 PM - 5 PM; Admis adults $3, students & senior citizens $2; Estab 1992 - to offer a synoptic vision of the history, art & culture of the Americas; Four permanent exhibs; Average Annual Attendance: 30,000
Activities: Classes for adults & children; concerts; gallery talks; tours

VIEQUES

M **INSTITUTE OF PUERTO RICAN CULTURE,** Museo Fuerte Conde de Mirasol, PO Box 71, Vieques, PR 00765; Magnolia 471, Vieques, PR 00765. Tel 787-741-1717; Fax 787-741-1717; Elec Mail bieke@prdigital.com; Internet Home Page Address: enchanted-isle.com/elfortin/; *Dir* Robert L Rabin Siegal
Open Wed - Sun 10 AM - 4 PM; Admis adult $2, children $1, in excursions $1; Estab 1989 for the preservation of local culture; Two galleries for itinerant exhibs, 20 x 50 ft; Average Annual Attendance: 15,000
Special Subjects: Architecture, Graphics, Hispanic Art, Latin American Art, Photography, Prints, Sculpture, Watercolors, Anthropology, Archaeology, Pre-Columbian Art, Ceramics, Crafts, Folk Art, Decorative Arts, Manuscripts, Posters, Historical Material, Maps, Coins & Medals
Collections: Archaeology, architecture, history, silkscreens & photography of Vieques; other art of Puerto Rico & Vieques
Exhibitions: La Naturaleza de Vieques: 100 Millones de Anos de Historia (The Nature of Vieques: One Hundred Million Years of History) Flora, Fauna, Geologic Formation
Activities: Classes for adults & children; docent training; student guide prog; school conferences; lects open to pub, 10 vis lectrs per yr; concerts; tours; book traveling exhibs 6 per yr; originate traveling exhibs 6 per yr; sales shop sells books, original art, prints, crafts & t-shirts

RHODE ISLAND

BRISTOL

L **ROGER WILLIAMS UNIVERSITY,** Architecture Library, One Old Ferry Rd, Bristol, RI 02809-2921. Tel 401-254-3833; Fax 401-254-3565; Elec Mail jschlinke@rwu.edu; *Circ Supv* Claudia DeAlmeida; *Architecture Art Librn* John Schlinke
Open during acad semester Mon-Thurs 8AM-12AM; Fri 8AM-6PM; Sat noon-5PM; Sun noon-12AM; No admis fee; Estab 1987; Circ 18,000 vols
Library Holdings: Book Volumes 22,000; Maps 150; Pamphlets; Periodical Subscriptions 200; Slides 80,000
Special Subjects: Art History, Landscape Architecture, Maps, Historical Material, Industrial Design, Interior Design, Furniture, Drafting, Restoration & Conservation, Architecture
Collections: Architecture; historic preservation

KINGSTON

A **SOUTH COUNTY ART ASSOCIATION,** Helme House, 2587 Kingstown Rd, Kingston, RI 02881. Tel 401-783-2195; Internet Home Page Address: www.southcountyart.org; *Pres* Alan Wynne; *1st VPres* Mary Papenfoth; *Recording Secy* Judith Kaplin; *Treas* Peter Anderson; *Cur & Caretaker* Jim Duffy; *Dir* Rhonda Shumaker; *2nd VPres* Stephen Palmer
Open Wed - Sun 1 - 5 PM during exhibs; No admis fee; Estab 1929 to promote an interest in art & to encourage artists & to support, in every way, the aesthetic interests of the community; 1802 building, modern gallery space, 900 sq ft; Average Annual Attendance: 800; applicants for membership must submit three paintings and be accepted by a comt; dues lay member & artist $50; annual meeting Oct; artist must be accepted in juried show
Collections: No large permanent coll; paintings by early mems, usually not on display
Exhibitions: 13 varied exhibs per year
Publications: Newsletter, 6 issues

Activities: Classes for adults & children; lect open to pub, 4 vis lectrs per yr; gallery talks; competitions with awards; schols; original objects of art lent to other art assns; lending coll contains books, lantern slides, sculpture, original art works & slides

M **UNIVERSITY OF RHODE ISLAND,** Fine Arts Center Galleries, 105 Upper College Rd Kingston, RI 02881-0820. Tel 401-874-2775/2627; Fax 401-874-2007; Elec Mail shar@uri.edu; Internet Home Page Address: www.uri.edu/artgalleries; *Galleries Dir* Judith Tolnick; *Asst to Dir* Sharon Clark; *Interim Chair Art & Art History* Prof Robert Dilworth
Open Main Gallery Tues - Fri Noon - 4 PM & 7:30 - 9:30 PM, Sat 1 - 4 PM, Photography Gallery Tues - Fri Noon - 9 PM, Sat 1 - 4 PM, Corridor Gallery, Mon - Fri 9 AM - 5 PM; No admis fee; Estab 1970 to expose university & Southern New England communities to contemporary & historical art; Average Annual Attendance: 20,000
Income: Financed through university & outside grants
Special Subjects: Architecture, Drawings, Painting-American, Photography, Prints, Sculpture, American Indian Art, American Western Art, Afro-American Art, Collages
Exhibitions: 18-20 ongoing exhibs per yr
Publications: Exhibition catalogues
Activities: Educ dept; classes for adults; lect open to public, 5-10 vis lectrs per yr; concerts; gallery talks; sponsor competitions; originate traveling exhibs to university museums & galleries nationally

NEWPORT

M **NATIONAL MUSEUM OF AMERICAN ILLUSTRATION,** Vernon Court, 492 Bellevue Ave Newport, RI 02840-4127. Tel 401-851-8949; Fax 401-851-8974; Elec Mail art@americanillustration.org; Internet Home Page Address: www.americanillustration.org; *Dir* Judy AG Cutler; *Chmn* Laurence S Cutler; *Asst to Chmn/Arts Admin* Eric Brocklehurst; *Interiors Admin* Jill Perkins; *Caretaker Bldgs & Grounds* Craig Knowles; *Asst to Dir* Sara Bliss
Open by appointment; Admis adults $18, seniors $16, discounts to military, groups & gratis to AAM, NEMA, & National Arts Club members; 1998 to present the American Imagist Collection to the public in perpetuity; Golden Age American illustration art exhibited in Gilded Age architecture
Library Holdings: Auction Catalogs; Book Volumes 2,000; CD-ROMs; Cards; Clipping Files; Compact Disks; DVDs; Exhibition Catalogs; Framed Reproductions; Memorabilia; Original Art Works; Original Documents; Photographs; Prints; Reproductions; Sculpture; Slides
Special Subjects: Decorative Arts, Drawings, Etchings & Engravings, Historical Material, Landscapes, Marine Painting, Architecture, Portraits, Painting-American, Prints, Period Rooms, Graphics, Sculpture, Bronzes, Posters, Furniture, Carpets & Rugs, Cartoons, Reproductions
Collections: works by illustrators including Norman Rockwell, Maxfield Parrish, NC Wyeth, JC Leyendecker & 150 other luminaries; John Rogers sculpture collection
Exhibitions: current - Norman Rockwell: American Imagist; Norman Rockwell & his mentor JC Leyendecker; Maxfield Parrish: The Retrospective; Howard Pyle & the Brandywine; author Tom Wolfe's 'In Our Time'; N.C. Wyeth & Howard Pyle; The American Muse; Norman Rockwell's America & others
Publications: newsletter; guidebook, The Grand Tour; MuseNews; YouTube; Twitter; Facebook; Norman Rockwell and his mentor JC Leyendecker exhib catalog; Norman Rockwell's America in England; Norman Rockwell's America in Birmingham
Activities: Docent training; lects open to pub; 4-6 vis lectrs per yr; intern prog; gallery talks; tours; American Civilization Foundation Awards for contributors to popular culture; Lend original objects of art to Birmingham Art Mus, Naples Art Mus, Dulwich Picture Gallery - London; organize traveling exhibs throughout USA, UK, Italy, France, Japan; mus shop sells books, magazines, original art, reproductions & prints, stained glass products, floor tiles with illustration images, CDs, Tru-chrome prints

M **NAVAL WAR COLLEGE MUSEUM,** 686 Cushing Rd, Newport, RI 02841-1207. Tel 401-841-4052/2101/7276; Fax 401-841-7074; Elec Mail museum@usnwc.edu; Internet Home Page Address: www.visitnewport.com/buspages/navy/; Internet Home Page Address: www.usnwc.edu/about/nwc-museum.aspx; *Cur* Robert Cembrola; *Mus Shop Mgr* Julia Koster; *Dir* John B. Hattendorf; *Secy* Kelly Folger; *Cur* John Pentangelo; *Educ/Outreach* John W. Kennedy
Open Mon - Fri 10 AM - 4:30 PM, Sat & Sun Noon - 4:30 PM (June 1-Sept 30); No admis fee; Estab 1978, Themes: history of naval warfare, history of Navy in Narragansett Bay; 7000 sq ft on two floors of Founder Hall, a National Historic Landmark; Average Annual Attendance: 39,000
Income: Financed by Federal Navy & Naval War College Foundation, Inc
Special Subjects: Costumes, Manuscripts, Marine Painting, Historical Material, Maps, Miniatures, Military Art
Collections: Paintings, Sculpture (statuary, busts), Prints; Ship models
Publications: Exhibition catalogs - Faces of the Naval War College (2009)
Activities: Staff talks on themes & exhibits; lect open to pub, 2 vis lectrs per yr; gallery talks; tours; retail store sells books, reproductions, prints, clothing, & costume jewelry

M **NEWPORT ART MUSEUM AND ASSOCIATION,** 76 Bellevue Ave, Newport, RI 02840-7411. Tel 401-848-8200; Fax 401-848-8205; Elec Mail info@newportartmuseum.edu; Internet Home Page Address: www.newportartmuseum.org; *Dir Educ* Judy Hambleton; *Grants* Judy Blake; *Cur* Nancy Grinnell; *Vol Coordr* Suzanne Hauerstein; *Dir Opers* John Schneider; *Exec Dir* Elizabeth Goddard; *Mem* Larry Bacon; *Office Mgr* Diane Montenegro; *Dir Finance & Admin* Jim Hockhousen
Open summer Tues - Sat 10 AM - 5 PM, Sun & most holidays Noon - 5 PM, winter Tues - Sat 11 AM - 4 PM, Sun & most holidays Noon - 4 PM, cl Christmas, New Year's Day, Thanksgiving, & July 4th; Admis adults $10, seniors & students $8, children 12 & under, mems free, students and military $6; Estab 1912, Collects, preserves, exhibits, and interprets contemporary and historic visual arts with an emphasis on the rich heritage of the Newport region, and integrates appreciation for the arts and art-making into all programs. The Griswold House is a National Historic Landmark; Buildings contain 16 galleries in 2 bldgs exhibiting contemporary visual arts, historic & regional exhibits; Average Annual Attendance: 25,000; Mem: 1850; dues $25 & up; annual meeting in Fall
Income: Financed by donations, endowment, mem, classes & admis
Special Subjects: Drawings, Painting-American, Photography, Prints, Sculpture, Watercolors, Woodcuts, Etchings & Engravings, Period Rooms
Collections: Drawings, Paintings, Photographs, Prints, Sculpture
Exhibitions: Changing & permanent exhibs, all media
Publications: Members' newsletters, quarterly; school class brochure
Activities: Day & evening classes for adults & children; docent training; outreach programs in house & off site; lect open to pub & some for mems only, 6-20 vis lectrs per yr; concerts; gallery talks; tours; awards; competitions; annual juried mems show awards in 6 categories; awards in 6 categories for annual school exhibs; schols offered; outreach dept serves area schools & underserved populations; individual paintings & original objects of art lent to other museums; originate traveling exhibs; sales shop sells books, original art, reproductions, and consignment antiques and collectibles, jewelry

A **NEWPORT HISTORICAL SOCIETY & MUSEUM OF NEWPORT HISTORY,** 82 Touro St, Newport, RI 02840-2978. Tel 401-846-0813; Fax 401-846-1853; Elec Mail info@newporthistorical.org; Internet Home Page Address: www.newporthistorical.org; *Pres* John J Salesses; *1st VPres* Dennis McCoy; *2nd VPres* Richard Burnham; *Secy* Hope P Alexander; *Treas* Paul Steinbrenner; *Pres Emeritus* Bradford A Brecken; *Pres Emeritus* Kenneth H Lyons; *Exec Dir* Scott W Loehr; *Financial Adminr* Janet W Boyes; *Dir Educ & Pub Programming* C Morgan Grefe Ph.D.; *Dir Mktg* Leslie Lindeman; *Registrar* Kim A Krazer; *Reference Librn & Genealogist* Bert Lippincott III, C.G.; *Mem Secy* Judy Kelley; *Historic Sites & Colls Mgr* Adams Taylor; *Newsletter Ed* James Yarnall; *Admin Asst* Cheryl Carvalho
Mus Open May 5 - June 12 Thurs - Sat, 10 AM - 4 PM, Sun 1 - 4 PM; June 15 - Sept 5 daily 10 AM - 4 PM; call for other hours; Suggested mus admis adults $4, children over age 5 $2; Estab 1853 to collect & preserve items of historical interest pertaining to the city; Maintains gallery & also owns & exhibits the first Seventh Day Baptist Church in America (1729); the Wanton-Lyman-Hazard House (1675), the first home to be restored in Newport; the Friends Meeting House (1699), site of the annual New England Quakers Meeting for over 200 years & mus of Newport History. Maintains reference library; Average Annual Attendance: 20,000; Mem: 1250; dues 1854 Society $1,000; Sponsor $500; Contributor $100; Indiv $50; Library/Mus $35; Student $25
Income: Financed by endowment, mem, state appropriation & other contributions
Special Subjects: Architecture, Costumes, Drawings, Graphics, Historical Material, Landscapes, Manuscripts, Photography, Sculpture, Silver, Textiles, Painting-American, Decorative Arts, Dolls, Furniture, Glass, Jewelry, Marine Painting, Period Rooms, Maps
Collections: Artifacts, china, Colonial silver, dolls, glass, furniture, Newport scenes & portraits, pewter & toys, photographs; ship models; paintings; printing press used by James Franklin; ball gown worn by a member of the Summer Colony; figurehead from the yacht Aloha; 18th century women's shoe exhibit
Exhibitions: Numerous changing exhibits
Publications: Newport History, quarterly; Newport Historical Society Newsletter, 6 times per yr
Activities: Educ dept; lect open to pub, 12 vis lectrs per yr; gallery talks; tours; audio-visual progs; competitions with awards; mus shop sells books & prints

L **Library,** 82 Touro St, Newport, RI 02840. Tel 401-846-0813; *Librn* Bertram Lippincott III
Open Tues - Fri 9:30 AM - 4:30 PM, Sat 9 AM - Noon, summers, Sat 9:30 AM - 4:30 PM; Estab 1853 to provide resource materials; For reference only
Library Holdings: Audio Tapes; Book Volumes 9000; Clipping Files; Exhibition Catalogs; Fiche; Kodachrome Transparencies; Manuscripts; Memorabilia; Original Art Works; Pamphlets; Periodical Subscriptions 10; Photographs; Prints; Reels; Sculpture; Slides; Video Tapes
Special Subjects: Art History, Landscape Architecture, Decorative Arts, Maps, Painting-American, Historical Material, Ceramics, Furniture, Period Rooms, Costume Design & Constr, Stained Glass, Dolls, Restoration & Conservation, Silver, Silversmithing, Textiles, Pewter, Architecture
Activities: Walking tour; school progs; Explore the Newport National Historic Landmark District through interactive computer progs; video tour of Bellevue Ave

L **REDWOOD LIBRARY & ATHENAEUM,** 50 Bellevue Ave, Newport, RI 02840-3292. Tel 401-847-0292; Fax 401-841-5680; Elec Mail redwood@redwoodlibrary.org; Internet Home Page Address: www.redwoodlibrary.org; *Dir* Ken Brockway; *Spec Coll Librn* Whitney Pape; *Dir Develop* Beth Watson; *Coll Develop* Robert E Kelly; *Technical Servs* Lori Brosrven
Open Mon - Wed, Fri & Sat 9:30 AM - 5:30 PM, Thurs 9:30 AM - 8 PM, Sun (summer only) 1-5 PM; No admis fee; Estab 1747 as a general library; Average Annual Attendance: 20,000; 13,000 vis per yr; Mem: 1400; dues $100; annual meeting in Aug
Income: Financed by endowment, mem, ann giving, grants
Library Holdings: Auction Catalogs; Audio Tapes 300; Book Volumes 172,000; Clipping Files; Compact Disks 2,000; DVDs 300; Exhibition Catalogs; Manuscripts; Maps; Memorabilia; Original Art Works; Original Documents; Periodical Subscriptions 95; Photographs; Sculpture 40; Slides; Video Tapes
Special Subjects: Decorative Arts, Sculpture
Collections: 150 paintings, largely portraits; 40 sculptures; 50 pieces of furniture & other decorative arts items; those on display include portraits by Washington Allston, Robert Feke, G P A Healy, Charles Willson Peale, Rembrandt Peale, John Smibert, Gilbert Stuart, Thomas Sully; many paintings by Charles Bird King, historical & classical busts, & early Newport furniture
Exhibitions: rotating exhibs
Publications: To Preserve Hidden Treasures: From the Scrapbooks of Charles Bird King; Vitruvius Americanus
Activities: Classes for children; dramatic progs; lects open to pub; 10 vis lectrs per yr; concerts; gallery talks; group tours by prior arrangement; individual paintings & original objects of art lent to Preservation Society of Newport County & other mus; sales shop sells books, slides, cards & bookbags

M ROYAL ARTS FOUNDATION, Belcourt Castle, 657 Bellevue Ave, Newport, RI 02840-4280. Tel 401-846-0669, 849-1566; Fax 401-846-5345; Elec Mail royalarts@aol.com; Elec Mail belcourtcastle@aol.com; Internet Home Page Address: www.belcourtcastle.com; *Exec Dir* Harle Tinney; *Pres* Mark P Malkovich III
Open Mar - Jun, & Nov - Dec, Thur - Mon Noon to 4 PM (5 PM summers); Jul - Oct, Wed - Mon Noon - 4 PM; Dec holiday prog Sun 1 - 4 PM; Feb weekends & daily during Newport Winter Festival; cl Tues, Thanksgiving Day & Christmas; Admis adult $12, seniors 65+ & college student $8, student (ages 13-18) $7, child (ages 6-12) $5, children under 5 free; Estab 1957; 60-room private residence of the Tinney family open to visitors under the auspices of the Royal Arts Foundation; Average Annual Attendance: 30,000; Mem: annual meeting in Jan
Income: $300,000 (financed by admis fees)
Special Subjects: Architecture, Painting-American, Sculpture, Textiles, Costumes, Ceramics, Painting-European, Furniture, Jewelry, Porcelain, Oriental Art, Asian Art, Silver, Antiquities-Byzantine, Painting-British, Historical Material, Tapestries, Renaissance Art, Period Rooms, Embroidery, Antiquities-Oriental, Antiquities-Persian, Antiquities-Egyptian, Gold, Stained Glass
Activities: Lect open to pub, 4 vis lectrs per yr; guided & specialty tours (reservations by phone or web); mus shop sells books & magazines

M UNITED STATES NAVY SUPPLY CORPS SCHOOL, US Navy Supply Corps Museum, 1378 Porter Ave, Newport, RI 02841-1208. Elec Mail dan.roth@cnet.navy.mil; Internet Home Page Address: www.nscs.snet.navy.mil; *Cur & Dir* Dan Roth
Open Mon - Fri 9 AM - 5:15 PM, cl federal holidays; No admis fee; Estab 1974. Exhibits depict the history & activities of US Navy Supply Corps & commemorate noteworthy individuals assoc with the Corps; Mus housed in National Register Carnegie Library building (c1910); Average Annual Attendance: 2,000
Income: Financed by federal appropriation
Special Subjects: Historical Material, Military Art
Collections: Nautical paintings, ship models, gallery gear, navigational equipment, uniforms, personal memorabilia; Archives: official records, manuals, photographs, yearbooks, scrap books, newsletter, directories
Publications: Base guide; museum brochure
Activities: Sales shop operates out of Navy Supply Corps Foundation Office

PAWTUCKET

A RHODE ISLAND WATERCOLOR SOCIETY, Armistice Blvd, Slater Memorial Park Pawtucket, RI 02861. Tel 401-726-1876; Elec Mail riwsgallery@verizon.net; Internet Home Page Address: www.riws.org; *VPres* Jacqueline Cauna; *Treas* Frank R Robertson; *Pres* Lisa G Bailey; *Dir Gallery* Kristina N Occhino; *Receptionist* Alice Broadbeut; *Receptionist* Roberta Remieres
Open Tues - Sat 10 AM - 4 PM, Sun 1 - 5 PM; cl Jan & every Mon; No admis fee; Estab 1896 to encourage & promote the advancement of watercolor painting; Large carpeted upper & lower tiled gallery. Lower level gallery open for classes & exhibs; Mem: 350; dues $60 - $75; annual meeting Apr; assoc mem open to all
Income: Financed by dues, commissions, contributions & progs
Exhibitions: Annual Exhibition of Member's work; Annual Christmas Exhibition; Annual National Open Juried Watermedia Show; Annual New Members Show; 12 or more mem exhibs per yr
Publications: Member newsletter
Activities: Classes for adults; workshops; lect & demonstrations, open to members & guests; competitions with prizes; sales shop sells wrapped matted paintings from bins, reproductions, original art & prints

M SLATER MILL, (Old Slater Mill Association) Old Slater Mill Association, 67 Roosevelt Ave, Pawtucket, RI 02860-2127; PO Box 696, Pawtucket, RI 02862-0696. Tel 401-725-8638; Fax 401-722-3040; Elec Mail info@slatermill.org; Internet Home Page Address: www.slatermill.org; *Cur* Adrian Paquette; *Exec Dir* Susan A Whitney
Open Mar & Apr: Sat - Sun 11 AM - 3 PM, May - Oct: Tues - Sun 10 AM - 4 PM, cl Mon; Nov - Feb group tours by appointment; Admis adults (13-64) $10, seniors $9, children (6-12) $8, children under 6 free; Estab 1921; Visitor Center Gallery for temporary exhibits including history, art & craft shows. Three permanent galleries in historic buildings; Average Annual Attendance: 50,000; Mem: dues $50; annual meeting in June; approx 500 mems
Income: $500,000 (financed by endowment, mem & city appropriation)
Library Holdings: Book Volumes; Clipping Files
Special Subjects: Painting-American, Archaeology, Textiles, Costumes, Decorative Arts, Manuscripts, Furniture, Laces
Collections: Machine tools; manuscripts; photographs; textiles; textile machinery
Publications: Quarterly flyer; e-newsletter, monthly
Activities: Classes for adults & children; docent progs; lects open to pub; tours; gallery talks; traveling educ progs; originate traveling exhibs; sales shop sells books, prints, slides, photographs & local artists works

PROVIDENCE

ASSOCIATION OF INDEPENDENT COLLEGES OF ART & DESIGN
For further information, see National and Regional Organizations

M BERT GALLERY, 540 S Water St, Providence, RI 02903-4322. Tel 401-751-2628; Elec Mail info@bertgallery.com; Internet Home Page Address: www.bertgallery.com
Open Tues-Fri 11AM-5PM, Sat noon-4PM, other times by appointment
Collections: paintings; drawings; woodcuts; sculpture

M BROWN UNIVERSITY, David Winton Bell Gallery, 64 College St, Providence, RI 02912. Tel 401-863-2932; Fax 401-863-9323; Internet Home Page Address: www.brown.edu/bellgallery; *Dir* Jo-Ann Conklin; *Adminr* Terrence Abbott; *Preparator* Cameron Shaw; *Cur* Maya Allison
Open Sept - June Mon - Fri 11 AM - 4 PM, Sat & Sun 1 - 4 PM, cl major holidays; No admis fee; Estab 1971 to present exhibs of interest to the univ & community; The gallery is modern, covers 2625 sq ft, 14 ft ceilings & has track lighting; Average Annual Attendance: 8,000
Income: Financed by endowment & univ funds
Special Subjects: Photography, Painting-American, Prints, Woodcuts
Collections: Print & photography collection of historical & modern masters; selected color field paintings & modern sculpture
Exhibitions: Mall media juried student & faculty exhibs; International contemporary art
Publications: Exhibition catalogs
Activities: Lects open to pub; art work lent to exhibs mounted by museums & galleries; permanent coll contains 5000 original prints & photographs, over 100 modern paintings & sculptures; originates traveling exhibs

M Annmary Brown Memorial, 21 Brown St, Box A Providence, RI 02912-9005. Tel 401-863-1518; *Friends of the Library Coordr* Christy Law Blanchard; *Bldg Contact* Barbara Schulz
Open Mon - Fri 1 - 5 PM; No admis fee; Estab 1905 to offer representatives of schools of European & American painting; There are three galleries which house the art collection of the founder & his wife, & portraits of the Brown family & Mazansky collection of British swords; Average Annual Attendance: 3,000

L Art Slide Library, 64 College St, Providence, RI 02912-9021. Tel 401-863-3218; Fax 401-863-9589; Internet Home Page Address: www.brown.edu/facilities/University_Library/libs/art/index.html; *Assoc Cur* Karen Bouchard; *Cur* Norine Duncan
Open Mon - Fri 8:30 AM - 5 PM; Estab to serve Brown Univ students, faculty & alumni; Circ 35,000; Reference books do not circulate
Income: $200,000 (financed by university funds)
Library Holdings: Book Volumes 550; Exhibition Catalogs; Fiche; Photographs 30,000; Reproductions; Slides
Special Subjects: Art History, Folk Art, Decorative Arts, Photography, Drawings, Etchings & Engravings, Manuscripts, Portraits, Industrial Design, Asian Art, Ivory, Mosaics, Metalwork, Religious Art, Landscapes, Architecture

M Haffenreffer Museum of Anthropology, 21 Prospect St, Box 1965 Providence, RI 02912. Tel 401-863-2065; Fax 401-253-1198; Internet Home Page Address: www.brown.edu/facilities/haffenreffer/; *Deputy Dir & Cur* Kevin P Smith; *Assoc Cur & Coll Mgr* Thierry Gentis; *Cur* Robert Preucel; *Cur Progs & Educ* Geralyn Hoffman; *Exhib Designer & Photo Archivist* Rip Gerry
Open Tues - Sun 10 AM - 4 PM, cl Mon & university holiday; Admis free; Estab 1955 to educate Brown Univ Students & the general pub through anthropological research on humankind, about cultural differences & human similarities & to serve its constituencies with excellence; Average Annual Attendance: 10,000; Mem: Dues: Student $15, Individual $25, Dual & Couple $30, Family $35, Contributing $50-$99, Saville Society $100-$249, Giddings Society $250-$499, Mount Hope Society $500-$999, Haffenreffer Society $1,000 & up
Special Subjects: Archaeology, Pottery, Sculpture, Mexican Art, American Indian Art, African Art, Anthropology, Ethnology, Southwestern Art, Textiles, Costumes, Ceramics, Primitive art, Eskimo Art, Asian Art, Ivory, Antiquities-Egyptian, Antiquities-Greek, Antiquities-Etruscan
Exhibitions: Various exhibs, call for details
Activities: Classes for adults & children; docent training; lect open to pub, 8-10 vis lectrs per yr; gallery talks; tours; fels; artmobile; book traveling exhibs 1 per yr; originate traveling exhibs; mus shop sells books, magazines, original art, reproductions, prints, slides & objects related to the colls

M CITY OF PROVIDENCE PARKS DEPARTMENT, Roger Williams Park Museum of Natural History, 1000 Elmwood Ave, Providence, RI 02907-3655. Tel 401-785-9450; Fax 401-461-5146; Elec Mail mmassaro@musnathist.com; Internet Home Page Address: www.osfn.org/museum; *Cur* Marilyn R Massaro; *Dir* Tracey Keough; *Asst Cur* Shara Chase
Open daily 10 AM - 5 PM; Admis adult $2, children $1; Estab 1896; 5 exhibit galleries (one rotates); Average Annual Attendance: 15,000
Income: Financed by state appropriations, admis & donations
Library Holdings: Auction Catalogs; Book Volumes; Exhibition Catalogs; Kodachrome Transparencies; Lantern Slides; Original Documents; Photographs; Slides
Special Subjects: Anthropology, Archaeology, Ethnology, Folk Art
Collections: Natural history, Native American, Oceanic, African ethnography
Exhibitions: All Things Connected (Native American Collection); Natural Selections (Victorian Natural History); Circle of the Sea (Oceana); rotating exhibit
Publications: Exhibit catalogs (Native American, Oceana)
Activities: Children's classes; lect open to pub; mus shop sells books, children's items, exhibit-related

L Library,
Estab 1896
Library Holdings: Book Volumes 10,000; Clipping Files; Exhibition Catalogs; Kodachrome Transparencies; Lantern Slides; Photographs; Slides

A PROVIDENCE ART CLUB, 11 Thomas St, Providence, RI 02903-1314. Tel 401-331-1114; Fax 401-521-0195; Elec Mail galleries@providenceartclub.org; Internet Home Page Address: www.providenceartclub.org; *Pres* Daniel Mechnig; *Gallery Coordr* Kristin Grimm; *Gen Mgr* Seb Borges; *Admin Coordr & Archivist* Angel Dean
Open Mon - Fri 12 PM - 4 PM, Sat & Sun 2 - 4 PM; No admis fee; Estab 1880 for art culture & to provide exhibition space for artists; Galleries maintained in two 18th century buildings on historic Thomas Street in Providence; Average Annual Attendance: 12,000; Mem: 650; to qualify, artists' work must pass a board of artists; personal qualifications for non-artists; dues non-artist $764, artist $572; initiation fee: artist $1,280, non-artist $1,600; ann meeting first Wed in June
Income: Financed by endowment & mem
Collections: Small permanent collection of paintings & sculpture by Club members since 1880
Exhibitions: Forty shows a season of which 2 - 3 are juried open shows
Publications: Newsletter for members, monthly
Activities: Lect for mems & guests; gallery talks; competitions with awards; tours; schols offered

M PROVIDENCE ATHENAEUM, 251 Benefit St, Providence, RI 02903-2799. Tel 401-421-6970; Fax 401-421-2860; Elec Mail mbrower@providenceathenaeum.org; Internet Home Page Address: www.providenceathenaeum.org; *Exec Dir* Alison Maxwell; *Bus Mgr* Ken Garrepy
Open Mon - Thurs 9 AM - 7 PM, Fri 9 AM - 5 PM, Sat 9 AM - 5 PM, Sun 1 - 5 PM, cl Sat & Sun, from mid - June to Labor Day; No admis fee; Estab 1753 to provide cultural services, information, rare & current materials in an historic setting; Maintains a rare book library; Mem: Estab 1367; dues $25 - $150 annual meeting in the Fall
Income: $303,544 (financed by endowment & mem)
Purchases: $40,000
Collections: Strength in the 19th century
Exhibitions: Exhibs vary each month; local artists' works shown
Publications: The Athenaeum Bulletin, summer; Annual Report, Fall
Activities: Dramatic progs; film progs; lects open to pub; tours; festivals; concerts; day trips; original objects of art lent to bona fide institutions, libraries or societies; lending coll contains books, periodicals, records, videotapes, cassettes; sales shop sells Audubon prints in limited editions, stationery, t-shirts & Athenaeum cookbooks

L Library, 251 Benefit St, Providence, RI 02903. Tel 401-421-6970; Fax 401-421-2860; Elec Mail info@providenceathenaeum.org; Internet Home Page Address: www.providenceathenaeum.org; *Coll Librn* Kate Wodehouse; *Reference Librn* Carol Tation; *Librn* Lindsay Shaw
Open Mon - Thurs 9 AM - 7 PM, Fri & Sat 9 AM - 5 PM, Sun 1 - 5 PM, cl Sun in summer, July & Aug; No admis fee; Estab 1753 to provide cultural services, information rare & current materials in a historic setting; Circ 106,000; Mem: Dues $35 - $185; annual meeting in spring
Income: endowment, mem fees, ann appeal
Library Holdings: Audio Tapes; Book Volumes 161,486; Cassettes; Exhibition Catalogs; Manuscripts; Memorabilia; Original Art Works; Other Holdings Posters; Pamphlets; Periodical Subscriptions 133; Prints; Records; Sculpture; Video Tapes
Special Subjects: Art History
Collections: 19th century Robert Burns coll; 19th century library - rare book library; Audubon, Old Fiction, Holder Borde Bowen coll
Activities: Children's progs; film progs; festivals; readings & lects; tours; trips

L PROVIDENCE PUBLIC LIBRARY, Art & Music Services, 150 Empire St, Providence, RI 02903-3219. Tel 401-455-8005; Fax 401-455-8013; Elec Mail mchevian@provlib.org; Internet Home Page Address: www.provlib.org; *Coordr* Margaret Chevian
Open Mon & Thurs 1-9PM, Tues 10 AM - 6 PM, Fri & Sat 12:30AM - 5:30 PM, Sun Sept-May cl Wed; Estab 1875 to serve needs of the public
Income: financed by endowment, city and state appropriations and federal funds
Library Holdings: Book Volumes 43,000; Clipping Files; Compact Disks; DVDs; Framed Reproductions; Original Art Works; Other Holdings Posters; Periodical Subscriptions 85; Photographs; Prints; Records; Video Tapes
Special Subjects: Landscape Architecture, Decorative Arts, Illustration, Photography, Commercial Art, Drawings, Graphic Design, Painting-American, Painting-British, Sculpture, Ceramics, Crafts, Advertising Design, Cartoons, Interior Design, Furniture, Costume Design & Constr, Handicrafts, Pottery, Silversmithing, Architecture
Collections: Nickerson Architectural Collection; art & music books

M RHODE ISLAND COLLEGE, Edward M Bannister Gallery, 600 Mount Pleasant Ave, Providence, RI 02908-1940. Tel 401-456-9765; Fax 401-456-8269; Elec Mail bannistergallery@ric.edu; Internet Home Page Address: www.ric.edu/bannister; *Gallery Dir* James Montford
Open Tues - Fri noon - 8 PM; No admis fee; Estab 1978 to provide the Rhode Island community with a varied & progressive exposure to the visual arts, to offer to the col community, with its liberal arts perspective, access to top quality exhibits, artists & workshops; View map on web site; Average Annual Attendance: 5,000
Income: Financed by state appropriation, student organizations & RIC Foundation
Collections: Teaching collection of works purchased from exhibiting artists
Publications: Brochures; semiannual calendars; monthly exhibit announcements
Activities: Lects open to pub; average of 12 vis lectrs per yr; gallery talks

A RHODE ISLAND HISTORICAL SOCIETY, 110 Benevolent St, Providence, RI 02906-3103. Tel 401-331-8575; Fax 401-351-0127; Internet Home Page Address: www.rihs.org; *Exec Dir* Bernard P Fishman; *Educ Dir* C Morgan Grefe; *Coll Cur* Kirsten Hammerstrom
Aldrich House Offices: Mon - Fri 9 AM - 5 PM; John Brown House Museum: Tues - Sat 10 AM - 4 PM, winter hours Fri & Sat 10 AM - 4 PM; Library: Wed - Fri 10 AM - 5 PM, 2nd Sat of mo 12 - 5 PM; Museum of Work & Culture: Tues - Sat 10 AM - 5 PM, Sun 1 - 4 PM; Admis $7; Estab 1822 to preserve, collect & interpret Rhode Island historical materials, including books, manuscripts, graphics, films, furniture & decorative arts; Art exhibits at John Brown House Mus, Mus of Work & Culture; Average Annual Attendance: 30,000; Mem: 1,500; dues $40; annual meeting in Nov
Income: Financed by endowment, mem, city & state appropriation, earned income
Library Holdings: Auction Catalogs; Audio Tapes; Book Volumes; CD-ROMs; Cards; Cassettes; Clipping Files; Compact Disks; DVDs; Exhibition Catalogs; Fiche; Filmstrips; Kodachrome Transparencies; Lantern Slides; Manuscripts; Maps; Memorabilia; Micro Print; Motion Pictures; Original Art Works; Original Documents; Other Holdings; Pamphlets; Periodical Subscriptions; Photographs; Prints; Records; Reels; Reproductions; Sculpture; Slides; Video Tapes
Special Subjects: Architecture, Costumes, Drawings, Embroidery, Etchings & Engravings, Graphics, Historical Material, Landscapes, Manuscripts, Photography, Porcelain, Prints, Religious Art, Sculpture, Silver, Textiles, Watercolors, Painting-American, Pottery, Decorative Arts, Folk Art, Pewter, African Art, American Indian Art, Ceramics, Crafts, Hispanic Art, Portraits, Archaeology, Dolls, Furniture, Glass, Laces, Jewelry, Marine Painting, Ethnology, Period Rooms, Maps, Islamic Art, Painting-European, Carpets & Rugs, Flasks & Bottles, Dioramas, Painting-British, Coins & Medals
Exhibitions: Changing exhibitions on Rhode Island history & decorative & graphic arts
Publications: American Paintings in the Rhode Island Historical Society, (catalogue); The John Brown House Loan Exhibition of Rhode Island Furniture;

Nathanael Green Papers; Rhode Island History, bi-annual; Roger Williams Correspondence; occasional monographs; newsletter
Activities: Classes for adults & children; teacher education; exhibits; children's tours; film progs; lects open to pub, 8-10 vis lectrs per yr; concerts; gallery talks; tours; lending coll contains 10,000 prints for reference and copying; originates traveling exhibs; museum shop sells books, magazines & original art

M John Brown House, 110 Benevolent St, Providence, RI 02906. Tel 401-331-8575; Tel 401-273-7507; Fax 401-351-0127; Internet Home Page Address: www.rihs.org; *Cur* Kirsten Hammerstrom; *Exec Dir* Bernard P Fishman; *Dir Goff Institute* Morgan Grefe; *Educ Mgr* Dan Santos
Open Tues - Sat 10 AM - 5 PM, Sun Noon - 4 PM, cl weekdays Jan - Mar except by appointment; Admis adults $12, seniors & mems $10, children 12 & under $6; Estab 1942, the 1786 house carefully restored & furnished with fine examples of RI & period materials; Average Annual Attendance: 9,000; Mem: 1,700; basic mem $40
Income: RIHS Institutional budget, $2.2 million (2006)
Purchases: RIHS does purchase material related to history of John Brown House & important RI archives & objects
Library Holdings: Auction Catalogs; Audio Tapes; Book Volumes; CD-ROMs; Cards; Cassettes; Clipping Files; Compact Disks; DVDs; Exhibition Catalogs; Filmstrips; Lantern Slides; Manuscripts; Maps; Memorabilia; Motion Pictures; Original Art Works; Original Documents; Other Holdings; Pamphlets; Periodical Subscriptions; Photographs; Prints; Records; Reels; Sculpture; Slides; Video Tapes
Special Subjects: Painting-American, Watercolors, Textiles, Costumes, Ceramics, Crafts, Etchings & Engravings, Landscapes, Decorative Arts, Portraits, Dolls, Furniture, Glass, Jewelry, Porcelain, Silver, Marine Painting, Carpets & Rugs, Historical Material, Maps, Coins & Medals, Miniatures, Period Rooms, Embroidery, Pewter
Collections: Carrington Collection of Chinese export objects; McCrillis Collection of Antique Dolls; furniture by Rhode Island cabinetmakers, some original to the house; major archival colls on Rhode Island subjects
Exhibitions: A Passion for the Past (by C Morgan Grefe, B Fishman & J K Hammerstrom)
Publications: Rhode Island History, Papers of Nathanael Greene
Activities: Educ prog; classes for adults; concerts; gallery talks; tours; schols; history makers awards; lending of original objects of art to qualified non-profit educational institutions; mus shop sells books, magazines, prints

M Aldrich House, 110 Benevolent St, Providence, RI 02906. Tel 401-331-8575; *Contact* Renata Luong; *Dir Educ* C Morgan Grefe, Ph.D.; *Exec Dir* Bernard P Fishman
Open Tues - Fri 8:30 AM - 5:30 PM, cl Sun & Mon; Admis adults $2, seniors & students $1; Estab 1974; Galleries for changing exhibs of RI artists & history
Income: Financed by endowment, state & local funds, grants (state & federal) & admis rates

L Library, 121 Hope St, Providence, RI 02906-2098. Tel 401-273-8107; Fax 401-751-7930; Elec Mail reference@rihs.org; Internet Home Page Address: www.rihs.org; *Deputy Dir Colls* Kirsten Hammerstrom; *Reference Librn* Lee Teverow; *Asst Reference Librn* Jordan Goffin; *Printed Art Conservation Librn* Phoebe Simpson Bear; *Spec Coll Cur* Karen Eberhart
Open Wed - Fri & second Sat of month 10 AM - 5 PM; Admis to out of state non-mems $5 per day; Estab 1822 to collect, preserve & make available materials relating to state's history & development; Galleries at John Brown & Aldrich Houses; Average Annual Attendance: 4,000; Mem: 1,400; dues individual $40; ann meetings in Sept
Income: $700,000 (financed by endowment, mem & state appropriation)
Library Holdings: Book Volumes 88,000; Manuscripts 6,696; Maps 200; Memorabilia 866; Motion Pictures 9,000,000 ft; Periodical Subscriptions 2600; Photographs 100,000
Special Subjects: Manuscripts, Maps, Historical Material, Architecture
Collections: 5000 manuscripts colls dating from 17th century; Rhode Island Imprints, 1727-1800; Rhode Island Broadsides; Providence Postmaster Provisional Stamps; Rhode Island Post Office Covers; genealogical sources, all state newspapers, maps, films, TV news films and movies, graphics, architectural drawings; 150,000 reference volumes; 200,000 photographs; bus archives; oral history tapes
Publications: Rhode Island History, twice yearly
Activities: Workshops for adults; lects open to pub; vis lectrs 6 per yr; tours; mus shop sells books, magazines, prints, genealogical charts

M RHODE ISLAND SCHOOL OF DESIGN, Bayard Ewing Building Gallery, 231 S Main St, Providence, RI 02903; 2 College St, Providence, RI 02903-2717. Tel 401-454-6281; Fax 401-465-6299; *Gallery Dir* James Barnes
Call for hours; No admis fee; Estab 1979 to show rotating exhibs & student work; Single space; Average Annual Attendance: 2,000
Income: Financed via school budget
Collections: paintings; photographs; sculpture
Activities: Lects open to pub; gallery talks; originates traveling exhibs

M RHODE ISLAND SCHOOL OF DESIGN, Museum of Art, 224 Benefit St, Providence, RI 02903-2723. Tel 401-454-6500; Fax 401-454-6556; Elec Mail museum@risd.edu; Internet Home Page Address: www.risdmuseum.org; *Interim Dir* Ann Woolsey; *Cur Ancient Art* Gina Borromeo; *Cur Contemporary Art* Judith Tannenbaum; *Dept Head & Cur Costumes & Textiles* Kate Irvin; *Cur Costumes & Textiles* Joanne Dolan Intersoll; *Dir Educ* Sarah Ganz; *Cur Painting & Sculpture* Maureen O'Brien; *Cur Prints, Drawings & Photos* Jan Howard; *Registrar* Tara Emsley; *Dir Devel* Suzanne Fortier; *Dir Mktg* Donna Desrochers
Open Tues - Sun 10 AM - 5 PM, Thurs until 9 PM, cl Mon, Aug. & holidays; Admis adults $10, seniors 62+ $7, college students w/ID & youth 5-18 $3, mems, RISD & Brown students, faculty, staff & children under 5 free; pay what you wish every Sun 10 AM - 1 PM, 3rd Thurs of month 5-9 PM & last Sat of month free (except Dec); Estab 1877 to collect & exhibit art for general educ of RISD students & the pub; Present buildings opened in 1897, 1906, 1926 & 1990, 2008; Average Annual Attendance: 100,000; Mem: 3500
Income: Financed by endowment, mem, state & federal appropriation, pvt & corporate contributions
Special Subjects: Drawings, Ceramics, Glass, Metalwork, Mixed Media, Furniture, Photography, Silver, Textiles, Bronzes, Painting-British,

Painting-European, Painting-French, Sculpture, Tapestries, Graphics, Painting-American, Prints, Watercolors, Pre-Columbian Art, Costumes, Woodcarvings, Decorative Arts, Furniture, Jade, Jewelry, Porcelain, Oriental Art, Asian Art, Carpets & Rugs, Ivory, Coins & Medals, Renaissance Art, Embroidery, Antiquities-Greek, Antiquities-Roman, Mosaics
Collections: Lucy Truman Aldrich Collection of European porcelains & Oriental textiles; Ancient Oriental & ethnographic art; American painting; contemporary graphic arts; Nancy Sayles Day Collection of modern Latin American art; English watercolors; 15th - 18th century European art; 19th & 20th century French art from Romanticism through Surrealism; Albert Pilavin Collection of 20th century American Art; Pendleton House collection of 18th century American furniture & decorative arts; Abby Aldrich Rockefeller coll of Japanese prints
Publications: Gallery guides for select exhibits; catalogs
Activities: Classes for adults & children; docent training; lect open to pub; lects for mems only; gallery talks; concerts; tours; fels; competitions with awards; outreach programs serve schools, nursing homes & hospital children's ward in the area; books traveling exhibs 1 per yr; originates traveling exhibs nationally & internationally; mus shop sells books, original art, reproductions, prints, jewelry, posters & postcards

L **Fleet Library at RISD,** 15 Westminster St, Providence, RI 02903-2784; 2 College St, Providence, RI 02903-2784. Tel 401-709-5900; Fax 401-709-5903; Elec Mail risdlib@risd.edu; Internet Home Page Address: library.risd.edu; *Dir* Carol Terry; *Readers' Svcs Librn* Claudia Covert; *Spec Coll Librn* Laurie Whitehill Chong; *Archivist* Andy Martinez; *Visual Resources Librn* Mark Pompelia; *Technical Svcs Librn* Robert Garzillo; *Reference Librn* Ellen Petraits; *Interlibrary Loan* Gail Geisser; *Catalog/Reference Librn* Elinor Nacheman
Open Mon - Fri 8:30 AM - 5 PM, Sat 10 AM - 5 PM, Sun noon - 5 PM; summer and holiday hours vary; Circ 56,000; Open to the pub for reference & research (appointment recommended); Average Annual Attendance: 53,000; Mem: Dues $100
Library Holdings: Auction Catalogs 18,000; Book Volumes 167,500; CD-ROMs; Clipping Files 490,000; Compact Disks; DVDs; Exhibition Catalogs; Fiche; Lantern Slides 22,000; Motion Pictures; Other Holdings Artists' books; Postcards; Posters; Periodical Subscriptions 340; Photographs; Reproductions 19,000; Video Tapes 5,000
Special Subjects: Architecture
Collections: Artists' books, Lowthorpe coll on landscape; Architecture, Gorham Design Library, miniature books; Walter Lorraine Coll of Children's Books

SAUNDERSTOWN

M **GILBERT STUART MEMORIAL ASSOCIATION, INC,** Gilbert Stuart Birthplace & Museum, 815 Gilbert Stuart Rd, Saunderstown, RI 02874-2911. Tel 401-294-3001; Fax 401-294-3869; Elec Mail info@gilbertstuartmuseum.org; Internet Home Page Address: www.gilbertstuartmuseum.org; *Exec Dir* Margaret O'Connor; *Pres* Daniel Bell
Open early May - mid-Oct Thurs - Mon 11 AM - 4 PM, Sun Noon - 4 PM, cl Tues & Wed; Admis adults $7, children 6 - 12 $4, children under 6 no admis fee; Designated 1966 as a national historic landmark, the furnished birthplace of America's foremost portrait painter; the home was built 1751; Restored home with grist mill & snuff mill; Average Annual Attendance: 4,500; Mem: 425; dues $50 family, $35 individual; annual meeting in May
Income: Financed by endowment, admis fees, grants, mem
Library Holdings: Clipping Files; Compact Disks; Memorabilia; Photographs; Prints
Special Subjects: Portraits
Collections: Collections of artifacts, period tools & prints; Artifacts; Period Tools; Prints
Exhibitions: Artist in residence
Activities: Classes for adults; docent training, children trained as jr docents who give weekend tours and hold spec events; dress in colonial costume ages 8-20; guided tours of the home; sales of books, reproductions, prints, cards

WAKEFIELD

M **HERA EDUCATIONAL FOUNDATION,** Hera Gallery, 10 High St, Wakefield, RI 02879-7403; PO Box 336, Wakefield, RI 02880-0336. Tel 401-789-1488; Elec Mail info@heragallery.org; Internet Home Page Address: www.heragallery.org; *Pres* Barbara Pagh; *VPres* Mara Trachtenberg
Open Wed - Fri 1 - 5 PM, Sat 10 AM - 4 PM, or by appointment; No admis fee; Estab 1974 as a women's cooperative gallery exhibiting the work of mems & non-mems; 30 ft x 40 ft in dimension with 9 ft ceiling; Average Annual Attendance: 1,500; Mem: Dues $185 - $480; monthly meetings second Wed; reduced fees for bd mems; membership based on artistic merit
Income: Financed by mem, contributions, grants & schols
Library Holdings: Slides of mems
Exhibitions: 10 - 11 exhibs per yr; Curated, juried & member exhibitions
Activities: Classes for children; readings; critiques; film festivals; lect open to pub on contemporary culture, 2-3 vis lectrs per yr; gallery talks by artists; juried competition with cash award; symposia; critique group; concerts; exten prog serves Rhode Island; artmobile; sales shop sells reproductions, prints

WARWICK

M **COMMUNITY COLLEGE OF RHODE ISLAND,** Knight Campus Art Gallery, 400 East Ave, Knight Campus Warwick, RI 02886-1805. Tel 401-825-2220; Fax 401-825-1148; Elec Mail knightgallery@ccri.edu; Internet Home Page Address: www.ccri.edu/art/galleries.shtml; *Dir* Viera Levitt
Open Mon & Sat 11 AM - 4 PM, Tues, Wed, Fri 10 AM - 4 PM, Thurs 10 AM - 7 PM; No admis fee; Estab 1972; Maintains reference library; Average Annual Attendance: 1,000
Exhibitions: Exhibs are changed monthly
Activities: Lects open to public, 10 vis lectrs per yr; concerts; gallery talks; tours; competitions with awards; exten dept; individual paintings & original objects of

art lent; lending collection contains 300 color reproductions, 20 filmstrips, 10,000 Kodachromes, motion pictures & clippings & small prints; originate traveling exhibs

M **Flanagan Valley Campus Art Gallery,** 1762 Louisquisset Pike, Lincoln, RI 02865-4585. Tel 401-333-7000; Fax 401-825-2265; Elec Mail flanagangallery@ccri.edu; Internet Home Page Address: www.ccri.edu/art/galleries.shtml; *Dir & Librn* Tom Morrissey
Open Mon - Fri 10 AM - 2 PM; No admis fee; Estab 1974; 26 sq ft space with track lighting; Average Annual Attendance: Over 5,000
Exhibitions: Exhibitions are changed bi-monthly
Activities: Lects open to pub, 10 vis lectrs per yr; concerts; gallery talks; tours; competitions with awards; exten dept; individual paintings & original objects of art lent; originating traveling exhibs

M **WARWICK MUSEUM OF ART,** 3259 Post Rd, Warwick, RI 02886-7145. Tel 401-737-0010; Elec Mail taylor@warwickmuseum.org; Internet Home Page Address: www.warwickmuseum.org; *Pres* Deborah O Mercer; *VPres* Pam Unwin-Barkley; *2nd VPres* Diane Newman-Goins; *Treas* Teresa Hamel; *Secy* Michelle Place-Gleason; *Office Mgr* Taylor Terreri
Open Wed, Fri & Sat 12:30 PM - 4:30 PM, Tues & Thurs 12:30 PM - 7:30 PM; Estab 1976 to promote a dynamic resource for all aspects of the cultural arts; Small gallery, formerly the Kentish Artillery built in 1912; Average Annual Attendance: 3,000
Income: $40,000 (financed by mem & city & state appropriation)
Exhibitions: Rhode Island Open Juried Exhibit (all media); RI State Council on the Arts Exhibits; Spring Juried Exhibit (themes change); Group shows
Activities: Art classes for adults & children; art exhibits that change every 6-8 wks; children's summer art camp; gallery talks; special events; comedy peformances wkly; excellence awards for RI Open Juried exhib

WESTERLY

M **WESTERLY PUBLIC LIBRARY,** Hoxie Gallery, 44 Broad St, Westerly, RI 02891-6009. Tel 401-596-2877; Fax 401-596-5600; Elec Mail ktaylor@westerlylibrary.org; Internet Home Page Address: www.westerlylibrary.org; *Dir* Kathryn T Taylor; *Community Svcs* Jane Johnson
Open Mon - Wed 9 AM - 9 PM, Thurs & Fri 9 AM - 6 PM, Sat 9 AM - 4 PM, Sun Oct - May Noon - 4 PM; No admis fee; Estab 1892 as a memorial to soldiers of the Civil War & to provide a library & activities center for the community; Art gallery maintained, 30 x 54 ft, 16 ft ceiling, with incandescent track lighting; Average Annual Attendance: 5,000
Income: Financed by endowment, city & state appropriation
Collections: Margaret Wise Brown Archive; Children's Book Week Posters
Exhibitions: Ten - twelve exhibs scheduled per yr; local artists exhib
Activities: Lect open to pub; library tours

SOUTH CAROLINA

AIKEN

M **AIKEN COUNTY HISTORICAL MUSEUM,** 433 Newberry St SW, Aiken, SC 29801-4844. Tel 803-642-2015; Fax 803-642-2016; Elec Mail museum@aikencountysc.gov; *Dir* Carolyn Miles; *Mus Shop Mgr* Nancy Johnson; *CEO* Owen Clary
Open Tues - Fri 10 AM - 5 PM, Sat & Sun 2 - 5 PM; Admis donations requested; Open 1970 to document local history; Average Annual Attendance: 7,500; Mem: 350; mem open to residents; dues $10 & up; ann meeting in Oct
Income: $71,000 (financed by endowment, mem, county subsidiary)
Collections: Agricultural-implements; Dairy-implements; log cabins; military; Savannah River Site (nuclear); Schools-furniture & winter items; Winter Colony-furniture
Exhibitions: Selections from permanent collection
Activities: Children's classes; docent progs; book traveling exhibs 10 per yr; retail store sells books & prints

ANDERSON

A **ANDERSON COUNTY ARTS COUNCIL,** 405 N Main St, Anderson, SC 29621-5614. Tel 864-224-8811; Fax 864-224-8864; *Exec Dir* Kimberly Spears; *Admin Dir* Annette Buchanan
Open Mon - Fri 9:30 AM - 5 PM, cl Sat, Sun & holidays; No admis fee; Estab 1972 as a nonprofit institution, encouraging & stimulating the practice & appreciation of the arts among the people living in the County of Anderson & the State of South Carolina; Gallery rotates exhibits monthly, featuring locally, regionally & nationally known artists; Average Annual Attendance: 10,000; Mem: 550; dues $1000, $500, $100, $50, $30; annual meeting last Tues of Sept
Income: Financed by mem, foundations, donations, county appropriation & grants
Exhibitions: Anderson Artist Guild Members Show; Soiree Clay Invitational; Youth Art Month; Changes
Publications: Calendar of events; newsletter; annual report
Activities: Classes for adults & children; gallery talks; tours

BEAUFORT

M **UNIVERSITY OF SOUTH CAROLINA BEAUFORT ART GALLERY,** Univ S Carolina, 801 Carteret St Beaufort, SC 29902. Tel 843-521-4145; Elec Mail info@beaufortarts.com; Internet Home Page Address: www.beaufortarts.com; *Prog Coordr* Sarah Van Winkle; *Exec Dir* Eric V Holowacz
Open daily 9 AM - 5 PM; No admis fee; Estab 1990; Two-room community art gallery in Performing Arts Center at the University of South Carolina Beaufort; Average Annual Attendance: 10,000; Mem: 700; dues $10-$1000; ann meeting in May

Income: $150,000 (financed by mem, city & state appropriations)
Activities: Classes for adults; dramatic progs; lects open to pub, 1 - 4 vis lectrs per yr; book traveling exhibs 2-4 per yr

BELTON

M   **BELTON CENTER FOR THE ARTS,** 306 City Sq, Belton, SC 29627; PO Box 368, Belton, SC 29627-0368. Tel 864-338-8556; Fax 864-338-0280; *Contact* Betsy Chapman

CHARLESTON

M   **CAROLINA ART ASSOCIATION,** Gibbes Museum of Art, 135 Meeting St, Charleston, SC 29401-2217. Tel 843-722-2706; Fax 843-720-1682; Internet Home Page Address: www.gibbesmuseum.org; *Exec Dir & Chief Cur* Angela D Mack; *Registrar* Zinnia Willits; *Asst to Exec Dir & Mem Coord* Wendi Ammons; *Pub Rels, Mktg Mgr & Dir Communs* Maria Loftus; *Admin* Eliza Buxton
Open Tues - Sat 10 AM - 5 PM, Sun 1 - 5 PM; cl national holidays; Admis $9 adults; $7 seniors, students & military; $5 children (6-18); children under 6 - free; Estab 1858 as an art gallery & mus; Circ non-circulation; Beau-Arts style building erected in 1905, renovated in 1978; gallery is 31,000 sq ft; Average Annual Attendance: 60,000; Mem: 4,000; dues $35 & up; annual meeting 3rd Mon in Oct
Income: $1,300,000 (financed by endowment, mem, city & county appropriation, grants & contributions)
Purchases: Contemporary & historical paintings, sculpture, prints, drawings & photographs
Library Holdings: Book Volumes; Clipping Files; Exhibition Catalogs; Lantern Slides; Manuscripts; Maps; Memorabilia; Original Art Works; Original Documents; Other Holdings; Pamphlets; Photographs; Slides
Special Subjects: Painting-American, Prints, Woodcuts, Portraits, Oriental Art, Miniatures
Collections: American Colonial, Federal & Contemporary Paintings & Prints; Miniature Portraits; American art related to Charleston; Japanese Woodblock prints
Exhibitions: Approx 14 per yr
Publications: Bulletins, quarterly; books; exhibit catalogs & brochures
Activities: Docent training; lects open to pub, 2 vis lectrs per yr; gallery talks; tours; exten dept serves tri-county area; individual paintings & original objects of art lent to museums; 8 per yr; originate traveling exhibs, regional & national venues to mus; mus store sells books, magazines, original art, reproductions, prints, original crafts, jewelry & various mus related products
L   **Library,** 135 Meeting St, Charleston, SC 29401. Tel 843-722-2706; *Dir* Angela Mack
Open Tues - Sat 10 AM - 5 PM, Sun 1 PM - 5 PM; Admis adults $9, seniors, students & military $7, children ages 6-12 $5; 1858; Open to scholars for reference only, by appointment; Average Annual Attendance: 25,000
Income: Financed by pub & pvt support
Library Holdings: Book Volumes 3709; Clipping Files; Exhibition Catalogs; Kodachrome Transparencies; Manuscripts; Original Art Works; Pamphlets; Periodical Subscriptions 26; Photographs; Records; Sculpture; Video Tapes
Collections: Painting; Sculpture; Works on paper; Miniature portraits
Activities: Classes for adults & children; Lect open to public, 4 vis lectrs per year, gallery talks, tours; Originate Traveling Exhibs to Mus; Mus shop sells books, reproductions, prints

M   **CHARLESTON MUSEUM,** 360 Meeting St, Charleston, SC 29403-6297. Tel 843-722-2996; Fax 843-722-1784; Elec Mail info@charlestonmueum.com; Internet Home Page Address: www.charlestonmuseum.org; *Pres* Hugh C Lane Jr; *Cur Historic Archaeology* Martha Zierden; *Cur History* Christopher Loeblein; *Cur Historic Houses* Karen King; *Cur Natural History* Albert E Sanders; *Registrar* Jan Hiester; *Cur Ornithology* Dr William Post; *Archivist* K Sharon Bennett; *Dir* Dr John R Brumgardt; *Asst Archivist* Julia Logan
Open daily Mon - Sat 9 AM - 5 PM, Sun 1 - 5 PM; Admis adults $5, children $2; Estab 1773 as a mus & library to diffuse knowledge of history, decorative arts, art, natural history, anthropology & technology; also to preserve houses & monuments; It is the oldest mus in the United States; Average Annual Attendance: 22,000; Mem: 550; dues $15 & up; annual meeting in Feb
Income: Financed by mem, city & county appropriations, admis & sales
Special Subjects: Textiles, Ceramics, Decorative Arts, Furniture, Glass
Collections: Ceramics, decorative arts, furniture, glass, maps, photos, prints & textiles, art of northern BC
Publications: Bimonthly newsletter
Activities: Tours for adults & children; docent training; 8 lects per yr; concerts; sales shop sells books, magazines & prints related to collections
L   **Library & Archives,** 360 Meeting St, Charleston, SC 29403-6297. Tel 843-722-2996; Fax 843-722-1784; Elec Mail info@charlestonmuseum.org; Internet Home Page Address: www.CharlestonMuseum.org; *Archivist* Jennifer Scheetz; *Asst Archivist* Jennifer McCormick
Open Mus: Mon - Sat 9 AM - 5 PM, Sun 1 - 5 PM; Archives & Library by appointment only; Admis $10; Estab 1773 as an educational institution, collects, preserves & uses artifacts of natural history, history, anthropology & decorative arts for staff & scholarly research; Mem: Dues $40
Library Holdings: Book Volumes 5000; Clipping Files; Exhibition Catalogs; Manuscripts; Maps; Memorabilia; Original Art Works; Original Documents; Other Holdings Maps; Pamphlets; Periodical Subscriptions 120; Photographs; Prints; Records; Reproductions
Special Subjects: Photography, Drawings, Etchings & Engravings, Manuscripts, Maps, Prints, Historical Material, Archaeology, Anthropology, Furniture, Pottery, Silver, Textiles
Activities: Classes for adults & children; lect open to the pub; gallery talks; tours; mus shop
M   **Heyward-Washington House,** 360 Meeting St, Charleston, SC 29403-6235. Tel 843-722-0354; Fax 843-722-1784; Elec Mail info@chrlestonmuseum.org; Internet Home Page Address: www.charlestonmuseum.org; *Chief Interpreter* Melanie Wilson

Open daily 10 AM - 5 PM; Sun 1 - 5 PM; Admis adults $10, children $5; Built 1772; home of Thomas Heyward, Jr; purchased by the Mus in 1929; Mus is furnished with Charleston-made furniture of the period; a National Historic Landmark
Collections: House furnishings; 18th century Chippendale & Charleston made furniture
Activities: Classes for children; lects open to pub; daily tours
M   **Joseph Manigault House,** 360 Meeting St, Charleston, SC 29403-6235. Tel 843-722-2996; Fax 843-722-1784; Elec Mail info@charlestonmuseum.org; Internet Home Page Address: www.CharlestonMuseum.org; *Chief Interpreter* Melanie Wilson
Open Mon - Sat 10 AM - 5 PM, Sun 1 - 5 PM; Admis adults $10, children 3 - 12 $5; Estab 1773 to preserve & interpret Charleston natural & social history; This house was built in 1803 & is a premier example of Adam style, or Federal architecture; Average Annual Attendance: 50,000; Mem: 2200; dues varies
Special Subjects: Architecture, Decorative Arts, Furniture, Glass
Collections: American, English, French furnishings of the period capture the lifestyle of the wealthy rice-planting Manigault family
Activities: Classes for children; gallery talks; Tours; mus shop sells books, reproductions, prints & other local crafts in neighboring (patron) mus

M   **CITY OF CHARLESTON,** City Hall Council Chamber Gallery, 80 Broad St, Charleston, SC 29401-2225. Tel 843-724-3799; Fax 843-720-3827; *Cur* Carol Ezell-Gilson
Open Mon - Fri 9 AM - 5 PM; No admis fee; Estab 1818 to preserve for the citizens of Charleston a portrait coll of the city's history; A unique collection of American portraits housed in the 2nd oldest city council chamber in continuous use in the US; Average Annual Attendance: 20,000
Income: Financed by city
Collections: Washington Trumbull, 1791; J Monroe Samuel Morse, 1819; A Jackson John Vanderlyn, 1824; Zachary Taylor James Beard, 1848; Marquis de Lafayette Charles Fraser, 1825; Pierre Beauregard George Healy, 1861; C Gaddsen-R Peale; portraits by Jarvis, Savage, John Blake White, James Earle, G Whiting Flagg
Publications: Catalog of paintings & sculpture
Activities: Lect open to pub; tours

M   **COLLEGE OF CHARLESTON SCHOOL OF ARTS,** Halsey Institute of Contemporary Art, 161 Calhoun St, Charleston, SC 29424. Tel 843-953-4422; Fax 843-953-7890; Elec Mail halsey@cofc.edu; Internet Home Page Address: www.halsey.cofc.edu; *Gallery Dir* Mark Sloan; *Prog Coordr* Rebecca Silberman; *Educ & Outreach Coordr* Lizz Biswell; *Mem Coordr* Elizabeth Reed
Open Mon - Sat 11 AM - 4 PM; No admis fee; Estab 1978 as a col gallery with focus on contemporary art; New & improved facilities with two inter-linked galleries as well as a lib resource room, media room, offices & storage; Average Annual Attendance: 8,000
Income: $175,000 (financed by state appropriation, earned income, grants & contributions)
Library Holdings: Auction Catalogs; Book Volumes; Exhibition Catalogs; Periodical Subscriptions
Publications: Periodic catalogs & gallery guides; Evon Streetman in Retrospect; Hung Liu: Washington Blues; The Right to Assemble; With Beauty Before Us: The Navajo of Chil Chin Beto; Appropriate to the Moment: Michael Tyzack; Cheryl Goldsleger: Improvisations; Force of Nature: Site Installations by Ten Japanese Artists; Alive Inside: The Lure & Lore of the Sideshow; Aldwyth: work v./work n. -Collage & Assemblage 1991-2009; Palmetto Portraits Project
Activities: Lect open to pub, 2-10 vis lectrs per yr; gallery talks; tours; concerts; juried student competitions; contemporary, emerging, & mid-career artists from all over the world; film series; artist in residence; AAM Design Publication Award 2010; book traveling exhibs 0-2 per yr; originate traveling exhibs to South east

CLEMSON

M   **CLEMSON UNIVERSITY,** Rudolph E Lee Gallery, Lee Hall, Clemson, SC 29634-0001. Tel 843-656-3883; Fax 843-864-656-7523; Elec Mail woodwaw@exchange.clemspm/edi; *Dir* Denise Woodward-Detrich
Open Mon - Fri 9 AM - 4:30 PM, Sun 2 - 5 PM, cl Sat; No admis fee; Estab 1956 to provide cultural & educational resources; to collect, preserve, interpret & display items of historical, educational & cultural significance; Average Annual Attendance: 20,000
Income: Financed by state appropriation
Special Subjects: Architecture, Painting-American, Graphics
Collections: Clemson Architectural Foundation Collection; Contemporary American Paintings & Graphics
Publications: Exhibition Bulletin, annually; Posters on Exhibits, monthly
Activities: Lect open to pub, 3-5 vis lectrs per yr; gallery talks; tours; exten dept servs Southeast United States; individual paintings & original objects of art lent to museums, universities; lending collection contains original prints, paintings, sculpture; originate traveling exhibs
L   **Emery A Gunnin Architectural Library,** Lee Hall, Clemson, SC 29634-0001. Tel 864-656-3933; Fax 864-656-3932; Internet Home Page Address: www.clemson.edu/gunnin/; *Media Resources Cur* Christopher Chapman; *Branch Head* Gypsey Teague; *Ref Librn* Kathy Edwards
Open during school yr Sun 2 -10PM, Mon - Thurs 7:30AM - 10PM, Fri 7:30AM - 5PM; No admis fee; For reference only for univ & pub use; Average Annual Attendance: 91,000
Library Holdings: Audio Tapes; Book Volumes 45,000; CD-ROMs; Exhibition Catalogs; Pamphlets; Periodical Subscriptions 212; Slides 150,000; Video Tapes
Special Subjects: Art History, Constructions, Landscape Architecture, Decorative Arts, Photography, Commercial Art, Drawings, Sculpture, Ceramics, Conceptual Art, Crafts, Archaeology, Drafting, Aesthetics, Pottery, Architecture
Collections: Rare Book Collection; South Carolina City & Regional Planning Documents
M   **Fort Hill Plantation,** Fort Hill St, Clemson, SC 29634-5605; 109 Daniel Dr, Clemson Univ Visitor Center Clemson, SC 29631-3006. Tel 864-656-3311,

656-2475; Fax 864-656-1026; *Dir Historic Houses & Cur* Will Hiott; *Dir Visitor Services* Helen Adams
Open Mon - Fri 10 AM - 5 PM, Sat 10 AM - 5 PM, Sun 2 - 5 PM, cl holidays & Christmas week; Admis by donation; A historic house mus located in the home of John C Calhoun. Restoration of the house & furnishings are an on-going project of the John C Calhoun Chap of the United Daughters of the Confederacy & Clemson University
Income: Financed by Clemson University
Special Subjects: Decorative Arts, Furniture, Portraits, Painting-Flemish, Period Rooms
Publications: Fort Hill, brochure
Activities: Lect; guided tours

COLUMBIA

M **COLUMBIA MUSEUM OF ART,** 1515 Main St, Columbia, SC 29201; PO Box 2068, Columbia, SC 29202-2068. Tel 803-799-2810; Fax 803-343-2150; Elec Mail ewoodoff @columbiamuseum.org; Internet Home Page Address: www.columbiamuseum.org; *Exec Dir* Karen Brosius; *Chief Cur* Dr Todd Herman; *Dir Educ* Ali Borchardt; *Dir Facility Opers* Michael Roh; *Dir Develop* Scott Nolan; *Dir Mktg & Comms* Ellen Woodoff; *Mgr Human Resources* Teri Keener Seybt; *Deputy Dir* Joelle Ryan-Cook
Open Tues - Fri 11 AM - 5 PM, Sat 10 AM - 5 PM, Sun noon - 5 PM, 1st Fri of month until 8 PM; Admis adults $10, military & seniors $8, students $5, children under 5, members & Sun no charge, discounts to AAM, ICOM & SEMC members; Estab 1950 to extend & increase art understanding, to assist in the conservation of a valuable cultural heritage & to recognize & assist contemporary art expression; Library for reference only; Average Annual Attendance: 120,000; Mem: 3,500; dues individual $45, dual $65, household $75, patron $200, Premier Society $500 & above; annual meeting in May
Income: $2,572,500 supported by citizens and corporations of the Midlands, City of Columbia, Richland County, SC Arts Commission, Cultural Council of Richland & Lexington Counties
Purchases: Works of art on paper, Southeastern artists, textiles, paintings & decorative arts
Library Holdings: Auction Catalogs; Book Volumes; Clipping Files; Exhibition Catalogs; Original Documents; Periodical Subscriptions
Special Subjects: Graphics, Painting-American, Textiles, Decorative Arts, Painting-European, Furniture, Renaissance Art, Painting-Italian
Collections: Kress Collection of Renaissance Paintings; International coll of fine & decorative arts from Medieval to present included Renaissance & Baroque Old Masters; Seibels Collection of Renaissance Art; Scotese Collection of Graphics; Turner Collection of Asian Art
Publications: Annual report; Collections Magazine, bimonthly; exhibition brochures
Activities: Educ progs for adults & children; docent training; lects open to pub, 6 vis lectrs per yr; concerts; gallery talks; tours; schols offered; lending coll of original art objects; mus shop sells books, reproductions, prints, ceramics, glass, jewelry, original art & other items

L **Lee Alexander Lorick Library,** PO Box 2068, Columbia, SC 29202. Tel 803-799-2810, 343-2155, 343-2156; Fax 803-343-2219; Elec Mail nrice@columbiamuseum.org; Internet Home Page Address: www.colubiamuseum.org; *Curatorial Asst* Noelle Rice
Open by appointment only; Admis adults $10, military & seniors 65+ $8, students $5; under 5 yrs no admis fee; Estab 1950; Open to mems & pub for reference only; Average Annual Attendance: 119,552; Mem: Various mem levels & meetings
Income: $10,000 (financed by mus)
Library Holdings: Audio Tapes; Book Volumes 14,000; Cassettes; Clipping Files; Exhibition Catalogs; Memorabilia; Other Holdings Vertical files; Pamphlets; Periodical Subscriptions 50; Video Tapes
Special Subjects: Art History, Collages, Decorative Arts, Illustration, Photography, Drawings, Etchings & Engravings, Islamic Art, Manuscripts, Maps, Painting-American, Painting-British, Painting-Dutch, Painting-Flemish, Painting-French, Painting-Italian, Pre-Columbian Art, Sculpture, Historical Material, History of Art & Archaeology, Watercolors, Ceramics, Conceptual Art, Crafts, Latin American Art, American Western Art, Bronzes, Art Education, Asian Art, American Indian Art, Porcelain, Furniture, Southwestern Art, Ivory, Jade, Glass, Stained Glass, Enamels, Oriental Art, Religious Art, Silver, Textiles, Woodcuts, Landscapes, Antiquities-Egyptian, Antiquities-Greek, Antiquities-Roman, Architecture, Folk Art, Portraits, Pottery, Woodcarvings
Activities: Ten visiting lectrs per year; concerts; gallery talks; tours; sponsoring of competitions; extension progs serve boys & girls clubs of the Midlands; lending of original art to various mus at various times; mus shop sells books, original art, jewelry, stationary, organizers etc

M **PONDER FINE ARTS GALLERY-BENEDICT COLLEGE,** 1600 Harden St, Columbia, SC 29204. Tel 803-253-5000;
Open Mon-Fri 10AM-4PM; No admis fee
Collections: paintings; photographs, sculpture

A **SOUTH CAROLINA ARTS COMMISSION,** 1026 Sumter St Rm 102, Columbia, SC 29201-3746. Tel 803-734-8696; Fax 803-734-8526; Elec Mail info@arts.sc.gov; Internet Home Page Address: www.southcarolinaarts.sc.gov; *Dir Visual Arts* Harriett Green; *Exec Dir* Ken May; *Dir Literary Arts* Sara June Goldstein; *Dir Traditional Arts* Julianne Carroll; *Dir Performing Arts* Laurel Posey
Open Mon - Fri 8:30 AM - 5 PM; No admis fee; State Agency estab 1967 to promote & develop the arts in South Carolina
Income: $1.8M (financed primarily by state & federal income)
Collections: State Art Collection
Activities: Educ programming; lect open to pub, gallery talks; competitions with awards, Folk Heritage Award, Verner Award; artists' workshops; grants-in-aid & fels offered; exten dept serves state; individual paintings & original objects of art lent to other galleries & museums; lending coll contains 446 original art works, paintings, photographs, sculpture, slides; originate traveling exhibs, circulates to 6 sites in South Carolina

L **Media Center,** 1026 Sumter St Rm 102, Columbia, SC 29201-3746. Tel 803-734-8696; Fax 803-734-8526; Elec Mail sleonard@arts.state.sc.us; *Dir* Susan Leonard
Open Mon - Fri 8:30 AM - 5 PM
Income: Financed by state & federal income
Library Holdings: Audio Tapes; Cassettes; Motion Pictures; Slides; Video Tapes
Special Subjects: Film

M **SOUTH CAROLINA STATE MUSEUM,** 301 Gervais St, Columbia, SC 29201-3041. Tel 803-898-4921; Fax 803-898-4969; Internet Home Page Address: www.museum.state.sc.us; *Deputy Dir Prog* Shelia Reily; *Dir Exhibits* Michael Fey; *Dir Tut* Underwood; *Exec Dir* William Calloway; *Chief Cur Art* Polly Laffitte; *Exec Dir* Overton G Ganong; *Dir Science & Outreach* Tom Falvey; *Deputy Dir Admin* Tony Shealy; *Store Mgr* Scottie Ash; *Chief Cur Natural History* James Knight; *Registrar* Michelle Baker; *Chief Cur Art* Paul Matheny; *Asst Dir Exhibits* James M Brown; *VChmn* Gary Culbreath; *Cultural History Chief Cur* Fritz Hamer; *Dir Educ Progs* Meika Samuel; *History Cur* Elaine Nichols
Open Mon - Sat 10 AM - 5 PM, Sun 1 - 5 PM; Estab 1973; Four large floors in a renovated textile mill with exhibits in art, history, natural history & science & technology; Average Annual Attendance: 250,000; Mem: 6500; ann meeting in June
Income: Financed by admis, state appropriations, store revenue & supplement state money
Special Subjects: Hispanic Art, Painting-American, Photography, Sculpture, Textiles, Crafts, Folk Art, Afro-American Art, Decorative Arts, Juvenile Art, Miniatures
Collections: Art - all media; Cultural History; Natural History; Science & Technology
Exhibitions: Art - South Carolina/Kentucky Exchange; History - The Palmetto State Goes Tower: WW II & South Carolina; Natural History - Fossil Collectors & Collections; 100 Years/100 Artists: A View of 20th Century South Carolina Art
Publications: Annual report; Images, quarterly
Activities: Docent progs; lect open to pub; lending coll contains 500 paintings; book traveling exhibs 10 per yr; originate traveling exhibs 4 per yr; retail store sells books & slides

M **UNIVERSITY OF SOUTH CAROLINA,** McKissick Museum, 816 Bull St, Columbia, SC 29208-0001. Tel 803-777-7251; Fax 803-777-2829; Elec Mail mcksmail@sc.edu; Internet Home Page Address: www.cla.sc.edu/mcks; Internet Home Page Address: www.cas.sc.edu/mcks/; *Chief Cur Exhibs* Jason Shaiman; *Bus Mgr* Peggy Nunn; *Cur Educational Servs* Alice Bouknight; *Cur Folk Art & Research* Saddler Taylor; *Dir* Lynn Robertson; *Cur Colls* Jill Koverman; *Asst Cur* Noelle Rice
Open Mon - Fri 8:30 AM - 5 PM, Sat 11 AM - 3 PM, Sun 1 - 5 PM, cl July 4th, Labor Day, Thanksgiving & day after, Dec 25, Jan 1; No admis fee; Estab 1976 to centralize the university's mus colls; Contains 4 major gallery areas for temporary & changing exhibs in art, science & history; Average Annual Attendance: 70,000
Income: Financed by state appropriation & donations
Purchases: Southern Folk Art
Special Subjects: Silver
Collections: Bernard Baruch Collection of 18th Century Silver; Movietonews News Reels; James F Byrnes Collection; Howard Gemstone Collection; Richard Mandell: Art Nouveau Collection; Colburn Gemstone Collection; university memorabilia; southeastern folk art; minerals, fossils, rocks & meteorites; contemporary art works
Exhibitions: A Portion of the People: Three Hundred Years of Jewish Life in South Carolina; student & faculty art
Publications: Exhibition catalogs; Calendar of events (quarterly)
Activities: Docent training; lect open to pub, 4-5 vis lectrs per yr; concerts; gallery talks; tours; competitions; slide-tape progs & classes for students & senior citizens; community outreach to senior citizen groups & children's hospital wards; originate traveling exhibs

L **Slide Library,** 1615 Senate St, McMaster Gallery Columbia, SC 29201. Tel 803-777-4236; Fax 803-777-0535; *Librn* Linda D Morgan
Not open to pub; No admis fee; Estab as a major teaching resource for the Art Department; Circ 200,000 holdings, 50,000 circulation
Library Holdings: Book Volumes 3000; Cassettes; Clipping Files; Exhibition Catalogs; Manuscripts; Motion Pictures; Other Holdings Slide-tape Programs & Digital Collection 21,000; Pamphlets; Periodical Subscriptions 17; Photographs; Slides 125,000; Video Tapes
Special Subjects: Art History, Folk Art, Drawings, Etchings & Engravings, Crafts, American Western Art, Bronzes, Advertising Design, Art Education, American Indian Art, Furniture, Afro-American Art, Carpets & Rugs, Antiquities-Assyrian, Architecture

DUE WEST

M **BOWIE ARTS CENTER,** 2 Washington St, Erskine College Due West, SC 29639. Tel 864-379-8867; Fax 864-379-2167
Open Aug - June: Mon - Sat & 1st Sun of the month 2 PM - 4 PM; No admis fee
Collections: Antique mechanical musical instruments; clocks; decorative arts; glass & porcelain; furnishings from the 19th & early 20th centuries; photographs

FLORENCE

M **FLORENCE MUSEUM,** 558 Spruce St, Florence, SC 29501-5152. Tel 843-662-3351; Elec Mail contact@florencemuseum.org; Internet Home Page Address: florencemuseum.org; *VChmn* Hunter Stokes; *VPres* Vicki Stokes; *Dir* Andrew R Stout; *Cur Coll* Stephen Motte; *Cur Educ* Heather Dillon
Open Tues - Sat 10 AM - 5 PM, Sun 2 - 5 PM, cl Mon & major holidays; Admis general $1, mems free; Estab 1924 (incorporated in 1936) as a general mus of art, natural science & history of South Carolina, with emphasis on the region known as the Pee Dee to acquaint the pub with fine art; Changing art exhibs, main galleries; Average Annual Attendance: 25,000; Mem: 450; dues benefactor $1000, patron $500, donor $250, sustaining $100, sponsor $50, family $30, individual $15

Income: $200,000 (financed by mem, county & city appropriation & donations)
Library Holdings: Auction Catalogs; Book Volumes; Clipping Files; Exhibition Catalogs; Manuscripts; Maps; Memorabilia; Original Art Works; Photographs; Prints; Reels; Reproductions; Slides; Video Tapes
Special Subjects: Archaeology, Architecture, Portraits, Pre-Columbian Art, Prints, Silver, Textiles, Woodcuts, Manuscripts, Painting-British, Painting-European, Painting-French, Painting-Japanese, Tapestries, Drawings, Graphics, Painting-American, Watercolors, American Indian Art, Pre-Columbian Art, Southwestern Art, Religious Art, Ceramics, Pottery, Primitive art, Woodcarvings, Etchings & Engravings, Landscapes, Afro-American Art, Decorative Arts, Judaica, Collages, Furniture, Glass, Jade, Jewelry, Oriental Art, Asian Art, Antiquities-Byzantine, Carpets & Rugs, Historical Material, Ivory, Coins & Medals, Restorations, Miniatures, Painting-Flemish, Renaissance Art, Embroidery, Antiquities-Oriental, Antiquities-Persian, Islamic Art, Antiquities-Egyptian, Antiquities-Greek, Antiquities-Roman, Military Art, Antiquities-Etruscan
Collections: Permanent Collection includes: African, Asian, Southwestern American Indians, Catawba Indian Collections, Greek & Roman Archaeological material; historical artifacts; works of local Black artist William H Johnson; works of local & regional artists; Museum Permanent Collection, Regional Artists; Native American Art
Exhibitions: PeeDee Regional Art Competition
Publications: Florence Museum magazine, biannual
Activities: Classes for adults & children; docent training; lects open to pub, 4 vis lectrs per yr; gallery talks; self-guided tours; art competitions with prizes; schols; book traveling exhibs; original art

GREENVILLE

M **BOB JONES UNIVERSITY MUSEUM & GALLERY INC,** (BJU Museum & Gallery) 1700 Wade Hampton Blvd, Greenville, SC 29614-0001. Tel 864-770-1331; Fax 864-770-1306; Elec Mail contact@bjumg.org; Internet Home Page Address: www.bjumg.org; *Chmn Bd* Bob Jones III; *Dir* Erin Jones; *Cur* John Nolan; *Dir Educ* Donnalynn Hess; *Registrar* Barbara Sicko; *Dir Security & Plant Operations* James Jackson; *Events Coordr* Amy Basinger; *Guest Svcs* Rebekah Cobb; *Resource Devel* Frank Richards
Open Tues - Sun 2 - 5 PM, cl Mon, mid-Dec - mid-Jan, New Year's Day, July 4, Thanksgiving weekend & Commencement weekend in May. Satellite location open Tues - Sat 10 AM - 5 PM, Sun 2 PM - 5 PM, cl Mon, Dec 24 - 25, Jan 1, July 4 & Thanksgiving Day; Admis Adults $5; Seniors (60+) $4; Students $3; Children 12 & under & members free; Estab 1951 to show the development of 14th - 19th century Old Masters paintings; 30 elegant galleries filled with art; tapestries, furniture, sculpture, & architectural motifs from the 13th through 19th centuries. Satellite location has rotating Old Masters exhibit & Learning Ctr with hands-on interactive displays; Average Annual Attendance: 20,000; Mem: Dues: mem levels - family/dual $150, individual $50
Income: Gifts from mems, donations, grants & admissions
Library Holdings: Auction Catalogs; Book Volumes; Exhibition Catalogs
Special Subjects: Antiquities-Assyrian, Painting-American, Sculpture, Bronzes, Archaeology, Textiles, Religious Art, Ceramics, Woodcarvings, Etchings & Engravings, Decorative Arts, Painting-European, Portraits, Furniture, Porcelain, Oriental Art, Silver, Painting-British, Painting-Dutch, Painting-French, Ivory, Coins & Medals, Tapestries, Baroque Art, Painting-Flemish, Renaissance Art, Period Rooms, Embroidery, Medieval Art, Painting-Italian, Antiquities-Persian, Antiquities-Egyptian, Antiquities-Greek, Antiquities-Roman, Mosaics, Stained Glass, Painting-German, Painting-Russian, Enamels
Collections: Religious art by the Old Masters from the 14th-19th centuries including Botticelli, Cranach the Elder, G David, Murillo, Ribera, Rubens, Tintoretto, Veronese, Zurbaran; Revealed Religion by Benjamin West, 7 paintings; Bowen Collection of biblical antiquities & illustrative material from the Holy Land
Exhibitions: (08/2013-12/2014) Charles Dickens: The Continuing Victorian Narrative
Publications: Catalogs; illustrated booklets; gallery newsletter, calendar of events
Activities: Classes for children; educator seminars; dramatic progs; docent training; lectrs open to pub; concerts; gallery talks; tours for school & adult groups by appointment; awards, Certificate of Excellence 2012 Exhib Competition; Certificate of Excellence 2013 Trip Advisor; individual paintings lent to other galleries in the US & abroad; progs for pub & pvt local schools; gift shop sells books, reproductions, prints, postcards, gift items & educational products

M **GREENVILLE COUNTY MUSEUM OF ART,** 420 College St, Greenville, SC 29601-2099. Tel 864-271-7570; Fax 864-271-7579; Elec Mail info@greenvillemuseum.org; Internet Home Page Address: www.greenvillemuseum.org; *Registrar Pub Rels* Claudia Beckwith; *Dir* Thomas W Styron; *Develop* Mary Lawson; *Pub Rels* Mary McCarthy; *Comptroller* Jeanne Marsh
Open Tues - Sat 11 AM - 5 PM, Sun 1 - 5 PM, cl Mon & major holidays; No admis fee, donations accepted; Estab 1958 for the coll & preservation of American Art; Seven major galleries devoted to permanent collections of American art from the colonial to the contemporary, changing & traveling exhibitions. Colls featuring Andrew Wyeth, Jasper Johns; Average Annual Attendance: 123,000; Mem: 1250; dues $50 - $10,000
Income: Financed by mem, donations & county appropriation
Special Subjects: Painting-American, Afro-American Art, Portraits
Collections: Pre World War II Southern Art; Andrew Wyeth, Watercolors; contemporary art
Exhibitions: Andrew Wyeth: Friends & Family; Southern Scenes; local artists
Publications: Exhibit catalogs
Activities: Classes for adults & children; docent training; Museum School of Art; lect open to pub, 6-10 vis lectrs per yr; gallery talks; tours; exten dept serves Greenville County schools; lending coll contains slides; mus shop sells books, original art, slides, prints, children's educ toys, regional crafts & cards

C **LIBERTY LIFE INSURANCE COMPANY,** 2000 Wade Hampton Blvd, Greenville, SC 29615-1036; PO Box 789, Greenville, SC 29602-0789. Tel 864-609-8111; *Pres* Francis M Hipp
Open during normal bus hours by appointment; Estab 1978 to collect textile art selections from various cultures & historical periods; Collection displayed throughout corporate headquarters
Collections: Limited edition prints, graphics & silkscreens; textile art works from around the world
Publications: The Liberty Textile Collection
Activities: Individual paintings & original objects of art lent to regional & national museums & galleries

GREENWOOD

M **THE MUSEUM,** (Greenwood Museum) 106 Main St, Greenwood, SC 29646-2763; PO Box 3131, Greenwood, SC 29648-3131. Tel 864-229-7093; Fax 864-229-9317; Elec Mail greenwoodmuseumdirector@gmail.com; Internet Home Page Address: www.greenwoodmuseum.org; *Exec Dir* Stacey Thompson; *Pres* Pam Hunley
Open Wed - Sat 10 AM - 5 PM, cl Mon & Tues; Admis free; Estab 1967 for educ purposes; Average Annual Attendance: 10,000; Mem: 400; dues $35 & up
Income: Financed by mem, contributions & grants
Special Subjects: Drawings, Historical Material, Art Education, Flasks & Bottles, Furniture, Mexican Art, Painting-American, Photography, Sculpture, African Art, Anthropology, Archaeology, Ethnology, Textiles, Costumes, Ceramics, Crafts, Folk Art, Pottery, Primitive art, Woodcarvings, Dolls, Glass, Porcelain, Asian Art, Carpets & Rugs, Historical Material, Ivory, Scrimshaw, Coins & Medals, Dioramas, Period Rooms, Embroidery, Laces, Antiquities-Oriental, Antiquities-Egyptian, Antiquities-Greek, Antiquities-Roman, Pewter
Collections: Main Street Timeline 1800s-1950; Arrowheads, Thomas Edison, Carriages and Coaches; Railroad memorabilia & 7 vintage train cars
Exhibitions: Traveling exhibs, regional & international
Publications: Newsletter, quarterly
Activities: Classes for adults & children; lect open to pub, gallery talks, tours; book traveling exhibs 1 major show per yr; sales shop sells books, original art, reproductions & prints

HARTSVILLE

M **COKER COLLEGE,** Cecelia Coker Bell Gallery, Coker College, Gladys C Fort Art Bldg Hartsville, SC 29550; 300 E College Ave, Hartsville, SC 29550-3797. Tel 843-383-8156; Fax 843-383-8048; Elec Mail artgallery@coker.edu; Internet Home Page Address: www.ceceliacokerbellgallery.com; *Dir* Larry Merriman
Open Mon - Fri 10 AM - 4 PM (when classes are in session); No admis fee; Estab 1983 to serve campus & community; 30 ft x 40 ft self-contained, movable partitions, track light, security system; Average Annual Attendance: 5,000
Exhibitions: Area artists; annual student juried show; senior students show; vis artists; 5 solo national & international exhibitions; (11/18/2013-11/26/2013) 41st Annual Student Show: various media; (12/02/2013-12/12/2013) Senior Exhibition: design; (01/16/2014-01/31/2014) 41st Annual Faculty Show: various media; (02/03/2014-02/28/2014) Laura Carpenter Truitt: painting; (03/03/2014-03/28/2014) Dawn Gettler: mixed media installation; (03/31/2014-05/09/2014) Senior Exhibitions: various media; (05/20/2014-08/22/2014) Annual Student Summer Show: various
Publications: Collection catalog
Activities: Lect open to public, 3 - 5 vis lectrs per yr; gallery talks; student juried competitions with awards

MURRELLS INLET

M **BROOKGREEN GARDENS,** 1931 Brookgreen Gardens Dr, Murrells Inlet, SC 29576; P. O. Box 3368, Pawleys Island, SC 29585-3368. Tel 843-235-6000; Tel 800-849-1931 (Toll Free); Fax 843-237-6039; Elec Mail info@brookgreen.org; Internet Home Page Address: www.brookgreen.org; *CEO & Pres* Robert Jewell; *CFO & VPres Human Resources* Alexandra Kempe; *VPres Horticulture & Conservation* George Weich; *VPres Devel* Phillip A Tukey; *VPres Mktg* Helen Benso; *Vol Mgr* Kelly Callahan; *Mus Shop Mgr* Barbara Harrison
Open daily 9:30 AM - 5 PM, cl Christmas; Admis adults $12, seniors $10, children 6-12 $5, children 5 & under & members free; Estab 1931 to exhibit the flora & fauna of South Carolina & to exhibit objects of art; The outdoor mus exhibits American sculpture & has changing sculpture exhibitions in indoor galleries; Average Annual Attendance: 207,500; Mem: 3000; dues individual $60, family $90, President's Council $250, Chairman's Council $1,000, Huntington Society $2,500, Atalay Society $5,000
Income: Financed by endowment, mem, gifts, grants & admis
Special Subjects: Sculpture, American Western Art, Bronzes, Historical Material, Coins & Medals
Collections: Collection of American figurative, sculpture, pieces by sculptors; Art Education; Art History; Landscape Architecture; Exploring American Sculpture
Publications: Brookgreen Journal, biannual; The Garden Path, biannual; exhibition catalogues
Activities: Classes for adults & children; docent training; workshops; gallery talks; tours; awards; originate traveling exhibs; mus shop sells books, magazines, original art, reproductions, prints, postcards, pamphlets, sculpture, jewelry & gifts

L **Library,** 1931 Brookgreen Garden Dr, Murrells Inlet, SC 29576; PO Box 3368, Pawleys Island, SC 29585-3368. Tel 843-237-4218; Fax 843-237-1014; Elec Mail rsalmon@brookgreen.org; Internet Home Page Address: www.Brookgreen.org; For reference only to staff
Library Holdings: Audio Tapes; Book Volumes 2200; Cassettes; Clipping Files; Exhibition Catalogs; Filmstrips; Framed Reproductions; Kodachrome Transparencies; Manuscripts; Memorabilia; Motion Pictures; Other Holdings Architectural & engineering drawings & prints; Maps; Pamphlets; Periodical Subscriptions 50; Photographs; Prints; Reels; Slides; Video Tapes

PICKENS

M **PICKENS COUNTY MUSEUM OF ART & HISTORY,** 307 Johnson St, Pickens, SC 29671-2463. Tel 864-898-5963; Fax 864-898-5580; Elec Mail picmus@co.pickens.sc.us; Internet Home Page Address: www.co.pickens.sc.us/culturalcommission; *Exec Dir* C Allen Coleman; *Chmn* Mr Susan Benjamin; *Cur* Helen Hockwelt; *Mill Site Mgr* Ed Bolt; *Mus Shop Mgr* Den Keys
Open Tues - Wed & Fri 9 AM - 5 PM, Thurs 9 AM - 7:30 PM, Sat 9 AM - 4:30 PM; No admis fee; Estab 1975 as a general mus; Average Annual Attendance: 35,000

Collections: regional 20th & 21st century art; photographs
Publications: newsletter, Old Gaol Gazette
Activities: Educ progs; workshops; classes; guided tours; lect; gallery talks; concerts

ROCK HILL

M **MUSEUM OF YORK COUNTY,** 4621 Mount Gallant Blvd, Rock Hill, SC 29732-9905. Tel 803-329-2121; Fax 803-329-5249; Elec Mail information@chmuseum.org; Internet Home Page Address: http://chmuseums.org/myco/; *Exec Dir* Van W Shields
Open Mon - Sat 10 AM - 5 PM, Sun 1 - 5 PM; Admis $5, seniors $4, youth $3, children under 3 & mems free, no admis fee Sun; Estab 1948; Spring, Alternative & Lobby galleries (changing art exhibits); Average Annual Attendance: 50,000; Mem: 1248; dues vary
Income: $1,383,225 (financed by mem, admis & county appropriation)
Special Subjects: Painting-American, Sculpture, African Art, Anthropology, Archaeology, Ethnology, Textiles, Costumes, Ceramics, Woodcarvings, Decorative Arts, Posters, Historical Material, Dioramas
Collections: African animals - mounted specimens; African art & ethnography; local art; local history & archaeology; local natural history specimens
Publications: Quarterly, bi-monthly; Teacher's Guide, annual
Activities: Classes for adults & children; docent progs; lect open to pub, 10 vis lectrs per yr; competitions with purchase awards; exten dept servs county; book traveling exhibs 5 per yr; retail store sells books & prints
L **Staff Research Library,** 4621 Mount Gallant Rd, Rock Hill, SC 29732-9637. Tel 803-329-2121; Fax 803-329-5249; *Cur Coll* Anne Lane
For research
Income: Financed by departmental budgets
Library Holdings: Audio Tapes; Cassettes; Exhibition Catalogs; Pamphlets; Video Tapes
Special Subjects: Photography, Crafts, Archaeology, Ethnology, Art Education, American Indian Art, Primitive art, Anthropology, Restoration & Conservation

M **WINTHROP UNIVERSITY GALLERIES,** 133 McLaurin Hall, Rock Hill, SC 29733-0001. Tel 803-323-2493; Fax 803-323-2333; Elec Mail derksenk@winthrop.edu; Internet Home Page Address: www.winthrop.edu/vpa/; *Dir* Tom Stanley; *Asst Gallery Dir* Karen Derksen
Open Mon - Fri 9 AM - 5 PM; No admis fee; Housed within Rutledge Bldg, the Col of Visual & Performing Arts at Winthrop University. Presents temporary visual art & design exhibs for the enhancement of acad achievement & understanding within the col community; Gallery is 3500 sq ft; Average Annual Attendance: 15,000
Income: Financed by state appropriation
Collections: Paintings & photographs; art exhibitions
Exhibitions: Student Exhibs; South Carolina State Art Collection; one-person shows; invitational exhibs in photo, drawing, painting, printmaking, textiles, design, ceramics & glass; Portraits et Personages: Selected Works from the Collection de l'Art Brut
Activities: lect open to pub; concerts; gallery talks; schols & fels offered; originate traveling exhibs

SPARTANBURG

A **ARTS PARTNERSHIP OF GREATER SPARTANBURG, INC,** Chapman Cultural Center, 200 E St John St, Spartanburg, SC 29306. Tel 864-583-2776; Fax 864-948-5353; Elec Mail info@spartanarts.org; Internet Home Page Address: www.chapmanculturalcenter.org; *Pres & COO* Jennifer Evins; *Dir Arts Educ* Ava Hughes; *Dir Outreach* Karen Parrott; *Dir Facilities* Jeff Pickens
Open Mon - Sat 9 AM - 5:30 PM; No admis fee; Estab 1993 to coordinate & develop all cultural activities in the area; Average Annual Attendance: 250,000; Mem: Ann meetings in May
Special Subjects: Historical Material, Sculpture, Textiles, Watercolors, Decorative Arts
Exhibitions: Changing exhibits
Publications: Membership Brochure, ann; Spartanburg Arts Calendar, monthly
Activities: Artist residences in schools; performances in school; David W Reid Award for Achievement in Excellence in the Arts in Spartanburg County; schools offered

M **CONVERSE COLLEGE,** Milliken Art Gallery, 580 E Main, Spartanburg, SC 29302. Tel 864-596-9177; Fax 864-596-9606; Elec Mail artdesign@converse.edu; Internet Home Page Address: www.converse.edu; *Dir* Kathryn Boucher
Open Mon - Fri 9 AM - 5 PM, Sun 2 - 5 PM, cl holidays; No admis fee; Estab 1971 for educational purposes; A brick & glass structure of 40 x 60 ft; movable panels 4 x 6 ft for exhibition of work, 16 panels, 12 sculpture stands; Average Annual Attendance: 2,400
Income: Financed by endowment
Exhibitions: Invitational exhibits of regional artists; annual juried student show; senior exhibit
Activities: Educ dept; lect open to public, 5-6 vis lectrs per year; gallery talks; tours

M **SPARTANBURG ART MUSEUM,** 200 E St John St, Spartanburg, SC 29306. Tel 864-582-7616; Fax 864-948-5353; Elec Mail museum@spartanarts.org; Internet Home Page Address: www.spartanburgartmuseum.org; *Exhibs Coordr* Casey Rigby; *Art School Dir* Addie Hutchins; *Colors Coordr* Kathy Wofford
Open Tues - Wed & Fri - Sat 10 AM - 5 PM, Thurs 10 AM - 8 PM; No admis fee; Estab 1969 to promote the works of contemporary artists in the southeastern United States; Gallery is located in the Chapman Cultural Center & contains both a permanent sales section & a changing exhibit area; Average Annual Attendance: 16,000; Mem: 500; dues $35 - $5,000
Income: Financed by endowment & mem
Library Holdings: Clipping Files; Exhibition Catalogs; Memorabilia

Special Subjects: Painting-American, Photography, Prints, Sculpture, Watercolors, Textiles, Ceramics, Folk Art, Pottery, Woodcarvings, Landscapes, Portraits, Juvenile Art
Collections: Contemporary Southeastern Artists
Exhibitions: Annual Juried Exhibit; Sidewalk Art Show - Sept; 15 changing exhibs annually
Publications: Quarterly newsletter
Activities: Classes for adults & children; docent training; lect open to pub, 5 vis lectrs per yr; lects for mems only; gallery talks; tours; competitions with awards; Colors-a free afterschool art studio for at-risk youth-Mon-Thurs 3-6pm; mus shop sells original art, books, prints, pottery & jewelry

M **UNIVERSITY OF SOUTH CAROLINA AT SPARTANBURG,** Art Gallery, 800 University Way, Division of Fine Arts, Languages & Literature Spartanburg, SC 29303-4932. Tel 864-503-5689; Fax 864-503-5835; *Dir Gallery* Jane Nodine
Open daily 10 AM - 4 PM; No admis fee; Estab 1982, primarily as a teaching gallery. Contemporary art displayed; 800 sq ft of carpeted wall space with windows along one wall, located across from Performing Arts Center
Income: $1200 (financed by Student Affairs Office of University)
Exhibitions: Annual Student Art Exhib; Exhibs of Regional Artists
Publications: Exhibition announcements
Activities: Lect open to pub, 4-6 vis lectrs per yr; competitions; book traveling exhibs 5 per yr; originate traveling exhibs 1 per yr

M **WOFFORD COLLEGE,** Sandor Teszler Library Gallery, 429 N Church St, Spartanburg, SC 29303-3663. Tel 864-597-4300; Fax 864-597-4329; Internet Home Page Address: www.wofford.edu; *Dir* Oakley H Coburn
Open during school yr Mon-Thurs 8 AM - 12 AM, Fri 8 AM - 7 PM, Sat 10 AM - 5 PM, Sun 1 PM - 12 AM; Estab 1969 to support educ & cultural activities of the col; Gallery located within col library; Average Annual Attendance: 100,000
Collections: Hungarian Impressionist
Exhibitions: Various exhib
Activities: Book traveling exhibs, 1-2 per yr

SUMTER

M **SUMTER GALLERY OF ART,** 200 Hasel St, Sumter, SC 29150-4506; PO Box 1316, Sumter, SC 29151-1316. Tel 803-775-0543; Fax 803-778-2787; Elec Mail director@sumtergallery.org; Internet Home Page Address: www.sumtergallery.org; *Exec Dir* Karen Watson; *Asst Dir & Cur* Frank McCauley; *Art Educ Dir* Amanda Cox
Open Tues - Fri 11 AM - 5 PM, Sat 1:30 - 5 PM, cl Easter, Thanksgiving, Christmas & month of July; No admis fee; Estab 1970 to bring to area exhibits of works of recognized artists, to provide an outlet for local artists for showing & sale of their work & to serve as a facility where visual art may become a part of life & educ of the people, particularly children of this community; The Gallery is the 1850 home of the late Miss Elizabeth White, well-known artist of Sumter, which was deeded to the gallery in 1977 under the terms of her will. Presently using hall, four downstairs rooms, back studio & rooms upstairs; Average Annual Attendance: 8,500; Mem: 460; dues commercial patron & patron $100, family $40, individual $25; annual meeting in May
Income: $100,000 (financed by mem, earned income, exhibit sponsors, donations, County Council)
Collections: 62 paintings, etchings & drawings of Elizabeth White given to the gallery by trustees of her estate
Exhibitions: Annual Young People's Exhibit; Individual & group exhibits of paintings, sculpture, collages, photography & crafts by recognized artists primarily from Southeast; Touchable exhibit for the blind & visually impaired; Sumter Artist Guild Exhibit; Annual Sumter Teacher Exhibit
Publications: Newsletter, 2 times per year
Activities: Classes & workshops for adults & children; docent training; lect open to pub; competitions; awards given; gallery talks; tours; schols; gallery gift shop primarily sells works by South Carolinian artists. Also on sale art to wear including jewelry; reproductions; prints

WALTERBORO

M **SOUTH CAROLINA ARTISANS CENTER,** 318 Wichman St, Walterboro, SC 29488-2921. Tel 843-549-0011; Fax 843-549-7433; Elec Mail artisan@lowcountry.com; Elec Mail info@scartisanscenter.com; Internet Home Page Address: www.scartisanscenter.com
Open Mon - Sat 10 AM - 6 PM, Sun 1 - 6 PM; No admis fee; Estab 1994 to provide a showcase & market for the handcrafted work of the state's leading artisans; Housed in restored nine-room Victorian cottage; 2800 sq ft retail facility; Average Annual Attendance: 26,000
Special Subjects: Afro-American Art, American Indian Art, Metalwork, Photography, Pottery, Painting-American, Prints, Textiles, Sculpture, Drawings, Watercolors, Ceramics, Crafts, Folk Art, Woodcarvings, Woodcuts, Decorative Arts, Collages, Dolls, Furniture, Glass, Jewelry, Porcelain, Carpets & Rugs, Stained Glass, Pewter, Leather, Reproductions, Bookplates & Bindings
Exhibitions: Sweetgrass Baskets; Live demonstrations (3rd Sat. every month); Mary Whyte author/artist - Life of Alfreda
Publications: Hands On, newsletter monthly
Activities: Classes for adults & children; demonstrations; workshops; classes for artists; summer art camp; lect open to pub; 4 vis lectrs per yr; tours; sponsoring of competitions; schols; Made in SC: standardized curriculum; rural SC communities; sales shop sells books, original art & original crafts; magazines; reproductions; prints; SC food products

SOUTH DAKOTA

ABERDEEN

M **DACOTAH PRAIRIE MUSEUM,** Lamont Art Gallery, 21 S Main St, Aberdeen, SD 57402-4218. Tel 605-626-7117; Fax 605-626-4026; Elec Mail dpm@brown.sd.us; Internet Home Page Address: www.dacotahprairiemuseum.com; *Cur Educ* Sherri Rawstern; *Cur Exhib* Lora Schaunam; *Dir* Sue Gates; *VPres* Kim Lien
Open Tues - Fri 9 AM - 5 PM, Sat & Sun 1 - 4 PM; No admis fee; Estab 1969 to preserve the heritage of the peoples of the Dakotas; Average Annual Attendance: 60,000; Mem: 300 foundation mems
Income: Financed by county funds
Special Subjects: American Indian Art, Historical Material
Collections: Sioux & Arikara Indian artifacts; local & regional artists; photography
Publications: Annual Report; Dacotah Prairie Times, 3 per yr
Activities: Classes for adults & children; gallery talks; tours; individual paintings & original objects of art lent to museums, art centers & some materials to schools; book traveling exhibs 12 per yr; mus shop sells books, magazines, prints, original art & reproductions

L **Ruth Bunker Memorial Library,** 21 S Main St, Aberdeen, SD 57401-4218. Tel 605-626-7117; Fax 605-626-4026; Internet Home Page Address: www.brown.sd.us/museum; *Cur Coll* Michele Porter; *Dir* Sue Gates
Open Tues - Fri 9 AM - 5 PM, Sat & Sun 1 - 4 PM, cl national holidays; Estab 1980 to store books, archives, maps, blueprints, etc; Circ Non-circulating; Reference for staff & academia only
Income: Financed by county funds
Library Holdings: Audio Tapes; Book Volumes 2800; Clipping Files; Exhibition Catalogs; Manuscripts; Original Art Works; Pamphlets; Photographs; Prints; Reproductions; Sculpture; Slides
Activities: Special classes; lect open to pub; gallery talks; tours; book traveling exhibs; originate traveling exhibs in midwest

M **NORTHERN STATE UNIVERSITY,** Northern Galleries, 1200 S Jay St, Aberdeen, SD 57401-7198. Tel 605-626-7766; Fax 605-626-2263; Elec Mail hoarw@northern.edu; Internet Home Page Address: www.northern.edu/galleries; *Dir Gallery* Rebecca Mulvaney
Open 8 AM - 5 PM; No admis fee; Estab 1902 to support Univ program; Four galleries: Lincoln professional secure setting, Union - student area, two hallway locations; Average Annual Attendance: 3,000
Income: $6,000 (financed by state appropriation)
Collections: Drawings, painting, photography, prints, sculpture
Exhibitions: Rotating exhibits
Activities: Educ dept; lect open to pub, 3 vis lectrs per yr; gallery talks; tours; competitions with prizes; individual paintings & original objects of art lent to regional locations; lending coll contains framed reproductions, original prints, paintings, photographs; book traveling exhibs 2 per yr

M **WEIN GALLERY,** Presentation College, 1500 N Main St Aberdeen, SD 57401-1280. Tel 605-229-8577; Fax 605-229-8518; Elec Mail brad.tennant@presentation.edu; Internet Home Page Address: www.presentation.edu/weingallery; *Dir* Brad Tennant
Open Mon - Fri 8 AM - 8 PM, Sat 1 PM - 7 PM; No admis fee; Estab 1971
Collections: Artwork by local artists.

BROOKINGS

M **SOUTH DAKOTA STATE UNIVERSITY,** South Dakota Art Museum, 936 Medary Ave at Harvey Dunn St, Brookings, SD 57007-0999; PO Box 2250, Brookings, SD 57007. Tel 605-688-5423; 866-805-7590; Fax 605-688-4445; Elec Mail sdsu.sdam@sdstate.edu; Internet Home Page Address: www.southdakotaartmuseum.com; *Cur Coll* Lisa Scholten; *Cur Exhibs* Jodi Lundgren; *Dir* Lynn Verschoor; *Marketing & Develop* Stacy Buehner; *Store Mgr* Pam Adler
Open Mon - Fri 10 AM - 5 PM, Sat 10 AM - 4 PM, Sun Noon - 4 PM; No admis fee; Estab 1970 as the state center for visual arts with various programs; The facility was designed by Howard Parezo, AIA, Sioux Falls, & occupies 112 x 90 ft site. There are seven galleries & a 147-seat auditorium; Average Annual Attendance: 150,000; Mem: 800, dues $30
Income: Financed by state appropriation, endowment, gifts & grants
Special Subjects: Afro-American Art, Decorative Arts, Folk Art, Art Education, Glass, Mixed Media, Furniture, Photography, Pottery, Textiles, Woodcuts, Sculpture, Tapestries, Drawings, Graphics, Painting-American, Prints, Watercolors, American Indian Art, American Western Art, Southwestern Art, Textiles, Ceramics, Pottery, Woodcarvings, Landscapes, Portraits, Posters, Eskimo Art, Jewelry, Porcelain, Carpets & Rugs, Historical Material, Embroidery, Mosaics, Stained Glass, Reproductions
Collections: American Art; Harvey Dunn Paintings; Oscar Howe Paintings; Marghab Linens; Native American Art; Native American Tribal Art
Publications: Exhibition catalogs; newsletter; brochures
Activities: Classes for adults & children; docent training; lect open to pub, 2-4 vis lectrs per yr; gallery talks; tours; individual paintings & original objects of art lent to professionally run museums with excellent facilities; originates traveling exhibs to other art galleries & mus; mus shop sells books, magazines, original art, reproductions, prints, jewelry, international items, pottery, Native American art, Christmas, textiles, fiber arts, CDs, cards & stationery

L **Hilton M. Briggs Library,** Box 2115, Brookings, SD 57007. Tel 605-688-5106; Fax 605-688-6133; Elec Mail kkristi.tornquist@sdstate.edu; Internet Home Page Address: www.sdstate.edu/library; *Chief Univ Librn* Kristi Tornquist; *Head of Pub Servs* Chris Schafer; *Univ Archivist* Michele Christian
Open Mon - Thurs 7:45 AM - Midnight, Fri 7:45 AM - 9 PM, Sat 10 AM- 9 PM, Sun 1 PM - Midnight; Open to the pub for lending through the main library
Income: Financed by state appropriation, endowment, gifts & grants

Library Holdings: Book Volumes 4,500; Exhibition Catalogs; Original Art Works; Photographs; Slides; Video Tapes
Collections: Daschle Career Papers

CRAZY HORSE

M **CRAZY HORSE MEMORIAL,** Indian Museum of North America, Native American Educational & Cultural Center & Crazy Horse Memorial Library (Reference), 12151 Ave of the Chiefs, Crazy Horse, SD 57730-8900. Tel 605-673-4681; Fax 605-673-2185; Elec Mail memorial@crazyhorsememorial.org; Internet Home Page Address: www.crazyhorse.org; *CEO & Pres* Ruth Ziolkowski; *Mus Registrar* Janeen Melmer; *Head Librn* Marguerite Cullum
Open 8 AM - dark; Admis memorial $27 per car, $10 per person, under 6 free, mus & center free; Memorial estab 1947, mus estab 1974, Center estab 1995, for preservation of the culture of the North American Indian; Three wings; Average Annual Attendance: 1,100,000
Income: Financed by Crazy Horse Memorial Foundation
Library Holdings: Auction Catalogs; Audio Tapes; Book Volumes; CD-ROMs; Cassettes; Clipping Files; Framed Reproductions; Memorabilia; Original Art Works; Photographs; Prints; Sculpture
Special Subjects: Painting-American, Sculpture
Collections: North American Indian Artifacts; Mountain Sculpture/Carving Displays; Pioneer memorabilia; Paintings & Sculptures; North American Artifacts; Mountain Sculpture-Carving
Exhibitions: Gift from Mother Earth Art Show (ann, second weekend in June)
Publications: Memorial: Progress; Mus: Indian Museum of North America; Crazy Horse Coloring Book
Activities: Classes for adults; lect open to pub; 2-3 vis lectr; concerts; schols offered; book traveling exhibs; mus shop sells books, prints, original art, reproductions

CUSTER

M **GLORIDALE PARTNERSHIP,** National Museum of Woodcarving, Hwy 16 W, Custer, SD 57730; PO Box 747, Custer, SD 57730-0747. Tel 605-673-4404; Internet Home Page Address: www.blackhills.com/woodcarving; *Owner* Dale E Schaffer
Open May - Oct, daily 9 AM -7PM, cl Nov - May; Admis adults $8.99, seniors $8.50, children 5 - 14 $6.99, group rates available; Estab 1972 in order to elevate the art of woodcarving; Average Annual Attendance: 70,000
Income: $250,000 (financed by mus admis)
Purchases: $100,000 for gallery & gift shop
Library Holdings: Cards; DVDs; Framed Reproductions; Original Art Works; Prints; Reproductions; Sculpture; Video Tapes
Special Subjects: Historical Material, American Western Art, Painting-American, Sculpture, Religious Art, Woodcarvings, Reproductions
Collections: Wooden Nickel Theater; 36 scenes by original animator of Disneyland; carving studio
Exhibitions: Area woodcarvers & artists
Activities: Classes for adults; lects open to pub; tours; schols & fels offered; exten dept serves Custer Community School; mus shop sells books, magazines, original art, reproductions & USA woodcarvings

HOT SPRINGS

M **PIONEER HISTORICAL MUSEUM OF SOUTH DAKOTA,** 300 N Chicago, Hot Springs, SD 57747. Tel 605-745-5147; Elec Mail pioneer@pioneer-museum.com; Internet Home Page Address: www.pioneer-museum.com; *Pres* Paul Hickok; *VPres* Bob Brown; *Treas* Ken Wilcox; *Secy* Niona Case
Open June - Sept Mon - Sat 9 AM - 5 PM; Admis discount to families; Built in 1893 & used as a school until 1961, this historic sandstone bldg now houses a coll which includes 25 exhibit areas showcasing pioneer life in Hot Springs/Fall River County. handicapped-accessible with elevator to 25 exhibit areas; Mem: Dues Lifetime $100; Bus $25 (ann); Family $10 (ann); Individual $5 (ann)
Special Subjects: Historical Material, Furniture, Period Rooms
Collections: over 600 historical pieces of original artwork, tapestries, famous prints & photos; authentic 19th century classroom; recreated doctor's office; old washing machines, wood cook stoves, kerosene lamp & many other historical items
Activities: Ann Mem Drive; Pioneer Days & Mus Tour; mus related books & gift items for sale

LEMMON

M **GRAND RIVER MUSEUM,** 114 10th St W, Lemmon, SD 57638-2202. Tel 605-374-3911; Tel 605-374-7574; Elec Mail grmuseum@sdplains.com; Internet Home Page Address: www.grandrivermuseum.org/index.htm; *Bd Dir* Edward Schmidt; *Bd Dir* Phyllis Schmidt; *Pres, Bd Dir* Stuart Schmidt; *Bd Dir* Lisa Schmidt; *Bd Dir* John Lopez; *Bd Dir* Kim Petik; *Bd Dir* Jim Petik
Open May - Sep, Mon - Sat 9AM-6PM, Sun Noon - 5PM; Admis by suggested donations; Founded 1998 to establish a forum with topics devoted to culture & paleontology, with an emphasis on the Grand River area. Nonprofit org; Large display of dinosaur fossils & displays of cowboy, ranching & Native Am artifacts from the local area; Average Annual Attendance: 4,500; Mem: Donor levels Bus 250 & over; Sponsor $100; Family $35
Library Holdings: Photographs; Prints
Special Subjects: American Indian Art, Historical Material, Photography, Ethnology, Historical Material
Collections: Dinosaur & fossil room; Native American room; Early ranching room; exhibs on creation science
Exhibitions: John Lopez Art Show-periodically
Publications: newsletter, quarterly

Activities: School & teacher progs, cultural exchange, community involvement & cooperation with other similar institutions; one vis lectr per yr; tours; mus shop sells book; clothing-memorabilia

MITCHELL

M MIDDLE BORDER MUSEUM & OSCAR HOWE ART CENTER, 1300 McGovern Ave, Mitchell, SD 57301-7901; PO Box 1071, Mitchell, SD 57301-7071. Tel 605-996-2122; Fax 605-996-0323; Elec Mail mbm-ohac@santel.net; Internet Home Page Address: www.oscarhowe.com; Exec Dir Lori Holmberg
Open Mon - Sat 9 AM - 5 PM; No admis fee; Estab 1939 for historical preservation of pioneer & Native American way of life & to promote local and regional artists as well as the Mitchell community; Housed in 4 historic buildings on grounds of Dakota Wesleyan University campus; handicapped accessible; Average Annual Attendance: 4,800; Mem: 300; dues $25 & up
Income: Financed by pvt & pub funds
Special Subjects: American Indian Art, Etchings & Engravings, Historical Material, Architecture, Glass, American Western Art, Furniture, Photography, Porcelain, Pottery, Painting-American, Prints, Period Rooms, Textiles, Bronzes, Maps, Sculpture, Watercolors, Dolls, Embroidery
Collections: Paintings by Sioux artist & South Dakota artist laureate, Oscar Howe; Charles Hargens Western art; Harvey Dunn
Exhibitions: Youth Art Exhibit (March)
Activities: Classes for adults & children; lects open to pub, 1-2 vis lectrs per yr; gallery talks; tours; awards (Youth Art); individual paintings & original objects of art lent to other galleries; lending coll contains paintings; book traveling exhibs; mus shop sells books, original art, reproductions, prints, jewelry, pottery Native American crafts & quilts

MOBRIDGE

M KLEIN MUSEUM, 1820 W Grand Crossing, Mobridge, SD 57601-1114. Tel 605-845-7243; Elec Mail kleinmuseum@westriv.com; Mus Shop Mgr Diane Kindt; VChmn & VPres Ervin Dupper
Open daily 9 AM - Noon & 1 - 5 PM, cl Tues; Admis adult $2, student $1; Estab 1975; Average Annual Attendance: 4,500; Mem: 225; dues bus $35, family $10; ann meeting in Apr
Income: $29,000 (financed by mem & donations)
Special Subjects: Drawings, American Indian Art, American Western Art, Archaeology, Dolls, Glass
Collections: Native American; Pioneer; Native American Artifacts
Exhibitions: Native American Beadwork; Sitting Bull Pictorial Display; Prairie Period Rooms
Activities: Sales shop sells books & prints

PIERRE

M MOODY COUNTY HISTORICAL SOCIETY, Moody County Museum, 706 E Pipestone Pierre, SD 57501-2217; PO Box 25, Flandreau, SD 57028-0025. Tel 605-997-3191; Elec Mail mchsmus1@knology.net; Internet Home Page Address: www.sdhistory.org/mus/museum.htm; Dir Dale Johnson; Pres Carole Hurley
Open Memorial Day - Labor Day: Tues - Sat Noon - 5 PM; No admis fee; Estab 1965 to promote understanding of history of Moody County, South Dakota; Jones' one-room school; 1880 depot; 1871 Santee Sioux Riverbend Meeting House, historic first frame building in Flandreau, Moody County; Average Annual Attendance: 900; Mem: 392; dues $20; annual meeting second Mon in Jan
Income: $17,000 (financed by county & city appropriation, donations, memorials & mem)
Library Holdings: Book Volumes; CD-ROMs; DVDs; Maps; Memorabilia; Original Documents; Pamphlets; Photographs; Video Tapes
Special Subjects: Historical Material, Landscapes, Glass, Furniture, Photography, Portraits, Pottery, Period Rooms, Textiles, Manuscripts, Maps, Costumes, Religious Art, Crafts, Dolls, Carpets & Rugs, Laces, Leather, Military Art
Collections: County artifacts, census records on microfilm, newspapers, photographs (available for reproduction), postcards; Indian Artifacts (1890-1927)
Exhibitions: Fourth of July Festival; Christmas Tree Festival-Thanksgiving to New Year
Publications: Trekking thru Trent newsletter, quarterly; Trent Moody County, SD, book; Echoes of Egan, Egan, Moody Co, SD; Annual of the Ages, Flandreau SD 2009 All-School Reunion
Activities: Classes for adults & children; Brown Bag luncheons from Sept - May; lect open to pub, 2 vis lectrs per yr; gallery talks; bus tours; competitions with prizes; contests; sales shop sells note papers; 1896, 1908 & 1915 Plat Books; histories of county communities, prints & collages of Flandreau, SD history

M SOUTH DAKOTA NATIONAL GUARD MUSEUM, 301 E Dakota Ave, Pierre, SD 57501-3225. Tel 605-224-9991; Internet Home Page Address: ngmuseum.sd.gov; Dir Robert L Kusser; Cur Seb Axtman
Open Mon - Fri 9 AM - 4 PM; cl weekends & holidays; group tours avail other times by appt; No admis fee, donations accepted; Originated as the 147th Field Artillery Historical Society in 1975; Mus estab 1983 to provide a facility for memorabilia & historical documents pertaining to the SD National Guard. The mus is a repository of historical info for both the Army & Air National Guard; Nonprofit org; ADA accessible; Mem: dues Adjutants Gen Club $500 & up, Charter Life $100, Sustaining Org $1 per mem per yr, Indiv Sustaining $10 per yr
Collections: Historical documents; military equipment; records; relics & memorabilia from Civil War, Spanish American War, WWI & WWII, Korean War, Desert Storm & Bosnian Peace-Keeping Mission; Sherman Tank; Armored Personnel Carrier; 75mm cannon; 105mm Howitzer; anti-aircraft guns; A-7-D Jet

PINE RIDGE

M HERITAGE CENTER, INC, 100 Mission Dr, Red Cloud Indian School Pine Ridge, SD 57770-2100. Tel 605-867-8257, 867-5491 (218); Fax 605-867-1291; Elec Mail heritagecenter@redcloudschool.org; Internet Home Page Address: www.redcloudschool.org/museum; Pres Peter J Klink; VPres Alvin Tibbitts; Dir Peter Strong; Cur Mary Bordeaux
Open Winter Mon - Fri 8 AM - 5 PM; Summer Mon - Fri 8 AM - 6 PM, Sat -

Sun 8 AM - 5 PM; No admis fee; Estab 1974 to exhibit Indian art & culture; Mus has four changing galleries of American & Canadian Native American art. Mainly paintings & sculpture; Average Annual Attendance: 11,000
Income: Financed by donations & grants
Special Subjects: Anthropology, Decorative Arts, Drawings, Etchings & Engravings, Historical Material, Landscapes, Ceramics, Collages, Portraits, Pottery, Prints, Silver, Textiles, Sculpture, Graphics, Painting-American, Watercolors, American Indian Art, Ethnology, Southwestern Art, Folk Art, Woodcarvings, Eskimo Art, Painting-Canadian, Dolls, Jewelry, Leather
Collections: Native American paintings & prints; Native American sculpture; star quilts & tribal arts
Exhibitions: Selections from permanent collection; Eskimo prints; Northwest coast prints; Annual Red Cloud Indian Art Show
Activities: Docent training; tours; awards; individual paintings & original objects of art are lent to other museums & art centers; book traveling exhibs 4-6 per yr; originate traveling exhibs; mus shop sells books, original art, reproductions & prints

RAPID CITY

M INDIAN ARTS & CRAFTS BOARD, US DEPT OF THE INTERIOR, Sioux Indian Museum, 222 New York St, Rapid City, SD 57701-1199. Tel 605-394-2381; Fax 605-348-6182; Internet Home Page Address: www.iacb.doi.gov; Mus Aid Marshall Burnette; Interim Cur Paulette Montileaux
Open 9 AM - 6 PM daily (Memorial Day - Labor Day), Mon - Sat 10 AM - 5 PM, Sun 1 - 5 PM (Labor Day - Memorial Day); Admis adults (18-61) $8, seniors(62+) $6.90, children (11-17) $5.75, children 10 & under free; Estab 1939 to promote the development of contemporary Native American arts & crafts of the United States; Average Annual Attendance: 45,000; Mem: (see www.journeymuseum.org)
Income: Financed by federal appropriation
Special Subjects: American Indian Art, Crafts
Collections: Contemporary Native American arts & crafts of the United States; Historic works by Sioux craftsmen
Exhibitions: Continuing series of one-person exhibitions
Publications: One-person exhibition brochure series, bimonthly
Activities: Lect; tours; sales shop sells original arts & crafts

M RAPID CITY ARTS COUNCIL, Dahl Arts Center, 713 Seventh St, Rapid City, SD 57701. Tel 605-394-4101; Fax 605-394-6121; Elec Mail contact@thedahl.org; Internet Home Page Address: www.thedahl.org; Cur Mary Maxon; Exec Dir Linda Anderson; Visual Art Educ Victoria Ledford; Community Serv Dir Barbara Evanson
Open Tues, Wed &- Fri. 10 AM - 6 PM, Thurs 10 AM - 8 PM, Sat & Sun 1 - 5 PM, cl Mon; Admis $2.50; Estab 1974 to promote & nourish creativity through the arts; The art center contains 3 galleries: Cyclorama Gallery, a 200 ft oil mural of American history; Central Gallery, touring & invitational exhibitions; Ruth Brennan Gallery, the main educ gallery; Average Annual Attendance: 60,000; Mem: Ann meeting fourth Mon in July
Income: $4,280,000 (financed by earned income, city appropriation, rentals, grants & contributions)
Special Subjects: Painting-American, Prints, Watercolors
Collections: Grace & Abigail French Collection, oils & watercolors; Hazel Schwentker Collection, watercolors, inks & washes; contemporary original work by regional artists
Activities: Classes for adults & children; dramatic progs; docent training; lect open to pub, 3 lect per yr; concerts; gallery talks; tours; sponsoring of competitions; schols offered; individual paintings & original objects of art lent; originate traveling exhibs to museums, galleries, colleges & art centers

SIOUX FALLS

A AMERICAN INDIAN SERVICES, 817 N Elmwood Ave, Sioux Falls, SD 57104-1942. Tel 605-334-4060; Fax 605-334-8415; Internet Home Page Address: www.aissiouxfalls.org/programs; WATS 800-658-4797; Exec Dir Marilyn Meyer
Estab 1979; Northern Plains Art Gallery; Mem: Member federally recorded tribe, proof of descendancy
Income: Financed by mem, state appropriation & individual donations
Activities: Local school shows

M AUGUSTANA COLLEGE, Eide-Dalrymple Gallery, 30th St & Grange Ave, Center for Visual Arts, Augustana College Sioux Falls, SD 57197; Eide-Dalrymple Gallery, 2001 S Summit Ave Sioux Falls, SD 57197. Tel 605-274-4006; Fax 605-274-5323; Elec Mail lindsay.twa@augie.edu; Internet Home Page Address: www.augie.edu/dept/art/art/eidedalrymplegallery.htm; Dir Lindsay Twa PhD; Gallery Coordr John Peters
Open Mon-Fri 10AM-5PM, Sat noon-5PM; No admis fee; Estab 1960 to serve as active force in art educ by presenting art within a cross-cultural perspective; Located on campus, featuring changing exhibits of works by professional artists in the region as well as occasional ethnographic shows, houses permanent coll of signed original prints; Average Annual Attendance: 3,000
Income: Financed by College appropriation & gifts
Purchases: Japanese woodcuts, European signed prints, New Guinea masks & objects
Special Subjects: Prints, Primitive art
Collections: Ethnographic & primitive art; original prints of European & American artists; Andy Warhol photographs
Exhibitions: Monthly changing exhibitions of contemporary, ethnographic, student art
Activities: Art & mus classes; lects open to pub, 6 vis lectrs per yr; concerts; gallery talks; tours; sponsoring of competitions; scholarships; mus shop sells original art

A AUGUSTANA COLLEGE, Center for Western Studies, 2121 S Summit Ave, Sioux Falls, SD 57197; 2001 S. Summit Ave, Sioux Falls, SD 57197. Tel 605-274-4007; Fax 605-274-4999; Elec Mail cws@augie.edu; Internet Home Page Address: augie.edu/CWS; Exec Dir Harry F Thompson, PhD; Colls Asst Elizabeth Thrond; Educ Asst Kristi Thomas; Office Coordr Amy Nelson
Open Mon - Fri 8 AM - 5 PM; Sat 10 AM - 2 PM; No admis fee; Estab 1970 for

coll & preservation of historic & cultural material for understanding of Northern Plains region; Artists of the Plains Gallery, original oils, watercolors, bronzes & prints by regional artists; Average Annual Attendance: 6000; Mem: 700; dues $50 & up; ann meeting in Dec
Income: Financed by endowment, mem, gifts, grants & book sales
Purchases: Four Feathers by Richard Red Owl
Library Holdings: Audio Tapes; Book Volumes; CD-ROMs; Cassettes; Compact Disks; DVDs; Manuscripts; Maps; Memorabilia; Original Documents; Periodical Subscriptions; Photographs; Prints; Sculpture; Slides; Video Tapes
Collections: South Dakota Art; historical manuscripts; photos; art by regional artists; Blue Cloud Abbey
Exhibitions: 3-4 exhibits per year featuring South Dakota & Northern Plains Artists
Publications: An Illustrated History of the Arts in South Dakota; Poems & Essays of Herbert Krause; Lewis & Clark Then and Now: A New South Dakota History; A Harvest of Words: Contemporary South Dakota Poetry
Activities: Boe Forum on Public Affairs; lect open to pub, 6 vis lectrs per yr; gallery talks; tours; competitions with awards; individual paintings & original objects of art lent to other offices on campus; book traveling exhibs 6-8 per yr; mus shop sells books, original art, prints, reproductions

M **WASHINGTON PAVILION OF ARTS & SCIENCE,** Visual Arts Center, 301 S Main Ave, Sioux Falls, SD 57104-6311. Tel 605-367-7397; Fax 605-367-7399; Elec Mail info@washingtonpavilion.org; Internet Home Page Address: www.washingtonpavilion.org; WATS 877-WASH-PAV; *Pres/CEO* Gary Wood; *Dir Develop* Allison Hauck; *Dir Opers* Jen Loos
Visit website for hours; No admis fee; Estab 1961 as a contemporary mus; Six galleries; Average Annual Attendance: 75,000; Mem: 1250; visit website for dues
Income: Financed by state appropriations, mem, gifts, contributions
Collections: Historical & contemporary interest, monthly 2-D work; National Printmakers collection
Publications: Monthly newsletter
Activities: Classes for adults & children; lect open to pub, receptions; concerts; gallery talks; tours; individual paintings & original art lent; mus shop sells books, magazines, original art, prints, reproductions, pottery & cards; children's studio on site
L **Library,** 301 S Main Ave, Sioux Falls, SD 57104. Tel 605-367-7397; Internet Home Page Address: www.washingtonpavilion.org
Call for hours; Open to mems only
Income: Financed by state appropriations, mem, gifts, contributions
Library Holdings: Book Volumes 320
Publications: Art News

SPEARFISH

M **BLACK HILLS STATE UNIVERSITY,** Ruddell Gallery, 1200 University, Spearfish, SD 57799-0002. Tel 605-642-6104, Ext 6111, 642-6852; Fax 605-642-6105; Internet Home Page Address: www.bhsu.edu; *Dir* Jim Knutsen
Open Mon - Fri 8 AM - 4 PM, Sat & Sun by appointment; Estab 1936 to encourage art expression & greater appreciation in the Black Hills area. Work of the art center is promoted jointly by Black Hills State College Art Department & the Student Union; Average Annual Attendance: 2,000; Mem: 500; dues $5 & up
Exhibitions: Photography, regional & vis artists
Activities: Lect open to pub, 3 vis lectrs per yr; competitions with awards; individual paintings & original objects of art lent to other colleges & universities; sales shop sells original art
L **Library,** 1200 University, Spearfish, SD 57799. Tel 605-642-6833; Fax 605-642-6105; *Dir Library* Edmund Erickson
Open Mon - Thurs 7:30 AM - 11:30 PM, Fri 7:30 AM - 5 PM, Sat 10 AM - 5 PM, Sun 2 PM - 11 PM
Library Holdings: Book Volumes 300; Motion Pictures; Reproductions
Collections: Carnegie gift library containing 1000 prints and 150 books

VERMILLION

M **UNIVERSITY OF SOUTH DAKOTA,** (University of South Dakota Art Galleries) University Art Galleries, W M Lee Ctr for the Fine Arts, Vermillion, SD 57069; 414 E Clark St, Vermillion, SD 57069-2390. Tel 605-677-3177; Elec Mail alison.erazmus@usd.edu; Internet Home Page Address: www.edu/fine-arts/university-art-galleries/index.cfm; *Dir* Alison Erazmus
Open Mon - Fri 8 AM - 5 PM; No admis fee; Estab 1976. Primary mission is educational, serving specifically the needs of the col & augmenting the university curriculum as a whole; There are three galleries; The John A. Day Gallery has rotating contemporary art exhibs, retrospectives, & student art exhibs. 50' x 50' located in the Fine Arts Center. The second houses the university collection of works by Oscar Howe, a Native American painter. This facility is approx 30' x 20'. The third is a small changing gallery approx 18' x 20'; Average Annual Attendance: 15,000
Income: $110,000 (financed by state appropriation & student fee allotment)
Purchases: $5,000
Special Subjects: American Indian Art
Collections: 60 Works by Oscar Howe; variety of media by contemporary artists; Northern Plains Native American Fine Arts, faculty & student colls, African masks & sculptures, German Expressionist
Exhibitions: Varied by year
Publications: Catalogues for major exhibs
Activities: Educ prog; docent training; lect open to pub; 2 lectrs per year; exten dept serves 300 miles in general region; individual paintings & original objects of art lent to professional museums & galleries; book traveling exhibs 2 per yr; organize traveling exhibs to regional art mus focusing on Regionalist & Native American Art; mus shop sells reproductions, prints, Oscar Howe

WALL

M **WOUNDED KNEE MUSEUM,** 217 10th Ave, Wall, SD 57790. Tel 605-279-2573 (Seasonal); Tel 970-226-3218 (Admin office); Elec Mail info@woundedkneemuseum.org; Internet Home Page Address: www.woundedkneemuseum.org
Open seasonally to Oct 12: daily 8:30 AM - 5:30 PM; call for extended hours;

Admis adults $5, seniors 60 & over $4, children under 12 no admis fee; tour groups please call or email for more info; Mus tells the story of a small band of Lakota families who became the focus of the last major military operation of the US Army in its centuries-long effort to subdue the Native American tribes. Handicapped-accessible
Special Subjects: Historical Material, Photography, American Indian Art
Collections: Exhibs & photos surrounding the Wounded Knee Massacre; trading post
Exhibitions: Smothering the Seven Fires; Wovoka's Ghost Dance; Words That Killed; Big Foot's Trail; The Adaptable Lakota; Treaty of 1868
Publications: A Sioux Chronicle, by George E Hyde; The Ghost Dance Religion and the Sioux Outbreak of 1890, by James Mooney; Bury My Heart at Wounded Knee, by Dee Brown; Lost Bird of Wounded Knee, by Renee Samsom Flood
Activities: Group tours & self-guided tours; educ progs; memorial movie on the Lakota people; books & mus related items for sale

YANKTON

M **BEDE ART GALLERY,** Mount Mary College, Art Office, 1105 W 8th St Yankton, SD 57078-3725. Tel 605-668-1574; Elec Mail dkahle@mtmc.edu; Internet Home Page Address: www.mtmc.edu; *Dir* David Kahle
Open Mon - Fri 8 AM - 8 PM; No admis fee
Collections: Student artwork

M **YANKTON COUNTY HISTORICAL SOCIETY,** Dakota Territorial Museum, 610 Summit St, Yankton, SD 57078-3858. Tel 605-665-3898; Internet Home Page Address: dakotaterritorialmuseum.org; *Dir & Cur* Crystal Nelson; *Pres* Joan Neubauer
Open Mon - Fri 10 AM - 5 PM; Sun Noon - 4 PM (May - Sep 30); Mon - Sun noon - 4 PM (Oct - Apr 30); No admis fee; Estab 1961 as an historical museum; Average Annual Attendance: 6,000; Mem: 250; dues vary; annual meeting in Oct
Income: $20,000 (financed by city & county appropriation)
Special Subjects: Historical Material, Furniture, Dolls
Collections: Paintings by Louis Janousek; sculptures by Frank Yaggie; historic photographs
Exhibitions: Rotating
Activities: Educ progs; riverboats; roads; & rails in June; lects open to pub; free monthly brown bag; gift shop sells books, reproductions, prints, jewelry, kids items & t-shirts

TENNESSEE

CHATTANOOGA

L **CHATTANOOGA-HAMILTON COUNTY BICENTENNIAL LIBRARY,** Fine Arts Dept, 1001 Broad St, Chattanooga, TN 37402-2620. Tel 423-757-5310; Elec Mail library@lib.chattanooga.gov; Internet Home Page Address: www.lib.chattanooga.gov/finearts.html; *Head of Dept* Barry Bradford
Open Mon - Thurs 9 AM - 9 PM, Fri - Sat 9 AM - 6 PM, Sept - May; No admis fee; Estab 1888, dept estab 1976
Income: Financed by city, county & state appropriation
Library Holdings: Audio Tapes; Cassettes; Clipping Files; DVDs; Motion Pictures; Periodical Subscriptions 63; Video Tapes
Special Subjects: Art History, Film, Painting-American, Painting-British, Pre-Columbian Art, Historical Material, Furniture
Collections: Collection of books, cassette tapes, compact discs, music books, phono records, 16mm film & video VHS tapes

M **HOUSTON MUSEUM OF DECORATIVE ARTS,** 201 High St, Chattanooga, TN 37403-1185. Tel 423-267-7176; Elec Mail houstonmuseumchattanooga@gmail.com; Internet Home Page Address: www.thehoustonmuseum.org; *Mus Mgr* Amy Autenreith; *Pres* Barbara Wofford
Open Thurs, Fri, Sat & Sun 12 noon - 4 PM; Admis adults $9, discount to AAA members, children 4-17 $3.50; Estab 1961, incorporated 1949; Average Annual Attendance: 20,000; Mem: 500; dues $5000, $2500, $1000, $100, $50, $45, $35, $25; ann meeting in May
Income: Financed by mem dues, foundation cook book sales, profits from antiques show, parking lot & admis fees, gift shop profits, individual & corporate donations
Special Subjects: Decorative Arts, Dolls, Furniture, Glass
Collections: Coverlet coll; Early American furniture; rare coll of pressed glass (5,000 pitchers, 600 patterns of pressed glass, all types of art glass, steins & Tiffany glass); ceramics, dolls, porcelains
Publications: Always Paddle Your Own Canoe: The Life, Legend & Legacy of Ann Safley Houston; Fabulous Houston; Houston Museum of Decorative Arts Coverlet Collection
Activities: Docent training; lect open to pub, 1-2 vis lectrs per yr; tours; mus shop sells books, reproductions, prints, decorative art objects & items reflective of pieces in permanent coll

M **HUNTER MUSEUM OF AMERICAN ART,** 10 Bluff View, Chattanooga, TN 37403-1197. Tel 423-267-0968; Fax 423-267-9844; Elec Mail mphlaum@huntermuseum.org; Internet Home Page Address: www.huntermuseum.org; *Dir Develop* Caroline Von Kessler; *Pub Rels & Mktg Dir* Katrina Craven; *Cur Educ* Adera Causey; *Chief Cur* Ellen Simak
Open Mon - Tues & Fri - Sat 10 AM - 5 PM, Wed & Sun noon - 5 PM, Thurs 10 AM - 8 PM; Admis adults $9.95, children 3-17 $4.95, mems & children under 3 free, 1st Sun of month free; Estab 1952 to present a visual arts program of high quality, maintain a fine coll of American art & to carry out a vigorous educational program in the community & the schools; The permanent coll of American art is housed in the George Thomas Hunter Mansion constructed in 1904, an addition was opened in 1975, and a second addition was opened in 2005; Average Annual Attendance: 58,000; Mem: 1800; dues individual $45, family $65, donor $100,

sponsor $350, Chairman's Circle Member $1,000, Chairman's Circle Benefactor $2,500, Chairman's Circle Grand Benefactor $5,000
Library Holdings: Cards; Cassettes; Clipping Files; Memorabilia; Original Documents; Pamphlets; Periodical Subscriptions; Photographs
Special Subjects: Portraits, Pottery, Silver, Textiles, Tapestries, Painting-American, Photography, Prints, Sculpture, Watercolors, Woodcarvings, Posters, Glass, Stained Glass
Collections: American paintings, later 18th century to present, including works by Bierstadt, Benton, Burchfield, Cassatt, Durand, Hassam, Henri, Inness, Marsh, Miller, Twachtman, Whistler & others; contemporary works including Beal, Bechtle, Fish, Frankenthaler, Golub, Goodman, Johns, LeWitt, Park, Pearlstein, Rauschenberg, Schapiro, Stackhouse, Wesselman, Wonner & Youngerman; contemporary American prints; sculpture by Calder, Hunt, Nevelson, Segal, Snelson & others; glass by Chihuly, Littleton, Morris, Zinsky
Publications: Brochures & announcements; bulletin, quarterly; A Catalogue of the American Collection, Hunter Museum of Art, 1985, 300-page illustrated focus on pieces in the permanent collection
Activities: Classes for adults, teens & children; docent training; internships; Designing Innovation prog; community partnerships; student gallery; lect open to pub; gallery talks; concerts; tours; individual paintings are lent to other museums; book traveling exhibs 6-8 per yr; originate traveling exhibs which circulate to qualified galleries & art museums; mus shop sells books, reproductions, gift items, jewelry

L Reference Library, 10 Bluff View, Chattanooga, TN 37403. Tel 423-267-0968; Fax 423-267-9844; Internet Home Page Address: www.huntermuseum.org; *Dir* Robert A Kret
Open by appointment only; Estab 1958 as reference source for staff only; Circ Non-circulating
Library Holdings: Book Volumes 1500; Cards; Cassettes; Clipping Files; Exhibition Catalogs; Memorabilia; Motion Pictures; Original Art Works; Pamphlets; Periodical Subscriptions 8; Photographs; Prints; Sculpture; Slides
Special Subjects: Architecture

M TANNER HILL GALLERY, 3069 S Broad St Ste 3, Chattanooga, TN 37408-3083. Tel 404-580-4299; *Dir* Angela Usrey; *Dir* Annie Harpe
Open Thurs - Fri noon - 5 PM (during exhibs & by appointment)
Collections: paintings; sculpture

M UNIVERSITY OF TENNESSEE AT CHATTANOOGA, Cress Gallery of Art, Fine Arts Ctr, 752 Vine St Chattanooga, TN 37043; 615 McCallie Ave, Dept of Art # 1301 Chattanooga, TN 37403-2504. Tel 423-425-4600; Tel 423-304-9789; Fax 423-425-2101; Elec Mail ruth-grover@utc.edu; Internet Home Page Address: www.utc.edu/cressgallery; *Dir & Cur* Ruth Grover
Open Mon - Fri 9:30 AM - 7:30 PM; No admis fee; Estab 1980 as a teaching gallery for art department, campus & community; 2-room gallery, main 116+ running ft, auxiliary 54 running ft; Average Annual Attendance: 8,000
Income: School funding, grants and donations
Library Holdings: Exhibition Catalogs; Kodachrome Transparencies; Lantern Slides; Original Art Works; Other Holdings teaching collection with Western art & archit; Prints; Sculpture; Slides; Video Tapes
Collections: Graphics; paintings; sculpture
Exhibitions: 6 - 7 temporary exhibitions per year
Activities: Lect open to pub; 4 vis lectrs per yr; gallery talks; tours on request; individual paintings & original objects of art lent to various campus areas; lending coll contains original prints & paintings; temporary and traveling exhibs

CLARKSVILLE

M AUSTIN PEAY STATE UNIVERSITY, Margaret Fort Trahern Gallery, Trahern Bldg, College & 8th St Clarksville, TN 37044; PO Box 4677 Clarksville, TN 37044. Tel 931-221-7333; Fax 931-221-7432; Elec Mail holteb@apsu.edu; Internet Home Page Address: www.apsu.edu/art/gallery/trahern.html; *Dir* Bettye Holte
Open Mon - Fri 9 AM - 4 PM; Sat 10 AM - 2 PM; Sun 1 - 4 PM; No admis fee; Estab 1962 as a univ community service to exhibit a variety of visual media; Average Annual Attendance: 8,000
Income: Financed by univ appropriations
Exhibitions: Average 10-12 per year
Publications: Announcements of shows & artist biographies
Activities: Lect open to pub, 6-8 vis lectrs per yr; gallery talks; tours; competitions with awards; schols offered

L Art Dept Library, 601 College St, Dept of Art Austin Peay State University Clarksville, TN 37044. Tel 931-221-7333; Internet Home Page Address: www.apsu.edu; *Dean College Arts & Letters* Dixie Webb; *Dept Chair* Gregg Schlanger; *Gallery Dir* Warren Greene
Collections: Larson Drawing Collection

M Mabel Larsen Fine Arts Gallery, PO Box 4677, Clarksville, TN 37044-0001. Tel 931-221-7334; Fax 931-221-7432; Elec Mail holteb@apsuoz.edu; *Dir* Bettye S Holte
Open Mon - Fri 8 AM - 4 PM, cl holidays; No admis fee; Estab 1994 to house Austin Peay State Univ permanent art colls; Average Annual Attendance: 5,000
Income: Financed by state funds
Library Holdings: Original Art Works
Collections: Larson Drawing Collection; Hazel Smith Collection; Center of Excellence Student Collection
Exhibitions: Changing exhibits of the University permanent collection
Activities: Gallery talks; competitions

COOKEVILLE

A CUMBERLAND ART SOCIETY INC, Cookeville Art Gallery, 186A S Walnut, Cookeville, TN 38501. Tel 931-526-2424; Elec Mail cumberlandartsociety@yahoo.com; Internet Home Page Address: cumberlandartsociety.com; *Pres* Adele Seitzinger; *1st Vice Pres* Chuck Becker; *2nd Vice Pres* Nadine Armstrong; *Treas* Rose Dahms; *Sec* Bonnie Masters
Open Mon - Fri & Sun 1 - 4 PM; No admis fee; Estab 1961 to promote arts in the community & area; A new building with adequate gallery & studio space. The

gallery is carpeted & walls are finished with wallscape & track lighting; Average Annual Attendance: 3,000; Mem: 125; dues $30, renewal $30, students $15; meeting quarterly
Income: Financed by mem, city & state appropriations
Exhibitions: Changing exhibits, monthly
Activities: Classes for children & adults; art educ for elementary school age children; lect open to pub, 6 vis lectrs per yr; gallery talks; tours; competitions with awards

HENDERSONVILLE

A HENDERSONVILLE ARTS COUNCIL, Monthaven Mansion, 1154 W Main St, Hendersonville, TN 37077-2823; PO Box 64, Hendersonville, TN 37077-2823. Tel 615-822-0789; Elec Mail artscouncil@monthaven.org; Internet Home Page Address: www.hendersonvillearts.org; *Interim Exec Dir* Jerry Tachora
Open 9 AM - 3 PM; No admis fee; Estab 1975 to promote & educate through the arts; Galleries are located in 200 yr old home; Average Annual Attendance: 10,000
Income: non-profit, funding through grants/fundraisers
Exhibitions: Monthly changing exhibits
Publications: News d'Art, quarterly
Activities: Classes for adults & children; dramatic progs; concerts; gallery talks; gift shop sells local crafts & prints

JOHNSON CITY

M EAST TENNESSEE STATE UNIVERSITY, The Reece Museum, PO Box 70660, Johnson City, TN 37614-1701. Tel 423-439-4392; Fax 423-439-4283; Elec Mail reecemus@etsu.edu; Internet Home Page Address: www.etsu.edu/reece; *Dir* Theresa Burchett; *Secy* Pamela Marston; *Coll Mgr* Kirsti Giles
Open Tues & Wed & Fri 9 AM - 4 PM, Thurs 9 AM - 7 PM; No admis fee, donations accepted; Estab 1965 to enhance the cultural & educational advantages of the University & the people of upper East Tennessee; The purpose of Friends of the Reece Museum is to support programs of the mus; Mem: 250; dues President's Trust $10,000 plus, Benefactor $500, Sustaining $250, Patrons $100, Supporting $50, Family $30, Individual $20, Student $10
Income: Financed through the state of TN
Special Subjects: American Indian Art, Archaeology, Historical Material, Ceramics, Pre-Columbian Art, Painting-American, Prints, Period Rooms, African Art, Anthropology, Crafts, Asian Art, Cartoons
Collections: Southern Appalachian Art; historical Appalachian artifacts from frontier settlement to present day; pre-historic and archaeological artifacts; East Tennessee politics; Appalachian music and crafts; East Tennessee State University coll; paintings and prints by national and international artists
Exhibitions: Annual Alumni Exhibit; Annual Holiday Exhibit; Rotating exhibs
Publications: CRM Calendar, quarterly, gallery guides with exhibitions
Activities: classes for adults; gallery talks; tours; competitions with awards; concerts; lects; Lets Learn about Coal-Teacher's Trunk program; books traveling exhibs 1-2 per yr; originates traveling exhibs nationally; mus shop sells books & magazines

KINGSPORT

A ARTS COUNCIL OF GREATER KINGSPORT, Renaissance Center Main Gallery, 1200 E Center St, Kingsport, TN 37660-4958. Tel 423-392-8420; Fax 423-392-8422; Elec Mail info@kingsportarts.org; Internet Home Page Address: www.kingsportarts.org; *Pres* Bob Lawrence; *Pres Elect* Elaine Barker
Open Mon - Fri 8 AM - 5 PM; No admis fee, charge for special events; Estab 1968 to promote & present all the arts to all the people in area; this includes performing arts, visual arts & classes; One gallery with monthly shows; Average Annual Attendance: 20,000; Mem: 400; dues $20 - $500
Income: Financed by mem & grants
Activities: Classes for adults & children; lect open to pub, 3 vis lectrs per yr; concerts; competitions with awards; schols; originate traveling exhibs through Southern Arts Federation

KNOXVILLE

M BECK CULTURAL EXCHANGE CENTER, INC, 1927 Dandridge Ave, Knoxville, TN 37915-1909. Tel 865-524-8461; Fax 865-524-8462; Elec Mail beckcenter@beckcenter.net; Internet Home Page Address: www.beckcenter.net; *Dir & CEO* Avon William Rollins Sr
Open Tues - Sat 10 AM - 6 PM; No admis fee, donations accepted; Estab 1975 to encourage, collect, preserve & display local, regional, & national Black history; Average Annual Attendance: 35,000; Mem: 1,000; annual meeting in Sept
Income: $90,000 (financed by mem, city, county & state appropriations)
Library Holdings: Audio Tapes; Cassettes; Clipping Files; Compact Disks; Original Art Works; Original Documents; Records; Sculpture; Slides; Video Tapes
Special Subjects: African Art, Afro-American Art, Cartoons
Exhibitions: Federal Judge William H Hastie Room; Library of Books & Recordings; oral histories; weekly newspapers of the local Black experience; Senior Citizens Story Writing Contest
Publications: 200 Year History of Knoxville & 125 Year History of Knoxville College; State of Black Economy in Tennessee
Activities: Classes for adults & children; school & community presentations; docent progs; lects open to pub; competitions with cash awards; traveling slide presentations; mus shop sells books, prints, music & clothing

M KNOXVILLE MUSEUM OF ART, 1050 World's Fair Park Dr, Knoxville, TN 37916-1653. Tel 865-525-6101; Fax 865-546-3635; Elec Mail info@knoxart.org; Internet Home Page Address: www.knoxart.org; *Exec Dir* David Butler; *Cur* Stephen Wicks; *Asst Cur* Clark Gillespie; *Dir Develop* Donna Dempster; *Dir Mktg* Angela Thomas; *Dir Finance* Joyce Jones
Open Tues-Thurs & Sat 10AM-5PM, Fri 10AM-8PM, Sun 1PM-5PM; Admis general $5; group & school tours available; please call 865-6101 ext. 226 to

arrange for more information; Estab 1961 as a nonprofit private corporation. Grand opening was held in 1990. Located on the former World's Fair site downtown; New state-of-the-art 53,000 sq ft facility. Maintains reference library; Average Annual Attendance: 117,000; Mem: 4300; dues $40 - $1000

Income: Financed by mems, contributions, sponsorships, foundations & local, state & federal grants

Purchases: Therman Statom's 'Antartica'; John Wilson's 'Martin Luther King, Jr'; Warrington Colescott's 'Jazz Piano'

Library Holdings: Auction Catalogs; Book Volumes; CD-ROMs; Exhibition Catalogs; Original Documents; Pamphlets; Periodical Subscriptions; Slides; Video Tapes

Special Subjects: Drawings, Hispanic Art, Latin American Art, Mexican Art, Painting-American, Photography, Prints, Sculpture, Watercolors, American Indian Art, American Western Art, Bronzes, Folk Art, Woodcuts, Etchings & Engravings, Landscapes, Afro-American Art, Decorative Arts, Painting-European, Portraits, Porcelain, Miniatures, Period Rooms, Medieval Art

Collections: Modern & contemporary art in all media; Works by artists who worked during & after the 20th century in painting, photography, sculpture & works on paper

Publications: Bi-monthly calendar; exhibition catalogs; newsletter

Activities: Classes for adults & children; docent preparation; artists in the classrooms; school outreach; lects open to pub, 5-8 vis lectrs per yr; concerts; gallery talks; tours; competitions with awards; scholarships & fels offered; exten dept serves 9 county region; lending collection contains books, cassettes, color reproductions & slides; Art2Go; suitcases for classroom use; originate traveling exhibs; mus shop sells books, original art, reproductions, prints, jewelry, accessories (apparel), greeting cards, calendars, toys, t-shirts & art-related gifts; Exploratory Gallery on-site for students & families

M **UNIVERSITY OF TENNESSEE,** McClung Museum of Natural History & Culture, 1327 Circle Park Dr, Knoxville, TN 37996-3200. Tel 865-974-2144; Fax 865-974-3827; Elec Mail museum@utk.edu; Internet Home Page Address: www.mcclungmuseum.utk.edu; *Exhib Coordr* Steve Long; *Registrar & Colls Mgr* Robert Pennington; *Dir* Jefferson Chapman; *Cur Archaeology* Dr Timothy Baumann; *Media Productions Coordr* Lindsay Kromer; *Mus Educator* Deborah Woodiel; *Asst Cur* Catherine Shteynberg

Open Mon - Sat 9 AM - 5 PM, Sun 1 - 5 PM; No admis fee; Estab 1961 to collect, maintain & interpret paintings, works of art, items of natural history & historical objects with emphasis placed on the Tennessee area. A major purpose is to provide research materials for students & faculty of the university; Average Annual Attendance: 50,000; Mem: 520; dues $30-2,500

Income: Financed by state appropriations & private contributions

Library Holdings: Auction Catalogs; Photographs; Slides

Special Subjects: American Indian Art, Anthropology, Archaeology, Decorative Arts, Prints, Pottery, Porcelain, Oriental Art, Asian Art, Historical Material, Antiquities-Egyptian

Collections: Eleanor Deane Audigier Art Collection; Frederick T Bonham Collection (18th - 20th Century furniture, art objects); Lewis-Kneberg Collection (Tennessee archaeology); Malacology Collection (marine species & fresh water North American mollusks)

Exhibitions: The Decorative Experience; Ancient Egypt: The Eternal Voice; Archaeology & the Native Peoples of Tennessee; Geology and the Fossil History of Tennessee; Human Origins; Battle of Ft Sanders; Freshwater Mussels

Publications: Museum member newsletter; occasional papers

Activities: Classes for children; docent training; lects open to pub, 3-5 vis lectrs per yr; individual paintings & original objects of art lent; book traveling exhibs, 1-3 per yr; mus shop sells books, original art, reproductions & slides

M **Ewing Gallery of Art and Architecture,** 1715 Volunteer Blvd, Knoxville, TN 37996-0001. Tel 865-974-3200; Fax 865-974-3198; Elec Mail spangler@utk.edu; *Registrar* Cindy Spangler; *Dir* Sam Yates

Open Mon - Thurs 8:30 AM - 8 PM, Fri 8:30 AM - 4:30 PM, Sun 1 - 4 PM; No admis fee; Estab 1981 to provide quality exhibitions focusing on contemporary art & architecture; Gallery consists of 3,500 sq ft exhibition space; Average Annual Attendance: 6,000

Collections: Contemporary American prints, paintings & drawings; Japanese prints; Joseph Delaney

Activities: Lects open to pub, 12 vis lectrs per yr; gallery talks; tours; sponsor competitions; scholarships offered; lending collection contains individual & original objects of art; originate traveling exhibs

A **Visual Arts Committee,** 305 University Center, Knoxville, TN 37996-4800. Tel 423-974-5455; Fax 423-974-9252; Elec Mail vac@utk.edu; Internet Home Page Address: www.activities.utk.edu; *Prog Dir* Ashleigh Moyer; *Asst Dir* Philip Smith; *Grad Advisor* Meghan Terry

Open Mon - Fri 7:30 AM - 10:30 PM, Sat 7 AM - 10 PM, Sun 1 - 6 PM; No admis fee; Estab to provide visual arts for the students of the univ & vis artist lectr series; Two major galleries: Gallery Concourse has 300 running ft; Average Annual Attendance: 20,000

Income: Financed by student activities fees

Exhibitions: 8 exhibits per year; student shows

Publications: Visual Arts Comt Ann Catalog

Activities: Lects open to pub; 6 vis lectrs per yr; competitions

MARYVILLE

M **MARYVILLE COLLEGE,** Fine Arts Center Gallery, 502 E Lamar Alexander Pkwy, Maryville, TN 37804-5907. Tel 865-981-8150, 981-8000; Fax 865-273-8873; Elec Mail sowders@maryvillecollege.edu; Internet Home Page Address: www.maryvillecollege.edu; *Chmn* Mark Hall

Open Mon - Fri during school year 9 AM - 5 PM; No admis fee; Located in fine arts center

Income: School funding

Exhibitions: Monthly rotating exhibitions

Activities: Gallery programs in connection with circulating exhibitions; art movies, four times a year

MC MINNVILLE

M **SOUTHERN MUSEUM & GALLERIES OF PHOTOGRAPHY,** 210 E Main St, Mc Minnville, TN 37111-2508. Tel 931-507-8102; *Southern Standard Staff Reporter* Monty Wanamaker

Open Wed & Fri - Sat 10 AM - 4 PM

Collections: Photographs

MEMPHIS

AUTOZONE
For further information, see National and Regional Organizations

M **BELZ MUSEUM OF ASIAN & JUDAIC ART,** 119 S Main St, Memphis, TN 38103-3647. Tel 901-523-ARTS; Elec Mail info@belzmuseum.org; Internet Home Page Address: www.belzmuseum.org; *Dir* Nancy Knight; *Guest Svcs Admin* Melanie Miller; *Research Assoc* Daniel Graubman; *Research Asst* Michelle Williams

Open Tues-Fri 10AM-5:30PM, Sat-Sun noon-5PM; cl New Year's Day, Easter, Independence Day, Thanksgiving, Christmas; Admis adults $6, seniors $5, students $4

Collections: Asian art pertaining to China's Quing Dynasty, including works in jade and ivory; Chinese puppets; historic and literal pieces relating to Judaism

A **CENTER FOR SOUTHERN FOLKLORE,** 119 S. Main St, Peabody Place Trolley Shop Memphis, TN 38103-3647. Tel 901-525-3655; Fax 901-525-3945; Elec Mail info@southernfolklore.com; Internet Home Page Address: www.southernfolklore.com; *Exec Dir* Judy Peiser

Open Mon & Thurs 10 AM - 8 PM, Fri & Sat 10 AM - Noon, Sun 1 - 8 PM; Admis $2; Estab 1972 as a nonprofit organization which archives, documents & presents folk art, culture & music through film, photography, exhibits & lectures; Mem: 800; dues $25

Income: $350,000 (financed by mem, state appropriation & national endowment)

Collections: African - American Quilt; Contemporary Slides - Folk Art & Culture; Folk Art; Historical & Contemporary Photographs

Activities: Classes for adults & children; cultural tourism; lect open to public; lending collection contains 50 paintings & art objects; retail store sells books, magazines & original art

M **THE DIXON GALLERY & GARDENS,** 4339 Park Ave, Memphis, TN 38117-4698. Tel 901-761-5250; Fax 901-682-0943; Elec Mail jduggan@dixon.org; tdumas@dixon.org; Internet Home Page Address: www.dixon.org; *Dir* Kevin Sharp; *Dir Horticulture* Dale Skaggs; *Dir Develop* Susan Johnson; *Dir Communs* Emily Halpern; *Cur Educ* Margarita Sandino; *Vis Svcs* Jenny Duggan; *Vis Svcs* Tanya Dumas

Open Tues - Fri 10 AM - 4 PM, Sat 10 AM - 5 PM, Sun 1 PM - 5 PM, & Thurs 9 PM, cl Mon, New Years Day, July 4, Thanksgiving Day, Christmas Eve & Day; Admis adults $7, students 18 & older w/ID & seniors $5, children 7-17 yrs $3, mems & children 6 & under free, Tues 10 AM - 4 PM pay what you wish, Sat 10 AM - Noon free; group rates apply, school groups with advance registration free; Estab 1976 as a bequest to the pub from the late Margaret & Hugo Dixon. Their Impressionist Art Collection & their Georgian-style home & gardens, situated on 17 acres of landscaped woodland, serve as the museum's foundation; Two wings added in 1977 & 1986 house the developing permanent collection & accommodate loan exhibitions. Formal & informal gardens, conservatory & greenhouses are located on the site; Average Annual Attendance: 70,000; Mem: 3000; dues sustainer $1000, patron $500, cosmopolitans $300, donor $250, young at art $150, sponsor $125, family $60, individual $45

Income: Financed by endowment, contributions, mem, & corporate sponsorships

Library Holdings: Auction Catalogs; Book Volumes; DVDs; Exhibition Catalogs; Kodachrome Transparencies; Original Documents; Photographs; Video Tapes

Special Subjects: Ceramics, Painting-British, Painting-American, Prints, Watercolors, Decorative Arts, Porcelain, Painting-French, Pewter

Collections: French Impressionist painting; Barbizon, Post-Impressionist & related schools; 18th century British paintings; Warda Stevens Stout Collection of 18th century German porcelain; 18th & 19th centuries works by Pierre Bonnard, Eugene Boudin, Theodore Earl Butler, A F Cals, Jean-Baptiste Carpeaux, Mary Cassatt, Paul Cezanne, Marc Chagall, William Merritt Chase, John Constable, J B C Corot, Kenyon Cox, Henri-Edmond Cross, Charles Francois Daubigny, Edgar Degas, Julien Dupre, Sir Jacob Epstein, Henri Fantin-Latour, Thomas Gainsborough, Paul Gauguin, Edmond Grandjean, Francesco Guardi, Paul Guigou, Armand Guillaumin, Henri Joseph Harpignies, William James, Johan Jongkind, S V E Lepine, Maximilien Luce, Albert Marquet, Paul Mathey, Henri Matisse, Claude Monet; Berthe Morisot, Henriette A Oberteuffer, Ludovic Piette, Camille Pissarro, Sir Henry Raeburn, J F Raffaelli, Auguste Renoir, Sir Joshua Reynolds, Henri Rowart, Paul Singer Sargent, Paul Signac, Alfred Sisley, Allen Tucker, J M W Turner, Horatio Walker and Richard Wilson; Gardens & Gardening; The Adler Pewter Collection; Jean-Louis Forain Collection; The Charlotte Stuart Hooker Collection of English Ceramics; The Noufflard Collection

Publications: Exhibition catalogs; quarterly newsletter

Activities: Classes for adults; workshops; progs for children; docent training; mobile art educ in Art-to-Grow van; teacher resources; internships; lects open to pub; concerts; gallery talks; film series; individual paintings & original objects of art lent to mus & galleries; lending collection contains original paintings, prints, sculpture & porcelain; originate 1-3 book traveling exhibs per yr; originate traveling exhibs to mus; mus shop sells art & garden books, prints, jewelry, notecards & garden items

L **Library,** 4339 Park Ave, Memphis, TN 38117. Tel 901-761-5250; Fax 901-682-0943; Elec Mail info@dixon.org; Internet Home Page Address: www.dixon.org; *Librn* Janice Tankersley

Open Tues - Sat 10 AM - 5 PM, Sun 1 - 5 PM; Admis adults $5, seniors $4, students & children free; Circ 3500; Open to members during mus hours, for reference only; Average Annual Attendance: 50,000

Income: $10,000 (financed by mem, corporate & private sponsorship & the Hugo Dixon Foundation)

Library Holdings: Auction Catalogs; Book Volumes; Cards; Clipping Files; DVDs; Exhibition Catalogs; Manuscripts; Pamphlets; Periodical Subscriptions 15; Photographs; Slides; Video Tapes
Special Subjects: Decorative Arts, Painting-French, Ceramics, Pewter
Collections: French and American Art in the 19th and 20th centuries
Activities: Classes for adults & children; dramatic training; concerts; gallery talks; exten dept serves school outreach, 18,000 students per yr; originate traveling exhibs; mus shops sells books, reproductions, & prints

C FIRST HORIZON NATIONAL CORP, (First Tennessee National Corp) First Tennessee Heritage Collection, 165 Madison Ave, Memphis, TN 38103-2723. Tel 901-523-4291; Fax 901-523-4354; *CEO* Bryan Jordan; *Tours* Lizzy Haymond
Mus open Mon - Fri 8:30 AM - 6 PM, Sat 9 AM - Noon; Estab 1979 to depict Tennessee's heritage & history through art; Gallery, with over 150 original works, is located in First Tennessee's corporate headquarters; Average Annual Attendance: 5,000
Income: Financed by corporation
Special Subjects: Etchings & Engravings, Sculpture, Watercolors, Painting-American, Prints
Collections: Engravings, etchings, lithographs, murals, paintings, sculpture, watercolors
Exhibitions: Permanent collection
Activities: Educ dept

C FIRST TENNESSEE BANK, 165 Madison Ave, Memphis, TN 38103. Tel 901-523-4352 (Communs Dept); Fax 901-523-4354 (Communs Dept); *In Charge Art Coll* Kathy Alexander; *Office Mgr* Nancy Bradfield
Estab to provide community interest in the arts; to aid participating artists; to enhance lobby; Supports local artists & art forms on display that lend an interest to the community
Collections: Paintings by local artists in a variety of media
Activities: Sponsors Wildlife Artist Guy Coheleach

M MEMPHIS BROOKS MUSEUM OF ART, 1934 Poplar Ave, Memphis, TN 38104-2765. Tel 901-544-6200; Fax 901-725-4071; Internet Home Page Address: www.brooksmuseum.org; *Cur Educ* Marina Pacini; *Registrar* Kip Peterson; *Chief Preparator* Bert Sharp III; *Asst Preparator* Paul Tracy; *CFO* Barbara Mullins; *Facilities Mgr* Nicolas Carranza; *Mus Shop Mgr* Daphne Hewett; *Dir Develop* Debbie Litch; *Assoc Dir Develop* Andrew Trippel; *Exec Asst Dir* Peter Dandridge; *VChmn* Joe Weller; *Assoc Registrar* Marilyn Masler; *Dir Media & Pub* Jan Bauman; *Dir* Cameron Kitchin
Open Wed & Fri 10AM-4PM, Thurs 10AM-8PM, Sat 10AM-5PM, Sun 11:30AM-5PM; Admis adults $7, seniors $6, youth & students $3, children under 6 free; Estab 1912 to exhibit, preserve & elucidate works of art; The original building was opened in 1916 with additions in 1955 and 1973. Maintained by the city of Memphis, Public Service Department; Average Annual Attendance: 125,000; Mem: 3156; dues $35 & up
Income: $1,000,000 (financed by city appropriation & Friend's Foundation)
Special Subjects: Painting-British, Painting-French, Painting-American, Sculpture, Textiles, Glass, Porcelain, Oriental Art, Asian Art, Painting-Dutch, Painting-Flemish, Renaissance Art, Painting-Italian
Collections: American Paintings & Sculpture, 18th-20th centuries; Dutch & Flemish Paintings, 16th-18th centuries: Eastern & Near-Eastern Decorative Arts Collection (Han, Tang & Ching Dynasty); English Paintings, 17th-19th centuries; French Paintings, 16th-19th centuries; International Collection of Paintings & Sculpture, 19th & 20th centuries; Kress Collection of Italian Paintings & Sculptures, 13th-18th centuries; Mid-south Collection of 20th century paintings & sculptures; glass, textile & porcelain collection; Dr Louis Levy Collection of American Prints
Exhibitions: 4 rotating exhibitions per year
Publications: Bimonthly newsletter
Activities: Classes for adults & children; docent training; outreach prog & studio art activities for student groups; lects open to pub, 9 vis lectrs per yr; concerts; gallery talks; tours; competitions; awards; individual paintings & original objects of art lent; book traveling exhibs 7-10 per yr; originate traveling exhibs; mus shop sells books, reproductions, prints, slides, mus replicas, jewelry & regional pottery
L Library, 1934 Poplar Ave, Overton Park Memphis, TN 38104-2765. Tel 901-544-6200; Fax 901-725-4071; Elec Mail brooks@brooksmuseum.org; Internet Home Page Address: www.brooksmuseum.org
By appointment only; No admis fee; Estab 1912; Reference only; Average Annual Attendance: varies; Mem: Part of museum
Income: financed by city appropriations, memberships
Library Holdings: Book Volumes 6134; Clipping Files 4223; Exhibition Catalogs 2367; Periodical Subscriptions 24

L MEMPHIS COLLEGE OF ART, G Pillow Lewis Memorial Library, 1930 Poplar Ave, Memphis, TN 38104-2764. Tel 901-272-5130; Fax 901-272-5104; Elec Mail mstrawder@mca.edu; Internet Home Page Address: www.mca.edu; *Pres* Jeffrey D Nesin; *Dean* Ken Strickland; *Head Librn* Maxine Strawder; *Visual Resources Cur* Karla Strickland
Open Mon - Thurs 8 AM - 8 PM, Fri 8 AM - 5PM, Sat 10 AM - 3 PM, summer hours Mon - Fri 8:30 AM -4:30 PM; No admis fee; Estab 1936 as an adjunct educational program; The Standing Committee on Exhibitions arranges visiting shows
Library Holdings: Auction Catalogs; Book Volumes 17,000; Clipping Files; Exhibition Catalogs; Periodical Subscriptions 110; Prints; Reproductions; Slides
Special Subjects: Art History, Illustration, Mixed Media, Photography, Calligraphy, Drawings, Graphic Arts, Graphic Design, History of Art & Archaeology, Printmaking, Art Education, Bookplates & Bindings, Metalwork, Jewelry, Pottery
Collections: Jacob Marks Memorial Collection; works by college graduates & faculty; Dennis Sexsmith Visual Resources Collection
Exhibitions: Juried student shows; one & two-person faculty shows; senior exhibition; summer student show; traveling exhibitions
Publications: Exhibition catalogs

Activities: Classes for adults, children, undergraduate & graduate college students; lect; guided tours; films; competitions; book traveling exhibitions

L MEMPHIS-SHELBY COUNTY PUBLIC LIBRARY & INFORMATION CENTER, Dept of Art, Music & Films, 3030 Poplar Ave, Memphis, TN 38111-3527. Tel 901-415-2749; Fax 901-323-7206; Elec Mail mcclyok@memphislibrary.org; Internet Home Page Address: www.memphislibrary.org; *Dir* Judith Drescher; *Deputy Dir* Sallie Johnson; *Sr Mgr Humanities* Gina Milburn; *Dir Libraries* Keenan McCloy
Open Mon - Thurs 9 AM - 9 PM, Fri & Sat 9 AM - 6 PM, Sun 1 - 5 PM; Estab 1895 to serve the reference, informational, cultural & recreational needs of residents of Memphis-Shelby County; Turner-Clark Gallery exhibits promising & established local & regional artists of various media
Income: Financed by city & state appropriation
Library Holdings: Book Volumes 63,000; Cassettes 800; Motion Pictures 3000; Periodical Subscriptions 245; Records 35,000; Video Tapes 3000

M MISSISSIPPI RIVER MUSEUM AT MUD-ISLAND RIVER PARK, 125 N Front St, Memphis, TN 38103-1713. Tel 901-576-7241; Fax 901-576-6666; Internet Home Page Address: www.mudisland.com; *Gen Mgr* Trey Giuntini; *Museum Mgr* Alisa Bradley
Open Apr 14 - Oct 31 10 AM - 5 PM; cl Mon; Admis adults $4, children 3-11 & seniors $3; Estab 1978 to interpret the natural & cultural history of the Mississippi River Valley; Maintains reference library; Average Annual Attendance: 150,000
Income: $350,000 (financed by city appropriation)
Special Subjects: Architecture, Graphics, American Indian Art, Anthropology, Archaeology, Costumes, Folk Art, Pottery, Afro-American Art, Manuscripts, Furniture, Glass, Jewelry, Carpets & Rugs, Historical Material, Maps, Coins & Medals, Dioramas, Period Rooms, Laces
Collections: 2-D & 3-D pieces that interpret the natural & cultural history of the lower Mississippi River
Activities: Classes for children; dramatic prog; docent training; lects open to pub; gallery talks; tours; competitions with prizes; book traveling exhibs 3-5 per yr; originate traveling exhibs; mus shop sells books, magazines, reproductions & prints

M RHODES COLLEGE, Clough-Hanson Gallery, 2000 N Parkway, Clough Hall Memphis, TN 38112-1624. Tel 901-843-3442; Fax 901-843-3727; Elec Mail pacini@rhodes.edu; Internet Home Page Address: www.rhodes.edu/academics/5264.asp; *Dir & Cur* Marina Pacini
Open Tues - Sat 11 AM - 5 PM; Estab 1970 to exhibit local, regional & national artists & mount student exhibitions; Average Annual Attendance: 2,200
Special Subjects: Textiles, Woodcarvings
Collections: Jessie L Clough Art Memorial for Teaching; Asian & European textiles; Japanese & woodblock prints; 20th Century American Prints
Exhibitions: Changing exhibitions
Publications: Annual exhibit catalog
Activities: Lect open to public; gallery talks; 1 book traveling exhibition per year

M UNIVERSITY OF MEMPHIS, Art Museum, 3750 Norriswood, 142 Communication & Fine Arts Bldg Memphis, TN 38152-3200. Tel 901-678-2224; Fax 901-678-5118; Elec Mail artmuseum@memphis.edu; Internet Home Page Address: www.memphis.edu/amum; *Dir* Leslie L Luebbers, PhD; *Asst Dir* Lisa Francisco-Abitz; *Exhibit Specialist/Preparator* Eric Bork; *Mus Media Specialist* Jason Miller; *Admin Secy* Anita Huggins
Open Mon - Sat 9 AM - 5 PM year round except between changing exhibits; closed Univ Holidays; No admis fee; Estab 1981 to sponsor programs & mount temporary exhibitions to expand knowledge about all periods of art with a special emphasis on contemporary art; Mus has 7000 sq ft of exhibition space including one permanent exhibit of ancient Egyptian art; Average Annual Attendance: 11,502; Mem: 200
Income: Financed by state appropriation, pub & private support
Special Subjects: Anthropology, Archaeology, Drawings, Etchings & Engravings, Folk Art, Architecture, Photography, Painting-American, Prints, Period Rooms, Woodcuts, Sculpture, Graphics, Woodcarvings, Antiquities-Egyptian
Collections: Egyptian Hall: antiquities from 3500 BC - 7th century AD; Print Collection: contemporary prints; collection of over 250 prints, an overview; African Art Coll from Martha & Robert Fogelman coll
Exhibitions: Changing contemporary shows
Publications: AM Edition Newsletter, quarterly
Activities: Lects open to pub, 5 vis lectrs per yr; tours; competitions with awards; schols offered; permanent collections lent to other institutions with proper facilities; originate traveling exhibs
L Visual Resource Collection, 220 Jones Hall, Memphis, TN 38152-3306. Tel 901-678-2938; Fax 901-678-2735; Elec Mail slsandrs@memphis.edu; Internet Home Page Address: www.uom.edu; *Colls Cur* Susan L Sanders
Open Mon - Sat 9 AM - 6 PM except when exhibitions are being changed; No admis fee; Estab 1967 to provide slides for Art Faculty, University Faculty, & some outside organizations; Circ 160,000; Maintains Egyptian Museum, the Gallery Museum & a student-run museum
Income: Financed by the university
Library Holdings: Audio Tapes; Book Volumes 218; CD-ROMs; Cassettes; Clipping Files; Compact Disks; DVDs; Exhibition Catalogs; Filmstrips; Original Art Works; Periodical Subscriptions 160; Prints; Records; Reproductions; Sculpture; Slides; Video Tapes
Special Subjects: Art History, Archaeology, American Western Art, Art Education, American Indian Art, Afro-American Art, Antiquities-Oriental, Antiquities-Persian, Antiquities-Assyrian, Antiquities-Byzantine, Antiquities-Egyptian, Antiquities-Etruscan, Antiquities-Greek, Antiquities-Roman, Architecture
Collections: 35 mm slides of history of Western art, photography, non-Western art; Western Art; African Art; Native American Art; Murname Collection of Egyptian Slides; Collection of 17th-19th century American Architecture
Activities: Educ program; lects open to pub; 10-15 vis. lectrs per yr; concerts; gallery talks; tours; competitions; schols offered; exten prog includes Family Day prog

MORRISTOWN

A **ROSE CENTER & COUNCIL FOR THE ARTS,** 442 W Second North St, Morristown, TN 37814-4026; PO Box 1976, Morristown, TN 37816-1976. Tel 423-581-4330; Fax 423-581-4307; Elec Mail info@rosecenter.org; Internet Home Page Address: www.rosecenter.org; *Exec Dir* Drew Ogle; *Operations Mgr* Patty Gracey; *Educ & Special Events* Beccy Hamm; *Facilities Mgr* Ray James
Open Mon - Wed & Fri 9 AM - 5 PM, Thurs 9 AM - 7 PM; No admis fee; Estab 1975 to promote, implement, & sustain historical, educational & cultural activities & projects of both local & national importance; to preserve & maintain Rose School as a museum & cultural center; Circ 1,000; Art gallery, historic gallery, children's touch mus, historical classroom; Average Annual Attendance: 75,000; Mem: 450
Income: Financed by endowment, mem, city, county & state appropriation, class instruction
Library Holdings: Book Volumes; Original Art Works; Other Holdings; Photographs; Slides
Special Subjects: Historical Material, Photography, Textiles, Painting-American, Decorative Arts, Folk Art, Crafts
Collections: Local historical material, crafts & art; clothing
Publications: Monthly newsletter; Qtr calendar
Activities: Classes for adults & children; dramatic progs; art camps; lects open to pub; 5 vis lectrs per yr; concerts; gallery talks; tours; school progs; competition sponsoring; schols; Rose Art award; book traveling exhibs 1 per yr; originates traveling exhibs of various fine art; mus shop sells books & crafts, books & reproductions

MURFREESBORO

M **MIDDLE TENNESSEE STATE UNIVERSITY,** Baldwin Photographic Gallery, PO Box 305, Murfreesboro, TN 37132-0001. Tel 615-898-2300; Fax 615-898-5682; Elec Mail tjimison@mtsu.edu; *Cur* Tom Jimison
Open Mon - Fri 8 AM - 4:30 PM, Sat 8 AM - Noon, Sun 6 - 10 PM; No admis fee; Estab 1970 for the exhibition of outstanding photographers; Gallery has 193 running ft of display area; Average Annual Attendance: 30,000
Income: Financed by the university
Purchases: Purchase work from exhibiting photographers
Special Subjects: Photography
Collections: Ansel Adams; Shelby Lee Adams; Richard Avedon; Harold Baldwin; Harry Callahan; Marrie Camhi; Geri Della Rocea de Candal; Barbara Crane; Jim Ferguson; Dore Gardner; Philip Gould; Tom Jimison; Builder Levy; Minor White & others; Jim Norton; April Ottey; John Pfahl; Walter Rosenblum; John Schulze; Aaron Sisking; Marianne Skogh; H H Smith; Michael P Smith; Jerry Velsman; Ed Weston by Cole; Jack Wilgus; Sean Wilkinson; Kelly Wise
Publications: Lightyear, annually
Activities: Lects open to pub; 4 vis lectrs per yr; original objects of art lent to responsible organizations; lending collection contains photographs; book traveling exhibs 3 per yr; originate traveling exhibs to university galleries

NASHVILLE

M **BOARD OF PARKS & RECREATION,** The Parthenon, Centennial Park, West End Ave Nashville, TN 37203; P.O. Box 196340, Nashville, TN 37219-6340. Tel 615-862-8431; Fax 615-880-2265; Elec Mail parthenon@nashville.org; Internet Home Page Address: www.parthenon.org; *Mus Store Mgr* Timothy Cartmell; *Dir* Wesley M Paine; *Dir Opers* Lauren Bufferd; *Cur* Susan Shockley; *Registrar & Asst Cur* Brenna Cothran; *Dir Educ* DeeGee Lester; *Event Coordr & Gallery Asst* Laura Carrillo
Open yr round Tues - Sat 9 AM - 4:30 PM, June - Aug Sun 12:30 -4:30 PM, cl Sun, Mon & legal holidays; Admis adults $6.00, children (4-17) & seniors $4; Estab 1897 to offer Nashville residents & tourists quality art for viewing in a Historical setting of significance & beauty; 2 changing exhibit galleries & James M Cowan Gallery of American Art; Average Annual Attendance: 150,000+; Mem: 600 mem; dues seniors & students $25; individual $35; family $50
Income: Financed by city & county taxes, donations & memberships
Special Subjects: Architecture, Painting-American, Sculpture
Collections: Cowan Collection, sixty three paintings by 19th & 20th century American artists, donated by James M Cowan; Century III Collection, sixty two art works, purchased from area artists, juried by John Canaday in celebration of Nashville's bicentennial
Exhibitions: Exhibitions change every 4 months
Publications: Century III Catalog; The Cowan Catalog; A Tale of Two Parthenons; Winslow Homer: An American Genius at the Parthenon; Carlton Wilkinson-Coming Home: A Retrospective
Activities: Docent training; lect open to public, 9 vis lectrs per year; concerts; gallery talks; guided tours; lending of original objects of art to Farnsworth Museum, ME; Berry-Hill Galleries, NY; book traveling exhibitions 1-2 per yr; sales shop sells books, souvenirs, prints & slides

M **CHEEKWOOD-TENNESSEE BOTANICAL GARDEN & MUSEUM OF ART,** 1200 Forrest Park Dr, Nashville, TN 37205-4242. Tel 615-356-8000; Fax 615-353-0919; Elec Mail info@cheekwood.org; Internet Home Page Address: www.cheekwood.org; *Registrar* Kaye Crouch; *Preparator* Todd McDaniel; *Chief Cur* Celia Walker; *Pub Information* Carolyn Lawrence; *Dir Educ* Mary Grissom; *Pres & CEO* Dr Jack Becker; *Dir Exhibs & Prog* Allison Reid
Open Tues - Sat 9:30 AM - 4:30 PM, Sun 11 AM - 4:30 PM, cl Mondays, Thanksgiving, Christmas Eve, Christmas, New Year's Eve & New Year's Day; Admis adults $10, seniors $8, children 7-17 $5, children under 7 free; Estab 1957 to collect, preserve & interpret American art. Mus opened to pub in 1960 in a Georgian-style mansion built in 1929 by Mr & Mrs Leslie Cheek. The site underwent further renovation & adaptation in 1980 & 1998; Circ Non-circulating; Galleries contain 12,000 sq ft of exhibition space, divided almost equally between installation of permanent collection & traveling exhibitions. Permanent exhibitions include the American Experience fine art from the collection, Worcester porcelain collection, American and European silver and snuff bottle collection. Separate facility for modern and contemporary art. Outdoor sculpture trail (approx 1 mile) contains regional, national and international sculpture from the collection; Average Annual Attendance: 170,000; Mem: 8700; dues supporting $125, family $65, individual $40,senior (65 & over) $40, student educator $25; annual meeting 3rd Wed in June
Income: Financed by mem, admis, corporate & foundation grants, private gifts, several fundraising events
Library Holdings: Auction Catalogs; Audio Tapes; Book Volumes; CD-ROMs; Exhibition Catalogs; Pamphlets; Periodical Subscriptions; Video Tapes
Special Subjects: Graphics, Painting-American, American Western Art, Decorative Arts, Porcelain
Collections: American paintings; contemporary art; European & American decorative arts; William Edmondson Collection
Exhibitions: Andrew Wyeth Helga Pictures; A Century of Progress: 20th Century Painting in Tennessee; Glass of the Avant-Garde from Vienna Secession to Bauhaus; Young America from the National Museum of American Art
Publications: Brochures, catalogues, checklists, monographs, monthly newsletter, posters
Activities: Classes for adults & children; docent training; lects open to pub; concerts; tours; workshops; individual paintings & original objects of art lent to other mus; book traveling exhibs 5-6 per yr; originate traveling exhibs; mus shop sell books, prints & posters; junior mus

L **Museum of Art,** 1200 Forrest Park Dr, Nashville, TN 37205-4242. Tel 615-356-8000; Fax 615-353-0919; Internet Home Page Address: www.cheekwood.org; *Cur* Jochen Wierich; *Registrar* Kaye Crouch; *Dir* Jack Becker
Open by appointment; Estab 1960
Library Holdings: Book Volumes 5000; Periodical Subscriptions 58
Special Subjects: Art History, Folk Art, Decorative Arts, Photography, Graphic Arts, Painting-American, Pre-Columbian Art, Prints, Sculpture, History of Art & Archaeology, American Western Art, Printmaking, Afro-American Art, Restoration & Conservation, Architecture
Collections: Mainly American Art (paintings, drawings & sculpture); American & European decorative arts
Activities: Classes for adults & children; dramatic progs; docent training; lects open to pub; 2 vis lectrs per yr; concerts; gallery talks; tours; sponsoring of competitions; lending of original objects of art to other mus; mus shop: books, magazines; reproductions; prints

L **Botanic Hall Library,** 1200 Forrest Park Dr, Nashville, TN 37205-4242. Tel 615-353-2148; Fax 615-353-2731; *Librn* Ida Galehouse
Library Holdings: Book Volumes 5000

M **FISK UNIVERSITY,** Carl Van Vechten Gallery, 1000 17th Ave N, Nashville, TN 37208-3051. Tel 615-329-8720; Fax 615-329-8544; Elec Mail galleries@fisk.edu; Internet Home Page Address: www.fisk.edu; *Admin Asst* T Williams; *Interim Dir* Sarah Burroughs
Open during acad yr Mon - Fri 10 AM - 5 PM, cl weekends & univ holidays; Admis adults $10, seniors 60+ $6, college students w/ID $5, children 18 & under free, group 10 or more $6/person; Estab 1949 as an educ resource center for the Fisk & Nashville communities & for the promotion of the visual arts; Neo-Romanesqu structure built 1888 as a church, served as univ gym 1903-1949, converted to art gallery & opened 1949, renovated early 1980's & rededicated 1984; Gallery 1 features rotating traveling exhibs & Gallery 2 houses the permanent Stieglitz Collection; Average Annual Attendance: 24,000
Income: Financed through the university, state appropriations, grants & private donations
Special Subjects: Afro-American Art, Drawings, Folk Art, Photography, Painting-American, Prints, Painting-French, African Art
Collections: African-American Collection; European & American prints & drawings; Traditional & Contemporary African Art Collection; Carl Van Vechten Collection of Photographs; Alfred Stieglitz Collection of Modern American & European Art; Cyrus Baldridge Drawings
Publications: Fisk Art Report, annually
Activities: Lects open to public, 4-6 vis lectrs per yr; gallery talks; tours; book traveling exhibs; originates traveling exhibs; sales shop sells books & reproductions

M **Aaron Douglas Gallery,** 1000 17th Ave N, Nashville, TN 37208. Tel 615-329-8685; Internet Home Page Address: www.fisk.edu
Open Mon - Fri 10 AM - 5 PM, cl Sat & Sun & university holidays; Admis free; Estab 1949; Located in John Hope & Aurelia E Franklin Univ Library, 3rd fl; Special Collections located on 2nd fl
Special Subjects: Afro-American Art, Drawings, Folk Art, Photography, Painting-American, Prints, Painting-European, Sculpture, African Art
Exhibitions: Changing exhibs from the permanent collection of classical & contemporary African art, modern & contemporary African-American art, & American & European art

L **Library,** 17 Ave N, North Nashville, TN 37208; 1000 17th Ave, North Nashville, TN 37208. Tel 615-329-8720; Fax 615-329-8544; Elec Mail jcsmith@fisk.edu; Internet Home Page Address: www.fisk.edu; *Dir* Opal Baker; *Univ Librn* Jessie Carney Smith; *Ref Librn Special Collections* Beth Howse
Open Mon - Thurs 7:45 AM - 10 PM, Fri 7:45 AM - 5 PM, Sat 1-5 PM, Sun 2-10 PM; hours subject to change during exam periods & univ holidays; No admis fee; Estab 1949; Publications are used by students & instructors for research
Library Holdings: Audio Tapes; Book Volumes 1100; Clipping Files; Exhibition Catalogs; Filmstrips; Kodachrome Transparencies; Lantern Slides; Manuscripts; Motion Pictures; Original Art Works; Original Documents; Pamphlets; Photographs; Reproductions; Slides
Collections: Multiple collections consisting of primary & secondary materials on African-American themes; Aaron Douglas Collection: general & personal correspondence (1921-1974) with the Metropolitan Mus of Art & the Harmon Foundation, early drawings, sketches & watercolors, lectures, speeches, programs, photographs, newspaper clippings (1930-1973)

M GENERAL BOARD OF DISCIPLESHIP, THE UNITED METHODIST CHURCH, The Upper Room Chapel & Museum, 1908 Grand Ave, Nashville, TN 37212-2129. Tel 615-340-7207; Fax 615-340-7293; Elec Mail kkimball@upperoom.org; Internet Home Page Address: www.chapel.upperroom.org; *Upper Room Cur* Kathryn Kimball
Open Mon - Fri 8 AM - 4:30 PM; No admis fee, contributions encouraged; Estab 1953 as a religious mus reflecting universal Christianity; Average Annual Attendance: 10,000
Income: Self supporting
Library Holdings: Book Volumes; Fiche; Periodical Subscriptions
Special Subjects: Decorative Arts, Historical Material, Art History, Painting-British, Painting-French, Hispanic Art, Mexican Art, Painting-American, Sculpture, American Indian Art, Bronzes, African Art, Textiles, Religious Art, Ceramics, Folk Art, Woodcarvings, Afro-American Art, Judaica, Manuscripts, Painting-European, Painting-Japanese, Furniture, Porcelain, Asian Art, Antiquities-Byzantine, Painting-Dutch, Carpets & Rugs, Coins & Medals, Tapestries, Calligraphy, Painting-Flemish, Renaissance Art, Embroidery, Painting-Spanish, Painting-Italian, Stained Glass, Reproductions, Painting-Russian
Collections: Bibles from 1577; 2/3 Lifesize Woodcarving of da Vinci's Last Supper; Nativity Scenes; Ukrainian Eggs; furniture; illuminated manuscripts; oriental rugs; porcelain; Nativity Scenes (over 100 sets)
Exhibitions: Woodcarving; Porcelains; Furniture; Manuscripts from 1300-1800s; Paintings-copies from several masterworks of Raphael, da Vinci, Ruebens
Publications: Upper Room Devotional Guide, every 2 months; books; magazines
Activities: Docent training; gallery talks; tours; sales shop sells books, magazines, slides, postcards of woodcarving, original art, reproductions, prints

A TENNESSEE HISTORICAL SOCIETY, 300 Capitol Blvd., War Memorial Bldg, Ground Flr Nashville, TN 37243. Tel 615-741-8934; Fax 615-741-8937; Elec Mail tnhissoc@tennesseehistory.org; Internet Home Page Address: www.tennesseehistory.org; *CEO* Ann Toplovich; *VPres* William P Morrelli; *Secy* Carole S Bucy
Open Mon - Fri 8 AM - 5 PM; cl national holidays; No admis fee; Estab 1849 to preserve & interpret the history of all Tennesseans; Average Annual Attendance: 700, does not include museum attendance; Mem: 2000; dues John Haywood Society $250, sustaining $75, regular $35; annual meeting in May
Income: Financed by mem dues, grants & gifts
Collections: Art, decorative art & artifacts related to Tennessee culture, history & pre-history.
Publications: Tennessee Historical Quarterly
Activities: Lect provided, 7 vis lectrs per year

M TENNESSEE STATE MUSEUM, 505 Deaderick St, Polk Cultural Ctr Nashville, TN 37243-1402. Tel 615-741-2692; Tel 800-407-4324 (toll free); Fax 615-741-7231; Elec Mail museuminfo@tnmuseum.org; Internet Home Page Address: www.tnmuseum.org; *Exec Dir* Lois Riggins-Ezzell; *Deputy Exec Dir* Evadine McMahan; *Dir Coll* Dan Pomeroy; *External Affairs* Leigh Hendry; *Dir Exhib* Philip Kreger; *Dir Opers* Patricia Rasbury; *Dir Pub Rels* Paulette Fox; *Pub Rels Coordr* Randal Jones; *Sr Cur Art & Architecture* James Hoobler
Open Sun 1 - 5 PM, Tues - Sat 10 AM - 5 PM, cl Mon, Christmas, Easter, Thanksgiving, New Year's Day; No admis fee; Estab 1937 to preserve & interpret the historical artifacts of Tennessee through mus exhibits & statewide outreach & educational programs; A military history mus in the War Memorial Building depicts Tennessee's involvement in modern wars (Spanish-American to World War II). Exhibits highlight life in Tennessee from early man through 1920. Gallery houses changing art & history exhibits. Maintains small reference library; Average Annual Attendance: 200,000; Mem: 1500; dues $25 & up
Income: Financed by state appropriation
Purchases: Tennessee related early 19th century paintings & prints; 19th century Tennessee made silver; 19th century Tennessee made firearms
Special Subjects: Historical Material
Collections: Objects relating to Tennessee history from pre-historic times to the present, Tennessee Historical Society; portraits & paintings of & by prominent Tennesseans; contemporary Tennessee related artists' works
Publications: Exhibition catalogs; quarterly newsletter
Activities: Docent training, dramatic progs; lects open to pub, gallery talks, tours, sponsors competitions; exten dept serving statewide; individual paintings & original objects of art; book traveling exhibs; originate traveling exhibs; mus shop sells books, Tennessee crafts, items relating to the collection; junior mus
L Library, 505 Deaderick St, Nashville, TN 37243-1402. Tel 615-741-2692; Fax 615-741-7231; *Dir Coll* Dan Pomeroy
Open Tues - Fri 10 AM - 5 PM, by appt
Income: Financed by State Appropriation
Library Holdings: Book Volumes 1700; Exhibition Catalogs; Pamphlets; Periodical Subscriptions 15; Photographs; Slides; Video Tapes
Special Subjects: Folk Art, Decorative Arts, Painting-American, Historical Material, Ceramics, Crafts, American Indian Art, Costume Design & Constr, Glass, Dolls, Handicrafts, Jewelry, Coins & Medals, Flasks & Bottles, Laces

M VANDERBILT UNIVERSITY, Vanderbilt University Fine Arts Gallery, Cohen Memorial Hall, 1220 21st Ave S Nashville, TN 37203; 230 Appleton Pl, PMB 0273 Nashville, TN 37203-5721. Tel 615-322-0605; Fax 615-343-1382; Internet Home Page Address: www.vanderbilt.edu/gallery; *Dir* Joseph S Mella; *Art Cur Asst* Amy Bridgeman
Open Mon - Wed & Fri Noon - 4 PM, Thurs Noon - 8 PM, Sat & Sun 1 - 5 PM (subject to school calendar); No admis fee; Estab collection 1956, gallery 1961, to provide exhibitions for the university & Nashville communities, & original art works for study by Vanderbilt students & gen pub; The gallery is housed in the historic Cohen Memorial Hall built in 1928 ; Average Annual Attendance: 3,000
Income: Financed by university resources
Special Subjects: Painting-American, Drawings, Prints, Painting-European, Renaissance Art, Painting-Italian
Collections: Herman D Doochin Collection of Asian Art; Anna C Hoyt Collection of Old Master Prints; former Peabody College Art Collection including Kress Study Collection of Italian Renaissance Paintings; Harold P Stern Collection of Oriental Art & Rare Books; Contemporary Works on Paper and other Multiples; Samuel H Kress Collection

Exhibitions: Rotating exhibits every 2-4 months
Publications: Far From the Sea: October Foundation 1998-2003; Of Rage And Redemption: The Art of Oswaldo Guayasamín; Reflections of the Dutch Golden Age Etchings by Adriaen van Ostade; Reading Pictures: Text & Contemporary Art; Maria Magdalena Campos-Pons : Mama/Reciprocal Energy
Activities: Lects open to public; gallery talks; tours; individual paintings & original objects of art lent to museums & galleries; book traveling exhibs 2-3 per yr; originate traveling exhibits

A WATKINS COLLEGE OF ART, DESIGN & FILM, Brownlee O Currey Gallery, 2298 Rosa L Parks Blvd Nashville, TN 37228-1306. Tel 615-383-4848; Fax 615-383-4849; Internet Home Page Address: www.watkins.edu; *Dean Acad Affairs* John Sullivan; *Pres* Ellen L Meyer; *VPres Inst Advancement* Hilary Brown; *VPres Fin* Mary Ellen Lothamer
Open Mon-Fri 8:30 AM - 9 PM, cl Sat & Sun, Christmas, New Years, July 4, Labor Day, Thanksgiving Day; No admis fee; Estab 1885 as an adult educ center for art, interior design, adult evening high school & courses of a gen nature; currently a 4 yr undergrad BFA col of visual arts
Income: Financed by rent from bus property
Collections: All-State Artist Coll (oldest coll of Tennessee art in the state); this is a purchase-award coll of oil, pastels, watercolors, graphics and sculpture; several other colls of lesser value
Exhibitions: Ten exhibitions per year
Publications: Art brochure; qtr catalogue listing courses
Activities: Classes for adults & children; lects open to pub, 6-8 vis lectrs per yr; competitions; Student Exhib Awards; individual paintings lent to schools; original objects of art lent; originates traveling exhibs
L Library, 2298 MetroCenter Blvd, Nashville, TN 37228. Tel 615-383-4848 (main), 277-7426 (library); Fax 615-383-4849; Internet Home Page Address: www.watkins.edu; *Librn* Beverly Starks
Open 8:30 AM - 9 PM; Estab 1885
Library Holdings: Book Volumes 12,000; Filmstrips; Periodical Subscriptions 15; Slides; Video Tapes

OAK RIDGE

A OAK RIDGE ART CENTER, 201 Badger Rd, Oak Ridge, TN 37830-6216. Tel 423-482-1441; *Dir* Leah Marcum-Estes; *Pres* William Capshaw
Open Tues - Fri 9 AM - 5 PM, Sat - Mon 1 - 4 PM; No admis fee; Estab 1952 to encourage the appreciation & creation of the visual arts; Two galleries house temporary exhibitions & permanent collection exhibitions, one rental gallery, classrooms & library; Average Annual Attendance: 20,000; Mem: 450; dues $35; meetings 2nd Mon of month
Income: $130,000 (financed by mem & grants)
Collections: The Mary & Alden Gomez Collection; Contemporary Regional Works; European Post World War II
Exhibitions: Open Show, Juried Competition (all media); monthly exhibit
Publications: Art Matters, monthly bulletin
Activities: Classes for adults & children; docent training; forums; workshops; lect open to public, 6-8 vis lectrs per year; gallery talks; tours; competitions with awards; individual paintings & original objects of art rented to individuals & bus on semi-annual basis; lending collection contains original art works, VCR tapes, 2000 books & 1000 slides
L Library, 201 Badger Rd, Oak Ridge, TN 37830-6216. Tel 423-482-1441; *Dir* Leah Marcum-Estes
Open Tues - Fri 9 AM - 5 PM; Open to members for lending & reference
Income: financed by members & grants
Library Holdings: Audio Tapes; Book Volumes 2000; Exhibition Catalogs; Filmstrips; Memorabilia; Original Art Works; Slides; Video Tapes
Special Subjects: Pottery
Publications: Monthly newsletter

PURYEAR

A INTERNATIONAL SOCIETY OF MARINE PAINTERS, 1800 Goldston Springs Rd, Puryear, TN 38251-3711. Tel 406-293-8447; Elec Mail dlarge@schoonerlinks.com; Internet Home Page Address: www.ismpart.com; *Pres* David Large; *VPres* Richard Levesque
Estab 1984; Mem: mem $15 - $25
Income: Financed by dues & contributions
Special Subjects: Marine Painting
Exhibitions: Annual Marine Artist Breakfast in Gloucesster, MA & Bradenton, FL
Publications: Seascaped, every 3 months
Activities: Originate traveling exhibs to major art galleries, art centers & marine museums

SEWANEE

L UNIVERSITY OF THE SOUTH, Jessie Ball duPont Library, 29 Alabama Ave, Sewanee, TN 37383-0001. Tel 931-598-1664; Fax 931-598-1145; Elec Mail cpfeiff@sewanee.edu; *Dir* Cheryl Pfeiffer
Open Mon - Thurs 7:45 AM - 1 AM, Fri 7:45 AM - 9 PM, Sat 9 AM - 6 PM, Sun 10 AM - 1 AM; Estab 1863
Special Subjects: Collages, Drawings, Etchings & Engravings, Manuscripts, Bronzes, Furniture, Ivory, Glass, Carpets & Rugs, Embroidery, Enamels, Gold, Jewelry, Landscapes, Coins & Medals

M UNIVERSITY OF THE SOUTH, University Art Gallery, 68 Georgia Ave Sewanee, TN 37383. Tel 931-598-1223; Fax 931-598-3335; Elec Mail sjmaclar@sewanee.edu; Internet Home Page Address: www.sewanee.edu/gallery/; *Gallery Dir* Shelly MacLaren
Open Tues - Fri 10 AM - 5 PM, Sat & Sun Noon - 4 PM, holidays & acad holidays by appointment; No admis fee; Estab 1938 to provide exhibits of interest

to students & local & regional audiences; One large space with balcony, one main entry door, carpeted walls, track lighting; Average Annual Attendance: 3,000-5,000
Income: Financed by college funds, contributions & gifts
Library Holdings: CD-ROMs; Compact Disks; DVDs; Lantern Slides; Original Art Works; Photographs; Prints; Sculpture; Slides; Video Tapes
Special Subjects: Prints, Sculpture, Drawings, Graphics, Painting-American, Photography, Watercolors, Etchings & Engravings, Manuscripts, Furniture, Silver, Historical Material, Stained Glass
Exhibitions: 5 exhibitions during school year
Activities: Lects open to public; concerts; gallery talks; sponsor competitions; original objects of art lent to qualified venues; book traveling exhibs (occasional)

TRENTON

M **PORCELAIN VEILLEUSES-THEIERES MUSEUM,** 309 S College St, Trenton City Hall Trenton, TN 38382-2171. Tel 731-855-2013; Fax 731-855-1091; Internet Home Page Address: www.teapotcollection.com

TULLAHOMA

M **TULLAHOMA FINE ARTS CENTER REGIONAL MUSEUM OF ART,** 401 S Jackson St, Tullahoma, TN 37388-3469. Tel 931-455-1234; Fax 931-455-1234; Elec Mail lucy@tullahomafinearts.org; Internet Home Page Address: www.tullahomafinearts.org

TEXAS

ABILENE

M **CENTER FOR CONTEMPORARY ARTS,** 220 Cypress St, Abilene, TX 79601. Tel 925-677-8389; Fax 925-677-1171; *Exec Dir* Darla Harmon
Open Tues-Sat 11AM-5PM
Collections: works by contemporary artists; paintings; sculpture; photographs

M **GRACE MUSEUM, INC,** PO Box 33, Abilene, TX 79604-0033. Tel 915-673-4587; Fax 915-675-5993; Elec Mail info@thegracemuseum.org; Internet Home Page Address: www.thegracemuseum.org; *Develop Dir* Kimberly Snyder; *Cur Educ* Kathryn Best; *Pres & CEO* Judith Godfrey; *Coordr Educ Prog* Pam Harman; *Dir Finance* Vicki Hooker; *Cur Coll* Holly North; *Dir Mktg & Pub Rels* Heather Kuhu; *Office Mgr* Patricia Ditmore
Open Tues - Sat 10 AM - 5 PM, Thurs 10 AM - 8 PM, cl Sun & Mon; Admis adults $5, children $3; Estab 1937 as an art & history educ institution; Contemporary, neutral spaces; Average Annual Attendance: 80,000; Mem: 1200; dues $50 & up
Income: Financed by mem, grants, fund-raising events, sponsors & endowment
Special Subjects: Painting-American, Prints
Collections: American Paintings & Prints; Local History; T&P Railway Collection; Texas Heritage: Peter Searcy, Allen Houser, Fidencio Duran, Maxine Rerini; Photography Collection by Bill Wright
Exhibitions: Regular schedule of temporary & long-term exhibitions, including contemporary art
Publications: Brochures; biannual newsletter
Activities: Classes for adults & children; docent training; lects open to public, 2-5 vis lectrs per year; gallery talks; tours; individual paintings & original works of art lent to other museums; lending collection contains original art works, original prints, paintings, photographs, sculptures, slides; book traveling exhibitions 2-3 per year; museum shop sells books, magazines, reproductions, prints, slides, games, toys, crafts, note cards & decorative arts

M **MCMURRY UNIVERSITY,** Ryan Fine Arts Center, 514th & Sayles Blvd, Abilene, TX 79697; PO Box 8, Abilene, TX 79697-0001. Tel 915-793-3823; Fax 915-793-4662; Internet Home Page Address: www.mcm.edu
Open Mon - Fri 8 AM - 5 PM, cl Sat & Sun; No admis fee; Estab 1970 when building was completed; Large room overlooking larger sculpture garden; Average Annual Attendance: 2,500
Income: Financed by college art budget
Exhibitions: Varied exhibitions, changing monthly, of national, regional & area artists
Activities: Classes for adults in photography; lect open to public; gallery talks; competitions; individual paintings & original objects of art lent to college offices

ALBANY

M **THE OLD JAIL ART CENTER,** 201 S Second St, Albany, TX 76430. Tel 325-762-2269; Fax 325-762-2260; Elec Mail info@theoldjailartcenter.org; Internet Home Page Address: www.theoldjailartcenter.org; *Exec Dir* Margaret Blagg; *Registrar* Amy Kelly; *Dir Educ* Erin Whitmore; *Archivist & Librn* Molly Sauder
Open Tues - Sat 10 AM - 5 PM, Sun 2 - 5 PM; No admis fee; Estab 1980 to collect & display art of US & Europe, Asian & Pre-Columbian art; Four galleries in old 1877 jail. 8 additional galleries plus Stasney Center for Educ. Marshall R Young Courtyard for outdoor sculpture; Average Annual Attendance: 12,000; Mem: 800; dues $25
Library Holdings: Book Volumes; Exhibition Catalogs; Periodical Subscriptions; Video Tapes
Special Subjects: Architecture, Drawings, Painting-American, Photography, Prints, Sculpture, Watercolors, Bronzes, Pre-Columbian Art, Ceramics, Woodcuts, Manuscripts, Furniture, Painting-French, Carpets & Rugs, Historical Material, Maps, Antiquities-Oriental, Painting-Spanish, Painting-Italian, Painting-German
Collections: Antique Furniture & Pre-Columbian; Sculpture; Paintings & graphics; Photography; Asian pottery & Chinese tomb figures; British Contemporary Paintings

Publications: Exhibit catalogs; newsletter, semi-annual
Activities: Classes for adults & children; dramatic progs; docent training; distance learning making classrooms nationally & internationally; lects for members only, 2 vis lectrs per yr; gallery talks; tours; schols offered; individual paintings & original objects of art lent; lending collection contains 400 paintings & some sculpture; book traveling exhibs annually; originate traveling exhibs; mus shop sells books, reproductions, notecards, plus other items

L **Green Research Library,** 201 S Second St, Albany, TX 76430. Tel 325-762-2269; Fax 325-762-2260; Elec Mail archivist@theoldjailartcenter.org; Internet Home Page Address: www.theoldjailartcenter.org; *Registrar* Rebecca Bridges; *Exec Dir* Thomas Jones; *Archivist/Librn* Molly Sauder
Open Tues - Sat 10 AM - 5 PM, Sun 2 - 5 PM; No admis fee; Estab 1984; For reference only
Library Holdings: Book Volumes 2000; Periodical Subscriptions 4
Special Subjects: Art History, Illustration, Photography, Drawings, Pre-Columbian Art, Sculpture, History of Art & Archaeology, American Western Art, Art Education, Asian Art, American Indian Art, Mexican Art, Oriental Art, Antiquities-Egyptian, Antiquities-Greek, Architecture

AMARILLO

A **AMARILLO ART ASSOCIATION,** Amarillo Museum of Art, 2200 S Van Buren St, Amarillo, TX 79109-2407; PO Box 447, Amarillo, TX 79105-0447. Tel 806-371-5050; Fax 806-373-9235; Internet Home Page Address: www.amarilloart.org; *Dir & Cur* Patrick McCracken; *Cur Educ* Mark Morey; *Admin Asst* Liz Seliger; *Admin Asst* Cindy Mote; *Coll Mgr* Reba Jones
Open Tues - Fri 10 AM - 5 PM, Sat & Sun 1 - 5 PM; No admis fee; Estab 1972 for visual arts; Gallery 100, 90 x 30 ft, atrium area 45 ft; Gallery 200 & 203, 90 x 32 ft, 11 ft ceiling; Gallery 305 & 307, each 32 x 28 ft, 10 ft ceiling; Average Annual Attendance: 60,000; Mem: 1800; dues $50-$500
Income: Financed by mem, college, endowment sponsorship program & exhibition underwriting
Collections: Contemporary American drawings, paintings, prints & sculpture; Asian Art Collection
Publications: Annual Report; brochures, as needed; Calendar of Events, bimonthly; catalogs on exhibits
Activities: Classes for adults & children; docent training; lectrs open to pub, 2 vis lectrs per yr; gallery talks; tours; individual paintings & original objects of art lent to qualified institutions; originate traveling exhibs; mus shop sells books, original art, reproductions, prints, posters, crafts

L **Library,** 2200 S Van Buren St, Amarillo, TX 79109-2407; PO Box 447, Amarillo, TX 79105-0447. Tel 806-371-5050; Fax 806-373-9235; Internet Home Page Address: www.amarilloart.org; *Librn* Dru Scamahorn
Open Tues-Fri 10AM-5PM, Sat & Sun 1-5PM; Circ Non-circulating; For reference only
Library Holdings: Book Volumes 1500; Periodical Subscriptions 18

ARLINGTON

M **ARLINGTON MUSEUM OF ART,** PO Box 114, Arlington, TX 76004-0114. Tel 817-275-4600; Fax 817-860-4800; Elec Mail ama@arlingtonmuseum.org; Internet Home Page Address: www.arlingtonmuseum.org; *Pres* Walter Virden; *Secy* Lynda Freeman; *Bd Mem* Susan Fuller-Sutherland
Open Wed 1 PM - 5 PM, Thurs - Fri 1 PM - 5 PM, Sat 10 AM - 5 PM, Sun 1 PM - 5 PM; No admis fee; Estab 1989 to provide access to art for the cultural enrichment and development of the community; Large converted J C Penney's with Mezzanine galleries; Average Annual Attendance: 18,000; Mem: 400; dues $25-$10,000
Income: Financed by endowment, mem, city appropriation & reception rental
Collections: Texas Contemporary Art
Publications: Artifaces, quarterly; AMA News, biannual; exhib catalogs
Activities: Classes for adults & children; docent training; lects series open to pub; gallery talks; tours; originate traveling exhibs

M **UNIVERSITY OF TEXAS AT ARLINGTON,** Gallery at UTA, 502 S Cooper St, Fine Arts Bldg Arlington, TX 76010. Tel 817-272-3110; Fax 817-272-2805; Elec Mail bhuerta@uta.edu; Internet Home Page Address: www.uta.edu/gallery; *Dir & Cur* Benito Huerta; *Asst Cur* Patricia Healy
Open Mon-Fri 10 AM - 5 PM, Sat Noon - 5 PM, cl acad holidays & summers; No admis fee; Estab 1975 on completion of Fine Arts Complex. The Gallery serves the entire university; exhibitions are contemporary; Main Gallery is air-cooled, 4000 sq ft with incandescent light; Average Annual Attendance: 15,000
Income: $25,000 (financed by state appropriation, private gifts & grants)
Special Subjects: Painting-American
Publications: Tri-fold color brochures on exhibs from past 5 years; exhib catalog; Celia Muñoz: Stories Your Mother Never Told You
Activities: Undergraduate course on museum techniques; lect open to public, 6 vis lectrs per year; gallery talks; catalogs on sale

AUSTIN

M **AUSTIN CHILDREN'S MUSEUM,** 201 Colorado, Austin, TX 78701-3922. Tel 512-472-2499; Fax 512-472-2495; Internet Home Page Address: www.austinkids.org; *Exec Dir* Mike Nellis; *Exec Asst* Pam Paine
Open Mon 9 AM - noon (children under 3 yrs only), Tues - Sat 10 AM - 5 PM, Wed 5 - 8 PM (community night), Sun noon - 5 PM (4 - 5 PM no charge), cl New Year's Day, Easter, Memorial Day, Independence Day, Labor Day, Thanksgiving Day & Christmas Day; Admis adult & children 2 yrs & up $6.50, children 12 - 23 months $4.50, children under 12 months no charge; Estab 1983 to create innovative learning experiences for children & families that equip & inspire the next generation of creative problem solvers; Offers a variety of hands-on exhibits for children of all ages; Average Annual Attendance: 210,000; Mem: 2,700; dues $75 - 1,000
Income: Financed through mem, donations & grants

Exhibitions: Global City, Tinkerer's Workshop, Austin Kiddie Limits, Kid Metro, Funstruction Zone, Rising Star Ranch

M **CITY OF AUSTIN PARKS & RECREATION,** O. Henry Museum, 409 E Fifth St, Austin, TX 78701. Tel 512-472-1903; Fax 512-472-7102; Elec Mail ohenrymuseum@austintexas.gov; Internet Home Page Address: www.ohenrymuseum.org; *Educ Coordr* Michael Hoinski; *Asst Cur* Quinn Argall
Open Wed - Sun Noon - 5 PM; No admis fee, donations accepted; Estab 1934 to preserve O Henry's works; The 1891 historic home of the famous short story writer. The home exhibits artifacts & memorabilia relating to the author; Average Annual Attendance: 10,000; Mem: 30; dues $25; annual meeting in Jan
Income: $112,000 (financed by mem, city appropriations & programs)
Special Subjects: Historical Material, Porcelain, Pottery, Textiles, Decorative Arts, Manuscripts, Furniture, Restorations, Period Rooms
Exhibitions: Annual O Henry PUN-OFF Festival of Wit & Puns; O Henry Writing Club
Activities: Classes for adults & children; lects open both to mems & pub, 1 vis lectr per yr; book traveling exhibs 1 per yr; originate traveling exhibs 1 per yr; mus shop sells books

M **CITY OF AUSTIN PARKS & RECREATION DEPARTMENT,** Julia C Butridge Gallery, Dougherty Arts Ctr, 1110 Barton Springs Rd Austin, TX 78704-1150. Tel 512-397-1455; Fax 512-397-1460; Elec Mail megan.weiler@ci.austin.tx.us; Internet Home Page Address: www.ci.austin.tx.us/dougherty/butridge.htm; *Art in Pub Places Mgr* Martha Peters; *Art in Pub Places Coordr* Megan Weiler
Open Mon - Thurs 9 AM - 9:30 PM, Fri 9 AM - 5:30 PM, Sat 10 AM - 2 PM, cl Sun; No admis fee; Estab to preserve & enrich the cultural life of the city; 1800 sq ft of space in a multi-use arts facility available to organizations & artists in the Austin area
Income: Financed by city appropriation
Exhibitions: Rotating schedule presented by local artists & art organizations (all media & subject matter)
Activities: Gallery talks

M **THE CONTEMPORARY AUSTIN,** (Austin Museum of Art) Laguna Gloria, 3809 W 35th St Austin, TX 78703-1001; Jones Center, 700 Congress Ave Austin, TX 78701. Tel 512-453-5312 (Jones Center); Tel 512-458-8191 (Laguna Gloria); Elec Mail info@thecontemporaryaustin.org; Internet Home Page Address: thecontemporaryaustin.org; *Exec Dir* Louis Grachos; *Dir Develop* Tery Quinn; *Art School Dir* Judith Sims; *Sr Cur* Heather Persanti
Open Tues - Sat 11 AM - 7 PM, Sun Noon - 5 PM (Jones Center); Tues - Sun 10 AM - 4 PM (Laguna Gloria); Admis adults $5, seniors & students $3, under 18, military, mems & Tues free; Estab 1911 to reflect the spectrum of contemporary art through exhibs, commissions, educ & colls; 9000 sq ft (Jones Center) 2200 sq ft (Laguna Gloria); Average Annual Attendance: 125,000; Mem: Dues $35 - $5,000
Income: Financed by corporate & individual donations, special events, grants, ann fund, mem, City of Austin
Library Holdings: Auction Catalogs; Audio Tapes; Book Volumes; CD-ROMs; Cassettes; Exhibition Catalogs; Kodachrome Transparencies; Periodical Subscriptions; Slides; Video Tapes
Special Subjects: Latin American Art, Mexican Art, Photography, Afro-American Art
Collections: 20th century painting, sculpture, photographs, prints & drawings; contemporary art
Exhibitions: Changing exhibitions of contemporary art from throughout the world
Publications: Monthly newsletter & exhib catalogues
Activities: Art School classes for adults & children; cultural & educational progs in conjunction with exhibs, docent tours; lects open to pub, 12 vis lectrs per yr; gallery talks; tours; awards, Texas prize; schols offered; individual paintings & original objects of art lent to mus; book traveling exhibs 3-4 per yr; originate traveling exhibs

M **ELISABET NEY MUSEUM,** 304 E 44th St, Austin, TX 78751-3813. Tel 512-458-2255; Fax 512-453-0638; Elec Mail enm@ci.austin.tx.us; Internet Home Page Address: www.ci.austin.tx.us/elisabetney; *Dir* Mary Collins Blackmon
Open Wed - Sun Noon - 5 PM; No admis fee, donations accepted; Estab 1911 to preserve the memory and legacy of 19th C. portrait sculptor, Elisabet Ney (1833-1907). Elisabet Ney portraits and personal memorabilia displayed in the artists 1892 Austin, TX studio; One of five 19th-century American sculpture studios to survive with its contents, the museum is a national, state & historic landmark comprised of artists former studio bldg, 2.5 acres of original 6 acre site & 508 piece coll on permanent loan from Harry Ransom Humanities Research Ctr of Univ TX at Austin; Average Annual Attendance: 10,000
Income: $100,000 (financed by city appropriation, grants & donations)
Special Subjects: Architecture, Sculpture, American Western Art, Portraits, Historical Material, Restorations
Collections: Portrait sculptures of 19th-century European & Texas notables by Elisabet Ney in plaster & marble, tools, furnishings & personal memorabilia
Activities: Summer progs for children; school outreach progs; progs for at-risk children & youth; concerts; gallery talks; tours

L **Library,** 304 E 44th, Austin, TX 78751. Tel 512-458-2255; Fax 512-453-0638; *Dir* Mary Collins Blackmon
Open Wed - Sat 10 AM - 5 PM, Sun Noon - 5 PM; Estab 1908 to collect background material on subjects relevant to the museum's history & period; For reference only
Library Holdings: Book Volumes 330; Clipping Files; Exhibition Catalogs; Manuscripts; Memorabilia; Original Art Works; Other Holdings Letters; Pamphlets; Periodical Subscriptions 7; Photographs; Slides
Special Subjects: Art History, Manuscripts, Sculpture, Historical Material, Portraits, Bronzes, Art Education, Furniture
Exhibitions: A Life in Art; Elizabet Ney in Austin
Publications: SURSUM, collected letters of Elizabet Ney
Activities: Classes for adults & children; dramatic progs; docent training; AV programs; lects open to pub, 3-5 vis lectrs per yr; concerts; gallery talks; tours; exten dept serves Austin area school systems

A **MEXIC-ARTE MUSEUM,** 419 Congress Ave, Austin, TX 78768; PO Box 2273, Austin, TX 78768-2273. Tel 512-480-9373; Fax 512-480-8626; Elec Mail info@mexic-artemuseum.org; Internet Home Page Address: www.mexic-artemuseum.org; *Exec Dir* Sylvia Orozco; *Pres* John Hogg, MD; *Dir Develop* Frank M Rodriguez; *VPres Pub Affairs* Luis Patino; *VPres Mem* Annabelle Arteaga, PhD
Open Mon - Thurs 10 AM - 6 PM; Fri & Sat 10 - 5 PM; Sun noon - 5 PM; Admis adults $5, seniors & students $4, children 12 & under $1, mems no charge; Estab 1984; dedicated to cultural enrichment & educ through the presentation & promotion of traditional & contemporary Mexican, Latino American art and Culture; 4500 sq ft; Average Annual Attendance: 100,000; Mem: 400
Income: 600,000
Library Holdings: Audio Tapes; Book Volumes; Cassettes; Exhibition Catalogs; Records; Video Tapes
Special Subjects: Prints, Woodcuts, Hispanic Art, Latin American Art, Mexican Art
Collections: Graphic prints from workshop of popular graphics from Mexico; Contemporary art work in all disciplines with a focus on Mexican & Latino art; Masks from the State of Guerrero; The Serie Print Project; The Ernest De Soto Collection
Activities: Classes for children; children's hands-on activities; panel discussions; docent training; lect open to public; gallery talks; awards; tours; three vis lectrs; original objects of art lent to other arts facilities; lending collection; museums; mus shop sells books, magazines, reproductions, folk art

M **SAINT EDWARD'S UNIVERSITY,** Fine Arts Gallery, 3001 S Congress Ave, Austin, TX 78704-6489. Tel 512-492-3159; Fax 512-448-8492; Elec Mail arts_gallery@stedwards.edu; Internet Home Page Address: www.think.stedwards.edu/fineartsgallery; *Dir* Hollis Hammonds
Open Mon - Fri 9 AM - 5 PM; No admis fee; Estab 1961 to present for the university population & general pub a monthly schedule of exhibits in the visual arts, as a means of orientation toward established & current trends in art styles in terms of their historical-cultural significance & aesthetic value, through teaching exhibitions, pub & private collections from distributing & compiling agencies, museums, galleries, artists & exhibs by regional, nat & international artists; Average Annual Attendance: 10,000
Income: Financed by the college
Exhibitions: Annual student & faculty exhibitions; Fall term exhibits by vis artists; local, nat & international
Activities: Classes; lects, 3-5 vis lectrs per yr; gallery talks; tours; literature

M **UMLAUF SCULPTURE GARDEN & MUSEUM,** 605 Robert E Lee Rd, Austin, TX 78704-1453. Tel 512-445-5582; Fax 512-445-5583; Elec Mail info@umlaufsculpture.org; Internet Home Page Address: www.umlaufsculpture.org; *Dir Opers* Joelle Geisler; *Dir Educ* Sheila Fox; *Exec Dir* Nelie Plourde
Open Wed - Fri 10 AM - 4:30 PM, Sat & Sun 1 - 4:30 PM; Admis general $3.50, seniors $2.50, student $1; Estab 1991 to provide educational programs & experiences that encourage the appreciation of sculpture; Average Annual Attendance: 27,000; Mem: Friends of the UMLAUF Sculpture Garden
Income: Financed by endowment, garden rentals for weddings, receptions & parties, fundraiser The Garden Party
Library Holdings: Auction Catalogs; Audio Tapes; Book Volumes; Clipping Files; DVDs; Exhibition Catalogs; Filmstrips; Kodachrome Transparencies; Manuscripts; Memorabilia; Motion Pictures; Original Art Works; Original Documents; Photographs; Prints; Sculpture
Special Subjects: Drawings, Painting-American, Sculpture, Watercolors, Bronzes, Religious Art, Ceramics, Woodcarvings
Collections: Charles Umlauf Collection: sculptures & drawings; original drawings & paintings; sculptures in exotic woods, terra cotta, cast stone, bronze, alabaster & marble in detailed realism & abstractions
Publications: Garden Grapevine, Newsletter biannual
Activities: Docent training; sculpture tours & workshops for students; lects open to pub, 6-8 vis lectrs per yr; gallery talks; original objects of art lent to other mus that fit borrowing criteria; mus shop sells books, postcards, notecards, mugs & t-shirts

L **UNIVERSITY OF TEXAS AT AUSTIN,** Fine Arts Library, Doty Fine Arts Bldg 3-200, 23rd & Trinity Austin, TX 78713-8916; PO Box P, Austin, TX 78713-8916. Tel 512-495-4480, 495-4481; Fax 512-495-4490; Elec Mail lschwartz@austin.utexas.edu; Internet Home Page Address: www.lib.utexas.edu/fal; *Head Librn* Laura Schwartz; *Music Librn* David Hunter; *Theatre & Dance Librn* Beth Kerr; *Media Coordr, Audio Visual* Gary Lay; *Media Coordr, Images* Sydney Kilgore
Open Mon - Thurs 8 AM - 10 PM; Fri 8 AM - 5 PM; Sat noon - 5 PM; Sun noon - 5 PM; Estab 1948 to support teaching & research in Fine Arts fields including PhD level in art history & to the master's level in art educ & studio art; Circ 180,000; For lending; Average Annual Attendance: 160,000
Income: Financed by state appropriation
Library Holdings: Auction Catalogs; Audio Tapes; Book Volumes 300,000; CD-ROMs; Cassettes; Compact Disks; DVDs 15,000; Exhibition Catalogs; Fiche 24,000; Other Holdings 17,000; Periodical Subscriptions 400; Records 100,000; Reels 4500; Slides 550,000; Video Tapes 16,000
Special Subjects: Art History, Theatre Arts, Art Education, Textiles

M **Blanton Museum of Art,** 1 University Station D1303, Austin, TX 78712. Tel 512-471-7324; Fax 512-471-7023; Elec Mail info@blantonmuseum.org; Internet Home Page Address: www.blantonmuseum.org; *Dir* Ned Rifkin; *Sr Cur* Jonathan Bober; *Dep Dir Arts & Progs* Annette DiMeo Carlozzi; *Dep Dir External Affairs* Simone Wicha
Open Tues - Fri 10 AM - 5 PM, third Thurs 10 AM - 9 PM, Sat 11 AM - 5 PM, Sun 1 PM - 5 PM, cl Mon; Admis Adults $7, seniors (65 & over) $5, college students & youth (13-21) $3, current faculty, students, staff & children under 12 free; Estab 1963 to serve the students & faculty of the university & the general pub; 57 Renamed the Jack S Blanton Museum of Art in 98; Average Annual Attendance: 240,000; Mem: 7253; dues $45 & up
Special Subjects: Portraits, Painting-European, Drawings, Hispanic Art, Latin American Art, Mexican Art, Painting-American, Prints, Sculpture, Watercolors,

American Western Art, Southwestern Art, Textiles, Religious Art, Woodcarvings, Woodcuts, Etchings & Engravings, Afro-American Art, Baroque Art, Renaissance Art, Antiquities-Greek, Reproductions
Collections: Suida-Manning Collection; 19th & 20th Century American paintings, including Mari & James A Michener Collection of 20th Century American Art & the C R Smith Collection of Art of the American West; Leo Steinberg Collection
Exhibitions: Masterpieces of European Painting - Permanent Installation
Publications: Exhibition catalogues
Activities: Classes for adults & children; docent training; lects open to public, 5-15 vis lectrs per yr; concerts; gallery talks; tours; school tours K - 12; symposia; vis artists; film & video series; exten dept serves Texas & the region; individual paintings & original objects of art lent to educational exhibiting organizations (universities & college museums); originate traveling exhibs to other university art museums & city museums; mus shop sells books, magazines, original art, reproductions & prints

L **Harry Ransom Humanities Research Center,** 21st & Guadalupe, Austin, TX 78713-7219; PO Box 7219, Austin, TX 78713-7219. Tel 512-471-8944; Fax 512-471-9646; Elec Mail info@hrc.utexas.edu; Internet Home Page Address: www.hrc.utxas.edu; *Dir* Thomas F Staley PhD; *Registrar* Sonja Reid, MSIS; *Assoc Dir* Richard W Oram, PhD; *Assoc Dir* James Stroud; *Assoc Dir* Cathy Henderson, MLS; *Assoc Dir* Margie Rine
Gallery open Tues, Wed & Fri 10 AM - 5 PM, Thurs 10 AM - 7 PM, Sat - Sun 12 PM - 5 PM; No admis fee; Library estab 1957; Circ Non-circulating; Feature rotating exhibitions drawn from the Center's collection; Average Annual Attendance: 75,000; Mem: 900; dues $50 - $1,000
Income: Financed by endowment, mem & state appropriation
Library Holdings: Book Volumes 1,000,000; Manuscripts; Maps; Memorabilia; Original Art Works; Original Documents; Other Holdings; Photographs; Prints; Sculpture
Special Subjects: Film, Drawings, Manuscripts, Latin American Art, Industrial Design, Costume Design & Constr, Bookplates & Bindings
Collections: manuscripts, rare books, photography, film, performing arts
Activities: Research library docent training; lects open to public, 8 vis lectrs per yr; gallery talks; tours; fels offered; individual paintings & original objects of art lent

L **Architecture & Planning Library,** Battle Hall 200, Austin, TX 78713-8916; PO Box P, Austin, TX 78713-8916. Tel 512-495-4620; Elec Mail apl@lib.utexas.edu; Internet Home Page Address: www.lib.utexas.edu/apl; *Head Librn & Cur Alexander Architectural Archive* Beth Dodd; *Archit & Planning Librn* Martha Gonzalez Palacios
Open fall & spring semesters Mon-Thurs 9 AM - 10 PM, Fri 9 AM - 7 PM, Sat Noon - 6 PM, Sun 1 PM - 10 PM, reduced hours during summer sessions & intersessions; Estab 1925; Circ 172,700; Average Annual Attendance: 97,500
Library Holdings: Auction Catalogs; Audio Tapes 31; Book Volumes 96,000; CD-ROMs 33; Cards; Cassettes; Clipping Files; Exhibition Catalogs; Fiche 25,042; Filmstrips 1; Kodachrome Transparencies; Lantern Slides; Manuscripts 1,600 linear ft; Maps 160; Memorabilia; Motion Pictures 1; Original Art Works; Original Documents; Other Holdings; Pamphlets; Periodical Subscriptions 240; Photographs; Prints; Reels 499; Reproductions; Sculpture; Slides 155,311; Video Tapes
Special Subjects: Constructions, Landscape Architecture, Decorative Arts, Historical Material, Interior Design, Furniture, Drafting, Period Rooms, Stained Glass, Carpets & Rugs, Restoration & Conservation, Tapestries, Architecture
Collections: Alexander Architectural Archive
Exhibitions: Blake's Choice web exhibit (ongoing); Texas Architecture: A Visual History from the Marian Davis & Doug Blakeley Alexander Collections; Spanish Colonial Architecture in the Alexander Architectural Archive; The Architectural Legacy of Herbert Miller Greene
Activities: Classes for adults & children; tours; lending of original objects of art for exhibs

A **WOMEN & THEIR WORK,** 1710 Lavaca, Austin, TX 78701-1316. Tel 512-477-1064; Fax 512-477-1090; Elec Mail info@womenandtheirwork.org; Internet Home Page Address: www.womenandtheirwork.org; *Exec Dir* Chris Cowden; *Prog Dir* Rachel Koper
Open Mon - Fri 10 AM - 6 PM, Sat 12 - 5 PM; No admis fee, donations appreciated; Estab 1978 to promote recognition & appreciation of women's art; 2000 sq ft of exhib space & a gallery gift shop; Average Annual Attendance: 25,000; Mem: 1000; dues $50
Income: $500,000 (financed by endowment, mem, city & state appropriation, private foundations, corporations & gallery gift shop)
Exhibitions: Visual Arts Exhibs - Juried and curated exhibs of Tex artists & touring exhibs from outside the region; Gallery Artist Sers - Solo exhibs showcasing emerging & mid-career visual artists selected from an ann selection panel; Artist Commissions & Fees - Direct financial support for visual & performing artists through honoraria & grants; Dance, Music & Theater Performances - A member of the National Performance Network, Women & Their Work produces events featuring local, regional, and national performing artists, often in collaborative venues
Publications: Artists Brochures every 7 wks
Activities: Classes for adults & children; docent training; workshops & symposia for teachers; lects open to pub, 4 vis lectrs per yr; gallery talks; tours; originate traveling exhibs all over Texas & other sites outside the state; mus shop sells books, original art, reproductions, prints, craft items, jewelry

BANDERA

M **FRONTIER TIMES MUSEUM,** 510 13th St, Bandera, TX 78003; PO Box 1918, Bandera, TX 78003-1918. Tel 830-796-3864; Elec Mail information@frontiertimesmuseum.org; Internet Home Page Address: www.frontier-timesmuseum.org; *Exec Dir* Rebecca Huffstutler Norton; *Pres* George T Sharman; *Secy* Claire Jo Anderson; *Treas* Theresa Helbert; *Receptionist* Rose Greenwalt; *Receptionist* Darla Hinton; *Admin Asst* Cerise Ripps
Open Mon - Sat 10 AM - 4:30 PM; Admis adults $5, seniors $3, children under 12 years $2; Estab 1933 to preserve records, photographs & artifacts of the American West with emphasis on the local Texas hill country area; Doane Gallery - Western & Tex regional art; Average Annual Attendance: 12,000; Mem: 25; Board of Dir meets 11 times a yr
Income: $20,000 (financed by endowment, $10,000 from F B Doane Foundation)
Special Subjects: Anthropology, Decorative Arts, Drawings, Etchings & Engravings, Historical Material, Flasks & Bottles, Furniture, Photography, Portraits, Pottery, Prints, Textiles, American Western Art, Folk Art, Dolls, Coins & Medals
Collections: F B Doane Collection of Western Paintings; Louisa Gordon Collection of Antiques, including bells from around the world; J Marvin Hunter Collection of Photographs, Artifacts, Memorabilia of American West and the Texas Hill Country; Photograph Collection; Western Hat Collection
Activities: Free admis to educational groups; living history - Cowboys on Main St; lects open to pub, 6 vis lectrs per yr; tours; Texas Heroes Hall of Honor; mus shop sells books, magazines, reproductions & prints, jewelry, decorative arts

BEAUMONT

M **ART MUSEUM OF SOUTHEAST TEXAS,** 500 Main St, Beaumont, TX 77701; PO Box 3703, Beaumont, TX 77704-3703. Tel 409-832-3432; Fax 409-832-8508; Elec Mail info@amset.org; Internet Home Page Address: www.amset.org; *Registrar* Tim Robtoy; *Cur Educ* Sandra Laurette; *Events Coordr* Christle Fengin; *Pub Rels* Menique Sennett; *Exec Dir* Lynn Castle; *Cur Art* Caitlin Williams
Open Mon - Fri 9 AM - 5 PM, Sat 10 AM - 5 PM, Sun Noon - 5 PM, cl major holidays; No admis fee; Estab 1950 as a non-profit institution to serve the community-through the visual experience & its interpretation as an instrument for educ, cultural enrichment & aesthetic enjoyment; The mus has 2400 sq ft of exhibition space, four galleries; Average Annual Attendance: 65,000; Mem: 850; dues individual $30; annual meeting in Sept
Income: Financed by endowment, mem, city appropriation, fund raisers, grants, mus shop & contributions
Purchases: Regional contemporary art
Library Holdings: Auction Catalogs; Audio Tapes; Book Volumes; Exhibition Catalogs; Periodical Subscriptions; Slides; Video Tapes
Special Subjects: Decorative Arts, Drawings, Etchings & Engravings, Folk Art, Landscapes, Photography, Painting-American, Prints, Sculpture, Graphics, Painting-American, Photography, Sculpture
Collections: 19th & 20th century American folk art, painting, sculpture, graphics & photography; James Whistler etchings & engravings
Publications: Qtr newsletter; see website for listing of other publications www.amset.org
Activities: Educ prog; classes for adults & children; docent training; lects open to pub, 9 vis lectrs per yr; Power Point lect; gallery talks; tours; sponsors competitions with awards; scholarships offered; individual paintings & original objects of art lent to other institutions; originates traveling exhibs; mus shop sells books, original art & reproductions

A **THE ART STUDIO INC,** 720 Franklin, Beaumont, TX 77701. Tel 409-838-5393; Fax 409-838-4695; Elec Mail artstudio@artstudio.org; Internet Home Page Address: www.artstudio.org; *Dir* Greg Busceme; *Admin Asst* Elizabeth French
Open Tues - Sat 2 PM - 5 PM; No admis fee; Estab 1983 to provide workspace for area artist/community outreach; One gallery 60 x 30 for exhibitions; one sales gallery; 2-D & 3-D work specializing in ceramics; Average Annual Attendance: 8,000; Mem: 1700; dues minimum $35
Income: $70,000 (financed by mem, individual contributions & private foundations)
Library Holdings: Book Volumes; Exhibition Catalogs; Manuscripts; Memorabilia; Original Art Works; Original Documents; Periodical Subscriptions
Special Subjects: Architecture, Drawings, Etchings & Engravings, Historical Material, Metalwork, Photography, Porcelain, Sculpture, Watercolors, Pottery, Stained Glass, American Western Art, Asian Art, Bronzes, Decorative Arts, Folk Art, Woodcuts, Afro-American Art, American Indian Art, Ceramics, Collages, Crafts, Pre-Columbian Art, Furniture, Glass, Jewelry, Enamels, Calligraphy, Primitive art
Collections: Permanent ceramic collection of local & international artists' work
Exhibitions: 9 per yr, Feb - June & Sept - Dec, opening first Sat evening featuring local artists
Publications: Issue
Activities: Classes for adults & children; juvenile & adult probation progs; dramatic progs; lects open to pub; concerts; gallery talks; tours; exten dept serves Juvenile Probation Dept, low income, fixed income

M **BEAUMONT ART LEAGUE,** 2675 Gulf St, Beaumont, TX 77703-4417. Tel 409-833-4179; Elec Mail bal-dana@gtbizclass.com; Internet Home Page Address: www.beaumontartleague.org; *Pres* Sue Bard; *Dir* Dana Dorman
Open Tues - Fri 10 AM - 4 PM, Sat 10 AM - 2 PM by appointment, cl New Year's Day, Independence Day, Thanksgiving & Christmas; No admis fee, donations accepted; Estab 1943 to promote fine art through exhibitions & art educ; Two spacious galleries with color corrected lighting & spot lights; Average Annual Attendance: 1,000; Mem: 325; dues student $20, individual $35, family $45, friend $50, patron $100, benefactor $500, lifetime $1,000; annual meeting in May
Income: $26,000 (financed by mem, donations & fundraising), grants
Purchases: Five paintings through purchase awards from juried competition
Library Holdings: Book Volumes 500; Video Tapes 20
Special Subjects: Painting-American, Sculpture, Woodcarvings, Collages
Collections: Permanent collection of paintings, photography & sculpture (93 pieces)
Exhibitions: Portrait Show; 3-D Show; Neches River Festival Exhibition; Gulf Coast Educators; Photography; Beaumont National Juried Exhibition, Membership Show; Tri-State Plus
Publications: Newsletters, 12 per year; class schedules, 4 per year; show entry forms & invitations
Activities: Classes for adults; lects open to pub, 1-2 vis lectrs per yr; gallery talks; competitions with awards; BAL National Purchase Award; Frank Gerritts Purchase Award; lending collection contains books; mus shop sells original art

M LAMAR UNIVERSITY, (Dishman Art Museum) Dishman Art Museum, 1030 E Lavaca, Beaumont, TX 77705; PO Box 10027, Beaumont, TX 77710-0027. Tel 409-880-8959; Fax 409-880-1799; Internet Home Page Address: www.lamar.edu/dishman; *Dir* Dr Megan K Young
Open Mon - Fri 8 AM - 5 PM, cl New Year's Day, Good Friday, Memorial Day, Labor Day, Thanksgiving & Christmas Day; No admis fee; Estab 1983; 6,000 sq ft exhibition space; Average Annual Attendance: 4,000
Library Holdings: Book Volumes 500
Special Subjects: Decorative Arts, Ceramics, Painting-American, Prints, Tapestries, Watercolors, African Art, Primitive art, Woodcarvings, Woodcuts, Carpets & Rugs
Collections: African & New Guinea masks & shields; 19th century painting; 19th-century porcelain; contemporary painting, prints & ceramics; Eisenstadt Collection; Robert Willis Print Collection
Activities: Lects open to pub; gallery talks; tours; schols

M MAMIE MCFADDIN WARD HERITAGE HISTORIC FOUNDATION INC, 725 Third St, Beaumont, TX 77701; 1906 McFaddin Ave, Beaumont, TX 77701. Tel 409-832-1906; Fax 409-832-3483; Elec Mail info@mcfaddin-ward.org; Internet Home Page Address: www.mcfaddin-ward.org; *Cur Coll* Sherri Birdsong; *Buildings & Grounds Supv* Felix McFarland; *Dir* Matthew White; *Admin/Deputy Dir* William Stark Jr; *Educ Coordr* Janis Becker; *Mgr Visitor Center* Becky Fertitta
Open Tues - Sat 10 AM - 4 PM, Sun 1 - 4 PM, cl Mon; Admis adults $3, seniors $1.50, children under 8 not admitted; Estab 1982 to preserve, publish, exhibit & present knowledge of the period; Historic house mus with original collections of decorative arts of the period 1890-1950 as left by original owners; 17 rooms, 12,800 sq ft wood frame Beaux Arts Colonial Home with carriage house; Average Annual Attendance: 10,000
Income: $950,000 (financed by endowment)
Special Subjects: Decorative Arts, Period Rooms
Collections: American-made furniture; Continental European ceramics; Oriental rugs; period glass; period silver & porcelain
Publications: Brochure; souvenir booklet; Viewpoints, quarterly
Activities: Classes for children; docent training; family open house; lects open to pub, 4-6 vis lectrs per yr; mus shop sells books, magazines, prints & slides
L McFaddin-Ward House, 1906 McFaddin Ave, Beaumont, TX 77701. Tel 409-832-1906; Fax 409-832-3483; Elec Mail info@mcfaddin-ward.org; *Dir* Matthew White
Open Tues - Sat 10 AM - 4 PM, Sun 1 - 4 PM; Admis adults $3; Estab 1982 for staff & docent study; For reference only; Average Annual Attendance: 10,000
Income: Foundation funded
Library Holdings: Audio Tapes; Book Volumes 700; Clipping Files; Memorabilia; Pamphlets; Periodical Subscriptions 100; Photographs; Slides; Video Tapes
Collections: Decorative arts
Activities: Classes for adults & children; docent training; lects open to pub, 3 vis lectrs per yr; mus shop sells books, magazines, slides

BROWNSVILLE

M BROWNSVILLE ART LEAGUE, Brownsville Museum of Fine Art, 660 E Ringgold St, Brownsville, TX 78520-7974. Tel 956-542-0941; Fax 956-542-6931; Elec Mail marcela@brownsvillemfa.org; Internet Home Page Address: www.brownsvillemfa.org; *Dir* Tina Garbo Bailey; *Pres* Bertha Garza; *Admin Dir* Tencha Sloss; *Bookkeeper* Dee Ramirez; *Mktg* Adriana Contreras; *Rentals* Dora Duarte
Open Tues, Thurs - Sat 10 AM - 4 PM, Wed 10 AM - 8 PM, cl New Years, Easter, Labor Day, Thanksgiving & Christmas; Admis adults $5, seniors, students with ID & children $3, children under 6 no charge; Estab 1935, mus opened 1957 to offer cultural advantages to lower Rio Grande Valley; Permanent collection on rotating basis housed in the Brownsville Mus of Fine Art; Average Annual Attendance: 10,000; Mem: 300; dues $60; $65; $120; family $150; meetings 2d Tues of each month
Income: Financed by donations, fundraisers, mem dues
Library Holdings: Audio Tapes; Book Volumes; CD-ROMs; Cards; Clipping Files; Lantern Slides; Original Art Works; Records; Slides
Collections: Paintings by Marc Chagall, H A DeYoung, M Enagnit, William Hogarth, Augustus John, Dale Nichols, Jose Salazar, Ben Stahl, Fredric Taubes, Hauward Veal, James McNeil Whistler, N C Wyeth, Milford Zornes
Exhibitions: International Art Show
Publications: Brush Strokes, six per year
Activities: Classes for adults & children; workshops by vis artists; docent training; music classes; painting classes; lects open to pub; 4 vis lectrs per yr; concerts; gallery talks; tours; sponsoring of competitions; schols; awards: $5,000 Int Art Show, $400 Student Art Show; individual paintings lent to schools; originate traveling exhibs; mus shop sells books, original art, reproductions, prints, jewelry, pillows, notecards & other items

CANYON

M PANHANDLE-PLAINS HISTORICAL MUSEUM, 2503 4th Ave, WTAMU Box 60967, Canyon, TX 79015. Tel 806-651-2244; Fax 806-651-2250; Elec Mail museum@pphm.wtamu.edu; Internet Home Page Address: www.panhandleplains.org; *Dir* Guy C Vanderpool; *Art Cur* Michael R Grauer; *Mktg Mgr* Stephanie Price
Open June - Aug, Mon - Sat 9 AM - 6 PM, Sun 1 PM - 6 PM; Sept - May, Mon - Sat 9 AM - 5 PM, Sun 1 PM - 6 PM; cl New Years Day, Thanksgiving, Christmas Eve & Day; Admis adults $10, seniors $9, children 4-12 $5, under 4 yrs free; Estab 1933 to preserve history of the region, including all phases of history, fine arts & natural sciences; Five galleries for American, European, Texas & Frank Reaugh art & changing exhibitions; 22 galleries for art, archaeology, petroleum, textiles, western heritage, paleontology & transportation; Average Annual Attendance: 75,000; Mem: 1000; dues Goodnight Circle $1000, patron $500, supporter $250, contributor $100, family $75, friend $50

Income: $1,800,000 (financed by state, endowment & membership)
Library Holdings: Audio Tapes; Book Volumes; Cards; Clipping Files; DVDs; Fiche; Filmstrips; Manuscripts; Maps; Memorabilia; Original Documents; Periodical Subscriptions; Photographs; Prints; Records; Slides
Special Subjects: Afro-American Art, Drawings, Etchings & Engravings, Folk Art, Historical Material, Landscapes, Marine Painting, Glass, Metalwork, Flasks & Bottles, Gold, Pottery, Pre-Columbian Art, Painting-American, Textiles, Woodcuts, Manuscripts, Painting-British, Painting-European, Tapestries, Architecture, Graphics, Hispanic Art, Latin American Art, Mexican Art, Photography, Prints, Sculpture, Watercolors, American Indian Art, American Western Art, Bronzes, Anthropology, Archaeology, Ethnology, Southwestern Art, Costumes, Religious Art, Ceramics, Crafts, Primitive art, Woodcarvings, Decorative Arts, Painting-Japanese, Portraits, Posters, Eskimo Art, Dolls, Furniture, Jade, Jewelry, Porcelain, Oriental Art, Asian Art, Silver, Painting-Dutch, Painting-French, Carpets & Rugs, Ivory, Maps, Coins & Medals, Restorations, Baroque Art, Calligraphy, Miniatures, Painting-Flemish, Painting-Polish, Renaissance Art, Dioramas, Period Rooms, Embroidery, Medieval Art, Painting-Spanish, Painting-Italian, Islamic Art, Antiquities-Egyptian, Antiquities-Roman, Mosaics, Cartoons, Stained Glass, Painting-German, Pewter, Leather, Military Art, Reproductions, Painting-Russian, Enamels, Painting-Scandinavian, Bookplates & Bindings
Collections: Over 1300 paintings by 19th & early 20th century American Painters; 16th-19th century European painters
Exhibitions: Exhibitions rotate & change
Publications: Panhandle-Plains Historical Review, annually
Activities: Events for adults & children; docent training; outreach progs for pub schools; podcasts; lects open to pub; 5-6 vis lectrs per yr; gallery talks, tours; Pioneer Spirit Award; originate traveling exhibs to mus with Texas & Southwestern art interest; mus shop sells books, mag, & gifts; Panhandle-Plains Western Art Show & Sale, Summer Institute
L Research Center, 2401 Fourth Ave, Canyon, TX 79015. Tel 806-651-2261; Fax 806-651-2250; *Archivist & Librn* Betty Bustos
Open June - Aug Mon - Sat 9 AM - 6 PM; Sept - May Tues - Sat 9 AM - 5 PM; For reference only
Library Holdings: Audio Tapes; Book Volumes 2000; Cards; Cassettes; Clipping Files; Exhibition Catalogs; Fiche; Framed Reproductions; Kodachrome Transparencies; Lantern Slides; Manuscripts; Memorabilia; Micro Print; Motion Pictures; Pamphlets; Periodical Subscriptions 40; Photographs; Records; Reels; Reproductions; Slides; Video Tapes
Special Subjects: Art History, Decorative Arts, Commercial Art, Ceramics, Crafts, Archaeology, American Western Art, Cartoons, Art Education, American Indian Art, Anthropology, Antiquities-Oriental, Carpets & Rugs, Antiquities-Egyptian, Architecture

COLLEGE STATION

M TEXAS A&M UNIVERSITY, J Wayne Stark University Center Galleries, 4229 Tamu, College Station, TX 77843-0001. Tel 979-845-6081; Fax 979-862-3381; Elec Mail uart@stark.tamu.edu; Internet Home Page Address: stark.tamu.edu; *Dir* Catherine A Hastedt; *Admin Secy* Beverly Wagner
Open Tues - Fri 9 AM - 8 PM, Sat - Sun Noon - 6 PM; No admis fee; Estab 1974 to bring art exhibits of state & national significance to Texas A & M University; Average Annual Attendance: 45,000
Income: Financed by university funds
Special Subjects: Art Education, Art History, Painting-American
Collections: Paintings by Texas artists
Activities: Classes for adults & children; docent training; lects open to pub; gallery talks; tours; book traveling exhibs; organize traveling exhibs; mus shop sells books & prints
A MSC Visual Arts Committee, 1237 TAMU, Memorial Student Ctr College Station, TX 77843-1237. Tel 979-845-9252; Fax 979-845-5117; Elec Mail kelli@msc.tamu.edu; Internet Home Page Address: www.vac.tamu.edu; Open daily 9 AM - 8 PM, Sat & Sun Noon to 6 PM; No admis fee; Estab 1989; Gallery is 16 x 60 ft with lighting; windows to interior hallway for partial viewing after hours; Average Annual Attendance: 8,000; Mem: 30
Income: Financed by student service fees allotment, donations & art sales
Exhibitions: Annual Juried Student Competition
Publications: Exhibition brochures
Activities: Lects open to pub, 1 vis lectrs per yr; gallery talks; tours; sponsor competitions; book traveling exhibs 7-8 per yr

COLORADO CITY

M HEART OF WEST TEXAS MUSEUM, 340 E 3rd St, Colorado City, TX 79512-6408. Tel 325-728-8285; Fax 325-728-8944; Elec Mail museum@cityofcoloradocity.org; Internet Home Page Address: www.coloradocitytexas.org; *Pres* Gay Houston; *Dir* Patty Pharis
Open Tues - Fri noon - 5 PM, cl Sat, Sun & Mon; No admis fee
Income: Financed by city appropriation
Library Holdings: Clipping Files; Maps; Memorabilia; Original Documents; Photographs; Prints; Records; Slides
Special Subjects: Historical Material, Glass, Furniture, Anthropology, Archaeology, Dolls, Period Rooms
Exhibitions: Mammoth exhibit (found nearby); Antiquus Bison exhibit (found nearby)

COMMERCE

M TEXAS A&M UNIVERSITY - COMMERCE, University Gallery, PO Box 3011, Commerce, TX 75429-3011. Tel 903-886-5208; Fax 903-886-5987; Elec Mail barbara_frey@tamu-commerce.edu; *Dir* Barbara Frey
Open Mon - Fri 1 PM - 5 PM; No admis fee; Estab 1979 to provide exhibitions of interest to the University & local community; Gallery 37 x 30 ft; running ft 206, sq ft 1460; track lighting; floor electrical outlets, climate control, security system; Average Annual Attendance: 3,000
Income: Financed by state appropriation

Collections: Collection of Student Work
Exhibitions: New American Talent 23rd Exhibition; Michael Peven: Good Dog/Bon Chien; Ann Holiday Art Sale; MFA Thesis Exhibition; A&M Corpus Christi Art Faculty Exhibition; Piero Fenci & Elizabeth Alcamatsu; Graduating Senior show
Activities: Lect open to public; 4 vis lectrs per yr; gallery talks; tours; ann juried student art exhib award; assistantships offered; individual paintings & original objects of art lent to regional citizens & University facilities; originate book traveling exhib

CORPUS CHRISTI

M ART COMMUNITY CENTER, Art Center of Corpus Christi, 100 Shoreline, Corpus Christi, TX 78401. Tel 361-884-6406; Fax 361-884-8836; Elec Mail info@artcentercc.org; Internet Home Page Address: artcentercc.org; *Dir* Bob Baker; *Admin Asst* Malissa Kay Baker; *Rental Coordr* Sarah Norris
Open Tues - Sun 10 AM - 4 PM; No admis fee; Estab 1972 to promote & support local artists; 5 galleries, all media; Average Annual Attendance: 7,500; Mem: 700; dues $30-$50
Special Subjects: Drawings, Etchings & Engravings, Landscapes, Marine Painting, Ceramics, Glass, Mexican Art, Porcelain, Portraits, Pottery, Painting-American, Sculpture, Graphics, Hispanic Art, Latin American Art, Photography, Watercolors, Metalwork, Juvenile Art, Mosaics, Stained Glass
Exhibitions: Monthly exhibits by member groups; Annual Dimension Show
Publications: Artbeat, bimonthly newsletter
Activities: Classes for adults & children; gallery talks; tours; lect open to public; Dimension, all-mem awards; sales gift shop sells books, original art, prints, clay & jewelry

M BILLIE TRIMBLE CHANDLER ARTS FOUNDATION, Texas State Museum of Asian Cultures, 1809 N Chaparral St, Corpus Christi, TX 78401-1111. Tel 361-882-2641; Fax 361-882-5718; Elec Mail asiancm@yahoo.com; Internet Home Page Address: www.geocities.com/asiancm; *Mng Dir* Joye LaBarrett; *Admin Asst* Nozomi Lundberg
Open Tues - Sat 10 AM - 4 PM, cl New Years, Easter, Memorial Day, July 4, Labor Day, Thanksgiving & Christmas; Admis adults $6, students, seniors & military $4, children (3-12) $3, children under 3 yrs no admis fee; Estab 1973; Exhibits artifacts from Asian countries. Asian gift shop on site, gallery rental space for exhibits & events
Income: Financed by private donations, grants & memberships
Library Holdings: Framed Reproductions; Original Art Works; Periodical Subscriptions; Photographs; Reproductions; Slides; Video Tapes
Special Subjects: Ceramics, Woodcuts, Watercolors, Bronzes, Costumes, Pottery, Woodcarvings, Painting-Japanese, Dolls, Jade, Jewelry, Oriental Art, Asian Art, Ivory, Calligraphy, Dioramas, Embroidery, Antiquities-Oriental
Collections: Buddhist decorative arts; Asian & decorative arts including Hakata dolls, porcelains, metal ware, cloisonne & lacquerware; oriental fan coll; jade & ivory
Activities: Educ dept; classes for adults & children; docent training; special events monthly, Asia After Five each first Fri of month; lects open to pub; gallery talks; tours; sponsoring of competitions; sales shop sells general gift items Asian influenced, books, magazines, original art, reproductions, prints, toys & games

M DEL MAR COLLEGE, Joseph A Cain Memorial Art Gallery, 101 Baldwin, Corpus Christi, TX 78404-3897. Tel 361-698-1216; Fax 361-698-1511; Elec Mail krosier@delmar.edu; Internet Home Page Address: www.delmar.edu; *Chair Art & Drama Dept* Ken Rosier; *Gallery Dir* Randy Flowers
Open Mon - Thurs 9 AM - 4 PM, Fri 9 AM - Noon; No admis fee; Estab 1932 to teach art & provide exhib showcase for col & community; Gallery consists of 1750 sq ft plus other smaller areas; Average Annual Attendance: 3,300
Income: Financed by state appropriation & private donations
Special Subjects: Drawings, Sculpture
Collections: Purchases from Annual National Drawings and Small Sculpture Show
Exhibitions: Annual Juried Exhibition open to any U.S. artist
Publications: Exhibition mailer & catalog

M SOUTH TEXAS INSTITUTE FOR THE ARTS, Art Museum of South Texas, 1902 N Shoreline Blvd, Corpus Christi, TX 78401-1138. Tel 361-825-3500; Fax 361-825-3520; Elec Mail artmuseum@tamucc.edu; Internet Home Page Address: www.artmuseumofsouthtexas.org; *Assoc Dir* Sara Morgan; *Cur* Deborah Fullerton; *Dir* Joe Schenk; *Cur Educ* Linda Rodriguez; *Mktg Dir* Cynthia Anderson
Open Tues - Sat 10 AM - 5 PM; Sun 1 PM - 5 PM, Thurs 10 AM - 9 PM, cl Mon, New Year's, Christmas, Thanksgiving; Admis fee adults $8, seniors, students and military $6, 12 & under free; Estab 1960 as a nonprofit organization to stimulate & encourage the fullest possible understanding & appreciation of the fine arts in all forms with particular interest in the region; Average Annual Attendance: 100,000; Mem: 85,000; dues $15-$5000
Income: $900,000 (financed by mem, city & state appropriations, school district)
Special Subjects: Prints
Collections: 1400 piece permanent coll
Exhibitions: Varies, call for details
Publications: Exhibition catalogs
Activities: Classes for adults & children; docent training; filmstrips; lects open to pub, 10 vis lectrs per yr; concerts; gallery talks; tours; competitions; book traveling exhibs; mus shop sells books, magazines, original art & artifacts related to exhibits
L Art Museum of South Texas, 1902 N Shoreline Blvd, Corpus Christi, TX 78401. Tel 361-825-3500; Fax 361-825-3520; Elec Mail deborah.fullerton@tamucc.edu; Internet Home Page Address: www.artmuseumofsouthtexas.org; *Cur Exhibs* Deborah Fullerton; *Dir* Joe Schenk
Open Tues - Fri 10 AM - 5 PM; Admis fee adults $8, seniors, students & military $4, 12 & under free; Estab 1965, to provide reference information for visitors to mus & docent students; For reference only; Average Annual Attendance: 75,000; Mem: 1,200
Income: $2723

Library Holdings: Audio Tapes; Book Volumes 8000; Cassettes; Clipping Files; Exhibition Catalogs; Kodachrome Transparencies; Pamphlets; Periodical Subscriptions 40; Photographs; Reproductions; Slides; Video Tapes
Special Subjects: Photography, Painting-American, Pre-Columbian Art, Prints, Sculpture, Historical Material, Watercolors, American Western Art, Southwestern Art, Woodcarvings, Woodcuts, Landscapes, Pottery

M TEXAS A&M UNIVERSITY-CORPUS CHRISTI, Weil Art Gallery, 6300 Ocean Dr, Ctr for the Arts Corpus Christi, TX 78412-5815. Tel 361-825-2314, 825-2317; Fax 361-994-6097; Elec Mail anderson@falcon.tamucc.edu; Internet Home Page Address: www2.tamurc.edu/~dvpa/artsite/gallery/default; *Dir* Mark Anderson
Open Mon - Fri, call for hours (different times for each exhibit), cl school holidays; No admis fee; Estab 1979 to provide high quality art exhibitions to the university & the pub; Average Annual Attendance: 10,000
Income: Financed by private & state funding
Collections: The Lee Goodman Collection
Exhibitions: Contemporary Texas & Mexican Artists
Publications: Exhibition catalogs
Activities: Classes for adults & children; dramatic progs; docent training; lects open to pub; gallery talks; tours; schols offered; exten dept serves regional & local communities

CORSICANA

L NAVARRO COLLEGE, Gaston T Gooch Library & Learning Resource Center, 3200 W Seventh Ave, Corsicana, TX 75110-4818. Tel 903-874-6501; Fax 903-874-4636; Elec Mail dbeau@nav.cc.tx.us; Internet Home Page Address: www.nab.cc.ts.us.org; *Dean* Darrell Beauchamp PhD
Open Mon - Thurs 8 AM - 9 PM, Fri 8 AM - 5 PM, Sun 5 - 8 PM; No admis fee; Estab 1996 to inform & educate regarding the US Civil War; Open viewing of documents in cases
Income: Financed by endowment
Purchases: $1,000,000
Special Subjects: Art History, Intermedia, Commercial Art, Historical Material, Advertising Design, American Indian Art, Drafting, Woodcarvings
Collections: Samuels Hobbitt Collection, woodcarvings; Pearce Civil War Documents Collection; Pearce Western Art Collection; Reading Indian Artifacts Collection; Roe & Ralston Library, documents
Exhibitions: Civil War Documents & Memorabilia; Native American Artifacts; Woodcarvings of Artist Ludwig Kieninger

DALLAS

M AFRICAN AMERICAN MUSEUM, 3536 Grand Ave, Dallas, TX 75315-0157; PO Box 150157, Dallas, TX 75315-0157. Tel 214-565-9026; Fax 214-421-8204; Internet Home Page Address: www.aamdallas.org; *Chief Cur* Phillip Collins; *Opers Mgr* Barry Jones; *Mgr Mktg, Commun & Events* Mark Smith; *Pres & CEO* Dr Harry Robinson Jr; *Pub Rels Coordr* Lee Taylor
Open Tues - Fri 12 PM - 5 PM, Sat 10 AM - 5 PM, Sun 1 PM - 5 PM; Admis for groups of 10 or more, adults $2, children & seniors $1; Average Annual Attendance: 201,000
Library Holdings: Book Volumes 1,500
Collections: African American fine art & folk art; Texas Black history
Publications: Quarterly newsletter
Activities: Educ prog; docent prog; lects; book traveling exhibs

M THE DALLAS CONTEMPORARY, Dallas Visual Art Center, 161 Glass St, Dallas, TX 75207-6903. Tel 214-821-2522; Fax 214-821-9103; Elec Mail info@thecontemporary.net; Internet Home Page Address: www.thecontemporary.net; *Dir & Cur* Joan Davidow; *Operations Coordr* Maureen Doane; *Prog Coordr* Leslie Connally; *Mem Coordr* Chris Elam; *Events Coordr* Taylor McDaniel; *Educ Coordr* Lydia Regalado
Open Tues - Sat, 10 AM - 5 PM, cl Sun; No admis fee; Estab 1981 to provide exhibition, educ & information opportunities for visual artists & art appreciators in North Texas; 5 galleries totaling 12,000 sq ft, natural light; track lighting; Average Annual Attendance: 15,000; Mem: 800; dues $50-$2500; mem open to artists & art appreciators
Income: Financed by donations, grants, facility use fees, mem & fundraising
Exhibitions: Theme & solo exhibitions open to the public with both private & public openings; Annual Membership Exhibition
Publications: Exhibition programs & catalogs; newsletter, monthly
Activities: Tours for adults & children; self guided tours; drawing classes; off-site progs for students; classes for adults; tours & classes for children; gallery talks; Legends, in it's 12th yr, honors the artist, professional, patron; traveling exhibs; galleries, mus in Texas & in the Southwest

A DALLAS HISTORICAL SOCIETY, Hall of State, 3939 Grand Ave, Dallas, TX 75315; PO Box 150038, Fair Park Dallas, TX 75315-0038. Tel 214-421-4500; Fax 214-421-7500; Elec Mail jack@dallashistory.org; Internet Home Page Address: www.dallashistory.org; *Exec Dir* Jack Bonning; *Dir Colls* Alan Olson
Open Tues - Sat 9 AM - 5 PM, Sun 1 - 5 PM, cl Mon; No admis fee; Estab 1922 to collect & preserve materials relative to the history of Texas & Dallas; The Hall of State is an example of Art-Deco architecture; exhibition space totals 5000 sq ft; Average Annual Attendance: 130,000; Mem: dues $50; annual meeting in Apr
Income: Financed by mem & city appropriation, private donations
Library Holdings: Auction Catalogs; Audio Tapes; Book Volumes; Cards; Cassettes; Clipping Files; Exhibition Catalogs; Fiche; Filmstrips; Framed Reproductions; Kodachrome Transparencies; Lantern Slides; Manuscripts; Maps; Memorabilia; Micro Print; Motion Pictures; Original Art Works; Original Documents; Other Holdings; Pamphlets; Periodical Subscriptions; Photographs; Prints; Records; Reels; Reproductions; Sculpture; Slides; Video Tapes
Collections: Texas/Dallas Gallery; Frank Reaugh, Bound for Texas, White House in Miniature

Publications: Dallas Historical Society Register, newsletter biannual; Dallas Rediscovered: A Photographic Chronicle of Urban Expansion; When Dallas Became a City: Letters of John Milton McCoy, 1870-1881; A Guide to Fair Park, Dallas
Activities: In-class progs; classes for adults & children; dramatic progs; docent training; summer children's workshops; lects open to pub, 2 vis lectrs per yr; gallery talks; tours; awards; book signings; historic & current affairs open forums; sponsor local Awards for Excellence; Stanley Marcus Gale for fashion design achievement; exten dept; individual & original objects of art lent to local school & Houston Museum of Fine Arts; book traveling exhibs 6 per yr; originate traveling exhibs; sales shops sells books, magazines, reproductions, prints, slides, photos

L **Research Center Library,** Hall of State, Fair Park, PO Box 150038 Dallas, TX 75315-0038. Tel 214-421-4500; Fax 214-421-7500; Internet Home Page Address: www.dallashistory.org; *Dir Colls* Alan Olson; *Archives Dir* Rachel Roberts
Open Wed - Fri 1 - 5 PM by appointment only; For reference only
Library Holdings: Book Volumes 1600; Cards; Cassettes; Clipping Files; Exhibition Catalogs; Filmstrips; Framed Reproductions; Lantern Slides; Manuscripts; Maps; Memorabilia; Motion Pictures; Original Art Works; Other Holdings Archives, pages 2,000,000; Pamphlets; Periodical Subscriptions 20; Photographs; Prints; Records; Reels; Reproductions; Sculpture; Slides; Video Tapes
Special Subjects: Manuscripts, Maps, Historical Material
Collections: R M Hayes Photographic Collection of Texas Historic Sites; J J Johnson & C E Arnold Photographs of Turn-of-the-Century Dallas; Frank Reaugh Paintings; Allie Tennant Papers; Texas Centennial Papers; WWI & WWII posters
Exhibitions: All Together; WWI Posters of the Allied Nations; Fair Park Moderne: Art & Architecture of the 1936 Texas Centennial Exposition
Publications: Exhibit catalogs
Activities: Activities for school children; docent training; city tours

M **DALLAS MUSEUM OF ART,** 1717 N Harwood St, Dallas, TX 75201-2315. Tel 214-922-1200; Fax 214-922-1350; Elec Mail gkalenik@dallasmuseumofart.org; Internet Home Page Address: www.dallasmuseumofart.org; *Cur Arts of the Americas & the Pacific* Carol Robbins; *Dir Mktg & Commun* Judy Conner; *Cir Collections Mgmt* Gabriella Truly; *Dir Human Resources* Pamela Autry; *Dir Develop* Diana Duke Duncan; *Dir* Bonnie Pitman; *Mus Shop Mgr* Janet Stieve; *Dir Exhibs & Publs* Tamara Woofon-Bonner; *Sr Cur European Art* Dr Dorothy Kosinski; *Assoc Cur Contemporary Art* Suzanne Weaver; *Sr Cur Arts of Africa, Pacific & Americas* Dr Roslyn A Walker; *Assoc Cur American Art* Dr William Keyse Rudolph; *Cur Decorative Arts & Design* Kevin W Tucker; *Cur Contemporary Art* Charles Wylie; *Dir Educ* Gail Davitt; *Dir Pub Rels* Jill Bernstein
Open Tues - Sun 11 AM - 5 PM, Thurs until 9 PM, Late Night Fridays on 3rd Fri of all months except Dec open until Midnight, cl Mon, New Year's Day, July 4, Thanksgiving & Christmas; Admis adults $10, seniors & military $7, students $5, mems free, 1st Tues of month free, special exhibition admis varies; group rates available; Estab 1903 to purchase and borrow works of art from all periods for the aesthetic enjoyment and educ of the pub; Fifteen galleries for permanent collection; 14,000 sq ft for temporary exhibition; Average Annual Attendance: 550,000; Mem: 22,000 dues $30 - $10,000; annual meeting May
Income: $8,900,000 (financed by endowment, mem & city appropriation)
Purchases: $1,000,000
Special Subjects: Architecture, Drawings, American Indian Art, American Western Art, Bronzes, African Art, Archaeology, Ceramics, Crafts, Afro-American Art, Decorative Arts, Collages, Asian Art, Antiquities-Byzantine, Carpets & Rugs, Coins & Medals, Baroque Art, Calligraphy, Antiquities-Oriental, Antiquities-Persian, Antiquities-Egyptian, Antiquities-Greek, Antiquities-Roman, Antiquities-Etruscan, Antiquities-Assyrian
Collections: European & American painting & sculpture; ancient Mediterranean & Pre-Columbian art; African, Oceanic & Japanese art; drawings; prints; American & European decorative arts; Audio-Visual Installations; Texas Regional Art
Publications: Annual report; exhibition catalogs; President's newsletter; quarterly newsletter
Activities: Classes for adults & children; workshops; Family Celebrations; weekends at the Museum; Late Nights; summer camps; school outreach; docent training; lects open to pub, 50 vis lectrs per yr; concerts; Jazz series Thursday Night Live; film series; gallery talks; tours; exten dept serving Dallas County; artmobile; individual paintings & original objects of art lent to other mus; book traveling exhibs 3-4 per yr; originate traveling exhibs; mus shop sells books, magazines, original art, prints, slides, jewelry, toys, cards & puzzles

L **Mildred R & Frederick M Mayer Library,** 1717 N Harwood St, Dallas, TX 75201-2398. Tel 214-922-1277 (Library); Tel 214-922-1367 (Archives); Elec Mail library@dallasmuseumofart.org; Elec Mail archives@dallasmuseumofart.org; Internet Home Page Address: www.dm-art.org/Research/index.htm; *Reference Librn* Mary Leonard; *Head of Library* Jackie Allen
Open Tues, Wed & Fri Noon - 4:30 PM, Thurs Noon - 6:45 PM & Sat 1 - 4:30 PM; For reference only, open to pub for research only
Income: Financed by city & private endowment
Library Holdings: Book Volumes 32,000; Exhibition Catalogs; Other Holdings Artist File; Periodical Subscriptions 105
Special Subjects: Art History, Decorative Arts, Pre-Columbian Art

L **J ERIC JOHNSON LIBRARY,** Fine Arts Division, 1515 Young St, Dallas, TX 75201-5411. Tel 214-670-1643; Fax 214-670-1646; Internet Home Page Address: www.dallaslibrary.org; *Mgr Fine Art Div* Victor Kralisz; *Music Librn* Tina Murdock; *Art Librn* Gwen Dixie; *Theater/Film Librn* Cathy Ritchie; *Asst Mgr* Julie Travis
Open Mon - Thurs 9 AM - 9 PM; Fri & Sat 9 AM - 5 PM; Sun 1 PM - 5 PM; No admis fee; Estab 1901 to furnish the citizens of Dallas with materials and information concerning the arts; 42 ft x 32 ft; Average Annual Attendance: 1,500
Income: Financed by city appropriation, federal & state aid, Friends of the Library, endowment
Library Holdings: Auction Catalogs; Audio Tapes; Book Volumes 88,000; Clipping Files 81 drawers; Compact Disks 11,500; DVDs 2,900; Exhibition Catalogs 750; Fiche; Memorabilia; Other Holdings 19,000 Music Scores; Periodical Subscriptions 375; Photographs; Prints; Records 39,000; Video Tapes 4,500
Collections: W E Hill Collection (history of American theater); Lawrence Kelly Collection of Dallas Civic Opera Set & Costume Designs; Manuscript Archives (music); Margo Jones Theater Collection; original fine print coll; John Rosenfield Collection (art and music critic); Interstate Theatre Collection; USA Film Festival Files; Local Archival Material in Film, Dance, Theatre & Music; Dallas Theater Archives; Dallas Theater Center & other local theater colls; Undermain Theater
Exhibitions: "First Timers": Students, Schools, Less Established Artists
Activities: Dramatic progs, dance progs; concerts; sales shop sells books & magazines

M **THE MCKINNEY AVENUE CONTEMPORARY (THE MAC),** 3120 McKinney Ave, Dallas, TX 75204. Tel 214-953-1212; Fax 214-953-1873; Elec Mail macmembership@the-mac.org; Internet Home Page Address: www.the-mac.org; *Dir* Lisa Hees; *Mem & Vol Coordr* Claire Roseland; *Develop Coordr* Laura Lee Brott; *Facility & Gallery Liaison* Leslie Connally
Open Wed - Sat 11 AM - 9 PM; No admis fee; Estab 1994; non-profit supporting emerging & established artists; 18,000 sq ft bldg including 2,800 sq ft visual exhib space, 900 sq ft New Works Space, black box theater & additional theater; Average Annual Attendance: 11,000; Mem: 500
Income: (financed by mem, sponsorships, donations & grants)
Exhibitions: Annual Membership Exhib
Activities: Lects open to pub; concerts; gallery talks; art talks; community events; mus shop sells books, magazines, original art & prints

M **MIRACLE AT PENTECOST FOUNDATION,** Biblical Arts Center, 7500 Park Ln, Dallas, TX 75225-2025; PO Box 12727, Dallas, TX 75225-0727. Tel 214-691-4661; Fax 214-691-4752; Internet Home Page Address: www.biblicalarts.org; *Dir* Ronnie L Roese; *Cur* Susan E Metcalf
Open Tues - Sat 10 AM - 5 PM, Thurs evenings by appointment, Sun 1 - 5 PM, cl New Years Day, Thanksgiving, Christmas Eve & Christmas Day; Admis adults $4, seniors $3.50, students 13-18 $3, children 6-12 $2.50, exhibition galleries free; Estab 1966 to provide a place where people of all faiths may have the opportunity to witness the Bible as it inspires mankind in the arts; Average Annual Attendance: 45,000
Income: Financed by private foundation
Special Subjects: Religious Art
Collections: Joseph Boggs Beale's Biblical Illustrations; founder's collection of oriental art; Torger Thompson's Miracle at Pentecost painting & Miracle at Pentecost pilot painting; Biblical art
Exhibitions: Annual Children's Juried Art Show
Publications: Books, Creation of a Masterpiece, Videotape, Pentecost: Gift from God, Christianity and the Arts Magazine
Activities: Educ progs; docent training; gallery talks; competitions; individual paintings & original objects of art lent; book traveling exhibs 8-12 per yr; originate traveling exhibs to other mus; mus shop sells books, reproductions, prints, slides

L **SOUTHERN METHODIST UNIVERSITY,** Hamon Arts Library, 6100 Hillcrest Ave, Dallas, TX 75275-0356; PO Box 750356, Dallas, TX 75275-0356. Tel 214-768-2796; Fax 214-768-1800; Elec Mail bmitchel@smu.edu; Internet Home Page Address: www.smu.edu/cul/hamon; *Dir* Alisa Rata Stutzbach; *Art Librn* Beverly Mitchell; *Head Bywaters Spec Coll* Sam Ratchlifle; *Cur* Ellen Buie Niewyk; *Cur Asst* Emily Grubbs
Open Mon - Thurs 8 AM - 12 AM, Fri 8 AM - 6 PM, Sat 9 AM - 5 PM, Sun 1 PM - 12 AM; No admis fee; Estab to support educational curriculum of art & art history department of university; Circ 42,500; Average Annual Attendance: 150,000
Library Holdings: Audio Tapes; Book Volumes 152,000; Cassettes; Compact Disks 10,000; DVDs 200; Exhibition Catalogs; Fiche; Original Art Works; Other Holdings Music scores; Pamphlets; Periodical Subscriptions 269; Reels; Video Tapes 1,100
Special Subjects: Art History, Film, Etchings & Engravings, Painting-American, Painting-British, Painting-Spanish, Painting-European, Ceramics, Costume Design & Constr, Antiquities-Byzantine, Antiquities-Egyptian, Antiquities-Etruscan, Antiquities-Greek, Antiquities-Roman, Coins & Medals, Architecture
Activities: Lects open to pub

M **Meadows Museum,** 5900 Bishop Blvd, Dallas, TX 75275-0357; PO Box 750357, Dallas, TX 75275-0357. Tel 214-768-2516; Fax 214-768-1688; Internet Home Page Address: smumeadows.edu; *Dir* Mark Roglan; *Mus Accnt* Roni Arifin; *Mem Mgr* Catherine Baetz; *Mktg Coordr* Chris Byrd; *Asst to Dir* Irene Davies; *Events Mgr* Marin Fiske; *Opers Mgr* Charlie Guijarro; *Deputy Dir* Elizabeth Hunt Blanc; *Security Supv* Brenda Laury; *Colls Mgr & Cur Exhibs* Bridget Marx; *Dir Educ* Carmen Smith; *Educ Coordr* Tamytha Smith; *Asst Cur Educ* Scott Winterrowd
Open Tues-Sat 10AM-5PM, Thurs until 8PM, Sun noon-5PM; No admis fee, donations accepted; Estab 1965 to preserve & study the art of Spain; Average Annual Attendance: 50,000
Income: 3 million; financed by endowment, gifts, tuition allocation, and museum revenue
Special Subjects: Sculpture, Religious Art, Etchings & Engravings, Landscapes, Baroque Art, Medieval Art, Painting-Spanish
Collections: Paintings: Fernando Yanez de la Almedina (active 1505-1531); Saint Sebastian (1506), Juan de Borgona (active 1508-1514); Juan Carreno de Miranda (1614-1685); The Flaying of Saint Bartholomew (1666); Bartolome Esteban Murillo (1618-1682); The Immaculate Conception (ca 1655); Jacob Laying the Peeled Rods Before the Flocks of Laban (ca 1665); Jusepe de Ribera (1591-1652); Portrait of a Knight of Santiago (ca 1630-40); Diego Rodriguez de Silva y Velazquez (1599-1660); Sibyl With Tabula Rasa (ca 1644-1648); Francisco de Goya (1746-1828); The Madhouse at Saragossa (1794); Joan Miro (1893-1983); Queen Louise of Prussia (1929); Pablo Picasso (1881-1973); Still Life in a Landscape (1915); Antoni Tapies Grand Noir (Great Black Relief) (1973); Sculpture: Alejo de Vahia (active ca 1480-1510); Pieta (1490-1510); Juan Martinez Montanes (1568-1649); Saint John the Baptist (ca 1630-1635); Anonymous (Follower of Pedro de Mena); Saint Anthony of Padua Holding the Christ Child (ca 1700); El Grecco: St Francis Kneeling in Meditation; Elizabeth Meadows Sculpture Collection; University Art Collection
Publications: Exhibition Catalogue; Submissions Members Publication
Activities: Classes for adults & children; docent training; outreach prog, university initiatives; lects open to pub; lects for mems only; vis lectrs 25 per yr; concerts;

tours; gallery talks; Moss/Chumley Award; competitions with awards, family days; internships & apprenticeships offered; individual paintings & original objects of art lent to other museums & galleries in US & Europe for scholarly exhibs, SMU continuing studies; originates traveling exhibs; mus shop sells books, reproductions, prints, catalogs, jewelry, and various items

DENTON

M TEXAS WOMAN'S UNIVERSITY ART GALLERY, PO Box 425469, Denton, TX 76204-5469. Tel 817-898-2530; Fax 817-898-2496; Elec Mail visualarts@twu.edu; Internet Home Page Address: www.twu.edu/as/va/gallery.html; *Dir* Corky Stuckenbruck; *Chair* John L Weinkein
Open Mon - Fri 9 AM - 4 PM, Sat 1 - 4 PM & Sun upon request; No admis fee; Fine Arts Building consists of two galleries, each consisting of 3000 sq ft; Average Annual Attendance: 4,000
Income: Financed by Art Department & student activities fees
Exhibitions: Departmental galleries have approx twelve exhibits per school yr
Activities: Concerts; gallery talks; tours; competitions with awards; scholarships offered

M UNIVERSITY OF NORTH TEXAS, Art Gallery, 1155 Union Circle # 305100, College of Visual Arts and Design Arts Bldg Room 17 Denton, TX 76203-5100. Tel 940-565-2000, 565-4316; Fax 940-565-4717; *Gallery Dir* Diana Block
Open Mon & Tues Noon - 8 PM, Wed - Sat Noon - 5 PM, cl Thanksgiving; No admis fee; Estab 1960 as a teaching gallery directed to students of University of North Texas, the Denton Community & Dallas/Fort Worth area; The gallery covers 193 running ft of exhibition wall space, approx 10 ft high, which may be divided into smaller spaces by the use of semi-permanent portable walls; the floor is carpeted-terrazzo; Average Annual Attendance: 10,000
Income: Financed by state appropriation
Collections: Voertman Collection (student purchases); permanent coll
Publications: Exhibition announcements
Activities: Lects open to public, 4-8 vis lectrs per yr; tours; competitions; individual paintings & original objects of art lent to the university offices; originate traveling exhibs to other universities & museums
L Visual Resources Collection, 1155 Union Circle #305100, College of Visual Arts and Design Arts Bldg Room 107 Denton, TX 76203-5100. Tel 940-565-4019; Fax 940-565-4717; Elec Mail graham@unt.edu; *Visual Resources Cur* Ann Graham, MFA; *Asst Cur* Jennifer Richmond, MA
Estab to provide art images for instruction; For reference only
Purchases: $6000
Library Holdings: DVDs 500; Lantern Slides; Other Holdings Interactive CD 50; Laserdiscs 10, Image Database; Video Tapes 700
L Libraries, 1155 Union Circle #305190, Denton, TX 76203-5017. Tel 940-565-2413, 565-3025, 565-2696; Fax 940-369-8760; Elec Mail dgrose@library.unt.edu; Internet Home Page Address: www.library.unt.edu; *Dean* Donald Grose; *Asst Dean* Sandra Atchison
Open Mon - Thurs 7:30 AM - 2 AM; Fri 7:30 AM - 12 AM; Sat 9 AM - 12 AM, Sun 1 PM - 2 AM; Estab 1903 to support the acad progs & faculty & student research
Income: Financed by state appropriation
Library Holdings: Audio Tapes; Book Volumes 50,000; Cassettes; Exhibition Catalogs; Fiche; Filmstrips; Motion Pictures; Original Art Works; Periodical Subscriptions 186; Prints; Records; Reels; Reproductions; Slides; Video Tapes
Special Subjects: Art History, Photography, Sculpture, Ceramics, Printmaking, Advertising Design, Art Education, Textiles
Collections: Art auction sales catalogs & information

EDINBURG

M HIDALGO COUNTY HISTORICAL MUSEUM, 121 E McIntyre St, Edinburg, TX 78541-3537. Tel 956-383-6911; Fax 956-381-6911; Elec Mail hchm@hiline.net; Internet Home Page Address: www.riograndeborderlands.org; *Exec Dir* Mrs Shan Rankin; *Asst Dir & Cur Exhibits* Thomas A Fort; *Cur Archives & Coll* David J Mycue; *Develop Officer* Lynne Beeching; *Educ* Rachel Brown; *Pub Rels Officer* Jim McKone; *Coll & Exhib* Robert Garcia; *Programming Officer* Mia Marisol Buentello; *Archival Asst* Esteban Lomas; *Maintenance* Nazario Reyna; *Chmn Board Trustees* Danny Gurwitz; *Admin Asst* Marisela Saenz; *Receptionist* Sandra Luna
Open Tues - Fri 9 AM - 5 PM, Sat 10 AM - 5 PM, Sun 1 - 5 PM; Admis adults $2, seniors $1.50, students $1, children $.50; Estab 1967 to preserve & present the borderland heritage of south Texas & northeastern Mexico; Maintains reference library; Average Annual Attendance: 25,000; Mem: 800; dues $25-$1000
Income: $800,000 (financed by endowment, mem, county & city appropriation, fundraising)
Special Subjects: Graphics, Hispanic Art, Latin American Art, Mexican Art, Photography, American Indian Art, American Western Art, Anthropology, Manuscripts, Portraits, Posters, Maps
Collections: Historic Artifacts of Region
Exhibitions: Regional Emphasis: Early Spanish Settlement; Mexican American War; Civil War; Ranching; Steamboat Era; Hanging Tower; Early Agriculture; Revolution on the Rio Grande
Publications: Exhibition catalogs
Activities: Classes for adults & children; dramatic progs; docent training; lects open to pub, 15-20 vis lectrs per yr; tours; mus shop sells books, gifts & toys

M UNIVERSITY OF TEXAS PAN AMERICAN, Charles & Dorothy Clark Gallery; University Gallery, Fine Arts Complex, 1201 W University Dr Edinburg, TX 78539. Tel 956-381-2655; Fax 956-384-5072; Elec Mail galleries@utpa.edu; Internet Home Page Address: www.utpa.edu/dept/art/pages/artgall.html; *Gallery Dir* Patricia Ballinger
Open Mon - Fri 9 AM-5 PM, nights and weekends for theater performances; No admis fee; To serve our growing students body & community-at-large; 2 art galleries on campus of University of Texas Pan-American; Average Annual Attendance: 10,000

Income: University funding
Special Subjects: Ceramics, Prints, Sculpture, Posters
Collections: Coll includes pieces by: Josef Albers; Salvador Dali; Honore Daumier; Francisco Goya; Rudolf Hausner; Roy Lichtenstein; Georges Rouault; permanent coll of ceramics, modern sculpture, paintings, posters, pre-Columbian artifacts, prints
Exhibitions: Temporary exhibitions by contemporary artists from around the United States & Mexico; BFA student shows; MFA shows
Activities: Lects open to pub; gallery talks; tours; sponsoring of competitions; Ann Student Art Show awards; lending of original objects of art to Univ offices and buildings

M UTPA Art Galleries, Communications Arts & Sciences Bldg, 1201 W University Dr Edinburg, TX 78539-2970. Tel 956-381-2655; Fax 956-384-5072; Elec Mail galleries@utpa.edu; Internet Home Page Address: www.utpa.edu/dept/art/pages/artgall.html; *Gallery Dir* Patricia Ballinger
Open Mon - Thurs 10 AM - Noon, Tues & Thurs 1 - 3 PM; No admis fee; Estab 1986 to serve the university student body as well as the community at large; Average Annual Attendance: over 10,000 per yr
Income: Univ funding
Special Subjects: Prints, Sculpture, Ceramics, Posters
Collections: Coll includes pieces by: Joseph Albers; Salvador Dali; Honore Daumier; Francisco Goya; Rudolf Hausner; Roy Lichtenstein; Georges Rouault; permanent coll of ceramics, modern sculpture, paintings, posters, pre-Columbian artifacts, prints
Exhibitions: Temporary exhibitions by contemporary artists from around the United States & Mexico; BFA student shows; Masters Fine Arts Exhibitions
Activities: Lects open to pub; gallery tours; student competitions

EL PASO

M CASASOLA MUSEUM, 619 Prospect St, El Paso, TX 79902; PO Box 922, Sunland Park, TX 88063-0922. Tel 505-312-0257; *Contact* Carlos Vigueras
Open daily 10 AM - 5 PM
Collections: History & culture; paintings; photographs
Activities: Educ progs

M CITY OF EL PASO, One Arts Festival Plaza, El Paso, TX 79901-1135. Tel 915-532-1707; Fax 915-532-1010; Elec Mail tomormx@elpasotexas.gov; Internet Home Page Address: www.elpasoartmuseum.org; *Dir* Michael A Tomor Ph.D.; *Cur of Coll* William R Thompson; *Registrar* Elizabeth A Schorr; *Asst Cur* Jerry Medrano; *Cur Educ* Lori Eklund; *Asst Cur Educ* Ann Camp
Open Tues - Sat 9 AM - 5 PM, Sun noon - 5 PM, cl Mon; Admis general $1, students & children $.50, free on Sun; Estab 1960 as a cultural & educational institution; Tom Lea Gallery, De Wetter Gallery, Contemporary Gallery, Samuel H. Kress Gallery; Average Annual Attendance: 80,000; Mem: 750; dues $15-$5000
Income: Financed by mem & city appropriation
Library Holdings: Auction Catalogs; Exhibition Catalogs; Pamphlets; Periodical Subscriptions
Special Subjects: Graphics, Hispanic Art, Latin American Art, Mexican Art, Painting-American, Photography, Watercolors, American Western Art, Pre-Columbian Art, Southwestern Art, Woodcuts, Afro-American Art, Painting-European, Painting-French, Baroque Art, Painting-Flemish, Renaissance Art, Painting-Spanish, Painting-Italian
Collections: Kress Collection of Renaissance & Baroque Periods; 19th & 20th century American painting; contemporary American & Mexican; Mexican Colonial paintings; works on paper, American & European; Samuel H Kress Collection
Publications: Members' newsletter, teacher newsletter
Activities: Classes for adults & children; docent training; lects open to pub, concerts; gallery talks; tours; individual paintings & original objects of art lent to other mus & institutions on request; originate traveling exhibs to accredited mus & university galleries; mus shop sells unique gifts, mus catalogs, souvenirs, books, reproductions, slides, jewelry, toys, home & office products
L El Paso Museum of Art, One Arts Festival Plaza, El Paso, TX 79901-1135. Tel 915-532-1707; Fax 915-532-1010; Internet Home Page Address: www.elpasoartmuseum.org; *Cur Coll* Amy Grimm; *Cur Coll* Christian Gerstheimer; *Registrar* Michelle Ryden; *Cur Educ* Amy Reed; *Asst Cur Coll* Ben Fyffe
Open Tues, Wed, Fri & Sat 9 AM - 5 PM, Thurs 9 AM - 9 PM, Sun Noon - 5 PM, cl Mon & city holidays; No admis fee; Estab 1947; Open to the pub & mem for reference only; Average Annual Attendance: 100,000; Mem: 900
Library Holdings: Auction Catalogs; Book Volumes 1500; Cards; Exhibition Catalogs; Kodachrome Transparencies; Periodical Subscriptions 8; Slides
Special Subjects: Art History, Photography, Painting-American, Painting-Flemish, Painting-French, Painting-German, Painting-Italian, Painting-Spanish, Prints, Painting-European, Latin American Art, American Western Art, American Indian Art, Mexican Art, Aesthetics, Afro-American Art
Collections: 19th- & 20th-century American Art; Colonial Mexican Art; Samuel H Kress Collection
Publications: James Surls: Walking with Diamonds, 99; Eugene Thurston: The Majesty of the Southwestern Landscape, 2000
Activities: Classes for adults & children; dramatic progs; docent training; lects open to pub, 25 vis lectrs per yr; concerts; gallery talks; tours; Design Awards, TX Assoc Museums; exten prog lends original objects of art to mus; book traveling exhibs; originate traveling exhibs to regional mus; mus shop sells books, slides & original art
M El Paso Museum of Archaeology, 4301 Transmountain Rd, El Paso, TX 79924. Tel 915-755-4332; Fax 915-759-6824; Elec Mail archaeologymuseum@elpasotexas.gov; Internet Home Page Address: www.elpasotexas.gov/arch_museum/; *Dir* Marc Thompson PhD; *Cur* Jason Jurgena; *Educ Cur* Lora Jackson
Open Tues - Sat 9 AM - 5 PM, Sun 12 noon - 5 PM; No admis fee; Estab 1977 as an archaeological mus to show human adaptation to a desert environment; Mus contains replica of Olla Cave, a Mogollon cliff dwelling & four other prehistoric dioramas & artifacts from the US Southwest & Mexico; Average Annual Attendance: 45,000; Mem: Student $15, individual $25, family $40
Income: Financed by city appropriation

Special Subjects: American Indian Art, Archaeology
Collections: Five dioramas depict life styles & climate changes of Paleo Indians including the hunting & gathering area & the Hueco Tanks site; Pre-Columbian (Casas Grandos) & Mogollon archaeological artifacts; Apache, Tarahumara artifact colls
Activities: Classes for children; slide lect demonstrations at schools & civic organizations; docent training; lects open to pub; tours, sponsor competitions; book traveling exhibs annually; sales shop sells books, reproductions & prints

M **INTERNATIONAL MUSEUM OF ART,** 1211 Montana Ave, El Paso, TX 79902-5511. Tel 915-543-6747; Fax 915-543-9222; Elec Mail iavatx@aol.com; Internet Home Page Address: www.internationalmuseumofart.net; *Mgr* Debbie Horn; *Admin Asst* Carolyn Casarez
Open Thurs-Sun 1PM-5PM; No admis fee; Estab 1991; Average Annual Attendance: 3,000; Mem: 250; dues $25
Collections: collections from Asia & Africa; Mexican Revolution collection including a replica of Pancho Villa's death mask & a replica of a Mexican casita
Activities: Classes for adults; art classes; mus shop sells reproductions, prints

M **UNIVERSITY OF TEXAS AT EL PASO,** Stanlee & Gerald Rubin Center for the Visual Arts, 500 W University Ave, Department of Art El Paso, TX 79902-5816. Tel 915-747-6151; Fax 915-747-6067; Elec Mail rubincenter@utep.edu; Internet Home Page Address: www.rubincenter.utep.edu; *Dir* Kate Bonansinga; *Asst Dir* Kerry Doyle; *Preparator* Daniel Szwaczkowski; *Admin Asst* Victoria Aviles
Open Tues, Wed, & Fri 10AM-5PM, Thurs 10AM-7PM, Sat Noon-5PM; No admis fee; University estab 1914, Department of Art established 1940, Rubin Center est 2004; 3 galleries: 1900, 1100, and 550 sq ft; Average Annual Attendance: 50,000
Income: Public and private gifts and grants
Special Subjects: Painting-American, Prints, Crafts
Exhibitions: Contra Flujo: Independence & Revolution; Fernando Llanos: Revolutionary Imaginary
Publications: Exhibition catalogs
Activities: Classes for adults & children; lect open to public; 10 vis lectrs per yr; 2-4 gallery talks per year; tours; competitions; gallery tours; exten work offered through university exten service to anyone over high school age; fees vary; 1 book traveling exhib per yr; Originates traveling exhibitions that circulate to other museums and galleries

FORT WORTH

M **AMON CARTER MUSEUM OF AMERICAN ART,** 3501 Camp Bowie Blvd, Fort Worth, TX 76107-2695. Tel 817-738-1933; Fax 817-989-5099; Internet Home Page Address: www.cartermuseum.org; Internet Home Page Address: www.acmaa.worldcat.org; *Dir* Ron Tyler; *Exec Asst to Dir* Trish Williamson; *CFO* Randy S Ray; *Registrar* Marci Caslin; *Cur Paintings & Sculpture* Rebecca Lawton; *Asst Cur Photographs* Jessica May; *Asst Cur Paintings & Sculpture* Shirley Reece-Hughes; *Sr Cur Photographs* John Rohrbach; *Sr Cur Western Paintings & Sculpture* Rick Stewart; *Library Dir* Samuel Duncan; *Archivist & Reference Serv Mgr* Jonathan Frembling; *Dir Publ* Will Gillham; *Dir Develop* Carol Noel; *Head Educ* Stacy Fuller; *Mus Events Mgr* Lauri Lawrence; *COO* Lori Eklund; *Pub Information* Tracy Greene
Open Tues - Sat 10 AM - 5 PM, Thurs until 8 PM, Sun Noon - 5 PM, cl Mon & major holidays; No admis fee; Estab 1961 for the study & documentation of nineteenth & early twentieth century American art through permanent collections, exhibitions & publications; Main gallery plus eleven smaller galleries; Average Annual Attendance: 100,000; Mem: 800; dues $50 - $500
Income: Financed by endowment, grants & contributions
Special Subjects: Afro-American Art, American Indian Art, Folk Art, Historical Material, Landscapes, Art History, Photography, Prints, Sculpture, Drawings, Painting-American, Photography, Prints, Watercolors, American Western Art, Bronzes, Southwestern Art, Woodcuts, Etchings & Engravings, Landscapes, Restorations, Reproductions
Collections: American paintings & sculpture; print coll; photographs; illustrated books; works on paper; Remington & Russell
Publications: Monthly Calendar of Events, bi-annual Program & active publication program in American art & history
Activities: Classes for adults & children; docent training; lects open to public, 10 vis lectrs per yr; gallery talks; tours; individual paintings & original objects of art lent to national art mus; lending collection contains original art works, paintings, photographs, sculpture & ephemera material; book traveling exhibs 2-3 per yr; originate traveling exhibs 2-3 to national art mus; mus shop sells books, prints & gift items

L **Research Library,** 3501 Camp Bowie Blvd, Fort Worth, TX 76107-2062. Tel 817-989-5040; Fax 817-989-5032; Elec Mail library@cartermuseum.org; Internet Home Page Address: www.cartermuseum.org/library; library.tcu.edu/cdlccat (catalog); *Library Dir* Samuel Duncan; *Archivist & Reference Serv Mgr* Jonathan Frembling; *Library Technical Servs Coordr* Mary Jane Harbison
Open Wed & Fri 11 AM - 4 PM, Thurs 11 AM - 7 PM, Sat 11 AM - 4 PM Sept thru May; Estab 1961
Library Holdings: Auction Catalogs; Book Volumes 55,000; Clipping Files; Exhibition Catalogs; Fiche 60,000; Maps; Original Documents Archives of American Art; Pamphlets; Periodical Subscriptions 140; Photographs; Prints; Reels 7000; Reproductions
Special Subjects: Art History, Illustration, Photography, Drawings, Etchings & Engravings, Graphic Arts, Maps, Painting-American, Prints, Sculpture, Historical Material, History of Art & Archaeology, Watercolors, Ethnology, American Western Art, Bronzes, Printmaking, American Indian Art, Southwestern Art, Afro-American Art, Bookplates & Bindings, Restoration & Conservation, Woodcarvings, Woodcuts, Landscapes, Reproductions, Architecture, Folk Art
Collections: exhibition catalogs, monographs, catalogues raisonnes, reference material, periodicals, auction catalogs, ephemera, and electronic resources on American art, history, and photography, with emphasis on the history and visual record of the Western US; Microform holdings include large nineteenth-century U.S. newspaper coll, city directories, Western Americana: Frontier History of the Trans-Mississippi West, 1550-1900, New York Public Library artists and print files, History of Photography periodicals, Knoedler Library, and Archives of American Art; fine examples of rare and illustrated books; archival holdings include museum institutional records and artist archival, including Laura Gilpin, Eliot Porter, Karl Struss, and the records of the Roman Bronze Works

C **BANK ONE FORT WORTH,** 500 Throckmorton, Fort Worth, TX 76102-3708; PO Box 2050, Fort Worth, TX 76113-2050. Tel 817-884-4000; Fax 817-870-2454; *Property Mgr* Lew Massey
Estab 1974 to enhance the pub areas of bank lobby & building; to provide art for offices of individual bank officers; Collection displayed throughout bank building, offices & public space
Collections: Alexander Calder sculpture; more than 400 pieces of drawings, graphics, paintings, prints, sculpture & tapestries, focusing on art of the Southwest, including artists throughout the nation & abroad
Activities: Tours for special groups only; sponsor two art shows annually; provide cash prizes; scholarships offered

L **FORT WORTH PUBLIC LIBRARY ARTS & HUMANITIES,** Fine Arts Section, 500 W 3rd, Fort Worth, TX 76102. Tel 817-871-7737; Fax 817-871-7734; Elec Mail tstone@fortworthlibrary.org; Internet Home Page Address: www.fortworthgov.org/library; *Unit Mgr* Thelma Stone; *Librn* Elmer Sackman; *Libr Asst* Gayle Mays; *Librn Asst* D Metcalf
Open Mon - Thurs 9 AM - 9 PM, Sat 10 AM - 6 PM, Sun Noon - 6 PM; No admis fee; Estab 1902
Income: Financed by appropriation
Library Holdings: Cassettes; Clipping Files; Fiche; Original Art Works; Other Holdings Articles, Books, Music scores, Pamphlets & programs, Sheet music, Special clipped picture files; Pamphlets; Photographs; Prints; Records; Video Tapes
Special Subjects: Cartoons, Bookplates & Bindings
Collections: Hal Coffman Collection of original political cartoon art; Nancy Taylor Collection of bookplates; historic picture & photograph collection autographed by various celebrities; rare books
Exhibitions: Antiques, crafts, prints, original photographs & original works; also art gallery exhibs of paintings, sculpture, photographs, folk crafts
Publications: Bibliographies; catalogs; monthly Focus
Activities: Tours

M **KIMBELL ART FOUNDATION,** Kimbell Art Museum, 3333 Camp Bowie Blvd, Fort Worth, TX 76107-2792. Tel 817-332-8451; Fax 817-877-1264; Elec Mail curators@kimbellart.org; Internet Home Page Address: www.kimbellart.org; *Dir* Eric M Lee; *Deputy Dir* George TM Shackelford; *Cur European Art & Head Acad Svcs* Nancy Edwards; *Chief Conservator* Claire M Barry; *Librn* Chia-Chun Shih; *Dir Finance & Admin* Susan R Drake; *Mktg & Pub Rels* Jessica Brandrup; *Cur of Asian & non-Western Art* Jennifer Casler Price; *Mgr Publications* Wendy P Gottlieb; *Registrar* Patricia Decoster; *Spec Events & Mem Mgr* Robert McAn; *Cur Emer Architecture/Archivist* Patricia Cummings Loud; *Opers Mgr* Larry Eubank; *Security Mgr* David McMillan; *Mgr Food Svcs* Shelby Schafer
Open Tues - Thurs & Sat 10 AM - 5 PM, Fri Noon - 8 PM, Sun Noon - 5 PM, cl Mon, July 4, Thanksgiving, Christmas & New Year's; No admis fee to permanent coll; fees apply to special exhibs, half-price offered Tues all day & Fri 5-8 PM; Open to public 1972 for the collection, preservation, research, publication & public exhibition of art of all periods; Average Annual Attendance: 300,000; Mem: 24,000; dues $40-$10,000
Income: Financed by foundation
Library Holdings: Auction Catalogs; Book Volumes; Exhibition Catalogs; Periodical Subscriptions
Special Subjects: Sculpture, African Art, Pre-Columbian Art, Painting-European, Asian Art, Antiquities-Egyptian, Antiquities-Greek, Antiquities-Roman, Antiquities-Assyrian
Collections: European paintings & sculpture from Renaissance to early 20th century; Mediterranean antiquities; African sculpture; Asian sculpture, paintings & ceramics; Pre-Columbian sculpture & ceramics; Antiquities - Cycladic; Oceanic Art
Publications: In Pursuit of Quality: The Kimbell Art Museum/An Illustrated History of the Art & Architecture; Light is the Theme: Louis I Kahn & the Kimbell Art Museum; biannual calendar; exhibition catalogs
Activities: Classes for adults & children, hearing impaired & sight impaired; docent training; summer camps; family festivals & gallery guides; lects open to pub; gallery talks; tours; films; book discussion club; original objects of art & individual paintings lent to other mus organizing important international loan exhibs; book traveling exhibs; originate traveling exhibs to other mus; mus shop sells books, magazines, reproductions, slides, art related videotapes, puzzles, posters

L **Library,** 3333 Camp Bowie Blvd, Fort Worth, TX 76107-2792. Tel 817-332-8451; Fax 817-877-1264; Internet Home Page Address: www.kimbellart.org; *Librn* Chia-Chun Shih
Open by appointment only; No admis fee; Estab 1967 to support museum staff, docents & research in area; For reference use of curatorial staff
Library Holdings: Auction Catalogs 11,600; Book Volumes 37,000; Exhibition Catalogs; Fiche 20,500; Motion Pictures; Periodical Subscriptions 154; Reels; Slides
Collections: European art from ancient to early 20th century, Oriental, Pre-Columbian & African art; Witt Library on microfiche

M **MODERN ART MUSEUM,** (Fort Worth Art Association) 3200 Darnell St, Fort Worth, TX 76107-2872. Tel 817-738-9215; Tel 866-824-5566; Fax 817-735-1161; Elec Mail info@themodern.org; Internet Home Page Address: www.themodern.org; *Chief Cur* Michael Auping; *Cur Educ* Terri Thornton; *Mem & Spec Events* Suzanne Woo; *Registrar* Rick Floyd; *Secy* Claudia Carrillo; *Pub Information Officer* Kendal Smith Lake; *Admin Asst to Cur* Susan Colegrove; *Head Design & Installation* Tony Wright; *Bus Mgr* Jo Garwood; *Computer Systems Mgr* Jim Colegrove; *Bldg Engineer* Scott Grant; *Museum Store Mgr* Lorri Wright; *Dir* Marla Price; *Cur* Andrea Karnes
Open Tues - Sun 10 AM - 5 PM, Fri until 8 PM, cl Mon & holidays; Admis general (13-adult) $10, students w/ID & seniors (60 +) $4, mems & children 12 &

under & 1st Sun ea month free, Wed half price; Modern & contemporary art; Average Annual Attendance: 200,000; Mem: 5,500; Benefactor $25,000, Chmn's Cir $10,000 President's Cir $5,000; Patron $1,200; Contributor $500; Sustainer $200; Family $150; Assoc $125; Basic $65
Special Subjects: Architecture, Hispanic Art, Latin American Art, Mexican Art, Painting-American, African Art, Ceramics, Landscapes, Afro-American Art, Collages, Painting-European, Painting-Japanese, Painting-Canadian, Furniture, Glass, Metalwork, Painting-British, Painting-Dutch, Painting-French, Painting-Flemish, Painting-Italian, Painting-Australian, Painting-German, Painting-Israeli, Painting-New Zealand
Collections: Works by modern & contemporary masters, notably Picasso, Kandinsky, Still, Rothko, Judd, Marden, Dine, Rauschenberg, Oldenburg, Lichtenstein, Warhol, Hodgkin, Avery, Scully & Motherwell; Post 1940's art from all countries, paintings, sculpture, drawings, prints & gifts; Photography by Cindy Sherman, Carrie May Williams, Bill Viola
Publications: Biannual calendar; Art the Modern (Magazine)
Activities: Classes for adults, teens & children; teacher workshops; internships; lects open to pub & for members only, 20 vis lectrs per yr; gallery talks; tours; concerts; scholarships; originate traveling exhibs; mus shop sells books, magazines & reproductions

M **SID W RICHARDSON FOUNDATION,** Sid Richardson Museum, 309 Main St, Fort Worth, TX 76102-4006. Tel 817-332-6554; 888-332-6554; Fax 817-332-8671; Elec Mail info@sidrichardsonmuseum.org; Internet Home Page Address: www.sidrichardsonmuseum.org; *Dir* Mary Burke; *Dir Tour Progs* Katherine Yount
Open Mon - Thurs 9 AM - 5 PM, Fri - Sat 9 AM - 8 PM, Sun 12 AM - 5 PM, cl major holidays; No admis fee; Estab 1982; totally renovated in 2006, the museum exhibits paintings by Frederic Remington & Charles M. Russell. Educ programs & museum store; Average Annual Attendance: 40,000
Income: Financed by the Sid W Richardson Foundation
Special Subjects: Painting-American, Watercolors, American Western Art, Bronzes
Collections: Frederic Remington Collection; Charles M Russell Collection
Exhibitions: Permanent exhibit of paintings by Frederic Remington, Charles M Russell & other Western artists
Publications: Remington & Russell, The Sid Richardson Collection
Activities: Classes for adults & children; gallery talks; tours; mus shop sells books, prints, postcards, note cards, posters, reproduction bronzes & prints on canvas

M **TEXAS CHRISTIAN UNIVERSITY,** University Art Gallery, Campus Box 298000, Dept of Art & Art History Fort Worth, TX 76129-0001. Tel 817-257-7643; Fax 817-257-7399; Elec Mail rwatson@tcu.edu; Internet Home Page Address: www.artanddesign.tcu.edu; *Dir* Ronald Watson
Open Mon 11 AM - 6 PM, Tues - Fri 11 AM - 4 PM, Sat & Sun 1 - 4 PM; No admis fee; Estab to present the best art possible to the student body; to show faculty & student work; Gallery consists of one large room, 30 x 40 ft, with additional movable panels; Average Annual Attendance: 10,000
Income: Financed by college funds
Collections: Japanese 18th Century Prints & Drawings; Contemporary Graphics; Art in the Metroplex; juried local artists
Publications: Exhibition notes, mailers & posters
Activities: Classes for adults; lect open to public, 15 vis lectrs per year; gallery talks; competitions
M **Moudy Gallery,** Moudy Bldg N, 2805 S University Dr Fort Worth, TX 76129. Tel 817-257-2588; Elec Mail theartgalleries@tcu.edu; Internet Home Page Address: www.theartgalleries.tcu.edu; *Dir* Anne Bothwell
Open acad yr Mon 11AM-6PM, Tues-Fri 10AM-4PM, Sat 1PM-4PM; No admis fee
Collections: works by students & professional artists

M **UNIVERSITY OF NORTH TEXAS HEALTH SCIENCE CENTER FORT WORTH,** Atrium Gallery, 3500 Camp Bowie Blvd, Fort Worth, TX 76109-2644. Tel 817-735-0301; Elec Mail shea.pattersonyoung@unthsc.edu; Internet Home Page Address: www.hsc.unt.edu/atriumgallery/; *Cur* Shea Patterson Young
Open Mon - Fri 8 AM - 5 PM; No admis fee; Estab 1986 as a nonprofit, pub service gallery; Three-story pub service gallery in North Texas featuring international groups like The SFA & SWA, PSH works in all media by a variety of artists; Average Annual Attendance: 2,000
Income: Financed by state appropriation
Collections: Permanent Collection of the Society of Watercolor Artists
Exhibitions: Annual 12-County High School Art Competition; changing monthly exhibits; Colored Pencil Society of America
Activities: Teacher workshops; competitions with prizes; 12 vis lectrs per yr; sponsoring of competitions; scholarships

FREDERICKSBURG

M **JOE GISH'S OLD WEST MUSEUM,** (Old West Museum) 502 N Miliam St, Fredericksburg, TX 78624. Tel 940-872-9698; 830-997-2794; Fax 940-872-8504; Elec Mail sunsettradingpost@earthlink.net; Internet Home Page Address: www.cowboymuseum.net; *Owner & Cur* Jack Glover; *Co-Owner* Cherie Glover; *Owner* Joe Gish
No regular hours; call for hours; Admis no charge; Estab 1987; 2 room log building 2 1/2 blocks off Main St in St. Fredericksburg Texas; Average Annual Attendance: 67,000; Mem: 300; dues $35
Income: Financed by endowment & mem
Special Subjects: Architecture, Painting-American, Photography, Prints, Sculpture, American Western Art, Textiles, Costumes, Posters, Restorations
Collections: Historic clothing; sculpture; western art
Exhibitions: Western Art Show & Sale; Western Spirit Art Show
Publications: Stageline, quarterly
Activities: Classes for adults & children; docent training; lects open to pub, 10 vis lectrs per yr; competitions; book traveling exhibs, 2 per yr; sales shop sells books, reproductions, prints

GAINESVILLE

L **NORTH CENTRAL TEXAS COLLEGE,** Library, 1525 W California St, Gainesville, TX 76240-4636. Tel 940-668-7731, Ext 338; Fax 940-668-6049; *Dir Library Svcs* Dana Pearson
Open Mon - Thurs 8 AM - 9:30 PM, Fri 8 AM - 4:30 PM, Sun 2 - 5 PM; Estab 1924 to serve the needs of the admin, faculty & students; Circ 500
Purchases: $1500
Library Holdings: Audio Tapes; Book Volumes 50,000; Cards; Cassettes; Clipping Files; Fiche; Filmstrips; Lantern Slides; Motion Pictures; Pamphlets; Periodical Subscriptions 175; Prints; Records; Reproductions; Slides; Video Tapes
Activities: Brownbook reviews

GALVESTON

L **ROSENBERG LIBRARY,** 2310 Sealy Ave, Galveston, TX 77550. Tel 409-763-8854; Fax 409-763-0275; Elec Mail jaugelli@rosenberg-library.org; Internet Home Page Address: www.rosenberg-library.org; *Head Spec Coll* Casey Greene; *Museum Cur* Eleanor Clark; *CEO, Exec Dir* John Augelli; *Pres* Jan Coggeshall
Open Mon - Sat 9 AM - 5 PM; cl Sun & national holidays; No admis fee; Estab 1904 to provide library services to the people of Galveston, together with lectures, concerts, exhibitions; Library includes the Harris Art Gallery, The James M Lykes Maritime Gallery, The Hutchings Gallery, together with miscellaneous art & historical exhibit galleries & halls
Income: $55,000,100 (financed by endowment, city & state appropriation)
Library Holdings: Book Volumes 250,000; Compact Disks; DVDs; Fiche; Manuscripts; Maps; Memorabilia; Motion Pictures; Original Art Works; Original Documents; Periodical Subscriptions 500; Photographs; Prints; Sculpture
Collections: Historical objects relating to Galveston & Texas; photographic & manuscript colls; historic maps & architectural drawings; large coll of paintings with a focus on regional artists & maritime subjects; large colls of American & European decorative glass, textiles, silver & Native American crafts
Exhibitions: Permanent exhibit of Galveston maritime history; rotating exhibits of framed art, decorative arts, photographs & other historic objects
Activities: Historical lect & presentations; book signings; public prog; gallery tours; joint exhibs with other local mus; active loan prog

GLEN ROSE

M **BARNARD'S MILL ART MUSEUM,** 307 SW Barnard St, Glen Rose, TX 76043; PO Box 2537, Glen Rose, TX 76043-2537. Tel 254-897-7494; *Dir* Richard Moore; *Chmn* SC Coconaur; *Treas* David Morrow; *Cur* Hollis Taylor
Open Sat 10 AM - 5 PM, Sun 1 - 5 PM; No admis fee; Average Annual Attendance: 650
Library Holdings: Book Volumes
Collections: 200 paintings, bronzes & etchings
Activities: Educ prog for college students affiliated with Tarleton State Univ; guided tours

HOUSTON

A **ART LEAGUE OF HOUSTON,** 1953 Montrose Blvd, Houston, TX 77006-1243. Tel 713-523-9530; Fax 713-523-4053; Elec Mail artleagh@neosoft.com; Internet Home Page Address: www.hfac.uh.edu/freeland/ALH; *Pres (V)* Margaret Poisaant; *Exec Dir* Claudia Solis
Open Mon - Fri 9 AM - 5 PM, Sat 11 AM - 5 PM; No admis fee; Estab 1948 to promote pub interest in art & the achievements of Houston area artists; Gallery maintained for monthly exhibits; Average Annual Attendance: 20,000; Mem: 1500; dues $25-$1000; annual meeting in May/June
Income: $300,000 (financed by grants, mem & fundraising functions)
Exhibitions: Monthly exhibits; Regional exhibitions; The Gala, Sharon Koprova
Publications: Exhibition catalogs; newsletter, monthly
Activities: Classes for adults & children; Cameron Foundation Artpresence docent Program; HIV & Art Outreach Program; Multiple Sclerosis Outreach Program; lect open to public; competitions with prizes; workshops, gallery talks; tours; sales shop sells calendars, craft items, original art, print reproductions

M **ART MUSEUM OF THE UNIVERSITY OF HOUSTON,** Blaffer Gallery, Entrance 16 off Cullen Blvd, Fine Arts Bldg Houston, TX 77204-4891; 120 Fine Arts Bldg, University of Houston Houston, TX 77204-4018. Tel 713-743-9521; Fax 713-743-9525; Internet Home Page Address: www.class.uh.edu/blaffer/; *Dir & Chief Cur* Claudia Schmuckli; *Dir External Affairs* Susan Conaway; *Cur Educ* Katherine Veneman; *Admin* Karen Zicterman; *Asst Cur Educ* Viola Chavez; *Asst Dir External Affairs* Jeffrey Bowen; *Assoc Cur* Rachel Hooper; *Registrar* Youngmin Chung; *Mus Preparator* Jonathan Hopson; *Deputy Dir* James Rosengren
Open Tues - Sat 10 AM - 5 PM; cl Sun, Mon, univ & major holidays; No admis fee; Estab 1973 to present a broad spectrum of visual arts, utilizing the interdisciplinary framework of the University, to the acad community and to the rapidly increasing diverse population of greater Houston; Main gallery is 3,760 sq ft, ceiling height varies from 10-25 ft; Second floor gallery is 2,980 sq ft; Average Annual Attendance: 45,000
Income: Financed by state appropriation, university, local funds, grants, gifts
Special Subjects: Graphics, Latin American Art, Mexican Art, Painting-American, Photography, Afro-American Art, Decorative Arts, Painting-Japanese, Asian Art, Painting-British, Painting-French, Painting-Spanish, Painting-Italian, Painting-Australian, Painting-German
Exhibitions: Exhibitions change quarterly, call for details
Publications: Exhibition catalogs on originating shows
Activities: Outreach school progs; workshops; videos; docent training; lects open to pub, 6-10 vis lectrs per yr; concerts; gallery talks; tours; competitions with awards; book traveling exhibs 3-4 per yr; originate traveling exhibs 1 per yr to various contemporary art mus; mus shop sells books & gift items

L **William R Jenkins Architecture & Art Library,** 114 University Libraries, Houston, TX 77004-2000. Tel 713-743-2340; Elec Mail archlib@mail.uh.edu; Internet Home Page Address: info.lib.uh.edu/aa; *Libr Coordr* Catherine Essinger; *Libr Supv* Tina McPherson; *Sr Libr Asst* Chris Conway; *Libr Specialist* Donovan Parker
Open Mon - Thurs 8 AM - 8 PM, Fri 8 AM - 5 PM, Sat 10 AM - 5 PM, cl Sun; No admis fee; For reference only, students & faculty
Income: Financed by state appropriation
Library Holdings: Book Volumes 70,000; Fiche 15,683; Pamphlets; Periodical Subscriptions 230; Reels 182
Special Subjects: Art History, Photography, Architecture

M **CONTEMPORARY ARTS MUSEUM HOUSTON,** (Contemporary Arts Museum) 5216 Montrose Blvd, Houston, TX 77006. Tel 713-284-8250; Fax 713-284-8275; Elec Mail info@camh.org; Internet Home Page Address: www.camh.org; *Dir* Bill Arning; *Deputy Dir Facilities & Risk Management* Mike Reed; *Registrar* Tim Barkley; *Dir Community Engagement* Connie McAllister; *Sr Cur* Valerie Cassel Oliver; *Deputy Dir Finance & Admin* Amber Winsor; *Cur* Dean Daderko; *Educ & Pub Progs Mgr* Daniel Atkinson; *Educ Assoc* Jamal Cyrus; *Retail Operations Dir* Sue Pruden; *Asst Develop Dir* Amanda Bredbenner; *Preparator* Jeff Shore; *Gallery Supervisor* Kenya Evans
Open Tues, Wed & Fri 10 AM - 7 PM, Thurs 10 AM - 9 PM, Sat 10 AM - 6 PM, Sun noon - 6 PM, cl Mon, Thanksgiving & Christmas Days; No admis fee; Estab 1948 to provide a forum for art with an emphasis on the visual arts of the present & recent past, to document new directions in art through changing exhibitions & publications, to engage the public in a lively dialogue with today's art & to encourage a greater understanding of contemporary art through educational programs; the mus is a non-collecting institution; Current bldg was designed by Gunnar Birkerts & opened in 1972; comprises one large gallery of 10,500 sq ft and a smaller gallery of 1500 sq ft; Average Annual Attendance: 91,000; Mem: 700; dues $35 & up
Activities: Progs for families; teacher resources; Teen Council; lects open to pub, 6-12 vis lectrs per yr; concerts; gallery talks; tours; originate traveling exhibs to other art mus; mus shop sells books & gifts

M **DIVERSE WORKS,** 4102 Fannin St #200, Houston, TX 77004-4808. Tel 713-223-8346; Fax 713-223-4608; Elec Mail info@diverseworks.org; Internet Home Page Address: www.diverseworks.org; *Co-Dir* Diane Barber; *Co-Dir* Sixto Wagan; *Opers Mgr* Jon Read; *Pub Relations & Mktg Mgr* Shawna Forney; *Admin Mgr* Tracey Morton
Open Mon - Sat Noon - 6 PM; No admis fee; Estab 1983 to present work by contemporary artists working in all arts media & residencies; Main gallery 40 ft x 70 ft, small gallery 20 ft x 30 ft; Average Annual Attendance: 30,000
Income: $500,000 (financed by individual & foundation contributions, federal & city funds, earned income)
Exhibitions: 10-15 exhibitions a year of Texas & National Artists; 25 exhibitions per year of dance, music, performance & theatre
Activities: Classes for adults; Lect open to public, 20 vis lectrs per year; concerts; tours

A **FOTO FEST INTERNATIONAL,** 1113 Vine St Ste 101, Houston, TX 77002-1043. Tel 713-223-5522; Fax 713-223-4411; Elec Mail info@fotofest.org; Internet Home Page Address: www.fotofest.org; *Chmn & Co-Founder* Fred Baldwin; *Artistic Dir & Co-Founder* Wendy Watriss; *Exhib Coordr* Jennifer Ward
Open Mon - Fri 10 AM - 5 PM (during exhibs), Thurs 10 AM - 7 PM, Sat noon - 5 PM; No admis fee; Estab to promote public appreciation for photographic art, international & cross-cultural exchange & literacy through photography
Special Subjects: Photography
Exhibitions: All exhibs held at FotoFest HQ, Houston unless indicated otherwise
Activities: Educ prog; gallery talks; tours; sales shop sells books

M **HOUSTON BAPTIST UNIVERSITY,** Museum of American Architecture and Decorative Arts, 7502 Fondren Rd, Houston, TX 77074-3298. Tel 281-649-3997; *Dir* Suzie Snoddy
Open Mon - Sat 10 AM - 4 PM, cl holidays & Sun; Admis adults $6, seniors $5, children $4; Estab 1969 to depict social history of Americans & diverse ethnic groups who settled in Texas; Average Annual Attendance: 9,000; Mem: 125; dues $25
Income: Financed by mem & donations
Special Subjects: Architecture, Portraits, Period Rooms, Maps, Decorative Arts, Dolls, Furniture, Miniatures
Collections: Theo Redwood Blank Doll Collection; Schissler Antique Miniature Furniture Collection; Dolls; European Decorative Miniature Furniture; Dog-Trot Log Cabin
Activities: Docent training; lect open to public, 2-4 vis lectrs per year; tours

A **HOUSTON CENTER FOR PHOTOGRAPHY,** 1441 W Alabama, Houston, TX 77006-4103. Tel 713-529-4755; Fax 713-529-9248; Elec Mail info@hcponline.org; Internet Home Page Address: www.hcponline.org; *Exec Dir* Bevin Bering Dubrowski; *Exec Asst* Sandy Vitrano; *Asst Dir Educ* Juliana Forero; *Exhibs Coordr* Jason Dibley
Open Wed & Sun 11 AM - 5 PM, Thurs 11 AM - 9 PM; No admis fee; Estab 1981; Maintains reference library; Average Annual Attendance: 15,000; Mem: 800; dues $35 & up
Income: $175,000 (financed by endowment, mem, city & state appropriation, NEA & private gifts)
Special Subjects: Photography
Exhibitions: Membership & Fellowship exhibitions
Publications: Spot, bi-annual
Activities: Classes for adults & children; outreach prog; lects open to pub; gallery talks; tours; competitions; fels; book traveling exhibs; originate traveling exhibs to mus & non-profit galleries

L **HOUSTON PUBLIC LIBRARY,** 500 McKinney St, Fine Arts & Recreation Dept Houston, TX 77002-2530. Tel 713-236-1313; Fax 713-247-3302; Elec Mail jharvath@hpl.lib.tx.us; Internet Home Page Address: www.houstonlibrary.org; *Mgr Fine Arts & Recreation* John Harvath; *Asst Mgr* Sandra Stuart
Open Mon - Fri 9 AM - 9 PM, Sat 9 AM - 6 PM, Sun 2 - 6 PM; Estab 1848 as a private library for the Houston Lyceum & opened to the pub in 1895; Circ 142,651; Monthly exhibits, including art shows are spread throughout the Central Library Building
Income: Financed by endowment, city appropriation & Friends of the Library
Library Holdings: Book Volumes 160,110; Clipping Files 24,131; Exhibition Catalogs; Other Holdings Auction Catalogs 6742; Compact Discs 9500; Sheet Music 15,325; Pamphlets; Periodical Subscriptions 400; Records
Special Subjects: Decorative Arts, Oriental Art
Activities: Lect open to public; tours; lending collection contains 9500 compact discs

M **LAWNDALE ART CENTER,** 4912 Main St, Houston, TX 77002. Tel 713-528-5858; Fax 713-528-4140; Elec Mail askus@lawndaleartcenter.org; Internet Home Page Address: www.lawndaleartcenter.org; *Exec Dir* Christine Jelson West; *Exhibs & Programming Dir* Dennis Nance; *Community Relations Coordr* Emily Link; *Office Mgr* Kelly Montana; *Exhibs Asst* Daniel Bertalot
Open Mon-Fri 10 AM- 5 PM; Sat noon - 5 PM; No admis fee; Estab 1979; Develops local contemporary artists & the audience for their art; Average Annual Attendance: 18,000
Exhibitions: Over 20 exhibs ann by local & regional artists

M **MENIL FOUNDATION, INC,** (Menil Collection) The Menil Collection, 1533 Sul Ross, Houston, TX 77006-4729; 1511 Branard St, Houston, TX 77006-4797. Tel 713-525-9400; Fax 713-525-9444; Elec Mail info@menil.org; Internet Home Page Address: www.menil.org; *Chmn* Louisa S Sarofim; *Dir* Josef Helfenstein; *Information Technology* Buck Bakke; *Cur* Toby Kamps; *Cur* Michelle White; *Chief Conservator* Brad Epley; *Librn* Eric Wolf; *Registrar* Anne Adams; *Pres* Janet Hobby; *Pub Rels* Vance Muse; *Deputy Dir & COO* Sheryl Kolasinski; *CFO* Michael Cannon
Open Wed - Sun 11 AM - 7 PM, cl Mon & Tues, New Year's Day, Easter, Independence Day, Thanksgiving Day, Christmas Day; No admis fee; Opened in 1987, estab to organize & present art exhibitions & progs; two landmark bldgs designed by Renzo Piano; Average Annual Attendance: 175,000; Mem: 1500; dues student $25, levels $100 - $10,000
Income: Financed by pvt foundation and pvt endowment & mems
Library Holdings: Auction Catalogs; Book Volumes; Clipping Files; Photographs; Prints
Special Subjects: Afro-American Art, Photography, Pre-Columbian Art, Prints, Drawings, Painting-American, African Art, Religious Art, Primitive art, Antiquities-Byzantine, Renaissance Art, Medieval Art, Antiquities-Oriental, Antiquities-Persian, Antiquities-Egyptian, Antiquities-Greek, Antiquities-Roman, Antiquities-Etruscan, Antiquities-Assyrian
Collections: Antiquities from the Paleolithic to the pre-Christian eras; Art of Africa; Medieval & Byzantine art; Oceanic & Pacific Northwest tribal cultures; 20th century drawings, paintings, photographs, prints & sculpture; Permanent collection at 16,000
Publications: Exhibition catalogs
Activities: Classes for children; lects open to pub, lects for mems only; concerts; gallery talks; tours; Walter Hopps Award for Curatorial Achievement; fels; originate traveling exhibs; mus shop sells books, magazines & original art

M **MIDTOWN ART CENTER,** 3414 La Branch St, Houston, TX 77004-3841. Tel 713-521-8803; Fax 713-521-9003; Elec Mail midtownartcenter@hotmail.com; Internet Home Page Address: www.midtownartcenter.com; *Dir* Ida Thompson
Call for hours; No admis fee; Estab 1982 as a multi-cultural, multi-disciplinary art center serving grassroots artists
Income: Financed by mem & donations
Exhibitions: Local artist exhibitions throughout the year;
Activities: Classes for adults & children

M **MUSEUM OF FINE ARTS HOUSTON,** Bayou Bend Collection & Gardens, 6003 Memorial Dr, Houston, TX 77007; PO Box 6826, Houston, TX 77265-6826. Tel 713-639-7750; Fax 713-639-7770; Elec Mail bayoubend@mfah.org; Internet Home Page Address: www.mfah.org/bayoubend; *Cur* Michael K Brown; *Dir Educ* Jennifer Hammond; *Conservator* Steven Pine; *Cur Gardens* Bart Brechter; *Exec Asst* Caryn Fulda; *Admin Asst, BB* Janet Marshall; *Dir BB Library* Margaret Culbertson; *Prog Mgr* Joey Milillu; *Visitor Servs Mgr* Lavinia Ignat; *Shop Supervisor* Lisa Sugita; *Hill Archive Proj Mgr* Marie Wise
Open Aug (self guided tours) Tues - Sat 10 AM - 5 PM, Sun 1 - 5 PM (last admis 4 PM); Admis gen admis $12.50 -$15, students & seniors (ID required) $11-$13.50, children 10-17 $6.25-7.50, gardens only $5, children under 9 no charge; Estab 1957 dedicated to serving all people by pursuing excellence in art & horticulture through collection, exhibition & education; Twenty-eight room settings that trace the evolution of American style from 1620's to 1870's & an area focused on 19th century Texas furniture, pottery & decorative arts. Affiliate of Museum of Fine Arts, Houston; Average Annual Attendance: 100,000; Mem: Board meetings Sep - Nov & Jan - May
Library Holdings: Auction Catalogs; Book Volumes; Exhibition Catalogs
Special Subjects: Decorative Arts, Etchings & Engravings, Folk Art, Historical Material, Landscapes, Ceramics, Glass, Metalwork, Flasks & Bottles, Furniture, Porcelain, Portraits, Pottery, Painting-American, Prints, Period Rooms, Textiles, Sculpture, Drawings, Watercolors, American Western Art, Woodcarvings, Jewelry, Silver, Carpets & Rugs, Maps, Embroidery, Pewter
Collections: Bayou Bend Collection of American decorative arts & paintings
Publications: Bayou Bend Gardens: A Southern Oasis; America's Treasures at Bayou Bend: Celebrating Fifty Years; American Material Culture and the Texas Experience: The David B. Warren Symposium
Activities: lects open to pub, 2 vis lectrs per yr; concerts; gallery talks; tours; schols & fels offered; mus shops sells books & gifts

M **MUSEUM OF FINE ARTS, HOUSTON,** (Rienzi Center for European Decorative Arts) Rienzi Center for European Decorative Arts, 1406 Kirby Dr, Houston, TX 77019-1412; Rienzi MFAH, PO Box 6826 Houston, TX 77265-6826. Tel 713-639-7800; Fax 713-639-7810; Elec Mail rienzi@mfah.org; Internet Home Page Address: www.mfah.org/rienzi; *Dir* Katherine S Howe; *Assoc Cur Decorative Arts* Christine Gervais; *Curatorial Asst* Caroline Cole; *Docent Prog Mgr* Stephenie Niemeyer; *Pub Progs Mgr* Sara Foley Edwards; *Exec Asst* Adriana Rubio; *Educ Asst* Casey Monahan; *Facilities Coordr* Juan Alonzo
Ctr open to guided tours only, Wed - Fri 10 AM - 5 PM, Sat 10 AM - 4 PM, Sun 1-5 PM; gardens open Wed - Sun 10 AM - 4:30 PM; Reinzi cl Aug & most natl

holidays; Admis to Ctr, advance ticket purchase req: adults $8, seniors & students with ID $5, MFAH mem $4, group rates available, admis to Gardens free; Affiliate of Museum of Fine Arts, Houston; Average Annual Attendance: 20,000
Special Subjects: Decorative Arts, Drawings, Ceramics, Glass, Metalwork, Furniture, Porcelain, Portraits, Silver, Painting-European, Sculpture, Hispanic Art, Textiles, Painting-British, Baroque Art, Miniatures, Painting-Spanish
Collections: Rienzi Collection of European Decorative Arts & Paintings; Portrait Miniatures from the Caroline A Ross Collection
Exhibitions: The Wedding Dress; Rienzi Begins: John F Staub & the Mastersons
Publications: Rienzi: European Decorative Arts & Paintings, Katherine S. Howe et al
Activities: Docent training; family art workshops; sketching; tea & tour events; salons; concerts; gallery talks; tours; lects open to pub; book club; story time; family days/ 4 vix lects per yr

M **MUSEUM OF FINE ARTS, HOUSTON,** 1001 Bissonnet St, Houston, TX 77005-1803; PO Box 6826, Houston, TX 77265-6826. Tel 713-639-7771; Fax 713-639-7399; Elec Mail guestservices@mfah.org; Internet Home Page Address: www.mfah.org; *Dir* Gary Tinterow; *Assoc Dir, Admin* Willard Holmes; *Assoc Dir Develop* Amy Purvis; *CFO* Eric Anyah; *Asst Dir Exhibs* Deborah Roldan
Open Tues - Wed 10 AM - 5 PM, Thurs 10 AM - 9 PM, Fri & Sat 10 AM - 7 PM, Sun 12:15 - 7 PM, cl Mon, except Mon holidays, Thanksgiving & Christmas Days; Admis adults $15, seniors $10, military $10, students & youth $7.50, 12 & younger free, mems free & Thurs free, group rates available; Estab 1900 as an art mus containing works from prehistoric times to the present; Exhibition space totals 325,000 sq ft; Average Annual Attendance: 900,000; Mem: 35,000; dues $45-$1,500
Library Holdings: Auction Catalogs; Book Volumes; CD-ROMs; Clipping Files; DVDs; Exhibition Catalogs; Fiche; Other Holdings; Pamphlets; Periodical Subscriptions
Special Subjects: Decorative Arts, Flasks & Bottles, Photography, Drawings, Latin American Art, Prints, African Art, Asian Art, Baroque Art, Renaissance Art, Embroidery, Islamic Art
Collections: Coll of world art in all media, spanning 5,000 years; 2 house museums; Bayou Bend Collection & Gardens; Rienzi Center for European Decorative Arts
Publications: Annual report; calendar of events, bimonthly; catalogs of exhibitions
Activities: Classes for adults & children; docent training; progs specifically for educators; lects open to pub, 100 vis lectrs per yr; concerts; gallery talks; tours; internships available; individual paintings & objects lent to other art institutions; originate traveling exhibs to qualified mus; mus shop sells books, magazines, prints

L **Hirsch Library,** 1001 Bissonnet St, Houston, TX 77005-1803; PO Box 6826, Houston, TX 77265-6826. Tel 713-639-7325; Fax 713-639-7399; Elec Mail hirsch@mfah.org; Internet Home Page Address: www.mfah.org/library/home.asp; *Dir* Margaret Culbertson; *Catalog Librn* Edward Lukasek; *Ref Librn* Jon Evans; *Tech Svcs Librn* Margaret Ford
Not open to gen pub; open to researchers Tues - Fri 10 AM - 5 PM, Thurs until 9 PM, Sat Noon - 5 PM, phone or email svc only on Mon, cl Sun; No admis fee; Estab 1900; For reference only
Income: Financed by Hirsch Endowment
Library Holdings: Book Volumes 100,000; Clipping Files; Compact Disks; DVDs; Exhibition Catalogs; Fiche; Other Holdings Archival Records; Artists' Ephemera Files; Museum Files; Pamphlets; Periodical Subscriptions 250; Prints; Reels; Slides; Video Tapes
Special Subjects: Art History, Decorative Arts, Film, History of Art & Archaeology, Latin American Art, Fashion Arts, Art Education, Asian Art, American Indian Art, Furniture, Costume Design & Constr, Glass, Afro-American Art, Gold, Jewelry
Collections: Collection of world art in all media, spanning 5000 years; 2 house museums for American decorative arts & European decorative arts
Publications: MFAH Houston Visitor Guide; numerous exhibition catalogs; MFAH Today, bimonthly member publication
  —**Bayou Bend Collection & Gardens,**
See separate listing in Houston, Tx
  —**Glassell School of Art,**
See separate listing under US Art Schools in Houston, TX
  —**Rienzi Center for European Decorative Arts,**
See separate listing in Houston, Tx

M **MUSEUM OF SOUTHERN HISTORY,** Houston Baptist University, Cultural Arts Ctr, 7502 Fondren Rd Houston, TX 77074-3204. Tel 281-649-3997; Elec Mail ssnoddy@hbu.edu; Internet Home Page Address: www.hbu.edu/hbu/museum_of_southern_history; *Pres Emeritus* Joella Morris; *Admin* Suzie Snoddy
Open Mon - Sat 10 AM - 4 PM, cl univ holidays & holiday weekends; Admis adults $6, seniors $5, children $4; Estab 1978; Average Annual Attendance: 5,000; Mem: 300; $25, $50, $75 & $100
Income: nonprofit donations
Special Subjects: Photography, Portraits, Prints, Silver, Maps, Tapestries, Painting-American, Watercolors, Costumes, Decorative Arts, Furniture, Jewelry, Historical Material, Period Rooms, Military Art
Collections: Antique handguns; Confederacy-money & uniforms; Medical exhibit, late 1800's; quilts; Sharecropper's Cabin; Terry's Texas Rangers; various oils, historic paintings
Publications: Quarterly newsletter
Activities: Docent training; lects open to pub; 5 vis lectrs per yr; book traveling exhibs; mus shop sells books

L **RICE UNIVERSITY,** Brown Fine Arts Library, 6100 Main St, Rice Univ Houston, TX 77005; PO Box 1892, Brown Fine Arts Library Fondren Library MS 44 Houston, TX 77005-1892. Tel 713-348-5691; Internet Home Page Address: library.rice.edu; *Art & Architecture Librn* Jet M Prendeville; *Music Librn* Mary Brower
Open acad yr 24 hrs starting Noon Sun & closing 10 PM Fri, Sat 9 AM - 10 PM, holiday hrs vary; Estab 1964 combined art, architecture, music collections in the Alice Pratt Brown Library estab 1986; Located in Fondren Library, 3rd fl

Income: Financed by Rice Univ
Library Holdings: Book Volumes 190,000; Cassettes; DVDs; Exhibition Catalogs 6000; Other Holdings Scores; Periodical Subscriptions; Records
Special Subjects: Art History, Film, Photography, Architecture
Collections: Brown Fine Arts Collection

M **Rice Gallery,** 6100 Main St, 352 Sewall Hall Houston, TX 77005; PO Box 1892, Rice Univ Art Gallery MS-59 Houston, TX 77251-1892. Tel 713-348-6069; Fax 713-348-5980; Elec Mail ruag@rice.edu; Internet Home Page Address: www.ricegallery.org; *Dir & Chief Cur* Kimberly Davenport; *Asst Cur* Joshua Fischer; *Mgr* Christine Medina; *Preparator* David Krueger; *Designer* Antonio Manega; *Photographer* Nash Baker
Open Tues - Sat 11 AM - 5 PM & Thurs 11 AM - 7 PM, Sun Noon - 5 PM, cl Mon; No admis fee; Support the education & research mission of Rice Univ & serve as an artistic resource for the Rice & Houston communities by commissioning & presenting site-specific installations & related programming; 40 x 44 ft white box with one glass wall; Average Annual Attendance: 25,000; Mem: 150; dues student, artist & educator $25, catalyst $50, friend $100, advocate $250, assoc $500, partner $1000, patrons $3000+
Income: Rice University, Rice Patrons & Members, The Brown Foundation Inc, the City of Houston, the Robert J Card, M.D. & Karol Kreymer Catalogue Endowment, & the Leslie & Brad Bucher Artist Residency Endowment
Purchases: $450,000; non-collecting institution
Publications: Exhibit catalogs
Activities: Opportunity to work with artists during their residencies; lect & panel discussions, 5+ vis lectrs per yr; symposia & performances are free & open to public; gallery talks; tours; gallery store sells publications, clothing, accessories, stationery, posters

INGRAM

A **HILL COUNTRY ARTS FOUNDATION,** Duncan-McAshan Visual Arts Center, Hwy 39, Ingram, TX 78025; PO Box 1169, Ingram, TX 78025-1169. Tel 830-367-5121, 367-5120; Fax 830-367-5725; Elec Mail visualarts@hcaf.com; Internet Home Page Address: www.hcaf.com; *Art Dir* Jennifer Haynes
Gallery open Mon - Fri 9 AM - 5 PM, Sat 1 - 4 PM; No admis fee except for special events; Estab 1958 to provide a place for creative activities in the area of visual arts & performing arts; also to provide classes in arts, crafts & drama; 1800 sq ft; Average Annual Attendance: 35,000; Mem: 600; dues $40 & up; annual meeting first Sat in Dec
Income: Financed by endowment, mem, benefit activities, donations & earned income
Library Holdings: Auction Catalogs; Audio Tapes; Filmstrips; Motion Pictures; Original Art Works; Original Documents; Other Holdings; Sculpture; Slides; Video Tapes
Collections: 50+ pieces - contemporary paintings, prints, photographs & sculpture
Exhibitions: 8 rotating exhibits per yr; Regional Christmas Show
Publications: Spotlight, quarterly newsletter
Activities: Classes for adults & children; dramatic progs; lects open to pub, 2 vis lectrs per yr; concerts; national juried competitions with awards; scholarships offered; mus shop sells books, magazines, original art & prints

IRVING

M **IRVING ARTS CENTER,** Galleries & Sculpture Garden, 3333 N MacArthur Blvd, Irving, TX 75062-8026. Tel 972-252-7558; Fax 972-570-4962; Elec Mail minman@cityofirving.org; Internet Home Page Address: www.irvingartscenter.com; *Exec Dir* Richard E Huff; *Dir Exhibs & Educ Progs* Marcie J Inman; *Chmn* Jo-Ann Bresowar
Open Mon - Wed & Fri 9 AM - 5 PM, Thurs 9 AM - 8 PM, Sat 10 AM - 5 PM, Sun 1 - 5 PM; No admis fee; Estab 1990
Income: Financed by hotel/motel occupancy tax
Special Subjects: Painting-American, Photography, Sculpture, Watercolors, Pottery, Woodcuts
Collections: Permanent installations by James Surls, Jesus Moroles & Michael Manjarris in Sculpture Garden
Activities: Classes for children; dramatic progs; docent training; lect open to public, 2-3 vis lectrs per yr; concerts; gallery talks; tours; sponsor competitions; book traveling exhibitions 4-6 per yr

JOHNSON CITY

M **THE BENINI FOUNDATION & SCULPTURE RANCH,** 377 Shiloh Rd, Johnson City, TX 78636-4584. Tel 830-868-5244; Internet Home Page Address: www.sculptureranch.com; *Pres* Lorraine Benini
No admis fee; Estab 1984
Special Subjects: Sculpture
Collections: Contemporary Italian paintings & sculpture

KERRVILLE

M **L D BRINKMAN FOUNDATION,** 444 Sidney Baker S, Kerrville, TX 78028. Tel 830-257-2000; Fax 830-257-2030; *Cur* Mel Vick-Knueiper; *Trustee* Charles Thomas; *Trustee* L.D. Brinkman
Open weekdays by appointment; No Admis fee; Estab 1985 to promote western art; Average Annual Attendance: 900
Special Subjects: Painting-American, Watercolors, American Indian Art, American Western Art, Bronzes, Southwestern Art
Collections: American Western Art (1870's - Present): works on paper, paintings & sculpture, including Cowboy Artists of America
Activities: Individual paintings & original objects of art lent

M THE MUSEUM OF WESTERN ART, 1550 Bandera Hwy, Kerrville, TX 78028-9547; PO Box 294300, Kerrville, TX 78029-4300. Tel 830-896-2553; Fax 830-257-5206; Internet Home Page Address: www.museumofwesternart.org; *Operations Mgr* Gladys Simon
Open Tues - Sat 10 AM - 4 PM; Admis adults $7, seniors $6, children adolescents 9-17, col students with ID & adult groups 15 or more $5, children 8 & under & school tours k-12 with reservations free; Estab 1983 to display contemporary art of American West; Average Annual Attendance: 45,000; Mem: dues $35-$10,000
Income: Financed by mem dues, contributions, entrance fees, sales in mus shop & grants
Library Holdings: Auction Catalogs; Book Volumes; Clipping Files; Exhibition Catalogs; Memorabilia; Original Art Works; Pamphlets; Photographs; Prints; Reels; Sculpture; Slides; Video Tapes
Collections: Permanent coll of Western American Realism from mid 20th c to present
Publications: Visions West: History of the Cowboy Artists Museum
Activities: Classes for young serious art students, adults, children & students; docent progs & training; lect talks; gallery talks; schols offered; original objects of art lent to other mus; book traveling exhibs 2 per yr; originate traveling exhibs; mus shop sells books, magazines, original art, reproductions & prints

L **Museum of Western Art & Research Library,** 1550 Bandera Hwy, Kerrville, TX 78028; PO Box 294300, Kerrville, TX 78029-4300. Tel 830-896-2553, Ext. 226; Fax 830-896-2556; Elec Mail library3@mowatx.com; Internet Home Page Address: www.museumofwesternart.org; *Librn* Fred R Egloff
Open by appointment during museum hours Tues - Sat 10 AM - 4 PM; Admis $7; 1983; For reference only; Average Annual Attendance: 25,000
Income: Financed by donations & mem
Library Holdings: Book Volumes 3,000; Cards; Clipping Files; Exhibition Catalogs; Framed Reproductions; Manuscripts; Memorabilia; Original Art Works; Pamphlets; Periodical Subscriptions 10; Photographs; Prints; Slides
Special Subjects: Art History, Illustration, Painting-American, Prints, Sculpture, Historical Material, History of Art & Archaeology, American Western Art, Bronzes, Printmaking, Art Education, American Indian Art
Activities: Classes for adults & children; Western Art Academy; vis lectrs 2 per yr; gallery talks; tours; sales shop sells books, magazines, reproductions, prints, gifts, original art; Journey West Gallery

KINGSVILLE

M TEXAS A&M UNIVERSITY, Art Gallery, 700 University Blvd, Art Dept Kingsville, TX 78363-8203. Tel 361-593-2619, 593-2111; *Dir* Santa Barraza
Open Mon - Fri 9 AM - 4 PM; No admis fee; Estab to exhibit art work of students, as well as visitors; Average Annual Attendance: 3,000
Income: Financed by state appropriations
Exhibitions: Student Art Exhibts

LAREDO

M LAREDO CENTER FOR THE ARTS, 500 San Agustin, Laredo, TX 78040. Tel 956-725-1715; Fax 956-725-1741; Elec Mail info@laredoartcenter.org; Internet Home Page Address: www.laredoartcenter.org
Open call for hours
Collections: works by local & international artists
Activities: Workshops

LONGVIEW

M LONGVIEW MUSEUM OF FINE ART, (Longview Art Museum) 215 E Tyler St, Longview, TX 75601; PO Box 3484, Longview, TX 75606-3484. Tel 903-753-8103; Fax 903-753-8217; Internet Home Page Address: www.lmfa.org; *Dir* Renee Hawkins; *Events Coordr* Paula Davis; *Publicist* Zoe Glascock; *Admin Asst* Aimee Klein
Open Tues - Fri 10 AM - 4 PM, Sat Noon - 4 PM; No admis fee; Estab 1958 by Junior Service League for the purpose of having a contemporary art museum in the community; Circ 1000; East Gallery 15, 000 sq ft in 3 open rooms; Average Annual Attendance: 20,000; Mem: 500; $10 - $5000, $50 family; Board of Trustees monthly meetings
Income: Financed by mem & guild projects, donations & grants
Library Holdings: Book Volumes
Special Subjects: Painting-American, Photography, Prints, Sculpture, Watercolors, Ceramics, Woodcuts, Etchings & Engravings, Landscapes, Afro-American Art, Collages, Portraits, Posters, Painting-Australian
Collections: Regional Artists Collection formed by purchases from Annual Invitational Exhibitions over the past 35 years; work by contemporary Texas artists
Exhibitions: (spring) Annual Invitational Exhibit; (fall) Annual Winners Exhibit, (Apr) Annual Student Art
Publications: Exhibition catalogs
Activities: Classes for adults & children; docent training; day at museum with artist in residence for all 4th grade students; artworks creative learning center; lects open to pub, 4-6 vis lectrs per yr; talks; competitions with cash awards; individual paintings & original objects of art lent; originate traveling exhibs; mus shop sells prints, mus quality crafts & gifts, glasswork & jewelry

LUBBOCK

M CITY OF LUBBOCK, Buddy Holly Center, 1801 Crickets Ave, Lubbock, TX 79401-5128. Tel 806-775-3560; Fax 806-767-0732; Elec Mail bwitcher@mylubbock.us; Internet Home Page Address: www.buddyhollycenter.org; *Sales & Mktg* Vassandra Okoruwa; *Educ Coordr* Lisa Howe; *Asst Dir* Eddy Grigsby; *Gift Shop Mgr* David Seitz; *Cur* Jacqueline Bober
Open Tues - Fri 10 AM - 5 PM, Sat 10 AM - 5 PM, Sun 1 PM - 5 PM; Estab 1984; Fine Art Gallery; Foyer Gallery; Buddy Holly Gallery
Collections: Buddy Holly memorabilia; Contemporary art

Exhibitions: Buddy Holly; Illuminance; Celebration; crafts
Activities: Classes for adults & children; docent training; dramatic progs; lects open to pub; concerts; gallery talks; tours; sponsoring of competitions; organize traveling exhibs to mus & univ; mus shop sells books, magazines, original art, reproductions

M LOUISE HOPKINS UNDERWOOD CENTER FOR THE ARTS, 511 Ave K, Lubbock, TX 79401. Tel 806-762-8606; *Exec Dir* Karen Wiley
Open Tues-Sat 9AM-5PM
Collections: works by contemporary artists; sculpture; paintings

M TEXAS TECH UNIVERSITY, Museum of Texas Tech University, Fourth St & Indiana Ave, Lubbock, TX 79409; PO Box 43191, Lubbock, TX 79409-3191. Tel 806-742-2442; Fax 806-742-1136; Elec Mail museum.texastech@ttu.edu; Internet Home Page Address: www.museum.ttu.edu; *Assoc Dir Operations* David K Dean; *Cur History* Henry B Crawford; *Cur Anthropology* Dr Eileen Johnson; *Cur Ethnology & Textiles* Mei Wan Campbell; *Cur Natural Science Research Lab* Dr Robert Baker; *Cur Vertebrate Paleontology* Dr Sankar Chatterjee; *Coll Mgr (Sciences) & Cur of Coll (Sciences)* Richard Monk; *Coll Mgr (Anthropology)* Susan Baxevanis; *Registrar* Nicola Ladkin; *Exec Dir* Gary Edson; *Educ Prog Mgr* Dr Lee Brodie; *Exhibit Design Mgr* Denise Newsome
Open Main Building Tues - Sat 10 AM - 5 PM, Thurs 10 AM - 8:30 PM, Sun 1 - 5 PM, cl Mon; Moody Planetarium Tues - Fri, 3:30 - 7:30 PM, Sat & Sun 2 - 3:30 PM; Lubbock Lake Landmark Tues - Sat 9 AM - 5 PM, Sun 1 - 5 PM, cl Mon; No admis fee for Museum & Lubbock Lake Landmark; Moody Planetarium adults $1, student $.50, children under 5 and adults 65 & older free; Estab 1929 for pub service, research & teaching. Mus mission: collect, preserve & interpret knowledge about Texas, the Southwest & other regions as related by natural history, heritage & climate; 12 permanent galleries for art; 5 temporary galleries in Main Building, 1 gallery at Landmark; Average Annual Attendance: 150,000; Mem: 1,000; dues MTTUA $20, $40 & $60; annual meetings MTTUA in July & Nov
Income: Financed by state appropriations, Museum of Texas Tech University Assn, private donations, local, regional, national research grants
Special Subjects: Folk Art, Ceramics, Flasks & Bottles, Pottery, Drawings, Hispanic Art, Latin American Art, Painting-American, Photography, Prints, Sculpture, Watercolors, American Western Art, Bronzes, African Art, Anthropology, Archaeology, Ethnology, Pre-Columbian Art, Southwestern Art, Textiles, Costumes, Religious Art, Crafts, Woodcarvings, Etchings & Engravings, Landscapes, Portraits, Dolls, Furniture, Glass, Jade, Historical Material, Ivory, Embroidery, Laces, Leather
Collections: Archaeology; ceramics; contemporary paintings; ethnology; graphics; history; Texas contemporary artists; Diamond M Fine Art; sciences; paleontology
Exhibitions: Changing exhibitions of art, sciences, photography & history; permanent exhibitions of anthropology, archaeology & history; Paleo/Indian archaeological site, Lubbock Lake Landmark
Publications: MuseNews newsletter, quarterly; Museum Journal, annually; occasional papers, as needed; Museology, as needed
Activities: Classes for adults & children; docent training; lects open to pub, 8-9 vis lectrs per yr; concerts; gallery talks; tours; sponsoring of competitions; scholarships offered; individual paintings & original objects of art lent to other mus; exten program serves local school districts, hostels, MHMR; book traveling exhibs 8-10 per yr; originate traveling exhibs usually within Texas; two mus shops sell books, magazines, original art, reproductions, prints & slides

L **School of Art Visual Resource Center,** Box 2081, Texas Tech University School of Art Visual Resource Center Lubbock, TX 79408-2081. Tel 806-742-2887 exten 239; Fax 806-742-1971; Elec Mail ybprw@ttacs.ttu.edu; Internet Home Page Address: www.art.ttu.edu/artdept/artdepinfo/vrc/; *Visual Resource Cur* Philip Worrell; *Sr Office Asst* Elissa Steinert
Open Mon - Thurs 7:30 AM - 5:00 PM, Fri 8 AM - 5 PM, summer hours vary; Reference & teaching library
Income: $10,000 (financed by state legislature appropriation, private donations & grants)
Library Holdings: Book Volumes 4000; Compact Disks; DVDs; Other Holdings CD-Roms; Periodical Subscriptions 50; Slides 110,000; Video Tapes 190
Special Subjects: Art History, Calligraphy, Advertising Design, Art Education, Asian Art, American Indian Art, Aesthetics, Antiquities-Oriental, Antiquities-Persian, Antiquities-Assyrian, Antiquities-Byzantine, Antiquities-Egyptian, Antiquities-Etruscan, Antiquities-Greek, Antiquities-Roman

LUFKIN

A MUSEUM OF EAST TEXAS, 503 N Second St, Lufkin, TX 75901. Tel 409-639-4434; Fax 936-639-4435; Elec Mail jmcdonald@metlufkin.org; *Exec Dir* J P McDonald; *Admin Asst* Claudine Lovejoy; *Cur Coll* Kyley Cantwell; *Cur Educ* Ann N Reyes
Open Tues - Fri 10 AM - 5 PM, Sat - Sun 1 - 5 PM, cl Independence Day, Thanksgiving & Christmas; No admis fee; Estab 1975 by the Lufkin Service League to bring the fine arts to East Texas & to cultivate an interest in regional history; Average Annual Attendance: 12,000; Mem: 500; dues President's Circle $1000, patron $500, sustainer $250, sponsor $150, contributor $100, family $50, individual $25
Income: financed by mem & grants
Exhibitions: East Texas Art; Exhib change every 4 months
Publications: Bi-monthly newsletter
Activities: Classes for adults & children; docent training; trips; lect open to public; gallery talks; tours; competitions with awards; traveling trunks; mus shop sells books, prints & various items

MARFA

M CHINATI FOUNDATION, One Cavalry Row, Marfa, TX 79843; PO Box 1135, Marfa, TX 79843-1135. Tel 432-729-4362; Fax 432-729-4597; Elec Mail information@chinati.org; Internet Home Page Address: www.chinati.org; *Dir* Thomas Kellein, PhD; *Pres* Arlene Dayton
Open Wed - Sun first 1/2 of tour 10 AM, 2nd 1/2 of tour 2 PM; Admis adults $10, seniors & students $5, members free; Estab 1986; Non profit pub foundation,

permanent installations by limited number of artists; Average Annual Attendance: 10,000; Mem: 1,200
Income: financed by mem, grants & donations
Library Holdings: Cards; Exhibition Catalogs; Slides
Special Subjects: Architecture, Sculpture
Collections: Carl Andre Collection of Poems; John Chamberlain Collection: 23 sculptures; Donald Judd Collection: 100 mill aluminum sculptures & 15 concrete outdoor works; Ilya Kabakov Collection: mixed media installation; Claes Oldenburg Collection: aluminum/fiberglass outdoor work; Dan Flavin works in fluorescent light
Exhibitions: Permanent installation: six buildings of work in fluorescent light by Dan Flavin
Publications: Art in the Landscape, 1997; Chinati Foundation Newsletter, annual
Activities: Classes for children; docent training; artist residencies; intern training; lect open to public, 7 per biennial symposium, tours; sales shop sells books; prints; reproductions; t-shirts & caps

MARSHALL

M **HARRISON COUNTY HISTORICAL MUSEUM,** 707 N Washington, Marshall, TX 75670; PO Box 1987, Marshall, TX 75671-1987. Tel 903-938-2680; Fax 903-927-2534; Elec Mail museum@shreve.net; Internet Home Page Address: www.cets.sfasu.edu/Harrison/; *Pres* Alex Liebling; *CEO* Carrol Fletcher; *Mus Shop Mgr* Gwen Nolan Warren
Open Tues - Sat 10 AM - 4 PM, cl Sun & Mon; Admis adults $1; Gallery is housed in Ginocchio Hotel, built in 1896; Average Annual Attendance: 11,000; Mem: 375; dues family $35, individual $25, students $10
Income: Financed by mem, donations, admis & endowment
Special Subjects: Ceramics, Historical Material
Collections: Cut & Pressed Glass; 400 BC - 1977 Ceramics; Hand-painted China; Historical Material; Religious Artifacts; etchings; jewelry; paintings; porcelains; portraits; Pioneer implements; transportation
Publications: Historical Newsletter, quarterly
Activities: Guided tours; genealogical records researched; competitions with awards

M **MICHELSON MUSEUM OF ART,** 216 N Bolivar, Marshall, TX 75670; PO Box 8290, Marshall, TX 75671-8290. Tel 903-935-9480; Fax 903-935-1974; Elec Mail info@michelsonmuseum.org; Internet Home Page Address: www.michelsonmuseum.org; *Educ Dir* Bonnie Spangler; *Dir* Susan Spears; *VPres* Steve Lewis
Open Tues - Fri 10 AM - 4 PM, Sat 1 - 4 PM, cl holidays; No admis fee; Estab 1985 to exhibit works of Leo Michelson & special exhibits; Three galleries, one exhibits permanent collection of works by Leo Michelson & other American artists; Average Annual Attendance: 8,000; Mem: 400; dues $35 & up
Income: $360,000 (financed by mem, city & state appropriations)
Library Holdings: Book Volumes; Prints
Special Subjects: Drawings, Painting-American, Prints, Watercolors, African Art, Woodcuts, Eskimo Art, Painting-French, Painting-German, Painting-Russian
Exhibitions: Leo Michelson (1887 - 1978 Russian/American); Selections from the permanent collection
Activities: Classes for adults & children; docent training; lects open to pub; vis lectrs 1 per yr; gallery talks; tours; concerts; book traveling exhibs 4 per yr; mus shop sells books, original art, reproductions & prints

MCALLEN

M **INTERNATIONAL MUSEUM OF ART & SCIENCE,** 1900 Nolana, McAllen, TX 78504. Tel 956-682-1564; Fax 956-686-1813; Elec Mail infor@imasonline.org; Internet Home Page Address: www.mcallenmuseum.org; *Exec Dir* Joseph Bravo; *Cur* Maria Elena Macias
Open Tues, Wed, Fri & Sat 9 AM - 5 PM, Thurs 9 AM - 8 PM, Sun 1 PM - 5 PM; Admis adults $7, seniors & students $5, children 4-12 $4, children 3 & under free; Estab 1967; Open to staff, volunteers & researchers for reference only; Average Annual Attendance: 80,000; Mem: Mem start at $42
Special Subjects: Folk Art, Art Education, Art History, Woodcuts, Painting-American, Photography, Prints, Watercolors, Textiles, Woodcarvings, Painting-European
Collections: Local, state & regional artists; Mexican folk art; Mexican Prints; US & European paintings
Exhibitions: Abstract Works from the MIM Collection; Christmas Tree Forest; Nightscapes; Arte Rio Grande, Francis Valesco
Publications: Bulletins & brochures periodically; Newsletter, monthly
Activities: Classes for adults & children; lects open to pub, gallery talks; tours; mus shop sells books, original art, prints

MIAMI

M **ROBERTS COUNTY MUSEUM,** PO Box 306, Miami, TX 79059-0306; 120 E Commercial St, Miami, TX 79059. Tel 806-868-3291; Fax 806-868-3381; Elec Mail robertscomuseum@amaonline.com; Internet Home Page Address: www.robertscountymuseum.org; *Dir* Emma Bowers; *Exec Dir* Cecil Gill
Open Tues - Fri 10 AM - 5 PM, weekends by appointment, cl Mon & holidays; No admis fee; Estab 1979; Average Annual Attendance: 3,000
Library Holdings: Book Volumes; Maps; Original Art Works; Original Documents; Other Holdings; Pamphlets; Periodical Subscriptions; Photographs; Prints; Records
Special Subjects: American Indian Art, Anthropology, Archaeology, Furniture
Collections: Locke Collection of Indian artifacts; Mead Collection of mammoth bones & fossils; Historical Museum of early Miami; Native American Art Collection; Miami Mammoth Kill Site
Exhibitions: Annual Nat Cow-Calling Contest with Art Show first Sat in June
Activities: Classes for children; quilting demonstrations daily; lects open to pub; tours; mus shop sells books, T-shirts, jewelry & keychains, traveling exhibs

MIDLAND

M **MUSEUM OF THE SOUTHWEST,** 1705 W Missouri, Midland, TX 79701-6516. Tel 432-683-2882; Fax 432-684-9151; Elec Mail info@museumsw.org; Internet Home Page Address: www.museumsw.org; *Exec Dir* Brian Lee Whisenhunt
Open Tues - Sat 10 AM - 5 PM, Sun 2 - 5 PM, cl Mon; No admis fee; $3 Children's Mus & $3 planetarium, additional cost for shows; Incorporated 1965 as an art & history mus with a separate planetarium providing various science exhibits; children's mus; Six galleries exhibiting traveling exhibs & permanent colls; Average Annual Attendance: 100,000; Mem: 800; dues $40-$1200; board meeting third Wed monthly
Income: Financed by mem, contributions & grants
Special Subjects: Historical Material, Landscapes, Ceramics, American Western Art, Photography, Pottery, Pre-Columbian Art, Painting-American, Prints, Textiles, Bronzes, Sculpture, Drawings, Watercolors, American Indian Art, Archaeology, Southwestern Art, Etchings & Engravings
Collections: Art & archaeological materials of the Southwest; Indian art coll; permanent art coll
Publications: Annual Report; Intersections, twice yearly
Activities: Classes for adults & children; docent training; arts & crafts classes; video showings; lects open to pub & for members only, 204 vis lectrs per yr; concerts; gallery talks; tours; individual paintings lent to other mus; book traveling exhibs 6-8 per yr; mus shop sells books, jewelry, gifts & original clothing

NACOGDOCHES

M **STEPHEN F AUSTIN STATE UNIVERSITY,** SFA Galleries, 208 Griffith Fine Arts Bldg, Stephen F Austin State University Nacogdoches, TX 75962. Tel 936-468-1131; Fax 936-468-2938; Elec Mail baileysl@sfasu.edu; *Dir* Shannon Bailey
Open Tues - Sun 12:30 - 5 PM; No admis fee; Estab as a teaching gallery & to bring in art from outside this area for our students & the East Texas community; One room approx 56 x 22 ft, plus storage; Average Annual Attendance: 5,000
Income: Financed by state educ funds & private contributions
Activities: Classes for children; docent training; workshops; lect open to public; gallery talks; tours; museum trips; competitions with awards

ODESSA

M **ELLEN NOEL ART MUSEUM OF THE PERMIAN BASIN,** 4909 E University Blvd, Odessa, TX 79762-8144. Tel 432-550-9696; Fax 432-550-9226; Internet Home Page Address: www.noelartmuseum.org; *Collection Mgr* Letha Hooper; *Dir* George Jacob; *Develop Officer* Judith Motyka; *Publicity* Jessica Smith; *Admin* Stacy Benavides; *Security/Facilities Technician* Willie Sturgeon; *Cur Educ* Doylene Land; *Educ Coordr* Annie Stanley; *Vis Servs Coordr* Daniel Zies
Open Tues - Sat 10 AM - 5 PM, Sun 2 - 5 PM, cl Mon; No admis fee; Estab 1985 to increase public awareness & appreciation of art through exposure & education; Accessible galleries & sculpture garden; Average Annual Attendance: 20,000; Mem: 475; dues $30 & up; annual meeting in May
Income: $210,000 (financed by mem, grants, donations & fund raisers)
Library Holdings: Book Volumes; Clipping Files; Exhibition Catalogs; Original Documents; Pamphlets; Periodical Subscriptions; Prints; Records
Special Subjects: Drawings, Hispanic Art, Mexican Art, Photography, Prints, Sculpture, Watercolors, American Western Art, Bronzes, Southwestern Art, Religious Art, Ceramics, Folk Art, Woodcarvings, Etchings & Engravings, Landscapes, Collages, Portraits, Posters, Jewelry, Porcelain, Silver, Juvenile Art, Renaissance Art, Embroidery
Collections: Permanent collection of American art since 1860
Exhibitions: Rotating exhibitions, 20 per yr
Activities: Classes for adults & children; workshops; demonstrations; videos; community art days; lects open to pub, lects for mems; gallery talks; tours; schols offered; exten dept; lending collection, contains paintings; internships, related course at Univ of Texas of the Permian Basin; mus shop sells art related books, magazines, original art, Smithsonian merchandise, children's art activities

M **PRESIDENTIAL MUSEUM & LEADERSHIP LIBRARY,** 4919 E University Blvd, Odessa, TX 79762-8144. Tel 432-363-7737; Elec Mail president.museum@att.net; Internet Home Page Address: www.thepresidentialmuseum.com; *Adminr* Charles Cotten; *Assoc Adminr* Gail Barnes
Open Tues - Sat 10 AM - 5 PM; Donations accepted; Estab 1965 & dedicated to the office of the Pres, electoral process & pub serv; Average Annual Attendance: 5,000
Income: Financed by grants and donations
Library Holdings: Audio Tapes; Book Volumes 5,000; Cassettes; Clipping Files; Exhibition Catalogs; Memorabilia; Pamphlets; Periodical Subscriptions 15; Records; Reproductions; Sculpture; Slides; Video Tapes
Special Subjects: Portraits, Dolls
Collections: Campaign memorabilia; original signatures; portraits; First lady inaugural gowns coll
Exhibitions: Long-term exhibitions on the presidency & first ladies; special temporary exhibitions
Activities: Present a brief history of the United States as seen through the presidency

ORANGE

M **NELDA C & H J LUTCHER STARK FOUNDATION,** Stark Museum of Art, 712 Green Ave, Orange, TX 77630-5721. Tel 409-886-2787; Fax 409-883-6361; Elec Mail info@starkmuseum.org; Internet Home Page Address: www.starkmuseum.org; *Pres & CEO Stark Foundation* Walter Riedel; *Coll Mgr* Terri Fox; *Chief Security Officer* Tom Parks; *Librn* Jenniffer Hudson-Connors; *Dir Stark Mus of Art* Sarah E Boehme PhD; *Chief Educ* Elena Ivanova, Ph.D; *Educ Studio & Family Progs* Amelia Wiggins; *Registrar* Allison Evans; *Admin Asst* Alicia Benitez-Booker
Open Tues - Sat 9 AM - 5 PM; Estab 1978 to preserve & display the Stark collection of art & promote interests in subjects relative to the same through

exhibitions, publications & educational programs; Five galleries & lobby, 18,000 sq ft of total exhibition area; Average Annual Attendance: 14,000
Income: Financed by endowment
Library Holdings: Auction Catalogs; Audio Tapes; Book Volumes; CD-ROMs; Clipping Files; DVDs; Exhibition Catalogs; Kodachrome Transparencies; Manuscripts; Original Art Works; Original Documents; Periodical Subscriptions; Photographs; Prints; Sculpture; Video Tapes
Special Subjects: Drawings, Painting-American, Prints, American Indian Art, American Western Art, Bronzes, Southwestern Art, Etchings & Engravings, Decorative Arts, Manuscripts, Furniture, Glass, Porcelain, Carpets & Rugs, Restorations
Collections: Art relating to American West 1830-1965, special emphasis on artist explorers, illustrators & New Mexico artists; Native American Art (Plains, Southwest Northwest Coast, decorative arts, glass); rare books & manuscripts
Publications: Exhibition catalogs; Stark Museum of Art: A Guide to the Galleries, Orange, TX, David C. Hunt; Stark Foundation 1998, Nelda C & HJ Lutcher; Stark Museum of Art: Taos Portfolio, Orange, TX, David C Hunt; Stark Foundation 2001, Nelda C & HJ Lutcher
Activities: Classes for adults & children; dramatic progs; docent training; tours for school children and adults; lect open to public; gallery talks; tours; 1-2 book traveling exhibs per yr; mus shop sells books, prints & Christmas ornaments based on colls

PANHANDLE

M   **CARSON COUNTY SQUARE HOUSE MUSEUM,** Fifth & Elsie Sts, PO Box 276 Panhandle, TX 79068; PO Box 276, Panhandle, TX 79068-0276. Tel 806-537-3524; Fax 806-537-5628; Elec Mail shm@squarehousemuseum.org; Internet Home Page Address: www.squarehousemuseum.org; *Interim Dir* Dr Bill Green; *Admin Asst & Mus Store Mgr* Janie Plumlee; *Bus Mgr* Shirlyn Grantham
Open Mon - Sat 9 AM - 5 PM, Sun 1 - 5 PM, cl Thanksgiving, Christmas Eve, Christmas, New Years & Easter; No admis fee; Estab 1965 as a general mus with art galleries, area & State & National historical displays; Wildlife building & displays; Historic house, listed in National Register of Historic Places; Two enclosed security controlled art galleries, an educ center & art gallery; Average Annual Attendance: 30,000
Income: Financed by endowments, income & pub contributions
Special Subjects: Drawings, Painting-American, Photography, Prints, American Indian Art, Bronzes, Anthropology, Archaeology, Ethnology, Costumes, Crafts, Folk Art, Primitive art, Etchings & Engravings, Decorative Arts, Manuscripts, Dolls, Furniture, Carpets & Rugs, Historical Material, Maps, Dioramas, Period Rooms, Laces, Leather
Collections: Paintings of area pioneers by Marlin Adams; sculpture & bronze by Jim Thomas, Grant Speed & Keith Christi; Kenneth Wyatt paintings; Ben Carlton Mead & Harold Bugbee paintings; contemporary Native American art, Native American beadwork, Acoma pottery; costumes; antiques; Native American Art
Publications: A Time To Purpose, county history book; Land of Coronado, coloring book; The Square House Cook Book; Voices of the Square House, poems
Activities: Classes for adults & children; dramatic progs; docent training; lects open to pub, 1 vis lectrs per yr; concerts; gallery talks; tours; mus shop sells books, reproductions, prints & mus related gift items

PARIS

M   **HAYDEN MUSEUM OF AMERICAN ART,** 930 Cardinal Lane, Paris, TX 75460. Tel 903-785-1925; Fax 903-784-7631; *Dir & Pres* William Hayden, MD
Open by appointment; No admis fee; Average Annual Attendance: 2,500
Library Holdings: Book Volumes
Collections: paintings; decorative arts; prints; photographs; sculpture; American art history
Activities: Seminars; lect

ROUND TOP

M   **JAMES DICK FOUNDATION,** Festival - Institute, PO Box 89, 248 Jaster Rd Round Top, TX 78954-0089. Tel 979-249-3129; Fax 979-249-5078; Elec Mail lamarl@festivalhill.org; Internet Home Page Address: www.festivahill.org; *Founder & Dir* James Dick; *Managing Dir* Richard R Royall; *Dir Library & Mus* Lamar Lentz
Open by appointment; Tours $5, summer concerts $20 per person, chamber music $10 per person; Estab 1971 as a center for music, the arts & humanities; Guion Room, Oxehufwud Room, Historic House Collection. Maintains reference library; Average Annual Attendance: 40,000-50,000
Income: Financed through ticket sales & donations
Library Holdings: Auction Catalogs; Book Volumes; Clipping Files; Compact Disks; DVDs; Exhibition Catalogs; Manuscripts; Memorabilia; Motion Pictures; Original Art Works; Photographs; Prints; Records; Reels
Special Subjects: History of Art & Archaeology, Interior Design, Landscape Architecture, Art History, Furniture, Architecture, Graphics, Painting-American, Photography, American Western Art, Southwestern Art, Costumes, Ceramics, Crafts, Folk Art, Landscapes, Decorative Arts, Manuscripts, Furniture, Glass, Jewelry, Porcelain, Carpets & Rugs, Historical Material, Maps, Coins & Medals, Period Rooms, Laces, Pewter, Painting-Russian, Painting-Scandinavian
Collections: British Country Houses, Decorative Arts, Historic House Collection, Music Instruments, Painting, Swedish Decorative Arts - 16th century to present, Texas History, 20th-century photography
Activities: Classes for students; docent training; lect open to public; 16 vis lectrs per yr; concerts; gallery talks; tours; scholarships offered to music students; sales shop

SAN ANGELO

M   **ANGELO STATE UNIVERSITY,** Houston Harte University Center, PO Box 11027, San Angelo, TX 76909-0001. Tel 915-942-2062; Fax 915-942-2354; *Dir Prog* Rick E Greig
Open Mon - Fri 8 AM - 10:30 PM, Sat 9 AM - 10:30 PM, cl Sun; No admis fee; Estab 1970 to provide entertainment & informal educ for the students, faculty & staff; Gallery is maintained

Income: $3000 (financed by city & state appropriations)
Collections: Wax drawings done by Guy Rowe for illustration of the book In Our Image by Houston Harte
Exhibitions: Historical artifacts; modern drawings; photography; pottery; weaving; children, students and faculty exhibitions
Activities: Lects open to public, 2 vis lectrs per yr; gallery talks; tours; concerts; dramatic progs; competitions

M   **SAN ANGELO ART CLUB,** Helen King Kendall Memorial Art Gallery, 119 W First St, San Angelo, TX 76903. Tel 915-653-4405; *Pres* Mary Taylor; *1st VPres* Mary Kollmeyer; *Secy* Sue Meacham; *Treas* Patty Towler
Open Wed 9 AM - 2 PM, Sat & Sun 1 - 4 PM; No admis fee; Club estab 1928 & gallery estab 1948 to promote the visual fine arts in San Angelo; Average Annual Attendance: 1,500; Mem: 90; dues $30; meeting first Mon each month
Income: $8,000 (financed by Memorial Endowment Fund)
Collections: Paintings by George Biddle, Gladys Rockmore Davis, Xavier Gonzales, Iver Rose & Frederick Waugh, Hazel Janick; Karl Albert, Joseph Sharp, Willard Metcalf, Robert Woods, Dwight Holmes
Exhibitions: Monthly exhibits from area artists; The Gallery supports the local art community with exhibs including an annual HS art show and an annual exhibit which supports the Concho Valley Assn for the blind
Publications: Splashes, monthly newsletter
Activities: Classes for adults & children & dramatic progs; tours; competitions with awards; individual paintings & original objects of art lent to libraries, churches & bus

M   **SAN ANGELO MUSEUM OF FINE ARTS,** One Love St, San Angelo, TX 76903. Tel 325-653-3333; Fax 325-658-6800; Elec Mail museum@samfa.org; Internet Home Page Address: www.samfa.org; *Pres* Debbie Cross; *VPres* Jeff Curry; *Dir* Howard J Taylor; *Coll Mgr* Laura Romer Huckaby; *Exec* Gracie Fernandez; *Preparator* John Mattson; *Asst Educ* Rebekah Coleman; *Gift Shop Mgr* Betty Connally; *Maintenance Chief/Security* Joel Quintella
Open Tues - Sat 10 AM - 4 PM, Thurs until 6 PM & Fri until 9 PM, Sun 1 - 4 PM, cl Mon & major holidays; Admis adults $2, sr citizens $1, members, local students, military & children & adults with children free; Estab 1981 to provide quality visual arts exhibits & stimulating programs for educational & cultural growth; 30,000 sq ft bldg designed by architect Malcolm Holzman & contains three gallery spaces; Average Annual Attendance: 65,000; Mem: Dues $10 and up
Income: $600,000 (financed by endowment, sales, admis & grants
Library Holdings: Auction Catalogs; Audio Tapes; Book Volumes; CD-ROMs; Clipping Files; Compact Disks; DVDs; Exhibition Catalogs; Kodachrome Transparencies; Slides; Video Tapes
Special Subjects: Ceramics, Mexican Art
Collections: Texas art (1942-present); American crafts (1945-present), particularly ceramics; American paintings & sculpture of all eras; Mexican & Mexican-American art of all eras; Selected European, Oriental & African art; Spanish Colonial Art
Exhibitions: (Biennial) San Angelo National Ceramic Competition
Publications: Exhibit catalogs
Activities: Classes for adults & children; outreach progs; docent training; concerts; gallery talks; tours; lects open to pub, 15 vis lectrs per yr; sponsoring competitions with awards; National Museum Service Award; exten dept serves 14 counties in W Texas; book traveling exhibs, 2 - 3 per yr; originate traveling exhibs to mus; mus shop sells books, magazines, original art, reproductions, prints, educational toys, paper goods, jewelry & ceramics & other gift items

SAN ANTONIO

M   **BLUE STAR CONTEMPORARY ART CENTER,** (Contemporary Art for San Antonio Blue Star Art Space) 116 Blue Star, San Antonio, TX 78204-1713. Tel 210-227-6960; Fax 210-229-9412; Elec Mail giselle@bluestarart.org; Internet Home Page Address: www.bluestarart.org; *Pres/Exec Dir* Bill FitzGibbons; *Exhib & Prog Mgr* Zinnia Salcedo; *Gal Liaison* Krisanne Frost; *IT Specialist* Kyle Olson; *Studio Mgr & Art Instr* Alex Rubio; *Exec Asst & Office Mgr* Giselle Reinhardt-Gillis; *Asst Prep* Joseph Duarte; *Dir Develop* Lara Luce
Open Tues - Sat Noon - 6 PM, Thurs Noon - 8 PM; No admis fee, donations accepted; Estab 1986 to advance contemporary art by presenting culturally diverse exhibitions and programs to broaden San Antonio's local contemporary art experience by nurturing and showcasing local talent and participating in a diverse exchange on regional, nat & international levels; 13,000 sq ft warehouse; Average Annual Attendance: 125,000; Mem: 65; Society de Cien $1,000, Blue Star contemporaries $250, family contemporaries $350, Blue Star $40, family Blue Star $60, artist $25, family artist $35
Income: Financed by an oper endowment, mem, community educational prog & activities, Board dues, city & state grants, grants from pub & private foundations & trusts
Collections: Contemporary multimedia painting, prints, sculpture, photographs
Publications: BS, Blue Star mem quarterly newsletter; small exhib pamphlets & catalogues
Activities: Educ prog for adults & school children; docent training; lects open to pub; 4-5 vis lectrs per yr; gallery talks; tours; concerts; awards for supporting SA Express-News Literacy Prog; consistently recognized by local journals at best contemp art gallery in town; schols offered; satellite exhib sites; senior art classes at satellite & other venues; book traveling exhibs 1-2 per yr to local & regional art & educ organizations; mus shop sells books, original art, reproductions, prints, T-shirts, posters; on-line purchasing

L   **CENTRAL LIBRARY,** Dept of Fine Arts, 600 Soledad St, San Antonio, TX 78205-1208. Tel 210-207-2500; Fax 210-207-2552; *Asst Dir* Nancy Gandara; *Dept Head* Mary A Wright; *Art Coll Develop Specialist* Beth Shorlemer; *Dir* Laura Isenstein
Open Mon - Fri 9 AM - 9 PM, Sat 9 AM - 5 PM, Sun 11 AM - 5 PM; Estab to provide art reference & lending materials to the residents of Bexar County; Art gallery is maintained. Also serves as a major resource center to regional libraries in South Texas
Income: Financed by city, state & federal appropriation

Purchases: $250,000
Library Holdings: Audio Tapes; Cassettes; Clipping Files; Compact Disks; Exhibition Catalogs; Fiche; Filmstrips; Memorabilia; Motion Pictures; Pamphlets; Photographs; Records; Reels; Reproductions; Video Tapes
Exhibitions: Regular Exhibition of local & National artists
Activities: Classes for children; dramatic progs; lects open to pub, 2 vis lectrs per yr; concerts; gallery talks; tours; competitions with awards; exten dept; lending collection contains 320,000 books, 400 video cassettes, 10,000 audio cassettes, 15,000 motion pictures; book traveling exhibs

A **CENTRO CULTURAL AZTLAN,** 1800 Fredericksburg Rd, Deco Bldg, Ste 103 San Antonio, TX 78201. Tel 210-432-1896; Fax 210-432-1983; Elec Mail ccaztlan@swbell.net; Internet Home Page Address: www.centroculturalaztlan.org; *Exec Dir* Malena Gonzalez-Cid; *Arts Prog Dir* Ruth M. Guajardo
Open Mon - Fri 9 AM - 5 PM; No admis fee; Estab 1977 to support & strengthen Chicano/Latino culture & identity; Expression Fine Art Gallery mounts 10 art exhibits per year to showcase visual artists; Average Annual Attendance: 62,000
Special Subjects: Metalwork, Folk Art, Ceramics, Hispanic Art, Jewelry
Exhibitions: Annual Lowrider Car Exhibition, held annually 1st Sun in Apr
Publications: ViAztlan, quarterly journal of contemporary arts & letters
Activities: Classes for children; gallery talks; guest lectr; reading recitals; mus shop sells original art, prints

M **CITY OF SAN ANTONIO,** (Spanish Governor's Palace) 105 Plaza de Armas, San Antonio, TX 78205-2412. Tel 210-224-0601; Fax 210-223-5562; Elec Mail charlotte.boord@sanantonio.gov; Internet Home Page Address: www.spanishgovernorspalace.org; *Mus Supv* Charlotte Boord
Open Tues - Sat 9 AM - 5 PM, Sun 10 AM - 5 PM; Admis adults $4, children under 14 $2, military & seniors $3; Estab 1749; Historic site with period furnishings; Average Annual Attendance: 25,000
Income: $65,000 (financed by city appropriation)
Special Subjects: Historical Material, Architecture, Maps, Hispanic Art, Textiles, Religious Art, Folk Art, Pottery, Furniture, Restorations, Period Rooms
Collections: Spanish-colonial furnishings, paintings, earthenware, brass & copper pieces from 16th - 17th century
Publications: Spanish Governor's Palace brochure
Activities: Mus shop sells notecards, key chains, histories, courtyard sketches, postcards

A **COPPINI ACADEMY OF FINE ARTS,** Elizabeth di Barbieri, 115 Melrose Pl, San Antonio, TX 78212-1924. Tel 210-824-8502; Elec Mail webmaster@coppini.us; Internet Home Page Address: www.coppini-us; *Pres* Janice Yow
Open by appointment; No admis fee; Estab 1945 to promote classic & representational art; to encourage worthy accomplishment in the field of art & to serve as a means of public exhibition for the work of active members & guests; Hosted & mem exhibits; Average Annual Attendance: 1,000; Mem: dues per annum; ann meeting third Sun of Nov
Income: Membership & trust
Collections: Oil paintings by Rolla Taylor; sculpture & paintings by Waldine Tauch & Pompeo Coppini
Exhibitions: Annual May Garden Show. Monthly changing exhibits in upper gallery by members; (exhibs listed on website)
Publications: Coppini News Bulletin, monthly newsletter distributed to members
Activities: Classes for adults & children; lects open to pub, 6 vis lectrs per yr; gallery talks; tours; competitions; Artist of the Year award; scholarships offered; individual paintings & original objects of art lent; originate traveling exhibs; mus shop sell reproductions

L **Library,** 115 Melrose Pl, San Antonio, TX 78212. Tel 210-824-8502; Elec Mail coppini1@sbcglobal.net; Internet Home Page Address: www.coppiniacademy.org; *Pres* Dr Hal Martin; *1st VPres* Donna Bland; *Secy* Sussanne Clark; *Treas* Ron Watkins; *Art Dir* Louis Mar
Estab 1945 to promote classical art; Circ 1500; Monthly exhibits of membership & museum coll; Average Annual Attendance: 1,000; Mem: dues $35; monthly meeting 3rd Sun
Income: Trust & fund raising
Library Holdings: Book Volumes 200; Clipping Files; Original Art Works; Periodical Subscriptions 50; Photographs; Sculpture; Slides; Video Tapes
Special Subjects: Sculpture
Activities: Classes for adults & children; lects open to pub; Awards - Artist of the Year; ann Schols $3000, HS Sr Art Major, 1 year

A **GUADALUPE CULTURAL ARTS CENTER,** 1300 Guadalupe St, San Antonio, TX 78207-5514. Tel 210-271-3151; Internet Home Page Address: www.guadalupeculturalarts.org; *Exec Dir* Patty Ortiz; *Develop Dir* Brad Carlin; *Mktg & Pub Rels Dir* Lorraine Pulido; *Exhibs Coordr* Chris Davila
Open 9 AM - 5 PM & spec events as scheduled; Admis fee varies; Estab 1979, non-profit, multi-disciplinary arts organization dedicated to the development, preservation & promotion of Latino arts & to facilitating a deeper understanding & appreciation of Chicano/Latino & Native American cultures; Center manages the beautifully restored, historic Guadalupe Theatre, a 410 seat, handicapped accessible, multi-purpose facility that houses the Theater Gallery, a large auditorium, a proscenium stage & equipment for theatrical & cinematic presentations; maintains Guadalupe Gallery & Cesar Chavez Project Space; Average Annual Attendance: 150,000
Income: $1,700,000
Exhibitions: Annual Tejano Conjunto Festival; Annual San Antonio Inter-Americas Bookfair; Annual Juried Women's Art Exhibit; Annual Student Exhibit; Hecho a Mano/Made by Hand (annual fine arts & crafts market)
Activities: Visual arts prog; classes & workshops; creative dramatics classes; dance prog; media prog; classes for adults & children; 4-6 vis lectrs per yr; fels & schols available; sales shop

M **MCNAY ART MUSEUM,** 6000 N New Braunfels Ave, San Antonio, TX 78209-4618. Tel 210-805-1727; Elec Mail library@mcnayart.org; Internet Home Page Address: www.mcnayart.org; *Pres* J R Hurd; *Dir* William J Chiego; *Cur Educ* Rose M Glennon; *Cur Tobin Theatre Coll & Library* Jody Blake; *Coll Mgr* Heather Lammers; *Librn* Ann Jones; *Dir Develop* Colleen M Kelly; *Museum Store Mgr* Janet D Goddard; *Assoc Cur Prints & Drawings* Lyle Williams; *Pub Rels* Daniela Oliver; *Chief Cur & Cur Art after 1945* Rene Paul Barilleaux
Open Tues -& Wed 10 AM - 4 PM, Thurs 10 AM - 9 PM, Sat 10 AM - 5 PM, Sun Noon - 5 PM, cl Mon, Jan 1, July 4, Thanksgiving & Christmas; Admis adults $8, students with ID, seniors 65 & over, & active military $5, children 12 & under & mems free; extra admis during special exhibs; Estab 1954 for the encouragement & development of modern art; 30,000 vol art history reference library; Robert L B Tobin Theatre Arts Library; 23 acres of gardens; 300-seat auditorium; McNay Mus Store; handicap accessibility, 200 seat lect hall, 45,000 sq ft new exhib hall, Jane & Arthur Stieren Ctr for Exhibs; Average Annual Attendance: 125,000; Mem: Dues assoc $1,500, patron $750, sustaining $500, contributing $250, supporting $150, family/dual $75, individual $45
Income: Financed by endowment, mem & private gifts
Special Subjects: American Indian Art, Decorative Arts, Graphics, Painting-American, Sculpture, Painting-European, Medieval Art
Collections: Oppenheimer Collection of late medieval & early Renaissance sculpture & paintings; Tobin Theatre Arts Collection related to opera, ballet & musical stage
Publications: Annual report; exhibition catalogues & brochures; Impressions, quarterly newsletter
Activities: Teen workshops; family activities; teacher resources; docent training; lects open to pub, 8 vis lectrs per yr; concerts; gallery talks; tours; individual paintings & original objects of art lent to other mus; book traveling exhibs 2 per yr; originates traveling exhibs; mus shop sells books & original art

L **McNay Art Museum Library & Archives,** 6000 N New Braunfels St, San Antonio, TX 78209; PO Box 6069, San Antonio, TX 78209. Tel 210-824-5368, 805-1727; Fax 210-805-1760; Elec Mail info@mcnayart.ort; Internet Home Page Address: www.mcnayart.org; *Librn* Ann Jones
Open to the pub Tues - Fri 10 AM - 4 PM, Thurs until 9 PM, Sat 10 AM - 5 PM, Sun noon - 5 PM; Admis adults $8, students with ID, seniors & active military $5, mems & children 12 & under free; Estab 1954 as an adjunct to the mus; Circ non-circulating
Income: Financed by endowment & gifts
Library Holdings: Auction Catalogs; Book Volumes 30,000; CD-ROMs; Clipping Files; Compact Disks; DVDs; Exhibition Catalogs; Fiche; Original Documents; Other Holdings Vertical Files: 27,000; Pamphlets; Periodical Subscriptions; Photographs; Records; Video Tapes
Special Subjects: Art History, Collages, Decorative Arts, Photography, Drawings, Etchings & Engravings, Graphic Arts, Painting-French, Painting-German, Painting-Russian, Prints, Sculpture, Painting-European, Stage Design, Watercolors, Latin American Art, Theatre Arts, Printmaking, Mexican Art, Southwestern Art, Costume Design & Constr, Glass, Handicrafts, Oriental Art, Woodcuts
Collections: Monographs; museum publications; magazines & periodicals; indexes; catalogues raisonnes; Rare Book Collection; Archives incl: admin records, McNay publications, catalogs of visiting exhibs, images, papers & records of Marion Koogler McNay, papers & records of museum affiliated persons & organizations

A **SAN ANTONIO ART LEAGUE,** San Antonio Art League Museum, 130 King Williams St, San Antonio, TX 78204. Tel 210-223-1140; Fax 210-223-2826; Elec Mail saalm@idworld.net; Internet Home Page Address: www.saalm.org; *Pres* Nancy M Bacon
Open Tues - Sat Noon - 6 PM; No admis fee; Estab 1912 as a pub art gallery for San Antonio & for the promotion of a knowledge & interest in art by means of exhibitions; 4 rooms & large hall capable of hanging 150 paintings; Mem: 820; dues $15-$500; meetings monthly Oct - May
Income: Financed by mem & fundraising projects
Special Subjects: Prints, Sculpture, Crafts
Collections: Davis Collection, 1920 American Art; focus on San Antonio & Texas artist
Exhibitions: Rotating exhibits
Publications: Exhibition catalogs; monthly calendar of events
Activities: Educ dept; lects open to public, 3 vis lectrs per year; gallery talks; tours; paintings & original art objects lent

L **Library,** 130 King Williams St, San Antonio, TX 78204. Tel 210-223-1140; Elec Mail saalm@idworld.net; Internet Home Page Address: www.saalm.org; *Pres* Louise Cantwell
Open Tues - Sat 12 PM - 6 PM; For reference only
Income: Financed by mem & fundraising
Library Holdings: Book Volumes 350

M **SAN ANTONIO MUSEUM OF ART,** 200 W Jones Ave, San Antonio, TX 78215-1406. Tel 210-978-8111; Fax 210-978-8182; Elec Mail maly.menier@samuseum.org; Internet Home Page Address: www.samuseum.org; *Dir* Dr Marion Oettinger Jr, PhD; *Consulting Cur Ancient Art* Dr Jessica Davis Powers; *Adjunct Cur Decorative Arts* Merribell Parsons; *Dir Operations* Dan Walton; *Deputy Dir* Emily Jones; *Dir Finance & Admin* Polly Vidaurri; *Dir Educ* Olga Samples-Davis; *Registrar* Karen Z Baker; *Commun Mgr* Leigh Baldwin; *Gift Shop Mgr* Arleen West; *Spec Events Liaison* Bill Wolff; *Cur Asian Art* Martha Blackwelder; *Chmn Bd Trustees* Karen Hixon
Open Wed - Sat 10 AM - 5 PM, Tues 10 AM - 8 PM, Sun Noon - 6 PM, cl Mon; Admis adult $8, sr citizen $7, students with ID $5, children 4-11 $3, mem, children under 4 & Tues 4 - 8 PM free; Estab 1981; a renovation project, the Brewery was originally chartered in 1883; Anheuser-Busch Brewing Assoc of St Louis, during the early 1900's replaced the original wooden structures with a castle-like brick complex. 70,959 sq ft of exhibition pace; Average Annual Attendance: 110,000; Mem: 2,000; dues vary
Library Holdings: Auction Catalogs; Book Volumes; Exhibition Catalogs; Periodical Subscriptions
Special Subjects: Prints, Hispanic Art, Latin American Art, Mexican Art, Painting-American, Pre-Columbian Art, Folk Art, Painting-European, Oriental Art, Asian Art, Silver, Antiquities-Oriental, Antiquities-Egyptian, Antiquities-Greek

Collections: American photography since 1920; contemporary & modern art; 18th-20th century paintings & sculpture; European & American paintings & decorative art; Greek & Roman antiquities; Mexican folk art; Pre-Columbian art; Spanish colonial art; Asian art; Islamic art; Oceanic art
Publications: Exhibition catalogues
Activities: Classes for adults & children; docent training; teacher workshops; parent-child classes; lects open to pub, 10-20 vis lectrs per yr; concerts; gallery talks; tours; individual paintings & original objects of art lent to other art institutions for special exhibitions; originate traveling exhibs to other art mus; mus shop sells books, reproductions prints, general art-interest merchandise, t-shirts, jewelry

A **SOUTHWEST SCHOOL OF ART,** 300 Augusta St, San Antonio, TX 78205-1216. Tel 210-224-1848; Fax 210-224-9337; Elec Mail information@swschool.org; Internet Home Page Address: www.swschool.org; *Pres* Paula Owen; *Sales Gallery Mgr* Clare Watters; *Cur/Assoc* Kathy Armstrong-Gillis
Exhib spaces open Mon - Sat 9 AM - 5 PM; gallery shop open Mon-Sat 10 AM - 5 PM; No admis fee; Estab 1965; non-profit/community-based art school for all ages & skill levels; Russell Hill Rogers Galleries Constitute 3,500 sq ft of Exhib space for contemporary art. The Ursuline Gallery displays local & regional artists; Average Annual Attendance: 250,000; Mem: 700; dues $45 & up
Income: Financed by pvt donors, earned income from art school & City of San Antonio Office of Cultural Affairs
Exhibitions: 12 changing exhibs per year-contemporary art and craft
Publications: Opening Invitations; handouts for all exhibitions including photo of artists, cur essay, exhibition checklist; catalogues of classes
Activities: Classes for adults & children; arts workshop progs with vis artists; lects open to pub, 10 vis lectrs per yr; tours; gallery talks; schols offered; gallery shop sells original art, etc

M **THE UNIVERSITY OF TEXAS AT SAN ANTONIO,** (The University of Texas) Institute of Texan Cultures, 801 E Durango Blvd, San Antonio, TX 78205-3209. Tel 210-458-2300; Fax 210-458-2380; Elec Mail itcweb@utsa.edu; Internet Home Page Address: www.texancultures.com; *Exec Dir* Timothy J Gette; *Librn* Yu Li; *Photo Archivist* Tom Shelton; *Dir Educ & Interpretation* Lupita Barrera; *Mktg* Denise L. Orozco; *Dir Exhib & Coll* Bryan Howard; *COO* Aaron Parks; *Pub Affairs* James Benavides
Open Mon - Sat 9 AM - 5 PM, Sun 12 PM - 5 PM; Admis adults $8, seniors 65 & older $7, children 3-11 & military with ID $6; Estab 1968; Maintains reference library; Average Annual Attendance: 200,000; Mem: See website for mem info
Income: $4,500,000 (financed by endowment, mem, state appropriation, gifts & sales)
Library Holdings: Audio Tapes; Fiche; Photographs
Special Subjects: Anthropology, Ethnology, Folk Art, Afro-American Art
Collections: Ethnic culture including Anglo, Belgian, Black, Chinese, Czech, Danish, Dutch, English, Filipino, French, German, Greek, Hungarian, Indian, Irish Italian, Japanese, Jewish, Lebanese, Mexican, Norwegian, Polish, Scottish, Spanish & Swedish (all Texans); one room school house, barn, windmill, fort & log house
Activities: Classes for adults & children; dramatic progs; docent progs; oral histories; lects open to pub; concerts; gallery talks; tours; festivals; traveling exhibs 2-3 per yr; sales shop sells books, prints, original art, reproductions & international gift items

M **WITTE MUSEUM,** 3801 Broadway, San Antonio, TX 78209. Tel 210-357-1881; Fax 210-357-1882; Elec Mail witte@wittemuseum.org; Internet Home Page Address: www.wittemuseum.org; *Pres & Exec Dir* James C McNutt; *Dir Prog & Coll* Elisa Phelps; *Exhibits Mgr* John Edmundson; *VChmn* Margaret F Anderson; *Cur History & Textiles* Michaele Haynes; *Exec VPres* Mimi Quintanilla; *Cur Archives & Registrar* Rebecca Huffstutler; *Dir Admin Servs* Bea Abercrombie; *Dir Pub Rels* Irma Guerrero; *Dir Retail Svcs* Barbara Bowie
Open Mon, Wed & Sat 10 AM - 5 PM, Tues 10 AM - 9 PM, Sun Noon - 5 PM; summer until 6 PM; Admis adults $5.95, seniors 65 & older $4.95, children 4-11 $3.95, children 3 & under free; group discount rates; Tues free from 3 - 9 PM; Estab 1926 by Ellen Schulz (later Quillin); Historical building located on the edge of the 450 acre Brackenridge Park on the banks of the San Antonio River & ancient Indian encampment area. Three restored historic homes on the grounds-the Ruiz, Navarro & Twohig houses; Average Annual Attendance: Over 250,000; Mem: 3000; dues family $60, individual $35
Special Subjects: Painting-American, American Indian Art, Anthropology, Textiles, Costumes, Folk Art, Decorative Arts, Dolls, Furniture, Silver, Historical Material, Embroidery, Laces
Exhibitions: Various exhibitions; call for details
Activities: Classes for adults & children; dramatic progs; docent training; lects open to pub; concerts; gallery talks; tours; camp-ins; family days; hands-on activities; behind-the-scenes tours; book traveling exhibs

SHERMAN

M **AUSTIN COLLEGE,** Ida Green Gallery, 900 N Grand Ave, Sherman, TX 75090-4400. Tel 903-813-2251; Fax 903-813-2273; Internet Home Page Address: www.dustincollege.edu; *Chair* Mark Monroe
Open 9 AM - 5 PM weekdays; No admis fee; Estab 1972 to serve campus and community needs; Selected exhibitions of contemporary art by regional & national artists; Average Annual Attendance: 7,000
Income: Financed by endowment
Purchases: Occasional purchases of outdoor sculpture
Special Subjects: Prints
Collections: Prints
Exhibitions: Monthly, except summer
Activities: Classes for adults & children; lect open to public, 20 vis lectrs per year; gallery talks; tours; competitions; scholarships offered

SPRING

M **PEARL FINCHER MUSEUM OF FINE ARTS,** 6815 Cyrpresswood Dr, Spring, TX 77379-7705. Tel 281-376-6322; Fax 281-376-2944; Open Tues-Wed & Sat 10AM-5PM, Thurs 10AM-8PM, Fri 10AM-6PM, Sun noon-5PM; Suggested donation $5

Collections: paintings, drawings, sculptures

TYLER

M **TYLER MUSEUM OF ART,** 1300 S Mahon Ave, Tyler, TX 75701-3438. Tel 903-595-1001; Fax 903-595-1055; Elec Mail info@tylermuseum.org; Internet Home Page Address: www.tylermuseum.org; *Head Educ Cur* Ken Tomio; *Facilities & Spec Events* Robert Owen; *Dir* Kimberley Bush Tomio; *Pres* Verna Hall; *Pub Rel & Mktg* Caleb Bell; *Accnt & HR Mgr* Kerry Moses
Open Tues - Sat 10 AM - 5 PM, Sun 1 - 5 PM; No admis fee, donations accepted; some special exhibs ticketed; Estab 1971 as a museum of art from 19th century to the present & specializing in early to contemp Texas art; Two galleries are 40 x 60 ft with 20 ft ceilings; Average Annual Attendance: 26,000; Mem: 700; dues $10 - $25,000
Income: $1.1 million (financed by endowment, memberships & donations)
Library Holdings: Auction Catalogs; Book Volumes; DVDs; Exhibition Catalogs; Kodachrome Transparencies; Other Holdings Harry Worthman Archives; Periodical Subscriptions; Photographs; Slides; Video Tapes
Special Subjects: Mexican Art, Photography, Painting-American, Sculpture, Asian Art
Collections: 1,700 works: special focus on early to contemporary Texas art; artists represented: Keith Carter, Joseph Glaso, Al Souza, Porfirio Salinas, Clyde Connell, Vernon Fisher, Terry Allen, Graydon Parrish & Norman Rockwell; contemporary Mexican folk art
Publications: Harry Worthman: A Life in Art, 2005; L O Griffith: Painting the Texas Landscape (2010); The Wyeths Across Texas (2012)
Activities: Classes for children; docent training; lects open to pub, 4 vis lectrs per yr; gallery talks; tours; high school student annual art exhib awards; exten prog serves local school district (elementary school); originate traveling exhibs to regional mus; mus shop sells books, assoc items, notecards, gift items relating to Texas & special exhib

L **Reference Library,** 1300 S Mahon Ave, Tyler, TX 75701. Tel 903-595-1001; Fax 903-595-1055; Elec Mail info@tylermuseum.org; Internet Home Page Address: www.tylermuseum.org; *Dir* Kimberley Bush Tomio; *Spec Events & Facilities Mgr* Robert Owen; *Cur & Head Educ* Ken Tomio; *Develop Officer* Caroline Wylie; *Registrar* Toni Lee Kraft
Open Tues - Sat 10 AM - 5 PM, Sun 1 - 5 PM; No admis fee for most exhibitions; Estab 1971 as an educational & cultural center to enrich the lives of East Texas citizens & visitors through the collection, preservation, study, exhibition, interpretation & celebration of the visual arts; Circ Non-circulating; 2 galleries; Average Annual Attendance: 30,000; Mem: 800
Income: $750,000 (financed by memberships, private donations, grants & city appropriation)
Library Holdings: Book Volumes 2,000; Clipping Files; Exhibition Catalogs; Kodachrome Transparencies; Periodical Subscriptions 6; Photographs; Slides; Video Tapes
Special Subjects: Folk Art, Photography, Drawings, Painting-American, Painting-French, Painting-German, Prints, Sculpture, Watercolors, Ceramics, Bronzes, Porcelain, Woodcuts, Landscapes, Portraits
Collections: 19th, 20th & 21st century Contemporary art
Publications: The Preview mag semi-annually
Activities: Classes for adults & children; docent training; summer art camp for children; school tours; family days; lects open to pub; 7-8 vis lectrs per yr; gallery talks; tours; performances; artist demonstrations; mus shop sells books, original art, reproductions, prints, postcards & other cards

VAN HORN

M **CULBERSON COUNTY HISTORICAL MUSEUM,** PO Box 231, Van Horn, TX 79855-0231. Tel 915-283-8028; *Secy* Ellen Lipsey; *Pres* Larry Simpson
Open Mon - Fri 2 - 5 PM, Sat by appointment; No admis fee, donations accepted; Estab 1972; history of Culberson County & original settlers; Mem: 50; dues $10; monthly meetings
Income: Donations
Special Subjects: Archaeology, Drawings, American Indian Art, American Western Art, Southwestern Art, Costumes, Folk Art, Manuscripts, Dolls, Furniture, Maps, Restorations, Period Rooms, Leather
Collections: Collections from old ranch families of Culberson County
Exhibitions: 1890s saloon, saddles & cowboy gear; Native American artifacts; Frontier Day

VERNON

M **RED RIVER VALLEY MUSEUM,** 4600 College Dr W, Vernon, TX 76385-4052; PO Box 2004, Vernon, TX 76385-2004. Tel 817-553-1848; Fax 817-553-1849; Elec Mail director@redrivervalleymuseum.org; Internet Home Page Address: www.redrivervalleymuseum.org; *Exec Dir* Sherillyn Yoakum; *Asst Dir* Carolyn Trafton; *Pres Bd Dirs* Stanley Heatly; *VPres* Bobby Burrus
Open Tues - Sun 1 - 5 PM; No admis fee, donations accepted (large groups $2 per person); Estab 1963 to provide for & preserve local heritage while maintaining national exhibits in the arts, history & science programs; Two galleries with one hundred linear ft of hanging space; Average Annual Attendance: 8,000
Income: Financed by contributions, hotel/motel tax & donations
Special Subjects: American Indian Art, Historical Material, Sculpture, Dolls, Reproductions
Collections: Electra Waggoner Biggs Sculpture Collection; J Henry Ray American Indian Artifacts Collection; Taylor Dabney Gems, Rocks & Minerals Collection; Bill Bond Wild Game Trophies; Western Cattle Trail; annual Quilt Show - Oct/Nov; Red River Valley International Juried Art Exhibition - May/June
Publications: Museum Newsletter, quarterly
Activities: Classes for children, docent training; lects open to pub; 1-2 vis lectrs; gallery talks; tours; volunteer of the year award; book traveling exhibs; mus shop sells books, magazines, brochures, prints, collector's items, reproductions

WACO

M THE ART CENTER OF WACO, 1300 College Dr, Waco, TX 76708-1497. Tel
254-752-4371; Fax 254-752-3506; Elec Mail director@artcenterwaco.org;
officemanager@artcenterwaco.org; Internet Home Page Address:
www.artcenterwaco.org; *Exec Dir* Mark Arnold; *Bus Office Mgr* Jennifer Warren
Open Tues - Sat 10 AM - 5 PM, Sun 1 - 5 PM; Suggested donation $2; Estab
1972 to provide a variety of exhibitions for appreciation & classes for
participation; Former residence of William Cameron, now renovated & contains
one large main gallery & a small adjacent gallery, also additional exhibition space
on the second floor; Average Annual Attendance: 120,000; Mem: 900; dues $20 -
$1,000; accredited by the Assoc of American Mus since 1991
Income: $200,000 (financed by endowment, mem & grants)
Exhibitions: Exhibitions vary, call for details
Publications: Catalogs; exhibit brochures; newsletter
Activities: Classes for adults & children; docent training; lects open to pub, 2-3
vis lectrs per yr; concerts; gallery talks; tours; competitions; exten dept serves
ethnic minorities & low socio-economic groups; originates traveling exhibs; mus
shop sells books, reproductions, glass, pewter & gift items
L Library, 1300 College Dr, Waco, TX 76708. Tel 254-752-4371; Fax
254-752-3506; Elec Mail info@artcenterwaco.org; Internet Home Page Address:
www.artcenterwaco.org; *Exec Dir* Mark Arnold; *Bus Office Mgr* Jennifer Warren
Open Tues - Sat 10 AM - 5 PM, Sun 1 - 5 PM; Admis $2 suggested donation;
Estab 1976 as a source for staff, faculty, patrons of the Art Center & children to
enhance artistic creativity through instruction & research; Former residence of
William Cameron; Average Annual Attendance: 120,000; Mem: 900; dues $20 -
$1,000
Income: Financed by mem, class fees, grants etc.
Library Holdings: Book Volumes 1,000; Exhibition Catalogs; Periodical
Subscriptions 18
Special Subjects: Art History, Folk Art, Calligraphy, Commercial Art, Drawings,
Etchings & Engravings, History of Art & Archaeology, Ceramics, Latin American
Art, American Western Art, Art Education, Asian Art, American Indian Art,
Afro-American Art, Landscapes
Exhibitions: Rotating exhibitions
Activities: Classes for adults & children; docent training; lects open to the public;
lects for mems; gallery talks; tours; schols awarded
Courses: Regional Art

M BAYLOR UNIVERSITY, Martin Museum of Art, 1401 S University Parks Dr,
Waco, TX 76798-7263; 1 Bear Pl, #97344 Waco, TX 76798-7344. Tel
254-710-1867; Fax 254-710-1566; Elec Mail heidihornik@baylor.edu; Internet
Home Page Address: www.baylor.edu/art; *Dir* Dr Heidi Hornik
Open Tues - Fri 10 AM - 5 PM, Sat Noon - 5 PM; No admis fee; Estab 1967 as a teaching arm of the university to serve the area; Gallery contains
one large room with storage & preparation room; Average Annual Attendance:
7,000
Income: Financed through the art dept
Purchases: Contemporary American Art
Special Subjects: Drawings, Glass, Painting-American, Prints, Sculpture,
Graphics, Watercolors, African Art
Collections: Contemporary painting & sculpture; graphics; local artists; prints;
sculpture from Sepik River area in New Guinea, Africa
Activities: Lects open to pub, 4 vis lectrs per yr; gallery talks
L Armstrong Browning Library, Eighth & Speight Sts, Waco, TX 76798-7152;
One Bear Place #97152, Waco, TX 76798-7152. Tel 254-710-3566; Fax
254-710-3552; Internet Home Page Address: www.browninglibrary.org; *Dir & Cur
Manuscripts* Rita S Patteson; *Cur Books & Printed Material* Cynthia A Burgess;
Coordr Avery Sharp
Open to visitors Mon - Fri 9 AM - 5 PM, Sat 10 AM - 2 PM; open for research
Mon - Fri 9 AM - 5 PM, Sat by appointment; No admis fee; Estab 1918 to
provide a setting for the personal possessions of the Brownings' & to have as
complete as is possible a collection for the use of Browning scholars; Gallery is
maintained; Average Annual Attendance: 22,000; Mem: dues individual $50
Income: Financed by endowment & private university
Library Holdings: Auction Catalogs; Audio Tapes; Book Volumes 25,000;
Cassettes; Clipping Files; Filmstrips; Manuscripts 10,000; Memorabilia; Motion
Pictures; Original Art Works; Original Documents; Other Holdings; Pamphlets;
Periodical Subscriptions; Photographs; Prints; Records; Reels; Reproductions;
Sculpture; Slides; Video Tapes
Collections: Kress Foundation Study Collection; Pen Browning Paintings;
portraits of Robert Browning & Elizabeth Barrett Browning; portraits of donors;
Julia Margaret Cameron, photographs; Wedgwood; Dresden; Joseph Milsand
Collection
Publications: Armstrong Browning Library Newsletter, semi-annual; Baylor
Browning Interests, irregular; Studies in Browning & His Circle, annual; More
Than Friend, The Letters of Robert Browning to Katharine DeKay Bronson; EBB
at the Mercy of Her Publishers; Elizabeth Barrett Browning: Life in a New
Rhythm, An exhibition held at the Grolier Club, 15 Dec 1993 through 19 February
1994; The Pied Piper: A Tale of Two Ditties; Armstrong Browning Library
Souvenir booklet
Activities: Lects open to pub, 2 vis lectrs per yr; concerts; tours; fels offered;
sales shop sells books, postcards, Victorian style mementoes

MIDWEST ART HISTORY SOCIETY
For further information, see National and Regional Organizations

M TEXAS RANGER HALL OF FAME & MUSEUM, 100 Texas Ranger Trl,
Waco, TX 76706; PO Box 2570, Waco, TX 76702-2570. Tel 254-750-8631; Fax
254-750-8629; Elec Mail info@texasranger.org; Internet Home Page Address:
www.texasranger.org; *Exec Dir* Byron Johnson; *Deputy Dir Opers* Christina
Stopka; *Colls Asst* Tina Brumm; *Colls Mgr* Shelly Crittenden
Open daily 9 AM - 5 PM, cl Thanksgiving, Christmas, New Year's Day; Admis
adults $7, children (6 & up) $3; 1968; Average Annual Attendance: 50,000; Mem:
Dues individual, student & senior $35
Income: Financed by contributions, gifts, grants, mem & state appropriations

Special Subjects: American Western Art, Photography, Painting-American,
Sculpture, American Indian Art, Southwestern Art
Collections: Texas Ranger items; Western history; paintings & sculpture
Publications: The Texas Ranger Dispatch; The Online Journal of Texas Ranger
History
Activities: Educ prog; Lect; research on Texas Rangers; mus shop
L Texas Ranger Research Center, PO Box 2570, Waco, TX 76702-2570. Tel
254-750-8631; Fax 254-750-8629; Elec Mail trhf@eramp.net; Internet Home Page
Address: www.texasranger.org; *Head* Christina Stopka
Open Mon - Sat 9 AM - Noon, 1-3 PM; Estab 1976; For reference only
Income: Financed by City of Waco
Library Holdings: Book Volumes 1,600; Cassettes; Clipping Files; Manuscripts;
Memorabilia; Photographs; Reels; Video Tapes
Activities: Mus shop

WAXAHACHIE

M ELLIS COUNTY MUSEUM INC, 201 S College St, Waxahachie, TX
75165-3711; PO Box 706, Waxahachie, TX 75168-0706. Tel 972-937-0681; Fax
972-937-0681; Elec Mail ecmuseum@sbcglobal.net; Internet Home Page Address:
www.elliscountymuseum.org; *Cur* Shannon Simpson
Open Mon-Sat 10 AM - 5 PM, Sun 1 - 5 PM; No admis fee, donations accepted;
Estab 1969 to collect & maintain artifacts relating to county's history; Average
Annual Attendance: 10,000-12,000; Mem: 275; dues benefactor $1000, sponsor
$200, patron $100, bus $50, family $25 individual $15
Income: $70,000 (financed by annual fundraiser)
Special Subjects: Decorative Arts, Furniture
Collections: Decorative Arts, Clothing, Furniture; Folding Fans; Photographs,
Memorabilia; Technological Implements; Weaponry
Exhibitions: Artifacts relating to county's history
Activities: Retail store sells books, reproductions, prints

WICHITA FALLS

M KEMP CENTER FOR THE ARTS, 1300 Lamar, Wichita Falls, TX 76301. Tel
940-767-2787; Fax 940-767-3956; Elec Mail info@kempcenter.org; Internet Home
Page Address: www.kempcenter.org; *Dir* Carlana Fitch; *Pres* Michael Koen; *Mus
Shop Mgr* Pat Wearth
Open Mon - Fri 9 AM - 5 PM, cl New Year's Day, Independence Day, Labor Day,
Christmas; No admis fee; Average Annual Attendance: 32,000
Collections: works by regional artists
Publications: quarterly newsletter; annual sculpture catalogue
Activities: classes; mus shop

M WICHITA FALLS MUSEUM & ART CENTER, Two Eureka Circle, Wichita
Falls, TX 76308. Tel 940-692-0923; Fax 940-696-5358; Elec Mail
wfma@mwsu.edu; Internet Home Page Address: www.mwsu.edu/wfma; *Cur Coll
& Exhib* Danny Bills; *Dir* Cohn Drennan
Open Tues - Fri 9:30 AM - 5 PM, Thurs until 7PM, Sat 10:30 AM - 5 PM, cl Sun
& Mon; Admis fee varies with exhibits; Estab 1964 for the purpose of serving the
community; Three galleries house art exhibits, two galleries house science
exhibits; Average Annual Attendance: 50,000; Mem: 800; dues $30 - $1,000
Income: Financed by endowment, mem & city appropriation
Special Subjects: Prints
Collections: American prints; Photography/Lester Jones; Caldecott Collection of
children's book illustrations
Publications: Events calendar, Sept, Jan, May
Activities: Classes for adults & children; dramatic progs; docent training; lects
open to pub, concerts; tours, competitions; lending collection of original prints to
Midwestern State University; originate traveling exhibs

WIMBERLEY

M PIONEER TOWN, Pioneer Museum of Western Art, 333 Wayside Dr, Wimberley,
TX 78676-5117. Tel 512-847-3289; Fax 512-847-6705; *Dir* Raymond L Czichos;
Secy Kasia Zinz; *Dir Video* C L Czichos; *Secy & Treas* John D White
Open Memorial Day - Labor Day by appointment only (512-847-3289); Estab
1956 as a village & art museum
Income: Financed by donations
Special Subjects: Architecture, Sculpture, American Western Art, Bronzes, Crafts,
Decorative Arts, Metalwork
Collections: Remington Bronze Collection; Jack Woods Collection

UTAH

BLANDING

M THE DINOSAUR MUSEUM, 754 S 200 W, Blanding, UT 84511-3909. Tel
435-678-3454; Elec Mail dinos@dinosaur-museum.org; Internet Home Page
Address: www.dinosaur-museum.org
Open Apr 15 - Oct 15 Mon - Sat 9 AM - 5 PM; cl Sun; Admis adults $3.50,
seniors $2.50, children $2; 1992; Mus covers history of the world of dinosaurs,
complete with skeletons, fossilized skin, eggs, footprints, feathered dinosaurs &
dinosaurs in the movies, state-of-the-art graphics and realistic. sculptures.
Nonprofit org
Special Subjects: Historical Material, Sculpture
Collections: Herrerasaurus from Argentina; Plateosaurus from Germany; life-size
dinosaur sculptures; Tarbosaurus from Mongolia; Permian logs from Utah;
mummified Edmontosaurus from Wyoming, Feathered Dinosaurs Hall; original
dinosaur movie posters & memorabilia

Exhibitions: The Art and Science of Dinosaurs in Movies: traces the changing image of the motion picture dinosaur from the silent 1919 Ghost of Slumber Mountain to present day blockbusters; Feathered Dinosaurs
Publications: Feathered Dinosaurs and the Origin of Flight, edited by Sylvia J Czerkas; Cine-Saurus the History of Dinosaurs in the Movies, Stephen Czerkas author 2006
Activities: Guided tours by appt; research projects; originates traveling exhibs to mus in USA & Canada; mus shop sells books, magazines, reproductions

BRIGHAM CITY

M **BRIGHAM CITY CORPORATION,** Brigham City Museum & Gallery, 24 N 300 W, Brigham City, UT 84302-2030; PO Box 583, Brigham City, UT 84302-0583. Tel 435-226-1439; Elec Mail bcmuseum@brighamcity.utah.gov; Internet Home Page Address: www.brighamcitymuseum.org; *Dir* Kaia Landon; *Publicity & Heritage Writer* Mary Alice Hobbs
Open Tues - Fri 11 AM - 6 PM, Sat 1 - 5 PM, cl Sun & Mon; No admis fee; Estab 1970 to document local history & host traveling exhibitions; Rotating gallery 2,500 sq ft, History Area 1,700 sq ft; Average Annual Attendance: 13,000
Income: Financed by Brigham City Corporation
Special Subjects: Anthropology, Decorative Arts, Drawings, Historical Material, Landscapes, American Western Art, Furniture, Pottery, Painting-American, Photography, Prints, American Indian Art, Southwestern Art, Ceramics, Folk Art, Portraits, Glass
Collections: Ceramics; crystal & glass; fibers; folk art; 19th century clothing, artifacts & furniture; painting; printmaking; pioneer furniture of Brigham City
Publications: Historic Tour of Brigham City; Mayors of Brigham City
Activities: Educ dept for research, & oral histories; lects open to public; gallery talks; tours; competitions; awards; 1-2 book travelling exhibs per yr; monthly rotating exhibs of art & varied collections; mus shop sells books

CEDAR CITY

M **SOUTHERN UTAH UNIVERSITY,** Braithwaite Fine Arts Gallery, 351 W Center St, Cedar City, UT 84720-2470. Tel 435-586-5432; Fax 435-865-8012; Elec Mail museums@suu.edu; Internet Home Page Address: www.suu.edu/pva/artgallery; *Dir* Lydia Johnson
Open Tues-Sat Noon - 7 PM; No admis fee; Estab 1976 to provide a quality visual arts forum for artists' work and the viewing public; The gallery has 2,500 sq ft of space with 300 linear ft of display surface; it is equipped with facilities for two & three-dimensional media with electronic security system; Average Annual Attendance: 10,000; Mem: 100; dues $50 - $500
Income: Financed by city and state appropriations and private donations
Special Subjects: Painting-American
Collections: 18th, 19th & 20th century American art
Publications: Exhibition announcements, quarterly; newsletter, quarterly
Activities: Gallery talks; tours; competitions; book traveling exhibitions 6 per year

EPHRAIM

M **SNOW COLLEGE ART GALLERY,** 150 E College Ave, Ephraim, UT 84627-1550. Tel 435-283-7416; Elec Mail adam.larsen@snow.edu; Internet Home Page Address: www.snow.edu/art/gallery/index.html; *Dir* Adam Larsen
Open Mon-Fri 9AM-5PM, other times by appointment
Collections: student & faculty artwork

FILLMORE

M **UTAH DEPARTMENT OF NATURAL RESOURCES, DIVISION OF PARKS & RECREATION,** Territorial Statehouse State Park Museum, 50 W Capitol Ave, Territorial Statehouse State Park Museum Fillmore, UT 84631-5556. Tel 435-743-5316; Fax 801-435-743-4723; Elec Mail parkcomment@utah.gov; Internet Home Page Address: stateparks.utah.gov; *Cur* Carl Camp
Open Mon - Sat 9 AM - 5 PM, cl Sun, Thanksgiving, Christmas & New Years Day; Admis $2 per person, children 6 - 11 $1; Estab 1930, as a museum for pioneer relics; Restored by the state & local Daughters of Utah Pioneers; owned & operated by Utah State Division of Parks & Recreation; Average Annual Attendance: 35,000
Income: Financed by state appropriations
Library Holdings: Book Volumes; Manuscripts; Original Documents
Special Subjects: Historical Material, American Western Art, Furniture, Porcelain, Portraits, Pottery, Painting-American, Textiles, Manuscripts, Photography, Prints, Ceramics, Posters, Period Rooms
Collections: Charcoal & pencil sketches; paintings by Utah artists; photograph prints coll; pioneer portraits in antique frames; silk screen prints; rooms arranged in period settings
Exhibitions: Rotating exhibits
Activities: Educ dept; 3 day youth camps with pioneer activities; 1 day family reunion activities; lect; gallery talks; tours; Arts & Living History Festival; mus shop sells books, postcards, kids' toys, old time toys & candy

KANAB

M **KANAB HERITAGE MUSEUM & JUNIPER FINE ARTS GALLERY,** 13 S 100 E, Kanab, UT 84741. Tel 435-644-3966; Tel 435-644-3898; *Cur* Deanna Tait Glover; *Cur* Win Barney
Open Summer: Mon - Fri 1 PM - 5 PM; No admis fee
Collections: Local history & culture; period furnishings; photographs; personal artifacts; works by local artists; William Cody "Buffalo Bill" camp table
Exhibitions: John Wesley Powell artifacts; Maynard Dixon & Milford Zornes exhibits
Activities: Western Legends Roundup award; mus shop sells books & prints

LOGAN

M **UTAH STATE UNIVERSITY MUSEUM OF ART,** Nora Eccles Harrison Museum of Art, 4020 Old Main Hill, Utah State Univ Logan, UT 84322-4020. Tel 435-797-0163; Fax 435-797-3423; Elec Mail NEHMA@usu.edu; Internet Home Page Address: artmuseum.usu.edu; *Exec Dir & Chief Cur* Victoria Rowe Berry; *Educ Cur* Nadra E Haffar; *Bus Mgr* Rachel Hamm; *Registrar* Casey Alen; *Cur Exhibs, Progs & Webmaster* Deb Banerjee; *Arts Bridge Prog Dir* Laurie Baefsky
Open Mon - Fri 10 AM - 5 PM, Sat 11 AM - 4 PM; cl Sun & holidays; No admis fee; Estab 1982; Over 10,000 sq ft of exhibition area, mostly devoted to permanent exhibits; Average Annual Attendance: 30,000; Mem: 100; dues $10 - $500
Purchases: $300,000
Special Subjects: American Indian Art, American Western Art, Ceramics
Collections: Native American art; 20th century American art, with emphasis on Western US artists; 20th century American ceramics
Publications: Exhibition catalogs; Insight, newsletter, three times per yr
Activities: Educ prog; lects open to pub, 2-4 vis lectrs per yr; gallery talks; schols & fels offered

MOUNT CARMEL

M **THUNDERBIRD FOUNDATION FOR THE ARTS,** 2002 State St, Mount Carmel, UT 84755; Maynard Dixon Home & Studio, Hwy 89-mile Marker 84 Mount Carmel, UT 84755. Tel 435-648-2653; Tel 801-533-5330; Internet Home Page Address: www.thunderbirdfoundation.com; *Dir* Susan Bingham
Open May - Oct Mon - Sun 10 AM - 4 PM, and by appointment; Estab 2001; Average Annual Attendance: 3,000

OGDEN

A **ECCLES COMMUNITY ART CENTER,** 2580 Jefferson Ave, Ogden, UT 84401-2411. Tel 801-392-6935; Fax 801-392-5295; Elec Mail eccles@ogden4arts.org; Internet Home Page Address: www.ogden4arts.org; *Gift Shop Mgr* Arlene Muller; *Dir* Patrick E Poce; *Cur of Educ* Jill S Sioblom; *Asst Dir* Debra Muller
Open Mon - Fri 9 AM - 5 PM, Sat 9 AM - 3 PM, cl Sun & holidays; No admis fee; Estab 1959 to serve as focal point for community cultural activities & to promote cultural growth; Maintains an art gallery with monthly exhibits; Average Annual Attendance: 25,000; Mem: 600; dues $25 - $100; annual meeting in Nov
Income: $100,000 (financed by mem, state appropriation & fund raising)
Collections: Utah Artists (historic & contemporaries)
Exhibitions: Utah Pastel Society 28th Annual Statewide Competition; paintings by Jamaica Jensen; other Utah artists
Publications: Newsletter, quarterly
Activities: Classes for adults & children; docent training; lects open to pub, 6 vis lectrs per yr; concerts; gallery talks; tours; competition with awards; schols offered; book traveling exhibs; sales shop sells original art, reproductions, prints, ceramics, jewelry & artist produced cards

M **OGDEN UNION STATION,** Myra Powell Art Gallery & Gallery at the Station, 2501 Wall Ave, Ogden, UT 84401-1359. Tel 801-393-9880; Fax 801-621-0230; Elec Mail rebeverlyous@msn.com; Internet Home Page Address: www.theunionstation.org/galleries.html; *Exec Dir* Roberta Beverly
Open Mon - Sat 10 AM - 5 PM; No admis fee; Estab 1979 to acquaint more people with the visual arts & to heighten awareness of art; 12.5 ft x 113 ft; 39 panels 6 ft x 4 ft; Average Annual Attendance: 2,500; Mem: Practicing Artists
Income: Financed by endowment & donations
Collections: Non-objective painting, Indian Design, Landscape, Navajo Sand Painting, Aluminum Sculpture
Exhibitions: Exhibs change monthly
Activities: Lects open to public; 6 vis lectrs per yr; competitions with awards; schols & fellowships offered; individual paintings & original objects of art lent

M **Union Station Museums,** 2501 Wall Ave, Ogden, UT 84401. Tel 801-393-9886; Internet Home Page Address: www.theunionstation.org; *Exec Dir* Roberta Beverly; *Mus Mgr* Amanda Felix
Open Mon - Sat 10 AM - 5 PM; Admis adults $5, sr citizens $4, children under 12 $3; Estab 1976 to serve as a cultural & civic center for Ogden, Utah; Average Annual Attendance: 40,000; Mem: Dues $50
Income: 501 (c) (3) non-profit
Library Holdings: Audio Tapes; Book Volumes; CD-ROMs; Cassettes; DVDs; Framed Reproductions; Manuscripts; Maps; Memorabilia; Original Documents; Other Holdings; Periodical Subscriptions; Photographs; Prints; Reproductions
Special Subjects: Historical Material, American Western Art, Furniture, Maps, Dioramas
Collections: Railroad memorabilia
Exhibitions: Browning Firearms; Classic Cars; Wattis-Dumke Model Railroad; Myra Powell Gallery; Utah State Railroad Museum; Utah Cowboy & Western Heritage Museum
Publications: Union Station-monthly via e-mail; Union Station Annual Publication
Activities: Concerts; gallery strolls; mus shop sells books, reproductions, prints, gifts

OREM

M **UTAH VALLEY UNIVERSITY,** Woodbury Art Museum, 575 E University Pkwy, #250, Orem, UT 84097-7400. Tel 801-863-4200; Elec Mail uvmuseum@uvu.edu; Internet Home Page Address: www.uvu.edu/museum; *Interim Dir* Melissa Hempel; *Admin* Katherine Hall; *Graphic Designer* Amanda Luker; *Registrar* Rebekah Monahan
Open Wed - Sat 11 AM - 5 PM, Tues 11 AM - 8 PM; No admis fee
Collections: artwork
Activities: Museum studies class through UVU

PARK CITY

A KIMBALL ART CENTER, 638 Park Ave, Park City, UT 84060-5106; PO Box 1478, Park City, UT 84060-1478. Tel 435-649-8882; Fax 435-649-8889; Internet Home Page Address: www.kimball-art.org; *Dir* Robin Rankin; *Art Educ Coordr* Jenny Diersen; *Develop Dir* Konstantine Deslis; *Exhib Coordr* Erin Linder; *Pub Rels* Corinne Humphrey
Open weekdays 10 AM - 5 PM, Sat noon - 7 PM, Sun noon - 5 PM; No admis fee; Estab 1976 for monthly gallery shows & workshops in arts & crafts, fine arts; Main gallery has movable walls & is 80 x 180 ft; Badami gallery measures 17 x 20 ft; Average Annual Attendance: 250,000; Mem: 600; dues individual $40, family $70
Income: $700,000 (financed by endowment, mem & contributions)
Exhibitions: Twenty four exhibits annually in various styles & mediums
Activities: Classes for adults & children; docent training; lects open to public, 6 vis lectrs per year; gallery talks; tours; competitions; opening receptions with exhibiting artists; ann art festival; awards, 2013 P/A (Progressive Architecture) Award for new building design; book traveling exhibitions; sales shop sells original art, reproductions & prints

PRICE

M COLLEGE OF EASTERN UTAH, Gallery East, 451 E Fourth N, Price, UT 84501. Tel 435-637-2120; Fax 435-637-4102; Internet Home Page Address: www.ceu.edu; *Gallery Coordr* Karen Green
Open Mon - Fri 8:30 AM - 5 PM; No admis fee; Estab 1976 to provide an educational & aesthetic tool within the community; 2,300 sq ft; maintains reference library; Average Annual Attendance: 15,000
Income: $1,600 (financed by school appropriation)
Special Subjects: Painting-American, Prints
Exhibitions: Changing exhibits
Activities: Classes for adults; docent training; lects open to pub, 4-5 vis lectrs per yr; gallery talks; tours; competitions with awards; scholarships offered; originates traveling exhibs to colleges

PROVO

M BRIGHAM YOUNG UNIVERSITY, B F Larsen Gallery, A-41 ASB, Provo, UT 84602. Tel 801-378-2881; Fax 801-378-5964; Elec Mail gallery303@byu.edu; Internet Home Page Address: visualarts.byu.edu; *Gallery Dir* Todd Frye
Open 9 AM - 5 PM; No admis fee; Estab 1965 to bring to the University students & faculty a wide range of new experiences in the visual arts; B F Larsen Gallery is a three story atrium shaped gallery with exhibition areas in center floor & upper levels; Gallery 303 is large room with foyer & single entrance-exit; total exhibition space 15,260 sq ft; Average Annual Attendance: 55,000 Gallery 303; 100,000 Larsen
Income: Financed by university
Special Subjects: Drawings, American Western Art, Painting-American, Prints, Manuscripts, Sculpture
Collections: Maynard Dixon Collection; Mahonri Young Collection of Manuscripts; J Alden Weir Collection
Exhibitions: Invitational exhibits; exhibits by students & faculty, curated exhibits of contemporary artists & circulating exhibits
Activities: Lects open to pub; competitions; monetary & cert awards; individual paintings & original objects of art lent to university executive, faculty & university library; book traveling exhibits monthly
L Harold B Lee Library, PO Box 26800, Provo, UT 84602-6800. Tel 801-378-4005; Fax 801-378-6708; Internet Home Page Address: www.lib.byu.edu; *Dir Libraries* Sterling Albrecht; *Fine Arts Librn* Christiane Erbolato-Ramsey
Open Mon - Sat 7 AM - Midnight; No admis fee; Estab 1875 to support the university curriculum
Income: Financed by endowment, mem & Latter-day Saints church funds
Library Holdings: Audio Tapes; Book Volumes 3,677,805; CD-ROMs; Cassettes; Compact Disks; Exhibition Catalogs; Fiche; Filmstrips; Memorabilia; Motion Pictures; Pamphlets; Periodical Subscriptions 16,487; Photographs 12,000; Prints; Reels; Slides; Video Tapes
Special Subjects: Photography, Graphic Arts, American Western Art
Collections: 15th & 16th century graphic art coll; Vought indexed & mounted art reproduction collection; George Anderson Collection of early Utah photographs; C R Savage Collection
Activities: Tours
M Museum of Art, North Campus Dr, Provo, UT 84602-1400. Tel 801-422-8287; Fax 801-422-0527; Elec Mail moa@byu.edu; Internet Home Page Address: moa.byu.edu; *Interim Dir & Assoc* Ed Lind; *Head Cur* Cheryl May
Open Mon, Sat 10 AM - 6 PM, Thurs & Fri evenings 6 PM - 9 PM; No admis fee; Estab 1993 to educate patrons & community; 11 galleries; study & general purpose sculpture garden; Average Annual Attendance: 135,000+
Special Subjects: Drawings, Painting-American, Prints, Sculpture, Watercolors, American Western Art, Bronzes, Religious Art, Ceramics, Pottery, Woodcarvings, Woodcuts, Etchings & Engravings, Landscapes, Portraits, Posters, Marine Painting, Painting-French, Carpets & Rugs, Renaissance Art, Cartoons
Collections: American Art-Hudson River School of American Impressionism; Collections include: Maynard Dixon, Mahonri Young, J. Alden Weir
Publications: InSite, Biannual online magazine
Activities: Classes for adults & children; docent progs; acad & pub progs; lects open to pub, 5-6 vis lectrs per yr; concerts; gallery talks; tours; lending collection contains 17,000 items, including individual paintings & original objects of art; book traveling exhibs 2-3 per yr; mus shop sells books, magazines, prints, reproductions & slides

SAINT GEORGE

M DIXIE STATE COLLEGE, Robert N & Peggy Sears Gallery, 225 S 700 East, Saint George, UT 84770. Tel 435-652-7500; Fax 435-656-4131; Internet Home Page Address: new.dixie.edu; *VPres Cultural Affairs* George Whitehead; *Cur & Collections Mgr* Kathy C Cieslewicz
Open Mon - Fri 9 AM - 5 PM, cl school holidays; No admis fee; Estab 1960 to serve southwestern Utah as a visual arts exhibit center; Gallery is located in the Eccles Fine Art Center; Average Annual Attendance: 10,000-15,000
Income: Financed by state appropriation & 35% of sales from monthly shows
Special Subjects: American Indian Art, Drawings, American Western Art, Photography, Pottery, Prints, Bronzes, Woodcuts, Painting-American, Sculpture, Watercolors, Ceramics, Etchings & Engravings, Landscapes, Portraits, Carpets & Rugs
Collections: Early & contemporary Utah painters; Ceramics; Artifacts; Contemporary Native American
Exhibitions: Dixie State College, Sears Invitational Show & Sale; Art Dept Showcase, plus 3 curated exhibs
Activities: Classes for adults; dramatic progs; lects open to pub, vis lectrs; concerts; gallery talks

M ST GEORGE ART MUSEUM, 47 E 200 N, Saint George, UT 84770-2845. Tel 435-627-4525; Fax 435-627-4526; Elec Mail museum@sgcity.org; Internet Home Page Address: www.sgartmuseum.org; *Dir* Deborah Reeder
Open Mon-Sat 10AM-5PM, 3rd Thurs of month 10AM-9PM with art conversations at 7PM; Admis adults $3, children 3 - 11 $1, children under 3 & mems no admis fee; Estab 1991; Mus houses work of Utah artists; mus is located in a fully-restored sugar beet storage structure that is part of the St George's historic district; Average Annual Attendance: 10,000; Mem: Dues Pres Circle/Corporate Sponsor $1000; Benefactor $750; Friend $500; Patron $250; Contributor $100; Indiv $50
Income: City of St. George municipal, non-profit
Library Holdings: Audio Tapes; Book Volumes; Cassettes; Exhibition Catalogs; Periodical Subscriptions; Video Tapes
Special Subjects: Historical Material, Painting-American
Collections: Permanent collection available online
Publications: A Century of Sanctuary, the Art of Zion National Park
Activities: Art Festival; 3rd Thurs Conversations at 7 PM; docent training; family discovery center; lects open to pub; 10 vis lectrs per yr; tours, gallery talks; sponsoring of competitions; books traveling exhibs varies per yr; mus shop sells books, magazines, prints & related merchandise

SALT LAKE CITY

M CHURCH OF JESUS CHRIST OF LATTER-DAY SAINTS, Museum of Church History & Art, 45 N West Temple St, Salt Lake City, UT 84150-0902. Tel 801-240-4615; Fax 801-240-5342; Internet Home Page Address: www.lds.org; *Dir* Glen Leonard
Open Mon - Fri 9 AM - 9 PM, Sat, Sun & holidays 10 AM - 7 PM, cl Easter, Thanksgiving, Christmas & New Year's Day; No admis fee; Estab 1869 to disseminate information & display historical memorabilia, artifacts & art to the vis pub; Assists in restorations & furnishing of Church historic sites; Average Annual Attendance: 250,000
Income: Financed by Church
Special Subjects: Bronzes, Architecture, Painting-American, Photography, Sculpture, Watercolors, American Indian Art, American Western Art, Southwestern Art, Textiles, Costumes, Religious Art, Folk Art, Pottery, Primitive art, Woodcarvings, Landscapes, Decorative Arts, Portraits, Furniture, Historical Material, Stained Glass
Collections: Mostly 19th & 20th century Mormon art & historical artifacts: portraits, paintings, drawings, sculpture, prints, American furniture, china, pottery, glass; Mormon quilts & handwork; decorative arts; clothing & textiles; architectural elements & hardware; Oceanic & American Indian pottery, basketry & textiles; Mormon Collection
Publications: Exhibition catalogs; brochures; Image of Faith: Art of the Latter-day Saints (1995)
Activities: Docent training; seminars; gallery demonstrations; school outreach; lects open to pub; gallery talks tours; International Art Competition; individual paintings & original objects of art lent; mus shop sells books, prints, slides & postcards
L Art Library, 45 N West Temple, Salt Lake City, UT 84150-9006. Tel 801-240-4604; Fax 801-240-5342; Internet Home Page Address: www.lds.org; *Librn* Ron Read
Open hours vary, by appointment; Estab as reference source for historical information on Latter-Day Saints; Reference library
Income: Financed by church
Library Holdings: Audio Tapes; Book Volumes 2,200; Cassettes; Clipping Files; Exhibition Catalogs; Fiche; Memorabilia; Motion Pictures; Original Art Works; Pamphlets; Periodical Subscriptions 25; Photographs; Reels; Sculpture; Slides; Video Tapes

M MUSEUM OF UTAH ART & HISTORY, 825 N 300 W Ste W109, Salt Lake City, UT 84103-1428. Tel 801-355-5554; Fax 801-355-5222; Elec Mail ksteadman@muahnet.org; Internet Home Page Address: www.muahnet.org; *Dir* Kandace Steadman
Open Tues - Sat 11 AM - 3 PM; No admis fee; Estab 2000; Average Annual Attendance: 7,000

A SALT LAKE ART CENTER, Utah Museum of Contemporary Art, 20 S W Temple, Salt Lake City, UT 84101. Tel 801-328-4201; Fax 801-322-4323; Elec Mail info@utahmoca.org; Internet Home Page Address: www.utahmoca.org; *Exec Dir* Adam Price; *Communs Dir* Danica Farley; *Cur Exhibs* Aaron Moulton; *Educ Dir* Jared Steffensen
Open Tues - Thurs 11AM-6PM, Fri 11AM-9PM, Sat 11AM-6PM; No admis fee; Estab 1931 to educate the community in the contemporary visual arts through exhibitions & classes; UMOCA has five exhib spaces; Average Annual Attendance: 48,000; Mem: 1,560; dues Basic $40, Deluxe $150, annual meeting in June
Income: Financed by mem, city & state appropriation, earned income, gifts, private & corporate contributions
Collections: Utah artists (1930-Present); contemporary art
Activities: Classes for adults & children; docent training; studio & lect courses; lects open to pub, 10 vis lectrs per yr; gallery talks; tours; 2 - 3 book traveling

exhibs per yr; mus shop sells books, jewelry, ceramics, cards, journals, magazines, original art, prints & textiles

L SALT LAKE CITY PUBLIC LIBRARY, Fine Arts & Audiovisual Dept and Atrium Gallery, 210 E 400 St, Salt Lake City, UT 84111-2849. Tel 801-524-8200; Fax 801-524-8272; *Head Fine Arts & Av Dept* Carolyn Dickinson; *Dir* Beth Elder; *Asst Mgr* Howard Brough
Open Mon - Thurs 9 AM - 9 PM, Fri - Sat 9 AM - 6 PM, Sun 1 - 5 PM; No admis fee; Estab 1898; Maintains an art gallery with monthly exhibitions
Income: Financed by city appropriation
Library Holdings: Book Volumes 400,000; Exhibition Catalogs; Filmstrips; Original Art Works; Records; Reproductions; Slides; Video Tapes
Special Subjects: Film
Collections: Art of Western United States; Utah Artists; American & European Works on Paper
Publications: Brochures accompanying individual exhibitions; Permanent Art Collection Catalogue
Activities: Films; gallery talks; tours; demonstrations; slide presentations; individual paintings & original objects of art lent to museums & non-profit galleries; originate traveling exhibs

M UNIVERSITY OF UTAH, Utah Museum of Fine Arts, 410 Campus Center Dr., Marcia & John Price Museum Bldg Salt Lake City, UT 84112-0350. Tel 801-581-7332; Fax 801-585-5198; Elec Mail umfa.publicrelations@utah.edu; Internet Home Page Address: www.umfa.utah.edu; *Cur Educ* Virginia Catherall; *Cur Educ* Megan Hallett; *Cur* Jill Dawsey; *Dir Coll & Exhibs* David Carroll; *Exec Dir* Gretchen Dietrich; *Dir Finance & Opers* George Lindsey
Open Tues, Thurs, Fri 10 AM - 5 PM, Wed 10 AM - 8 PM, Sat & Sun 11 AM - 5 PM, cl Mon & holidays; Admis adults $7, seniors & students $5, UFA mems & children under 6 free; Estab to engage visitors in discovering meaningful connections with the artistic expressions of the world's cultures; Average Annual Attendance: 110,000; Mem: 2,500; patron $100, dues family $65, senior $30, individual $20, student $15,
Income: Financed by university & private gifts
Special Subjects: Drawings, Landscapes, Glass, Flasks & Bottles, Furniture, Painting-American, Silver, Sculpture, Graphics, Hispanic Art, Latin American Art, Mexican Art, Photography, Watercolors, American Indian Art, Bronzes, African Art, Pre-Columbian Art, Southwestern Art, Textiles, Costumes, Religious Art, Ceramics, Primitive art, Woodcarvings, Woodcuts, Painting-European, Painting-Japanese, Portraits, Furniture, Jade, Jewelry, Porcelain, Oriental Art, Asian Art, Silver, Painting-British, Painting-Dutch, Painting-French, Carpets & Rugs, Ivory, Juvenile Art, Tapestries, Baroque Art, Painting-Flemish, Renaissance Art, Embroidery, Medieval Art, Painting-Spanish, Painting-Italian, Antiquities-Egyptian, Antiquities-Greek, Mosaics, Painting-German
Collections: Winifred Kimball Hudnut Collection; Natacha Rambova Egyptian Collection; Marion Sharp Robinson Collection; Trower & Michael Collections of English, American & Peruvian Silver; Bartlett Wicks Collection
Activities: Classes for children & adults; docent training; lect open to public, some for mem only; concerts; gallery talks; tours; organize traveling exhibs to BBHC in Cody WY; Missouri History Mus; museum shop sells reproductions, prints, jewelry & apparel, films, & cafe
L Katherine W Dumke Architecture Library, Marriott Library, 295 S 1500 E, Salt Lake City, UT 84112-0860. Tel 801-581-8104; Internet Home Page Address: www.lib.utah.edu/fa; *Head Fine Arts* Greg Hatch; *Fine Arts Librn* Luke Leither
Open Mon - Thurs 7 AM - 2 AM, Fri & Sat 7 AM - 8 PM, Sun noon - 2 AM; Estab 1967 to serve the students & faculty of the University with research materials & specialized services; For lending & reference
Income: Financed by state appropriation
Purchases: $60,000 per yr for fine arts books
Library Holdings: Auction Catalogs; Audio Tapes; Book Volumes 2,000,000; CD-ROMs; Cassettes; Clipping Files; Compact Disks; DVDs; Exhibition Catalogs; Fiche; Manuscripts; Memorabilia; Motion Pictures; Original Art Works; Original Documents; Other Holdings; Periodical Subscriptions 17,000; Photographs; Prints; Reproductions; Slides; Video Tapes
Special Subjects: Art History, Folk Art, Photography, Graphic Arts, Graphic Design, Painting-American, Painting-British, Painting-Dutch, Painting-Flemish, Painting-European, American Western Art, Advertising Design, Art Education, Asian Art, Furniture, Southwestern Art, Glass, Aesthetics, Afro-American Art, Bookplates & Bindings, Architecture, Folk Art
Activities: Library supports in-house traveling exhibits & research & curriculum needs of the Univ; lects open to pub; book traveling exhibs; organize traveling exhibs

M UTAH ARTS COUNCIL, Chase Home Museum of Utah Folk Arts, 600 E. 1100 S. in Salt Lake City's Liberty Park, Salt Lake City, UT 84105; 617 E South Temple, Salt Lake City, UT 84102-1177. Tel 801-236-7555; Fax 801-236-7556; Elec Mail cedison@utah.gov; Internet Home Page Address: arts.utah.gov; *Exec Dir* Margaret Hunt; *Asst Dir* Lynnette Hiskey; *Visual Arts Mgr* Lila Abersold; *Commus Mgr* Lydia Durand; *Folk Arts Mgr* Carol Edison; *Pub Arts & Design Arts Mgr* Jim Glenn; *Community Outreach Mgr* Anna Boulton; *Performing Arts Coordr* Jason Bowcutt; *Arts Educ Initiatives Dir* Janet Wolf
Open spring & fall Sat - Sun Noon - 5 PM, Memorial Day - Labor Day Mon - Thurs Noon - 5 PM, Fri - Sun 2 PM - 7 PM; No admis fee; Estab 1986 to showcase folk art in the State Art Collection; Four small galleries, one small reception area & two hallways for display in a 19th century two-story farmhouse; Average Annual Attendance: 25,000
Income: Financed by state & federal appropriations
Library Holdings: Audio Tapes; Book Volumes 600; Cassettes; Clipping Files; Motion Pictures; Pamphlets; Periodical Subscriptions 5; Photographs; Prints; Records; Slides
Special Subjects: Photography, Sculpture, Crafts, Folk Art
Collections: Ethnic; Familial; Occupational; Religious; Regional with an emphasis on traditional work by living folk artists; Native American
Exhibitions: Annual exhibit of Utah folk art; rotating exhibits
Publications: Publications & recordings featuring old-time social dance, Navajo baskets, Hispanic traditions
Activities: Lects open to pub; concerts; group tours; originates traveling exhibs; mus shop sells books & folk art music

A UTAH LAWYERS FOR THE ARTS, 170 S Main St, Ste 1500, Salt Lake City, UT 84101-1644. Tel 801-521-3200; Fax 801-328-0537; Internet Home Page Address: www.vlany.org; *Pres* James W Stewart; *Contact Person* Andrew Deiss; *Mktg Dir* Micquelle Corry
Estab 1983 to provide pro bono legal services; Mem: 36; mem open to attorneys & law students; $30 annual fee, $15 student fee
Income: Financed by mem
Publications: Art/Law News, quarterly newsletter

SANDY

M HILL GALLERY AND SCULPTURE PARK, 9045 S 1300 E, Canyon Ridge Center Sandy, UT 84094-3134. Tel 801-562-9242; Internet Home Page Address: www.danhillsculpture.com/sculpturepark.phtml
Open Tues-Fri noon-5PM, other times by appointment
Collections: life-size monumental outdoor sculptures, carvings, paintings, giclee prints, photographs, kaleidoscopes, lamps, baskets, cards & books by local and regional artists

SPRINGVILLE

M SPRINGVILLE MUSEUM OF ART, 126 E 400 South, Springville, UT 84663. Tel 801-489-2727; Fax 801-489-2739; Internet Home Page Address: www.smofa.org; *Assoc Dir* Natalie Petersen; *Asst Dir & Cur Educ* Virgil E Jacobsen; *Dir* Dr. Vern Swanson
Open Tues - Sat 10 AM - 5 PM, Wed 10 AM - 9 PM, Sun 3 - 6 PM, cl Mon & holidays; No admis fee; Estab 1903 for the collection & exhibition of Utah fine arts & as educational resource; Built in Spanish Colonial style in 1937 with 28 galleries and sculpture garden; Average Annual Attendance: 120,000; Mem: 350; dues family $40, individual $25, student $15; annual meeting in Apr
Income: $1,000,000 (financed by donations, bookstore, mem, city & state appropriations)
Purchases: varies
Special Subjects: American Western Art, Photography, Pottery, Period Rooms, Painting-British, Painting-American, Watercolors, Bronzes, Southwestern Art, Religious Art, Portraits, Carpets & Rugs, Reproductions, Painting-Russian
Collections: Artwork by Cyrus Dallin & John Hafen; 20th Century American Realism, Soviet Realism; Utah artists from 1850 to present of all styles
Exhibitions: Annual Spring Salon (Utah Invitational Fine Art); Annual Utah Autumn Exhibit; High Schools of Utah Show; National Quilt Show;
Publications: Annual exhibition catalogues
Activities: Educ prog; docent progs; children's progs; art teacher in-service progs earn cr toward teaching cert; classes for children; lects open to pub, 6 vis lectrs per yr; concerts; gallery talks; tours; competitions with awards; individual paintings & original objects of art lent to professional, governmental & educational institutions & mus; lending collection contains paintings & sculpture; originate traveling exhibs to Utah Arts Council, other mus & to schools; mus shop sells books, magazines, reproductions, prints & catalogues

VERMONT

BARRE

M STUDIO PLACE ARTS, 201 N Main St, Barre, VT 05641-4125. Tel 802-479-7069; Elec Mail info@studioplacearts.com; Internet Home Page Address: www.studioplacearts.com; *Exec Dir* Sue Higby
Open Tues - Fri 10 AM - 5 PM, Sat noon - 4 PM; No admis fee; Three gallery exhibs that change every six weeks yr round; Average Annual Attendance: 8,000; Mem: 1,800; dues $35 yr
Income: $150,000 (private donations)
Collections: paintings; photographs; sculpture
Exhibitions: See website for archive of exhibs
Activities: Classes for adults & children; lects open to pub; 5-8 vis lectrs per yr; gallery talks

BARTON

M BREAD & PUPPET THEATER, (Bread & Puppet Theater Museum) Bread & Puppet Museum, 753 Heights Rd, Rt 122 Barton, VT 05839-9637. Tel 802-525-6972/3031; *Artist* Peter Schumann; *Mgr* Elka Schumann
Open June - Oct daily 10 AM - 6 PM; No admis fee, donations welcome; Estab 1975 to exhibit & promote the art of puppetry; 100 ft long, 2-storied former dairy barn; Average Annual Attendance: 20,000
Income: $10,000 (financed by donations, sales of publications & art & by the Bread & Puppet Theater)
Special Subjects: Sculpture, Graphics
Collections: giant puppets; masks; graphics of The Bread and Puppet Theater
Publications: The Radicality of Puppet Theater; Bread & Puppet Museum catalog
Activities: Free mus tour, Sun 1 PM July - Aug; lends art to various exhibits; sales shop sells books, prints, original art, reproductions, posters & postcards, video & audio merchandise

BENNINGTON

M BENNINGTON MUSEUM, 75 Main St, Bennington, VT 05201-2885. Tel 802-447-1571; Fax 802-442-8305; Elec Mail info@benningtonmuseum.org; Elec Mail sperkins@benningtonmuseum.org; Internet Home Page Address: www.benningtonmuseum.org; *Librn* Tyler Resch; *Exec Dir* Stephen Perkins; *Cur Coll* Jamie Franklin; *Colls Mgr* Callie Stewart; *Pub Programs Dir* Deana Mallory; *Vis Scvs* Karen Harrington; *Mktg & Pub Rels* Susan Strano; *Develop Assoc* Joy Danila
Open daily 10AM - 5PM, open seven days a week in Sept & Oct, cl Wed; Admis adults $10, students and senior citizens $9, children under 12 free; Estab 1875 as

resource for history and fine and decorative arts of New England; Local historical mus with 11 galleries, Grandma Moses Schoolhouse Mus; Average Annual Attendance: 35,000; Mem: 700; dues $40 - $1500; annual meeting in May
Income: Financed by dues, donations, admissions & grants
Special Subjects: Glass, Pottery, Painting-American, Sculpture, Drawings, Costumes, Ceramics, Folk Art, Decorative Arts, Dolls, Furniture, Coins & Medals, Embroidery
Collections: Bennington pottery; Bennington Flag; Grandma Moses Paintings; rare documents
Publications: Exhibition catalogs
Activities: Classes for adults & children; docent training; lects open to pub, 4 vis lectrs per yr; gallery talks; tours; individual paintings & original objects of art lent to other qualifying organizations; book traveling exhibs; originate traveling exhibs to other northern New England mus; mus shop sells books, magazines, original art, reproductions, prints & decorative arts

BRATTLEBORO

M **BRATTLEBORO MUSEUM & ART CENTER,** 10 Vernon St Brattleboro, VT 05301-3623. Tel 802-257-0124; Fax 802-258-9182; Elec Mail info@brattleboromuseum.org; Internet Home Page Address: www.brattleboromuseum.org; *Dir* Danny Lichtenfeld; *Educ Cur* Susan Calabria; *Chief Cur* Mara Williams; *Opers Mgr* Teta Hilsdon
Open 11AM-5PM Thurs-Mon; Admis adults $8, seniors $6, students $4, children under 6 & members free; Estab 1972 to present art & ideas in ways that inspire, educate & engage people of all ages; The museum is located in a railroad station built in 1915, now a registered historic site. Six galleries with changing exhibitions & museum gift shop; Average Annual Attendance: 20,000; Mem: 800; dues family $80, individual $45, senior $40; annual meeting in May
Income: $400,000 (financed by mem, donations, town, state, federal grants, corporate sponsorships, program fees & gift shop sales)
Exhibitions: Approx 15 exhibits annually
Publications: Built Landscapes Gardens of the Northeast; Seeing Japan; The Art of Frank Stout; Artful Jesters; Wolf Kahn Landscape of Light; From Street to Studio; Call & Response; Cecily Kahn; Sleight of Hand: Eric Sealine; Brattleboro: Past, Present, Future; Jules Olitski: An Inside View
Activities: Classes for adults; docent training; progs for school groups; family workshops; lects open to pub, 12 vis lectrs per yr; concerts; gallery talks; tours; Scholastic Arts Writing Awards exhib (Vermont); organize traveling exhibs for museums & galleries; mus shop sells books, notecards, postcards

BURLINGTON

M **UNIVERSITY OF VERMONT,** Robert Hull Fleming Museum, 61 Colchester Ave, Burlington, VT 05405-0001. Tel 802-656-0750; Fax 802-656-8059; Elec Mail fleming@uvm.edu; Internet Home Page Address: www.flemingmuseum.org; *Dir* Janie Cohen; *Cur* Aimee Marcereau DeGalan
Open Labor Day- Apr 30 Tues - Fri 9AM - 4PM, Wed until 8PM, Sat - Sun 1 - 5PM; Admis family $10, adults $5, senior & students $3; Estab 1931; contains 20,000 objects; Average Annual Attendance: 14,000; Mem: 400; dues Fleming Soc $1,000, benefactor $500-$999, patron $250-$499 supporting $100-$249 contributing $50-$99, family $30, individual $20, student $10
Income: Financed by mem, university appropriations & grants, private gifts
Special Subjects: Drawings, Prints, Ethnology, Costumes, Oriental Art, Medieval Art, Antiquities-Greek, Antiquities-Roman
Collections: over 20,000 objects
Exhibitions: American historic & contemporary; Asian; Ethnographic; Medieval & Ancient; European; Egyptian
Publications: Exhibition catalogs; newsletter-calendar, 3 per yr
Activities: Classes for adults & children; docent training; lects open to pub, 12 vis lectrs per yr; concerts; gallery talks; tours; community outreach serves all Vermont; individual paintings & original objects of art lent to mus community; annual family day; annual heirloom appraisal day; book traveling exhibs; originate traveling exhibs; mus shop sells books, magazines, reproductions, prints, publications, kids merchandise & Vermont crafts

M **Francis Colburn Gallery,** Williams Hall, Burlington, VT 05405-0001. Tel 802-656-2014; Fax 802-656-2064;
Open Sept - May 9 AM - 5 PM; No admis fee; Estab 1975
Exhibitions: Student, faculty & visiting artist works

M **VERMONT STATE CRAFT CENTER AT FROG HOLLOW,** 85 Church St, Burlington, VT 05401-4420. Tel 802-388-3177, 863-6458; Fax 802-860-6506; Elec Mail information@froghollow.org; Internet Home Page Address: www.froghollow.org; *Gallery Mgr* Barbara Cunningham; *Sales Mgr* Amy Bourgeois; *Pub Rels* Michael Giorgio; *Exec Dir* William F Brooks Jr
Open Mon - Sat 9:30 AM - 5:30 PM, Sun afternoon spring - fall; No admis fee; Estab 1971 to provide craft educational, informational & marketing services to school children, adults & professionals; Sales gallery exhibits the work of over 250 juried Vermont crafts people, also hosts yearly exhibition schedule featuring the work of noted crafts people world wide; Average Annual Attendance: 200,000; Mem: 1,200; dues $30 - $250; annual meeting in Nov; exhibiting members are juried into the gallery
Income: Financed by mem, federal & state grants, fundraising activities, consignment receipts & tuition
Special Subjects: Crafts
Collections: Vermont Crafts
Publications: Information services bulletin; calendar; show announcements; course brochures
Activities: Classes for adults & children; craft demonstrations; professional workshops for crafts people; pottery facility; resident potter studios; lects open to public, 4 vis lectrs per yr; tours; original objects of fine craft lent to Vermont State Senate office in Washington; originates traveling exhibs; gallery shop sells books & Vermont crafts

CAMBRIDGE

M **BRYAN MEMORIAL GALLERY,** 180 Main St, Cambridge, VT 05444; PO Box 340, Jeffersonville, VT 05464-0340. Tel 802-644-5100; Fax 802-644-8342; *Exec Dir* Mickey Myers
Open Feb-Mar, Oct-Dec Thurs - Sun 11AM - 4 PM; July-Sept daily 11 AM to 5 PM; Estab 1984; preserving & exhibiting New England landscape painting; Average Annual Attendance: 5,000; Mem: Mem dues $30 per yr
Special Subjects: Landscapes, Painting-American
Collections: Paintings
Activities: Classes for adults; workshops; educational progs; gallery talks; competitions; Alden Bryan medal for landscape painting; sales hop sells books & cards

COLCHESTER

M **MCCARTHY GALLERY,** McCarthy Arts Center, 1 Winooski Park Colchester, VT 05439-1000. Tel 802-654-2246;
Open Mon-Fri 3PM-5PM & 7:30PM--9:30PM, Sat-Sun 1PM-5PM
Collections: paintings; photographs; sculpture

FERRISBURGH

A **ROKEBY MUSEUM,** 4334 Route 7, Ferrisburgh, VT 05456-9779. Tel 802-877-3406; Fax 802-877-3406; Elec Mail rokeby@comcast.net; Internet Home Page Address: www.rokeby.org; *Dir* Jane Williamson
Open May - Oct Thurs - Sun 11 AM - 3 PM, open by appointment only remainder of yr; Admis fees Adult $6, seniors & students $4, children under 13 $2; Estab 1963 to exhibit & interpret lives & works of the Robinson family; Robinson family (prolific artists) art is displayed throughout the house. Work of Rachael Robinson Elmer (1878 - 1919), student at Art Students League, is most prominent. She & her father, Rowland E Robinson (1833 - 1900), were published artists; Average Annual Attendance: 2,400; Mem: 250; dues life $500, family $40, individual $25, student $10; ann meeting in mid-May
Income: Financed by mem, contributions & grants
Special Subjects: Costumes, Manuscripts, Textiles, Watercolors, Hispanic Art, Furniture, Period Rooms
Collections: Art, oils & watercolor sketches; books & manuscripts; 17th - 20th century furnishings; textiles & costumes
Publications: Messenger
Activities: Classes for children; docent training; lects open to pub; mus shop sells books & prints

HARDWICK

M **GRASS ROOTS ART & COMMUNITY EFFORT (GRACE),** Firehouse Gallery, 59 Mill St, Hardwick, VT 05843; PO Box 960, Hardwick, VT 05843-0960. Tel 802-472-6857; Fax 802-472-9578; Elec Mail grace@vtlink.net; Internet Home Page Address: www.graceart.org; *Mng Dir* Carol Putnam; *Exhib Dir* Kathy Stark; *Develop Coordr* Mimi Smyth
Open Tues - Thurs 10 AM - 4 PM; No admis fee; 1975; Average Annual Attendance: 500
Special Subjects: Folk Art, Painting-American, Watercolors
Collections: Estate of Gayleen Aiken
Publications: States of Grace; Moonlight & Music: The Enchanted World of Gayleen Aiken
Activities: Classes for adults & children; sales shop sells books, original art & prints

JERICHO

M **EMILE A GRUPPE GALLERY,** 22 Barber Farm Rd, Jericho, VT 05465-9795. Tel 802-899-3211; Internet Home Page Address: www.emilegruppegallery.com
Open Thurs-Sun 10AM-3PM; other times by appointment
Collections: paintings; photographs

A **JERICHO HISTORICAL SOCIETY,** 4A Red Mill Dr, Jericho, VT 05465; PO Box 35, Jericho, VT 05465-0035. Tel 802-899-3225; Fax 802-899-3027; Internet Home Page Address: www.jerichohistoricalsociety.org; *Pres* Ann Squires; *Sales Shop Mgr* Gail Prior; *Archives Chmn* Wayne Howe
Open Apr - Dec Mon - Sat 10 AM - 5 PM, Sun 11:30 AM - 4 PM, Jan - Mar Wed & Sat 10 AM - 5 PM, Sun 11:30 AM -4 PM; cl Sun July & Aug; No admis fee; Estab 1978
Income: Financed by mem & contributions
Collections: Milling Machinery; Slides of Snow Flakes & Ice Crystals (video tape)
Exhibitions: Machinery, permanent exhibit; Snowflake Bentley Exhib, permanent

JOHNSON

M **JACOB WALKER ART GALLERY,** Route 15, Johnson, VT 05656. Tel 802-849-6185
Open Thurs - Sun 10AM - 4PM
Collections: paintings; drawings

M **JULIAN SCOTT MEMORIAL GALLERY,** 337 College Hill, Johnson State College, Dibden Center Johnson, VT 06565. Tel 800-635-2356; *Dir* Leila Bandar
Open Summer Tues-Fri noon-6PM, Sat noon-4PM; Winter call for hours
Collections: paintings; drawings; sculptures

M   **VERMONT STUDIO CENTER,** Red Mill Gallery, 80 Pearl St, Johnson, VT 05656; PO Box 601, Johnson, VT 05656-0613. Tel 802-635-2727

LUDLOW

M   **BLACK RIVER ACADEMY MUSEUM & HISTORICAL SOCIETY,** (Black River Historical Society) Black River Academy Museum, High St, Ludlow, VT 05149-1091; PO Box 73, Ludlow, VT 05149-0073. Tel 802-228-5050; Elec Mail glbrehm@tds.net; Internet Home Page Address: bramvt.org; *Dir* Georgia L Brehm; *Asst* Linda L Tucker
Open Noon - 4 PM, summer only; Admis $2; Estab 1972; 3-story brick building built in 1889; Average Annual Attendance: 1,200; Mem: 200; dues family $45, single $25
Income: $25,000 (financed by endowment)
Library Holdings: Manuscripts; Maps; Memorabilia; Original Documents; Pamphlets; Photographs
Special Subjects: Glass, Furniture, Maps
Collections: School memorabilia, farming implements, domestic items - 19th century, furnishings, clothing; Calvin Coolidge School Days Memorabilia; Fiber-R Arts Spinning Wheels/Weaving Looms; Barns of Ludlow
Publications: History of Ludlow, VT, J Harris (monograph); Black River Academy Booklet; Village Walking Tour Booklet
Activities: Dramatic progs; classes for adults & children; docent training; lects open to pub, 200 vis lectrs per yr; concerts; tours on holidays; VT Historical Society Educational Awards; schols; traveling exhibs 2 per yr; sales shop sells books, reproductions

LYNDON CENTER

M   **SHORES MEMORIAL MUSEUM,** (Shores Memorial Museum and Victoriana) Main St, Lyndon Center, VT 05850; PO Box 85, Lyndon Center, VT 05850-0085. Tel 802-626-3265; Internet Home Page Address: www.shoresmuseum.org; *Cur* Christopher Raymond; *Pres* Eric Paris
Summers by appt; No admis fee, donations accepted; Mus portrays a working man's home of the late Victorian era. Completed in 1896, this Queen Anne-style house was home to the Shores family of Lyndon Center, VT; Mem: 180; dues $5 ann
Library Holdings: Clipping Files; Memorabilia; Original Documents; Photographs
Special Subjects: Historical Material, Photography, Period Rooms, Costumes, Dolls, Furniture
Collections: Photographs, organs; kitchen & pantry exhib which demonstrates the time in which food preparation meant hours of hand labor. Coll includes wooden plates & bowls, a mortar & pestle, wire basket for egg collecting, long-handled bedwarmer, and a sadiron for pressing clothes; upstairs room features period clothing, exhib of war memorabilia & a doll exhib
Publications: Mr. Vail Comes to Town (Biog of Theodore N Vail)
Activities: Resource room for historical research; classes for children; tours

MANCHESTER

A   **SOUTHERN VERMONT ART CENTER,** 2522 West Rd, Manchester, VT 05254; PO Box 617, Manchester, VT 05254-0617. Tel 802-362-1405; Fax 802-362-3279; Elec Mail info@svac.org; Internet Home Page Address: www.svac.org; *Pres* Charles M Ams III; *Dir* Christopher Madkour; *Dir Pub Rels* Margaret Donovan
Open Tues - Sat 10 AM - 5 PM, Sun Noon - 5 PM, cl July 4th; Admis adults $8, students $3, free admis Sun; members and children under 13 free; Estab 1929 to promote educ in the arts & to hold exhibitions of art in its various forms; 10 galleries; sculpture garden; Average Annual Attendance: 25,000; Mem: Dues $55 - $75; annual meeting in Sept
Income: Financed by mem & contributions
Collections: Contemporary American sculptors & painters; loan coll
Exhibitions: Annual exhibitions for members; Fall Show; one-man & special exhibitions
Publications: Annual catalog & brochures
Activities: Classes for adults & children in painting, drawing, graphic arts, photography, sculpture & pottery; concerts; scholarship & fels offered
L   **Library,** PO Box 617, West Rd, Manchester, VT 05254. Tel 802-362-1405; *Dir* Christopher Madkour
Open Tues - Fri 10 AM - 5 PM
Income: Income from contributions
Library Holdings: Book Volumes 500

MIDDLEBURY

M   **HENRY SHELDON MUSEUM OF VERMONT HISTORY AND RESEARCH CENTER,** (Sheldon Museum) One Park St, Middlebury, VT 05753. Tel 802-388-2117; Fax 802-388-2112; Elec Mail info@henrysheldonmuseum.org; Internet Home Page Address: www.henrysheldonmuseum.org; *Exec Dir* Jan Albers; *Coll Mgr* Mary Towle-Hilt; *Educ Coordr* Susan Peden; *Librn* Orson Kingsley; *Assoc Dir* Mary Manley
Open Mon - Sat 10 AM - 5 PM; Admis family $12, adults $5, seniors & students $4.50, youth $3; Estab 1882 for the preservation of furniture, portraits, decorative arts, artifacts & archival material of Middlebury & Addison County, VT; Museum housed in 1829 marble merchants home and with a gallery; Average Annual Attendance: 4,000; Mem: 650; dues $10 & up
Library Holdings: Book Volumes; Manuscripts; Maps; Original Documents; Pamphlets; Photographs
Special Subjects: Architecture, Glass, Furniture, Porcelain, Pottery, Painting-American, Manuscripts, Maps, Textiles, Costumes, Ceramics, Decorative Arts, Portraits, Posters, Historical Material, Period Rooms, Pewter
Collections: China; furniture; glass; historical material; landscapes; pewter; portraits; prints

Exhibitions: Changing art and history exhibits in the Cerf Gallery; permanent exhibits of 19th Century home & furnishings
Publications: Marble in Middlebury; Walking History of Middlebury; annual report; newsletter
Activities: Traditional craft classes for adults and workshops for children; lects open to pub; guided tours; gallery talks; tours; one concert annually; out-reach program to county schools; mus shop sells gifts, home accessories, jewelry, toys, games, reproductions, prints & books on Vermont history

M   **MIDDLEBURY COLLEGE,** Museum of Art, Rte 30, Mahaney Center for the Arts Middlebury, VT 05753-6177. Tel 802-443-5007, 443-5235; Fax 802-443-2069; Elec Mail deperkin@middlebury.edu; Internet Home Page Address: museum.middlebury.edu; *Chief Cur* Emmie Donadio; *Cur Educ* Sandra Olivo; *Dir* Richard Saunders; *Registrar* Margaret Wallace; *Designer* Ken Pohlman; *Admin Opers Mgr* Douglas Perkins; *Events Outreach Coordr* Mikki Lane
Open Tues - Fri 10 AM - 5 PM, Sat & Sun Noon - 5 PM, cl Mon & holidays; No admis fee; Estab 1968 as a teaching collection. Now also presents loan exhibitions, work by individuals & groups, student exhibits; In 1992 moved to new Middlebury College Center for the Arts, designed by Malcolm Holzman of Hardy, Holzman & Pfeiffer Assoc; Average Annual Attendance: 15,000 - 17,000; Mem: 350; dues vary on 7 levels; annual meeting in Apr, triannual board meetings
Income: Financed through College, Friends of Art & grants
Special Subjects: Drawings, Painting-American, Photography, Prints, Sculpture, Watercolors, American Western Art, Bronzes, Woodcarvings, Etchings & Engravings, Decorative Arts, Painting-European, Portraits, Asian Art, Coins & Medals, Calligraphy, Period Rooms, Antiquities-Oriental, Antiquities-Greek, Antiquities-Roman, Antiquities-Assyrian
Collections: Asian art; drawings; paintings; photographs; prints; sculpture; antiquities
Publications: Gallery brochure; exhibition catalogues & brochures; exhibitions & events calendars
Activities: Classes for children; docent training; family workshops; teacher workshops; lects open to pub, 2-3 vis lectrs per yr; gallery talks; Friends of Art sponsor Annual Arts Awards given to members of the local community; book traveling exhibs 6-7 per yr; originate traveling exhibs; mus shop sells books, prints, notecards, postcards, posters

MONTPELIER

M   **T W WOOD GALLERY & ARTS CENTER,** 46 Barre St, Montpelier, VT 05602-3508. Tel 802-828-8743; Fax 802-828-8645; Elec Mail info@twwoodgallery.org; Internet Home Page Address: twwoodgallery.org; Open Tues - Sun Noon - 4 PM; Admis by donation; Estab 1895 by 19th century genre & portrait artist T W Wood to house & exhibit a portion of his works. Gallery acts as archive for information about T W Wood; 3 gallery spaces: 2,700 sq ft, 800 sq ft, 500 sq ft, 15 ft high ceilings; in newly renovated 1870 College Hall on Vermont College campus; Average Annual Attendance: 10,000; Mem: 200; dues $35 - $100
Income: Financed by endowment, city appropriation, grants & mem
Special Subjects: Painting-American
Collections: Oil paintings, watercolors, prints by T W Wood, A B Durand, J G Brown, A Wyant, Edward Gay; 100 works from the 1920s & 30s, some by WPA painters Reginald Marsh, Louis Boucher, Paul Sample, Joseph Stella; early 19th century American portraits
Publications: Monograph on the Wood Collection
Activities: Classes for children; docent training; children's art camp; lects open to pub, 8 vis lectrs per yr; concerts; gallery talks; tours; individual paintings & original objects of art lent to local organizations, bus & other mus with appropriate security systems; lending collection includes original prints & photographs; mus shop sells books, original art, reproductions, slides, gifts & cards

M   **VERMONT HISTORICAL SOCIETY,** Museum, 109 State St, Montpelier, VT 05609-0901. Tel 802-828-2291; Fax 802-828-1415; Elec Mail vhs-info@state.vt.us; Internet Home Page Address: www.vermonthistory.org; *Cur* Jacqueline Calder; *Registrar* Mary Labate Rogstad; *Mus Prog Mgr* Geraldine Brown; *Mus Asst* Polly Bentley
Open Tues - Fri 10AM - 4PM, cl state and federal holidays; Admis adults $3, seniors & students $2; Estab 1838 to collect, preserve and make available for study items from Vermont's past; Average Annual Attendance: 22,000; Mem: 2,600; dues $25 - $600; annual meeting in Aug or Sept
Income: Financed by endowment, mem, state appropriation & contributions
Collections: Collection of fine arts, decorative arts, tools & equipment and work of Vermont artists; genealogy
Exhibitions: Generation of Change; Vermont, 1820-1850; All the Precious Past; Baseball in VT
Publications: Vermont History, 2 times per year; Vermont History News, bi-monthly
Activities: Lects open to pub; fellowships offered; mus shop sells books, prints, gifts & postcards
L   **Library,** 109 State St, Montpelier, VT 05609-0901. Tel 802-828-2291; Fax 802-828-3638; Elec Mail vhs@vhs.state.vt.us; Internet Home Page Address: www.state.vt.us/vhs; *Dir* Gainor B Davis; *Asst Librn* Marjorie Strong; *Library Asst* Claire Gilbertson; *Library Asst* Bernadette Harrington
Open Tues - Fri 9 AM - 4 PM, Wed until 8 PM, second Sat of each month 9 AM -4 PM; Admis user fee $5; Estab 1838; Reference Library
Income: Financed by endowment, mem, state & contributions
Purchases: $4900
Library Holdings: Audio Tapes; Book Volumes 150,000; Cassettes; Manuscripts; Motion Pictures; Pamphlets; Photographs; Reels; Video Tapes
Special Subjects: Folk Art, Landscape Architecture, Decorative Arts, Manuscripts, Historical Material, Ceramics, Crafts, Archaeology, Advertising Design, Interior Design, Furniture, Costume Design & Constr, Glass, Bookplates & Bindings, Dolls, Embroidery, Handicrafts, Landscapes, Coins & Medals, Flasks & Bottles, Architecture

MOSCOW

M **LITTLE RIVER HOTGLASS STUDIO & GALLERY,** 593 Moscow Rd, Moscow, VT 05662; PO Box 1504, Stowe, VT 05672-1504. Tel 802-253-0889; Fax 802-253-4128
Open Wed-Mon 10AM-5PM
Collections: blown glass sculptures

PITTSFORD

M **NEW ENGLAND MAPLE MUSEUM,** Rte 7, Pittsford, VT 05763; PO Box 131, Pittsford, VT 05763-0131. Tel 802-483-9414; Fax 802-483-2101; Elec Mail newenglandmaplemuseum@yahoo.com; Internet Home Page Address: www.maplemuseum.com; *Pres* Michael Blanchard; *Cur, Mgr & Purchasing* Mary Blanchard; *Asst Mgr* Laura Goodrich
Open daily 9:30 AM - 5:30 PM (May 20 - Oct 31), 10 AM - 4 PM (Nov 1 - Dec 23 & mid-Mar - May 19); Admis adults $5, seniors $4, children between 6 - 12 $1, children under 6 free; Estab 1977 to present the complete history of maple sugaring; Photographs, paintings, carvings, dioramas; Average Annual Attendance: 35,000
Income: $400,000 (financed by gift shop sales & admis)
Purchases: $2,000 per yr, mainly maple sugaring antiques
Library Holdings: Photographs; Slides; Video Tapes
Special Subjects: Drawings, Historical Material, Photography, Painting-American, Ceramics, Crafts, Folk Art, Woodcarvings, Dioramas
Collections: Oil paintings on maple sugaring by Paul Winter; oil murals on early maple sugaring by Vermont artist Grace Brigham; Photo Collection 1900-1938 Maple sugaring in Vermont
Exhibitions: Permanent collection
Activities: Tours; Mus shop sells books, magazines, original art, reproductions, prints, slides, travel videos, pottery, jewelry, Vermont crafts & specialty foods

RUTLAND

M **NORMAN ROCKWELL MUSEUM OF VERMONT,** 654 Route 4 E, Rutland, VT 05701. Tel 877-773-6095; Fax 802-775-2440; Elec Mail sales@normanrockwellvt.com; Internet Home Page Address: www.normanrockwellvt.com
Open every day 9 AM - 5 PM; Admis adults $6.50, seniors $6, children $2.50; Estab in 1976 to commemorate Norman Rockwell's Vermont years & the entire span & diversity of the artist's career which ran from 1911-1978; Located in Rutland, near the corners of Rt 4 and Rt 7, two miles east on Rte 4
Special Subjects: Folk Art, Prints, Painting-American, Posters
Collections: Chronological display of more than 2,500 Rockwell magazine covers, advertisements, calendars & other publ works which shows his develop as an illustrator & links his works to the political, economic & cultural history of the US; featured works of artist Robert Duncan, member of the Cowboy Artists of America
Activities: mus shop sells books, magazines, reproductions, prints, figurines, plates, puzzles & mugs

A **RUTLAND AREA ART ASSOCIATION,** Chaffee Art Center, 16 S Main St, Rutland, VT 05701-4136; PO Box 1447, Rutland, VT 05701-1447. Tel 802-775-0356; Fax 802-775-6242; Elec Mail mary@chaffeeartcenter.org; Internet Home Page Address: www.chaffeeartcenter.org; *Exec Dir* Mary Mitigay
Open Wed - Sat 10 AM - 5 PM, Sun Noon - 4 PM, cl Mon & Tues; No admis fee; donations accepted; Estab & incorporated 1961 to promote & maintain an educational & cultural center in the central Vermont region for the area artists, all artistic mediums presented; 1896 Queen Anne Victorian mansion listed on state & national register; Average Annual Attendance: 30,000; Mem: 400; juried artists; dues $50; annual meeting in Feb
Income: Financed by mem, special funding, contributions, grants, foundations, activities & spec events
Exhibitions: Annual Members Exhibit, juried; Art-in-the-Park outdoor festivals; group & invitational exhibits; featured artists exhib
Publications: Calendar of events, annually; exhibition posters
Activities: Classes for adults & children; docent training; lects open to pub, 4 vis lectrs per yr; concerts; gallery talks; tours; competition with awards; schols offered; individual printings lent to local banks, corporations & other area cultural organizations; all original artwork & prints for sale

SAINT JOHNSBURY

M **FAIRBANKS MUSEUM & PLANETARIUM,** 1302 Main St, Saint Johnsbury, VT 05819-2224. Tel 802-748-2372; Fax 802-748-1893; Internet Home Page Address: www.fairbanksmuseum.org; *Dir* Charles C Browne
Open Tues - Sat 9 AM - 5 PM, Sun 1 - 5 PM, extended summer hours; Admis families $12, adults $5, students & sr citizens $4, children $3, group rates available; Estab 1889 as a center for exhibits, special exhibitions & programs on science, technology, the arts & the humanities; Average Annual Attendance: 90,000; Mem: 800; dues $35; monthly meeting
Income: $500,000 (financed by admis income, grants, endowment, mem & municipal appropriations)
Special Subjects: Photography, Watercolors, American Indian Art, African Art, Archaeology, Ethnology, Textiles, Costumes, Folk Art, Eskimo Art, Dolls, Oriental Art, Asian Art, Historical Material, Ivory, Maps, Coins & Medals, Dioramas, Islamic Art, Antiquities-Egyptian, Military Art
Collections: natural science, history & anthropology colls; Oceanic Art
Publications: Exhibit catalogs; quarterly newsletter
Activities: Classes for adults & children; docent training; lects open to pub, 20 vis lectrs per yr; concerts; gallery talks; tours; exten dept serving Northeast Vermont; artmobile; individual paintings & original objects of art lent to other accredited mus; lending collection contains 500 nature artifacts, 50 original art works, 10

paintings & 500 photographs; book traveling exhibs one per yr; mus shop sells books, magazines, original art, reproductions, prints & science-related items; junior mus

M **NORTHEAST KINGDOM ARTISANS GUILD,** 430 Railroad St, Number 2 Saint Johnsbury, VT 05819-1727. Tel 802-748-0158; Elec Mail nekguild@kingcon.com; Internet Home Page Address: www.nekartisansguild.com
Open Mon-Sat 10:30AM-5:30PM; Estab in 1997 featuring a variety of fine traditional & contemporary craft by Vermont artisans
Collections: handmade crafts & fine arts including baskets, clay, fiber, glass, metal, paper, & wood; prints; watercolors; oils; photographs

M **SAINT JOHNSBURY ATHENAEUM,** 1171 Main St Saint Johnsbury, VT 05819. Tel 802-748-8291; Fax 802-748-8086; Elec Mail inform@stjathenaeum.org; Internet Home Page Address: www.stjathenaeum.org; *Library Dir* Lisa Von Kann; *Exec Dir* Mathew Powers
Open Mon-Fri 10 AM - 5:30 PM, Sat 9:30 AM - 4PM; Admis $5 to gallery for non-residents; donations accepted; Estab 1873 & maintained as a 19th century gallery; given to the townspeople by Horace Fairbanks; It is the oldest art gallery still in its original form in the United States; the only art-related nat historic landmark in the state of Vermont; Average Annual Attendance: 10,000
Income: Financed by endowment, town appropriation & annual giving
Special Subjects: Landscapes, Architecture, Portraits, Painting-American, Period Rooms, Manuscripts, Maps, Painting-European, Sculpture, Religious Art
Collections: 19th century American landscape paintings of the Hudson River School (Bierstadt, Colman, Whittredge, Cropsey, Gifford, Hart brothers); copies of masterpieces; sculpture
Exhibitions: Permanent Collection
Publications: Art Gallery Catalogue
Activities: Docent training; youth progs; lect open to public; gallery talks; tours; concerts; mus shop sells books, reproductions, art card-reproductions, prints & posters

M **STEPHEN HUNECK GALLERY AT DOG MOUNTAIN,** 143 Parks Rd, Saint Johnsbury, VT 05819-8907. Tel 800-449-2580; 802-748-2700; Fax 802-748-3075; Elec Mail info@dogmt.com; Internet Home Page Address: www.dogmt.com; *Gallery Mgr* Amanda McDermott; *Art Dir* Gwendolyn Huneck; *Sales Mgr* Jill Brown
Open Mon-Sat 10AM-5PM, Sun 11AM-4PM; No admis fee; Estab 2000; Gallery is the home of the artwork of the late Stephen Huneck & the only Dog Chapel in the world; Average Annual Attendance: 5,000+
Collections: sculptures; paintings; photographs
Activities: Hiking trails; dog ponds; dog chapel; sales shop sells books, original art, reproductions, prints, sculptures, dog toys, clothing

SHELBURNE

M **FURCHGOTT SOURDIFFE GALLERY,** 86 Falls Rd, Shelburne, VT 05482-6208. Tel 802-985-3848
Open Tues-Fri 9:30AM-5:30PM; Sat 10AM-5PM
Collections: paintings; pottery

M **SHELBURNE MUSEUM,** Museum, 6000 Shelburne Rd, Shelburne, VT 05482; PO Box 10, Shelburne, VT 05482-0010. Tel 802-985-3346; Fax 802-985-2231; Elec Mail info@shelburnemuseum.org; Internet Home Page Address: www.shelburnemuseum.org; *Dir Coll* Catherine Comar
Open Mon-Sat 9AM-5PM, Sun 1PM-5PM; Admis call for rates, group rates available; Estab 1947 exhibits American fine, decorative & utilitarian arts, particular emphasis on Vermont and New England heritage; 37 buildings on 45 acres; Average Annual Attendance: 160,000; Mem: Dues $30 - $75
Income: Financed primarily by admissions & fundraising from members
Special Subjects: Painting-American, Ethnology, Textiles, Ceramics, Folk Art, Decorative Arts, Painting-European, Dolls, Period Rooms
Collections: American paintings, folk art, decoys, architecture, furniture, quilts & textiles, dolls, sporting art & sculpture, ceramics, tools, sleighs & carriages, toys, farm & home implements; seven period houses; European material: Impressionist & Old Master paintings; English furniture & architectural elements; Native American ethnographic artifacts; Sidewheeler Ticonderoga, railroad memorabilia including steam train, circus material & carousel animals
Activities: Classes for children; docent training; lect open to public, 5 vis lectrs per year; concerts; gallery talks; tours; exten dept serves Vermont; book traveling exhibitions annually; mus shop sells books, reproductions, prints, slides & original art

L **Library,** PO Box 10, Shelburne, VT 05482-0010. Tel 802-985-3346; Fax 802-985-2331; Elec Mail info@shelburnemuseum.org; Internet Home Page Address: www.shelburnemuseum.org; *Librn* Polly Darnell; *Sr Cur* Jean Burks
Open May - Oct 10 AM - 5 PM; Admis Adults $18, children $9; Estab 1947, art & Americana; Open to pub by appointment; Average Annual Attendance: 120,000; Mem: 5,500 members
Income: Financed by grants & contributions, admissions & earned income
Library Holdings: Audio Tapes; Book Volumes 6,000; Cassettes; Clipping Files; Exhibition Catalogs; Filmstrips; Kodachrome Transparencies; Manuscripts; Memorabilia; Motion Pictures; Pamphlets; Periodical Subscriptions 66; Photographs; Prints; Records; Slides; Video Tapes
Special Subjects: Art History, Folk Art, Decorative Arts, Drawings, Etchings & Engravings, Painting-American, Painting-French, Painting-European, Historical Material, Ceramics, American Western Art, Asian Art, American Indian Art, Porcelain, Furniture, Period Rooms, Glass, Carpets & Rugs, Dolls, Handicrafts, Miniatures, Pottery, Marine Painting, Landscapes, Pewter, Flasks & Bottles, Scrimshaw, Laces, Architecture, Embroidery, Textiles, Woodcarvings
Collections: Art & Americana from the 17th - 20th centuries
Activities: Classes for adults & children; docent training; lects open to public; concerts; gallery talks; tours; fellowships; mus shop sells books, magazines, reproductions, prints

SPRINGFIELD

A SPRINGFIELD ART & HISTORICAL SOCIETY, The Miller Art Center, 9 Elm St, Springfield, VT 05156; PO Box 313, Springfield, VT 05156-0313. Tel 802-885-2415; Elec Mail info@millerartcenter.com; *Pres* Leonard K Bolduc; *VPres* John Swanson; *Dir* Maureen Bolduc
Open Thurs & Fri 11 AM - 4 PM, Sat 11 AM - 3 PM; Admis $3; Estab 1956 for the purpose of presenting history, arts & sciences of Springfield & environs; Gallery located in a Victorian mansion built in 1861 & is maintained for monthly exhibits; Average Annual Attendance: 1,200; Mem: 250; dues $50, $35 & $20; ann meeting in Nov
Income: $25,000 (financed by endowment & mem)
Library Holdings: Audio Tapes; Book Volumes; CD-ROMs; Cassettes; Clipping Files; Manuscripts; Maps; Memorabilia; Original Art Works; Original Documents; Photographs; Prints; Sculpture; Slides; Video Tapes
Special Subjects: Architecture, Costumes, Drawings, Historical Material, Landscapes, Manuscripts, Photography, Prints, Sculpture, Textiles, Watercolors, Painting-American, Pottery, Decorative Arts, Pewter, Portraits, Dolls, Period Rooms, Maps
Collections: Primitive portraits by H Bundy, Aaron D Fletcher & Asahel Powers; Richard Lee, pewter; Bennington pottery; paintings by local artists; toys, costumes, sculpture, crafts; machine tool industry
Exhibitions: Historical exhibs: costumes; toys; photography; fine arts; student & mem art exhibs
Publications: Annual schedule of events & monthly notices; members quarterly newsletter
Activities: Classes for adults & children; civil war living history group; lects open to pub, 4 vis lectrs per yr; concerts; gallery talks; competitions with awards; individual paintings & objects of art lent to local galleries; lending collection contains original art work, paintings, photographs, sculpture, slides; living history - Sanitary Commission - Civil War group presentations; mus shop sells books, original art, slides, prints, magnets, post cards

STOWE

M CLARKE GALLERIES, 51 S Main St, PO Box 777 Stowe, VT 05672-0777. Tel 917-454-8779; Elec Mail clarkegalleries@gmail.com;
Call for hours; Average Annual Attendance:
Collections: American & European paintings and sculpture from 1800s to present; photographs; prints

M GREEN MOUNTAIN FINE ART GALLERY, 64 S Main St, Stowe, VT 05672; PO Box 1384, Stowe, VT 05672-1384. Tel 802-253-1818; Fax 802-253-6837
Open Wed-Mon 10AM-6PM
Collections: watercolors; oils; pastels; prints; mixed media; photography

M ROBERT PAUL GALLERY, 394 Mountain Rd, Stowe, VT 05672; PO Box 1413, Stowe, VT 05672-1413. Tel 800-873-3791
Open Mon-Sat 10AM-6PM, Sun 10AM-5PM
Collections: sculpture; photography

M WEST BRANCH GALLERY & SCULPTURE PARK, 17 Towne Farm Ln, Stowe, VT 05672-4138; PO Box 250, Stowe, VT 05672-0250. Tel 802-253-8943; Internet Home Page Address: www.westbranchgallery.com
Open Wed-Sun 11AM-6PM, other times by appt; No admis fee; Estab 2004; Contemporary paintings & sculpture
Collections: paintings; sculptures

WEST RUTLAND

M CARVING STUDIO AND SCULPTURE CENTER, 636 Marble St, West Rutland, VT 05777; PO Box 495, West Rutland, VT 05777-0495. Tel 802-438-2097; Fax 802-438-2020; Elec Mail info@carvingstudio.org; Internet Home Page Address: www.carvingstudio.org
Call for hours
Collections: sculptures

WHITE RIVER JUNCTION

M MAIN STREET MUSEUM, 58 Bridge St, White River Junction, VT 05001-7040. Tel 802-356-2776
Open Thurs-Sun 1PM-6PM; Average Annual Attendance:
Collections: local history & culture; photographs; sculptures; paintings

VIRGINIA

ALEXANDRIA

A THE ART LEAGUE GALLERY & SCHOOL, 105 N Union St, Alexandria, VA 22314-3217. Tel 703-683-2323, 683-1780; Fax 703-683-0167; Elec Mail info@theartleague.org; Internet Home Page Address: www.theartleague.org; *Pres* Betsy Anderson; *Exec Dir* Linda Hafer; *Deputy Exec Dir* Suzanne Bethel; *Treas* Ellen Fishbein; *VPres* Nancy Fortwengler; *Gallery Dir* Rose O'Donnell; *VPres* Jane McElvaney Coonce; *Dir School* Kathi Cohen
Open Mon - Sat 10 AM - 6PM, Sun Noon - 6 PM; No admis fee; Estab 1954 to promote & maintain standards of art through mem juried exhibs & a large school which teaches all facets of the fine arts & some high skill crafts; Sixteen classrooms total; three classrooms in the Torpedo Factory Art Center in Old Town Alexandria, Virginia; three gallery rooms & thirteen classrooms in two annexes;

Average Annual Attendance: 500,000; Mem: 1,200; dues $70; annual meeting in June; open to all
Income: program income, grants & contributions, member dues
Library Holdings: Book Volumes 1665; Periodical Subscriptions
Exhibitions: Monthly juried shows for members; solo shows monthly; Annual Student Faculty Show; Art in City Hall
Activities: Classes for adults & children; foreign & domestic art-travel workshops; lect open to public; gallery talks; tours; sponsors competitions with monthly Best in Show cash awards & other recognition awards; sales shop sells art supplies

ART SERVICES INTERNATIONAL
For further information, see National and Regional Organizations

M GALLERY WEST LTD, 1213 King St, Alexandria, VA 22314-2926. Tel 703-549-6006; Elec Mail gallerywest@verizon.net; Internet Home Page Address: www.gallery-west.info/; *Pres* Judith Smith; *VP* Mary B Allen; *Treas* Cindi Lewis
Open Jan - Mar Wed - Sun 11 AM - 5 PM, Apr - Dec Wed - Sun 11 AM - 6 PM; No admis fee; Estab 1979 to showcase artists of all media in the Washington DC metro area

M GEORGE WASHINGTON MASONIC MEMORIAL, 101 Callahan Dr, Alexandria, VA 22301-2751. Tel 703-683-2007; Fax 703-519-9270; Internet Home Page Address: www.gwmemorial.org; *Exec Secy & Treas* George D Seghers; *Exec Adminr* JoAnn Guthrie; *Cur* Stephen Patrick
Open daily 10 AM - 4 PM; No admis fee, observation deck admis $5; Estab 1932; Maintains a reference library; 12 exhibition rooms; auditorium; 3 museums; Average Annual Attendance: 60,000 - 70,000; Mem: 1.8 million; voluntary contributions; annual meeting Feb 22
Income: Privately funded charitable organization
Library Holdings: Book Volumes; Compact Disks; DVDs; Fiche; Framed Reproductions; Maps; Memorabilia; Original Documents; Pamphlets; Periodical Subscriptions; Photographs; Reproductions
Special Subjects: Painting-American, Portraits, Furniture, Coins & Medals, Dioramas, Stained Glass
Collections: George Washington Portraits & Relics; Masonic & related artifacts
Exhibitions: Relics & portraits of George Washington, murals, Lafayette & Intimates of Washington; Art & Architecture 1900 - 1930
Publications: Light, quarterly
Activities: Dramatic programs; lects open to pub, 3 vis lectrs per yr; concerts; tours; George Washington Memorial Award; mus shop sells books, reproductions, prints

A NORTHERN VIRGINIA FINE ARTS ASSOCIATION, The Athenaeum, 201 Prince St, Alexandria, VA 22314-3313. Tel 703-548-0035; Fax 703-948-0456; Elec Mail admin@nvfaa.org; Internet Home Page Address: www.nvfaa.org; *Exec Dir* Catherine Asel Ford; *Events Coordr* Kevin Peck
Open Thurs, Fri & Sun 12 noon - 4 PM, Sat 1 PM - 4 PM, cl Mon, Tues, Wed & holidays; No admis fee; Estab 1964 to promote education, appreciation, participation & pursuit of excellence in all forms of art & crafts; to enrich the cultural life of the metropolitan area & Northern Virginia; Main gallery space on main floor, with additional area available; Average Annual Attendance: 10,000; Mem: 70; dues $40-$500
Income: Financed by mem, fundraisers & grants
Exhibitions: Annual Joint Art League/Athenaeum Multi-media Juried show; Five Virginia Photographers: Sally Mann, E Gowen & Others; Thomas Hart Benton; Washington Color School: Stars & Stripes; Kathleen Ewing's Dog Days Dog Show; Portent curated by Richard Dana; Networked curated by J.T.Kirtland; Waxworks curated by Ellen Weiss; Hair Apparent curated by Twis Murray
Publications: Quarterly newsletter
Activities: Dance classes for adults & children; dramatic progs; docent training; lects open to pub, gallery talks; tours; sponsoring of competitions; schols offered; exten prog serving Northern Virginia

SPECIAL LIBRARIES ASSOCIATION
For further information, see National and Regional Organizations

ARLINGTON

M ARLINGTON ARTS CENTER (AAC), 3550 Wilson Blvd, Arlington, VA 22201-2348. Tel 703-248-6800; Fax 703-248-6849; Elec Mail information@arlingtonartscenter.org; Internet Home Page Address: www.arlingtonartscenter.org; *Exec Dir* Stefanie Fedor
Open Wed - Fri 12-7 PM, Sat & Sun Noon - 5 PM; No admis fee; Estab to present new work by emerging & established artists from the region (Virginia, Maryland, Washington DC, West Virginia, Pennsylvania & Delaware); 17,000 sq ft venue for contemporary art; Average Annual Attendance: 11,000
Special Subjects: Calligraphy
Activities: Classes for adults, teens & children; studio res prog; workshops; lects open to pub; gallery talks; tours; vis artist prog; juried exhibs

L ARLINGTON COUNTY DEPARTMENT OF PUBLIC LIBRARIES, Fine Arts Section, 1015 N Quincy St, Arlington, VA 22201-4603. Tel 703-228-5990; 228-5996; Fax 703-228-5692; Elec Mail ikauff@arlingtonva.us; Internet Home Page Address: www.arlingtonva.us/library; *Branch Librn* Margaret Brown; *Head Art Prog* Ingrid Kauffman
Open Mon - Thurs 10 AM - 9 PM, Fri & Sat 10 AM - 5 PM, Sun 1 - 9 PM; No admis fee; Estab 1935 to serve needs of an urban-suburban population in all general subjects; Juried shows of 4-5 artists change monthly
Income: Financed by county & state appropriations
Purchases: Jeff Wilson - Blue Lids
Library Holdings: Book Volumes 3,000; Other Holdings Total holdings: 323,000; Periodical Subscriptions 15
Exhibitions: Local artists, crafts people & photographers have exhibitions at the central library each month; additional exhibs at Shirlington Branch library; see website for addition exhib info

Activities: Lects open to pub, 10 vis lectrs per yr; workshops; film shows; extended learning institute video tapes from Northern Virginia Community Col available

M **BLUEMONT HISTORICAL RAILROAD JUNCTION,** Blueprint Junction Park, 601 N Manchester St Arlington, VA 22203; 2100 Clarendon Blvd, Ste 201 Arlington, VA 22201-5447. Tel 703-228-3323; Fax 703-228-3328; Elec Mail prcr@arlingtonva.us; *Ranger* Sedgwick Moss; *Ranger Coordr* Lynne Everly; *Vol Pub Rels* Stephen Patrick; *Park Ranger II* Lynda Kersey
Open May - Sept Sat & Holidays 10 AM - 6 PM, Sun 1 - 5 PM; No admis fee, donations accepted; Estab 1992; Arlington & Alexandria's only railway mus interprets the history of these communities that grew up around the lines; housed on former southern railway caboose X-441, built in 1972; Average Annual Attendance: 2,500
Income: A feature of Arlington County parks and recreation
Collections: Photos & objects from local railway history
Activities: Guided tours

M **LEE ARTS CENTER,** 5722 Lee Hwy, Arlington, VA 22207. Tel 703-228-0560; Fax 703-228-0559; Elec Mail leearts@arlingtonva.us; Internet Home Page Address: www.arlingtonarts.org; *Contact* Steven Munoz

ASHLAND

M **FLIPPO GALLERY,** 211 N Center St, Randolph Macon College, Pace-Armistead Hall Ashland, VA 23005. Tel 804-752-7200
Open Mon - Fri 10 AM - 4 PM, Sat - Sun by appointment
Collections: Student & faculty artwork; exhibits by national & state artists

BLACKSBURG

A **BLACKSBURG REGIONAL ART ASSOCIATION,** PO Box 525, Blacksburg, VA 24063-0525. Elec Mail braa-info@bev.net; Internet Home Page Address: www.braa.arts.bev.net; *Pres* Roberta Sallee; *Mem Chmn* Tom Barnhart; *Treas* Jeanette Bowker; *VPres* Nancy Norton; *VPres* Danie Janov
No admis fee; contributions; Estab 1950, affiliated with the Virginia Museum of Fine Arts, dedicated to the encouragement & enjoyment of the arts; 11 galleries in merchant venues; Mem: 130; dues individual $20, family $25; annual meeting in Apr
Income: Financed by mem & patron contributions
Library Holdings: DVDs
Exhibitions: 11 rotating exhibitions per yr & juried exhibits
Publications: BRAA newsletter, monthly
Activities: Art classes for pub & members only; lects open to pub & members only, 3 vis lectrs per yr; competitions; sponsored shows; art sales events

M **VIRGINIA POLYTECHNIC INSTITUTE & STATE UNIVERSITY,** Armory Art Gallery, 201 Drapper Rd, Blacksburg, VA 24061-0103. Tel 540-231-4859, 231-5547; Fax 540-231-7826; *Art Chair & Interim Staff Dir* Bailey Van Hook; *Gallery Coordr* Francis Thompson
Open Mon - Fri Noon - 5 PM, Sat Noon - 4 PM; No admis fee; Estab 1969 to serve needs of art department as a teaching gallery as well as to meet community needs in an area where there are few large art centers & museums; Gallery is located in same building as Art Department; exhibition area is approx 16 x 40 ft; Average Annual Attendance: 2,000 plus student use
Income: Financed through special university budget
Exhibitions: Special invited exhibitions & exhibitions by Virginia artists, students & visiting artists
Publications: Exhibition calendar; gallery announcements
Activities: Docent training to college students; lects open to public, 3 vis lectrs per yr; gallery talks; individual paintings & original objects of art lent to faculty & staff offices on campus, as well as library & continuing educ center; originate traveling exhibs

M **Perspective Gallery,** 118 N Main St, Squires Student Ctr Blacksburg, VA 24060-3939. Tel 540-231-5431; Fax 540-231-5430; *Art Dir* Tom Butterfield
Open Tues - Fri Noon - 10 PM, Sat & Sun 2 - 10 PM, cl Mon; No admis fee; Estab 1969 to provide a broad arts experience for the students, faculty & the university community; Average Annual Attendance: 50,000
Income: Financed by university unions & student activities

L **Art & Architecture Library,** 302 Cowgill Hall, Blacksburg, VA 24062; PO Box 90001, Blacksburg, VA 24062-9001. Tel 540-231-9271; Elec Mail h.ball@vt.edu; Internet Home Page Address: www.lib.vt.edu; *Librn* Heather Ball; *Visual Resources Cur* Brian Shelburne
Open Mon - Thurs 8 AM - 11 PM, Fri 8 AM - 5 PM, Sat 1 - 5 PM, Sun 2 - 11 PM; Estab 1928 to provide service to the College of Architecture & Urban Studies & the other divisions of the university; Circ 60,000
Income: Financed by state appropriation & gifts
Purchases: $69,500
Library Holdings: Book Volumes 65,000; CD-ROMs; Cassettes; Clipping Files; DVDs; Exhibition Catalogs; Fiche; Pamphlets; Periodical Subscriptions 300; Reels; Slides 70,000; Video Tapes
Special Subjects: Landscape Architecture, Architecture

BROOKNEAL

M **PATRICK HENRY MEMORIAL FOUNDATION,** Red Hill National Memorial, 1250 Red Hill Rd, Brookneal, VA 24528-3302. Tel 804-376-2044; Fax 804-376-2647; Internet Home Page Address: www.redhill.org; *Admin Asst* Lynn Davis; *Exec Dir* Dr Jon Kukla; *Cur* Edith Poindexter; *Assoc Cur* Karen Gorham-Smith
Open 9 AM - 5 PM, winter, 9 AM - 4 PM; Admis fee $6; Estab 1944 to preserve & develop a memorial to Patrick Henry; One room with Rothermel painting as focal point; Average Annual Attendance: 11,000; Mem: dues $25 & up; annual meeting in May

Income: $250,000 (financed by endowment, mem, county & state appropriation)
Library Holdings: Audio Tapes; Clipping Files; Framed Reproductions; Manuscripts; Maps; Memorabilia; Motion Pictures; Original Art Works; Original Documents; Pamphlets; Photographs; Sculpture; Video Tapes
Special Subjects: Landscape Architecture, Architecture, Furniture, Photography, Portraits, Silver, Sculpture
Collections: Patrick Henry images; decorative arts; furniture & memorabilia
Exhibitions: Patrick Henry Before the Virginia House of Burgesses by P F Rothermel; Patrick Henry Memorabilia
Publications: Quarterly newsletter
Activities: Classes for adults & children; docent progs; lects open to pub; 2 vis lectrs per yr; tours; schols offered; National Forensic League Annual Competition; mus shop sells reproductions

CHANTILLY

M **NATIONAL AIR AND SPACE MUSEUM,** Steven F Udvar-Hazy Center, 14390 Air & Space Museum Pkwy, Chantilly, VA 20151-3002. Tel 703-572-4118; Elec Mail NASM-VisitorServices@si.edu; Internet Home Page Address: www.nasm.si.edu/udvarhazy; *NASM Dir* John R Dailey
Open daily 10 AM - 5:30 PM, cl Dec 25; extended summer hrs until 7 PM; No admis fee; pub parking $15, free after 4 PM; Bldg opened 2003 to provide extra exhib space unavailable to National Air & Space Mus on National Mall; James S. McDonnell Space Hangar opened 2004; Comprised of Boeing Aviation Hangar, James S McDonnell Space Hangar, Donald D Engen Observation Tower & Airbus IMAX Theater. Bureau of the Smithsonian Institution in Washington, DC
Collections: National Aviation & Space Exploration Wall of Honor; Aircraft & Engines; Aerial Cameras; International Space; Awards & Insignia; Propulsion; Rocketry
Exhibitions: Applications Satellites; Human Spaceflight; Rockets & Missiles; Space Science; Flight Simulator; Aerobatic Flight; Business Aviation; Cold War Aviation; Commercial Aviation; General Aviation; Korea & Vietnam Aviation; Modern Military Aviation; Pre-1920 Aviation; Sport Aviation; Ultralight Aircraft; Vertical Flight; World War II Aviation; World War II German Aviation
Activities: Educ progs; school group activities; tours; mus store

M **Donald D Engen Tower,** 14390 Air & Space Museum Pkwy, Chantilly, VA 20151-3002. Tel 703-572-4118; Elec Mail NASM-VisitorServices@si.edu; Internet Home Page Address: http://www.nasm.si.edu/visit/concessions/tower.cfm
Hours available at Mus Welcome Ctr; Tower closes before rest of bldg; No admis fee; Two levels incl observation accessible by elevator
Exhibitions: Lower Level Exhib: air traffic control workstation, equipment, & artifacts; Observation Level Exhib: explains basic features of an airport

CHARLES CITY

M **SHIRLEY PLANTATION FOUNDATION,** 501 Shirley Plantation Rd, Charles City, VA 23030-2907. Tel 804-829-5121; Fax 804-829-6322; Elec Mail info@shirleyplantation.com; Internet Home Page Address: www.shirleyplantation.com; *Owner* Charles Hill Carter Jr; *Dir* Janet L Appel; *Deputy Dir* Randy Carter
Open daily 9:30 AM - 4:30 PM; cl Thanksgiving and Christmas; Admis adults $11, discounts for AAA, military & seniors 60 & up, & youth; Estab 1613 to share the history of one distinguished family from colonial times to the present; oldest family-owned bus in North America; Oldest Virginia Plantation continuous home to the Hill Carter Family, currently 10th & 11th generations; maintains 8 original colonial outbuildings circa 1730's & 1750's; Average Annual Attendance: 45,000
Special Subjects: Etchings & Engravings, Prints, Silver, Textiles, Painting-French, Architecture, Drawings, Painting-American, Anthropology, Archaeology, Ceramics, Pottery, Woodcarvings, Woodcuts, Landscapes, Decorative Arts, Manuscripts, Painting-European, Portraits, Furniture, Glass, Porcelain, Metalwork, Painting-British, Historical Material, Maps, Coins & Medals, Restorations, Painting-Flemish, Period Rooms, Antiquities-Oriental, Pewter, Reproductions, Bookplates & Bindings
Collections: 18th century English silver & oil portraits; 18th & 19th century furniture & handcarved woodwork; Civil War, culinary, gardens, genealogy, trees
Exhibitions: Timeline, permanent exhib
Publications: Shirley Plantation booklet
Activities: Classes for adults & children; dramatic progs, thematic seasonal progs; tours; lending collections contain books, original art works, original prints, photographs & over 18,000 documents on permanent loan to Colonial Williamsburg; mus shop sells books, reproductions, prints, silver & porcelain

M **WESTOVER PLANTATION,** (Westover) 7000 Westover Rd, Charles City, VA 23030-3329. Tel 804-829-2882; Fax 804-829-5528; Elec Mail info@westover-plantation.com; Internet Home Page Address: westover-plantation.com; *Mgr* Andrea F Erda
Grounds & garden open daily 9 AM - 6 PM; Admis $5, children $3; house interior open by appointment; Built about 1730 by William Byrd II, Founder of Richmond, the house is considered one of the finest example of Georgian architecture in America, with steeply sloping roof, tall chimneys in pairs at both ends, elaborate Westover doorway, a three story central structure with two end wings. The path from the Caretakers House to the house is lined with tulip poplars over 100 years old; former kitchen is a separate small brick building. East of the house (open to visitors) is the Necessary House, an old icehouse & a dry well with supposed passageways leading under the house to the river. The Westover gates of delicate ironwork incorporate initials WEB; lead eagles on the gateposts, fence column topped with stone finials cut to resemble pineapples, beehives, & other symbolic designs. Long estab boxwood garden with tomb of William Byrd II. Members of his family, & Captain William Perry, who died Aug 1637, are buried in old church cemetery one-fourth mile west of house
Special Subjects: Architecture

CHARLOTTESVILLE

M **SECOND STREET GALLERY,** 115 Second St SE, Charlottesville, VA 22902. Tel 434-977-7284; Fax 434-979-9793; Elec Mail ssg@secondstreetgallery.org; Internet Home Page Address: www.secondstreetgallery.org; *Pres* Steve Taylor; *VPres* Steve Delgado; *Treas* Ryan Ford; *Secy* Mary M Murray; *Exec Dir* Rebecca Young Schoenthal; *Gallery Opers & Outreach* Andrew M Greeley; *Mem & Develop Assoc* Amanda Currie Jones
Open Tues - Sat 11 AM - 6 PM; No admis fee; Estab 1973 as an alternative arts space to present emerging & accomplished contemporary artists from regional & national localities and to promote an appreciation of contemporary art and culture by educating the public; Two galleries: main gallery 1520 sq ft, Dove gallery 360 sq ft; Average Annual Attendance: 15,000; Mem: 375; dues benefactor $1,000, Patron $500, sponsor $250, friend $100, individual $35
Income: Financed by individual, corporate & foundation contributions & grants from the Virginia Commission for the Arts & fundraising activities
Publications: The Second Glance, quarterly newsletter; exhibit catalogs
Activities: Adult educ; Lect; tours; literary readings; in-school workshops; grant support from the Andy Warhol Foundation for the Visual Arts

M **THOMAS JEFFERSON FOUNDATION, INC,** Monticello, PO Box 316, Charlottesville, VA 22902-0316. Tel 434-984-9801, 434-984-9822; Fax 434-977-7757; Elec Mail administration@monticello.org; Internet Home Page Address: www.monticello.org; *Pres* Leslie Greene Bowman
Open Mar - Oct Mon - Sun 8 AM - 5 PM, Nov - Feb Mon - Sun 9 AM - 4:30 PM, cl Christmas; Admis adults $17 Nov-Feb $22 March-Oct, children 6-11 $8; Estab 1923 to preserve education; Monticello is owned & maintained by the Thomas Jefferson Foundation, a nonprofit organization founded in 1923. The home of Thomas Jefferson, designed by him & built 1769-1809, contains many original furnishings & art objects; Average Annual Attendance: 525,000
Income: Pvt
Library Holdings: Audio Tapes; Book Volumes; CD-ROMs; Cards; Cassettes; Clipping Files; Compact Disks; DVDs; Exhibition Catalogs; Fiche; Filmstrips; Manuscripts; Maps; Memorabilia; Original Documents; Other Holdings; Pamphlets; Periodical Subscriptions; Photographs; Prints; Reproductions; Slides; Video Tapes
Special Subjects: Afro-American Art, American Indian Art, Archaeology, Landscapes, Architecture, Ceramics, Portraits, Maps, Sculpture, Drawings, Painting-American, Religious Art, Etchings & Engravings, Decorative Arts, Manuscripts, Furniture, Historical Material, Restorations, Reproductions
Activities: Classes for children; lects open to pub; concerts; talks, fels; mus shop sells books, reproductions & prints

M **UNIVERSITY OF VIRGINIA,** The Fralin Museum of Art at the University of Virginia, 155 Rugby Rd, Charlottesville, VA 22904-4119; PO Box 400119, Charlottesville, VA 22904-4119. Tel 434-924-3592, 434-243-2050 (tours); Fax 434-924-6321; Internet Home Page Address: www.virginia.edu/artmuseum; *Cur Exhibs* Jennifer Farrell; *Coll Mgr* Jean Collier; *COO* David Chennault; *Dir Develop* Elizabeth Wright; *Preparator* Andrew Hersey; *Dir* Bruce Boucher; *Exhibs Coordr* Ana Marie Liddell; *Acad Cur* M Jordan Love; *Docent Coordr* Virginia Soenksen; *Accounting Specialist* Diana Garnett; *Cur Asst* Katelyn Hobbs; *Dir Annual Giving* Sarah Mullen; *Mktg Mgr* Emelia Meckstroth; *Asst Registrar* Rachael Salisbury; *Digital Colls Coordr* William Auten; *Asst to Dir* Laurie Hilsinger; *Assoc Acad Cur* Aimee Hunt
Open Tues - Sun noon - 5 PM, cl Mon; No admis fee, donations accepted; Estab 1935 to make original works of art available to the university community & to the general pub; Perm coll & temp exhibitions; teaching museum; more than 12,000 works; Average Annual Attendance: 28,000; Mem: 2,200; dues dir circle $5,000, cur circle $2,500, benefactor $1,000, patron $500, sponsor $200, basic $75, seniors $40, student free
Income: Financed by mem, state appropriation & gifts
Special Subjects: American Indian Art, Etchings & Engravings, Landscapes, Ceramics, American Western Art, Photography, Porcelain, Portraits, Pottery, Pre-Columbian Art, Painting-French, Painting-Japanese, African Art, Posters, Asian Art, Antiquities-Byzantine, Coins & Medals, Baroque Art, Painting-Flemish, Antiquities-Oriental, Painting-Italian, Antiquities-Greek, Antiquities-Roman, Painting-German, Antiquities-Etruscan
Collections: American art; European & American Art in the age of Jefferson; Old Master prints; East Asian art; contemporary art; American Indian art; Oceanic Art; prints, drawings, photographs, Roman Coins; Ancient Mediterranean
Exhibitions: Various rotating exhibitions, call for schedule
Publications: exhibition brochures; calendar
Activities: Educ progs for adults, students, children; docent training; lects open to pub, 5+ vis lectrs per yr; gallery talks; tours; fels & internships offered; original works of art lent; book traveling exhibs 1-3 per yr; mus shop sells books & cards
L **Fiske Kimball Fine Arts Library,** Bayly Dr, Charlottesville, VA 22903; PO Box 400131, Charlottesville, VA 22904-4131. Tel 804-924-7024; Fax 804-982-2678; Elec Mail jsr8s@virginia.edu; Internet Home Page Address: www.lib.virginia.edu/fine-arts/index.htm/; *Asst Librn & Pub Services* Barbara Jackson
Open school year Mon - Thurs 8 AM - Midnight, Fri 8 AM - 8 PM, Sat 10 AM - 8 PM, Sun Noon-Midnight; Estab 1970; combination of existing art & architecture libraries to provide a research facility providing printed, microform, audio visual & electronic materials for the art, architecture & drama curriculum; Circ 115,000; Fifty percent of collection is non-circulating
Income: $212,000
Library Holdings: Audio Tapes; Book Volumes 127,000; Cassettes; Exhibition Catalogs; Fiche; Filmstrips; Kodachrome Transparencies; Manuscripts; Periodical Subscriptions 285; Photographs; Reels; Slides 171,000
Special Subjects: Art History, Film, Photography, Archaeology, Architecture
Collections: Francis Benjamin Johnson Photographs of Virginia Architecture; Rare books
Publications: Bibliography of the Arts: Including Fine & Decorative Arts, Architecture, Design & the Performing Arts, updated quarterly; Guide To Sources, irregular serial; Notable Additions to the library collection, quarterly

CHESAPEAKE

M **PORTLOCK GALLERIES AT SONO,** 3815 Bainbridge Blvd, Chesapeake, VA 23324-1607. Tel 727-502-4901; Elec Mail nbenson@cityofchesapeake.net; Internet Home Page Address: www.portlockgalleries.com; *Gallery Dir* Nicole Benson
Open Tues - Fri 10 AM - 5 PM, Sat - Sun 1 PM - 5 PM; cl holidays; No admis fee
Collections: Paintings & photographs; art exhibitions

CHRISTIANBURG

M **MONTGOMERY MUSEUM & LEWIS MILLER REGIONAL ART CENTER,** 300 S Pepper St, Christiansburg, VA 24073. Tel 540-382-5644; Fax 540-382-9127; Elec Mail info@montgomerymuseum.org; Internet Home Page Address: www.montgomerymuseum.org; *Dir* Shearon Campbell; *Pres (Vol)* Robert L Puff
Open Mon - Sat 10:30 AM - 4:30 PM, Sun 1:30 - 4:30 PM; Admis adult $1, children $.50; Estab 1983; Average Annual Attendance: 3,500
Income: Financed by grants, gifts & members
Library Holdings: Book Volumes; Clipping Files; Memorabilia; Original Art Works; Pamphlets; Photographs; Prints; Slides
Collections: Lewis Miller Art; clothing; family genealogy; photographs; dolls, local history books, old photo albums, household items, bus machines, weaving loom
Exhibitions: Rotating exhibits
Publications: Quarterly newsletter; Montgomery Museum newsletter; booklets
L **Library,** 300 S Pepper St, Christiansburg, VA 24073. Elec Mail info@montgomerymuseum.org; Internet Home Page Address: www.montgomerymuseum.org; *Dir* Linda L Martin
Open Mon - Sat 10:30 AM - 4:30 PM, Sun 1:30 - 4:30 PM; Admis adult $2, children 12 & under $1, free to members; Reference
Library Holdings: Book Volumes 300; Clipping Files; Memorabilia; Original Art Works; Other Holdings; Pamphlets; Photographs; Prints; Slides
Special Subjects: Folk Art, Photography, Prints, Historical Material, Crafts, Dolls

COURTLAND

M **RAWLS MUSEUM ARTS,** 22376 Linden St Courtland, VA 23837. Tel 757-653-0754; Fax 757-653-0341; Elec Mail rma@beldar.com; Internet Home Page Address: www.rawlsarts.cjb.net; *Exec Dir* Barbara Easton-Moore; *Educational Outreach Coordr* Elizabeth Fox; *VPres* Dorothy Council
Open Tues - Fri 10 AM - 4 PM, Sat Noon - 4 PM; No admis fee; Estab 1958 to promote the arts in the city of Franklin & the counties of Isle of Wight, Southampton, Surry & Sussex; Main gallery is 45 ft x 50 ft, 12 ft high with track lighting, adjunct Francis Gallery also has track lighting; Average Annual Attendance: 7,500; Mem: 248; dues $15 - $42, annual meeting in June, Board of Dir meet monthly
Income: $40,000 (financed by endowment, mem & grants)
Special Subjects: Portraits, Pottery, Drawings, Painting-American, Photography, Watercolors, Crafts, Posters, Glass, Silver
Collections: Antique glass & silver; Southeastern Virginia Artists; drawings, paintings, lithographs
Exhibitions: Annual Regional Photography Exhibition; two Annual Student Art Shows; regular group exhibitions by area artists; Virginia Museum of Fine Arts Traveling Exhibitions; annual regional exhibition
Publications: R M A Bulletin
Activities: Classes for adults & children; family fun events; intensive 4-6 hour educ outreach classes addressing SOL's for four school systems; lects open to pub, 4 vis lectrs per yr; concerts; gallery talks; tours; sponsoring of competitions; schols offered; paintings & art objects lent to mus & libraries; mus shop sells books, original art & prints

DANVILLE

M **DANVILLE MUSEUM OF FINE ARTS & HISTORY,** 975 Main St, Danville, VA 24541-1822. Tel 434-793-5644; Fax 434-799-6145; Elec Mail artandhistory@danvillemuseum.org; Internet Home Page Address: www.danvillemuseum.org; *Pres* Jack Neal Jr; *Exec Dir* Lynne Bjarnesen; *Office Mgr* Geraldine Scearce; *Museum Shop Mgr* Tim Stowe; *Educ Coordr* Sharon Hughes; *Arts Prog Coordr* Shawn Jones; *Develop Coordr* Katherine Milam
Open Tues - Fri 10 AM - 5 PM, Sat & Sun 2 - 5 PM; No admis fee; Estab 1974; Museum has two galleries: 27 x 35 ft with track lighting; one smaller gallery 24 x 17 ft with track lighting; Average Annual Attendance: 20,000; Mem: 600; dues $20 - $1,000
Income: Financed by mem, grants, fundraisers, class fees
Library Holdings: Auction Catalogs; Audio Tapes; Book Volumes; CD-ROMs; Exhibition Catalogs
Special Subjects: Architecture, Drawings, Graphics, Painting-American, Sculpture, Watercolors, Textiles, Costumes, Folk Art, Woodcarvings, Woodcuts, Etchings & Engravings, Decorative Arts, Painting-European, Portraits, Historical Material, Maps, Tapestries, Period Rooms, Laces
Collections: American Costume Collection including 2 locally made crazy quilts; Civil War; emphasis on works by contemporary Southern & Mid-Atlantic Artists; historic artifacts & documents pertaining to the history of Danville; 19th & 20th century decorative arts including furniture, silver, porcelain; Victorian American paintings & works on paper 1932 - present
Exhibitions: Rotating schedule of art & history exhibitions; Survey shows highlighting historic & modern artists in movement; Historic exhibit includes restored period rooms, a Victorian parlor, bedroom & library; Between the Lines: 1861-1865
Publications: Last Capital of the Confederacy, book; Activities Report, quarterly newsletter

Activities: Classes for adults & children; docent training; hands-on school progs; lects open to pub, 3 vis lectrs per yr; gallery talks; tours; mus shop sells books, magazines, original art, prints & reproductions

FAIRFAX

L   PROVISIONS LIBRARY, Provisions Research Center for Arts & Social Change, Art & Design Bldg Ste L002, George Mason University Fairfax, VA 22030. Tel 202-670-7768; Elec Mail provisionslibrary@gmail.com; Internet Home Page Address: www.provisionslibrary.com; *Pres* Ethelbert Miller; *Dir & Cur* Donald Russell; *Dir Arts & Media* Niel Van Tomme
Open Tues - Fri noon - 5 PM; No admis fee, donations accepted; Estab 1993; Circ Non-circulating; Library, exhibs & educ progs linking contemporary global arts with social change issues; Average Annual Attendance: 10,000 - 49,999 by estimate
Library Holdings: Audio Tapes 300; Book Volumes 5000; Compact Disks 200; DVDs 200; Other Holdings 400 DVDs; Periodical Subscriptions 200; Video Tapes 200
Special Subjects: Intermedia, Photography, Graphic Arts, Conceptual Art, Latin American Art, Cartoons, Art Education, Video, Afro-American Art
Collections: Books, periodicals, audiovisuals & films on global social issues
Exhibitions: Close Encounters: Acts of Social Imagination; Revisiting Histories
Publications: Exhib catalogs
Activities: Research on global social change; formal educ progs for adults & col students; training progs for professional mus workers; guided tours; hobby workshops; participatory exhibs; study clubs; lects open to pub; 15 vis lectrs per yr; films; arts festivals; floating mus project; originate traveling exhibs to museums, universities & art centers

FARMVILLE

A   LONGWOOD CENTER FOR THE VISUAL ARTS, 129 N Main St, Farmville, VA 23901-1305. Tel 804-395-2206; Fax 804-392-6441; Internet Home Page Address: www.longwood.edu/lcva/; *Dir* Kay Johnson Bowles; *Prog Mgr* Beth Cheuk; *Colls Mgr* Ashley Webb; *Cur Educ* Emily Greshem; *Exhib Mgr* Alex Grabiec; *Mus Registrar* Robin Sedgwick; *Preparator* Brian Carley
Open Mon - Sat 11 AM - 5 PM; Admin offices open Mon - Fri 8:30 AM - 5 PM; No admis fee; Estab 1978; 27,000 sq ft facility incl the Miller Gallery, Bishop Gallery, Sully Gallery, & Main St Gallery as well as a Kids Activity room, classroom & multi-purpose room; Mem: Dues friend $1 - $99, advocate $100 - $249, fellow $250 - $499, collector $500 - $749, connoisseur $750 - $1249, benefactor $1250 - $2499, champion $2500 - 4999, patron $5000+
Special Subjects: Drawings, Photography, Porcelain, Prints, Sculpture, Painting-American, Pottery, Asian Art, Decorative Arts, Folk Art, African Art, Glass, Woodcarvings
Collections: Virginia Artists Collection: incl work by Theresa Pollak, Gene Davis, Nell Blaine, Sally Mann, Willie Ann Wright, Nancy Witt, Miles Carpenter, Marion Line & Kent Ipson; African Art Collection: incl statues, masks, drums, baskets & garments; American Art Collection: 400+ works by Thomas Sully, James McNeill Whistler, Robert Raushenberg, Gene Davis, Anna Hyatt Huntingdon, Lilly Martin Spencer, Sam Maloof, John Garland Brown, Albert Pinkham Ryder, Homer Martin Dodge, John Neagle & Eastman Johnson; Jackson L Blanton Collection: 450+ works by a variety of VA artists; Waverly Manson Cole Collection of 19th c Decorative Arts; William & Ann Oppenheimer Collection of Folk Art; Rowe Collection of Chinese Art
Activities: Classes for adults & children; lects open to pub; gallery talks; tours; slide presentation; originate traveling exhibs to rural communities in Southside Virginia

FREDERICKSBURG

M   JAMES MONROE MUSEUM, 908 Charles St, Fredericksburg, VA 22401-5810. Tel 540-654-1043; Fax 540-654-1106; Internet Home Page Address: www.jamesmonroemuseum.mwc.edu; *Cur* David B Voelkel
Open Mar 1 - Nov 30 daily 10 AM - 5 PM, Dec 1 - Feb 28 daily 10 AM - 4 PM, cl Thanksgiving, Dec 24, 25, 31 & Jan 1; Admis adults $5, children 6-18 $1, children under 5 free; Estab 1927 to keep in memory the life & service of James Monroe & of his contribution to the principles of government, to preserve his treasured possessions for present & future generations; Open to the pub in 1928; owned by Commonwealth of Virginia & under the control of Mary Washington College; a National Historic Landmark; Average Annual Attendance: 12,000; Mem: $25 & up
Income: financed by state funds
Special Subjects: Sculpture, Ceramics, Portraits, Furniture, Jewelry, Silver
Collections: Louis XVI furniture purchased by the Monroes in France in 1794 & later used by them in the White House; portraits; sculpture; silver; china; jewelry; books; documents
Exhibitions: Rotating exhibs
Publications: Images of a President: Portraits of James Monroe, catalog Library of James Monroe; catalog; A Presidential Legacy
Activities: Docent training; workshops; lects open to pub; gallery talks; tours; scholarships offered; exten dept serves Mary Washington College University of VA area; mus shop sells books, magazines, reproductions, prints, slides, history related objects & exclusive items from local crafts people
L   James Monroe Memorial Library, 908 Charles St, Fredericksburg, VA 22401. Tel 540-654-1043; Fax 540-654-1106; Internet Home Page Address: www.jamesmonroemuseum.mwc.edu; *Dir* John N Pearce; *Cur* David Voelkel
Open by appointment only; Admis adults $5, children 6-18 $1, children under 5 free; Estab 1927 as a presidential mus & library; Open to pub; archival resources available by appointment only; Average Annual Attendance: 12,000
Income: Financed by state allocations & revenues
Library Holdings: Book Volumes 10,000; Manuscripts 27,000; Other Holdings Documents; Letters

M   UNIVERSITY OF MARY WASHINGTON, (Mary Washington College) Gari Melchers Home and Studio, 224 Washington St, Fredericksburg, VA 22405-2360. Tel 540-654-1015; Fax 540-654-1785; Elec Mail garimelchers@umw.edu; Internet Home Page Address: www.garimelchers.org; *Cur* Joanna D Catron; *Dir* David Berreth
Open daily 10 AM - 5 PM; Admis adults $10, seniors $9, adult groups $8, children between 6 & 18 $5; Estab 1975 to exhibit, preserve & interpret the works of art & memorabilia of the late American artist Gari Melchers, in his former estate & studio; Studio consists of four gallery rooms, a work room & storage rooms; Average Annual Attendance: 13,000
Income: $800,000 (financed by endowment & state appropriation)
Library Holdings: Auction Catalogs; Exhibition Catalogs; Manuscripts; Memorabilia; Original Documents; Photographs
Special Subjects: Decorative Arts, Drawings, Landscapes, Furniture, Photography, Painting-American, Period Rooms, Sculpture, Watercolors, Porcelain, Painting-Dutch, Painting-Italian, Painting-German
Collections: Over six hundred works of art, paintings, drawings & etchings by Gari Melchers; Over 1,000 sketches & studies by Gari Melchers; Paintings & drawings by Berthe Morisot, Franz Snyders, Puvis de Chavannes & others; Furnishings from Europe & America
Publications: Exhibition catalogs
Activities: Docent training; educ prog; classes for adults & children; aesthetics tours for school groups; outreach progs for school & nursing homes; lects open to pub; 3 vis lectrs per year; gallery talks; tours; individual paintings & original objects of art lent; mus shop sells books, reproductions & prints
M   University of Mary Washington Galleries, 1301 College Ave, at Seacobeck St Fredericksburg, VA 22401-5300. Tel 540-654-1013; Fax 540-654-1171; Internet Home Page Address: www.umw.edu/umw-galleries; *Office Mgr* Angela Whitley; *Dir* Anne Timpano; *Asst Cur & Registrar* Kyra Swanson; *Vis Svcs Coordr* Justin Geiger
Open Mon, Wed & Fri 10 AM - 4 PM, Sat & Sun 1 - 4 PM; No admis fee; Estab 1956 for educ in art history & cultural history; Average Annual Attendance: 5,000
Special Subjects: Drawings, Etchings & Engravings, Landscapes, Photography, Portraits, Painting-American, Prints, Watercolors, Woodcuts, Asian Art
Collections: 19th & 20th Century American art; Asian Art
Exhibitions: Contemporary art; exhibs from permanent collection; faculty & student
Publications: Booklets; catalogs
Activities: Lects open to pub; 5 vis lectrs per yr; concerts; gallery talks; tours

GLEN ALLEN

M   COUNTY OF HENRICO, Meadow Farm Museum, 3400 Mountain Rd, Glen Allen, VA; PO Box 27032, Richmond, VA 23273-7032. Tel 804-501-5520; Fax 804-501-5284; Internet Home Page Address: www.co.henrico.va.us/rec; *Historic Preservation Supv* Chris Gregson; *Coll Mgr* Kimberly Sicola; *Asst Site Mgr* Linda Eikmeier
Open Tues - Sun Noon - 4 PM; No admis fee; Estab 1981 to exhibit works of 20th century American folk artists; 20 ft x 20 ft, AV room; Average Annual Attendance: 50,000
Income: Financed by Henrico County
Special Subjects: Architecture, Archaeology, Ceramics, Crafts, Folk Art, Afro-American Art, Decorative Arts, Furniture, Carpets & Rugs, Embroidery
Collections: 19th & 20th Century folk art
Exhibitions: Annual Folk-Art Exhibit
Publications: Exhibition flyers, annually
Activities: Children's classes; lect open to public, 4 vis lectrs per year; tours; individual paintings & original objects of art lent to Virginia Beach Art Center; lending collection contains original art works, paintings & sculptures; sales shop sells books & reproductions
L   Library, 3400 Mountain Rd, Glen Allen, VA 23060; PO Box 27032, Richmond, VA 23273. Tel 804-501-5520; Fax 804-501-5284; *Site Mgr* Anna Beegles
Open by appointment only; for reference only
Library Holdings: Audio Tapes; Book Volumes 100; Clipping Files; Exhibition Catalogs; Kodachrome Transparencies; Periodical Subscriptions 10; Photographs; Slides; Video Tapes

M   THE CULTURAL ARTS CENTER AT GLEN ALLEN, 2880 Mountain Rd, Glen Allen, VA 23060; PO Box 1249, Glen Allen, VA 23060-1249. Tel 804-261-2787; Fax 804-261-6217; Elec Mail info@glenallen.com; Internet Home Page Address: www.artsglenallen.com; *Pres & Dir Programming* K Alferio; *Performing Arts Mgr & Technical Dir* Richard Koch; *Visual Arts Mgr* Lauren Hall; *Dir Develop* Nellie Blair; *Dir Mktg & Pub Rels* Anita Waters
Call for hours; No admis fee with some ticketed events; Estab 1999; Two galleries feature regional, national, & international artists; Average Annual Attendance: 100,000
Collections: Paintings & photographs; art exhibitions

HAMPTON

A   CITY OF HAMPTON, Hampton Arts Commission, 4205 Victoria Blvd, Hampton, VA 23669; 125 E Mellen St, Hampton, VA 23663-1711. Tel 757-722-2787; 757-727-1621; Fax 757-727-1167; Elec Mail amtheater@city.hampton.va.us; Internet Home Page Address: www.amtheatre.com; *Dir* Michael P Curry; *Arts Coordr* Debra Burrell; *Production Mgr* Mary Blackwell; *Box Office Mgr* Mildred Williams
Art Ctr open year round Tues - Fri 10 AM - 6 PM, Sat - Sun 1 - 5 PM, cl major holidays; theatre open Mon - Fri 9 AM - 5:30 PM; No admis fee; Created in Dec, 1987, housed in the Charles H Taylor Arts Center
Income: Financed by municipal funds & contributions
Library Holdings: Cards
Exhibitions: Regional artists presented at Charles H Taylor Arts Center, monthly; special events art shows; performances by international artists presented at the American Theatre

Activities: Classes for adults & children; master classes in drama & music; dramatic progs; workshops; demonstrations; lects open to pub; lects for mem only; 12 vis lectrs per yr; concerts; gallery talks; tours; competitions with awards; lending to selected bus; 1 - 2 book traveling exhibs

M **HAMPTON UNIVERSITY,** University Museum, 11 Frissell Ave, Hampton, VA 23663-2340. Tel 757-727-5308; Fax 757-727-5170; Elec Mail museum@hamptonu.edu; Internet Home Page Address: www.hamptonu.edu/museum; *Dir* Vernon S Courtney; *Cur Colls* Vanessa Thaxton-Ward
Open Mon - Fri 8 AM - 5 PM, Sat & Sun Noon - 4 PM, cl Sun; No admis fee; Estab 1868 as a museum of traditional art & artifacts from African, Asian, Oceanic & American Indian cultures & contemporary & traditional African-American Art; Average Annual Attendance: 60,000; Mem: Dues start at $25, students $15
Income: Financed by college funds
Special Subjects: American Indian Art, African Art, Afro-American Art
Collections: African, Asian, Oceanic & American Indian Art; Contemporary & traditional African-American Art; artwork & objects relating to history of university; university archives
Publications: The Internat Journal of African American Art
Activities: Educ dept; lects open to pub; gallery talks; group tours by appointment; Governor's Award for Artistic Org 2008-2009; individual paintings & original objects of art lent to other mus & art galleries with appropriate security; sales shop sells books, magazines & prints

M **HEADQUARTERS FORT MONROE, DEPT OF ARMY,** Casemate Museum, 20 Bernard Rd, Hampton, VA 23651-1004; PO Box 51341, Hampton, VA 23663-0341. Tel 757-788-3935; Fax 757-788-3886; Elec Mail claire.samuelson@us.army.mil; *Cur* Claire Samuelson; *Mus Specialist* David J Johnson
Open daily 10:30 AM - 4:30 PM; No admis fee; Estab 1951 to depict history of Fort Monroe; Average Annual Attendance: 40,000; Mem: 250; dues one-time-only fee based on plateaus: annual meeting in mid-Jan
Income: Financed by federal & state appropriation
Library Holdings: Micro Print; Motion Pictures; Original Art Works; Photographs; Prints; Sculpture; Slides
Special Subjects: Decorative Arts, Architecture, Pottery, Drawings, Graphics, Painting-American, Photography, Prints, Watercolors, Ceramics, Etchings & Engravings, Manuscripts, Posters, Furniture, Glass, Porcelain, Silver, Historical Material, Maps, Coins & Medals, Period Rooms, Cartoons, Stained Glass, Leather, Military Art, Reproductions
Collections: Military Posters; Jack Clifton Paintings Collection
Exhibitions: Civil War Artifacts; Coast Artillery Guns in Action; Glass Bottles
Publications: Exhibition catalogs
Activities: Docent training; lects provided upon request to local organizations; tours; originate traveling exhibs 3 per yr; mus shop sells books, reproductions, prints

HARRISONBURG

M **JAMES MADISON UNIVERSITY,** Sawhill Gallery, MSC 7101, 820 S Main St, Duke Hall, Rm 101 Harrisonburg, VA 22807. Tel 540-568-6407; Fax 540-568-5862; Elec Mail freebugl@jmu.edu; Internet Home Page Address: www.jmu.edu/artandarthistory; *Gallery Dir* Gary Freeburg
Open Sept - Apr, Mon - Fri 10 AM -5PM, Sat noon - 5PM, May - Aug call for summer schedule & hours; No admis fee; Estab 1967 to schedule changing exhibitions for the benefit of students & citizens of this area; One-room gallery of 1040 sq ft with movable panels; Average Annual Attendance: 10,000 - 12,000
Income: Financed by state appropriation, and is part of operation in Art Dept budget
Special Subjects: Asian Art, Antiquities-Greek, Antiquities-Roman
Collections: Sawhill Collection, mainly artifacts from classical civilizations; Staples Collection of Indonesian Art
Exhibitions: Rotating exhibitions
Activities: Competitions

VIRGINIA QUILT MUSEUM, 301 S Main St, Harrisonburg, VA 22801-2606. Tel 540-433-3818; Fax 540-433-3818
Open Feb-Dec Tues-Sat 10AM-4PM; cl major holidays; Admis adults $5, students 12-18 $3, youth 5-11 $2, children under 5 free
Collections: early & contemporary quilts; quilting; sewing machines

HERNDON

INDUSTRIAL DESIGNERS SOCIETY OF AMERICA
For further information, see National and Regional Organizations

LEESBURG

M **OATLANDS PLANTATION,** (Oatlands, Inc) 20850 Oatlands Plantation Lane, Leesburg, VA 20175. Tel 703-777-3174; Fax 703-777-4427; *Events Coordr* Jeannie Whitty; *Mgr* David Boyce
Open Apr - Dec, Mon - Fri 10 AM - 5 PM, Sat 9:30 AM - 5 PM, Sun 1 - 5 PM, cl Thanksgiving Day, Christmas, New Years; Admis adults $8, seniors & youths (7-18) $7, children (5- 11) $1; special events at special rates, group rates by arrangement, free to National Trust members & friends except for special events; Oatlands is a Classical Revival Mansion constructed by George Carter, son of Robert (Councillor) Carter (c 1800-06). It was partially remodeled in 1827 when the front portico with hand carved Corinthian capitals was added. Confederate troops were billeted here during part of the Civil War. The home remained in possession of the Carters until 1897. In 1903 Mr & Mrs William Corcoran Eustis, of Washington DC, bought Oatlands. Their daughters gave the property to the National Trust for Historic Preservation; the property is protected by preservation

easements which help ensure the estates continuing role as a center for equestrian sports & cultural events which are produced by Oatlands & various groups
Income: $600,000 (financed by grants, endowments, admis, fundraising events & shop sales)
Special Subjects: Furniture, Period Rooms
Collections: Greek-Revival ornaments adorn interior; Carter & Eustis Collection of Furniture
Exhibitions: Annual needlework Show; Christmas at Oatlands; semi annual Antique Show
Publications: Oatlands Column, quarterly newsletter
Activities: Special events

LEXINGTON

M **WASHINGTON & LEE UNIVERSITY,** Gallery of DuPont Hall, 204 W Washington St, Lexington, VA 24450-2116. Tel 540-463-8861; Fax 540-463-8104; Internet Home Page Address: www.wlu.edu; *Dir* Kathleen Olsen; *Chmn Dept Art* Pamela Simpson
Open Mon - Fri 9 AM - 5 PM, Sat 11 AM - 3 PM, Sun 2 - 4 PM; No admis fee; Estab 1929 in separate gallery as teaching resource of art; One room, 30 x 60 ft, is maintained for temporary exhibits; also maintained one storeroom; Average Annual Attendance: 40,000
Income: Financed through the university
Exhibitions: Annual faculty show; annual student show; monthly exhibitions; traveling exhibitions
Publications: Exhibition catalogs
Activities: Lect open to public, 5 vis lectrs per year; gallery talks; tours; book traveling exhibitions 3 per year

L **Leyburn Library,** 204 W Washington St, Lexington, VA 24450-2116. Tel 540-458-8644; Fax 540-458-8964; Elec Mail merrilly@wlu.edu; Internet Home Page Address: www.library.wlu.edu; *Art Librn* Yolanda Merrill; *Head Librn* John Tombarge; *Sr Reference Librn* Dick Grefe
Open 24 hours a day during school yr, summer Mon - Fri 8:30 AM - 4:30 PM; Open for reference to students, scholars, public; this library is part of the main university library
Collections: Rare books, 17th - early 20th centuries

M **Lee Chapel & Museum,** 204 W Washington St, Lexington, VA 24450-2116. Tel 540-463-8768; Internet Home Page Address: www.leechapel.wlu.edu; *Dir* Patricia Hobbs
Open Apr 1- Oct 31 Mon - Sat 9 AM - 5 PM, Sun 1 - 5 PM, Nov 1-Mar 31 Mon - Sat 9 AM - 4 PM, Sun 1 PM - 4 PM; No admis fee; Estab 1868 as a part of the university. It is used for concerts, speeches & other events; Museum relates the history of the university and its ties to its namesakes and is used also to display the paintings, collections & personal items of the Washington & Lee families. The Lee Chapel is a National Historic Landmark; Average Annual Attendance: 55,000
Income: Financed through the university
Special Subjects: Historical Material, Painting-American, Portraits, Period Rooms
Collections: Washington-Custis-Lee Art Collection; Lee archives; Lee family crypt; Lee's office; recumbent statute of General Lee by Valentine
Publications: Brochure
Activities: Mus shop sells books, reproductions, prints & related merchandise

LORTON

M **LORTON ARTS FOUNDATION,** (Workhouse Arts Center) Workhouse Arts Center, 9601 Ox Rd, Lorton, VA 22079. Tel 703-584-2900; Fax 703-690-1880; Elec Mail info@workhousearts.org; Internet Home Page Address: www.workhousearts.org; *Pres & CEO* John Mason; *Dir Visual Arts* Brett John Johnson
Open Wed - Sat 11 AM - 6 PM, Sun noon - 5 PM; No admis fee; Estab 2008; cultural arts center; A unique arts center that provides visual & performing arts, arts educ & entertainment; Average Annual Attendance: 173,000
Exhibitions: Ongoing monthly exhibits
Activities: Classes for adults & children; dramatic progs; docent training; lects open to pub; 6-10 vis lectrs per yr; concerts; gallery talks; tours; sponsoring of competitions; schols; extension prog to northern VA & DC; sales shop sells original art, reproductions & prints

LYNCHBURG

A **ACADEMY OF FINE ARTS,** (Lynchburg Fine Arts Center Inc) 600 Main St, Lynchburg, VA 24504-1322. Tel 434-528-3256; Fax 434-528-5841; Elec Mail Info@AcademyFineArts.com; Internet Home Page Address: www.academyfinearts.com; *Exec Dir* Richard S Kordos; *Dir Educ* Kelly Allen; *Exhib Cur* Ted Batt
Open Mon - Fri 9 AM - 5 PM, Sat by appt; Estab 2003 through merger of Lynchburg Fine Arts Ctr & Academy of Music; Maintains Academy Gallery & Art UpFront at 600 Main St, & mixed media exhibits in the lobby of The Arts and Education Bldg at Commerce & 5th Streets in historic Downtown Lynchburg

L **JONES MEMORIAL LIBRARY,** 2311 Memorial Ave, Lynchburg, VA 24501-2648. Tel 804-846-0501; *Dir* Edward Gibson
No admis fee; Estab 1907; For reference
Income: $180,000 (financed by endowment & donations)
Purchases: $5,000
Library Holdings: Book Volumes 20,000; Clipping Files; Exhibition Catalogs; Manuscripts; Memorabilia; Original Art Works; Other Holdings Architectural drawings; Periodical Subscriptions 45; Photographs; Sculpture
Special Subjects: Drawings, Historical Material, Architecture
Collections: Lynchburg Architectural Archives

M **LYNCHBURG COLLEGE,** Daura Gallery, 1501 Lakeside Dr, Lynchburg, VA 24501-3113. Tel 804-544-8343; Fax 804-544-8277; Elec Mail rothermel@lynchburg.edu; Internet Home Page Address: www.lynchburg.edu/daura; *Dir* Barbara Rothermel; *Asst Dir* Steve Riffee; *Admin Asst* Laurie Cassidy
Open Mon - Fri 9 AM - 4 PM, select Sun 1 - 4 PM (acad yr) or by appointment; No admis fee; Estab 1974 to supplement & support the acad curriculum of Lynchburg College; Average Annual Attendance: 5,000; Mem: 200

Income: Financed by endowment & Lynchburg College
Library Holdings: Book Volumes; Exhibition Catalogs
Special Subjects: Drawings, Painting-American, Sculpture, Etchings & Engravings, Painting-Spanish
Collections: American & Virginia Art; Pierre Daura (paintings, sculpture, works on paper); Waves on Paper; African art
Publications: Exhibit brochures, 3-4 per year
Activities: Lects open to pub, 6 vis lectrs per yr; gallery talks; tours; book traveling exhibs, 1 per yr; circulate through Virginia Museum of Fine Arts, Statewide Exhibits Prog, AAMG, VAM, all others by request

M **RANDOLPH COLLEGE,** Maier Museum of Art, 2500 Rivermont Ave, Lynchburg, VA 24503-1526. Tel 434-947-8136; Fax 434-947-8726; Elec Mail museum@randolphcollege.edu; Internet Home Page Address: www.maiermuseum.org; *Dir* Martha K Johnson; *Registrar* Deborah Spanich; *Mus Preparator* John Spanich
Open Sept - May Tues - Sun 1 - 5 PM, cl Mon; open Jun - Aug Wed - Sun 1 - 4 PM; No admis fee; American Art Collection estab 1920 to promote scholarship through temporary exhibitions & collection; Building currently housing collection built in 1952. 5 galleries contain more than 75 paintings from the permanent collection by American artists. One gallery is used for the 6 to 8 temporary exhibitions displayed each acad yr; Average Annual Attendance: 7,400; Mem: 125; dues $35+
Income: Financed by endowment
Purchases: Joseph Cornell (collage); Jamie Wyeth (watercolor); John Frederick Peto (oil); Jennifer Bartlett (work on paper)
Special Subjects: Landscapes, Marine Painting, Photography, Painting-American, Prints, Drawings, Textiles, Religious Art, Ceramics, Folk Art, Woodcarvings, Etchings & Engravings, Collages, Portraits
Collections: collection of 19th & 20th Century American paintings; European & American graphics
Exhibitions: Rotating exhibits, exhibit featuring pieces from collection; Annual exhib of contemporary art, Sept-Dec
Publications: Annual exhibition catalogue; biannual newsletter
Activities: Docent training; lects open to pub, 3-5 vis lectrs per yr; concerts; gallery talks; tours; Calvert Writing Award; objects of art lent to other mus; originate traveling exhibs; mus shop sells books, exhib catalogs, stationary & reproductions

MARTINSVILLE

M **PIEDMONT ARTS ASSOCIATION,** 215 Starling Ave, Martinsville, VA 24112-3832. Tel 276-632-3221; Fax 276-638-3963; Elec Mail paa@piedmontarts.org; Internet Home Page Address: www.piedmontarts.org; *Dir Finance & Facility* Pam Allen; *Admin Asst* Barbara Bradshaw; *Asst Dir & Dir Exhib* Branden Adams; *Exec Dir* Kathy Rogers; *Dir Mktg* Bernadette Moore; *Dir Programs* Barbara Parker; *Educ Coordr* Heidi Pinkston
Open Mon - Fri 10 AM - 5 PM, Sat 10 AM - 3 PM, Sun 1:30 - 4:30 PM, cl Mon; No admis fee; Estab 1961 to encourage & develop awareness & appreciation of the arts & provide an opportunity for participation in the arts; Five professionally furnished galleries: two feature artists with extensive show experience & reputation, one features work by both established & emerging artists, one features work by students from local schools & one features small exhibitions of local interest; Average Annual Attendance: 35,000; Mem: 1,000; dues patrons $150 & up, family $50, single $35, senior & student $25
Income: $350,000 (financed by endowment, mem, city & state appropriations, federal government & grants from foundations)
Special Subjects: Painting-American, Photography, Prints, Sculpture, Watercolors, American Indian Art, American Western Art, African Art, Southwestern Art, Textiles, Religious Art, Pottery, Afro-American Art, Painting-European, Portraits, Posters, Porcelain, Silver, Painting-British, Painting-French, Painting-Flemish, Stained Glass, Painting-German, Reproductions, Painting-Israeli
Exhibitions: Rotating exhibits
Publications: The Arts & You, bi-monthly newsletter
Activities: Classes for adults & children; dramatic progs; docent training; performing arts series; lects open to pub, 1 vis lectrs per yr; concerts; gallery talks; tours; sponsoring of competitions with awards; schols offered; book traveling exhibs 5-6 per yr

MASON NECK

M **GUNSTON HALL PLANTATION,** 10709 Gunston Rd, Mason Neck, VA 22079-3901. Tel 703-550-9220; Fax 703-550-9480; Elec Mail historic@gunstonhall.org; Internet Home Page Address: www.gunstonhall.org; *Asst Dir* Susan A Borchardt; *Dir* Thomas A Lainhoff
Open daily 9:30 AM - 5 PM, cl Thanksgiving, Christmas, New Years Day; Admis adults $7, seniors/groups $6, children (6-18) $3; Estab 1950 to acquaint the pub with George Mason, colonial patriot & his 18th century house & gardens, covering 555 acres; Owned & operated by the Commonwealth of Virginia; Average Annual Attendance: 50,000; Mem: 2,200
Income: Financed by state appropriation & admis fee
Special Subjects: Painting-British, Painting-American, Decorative Arts, Furniture, Historical Material, Restorations
Collections: 18th & 19th century family pieces
Activities: Classes for children; docent training; lect open to public, 8-12 vis lectrs per year; tours; individual paintings & original objects of art lent to other museums; sales shop sells books, reproductions; Children's Touch Museum located in basement

L **Library,** 10709 Gunston Rd, Mason Neck, VA 22079. Tel 703-550-9220; Fax 703-550-9480; Elec Mail library@gunstonhall.org; Internet Home Page Address: www.gunstonhall.org; *Dir* David Reese; *Cur* Susan Borchardt; *Librn* Mark Whatford; *Cur* Caroline Riley
Open Mon - Fri 9:30 AM - 5 PM & by appointment, cl Thanksgiving, Christmas & New Years Day; Estab 1950 to recreate the 18th Century home of George Mason IV as a research source plus acquiring a working reference collection on George Mason, early Virginia history & the decorative arts; Average Annual Attendance: 50,000
Income: Financed by endowment
Library Holdings: Auction Catalogs; Book Volumes 11,000; Cassettes; Exhibition Catalogs; Fiche; Filmstrips; Manuscripts; Memorabilia; Motion Pictures; Other Holdings Original documents; Pamphlets; Periodical Subscriptions 50; Photographs; Reels; Reproductions
Special Subjects: Decorative Arts, Manuscripts, Prints, Historical Material, Portraits, Archaeology, Porcelain, Furniture, Period Rooms, Restoration & Conservation, Silver, Textiles, Pewter, Architecture
Collections: Robert Carter Collection; Pamela C Copeland Collection; Elizabeth L Frelinghuysen Collection; Mason-Mercer Rare Book Collection

MIDDLETOWN

M **BELLE GROVE INC.,** Belle Grove Plantation, 336 Belle Grove Rd, Middletown, VA 22645; PO Box 537, Middletown, VA 22645-0537. Tel 540-869-2028; Fax 540-869-9638; Elec Mail info@bellegrove.org; Internet Home Page Address: www.bellegrove.org; *Exec Dir* Elizabeth McClung; *Admin Asst* Betsey Anderson; *Visitor Svcs Clerk* Sally Humphrey; *Bookkeeper* Renee Maines; *Maintenance Tech* Dennis Campbell; *Prog & Develop Asst* Sarah Ainsworth; *Shop Assoc* Kelly DeTample
Open Apr - Oct Mon - Sat 10 AM - 4 PM, Sun 1 - 5 PM; Admis adults $8, seniors $7, student $4, special rates for groups; Open to the pub in 1967, it is preserved as a historic house & is the property of the National Trust for Historic Preservation & managed by Belle Grove, Inc, an independent local nonprofit organization. It serves as a local preservation center & resource for the interpretation of regional culture in the Shenandoah Valley; Built in 1797 for Major Isaac Hite, Jr, a Revolutionary War officer & bro-in-law of James Madison, Belle Grove was designed with the help of Thomas Jefferson. During the Battle of Cedar Creek in 1864, the house served as headquarters to General Phillip Sheridan. The property is a working farm & Belle Grove maintains an active prog of events for the visiting pub; Average Annual Attendance: 15,000
Library Holdings: Book Volumes; Cassettes; Clipping Files; Maps; Memorabilia; Original Art Works; Original Documents; Pamphlets; Periodical Subscriptions; Photographs; Prints; Reproductions; Video Tapes
Special Subjects: Decorative Arts, Architecture, Furniture, Portraits, Painting-American, Period Rooms, Restorations
Collections: Antique collectibles
Exhibitions: Four Portraits by Charles Peal Polk: Colonel James Madison, Nelly Conway Madison-Hite, Major Isaac Hite, Mrs James Madison
Publications: The Women of Belle Grove
Activities: Docent training; lect open to public; 1-2 vis lectrs per year; tours; mus shop sells books, reproductions, prints, gifts

MOUNT VERNON

M **FRANK LLOYD WRIGHT POPE-LEIGHEY HOUSE,** 9000 Richmond Hwy, Mount Vernon, VA 22309; PO Box 15097, Alexandria, VA 22309-0097. Tel 703-780-4000; Fax 703-780-8509; Internet Home Page Address: www.nationaltrust.org; *Asst Dir* Gail Donahue; *Dir* Ross Randall
Open Mar - Dec, daily 10 AM -5 PM, cl New Years, Thanksgiving & Christmas; Admis adults $6, seniors & students $5, group rates by arrangement; Estab 1964; Frank Lloyd Wright's Pope-Leighey House is a property of the National Trust for Historic Preservation, located on the grounds of Woodlawn Plantation. This residence was designed in 1939 by Frank Lloyd Wright for his clients, the Loren Pope Family. Built of cypress, brick and glass, the Usonian structure contains such features as a flat roof, radiant heat, indirect lighting, carport & custom furniture, all designed by Frank Lloyd Wright, as an example of architecture for the average-income family. Threatened by construction of an interstate highway in 1964, Mrs Marjorie Folsom Leighey, second owner, presented the property to the National Trust for Historic Preservation. It was then moved to the Woodlawn grounds; Average Annual Attendance: 28,000; Mem: 350, dues family $40
Special Subjects: Architecture
Collections: Pope & Leighey Family Collections
Exhibitions: Christmas at Pope-Leighey House; annual World War II exhibits; Annual Wright Birthday June 8
Publications: Brochure and paperback history of house
Activities: Classes for adults & children; docent training; lects open to pub; 9 vis lectrs per month; tours daily; mus shop sells books, reproductions & prints

M **MOUNT VERNON LADIES' ASSOCIATION OF THE UNION,** PO Box 110, George Washington's Mt Vernon Estate & Gardens Mount Vernon, VA 22121-0110. Tel 703-780-2000; Fax 703-799-8698; Internet Home Page Address: www.mountvernon.org; *Regent* Mrs Ann Bookout; *Cur* Susan Schoelwer; *Pres & CEO* Curt Viebranz; *Sr Cur & VPres* Carol Cadou; *COO* Barton Groh
Open daily 8 AM - 5 PM: entrance gate closes Mar 1 - Oct 1 at 5 PM, Oct 2 - Mar 2 at 4PM; Admis annual pass $25, adults $15, $7.50 for groups of 12 or more children or groups of 20 or more adults, student groups $4.50, adults over 62 $14, children 6-11 $7, children under 6 free; Estab 1853; The home of George Washington, purchased in 1858 from his great-grand-nephew by the Mount Vernon Ladies Assoc of the Union, which maintains it. The estate includes Washington's private residence, restored flower & kitchen gardens, the tombs of George & Martha Washington, a four acre farm site with a reconstruction of Washington's sixteen sided treading barn & a new state-of-the-art Ford Orientation Center & Donald W Reynolds Mus & Educ Center. Mount Vernon also maintains Washington's Gristmill & Distillery & library for the study of George Washington; Average Annual Attendance: 1,000,000; Mem: Semi-annual meeting Oct & Apr
Income: Financed by admis fees & donations
Library Holdings: Auction Catalogs; Book Volumes; Clipping Files; DVDs; Exhibition Catalogs; Fiche; Lantern Slides; Manuscripts; Maps; Original Documents; Pamphlets; Periodical Subscriptions; Photographs
Special Subjects: Decorative Arts, Period Rooms
Collections: Mansion is fully furnished with original & period furniture, silver, portraits & prints; large coll of original Washington memorabilia, manuscripts & books; George Washington Memorabilia

Publications: Annual Report; The Gardens & Grounds at Mount Vernon; George Washington, A Brief Biography; The Last Will & Testament of George Washington; The Maxims of Washington; Mount Vernon; The Mount Vernon Coloring Book; The Mount Vernon Cookbook; The Mount Vernon Gardens; Mount Vernon Handbook; Nothing More Agreeable: Music in George Washington's Family; George Washington: Citizen - Soldier

Activities: Educ prog; teacher Institute; lects open to pub; lects for mems only; 3 vis lectrs per yr; concerts; tours; awards include Washington Book Prize; Mount Vernon History Teacher of the Year Award; Fred W Smith National Library Fellowship; book traveling exhibs; Sales shop sells books, reproductions, prints, coloring books, t-shirts, food & Christmas items

L **Library,** PO Box 110, George Washington Pky S Mount Vernon, VA 22121-0110. Tel 703-799-8639, 799-5085; Fax 703-799-8698; Elec Mail bmcmillan@mountvernon.org or jkittlaus@mountvernon.org; Internet Home Page Address: www.mountvernon.org; *Librn* Barbara McMillan; *Library Asst* Jennifer Kittlaus; *Spec Projects Mgr* John Rudder
Open by appointment; Reference library only
Library Holdings: Auction Catalogs; Audio Tapes; Book Volumes 12,000; Clipping Files; Compact Disks; DVDs; Exhibition Catalogs; Filmstrips; Framed Reproductions; Kodachrome Transparencies; Lantern Slides; Manuscripts; Maps; Memorabilia; Motion Pictures; Original Art Works; Pamphlets; Periodical Subscriptions 85; Photographs; Prints; Records; Reproductions; Sculpture; Slides; Video Tapes
Special Subjects: Landscape Architecture, Decorative Arts, Manuscripts, Painting-American, Painting-British, Prints, Historical Material, Portraits, Archaeology, Printmaking, Furniture, Period Rooms, Restoration & Conservation, Textiles, Architecture
Collections: American Revolution; 18th Century Agriculture; Mount Vernon; Virginia slavery; Washington family; George Washington
Publications: Annual report

L **The Fred W Smith National Library for the Study of George Washington,** 3500T Mt Vernon Memorial Hwy, Mount Vernon, VA 22121. *Libr Dir* Douglas Bradburn; *Chief Librn* Mark Santangelo
Library Holdings: Book Volumes; Clipping Files; DVDs; Exhibition Catalogs; Fiche; Lantern Slides; Manuscripts; Maps; Original Art Works; Pamphlets; Periodical Subscriptions; Photographs
Special Subjects: Landscape Architecture, Decorative Arts, Manuscripts, Maps, Painting-American, Historical Material, Archaeology, Furniture

M **WOODLAWN/THE POPE-LEIGHEY,** (Woodlawn Plantation) PO Box 37, Mount Vernon, VA 22121-0037. Tel 703-780-4000; Fax 703-780-8509; *Asst Dir* Gail Donahue; *Dir* Ross Randall
Open 10 AM - 5 PM, cl New Years; Admis adults $6, seniors & students $5, group rates by arrangement; Estab 1805; Land originally part of Mount Vernon. Built in 1800-05 for George Washington's granddaughter upon her marriage to Lawrence Lewis, Washington's nephew. It was designed with central pavilion & flanking wings by Dr William Thornton, winner of the architectural competition for the design of the United States Capitol. A group of Quakers, a pioneer anthropologist, a playwright & Senator Oscar W Underwood of Alabama were among Woodlawn's residents after the Lewis'. In 1951 the foundation's trustees decided that the visiting public would be better served if Woodlawn was administered by the National Trust. The mansion furnishings are largely from the Federal & early Empire periods & include Lewis family furniture; Average Annual Attendance: 60,000; Mem: 350; dues family $40
Special Subjects: Architecture, Drawings, Painting-American, Sculpture, Watercolors, Archaeology, Textiles, Costumes, Ceramics, Etchings & Engravings, Decorative Arts, Portraits, Furniture, Glass, Jewelry, Porcelain, Silver, Painting-British, Carpets & Rugs, Historical Material, Maps, Coins & Medals, Restorations, Miniatures, Period Rooms, Embroidery, Pewter, Leather
Exhibitions: Needlework Exhibit; A Woodlawn Christmas in Dec; Haunted History Tours
Publications: Friends of Woodlawn Newsletter, quarterly; Welcome to Woodlawn, booklet
Activities: Classes for adults & children; dramatic progs; docent training; special events; lects open to pub; tours; individual paintings & original objects of art lent to qualified mus; lending collection consists of original prints, paintings, furnishings & textiles; mus shop sells books, reproductions, prints, antiques, foods, toys

NEWPORT NEWS

M **THE MARINERS' MUSEUM,** 100 Museum Dr, Newport News, VA 23606-3759. Tel 757-596-2222; Fax 757-591-7311; Elec Mail info@mariner.org; Internet Home Page Address: www.mariner.org; WATS 800-581-7245; *VPres Finance & Admin* Gary Egan; *VPres Facilities Management* John Cannup; *VPres Develop* Marguerite K Vail; *Pres* John B Hightower; *Mus Shop Mgr* Georgia Mamangakis; *Dir Educ* Anna G Holloway; *VPres Develop* Mita Vail; *Chmn* Lloyd U Noland; *VPres Mktg* Karen P Grinnan
Open daily 10 AM - 5 PM, cl Thanksgiving Day & Christmas Day; Admis adults $6.00, students $4.00 (ID required for students 18 & older), children ages 5 & under free, discounts offered for active duty military, AAA members & sr citizens, group rate for party of 10 or more; Estab 1930 as an educational, nonprofit institution accredited by the American Assoc of Museums, preserves & interprets maritime history & other maritime artifacts. Costumed interpreters & film Mariner, help maritime history come alive; Located in a 550 acre park which features the 5 mile Noland Trail. Museum has twelve permanent galleries, including Age of Exploration & Chesapeake galleries; paintings & decorative arts; Crabtree Collection of miniature ships; collection of International Small Craft; Great Hall of Steam; William F Gibbs: Naval Architect Gallery. Maintains reference library; Average Annual Attendance: 100,000; Mem: 2,500
Special Subjects: Drawings, Graphics, Painting-American, Photography, Prints, Sculpture, Watercolors, Anthropology, Ethnology, Pre-Columbian Art, Ceramics, Crafts, Folk Art, Pottery, Primitive art, Woodcarvings, Woodcuts, Etchings & Engravings, Decorative Arts, Manuscripts, Painting-Japanese, Portraits, Posters, Marine Painting, Painting-Dutch, Painting-French, Historical Material, Ivory, Maps, Scrimshaw, Coins & Medals, Dioramas, Stained Glass, Military Art, Bookplates & Bindings

Collections: Crabtree Collection of miniature ships; thousands of marine artifacts; over 1,000 paintings; over 1,000 ship models
Publications: Mariners' Museum Pipe, quarterly newsletter; Mariners' Museum Annual, annual journal
Activities: Classes for adults & children; docent training; lects open to members, 6 vis lectrs per yr; concerts; gallery talks; tours; competitions with awards; schols & fellowships offered; individual paintings & original objects of art lent to mus; collection contains 120 motion pictures, 2,000 original art works, 8,000 original prints, 1,300 paintings; mus shop sells books, magazines, reproductions, prints, slides, jewelry & other maritime related items

L **Library,** 100 Museum Dr, Newport News, VA 23606-3759. Tel 757-591-7782; Fax 757-591-7310; Elec Mail library@marinersmuseum.org; Internet Home Page Address: www.marinersmuseum.org; *Librn* Cathy Williamson; *Librn, Tech Svcs* Jennifer Anielski; *Asst Archivist* Bill Barker
Open Mon - Fri 10 AM - 5 PM, cl Sat & Sun; No admis fee; Estab 1930; For reference only
Income: Financed by endowment
Library Holdings: Auction Catalogs; Book Volumes 75,000; Clipping Files; Exhibition Catalogs; Manuscripts; Memorabilia; Other Holdings Original documents; Pamphlets; Periodical Subscriptions 150; Photographs 350,000; Prints
Special Subjects: Art History, Decorative Arts, Manuscripts, Maps, Painting-American, Painting-British, Painting-Dutch, History of Art & Archaeology, Crafts, Archaeology, Anthropology, Eskimo Art, Drafting, Handicrafts, Marine Painting, Flasks & Bottles, Scrimshaw

A **PENINSULA FINE ARTS CENTER,** 101 Museum Dr, Newport News, VA 23606-3758. Tel 757-596-8175; Fax 757-596-0807; Elec Mail info@pfac.va.org; Internet Home Page Address: www.pfac-va.org; *Pres* Chris Stuart; *Treas* Patricia Melochick; *Cur* Michael Preble; *Exec Dir* Courtney Gardner; *Mktg Dir* Amber Kennedy
Open Tues - Sat 10 AM - 5 PM, Sun 1 - 5 PM; Admis adults $7.50, students, seniors, & AAA $6, children 6-12 $4, children 5 & under free; Estab 1962 to promote an appreciation of the fine arts through changing exhibitions with works from the Virginia Mus, other institutions & outstanding artists, both emerging & estab; Three galleries maintained with changing exhibitions; Average Annual Attendance: 40,000; Mem: 1,200+; dues family (incl mem) $60, individual $40
Income: Financed by mem
Exhibitions: Biannual exhibs; local, regional, & international art; Diverse rotating exhibition schedule that includes works ranging from historic to contemporary in a range of media
Publications: Art class schedules; e-newsletter to members, monthly; notification of spec events
Activities: Classes for adults & children; lect open to public, 4 vis lectrs per year; concerts, gallery talks, tours; competitions with awards; cash awards & cert of distinction for college & high school art; originates traveling exhibs to schools, libraries & other art organizations; mus shop sells books, original art, prints, jewelry, accessories & crafts

NORFOLK

M **CHRYSLER MUSEUM OF ART,** 245 W Olney Rd, Norfolk, VA 23510-1587. Tel 757-664-6200; Fax 757-664-6201; Elec Mail info@chrysler.org; Internet Home Page Address: www.chrysler.org; *Dir* Jeff Harrison; *Dir Devel* Edwina Bell; *Dir Fin & CFO* Dana Fuqua; *Deputy Dir Opers* Catherine Jordan Wass; *Exhib Mgr* Willis Potter; *Chief Preparator & Installation Coordr* Susan Christian; *Historic Houses Mgr* John Christianson; *Dir Visitor Svcs* Colleen Higginbotham; *Dir Educ & Pub Progs* Scott Howe
Open Wed 10 AM - 9 PM, Thurs - Sat 10 AM - 5 PM, Sun Noon - 5 PM, cl Mon, Tues & major holidays; No admis fee for permanent coll, donations accepted; fees apply to special exhibs; Mus originates from a memorial assoc estab in 1901 to house a coll of tapestries & paintings donated in memory of & by Irene Leache. The Norfolk Society of Arts was founded in 1917, which raised funds throughout the 1920s to erect a building to permanently hold the coll; A Florentine Renaissance style building, named the Norfolk Museum of Arts & Sciences, opened to the pub in 1933. The Houston Wing, housing the Museum Theatre & Lounge, was added in 1956, the Centennial Wing in 1976 & another wing to house the library & additional galleries was opened in 1989. The building has been designated the Chrysler Museum since 1971, when a large portion of the collection of Walter P Chrysler, Jr was given to Norfolk. Mus contains 140,000 sq ft; Average Annual Attendance: 200,000; Mem: 4,500; dues Masterpiece Society Benefactor $10,000; Masterpiece Society Patron $5,000; Masterpiece Society Sponsor $2,500; Dir Circle $1,000; Patron $500; Assoc $100; Household $60 (seniors 65 & up, students, teachers & active-duty military $50); Individual $45 (seniors age 65 & up, students, teachers and active-duty military $35); Corporate memberships available
Income: Financed by municipal appropriation & state appropriations as well as federal grants
Library Holdings: Auction Catalogs; Book Volumes; Clipping Files; Exhibition Catalogs; Manuscripts; Memorabilia; Original Documents; Pamphlets; Periodical Subscriptions; Video Tapes
Special Subjects: Decorative Arts, Photography, Sculpture, Painting-American, Glass, Oriental Art, Painting-Dutch, Painting-French, Painting-Flemish, Painting-Italian, Antiquities-Greek, Antiquities-Roman
Collections: African artists; American art from 18th century primitives - 20th century Pop Art, incl painting & sculpture; Bernini's Bust of the Savior; Francoise Boucher, The Vegetable Vendor; Mary Cassatt, The Family; Thomas Cole, The Angel Appearing to the Shepherds; Decorative arts including furniture, silver, gold, enameled objects & Worcester porcelain; 18th century English paintings; 14th-18th century Italian paintings; 15th-18th century Netherlandish & German works; Gaugin's Loss of Virginity; Bernice Chrysler Garbisch & Edgar William Garbish Native American paintings; Institute of Glass; Matisse, Bowl of Apples on a Table; Near & Far East Artists; Oriental artists; photography coll including Alexander Gardner, Lewis W Hine, Walker Evans, Ansel Adams, W Eugene Smith & contemporaries Joel Meyerowitz & Sheila Metzner; Pre-Columbian artists; Reni, The Meeting of David & Abigail; 16th - 20th century French paintings; works from Spanish school; 8,000 object glass coll including Tiffany glass, English cameo glass & contemporary glass sculpture

Exhibitions: Connoisseurs & Souvenirs: Silver from the Permanent Collection
Publications: Monthly members' newsletter; exhibition catalogues; Annual Report
Activities: Educ prog; family progs; docent training; teacher workshops; outreach information packages; lects open to pub, 15-20 vis lectrs per yr; concerts; gallery talks; tours; competitions (juried); exten dept operates three historic homes; individual paintings & original objects of art lent to accredited mus; Hampton Roads; book traveling exhibs; originates traveling exhibs; mus shop sells books, prints

L **Jean Outland Chrysler Library,** 245 W Olney Rd, Norfolk, VA 23510-1587. Tel 757-965-2035; Fax 757-664-6291; Elec Mail lchristiansen@chrysler.org; Internet Home Page Address: www.chrysler.org; *Dickson Librn* Laura Christiansen; *Library Asst* Sara Mason
Open Wed - Fri 10 AM - 4:45 PM, Wed evening by appt; No admis fee; Estab 1933 to collect materials in support of the collections of the Chrysler Mus; Circ Non-circulating; Open to the pub for reference only; Average Annual Attendance: 2,000
Income: Financed partially by endowment
Library Holdings: Auction Catalogs; Audio Tapes; Book Volumes 106,000; CD-ROMs; Clipping Files; DVDs; Exhibition Catalogs; Fiche; Manuscripts; Original Documents; Other Holdings; Pamphlets; Periodical Subscriptions 200; Video Tapes
Special Subjects: Art History, Decorative Arts, Photography, Painting-American, Painting-British, Painting-Dutch, Painting-Flemish, Painting-French, Painting-German, Painting-Italian, Painting-Japanese, Painting-Russian, Painting-Spanish, Pre-Columbian Art, Sculpture, Painting-European, Historical Material, Portraits, Art Education, Glass, Aesthetics, Restoration & Conservation, Painting-Scandinavian
Collections: Monographs: 50,000; vertical files on artists & art-related topics; Audio Visual Colls; Rare Books; Archives
Activities: Docent training; internships; lects open to pub; tours; Fels

M **HERMITAGE FOUNDATION MUSEUM,** 7637 N Shore Rd, Norfolk, VA 23505-1730. Tel 757-423-2052; Fax 757-423-1604; Elec Mail info@hermitagefoundation.org; Internet Home Page Address: www.hermitagefoundation.org; *Pres Bd* William Hull; *Admin Asst* Jean Turmel; *Mgr, Mus Coll* Kristin C Law; *Site Mgr* Andrea Prosser; *Asst to Dir Admin & Develop* Karen Perry
Open daily 10 AM - 5 PM (cl Wed), Sun 1 - 5 PM, cl New Years Day, Thanksgiving Day, Christmas Day; Admis adults $4, children 6-18 $1; no fee for activity military; Estab 1937 to disseminate information concerning arts & maintain a collection of fine art materials; Large Tudor-style historic house on 12-acre estate houses major collections as well as two small changing exhibition galleries; Average Annual Attendance: 20,000; Mem: 400; dues $30; meeting four times per yr
Special Subjects: Drawings, Landscapes, Ceramics, Glass, Mexican Art, Antiquities-Assyrian, Photography, Pottery, Painting-American, Prints, Textiles, Maps, Painting-European, Painting-French, Sculpture, Bronzes, Southwestern Art, Costumes, Religious Art, Crafts, Primitive art, Woodcarvings, Decorative Arts, Furniture, Jade, Oriental Art, Antiquities-Byzantine, Carpets & Rugs, Coins & Medals, Tapestries, Embroidery, Antiquities-Oriental, Antiquities-Persian, Antiquities-Egyptian, Antiquities-Roman, Stained Glass, Reproductions, Enamels
Collections: English oak & teakwood woodcarvings; Major coll of decorative arts from various periods & countries; Oriental coll of Chinese bronzes & ceramic tomb figures, lacquer ware, jades & Persian rugs; Spanish & English furniture; individual paintings & original objects of art lent to institutions; lending coll contains original art works, paintings, records & sculpture
Exhibitions: American Illustrator; Art on Paper; Isabel Bishop; Bernard Chaet (paintings); Contemporary American Graphics; Currier & Ives; Export Porcelain from a Private Collection; Freshwork (Virginia photographers); Alexandra Georges (photographs); The Photographs of Wright Morris; Henry Pitz (one man show); student exhibitions from summer workshops
Activities: Classes for adults & children; dramatic progs; lects open to pub & auxiliary lects for members only, 10-12 vis lectrs per yr; concerts; tours; Best of Norfolk awards; individual paintings & original objects of art lent to institutions; lending collection contains 750 original art works, 300 paintings, 150 records & 50 sculpture; book traveling exhibs; originate traveling exhibs; mus shop sells original art, t-shirts & umbrellas

L **Library,** 7637 N Shore Rd, Norfolk, VA 23505. Tel 757-423-2052; Fax 757-423-1604; Elec Mail info@hermitagefoundation.org; Internet Home Page Address: www.hermitagefoundation.org; *Mgr Mus Coll* Kristin C Law; *Site Mgr* Andrea Prosser; *Asst to Dir Admin & Develop* Karen Perry
Open Mon - Sat 10 AM - 5 PM, Sun 1 - 5 PM, cl Wed; Admis donations for use & research; Estab 1937 for the advancement of art education; Open to students and staff for reference only
Library Holdings: Auction Catalogs; Book Volumes 800; Exhibition Catalogs; Original Documents; Periodical Subscriptions; Photographs
Special Subjects: Art History, Folk Art, Decorative Arts, Islamic Art, Painting-American, Sculpture, Historical Material, Ceramics, Crafts, Bronzes, Art Education, American Indian Art, Porcelain, Primitive art, Furniture, Ivory, Jade, Glass, Antiquities-Oriental, Antiquities-Persian, Carpets & Rugs, Embroidery, Oriental Art, Pottery, Religious Art, Restoration & Conservation, Silver, Tapestries, Textiles, Woodcarvings, Antiquities-Byzantine, Antiquities-Egyptian, Antiquities-Greek, Coins & Medals, Pewter, Laces, Architecture
Collections: Personal letters & information on Douglas Volk, Helen M Turner, Harriet W Frishmuth, C T Loo, D Kelekian, Charles Woodsend & Karl von Rydingsvard

M **MACARTHUR MEMORIAL,** MacArthur Sq, Norfolk, VA 23510. Tel 757-441-2965; Fax 757-441-5389; Elec Mail macarthurmemorial@norfolk.gov; Internet Home Page Address: www.macarthurmemorial.org; *Dir* William J Davis; *Cur* Charles R Knight; *Admin Asst* Janice Stafford Dudley; *Archivist* James W Zobel
Open Mon - Sat 10 AM - 5 PM, Sun 11 AM - 5 PM, cl Thanksgiving, Christmas, New Years Day; No admis fee; Estab 1964 to memorialize General Douglas MacArthur; Located in the 1850 Court House which was rebuilt in 1962; nine galleries contain memorabilia; Average Annual Attendance: 51,074
Income: $563,312 (financed by city appropriation & the General Douglas MacArthur Foundation)

Special Subjects: Photography, Portraits
Exhibitions: 1-2 rotating exhibitions per year
Activities: Concerts; gallery talks; tours; research assistance grants & fellowships offered; individual paintings and original objects of art lent to mus; mus shop sells books, reproductions, prints, slides

L **Library & Archives,** 1 MacArthur Sq, Norfolk, VA 23510-2382. Tel 757-441-2965; Fax 757-441-5389; Internet Home Page Address: www.sites.communitylink.org/mac; *Archivist* James W Zobel
Open 8:30 AM - 5 PM; No admis fee; Estab 1964; Research library; Average Annual Attendance: 1,000
Income: Financed by the City of Norfolk & the General Douglas MacArthur Foundation as part of the MacArthur Memorial Museum
Library Holdings: Audio Tapes; Book Volumes 6000; Cassettes; Clipping Files; Fiche; Framed Reproductions; Manuscripts; Motion Pictures 130; Other Holdings Original documents 2,000,000, Photographs 80,000; Records; Reels; Slides; Video Tapes 120
Collections: Brigadier General Bonner F Fellers Collection: papers; Major General Courtney Whitney Collection: papers
Activities: Classes for adults & children; lects open to pub, 2-3 vis lectrs per yr; tours; competitions with prizes; schols offered

M **OLD DOMINION UNIVERSITY,** Art Dept, University Gallery, 350 W 21st St Norfolk, VA 23517; University Gallery, Visual Art Bldg, Rm 203 Norfolk, VA 23529-0001. Tel 757-683-4047, 683-2355; Fax 757-683-5923; Elec Mail khuntoon@odu.edu; Internet Home Page Address: www.odu.edu/al/artsandletters/gallery/index.html; *Art Chmn* Dr Robert Wojtowicz; *Dir Gallery* Katherine Huntoon
Open Tues - Thurs noon - 3 PM, Fri & Sat Noon - 5 PM, Sun 1 - 4 PM; No admis fee; Estab 1972 for the exhibition of contemporary work; also estab as a pub forum for contemporary artists, with student exposure; Average Annual Attendance: 3,000
Income: Financed by endowment & city appropriation
Library Holdings: Book Volumes 7000; Periodical Subscriptions 40
Exhibitions: Monthly exhibitions during calendar year
Activities: Lect open to public, 10 vis lectrs per year; gallery talks; tours; competitions; exten dept

L **Elise N Hofheimer Art Library,** Diehn Fine & Performing Arts Ctr, Rm 109 Norfolk, VA 23529. Tel 757-683-4059; Elec Mail dburritt@odu.edu; Internet Home Page Address: www.lib.odu.edu/artlib/index.htm; *Libr Specialist II* Deanna Burritt-Peffer
Open Mon - Fri 8 AM - 5 PM, Sat - Sun 1 - 5 PM; Estab 1963; Circ 15,930; Open to students & faculty; open to the public for reference; Average Annual Attendance: 22,000
Income: Financed by state, gifts & grants
Library Holdings: Auction Catalogs; Book Volumes 15,930; CD-ROMs; DVDs; Exhibition Catalogs; Periodical Subscriptions 36; Video Tapes
Special Subjects: Art History, Collages, Decorative Arts, Calligraphy, Etchings & Engravings, Ceramics, Conceptual Art, Cartoons, Aesthetics, Afro-American Art, Antiquities-Oriental, Antiquities-Byzantine, Antiquities-Greek, Antiquities-Roman, Architecture
Activities: Library instruction/orientation sessions; tours

ORANGE

M **ARTS CENTER IN ORANGE,** 129 E Main St, Orange, VA; 129 E Main St, PO Box 13 Orange, VA 22960-0011. Tel 540-672-7311; Internet Home Page Address: www.artscenterorange.org; *Exec Dir* Laura Thompson
Open call for hours
Collections: works by emerging artists
Activities: classes; mus shop

PETERSBURG

M **THE CITY OF PETERSBURG MUSEUMS,** 15 W Bank St, Petersburg, VA 23803-3213. Tel 804-733-2404; Fax 804-863-0837; Elec Mail petgtourism@earthlink.net; Internet Home Page Address: www.petersburg.va.org/tourism; *Coll Cur* Laura Willoughby; *Educ Coordr* Martha Atkinson
Hours seasonal. See website or call for hours; Admis adults $5, seniors, children & groups $4; Estab 1972 as a system of city museums; Three historic sites dating from 1735-1839. Maintains reference library; Average Annual Attendance: 25,000
Income: City of Petersburg, grants
Library Holdings: Auction Catalogs; Book Volumes; Clipping Files; Exhibition Catalogs; Lantern Slides; Manuscripts; Maps; Memorabilia; Original Art Works; Original Documents; Periodical Subscriptions; Photographs; Prints; Reproductions; Slides
Special Subjects: Archaeology, Architecture, Glass, Portraits, Painting-American, Prints, Manuscripts, Maps, Sculpture, Photography, Watercolors, Costumes, Ceramics, Decorative Arts, Furniture, Silver, Period Rooms, Embroidery, Stained Glass
Collections: City of Petersburg photographs & manuscripts; Military-Civil War; 19th century decorative arts; 15 Tiffany stained glass windows by Louis Comfort Tiffany Studio-Blandford Church; Period rooms 19th & early 20th century - Centre Hill Museum
Publications: Petersburg: Images of America Series; Petersburg: Postcard History Series
Activities: Docent training; lects open to pub; 4 vis lectrs per yr; tours; individual paintings & original objects of art lent to other mus; one book traveling exhib per yr, organized for libraries, schools, non-profits; mus shop sells books, postcards & children's merchandise

PORTSMOUTH

M **PORTSMOUTH MUSEUMS,** Courthouse Galleries, 400 High St, Portsmouth, VA 23704-3622; 521 Middle St., Portsmouth, VA 23704-3708. Tel 757-393-8543; Fax 757-393-5228; Elec Mail perryn@portsmouthva.gov; Internet Home Page Address: www.courthousegalleries.com; *Dir* Nancy S Perry; *Cur* Gayle Paul
Open Tues - Sat 10 AM - 5 PM, Sun 1 - 5 PM, cl Mon; Admis $9 to tour four municipal museums, general fee $3; mems free; Estab 1974 to offer a wide variety

of the visual arts to the citizens of Tidewater area & beyond; Average Annual Attendance: 25,000; Mem: 1200; dues mus contributor $1,000, Andalo's clubhouse $500, patron $250, conductor $100, planetarium (military, grandparent, sr couples) $45, passenger $30
Income: $53,000
Exhibitions: Up to 8 changing exhibitions per year; Ceramics, photography, sculpture, drawings/paintings
Publications: Quarterly newsletter
Activities: Classes for adults & children; workshops; school progs; family events & outreach; after school art progs in collaboration with Portsmouth pub schools; art camps; awards related to Outdoor Sculpture exhib; mus shop sells books, prints & gifts related to exhibs & holidays

PULASKI

M **FINE ARTS CENTER FOR THE NEW RIVER VALLEY,** 21 W Main St, Pulaski, VA 24301-5015; PO Box 309, Pulaski, VA 24301-0309. Tel 540-980-7363; Elec Mail info@facnrv.org; Internet Home Page Address: www.facnrv.org; *Exec Dir* Judy Ison
Open 10 AM - 4:30 PM; No admis fee; Estab 1978 to foster & furnish activities, programs & facilities to increase understanding of the arts; Gallery area 800 sq ft, classroom area 1800 sq ft; Average Annual Attendance: 16,000; Mem: 550; dues $10-$1000; annual meeting in Sept
Income: $129,000 (financed by mem, city & state appropriation & bus sponsorship)
Purchases: $80,000 (building in 1988)
Special Subjects: Painting-American, Ceramics, Crafts, Folk Art, Etchings & Engravings, Landscapes, Collages, Painting-European, Painting-Japanese, Glass, Jewelry, Asian Art, Painting-British, Painting-Dutch, Painting-French, Baroque Art, Calligraphy, Miniatures, Painting-Flemish, Painting-Polish, Painting-Italian, Painting-Australian, Painting-German, Painting-Russian, Painting-Scandinavian
Collections: Permanent collection established by donated pieces of art, sculpture & original paintings from the New River Valley Region
Exhibitions: Biennial Juried competition for artists living within a 100 mile radius; Rotating exhibits
Publications: Centerpiece, monthly newsletter
Activities: Classes for adults & children; dramatic progs; docent progs; lects open to pub; gallery talks; tours; competition with cash awards; schols & fels offered; artmobile serves New River Valley; lending collection; sales shop sells books, prints, original art, local craft items, reproductions, jewelry

RESTON

INTER-SOCIETY COLOR COUNCIL
For further information, see National and Regional Organizations

NATIONAL ART EDUCATION ASSOCIATION
For further information, see National and Regional Organizations

NATIONAL ASSOCIATION OF SCHOOLS OF ART & DESIGN
For further information, see National and Regional Organizations

RICHMOND

M **1708 GALLERY,** 319 W Broad St, Richmond, VA 23220; PO Box 12520, Richmond, VA 23241-0520. Tel 804-643-1708; Fax 804-643-7839; Elec Mail info@1708gallery.org; Internet Home Page Address: www.1708gallery.org; *Exec Dir* Emily Smith; *Asst. Dir.* Jolene Giandomenico
Open Tues - Fri 11 AM - 5 PM, Sat 11 AM - 4 PM, other times by appointment; No admis fee; Estab 1978 to offer an alternative presentation space to emerging & professional artists; Gallery is devoted to the presentation of contemporary art; Average Annual Attendance: 10,000
Library Holdings: Exhibition Catalogs
Special Subjects: Drawings, Painting-American, Photography, Prints, Sculpture, Etchings & Engravings
Activities: Educ dept; internship prog; juried exhibs; Monster Drawing Rally; lects, gallery talks; annual auction; books, catalogues (Inlight Richmond)

A **AGECROFT ASSOCIATION,** Agecroft Hall, 4305 Sulgrave Rd, Richmond, VA 23221-3256. Tel 804-353-4241; Fax 804-353-2151; Internet Home Page Address: www.agecrofthall.com; *Cur Educ* Alice D Young; *Exec Dir* Richard W Moxley
Open Tues - Sat 10 AM - 4 PM, Sun 12:30 PM - 5 PM; Admis adults $5, seniors $4.50, students $3, group rates by prior arrangements; Estab 1969 to exhibit 15th century Tudor Manor house brought over from Lancashire, England in 1926 & rebuilt in Richmond. Furnished with period objects of art; Average Annual Attendance: 20,000
Income: Financed by endowment & admis
Purchases: 1,560 portrait of William Dauntesey
Collections: 16th & early 17th century furniture & objects of art depicting Elizabethan lifestyle, when Agecroft Hall was at its pinnacle
Exhibitions: Permanent exhibit of British memorabilia 1890 - present
Activities: Classes for adults; docent training; lects open to pub; concerts; gallery talks; specialized tours; mus shop sells books & reproductions
M **Museum,** 4305 Sulgrave Rd, Agecroft Hall Richmond, VA 23221-3256. Tel 804-353-4241; Fax 804-353-2151; Internet Home Page Address: www.agecrofthall.com; *Cur Educ* Jill Pesesky; *Coll Mgr* Jefferson Collins; *Exec Dir* Richard W Moxley; *Mgr Tour Svcs* Ashley Hart
Open Tues - Sat 10 AM - 4 PM, Sun 12:30 - 5 PM; Admis adults $8, seniors $7, students $5, children under 6 free; Estab 1969 to interpret the material culture & social history of England (1485-1660); Rebuilt from 15th century English house, 7 period rooms & 2 exhibit galleries. Maintains reference library; Average Annual Attendance: 20,000
Special Subjects: Architecture, Textiles, Costumes, Ceramics, Pottery, Woodcarvings, Manuscripts, Painting-European, Portraits, Porcelain, Silver, Metalwork, Painting-British, Carpets & Rugs, Historical Material, Maps,

Restorations, Tapestries, Painting-Flemish, Renaissance Art, Period Rooms, Stained Glass, Pewter, Leather, Bookplates & Bindings
Collections: Bone & Ivory; Clocks; English Silver
Activities: Classes for adults & children; dramatic progs; quarterly living history events; workshops; summer Shakespeare festival; lects open to pub, 10-12 vis lectrs per yr; concerts; gallery talks; tours; original objects of art lent to Folger Shakespeare Library in Washington, DC; lending collection contains 3000 books, paintings, photographs & 500 decorative art holdings; mus shop sells books, reproductions, textiles, games, jewelry

M **ARTSPACE,** 31 E 3rd St, Richmond, VA 23224; Zero E 4th St, Richmond, VA 23224-4202. Tel 804-232-6464; Fax 804-232-6465; Elec Mail artspaceorg@gmail.com; Internet Home Page Address: www.artspacegallery.org; *Pres* Jessica Sims; *Treas* Martin McFadden; *Secy* Tiffany Floyd; *VPres* Jason Moore; *Adminr* Kathleen Westkaemper
Open Tues - Sun Noon - 4 PM; No admis fee; Estab 1988 as an assn of artists interested in exhibiting their own work & providing a space for other artists to reach a wider audience in the greater Richmond area; Two medium rooms & one large room; Average Annual Attendance: 19,000; Mem: 25; artists, photographers, sculptors must submit work to mem for admittance; dues $420; accepts proposal for anyone who wants to exhibit; monthly meetings
Income: $50,000 (financed by mem, fund raising, donations, city & state grants)
Special Subjects: Mixed Media, Drawings, Painting-American, Photography, Prints, Etchings & Engravings, Bookplates & Bindings
Exhibitions: Open new exhibit 4th Fri of every month
Publications: online publications on website
Activities: Classes for adults; dramatic progs; docent training; lects open to pub, 3-4 per yr; annual support from local arts foundations; concerts; gallery talks; lending contains 30-40 items to VA area; book traveling exhibs 2 per yr; originate traveling exhibs 2 per yr; sales shop sells original art & prints

M **CHASEN GALLERIES OF FINE ART,** 3554 W Cary St, Richmond, VA 23221-2729. Tel 804-204-1048; Tel 800-524-2736; Fax 804-204-1049; Elec Mail art@chasengalleries.com; Internet Home Page Address: www.chasengalleries.com; *Pres* Andrew Chasen; *VPres* Marc Cates; *Dir* Jeff Timlin
Open Mon - Sat 10AM - 6PM, Sun noon - 4PM (except Summer) ; No admis fee; Estab 1999; Large varied selection of artists, sculptors & glass artists from around the world

C **CRESTAR BANK,** Art Collection, 919 E Main St, Richmond, VA 23219-4625. Tel 804-782-5000; Fax 804-782-5469; Internet Home Page Address: www.suntrust.com; *Pres* C T Hill
Open daily 9 AM - 5 PM; No admis fee; Estab 1970; Collection displayed in banks and offices; separate gallery used for new exhibit each month
Collections: Contemporary Art
Activities: Competitions with awards

M **CROSSROADS ART CENTER GALLERY,** 2016 Staples Mill Rd, Richmond, VA 23230-3109. *Contact* Jenni Kirby

A **CULTUREWORKS,** (Art Council of Richmond, Inc) 1906 A N Hamilton St, Richmond, VA 23230-4113. Tel 804-340-5281; Fax 804-340-5285; Elec Mail leslie@richmondarts.org; *Pres* John Bryan; *Admin Mgr* Leslie Huffman
Open office Mon - Fri 9 AM - 5 PM; No admis fee; Estab 1949 to promote & support the arts & to provide arts programs & services to enhance the quality of city living
Income: Financed by grants, contributions & city appropriation
Publications: Arts Spectrum Directory, annually

M **FOLK ART SOCIETY OF AMERICA,** 1904 Byrd Ave, No 312, Richmond, VA 23230; PO Box 17041, Richmond, VA 23226-7041. Tel 804-285-4532; Elec Mail fasa@folkart.org; Internet Home Page Address: www.folkart.org; *Admin Asst* Barbara Hassett; *Pres* Ann Oppenhimer; *Financial Dir* William Oppenhimer
Open by appointment; No admis fee; Estab 1987; Maintains reference library; Mem: Dues $35 contribution minimum
Library Holdings: Auction Catalogs; Book Volumes; CD-ROMs; Clipping Files; DVDs; Exhibition Catalogs; Kodachrome Transparencies; Memorabilia; Original Documents; Periodical Subscriptions; Photographs; Slides; Video Tapes
Special Subjects: Latin American Art, Mexican Art, Painting-American, Southwestern Art, Religious Art, Folk Art, Woodcarvings, Afro-American Art, Eskimo Art, Historical Material
Collections: Books, files, magazines, videos; Constructions; Handicrafts; Restoration & Conservation
Publications: Folk Art Messenger, 3 times a yr
Activities: Lects open to pub, 1 vis lectr per yr; Awards of Distinction: to a scholar & to an artist

M **NATIONAL SOCIETY OF THE COLONIAL DAMES OF AMERICA IN THE COMMONWEALTH OF VIRGINIA,** Wilton House Museum, 215 S Wilton Rd, Richmond, VA 23226-2212. Tel 804-282-5936; Elec Mail wiltonhouse@mindspring.com; Internet Home Page Address: www.wiltonhousemuseum.org; *Cur* Dana Hand-Evans; *Office Mgr* Marianne Zwicker
Open Tues - Sat 1 - 4:30 PM, Sun 1:30 - 4:30 PM, cl Mon, group school tours 10 AM - 1 PM Tues - Fri; Admis $5; Estab 1935; 18th Century Georgian Mansion with period furnishings; Average Annual Attendance: 3,500
Income: Endowment, grants
Special Subjects: Architecture, Painting-American, Textiles, Ceramics, Decorative Arts, Portraits, Furniture, Glass, Silver, Maps, Period Rooms
Collections: 18th & 19th century furniture; 18th century decorative arts, porcelain; silver; textiles
Activities: Classes for adults & children; docent training; summer camps; lect open to pub, 5-7 vis lectrs per yr; school tours; mus shop sells books & reproductions

A **PRESERVATION VIRGINIA,** (Association for the Preservation of Virginia Antiquities) 204 W Franklin St, Richmond, VA 23220. Tel 804-648-1889; Fax 804-775-0802; Elec Mail ekostelny@ preservationvirginia.org; Internet Home Page Address: www.preservationvirginia.org; *Exec Dir* Elizabeth Kostelny; *Dir Properties* Louis J Malon; *Cur* Catherine Dean
Call for hours; Estab 1889 to acquire & preserve historic buildings, grounds & monuments in Virginia; Preservation VA owns & administers properties in Virginia. Among the properties: Historic Jamestown; Water Reed Birthplace, Gloucester County; Bacon's Castle & Smith's Fort Plantation, Surry County; John Marshall House, Richmond; Scotchtown, Hanover County; Mary Washington House, Hugh Mercer Apothecary Shoe & Rising Sun Tavern, St James Cottage, Fredericksburg; Smithfield Plantation, Blacksburg; Farmers Bank, Petersburg; Cape Henry Lighthouse, Virginia Beach; Hours & admis vary according to location; Average Annual Attendance: 650,000; Mem: 6,000; dues individual $40
Income: Financed by mem, endowment fund donations & grants
Special Subjects: Historical Material, Decorative Arts, Portraits, Furniture, Period Rooms
Collections: Decorative arts; 17th - 19th century furniture, glass, ceramics, metalwork & textiles
Publications: Ventures, biannually
Activities: Classes for adults & children; docent training; lect open to public; preservation awards; endangered sites list; individual paintings & objects of art lent to other nonprofit preservation organizations' exhibits; mus shop sells books, reproductions, prints, gifts, Virginia handicrafts

L **Library,** 204 W Franklin St, Richmond, VA 23220-5012. Tel 804-648-1889; Fax 804-648-1889; Elec Mail lmalon@apva.org; Internet Home Page Address: www.apva.org; *Dir Properties* Louis J Malon
Open by appointment only; For reference use only
Library Holdings: Book Volumes 3000; Clipping Files; Exhibition Catalogs; Pamphlets; Periodical Subscriptions 12; Photographs; Slides
Special Subjects: Decorative Arts, Historical Material, Architecture

M **John Marshall House,** 818 E Marshall St, Richmond, VA 23219-1917; PO Box 1098, Richmond, VA 23218. Tel 804-648-7998; Elec Mail johnmarshallhouse@preservationvirginia.org; Internet Home Page Address: www.preservationvirginia.org/marshall; *Site Coordr* Bobbie Leviness; *Exec Dir* Elizabeth Kostelny; *Assoc Dir Mus Operations & Educ* Jennifer Hurst-Wender
Open seasonally, see website for hours; Admis fee; Estab. 1911; Historical house mus built in 1790. Portrays John Marshall's life (1790-1835) in this historic Richmond home & his contribution to the nation; Average Annual Attendance: 5,000
Special Subjects: Architecture, Painting-American, Photography, Sculpture, Archaeology, Textiles, Costumes, Ceramics, Decorative Arts, Manuscripts, Portraits, Furniture, Glass, Porcelain, Historical Material, Restorations, Period Rooms, Embroidery, Laces
Collections: Decorative arts; period furniture 1790-1835; Marshall memorabilia
Activities: Classes for children; docent training; presentations for groups; lect open to public, some for members only; tours; mus shop sells books, reproductions, prints & Marshall items

M **UNIVERSITY OF RICHMOND,** University Museums, University of Richmond Museums, Richmond, VA 23173-0001. Tel 804-289-8276; Fax 804-287-1894; Elec Mail rwaller@richmond.edu; Elec Mail museums@richmond.edu; Internet Home Page Address: museums.richmond.edu; *Dir* Richard Waller; *Deputy Dir* N Elizabeth Schlatter; *Mus Preparator* Stephen Duggins; *Mus Preparator* Henley Guild; *Asst Coll Mgr* David Hershey; *Cur Mus Coll* Matthew Houle; *Cur Mus Progs* Heather Campbell; *Coordr Mus Visitor & Tour Srvcs* Denisse De Leon; *Mus Opers Mgr* Katreena Clark
Open Sun - Fri 1 - 5 PM, cl fall break, Thanksgiving wk, semester break & spring break; No admis fee; Estab 1968; 3 Mus: Joel & Lila Harnett Museum of Art; Joel & Lila Harnett Print Study Center; Lora Robins Gallery of Design from Nature; Average Annual Attendance: 12,000
Library Holdings: Exhibition Catalogs
Special Subjects: Decorative Arts, Etchings & Engravings, Folk Art, Landscapes, Marine Painting, Ceramics, Collages, Glass, Photography, Porcelain, Portraits, Pottery, Painting-American, Prints, Woodcuts, Maps, Sculpture, Drawings, Graphics, Watercolors, Bronzes, African Art, Pre-Columbian Art, Primitive art, Afro-American Art, Eskimo Art, Oriental Art, Asian Art, Silver, Antiquities-Byzantine, Ivory, Coins & Medals, Baroque Art, Calligraphy, Embroidery, Antiquities-Oriental, Antiquities-Egyptian, Antiquities-Greek
Collections: I Webb Surratt Jr Print Collection; Center Street Studio Archives
Publications: Exhibition catalogs
Activities: Classes for adults & children; docent training; lects open to pub; 10 vis lectrs per yr; concerts; gallery talks; tours; sponsoring of competitions; mus; lending of original art; originate book traveling exhibs; originate traveling exhibs to other mus; mus shop sells books

M **VALENTINE RICHMOND HISTORY CENTER,** (Valentine Museum/Richmond History Center) 1015 E Clay St, Richmond, VA 23219-1527. Tel 804-649-0711; Fax 804-643-3510; Elec Mail info@valentinemuseum.com; Internet Home Page Address: www.valentinemuseum.com; *Dir* William Martin
Open Mon - Sat 10 AM - 5 PM, Sun Noon - 5 PM; Admis adults $5, students $4, children 7-12 $3, children 3-6 $1, children under 3 free; Estab 1892 as a mus of the life & history of Richmond; Average Annual Attendance: 65,000; Mem: 500; dues individual $30
Income: Financed by endowment, mem, city & state appropriation & gifts
Special Subjects: Ceramics, Painting-American, Photography, Prints, Sculpture, Watercolors, Costumes, Decorative Arts, Glass, Jewelry, Silver, Laces
Collections: Conrad Wise Chapman Collection: oils, almost entire life works; William James Hubard Collection: drawings & oils; William Ludwell Sheppard Collection: drawings & watercolors; Edward Virginius Valentine Collection: sculpture; outstanding coll of Southern photographs; neo classical wall paintings
Exhibitions: Rotating exhibits
Publications: Valentine Newsletter, quarterly
Activities: Classes for adults & children; docent training; dramatic progs; lects open to pub; concerts; tours; exten dept serving city & area counties; originate traveling exhibs; mus & sales shops sell books, original art, reproductions, prints, slides & silver; Family Activity Center

L **Archives,** 1015 E Clay St, Richmond, VA 23219-1590. Tel 804-649-0711; Fax 804-643-3510; Elec Mail archives@richmondhistorycenter.com; Internet Home Page Address: www.richmondhistorycenter.com
Open to researchers Tues - Fri noon - 4 PM; Contact for applicable fees; Open to the pub by appointment only; non-lending, reference library
Income: Financed by gifts, mem, endowment
Library Holdings: Audio Tapes; Book Volumes 10,000; Clipping Files; Compact Disks; DVDs; Exhibition Catalogs; Lantern Slides; Manuscripts; Maps; Memorabilia; Original Art Works; Original Documents; Pamphlets; Periodical Subscriptions 20; Photographs 50,000; Prints 600; Reels; Reproductions; Slides; Video Tapes
Special Subjects: Photography
Activities: mus shop sells books

M **VIRGINIA COMMONWEALTH UNIVERSITY,** Anderson Gallery, 907 1/2 W Franklin St, Richmond, VA 23824-2514. Tel 804-828-1522; Fax 804-828-8585; Elec Mail artgallery@vcu.edu; Internet Home Page Address: www.vcu.edu/arts/gallery; *Dir* Ashley Kistler; *Exhib Mgr* Michael Lease; *Gallery Coordr* Traci Horne Garland
Open Tues - Fri 10 AM - 5 PM, Sat & Sun noon - 5 PM; No admis fee; Estab 1930, re-opened 1970 as the showcase for the contemporary arts in Richmond; to expose the university & community to a wide variety of current artistic ideas & expressions; Circ 2-4 exhib books publ yr; Gallery is situated on campus in a four-story converted stable. There are seven galleries with a variety of exhib spaces; Average Annual Attendance: 40,000; Mem: 275
Collections: Contemporary prints & paintings; cross section of prints from the 15th to 20th century covering most periods; vintage & contemporary photography
Publications: Catalogs; newsletters; posters & brochures
Activities: Lects open to pub, 4 vis lectrs per yr; concerts; gallery talks; tours; competitions; lending collection contains original art works, original paintings & photographs; originate traveling exhibs to other univ galleries, mus & non-profit art spaces; mus shop sells books

L **VIRGINIA DEPT HISTORIC RESOURCES,** Research Library, 2801 Kensington Ave, Richmond, VA 23221-2470. Tel 804-367-2323; Fax 804-367-2391; Elec Mail hhubbard@dhr.state.va.us; Internet Home Page Address: www.dhr.state.va.us; *Archivist* Quatro Hubbard
Open Mon - Fri 8:30 AM - Noon, 1 - 4:45 PM; Estab 1966; For reference only
Library Holdings: Book Volumes 4500; Clipping Files; Kodachrome Transparencies; Manuscripts; Maps; Periodical Subscriptions 75; Photographs; Slides; Video Tapes
Special Subjects: Decorative Arts, Maps, Historical Material, History of Art & Archaeology, Archaeology, Anthropology, Architecture
Collections: Archaeology; Architecture; Ethnography; History
Publications: Notes on Virginia; Preservation in Progress

A **VIRGINIA HISTORICAL SOCIETY,** PO Box 7311, Richmond, VA 23221-3307. Tel 804-358-4901; Fax 804-355-2399; Elec Mail charles@vahistorical.org; Internet Home Page Address: www.vahistorical.org; *COO, Assoc Dir* Robert Strohm; *Dir Mus* James Kelly; *CEO & Pres* Dr Charles F Bryan Jr; *Cur of Virginia Art* Dr William Rasmussen
Open Tues - Sat 10 AM - 5 PM, Mus Sun 1 - 5 PM; Admis $4, seniors (55+) $4, students and children $2, members free; Estab 1831 for collecting, preserving & making available to scholars research material relating to the history of Virginia, its colls include extensive holdings of historical portraiture; Ten galleries feature changing & permanent exhibits drawn from pub & pvt colls throughout Virginia; Average Annual Attendance: 60,000; Mem: 8000; dues $38 & up
Income: Financed by endowment & mem
Library Holdings: Auction Catalogs; Clipping Files; Exhibition Catalogs; Fiche; Kodachrome Transparencies; Lantern Slides; Manuscripts; Maps; Memorabilia; Micro Print; Motion Pictures; Original Art Works; Original Documents; Pamphlets; Periodical Subscriptions; Photographs; Prints; Records; Sculpture; Slides; Video Tapes
Collections: Books; Manuscripts; Museum Collection; Portraits
Exhibitions: The Story of Virginia, an American Experience (permanent); Virginians at Work (permanent); Silver in Virginia (permanent); The Virginia Manufactory of Arms (permanent); Arming the Confederacy (permanent)
Publications: Bulletin, quarterly; Virginia Magazine of History & Biography, quarterly
Activities: Classes for adults & children; docent training; teacher recertification; lects open to pub, 10 vis lectrs per yr; gallery talks; tours; William Rachel Award; fels offered; exten dept; individual paintings & original objects of art lent; lending collection contains paintings, original prints; book traveling exhibs 2-3 per yr; originates traveling exhibs 1-2 per yr in Virginia; mus shop sells books, prints, reproductions

L **Library,** 428 North Blvd, Richmond, VA 23221-0311; PO Box 7311, Richmond, VA 23221-0311. Tel 804-358-4901; Fax 804-342-9647; Elec Mail jguild@vahistorical.org; Internet Home Page Address: www.vahistorical.org; *Pres* Paul A Levengood; *Vice Pres Advancement* Pamela R Seay; *CFO* Richard SV Heiman; *Dir Lib Services* Frances Pollard; *VPres Prog* Nelson D Lankford; *VPres Coll* Lee Shepard; *Dir Educ* William Obrochta; *Dir Tech Services* Paulette Schwarting; *Cur Art* William Rasmussen; *Mktg & Pub Rels* Cynthia Moore; *Media Rel Spec* Jennifer Guild; *Mus Shop Mgr* Jessica Deruosi; *Va House Site Mgr* Tracy Bryan
Open Mon - Sat 10 AM - 5 PM Sun 1PM-5PM; No admis fee; Estab 1831 for the study of Virginia history; Circ Non-circulating; 3 permanent exhibit galleries, 5 changing exhibit galleries; Average Annual Attendance: 60000; Mem: 8,000
Income: 5.7 million annual budget, endowment, membership, gifts, earned income, grants, admissions
Library Holdings: Book Volumes 150000; CD-ROMs; Clipping Files; Compact Disks; DVDs; Exhibition Catalogs; Fiche; Filmstrips; Manuscripts; Maps; Memorabilia; Original Art Works; Original Documents; Pamphlets; Periodical Subscriptions 300; Photographs 100,000; Prints; Reels; Reproductions; Sculpture; Slides; Video Tapes
Special Subjects: Landscape Architecture, Decorative Arts, Photography, Manuscripts, Maps, Painting-American, Prints, Historical Material, Bookplates & Bindings, Silver, Architecture, Portraits

Collections: 150000 Volumes; 200,000 Photographs; 25000 Mus Paintings
Exhibitions: Story of Virginians Permanent Exhibit
Publications: History Notes, quarterly; Virginia Magazine of History & Biography, quarterly
Activities: Lects open to pub, 12 vis lectrs per yr; gallery talks; tours; fel; awards given, Brenton S. Halory Teaching Award, Bobby Chandler Student Award, W.M.M.E Rachel Award, President's Award for Excellence, Dist History Service Award; originates traveling exhibits to US and Canada; Mus shop sells books, magazines, reproductions, prints

M **VIRGINIA MUSEUM OF FINE ARTS,** 200 N Blvd, Richmond, VA 23220-4007. Tel 804-340-1400; Fax 804-340-1548; Elec Mail visitorservices@vmfa.museum; Internet Home Page Address: www.vmfa.museum; *Pres* Pamela Reynolds; *Dir & CEO* Alex Nyerges; *COO* Carol Amato; *Chief Cur Designate & Cur American Art* Dr Sylvia Yount; *Cur Chair & Cur S Asian & Islamic Art* Dr Joseph M Dye III; *Assoc Cur, S Asian & Islamic Art* John Henry Rice; *Cur African Art* Richard B Woodward; *Asst Cur Pre Columbian & Native American Art* Dr Lee Anne Hurt; *Cur Ancient Art* Dr Peter J Schertz; *Assoc Cur American Art* Dr Elizabeth O'Leary; *Asst Cur American Art* Dr Susan J Rawles; *Cur Decorative Arts 1890 to Present* Barry Shifman; *Cur E Asian Art* Li Jian; *Paul Mellon Cur & Head Dept European Art* Dr Mitchell Merling; *Cur Modern & Contemporary Art* John Ravenal; *Research Fel Modern & Contemporary Art* Emily Smith; *Deputy Dir Sales & Mktg* Alexis Vaughn; *Assoc Dir Communs & Mktg* Suzanne Hall; *Deputy Dir Educ & Statewide Partnerships* Sandra C Rusak; *Mgr Publ & Chief Graphic Designer* Sarah Lavicka; *Deputy Dir Exhibs* Robin Nicholson; *Mus Shop Mgr* Barbara Lenhardt
Open Sat - Wed 10 AM- 5 PM, Thurs & Fri 10 AM - 9 PM, cl Mon & Tues; No admis fee; Estab 1934; Participating in the museum's progs are the Fellows of the Virginia Mus, who meet yearly to counsel the mus on its future plans; The Council, which sponsors & originates special progs; the Collector's Circle, a group of Virginia art lovers which meets four times per yr to discuss various aspects of coll; the Corporate Patrons, state & local bus firms who lend financial support to mus progs; Maintains reference library, Pauley Ctr & studio school; Average Annual Attendance: 300,000; Mem: 20,000; dues $15 & up; annual meeting in May
Income: Financed by Commonwealth of VA
Special Subjects: Drawings, Graphics, Sculpture, Bronzes, Pottery, Etchings & Engravings, Decorative Arts, Painting-European, Furniture, Glass, Jade, Jewelry, Porcelain, Asian Art, Silver, Tapestries, Painting-Flemish, Renaissance Art, Painting-Italian, Islamic Art, Antiquities-Egyptian, Antiquities-Greek, Gold, Enamels
Collections: Lady Nancy Astor Collection of English China; Branch Collection of Italian Renaissance Paintings, Sculpture & Furniture; Ailsa Mellon Bruce Collection of 18th Century Furniture & Decorative Arts; Mrs Arthur Kelly Evans Collection of Pottery & Porcelain; Arthur & Margaret Glasgow Collection of Flemish & Italian Renaissance Paintings, Sculpture & Decorative Arts; Nasli & Alice Heeramaneck Collection of Art of India, Nepal, Kashmir & Tibet; T Catesby Jones Collection of 20th Century European Paintings & Drawings; Dr & Mrs Arthur Mourot Collection of Meissen Porcelain; The John Barton Payne Collection of Paintings, Prints & Portuguese Furniture; Lillian Thomas Pratt Collection of Czarist Jewels by Peter Carl Faberge; Adolph D & Wilkins C Williams Collection of Paintings, Tapestries, China & Silver; British Sporting Art; Art Deco Collection; Jerome & Rita Collection of English Silver; Cochrane Collection of American Art; Fischer Collection of Expressionism
Publications: The Arts of India; Dr Joseph M Dye III; James McNeil Whistler: Uneasy Pieces; Virginia Museum Calendar, bi-monthly; brochures; catalogs for spec exhibs & collections; programs
Activities: Classes for adults, teens & children; family progs; teacher workshops; docent training; lects open to pub, concerts; gallery talks; tours; fels offered 10 - 15 per yr to Virginia artists; internships; exten prog; statewide outreach across state of VA; book traveling exhibs, 67 go out to statewide partners; originate traveling exhibs throughout the state of Virginia; mus shop sells books, magazines, original art, reproductions, prints, toys, gifts, notecards, jewelry, apparel

L **Margaret R & Robert M Freeman Library,** 200 N Blvd, Richmond, VA 23220-4007. Tel 804-340-1495; Fax 804-340-1548; Elec Mail library@vmfa.museum; Internet Home Page Address: www.pandora.vmfa.museum; *Head Fine Arts Librn* Suzanne H Freeman; *Asst Librn* Courtney C Yevich; *Reference Librn* Lee B Viverette
Open Mon - Fri Noon - 5 PM; Estab 1935 for art history research for gen pub, academia & staff; Circ Non-circulating; For reference only; Average Annual Attendance: 1,500
Income: Financed by private funds
Library Holdings: Auction Catalogs 45,000; Book Volumes 143,000; CD-ROMs 22; Clipping Files; Exhibition Catalogs; Manuscripts; Memorabilia; Original Documents; Other Holdings Monographs; 82,000; Vertical Files: 40,000; Pamphlets; Periodical Subscriptions 234; Reels
Special Subjects: Art History, Decorative Arts, Sculpture, Crafts
Collections: Weedon Collection; Hayes Collection; Maxwell Collection of East Asian Art; McGlothlin Collection of American Art; Tucker Numismatics Collections; Lewis Decorative Art Collection; Pinkney Near West European Collection; Coopersmith Collection; Rare Books Coll; Archives
Exhibitions: Rotating exhibs of rare books & archival material located in libr atrium
Activities: Classes for adults; book club; docent training; internships

A **VISUAL ARTS CENTER OF RICHMOND,** 1812 W Main St, Richmond, VA 23220-4520. Tel 804-353-0094; Fax 804-353-8018; Elec Mail maggitinsley@visarts.org; Internet Home Page Address: www.visarts.org; *Prog Dir* Aimee Joyaux; *Fundraising* Susan Early; *Exhib Prog* Carolina Cobb Wright; *Mktg & Media* Maggi Tinsley; *Outreach* Sally Kemp
Open Mon - Fri 9AM - 9PM, Sat 10AM - 4PM, Sun 1 - 4PM; No admis fee; Estab 1963 as a nonprofit center for the visual arts committed to promoting artistic excellence through educational programs, gallery exhibs & artists services; Average Annual Attendance: 5,000; Mem: 750 mem, ann dues vary by category
Publications: Exhibition catalogs
Activities: Classes for adults & children; lect open to pub; gallery talks; tours; competitions with awards; schols offered for children only; originates traveling exhibs; sales shop sells magazines

ROANOKE

M **TAUBMAN MUSEUM OF ART,** 110 Salem Ave SE, Roanoke, VA 24011-1410. Tel 540-342-5760; Fax 540-342-5798; Elec Mail info@taubmanmuseum.org; Internet Home Page Address: www.taubmanmuseum.org; *Exec Dir* David Mickenberg; *Pres Bd Trustees* Dr Paul Frantz; *COO* Jim Becker; *Dir External Affairs* Kimberly Templeton; *Mus Shop Mgr* Marie Napoli; *Controller* Sheri Rock
Open Tues - Sat 10 AM - 5 PM, Thurs until 8 PM, Sun Noon - 5 PM; Admis adults $10.50, members no charge, Free Thurs 5PM - 8 PM; Estab 1951 as a general art mus with a focus on American art; 81,000 sq ft bldg houses 4 special exhib & 5 permanent coll galleries, educ spaces incl studio classroom & library, multipurpose auditorium, theatre, interactive gallery for children, museum shop & cafe; Average Annual Attendance: 85,000; Mem: 3,000; dues senior & student $35, individual $45, family $70, friend $100, sustainer $250, patron $500, benefactor $1,000
Income: Financed by mem earned income, donations & endowment
Collections: 19th & 20th c. American art; modern & contemporary art; Folk Art; Japanese Prints; Decorative Arts; Regional Art; Photography
Publications: Annual Report; Volunteer newsletter; exhib catalogs; quarterly newsletter
Activities: Classes for adults & children; docent training; art venture family interactive center; lects open to pub, 8-10 vis lectrs per yr; concerts; gallery talks; tours; artmobile; individual paintings & objects of art lent to qualified mus; book traveling exhibs 1-3 per yr; originate traveling exhibs; mus store selling books, original art, prints, reproductions, handmade crafts including jewelry & children's items; junior mus

SPRINGFIELD

L **VICANA (VIETNAMESE CULTURAL ASSOCIATION IN NORTH AMERICA) LIBRARY,** 6433 Northanna Dr, Springfield, VA 22150-1335. Tel 703-971-9178; Fax 703-719-5764; Elec Mail nnb726.nguyen@aol.com; *Pres* Nguyen Ngoc Bich; *Librn* Dao Thi Hoi, Ed.D
Open by special arrangement; No admis fee; Estab 1982
Income: Gifts, donations, exchanges
Purchases: $2,000 per yr
Library Holdings: Audio Tapes; Book Volumes 30000; CD-ROMs; Cassettes 50; Clipping Files; Compact Disks; DVDs 50; Exhibition Catalogs; Filmstrips; Framed Reproductions; Manuscripts 30; Original Documents; Pamphlets; Photographs; Records 100; Video Tapes 100
Special Subjects: Art History, Folk Art, Historical Material, History of Art & Archaeology, Ceramics, Crafts, Ethnology, Art Education, Asian Art, Aesthetics, Handicrafts, Oriental Art
Collections: Historical coll: Vietnamese, English, French; slides of Vietnamese life; Vietnamese cultural artifacts
Publications: Tet the Vietnamese New Year
Activities: Lects by invitation; 3-4 book traveling exhibs per yr

STAUNTON

A **STAUTON AUGUSTA ART CENTER,** 20 S New St, Staunton, VA 24401-4308. Tel 540-885-2028; Elec Mail info@saartcenter.org; Internet Home Page Address: www.saartcenter.org; *Exec Dir* Beth Hodge
Open Mon - Fri 10AM - 5 PM, Sat 10 AM - 4 PM, Sun 1 - 4 PM; No admis fee; Estab 1961 for art exposure & educ to area residents & visitors; state of the art exhibition galleries in a rehabilitated former hotel C 1895; Average Annual Attendance: 12,000; Mem: 550; dues $60 family, $40 individual
Income: $166,000 (financed by mem, city & state appropriations), gallery sales
Exhibitions: Annual Art in the Park; Christmas Art for Gifts; Art & fine craft exhibits change every six weeks
Activities: Classes for adults & children; lect open to public; gallery talks; vis lectrs 6 per yr; Art in the Park art award $1,500; schols; mus shop sells books, original art, reproductions, prints

M **WOODROW WILSON BIRTHPLACE FOUNDATION,** 20 N Coalter St, Staunton, VA 24402; PO Box 24, Staunton, VA 24402-0024. Tel 540-885-0897; Fax 540-886-9874; Internet Home Page Address: www.woodrowwilson.org; *Dir Coll* Edmund Potter
Open daily 9 AM - 5 PM Mar - Nov, 10 AM - 4 PM Dec - Feb, cl Thanksgiving, Christmas & New Year's Day; Admis adults $6, AAA discount & seniors $5.50, students age 13 & up or with ID $4, children 6-12 $2, children under 6 free; Estab 1938 for the interpretation & collection of life & times of Woodrow Wilson. Collection is housed in the 1846 Presbyterian Manse which was the birthplace of Woodrow Wilson; Mem: 700; dues $25 & up
Special Subjects: Painting-American, Decorative Arts, Historical Material, Period Rooms
Collections: Historical Material pertinent to the Wilson family; decorative arts, furniture, manuscripts, musical instruments, paintings, photographs, prints & drawings, rare books, textiles
Publications: Brochures; guides; newsletter, quarterly; pamphlets
Activities: Classes for children; lect open to public; tours; internships offered; original objects of art lent to museums & libraries; lending collection contains original art work & sculpture; sales shop sells books, magazines, reproductions, prints & slides

L **Woodrow Wilson Presidential Library,** 20 N Coalter St, Staunton, VA 24402; PO Box 24, Staunton, VA 24402-0024. Tel 540-885-0897; Fax 540-886-9874; Elec Mail woodrow@cfw.com; Internet Home Page Address: www.woodrowwilson.org; *Dir Coll* Edmund Potter; *Bus Mgr* Janet Campbell
Open daily 10 AM - 5 PM Mar - Nov, 10 AM - 4 PM Dec - Feb, cl Thanksgiving, Christmas & New Year's Day; Admis adults $7, AAA discount $6.25, students age 13 & up or with ID $4, children 6-12 $2, children under 6 free; Estab 1938 for the interpretation & collection of life & times of Woodrow Wilson. Collection is housed in the 1846 Presbyterian Manse which was the birthplace of Woodrow Wilson; Average Annual Attendance: 22,000; Mem: 700; dues $25 & up

Income: Financed by endowment, admis & grants
Library Holdings: Book Volumes 2000; Pamphlets; Photographs
Exhibitions: Women's History; Black History; Wedding Customs
Publications: Wilson Newsletters, quarterly
Activities: Mus shop sells books, original art, reproductions, prints

STRASBURG

M **STRASBURG MUSEUM,** 440 E King St, Strasburg, VA 22657-2433. Tel 540-465-3428; *VPres* Nicholas Racey; *Secy* Patricia Clem; *CEO, VChmn* John Adamson; *Mus Shop Mgr* Glenna Loving
Open May to Oct, daily 10 AM - 4 PM; Admis adults $2, children $.50; Estab 1970 to present the past of a Shenandoah Valley community & to preserve the pottery-making tradition of Strasburg; The mus is housed in the former Southern Railway Depot, which was originally built as a steam pottery; Average Annual Attendance: 4,000; Mem: 140; dues $30; annual meeting in Mar
Income: Financed by mem, admis fees & gifts
Collections: Artifacts & exhibits, farm & railroad crafts, pottery
Activities: Classes for adults & children in pottery making; mus shop selling books original art, pottery & other local crafts

SWEET BRIAR

L **SWEET BRIAR COLLEGE,** Mary Helen Cochran Library, 134 Chapel Rd, Sweet Briar, VA 24595-5001. Tel 804-381-6138; Fax 804-381-6173; Elec Mail lnjohnston@sbc.edu; Internet Home Page Address: www.cochran.sbc.edu; *Technical Svcs* Julie Kane; *Pub Svcs* Lisa N Johnston; *Bibliographic Instruction & Branch Librn* Joe Malloy; *Serials Librn* Liz Kent; *Dir* John G Jaffe
Open Mon - Thurs 8 AM - 1 AM, Fri 8 AM - 6 PM, Sat 10 AM - 6 PM, Sun 8 AM - 1 AM; Estab 1961, when it was separated from the main library, the library serves an undergraduate community; The Art Library is now located in the Mary Helen Cochran Library
Income: Financed by college funds
Library Holdings: Book Volumes 12,500; Cassettes; Exhibition Catalogs; Fiche; Kodachrome Transparencies; Lantern Slides; Original Art Works; Pamphlets; Periodical Subscriptions 60; Prints; Video Tapes
Special Subjects: Folk Art, Graphic Arts, Painting-American, Painting-British, Painting-Dutch, American Western Art, American Indian Art, Furniture, Glass, Aesthetics, Afro-American Art, Gold, Antiquities-Assyrian, Painting-Australian, Painting-Canadian

M **Art Collection & Galleries,** 134 Chapel Rd, Anne Gary Pannell Ctr Sweet Briar, VA 24595-5001. Tel 434-381-6248; Elec Mail klawson@sbc.edu; Internet Home Page Address: www.sbc.edu/art-galleries; *Dir* Karol Lawson; *Registrarial Asst* Nancy McDearmon
Open Mon-Thurs 10AM-5PM, Fri 10AM-2PM, Sun 1-4PM, cl Sat & col breaks; No admis fee; Estab 1985 to support the educational mission at Sweet Briar College through its exhibits, collections & educational programs; Average Annual Attendance: 4,000; Mem: 200; dues $25; annual meeting in Apr
Special Subjects: Afro-American Art, Drawings, Etchings & Engravings, Landscapes, Collages, Photography, Painting-American, Prints, Woodcuts, Graphics, Watercolors, African Art, Manuscripts, Posters, Asian Art, Antiquities-Greek, Antiquities-Roman
Collections: American & European drawings & prints & photographs; Japanese woodblock prints, 18th & 19th century paintings; Works on paper by female artists of the 20th & 21st centuries
Exhibitions: Rotating exhibits from permanent collection plus traveling exhibits; average 12 exhibs per yr
Publications: Visions: News from the Friends of Art newsletter-1 issues per yr; Women Artists of the Twentieth Century: Sweet Briar College Anne Gary Pannell Art Gallery Collection catalog
Activities: Tours for children; lects open to pub; 4 vis lectrs per yr; concerts; gallery talks; music; theater; dance performances in conjunction with exhibs

TRIANGLE

M **MARINE CORPS UNIVERSITY,** National Museum of the Marine Corps, 18900 Jefferson Davis Hwy, Triangle, VA 22172-1938; 2014 Anderson Ave, Quantico, VA 22134-5100. Tel 703-499-3185/ 898-8855; Fax 703-784-5856; Elec Mail info@usmcmuseum.org; Internet Home Page Address: www.usmcmuseum.com; *Mus Dir* Liz Ezell; *Dep Dir* Charlie Grow; *Supervisory Cur Art* Joan Thomas; *Art Cur* Vickie Stuart-Hill
Open daily 9 AM - 5 PM; cl Christmas Day; No admis fee; Estab 2006; Average Annual Attendance: 504,000
Library Holdings: Clipping Files; Framed Reproductions; Kodachrome Transparencies; Manuscripts; Original Art Works; Original Documents; Other Holdings; Sculpture
Special Subjects: Painting-American, Sculpture, Historical Material, Military Art
Publications: Exhibit publications
Activities: Docent training; gallery talks; lend art to other museums; traveling exhibs to other art mus & USMC commands

VIRGINIA BEACH

A **CONTEMPORARY ART CENTER OF VIRGINIA,** (Virginia Beach Center for the Arts) 2200 Parks Ave, Virginia Beach, VA 23451-4062. Tel 757-425-0000; Fax 757-425-8186; Elec Mail ragan@cacv.org; Internet Home Page Address: www.cavc.org; *Exec Dir* Debi Gray; *Chmn Board Trustees* Randy Sutton; *Accounting Mgr* Elaine Allen; *Dir Develop* Amy Walton; *Pub Rels Assoc* Erika Guess; *Spec Event Mgr* Tiffany Russell; *Develop Assoc* Margie Donovan; *Dir Opers* Kate Pittman; *Receptionist* Lindsay Horton; *Facilities Mgr* Irene Tavenner; *Secy* Louis Cross; *Dir Exhibs & Educ* Ragan Cole-Cunningham; *Cur Educ* Alison Byrne; *Registrar* Monee Bengston; *Youth Prog Mgr* Holly Ackiss; *Assoc Cur* Heather Hakimzadeh
Open Tues - Fri 10 AM - 5 PM, Sat 10 AM - 4 PM, Sun Noon - 4 PM, cl Mon, New Year's Day, Thanksgiving & Christmas Day; Admis adults $7, students,

seniors & military $2, members & children under 4 free; Estab 1952, as a nonprofit organization serving citizens of the greater Hampton Roads area with exhibits & programming in the visual arts; Exhibition space 5600 sq ft; Average Annual Attendance: 517,000; Mem: 3000, dues standard individual $50, student, senior, military, teacher & individual $30, standard household $65, student, senior, military, teacher household $55, assoc $125, patron $250, donor $500, Collector's Circle $1,250, Chairman's Circle $2,500; annual meeting in Sept
Income: Financed by mem, pub grants, private donations, various fundraising events
Collections: Best-in-Show winners from Boardwalk Art Show
Exhibitions: 10 exhibitions per year of contemporary art
Publications: ArtLetter, monthly; exhibition catalogues
Activities: Classes & workshops for adults & children; dramatic progs; docent training; film series; performing arts; lects open to pub; 15 vis lectrs per yr; concerts; gallery talks; tours; schols & fels offered; exten dept serves municipal employees; mus shop sells books, original art, reproductions, prints, crafts, jewelry, wearable art

WAVERLY

M **MILES B CARPENTER FOLK ART MUSEUM,** (Miles B Carpenter Museum) 201 Hunter St, Waverly, VA 23890-2631; PO Box 1376, Waverly, VA 23890-1376. Tel 804-834-3327; Tel 804-834-2151; *VPres* Frances B Gray; *Secy* Deborah A Davis; *Treas* Thelma W Wyatt; *Pres* Shirley S Yancey
Open Thurs - Mon 2 - 5 PM, other times by appointment; Admis by donation; Estab 1986 to maintain a museum in the home of nationally known folk artist Miles Burkholder Carpenter & to encourage art; Two-floor gallery; Average Annual Attendance: 6,000; Mem: 25 members; no dues; annual meeting last Sat in Jan
Income: $25,000 (financed by state grants & donations)
Special Subjects: Sculpture, Folk Art, Woodcarvings
Collections: Miles B Carpenter Permanent Collection of woodcarvings, tools & memorabilia
Exhibitions: Miles B Carpenter (woodcarvings, tools & memorabilia); Folk Art Paintings; Seven visiting exhibits
Publications: Cutting the Mustard
Activities: Classes for adults & children; dramatic progs; docent training; lects open to pub, 4 vis lectrs per yr; tours; schols

WILLIAMSBURG

M **COLLEGE OF WILLIAM & MARY,** Muscarelle Museum of Art, P.O. Box 8795, Williamsburg, VA 23187-8795. Tel 757-221-2700; Fax 757-221-2711; Elec Mail museum@wm.edu; Internet Home Page Address: www.wm.edu/muscarelle; *Registrar* Melissa Parris; *Cur Educ & New Media* Amy Gorman PhD; *Exhib Mgr* Kevin Gilliam; *Asst to Dir* Cindy Lucas; *Spec Projects Adminr* Ursula McLaughlin; *Mem Sec* Bronwen Watts; *Dir* Aaron H De Groft, PhD; *Mgr Institutional Advancement* Christina Carroll, JD
Open Tues - Fri 10 AM - 5 PM, Sat & Sun noon - 4 PM, cl Mon; Admis fee $5, additional fee for special exhibs, free to mems, William & Mary students, faculty, staff, & children under 12; Estab 1983; Average Annual Attendance: 65,000; Mem: 1,400; dues $40 & up
Income: Financed by endowments, state appropriations & donations
Special Subjects: Afro-American Art, Anthropology, Landscapes, Marine Painting, Metalwork, Gold, Portraits, Painting-American, Manuscripts, Maps, Painting-French, Drawings, Graphics, Painting-American, Photography, Prints, Sculpture, Watercolors, American Indian Art, Bronzes, Southwestern Art, Religious Art, Ceramics, Woodcuts, Etchings & Engravings, Landscapes, Collages, Painting-European, Posters, Eskimo Art, Furniture, Glass, Jade, Jewelry, Porcelain, Oriental Art, Asian Art, Silver, Metalwork, Painting-British, Painting-Dutch, Painting-French, Historical Material, Coins & Medals, Baroque Art, Calligraphy, Painting-Flemish, Painting-Polish, Renaissance Art, Medieval Art, Painting-Spanish, Painting-Italian, Islamic Art, Painting-Australian, Painting-German, Pewter, Painting-Russian, Enamels, Bookplates & Bindings
Collections: African Art; Asian Art; Native American Art; paintings & sculpture; Sixteenth-Twentieth Century American & European Works
Exhibitions: See www.wm.edu/muscarelle/exhibitions for current, upcoming & past exhibs
Publications: Newsletter, two times a year; exhibition catalogues
Activities: Classes for adults & children; docent training; school field trips; lect open to pub; lectrs for mems only; 5 vis lectrs per year; gallery talks; concerts; tours; Cheek Medal (for outstanding contributions in mus, performing or visual arts); sponsoring of competitions; schols; fels; individual paintings & original objects of art lent to special exhibs organized by other museums; book traveling exhibs, 2-9 per yr; originate traveling exhibs that circulate to other mus, art centers, colleges; national & international mus; mus shop sells books, original art, reproductions, notecards, T-shirts, prints

M **COLONIAL WILLIAMSBURG FOUNDATION,** PO Box 1776, Williamsburg, VA 23187-1776. Tel 757-229-1000; Fax 757-220-7286; Internet Home Page Address: www.history.org; *VPres Coll & Museums* Ronald Hurst; *Pres* Colin Campbell; *Dir Pub Rels* Tim Andrews
Open 9 AM - 5 PM; Estab 1927 the worlds largest outdoor mus, providing first hand history of 18th-century English colony during period of subjects becoming Americans; The colonial area of this 18th century capital of Virginia, encompassing 300 acres with nearly 500 homes, shops, taverns, dependencies, has been carefully restored to its original appearance. Included are 90 acres of gardens & greens. The work was initiated by John D Rockefeller, Jr. There are more than 40 exhibition homes, public buildings & craft shops where guides & craftsmen in colonial costumes show visitors the way of life of pre-Revolutionary Virginia. Incl are the historic Burton Parish Church, the Governor's Palace, Capitol, the Courthouse of 1770, Bassett Hall (local residence of the Rockefellers), the DeWitt Wallace Dec. Arts Mus & Abby Aldrich Rockefeller Folk Art Mus. The exhibition properties include 225 furnished rooms; Average Annual Attendance: 1,000,000

Income: Financed by admis, gifts & grants, real estate, products, restaurants & hotels
Collections: 18th-Century British & American Painting; English Pottery & Porcelains; Silver; Furniture; with frequent additions, include representative pieces, rare English pieces in the palace; exceptionally fine textiles & rugs; extensive collection of primary & secondary materials relating to British North America, the Colonial Period & the early National Period & American folk art.
Publications: The foundation publishes many books on a wide range of subjects; Colonial Williamsburg, quarterly journal
Activities: Classes & tours for adults & children; lects open to pub, 30 vis lectrs per yr; concerts; gallery talks; special focus tours; individual paintings & original objects of art lent; mus shop sells books, magazines, original art, reproductions, prints & slides

A **Visitor Center,** PO Box 1776, Williamsburg, VA 23187-1776. Tel 757-220-7645; Internet Home Page Address: www.history.org; *Dir* William Pfeifer
Open daily 8:30 AM - 8:30 PM; Estab 1927; Outside the historic area this modern center houses graphic exhibits of the restoration & colonial life. Continuous showings of a full-color, vista vision film, Williamsburg: The Story of a Patriot
Publications: Books & brochures on Williamsburg & colonial life; gallery book of the Folk Art Collection
Activities: Limited grant-in-aid prog for researchers; slide lect; annual events including Antiques Forum; Garden Symposium; regular performance of 18th century dramas, organ recitals & concerts

L **John D Rockefeller, Jr Library,** 313 First St, Williamsburg, VA 23185; PO Box 1776, Williamsburg, VA 23187-1776. Tel 757-565-8500; Fax 757-565-8508; Elec Mail jclark@cwf.org; Internet Home Page Address: www.research.history.org/JDRLibrary.cfm; *Office Mgr* Inge Flester; *Decorative Arts Librn* Susan Shames; *Reference Librn* Del Moore; *Circ Library Asst* Joann Proper; *Assoc Librn* Doug Mayo; *Pub Svcs Librn* Juleigh Clark; *Assoc Cur Architecture Coll* George Yetter; *System Adminr & Sr Cataloger* Julie Conlee; *Acquisitions Librn* Annette Parham; *Visual Resources Editorial Librn* Marianne Martin; *Dir* James Horn
Open Mon - Fri 9 AM - 5 PM, cl major holidays; No admis fee; Circ 10,000; Average Annual Attendance: 26,000
Library Holdings: Auction Catalogs 20,000; Book Volumes 76,053; Cards 800; Clipping Files; Compact Disks; DVDs; Fiche; Manuscripts 50,000; Maps 2,500; Other Holdings Architectural drawings 65,000; Compact discs-Music; Negatives 250,000; Periodical Subscriptions 380; Photographs 250,000; Reels 6000; Slides 250,000; Video Tapes 1000
Special Subjects: Folk Art, Painting-American, Painting-British, Archaeology, Furniture, Architecture
Collections: 18th Century Arts & Trades; Historical Preservation in America; History of the Restoration of Colonial Williamsburg; Decorative Arts, Folk Art, Architecture, Auction Catalogs
Publications: Exhibit catalogs

M **Abby Aldrich Rockefeller Folk Art Museum,** 326 W Francis St, Williamsburg, VA 21385; PO Box 1776, Williamsburg, VA 21387-1776. Tel 757-220-7724; Fax 757-565-8804; Elec Mail mcottrill@cwf.org; Internet Home Page Address: www.colonialwilliamsburg.com/do/artmuseums/; *Dir Mus Exhibs & Opers* Richard Hadley; *Mgr Mus Educ* Patricia Balderson; *Mgr Hennage Auditorium* Mary Cottrill; *Mgr Exhibits Planning* Jan Gilliam; *VPres Conservation, Colls & Mus* Ronald Hurst
Open Jan - Mar daily 10 AM- 5 PM, April - Dec: daily 10 AM - 7 PM; Admis adults $10, youth 6-17 $5, under 6 free; annual mus pass $20 adults, $10 youth; Estab 1957; Colonial & contemporary artists & craftspeople working outside the mainstream of academic art to record aspects of everyday life, making novel & effective use of the materials at hand. Bold colors, simplified shapes, & patterns can be seen in the variety of paintings, carvings, toys, & needleworks. Offers changing exhibs of American folk art from its permanent holdings and mus loan shows; Average Annual Attendance: 200,000
Income: part of Colonial Williamsburg Foundation
Special Subjects: Ceramics, Furniture, Pottery, Period Rooms, Textiles, Sculpture, Watercolors, Folk Art, Primitive art
Collections: 18th, 19th & 20th c. folk art incl decoys, painted furniture, paintings, sculptures, signs & textiles
Exhibitions: (06/29/2013-12/31/2013) Paper Trail: Documenting Rites of Passage in German-Speaking America; (2013) Tramp Art; (2013) American Folk Portraits; (2013) Quilts in the Baltimore Manner; (2013) Cross Rhythms: Folk Musical Instruments; (2013) Sidewalks to Rooftops: Outdoor Folk Art; (2013) Inspiration and Ingenuity: American Stoneware; (2013) Conserving the Carolina Room; (2013) Down on the Farm; (2013) Introduction to American Folk Art
Publications: Exhibition catalogs
Activities: Classes for adults & children; dramatic programs; docent & teacher training; lects open to pub, 12 vis lectrs per yr; gallery talks; concerts; tours; paintings & sculpture lent to other mus; book traveling exhibs, 1 per yr; originate traveling exhibs; mus shop sells books, reproductions, magazines, original art, prints, CDs music

M **DeWitt Wallace Decorative Arts Museum,** 326 W Francis St, Williamsburg, VA 23185; PO Box 1776, Williamsburg, VA 23187-1776. Tel 757-220-7724; Fax 757-565-8804; Elec Mail mcottnill@cwf.org; Internet Home Page Address: www.colonialwilliamsburg.com/do/art-museums/; *Dir Mus Exhibs & Opers* Richard Hadley; *Mgr Mus Educ* Patricia Balderson; *Mgr Hennage Auditorium* Mary Cottrill; *Mgr Exhibs Planning* Jan Gilliam; *VPres Conservation, Colls & Mus* Ronald Hurst
Open Jan - March 10 AM - 5 PM daily, April - Dec 10 AM - 5 PM daily; Admis adults $10, children 6-17 yrs old $5, under 6 free; annual museum pass $20 adults & $10 youth; Estab 1985; Extensive collections of American & British antiques; Average Annual Attendance: 200,000
Income: part of the Colonial Williamsburg Foundation, DeWitt Wallace Fund for Colonial Williamsburg
Special Subjects: Archaeology, Historical Material, Ceramics, Glass, Furniture, Porcelain, Portraits, Pottery, Painting-American, Prints, Silver, Textiles, Maps, Painting-British, Costumes, Decorative Arts, Jewelry, Coins & Medals, Baroque Art, Embroidery
Collections: English & American decorative arts from 1600-1830; furniture; metals; ceramics; glass; paintings; prints; firearms; kitchen equipment; textiles
Exhibitions: (03/03/2013-12/31/2013) Painters and Paintings in the Early American South; (05/25/2013-12/31/2013) Threads of Feeling; (11/28/2013) A Rich and Varied Culture: The Material World of the Early South; (2013) Dollars, Farthings & Fables: Money & Medals from the Colonial Williamsburg Collection; (2013) Lock, Stock, and Barrel; (2013) Richard Newsham's Fire Engine; (2013) Rebuilding Charlton's Coffeehouse; (2013) American Furniture: From Virginia to Vermont; (2013) Changing Keys: Keyboard Instruments for America, 1700-1830; (2013) Revolution in Taste; (2013) Treasure Quest: Great Silver Collections from Colonial Williamsburg; (2013) Identifying Ceramics: The Who, What and Ware
Publications: Exhibition catalogues; Painters & Paintings in the Early American South - March 2013
Activities: Educ dept; classes for adults & children, dramatic programs; docent & teacher training; lects open to pub, 12 vis lectrs per yr; concerts; gallery talks; tours; slide & video presentations; musical events; book traveling exhibs 1 per yr; mus shop sells books, reproductions, magazines, original art, DVDs, CDs, prints & slides

M **JAMESTOWN-YORKTOWN FOUNDATION,** Jamestown Settlement, PO Box 1607, Williamsburg, VA 23187-1607; Rte 31 S, Williamsburg, VA 23185. Tel 757-253-4838; Fax 757-253-5299; Internet Home Page Address: www.historyisfun.org; www.shophistoryisfun.org; *Capital Projects Admin* Michael S Shuflat; *Human Resources Mgr* Patrick G Teague; *Facilities Mgr* Douglas P Duval; *Dir Finance* Jean L Puckett; *Deputy Dir Admin* John J Lunsford; *Chief Develop Officer* Carter S Sonders; *Senior Develop Officer* Julie W Basic; *Exec Asst to Boards* Laura W Bailey; *Exec Dir* Philip G Emerson; *Media Relations Mgr* Deborah L Padgett; *Sr Sales & Promotions Mgr* Joan A Heikens; *Sr Retail Opers Mgr* Gary T Joyner; *Sr Dir Mktg & Retail Opers* Susan K Bak; *OESS Dir Educ* Pamela J Pettengel; *Exhib & Design Mgr* Rhonda R Tyson; *Dir Mus Educ* James S Holloway; *Curatorial Servs Mgr* Thomas E Davidson
Open daily 9 AM - 5 PM, cl Christmas & New Year's; Admis adults $15.50, children 6-12 $7.25 comb ticket adults $20, children 6-12 $10, American Heritage ann pass adults $35, children 6-12 $17.50; Estab 1957 as Jamestown Festival Park, renamed in 1990; Museum consists of indoor theater & gallery exhibs & outdoor living history prog; Average Annual Attendance: 90,639; Mem: 260; dues $25-$5000; annual meeting in Apr
Purchases: $20,000
Library Holdings: Auction Catalogs; Book Volumes; CD-ROMs; Fiche
Special Subjects: Archaeology, Etchings & Engravings, Ceramics, Glass, Furniture, Pottery, Silver, Textiles, Manuscripts, Maps, Prints, African Art, Anthropology, Folk Art, Portraits, Porcelain, Metalwork, Historical Material, Coins & Medals, Period Rooms, Pewter, Reproductions
Collections: 1,430 non-archaeological & approx 179,000 archaeological objects reflecting Jamestown's English origins; 16th & 17th century portraits, documents, furnishings, toys, ceremonial & decorative objects, tools & weapons
Publications: Series of biographies of Revolutionary Virginia leaders; brochures
Activities: Classes for adults & children; docent training; lects open to pub, 8 vis lectrs per yr; tours; outreach educ progs in 118 Virginia school districts; sales shop sells books, original art, reproductions

M **Yorktown-Victory Center,** 200 Water St, Yorktown, VA 23690; PO Box 1607, Williamsburg, VA 23187-1607. Tel 757-887-7116; Fax 757-887-1306; Internet Home Page Address: www.historyisfun.org; www.shophistoryisfun.org
Open daily 9 AM - 5 PM, cl Christmas Day & New Years Day; Admis adults $9.75, children 6-12 $5.50, comb ticket adults $20, children 6-12 $10, American Heritage ann pass adults $35, children 6-12 $17.50; Estab 1976, renovated in 1990's with new gallery exhibs; currently under renovation to become American Revolutionary Museum at Yorktown; Mus consists of timeline, exhib galleries & outdoor living history to recreate the history of the American Revolution
Collections: Approx 1,300 artifacts of 18th century, including documents, paintings, engravings, military equipment, nautical objects, medical tools, clothing, personal effects & household objects

M **THIS CENTURY ART GALLERY,** 219 N Boundary St, Williamsburg, VA 23187; PO Box 388, Williamsburg, VA 23187-0388. Tel 757-229-4949; Elec Mail thiscenturyartgallery@verizon.net; Internet Home Page Address: www.thiscenturyartgallery.org; *Pres* Michael Kirby; *VPres & Artistic Dir* Apryl MillerAltman
Open Tues - Sat 11 AM - 5 PM, Sun 1 - 5 PM, cl Thanksgiving, Christmas; No admis fee; Estab 1959; Average Annual Attendance: 4,800
Collections: arts & crafts of contemporary artists
Publications: annual brochure; quarterly newsletter
Activities: Educ prog; classes for adults & children; workshops; lect; members' show awards

WASHINGTON

BAINBRIDGE ISLAND

M **BAINBRIDGE ARTS & CRAFTS GALLERY,** 151 Winslow Way E, Bainbridge Island, WA 98110. Tel 206-842-3132; Fax 206-780-8149; Elec Mail gallery@bacart.org; Internet Home Page Address: bainbridgeartscrafts.org

A **BAINBRIDGE ISLAND ARTS COUNCIL,** 221 Winslow Way W, Ste 201, Bainbridge Island, WA 98110. Tel 206-842-7901; Fax 206-842-8825; Elec Mail admin@artshum.org; Internet Home Page Address: www.artshum.org; *Exec Dir* Morgan Smith; *Prog Dir* Devon Zotovich Phillips; *Prog Dir* Lindsay Latimore
Open Mon-Thurs 9 AM - 4 PM; Estab 1986
Income: Financed by city & state appropriations & donations
Activities: Artist grants offered

BELLEVUE

M **BELLEVUE ARTS MUSEUM,** 510 Bellevue Way NE, Bellevue, WA 98004-5014. Tel 425-519-0770; Fax 425-637-1799; Elec Mail info@bellevuearts.org; Internet Home Page Address: www.bellevuearts.org; *Dir Curatorial Affairs/Artistic Dir* Stefano Catalani; *Deputy Dir* Marsha Wolf; *Mktg & Pub Rels Dir* Tanja Baumann; *Controller* Jodi Scharlock; *Bd Pres* Anne Kilcup; *Retail Sales Mgr* Nancy Whittaker; *Managing Dir* Larry Wright
Office hours Mon - Fri, 9 AM - 5 PM; mus open Tues - Sun 11 AM - 5 PM, free first Fri 11 AM - 8 PM; Admis adults $10, seniors & students $7, children under 6

& mems no admis fee; family ticket (up to 2 adults & 4 children under 18) $25; Estab 1975 to be the Pacific Northwest's center for the exploration of art, craft & design; Maintains 6000 sq ft for changing & temporary exhibs; Average Annual Attendance: 52,000; Mem: 1,800; annual mem fee
Income: $2,900,000 (financed by mem, pvt contributions, store sales, grants, fundraising events, arts & crafts fair)
Special Subjects: Decorative Arts, Folk Art, Ceramics, Furniture, Gold, Porcelain, Pottery, Sculpture, Drawings, Textiles, Crafts, Woodcarvings, Furniture, Jewelry, Embroidery, Enamels
Exhibitions: Quarterly rotating exhibs; (08/16/2013-01/05/2014) Rick Araluce: The Minutes. the Hours, the Days; (11/21/2013-02/02/2014) A World of Paper: Isabelle de Borchgrave Meets Mariano Fortuny
Publications: Member newsletters; exhibition catalogs; posters; program brochures
Activities: Classes for adults & children; docent training; lects open to pub, 2-4 vis lectrs per yr; films; talks; tours; symposia; hands-on activities for children; awards through art & craft juries; competitions; originates traveling exhibs; mus store sells books, prints, jewelry, reproductions, cards & papers, original art & gifts

BELLINGHAM

M **WESTERN WASHINGTON UNIVERSITY,** Viking Union Gallery, 516 High St, VU Room 422 Bellingham, WA 98225-5946. Tel 360-650-6534, Exten 6534; Fax 360-650-7736; Elec Mail as.gallery@wwwu.edu; Internet Home Page Address: www.gallery.as.wwu.edu; *Dir* Hannah Fenske; *Adv* Casey Hayden
Open Mon - Fri 11 AM 5 PM; No admis fee; Estab 1969 to provide a wide variety of gallery exhibits for western students and the community; The gallery is a student run venue that strives to support local, student, and national artists; Average Annual Attendance: 5,000
Income: $8,500 (financed by student activity fees)
Collections: Matthew Curry
Exhibitions: Exhibitions change every month; Annual Beyond Borders International; Undergraduate Fine Art Competition; Annual Labyrinth Women's Exhibition & Literary Journal
Activities: Lects open to pub; sponsoring of competitions; awards to top 3 winners in Beyond Borders
M **Western Gallery,** Fine Arts Complex, WWU Bellingham, WA 98225-9068; 516 High St, MS9068, Western Washington University Bellingham, WA 98225. Tel 360-650-3900; Fax 360-650-6878; Elec Mail sarah.clarklangager@wwu.edu; Internet Home Page Address: www.westerngallery.wwu.edu; *Mus Spec* Paul Brower
Open Mon, Tues, Thurs & Fri 10 AM - 4 PM, Wed 10 AM - 8 PM, Sat Noon - 4 PM when university is in session; No admis fee; Old gallery estab 1950, new gallery estab 1989 to exhibit contemporary art; Washington Art Consortium office & collections based at Western Gallery. Rotating exhibitions on contemporary art, 3-4 per yr; Average Annual Attendance: 15,000
Income: Financed by state appropriation & endowment for exhibs
Special Subjects: Graphics, Sculpture
Collections: Outdoor Sculpture Collection WWU (contemporary sculpture since 1960); American drawings & prints; 20th Century Chair Collection
Exhibitions: Rotating exhibits every 6-8 weeks
Publications: Outdoor Sculpture Collection brochures; "Sculpture in Place: A Campus as Site" published by Western Washington University
Activities: Lects open to pub, 3 vis lectrs per year; gallery talks; tours of outdoor sculpture collection; Wed noon hour & evening discussions

M **WHATCOM MUSEUM,** (Whatcom Museum of History and Art) 250 Flora St Bellingham, WA 98225-4497; 121 Prospect St, Bellingham, WA 98225-4497. Tel 360-778-8930; Fax 360-778-8931; Elec Mail museuminfo@cob.org; Internet Home Page Address: www.whatcommuseum.org; *Dir* Patricia Leach; *Cur Art* Barbara Matilsky; *Educ* Mary Jo Maute; *Cur Coll* Janis Olson; *Educ* Elsa Lenz Kothe; *Develop Assoc* Kristin Costanza; *Exhib Designer* Scott Wallin; *Photo Archives Historian* Jeff Jewell; *Preparator* Curtis Mahle; *Store Mgr* Janet Ershig
Open Tues - Sun Noon - 5 PM, cl Mon & holidays; Admis adults $10, seniors & military $8, children $4.50; Estab 1940 to collect, preserve & use, through exhibits, interpretation & research, objects of historic or artistic value & to act as a multi-purpose cultural center for the Northwest Washington area providing presentations in all aspects of the arts; Three galleries (9,000 sq ft) in the new Leed Silver Lightcatcher bldg; 9 galleries plus permanent historical exhib spaces in the 1892 City Hall mus; Average Annual Attendance: 100,000; Mem: 1000; dues family $65, individual $50; annual meeting in Mar; open to pub
Income: Financed by pvt & pub funds
Special Subjects: Drawings, Painting-American, Photography, Sculpture, Watercolors, Ethnology, Textiles, Crafts, Folk Art, Woodcarvings, Landscapes, Portraits, Dolls, Historical Material, Dioramas, Period Rooms
Collections: Modern & Contemporary Northwest Art; Darius Kinsey, J Wilbur Sandison, Bert W Huntoon, Jack Carver & Galen Biary Historic Photographic Collections; Northwest Native American Artifacts; Regional Historic Photographs & Artifacts; H C Hanson Naval Architecture Collection
Exhibitions: Rotating exhibits every 4-6 months
Publications: Art & Events Calendar, quarterly; Exhibit catalogs; History texts
Activities: Classes for adults & children; docent training; lects open to pub, 60 vis lectrs per yr; concerts; gallery talks; tours; exten dept serves public school outreach & community outreach; book traveling exhibs; originate traveling exhibs; mus shop sells books, original art & reproductions; Lightcatcher Cafe
L **Library,** 121 Prospect St, Bellingham, WA 98225-4497. Tel 360-676-6981; Fax 360-738-7409; Elec Mail museuminfo@cob.org; Internet Home Page Address: www.city-govt.ci.bellingham.wa.us/museum.htm; *Photo Archivist* Toni Nagel; *CEO & Dir* Thomas Livesay; *Treas* Stan Miller; *Designer* Scott Wallin; *Educ Coordr* Richard Vanderway; *Mus Shop Mgr* Jenseen Brons; *Pres* Jeff McClure; *Accnt* Judy Frost; *Cur Coll* Janis Olson; *Cur Art* Kathleen Moles; *Dir Develop* Kathleen Iwerson
Open to pub by appointment only; Estab 1941; For reference only; Average Annual Attendance: 110,000; Mem: 1350
Income: Pvt and pub funds, municipal museum

Library Holdings: Book Volumes 500; Original Documents; Photographs; Prints; Records; Sculpture; Slides; Video Tapes
Special Subjects: Collages, Decorative Arts, Photography, Drawings, Painting-American, Posters, Prints, Sculpture, Historical Material, Watercolors, Ethnology, Eskimo Art, Period Rooms, Dolls, Woodcuts
Activities: Classes for adults & children; dramatic prog; docent training; lects open to pub; concerts; gallery talks; tours; sponsoring of competitions; mus shop sells books, reproductions, prints & photos; Whatcom Children's Museum

CHEHALIS

L **Library,** 599 NW Front Way, Chehalis, WA 98532. Tel 360-748-0831; Elec Mail director@lewiscountymuseum.org; Internet Home Page Address: www.lewiscountymuseum.net; *Dir* Steven A Skinner
Open Tues - Sat 10 AM - 5 PM; Admis adult $5, seniors & ages 6 -17 $4, under 6 free; Estab 1979; Reference library; Average Annual Attendance: 14,000; Mem: 350; dues individual $25; family $35
Library Holdings: Book Volumes 150; Clipping Files; Manuscripts; Memorabilia; Pamphlets; Reproductions
Special Subjects: Photography, Manuscripts, Maps, Historical Material, Fashion Arts, American Indian Art, Furniture, Period Rooms, Dolls, Pottery, Restoration & Conservation, Textiles, Dioramas, Flasks & Bottles, Display

CLARKSTON

A **VALLEY ART CENTER INC,** 842 Sixth St, Clarkston, WA 99403. Tel 509-758-8331; Elec Mail artcenter@cableone.net; *Dir* Paul Fuson; *Cur* Craig Whitcomb; *Treas* Stephanie Whitcomb
Open Tues - Thurs 9 AM - 3 PM, Fri noon - 6 PM, Sat 9 AM - 3 PM & by appointment; No admis fee, donations accepted; Estab 1968 to encourage & instruct in all forms of the visual arts & to promote the cause of art in the community; A portion of the center serves as the gallery; wall space for display of paintings or other art; showcases for colls & artifacts; Average Annual Attendance: 5,000-7,000; Mem: 200; dues $35; annual meeting in Jan
Income: Financed by mem & class fees
Library Holdings: Book Volumes; Video Tapes
Publications: Exhibit calendar
Activities: Classes for seniors, adults & children; lect open to public, 4 vis lectrs per year; gallery talks; tours; competitions with awards; scholarships offered; individual paintings & original objects of art lent to local bus & individuals, including artists; lending collection contains books, original prints, paintings, records & photographs; sales shop sells books, original art, sculpture, prints, pottery & soft goods

COUPEVILLE

A **PACIFIC NORTHWEST ART SCHOOL,** Gallery at the Wharf, 15 NW Birch St, Coupeville, WA 98239-3103. Tel 360-678-3396; Tel 866-678-3396; Fax 360-678-7420; Elec Mail info@pacificnorthwestartschool.com; Internet Home Page Address: www.pacificnorthwestartschool.com; *Exec Dir* Judy G Lynn; *Educ Dir* Soledad Sahdana-Melber; *Reg & Prog Dir* Jan Graham; *Prog Mgr* Cis Branaff
Open Mon - Fri 9 AM - 4 PM; No admis fee; Estab 1989 for arts educ; Average Annual Attendance: 1,400; Mem: 450; dues vary; annual meeting in Jan
Library Holdings: Auction Catalogs; Audio Tapes; Book Volumes; Cassettes; Exhibition Catalogs; Memorabilia
Collections: Paintings & photography donated by NFS faculty & students
Publications: Biannual catalog of visual arts workshops
Activities: Classes for adults & children; lects open to pub 3-4 times per year; scholarships offered; serves Whidbey Island and lends original objects of art to bus and libraries; sales shop sells prints and original art

ELLENSBURG

M **CENTRAL WASHINGTON UNIVERSITY,** Sarah Spurgeon Gallery, 400 E Eighth Ave, Ellensburg, WA 98926-7564. Tel 509-963-2665; Fax 509-963-1918; Elec Mail chinnm@cwu.edu; Internet Home Page Address: www.cwu.edu/~art; *Dir Art Gallery* James Sahlstrand
Open Mon - Fri 8 AM - 5 PM; No admis fee; Estab 1970 to serve as university gallery & hold regional & national exhibits; The gallery is a large, single unit; Average Annual Attendance: 20,000
Income: Financed by state appropriations
Exhibitions: Rotating exhibits
Publications: Catalogs for all National shows
Activities: Lect open to public; competitions

M **CLYMER MUSEUM OF ART,** 416 N Pearl St, Ellensburg, WA 98926-3112. Tel 509-962-6416; Fax 509-962-6424; Elec Mail clymermuseum@charter.net; Internet Home Page Address: www.clymermuseum.com; *Dir* Mia Merendino
Open Mon - Fri 10 AM - 5 PM, Sat 10 AM - 4 PM, Sun Noon - 4 PM, cl major holidays; No admis fee, donations accepted; Estab 1991 to preserve & promote the works of John F. Clymer; Two rooms with art from visiting artists; Average Annual Attendance: 21,280; Mem: 150; dues $35-$1000
Income: Financed by mem, gift shop sales & fund raisers
Collections: John Ford Clymer's Works of Art, illustration, historical, outdoor
Exhibitions: Life & Art of John F Clymer; exhibits of visiting artists change every two months
Publications: newsletter
Activities: Lects open to pub, 6 vis lectrs per yr; book traveling exhibs 1 per yr; mus shop sells books & prints

M **GALLERY ONE VISUAL ARTS CENTER,** 408 N Pearl St, Ellensburg, WA 98926-3112. Tel 509-925-2670; Elec Mail director@gallery-one.org; Internet Home Page Address: www.gallery-one.org; *Exec Dir* Carol Hassen; *Asst Dir* Monica Miller; *Arts Programmer* Renee Adams; *Retail Mgr* Sarah Haven; *Educ Coordr* Becky Parmenter
Open Mon - Fri 11 AM - 5 PM, Sat & Sun noon - 4 PM; No admis fee; Estab 1968 to offer quality artistic & educational experience to all ages; 3 exhib

galleries, gift gallery, 4 ed rooms, ceramics studio, 7 artists studios; Average Annual Attendance: 100,000; Mem: 350; dues $200-$500; meeting 3rd Mon each month

Income: $200,000 (financed by sales, mem & fundraisers)

Special Subjects: Drawings, Graphics, Painting-American, Photography, Prints, Sculpture, Bronzes, Ceramics, Crafts, Pottery, Etchings & Engravings, Landscapes, Decorative Arts, Collages, Dolls, Glass, Jewelry, Porcelain, Silver, Marine Painting, Metalwork, Scrimshaw, Stained Glass, Pewter, Enamels

Exhibitions: See website

Activities: Occasional classes for adults & children; lect open to public, 10 vis lectrs per yr; competitions with awards; gallery talks; tours; juried exhibs $2500 in awards; individual paintings are lent; lending collection contains original artworks, paintings & sculptures; sales shop sells books, original art, reproductions, prints, arts & crafts

A **WESTERN ART ASSOCIATION,** 309 N Pearl St, Ellensburg, WA 98926-3995. Tel 509-962-2934; Fax 509-962-8515; Elec Mail waa@elltel.net; Internet Home Page Address: www.westernartassoc.org; *Pres* Bill Phillip; *VPres* Larry MacGuffie; *Secy* Sandy Elliot; *Treas & Exec Dir* JoAnn Wise
Open third weekend in May Fri - Sat 10 AM - 10 PM, Sun 10 AM - 3 PM; Estab 1972 to promote western art, artifacts & heritage; Annual art show, sale & auction; Average Annual Attendance: 3,000 - 8,000; Mem: 275; dues family $50, individual $25; annual meeting in Aug

Income: $125,000 (financed by mem, Annual National Ellensburg Art Show & Auction, grants & sponsors)

Special Subjects: American Western Art

Activities: Lect open to pub; competitions with prizes; Best of Show; People's Choice; other media; schols offered; individual paintings & original objects of art lent; originate traveling exhibs 1 per yr; sales shop sells prints & original art

EVERETT

M **RUSSELL DAY GALLERY,** Parks Student Union Bldg, Rm 219, 2000 Tower St Everett, WA 98201-1352. Tel 435-388-9036; Elec Mail slepper@everettcc.edu; Internet Home Page Address: www.everettcc.edu/russelldaygallery; *Dir* Sandra Lepper
Open Mon - Wed 8 AM - 7 PM, Thurs - Fri 8 AM - 4 PM
Collections: Paintings

FRIDAY HARBOR

M **WESTCOTT BAY INSTITUTE,** Island Museum of Art & Westcott Bay Sculpture Park, 314 Spring St, Friday Harbor, WA 98250; PO Box 339, Friday Harbor, WA 98250-0339. Tel 360-370-5050; Fax 360-370-5805; Elec Mail kay@wbay.org; Internet Home Page Address: www.wbay.org; *Dir* Kay Kammerzell
Open Island Museum of Art: Tues - Sat 11 AM - 5 PM with extended summer hours, Westcott Bay Sculpture Park: daily dawn - dusk year-round; No admis fee for Island Museum of Art, Westcott Bay Sculpture Park: adults $5, children free; Estab 2000; Exhib of 2 & 3 dimensional art focusing on northwest & west coast contemp art; Average Annual Attendance: 50,000; Mem: 300

Income: Financed by grants & membership

Special Subjects: Glass, Sculpture, Bronzes, Woodcarvings, Metalwork

Activities: Classes for adults & children; tours; exhibitions; mus shop sells books & original art

GOLDENDALE

M **MARYHILL MUSEUM OF ART,** 35 Maryhill Museum Dr, Goldendale, WA 98620-4601. Tel 509-773-3733; Fax 509-773-6138; Elec Mail maryhill@maryhillmuseum.org; Internet Home Page Address: www.maryhillmuseum.org; *Dir* Colleen Schafroth; *CFO* Leslie Wetherwell; *Cur Art* Steven L. Grafe; *Cur Educ* Carrie Clark-Peck
Open daily 10 AM - 5 PM Mar 15 - Nov 15; Admis adults $9, seniors $8, students 7-18 $3, under 6 free; Estab 1923 as a museum of art; Chateau-style mansion with 4 stories of galleries on 26 acres of parklands plus full scale Stonehenge nearby; cafe & museum shop; Average Annual Attendance: 45,000; Mem: 450; dues $50 individual, $75 family

Special Subjects: Prints, Textiles, Sculpture, Drawings, Painting-American, American Indian Art, Ethnology, Religious Art, Etchings & Engravings, Decorative Arts, Furniture, Glass, Painting-British, Historical Material, Antiquities-Greek

Collections: American Indian Art; antique & modern chess sets; European & American paintings; Queen of Romania furniture & memorabilia; regional historic photographs; Rodin sculpture & watercolors; Russian icons; 1946 costumed French fashion mannequins, decorative arts; art nouveau glass; Romanian Folk textiles, contemporary sculpture

Publications: Brochure, souvenir & exhibition booklets

Activities: Classes for adults & children, performing arts progs, docent training; lects open to pub, 4 vis lectrs per yr; gallery talks; tours; lending collection contains individual paintings & original objects of art; book traveling exhibs, 2 - 3 annually; originate traveling exhibs to national & international mus; mus shop sells gift items & publications on collections

GREENBANK

M **ROB SCHOUTEN GALLERY,** 765 Wonn Rd, Greenbank Farm, C103 Greenbank, WA 98253. Tel 360-222-3070
Open Summer daily 10AM-5PM, Winter daily 11AM-4PM; Circ
Collections: works by Rob Schouten including oil paintings, etchings, & Giclee prints; works by other artists include paintings, drawings, printmaking, & sculpture

KENNEWICK

A **ARTS COUNCIL OF THE MID-COLUMBIA REGION,** 5 N Morain, Kennewick, WA. Tel 509-943-6702; Fax 509-943-6164; Elec Mail arts council@tcfn.org; Internet Home Page Address: www.owt.com/arts/artscouncil; *Exec Dir* Beth Perry
Open Mon - Fri 10 AM - 5 PM, Sat 11 AM - 3 PM; Estab Apr 1968 to advocate the arts in the Mid-Columbia Region; Average Annual Attendance: 17,000; Mem: 300; dues $35

Income: $130,000 (financed by city, corporate & private mem)

Publications: Calendar, weekly

Activities: Educ progs; lects open to pub, 5 vis lectrs per yr; gallery talks; tours; book traveling exhibs 1 per yr

KIRKLAND

KIRKLAND ARTS CENTER, 620 Market St, Kirkland, WA 98033-5421. Tel 425-822-7161; Fax 425-889-2963; Internet Home Page Address: www.kirklandartscenter.org; *Exec Dir* Christopher Shainin; *Exhibs Dir* Cable Griffith; *Educ Dir* Myra Kaha; *Develop Dir* Lauren Erlinger
Open Mon-Fri 11 AM-6 PM, Sat 11 AM-5 PM 2nd Thurs 6 PM-8 PM
Collections: paintings; sculpture; ceramics; prints

LA CONNER

M **MUSEUM OF NORTHWEST ART,** 121 S First St, La Conner, WA 98257; PO Box 969, La Conner, WA 98257-0969. Tel 360-466-4446; Fax 360-466-7431; Elec Mail marketing@museumofnwart.org; Internet Home Page Address: www.museumofnwart.org; *Exec Dir* Christopher Shainin; *Mktg & Develop Coordr* Christy Lyman; *Exhibs Dir* Lisa Young; *Educ Dir* Jasmine Valandani; *Outreach Dir* Christine Wardenburg-Skinner; *Interim Bus Mgr* Pat Hoover; *Mus Store Mgr* Jacque Chase
Store & galleries open Sun & Mon noon - 5 PM, Tues - Sat 10 AM - 5 PM; Admis $5, members free; Estab 1981 to preserve, protect & interpret the fine visual art of the Pacific Northwest; Average Annual Attendance: 15,000; Mem: 1000; dues $35-$1000

Income: $700,000 (financed by mem, admis, grants, donations & special events)

Special Subjects: Drawings, Landscapes, Marine Painting, Photography, Portraits, Painting-American, Prints, Textiles, Graphics, Latin American Art, Painting-American, Photography, Prints, Sculpture, Watercolors, Ceramics, Pottery, Woodcarvings, Woodcuts, Etchings & Engravings, Landscapes, Collages, Glass, Jewelry, Porcelain, Oriental Art, Metalwork, Historical Material

Collections: Northwest painting, drawing, sculpture & prints, studio glass

Publications: Catalogs; quarterly newsletter

Activities: Classes for adults & children; docent training; lects open to pub; 15 vis lectrs per yr; gallery talks; tours; Governor's Arts Award; book traveling exhibs 1 per yr; originate traveling exhibs 1 per yr; mus shop sells books, original art, reproductions, prints, jewelry, paper products, fiber art & sculpture

OLYMPIA

M **EVERGREEN STATE COLLEGE,** Evergreen Gallery, 2700 Evergreen Pkwy NW, Olympia, WA 98505. Tel 360-867-5125; Fax 360-867-6794; Elec Mail friedma@evergreen.edu; Internet Home Page Address: www.evergreen.edu/gallery; *Dir* Ann Friedman
Open Mon - Thurs Noon - 4 PM; No admis fee; Contemporary Gallery; Average Annual Attendance: 4,000

Income: grants, fellowship, donations

Special Subjects: American Indian Art, Drawings, Etchings & Engravings, Ceramics, Photography, Pottery, Painting-American, Prints, Textiles, Sculpture, Woodcuts

Collections: Evergreen State College Art Collection; black & white photography, prints, ceramics, paintings

Exhibitions: Contemporary West Coast & US art; Native American Art

Activities: Lects open to pub; concerts; gallery talks; tours; book traveling exhib 1 or 2 per yr

M **MONARCH CONTEMPORARY ART CENTER & SCULPTURE PARK,** 8431 Waldrick Rd SE, Olympia, WA 98501; 7332 Churchill Rd, Tenino, WA 98589. Tel 360-264-7777; Fax 360-264-4646; Elec Mail heernett@aol.com; Internet Home Page Address: www.monarchartcenter.org; *Contact* Chanelle Holbrook-Shaw
Open dawn to dusk; Admis donation; Estab 1998; showcasing art work; 1,200 sq ft with reception kitchen attached; Average Annual Attendance: 1,800

Income: Donations & grants, $15,000-$20,000 per yr

Collections: Valentine Wellman paintings & sculptures

M **STATE CAPITAL MUSEUM,** 211 21st Ave W, Olympia, WA 98501. Tel 360-753-2580; Fax 360-586-8322; Elec Mail dvalley@wshs.wa.gov; Internet Home Page Address: www.wshs.org; *Cur Exhib* Redmond Barnett; *Dir* Derek R Valley; *Cur Educ* Susan Rohrer; *Admin Asst* Helen Adams
Open Tues - Fri 10 AM - 4 PM, Sat Noon - 4 PM, cl Sun & Mon; Admis family $5, adults $2, seniors $1.75, children $1; Estab 1941 to interpret history of the State of Washington & of the capital city; The one-room museum presents changing monthly shows; Average Annual Attendance: 40,000; Mem: 400; dues family $12, individual $6; annual meeting in June

Income: Financed by city & state appropriation & local funds

Special Subjects: American Indian Art, Woodcuts, Etchings & Engravings

Collections: Etchings by Thomas Handforth; Winslow Homer Woodcuts; Northwest Indian serigraphs

Exhibitions: Rotating exhibits

Publications: Museum Newsletter, bi-monthly; Museum Calendar; every other month: lists all scheduled events; Columbia, The Magazine of Northwest History

Activities: Classes for adults & children; dramatic progs; docent training; lects open to pub; concerts; gallery talks; tours; individual paintings & original objects of art lent to State offices; lending collection contains original prints, paintings; originate traveling exhibs; sales shop sells books & slides

PORT ANGELES

M **CITY OF PORT ANGELES,** (Port Angeles Fine Arts Center) Port Angeles Fine Arts Center & Webster Woods Art Park, 1203 E Lauridsen Blvd, Port Angeles, WA 98362-6630. Tel 360-457-3532; Elec Mail pafac@olypen.com; Internet Home Page Address: www.pafac.org; *Educ Dir* Barbara Slavik; *Bd Trustees* Jake Seniuk; *VChmn* Vicci Rudin; *Foundation Pres* Linda Crow; *Endowment Pres* Harris Verner
Open Mar - Oct: Wed - Sun 11 AM - 5 PM, Nov - Feb: 10 AM - 4 PM; No admis fee, donations accepted; Estab 1986; 1950's NW contemporary semi-circular home designed by Paul Hayden Kirk, converted to gallery. Changing shows of contemporary art in all media. Panoramic views & integration of natural surroundings in gallery space via many glass walls. Five acre Webster Woods Art Park with over 125 works; Average Annual Attendance: 18,000; Mem: 300; dues $35 & up
Income: $175,000 (financed by endowment, mem, grants & corporate gifts)
Library Holdings: Exhibition Catalogs; Kodachrome Transparencies; Original Art Works; Photographs; Prints; Sculpture; Slides; Video Tapes
Special Subjects: Drawings, Ceramics, Glass, Painting-American, Woodcuts, Photography, Sculpture, Watercolors, Landscapes, Collages, Posters, Painting-Canadian
Collections: Esther Webster Art Collection; miscellaneous donated works; Art Park has numerous gifted & donated works
Exhibitions: Art outside - year round sculpture park; 6 original exhibs annually
Publications: On Center, quarterly
Activities: Classes for children; docent progs; lects open to pub, 4 vis lectrs per yr; concerts; readings; gallery talks; tours; sales shop sells books, handicrafts, magazines, original art, reproductions & prints

PORT TOWNSEND

A **CENTRUM ARTS & CREATIVE EDUCATION,** Fort Worden State Park, PO Box 1158 Port Townsend, WA 98368-0958. Tel 360-385-3102; Fax 360-385-2470; Elec Mail jmacelwee@centrum.org; Internet Home Page Address: www.centrum.org; WATS 800-733-3608; *Exec Dir* John A MacElwee; *Young Artist Proj Prog Mgr* Martha Worthley; *Dir Progs* Jodan Hartt; *Dir Opers* Lisa Werner
Open Mon - Fri 8:30 AM - 5 PM; Estab 1973 to assist those who seek creative & intellectual growth & to present visual, literary & performing arts to the pub; Average Annual Attendance: 38,500; Mem: 800; dues $25 & up
Income: Financed by donations, fees & grants
Collections: Collection of prints from artists in residence
Activities: Resident workshops for children; dramatic progs; lects open to pub, 20 vis lectrs per yr; concerts; awards; gallery talks; scholarships; artist in residence prog

M **NORTHWIND ARTS CENTER,** 2409 Jefferson St, Port Townsend, WA 98368-4637. TWX 360-379-1086

PULLMAN

M **WASHINGTON STATE UNIVERSITY,** Museum of Art, PO Box 647460, Pullman, WA 99164-7460. Tel 509-335-1910 (office); Fax 509-335-1908; Elec Mail artmuse@wsu.edu; Internet Home Page Address: www.museum.wsu.edu; *Dir* Chris Bruce; *Assoc. Dir* Anna-Maria Shannon; *Cur* Keith Wells; *Asst Cur* Zachary Mazur; *Dir Develop* Jill Aesoph; *Media/PR Mgr* Debby Stinson
Open Mon - Fri 10 AM - 4 PM, Thurs 10 AM - 7 PM, Sat & Sun 1 - 5 PM, cl Sun; No admis fee; Estab 1973 to contribute to the humanistic & artistic educational purpose & goal of the university for the direct benefit of the students, faculty & surrounding communities; Gallery covers 5000 sq ft & is centrally located on campus; Average Annual Attendance: 28,000; Mem: 400; dues $50-$1000; annual meeting in the spring
Income: Financed by the state of Washington, private & pub grants & contributions
Library Holdings: Audio Tapes; Book Volumes; Exhibition Catalogs; Kodachrome Transparencies; Memorabilia; Pamphlets; Slides; Video Tapes
Special Subjects: Painting-American, Photography, Prints
Collections: Late 19th century to present-day American art, with particular strength in the areas of the Ash Can School & Northwest regional art; contemporary American & British prints
Exhibitions: Annual; fine arts faculty & the master of fine arts thesis; permanent collection, rental/traveling
Activities: Classes for children and adults; docent training; lect open to public, 2-5 vis lectrs per year; concerts; gallery talks; tours; competitions; 2-4 book traveling exhibitions per year

RICHLAND

A **ALLIED ARTS ASSOCIATION,** Allied Arts Center & Gallery, 89 Lee Blvd, Richland, WA 99352-4222. Tel 509-943-9815; Fax 509-943-4068; Internet Home Page Address: www.alliedartsrichland.org; *Gallery Adminr* Penelope Walder; *Pres* Marion Goheen; *Pres* Judith Loomis
Open Tues - Sat 11 AM - 5 PM; No admis fee; Estab 1947 to stimulate interest in various forms of visual art; 4532 sq ft. Consists of the Townside Gallery, Motyka Room, Parkside Gallery & an Educational Wing; Mem: 400; dues $20; annual meeting in Nov
Income: $80,000
Library Holdings: Book Volumes 500
Exhibitions: Monthly Exhibitions; Annual Sidewalk Show

Activities: Classes for adults & children; docent progs; conferences; lects open to pub; Szulinski Award; schols & fels offered; sales shop sells original art, prints, pottery & fine crafts

SEATTLE

A **4 CULTURE,** (King County Arts Commission) 101 Prefontaine Pl S, Seattle, WA 98104-2672. Tel 206-296-8671; Fax 206-296-8629; Elec Mail jim.kelly@4culture.org; Internet Home Page Address: www.4culture.org; *Exec Dir* Jim Kelly
Open Mon - Fri 8:30 AM - 5:00 PM; Estab 1967 to provide cultural arts opportunities to the citizens of King County; 4Culture purchases & commissions many works of art for public buildings; annual grant program for organizations & artists in all artistic disciplines, also multi-cultural & disabled arts population; operates touring program of performing arts events in county locations; Mem: 16; 1 meeting per month
Income: $1,300,000 million (financed by county government, plus one percent for commissioned art in county construction projects)
Purchases: Occasional works commissioned for public art
Exhibitions: Rotating exhibits
Publications: The ARTS, bimonthly newsletter; The Touring Arts Booklet biennially; public art brochure; guide to programs, annually
Activities: Workshops; performances

A **911 MEDIA ARTS CENTER,** 909 NE 43rd St, Ste 206 Seattle, WA 98105-6020. Tel 206-682-6552; Elec Mail info@911media.org; Internet Home Page Address: www.911media.org; *Exec Dir* Steven Michael Vroom; *Commun Dir* Nichole Rathburn
Open Mon - Fri Noon - 6 PM; No admis fee; Estab 1981 as a film & video post-production center; Exhibition space; Average Annual Attendance: 15,000; Mem: 500; dues $50
Income: Financed by earned income, grants including McArthur Foundation, NEA, WASAC, SAC, KCAC, 4 Culture, Andy Warhol Foundation
Collections: Artists' video tapes
Publications: Film & video calendar, bimonthly
Activities: Workshops in film video making, video editing, grant writing & internet; educ prog; classes for adults & children; lects open to pub, 3 vis lectrs per yr; gallery talks; tours; awards Anne Focke Arts Leadership Award; schols & fel awarded

A **ALLIED ARTS OF SEATTLE,** 216 First Ave S #253, Seattle, WA 98104-2586; PO Box 4707, Seattle, WA 98194-0707. Tel 206-624-0432; Fax 206-624-0433; Elec Mail aarts@speakeasy.net; Internet Home Page Address: www.alliedarts-seattle.org; *Pres* David Yeaworth
Open Mon - Fri 9 AM - 4:30 PM; No admis fee; Estab 1954 to promote & support the arts & artists of the Northwest & to help create the kind of city that will attract the kind of people who support the arts; Mem: 500; dues $35 - $250 depending on category; annual meeting Jan
Income: $70,000 (financed by mem & fundraising events)
Publications: Access: The Lively Arts, directory of arts organizations in Puget Sound, biannual; Art Deco Seattle; Image of Imagination: Terra-Cotta Seattle

M **CENTER ON CONTEMPORARY ART,** 6413 Seaview Ave NW, Seattle, WA 98107-2666. Tel 206-728-1980; Fax 206-728-1980; Elec Mail coca@cocaseattle.org; *Exec Dir* Don Hudgins; *Chmn* Ethan Wing; *Pres* Dino Martini
Open Tues - Thurs 2 - 8 PM, Fri - Sun 12 - 5 PM; No admis fee; Average Annual Attendance: 15,000
Collections: contemporary art; performance art
Publications: COCA Newsletter
Activities: Multimedia & multidisciplinary prog; lects; guided tours; mus-related items for sale

A **CENTER ON CONTEMPORARY ART,** 6413 Seaview Ave NW, Seattle, WA 98107-2666. Tel 206-728-1980; Elec Mail coca@cocaseattle.org; Internet Home Page Address: www.cocaseattle.org; *Managing Dir* Steve Tremble; *Prog Dir* Katie J Kurtz
Open Memorial Day weekend - mid-Dec: Tues - Sat 10 AM - 6 PM, Sun 1 - 5 PM; Admis $5 suggested donation for nonmem, mems & children no charge; Estab 1980 to serve as a catalyst & forum for the advancement & understanding of contemporary art; Average Annual Attendance: 40,000; Mem: 1000; dues $15-$100
Exhibitions: Nirvana: Capitalism & the Consumed Image; Square Painting
Publications: Bimonthly newsletter
Activities: Lects open to pub, 3 vis lectrs per yr; concerts; gallery talks; competitions with awards, five $1000 for new annual artist; book traveling exhibs; mus shop sells items depending on exhib

M **CORNISH COLLEGE OF THE ARTS,** Fisher Gallery, 1000 Lenora St, Seattle, WA 98121-2707. Tel 206-726-5151; Elec Mail artdept@cornish.edu; Internet Home Page Address: www.cornish.edu/art/; *Dept Chair* Kent Devereaux; *Exhibition Cur* Jess Van Nostrand; *Production Coordr* Megan Campbell-Miller
L **Cornish Library,** 1000 Lenora St, Seattle, WA 98121. Tel 206-726-5145; Fax 206-315-5811; Elec Mail libraryref@cornish.edu; Internet Home Page Address: www.cornish.edu/library; *Dir Library Svcs* Hollis Near; *Librn* Heather Sheppard; *Cur Visual Resources* Bridget Nowlin; *Lib Specialist* Pamela Erskine
Open Mon - Fri 8 AM - 5 PM; Estab 1914; Circ 15,000; Open to students, staff & faculty; open to public for reference only
Library Holdings: Auction Catalogs 600; Book Volumes 20,500; Compact Disks 4,000; DVDs 768; Exhibition Catalogs 1000; Other Holdings CDs: 5,000; Periodical Subscriptions 184; Records 1,000; Slides 44,000; Video Tapes 1,000
Special Subjects: Theatre Arts
Activities: Four yr visual & performing arts col

A **CORPORATE COUNCIL FOR THE ARTS/ARTS FUND,** 10 Harrison St, Ste 200, Seattle, WA 98109. Tel 206-281-9050; Fax 206-281-9175; Elec Mail info@artsfund.org; Internet Home Page Address: www.cca-artsfund.org; *Pres* Peter Donnelly; *VPres Community Affairs* Dwight Gee; *Dir of Finance & Operations* Julie Sponsler; *Campaign Dir* Roxanne Shepherd
Open 8:30 AM - 5:30 PM; Estab 1968 as a clearinghouse for corporate

contributions to the arts, to monitor budgeting of art agencies & assess ability of bus to provide funding assistance; Gallery not maintained; Mem: 304 corporate mem & 1697 individual mem; ann meeting in Oct
Income: $2,885,897 (financed by mem)
Publications: Annual Report; brochures; periodic membership reports
Activities: Annual fundraising event & campaign

M **FRYE ART MUSEUM,** 704 Terry Ave, Seattle, WA 98104-2019. Tel 206-622-9250; Fax 206-223-1707; Elec Mail info@fryemuseum.org; Internet Home Page Address: www.fryemuseum.org; *Dir* Jo-Anne Birnie Danzker
Open Tues - Sun - 11 AM - 5 PM, Thurs 11 AM - 7 PM, cl Mon; No admis fee; Estab 1952; Average Annual Attendance: 100,000
Income: pvt financed
Purchases: American paintings, contemporary, German & Austrian 19th & 20th century
Library Holdings: Book Volumes; DVDs; Exhibition Catalogs; Pamphlets; Periodical Subscriptions; Video Tapes
Special Subjects: Etchings & Engravings, Painting-Japanese, Painting-American, Prints, Watercolors, Painting-Canadian, Painting-Dutch, Painting-French, Painting-Polish, Painting-Spanish, Painting-Italian, Painting-German, Painting-Russian, Painting-Scandinavian
Collections: American masters from the Colonial period to painters of today; 19th & 20th century American, German & French paintings; Bordin, Kaulbach, Koester, Lenbach, Leibl, Liebermann, Lhermitte, Max, Monticelli; Stuck, Winterhalter, Zugel, Zumbusch, American paintings by Pendergast, Hassam, Cassatt, Henri, Sargent, Wyeth, Homer, Eakins, Copley, Stuart
Publications: Frye magazine, 3 times per yr
Activities: Classes for adults & children; docent training; films; lects open to pub; 25 vis lectrs per yr; concerts; gallery talks; tours; individual paintings & objects of art lent to mus exhibs; 2 book traveling exhibs per yr; originate traveling exhibs; mus shop sells books, reproductions, prints, original art, posters, slides, videos, art catalogs, toys, jewelry & other gift items

A **GLASS ART SOCIETY,** 6512 23rd Ave NW Ste 329, Seattle, WA 98117-5728. Tel 206-382-1305; Fax 206-382-2630; Elec Mail info@glassart.org; Internet Home Page Address: www.glassart.org; *Exec Dir* Pamela Figenshow Koss; *Communs Mgr* Kristin Galioto; *Exec Asst* Patty Cokus; *Mem Servs/Registrar* Heather Kraft

M **HENRY GALLERY ASSOCIATION,** Henry Art Gallery, 15th Ave NE & NE 41st St, Seattle, WA 98195. Tel 206-543-2280; Fax 206-685-3123; Elec Mail info@u.washington.edu; Internet Home Page Address: www.henryart.org; *Dir* Sylvia Wolf; *Cur Coll* Judy Sourakli; *Chief Cur* Elizabeth Brown; *Communs Mgr* Betsey Brock; *Dir Finance* Anne Walsh; *Foundation & Corp Giving Mgr* Angela Lindou; *Develop Officer* Kathy Savory; *Opers Mgr* Owen Santos
Open Sat, Sun & Wed 11 AM - 4 PM, Thurs & Fri 11 AM - 9 PM, cl Mon & Tues; Admis general $10, seniors $6, mems & student w/ID free; Estab 1927 for modern & contemporary art; The Northwest's leading center for modern and contemporary art; Average Annual Attendance: 70,000; Mem: 2500; dues $25 - $10,000; ann meeting in the summer
Income: $3,800,000 (financed by endowment, mem, state appropriation & grants)
Library Holdings: Auction Catalogs; Book Volumes 2761; CD-ROMs 16; Cassettes; Clipping Files; Exhibition Catalogs; Video Tapes 101
Special Subjects: Decorative Arts, Ceramics, Porcelain, Pottery, Prints, Tapestries, Drawings, Graphics, Painting-American, Photography, Sculpture, Watercolors, Textiles, Costumes, Woodcuts, Etchings & Engravings, Landscapes, Posters, Painting-Canadian, Painting-French, Embroidery
Collections: Mixed Media, paintings, prints, photography, sculpture, textiles & costumes
Publications: Exhibition Catalogs
Activities: Classes for adults & children; docent training; film series; lects open to pub; 10 - 15 vis lectrs per yr; gallery talks; tours; sponsoring of competitions; fels; book traveling exhibs 1-2 per yr; originate traveling exhibs to other mus nationally & internationally; mus shop sells books, magazines, reproductions, jewelry, gifts, cards

M **LEGACY LTD,** 1003 First Ave, Seattle, WA 98104. Tel 206-624-6350; Fax 206-624-4108; Elec Mail legacy@drizzle.com; Internet Home Page Address: www.thelegacyltd.com; *Pres* Helen Carlson; *VPres* Paul Nicholson
Open Mon - Sat 10 AM - 6 PM; No admis fee; Estab 1933 for the coll & sale of Northwest Coast Indian contemporary & historic material
Exhibitions: Annual in-house special exhibits of historic contemporary Northwest Coast Indian & Eskimo art, ongoing exhibits of same
Activities: Sales shop sells books, magazines, original art & prints

M **PHOTO CENTER NW,** 900 12th Ave, Seattle, WA 98122. Tel 206-720-7222; Fax 206-720-0306; Elec Mail pcnw@pcnw.org; Internet Home Page Address: pcnw.org/gallery; *Gallery Dir* Ann Pallesen
Open Mon - Thurs 11 AM -10 PM, Fri - Sun noon - 8 PM; No admis, gallery open to pub; Estab mid 1980's; gallery, school, rental dark rooms; A renowned showcase of photography, exhibiting both contemporary & historic works from photographers around the world. The gallery exhibits photography & related media & operates in an educational institution; Average Annual Attendance: 1500; Mem: 400+; $75 basic
Special Subjects: Photography

A **PRATT FINE ARTS CENTER,** Gallery, 1902 S Main St, Seattle, WA 98144-2206. Tel 206-328-2200; Fax 206-328-1260; Elec Mail info@pratt.org; Internet Home Page Address: www.pratt.org; *Exec Dir* Michelle Bufano
Open daily 8:30 AM - 10 PM; No admis fee; admis fee for art classes; Estab 1976; Average Annual Attendance: 3,500
Exhibitions: Rotating monthly exhibits (glass, jewelry, painting, prints, metal, mixed media, sculpture)
Publications: Quarterly class schedule
Activities: Classes for adults & children; educ prog; lect open to public, 10 vis lectrs per year

M **SCIENCE FICTION MUSEUM AND HALL OF FAME,** Frank Gehry Bldg, 325 5th Ave Seattle, WA 98109-4630. Tel 206-724-3428; Fax 206-770-2727; Elec Mail info@sfhomeworld.org; Internet Home Page Address: www.sfhomeworld.org; *Dir* Donna Shirley
Open May 31 - Sept 6 daily 10 AM - 8 PM; Sept 7 - May 30 Tues - Thurs 10 AM - 5 PM, Fri - Sat 10 AM - 9 PM, Sun 10 AM - 6 PM; Admis adults $12.95, seniors, military & youth 7-17 $8.95, children 6 & under and mems free; 13,000 sq ft exhib space; Mem: dues Fam $75, Dual $60, Indiv $40
Activities: Lects; workshops; educ progs

M **SEATTLE ART MUSEUM,** Downtown, 1300 1st Ave, Seattle, WA 98101. Tel 206-654-3100; Fax 206-654-3135; Elec Mail webmaster@seattleartmuseum.org; Internet Home Page Address: www.seattleartmuseum.org; *Librn* Traci Timmons; *Mus Store Mgr* Brad Bigelow; *Asst Cur Modern Art* Marisa Sanchez; *Pres Bd* Maggie Walker; *CFO* Robert Cundall; *Cur African Art* Pamela McClusky; *Conservator* Nicholas Dorman; *Mgr Exhibitions* Zora Hutlova-Foy; *Chmn Bd* Charlie Wright; *Exhibitions Designer* Michael McCafferty; *Deputy Dir Art* Chiyo Ishikawa; *Controller* Nancy Zwieback; *Cur Drawings* Julie Emerson; *Vice Dir* Maryann Jordan; *Dir Educ* Sandra Jackson-Dumont; *Dir Pub Rels* Cara Egan
Open Wed - Sun 10 AM - 5 Pm, Thurs & Fri 10 AM - 9 PM, cl Mon, Tues & most major holidays; Admis adults $15, military & seniors $12, students & children 3-17 $9, mems & children 12 & under free, 1st Thurs of month free, 1st Fri free to seniors, 2nd Fri 5-9 PM free to teens ages 13-19; group rates available; Estab 1906, incorporated 1917, building opened 1933; gift to the city from Mrs Eugene Fuller & Richard Eugene Fuller, for recreation, educ & inspiration of its citizens; Average Annual Attendance: 400,000; Mem: 30,000
Income: Financed by state appropriations, grants, mem
Library Holdings: Auction Catalogs; Book Volumes; Clipping Files
Special Subjects: Painting-American, Prints, Primitive art, Painting-European, Painting-Japanese, Jade, Porcelain, Oriental Art, Asian Art, Antiquities-Greek, Antiquities-Roman
Collections: LeRoy M Backus Collection of Drawings & Paintings; Manson F Backus Collection of Prints; Norman Davis Collection of Classical Art; Eugene Fuller Memorial Collection: special emphasis on Japan, China, India, & including Egypt, Ancient Greece & Rome, European, Near Eastern, primitive & contemporary Northwest art, & Chinese Jades from Archaic - 18th century; Alice Heeramaneck Collection of Primitive Art; Henry & Martha Isaacson Collection of 18th Century European Porcelain; H Kress Collection of 14th - 18th Century European Paintings; Thomas D Stimson Memorial Collection (with special emphasis on Far Eastern art); Chinese & Indian Collection; 18th Century Drawing Room (furnished by the National Society of Colonial Dames of American in the State of Washington); major holdings in Northwest art, including Tobey, Callahan, Graves as well as all contemporary art, especially American artists Gorky, Pollock, Warhol & Lichtenstein; selected highlights on Asian coll on permanent display (with special emphasis on Japanese screens, paintings, sculpture and lacquers); Katherine C White Collection of African Art
Publications: Quarterly Newsletter; Art from Africa: Long Steps Never Broke a Back; Neri di Bicci and Devotional Painting in Italy; Spain in the Age of Exploration 1492-1819
Activities: Docent training; film progs; double lect course under the Museum Guild; adult art history classes; classes for children; lects open to pub & for mems only, 12 vis lectrs per yr; tours; program for senior citizens; concerts; gallery talks; mus shop sells books, gifts & jewelry

L **Dorothy Stimson Bullitt Library,** 1300 First Ave, Seattle, WA 98101-2003. Tel 206-625-3220; Elec Mail libraries@seattleartmuseum.org; Internet Home Page Address: www.seattleartmuseum.org; *Librn* Elizabeth de Fato; *Mus Store Mgr* Brad Bigelow; *Asst Cur Modern Art* Tara Young; *Mus Educator* Beverly Harding; *Mus Educator* Kathleen Peckham Allen; *CFO* Robert Cundall; *Mus Photography* Paul Macapia; *Cur African Art* Pamela McClusky; *Conservator* Nicholas Dorman; *Mgr Exhibitions* Zora Hutlova-Foy; *Sr Mus Educator* Sarah Loudon; *Cur European Painting* Chiyo Ishikawa; *Exhibitions Designer* Michael McCafferty; *Deputy Dir Art* Lisa Corrin; *Sr Deputy Dir* Gail Joice; *Controller* Debbi Lewang; *Ruth J Nutt Cur Drawings* Julie Emerson
Open Wed - Fri 10 AM - 4 PM; Archives of the Seattle Art Museum's records are held in the Special Collections of the University of Washington Libraries (for reference only)
Income: Financed by state appropriation, grants, mem
Library Holdings: Audio Tapes; Book Volumes 19,000; Exhibition Catalogs; Periodical Subscriptions 50; Slides 75,000; Video Tapes
Special Subjects: Historical Material
Collections: Books, catalogs, journals, videos & ephemera on Northwest Artists, Art of Africa, Oceana & the Americas, Decorative Arts, European Painting & Sculpture, Modern & Contemporary Art, American Art & Native American (Northwest Coast) Art; art reference coll; Northwest Artist Files: 6,000+ local & regional artists; publications & object files on objects in Mus permanent coll; resources for current exhibs; worldwide mus publications; vertical files on the history of the Seattle Art Mus, local arts organizations, galleries, museums & public art

M **Olympic Park,** 2901 Western Ave, Seattle, WA 98121; 1300 First Ave, Seattle, WA 98101-2003. Tel 206-332-1377; Fax 206-654-3135; Elec Mail webmaster@seattleartmuseum.org; Internet Home Page Address: www.seattleartmuseum.org; *Dir* Derrick R Cartwright
Open daily yr round from 30 min before sunrise to 30 min after sunset; PACCAR Pavilion open day after Labor Day - Apr 30 Tues - Sun 10 AM - 4 PM, cl Mon, May 1 - Labor Day Tues - Sun 10 AM - 5 PM, cl Mon; see website for Pavilion holiday closings; No admis fee; PACCAR Pavilion Garage parking fees apply; Purchased 1999, opened 2007; 9 acre former industrial area now a sculpture park and green space on Seattle's waterfront
Income: Financed by Seattle Art Museum
Special Subjects: Sculpture
Collections: PACCAR Pavilion; Gates Amphitheater; The Valley; Henry & William Ketcham Families Grove; Barry Ackerly Family East Meadow; Kreielsheimer North Meadow; The Shore
Activities: Tours

M **Seattle Asian Art Museum,** 1400 E Prospect St, Volunteer Park Seattle, WA 98112-3303. Tel 206-654-3100; Fax 206-324-2828; Elec Mail webmaster@seattleartmuseum.org; Internet Home Page Address:

www.seattleartmuseum.org; *Dir* Dr Kimberly Rorschach; *Foster Foundation Cur Chinese Art* Dr Josh Yiu; *Cur Japanese & Korean Art* Xiaojin Wu
Open Wed - Sun 10 AM - 5 PM, Thurs 10 AM - 9 PM, Tues & most major holidays; Admis adult $7, students w/ID, seniors & teens $5, mems & children 12 & under free, 1st Thurs of month free, 2nd Thurs of month 5-9 PM free, 1st Fri free to seniors, 1st Sat free for families; Opened 1994 in former location of Seattle Art Museum as a showcase for the Museum's Asian Art Collection & community hub for Asian culture; Maintains Gardner Center for Asian Art & Ideas
Special Subjects: Historical Material, Asian Art
Exhibitions: (Ongoing) Chinese Art: A Seattle Perspective; (Ongoing) Live Long & Prosper: Auspicious Motifs in East Asian Art; (Ongoing) Looking West, Finding East
Activities: Lects open to pub; Gardner Ctr lect series; tours

L **McCaw Foundation Asian Art Library,** 1400 E Prospect St, Volunteer Park Seattle, WA 98112-3303. Tel 206-654-3202; Fax 206-654-3191; Elec Mail libraries@seattleartmuseum.org; Internet Home Page Address: www.seattleartmuseum.org; *Dir* Derrick R Cartwright
Open Thurs & Fri 2-5 PM, Sat 10 AM - 5 PM; Sat summer hrs Jun - Aug 10 AM - 2 PM; No admis fee; Located on the Lower Level of the Seattle Asian Art Museum (For reference only)
Library Holdings: Auction Catalogs; Book Volumes; Other Holdings
Special Subjects: Historical Material, Asian Art
Collections: Books, catalogs & journals on Chinese, Japanese, Korean, Indian & Southeast Asian Art; art reference coll; publications & object files on objects in Seattle Asian Art Museum's permanent coll; resources for current exhibits

L **Ann P Wyckoff Teacher Resource Center,** 1400 E Prospect St, Volunteer Park Seattle, WA 98112-3303. Tel 206-654-3186; Fax 206-654-3191; Elec Mail trc@seattleartmuseum.org; Internet Home Page Address: www.seattleartmuseum.org; *Dir* Derrick R Cartwright
Open Thurs & Fri 2-5 Pm, Sat 10 AM - 5 PM, or by appt during mus hrs; Sat summer hrs Jun - Aug 10 AM - 2 PM; No admis fee; Lending libr available to educators. Located on the Lower Level of the Seattle Asian Art Museum
Library Holdings: Book Volumes; Compact Disks; DVDs; Video Tapes
Collections: 4,000+ art & culture related educational resources; curriculum guides; online art-information storage databases

L **SEATTLE PUBLIC LIBRARY,** Arts, Recreation & Literature Dept, 1000 Fourth Ave, Seattle, WA 98104. Tel 206-386-4636; Elec Mail arl@spl.org; Internet Home Page Address: www.spl.org; *Mgr* Barbara Armstrong
Estab 1889; Circ 181,772; Lending & reference library
Income: Financed by city tax dollars & foundation grants
Purchases: $26,000
Library Holdings: Audio Tapes; Book Volumes 147,202; Cassettes; Clipping Files; Exhibition Catalogs; Fiche; Framed Reproductions; Lantern Slides; Manuscripts; Original Art Works; Pamphlets; Periodical Subscriptions 310; Photographs; Prints; Records; Reproductions; Slides; Video Tapes
Special Subjects: Art History, American Western Art, Advertising Design, American Indian Art, Aesthetics, Afro-American Art, Antiquities-Oriental, Antiquities-Persian, Antiquities-Assyrian, Antiquities-Byzantine, Antiquities-Egyptian, Antiquities-Etruscan, Antiquities-Greek, Antiquities-Roman, Architecture

M **UNITED INDIANS OF ALL TRIBES FOUNDATION,** Daybreak Star Center Gallery, 3801 W Government Way, Discovery Park Seattle, WA 98199-1014; PO Box 99100, Seattle, WA 98199-0100. Tel 206-285-4425; Fax 206-282-3640; Elec Mail info@unitedindians.org; Internet Home Page Address: www.unitedindians.org; *Exec Dir* Marty Bluewater; *CFO* Michelle Sanidad
Open Mon - Fri 10 AM - 5 PM, Sat & Sun Noon - 5 PM; No admis fee; Estab 1977 to present contemporary American Indian fine art; Average Annual Attendance: 30,000
Collections: Collections of international American Indian tribes & cultures
Exhibitions: Permanent exhibit of different American Indian tribes & cultures as well as changing exhibitions of contemporary native art

M **UNIVERSITY OF WASHINGTON,** Henry Art Gallery, 15th Ave NE & NE 41st St, Seattle, WA 98195; PO Box 351410, Seattle, WA 98195-0001. Tel 206-543-2281; Fax 206-685-3123; Elec Mail info@henryart.org; Internet Home Page Address: www.henryart.org; *Foundations Government Relations Mgr* Angela Lindo; *Sr Cur* Elizabeth A Brown; *Cur Coll* Judy Sourakli; *Pub Information Mgr* Betsey Brock; *Dir* Sylvia Wolf; *Dir Develop* Robyn McIntire; *Dir Finance* Anne Walsh; *Human Resources* Ethelyn Abellanosa
Open Tues - Sun 11 AM - 5 PM, Thurs until 8 PM, cl Mon; Admis adults $10, seniors $6, students with ID & children under 13 free; Estab 1927; 8 galleries, 6000 sq ft of exhibition space; Average Annual Attendance: 800,000; Mem: 3500; dues $25 & up
Special Subjects: Drawings, Ceramics, Photography, Pottery, Prints, Textiles, Sculpture, Costumes, Crafts, Carpets & Rugs, Embroidery
Collections: 19th century American landscape painting; contemporary West Coast ceramics; works on paper, prints, drawings & photographs; 20th century Japanese folk pottery; Elizabeth Bayley Willis Collection of Textiles from India; western & ethnic textiles; 19th & 20th century western dress (formerly Costume & Textile Study Center)
Exhibitions: Masters of Fine Arts; 12-15 exhibs per yr focused on contemporary art
Publications: Books, exhibition catalogues
Activities: Educ programs; lects open to pub; gallery talks; tours; book traveling exhibs circulating in the US & abroad; originate traveling exhibs to mus in the United States & abroad; mus shop sells books & prints

L **Architecture-Urban Planning Library,** 334 Gould Hall, Seattle, WA 98195; PO Box 355730, Seattle, WA 98195-5730. Tel 206-543-4067; Internet Home Page Address: www.lib.washington.edu/aup; *Librn* Betty L Wagner
Open Mon - Thurs 8 AM - 9 PM, Fri 8 AM - 5 PM, Sat - Sun 1 - 5 PM; Estab 1923
Library Holdings: Book Volumes 45,000; CD-ROMs; Compact Disks; Exhibition Catalogs; Fiche 5246; Memorabilia; Pamphlets 1684; Periodical Subscriptions 300; Video Tapes

Special Subjects: Landscape Architecture, Architecture
Collections: Carl Gould Portrait

L **Univ of Washington Libraries, Special Collections,** PO Box 352900, Seattle, WA 98195-2900. Tel 206-543-1929 or 543-1879; Fax 206-543-1931; Elec Mail speccoll@u.washington.edu; Internet Home Page Address: www.lib.washington.edu/specialcoll/; *Head* Carla Rickerson; *Cur Visual Materials* Nicolette Bromberg; *Book Arts & Rare Books Cur* Sandra Kroupa; *Manuscripts & Spec Collections Cataloging Librn* Marsha Maguire; *Univ Archivist* John Bolcer; *Pacific Northwest Cur* Nicole Bouche
Classes in session, Mon - Fri 10 AM - 4:45 PM, Wed 10 AM - 7:45 PM, Sat 1 - 4:45 PM; interim, Mon - Fri 1 - 4:45 PM; No admis fee; Average Annual Attendance: 5,199
Library Holdings: Maps; Other Holdings Architectural plans, drawings & renderings 63,137; Pamphlets; Photographs; Prints
Special Subjects: Photography, Manuscripts, Bookplates & Bindings
Collections: Book arts coll; Northwest American Indian Art
Exhibitions: Best Western Books
Activities: Classes for adults; book traveling exhib 1 per yr

L **Art Library,** 101 Art Bldg, Seattle, WA 98195; PO Box 353440, Seattle, WA 98195-3440. Tel 206-543-0648; Elec Mail art@lib.washington.edu; Internet Home Page Address: www.lib.washington.edu/art; *Librn* Angela Weaver
Open Mon - Thurs 8 AM - 6 PM, Fri 8 AM - 5 PM, Sun 1 - 5 PM, cl Sat; Estab 1940 to provide resources for the instructional & research programs of the School of Art & serves as the Art Library for the university community
Income: Financed by state appropriation
Library Holdings: Book Volumes 44,000; Clipping Files; Exhibition Catalogs; Fiche; Periodical Subscriptions 200; Reproductions
Special Subjects: Art History, Photography, Sculpture, Ceramics, Printmaking, Industrial Design
—**Art Slide Library,** 120 Art Bldg, Seattle, WA 98195; PO Box 353440, Seattle, WA 98195-3440. Tel 206-543-0649; Fax 206-685-1657; Elec Mail jcmills@u.washington.edu; *Dir Visual Svcs* Jeanette C Mills; *Cur* Debra L Cox
Slide library is a teaching collection that is only available to University of Washington faculty, staff & students
Library Holdings: Slides 330,000
Collections: 35 mm art slides: Western, Asian, Tribal

M **Burke Museum of Natural History and Culture,** University of Washington Campus, Seattle, WA 98195; PO Box 353010, Burke Museum of Natural History & Culture Seattle, WA 98195-3010. Tel 206-543-5590; Fax 206-685-3039; Elec Mail theburke@u.washington.edu; Internet Home Page Address: www.burkemuseum.org; *Cur Native American Art* Robin Wright; *Cur Paleobotany* Caroline Stromberg; *Cur Invertebrate Paleontology* Elizabeth Nesbitt; *Cur Archaeology* Peter Lape; *Assoc Dir* Erin Younger; *Cur Genetic Resources* Adam Leache; *Cur Native Amer Ethnology* Deana Dart-Newton; *Cur Fishes* Theodore Pietsch; *Dir* Julie Stein; *Cur Botany* Richard Olmstead; *Cur Vertebrate Paleontology* Christian Sidor
Open daily 10 AM - 5 PM, First Thurs of the month 10 AM - 8 PM; Admis general $9.50, seniors $7.50, students $6, children under 5 free; call for spec admis fees; Estab 1885 for research & exhibs; 2 permanent exhibs & 1 temp exhib gallery; Average Annual Attendance: 105,000; Mem: 2,250; dues $20 - $55
Income: Financed by state, endowment, gifts, self-generated revenues
Collections: Natural & cultural history of Washington State, the Pacific Northwest & the Pacific Rim
Exhibitions: Life & Times of Washington; Pacific Volunteers; 3-6 temp exhibs
Activities: Classes for adults & children; docent training; lects open to pub & mem only, 8 vis lectrs per yr; gallery talks; tours; exten prog circulates study collection & serves Washington state schools, mus, community ctrs; Burkemobile; Burke in a Box; book traveling exhibs, 1-2 per yr; originates traveling exhibs nationally & statewide to mus; mus store sells books, magazines, reproductions, exhib merchandise & NW-themed gifts

M **WESTERN BRIDGE,** 3412 4th Ave S, Seattle, WA 98134-1905. Tel 206-838-7444; Elec Mail info@westernbridge.org; Internet Home Page Address: www.westernbridge.org; *Contact* Eric Fredericksen

M **WING LUKE ASIAN MUSEUM,** 719 S King St, Seattle, WA 98104-3035. Tel 206-623-5124, 623-5190 (tour desk); Fax 206-623-4559; Elec Mail folks@wingluke.org; Internet Home Page Address: www.wingluke.org; *Vol Coordr* Laura Shapiro; *Dir* Ron Chew
Open Tues - Fri 11 AM - 4:30 PM, Sat & Sun Noon - 4 PM; Admis adults $4, students & seniors $3, children $2; Estab 1966 to preserve & present the history, art & culture of Asian Pacific Americans & to bridge Asians, Asian Pacific Americans & Americans of other backgrounds; Changing exhib area; permanent exhib; Average Annual Attendance: 70,000; Mem: 1000; dues $30; annual meeting in Jan
Income: $500,000 (financed by endowment, mem, annual art auction, local & state commissions & grants for exhibits)
Special Subjects: Asian Art
Collections: Asian American Art; Historical Artifacts & Photos
Publications: Publishes exhibit catalogs
Activities: Classes for adults & children; lect open to public, 4 vis lectrs per year; tours

L **Governor Gary Locke Library and Community Heritage Center,** 719 S King St, Seattle, WA 98104. Tel 206-623-5124; Fax 206-623-4559; Elec Mail folks@wingluke.org; Internet Home Page Address: www.wingluke.org; *Cur Coll* Bob Fisher; *Dir* Ron Chew; *Assoc Dir* Beth Takekawa
Open Tues - Fri 11 AM - 4:30 PM, Sat & Sun Noon - 4 PM; Admis adults $4, seniors & students $3, ages 5-12 $2, 1st Thurs of every month free; Estab 1967; Mem: Dues $20
Income: Financed by contributions, endowment, grants & mem
Library Holdings: Book Volumes 5000; Clipping Files; Photographs; Slides 150; Video Tapes
Exhibitions: One Song, Many Voices: The Asian Pacific American Experience; The Densho: Japanese American Legacy Project; rotating exhibs

SHORELINE

M SHORELINE HISTORICAL MUSEUM, 749 N 175th St, Shoreline, WA 98133-4801; PO Box 55594, Shoreline, WA 98155-0594. Tel 206-542-7111; Elec Mail shorelinehistorical@juno.com; Internet Home Page Address: www.shorelinehistoricalmuseum.org; *VPres* Stephen Brown; *Cur* Keith Routley
Open Tues - Sat 10 AM - 4 PM; Admis by donation; Estab 1976 to preserve local history; Average Annual Attendance: 5,000; Mem: 360; dues family $25, annual $10, pioneer $5; annual meeting third Wed in Nov
Income: $35,000 (financed by mem, donations, room rentals & fundraising)
Special Subjects: Historical Material, Period Rooms
Exhibitions: School room, home room; vintage radios; blacksmith shop; transportation exhibit; post office; country store; other rotating exhibits
Publications: Newsletter, 4 times a year
Activities: Classes for children; docent training; lect open to public; tours; original objects of art lent; sales shop sells books, prints, postcards & area photo cards

SPOKANE

A CORBIN ART CENTER, 507 W 7th Ave, Spokane, WA 99204-2709. Tel 509-625-6677; Internet Home Page Address: www.spokaneparks.org/corbin
Open Mon - Thurs 9 AM - 4 PM; No admis fee
Collections: paintings
Activities: Classes for adults & children; camps

M EASTERN WASHINGTON STATE HISTORICAL SOCIETY, Northwest Museum of Arts & Culture, 2316 W First Ave, Spokane, WA 99201. Tel 509-456-3931; Fax 509-363-5303; Elec Mail themac@northwestmuseum.org; Internet Home Page Address: www.northwestmuseum.org; *Exec Dir* Forrest Rodgers; *Cur History* Marsha Rooney; *Dir Plateau Culture Ctr* Michael Holloman; *Cur of Collections* Val Wahl; *Cur of Special* Rose Krause; *Art at Work* Tammy Gabbert; *Mus Programs Mgr* Laura Thayer; *Mus Svcs Mgr* Lori Bertis; *Commns Mgr* Rebecca Bishop
Open Wed-Sat 10AM - 5PM; Admis $7 adult, $5 sr citizen & children, 5 & under free; Estab 1916 to collect & preserve Pacific Northwest History, art & American Indian materials; 5 galleries of 15,000 sq ft, auditorium, library & archives, outdoor amphitheater, Cafe MAC; Average Annual Attendance: 100,000; Mem: 2500; dues $25-5,000
Income: Financed by mem, state appropriations, fundraising, endowment & contributions
Library Holdings: Audio Tapes; CD-ROMs; Cassettes; Clipping Files; Exhibition Catalogs; Fiche; Filmstrips; Kodachrome Transparencies; Lantern Slides; Manuscripts; Maps; Memorabilia; Motion Pictures; Original Documents; Other Holdings; Pamphlets; Periodical Subscriptions; Photographs; Slides; Video Tapes
Special Subjects: Architecture, Painting-American, Photography, Prints, American Indian Art, Woodcarvings, Manuscripts, Historical Material, Maps
Collections: American Indian, regional history, Northwest modern contemporary art; Historic house of 1898 by architect Kirtland K Cutter, interior designed & decorated with period furnishings; 19th & 20th century American & European art; representative works of Pacific Northwest artists
Exhibitions: Exhibits change regularly
Activities: Classes for adults & children; docent training; lects open to pub; gallery talks; tours; individual paintings & original objects of art lent to professional nonprofit institutions nationally; lending collection contains books, original art works; original prints, paintings, sculptures & 135,000 photographs; book traveling exhibs; originates traveling exhibs; mus shop sells books, & gift items

M GONZAGA UNIVERSITY, Art Gallery, 502 E Boone Ave, Spokane, WA 99258-1774. Tel 509-328-4220, Ext 6611; Fax 509-323-5525; Elec Mail patnode@calvin.gonzaga.edu; Internet Home Page Address: www.Gen.Gonzaga.Edu/Jundt; *Asst Cur* Paul Brekke; *Prog Coordr* Anita Martello
Open Mon - Fri 10 AM - 4 PM, Sat Noon - 4 PM, through acad yr; No admis fee; Estab 1971 to service the Spokane Community, art department & general university population at Gonzaga University; Jundt Gallery estab 1995; Jundt Gallery 2720 sq ft. Arcade Gallery 1120 sq ft; Average Annual Attendance: 30,000
Income: Financed by parent institution
Purchases: Jacob Lawrence, Wayne Thiebaud & Sylvia Wald prints
Special Subjects: Drawings, Mexican Art, Painting-American, Prints, Sculpture, Bronzes, Religious Art, Ceramics, Pottery, Woodcuts, Etchings & Engravings, Afro-American Art, Glass, Tapestries
Collections: Dale Chihuly Glass Installation (Chandelier); Rodin Sculpture Coll; Contemporary & old master print coll; student art coll
Activities: Educ dept; docent training; lect open to public, 6 vis lectrs per year; gallery talks; tours; student purchase awards; individual paintings lent to museums, art centers & university galleries; lending collection contains paintings, photographs, sculptures & 3000 original prints; book traveling exhibitions 3 per year

M JUNDT ART MUSEUM, Gonzaga Univ, E 502 Boone Ave Spokane, WA 99258-0001. Tel 509-313-6611; Fax 509-313-5525; Elec Mail manoguerra@gonzaga.edu; Internet Home Page Address: www.gonzaga.edu/jundt; *Dir & Cur* Dr Paul Manoguerra; *Asst Cur Educ* Karen Kaiser; *Prog Coordr* Anita Martello
Open Winter Mon - Sat 10 AM - 4 PM, Summer call for hours, cl univ holidays; No admis fee; Average Annual Attendance: 25,000
Collections: student prints; Old Master's prints; photography prints; contemporary prints; Auguste Rodin sculptures; Chihuly glass
Activities: Docent training; lect; gallery talks

L SPOKANE PUBLIC LIBRARY, 906 W Main St, Spokane, WA 99201. Tel 509-444-5300; *Dir* Pat Partovi
Open Tues - Wed 10 AM - 8 PM, Thurs - Sat 10 AM - 6 PM; No admis fee; Estab 1894 basically to meet citizens educ, information, recreation & cultural lifelong learning needs through a variety of programs & facilities; Gallery maintained for special exhibitions
Library Holdings: Audio Tapes; Cassettes; Clipping Files; Compact Disks; DVDs; Exhibition Catalogs; Fiche; Filmstrips; Kodachrome Transparencies; Manuscripts; Maps; Micro Print; Motion Pictures; Original Art Works; Other Holdings Original documents; Pamphlets; Periodical Subscriptions; Photographs; Records; Reels; Slides; Video Tapes
Collections: AV; children's & young adult; fiction; genealogy; non-fiction; northwest; periodicals; rare books
Publications: Previews, monthly
Activities: Classes for adults & children; dramatic progs; lects open to pub; concerts

TACOMA

M TACOMA ART MUSEUM, 1701 Pacific Ave, Tacoma, WA 98402-3214. Tel 253-272-4258; Fax 253-627-1898; Elec Mail info@tacomaartmuseum.org; Internet Home Page Address: www.tacomaartmuseum.org; *Dir* Stephanie Stebich; *Deputy Dir & Dir Admin & Fin* Cameron Fellows; *Dir Devel* Kara Hefley; *Dir Educ* Courtney Vowels; *Dir Cur Admin & Cur Contemporary & Northwest Art* Rock Hushka; *Commns Coordr* Lisa McKeown
Open Wed - Sun 10 AM - 5 PM, 3rd Thurs until 8 PM, cl Mon, Tues, Thanksgiving, Christmas, New Years, MLK Jr Day & Jul 4; Admis adults $10, seniors 65+, students & military $8, mems & children under 5 free; 3rd Thurs of month 5-8 PM free; group & family rates available; Founded 1935; 12,000 sq ft of galleries are open and airy, highlighting the work on view; eight exhibs spaces; maintains art reference library. Member of the Washington Art Consortium; Average Annual Attendance: 80,000; Mem: 1900; dues $20-$2500
Income: $1,000,000 (financed by contributions, grants, mem & carried income)
Library Holdings: Book Volumes 6000; Clipping Files 4000; DVDs 36; Exhibition Catalogs; Pamphlets; Periodical Subscriptions 12; Video Tapes 40
Special Subjects: American Indian Art, Etchings & Engravings, Landscapes, Architecture, Ceramics, Photography, Portraits, Prints, Painting-British, Painting-European, Painting-Japanese, Sculpture, Painting-American, Prints, Sculpture, Woodcarvings, Woodcuts, Glass, Jewelry, Asian Art, Painting-French, Reproductions
Collections: American & French paintings; American sculpture; Chinese Textiles; 19th & 20th Century American Art; European & Asian Works of art; European Impressionism; Japanese Woodblock prints; Dale Chihuly Glass; Northwest Art; Studio Art Jewelry; Works on Paper
Publications: Museum Notes, quarterly to mems; exhib catalogs; Northwest Biennial, catalog
Activities: Educ prog; classes for adults & children; youth summer camp; docent training; lects open to pub, 20 vis lectrs per yr; gallery talks; tours; concerts; performances; film screenings; poetry & book readings; biennial competition with awards; individual paintings & original objects of art lent to other professional mus; mus shop sells books, original art, reproductions, prints, cards, jewelry, concerts & films

L TACOMA PUBLIC LIBRARY, Handforth Gallery, 1102 Tacoma Ave S, Tacoma, WA 98402-2098. Tel 253-591-5666; Fax 253-627-1693; Internet Home Page Address: www.tpl.wa.us; *Mgr Community Rels* David Domkoski
Open Mon - Thurs 9 AM - 9 PM, Fri & Sat 9 AM - 6 PM; Estab 1952 to extend library services to include exhibits in all media in the Thomas S Handforth Gallery; Circ 1,237,000; Average Annual Attendance: 20,000
Income: Financed by city appropriation
Library Holdings: Audio Tapes; Book Volumes 800,000; Cassettes; Clipping Files; Exhibition Catalogs; Framed Reproductions; Memorabilia; Motion Pictures; Original Art Works; Other Holdings Audio compact discs; Pamphlets; Periodical Subscriptions 1600; Photographs; Prints; Records; Reels; Video Tapes
Special Subjects: Photography, Manuscripts
Collections: Art book; city, county, federal & state documents; rare books
Exhibitions: 8 monthly changing exhibits; exhibits featuring local & regional artists; educ & historic exhibits
Activities: Classes for children; dramatic progs; lects open to pub, 3-4 vis lectrs per yr; originate traveling exhibs

M UNIVERSITY OF PUGET SOUND, Kittredge Art Gallery, 1500 N Warner, CM 1072 Tacoma, WA 98416-0005. Tel 253-879-3701; Fax 253-879-3500; Internet Home Page Address: www.pugetsound.edu/about/campus/the northwest/kittredge gallery
Open Mon - Fri 10 AM - 5 PM, Sat noon - 5 PM; No admis fee; Estab 1961 for showing of student & professional works; Exhibition space consists of 2 galleries: Small Gallery with 80 ft of running wall space & Kittredge Gallery with 160 ft of running wall space; track lighting; security alarms; Average Annual Attendance: 3,900
Collections: Abby Williams Hill, painter of Northwest scenes from 1880s to 1930s; contemporary west coast ceramics; Northwest paintings, American prints
Activities: Lect open to pub, 4-6 vis lectrs per yr; gallery talks; individual paintings & original works of art lent to professional art museums & historical museums; lending coll contains original prints, paintings & ceramic works

M WASHINGTON STATE HISTORICAL SOCIETY, (Washington State History Museum) 1911 Pacific Ave, Tacoma, WA 98402-3109. Tel 253-272-3500; Fax 253-272-9518; Internet Home Page Address: www.wshs.org; *Dir* David Nicandri
Call for hours; Admis adults $7, seniors $6.25, students $5, members & children under 5 free; Estab 1891 to research, preserve & display the heritage of Washington State; Soc owns three buildings; art gallery under the direction of the Soc; two floors of exhibits (Washington State, Native American Artifacts, temporary exhibits); Average Annual Attendance: 125,000; Mem: 3000; dues $38- $48; annual meeting in Aug
Income: Financed by mem, state appropriations & gifts
Special Subjects: Photography, Manuscripts, Posters, Historical Material, Maps
Collections: Pre-historic relics; Indian & Eskimo artifacts, baskets, clothing, utensils; Oriental items; Washington-Northwest pioneer relics; archives
Exhibitions: Train Exhibit (permanent); rotating exhibits

Publications: History Highlights (newsletter), quarterly; Columbia (popular historical journal), quarterly
Activities: Classes for adults & children; docent training; lects open to pub, 15 vis lectrs per yr; tours; interpretative programs; concerts; dramatic programs with awards; schols offered; individual paintings & original objects of art lent to comparable mus & cultural institutions; lending collection contains natural artifacts, photographs & sculpture; originates traveling exhibs; mus shop sells books, magazines, reproductions, prints, postcards & stationery

L   **Research Center,** 315 Stadium Way, Tacoma, WA 98403. Tel 253-798-5914; Fax 253-597-4186; Elec Mail jwerlink@wshs.wa.gov; Internet Home Page Address: www.washingtonhistory.org; *Asst Cur Photo* Joy Werlink; *Cur Art* Lynette Miller
Open Tues, Wed & Thurs 12:30 - 4:30 PM by appointment; No admis fee; Estab 1941 for research in Pacific Northwest history; For reference only
Income: Financed by mem, state appropriations & gifts
Library Holdings: Book Volumes 12,000; Clipping Files; Manuscripts 4,500,000; Maps 3,200; Memorabilia; Original Art Works 3,800; Pamphlets; Photographs 500,000; Prints 30,000; Reels; Sculpture 350
Special Subjects: Collages, Decorative Arts, Photography, Drawings, Etchings & Engravings, Manuscripts, Maps, Painting-American, Posters, Sculpture, Historical Material, Watercolors, Ceramics, Crafts, Archaeology, Ethnology, Bronzes, Asian Art, American Indian Art, Anthropology, Eskimo Art, Furniture, Glass, Dolls, Jewelry, Silver, Woodcarvings, Landscapes, Coins & Medals, Embroidery, Portraits, Pottery, Textiles
Collections: Asahel Curtis Photograph Collection; Paintings, prints, drawings by Washington State & NW artists
Publications: Columbia Magazine, quarterly

VANCOUVER

M   **CLARK COLLEGE,** Archer Gallery/Gaiser Hall, 1933 Fort Vancouver Way, Vancouver, WA 98663-3598. Tel 360-992-2246; Fax 360-992-2888; Elec Mail mhirsch@clark.edu; Internet Home Page Address: www.clark.edu; *Dir* Marjorie Hirsch
Open Tues - Thurs 9 AM - 8 PM, Fri 9 AM - 4 PM, Sat & Sun 1 - 5 PM; No admis fee; Gallery has 2,000 sq ft; Average Annual Attendance: 5,000
Exhibitions: Six exhibs during acad yr
Activities: Gallery talks; Lect open to public, 3 - 4 vis lectrs per year

WENATCHEE

M   **CHELAN COUNTY PUBLIC UTILITY DISTRICT,** Rocky Reach Dam, US 97A Chelan Hwy, Wenatchee, WA 98807; PO Box 1231, Wenatchee, WA 98807-1231. Tel 509-663-8121; Visitor Center: 663-7522; Fax 509-664-2874; *CEO & Gen Mgr* Roger Braden
No admis fee; Estab 1961 as a landscape ground & exhibit galleries; History of Electricity & Edisonia, Geology, Anthropology - Local Indian & Pioneer History; Average Annual Attendance: 100,000
Income: Financed by Hydro Electric revenue
Special Subjects: Graphics, American Indian Art, Anthropology, Archaeology, Portraits, Historical Material
Collections: Electrical artifacts; Indian Artifacts (Central Columbia River Region); Nez Perce Indian Portraits
Exhibitions: Monthly art exhibits
Activities: Educ dept; teacher seminars; seasonal tours; science camp

M   **NORTH CENTRAL WASHINGTON MUSEUM,** Wenatchee Valley Museum & Cultural Center, 127 S Mission, Wenatchee, WA 98801. Tel 509-888-6240; Elec Mail info@wvmcc.org; Internet Home Page Address: www.wenatcheevalleymuseum.com; *Cur* Mark Behler; *Dir Pub Rels* Chris Rader; *Exhibits Coordr* Bill Rietveldt; *Dir Brenda* Abney
Open Tues - Sat 10 AM - 4 PM, cl Sun & major holidays; Admis adults $5, students & seniors $4, youth $2; Estab 1939 to preserve & present history & the arts. Gallery program offers exhibits of regional, national & international importance; 4500 sq ft changing exhibition gallery features 6-8 shows per yr; Average Annual Attendance: 30,000; Mem: 700; dues $25 & up; annual meeting & monthly board meetings
Income: Financed by public-private partnership with city of Wenatchee & non-profit museum assn
Special Subjects: Prints, Ceramics, Historical Material
Collections: International Ceramics Coll; 19th Century Japanese Woodblock Prints; local historical colls
Exhibitions: Rotating art exhibits; rotating historical exhibits; permanent history exhibits, including Pioneer Living & Apple Industry Exhibit
Publications: The Confluence, quarterly; Museum News, quarterly; books, River of Memory: The Everlasting Columbia by William Layman
Activities: Classes for adults & children; educational kits available on variety of subjects; lects open to pub; 20 vis lectrs per yr; concerts; gallery talks; tours; 2 book traveling exhibs per yr; originates traveling exhibs to Pacific NW & Canada; mus shop sells books, original art, prints, original Apple Box Labels, stationery, jewelry & toys

M   **WENATCHEE VALLEY COLLEGE,** Robert Graves Gallery, 1300 Fifth St, Wenatchee, WA 98801. Tel 509-682-6776; Elec Mail robertgravesgallery@wvc.edu; Internet Home Page Address: www.ctc.edu (select Wenatchee Campus); *Pres* John Crew
Open Mon 8 AM - 8 PM, Tues - Thurs 9 AM - 1 PM, Fri & week-ends by appointment; No admis fee, donations accepted; Estab 1976 to serve a rural, scattered population in North Central Washington State, which without Robert Graves Gallery, would not have access to a non-sales gallery; Non-profit community art gallery housed in Sexton Hall on Wenatchee Valley College Campus; Average Annual Attendance: 4,000; Mem: 150; dues $20-$100
Income: $20,000 (financed by mem, grants, donations, fundraising events & art classes/workshops)
Library Holdings: Book Volumes; Original Art Works
Collections: Paintings, prints & sculpture (25 pieces total)

Publications: Gallery News, quarterly
Activities: docent training; poetry slam; lect open to public, gallery talks; tours; Invitational Exhibit for member artists; awarded Peoples Choice at Members Exhibit

WOODINVILLE

A   **NORTHWEST WATERCOLOR SOCIETY,** 14519 NE 174th St, Woodinville, WA 98072; PO Box 50387, Bellevue, WA 98015-0387. Tel 425-822-6552; Elec Mail molly@mollymurrah.com; Internet Home Page Address: www.nwws.org; *VPres* Shirley Jordan; *Treas* Peggy Meyers; *Pres* Molly Murrah; *Rec Secy* Wanda Hickman; *Corresp Secy* Seiko Konya
Exhibs open Mon - Fri 9 AM - 5 PM at Seattle Design Ctr; Admis free; Estab 1939 to promote interest in & appreciation for watercolor as an artistic medium; Average Annual Attendance: 1,000; Mem: 900; dues $40; Assoc Mems $40 per yr; Signature mems must exhibit in Juried open & waterworks shows (2 open or 1 open plus 2 waterworks shows) & be current on dues; monthly meetings Sept-May
Income: Financed by members
Library Holdings: CD-ROMs; DVDs; Exhibition Catalogs
Collections: Fred Hutchison Cancer Hospital - permanent coll
Exhibitions: Annual International Juried Show; Waterworks-Juried Members Show; Signature Show
Publications: Hot Press Newsletter, bimonthly
Activities: Educ dept; workshops; lect/demos open to public; free exhibs open to pub; 8 vis lectrs per yr; competitions with awards - Open $10,000, Waterworks $4,000; scholarships offered, funded by the Northwest Watercolor Foundation Charitable Fund; lending collection contains over 50 videos

YAKIMA

A   **ALLIED ARTS OF YAKIMA VALLEY,** (The Peggy Lewis Gallery at the Allied Arts Center) The Peggy Lewis Gallery, 5000 W Lincoln Ave, Yakima, WA 98908-2657. Tel 509-966-0930; Fax 509-966-0934; Elec Mail Info@alliedartsyakima.org; Internet Home Page Address: www.alliedartsyakima.org; *Exec Dir* Elizabeth Miller; *Exec Dir* Jessica Moskwa
Open Mon - Fri 9 AM - 5 PM; No admis fee; Estab 1962 to encourage, promote & coordinate the practice & appreciation of the arts among the people of Yakima Valley; General gallery shows changing monthly exhibits; Average Annual Attendance: 20,000; Mem: 600; dues $25 - $500; annual meeting in Sept
Income: Financed by mem
Exhibitions: Monthly exhibits by local and area artists; annual juried exhibit
Publications: Artscope (arts calendar) monthly
Activities: Classes for adults & children; dramatic progs; lects open to pub, 1-3 vis lectrs per yr; concerts; gallery talks; tours; competitions with awards; sales shop sells original art

M   **YAKIMA VALLEY COMMUNITY COLLEGE,** Larson Gallery, 16th & Nob Hill Blvd, Yakima, WA 98907; PO Box 22520, Yakima, WA 98907-2520. Tel 509-574-4875; Fax 509-574-6826; Elec Mail gallery@yvcc.edu; Internet Home Page Address: www.larsongallery.org; *Dir* David Lynx; *Asst Dir* Denise Olsen; *Office Admin* Debby Bailey; *Gallery Asst* Haylee Olsen
Open Tues - Fri 10 AM - 5 PM, Sat 1 PM - 5 PM; cl Sun & Mon, July & Aug; No admis fee; Estab 1949; Fine arts gallery; Average Annual Attendance: 15,000; Mem: 360; dues $25-$1000
Income: $100,000 (financed by endowment, mem & fundraising)
Collections: Contemporary art, primarily 2-D
Exhibitions: Rotating exhibitions
Activities: Classes for adults; docent progs; workshops June & July; lects open to pub, 4-6 vis lectrs per yr; Central Washington Artist Exhibition (5,000 awards annually); Photo Exhibition (5,000 awards biennially); Fiber Exhibition (2,000 awards biennially); gallery talk; tours; book 1 traveling exhib per yr; sales shop sells books, original art & notecards

WEST VIRGINIA

CHARLESTON

M   **AVAMPATO DISCOVERY MUSEUM,** (Sunrise Museum, Inc) The Clay Center for Arts & Sciences, 300 Leon Sullivan Way, Charleston, WV 25301; 1 Clay Sq, Charleston, WV 25301-2424. Tel 304-561-3500; Fax 304-561-3552; Internet Home Page Address: www.theclaycenter.org; *Colls Mgr* Denise Deegan; *Dir Exhibs/Cur Art* Richard Ambrose; *CEO/Pres* Dr Judith Wellington; *Dir Performing Arts* Lakin Cook; *VPres Opers* Sarah Martin
Open Wed - Sat 10 AM - 5 PM, Sun Noon - 5 PM, cl Mon, Tues & national holidays; Admis adults $6.50, students, teachers & seniors $5, children under 3 free; Estab 1960; Circ 3,000; Formerly Sunrise Museum moving to new location in 2003. The museum will house performing arts theatre & symphony; Dual Focus in arts & science. Merged with the Clay Center, July 2006; Average Annual Attendance: 120,000; Mem: dues Benefactors' Circle $1000, patron $500, supporting $250, contributing $100, participating $75 & individual $45
Income: $5.5M (financed by endowment, mem, earned income, corporate & bus contributions)
Library Holdings: Book Volumes; Exhibition Catalogs
Special Subjects: Painting-American, Sculpture, Decorative Arts
Collections: 17th through 20th century American paintings, prints & sculpture; works on paper: emphasis on 20th & 21st century American art
Exhibitions: Numerous regional & international exhibits held throughout the year
Publications: quarterly newsletter
Activities: Classes for adults & children; dramatic progs; docent training; lects open to pub; 6 vis lectrs per yr; guided tours; planetarium & film programs; concerts; gallery talks; STARLAB portable planetarium; individual & original

objects of art lent to other mus & pub institutions; 2 or more book traveling exhibs per yr; mus shop sells books, prints & variety of scientific, educational & decorative gift items including jewelry

HUNTINGTON

M HUNTINGTON MUSEUM OF ART, 2033 McCoy Rd, Huntington, WV 25701-4999. Tel 304-529-2701; Fax 304-529-7447; Elec Mail ltipton@hmoa.org; Internet Home Page Address: www.hmoa.org; *Sr Cur* Jenine Culligan; *Dir Educ* Lisa Geelhood; *Pub Rels* John Gillispie; *Comp* Kathy Saunders; *Dir* Margaret A Skove; *Dir Develop* Margaret Mary Layne
Open Tues - Sat 10 AM - 5 PM, Sun Noon - 5 PM; cl Mon; No admis fee; Estab 1952 to own, operate & maintain an art museum for the collection of paintings, prints, bronzes, porcelains & all kinds of art & utility objects; to permit the study of arts & crafts & to foster an interest in the arts; Three building complex on 52-acre site includes ten galleries, two sculpture courts, seven studio workshops, a 10,000 volume capacity library, 300 seat auditorium, two & one-half miles of nature trails & an amphitheatre; Average Annual Attendance: 75,000; Mem: dues vary; annual meeting in June
Income: Financed by endowment, mem, city, state & county appropriations
Special Subjects: Graphics, Painting-American, Photography, American Western Art, Ethnology, Ceramics, Crafts, Folk Art, Afro-American Art, Decorative Arts, Collages, Painting-Canadian, Furniture, Glass, Antiquities-Byzantine, Painting-British, Painting-Dutch, Carpets & Rugs, Coins & Medals, Period Rooms, Painting-Spanish, Antiquities-Persian, Military Art, Painting-Russian, Antiquities-Assyrian, Painting-Scandinavian
Collections: American & European Paintings & Prints; American Decorative Arts; Georgian silver; firearms; historical and contemporary glass; Turkish prayer rugs; Georgian Silver Collection
Publications: Exhibit catalogs; quarterly newsletter
Activities: Classes & workshops for adults & children; docent training; pub lectrs; concerts; theatre productions; gallery talks; tours; individual paintings & original objects of art lent to mus; tri-state area of Ohio, Kentucky, West Virginia in 75-mile radius; originates traveling exhibs; mus shop sells books, original art, reproductions, prints & crafts; Junior Art Mus

MARTINSBURG

M ASSOCIATES FOR COMMUNITY DEVELOPMENT, The Arts Center, Inc, 300 W King St, Martinsburg, WV 25401-3202. Tel 304-263-0224; *VPres Bd Dir* Mary Boyd Kearse; *Pres Bd & Dir* Barbara Gibson
Open Mon - Fri 10 AM - 4 PM; No admis fee; Estab 1987 to exhibit the work of local & regional artists & craftsmen; Mem: 200; dues $20-$1,000; quarterly meetings
Income: $88,000 (financed by mem, city appropriation, state appropriation & exhibit sponsors)
Special Subjects: Photography, Sculpture, Crafts
Exhibitions: Changing exhibits featuring a variety of arts & crafts including photography, sculpture, oil, acrylic, watercolor by local artisans; Youth Art Month Exhibit
Publications: Boarman Newsletter, quarterly; annual brochure; show invitations, 7 per year
Activities: Classes for adults & children; artist-in-residence young artists summer workshop; Christmas Show & Sale; lect open to public, 4 vis lectrs per year; competitions with awards; schols & fels offered; book traveling exhibitions 1 per year; sales shop sells books, prints, original art & handcrafts

MORGANTOWN

L WEST VIRGINIA UNIVERSITY, Evansdale Library, PO Box 6105, Morgantown, WV 26506-6105. Tel 304-293-5039; Fax 304-293-7330; Internet Home Page Address: www.libraries.wvu.edu; *Head Librn* Jo Ann Calzonetti
Open Mon - Thurs 8 AM - 12 AM, Fri 8 AM - 5 PM, Sat 9 AM - 5 PM, Sun 6 - 10 PM
Library Holdings: Book Volumes 260,000; Periodical Subscriptions 2250
Special Subjects: Art History, Landscape Architecture, Art Education
M Laura & Paul Mesaros Galleries, PO Box 6111, Creative Arts Ctr Morgantown, WV 26506-6111. Tel 304-293-4841, ext 3210; Fax 304-293-5731; Elec Mail kolson@wvu.edu; Internet Home Page Address: www.wvu.edu; *Cur* Kristina Olson
Open during acad yr Mon - Sat Noon - 9:30 PM, cl Sun & university holidays; No admis fee; Estab 1867
Collections: Costumes; music; paintings; theatre
Exhibitions: Call for exhibit information
Activities: Lect; gallery talks; tours; concerts; drama; competitions; temporary traveling exhibitions

PARKERSBURG

A THE CULTURAL CENTER OF FINE ARTS, Art Gallery, 725 Market St, Parkersburg, WV 26101-4628. Tel 304-485-3859; Fax 304-485-3850; Elec Mail ekge@earthlink.net; Internet Home Page Address: www.wvfinearts.com; *CEO & Exec Dir* Ed Pauley; *Pres (V)* Harry Schranom
Open Tues - Sat 10 AM - 5 PM, Sun 1 - 5 PM; No admis fee for members, non-members $2, cl nat holidays; Estab 1938 for the operation & maintenance of an art center & mus facility for the appreciation & enjoyment of art, both visual & decorative, as well as art history, crafts & other related educational or cultural activities; Main gallery 7,500 sq ft & upper gallery 3,000 sq ft, completely carpeted, air conditioned & climate controlled; Average Annual Attendance: 25,000; Mem: 500; dues supporting or patron $250, sustaining $100, family $30, individual $20; annual meeting in June; rate schedule upon request
Income: $160,000 (financed by endowment, mem & state appropriation)

Library Holdings: Book Volumes; Clipping Files; Exhibition Catalogs; Framed Reproductions; Memorabilia; Periodical Subscriptions; Reproductions; Slides; Video Tapes
Collections: Advice of Dreams (oil by Beveridge Moore); Amish & African Artifacts; The Hinge (watercolor by Rudolph Ohrning); Parmenides (sculpture by Beverly Pepper); Permanent collection of over 200 2D & 3D works
Exhibitions: Six exhibs per yr
Publications: Calendar of events, bimonthly; annual report; exhibition catalogs
Activities: Classes for adults & children; docent training; workshops; outreach prog, Arts-in-the-parks; 3 major fundraisers; educational programming; lects open to pub, 6 vis lectrs per yr; concerts; gallery talks; tours; competition with awards; $8,000 for Realism competition, others vary by exhibit; book traveling exhibs; originate traveling exhibs; mus shop sells books, original art, prints, local art, jewelry, Don Whitlatch "Spring Break" print

ROMNEY

L HAMPSHIRE COUNTY PUBLIC LIBRARY, 153 W Main St, Romney, WV 26757-1694. Tel 304-822-3185; Fax 304-822-3955; Internet Home Page Address: www.wvculture.org; *Librn* Brenda Riffle
Open Mon & Fri 10 AM - 8 PM, Tues - Thurs 10 AM - 6 PM, Sat 10 AM - 4 PM; No admis fee; Estab 1942; 7 Display cases changed every month; Average Annual Attendance: 45,000; Mem: 11,000
Income: $128,000 financed by state, donations, mem
Purchases: $32,000
Library Holdings: Audio Tapes; Book Volumes 38,000; Cassettes; Clipping Files; Maps; Original Documents; Pamphlets; Periodical Subscriptions 96; Photographs; Prints; Records; Reels; Video Tapes
Collections: books
Exhibitions: Children's art; private collections of rocks, antiques, displays of items of other countries; various local artists collection; weaving
Activities: Classes for adults & children; lect open to public; concerts; tours; plays; antique show; competitions with awards; individual paintings lent

WESTON

M MUSEUM OF AMERICAN GLASS IN WV, (WV Museum of American Glass) 230 Main Ave, Weston, WV 26452-2044; PO Box 574, Weston, WV 26452-0574. Tel 304-269-5006; Elec Mail wvmag@ma.rr.com; Internet Home Page Address: www.magwv.com; *Exec Dir* Dean Six; *Archivist* Tom Felt
Open winter hours: Mon - Tues & Thurs - Sat 12 PM - 4 PM; Memorial Day to Labor Day open daily noon - 4 PM; No admis fee, donations accepted; Estab 1993; Located on Main Ave in downtown Weston, WV. Mus has the mission of sharing the diverse & rich heritage of glass as a product & historical object telling of the lives of glass workers, their families & communities, and of the tools & machines they used in glass houses; Average Annual Attendance: 2,500; Mem: Dues Benefactor $500 & up; Patron $100; Sustaining $50; Supporting $35; Ann $25
Special Subjects: Historical Material, Glass, Prints
Collections: Diverse & beautiful glass objects produced by factories during this century; five large covered jars designed by Fritz Driesbach and executed by the Blenko Glass Co, Milton, WV; three Tiffany decorative glass tiles (one signed); hand-painted Top Hat tumbler, a product of the WV Glass Specialty Co, Weston WV, signed by the artist, Al Erbe; commemorative glass bust of M J Owens, a native of WV and inventor of the automatic bottle-making machine; national marble museum; studio art glass by Kelsey Murphy, Roberto Moretti, Dominick Labino & other artists
Publications: Black Glass Book, published by WVMAG; All About Glass, quarterly magazine for mems
Activities: Research library; events such as The Marble Festival; educational interactive displays for children; annual glass gathering; mus shop sells books, magazines & glassware

WHEELING

A OGLEBAY INSTITUTE, Stifel Fine Arts Center, 1330 National Rd, Wheeling, WV 26003-5706. Tel 304-242-7700; Elec Mail inspire@oionline.com; Internet Home Page Address: www.oionline.com/arts; *Dir* Rick Morgan; *Exhibs Dir* Brad Johnson; *Educ Dir* Jessica Leach
Open Mon - Fri 9 AM - 5 PM, Sat 10 AM - 4 PM; No admis fee; Estab 1930 to present art exhibitions & to provide the opportunity for life-long learning in the fine arts fields; Circ 8; Three galleries located in the Stifel Mansion occupy the center of the facility on both floors; Average Annual Attendance: 6,000; Mem: 1450; dues $15 & up
Activities: Classes for adults & children; dramatic progs; docent training; school progs; lect open to public; concerts; gallery talks; tours; schols
M Mansion Museum, 1330 National Rd, Oglebay Park Wheeling, WV 26003-5706. Tel 304-242-7272; Fax 304-242-4203; Internet Home Page Address: www.oionline.com/museum; *Dir* Holly McCluskey; *Sr Cur* John A Artzberger
Open Mon - Sat 9:30 AM - 5 PM, Sun & holidays Noon - 5 PM; Admis $5, 55 & over $4.25, students $2, children under 12 free with paying adults; Estab & incorporated 1930 to promote educational, cultural & recreational activities in Wheeling Tri-State area; Building & ground are the property of the city; an exhibition wing adjoins the main house; annual Christmas decorations; Average Annual Attendance: 83,394; Mem: 1450; dues $15 & up
Special Subjects: Porcelain, Glass, Period Rooms, Pewter
Collections: Early 19th century china; early glass made in Wheeling & the Midwest
Exhibitions: Current exhibits of art & other allied subjects change periodically; decorative arts
Activities: Antique show & sales; antique classes; gallery talks; self-guided & prearranged group tours
L Library, 1330 National Rd, Oglebay Park Wheeling, WV 26003-5706. Tel 304-242-7272; Fax 304-242-4203; *Sr Cur* John A Artzberger

Open by appointment only; Founded 1934; Highly specialized on the early history of the area
Library Holdings: Book Volumes 800; Micro Print 20; Other Holdings Documents bound 100, Maps, VF 4; Slides
Special Subjects: Decorative Arts, Historical Material
Collections: Brown Collection of Wheeling History, photographs; Wheeling City Directories; Wheeling & Belmont Bridge Company Papers
Activities: Classes for adults & children; docent training; 2 vis lectrs per yr; exten prog, 75 mile radius of Wheeling

WISCONSIN

APPLETON

M **LAWRENCE UNIVERSITY,** Wriston Art Center Galleries, 711 E Boldt Way, Appleton, WI 54911-5690. Tel 920-832-6621; Fax 920-832-7362; Elec Mail odonnelp@lawrence.edu; Internet Home Page Address: www.lawrence.edu; *Cur & Dir* Frank Lewis
Open Tues - Fri 10 AM - 4 PM, Sat & Sun Noon - 4 PM, cl Mon; No admis fee; Estab 1950 for teaching & community exhibitions. Wriston Art Center opened Spring 1989; Three exhibitions galleries for changing exhibits of contemporary & historical shows; Average Annual Attendance: 5,000
Special Subjects: Drawings, Prints, Graphics, Oriental Art, Asian Art
Collections: American regionalist art; Japanese prints & drawings; Ottilia Buerger Collection of Ancient Coins; Pohl Collection-German Expressionism
Exhibitions: Various exhib
Activities: Lect open to public, 3-6 vis lectrs per year; individual paintings & original works of art lent for exhibitions in other museums

BELOIT

M **BELOIT COLLEGE,** Wright Museum of Art, 700 College St, Beloit, WI 53511-5595. Tel 608-363-2677; Fax 608-363-2718; Internet Home Page Address: www.beloit.edu/wright; *Dir* Joy Beckman; *Coll Mgr* James Pearson; *Asst* Aaron Wilson
Open Tues - Sun 11 AM - 4 PM; No admis fee; Estab 1893; Wright Art Hall built 1930 to house the coll for the enrichment of the col & community through exhib of permanent coll & traveling & temporary art exhibs of cultural & aesthetic value; A Georgian building architecturally styled after the Fogg Mus in Cambridge, Massachusetts. Three galleries on main floor, on a large center ct; Art Department shares other floors in which two student galleries are included; Average Annual Attendance: 20,000
Purchases: 17th - 20th century graphics; Asian decorative arts
Special Subjects: Decorative Arts, Painting-European, Sculpture, Architecture, Graphics, Latin American Art, Painting-American, Photography, Anthropology, Archaeology, Portraits, Jade, Jewelry, Porcelain, Oriental Art, Asian Art, Metalwork, Painting-British, Ivory, Baroque Art, Calligraphy, Medieval Art, Antiquities-Oriental, Antiquities-Egyptian, Antiquities-Greek, Antiquities-Roman, Gold, Painting-German, Bookplates & Bindings
Collections: European & American (paintings, sculpture & decorative arts); Fisher Memorial Collection of Greek Casts; graphics, emphasis on German Expressionist & contemporary works; Gurley Collection of Korean Pottery, Japanese Sword Guards, Chinese Snuff Bottles & Jades; Morse Collection of Paintings & Other Art Objects; Neese Fund Collection of Contemporary Art; Prints by Durer, Rembrandt, Whistler & others; 19th century photographs; Pitkin Asian Art Collection
Publications: Exhibition catalogs
Activities: Classes; supportive progs; docent training; lects open to pub; gallery talks; tours; originates traveling exhibs; mus shop sells books, original art & reproductions

BROOKFIELD

M **WILSON CENTER,** Ploch Art Gallery, 19805 W Capitol Dr, Brookfields Mitchell Park Brookfield, WI 53045-2722. Tel 262-781-9470; Fax 262-781-9798; Elec Mail rsvp@wilson-center.com; Internet Home Page Address: www.wilson-center.com

CEDARBURG

A **WISCONSIN FINE ARTS ASSOCIATION, INC,** Ozaukee Art Center, W62 N718 Riveredge Dr, Cedarburg, WI 53012. Tel 262-377-8290; *Art Dir* Paul Yank
Open Wed - Sun 1 - 4 PM, or by appointment; No admis fee; Estab 1971; Historical landmark with cathedral ceiling; Average Annual Attendance: 10,000; Mem: 600; dues bus patron $500, patron $200, sustaining $100, assoc sustaining $50, family $30, individual $22, family $10; annual meeting in Oct
Income: Mem contributions, state appropriations
Collections: Paintings, sculpture, prints, ceramics
Exhibitions: Ozaukee County Show; Harvest Festival of Arts
Publications: Monthly newsletter
Activities: Classes for adults and children; docent training; lects open to public, 2 vis lectrs per year; concerts; gallery talks; tours; competitions with awards; arts festivals

EAU CLAIRE

M **UNIVERSITY OF WISCONSIN-EAU CLAIRE,** Foster Gallery, 121 Water St, Eau Claire, WI 54701-4811; PO Box 4004, Eau Claire, WI 54702-4004. Tel 715-836-2328; Fax 715-836-4882; Elec Mail wagenetk@uwec.edu; Internet Home Page Address: www.uwec.edu/art/foster; *Dir* Thomas Wagener
Open Foster Gallery: Mon - Fri 10 AM - 4:30 PM, Thurs 6 PM - 8 PM, Sat & Sun 1 - 4:30 PM; No admis fee; Estab 1970 to show finest contemporary art in all media; State University Gallery in Fine Arts Center; Average Annual Attendance: 24,000

Income: Funded by state appropriation
Special Subjects: Drawings, Etchings & Engravings, Painting-American, Prints, Graphics, Photography, Sculpture, Watercolors, Ceramics, Woodcuts, Collages
Collections: Eau Claire Permanent Art Collection; 20th Century Artists
Exhibitions: (01/23/2014-02/13/2014) Art + Tech; (02/20/2014-03/13/2014) Shading; (04/03/2014-04/24/2014) 57th Annual Juried Student Art Show; (05/01/2014-05/11/2014) Bachelor of Fine Arts Senior exhib
Activities: Lect open to public, 4-5 vis lectrs per year; competition with awards; gallery talks; book traveling exhibitions 3-4 per year

FISH CREEK

M **FRANCIS HARDY GALLERY,** 3038 Anderson Ln, Fish Creek, WI 54212; PO Box 394, Ephraim, WI 54211-0394. Tel 920-854-5535; Internet Home Page Address: thehardy.org; *Contact* Elizabeth Meissner

FOND DU LAC

M **WINDHOVER CENTER FOR THE ARTS,** 51 Sheboygan St, Fond Du Lac, WI 54935-4219. Tel 920-921-5410; Elec Mail info@windhovercenter.org; Internet Home Page Address: www.windhovercenter.org; *Contact* Kevin Miller

GREEN BAY

M **NEVILLE PUBLIC MUSEUM OF BROWN COUNTY,** 210 Museum Pl, Green Bay, WI 54303-2780. Tel 920-448-4460; Fax 920-448-4458; Elec Mail bc_museum@co.brown.wi.us; Internet Home Page Address: www.nevillepublicmuseum.org; *Dir* Rolf Johnson; *Cur Science* John Jacobs; *Cur Colls* Louise Pfotenhauer; *Cur of Educ* Matt Welter; *Cur Art* Marilyn Stasiak; *AV Technician* Larry La Malfa; *Office Mgr* Kathy Rosera; *Exhib Technician* Maggie Dernehl; *Guest Svcs Coordr* Jessica Day; *Clerk Typist* Tammy Ayotte; *Dir Develop Mktg* Mauree Childress; *Mktg Asst* Jenny Seim
Open Mon, Tues, Thurs, Fri, Sat 9 AM - 5 PM, Wed 9 AM - 8 PM, Sun Noon - 5 PM; Adm adult $5, children ages 5 & under free; special rates for school & youth groups available; Estab 1915 as Green Bay Pub Mus; names changed 1926, estab to interpret the collections & educate through exhibits, educational programming, research & publications; Art gallery presently in use, largest 3000 sq ft. Maintains reference library; Average Annual Attendance: 66,000; Mem: 700; dues Individual $30, Family $50
Income: Financed by county appropriation & private donations
Special Subjects: Drawings, Painting-American, Photography, Prints, Sculpture, Watercolors, Costumes, Folk Art, Etchings & Engravings, Dolls, Furniture, Glass, Porcelain, Embroidery
Collections: Victoriana, antique furniture, china, glass, costumes, accessories; contemporary & historical paintings; drawings; prints & sculpture; archeology, geology, photographs, news film from local TV stations; David Belasco Collection
Exhibitions: On the Edge of the Inland Sea
Publications: Musepaper, 4 times per yr
Activities: Classes for adults & children; docent training; lects open to pub, vis lectrs; concerts; gallery talks; tours; competitions with awards; schols offered; individual paintings & original objects of art lent to other mus; book traveling exhibs; mus shop sells books, magazines, original art, reproductions, prints, gifts & cards

L **Research Library, Photo & Film Collection,** 210 Museum Pl, Green Bay, WI 54303. Tel 920-448-4460; Fax 920-448-4458; Elec Mail mean_jm@co.brown.wi.us; Internet Home Page Address: www.nevillepublicmuseum.org; *Recorder* Jeanine Mead
Open by appointment; Open to the public for reference by appt only
Library Holdings: Audio Tapes; Book Volumes 5000; Clipping Files; Exhibition Catalogs; Fiche; Kodachrome Transparencies; Memorabilia; Motion Pictures; Pamphlets; Periodical Subscriptions 20; Photographs; Reels; Slides; Video Tapes

M **UNIVERSITY OF WISCONSIN, GREEN BAY,** Lawton Gallery, 2420 Nicolet Dr, Green Bay, WI 54311-7001. Tel 920-465-2271, 465-2916; Fax 920-465-2890; Elec Mail perkinss@uwgb.edu; Internet Home Page Address: www.uwgb.edu/lawton; *Acad Cur Art* Dr Stephen Perkins; *Asst Cur* Erin Rose
Open Tues - Sat 10 - 3 PM, cl Sun & Mon; No admis fee; Estab 1974 to show changing exhibs of contemporary & 20th century art, student & faculty work; Gallery is 2,000 sq ft; Average Annual Attendance: 3,000
Income: $5,000
Purchases: Limited purchases & donations to Univ Wisc-Green Bay permanent coll
Collections: Contemporary art & prints; student & faculty work; Native American coll; 160 Andy Warhol Photographs
Exhibitions: Graduating Seniors Exhibition
Publications: Exhibition catalogs
Activities: Gallery & museum practices minor for undergraduates; workshops related to exhibs; lects open to pub; 2-3 vis lectrs per semester; competitions; gallery talks; assorted awards for student juried art exhibition; Lawton Gallery Award for excellence 2D & 3D; schols; exten prog loaned to university departments & offices; learning in retirement; originates traveling exhibs to other university galleries

GREENBUSH

M **WADE HOUSE HISTORIC SITE-WISCONSIN HISTORICAL SOCIETY,** (Wade House & Wesley W Jung Carriage Museum) Wesley W. Jung Carriage Museum, W 7824 Center St, Greenbush, WI 53026; PO Box 34, Greenbush, WI 53026-0034. Tel 920-526-3271; Fax 920-526-3626; Elec Mail wadehouse@wisconsinhistory.org; Internet Home Page Address: www.wadehouse.org; *Dir* David Simmons; *Cur Interpretation* Jeffery Murray
Open mid-May - mid-Oct 10 AM -5 PM; Admis family rate $30, adults $11, seniors $9.25, child $5.50 (includes carriage ride); Estab 1953 to educate public concerning 1860s Wisconsin Yankee town life; Average Annual Attendance: 23,000

Income: $500,000 (financed by state appropriation, admis fees)
Special Subjects: Architecture, Archaeology, Ceramics, Crafts, Decorative Arts, Furniture, Historical Material, Period Rooms
Collections: Wisconsin made Carriages; 1860s Household Furnishings
Exhibitions: 1860s Historic Stagecoach Inn Tour; Working Water-powered Sawmill; Blacksmith Shop
Activities: Classes for adults & children; docent training; spec events; lects open to pub, vis lectrs; tours; mus shop sells books, reproductions, original art & prints

HUDSON

M **THE PHIPPS CENTER FOR THE ARTS,** Galleries, 109 Locust St, Hudson, WI 54016-1518. Tel 715-386-8409; Elec Mail info@thephipps.org; Internet Home Page Address: www.thephipps.org

KENOSHA

M **KENOSHA PUBLIC MUSEUMS,** 5500 1st Ave, Kenosha, WI 53140-3778. Tel 262-653-4140; Fax 262-653-4437; Elec Mail djoyce@kenosha.org; Internet Home Page Address: www.kenoshapublicmuseum.org; *Dir* Daniel Joyce; *Vol Pres* Sally Heideman; *Deputy Dir* Peggy Gregorski; *Cur Exhibits* Rachel Klees Andersen; *Cur Collections* Gina Radandt; *Sr Cur Educ* Nancy Matthews; *Coordr Opers* Ken Ade
Open Sun - Mon noon - 5 PM, Tues - Sat 9 AM - 5 PM; cl New Year's Eve & Day; Martin Luther King Jr Day; Good Friday; Memorial Day; Independence Day; Labor Day; Thanksgiving; Christmas Eve & Day; No admis fee; Estab 1935 to promote interest in general natural history & regional art; The gallery has 8,000 sq ft of permanent exhib space & 8,000 sq ft for temporary exhibits; Average Annual Attendance: 132,839; Mem: 2600 households, $25 individuals, $40 family
Income: $1,500,000 (financed by city appropriation)
Purchases: $2200
Library Holdings: Book Volumes 5,000; Original Documents; Prints
Special Subjects: American Indian Art, Archaeology, Drawings, Etchings & Engravings, Historical Material, Landscapes, Glass, Flasks & Bottles, Furniture, Photography, Pre-Columbian Art, Painting-American, Prints, Silver, Textiles, Manuscripts, Maps, Painting-European, Painting-Japanese, Graphics, Hispanic Art, Latin American Art, Mexican Art, Sculpture, Watercolors, Bronzes, African Art, Anthropology, Ethnology, Southwestern Art, Costumes, Religious Art, Ceramics, Crafts, Folk Art, Pottery, Primitive art, Woodcarvings, Woodcuts, Decorative Arts, Portraits, Posters, Eskimo Art, Dolls, Jade, Jewelry, Porcelain, Oriental Art, Asian Art, Metalwork, Carpets & Rugs, Ivory, Juvenile Art, Coins & Medals, Calligraphy, Miniatures, Dioramas, Islamic Art, Antiquities-Greek, Antiquities-Roman, Mosaics, Stained Glass, Leather, Military Art, Reproductions, Enamels
Collections: Civil War; Paleontology; Natural History; Art
Publications: Newsletter, bimonthly; Wisconsin Folk Pottery Book
Activities: Classes for adults & children; dramatic progs; docent training; lect open to pub, 20 vis lectrs per yr; concerts; gallery talks; tours; competitions; films; lending collection contains color reproductions, 30 framed reproductions, 280 motion pictures, nature artifacts & slides; originate traveling exhibs; mus shop sells books, crafts, ethnic jewelry, earrings, magazines, original art, reproductions, prints, toys & collectibles

LA CROSSE

M **VITERBO UNIVERSITY,** Art Gallery, 815 S Ninth St, La Crosse, WI 54601. Tel 608-796-3000 (Main), 796-3757; Fax 608-796-3736; *Dir* Joseph E Miller
Open Mon - Fri 10 AM - 5 PM; No admis fee; Estab 1964 to exhibit arts & crafts which will be a valuable supplement to courses offered; Gallery is located in the center of the Art Department; 100 running feet; soft walls; good light
Income: Financed by school appropriation
Collections: Mrs Lynn Anna Louise Miller, Collection of the contemporary United States primitive; Peter Whitebird Collection of WPA project paintings
Activities: Classes for adults & children; dramatic progs; lects open to pub; gallery talks; 2-5 vis lectrs per yr; schols

LAC DU FLAMBEAU

A **DILLMAN'S CREATIVE ARTS FOUNDATION,** 3305 Sand Lake Lodge Ln, Lac Du Flambeau, WI 54538; PO Box 98, Lac Du Flambeau, WI 54538-0098. Tel 715-588-3143; Fax 715-588-3110; Elec Mail dillmans@newnorth.net; Elec Mail vacations@dillmans.com; Internet Home Page Address: www.dillmans.com; *VPres* Sue Robertson; *Pres* Dennis Robertson
Open 24 hours May - Oct; Admis varies, see website; Estab 1987 to offer educational experience; Display on Dillman Lodge walls, hallway, studios & rack in gift shop; Average Annual Attendance: 500
Publications: Annual brochure
Activities: Classes for adults & children; lects open to pub, 100 vis lectrs per yr; schols & fels offered; exten dept serves faculty; lending collection contains books; book traveling exhibs 12-15 per yr; originate traveling exhibs 12-15 per yr; sales shop sells books, original art & prints
L **Tom Lynch Resource Center,** 3305 Sand Lake Lodge Ln, Box 98, Lac du Flambeau, WI 54538. Tel 715-588-3143; Fax 715-588-3110; Elec Mail dillmans@newnorth.net; Internet Home Page Address: www.dillmans.com; *Pres* Dennis Robertson; *VPres* Sue Robertson; *Secy* Betsy Behnke
Open May - Oct; Admis fees vary by workshop; Estab 1977 for education; Lends books and tapes; sale of art works; Average Annual Attendance: 500
Income: Income from workshop fees
Library Holdings: Audio Tapes 20; Book Volumes 500; Exhibition Catalogs; Framed Reproductions 20; Original Art Works 100; Prints 4000; Reproductions 100; Video Tapes 20
Activities: Classes for adults & children; awards from Midwest Watercolor Soc & Oil Painters of Am; schols offered; workshops in Europe; mus shop sells books, original art, reproductions & prints

M **LAC DU FLAMBEAU BAND OF LAKE SUPERIOR CHIPPEWA INDIANS,** George W Brown Jr Ojibwe Museum & Cultural Center, 603 Peace Pipe, Lac Du Flambeau, WI 54538; PO Box 804, Lac du Flambeau, WI 54538-0804. Tel 715-588-3333, 588-2139; Fax 715-588-2355; Elec Mail bearpawn@hotmail.com; *Mus Dir* Christina Breault; *Mus Mgr* Teresa Mitchell; *Colls Technician* Nina Isham
Open May - Oct Mon - Sat 10 AM - 4 PM & Nov - Apr Mon - Fri 10 AM - 2 PM; Admis adult $3, children $2, seniors $2, tour group $4 per person; Estab 1988 to collect, preserve, protect & promote the cultural history of the Lac du Flambeau Ojibwe; Main floor: Four seasons exhibit featuring the harvesting cycle of the traditional ways of the Ojibwe Indian people plus numerous objects of the Ojibwe; Average Annual Attendance: 6,500
Income: $100,000 (financed by Tribal appropriation)
Purchases: Various historical, cultural objects, photos & documents
Library Holdings: Auction Catalogs; Audio Tapes; Cards; Cassettes; Compact Disks; Kodachrome Transparencies; Manuscripts; Maps; Memorabilia; Original Art Works; Photographs; Prints; Reproductions; Slides; Video Tapes
Special Subjects: Drawings, Photography, American Indian Art, Archaeology, Ethnology, Textiles, Costumes, Crafts, Folk Art, Woodcarvings, Etchings & Engravings, Decorative Arts, Manuscripts, Posters, Dolls, Jewelry, Carpets & Rugs, Historical Material, Maps, Dioramas, Embroidery, Leather
Collections: Manuscripts, documents & photography of the Lac du Flambeau Band of the Lake Superior Ojibwe; Objects of the cultural history of The Lake Superior Ojibwe; Lake Superior Ojibwe Collection
Exhibitions: Various exhibits of the cultural ways of the Lac du Flambeau Ojibwe
Activities: Classes for adults & children; interactive TV progs area schools; dramatic progs; lects open to pub, 3 vis lectrs per yr; cultural sharing prog; community art display; history topics; individual paintings lent throughout Wisconsin; mus shop sells books, magazines, original art, reproductions, prints, Ojibwe arts & crafts & food

MADISON

M **EDGEWOOD COLLEGE,** DeRicci Gallery, 1000 Edgewood College Dr, Madison, WI 53711-1997. Tel 800-444-4861 Exten 2263; Elec Mail pprindle@edgewood.edu; Internet Home Page Address: http://art.edgewood.edu/gallery.html; *Gallery Dir* Paul Baker Prindle, MA, MFA
Open daily 10 AM - 6 PM

M **MADISON MUSEUM OF CONTEMPORARY ART,** (Madison Art Center) 227 State St, Madison, WI 53703-2214. Tel 608-257-0158; Fax 608-257-5722; Elec Mail info@mmoca.org; Internet Home Page Address: www.mmoca.org; *Registrar* Marilyn Sohi; *Bus Mgr* Michael Paggie; *Technical Svcs Supvr* Mark Verstegen; *Gallery Shop Mgr* Leslie Genszler; *Cur Educ & Pub Programming* Sheri Castelnuovo; *Pub Information* Katie Kazan; *Gallery Operations Mgr* Mary Kolar; *Dir* Stephen Fleischman; *Exhib Cur* Jane Simon; *Exhib Cur* Rick Axsom
Open Tues - Thurs & Sun Noon- 5 PM, Fri Noon - 8 PM, Sat 10 AM- 8 PM, cl Mon; No admis fee, donations accepted; Estab 1901 to exhibit and collect modern & contemporary art; Circ non-circulating; Within Overture Center for the Arts; Average Annual Attendance: 150,000; Mem: 2000; dues $40 & up; annual meeting in May
Income: $2,220,000 (financed by mem, grants, gifts & earned revenue)
Library Holdings: Book Volumes; Clipping Files; Exhibition Catalogs; Original Documents; Periodical Subscriptions
Special Subjects: Mexican Art, Photography, Painting-American, Prints, Drawings, Sculpture
Collections: Emphasis on contemporary America; large print & drawing coll (Japanese, European, Mexican & American); paintings; photographs
Publications: Catalogs & announcements usually accompany each exhibition; quarterly newsletter
Activities: Docent training; youth progs; lects open to public; film series; gallery talks; tours; originate traveling exhibs; mus store sells books, reproductions, prints, fine craft

M **STEEP & BREW GALLERY,** 544 State St, Madison, WI 53703-5500. Tel 608-256-2902; Elec Mail mduerr@madison.k12.WI.us; *Dir* Mark Duerr
Open Mon - Thurs 8 AM - 10 PM, Fri & Sat 9 AM - 11 PM, Sun 11 AM - 8 PM; No admis fee; Estab 1985 as a gallery showing emerging & experimental local artists; Store front street level gallery with 1700 sq ft of space
Income: $4000 (financed by exhibition fees & commission on sales)
Purchases: Ray Esparsen, Theron Caldwell Ris, Randy Arnold
Exhibitions: Regular exhibits by various local artists
Activities: Concerts; gallery talks

M **UNIVERSITY OF WISCONSIN-MADISON,** Wisconsin Union Galleries, 800 Langdon St, Rm 5210 Madison, WI 53706-1419; 1308 W Dayton St, Rm 235, Madison, WI 53715. Tel 608-262-7592 (committee); 890-4432 (advisor); Fax 608-890-4411; Elec Mail schmoldt@wisc.edu; Elec Mail art@union.wisc.edu; Internet Home Page Address: www.union.wisc.edu/art; *Union Dir* Mark Guthier; *Art Advisor & Art Coll Mgr* Robin Schmoldt
Open 10 AM - 8 PM; No admis fee; Estab 1907 to provide a cultural program for the members of the university community; Owns two fireproof buildings with four separate galleries 1700 sq ft: Memorial Union, 800 Langdon; Union South, 1308 W Dayton St; Average Annual Attendance: 320,000; Mem: 50,000 faculty, alumni & townspeople, plus 45,000 students; dues $50
Special Subjects: Decorative Arts, Drawings, Etchings & Engravings, Folk Art, Landscapes, Ceramics, Collages, Glass, Metalwork, Photography, Portraits, Pottery, Painting-American, Prints, Woodcuts, Graphics, Watercolors, Woodcarvings
Collections: Oil & watercolor paintings, photographs, drawings, prints & sculptures, mostly by Wisconsin artists
Publications: A Reflection of Time: The WI Union Art Collection
Activities: Informal classes in arts & crafts; dramatic progs; lects open to pub, 10-12 vis lectrs per yr; gallery talks; competitions with prizes; annual student art show with purchase awards; Annual Purchase Awards; book traveling occasionally

M **Chazen Museum of Art,** 750 University Ave, Madison, WI 53706-1479. Tel

608-263-2246; Fax 608-263-8188; Internet Home Page Address: www.chazen.wisc.edu; *Dir* Russell Panczenko; *Cur Paintings, Sculpture, Decorative Arts* Maria Saffiotti Dale; *Cur Prints, Drawings, Photos* Andrew Stevens; *Cur Educ* Anne Lambert; *Exhib Designer & Chief Preparator* Jerl Richmond; *Exhib Coordr* Mary Ann Fitzgerald; *Preparator* Steve Johanowicz; *Registrar* Andrea Selbig; *Registrar* Ann Sinfield; *Preparator* Kate Wanberg; *Develop Specialist* Amy Guthier

Open Tues - Fri 9 AM - 5 PM, Sat - Sun 11 AM - 5 PM, cl Mon; No admis fee; Estab 1970 as a cultural resource for the state & region & to support the educ & serv mission of the Univ of Wisconsin-Madison; 20 permanent galleries, 16 display niches & 3 temporary exhib halls present over 2,000 objects in over 42,000 sq ft of exhibit space; Average Annual Attendance: 140,000; Mem: 1,300; dues $25-$1000

Income: Financed by endowment, mem, state appropriation & private sources
Purchases: $500,000
Special Subjects: Afro-American Art, American Indian Art, Drawings, Etchings & Engravings, Landscapes, Marine Painting, Architecture, Ceramics, Glass, Metalwork, Furniture, Photography, Porcelain, Portraits, Pottery, Pre-Columbian Art, Prints, Textiles, Bronzes, Manuscripts, Painting-British, Painting-French, Painting-Japanese, Sculpture, Graphics, Hispanic Art, Latin American Art, Mexican Art, Painting-American, Watercolors, African Art, Archaeology, Southwestern Art, Religious Art, Primitive art, Decorative Arts, Painting-European, Posters, Eskimo Art, Jade, Jewelry, Oriental Art, Asian Art, Silver, Antiquities-Byzantine, Metalwork, Painting-Dutch, Ivory, Coins & Medals, Baroque Art, Calligraphy, Miniatures, Painting-Flemish, Painting-Polish, Renaissance Art, Medieval Art, Antiquities-Oriental, Painting-Spanish, Painting-Italian, Islamic Art, Antiquities-Greek, Antiquities-Roman, Mosaics, Stained Glass, Painting-Australian, Painting-German, Antiquities-Etruscan, Painting-Russian, Enamels, Painting-Scandinavian
Collections: Joseph E Davies Collection of Russian Icons, Russian & Soviet Paintings; Vernon Hall Collection of European Medals; Edward Burr Van Vleck Collection of Japanese Prints; Ernest C & Jane Werner Watson Collection of Indian Miniatures; Samuel & Rosemary Chen Coll Chinese paintings; Terese & Alvin Lane Coll Modern Sculpture & Drawings; Andrew Laurie Stengel Coll European Medals; Alexander & Henrietta W Hollaender Coll Contemporary art; Janice & Jean-Pierre Golay Coll Contemporary Art
Exhibitions: 4-6 major temp exhibs, 8-10 rotating exhibits per yr
Publications: Biennial bulletin; calendar, bimonthly; spec exhibition catalogs; newsletter
Activities: Classes for adults & children; docent training; lects open to pub; 10-15 vis lectrs per yr; concerts; gallery talks; tours; ann outstanding MFA student award; individual paintings & original objects of art lent to other mus; book traveling exhibs 2-4 per yr; originate traveling exhibs; sales shop sells books, magazines, original art, prints, reproductions & toys

L **Kohler Art Library,** 160 Conrad A Elvehjem Bldg, Univ Wisconsin Madison Madison, WI 53706; 800 University Ave, Madison, WI 53706-1414. Tel 608-263-2258; Fax 608-263-2255; Elec Mail lkorenic@library.wisc.edu; Internet Home Page Address: art.library.wisc.edu; *Dir* Lyn Korenic; *Reference Librn* Linda Duychak; *Circ/Reserves* Soren Schoff; *Tech Svcs* Kelly Tourdot
Open hrs vary seasonally, see website; Estab 1970 to support the teaching & research needs of the Art & Art History Departments & the Chazen Mus of Art; Circ 50,000; Average Annual Attendance: 60,000
Income: Financed by state appropriation & private funding
Library Holdings: Auction Catalogs; Book Volumes 185,000; CD-ROMs; Cassettes 50; Clipping Files; Compact Disks; DVDs; Exhibition Catalogs; Fiche 21,000; Micro Print; Pamphlets; Periodical Subscriptions 460; Reels 400; Video Tapes
Special Subjects: Decorative Arts
Exhibitions: Regular exhibs of materials from library collections
Activities: Tours

M **WISCONSIN ACADEMY OF SCIENCES, ARTS & LETTERS,** Steenbock Gallery, 1922 University Ave, Madison, WI 53726-4013. Tel 608-263-1692; Fax 608-265-3039; Internet Home Page Address: www.wisconsinacademy.org
Open Mon - Fri 8:30 AM - 4:30 PM
M **James Watrous Gallery,** 201 State St Fl 3, Overture Ctr for the Arts Madison, WI 53703-2214. Tel 608-265-2500; Fax 608-265-3039; Internet Home Page Address: www.wisconsinacademy.org; *Dir* Martha Glowacki
Open Tues - Thurs 11 AM - 5 PM, Fri & Sat 11 AM - 9 PM, Sun 1 PM - 5 PM; No admis fee; Dedicated to Wisconsin artists
Activities: Lects open to pub; gallery talks

M **WISCONSIN HISTORICAL SOCIETY, WISCONSIN HISTORICAL MUSEUM,** 30 N Carroll St, Madison, WI 53703-2707. Tel 608-264-6555; Fax 608-264-6575; Internet Home Page Address: www.wisconsinhistory.org/museum; *Dir* Ellsworth Brown; *Cur Art Coll* Joseph Kapler; *Cur Visual Materials* Andy Kraushaar; *Cur Native American* Jennifer Kolb; *Cur Costumes & Textiles* Leslie Bellais; *Cur Political, Armaments* Paul Bourcier; *Cur Bus & Technology* David Driscoll; *Cur Archaeology* Denise Wiggins
Open Tues - Sat 9 AM - 4 PM; Estab 1846, mus added 1854; organized to promote a wider appreciation of the American heritage, with particular emphasis on the collection, advancement & dissemination of knowledge of the history of Wisconsin & of the Middle West; Average Annual Attendance: 71,600; Mem: 12,000; dues $30 & up
Income: Financed by state appropriation, earnings, gifts & federal grants
Special Subjects: Architecture, Drawings, Graphics, Painting-American, Prints, American Indian Art, American Western Art, Anthropology, Archaeology, Costumes, Ceramics, Crafts, Folk Art, Woodcarvings, Etchings & Engravings, Portraits, Furniture, Jewelry, Silver, Carpets & Rugs, Coins & Medals, Cartoons, Pewter, Leather, Military Art
Collections: American Historical & Native American material; iconographic coll; ceramics, coins, costumes, dolls, furniture, paintings, prints, photographs, & slides
Exhibitions: Special case and gallery exhib
Publications: Wisconsin Magazine of History, quarterly
Activities: Educ prog; classes for children; docent training; lect open to public; concerts; tours; gallery talks; individual paintings & original objects of art lent to other museums & individuals for educational purposes; book traveling exhibitions;

mus shop sells books, magazines, original art, reproductions, prints, clothing, toys, cards, CDs & DVDs
L **Archives,** 816 State St, Madison, WI 53706-1482. Tel 608-264-6460; Fax 608-264-6472; Elec Mail archref@mail.shsw.wisc.edu; Internet Home Page Address: www.shsw.wisc.edu; *Dir & Archivist* Peter Gottlieb
Open Mon - Fri 8 AM - 5 PM, Sat 9 AM - 4 PM; Average Annual Attendance: 1,846
Income: Financed by state
Library Holdings: Book Volumes; Cassettes; Fiche; Kodachrome Transparencies; Lantern Slides; Manuscripts; Maps; Memorabilia; Motion Pictures; Original Art Works; Original Documents; Other Holdings Original documents; Maps; Photographs; Prints; Records; Reels; Reproductions; Slides; Video Tapes

MANITOWOC

M **RAHR-WEST ART MUSEUM,** 610 N 8th St, Manitowoc, WI 54220-3998. Tel 920-683-3090; Fax 920-683-5047; Elec Mail rahrwest@manitowoc.org; Internet Home Page Address: rahrwestartmuseum.org; *Asst Dir* Daniel Juchniewich; *Dir* Barbara Bundy-Jost; *Admin Asst* Elaine Schroeder
Open Mon, Tues, Thurs & Fri 10 AM - 4 PM, Wed 10 AM - 8 PM, Sat & Sun 11 AM - 4 PM, cl holidays; No admis fee; Estab 1950 as city art museum and civic center to serve the city of Manitowoc. Transitional gallery in new wing built 1975; period rooms in Victorian Rahr Mansion built c 1991; a Registered Historic home; American art wing built in 1986; Ruth West Gallery 48' x 63'; Corridor Gallery, for changing exhibits; Permanent Collections Gallery; Average Annual Attendance: 22,000; Mem: 600; dues $40 individual
Income: $250,000 (financed by mem & city appropriation)
Library Holdings: Book Volumes 1500; Exhibition Catalogs; Periodical Subscriptions; Video Tapes
Special Subjects: Porcelain, Drawings, Graphics, Painting-American, Prints, Watercolors, Furniture, Glass, Ivory, Period Rooms
Collections: 19th & 20th Century American Paintings & Prints; Schwartz Collection of Chinese Ivories; contemporary art glass; works by Francis, Johns Lichtenstein & O'Keeffe; Schuette Woodland Indian Collection
Exhibitions: Monthly changing exhibitions; Annual exhibitions of community generated art; Traveling exhibitions of a changing schedule each yr
Publications: Catalogues of collections & exhibitions
Activities: Classes for adults & children; docent training; family activities; lects open to pub; concerts; gallery talks; tours; scholarships offered

MARSHFIELD

M **NEW VISIONS GALLERY, INC,** 1000 N Oak Ave, Marshfield Clinic Marshfield, WI 54449-5703. Tel 715-387-5562; Fax 715-387-5506; Elec Mail newvisions.gallery@frontier.com; Internet Home Page Address: www.newvisionsgallery.org; Internet Home Page Address: facebook.com/newvisionsgallery; *Dir* Betsy Bostwick; *Office Mgr* Tamara Mess; *Asst Dir* James Machtan
Open Mon - Fri 9 AM - 5:30 PM; No admis fee; Estab 1975 for the education, awareness & appreciation of visual arts; 1500 sq ft exhib space, track lighting, moveable display panels, sculpture stands; Average Annual Attendance: 75,000; Mem: 375; dues $25 - $1000 & up
Income: $150,000 (financed by mem, earned income, fundraising & gifts)
Library Holdings: Auction Catalogs; Audio Tapes; Book Volumes; CD-ROMs; Cassettes; Exhibition Catalogs; Video Tapes
Special Subjects: Drawings, Graphics, Painting-American, Photography, Prints, Sculpture, Watercolors, American Indian Art, African Art, Southwestern Art, Ceramics, Crafts, Pottery, Woodcuts, Etchings & Engravings, Decorative Arts, Painting-Japanese, Posters, Glass, Porcelain, Oriental Art, Asian Art, Carpets & Rugs, Juvenile Art, Painting-Australian
Collections: Australian Aboriginal Art Collection; Haitian Painting Collection; West African Art Collection; original prints
Exhibitions: Emerging Talents; New Visions' Culture & Agriculture; Annual Marshfield Art Fair; Rotating exhibs of professional artists & permanent collections
Publications: Brochures, every 6 wks; catalogs
Activities: Classes for adults; docent training; lects open to pub, gallery talks; tours; competitions with awards; lending collection contains books; book traveling exhibs 2 annually; mus shop sells gifts produced by artists or craft studios, jewelry, pottery, card, reproduction & prints

MENOMONIE

M **UNIVERSITY OF WISCONSIN-STOUT,** J Furlong Gallery, 410A 10th Ave, Dept of Art & Design, Micheels Hall Menomonie, WI 54751-2506. Tel 715-232-2261; Elec Mail furlong@uwstout.edu; *Cur* Chris Zerendow
Open Mon - Fri 10 AM - 4 PM, Tues 6 - 9 PM, Sat Noon - 3PM; No admis fee; Estab 1966 to serve university & local community with exhibits of art; A single room gallery; track lighting; Average Annual Attendance: 1,500
Income: Financed by state appropriation
Special Subjects: Drawings, Painting-American, Prints, Sculpture, African Art
Collections: African Art; paintings including works by Warrington Colescott, Roy Deforest, Walter Quirt, George Roualt & Raphael Soyer; drawings; prints; sculpture
Exhibitions: Changing exhibits
Activities: Classes for children; gallery talks; individual paintings & original objects of art lent to faculty, staff & campus offices

MEQUON

M **CONCORDIA UNIVERSITY WISCONSIN,** Fine Art Gallery, 12800 N Lake Shore Dr, Mequon, WI 53092-2418. Tel 262-243-5700; Fax 262-243-4351; Internet Home Page Address: www.cuw.edu; *Acad Dean* Dr David Eggebrecht; *Gallery Dir* Prof Jeffrey Shawhan
Open Sun, Tues, Wed & Fri 1 - 4 PM, Thurs 5 - 7 PM; No admis fee; Estab 1972 to exhibit work of area & national artists as an educational arm of the col; Average Annual Attendance: 1,000

Income: Financed through college budget
Special Subjects: Graphics, Bronzes, Painting-Russian
Collections: Graphics include Roualt, Altman & local artists; American landscape; religious art; Russian bronzes & paintings; John Doyle Lithographs; John Wiley Collection
Publications: Annual schedule
Activities: Classes for adults & children; lects for members only, 2-3 vis lectrs per year; gallery talks

MILWAUKEE

M **ALVERNO COLLEGE GALLERY,** Art and Cultures Gallery, 3401 S 39th St, Milwaukee, WI 53215-4020; PO Box 343922, Milwaukee, WI 53234-3922. Tel 414-382-6142; Fax 414-382-6354; Elec Mail linda.sommers@alverno.edu; Internet Home Page Address: www.alverno.edu; *Dir Gallery* Lynda J Sommers
Open Wed - Sat 12 PM - 5 PM, Thurs 12 PM - 7 PM; No admis fee; Estab 1954 for the aesthetic enrichment of community & the aesthetic educ of students
Income: $2000
Exhibitions: Senior Show; Juried Student Exhibition
Activities: Docent training; lects open to pub, 4 vis lectrs per yr; concerts; gallery talks; tours; competitions with awards; book traveling exhibs 1-2 per yr

L **ASCENSION LUTHERAN CHURCH LIBRARY,** 1236 S Layton Blvd, Milwaukee, WI 53215-1694. Tel 414-645-2933; Fax 414-645-0218; *Opers Mgr* Heidi Barret
Open Sun 8:30 - 11 AM & upon request; No admis fee; Estab 1954
Income: Financed by church budget, donations & bequests
Library Holdings: Audio Tapes; Book Volumes 13,000; Cassettes; Filmstrips; Framed Reproductions; Periodical Subscriptions 30; Video Tapes 40
Special Subjects: Decorative Arts, Crafts, Embroidery, Religious Art
Collections: Classic Art, framed pictures, organ music

C **BANK ONE WISCONSIN,** 111 E Wisconsin Ave, Milwaukee, WI 53202-4815. Tel 414-765-3000; *Facilities Mgr* Cheri Eddy
Estab to encourage Wisconsin art & artists; Collection displayed in offices, conference rooms & corridors within Bank One Plaza
Collections: Acrylics, batik, bronze sculpture, lithographs, oils, wall sculpture, watercolors by Wisconsin artists

M **CARDINAL STRITCH UNIVERSITY,** NM Gallery, 6801 N Yates Rd, Milwaukee, WI 53217-3985. Tel 414-414-4000; Internet Home Page Address: www.stritch.edu; *Chmn Art Dept* Timothy Abler; *Gallery Dir* Shana McCaw
Open Tues - Fri noon - 4 PM, Sat 1 - 4 PM; No admis fee; Estab 1947 to encourage creative art in each individual; educ gallery featuring student work & local & nat artists
Income: Financed by endowment, city & state appropriations & tuition
Activities: Gallery talks; mus shop sells original art

M **CHARLES ALLIS ART MUSEUM,** 1801 N Prospect Ave, Milwaukee, WI 53202; 1630 E Royal Pl, Milwaukee, WI 53202. Tel 414-278-8295; Fax 414-278-0335; Elec Mail akolata@cavtmuseums.org; Internet Home Page Address: www.cavtmuseums.org; *Exec Dir* Sarah Staider; *Cur Exhibitions* Laurel Turner; *Events Mgr* Judith Hooks; *Mgr Mktg* Ava Berry
Open Wed - Sun 1 - 5 PM; Admis general pub $5, seniors & students $3, members & children under 12 free; Estab 1947 as a house-mus with 850 art objects from around the world & spanning 2500 years, collected by Charles Allis, first president of the Allis-Chalmers Company & bequeathed to the people of Milwaukee. The mus is part of the Milwaukee County War Memorial Complex; Average Annual Attendance: 30,000; Mem: 500; dues student $25, senior individual $35, individual $45, senior couple $55, family $60, sustainer $75-$124, patron $125-$249, sponsor $250-$499, benefactor $500-$999, philanthropist $1,000 & up ; ann meetings in Oct
Income: $575,000 (combined budget) financed by endowment, private & public contributions & rental revenue
Special Subjects: Painting-American, Ceramics, Painting-French, Renaissance Art
Collections: Chinese, Japanese & Persian ceramics; Greek & Roman antiquities; 19th century French & American paintings; Renaissance bronzes
Publications: Exhibition catalogs; quarterly newsletter
Activities: Docent training; lects open to pub, 10 vis lectrs per yr; concerts; gallery talks; tours; film series; sponsoring of competitions

M **GROHMANN MUSEUM,** 1000 N Broadway, Milwaukee, WI 53202-3110; 1025 N Broadway, Milwaukee, WI 53202-3109. Tel 414-277-2300; Elec Mail grohmannmuseum@msoe.edu; Internet Home Page Address: www.msoe.edu

M **MARQUETTE UNIVERSITY,** Haggerty Museum of Art, 530 N 13th St, Milwaukee, WI 53233-2205; PO Box 1881, Milwaukee, WI 53201-1881. Tel 414-288-7290; Fax 414-288-5415; Elec Mail haggertym@marquette.edu; Internet Home Page Address: www.marquette.edu/haggerty; *Registrar* John Loscuito; *Admin Asst* Mary Wagner; *Communs Asst* Mary Dornfeld; *Preparator Asst* Rick Stultz; *Asst Cur* Jerome Fortier; *Assoc Dir* Lee Coppernoll; *Assoc Cur* AnneMarie Sawkins; *Cur Educ* Lynne Shumow; *Head Preparator* Dan Herro; *Dir* Wally Mason
Open Mon - Wed, Fri & Sat 10 AM - 4:30 PM, Thurs 10 AM -8 PM, Sun Noon - 5 PM; No admis fee; Estab 1984 to provide exhibitions of art from Old Masters to the present; 20,000 sq ft. A modern free standing building with security & climate control. Maintains reference library; Average Annual Attendance: 40,000; Mem: 500; dues $50-$5000; annual meeting in Sept
Income: Financed through private contributions & the university
Library Holdings: Auction Catalogs; Book Volumes; Clipping Files; Exhibition Catalogs
Special Subjects: Drawings, Latin American Art, Painting-American, Prints, American Indian Art, African Art, Religious Art, Etchings & Engravings, Landscapes, Decorative Arts, Painting-European, Posters, Dolls, Furniture, Glass, Porcelain, Painting-British, Painting-Dutch, Painting-French, Carpets & Rugs, Painting-Flemish, Renaissance Art, Painting-Spanish, Painting-Italian, Painting-German
Collections: Old Master, Modern, Contemporary paintings; prints, photography; decorative arts; tribal arts; German art, 1920s - 1930s
Publications: Exhibit catalogs; Italian Renaissance Masters
Activities: Educ dept; docent training; lects & workshops open to pub, 15-20 vis lectrs per yr; gallery talks; tours; awards; concerts; individual paintings & original objects of art lent to mus; originate traveling exhibs; mus shop sells books, reproductions, merchandise cards

M **MILWAUKEE ART MUSEUM,** 700 N Art Museum Dr, Milwaukee, WI 53202-4007. Tel 414-224-3200; Fax 414-271-7588; Elec Mail mam@mam.org; Internet Home Page Address: www.mam.org; *Pres Bd Trustees* Raymond R Krueger; *Exec Dir* Daniel T Keegan; *Chief Educ* Barbara Brown Lee; *Dir Pub Progs* Fran Serlin; *Sr Dir Devel* Mary Albrecht; *Sr Dir Communs* Vicki Scharfberg; *Dir Visitor Experience* Bambi Grajek-Specter; *Dir Human Resources* Jan Schmidt; *Chief Cur* Brady Roberts; *Dir Exhibs & Sr Cur European Art* Laurie Winters; *Sr Conservator* Jim De Young; *Cur Photographs* Lisa Hostetler; *Asst Cur 20th c Design* Mel Buchanon; *Assoc Conservator* Terri White; *Asst Cur Modern & Contemporary Art* John McKinnon; *Assoc Cur Prints & Drawings* Mary Weaver Chapin; *Chief Preparatory* Larry Stadler; *Librn & Archivist* Heather Winter
Open Tues - Sun, 10 AM - 5 PM, Thurs until 8 PM, cl Mon, Thanksgiving Day, Christmas Day; Admis adults $14, military, seniors & students w/ID $12, mems & children under 12 free, 1st Thurs of month free; Estab 1888 to create an environment for the arts that will serve the people of the greater Milwaukee community; Large flexible galleries, including a sculpture ct & outdoor display areas. Fine arts & decorative arts are mixed to create an overview of a period, especially in the fine American Wings; small galleries provided for specific or unique collections; Average Annual Attendance: 150,000; Mem: 11,000; dues student $25, individual $60, family/ dual $75, art advocate $150, donor $350, patron $500, partner $1000, benefactor $2500 - $4999, philanthropist $5000 - $9999, sustaining philanthropist $10,000 - $24,999, dir patron circ $25,000 - $49,999, Calatrava Society $50,000 - $99,999, Peg Bradley Society $100,000+
Income: Financed by endowment, mem, county & state appropriations & fund drive
Special Subjects: Architecture, Painting-American, Painting-European, Antiquities-Egyptian, Antiquities-Greek, Antiquities-Roman, Painting-German
Collections: 19th & 20th Century American & European Art, including the Bradley & Layton Collections: The American Ash Can School & German Expressionism are emphasized; All media from Ancient Egypt to Modern America; The Flagg Collection of Haitian Art; Michael & Julie Hall Collection of American Folk Art; a study collection of Midwest Architecture - The Prairie Archives; Layton Collection; Rene Von Schleinitz Collection; Mrs Harry L Bradley Collection; American Decorative Arts & the Chipstone Foundation; Marcia & Granvil Specks Collection; Floyd & Josephine Segel Collection of Photography; Maurice & Esther Leah Ritz Collection
Exhibitions: Rotating exhibits & exhibits from permanent collection
Publications: Exhibs & program brochure, 3 per yr; numbers calendar, bimonthly
Activities: Classes for adults & children; docent training; lects open to pub, 4-6 vis lectrs per yr; concerts; gallery talks; tours; competitions; films; scholastic art prog; originate traveling exhibs; mus shop sells books & magazines

L **George Peckham Miller Art Research Library,** 700 N Art Museum Dr, Milwaukee, WI 53202-4007. Tel 414-224-3270; Elec Mail library@mam.org; Internet Home Page Address: www.mam.org/collection/library.php; *Archivist & Librn* Heather Winter; *Audio Visual Librn* Beret Balestrieri Kohn
Open Sep - May Tues & Web 2-4 PM or by appt, Jun - Aug by appt only; No admis fee; photocopying fees apply; Estab 1916; Circ Non-circulating
Library Holdings: Auction Catalogs; Book Volumes 20,000; Clipping Files; Exhibition Catalogs; Original Documents; Other Holdings; Pamphlets; Periodical Subscriptions 60
Collections: National & international museum & gallery publications, incl Milwaukee Art Mus publications; monographs on art & artists; catalogue raisonnes; auction sales catalogues; artist files; Rare Books Collection
Activities: Classes for adults & children; docent training; lects open to the pub; gallery talks; tours; mus shop sells books, prints

M **MILWAUKEE COUNTY WAR MEMORIAL INC.,** Villa Terrace Decorative Arts Museum, 2220 N Terrace Ave, Milwaukee, WI 53202-1216. Tel 414-271-3656; Fax 414-271-3986; Elec Mail ehaouchine@cavtmuseums.org; Internet Home Page Address: www.villaterracemuseum.org; *Cur Exhibs & Coll* Martha Monroe; *Events Mgr* Katie Shorts; *Mgr Mktg* Erica Passey
Open Wed - Sun 1 - 5 PM; Admis $5, seniors (over 62) & students $3, members & children under 12 free; Estab 1967; Art mus & formal gardens; Average Annual Attendance: 30,000; Mem: 500; dues $40, srs $35
Income: $575,000 financed through pvt & pub contributions and rental revenue
Special Subjects: Landscape Architecture, Architecture, Ceramics, Glass, Metalwork, Porcelain, Pottery, Period Rooms, Silver, Bronzes, Sculpture, Decorative Arts, Furniture, Jade, Oriental Art, Asian Art, Ivory, Maps, Restorations, Renaissance Art, Stained Glass, Enamels
Collections: Decorative arts; furniture; glassware; paintings; wrought iron; Cyril Colnik Archive
Publications: Exhibition catalogs
Activities: Classes for adults & children; docent training; lects open to public; 3-6 vis lectrs per year; concerts; gallery talks; tours; ongoing temporary exhibitions; garden tours; Mayor's Landscape award

L **MILWAUKEE INSTITUTE OF ART & DESIGN,** Library, 273 E Erie St, Milwaukee, WI 53202-6003. Tel 414-847-3342; Fax 414-291-8077; Internet Home Page Address: www.miad.edu/; *Asst Dir, Library Serv* Nancy Siker; *Circ Coordr* Cathryn Wilson
Open Mon - Fri 8 AM - 5 PM; Estab 1974 as an Art & Design Library for the art school
Income: Financed by institution & private grants
Library Holdings: Book Volumes 26,000; DVDs 250; Other Holdings Postcards 2,440; Pamphlets; Periodical Subscriptions 125; Slides 32,000; Video Tapes 500
Special Subjects: Decorative Arts, Photography, Graphic Design, Advertising Design, Industrial Design, Interior Design

Collections: Member of Switch Consortium

L　**MILWAUKEE PUBLIC LIBRARY,** Art, Music & Recreation Dept, 814 W Wisconsin Ave, Milwaukee, WI 53233-2385. Tel 414-286-3000; Fax 414-286-2137; Internet Home Page Address: www.mpl.org; *Library Dir* Paula Kiely; *Dir Central Library Svcs* Joan Johnson; *Coordr Humanities, Arts & Special Colls* Mary Milinkovich
Open Mon noon - 8 PM, Tues - Sat 9 AM - 4 PM; No admis fee; Estab 1878
Income: Financed by budgeted funds & endowments
Library Holdings: Auction Catalogs; Audio Tapes; Book Volumes 2,400,000; CD-ROMs; Cassettes; Clipping Files; Compact Disks; DVDs; Exhibition Catalogs; Fiche; Manuscripts; Maps; Original Documents; Pamphlets; Periodical Subscriptions; Photographs; Records; Video Tapes
Special Subjects: Art History, Landscape Architecture, Decorative Arts, Posters, Crafts, Coins & Medals, Architecture
Collections: Auction catalogs; Audubon Prints - complete

M　**MILWAUKEE PUBLIC MUSEUM,** 800 W Wells St, Milwaukee, WI 53233-1404. Tel 414-278-2702; Fax 414-278-6100; Elec Mail smedley@mpm.edu; Internet Home Page Address: www.mpm.edu; *VPres Mktg & Communs* Mary Bridges; *Sr VPres Mus Progs* Ellen Censky; *Dir Information Servs & Electronic Systems* Linda Gruber; *Communs Mgr* Carrie Trousil; *Sr VPres Finance* Michael Bernatz; *Dir Exhib Program* James Kelly; *Dir Human Resources & Labor Relations* Judith Atkinson; *Pres & CEO* Jay Williams
Open Mon & Wed - Sun 9 AM - 5 PM, cl Tues, Independence Day, Thanksgiving, Christmas; Admis adults $14, sr citizens (60 & over, col students with ID, teens (13-12 $11, children 3-12 $10, children 3 & under, mems with card & AAM, ASTC mems with card no charge; Estab 1883 as a natural history mus; Steigledor-special exhibits gallery, Erwin C Uihlern-smaller exhibits, Clinton B Rose exhibit case; Average Annual Attendance: 413,000; Mem: 7400
Special Subjects: Photography, Anthropology, Folk Art, Decorative Arts
Collections: All major sub-disciplines of anthropology, botany, ethnology, natural history outreach, geology-paleontology; invertebrate & vertebrate zoology; decorative, fine & folk arts; film, photographs & specimen collection
Activities: Classes for children (school groups only), spec events, workshops, summer camps, IMAX dome theatre; lects open to pub & mems; vis lectrs ann; sales shop sells pottery, jewelry, stationery, ornaments, models, games, dolls

M　**MOUNT MARY COLLEGE,** Marian Gallery, 2900 Menomonee River Pkwy, Milwaukee, WI 53222. Tel 414-258-4810; Fax 414-256-1224; Elec Mail gastone@mtmary.edu; Internet Home Page Address: www.mtmary.edu; *Dir Gallery* Barbara Heimsch; *Cur* Elizabeth Gaston; *Prog Dir Fine Art* Debra Heermans; *Prog Dir Graphic Design* Nancy Lohmiller; *Prog Dir Fashion Design* Sandra Keiser; *Prog Dir Art Therapy* Bruce Moon; *Prog Dir Interior Design* Pam Steffen; *Prog Dir Interior Design* Leona Knobloch-Nelson
Open Mon - Fri 9 AM - 4:30 PM, Sat 7 Sun 1 - 4 PM; No admis fee; Estab 1940 to provide both students & local community with exposure to art experiences & to provide artists, both estab professionals & aspirants with a showplace for their work; Average Annual Attendance: 1,000
Income: Financed by private funds
Special Subjects: Prints, Costumes, Etchings & Engravings, Furniture
Collections: Antique furniture, 16th Century & Victorian period; contemporary print collection; historic costume collection; watercolors by Wisconsin artists
Activities: Classes for adults & children; lects open to pub, 6 vis lectrs per yr; concerts; gallery talks; tours; competitions & awards; schols offered

M　**UNIVERSITY OF WISCONSIN,** Institute of Visual Arts, (INOVA), 3253 N Downer Ave, Milwaukee, WI 53211-3153; PO Box 413, Milwaukee, WI 53201-0413. Tel 414-229-6509; Fax 414-229-6785; Elec Mail inova@cd.uwm.edu; Internet Home Page Address: www.uwm.eduSOA/inova; *Sr Cur* Marilu Knode; *Dir* Peter Doroshenko
Open Wed - Sun Noon - 5 PM, cl holidays; No admis fee; Estab 1982 to function as university museum; also oversees operations of art history gallery & fine arts galleries with international contemporary ar
Income: Financed by state appropriation
Special Subjects: Photography, Painting-American, Prints, Sculpture, Graphics, Religious Art, Oriental Art
Collections: INOVA presents its global audience with work by the most important dynamic & controversial local, national & international contemporary artists. INOVA commissions new site-specific work presenting artists in the region or the country for their first one-person exhibition
Publications: Catalogs; checklists; handouts
Activities: Lects open to public, 4 - 5 vis lectrs per yr; gallery talks; tours; originate traveling exhibs 1 - 2 per yr

M　**Union Art Gallery,** 2200 E Kenwood Blvd, Milwaukee, WI 53211; PO Box 413, Milwaukee, WI 53201-0413. Tel 414-229-6310; Fax 414-229-6709; Elec Mail art_gallery@aux.uwm.edu; Internet Home Page Address: www.aux.uwm.edu/union/artgal.htm; *Gallery Mgr* Steven D Jaeger; *Gallery Guard* Alicia Boll; *Gallery Guard* Richard Klein
Open Mon, Tues, Wed & Fri 11 AM - 3 PM, Thurs 11 AM - 7 PM, cl Sat & Sun; No admis fee; Estab 1972 to provide space for local & regional artists, along with student art, primarily undergraduate, to be shown in group exhibits established by peer selection and apart from faculty selection; 2500 sq ft, two stories high with more than 250 running feet of exhibit wall space; Average Annual Attendance: 16,500
Income: Union programming budget
Collections: Permanent Collection incl 2 & 3-D
Activities: Classes for adults; lects open to pub; concerts; competitions with awards; gallery talks; sale shop sells original art

A　**WALKER'S POINT ARTISTS ASSOC INC,** Gallery 218, 207 E Buffalo St, Ste 218, Milwaukee, WI 53202. Tel 414-643-1732; Elec Mail director@gallery218.com; Internet Home Page Address: www.gallery218.com; *Artist & Pres* Judith Hooks; *Artist* Bernie Newman; *Artist* Kathryn Kmet; *Artist* Jean Marc Richel; *Artist* Josh Hintz; *Artist* Sam Lux; *Artist* Mike Smith
Open Thurs - Sun noon - 5 PM; open late for special events; Estab 1991 to provide opportunities for local artists; Multidisciplinary cooperative gallery

presenting contemporary works by members; Average Annual Attendance: 6,000; Mem: Qualifications: resume, work samples, artist statement
Income: Financed by membership dues, individual donations, & commissions from sales
Library Holdings: Pamphlets; Periodical Subscriptions; Photographs; Prints; Sculpture; Slides
Special Subjects: Drawings, Etchings & Engravings, Photography, Prints, Sculpture, Watercolors, Painting-American, Asian Art, Collages, Latin American Art, Medieval Art, Calligraphy, Painting-European, Painting-Japanese
Exhibitions: Eight exhibs per yr - group
Activities: Lects open to pub & mems, 1 vis lectr per yr; competitions with prizes; poetry readings; gallery talks; sponsoring of competitions; gallery nights; film screenings; live music; sales shop sells books, prints, magazines, original art

M　**WALKER'S POINT CENTER FOR THE ARTS,** 839 S 5th St, Milwaukee, WI 53204-1730. Tel 414-672-2787; *Exec Dir* Gary Tuma

MONROE

M　**MONROE ARTS CENTER,** 1315 11th St, Monroe, WI 53566-1744; PO Box 472, Monroe, WI 53566-0472. Tel 608-325-5700; Fax 608-325-5701; Elec Mail info@monroeartscenter.com; Internet Home Page Address: monroeartscenter.com

NEENAH

M　**BERGSTROM-MAHLER MUSEUM,** 165 N Park Ave, Neenah, WI 54956-2956. Tel 920-751-4658; Fax 920-451-4755; Elec Mail info@paperweightmuseum.com; Internet Home Page Address: www.bergstrom-mahlermuseum.com; *Exec Dir* Alex Vance; *Cur* Jami Severstad; *Mgr Communs* Wendy Lloyd
Open Tues-Fri 10AM-4:30PM, Sat 9AM-4:30PM, Sun 1-4:30PM; No admis fee; Estab 1959 to provide cultural & educational benefits to the pub; Average Annual Attendance: 29,000
Income: $200,000 (financed by endowment, state & county appropriations & gifts)
Special Subjects: Painting-American, Sculpture, Glass
Collections: Over 1900 contemporary & antique paperweights; Victorian Glass Baskets; Germanic Glass; paintings; Ernst Mahler Collection of Germanic Glass
Exhibitions: Monthly exhibitions in varied media
Publications: Museum Quarterly; Glass Paperweights of Bergstrom - Mahler Museum Collection Catalogue; Paul J Stankard: Poetry in Glass
Activities: Classes for adults & children; docent training; lects open to pub; gallery talks; tours; individual paintings & original objects of art lent to mus; mus shop sells glass paperweights & glass items, original art

L　**Library,** 165 N Park Ave, Neenah, WI 54956-2956. Tel 920-751-4658; Fax 920-751-4755; Elec Mail info@paperweightmuseum.com; Internet Home Page Address: bergstrom-mahlermuseum.com; *Exec Dir & Cur* Mirenda Smith; *Educ Dir* Chelisa Herbrich; *Shop Mgr* Kathy Smits; *Mktg & Dev Dir* Jen Bero
Open Tues - Sat 10 AM - 4:30 PM, Sun 1 PM - 4:30 PM; No admis fee, donations accepted; 1959-Visual Arts Based Educ Org; Average Annual Attendance: 20000; Mem: 4500
Income: Endowed
Library Holdings: Book Volumes 2000; Memorabilia; Periodical Subscriptions 10; Slides
Special Subjects: Art History, Etchings & Engravings, Painting-German, Historical Material, Glass
Collections: Antique Paperweights and Germanic Contemporary Glass; Drinking Vessels; Victorian Glass Baskets
Activities: Classes for adults & children; arts festival on the 3rd Sun in July; Lect open to the public; gallery talks; sponsoring of competitions; Mus shop sells original art

NEW GLARUS

M　**CHALET OF THE GOLDEN FLEECE,** 618 2nd St, New Glarus, WI 53574-9626. Tel 608-527-2614; Tel 800-527-6838; *Cur* Helen Altmann
Open May - Oct Fri - Mon 10 AM - 4 PM; groups with advanced reservations; Admis adults $5, students 6-17 $2; Estab 1955; Authentic Swiss style chalet which was once a private residence; collection from around the world; Average Annual Attendance: 5,000
Income: Financed by admis fees & village of New Glarus
Collections: Swiss wood carvings & furniture; antique silver & pewter samplers; prints; exceptional glass & china; coins; stamps; paintings; etchings; Swiss dolls
Activities: Lect open to public; tours

OSHKOSH

M　**OSHKOSH PUBLIC MUSEUM,** 1331 Algoma Blvd, Oshkosh, WI 54901-2799. Tel 920-424-4731; Fax 920-424-4738; Elec Mail info@publicmuseum.oshkosh.net; Internet Home Page Address: www.publicmuseum.oshkosh.net; *Activities Coordr* Paul Poeschl; *Registrar* Joan Lloyd; *Cur* Debra Daubert; *Staff Artist* Don Oberweiser; *Dir* Bradley Larson; *Pres* Eugene Winkler; *Asst Dir* Michael Breza; *Archivist* Scott Cross
Open Tues - Sat 10 AM - 4:30 PM, Sun 1 - 4:30 PM, cl Mon & major holidays; No admis fee; Estab 1924 to collect & exhibit historical, Indian & natural history material relating to the area & fine & decorative & folk arts. 1908 converted home with new wing, Steiger Memorial Wing, opened in 1983 for additional exhibition space; Mus housed in city owned mansion near university campus; Average Annual Attendance: 65,000; Mem: 450; dues $25
Income: Financed by city appropriation
Library Holdings: Audio Tapes; Book Volumes; Manuscripts; Maps; Motion Pictures

Special Subjects: Painting-American, Sculpture, Archaeology, Costumes, Crafts, Folk Art, Pottery, Landscapes, Decorative Arts, Manuscripts, Portraits, Posters, Glass, Historical Material, Maps, Embroidery
Collections: American Artists: archeology; firearms; Indian Artifacts; Local & Wisconsin History; Natural History; Pressed Glass; period textiles
Exhibitions: Monthly changing exhibits; permanent exhibits; Annual Art Fair
Publications: Like A Deer Chased by the Dogs, The Life of Chief Oshkosh; Voices of History, 1941-1945
Activities: Classes for adults & children; lects open to pub; 5 vis lectrs per yr; individual paintings & original objects of art lent to mus; book traveling exhibs 1 per yr; mus shop sells books & reproductions

L **Library,** 1331 Algoma Blvd, Oshkosh, WI 54901-2799. Tel 920-236-5762; Fax 920-424-4738; Elec Mail info@publicmuseum.oshkosh.net; Internet Home Page Address: www.publicmuseum.oshkosh.net; *Archivist* Scott Cross; *Cur* Debra Daubert; *Registrar* Joan Lloyd; *Cur* Bradley Larson
Open Tues - Sat 10AM - 4:30PM; Sun 1 - 4:30 PM, cl Mon & major holidays; Admis adults $7, children 6-16 $3.50, children 5 & under free; Estab 1923. Research for mus exhibits & general pub; For reference only; Average Annual Attendance: 42,000; Mem: 700 members; dues $20.00/no meetings
Income: Financed by appropriations, donations, & admissions
Library Holdings: Audio Tapes; Book Volumes 2500; Cassettes; Clipping Files; Exhibition Catalogs; Filmstrips; Kodachrome Transparencies; Lantern Slides; Manuscripts; Maps; Memorabilia; Motion Pictures; Original Art Works; Original Documents; Other Holdings Maps; Pamphlets; Periodical Subscriptions 5; Photographs; Prints; Records; Sculpture; Slides; Video Tapes
Special Subjects: Archaeology
Publications: Exhibition catalogs
Activities: Lects open to pub, 2-4 vis lectrs per yr; mus shop sells books, reproductions, & photographs

A **PAINE ART CENTER & GARDENS,** (Paine Art Center & Arboretum) 1410 Algoma Blvd, Oshkosh, WI 54901-7708. Tel 920-235-6903; Fax 920-235-6303; Elec Mail mmueller@paineartcenter.com; Internet Home Page Address: www.paine.artcenter.com; *Financial Bus Mgr* Doris Peitz; *Cur Horticulture* Sheila Glaske; *Exec Dir* Barbara Hirschfeld; *Cur Coll & Educ* Laurel Spencer Forsythe; *Vol/Educ* Bobbie Scott; *Mus Serv Coordr* Mitzi Mueller
Open Tues - Sun 11 AM - 4 PM & national holidays; Admis adults $5, students with ID $2, seniors $2.50, children & members free; Estab 1947 as a nonprofit corporation to serve the needs of the upper Midwest by showing fine & decorative arts & horticulture; Average Annual Attendance: 30,000; Mem: 900; dues contributing $50, general $35, senior citizens $15
Income: Financed by endowment, mem & donations
Collections: American glass; decorative arts; icons; 19th & 20th century American paintings & sculpture; 19th century English & French paintings; period rooms; oriental rugs; American silver; arboretum contains displays of native & exotic trees, shrubs & herbaceous plants
Exhibitions: Temporary exhibitions drawn from sources, coast to coast
Publications: Exhib catalogues; bimonthly newsletter; class schedules
Activities: Classes for adults & children; docent training; lects open to pub, 3-6 vis lectrs per yr; concerts; gallery talks; tours; individual paintings & original objects of art lent to other mus & institutions; originates traveling exhibs; sales shop sells books, reproductions & jewelry

L **George P Nevitt Library,** 1410 Algoma Blvd, Oshkosh, WI 54901. Tel 920-235-6903; Fax 920-235-6303; Internet Home Page Address: www.thepaine.org; *Exec Dir* Aaron Sherer
Open Tues - Sun 11 AM - 4 PM, cl Mon; No admis fee for members, family $18, adults $7, seniors $6, students $5, children 5-12 $4, children under $3; Estab primarily for staff use as an art reference but also open to pub by appointment; Circ 3,000; For reference only; Average Annual Attendance: 30,000; Mem: 542; dues $40 & up; annual meeting in Apr
Library Holdings: Book Volumes 5,200; Cassettes; Clipping Files; Exhibition Catalogs; Kodachrome Transparencies; Memorabilia; Original Art Works; Pamphlets; Photographs; Slides
Special Subjects: Art History, Decorative Arts, Photography, Drawings, Etchings & Engravings, Painting-American, Sculpture, History of Art & Archaeology, Ceramics, Interior Design, Asian Art, Period Rooms, Goldsmithing, Oriental Art, Architecture
Collections: French Barbizon and American landscape paintings
Activities: Classes for adults and children; docent training; horticultural progs; 2-3 vis lectrs per yr; gallery talks; tours; mus shop sells books, original art

M **UNIVERSITY OF WISCONSIN OSHKOSH,** Allen R Priebe Gallery, 800 Algoma Blvd, Arts & Communication Bldg Oshkosh, WI 54901-3551. Tel 920-424-2235; Fax 920-424-1738; Internet Home Page Address: www.uwosh.edu/apgallery; *Dir* Andrew Redington
Open Mon - Fri 10:30 AM - 4 PM, Mon - Thurs 7 - 9 PM, Sat & Sun 1 - 4 PM, Sept thru May; No admis fee; Estab 1971 for the purpose of offering exhibits which appeal to a wide range of people; Gallery is 60 x 40 with additional wall space added with partitions, a skylight along back ceiling; Average Annual Attendance: 15,000
Income: Financed by student allocated monies & Dept of Art
Purchases: $1500
Special Subjects: Drawings, Prints
Exhibitions: Various exhib
Activities: Lects open to pub, 2-4 vis lectrs per yr; gallery talks; tours; competitions with awards; individual paintings & original objects of art lent to Univ staff & area mus

PLATTEVILLE

M **UNIVERSITY OF WISCONSIN - PLATTEVILLE,** Harry & Laura Nohr Gallery, One University Plaza, Platteville, WI 53818. Tel 608-342-2787; Fax 608-342-1737; Elec Mail nohr_galalery@uwplatt.edu; *Dir* Michael Breitner; *Asst Dir* Catherine Kutka
Open Mon - Fri 9 AM - 4 PM, Sat 10 AM - 2 PM; No admis fee; Estab 1978; Average Annual Attendance: 9,000

Income: Financed by student fees & state funds
Collections: Pottery, paintings, sculptures
Activities: Lects open to pub, 4 vis lectrs per yr; gallery talks; tours; competitions with awards; book traveling exhibs

RACINE

A **RACINE ART MUSEUM,** 441 Main St, Racine, WI 53403; PO Box 187, Racine, WI 53401-0187. Tel 262-638-8300; Fax 262-898-1045; *CEO* Bruce Pepich; *Pres* Bruce Bernberg; *Dir Develop* Laura D'Amato
Open Tues - Sat 10 AM - 5 PM, Sun 10 AM - 5 PM, cl federal holidays; Admis adults $5, discounts to AAM members, members free
Library Holdings: Book Volumes 3,500
Collections: American contemporary art; 20th century American crafts
Publications: exhibition brochures & catalogues
Activities: Educ prog; hobby workshops; guided tours; lects; gallery talks; mus shop

A **WUSTUM MUSEUM ART ASSOCIATION,** 2519 Northwestern Ave, Racine, WI 53404-2242. Tel 262-636-9177; Fax 262-636-9231; *Dir* Bruce W Pepich
Open daily 1 - 5 PM, Mon & Thurs 1 - 9 PM; No admis fee; Estab 1941 to foster & aid the estab & development to pub art galleries & museums, progs of educ & training in the fine arts & to develop pub appreciation & enjoyment of the fine arts; Estab 1846 Italianate farmhouse, 2 stories, 6-room classroom addition, 13 acres of parkland, Boerner-designed formal gardens. Maintains library; Average Annual Attendance: 50,000; Mem: 650; dues $20 & up; ann meeting in May
Income: $500,000 (financed by mem, grants & fundraising)
Special Subjects: African Art, Furniture, Glass, Eskimo Art
Collections: 300 works WPA; 20th century works on paper, studio glass, ceramics, fibers; 19th century African jewelry, metals, artists books, paintings
Exhibitions: Watercolor Wisconsin (annual); Wisconsin Photography (triennial); Annual Nationwide Thematic Show (summer); Area Arts
Publications: Exhibit brochures & catalogs; Vue, quarterly newsletter
Activities: Classes for adults & children; docent training; outreach for local school children; gang intervention progs; lects open to pub, 6-10 vis lectrs per yr; gallery talks; tours; competitions with awards; individual paintings & original art objects lent to mus; lending collection contains books, nature artifacts, original art works; original prints & paintings; book traveling exhibs; originate traveling exhibs; mus shop sells books & original art, gifts & collectibles

M **Charles A Wustum Museum of Fine Arts,** 2519 Northwestern Ave, Racine, WI 53404. Tel 262-636-9177; Fax 262-636-9231; Internet Home Page Address: www.wustum.org; *Dir* Bruce W Pepich
Open Tues - Sat 10 AM - 5 PM, cl Sun, Mon, Federal holidays & Easter; No admis fee; Estab 1940 to serve as cultural center for greater Racine community; Mus contains six galleries located in 1856 Wustum homestead & 1996 addition; Average Annual Attendance: 45,000
Income: $500,000 (financed by endowment, city & county appropriations, private gifts & programs)
Purchases: $500-$1000
Special Subjects: Painting-American, Prints, Watercolors
Collections: Contemporary Wisconsin Watercolors; WPA Project paintings & prints; contemporary graphics; works on paper, ceramic sculpture, glass sculpture, all post-1850 & primarily American
Exhibitions: Rotating exhibits
Activities: Classes for adults & children; docent training; lects open to pub, 2-3 vis lectrs per yr; gallery talks; tours; competitions with awards; film progs; individual paintings & original objects of art lent to other institutions; lending collection contains 2500 original art works, 700 original prints, 400 paintings, 200 photographs, 250 sculptures, 700 crafts & artist-made books; book traveling exhibs; originate traveling exhibs; mus shop sells books, original art, stationery, arts & crafts

L **Wustum Art Library,** 2519 Northwestern Ave, Racine, WI 53404. Tel 262-636-9177; Fax 262-636-9231; Internet Home Page Address: www.wustum.org; *Librn* Nancy Elsmo; *Dir* Bruce W Pepich
Open Sun - Sat 1 - 5 PM, Mon & Thurs 1 - 9 PM; Estab 1941 to provide mus visitors & students with exposure to art history & instructional books; For reference only to pub, members may check out books
Income: $2500
Library Holdings: Book Volumes 1500; Exhibition Catalogs; Pamphlets; Periodical Subscriptions 12; Video Tapes
Special Subjects: Photography, Prints, Sculpture, Watercolors, Printmaking, Porcelain, Pottery, Textiles, Woodcarvings
Publications: Quarterly catalogues

RHINELANDER

L **RHINELANDER DISTRICT LIBRARY,** 106 N Stevens St, Rhinelander, WI 54501-3158. Tel 715-369-1070; Fax 715-365-1076; *Dir* Steve Kenworthy
No admis fee; Estab 1903
Income: financed by endowment
Library Holdings: Book Volumes 1500; Photographs; Sculpture; Video Tapes
Special Subjects: Art History, Folk Art, Photography, Calligraphy, Etchings & Engravings, Painting-American, Painting-Dutch, Painting-Flemish, Painting-French, Painting-German, Painting-Italian, Sculpture, Painting-European, American Western Art, Asian Art, Architecture
Collections: Architecture; arts & crafts; books & videos; Bump Art Collection; European & American Artists; photography

RICHLAND CENTER

M **FRANK LLOYD WRIGHT MUSEUM,** AD German Warehouse, 300 S Church St, Richland Center, WI 53581; PO Box 6339, Madison, WI 53716-0339. Tel 608-647-2808; *Co-Owner, Mgr & Dir* Harvey W Glanzer; *Co-Owner & Creative Dir* Beth Caulkins
Open by request May - Nov, call ahead; Admis adult $10, children $5, group rates by arrangement; Estab 1915; Warehouse is a red brick structure topped by a

Mayan concrete frieze. It employs a structural concept known as the Barton Spider-web system. Interior grid of massive concrete columns provide structural support for floors & roof. Elimination of interior walls allows maximum freedom of interior space. Gift shop on first & lower level, mus & gallery on second floor
Exhibitions: Large 8 ft x 8 ft Photographic Murals of Wright's Work; Engineering scale model of Monona Terrace in Madison

RIPON

M RIPON COLLEGE CAESTECKER ART GALLERY, 300 Seward St, PO Box 248 Ripon, WI 54971. Tel 920-748-8110, 748-8115; Elec Mail kaineu@ripon.edu; *Dir* Rafael Salas
Open Tues - Fri 1 - 4 PM & 7 - 9PM, Sat - Sun 2 - 6
Income: Financed by the college
Collections: Paintings, print, sculpture, multi-media
Exhibitions: Rotating exhibits
Activities: Individual paintings lent to schools

RIVER FALLS

M UNIVERSITY OF WISCONSIN, Gallery 101, 410 S Third St, Art Dept, Office 172KFA River Falls, WI 54022-5010. Tel 715-425-3266, 425-3911 (main); Elec Mail michael.a.padgett@uwrf.edu; Internet Home Page Address: www.uwrs.edu; *Dir Gallery* Michael Padgett
Open Mon - Fri 9 AM - 5 PM & 7 - 9 PM, Sun 2 - 4 PM; No admis fee; Estab 1973 to exhibit artists of regional & national prominence & for educational purposes; Maintains one gallery; Average Annual Attendance: 21,000
Income: Financed by state appropriation & student activities funds
Collections: National & International Artists; Regional Artists; WPA Artists
Exhibitions: Rotating exhibits
Activities: Lects open to public; gallery talks; originate traveling exhibs

SHEBOYGAN

C KOHLER CO, John Michael Kohler Arts Center - Arts/Industry Program, 608 New York Ave, Sheboygan, WI 53081-4507. Tel 920-458-6144; Fax 920-458-4473; Internet Home Page Address: www.jmkac.org; *Dir* Ruth Kohler; *Coordr* Michael Ogilvie
Open Mon, Wed, Fri 10 AM - 5 PM, Tues & Thurs 10 AM - 8 PM, Sat & Sun 10 AM - 4 PM; No admis fee, donations accepted; Estab 1973; Exhibition of collections made by artists in residence; Average Annual Attendance: 200,000
Income: Financed by Kohler Co
Library Holdings: Other Holdings Metalwork; Sculpture
Special Subjects: Ceramics, Sculpture
Collections: Original art pieces created in Kohler Co facilities by resident artists in the Art Industry Program
Activities: Lectrs open to the public; 6 vis lectrs per year

A SHEBOYGAN ARTS FOUNDATION, INC, John Michael Kohler Arts Center, 608 New York Ave, Sheboygan, WI 53081-4507. Tel 920-458-6144; Fax 920-458-4473; Internet Home Page Address: www.jmkac.com; *Dir* Ruth DeYoung Kohler; *Cur* Leslie Umberger
Open Mon, Wed & Fri 10 AM - 5 PM, Tues & Thurs 10 AM - 8 Sat & Sun Noon - 4 PM; No admis fee, donations accepted; Estab 1967 as a visual & performing arts center focusing on contemporary American crafts & works which break barriers between art forms; Contains ten exhibition galleries, the largest being 60 ft x 45 ft, theatre, four studio-classrooms, library, sales gallery; Average Annual Attendance: 135,000; Mem: 1600; dues family $60, individual $48, senior $40; student $30
Income: Financed by mem, grants, corporate-foundation donations, sales gallery, ticket sales
Collections: Contemporary Ceramics; Contemporary Visionary Art; Historical Decorative Arts
Publications: Biennial Report; Exhibition Checklist 6-10 annually; Exhibition Catalogues, 2-4 annually; Newsletter, bimonthly
Activities: Classes for adults & children; dramatic progs; docent training; artists-in-residence progs; demonstrations; lects open to pub, 18-20 vis lectrs per yr; concerts; gallery talks; tours; competitions with awards; scholarships & fels offered; individual paintings & original objects of art lent to other arts institutions which meet the loan requirements, lending collection includes 6000 original art works & 100 paintings; book traveling exhibs; originates traveling exhibs which circulate to mus & artists organizations; sales shop sells magazines, original art, slides, postcards & notecards

STEVENS POINT

M UNIVERSITY OF WISCONSIN-STEVENS POINT, Carlsten Art Gallery, 1800 Portage St, Noel Fine Arts Center Stevens Point, WI 54481-1925. Tel 715-346-4797; Elec Mail cheft@uwsp.edu; Internet Home Page Address: www.uwsp.edu/art-design/carlsten; *Dir* Caren Heft
Open Mon - Fri 10 AM - 4 PM, Sat & Sun 1 - 4 PM, Thurs 7 - 9 PM; No admis fee; Estab 1971; 2,000 sq ft; Average Annual Attendance: 12,000
Income: Financed through university
Exhibitions: Tom Bamberger; Juried Student Exhibition; Drawing on the Figure; BFA Exhibition; Exhibitions rotate every three weeks

STURGEON BAY

M MILLER ART CENTER FOUNDATION INC, Miller Art Museum, 107 S Fourth Ave, Sturgeon Bay, WI 54235. Tel 920-746-0707 (office), 743-6578 (gallery); Elec Mail bmam@dcwis.com; Internet Home Page Address: www.millerartmuseum.org; *Cur* Deborah Rosenthal; *Dir* Bonnie Hartmann; *Mus Asst* Michael Nitsch
Open Mon 10 AM - 5 PM, Mon evenings until 8 PM; No admis fee; Estab 1975; Gallery is 5000 sq ft; 4 galleries; Average Annual Attendance: 18,000; Mem: 168; dues assoc $20, active $10; annual meeting second Thurs in Nov

Income: Financed by endowment, mem, county funds, sustaining, mem & grants
Special Subjects: Drawings, Etchings & Engravings, Landscapes, Collages, Portraits, Painting-American, Prints, Woodcuts, Photography, Watercolors
Collections: permanent coll contains over 600 paintings, emphasis on paintings, prints & drawings by 20th century Wisconsin artists
Exhibitions: Salon of High School Art, Wis; Wildlife Biennial Invitational; Juried Annual; Abstractions, James J Ingiversen: Master Painter; Holiday Theme Exhibit - Local Artists
Activities: Classes for adults & children; docent training; art library for mems & vols; lects open to pub, 6 vis lectrs per yr; concerts; gallery talks; tours; competitions with awards; individual paintings lent to other mus & art centers; lending coll contains 600 original art works; exten prog serves Master Artists K-5th gr; sales shop sells books, original art, prints, reproductions, jewelry, cards & pottery

WAUSAU

M CENTER FOR THE VISUAL ARTS, Gallery, 427 N 4th St, Wausau, WI 54403-5420. Tel 715-842-4545; Elec Mail cva@cvawausau.org; Internet Home Page Address: www.cvawausau.org; *Contact* Katie Crotteau

M LEIGH YAWKEY WOODSON ART MUSEUM, 700 N 12th St, Wausau, WI 54403-5007. Tel 715-845-7010; Fax 715-845-7103; Elec Mail museum@lywam.org; Internet Home Page Address: www.lywam.org; *Cur Educ* Jayna Hintz; *Cur Educ* Catie Anderson; *Dir* Kathy Kelsey Foley; *Registrar & Cur Colls* Jane Weinke; *Cur Exhibs* Andy McGivern
Open Tues - Fri 9 AM - 4 PM, Sat & Sun Noon - 5 PM; first Thurs every month 9 AM - 7:30PM; No admis fee; Estab 1976; Average Annual Attendance: 60,000
Collections: Contemporary & historic paintings, drawings & sculptures with birds as the main subject
Exhibitions: (Labor Day - Oct/Nov) Birds in Art
Publications: Birds in Art, annual exhibition catalog
Activities: Docent progs; classes for adults, children; lects open to pub; gallery talks; tours; book traveling exhibs 3-4 per yr; originate traveling exhibs to art, natural history & science mus

WEST ALLIS

M INTERNATIONAL CLOWN HALL OF FAME & RESEARCH CENTER, INC, State Fair Park, 640 S 84th St #526 West Allis, WI 53214-1438. Tel 414-290-0105; Fax 414-290-0106; Elec Mail mirthcon@juno.com; Internet Home Page Address: www.theclownmuseum.org; *Exec Dir* James D Mejchar
Open Mon - Fri 10 AM - 4 PM; No admis fee; donations accepted; Estab 1986 to promote & advance the art of clowning through preservation & education; Average Annual Attendance: 15,000; Mem: 500; dues $35-$1000; annual meeting 1st weekend in Aug
Income: $150,000 (financed by endowment, mem, gift shop & admis)
Library Holdings: Cassettes; Clipping Files; DVDs; Kodachrome Transparencies; Memorabilia; Original Art Works; Photographs; Records; Slides; Video Tapes
Special Subjects: Historical Material, Prints, Costumes, Crafts, Posters, Dolls, Miniatures
Publications: Let the Laughter Loose, quarterly newsletter
Activities: Classes for adults & children; dramatic progs; docent training; lects open to pub, 25 vis lectrs per yr, gallery talks, tours; sales shop sells books, magazines, prints, reproductions & clown novelties

WEST BEND

M MUSEUM OF WISCONSIN ART, 205 Veterans Ave, West Bend, WI 53095-3312. Tel 262-334-9638; Fax 262-334-8080; Elec Mail info@wisconsinart.org; Internet Home Page Address: www.wisconsinart.org; *Pres* Dale Kent; *Exec Dir & CEO* Laurie Winters; *Chief Operating Officer* Jeanne Laska; *Dir Colls & Exhibs* Graeme Reid; *Dir Develop* Heidi Winter; *Dir Mktg & Pub Rels* Brittani Mattke; *Dir Edu & Pub Progs* Faith Rockenstein; *Controller* Jami Wild; *Coll Information Mgr* Chris Anderson; *Graphic Designer* Amy Hafemann; *Facilities Mgr* Ebon Heimerman; *MOWA Shop Mgr* Julie Jackson; *Facility Rental Mgr* Megan Johnson; *Mem Coordr* Liz Knopke; *Educ Asst* Jessica Lemberg; *Preparator & Exhib Designer* August Peter; *Assoc Cur* Erika Petterson; *Exec Asst* Jennifer Suelflow; *Registrar* Andrea Waala
Open Tues - Sun 10 AM - 5 PM, Thurs 10 AM - 8 PM, cl Mon; Free to MOWA mems; Estab 1961; one of America's great regional art museums; state of the art bldg contains nine galleries featuring the work of today's hottest Wisconsin artists, as well as Wisconsin art from the ages including Carl von Marr's masterpiece The Flagellants; The modern & contemporary new bldg includes nearly 12,000 sq ft of gallery space, qpprox 7,000 sq ft of facility rental space for special events, a unique gift shop with Wisconsin-made items, two education studios & an outdoor sculpture garden; Average Annual Attendance: 25,000; Mem: 5,000; dues individual $12, 2 people $24, household 3 or more with children 17 & under $50
Income: Financed by endowment, mem & donations
Library Holdings: Audio Tapes; Book Volumes; Cassettes; Clipping Files; Compact Disks; DVDs; Original Art Works; Original Documents; Photographs; Records; Reproductions
Special Subjects: Decorative Arts, Etchings & Engravings, Furniture, Drawings, Painting-American, Sculpture, Watercolors
Collections: Carl von Marr Collection; Wisconsin Art History 1850-1960; 1800-2000 Contemporary Wisconsin Art
Exhibitions: (10/01/2013-01/05/2014) Edward S. Curtis and the Vanishing Race (Main Gallery); (01/17/2014-03/02/2014) WVA Biennial (Main Gallery); (03/21/2014-06/08/2014) Milwaukee Handicrafts Project (Main Gallery); (06/19/2014-09/04/2014) John Steuart Curry: At Home in Wisconsin (Main Gallery); (10/02/2014-01/11/2015) Tom Loeser: Masterworks (Main Gallery); (12/06/2013-01/26/2014) Laurel Lueders: The Rebellion of Systems (One Gallery); (02/07/2014-04/13/2014) Beth Lipman- Precarious Possessions (One Gallery); (04/25/2014-07/27/2014) Carl Corey: For Love and Money (One Gallery);

(08/07/2014-11/09/2014) Marc Sijan (One Gallery); (12/06/2013-01/05/2014) The 2013 Great and Wonderful MOWA Members Show (State Gallery); (01/17/2014-04/13/2014) Wisconsin Pastel Artists (State Gallery); (04/25/2014-07/20/2014) Coalition of Photographic Arts (State Gallery); (08/07/2014-11/16/2014) Madison Art Guild 100th Anniversary Exhibition (State Gallery)
Publications: Carl Von Marr, American-German Artist (1858-1936); quarterly printed newsletter; monthly e-newsletter
Activities: Classes for adults and children; docent training; lects open to public; lects for mems only; 12 vis lects per yr; tours; gallery talks; sponsored competitions; Art Aware an educational outreach (art appreciation) service to local schools; MOWA On the Lake - serving Saint John's On The Lake in Milwaukee, WI; traveling exhibs, 1-3 per yr; originate traveling exhibs; mus shop sells books, reproductions, prints from collection

WHITEWATER

M **UNIVERSITY OF WISCONSIN-WHITEWATER,** Crossman Gallery, 800 W Main St, Whitewater, WI 53190-1705. Tel 262-472-1207, 472-5708; Fax 262-472-2808; Elec Mail flanagam@mail.uww.edu; Internet Home Page Address: blogs.uww.edu/crossman/; *Dir* Michael Flanagan
Open Mon - Fri 10 AM - 5PM & 6 - 8 PM, Sat 1 - 4 PM, cl Sun; No admis fee; Estab 1965 to provide professional exhibits; 47 ft x 51 ft, secure alarmed facility; Average Annual Attendance: 10,000
Income: $7000 (financed by segregated student fee appropriation)
Collections: American Folk Art Collection; Regional Art Collection; Early 20th century German works on paper
Exhibitions: Ceramic Invitational; Artassa Collaboration; Chronicles of Latin America; Contemporary sculpture
Activities: Classes for adults & children; student training in gallery management; lects open to public, 3 vis lectrs per year; concerts; gallery talks; tours; student juried show

WYOMING

BIG HORN

M **BRADFORD BRINTON MEMORIAL & MUSEUM,** 239 Brinton Rd, Big Horn, WY 82833; PO Box 460, Big Horn, WY 82833-0460. Tel 307-672-3173; Fax 307-672-3258; Elec Mail kls_bbm@vcn.com; Internet Home Page Address: www.bradfordbrintonmemorial.com; Internet Home Page Address: www.BBMandM.org; *Dir & Chief Cur* Kenneth L Schuster; *Registrar* Barbara R Schuster
Open Memorial Day weekend - Labor Day Mon - Sat 10 AM - 4 PM, Sun noon - 4 PM; please call for off-season hours; Admis adults $4, students over 13 & sr citizens over 62 $3; Estab 1961 to show a typical Gentleman's working ranch of the 1920s complete with Western art & original furnishings; Reception Gallery with changing exhibs; Ranch House with original displays (art by Russell, Remington, Borein, F T Johnson); Average Annual Attendance: 10,000; Mem: 300; dues $15 & up
Special Subjects: American Western Art, Porcelain, Silver, Hispanic Art, Painting-American, Prints, Sculpture, Southwestern Art, Ceramics, Crafts, Decorative Arts, Furniture, Jewelry, Painting-British, Period Rooms
Collections: Plains Indians Artifacts; Western American Art by Frederic Remington & Charles M Russell; American art & a few pieces of European art, largely of the 19th & 20th century
Publications: Monographs on artists in the collection from time to time, brochures on exhibitions curated
Activities: Educ dept; lects open to pub, 4 vis lectrs per yr; tours; mus shop sells books, magazines, original art, prints, American Indian jewelry & crafts

CASPER

M **NICOLAYSEN ART MUSEUM & DISCOVERY CENTER,** Children's Discovery Center, 400 E Collins Dr, Casper, WY 82601-2815. Tel 307-235-5247; Fax 307-235-0923; Internet Home Page Address: www.thenic.org; *Acting Dir* Valerie Kulhavy; *Cur* Lisa Hatchadoorian; *Develop Dir* Amanda Helm; *Admin Coordr* Lori Klatt; *Registrar* Ingrid Burnett; *Mus Shop Mgr* Jan Debeer; *Pub Relations* Clay Anthony
Open Tues - Sat 10 AM - 5 PM, Sun Noon-4 PM; Admis non mems $5, children $3; Estab 1967 to exhibit permanent collection, nationwide traveling exhibits & provide school tours, art classes & workshops; Two galleries, 2500 sq ft and 500 sq ft; Average Annual Attendance: 40,000; Mem: 1,500; dues individual $35, family $60, annual meeting last Wed of Mar
Income: $900,000 (financed by mem, grants & fundraising events)
Collections: Carl Link Drawings; Artists of the Region; Conrad Schwiering Studio
Exhibitions: Twenty per year.
Publications: Historic Ranches of Wyoming
Activities: Classes for adults & children; docent training; lects open to pub, 5-10 vis lectrs per yr; concerts; gallery talks; competitions with cash awards; individual paintings & original objects of art lent to qualified exhibiting institutions; lending collection contains 2500 original art works; book traveling exhibs; originate traveling exhibs; mus shop sells books, original art & gifts; children's mus

L **Museum,** 400 E Collins Dr, Casper, WY 82601. Tel 307-235-5247; Fax 307-235-0923; *Discovery Center Coordr* Val Martinez; *Registrar* Debbie Oliver; *Dir* Joe Ellis
Open Tues - Sat 10 AM - 5 PM, Thurs 10 AM-8 PM, Sun Noon-4 PM; Admis adults $2, children under 12 $1, free Thurs, Sat & Sun; Estab 1967 to collect & exhibit regional contemporary art; 8000 sq ft including 6 small and 1 large gallery. Computer controlled temperature & humidity. Hands on discovery center for children; Average Annual Attendance: 60,000; Mem: 700; dues $50; annual meeting 3rd Tues May

Income: $235,000 (financed by donations & fundraising events)
Library Holdings: Book Volumes 66; Exhibition Catalogs; Pamphlets; Periodical Subscriptions 8; Slides
Collections: Carl Link Collection; Regional Contemporary Pottery
Activities: Classes for children; dramatic progs; lects open to pub, 2000 lectrs per yr; gallery talks; tours; juried regional competitions; book traveling exhibs 1-2 per yr; mus shop sells books, original art, prints, pottery, glass, jewelry & cards

CHEYENNE

M **DEPARTMENT OF COMMERCE,** Wyoming Arts Council Gallery, 2320 Capitol Ave, Cheyenne, WY 82002-0001. Tel 307-777-7742; Fax 307-777-5499; Elec Mail lfranc@missc.state.wy.us; Internet Home Page Address: www.wyoarts.state.wy.us; *Visual Arts Prog Mgr* Liliane Francuz
Open Mon - Fri 8 AM - 5 PM, cl holidays; Estab 1990 to exhibit work of artists living & working in Wyoming; Average Annual Attendance: 1,200
Exhibitions: 4-5 exhibits annually, work of Wyoming artists in all media
Activities: Lects open to pub, gallery talks; originates traveling exhibs to state of Wyo non-profit organizations

M **WYOMING STATE MUSEUM,** 2301 Central Ave, Cheyenne, WY 82002-0001. Tel 307-777-7022 (museum), 7021 (tours), 5320 (store), 5427 (collections); Fax 307-777-5375; Elec Mail wsm@state.wy.us; Internet Home Page Address: www.wyomuseum.state.wy.us; *Dir* Marie Wilson-McKee
Open May - Oct Tues-Sat 9 AM-4:30 PM, Nov - Apr Tues - Fri 9 AM - 4:30 PM, Sat 10 AM - 2 PM, cl Sun and holidays; No admis fee; Estab 1895 to collect, preserve & to exhibit the work of Wyoming & Western artists; Average Annual Attendance: 34,000
Income: Financed by state appropriation
Special Subjects: American Indian Art, American Western Art, Decorative Arts
Collections: Wyoming artists, historical & contemporary including Historical Hans Kleiber, William Gollings, M D Houghton, Cyrenius Hall, William H Jackson, J H Sharp
Exhibitions: Regional & Wyoming contemporary art, western art; Governor's Annual Art Exhibition, June - Aug ann
Activities: Classes for children; lects open to pub, 9 vis lectrs per yr; gallery talks; tours; individual paintings & original objects of art lent to institutions belonging to AAM, Colo-Wyo Assn of Museums (CWAM) & Mount Plains Museums Assn; mus shop sells books, original art, reproductions

CLEARMONT

M **UCROSS FOUNDATION,** Big Red Barn Gallery, 30 Big Red Ln, Clearmont, WY 82835-9723. Tel 307-737-2291; Fax 307-737-2322; Elec Mail ucross@wyoming.com; *Pres* Elizabeth Guheen; *Exec Dir* Sharon Dynak
Open Mon - Fri 9 AM - 4 PM; No admis fee; Estab 1981; Gallery is located in a renovated barn on the grounds of an artists' & writers' residency program
Special Subjects: Painting-American, Sculpture, Watercolors, Textiles
Exhibitions: Quilts by Linda Behar; 4-6 group & solo shows a year; 4 exhibits annually in winter, spring, summer & fall
Publications: Ucross newsletter, annually
Activities: Sales shop sells books, postcards & gifts

CODY

M **BIG HORN GALLERIES,** 1167 Sheridan Ave, Cody, WY 82414-3627. Tel 307-527-7587; Fax 307-527-7586
Call for hours
Collections: Western & wildlife art and landscapes

A **BUFFALO BILL MEMORIAL ASSOCIATION,** Buffalo Bill Historical Center, 720 Sheridan Ave, Cody, WY 82414-3428. Tel 307-587-4771; Fax 307-587-5714; Elec Mail leeh@bbhc.org; Internet Home Page Address: www.bbhc.org; *Chmn* Alan Simpson; *Exec Dir* Robert Price Shimp; *Cur Plains Indian Museum* Emma Hanson; *Dir Educ* Maryanne Andrus; *Registrar* Elizabeth Holmes; *Assoc Dir* Wally Reber; *Cur Buffalo Bill Mus* Juti Winchester; *Cur Draper Mus of Natural History* Charles Preston; *Librn* Mary Robinson; *Dir Pub Rels* Lee Haines; *Cur McCracken Research Library* Kurt Graham
Open Apr 10 AM - 5 PM, May 8 AM - 8 PM, June - Sept 15 8 AM - 8 PM, Sept 16 - Oct 8 AM - 5 PM, Nov - Mar 10 AM - 3 PM, cl Mon; Admis Adults $15, sr citizens $13 & special group rate; Estab 1917 to preserve & exhibit art, artifacts & memorabilia of the Old West; to operate Buffalo Bill Mus, Plains Indian Mus, Whitney Gallery of Western Art & Cody Firearms Mus & Draper Mus of Natural History; Average Annual Attendance: 250,000; Mem: Dues $38 & up
Income: Financed by admis & private funds
Publications: Annual exhibition catalogues; quarterly newsletter
Activities: Classes for adults & children; docent training; lects open to pub; gallery talks; tours; schols offered; individual paintings & original objects of art lent to other institutions; book traveling exhibs; originate traveling exhibs around the US; mus shop sells books, original art, reproductions, prints, slides, jewelry, collectible items, Indian crafts & Kachina dolls

L **Harold McCracken Research Library,** 720 Sheridan Ave, Cody, WY 82414. Tel 307-587-4771; Fax 307-587-5714, 307-527-6042; Internet Home Page Address: www.bbhc.org; *House Cur* Nathan Bender; *Librn* Frances Clymer
Open Mon - Fri 8 AM - 5 PM (summer), Tues, Fri 10 AM - 3 PM (winter); Estab 1980 for research in Western history & art; Circ non circulating; Open to the pub for reference only; Average Annual Attendance: 250,000
Library Holdings: Audio Tapes 1500; Book Volumes 15,000; Cassettes; Clipping Files; Exhibition Catalogs; Fiche; Filmstrips 1300; Kodachrome Transparencies; Lantern Slides; Manuscripts; Memorabilia 300; Motion Pictures; Other Holdings Engraving & Architectural Drawings 200; Pamphlets; Periodical Subscriptions 86; Photographs; Prints; Records; Reels 7000; Reproductions; Slides 6500; Video Tapes

Special Subjects: Art History, Folk Art, Photography, Commercial Art, Etchings & Engravings, Manuscripts, Maps, Painting-American, Archaeology, Ethnology, American Western Art, Art Education, American Indian Art, Anthropology, Landscapes
Collections: WHD Koerner Archives; Buffalo Bill Cody Archives; Photo Collections; Rare Books
Activities: Classes for adults & children; dramatic progs; docent training; lects open to pub, 20 vis lectrs per yr; concerts; gallery talks; tours; mus shop sells books, magazines, original art, reproductions & prints

A   **CODY COUNTRY ART LEAGUE,** 836 Sheridan Ave, Cody, WY 82414-3411. Tel 307-587-3597; Elec Mail office@codycountryartleague; Internet Home Page Address: www.codycountryartleague.com; *Pres* Shirley Barhaug; *Treas* Lynn Mowery
Open summer: Mon - Sat 9 AM -5 PM, Sun 10 AM - 3 PM, winter: Mon - Fri 9 AM - 5 PM; No admis fee; Estab 1964 for promotion of artistic endeavor among local & area artists; also established for exhibits, displays & sales; Average Annual Attendance: 25,000; Mem: 250; dues $40 (artist), annual meeting in Jan; must be juried in
Income: Financed by mem dues, yearly auction, sponsors & events
Special Subjects: Drawings, Landscapes, Metalwork, Mosaics, Photography, Watercolors, Pottery, Stained Glass, American Western Art, Bronzes, Ceramics, Furniture, Glass, Woodcarvings
Exhibitions: Ann Art Show June-July; Ann Garden Tour July
Activities: Classes for adults & children; dramatic progs; films; workshops; community events; lects open to pub, 2-3 vis lectrs per yr; competitions; sales shop sells books, original art,& prints

M   **SIMPSON GALLAGHER GALLERY,** 1161 Sheridan Ave, Cody, WY 82414-3627. Tel 307-587-4022
Call for hours
Collections: Paintings; wildlife sculpture; western intaglios

JACKSON

M   **NATIONAL MUSEUM OF WILDLIFE ART OF THE UNITES STATES,** 2820 Rungius Rd, Jackson, WY 83001; PO Box 6825, Jackson, WY 83002-6825. Tel 307-733-5771; Fax 307-733-5787; Elec Mail info@wildlifeart.org; Internet Home Page Address: www.wildlifeart.org; *Pres & CEO* James C McNutt, PhD; *Cur Art* Adam D Harris, PhD; *Cur Educ* Jane Lavino; *CFO* Lisa Holmes; *Dir Facility & Security* Joe Bishop; *Dir Opers* Steve Seamons; *Dir Develop & Mktg* Ponteir Sackrey; *Dir Digital Communs* Zeenie Scholz
Open Summer 9 AM - 5 PM; Spring/Fall/Winter Mon - Sat 9 AM - 5 PM, Sun 11 AM - 5 PM; Admis $12 adults, seniors $10, children 5-18 $6; Estab 1987 devoted to Fine Wildlife Art; collection includes work from 2500 BC to present; Circ Non-circulating; Facility has 14 galleries, cafe, museum shop, 2 classrooms, 200 seat auditorium & library; galleries house traveling exhibits & permanent colls; Average Annual Attendance: 77,000; Mem: Annual dues $35 individual
Income: Financed by endowment, mem & admis
Library Holdings: Auction Catalogs; Book Volumes; Clipping Files; Compact Disks; DVDs; Memorabilia; Motion Pictures; Periodical Subscriptions; Photographs; Slides; Video Tapes
Special Subjects: Drawings, Folk Art, Prints, Bronzes, Manuscripts, Maps, Painting-British, Painting-American, Photography, Sculpture, Watercolors, American Indian Art, American Western Art, Anthropology, Pre-Columbian Art, Southwestern Art, Etchings & Engravings, Landscapes, Painting-European, Painting-Canadian, Painting-Dutch, Painting-French, Historical Material, Miniatures, Medieval Art, Painting-Scandinavian
Collections: Wildlife Art Collection
Exhibitions: Special Grand Opening exhibits
Publications: Call of the Wild magazine, annual; eNews
Activities: Classes for adults & children; dramatic progs; docent training; paid internships; lects open to pub, 10 vis lectrs per yr; tours; competitions; awards: Rungius Medal, Bull-Bransom Award, Western Visions People's Choice Award, Western Visions Red Smith Award, Western Visions Trustees Purchase Award, Western Visions Robert Kuhn Award; schols available; lend orig objects of art to other museums; book traveling exhibs 1-2 per yr; originates traveling exhibs; mus shop sells books, prints, magazines, reproductions, gifts, housewares, apparel & jewelry

L   **Library,** 2820 Rungius Rd, PO Box 6825 Jackson, WY 83002-6825. Tel 307-733-5771, 800-313-9553; Fax 307-733-5787; Elec Mail info@wildlifeart.org; Internet Home Page Address: www.wildlifeart.org; *Dir* Francine Carraro
Open Mon - Fri 9 AM - 5 PM (Summer & Winter), Mon-Fri 9 AM - 5 PM, Sat 1 - 5 PM (Spring & Fall); Admis family $16, adults $8, seniors & students $7; Estab 1987 to enrich & inspire pub appreciation & knowledge of fine art & to explore humanity's relationship with nature by collecting fine art focused on wildlife & presenting exceptional exhibs & educational progs; 12 galleries including 6 changing exhib galleries; Mem: dues $35 - $2500
Library Holdings: Auction Catalogs; Audio Tapes; Book Volumes 1000; Clipping Files; Exhibition Catalogs; Motion Pictures; Pamphlets; Slides; Video Tapes
Special Subjects: Art History, Film, Illustration, Photography, Drawings, Etchings & Engravings, Maps, Painting-American, Painting-British, Painting-German, Sculpture, Painting-European, Watercolors, American Western Art, Bronzes, Printmaking, Art Education, American Indian Art, Southwestern Art, Metalwork, Miniatures, Restoration & Conservation, Woodcuts, Landscapes, Painting-Canadian, Architecture, Folk Art
Collections: JKM Collection; American Bison Collection; John Clymer Studio Collection; Carl Rungius Collection; Over 300 works of art by over 200 artists
Publications: Call of the Wild triannual newsletter & spec exhib catalogs
Activities: Classes for adults & children; docent training; lects open to pub; concerts, gallery talks; tours; Rungius Award; Red Smith Award; book traveling exhibs, 6 per yr; mus shop sells books, magazines, reproductions & prints

LARAMIE

M   **UNIVERSITY OF WYOMING,** University of Wyoming Art Museum, 2111 Willett Dr, Laramie, WY 82071-2000; 1000 E University Ave, Dept 3807 Laramie, WY 82071-2000. Tel 307-766-6622; Fax 307-766-3520; Elec Mail uwartmus@uwyo.edu; Internet Home Page Address: www.uwyo.edu/artmuseum; *Dir & Chief Cur* Susan Moldenhauer; *Cur Educ* Wendy Bredehoft; *Cur Coll* Nicole Crawford; *Reg* Fay Bisbee; *Master Teacher* Heather Bender; *Asst Cur* Rachel Miller; *Mktg Assoc* Molly Dunnell; *Chief Prep* Sterling Smith; *Prep* Conor Mullen; *Visitor Serv Assoc* Janine Reinhardt; *Accnt* Abbie Connally; *Admin Asst* Joyce Gore
Open Mon - Sat 10 AM - 5 PM; Mon until 9 PM Sept - Nov, Feb -Apr; No admis fee; Estab 1972 to serve as an art resource center for faculty, students & the general public; Exhibition space consists of 9 galleries & outdoor sculpture terrace; Average Annual Attendance: 90,000; Mem: 500; dues $40 & up
Income: Financed by state appropriation, friends organization, individual and corporate gifts & grants
Special Subjects: American Indian Art, Drawings, Etchings & Engravings, American Western Art, Photography, Painting-American, Prints, Painting-British, Painting-French, Sculpture, Painting-American, Prints, Sculpture, Primitive art, Woodcuts, Painting-European, Portraits
Collections: Collection of 7000 paintings, sculptures, works on paper, photographs, crafts & ethnographic materials, primary 17th to 20th century
Publications: Exhibition catalogs
Activities: Classes for adults & children; docent training; Summer Teaching Institute; lects open to pub, 4 vis lectrs per yr; concerts; gallery talks; tours; student exhib awards; individual paintings and original objects of art lent to other museums regionally and nationally; artmobile; collection contains 7000 original art works; originates traveling exhibs; mus shop sells logo items, mus publs

MOOSE

A   **GRAND TETON NATIONAL PARK SERVICE,** Colter Bay Indian Arts Museum, PO Drawer 170, Moose, WY 83013. Tel 307-739-3594; *Cur* Alice Hart; *Naturalist* Laine Thom
Open May 8 AM - 5 PM, June - Sept 8 AM - 8 PM, cl Oct - Apr; No admis fee; Estab 1972; Average Annual Attendance: 300,000
Special Subjects: American Indian Art
Collections: David T Vernon Indian Arts Collection
Exhibitions: Native American Guest Artist's Demonstration Program; David T Vernon Indian Arts Collection
Activities: Tours open to public; sales shop sells books & prints

ROCK SPRINGS

A   **SWEETWATER COUNTY LIBRARY SYSTEM AND SCHOOL DISTRICT #1,** Community Fine Arts Center, 400 C St, Rock Springs, WY 82901-6225. Tel 307-362-6212; Fax 307-352-6657; Elec Mail cfac@sweetwaterlibraries.com; Internet Home Page Address: www.cfac4art.com; *Asst to Dir* Jennifer Messer; *Dir* Debora Thaxton Soule; *Receptionist* Margaret Russell
Open Mon - Thurs 10 AM - 6 PM, Fri & Sat Noon - 5 PM; No admis fee; Estab 1966 to house permanent art collection and hold various exhibits during the year; Halseth Gallery houses permanent art coll owned by local school dist; Circ 200+; 19th - 21st century American art - collection owned by local school district; Average Annual Attendance: 8,000
Income: Financed by grants, city appropriation, county funds & school district No 1
Library Holdings: Book Volumes; DVDs; Periodical Subscriptions; Video Tapes
Special Subjects: Drawings, Etchings & Engravings, Landscapes, Mosaics, Photography, Prints, Watercolors, Painting-American, Pottery, American Western Art, Folk Art, Woodcuts, American Indian Art, Ceramics, Collages, Woodcarvings
Collections: Over 550 pieces of original art including Norman Rockwell, Grandma Moses, Raphael Soyer among others
Publications: Calendar of events; catalogue brochure
Activities: Classes for adults & children; art workshops for children & students; dramatic progs; 3-4 concerts per yr; 1-2 gallery talks per yr, large tours by appointment; competitions; high school awards; book 2-3 traveling exhibs per yr

M   **WESTERN WYOMING COMMUNITY COLLEGE ART GALLERY,** 2500 College Dr, Rock Springs, WY 82902; PO Box 428, Rock Springs, WY 82902. Tel 307-382-1723
Call for hours
Collections: Paintings; sculpture; photographs

SUNDANCE

M   **CROOK COUNTY MUSEUM & ART GALLERY,** PO Box 63, Sundance, WY 82729-0063. Tel 307-283-3666; Fax 307-283-1192; Elec Mail ccmuseum@rangeweb.net; Internet Home Page Address: www.crookcountymuseum.com; *Dir* Rocky Courchaine
Open Mon - Fri 8 AM - 5 PM, cl holidays; No admis fee; Estab 1971 to preserve & display Crook County history, display County artists & provide a showcase for county residents' collections; Local art; Average Annual Attendance: 6,000; Mem: 60; corporate $500, bus $150, family $75, couple $40, individual $25
Income: Financed by County appropriation
Special Subjects: Archaeology, Drawings, Folk Art, Glass, Flasks & Bottles, Furniture, Painting-American, Period Rooms, Textiles, Bronzes, Manuscripts, Maps, Watercolors, American Western Art, Anthropology, Crafts, Woodcarvings, Posters, Dolls, Jewelry, Historical Material, Coins & Medals, Dioramas, Embroidery, Laces, Leather
Collections: Furniture, pictures, Western historical items
Publications: Brochure
Activities: Docent training; tours for school children; gallery talks; originates traveling exhibs; mus shop sells books

WHEATLAND

M **WYOMING TRAILS GALLERY,** 1004 16th St, Wheatland, WY 82201-2530. Tel 307-322-3300
Open Wed - Sat 9 AM - 4 PM; other times by appointment
Collections: Paintings; bronze; pottery; jewelry; folk arts

PACIFIC ISLANDS

PAGO PAGO, AMERICAN SAMOA

M **JEAN P HAYDON MUSEUM,** PO Box 1540, Pago Pago, American Samoa, PI 96799-1540. Tel 684-633-4347; Fax 684-633-2059; *Chmn Board Trustees* Lauti Simona; *Exec Dir & Cur* Leleala E Ppili
Open Mon-Fri 7:30AM-4PM; No admis fee; Estab 1971 to establish, maintain, acquire & supervise the collection, study preservation, interpretation & exhibition of fine arts objects & such relics, documents, paintings, artifacts & other historical & related materials as well as evidence that illustrate the history of the Samoan Islands & the culture of their inhabitants, particularly of American Samoa; new extension of the mus is an art gallery displaying local artists work & student arts; Average Annual Attendance: 74,000
Income: Financed by city or state appropriations and grants from NEA
Collections: Natural Sciences; Polynesian Artifacts; Samoan Village Life; US Navy History; paintings, drawings, slides, photographs, artifacts
Exhibitions: Various
Activities: Classes for adults & children; dramatic progs; lects open to pub, 3 vis lectrs per yr; artmobile; duplicate but not original objects of art lent to schools & individuals; lending collection contains books, paintings & photographs; mus & sales shop sells books, reproductions, prints, handicrafts & postcards

O **ART DEALERS ASSOCIATION OF CANADA,** 511 King St W, Ste 302 Toronto, ON M5V 1K4 Canada. Tel 416-934-1583; Fax 416-934-1584; Elec Mail info@ad-ac.ca; Internet Home Page Address: www.ad-ac.ca; *Pres* Michael Gibson; *VPres & Treas* Jeanette Langmann; *Secy* Monte Clark; *Exec Dir* Brady Schmidt; *Mgr Appraisals & Programs* Johanna Robinson
Estab 1966 for the promotion of art & artists of merit in Canada; Mem: 70, mems must have five yrs in operation plus approved reputation, financial integrity; dues vary; ann meeting in board
Income: Financed by mem & appraisal fees
Publications: Benefits of donation brochure; gen information brochure; mem directory; print brochure
Activities: Schols offered

O **ASTED INC,** 2065 rue Parthenais, bureau 387, Montreal, QC H2K 3T1 Canada. Tel 514-281-5012; Fax 584-281-8219; Elec Mail info@asted.org; Internet Home Page Address: www.asted.org; *Exec Dir* Louis Cabral; Nadia Riffi
Estab 1974 for the professional development of French-speaking information & documentation specialists nationwide; Mem: 500; varies; Oct meetings
Income: financed by government assistance
Exhibitions: Ann exhibits
Publications: Dewey Decimal Classification, 21st French edition; Documentation et Bibliotheques, 4 times per yr
Activities: Schols offered; originate traveling exhibs

O **CANADIAN ART FOUNDATION,** 215 Spadina Ave, Ste 320 Toronto, ON M5T 2C7 Canada. Tel 416-368-8854; Fax 416-368-6135; Elec Mail info@canadianart.ca; Internet Home Page Address: www.canadianart.ca; *Exec Dir & Interim Publr* Ann Webb; *Art Dir* Barbara Solowan; *Mgr Dir* Bryne McLaughlin; *Assoc Ed* Claire Crighton; *Asst Ed* David Balzer; *Mktg & Communs* Elaine Gaito; *Advertising Asst* Elena Potter; *Assoc Ed* Leah Sandals; *Office Mgr* Liana Schmidt; *Event Mgr* Megan Kalaman; *Admin Asst* Rachael Watson; *Ed* Richard Rhodes
Open Mon - Fri 9 AM - 5 PM; Estab 1984 as a charitable organization that fosters and supports the visual arts in Canada; Circ 22,000
Publications: Canadian Art, quarterly
Activities: Educ prog; school hop; lects open to pub 2-3 per yr, gallery talks, tours, sponsoring competitions; awards, writing prize

O **CANADIAN CONFERENCE OF THE ARTS,** 406-130 Slater St, Ottawa, ON K1P 6E2 Canada. Tel 613-238-3561; Fax 613-238-4849; Elec Mail info@ccarts.ca; Internet Home Page Address: www.ccarts.ca; *National Dir* Alain Pineau; *Admin Asst* Louise Rochon; *Assoc Dir & Sr Policy Advisor* Anne-Marie Des Roches; *Admin Dir* Manon Charron; *Communs & Research Officer* Kimberly Wilson; *Mem & Develop Coordr* Judith Haney; *Mem & Develop Coordr* Alessia Bongiovanni
Open 9 AM - 5 PM; No admis fee; Estab 1945 as a national nonprofit assoc to strengthen pub & pvt support to the arts & enhance the awareness of the role & value of the arts; Mem: 850; dues affiliate mem $2,205; patron $200; individual mem $50; friend $20; ann meeting June
Income: Financed by mem, grants & contracts
Publications: Blizzart, quarterly; Handbook Series: Directory of the Arts; Who Teaches What; policy papers & reports
Activities: Awards-Diplome d'Honneur to persons who have contributed outstanding service to the arts in Canada; Financial Post Awards: in collaboration with The Council for Business & the Arts in Canada, encourages the corporate sector's involvement with the visual & performing arts in Canada & recognizes those corporations whose involvement is already at a high & productive level; Rogers Communications Inc Media Award; Keith Kelly Award for Cultural Leadership; Diplîe d'honneur; Rogers Communications Inc Media Award for Coverage

O **CANADIAN MUSEUMS ASSOCIATION,** Association des Musees Canadiens, 280 Metcalfe St, Ste 400, Ottawa, ON K2P 1R7 Canada. Tel 613-567-0099; Fax 613-233-5438; Elec Mail info@museums.ca; Internet Home Page Address: www.museums.ca; *Exec Dir* John G McAvity; *Finance Dir* Sue Lamothe; *Mgr, Mem Develop* Eveline Callupe; *Pres* William (Bill) Greenlaw; *Pub Affairs Dir* Audrey Vernette; *Mgr Communs* Julie Cormier Doiron
Estab 1947 to advance pub mus services in Canada, to promote the welfare & better admin of museums & to foster a continuing improvement in the qualifications & practices of mus professions; Mem: 2000; dues voting individual $85, senior $50; non-voting affiliate & foreign $100, corporate $250; ann meeting in Apr
Income: Financed by mem & government grants
Publications: Muse, bimonthly
Activities: Educ prog; professional develop activities; CMA Awards; bursary program; travel grants

O **CANADIAN SOCIETY FOR EDUCATION THROUGH ART,** National Office-University of Victoria, Faculty of Education, Dept of Curriculum & Education, PO Box 3010 STN CSC Victoria, BC V8W 3N4 Canada. Tel 250-721-7896; Fax 250-721-7598; Elec Mail office.csea@gmail.com; Internet Home Page Address: www.csea-scea.ca; *Secy Gen* Mary-Jane Emme
Estab 1955; voluntary assn founded in Quebec City. Mems dedicated to the advancement of art educ, the publication of current thinking & action in art educ & the promotion of higher standards in the teaching of art; Average Annual Attendance: 400; Mem: 700; dues professional $65 (CN); student/retired $30 (CN)
Income: Financed by mem
Collections: Historical Canadian Art; Children's Art
Publications: Canadian Review of Art Education, 1-2 times per ye; Journal, 1-2 times per yr; newsletter, quarterly; spec publs
Activities: Workshops; research; lect open to public; gallery talks; tours; awards; scholarships offered

O **CANADIAN SOCIETY OF PAINTERS IN WATERCOLOUR,** 80 Birmingham St., Unit B3, Toronto, ON M8V 3W6 Canada. Tel 416-533-5100; Elec Mail info@cspwc.com; Internet Home Page Address: www.cspwc.com; *Pres* William Rogers; *Past Pres* Katherine McOstrichZarull; *CSPWC Adminr* Anita Cotter
Admis assoc mem $35 ann; Estab 1925 to promote watercolour painting in Canada; AIRD Gallery, MacDonald Block, Queen's Park - shared on a rotating basis with five other societies; monthly exhibs; Mem: 260 & 175 assoc; dues $125; ann meeting in May. Mem qualifications: digital images sent to national mem comt (details listed on website)
Income: financed by mems dues, assoc, commissions on sale of work & book sales
Library Holdings: Clipping Files; Exhibition Catalogs; Memorabilia; Original Art Works; Photographs; Slides
Collections: Dipl Collection at Art Gallery of Peel, Brampton, Ontario; Portfolio of 75 works in collection of Her Majesty the Queen at Windsor Castle
Exhibitions: Annual Open Juried Exhibition; Members' Exhibitions; International Exchanges; International Waters with AWS & RWS
Publications: Aquarelle; Quarterly newsletter (quarterly)
Activities: Classes for adults; lect open to mems; competitions with awards; awards at ann open juried exhib, Open Water; originates traveling exhibs across Canada to galleries; internationally to fellow arts organizations; national watercolor weekend of demonstrations & discussions

O **INTERNATIONAL ASSOCIATION OF ART CRITICS,** AICA Canada, Inc, 172 Roselawn Ave, Toronto, ON M4R 1E6 Canada. Tel 416-925-5564; Fax 416-925-2972; Elec Mail kcarpent@yorku.ca; Internet Home Page Address: www.aica-int.org; *Pres (Toronto)* Prof Ken Carpenter; *VPres (Toronto)* Prof Gerald Needham; *Treas & Mem (Toronto)* Hedwidge Asselin; *Secy (Toronto)* Sarah Parsons
Estab 1970; Mem: 50; mems must be practicing published activities in accepted art press
Income: Financed by mem fees
Activities: Annual International Conference of Art Critics

O **ORGANIZATION OF SASKATCHEWAN ARTS COUNCILS (OSAC),** 1102 Eighth Ave, Regina, SK S4R 1C9 Canada. Tel 306-586-1250; Fax 306-586-1550; Elec Mail info@osac.sk.ca; Internet Home Page Address: www.osac.sk.ca; *Exec Dir* Kevin Korchinski; *Visual & Media Arts Coordr* Rob Bos; *Visual & Media Arts Asst* Zoe Schneider; *Operations* Catherine Tomczak; *Performing Arts Coordr* Marianne Woods; *Performing Arts Coordr* Carol Cairns
Open Mon - Fri 8:30 AM - 5 PM; Estab 1969 to tour exhibs of Saskatchewan artists work & tour performers from across Canada, US & of international stature; Organization that enables community arts councils & schools to tour & hold live musical & theatre performances, visual art exhibs, work shops & special events across Saskatchewan; Mem: 50 Arts Councils, 100 School Center members, ann conference in Oct
Library Holdings: Audio Tapes; Book Volumes 175; CD-ROMs; Cassettes; Clipping Files; Compact Disks; DVDs; Exhibition Catalogs; Kodachrome Transparencies; Manuscripts; Pamphlets; Periodical Subscriptions 10; Records; Reproductions; Slides; Video Tapes
Activities: Classes for adults & children; dramatic progs; docent training; lects open to pub; exten dept serves lending coll

O **QUICKDRAW ANIMATION SOCIETY,** 351 11th Ave SW, Ste 201, Calgary, AB T2R 0C7 Canada. Tel 403-261-5767; Fax 403-261-5644; Elec Mail qas@shaw.ca; Internet Home Page Address: qas.awn.com; *Exec Dir* Sharon Adams; *Film Production Coordr, Instr (Tour de Film)* Richard Reeves; *Digital Production Coordr, Instr* Alan Ferguson; *Programming & Commun Coordr* Keith Murray; *Librn, Animation Instr (Quick Kids)* Jean-Francois Cote; *Career & Life Counselor (YA! Project)* Ramin Eshraghi-Yazdi; *Production Technician (YA! Project)* Anne Koizumi; *Animation Instr (YA! Project)* Chris Markowsky
Open Tues - Sat 10 AM - 5 PM; Estab 1984 to promote study of animation &

provide equipment for the production of independent animated film; Mem: 150; dues subscription $15, assoc $25, Quick Kid $30, producing $50; ann meeting in Apr
Income: $150,000 from Federal, Provincial, municipal funding, mem fees, courses & workshop fees
Library Holdings: Book Volumes; Video Tapes
Exhibitions: Animated film festivals
Publications: Quickdraw Quarterly
Activities: Classes for adults; lects open to pub; Artist in Residence award; schols; lending coll contains books, videotapes, equipment for use in animated film production

O **ROYAL ARCHITECTURAL INSTITUTE OF CANADA,** 330-55 rue Murray St, Ottawa, ON K1N 5M3 Canada. Tel 613-241-3600; Fax 613-241-5750; Elec Mail info@raic.org; Internet Home Page Address: www.raic.org; *Exec Dir* Jon F Hobbs; *Professional Develop & Exec Svcs Coordr/Privacy Officer* Chantal Bedard; *Awards & Honors Mgr/College of Fellows, Foundation Coordr* Chantal Charbonneau; *Adminr Asst/Receptionist/Document Orders* Nicole Pelletier; *Commun & Mem* Sylvie Powell; *Commun & Outreach* Denise MacDonald; *Graphic/Web Designer/Coordr* Etienne Sicotte; *Mem Coordr* Chantal Fredette; *Financial Officer* Jonathan Ouellette
Open daily 8:30 AM - 5 PM, summer hours Fri 8:30 AM-12:30 PM; Estab 1908 to promote a knowledge & appreciation of architecture & of the architectural profession in Canada & to represent the interests of Canadian architects; Mem: 3800; mem open to architectural grads; dues $220
Publications: RAIC Directory, annually
Activities: Lect open to pub; awards given; schols offered
L **Library,** 55 Murray St, Ottawa, ON K1N 5M3 Canada. Tel 613-241-3600; Elec Mail info@raic.org; Internet Home Page Address: www.raic.org; *Exec Asst* Judy Scott
Open daily 8:30 AM - 5 PM, summer hours Fri 8:30 AM - 12:30 PM; Estab for archival info only; Circ Non-circulating
Library Holdings: Book Volumes 200
Special Subjects: Architecture

O **ROYAL CANADIAN ACADEMY OF ARTS,** 401 Richmond St W, Ste 375, Toronto, ON M5V 3A8 Canada. Tel 416-408-2718; Fax 416-408-2286; Elec Mail rcaarts@interlog.com; Internet Home Page Address: www.rca-arc.ca; *Pres* Ann McCall; *VPres* Barbara Vogel; *Treas* Joseph Richard Veilleux; *Office Admin* Raenel Leppky
Estab 1880 to better the visual arts field in Canada through exhibs, assistance to young artists & to museums; Mem: 700; honor soc; mem open to visual artists who demonstrated excellence in their own medium; dues $200; AGA ann meeting in May
Income: Nonprofit assoc financed by mem & donations
Exhibitions: Special exhibs of the History of the Royal Canadian Academy 1880-1980; national, multi-disciplined, juried exhib
Publications: Passionate Spirits: A History of the Royal Canadian Academy of Arts 1880-1980; Self Portrait Project
Activities: Originate traveling exhibs

O **SASKATCHEWAN ARTS BOARD,** 1355 Broad St, Regina, SK S4R 7V1 Canada. Tel 306-787-4056; Fax 306-787-4199; Elec Mail info@artsboard.sk.ca; Internet Home Page Address: www.artsboard.sk.ca; *Exec Dir* Jeremy Morgan; *Dir Operations* Peter Sametz; *Communs Strategist* Sabrina Cataldo; *Exec Asst* Sandi Desjatlais
Open 8 AM - 4:30 PM; Estab 1948, the Arts Board is an arms-length agency of govt with a mandate to promote, support & facilitate public understanding, access

to and participation in the arts, and to support the development of the Saskatchewan arts community and individual artists
Income: Financed by ann provincial government grant
Collections: Permanent Collection containing over 2500 works by Saskatchewan artists & artisans only, dating from 1950 to present
Exhibitions: Clearing a Path: An Exhibition of Traditional Indigenous Art
Publications: Ann Report; website; Business Development Plan; Saskatchewan...Our Place poster kit & teacher's guide
Activities: Grants are provided to individual artists, organizations, galleries and in support of project-based activity in Saskatchewan. The Arts Board is a critical advocacy organization for arts in the Saskatchewan; provides awards for outstanding achievement in the arts

O **SCULPTOR'S SOCIETY OF CANADA,** Canadian Sculpture Centre, 500 Church St, Toronto, ON M4Y 2C8 Canada. Tel 416-533-0126; Tel 647-435-5858; Elec Mail gallery@cansculpt.org; Internet Home Page Address: www.cansculpt.org; *Pres & Gallery Co Dir* Dodi Michelle Young; *VPres & Gallery Co Dir* Richard McNeill; *Treas* J Young; *Secy* Bastien Martel; *Pres Emeritus & Gallery Co Dir* Judi Michelle Young
Open Tues - Fri noon - 6 PM, Sat 11 AM - 4 PM, cl holiday weekends; No admis fee; Estab 1928 to promote the art of sculpture, to present exhibs (some to travel internationally), to educate the pub about sculpture; 1000 sq ft exhib space; Average Annual Attendance: 2,500; Mem: 150; to qualify for mem, sculptors must submit CD of work for jury approval; dues $150; 2 general meetings per yr, exec comt meetings, 12 per yr
Income: Financed by mem & sales commission
Purchases: Ann selection comt (deadline Sep 15)
Library Holdings: CD-ROMs; Exhibition Catalogs; Pamphlets; Periodical Subscriptions
Exhibitions: Annual Graduating Students Juried Exhibition; Canadian National Exhibition; McMichael Canadian Collection; Member Show; Sculptures for the Eighties; 70th Anniversary Exhibition; Annual Emerging Artist Exhibition; Art of Collecting Exhibition
Publications: Exhibition catalogues
Activities: Workshops; lects open to pub; gallery talks; tours; 4-6 vis lectrs per yr; competitions with awards of student exhibs, A&M Green FDN Award, Artcast Inc Award, & MST Bronze LTD Award; originate traveling exhibs to international cultural centres, embassy galleries; sculpture gallery sells books & original art

O **SOCIETY OF CANADIAN ARTISTS,** Box 54029, Lawrence Plaza PO, 500 Lawrence Ave W Toronto, ON M6A 3B7 Canada. Elec Mail info@societyofcanadianartists.com; Internet Home Page Address: www.societyofcanadianartists.com; *VPres Mem* Ed Yaghdjian; *VPres Exhibs* Andrew Sookrah; *VPres Finance* Dorothy Chisholm; *VPres Commun* Gilbert Strudwick
Estab in 1957 as the Soc of Cooperative Artists & operated the first cooperative gallery in Toronto. In 1967 the name was changed to the Soc of Canadian Artists, registered as a nonprofit organization in 2007; Mem: 270, elected mem by jury, assoc mem open to artists throughout Canada
Income: Financed by mem & commissions on sale
Exhibitions: 2 shows per yr, open juried & mem only
Publications: Quarterly newsletter, exhib catalogues
Activities: Sponsorship of art conferences & workshops; promotion of Canadian artists

Canadian Museums, Libraries & Associations

ALBERTA

BANFF

M BANFF CENTRE, Walter Phillips Gallery, 107 Tunel Mountain Dr, Banff, AB T1L 1H5 Canada; PO Box 1020, Station 14 Banff, AB T1L 1H5 Canada. Tel 403-762-6281; Fax 403-762-6659; Elec Mail walter_phillipsgallery@banffcentre.ca; Internet Home Page Address: www.banffcentre.ca/wpg; *Preparator* Mimmo Maiolo; *Cur* Maomi Potter; *Cur Asst* Stephanie Kolla; *Prog Asst* Shauna Thompson; *Pres & CEO* Mary Hoftstetter
Open Wed - Sun 12:30 PM - 5 PM, Thurs 12:30 PM - 9 PM; No admis fee; Estab 1977 to serve the community & artists in the visual arts prog at The Banff Centre, School of Fine Arts. Contemporary exhibits are presented; Gallery is 15.24 x 21.34 m with 325.5 sq m of running space; Average Annual Attendance: 20,000
Income: Financed by provincial & pub funding
Collections: Walter J Phillips Collection
Publications: Exhib catalogs
Activities: Lect open to pub; concerts; gallery talks; tours; original objects of art lent to other galleries & museums; book traveling exhibs 1 per yr; originate traveling exhibs to Canadian & international galleries; mus shop sells books & original art

L Paul D Fleck Library & Archives, PO Box 1020, Sta 43, Banff, AB T0L 0C0 Canada. Tel 403-762-6265; Fax 403-762-6266; Elec Mail library@banffcentre.ca; *Music Librn* Kyla Jemison
Open Mon - Fri 9 AM - 5 PM; For reference only
Library Holdings: Book Volumes 32,000; CD-ROMs; Cassettes; Compact Disks; DVDs; Exhibition Catalogs; Fiche; Motion Pictures; Periodical Subscriptions 125; Records 12,000; Slides 27,000; Video Tapes 1100
Special Subjects: Intermedia, Film, Photography, Painting-American, Conceptual Art, Art Education, Primitive art, Furniture, Costume Design & Constr, Aesthetics, Pottery, Painting-Canadian, Architecture

M PETER & CATHARINE WHYTE FOUNDATION, Whyte Museum of the Canadian Rockies, PO Box 160, 111 Bear St Banff, AB T1L 1A3 Canada. Tel 403-762-2291; Fax 403-762-8919; Elec Mail info@whyte.org; Internet Home Page Address: www.whyte.org; *Exec Dir & Chief Cur* Michale Lang; *Pres* Tristan White Jones; *Mktg & Communs* Pamela Challoner; *Chief Financial & Operating Officer* Graeme Nunn
Open Mon - Sun 10 AM - 5 PM, cl Christmas & New Year's Day; Admis family $15, adults $6, students & seniors $3.50, children 5 & under free; Acquires, preserves, interprets & makes accessible the history & culture of the Rocky Mountains of Canada inspiring & cultivating the exchange of knowledge & ideas through our collections, programs & exhibitions; Gallery consists of the Main Gallery, Rummel Room & Swiss Guides Room; Average Annual Attendance: 50,000; Mem: 600; dues $30
Income: Financed by endowment, federal & provincial special activities grants, pvt funding, admis & sales
Special Subjects: Historical Material, Prints, Textiles, Woodcuts, Manuscripts, Maps, Photography, Sculpture, Watercolors, Painting-Canadian
Collections: Historical & contemporary art by artists of the Canadian Rockies; Cultural history colls of Canadian Rockies
Exhibitions: Visit www.whyte.org for upcoming exhibs
Publications: The Cairn, biannually; Calendar of Events
Activities: Classes for adults & children; lects open to pub, 20 vis lectrs per yr; concerts; gallery talks; tours; films; individual paintings & original objects of art lent to cert mus & art galleries; book traveling exhibs; originate traveling exhibs to other cert mus & art galleries; mus shop sells books, original art, reproductions & prints

CALGARY

M ALBERTA COLLEGE OF ART & DESIGN, Illingworth Kerr Gallery, 1407 14th Ave NW, Calgary, AB T2N 4R3 Canada. Tel 403-284-7632; Fax 403-289-6682; Elec Mail ron.moppett@acad.ab.ca; Internet Home Page Address: www.acad.ab.ca; *Dir & Cur* Ron Moppett; *Asst Cur* Richard Gordon; *Technician* Valerie Dowhaniuk
Open Tues - Sat 10 AM - 6 PM; No admis fee; Estab 1958 as an acad didactic function plus general visual art exhib service to pub; Two galleries: 425 sq meters of floor space; 125 meters running wall space; full atmospheric & security controls; Average Annual Attendance: 20,000
Library Holdings: Book Volumes 35,645; Clipping Files; DVDs 1,052; Other Holdings Digital Images 40,000
Special Subjects: Ceramics, Graphics, Photography, Sculpture, Jewelry
Collections: Permanent collection of ceramics, graphics, paintings, photography, student honors work

Exhibitions: Contemporary art in all media by regional, national & international artists
Publications: Exhib catalogs; posters
Activities: Lects open to pub, 20 vis lectrs per yr; gallery talks; individual paintings & objects of art lent to other galleries; lending coll contains original art works; book traveling exhibs 3-4 per yr

L Luke Lindoe Library, 1407 14th Ave NW, Calgary, AB T2N 4R3 Canada. Tel 403-284-7631; Fax 403-289-6682; Elec Mail christine.sammon@acad.ca; Internet Home Page Address: www.acad.ab.ca; *Library Dir* Christine E Sammon; *Librn* Adrienne Connelly
Open Mon - Thurs 8:30 AM - 8 PM, Fri 8:30 AM - 4:30 PM, Sat 11 AM - 5 PM; Estab 1926; Circ 27,836; Average Annual Attendance: 57,646; Mem: $25 ann fee for community borrowers
Purchases: $85,000
Library Holdings: Book Volumes 35,645; Clipping Files; DVDs 1,052; Exhibition Catalogs; Other Holdings Digital Images: 40,000; Periodical Subscriptions 111
Special Subjects: Art History, Illustration, Photography, Commercial Art, Drawings, Etchings & Engravings, Painting-American, Advertising Design, Art Education, Glass, Aesthetics, Metalwork, Goldsmithing, Antiquities-Assyrian, Architecture

A ALBERTA SOCIETY OF ARTISTS, #305-1235 26th Ave SE, Calgary, AB T2G 1R7 Canada. Tel 403-265-0012; Fax 403-263-4610; Elec Mail coordinator@albertasocietyofartists.com; Internet Home Page Address: www.artists-society.ab.ca; *Pres* Barbara J West; *Treas* Donna Jo Massie; *Past Pres* Joanna Moore; *Provincial Exhibs Chmn* Mali Docktor; *Advocacy Chmn* Greg Pyra; *Mem Chmn* Ilse Anysas-Salkauskas; *Councilor at Large* Randall Talbot; *Councilor at Large* Joel Sinclair; *Edmonton Branch Chmn* Donna Miller; *Calgary Branch Chmn* Deborah Catton; *Lethbridge Branch Chmn* Sherry Chanin
Estab 1926 as an assn of professional artists designed to foster and promote the development of visual and plastic fine arts primarily within the province; Mem: Approx 250; dues $60 each yr; AGM: Apr. New members are juried in annually based on slides or digital images of artwork
Exhibitions: Exhib organized annually by provincial & the Calgary & Edmonton branch
Publications: Highlights (newsletter), bimonthly
Activities: Through exhib, educ & commun, the ASA strives to increase pub awareness & appreciation of the visual arts in Alberta; classes for adults; lects open to pub 8 vis lectrs per yr; scholarships; originates traveling exhibs to art galleries in Alberta & other regions of Canada

M ART GALLERY OF CALGARY, 117 8th Ave SW, Calgary, AB T2B 1B4 Canada. Tel 403-770-1350; Fax 403-264-8077; Elec Mail info@artgallerycalgary.org; Internet Home Page Address: www.artgallerycalgary.org; *Pres & CEO* Valerie Cooper; *Sr Cur* Marianne Elder; *Cur* Lori Ellis; *Cur* Sarah Songhurst-Thonet; *Mktg & Commun* Heidi Drewett; *Admin* Katie Fisher
Open Tues - Sat 10 AM - 5 PM, first Thurs 10 AM - 9 PM; Admis adults $5, student, youth & senior $2.50, under 12 free; Estab 1978 to exhibit the works of emerging & estab western Canadian artists; Top floor of the restored Memorial Park Library (old Carnegie Library); Average Annual Attendance: 90,000; Mem: 500; dues family $30, individual $20, students & srs $15; ann meeting in Apr
Income: $550,000 (financed by mem, city & provincial appropriation, grants, pvt donations & corporate funds)
Special Subjects: Architecture, Drawings, Graphics, Ceramics, Folk Art, Etchings & Engravings, Landscapes, Collages, Furniture, Glass, Jewelry, Metalwork, Carpets & Rugs, Juvenile Art, Gold
Publications: Quarterly exhibit catalogues; quarterly newsletter; semiannual exhibition brochures
Activities: Classes for adults & children; professional develop; lects open to pub, 10 vis lectrs per yr; gallery talks; tours; family days; art appreciation club; exten dept serves city of Calgary; book traveling exhibs 6 per yr; originate traveling exhibs to Southern Alberta; sales shop sells books, t-shirts & cards

M CALGARY CONTEMPORARY ARTS SOCIETY, Triangle Gallery of Visual Arts, c/o The Calgary Contemporary Arts Society, 104, 800 Macleod Trail Se Calgary, AB T2G 2M3 Canada. Tel 403-262-1737; Fax 403-262-1764; Elec Mail info@trianglegallery.com; Internet Home Page Address: www.trianglegallery.com; *Dir & Cur* Jacek Malec; *Gallery Admin* Rhonda Barber
Open Tues - Fri 11 AM - 5 PM, Sat 12 PM - 4 PM; Admis adults $2, seniors & students $1, family $5, mem & Thurs free; Estab 1988 to exhibit contemporary art in all media & provide exten progs for pub; 2,571 sq ft, 264 running feet of wall space, 60 ft flexible wall system; Average Annual Attendance: 10,000; Mem: 500; dues $25; ann meeting in Nov
Income: $150,000 (financed by mem, city & state appropriation, corporate & pvt donations, fundraising events)
Collections: Artist circle, donated works

Exhibitions: Rotate 10-12 exhibits per yr
Publications: Update, monthly newsletter; exhibition brochures & catalogs
Activities: Docent training; workshops; lects open to pub, 20-30 vis lectrs per yr; performances; exten servs provides paintings & art rentals; book traveling exhibs 3-6 times per yr

L CALGARY PUBLIC LIBRARY, Arts & Recreation Dept, 616 Macleod Trail SE, Calgary, AB T2G 2M2 Canada. Tel 403-260-2600; Fax 403-262-5929; Elec Mail arts&rec@calgarypubliclibrary.com; Internet Home Page Address: www.calgarypubliclibrary.com
Open Mon - Thurs 10 AM - 9 PM, Fri & Sat 10 AM - 5 PM, Sun Noon - 5 PM; No admis fee; Estab to provide information & recreational materials for the gen pub
Purchases: $70,000 Canadian
Library Holdings: Book Volumes 85,000; Clipping Files; Compact Disks; DVDs; Exhibition Catalogs; Periodical Subscriptions 250; Records; Video Tapes
Special Subjects: Art History, Film, Photography, Graphic Arts, Crafts, Theatre Arts, American Western Art, Fashion Arts, Video, American Indian Art, Painting-Canadian, Architecture
Collections: Clipping files on local artists
Exhibitions: Rotating exhibit cases

M GLENBOW MUSEUM, 130 Ninth Ave SE, Calgary, AB T2G 0P3 Canada. Tel 403-268-4100; Fax 403-265-9769; Elec Mail info@glenbow.org; Internet Home Page Address: www.glenbow.org; *Pres & CEO* Kirstin Evenden; *VPres Develop* Ken Lima-Coelho; *Mgr Colls* Daryl Betania; *Registrar* Lia Melemenis; *Traveling Exhibs* Rebecca Derry; *Dir Indigenous Studies* Dr Gerald Conaty; *VPres Access Colls & Exhibs* Melanie Kjorlien; *VPres Central Servs* Marion Shill; *Dir Library & Archives* Doug Cass
Open Mon - Sat 9 AM - 5 PM, Sun noon - 5 PM; Admis family $28, adults $14, senior $10, student & youth $9, under 6 free; Estab 1966 for art, books, documents, Indian & pioneer artifacts that lead to the preservation & better understanding of the history of western Canada; Circ 90; Mus has three exhib floors; 93,000 sq ft of exhib space; Average Annual Attendance: 200,000; Mem: 5000; dues family $90, $160/2 yrs, individual $55, $100/2 yrs, student $35, $60/2 yrs
Income: $10,300 (financed by endowment, provincial & federal appropriation, self-generated revenue)
Purchases: $100,000
Special Subjects: Historical Material
Collections: Art: Representative colls of Canadian historical & contemporary art, Indian & Inuit, & works of art on paper; Ethnology: Large coll of material relating to Plains Indians; representative holdings from Africa, Australia, Oceania, Central & South America, Inuit & Northwest Coast; Library & Archives: Western Canadian historical books, manuscripts & photographs; Military history; Cultural History
Publications: Chautauqua in Canada; Max Ernst; Four Modern Masters; exhib catalogs
Activities: Classes for adults & children; dramatic progs; docent training; lect open to pub; gallery talks; tours; exten dept; individual paintings & original objects of art lent to pub museums & galleries; lending coll contains 15,000 works on paper, 5000 paintings, sculpture & 5000 items of decorative art; book traveling exhibs 25 per yr; originate traveling exhibs; mus shop sells books, magazines, reproductions & prints
L Library, 130 Ninth Ave SE, Calgary, AB T2G 0P3 Canada. Tel 403-268-4197; Fax 403-232-6569; Elec Mail glenbow@glenbow.org; Elec Mail dcass@glenbow.org; Elec Mail lmoir@glenbow.org; Internet Home Page Address: www.glenbow.org; *Librn* Lindsay Moir; *Archivist* Jim Bowman
Open Tues - Fri 10 AM - 5 PM; Circ Non-circulating; Open for reference
Income: Financed by endowment & government of Alberta
Library Holdings: Auction Catalogs; Book Volumes 90,000; CD-ROMs; Cards; Clipping Files; Exhibition Catalogs; Fiche; Manuscripts; Maps; Pamphlets; Periodical Subscriptions 100; Photographs; Reels
Special Subjects: Illustration, Manuscripts, Maps, Painting-British, Prints, Printmaking, Textiles, Painting-Canadian
Collections: Western Canadian Art; Historic Canadian Art

C PETRO-CANADA, Corporate Art Programme, 1504 8th Ave. S.E., Calgary, AB T2G 0N3 Canada. Tel 403-262-7399; Fax 403-296-4990; *Art Cur* Pauline Lindland
Estab 1984 for encouragement of Canadian art
Income: $120,000 (financed by corporation)
Collections: 1600 2-D works in all media by contemporary Canadian artists

QUICKDRAW ANIMATION SOCIETY
For further information, see National and Regional Organizations

C SHELL CANADA LTD, 400 Fourth Ave SW, PO Box 100, Sta M Calgary, AB T2P 2H5 Canada. Tel 403-691-3111; Fax 403-691-4350; *Coordr Coll* Dianne Engel
Collections: Works of contemporary Canadian artists with media concentrations in painting, sculpture, graphics, mixed media & works on paper

A TRUCK CONTEMPORARY ART IN CALGARY, The Grain Exchange (Lower Level), 815 1st St SW Calgary, AB T2P 1N3 Canada. Tel 403-261-7702; Fax 403-264-7737; Elec Mail info@truck.ca; Internet Home Page Address: www.truck.ca
No admis fee

M UNIVERSITY OF CALGARY, Nickle Galleries, 2500 University Dr NW, Calgary, AB T2N 1N4 Canada. Tel 403-220-7234; Fax 403-282-3075; Elec Mail nickle@ucalgary.ca; Internet Home Page Address: www.ucalgary.ca/~nickle; *Cur Decorative Arts* Michele Hardy; *Cur Art* Christine Sowiak; *Registrar* Lisa Tillotson; *Cur Numismatics* Geraldine Chimirri-Russell; *Dir* John Wright
Open Mon - Fri 10 AM - 5 PM; No admis fee; Estab 1970, an Alberta pioneer, Samuel C Nickle, gave the University a gift of one million dollars & the mus was opened in 1979. His son, Carl O Nickle, presented the University with an immensely valuable coll of some 10,000 ancient coins, covering over 2500 yrs of human history which is housed in the Numismatics dept of the mus; Circ yes; Mus houses the permanent collection of the University; exhibs of art, numismatics and textiles are presented on a temporary basis in 3 galleries.; Average Annual Attendance: 15,000; Mem: 250; dues $10 - $40
Income: Financed by state appropriation through the University, donations, earned income & grants
Purchases: $100,000
Library Holdings: Book Volumes 200
Special Subjects: Ceramics, Drawings, Photography, Prints, Sculpture, Watercolors, Textiles, Painting-Canadian, Carpets & Rugs, Coins & Medals
Collections: Coins & bills covering 2500 years of Human History; Jean & Marie Erikson Rug & Textile Collection; Modern Contemporary Western Canadian Art
Exhibitions: Local, national & international exhibs are presented on a continuous basis
Publications: Exhib catalogs
Activities: Liaise with faculties at universities; lects open to pub, 10-20 vis lectrs per yr; gallery talks; tours; individual paintings & original objects of art lent to other museums & art galleries; book traveling exhibs 2 per yr; originate traveling exhibs to Canadian mus; mus shop sells books, jewelry & other gift items
L Faculty of Environmental Design, 2500 University Dr, PFA 2182 Calgary, AB T2N 1N4 Canada. Tel 403-220-6601; Fax 403-284-4399; Elec Mail johnstoa@ucalgary.ca
Open Mon - Fri 9:30 AM - 4:30 PM; No admis fee; Estab 1973 as a resource facility for students & faculty in 5 prog areas: architecture, urban planning, industrial design, environmental science & environmental design; Small gallery for display of student works & traveling exhibs; workshop; photo lab facilities
Library Holdings: Audio Tapes; Book Volumes 500; Cassettes; Manuscripts; Memorabilia; Other Holdings Drawings; Models; Periodical Subscriptions 30; Slides; Video Tapes
Special Subjects: Industrial Design, Interior Design, Architecture

CZAR

M SHORNCLIFFE PARK IMPROVEMENT ASSOC, Prairie Panorama Museum, PO Box 60, Czar, AB T0B 0Z0 Canada. Tel 780-857-2435; *Cur* Helena Lawrason
Open Sun 2 - 6 PM, other days by appointment; No admis fee; Estab 1963 for the enjoyment of the pub; Average Annual Attendance: 580
Income: Finances by government grant & donations
Collections: Indian artifacts, clothing, tools, dolls, books; Salt & Pepper Coll; Two 1926 coffeemakers, homemade snowshoes (1920), Cajun accordion
Activities: Classes for children

EDMONTON

A ALBERTA CRAFT COUNCIL, 10186 106th St, Edmonton, AB T5J 1H4 Canada. Tel 780-488-6611; Fax 780-488-8855; Elec Mail acc@albertacraft.ab.ca; Internet Home Page Address: www.albertacraft.ab.ca; *Exec Dir* Tom McFall; *Mem Svcs* Joanne Hamel; *Mgr Admin* Nancy St Hilaire
Open Mon - Sat 9 AM - 5 PM; No admis fee; Estab 1980 to promote craft; Gallery exhibits 12 shows per yr of craft in these 5 media: clay, glass, wood, metal & fiber; Mem: Dues vary
Income: Financed by mem
Exhibitions: 12 shows per yr
Publications: Alberta Craft Magazine, 4 per year
Activities: Annual Alberta Craft Council Awards; book traveling exhibs 1 per yr; originate traveling exhibs 1 every 4 yrs circulating nationally & internationally; sales shop sells crafts

A ALBERTA FOUNDATION FOR THE ARTS, 10708 105 Ave, Edmonton, AB T5H 0A1 Canada. Tel 780-427-9968; Fax 780-422-9132; Internet Home Page Address: www.affta.ab.ca; *Chmn* John C Osler; *Arts Prog Coordr* Ross Bradley; *Exec Dir* Jeffrey Anderson
Open Mon - Fri 8:15 AM - 4:30 PM; No admis fee; Estab 1972 to collect & to exhibit art works produced by Alberta artists; to provide financial assistance to Alberta pub, institutional & commercial art galleries, art groups & organizations for progs & special projects; to assist other galleries in Edmonton
Income: Financed by Alberta Lotteries
Collections: Alberta Foundation for the Arts Collection
Exhibitions: Exhibits are provided through a consortium of Alberta pub galleries. The progs vary from yr to yr & from region to region; Spaces & Places; Little by Little
Publications: Ann Report; exhib catalogs
Activities: Acquisition of art works by Alberta artists; exhib prog in and outside Canada; Jon Whyte Memorial Prize, Tommy Banks Award; scholarships & fels offered; individual paintings & original objects of art lent to pub government buildings; book traveling exhibs; sales shop sells books

M ART GALLERY OF ALBERTA, 2 Sir Winston Churchill Sq, Edmonton, AB T5J 2C1 Canada. Tel 780-422-6223; Fax 780-426-3105; Elec Mail info@youraga.ca; Internet Home Page Address: www.youraga.ca; *Exec Dir & Chief Cur* Catherine Crowston
Open Tues, Thurs, Fri, Sat & Sun 11AM - 5PM, Wed 11AM - 9PM, cl Mon; Admis adults $12.50, seniors (65+) & students $8.50, children 6 & under free; Estab 1924 to collect & exhibit paintings, sculptures, photographs & other works of visual art & to teach art appreciation; Gallery covers 80,000 sq ft; exhibition area 30,000 sq ft; Average Annual Attendance: 100,000 (est)
Special Subjects: Painting-American, Photography, Sculpture, Watercolors, Religious Art, Woodcuts, Painting-European, Portraits, Painting-Canadian
Collections: Contemporary Canadian art; contemporary & historical photography; contemporary international art; historical Canadian art; historical European & American art
Exhibitions: 29 in-house exhibitions & 23 extension shows
Publications: Take part magazine, 3 times per yr; exhibition catalogues

Activities: Classes for adults & children; lects open to pub; lects for mems only; gallery talks & tours; 8 vis lectrs per yr; concerts; book traveling exhibs; originate traveling exhibs; mus shop; junior mus called The Children's Gallery

A LATITUDE 53 CONTEMPORARY VISUAL CULTURE, (Latitude 53 Society of Artists) 10248 106th St, Edmonton, AB T5J 1H5 Canada. Tel 780-423-5353; Fax 780-424-9117; Elec Mail info@latitude53.org; Internet Home Page Address: www.latitude53.org; *Exec Dir* Todd Janes; *Prog Officer* Robert Harpin; *Develop Coordr* Tyler Sherard; *Outreach Coordr* Jaye Benoit
Open Tues - Fri 11 AM - 7 PM, Sat 11 AM - 5 PM, cl Sun & Mon; No admis fee; Estab 1973 to encourage & promote the artistic endeavours of contemporary artists & to build a pub awareness of current & experimental cultural developments; Visual, installations, performance & video. Resource center for grants & contracts; Average Annual Attendance: 26,000; Mem: 300; dues $25; ann meeting third Mon in Oct
Income: $300,000 (financed by grants, donations, pub & pvt funding, mem & fundraising events)
Library Holdings: Cassettes; Clipping Files; Exhibition Catalogs; Periodical Subscriptions
Publications: Exhib catalogues
Activities: Lects open to pub, 9 vis lectrs per yr; concerts; gallery talks & tours; discussion groups; performance art festival; pub art projects; book traveling exhibs 10 per yr; originate traveling exhibs for other art centers; sales shop sells books, magazines

M MINISTRY OF ALBERTA CULTURE, (Department of Culture & Community Spirit) Royal Alberta Museum, 12845 102nd Ave, Edmonton, AB T5N 0M6 Canada. Tel 780-453-9100; Fax 780-454-6629; Internet Home Page Address: www.royalalbertamuseum.ca; *Exec Dir* Chris Robinson; *Dir Colls* Albert Finnamore; *Dir Visitor Experience* Karen Mackie; *Dir Bus Opers* Bruce Bolton; *Dir Mus Renewal* Tom Thurston
Open daily 9 AM - 5 PM; Admis families $28, adults $10, sr $8, student $7, youth (7-17) $5, under 6 free; Estab 1967 to preserve & interpret the human & natural history of the Alberta region; Four major exhibit areas divided equally into human & natural history under broad themes of settlement history, archaeology & anthropology, natural history & habitats; Average Annual Attendance: 200,000 - 250,000; Mem: 1200; dues $12 - $19; ann meeting in June
Income: $5,154,000 (financed by provincial government, mus shop, facility rentals, progs, special exhibits & admis)
Library Holdings: Auction Catalogs; Audio Tapes; Book Volumes; CD-ROMs; Cassettes; Clipping Files; Compact Disks; DVDs; Exhibition Catalogs; Fiche; Framed Reproductions; Lantern Slides; Maps; Memorabilia; Original Art Works; Original Documents; Pamphlets; Periodical Subscriptions; Photographs; Prints; Records; Reels; Reproductions; Sculpture; Slides; Video Tapes
Special Subjects: Archaeology, Decorative Arts, Folk Art, Historical Material, Furniture, Ethnology, Eskimo Art, Dolls, Jewelry, Coins & Medals, Dioramas, Embroidery
Collections: Archaeological, ethnographical; fine & decorative arts; folk life; geology; historical; invertebrate zoology; mammalogy; palaeontology; ornithology; vascular & non vascular plants; ichthyology & herpetology; military & political history; pollen & seeds; numismatics
Exhibitions: Approx 10 feature exhibits
Publications: Occasional papers; occasional series; publ series; exhibit catalogs; teacher guides
Activities: Classes for children; dramatic progs; docent training; lects open to pub, 6-20 vis lectrs per yr; gallery talks; tours; concerts; schols offered; exten dept serves western Canada; individual paintings & original objects of art lent to other museums; outreach sr program; loans artifacts & specimens to pub & educational facilities; book traveling exhibs 5 times per yr; originate traveling exhibs to mems of Alberta Exhibit Network; other museums in Canada; mus shop sells books, children's articles, jewelry, logo pins, original art, reproductions, prints, slides & t-shirts

L Provincial Archives of Alberta, 8555 Roper Rd, Edmonton, AB T6E 5W1 Canada. Tel 780-427-1750; Fax 780-427-4646; Elec Mail paa@gov.ab.ca; Internet Home Page Address: www.culture.alberta.ca/paa/; *Provincial Archivist* Leslie Latta; *Dir Colls Mgmt* Wayne Murdoch; *Dir Access & Pres Servs* Susan Stanton; *Team Leader Private Records* Tom Anderson; *Team Leader Government Records* Glynys Hohmann
Open Tues - Fri 9 AM - 4:30 PM, Wed evening until 9 PM, Sat 9 AM - 4:30 PM; Estab 1967 to identify, evaluate, acquire, preserve, arrange & describe & subsequently make available for pub research, reference & display those diversified primary & secondary sources that document & relate to the overall history & develop of Alberta; Small gallery which rotates 3-4 exhibs per yr; Average Annual Attendance: 8,000
Income: Financed by provincial appropriation
Library Holdings: Audio Tapes; Book Volumes 10,000; Cassettes; Clipping Files; Fiche; Manuscripts; Motion Pictures; Original Art Works; Other Holdings Original documents; Pamphlets; Periodical Subscriptions 100; Photographs; Prints; Records; Reels; Slides
Collections: Includes: government & private textual records; maps, plans & drawings; photographs; audiovisual images; 14,000+ vol reference library
Exhibitions: Several small displays each year highlighting recent accessions or historical themes; periodic major exhibs
Publications: Exhib catalogues; guides to colls; information leaflets; occasional papers
Activities: Lects open to pub; organize traveling exhibs via the Alberta Trex travelling exhibs prog to schools, libraries & other small venues throughout the province; sales shop sells books, reproductions, prints & archival presentation products

M UKRAINIAN CANADIAN ARCHIVES & MUSEUM OF ALBERTA, 9543 110th Ave, Edmonton, AB T5H 1H3 Canada. Tel 780-424-7580; Fax 780-420-0562; Elec Mail ucama@shaw.ca; Internet Home Page Address: www.ucama.ca; *Pres* Paul Teterenko; *1st VP* Nestor Makuch; *2nd VP* Khrystia Kohut
Open Tues - Fri 10 AM - 5 PM, Sat Noon - 5 PM, cl Mon & Sun; Admis $5; Estab 1972; 3 stories, library & mus; Mem: Dues family $40, individual $25

Income: Financed by mem, donations & casinos
Special Subjects: Decorative Arts, Folk Art, Landscapes, Ceramics, Furniture, Photography, Portraits, Pottery, Prints, Textiles, Woodcuts, Watercolors, Costumes, Religious Art, Crafts, Posters, Dolls, Carpets & Rugs, Historical Material, Embroidery
Collections: Drawings, historical material, national costumes, paintings, prints, sculpture & textiles
Activities: Guided tours; displays

M WHERE EDMONTON COMMUNITY ARTISTS NETWORK SOCIETY, Harcourt House Arts Centre, 10215 112 St, Edmonton, AB T5K 1M7 Canada. Tel 780-426-4180; Fax 780-425-5523; Elec Mail harcourt@telusplanet.net; Internet Home Page Address: www.harcourthouse.ab.ca; *Exec Dir* Vince Gasparri; *Admin Coordr* Marilyn Glen
Open Mon - Fri 10 AM - 5 PM, Sat 12 PM - 4 PM; No admis fee; Estab 1988; A not-for-profit arts center which includes a pub gallery, art educ prog, & artists' studios. Two gallery spaces include the main space local, national, international (828.5 sq ft) & front room space (536.5 sq ft) for mems & local artists to display their work, open to Alberta, Canada venues only; Average Annual Attendance: 8,000; Mem: 300; dues $25; ann meeting in Apr
Income: Financed by mem, city & state appropriations
Exhibitions: Rotating exhibits
Publications: Harcourt Expressed, quarterly
Activities: Classes for adults & children; lects open to pub, 6 vis lectrs per yr; originate traveling exhibs 8 per yr

GRANDE PRAIRIE

M PRAIRIE ART GALLERY, 98 39-103 Ave, Grande Prairie, AB T8V 6M7 Canada. Tel 780-532-8111; Fax 780-539-9522; Elec Mail info@prairiegallery.com; Internet Home Page Address: www.prairiegallery.com; *Exec Dir & Cur* Robert Steven; *Traveling Exhib Cur* Todd Schaber; *Community Experience Mgr* Sabine Schneider
Open Mon - Thurs 10 AM - 5 PM, Fri 10 AM - 9 PM, Sat - Sun 10 AM - 5 PM; No admis fee; Estab 1975 as a pub art mus; Maintains reference library; Average Annual Attendance: 54,000; Mem: 300; dues $40
Income: $700,000 (financed by mem, city appropriation, provincial & federal government grants)
Special Subjects: Painting-American, Folk Art, Decorative Arts, Painting-European, Painting-Canadian, Painting-Dutch, Painting-French, Historical Material, Painting-Flemish, Painting-Spanish, Cartoons, Painting-German, Painting-New Zealand
Collections: Alberta Art; Contemporary Western Canadian Art
Exhibitions: 6 - 8 per yr
Publications: 3-6 per yr
Activities: Classes for adults & children; lects open to pub, 3-6 vis lectrs per yr; tours; Euphemia McNaught Award; Evy McBryan Award; schols offered; extension prog serves Northwestern Alberta; book traveling exhibs 1-2 per yr; originate traveling exhibs to remote & rural communities in Northwestern Alberta

LETHBRIDGE

A ALLIED ARTS COUNCIL OF LETHBRIDGE, Bowman Arts Center, 811 Fifth Ave S, Lethbridge, AB T1J 0V2 Canada. Tel 403-327-2813; Fax 403-327-6118; Elec Mail darcy@artslethbridge.org; Internet Home Page Address: www.artslethbridge.org; Internet Home Page Address: www.communityartscentre.org; *Pres* Barb Cunningham; *Exec Dir* Suzanne Lint; *Gallery Svcs Coordr* Darcy Logan
Open Mon - Fri 9 AM - 9 PM, Sat 10 AM - 4 PM, cl Sun, summer hours Mon - Fri 9 AM - 5 PM, Sat 10 AM - 4 PM, cl Sun; No admis fee; Estab 1958 to encourage & foster cultural activities in Lethbridge, to provide facilities for such cultural activities & to promote the work of Alberta & western Canadian artists; Average Annual Attendance: 20,000; Mem: 300; dues $25, ann meeting in Feb
Income: $67,000 (financed by mem & city appropriation, Alberta Culture granting & fundraising)
Exhibitions: Local & regional exhibs: Children's art, fabric makers, painters, potters; one-man shows: Paintings, photography, prints, sculpture, silversmithing; provincial government traveling exhibits
Publications: Calendar of Arts, weekly
Activities: Classes for adults & children; dramatic progs; concerts; competitions; schols offered; originates traveling exhibs; sales shop sells original art

M CITY OF LETHBRIDGE, Sir Alexander Galt Museum, 502 First St S, Lethbridge, AB T1J 0P6 Canada; 910 Fourth Ave S, Lethbridge, AB T1J 0P6 Canada. Tel 403-320-3898 (mus), 329-7302 (archives); Elec Mail info@galtmuseum.com; Internet Home Page Address: www.galtmuseum.com; *Display Artist* Brad Brown; *Exec Dir & CEO* Susan Burrows-Johnson; *Cur* Wendy Aitkens; *Archivist* Greg Ellis; *Mktg & Commun* Anine Vonkeman; *Finance Officer* Evelyn Yackulic; *Visitor Svcs* Belinda Crowson
Open May 15 - Aug 31 daily 10 AM - 8 PM, Sept 1 - May 14 Mon - Sat 10 AM - 4:30 PM, Sun 1 PM - 4:30 PM, cl holidays; Admis families $12, adults $5, seniors & students $4, youth (7-17) $3, under 6 free; Estab 1964 to promote the study of human history in southern Alberta; Five Galleries; One gallery is for community use; 800 sq ft & 100 ft running wall space; Average Annual Attendance: 25,000
Income: $247,000
Collections: Historical artifact coll; Archives Coll: photos, manuscripts, books, tapes, films
Exhibitions: Rotate 6-8 exhibits per yr
Activities: Children's classes; docent progs; lects open to pub, 10 vis lectrs per yr; tours; book traveling exhibs 8 per yr; originate traveling exhibs to area schools, institutions, fairs; mus shop sells books & locally handcrafted items

L LETHBRIDGE PUBLIC LIBRARY, Art Gallery, 810 Fifth Ave S, Lethbridge, AB T1J 4C4 Canada. Tel 403-380-7310; Fax 403-329-1478; Elec Mail lpl@lethbridgepubliclibrary.ca; Internet Home Page Address: www.lethbridgepubliclibrary.ca; *Dir* Liz Rossnagel
Open Mon - Sat 9:30 AM - 9 PM, Sun 1:30 PM - 5:30 PM; No admis fee; Estab 1974 to expand human experience, to encourage people to look at art as well as

read & attend library progs; Gallery 900 sq ft wall space for each exhibit, 110 linear ft wall space; Average Annual Attendance: 8,000
Income: Financed by city appropriations
Library Holdings: Book Volumes 193,243; Periodical Subscriptions 500
Activities: Lects open to pub, 8-10 vis lectrs per yr; tours; lending coll contains 250,000 books, 250,000 cassettes, CDs & talking books; book traveling exhibs 6 per yr; originate traveling exhibs

M **SOUTHERN ALBERTA ART GALLERY,** 601 Third Ave S, Lethbridge, AB T1J 0H4 Canada. Tel 403-327-8770; Fax 403-328-3913; Elec Mail info@saag.ca; Internet Home Page Address: www.saag.ca; *VPres* Eric Hillman; *Pub Prog Cur* Anine Vonkeman; *Pres* Dan Westwood; *Dir* Marilyn Smith; *Cur Spec Projects* Joan Stebbins; *Preparator* Paul Smith; *Cur* Ryan Doherty; *Asst Cur* Hannah Wigle; *Educ Coordr* Ambert Watt; *Pub Rels Mgr* Christina Cuthbertson; *Vis Svcs Mgr* Sue Black
Open Tues - Sat 10 AM - 5 PM, Sun 1 - 5 PM; Admis adults $5, student & senior $4, groups $3 (per person), under 12, mem & Sun free; Estab 1976 to present historical & contemporary art programs designed to further the process of art appreciation; Three gallery spaces contained in historical Lethbridge building remodeled as art gallery; Average Annual Attendance: 30,000; Mem: 325; dues family $35, single $20, artist & student $10; ann meeting in Feb
Income: Financed by mem, city, provincial & federal appropriation
Collections: Donald Buchanan Art Collection of City of Lethbridge containing mid-20th Century Canadian work & various international pieces
Exhibitions: Historical and contemporary art changing monthly
Publications: Exhib catalogues; quarterly newsletter
Activities: Classes for children; docent training; professional development series; lects open to pub, numerous vis lectrs per yr; gallery talks; tours; artmobile; originate traveling exhibs; sales shop sells magazines & reproductions

L **Library,** 601 Third Ave S, Lethbridge, AB T1J 0H4 Canada. Tel 403-327-8770; Fax 403-328-3913; Internet Home Page Address: www.saag.ca; *Librn* Joseph Anderson; *Asst Cur* David Diviney; *Dir* Marilyn Smith; *Cur* Joan Stebbins; *Head Pub Rels* Anine Vonkeman; *Develop Mgr* Karin Champion; *Educ Coordr* Marsha Reich; *Visitors Svcs Mgr* Sue Black; *Librn* Elspeth Nickle
Open Tues - Sat 10 AM - 5 PM, Sun 1 - 5 PM; No admis fee; Estab 1976; Contemporary pub art gallery; Average Annual Attendance: 32,000; Mem: 400+ mem
Library Holdings: Audio Tapes; Book Volumes 4000; Cassettes; Clipping Files; Exhibition Catalogs; Filmstrips; Manuscripts; Pamphlets 3200; Periodical Subscriptions 12; Reproductions; Slides; Video Tapes
Exhibitions: 15 exhibs annually
Publications: 6-8 publs annually
Activities: Classes for adults & children; lects open to pub, 25 - 30 vis lectrs per yr; concerts; gallery talks; tours; video competitions; exten dept serves southern & central Alberta; lending collection contains 520 books, 22 cassettes, 56 videos (in house viewing only); book traveling exhibs; originate traveling exhibs; sales shop sells books, magazines, original art, prints & reproductions

M **UNIVERSITY OF LETHBRIDGE,** Art Gallery, 4401 University Dr, W600, Centre for the Arts Lethbridge, AB T1K 3M4 Canada. Tel 403-329-2666; Fax 403-382-7115; Elec Mail josephine.mills@uleth.ca; Internet Home Page Address: www.uleth.ca/artgallery; *Chief Preparator* Jane Edmundson; *Registrar* Juliet Graham; *Dir & Cur* Josephine Mills; *Admin Mgr* Fred Greene; *Curatorial Researcher & Preparator* Jane Edmundson; *Fine Arts Technician* Chad Patterson
Open Mon - Fri 10 AM - 4:30 PM, Thurs 10 AM - 8:30 pm; No admis fee; Estab 1968 for pub service & the teaching mechanism; 29 ft x 42 ft gallery; Visual Arts Study Centre, 8:30 - 4:30 PM Mon - Fri, where any work from the coll will be made available for viewing, Helen Christou Gallery, Project channel Video Gallery
Income: Financed by univ & government appropriations
Collections: Permanent Coll consists of 19th century art (primarily Canadian), 20th century international art; Inuit
Exhibitions: Exhibs with exception of the Annual BFA show are curated from the permanent collection; approx 10 shows per yr
Activities: Lects open to pub, 10-15 vis lectrs per yr; gallery talks; tours; individual paintings & original objects of art lent to pub & commercial galleries & corporations; organize traveling ehibs nationally & internationally

MEDICINE HAT

M **ESPLANADE ARTS & HERITAGE CENTRE,** 401 First St SE, Medicine Hat, AB T1A 8W2 Canada. Tel 403-502-8580 (main), 502-8581 (mus), 502-8583 (gallery); Fax 403-502-8589; Elec Mail esplanade@medicinehat.ca; Internet Home Page Address: www.esplanade.ca; *Dir* Carol Beatty; *Cur Art* Joanne Marion
Open Mon - Fri 10 AM - 5 PM, Sat - Sun & holidays 12 PM - 5 PM; Admis family $12, adults $4, youth & student $3, under 6 free; Estab 1951; Circ 85; Gallery has 3,000 sq ft on main floor; Average Annual Attendance: 18,500; Mem: 250; dues supporting $50, bus $50, family $20, individual $10
Income: Financed by memberships, donations, fund raising & federal appropriation
Collections: Pioneer artifacts of city & the district; Indian artifacts; Regional, Canadian Modern & Contemporary art
Exhibitions: Rotate 12 per yr
Publications: exhib catalogues, several ann
Activities: Classes for children; docent training; films; gallery talks tours; exten prog serves southeastern Alberta; lending of original objects of art to pub galleries in Canada; organize traveling exhibs to pub galleries in Canada; mus shop sells books, magazines, original art, reproductions, prints

L **MEDICINE HAT PUBLIC LIBRARY,** 414 First St SE, Medicine Hat, AB T1A 0A8 Canada. Tel 403-502-8525; Fax 403-502-8529; Elec Mail library@city.medicine-hat.ab.ca; Internet Home Page Address: www.shortgrass-lib.ab.ca/mhpl; *Head Reference Svcs* Sheila Drummond; *Chief Librn* Rachel Sarjeant-Jenkins; *Head Adult Servs* Hilary Munro
Open Mon - Thurs 10 AM - 9 PM, Fri & Sat 10 AM - 5:30 PM, Sun 1 - 5:30 PM; Library has a display area for traveling and local art shows; 600 sq ft room with track lighting and alarm system

Library Holdings: Book Volumes 165,589; CD-ROMs 30; Cassettes 3224; Clipping Files; Compact Disks 3393; Motion Pictures 50; Original Art Works 30; Other Holdings Talking Books 1904; Pamphlets 3317; Periodical Subscriptions 243; Prints; Records; Reels 50; Sculpture; Video Tapes 2437
Exhibitions: Art loans from Alberta Foundation for the Arts; Exhibits of local artists
Activities: Dramatic progs; lects open to pub, 10 vis lectrs per yr; concerts

RED DEER

M **RED DEER & DISTRICT MUSEUM & ARCHIVES,** 4525 47A Ave, Red Deer, AB T4N 6Z6 Canada. Tel 403-309-8405; Fax 403-342-6644; Elec Mail museum@reddeer.ca; Internet Home Page Address: www.museum.red-deer.ab.ca; *Prog Coordr* Rod Trentham; *Exhibits Coordr* Diana Anderson; *Coordr Coll* Valerie Miller; *Office Mgr* Lorraine Evans-Cross; *Vol Coordr* Dorothy Reso-Hickman; *Mgr* Lorna Johnson; *Commun & Mktg Coordr* Lynn Norman
Open Mon - Sun 12 PM - 5 PM, Wed 12 PM - 9 PM; Admis by donation; Estab 1978 to present the human history of the region through an on-going series of exhibs & interpretive progs; Stewart Room has 64 running ft of exhib space; Volunteer's Gallery has 124 running ft of exhibition space; Donor's Gallery has 160 running ft of exhib space; 2500 sq ft total area of circulating exhib space; 4100 sq ft of permanent exhib space; Average Annual Attendance: 60,000; Mem: 1000; dues family $15, individual $10
Income: Financed by municipal, provincial & federal grants
Special Subjects: Photography, Textiles, Primitive art, Painting-Canadian, Porcelain, Restorations, Period Rooms
Collections: Bower Collection of archaeological specimens from Central Alberta; Central Alberta human history; Inuit carving, prints & related material; Swallow Collection of Inuit & Indian Art; permanent art coll, clothing & textiles
Exhibitions: Programs featuring local, international, national & provincial artists; Alberta Community Art Clubs Assoc; Alberta Wide Juried Exhibition; Central Alberta Photographic Society Annual Exhibit; Red Deer College Student Show
Publications: Quarterly newsletter, Inventive Spirit (compendium & database of Alberta inventions)
Activities: Classes for children; mus-kits; lect open to pub; concerts; gallery talks; tours; originate traveling exhibs provincially, nationally to museums & art galleries; mus shop sells books, magazines, original art, prints, coloring books, learning tools, souvenirs, postcards, stationery & gifts; children's discovery zone

STONY PLAIN

M **MULTICULTURAL HERITAGE CENTRE,** Public Art Gallery, 5411 51st St, Box 2188 Stony Plain, AB T7Z 1X7 Canada. Tel 780-963-2777; Fax 780-963-0233; Elec Mail info@multicentre.org; Internet Home Page Address: www.multicentre.org; *Cur* John Maywood; *Exec Dir* Judy Unterschultz
Open Mon - Wed 10 AM - 4 PM, Thurs - Sun 10 AM - 8 PM; No admis fee; Estab 1974 to provide exposure to high quality art with priority given to local Alberta artists, to develop an appreciation for good art, to provide exposure for upcoming artists; Gallery has 2000 sq ft of exhib space; Multicultural Heritage Centre also consists of Öppertshauser House on same site; maintains reference library; Average Annual Attendance: 85,000; Mem: 100; dues $20, ann meeting Jan
Income: Financed by government grants, free for children & adult program, commissions from store sales, Homesteaders Kitchen revenue & fundraising
Special Subjects: Historical Material
Collections: Area history; family histories; photographs
Exhibitions: 20 exhibs per year
Publications: Monthly newsletter
Activities: Classes adults & children, dramatic progs; lects open to pub, 10 vis lectrs per yr; concerts; sales shop sells books, original art, reproductions & prints

BRITISH COLUMBIA

BURNABY

M **BURNABY ART GALLERY,** 6344 Deer Lake Ave, Burnaby, BC V5G 2J3 Canada. Tel 604-297-4422; Fax 604-205-7339; Elec Mail gallery@burnaby.ca; Internet Home Page Address: www.burnabyartgallery.ca; *Dir & Cur* Darrin Martens; *Exhib Coordr & Preparator* Robert MacIntyre; *Educ Programmer, Sch* Theresa Carroll
Open Tues - Fri 10 AM - 4:30 PM, Sat - Sun 12 PM - 5 PM, cl Mon; No admis fee, donations accepted; Estab 1967 to collect & exhibit Canadian art, with continually changing exhibs of prints & works of art on paper; Gallery is housed in Ceperley Mansion in Deer Lake Park; Average Annual Attendance: 25,000
Income: Financed by municipal, provincial & federal grants, pub & pvt donations
Library Holdings: Clipping Files; Exhibition Catalogs; Pamphlets
Special Subjects: Prints
Collections: 20th Century prints including contemporary artists; Works on paper; Contemporary Art
Exhibitions: Tracing Culture IV; Day Without Art (video)
Publications: Catalogues & brochures to accompany exhibs
Activities: Classes for adults & children; docent training; workshops for schools; lects open to pub; 4-6 lectrs per yr; gallery talks; tours; exten dept serves BC; Metro Vancouver; individual paintings & original objects of art lent to other exhib centers pub & corp; lending collection contains 600 original prints & drawings; organize traveling exhibs to Canadian institutions

M **SIMON FRASER UNIVERSITY,** Simon Fraser University Gallery, 8888 University Dr, AQ3004 Burnaby, BC V5A 1S6 Canada. Tel 778-782-4266; Fax 778-782-3029; Elec Mail gallery@sfu.ca; Internet Home Page Address: www.sfu.ca/gallery; *Coordr* Veronika Klaptocz; *Dir & Cur* Bill Jeffries; *Coordr* Adriana Contreras; *Colls Mgr* Nadine Power
Open Tues - Fri 10 AM - 5 PM, Sat 12 PM - 5 PM, cl holiday weekends; No admis fee; Estab 1971 to collect, conserve & display original works of art,

principally contemporary Canadian; Gallery is 150 to 310 running ft, 1200 sq ft. Permanent works are installed throughout the univ campus; Average Annual Attendance: 10,000

Income: Financed by pub univ appropriations, government grants & corporate donations

Special Subjects: Graphics

Collections: Simon Fraser Collection, including contemporary & Inuit graphics; international graphics

Publications: Biannual report

Activities: Lects open to public; gallery talks; tours; individual paintings & original objects of art loaned to art galleries

L **W A C Bennett Library,** Burnaby, BC V5A 1S6 Canada. Tel 778-782-3869; Fax 778-782-3023; Internet Home Page Address: www.lib.sfu.ca; *Univ Librn* Chuck Eckman

Open Mon-Thurs 8 - 11:45 AM, Fri 8 AM - 10 PM, Sat & Sun 10 AM - 10 PM; Reference material available in library & University Archives

Library Holdings: Audio Tapes; Book Volumes 1,000,000; DVDs; Exhibition Catalogs; Fiche; Filmstrips; Manuscripts; Motion Pictures; Other Holdings CD-ROM; Compact discs; Pamphlets; Periodical Subscriptions 11,500; Records; Reels; Slides; Video Tapes

CHILLIWACK

A **CHILLIWACK COMMUNITY ARTS COUNCIL,** Community Arts Centre, 9201 Corbould St, Chilliwack, BC V2P 2A4 Canada. Tel 604-392-8888; Fax 604-392-8008; Elec Mail info@chilliwackculturalcentre.ca; Internet Home Page Address: www.chilliwackartscouncil.com; *Exec Dir* Michael Cade; *Rentals Mgr* Theresia Reid; *Mktg Mgr* Ann Goudswaard; *Office Mgr* Chrissie Hood

Open Mon - Fri 9 AM - 5 PM, cl weekends & holidays; box office: Mon - Fri 9:30 AM - 9 PM, Sat - Sun 9:30 AM - 5 PM; No admis fee; Estab 1959 as Arts Council, Arts Centre estab 1973 to encourage all forms of art in the community; 1 large gallery; Average Annual Attendance: 10,000; Mem: 5000; dues group & family $25, organizational $15, individual $15; annual meeting Sept

Income: Financed by endowment, mem & grants

Exhibitions: Christmas Craft Market

Publications: Arts Council Newsletter, 11 per yr

Activities: Classes for adults & children; dramatic progs; concerts; schols offered

COQUITLAM

A **PLACE DES ARTS AT HERITAGE SQUARE,** 1120 Brunette Ave, Coquitlam, BC V3K 1G2 Canada. Tel 604-664-1636; Fax 604-664-1658; Elec Mail info@placedesarts.ca; Internet Home Page Address: www.placedesarts.ca; *Dir* Joan Roberts; *Asst to Exec Dir* Stanley Quek; *Communs Coordr* Kate Lancaster; *Visual Arts Coordr* Katrina Driver

Open early Sept to late Jun Mon - Fri 9 AM - 9 PM, Sat 9 AM - 5 PM, Sun 1 PM - 5 PM; see website for summer hours. ; No admis fee; Estab 1972 as a cultural, community crafts & resource center, an art centre & music school; 3 galleries - 3 shows monthly; Average Annual Attendance: 58,000

Income: Financed by municipal grant

Exhibitions: Monthly shows of emerging artists, artists & craftsmen throughout the year

Publications: Prog Sept - June; summer prog Jul - Aug

Activities: Satellite courses for school children; classes for adults & children; visual arts, music, drama, dance; lect open to pub; concerts; gallery talks; schols offered

COURTENAY

M **COMOX VALLEY ART GALLERY,** 580 Duncan Ave, Courtenay, BC V9N 2M7 Canada. Tel 250-338-6211; Fax 250-338-6287; Elec Mail contact@comoxvalleyartgallery.com; Internet Home Page Address: www.comoxvalleyartgallery.com; *Exec Dir* Sharon Karsten; *Cur* Anh Le; *ShopMgr* Rhonda Burden

Open Tues - Sat 10 AM - 5 PM; Admis $2 donation; Estab 1974; contemporary art/feature local artists; Contemporary & community galleries; Average Annual Attendance: 22,000; Mem: 288; dues $25 per yr

Income: Financed through grants, fundraisers & gift shop sales

Exhibitions: See website

Activities: Art educ progs; pub outreach; classes for adults & children; youth media workshops; lects open to pub; approx 8 vis lectrs per yr; concerts; gallery talks; tours; Nonny Milne schol for youth; sales shop sells books, magazines, original art, reproductions, prints, pottery, jewelry, glass

DAWSON CREEK

M **SOUTH PEACE ART SOCIETY,** Dawson Creek Art Gallery, 101-816 Alaska Ave, Dawson Creek, BC V1G 4T6 Canada. Tel 250-782-2601; Fax 250-782-8801; Elec Mail curator@dcartgallery.ca; Internet Home Page Address: www.dcartgallery.ca; *Dir* Ellen Corea; *Treas* Barbara Swail; *Pres* Barb Handysides; *Gift Shop Mgr & Admin Asst* Alana Hall

Open June - Aug daily 9 AM - 5 PM; Sept - May, Tues - Fri 10 AM - 5 PM, Sat 12 PM - 4 PM; Admis by donation; Estab 1961 to promote art appreciation in community; Art Gallery in elevator annex in NAR Park. NAR Park includes mus & Tourist Information Office; Average Annual Attendance: 65,000; Mem: 100; dues $35; ann meeting third Thurs of Mar

Income: $130,000 (financed by municipal building & ann sponsorship, commission from sales, provincial cultural grant, federal grant Canada council)

Library Holdings: Book Volumes; Exhibition Catalogs; Original Art Works

Exhibitions: Approx 13 per yr, local & traveling

Publications: Newsletter, quarterly

Activities: Classes for adults & children; lects open to pub, 3 vis lectrs per yr; gallery talks; individual paintings lent to mems, bus, pvt homes; lending coll contains color reproductions, slides, 145 books & 350 original prints; book

traveling exhibs 4-6 per yr; circulate to galleries in British Columbia; sales shop sells original art, pottery, metal, woodwork, jewelry, stained glass, oils, soaps, weaving, cards & other items

HOPE

M **JOHN WEAVER SCULPTURE COLLECTION,** 19255 Silverhope Rd, Hope, BC Canada; PO Box 1723, Hope, BC V0X 1L0 Canada. Tel 604-869-5312; Elec Mail henryweaver@johnweaverfinearts.com; Elec Mail saraleszstak@johnweaverfinearts.com; Internet Home Page Address: www.johnweaverfinearts.com; *Pres, Cur & Sculpture* Henry C Weaver; *Cur* Sara Lesztak; *Exec Asst* Noni Weaver; *Sculptor* Elizabeth Lesztak

Open by appointment; 1977; Artist copy collection/sales gallery

Income: Financed by sales of editions of bronzes

Library Holdings: Cassettes; Clipping Files; Original Documents; Pamphlets; Photographs; Sculpture

Special Subjects: Folk Art, Drawings, Painting-American, Sculpture, Watercolors, Bronzes, Woodcarvings, Woodcuts, Portraits, Historical Material, Military Art

Collections: Mythology; Technology & Man; Bronze sculptures; oil paintings & watercolors by John Bruce Weaver, Jesse Bruce Weaver, Betty Menke; sketches by John Barney Weaver

Publications: Brochures, postcards & portfolios; Weaver Fine Art Bronze, 2007; Sculpture of John Weaver, 1968

Activities: Classes for adults & children as requested by student or art assn; Lects open to pub; tours; demonstrations; vis lectrs open by personal request to artist; lending coll contains sculptures; originate traveling exhibs; sales shop sells books & original art

KAMLOOPS

M **KAMLOOPS ART GALLERY,** 101 - 465 Victoria St, Kamloops, BC V2C 2A9 Canada. Tel 250-377-2400; Fax 250-828-0662; Elec Mail kamloopsartgallery@kag.bc.ca; Internet Home Page Address: www.kag.bc.ca; *Exec Dir* Jann L M Bailey; *Mgr, Financial & Facility Svcs* Wendy Lysak; *Registrar & Coll Coordr* Trish Keegan; *Financial Asst* Shauna Bell; *Mgr Admin Svcs* Beverley Clayton; *Interim Cur* Jordan Strom; *Asst Cur* Craig Willms; *Exhibition Designer/Preparator* Matthew Tremblay; *Gallery Store Buyer* Patti Procknow; *Prog Coordr* Linda Favrholdt; *Mktg Coordr* James Gordon; *Admis/Gallery Store Coordr* Nicole Baker; *Events Coordr* Judy Basso

Open Mon - Wed, Fri & Sat 10 AM - 5 PM, Thurs 10 AM - 9 PM, Sun Noon - 4 PM; Admis various; Estab 1978; pub art mus; Exhib gallery, 4400 running ft, total area of gallery 14,225 ft; Average Annual Attendance: 30,000; Mem: 600; dues family $45, individual $30, senior citizens, artists & students $15, child $10; ann meeting in Apr

Income: $1,400,000 (operating & prog grants, fundraising, sponsorships & donations)

Library Holdings: Auction Catalogs; Clipping Files; Exhibition Catalogs

Special Subjects: Drawings, Photography, Prints, Sculpture, Watercolors, Etchings & Engravings, Painting-Canadian

Collections: Contemporary Canadian Art; Canadian Prints & Drawings; photography; sculpture; Contemporary Canadian Art Collection

Exhibitions: Monthly National & International Exhibs

Publications: Newsletter, 4 times per yr; exhib catalogs

Activities: Classes for adults & children; lects open to pub, 10-12 vis lectrs per yr; concerts; gallery talks; tours; book traveling exhibs; originate traveling exhibs; mus shop sells books, magazines, original crafts, reproductions, prints & gifts

KELOWNA

M **OKANAGAN HERITAGE MUSEUM,** (Kelowna Museum) 470 Queensway Ave, Kelowna, BC V1Y 6S7 Canada. Tel 250-763-2417; Fax 250-763-5722; Elec Mail info@kelownamuseum.ca; Internet Home Page Address: www.kelownamuseum.org; *Pres* Jim Grant; *Dir & Cur* Wayne Wilson; *Assoc Dir Admin* Krista Stokall; *Assoc Dir Laurel Opers* Nathalie Bomberg; *Conservator* Marta Leskard; *Exhib Coordr* Dennis Domen; *Archivist* Donna Johnson

Open Mon - Fri 10 AM - 5 PM, Sat 10 AM - 4 PM, cl Sun; Admis by donation; Estab 1936 as a community mus where traveling exhibits are received & circulated; 12,000 sq ft of display plus storage, workshop & archives; permanent galleries: Natural History, Local History, Ethnography, two exhibit galleries; Average Annual Attendance: 35,000; Mem: 200; dues $25; ann meeting in Mar

Income: Financed by mem, city & state appropriation

Special Subjects: Drawings, Latin American Art, Painting-American, American Indian Art, Bronzes, African Art, Archaeology, Ethnology, Textiles, Costumes, Ceramics, Crafts, Folk Art, Decorative Arts, Eskimo Art, Furniture, Glass, Jewelry, Asian Art, Silver, Metalwork, Miniatures, Antiquities-Egyptian, Antiquities-Greek, Antiquities-Roman

Collections: Coins & medals; decorative arts; ethnography; general history; Kelowna History; natural history

Exhibitions: Changing exhibs every 3 months

Publications: The Games Grandpa Played, Early Sports in BC; Nan, A Childs Eye View of Okanagan; Lak-La-Hai-Ee Volume III Fishing; A Short History of Early Fruit Ranching Kelowna; Sunshine & Butterflies

Activities: Classes for adults & children; lects open to pub, 6 vis lectrs per yr; tours; gallery talks; individual paintings & original objects of art lent to qualified mus; book traveling exhibs 7-8 per yr; originate traveling exhibs; mus shop sells books, original art, reproductions, prints

L **Kelowna Public Archives,** 470 Queensway Ave, Kelowna, BC V1Y 6S7 Canada. Tel 250-763-2417; Fax 250-763-5722; Elec Mail archivevs@kelownamuseums.ca; Internet Home Page Address: www.kelownamuseums.ca; *Archivist* Donna Johnson

Open by appointment only; Circ Non-circulating

Library Holdings: Cassettes; Clipping Files; Fiche; Manuscripts; Maps; Micro Print; Motion Pictures; Original Art Works; Original Documents; Periodical Subscriptions; Photographs; Prints; Slides; Video Tapes

Collections: Photograph Collection; reference library, reference files, maps

Activities: Classes for adults & children, docent training; lectrs open to pub, gallery talks, tours; Museum shop, books, reproductions, gift items; junior museums located at 1304 Ellis St, 1424 Ellis St

NANAIMO

M **MALASPINA COLLEGE,** Nanaimo Art Gallery, 900 Fifth St, Nanaimo, BC V9R 5S5 Canada. Tel 250-755-8790; Fax 250-741-2214; Elec Mail info@nanaimogallery.ca; Internet Home Page Address: www.nanaimoartgallery.com; *Pres* Ian Niamath; *VPres* Sasha Koerbler; *Treas* Irene Berg; *Secy* Wendy Williston; *Gallery Mgr* Ed Poli; *Cur* Fran Benton; *Admin Dir* Chris Kuderle; *Gallery Asst & Cur Tech* Stephen Laidlaw
Open Mon - Fri 10 AM - 5 PM, Sat 12 PM - 4 PM; Admis $2 suggested donation; Estab 1976 to exhibit the works of contemporary visual artists; Two Galleries: gallery I is 1300 sq ft with 11 ft ceilings; gallery II is 775 sq ft with 10 ft ceilings; Average Annual Attendance: 20,000; Mem: 386; dues $10 & up; ann meeting in Apr
Income: Financed by mem, earned gallery shop, city & state appropriations; schools & school districts
Collections: Works by contemporary artists primarily regional but some national & international; Contemporary Art
Exhibitions: Contemporary Art, Historical & Scientific exhibits; Street Banner Painting Competition; rotate 9 exhibs per yr on campus, 12 per yr downtown facility
Publications: Nanaimo Art Gallery newsletter, 3 per yr
Activities: Classes for adults & children; docent training; lects open to pub, 6-8 vis lectrs per yr; gallery talks; tours; competitions with awards; exten dept serves local elementary schools; individual paintings & original objects of art lent; lending coll contains original art work, original prints, paintings & sculpture; book traveling exhibs 1-2 per yr; mus shop sells books, original art & local crafts

PENTICTON

M **THE PENTICTON ART GALLERY,** (Art Gallery of South Okanagan) 199 Front St, Penticton, BC V2A 1H3 Canada. Tel 250-493-2928; Fax 250-493-3992; Elec Mail agso@vip.net; Internet Home Page Address: www.galleries.bc.ca/agso; *Dir* Geraldine Parent
Open Tues - Fri 10 AM - 5 PM, Sat & Sun noon - 5 PM, cl Mon & Statutory Holidays; Admis adults & non-members $2, children & students free, Sat & Sun no admis fee

PRINCE GEORGE

M **PRINCE GEORGE ART GALLERY,** 725 Civic Plaza, Prince George, BC V2L ST1 Canada. Tel 250-614-7800; Fax 250-563-3211; Elec Mail art@tworiversartgallery.com; Internet Home Page Address: www.tworiversartgallery.com; *Cur* George Harris; *Admin Asst* Jeanne Hodges; *Mng Dir* Peter Thompson; *Pub Prog Mgr* Carolyn Holmes; *Shop Mgr* Brigid Ryder
Open Mon - Sat 10 AM - 5 PM, Thurs 10 AM - 9 PM, Sun 1 PM - 4 PM, Holiday Mon 12 PM - 5 PM; Admis family $10, adults $5, sr citizens & students $4, children 5-12 $2, under 5 free; Estab 1970 to foster development of arts & crafts in the community; to foster & promote artists; New Building, 2 floors, art rental section, two sq ft galleries, offices, storage, gift shop, large foyer & sculpture ct; Average Annual Attendance: 26,000; Mem: 382; dues family $43, individual $27, sr citizens & students $22; ann meeting in Feb
Income: Financed by provincial & municipal grants, pvt donations
Special Subjects: Sculpture, Painting-Canadian
Collections: Original paintings by British Columbia artists
Exhibitions: Exhibitions held every 10-12 weeks, primarily Canadian Artists; three ann fundraisers
Publications: Quarterly newsletter
Activities: Classes for adults & children; docent training; lects open to pub, 6-10 vis lectrs per yr; gallery talks; tours; exten dept serves regional district; individual paintings & original objects of art rented to mems; book traveling exhibs 2 per yr; sales shop sells original paintings, drawings, pottery, handicrafts, prints, cards

PRINCE RUPERT

M **MUSEUM OF NORTHERN BRITISH COLUMBIA,** Ruth Harvey Art Gallery, 100 First Ave W, PO Box 669 Prince Rupert, BC V8J 3S1 Canada; 100-1st Ave West, Prince Rupert, BC V8J 1A8 Canada. Tel 250-624-3207; Fax 250-627-8009; Internet Home Page Address: www.museumofnorthernbc.com; *Cur* Susan Marsden; *Gift Shop Mgr* Irene Fernandes; *Colls Mgr* Erin Alger; *Performance Coordr* Sampson Bryant
Open Oct-May Tues-Sat 9AM-5PM, June-Aug daily 9AM-5PM, Sept daily 9AM-5PM; Admis adults $6, Teens 13-19 $3, Child 6-12 $2, Young Child under 5 $1; Estab 1924, new building opened 1958, to collect, maintain & display the history of the peoples of the north coast, particularly of the Prince Rupert area; especially the Tsimshian, the First Nations group in this area who have occupied the northwest coast for approx 10,000 yrs; Large main gallery, Treasures Gallery, Hallway of Nations, Monumental Gallery, Ruth Harvey Art Gallery; Average Annual Attendance: 80,000; Mem: 280; dues corporate $75, family $20, individual $15, sr citizen & student $10; ann meeting in May
Income: $250,000 (financed primarily by municipality & province)
Library Holdings: Clipping Files; Manuscripts; Maps; Memorabilia; Original Documents; Pamphlets; Reproductions
Special Subjects: Photography, Prints, Graphics, Anthropology, Archaeology, Ethnology, Textiles, Ceramics, Crafts, Primitive art, Woodcarvings, Portraits, Painting-Canadian, Jewelry, Porcelain, Historical Material, Maps, Coins & Medals, Gold
Collections: Contemporary North Coast First Nations; historical colls; native First Nations colls; natural history; photographs

Exhibitions: A continually changing display prog; fine arts exhibs from large galleries; local artists exhibs
Publications: Library contains 800 vols, 50 rare
Activities: Classes for adults & children; dramatic progs; lects open to pub, 3-4 vis lectrs per yr; gallery talks; tours; competitions; book traveling exhibs; mus shop sells books, native art, original art, reproductions, prints & souvenirs

L **Library,** 100 First Ave W, Prince Rupert, BC V8J 1A8 Canada. Tel 250-624-3207; Fax 250-627-8009; Internet Home Page Address: www.museumofnorthernbc.com; *Colls Mgr* Erin Alger; *Performance Coordr* Sampson Bryant; *Dir* Robin Weber; *Cur* Susan Marsder
Open June - Aug daily - 9 AM - 5 PM, Sept daily 9 AM - 5 PM, Oct - May Tues - Sat 9 AM - 5 PM, cl Sun, Mon, & holidays; No admis fee for use of reference library; appointments required; Small reference library for staff & researchers
Income: $280,000 (financed by city, province, donations & gift shop)
Library Holdings: Audio Tapes; Book Volumes 1000; Clipping Files; Exhibition Catalogs; Manuscripts; Other Holdings Archival materials; Pamphlets; Periodical Subscriptions 10; Photographs; Video Tapes
Special Subjects: Prints, Historical Material, Ceramics, Archaeology, Ethnology, Porcelain, Primitive art, Anthropology, Eskimo Art, Restoration & Conservation, Tapestries, Textiles, Coins & Medals, Painting-Canadian
Publications: Library contains 800 vols, 50 rare
Activities: Educ dept; lects open to pub; mus shop sells books, original art, reproductions & prints

REVELSTOKE

A **REVELSTOKE VISUAL ARTS CENTRE,** 320 Wilson St, PO Box 2655 Revelstoke, BC V0E 2S0 Canada. Tel 250-814-0261; Elec Mail info@revelstokevisualarts.com; Internet Home Page Address: www.revelstokevisualarts.com; *Chmn* Joanne Stacey; *Treas* Margaret Pacaud
Admis by donation; Estab 1949 to promote & stimulate interest in art by studying art, artists methods & work, developing local interest & interchanging ideas; Average Annual Attendance: 500; Mem: 45; dues $10; ann meeting in Apr
Income: Grants, sales & donations
Collections: Centennial coll contains 10 watercolors, acrylics & oils by Sophie Atkinson
Exhibitions: Weaving & Pottery by Local Artisans; Sr Citizens' Paintings; Snowflake Porcelain Painters; Works by members of the Revelstoke Art Group - summer
Activities: Classes for adults & children

RICHMOND

A **RICHMOND ARTS CENTRE,** 180-7700 Minoru Gate, Richmond, BC V6Y 1R9 Canada. Tel 604-247-8300; Fax 604-247-8301; Elec Mail artscentre@richmond.ca; Internet Home Page Address: www.richmond.ca; *Arts Coordr* Suzanne E Greening; *Arts Programmer* Lenore Clemens
Open Mon - Fri 9 AM - 9:30 PM, Sat & Sun 10 AM - 5 PM; No admis fee; Estab 1967 to provide stimulation & nourishment to the arts in the community
Income: Financed by city appropriation
Activities: Classes for adults & children in visual & dramatic arts, ballet & jazz; concerts; special events & festivals; art truck, takes the arts out to the community; sales shop sells original art & music CDs

SOOKE

M **SOOKE REGION MUSEUM & ART GALLERY,** 2070 Phillips Rd, Sooke, BC V0S 1N0 Canada; PO Box 774, Sooke, BC V9Z 1H7 Canada. Tel 250-642-6351; Fax 250-642-7089; Elec Mail info@sookeregionmuseum.com; Internet Home Page Address: www.sookeregionmuseum.com; *Exec Dir* Terry Malone
Open winter Tues - Sun 9 AM - 5 PM, cl Mon, summer daily 9 AM - 5 PM; Admis donation; Estab 1977 to advance local history & art; Exhibit changes monthly featuring a different local artist or artist group, or segment of mus coll; Average Annual Attendance: 30,000
Income: Financed by donations
Special Subjects: American Indian Art, Archaeology, Ethnology, Costumes, Crafts, Dolls, Period Rooms
Collections: Fishing, Logging & Mining Artifacts; Native Indian Crafts (post & pre-contact); Pioneer Implements
Exhibitions: Polemaker's Shack; Moss Cottage; Wreck of Lord Western
Activities: Children classes; docent training; lects open to pub, 4 vis lectrs per yr; tours; competitions with awards; retail store sells books & original art

SURREY

M **SURREY ART GALLERY,** 13750 88th Ave, Surrey, BC V3W 3L1 Canada. Tel 604-501-5566; Fax 604-501-5581; Elec Mail artgallery@surrey.ca; Internet Home Page Address: www.arts.surrey.ca; Internet Home Page Address: www.surreytechlab.ca; *Dir* Liane Davison; *Cur Progs* Ingrid Kolt; *Cur* Jordan Strom
Open Mon - Wed & Fri 9 AM - 5 PM, Tues - Thurs 9 AM - 9 PM, Sat 10 AM - 5 PM, Sun Noon - 5 PM; Admis by donation; Estab 1975; Contemporary art; Average Annual Attendance: 50,000
Income: Financed by city & provincial appropriation, special private foundations grants & federal grants per project application
Purchases: $10,000
Library Holdings: Book Volumes; Clipping Files; Exhibition Catalogs; Manuscripts; Original Documents; Periodical Subscriptions
Special Subjects: Sculpture, Photography, Prints, Painting-Canadian
Collections: Contemporary Canadian Art
Publications: Exhib catalogues; Surrey Arts Center Calendar, bimonthly
Activities: Classes for adults & children; docent training; lects open to pub, 10 vis lectrs per yr; concerts; gallery talks; tours; individual paintings & original objects of art lent to other institutions; book traveling exhibs 1 or more per yr; originates

traveling exhibs; sales shop sells original art, locally made jewelry, arts & crafts, glasswork, woodwork & cards

L **Library,** 13750 88th Ave, Surrey, BC V3W 3L1 Canada. Tel 604-501-5566; Fax 604-501-5581; Elec Mail artgallery@surrey.ca; Internet Home Page Address: www.surrey.ca/culture-recreation/1537.aspx; *Dir* Liane Davison; *Cur Prog* Ingrid Kolt; *Cur Exhib & Coll* Jordan Strom; *Librn* Urmilla Das; *Asst Cur* Brian Foreman
Open Mon - Fri 9 AM - 5 PM, Sat 10 AM - 5 PM, Sun Noon - 5 PM, Thurs evenings 5 - 9 PM, cl statutory holidays; Admis by donation; Estab 1975 for exhibs & educ in contemporary art. Reference library for staff & docents only; Contemporary art museum; Average Annual Attendance: 50,000
Income: Financed by municipal
Purchases: $1000
Library Holdings: Book Volumes 550; Cards; Clipping Files; Exhibition Catalogs; Periodical Subscriptions 20; Slides
Collections: Contemporary art
Activities: Docent training; lects open to pub; tours; exten prog serves Surrey & region; lending original objects of art to mus

VANCOUVER

M **BILL REID GALLERY OF NORTHWEST COAST ART,** 639 Hornby St, Vancouver, BC V6C 2G3 Canada. Tel 604-682-3455; Fax 604-682-3310; Elec Mail info@billreidgallery.ca; Internet Home Page Address: www.billreidgallery.ca; *Exec Dir* Mike Robinson; *Dir Mktg* Paula Fairweather
Open Wed - Sun 11 AM - 5 PM, cl Mon & Tues; Admis adult $10, senior & student (18+ with valid ID) $7, children (5-17) $5; Estab 2008 as a public gallery for contemporary aboriginal art of the northwest coast; Home to the Bill Reid coll & changing exhibs of contemporary Aboriginal Art of the northwest coast; Mem: Dues seniors & students $20, adults $30, couple $40, family $45
Income: Nonprofit
Collections: Bill Reid Collection
Exhibitions: Permanent exhib, Restoring Enchantment: Gold & Silver Masterworks by Bill Reid; Core exhibs & up to 3 temporary exhibs per yr
Publications: Bill Reid & the Haida Canoe & Camping or Irregardless: Humor in Contemporary Northwest Coast Art
Activities: Educ prog; docent training; pub progs associated with exhibs; lects open to pub, 3-4 vis lectrs per yr; gallery talks; tours; originate traveling exhibs; gallery shop sells books, original art, reproductions, prints, jewelry, accessories

A **COMMUNITY ARTS COUNCIL OF VANCOUVER,** 440-111 W Hasting St, Vancouver, BC V6B 1H4 Canada. Tel 604-683-4358, 683-8099; Fax 604-683-4394; Elec Mail info@carv.bc.ca; Internet Home Page Address: www.cacv.ca; *Pres* Hamish Malkin; *Asst* Karen Benbassat
Open 9 AM - 5 PM; No admis fee; Estab 1946 as a soc dedicated to the support of arts, with a wide range of interest in the arts; to promote standards in all art fields including civic arts; also serves as a liaison centre; Exhib Gallery shows works of semi-professional & emerging artists; 2200 sq ft on two levels, street level entrance; Average Annual Attendance: 40,000; Mem: 500; dues $15; ann meeting in Sept
Income: Financed by British Columbia Cultural & Lotteries Fund, City of Vancouver, mem & donations
Exhibitions: Two shows per month
Publications: Arts Vancouver Magazine, 4 issues per year
Activities: Lect open to pub; performances; workshops; concerts; gallery talks; competitions; schols & fels offered

M **CONTEMPORARY ART GALLERY,** (Toronto Centre for Contemporary Art) 555 Nelson St, Vancouver, BC V6B 6R5 Canada. Tel 604-681-2700; Fax 604-683-2710; Elec Mail cagart@rogerg.com; Internet Home Page Address: Contemporaryartgalleries.com; *Dir* Sonja Dagon; *Gallery Mgr* Zoya Boruchov
Open Tues - Sun noon - 6 PM; cl BC statutory holidays; No admis fee; Estab 1969
Collections: Permanent collections of contemporary art in Toronto's public schools; Contemporary Art
Exhibitions: Rotating exhibits monthly

M **CONTEMPORARY ART GALLERY SOCIETY OF BRITISH COLUMBIA,** 555 Nelson St, Vancouver, BC V6B 6R5 Canada. Tel 604-681-2700; Fax 604-683-2710; Elec Mail info@contemporaryartgallery.ca; Internet Home Page Address: www.contemporaryartgallery.ca; *Exec Dir* Nigel Prince; *Cur* Jenifer Papararo; *Prog Coordr* Lisa Fedorak; *Head Develop & Communs* Susan Lavitt; *Gallery Coordr* Jill Henderson; *Book-Keeper* Uli Hobruecker; *Preparator* Phil Dion
Open Tues - Sun noon - 6 PM; No admis fee; Estab 1971 as an exhib space for regional, national & international contemporary art; The Gallery has 1,700 sq ft exhib area; Average Annual Attendance: 16,000; Mem: 300; dues $39
Income: Financed by Federal Government, British Columbia Arts Council, City of Vancouver, mem fees & fundraising
Library Holdings: Auction Catalogs; CD-ROMs; Clipping Files; Compact Disks; DVDs; Exhibition Catalogs; Pamphlets; Periodical Subscriptions; Slides
Collections: City of Vancouver Art Collection; Contemporary Gallery Society of B C Art Collection
Publications: Exhibition brochure & catalogs
Activities: Classes for children; educ prog; docent training; online teaching resources; lects open to pub, 6 vis lectrs per yr; gallery talks; tours; Visual Arts Develop Award; individual paintings & original objects of art lent to civic agencies; lending coll contains 3400 works; organize traveling exhibs to mus & galleries nat & international; mus shop sells books, prints, original art

M **EMILY CARR INSTITUTE OF ART & DESIGN CHARLES H SCOTT GALLERY,** The Charles H Scott Gallery, 1399 Johnston St, Charles H. Scott Gallery-Emily Carr Institute Vancouver, BC V6H 3R9 Canada. Tel 604-844-3809; Fax 604-844-3801; Elec Mail scottgal@eciad.ca; Internet Home Page Address: http://www.ecuad.ca/resources/galleries/chscott; *Cur* Greg Bellerby; *Cur* Cate Rimmer; *Pres* Ron Burnett
Open Mon - Fri 12 PM - 5 PM, Sat - Sun 10 AM - 5 PM; No admis fee; Estab 1980 to provide mus quality exhibs & publs of critically significant visual art; 3000 sq ft gallery with all environmental & security safeguards; Average Annual Attendance: 30,000
Income: $95,000 (financed by provincial appropriation)
Exhibitions: Social Process - Collective Action, Mary Kelly 1970-75
Publications: Exhib catalogues
Activities: Tours upon request; book traveling exhibs 1-2 per yr; originate traveling exhibs; sales shop sells exhib catalogues

L **Library,** 1399 Johnston St, Vancouver, BC V6H 3R9 Canada. Tel 604-844-3840; Fax 604-844-3801; *Librn* Donna Zwierciadlowski; *Library Dir* Sheila Wallace
Open May - Aug Mon - Fri 8:30 AM - 5 PM, Sept - Apr Mon - Thurs 8:30 AM - 9 PM, Fri & Sat 8:30 AM - 5 PM; Circ 65,000
Income: Financed by government funding
Library Holdings: Audio Tapes; Book Volumes 18,000; Clipping Files; Exhibition Catalogs; Fiche; Periodical Subscriptions 165; Records; Slides 134,000; Video Tapes 1900
Special Subjects: Film, Photography, Graphic Design, Painting-American, Posters, Pre-Columbian Art, Prints, Sculpture, Painting-European, Printmaking, Industrial Design, Video, Primitive art, Pottery, Woodcarvings, Painting-Canadian

M **MUSEUM OF VANCOUVER,** (Vancouver Museum Commission) 1100 Chestnut St, Vanier Park Vancouver, BC V6J 3J9 Canada. Tel 604-736-4431; Fax 604-736-5417; Elec Mail guestservices@vanmuseum.bc.ca; Internet Home Page Address: www.vanmuseum.bc.ca; *CEO* Nancy Noble; *Cur Anthropology* Lynn Maranda; *Cur Asian Studies* Paula Swart; *Cur History* Joan Seidl; *Conservator* Carol Brynjfson
Open Tues - Sun 10 AM - 5 PM, Thurs 10 AM - 9 PM; Admis families $32, adults $11, students & seniors $9, youth (5-17) $7, under 5 free; Estab 1894 to collect, preserve & interpret natural & cultural history of Vancouver area; Permanent exhibs tell Vancouver's stories from the early 1900s to the late 70s complimented by contemporary ground breaking feature exhibs; Average Annual Attendance: 70,000; Mem: 500
Income: Financed by city of Vancouver, government grants, fundraising & gift shop sales
Special Subjects: Drawings, American Indian Art, African Art, Anthropology, Archaeology, Ethnology, Costumes, Ceramics, Folk Art, Etchings & Engravings, Decorative Arts, Eskimo Art, Dolls, Furniture, Glass, Jade, Jewelry, Asian Art, Historical Material, Ivory, Coins & Medals, Antiquities-Oriental, Antiquities-Egyptian, Antiquities-Greek, Antiquities-Roman
Collections: Vancouver Stories; Anthropology, Asian Studies, History and Natural History Colls
Exhibitions: Vancouver history exhibs; changing temporary exhibs
Publications: Occasional exhib catalogues
Activities: Classes for adults & children; docent progs; lects open to pub; gallery talks; tours; competitions; originate traveling exhibs to mus; mus shop sells books, original art, reproductions & prints

L **Museum of Vancouver Library,** 1100 Chestnut St, Vancouver, BC V6J 3J9 Canada. Tel 604-736-4431; Fax 604-736-5417; Internet Home Page Address: www.museum of vancouver.ca; *CEO* Nancy Noble
Open by appointment only; Circ Non-circulating; For reference
Library Holdings: Audio Tapes; Book Volumes 9000; Cassettes; Clipping Files; Exhibition Catalogs; Pamphlets; Periodical Subscriptions 30; Video Tapes
Special Subjects: Folk Art, Decorative Arts, Historical Material, Archaeology, Asian Art, American Indian Art, Porcelain, Anthropology, Eskimo Art, Mexican Art, Stained Glass, Oriental Art, Painting-Canadian
Collections: Vancouver history & culture, Northwest Coast First Nations
Activities: Classes for adults & children; Lects open to pub

M **UNIVERSITY OF BRITISH COLUMBIA,** Morris & Helen Belkin Art Gallery, 1825 Main Mall, Vancouver, BC Canada. *Dir & Cur* Scott Watson; *Adminr* Annette Wooff; *Prog Coordr* Naomi Sawada; *Preparator & Colls Mgr* Owen Sopotiuk; *Archivist* Krisztina Laszio
Open Tues - Fri 10 AM - 5 PM, Sat & Sun Noon - 5 PM, cl Mon & civic holidays; No admis fee; Estab 1948, The gallery has a mandate to encourage projects conceived for its special content. Our programming emphasizes contemporary art & also projects which serve to further understanding of the history of Avant-Garde; Gallery covers 27,000 sq ft; Average Annual Attendance: 15,000; Mem: No mem prog
Income: Financed by departmental funds
Publications: Announcements; exhib catalogues

L **Art & Architecture Planning, UBC Library,** 1961 East Mall, Irving K. Barber Learning Centre Vancouver, BC V6T 1Z1 Canada. Tel 604-822-3943; Internet Home Page Address: www.library.ubc.ca/aarp; *Head Librn* D Vanessa Kam; *Reference Librn* Paula Farrar
Open Mon - Thurs 8 AM - 10 PM, Fri 8 AM - 6 PM, Sat 10 AM - 6 PM, Sun Noon - 8 PM; No admis fee; Estab 1948 to serve students & faculty in all courses related to fine arts, architecture & planning
Library Holdings: Auction Catalogs; Book Volumes 230,000; CD-ROMs; Clipping Files; Exhibition Catalogs; Pamphlets; Periodical Subscriptions; Reproductions
Special Subjects: Art History, Landscape Architecture, Decorative Arts, Illustration, Photography, Drawings, Etchings & Engravings, Graphic Arts, Painting-American, Painting-British, Painting-French, Posters, Pre-Columbian Art, Prints, Sculpture, Painting-European, Historical Material, History of Art & Archaeology, Watercolors, Conceptual Art, Latin American Art, Printmaking, Interior Design, Asian Art, Furniture, Costume Design & Constr, Restoration & Conservation, Woodcarvings, Woodcuts, Antiquities-Byzantine, Antiquities-Roman, Reproductions, Painting-Canadian, Architecture
Activities: Library instruction, reference servs

M **Museum of Anthropology,** 6393 NW Marine Dr, Vancouver, BC V6T 1Z2 Canada. Tel 604-822-5087; Fax 604-822-2974; Internet Home Page Address: www.moa.ubc.ca; *Dir & Prof* Dr Ruth Phillips; *Cur Northwest Coast* Alexia Bloch; *Cur of Educ & Pub Prog* Jill Baird; *Cur of Ethnology & Media* Pam Brown; *Cur Ethnology & Document* Elizabeth Johnson; *Cur Ethnology & Ceramics* Carol Mayer; *Sr Conservator* Miriam Clavir; *Conservator* Heidi Swierenga; *Project Mgr Conservation* Darrin Morrison; *Mgr Admin* Moya Waters; *Mgr Admin* Anna Pappalardo; *Shop Mgr Wholesale & Supvr Admin* Salma Mawani; *Shop Mgr Retail* Deborah Tibbel; *Communs Mgr* Jennifer Webb; *Coll*

Mgr Ann Stevenson; *Mgr Loans & Proj* Allison Cronin; *Asst Coll Mgr* Nancy Bruegeman; *Mgr Directed Studies & the Critical Curatorial Studies Prog* Kersti Krug; *Mgr Design & Photog* Bill McLennan; *Mgr Design & Exhibits* David Cunningham; *Mgr Design & Production* Skooker Broome; *Archaeology Asst Cur* Joyce Johnson; *Booking Coordr* Gwilyn Timmers; *Asst to Dir* Nina Chatelain; *Librn* Justine Dainard; *Archivist* Krisztina Laszlo
Open Sept - May Tues 11 AM - 9 PM, Wed - Sun 11 AM - 5 PM, May - Sept daily 10 AM - 5 PM, Tues 10 AM - 9 PM; Admis family $20, adults $7, sr citizens $5, students & children $4, group rates for 10 or more, Tues free 5 - 9 PM; Estab 1947 to develop a high quality institution that maximizes pub access & involvement while also conducting active progs of teaching, research & experimentation; Average Annual Attendance: 170,000; Mem: 750; dues family $50, individual student & sr couple $30, student & sr citizens $20
Library Holdings: Auction Catalogs; Book Volumes; Exhibition Catalogs; Pamphlets; Periodical Subscriptions
Special Subjects: Architecture, American Indian Art, American Western Art, Anthropology, Archaeology, Ethnology, Textiles, Ceramics, Crafts, Folk Art, Woodcarvings, Decorative Arts, Oriental Art, Asian Art, Historical Material, Coins & Medals, Antiquities-Oriental, Antiquities-Greek, Antiquities-Etruscan
Collections: Ethnographic areas around the world, especially the northwest coast of British Columbia; European ceramics; mus journals; oriental art & history
Activities: Classes for adults & children; volunteer training; lects open to pub, 20-30 vis lectrs per yr; gallery talks; tours; competitions with awards; exten dept; original objects of art lent to institutions for special exhibs; book traveling exhibs; originate traveling exhibs; mus shop sells books, original art, jewelry, reproductions, prints, slides, postcards, note cards & t-shirts

M **VANCOUVER ART GALLERY,** 750 Hornby St, Vancouver, BC V6Z 2H7 Canada. Tel 604-662-4719, 662-4700 (Admin Offices); Fax 604-682-1086; Elec Mail curatorial@vanartgallery.bc.ca; Internet Home Page Address: www.vanartgallery.bc.ca; *Chair* Bruce Wright; *Dir* Kathleen Bartels; *Chief Cur* Daina Augaitis; *Sr Cur* Bruce Grenville; *Dir Mktg* Stephen Webster; *Conservator* Monica Smith; *Registrar* Jenny Wilson; *Librn* Cheryl Siegel; *Assoc Dir* Paul Larocque; *Dir Develop* Scott Elliott; *Sr Cur* Ian Thom; *Sr Cur* Grant Arnold
Open daily 10 AM - 5 PM, Tues 10 AM - 9 PM; Admis adults $17.50, sr citizens $12.50, students with cards $12.50, children 5-12 $6.25, under 5 free; Estab 1931 to foster the cultural development of the community & a pub interest in the arts; Gallery moved in 1983 into a reconstructed 1907 classical courthouse which had been designed by Francis Rattenbury. The building contains 41,400 net sq ft of gallery space. Complex contains a total gross area of 164,805 sq ft; Average Annual Attendance: 300,000; Mem: 40,000; dues family $120, individual $75
Income: Financed by city, provincial & federal government grants, pvt & corporate donations, endowment
Library Holdings: Auction Catalogs 500; Audio Tapes 400; Book Volumes 46,000; CD-ROMs; Clipping Files 6,000; Exhibition Catalogs; Periodical Subscriptions 150; Slides 30,000
Special Subjects: Landscapes, Architecture, Photography, Portraits, Painting-American, Prints, Textiles, Painting-British, Sculpture, Drawings, Painting-Canadian, Asian Art, Painting-Dutch
Collections: 10,000 works, including drawings, film, objects, paintings, photographs
Publications: Ann Report; Calendar, 5 times per annum; Exhib Catalogues; biannual mems newsletter
Activities: Classes for adults & children; docent training; lect open to pub, 10 vis lectrs per yr; gallery talks; tours; concerts; individual paintings & original objects of art lent to museums who comply with security & climate control standards; originate traveling exhibs to major art mus across Canada & internationally; mus shop sells books, magazines, reproductions, postcards, posters, prints, native Indian art, jewelry, goods in leather, paper & wood by local artisans, non-circulating reference library open to the public

L **Library,** 750 Hornby St, Vancouver, BC V6Z 2H7 Canada. Tel 604-662-4709; Fax 604-682-1086; Elec Mail casiegel@vanartgallery.bc.ca; Internet Home Page Address: www.vanartgallery.bc.ca; *Librn* Cheryl A Siegel; *Librn* Lynn Brockington
Open Mon - Fri 1 - 5 PM; Estab 1931 to serve staff, docents, students & the public; For reference only; Average Annual Attendance: 3,000
Library Holdings: Auction Catalogs 500; Audio Tapes 400; Book Volumes 42,000; Clipping Files 6,000; Memorabilia; Pamphlets; Periodical Subscriptions 150; Photographs
Collections: Fine arts specializing in Canadian & contemporary art

L **VANCOUVER CITY ARCHIVES,** 1150 Chestnut St, Vancouver, BC V6J 3J9 Canada. Tel 604-736-8561; Fax 604-736-0626; Elec Mail archives@vancouver.ca; Internet Home Page Address: vancouver.ca/archives; *Dir* Leslie Mobbs; *City Archivist* Heather M Gordon
Open Mon - Fri 9 AM - 5 PM, cl weekends & legal holidays; No admis fee; Estab 1933
Income: Financed by city appropriation
Library Holdings: Clipping Files; Fiche; Kodachrome Transparencies; Lantern Slides; Manuscripts; Maps; Memorabilia; Motion Pictures; Original Art Works; Original Documents; Other Holdings Charts; Civic Records; Drawings; Maps; Paintings; Pamphlets; Photographs; Slides; Video Tapes
Special Subjects: Photography, Maps, Painting-Canadian
Exhibitions: Temporary exhibs
Activities: Lect open to pub; tours

M **VANCOUVER PUBLIC LIBRARY,** Fine Arts & Music Department, 350 W Georgia St, Vancouver, BC V6B 6B1 Canada. Tel 604-331-3603; Fax 604-331-3701; Elec Mail info@vpl.ca; Internet Home Page Address: www.vpl.ca; *Mgr Colls* C Middlemass
Open Mon - Thurs 10 AM - 9 PM, Fri & Sat 10 AM - 6 PM, Sun Noon - 5 PM; Library estab 1887 as Vancouver Reading Room. Fine Arts coll estab 1930; Circ 255,900; Mem: 274,700; members free to those living in the region
Library Holdings: Auction Catalogs; Book Volumes 115,400 & 14,300 song books & performance scores; CD-ROMs 90; Compact Disks 17,900; DVDs 9,800; Exhibition Catalogs; Other Holdings Documentation files for British Columbia artists; Periodical Subscriptions 225
Special Subjects: Decorative Arts, Furniture, Porcelain, Silver, Textiles, Silversmithing, Costumes, Painting-Canadian, Jewelry
Activities: Educ progs; ebook, email & internet training for adults; author readings; progs co-sponsored with community groups

VERNON

M **VERNON ART GALLERY,** 3228 31st Ave, Vernon, BC V1T 9G9 Canada. Tel 250-545-3173; Fax 604-545-9096; Elec Mail vernonartgallery@home.com; Internet Home Page Address: www.galleries.bc.ca/vernon; *Exec Dir* Renee Lapierre; *Curatorial Dir* Lubos Culen; *Preparator* Joanne Sale-Hook
Open Mon - Fri 10 AM - 5 PM, Sat 11 AM - 4 pm, cl Sun; No admis fee; Estab 1967 for the coll & exhib of art work by Okanagan, national & international artists; Two gallery spaces professionally designed & measure 5500 sq ft, also reception area, gift shop & admin & kitchen area; Average Annual Attendance: 27,000; Mem: 420; dues family $35, individual $25, sr citizens & students $20
Income: Financed by mem, city appropriation & grants
Collections: Permanent coll consists of ceramics, paintings, prints, sculpture and serigraphs
Exhibitions: 20 exhibits ann
Publications: Art Quarterly
Activities: Classes for adults & children; docent training; lects, 3 vis lectrs per yr; gallery talks; concerts; tours; performances; competitions; book traveling exhibs 3-4 per yr; originate traveling exhibs; mus shop sells books, magazines, original art, reproductions & local crafts

VICTORIA

M **ART GALLERY OF GREATER VICTORIA,** 1040 Moss St, Victoria, BC V8V 4P1 Canada. Tel 250-384-4101; Tel 250-384-4171 (Admin); Fax 250-361-3995; Elec Mail mloria@aggv.bc.ca; Internet Home Page Address: www.aggv.bc.ca; *Dir* Jon Tupper; *Cur Asian Art* Barry Till; *Mgr Pub Affairs & Dir Develop* Mark Loria; *Dir Finance & Admin* Barb Lucas; *Pres* Lorrainne Dixon; *Assoc Cur* Nicole Stanbridge; *Coll Mgr* Stephen Topfer; *Chief Cur* Mary Jo Hughes
Open Mon - Sun 10 AM - 5 PM, Thurs - 10 AM - 9 PM; winter Tues - Sat 10 AM - 5 PM, Thurs 10 AM - 9 PM, Sun 12 PM - 5 PM, cl Mon; Admis adults $12, seniors & students $10, children (6-17) $2, under 5 free; admis donation first Tues; Estab 1947; Six modern galleries adjoin 19th Century Spencer Mansion-Japanese Garden; Average Annual Attendance: 56,500; Mem: 1950; dues family $70, individual $50, student & non-resident $25; ann meeting 2nd wk of June
Income: $2,000,000 (financed by mem, city, federal & provincial grants)
Special Subjects: Painting-British, Primitive art, Decorative Arts, Painting-European, Painting-Canadian, Oriental Art, Asian Art
Collections: Chinese, Indian, Persian & Tibetan Art; Contemporary Canadian, American & European; European Painting & Decorative Arts from 16th-19th centuries; Japanese Art from Kamakura to Contemporary; Primitive Arts
Exhibitions: Approx 35 exhibs in 6 exhib halls, changing every 6 wks
Publications: Mem newsletter, 4 times per yr
Activities: Classes for adults & children; docent training; gallery in the schools prog; workshops; lects open to pub, 12 vis lectrs per yr; concerts; tours; gallery talks; exten dept serves BC; individual paintings & original objects of art lent to mus & local pub bldgs; lending colls contains cassettes, original art works, sculpture, scrolls, 4800 books, 5000 original prints, 2000 slides; book traveling exhibs 5-20 per yr; originate traveling exhibs; sales shop sells books, magazines, reproductions, stationery, jewelry, pottery, ornaments, glass & prints

L **Library,** 1040 Moss St, Victoria, BC V8V 4P1 Canada. Tel 250-384-4171; Fax 250-361-3995; Elec Mail library@aggv.bc.ca; Internet Home Page Address: www.aggv.ca; *Librn* Ms J Thompson; *Chief Cur* M Jacques
Open 10 AM - 5 PM; Estab 1951; Circ Non-circulating
Library Holdings: Book Volumes 7,000; Cassettes 25; Clipping Files 1,000; Compact Disks 50; DVDs 20; Exhibition Catalogs 2,500; Photographs 200; Slides 300; Video Tapes 50
Special Subjects: Art History, Folk Art, Landscape Architecture, Decorative Arts, Mixed Media, Photography, Drawings, Etchings & Engravings, Graphic Arts, Painting-American, Painting-British, Painting-Dutch, Painting-French, Painting-German, Painting-Italian, Painting-Japanese, Prints, Sculpture, Painting-European, History of Art & Archaeology, Watercolors, Ceramics, Interior Design, Art Education, Asian Art, Porcelain, Jade, Glass, Antiquities-Oriental, Antiquities-Persian, Embroidery, Oriental Art, Pottery, Silver, Silversmithing, Tapestries, Textiles, Woodcarvings, Woodcuts, Antiquities-Assyrian, Antiquities-Byzantine, Antiquities-Egyptian, Antiquities-Etruscan, Antiquities-Greek, Antiquities-Roman, Painting-Canadian, Architecture

A **BRITISH COLUMBIA MUSEUMS ASSOCIATION,** 201-645 Fort St, Victoria, BC V8W 1G2 Canada. Tel 250-356-5700; Fax 250-387-1251; Elec Mail bcma@museumsassn.bc.ca; Internet Home Page Address: www.museumsassn.bc.ca; *Exec Dir* Jim Harding; *Mem Svcs Coordr* Shelley Gauthier

CANADIAN SOCIETY FOR EDUCATION THROUGH ART
For further information, see National and Regional Organizations

M **CRAIGDARROCH CASTLE HISTORICAL MUSEUM SOCIETY,** 1050 Joan Crescent, Victoria, BC V8S 3L5 Canada. Tel 250-592-5323; Fax 250-592-1099; Elec Mail info@thecastle.ca; Internet Home Page Address: www.craigdarrochcastle.com; *Registrar & Technician* Delphine Castle; *Cur* Bruce Davies; *Vol Coordr* Robert Rathwell; *Exec Dir* Trish Chan; *Restoration Mgr* Frank Tosczak; *Mus Store Mgr* Karen Kinney
Open 10 AM - 4:30 PM; June 15 - Sept 1, 9 AM - 7 PM; Admis adults $11.75, senior $10.75, student $7.75, child $3.75, 5 and under free; Estab 1959 for conservation & restoration of house; Average Annual Attendance: 150,000; Mem: 500; dues $25; ann meeting in the spring
Income: $1.4 mil (financed by progs & visitation)
Library Holdings: Auction Catalogs; Audio Tapes; Exhibition Catalogs; Kodachrome Transparencies; Photographs

Special Subjects: Architecture, Painting-American, Textiles, Ceramics, Painting-Canadian, Dolls, Furniture, Carpets & Rugs, Historical Material, Restorations, Period Rooms, Embroidery, Stained Glass
Collections: Historical objects pertaining to the years 1890-1908; 5000 objects used to furnish an historical turn of the century mansion
Publications: Castle Quarterly, newsletter, annual report
Activities: Classes for children; dramatic progs; docent training; lects open to pub, 2 vis lectrs per yr; gallery talks; tours; individual paintings & original objects of art lent to other qualified cultural institutions; lending coll contains books, original art works, prints & paintings; mus shop sells books & souvenirs

A OPEN SPACE, 510 Fort St, Fl 2 Victoria, BC V8W 1E6 Canada. Tel 250-383-8833; Elec Mail openspace@openspace.ca; Internet Home Page Address: www.openspace.ca; *Exec Dir* Helen Marzolf; *New Music Coordr* Christopher Reiche; *Prog Coordr* Doug Jarvis; *Technician* Miles Geisbrecht; *Admin Asst* Jacquelyn Bortolussi
Open Tues - Sat Noon - 5 PM, cl Mon & Sun; Admis by donation; Estab 1972, open space is dedicated to contemporary art through visual art, new music, performance, literature & new media; Circ 20,000; Gallery has 3000 sq ft, 220 running ft with full light grid controlled to level for works of art & for performance progs; Average Annual Attendance: 25,000; Mem: 150; dues $15 - $30
Income: $400,000 (financed by federal & provincial appropriations, city grants, donations, mem fees & self-generated revenue)
Library Holdings: Audio Tapes; Book Volumes; CD-ROMs; Exhibition Catalogs; Memorabilia; Original Art Works; Original Documents; Other Holdings; Periodical Subscriptions; Photographs; Slides; Video Tapes
Exhibitions: 10-12 contemporary visual art exhibs per yr
Publications: catalogues & monographs published for all exhibs (list available on request)
Activities: Teacher-in-residence prog; Lects open to pub, 8 vis lectrs per yr; concerts; gallery talks; tours; awards for music composers of international stature; visual art lects, new music, performance, new medium, interarts, readings; artist residencies; organize traveling exhibs as requested; mus shop sells books

L ROYAL BRITISH COLUMBIA MUSEUM, BC Archives, 675 Belleville St, Victoria, BC V8W 9W2 Canada. Tel 250-387-1952; Fax 250-387-2072; Elec Mail access@bcarchives.bc.ca; Internet Home Page Address: www.bcarchives.gov.bc.ca/index.htm; *Provincial Archivist & Dir* Gary A Mitchell
Open Mon - Fri 10 AM - 4 PM; Estab 1893 to collect & preserve all records relating to the historical development of British Columbia; Archival coll; 10,000 historical works documenting British Columbia
Income: Financed by provincial appropriation
Library Holdings: Audio Tapes; Book Volumes 70,380; Clipping Files; Exhibition Catalogs; Manuscripts; Original Art Works; Other Holdings Original documents; Maps; Pamphlets; Periodical Subscriptions 100; Photographs; Reels
Publications: Art reproductions

M UNIVERSITY OF VICTORIA, The Legacy Art Gallery, 630 Yates St, Victoria, BC V8W 1K9 Canada. Tel 250-721-6562; Fax 250-721-6607; Elec Mail curator@uvic.ca; Internet Home Page Address: www.uvac.uvic.ca; *Dir* Mary Jo Hughes; *Pres* Dr David Turpin; *Cur* Caroline Reidel; *Secy of Gallery* Cheryl Robinson; *Coll Coordr* Cindy Vance
Open Wed - Sat 10 AM - 4 PM; No admis fee; Estab 1963 to collect, preserve & exhibit the decorative arts, maintain teaching colls for the univ; Gallery has 3000 sq ft of environmentally controlled exhib space, three galleries programmed, loan exhibits & from coll permanent exhibit. Maintains reference library; Average Annual Attendance: 100,000
Income: $200,000 (financed by endowment & state appropriation)
Purchases: $500
Special Subjects: Architecture, Drawings, Graphics, Photography, American Indian Art, American Western Art, Anthropology, Archaeology, Ethnology, Costumes, Ceramics, Crafts, Folk Art, Primitive art, Etchings & Engravings, Decorative Arts, Portraits, Jewelry, Porcelain, Oriental Art, Asian Art, Ivory, Renaissance Art, Medieval Art, Islamic Art
Collections: Maltwood Collection of Decorative Art; contemporary art (Canadian); Ethnographic & design art; Pacific Northwest modern & contemporary
Exhibitions: Permanent collections, continuing and rotating
Publications: Collections related exhib catalogues
Activities: Lects open to pub, 10 vis lectrs per yr; gallery talks; tours; individual paintings lent to offices & pub spaces on campus; lending coll contains 3000 original prints, 1000 paintings & sculpture; lend original art objects to on & off campus borrowers; book traveling exhibs 5 per yr; originate traveling exhibs to local mus; mus shop sells books, original art, reproductions & prints

WHITE ROCK

M ARNOLD MIKELSON MIND & MATTER ART GALLERY, 13743 16th Ave, White Rock, BC V4A 1P7 Canada. Tel 604-536-6460; Elec Mail mary@mindandmatterart.com; Internet Home Page Address: www.mindandmatterart.com; *Pres* Mary Mikelson; *Asst Dir* Myra Mikelson; *Mgr* Arnold Mikelson; *Asst Mgr* Sapphire Mikelson
Open Noon - 6 PM or by appointment; No admis fee; Estab 1965; 2000 sq ft gallery on three acres, upper flr mus, main flr continues exhibs of Canadian artists; Average Annual Attendance: 15,000
Income: Funded by the Mikelson Family
Special Subjects: Folk Art, Landscapes, Marine Painting, Pottery, Sculpture, Watercolors, Woodcarvings, Jewelry
Collections: Showcase wood sculpture by the late Arnold Mikelson; Arnold Mikelson Wood Sculpture
Exhibitions: Metal art, modern landscape, painting, stone sculpture, wildlife, wood sculpture; Nov-Dec, Annual Art for X-mas; July, Arnold Mikelson Festival of Arts
Activities: Classes for children; lects open to pub, 25-30 lectrs per yr; gallery talks; schols; mus shop sells original art

MANITOBA

BOISSEVAIN

M MONCUR GALLERY, PO Box 1241, Boissevain, MB R0K 0E0 Canada. Tel 204-534-6478 or 534-6689; Fax 204-534-3710; Elec Mail info@moncurgallery.org; Internet Home Page Address: www.moncurgallery.org; *Chmn* Shannon Moncur; *Secy* Phyllis Hallett; *Treas* Audrey Hicks
Open Tues - Sat 10 AM - 5 PM; Admis adults $3, children $2; Estab 1986; Native History; Average Annual Attendance: 500-1,000
Income: $8,000 (financed by city & state appropriation)
Special Subjects: Archaeology
Collections: Aboriginal artifacts dating back 10,000 years collected in the Turtle Mountain area; Aboriginal Artifacts

BRANDON

A THE ART GALLERY OF SOUTHWESTERN MANITOBA, 710 Rosser Ave Unit 2, Brandon, MB R7A 0K9 Canada. Tel 204-727-1036; Fax 204-726-8139; Elec Mail info@agsm.ca; Internet Home Page Address: http://agsm.ca/; *Dir* Gordon McDonald; *Cur* Chris Reid
Open Mon & Thurs 10 AM - 9 PM, Tues, Wed & Fri 10 AM - 5 PM, Sun 2 - 5 PM; No admis fee; Estab 1960 to promote & foster cultural activities in western Manitoba; Average Annual Attendance: 2,400; Mem: 400; dues $6 - $20; ann meeting May
Income: Financed by mem, city & provincial appropriations & federal grants
Exhibitions: Exhibitions of regional, national & international significance
Publications: Bulletin, every 2 months
Activities: Classes for adults & children; lects open to pub, 2 vis lectrs per yr; gallery talks; tours; competitions; individual paintings & original objects of art lent to mems; lending coll contains original art works, original prints, paintings, weaving

L Brandon Public Library, 710 Rosser Ave Unit 1, Brandon, MB R7A 0K9 Canada. Tel 204-727-6648; Fax 204-726-8139; Elec Mail wmrlibrary@wmrlibrary.mb.ca; Internet Home Page Address: http://www.wmr1.ca/bpl.html; *Chief Librn* Kathy Thornborough
Open Mon & Thurs 10 AM - 9 PM, Tues, Wed & Fri 10 AM - 5 PM, Sun 2 - 5 PM; Circ Non-circulating; Open to mems
Library Holdings: Book Volumes 78,000

CHURCHILL

M ESKIMO MUSEUM, 242 La Verendrye, PO Box 10 Churchill, MB R0B 0E0 Canada. Tel 204-675-2030; Fax 204-675-2140; *Dir* Bishop Reynald Rouleau; *Asst Cur* Cathy Widdowson; *Cur* Lorraine Brandson
Open June - Nov 8: Mon 1 - 4:30 PM, Sat 9 AM - Noon & 1 - 5 PM, Nov 9 - May 31: Mon 1 - 4:30 PM, Tues - Fri 10:30 AM - Noon & 1 - 4:30 PM, Sat 1 - 4 PM; No admis fee; Estab 1944 to depict the Eskimo way of life through the display of artifacts; Mus has large single display room; Average Annual Attendance: 10,500
Income: Administered & funded by the Roman Catholic Episcopal Corporation of Churchill Hudson Bay
Special Subjects: Sculpture, Ethnology, Eskimo Art
Collections: Contemporary Inuit carvings; ethnographic collections; prehistoric artifacts; wildlife specimens
Publications: Carved From the Land by Lorraine Brandson 1994
Activities: Films & slide shows for school groups upon request; tours upon request; original objects of art lent to special exhibs & galleries; mus shop sells books, original art, art cards, postcards & northern theme clothing (t-shirts, sweatshirts & caps)

L Library, 242 La Verendrye, PO Box 10 Churchill, MB R0B 0E0 Canada. Tel 204-675-2030; Fax 204-675-2140; *Cur* Lorraine Brandson; *Asst Cur* Diann Elliott
Open by appointment only; Circ Non-circulating; Estab mainly for Arctic Canada material
Purchases: $1,000
Library Holdings: Book Volumes 500; Clipping Files; Exhibition Catalogs; Maps; Photographs; Video Tapes
Special Subjects: Crafts, Archaeology, Ethnology, Eskimo Art, Handicrafts, Restoration & Conservation

DAUPHIN

M DAUPHIN & DISTRICT ALLIED ARTS COUNCIL, Watson Art Centre, 104 First Ave NW, Dauphin, MB R7N 1G9 Canada. Tel 204-638-6231; Fax 204-638-6231; Elec Mail info@watsonartcentre.com; Internet Home Page Address: www.watsonartcentre.com; *Adm\`nr* Ruth E Lowe; *Pres* Michelle NyQuist; *Treas* Jenna Alexander; *Secy* Maureen Neabel
Open Mon - Fri Noon - 5 PM; No admis fee; Estab 1973 to provide a home for the arts in the Dauphin District; 1 large gallery; Average Annual Attendance: 20,000; Mem: Dues assoc $100, family $20, individual $15; ann meeting in Mar
Income: $100,000 (financed by mem, town appropriation, provincial appropriation, donations)
Exhibitions: Rotate several exhibits per month
Publications: Arts council newsletter, quarterly
Activities: Classes for adults & children; dramatic progs; concerts; gallery talks; tours; lending coll contains paintings & art objects; book traveling exhibs 1 or 2 per yr; originate traveling exhibs; mus shop sells books & original art

PORTAGE LA PRAIRIE

A PORTAGE AND DISTRICT ARTS COUNCIL, Portage Arts Centre, 11-2nd St NE, Portage la Prairie, MB R1N 1R8 Canada. Tel 204-239-6029; Fax 204-239-1472; Elec Mail pdac@mts.net; Internet Home Page Address: www.portageartscentre.ca; *Mgr* Jean Armstrong; *Arts Promotion Coordr* Lori Blight
Open Tues - Sat 11 AM - 5 PM; 200 ft running wall space & 1,700 sq ft floor space; classroom; pottery studio; dance studio; library; Mem: dues students $20, adult $25, family $45, group $75

Activities: Classes; workshops; gift shop sells art supplies, original art

WINNIPEG

L ARCHIVES OF MANITOBA, 130-200 Vaughan St, Winnipeg, MB R3C 1T5 Canada. Tel 204-945-3971; Fax 204-948-2008; Elec Mail archives@gov.mb.ca; Internet Home Page Address: www.gov.mb.ca/chc/index.html
Open Mon - Fri 9 AM - 4 PM; No admis fee; Estab 1952 to gain access to Manitoba's documentary heritage; to preserve the recorded memory of Manitoba
Income: Financed by provincial appropriation through the Minister of Culture, Heritage & Tourism
Collections: Hudson's Bay Company Archives; Documentary & archival paintings, drawings, prints & photographs relating to Manitoba
Activities: Individual paintings & original objects of art lent to pub institutions with proper security; book traveling exhibs

A MANITOBA ASSOCIATION OF ARCHITECTS, 137 Bannatyne Ave, 2nd Flr, Winnipeg, MB R3B 0R3 Canada. Tel 204-925-4620; Fax 204-925-4624; Elec Mail info@mbarchitects.org; Internet Home Page Address: www.mbarchitects.org; *Exec Dir* Judy Pestrak
Open Mon - Fri 9 AM - 5 PM; Estab 1906 as a Provincial Architectural Registration Board & professional governing body; Mem: 350; dues $375; ann meeting in Mar
Income: Financed by ann mem dues
Publications: Columns, quarterly

M MANITOBA HISTORICAL SOCIETY, Dalnavert Museum, 61 Carlton St, Winnipeg, MB R3C 1N7 Canada. Tel 204-943-2835; Fax 204-943-2565; Elec Mail dalnavert@mhs.mb.ca; Internet Home Page Address: www.mhs.mb.ca; *Pres* Dr Harry W Duckworth; *Chief Admin Officer* Jacqueline Frieseu; *Chief Prog Officer & Cur* Jennifer Bisch
Open Wed - Fri 10 AM - 5 PM, Sat 11 AM - 6 PM, Sun 12 PM - 4 PM; Admis family $12, adults $5, sr citizens $4 youth $3, under 5 free; Estab 1975 to preserve & display the way of life of the 1895 well-to-do family; Average Annual Attendance: 2,000
Income: $200,000 (financed by municipal, provincial & federal funding, admissions, programming & donations)
Special Subjects: Decorative Arts, Drawings, Etchings & Engravings, Historical Material, Architecture, Art History, Ceramics, Glass, Metalwork, Furniture, Costumes, Crafts, Painting-Canadian, Dolls, Jewelry, Carpets & Rugs, Ivory, Coins & Medals, Embroidery, Laces, Leather
Collections: Home furnishings of the 1895 period: clothing, decorative arts material, furniture, household items, paintings & original family memorabilia
Activities: Educ prog; classes for adults & children; dramatic progs; docent training; lect open to pub; concerts; tours; mus shop sells books, magazines, original art, heritage seeds & work by local artisans

A MANITOBA SOCIETY OF ARTISTS, PO Box 21056, Winnipeg, MB R3R 3R2 Canada. Tel 204-832-3045; Elec Mail president@mbsa.ca; Internet Home Page Address: www.mbsa.ca; *Pres* Bonnie Taylor; *VPres* Tony Kuluk; *Mem Chair* Rosella Farmer; *Webmaster* Garth Palanuk; *Secy* Lois Hogg
Estab 1901 to further the work of the artist at the local & community levels; Mem: 105; dues $50; ann meeting Oct
Income: Financed by mem & commission on sales, donations
Special Subjects: Drawings, Etchings & Engravings, Landscapes, Posters, Prints, Sculpture, Watercolors, Pottery, Woodcuts, Afro-American Art, Crafts, Miniatures, Portraits, Oriental Art, Calligraphy, Dioramas
Exhibitions: annual competition & exhibition open to all residents of Manitoba; Fresh Paint! annual mems exhib & sale (mem only)
Publications: Newsletter
Activities: Educ aspects include teaching by mems in rural areas & artist-in-residence work in pub schools; workshops; how to hang exhibs; annual art history conference; lect open to pub; gallery talks; tours; competitions with awards; awards in memory of deceased mems; Bursary to post secondary students in fine arts or graphics; schols offered; originate traveling exhibs

M PLUG IN, Institute of Contemporary Art, 460 Portage Ave, Unit 1 Winnipeg, MB R3C 0E8 Canada. Tel 204-942-1043; Fax 204-944-8663; Elec Mail info@plugin.org; Internet Home Page Address: www.plugin.org; *Dir* Anthony Kiendl; *Gallery Asst* Karin Streu; *Mng Dir* Heather Laser; *Asst Cur* Cassidy Richardson; *Admin & Events Coordr* Janique Vigier
Open Tues 12 PM - 5 PM, Wed 12 PM - 9 PM, Fri 12 PM - 7 PM, Sat 9 AM - 7 PM, Sun 9 AM - 5 PM, cl Mon; No admis fee; Estab 1974; 5,000 sq ft; 200 linear ft of gallery wall; renovated street-level gallery in historic Exchange District; Average Annual Attendance: 30,000; Mem: 350; dues $50 regular, $25 artists
Income: $650,000 (financed by mem, federal, city & state appropriation)
Library Holdings: Book Volumes; Exhibition Catalogs; Pamphlets; Periodical Subscriptions
Publications: Memories of Overdevelopment: The Philippine Diaspora in Contemporary Art (1998); Marcel Dzama: More Famous Drawings, Beck & Al Hanson: Playing with Matches, The Paradise Institute - Janet Cardiff & George Bures-Miller, Shaan Syed: Crowds & Constellations, Micah Lexier: David Then & Now, Mitch Robertson: 567 Economies of Good & Evil
Activities: Classes for children; lects open to pub, 10-20 vis lectrs per yr; gallery talks; tours; book traveling exhibs 4 per yr; originate traveling exhibs 4 per yr to galleries & artist-run centers; circulating internationally; mus shop sells books, magazines, original art & prints

M UKRAINIAN CULTURAL & EDUCATIONAL CENTRE, 184 Alexander Ave E, Winnipeg, MB R3B 0L6 Canada. Tel 204-942-0218; Fax 204-943-2857; *Pres Board Dirs* Paul Stanicky
Open Mon - Sat 10 AM - 4 PM; No admis fee; Estab as the largest Ukrainian cultural resource centre & repository of Ukrainian historical & cultural artifacts in North America; Mem: 2000; dues $15, ann meeting June
Income: $216,328 (financed by province of Manitoba, federal government, donations, mem, trust fund, fundraising events)

Collections: Ukrainian Folk Art; folk costumes; embroidery; weaving; pysanky (Easter eggs); woodcarving; ceramics; coins, postage stamps and documents of the Ukrainian National Republic of 1918-1921; works of art by Ukrainian, Ukrainian-Canadian and Ukrainian-American artists: prints, paintings, sculpture; archives: Ukrainian immigration to Canada, music colls
Publications: Visti Oseredok/News from Oseredok, members' bulletin, 2-3 times per yr
Activities: Lect open to pub; gallery talks; tours; competitions; schols offered; individual paintings & original objects of art lent to educ institutions, galleries & museums; lending coll contains color reproductions, framed reproductions, motion pictures, phonorecords, 40,000 photographs, 2000 slides; book traveling exhibs ann; originate traveling exhibs; sales shop sells books, original art, reproductions, prints, folk art, phonorecords, cassettes

M Gallery, 184 Alexander Ave E, Winnipeg, MB R3B 0L6 Canada. Tel 204-942-0218; Fax 204-943-2857; Elec Mail ucec@mts.net; Internet Home Page Address: www.oseredok.org; *Board Dirs* Paul Stanicky
Open Mon - Sat 10 AM - 4 PM, Sun 1 PM - 4 PM (July - Aug); No admis fee; Mem: Dues family & organization $25, individual $15, student & sr citizen $5
Collections: 18th Century Icons; Contemporary Graphics (Archipenko, Gritchenko, Trutoffsky, Krycevsky, Hluschenko, Pavlos,; Kholodny, Hnizdovsky, Mol, Levytsky, Shostak, Kuch); Contemporary Ukrainian; Canadian Coll

L Library & Archives, 184 Alexander Ave E, Winnipeg, MB R3B 0L6 Canada. Tel 204-942-0218; Fax 204-943-2857; *Pres Board Dirs* Paul Stanicky
Open Tues & Thurs 10 AM - 11 AM; For reference only; lending to mems
Library Holdings: Book Volumes 30,000; Cassettes; Clipping Files; Exhibition Catalogs; Motion Pictures; Other Holdings Ukrainian newspapers & periodicals; Pamphlets; Photographs; Records; Slides; Video Tapes
Publications: Visti, ann newsletter

M UNIVERSITY OF MANITOBA, School of Art Gallery, School of Art, 212 Art Lab Winnipeg, MB R3T 2N2 Canada. Tel 204-474-9322; Fax 204-474-7605; Elec Mail mary-reid@ms.umanitoba.ca; Internet Home Page Address: www.umanitoba.ca/schools/art; *Gallery Dir* Mary Reid; *School of Art Dir* Paul Hess
Open Mon - Fri 9 AM - 4 PM; No admis fee; Estab 1965; Circ 95; School of art gallery estab 1965 to provide exhibs of contemporary art & activities on the univ campus; exhibitions open to the pub; Average Annual Attendance: 20,000
Collections: Contemporary Canadian & American painting, prints & sculpture; L L Fitzgerald Study Collection
Exhibitions: Exhibs of Canadian, European & American Art, both contemporary & historical; special exhibs from other categories; ann exhibs by the graduating students of the School of Art
Publications: Exhib catalogues
Activities: Discussion groups; workshops; lects open to pub, 3-6 vis lectrs per yr; gallery talks; individual paintings & original objects of art lent; book traveling exhibs, 2-4 per yr; originate traveling exhibs

M Faculty of Architecture Exhibition Centre, 215 Architecture, 2 Bldg Winnipeg, MB R3T 2N2 Canada; 201 Russell Bldg, Winnipeg, MB R3T 2N2 Canada. Tel 204-474-9558; Fax 204-474-7532; Internet Home Page Address: www.umanitoba.ca; *Co-Dir* Prof Michael Cox; *Co-Dir & Prof* Patrick Harrop
Open Mon - Fri 8:30 AM - 4:30 PM, weekend by special arrangements; Estab 1959 with the opening of the new Faculty of Architecture Building to provide architectural & related exhibs for students & faculty on the univ campus; 760 sq ft, secured climate controlled; over 900 linear ft of hanging space; Average Annual Attendance: 7,500
Income: Financed by endowments, grants & pvt sponsorships
Special Subjects: Architecture, Drawings, Painting-American, Photography, Prints, Sculpture, Watercolors, Archaeology, Textiles, Ceramics, Pottery, Etchings & Engravings, Decorative Arts, Manuscripts, Portraits, Painting-Canadian, Furniture, Painting-French, Historical Material, Tapestries, Antiquities-Greek, Antiquities-Roman, Mosaics, Painting-German, Reproductions
Collections: An extensive coll of drawings, prints, paintings, sculpture, ceramics, furniture & textiles (tapestries)
Exhibitions: Exhibs from a diversity of pvt & pub sources; annual exhibs by the students in the Faculty of Architecture
Activities: Lects open to pub, 6 vis lectrs per yr; gallery talks; symposia; individual paintings & original objects of art lent to recognized institutions; lending coll contains original art works, original prints, paintings, photographs, sculptures, furniture, textiles & ceramics

L Architecture & Fine Arts Library, 206 Russell Bldg, Univ Manitoba Winnipeg, MB R3T 2N2 Canada. Tel 204-474-9216; Fax 204-474-7539; Elec Mail mary_lochhead@umanitoba.ca; Internet Home Page Address: www.umanitboa.ca/libraries/units/archfa/; *Head* Mary Lochhead; *Reference Librn* Liv Valmestad
Open Mon - Thurs 8:30 AM - 9 PM, Fri 8:30 AM - 5 PM, Sat & Sun 12 PM - 5 PM, May - Aug Mon - Fri 8:30 AM - 4:30 PM; Estab 1916 to serve the needs of students & faculty in the areas of architecture, fine arts, landscape architecture, environmental design, city & regional planning, graphic design, interior design & photography; Circ 100,000; Average Annual Attendance: 68,645
Income: Financed primarily by provincial government
Library Holdings: Audio Tapes 75; Book Volumes 87,395; CD-ROMs 94; Cassettes 88; Clipping Files; Fiche 560; Lantern Slides 13,000; Maps 200; Other Holdings; Pamphlets; Periodical Subscriptions 250; Photographs; Reels 210; Slides 123,000; Video Tapes 294
Special Subjects: Landscape Architecture, Photography, Interior Design, Architecture

M THE WINNIPEG ART GALLERY, 300 Memorial Blvd, Winnipeg, MB R3C 1V1 Canada. Tel 204-786-6641; Fax 204-788-4998; Elec Mail inquiries@wag.mb.ca; Internet Home Page Address: www.wag.ca; *Dir* Stephen D Borys, PhD, MBA; *Chief Cur & Cur Decorative Art & Fine Art, Head Mus Servs* Helen Delacretaz; *Cur Historical Art* Andrew Kear; *Cur Inuit Art* Darlene Coward Wight; *Head Educ* Anna Wiebe; *Conservator* Radovan Radulovlic; *Registrar* Karen Kisiow; *Colls Mgr* Lisa Quirion; *Develop Dir* Pam Simmons; *Mgr Communs & Mktg* Catherine Maksymiuk; *Mgr Bus Opers & Servs* Bill Elliott; *Human Resources Mgr* Mike Malyk; *Accounting Mgr* Hugh Hansen; *Gallery Shop & Art Rental & Sales Mgr* Sherri Van Went
Open Tues - Sun 11 AM - 5 PM, Fri 11 AM - 9 PM; Admis family $25, adults

$10, sr citizens & students $8, children under 6 free; Estab 1912, incorporated 1963. Rebuilt & relocated 1968, opened 1972, to present a diversified, quality level prog of art in all media, representing various cultures, past & present; Circ Reference only; Building includes 9 galleries as well as displays on mezzanine level, sculpture ct & main foyer; Average Annual Attendance: 142,000; Mem: 4400; dues family $50, individual $35, senior citizen couples $30, student & senior citizens $20; annual meeting in Aug

Income: $3,500,000 (financed by endowment, mem, city, state & federal appropriation)

Special Subjects: Decorative Arts, Drawings, Photography, Prints, Painting-American, Sculpture, Eskimo Art, Painting-Canadian

Collections: Contemporary Canada; contemporary Manitoba; Gort Collection; Master prints & drawings

Exhibitions: The changing exhibition includes contemporary & historical works of art by Canadian, European & American artists

Publications: Tableau (calendar of events), monthly; exhibition catalogs

Activities: Classes for adults & children; docent training; lects open to pub, 10 vis lectrs per yr; concerts; gallery talks; tours; exten dept serves Manitoba, Canada, United States & Europe; individual paintings & original objects of art lent to centres & mus; book traveling exhibs 4 per yr; originate traveling exhibs; mus shop sells books, magazines, original art, reproductions & prints

L **Clara Lander Library,** 300 Memorial Blvd, Winnipeg, MB R3C 1V1 Canada. Tel 204-786-6641, Ext 237; Fax 204-788-4998; Elec Mail kcollins@wag.ca; Internet Home Page Address: www.wag.ca; *Librn* Kenlyn Collins
Open Tues - Fri 11 AM - 4:30 PM; Estab 1954 to serve as a source of informational & general interest materials for members & staff of the Winnipeg Art Gallery & to art history students; Circ Reference only
Income: Financed by mem, city & provincial appropriations
Purchases: $10,000
Library Holdings: Auction Catalogs; Audio Tapes; Book Volumes 30,000; CD-ROMs; Clipping Files 10,000; Exhibition Catalogs; Lantern Slides; Manuscripts; Memorabilia; Original Documents; Pamphlets; Periodical Subscriptions 60; Photographs; Reels; Slides
Special Subjects: Art History, Decorative Arts, Photography, Ceramics, American Western Art
Collections: Archival material pertaining to Winnipeg Art Gallery; Rare Books on Canadian & European Art; George Swinton Collection on Eskimo & North American Indian art & culture; Artists' Files Collection; Special collections

NEW BRUNSWICK

CAMPBELLTON

M **GALERIE RESTIGOUCHE GALLERY,** 39 Andrew St, Campbellton, NB E3N 3H1 Canada; PO Box 674, Campbellton, NB E3N 3H1 Canada. Tel 506-753-5750; Fax 506-759-9601; Elec Mail rgaleri@nbnet.nb.ca; *Dir* Charlene Lanteigne
Open Tues - Sat 10AM-4PM Sept to June, Summer 9AM-5PM, cl Sun & Mon; No admis fee; exhibitions in Jeanette MacDonald Room $3.00, Guided tour of Athol House Museum $6.00; Estab 1975 for exhibitions & activities; Building has 4800 sq ft; Exhibition hall is 1500 sq ft, small gallery 400 sq ft; 230 running feet; Average Annual Attendance: 25,000; Mem: 185; dues $20 single membership, $30 family, $50 assoc
Income: $60,000 (financed by provincial & city appropriations & private donations)
Collections: Athol House Museum Collection in Three Show Cases
Exhibitions: Hands on Signs
Publications: Exhibitions catalogues; Restigouche Gallery brochure
Activities: Classes for adults & children; art & craft workshops; lects open to public, 10 vis lectrs per yr; concerts; gallery talks; tours; book and cd launches; artists days; cultural center as well; traveling exhibs exten service; originate traveling exhibs; mus shop sells books, original art, reproductions, prints, cards, tourist items

FREDERICTON

M **BEAVERBROOK ART GALLERY,** 703 Queen St, Fredericton, NB E3B 5A6 Canada; PO Box 605, Fredericton, NB E3B 5A6 Canada. Tel 506-458-8545, 458-2028; Fax 506-459-7450; Elec Mail lglenn@beaverbrookartgallery.org; Elec Mail emailbag@beaverbrookartgallery.org; Internet Home Page Address: www.beaverbrookartgallery.org; *Art Educ & Mgr Pub Progs* Adda Mihailescu; *Mgr Communs & Outreach* Laurie Glenn Norris; *Fin Adminstr* Tanya Belanger; *Dir & CEO* Bernard Riordon; *Cur & Deputy Dir* Terry Graff
Open year round, 9 AM - 5:30 PM, Thurs 9 AM - 9 PM, Sun & holidays noon - 5:30 PM; cl Mon Jan 1-May 31; Admis adults $8, seniors $6, students $3, children under 6 free, family of 4 $18; Thurs 5:30 PM - 9 PM, pay as you wish; Estab 1959 to foster & promote the study & the pub enjoyment & appreciation of the arts; Major galleries upstairs; British, Canadian, High Galleries & Marion McCain Atlantic Gallery. East wing galleries: Hosmer, Pillow-Vaughan Gallery, Sir Max Aitken Gallery & Vaulted Corridor Gallery. Downstairs galleries: Joseph & Fanry Oppenheimer Gallery & foyer Gallery; Average Annual Attendance: 45,000; Mem: 1000; dues family $60, individual $50
Library Holdings: Auction Catalogs; Book Volumes; Exhibition Catalogs; Pamphlets; Periodical Subscriptions; Video Tapes
Special Subjects: Decorative Arts, Furniture, Portraits, Painting-European, Tapestries, Religious Art, Painting-Canadian, Porcelain, Painting-British, Painting-Flemish, Renaissance Art, Medieval Art, Painting-Spanish
Collections: Hosmer-Pillow-Vaughan coll of continental European fine & decorative arts from the 14th & 19th century; Works by Dali, Constable, Gainsborough, Hogarth, Cornelius Krieghoff, Reynolds, Sutherland & Turner; 16th-20th century English paintings; 18th & early 19th century English porcelain; 19th & 20th century Canadian & New Brunswick paintings; Contemporary modern & historical Canadian & British art

Publications: Tableau; The magazine of the Beaverbrook Art Gallery ann report, exhib catalogues
Activities: Classes for adults & children; lects open to pub; approx 12 vis lectrs per yr; gallery talks; films; tours; exten dept serving New Brunswick & Atlantic region; individual paintings lent to recognized art galleries; collection contains 3000 original art works, sculpture; 8-10 book traveling exhibs per yr; originate traveling exhibs throughout Canada & within N America; sales shop sells books, magazines & prints

L **Library,** 703 Queen St, Fredericton, NB E3B 5A6 Canada; PO Box 605, Fredericton, NB E3B 5A6 Canada. Tel 506-458-8545; Fax 506-459-7450; Internet Home Page Address: www.beaverbrookartgallery.org; *Librn* Barry Henderson
Open to gallery personnel only, for reference
Library Holdings: Exhibition Catalogs; Video Tapes
Special Subjects: Decorative Arts, Painting-British, Painting-Flemish, Painting-Spanish, Painting-European, Portraits, Porcelain, Furniture, Religious Art, Tapestries, Painting-Canadian
Publications: Auction Catalogs

M **NEW BRUNSWICK COLLEGE OF CRAFT & DESIGN,** Gallery, 457 Queen St, Fredericton, NB E3B 5H1 Canada; PO Box 6000, Fredericton, NB E3B 5H1 Canada. Tel 506-453-2305; Fax 506-457-7352; Elec Mail nbccd.email@gnb.ca; Internet Home Page Address: www.nbcc.ca/nbccd; *Prin* Luc Paulin; *Registrar* Louise Neveu
Open Sept - May, Mon - Fri 9AM - 4:30 PM; No admis fee; Estab 1938 to educate students as professional crafts people & designers; Maintains reference library
Income: Financed by provincial government
Exhibitions: Student & staff juried shows; periodic vis exhibitions
Activities: Classes for adults & children; lects open to pub, 10 vis lectrs per yr; awards; lending coll contains original art works, video tapes, slides & 3000 books

L **Library,** 457 Queen St, PO Box 6000 Fredericton, NB E3B 5H1 Canada; PO Box 6000, Fredericton, NB E3B 5H1 Canada. Tel 506-453-5938; Elec Mail julie.mcdonald@gnb.ca; *Library Coordr* Julie Lumbria-McDonald; *Prin* Robert Kavanagh; *Dir Admin* Stephen Goudey
Open Mon - Fri, 8:15 AM - 4:30 PM; A very small but growing library which is primarily for students & craftsmen
Income: Financed by government & book donations
Library Holdings: Book Volumes 3000; Clipping Files; Exhibition Catalogs; Filmstrips; Pamphlets; Periodical Subscriptions 60; Slides; Video Tapes 300
Special Subjects: Art History, Collages, Folk Art, Decorative Arts, Film, Illustration, Mixed Media, Photography, Calligraphy, Commercial Art, Drawings, Graphic Arts, Graphic Design, Posters, Prints, Sculpture, Watercolors, Ceramics, Conceptual Art, Latin American Art, American Western Art, Printmaking, Advertising Design, Cartoons, Fashion Arts, Interior Design, Lettering, Art Education, Asian Art, American Indian Art, Primitive art, Mexican Art, Costume Design & Constr, Aesthetics, Afro-American Art, Metalwork, Antiquities-Oriental, Carpets & Rugs, Goldsmithing, Handicrafts, Jewelry, Oriental Art, Pottery, Religious Art, Silversmithing, Tapestries, Textiles, Antiquities-Egyptian, Antiquities-Greek, Antiquities-Roman, Display, Architecture
Publications: Computerized catalogue

M **ORGANIZATION FOR THE DEVELOPMENT OF ARTISTS,** Gallery Connexion, 440 York St, Chestnut Complex Fredericton, NB Canada; PO Box 696, Fredericton, NB E3B 5B4 Canada. Tel 506-454-1433; Fax 506-454-1401; Elec Mail connex@nbnet.nb.ca; Internet Home Page Address: www.galleryconnexion.ca; *Dir* John Edward Cushnie; *Pres* Mary-Ellen Green
Open Tues - Fri noon - 6 PM, Sat noon - 4 PM; No admis fee; Estab 1984 to show contemporary experimental work; Maintains a reference library; Average Annual Attendance: 2,600; Mem: 110; dues full mem $30, assoc $20, students $15; ann meeting in March
Income: $50,000 (financed by mem, provincial appropriation & Canada Council)
Library Holdings: Exhibition Catalogs; Periodical Subscriptions; Video Tapes
Exhibitions: 6 shows per yr
Publications: Connexionews, monthly
Activities: Classes for adults; lects open to pub; 6-10 vis lectrs per yr; concerts; book traveling exhibs 6-10 per yr; originate traveling exhibs 1 per yr

M **UNIVERSITY OF NEW BRUNSWICK,** Art Centre, Memorial Hall, Bailey Ave, PO Box 4400 Fredericton, NB E3B 5A3 Canada. Tel 506-453-4623; Fax 506-453-5012; Elec Mail artists@unb.ca; *Dir* Marie Maltais
Open Mon - Fri 9 AM - 4:30 PM; summer Mon - Fri 9 AM - 4 PM; No admis fee; Estab 1940 to broaden the experience of the univ students & serve the city & province; Two galleries, each with approx 100 running ft of wall space; display case; Average Annual Attendance: 5,000
Income: Financed by provincial univ & grants for special projects
Purchases: $7,000
Library Holdings: Original Art Works; Photographs; Prints; Sculpture
Special Subjects: Etchings & Engravings, Photography, Portraits, Prints, Prints, Sculpture, Watercolors, Textiles, Pottery, Woodcuts, Painting-Canadian, Stained Glass
Collections: Chiefly New Brunswick Artists; some Canadian (chiefly printmakers)
Publications: Chiefly New Brunswick Artists; Canadian artists
Activities: Classes for adults & children; lects open to pub, 4 vis lectrs per yr; gallery talks; tours; individual paintings & original objects of art lent to pub but secure areas on this campus & the univ campus in Saint John & reproductions to students; lending coll contains framed reproductions, original prints, paintings, photographs, sculptures & slides; book traveling exhibs 4 per yr; originate traveling exhibs provincially to nationally

HAMPTON

M **KINGS COUNTY HISTORICAL SOCIETY & MUSEUM,** 27 Centennia Rd, Box 1813 Hampton, NB E5N 6N3 Canada. Tel 506-832-6009; Elec Mail kingscm@nbnet.nb.ca; Internet Home Page Address: www.kingscountymuseum.com; *Pres* Louise Fyffe; *Treas* Faye Pearson; *Genealogist* John R Elliott; *Co-Genealogist* Richard Thorne; *Dir* Christine White
Open Mon - Fri 8:30 AM - 4:30 PM (July-Aug); Mon, Wed & Fri 9 AM - 2 PM (Sept-June); Admis adults $2, children $1; Estab 1968 to preserve loyalist history

& artifacts; Maintains small reference library & research archives; Average Annual Attendance: 1,400; Mem: 300; dues society $20 & $ 25; ann meeting in Nov
Income: $2,250 (financed by provincial & student grants, dues, fairs & book sales)
Library Holdings: Fiche; Maps; Original Documents; Photographs
Special Subjects: Folk Art, Metalwork, Flasks & Bottles, Porcelain, Portraits, Pottery, Prints, Period Rooms, Woodcuts, Manuscripts, Sculpture, Tapestries, Photography, Watercolors, Ethnology, Textiles, Costumes, Ceramics, Decorative Arts, Painting-Canadian, Dolls, Furniture, Glass, Jewelry, Silver, Carpets & Rugs, Historical Material, Ivory, Maps, Scrimshaw, Coins & Medals, Embroidery, Pewter
Collections: Coin; dairy; glass; jewelry; quilts; Brass Measures (1854); tools; furniture; pottery; textiles; military
Exhibitions: The Mysterious Stranger, static display; The Home Children; Crime & Punishment: 200 Years in the Kings County Gaol
Publications: Memories newsletter, 7 per yr
Activities: Classes for adults & children; docent training; lects open to pub, 7 vis lectrs per yr; tours; life memberships; appreciation cert; mus shop sells books

MONCTON

M **GALERIE D'ART DE L'UNIVERSITE DE MONCTON,** 85th Edific Clement Cormier, Moncton, NB E1A 3E9 Canada. Tel 506-858-4088; Fax 506-858-4043; Internet Home Page Address: www.umoncton.ca/gaum/; *Secy* Necol LaBlanc; *Technician* Paul Bourque; *Dir* Luc Charette
Open summer Mon - Fri 10 AM - 5 PM, Sat & Sun 1 - 5 PM; winter Tues - Sat 1 - 4:30 PM; Sat & Sun 1 - 4 PM; No admis fee; Estab 1965 to offer outstanding shows to the univ students & to the pub; 400 linear ft wall space, 3500 sq ft vinyl plywood walls, controlled light, temperature, humidity systems, security system; Average Annual Attendance: 13,000
Income: $100,000 (financed through univ)
Collections: Artists represented in permanent coll: Bruno Bobak; Alex Colville; Francis Coutellier; Tom Forrestall; Georges Goguen; Hurtubise; Hilda Lavoie; Fernand Leduc; Rita Letendre; Toni Onley; Claude Roussel; Romeo Savoie; Pavel Skalnik; Gordon Smith
Exhibitions: Rotating exhibits
Activities: Classes for children; dramatic progs; lects open to pub, 10 vis lectrs per yr; concerts; gallery talks; tours; individual paintings & original objects of art lent to univ personnel & art galleries & mus; lending coll contains 500 reproductions, 300 original art works, 180 original prints, 30 paintings, 20 sculpture

M **RADIO-CANADA SRC CBC,** Georges Goguen CBC Art Gallery, 250 University Ave, PO Box 950 Moncton, NB E1C 8N8 Canada. Tel 506-382-8326; Fax 506-867-8031; Elec Mail ghg@nbnet.nb.ca; Internet Home Page Address: www.radio-canada.ca/atlantique; *Dir* George Goguen
Open Mon - Fri 9 AM - 5 PM, Sat 9 AM - 1 PM; No admis fee; Estab 1972 for maritime artists; Gallery size 15 x 25, track lighting; Average Annual Attendance: 500
Library Holdings: CD-ROMs; Cassettes; Video Tapes
Special Subjects: Painting-American, Photography, Prints, Sculpture, Watercolors, Religious Art, Woodcarvings, Woodcuts, Painting-European, Posters, Painting-Canadian, Painting-French
Activities: Classes for children; 500 vis lectrs per yr; gallery talks; tours

SACKVILLE

M **MOUNT ALLISON UNIVERSITY,** Owens Art Gallery, 61 York St, Sackville, NB E4L 1E1 Canada. Tel 506-364-2574; Fax 506-364-2575; Elec Mail owens@mta.ca; Internet Home Page Address: www.mta.ca/owens; Telex 014-2266; *Fine Art Conservator* Jane Tisdale; *Registrar/Preparator* Roxie Ibbitson; *Dir* Gemey Kelly; *Cur Educ* Lucy MacDonald
Open Mon - Fri 10 AM - 5 PM, Sat - Sun 1 PM - 5 PM; No admis fee; Estab 1895, rebuilt 1972; Building includes five gallery areas; conservation laboratory; Average Annual Attendance: 13,000
Income: Financed by Mount Allison University, government, corporate & pvt assistance
Special Subjects: Graphics, Painting-American, Sculpture
Collections: Broad coll of graphics, paintings, works on paper; 19th & 20th century Canadian, European & American Art, Contemporary Canadian
Publications: Exhib catalogs
Activities: Family Sundays; lects open to pub, 15 vis lectrs per yr; gallery talks; tours; individual paintings lent to other galleries & museums; book traveling exhibs 5 per yr; originate national traveling exhibs

M **STRUTS GALLERY,** 7 Lorne St, Sackville, NB E4L 3Z6 Canada. Tel 506-536-1211; Fax 506-536-4565; Elec Mail info@strutsgallery.ca; Internet Home Page Address: www.strutsgallery.ca; *Coordr* John Murchie; *Mgr Faucet Media Arts* Paul Henderson; *Production Supvr, Faucet Media Arts* Amanda Dawn Christie
Open 1 PM - 5 PM daily; No admis fee; Estab 1982; 1,000 sq ft; Average Annual Attendance: 1,500; Mem: Open to professional artist, assoc or student; dues professional $35, assoc & student $15; ann meeting in Oct
Income: $100,000 (financed by mem, Canada Council, Province of New Brunswick)
Exhibitions: Show work by contemporary living artists & a broad range of experimental art works
Activities: Lects open to pub, 2-5 vis lectrs per yr

SAINT ANDREWS

M **ROSS MEMORIAL MUSEUM,** 188 Montague St, Saint Andrews, NB E5B 1J2 Canada. Tel 506-529-5124; Fax 506-529-5183; Elec Mail rossmuse@nb.aibn.com; Internet Home Page Address: www.rossmemorialmuseum.ca; *Dir* Margot Magee Sackett
Open early June to Thanksgiving Mon - Sat 10 AM - 4:30 PM; Admis by donation in season ($3 off-season); Estab 1980; One decorative arts collection in historic house; Average Annual Attendance: 8,000

Special Subjects: Architecture, Painting-American, Watercolors, American Western Art, Bronzes, Ceramics, Landscapes, Decorative Arts, Portraits, Painting-Canadian, Furniture, Carpets & Rugs
Collections: New Brunswick Furniture Collection; Ross Decorative Art Collection
Exhibitions: Special summer exhibit
Activities: Classes for children; lect open to pub

A **SUNBURY SHORES ARTS & NATURE CENTRE, INC,** Gallery, 139 Water St, Saint Andrews, NB E5B 1A7 Canada. Tel 506-529-3386; Fax 506-529-4779; Elec Mail info@sunburyshores.org; Internet Home Page Address: www.sunburyshores.org; *Pres* Muriel Jarvis; *Dir* Cara Coes; *Exec Dir* James Steel
Open July - Aug 8:30 AM - 5 PM daily; Sept - June, Mon - Fri 9 AM - 4:30 PM; No admis fee; Estab 1964, to function as a link for & harmonize views of scientists, artists & industrialists; Gallery maintained, 200 running ft, fire & burglar protection, security during hours, controllable lighting & street frontage; Average Annual Attendance: 5,000; Mem: 400; dues family $50, individual, students & sr citizens $30; ann meeting in June/July
Income: Financed by endowment, mem, grants, revenue from courses & activities, including special projects
Collections: Instructor Artwork
Exhibitions: Exhibits change frequently throughout the yr
Publications: Brochure, summer annually; Sunbury Notes, quarterly; weekly newspaper column
Activities: Courses in fine arts & nature; lects open to pub, 10-15 vis lectrs per yr; concerts; gallery talks; Sunbury Shores Awards of Excellence; schols offered; mus shop sells books, original art, reproductions & prints

L **Library,** 139 Water St, Saint Andrews, NB E5B 1A7 Canada. Tel 506-529-3386; Fax 506-529-4779; Elec Mail sunshore@nbnet.nb.ca; Internet Home Page Address: www.sunburyshores.org; *Dir* Lois Fenety
Open Mon-Fri 9 AM - 4:30 PM, cl Sat & Sun; No admis fee; Circ Non-circulating; Open to pub; primarily for reference
Income: Financed by mem
Library Holdings: Book Volumes 600; Exhibition Catalogs; Periodical Subscriptions 10

SAINT JOHN

M **NEW BRUNSWICK MUSEUM,** 1 Market Sq, Saint John, NB E2L 4Z6 Canada; 277 Douglas Ave, Saint John, NB E2K 1E5 Canada. Tel 506-643-2300; Tel 888-268-9595; Fax 506-643-6081; Elec Mail nbmuseum@nbm-mnb.ca; Internet Home Page Address: www.nbm-mnb.ca; *Controller* Lane Atkinson; *History & Technology Cur* Gary Hughes; *Mgr Temporary Exhibits* Regina Mantin; *CEO* Jane Fullerton; *Cur Zoology* Dr Donald McAlpine; *Cur Geology* Dr Randy Miller; *Cur New Brunswick Cultural History & Art* Peter Larocque; *Cur Botany* Dr Stephen Clayden; *Mgr Programming* Rose Poirier
Open Mon - Wed & Fri 9 AM - 5 PM, Thurs 9 AM - 9 PM, Sat 10 AM - 5 PM, Sun Noon - 5 PM; cl Mon Nov to mid-May; Admis families $17, adults $8, seniors $6, students $4.50, children 3 & under free; Estab 1842 to collect, conserve, exhibit & interpret the Human & Natural history of New Brunswick in relation to itself & to the outside world; Twelve major galleries for permanent exhibits, three galleries for changing temporary exhibits; 62,000 sq ft gallery space; Average Annual Attendance: 75,000; Mem: 500; dues $16 - $500
Income: $1,600,000 (financed by municipal, federal & provincial appropriations)
Special Subjects: Drawings, Historical Material, Marine Painting, Ceramics, Flasks & Bottles, Prints, Textiles, Woodcuts, Sculpture, Tapestries, Painting-American, Watercolors, American Indian Art, African Art, Ethnology, Costumes, Crafts, Folk Art, Woodcarvings, Etchings & Engravings, Landscapes, Decorative Arts, Judaica, Manuscripts, Collages, Eskimo Art, Painting-Canadian, Dolls, Furniture, Glass, Jewelry, Metalwork, Painting-British, Carpets & Rugs, Maps, Coins & Medals, Miniatures, Period Rooms, Embroidery, Laces, Antiquities-Greek, Antiquities-Roman, Gold, Pewter, Leather, Military Art, Enamels
Collections: 3 galleries: Canadian Art, International Art; New Brunswick Art; Decorative Arts
Exhibitions: Various exhibitions
Activities: Educ prog; classes for adults & children; docent training; lects open to pub; 6-8 vis lectrs per yr; gallery talks; tours; competitions sponsored in schools; schols & fels offered; individual paintings & original objects of art lent to mus & galleries; book traveling exhibs 4-6 per yr; originate traveling exhibs nationally & internationally; mus shop sells books, original art & reproductions

L **Archives & Research Library,** 277 Douglas Ave, Saint John, NB E2K 1E5 Canada. Tel 506-643-2322; Fax 506-643-2360; Elec Mail archives@nbm-mnb.ca; Internet Home Page Address: www.nbm-mnb.ca; *Head, Archives & Research Library* Felicity Osepchook; *Library & Archives Asst* Jennifer Longon; *Library & Archives Asst* Christine Little
Open Tues - Fri 10 AM - 4:30 PM; Circ Non-circulating; Open to the pub for reference only
Income: nonprofit, government funded
Library Holdings: Auction Catalogs; Book Volumes 20,000; Clipping Files; Exhibition Catalogs; Fiche; Manuscripts; Original Documents; Periodical Subscriptions 75; Photographs; Reels
Special Subjects: Art History, Decorative Arts, Photography, Calligraphy, Etchings & Engravings, Maps, Painting-American, Painting-British, Prints, Watercolors, Ceramics, Crafts, Archaeology, American Western Art, Bronzes, Printmaking, Cartoons, Art Education, Asian Art, American Indian Art, Porcelain, Anthropology, Eskimo Art, Furniture, Costume Design & Constr, Aesthetics, Afro-American Art, Bookplates & Bindings, Metalwork, Carpets & Rugs, Gold, Goldsmithing, Jewelry, Miniatures, Oriental Art, Pottery, Restoration & Conservation, Silver, Silversmithing, Textiles, Marine Painting, Antiquities-Assyrian, Scrimshaw, Painting-Canadian, Architecture, Folk Art, Portraits

NEWFOUNDLAND

CORNER BROOK

M MEMORIAL UNIVERSITY OF NEWFOUNDLAND, Sir Wilfred Grenfell College Art Gallery, University Dr, Fine Arts Bldg Corner Brook, NF A2H 6P9 Canada. Tel 709-637-6209; Fax 709-637-6203; Elec Mail gtuttle@swgc.mun.ca; Internet Home Page Address: www2.swgc.mun.ca/artgallery; *Dir & Cur* Gail Tuttle
Open Tues - Sat 11 AM - 5 PM; No admis fee; Estab 1988; 2,000 sq ft, 324.2 running ft, white walls, neutral carpet; Average Annual Attendance: 6,000; Mem: 300
Income: $100,000 (financed by univ & Canada Council)
Collections: Drawings, paintings, photography & prints (mainly contemporary Canadian)
Exhibitions: Changing contemporary exhibs every 7 wks
Publications: Exhibition catalogues
Activities: Docent progs; lects open to pub, 8 vis lectrs per yr; lending coll; book traveling exhibs 3 per yr; originate traveling exhibs 1 per yr; sales shop sells catalogues

SAINT JOHN'S

A CRAFT COUNCIL OF NEWFOUNDLAND & LABRADOR, (Newfoundland & Labrador Crafts Development Association) Devon House, 59 Duckworth St Saint John's, NF A1C 1E6 Canada. Tel 709-753-2749; Fax 709-753-2766; Elec Mail info@crafcouncil.nl.ca; Internet Home Page Address: www.craftcouncil.nl.ca; *Gallery Coordr* Sharon LeRiche; *Shop Mgr* Shannon Reid; *Exec Dir* Anne Manuel
Open Mon - Sat 10 AM - 5 PM, Sun 1 PM - 5 PM; No admis fee; Estab 1991 to promote innovation & excellence in craft; The only gallery in Newfoundland & Labrador dedicated to the promotion & sale of fine craft. It encourages excellence & innovation & promotes craft as a valuable part of our cultural heritage. Maintains lending & reference library; Average Annual Attendance: 50,000; Mem: 300
Income: $80,000 (financed by federal government, foundations, fund raising & earned revenue)
Special Subjects: Embroidery, Metalwork, Textiles, Pottery, Stained Glass, Pewter, Ceramics, Crafts, Dolls, Furniture, Jewelry, Leather, Scrimshaw, Enamels, Tapestries
Collections: Craft Collection
Exhibitions: Revolving theme & solo exhibitions, 6-8 per year
Publications: Newsletter, 6 per yr
Activities: Classes for adults & children; lect open to pub; ann awards of excellence; juried; schols offered; sales shop sells high quality craft

M MEMORIAL UNIVERSITY OF NEWFOUNDLAND, The Rooms Provincial Art Gallery, Allandale Rd & Prince Philip Dr, Saint John's, NF A1C 5S7 Canada; PO Box 1800, Station C, 9 Bonaventure Ave Saint John's, NL A1C 5P9 Canada. Tel 709-757-8040; Fax 709-757-8041; Elec Mail information@therooms.ca; Internet Home Page Address: www.therooms.ca; *Cur* Caroline Stone; *Mgr Opers* Wanda Mooney; *Registrar* Chris Batten; *Cur* Bruce Johnson; *Art Gallery Educ* Jason Sellars; *Coll Mgmt Tech* Keith White; *CEO* Dean Brinton; *Gen Prog Officer* Perry Chafe
Open June - Oct Mon - Sat 10 AM - 5 PM, Wed & Sat 10 AM - 9 PM, Sun 12 PM - 5 PM; Oct - May, cl Mon; Admis family $15, adults $5, seniors & students $4, youth (6-16) $3, under 5 free; Estab 1961 to display contemporary Canadian art, with an emphasis on Newfoundland work & provide visual art educ progs; Four galleries with 130 running ft each; Average Annual Attendance: 30,000
Income: Financed through the univ, federal funding & revenue generation
Collections: Newfoundland Contemporary, Folk & Historic Art; Post 1960 Canadian Art
Exhibitions: Contemporary art rotating exhibit
Publications: Catalogs of in-house exhibitions
Activities: Educ dept; docent training; lects open to pub, 10-12 vis lectrs per yr; concerts; gallery talks; tours; exten dept serves east coast of province; book traveling exhibs 8-10 per yr; originate traveling exhibs to Canadian & international pub art mus; sales shop sells books, art coll products, t-shirts, bags & cards

M THE ROOMS CORPORATION OF NEWFOUNDLAND & LABRADOR, (Provincial Museum of Newfoundland & Labrador) 1800 Stn C, Saint John's, NF A1C 5P9 Canada. Tel 709-757-8000; Fax 709-757-8017; Elec Mail information@therooms.ca; Internet Home Page Address: www.therooms.ca
Open June - Oct Mon - Tues & Thurs - Sat 10AM-5PM, Wed 10AM-9PM, Sun 12PM-5PM, Oct-May cl Mon, Tues & Fri - Sat 10AM-5PM, Wed & Thurs 10AM-9PM, Sun noon to 5PM; Admis families $20, adults $7.50, seniors & students $5, youth (6-16) $3, under 5 free & free admis Wed nights 6PM-9PM; Estab 1878 as the Athenaeum for the preservation of Provincial Heritage; The Provincial Mus houses colls & exhibs reflecting the human & natural history of Newfoundland & Labrador. Branches at The Provincial Seamen's Mus at Grand Bank & The Mary March Provincial Mus at Grand Falls; Average Annual Attendance: 60,000; Mem: Ind $40, Family $70, Students and Seniors $ 30
Income: Financed by federal & provincial appropriations
Special Subjects: Photography, Archaeology, Ethnology, Textiles, Costumes, Ceramics, Crafts, Folk Art, Pottery, Eskimo Art, Dolls, Furniture, Glass, Jewelry, Porcelain, Marine Painting, Scrimshaw, Coins & Medals, Dioramas, Embroidery, Gold, Pewter, Leather
Collections: Beothuk, Thule, Maritime Archaic, pre-Dorset, Dorset, Innu, Inuit and Micmac artifacts; history material; maps; naval and military; 19th century Newfoundland domestic artifacts, maritime, natural history, mercantile; 18th - 20th century Newfoundland material, outport furniture, textiles, navigational instruments, ship portraits, watercolors, prints, drawings
Exhibitions: Rotating exhibits; Native Peoples gallery; Natural History Gallery-permanent

Publications: Museum Notes; exhib catalogues; technical bulletins; Archeology in Newfoundland & Labrador, Natural History Curatorial Reports
Activities: Classes for adults & children; lects open to pub, 12 vis lectrs per yr; tours; gallery talks; concerts; book 3 traveling exhibs per yr; originate traveling exhibs to nat and international mus

NOVA SCOTIA

DARTMOUTH

M DARTMOUTH HERITAGE MUSEUM, (Regional Museum of Cultural History) 26 Newcastle St, Evergreen House Dartmouth, NS B2Y 3M5 Canada. Tel 902-464-2300; Fax 902-464-8210; Elec Mail museum@bellaliant.com; Internet Home Page Address: www.dartmouthheritagemuseum.ns.ca; *Cur* Crystal Martin; *Ed* Bonnie Elliott
Open summer Tues-Sun 10AM - 5PM, winter Tues-Sat 10AM - 5PM, cl Sat & Sun 1-2PM; Admis $2, under 12 free; Estab 1967 to collect & preserve the history & heritage of the Dartmouth & area; Average Annual Attendance: 15,000; Mem: 110 mems, $20 yr dues Aug-June
Income: Financed by city appropriation, provincial funds & fundraising
Special Subjects: Graphics, Photography, Prints, Watercolors, Textiles, Costumes, Ceramics, Pottery, Painting-European, Portraits, Posters, Painting-Canadian, Dolls, Furniture, Glass, Porcelain, Scrimshaw, Embroidery
Collections: Local history collection including art, archival, textile/costume & general social history material
Exhibitions: Four exhibitions scheduled per year
Activities: Classes for adults & children; gallery talks; tours; exten dept serves historic houses; mus shop sells CDs, calendars & note cards

L SOCIETY FOR THE PROTECTION & PRESERVATION OF BLACK CULTURE IN NOVA SCOTIA, Black Cultural Center for Nova Scotia, 1149 Main St, Dartmouth, NS B2Z 1A8 Canada. Tel 902-434-6223; Fax 902-434-2306; Elec Mail bccns@istar.ca; Internet Home Page Address: www.bccns.com; *Cur* Henry Bishop
Open Sept 1 - May 31, Mon - Fri 9 AM - 5 PM; June 1 - Sept 1, Mon - Fri 9 AM - 5 PM, Sat 10 AM - 3 PM; Admis families $20, adults $6, students & seniors $4, under 5 free; Estab 1984; For reference only; Average Annual Attendance: 10,000; Mem: Dues $15 & up
Income: Financed by provincial & federal government
Library Holdings: Audio Tapes; Book Volumes 3000; Cassettes; Clipping Files; Framed Reproductions; Lantern Slides; Manuscripts; Memorabilia; Original Art Works; Pamphlets; Prints; Records; Reproductions; Slides; Video Tapes
Collections: African Nova Scotians
Exhibitions: African Canadians
Publications: Newsletter Preserver
Activities: Lect open to public; school tours; presentations; sales shop sells books

HALIFAX

M ART GALLERY OF NOVA SCOTIA, 1723 Hollis St, Halifax, NS B3J 3C8 Canada. Tel 902-424-7542; Fax 902-424-7359; Internet Home Page Address: www.ednet.ns.ca/educ/heritage/agns; *Chief Exec Officer & Dir* Ray Cronin; *Cur Colls* Shannon Parker; *Fine Arts Conservator* Laurie Hamilton; *Corp Controller* Nil D'entremont
Open daily 10 AM - 5 PM, Thurs 10 AM - 9 PM; Admis adults $10, sr citizens & students with ID $8, children under 12 & members free; Estab 1975 to replace the Nova Scotia Mus of Fine Arts, dedicated to serving the pub by bringing the visual arts & people together in an environment which encourages exploration, dialogue & enjoyment; Thirty-five galleries, for permanent collection & temporary exhibitions; Average Annual Attendance: 85,000; Mem: 3500; dues life members $2000, family $75, individual $50, senior couple $55, senior individual $35, young member/student $20
Income: Financed by Nova Scotia Dept of Tourism, Culture & Heritage, Dept of Canadian Heritage, The Canada Council, municipal governments, private foundations & individual & corporate supporters
Purchases: $150,000
Special Subjects: Decorative Arts, Etchings & Engravings, Illustration, Landscapes, Marine Painting, Photography, Porcelain, Portraits, Painting-American, Textiles, Woodcuts, Maps, Painting-European, Sculpture, Tapestries, Drawings, Graphics, Prints, Watercolors, Religious Art, Ceramics, Crafts, Folk Art, Pottery, Woodcarvings, Eskimo Art, Painting-Canadian, Oriental Art, Painting-British, Historical Material, Renaissance Art, Embroidery, Medieval Art, Reproductions
Collections: Canadian Historical & Contemporary Art Collection drawings, paintings, prints, sculpture, ceramics & international art; Nova Scotia Folk Art Collection; Nova Scotian Collection
Exhibitions: Rotating exhibits
Activities: Classes for adults & children; docent training; outreach; lects open to pub, 5-10 vis lectrs per yr; gallery talks; tours; family Sundays, family weekends; Black Tie Gala; Pick of the Month; Sobey Art Award; exten dept serves Province of Nova Scotia; artmobile; individual paintings & original objects of art lent to Province & Government House; lending collection contains original art works, framed reproductions, original prints, paintings & sculpture; book traveling exhibs 2-3 per yr; originate traveling exhibs 10-15 per yr; mus & sales shop sells books, jewelry, magazines, original art, pottery, prints, reproductions, slides, crafts & also rental service

M DALHOUSIE UNIVERSITY, Dalhousie Art Gallery, 6101 University Ave, Halifax, NS B3H 3J5 Canada. Tel 902-494-2403, 494-2195; Fax 902-423-0591; Elec Mail art.gallery@dal.ca; Internet Home Page Address: artgallery.dal.ca; *Registrar & Preparator* Michele Gallant; *Commun & Design* Sym Corrigan; *Dir & Cur* Peter Dykhuis
Open Tues - Sun 11 AM - 5 PM, Wed 7 - 10 PM, cl Mon; No admis fee; Estab 1943 to collect, preserve, interpret & display works of art, primarily of Canadian

origin; Dalhousie Art Gallery is located in the Dalhousie Arts Centre and open to university community and local area; it contains 4 galleries, 400 running ft of wall space & 4000 sq ft floor space; Average Annual Attendance: 12,000
Income: Financed by university supplemented by government grants
Collections: Canadian works on paper; Atlantic Canadian artists all media
Exhibitions: Contemporary & historical exhibitions
Publications: Annual Report; Calendar of Events, 3 times per yr, exhibition catalogues & brochures
Activities: Classes for children; docent training; lects open to pub, 12 vis lectrs per yr; concerts; gallery talks; tours; exten dept serves regional & national area; individual paintings & original objects of art lent to professional galleries & campus areas; book traveling exhibs; originate traveling exhibs; sales shop sells gallery publications

M **EYE LEVEL GALLERY,** 2159 Gottinger St, Halifax, NS B3K 3B5 Canada. Tel 902-425-6412; Fax 902-425-0019; Elec Mail director@eyelevelgallery.ca; Internet Home Page Address: www.eyelevelgallery.ca; *Dir* Eryn Foster
Open Tues - Sat Noon - 5 PM; No admis fee; Estab 1974 to exhibit contemporary art in a non-museum setting; Ten 25 x 40 ft windows on one end; white, grey floor, 2 small pillars. Exhibiting every 4 wks (Sept-Apr) & every 2 wks during the summer; Average Annual Attendance: 10,000; Mem: 150; dues $6 & up; meetings in Feb, Mar, Apr, June, Aug & Nov
Income: $65,000 (financed by mem, Canada Council, Nova Scotia Arts Council)
Collections: Art Poster, 1974-Present; Artist Books Collection
Exhibitions: Cultural Competition; rotating exhibits
Publications: Exhibition catalogues
Activities: Lects open to pub, 5 vis lectrs per yr; competition with awards; sales shop sells books

M **MOUNT SAINT VINCENT UNIVERSITY,** MSVU Art Gallery, 166 Bedford Hwy, Halifax, NS B3M 2J6 Canada. Tel 902-457-6788, 457-6160; Fax 902-457-2447; Elec Mail art.gallery@msvu.ca; Internet Home Page Address: www.msvuart.ca; *Office Mgr* Traci Steylen; *Dir Art Gallery* Ingrid Jenkner; *Technician* David Dahms; *Prog Coordr* Katie Belcher
Open Tues - Fri 11 AM - 5 PM, Sat, Sun 1 - 5 PM, cl Mon & holidays; No admis fee; Estab 1970 & operating throughout the year with continuously-changing exhibitions of local, regional, national & international origin in the area of visual culture; Gallery situated on the main floor & mezzanine; Average Annual Attendance: 15,000
Income: Financed by university funds & Canada Council for the Arts
Special Subjects: Decorative Arts, Landscape Architecture, Ceramics, Collages, Textiles, Woodcuts, Tapestries, Graphics, Photography, Prints, Sculpture, Watercolors, Pottery, Etchings & Engravings, Painting-Canadian, Porcelain, Embroidery
Collections: The Art Gallery is custodian of a collection of pictures, ceramics & pottery of the late Alice Egan Hagen of Mahone Bay, noted Nova Scotia potter & ceramist; works by Atlantic region artists; contemporary Canadian art; women artists
Publications: Gallery News, biannual; exhib catalogs
Activities: Lects open to public, 4 vis lectrs per yr; gallery talks; tours; book traveling exhibs 2 per yr; originate traveling exhibs to Canadian art galleries

A **NOVA SCOTIA ASSOCIATION OF ARCHITECTS,** 1359 Barrington St, Halifax, NS B3J 1Y9 Canada. Tel 902-423-7607; Fax 902-425-7024; Elec Mail info@nsaa.ns.ca; Internet Home Page Address: nsaa.ns.ca; *Exec Dir* Diane Scott-Stewart; *Pres* Therese Leblanc
Open Mon - Fri 9 AM-5 PM; Estab 1932 to license & regulate architects of Nova Scotia; Mem: 200; annual meeting in Apr
Income: Financed by memberships
Publications: Newsletter, monthly

M **NOVA SCOTIA CENTRE FOR CRAFT & DESIGN,** Mary E Black Gallery, 1061 Marginal Rd, Halifax, NS B3H 4P6 Canada. Tel 902-492-2522; Fax 902-492-2526; Elec Mail info@craft-design.ns.ca; Internet Home Page Address: www.craft-design.ns.ca; *Dir* Susan MacAlpine Foshay; *Studio Coordr* Catherine Allen
Open Mon - Wed & Fri 9 AM - 5 PM, Thurs 9 AM - 8 PM, Sat 10 AM - 5 PM, Sun 12 PM - 5 PM; No admis fee; Estab 1990; 900 sq ft in Halifax's seawall develop area near Pier 21 national site. Meets Canadian Conservation Institute Standards for temporary exhibitions; Average Annual Attendance: 15,000
Collections: Permanent collection of crafts
Exhibitions: 6 contemporary, temporary shows of craft & design annually
Publications: Exhibition catalogues
Activities: Classes for adults; lects open to pub, 51 vis lectrs per yr; gallery talks; tours

M **NOVA SCOTIA COLLEGE OF ART AND DESIGN,** Anna Leonowens Gallery, 1891 Granville St, Halifax, NS Canada; 5163 Duke St, Halifax, NS B3J 3J6 Canada. Tel 902-494-8223; Fax 902-425-3997; Elec Mail tdirisio@nscad.ca; Internet Home Page Address: www.nscad.ca; *Dir* Tony DiRisio; *Pres* David Smith
Open Tues - Fri 11 AM - 5 PM, Mon evenings 5:30 - 7:30 PM, Sat Noon - 4 PM; No admis fee; Estab 1968 for educational purposes; 3 exhibition spaces; Average Annual Attendance: 20,000
Income: Financed by state appropriations & tuition
Special Subjects: Drawings, Graphics, Prints, Sculpture, Textiles, Ceramics, Crafts, Etchings & Engravings, Collages, Jewelry, Metalwork
Collections: NSCAD permanent coll; prints from NSCAD lithography workshop
Exhibitions: 120 exhibitions per yr
Publications: Ten books; exhibition catalogs, occasionally
Activities: Lects open to pub; 2 vis lectrs per yr; gallery talks
L **Library,** 5163 Duke St, Halifax, NS B3J 3J6 Canada. Tel 902-494-8181; Fax 902-425-1978; Elec Mail library@nscad.ca; Internet Home Page Address: www.nscad.ca; *Contact* Tanja Harrison
Open Mon - Fri 8:30 AM - 10 PM, Sat & Sun Noon - 8 PM; No admis fee; Estab 1887; Circ 30,000
Income: Financed by state appropriation & student fees
Purchases: $120,000

Library Holdings: Book Volumes 50,000; CD-ROMs; Cassettes; Compact Disks; DVDs; Exhibition Catalogs; Fiche; Motion Pictures; Pamphlets; Periodical Subscriptions 250; Records; Reels; Slides; Video Tapes

M **Seeds Gallery,** 1892 Hollis St, Halifax, NS Canada. Tel 902-494-8301; Elec Mail seedsagllery@nscad.ca; Internet Home Page Address: nscad.ca/seedsgallery
Open Tues - Sat 11 AM - 6 PM; Showcases diverse range of original artwork by students and alumni of the Nova Scotia College of Art & Design
Collections: Ceramics, jewelry, painting, photography, printmaking, sculpture, textiles

M **NOVA SCOTIA MUSEUM,** Maritime Museum of the Atlantic, 1675 Lower Water St, Halifax, NS B3J 1S3 Canada. Tel 902-424-7490; Fax 902-424-0612; Internet Home Page Address: museum.gov.ns.ca/mma/index.html; *Dir Mus Opers* Calum Ewing; *Cur Marine History* Dan Conlin; *Registrar* Lynn-Marie Richard; *Coordr Vis Svcs & Educational Programming* Christine Sykora; *Coordr Pub Progs, Info & Mktg* Jenny Nodelman; *Sr Preparator* Mark Scott; *Mgr* Kim Reinhardt; *Mgr Partnerships & Develop* John Hennigar-Shuh
Open May 1 - Oct 31 Mon & Wed - Fri 9:30 AM - 5:30 PM, Tues 9:30 AM - 8 PM, Sun (May - Oct) 1 PM - 5:30 PM (June - Sept) 9:30 AM - 5:30 PM; Nov 1 - Apr 30, Tues 9:30 AM - 8 PM, Wed - Fri 9:30 AM - 5 PM, Sun 1 PM - 5 PM; Admis May - Oct: families $22.50, adults $8.75, senior $7.75, youth 6-17 $4.75, under 5 free; Nov - Apr: families $11, adults $4.75, senior $4, youth 6-17 $2.75, under 5 free; Estab 1948 to interpret maritime history of eastern coast of Canada; Gallery exhibits items from Days of Sail, Age of Steam, Navy, Small Craft, Shipwrecks, Underwater Archaeology, Titanic & Halifax Explosion; Average Annual Attendance: 175,000
Income: Financed by province of Nova Scotia Dept Tourism & Culture
Library Holdings: Book Volumes; Clipping Files; Photographs; Slides
Special Subjects: Crafts, Marine Painting
Collections: Halifax Explosion; Historical Marine Painting display; small craft, ship models, ship portraits, uniforms, marine artifacts; Titanic artifacts; WWII Atlantic convoys; Sable Island Canadian Navy
Exhibitions: Rotate 6-8 per yr
Activities: School progs; interpretive progs & tours; lects open to pub; gallery talks; concerts (sea shanties); tours; individual paintings & original objects of art lent to other institutions; mus shop sells books, reproductions, clothing, marine memorabilia & toys

M **ST MARY'S UNIVERSITY,** Art Gallery, 5865 Gorsebrook Ave, Halifax, NS B3H 3C3 Canada; 923 Robie St, Halifax, NS B3H 3C3 Canada. Tel 902-420-5445; Fax 902-420-5060; Elec Mail gallery@smu.ca; Internet Home Page Address: www.smuartgallery.ca; *Dir & Cur* Robin Metcalfe; *Office, Events & Commun Coordr* Erika Proctor; *Asst Cur* Pam Corell; *Colls Coordr* Harry Hamm
Open Tues - Fri 11 AM - 5 PM, Sat - Sun Noon - 5 PM; No admis fee; Estab 1970 to present a variety of exhibitions & performances of both regional & national interest & by contemporary artists; Average Annual Attendance: 12,000
Income: Financed by provincial appropriation
Collections: Works on paper by contemporary Canadian artists
Publications: Exhibit catalogues, 1-2 times per year
Activities: Adult drawing classes; lects open to public, 3-4 vis lectrs per year; concerts; gallery talks; tours; individual paintings & original objects of art lent; exten dept serves university; book traveling exhibs 1-2 per yr; originate 1 traveling exhib; circulated to the Atlantic Provinces of Canada; sales shop sells catalogs

A **VISUAL ARTS NOVA SCOTIA,** 1113 Marginal Rd Halifax, NS B3H 4P7 Canada. Tel 902-423-4694; Tel 866-225-8267 (toll free); Fax 902-422-0881; Elec Mail vans@visualarts.ns.ca; Internet Home Page Address: visualarts.ns.ca; *Exec Dir* Crystal Melville; *Prog Coordr* Becky Welter-Nolan; *Paints Coordr* Andrea Ritchie
Open daily 9 AM - 5 PM; No admis fee; Estab 1976 as a non-profit arts service organization to foster the development, awareness & understanding of the visual arts in Nova Scotia. Encourages the production, exhibition & appreciation of works by Nova Scotia's visual artists; 1 small gallery maintains slide registry, video library & archives & off-site exhib space - 5 small vitrines; Average Annual Attendance: 1,000; Mem: Over 600; dues corporate $65, couple/group/gallery $45, individual $35, senior $30, student $25
Income: $170,000 (financed by fund raising, mem & provincial appropriation)
Library Holdings: Audio Tapes; Book Volumes; Exhibition Catalogs; Pamphlets; Slides; Video Tapes
Exhibitions: Far & Wide: third biennial exhibition; biennial juried exhibitions, annual open exhibitions & occasional regional exhibitions
Publications: Visual Arts News, 3 times per yr
Activities: PAINTS (Professional Artists in the Schools); classes for adults; workshop prog; mentorship prog; educ prog; internships offered

LUNENBURG

M **LUNENBURG ART GALLERY SOCIETY,** 79 Pelham (corner Pelham & Duke), PO Box 1418 Lunenburg, NS B0J 2C0 Canada. Tel 902-640-4044; Fax 902-640-3035; Elec Mail lag@eastlink.ca; Internet Home Page Address: www.lunenburgartgallery.com; *Pres* Garry Woodcock; *Treas* Diana Dines; *Secy* Merrill Heubach; *Planning & Exhib* Jo McGee; *Members' Gallery* Patty Rhinelander; *Publicity & Gallery Mgr* Christine Umlah
Open Tues - Sat 10 AM-5 PM, Sun 1-5 PM, cl Mon; No admis fee; Estab 1977 to provide art appreciation to community & venue for artists; 1 exhib gallery & 1 members' gallery; Average Annual Attendance: 4,000; Mem: 150; dues supporters $20; exhibiting artists $30
Income: $30,000 (financed by mem & fundraising)
Purchases: Collection of Earl Bailly Paintings, Lunenburg Mouth Painter
Library Holdings: Cards; Clipping Files; Exhibition Catalogs; Framed Reproductions; Memorabilia; Original Art Works; Original Documents; Pamphlets; Periodical Subscriptions; Photographs; Prints; Reproductions; Sculpture
Collections: Meldrum Collection by Earl Bailly
Exhibitions: Exhibits rotate once per month with "opening receptions" on a Tues - 5 PM every month

Activities: Classes for children; art workshops, school progs; competitions; sales shop sell books, original art, reproductions, prints, cards & notes

WOLFVILLE

M ACADIA UNIVERSITY ART GALLERY, c/o Beveridge Arts Centre, Rm 129 Wolfville, NS B4P 2R6 Canada. Tel 902-585-1373; Fax 902-585-1070; Elec Mail artgallery@acadiau.ca; Internet Home Page Address: gallery.acadiau.ca; *Dir* Laurie Dalton
No admis fee; Estab 1978, art dept 1928, to exhibit contemporary & historical art particularly from the Atlantic region; Average Annual Attendance: 15,000; Mem: $10 membership
Income: $65,000 (financed by endowment & University funds)
Purchases: $15,000 (works by Atlantic region artists)
Collections: Contemporary & Historical Paintings, Drawings & Prints
Activities: Lects open to pub; 4 vis lectrs per yr; book traveling exhibs 8 per yr; originate traveling exhibs 4 per yr

YARMOUTH

M YARMOUTH COUNTY HISTORICAL SOCIETY, Yarmouth County Museum & Archives, 22 Collins St, Yarmouth, NS B5A 3C8 Canada. Tel 902-742-5539; Fax 902-749-1120; Elec Mail ycmuseum@eastlink.ca; Internet Home Page Address: www.yarmouthcountymuseum.ednet.ns.ca; *Pres* Aurel Mooney; *Dir* Bruce Bishop; *Cur* Nadine Gates; *Archivist* Jamie Serran
Open May 15 - Oct 14 9 AM - 5 PM, Oct 16 - May 14 2 - 5 PM, cl Mon; Admis adults $3, students $1, children $.50; Estab 1958 to display artifacts & paintings relating to Yarmouth's past; Located in former Congregational Church built in 1893; Average Annual Attendance: 14,000; Mem: 400; dues $25; meetings first Thurs each month
Income: $170,000 (financed by mem, admis & state appropriation)
Purchases: $500
Library Holdings: Audio Tapes; Book Volumes; CD-ROMs; Cassettes; Clipping Files; Compact Disks; DVDs; Exhibition Catalogs; Fiche; Manuscripts; Maps; Memorabilia; Original Art Works; Original Documents; Other Holdings; Pamphlets; Photographs; Prints
Special Subjects: Folk Art, Flasks & Bottles, Textiles, Drawings, Graphics, Photography, Ethnology, Costumes, Crafts, Folk Art, Etchings & Engravings, Landscapes, Decorative Arts, Manuscripts, Portraits, Painting-Canadian, Dolls, Furniture, Glass, Porcelain, Marine Painting, Historical Material, Ivory, Coins & Medals, Restorations, Period Rooms, Embroidery, Laces, Pewter, Military Art
Collections: Gen historical coll; paintings of & by Yarmouthians; coll of ship portraits of Yarmouth vessels & vessels commanded by Yarmouthians; gen & marine artifacts; marine drawings & portraits
Exhibitions: Various local exhibits
Publications: Monthly newsletter
Activities: Classes for children; lects open to pub, 12 vis lectrs per yr; concerts; gallery talks; tours; Heritage Awards; books traveling exhibs 1 per yr; mus shop sells books, prints, reproductions, local handicrafts, pewter jewelry

ONTARIO

ALMONTE

M MISSISSIPPI VALLEY CONSERVATION AUTHORITY, R Tait McKenzie Memorial Museum, 2854 Concession 8, RR#1, Mill of Kintail Conservation Area Almonte, ON K0A 1A0 Canada; 4175 Hwy 511, RR #2 Lanark, ON K0G 1K0 Canada. Tel 613-256-3610; Fax 613-256-5087; Elec Mail Kintail@trytel.com; Internet Home Page Address: www.mvc.on.ca; *Site Supv* Suzanne McFarlane; *Cur* Stephanie Kolsters; *Educ Coordr* Sarah O'Grady
Open May 1 - Thanksgiving (Canada) daily 10:30 AM - 4:30 PM; Admis $5 per car; Estab 1952 as a private mus, publicly owned since 1973 by Mississippi Valley Conservation Authority as a memorial to Dr R Tait McKenzie, Canadian sculptor, physical educator, surgeon & humanitarian. Home to Dr James Naismith, inventor of basketball, museum; Average Annual Attendance: 7,500
Income: Financed by provincial government grant
Library Holdings: Exhibition Catalogs; Manuscripts; Memorabilia; Original Art Works; Original Documents; Photographs; Sculpture
Special Subjects: Furniture, Photography, Sculpture, Carpets & Rugs
Collections: 70 Original Athletic, Memorial & Monumental Sculptures, nearly all in plaster; 600 Pioneer Artifacts, mostly collected by Dr McKenzie; Life & Times of Dr James Naismith; basketball artifacts
Exhibitions: Monthly art installations, local artists
Activities: Educ prog; classes for children; tours; gallery talks; scholarships offered; sales shop sells books, reproductions, postcards, gift notes, original art & prints

ATIKOKAN

L QUETICO PARK, John B Ridley Research Library, Quetico Park, 108 Saturn Ave Atikokan, ON P0T 1C0 Canada. Tel 807-929-2571 ext 224; Fax 807-929-2123; Elec Mail andrea.allison@ontario.ca; *Librn* Andrea Allison
Open year-round by appointment; Estab 1986; For reference only
Income: Financed by Ontario Parks
Purchases: $1500
Library Holdings: Book Volumes 4,800; Cassettes 380; Periodical Subscriptions 20; Photographs 8000; Slides 18,000; Video Tapes 100
Special Subjects: Archaeology
Collections: Natural history & cultural history displays on Quetico Park including archaeology, fur trade & voyageur history
Activities: Lect open to pub July - Aug

BANCROFT

M ART GALLERY OF BANCROFT INC, 10 Flint Ave, Bancroft, ON K0L 1C0 Canada; PO Box 398, Bancroft, ON K0L 1C0 Canada. Tel 613-332-1542; Elec Mail agb@nexicom.net; Internet Home Page Address: www.agb-weebly.com; *Pres* Diana Gurley; *VP* Richard Capener
Open Wed - Fri Noon - 5 PM, Sat 10 AM - 4 PM; Admis by donation; Estab 1980 to foster the fine arts in the area; Gallery & gift shop in a new location; Average Annual Attendance: 9,000; Mem: 155; dues $20; annual meeting in Sept
Income: Financed by corporate sponsorships, donations, gallery & gift shop sales
Special Subjects: Sculpture, Photography, Watercolors, Textiles, Pottery, Painting-Canadian, Jewelry, Stained Glass
Collections: Murray Schafer: Sound Sculptures; miscellaneous glass, fabric, paintings
Exhibitions: 12 exhibitions per year
Activities: Classes for children; gallery talks; competition with awards; annual juried & student exhib awards; shop sells original art, prints, crafts of all nature, pottery, stained glass, wood carvings & photographs

BELLEVILLE

M GLANMORE NATIONAL HISTORIC SITE OF CANADA, 257 Bridge St E, Belleville, ON K8N 1P4 Canada. Tel 613-962-2329; Fax 613-962-6340; Elec Mail rrustige@city.belleville.on.ca; Internet Home Page Address: www.glanmore.ca; *Educ* Melissa Wakeling; *Cur* Rona Rustige; *Secy* Darlene Rodgers; *Custodian* Mac Ellis; *Weekend Receptionist* Mary Jane Throop; *Database Coordr* Jen Gibson
Open June, July, Aug Tues - Sun 10 AM - 4:30 PM, Sept-May Tues - Sun 1 - 4:30 PM; Admis adults $6, seniors & students $5; children 5-12 $3.50; Estab 1973 to collect & interpret history of Belleville & 1880s nat historic site; Historic House with extensive collection of Victorian paintings, notably Horatio Henry Couldery, Bertram & Cecelia Couldery, copies of Gainsborough, Constable, Uens, Wilkie & Rembrandt; Average Annual Attendance: 8,000; Mem: 40; Friends of Glanmore; dues $10 per yr; meeting 1st Tues of month Sept - June
Income: Financed by corporation of City of Belleville & Ontario Ministry of Culture
Library Holdings: Book Volumes; Clipping Files; Lantern Slides; Maps; Original Art Works; Original Documents; Other Holdings; Pamphlets
Special Subjects: Etchings & Engravings, Porcelain, Portraits, Silver, Textiles, Bronzes, Maps, Sculpture, Architecture, Drawings, Photography, Watercolors, Ceramics, Landscapes, Decorative Arts, Manuscripts, Painting-Canadian, Dolls, Furniture, Glass, Jewelry, Oriental Art, Asian Art, Painting-British, Painting-French, Carpets & Rugs, Historical Material, Ivory, Coins & Medals, Restorations, Miniatures, Period Rooms, Embroidery, Gold, Pewter, Leather, Enamels
Collections: Couldery European Art Collection: (Cloisonne, paintings & furniture, typical of upper class turn of the century taste); Phillips-Burrows-Faulkner Collection; Regional History Collection; Manly McDonald Originals; Sir Mackenzie Bowell Collection; William Sawyer Collection; Dr Paul Lamp Collection
Publications: Exhibit catalog
Activities: Classes for adults & children; docent training; internships; student placements; education kits lent to schools & groups; lects open to pub; tours; gallery talks; sponsoring of competitions; individual paintings & original objects of art lent to mus, galleries; book traveling exhibs, annually; mus shop sells books, reproductions, artifacts, prints, & gift items related to Victoriana

BRACEBRIDGE

M MUSKOKA ARTS & CRAFTS INC, Chapel Gallery, 15 King St, PO Box 376 Bracebridge, ON P1L 1T7 Canada. Tel 705-645-5501; Fax 705-645-0385; Elec Mail info@muskokaartsandcrafts.com; Internet Home Page Address: www.muskokaartsandcrafts.com; *Cur* Elene J Freer
Open Tues - Sat 10 AM-1 PM & 2-5 PM; Admis donations accepted; Estab 1963, museum estab 1989; Average Annual Attendance: 10,000; Mem: 340; dues $20-$30; annual meeting in Oct
Income: Financed by mem & donations
Publications: Newsletter, 12 per year
Activities: Classes for adults & children; lects for mems only, 1-5 vis lectrs per yr; schols offered

BRAMPTON

M ART GALLERY OF PEEL, Peel Heritage Complex, 9 Wellington St E, Brampton, ON L6W 1Y1 Canada. Tel 905-791-4055; Fax 905-451-4931; Elec Mail HCResearch@peelregion.ca; Internet Home Page Address: www.region.peel.on.ca/heritage; *Cur* David Somers; *Develop Officer* Valerie Dowbiggin
Open Mon - Fri 10 AM - 4:30 PM, Thurs 6 - 9 PM, Sat & Sun Noon - 4:30 PM; Admis family $7, adults $2.50, seniors $1.50, students & children $1; Estab 1968 to promote & collect art & artifacts on regional & provincial level; Average Annual Attendance: 20,000; Mem: 200; dues corporate $150, family $45, individual $30; annual meeting in Feb
Collections: Permanent Collection of Canadian Artists, special focus on Peel Region; Works on paper; Caroline & Frank Armington Print Collection
Exhibitions: Eight exhibits per year (all mediums); Annual Open Juried Show; Regional Artists
Publications: Carolina & Frank Armington; Canadian Painter -Etchers in Paris; exhib catalogs
Activities: Classes for adults & children; docent training; lects open to pub, 2-3 vis lectrs per yr; gallery talks; tours; competitions with prizes; exten dept serves Southern Ontario; individual paintings & original objects of art lent to public buildings & other institutions; book traveling exhibs 1 per yr; originate traveling exhibs to libraries & other galleries; sales shop sells books, reproductions & prints
L Archives, 9 Wellington St E, Brampton, ON L6W 1Y1 Canada. Tel

905-791-4055; Fax 905-451-4931; Internet Home Page Address: www.region.peel.on.ca/heritage; *Archivist* Diane Kuster; *Cur* David Somers
Open Mon - Fri 10 AM - 4:30 PM, Sat 12 PM - 4:30 PM; Circ Non-circulating; Reference only
Library Holdings: Book Volumes 550; Clipping Files; Exhibition Catalogs; Memorabilia; Periodical Subscriptions 3

BRANTFORD

M **BRANT HISTORICAL SOCIETY,** Brant Museum & Archives, 57 Charlotte St, Brantford, ON N3T 2W6 Canada. Tel 519-752-2483; Fax 519-752-1931; Elec Mail information@brantmuseums.ca; Internet Home Page Address: www.brantmuseums.ca; *Exec Dir* John Robertson
Open Tues - Sat 10 AM - 4 PM, July & Aug Sun 1 - 4 PM; Admis by donation; Estab 1908 to preserve, interpret & display Brant County history; Average Annual Attendance: 9,200; Mem: 200; dues family $40, individual $25, student $20
Income: Financed by mem, provincial, county & city grants & fundraising
Library Holdings: Book Volumes; Clipping Files; Fiche; Filmstrips; Manuscripts; Maps; Original Art Works; Original Documents; Photographs; Prints; Slides
Special Subjects: Historical Material
Collections: Early Indian history; historical figures; portraits & paintings; Brant County history; Old maps & photographs of Brant County
Publications: Annual brochure; Brant County, the Story of its People, vol I & II; Grand River Navigation Company Newsletter, quarterly
Activities: Classes for children; docent training & Kids' camps; lectrs open to pub; tours; mus shop sells books, reproductions & prints

L **Library,** 57 Charlotte St, Brantford, ON N3T 2W6 Canada. Tel 519-752-2483; Fax 519-752-1931; Internet Home Page Address: www.brantmuseums.ca; *Exec Dir* Joan Kanigan-Fairen
Open Tues - Sat 10 AM - 4PM; Admis $8 (research fees); Estab for research only; Circ Non-circulating
Library Holdings: Book Volumes 500; Maps; Photographs
Special Subjects: Religious Art
Collections: First editions of history & archaeology; old Bibles available for research on premises under supervision of cur; rare books; Photographs of Brant County & old maps
Activities: Classes for adults & children; 8 vis lectrs per yr; mus shop sells books

M **GLENHYRST ART GALLERY OF BRANT,** 20 Ava Rd, Brantford, ON N3T 5G9 Canada. Tel 519-756-5932; Fax 519-756-5910; Elec Mail info@glenhyrst.ca; Internet Home Page Address: www.glenhyrst.ca; *Cur* Bryce Kanbara
Open Tues - Fri 10 AM - 5 PM, Sat & Sun 12 - 5 PM; No admis fee; Estab 1957 as a nonprofit pub arts center serving the citizens of Brantford & Brant County; Situated on 16 picturesque acres, the gallery offers rotating exhib of contemporary art; Average Annual Attendance: 19,000; Mem: 425; dues family $40, individual $30, student & senior citizen $20; annual meeting in Feb
Income: Financed by mem, municipal, provincial & federal appropriations & local foundations
Library Holdings: Book Volumes 140; CD-ROMs; Clipping Files 200; Exhibition Catalogs 200; Periodical Subscriptions 10
Special Subjects: Prints, Painting-Canadian
Collections: Contemporary Canadian graphics/works on paper; historical works by R R Whale & descendants, outdoor sculpture
Exhibitions: Biennial juried exhib
Activities: Classes for adults & children; lect open to pub; tours; gallery talks; individual paintings lent to public art galleries & museums/Brantford and Brant

BURLINGTON

M **BURLINGTON ART CENTRE,** 1333 Lakeshore Rd at Brock, Burlington, ON L7S 1A9 Canada. Tel 905-632-7796; Fax 905-632-0278; Elec Mail info@BurlingtonArtCentre.on.ca; Internet Home Page Address: www.burlingtonartcentre.on.ca; *Exec Dir* Ian D Ross; *Dir Programs* George Wale; *Dir Develop & Mktg* Sandra Baker; *Cur Educ* Laura Arseneau
Open Mon - Thurs 9 AM - 10 PM, Fri - Sat 9 AM - 5 PM, Sun 12 PM - 5 PM; No admis fee; Estab 1978; Maintains reference library, main gallery, F R Perry Gallery; permanent collection corridor courtyard; Average Annual Attendance: 90,000; Mem: 1200; dues $30-$65; annual meeting in Mar
Income: $1,150,000 (financed by mem, city appropriation, province appropriation, earned revenues, fund raising, donations & sponsorship)
Purchases: $10,000
Collections: Contemporary Canadian Ceramic Art
Activities: Classes for adults & children; docent training; hands-on progs; lects open to pub, 2 vis lectrs per yr; tours; exten dept; original objects of art lent; book traveling exhibs 1 per yr; originate traveling exhibs 20 per yr; mus shop sells original art & jewelry

CAMBRIDGE

L **CAMBRIDGE PUBLIC LIBRARY AND GALLERY,** 1 North Sq, Cambridge, ON N1S 2K6 Canada. Tel 519-621-0460; Fax 519-621-2080; Elec Mail galleriesinfo@cambridgegalleries.ca; Internet Home Page Address: www.cambridgelibraries.ca/main.cfm; *Gallery Dir* Mary Misner; *Chief Librn* Greg Hayton
Open Mon - Thurs 9:30 AM - 8:30 PM, Fri & Sat 9:30 AM - 5:30 PM; Sept - May open Sun 1 - 5 PM; No admis fee; Estab 1969; Gallery on second floor with 2000 sq ft, 250 linear ft; Average Annual Attendance: 25,000
Income: Financed by provincial appropriation, federal & private
Library Holdings: Book Volumes 150,000; Periodical Subscriptions 100
Collections: Regional Artists
Exhibitions: Rotate 6 - 8 per yr
Publications: Bi-monthly newsletter

Activities: Classes for adults & children; lects open to pub, 10 vis lectrs per yr; concerts; gallery talks; tours; competitions with awards; individual paintings & original objects of art lent; originate traveling exhibs
Courses: Fiber Art

CHATHAM

A **THAMES ART GALLERY,** 75 William St N, Chatham, ON N7M 4L4 Canada. Tel 519-354-8338; Fax 519-354-4170; Elec Mail ccc@chatham-kent.ca; Internet Home Page Address: www.city.chatham-kent.ca/tag; Internet Home Page Address: www.theculturalcentre.com; *Dir & Cur* Carl Lavoy; *Cur Asst* Sonya Blazek
Open daily 1 PM - 5 PM; No admis fee; Estab 1963 to operate as a regional arts centre, to advance knowledge & appreciation of & to encourage, stimulate & promote interest in the study of culture & the visual arts; Gallery maintained; designated National Exhibition Centre for the presentation of visual art works & museum related works, to the public of this country; Average Annual Attendance: 15,000; Mem: $50 Culture Vulture mem
Income: Financed by mem, municipal, & federal governments; Ontario Arts Council, & the Canada Council for the Arts
Library Holdings: Book Volumes; CD-ROMs; Exhibition Catalogs; Original Art Works; Periodical Subscriptions; Photographs; Prints; Sculpture; Slides; Video Tapes
Collections: Local Artists; regional contemporary artists
Exhibitions: Ten various historical and contemporary exhibs per yr
Publications: At the Centre, 10 per yr
Activities: Classes for adults & children; docent training; lects open to public, 9 vis lectrs per yr; concerts; gallery talks; tours; juried fine art shows; individual & original objects of art lent to accredited galleries & museums; lending collection contains 2100 slides; serves Chatham-Kent; 1-2 book traveling exhibs; originate traveling exhibs to other accredited galleries

CORNWALL

M **CORNWALL GALLERY SOCIETY,** Cornwall Regional Art Gallery, 168 Pitt St Promenade, Cornwall, ON K6J 3P4 Canada. Tel 613-938-7387; Fax 613-938-9619; Elec Mail info@cornwallregionalartgallery.ca; Internet Home Page Address: cornwallregionalartgallery.ca; *Exec Dir* Sylvie Lizotte
Open Tues - Sat 10 AM - 5 PM, cl Sun & Mon; No admis fee; Estab 1982 to promote interest in & study of visual arts; Main gallery has 3 display walls measuring 44.5 ft, 30 ft & 10 ft 9 inches; walls 12 ft; Gallery Shoppe where local art is sold; Average Annual Attendance: 15,000; Mem: 200; dues $20 & up; annual meeting in June
Income: $90,000 - $100,000 (financed by mem & city appropriation)
Special Subjects: Drawings, Photography, Prints, Sculpture, Watercolors, Religious Art, Ceramics, Crafts, Folk Art, Pottery, Decorative Arts, Portraits, Painting-Canadian, Porcelain, Embroidery, Laces
Collections: Contemporary Canadian Art
Exhibitions: Annual Juried Exhibition; rotate exhibits from Canadian artists once per month
Publications: Newsletter, tri-annually
Activities: Classes for adults & children; individual paintings lent; mus shop sells original art

DON MILLS

C **ROTHMANS, BENSON & HEDGES,** Art Collection, 1500 Don Mills Rd, Don Mills, ON M3B 3L1 Canada. Tel 416-449-5525; Fax 416-449-4486; *Mgr Gen Servs* John Bird
Open to public; Estab 1967; Collection displayed at head office
Special Subjects: Eskimo Art
Collections: Contemporary Canadian art from last decade
Activities: Awards for Toronto Outdoor Art Exhibition each yr; individual objects of art lent to traveling or special exhibs; originate traveling exhibs to all major public galleries in Canada

DURHAM

M **DURHAM ART GALLERY,** 251 George St E, PO Box 1021 Durham, ON N0G 1R0 Canada. Tel 519-369-3692; Fax 519-369-3327; Elec Mail info@durhamart.on.ca; Internet Home Page Address: www.durhamart.on.ca; *Pres* Trevor Crilly; *Dir* Ilse Gassinger
Open Tues - Fri 10 AM - 5 PM, Sat - Sun 1 PM - 4 PM, Thurs 7 AM - 8 PM; Estab 1978

GUELPH

M **MACDONALD STEWART ART CENTRE,** 358 Gordon St, Guelph, ON N1G 1Y1 Canada. Tel 519-837-0010; Fax 519-767-2661; Elec Mail info@msac.ca; Internet Home Page Address: www.msac.ca; *Asst Cur* Dawn Owen; *Pub Programming Asst* Aiden Ware; *Gallery Coordr* Verne Harrison
Open Tues - Sun Noon - 5 PM; Admis by donation; Estab 1978 by University of Guelph, city, county & board of educ to collect & exhibit works of art; maintain & operate a gallery & related facilities for this purpose fulfilling a pub role in city & county; 30,000 sq ft building comprising galleries, lecture room, studio, meeting rooms, resource centre, gift shop & rental service. Restored & renovated in 1980; Average Annual Attendance: 25,000; Mem: 600; dues family $30, individual $20, senior & student $10; annual meeting Sept-Oct
Income: Financed by university, city, county, board of educ, provincial & federal grants, mem & donations
Purchases: Canadian art
Special Subjects: Prints, Decorative Arts, Eskimo Art

Collections: Historical & contemporary Canadian art; historical & contemporary international prints; Inuit Collection; contemporary sculpture; outdoor sculpture (Donald Forster Sculpture Park)
Publications: Catalogue of permanent collection of University of Guelph 1980; exhibition catalogues, 6 per yr; quarterly newsletter
Activities: Classes for children; docent training; workshops; lects open to pub; gallery talks; school & group tours; concerts; tours; exten dept serves Wellington County & other Canadian public galleries, also have circulated in US & Europe; individual paintings lent to institutions & public galleries; art rental to gallery members; lending collection contains 500 original paintings, 400 prints, photographs & 50 sculptures; book traveling exhibs 4-6 per yr; originate traveling exhibs 1-2 per yr for museums in Canada & abroad; sales shop sells books, magazines, reproductions, toys, pottery, textiles, jewelry & catalogues

HAILEYBURY

M **TEMISKAMING ART GALLERY,** 325 Farr Dr, Haileybury, ON P0J 1K0 Canada; PO Box 1090, Haileybury, ON P0J 1K0 Canada. Tel 705-672-3706; Fax 705-672-5966; Internet Home Page Address: www.temiskamingartgallery.ca; *Dir & Cur* Peter Greyson
Open Tues - Fri 10 AM - 4 PM, Sat 12 PM - 4 PM; No admis fee; Estab 1980 to educate; 1 large gallery; Mem: Dues $15 & up; Annual meeting May
Income: Financed by mem & city appropriation &Ontario Arts Council
Special Subjects: Drawings, Etchings & Engravings, Landscapes, Ceramics, Collages, Photography, Portraits, Pottery, Sculpture, Watercolors, Painting-Japanese, Painting-Canadian
Collections: North Ontario Collection
Exhibitions: Rotating exhibits
Activities: Classes for adults & children; lects open to pub, 5 vis lectrs per yr; gallery talks; artmobil; lendig of original art to city hall staff

HAMILTON

M **ART GALLERY OF HAMILTON,** 123 King St W, Hamilton, ON L8P 4S8 Canada. Tel 905-527-6610; Fax 905-577-6940; Elec Mail info@artgalleryofhamilton.com; Internet Home Page Address: www.artgalleryofhamilton.com; *Pres & CEO* Louise Dompierre; *Dir Curatorial Affairs* Dr Benedict Leca; *Educator* Laurie Kilgour-Walsh; *Dir Mktg & Communs* Janet Mowat; *Dir Commercial Activities* Mark Stewart
Open Tues & Wed 11 AM - 6 PM, Thurs 11 AM - 8 PM, Fri 11 AM - 6 PM, Sat & Sun Noon - 5 PM, cl Mon; Admis to ticketed exhibs: adults $10, students & seniors $8, children 6-17 $4; Estab Jan 1914 to develop & maintain a centre for the study & enjoyment of the visual arts; new gallery opened Oct 1977; renovated & reopened May 2005; Building is 76,000 sq ft, 24,000 sq ft of exhibition space; Average Annual Attendance: 150,000+; Mem: 2000; dues family $90, single $55; annual meeting in June. Expect partial closures due to major rennovations Oct. 2003 to April 2005
Income: Earned revenue endowment, mem, city & provincial appropriation & federal grants
Special Subjects: Graphics, Painting-American, Photography, American Western Art, Religious Art, Woodcarvings, Etchings & Engravings, Painting-European, Eskimo Art, Painting-British, Baroque Art
Collections: Complete graphics of Karel Appel; Canadian fine arts; American, British & European fine arts; historical, modern & contemporary coll; Joey and Toby Tanenbaum Collection (19th century European)
Exhibitions: Twenty-nine exhibitions scheduled per yr
Publications: Insights, 3 times per yr
Activities: Educ prog; classes for adults & children; docent training; lects open to pub, 10-20 per yr; concerts; gallery talks; tours; 2000 Lieutenant Governor's award for the arts; individual paintings & original objects of art lent to other galleries & mus; lending collection contains 7800 art works; book traveling exhibs; originate traveling exhibs to provincial galleries & art ctrs; internat. art galleries; mus shop sells books, magazines, original art, reproductions & giftware

L **Muriel Isabel Bostwick Library,** 123 King St W, Hamilton, ON L8P 4S8 Canada. Tel 905-527-6610 ext 230; Fax 905-577-6940; Internet Home Page Address: www.artgalleryofhamilton.on.ca; *Librn* Helen Hadden; *Sr Cur* Shirley Madill
Open Tues - Sun 11 AM - 5PM, Thurs 11 AM - 9 PM; Open to gallery members & researchers for reference
Library Holdings: Book Volumes 4800; Clipping Files; Exhibition Catalogs; Periodical Subscriptions 14; Photographs
Special Subjects: Art History, Mixed Media, Painting-American, Prints, Sculpture, Painting-European, Portraits, Printmaking, Oriental Art, Restoration & Conservation
Collections: References on Canadian art history; exhibition catalogues

M **DUNDURN CASTLE,** 610 York Blvd Hamilton, ON L8R 3H1 Canada. Tel 905-546-2872; Fax 905-546-2875; Elec Mail dundurn@hamilton.ca; Internet Home Page Address: www.city.hamilton.on.ca/culture-and-rec; *Cur Asst* Elizabeth Wakeford; *Cur* Bill Nesbitt
Open July 1 - Sept 1 daily 10 AM - 4 PM; Sept 2 - June 30 Tues - Sun 12 PM - 4 PM, cl holidays; Admis family $25, adults $10, sr citizens & students $8, children $5, children under 5 free, discounts on group rates for over 20 people; Dundurn, the home of Sir Allan Napier MacNab; Hamilton's Centennial Project was the restoration of this historic house; built in 1832-35, it was tenured by MacNab until his death in 1862. The terminal date of the furnishings is 1855; Approx 43 rooms are shown; two-room on-site exhibit area; Average Annual Attendance: 70,000
Income: Financed by city of Hamilton, owner & operator
Special Subjects: Architecture, Photography, Prints, Watercolors, Archaeology, Textiles, Religious Art, Pottery, Woodcarvings, Etchings & Engravings, Portraits, Painting-Canadian, Furniture, Glass, Porcelain, Silver, Carpets & Rugs, Coins & Medals, Restorations, Tapestries, Calligraphy, Period Rooms, Stained Glass, Pewter, Reproductions

Collections: Regency & mid-Victorian furnishings depicting the lifestyle of an upper class gentleman living in upper Canada in the 1850s; restored servants quarters
Exhibitions: Historical Crafts Fair, Harvest Home-baking & preserving competitions; Victorian Christmas
Activities: Classes for adults & children; docent training; lects open to pub; concerts; gallery talks, tours; individual paintings & original objects of art lent; mus shop sells books, reproductions, prints & slides, tea room & food service facilities

M **MCMASTER UNIVERSITY,** McMaster Museum of Art, Alvin A Lee Bldg, 1280 Main St W Hamilton, ON L8S 4L6 Canada. Tel 905-525-9140, Ext 23081; Fax 905-527-4548; Elec Mail museum@momaster.ca; Internet Home Page Address: www.mcmaster.ca/museum; *Dir & Chief Cur* Carol Podedworny; *Preparator* Jennifer Petteplace; *Communs Officer* Rose Anne Prevec; *Admin Asst* Jude Levett; *Information Officer* Nicole Knibb; *Information Officer* Teresa Gregorio; *Monitor/Display Provider* Hamish Shea-Pelletier; *Monitor/Technical Asst* Feng Guo; *Colls Administrator* Julie Bronson; *Sr Cur* Ihor Holubizky
Open Tues - Wed 11 AM - 5 PM, Thurs 11 AM - 7 PM, Sat Noon - 5 PM, cl Mon & Sun; Admis fee donations; Estab 1967 to provide the university & pub with exhibitions of historical & contemporary art from Canada & other countries; Houses the University's collection of 6000 works of art and present exhibs; Average Annual Attendance: 25,000
Income: $1,000,000 (financed by university & private endowment, corporate & individual support)
Library Holdings: Auction Catalogs; Book Volumes; CD-ROMs; Clipping Files; Exhibition Catalogs; Manuscripts; Maps; Memorabilia; Original Art Works; Original Documents; Pamphlets; Periodical Subscriptions; Photographs; Prints; Sculpture; Slides; Video Tapes
Special Subjects: American Indian Art, Etchings & Engravings, Landscapes, Flasks & Bottles, Photography, Maps, Sculpture, Drawings, Painting-American, Prints, Watercolors, Bronzes, Religious Art, Woodcuts, Painting-European, Painting-Canadian, Glass, Asian Art, Painting-British, Painting-Dutch, Painting-French, Coins & Medals, Painting-Flemish, Painting-Italian, Antiquities-Egyptian, Antiquities-Roman, Painting-German, Painting-Russian
Collections: Levy Collection, impressionist & post-impressionist, paintings & early Dutch panels; American & Canadian Art; European paintings, prints & drawings; Expressionist Prints
Exhibitions: Presents 12-15 exhibitions ann
Publications: The Art Collection of McMaster University; Levy legacy and various exhibition catalogues
Activities: Classes for adults & children; classroom facilities; docent training; lects open to pub; concerts; gallery talks; artist talks; 7 vis lectrs per yr; tours; receptions; individual paintings and original objects of art lent to National Gallery of Canada, Art Gallery of Ontario & other Canadian institutions; originates 5 book traveling exhibs per yr; originate traveling exhibs to other univs or public galleries

JORDAN

M **JORDAN HISTORICAL MUSEUM OF THE TWENTY,** 3800 Main St, Jordan, ON L0R 1S0 Canada. Tel 905-562-5242; Fax 905-562-7786; Elec Mail museum@lincoln.ca; Internet Home Page Address: www.lincoln.ca; *Cur & Dir* Helen Booth; *Asst Dir* Sylvia Beben
Open summer Tues - Sun 10 AM - 5 PM; winter Mon - Fri 8:30 AM - 4:30 PM, Sat 1 PM - 4 PM; Admis fee suggested donation; Estab 1953 to preserve the material & folklore of the area known as The Twenty, Mile Creek vicinity; Average Annual Attendance: 10,000; Mem: 100; dues corp with over 15 employees $50, under 15 $35, family $25, individual $15
Income: Financed by admis, provincial grants, municipal grants, internal fund raising activities & donations
Special Subjects: Historical Material, Period Rooms
Collections: Archives; furniture; historical material & textiles
Exhibitions: Special annual exhibits; Pioneer Day
Activities: Classes for children; special displays as requested by the community; Pioneer Day first Sat after Canadian Thanksgiving holiday; lects open to pub, 1 vis lectr per yr; individual paintings & original objects of art lent; sales shop sells books, original art, prints, pottery, textiles & local craft items

KINGSTON

M **QUEEN'S UNIVERSITY,** Agnes Etherington Art Centre, 99 University Ave, Bader Ln Kingston, ON K7L 3N6 Canada. Tel 613-533-2190; Fax 613-533-6765; Elec Mail aeac@post.queensu.ca; Internet Home Page Address: www.aeac.ca; *Chief Cur & Cur Contemporary Art* Jan Allen; *Pub Prog Officer* Pat Sullivan; *Dir* Janet M Brooke; *Preparator* Nigel Barnett; *Financial Coordr* Barry Fagan; *Bader Cur European Art* David de Witt; *Admin Coordr* Matthew Hills; *Coll Mgr & Exhib Coordr* Jennifer Nicoll
Open Tues - Fri 10 AM - 4:30 PM, Sat - Sun 1 PM - 5 PM; Admis adults $4, seniors $2.50, students & children free; Estab 1957 to provide the services of a pub art gallery & mus for the community & region; Gallery has approx 8000 sq ft of display space, in eight galleries showing a balanced program of exhibitions of contemporary & historical, national, international & regional art; Average Annual Attendance: 30,000; Mem: 900; dues $15-$200; annual meeting in Sept (Gallery Assn)
Income: $1,000,000 (financed by endowment, city & provincial appropriation, University & Canada Council funds)
Purchases: $100,000
Special Subjects: Graphics, Prints, Sculpture, Ethnology, Antiquities-Greek, Antiquities-Roman
Collections: African Art; Canadian Dress Collection; Canadian Paintings; Prints, Sculpture, Historical & Contemporary; Decorative Objects; Ethnological Collection; European Graphics; European 17th Century; Old Master Paintings; Quilts; Silver
Exhibitions: About 30 exhibitions mounted each year

Publications: Currents, quarterly; annual report; exhibition publications & catalogues; studies

Activities: Docent training regarding tours for school & other groups; lects open to public, 10 vis lectrs per yr; gallery talks; tours; artwork rented by Gallery Assn Art Rental to private individuals & bus; originate traveling exhibs to other cultural institutions; museum shop sells books, reproductions, prints & gift items including ceramics, jewelry, glassware

L **Stauffer Library Art Collection,** 101 Union St, Kingston, ON K7L 5C4 Canada. Tel 613-533-6929; Fax 613-533-6765; Elec Mail lucinda.walls@queensu.ca; Internet Home Page Address: http://library.queensu.ca/webart/; *Librn* Lucinda Walls
Open (see website); Estab 2003; Open to students, faculty & staff; open to public for reference only
Library Holdings: Book Volumes 50,000; Exhibition Catalogs 14,000; Fiche 1400; Other Holdings Reference bks; Periodical Subscriptions 140; Photographs; Reels 300; Video Tapes 215
Special Subjects: Art History

M **ST LAWRENCE COLLEGE,** Art Gallery, 100 Portsmouth Ave, PO Box 6000 Kingston, ON K7L 5A6 Canada. Tel 613-544-5400, Ext 1283; Fax 613-545-3923; Internet Home Page Address: www.sl.on.ca; *Dept Coordr* Terry Pfliger; *Gallery Coordr* Michael Shumate, BFA
Open Noon - 4 PM; No admis fee; College estab 1968, mus estab 1973 to augment the creative art program with shows, visiting artists; Average Annual Attendance: 4,000

KITCHENER

M **HOMER WATSON HOUSE & GALLERY,** 1754 Old Mill Rd, Kitchener, ON N2P 1H7 Canada. Tel 519-748-4377; Fax 519-748-6808; Internet Home Page Address: www.homerwatson.on.ca; *Exec Dir* Faith Hieblinger; *Cur* Sandu Sindile; *Dir Educ & Pub Progs* Chandra Erlendson; *Develop Officer* Kate Macpherson; *Mktg & PR Coordr* Helena Ball; *Research & Archive Coordr* Laura Mabee
Open Tues - Sun Noon - 4:30 PM; Admis $5; Estab 1981 as Homer Watson Memorial; Three studios for contemporary art - total of 155 running ft; Average Annual Attendance: 6,000; Mem: 250; dues family $30, individual $18; annual meeting 2nd Tues in June
Income: $500,000 (financed by mem, city appropriation, workshops & classes)
Purchases: $6,000
Collections: Watson Family Artifacts; Homer Watson Paintings
Exhibitions: Contemporary art-regional & provincial artists
Activities: Classes for adults & children; lects open to pub; 4 vis lectrs per year; concerts; gallery talks; tours; mus shop sells books, original art, reproductions, prints, confectionery, t-shirts

M **KITCHENER-WATERLOO ART GALLERY,** 101 Queen St N, Kitchener, ON N2H 6P7 Canada. Tel 519-579-5860; Fax 519-578-0740; Elec Mail mail@kwag.on.ca; Internet Home Page Address: www.kwag.ca; *Pres* Rita Ross; *VPres Finance & Treas* Jim Stinson; *Exec Dir* Shirley Madill; *Cur* Crystal Mowry; *Registrar* Jennifer Bullock; *Preparator* Ian Newton; *Mgr Finance & Admin* Shelly Mitchell; *Dir Pub Prog* Nicole Neufeld; *Dir Develop & Mktg* Caroline Oliver; *Graphic Designer* Liz Dorant; *Develop Assoc* Eleanor Mueller
Open Mon - Sat 9:30 AM - 5 PM, Thurs until 9 PM, Sun 1 PM - 5 PM; No admis fee; Estab 1956, the Kitchener-Waterloo Art Gallery is a pub institution interested in stimulating an appreciation of the visual arts & dedicated to bringing to the community exhibitions, art classes, lectures, workshops & special events; Average Annual Attendance: 40,000; Mem: 820; dues bus $100, family $40, individual $30, senior citizens & students $15
Income: Financed by government grants, foundation grants, corporate & individual donations, special events, mem dues, voluntary admis & sales of publication
Library Holdings: Exhibition Catalogs; Original Art Works
Special Subjects: Photography, Prints, Painting-European, Sculpture, Drawings, Prints, Watercolors, Painting-Canadian, Painting-German
Collections: Homer Watson Collection
Publications: Calendar, quarterly; exhibition catalogs, quarterly
Activities: Art classes for adults & children; docent training; lects open to public; lects for mems only; gallery talks; tours; art travel tours; schol progs

KLEINBURG

M **MCMICHAEL CANADIAN ART COLLECTION,** 10365 Islington Ave, Kleinburg, ON L0J 1C0 Canada. Tel 905-893-1121; Fax 905-893-0692; Elec Mail info@mcmichael.com; Internet Home Page Address: www.mcmichael.com; *Exec Dir & CEO* Tom Smart; *Dir Finance & Human Resources* Mary Benvenuto; *Dir Devel* Peter Ross; *Dir Opers* Alexander Meadu; *Dir Educ & Prog* Scott MacDonald; *Registrar* Janine Butler; *Conservator* Alison Douglas; *Mgr Spec Projects & Bd Svcs* Rebecca Couch; *Treas* Edwin F Hawken; *Secy* Robert C Dowsett; *Chmn* Michael W Johnston
Open Mon - Sat 10 AM - 4 PM, May 4 - Oct 26, Sun 10 AM - 5 PM; Admis family $30, adults $15, students & sr citizens $12; Estab 1965
Collections: Focus of the coll is the works of art created by Indian, Inuit & Metis artists, the artists of the Group of Seven & their contemporaries & other artists who have made or make a contribution to the development of Canadian Art
Exhibitions: Temporary exhibitions lasting from 1 to 3 months
Publications: Permanent collection catalogue; exhibition catalogues; quarterly newsletters
Activities: Comprehensive educ progs at the elementary & secondary school levels; guided group tours by appointment; exten progs & temporary exhibition progs; progs for kindergarten & special interest groups

L **Library & Archives,** Islington Ave, Kleinburg, ON L0J 1C0 Canada. Tel 905-893-1121; Fax 905-893-2588; Elec Mail library@mcmichael.com; Internet Home Page Address: www.mcmichael.com; *Librn & Archivist* Linda Morita
Open by appointment

Library Holdings: Auction Catalogs; Audio Tapes; Book Volumes 5000; Cassettes; Clipping Files; Exhibition Catalogs; Fiche; Manuscripts; Memorabilia; Original Art Works; Original Documents; Other Holdings Archival material; Pamphlets; Periodical Subscriptions 30; Photographs; Reproductions; Slides; Video Tapes
Special Subjects: Art History, Prints, Printmaking, Eskimo Art, Landscapes, Painting-Canadian

LINDSAY

M **THE LINDSAY GALLERY INC,** 190 Kent St W, Fl 2 Lindsay, ON K9V 2Y6 Canada. Tel 705-324-1780; Fax 705-324-9349; Elec Mail art@thelindsaygallery.com; Internet Home Page Address: www.thelindsaygallery.com; *Board Chmn* Mary Jeffery
Open Tues - Sat 10 AM - 11:30 AM & 12 PM - 4 PM; No admis fee; Estab 1976; half of 2d floor of library, Lindsay branch; Average Annual Attendance: 6,000; Mem: 300; family $40, individual $25, senior citizens & student $20
Income: $76,000 (financed by mem, fund raising, & corporate sponsorship)
Special Subjects: Sculpture, Painting-Canadian
Collections: Historical & contemporary Canadian
Publications: Bimonthly Newsletter
Activities: Art classes for adults & children; lects open to pub, 2 vis lectrs per yr; Awards, art student bursary, memorial award to a secondary school student at juried show; book traveling exhibs 1-2 times per yr; 12 Exhibs per yr; Summer Art in the Park; sales shop sells original art, prints, original crafts & artists jewelry

LONDON

M **MUSEUM LONDON,** 421 Ridout St N, London, ON N6A 5H4 Canada. Tel 519-661-0333; Fax 519-661-2559; Elec Mail omercer@museumlondon.ca; Internet Home Page Address: www.museumlondon.ca; *Cur Educ* Steve Mavers; *Cur Contemporary Art & Head Exhibitions and Collections* Melanie Townsend; *Dir Finance* Gail Roberts; *Cur Pub Programs* Paul Walde; *Partnerships Mgr* Carol Kehoe; *Exec Dir* Brian Meehan; *Head Admin* Cynda Mercer; *Registrar* Kevin Zacher; *Registrar* Jeanette Cousins Ewan; *Gallery Svcs Coordr* Heidi Sura
Open June 1 - Aug 31, Tues - Sun 11 AM - 5 PM, Thurs 11 AM - 9 PM; Sept - July, Tues - Sun 12 PM - 5 PM, Thurs 12 PM - 9 PM, cl Mon; Admis by donation; Estab 1940; New bldg open 1980 containing 26,500 sq ft of exhibition space, 150 seat auditorium; maintains reference library; Average Annual Attendance: 125,000; Mem: 600; family $65, individual $40, senior citizens & students $20; annual meeting in Apr
Income: $2,992,285 (financed municipal, provincial & fed govts, donations, memberships, sponsorships & fundraising)
Collections: Permanent Collection stresses regional & local artists, who have become internationally & nationally recognized such as Jamelie Hassan, Paterson Ewan, Jack Chambers, Greg Curnoe & Paul Peel; The Moore Collection; a collection of historical art & artifacts, primarily of London & region; Hamilton King Meek Memorial Collection; F B Housser Memorial Collection
Exhibitions: Works of art - international, national & regional; programs of multi-media nature, including performing arts, exhibitions of historical artifacts & art
Publications: Exhibition catalogues; Quarterly magazine
Activities: Classes for adults & children; docent training; workshops; lects open to pub; 40 vis lectrs per yr concerts; gallery talks; tours; individual paintings & original objects of art lent to other art institutions; originate traveling exhibs; mus shop sells books, original art, reproductions, prints & jewelry

M **UNIVERSITY OF WESTERN ONTARIO,** McIntosh Gallery, London, ON N6A 3K7 Canada. Tel 519-661-3181; Fax 519-661-3059; Elec Mail mcintoshgallery@uwo.ca; Internet Home Page Address: mcintoshgallery.ca; *Cur & Educ Dir* Catherine Elliot Shaw; *Installations Officer & Registrar* David Falls; *Acting Dir* Judith Roger
Open Tues - Thurs Noon - 7 PM, Fri - Sun Noon - 4 PM, cl Mon; No admis fee; Estab 1942; Three galleries with a total of 2960 sq ft; Average Annual Attendance: 14,000; Mem: 155
Income: Financed by endowment, mem, provincial appropriation, special grants & University funds
Collections: Canadian Art
Exhibitions: 12 to 14 exhibitions per year
Publications: Newsletter, 3 times a yr; exhibition catalogues
Activities: Docent training; lects open to public, 6-10 vis lectrs per yr; gallery talks; tours; individual paintings & original objects of art lent to galleries; lending collection contains books, cassettes, framed reproductions, original art works & prints, paintings, photographs & sculpture; book traveling exhibs 1-3 per yr; originate traveling exhibs

L **The D B Weldon Library,** 1151 Richmond St, Ste 2, London, ON N6A 3K7 Canada. Tel 519-661-3162; Fax 519-661-3911; Internet Home Page Address: www.lib.uwo.ca; *Dir* Catherine Wilkins
Open Mon - Thurs 8 AM - 11:30 PM, Fri 8 AM - 9 PM, Sat 11 AM - 9 PM, Sun 11 AM - 11:30 PM; Open to all university staff, faculty & students for research & borrowing. Open to the public for in-house research; Average Annual Attendance: 1,700,000
Library Holdings: Book Volumes 1,439,855; Clipping Files; Exhibition Catalogs; Fiche; Pamphlets; Periodical Subscriptions 4,956; Reels
Special Subjects: Art History, Decorative Arts, Maps, Painting-American, History of Art & Archaeology, Archaeology, American Western Art, Eskimo Art, Metalwork, Carpets & Rugs, Antiquities-Byzantine, Antiquities-Etruscan, Antiquities-Greek, Antiquities-Roman, Painting-Canadian

MIDLAND

M **HURONIA MUSEUM,** Gallery of Historic Huronia, 549 Little Lake Park, PO Box 638 Midland, ON L4R 4P4 Canada. Tel 705-526-2844; Fax 705-527-6622; Elec Mail info@huroniamuseum.com; Internet Home Page Address: www.georgianbaytourism.on.ca; Internet Home Page Address: www.huroniamuseum.com; *Dir* James Hunter; *Photographer & Cur* Genevieve Carter; *Educ* Gillian Ross; *Admin* Nahamni Born
Open Nov 1 - Mar 31 Mon - Fri 9 AM-5 PM, Apr 1 - Oct 31 daily 9 AM-5 PM;

Admis adult $8, sr citizens $7, children 5 - 17 $5, under 5 free; Estab 1947 to collect art of Historic Huronia; Several large galleries dealing with local contemporary artists, historical regional artists, design exhibit on Thor Hansen & other designers; Average Annual Attendance: 20,000; Mem: Dues family $30, individual $20; annual meeting last Thurs in May

Income: $400,000 (financed by endowment, mem, admis, sales, fundraising, grants)

Purchases: $10,000 (Ted Lord Art Collection); $400,000 (Cultural Properties Donation; Ferguson Collection)

Library Holdings: Auction Catalogs; Book Volumes; Clipping Files; DVDs; Exhibition Catalogs; Kodachrome Transparencies; Lantern Slides; Manuscripts; Maps; Memorabilia; Original Art Works; Original Documents; Pamphlets; Periodical Subscriptions; Photographs; Records; Reproductions; Sculpture; Slides

Special Subjects: Historical Material, Furniture, Photography, Drawings, American Indian Art, Archaeology, Ethnology, Costumes, Ceramics, Crafts, Folk Art, Etchings & Engravings, Decorative Arts, Eskimo Art, Painting-Canadian, Dolls, Glass, Coins & Medals, Bookplates & Bindings

Collections: Mary Hallen Collection (watercolors); Frans Johnston Collection (oils, watercolors); Ted Lord Collection (paintings, prints, watercolors); Bill Wood Collection (etchings, oils, watercolors); General Collection (carvings, oil, watercolors); Lucille Oille Wells; Alex Jackson Collection; Norval Morrisseau Native Art Collection

Exhibitions: A Photographic History of the Georgian Bay Lumber Co 1871-1942; art shows once a month

Publications: Exhibition catalogues, ann report on activities

Activities: Classes for adults & children; educ prog; docent training; lects for Mems only, 6 vis lectrs per yr; concerts; gallery talks; tours; fels; Huronia Heritage Award ann award; lending collection contains paintings to other institutions who put together exhibs; originate traveling circulating to other local mus & galleries; mus shop sells books, original art, magazines, reproductions & prints

MISSISSAUGA

M **ART GALLERY OF MISSISSAUGA,** 300 City Centre Dr, Mississauga, ON L5B 3C1 Canada. Tel 905-896-5088; Fax 905-615-4167; Elec Mail robert.freeman@mississauga.ca; Internet Home Page Address: www.artgalleryofmississauga.com; *Exec Dir & Cur* Robert Freeman; *Gallery Asst* Jaclyn Qua-Hiansen; *Opers Mgr* Gail Farndon; *Weekend Attendant* Joe Vinski Open Mon - Fri 10 AM - 5 PM, Thurs until 8 PM, Sat & Sun Noon - 4 PM; No admis fee; Estab 1987 to promote awareness and the appreciation of the visual arts through the operation, development and growth of a public, not-for-profit art gallery; 3000 sq ft divided into four galleries: Main, Community, Member's & Chapel; Average Annual Attendance: 20,000; Mem: 400; dues $40-$5,000; annual meeting in Apr

Income: Financed by mem, city appropriation, federal & provincial government

Collections: Permanent collection

Exhibitions: 11 exhibitions per year, 6 week average per exhibition

Publications: Brush Up

Activities: Lects open to pub, 5 vis lectrs per yr; 10-15 outreach programs per yr; gallery talks; tours; individual paintings & original objects of art lent to other public art galleries; exten prog serving Mississauga; book traveling exhibs 1-2 per yr; originate traveling exhibitions to Ontario

L **MISSISSAUGA LIBRARY SYSTEM,** 301 Burnhamthorpe Rd W, Mississauga, ON L5B 3Y3 Canada. Tel 905-615-3500; Fax 905-615-3625; Internet Home Page Address: www.mississauga.on.ca/library; *Dir Library Svcs* Don Mills Open: Hours vary according to branch; No admis fee; Outlet for local artists at branch galleries; present more widely recognized artists at Central & Burnhamthrope Galleries; Total of eleven galleries in system, 90 running ft each, often multi-purpose rooms

Collections: Permanent collection of 135 paintings and prints by Canadian artists, emphasis on prints (all framed)

Publications: Link News Tabloid Format, quarterly

Activities: Lect open to public; competitions with cash prizes; lending collection contains books & motion pictures; book traveling exhibitions

L **Central Library, Arts Dept,** 301 Burnhamthorpe Rd W, Mississauga, ON L5B 3Y3 Canada. Tel 905-615-3500; Fax 905-615-3625; Elec Mail library.info@mississauga.ca.; Internet Home Page Address: www.mississauga.ca/portal/residents/centrallibrary; *Dir Library Svcs* Don Mills Open Mon - Fri 9 AM - 9 PM, Sat 9 AM - 5 PM, Sun 1 - 5 PM, cl Victorian Day

Income: $7,000,000 (financed by Municipal & Provincial funds)

Library Holdings: Book Volumes 38,000; Cassettes; Exhibition Catalogs; Filmstrips; Other Holdings Compact Discs; Periodical Subscriptions 29; Video Tapes

M **UNIVERSITY OF TORONTO AT MISSISSAUGA,** (Erindale College, University of Toronto at Mississauga) Blackwood Gallery, 3359 Mississauga Rd N, Mississauga, ON L5L 1C6 Canada. Tel 905-828-3789; Fax 905-569-4262; Elec Mail bfischer@credit.erin.utoronto.ca; Internet Home Page Address: www.utm.utoronto.ca; *Dir & Cur* Christof Migone; *Curatorial Asst* Juliana Zalucky; *Outreach Programmer* Suzanne Carte-Blanchenot Open Sun 11AM - 5PM; No admis fee; Estab 1969 to educate the public & present contemporary art; Gallery has four walls with various dividers & floor space of 36 x 30 ft; Average Annual Attendance: 5,000

Collections: Acrylics, drawings, oils, pen sketches & prints, sculpture, water colour, multiples

Publications: exhib catalogs

Activities: Classes for children; lect open to public; presentation of 6-8 exhibs of contemporary art per year; gallery talks; tours; competitions with awards, Blackwood Gallery Award; individual paints & original objects of art lent in house & to public art galleries; book 1 traveling exhib per yr; originates traveling exhibs for small to medium sized galleries & museums; mus shop sells exhibs catalogue

OAKVILLE

M **OAKVILLE GALLERIES,** Centennial Square and Gairloch Gardens, 1306 Lakeshore Rd E, Oakville, ON L6J 1L6 Canada. Tel 905-844-4402; Fax 905-844-7968; Elec Mail info@oakvillegalleries.com; Internet Home Page Address: www.oakvillegalleries.com; *Cur Contemporary Art* Marnie Fleming; *Dir* Matthew Hyland; *Asst Cur* Rose Bouthillier; *Office Mgr* Maria Zanetti; *Develop Assoc* Brady Schmidt; *Commun Specialist* Gabby Moser; *Community Arts Programmer* Sarah Febraro; *Bilingual Educ Officer* Emily Gove Centennial Square open Tues - Thurs Noon - 9 PM, Fri Noon - 5 PM, Sat 10 AM - 5 PM, Sun 1 - 5 PM; Gairloch Garden open Tues - Sun 1 - 5 PM; Admis by donation; Estab Centennial 1967, Gairloch 1972, to exhibit contemporary visual arts; Oakville Galleries is a not-for-profit public art gallery committed to contemporary art; Average Annual Attendance: 48,000; Mem: 500

Collections: Contemporary Canadian painting, sculpture, photographs, drawing & prints; contemporary outdoor sculpture

Publications: Exhibition catalogues

Activities: Art classes for adults & children; lects series open to pub; tours; gallery talks; 12 vis lectrs per yr; originate various traveling exhibs; mus shop sells original art and crafts

L **SHERIDAN COLLEGE OF APPLIED ARTS AND TECHNOLOGY,** Trafalgar Campus Library, 1430 Trafalgar Rd, Oakville, ON L6H 2L1 Canada. Tel 905-845-9430, Ext 2482; Fax 905-815-4123; Internet Home Page Address: www1.sheridaninstitute.ca; *Dir Library Svcs* Shahida Rashid; *Reference* Janet Fear; *Circ* Geraldine Venn; *Librn Colls Liaison* Ahtasham Rizvi Open Sept - June, Mon - Thurs 8:30 AM - 10 PM, Fri 8:30 AM - 4:30 PM, Sat - Sun 11 AM - 4 PM; July & Aug, Mon - Fri 8:30 AM - 4:30 PM, Sat - Sun 11 AM - 4 PM; Estab 1970 to serve the students & faculty of School of Animation, Art & Design; Circ 23,000

Income: Financed by the college

Library Holdings: Book Volumes; Clipping Files; Exhibition Catalogs; Periodical Subscriptions 96; Slides 27,809; Video Tapes 50

Special Subjects: Art History, Illustration, Photography, Graphic Design, Crafts

ORILLIA

M **ORILLIA MUSEUM OF ART & HISTORY,** 30 Peter St S, Orillia, ON L3V 5A9 Canada. Tel 705-326-2159; Elec Mail admin@orilliamuseum.org; Internet Home Page Address: www.orilliamuseum.org; *Exec Dir* Ninette Gyorody; *Exhibs Mgr* Matt Macintosh; *Colls Mgr* Sheena Westcott-Sykes Open Tues - Sat 10 AM - 4 PM; Donations accepted; Estab 1999 to share art & history of region; Art & history mus; Average Annual Attendance: 11,000; Mem: 500 mems

Collections: Art; local artifacts

Exhibitions: See website

Activities: Classes for adults & children; lects open to pub; schols; mus shop sells books, reproductions, prints, original one of a kind art

OSHAWA

M **THE ROBERT MCLAUGHLIN GALLERY,** 72 Queen St, Civic Centre Oshawa, ON L1H 3Z3 Canada. Tel 905-576-3000; Fax 905-576-9774; Elec Mail communications@rmg.on.ca; Internet Home Page Address: www.rmg.on.ca; *Exec Dir* David Aurandt; *Cur* Linda Jansma; *Admin* Olinda Casimiro; *Bookkeeper* Colleen Lush; *Preparator* Jason Dankel; *Educ Outreach Coordr* Joel Campbell Open Mon, Tues, Wed & Fri 10 AM - 5 PM, Thurs 10 AM - 9 PM, Sat & Sun Noon - 4 PM; No admis fee; Estab Feb 1967 as The Art Gallery of Oshawa, in May 1969 as the Robert McLaughlin Gallery; R S McLaughlin Gallery 77 x 38 x 15 ft; Isabel McLaughlin Gallery 77 x 38 x 13 ft; Alexandra Luke Gallery (no 1) 62 x 48 x 9 1/2 ft; Alexandra Luke Gallery (no 2) 46 x 27 x 13 ft; E P Taylor Gallery 23 x 37 x 9 ft; General Motors Gallery 25 x 37 x 9 ft; Corridor Ramp (Isabel McLaughlin Gallery) 48 x 8 x 10 ft; Corridor (Alexandra Luke) 68 x 5 1/2 x 8 ft with Foyer & Dir Office; Average Annual Attendance: 40,000; Mem: 500; dues family $45, single $35, student $20; annual meeting in May

Income: Financed by membership, city appropriation, Canada Council, Ministry Culture & Recreation & Ontario Arts Council

Special Subjects: Photography, Prints, Sculpture, Watercolors, Woodcuts, Portraits, Painting-Canadian

Collections: Canadian 19th & 20th century drawings, paintings, prints & sculpture; major coll of works by Painters Eleven

Publications: Annual Report; bi-monthly bulletin; Calendar of Events, annually; exhibition catalogs

Activities: Classes for adults and children; docent training; lects open to pub, 6 vis lectrs per yr; gallery talks; tours; schols & fels offered; original objects of art lent to schools, institutions & industries; lending coll contains cassettes, 300 color reproductions, framed reproductions, original art works, 10,000 slides & 5100 books; sales shop sells books, reproductions, prints & local crafts

L **Library,** 72 Queen St, Civic Centre Oshawa, ON L1H 3Z3 Canada. Tel 905-576-3000; Fax 905-576-9774; Elec Mail bduff@rmg.on.ca; Internet Home Page Address: www.rmg.on.ca; *Coordr Library Svcs* Barb Duff; *Asst Curator* Sonja Jones Open Mon, Tues, Wed & Fri 10 AM - 5 PM, Thurs 10 AM - 9 PM, Sat & Sun Noon - 4 PM; Admis donations accepted; Open to pub, mem available

Library Holdings: Auction Catalogs; Audio Tapes; Book Volumes 8000; Cassettes; Clipping Files; Exhibition Catalogs; Manuscripts; Original Documents; Pamphlets; Periodical Subscriptions; Photographs; Slides; Video Tapes

Collections: Canadian contemporary art books

Activities: Classes for adults & children; docent training; mus shop sells books & original art

OTTAWA

A **CANADA COUNCIL FOR THE ARTS,** Conseil des Arts du Canada, 350 Albert St, PO Box 1047 Ottawa, ON K1P 5V8 Canada. Tel 613-566-4414; Fax 613-566-4390; Internet Home Page Address: www.canadacouncil.ca; WATS 800-263-5588; *Dir* Robert Sirman; *Chmn* Karen Kain; *Media & Pub Rels* Grace Thrasher Open daily 8:45 AM-5 PM, cl Sat & Sun; Estab 1957 to foster & promote the

arts. The Council provides a wide range of grants & services to professional Canadian artists & art organizations in dance, media arts, music, opera, theatre, writing, publishing & the visual arts. Also Art Bank; Estab 1957, the Council is a national arm's-length agency which provides grants & services to professional Canadian artists & arts organizations in dance, media arts, music, theatre, writing & publishing, interdisciplinary work & performance art, & the visual arts. The Art Bank of the Canada Council rents contemporary Canadian art to the pub & private sectors across Canada. The Council also maintains the secretariat for the Canadian Commission for UNESCO, administers the Killam Program of scholarly awards & prizes, & offers a number of other prestigious awards. The Public Lending Right (PLR) Commission, which is operated by the Canada Council, administers a program of payments to Canadian authors for their eligible books catalogued in libraries across Canada. The Canada Council for the Arts is funded by & reports to Parliament through the Minister of Canadian Heritage
Income: Financed by Parliament of Canada, endowment fund & private individuals
Activities: Prizes awarded; grants & fels offered

M **CANADA SCIENCE AND TECHNOLOGY MUSEUM,** 1867 St Laurent Blvd, PO Box 9724, Sta T Ottawa, ON K1G 5A3 Canada. Tel 613-991-3044; Fax 613-990-3636; Elec Mail cts@technomuses.ca, info@technomuses.ca; Internet Home Page Address: www.sciencetech.technomuses.ca; Others 613-991-9207; *Promotion* Leeanne Akehurst; *Dir Gen* Claude Faubert; *Dir Exhibs* Ginette Beriault; *Dir Curatorial* Geoff Rider
Open Daily 9 AM - 5 PM (May - Labor Day), winter hours Tues - Sun 9 AM - 5 PM, cl Mon; Admis adult $7.50, sr citizens & students $5, children 4-14 $3.50, under 4 free, family $18; Estab 1967 to foster scientific & technological literacy throughout Canada by establishing & maintaining a collection of scientific & technological objects; Main exhib areas showcase astronomy, Canada in space, communications, computer technology, household appliances, physics & land & marine transportation; Average Annual Attendance: 400,000; Mem: Dues $25 & up
Income: Financed by treasury board appropriations, admis fees & sales
Collections: Agriculture, Energy, Land & Marine Transportation, Physical Sciences, Printing, Space Communications; Science & Technology
Exhibitions: Canada in Space; Connexions; Love, Leisure & Laundry; Locomotives; Canadian SC & Engineering Hall of Fame; LOG On; More Than A Machine; Rotate 2-8 exhibitions per yr
Publications: Material History Bulletin
Activities: Classes for adults & children; astronomy progs (evening); March break and summer day camps for children; originate traveling exhibs; mus shop sells books, magazines, models, shirts, mugs, maps & educational toys

CANADIAN CONFERENCE OF THE ARTS
For further information, see National and Regional Organizations

M **CANADIAN MUSEUM OF CONTEMPORARY PHOTOGRAPHY,** 380 Sussex Dr, Ottawa, ON K1N 9N4 Canada; PO Box 465, Sta A, Ottawa, ON K1N 9N6 Canada. Tel 613-990-1985; Tel 800-319-2787; Fax 613-993-4385; Elec Mail cmcp@ngc.chin.gc.ca; Internet Home Page Address: www.cmcp.gallery.ca; *Nat & International Prog Mgr* Anne Jolicoeur; *Assoc Cur* Pierre Dessureault; *Prog Mgr* Maureen McEvoy; *Dir* Martha Hanna
Open May 1 - Sept 30 daily 10 AM - 5 PM, Thurs 10 AM - 8 PM; Oct 1 - Apr 30 Tues - Sun 10 AM - 5 PM, Thurs 10 AM - 8 PM; Admis adults $9, seniors & students $7, youth (12-19) $4, family $18, under 12 free; Estab 1985 as an affiliate of the National Gallery of Canada; Reconstructed railway tunnel houses 354 sq meters of exhibition galleries specially lit for photography, a theatre designed for flexible programming, a boutique & a research centre; exhibitions change quarterly
Income: Financed by federal government, National Gallery of Canada (Crown Corporation)
Special Subjects: Photography, Prints, Landscapes, Portraits, Reproductions
Collections: 158,000 images by Canadian photographers
Exhibitions: Over 40 exhibitions, solo & group, are available for loan
Publications: Exhibition catalogues
Activities: Family progs; teacher workshops; educational exhibitions; interpreter training; didactic printed materials; evaluation studies; lects open to pub, 10-12 vis lectrs per yr; gallery talks; tours for adults & children; original objects of art lent to other mus & galleries for use in exhibs; book traveling exhibs 1-2 per yr; originate traveling exhibs to other mus, art galleries or spaces that meet conservation requirements across Canada & abroad; mus shop sells books, prints, photo related jewelry, children's gifts & postcards

M **CANADIAN MUSEUM OF NATURE,** Musee Canadien de la Nature, 240 McLeod St, Ottawa, ON K2P 2R1 Canada; PO Box 3443, Station D Ottawa, ON K1P 6P4 Canada. Tel 613-566-4700; Fax 613-566-4798; Elec Mail questions@mus-nature.ca; Internet Home Page Address: nature.ca; *Interim Pres & CEO* Margaret Beckel; *Dir Fin Mgmt Svcs & Interim VP* Michel Houle; *Dir Coll Svcs* Roger Baird; *Dir Facilities Mgmt Svcs* Marc Chretien; *Dir Research Svcs* Mark Graham, PhD; *Dir Human Resources* Diane McCullagh; *Dir Community Svcs* Marie Lasnier; *Dir Commun Svcs* Elizabeth McCrea; *Dir Info & Tech Svcs* Greg Smith; *Acting Mgr Exhib Svcs & Proj Mgr Temp Exhib* Carol Campbell; *Coordr Traveling Exhibs* Rachel Gervais; *Sr Media Rels Officer* Dan Smythe; *Head Archives, Records & Libr* Chantal Dussault
Open Sept - Apr daily 9 AM - 5 PM & Thurs 9 AM - 8 PM, cl Mon, May - Sept daily 9 AM - 6 PM, Thurs & Fri 9 AM - 8 PM, cl Mon; Admis families $25, individuals $10, children 3 and under free; Estab 1856 to disseminate knowledge about the natural sciences, with particular but not exclusive reference to Canada; Canada's national museum of natural history & natural sciences; Average Annual Attendance: 450,000; Mem: Dues family $85; adult $45; student $35
Income: Financed by donations, government & self generated revenue
Library Holdings: Audio Tapes; Book Volumes; CD-ROMs; Cards; Cassettes; DVDs; Original Art Works; Periodical Subscriptions; Sculpture
Special Subjects: Drawings, Photography, Prints, Watercolors, Costumes, Ceramics, Crafts, Woodcarvings, Posters, Painting-Canadian, Dioramas
Collections: Prints; Paintings, Sculpture; over ten million specimens
Exhibitions: Talisman Energy Fossil Gallery; Mammal Gallery; Bird Gallery; RBC Blue Water Gallery; Vale Earth Gallery; Animalium
Activities: Classes for children; school progs (primary & secondary); volunteer training; lects, film series; demonstrations & workshops dealing with natural history subjects

CANADIAN MUSEUMS ASSOCIATION
For further information, see National and Regional Organizations

M **CANADIAN WAR MUSEUM,** 1 Vimy Pl, Ottawa, ON K1A 0M8 Canada. Tel 819-776-8600; Fax 819-776-8623; Elec Mail information@warmuseum.ca; Internet Home Page Address: www.warmuseum.ca; *Dir Gen* James Whitham; *Acting Dir Research* Dr Laura Brandon; *Dir Colls* Tony Glen
Open May 1 - June 30 Mon - Wed 9 AM - 6 PM, Thurs 9 AM - 8 PM, Sat & Sun 9:30 AM - 6 PM; July 1 - Sept 1 daily 9 AM - 6 PM, Thurs & Fri 9 AM - 9 PM; Sept 2 - Oct 13 daily 9:30 AM - 6 PM, Thurs 9:30 AM - 8 PM; Oct 14 - Apr 30 Mon - Sun 9:30 AM - 5 PM, Thurs 9 AM - 8 PM; Admis family $32, adult $15, sr citizen $11, student $10, children 3-12 $8; Estab 1880 to collect, preserve & display objects relevant to Canadian military history. Promote public understanding of Canada's military history in its personal, national and international dimensions; Average Annual Attendance: 400,000
Income: Financed by government funds
Library Holdings: Auction Catalogs; Audio Tapes; Book Volumes; CD-ROMs; Cassettes; Clipping Files; Compact Disks; DVDs; Exhibition Catalogs; Framed Reproductions; Kodachrome Transparencies; Lantern Slides; Manuscripts; Maps; Motion Pictures; Original Documents; Pamphlets; Periodical Subscriptions; Photographs; Prints; Records; Slides; Video Tapes
Special Subjects: Historical Material, Painting-Canadian, Coins & Medals
Collections: Uniforms & accoutrements; medals & insignia; equipment; vehicles; art; archives; photographs; weapons
Exhibitions: Canadian Experience Galleries-permanent exhibition; Trench Culture (12/07-3/29/08)
Activities: Educ dept & prog; classes for adults & children; lect presentations open to pub; tours; gallery talks; concerts; fels offered; lending collection contains 13,000 books; artwork lent to other mus & galleries, educational institutions, national exhib centers; originate traveling exhibs to mus & galleries; mus shop sells books, reproductions, prints, slides, shirts & models

M **CANADIAN WILDLIFE & WILDERNESS ART MUSEUM,** PO Box 98, Sta B, Ottawa, ON K1P 6C3 Canada. Tel 613-237-1581; Fax 613-237-1581; Elec Mail cawa@magma.ca; Internet Home Page Address: www.magma.ca/cawa; *Co-Dir* Cody Sadler; *Dir* Gary Slimon
Open Mon - Sun 10 AM - 5 PM; Admis $3; Estab 1987; Museum exhibits paintings, sculptures & carvings of wildlife themes; Mem: Dues $50-$1000; annual meeting in Jan
Income: Financed by endowment, mem, state appropriation, mus proceeds
Special Subjects: Painting-American, Sculpture
Collections: Wildlife & wilderness paintings, sculpture, carvings & decoys
Publications: Brochure; newsletter
Activities: Classes for children; 'how-to' seminars; lects open to pub, 4 vis lectrs per yr; individual paintings & original objects of art lent to mus with similar mandates; lending collection contains original art work paintings & sculpture; book traveling exhibs 1 per yr; originate traveling exhibs; mus shop sells books, magazines, prints, slides

L **Library,** PO Box 98, Sta B, Ottawa, ON K1P 6C3 Canada. Tel 613-237-1581 (and fax); Elec Mail cawa@bell.net; Internet Home Page Address: www.magma.ca/cawa/; *Co-Dir* Cody Sadler; *Dir* Gary Slimon
Library mainly for research for member artists
Library Holdings: Exhibition Catalogs; Other Holdings Magazines; Slides
Special Subjects: Commercial Art, Graphic Arts, Painting-American, Painting-French, Pre-Columbian Art, Prints, Sculpture, Painting-European, Historical Material, Watercolors, Latin American Art, Ethnology, American Western Art, Printmaking, Art Education, Video, American Indian Art, Eskimo Art, Mexican Art, Southwestern Art, Woodcarvings, Landscapes, Reproductions, Painting-Canadian, Portraits

A **DEPARTMENT OF CANADIAN HERITAGE,** Canadian Conservation Institute, 1030 Innes Rd, Ottawa, ON K1A 0M5 Canada. Tel 613-998-3721; Fax 613-998-4721; Elec Mail cci-library@pch.gc.ca (English) or icc-biblio@pch.gc.ca (French); Internet Home Page Address: www.cci-icc.gc.ca; *Chief Library Svcs* Joy Patel; *Dir Gen & COO* Jeanne Inch; *Assoc Dir Gen & Dir Conserv* Charlie Costain; *Dir Bus Planning* Lise Perron-Croteau; *Mgr Conserv Research Svcs* David Grattan; *Mgr Fine Arts, Papers & Textiles* James Bourdeau
Open Tues - Fri 9 AM - 4 PM; No admis fee; Estab 1972; Delivers wide range of services and products, research & preservation
Income: Financed by state appropriation
Library Holdings: Audio Tapes 17; Book Volumes 10,000; Clipping Files; Fiche 139; Pamphlets; Periodical Subscriptions 300; Video Tapes 175
Collections: Conservation of cultural property; conservation research
Publications: CCI Newsletter, biannual; CCI Notes, irregular; CCI Technical Bulletins, irregular

M **ENVIRONMENT CANADA - PARKS CANADA,** Laurier House, National Historic Site, 335 Laurier Ave E, Ottawa, ON K1N 6R4 Canada. Tel 613-992-8142; Fax 613-947-4851; Elec Mail laurier.house@pc.gc.ca; Internet Home Page Address: www.pc.gc.ca/lhn-nhs/on/laurier; *Visitor Experience Mgr* Anne-Marie Johnson
Open May 24 - June 30 Wed - Mon 9 AM - 5 PM, July 1 - Sept 3 daily 9 AM - 5 PM, Sept 4 - Oct 8 Thurs - Mon 9 AM - 5 PM; Admis family $9.80, adults $3.90, sr citizens $3.40, youth $1.90, under 6 free; Estab 1951; This is a historic house & former residence of Two Prime Ministers, Sir Wilfrid Laurier & the Rt Honorable William Lyon Mackenzie King containing furniture & memorabilia. The house is primarily furnished in the style of its last occupant, the Rt Honorable William Lyon Mackenzie King, with space given to the Laurier Collection; Average Annual Attendance: 8,014
Income: Financed by federal government & trust fund
Special Subjects: Decorative Arts, Drawings, Glass, Furniture, Portraits, Silver, Textiles, Sculpture, Religious Art, Landscapes, Painting-Japanese, Painting-Canadian, Jewelry, Painting-Dutch, Period Rooms, Painting-Italian, Reproductions

Exhibitions: Visitor Centre Exhibit
Publications: Main Park Brochure provided to visitors
Activities: Guided tours

M **MUSEUM FOR TEXTILES,** Canada Aviation Museum, 11 Aviation Pkwy, Ottawa, ON K1K 4R3 Canada; PO Box 9724, Station T Ottawa, ON K1G 5A3 Canada. Tel 613-993-2010; Fax 613-990-3655; Elec Mail aviation@technomuses.ca; Internet Home Page Address: www.aviation.technomuses.ca; *Dir* Francine Poirier; *Cur* A J (Fred) Shortt
Open May 1 - Labour Day daily 9 AM - 5 PM; after Labour Day - Apr 30 Wed - Sun 10 AM - 5 PM, cl Mon & Tues; Admis families $14, adults $6, seniors & students with ID $5, children 4-15 $3, under 4 free; Estab 1960 to illustrate the evolution of the flying machine & the important role aircraft played in Canada's development; Average Annual Attendance: 250,000; Mem: 2000; dues $20-$80
Collections: More than 120 aircraft plus thousands of aviation related artifacts
Activities: Classes for adults & children; lect open to public; tours; sales shop sells books, magazines & prints

L **NATIONAL ARCHIVES OF CANADA,** Art & Photography Archives, 395 Wellington St, Ottawa, ON K1A 0N4 Canada. Tel 613-996-7766; Fax 613-995-6575; Internet Home Page Address: www.collectionscanada.gc.ca; *National Archivist* Ian Wilson; *Dir & Custodian Holdings* Elizabeth Moxley; *Chief Coll Consultation* Robert Grandmaitre; *Documentary Art & Photo Acquisition* Jim Barant; *Descriptive Servs Section* Jennifer Svarckopf
Open daily 9 AM - 4:45 PM; No admis fee; Estab 1905 to acquire & preserve significant Canadian archival material in the area of visual media, including paintings, watercolours, drawings, prints, medals, heraldry, posters & photography relating to all aspects of Canadian life, to the development of the country, to provide suitable research services, facilities to make this documentation available to the pub by means of exhibitions, publications & pub catalogue
Income: Financed by federal appropriation
Purchases: $80,000
Library Holdings: Auction Catalogs; Book Volumes 4000
Special Subjects: Photography, Drawings, Etchings & Engravings, Painting-British, Painting-Italian, Posters, Prints, Portraits, Watercolors, American Indian Art, Miniatures, Landscapes, Coins & Medals, Reproductions, Painting-Canadian
Collections: 1800 paintings; 22,000 watercolours & drawings; 90,000 prints; 30,000 posters; 16,000 medals; 7000 heraldic design & seals; 80,000 caricatures; 22 million photographs
Publications: Catalog of publications available on request
Activities: Lect open to pub; Tours; original art lent to mus & galleries; sales shop sells reproductions & slides

M **NATIONAL GALLERY OF CANADA,** 380 Sussex Dr, PO Box 427, Sta A Ottawa, ON K1N 9N4 Canada. Tel 613-990-1985; Fax 613-993-4385; Elec Mail info@gallery.ca; info@beaux-arts.ca; Internet Home Page Address: www.museebeaux-arts.ca; *Deputy Dir, Chief Cur Colls & Research, Cur Prints & Drawings* Dr David Franklin; *Deputy Dir Exhibs & Installations* Karen Colby-Stothart; *Cur, Contemp Art* Josee Drouin-Brisebois; *Cur, Canadian Art* Charlie Hill; *Audain Cur Indigenous Art* Greg A Hill; *Cur, Photography* Ann Thomas; *Dir* Marc Mayer; *Deputy Dir & Chief Cur* Paul Lang
Open May - Sept 10 AM - 5 PM, Thurs 10 AM - 8 PM; Oct - Apr Tues - Sun 10 AM - 5 PM, Thurs 10 AM - 8 PM, cl Dec 25, Jan 1; Admis adults $15 for special exhibitions, $9 for permanent collection, children under 12 free; Founded 1880 under the patronage of the Governor-General, the Marquess of Lorne & his wife the Princess Louise; first inc 1913 to develop, maintain, and promote works of contemporary & modern art with special, but not exclusive, reference to Canada; On May 21 1988, the first permanent home of National Gallery of Canada opened to the pub & to critical & popular acclaim. Overlooking the Ottawa river & steps away from Parliament Hill, the gallery is a landmark in the Capital's skyline. Light, spacious galleries & quiet courtyards lead the visitors on a voyage of discovery of Canada's exceptional art coll; Average Annual Attendance: 500,000; Mem: 10,000 - 12,000; dues individual $80, family $95
Purchases: $3,000,000
Library Holdings: Audio Tapes; Book Volumes; CD-ROMs; Cards; Cassettes; Clipping Files; Exhibition Catalogs; Fiche; Filmstrips; Framed Reproductions; Kodachrome Transparencies; Manuscripts; Original Documents; Other Holdings; Periodical Subscriptions; Photographs; Prints; Records; Slides; Video Tapes
Special Subjects: Drawings, Graphics, Painting-American, Photography, Bronzes, Etchings & Engravings, Landscapes, Decorative Arts, Collages, Painting-European, Portraits, Painting-Canadian, Furniture, Asian Art, Painting-British, Painting-Dutch, Painting-French, Baroque Art, Painting-Flemish, Medieval Art, Painting-Spanish, Painting-Italian, Painting-German, Painting-Russian, Bookplates & Bindings
Collections: Over 45,000 works in entire coll, over 1200 on display in permanent coll galleries; contemporary Inuit artists work; historical & contemporary Canadian art; media arts in the world over 600 titles, totaling more than 10,000 hours of video & film; 19,000 photography works; 20th century American art; western European art 14th-20th centuries; Inuit Art; Indigenous Art
Exhibitions: Exhibitions from permanent coll, private & pub sources are organized & circulated in Canada & abroad
Publications: Annual report (incorporating annual review, with current acquisition lists); catalogues of permanent coll; CD-Rom on the Canadian coll; documents in the history of Canadian Art; exhibition books & catalogues; masterpieces in the National Gallery of Canada
Activities: Classes for adults & children; docent training; dramatic progs; film series; workshops for physically & mentally challenged, teen council; lects open to pub, 20 vis lectrs per yr; concerts; gallery talks; tours; schols & fels offered; individual paintings & original objects of art lent to art museums & galleries in Canada & abroad, subject to the same environmental conditions (other conditions apply); book traveling exhibs 25 per yr; originate traveling exhibs to Canadian & international venues; mus shop sells books, magazines, reproductions, prints, jewelry; affiliate Canadian Museum of Contemporary Photography

L **Library,** 380 Sussex Dr, PO Box 427, Sta A Ottawa, ON K1N 9N4 Canada. Tel 613-998-8949; Fax 613-990-9818; Elec Mail erefel@gallery.ca; Internet Home Page Address: www.gallery.ca; *Chief Librn* Jonathan Franklin; *Head Archives* Cyndie Campbell; *Bibliographer* Jo Beglo; *Head Reader Serv* Peter Trepanier; *Head Colls & Database Mgr* Lisa DiNoble
Open Wed - Fri 10 AM - 4:45 PM, cl holidays; Estab 1918 to support the research & information requirements of gallery personnel; to make its collections of resource materials in the fine arts available to Canadian libraries & scholars; to serve as a source of information about art & art activities in Canada; Circ 35,000; For reference only; Average Annual Attendance: 9,000
Library Holdings: Auction Catalogs; Audio Tapes; Book Volumes 300,000; CD-ROMs; Cards; Cassettes; Clipping Files; Compact Disks; Exhibition Catalogs; Fiche; Filmstrips; Kodachrome Transparencies; Lantern Slides; Manuscripts; Memorabilia; Motion Pictures; Original Documents; Other Holdings Auction catalogues; Illustrated books; Rare books; Pamphlets; Periodical Subscriptions 1100; Photographs; Records; Reels; Slides; Video Tapes
Special Subjects: Art History, Film, Drawings, Graphic Arts, Conceptual Art, Printmaking, Video, Eskimo Art, Aesthetics, Painting-Canadian, Architecture
Collections: Art Documentation; Canadiana; Art Metropole
Exhibitions: Various, see website
Publications: Artists in Canada; Reference Database (CHIN); Library and Archives, occasional paper series 1-8; library and archives, exhibition 1-42
Activities: Library tours, exhibs

L **OTTAWA PUBLIC LIBRARY,** Fine Arts Dept, 120 Metcalfe St, Ottawa, ON K1P 5M2 Canada. Tel 613-236-0301; Fax 613-567-4013; Internet Home Page Address: www.opl.on.ca; *Admin Dir* Jean Martel; *Dir* Barbara Clubb
Open Mon - Thurs 10 AM - 9 PM, Fri 10 AM - 6 PM, Sat 9:30 AM - 5 PM, Sun 1 - 5 PM (winters); No admis fee; Estab 1906 to serve the community as a centre for general & reliable information; to select, preserve & administer books & related materials in organized collections; to provide opportunity for citizens of all ages to educate themselves continuously
Income: $8,808,600 (financed by city, province, other)
Library Holdings: Book Volumes 12,000; Cassettes; Clipping Files; Fiche; Filmstrips; Pamphlets; Periodical Subscriptions 85; Reels
Exhibitions: Monthly exhibits highlighting local artists, craftsmen, photographers & collectors
Activities: Lect open to public; library tours

OWEN SOUND

M **OWEN SOUND HISTORICAL SOCIETY,** Marine & Rail Heritage Museum, 1155 First Ave W, Owen Sound, ON N4K 4K8 Canada. Tel 519-371-3333; Elec Mail marinerail.museum@e-owensound.com; Internet Home Page Address: www.marinerail.com; *Pres* Jim Henderson; *Cur* Neil Garneau
Open Sept - May Tues - Fri 10 AM - 4 PM; Sept - Nov Sat 11:30 AM - 3:30 PM, cl Sun; Jun, July & Aug Mon - Sat 10 AM - 4 PM, Sun & holiday Mon 11 AM - 4 PM; Admis adults $4, children 3 - 13 $2, under 2 yrs free, family $10; Estab 1985 for the preservation of Owen Sound's marine, rail & industrial history; Mem: Dues $10 & up
Income: Financed by mem, donations & government grant
Special Subjects: Historical Material
Collections: Charts, timetables, railway artifacts & models; Corvette HMCS Owen Sound artifacts; Dug-out & Birch-bark canoes; house flags of Marine Transport Coys; lifeboat from the Paul Evans; marine & railway uniforms; patterns from local foundry in production of propellers & shipbuilding; scale models of ships that sailed the Great Lakes
Activities: Lects open to pub, 6 vis lectrs per yr; children's competition with prizes; lending coll contains books

M **TOM THOMSON MEMORIAL ART GALLERY,** 840 First Ave W, Owen Sound, ON N4K 4K4 Canada. Tel 519-376-1932; Fax 519-376-3037; Elec Mail ttag@e-owensound.com; Internet Home Page Address: www.tomthomson.org; *Dir* Stuart Reid; *Mgr Pub Progs* David Huff; *Mgr Devel* Pauline Macleod Farley; *Colls Mgr* Rachel Monckton
Open Sept - June Tues - Fri 11 AM - 5 PM, Wed 11 AM - 5 PM, Sat & Sun Noon - 5 PM; July & Aug Mon - Sat 10 AM - 5 PM, Sun Noon - 5 PM; No admis fee; Estab 1967 to collect & display paintings by Tom Thomson, a native son & Canada's foremost landscape artist; to educate the public; Paintings by Tom Thomson on permanent display, plus 2 galleries of changing exhibitions; Average Annual Attendance: 30,000; Mem: 300; dues family $25, individual $15, senior citizens & students $10
Income: Financed by city appropriation & provincial grants & fundraising
Collections: Tom Thomson; Historic & Contemporary Canadian Artists; Group of Seven
Publications: Bulletin, six per year; exhibition catalogs 3 per year
Activities: Classes for adults & children; docent training; lects open to pub; gallery talks; tours; films; competitions with awards; concerts; exten dept serves city bldgs; mus shop sells books, reproductions, prints & postcards

L **Library/Archives,** 840 First Ave W, Owen Sound, ON N4K 4K4 Canada. Tel 519-376-1932; Fax 519-376-3037; Internet Home Page Address: www.tomthomson.org; *Dir* Stuart Reid; *Educ* David Huff
Open by appointment only; Circ Non-circulating; Open for reference of Tom Thomson files
Library Holdings: Book Volumes 400; Exhibition Catalogs; Periodical Subscriptions 6
Collections: Files on Tom Thomson

PETERBOROUGH

M **ART GALLERY OF PETERBOROUGH,** 250 Crescent St, Peterborough, ON K9J 2G1 Canada. Tel 705-743-9179; Fax 705-743-8168; Elec Mail gallery@agp.on.ca; Internet Home Page Address: www.agp.on.ca; *Cur* Carla Garnet; *Gallery Opers Asst* Janice Fortune; *Dir* Celeste Scopelites; *Educ & Prog Coordr* Jane Wild; *Admin Clerk* Susanne Lloyd
Open Tues - Sun 11 AM - 5 PM; office Mon - Fri 9 AM - 5 PM; No admis fee; Estab 1974; Gallery situated along a lake & in a park; new extension added & completed June 1979; Average Annual Attendance: 16,000; Mem: 700; dues family $35, individual $25, sr citizens $20, student $15; annual meeting June
Income: Financed by mem, fundraising & provincial, federal, municipal grants

Library Holdings: Book Volumes; Exhibition Catalogs
Collections: European and Canadian works of art
Publications: Catalogues on some exhibitions; pamphlets on artists in exhibitions
Activities: Classes for adults & children; docent training; workshops; art prog to pub schools; lects open to pub; 6 vis lects per yr; gallery talks; tours; individual paintings & original objects of art lent to other galleries; 1 to 2 book travelling exhibs per yr; organize travelling exhibs to public galleries across Canada; sales shop sells books, crafts & fine art

SAINT CATHARINES

A **RODMAN HALL ARTS CENTRE,** 109 St Paul Crescent, Saint Catharines, ON L2S 1M3 Canada. Tel 905-684-2925; Fax 905-682-4733; Elec Mail rodmanhall@brocku.ca; Internet Home Page Address: www.brocku.ca/rodmanhall; *Interim Dir* Debbie Slade; *Asst Cur* Marcie Bronson; *Admin Asst* Susan Dickinson; *Vol Svcs Coordr* Patricia Hodge; *Preparator* Matt Harley
Open summer Tues - Sun 12 PM - 5 PM; fall Tues - Thurs 12 PM - 9 PM, Fri - Sun 12 PM - 5 PM; No admis fee; Estab 1960, art gallery, cultural centre & visual arts exhibitions; Four galleries in an 1853, 1960 & 1975 addition. 1975 - A1 - National Museums of Canada. Maintains reference library; Average Annual Attendance: 45,000; Mem: 800; dues tax receipt $75 or more, family $40, individual $25; annual meeting in Sept
Income: Financed by mem, city, province & government of Canada
Collections: American graphics & drawings; Canadian drawings, paintings, sculpture & watercolours; international graphics & sculpture
Exhibitions: Monthly exhibitions featuring painting, photographs, sculpture & other art
Publications: Catalogue - Lord and Lady Head Watercolours; monthly calendar; Rodman Hall Arts Center (1960-1981)
Activities: Classes for adults & children; dramatic progs; docent training; workshops; films; lects open to pub, 6 vis lectrs per yr; concerts; gallery talks; tours; individual paintings & original objects of art lent to city hall & other art galleries; book traveling exhibs 16 per yr; book traveling exhibs 5 per yr; mus shop sells books, original art, gifts, pottery, glassware & jewelry
L **Library,** 109 St Paul Crescent, Saint Catharines, ON L2S 1M3 Canada. Tel 905-684-2925; Fax 905-682-4733; *Librn* Debra Attenborough
Open Tues - Fri 9 AM - 5 PM; Estab 1960; Reference library
Library Holdings: Book Volumes 3500; Cards; Cassettes; Clipping Files; Exhibition Catalogs; Pamphlets; Periodical Subscriptions 7; Photographs; Reproductions; Slides; Video Tapes

SAINT THOMAS

M **ST THOMAS-ELGIN PUBLIC ART CENTRE,** (St Thomas Elgin Art Gallery) 301 Talbot St, Saint Thomas, ON N5P 1B5 Canada. Tel 519-631-4040; Fax 519-631-4057; Elec Mail info@stepac.ca; Internet Home Page Address: www.stepac.ca; *Exec Dir & Cur* Laura Woermke; *Educ & Events Coordr* Eleanor McAlpine; *Admin Asst* Jenny Couse
Open Sun 12 PM - 3 PM, Tues - Wed 10 AM - 4 PM, Thurs - Fri 10 AM - 9 PM, Sat 12 PM - 4 PM; No admis fee; Estab 1969; Pub gallery; Average Annual Attendance: 10,000; Mem: 658; dues senior citizens $15, family $30, single $20; annual meeting in March
Income: $150,000 (financed by endowment, mem, municipality, donations, & earned revenues)
Library Holdings: Book Volumes; Exhibition Catalogs; Original Art Works; Photographs; Slides; Video Tapes
Collections: Fine Art Works by Canadian Artists
Publications: Info brochures; gallery newsletter 3 per year
Activities: Educ prog in art for all adults & children; lects open to pub; tours, sponsor competitions; schols offered; lending of original art to other galleries; originate traveling exhibs; gift shop sells original art & promotional items

SCARBOROUGH

M **CITY OF SCARBOROUGH,** Cedar Ridge Creative Centre, 225 Confederation Dr, Scarborough, ON M1G 1B2 Canada. Tel 416-396-4026; Fax 416-396-7044; Elec Mail crcc@toronto.ca; *Coordr Cultural Progs* Ann Christian
Open 9 AM - 9 PM; No admis fee; Estab 1985 as a gallery & teaching studio; 3-interconnecting rooms & solarium with oak paneling, 18' x 22', 18' x 28', 16' x 26'; Average Annual Attendance: 1,300; Mem: Annual dues $10 (it entitles member to rent gallery for one week for $39)
Exhibitions: Contemporary Art Show
Activities: Classes for adults & children; one day workshops in arts & crafts; lects open to pub, 2 vis lectrs per yr

SIMCOE

A **LYNNWOOD ARTS CENTRE,** 21 Lynnwood Ave, PO Box 67 Simcoe, ON N3Y 4K8 Canada. Tel 519-428-0540; Fax 519-428-0549; Elec Mail lynnwood@kwic.com; *Dir* Rod Demerling; *Office Mgr* Gail Smalley; *Chmn* Hazel Andrews
Open Wed - Thurs & Sun Noon-4 PM, Fri Noon-8 PM, Sat 10 AM-4 PM; No admis fee; Estab 1973 to provide a focal point for the visual arts in the community; Built in 1851 - Greek Revival Architecture; orange brick with ionic columns & is a National Historic Site; Average Annual Attendance: 8,800; Mem: 300; dues family $30, individual $25, student & senior citizen $20; annual meeting in Mar
Income: $140,000 (financed by mem, patrons-private & commercial, Ontario Arts Council)
Collections: Contemporary Canadian Art
Exhibitions: Exhibitions of contemporary art & permanent collection works; Local artists
Publications: Quarterly newsletter

Activities: Classes for adults & children; docent training; lects open to pub, 15 lectrs per yr; concerts; gallery talks; tours; seminars; juried art exhibs (every two years) with purchase awards; sales shop sells books & hand-crafted items

L **Eva Brook Donly Museum & Archives,** 109 Norfolk St S, Simcoe, ON N3Y 2W3 Canada. Tel 519-426-1583; Fax 519-426-1584; Elec Mail office@norfolklore.com; Internet Home Page Address: www.norfolkore.com; *Cur* Helen Bartens
Open Tues - Sat 10 AM - 4:30 PM; Admis by donation; research admis $10 per person; Estab 1900 to promote awareness and understanding of all aspects of the County of Norfolk's Heritage and History and to develop commitment to the preservation of artifacts and archives; Reference & a photograph collection for display; Average Annual Attendance: 6,000; Mem: 425; dues $40-$1,000
Income: Admissions, fundraising, grants, research, mems, progs, gift shop sales, donations
Library Holdings: Audio Tapes; Book Volumes 2000; Cassettes; Clipping Files; Compact Disks; Fiche; Kodachrome Transparencies; Lantern Slides; Manuscripts; Maps; Memorabilia; Micro Print; Original Art Works; Original Documents; Periodical Subscriptions; Photographs; Prints; Reels; Sculpture; Slides; Video Tapes
Special Subjects: Decorative Arts, Mixed Media, Photography, Drawings, Etchings & Engravings, Manuscripts, Maps, Painting-American, Painting-British, Posters, Pre-Columbian Art, Prints, Sculpture, Historical Material, Portraits, Watercolors, Ceramics, Archaeology, Advertising Design, Cartoons, Porcelain, Furniture, Mexican Art, Period Rooms, Costume Design & Constr, Glass, Bookplates & Bindings, Metalwork, Dolls, Embroidery, Jewelry, Restoration & Conservation, Silver, Marine Painting, Landscapes, Coins & Medals, Flasks & Bottles, Laces, Painting-Canadian, Architecture, Folk Art, Pottery, Textiles
Collections: over 500 works by W.E. Cantelon; Art by Eva Brook Donly & Wiliam Pope; archaeological collections; historical artifacts
Publications: Norfolore, quarterly newsletter
Activities: Classes for adults & children; docent training; lects open to pub; 2-5 vis lectrs per year; gallery talks; tours; museum shop sells books & original art

ST CATHARINES

M **NIAGARA ARTISTS' COMPANY,** 354 St Paul St, St Catharines, ON L2R 3N2 Canada. Tel 905-641-0331; Fax 905-641-4970; Elec Mail artists@nac.org; Internet Home Page Address: www.nac.org; *Dir Opers & Programming* Stephen Remus; *Dir Outreach & Publ* Natasha Pedros; *Pres* Roslyn Pivarnyik; *VPres* John Venditti
Open Wed - Fri 10 AM - 5 PM, Sat 12 PM - 4 PM; No admis fee; Estab 1969; Main gallery has 2400 sq ft, 2nd gallery has 500 sq ft; Average Annual Attendance: 6,100; Mem: 135; mem open to volunteers for exhibits & fundraisers; dues $15-$50; annual meeting mid-July
Income: $120,000 (financed by mem, Ontario government, federal government & sponsorship)
Exhibitions: rotate 6-8 exhibits per yr
Publications: NAC News, monthly
Activities: Lect open to public

STRATFORD

M **GALLERY STRATFORD,** 54 Romeo St S, Stratford, ON N5A 4S9 Canada. Tel 519-271-5271; Fax 519-271-1642; Elec Mail info@gallerystratford.on.ca; Internet Home Page Address: www.gallerystratford.on.ca; *Office Mgr* Christine Lee; *Exec Dir* Zhe Gu
Open Sept - May Tues - Sun 1 PM - 4 PM; summer hours June - Sept Tues - Sun 10 AM - 5 PM; bus hours weekdays 9 AM - 5 PM; Admis $5, sr citizens & students $4, children under 12 free; Estab 1967 as a nonprofit permanent establishment open to the pub & administered in the pub interest for the purpose of studying, interpreting, assembling & exhibiting to the pub; public art gallery; Average Annual Attendance: 25,000; Mem: 400; annual meeting in Mar
Income: $348,743 (financed by mem, city appropriation, provincial & federal grants & fundraising)
Collections: Works of art on paper
Exhibitions: Changing exhibits, geared to create interest for visitors to Stratford Shakespearean Festival; during winter months geared to local municipality
Publications: Catalogs; calendar of events
Activities: Classes for adults & children; docent training; lects open to pub; gallery talks; tours; visual art award for grade 12; scholarships offered; originates traveling exhibs; gift shop sells Canadian craft, glass, jewelry, pottery, silk scarves & cards

SUDBURY

M **LAURENTIAN UNIVERSITY,** Museum & Art Centre, 251 John St, Sudbury, ON P3E 2Z7 Canada. Tel 705-674-3271; Tel 705-675-4871; Fax 705-674-3065; Internet Home Page Address: www.artsudbury.org; *Dir* Bill Huffman
Open Tues & Wed Noon - 5 PM, Thurs & Fri Noon-9PM, Sat & Sun Noon-5PM, mornings by appointment, cl Mon; Admis fee voluntary; Estab 1968 to present a continuous program of exhibitions, concerts & events for the people of Sudbury & the district; Gallery has two floors of space: 124 running ft in one & 131 running ft in the second gallery & 68.5 running ft in third gallery; Average Annual Attendance: 30,000; Mem: 400; dues family $26.75, single $16.05, student & senior citizen $8.56; annual meeting in June
Income: Financed by endowment, mem, city & provincial appropriations, government & local organizations
Special Subjects: Painting-American, Painting-Canadian, Painting-Polish
Collections: Canadian coll dating from the late 1800s & early 1900s to contemporary. The Group of Seven, Eskimo sculptures & prints as well as works of historical Canadian artists comprise the coll; Indian works from northern Ontario
Publications: Communique, every eight weeks

Activities: Lects open to pub, 10 vis lectrs per yr; concerts; gallery talks; tours; lending collection contains 1300 original art works & 8300 slides; book traveling exhibs 2-4 per yr; mus shop sells magazines, catalogues, postcards, posters, prints & gift items

L **Art Centre Library,** 251 John St, Sudbury, ON P3E 2Z7 Canada. Tel 705-675-4871; Fax 705-674-3065; Elec Mail gallery@artsudbury.org; Internet Home Page Address: www.artsudbury.org; *Dir & Cur* Bill Huffman; *Curatorial Asst* Leeann Lahaie
Open Tues, Wed, Sat & Sun Noon-5PM, Thurs & Fri Noon-9PM; Admis $2 donation; Estab 1977; For reference only; Average Annual Attendance: 25,000
Purchases: Contemporary Canadian, new media
Library Holdings: Book Volumes 5000; Cards; Cassettes; Clipping Files; Exhibition Catalogs; Lantern Slides; Pamphlets; Periodical Subscriptions 78; Photographs; Slides 8300; Video Tapes
Activities: Classes for adults & children; lects open to pub; concerts; gallery talks; tours; exten prog serves area schools; artmobile; lending of original objects of art; originate 2 traveling exhibs per yr; mus shop sells books & magazines

TORONTO

M **A SPACE,** 401 Richmond St W, Ste 110, Toronto, ON M5V 3A8 Canada. Tel 416-979-9633; Fax 416-979-9683; Elec Mail aspace@interlog.com; Internet Home Page Address: www.aspacegallery.org; *Admin Dir* Bill Huffman; *Dir Prog* Ingrid Mayrhofer
Open Tues - Fri 11 AM - 6 PM, Sat Noon - 5 PM, cl Sun & Mon; No admis fee; Estab 1971; 1,000 sq ft of gallery space & hardwood floors. Maintains reference library; Average Annual Attendance: 15,000; Mem: 150; dues $15; 4 meetings yearly
Income: $171,000 (financed by endowment, mem, city & state appropriation)
Collections: Contemporary Visual Art
Exhibitions: Artists' submissions to gallery
Publications: Addendum-A Space Community Newsletter, quarterly
Activities: Lects open to pub, 5 vis lectrs per yr; concerts; gallery talks; tours; book traveling exhibs; originate traveling exhibs; mus shop sells books

M **ART GALLERY OF ONTARIO,** 317 Dundas St W, Toronto, ON M5T 1G4 Canada. Tel 416-979-6623; Fax 416-979-6648; Internet Home Page Address: www.ago.net; *Exec Dir Develop* Sean St Michael; *Dir & CEO* Matthew Teitelbaum; *Chief Cur* Dennis Reid; *Dir Mktg & Communs* Arlene Small; *Dir Pub Affairs* Susan Bloch-Nevitte; *Pres* A Charles Braille
Admis adults $15, students $12, special exhibs $18; Estab 1900 to cultivate & advance the cause of the visual arts in Ontario; to conduct programmes of educ in the origin, development, appreciation & techniques of the visual arts; to collect & exhibit works of art & displays & to maintain & operate a gallery & related facilities as required for this purpose; to stimulate the interest of the pub in matters undertaken by the Gallery; Cl Oct 7, 2007 to Nov 14, 2008 due to renovation; 583,000 sq ft new facility; Average Annual Attendance: 317,066; Mem: Student dues $40, nonres $60, individual $75, family $100, contributing $150 - $249, Supporting $250 - $499, Sustaining $500 - $999, Cur's Circle $1500
Income: Financed by mem, provincial, city & federal appropriations & earned income
Purchases: $1,000,000
Library Holdings: Auction Catalogs; Audio Tapes; Book Volumes; CD-ROMs; Cards; Clipping Files; DVDs
Special Subjects: Painting-American, Sculpture, African Art, Painting-European
Collections: American & European Art (16th century to present); Canadian Historical & Contemporary Art; Henry Moore Sculpture Center, Prints & Drawings; Henry Moore Sculpture Collection
Exhibitions: Swing Space: Wallworks-Contemporary Art in Unexpected Places
Publications: Art Matters Journal, eleven times per year; annual report; exhibition catalogs
Activities: Classes for adults & children; docent training; lect open to public; gallery talks; tours; individual paintings & original objects of art loaned; sales shop sells books, reproductions, prints & jewelry; art rental shop for members to rent original works of art; Teens Behind the Scenes

L **Edward P Taylor Research Library & Archives,** 317 Dundas St W, Toronto, ON M5T 1G4 Canada. Tel 416-979-6642; Fax 416-979-6602; Elec Mail library_archives@ago.net; Internet Home Page Address: www.ago.net/ago/library; *Deputy Librn* Larry Pfaff; *Chief Librn* Karen McKenzie; *Archivist Spec Coll* Amy Marshall
Open Wed - Fri 1 - 4:45 PM; No admis fee; Estab 1933 to collect printed material for the documentation & interpretation of the works of art in the Gallery's collection, to provide research & informational support for the Gallery's programs & activities; to document the art & artists of Ontario, Toronto & Canada, Includes Museum's archives and Canadian art archives
Income: Financed by parent institution, donations, grants
Library Holdings: Auction Catalogs; Audio Tapes; Book Volumes 140,000; CD-ROMs; Clipping Files; DVDs; Exhibition Catalogs; Fiche; Manuscripts; Original Documents; Other Holdings Auction catalogs; Pamphlets; Periodical Subscriptions 650; Photographs; Reels; Reproductions
Special Subjects: Art History, Decorative Arts, Mixed Media, Etchings & Engravings, Graphic Arts, Painting-American, Painting-British, Painting-Dutch, Painting-Flemish, Painting-French, Conceptual Art, Latin American Art, Eskimo Art, Marine Painting, Landscapes, Painting-Canadian
Collections: Canadian Illustrated Books; Garrow Collection of British Illustrated Books & Wood Engravings of the 1860s; Canadian Book-Plates; International Guide Books; McIntosh Collection of Books on Sepulchral Monuments; Muldoon Collection of Aesop Editions

M **ART METROPOLE,** 1490 Dundas St W, Toronto, ON M6K 1T5 Canada. Tel 416-703-4400; Fax 416-703-4404; Elec Mail info@artmetropole.org; Internet Home Page Address: www.artmetropole.org; *Dir* Corinn Gerber; *Registrar* Yan Wu; *Shop Mgr* Cheyanne Tarions
Open Wed - Sat 11 AM - 6 PM; No admis fee; Estab 1974 to document work by artists internationally working in non-traditional & multiple media; 900 sq ft
Income: Financed by sales & government funding

Special Subjects: Conceptual Art, Costumes
Exhibitions: Exhibits rotate every 2 months
Activities: Gallery talks; Mus shop sells books, magazines, original art, artists' books & multiples

A **ARTS AND LETTERS CLUB OF TORONTO,** 14 Elm St, Toronto, ON M5G 1G7 Canada. Tel 416-597-0223; Fax 416-597-9544; Elec Mail info@artsandlettersclub.ca; Internet Home Page Address: www.artsandlettersclub.ca; *Pres* Diane Kruger; *Cur* Barbara Mitchell; *Librn* William Denton; *Archivist* Scott James
Admis by appointment; Estab 1908 to foster arts & letters in Toronto; Mem: 580; annual meeting May
Library Holdings: Book Volumes; Exhibition Catalogs
Special Subjects: Painting-Canadian
Collections: Club Collection - art by members & others; Heritage Collection - art by members now deceased
Activities: Arts & Letters Award

L **Library,** 14 Elm St, Toronto, ON M5G 1G7 Canada. Tel 416-597-0223; *Librn* Margaret Spence; *Gen Mgr* Jason Clarke
Open by appointment; Open to club members & researchers for reference
Library Holdings: Audio Tapes; Book Volumes 2500; Cassettes; Clipping Files; Exhibition Catalogs; Kodachrome Transparencies; Manuscripts; Memorabilia; Motion Pictures; Original Art Works; Periodical Subscriptions 40; Prints; Sculpture; Slides; Video Tapes
Special Subjects: Sculpture, Theatre Arts, Architecture

M **BAU-XI GALLERY,** 340 Dundas St W, Toronto, ON M5T 1G5 Canada. Tel 416-977-0600; Fax 416-977-0625; Elec Mail toronto@bau-xi.com; Internet Home Page Address: www.bau-xi.com; *Dir* Tien Huang
Open Mon - Sat 10 AM - 5:30 PM, Sun 11 AM - 5:30 PM; No admis fee; Estab 1965; Locations in Toronto & Vancouver, representing a broad spectrum of artists; three floors of artwork
Income: Financed by pvt funding
Collections: Contemporary Canadian Art
Exhibitions: Changing exhibition schedule showcasing gallery artists including: estate of Alistair Bell, Tom Burrows, Tom Campbell, Robert Cadotte, Darlene Cole, Jamie Evrard, Ted Fullerton, Ted Godwin, Fred Hagan, Don Jarvis, Brian Kipping, Ken Lochhead, Hugh Mackenzie, Casey McGlynn, Robert Marchessault, Pat O'Hara, Andre Petterson, Joseph Plaskett, Jack Shadbolt, Shi Le, Stuart Slind, Alex Cameron, Steven Nederveen; rotate 14 - 15 per yr
Activities: Art sales

M **BAYCREST CENTRE FOR GERIATRIC CARE,** The Morris & Sally Justein of Baycrest Heritage Museum, 3560 Bathurst St, Toronto, ON M6A 2E1 Canada. Tel 416-785-2500, Ext 2802, Ext 2645 (pub affairs); Fax 416-785-2464; Elec Mail pdickinson@baycrest.org; Internet Home Page Address: www.baycrest.org/museum; *Coordr* Pat Dickinson
Open Thurs - Sun 9 AM - 9 PM, Fri 9 AM - sunset; cl Sat; No admis fee; Estab 1972; Displays permanent coll of Judaica or temporary exhibs on Jewish themes
Special Subjects: Historical Material, Judaica
Collections: Judaica: ceremonial objects, domestic artifacts, memorabilia, books, photos, documents & works on paper
Exhibitions: Regular temporary exhibs. Contact museum or visit website for current exhibs

CANADIAN ART FOUNDATION
For further information, see National and Regional Organizations

CANADIAN SOCIETY OF PAINTERS IN WATERCOLOUR
For further information, see National and Regional Organizations

M **CITY OF TORONTO CULTURE,** The Market Gallery, 95 Front St E, Toronto, ON M5E 1C2 Canada. Tel 416-392-7604; Fax 416-392-0572; Internet Home Page Address: www.toronto.ca/culture/the_market_gallery.htm; *Cur* Pamela Wachna; *Exhib & Outreach Technician* Michael Dowbenka; *Gallery Clerk* Jacquie Gardner
Open Tues - Fri 10 AM - 4 PM, Sat 9 AM - 4 PM, cl Sun & Mon; No admis fee; Estab 1979 to bring the art & history of Toronto to the public; Located in original 19th century Toronto City Hall; Average Annual Attendance: 25,000; Mem: Municipal Government
Library Holdings: Exhibition Catalogs; Kodachrome Transparencies; Original Documents
Special Subjects: Prints, Watercolors, Landscapes, Portraits, Painting-Canadian, Marine Painting, Historical Material
Collections: City of Toronto Fine Art Collection (oil, watercolor, prints & sculpture)
Exhibitions: Various exhibitions on Toronto's art, culture & history presented on an on-going basis
Publications: Exhibit catalogs
Activities: Classes for adults & children; lect open to public; gallery talks; paintings lent

A **CITY OF TORONTO MUSEUM SERVICES,** (Heritage Toronto) Historic Fort York, 100 Garrison Rd, Toronto, ON M5V 3K9 Canada; 55 John St, 8th Fl Toronto, ON M5V 3C6 Canada. Tel 416-392-6907; Fax 416-392-6917; Elec Mail fortyork@toronto.ca; Internet Home Page Address: www.fortyork.ca; *Cur* Wayne Reeves; *Mus Adminr* David O'Hara
Open Sept - May, Mon - Fri 10 AM - 4 PM, Sat - Sun 10 AM - 5 PM; May - Sept, Mon - Sun 10 AM - 4 PM; Admis adults $7.62, sr citizens & youth (13-18) $3.81, children (4-12) $2.86; Estab 1934 to tell the story of the founding of Toronto & the British Army in the 19th century; All buildings have permanent or temporary exhibits & period - room settings; maintains reference library; Average Annual Attendance: 55,000
Income: Financed by city appropriation
Special Subjects: Historical Material
Collections: 19th century Military; Original War of 1812 Buildings; Original War of 1812 Uniforms; Original War of 1812 Weapons

Activities: Classes for adults & children; lect open to public; sales shop sells books, prints & reproductions

M **DELEON WHITE GALLERY,** 1096 Queen St W, Toronto, ON M6J 1H9 Canada; PO Box 41120, Mississauga, ON L4W 1V5 Canada. Tel 647-836-0496; Fax 416-597-9455; Elec Mail info@ecotecturecanada.org; Internet Home Page Address: www.ecotecturecanada.org; *Cur* Virginia MacDonnell; *Dir* Stephen White
Open Thurs - Fri 2 PM - 8 PM, Sat - Sun 12 PM - 6 PM; No admis fee; Estab 1995
Special Subjects: Architecture, Drawings, Mexican Art, Painting-American, Photography, Prints, Sculpture, Watercolors, Bronzes, Woodcuts, Landscapes, Collages, Painting-Japanese, Painting-Canadian, Painting-French, Painting-German
Collections: Contemporary Ecological Art; Outdoor Environmental Art
Exhibitions: Alan Sonfist, Ian Lazarus
Publications: DeLeon White Gallery News, quarterly
Activities: Lects open to pub; book traveling exhibs 2 per yr; originate traveling exhibs 2 per yr; sales shop sells books, magazines, original art, prints & slides

A **FUSION: THE ONTARIO CLAY & GLASS ASSOCIATION,** Fusion Clay & Glass Association, 1444 Queen St E, Toronto, ON M4L 1E1 Canada. Tel 416-438-8946; Fax 416-438-0192; Elec Mail fusion@clayandglass.on.ca; Internet Home Page Address: www.clayandglass.on.ca; *Pres* Vickie Salinas; *Office Adminr* Jenanne Longman; *Finance* Deborah Freeman
Open Mon - Fri 9 AM - 4 PM; No admis fee; Estab 1975; Ashbridge House; Mem: Dues $60 per yr
Income: Financed by mem
Special Subjects: Decorative Arts, Ceramics, Crafts, Glass
Collections: Permanent collection housed at Burlington Art Ctr
Exhibitions: Fireworks (biennial juried traveling exhib); Silent Auction (biennial fundraiser)
Publications: Fusion Magazine, 3 per year; Fusion News Magazine, 3 per year
Activities: Classes for adults; workshops; lects open to pub; schols; awards (student exhibs, design awards); originates traveling exhibs to galleries within Ont

M **GALLERY MOOS LTD,** 305-722 College St, Toronto, ON M6G 1C4 Canada. Tel 416-504-5445; Fax 416-504-5446; Elec Mail gallerymoos@rogers.com; Internet Home Page Address: www.gallerymoos.com; *Pres* Walter A Moos; *Adminr* Svetlana Novikova; *Asst* Bryan Almas
Open Tues - Sat 11 AM - 6 PM; No admis fee; Estab 1959; Maintains reference library, contemporary art gallery
Income: Financed by pvt funding
Library Holdings: Auction Catalogs
Special Subjects: Painting-American, Prints, Sculpture, Painting-Canadian
Collections: Contemporary Canadian & international art artists include: Karel Appel, Ken Danby, Sorel Etrog, Gershon Iskowitz, Jean-Paul Riopelle, Antoni Tapies, Lester Johnson, WIlliam Scott, Robert Hedrick, Mark Ash, Josue Demarche, Evan Levy, Dennis Geden, Leonidas Correa, Rose Lindzon, Sandra Manzi, Burton Kramer, Scott Ellis, David Urban, Burton Kramer

M **GEORGE R GARDINER MUSEUM OF CERAMIC ART,** 111 Queen's Park, Toronto, ON M5S 2C7 Canada. Tel 416-586-8080; Fax 416-586-8085; Elec Mail mail@gardinermuseum.com; Internet Home Page Address: www.gardinermuseum.on.ca; *Exec Dir* Alexandra Montgomery; *Coll Mgr* Christina Green; *Preparator* Cindy Koh; *Exec Asst* Sheila Snelgrove; *Assoc Cur* Rachel Gotlieb; *Assoc Cur* Elisa Saui; *Interim Chief Cur* Peter Kaellgren
Open Mon - Thurs 10 AM-6 PM, Fri 10 AM - 9 PM, Sat & Sun 10 AM-5 PM; Admis adults $12, sr citizens $8, students & children $6; Estab 1984 as the only specialized museum of ceramics in Canada; Museum houses one of the world's greatest collections of ceramic art from the early 15th century to the 20th century; Average Annual Attendance: 60,000; Mem: 1145
Income: Endowment
Library Holdings: Auction Catalogs; Audio Tapes; Clipping Files; Exhibition Catalogs; Periodical Subscriptions
Special Subjects: Ceramics
Collections: English delftware; European porcelain; Italian maiolica; Ancient Americas pottery; Chinese porcelain; Minton contemporary ceramics; Japanese porcelain
Activities: Clay classes for adults & children; school prog; docent progs; lects open to pub; gallery talks; tours; RBC Emerging Artist Award ($10,00 Can); book traveling exhibs 3 per yr; retail store sells books, original art, ceramics & artist design objects

M **HARBOURFRONT CENTRE,** (The Power Plant) The Power Plant Contemporary Art Gallery, 231 Queens Quay W, Toronto, ON M5J 2G8 Canada. Tel 416-973-4949; Elec Mail info@thepowerplant.org; Internet Home Page Address: www.thepowerplant.org; *Dir* Gaetane Verna
Open Tues, Wed, Fri, Sat & Sun -10 AM - 5 PM, Thurs 10 AM- 8 PM; Admis free; Estab 1987; Pub gallery devoted to contemporary visual art; Average Annual Attendance: 70,000
Activities: Classes for children; lects open to pub; gallery talks; tours; mus shop sells books, original art

M **JOHN B AIRD GALLERY,** 900 Bay St, 1st Fl, Macdonald Block Toronto, ON M7A 1C2 Canada. Tel 416-928-6772; Elec Mail director@airdgallery.org; Internet Home Page Address: http://www.airdgallery.org/; *Dir* Dale Barrett
Open Mon - Fri 10 AM - 6 PM; Nonprofit, non-collecting exhib ctr
Special Subjects: Photography, Sculpture, Watercolors, Textiles, Pottery, Woodcarvings, Woodcuts, Silver, Tapestries, Stained Glass
Collections: Printmaking; Silversmithing
Exhibitions: 12 ann exhibs

M **KOFFLER CENTRE OF THE ARTS,** (Bathurst Jewish Community Centre) Koffler Gallery, 4588 Bathurst St, Toronto, ON M2R 1W6 Canada. Tel 416-638-1881, Ext 4296; Fax 416-638-5813; Elec Mail lstarr@kofflerarts.org; Internet Home Page Address: www.kofflerarts.org; *Exec Dir* Lori Starr; *Cur* Mona Filip; *Head Progs & Exhib* Evelyn Tauben; *Head Communs* Tony Hewen; *Educ Coordr* Anya Laskin; *Dir Develop* Debbie Esdrin
Open Tues - Fri 10 AM - 4 PM, Sun noon - 4 PM; No admis fee; Estab 1976; 4,000 sq ft, contemporary program; 40,000 sq ft in new ctr under construction; Average Annual Attendance: 100,000

Income: $400,000 (financed by government grants, pvt donations & various institutions)
Library Holdings: CD-ROMs; Clipping Files; DVDs; Exhibition Catalogs; Slides
Special Subjects: Manuscripts
Publications: Catalogues & exhibitions brochures
Activities: Classes for adults & children; dramatic progs; school workshops; docent training; lects open to pub; 20 artist talks per yr; concerts; gallery talks; tours; sponsoring of competitions; visiting artists; schols available; book traveling exhibs, 2 per yr; originate traveling exhibs 1 per yr

M **MASLAK MCLEOD GALLERY,** 192 Davenport Rd, Toronto, ON M5R 1J2 Canada. Tel 416-944-2577; Fax 416-922-1636; Elec Mail gallery@masiakmcleod.com; Internet Home Page Address: www.maslakmcleod.com; *Cur* Joseph McLeod PhD; *Asst Cur* Kersti McLeod; *Asst Cur* Christian McLeod
Open daily 10 AM - 5 PM; No admis fee; Estab 1968; Gallery exhibits fine art, Indigenia Canada, international exhibits; Average Annual Attendance: 20,000; Mem: ADAC; recommendation from mems, Morrisseau Family Foundation, Canadian Professional Appraisers
Income: pvt
Purchases: Directly from artists or collections
Library Holdings: Auction Catalogs; Audio Tapes; Book Volumes; Cassettes
Special Subjects: American Indian Art, American Western Art, Anthropology
Collections: Native Art; North American Art; International
Exhibitions: Joseph Jacobs; Norval Morrisseau; Inuit Sculptures; Governors Gallery Santa Fe, Iaia Mus Santa Fe; Geronimo, Munich, Germany; Paces Strange, Halifax
Publications: catalogs
Activities: Classes for adults; lects open to pub; lects for mems only; gallery talks; awards connected to exhibits

M **MERCER UNION,** A Centre for Contemporary Art, 1286 Bloor St W, Toronto, ON M6H 1N9 Canada. Tel 416-536-1519; Fax 416-536-2955; Elec Mail info@mercerunion.org; Internet Home Page Address: www.mercerunion.org; *Dir Opers* York Lethbridge; *Dir Exhibs* Georgina Jacuson; *Exhib Tech* Jon Sasaki
Open Tues - Sat 11 AM - 6 PM; No admis fee; Estab 1979 is an artist-run centre committed to the presentation & examination of Canadian & contemporary Visual art & related cultural practices; 1500 sq ft; Average Annual Attendance: 15,000; Mem: 200; dues arts supporter $500-$1000, sustaining $100, supporting $50, educational $30, assoc $25, students $15; monthly board meetings
Income: $280,000 (financed by endowment, mem, city & state appropriations, Canada Council, Ontario Arts Council & Toronto Arts Council)
Library Holdings: Exhibition Catalogs
Collections: Michael Buchanan; Patricia Galimente, Gretchen Sankey; Contemporary Art
Exhibitions: rotate every 6 wks
Publications: Exhibition catalogues
Activities: Lects open to pub,10 vis lectrs per yr; gallery talks; sales shop sells books & catalogues, multiples

M **MUSEUM OF CONTEMPORARY CANADIAN ART,** (Art Gallery of North York) 952 Queen St W, Toronto, ON M6J 1G8 Canada. Tel 416-395-7490; Fax 416-395-7598; Elec Mail info@mocca.ca; Internet Home Page Address: www.mocca.ca; *Artistic Dir & Cur* David Liss; *Asst Cur* Su-Ying Lee; *Head Communs & Mktg* Fayiaz Chundra; *Mgr Membership & Develop* Katy Laird; *Managing Dir* Yves Theoret; *Exec Asst Office Artistic Dir & Cur* Rachel Solomon
Open Tues - Sun 11 AM - 6 PM; No admis fee; Estab 1994 to collect & exhibit Canadian contemporary art from 1985 - present; One floor, 6000 sq ft with 6 exhibitions per year of some of the most challenging art being produced in Canada today; Average Annual Attendance: 65,000
Special Subjects: Sculpture, Painting-Canadian
Collections: Contemporary Canadian Art
Activities: Lects open to pub

M **OCAD UNIVERSITY,** Student Gallery, 285 Dundas St W, Toronto, ON M5T 1W2 Canada; 100 McCaul St, Toronto, ON M5T 1W1 Canada. Tel 416-977-6000, Ext 262; Fax 416-977-6006; Internet Home Page Address: www.ocad.ca; *Exhibitions Coordr* Christine Swiderski; *Asst Coordr* Lisa Deanne Smith
Open Wed - Sat Noon - 6 PM; No admis fee; Estab 1970 for faculty & student exhibs & to exhibit outside work to benefit the col; Average Annual Attendance: 15,000
Income: Financed by College
Exhibitions: Exhibiting student works, rotate every 3 weeks
Publications: Invitations; small scale catalogs

L **Dorothy H Hoover Library,** 100 McCaul St, Toronto, ON M5T 1W1 Canada. Tel 416-977-6000; Fax 416-977-6006; Elec Mail jpatrick@ocad.ca; Internet Home Page Address: www.ocad.ca; *Dir Library Svcs* Jill Patrick; *Head Library Systems & Technical Svcs* James Forrester; *Technical Svcs Librn* Maureen Carter; *Archivist & Records Officer* Lynn Austin; *Head Reference, Information & Access Svcs* Daniel Payne; *Reference & Access Svcs Librn* Robert Fabbro
Open Apr 28 - May 13 Mon - Fri 9 AM - 4:45 PM, cl Sat - Sun; May 14 - Aug 3 Mon - Fri 9 AM - 6 PM, cl Sat, Sun, May 21, July 2 & Aug 6; Aug 4 - Dec 17, Mon - Fri 8 AM - 8:45 PM, Sat 11 AM - 5:45 PM, cl Sun; Dec 18 - Dec 21 Tues - Fri 9 AM - 5:45 PM, cl Sat, Sun, Dec 22 - New Years; Library formed in 1922, estab to support the curriculum; Circ 116,212; Average Annual Attendance: 400,000
Income: Financed through the College
Purchases: $250,000
Library Holdings: Book Volumes 30,000; Cassettes 620; Clipping Files; Exhibition Catalogs; Fiche; Filmstrips; Kodachrome Transparencies; Lantern Slides; Motion Pictures 75; Other Holdings Pictures 40,000; Vertical files 43,000; Pamphlets; Periodical Subscriptions 225; Records; Reels; Slides 85,000; Video Tapes 1000
Special Subjects: Art History, Decorative Arts, Film, Illustration, Mixed Media, Commercial Art, Drawings, Graphic Arts, Graphic Design, Ceramics, Conceptual Art, Archaeology, American Western Art, Advertising Design, Industrial Design,

Art Education, American Indian Art, Anthropology, Aesthetics, Afro-American Art, Jewelry, Architecture

A ONTARIO ASSOCIATION OF ART GALLERIES, 111 Peter St, Ste 617 Toronto, ON M5V 2H1 Canada. Tel 416-598-0714; Fax 416-598-4128; Elec Mail oaag@oaag.org; Internet Home Page Address: www.oaag.org; *Exec Dir* Demetra Christakos; *Project Coordr* Barbara Gilbert
Open 9 AM - 5 PM; Estab in 1968 as the provincial nonprofit organization representing pub art galleries in the province of Ontario. Institutional mem includes approx 84 pub art galleries, exhibition spaces & arts related organizations. Mem is also available to individuals; Gallery not maintained; Mem: 83; annual meeting in June
Income: Financed by mem, Ontario Arts Council, Ontario Ministry of Culture, Tourism & Recreation, Department of Canadian Heritage
Publications: Context, bimonthly newsletter
Activities: Professional development seminars & workshops; awards; active job file & job hot-line

M ONTARIO CRAFTS COUNCIL, OCC Gallery, 990 Queen St W, Toronto, ON M6J 1H1 Canada. Tel 416-925-4222; Fax 416-925-4223; Elec Mail gallery@craft.on.ca; Internet Home Page Address: www.craft.on.ca; *Exec Dir* Emma Quin; *Accounts & Opers Mgr* Paul Wilson; *Mem Svcs Coordr* Grace Donati; *Commun Officer* Maxine Bell; *Cur* Janna Hiemstra
Open Mon - Sat 11 AM - 6 PM; No admis fee; Estab 1976 to foster crafts & crafts people in Ontario; Maintains an art gallery; Average Annual Attendance: 8,000; Mem: 1,500; dues $130; annual meeting in June; see website for additional information
Income: Financed by mem & provincial appropriation, The Guild Shop, fundraising & publications
Exhibitions: Ontario Crafts Regional Juried Exhibition; bimonthly exhibitions in craft gallery
Publications: Studio magazine
Activities: Lects open to pub; gallery talks; tours; Sales shop sells books, original craft, Inuit art, sculpture & prints

L Craft Resource Centre, 990 Queen St W, Toronto, ON M6J 1H1 Canada. Tel 416-925-4222; Fax 416-925-4223; Elec Mail info@craft.on.ca; Internet Home Page Address: www.craft.on.ca; *Portfolio of Makers Mgr* Carol Ann Casselman; *Outreach Coordr* Rommy Rodriguez A
Open Wed - Fri Noon - 5 PM; No admis fee; Estab 1976. A comprehensive, special library devoted exclusively to the field of crafts. It is a primarily mem-funded not-for-profit organization & is available as an information service to the general pub & Ontario crafts Council members. Has an extensive portfolio registry featuring Canadian craftspeople; For reference only; Average Annual Attendance: 6,000; Mem: 3,000; dues $40; annual meeting in June
Library Holdings: Book Volumes 3000; Clipping Files; Exhibition Catalogs; Manuscripts; Other Holdings Portfolios of craftspeople 530; Periodical Subscriptions 350; Slides 100,000; Video Tapes
Special Subjects: Glass, Metalwork, Enamels, Pottery
Activities: Educ dept; tours; schols & fels offered; slide rental; publishing; Portfolio Makers Prog; Sales shop sells books, magazines, contemporary Canadian crafts

A Artists in Stained Glass, 151 Bloor St West, 5th Fl Toronto, ON M5S 1T6 Canada. Tel 416-690-0031; Internet Home Page Address: www.arts.on.ca; *Ed* Brigitte Wolf; *Pres* Robert Browne
Estab 1974 to encourage the development of stained glass as a contemporary art form in Canada; Maintains slide file library through the Ontario Crafts Council; Mem: 130; dues $25-$70; annual meeting in Nov
Income: $6,000 (financed by mem & state appropriation)
Publications: Flat Glass Journal, quarterly; Leadline, occasionally
Activities: Classes for adults; lects open to pub, 5 vis lectrs per yr

A THE PHOTON LEAGUE OF HOLOGRAPHERS, 401 Richmond St W, Ste B03, Toronto, ON M5V 3A8 Canada. Tel 416-599-9332, 203-7243; Internet Home Page Address: www.photonleague.org; *Dir* C Abrams
Open by appointment only; Estab 1985 for holography production. The Photon League is committed to providing affordable access to a professional level holography facility, educ about holography through workshops, encouragement & support of artistic production & dialogue in the field of holography. As a resource center, The Photon League organizes & curates exhibs, maintains an archive of holographic work & fosters the exploration of relevant technologies; Holography studio includes: 50 mw Helium Neon laser, 3 mw Helium Neon laser, 2 mw Helium Neon laser, 8 x 16 ft floating table, darkroom, computer controlled stereogram, optics & mounts; Mem: 15; dues international $75, core $60, student $20, assoc $15
Income: Financed by mem
Exhibitions: Ann exhibits at local locations
Publications: Quarterly newsletter
Activities: Classes for adults & children; artist-in-residence; workshops; panel discussions; open house; discussion group; lect open to public; lending collection contains original objects of art; sales shop sells holograms & T-shirts

M REDHEAD GALLERY, 401 Richmond St W, Toronto, ON M5V 3A8 Canada. Tel 416-504-5654; Fax 416-504-2421; Elec Mail art@redheadgallery.org; *Dir* Christy Thompson
Open Wed - Fri Noon - 5 PM, Sat Noon - 6 PM; No admis fee; Estab 1990 as an artist run culture; There are 2 exhibition spaces. One main space is primarily reserved for mem. Annual programming will include exhibitions by visiting artists. Two window spaces are rented on a monthly basis to emerging artists. Also hold poetry reading, exhibits permitting; Average Annual Attendance: 5,400; Mem: 19; dues $1,320
Income: financed by mem
Collections: Contemporary Art
Exhibitions: Contemporary Art; rotating exhibits

M ROYAL ONTARIO MUSEUM, 100 Queen's Park, Toronto, ON M5S 2C6 Canada. Tel 416-586-8000; Fax 416-586-5863; Internet Home Page Address: www.rom.on.ca; *Dir Human Resources* Chris Koester; *Dir & CEO* William Thorsell; *Deputy Dir Opers* Glenn Dobbin; *Deputy Dir Coll & Res* Mark Engstrom; *Exec Dir Mktg & Commercial Devel* Kelvin Browne; *CFO* Bill Graesser; *VPres Exhibits, Educ & New Media* Anthony Hushion; *Exec Dir Vis Rels* Ania Kordiuk; *Exec Dir Gallery Devel* Dan Rahimi
Open Mon - Thurs 10 AM - 5:30 PM, Fri 10 AM - 9:30 PM, Sat - Sun 10 AM - 5:30 PM; Admis adults $22, senior & student $19, child (4-14) $15, under 3 free; Estab 1912 & includes 20 curatorial departments in the fields of fine & decorative arts, archaeology & the natural & earth sciences; Average Annual Attendance: 1,000,000; Mem: 42,000; dues individual $65
Income: $25,000,000 (financed by federal grants, provincial grants, mus income, mem, bequests, grants & donations)
Special Subjects: Architecture, Hispanic Art, African Art, Anthropology, Archaeology, Pre-Columbian Art, Southwestern Art, Primitive art, Asian Art, Historical Material, Medieval Art
Collections: Far Eastern coll
Publications: Rotunda, quarterly magazine; numerous acad publications; gallery guides; exhibition catalogs; publications in print
Activities: Classes for adults & children; throughout the school yr, prebooked classes receive lessons in the mus; non-conducted classes can also be arranged with the mus at a cost of $3 per student; lects open to pub with vis lectrs, special lects for members only; concerts; gallery talks; tours; competitions; outreach dept serves Ontario; individual paintings & original objects of art lent to mus & galleries; originate traveling exhibs; mus shop sells books, magazines, reproductions, prints & slides

L Library & Archives, 100 Queen's Park, Toronto, ON M5S 2C6 Canada. Tel 416-586-5595; Fax 416-586-5519; Elec Mail library@rom.on.ca; Internet Home Page Address: www.rom.on.ca; *Library Mgr* Arthur Smith; *Far Eastern Librn* Jack Howard
Open to staff & pub viewing; No admis fee; Estab 1960 for curatorial research; Circ Non-circulating; Average Annual Attendance: 5,000
Income: $600,000 (operating grant)
Purchases: $95,000
Library Holdings: Book Volumes 156,769; Compact Disks 48; DVDs; Exhibition Catalogs; Fiche 531; Manuscripts; Memorabilia; Original Art Works; Original Documents; Pamphlets; Periodical Subscriptions 363; Photographs; Sculpture; Video Tapes 15
Special Subjects: Art History, Decorative Arts, Illustration, Photography, Etchings & Engravings, Graphic Arts, Islamic Art, Painting-American, Painting-British, Pre-Columbian Art, Prints, Sculpture, Painting-European, Historical Material, History of Art & Archaeology, Judaica, Portraits, Watercolors, Ceramics, Crafts, Archaeology, Ethnology, Printmaking, Fashion Arts, Asian Art, American Indian Art, Porcelain, Primitive art, Anthropology, Eskimo Art, Ivory, Jade, Period Rooms, Costume Design & Constr, Glass, Mosaics, Stained Glass, Metalwork, Antiquities-Oriental, Antiquities-Persian, Carpets & Rugs, Embroidery, Enamels, Gold, Goldsmithing, Handicrafts, Jewelry, Miniatures, Oriental Art, Religious Art, Restoration & Conservation, Silver, Silversmithing, Tapestries, Textiles, Woodcarvings, Woodcuts, Antiquities-Assyrian, Antiquities-Byzantine, Antiquities-Egyptian, Antiquities-Etruscan, Antiquities-Greek, Antiquities-Roman, Dioramas, Coins & Medals, Pewter, Scrimshaw, Laces, Painting-Canadian, Architecture, Pottery
Collections: Rare book coll; far eastern coll; J H Fleming Collection; Charles Rennie MacKintosh Collection
Activities: Classes for adults; dramatic progs; lects open to pub; concerts

M Dept of Western Art & Culture, 100 Queen's Park, Toronto, ON M5S 2C6 Canada. Tel 416-586-5524; Fax 416-586-5516; *Dept Head* Paul Denis
Open Mon - Thurs & Sat 10 AM - 6 PM, Fri 9 AM - 9:30 PM, Sun 11 AM - 6 PM; No admis fee; Estab 1951 to collect, exhibit & publish material on Canadian historical paintings & Canadian decorative arts; Canadian Gallery has three galleries: first gallery has six rooms showing English Colonial, French, Maritime, Ontario & German-Ontario furniture, also silver, glass, woodenware; second gallery has ceramics, toys, weathervanes, religious carving, early 19th century Quebec paneled room; third is a picture gallery for changing exhibitions; Average Annual Attendance: 45,000; Mem: 42,000
Special Subjects: Decorative Arts, Portraits, Coins & Medals
Collections: Canadian 18th & 19th centuries decorative arts - ceramics, coins & medals books, furniture, glass, guns, silver, woodenware; 16th-18th centuries exploration; portraits of Canadians & military & administrative people connected with Canada; 18th & 19th centuries topographic & historical Canadian views; 19th century travels
Exhibitions: Various exhibitions
Publications: William Berczy; D B Webster Brantford Pottery; Canadian Watercolors & Drawings; The William Eby Pottery, Conestogo, Ontario 1855 - 1970; English Canadian Furniture of the Georgian Period; An Engraver's Pilgrimage: James Smillie Jr in Quebec, 1821-1830; Georgian Canada: Conflict & Culture, 1745 - 1820; Printmaking in Canada: The Earliest Views & Portraits

L RYERSON UNIVERSITY, Ryerson University Library, 350 Victoria St, Toronto, ON M5B 2K3 Canada. Tel 416-979-5055; Fax 416-979-5215; Elec Mail libweb@ryerson.ca; Internet Home Page Address: www.library.ryerson.ca; *Chief Librn* Madeline Sefebvre
Open Mon - Fri 8 AM - Midnight, Sat - Sun 10 AM - Midnight; No admis fee; Estab 1948
Income: Financed by provincial appropriation & student fees
Library Holdings: Audio Tapes; Book Volumes 403,897; Cassettes; Fiche; Filmstrips; Micro Print; Motion Pictures; Pamphlets; Periodical Subscriptions 3888; Records; Reels; Slides; Video Tapes
Special Subjects: Film, Photography, Graphic Arts, Theatre Arts, Fashion Arts, Interior Design, Architecture
Collections: Kodak Canada Collection; Camera Collection; Historical Photograph Collection
Exhibitions: Rotate periodically

M **STEPHEN BULGER GALLERY,** 1026 Queen St W, Toronto, ON M6J 1H6 Canada. Tel 416-504-0575; Fax 416-504-8929; Elec Mail info@bulgergallery.com; Internet Home Page Address: www.bulgergallery.com; *Dir* Stephen Bulger; *Dir Opers* Natalie Spagnol; *Dir Sales* Sarah Burtscher
Open Tues - Sat 11 AM - 6 PM; No admis fee; Estab 1995; Gallery displays historical & contemporary photography; Average Annual Attendance: 20,000
Income: pvt
Special Subjects: Photography
Collections: Canadian & International Photography Collection
Exhibitions: Month-long exhibitions, either solo or thematic group shows
Publications: World's Greatest, Pete Doherty
Activities: Lects open to pub; classes for adults; 6 vis lectrs per yr; occasional gallery talks; free film screenings on Sat afternoons; original objects of art lent; lending coll contains 2000 books & 15,000 photographs; book traveling exhibs; originates traveling exhibs to pub and commercial galleries; sales shop sells books

M **TEXTILE MUSEUM OF CANADA,** 55 Centre Ave, Toronto, ON M5G 2H5 Canada. Tel 416-599-5321; Fax 416-599-2911; Elec Mail info@textilemuseum.ca; Internet Home Page Address: www.textilemuseum.ca; *Exec Dir* Shauna McCabe; *Cur Dir* Sarah Quinton; *Opers Mgr* Pat Neal
Open daily 11 AM - 5 PM, Wed until 8 PM; Admis family $30, general $15, seniors $10, youth & student $6, children under 5 free; Estab 1975; 15,000 sq ft of gallery space where 6-8 exhibitions are mounted each yr. Maintains reference library; Average Annual Attendance: 36,000; Mem: 1200; dues $65; annual meeting in May
Income: $400,000 (financed by mem, corporate & private sponsorship, fund raising, shop & attendance revenues)
Library Holdings: Exhibition Catalogs; Pamphlets; Periodical Subscriptions; Video Tapes
Special Subjects: Textiles, Carpets & Rugs, Laces
Collections: Artifacts Collection, 12000 textiles from all over the world
Exhibitions: Rotating exhibitions
Publications: Exhibition catalogues, 2-3 per year
Activities: Classes for adults & children; docent training; workshops; symposia; lects open to pub; gallery talks; tours; original objects of art lent; lending collections contains 12000 art objects; sales shop sells books, magazines, original art, reproductions, vintage & contemporary ethnographic textiles, gifts

C **TORONTO DOMINION BANK,** Toronto Dominion Ctr, PO Box 1 Toronto, ON M5K 1A2 Canada. Tel 416-982-8473; Fax 416-982-6335; *Cur Art* Natalie Ribkoff
Contemporary Art Collection is available for viewing by appointment only. The Inuit Gallery is open Mon - Fri 8 AM - 6 PM, Sat & Sun 10 AM - 4 PM; No admis fee; The Contemporary Art Collection is shown throughout branch offices in Canada & internationally; the Inuit Art Collection has its own gallery in the Toronto-Dominion Centre
Collections: Inuit Collection: a selection of prints, as well as stone, bone & ivory carvings; the Contemporary Collection: an ongoing project focusing on the art of emerging & mature Canadian artists, including original prints, paintings, sculpture & works on paper

L **TORONTO PUBLIC LIBRARY BOARD,** (Metropolitan Toronto Library Board) Library, 789 Yonge St, Toronto, ON M4W 2G8 Canada. Tel 416-393-7131; Fax 416-393-7030; Internet Home Page Address: www.torontopubliclibrary.ca; *City Librn* Jo Bryant; *Dir Research & Reference* Linda Mackenzie
Open Mon - Thurs 9:30 AM - 8:30 PM, Fri 9:30 AM - 5:30 PM, Sat 9 AM - 5 PM, Sun Sep 9 - end of June 1:30 - 5 PM; Estab 1959 for public reference
Income: Financed by city appropriation
Library Holdings: Auction Catalogs; Book Volumes 66,000; Clipping Files; DVDs; Exhibition Catalogs; Fiche; Periodical Subscriptions 315; Photographs; Prints; Reels; Reproductions; Video Tapes
Special Subjects: Decorative Arts
Collections: Postcards, scenic & greeting; printed ephemera; private presses with emphasis on Canadian; 1,000,000 picture clippings; theatre arts & stage design

M **TORONTO SCULPTURE GARDEN,** 115 King St E, Toronto, ON M4T 2L7 Canada; PO Box 65, Station Q Toronto, ON M4T 2L7 Canada. Tel 416-515-9658; Fax 416-515-9655; Elec Mail info@torontosculpturegarden.com; Internet Home Page Address: www.torontosculpturegarden.com; *Dir* Rina Greer
Open 8 AM - dusk; No admis fee; Estab 1981; Outdoor park featuring exhibitions of site-specific work commissioned for the site
Exhibitions: 2-3 exhibits per yr
Publications: Toronto Sculpture Garden; exhibition brochures

M **UNIVERSITY OF TORONTO,** (University of Toronto Art Centre) University of Toronto Art Centre, 15 King's College Circle, Toronto, ON M5S 3H7 Canada. Tel 416-978-1838; Fax 416-971-2059; Elec Mail liz.wylie@utoronto.ca; Internet Home Page Address: www.utac.utoronto.ca; *Dir* Niamh O'Laughaire; *Bus & Progs Coordr* Maureen Smith; *Coll Mgr* Heather Darling Pigat; *Cur* Matthew Brower; *Student & Educ Coordr* Sunny Kerr
Open Tues - Fri noon - 5 PM, Sat noon - 4 PM; No admis fee; Estab 1996; There are nine galleries each displaying selections from the three collections. Maintains reference library; Average Annual Attendance: 15,000; Mem: 200; dues $50 & up
Income: $260,000 (financed by endowment, mem & the University
Special Subjects: Drawings, Graphics, Painting-American, Bronzes, Ceramics, Etchings & Engravings, Landscapes, Manuscripts, Collages, Eskimo Art, Furniture, Oriental Art, Asian Art, Antiquities-Byzantine, Marine Painting, Metalwork, Painting-British, Carpets & Rugs, Ivory, Embroidery, Medieval Art, Antiquities-Oriental, Antiquities-Egyptian, Antiquities-Greek, Antiquities-Roman
Collections: Malcove Collection; University College Collection; University of Toronto Collection
Exhibitions: Selections from the Malcove Collection, University College Collection & the University of Toronto Collection
Publications: Partners Newsletter, biannual
Activities: Docent training; lects open to pub, 2 vis lectrs per yr; concerts; gallery talks; tours; individual paintings & original objects of art lent to other institutions/galleries; 2-3 book traveling exhibs per yr; sales shop sells books, reproductions & cards

M **UNIVERSITY OF TORONTO,** Justina M Barnicke Gallery, 7 Hart House Circle, Toronto, ON M5S 3H3 Canada. Tel 416-978-8398; Fax 416-978-8387; Elec Mail jmb.gallery@utoronto.ca; Internet Home Page Address: www.jmbgallery.ca; *Dir & Cur* Barbara Fischer; *Cur in Res* Maiko Tanaka
Open Mon - Wed 11 AM - 5 PM, Thurs 11 AM - 8 PM, Sat - Sun 1 - 5 PM; No admis fee; Estab 1919 to present contemporary art in Canada; Gallery 2,000 sq ft & total wall space of 350 running ft; produces offsite events; Average Annual Attendance: 12,000
Income: Financed by Hart House
Purchases: Canadian art
Collections: Canadian Art (historical & contemporary)
Exhibitions: Temporary exhibitions of historical & contemporary Canadian art
Activities: Classes for adults; docent training; university students/outreach progs; lects open to pub, 5-10 vis lectrs per yr; concerts; gallery talks; tours; writing award for art criticism; individual paintings & original objects of art lent; book traveling exhibs, 1-2 per yr; originate traveling exhibs; mus shop sells prints & slides & catalogues

L **Fine Art Library,** Sidney Smith Hall, 100 St George St Toronto, ON M5S 3G3 Canada. Tel 416-978-5006; Fax 416-978-1491; Internet Home Page Address: www.library.utoronto.ca/fine_art/library/refinfo.html; *Library Asst* Catherine Spence
Open Mon, Tues, Fri 9:30 AM - 5 PM, Wed - Thurs 9:30 AM - 8 PM ; No admis fee; Estab 1936 for reference only
Income: Financed by state appropriation & Department of Fine Art
Library Holdings: Book Volumes 5,000; Exhibition Catalogs 30,000; Photographs 90,000
Special Subjects: Art History, Archaeology
Collections: Catalog materials including temporary, permanent, dealer catalogs; photographic archives in various fields of Western art
Publications: Canadian Illustrated News (Montreal); Index to Illustrations, quarterly

A **VISUAL ARTS ONTARIO,** 1153A Queen St W, Toronto, ON M6J 1J4 Canada. Tel 416-591-8883; Fax 416-591-2432; Elec Mail info@vao.org; Internet Home Page Address: www.vao.org; *Coordr Art Placement* Tracey Bowen; *Project Officer* David McClyment; *Bookkeeper* Frima Yolleck; *Exec Dir* Hennie L Wolff; *Sr Project Officer* Avril Loret; *Program Coordr* Jocelyn De Backere; *Mem Coordr* Mitchell Chan
Open Tues - Fri 9 AM - 5 PM, Sat 12 PM - 5 PM; Estab 1974, Visual Arts Ontario is a nonprofit organization dedicated to furthering the awareness & appreciation of the visual arts; Mem: 2000; dues 2 year $65, 1 year $35
Income: Financed by mem, fundraising, municipal, provincial & federal grants, attendance at events
Collections: Resource Center; Slide Registry of Ontario artists
Publications: Agenda, quarterly newsletter; Art in Architecture; Art for the Built Environment in the Province of Ontario; The Guidebook to Competitions & Commissions; Perfect Portfolio on Your Own; Visual Arts Handbook
Activities: Workshops for professional artists; lects open to public; seminars & conferences; special projects; individual paintings & original objects of art lent to Ontario Government Ministries & corporations; originate traveling exhibs; offers on-line course "Perfect Portfolio" a learning course in professional portfolio development

A **WOMEN'S ART ASSOCIATION OF CANADA,** Dignam Gallery, 23 Prince Arthur Ave, Toronto, ON M5R 1B2 Canada. Tel 416-922-2060; Elec Mail waac@womensartofcanada.ca; Internet Home Page Address: www.womensartofcanada.ca; *Pres* Dale Butterill; *VP* Valentina Deek; *Accnt* Marina Bushuev; *Office Admin* Cal Lorimer
Open to pub for scheduled exhibitions & lectures; Estab 1886 to encourage women in the arts; branches in Toronto, Hamilton, St Thomas & Peterborough; Victorian House Gallery & Studios; Average Annual Attendance: 5,000+; Mem: 180; dues $250, qualifications: interest in the arts, nominated & seconded by members; annual meeting in Apr
Income: Donations
Library Holdings: Book Volumes; Clipping Files; DVDs; Framed Reproductions; Manuscripts; Memorabilia; Original Art Works; Original Documents; Other Holdings; Photographs; Prints; Reproductions; Sculpture; Video Tapes
Collections: Canadian Art Collection
Exhibitions: Throughout yr
Activities: Classes for adults; lects open to pub, 25+ vis lectrs per yr; concerts; gallery talks; tours; competitions with awards; schols given to Ontario College of Art, Royal Conservatory of Music, Nat Ballet School, Univ of Toronto Faculty of Music, Unwers Hy of Toronto, George Brown Theatre School; Sheridan Art & Design; individual paintings & original objects of art lent

L **Library,** 23 Prince Arthur Ave, Toronto, ON M5R 1B2 Canada. Tel 416-922-2060; Fax 416-922-4657; *Librn* Isabelle Johnson
Open during exhibs & lects only; Circ Non-circulating
Library Holdings: Book Volumes 1000

M **WYNICK TUCK GALLERY,** 401 Richmond St W, Ste 128, Ground Flr Toronto, ON M5V 3A8 Canada. Tel 416-504-8716; Fax 416-504-8699; Elec Mail wtg@wynicktuckgallery.on.ca; Internet Home Page Address: www.wynicktuckgallery.ca; *Co-Dir* David Tuck; *Asst Dir* Gina Facchini; *Co-Dir* Lynne Wynick
Open Tues - Sat 11 AM - 5 PM, cl Sun & Mon; No admis fee; Estab 1968 to represent contemporary Canadian artists as well as some international artists featuring paintings, sculptures, works on paper & photos; 4000 sq ft
Income: Financed by pvt funding
Exhibitions: Exhibitions rotate monthly
Activities: Sales shop sells original art

M **YORK UNIVERSITY,** Glendon Gallery, Glendon Hall, Glendon Col, York Univ, 2275 Bayview Ave Toronto, ON M4N 3M6 Canada. Tel 416-487-6721; Fax 416-487-6779; Elec Mail gallery@glendon.yorku.ca; Internet Home Page Address: www.glendon.yorku.ca/gallery; *Dir* Martine Rheault; *Cur* Marc Audette; *Mktg & Promotions* Christina Breger
Open Tues - Fri Noon-3 PM, Sat 1-4 PM; No admis fee; Estab 1977, focus on contemporary visual arts; 107.2 ft of running wall space, dark hardwood flooring,

natural sunlight & halogen track lighting; ground floor of Glendon Hall; Average Annual Attendance: 2,000
Income: $141,868 (financed by mem, York University & granting agencies)
Publications: Bilingual exhibition catalogue
Activities: Classes for children; lects open to pub, 5 vis lectrs per yr; concerts; gallery talks; tours; book traveling exhibs

M **YORK UNIVERSITY,** Art Gallery of York University, 4700 Keele St, Ross Bldg N145 Toronto, ON M3J 1P3 Canada; 4700 Keele St, Accolade East Bldg Toronto, ON M3J 1P3 Canada. Tel 416-736-5169; Fax 416-736-5985; Elec Mail agyu@yorku.ca; Internet Home Page Address: www.yorku.ca/agyu; *Dir & Cur* Philip Monk; *Asst Dir & Cur* Emelie Chhangur; *Asst Cur* Michael Maranda; *Coll & Educ Asst* Allyson Adley; *Admin Asst* Karen Pellegrino
Open Mon - Fri 10 AM - 4 PM, Wed 10 AM - 8 PM, Sun noon - 5 PM, cl July & Aug; Admis donations welcomed; Estab 1970 to maintain a program of exhibitions covering a broad spectrum of the contemporary visual arts; Gallery is 3600 sq ft, exhibition space 2800 sq ft, including program space & support space 750 sq ft; Average Annual Attendance: 15,000
Income: Financed by university, federal, provincial & municipal grants & private donations
Special Subjects: Painting-American, Sculpture, Eskimo Art, Painting-Canadian
Collections: Approx 750 works including ethnographical items & artifacts, approx 550 of the works are by Canadian artists. Current emphasis & expansion of outdoor sculpture coll
Publications: Exhibit catalogs
Activities: Lects open to pub, 3-4 vis lectrs per yr; gallery talks; tours; sponsoring of competitions; Critical Writing award; individual paintings & original objects of art lent for major shows or retrospectives to other members of the University & faculty for their offices; book traveling exhibs; originate traveling exhibs; mus shop sells books

L **Fine Arts Phase II Slide Library,** 4700 Keele St, Rm 274, North York, ON M3J 1P3 Canada. Tel 416-736-5534; Fax 416-736-5447; Internet Home Page Address: www.library.yorku.ca; *Cur* M Metraux; *Slide Librn* Marie Holubec; *Slide Librn* Lillian Heinson; *Subject Librn* Mary Kandiuk
Open 8 AM - 4:30 PM daily; cl weekends; Estab for reference only, students & faculty; Circ Slides circulate for staff & faculty
Income: Financed through university
Library Holdings: Periodical Subscriptions; Slides 250,000

M **YYZ ARTISTS' OUTLET,** 401 Richmond St W, No 140, Toronto, ON M5V 3A8 Canada. Tel 416-598-4546; Elec Mail yyz@interlog.com; Internet Home Page Address: www.interlog.com/~yyz; *Co-Dir* Dionne McAffee; *Co-Dir* Lisa Deanne Smith
Open Tues-Sat 11 AM - 5 PM; No admis fee; Estab 1979; Exhibs and pubs books on contemporary art; Average Annual Attendance: 3,000
Library Holdings: Exhibition Catalogs; Memorabilia; Original Documents; Pamphlets
Collections: Contemporary Art
Activities: Lects open to public, 5 vis lectrs per year; sales shop sells books, magazines, original art, multiples

WATERLOO

M **CANADIAN CLAY AND GLASS GALLERY,** 25 Caroline St N, Waterloo, ON N2L 2Y5 Canada. Tel 519-746-1882; Fax 519-746-6396; Elec Mail info@canadianclayandglass.ca; Internet Home Page Address: www.canadianclayandglass.ca; *Dir* Bill Poole; *Cur* Christian Bernard Singer; *Bookkeeper* Charmayne Greig; *Pub Rels* William Hlowatzki; *Retail Mgr* Emily Jull; *Dir Educator* Sheila McMath
Open Tues - Sat 11 AM- 6 PM, Sun 1-5 PM, cl Mon; No admis fee; Estab 1993; 4 galleries; Average Annual Attendance: 25,000; Mem: 450; dues family dual $45, adults, $35, artist, seniors, students (18+) $25
Income: Grants retail sales, donations, facility rental, fundraising, education progs, admis, exhibs, mems
Library Holdings: Audio Tapes; Book Volumes; CD-ROMs; Clipping Files; Compact Disks; DVDs; Exhibition Catalogs; Kodachrome Transparencies; Original Art Works; Original Documents; Other Holdings; Pamphlets; Periodical Subscriptions; Photographs; Prints; Records; Sculpture; Slides; Video Tapes
Special Subjects: Decorative Arts, Drawings, Etchings & Engravings, Historical Material, Architecture, Conceptual Art, Flasks & Bottles, Porcelain, Pottery, Sculpture, Bronzes, Ceramics, Crafts, Folk Art, Collages, Eskimo Art, Glass, Asian Art, Baroque Art, Dioramas, Stained Glass, Enamels
Collections: Contemporary Canadian & International clay, glass, stained glass & enamel. Holdings include: Paul Stankard, John Khun, William Morris, Marilyn Levine, Joe Fafard, Ruth McKinley, Richard Gomez. Paperweights by Bacarat, Banford, Clichy, St Louis, Whitefriars, Ysart, Heilman, Perthshire & Trabucco, Carl Beam, Julie Oakes, Tim Whiten, Aganetha Dyck
Exhibitions: Rotating every three months, presenting contemporary clay & glass, Artist include: Mary Anne Barkhouse, Christian Bernard Singer, Sarah Saunders, Ruth Chambers, Maurice Savoie, Judy Chicago, Donald Maynard, Yuichiro Komatsu, Julie Oakes, Bruce Taylor, Alfred Engerer, Andre Fournelle, Sadashi Inuzuka, Joan Brigham, Ann Roberts
Publications: Aspects & Excess: Shary Boyle; Boreal Baroque: Mary Anne Barkhouse; Ceramic Work from Rankin Inlet: Roger Aksadjuak, Pierre Aupilardjuk, John Kurok, Yvo Samguhak, Lucy Sanertanut, Jack Nuviak & Leo Napayok; Chicago in Glass: Judy Chicago; It's All Relative: Carl Beam, Ann Beam & Anong Migwans Beam; Ornamenta: Lyndal Osborne; Broken but Still Standing, Louise Pentz; Lucid Dreaming, Bruce Taylor; Glass Factor: Luminaries in the Canadian Art Glass Scene; Swounds: Julie Oakes
Activities: Classes & tours for adults, youth & children; art talks; docent training; play with clay Sundays; lects open to pub, 1 vis lectrs per yr; gallery talks; tours; sponsoring of competitions; Winifred Shantz award for ceramists; Royal Bank Canada (RBC), Award for Glass; fels available; lending of original objects of art to Canadian pub galleries & mus; book traveling exhibs, never more than 1; organize traveling exhibs to other Canadian pub galleries & mus; mus shop sells books, original art, & other decorative ceramic & glass art objects

M **UNIVERSITY OF WATERLOO,** University of Waterloo Art Gallery, 200 University Ave W, Waterloo, ON N2L 3G1 Canada. Tel 519-888-4567, Ext 36741; Fax 519-746-4982; Elec Mail ijurakic@uwaterloo.ca; Internet Home Page Address: uwag.uwaterloo.ca; *Dir & Cur* Ivan Jurakic
Open Sep - June Tues - Sat noon - 5 PM; cl July & Aug; No admis fee; Estab 1962; 4,000 sq ft, 350 running ft, concrete floors, drywall, 18 ft ceilings; Average Annual Attendance: 5,000; Mem: Alumni
Income: Financed by university & arts council grants from Canada; corporate sponsorship
Collections: Contemporary Canadian Art
Exhibitions: Changing temporary exhibits, 6-10 per yr
Publications: Exhibit catalogues
Activities: Lect open to public; in-gallery visitor-directed learning opportunities; gallery talks; tours; workshops; 3-4 vis lectrs per yr; exten dept serves Canada and U.S.; lending collections contains original objects of art; 1-2 book traveling exhibs per yr; originates traveling exhibs to Canadian galleries

L **Dana Porter Library,** 200 University Ave W, Waterloo, ON N2L 3G1 Canada. Tel 519-885-1211, Ext 5763; Fax 519-888-4320; Internet Home Page Address: www.uwaterloo.ca; Telex 069-5259; *Spec Coll Librn* Susan Bellingham; *Reference & Coll Develop Librn - Fine Arts & Archit* Michele Sawchuk; *Univ Librn* Murray Shepherd
Open Mon - Fri 9 AM - noon & 1 - 4 PM; Estab 1958 to provide access to information appropriate to the needs of the acad community
Library Holdings: Book Volumes 26,770; Clipping Files; Exhibition Catalogs; Fiche; Periodical Subscriptions 160; Records; Reels
Special Subjects: Etchings & Engravings, Printmaking
Collections: The Dance Collection (monographs, periodicals & pamphlets from 1535 to date relating to the history of dance-ballet); B R Davis Southey Collection; Euclid's Elements & History of Mathematics; Eric Gill Collection; Lady Aberdeen Library of Women; George Santayana Collection; Private Press Collection; Rosa Breithaupt Clark Architectural History Collection
Publications: Library publishes four bibliographic series: Bibliography, Technical Paper, Titles & How To
Activities: Undergraduate curriculum in architecture, art history & studio

M **WILFRID LAURIER UNIVERSITY,** Robert Langen Art Gallery, 75 University Ave W, Waterloo, ON N2L 3C5 Canada. Tel 519-884-0710, Ext 3801; Fax 519-886-9721; Elec Mail sluke@wlu.ca; *Pres* Dr Robert Rosehart; *Cur & Mgr* Suzanne Luke
Open Sep - Apr, Wed - Sat 12 PM - 5 PM; No admis fee; Estab 1969 to exhibit for the students, staff & faculty; The gallery has its own space in the John Aird Building & has 18 x 50 ft rectangular space incl various modular mounts; Average Annual Attendance: 50,000
Income: Financed by the university
Purchases: $16,000
Special Subjects: Drawings, Painting-American, Photography, Prints, Sculpture, Watercolors, Textiles, Woodcarvings, Woodcuts, Etchings & Engravings, Landscapes, Painting-European, Portraits, Eskimo Art, Painting-Canadian, Oriental Art, Marine Painting, Metalwork, Painting-British, Historical Material, Restorations, Tapestries
Collections: 2000 pieces of original art works & prints
Exhibitions: Student, staff & faculty show; the gallery mounts 10 exhibitions each year, mostly shows by artists in local area
Publications: Buried Treasure (75th Anniversary of WLU 1986)
Activities: Classes for adults; docent training; lects open to pub, 1-5 vis lectrs per yr; gallery talks; competitions; individual paintings & original works of art lent to campus offices & public areas; originate traveling exhibs

WINDSOR

M **ART GALLERY OF WINDSOR,** 401 Riverside Dr W, Windsor, ON N9A 7J1 Canada. Tel 519-977-0013; Fax 519-977-0776; Internet Home Page Address: www.agw.ca; *Dir* Catherine Mastin; *Information Coordr* Otto Buj; *Cur* Srimoyee Mitra
Open Wed - Sun 11 AM - 5 PM; cl Mon & Tues; No admis fee; Estab 1943 for collection & exhibition of works of art, primarily Canadian, for the study & enjoyment of the Windsor-Detroit area; Average Annual Attendance: 50,000; Mem: Gallery family $90, friend $65; seniors & students $30; annual meeting in March
Income: $1,300,000 (financed by mem, city appropriation & federal & provincial grants)
Collections: Primarily Canadian drawings, paintings, prints & sculpture 18th century to present; Inuit prints & sculpture; non-Canadian paintings & sculpture
Exhibitions: Approx 20 exhibitions a year, besides installation of permanent collection, of mostly Canadian historic & contemporary art works, paintings & graphics
Publications: Quarterly bulletin & catalogues for exhibitions organized by this gallery, 4 times a year
Activities: Docent training; educ prog; classes for adults & children; lects open to pub, 20 vis lectrs per yr; gallery talks; tours; book traveling exhibs approx 20 per yr; originate traveling exhibs; Education Gallery

L **Reference Library,** 401 Riverside Dr West, Windsor, ON N9 A 7J1 Canada. Tel 519-977-0013; Fax 519-977-0776; Elec Mail agw@mnsi.net; Internet Home Page Address: www.artgalleryofwindsor.com; *Librn* Janine Butler
Open Mon-Fri 9 AM - 5 PM; Estab 1966; Circ Non-circulating; Reference for staff, members & public
Income: Financed by mem
Library Holdings: Book Volumes 2500; Clipping Files; Exhibition Catalogs; Other Holdings Catalogs & museum bulletins; Pamphlets; Periodical Subscriptions 30; Video Tapes

WOODSTOCK

M **CITY OF WOODSTOCK,** Woodstock Art Gallery, 449 Dundas St, Woodstock, ON N4S 1C2 Canada; PO Box 1539, Woodstock, ON N4S 0A7 Canada. Tel 519-539-2382 ext 2801; Fax 519-539-2564; Elec Mail gallery@city.woodstock.on.ca; Internet Home Page Address: www.woodstock.on.ca; *Acting Cur* Patricia Deadman; *Educ Officer* Stephanie Porter; *Registrar* Roberta Grosland
Open Tues - Fri 11 AM - 5 PM, Sat 10 AM - 5 PM; No admis fee; Estab 1967 as

a community art gallery; Moved into neo-Georgian building (c1913) in 1983. Four gallery spaces: Carlyle Gallery (313 sq ft); Verne T Ross Gallery (464 sq ft); Nancy Rowell Jackman Gallery (323) sq ft); East Gallery (1303.75 sq ft); Average Annual Attendance: 18,500; Mem: 400; dues, life member $300, corporate $50, family $30, individual $20, senior citizen, $15, children $10
Income: Financed by City of Woodstock, Ministry of Citizenship & Culture, Ontario Arts Council, mem & donations
Collections: 290 works coll of Canadian Art, concentrating on Florence Carlyle contemporary Canadian regional artists
Publications: Newsletter 4 times per year; educational handouts on current exhibitions; monthly bulletin
Activities: Educ prog, classes for adults & children; dramatic progs, open studio evenings (family), junior cur group, teen film group; lects open to pub, 6-7 vis lectrs per yr; concerts; gallery talks; tours; competitions with awards; schols offered; art rental paintings are leased to residents of Oxford County & bus firms; lending collection contains paintings; lending of original objects of art to other galleries upon request & completion of stand facilities report; originate traveling exhibs to circulate southwestern Ontario & Toronto vicinities; gift shop sells cards, wrapping & writing paper, pottery, jewelry, weaving

PRINCE EDWARD ISLAND

CHARLOTTETOWN

M CONFEDERATION CENTRE ART GALLERY AND MUSEUM, 145 Richmond St, Charlottetown, PE C1A 1J1 Canada. Tel 902-628-6142; Fax 902-566-4648; Elec Mail artgallery@confederationcentre.com; Internet Home Page Address: www.confederationcentre.com/artgallery; *CEO* Jessie Inman; *Art Gallery Dir & Cur Hist Art* Kevin Rice; *Cur Contemp Art* Pan Wendt; *Preparator* Ben Kinder; *Registrar* Sandi Hartling; *CFO* Jodi Zver; *COO* Mike Cochrane; *Dir Mktg* Penny Walsh
Open Oct 13 - May 9: Tues - Sat 11 AM - 5 PM, Sun 1 PM - 5 PM, May 10 - Oct 12: daily 9 AM - 5 PM; Admis donation; Estab 1964 as a nat coll devoted to Canadian art & fine crafts; Average Annual Attendance: 90,000; Mem: 200; group $20, family $5, individual $3
Income: Financed by federal, provincial, city & private sector
Special Subjects: Decorative Arts, Drawings, Prints, Crafts, Painting-Canadian
Collections: 19th & 20th century Canadian paintings, drawings & decorative arts; paintings & drawings by Robert Harris
Exhibitions: Twenty-five exhibitions
Activities: Classes for adults & children, 6 vis lectr per year; gallery talks; tours; concerts; lects open to pub; tours; concerts; originate traveling exhibs; junior mus
L Library, 145 Richmond St, Charlottetown, PE C1A 1J1 Canada. Tel 902-368-4642; Fax 902-368-4652; Internet Home Page Address: www.library.pe.ca Open Tues-Thurs 10 AM - 9 PM, Fri & Sat 10 AM - 5 PM, Sun 1 - 5 PM, cl Mon; Open for reference
Library Holdings: Audio Tapes 30; Book Volumes 3500; Filmstrips 60; Periodical Subscriptions 35; Photographs; Slides 5000; Video Tapes

A PRINCE EDWARD ISLAND MUSEUM & HERITAGE FOUNDATION, 2 Kent St, Charlottetown, PE C1A 1M6 Canada. Tel 902-368-6600; Fax 902-368-6608; Elec Mail mhpei@gov.pe.ca; Internet Home Page Address: www.peimuseum.com; *Exec Dir* Dr David Keenlyside; *Cur Colls* Linda Berko; *Cur History* Boyde Beck
Open June - Sep at four of seven sites; call for hours after Aug; Admis charged; Estab 1970 for the human & natural history of Prince Edward Island; Seven sites, 3 open yr round; Average Annual Attendance: 120,000; Mem: 500, dues family $40, individual $25
Income: Financed by mem, provincial & federal appropriations
Special Subjects: Costumes, Embroidery, Etchings & Engravings, Historical Material, Decorative Arts, Crafts, Dolls, Furniture, Glass, Period Rooms, Maps, Carpets & Rugs, Coins & Medals
Collections: Provincial coll, 90,000 artifacts
Exhibitions: Rotate 4-5 exhibits per yr
Publications: The Island Magazine, semi-annual
Activities: Lects open to pub; gallery talks; awards: Pet Heritage Awards every Feb; mus shop sells books, magazines, original art, reproductions, prints & other gift items

QUEBEC

DORVAL

A DORVAL CULTURAL CENTRE, 1401 Lakeshore Dr, Dorval, PQ H9S 2E5 Canada. Tel 514-633-4180; Fax 514-633-4177; Internet Home Page Address: www.city.dorval.qc.ca
Open Mon - Thurs 2 - 5 PM & 7 - 9 PM, Fri, Sat & Sun 2 - 5 PM; No admis fee; Estab 1967 to promote culture and art; Maintains an art gallery
Income: Financed by city appropriation
Publications: Calendar, biannually
Activities: Classes for adults and children; dramatic progs; lects open to pub; gallery talks; tours; concerts

GATINEAU

M CANADIAN MUSEUM OF CIVILIZATION, 100 Laurier St, Gatineau, PQ K1A 0M8 Canada. Tel 819-776-7000; Fax 819-776-8300; Elec Mail web@civilization.ca; Internet Home Page Address: www.civilization.ca; *Pres & CEO* Dr Victor Rabinovitch; *Chief Operating Officer* David Loye; *VPres Exhib & Programs* Jean-Marc Blais; *Dir Gen Canadian War Mus* Mark O'Neill; *Chief Financial Officer* Gordon Butler; *VPres Research & Coll* Moira McCaffrey; *VPres Pub Affairs & Publishing* Chantel Schryer; *Dir Spec Projects* Michel Cheff; *VPres Human Resources* Elizabeth Goger
Open May 1 - June 30 & Sep 2 - Oct 13 daily 9 AM - 6 PM, Thurs 9 AM - 9 PM; July 1 - Sept 1 daily 9 AM; Oct 14 - Apr 30 Tues - Fri 9 AM - 5 PM, Thurs 9 AM - 8 PM; Sat & Sun 9:30 AM - 5 PM; cl Mon; Admis family $25, adults $10, seniors & students $8, children (3 - 12) $6; Estab 1856 to promote the advancement of historical & intercultural understanding & make known the cultural legacy with special, but not exclusive, reference to Canada; The Canadian Mus of Civilization was formerly known as the National Mus of Man. It is located on a 24-acre site in Gatineau, Quebec, on the Ottawa River, directly opposite Parliament Hill. The building has 1,076,430 sq ft & designed in two distinct structures: the mus bldg, the pub exhibition wing with over 177,611 sq ft of display space children's mus; Imax 295 seat theatre & the curatorial bldg, housing the collections (3 million artifacts), plus conservation labs & admin. Canadian War Mus is part of corp mus; Average Annual Attendance: 1,300,000; Mem: 4,500 mems; one-year DUO adult $85, one-year DUO family $99
Income: The mus generates $12,000,000 a yr & receives over $50,000,000 a yr from the federal government
Library Holdings: Audio Tapes; Book Volumes 70,000; CD-ROMs; Cards; Cassettes; Compact Disks; DVDs; Exhibition Catalogs; Fiche; Filmstrips; Manuscripts; Maps; Memorabilia; Micro Print; Motion Pictures; Original Art Works; Original Documents; Photographs; Prints; Records; Reels; Sculpture; Slides; Video Tapes
Special Subjects: Anthropology, Drawings, Etchings & Engravings, Folk Art, Historical Material, Landscapes, Marine Painting, Ceramics, Collages, Metalwork, Flasks & Bottles, Gold, Porcelain, Portraits, Prints, Period Rooms, Textiles, Sculpture, Tapestries, Graphics, Photography, Watercolors, Bronzes, Archaeology, Ethnology, Costumes, Religious Art, Folk Art, Pottery, Primitive art, Woodcarvings, Woodcuts, Decorative Arts, Manuscripts, Posters, Eskimo Art, Painting-Canadian, Dolls, Furniture, Glass, Jewelry, Silver, Carpets & Rugs, Historical Material, Ivory, Maps, Juvenile Art, Coins & Medals, Restorations, Calligraphy, Dioramas, Embroidery, Laces, Mosaics, Stained Glass, Pewter, Leather, Military Art, Reproductions, Enamels, Bookplates & Bindings
Collections: Archaeological Collection; Ethnographic Collection; Folk Culture Collections; Historical Collection; Military History Collection; Canadian Children's Mus Coll; Canadian Postal Mus Coll
Exhibitions: Permanent exhibitions: Grand Hall, First Peoples Hall; Face to Face: The Canadian Personalities Hall; Canada History Hall, The Canadian Experience Galleries at the War Mus; Approximately 14 temporary exhibs ann
Publications: Several series of publications & periodicals, 102 titles published in-house in last six years
Activities: Classes for adults & children; dramatic progs; docent training; lects open to pub, several vis lectrs per yr; concerts; gallery talks; tours; sponsoring of competitions; exten dept; original artifacts lent to mus & other institutions meeting specifications regarding security, environment, etc in Canadian Museums; awards, the William E Taylor Research Award Fund; 10 book traveling exhibs per yr; originate traveling exhibs to Mus across Canada & internationally; the boutiques stock a vast range of gift & educational articles; Kidshoppe; Bookstore/Collector's shop offers selection of books & fine crafts including folk art pieces & Native artwork; Canadian Children's Museum 100 Laurier St, PO Box 3100, Sta B Gatineau, QC J8X 4H2 Canada

M GALERIE MONTCALM, 25 Laurier St, PO Box 1970, Stn Hull Gatineau, PQ J8X 3Y9 Canada. Tel 819-595-7488; Fax 819-595-7492; Elec Mail galeriemontcalm1@gatineau.ca; Internet Home Page Address: www.gatineau.ca/galeriemontcalm; *Dir* Dominique Laurent; *Coordr Permanent Coll* Valerie Camden
Open Mon-Fri 9AM-4PM, Thurs 9AM-8PM, Sun Noon-5PM, cl Sat; No admis fee; Estab 1980, to present the art of local artists & national exhibitions, multi-disciplinary; One gallery, 2505 sq ft; Average Annual Attendance: 8,000
Income: $145,500 (financed by City of Gatineau)
Library Holdings: Book Volumes; Cards; Exhibition Catalogs; Original Art Works; Pamphlets; Reproductions; Sculpture
Special Subjects: Decorative Arts, Drawings, Landscapes, Collages, Porcelain, Pottery, Painting-American, Prints, Textiles, Bronzes, Woodcuts, Painting-French, Painting-Japanese, Sculpture, Graphics, Latin American Art, Watercolors, Crafts, Primitive art, Woodcarvings, Portraits, Posters, Painting-Canadian, Metalwork, Miniatures, Painting-Polish, Cartoons, Painting-Scandinavian
Collections: City of Gatineau (permanent coll); heritage artifacts; paintings; photographs; prints; sculpture; public art
Publications: Exhibition catalogs
Activities: Classes for children; workshops; lects open to pub, 1560 vis lectrs per yr; concerts; gallery talks; tours of the permanent coll; competitions with awards; retail store sells books, prints, original art

JOLIETTE

M MUSEE D'ART DE JOLIETTE, 145 rue Pere-Wilfrid-Corbeil, Joliette, PQ J6E 4T4 Canada. Tel 450-756-0311; Fax 450-756-6511; Elec Mail info@museejoliette.org; Internet Home Page Address: www.museejoliette.org; *Exec Dir* Gaetane Verna; *Cur Contemporary Art* Marie-Claude Landry; *Cur Educ* Annick Deblois; *Registrar* Marie-Helene Foisy; *Head Visitor Svcs* Danielle Chevalier
Open Tues - Sun noon - 5 PM; Admis adults $10, sr citizens & students $8, children $6; Estab 1967 for educational purposes; preservation of the collections; save local patrimony; Circ 75,000; 5 rooms of temporary exhibitions; permanent exhib room: fourteen century to present; Average Annual Attendance: 14,000; Mem: 600; dues family $80, individual $50; annual meeting in Sep
Income: $980,000 (financed by government grants & pvt funds), $256,000 (revenues)
Library Holdings: Book Volumes; Exhibition Catalogs; Kodachrome Transparencies; Photographs; Slides
Special Subjects: Pre-Columbian Art, Religious Art, Painting-European
Collections: Canadian art; European art; sacred art of Quebec; painting & sculpture
Exhibitions: 12 exhibitions per year
Publications: Catalog & pamphlet entitled Le Musee d'art de Joliette; catalogs of temporary exhibits
Activities: Classes for adults & children; docent training; educ program; lects open to pub, 6 vis lectrs per yr; concerts; gallery talks; tours; films; book traveling

exhibs, 2 per yr; originate traveling exhibs 2 per yr to museums & libraries; sales shop sells books, magazines, original art, postcards, reproductions & prints

JONQUIERE

M INSTITUT DES ARTS AU SAGUENAY, Centre National D'Exposition a Jonquiere, 4160 du Vieux Pont (Mont Jacob), CP 605, Ville de Saguenay Jonquiere, PQ G7X 7W4 Canada. Tel 418-546-2177; Fax 418-546-2180; Elec Mail info@centrenationalexposition.com; Internet Home Page Address: www.centrenationalexposition.com; *Pres* Lionel Brassard; *VPres* Therese Ouellet; *Treas* Sylvie Bergeron; *Secy* Claire Simard; *Dir* Manon Guerin
Open Sep - June, Mon - Fri 9 AM - 5 PM, Sat - Sun 10 AM - 6 PM; July - Aug, 10 AM - 6 PM; No admis fee; Estab 1979 as an art exposition; 3 galleries; Average Annual Attendance: 20,000; Mem: 150; open to all interested in Au Milieu Des Arts; dues $25; annual meeting in June
Income: $350,000 (financed by endowment, mem, city & state appropriation)
Activities: Classes for adults & children; gallery talks; tours; fellowships offered; book traveling exhibitions 3-4 per year

KAHNAWAKE

M KATERI TEKAKWITHA SHRINE/ST. FRANCIS XAVIER MISSION, PO Box 70, Mission St.Francis Xavier Kahnawake, PQ J0L 1B0 Canada. Tel 450-638-1546; Tel 450-638-6030; Fax 450-632-6031; Elec Mail kateritekakwithasanctuary@yahoo.ca; Elec Mail katericausecenter@gmail.com; Internet Home Page Address: www.kateritekakwitha.net; Internet Home Page Address: www.katericenter.com; *Pastor* Fr Raymond Vincent Esprit FMI; *Deacon* Ron Boyer
Open Mon - Fri 9 AM - 4 PM; weekends: please call; No admis fee; Estab as a mission in 1667; Large mission & fort with tomb of Kateri Tekakwitha, museum & gift shop; Average Annual Attendance: 5,000
Income: Financed by donations
Special Subjects: American Indian Art, Period Rooms, Painting-French, Religious Art
Collections: Archives, French & Canadian church silver, historic church, rectory & fort, old paintings, religious artifacts; Shrine of Saint Kateri Tekakwitha, Mohawk woman on threshold of becoming a saint, relics are in tomb in church, old known painting of Kateri (1690)
Publications: Kateri, quarterly
Activities: Concerts; tours; individual paintings & original objects of art lent; containing Kodachromes & sculptures; originate traveling exhibs; sales shop sells books, reproductions, religious & Kateri Tekakwitha articles & relic medals

MONTREAL

L ARTEXTE INFORMATION CENTRE, (Artexte Information & Documentation Centre) Documentation Centre, 460 Sainte Catherine West, Rm 508, Montreal, PQ H3B 1A7 Canada. Tel 514-874-0049; Elec Mail info@artexte.ca; Internet Home Page Address: www.artexte.ca; *Dir* Francois Dion; *Information Specialist* Felicity Tayler; *Information Specialist* John Latour; *Pres* Louise Dery
Open Wed - Sat 10:30 AM - 5:30 PM, cl Sun & Mon; No admis fee; Institution estab 1980, libr estab 1982; Documentation of contemporary visual arts, from 1965 - present with particular emphasis on Canadian art, consultation only; Average Annual Attendance: 1,500
Income: $350,000 (financed by city & state grants, donations)
Purchases: $15,500
Library Holdings: Book Volumes 2000; CD-ROMs; Cassettes; Clipping Files 8700; Compact Disks; DVDs; Exhibition Catalogs 10,500; Memorabilia; Pamphlets; Periodical Subscriptions 100; Photographs; Slides; Video Tapes
Publications: Artextes editions; Artexte info

A ASSOCIATION PROFESSIONNELLE DES DESIGNERS D'INTERIEUR DU QUEBEC, 465 Saint-Jean, Ste 101 Montreal, PQ H2Y 2R6 Canada. Tel 514-284-6263; Elec Mail info@apdiq.com; Internet Home Page Address: www.apdiq.com; *Pres* Andre Lapointe
Not open to Pub; Estab 2003 as a nonprofit professional assn; Mem: 500 (approx)
Exhibitions: Traveling exhibitions in the Province of Quebec
Publications: Journal magazine, monthly; News Bulletin, 5 issues per year
Activities: Educ Comt to improve the level of teaching in interior design; lects for mems only, 5-8 vis lectrs per yr; book traveling exhibs

ASTED INC
For further information, see National and Regional Organizations

L CANADIAN CENTRE FOR ARCHITECTURE, Library, 1920 Baile St, Montreal, PQ H3H 2S6 Canada. Tel 514-939-7000; Fax 514-939-7020; Elec Mail ref@cca.qc.ca; Internet Home Page Address: www.cca.qc.ca; *Founding Dir* Phyllis Lambert; *Dir* Mirko Zardini; *Assoc Dir Coll* Martien de Vletter
Open by appointment Mon - Fri 11 AM - 5 PM; Estab 1979; Circ 15,000 vols per yr; Estab 1979; on-site & remote research; library catalog available via website; surrogates provided when possible
Library Holdings: Auction Catalogs; Audio Tapes; Book Volumes 200,400; CD-ROMs; Cards; Cassettes; Clipping Files; Compact Disks; DVDs; Exhibition Catalogs; Fiche; Filmstrips; Manuscripts; Maps; Memorabilia; Motion Pictures; Original Documents; Other Holdings 3-D Artifacts including architectural toys; Pamphlets; Periodical Subscriptions 700; Photographs; Prints; Records; Reels; Reproductions; Slides; Video Tapes
Special Subjects: Landscape Architecture, Decorative Arts, Photography, Stage Design, Archaeology, Industrial Design, Interior Design, Furniture, Architecture
Collections: 200,000 printed vols
Activities: Educ prog; lects open to pub; gallery talks; tours; sponsored competitions; fel offered; mus shop sells books

M CHATEAU RAMEZAY MUSEUM, 280 rue Notre-Dame Est, Montreal, PQ H2Y 1C5 Canada. Tel 514-861-3708; Fax 514-861-8317; Elec Mail info@chateauramezay.qc.ca; *Exec Dir & Cur* Andre Delisle; *Archivist & Exhib Coordr* Christine Brisson; *Educ & Commun Coordr* Marie-Helene Vendette
Open Jun 1 - Nov 27 10 AM - 6 PM, Nov 28 - May 31 Tues - Sun 10 AM - 4:30 PM; Admis families $18, adults $9 seniors $7, students $6, children (5-17) $4.50, 4 and under free; Estab 1895 in residence of Claude de Ramezay (1705), governor of Montreal; Average Annual Attendance: 60,000; Mem: 200; dues life $1000, individual $40
Special Subjects: Period Rooms
Collections: Canadian drawings, furniture, paintings, prints & sculptures; 18th, 19th & 20th century colls; Indian colls; Period Rooms to Victorian Era
Activities: Classes for children; docent training; lects open to pub & some for mems only, 6 vis lects per yr; gallery talks; tours; sales shop sells books, reproductions, prints & slides

L Library, 280 Notre-Dame E, Montreal, PQ H2Y 1C5 Canada. Tel 514-861-7182; Fax 514-861-8317; Internet Home Page Address: www.chateauramezay.qc.ca; *Librn* Judith Berlyn
Open by appointment only; Estab for research & reference only; Circ Non-circulating
Library Holdings: Book Volumes 2200; Original Documents

M CONCORDIA UNIVERSITY, Leonard & Bina Ellen Art Gallery, 1400 Blvd de Maisonneuve W, LB-165 Montreal, PQ H3G 1M8 Canada. Tel 514-848-2424 ext 4750; Fax 514-848-4751; Elec Mail ellengal@alcor.concordia.ca; Internet Home Page Address: ellengallery.concordia.ca; *Dir* Michele Theriault; *Max Stern Cur* Melanie Rainville; *Educ & Pub Prog Coordr* Marina Polosa; *Exhib Coordr* Jo-Anne Balcaen; *Tech Supvr* Paul Smith; *Admin Asst* Rosette Elkeslassi; *Commun* Anne-Marie Proulx
Open Tues - Fri 12 PM - 6 PM, Sat 12 PM - 5 PM, cl July, Aug, holidays; No admis fee; Estab 1962 for exhibitions of Canadian art, to provide a venue for a variety of significant touring exhibitions chosen from within the region & across Canada; to display the permanent collection, all with the idea of providing an important cultural arena both for the university & public alike; Five interconnected exhibition spaces with a total 3115.81 sq ft; Average Annual Attendance: 66,000
Income: Financed by university & governmental funds
Purchases: Historic, modern & contemporary Canadian art
Special Subjects: Drawings, Prints, Sculpture, Pre-Columbian Art, Etchings & Engravings, Landscapes, Painting-Canadian
Collections: Modern & Contemporary Canadian Art Collection
Exhibitions: Edge & Image; ChromaZone; John MacGregor: A Survey; The Photographs of Professor Oliver Buell (1844-1910); Goodridge Roberts: The Figure Works; Figure Painting in Montreal 1935-1955; Sickert, Orpen, John & their Contemporaries at the New English Art Club; Robert Bordo: New York + Montreal; Conservation: To Care for Art; Undergraduate Student Exhibition; Recent Acquisitions to the Collection: Selections from the Concordia Collection of Art; Michael Jolliffe: Paintings; Phillip Guston: Prints; John Arthur Fraser: Watercolours; Brian Wood: Drawings & Photographs; Barbara Astman: Floor Pieces; K M Graham: Paintings & Drawings 1971-1984; Robert Flaherty: Photographs; Work by Selected Fine Art Graduates: A 10th Anniversary Celebration; Joyce Wieland: A Decade of Painting; Francois Baillarge (1759-1830): A Portfolio of Acad Drawings; Faculty of Fine Arts Biennial; Murray MacDonald & R Holland Murray: Recent Sculptures; Jean Paul Lemieux: Honoured by the University; The Figurative Tradition In Quebec; Contemporary Works on Paper; Undergraduate Student Exhibition; Selections from the Concordia Collection of Art; Canadian Pacific Poster Art 1881-1955; Shelagh Keeley: Drawings; Bernard Gamoy: Paintings; Harold Klunder: Paintings; Marcel Bovis: Photographs; Neerland Art Quebec: an exhibition by artists of Dutch descent in Quebec; Canada in the Nineteenth Century: The Bert & Barbara Stitt Family Collection; Posters from Nicaragua; Betty Goodwin: Passages; Ron Shuebrook: Recent Work; Louis Muhlstock: New Themes & Variations 1980-1985; John Herbert Caddy 1801-1887: Expressions of Will: The Art of Prudence Heward; Riduan Tomkins: Recent Paintings; Undergraduate Student Exhibition; Selections from the Concordia Collection of Art; Concordia: The Early Years of Loyola & Sir George Williams; Porcelain: Traditions of Excellence; Francois Houde: Glass Work; Shelley Reeves: Relics; Pre-Columbian Art from the Permanent Collection: Josef Albers: Interaction of Color; Brian McNeil: Ironworks; Robert Ayre: The Critic & the Collection; Claude-Philippe Benoit: Interieur, Jour; A Decade of Collecting: A selection of Recent Acquisitions; Contemporary Montreal Sculpture & Installation from the Canada Council Art Bank: A Twentieth Anniversary Celebration; First Impressions: Views of the Natural History of Canada 1550-1850; Local Developments: 20th century Montreal Area Art from the Collection of the Universite de Montreal; Montreal Photo Album: Photographs from Montreal Archives; Joanne Tod: The (Dis) Order of Things; Undergraduate Student Exhibition; Temporal Borders: Image & Site; Faculty Exhibition; Alex Colville: Selected Drawings; Selections from the Permanent Collection; From the Permanent Collection: A Selection of Recent Acquisitions; Chris Cran; Tom Dean; Undergraduate Student Exhibition; Nina M Owens (1869-1959); In Habitable Places
Publications: Exhibition catalogues
Activities: Lects open to public, 3 vis lectrs per yr; originate traveling exhibs

L CONSEIL DES ARTS DU QUEBEC (CATQ), (Conseil des Arts Textiles du Quebec (CATQ))Diagonale, Centre des arts et des fibres du Quebec, 5455 rue de Gaspe, espace 203 Montreal, PQ H2T 3B3 Canada. Tel 514-524-6645; Elec Mail info@artdiagonale.org; Internet Home Page Address: www.artdiagonale.org; *Dir* Stephanie L'Heureux; *Pres* Lyne Girard; *Treas* Heloise Audy; *Secy* Marie-France Cournoyel; *Admin* Nicole Parreton; *Admin* Jessica Belarger
Open Wed - Sat Noon - 5 PM; Estab 1980; Specialized in contemporary fiber art exhibits; Average Annual Attendance: 1,000
Income: $60,000 (financed by endowment & mem)
Purchases: $1100
Library Holdings: Book Volumes 800; Cassettes 10; Other Holdings Artist CV (textile); Periodical Subscriptions 17; Slides 1000; Video Tapes 13
Exhibitions: 4 - 6 exhibits a yr
Publications: Diagonale 01; Diagonale 02

Activities: Artist talks; conferences; artists residencies; Artist exchanges; Quebec Univ programs; originates traveling exhibs to other nonprofit galleries across Canada, Quebec

A **GUILDE CANADIENNE DES METIERS D'ART,** Canadian Guild of Crafts, 1460-B Sherbrooke St W, Montreal, PQ H3G 1K4 Canada. Tel 514-849-6091; Fax 514-849-7351; Elec Mail info@canadianguild.com; Internet Home Page Address: www.guildecanadiennedesmetiersdart.com; Internet Home Page Address: www.canadianguildofcrafts.com; *Mng Dir* Diane Labelle; *Coordr Sales* Diana Perera; *Coordr-Communs* Carole Dussault
Open Tues - Fri 10 AM - 6:00 PM, Sat 10 AM - 5 PM; No admis fee; Estab 1906 to promote, encourage & preserve arts & crafts of Canada; Permanent Collection Gallery of Inuit & First Nations Art; Exhibition Gallery; Average Annual Attendance: 30,000; Mem: 107; dues $30 & up; annual meeting in Mar/Apr
Income: Income from retail sales & donations
Library Holdings: Exhibition Catalogs; Periodical Subscriptions; Prints
Collections: Permanent collection of Inuit & First Nations Arts and Crafts; Audio Video tapes
Exhibitions: Fine craft exhibitions every 5 weeks except Jan & Feb; Inuit & First Nations Art (contemporary) twice a yr
Activities: Educ dept; lects open to public, 6-8 vis lectrs per yr; gallery talks; tours; awards; individual paintings & original objects of art lent to accredited institutions; lending collection includes prints; sales shop sells books, original art, reproductions, prints & Canadian crafts

L **JARDIN BOTANIQUE DE MONTREAL,** Bibliotheque, 4101 Sherbrooke St E, Montreal, PQ H1X 2B2 Canada. Tel 514-872-1824; Fax 514-872-5167; Elec Mail jardin_botanique@ville.montreal.qc.ca; Internet Home Page Address: www2.ville.montreal.qc.ca/jardin; *Botanist & Librn* Celine Arseneault; *Library Tech* Guy Frenette; *Information Specialist* Steluta Ovesia; *Cur Slide Library* Lise Servant
Open Mon - Fri 9 AM - 4:30 PM, Sat 9 AM - noon & 1 PM - 4:30 PM; No admis fee; Estab 1931; For reference; Average Annual Attendance: 10,000
Income: Financed by city & donations
Library Holdings: Book Volumes 30,000; Cassettes 100; DVDs 50; Other Holdings Posters 300; Periodical Subscriptions 495; Photographs; Slides 100,000; Video Tapes 400
Special Subjects: Landscape Architecture, Asian Art
Exhibitions: Rotate exhibitions once per yr

M **LA CENTRALE POWERHOUSE GALLERY,** 4296 Blvd Saint-Laurent, Montreal, PQ H2W 1Z3 Canada. Tel 514-871-0268; Fax 514-871-9830; Elec Mail galerie@lacentrale.org; Internet Home Page Address: www.lacentrale.org; *Programming Asst* Onya Hogan-Finlay; *Programming Coordr* Roxanne Arsenault; *Admin Coordr* Elizabeth A Shea
Open Wed noon - 6 PM, Thurs - Fri noon - 9 PM, Sat - Sun 12 PM - 5 PM; No admis fee; Estab 1973 to promote & broadcast the work of women artists in all domains; Gallery has 1500 sq ft; Average Annual Attendance: 6,000; Mem: 35; dues subscribers $20, active $10; annual meeting in Sep
Income: $120,000 (financed by mem, grants from federal, provincial & city governments, corporate & private donations)
Collections: Women Artists
Exhibitions: 7 exhibitions per year; a mixture of local & other parts of the country, occasionally American
Publications: Exhibit catalogues
Activities: Lects open to pub, 2-3 vis lectrs per yr; concerts; gallery talks; originate traveling exhibs to Canadian Art Centers; sales shop sells catalogues & t-shirts

M **LE MUSEE MARC-AURELE FORTIN,** 118 ru Saint Pierre, Montreal, PQ H2Y 2L7 Canada. Tel 514-906-0230; Fax 514-845-6100; Elec Mail sodart@sodart.org; Internet Home Page Address: www.museemufortinorg.com; *Asst to Dir* Marcelle Trudeau; *Dir* Rene Buisson
Open 11 AM - 5 PM, cl Mon; Admis $5, seniors & students $2, children under 12 free; Estab 1984; Average Annual Attendance: 15,000; Mem: 400; dues individual $30, family $50
Income: $100,000 (financed by endowment, mem & sales of reproductions)
Purchases: $45,000
Exhibitions: Marc-Aurele Fortin; Professional Book-Binding; rotate 2-4 exhibitions per yr
Activities: Lect open to public

M **MAISON SAINT-GABRIEL MUSEUM,** 2146 Dublin Pl, Pointe-Saint-Charles Montreal, PQ H3K 2A2 Canada. Tel 514-935-8136; Fax 514-935-5692; Elec Mail msgrcip@globetrotter.qc.ca; Internet Home Page Address: www.maisonsaint-gabriel.qc.ca; *Gen Mgr* Madeleine Juneau
Open Apr 13 - June 21 & Sep 2 - Dec 19, Tues - Sun 1 PM - 5 PM; June 22 - Sept 2, Tues - Sun 11 AM - 6 PM; Admis families $16, adult $8, seniors $6, students $4, youth $2, under 6 free; Estab 1966
Special Subjects: Sculpture, Crafts, Furniture, Embroidery
Collections: Antique Tools, Embroidery, Paintings & Sculpture; Furniture, Crafts & Upholstery of 18th & 19th centuries located in a 17th century house
Exhibitions: From Root Cellar to Attic; Laces & Embroideries

M **MCCORD MUSEUM OF CANADIAN HISTORY,** 690 Sherbrooke St W, Montreal, PQ H3A 1E9 Canada. Tel 514-398-7100; Fax 514-398-5045; Elec Mail info@mccord.mcgill.ca; Internet Home Page Address: www.mccord-museum.qc.ca; *Cur Costume* Cynthia Cooper; *Dir Develop* Marie-Claude Landry; *Cur Decorative Arts* Conrad Graham; *Cur History & Archives* Francois Cartier; *Exec Dir* Dr Victoria Dickenson; *Dir Coll, Res & Progs* Nicole Vallieres, PhD; *Dir Strategic Initiatives & Corp Secy* Marguerite Stratford; *Cur Notman Photog Archives* Helene Samson; *Cur Material Culture* Guislaine Lemay; *Chief Conservator* Anne MacKay; *Head Coll Mgmt* Christian Vachon; *Head Educ & Prog* Annabelle Laliberte; *Head Exhib* Line Villeneuve; *Dir Mktg* Michel Pelletier; *Dir Opers* Philip Leduc
Open Tues - Fri 10 AM - 6 PM, Sat & Sun 10 AM - 5 PM, Mon, holiday weekends & summer months 10 AM - 5 PM; Admis family $26, adults $13, sr citizens $10, students $7, children 6-12 $5, children under 6 free; Estab 1919 as a museum of Canadian Ethnology & Social History; Average Annual Attendance: 100,000; Mem: 1600
Income: Financed by mems, government & donations
Special Subjects: Drawings, Graphics, Ethnology, Costumes, Ceramics, Folk Art, Etchings & Engravings, Landscapes, Decorative Arts, Manuscripts, Eskimo Art, Painting-Canadian, Dolls, Furniture, Glass, Jewelry, Metalwork, Painting-British, Painting-French, Historical Material, Maps, Miniatures, Embroidery, Laces, Cartoons
Publications: Exhibition catalogs & monographs; guides to collections for children
Activities: Classes for adults & children; docent training; lects open to pub, 2-3 vis lectrs per yr; concerts; gallery talks; tours; competitions; schols offered; individual paintings & original works of art lent to other mus; book traveling exhibs 3 per yr; originate traveling exhibs to other museological institutions in Canada; mus shop sells books, original art, reproductions, prints & giftware

L **MCGILL UNIVERSITY,** Blackader-Lauterman Library of Architecture and Art, 3459 McTavish St, Redpath Library Bldg, 3rd Fl Montreal, PQ H3A 1Y1 Canada. Tel 514-398-4742; Fax 514-398-6695; Elec Mail marilyn.berger@mcgill.ca; Internet Home Page Address: www.mcgill.ca/blackader; *Head Librn* Marilyn Berger
Open winter & summer Mon - Fri 9 AM - 5 PM; Estab 1922 to establish a special collection of architectural material
Library Holdings: Book Volumes 100,00; CD-ROMs 70; DVDs 50; Exhibition Catalogs; Other Holdings Drawings 250,000; Pamphlets; Periodical Subscriptions 317; Photographs 25,000
Collections: Canadian Architecture Collection
Publications: The Libraries of Edward & W S Maxwell in the Collection of the Blacker-Lauterman; Moshe Safdie: Buildings & Projects, 1967-1992; Sources in Iconography: An Annotated Bibliography

M **MONTREAL MUSEUM OF FINE ARTS,** PO Box 3000, Sta H, Montreal, PQ H3G 2T9 Canada. Tel 514-285-1600; Fax 514-844-6042 (pub relations); Elec Mail webmaster@mbamtl.org; Internet Home Page Address: www.mmfa.qc.ca; *Cur Contemporary Art* Stephane Aquin; *Cur Old Master, Prints & Drawings* Hilliard T Goldfarb; *Dir Admin* Paul Lavallee; *Cur Canadian Art* Jacques Des Rochers; *Dir* Guy Cogeval; *Chief Conservator* Natalie Bondil; *Cur Non-Canadian Decorative Arts* Rosalynd Pepall; *Dir Communs* Danielle Champagne
Open Tues & Thurs - Sun 11 AM - 5 PM, Wed 11 AM - 9 PM, cl Mon; Permanent collection, no admis fee; Temporary exhibits; adults $12, students & seniors $6, children 2-12 $3; Estab 1860 as an art assoc for the exhibition of paintings; mus estab 1916; Average Annual Attendance: 275,000; Mem: dues $7-$50; annual meeting in Sep
Income: Financed by endowment, mem & provincial appropriation
Library Holdings: Exhibition Catalogs
Special Subjects: Drawings, American Western Art, Bronzes, African Art, Archaeology, Ceramics, Etchings & Engravings, Decorative Arts, Eskimo Art, Furniture, Glass, Asian Art, Antiquities-Byzantine, Carpets & Rugs, Baroque Art, Embroidery, Antiquities-Oriental, Antiquities-Persian, Antiquities-Egyptian, Antiquities-Greek, Antiquities-Roman, Gold, Antiquities-Etruscan, Enamels, Antiquities-Assyrian
Collections: Collection of African art by Fr Gagnon; Chinese, Near Eastern, Peruvian, Inuit primitive art; European decorative arts; French, Spanish, Dutch, British, Canadian and other schools; Japanese incense boxes; The Parker Lace Collection; Harry T Norton Collection of ancient glass; Lucile Pillow Porcelain Collection; decorative arts, painting, sculpture from 3000 BC to the present; Saidye and Samuel Bronfman Collection of Contemporary Canadian Art
Exhibitions: Rotating exhibitions
Publications: Collage (a calendar of events)
Activities: Classes for adults & children; lects open to pub; mus shop sells books, magazines, original art, reproductions, prints

L **Library,** CP 3000, Succursale H, Montreal, PQ H3G 2T9 Canada. Tel 514-285-1600; Fax 514-285-5655; Elec Mail biblio@mbamtl.org; *Head Librn* Joanne Dery; *Librn Periodicals* Therese Bourgault; *Library Technician* Manon Tremblay
Open as reference svc to researchers only, cl to pub; Estab 1882 for a reference & research centre for art students, specialists & visitors
Library Holdings: Auction Catalogs 65,000; Audio Tapes; Book Volumes 90,000; CD-ROMs; Cassettes; Clipping Files; Compact Disks; DVDs; Exhibition Catalogs; Fiche; Manuscripts; Other Holdings Vertical files 17,069; Pamphlets; Periodical Subscriptions 900; Video Tapes 110
Special Subjects: Art History, Decorative Arts, Drawings, Sculpture, Painting-Canadian
Collections: Canadiana; decorative art

M **MUSEE D'ART CONTEMPORAIN DE MONTREAL,** 185 Saint Catherine St W, Montreal, PQ H2X 3X5 Canada. Tel 514-847-6226; Fax 514-847-6291; Elec Mail info@macm.org; Internet Home Page Address: www.macm.org; *Dir & Chief Cur* John Zeppetelli; *Traveling Exhib Officer* Emeren Garcia; *Dir Human Resource* Monique Bernier; *Foundation* Danielle Patenaude; *CEO* Richard Bellerose; *Interim Dir Commun & Mktg* Wanda Palma
Open Tues, Thurs - Sun 11 AM - 6 PM, Wed 11 AM - 9 PM; Admis family $24, adults $12, sr citizens 60 & over $10, students $8, under 12 free, no admis fee Wed 5 - 9 PM; Estab 1964. Conservation & information about contemporary art are the most important aspects of the mus; also to present contemporary artists to the general pub; Circ 26,315; Building is a medium-sized four-story, art mus, with an exhibition area of 2800 sq meters divided in eight galleries & a Multimedia room; Average Annual Attendance: 247,700
Income: Financed by provincial grants
Library Holdings: Auction Catalogs; Audio Tapes; Book Volumes; CD-ROMs; Cards; Cassettes; Clipping Files; Compact Disks; DVDs; Exhibition Catalogs; Fiche; Filmstrips; Periodical Subscriptions
Collections: Contemporary Art - Canadian, international & Quebecois: drawings, engravings, installations, paintings, photographs, sculptures, videos
Publications: Catalogs of exhibitions
Activities: Classes for adults & children; summer camp for children; lects open to pub, 15 vis lectrs per yr; concerts; gallery talks; tours; competitions; exten dept

serving Quebec province; originate traveling exhibs circulating Canada, internationally; mus shop sells design accessories

L Mediatheque/ Media Centre, Centre for Research & Documentation on Contemporary Art, 185 Saint Catherine St W, Montreal, PQ H2X 1Z8 Canada. Tel 514-847-6906; Fax 514-847-6916; Internet Home Page Address: media.macm.org; *Librn* Sylvie Alix
Open Tues - Fri 11 AM - 4:30 PM, Wed 11 AM - 8:30 PM; Estab 1965; Circ Non-circulating; For reference only; Average Annual Attendance: 1,700
Income: Partially financed by Quebec Government
Purchases: $22,000
Library Holdings: Audio Tapes 250; Book Volumes 30,015; CD-ROMs; Cassettes; Clipping Files 10,000; DVDs; Exhibition Catalogs 25,644; Framed Reproductions; Kodachrome Transparencies; Motion Pictures; Other Holdings Artists Books: 300; Periodical Subscriptions 359; Photographs; Records; Slides 40,000; Video Tapes 325
Special Subjects: Art History, Film, Mixed Media, Photography, Drawings, Etchings & Engravings, Graphic Arts, Graphic Design, Prints, Sculpture, Conceptual Art, Crafts, Printmaking, Art Education, Video, Metalwork, Textiles
Collections: Archives of Paul-Emile Borduas (Painter 1905-1960); about 12,500 items including writings, correspondence, exhibition catalogs, etc

M MUSEE DES MAITRES ET ARTISANS DU QUEBEC, 615 Sainte Croix Ave, Montreal, PQ H4L 3X6 Canada. Tel 514-747-7367; Fax 514-747-8892; Internet Home Page Address: www.mmaq.qc.ca; *Pres* Eric Devlin; *Dir* Pierre Wilson
Open Tues - Sun noon - 5 PM; Admis family $14, adults $7, sr citizen $5, student $4, under 6 free, no admis fee Wed; Estab 1962 to didactic exhibitions of traditional arts & crafts of Quebec; Mus situated in a Gothic chapel of the Victorian period, built in 1867 in Montreal & moved to Saint-Laurent in 1930. Besides its permanent collection, the mus presents periodical exhibitions illustrating various aspects of the Quebec cultural heritage; Average Annual Attendance: 15,000; Mem: 100
Income: Financed by memberships, provincial and municipal appropriations, fund raising
Library Holdings: Book Volumes; Exhibition Catalogs
Special Subjects: American Indian Art, Textiles, Ceramics, Crafts, Folk Art, Woodcarvings, Furniture, Silver, Metalwork
Collections: Traditional & folk art of French Canada from 17th - 19th century: ceramics, crafts, furniture, metalworks, paintings, sculpture, religious art, silver, textiles, tools & wood-carving
Exhibitions: Album: Email au Quebec: 1949 - 1989; La dentelle au fil des ans; Album: Un musee dans une eglise; Rotate every 3 months
Publications: Album: Images Taillees du Quebec; Album: Les eglises et le tresor de Saint Laurent; Album: Les cahiers du musee: Hommage a Jean Palardy; Les cahiers du musee: Premiere biennale de la reliure du Quebec; La main et l'outil; Tapis Crochetes; Tissus conjonctifs, Regards sur le Mobilier laurentien, Rencontres ceramiques; Elibekian: un nom, trois generations; Maurice Savoie, art, architecture, industry; Emergences Alger Montreal; Biou et modernite artistique; chaud devant! Naissance du verre d'art; Fibres Boreales: Cultures en Partage; Expo 6+1, Art contemporain chinois: Chicago; Les artisans d'autrefois: Les objects d'autrefois; Ivar Mendez: deux mondes, un esprit; Maitres ceramistes formes a l'ecole du meuble: Decouvrir le passe au present: au coeur du vieux-Saint-Laurent; L'immigrant, Stella Pace; Reflexion 10e anniversaire, Les artistes canadiennes asiatiques; Violette Dionne, Figures anciennes et nouvelles; Enid Kaplan, Retrospective; Les artistes de la ligne orange; Projets carre rouge: Savoir refaire un printemps; Les legendes d'autrefois; La vie d'autrefois; Les chaussures d'autrefois
Activities: Classes for adults & children; lects open to public; concerts; gallery talks; tours; mus shop sells books, original art & reproductions

A SAIDYE BRONFMAN CENTRE FOR THE ARTS, Liane & Danny Taran Gallery, 5170 Cote Ste-Catherine, Montreal, PQ H3W 1M7 Canada. Tel 514-739-2301; Fax 514-739-9340; Elec Mail gallery@saidyebronfman.org; Internet Home Page Address: www.saidyebronfman.org; *Asst Dir* Katia Meir; *Mng Dir* David Moss; *Cur* Sylvie Gilbert; *Exec Dir (SBC)* John Hobday; *Dir/Cur (gallery)* Renee Baert; *Asst to Dir/Cur* Meredith Carruthers
Open Mon - Thurs 9 AM - 9 PM, Fri 9 AM - 2 PM, Sun 10 AM - 5 PM, cl Sat; No admis fee; Estab 1967 as a nonprofit cultural centre for the promotion & dissemination of contemporary arts; 3000 sq ft gallery; Average Annual Attendance: 90,000
Income: Financed by government grants
Exhibitions: Five major exhibitions per year, special interest in contemporary art, local, national & international
Publications: Exhibition catalogs
Activities: Classes for adults & children; lects open to pub, 6-12 vis lectrs per yr; gallery talks; tours; originate traveling exhibs; sales shop sells exhib catalogues

M SAINT JOSEPH'S ORATORY, Museum, 3800 Queen Mary Rd, Montreal, PQ H3V 1H6 Canada. Tel 514-733-8211; Fax 514-733-3797; Elec Mail musee@osj.qc.ca; Internet Home Page Address: www.saint-joseph.org; *Museum Cur* Chantal Turbide, PhD; *Oratory Rector* Claude Grou, CSC
Open daily 10 AM - 4:30PM (museum); Admis adults $4, student & seniors $3, youth (6-17) $2, under 6 free; Shrine founded 1904, estab 1955 as art mus; St Joseph's Oratory is also a Montreal landmark, the highest point in this city (856 ft above sea level), a piece of art - architecture - with a history, style, etc of its own
Library Holdings: Cards; Pamphlets
Special Subjects: Decorative Arts, Drawings, Textiles, Bronzes, Painting-French, Sculpture, Graphics, Photography, African Art, Religious Art, Posters, Eskimo Art, Painting-Canadian, Porcelain, Silver, Ivory, Coins & Medals, Miniatures, Embroidery, Mosaics, Painting-German
Collections: Ancient & Contemporary Art; Nativity Scenes from around the world
Exhibitions: (10/15/2010 -) Brother Andre - The Saint of Mount Royal; (10/15/2010 -) Nativite, nativity, nativita
Publications: 290 Nativity Scenes from 110 Countries
Activities: Concerts; films; tours; mus shop sells books, reproductions, prints & DVDs

L Centre d'archives et de Documentation Roland-Guthier, 3800 Queen Mary Rd, Montreal, PQ H3V 1H6 Canada. Tel 514-733-8211, Ext 2341; Fax 514-733-9735;

Elec Mail hleblond@osj.qc.ca; Internet Home Page Address: www.saint-joseph.org; *Archiviste* Helene Leblond
Open Mon - Fri 8:30 AM - 4:30 PM; By appointment
Library Holdings: Book Volumes 15,000; Photographs

A SOCIETE DES MUSEES QUEBECOIS, 209 rue Sainte-Catherine E, Pavillon Sainte-Catherine, 5th Floor, V5205 Montreal, PQ H2X 1L2 Canada; CP 8888, Succursale Centre-Ville Montreal, PQ H3C 3P8 Canada. Tel 514-987-3264; Fax 514-987-3379; Elec Mail info@smq.qc.ca; Internet Home Page Address: www.musees.qc.ca; *Dir* Michel Perron
Open daily 9 AM - Noon & 1 - 5 PM; Estab 1958; Mem: 300; Annual meeting in Oct
Income: $1,300,000 (financed by pub grants & sponsorships)
Publications: Musees, once a year; Bulletin, 2 times a year; Museums to Discover, Quebec & Series of Electronic Guides / Museum Guide (2006); Enjeux
Activities: Classes for mus works; mus shop sells books & magazines

M THE STEWART MUSEUM, (David M Stewart) 20 chemin du Tour de l'Isle, The Fort, St Helen's Island Montreal, PQ H3C 0K7 Canada. Tel 514-861-6701; Fax 514-284-0123; Elec Mail info@stewart-museum.org; Internet Home Page Address: www.stewart-museum.org; *Dir & Chief Cur* Guy Vadeboncoeur; *Librn* Suzanne Morin; *Head Visitor Svcs* Louise Girard; *Cur Colls Mgmt* Sylvie Dauphin; *Cur Arms & Militaria* Philip Butler; *Head Educ & Cultural Progs* Alain Frechette; *Head Opers & Finance* Roberto Galtere
Open summer daily 10 AM - 5 PM, off season Wed - Mon 10 AM - 5 PM, cl Tues; Admis family $20, adults $10, student & senior $7, under 6 free; Estab 1955 to exhibit artifacts relating to Canada's history; located in an old British Arsenal, built between 1820-24; galleries cover theme chronologically & by collection; Average Annual Attendance: 75,000; Mem: annual meeting in June
Income: $2,000,000 (financed by grants & self generated sources)
Library Holdings: Book Volumes 8156; Maps 704; Original Art Works; Original Documents 407; Pamphlets 62; Periodical Subscriptions 50; Photographs; Prints; Reproductions; Slides; Video Tapes 97
Special Subjects: Drawings, Etchings & Engravings, Marine Painting, Metalwork, Portraits, Ethnology, Decorative Arts, Glass, Historical Material, Miniatures, Pewter, Military Art
Collections: Firearms; Kitchen & Fireplace, dating from 16th century; prints; maps, navigation & scientific instruments
Publications: Exhibition catalogs
Activities: Classes for children; during summer months 18th century military parades by La Compagnie Franche de la Marine & the 78th Fraser Highlanders; concerts; tours; originate traveling exhibs to interested museums; Mus shop sells books, reproductions, prints & slides

L Library, 20 chemin du Tour-de-l'Isle, Montreal, PQ H3C QK7 Canada. Tel 514-861-6701; Fax 514-861-2211; Elec Mail info@stewart-museum.org; Internet Home Page Address: www.stewart-museum.org; *Exec Dir & Chief Cur* Guy Vadeboncoeur; *Head of Colls* Sylvie Dauphin; *Colls Asst* Louise Girard
Open Library on appointment: Mon - Thurs 9 AM - 5 PM; Museum: Wed - Sun 11 AM - 5 PM; Admis adults $13, senior, student, children $10; Estab 1955 as an 18th century gentleman's library; pvt mus; Library of rare books & rare maps open to researchers & members for reference on appointment
Library Holdings: Book Volumes 8156; CD-ROMs; DVDs; Manuscripts; Maps 704; Original Art Works; Original Documents; Pamphlets; Periodical Subscriptions 50; Photographs; Prints 3501; Reproductions; Slides; Video Tapes
Special Subjects: Maps
Collections: Coll of rare books, maps, documents & prints; artworks, household objects, scientific objects, weaponry & militaria
Publications: Exhibition catalogs
Activities: Educ progs; mus shop sells books & reproductions

C UNITED WESTURNE INC, Art Collection, Ville Saint Laurent, 505 Locke St Montreal, PQ H4T 1X7 Canada. Tel 514-342-5181; Fax 514-342-5181; *Chmn* Herbert Chervrier; *Exec Asst Finance & Admin* Carol Valiquette
Open Mon - Fri 8 AM-5 PM; Estab 1977; Mem: 250
Collections: Sculptures, mixed media, works on canvas, works on paper
Publications: Selections from the Westburne Collection
Activities: Individual paintings & original objects of art lent

L UNIVERSITE DE MONTREAL, Bibliotheque d'Amenagement, Pavillon de la Faculte de l'amenagement, 2940 chemin de la Cote Ste-Catherine, Salle 1162 Montreal, PQ H3C 3J7 Canada; CP 6128 succursale Centre-ville, Montreal, PQ H3C 3J7 Canada. Tel 514-343-7177; Internet Home Page Address: www.bib.umontreal.ca/AM; *Chief Librn* Lyne Belanger
Open acad yr: Mon - Thurs 8:30 AM - 9 PM, Fri 8:30 AM - 5 PM, Sat - Sun noon - 5 PM; Admis Universite de Montreal users free; Estab 1964
Purchases: $100,000
Library Holdings: Audio Tapes; Book Volumes 53,679; DVDs; Exhibition Catalogs; Periodical Subscriptions 300; Photographs; Slides 81,000; Video Tapes
Special Subjects: Landscape Architecture, Industrial Design, Architecture
Collections: History of Landscape Architecture, urban planning, design

L UNIVERSITE DU QUEBEC, Bibliotheque des Arts, Pavillon Hubert-Aquin, local A-1200, 400 rue Sainte-Catherine E Montreal, PQ H3C 3P3 Canada; CP 8889, Succursale Centre-ville, Montreal, PQ H3C 3P3 Canada. Tel 514-987-6134; Fax 514-987-0262; Internet Home Page Address: www.bibliotheques.uqam.ca; *Dir* Daphne Dufresne; *Reference Librn* Patricia Black
Open Mon - Fri 8:30 AM - 10 PM, Sat - Sun 11 AM - 5 PM
Library Holdings: Book Volumes 65,000; CD-ROMs; Clipping Files; Exhibition Catalogs; Periodical Subscriptions 500; Slides
Special Subjects: Painting-American, Pre-Columbian Art, Sculpture, Watercolors, Advertising Design, Art Education, Video, Primitive art, Eskimo Art, Religious Art, Restoration & Conservation, Silver, Woodcarvings, Woodcuts, Architecture

POINTE CLAIRE

A **POINTE CLAIRE CULTURAL CENTRE,** Stewart Hall Art Gallery, Stewart Hall, 176 Bord du Lac Pointe Claire, PQ H9S 4J7 Canada. Tel 514-630-1254 ext 1776; Fax 514-630-1285; Elec Mail millarj@ville.pointe-claire.qc.ca; Internet Home Page Address: www.ville.pointe-claire.qc.ca; *Dir Art Gallery* Joyce Millar; *Gallery Asst* Amanda Johnston; *Gallery Asst* Manel Benehabane
Open Mon - Sun 1 - 5 PM, Wed 1 - 9 PM; cl Sat June - Aug; No admis fee; Estab 1963; Gallery is 25 x 120 ft; Average Annual Attendance: 11,000; Mem: Policy & Planning Board meets 6 times per year
Income: Financed by city
Purchases: Contemporary Canadian Art for city of Pointe Claire permanent collection
Collections: Permanent collection of contemporary Canadian art
Exhibitions: Approx eight per yr, local, provincial, national and international content
Publications: Bulletins; schedules of classes, study series, social events, approx 30 per yr
Activities: Classes for children; docent training; lects open to pub, 8-10 vis lectrs per year; concerts, gallery talks, tours; lending collection contains original prints, paintings & crafts to pvt and corporate clients; mus shop sells original art, art objects

QUEBEC

M **L'UNIVERSITE LAVAL,** Ecole des Arts Visuels, Edifice La Fabrique, 295 Charest Blvd E, Bureau 090 Quebec, PQ G1K 7P4 Canada. Tel 418-656-7631; Fax 418-656-7678; Elec Mail accueil@arv.ulaval.ca; Internet Home Page Address: www.arv.ulaval.ca; *Dir* Alain Rochon
Open Mon - Fri 8:30 AM - 7 PM; No admis fee; Estab 1970; Average Annual Attendance: 800
Library Holdings: Audio Tapes; Book Volumes; CD-ROMs; Compact Disks
Special Subjects: Graphics, Sculpture
Collections: Art color slides, decorative arts, graphics, paintings, sculpture
Exhibitions: Temporary exhibition, changing monthly
Activities: Classes for adults & children; originates traveling exhibs
L **Library,** Cite' Universitaire, Quebec, PQ G1K 7P4 Canada. Tel 418-656-2131, Ext 3451; Fax 418-656-7897; Internet Home Page Address: www.vol.laval.org; *Dir Art* Madeleine Robin; *Dir Gen Library System* Claude Bonnelly
Open Mon-Fri 8:30 - 11 PM; Open to the pub for use on the premises; original prints & works of art available for study
Library Holdings: Book Volumes 25,000

M **LA CHAMBRE BLANCHE,** 185 Christophe-Colomb E, Quebec, PQ G1K 3S6 Canada. Tel 418-529-2715; Fax 418-529-0048; Elec Mail info@chambreblanche.qc.ca; Internet Home Page Address: www.chambreblanche.qc.ca; *Gen Coordr* Francois Vallee; *Commun Agent* Nataliya Petkova; *Technician* Jeanne Landry-Belleau; Carol-Ann Belzil-Normand
Open Wed - Sun 1-5 PM; No admis fee; Estab 1978 for diffusion of installation & in situation art, web art lab; Mem: 125
Income: Financed by Canada Art Council, Quebec Art Council & Town of Quebec City
Library Holdings: Audio Tapes; Book Volumes; CD-ROMs; DVDs; Exhibition Catalogs; Periodical Subscriptions
Publications: Annual bulletin; Lani Maestro; Residence 1982-1993; Temporalité; Jamelie Hassan; Sur les toits; Largus; Le performatif du Web
Activities: Lects open to pub, 4-5 vis lectrs per yr; L@ Ch@mbre Bl@nche Prize; fels available; mus shop sells books and mus publs

L **LES EDITIONS INTERVENTION, INTER-LE LIEU,** Documentation Center, 345 Du Pont, Quebec, PQ G1K 6M4 Canada. Tel 418-529-9680; Fax 418-529-6933; Elec Mail lelieu@total.net; *Coordr* Richard Martel; *Inter Mag Mgr* Nathalie Perrault
Open daily 10 AM - 4 PM, cl Sat & Sun unless exhibitions showing; Estab 1978; For reference, possible lending & magazine exchanges; Average Annual Attendance: 10,000; Mem: dues $20 & up
Income: Financed by pub funds, donations & mem
Special Subjects: Constructions, Mixed Media, Photography, Conceptual Art, Video, American Indian Art, Architecture
Exhibitions: Rotate 8 per yr
Publications: Inter, Art Actuel, 3 per year
Activities: Lects open to public, 3 vis lectrs per yr

M **MUSEE DE L'AMERIQUE FRANCAISE,** 2 Cote de la Fabrique, Quebec, PQ G1R 3V6 Canada; PO Box 155, Sta B, 85 rue Dalhousie Quebec, PQ G1K 7A6 Canada. Tel 418-692-2843; Fax 418-646-9705; Elec Mail mcq@mcq.org; Internet Home Page Address: www.mcq.org; *Conservation & Management Dir* Danielle Poire; *Coll & Research* Andree Gendreau; *Gen Dir* Claire Simard
Open June 23 - Sep 2, Tues - Sun 10 AM - 5 PM, cl Mon; summer June 24 - Sept 1 daily 9:30 AM - 5 PM; Admis adults $8, sr citizen $7, students $5.50, children 12-16 $2, under 12 free; The Musee de l'Amerique francaise has been integrated to the Musee de la civilisation since 1995. The Musee de la civilisation is subsidized by the ministere de la Culture et des Communications, Gouvernement du Quebec; Average Annual Attendance: 100,000; Mem: dues $25
Income: Financed by Ministere, Gouvernement du Quebec, Gouvernement Federal
Collections: 18th & 19th centuries Canadian paintings; 17th & 18th centuries European paintings; Ethnology; Gold & Silver Objects; Scientific Instruments; Sketches & Prints; Sculpture; Coins & Medals; Zoology
Exhibitions: L'oeuvre du Seminaire de Quebec (Seminaire de Quebec: Widsom and Works); Partir sur la route des francophones (On the road: The Francophone Odyssey)
Activities: Lects open to public; concerts; gallery talks; tours; sales shop sells books, magazines, prints & slides

M **MUSEE DES AUGUSTINES DE L'HOTEL DIEU DE QUEBEC,** 32 rue Charlevoix, Quebec, PQ G1R 5C4 Canada. Tel 418-692-2492; Fax 418-692-2668; Elec Mail mahdq@augustines.ca; *Dir Mus* Sr Nicole Perron; *Guide* Jacques St-Arnaud
Open Tues - Sat 9:30 AM - Noon & 1:30 - 5 PM, Sun 1:30 - 5 PM ; No admis fee, donations appreciated; Estab 1958 in the Monastere des Augustines (1695); The Hotel Dieu relives three centuries of history of the French Canadian people; Average Annual Attendance: 11,000
Special Subjects: Drawings, Photography, American Indian Art, African Art, Religious Art, Ceramics, Pottery, Manuscripts, Painting-European, Portraits, Dolls, Furniture, Glass, Porcelain, Painting-French, Coins & Medals, Calligraphy, Painting-Flemish, Period Rooms, Embroidery, Painting-Spanish, Painting-Italian, Leather
Collections: Antique furniture; embroideries; medical instruments 17th-20th century; objects from everyday life, models & several other unique works; paintings; silver & pewter artifacts
Activities: Original objects of art lent to museums
L **Archive,** 32 rue Charlevoix, Convent Office Quebec, PQ G1R 5C4 Canada. Tel 418-692-2492, Ext 247; Fax 418-692-2668; *Archivist* Sr Marie-Paule Couchon; *Dir Mus* Sr Nicole Perron
Open by appointment only; Religious & medical books available for research upon special request
Library Holdings: Book Volumes 4000

M **MUSEE NATIONAL DES BEAUX ARTS DU QUEBEC,** Parc des Champs-de-Bataille, Quebec, PQ G1R 5H3 Canada. Tel 418-644-6460; Internet Home Page Address: www.mnba.qc.c; *Exec Dir* Line Ouellet; *Cur Early Quebec Art 1850-1900* Mario Beland; *Cur Contemporary Art* Eve-Lyne Beaudry; *Cur Modern Art* Michele Grandbois; *Dir Exhibs & Publs* Anne Eschapasse; *Dir Research & Coll* Paul Bourassa; *Cur Early Quebec Art before 1850* Daniel Drouin; *Cur Actual Art* Bernard Lamarche; *Dir Admin* Jean-Francois Fusey; *Dir Communication & Develop* Patrick Caux
Open Tues - Sun 10 AM - 5 PM (9 PM on Wed); cl Mon; Admis adults $18, seniors 65+ $16, children & young adults 13-30 $10, 12 & under free; Estab 1933 under Government of Province of Quebec; 12 galleries, 1 restaurant, 1 theatre, cafe; Average Annual Attendance: 300,000
Income: Financed by Quebec government appropriation
Library Holdings: Auction Catalogs; Audio Tapes; Book Volumes; CD-ROMs; Cards; Cassettes; Clipping Files; Compact Disks; DVDs; Exhibition Catalogs; Fiche; Filmstrips; Framed Reproductions; Prints
Special Subjects: Drawings, Painting-American, Photography, Sculpture, Bronzes, Woodcarvings, Decorative Arts, Portraits, Painting-Canadian
Collections: Quebec art from 18th century to present; Design, drawings, goldsmith's work, paintings, photography, sculpture, tapestry works; European art
Exhibitions: Rotating exhibitions
Publications: Exhibit catalogs
Activities: Classes for adults & children; lects open to pub; concerts; gallery talks; tours; schol offered; exten dept serves province of Quebec; individual paintings lent to government; originates traveling exhibs; mus shop sells books, magazines, original art, reproductions, prints & postcards; junior mus
L **Bibliotheque,** Parc des Champs-de-Bataille, Quebec, PQ G1R 5H3 Canada. Tel 418-644-6460 ext 3341; Fax 418-643-2478; Elec Mail bibliom@mnba.qc.ca; Internet Home Page Address: mnba.qc.ca; *Dir Colls Mngmt & Info* Pierre Landry; *Documentary & Archives Mngmt* Nathalie Thibault; *Documentation Tech* Lina Doyon; *Documentation Tech* Nicole Gastonguay; *Documentation Tech* Caroline Gauthier; *Reference Agent* Helene Godbout
Open only by appointment; Estab 1933
Income: $100,000 (financed by Quebec government appropriation)
Purchases: $36,000
Library Holdings: Auction Catalogs; Audio Tapes 144; Book Volumes 40,000; CD-ROMs 52; Clipping Files 13,000; Compact Disks 23; DVDs; Exhibition Catalogs; Fiche; Other Holdings CD-Rom; Periodical Subscriptions 123; Photographs; Reels; Slides 58,000; Video Tapes 423
Special Subjects: Art History, Decorative Arts, Photography, Art Education, Painting-Canadian

M **VU CENTRE DE DIFFUSION ET DE PRODUCTION DE LA PHOTOGRAPHIE,** 523, De Saint-Vallier Est, Quebec, PQ G1K 3P9 Canada. Tel 418-640-2585; Fax 218-640-2586; Elec Mail info@vuphoto.org; Internet Home Page Address: www.vuphoto.org; *Artist & Dir* Alexis Desgagnes; *Dir* Pascale Bureau
Open Wed - Sun Noon - 5 PM; No admis fee; Estab 1981; Gallery contains exhibition area, digital printing lab & darkrooms; Average Annual Attendance: 15,000; Mem: 200
Income: Financed by endowment, mem, city appropriation & special events
Library Holdings: Book Volumes; CD-ROMs; DVDs; Exhibition Catalogs; Pamphlets; Periodical Subscriptions
Special Subjects: Art History, Conceptual Art, American Western Art, Photography
Collections: Artist Residencies Program Collection
Publications: Complete catalog at website
Activities: Educ prog; exhibs; production facilities in digital & analog photography; publication of books on contemporary photography; lects open to pub, 3 vis lectrs per yr; gallery talks; commented visits on exhibs; mus shop sells books

RIMOUSKI

M **LE MUSEE REGIONAL DE RIMOUSKI,** Centre National d'Exposition, 35 St Germain W, Rimouski, PQ G5L 4B4 Canada. Tel 418-724-2272; Fax 418-725-4433; Elec Mail mrdr@globetrotter.net; Internet Home Page Address: www.museederimouski.qu.ca; *Dir Museum* Carl Johnson; *Contemporary Art Conservator* Bernard Lamarche; *Educ & Culture* France LeBlanc; *Material Resources Tech* Gervais Belzile; *Coll Archivist* Nathalie Langelier; *Commun* Josyka Levesque
Open Wed - Fri 9:30 AM - 8 PM, Sat - Tues 9:30 AM - 6 PM ; Admis family $10, adults $4, students & sr citizens $3, children 5 & under free; Estab 1972 for the diffusion of contemporary art, historic & scientific exhibitions; to present local, national & international exhibitions & organize itinerant exhibitions; An old church, built in 1823, now historical monument, completely restored inside with three floors of exhibitions; Average Annual Attendance: 15,000; Mem: 400; dues $40; annual meeting in May or June

Income: $237,000 (financed by federal, provincial & municipal appropriation)
Exhibitions: Scientific Exploration of the Sea
Publications: L'Esprit des lieux; L'Artiste au jardin; Messac; Opera, Les Nuits de Vitre; Cozic; exhibit catalogs
Activities: Classes for children; school progs; lects open to pub, 5 vis lectrs per yr; concerts; gallery talks; tours; originate traveling exhibs; mus shop sells magazines

L **Library,** 35 W St Germain, Rimouski, PQ G5L 4B4 Canada. Tel 418-724-2272; Fax 418-725-4433; Internet Home Page Address: www.museederimouski.qu.ca; *Dir Museum* Carl Johnson
Circ Non-circulating; Open to pub for reference, call for seasonal hours, cl statutory holidays
Library Holdings: Book Volumes 2500; Exhibition Catalogs; Other Holdings Documents 800; Pamphlets; Reproductions; Sculpture

SEPT-ILES

M **MUSEE REGIONAL DE LU COTE-NORD,** (Musee Regional de la Cote-Nord) 500 blvd Laure, Sept-Iles, PQ G4R 1X7 Canada. Tel 418-968-2070; Fax 418-968-8323; Elec Mail mrcn@mrcn.qc.ca; Internet Home Page Address: www.mrcn.qc.ca; *Educ* Christine Lebel; *Conservateur* Steve Dubreuil; *Dir* Christian Marcotte; *Art Cur* Valerie Gill; *Boutique Mgr* Sophie Levesque
Open winter Tues - Fri 10 AM-5 PM, Sat & Sun 1-5 PM, cl Mon; summer 9 AM - 5 PM daily; Admis adult $7, sr citizens & students $6, children under 12 free; Estab 1975. Protects, preserves, studies & exhibits the heritage of the Cote-Nord region, with particular emphasis on fishing, hunting, mining & archaeological activity; Contemporary art from province of Quebec; Average Annual Attendance: 22,000; Mem: 150; annual meeting in June
Income: Financed by mem, city & state appropriation
Library Holdings: Audio Tapes; Book Volumes; Cards; Compact Disks; DVDs; Exhibition Catalogs; Framed Reproductions; Maps; Memorabilia; Original Art Works; Photographs; Prints; Reproductions
Special Subjects: Drawings, Photography, Sculpture, Watercolors, Archaeology, Ethnology, Textiles, Ceramics, Pottery, Woodcarvings, Woodcuts, Landscapes, Portraits, Posters, Eskimo Art, Painting-Canadian, Furniture, Porcelain, Metalwork, Historical Material, Juvenile Art
Collections: Archaeology; art; ethnology; history
Activities: Classes for adults & children; docent progs; lects open to pub; book traveling exhibs 2 per yr; mus shop sells books, magazines, reproductions, prints, artcraft & regional foodies

SHAWINIGAN

A **SHAWINIGAN ART CENTER,** 2100 blvd des Hetres, Shawinigan, PQ G9N 8R8 Canada. Tel 819-539-1888; Fax 819-539-2400; Elec Mail corporationculturelle@shawinigan.ca; Internet Home Page Address: www.cultureshawinigan.ca; *Gen Dir* Louise Martin; *Communs Agent* Francois St Martin; *Admin Asst* Renee Vachon; *Secy* Nancy Gilbert
Open Mon & Fri 9 AM - noon & 1 PM - 4:30 PM; No admis fee; Estab 1967; Gallery is maintained; Average Annual Attendance: 36,000
Income: Financed by city appropriation & cultural ministry
Collections: Oils; pastels; watercolors; polyesters; reproductions; copper enameling; inks; sculpture; tapestries
Activities: Classes for adults & children; dramatic progs; concerts; lending collection contains original art works, original prints, paintings, sculpture, slides; sales shop sells original art

SHERBROOKE

M **BISHOP'S UNIVERSITY,** Foreman Art Gallery, 2600 College St, Sherbrooke, PQ J1M 1Z7 Canada. Tel 819-822-9600 ext 2260/2279; Fax 819-822-9703; Elec Mail gallery@ubishops.ca; Internet Home Page Address: www.ubishops.ca/foreman; *Dir & Cur* Vicky Chainey Gagnon; *Cur Asst* Nicole Rutberg
Open Sep - July Tues - Sat noon - 5PM; No admis fee; Estab 1992 to serve the University Community & the entire Eastern Townships by displaying regional, national & international art work; 154.5 sq m/1667sq ft exhib space located adjacent to the Foyer of Centennial Theatre; Average Annual Attendance: 5,200
Income: Bishop's Univ
Collections: paintings, prints, & sculptures
Publications: catalog of exhibs, yearly
Activities: Docent training; work study prog; workshops; lects open to pub, 5 vis lectrs per yr; gallery talks, sponsoring of competitions; graduating student exhib 3 awards per yr

M **UNIVERSITY OF SHERBROOKE,** Art Gallery, 2500 blvd de l'Universite, Sherbrooke, PQ J1K 2R1 Canada. Tel 819-821-7742; Fax 819-820-1000; Elec Mail jbrouill@courrier.usherb.ca; *Dir* Johanne Brouillet
Open Mon - Sat noon - 8:30 PM; No admis fee; Estab 1964 to introduce pub to the best art work being done in Canada & to place this work in a historical (European) & geographical (American) context; Gallery has three exhibition areas totaling 12,800 sq ft on university campus & serves the community; Average Annual Attendance: 30,000
Income: $300,000 (financed by state & city appropriation & university funds)
Special Subjects: Graphics
Collections: 90 per cent Contemporary Graphics & Paintings Quebec & 10 per cent international
Publications: Monthly bulletin; catalogue
Activities: Lects open to public, 20 vis lectrs per year; gallery talks; lending collection contains books, cassettes, color reproductions, Kodachromes, original prints, paintings, photographs, sculpture, slides & videos

SUTTON

M **COMMUNICATIONS AND HISTORY MUSEUM OF SUTTON,** (Eberdt Museum of Communications) South Sutton, PQ J0E 2K0 Canada. Tel 450-538-3222
Open Mon-Fri 9AM-5PM; Admis $2; Mem: 160; dues $10
Income: (financed by mem, city & state appropriation)

Special Subjects: Historical Material
Collections: History, art & communs coll; 2300 historic objects
Activities: Lects open to pub; mus shop sells books

TROIS RIVIERES

M **FORGES DU SAINT-MAURICE NATIONAL HISTORIC SITE,** 1000 Blvd des Forges, Trois Rivieres, PQ G9C 1B1 Canada. Tel 819-378-5116; Fax 819-378-0887; Elec Mail parkscanada-que@pc.gc.ca; Internet Home Page Address: www.pc.gc.ca/lhn-nhs/qc/saintmaurice; *Supt* Carmen D Le Page
Open May 10 - Sep 1, 9:30 AM - 5:30 PM; Sept 2 - Oct 13, 9:30 AM - 4:30 PM; Admis family $9.80, adult $3.90, senior $3.40, youth $1.90; Estab 1973 as the first iron & steel industry in Canada 1729-1883; 50 acres of land-2 main exhibition centers, the ironmaster's house & the blast furnace; Average Annual Attendance: 50,000
Special Subjects: Archaeology, Metalwork
Collections: Cast Iron Stoves from the 18th & 19th century; Metal objects found between 1973-1980
Exhibitions: Blast Furnace Permanent Exhibition

M **GALERIE D'ART DU PARC-MANOIR DE TONNANCOUR,** Manoir de Tonnancour, 864 rue des Ursulines, CP 871 Trois Rivieres, PQ G9A 5J9 Canada. Tel 819-374-2355; Fax 819-374-1758; Elec Mail galerie@galeriedart.duparc.qc.ca; Internet Home Page Address: www.galeriedartduparc.qc.ca; *Dir* Christiane Simoneau
Open Tues - Fri 10 AM-Noon & 1:30-5 PM, Sat & Sun 1-5 PM, cl Mon; No admis fee; Estab 1972 to promote visual arts; Nonprofit organization; 10-12 exhibitions in visual arts per year & permanent history exhibition; Average Annual Attendance: 19,000
Income: Financed by city appropriation & government
Exhibitions: Rotating exhibitions
Activities: Classes for adults & children; book traveling exhibs 1 per yr; originate traveling exhibs; mus shop sells original art & reproductions

A **MAISON DE LA CULTURE,** (Centre Culturel de Trois Rivieres) Centre d'exposition Raymond-Lasnier, 1425 Place de l'Hotel-de-Ville, CP 368 Trois Rivieres, PQ G9A 5H3 Canada. Tel 819-372-4611; Fax 819-372-4632; Elec Mail cerl@v3r.net; Internet Home Page Address: www.cer-l.ca; *Dir* Marie-Andree Levasseur
Open Tues - Sun noon - 5 PM; No admis fee; Estab 1967 to promote visual art; Gallery features 275 sq meters total area; Average Annual Attendance: 12,000
Income: Financed by city appropriation & a corporation
Purchases: regular contacts with visual arts
Collections: 700 pieces
Publications: Exhib catalogues
Activities: Classes for adults & children; guided group visits; educ prog; tours

VAUDREUIL-DORION

M **MUSEE REGIONAL DE VAUDREUIL-SOULANGES,** 431 Ave St Charles, Vaudreuil-Dorion, PQ J7V 2N3 Canada. Tel 450-455-2092; Fax 450-455-6782; Internet Home Page Address: www.mrvs.qc.ca; *Dir* Daniel Bissonnette
Open Tues - Fri 9:30 AM - 4:30 PM & 7 PM - 9:30 PM, Sat - Sun 1 PM - 4:30 PM, cl Mon ; Admis family $12, adults $5, students $3.50, children (6-12) $2, under 6 free; Estab 1953, nonprofit organization subsidized by the Direction des Musees et Centres d'Exposition of the Ministere des Affaires culturelles du Quebec. The collection consists of artifacts & artists production that have & still illustrate the traditional way of life in the counties of Vaudreuil & Soulanges, the surroundings & the Province of Quebec; Mus has four rooms for permanent collection & one for temporary & traveling exhibitions. A documentation centre is open for searchers & students & an animator will receive groups on reservation for a commented tour; Average Annual Attendance: 13,000; Mem: 300; dues $20; annual meeting in Apr
Income: Financed by endowment
Special Subjects: Painting-American, Sculpture, Pottery, Portraits, Furniture
Collections: Edison Gramophone 1915; antique pottery; historic documents & material; farming; furniture, paintings, portraits, sculpture & woodworking
Exhibitions: Various exhibitions
Publications: Musee de Vaudreuil Catalog (selectif); Vaudreuil Soulanges, Western Gateway of Quebec
Activities: Classes for children; concerts; original objects of art lent

L **Centre d'Histoire d'la Presqu'ile,** 431 Ave Chaud, Vaudreuil, PQ J7V 2N3 Canada. Tel 450-455-2092; Fax 450-455-6782; Internet Home Page Address: www.mrds.qu.ca; *Dir* Daniel Bissonnette
Open Mon-Fri 9:30 AM - 4:30 PM, cl Sat & Sun; Circ Non-circulating; Reference only
Library Holdings: Book Volumes 5200; Other Holdings AV cylinders 600; Photographs

SASKATCHEWAN

ALBERTA

M **IMHOFF ART GALLERY,** 4515 44th St Alberta, SK S9V 0T8 Canada; 4420 50th Ave Lloydminster, SK T9V 0W2 Canada. Tel 780-875-6184; Fax 306-825-9070; *Cur* Barbara McKeand
Open Wed - Fri Noon-5 PM, Sat & Sun 1-5 PM; Admis adults $4, students $3.50, children $1.50; Estab to exhibit 200 paintings done by Berthold Imhoff, who died in 1939; 1 large gallery
Income: Financed by municipal and provincial appropriations
Exhibitions: Rotating exhibits

ESTEVAN

M ESTEVAN NATIONAL EXHIBITION CENTRE INC, Estevan Art Gallery & Museum, 118 Fourth St, Estevan, SK S4A 0T4 Canada. Tel 306-634-7644; Fax 306-634-2940; Elec Mail eagm@sasktel.net; Internet Home Page Address: www.eagm.ca; *Dir & Cur* Griffith Aaron Baker; *Gallery Educator* Karly Millions
Open Tues - Fri 8:30 AM - 6 PM, Sat 1-4 PM; No admis fee; Estab 1978 to receive, display & interpret objects & collections, that would increase the communities access to culture; Two galleries; one 16 x 30 ft, the other 26 x 65 ft; North West Mounted Police Museum; Average Annual Attendance: 22,000; Mem: Board of Dir meet first Thurs each month at 6 PM, Ann Gen meeting May
Income: $260,000 (financed by provincial & city appropriation & private sector fundraising)
Purchases: Andrew King Block Printing Coll valued at $120,000
Library Holdings: Audio Tapes; Exhibition Catalogs; Kodachrome Transparencies; Memorabilia; Original Art Works; Original Documents; Photographs; Prints; Sculpture; Slides; Video Tapes
Special Subjects: Prints, Painting-Canadian
Collections: Saskatchewan artists print series; Saskatchewan painting collection; Two ceramic wall murals valued at 18,000
Exhibitions: Rotating exhibs every 6 wks
Publications: Annual Report; newsletter, quarterly
Activities: Educ prog; classes for adults, children & seniors; lects open to pub, 4 vis lectrs per yr; gallery talks; tours; children's & regional art show competitions; awards of merit; exten dept serves southeast Saskatchewan; lending of original objects of art to local bus; book traveling exhibs 13-18 per yr; originate traveling exhibs through Canada; sales shop sells books, original art & souvenirs

LLOYDMINSTER

A BARR COLONY HERITAGE CULTURAL CENTRE, 4420 50th Ave, Lloydminster, SK T9V 0U2 Canada; 4515 44th St, Lloydminster, SK S9V 0T8 Canada. Tel 306-825-5655; Fax 306-825-9070; Elec Mail bchcc@lloydminster.ca; *Cur* Barbara McKeand
Open daily May - Sept 10 AM - 8 PM, Sept - May Wed - Sun 1 - 6 PM; Admis family $5.75, adults $2.75, sr citizens & students $2, children 12 & under $1.50, school tours $.50; Estab 1963 to promote & support appreciation for & educ about local history & the arts; The center is comprised of 4 exhibit galleries (1000 sq ft), a mus bldg (24,000 sq ft) & classroom teaching space
Income: Financed by donations & city appropriations
Collections: Antique Museum; Fuchs' Wildlife; Imhoff Paintings; Berghammer Art Collection; over 5000 artifacts related to the Barr Colonists, the first settlers of the area
Exhibitions: Exhibits rotate 6-8 per yr
Activities: Gallery talks; tours; traveling exhibitions

MOOSE JAW

M MOOSE JAW ART MUSEUM, INC, Art & History Museum, Crescent Park, Moose Jaw, SK S6H 0X6 Canada. Tel 306-692-4471; Fax 306-694-8016; Elec Mail mjamchin@sasktel.net; Internet Home Page Address: www.mjmag.ca; *Cur* Heather Smith; *Bus Mgr* Joan Maier; *Educ Coordr* Christy Schweiger; *Preparator* Vivian Barber
Open gallery noon - 5 PM; offices Mon - Fri 8:30 AM - noon & 1 PM - 5 PM; No admis fee; Estab 1966 for preservation, educ, collection & exhibitions; Gallery has 4304 sq ft with movable walls, Mus has 3970 sq ft, Discovery Centre has 1010 sq ft; Average Annual Attendance: 30,000; Mem: 190; dues family $25, individual $15
Income: $260,000 (financed by city, province & national appropriations & self-generated revenues)
Purchases: $260,000
Special Subjects: American Indian Art, Ethnology, Costumes, Folk Art, Painting-Canadian
Collections: 723 Canadian Historical & Contemporary Art Collection; 4,700 Human History Artifacts Collection; Canadian Historical & Contemporary Art Collection; Human History Artifacts Collection
Exhibitions: Heritage Gallery has permanent exhibits; art gallery rotates exhibits every 6 wks
Publications: Annual catalogs; bi-annual newsletter
Activities: Classes for adults & children; docent training; school tours; Discovery Centre mini science ctr; lects open to pub, 10-15 vis lectrs per yr; gallery talks; tours; individual paintings & original objects of art lent to other professional public institutions that meet appropriate environmental standards; book traveling exhibs 5-10 per yr; originate traveling exhibs; mus shop sells books, original works of art, educational toys

NORTH BATTLEFORD

M ALLEN SAPP GALLERY, One Railway Ave E, PO Box 460 North Battleford, SK S9A 2Y6 Canada. Tel 306-445-1760; Fax 306-445-1694; Elec Mail sapp@accesscomm.ca; Internet Home Page Address: www.allensapp.com; Internet Home Page Address: www.virtualmuseum.ca/Exhibitions/allensapp; *Cur* Dean Bauche
Open fall & winter Wed - Sun 1 - 5 PM; spring & summer daily 11 AM - 5 PM; No admis fee; Estab 1989; 8,000 sq ft gallery built in 1916 contains state of the art equipment incl high tech av presentation equipment; Average Annual Attendance: 9,000; Mem: 200; dues $10
Income: $100,000 (financed by municipal & provincial grants & gift shop revenues)
Library Holdings: Auction Catalogs; Book Volumes; CD-ROMs; Cards; Clipping Files; Compact Disks; Exhibition Catalogs; Kodachrome Transparencies; Manuscripts; Memorabilia; Motion Pictures; Original Documents; Pamphlets; Periodical Subscriptions; Photographs; Prints; Records; Slides; Video Tapes
Collections: The Gonor Collection, paintings, photos, slides of art by renowned Cree artist Allen Sapp plus the work of other Canadian 1st Nations artist
Exhibitions: Rotate 2 exhibs per yr featuring powerful and sensitive images of the Northern Plains Cree
Publications: gallery catalog, biennial
Activities: Classes for adults & children; Native studies; lects open to pub, 4 vis lectrs per yr; 1999 & 2002 Attractions Canadian award; circulate exhibs to credited mus; mus shop sells books, reproductions, prints

PRINCE ALBERT

M JOHN M CUELENAERE PUBLIC LIBRARY, Grace Campbell Gallery, 125 12th St E, Prince Albert, SK S6V 1B7 Canada. Tel 306-763-8496; Fax 306-763-3816; Elec Mail library@jmcpl.ca; Internet Home Page Address: www.jmcpl.ca; *Dir* Alex Juorio
Open Mon - Thurs 9 AM - 9 PM, Fri & Sat 9 AM - 5:30 PM, cl Sun; No admis fee; Estab 1973; Gallery is 100 linear ft
Income: Financed by city appropriation
Activities: Tours

REGINA

A MUSEUMS ASSOCIATION OF SASKATCHEWAN, MAS Office, 424 McDonald St Regina, SK S4N 6E1 Canada. Tel 306-780-9279; Fax 306-780-9463; Elec Mail mas@saskmuseums.org; Internet Home Page Address: www.saskmuseums.org; *Exec Dir* Wendy Fitch; *Professional Develop Coordr* Dan Holbrow; *Dir Finance* Brenda Herman; *Communications Coordr* Brittany Knudson; *Mus Advisor* May-Lin Polk; *Admin Asst* Ele Radbourne
Open daily 8 AM-4 PM, cl Sat & Sun; Estab 1967; Mem: 450; dues vary with budget $40 - $410
Income: Financed by lotteries & mem
Publications: Bi-monthly newsletter

ORGANIZATION OF SASKATCHEWAN ARTS COUNCILS (OSAC)
For further information, see National and Regional Organizations

L REGINA PUBLIC LIBRARY, Art Dept, PO Box 2311, Regina, SK S4P 3Z5 Canada. Tel 306-777-6070; Fax 306-949-7260; Internet Home Page Address: www.rpl.regina.sk.ca; *Acting Dir & Librn* Sandy Cameron
Open Mon - Thurs 9:30 AM - 9 PM, Fri 9:30 AM - 6 PM, Sat 9:30 AM - 5 PM, Sun 1:30 - 5 PM, cl holidays; No admis fee; Estab 1947; Also operates Sherwood Village Branch Gallery
Library Holdings: Audio Tapes; Book Volumes 10,230; Cassettes; Clipping Files; Exhibition Catalogs 4000; Fiche; Filmstrips; Motion Pictures; Original Art Works; Pamphlets; Periodical Subscriptions 60; Photographs; Prints; Slides; Video Tapes

M Dunlop Art Gallery, 2311 12th Ave, Regina, SK S4P 3Z5 Canada; PO Box 2311, Regina, SK S4P 3Z5 Canada. Tel 306-777-6040; Fax 306-949-7264; Elec Mail dunlop@rpl.regina.sk.ca; Internet Home Page Address: www.dunlopartgallery.org; *Dir* Noreen Neu; *Preparator* John Reichert; *Cur Asst* Joyce Clark; *Secy* Bev Antal
Open Mon - Thurs 9:30 AM - 9 PM, Fri 9:30 AM - 6 PM, Sat 9:30 AM - 5 PM, Sun 1:30 - 5 PM, cl holidays; No admis fee; Estab 1949 to research practices & histories with visual culture, with emphasis on relationships between cultural production & social context; to present results of research in an informative & publicly accessible format including exhibitions, screenings, lectures, programs, publications & extension programs; to promote the Gallery's purpose scope & programs to the public; to communicate, consult & cooperate with individuals, groups & organizations having similar objectives; to collect research catalog & preserve works of contemporary & historical significance for the people of Regina & Saskatchewan; to acquire & maintain works of contemporary art for circulation through art rental service; Circ 110,897; 122 seat film theater with stage, preview room, meeting rooms, library van, woodworking shop, collections & services of the Regina library. Maintains art research resource centre; Average Annual Attendance: 100,000
Income: Financed by city appropriation, provincial & federal grants
Purchases: $10,000
Library Holdings: Book Volumes; Exhibition Catalogs; Original Documents; Pamphlets; Periodical Subscriptions; Slides; Video Tapes
Special Subjects: Photography, Sculpture, American Indian Art, Crafts, Folk Art, Landscapes, Painting-Canadian
Collections: Permanent collection of Saskatchewan art; Inglis Sheldon-Williams Collection; 205 works of historical & contemporary art including paintings, sculpture & graphic art by Saskatchewan artists; Feminism & Contemporary Visual Art; Popular Culture & Contemporary Visual Art; Art Rental Collection: 226 works of historical & contemporary paintings & graphic art by Canadian artists
Exhibitions: 15 exhibitions per year
Publications: At the Dunlop Newsletter, quarterly; brochures; exhibition catalogs
Activities: Docent training; gallery facilitators available to discuss exhibitions with members of public individually; lects open to pub, 6 vis lectrs per yr; gallery talks; tours; competitions; individual paintings & original objects of art lent to Regina Pub Library card holders through an art rental coll available to the pub & works from permanent coll lent to other galleries; lending coll contains original art works, original prints & drawings; book traveling exhibs; originate traveling exhibs to galleries & museums with acceptable museum standards; sales shop sells books, magazines, cards, catalogues, posters & exhibition catalogues

M UNIVERSITY OF REGINA, MacKenzie Art Gallery, 3475 Albert St, Regina, SK S4S 6X6 Canada. Tel 306-584-4250; Fax 306-569-8191; Elec Mail mackenzie@uregina.ca; Internet Home Page Address: www.mackenzieartgallery.ca; *Coll Mgr* Bruce Anderson; *Head Cur* Timothy Long; *Preparator* Marc Courtemanche; *Admin Mgr* Gaynor Novak; *Conservator* Brenda Smith; *Mgr Finance & Opers* Shari Sokochoff
Open Mon - Wed & Sat 10 AM - 5:30 PM, Thurs - Fri 10 AM - 9 PM, Sun 11 AM - 5:30 PM; No admis fee; Estab 1953 to preserve & expand the coll left to the gallery by Norman MacKenzie & to offer exhibs to the city of Regina; to offer

works of art to rural areas through the Outreach Prog; Eight discreet galleries totaling approx 1500 running ft of exhibition space; Average Annual Attendance: 100,000; Mem: 1079; dues $35; annual meeting in June
Income: $1,000,000 (financed by federal & provincial governments, University of Regina & city of Regina & private funds)
Special Subjects: Oriental Art
Collections: Contemporary Canadian & American work; contemporary Saskatchewan work; 19th & early 20th century works on paper; a part of the collection is early 20th century replicas of Eastern & Oriental artifacts & art
Exhibitions: Changing exhibitions from the permanent collection & traveling exhibitions
Publications: Exhibition catalogues; staff publications of a professional nature; Vista, quarterly
Activities: Docent training; community prog of touring exhibs in Saskatchewan; interpretive progs; school tours; lects open to pub, 8-10 vis lectrs per yr; concerts; gallery talks; tours; films; exten dept serves entire province of Saskatchewan; originate traveling exhibs nation-wide; gallery shop sells books, magazines, reproductions, cards & catalogues
　　—MacKenzie Art Gallery Resource Centre, 3475 Albert St, Regina, SK S4S 6X6 Canada. Tel 306-522-4242; Fax 306-569-8191;
Open Mon, Tues, Fri, Sat & Sun 11 AM - 7 PM, Wed & Thurs 11 AM - 10 PM; Estab 1970 to offer the community a resource for art information, both historical & current; For reference only
Collections: Regional press clippings from 1925
Exhibitions: Between Abstraction & Representation, George Glenn; Jana Sterbak; Jan Gerrit Wyels 1888-1973; The Asymmetric Vision; Philosophical Intuition & Original Experience in the Art of Yves Gaucher; Peace Able Kingdom, Jack Severson; Artists With Their Work; Ryan Arnott; Grant McConnell; Memory in Place
Publications: Exhibition catalog
Activities: Film program, twice a month
　　—Visual Resource Center, Fine Arts Dept, Regina, SK S4S 0A2 Canada. Tel 306-585-5579; Fax 306-585-5744; Elec Mail finearts@max.cc.uregina.ca; *Cur* Pat Matheson
Estab for the instruction of art history
Library Holdings: Audio Tapes; Slides 90,000; Video Tapes
Collections: Prehistoric - contemporary, eastern & western art
L　**Education/Fine Arts Library,** Univ of Regina Library, Regina, SK S4S 0A2 Canada; 3737 Wascana Pkwy, Regina, SK S45 OA2 Canada. Tel 306-585-5123; Fax 306-585-5115; *Vis Arts Librn* Donna Bowman; *Music Librn & Film Librn* Gillian Nowlan; *Theatre Librn* Larry McDonald
Open (semester) Mon - Thurs 8 AM - 11 PM, Fri & Sat 8 AM - 7:30 PM, Sun 8 AM - 11 PM; Education and Fine Arts Library amalgamated with main library in 2005; For both lending & reference
Library Holdings: Audio Tapes; Book Volumes 18,000; Cassettes; Clipping Files; Compact Disks; Exhibition Catalogs; Fiche; Pamphlets; Periodical Subscriptions 55; Records; Reels; Video Tapes

SASKATOON

M　**AKA ARTIST RUN CENTRE,** 424 20th St W, Saskatoon, SK S7M OX4 Canada. Tel 306-652-0044; Fax 306-652-0534; Elec Mail aka@sasktel.net; Internet Home Page Address: www.akagallery.org; *Prog Coordr* Cindy Baker; *Admin Coordr* Troy Gronsdahl
Open Mon - Sat Noon - 5 PM; No admis fee; Estab 1970, incorporated 1973 to encourage the development of photography as a creative visual art; Main gallery is 650 sq ft, & workshop gallery is 250 sq ft; Average Annual Attendance: 8,000; Mem: 100; dues $25; annual meeting first Sun in May
Income: $196,000 (financed by mem, province appropriation, federal grants & fundraising)
Special Subjects: Photography
Collections: Permanent Collection of 901 Contemporary Canadian photographs
Exhibitions: 7 main gallery exhibitions per year; 7 workshop gallery exhibitions per year
Publications: Backflash, quarterly magazine; members monthly newsletter
Activities: Classes for adults; lects open to pub, 12 vis lectrs per yr; tours; exten dept; workshops throughout the province; portable darkrooms travel with instructors; book traveling exhibs; originate traveling exhibs to pub galleries in Canada; sales shop sells books, postcards, t-shirts
L　**Library,** 424 20th St W, Saskatoon, SK S7M 0X4 Canada. Tel 306-244-8018; Fax 306-665-6568; *Program Coordr* Cindy Baker; *Admin Coordr* Troy Gronsdahl
Open Mon - Sat Noon - 5 PM; No admis fee; Estab 1970; Circ Non-circulating; For references mem only
Library Holdings: Audio Tapes; Book Volumes 1500; Cassettes; Clipping Files; Exhibition Catalogs; Manuscripts; Pamphlets; Periodical Subscriptions 10; Reproductions; Slides

M　**MENDEL ART GALLERY & CIVIC CONSERVATORY,** 950 Spadina Crescent E, Saskatoon, SK S7K 3L Canada; PO Box 569, Saskatoon SK S7K 3L6 Canada. Tel 306-975-7610; Fax 306-975-7670; Elec Mail jkoutecky@mendel.ca; Internet Home Page Address: www.mendel.ca; *Exec Dir & CEO* Gregory Burke; *Dir Finance & Opers* Angie Larson; *Admin Asst & Mgr Vol Resources* Judy Koutecky; *Chief Cur* Lisa Baldissera; *Assoc Cur* Jen Budney; *Assoc Cur* Sandra Fraser; *Pub Progs Coordr* Laura Kinzel; *Mgr Resource Develop* Sue Williams; *Communs Coordr* Sheila Robertson
Open daily 9 AM - 9 PM, cl Christmas Day; No admis fee; Estab 1964 to exhibit, preserve, collect & interpret works of art; to encourage the development of the visual arts in Saskatoon; to provide the opportunity for citizens to enjoy & understand & to gain a greater appreciation of the fine arts; Average Annual Attendance: 200,000; Mem: 700; dues Artist $25; Student $25; Senior $30; Individual $50; Family $60; Not-for-Profit $75; Corporate $500
Income: $2,000,000 (financed by grants, gift shop, mem, donations & other sources)
Special Subjects: Painting-American, Photography, Prints, Religious Art, Portraits, Painting-Canadian
Collections: Regional, National and International Art

Publications: Exhibition catalogues; Folio, gallery newsmagazine
Activities: Classes for adults & children; gallery theatre; dramatic progs; lects open to pub; gallery talks; tours; exten dept; individual paintings & original objects of art lent to other galleries; lending collection contains 7000 artworks; originate traveling exhibs; gallery shop sells books, magazines, original Inuit art, reproductions, prints & craft items, all with an emphasis on Canadian handcrafts
L　**Reference Library,** PO Box 569, Saskatoon, SK S7K 3L6 Canada. Tel 306-975-7610; Fax 306-975-7670; Elec Mail mendel@mendel.saskatoon.sk.ca
Open to public by appointment; No admis fee; Estab 1964 for art research; For staff use; open to pub by appointment; Average Annual Attendance: 175,000; Mem: 650; dues $30
Library Holdings: Audio Tapes; Book Volumes 10,057; Cassettes; Clipping Files; Exhibition Catalogs; Filmstrips; Manuscripts; Memorabilia; Pamphlets; Periodical Subscriptions 20; Photographs; Records; Slides; Video Tapes
Special Subjects: Art History, Constructions, Folk Art, Commercial Art, Graphic Arts, Painting-American, Painting-British, History of Art & Archaeology, Conceptual Art, American Western Art, Art Education, American Indian Art, Eskimo Art, Painting-Canadian, Architecture
Collections: Aboriginal/First Nation; Canadian Contemporary; Canadian Historical
Activities: Classes for adults & children; lects open to pub, 6 vis lectrs per yr; gallery talks; tours; individual paintings & original objects of art lent to galleries only; lending collection contains books, phono records & slides; book traveling exhibs 20 per yr; originate traveling exhibs; sales shop sells books, magazines, original art, reproductions, prints, ceramics & glass

L　**NUTANA COLLEGIATE INSTITUTE,** Memorial Library and Art Gallery, 411 11th St E, Saskatoon, SK S7N 0E9 Canada. Tel 306-683-7580; Fax 306-657-3951; Internet Home Page Address: schools.spsd.sk.ca/nutana; *VPrin* Doug Njah; *Prin* Bruce Bradshaw; *Librn* Ron Bernston
Open daily 8 AM - 4 PM, summer 9 AM - 3 PM; No admis fee; Estab 1919 to promote an appreciation for art; a memorial to students who lost their lives in the two world wars; Maintains an art gallery; Average Annual Attendance: 2,000
Income: Financed by the institute
Library Holdings: Audio Tapes; Book Volumes 8000; Cassettes; Clipping Files; Exhibition Catalogs; Filmstrips; Kodachrome Transparencies; Motion Pictures; Original Art Works; Pamphlets; Periodical Subscriptions 35; Records; Reels; Slides; Video Tapes
Collections: Paintings & wood cuts by Canadian artists

A　**SASKATCHEWAN ASSOCIATION OF ARCHITECTS,** 200-642 Broadway Ave, Saskatoon, SK S7N 1A9 Canada. Tel 306-242-0733; Fax 306-664-2598; Elec Mail saskarchitects@sasktel.net; Internet Home Page Address: www.saskarchitects.com; *Exec Dir* John Parry; *Mem Services Coordr* Natal Laycock
Open 9 AM - 5 PM weekdays; Estab 1911 to support member architects; Average Annual Attendance: 300; Mem: 111; dues $670; annual meeting in Feb-May; must be registered architect
Income: Financed by mem
Library Holdings: Book Volumes; CD-ROMs
Collections: Books 40's - 70's
Publications: E-newsletter
Activities: Docent training; continuing educ for members; prize given to architectural technology student at Saskatchewan Technical Institute, Moose Jaw (4 twice a year)

M　**SASKATCHEWAN CRAFT COUNCIL & AFFINITY GALLERY,** 813 Broadway Ave, Saskatoon, SK S7N 1B5 Canada. Tel 306-653-3616; Fax 306-244-2711; Elec Mail saskcraftcouncil@sasktel.net; Internet Home Page Address: www.saskcraftcouncil.org; *Exec Dir* Sherry Luther; *Mem Svcs Coordr* Amanda Bosiak; *Exhib & Educ Coordr* Leslie Potter; *Exhib & Educ Coordr* Stephanie Canning; *Admin Asst* Donna Potter; *Communs Coordr* Vivian Orr; *Bookkeeper* Lesley Sutherland
Open Mon-Sat 10 AM - 5 PM, late Thurs until 8 PM; No admis fee; Estab 1975 to support, promote, exhibit & develop excellence in Saskatchewan craft; 900 sq ft; Average Annual Attendance: 25,000; Mem: 420; dues $100; annual meeting in May
Income: $429,000 (financed by mem, city appropriation, provincial grants)
Exhibitions: 8 exhibitions yearly
Activities: Lects open to pub, 8 vis lectrs per yr; gallery talks; tours; open juried competition with award for Saskatchewan residents; book traveling exhibs 2 per yr; originate traveling exhibs to provincial galleries; sales shop sells original fine craft art

M　**UNIVERSITY OF SASKATCHEWAN,** Gordon Snelgrove Art Gallery, 3 Campus Dr, Rm 191, Murray Bldg Saskatoon, SK S7N 5A4 Canada. Tel 306-966-4208; Fax 306-966-4266; Elec Mail gary.young@usask.ca; Internet Home Page Address: www.usask.ca/snelgrove; *Gallery Cur* Gary Young
Open Mon - Fri 9 AM - 4:30 PM, Sat 11 AM - 5 PM; No admis fee; Estab approx 1960 for the educ of students & local pub; Gallery covers approx 3000 sq ft of floor space, 300 running ft of wall space; Average Annual Attendance: 12,000
Income: Financed by provincial & federal government appropriations & university funds
Collections: Contemporary art from western & midwestern Canada
Exhibitions: Constantly changing exhibitions of art works; internationally organized & traveling shows
Publications: Show announcements, every three weeks; catalogues for selected exhibits
Activities: Lects open to pub, 10 vis lectrs per yr; gallery talks; tours; individual paintings & original objects of art lent to recognized regional exhibs centres for one time presentation or tour; lending collection contains 150 original art works
M　**Diefenbaker Canada Centre,** 101 Diefenbaker Pl, Saskatoon, SK S7N 5B8 Canada. Tel 306-966-8384; Elec Mail dief.centre@usask.ca; Internet Home Page Address: www.usask.ca/diefenbaker; *Archivist* Rob Paul; *Office & Progs Mgr* Temesa Ann DeMong; *Acting Dir* M Teresa Carlson
Open Mon - Wed & Fri, 9:30 AM - 4:30 PM, Thurs 9:30 AM - 8 PM, Sat - Sun & Holidays 12 PM 4:30 PM; Admis adults $5, students, seniors & children $3, family $12.50; Estab 1980 to explore Canada's evolution with its citizens & their

visitors. Its focus is Canada's citizenship, leadership & the country's international role; 2,000 sq ft gallery with complete environmental controls; Average Annual Attendance: 15,000

Income: Financed by pub foundations, donations & endowments

Library Holdings: Audio Tapes; Book Volumes; Cards; Cassettes; Clipping Files; Fiche; Framed Reproductions; Manuscripts; Maps; Memorabilia; Original Art Works; Original Documents; Pamphlets; Periodical Subscriptions; Photographs; Prints; Records; Reels; Reproductions; Sculpture; Slides; Video Tapes

Special Subjects: Landscapes, Glass, Furniture, Portraits, Manuscripts, Maps, Sculpture, Drawings, Photography, Prints, Watercolors, Textiles, Costumes, Crafts, Etchings & Engravings, Decorative Arts, Posters, Eskimo Art, Painting-Canadian, Dolls, Jewelry, Silver, Historical Material, Coins & Medals, Dioramas, Period Rooms, Pewter, Leather, Reproductions

Collections: Priministal papers of the Rt Honourable J G Diefenbaker & related papers; John G Diefenbaker Memorabilia & Archives

Exhibitions: Canadian Politics focuses upon the country during the 10th decade of the Confederacy; international & national regional travel exhibits; Prime Ministers office & the Canadian Cabinet room

Publications: The Diefenbaker Legacy, 1998

Activities: Study of modern Canadian history; reference service; classes for children; curriculum-based programs on Canadian law, politics & government; Conferences; seminars; pub events; 5 vis lectrs per yr; gallery talks; tours; book traveling exhibs, 30 plus per yr; originate traveling exhibs provincially; retail store sells books, prints, slides, jewelry, scarves, gifts, souvenirs

SWIFT CURRENT

M ART GALLERY OF SWIFT CURRENT, 411 Herbert St E, Swift Current, SK S9H 1M5 Canada. Tel 306-778-2736; Fax 306-773-8769; Internet Home Page Address: www.artgalleryofswiftcurrent.org; *Dir & Cur* Kim Houghtaling; *Reparator/Registrar* David Tuttle
Open Mon - Thurs 1 PM - 5 PM & 7 PM - 9 PM, Fri - Sat 1 PM - 5 PM, Sun 1 PM - 4:30 PM, cl Sun in July & Aug; No admis fee; Estab 1974 to exhibit temporary art exhibitions; 1876 sq ft; Average Annual Attendance: 18,000

Income: $120,000 (financed by city & provincial appropriation & federal grant)

Special Subjects: Painting-Canadian

Exhibitions: Nine temporary exhibitions per year featuring Provincial, national & international artists

Activities: Classes for adults & children; gallery talks; art classes - various mediums; book traveling exhibs occasionally 1 per yr; originate traveling exhibs

WEYBURN

M WEYBURN ARTS COUNCIL, Allie Griffin Art Gallery, 45 Bison Ave, Weyburn, SK S4H 0H9 Canada; 424 10th Ave SE, Weyburn, SK S4H 2AI Canada. Tel 306-848-3922; Fax 306-848-3271; Elec Mail weyburnartscouncil@live.ca; Internet Home Page Address: www.weyburnartscouncil.ca; *Cur* Ron Ror
Open Mon - Thurs 9:30 AM - 8:30 PM, Fri & Sat 9:30 AM - 6 PM, Sun (Oct - May) 1 PM - 5 PM (cl Sun July thru Aug); No admis fee; Estab 1964 to showcase art & craft work by Weyburn artists, Saskatchewan artists from various large & small communities, nationally known artists & artisans as well as international exhibitions on tour from lending galleries; Public art gallery displaying Saskatchewan art; Average Annual Attendance: 5,000

Collections: City of Weyburn Permanent Collection; incl Courtney Milne: Visions of the Goddess

Exhibitions: Exhibits works from the Weyburn permanent collection at regular intervals throughout each year; Exhibs supplied by lending galleries from across Saskatchewan

Activities: James Weir People's Choice Award given annually; ann adjudicated exhib; book 6 traveling exhibs; originates traveling exhibs to Saskatchewan OSAC mems

YUKON TERRITORY

DAWSON CITY

M DAWSON CITY MUSEUM & HISTORICAL SOCIETY, PO Box 303, Dawson City, YT Y0B 1G0 Canada. Tel 867-993-5291; Fax 867-993-5839; Elec Mail dcmuseum@yknet.yk.ca; *Dir* Paul Thistle; *Dir Admin* Cheryl Thompson
Open May - Sept 10 AM - 6 PM; Admis families $16, adult $7, sr citizens & students $5; Estab 1959 to collect, preserve & interpret the history of the Dawson

City area; Two long term, two changing exhibition spaces featuring Dawson & Klondike gold fields; Average Annual Attendance: 20,000; Mem: 170; dues $30-$1000; annual meeting in Apr

Income: $300,000 (financed by mem, state appropriation, grants)

Special Subjects: Ethnology, Furniture, Glass, Scrimshaw, Coins & Medals

Collections: 30,000 piece coll including archives, cultural, ethnographic, household, industrial, paleontology, photographs; Industrial & Domestic Artifacts; Local history of Klondike region art & exhibits

Exhibitions: Gold Rush; Railway; natural history; mining; Han People

Publications: Newsletter, quarterly

Activities: Docent progs; lects open to pub, 10 vis lectrs per yr; book traveling exhibs; originate traveling exhibs 2 per yr; mus shop sells books, original art, jewelry & souvenirs

L Klondike History Library, PO Box 303, Dawson City, YT Y0B 1G0 Canada. Tel 867-993-5291; Fax 867-993-5839; Elec Mail info@dawsonmuseum.ca; Internet Home Page Address: www.dawsonmuseum.ca; *Exec Dir* Laura Mann
Open Mid-May - Mid-Sept 10 AM - 6 PM, other by appointment only; Admis family $16, adults $7, seniors & students $5; Estab 1959; Museum; Average Annual Attendance: 20,000; Mem: 145

Income: Financed by earned income & government grants

Library Holdings: Book Volumes 3500; Cassettes; Clipping Files; Lantern Slides; Photographs; Slides

Special Subjects: Mixed Media, Photography, Manuscripts, Maps, Historical Material, Industrial Design, Furniture, Glass, Gold, Restoration & Conservation, Scrimshaw

Collections: Klondike & Gold Rush History

Activities: Docent training; 7 lects per yr; tours; mus shop sells work of Yukon artisans, books & souvenirs

WHITEHORSE

M YUKON ARTS CENTRE GALLERY, 300 College Dr, Whitehorse, YT Y1A 5X9 Canada; PO 16, Whitehorse, YT Y1A 5X9 Canada. Tel 867-667-8485; Fax 867-393-6300; Internet Home Page Address: www.yukonartscentre.com
Open year round, weekdays: 11 AM - 5 PM, Weekends: Sep -May 1 - 4 PM, June - Aug noon - 5 PM, third Thurs of month 11 AM - 9 PM, cl Statutory Holidays during winter; No admis fee, donations accepted; Gallery is comprised of a 4200 square foot exhibition space, focusing on Contemporary Canadian Art

A YUKON HISTORICAL & MUSEUMS ASSOCIATION, 3126 3rd Ave, Whitehorse, YT Y1A 1E7 Canada. Tel 867-667-4704; Fax 867-667-4506; Elec Mail yhma@northwestel.net; Internet Home Page Address: heritageyukon.ca; *Exec Dir* Tracey Anderson; *Pres* Marc Johnston; *VPres* Janna Swales; *Secy* Sally Robinson
Open Mon - Fri 9AM - 5 PM; No admis fee; Estab 1977 as a national organization to preserve & interpret history; Mem: 100; dues individual $25, annual meeting in May

Income: Financed by mem, donations & fundraising

Special Subjects: Historical Material, Maps

Publications: Newsletters, tour booklet, Yukon Exploration by G Dawson

Activities: Lects open to pub, 4 or more vis lectrs per yr; tours; competitions with awards; lending collection contains books, photographs, audio equipment (oral history taping); originate traveling photo exhibs to Yukon communities; sales shop sells books, t-shirts, prints, heritage pins & reproductions of old Canadian expedition maps

II ART SCHOOLS

Arrangement and Abbreviations

Art Schools in the U.S.

Art Schools in Canada

Arrangement and Abbreviations
Key to Art Schools

ARRANGEMENT OF DATA

Name and Address of institution; telephone number, including area code.

Names and titles of key personnel.

Hours open; admission fees; date established and purpose; average annual attendance; membership.

Annual figures on income and purchases.

Collections with enlarging collections indicated.

Exhibitions.

Activities sponsored, including classes for adults and children, dramatic programs and docent training; lectures, concerts, gallery talks and tours; competitions, awards, scholarships and fellowships; lending programs; museum or sales shops.

Libraries also list number of book volumes, periodical subscriptions, and audiovisual and micro holdings; subject covered by name of special collections.

ABBREVIATIONS AND SYMBOLS

Acad—Academic
Admin—Administration, Administrative
Adminr—Administrator
Admis—Admission
A-tapes—Audio-tapes
Adv—Advisory
AM—Morning
Ann—Annual
Approx—Approximate, Approximately
Asn—Association
Assoc—Associate
Asst—Assistant
AV—Audiovisual
Ave—Avenue
Bldg—Building
Blvd—Boulevard
Bro—Brother
C—circa
Cert—Certificate
Chap—Chapter
Chmn—Chairman
Circ—Circulation
Cl—Closed
Col—College
Coll—Collection
Comt—Committee
Coordr—Coordinator
Corresp—Corresponding
Cr—Credit
Cur—Curator
D—Day
Den—Denominational
Dept—Department
Develop—Development
Dipl—Diploma
Dir—Director
Dist—District
Div—Division
Dorm—Dormitory
Dr—Doctor, Drive
E—East, Evening
Ed—Editor
Educ—Education

Elec Mail—Electronic Mail
Enrol—Enrollment
Ent—Entrance
Ent Req—Entrance Requirements
Est, Estab—Established
Exec—Executive
Exhib—Exhibition
Exten—Extension
Fel(s)—Fellowships
Fri—Friday
Fs—Filmstrips
Ft—Feet
FT—Full Time Instructor
GC—Graduate Course
Gen—General
Grad—Graduate
Hon—Honorary
Hr—Hour
HS—High School
Hwy—Highway
Inc—Incorporated
Incl—Including
Jr—Junior
Lect—Lecture(s)
Lectr—Lecturer
Librn—Librarian
M—Men
Maj—Major in Art
Mem—Membership
Mgr—Manager
Mon—Monday
Mss—Manuscripts
Mus—Museums
N—North
Nat—National
Nonres—Nonresident
Per subs—Periodical subscriptions
PM—Afternoon
Pres—President
Prin—Principal
Prof—Professor
Prog—Program
PT—Part Time Instructor

Pts—Points
Pub—Public
Publ—Publication
Publr—Publisher
Pvt—Private
Qtr—Quarter
Rd—Road
Rec—Records
Reg—Registration
Req—Requirements
Res—Residence, Resident
S—South
Sat—Saturday
Schol—Scholarship
Secy—Secretary
Sem—Semeseter
Soc—Society
Sq—Square
Sr—Senior, Sister
St—Street
Ste—Suite
Sun—Sunday
Supt—Superintendent
Supv—Supervisor
Thurs—Thursday
Treas—Treasurer
Tues—Tuesday
Tui—Tuition
TV—Television
Undergrad—Undergraduate
Univ—University
Vis—Visiting
Vol—Volunteer
Vols—Volumes
VPres—Vice President
V-tapes—Videotapes
Vols—Volumes
W—West, Women
Wed—Wednesday
Wk—Week
Yr—Year(s)

† Major offered
A Association
C Corporate Art Holding
L Library
M Museum
O Organization

ALABAMA

AUBURN

AUBURN UNIVERSITY, Dept of Art, 108 Biggin Hall, Auburn, AL 36849-5125. Tel 334-844-4373; Fax 334-844-4024; Internet Home Page Address: www.auburnuniversity.edu; *Interim Dean* Joseph P Ansell; *Interim Head* Mark M Graham
Estab 1928; Maintain nonprofit art gallery; Biggin Gallery; pub; D & E; 457 maj & non-maj
Ent Req: HS dipl, ACT, SAT
Degrees: BFA 4 yr, BA 4 yr
Courses: †Ceramics, †Drawing, †Graphic Design, †Illustration, †Painting, †Printmaking, †Sculpture
Summer School: Complete 10 wk program

BAY MINETTE

JAMES H FAULKNER COMMUNITY COLLEGE, Art Dept, 1900 US Hwy 31 S, Bay Minette, AL 36507. Tel 334-937-9581; Internet Home Page Address: www.faulkner.cc.ai.us; *Div Chmn of Art* Walter Allen, MFA
Estab 1965; FT 2; pub; D & E; Scholarships; SC 4, LC 3; D 35, E 40, non-maj 57, maj 18
Ent Req: HS dipl
Degrees: AA 2 yrs
Tuition: Res—undergrad $63 per cr hr; nonres $115 per cr hr; campus res—room & board $1428
Courses: †Art History, †Commercial Design, †Drawing, History of Art & Architecture, †Painting, †Printmaking, †Sculpture
Summer School: Dir, Milton Jackson. Courses—Art Appreciation

BIRMINGHAM

BIRMINGHAM-SOUTHERN COLLEGE, Art & Art History, 900 Arkadelphia Rd, Birmingham, AL 35254-0002; PO Box 549021, Birmingham, AL 35254-0002. Tel 205-226-4928; Fax 205-226-3044; Elec Mail jpandeli@bsc.edu; Internet Home Page Address: www.bsc.edu; *Art Chair Prof* Pamela Venz; *Prof* Steve Cole; *Art Chair Prof* Jim Neel; *Assoc Prof* Kathleen Spies; *Asst Prof* Timothy B Smith; *Asst Prof* Kevin Shook; *Art Instr* Cooper Spivey; *Office Mgr* Judy E Pandelis
Estab 1946; Art supplies may be purchased at BSC bookstore; FT 5; pvt; D, E; Scholarships, Financial aid; SC 22, LC 8, interim term courses of 4 or 8 wk, 4 req of each student in 4 yr period; 500, maj 50
Ent Req: HS dipl, ACT, SAT scores, C average
Degrees: AB, BS, BFA, BM and BME 4 yr
Courses: Aesthetics, Art Appreciation, Art Education, Art History, Collage, Constructions, Design, Drawing, Film, Graphic Design, History of Art & Architecture, Mixed Media, Painting, Photography, Printmaking, Sculpture, Video
Adult Hobby Classes: Enrl 30; 8 wk term. Courses—Art History, Basic Drawing, Basic Painting
Children's Classes: Enrl approx 20. Laboratory for training teachers
Summer School: Enrl 100; 8 wk beginning June 11 & Aug 10. Courses—Art History, Design, Drawing, Painting, Sculpture

SAMFORD UNIVERSITY, Art Dept, 800 Lakeshore Dr, Birmingham, AL 35229-0002. Tel 205-726-2840; Elec Mail lcvann@samford.edu; Internet Home Page Address: www.samford.edu; *Chmn* Dr Robin D Snyder
Estab 1841; maintain nonprofit art gallery; FT 4, PT 11; pvt; D; Scholarships; SC 24, LC 4
Ent Req: HS dipl, ent exam, ACT, SAT
Degrees: BA & BS 4 yrs
Courses: Advertising Design, Ceramics, Commercial Art, Costume Design & Construction, Drawing, †Fine Arts, Graphic Arts, †Graphic Design, Handicrafts, History of Art & Architecture, Interior Design, Painting, Photography, Sculpture, Stage Design, Teacher Training, Theatre Arts
Summer School: Dir, Lowell Vann. Enrl 30, 2 five week terms. Courses—Appreciation, Studio Arts

UNIVERSITY OF ALABAMA AT BIRMINGHAM, Dept of Art & Art History, 900 13th St S, 113 Humanities Bldg Birmingham, AL 35228; 1530 3rd Ave S, Humanities Bldg 113 Birmingham, AL 35294-0002. Tel 205-975-2836; Elec Mail evelee@uab.edu; Internet Home Page Address: www.uab.edu; *Prof* Sonja Rieger, MFA; *Prof* James Alexander, MFA; *Prof* Heather McPherson PhD, MFA; *Prof & Chmn* Gary Chapman, MFA; *Asst Prof* Katherine

McIver PhD, MFA; *Prof* Bert Brouwer, MFA; *Asst Prof* Derek Cracco, MFA; *Asst Prof* Jessica Dallow, PhD; *Assoc Prof* Erin Wright, MFA; *Instr* Doug Baulos, MFA; *Asst Prof* Audra Buck, MFA
Estab 1966, dept estab 1974; Maintain nonprofit art gallery, 1530 3rd Ave-HB113, Birmingham, AL 35294-1260; pub; D, E & weekend; Scholarships; SC 27, LC 15, GC 8; D 500, E 300, non-maj 250, maj 210, grad 12
Ent Req: HS dipl, ACT, SAT
Degrees: BA, BFA, MA Art History
Courses: Advertising Design, Art Appreciation, Art Education, Art History, †Art Studio, Ceramics, Design, Drawing, Graphic Arts, Graphic Design, Illustration, Mixed Media, Painting, Photography, Printmaking, Sculpture
Summer School: Courses—Range over all fields & are about one half regular offerings

BREWTON

JEFFERSON DAVIS COMMUNITY COLLEGE, Art Dept, PO Box 958, Brewton, AL 36427; 220 Alco Dr, Brewton, AL 36426-2716. Tel 334-867-4832; Fax 334-867-7399; Elec Mail slaing@acet.net; Internet Home Page Address: www.jeffdavis.cc.al.us/; *Instr* Sue Laing
Estab 1965; pub; D & E; SC 10, LC 1; D 700, E 332, maj 20
Ent Req: HS dipl or equiv
Degrees: AA & AS
Courses: Art Appreciation, Art History, Basic Design, Ceramics, Drawing, Introduction to Art, Painting, Photography
Summer School: Dir, Sue Laing. Enrl 200. Courses—Ceramics, Drawing, Introduction to Art, Art Appreciation

FLORENCE

UNIVERSITY OF NORTH ALABAMA, Dept of Art, UNA Box 5006, Florence, AL 35632-0001. Tel 256-765-4384; Fax 256-765-4511; Elec Mail cchen@una.edu; Internet Home Page Address: www.una.edu; *Prof* Fred Owen Hensley, MFA; *Assoc Prof* Dr Suzanne D Zurinsky, PhD; *Prof* John D Turner, MFA; *Prof* Ronald L Shady, MFA; *Prof* Wayne Sides, MFA; *Prof* Chiong-Yiao Chen, MFA; *Asst Prof* Lisa Kirch, PhD; *Asst Prof* Nanhee Kim, MFA
Estab 1830; dept estab approx 1930; Maintain nonprofit art gallery; Univ Art Gallery, Box 5006, Univ N Ala; on-campus shop sells art supplies; FT 8; pub; D; Scholarships; SC 34, LC 10, GC 1; D 7250, non-maj 500, maj 150
Ent Req: HS dipl, or GED, ACT
Degrees: BFA, BS & BA 4 yr
Courses: Art Appreciation, Art Education, Art History, †Ceramics, Design, †Digital Media, Drawing, †Painting, †Photography, Printmaking, †Sculpture
Summer School: Dir, Chiong-Yiao Chen. Enrl 90; tuition $1764 for 8 wk term beginning June 8. Courses—Art Appreciation, Digital Media, Painting, Ceramics, Photography, Art History

HUNTSVILLE

UNIVERSITY OF ALABAMA IN HUNTSVILLE, Dept of Art and Art History, Roberts Hall, Rm 313, Huntsville, AL 35899. Tel 256-824-6114; Fax 256-824-6438; Elec Mail art@email.uah.edu; Internet Home Page Address: uah.edu/html/academics/libarts/art; *Prof* David Stewart PhD, MFA; *Asst Prof* Lillian Joyce, PhD; *Asst Prof* Keith Jones, MFA; *Temp Asst Prof* Susan Truman-McGlohon, MFA; *Chmn Art & Art History Dept* Michael Crouse, MFA; *Prof* Glenn Dasher, MFA
Estab 1969 (as independent, autonomous campus), dept estab 1965; pub; D & E; Scholarships; SC 46, LC 14; D 150
Ent Req: HS dipl, ACT
Degrees: BA 4 yr
Courses: †Art History, †Art Studio, Graphic Design, Painting, Photography, Sculpture
Adult Hobby Classes: Tuition $411 per 3 hr course. Courses—Computer Graphics, other miscellaneous workshops offered through Div of Continuous Educ
Summer School: Limited number of courses offered in a two 6 wk mini-terms

JACKSONVILLE

JACKSONVILLE STATE UNIVERSITY, Art Dept, 700 Pelham Rd N, Jacksonville, AL 36265-1623. Tel 256-782-5626; Fax 256-782-5419; Elec Mail art@jsucc.jsu.edu; *Head* Charles Groover, MFA
Estab 1883; pub; D & E; Scholarships; SC 22, LC 8, GC 4; D 8000, E 24, non-maj 70, maj 170, grad 11, others 15
Ent Req: HS dipl, ACT

Degrees: BFA, BA 4 yr
Courses: Art Appreciation, Art History, Calligraphy, Ceramics, Commercial Art, Drawing, Graphic Arts, Graphic Design, History of Art & Architecture, Painting, Photography, Printmaking, Sculpture

LIVINGSTON

UNIVERSITY OF WEST ALABAMA, Division of Fine Arts, Sta 10, Livingston, AL 35470. Tel 205-652-3400 (main), 652-3510 (arts); Fax 205-652-3405; Internet Home Page Address: www.uwa.edu; *Chmn* Jason Guynes
Estab 1835; Maintain nonprofit gallery; pub; D; Scholarships; 1800
Degrees: BA, BS, BMus, MEd, MSc
Courses: Art Appreciation, †Ceramics, Design, †Design, Drawing, †Introduction to Art
Summer School: Chmn, Jason Guynes. Courses—Introduction to Art

MARION

JUDSON COLLEGE, Division of Fine and Performing Arts, 302 Bibb St, Marion, AL 36756. Tel 800-447-9472; Fax 334-683-5147; Elec Mail twhisenhunt@judson.edu; Internet Home Page Address: www.judson.edu; *Dept Head* Jamie Adams
Estab 1838; Maintain nonprofit art gallery; pvt, den, W; D & E; Scholarships, Grants, Loans; SC 23, LC 6; 450
Ent Req: HS grad, adequate HS grades & ACT scores
Degrees: BA 3-4 yr
Tuition: $3500 per sem
Courses: Commercial Art, Design, Drawing, Elementary Art, Painting, Perspective Drafting, Pottery, Sculpture, Special Courses
Adult Hobby Classes: Enrl 5. Courses—Painting, Studio Drawing
Children's Classes: Drawing, Painting
Summer School: Head Art Dept, Ted Whisenhunt. Courses vary

MOBILE

SPRING HILL COLLEGE, Department of Fine & Performing Arts, 4000 Dauphin St, Mobile, AL 36608-1780. Tel 251-380-3861; Fax 334-380-2119; Internet Home Page Address: www.shc.edu; *Chmn* Stephen Campbell, SJ; *Prof, Chmn Communs Div* Thomas Loehr, MFA; *Prof* Ruth Belasco, MFA
Estab 1830, dept estab 1965; den; D & E; SC 21, LC 3; D 163, non-maj 128, maj 35
Ent Req: HS dipl, ACT, CEEB, SAT
Degrees: BA
Courses: Advertising Design, Aesthetics, Art Appreciation, †Art Business, Art Education, Art History, Ceramics, Commercial Art, Costume Design & Construction, Design, Drawing, †Studio Art, Textile Printing, †Therapy
Adult Hobby Classes: Enrl 15. Courses—wide variety
Summer School: Enrl 15. Courses—wide variety

UNIVERSITY OF SOUTH ALABAMA, Dept of Art & Art History, 172 Visual Arts Bldg, Mobile, AL 36688-0002. Tel 334-460-6335; Fax 334-414-8294; Internet Home Page Address: www.southalabama.edu/art/; *Chmn & Graphic Design* Larry Simpson; *Graphic Design* Clint Orr; *Printmaker* Sumi Putman; *Art Historian* Robert Bantens; *Art Historian* Janice Gandy; *Art Historian* Philippe Oszuscik; *Sculptor* Pieter Favier; *Graphic Design* Patrick Miller
Estab 1963, dept estab 1964; pub; D & E; SC 32, LC 25; maj & 150
Ent Req: HS dipl, ACT
Degrees: BA, BFA and BA(Art History) 4 yrs
Courses: Art Appreciation, †Art History, †Ceramics, Design, Drawing, †Graphic Design, History of Art & Architecture, Illustration, Mixed Media, †Painting, Photography, †Printmaking, †Sculpture
Summer School: Chmn, Larry Simpson. Courses—Art Appreciation, Art History, Ceramics, Drawing, Graphic Design, Painting

MONROEVILLE

ALABAMA SOUTHERN COMMUNITY COLLEGE, Art Dept, PO Box 2000, Monroeville, AL 36461-2000. Tel 334-575-3156; Elec Mail sbrown@ascc.edu; Internet Home Page Address: www.ascc.edu; *Chmn* Dr Margaret H Murphy
Sch estab 1965, dept estab 1971; pub; D & E; SC 6, LC 1; D 25, E 8, non-maj 23, maj 3
Ent Req: HS dipl, GED
Degrees: AA & AS 2 yrs
Tuition: In state—$60 per cr; out of state—$104
Courses: Art Appreciation, Drafting, †Drawing, †Painting, Stage Design, Theatre Arts

MONTEVALLO

UNIVERSITY OF MONTEVALLO, College of Fine Arts, Station 6663, Dept of Art Montevallo, AL 35115. Tel 205-665-6400; Fax 334-460-2110; Internet Home Page Address: www.montevallo.edu; *Dean* Kenneth J Procter; *Chmn* Clifton Pearson
Estab 1896; Maintain nonprofit art gallery; Bloch Hall; art supplies available on-campus; pub; D & E; Scholarships, Work study; SC 25, LC 5, GC 7; Maj 200, others 3300
Ent Req: ACT
Degrees: BA, BS, BFA
Courses: †Advertising Design, Art Education, Art History, Ceramics, Commercial Art, Design, Digital Imaging, †Drawing, †Graphic Arts, †Painting, †Photography, †Printmaking, †Sculpture

Summer School: Chmn Clifton Pearson.

MONTGOMERY

ALABAMA STATE UNIVERSITY, Dept of Visual & Theatre Arts, 915 S Jackson, Montgomery, AL 36101. Tel 334-229-4474; Fax 334-229-4920; Internet Home Page Address: www.ASU.edu; *Acting Dept Chmn* Dr William E Colvin FT 10, PT 4; pub; D&E; Scholarships
Degrees: BA, BFA
Tuition: Res—undergrad $1260 per sem; nonres—undergrad $2520 per sem
Courses: Advertising Design, Art Appreciation, Art Education, Art History, Ceramics, †Computer Graphics, Design, Drawing, Graphics, Painting, Photography, Printmaking, Stage Design, Theatre Arts

AUBURN UNIVERSITY MONTGOMERY, Dept of Fine Arts, 7061 Senators Dr, 105 Goodwyn Hall Montgomery, AL 36117; PO Box 244023, Montgomery, AL 36124-4023. Tel 334-244-3377; Fax 334-244-3740; Elec Mail ashughes@aum.edu; Internet Home Page Address: www.aum.edu/indexm_ektid1090.aspx; *Dept Head* Dr Mark Benson

HUNTINGDON COLLEGE, Dept of Art, 1500 E Fairview Ave, Montgomery, AL 36106-2148. Tel 334-833-4536, 4497; *Chmn* Christopher Payne, MFA
Estab 1973; E; 119
Degrees: AA
Courses: Art Appreciation, Art Education, Art History, Art in Religion, Ceramics, Design, Drawing, Graphic Design, Painting, Photography, Printmaking, Teacher Training, Theatre Arts
Adult Hobby Classes: Enrl 119; tuition $80 per hr. Courses—Art Appreciation, Beginning Drawing, Ceramics, Painting
Summer School: Enrl 329; tuition $800 per term for 6 hrs in Art. Courses—Ceramics, Drawing, Painting, Photography

NORMAL

ALABAMA A & M UNIVERSITY, Art & Art Education Dept, PO Box 262, Normal, AL 35762. Tel 256-858-4072; Fax 256-851-5571; Internet Home Page Address: www.alabamaa&muniversity.edu; *Chmn* Hoarce Carney; *Interim Dean* Delores Price; *Asst Prof* Robert Bean; *Asst Prof* Fran Church; *Asst Prof* Jennie Couch; *Asst Prof* Cara Fuller; *Asst Prof* Scott Smith; *Asst Prof* Joe Washington
Estab 1875, dept estab 1966; pub; D & E; Scholarships; SC 18, LC 3; non-maj 430, maj 35, grad 10
Ent Req: HS dipl
Degrees: BS (Commercial Art & Art Education), MS, MEd (Art Educ)
Tuition: Res—undergrad $1388 per sem, grad $221 per sem; nonres—undergrad $2981 per sem, grad $375 per sem
Courses: †Advertising Design, Art Appreciation, †Art Education, †Commercial Art, Drawing, Fibers, Glass Blowing, Graphic Arts, Jewelry, Painting, Photography, Printmaking, Sculpture, Weaving
Adult Hobby Classes: Enrl 10 - 15; tuition $89 per sem. Courses offered in all areas
Children's Classes: Enrl 15 - 20; tuition $89 per sem. Courses offered in all areas
Summer School: Dir, Dr Clifton Pearson. Enrl 50; tuition $426 for 8 wk sem. Courses—Art Education, Art History, Ceramics

TANNER

JOHN C CALHOUN STATE COMMUNITY COLLEGE, Department of Fine Arts, 6250 US Hwy 31N, Tanner, AL 35671-4028; PO Box 2216, Decatur, AL 35609-2216. Tel 256-306-2500; Fax 205-306-2925; Internet Home Page Address: www.calhoun.cc.al; *Instr* William Godsey, MA; *Instr* Jimmy Cantrell, EDS; *Instr* William Provine, MBA; *Dept Chmn* John T Colagross, MBA, EdD; *Instr* Kristine Beadle, BFA; *Instr* Stephanie Furry, DMA; *Instr* Samuel Timberlake, MM
Estab 1963; pub; D, E & Weekend; Scholarships; SC 30, LC 8; D 80, E 22, non-maj 29, maj 70, others 3
Ent Req: HS dipl, GED
Degrees: AS, AA and AAS 2 yrs
Courses: †Art Appreciation, Art Education, Art History, †Ceramics, †Commercial Art, †Drawing, †Film, †Graphic Design, Illustration, Lettering, †Painting, †Photography, Printmaking, †Sculpture, †Video
Summer School: Courses are selected from regular course offerings

TROY

TROY STATE UNIVERSITY, Dept of Art & Classics, Malone Hall of Fine Arts, Rm 132 Troy, AL 36082. Tel 334-670-3391; Fax 334-670-3390; Elec Mail egreen@tsogan.troyst.edu; Internet Home Page Address: www.troyst.edu; *Asst Prof* Pamela Allen; *Asst Prof* S L Shillabeer; *Prof* Ed Noriega; *Prof* A J Olson; *Chmn* Jessy John
Estab 1957. University has 2 other campuses; FT 5; pub; Scholarships; SC 23, LC 11
Ent Req: HS grad, ent exam
Degrees: BA and BS (Arts & Sciences), MS
Courses: Art Education, †Art History, Commercial Art, Drawing, Graphic Arts, Handicrafts, Jewelry, Lettering, Museology, Painting, Photography, Pottery, Silversmithing, Teacher Training
Adult Hobby Classes: Courses—Basketry, Crafts, Matting & Framing
Children's Classes: Enrl 30. Courses—Summer Workshop
Summer School: Dir, Robert Stampfli. Enrl 100; tuition $600 for June 12-Aug 11 term. Courses—Art Appreciation, Art Education, Art History, Drawing, Painting

TUSCALOOSA

STILLMAN COLLEGE, Stillman Art Gallery & Art Dept, 3601 15th St, Tuscaloosa, AL 35404; PO Box 1430, Tuscaloosa, AL 35403-1430. Tel 205-349-4240, Ext 8860; Internet Home Page Address: www.stillman.edu; *Asst Prof* Keyser Wilson, MFA; *Prof* R L Guffin, MFA

Estab 1876, dept estab 1951; pvt den; D; SC 8, LC 2; D 73, non-maj 73
Ent Req: HS dipl, ent exam
Courses: Afro-American Art History, Art Education, Art History, Ceramics, Commercial Art, Design, Drawing, Mixed Media, Painting, Sculpture

UNIVERSITY OF ALABAMA, Dept of Art, 103 Garland Hall, Box 870270 Tuscaloosa, AL 35487-0270. Tel 205-348-5967; Fax 205-348-0287; Elec Mail cpagani@as.ua.edu; Internet Home Page Address: www.ua.edu; *Chair* Dr Catherine Pagani; *Dir Grad Studies Studio Art* Craig Wedderspoon; *Dir Grad Studies Art History* Mindy Nancarrow
Estab 1831, dept estab 1919; Maintains a nonprofit art gallery, Sarah Moody Gallery of Art at University of Alabama; on-campus shop where art supplies may be purchased; pub; D & E; Scholarships; SC 50, LC 20, GC 20; D & E 1500, maj 270, grad 18
Ent Req: HS dipl, ACT
Degrees: BA and BFA 4 yr, MFA 3 yr, MA (art) 2 yr
Tuition: Res—undergrad & grad $2640 per sem; nonres - $8260
Courses: Advertising Design, †Art History, †Ceramics, Constructions, Design, Drafting, Drawing, †Graphic Design, History of Art & Architecture, Intermedia, Mixed Media, Museum Staff Training, †Painting, †Photography, †Printmaking, †Sculpture
Summer School: Enrl 375; tuition $1500 per sem. Courses—Art History, Ceramics, Drawing, Design, Graphic Design, Painting, Photography, Sculpture

TUSKEGEE

TUSKEGEE UNIVERSITY, Liberal Arts & Education, 1200 W Montgomery Rd, Tuskegee, AL 36088. Tel 334-727-8913, 8011; Fax 334-724-4196; Internet Home Page Address: www.tusk.edu; *Instr* Carla Jackson-Reese; *Head Dept Art* Uthman Abdur-Rahman; *Chmn Fine & Performing Arts* Warren Duncan; *Dean Liberal Arts* Benjamin Benford, Dr
Estab 1881; pvt
Courses: Art Appreciation, Art Education, Design Foundation

ALASKA

ANCHORAGE

UNIVERSITY OF ALASKA ANCHORAGE, Dept of Art, 3211 Providence Dr, College of Arts and Sciences Anchorage, AK 99508-4614. Tel 907-786-1783; Fax 907-786-1799; Internet Home Page Address: www.uaa.alaska.edu; *Chmn* Sean Licka
FT 11, PT 15; Pub; D & E; Scholarships; SC 43, LC 7-9; College of Arts & Sciences FT 1310
Ent Req: open enrl
Degrees: BA in art, BFA 4 yr
Courses: †Art Education, †Ceramics, †Drawing, Graphic Design, Illustration, †Painting, †Photography, †Printmaking, †Sculpture
Adult Hobby Classes: Same as regular prog
Summer School: Dir, Dennis Edwards. One term of 10 wks beginning May or two 5 wk sessions. Courses—Art Appreciation, Art Education, Native Art History, Photography & various studio courses

FAIRBANKS

UNIVERSITY OF ALASKA-FAIRBANKS, Dept of Art, 310 Fine Arts Complex, Fairbanks, AK 99775; PO Box 755640, Fairbanks, AK 99775-5640. Tel 907-474-7530; Fax 907-474-5853; Elec Mail fyart@uaf.edu; Internet Home Page Address: www.uaf.edu/art/; *Assoc Prof* Wendy Ernst-Croskrey; *Prof* Todd Sherman; *Prof* Jim Brashear; *Assoc Prof* Michael Nakoneczny; *Dept Chmn & Assoc Prof* David Mollett; *Assoc Prof* Mary Goodwin; *Assoc Prof* Miho Aoki; *Asst Prof* Da-ka-xeen Mehner
Estab 1963; Maintains nonprofit gallery - UAF Art Dept Gallery, PO Box 5640, Fairbanks, AK 99775; art/architecture library; pub; D & E; Scholarships; SC 28, LC 4; D 312, E 60, maj 45, 5 graduate students
Purchases: On-campus shop with limited amt art supplies
Ent Req: HS dipl
Degrees: BA, BFA, MFA
Tuition: Res—$112 per cr hour (lower dist); nonres $343 per r hour; grad level $222/non-res $453
Courses: Aesthetics, Art Appreciation, Art History, Ceramics, Computer Art, †Drawing, †Jewelry Making, Metalsmithing, Native Art, †Painting, Photography, †Printmaking, †Sculpture, Textile Design
Children's Classes: Enrl 50. Courses—Ceramics, Drawing, Design, Metalsmithing, Painting, Sculpture. Under the direction of the downtown center
Summer School: Dir, Michelle Bartlett. Enrl 65; 6 wk term. Courses—Ceramics, Drawing, Printmaking, Sculpture, Native Art-Painting

ARIZONA

DOUGLAS

COCHISE COLLEGE, Art Dept, 4190 W Hwy 80, Douglas, AZ 85607-9724. Tel 520-364-7943, Ext 225; Internet Home Page Address: www.cochise.org; *Instr Dept Head* Monte Surratt; *Instr* Manual Martinez
Estab 1965; department estab 1965; PT 7; pub; D & E; Scholarships; SC 12, LC 2; D 280, E 225, maj 20
Ent Req: HS dipl, GED

Degrees: AA 2 yrs (Painting & Sculpture)
Courses: Appreciation, Art, Art History, Ceramics, Color & Design, Commercial Design, Drawing, Jewelry, Painting, Photography, Printmaking, Sculpture, Special Topics in Art
Adult Hobby Classes: Courses—Painting

FLAGSTAFF

NORTHERN ARIZONA UNIVERSITY, College of Arts & Letters, South San Francisco St, Flagstaff, AZ 86011; PO Box 4094, College of Arts & Letters Flagstaff, AZ 86011-4094. Tel 928-523-2395; Internet Home Page Address: www.nau.edu/cal; *Dean* Michael Vincent; *Assoc Dean* Jean Boreen
Estab 1899; pub; D & E; Scholarships; SC 56, LC 19, GC 8-10; D 400, E 100, non-maj 342, maj 300, grad 30
Ent Req: HS dipl, ACT, Sat I
Degrees: BA & BS 4 yr, MA(Art Educ)
Tuition: Res—undergrad $1078 per sem; nonres—undergrad $368 per cr hr, $4416 per sem (12 cr hr); campus res available
Courses: Art Education, Art History, Ceramics, Drawing, †Fine Arts, Interior Design, Jewelry, †Metalsmithing, Painting, Printmaking, Sculpture
Adult Hobby Classes: Most of the above studio areas
Children's Classes: Enrl 80; tuition $5 for 5 Sat. Courses—Ceramics, Drawing, Painting, Puppetry
Summer School: Dir, Richard Beasley. Enrl 150; tuition $46 per cr. Courses—Most regular courses

HOLBROOK

NORTHLAND PIONEER COLLEGE, Art Dept, 993 E Hermosa Dr, Holbrook, AZ 86025-2036; PO Box 610, Holbrook, AZ 86025-0610. Tel 520-524-6111; Fax 520-524-2772; Internet Home Page Address: www.northland.cc.az.us; *Dir* Pat Wolf, MS
Estab 1974; FT 2, PT 60; pub; D & E; SC 28, LC 2
Degrees: AA, Assoc of Applied Sci 2 yr
Courses: Art Appreciation, Art History, Calligraphy, Ceramics, Commercial Art, Crafts, Design, Drawing, Graphic Arts, Lettering, Painting, Photography, Printmaking, Sculpture, Textile Design, Weaving
Adult Hobby Classes: Courses—Same as above
Summer School: 4 wk session in June

MESA

MESA COMMUNITY COLLEGE, Dept of Art, 1833 W Southern Ave, Mesa, AZ 85202-4866. Tel 480-461-7524, 461-7000 (main); Fax 480-461-7350; Internet Home Page Address: www.mc.maricopa.edu; *Chmn Art Dept* Sarah Capawana, MFA; *Instr* Carole Drachler PhD; *Instr* Jim Garrison, MA; *Instr* Linda Speranza, MA; *Instr* Darlene Swain, MFA; *Instr* Robert Galloway, MFA; *Instr* Cynthia Greening
Estab 1965; pub; D & E; Scholarships; SC 10, LC 8; D 667, E 394
Ent Req: HS dipl or GED
Degrees: AA 2 yrs
Courses: †Advertising Design, Art Appreciation, †Art History, †Ceramics, Crafts, †Drawing, Film, Interior Design, Jewelry, †Painting, †Photography, Weaving

PHOENIX

GRAND CANYON UNIVERSITY, Art Dept, 3300 W Camelback Rd, Phoenix, AZ 85017-1097. Tel 602-249-3300, Ext 2840; Tel 800-800-9776 Ext 2840; Fax 602-589-2459; Elec Mail imorrison@gcu.edu; Internet Home Page Address: www.grand-canyon.edu; *Asst Prof Art* Esmeralda Delaney, MFA; *Assoc Prof Art* Gaylen Stewart, MFA; *Asst Prof Art, Chair* Ian Morrison, MA; *Asst Prof Art* Sheila Schumacher, BFA; *Art Instr* Lynn Karns, MA; *Art Hist Instr* Judy Moffit, PhD
Estab 1949; maintains an on-campus gallery - A. P. Tell Gallery; prv; D & E; Scholarships; SC 52, LC 9 (Art Dept); D 106, E 25, non-maj 75, maj 30 (Art Dept)
Ent Req: HS dipl
Degrees: (art) BA & other university colleges/majors/degrees
Courses: †Advertising Design, Aesthetics, †Art Appreciation, †Art Education, Art History, Ceramics, †Collage, †Commercial Art, †Conceptual Art, †Constructions, †Costume Design & Construction, †Design, †Drawing, †Goldsmithing, †Graphic Arts, †Graphic Design, †Jewelry, †Mixed Media, †Painting, †Photography, †Printmaking, Professional Artist Workshop, †Sculpture, †Silversmithing, †Stage Design, †Teacher Training, †Theatre Arts
Adult Hobby Classes: Watercolor, Printmaking
Children's Classes: Enrl 31; tuition $25. Courses—Ceramics, Composition, Drawing, Sculpture

PHOENIX COLLEGE, Dept of Art & Photography, 1202 W Thomas Rd, Phoenix, AZ 85013-4234. Tel 602-264-2492; Fax 602-285-7276; Internet Home Page Address: www.pc.maricopa.edu; *Coordr, Photograph Dept* John Mercer; *Chmn* Roman Reyes; *Coordr Computer Graphics* Virginia Brouch, Dr; *Art History* Pamela Reed
Estab 1920; FT 5, PT 22; pub; Scholarships
Ent Req: HS dipl
Degrees: AA & AG 2 yrs
Courses: Art Education, Basic Design, Ceramics, Commercial Art, Computer Design, Computer Graphics, Drawing, Painting, Photography, Sculpture
Adult Hobby Classes: Enrl 500; tuition $22.50 for 16 wks. Courses—Full range incl Computer Art
Summer School: Dir, John Mercer. Enrl 100; two 5 wk sessions. Courses—Intro to Art, Western Art

PRESCOTT

YAVAPAI COLLEGE, Visual & Performing Arts Div, 1100 E Sheldon, Prescott, AZ 86301. Tel 520-445-7300, 776-2035; Fax 520-776-2036; Internet Home Page Address: www.yavapai.cc.az.us; *Instr* Glen L Peterson, EdD; *Instr* Dr Will Fisher, MA; *Instr* Roy Breiling, MA
Estab 1966, dept estab 1969; pub; D & E; Scholarships; SC 50, LC 50; D 1650, E 1563
Ent Req: HS dipl
Degrees: AA 2 yr
Courses: Art History, Calligraphy, Ceramics, Collage, Commercial Art, Design, Drawing, Film, Goldsmithing, †Graphic Arts, Illustration, Jewelry, Lathe Turning, Metalsmithing & Jewelry, Painting, †Papermaking, Photography, †Printmaking, Sculpture, Silversmithing, Theatre Arts, Weaving, †Web Page Design, Wood
Adult Hobby Classes: Enrl open; tuition per course. Courses offered through Retirement College
Children's Classes: Enrl open. Courses—Ceramics, Drawing, Painting
Summer School: Dir, Donald D Hiserodt. Enrl open. Courses—Ceramics, Drawing, Jewelry, Painting, Photography, Printmaking

SCOTTSDALE

SCOTTSDALE ARTISTS' SCHOOL, 3720 N Marshall Way, Scottsdale, AZ 85251-5559. Tel 480-990-1422; Fax 480-990-0652; Internet Home Page Address: www.scottsdaleartschool.org; WATS 800-333-5707; *Exec Dir* David Tooker
Estab 1983; D & E; Scholarships; 2500
Courses: Drawing, Painting, Sculpture

TEMPE

ARIZONA STATE UNIVERSITY, School of Art, 51 E 10th St, Tempe, AZ 85281-5613; PO Box 871505, Tempe, AZ 85287-1505. Tel 480-965-3468; Fax 480-965-8338; Internet Home Page Address: www.herbergercollege.asu.edu.art; *Dir* Julie Codell PhD
Estab 1885; maintain nonprofit art gallery; Harry Wood Gallery & Northlight Gallery for Photog; pub; D & E; Scholarships, Fellowships; SC 88, LC 70, GC 116; D 44,500, maj 960, grad 175
Ent Req: HS dipl, ACT
Degrees: BA & BFA 4 yrs, MFA 3 yrs, MA 2 yrs, EdD 3 yrs
Tuition: Res—undergrad $1136 (12 credits) per sem, grad $1136 per sem; nonres—undergrad $4864 (12 credits) per sem, grad $4864 per sem; campus res—room & board $6000
Courses: Art Appreciation, †Art Education, †Art History, †Ceramics, Computer Art, †Drawing, Fibers, †Intermedia, Jewelry, †Painting, †Photography, †Printmaking, †Sculpture, Small Metals, †Textile Design, Video Art, †Weaving
Children's Classes: Enrl 400; tuition $35. Courses—Studio
Summer School: Asst Dir, Jon Sharer. Enrl 500; tuition $93 per sem hr. Courses—Varies
—College of Architecture & Environmental Design, PO Box 871605, Tempe, AZ 85287-1605. Tel 480-965-3536; Fax 480-965-0894; *Dean* John Meunier, MFA; *Dir Archit* Michael Underhill, MFA; *Dir Design* Robert L Wolf, MFA; *Chmn Planning* Frederick Steiner, MFA
Estab 1885, col estab 1949; pub; D & E; lower div 212, upper div 466, grad 135
Ent Req: HS dipl, SAT
Degrees: BA, MA
Tuition: Res—$914 per sem; nonres—$3717 per sem
Courses: Architecture, Graphics, History, Interior Design, Mixed Media, Photography, Sketching
Summer School: Courses—lower & upper div courses primarily in Design, Graphics, History, Sketching and Rendering

THATCHER

EASTERN ARIZONA COLLEGE, Art Dept, 600 Church St, Thatcher, AZ 85552. Tel 520-428-8233, 428-8460; Fax 520-428-8462; Elec Mail wilson@eac.cc.az.us; Internet Home Page Address: www.eac.cc.az.us; *Instr* Richard Green PhD; *Instr* James Gentry, MA
Estab 1888, dept estab 1946; PT 14; pub; D & E; Scholarships; SC 25, LC 3; D 105, E 202, maj 30
Ent Req: HS dipl or GED
Degrees: AA & AAS 2 yrs
Courses: Advertising Design, Airbrush, Art Appreciation, Art History, Calligraphy, Ceramics, Design, Drawing, Fibers, Gem Faceting, Lapidary, Life Drawing, Photography, Printmaking, Sculpture, Silversmithing, Stage Design, Stained Glass, Weaving, Wood Carving

TUCSON

UNIVERSITY OF ARIZONA, Dept of Art, 1031 N Olive Rd, J Gross Gallery Rm 101D Tucson, AZ 85721; PO Box 210002, Tucson, AZ 85721-0002. Tel 520-621-7570; Fax 520-621-2955; Elec Mail artinfo@cfa.arizona.edu; Internet Home Page Address: art.arizona.edu; *Dir* Dennis Jones
Estab 1891, dept estab 1893; pub; D; Scholarships; SC 30, LC 21, GC 32; D 3094, maj 600, grad 100
Ent Req: Res—undergrad $919 per 7 units; grad $942 per 7 units per sem; campus res available
Degrees: BFA(Studio), BFA(Art Educ) and BA(Art History) 4 yrs, MFA(Studio) and MA(Art History or Art Educ) 2-3 yrs
Tuition: Res—undergrad $1174 per 7 units, grad $1132 per 7 units per yr; campus res—available

Courses: Advertising Design, †Art Education, †Art History, †Ceramics, †Drawing, Fibers, †Graphic Design, †Illustration, New Genre, †Painting, †Photography, †Printmaking, †Sculpture, Teacher Training, Video, Weaving
Summer School: Presession & two sessions offered. Request catalog (available in Apr) by writing to: Summer Session Office, Univ of Arizona, Tucson, AZ 85721

ARKANSAS

ARKADELPHIA

OUACHITA BAPTIST UNIVERSITY, Dept of Visual Art, OBU Box 3665, Arkadelphia, AR 71998-0001. Tel 870-245-5559; Fax 870-245-5500; Elec Mail thompsonl@obu.edu; *Dean School Fine Arts* Charles Fuller; *Prof Dr Raouf* Halaby; *Chmn* Larry Thompson; *Prof* Ted Barnes; *Instr* Stephanie Smith; *Instr* Becky Spradun
Estab 1886, dept estab 1934; Maintain nonprofit art gallery; Mabee Fine Arts Gallery, Box 3633 OBU, Arkadelphia, AR 71998; Pvt; D&E; Scholarships; SC 15, LC 2; D 72, non-maj 130, maj 72
Ent Req: HS dipl, ACT
Degrees: BA, BSE, BS and BME 4 yr
Courses: Art Appreciation, Art Education, Art History, Ceramics, Commercial Art, Conceptual Art, Design, Drawing, Graphic Design, History of Art & Architecture, Illustration, Jewelry, Mixed Media, Painting, Photography, Public School Arts, Sculpture, Teacher Training, †Theatre Arts

CLARKSVILLE

UNIVERSITY OF THE OZARKS, Dept of Art, 415 College Ave, Clarksville, AR 72830. Tel 501-754-3839; Fax 501-979-1349; Internet Home Page Address: www.ozarks.edu; *Prof* Blaine Caldwell; *Chmn* David Strain
Estab 1836, dept estab 1952; den; D; Scholarships; SC 9, LC 2; D 83, non-maj 8, maj 17
Ent Req: HS dipl, ACT
Degrees: BA & BS 4 yr
Courses: Art Appreciation, Design, Sculpture
Summer School: Drawing, History of Contemporary Art, Sculpture, Watercolor

CONWAY

UNIVERSITY OF CENTRAL ARKANSAS, Department of Art, McAlister Hall, Rm 101, Conway, AR 72035. Tel 501-450-3113; Fax 501-450-5788; Elec Mail jyoung@uca.edu; Internet Home Page Address: www.uca.edu; *Prof Dr* Gayle Seymour; *Prof* Roger Bowman; *Prof* Bryan Massey; *Chair, Assoc Prof Dr* Jeff Young; *Prof Dr* Kenneth Burchett; *Assoc Prof* Liz Smith; *Assoc Prof* Deborah Kuster; *Assoc Prof* Donna Pinckley; *Assoc Prof* Reinaldo Morales; *Asst Prof* Jennifer Rospert; *Assoc Prof* Ray Ogar; *Asst Prof* Sandra Luckett; *Asst Prof* Holly Laws; *Asst Prof* Li Zeng
Estab 1908; Maintain nonprofit gallery, Baum Gallery of Art, McCastlain Hall, UCA, 201 Donaghey, Conway, AR 72035; on-campus shop where art supplies may be purchased; FT 13, PT 8; pub; D; Scholarships; SC 26, LC 16; non-maj 700, maj 210
Activities: Schols offered
Ent Req: HS dipl
Degrees: BFA, BA
Courses: Advanced Studio, Art Appreciation, †Art Education, †Art History, †Ceramics, Color, Design, Drawing, Figure, †Graphic Design, Mixed Media, †Painting, †Photography, †Printmaking, †Sculpture
Summer School: 80 students; drawing, design, 3-D design, watercolor I, art appreciation, art history

FAYETTEVILLE

UNIVERSITY OF ARKANSAS, Art Dept, 116 Fine Arts Ctr, Fayetteville, AR 72701-1201. Tel 479-575-5202; Fax 479-575-2062; Elec Mail artinfo@uark.edu; Internet Home Page Address: http://art.uark.edu/; *Prof* Lynn Jacobs PhD, MFA; *Dept Chair & Assoc Prof* Jeannie Hulen, MFA; *Assoc Prof* John Newman, MFA; *Prof Emeritus* Robert Ross, MFA; *Assoc Prof* Angela M LaPorte, PhD; *Instr* Joanne Jones, MFA; *Assoc Prof* Marilyn Nelson, MFA; *Assoc Prof* Jacqueline Golden, MFA; *Prof* Michael Peven, MFA; *Asst Prof* Larry Swartwood, MFA; *Instr* Shannon Mitchell; *Assoc Prof* Kristin Musgnug, MFA; *Assoc Prof* Leo Mazow, Phd, MA; *Asst Prof* Bethany Springer, MFA; *Asst Prof* Thomas Hapgood, MFA; *Asst Prof* Alissa Mazow, PhD, MA
Estab 1871; Dept maintains Fine Arts Center Gallery, sUgAR: Student Gallery University of Arkansas & Library; Pub; D, E & Online at Global Campus in Rogers, AR; Scholarships, Fellowships; SC 40, LC 16, GC 20; Non-maj 50, maj 370, grad 16
Ent Req: HS dipl, portfolio for MFA
Degrees: MFA 60 cr hours & BA & BFA 4 yrs
Tuition: Res-$4,344 per yr; non-res-$10,290; room & board $5000
Courses: Art Appreciation, †Art Education, †Art History, †Ceramics, †Design, †Drawing, †Graphic Design, †Painting, †Photography, †Printmaking, †Sculpture
Adult Hobby Classes: Enrl 10; tuition $620 per sem; Courses—Ceramics
Summer School: Dir, Jeannie Hulen. Enrl 150; 6 wk session. Courses—Ceramics, Drawing, Painting, Photography, 2-D Design, 3-D Design

HARRISON

NORTH ARKANSAS COMMUNITY-TECHNICAL COLLEGE, Art Dept, 1515 Pioneer Ridge, Harrison, AR 72601. Tel 870-391-3000; Fax 870-391-3250; Elec Mail sdomino@northark.edu; Internet Home Page Address: www.northark.edu; *Chmn Div of Communs & Arts* Bill Skinner; *Dir Art Dept* Dusty Domino

Estab 1974, dept estab 1975; pub; D & E; SC 7, LC 1; in art dept D 80, E 30-40, non-maj 45, maj 35
Ent Req: HS dipl
Degrees: AA 2 yrs, AFA 2 yrs
Courses: Art Appreciation, Ceramics, Commercial Art, Costume Design & Construction, Design, Drafting, Drawing, Elementary Art Education, Graphic Design, Painting, Theatre Arts, Video
Adult Hobby Classes: Various courses offered each sem through Continuing Education Program
Summer School: Enrl 20-30; tuition $30-$35 for term of 6-8 wks beginning June 1. Courses—open; Art Workshop on Buffalo National River

HELENA

PHILLIPS COMMUNITY COLLEGE AT THE UNIVERSITY OF ARKANSAS, (Phillips County Community College) Dept of English & Fine Arts, 1000 Campus Dr, Helena, AR 72342; PO Box 785, Helena, AR 72342-0785. Tel 870-338-6474; Fax 870-338-7542; Internet Home Page Address: www.pccua.cc.ar.us; *Art Instr* Susan Worrington; *Chmn Visual & Performing Arts* Kirk Whiteside
Estab 1966; Maintain nonprofit art gallery; pub; D & E; Scholarships; SC 8, LC 1; 55
Ent Req: HS dipl, ent exam, GED
Degrees: AA and AAS 2 yr
Courses: Drawing, Pottery, Sculpture

LITTLE ROCK

ARKANSAS ARTS CENTER, (The Arkansas Arts Center) Museum, 501 E 9th St, Little Rock, AR 72202; PO Box 2137, Little Rock, AR 72203-2137. Tel 501-372-4000; Fax 501-375-8053; Elec Mail info@arkarts.com; Internet Home Page Address: www.arkarts.com; *Cur Arts & Interim Dir* Joseph W Lampo; *Educ* Lou Palermo; *Dir Mktg* Heather Haywood; *Registrar* Thom Hall; *Bus Mgr* Laine Harber; *State Svcs* Ned Metcalf; *Dir Mem* Matt Cleveland; *Shop Mgr* Kim White; *Children's Theatre* Bradley Anderson; *Mgr (V)* Carol Isom; *Pres* Belinda Shults; *Develop Dir* Clay Mercer; *Mus School Mgr* Andi Tompkins
Estab 1960, dept estab 1965; Maintains art/architecture library - Elizabeth Prewitt Taylor Library; pub; D & E; Scholarships; SC 62, LC 3; D 350, E 300 children & adults
Ent Req: open to anyone age 4 through adult
Courses: Aesthetics, Art Appreciation, Art History, Ceramics, Drawing, †Fashion Arts, Jewelry, Mixed Media, Painting, Photography, Sculpture, Teacher Training, †Theatre Arts, Woodworking
Adult Hobby Classes: Enrl 1265; tuition $95-$125 for 10 wk term
Children's Classes: Enrl 1373; tuition $65-$75 for 10 wk term. Courses—Theater Arts, Visual Arts
Summer School: Same as above

UNIVERSITY OF ARKANSAS AT LITTLE ROCK, Dept of Art, 2801 S University Ave, Little Rock, AR 72204-1099. Tel 501-569-3182; Fax 501-569-8775; Internet Home Page Address: www.ulr.edu/artdept; *Chmn* Win Bruhl, MFA
Estab 1928; FT 12, PT 5; pub; D & E; Scholarships; SC, LC; Univ sem 10,200, dept sem 1200
Ent Req: HS grad
Degrees: BA 4 yr, MA(studio), MA(art history)
Tuition: Res—undergrad $1054, grad $1441; non-res— undergrad $2557, grad $2971
Courses: Art Appreciation, Art Education, Art History, Ceramics, Design, Drawing, Graphic Design, Illustration, Painting, Photography, Pottery, Printmaking, Sculpture
Summer School: Dean, Deborah Baldwin. Enrl 250; tuition $584 per sem. Courses—Art Appreciation, Art Education, Art History, Studio Art

MAGNOLIA

SOUTHERN ARKANSAS UNIVERSITY AT MAGNOLIA, Dept of Art & Design, 100 E University, Magnolia, AR 71753-5000. Tel 870-235-4000; Fax 870-235-5005; Elec Mail rsstout@saumag.edu; Internet Home Page Address: www.saumag.edu/art; *Prof* Steven Ochs, MFA; *Assoc Prof* Scotland Stout, MFA; *Chair* Dan May, MFA; *Asst Prof* Rebecca Glenn; *Instr* Ann Bittick
Estab 1909; Maintain nonprofit art gallery; on-campus shop where art supplies may be purchased; pub; D & E; Scholarships; SC 18, LC 4; D 240, non-maj 260, maj 40
Ent Req: HS dipl
Degrees: BA, BSE 4 yr, BFA
Tuition: $3,500 per yr
Courses: Advertising Design, †Animation, Art Appreciation, Art Education, Art History, †Calligraphy, †Ceramics, Commercial Art, †Conceptual Art, Design, Drafting, Drawing, †Film, Graphic Arts, †Graphic Design, †Lettering, †Mixed Media, †Motion Gaming Web, †Painting, †Photography, †Printmaking, †Sculpture, †Video
Adult Hobby Classes: Classes & courses open to all at regular tuition rates
Children's Classes: Enrl 30; tuition $30. Courses—Kinder Art
Summer School: Dir, Jerry Johnson. Enrl 60. Courses—Art, Fine Arts

MONTICELLO

UNIVERSITY OF ARKANSAS AT MONTICELLO, Fine Arts Dept, PO Box 3460, Monticello, AR 71656-3460. Tel 870-460-1078; Internet Home Page Address: www.cotton.uamont.edu/~richardt/art_index.html; *Chmn* Tom Richard
Dept estab 1909; Scholarships

Ent Req: HS dipl
Degrees: BA
Tuition: Res—undergrad $2680 per sem; waiver from MI, LA, TX
Courses: Art Appreciation, Ceramics, Design, Drawing, Graphic Arts, History of Art & Architecture, Mixed Media, Painting, Printmaking
Summer School: Enrl 25; tuition $65 per cr hr for June-July. Courses—Art Appreciation, Art Education

PINE BLUFF

UNIVERSITY OF ARKANSAS AT PINE BLUFF, Art Dept, 1200 N University Dr, Pine Bluff, AR 71601. Tel 870-575-8326, 575-8328; Elec Mail lintonhl@uapb.edu; Internet Home Page Address: www.uapb.edu; *Dept Chmn* Henri Linton
Leedell Morehead-Graham Gallery (nonprofit) on campus; pub; D & E; Scholarships
Ent Req: HS dipl
Degrees: BS
Courses: Art Appreciation, Art Education, Art History, Calligraphy, Ceramics, Design, Drawing, Handicrafts, Painting, Photography, Printmaking, Sculpture, Textile Design, Weaving

RUSSELLVILLE

ARKANSAS TECH UNIVERSITY, Dept of Art, 1505 N Boulder Ave, Russellville, AR 72801-8800. Tel 501-968-0244; Fax 501-968-0204; Elec Mail john.sullivan@mail.atu.edu; Internet Home Page Address: www.atu.edu; *Assoc Prof* John Sullivan, MFA; *Asst Prof* Ty Brunson; *Asst Prof* David Mudrinich, MFA
Estab 1909; pub; D & E; Scholarships; SC 28, LC 5, GC 1; D 200, non-maj 130, maj 88
Ent Req: ent req HS dipl, ACT, SAT
Degrees: BA 4 yr
Courses: Advertising Design, Art Education, Art History, Ceramics, †Commercial Art, Display, Drawing, †Fine Arts, †Graphic Design, Illustration, Intro to Art, Lettering, Packaging Design, Painting, †Photography, Printmaking, †Sculpture, Teacher Training
Adult Hobby Classes: Drawing, Oil Painting, Watercolor
Summer School: Head Dept, Ron Reynolds. Courses—Art Education, Art History, Ceramics, Design, Drawing, Painting

SEARCY

HARDING UNIVERSITY, Dept of Art & Design, 915 E Market Ave, Searcy, AR 72149-0001; PO Box 12253, Searcy, AR 72149-0001. Tel 501-279-4426; Fax 501-279-4717; Elec Mail art@harding.edu; Internet Home Page Address: www.harding.edu; *Chmn Dept* John Keller, PhD; *Prof* Faye Doran, EdD; *Prof* Paul Pitt, MFA; *Prof* Daniel Adams, MFA; *Asst Prof* Beverly Austin, MA; *Assoc Prof Art* Steven B Choate, Ph.D; *Dir Interior Design & Assoc Prof* Amy Cox, MBA; *Prof* Stacy Schoen, MFA; *Assoc Prof Art* Greg Clayton, MFA; *Asst Prof* Sarah Wilhoit, Ph.D
Estab 1924; Maintains nonprofit Art & Design Gallery, art/architecture library, & campus store for sale of art supplies; pvt; D; Scholarships; SC 27, LC 9, GC 7; D 103, non-maj 25, maj 103
Ent Req: HS dipl, ACT
Degrees: BA, BS and BFA 4 yrs, MEd 5-6 yrs
Tuition: $472 per sem hr; campus res—room & board $6,000 per yr
Courses: 2-D Design, Advertising Design, Aesthetics, Architecture, Art Appreciation, Art Education, Art History, Ceramics, Color Theory, Computer Graphics, †Design, Drafting, Drawing, †Graphic Design, Interior Design, †Interior Design, Painting, Photography, Printmaking, Sculpture, Silversmithing, †Teacher Training, Weaving
Summer School: Dean, Travis Thompson. Tuition per sem hr for two 16 wk sessions beginning Aug Courses—Vary depending upon the demand, usually Art Education, Art History, Ceramics, Drawing, Painting, Watercolor

SILOAM SPRINGS

JOHN BROWN UNIVERSITY, Art Dept, 2000 W University, Siloam Springs, AR 72761. Tel 501-524-3131, Ext 182; Fax 501-524-9548; Internet Home Page Address: www.jbu.edu; *Asst Prof* Peter Pohle; *Head Dept* Charles Peer
Estab 1919; FT 2; pvt; D; Scholarships; SC 9, LC 3
Ent Req: HS grad
Degrees: AS(Art)
Courses: Art Appreciation, Art Education, Composition, Crafts (copper tooling, Design & Color, Drawing, Painting, enameling, jewelry, macrame, mosaic, pottery, weaving)

STATE UNIVERSITY

ARKANSAS STATE UNIVERSITY, Dept of Art, PO Box 1630, State University, AR 72467-1630. Tel 870-972-3050; Fax 870-972-3932; Elec Mail csteele@aztec.astate.edu; Internet Home Page Address: www.astate.edu/; *Prof* Evan Lindquist, MFA; *Prof* William Allen PhD, MFA; *Prof* Steven L Mayes, MFA; *Prof* Tom Chaffee, MFA; *Prof* John Keech, MFA; *Assoc Prof* Roger Carlisle, MFA; *Assoc Prof* Curtis Steele, MFA; *Assoc Prof* Debra Satterfield, MFA; *Assoc Prof* John J Salvest, MFA; *Asst Prof* Dr Paul Hickman PhD, MFA; *Instr* Jean Flint; *Instr* Nadine Hawke; *Instr* Gayle Pendergrass, MFA; *Instr* William H Rowe, MFA
Estab 1909, dept estab 1938; FT 13; pub; D & E; Scholarships; SC 33, LC 10, GC 34; D 300, E 100, non-maj 800, maj 132, grad 10
Ent Req: HS dipl

Degrees: BFA, BSE 4 yr, MA
Courses: Art Appreciation, †Art Education, †Art History, Ceramics, Drawing, †Graphic Design, Illustration, Intermedia, Painting, Photography, †Studio Art
Adult Hobby Classes: 20; tuition $82 per sem hr. Courses—Art History, Ceramics, Drawing, Painting
Summer School: Dir, Curtis Steele. Enrl 100; tuition res—$490; nonres—$1260 per 5 wk term. Courses—Art History, Drawing, Painting, Photography, Sculpture

WALNUT RIDGE

WILLIAMS BAPTIST COLLEGE, Dept of Art, 60 W Fulbright, Walnut Ridge, AR 72476. Tel 870-886-6741; Fax 870-886-3924; Internet Home Page Address: www.wbeoll.edu/infranetstart.htm; *Instr* Melissa Christiano; *Instr* Jima Mickie; *Chmn* Dr David Midkiff
den; D & E; Scholarships
Degrees: BS (Art Educ) & BA
Courses: Art Education, Ceramics, Conceptual Art, Drawing, Painting, Theatre Arts
Summer School: Dir, Dr Jerrol Swaim. Tuition $925 for 12-16 hrs, &75 per hr

CALIFORNIA

ANGWIN

PACIFIC UNION COLLEGE, Art Dept, 100 Howell Mountain Rd Angwin, CA 94508; One Angwin Ave Angwin, CA 94508. Tel 707-965-6311; Elec Mail ctturner@pcu.edu; Internet Home Page Address: puc.edu; *Chmn* Tom Turner
Dept estab 1882; pvt; D&E; Scholarships
Degrees: AS, BA, BS
Tuition: $470 per unit, $5445 per qtr
Courses: Art History, Ceramics, †Collage, Design, Drawing, Graphic Design, Illustration, Painting, Photography, Printmaking, Sculpture, Stained Glass
Summer School: Dir, Gary Gifford. Courses—Art History, Photography

APTOS

CABRILLO COLLEGE, Visual & Performing Arts Division, 6500 Soquel Dr, Aptos, CA 95003-3198. Tel 831-479-6464; Fax 831-479-5095; Internet Home Page Address: www.cabrillo.cc.ca.us; *Chmn* Dan Martinez
Estab 1959; FT 12, PT 22; pub; D & E; Scholarships; SC 46, LC 7
Ent Req: HS dipl
Degrees: AA 2 yr
Courses: Art History, Ceramics, Color, Design, Drawing, Handicrafts, Jewelry, Painting, Photography, Printmaking, Sculpture, Textile Design

ARCATA

HUMBOLDT STATE UNIVERSITY, College of Arts & Humanities, Art Dept, 1 Harpst St, Arcata, CA 95521-8299. Tel 707-826-3624; Fax 707-826-3628; Elec Mail arts@humboldt.edu; Internet Home Page Address: www.humboldt.edu; *Chmn* Teresa Stanley; *Assoc Prof* Julia Alderson; *Prof* Don Anton; *Assoc Prof* Nicole Jean Hill; *Assoc Prof* Heather Madar; *Prof* Kris Patzlaff; *Prof* Keith Schneider; *Assoc Prof* Sondra Schwetman; *Assoc Prof* Sarah Whorf; *Asst Prof* Ricardo Febre; *Lectr* Lien Truong; *Lectr* Denton Crawford; *Lectr* Nancy Frazier; *Lectr* Mimi Djoka; *Lectr* Lisa Rosenstveicht
Estab 1913; Maintains nonprofit First St Gallery, 422 1st St, Eureka, CA 95501 & Reese Bullen Gallery on campus. Art supplies sold on-campus store; pub; D & E; Scholarships; SC 50, LC 11, Seminar; Maj 450
Degrees: BA 4 yr, BA with credential 5 yr
Tuition: Res—$4500 per yr; campus res available
Courses: Art Education, Art History, Ceramics, Display, Drawing, Graphic Design, Jewelry, †Museum & Gallery Practices, Painting, Photography, Printmaking, Sculpture, Teacher Training
Children's Classes: Children's Art Academy
Summer School: Chair, Teresa Stanley. Summer Prog in Afissos, Greece; tuition $200 per unit & prog costs

AZUSA

AZUSA PACIFIC UNIVERSITY, College of Liberal Arts, Art Dept, 901 E Alosta, Azusa, CA 91702-2701; PO Box 7000, Azusa, CA 91702-7000. Tel 626-969-3434; Fax 626-969-7180; Internet Home Page Address: www.apu.edu; *Assoc Prof* James Thompson, EdD; *Chmn Dept* William Catling, MFA; *Asst Prof* Dave McGill, BA; *Assoc Prof* Susan Ney, MA; *Assoc Prof* Guy Kinnear, MFA; *Asst Prof* Kieran Gaya, MA; *Assoc Prof* Kent Butler, MFA; *Asst Prof* David Carlson, MFA; *Assoc Prof* Melanie Weaver, MFA
Estab 1899, dept estab 1974; Azusa Pacific Art Gallery; dean; pvt; D & E; Scholarships; SC 54, LC 7; maj 190, non-maj 250
Ent Req: HS dipl, state test
Degrees: BA(Art) 4 yrs, MFA 3 yrs
Courses: Art Appreciation, Art Education, Art History, Ceramics, Drawing, Graphic Arts, Graphic Design, Painting, Photography, Printmaking, Sculpture, Textile Design, Video
Summer School: Dir, W Catling; Enrl varies; Courses—varies

BAKERSFIELD

BAKERSFIELD COLLEGE, Art Dept, 1801 Panorama Dr, Bakersfield, CA 93305-1299. Tel 661-395-4674; Fax 661-395-4078; Elec Mail dkoeth@bakersfieldcollege.edu; Internet Home Page Address:

www2.bakersfieldcollege.edu/art; *Chair, Prof Art* David M Koeth; *Prof Art* Nancy Magner; *Dir Jones Gallery* Margaret Nowling; *Assoc Prof* Emily Madigan; *Prof Art* Adel Shafik; *Assoc Prof Art* Kristopher Stallworth; *Assoc Prof* Laura Borneman; *Instr* Cameron Brian; *Instr* Angie Horton; *Instr* Nina Landgraff; *Instr* Cecilia Noyes; *Instr* Debora Rodenhauser; *Instr* Claire Putney
Estab 1913; Maintains a nonprofit art gallery, Wylie & May Jones Gallery, 1801 Panorama Dr, Bakersfield, CA 93305; art supplies sold at on-campus store; pub; D, E & online; Scholarships, Fellowships; SC 22, LC 4; D 860, E 330, maj 300
Ent Req: ent exam, open door policy
Degrees: AA 2 yr
Courses: Advertising Design, Art Appreciation, Art History, Ceramics, Design, †Digital Illustration, †Digital Photography, Drawing, Glassblowing, †Graphic Design, Jewelry, Painting, Photography, Printmaking, Sculpture, †Teacher Training, †Typography
Summer School: Courses—Art Appreciation, Drawing

CALIFORNIA STATE UNIVERSITY, BAKERSFIELD, Dept of Art, 9001 Stockdale Hwy, Bakersfield, CA 93311-1022. Tel 661-664-3031; Fax 661-665-3555; Internet Home Page Address: www.csub.edu; *Chair & Assoc Prof* Sarah Vanderup
Estab 1965; Maintains non-profit art gallery, The Todd Madigan Galleries & Walter Steirn Library; FT 5; pub; D&E; Scholarships; SC, LC
Ent Req: HS diploma
Degrees: BA
Courses: Art Education, Art History, Ceramics, Design, Drawing, Painting, Photography, Printmaking, Sculpture

BELMONT

NOTRE DAME DE NAMUR UNIVERSITY, Wiegand Gallery, 1500 Ralston Ave, Belmont, CA 94002-1997. Tel 650-508-3595; Fax 650-508-3488; Internet Home Page Address: www.ndnu.edu; *Art Dept Chair* Betty Friedman; *Gallery Dir* Robert Poplack
Estab 1951; Maintains nonprofit art gallery; FT 2, PT 6; pvt; D & E; weekends; Scholarships; SC 20, LC 8; D 200, E 100, maj 35
Ent Req: HS dipl, ent exam
Degrees: BA 3 1/2 - 4 yrs, BFA
Courses: 2-D & 3-D Design, Advertising Design, Art Education, Art History, Color, Commercial Art, Composition, Conceptual Art, Constructions, Costume Design & Construction, Design, Display, Drawing, Etching, Film, Gallery Techniques, Graphic Arts, Graphic Design, History of Art & Architecture, Interior Design, Lettering, Lithography, Mixed Media, Museum Staff Training, Painting, Photography, Printmaking, Sculpture, Stage Design, Teacher Training, Theatre Arts

BERKELEY

UNIVERSITY OF CALIFORNIA, BERKELEY, College of Letters & Sciences-Art Practice Dept, 345 Kroeber Hall, Mail Code 3750 Berkeley, CA 94720-3750. Tel 510-642-2582; Fax 510-643-0884; Elec Mail love2jr@uclink4.berkeley.edu; Internet Home Page Address: art.berkeley.edu; *Dept Mgr* Margaret Thalhuber, MFA; *Chair* Mary Lovelace O'Neil, MFA; *Chair* Shawn Brixey, MS; *Undergrad faculty adv* Squeak Carnwath, MS; *Undergrad faculty adv* Anne Healy, BA; *Grad & undergrad faculty adv* Richard Shaw, MA; *Grad & undergrad faculty adv* Katherine Sherwood, MFA; *Grad & undergrad advising asst* Delores Levister, MFA; *Grad & undergrad faculty adv* Wendy Sussman, MFA; *Admin Asst* Jude Bell
Estab 1915; pub; D; Scholarships
Degrees: BA, MFA (sculpture & painting)
Courses: Art Theory, Drawing, Painting, Sculpture
—College of Environmental Design, Hearst Field Annex, Bldg B, Landscape Archit & Environ Planning Dept Berkeley, CA 94720-2000; 202 Wurster Hall, Landscape Archit & Environ Berkeley, CA 94720-2000. Tel 510-643-9335; Fax 510-643-6166; Elec Mail maclark@vclink4.berkeley.edu; Internet Home Page Address: www.laep.ced.berkeley.edu/laep/index; *Chmn City & Regional Planning* Michael Southworth PhD; *Chair* Walter J Hood, MLA & MArch; *Prof Urban Design in Architecture, Head Grad Adviser & Head Master Urban Design Prog* Peter Bosselmann, MArch; *Chair, Dept Landscape Architecture & Environmental Planning & Prof Landscape Architecture & Urban Design* Linda Jewell, MLA
pub; D & E; Scholarships
Degrees: BA, MA, MSC, PhD
Tuition: Res—undergrad $2023.25 per sem, grad $2134.25 per sem; nonres—undergrad $7330.25 per sem, grad $7351.25 per sem
Courses: Computer-Aided Design, Drawing, Landscape Architecture

BURBANK

WOODBURY UNIVERSITY, Dept of Graphic Design, Media Culture & Design, 7500 Glenoaks Blvd Burbank, CA 91510-7846. Tel 818-767-0888; Fax 818-504-9320; Internet Home Page Address: www.woodburyu.edu; *Chmn Interior Design* Randall Stauffer; *Chmn Fashion Design* Penny Collins; *Chmn Graphic Design* Bill Keeney; *Chmn Animation* Jack Bosson; *Chmn Architecture* Norman Millar
Estab 1884; Maintain art/architecture library; art supplies available on-campus; pvt; D & E; Scholarships; SC 56, LC 18
Ent Req: HS dipl
Degrees: BFA 4 yrs, MRA 2 yrs, BArc 5 yrs
Courses: Advertising Design, Architecture, Art History, Costume Design & Construction, Design, Display, Fashion Arts, †Fashion Design, Graphic Design, Illustration, †Interior Architecture, Photography, Textile Design
Summer School: Regular session

CARSON

CALIFORNIA STATE UNIVERSITY, DOMINGUEZ HILLS, Art & Design Dept, 1000 E Victoria St, LCH-A111 Carson, CA 90747-0001. Tel 310-243-3310; Elec Mail jkeville@csudh.edu; Internet Home Page Address: www.csudh.edu;

Chmn & Assoc Prof Jim Keville; *Prof Emeritus* John Goders; *Prof Emeritus* Bernard Baker; *Prof* Michele Allan; *Instr* Patricia Gamon; *Instr* David Parsons; *Prof Emeritus* Dr Louise Ivers; *Asst Prof* Ellie Zenhari; *Instr* Elaine Brandt
Estab 1960; Maintain nonprofit Univ Art Gallery; Cain Educ Resources Ctr; pub; D & E; Scholarships; SC 35, LC 25; maj 130
Ent Req: 2.0 GPA
Degrees: BA 4 yr
Courses: †Advertising Design, Aesthetics, Art Appreciation, †Art History, Ceramics, Collage, Design, Drawing, †Graphic Design, History of Art & Architecture, Mixed Media, Painting, Sculpture, Studio Art
Children's Classes: Tuition $36 - $55 per unit for 4 - 8 wk term. Courses—Crafts
Summer School: Dir, Jim Keville. Enrl 40; tuition $36 - $55 per unit for 4 - 8 wk term. Courses—Crafts, Experiencing Creative Art, Ceramics

CHICO

CALIFORNIA STATE UNIVERSITY, CHICO, Department of Art & Art History, First & Normal, Chico, CA 95929-0820. Tel 530-898-5331; Fax 530-898-4171; Elec Mail tlcotner@csuchico.edu; Internet Home Page Address: www.csuchico.edu/art; *Chmn & Assoc Prof* Teresa Cotner, PhD; *Grad Adv & Prof* Cameron Crawford, MFA; *Prof* Sheri Simons, MFA; *Prof Emeritus* David Hoppe, MFA; *Prof* James Kuiper, MFA; *Prof Emeritus* Yoshio Kusaba PhD; *Prof Emeritus* Sharon Smith, EdD; *Instr* Jason Tannen, MFA; *Prof* Jean Gallagher, MFA; *Prof Emeritus* Michael Simmons, EdD; *Prof Emeritus* Karen VanDerpool, MFA; *Assoc Prof* Nanette Wylde, MFA; *Assoc Prof* Sue Whitmore, MFA; *Assoc Prof* Eileen Macdonald, MFA; *Assoc Prof* Robert Herhusky, MFA; *Prof* Matt Looper, PhD; *Asst Prof* Elise Archias, PhD; *Prof* Kijeong Jeon Mirch; *Prof* Michael Bishop, MFA; *Prof* Tom Patton, MFA; *Prof* Masami Toku, PhD; *Prof Emeritus* James McManus, MFA; *Prof Emeritus* Vernon Patrick, MFA; *Instr* J Pouwels, MFA; *Instr* Nancy Meyer, MA; *Asst Prof* Rouben Mohivddin; *Assoc Prof* Asa Mittman, PhD; *Instr* Michael Murphy, MFA; *Vis Resource Specialist* Erin Herzog, MFA, MLIS; *Technician* David Barta
Estab 1887; maintains nonprofit gallery, Dept of Art, CSU, Chico, Chico, CA 95928; pub; D & E; SC 39, LC 29, GC 29; non-maj & maj 1900, grad 59
Ent Req: Ent exam and test scores
Degrees: BA 4 yr, BFA 5 yr, MFA 3 yr, MA 1 1/2 yr minimum
Courses: Aesthetics, Art Appreciation, Art Education, †Art History, †Ceramics, Design, Display, †Drawing, Glass, †History of Art & Architecture, †Interior Design, Intermedia, Mixed Media, Museum Staff Training, †Painting, Photography, †Printmaking, †Sculpture, Teacher Training, †Weaving
Summer School: Chmn, Vernon Patrick. Enrl 50. Courses—Varies

CLAREMONT

CLAREMONT GRADUATE UNIVERSITY, Art Department, 251 E Tenth St, Claremont, CA 91711. Tel 909-621-8071; Fax 909-607-1276; Elec Mail art@cgu.edu; Internet Home Page Address: www.cgu.edu/art; *Chair* David Pagel
Estab 1925; maintain nonprofit art gallery; Claremont Graduate University/Art Galleries & Special Exhibs Progs, 251 East Tenth St, Claremont, CA 91711-3913; FT 4, PT 9; priv; D; Scholarships; non-maj 1, grad 60
Ent Req: BA, BFA or Equivalent
Degrees: MA 1 yr, MFA 2 yr
Tuition: 2011-2012 $18,187 per semester
Courses: Art History, †Studio Art

PITZER COLLEGE, Dept of Art, 1050 N Mills Ave, Claremont, CA 91711-6101. Tel 909-621-8217; Fax 909-621-8481; Internet Home Page Address: www.pitzer.edu; *Photog* Stephen Cahill; *Drawing* Kathryn Miller; *Prof Ceramics* David Furman; *Photog* Michael Honer
Estab 1963; pvt; D&E; Scholarships, Fellowships; SC 10, LC 6
Ent Req: HS dipl, various criteria, apply Dir of Admis
Degrees: BA 4 yr
Courses: Art History, Ceramics, Constructions, Drawing, Environments, Film, History of Art & Architecture, Mixed Media, Photography, Sculpture, Video
—**Pitzer Art Galleries,** Pitzer College, 1050 N Mills Ave Claremont, CA 91711-6101. Tel 909-607-3143; Elec Mail pitzer_galleries@pitzer.edu; Internet Home Page Address: www.pitzer.edu/galleries; *Dir* Ciara Ennis
Open Tues-Fri 12PM-5PM, other times by appointment
Collections: Nichols Gallery: works by nat & international artists; Lenzner Family Gallery: works by emerging artists

POMONA COLLEGE, Dept of Art & Art History, 145 E Bonita Ave, Claremont, CA 91711-4426. Tel 909-607-2221; Fax 909-621-8892; Internet Home Page Address: http://art.pomona.edu; *Prof* Judson Emerick, PhD; *Prof* George Gorse, PhD; *Prof* Sheila Pinkel, MFA; *Chmn & Prof* Frances Pohl, PhD; *Assoc Prof* Mercedes Teixido, MFA; *Assoc Prof* Phyllis Jackson, PhD; *Assoc Prof* Michael O'Malley, PhD; *Asst Prof* Mark Allen; *Asst Prof* Sandeep Mukherjee; *Asst Prof* Lisa Anne Auerbach
Estab 1889; Maintain Montgomery Gallery at Pomona College; pvt; D; Scholarships; SC 15, LC 25; D 330 maj 37
Ent Req: HS dipl
Degrees: BA 4 yrs
Courses: †Art History, Art Studio, Ceramics, Drawing, Graphic Design, Painting, Photography, Sculpture

SCRIPPS COLLEGE, Millard Sheets Art Center-Williamson Gallery, 1030 Columbia Ave, Claremont, CA 91711-3948. Tel 909-621-8000; Fax 909-607-7576; Internet Home Page Address: www.scrippscollege.edu; *Chmn Dept* Nancy Macko
Estab 1928, dept estab 1933; pub; D; Scholarships; D 580, non-maj 480, maj 100
Ent Req: HS dipl
Degrees: BA
Courses: Architecture, Art History, Ceramics, Drawing, Fiber Arts, Film, Mixed Media, Painting, Printmaking, †Sculpture, Typography

COALINGA

WEST HILLS COMMUNITY COLLEGE, Fine Arts Dept, 300 Cherry Lane, Coalinga, CA 93210. Tel 559-935-0801, Ext 328; Fax 559-935-5655; Internet Home Page Address: www.westhillscollege.com; *Instr* Marilyn Trouse
Estab 1935; pub; D & E; SC 15, LC 2; D 625, E 1250, non-maj 25, maj 10
Ent Req: HS dipl or equivalent
Degrees: AA 2 yrs
Tuition: $11 per unit in-state; $139 out-of-state
Courses: Art History, †Ceramics, Design, †Drawing, Fashion Arts, †Illustration, Lettering, †Museum Staff Training, †Painting, Printmaking, Sculpture

COMPTON

COMPTON COMMUNITY COLLEGE, Art Dept, 1111 E Artesia Blvd, Room E-26 Compton, CA 90221-5393. Tel 310-637-2660; Internet Home Page Address: www.compton.cc.ca.us; *Prof* Verneal De Silvo; *Dr* Cornelia Lyles
Estab 1929; FT 1; pub; D & E; Scholarships; SC 16, LC 6; D 3500, E 2000, maj 18
Ent Req: HS dipl, 18 yrs of age
Degrees: AA 2 yr
Courses: Advertising Design, Afro-American Art, Art Appreciation, Drafting, Drawing, History of Art & Architecture, Lettering, Painting, Photography, Showcard Writing, Theatre Arts
Summer School: Courses—Art Appreciation

COSTA MESA

ORANGE COAST COLLEGE, Visual & Performing Arts Division, 2701 Fairview, Costa Mesa, CA 92628. Tel 714-432-5629; Fax 714-432-5075; Internet Home Page Address: www.orangecoastcollege.com; *Div Dean* Joe Poshek; *Instr Life Draw* Holly Topping; *Prof Drawing & Painting* Roger Whitridge; *Prof Drawing & Painting* Tom Dowling; *Prof Ceramics* Kevin Myers; *Sculpture* Leland Means; *Art History* Irini Rickerson; *Foundations* Joan Sallinger
Estab 1946; Maintains nonprofit art gallery, Frank M Doyle Arts Pavilion & library, Orange Coast Col Learning Resource Center 2701 Fairview Rd, Costa Mesa, CA 92626; on-campus limited art supply store; FT 30, Adjunct 80; pub; D & E; Scholarships; SC 225, LC 25; D 4500, E 3500, maj 825
Ent Req: ent exam
Degrees: AA 2 yr
Tuition: $46 per unit
Courses: Advertising Design, †Art, Art Appreciation, Art History, Ceramics, Commercial Art, †Computer Graphics, Design, Display, †Display & Visual Presentation, Drawing, Film, Graphic Arts, Graphic Design, Illustration, Interior Design, Jewelry, Lettering, Mixed Media, †Music, Painting, Photography, Printmaking, Sculpture, Stage Design, Theatre Arts, Video
Summer School: Dir Joe Poshek. Six & eight wk sessions. Courses—same as regular session

CUPERTINO

DE ANZA COLLEGE, Creative Arts Division, 21250 Stevens Creek Blvd, Cupertino, CA 95014-5797. Tel 408-864-8832; Internet Home Page Address: www.deanza.fhda.edu; *Instr* William Geisinger; *Instr* Michael Cole; *Instr* Lee Tacang; *Instr* Michael Cooper; *Dean Creative Arts* Dr Nancy Canter
Estab 1967, dept estab 1967; pub; D & E; Scholarships
Ent Req: 16 yrs of age
Degrees: Certificates of Proficiency, AA 2 yrs
Courses: Aesthetics, Art History, Ceramics, Drafting, Drawing, Film, Graphic Arts, Graphic Design, Lettering, Painting, Photography, Printmaking, Sculpture, Stage Design, Theatre Arts, Video
Adult Hobby Classes: Tuition varies per class. Courses—Bronze Casting, Calligraphy, Museum Tours,
Children's Classes: Computer art camp
Summer School: Courses—Drawing, Painting, Printmaking

CYPRESS

CYPRESS COLLEGE, 9200 Valley View St, Fine Arts Division Cypress, CA 90630-5805. Tel 714-484-7000, Ext. 47139; *Fine Arts Mgr* Barbara Russo; *Chairperson* Charlene Felos
Estab 1966; pub; D & E, Sat; Scholarships; SC, LC; D 13,200
Ent Req: HS dipl
Degrees: AA 2 yrs
Courses: Advertising Design, Art Appreciation, Art History, Ceramics, Commercial Art, Design, †Display, Drawing, †Gallery Design, Graphic Arts, Graphic Design, †Metalsmithing, †Painting, †Printmaking
Adult Hobby Classes: Adults may take any classes offered both day & extended; also offer adult education classes
Summer School: Extended Day Coordr, Dr Evelyn Maddox

DAVIS

UNIVERSITY OF CALIFORNIA, DAVIS, Dept of Art & Art History, One Shields Ave, Davis, CA 95616-8528. Tel 530-752-0105; Fax 530-752-0795; Elec Mail lcday@ucdavis.edu; Internet Home Page Address: www.ucdavis.edu; *Chmn Art Studio* Gina Werfel, MFA; *Dir Art History* Jeffrey Ruda; *Prof Painting & Mixed Media* Conrad Atkinson; *Prof Painting* Mike Henderson, MFA; *Prof Electronic & Digital Arts* Lynn Hershman, MA; *Prof Painting & Drawing* David

Hollowell, MFA; *Cooperating Faculty Dept of Art* Malaquias Montoya, BA; *Prof Painting* Pardee Hearne, MFA; *Prof Sculpture* Lucy Puls, MFA; *Prof* Annabeth Rosen, MFA; *Prof Painting* Cornelia Schulz, MFA
Estab 1952; FT 16; pub; D; Scholarships; SC 28, LC 35; maj 130, others 900
Degrees: BA 4 yrs, MA(Art History), MFA(Art Studio)
Courses: Art Appreciation, †Art History, Ceramic Sculpture, Ceramics, Conceptual Art, Constructions, Drawing, Graphic Arts, History of Art & Architecture, Mixed Media, Painting, Photography, Sculpture

EL CAJON

GROSSMONT COLLEGE, Art Dept, 8800 Grossmont College Dr, El Cajon, CA 92020-1765. Tel 619-644-7000; Internet Home Page Address: www.grossmont.edu/art/
Courses: Art History, Photography, Sculpture, Video

EUREKA

COLLEGE OF THE REDWOODS, Arts & Languages Dept Division, 7351 Tompkins Hill Rd, Eureka, CA 95501-9300. Tel 707-445-6700, 476-4302 (Art Dept); Fax 707-441-5916; *Dean* Lea Mills
Estab 1964; FT 4, PT 8; pub; D & E; Scholarships; SC 15, LC 3 per sem; 8330, maj 160
Ent Req: HS grad
Degrees: AA & AS 2 yrs
Tuition: Nonres—$148 per unit plus $15 enrollment fee per unit
Courses: Art Fundamentals, Ceramics, Drawing, Fabrics, Jewelry Making, Photography, Weaving

FAIRFIELD

SOLANO COMMUNITY COLLEGE, Division of Fine & Applied Art & Behavioral Science, 4000 Suisun Valley Rd, Fairfield, CA 94534-4017. Tel 707-864-7000; Internet Home Page Address: www.solano.edu; *Instr* Jan Eldridge; *Instr* Kate Delos; *Instr* Marc Lancet; *Instr* Marilyn Tannenbaum; *Instr* Ray Salmon; *Instr* Rod Guyer; *Instr* Marc Pondone; *Instr* Debra Bloomfield; *Instr* Vera Grosowsky; *Instr* Christine Rydell; *Instr* Al Zidek; *Instr* Bruce Blondin; *Div Dean* Richard Ida
Estab 1945; pub; D & E; SC 16, LC 5; D 255, E 174, maj 429
Ent Req: HS dipl
Degrees: AA 2 yrs
Courses: †3-D Art, Art History, Ceramics, Commercial Art, Drawing, Fashion Illustration, Form & Composition, Fundamentals of Art, Illustration, Lettering, Painting, Papermaking, Photography, Printmaking, Raku, Sculpture, Silkscreen, Survey of Modern Art
Adult Hobby Classes: Tuition varies per class. Courses—Cartooning, Jewelry Design, Stained Glass
Summer School: Dean summer session, Dr Don Kirkorian

FRESNO

CALIFORNIA STATE UNIVERSITY, FRESNO, Art & Design, 5225 N Backer Ave, Mail-Stop No 65 Fresno, CA 93740-0001. Tel 559-278-4240, 278-2516; Fax 559-278-4706; Elec Mail info@csufresno.edu; Internet Home Page Address: www.csufresno.edu/art and design; *Chmn* Nancy K Brian
Estab 1911; dept estab 1915; FT 15; pub; E; Scholarships; SC 45, LC 9, GC 4; 1000
Ent Req: HS dipl, SAT or ACT
Degrees: BA 4 yrs, MA 2 yrs
Courses: Art Education, Art History, Ceramics, Crafts, Drawing, Film, †Graphic Design, †Interior Design, Metalsmithing, Painting, Photography, Printmaking, Sculpture, Teacher Training
Adult Hobby Classes: Tuition $35 unit. Courses—various
Summer School: Courses—Ceramics

FRESNO CITY COLLEGE, Art Dept, 1101 E University Ave, Fresno, CA 93741-0002. Tel 559-442-4600; Fax 559-485-3367; Internet Home Page Address: www.fcc.cc.ca.us; *Dean* Anthony Cantu
Estab 1910; dept estab 1955; pub; D & E; SC 13, LC 3; D 14,000, E 2000
Ent Req: none, open door policy
Degrees: AA 2 yrs
Courses: Art Appreciation, Art History, Ceramics, Drawing, Fiber Art, Gallery Practices, Interaction of Color, Painting, Printmaking, Sculpture
Adult Hobby Classes: Ceramics, Design, Drawing, Painting, Sculpture
Summer School: Art Appreciation, Art History, Ceramics

FULLERTON

CALIFORNIA STATE UNIVERSITY, FULLERTON, Art Dept, PO Box 6850, Fullerton, CA 92834-6850. Tel 714-278-3471; Fax 714-278-2390; Internet Home Page Address: www.art.fullerton.edu; *Dean School of Arts* Jerry Samuelson, MA; *Chmn Dept* Larry Johnson, MA
Estab 1957, dept estab 1959; Art supplies available on-campus; pub; D & E; Scholarships; SC 62, LC 27, GC 12; grad 110, undergrad 1200
Ent Req: HS dipl, SAT or ACT
Degrees: BA, BFA, MA, MFA
Courses: †Art Education, †Art History, †Ceramics, Collage, Conceptual Art, Constructions, Design, Display, †Drawing, Glass, †Graphic Design, †Illustration, Intermedia, †Jewelry, Museum Studies, †Painting, †Photography, †Printmaking, †Sculpture, Silversmithing, Video, Wood
Summer School: Enrl 100; tuition $145 per unit. Courses—Art History

FULLERTON COLLEGE, Division of Fine Arts, 321 E Chapman Ave, Art Dept Fullerton, CA 92832-2011. Tel 714-992-7000, 7298; Fax 714-447-4097; Internet Home Page Address: www.fullcoll.edu; *Dir* Kate Johnson
Estab 1913; pub; D & E; Scholarships
Ent Req: HS dipl, ent exam
Degrees: AA 2 yr
Courses: Art History, Ceramics, Computer Graphics, Drawing, Gallery Design & Exhibition, Graphic Arts, Graphic Design, Illustration, Jewelry, Museum Staff Training, Painting, Photography, Printmaking, Sculpture, Textile Design, Weaving

GILROY

GAVILAN COMMUNITY COLLEGE, Art Dept, 5055 Santa Teresa, Gilroy, CA 95020. Tel 408-846-4946; Fax 408-848-4801; Elec Mail jedberg@gavilan.edu; Internet Home Page Address: www.gavilan.cc.ca.us; *Adjunct Prof* Jane Rekedael; *Chmn & Prof* Jane Edberg; *Adjunct* Morrie Roizen; *Prof* Arturo Rosette
Estab 1919; Maintain nonprofit art gallery; art supplies available on-campus; FT 2, PT 3; pub; D & E, Weekends, Long Distance Learning; SC 12, LC 2; D 450, E 75, maj 30
Ent Req: HS dipl or 18 yrs of age
Degrees: AA 2 yrs
Courses: Aesthetics, Art Appreciation, Art History, Art of the Americas, Ceramics, Design, Drawing, Graphic Design, History of Art & Architecture, Painting, Sculpture, Teacher Training, Theatre Arts
Summer School: Dir Jane Edberg. Courses—Ceramics, Drawing, Painting, Photo, Art Appreciation, Art History

GLENDALE

GLENDALE COMMUNITY COLLEGE, Visual & Performing Arts Div, 1500 N Verdugo Rd, Glendale, CA 91208-2894. Tel 818-240-1000; Fax 818-549-9436; Internet Home Page Address: www.glendale.edu; *Prof of Art* Robert Kibler, MA; *Prof of Photog* Joan Watanabe, MFA; *Instr* Susan Sing, MA; *Instr* Annabelle Aylmer, MFA; *Instr* Caryl St Ama, MFA; *MFA* Rodger Dickes; *Assoc Prof of Media Art* Michael Petros, MA; *Instr Art History* Trudi Abram, PhD; *Instr Dance* Dora Krannig; *Instr Music* Peter Green, DMA; *Assoc Prof Music* Beth Pflueger, MM; *Prof Music* Ted Stern, PhD; *Instr* David Attyah, MFA; *Instr* Jayne Campbell, DMA; *Instr* Richard Coleman, MA; *Instr* Byron Delto, MM; *Instr* Jeanette Farr, MFA; *Instr* Rebecca Hillquist, MFA; *Instr* Mark Poore; *Instr* Melissa Randel, MA
Estab 1927; Maintain nonprofit art gallery; pub; D & E; SC 25, LC 7; D 4100, E 3900, nonmaj 800, maj 200
Ent Req: HS dipl, ent exam
Degrees: AA 2 yrs
Courses: †2-D & 3-D Art, †Advertising Design, †Art History, Ceramics, Costume Design & Construction, Design, Drawing, Film, †Graphic Design, Illustration, Lettering, †Media Arts Animation, Music, Painting, †Photography, Printmaking, Sculpture, Stage Design, Theatre Arts
Summer School: Supt, Dr Audrey Levy

GLENDORA

CITRUS COLLEGE, Art Dept, 1000 W Foothill, Glendora, CA 91740. Tel 626-914-8062, 914-8581; Elec Mail bbollinger@citrus.cc.ca.us; Internet Home Page Address: www.citrus.cc.ca.us; *Dean of Faculty* Ben Bollinger
Estab 1915; pub; D & E; Scholarships; SC 26, LC 7; D 400, E 175, non-maj 400, maj 175
Ent Req: HS dipl
Degrees: AA and AS 2 yrs
Courses: Advertising Design, Art Appreciation, Art History, Ceramics, Commercial Art, Computer Art, Design, Drafting, Drawing, Graphic Design, Illustration, Painting, Photography, Sculpture
Children's Classes: Animation, Art Appreciation, Art History, Clay Sculpture, Computer Art, Design, Figure Drawing, Graphic Design, Watercolor
Summer School: Dir, Tom Tefft. Courses—Art History, Ceramics

HAYWARD

CALIFORNIA STATE UNIVERSITY, HAYWARD, Art Dept, 25800 Carlos Bee Blvd, Hayward, CA 94542-3000. Tel 510-885-3111; Fax 510-885-2281; Internet Home Page Address: www.csuhayward.edu; *Interim Chmn* Michael Henninger
Estab 1957; Maintain nonprofit art gallery; University Art Gallery; pub; D & E; Scholarships; SC 30, LC 12; 9900
Ent Req: HS dipl, ent exam, ACT
Degrees: BA 4 yr
Courses: Art Appreciation, Art History, Ceramics, Computer Graphics, Design, Drawing, Electronic Arts, History of Art & Architecture, Intermedia, Painting, Photography, Printmaking, Sculpture
Adult Hobby Classes: Courses offered through Continuing Education Dept

HUNTINGTON BEACH

GOLDEN WEST COLLEGE, Visual Art Dept, 15744 Golden West St, Huntington Beach, CA 92647. Tel 714-895-8358; Fax 714-895-8784; *Dean* David Anthony; *Chmn & Instr* Roger Camp, MA, MFA; *Instr* P Donaldson, MFA; *Instr* D Ebert, MA; *Instr* C Glassford, MA; *Instr* N Tornheim, MA; *Instr* B Conley; *Instr* S Lee-Warren
Estab 1966; pub; D & E, weekends; Scholarships; SC 12, LC 6; D 13,820, E 9339
Ent Req: HS dipl
Degrees: AA 2 yrs

Courses: †Advertising Design, Art History, Calligraphy, Ceramics, Display, †Drafting, Drawing, Illustration, Interior Design, Jewelry, Lettering, Mixed Media, Painting, Photography, Printmaking, Sculpture, Silversmithing, Stage Design, †Theatre Arts, Video
Summer School: Dir, Dave Anthony. Enrl 250-300; classes vary

IDYLLWILD

IDYLLWILD ARTS ACADEMY, 52500 Temecula Dr, Idyllwild, CA 92549; PO Box 38, Idyllwild, CA 52549-0038. Tel 909-659-2171; Fax 909-659-5463; *Chmn Dance* Jean-Marie Martz; *Chmn Theater* William Scott; *Visual Arts Chmn* Greg Kennedy; *Humanities Chmn* Ned Barrett; *Chmn Math & Science* Jerry McCampbell; *Chmn Music* Laura Melton
Estab 1950; pvt; Idyllwild Arts Academy is a 14 wk summer program beginning in mid-June with courses in the arts for all ages; Scholarships
Degrees: not granted by the Idyllwild Campus, university cr earned through USC-LA Campus; documentation provided to high schools for cr
Tuition: Boarding students $25,000 per yr; day students $12,700 per yr
Courses: Ceramics, Fiber, Painting, Papermaking, Photography, Printmaking, Sculpture
Adult Hobby Classes: Enrl open; tuition $165 per wk
Children's Classes: Enrl open; tuition $90-$120 per wk, $65 for half day program. Day & Residential Children's Arts Program; also Youth Ceramics

IMPERIAL

IMPERIAL VALLEY COLLEGE, Art Dept, PO Box 158, Imperial, CA 92251-0158. Tel 760-355-6206; Internet Home Page Address: www.imperialcc.ca.us; *Chmn Dept Humanities* Richard Hann; *Asst Prof Art* Nannette Kelly
Scholarships
Degrees: AA
Tuition: $13 per unit
Courses: Art Appreciation, Art History, Ceramics, Drawing, Painting

IRVINE

CITY OF IRVINE, Irvine Fine Arts Center, 14321 Yale Ave, Irvine, CA 92604-1901. Tel 949-724-6880; Fax 949-552-2137; *Educ Coordr* Tim Jahns, MA; *Cur* Dori Rawlins, MA
Estab 1980; FT 3; pub; D & E; SC 35; D 600, E 600
Courses: Art Appreciation, Calligraphy, Ceramics, Drawing, Handicrafts, Jewelry, Mixed Media, Painting, Sculpture, Teacher Training
Children's Classes: Enrl 400. Tuition varies. Courses—Arts
Summer School: Enrl 40. Tuition varies. Courses—Arts

UNIVERSITY OF CALIFORNIA, IRVINE, Studio Art Dept, Claire Trevor School of the Arts, 3229 Art Culture & Technology Bldg Irvine, CA 92697-2775; 400 Mesa Rd, Claire Trevor School of the Arts Irvine, CA 92697-2775. Tel 949-824-6648; Fax 949-824-5297; Elec Mail stuart@uci.edu; Internet Home Page Address: www.arts.uci.edustudioart; *Prof Painting* Kevin Appel; *Assoc Prof Art History & Cur Studies* Juli Carson; *Chair & Assoc Prof Photog* Miles Coolidge; *Assoc Prof Interactive Installation, & Programming* Beatriz da Costa; *Assoc Prof Media Histories* Martha Gever; *Assoc Prof Video, African American Studies* Ulysses Jenkins Jr; *Assoc Prof Digital Media* Antoinette LaFarge; *Assoc Prof Contemporary Art History* Simon Leung; *Prof Critical Theory, Feminism, Photog* Catherine Lord; *Assoc Prof Painting* Monica Majoli; *Prof Pub Art, Sculpture* Daniel Martinez; *Prof Asian American Studies* Yong Soon Min; *Prof Ceramic Sculpture* Gifford C Meyers; *Prof Elec Intermedia, Tech & Culture* Robert Nideffer; *Prof Robotic Sculpture, Critical Theory* Simon Penny; *Prof & Bren Chair* Yvonne Rainer; *Prof Photog & Media Theory* Connie Samaras; *Prof Visual Studies, Culture* David Trend; *Prof Video, Film Theory, Exper Media* Bruce Yonemoto
Estab 1965; pub; D; Scholarships; SC 25, LC 5, GC 4
Ent Req: HS dipl
Degrees: BA(Studio Art) 4 yr, MFA(Art) 3 yr
Courses: Ceramics, Digital Imaging, Drawing, History of Art & Architecture, Installation, Painting, Photography, Sculpture, Video
Summer School: Ceramics, Drawing, Painting

KENTFIELD

COLLEGE OF MARIN, Dept of Art, 835 College Ave, Kentfield, CA 94904-2590. Tel 415-485-9480; *Chmn* Chester Arnold
Estab 1926; pub; D & E; SC 48, LC 8; D 5000
Ent Req: HS dipl, ent exam
Degrees: AA, AS 2 yrs
Courses: Architectural Design, Architecture, Art Gallery Design Management, Art History, Ceramics, Color Theory, Drawing, History of Art & Architecture, Interior Design, Jewelry, Painting, Photography, Printmaking, Sculpture, Textile Design
Adult Hobby Classes: Enrl 400. Courses—Calligraphy, Drawing, Illustration, Jewelry, Painting, Printing
Children's Classes: College for Kids
Summer School: Ceramics, Drawing, Painting, Sculpture

LA JOLLA

UNIVERSITY OF CALIFORNIA, SAN DIEGO, Visual Arts Dept, 9500 Gilman Dr, La Jolla, CA 92093-0327. Tel 858-534-2860; Fax 858-534-0091; Elec Mail dean-ah@ucsd.edu; *Dean* Seth Lerer
Estab 1967; pub; D & E; Scholarships; SC 55, LC 30, GC 15; Maj 350, grad 40
Ent Req: HS dipl

Degrees: BA(Studio Art, Art History/Criticism, & Media) 4 yrs, MFA(Studio or Art Criticism) 2-3 yrs
Tuition: Res—undergrad $1281.50 per qtr; nonres—undergrad $4818 per qtr
Courses: Art Criticism/Film Criticism
Summer School: Dir, Mary Walshok

LA MIRADA

BIOLA UNIVERSITY, Art Dept, 13800 Biola Ave, La Mirada, CA 90639-0001. Tel 562-903-4807; Fax 562-903-4748; Elec Mail loren.baker@biola.edu; Internet Home Page Address: www.biolart.org; *Chmn Dept & Asst Prof* Loren Baker, MFA; *Asst Prof* Murray McMillan, MFA; *Prof* Barry Krammes, MFA; *Instr* Christina Valentine, MA; *Assoc Prof* Daniel Callis, MFA; *Asst Prof* Kayo Nakamura, MA; *Instr* Patricia Riske, MFA; *Instr* Amanda Burks, BA; *Instr* Lisa Rinaldo, BS; *Instr* Dyanna Espinoza, BS; *Instr* Jenifer Hanen, BS
Estab 1908. dept estab 1971; Maintain nonprofit art gallery on-campus; art library; limited art supplies available on-campus; pvt; D & E; Scholarships; SC 28, LC 4; D 120, maj 120
Ent Req: HS dipl, SAT or ACT; portfolio
Degrees: BFA 4 yrs
Courses: 2-D Design, 3-D Design, 4-D Design, Aesthetics, Animation, Art Appreciation, Art History, Ceramics, Critical Thought, Culmination, Design, Drawing, Figure Studies, Graphic Arts, Graphic Design, Illustration, Installation & Performance, Lettering, Mixed Media, Painting, Photography, Sculpture, Video
Summer School: Dir, Barry A Krammes. six week courses. Courses—vary

LA VERNE

UNIVERSITY OF LA VERNE, Dept of Art, 1950 Third St, La Verne, CA 91750. Tel 909-593-3511, Ext 4273, 4763; Elec Mail johnson@ulv.edu; Internet Home Page Address: www.ulv.edu; *Prof Photog* Gary Colby; *Asst Prof Art* Keith Lord; *Asst Prof Art History* Andres Zervigon; *Dept Chmn, Prof Art* Ruth Trotter
Estab 1891; Maintain nonprofit art gallery; Harris Art Gallery; pvt; D & E; Scholarships; SC 12, LC 10; D 125, E 60, maj 12
Ent Req: HS dipl
Degrees: BA(Art) 4 yrs
Courses: †Advertising Design, †Art Appreciation, †Art Education, †Art History, †Conceptual Art, Contemporary Art Seminar, Drawing, †History of Art, Painting, Photography, Sculpture, †Teacher Training, Theatre Arts
Summer School: Terms of 3 and 4 wks

LAGUNA BEACH

ART INSTITUTE OF SOUTHERN CALIFORNIA, 2222 Laguna Canyon Rd, Laguna Beach, CA 92651-1136. Tel 949-376-6000; Fax 949-376-6009; Elec Mail admissions@aisc.edu; Internet Home Page Address: www.aisc.edu; *Dean Visual Commun* Jonathan Burke; *Dean Fine Arts* Betty Shelton; *Dean Liberal Arts* Helen Garrison; *Instr* Stephanie Taugner; *Instr* George Zebot; *Instr* Kim Owinell
Estab 1961; pvt; D & E; Scholarships; SC 81, LC 48; D 280, maj 4
Ent Req: SATI or ACT, 3.0 GPA, portfolio, letter reg, personal, state
Degrees: BFA
Courses: Animation, Art History, Drawing, Fine Arts, Graphic Arts, Graphic Design, Painting, Photography, Visual Communication
Adult Hobby Classes: 15 wk semesters. Courses—Studio & Lecture courses
Children's Classes: 15 wk semesters. Courses—Studio & Lecture courses
Summer School: Pres, Patricia Caldwell. Two 5 wk sessions. Courses—Studio & Lecture courses

LANCASTER

ANTELOPE VALLEY COLLEGE, Art Dept, Division of Fine Arts, 3041 W Ave K, Lancaster, CA 93536-5426. Tel 661-722-6300; Fax 661-722-6390; Internet Home Page Address: www.avc.edu; *Dean Fine & Performing Arts Div* Dr Dennis White, MFA; *Prof* Robert McMahan, MFA; *Prof* Richard Sim, MFA; *Prof* Patricia Crosby-Hinds, MFA; *Asst Prof* Cynthia Minet, MFA
Estab 1929; pub; D & E
Degrees: AA 2 yrs
Courses: Art History, Ceramics, Color & Design, Computer Graphics, Drawing, Graphic Arts, Jewelry, Painting, Photography, Sculpture

LONG BEACH

CALIFORNIA STATE UNIVERSITY, LONG BEACH, Art Dept, 1250 Bellflower Blvd, Long Beach, CA 90840-0004. Tel 562-985-4376; Fax 562-985-1650; *Chmn* Jay Kvapi
Estab 1949; FT 40, PT 57; pub; D & E; Scholarships, Fellowships; SC 164, LC 26, GC 23, for both locations; 5356 for both locations
Ent Req: HS grad, ent exam, SAT
Degrees: BA, BFA, MA, MFA
Courses: Art Education, Art History, Bio Medical Art, Ceramics, †Digital Media, Drawing, †Fiber Art, †Intermedia, †Metals, Museum Studies, Painting, Photography, Printmaking, Sculpture, †Studio Art, †Wood
Children's Classes: Ceramics, Drawing, Painting
Summer School: Dean, Dr Robert Behm. Tuition $150 per unit. Courses—Art Education, Art History, Ceramics, Drawing, Fiber, Graphic Design, Illustration, Painting, Special Topics, Photography
—Design Dept, 1250 Bellflower Blvd, Long Beach, CA 90840. Tel 562-985-5089; Fax 562-985-2284; *Dean* Wade Hobgood; *Chmn* Charles Leinbach
Estab 1949; FT 10, PT 9; pub; SC 164, LC 26, GC 23 for both locations; 5356 for both locations
Ent Req: HS grad, ent exam

Degrees: BF, BFA, BS, MA, MFA
Courses: Design, Industrial Design, Interior Design, Perspective, Rapid Visualization
Summer School: Dean, Dr Donna George

LONG BEACH CITY COLLEGE, Art & Photography Dept, 4901 E Carson St, Long Beach, CA 90808-1780. Tel 562-938-4319; Internet Home Page Address: www.art.lbcc.edu; *Instr* Larry White; *Instr* Linda King, MFA; *Instr* Rodney Tsukashima, MA; *Instr* Mike Daniel, MFA; *Instr* Stas Orlovski; *Dept Chmn* Ann Mitchell; *Instr* Colleen Sterritt; *Assoc Prof Jewelry & Metalwork, Program Coordr Applied Design* Kristin Beeler, MFA
Pub; D, E & W; Scholarships; SC 65, LC 26
Ent Req: HS dipl, ent exam
Degrees: AA & cert 2 yrs
Courses: Art History, Ceramics, Commercial Art, Computer Art & Design, Drawing, Illustration, Jewelry, Lettering, Mixed Media, Painting, Photography, Printmaking, Sculpture, Studio Crafts
Adult Hobby Classes: Enrl 1500; tuition $13 per unit sem. Courses—Art History, Ceramics, Computer Graphics, Drawing, Jewelry, Painting, Photography, Printmaking, Sculpture
Summer School: Tuition $13 for 4-8 wk sem. Courses—same as above

LOS ALTOS HILLS

FOOTHILL COLLEGE, Fine Arts & Communications Div, 12345 El Monte Rd, Los Altos Hills, CA 94022. Tel 650-949-7325; Internet Home Page Address: www.foothillcollege.edu; *Dean* Alan Harvey
College has three campuses; D; Scholarships
Degrees: AA, cert
Tuition: Res—undergrad & grad $30 per unit; nonres—grad $102 per unit
Courses: Advertising Design, Art Appreciation, Art History, Ceramics, Computer Graphics, Design, Drawing, Film, Illustration, Painting, Photography, Printmaking, Sculpture, Stage Design, Textile Design

LOS ANGELES

ACE GALLERY, 5514 Wilshire Blvd, Los Angeles, CA 90046-3829. Tel 323-935-4411; Fax 323-202-1082; Elec Mail acelosa@aol.com; *Dir* Douglas Chrismas
Estab 1955; pvt; D; Scholarships; SC 4, LC 4, GC 4; D 6, E 7, non-maj 2, maj 8, grad 3
Ent Req: art school dipl, ent exam
Courses: Architecture, Calligraphy, Collage, Design, Drafting, Drawing, Graphic Arts, History of Art & Architecture, †History of Art in Architecture, Intermedia, Lettering, Mixed Media, Painting, Photography, Printmaking, Sculpture, Stage Design

THE AMERICAN FILM INSTITUTE, Center for Advanced Film & Television, 2021 N Western Ave, Los Angeles, CA 90027-1625. Tel 323-856-7600; Fax 323-467-4578; Internet Home Page Address: www.afionline.org/nft; *Dir & COO* James Hindman; *Dir & CEO* Jean Firstenberg; *Chmn Bd Trustees* Howard Stringer; *Chmn (V)* Frederick S Pierce; *Chmn Bd Dirs* John Aunet
Estab 1969 to aid in the development & collaboration of making films; Scholarships
Degrees: MFA
Courses: †Cinematography, Digital Media, †Directing, †Editing, Film, †Producing, †Production Design & Screen Writing, Video
Adult Hobby Classes: Non degree evening & weekend classes

BRENTWOOD ART CENTER, 13031 Montana Ave, Los Angeles, CA 90049-4891. Tel 310-451-5657; Fax 310-395-5403; Internet Home Page Address: www.brentwoodart.com; *Dir* Edward Buttwinick, BA
Estab 1971; 25; pub & pvt; D & E; SC 40; D 400, E 100
Courses: Design, Drawing, Mixed Media, Painting, Sculpture
Adult Hobby Classes: Enrl 300; tuition $175-$225 per month. Courses—Basic Drawing, Design, Life Drawing, Mixed Media, Painting, Sculpture
Children's Classes: Enrl 300; tuition $100-$180 per month. Courses—Cartooning, Drawing, Mixed Media, Painting, Sculpture
Summer School: Dir, Ed Buttwinick. Enrl 400; tuition $300-$500 for nine wk prog. Courses—Drawing, Mixed Media, Painting, Sculpture

CALIFORNIA STATE UNIVERSITY, LOS ANGELES, Art Dept, 5151 State University Dr, Los Angeles, CA 90032-4226. Tel 323-343-4010; Fax 323-343-4045; Elec Mail eforde@calstatela.edu; Internet Home Page Address: www.calstatela.edu/; *Chmn* Ed Forde, MFA
Estab 1947; Maintains fine arts gallery; art supplies available on-campus; pub; D & E; Scholarships; SC 85, LC 12, GC 9; D 2500 (Art), non-maj 150, maj 324, grad 47 (per quarter)
Ent Req: HS dipl, ent exam
Degrees: BA(Art), MA(Art), MFA(Art)
Courses: Advertising Design, Architecture, Art Education, Art History, †Ceramics, †Commercial Art, †Computer Graphics, Costume Design, Costume Design & Construction, Design, †Design Theory, †Drawing, Fashion Illustration, Graphic Arts, History of Art & Architecture, †Illustration, Painting, †Photography, Printmaking, Sculpture, †Teacher Training, †Textile Design, Textiles

INNER-CITY ARTS, 720 Kohler St, Los Angeles, CA 90021-1518. Tel 213-627-9621; Fax 213-627-6469; Elec Mail info@inner-cityarts.org; Internet Home Page Address: www.inner-cityarts.org; *Co-Founder & Artistic Dir* Bob Bates; *Dir Opers* Susie Goliti; *Deputy Dir* Sharyn L Church; *Chief Financial Officer* Ofelia De Los Santos
Estab to enrich the lives of inner city children, through a total arts program; 4; pub; D

LOS ANGELES CITY COLLEGE, Dept of Art, 855 N Vermont Ave, Los Angeles, CA 90029-3588. Tel 323-953-4000; Internet Home Page Address: www.lacc.cc.ca.us; *Chmn* Norman Schwab; *Instr* Phyllis Muldavin; *Prof* Gloria Bohanon, MFA; *Prof* Gayle Partlow; *Prof* La Monte Westmoreland; *Prof* Lee Whitton
Estab 1929; PT 9; pub; D & E; Scholarships; SC 48, LC 8; D 450, E 150, non-maj approx 2/3, maj approx 1/3
Ent Req: HS dipl & over 18 yrs of age
Degrees: AA 2 yr
Courses: †Advertising Design, †Art History, Ceramics, †Commercial Art, Display, Drawing, †Graphic Design, Life Drawing, †Painting, Printmaking, Sculpture
Adult Hobby Classes: Enrl 2090; tuition approx $20 per class of 8 wks. Courses—Ceramics, Design, Drawing, Painting, Perspective, Printmaking, Sculpture
Summer School: Chmn, Phyllis Muldavin. Enrl 250; tuition $50 for term of 6 wks beginning July. Courses—basic courses only

LOYOLA MARYMOUNT UNIVERSITY, Dept of Art & Art History, 1 LMU Dr, MS 8346 Los Angeles, CA 90045-2659. Tel 310-338-7424, 338-5189; Fax 310-338-1948; Elec Mail mtang@imu.edu; Internet Home Page Address: www.lmu.edu; *Prof* Rudolf Fleck, MFA; *Prof* Terresa Munoz, MFA; *Assoc Prof* Katherine Harper, PhD; *Prof* Jane Brucker, MFA; *Prof* Michael Brodsky, MFA; *Asst Prof* Dmitry Kmelnitsky, MFA; *Asst Prof* Teresa Lenihan, MFA; *Asst Prof* Damon Willick, PhD; *Assoc Prof* Dr Kirstin Noreen, PhD; *Asst Prof* Garland Kirkpatrick, MFA; *Asst Prof* Diane Meyer, MFA; *Asst Prof* Han Dai-Yu, MFA
Estab as Marymount Col in 1940, merged with Loyola Univ 1968; Maintain nonprofit art gallery, Laband art gallery; FT 13, PT 24; pvt & den; D & E; Scholarships; SC 65, LC 20; Maj 200
Ent Req: HS dipl
Degrees: BA 4 yrs
Courses: Advertising Design, Aesthetics, Art Appreciation, †Art Education, Art History, Ceramics, Computer Animation, Computer Graphics, †Conceptual Art, Design, Drawing, Graphic Arts, Graphic Design, Illustration, Jewelry, Lettering, †Mixed Media, †Museum Staff Training, Painting, Photography, Printmaking, Sculpture, Silversmithing
Adult Hobby Classes: Ceramics, Jewelry
Summer School: Dir, Chris Chapple, PhD. Courses— Ceramics, Computer Graphics, Jewelry, Art History, Water Color
  —**Laband Art Gallery,** One LMU Dr MS 8346, Los Angeles, CA 90045-2659.
  —**Von Der Ahe Library,** One LMU Dr MS 8203, Los Angeles, CA 90045-2659.

MOUNT SAINT MARY'S COLLEGE, Art Dept, 12001 Chalon Rd, Los Angeles, CA 90049-1599. Tel 310-954-4000, 954-4361 (art); Elec Mail adm@mscm.la.edu; Internet Home Page Address: www.msmc.la.edu; *Chmn & Prof* Jody Baral
Estab as Chalon Campus in 1925, also maintains Doheny Campus estab 1962; den; D & E; Scholarships; D 60, non-maj 31, maj 29
Ent Req: HS dipl
Degrees: BA and BFA 4 yrs
Courses: †Art Education, †Art History, Ceramics, †Collage, †Conceptual Art, †Constructions, Drawing, Fiber Design, †Graphic Arts, †Graphic Design, †Illustration, †Intermedia, †Mixed Media, Painting, Photography, †Printmaking, Sculpture, †Textile Design

OCCIDENTAL COLLEGE, Dept of Art History & Visual Arts, 1600 Campus Rd M-2, Los Angeles, CA 90041-3314. Tel 323-259-2749; Fax 323-259-2930; Elec Mail admissions@oxy.com; Internet Home Page Address: www.oxy.edu; *Chmn* Louise Yuhas, PhD; *Prof* Eric Frank, PhD; *Prof* Amy Lyford, PhD; *Prof* Esther Yau, PhD; *Prof* Broderick Fox, MFA, PhD; *Prof* Linda Besemer, MFA; *Prof* Linda Lyke, MFA; *Prof* Mary Beth Heffernan, MFA
Estab 1887; FT 7, PT 2; pvt; D & E; Scholarships, Grants; SC 19, LC 25, GC 5; maj 40, others 300
Ent Req: HS dipl, col transcript, SAT, recommendations
Degrees: BA 4 yrs
Courses: Aesthetics, †Art History, Ceramics, †Drawing, †Film, †Film & Media Studies, †Graphics, Mixed Media, †Painting, †Printmaking, †Sculpture
Adult Hobby Classes: Fundamentals

OTIS COLLEGE OF ART & DESIGN, Fine Arts, 9045 Lincoln Blvd, Los Angeles, CA 90045-3505. Tel 310-665-6885; Fax 310-665--6821; Elec Mail finearts@otis.edu; Internet Home Page Address: www.otis.edu; *Chmn* Meg Cranston; *Asst Chmn* Alex Slade; *Prog Dir Painting* Scott Grieger; *Prog Dir Photog* Soo Kim; *Prog Dir Sculpture/New Genres* Jacci den Hartog
Estab 1918; Maintains nonprofit art gallery & Millard Sheets Library; Pvt; D & E; Scholarships; SC 276, LC 117, GC 31; D 1,043, E 550, maj 1,043, grad 46
Degrees: BFA 4 yrs, MFA 2 yrs
Tuition: $14,473 per sem
Courses: Architecture/Landscapes/Interiors, Art Education, Communication Design, Digital Media, Environmental Arts, †Fashion Design, Fine Arts, Graphic Design, Illustration, Interactive Product Design, Photography, Toy Design
Adult Hobby Classes: Enrl 2,400; tuition varies
Children's Classes: Enrl 300. Tuition & courses vary
Summer School: Coordr K-12 Prog, Rosina Catalano. Tuition & courses vary

SOUTHERN CALIFORNIA INSTITUTE OF ARCHITECTURE, 960 E 3rd St, Los Angeles, CA 90013-1822. Tel 213-613-2200; Fax 213-613-2260; Elec Mail admissions@sciarc.edu; Internet Home Page Address: www.sciarc.edu; *Dir* Eric Owen Moss; *Dir Asst* Bijal Shah; *Acad Prog Asst* Paul Holliday; *Undergrad Dir* Chris Genik; *Grad Dir* Ming Fung
Estab 1972; Maintain a nonprofit art gallery, SCI-Arc Gallery, 960 E 3rd St, Los Angeles, CA 90013; pvt; D & E
Degrees: BArch, MArch
Courses: Architecture
Summer School: Summer Foundation Program in Architecture: Making & Meaning, $2,840

UNIVERSITY OF CALIFORNIA, LOS ANGELES, Dept of Art, 1300 Dickson Art Ctr, Los Angeles, CA 90095; Box 951615, Los Angeles, CA 90095-1615. Tel 310-825-3281; Fax 310-206-6676; Internet Home Page Address: www.arts.ucla.edu; *Chmn* Barbara Drucker
Scholarships, Fellowships
Degrees: BA, MA, MFA
Courses: Ceramics, Critical & Curatorial Studies, Drawing, Interdisciplinary Studio, New Genres, Painting, Photography, Sculpture
—Dept of Design & Media Arts, PO Box 951456, Broad Art Center Ste 2275 Los Angeles, CA 90095-1615. Tel 310-825-9007; Fax 310-206-6676; Internet Home Page Address: www.design.ucla.edu; *Chmn* Casey Reas
pub; D; SC, LC, GC
Ent Req: Dept and UCLA Application
Degrees: BA, MA, MFA
Tuition: Res—undergrad $1252 per quarter, grad $1420 per quarter; nonres—undergrad $3819.50 per quarter, grad $3987 per quarter
Courses: Art Education, Ceramics, Computer Imagery, Design, Fiber Textile, Graphic Design, Industrial Design, Interior Design, Video
—Dept Art History, PO Box 9511417, 100 Dodd Hall Los Angeles, CA 90095-1417. Tel 310-206-6905; Internet Home Page Address: www.ucla.edu; *Dept Chmn* Anthony Vidler
Scholarships, Fellowships
Degrees: BA, MA, PhD
Tuition: Res—undergrad $1252 per quarter, grad $1420 per quarter; nonres—undergrad $3819.50 per quarter, grad $3987 per quarter
Courses: †Art History

UNIVERSITY OF JUDAISM, Dept of Continuing Education, 15600 Mulholland Dr, Los Angeles, CA 90077-1599. Tel 310-476-9777; Fax 310-471-1278; Internet Home Page Address: www.uj.edu; *Dir* Gady Levy
Estab 1947; den; SC 14, LC 6
Degrees: units in continuing education only
Courses: Art History, Book Illustration, Calligraphy, Drawing, History of Jewish Art, Interior Design, Painting, Photography, Picture Book Making for Children, Sculpture, Tile Painting
Adult Hobby Classes: Enrl 8; tuition $127 per sem
Summer School: Courses offered

UNIVERSITY OF SOUTHERN CALIFORNIA, College of Letters, Arts & Sciences, Von KleinSmid Center-VKC 351, University of Southern California Los Angeles, CA 90089-0047. Tel 213-740-4552; Fax 213-740-8971; Elec Mail arthist@college.usc.edu; Internet Home Page Address: http://college.usc.edu/ahis/home/; *Chair* Carolyn Malone
Estab 1887, school estab 1979
Courses: †Art History

MALIBU

PEPPERDINE UNIVERSITY, SEAVER COLLEGE, Dept of Art, 24255 Pacific Coast Hwy, Malibu, CA 90263-3999. Tel 310-506-4000; Fax 310-506-7403; Elec Mail admission-seaver@pepperdine.edu; Internet Home Page Address: seavers.pepperdine.edu/finearts; *Prof* Avery Falkner; *Prof* Joe Piasentin; *Asst Prof* K Genevieve Freeman; *Assoc Prof* Cynthia Colburn; *Assoc Prof* Sonia Sorrell; *Chmn Fine Art* Gary Cobb
Estab 1937; Maintain nonprofit art gallery, Weisman Art Museum, Cultural Arts Center, Pepperdine University, Malibu, CA 90263; Church of Christ, pvt; D; Scholarships; SC & LC
Degrees: BA in Art
Tuition: Apartment $26,100; campus res—room & board $25,850 per yr
Courses: Art Appreciation, Art Education, Art History, Ceramics, Design, Drawing, Graphic Arts, Jewelry, Monotypes, Painting, Sculpture
Children's Classes: Children's classes are offered thru Weisman Museum (on campus), Dir Dr. Michael Zahian, Cultural Arts Center, Pepperdine Univ, Malibu, CA 90263
Summer School: Enrl 20; tuition $235 per unit. Courses—Jewelry, Mixed Media, Monotypes, Painting

MARYSVILLE

YUBA COLLEGE, Fine Arts Division, 2088 N Beale Rd, Marysville, CA 95901-7699. Tel 530-741-6700; Internet Home Page Address: www.yuba.cc.ca.us; *Assoc Dean* Michael Moyers
Estab 1927; FT 2; pub; D & E; Scholarships; SC 23, LC 2; total 1437, maj 493
Ent Req: HS grad or 18 yrs of age
Degrees: AA 2 yr
Summer School: Dean & Assoc Dean Community Educ, Cal Gower. Courses—Ceramics, Drawing

MENDOCINO

MENDOCINO ART CENTER, 45200 Little Lake St, Mendocino, CA 95460; PO Box 765, Mendocino, CA 95460-0765. Tel 707-937-5818; WATS 800-653-3328; *Exec Dir* Peggy Templer
Estab 1959; pvt; D & E; SC 24, LC 6; D 24
Publications: A&E Magazine, monthly
Ent Req: mutual interview, ceramics ROP 2 yr prog
Degrees: program in ceramics, sculpture, jewelry, textiles, computer arts, & fine arts
Courses: Calligraphy, †Ceramics, Drawing, Graphic Design, Jewelry, Lettering, Painting, Printmaking, Sculpture, Silkscreen, Silversmithing, Textile Design, Weaving
Summer School: Dir, Elaine Beldin-Reed. Enrl 6-15; tuition $175-$250 for 1 wk term. Courses—Acting, Ceramics, Fine Art, Jewelry, Weaving

MERCED

MERCED COLLEGE, Arts Division, 3600 M St - Stop 32, Merced, CA 95348-2898. Tel 209-384-6000; Fax 209-381-6469; Internet Home Page Address: www.merced.cc.ca.us; *Pres* Dr Ron Taylor; *Gallery Dir* Susanne French; *Dean* John Albano; *Prof 3-D Prog* Cheryl Barnett; *Prof 2-D Prog* Louisa Benhisen; *Digital Media Prog* Alana Perlin
Estab 1964; Maintain a non-profit art gallery & on-campus art supplies shop.; pub; D & E; Scholarships; SC 50, LC 10; D 4741, E 3187, non-maj 3700, maj 4228
Ent Req: 18 yrs & older
Degrees: AA & AS 2 yr
Courses: Art History, Ceramics, Costume Design & Construction, Design, †Digital Media, Drafting, Drawing, †Fine Art, Graphic Design, History of Art & Architecture, Illustration, †Music, Painting, †Photography, Printmaking, Sculpture, Stage Design, Teacher Training, †Theatre Arts
Summer School: Dir, Dr Ron Williams, Dean of Arts & Sciences.

MODESTO

MODESTO JUNIOR COLLEGE, Arts Humanities & Communications Division, 435 College Ave, Modesto, CA 95350-5800. Tel 209-575-6081; Fax 209-575-6086; Internet Home Page Address: www.gomjc.org; *Dean Div* Jim Johnson; *Instr* Richard Serroes; *Instr* Doug Smith; *Instr* Terry L Hartman, MA; *Instr* Gui Todd, MA; *Instr* Jerry M Reilly, MFA
Estab 1921, div estab 1964; pub; D & E; Scholarships; 16,024 total
Ent Req: grad of accredited high school, minor with California High School Proficiency Cert & parental permission, 11th & 12th graders with principal's permission, persons 18 or older who are able to profit from the instruction
Degrees: AA and AS 2 yrs
Courses: Advertising Design, Architecture, Art History, Ceramics, Display, Drafting, Drawing, Enameling, Film, Jewelry, Lapidary, Lettering, Painting, †Photography, Printmaking, Sculpture, †Silversmithing, Theatre Arts
Adult Hobby Classes: Courses—Arts & Crafts, Lapidary
Summer School: Dir, Dudley Roach. Tuition $6 health fee. Courses—a wide variety offered

MONTEREY

MONTEREY PENINSULA COLLEGE, Art Dept/Art Gallery, 980 Fremont St, Div of Creative Arts Monterey, CA 93940-4704. Tel 831-646-4200; Fax 831-646-3005; Internet Home Page Address: www.mpc.edu; *Chairperson Div Creative Arts* John Anderson; *Painting Instr* Robynn Smith; *Art Hist Instr* Richard Janick; *Jewelry & Metals Instr* Theresa Lovering-Brown; *Sculpture Instr* Gary Quinonez; *Graphics Instr* Darien Payne; *Adjunct* Skip Kadish; *Adjunct* Carol Holoday; *Graphics Instr* Jamie Dagdigian; *Ceramics Instr* Diane Eisenbach; *Photog Instr* Kevin Bransfield; *Art Gallery Dir* Melissa Pickford
Estab 1947; Monterey Peninsula College Art Gallery, nonprofit; Adjunct 20; pub; D & E; Scholarships; SC 17, LC 8; D 1,343, E 623, maj 160
Activities: Bookstore
Ent Req: HS dipl, 18 yrs or older
Degrees: AA & AS 2 yrs
Courses: †Architecture, Art Appreciation, Art History, †Ceramics, Collage, †Commercial Graphics, Costume Design & Construction, Design, Drafting, †Drawing, Film, Graphic Arts, Illustration, Intermedia, †Jewelry, Mixed Media, Museum Staff Training, †Painting, †Photography, Printmaking, †Sculpture, Silversmithing, †Studio Art, Video, Weaving
Summer School: Dir, Thorne Hacker. Term of 6 wks beginning June. Courses are limited

MONTEREY PARK

EAST LOS ANGELES COLLEGE, Art Dept, 1301 Avenida Cesar Chavez, Monterey Park, CA 91754-6001. Tel 323-265-8842; Fax 323-780-6847; Elec Mail kallanlp@elac.edu; *Dept Chmn* Linda Kallan; *Prof* Mike Owens; *Prof* Marie Alanen; *Assoc Prof* Surana Singh-Bischofberger; *Prof* Jim Uyekawa; *Assoc Prof* Steve Monau; *Prof* Christopher Turk
Estab 1949; Maintain nonprofit art gallery, Vincent Price Art Museum; FT 7; pub; D & E; Scholarships; SC 43, LC 10; D 486, E 160, maj 646
Degrees: AA 2 yr
Courses: †Advertising Design, †Art Fundamentals, †Art Graphic Communications, †Art History, †Ceramics, †Computer Graphics, Design, Display, †Drawing, †Electronic Publishing, Graphic Arts, Graphic Design, Lettering, †Life Drawing, Mixed Media, †Painting
Children's Classes: Enrl 60. Courses—Ceramics, Direct Printing Methods, Drawing, Painting
Summer School: Dir, Carson Scott. Enrl 50; tuition $13 per unit for 6 wk term. Courses—Art 201, Beginning Drawing, Beginning 2-D Design

NAPA

NAPA VALLEY COLLEGE, Art Dept, 2277 Napa Vallejo Hwy, Napa, CA 94558-7555. Tel 707-253-3000; Internet Home Page Address: www.nvc.cc.ca.us; *Chmn & Dir* Jan Molen; *Prof* Jay Golik; *Prof* Carolyn Broodwell
Degrees: AA & AS
Tuition: $11 per unit up to 5 units
Courses: Art Appreciation, Art History, Ceramics, Design, Drawing, Painting, Photography, Printmaking, Sculpture
Adult Hobby Classes: Courses offered
Children's Classes: Courses offered
Summer School: Courses—Painting, Ceramics, Drawing

NORTHRIDGE

CALIFORNIA STATE UNIVERSITY, NORTHRIDGE, Dept of Art, 18111 Nordhoff St, College of Arts, Media & Communication Northridge, CA 91330-0001. Tel 818-677-2242; Fax 818-677-3046; Elec Mail art.dept@csun.edu; Internet Home Page Address: www.csun.edu/artdep; *Dept Chmn* Joe Lewis
Estab 1956; 48; pub; D & E; Scholarships; SC 13, GC 5; D & E 2231, grad 101
Ent Req: HS dipl, GRE, SAT
Degrees: BA 4-5 yrs, MA
Courses: †Animation, †Art Education, †Art History, †Ceramics, †Drawing, †Graphic Design, †Illustration, †Painting, †Photography, †Printmaking, Public Art, †Sculpture, †Textile Design, †Video
Summer School: Dir, Joe Lewis. Enrl 100; tuition $136 per unit for 6 wks beginning June 1. Courses—Art History, Graphic Design

NORWALK

CERRITOS COMMUNITY COLLEGE, Fine Arts & Communication Div, 11110 Alondra Blvd, Norwalk, CA 90650-6298. Tel 562-860-2451; Fax 562-653-7807; Elec Mail info@cerritos.edu; Internet Home Page Address: www.cerritos.edu/fac; *Instr Dean Fine Arts* Dr Barry Russell
Estab 1956; pub; D & E; SC 36, LC 12
Ent Req: HS dipl or 18 yrs of age
Degrees: AA 2 yrs
Courses: 2-D & 3-D Design, †Acting, Calligraphy, Ceramics, Commercial Art, †Communications, †Directing, Display, Drawing, Graphic Arts, Graphic Design, History of Art & Architecture, Jewelry, †Journalism, Museum Staff Training, †Photography, Printmaking, Sculpture, †Theater
Summer School: Dir Dr Barry Russell. 6 wks per session. Drawing, Painting, History, Design, Ceramics, Calligraphy

OAKLAND

HOLY NAMES COLLEGE, Art Dept, 3500 Mountain Blvd, Oakland, CA 94619-1699. Tel 510-436-1000, Ext 1458; Fax 510-436-1199; Internet Home Page Address: www.hnc.edu; *Chmn Dept* Robert Simon
Estab 1917; FT 2, PT 4; pvt; D & E; Scholarships; SC 24, LC 4
Ent Req: HS dipl
Degrees: BA and BFA 4 yrs
Courses: Art History, Calligraphy, Ceramics, Drawing, Jewelry, Painting, Photography, Printmaking, Sculpture

LANEY COLLEGE, Art Dept, 900 Fallon St, Oakland, CA 94607-4893. Tel 510-834-5740; Fax 510-464-3231; *Asst Dean* Carlos McLean; *Chmn* Carol Joy
Estab 1962; FT 8, PT 9; pub; D & E; SC 52, LC 8; D 1400, E 450
Ent Req: HS dipl
Degrees: AA 2 yrs
Courses: Advertising Design and Architectural Design Courses available through the Architectural Design Dept; Photography Courses available through the Photography Dept, Cartooning, †Ceramics, Color & Design, †Commercial Art, Design, Drawing, Etching, †Graphic Arts, Graphic Design, Handicrafts, History of Art & Architecture, Illustration, Lettering, Lithography, †Painting, Portraiture, Relief Printing, †Sculpture, Silkscreen
Summer School: Chmn, David Bradford. Enrl 250; tuition $10 per unit for 6 wk term

MERRITT COLLEGE, Art Dept, 12500 Campus Dr, Oakland, CA 94619-3196. Tel 510-531-4911; Internet Home Page Address: www.peralta.cc.ca.us; *Dir* Helmut Schmitt
Estab 1970; FT 2 PT 8; D & E
Degrees: AA
Tuition: Undergrad—$11 per unit
Courses: Art History, Ceramics, Design, Illustration, Life Drawing, Painting, Sculpture
Adult Hobby Classes: Dir, Helmut Schmitt
Summer School: Dir, Helmut Schmitt. Enrol 120; tuition $5 per unit; six week courses. Courses—Life Drawing, Painting

MILLS COLLEGE, Art Dept, 5000 MacArthur Blvd, Oakland, CA 94613-1301. Tel 510-430-2117; Fax 510-430-3148; Elec Mail studio_art@mills.edu; Internet Home Page Address: www.mills.edu; *Prof* Hung Liu, MFA; *Prof* Anna Valentina Murch; *Prof* Catherine F Wagner; *Prof* Ken Burke; *Prof* Mary-Ann Milford; *Prof* Moira Roth
Estab 1852; Maintain nonprofit art gallery, Mills College, 5000 MacArthur Blvd Oakland, CA 94613; pvt, MFA coed, undergraduate women only; grad, coed; D & E; Scholarships; SC 23, LC 22, GC 20; grad 24
Ent Req: HS dipl, SAT, Advanced Placement Exam for undergrads
Degrees: BA 4 yrs, MFA 2 yrs
Tuition: $35,000 per yr; MFA $30,072 per yr; campus res—room & board $5,000 - $7,000 depending on type of room
Courses: 3-D Design, Aesthetics, †Art Education, Art History, Ceramics, †Conceptual Art, Drawing, †Electronic Arts, †History of Art & Architecture, Mixed Media, †Museum Staff Training, Painting, Photography, †Restoration & Conservation, Sculpture, Video

OCEANSIDE

MIRACOSTA COLLEGE, Art Dept, 1 Barnard Dr, Oceanside, CA 92056-3899. Tel 760-757-2121; Fax 760-795-6817; Internet Home Page Address: www.miracosta.cc.ca.us; *Instr* Erik Growborg, MA; *Instr Digital Art* Peggy Jones; *Art History Instr* Susan Delaney
Estab 1934; pub; D & E; Scholarships; SC 12, LC 4; maj 200
Ent Req: HS dipl

Degrees: AA and AS normally 2 yrs
Courses: Aesthetics, †Architecture, Art Appreciation, Art Education, †Art History, Ceramics, Collage, Computer Art, Conceptual Art, Constructions, †Costume Design & Construction, Design, †Drafting, Drawing, Figure Painting, Figure Sculpture, Film, †Graphic Design, History of Art & Architecture, Interior Design, Landscape Architecture, Mixed Media, †Painting, †Photography, †Printmaking, †Sculpture, †Stage Design, Teacher Training, †Theatre Arts
Children's Classes: Enrl 200; tuition small fees. Courses—Art, Theater
Summer School: Enrl 2000; tuition $15. Courses—Various subjects

ORANGE

CHAPMAN UNIVERSITY, Art Dept, 333 N Glassell, Orange, CA 92666. Tel 714-997-6729; Fax 714-997-6744; Internet Home Page Address: www.chapman.edu; *Chmn* David Kiddie, MFA; *Prof* Jane Sinclair, MFA; *Prof* Richard Turner, MFA; *Prof* Sharon Corey, MFA; *Prof* Denise Weyhrich, MFA; *Prof* Stephen Berens, MFA; *Prof* Wendy Salmond PhD, MFA
Estab 1918, branch estab 1954; den; D & E; Scholarships; SC 20, LC 15; D 275, non-maj 75
Ent Req: HS dipl, ACT, SAT or CLEP
Courses: Advertising Design, Art Appreciation, Art Education, Art History, Ceramics, Computer Graphics, Design, Drawing, Film, Graphic Arts, Graphic Design, Illustration, Lettering, Painting, Photography, Sculpture, Stage Design, Theatre Arts, Video
Children's Classes: Courses—workshops in connection with art education classes
Summer School: Courses—Ceramics

ORANGE CITY

NORTHWESTERN COLLEGE, Art Dept, 101 7th St SW, Orange City, CA 51041. Tel 712-737-7003, 737-7004; *Chmn, Prof* Phil Scorza, MFA
Estab 1882, dept estab 1965; pvt, affil Reformed Ch Am; D & E; Scholarships; SC 25, LC 3-4; D 200, non-maj 250, maj -25
Ent Req: HS dipl
Degrees: BA 4 yr
Tuition: Campus residency available
Courses: †Art Education, Art History, Ceramics, †Computer Design, Design, †Directed Studies, Drawing, Painting, Photography, Printmaking, Sculpture, †Student Initiated Majors

OROVILLE

BUTTE COLLEGE, Dept of Fine Arts and Communication Tech, 3536 Butte Campus Dr, Oroville, CA 95965-8399. Tel 530-895-2404; Fax 530-895-2346; Internet Home Page Address: www.butte.cc.ca.us; *Chmn & Ceramic Coordr* Idie Adams; *Dean Instruction* Dan Walker; *Instr* Will Stull; *Instr* Geoff Fricker; *Instr* Adrian Carrasco-Zanini; *Instr* David Cooper; *Instr* Mark Hall; *Instr* Simone Senat
Estab 1968; pub; D & E; Scholarships; SC 21, LC 4; D 3988, E 4194
Ent Req: HS dipl or 18 yrs or older
Degrees: AA
Courses: Ceramics, Commercial Photography, Fine Arts, Graphic Arts
—Dept of Performing Arts, 3536 Butte Campus Dr, Oroville, CA 95965. Tel 530-895-2581; Fax 530-895-2532; Internet Home Page Address: www.butte.cc.ca.us; *Head Dept* Margaret Hughes
Degrees: transfer major
Tuition: Res—$12 per unit; nonres—$208 per unit
Courses: Acting, Adaptive Dramatics, Set Design & Construction, Theater Arts Appreciation, Theater for Children

PALM DESERT

COLLEGE OF THE DESERT, Art Dept, 43-500 Monterey Ave, Palm Desert, CA 92260. Tel 760-773-2574; Fax 760-776-7310; Internet Home Page Address: www.collegeofthedesert.edu; *Chmn* Doug Walker
Estab 1962; College also has High Desert Campus; FT 3, PT 5; pub; D & E; Scholarships; SC 10, LC 3; D 150, E 150, maj 15
Ent Req: HS dipl, ent exam
Degrees: AA 2 yrs
Courses: Advertising Art, Art History, Ceramics, Design, Drawing, Introduction to Art, Oriental Brush Painting, Painting, Photography, Printmaking, Sculpture
Summer School: Six wk session. Courses—Art History, Ceramics, Painting, Sculpture

PASADENA

ART CENTER COLLEGE OF DESIGN, 1700 Lida St, Pasadena, CA 91103-1924; PO Box 7197, Pasadena, CA 91109-7197. Tel 626-396-2200; Fax 626-405-9104; Elec Mail swing.reception@artcenter.edu; Internet Home Page Address: www.artcenter.edu; *Pres* Richard Halushak, MA; *Fine Arts Dept Chmn* Laurence Drieband, MFA; *Film Dept Chmn* Robert Peterson, BFA; *Photog Dept Chmn* Jeff Atherton, BFA; *Transportation Design Chmn* Ken Okuyama, BS; *Liberal Arts, Science, Grad & Acad Studies Chmn* Mark Breitenberg, MArch; *Computer Graphics Chmn* Fred Fehlau; *Illustration Chmn* Philip Hays, BFA; *Product Design Chmn* C Martin Smith, BFA; *Chmn Environmental Design* Patricia Oliver, MArch; *Co-Chmn* Peter DiFabatino
Estab 1930; pvt; D & E; Scholarships; SC 168, LC 82, GC 22; D 1200, E 200, non-maj 200, maj 1200, grad 60
Library Holdings: Book Volumes 40,000
Ent Req: HS dipl, ACT, SAT if no col background, portfolio required, at least 12 samples of work in proposed maj
Degrees: BFA, BS, MFA, MS

Courses: †Advertising Design, †Advertising Illustration, Aesthetics, Architecture, Art History, Calligraphy, Collage, Commercial Art, Conceptual Art, †Critical Theory, Design, Drafting, Drawing, †Environmental Design, Fashion Arts, †Fashion Illustration, †Film, Graphic Arts, †Graphic Design, †Graphic Packaging, History of Art & Architecture, †Illustration, Interior Design, Intermedia, Mixed Media, New Media, †Painting, †Photography, Printmaking, †Product Design, †Transportation Design, Video
Adult Hobby Classes: Enrl 550, tuition $650 per class for 14 wk term. Courses—Advertising, Computer Graphics, Film, Fine Arts, Graphics, Illustration, Industrial Design, Liberal Arts & Sciences, Photography
Children's Classes: Enrl 230; tuition $175 per class for 10 wks; Sat classes for high school

PASADENA CITY COLLEGE, Visual Arts and Media Studies Division, 1570 E Colorado Blvd, Rm 118 Pasadena, CA 91106-2003. Tel 626-585-7238; Fax 626-585-7914; Elec Mail ajkritselis@pasadena.edu; Internet Home Page Address: http://www.pasadena.edu/; *Acting Area Head Design* Jerrold Graves, BA; *Acting Area Head Photog* Victoria Martin, MFA; *Acting Area Head History* Sandra Haynes, MA; *Acting Area Head Jewelry* Kay Yee, MFA; *Acting Area Head Ceramics* Alfred James Gonzalez, MA; *Div Dean* Alexander Kritselis, MFA; *Acting Area Head History* Joseph Futtner, MA
Estab 1902, dept estab 1916; Maintain a nonprofit art gallery; on-campus shop where art supplies may be purchased; pub; D & E; Scholarships; SC 159; D 2000, E 1200, non-maj 3200, maj 400
Ent Req: HS dipl
Degrees: AA 2 yrs, cert
Courses: Advertising Design, Art History, Ceramics, Commercial Art, Drawing, Film Art, Filmmaking, Graphic Arts, Graphic Design, Illustration, Jewelry, Lettering, Painting, Photography, Printmaking, Product Design, Sculpture
Summer School: Alexander Kritselis, Dean. Enrl 500; tuition $26 per unit for 6 wk sessions. Courses—Art History, Ceramics, Cinema, Design, Jewelry, Photography, Studio Arts, Film making

PLEASANT HILL

JOHN F KENNEDY UNIVERSITY, Department of Arts & Consciousness, 100 Ellinwood Way, Pleasant Hill, CA 94523-4817. Tel 510-647-2042; Elec Mail ksjoholm@jfku.edu; Internet Home Page Address: www.jfku.edu; *Chair* Karen Sjoholm; *Faculty* Robbyn Alexander

POMONA

CALIFORNIA STATE POLYTECHNIC UNIVERSITY, POMONA, Department of Art, 3801 W Temple Blvd, College of Environmental Design Pomona, CA 91768-2557. Tel 909-869-3508; Fax 909-869-4939; Elec Mail pmartinez@csupomona.edu; Internet Home Page Address: www.csupomona.edu; *Prof Emer* Dr Maren Henderson PhD; *Prof Emer* Charles Fredrick, MFA; *Prof* Joe Hannibal, MFA; *Prof* Babette Mayor, MFA; *Chair, Prof* Sarah Meyer, MFA; *Prof* David Hylton, MA; *Lectr* Joyce Hesselgrave, MFA; *Lectr* Ann Phong, MFA; *Lectr* Wendy E Slatkin, PhD; *Lectr* Karen Sullivan, MFA; *Lectr* Deane Swick, MFA; *Assoc Prof* Yachin Crystal Lee, MFA; *Assoc Prof* Alison Pearlman, PhD; *Assoc Prof* Chari Pradel, PhD; *Lectr* Desmond McVay, MFA; *Asst* Melissa Flicker, MFA; *Lectr* Barbara Thomason, MFA; *Assoc Prof* Ray Kampf, MFA; *Assoc Prof* Alyssa Lang, MFA; *Asst Prof* Anthony Acock
Estab 1966; Maintains nonprofit Kellogg Univ Art Gallery; art/architecture library; on campus shop to purchase art supplies; pub; D & E; SC 66, LC 15; enrl D 350, E 50, non-Maj 470, maj 350
Ent Req: HS dipl, plus testing
Degrees: BA & BFA, 4 yrs
Courses: †Advertising Design, †Art Appreciation, †Art Education, †Art History, †Ceramics, Design, †Drafting, †Drawing, †Fine Arts, †Graphic Arts, †Graphic Design, †History of Art & Architecture, †Illustration, †Lettering, †Painting, Photography, †Printmaking, †Sculpture, †Studio Crafts, †Teacher Training
Adult Hobby Classes: Courses offered through Office of Continuing Education
Summer School: Courses—usually lower division, 10 & 5 wk quarter offerings

PORTERVILLE

PORTERVILLE COLLEGE, Dept of Fine Arts, 100 E College, Porterville, CA 93257. Tel 559-791-2200; Fax 559-784-4779; Elec Mail Thowell@pc.cc.ca.us; Internet Home Page Address: www.pc.cc.ca.us; *Chmn* Tom Howell
Estab 1927; FT 2, PT 6; pub; D & E; SC 18, LC 3; D 300, E 78, non-maj 320, maj 58
Ent Req: HS dipl or over 18 yrs of age
Degrees: AA & AS 2 yrs
Courses: Airbrush, Art History, Ceramics, Design, Drawing, Handicrafts, Jewelry, Painting, Photography, Sculpture, Textile Design, Theatre Arts, color, weaving
Adult Hobby Classes: Courses—Jewelry, Weaving
Summer School: Dir, Nero Pruitt. Enrl 700 Term of 6 wks beginning June 13. Courses—Ceramics, Jewelry, Weaving

QUINCY

FEATHER RIVER COMMUNITY COLLEGE, Art Dept, 570 Golden Eagle Ave, Quincy, CA 95971-9124. Tel 530-283-0202; Internet Home Page Address: www.frcc.cc.ca.us; *Chmn* Diane Lipscomb; *Adjunct* Linda Hale; *Instr* Roxanne Valladao; *Adjunct* Russ Flint; *Adjunct* Allen Stentzel; *Adjunct* Lance Barker; *Adjunct* Maureen McPhee
FT 25 PT 65; pub; D&E; Scholarships; SC 25, LC 3, ; 200; non-maj, maj
Ent Req: HS GED
Degrees: AS, AA
Tuition: Res—$22 per unit; nonres—$195 per unit

Courses: Art Appreciation, Art History, Business of Art, Ceramics, Color Theory, Design, Drawing, †History of Art & Architecture, Painting, †Photography, †Printmaking, Sculpture, Textile Design, Weaving
Adult Hobby Classes: spinning & weaving

RANCHO CUCAMONGA

CHAFFEY COMMUNITY COLLEGE, Art Dept, 5885 Haven Ave, Rancho Cucamonga, CA 91737-9400. Tel 909-987-1737; Internet Home Page Address: www.chaffey.edu/; *Dept Chmn* Jan Raithel
E; Scholarships
Ent Req: HS dipl or equivalent
Degrees: AA
Tuition: Res—$11 per unit; non res— $155 per unit
Courses: Art History, Ceramics, Design, Drawing, Graphic Arts, Graphic Design, Illustration, Interior Design, Mixed Media, Museum Staff Training, Painting, Photography, Sculpture, Theatre Arts
Summer School: Dir, Byron Wilding. Enrl 200; tuition $13 for 6 wk courses. Courses—Art History, Ceramics, Design, Drawing, Graphic Computer Design

REDDING

SHASTA COLLEGE, Arts, Communications & Social Sciences Division, 11555 Old Oregon Trail, Redding, CA 96003; PO Box 496006, Redding, CA 96049-6006. Tel 530-242-7730; Fax 530-225-4763; Internet Home Page Address: www.shastacollege.edu; *Dean Div Arts, Commun & Soc Sciences* Ralph W Perrin, DrPH; *Instr & Gallery Dir* Susan Schimke; *Instr & Gallery Dir* David Gentry; *Admin Asst* Terri Casolary; *Instr* Andrew Patterson-Tutschka
Estab 1950; Maintains a nonprofit art gallery on campus; 2; pub; D & E; Scholarships; SC 28, LC 5
Ent Req: HS dipl
Degrees: AA 2 yr
Courses: Art Appreciation, Art Education, Art History, Ceramics, †Design, Drawing, Glass, Graphic Arts, Graphic Design, Mixed Media, Painting, Photography, Printmaking, Sculpture, †Stage Design, †Theatre Arts
Summer School: Dir, Dean Summer Prog. Enrl 150; tuition same as regular sem

REDLANDS

UNIVERSITY OF REDLANDS, Dept of Art, 1200 E Colton Ave, Redlands, CA 92373-3720. Tel 909-793-2121, Ext 3663; Elec Mail brownfie@uor.edu; Internet Home Page Address: www.redlands.edu; *Chmn* John Brownfield
Estab 1909; pvt; D & E; Scholarships, Fellowships; SC 18, LC 12; 1500
Ent Req: HS grad, ent exam
Degrees: BA and BS 4 yr, MA, ME, MAT
Courses: Art History, Ceramics, Drawing, Ethnic Art, Graphic Arts, Painting, Teacher Training

RIVERSIDE

CALIFORNIA BAPTIST UNIVERSITY, Art Dept, 8432 Magnolia Ave, Riverside, CA 92504-3297. Tel 909-689-5771. Ext 270; Internet Home Page Address: www.calbaptist.edu; *Chmn* Mack Branden
Scholarships
Degrees: BA
Tuition: $420 per unit
Courses: Art Appreciation, Art History, Ceramics, Design, Drawing, Painting, Printmaking, Sculpture

LA SIERRA UNIVERSITY, Art Dept, 4700 Pierce, Riverside, CA 92515. Tel 909-785-2170; Internet Home Page Address: www.lasierra.cc.ca.us; *Chmn Prof* Susan Patt; *Instr* Jan Inman; *Prof* Peter Erhard; *Prof* Beatriz Mejia-Krumbein; *Instr* Katrin Weise; *Instr* Donna Adrian; *Instr* Stephne Patt
Estab 1905; den; D & E; SC 29, LC 8, GC 1; D 2354
Ent Req: HS dipl, SAT
Degrees: BA, BS 4 yrs
Courses: Art History, Calligraphy, †Ceramics, Computer Graphics, Drawing, †Graphic Design, Illustration, Lettering, Occupational Therapy, †Painting, †Photography, †Printmaking, †Sculpture
Adult Hobby Classes: Enrl 35 per wk; tuition $330 per wk for 4 wk term. Courses—Watercolor Workshop
Summer School: Chmn, Roger Churches. 6 wk, 2-4 units. Courses—Art in the Elementary & Secondary School

RIVERSIDE COMMUNITY COLLEGE, Dept of Art & Mass Media, 4800 Magnolia Ave, Riverside, CA 92506-1201. Tel 909-222-8000; Fax 909-222-8740; Internet Home Page Address: www.rccd.cc.ca.us; *Dance Chmn* Jo Dierdorff; *Media Chmn* Charles Richard; *Chmn Performing Arts & Media* Kevin Mayse; *Chmn Art Dept* Dayna Peterson Mason
Estab 1917; FT8; pub; D & E; 37; D 910, E 175
Ent Req: HS dipl or over 18 yrs of age
Degrees: AA 2 yrs & Certs
Courses: 3-D Design, Advertising Design, Art Appreciation, Art History, Ceramics, †Computer Art, Design, Drawing, †Gallery-Exhib Design & Animation, Painting, Printmaking, Sculpture, Teacher Training
Summer School: Dir Dayna Peterson Mason. Courses—Art for Elementary Teachers, Art History, Ceramics, Drawing, Painting, Sculpture

UNIVERSITY OF CALIFORNIA, RIVERSIDE, Dept of the History of Art, 900 University Ave, Riverside, CA 92507-4600. Tel 951-827-4634; Fax 951-827-2331; Elec Mail arthist@ucr.edu; Internet Home Page Address: http://arthistory.ucr.edu; *Prof* Jonathan W Green, MA; *Prof Emeriti* Francoise

Forster-Hahn PhD, MA; *Prof Emeriti* Dericksen M Brinkerhoff PhD, MA; *Prof* Conrad Rudolph PhD, MA; *Chmn & Assoc Prof* Patricia M Morton PhD, MA; *Asst Prof* JP Park, PhD MA; *Asst Prof* Kristoffer Neville, PhD, MA; *Assoc Prof* Jeanette Kohl, PhD, MA; *Assoc Prof* Liz Kotz, PhD, MA; *Asst Prof* Susan Laxton, PhD, MA; *Prof* Malcolm Baker, PhD, MA; *Asst Prof* Jason Weems, PhD, MA
Estab 1968; Maintains a non-profit art gallery, Sweeney Gallery, 3824 Main St, Riverside, CA 92501; pub; D; LC 18, GC 5; maj 62, grad 26
Activities: Fels offered
Ent Req: HS dipl, res grad-point average 3.1, nonres grade-point average 3.4
Degrees: BA, MA, PhD
Tuition: Res—undergrad $6684, grad $8145; nonres—undergrad $23,640, grad $23,085
Courses: Art History, History of Art & Architecture, History of Photography
—**Dept of Art,** 1107 Olmsted Hall, Riverside, CA 92521. Tel 909-787-4634; Elec Mail jdivola@earthlink.net; *Prof* John Divola; *Chmn* Erika Suderburg; *Prof* Uta Barth; *Prof* James S Strombotne, MFA; *Lectr* Gordon L Thorpe, MA
Estab 1954; maintain nonprofit art gallery, Sweeny Art Gallery, UC Riverside, UCR California Museum of Photography, 3824 Main St, Riverside, CA 92507; pub; D; SC 14, LC 2; maj 58
Ent Req: HS dipl
Degrees: BA
Tuition: Res—undergrad $1500 per qtr, grad $1603; nonres—undergrad $3930 per qtr, grad $4163
Courses: Drawing, Painting, Photography, Printmaking, Video

ROCKLIN

SIERRA COMMUNITY COLLEGE, Art Dept, 5000 Rocklin Rd, Liberal Arts Division Rocklin, CA 95677-3337. Tel 916-624-3333, 789-2866 (Art Dept); Fax 916-789-2854; Internet Home Page Address: www.sierracollege.org; *Dean Humanities* Bill Tsuji; *Instr* Pam Johnson, MA; *Instr* Dottie Brown, MA; *Instr* Rebecca Gregg; *Instr* Tom Fillebrown; *Instr* Randy Snook; *Dept Tech Dir* Anthony Gilo
Estab 1914; pub; D & E; SC 18, LC 4; D & E approx 9000
Ent Req: English Placement Test
Degrees: AA
Courses: Art Education, Art History, Ceramics, Drawing, Painting, Photography, Printmaking, Sculpture
Summer School: Ceramics, Painting

ROHNERT PARK

SONOMA STATE UNIVERSITY, Art & Art History Dept, 1801 E Cotati Ave, Rohnert Park, CA 94928-3609. Tel 707-664-2364, 664-2365; Fax 707-664-4333; Internet Home Page Address: www.sonoma.edu/art; *Art Chmn* Michael Schwager
Estab 1961; dept estab 1961; pub; D & E; SC 38, LC 17; D 6000
Ent Req: HS dipl, SAT, eligibility req must be met
Degrees: BA & BFA
Courses: Art Education, Art History, Ceramics, Drawing, Painting, Papermaking, Photography, Printmaking, Sculpture, Teacher Training
Adult Hobby Classes: Various classes offered through Extended Educ
Summer School: Various classes offered through Extended Educ

SACRAMENTO

AMERICAN RIVER COLLEGE, Dept of Art/Art New Media, 4700 College Oak Dr, Sacramento, CA 95841-4286. Tel 916-484-8433; *Instr* Ken Magri, MA; *Spokesperson* Pam Maddock, MFA; *Instr* Tom J Brozovich, MA; *Instr* Gary Pruner, MFA; *Instr* Craig Smith, MFA; *Instr* Laura Parker, MAT; *Instr* Diane Richey-Ward, MFA; *Instr* Judy Hiramoto, MFA
Estab 1954; pub; D & E; Scholarships; SC 65, LC 12; D 10,000, E 10,000, non-maj 5000, maj 5000
Ent Req: HS dipl
Degrees: AA 2 yrs or more
Courses: Art Appreciation, Art History, Ceramics, Commercial Art, Design, Drawing, Film, Gallery Management, Graphic Arts, Graphic Design, Illustration, Interior Design, Jewelry, Lettering, Painting, Photography, Printmaking, Sculpture
Summer School: Area Dean, Sheryl Gessford. Enrl 120; tuition $11 per unit June-Aug. Courses—Ceramics, Design, Drawing, Introduction to Art, Photography

CALIFORNIA STATE UNIVERSITY, SACRAMENTO, Dept of Art, 6000 J St, Sacramento, CA 95819-6000. Tel 916-278-6166; Fax 916-278-7287; Internet Home Page Address: www.csus.edu/art; *Chmn* Catherine Turrill
Estab 1950; FT 20; pub; D; Scholarships; SC 40, LC 18, GC 12; maj 585
Ent Req: HS dipl, ent exam
Degrees: BA 4 yr, MA
Courses: Art Education, Art History, Arts with Metals, Ceramics, Computer Art, Drawing, Jewelry, Painting, Printmaking, Sculpture
Summer School: Enrl 225; 3 & 6 wk sessions

SACRAMENTO CITY COLLEGE, Art Dept, 3835 Freeport Blvd, Sacramento, CA 95822-1386. Tel 916-558-2551; Fax 916-558-2190; Internet Home Page Address: www.scc.losrios.cc.ca.us; *Dir Humanities & Fine Arts* Chris Iwata; *Instr* Laureen Landau, MFA; *Instr* F Dalkey, MFA; *Instr* Darrell Forney, MFA; *Instr* George A Esquibel, MA; *Instr* B Palisin, MA; *Instr* Mimi Fong; *Instr* Jennifer Griffin; *Instr* Robert Leach; *Instr* Christine Reading; *Instr* Teiko Sasser; *Instr* Isabel Shaskan; *Instr* Frank Zamora
Estab 1916; pub; D & E; Scholarships; SC 17, LC 9; D 880, E 389
Ent Req: HS dipl
Degrees: AA 2 yr
Courses: Ceramics, Commercial Art, Drawing, Jewelry, Modern Art, Painting, Photography, Sculpture, Technology, Theatre Arts

Summer School: Chmn, George A Esquibel. Courses—Art History, Design, Drawing, Oil-Acrylic, Watercolor

SALINAS

HARTNELL COLLEGE, Art & Photography Dept, 156 Homestead Ave, Salinas, CA 93901. Tel 831-755-6905; Fax 831-759-6052; Internet Home Page Address: www.hartnell.cc.ca.us; *Dean Fine Arts* Dr Daniel A Ipson
Estab 1922; FT 5, PT 18; pub; D & E; Scholarships; SC 14, LC 3; D 350 E 160, major 30
Ent Req: HS dipl
Degrees: AA 2 yr
Courses: †Calligraphy, Ceramics, Drafting, Drawing, Foundry, Gallery Management, Graphic Arts, History of Art & Architecture, †Jewelry, Metalsmithing, Painting, Photography, Sculpture, Stage Design, Theatre Arts, Video, Weaving
Summer School: Courses—Art Appreciation, Ceramics, Drawing, Film Making, Photography

SAN BERNARDINO

CALIFORNIA STATE UNIVERSITY, SAN BERNARDINO, Dept of Art, 5500 University Pkwy, Visual Arts Center San Bernardino CA 92407-2393. Tel 909-880-5802; Fax 909-880-7068; Internet Home Page Address: www.csusb.edu; *Chmn Dept & Instr* Joe Moran, MFA; *Dir Mus* Eva Kirsch; *Instr* Leo Doyle, MFA; *Instr* Don Woodford, MFA; *Instr* Billie Sessions, MFA; *Instr* Julius Kaplan PhD, MFA; *Instr* George McGinnis, MFA; *Instr* Sant Khalsa, MFA; *Instr* Kurt Collins, MS; *Instr* Susan Beiner; *Instr* Thomas McGovern
Estab 1965; pub; D & E; Scholarships; D 13,500, maj 220
Ent Req: HS dipl, SAT
Degrees: BA 4 yr, MA 2 yr
Courses: Advertising Design, Art Education, †Art History, Ceramics, Drawing, †Furniture Design, Glassblowing, Glasscasting, †Graphic Design, Painting, Photography, Printmaking, Sculpture, Woodworking

SAN BERNARDINO VALLEY COLLEGE, Art Dept, 701 S Mount Vernon Ave, San Bernardino, CA 92410-2798. Tel 909-888-6511; Internet Home Page Address: www.sbcc.cc.ca.us; *Head Dept* David Lawrence
Estab 1926; FT 5, PT 7; pub; D & E; Scholarships; D 750, E 400, maj 230
Ent Req: HS dipl or 18 yrs of age
Degrees: AA and AS 2 yrs
Courses: Advertising Art, Architecture, Art History, Basic Design, Ceramics, Commercial Art, Computer Graphics, Designs in Glass, Drafting, Drawing, Film, Glass Blowing, Lettering, Life Drawing, Painting, Photography, Sculpture, Theatre Arts

SAN DIEGO

SAN DIEGO MESA COLLEGE, Fine Arts Dept, 7250 Mesa College Dr, San Diego, CA 92111-4999. Tel 619-388-2829; Internet Home Page Address: www.sdccd.net; *Chmn* Richard Lou; *Instr* Barbara Blackmun PhD; *Instr* Ross Stockwell, MA; *Instr* Anita Brynolf, MA; *Instr* Jeorgia Laris, MA; *Instr* John Conrad, MA
Estab 1964; pub; D & E; Scholarships; SC 20, LC 7; D 15,000, E 8,000, maj 300
Ent Req: HS dipl or age 18
Degrees: AA 2 yrs
Courses: Art Appreciation, Art Education, Art History, Book Arts, Ceramics, Design, Drawing, Gallery Studies, Painting, Photography, Printmaking, Sculpture, Studio Arts
Summer School: Enrl 200; tuition & courses same as regular sem

SAN DIEGO STATE UNIVERSITY, School of Art, Design & Art History, 5500 Campanile Dr, San Diego, CA 92182-4805. Tel 619-594-6511; Fax 619-594-1217; Elec Mail artinfo@mail.sdsu.edu; Internet Home Page Address: www.sdsu.edu/art; *Studio Grad Coordr* David Hewitt; *Art History Grad Coordr* Jo-Anne Berelowitz, PhD; *Dir* Arthur Ollman, MFA
Estab 1897; Maintains University Art Gallery on campus, & SDSU Downtown Gallery, 725 W Broadway, San Diego, CA 92101; art supplies sold on-campus store; pub; D & E; Scholarships; SC 140, LC 35, GC 30; maj 982
Ent Req: HS dipl
Degrees: BA 4 yrs, MA, MFA
Courses: Art Education, †Art History, †Ceramics, †Drawing, †Furniture Design, †Gallery Design, †Graphic Design, History of Art & Architecture, Illustration, †Interior Design, Intermedia, †Jewelry, Mixed Media, †Painting, Photography, †Printmaking, †Sculpture, †Silversmithing, †Textile Design

UNIVERSITY OF SAN DIEGO, Art Dept, 5998 Alcala Park, San Diego, CA 92110-2492. Tel 619-260-4600; Fax 619-260-4619, Ext 4486; Internet Home Page Address: www.usd.ca.ca.us; *Chmn* Patricia Drinan
Estab 1952; FT 4; pvt; D & E; Scholarships; SC 19, LC 7; univ 5300, maj 50
Ent Req: HS dipl, SAT
Degrees: BA 4 yrs
Courses: †Art History, †Art Management, †Art in Elementary Education, †Ceramics, †Design, †Drawing, †Enameling, †Exhibition Design, †Museum Internship, †Painting, †Photography, †Printmaking, †Sculpture, †Weaving

SAN FRANCISCO

ACADEMY OF ART UNIVERSITY, Fine Arts Dept, 625 Sutter, San Francisco, CA 94102-1017. Tel 415-274-2200, 800-544-2787; Fax 415-618-6287; Internet Home Page Address: www.academyart.edu; *Dir Liberal Arts & Grad Studies* Eileen Everett

Estab 1929; FT 2, PT 8; pvt; D & E; Scholarships; SC 200, LC 100; D 2000, E 150, grad 20
Ent Req: HS dipl
Degrees: BFA 4 yrs, MFA 2 yrs
Tuition: Res—undergrad $12,300 per yr, grad $14,200 per yr; campus res available
Courses: Advertising Design, Aesthetics, Architecture, Art History, Ceramics, Collage, Commercial Art, Design, Drawing, Fashion Arts, Film, Graphic Arts, Graphic Design, Illustration, Industrial Design, Interior Design, Jewelry, Mixed Media, Painting, Photography, Printmaking, Sculpture, Video
Adult Hobby Classes: Enrl 75; tuition $350 per unit. Courses—Basic Painting, Ceramics, Portrait Painting, Pottery
Summer School: Term of 6 wks beginning June 23. Courses—Commercial & Fine Art

CALIFORNIA COLLEGE OF THE ARTS, (California College of Arts & Crafts) 1111 8th St, San Francisco, CA 94107-2247. Tel 415-703-9500; Fax 415-703-9539; Elec Mail info@cca.edu; Internet Home Page Address: www.cca.edu; Internet Home Page Address: www.cca.edu/academics/faculty (faculty directory); *Pres* Stephen Beal; *Office Mgr* Gail Davies; *Exec Asst* Ann Lajoie
Estab 1907; Non-profit art gallery: Wattis Institute for Contemporary Arts, 360 Kansas St, San Francisco, CA 94103; 500; pvt; D & E; Scholarships; undergrad 384; grad 110; lecture 123; Total: $1,450 undergrad/467 grad
Ent Req: HS dipl, Portfolio, SAT or ACT recommended, C grade-point average, 2 letters of recommendation
Degrees: BArch 4 yrs, BFA 4 yrs, BA 4 yrs, MFA 2 yrs, MA 2 yrs, MBA 2 yrs & MArch 3 yrs
Tuition: UG $39,984; Grad $1,389 per unit
Courses: †Animation, †Architecture, †Ceramics, †Comics, †Community Arts, †Curatorial Practice, †Design Strategy (MBA), †Fashion Arts, †Fashion Design, †Film, †Fine Arts, †Glass, Graphic Arts, †Graphic Design, Illustration, †Industrial Design, †Interaction Design, †Interior Architectural Design, †Interior Design, †Jewelry, †Metal Arts, Mixed Media, †Painting, †Photography, †Printmaking, †Sculpture, †Textiles, †Video, †Visual Criticism, †Visual Studies, †Woodwork & Furniture Design, †Writing & Literature
Adult Hobby Classes: Enrl 1400; tuition $45-395. Courses—Vary
Children's Classes: Pre-College (students completed 10, 11 & 12th grade) Enrl 230; tuition $2,750 4 wk, 3 college credit July program; housing $875; Courses: Architecture, Creative Writing, Drawing, Fashion Design, Graphic Design, Illustration, Industrial Design, Jewelry/Metal Arts, Painting, Photography (Black & White, Digital), Printmaking, Sculpture, Animation, Film
Summer School: Summer Atelier (students who complete 9th gr) - enrl 32; tuition $2,000, 3 wk prog July or July/Aug, courses: graphic novel, drawing; Young Artist Studio Prog (stud who complete 6, 7 & 8th gr) -enrl 200, tuition $620 for 2 wk prog June or Aug, Courses: Animation, Architecture, Computer Graphic, Graphic Design, Drawing, Hat Design, Jewelry Design, Mosaic Design, Painting, Photography, Printmaking, Sculpture, Woodworking; Dir, Nina Sadek. Enrl 300; tuition $1,453 per unit. Courses - Vary

CITY COLLEGE OF SAN FRANCISCO, Art Dept, 50 Phelan Ave, 118 Visual Arts Building San Francisco, CA 94112. Tel 415-239-3157; Fax 415-239-3131; Elec Mail mchereme@ccsf.edu; Internet Home Page Address: www.ccsf.edu/Departments/Art/; *Dept Chair* Anna Asebedo
Estab 1935

SAN FRANCISCO ART INSTITUTE, 800 Chestnut St, Admissions Office San Francisco, CA 94133-2206. Tel 415-749-4500; Fax 415-749-4592; Elec Mail admissions@sfai.edu; Internet Home Page Address: www.sfai.edu; *Dir Admissions* Renee Talmon
Estab 1871; Maintain nonprofit art gallery; Walter & McBean Galleries, 800 Chestnut St, San Francisco, CA 94133; pvt; D & E; Scholarships; SC 80, LC 22, GC 11; maj 466 grad 208
Ent Req: HS dipl or GED
Degrees: BFA 4 yrs, MFA 2 yrs
Courses: Art History, †Ceramics, †Conceptual Art, †Digital Media, †Drawing, †Film, †Painting, †Performance/Video, †Photography, †Printmaking, †Sculpture
Adult Hobby Classes: Tuition $290 for 4-11 wk session (per course). Courses—Variety of studio courses year round
Children's Classes: Enrl 40; tuition 8 wk session. Courses—Variety of studio courses, summers only
Summer School: Dir, Kate Eilertsen. Tuition 2-8 wk sessions $1800 course. Courses—Variety of studio courses

SAN FRANCISCO STATE UNIVERSITY, Art Dept, 1600 Holloway, San Francisco, CA 94132. Tel 415-338-2176; Fax 415-338-6537; Elec Mail artdept@sfsu.edu; Internet Home Page Address: www.sfsu.edu; *Dean* Morrison Keith; *Chmn* Candace Crockett
Estab 1899; Maintains nonprofit gallery, San Francisco State Univ Art Dept Gallery, 1600 Holloway Ave, San Francisco, CA 94132; art supplies available at on-campus shop; FT 23, PT 10; pub; D & E; Scholarships; SC 80, LC 20, GC 15; D 450, maj 600, grad 30
Ent Req: HS dipl
Degrees: BA 4 yrs, MFA 3 yrs, MA 2 yrs
Courses: Art Education, Art History, Ceramics, Conceptual/Information Arts, Mixed Emphasis, Painting, Photography, Printmaking, Sculpture, Textile
Summer School: Not regular session. Self-supporting classes in Art History, Ceramics, Drawing & Painting, Art Educ

SAN JACINTO

MT SAN JACINTO COLLEGE, Art Dept, 1499 N State St, San Jacinto, CA 92583-2399. Tel 951-487-3580; Elec Mail srobinso@msjc.cc.ca.us; Internet Home Page Address: www.msjc.edu; *Dept Chair* Eileen Doktorski; *Dept Chair* John Seed; *Dept Chair* Jason Bader; *Gallery Dir* Brandelyn Dillaway

Estab 1964; Maintains nonprofit art gallery; Mt San Jacinto College Art Gallery; art supplies sold at on-campus shop; pub; D & E; SC 8, LC 2; D 250, E 420, non-maj 400, grad 50
Ent Req: HS dipl
Degrees: AA & AS
Courses: Art History, Basic Design, Ceramics, †Graphic Design, Painting, Sculpture
Adult Hobby Classes: Courses—Community Educ Ceramics
Children's Classes: Studio courses
Summer School: Courses—Drawing

SAN JOSE

SAN JOSE CITY COLLEGE, School of Fine Arts, 2100 Moorpark Ave, San Jose, CA 95128-2799. Tel 408-298-2181; Fax 408-298-1935; Internet Home Page Address: www.sjcc.edu; *Dean Humanities & Social Science* Dr Patrick Gierster; *Instr* Judith Bell; *Interim Pres* Chui L Tsang; *Coordr Fine Arts* Eve Page Mathias; *Instr* Ciaran Maegowan
Estab 1921; pub; D & E; SC 7, LC 2; D 320, E 65
Ent Req: HS dipl or 18 yrs of age or older
Degrees: AA 2 yrs
Courses: 2-D & 3-D Design, Art History, Ceramics, Color, Drawing, Expressive & Representational Drawing, Life Drawing, Painting, Photography, Theatre Arts

SAN JOSE STATE UNIVERSITY, School of Art & Design, One Washington Sq, San Jose, CA 95192-0089. Tel 408-924-4320; Fax 408-924-4326; Elec Mail rwmilnes@sjsu.edu; Internet Home Page Address: ad.sjsu.edu; *Chmn Dept of Art* Brian Taylor; *Chmn Dept of Design* Randall Sexton
Estab 1857, dept estab 1911; Maintains Natalie and James Thompson Art Gallery, School of Art & Design SJSU, One Washington Square, San Jose, CA 95192-0089; pub; D & E; Scholarships, Fellowships; SC 200+, LC 30+, GC 10+; D 4529, maj 1800, grad 100
Ent Req: ACT & grade point average, SAT
Degrees: BA(Art), BA(Art History) 4 yrs, BFA(Graphic Design), BS(Industrial Design), BFA(Interior Design) & BFA(Art-Animation, Illustration, Digital Media, Pictorial Art, Spatial Art, Photography) 4 1/2 yrs, MA(Art History), 1 yr, MFA(Pictorial Arts), MFA(Photography), MFA(Spatial Arts) & MFA(Digital Media Arts) 3 yrs
Tuition: Res—(undergrad) $899 - $1328 per sem; nonres—$899 - $1328 plus $282/unit/per sem (non-res undergrad)
Courses: †Animation, †Art Education, †Art History, Ceramics, †Crafts (Jewelry), †Digital Media Art, Drawing, †Graphic Design, Illustration, †Industrial Design, †Interior Design, Jewelry, †Photography, Printmaking, †Sculpture, Teacher Training, Textiles
Summer School: Dean Continuing Educ, Mark Novak. Tuition $160 per unit for three summer sessions of 3 & 6 wks; 3 wk Jan session. Courses—Vary according to professors available & projected demand

SAN LEANDRO

CHABOT COLLEGE, Humanities Division, 2300 Davis St, San Leandro, CA 94577-2206. Tel 510-723-6600; Internet Home Page Address: www.chabot.org; *Chmn* Dr Sally Fitzgerald
Estab 1961; FT 21, PT 50; pub; D & E; Scholarships; SC 27, LC 5
Ent Req: HS dipl
Degrees: AA 2 yr
Courses: Advertising Design, Cartooning, Ceramics, Costume Design & Construction, Drafting, Drawing, History of Art & Architecture, Illustration, Lettering, Painting, Sculpture, Stage Design, Theatre Arts
Summer School: Dir, Robert Hunter. Enrl 72-100; tuition $2-$100 per 6 wks. Courses—Art History, Drawing, Introduction to Art, Sculpture, Watercolor

SAN LUIS OBISPO

CALIFORNIA POLYTECHNIC STATE UNIVERSITY AT SAN LUIS OBISPO, Dept of Art & Design, 1 Grand Ave, San Luis Obispo, CA 93407-9000. Tel 805-756-1111; Internet Home Page Address: www.artdesign.libart.calpoly.edu; *Asst Prof Art History* Elizabeth Adan; *Dept Chmn, Prof Photog* Sky Bergman; *Asst Prof Digital Media* Enrica Lovaglio Costello; *Asst Prof Studio Art* Daniel Dove; *Asst Prof Art History* Giancarlo Fiorenza; *Asst Prof Studio Art* Tera Galanti; *Prof Photog* Robert Howell; *Asst Prof* Joseph Coates; *Prof* Keith Dills; *Prof Studio Art* George Jercich; *Prof Photog* Eric Johnson; *Prof Graphic Design* Mary LaPorte; *Asst Prof Graphic Design* Charmaine Martinez; *Asst Prof Graphic Design* Kathryn McCormick; *Prof Studio Art* Michael Barton Miller; *Lectr Studio Art* Brian James Priest; *Assoc Prof Art History* Jean Wetzel
Estab 1901, dept estab 1969; FT 12; pub; D & E; SC 40, LC 12; D 1000, E 100, non-maj 1100, maj 220
Ent Req: HS dipl, portfolio review
Degrees: BS (Art & Design) 4 yrs
Tuition: Res—undergrad $3640 per yr; nonres—undergrad $5893 per yr; campus res—room & board $4366 per yr
Courses: Advertising Design, Art History, Ceramics, Design History, Drawing, Glass, Graphic Arts, Graphic Design, Metalsmithing, Painting, Photography, Printmaking, Sculpture
Summer School: Chair, Chuck Jennings. Enrl 215; tuition $740 for term June 20-Sept 2. Courses—Basic b/w Photography, Ceramics, Fundamentals of Drawing, Intermediate Drawing

CUESTA COLLEGE, Art Dept, PO Box 8106, San Luis Obispo, CA 93403-8106. Tel 805-546-3201; Fax 805-546-3995; *Chmn Fine Arts Div & Instr* Bob Pelfrey; *Instr* Guyla Amyx; *Instr* Barry Frantz; *Instr* Marian Galczenski; *Instr* David Prochaska
Estab 1964; pub; D & E; Scholarships

Ent Req: HS dipl or Calif HS Proficiency Exam
Degrees: AA and AS
Courses: Art Appreciation, Art History, Camera Art, Ceramics, Design, Display, Drawing, Graphic Design, Painting, Printmaking, Sculpture, Video
Summer School: Chmn Div Fine Arts, Bob Pelfrey. Courses—Drawing, Art History, Ceramics

SAN MARCOS

PALOMAR COMMUNITY COLLEGE, Art Dept, 1140 W Mission Rd, San Marcos, CA 92069-1487. Tel 760-744-1150, Ext 2302; Fax 760-744-8123; Internet Home Page Address: www.palomar.cc.ca.us; *Assoc Prof & Dir* Harry E Bliss, MFA; *Assoc Prof* Jay Shultz, MA; *Assoc Prof* James T Saw, MA; *Assoc Prof* Michael Steirnagle, MA; *Assoc Prof* Steve Miller, MA; *Chmn* Doug Durrant
Estab 1950; pub; D & E; Scholarships; SC 31, LC 4; D 775, E 200
Ent Req: ent exam
Degrees: AA 2 yr
Courses: †Animation, Art History, †Ceramics, Collage, †Commercial Art, Design Composition, †Drawing, Glassblowing, Graphic Arts, Graphic Design, Handicrafts, Illustration, †Jewelry, Lettering, Life Drawing, †Painting, †Printmaking, Sculpture, †Silversmithing, Stained Glass
Summer School: Courses—basic courses except commercial art and graphic design

SAN MATEO

COLLEGE OF SAN MATEO, Creative Arts Dept, 1700 W Hillsdale Blvd, San Mateo, CA 94402-3784. Tel 650-574-6161; Internet Home Page Address: www.gocsm.net; *Prof, Art History* Janet Black; *Pres* Michael Claire; *Prof 2D Art* Jude Pittman; *Prof 3D Sculpture & Ceramics* Rory Nakata; *Prof Photog* Lyle Gomes
Pub; D & E
Degrees: AA 2 yr
Tuition: Res—$11 per unit, nonres—$130 per unit; no campus res
Courses: †Architecture, Art History, Ceramics, †Commercial Art, Design, Drafting, Drawing, †Film, †General Art, Graphic Arts, Graphic Design, Painting, Photography, Printmaking, Sculpture, Video

SAN PABLO

CONTRA COSTA COMMUNITY COLLEGE, Dept of Art, 2600 Mission Bell Dr, San Pablo, CA 94806-3195. Tel 510-235-7800, Ext 4261; Fax 510-236-6768; Internet Home Page Address: www.contracosta.cc.ca.us; *Dept Head* Rich Akers
Estab 1950; pub; D & E; SC 10, LC 16; D 468, E 200
Ent Req: HS dipl or 18 yrs old
Degrees: Cert of Achievement 1 yr, AA and AS 2 yrs
Courses: Art History, Ceramics, Drawing, Painting, Photography, Sculpture, Silkscreen
Summer School: Assoc Dean Continuing Educ, William Vega. Enrl 50; tuition free for term of 8 wks beginning June 26. Courses—Art, Art Appreciation

SAN RAFAEL

DOMINICAN COLLEGE OF SAN RAFAEL, Art Dept, 50 Acacia Ave, San Rafael, CA 94901-2230. Tel 415-457-4440; Fax 415-485-3205; Internet Home Page Address: www.dominican.edu; *Chmn* Edith Bresnahan
Estab 1890; Scholarships
Degrees: BA, MA 4 yr
Tuition: Undergrad—$8628 per sem
Courses: Advertising Design, Art Appreciation, Art Education, Art History, Calligraphy, Ceramics, Design, Drawing, Handicrafts, Painting, Photography, Pottery, Printmaking, Sculpture, Stage Design, Textile Design, Theatre Arts, Weaving

SANTA ANA

SANTA ANA COLLEGE, (Rancho Santiago College) Art Dept, 1530 W 17th St, Santa Ana, CA 92706-3398. Tel 714-564-5600; Internet Home Page Address: www.sac.edu/academic_progs/art/; *Dean of Fine & Performing Arts* Sylvia Turner; *Co-Chair* Sharon Brown; *Co-Chair* Irene Soriano; *Ceramics* Patrick S Crabb, MA; *Painting* Estelle Orr, MA; *3D Animation & Modeling* Patricia Waterman
Estab 1915, dept estab 1960; pub; D & E; Scholarships; SC 21, LC 5; D 280, E 160, maj 57
Ent Req: HS dipl
Degrees: AA 2 yr
Tuition: Res—$11 per unit; nonres—$138 per unit
Courses: Advertising Design, Architecture, Art History, Ceramics, Commercial Art, Computer Graphics, Display, Drawing, Glass Blowing, Graphic Arts, Graphic Design, Handicrafts, Interior Design, Jewelry, Museum Staff Training, Painting, Sculpture
Adult Hobby Classes: Ceramics, Stained Glass
Summer School: Dir, Dean Thom Hill. Enrl 3000; tuition free for term of 6-8 wks beginning early June. Courses—Art Concepts, Ceramics, Design, Drawing, Painting

SANTA BARBARA

BROOKS INSTITUTE OF PHOTOGRAPHY, 27 E Cota St, Santa Barbara, CA 93101-1641. Tel 805-966-3888; Fax 805-564-1475; Elec Mail library@brooks.edu; *Librn* Susan Shiras

Open Mon - Fri 8 AM - 5 PM; Lend to students only, reference to non-students
Income: Financed by school tuition
Library Holdings: Book Volumes 7367; CD-ROMs 28; Filmstrips; Periodical Subscriptions 91; Video Tapes 234
Special Subjects: Film, Illustration, Mixed Media, Photography, Architecture
Exhibitions: Various student exhib
Activities: Online instruction for cyber libraries, research instruction

SANTA BARBARA CITY COLLEGE, Fine Arts Dept, 721 Cliff Dr, Santa Barbara, CA 93109-2394. Tel 805-965-0581; Fax 805-963-7222; Internet Home Page Address: www.sbcc.net; *Chmn* Diane Handsloser
Pub; D&E; Scholarships
Degrees: AA
Tuition: In-state—$12 per unit
Courses: Advertising Design, Architecture, Art Appreciation, Art History, Calligraphy, Cartooning, Ceramics, Design, Drawing, Fashion Arts, Film, Glassblowing, Handicrafts, Industrial Design, Interior Design, Jewelry, Painting, Printmaking, Sculpture, Stage Design, Textile Design, Weaving

UNIVERSITY OF CALIFORNIA, SANTA BARBARA, Dept of Art Studio, 552 University Rd, Ellison Hall, Rm 2838 Santa Barbara, CA 93106-0002. Tel 805-893-3138; Fax 805-893-7206; Internet Home Page Address: www.arts.ucsb.edu; *Chmn Dept* Kim Yasuda
Estab 1868, dept estab 1950; pub; D&E; Scholarships; SC 30, LC 7, GC 7; D 479, grad 60
Ent Req: HS dipl
Degrees: BA 4 yrs, MFA 2 yrs, PhD 7 yrs
Courses: †Art Theory, Ceramics, Drawing, Painting, †Performance Art, Photography, Printmaking, Sculpture
Summer School: Dir Loy Lytle

SANTA CLARA

SANTA CLARA UNIVERSITY, Dept of Art & Art History, 500 El Camino Real, Santa Clara, CA 95053-0264. Tel 408-554-4594; Fax 408-554-4809; Elec Mail artinfo@scu.edu; Internet Home Page Address: www.scu.edu/art; *Prof* Sam Hernandez, MFA; *Assoc Prof* Kathleen Maxwell PhD; *Assoc Prof* Andrea Pappas, PhD; *Lectr* Pancho Jimenez, MFA; *Chmn, Assoc Prof* Blake de Maria, PhD; *Assoc Prof* Katherine Aoki, MFA; *Assoc Prof* Katherine Morris, PhD; *Asst Prof* Ryan Reynolds, MFA; *Asst Prof* Don Fritz, MFA; *Chmn, Prof* Kelly Detweiler, MFA; *Asst Prof* Karen Fraser, PhD; *Lectr* David Pace, MFA; *Lectr* Renee Billingslea, MFA; *Lectr* Marco Marquez, MFA; *Prof Emerita* Brigid Barton; *Lectr* Julie Hughes, MFA; *Asst Prof* Tobias Woffard, PhD; *Asst Prof* Takeshi Moro, MFA
Estab 1851, dept estab 1972; Maintain a nonprofit art dept gallery (same address); basic art supplies found at the campus bookstore; Pvt; D, E; Scholarships; SC 61, LC 36; D 700, non-maj 700, maj 100
Ent Req: HS dipl
Degrees: BA Art, Art History
Tuition: $37,000 per yr; campus res—rm & bd $11,000 per yr
Courses: †Art History, Ceramics, †Commercial Art, Computer Art, †Design, Drawing, †Graphic Design, †History of Art & Architecture, Mixed Media, †Museum Staff Training, Painting, Photography, Printmaking, Sculpture
Summer School: Dir, Rafael Ulate. Enrl 15 per class; 5 wk term. Courses—Ceramics, Intro to Art History, Painting, Drawing, Photography, Graphic Design, Computer Imaging

SANTA CLARITA

COLLEGE OF THE CANYONS, Art Dept, 26455 Rockwell Canyon Rd, Santa Clarita, CA 91355-1899. Tel 661-259-7800; Fax 661-259-8362; Elec Mail lorigan-j@mail.coc.cc.ca.us; Internet Home Page Address: www.coc.cc.ca.us; *Instr* Robert Walker, MFA; *Chair* Jim Lorigan, MFA; *Adjunct* Larry Arbino; *Adjunct* Denise Delavaux; *Adjunct* Rebecca Edwards; *Adjunct* Amy Green; *Adjunct* Mercedes McDonald; *Adjunct* Ron Petrosky; *Adjunct* Laura Shurley-Olivas; *Adjunct* Larry Hurst; *Adjunct* Joy Von Wolffersdorff
Estab 1970, dept estab 1974; Maintain nonprofit art gallery at Col of Canyons, Santa Clarita, CA; art supplies available on-campus; pub; D & E, Sat; Scholarships; SC 11, LC 4; D 300, E 300, maj 50
Ent Req: must be 18 yrs of age
Degrees: AA & AS 2 yrs
Courses: 2-D Design, 3-D Design, Advertising Design, Art Appreciation, Art History, Computer Graphics, Drawing, Gallery Practices, Illustration, Painting, Photography, Printmaking, Sculpture, Watercolor
Adult Hobby Classes: Tuition $10 plus lab fees usually another $10 per sem
Children's Classes: Classes offered in continuing educ under child development
Summer School: Dir Carole Long

SANTA CRUZ

UNIVERSITY OF CALIFORNIA, SANTA CRUZ, Art Dept, 1156 High St, E104 Baskin Visual Arts Santa Cruz, CA 95064-1077. Tel 831-459-2272; Fax 831-459-3793; Internet Home Page Address: www.arts.ucsc.edu; *Chmn* Norman Locks
Pub; D; SC per quarter 11, LC per quarter 3; D approx 7000, maj 80
Ent Req: HS dipl
Degrees: BA 4 yrs
Courses: Aesthetics, Book Arts, Drawing, Electronic Art, Intaglio Printmaking, Intermedia, Lithography, Metal Sculpture, Painting, Photography, Sculpture

SANTA MARIA

ALLAN HANCOCK COLLEGE, Fine Arts Dept, 800 S College Dr, Santa Maria, CA 93454-6399. Tel 805-922-6966, Ext 3252; Fax 805-928-7905; Internet Home Page Address: www.hancock.cc.ca.us; *Head* Steve Lewis

Estab 1920. College has three other locations; FT 10, PT 20; pub; D & E; Scholarships; SC 24, LC 4; D 800, E 220, maj 115
Ent Req: HS dipl, over 18 and educable
Degrees: AA 2 yrs
Courses: Art Appreciation, Art History, Ceramics, Costume Design & Construction, Dance, Design, Drawing, †Film, †Graphic Arts, Graphic Design, History of Art & Architecture, Life Drawing, Music, Painting, †Photography, Sculpture, Silk Screen, †Theatre Arts, †Video, Video Production
Adult Hobby Classes: Enrl 100. Courses—Drawing, Watercolor
Children's Classes: Enrl 20. Courses—Drawing
Summer School: Enrl 230; term of 6-8 wks beginning June. Courses—Animation, Art, Computer Graphics, Dance, Drama, Electronic Music, Film, Video, Graphics, Music, Photography

SANTA ROSA

SANTA ROSA JUNIOR COLLEGE, Art Dept, 1501 Mendocino Ave, Santa Rosa, CA 95401-4395. Tel 707-527-4259; Fax 707-527-8416; Internet Home Page Address: www.santarosa.edu; *Chmn* Deborah Kirklin
Estab 1918, dept estab 1935; pub; D & E; Scholarships; SC 40, LC 8; D approx 800, E approx 1000
Ent Req: HS dipl
Degrees: AA 2 yrs
Courses: 3-D Design, Art Appreciation, Art History, Ceramics, Computer Graphics, Drawing, Etching, Graphic Design, Jewelry, Layout, Lettering, Painting, Photography, Poster Design, Pottery, Principles of Color, Printmaking, Sculpture, Silkscreen, Watercolor
Summer School: Chmn, Donna Larsen. Courses—Art History, Ceramics, Design, Drawing, Jewelry, Painting, Printmaking, Sculpture, Watercolor

SARATOGA

WEST VALLEY COLLEGE, Art Dept, 14000 Fruitvale Ave, Saratoga, CA 95070-5698. Tel 408-741-2014; Fax 408-741-2059; *Chmn* Morry Roizen
Estab 1964; Maintain nonprofit art gallery; Viking Art Gallery; FT 5, PT 8; pub; D & E; SC 51, LC 12; D 1260, E 801
Ent Req: HS dipl or 18 yrs of age
Degrees: AA, 2 yrs
Courses: Aesthetics, †Ceramics, Costume Design & Construction, †Design, Digital Graphics & Animation, †Drawing, †Etching, †Graphic Arts, †History of Art & Architecture, †Jewelry, †Lithography, †Metal Casting, Museum Staff Training, †Occupational Work Experience, †Painting, †Papermaking, †Sculpture, Stage Design, Stained Glass, Theatre Arts
Adult Hobby Classes: Tuition varies. Courses—many classes offered by Community Development Dept
Summer School: Dir, Moises Roizen. Enrl 200-250; tuition $35-$50. Courses—Art Appreciation, Art History, Ceramics, Drawing, Painting

SONORA

COLUMBIA COLLEGE, Fine Arts, 11600 Columbia College Dr, Sonora, CA 95370-8560. Tel 209-588-5100, 588-5150; Fax 209-588-5104; Internet Home Page Address: columbia.yosemite.cc.ca.us; *Instr* Li Ching Accurso; *Instr* Laurie Sylwester
Estab 1968; pub; D & E; Scholarships; SC 50, LC 4; D 100, E 75, non-maj 90, maj 10
Ent Req: HS dipl or over 18 yrs old
Degrees: AA 2 yrs
Courses: Art History, Ceramics, †Design, Drafting, Drawing, Film, History of Art & Architecture, Painting, Photography, Sculpture, Theatre Arts, Video
Adult Hobby Classes: Quilting; Watercolor (variable or no fee)
Summer School: Courses—Ceramics, Drawing

SOUTH LAKE TAHOE

LAKE TAHOE COMMUNITY COLLEGE, Art Dept, One College Dr South Lake Tahoe, CA 96150. Tel 530-541-4660, Ext 228; Fax 530-541-7852; Elec Mail foster@ltcc.edu; Internet Home Page Address: www.ltcc.ca.us; *Painting Instr* Phyllis Shafer, MFA; *Chmn Art Dept* David Foster, MA; *Instr* Ellen Manaffey
Estab 1975; Maintain nonprofit art galleries: Foyer Gallery, Fine Arts Bldg, Lake Tahoe Community Ctr; Main Gallery, Main Bldg. Art supplies available for purchase on campus; pub; D, E & weekends; Scholarships; SC 22, LC 6; D 375, E 150, non-maj 300, maj 75
Ent Req: HS dipl
Degrees: AA 2 yrs
Courses: Art Appreciation, Art History, Bronze Casting, Ceramics, Color, Design, Digital Art, Drawing, Painting, Photography, Printmaking, Sculpture, Theatre Arts
Summer School: Dean Humanities Mrs Diane Rosner. Enrl 100; tuition undergrad $7 per unit, grad $33 per unit. Courses—Art History, Bronze Casting, Ceramics, Design, Intro to Art, Landscape Drawing, Life Drawing, Painting, Photography, Raku Pottery, Sculpture, Watercolor

STANFORD

STANFORD UNIVERSITY, Dept of Art & Art History, Cummings Art Bldg, Rm 101 Stanford, CA 94305-2018; 435 Lasuen Mall, Stanford, CA 94305-2018. Tel 650-723-3404; Fax 650-725-0140; Elec Mail art_questions@lists.stanford.edu; Internet Home Page Address: art.stanford.edu; *Sr Admin* Elis Imboden
Estab 1891; FT 19; pvt; D; Scholarships; SC 48, LC 63, GC 37 (seminars); 3200, maj 70, grad 40
Ent Req: HS dipl

Degrees: BA 4 yrs, MA 1 yr, MFA 2 yrs, PhD 5 yrs
Tuition: $25,000 per yr; campus res—room & board $7105 per yr
Courses: Art History, Drawing, Painting, Photography, Printmaking, Sculpture
Adult Hobby Classes: Offered through Stanford Continuing Education
Children's Classes: Enrl 250. Courses—Offered through Museum
Summer School: Enrl 100; eight wk term. Courses—Art History, Drawing, Painting, Photography, Printmaking

STOCKTON

SAN JOAQUIN DELTA COLLEGE, Arts & Communication, 5151 Pacific Ave, Stockton, CA 95207-6370. Tel 209-954-5209; Fax 209-954-3747; Elec Mail mwamhoff@deltacollege.edu; Internet Home Page Address: www.deltacollege.edu; *Fine Arts Div Dean* Dr Meryl Wamhoff; *Instr* Jennifer Barrows; *Instr* Gary Carlos; *Instr* Joe Mariscal; *Instr* Mario Moreno; *Instr* Ruth Santee
Estab 1935: Maintains nonprofit art gallery, L H Horton, Jr. Art Gallery San Joaquin Delta College 515 Pacific Ave Stockton CA 92507; maintains on-campus supplies shop; Pub; D & E; SC 12, LC 2; D 7,000, E 6,000, Maj 100
Ent Req: HS dipl
Degrees: AA 2 yrs
Courses: Advertising Design, †Architecture, Art Appreciation, Art History, Calligraphy, Ceramics, Collage, Commercial Art, Costume Design & Construction, Design, Drafting, Drawing, Fashion Arts, Film, Graphic Arts, Graphic Design, History of Art & Architecture, Interior Design, Landscape Architecture, Lettering, Painting, Photography, Printmaking, Sculpture, Stage Design, Textile Design, Theatre Arts, Video
Summer School: MJ Wamhoff, Dean. Enrl 8,000; Six week session. Courses—Same as regular sessions

UNIVERSITY OF THE PACIFIC, College of the Pacific, Dept of Art & Art History, 3601 Pacific Ave, Stockton, CA 95211-0197. Tel 209-946-2241; Fax 209-946-2518; Internet Home Page Address: www.uop.edu; *Chmn* Barbara Flaherty
Estab 1851; FT 9; pvt; Scholarships; 37 (3 unit) courses & 14 (4 unit) courses available over 4 yrs, independent study; maj 55-70
Ent Req: HS grad with 20 sem grades of recommending quality earned in the 10th, 11th and 12th years in traditional subjects, twelve of these grades must be in acad subj
Degrees: BA & BFA
Courses: Art Education, †Art History, †Arts Administration, Ceramics, Commercial Design, Computer Art, Design, Drawing, Graphic Arts, †Graphic Design, Illustration, Lettering, Painting, Photography, Printmaking, Sculpture, †Studio Art
Summer School: Two 5 wk sessions

TAFT

TAFT COLLEGE, Art Department, 29 Emmons Park Dr, Taft, CA 93268-2317. Tel 661-763-4282; Fax 661-763-7705; Internet Home Page Address: www.tafp.cc.ca.uf; *Chmn* Sonja Swenson-Wolsey
Estab 1922; pub; D & E; Scholarships; SC 67, LC 6; 1500 total
Ent Req: HS grad or 18 yrs old
Degrees: AA 2 yrs
Courses: Architecture, †Art History, Basic Design, Ceramics, Commercial Art, Conceptual Art, †Drafting, Drawing, Graphic Arts, Graphic Design, †History of Art & Architecture, Illustration, Painting, †Photography, Sculpture
Adult Hobby Classes: Courses—Ceramics, Graphic Arts, Jewelry, Painting, Photography
Summer School: Dean, Don Zumbro. Term of 6-8 wks. Courses—vary

TEMECULA

DORLAND MOUNTAIN ARTS COLONY, PO Box 6, Temecula, CA 92593-0006. Tel 909-302-3837; Elec Mail info@dorlandartscolony.org; Internet Home Page Address: www.dorlandartscolony.org; *Exec Dir* Jill Roberts
Estab 1979; non-profit; Grants
Tuition: $450 per month
Courses: Architecture & Design, Mixed Media, Music, Performance, Photography, Sculpture, Theatre Arts, Visual Arts, Weaving, Writing, dance

THOUSAND OAKS

CALIFORNIA LUTHERAN UNIVERSITY, Art Dept, 60 W Olson Rd, Thousand Oaks, CA 91360. Tel 805-493-3450; Fax 805-493-3479; Internet Home Page Address: www.callutheran.edu; *Prof* Larkin Higgins; *Chmn* Nathan Tierney, PhD; *Asst Prof* Christine Sellin, PhD; *Asst Prof* Michael Pearce; *Asst Prof* Barry Burns; *Asst Prof* Brian Sethem
Estab 1961; maintains a nonprofit art gallery; Kwan Fong Art Gallery, Thousand Oaks, Calif; pvt; D & E; Scholarships; SC 12, LC 7; D 110, non-maj 46, maj 40
Ent Req: HS dipl, SAT or ACT, portfolio suggested
Degrees: BA 4 yr; MA 1 - 2 yr; EdD 3 yr
Courses: Art Education, Art History, Ceramics, †Commercial Art, Design, †Display, Drawing, †Graphic Arts, Graphic Design, Medical Illustration, †Mixed Media, Painting, Photography, Printmaking, Sculpture, Stage Design, Teacher Training, Theatre Arts
Summer School: Asst Prof, Michael Pearce. Tuition $800 per unit for term June-July, July-Aug. Courses—Art Education, Design, Drawing, Painting, Pottery, Sculpture

TORRANCE

EL CAMINO COLLEGE, Division of Fine Arts, 16007 Crenshaw Blvd, Torrance, CA 90506-0003. Tel 310-660-3715; Fax 310-660-3792; Elec Mail cfitzsimons@elcamino.edu; Internet Home Page Address: www.elcamino.edu; *Dean Div* Constance Fitzsimons

Estab 1947; FT 35, PT 61; pub; D & E; Scholarships; SC 46, LC 6; D 1700, E 900, non-maj 2378, maj 222
Ent Req: HS dipl
Degrees: AA 2 yrs
Courses: †Advertising Design, †Art Appreciation, †Art History, †Ceramics, Drawing, Graphic Arts, Jewelry, †Lettering, Museum Staff Training, Painting, Photography, Printmaking, Sculpture
Children's Classes: Enrl 30. Courses—Exploration of Children's Art
Summer School: Enrl 400; tuition $11 per unit. Courses—Art Appreciation, Drawing, Painting

TUJUNGA

MCGROARTY CULTURAL ART CENTER, 7570 McGroarty Terrace, Tujunga, CA 91042. Tel 818-352-5285, 352-0865; Elec Mail director@mcgroartyartscenter.org; Internet Home Page Address: www.mcgroartyartscenter.org; *Dir* Laurelle Geils
Estab 1982; PT 24; pub; D & E; Scholarships; SC 40, LC 1; D 600, E 200
Courses: Cartooning, Ceramics, Dance, Drawing, †Fashion Arts, Life Drawing, Painting, Piano, Tai Chi Chuan, †Violin, †Yoga
Adult Hobby Classes: Enrl 10; $100; Courses—Ceramics & Painting
Children's Classes: Courses—Ceramics, Creative Drama, Dance, Music for Little People, Painting, Piano, Visual Arts, Violin

TURLOCK

CALIFORNIA STATE UNIVERSITY, Art Dept, 801 W Monte Vista Ave, Turlock, CA 95382. Tel 209-667-3431; Fax 209-667-3871; Elec Mail gsenior@csustan.edu; Internet Home Page Address: csustan.edu; *Chmn Dept* Gordon Senior, MFA; *Prof* John Barnett, MFA; *Prof* C Roxanne Robbin, PhD; *Prof* David Olivant, MFA; *Prof* Richard Savini, MFA; *Prof* Hope Werness, PhD; *Prof* Dean DeCoker, MFA; *Prof* Jessica Gomula, MFA
Estab 1963, dept estab 1967; Maintain nonprofit art gallery; Univ Art Gallery, 801 University Ave, Bldg D, Turlock, CA 95382; pub; D & E; Scholarships; SC 27, LC 6, GC 4; D 700, E 300, non-maj 350, maj 125, grad 20
Ent Req: HS dipl
Degrees: BA 4 yrs; Printmaking Cert Prog; BFA 5 yrs
Courses: Art History, †Drawing, †Gallery Management, Painting, †Printmaking, †Sculpture, Teacher Training
Summer School: Summer semester offered

VALENCIA

CALIFORNIA INSTITUTE OF THE ARTS, School of Art, 24700 McBean Pkwy, Valencia, CA 91355-2397. Tel 661-255-1050; Fax 661-259-5871; Internet Home Page Address: calarts.edu; *Pres* Dr Steven D Lavine; *Dean* Thomas Lawson
Estab 1970; maintains art library & nonprofit gallery, Gallery @ Redcat 631 W Second St Los Angeles CA 90012; FT 30; pvt; D & E; Scholarships; SC, LC, GC; D 285, maj 211, grad 90
Ent Req: portfolio
Degrees: BFA 4 yrs, MFA
Tuition: $37,684 per yr; campus res available
Courses: Aesthetics, Art History, Collage, Conceptual Art, Constructions, Critical Theory, Drawing, Film, Graphic Arts, †Graphic Design, †Integrated Media, Intermedia, †Mixed Media, †Painting, †Photography, †Post Studio, †Printmaking, †Sculpture, †Video, Visual Communication

VAN NUYS

LOS ANGELES VALLEY COLLEGE, Art Dept, 5800 Fulton Ave, Van Nuys, CA 91401-4062. Tel 818-781-1200; Fax 818-785-4672; Internet Home Page Address: www.lavalleycollege.com; *Chmn* Dennis Reed
Degrees: AA, cert
Courses: Advertising Design, Art History, Ceramics, Design, Drawing, Painting, Photography, Printmaking, Sculpture
Summer School: Beginning Design I, Drawing

VENTURA

VENTURA COLLEGE, Fine Arts Dept, 4667 Telegraph Rd, Ventura, CA 93003-3899. Tel 805-654-6400 ext 1280; Internet Home Page Address: www.vccca.net; *Chmn* Myra Toth
Estab 1925; FT 7, PT 26; pub; D & E; Scholarships; SC 50, LC 15; D 500, E 500, maj 300
Ent Req: HS dipl or 18 yrs of age
Degrees: AA and AS
Courses: Advertising Design, †Art, Art Appreciation, †Art History, †Ceramics, Collage, †Commercial Art, Costume Design & Construction, Design, Display, Drafting, Drawing, Fashion Arts, †Graphic Arts, Graphic Design, History of Art & Architecture, Illustration, Intermedia, Landscape Architecture, Mixed Media, Museum Staff Training, †Painting, †Photography, †Printmaking, †Sculpture, Stage Design, Textile Design, †Theatre Arts
Adult Hobby Classes: Enrl 500; Courses—Art
Summer School: Dir, Gary Johnson. Enrl 325; tuition same as regular courses. 4-8 wk term. Courses—Ceramics, Color & Design, Computer Graphics, Drawing, Photography

VICTORVILLE

VICTOR VALLEY COMMUNITY COLLEGE, Art Dept, 18422 Bear Valley Rd, Victorville, CA 92392-5849. Tel 935-245-4271; Fax 935-245-9745; Internet Home Page Address: www.vcconline.com; *Instructional Aide* Richard Ripley; *Chmn* Frank Foster

Estab 1961, dept estab 1971; pub; D & E; Scholarships; SC 20, LC 5; D 125, E 125, non-maj 200, maj 50
Ent Req: HS dipl
Degrees: AA 2 yrs
Courses: Art History, Commercial Art, Design, Drawing, Graphic Design, History of Art & Architecture, Painting, Photography
Adult Hobby Classes: Enrl 100; tuition $10 per 6 wks
Summer School: Dir, John F Foster. Enrl 75; tuition $13 per cr hr. Courses—Art Concepts, Art History, Design, Drawing, Photography

VISALIA

COLLEGE OF THE SEQUOIAS, Art Dept, 915 S Mooney Blvd, Fine Arts Division Visalia, CA 93277-2214. Tel 559-730-3700; Fax 559-730-3894; Internet Home Page Address: www.sequoias.cc.ca.us; *Instr* Richard Flores; *Instr* Gene Maddox; *Instr* Barbara Strong
Estab 1925, dept estab 1940; PT 12; pub; D & E; Scholarships; SC 12, LC 4; D 60, E37, maj 10
Ent Req: HS dipl, must be 18 yr of age
Degrees: AA 2 yr
Courses: Art Appreciation, Art History, Calligraphy, Ceramics, Commercial Art, Display, Drawing, Gallery Staff Training, Graphic Arts, Graphic Design, History of Art & Architecture, Illustration, Lettering, Painting, Photography, Printmaking, Sculpture, Stage Design, Textile Design, Theatre Arts, Video
Adult Hobby Classes: Ceramics, Painting, Photography
Summer School: Dir, Marlene Taber. Courses—Drawing, Painting

WALNUT

MOUNT SAN ANTONIO COLLEGE, Art Dept, 1100 N Grand Ave, Walnut, CA 91789-1399. Tel 909-594-5611; Fax 909-468-3954; Internet Home Page Address: www.mtsac.edu; *Chmn Art* Carolyn Alexander; *Chmn Art* Craig Deines; *Chmn Art* Kirk Peterson; *Chmn Animation* Don Shore
Estab 1945; FT 14, PT 10; pub; D & E; SC 24, LC 5; D 2254, E 852, maj 500
Ent Req: over 18 yrs of age
Degrees: AA and AS 2 yrs
Courses: Advertising Design, Art History, Ceramics, Commercial Art, Drafting, Drawing, Fibers, Graphic Arts, Illustration, Lettering, Life Drawing, Metals & Enamels, Painting, Photography, Printmaking, Sculpture, Theatre Arts, Woodworking
Summer School: Courses—Ceramics, Drawing

WEED

COLLEGE OF THE SISKIYOUS, Theatre Dept, 800 College Ave, Weed, CA 96094-2899. Tel 530-938-5257; Fax 530-938-5227; Internet Home Page Address: www.siskiyous.edu; *Area Dir* Dennis Weathers
Estab 1957; pub; D & E; Scholarships; SC 15, LC 2; D 1200, maj 20
Ent Req: HS dipl
Degrees: AA 2 yrs
Courses: Art History, Ceramics, Computer Graphics, Drafting, Drawing, Graphic Arts, History of Art & Architecture, Life Drawing, Painting, Photography, Printmaking, Sculpture

WHITTIER

RIO HONDO COLLEGE, Visual Arts Dept, 3600 Workman Mill Rd, Whittier, CA 90601-1699. Tel 562-908-3471; Fax 562-908-3446; Elec Mail jdowney@riohondo.edu; Internet Home Page Address: www.riohondo.edu; *Dean* Joanna Downey-Schilling; *Assoc Prof Painting & Drawing* Ada Pullini Brown; *Prof Photog* Chris Acuna-Hansen; *Asst Prof Painting & Drawing* Margaret Griffith; *Asst Prof 3D & 2D Design* Ron Reeder; *Instr Ceramics & Gallery Dir* Robert Miller; *Asst Prof Art History* Cynthia Lewis; *Prof Art* Dale Harvey; *Prof Art & Art History* Shelia Lynch; *Instr Animation* David Dawson; *Instr Photog* Ann Mansolino
Estab 1962; FT 8, PT 14; pub; D & E; SC 18, LC 3; D & E 19,000, non-maj 2100, maj 200
Ent Req: HS dipl
Degrees: AA 2 yrs
Courses: Advertising Design, Aesthetics, Architecture, Art Appreciation, Art History, Ceramics, Commercial Art, Conceptual Art, Design, Display, Drafting, Drawing, Graphic Arts, Graphic Design, History of Art & Architecture, Illustration, Lettering, Painting, Photography, Theatre Arts
Adult Hobby Classes: Courses—Calligraphy, Printmaking, Oriental Brush Painting, Tole & Decorative Painting
Summer School: Enrl 3468

WHITTIER COLLEGE, Dept of Art, 13406 Philadelphia St, Whittier, CA 90608-4413. Tel 562-693-0771, ext 4686; Fax 562-698-4067; Elec Mail dsloan@whittier.edu; Internet Home Page Address: www.whittier.edu/academic/art/arthome; *Chmn* Dr David Sloan
Estab 1901; pvt; D & E; Scholarships, Fellowships; SC 12, LC 12; 552-560 per sem
Ent Req: HS dipl, accept cr by exam CLEP, CEEBA
Degrees: BA 4 yrs
Courses: Art Education, Art History, Ceramics, Drawing, Painting, Printmaking
Adult Hobby Classes: Tuition $5. Courses—Classes for special students
Children's Classes: Tuition $5. Courses—Classes for special students
Summer School: Dir, Robert W Speier. Enrl 25; tui $140 per cr 1-7 cr, $125 per cr 7-up cr, May 31-June 17, June 20-July 29, Aug 1-Aug 19. Courses—Water Soluble Painting, Color & Basic Drawing

WILMINGTON

LOS ANGELES HARBOR COLLEGE, Art Dept, 1111 Figueroa Pl, Wilmington, CA 90744-2311. Tel 310-522-8200; Fax 310-834-1882; Internet Home Page Address: www.lahc.cc.ca.us; *Assoc Prof* John Cassone, MA; *Asst Prof* Nancy E Webber, MFA; *Instr* DeAnn Jennings, MA; *Instr* Jay McCafferty, MA; *Chmn* David O'Shaughnessy
Estab 1949; pub; D & E; SC 48, LC 11; D 10,000, E 4200
Ent Req: HS dipl
Degrees: AA 2 yrs
Courses: Architecture, Art History, Ceramics, Drawing, Fashion Arts, Painting, Photography, Printmaking, Stage Design, Theatre Arts
Summer School: Art Dept Chmn, DeAnn Jennings. Courses—Art Fundamentals, Art History and Photography

WOODLAND HILLS

PIERCE COLLEGE, Art Dept, 6201 Winnetka, Woodland Hills, CA 91371-0002. Tel 818-710-4366, 719-6475; Fax 818-710-2907; Elec Mail oshimad@pierce.laccd.edu; Internet Home Page Address: www.piercecollege.com/usr/art/; *Art Dept Chmn* David Oshima; *Prof* Constance Moffat, PhD; *Instr* Angelo Allen; *Instr* Larissa Bank; *Instr* Amy Blount; *Instr* Joane Byce; *Instr* Alex Carrillo; *Instr* Melody Cooper; *Instr* Camille Cornelius; *Instr* Greg Gilbertson; *Instr* David Glover; *Instr* Robert Kingston; *Instr* Lori Koefoed; *Instr* Eduardo Navas; *Instr* Brian Peshek; *Instr* Howell Pinkston; *Instr* Jill Poyourow; *Instr* Nancy Rizzardi; *Instr* Gerald Vicich; *Instr* Constance Kocs
Estab 1947, dept estab 1956; Maintains nonprofit art gallery, 6201 Winnetka Ave, Woodland Hills, CA 91371; pub; D & E; SC 20, LC 8; D & E 23,000
Ent Req: HS dipl 18 yrs and over
Degrees: AA 60 units
Courses: Advertising Design, Architecture, Art Appreciation, Art History, Ceramics, Design, Drawing, Fine Art, Graphic Arts, Graphic Design, Jewelry
Adult Hobby Classes: Offered through Community Services Dept
Children's Classes: Offered through Community Services Dept
Summer School: Dir, Paul Whelan

COLORADO

ALAMOSA

ADAMS STATE COLLEGE, Dept of Visual Arts, 208 Edgemont Blvd, Alamosa, CO 81102-0001. Tel 719-587-7823; Fax 719-587-7330; Elec Mail caravens@adams.edu; Internet Home Page Address: www.art.adams.edu; *Head Chair & Prof Art* Margaret Doell, MFA; *Prof Art* Eugene Schilling, MFA; *Asst Prof Art* Claire van der Plas, MFA; *Prof Art* Dana Provence, MFA; *Assoc Prof Art* Roger Eriksen, MFA; *PT Instr* Kris Gosar; *PT Instr* Laura Murphy, MA; *Asst Prof* Jenny Gawronski, MFA; *PT Instr* Linda Relyea, MA
Estab 1924; Nonprofit galleries: Cloyde Snook Gallery, Hatfield Gallery, 208 Edgemont Blvd, Alamosa, CO 81101; schls offered annually to undergrads & grads; On-campus shop where art supplies may be purchased; pub; D & E; Scholarships; SC 46, LC 6, GC 11; D 450, non-maj 200, maj 85, grad 15
Ent Req: HS dipl, ACT & SAT
Degrees: BA & BFA 4 yrs, MA 1-1/2 yrs
Tuition: Res—undergrad $3,724 per sem, grad $3,015 per sem; nonres—$9,040 per sem, grad $5,958 per sem; campus res—room & board $4,250
Courses: Art Appreciation, Art Education, Art History, Ceramics, Design, Drawing, Graphic Design, †Lettering, Metalsmithing, Painting, Photography, Printmaking, Sculpture, Weaving
Summer School: Tuition res—$306 per cr hr, nonres—$749 per cr hr. Courses—Art History, Ceramics, Drawing, Metals, Painting, Photography, Sculpture, Printmaking

BOULDER

UNIVERSITY OF COLORADO, BOULDER, Dept of Art & Art History, Sibell-Wolle Fine Arts Bldg, N198A Boulder, CO 80309; Campus Box 318, Boulder, CO 80309. Tel 303-492-3580; Fax 303-492-4886; Elec Mail finearts@colorado.edu; Internet Home Page Address: www.colorado.edu/arts; *Chmn* James Johnson
Estab 1861; FT 32, PT 10; pub; D & E; Scholarships; SC 63, LC 44, GC 31, internships 2; D 800, grad 50, others 100
Ent Req: HS dipl
Degrees: BA or BFA (Art History & Studio Arts) 4 yrs, MA (Art History) 2 yrs, MFA (Studio Arts) 3 yrs
Courses: Art History, Ceramics, †Digital Arts, Drawing, Painting, Photography, Printmaking, Sculpture, Video
Summer School: Dir, James Johnson. Enrl 20-25 per course. Courses—Art History, Drawing, Painting, Photography, Printmaking, Sculpture, Special Topics, Watermedia, Digital Arts, Video

COLORADO SPRINGS

COLORADO COLLEGE, Dept of Art, 14 E Cache la Poudre St, Colorado Springs, CO 80903-3243. Tel 719-389-6366; Fax 719-389-6882; Internet Home Page Address: www.coloradocollege.edu; *Chmn* Carl Reed, MFA; *Prof* James Trissel, MFA; *Assoc Prof* Gale Murray PhD, MFA; *Prof* Bougdon Swider, MFA; *Assoc Prof* Edith Kirsch PhD, MFA
Estab 1874; pvt; D; Scholarships; SC 20, LC 20; D 1800, maj 40
Ent Req: HS dipl or equivalent & selection by admis comt
Degrees: BA & MAT 4 yr

Courses: 3-D Design, Art History, Art Studio, Drawing, Graphic Design, Painting, Photography, Printmaking, Sculpture
Summer School: Dean, Elmer R Peterson. Courses—Architecture, Art Education, Photography

UNIVERSITY OF COLORADO-COLORADO SPRINGS, Visual & Performing Arts Dept (VAPA), 1420 Austin Bluffs Pkwy, Colorado Springs, CO 80918-3733. Tel 719-255-4065; Fax 719-255-4066; Elec Mail bkiselic@uccs.edu; Internet Home Page Address: http://web.uccs.edu/vapa/index.shtml; Internet Home Page Address: www.galleryuccs.org; *Prof & Dir Film Studies* Robert von Dassanowsky, PhD; *Assoc Prof, Film Studies & Visual & Performing Arts* Teresa Meadows, PhD; *Instr Theater* Murray Ross; *Instr Music* Curtis Smith; *Chair, Visual & Performing Arts* Suzanne MacAulay, PhD; *Asst Prof & Dir Music* Glen Whitehead, MDA; *Assoc Prof Visual Arts* Elissa Auther, PhD; *Assoc Prof Visual Arts & Dir* Valerie Brodar, MFA; *Asst Prof & Dir Theatre* Kevin Landis, MFA; *Asst Prof Visual Arts* Matt Barton, MFA; *Asst Prof Visual Arts* Corey Dreith, MFA; *Instr Theatre* Leah Chandler-Mills, MA; *Instr Visual Arts* Carol Dass, MA; *Instr Visual Arts* Pauline Foss, MA
Estab 1965, dept estab 1970; Maintain nonprofit gallery, Gallery of Contemporary Art (GOCA) same address as campus & 2nd gallery GOCA located at, 121 S Tejon, Colorado Springs. Maintain art library, VAPA-Visual Resource Center, COH 2012 (same address as campus); FT 5 PT 15; pub; D & E; SC 18 LC 16; maj 100
Ent Req: HS dipl, res-ACT 23 SAT 1000, nonres ACT 24 SAT 1050
Degrees: BA (Studio) 4 yr, BA (Art History) 4 Yr, BA (Visual & Performing Arts) 4 yr, (Concentrations in music, art history, film studies, theatre, visual art
Courses: Aesthetics, †Art, Art Appreciation, Art History, Collage, Computer Art, †Costume Design & Construction, Drawing, †Film Studies, †History of Art & Architecture, Mixed Media, Painting, Photography, Sculpture, †Stage Design, †Theatre Arts
Summer School: Chair & Assoc Prof, Suzanne MacAulay

DENVER

ART INSTITUTE OF COLORADO, (Colorado Institute of Art) 1200 Lincoln St, Denver, CO 80203-2172. Tel 303-837-0825; Fax 303-860-8520; Elec Mail alcadm@aii.edu; Internet Home Page Address: www.aii.edu; *Dean Acad Affairs* Mitra Watts; *Pres* David Zorn
Estab 1952; Maintain nonprofit gallery; pvt; D & E; Scholarships; SC all; D1800
Ent Req: HS dipl
Degrees: Assoc 2 yr, BA 4 yr
Courses: Advertising Design, Commercial Art, Computer Animation, Costume Design & Construction, Culinary Arts, Design, Drafting, Fashion Arts, Graphic Arts, Graphic Design, Industrial Design, Interior Design, Multimedia, Video, Website Administration
Adult Hobby Classes: Part time prog available, nights & weekends
Summer School: Summer studio prog for HS Srs

METROPOLITAN STATE UNIVERSITY OF DENVER, Art Dept, PO Box 173362, Campus Box 59 Denver, CO 80204-3936. Tel 303-556-3090; Fax 303-556-4094; Internet Home Page Address: www.mscd.art.edu; *Chmn* Greg Watts
Estab 1963, dept estab 1963; Maintains a non-profit art gallery Center for Visual Art, 965 Santa Fe Dr., Denver, CO 80204; pub; D & E & F; Scholarships; SC 52, LC 8; D 650, E 325, maj 500
Ent Req: HS dipl or GED
Degrees: BFA 4 yrs
Courses: †Advertising Design, Aesthetics, Art Appreciation, Art Education, †Art History, †Ceramics, †Design, †Drawing, Electronic Media, Graphic Arts, Graphic Design, Illustration, †Jewelry, †Painting, Photography, Printmaking, Sculpture
Summer School: Same as regular session

REGIS UNIVERSITY, Fine Arts Dept, 3333 Regis Blvd, Denver, CO 80221-1099. Tel 303-458-3576, 458-4286; Internet Home Page Address: www.regis.edu; *Dept Chair* Gene Stewart
Estab 1880; FT 3, PT 6; pvt; D & E
Ent Req: HS dipl, ent exam
Degrees: BA, BS & BFA 4 yrs
Courses: Aesthetics, Art Appreciation, Art History, Design, Drawing, Film, Graphic Arts, Graphic Design, Painting, Photography, Sculpture, †Visual Arts

UNIVERSITY OF COLORADO AT DENVER, College of Arts & Media Visual Arts Dept, PO Box 173364, Campus Box 162 Denver, CO 80217-3364. Tel 303-556-4891; Fax 303-556-2355; Internet Home Page Address: www.cudenver.edu/CAM/visual/; *Prof* Ernest O Porps, MFA; *Asst Prof* Karen Mathews PhD, MFA; *Chmn* John Hull, MFA; *Painting & Drawing* Quinton Gonzales; *Painting & Drawing* James Elhenny; *Photo* Joan Brennan; *Sculpture* Scott Massey; *Multi-Media Study* Kent Homchick
Estab 1876, dept estab 1955; pub; D & E; Scholarships; SC 21, LC 13, GC 11; maj 168
Ent Req: HS dipl, ACT or SAT, previous acad ability and accomplishment
Degrees: BA and BFA 4 yrs
Courses: †Art History, †Creative Arts, †Drawing, †Painting, †Photography, †Sculpture, †Studio Arts
Summer School: Courses—Art History, Studio Workshops

UNIVERSITY OF DENVER, School of Art & Art History, 2121 E Asbury, Denver, CO 80208-0001. Tel 303-871-2846; Fax 303-871-4112; Elec Mail saah-interest@du.edu; Internet Home Page Address: www.du.edu/art; WATS 800-876-3323; *Prof Art History* Annette Stott; *Prof Sculpture* Lawrence Argent; *Sr Lectr Art History & Dir Mus Studies* Gwen Chanzit; *Assoc Prof Art History* Annabeth Headrick; *Assoc Prof Drawing & Painting* Deborah Howard; *Assoc Prof Drawing & Printmaking* Catherine Chauvin; *Prof Art History* M E Warlick; *Dir, Assoc Prof Foundations* Sarah Gjertson; *Assoc Prof Electronic Media Arts & Design* Rafael Fajardo; *Assoc Prof Electronic Media Arts & Design* Timothy Weaver; *Assoc Prof Photog* Roddy MacInnes; *Assoc Prof Art History* Scott Montgomery; *Assoc Prof* Mia Fetterman-Mulvey; *Adj Faculty Conservation* Carl

Patterson; *Adj Faculty Conservation* Sarah Melching; *Adjunct Faculty Mus Studies* Timothy Standring; *Adj Faculty Art History* Ron Otsuka; *Dir Gallery* Dan Jacobs; *Assoc Prof Electronic Media Arts & Design* Laleh Mehran; *Lectr Foundations* Susan Meyer
Estab 1864; Maintain nonprofit art gallery; Victoria H Myhren Gallery, 2121 East Asbury Ave, Denver, CO 80208 & Penrose Libr. Schol & fel offered in variable amounts to all qualified candidates for 1 yr annually; contact Dr M. E. Warlick; Pvt; D&E; Scholarships, Fellowships; SC 44, LC 34, GC 38; D 450, non-maj 170-200, maj 170, grad 50
Ent Req: HS dipl, ent exam, portfolio
Degrees: BA & BFA 4 yrs, MA & MFA 3 yrs; combined BA/MA 5 yrs
Tuition: $1,064 per qtr hr; campus res available
Courses: Art Appreciation, Art Education, Art History, Ceramics, Design, Digital Media, Drawing, History of Art & Architecture, Museum Studies, Painting, Photography, †Pre-Art Conservation, Printmaking, Restoration & Conservation, Sculpture, †Studio Art

DURANGO

FORT LEWIS COLLEGE, Art Dept, 1000 Rim Dr, Durango, CO 81301-3999. Tel 970-247-7167; Fax 970-247-7520; Internet Home Page Address: www.fortlewis.edu; *Asst Prof* Paul Booth; *Assoc Prof* Chad Colby; *Asst Prof* Jay Dougan; *Asst Prof* Anthony Holmquist; *Prof, chmn dept* Susan Moss; *Assoc Prof* Amy K Wendland
Estab 1956; 5 FT; pub; D & E; Scholarships; SC 30, LC 6; D 600, non-maj 450, maj 150
Ent Req: HS dipl, SAT
Degrees: BA & BS
Tuition: $1105 per sem; campus res available—$2528 room & board per sem
Courses: Aesthetics, Art History, Ceramics, Drawing, Handicrafts, Illustration, Industrial Design, Intermedia, Jewelry, Painting, Southwest Art
Summer School: Dean, Ed Angus. Enrl 1000. Courses—Art Education, Ceramics, Drawing, Mural Design, Painting

FORT COLLINS

COLORADO STATE UNIVERSITY, Dept of Art, G100 Visual Art Bldg, Fort Collins, CO 80523-9001. Tel 970-491-6774; Fax 970-491-0505; Internet Home Page Address: www.colostate.edu/depts/art; *Chmn* Phil Risbeck
Estab 1870, dept estab 1956; 34; pub; D; Scholarships; SC 55, LC 13, GC 5; D 547, non-maj 860, maj 547, grad 22
Ent Req: HS dipl, portfolio if by transfer
Degrees: BA(Art History & Art Education) and BFA 4 yr, MFA 60 hrs
Courses: Advertising Design, Aesthetics, Art Appreciation, †Art Education, †Art History, †Ceramics, †Drawing, †Fibers, Goldsmithing, Graphic Arts, †Graphic Design, History of Art & Architecture, Illustration, Jewelry, †Metalsmithing, †Painting, †Photography, †Pottery, †Printmaking, †Sculpture, Silversmithing, Teacher Training, Textile Design, Weaving
Children's Classes: Continuing education art offerings not on regular basis
Summer School: Dir, James T Dormer. Enrl 700. Courses—most regular session courses

GRAND JUNCTION

COLORADO MESA UNIVERSITY, Art Dept, 1100 North Ave, Grand Junction, CO 81501-3122. Tel 970-248-1833; Fax 970-248-1834; Elec Mail sgarner@coloradomesa.edu; Internet Home Page Address: coloradomesa.edu; *Dept Head* Teresa S Garner; *Prof* Carolyn I Quinn-Hensley; *Assoc Prof* Dr. W Steven Bradley; *Assoc Prof* Joshua Butler; *Lectr* Denise Wright; *Asst Prof* Eli M Hall; *Asst Prof* Araan Schmidt; *Asst Prof* Alison Harris; *Asst Prof* Heather Patterson McCullogh
Estab 1925; Maintain nonprofit art gallery, Johnson Gallery, Mesa State College, 1100 North Ave., Grand Junction, CO 81501; pub; D & E; Scholarships; SC 88, LC 14, Other 4
Ent Req: HS dipl, GED
Degrees: BFA
Courses: †Advertising Design, †Art Appreciation, †Art Education, Art History, Ceramics, Design, Drawing, Exhibitions & Management, †Graphic Design, History of Art & Architecture, Lettering, Mixed Media, Painting, Printmaking, Sculpture, Textile Design

GREELEY

AIMS COMMUNITY COLLEGE, Visual & Performing Arts, PO Box 69, Greeley, CO 80632-0069. Tel 970-330-8008; Fax 970-330-5705; Internet Home Page Address: www.aims.edu; *Dir Visual & Performing Arts* Alysan Broda; *Acad Dean Communs & Humanities* Susan Cribelli
Estab 1967; pub; D & E
Ent Req: HS dipl, equivalent
Degrees: AA
Courses: Art Appreciation, Art History, Ceramics, Design, Drawing, Fashion Arts, Interior Design, Jewelry, Painting, Photography, Sculpture, Textile Design, Weaving
Children's Classes: Courses offered
Summer School: Courses offered

UNIVERSITY OF NORTHERN COLORADO, School of Art & Design, 501 20th St, Greeley, CO 80639-6900. Tel 970-351-2143; Fax 970-351-2299; Internet Home Page Address: www.unco.edu; *Dir* Dennis Morimoto, Ed.D
Estab 1889; Maintains nonprofit art gallery: Mariani Gallery; FT 10; pub; D & E; Scholarships; SC 72, LC 20, GC 18 ; Non-maj 75, maj 361, grad 20
Ent Req: HS dipl, Portfolio

Degrees: BA 4 yr, MA
Courses: Art Education, Art History, Ceramics, †Computer Graphics, Drawing, Fiber Art, Graphic Design, Jewelry, Painting, Papermaking, Photographic Imaging, Photography, Printmaking, Sculpture
Summer School: Courses—Comparative Arts Program in Florence, Italy, Study of the Indian Arts of Mesa Verde, Mesa Verde workshop & on campus courses, Workshops in Weaving & Ceramics in Steamboat Springs, Colorado

GUNNISON

WESTERN STATE COLLEGE OF COLORADO, Dept of Art & Industrial Technology, 600 N Adam, Gunnison, CO 81231; Quigley Hall, Gunnison, CO 81231. Tel 970-943-0120, Ext 3090; Internet Home Page Address: www.western.edu; *Dept Chair* Heather Orr
Estab 1911; FT 40, PT 10-20; D & E; Scholarships; SC 29, LC 7; 2550
Ent Req: HS dipl, special exam
Degrees: BA & BFA, 4 yr
Courses: Art Appreciation, Art Education, Art History, Calligraphy, Ceramics, Commercial Art, Conceptual Art, Design, Drawing, Graphic Arts, Graphic Design, History of Art & Architecture, Indian Art, Introduction to Art, Jewelry, Mixed Media, Painting, Photography, Printmaking, Sculpture, Silversmithing, Studio Art, Textile Design, Weaving
Summer School: 4 & 8 wk courses. Courses—Drawing, Painting, Photography

LA JUNTA

OTERO JUNIOR COLLEGE, Dept of Arts, 1802 Colorado Ave, La Junta, CO 81050-3346. Tel 719-384-8721; Fax 719-384-6880; Internet Home Page Address: www.ojc.cccoes.edu; *Head Dept* Timothy F Walsh
Estab 1941; pub; D & E; Scholarships; SC 12, LC 3; 850
Ent Req: HS grad
Degrees: AA & AAS 2 yr
Courses: Art History, Creative Design, Drawing, Painting
Adult Hobby Classes: Enrl 60; tuition $47.50 per cr, non-credit courses vary. Courses—Art, Drawing, Painting

LAKEWOOD

RED ROCKS COMMUNITY COLLEGE, Arts Dept, 13300 W Sixth Ave, Lakewood, CO 80228. Tel 303-988-6160; Fax 303-914-6666; Internet Home Page Address: www.rrcc.cccoes.edu; *Art Instr* Susan Arndt; *Instr Pottery* James Robertson
Estab 1965; pub; D & E
Ent Req: HS dipl, equivalent
Degrees: AA
Courses: Art Appreciation, Art History, Ceramics, Design, Drawing, Electronic Studio, Painting, Photography, Printmaking, Sculpture
Summer School: Enrl 80; tuition $99 per 3 cr course per 10 wks. Courses—Ceramics, Drawing, Design, Watercolor

ROCKY MOUNTAIN COLLEGE OF ART & DESIGN, 1600 Pierce St, Lakewood, CO 80214-1897. Tel 303-753-6046; Fax 303-759-4970; Elec Mail admissions@rmcad.edu; Internet Home Page Address: www.rmcad.edu; WATS 800-888-2787; *Pres & Provost* Dr Maria Puzziferro; *Financial Aid* Tammy Dybdahl; *VPres Admis* John Meurer; *Dean Design & Communs Art* Lauren Pillote; *VPres Mktg* Rebecca Newman; *Dean Fine & Liberal Arts* Dan James
Estab 1963; Maintain nonprofit art gallery, Phillip J. Steele Gallery, Mary K Harris Bldg, 1600 Pierce St, Lakewood, CO 80214. Art supplies sold at on-campus store; FT 19, PT 41; pvt; D & E; Scholarships; SC 68%, LC 32%; D 610
Ent Req: HS grad or GED, portfolio, essay, GEST scores
Degrees: BFA
Tuition: $13,416 fulltime, $1,118 per cr hr incoming freshmen
Courses: †Animation, Art Education, Art History, Ceramics, Character Design, Design, Drafting, Drawing, Film, Game Art, Graphic Arts, †Graphic Design, †Illustration, †Interior Design, Mixed Media, †Painting, Photography, Printmaking, †Sculpture, Teacher Training, Video
Summer School: Enrl 276; tuition $13176 for full term. Courses—Same as regular term

PUEBLO

UNIVERSITY OF SOUTHERN COLORADO, Dept of Art, 2200 Bonforte Blvd, Pueblo, CO 81001-4990. Tel 719-549-2835; Fax 719-549-2120; *Asst Prof* Carl Jensen, MFA; *Chmn* Roy Sonnema, PhD; *Asst Prof* Maya Avina, MFA; *Asst Prof* Dennis Dalton, MFA; *Assoc Prof* Richard Hansen, MFA; *Assoc Prof* Victoria Hansen, MFA
Estab 1933; pub; D & E; Scholarships; SC 50, LC 18; D 700, E 50, non-maj 600, maj 175
Ent Req: HS dipl, GED, Open Door Policy
Degrees: BA and BS 4 yrs
Courses: Art History, Ceramics, Collage, Commercial Art, Computer Animation, Computer Imaging, Drawing, Exhibition Design, Graphic Design, Illustration, Painting, Photography, Printmaking, Sculpture, Teacher Training, Video
Summer School: Dir, Ed Sajbel. Enrl 125. Courses—Art Education, Art History, Ceramics, Introduction to Art, Painting

RANGELY

COLORADO NORTHWESTERN COMMUNITY COLLEGE, Art Dept, 500 Kennedy Dr, Rangely, CO 82648-3502. Tel 800-562-1105; Internet Home Page Address: www.cncc.edu; *Chair* Mary Karen Solomon

SALIDA

DUNCONOR WORKSHOPS, PO Box 416, Salida, CO 81201-0416. Tel
719-539-7519; *Head* Harold O'Connor
Estab 1976; pvt; D; SC; D 34
Ent Req: professional experience
Tuition: Varies by course
Courses: Design, Goldsmithing, Jewelry, Silversmithing
Adult Hobby Classes: Enrl 24; tuition $450 per wk. Courses—Jewelry Making
Summer School: Enrl 34; tuition $450 per wk. Courses—Jewelry Making

STERLING

NORTHEASTERN JUNIOR COLLEGE, Art Department, 100 College Ave,
Sterling, CO 80751-2345. Tel 970-522-6600, Ext 6701, 521-6701; Elec Mail
larry.prestwich@njc.edu; Elec Mail jaci.mathis@njc.edu; *Prof* Larry B Prestwich,
MA; *Instr* Peter L Youngers; *Instr* Joyce May; *Instr* Jaci Mathis, BA
Estab 1941; Maintain nonprofit art gallery on-campus, Peter L Youngers Fine Arts
Gallery; art supplies available on-campus; pub; D & E; Scholarships; SC 16, LC
2; D 100, E 24, non-maj 80, maj 20, others 10
Ent Req: HS dipl, GED
Degrees: AA 2 yr
Courses: Advertising Design, Art Appreciation, Art Education, Art History,
Ceramics, Commercial Art, Design, Drawing, Graphic Design, Lettering, Mixed
Media, Painting, Photography, Printmaking, Sculpture, Teacher Training
Adult Hobby Classes: Enrl 100. Courses—Basic Crafts, Ceramics, Drawing,
Macrame, Painting, Stained Glass

CONNECTICUT

BRIDGEPORT

HOUSATONIC COMMUNITY COLLEGE, Art Dept, 900 Lafayette Blvd,
Bridgeport, CT 06604-4704. Tel 203-332-5000; Fax 203-332-5123; Internet Home
Page Address: www.hcc.commnet.edu; *Faculty* Michael Stein, MFA; *Prog Coordr*
Ronald Abbe, MFA; *Faculty* John Favret, MFA
Estab 1967, dept estab 1968; maintains nonprofit gallery, Burt Chernow Gallery &
Housatonic Museum of Art; on-campus shop where art supplies may be
purchased; pub; D & E; Scholarships; SC 20, LC 5; D 200, E 170, maj 75
Ent Req: HS dipl
Degrees: AA Fine Art 2 yr, AA Graphic Design, AA Graphic Design Computer
Graphic Option
Courses: †Art History, †Ceramics, Computer Graphics, †Constructions, †Design,
†Drawing, †Film, †Graphic Arts, †Graphic Design, Mixed Media, †Painting,
†Photography, †Sculpture, †Stage Design, †Theatre Arts
Summer School: Dir, William Griffin. Courses—Same as regular session

UNIVERSITY OF BRIDGEPORT, Shintaro Akatsu School of Design, 84
Iranistan Ave, Bridgeport, CT 06604. Tel 203-576-4239, 576-4709; Fax
203-576-4653; *Dir* Thomas Julius Burger; *Assoc Prof* Donald McIntyre, MFA;
Assoc Prof Jim Lesko, MFA; *Assoc Prof* Sean Nixon, MFA; *Asst Prof* Ketti
Kupper, MFA
Estab 1927, dept estab 1947; pvt; D & E; Scholarships; SC 38, LC 24, GC 15; D
1150, E 200, non-maj 1070, maj 260, GS 22
Ent Req: portfolio for BFA candidates only, college boards
Degrees: BA, BS & BFA 4 yr
Courses: Advertising Design, Art History, Ceramics, †Graphic Design,
†Illustration, †Industrial Design, †Interior Design, Painting, Photography,
Printmaking, Sculpture, Theatre Arts, Weaving
Adult Hobby Classes: Enrl open; Courses—most crafts
Summer School: Chmn, Sean Nixon. Details from chairperson (203-576-4177)

DANBURY

WESTERN CONNECTICUT STATE UNIVERSITY, School of Visual &
Performing Arts, 181 White St, Danbury, CT 06810-6855. Tel 203-837-9401; Fax
203-837-8945; Internet Home Page Address:
www.wcsu.edu.ctstateu/artsci/homepage; *Dean* Dr Carol Hawkes; *Chmn Art Dept*
Terry Wells; *MFA Coordr* Margaret Grimes
Estab 1903; Maintains nonprofit art gallery; 181 White St, White Hall, 3rd Floor;
Haas Library Midtown Campus, 181 White St; art supplies available at book & art
store Midtown & Westside campus; FT 7; pub; D & E; Scholarships; SC 30, LC
3-6, GC 5; D 155, grad 11
Ent Req: HS dipl
Degrees: BA (graphic communications) 4 yr, MFA (painting & illustration) 2 yr
Courses: Animation Production, Ceramics, Design, Drawing, Graphic Arts,
†Graphic Design, History of Art & Architecture, †Illustration, Lettering,
†Museology, Painting, †Photography, Printmaking, Sculpture, Stage Design,
†Studio Art
Summer School: Dir Peter Serniak; Courses—same as regular session

FAIRFIELD

FAIRFIELD UNIVERSITY, Visual & Performing Arts, 1073 N Benson Rd,
Fairfield, CT 06824-5171. Tel 203-254-4000; Fax 203-254-4119; Internet Home
Page Address: www.fairfield.edu; *Prof, Chmn* Kathryn Jo Yarrington; *Acting Dean*
Dr Beverly Khan
Estab 1951; Priv; D & E, summer; Scholarships
Degrees: BA, Masters

Courses: Art History, Art of Film, Design, Drawing, Film Production, History of
Film, Painting, Photography, Printmaking, Sculpture, Video, Visual Design
Adult Hobby Classes: Enrl 2000; tuition $330 per 3 cr. Courses—Full Fine Arts
curriculum
Summer School: Dir, Dr Vilma Allen. Enrl 2000. Semester June - Aug

SACRED HEART UNIVERSITY, Dept of Art, 5151 Park Ave, Fairfield, CT
06432-1000. Tel 203-371-7737; Internet Home Page Address:
www.sacredheart.edu; *Prof* Virginia F Zic, MFA
Estab 1963, dept estab 1977; 8; pvt; D & E; Scholarships; SC 26, LC 5; D 300, E
100, non-maj 225, maj 70
Ent Req: HS dipl
Degrees: BA 4 yrs
Tuition: Campus res—available
Courses: Advertising Design, Art History, Computer Design, Design, Drawing,
†Graphic Design, History of Art & Architecture, †Illustration, †Painting
Summer School: Prof, Virginia Zic. Courses—Art History

FARMINGTON

TUNXIS COMMUNITY TECHNICAL COLLEGE, Graphic Design Dept, 271
Scott Swamp Rd, Farmington, CT 06032-3187. Tel 860-677-7701; Internet Home
Page Address: www.tunxis.commnet.edu; *Acad Dean* Sharon LeSuer; *Graphic
Design Coordr* Stephen A Klema, MFA; *Assoc Prof* William Kluba, MFA
Estab 1970, dept estab 1973; pub; D & E; SC 15, LC 4; non-maj 40, maj 90
Ent Req: HS dipl
Degrees: AS, AA (Graphic Design, Visual Fine Arts)
Courses: 2-D & 3-D Design, Color, Computer Graphics, Drawing, Graphic
Design, Illustration, Painting, Photography, Typography
Summer School: Dir Community Services, Dr Kyle. Courses—Computer
Graphics, Drawing, Painting, Photography

HAMDEN

PAIER COLLEGE OF ART, INC, 20 Gorham Ave, Hamden, CT 06514-3902.
Tel 203-287-3030; Fax 203-287-3021; Internet Home Page Address:
www.paiercollegeofart.edu; *Pres* Jonathan E Paier
Estab 1946; FT 36, PT 11; pvt; D & E; Scholarships; SC 10, LC 6 GC 1; D 185,
E 130
Ent Req: HS grad, presentation of portfolio, transcript of records,
recommendation
Degrees: BFA & AFA programs offered
Courses: Advertising Design, Architecture, Art Education, Art History,
Calligraphy, Conceptual Art, Design, Drafting, Drawing, Fine Arts, Graphic Arts,
†Graphic Design, History of Art & Architecture, †Illustration, †Interior Design,
Lettering, †Painting, †Photography, Printmaking, Textile Design
Summer School: Dir, Dan Paier. Enrl 50. Courses—CADD, Fine Arts, Graphic
Design, Illustration, Interior Design, Photography

HARTFORD

CAPITOL COMMUNITY TECHNICAL COLLEGE, Humanities Division &
Art Dept, 61 Woodland St, Hartford, CT 06105-2345. Tel 860-520-7800; Fax
860-520-7906; Internet Home Page Address: www.commnet.edu; *Chmn* John
Christi; *Prof* Thomas Werle
Estab 1967; FT 1, PT 2; D & E
Ent Req: HS dipl or equivalent
Degrees: AA & AS 2 yr
Courses: Art History, Ceramics, Design, Drawing, Figure Drawing, Painting,
Printmaking, Sculpture
Summer School: Courses offered

TRINITY COLLEGE, Dept of Studio Arts, 300 Summit St, Hartford, CT
06106-3186. Tel 860-297-2208; Fax 860-297-5349; Elec Mail
Joseph.Byrne@trincoll.edu; Internet Home Page Address:
www.trincoll.edu/depts/star/; *Prof Fine Arts* Robert Kirschbaum, MFA; *Asst Prof*
Pablo Delano, MFA; *Vis Assoc Prof* Nathan Margalit, MFA; *Asst Prof* Patricia
Tillman, MFA; *Chmn, Prof Fine Arts* Joseph Byrne
Estab 1823, dept estab 1939; pvt; D; Scholarships; SC 20, LC 22; D 400, non-maj
350, major 50
Ent Req: HS dipl
Degrees: MA
Courses: Design, Drawing, History of Art & Architecture, Painting, Photography,
Printmaking, Sculpture, †Studio Arts

MANCHESTER

MANCHESTER COMMUNITY COLLEGE, Fine Arts Dept, 60 Bidwell St,
Manchester, CT 06040-6449; PO Box 1046, Mail Sta 31 Manchester, CT
06045-1046. Tel 860-647-6272; Fax 860-647-6214; Internet Home Page Address:
www.mcc.commnet.edu; *Prof* John Stevens
Estab 1963, dept estab 1968; PT 4; pub; D & E; D & E 300, non-maj 240, maj 60
Ent Req: HS dipl, portfolio for visual fine arts prog
Degrees: AA & AS 2 yrs
Courses: Art History, Basic Design, Calligraphy, Ceramics, Drawing, Film,
Graphic Arts, History of Film, Lettering, Painting, Photography, Printmaking,
Sculpture, Sign Painting

MIDDLETOWN

MIDDLESEX COMMUNITY COLLEGE, (Middlesex Community Technical
College) Fine Arts Div, 100 Training Hill Rd, Middletown, CT 06457-4889. Tel
860-343-5800; Internet Home Page Address: www.mxcc.commnet.edu; *Head Dept,
Prof* Judith DeGraffenried; *Instr* Matthew Weber

Estab 1966; Maintain a nonprofit art gallery, Pegasus Gallery, Chapman Hall, Niche, Founders Hall; pvt; D & E

Degrees: AS

Courses: †Art Appreciation, Art History, Ceramics, Design, Drawing, †Graphic Arts, †History of Art & Architecture, Painting, †Photography, Sculpture, †Silversmithing

WESLEYAN UNIVERSITY, Dept of Art & Art History, Wesleyan Station, Middletown, CT 06459. Tel 860-685-2000; Tel 800-685-2682; Fax 860-685-2061; Internet Home Page Address: www.wesleyan.edu/art/; *Prof* David Schorr, MFA; *Prof* Jonathan W Best, PhD; *Prof* Clark Maines PhD, MFA; *Prof* Peter Mark PhD, MFA; *Assoc Prof* Jeffrey Schiff, MFA; *Assoc Prof, Dir* Tula Telfair, MFA; *Assoc Prof, Dir* Elizabeth Milroy PhD, MFA; *Assoc Prof* Phillip Wagoner PhD, MFA; *Chair* Joseph Siry
Estab 1831, dept estab 1928; pvt; D; SC 30, LC 25; in school D 3604, maj 94, undergrad 2667
Ent Req: HS dipl, SAT
Degrees: BA 4 yrs
Tuition: Campus res available
Courses: Architecture, Art History, Film, Film History, Film Production, Graphic Arts, History of Art & Architecture, History of Prints, Painting, Photography, Printmaking, Printroom Methods & Techniques, Sculpture, Theatre Arts, Typography
Summer School: Dir, Barbara MacEachern. Enrl 576; Term of 6 wks beginning July 5. Courses—grad courses in all areas

NEW BRITAIN

CENTRAL CONNECTICUT STATE UNIVERSITY, Dept of Art, 1615 Stanley St, New Britain, CT 06050-2439. Tel 860-832-3200; Fax 860-832-2634; Internet Home Page Address: www.ccsu.edu; *Chmn Dept* Dr M Cipriano
Estab 1849; FT 14, PT 15; pub; D & E; SC 36, LC 8, GC 20; D 200, E 150, non-maj 1000, maj 200, grad 200
Ent Req: HS dipl
Degrees: BA(Graphic Design), BA(Fine Arts) & BS(Art Educ) 4 yrs
Courses: Art Education, Art History, Ceramic Sculpture, Ceramics, Color Theory, Curatorship, Display, Drawing, Fibre Sculpture, Fine Arts, Gallery Management, Graphic Arts, Graphic Design, Handicrafts, Jewelry, Lettering, Painting, Photography, Printmaking, Sculpture, Serigraphy (Silk Screen), Stained Glass, Teacher Training
Children's Classes: Enrl 30, 5-17 yr olds. Courses—Crafts, Fine Arts
Summer School: Dean Continuing Educ, P Schubert. Enrl 200. Courses—Crafts, Design, Drawing, Fine Arts

NEW CANAAN

GUILD ARTS CENTER, Silvermine, 1037 Silvermine Rd, New Canaan, CT 06840-4337. Tel 203-866-0411, 966-6668; Fax 203-966-2763; Internet Home Page Address: www.silvermineart.org; *Dir School* Anne Connell
Estab 1949; Maintain nonprofit art gallery, Florence Schick School Exhib Gallery, for student work & the Silvermine Guild Gallery for Silvermine Guild Artists; pvt; D & E; SC 60, LC 1; 560
Ent Req: none
Degrees: none
Courses: Advertising Design, Art History, Ceramics, Computer Graphics, Drawing, Illustration, Painting, Photography, Printmaking, Sculpture, Sogetsu Ikebana, Youth Programs in Art
Adult Hobby Classes: Enrl 550-600. Courses offered
Children's Classes: Enrl 80-100. Courses offered
Summer School: Dir, Anne Connell. Courses—Same as above

NEW HAVEN

ALBERTUS MAGNUS COLLEGE, Visual and Performing Arts, 700 Prospect St, New Haven, CT 06511-1189. Tel 203-773-8546, 773-8550; Fax 203-773-3117; Internet Home Page Address: www.albertus.edu; *Prof Art* Jerome Nevins, MFA; *Chmn & Assoc Prof Art* Beverly Chieffo, MA; *Asst Prof Art Therapy* Marian Towne, MA
Estab 1925, dept estab 1970; pvt; D & E; Scholarships; SC 20, LC 9; D 120, non-maj 60, maj 40
Ent Req: HS dipl, SAT, CEEB
Degrees: BA, BFA 8 sem
Tuition: Campus res available
Courses: Aesthetics, Art Education, Art History, Art Therapy, Ceramics, Collage, Design, Drawing, Fabric Design & Construction, History of Art & Architecture, Mixed Media, Painting, Photography, Printmaking, Sculpture, Teacher Training, Weaving
Adult Hobby Classes: Courses offered
Summer School: Dir, Elaine Lewis. Courses—vary

SOUTHERN CONNECTICUT STATE UNIVERSITY, Dept of Art, 501 Crescent St, New Haven, CT 06515-1355. Tel 203-392-6653; Fax 203-392-6658; Internet Home Page Address: www.southernct.edu/undergrad/schas/ART/index; *Dept Head* Cort Sierpinski
Estab 1893; pub; D & E; SC 40, LC 18, GC 20; D 315, GS 100
Ent Req: HS dipl, SAT
Degrees: BS, MS(Art Educ), BA(Art History) & BA, BS(Studio Art) 4 yrs
Courses: Art Education, Art History, Ceramics, Graphic Design, Jewelry, Metalsmithing, Painting, Photography, Printmaking, Stained Glass, Teacher Training
Summer School: Dir, Keith Hatcher. Enrl 320. Courses—Art History, Crafts, Drawing, Graphic Design, Painting, Photography, Printmaking, Sculpture, Stained Glass

YALE UNIVERSITY, School of Art, Holcombe T Greene Jr Hall, 1156 Chapel St New Haven, CT 06520-8339; PO Box 208339, New Haven, CT 06520-8339. Tel 203-432-2600; Fax 203-436-4947; Internet Home Page Address: www.yale.eduart; *Dean* Richard Benson; *Prof* Rochelle Feinstein, MFA; *Prof* Tod Papageorge, MA; *Prof Emeritus* William Bailey, MFA; *Prof* Richard Lytle, MFA; *Prof* Sheila Levrant-Bretteville, MFA; *Prof* Robert Reed, MFA
Estab 1869; pvt; D; Scholarships; GC118
Ent Req: BFA, BA, BS or dipl from four year professional art school & portfolio
Degrees: MFA 2 yrs
Tuition: $14,600 per yr
Courses: Drawing, Graphic Design, Painting, Photography, Printmaking, Sculpture
Summer School: 8 wk undergrad courses in New Haven, 3 cr each; 5 wk Graphic Design Prog in Brissago, Switzerland; 8 wk Fel Prog in Norfolk
—**Dept of the History of Art,** 56 High St Rm 103, New Haven, CT 06520-8272; PO Box 208272, New Haven, CT 06520-8272. Tel 203-432-2667; Fax 203-432-7462; *Dir Grad Studies* Christopher Wood; *Prof* Mimi Yiengpruksawan; *Dir Undergrad Studies* Kelly Jones; *Chmn* Edward Cooke
Estab 1940; FT 27, PT 2; pvt; D; Scholarships, Fellowships, Assistantships
Ent Req: for grad prog—BA & foreign language
Degrees: PhD(Art History) 6 yr
Tuition: $26,770 per yr
Courses: †Art History
—**School of Architecture,** 180 York St, New Haven, CT 06520-8924. Tel 203-432-2296, 432-2288; Fax 203-432-7175; Internet Home Page Address: www.architecture.yale.edu; *Dean* Robert Stern
Estab 1869; pvt; Scholarships; 142 maximum
Ent Req: Bachelor's degree, grad record exam
Degrees: MEd 2 yr, MArchit 3 yr
Tuition: $24,500 per yr
Courses: Aesthetics, Architecture, Art History, Design, Drawing, Landscape Architecture, Photography

NEW LONDON

CONNECTICUT COLLEGE, Dept of Art, 270 Mohegan Ave, New London, CT 06320-4125; PO Box 5206, New London, CT 06320-4196. Tel 860-439-2740; Fax 860-439-5339; Internet Home Page Address: www.conncoll.edu/departments/art; *Prof* Peter Leibert; *Prof* David Smalley; *Prof* Barkley L Hendricks; *Prof* Maureen McCabe; *Assoc Prof* Pamela Marks; *Assoc Prof* Andrea Wollensak; *Assoc Prof* Ted Hendrickson; *Prof* Tim McDowell; *Vis Asst Prof* Matt Harle; *Vis Asst Prof* Denise Pelletier; *Acad Dept Asst* Heidi Shepard
Estab 1911; pvt; D & E; Scholarships; SC 25; D 1600, maj approx 20
Ent Req: HS dipl, ent exam
Degrees: BA 4 yrs
Tuition: $15,175 per yr; campus res—room & board $4800
Courses: Architecture, Arts & Technology, Ceramics, Collage, Computer Art, Design, Drawing, †Graphic Arts, Graphic Design, Mixed Media, Painting, Photography, Printmaking, Silversmithing, Video
Summer School: Acting Dir, Ann Whitlach. Courses—Vary
—**Dept of Art History, Architectural Studies & Museum Studies,** 270 Mohegan Ave, Box: Art New London, CT 06320. Tel 860-439-2740; Fax 860-439-5339; Internet Home Page Address: www.conncoll.edu; *Prof* Andrea Wollensak

OLD LYME

LYME ACADEMY COLLEGE OF FINE ARTS, (Lyme Academy of Fine Arts) 84 Lyme St, Old Lyme, CT 06371-2333. Tel 860-434-5232; Fax 860-434-8725; Elec Mail admission@lymeacademy.edu; Internet Home Page Address: www.lymeacademy.edu; *Pres* Debra Petke; *Registrar* Jim Falconer, MA; *Asst Dean Admis & Cont Ed* Jennifer Renko, MA; *Dean & VP Acad Affairs* Laura J Zarriw
Estab 1976; Maintain nonprofit art gallery, The Chauncey Stillman Gallery, 84 Lyme St, Old Lyme, CT 06371; maintains art/architecture library, The Krieble Library, 84 Lyme St, Old Lyme, CT 06371; on-campus shop were art supplies may be purchased; pvt; D & E; Scholarships, Fellowships; SC 83 LC 6; 97
Ent Req: HS dipl, portfolio
Degrees: Cert 3 yr, BFA 4 yr
Courses: Art History, †Drawing, †Illustration, †Painting, Printmaking, †Sculpture
Adult Hobby Classes: Visit website for details
Summer School: Varies, see website for details

STORRS

UNIVERSITY OF CONNECTICUT, Dept of Art & Art History, 830 Bolton Rd, Unit 1099 Storrs, CT 06269-1099. Tel 860-486-3930; Fax 860-486-3869; Elec Mail anne.dalleva@uconn.edu; Internet Home Page Address: www.art.uconn.edu; *Head Dept* Anne D'Alleva; *Assoc Head* Jean Givens; *Assoc Head* Ray DiCapua
Estab 1882, dept estab 1950; Dept has nonprofit Atrium Gallery, professional & teaching gallery - The Contemporary Art Galleries, Barry Rosenberg, Dir of Exhib; FT 24, PT 10; pub; D; Scholarships; SC 43, LC 32, GC 15; D 1600, maj 280, grad 10
Ent Req: HS dipl, SAT, Portfolio Review
Degrees: BA(Art History), BFA(Studio) 4 yrs, MFA 2 yrs, MA Art History 2 yrs
Courses: Art Appreciation, †Art History, Ceramics, †Communication Design, Drawing, †Illustration, †Painting, †Photography, †Printmaking, †Sculpture, †Video

WEST HARTFORD

UNIVERSITY OF HARTFORD, Hartford Art School, 200 Bloomfield Ave, West Hartford, CT 06117-1599. Tel 860-768-4393, 768-4827; Fax 860-768-5296; Elec Mail calafiore@mail.hartford.edu; Internet Home Page Address: www.hartfordartschool.org; *Assoc Dean* Thomas Bradley, MA; *Asst Dean* Robert Calafiore, MFA; *Prof* Lloyd Glasson, MFA; *Prof* Frederick Wessel, MFA; *Assoc*

Prof Gilles Giuntini, MFA; *Assoc Prof* Christopher Horton, MAT; *Assoc Prof* Jim Lee, MFA; *Assoc Prof* Patricia Lipsky, MFA; *Assoc Prof* Ellen Carey, MFA; *Assoc Prof* Walter Hall, MFA; *Assoc Prof* Mary Frey, MFA; *Assoc Prof* Stephen Brown, MFA; *Asst Prof* Douglas Andersen, MA; *Asst Prof* Mark Snyder, MFA; *Asst Prof* Hirokazu Fukawa, MFA; *Asst Prof* Susan Wilmarth-Rabineau, MFA; *Asst Prof* Gene Gort, MFA; *Asst Prof* Matthew Towers, MFA; *Dean* Stuart Schar, PhD; *Asst Prof* Bill Thomson; *Asst Prof* John Nordyke; *Asst Prof* Nancy Wynn; *Asst Prof* Jeremiah Patterson
Estab 1877; pvt; D & E; Scholarships; SC 70, LC 5, GC 32; D 375, E 100, non-maj 125, maj 375, grad 20
Ent Req: HS dipl, SAT, portfolio review
Degrees: BFA 4 yr, MFA 2 yr
Courses: Architecture, †Art History, †Ceramics, Glass, Illustration, Media Arts, †Painting & Drawing, †Photography, †Printmaking, †Sculpture, †Video, †Visual Communication Design
Summer School: Dir, Tom Bradley. Enrl 50-75. Courses—Ceramics, Drawing, Visual Comm Design, Photography, Printmaking, Sculpture

UNIVERSITY OF SAINT JOSEPH, CONNECTICUT, Dept of Fine Arts, 1678 Asylum Ave, West Hartford, CT 06117-2791. Tel 860-232-4571; Fax 860-233-5695; Elec Mail info@mercy.sjc.edu; Internet Home Page Address: www.usj.edu; *Chmn Dept* Dorothy Bosch Keller; *Adj* Patricia Weise; *Adj* Barbara DiOrio
Estab 1932; Saint Joseph College Art Gallery (same address); FT 1, PT 2; pvt; W; also weekend prog for adult learner (co-ed); D & E; weekend; summer; Scholarships; SC 5, LC 7; D 104
Activities: Schols offered
Ent Req: HS dipl, CEEB
Degrees: BA, BS and MA 4 yr (except for Art History or Studio Art), PhD (Pharmacy)
Tuition: $27,580 (24-36 cr) incoming freshman
Courses: †African American Art, American Architecture, Architecture, Art Appreciation, †Art History, †Design, Drawing, Egyptian Art, Fundamental of Design, Greek Art, History of American Antiques, History of American Art, History of Art & Architecture, History of Women Artists, Impressionism, †Latin American Art, †Museum Staff Training, Painting, †Pastel Drawing, †Printmaking, Renaissance, †Watercolor
Summer School: Chmn, D Keller. Enrl 400; tuition $250 per cr hr. Maj in art history offered

WEST HAVEN

UNIVERSITY OF NEW HAVEN, Dept of Visual & Performing Arts & Philosophy, 300 Boston Post Rd, West Haven, CT 06516-1916. Tel 203-932-7101; Internet Home Page Address: www.newhaven.edu; *Coordr of Arts* Christie Summerville; *Chmn* Michael G Kaloyanides
Estab 1927, dept estab 1972; FT 2, PT 8; pvt; D & E; SC 30, LC 5; D 350, E 110
Ent Req: HS dipl
Degrees: BA & BS 4 yrs, AS 2 yrs
Courses: †Advertising Design, Art History, Calligraphy, Ceramics, Commercial Art, Constructions, Dimensional Design, Drawing, Film Animation, Graphic Arts, Graphic Design, History of Art & Architecture, Illustration, Interaction of Color, Interior Design, Mixed Media, Painting, Photography, Printmaking, Sculpture
Summer School: Courses—Ceramics, Drawing, History of Art, Painting, Photography, Sculpture

WILLIMANTIC

EASTERN CONNECTICUT STATE UNIVERSITY, Fine Arts Dept, 83 Windham St, Willimantic, CT 06226-2211. Tel 860-465-5000; Fax 860-456-5508; Internet Home Page Address: www.ecsu.ctstate.edu; *Chmn* Lulu Blocton
Estab 1881; FT 4, PT 4; pub; D & E; Scholarships; D 300, E 75, maj 40
Ent Req: HS dipl
Degrees: BA(Fine Arts) & BS(Art) 4 yrs
Courses: Art History, Ceramics, Drawing, Enameling, Graphic Arts, Interior Design, Jewelry, Painting, Sculpture, Weaving
Summer School: Dir, Owen Peagler. Courses—Art & Craft Workshop

WINSTED

NORTHWESTERN CONNECTICUT COMMUNITY COLLEGE, Fine Arts Dept, 2 Park Pl, Winsted, CT 06098-1706. Tel 860-738-6300; Fax 860-379-4995; Internet Home Page Address: www.commnet.edu/nwctc; *Prof* Charles Dmytriw; *Prof* Janet Nesteruk; *Prof* Richard Fineman
Dept estab 1965; FT 3; D & E
Ent Req: HS dipl or equivalent
Degrees: AA (Arts)
Courses: Advertising Design, Art Appreciation, Art History, Ceramics, Design, Drawing, Graphic Arts, Painting, Photography, Printmaking, Sculpture, Video

DELAWARE

DOVER

DELAWARE STATE COLLEGE, Dept of Art & Art Education, 1200 N Depont Hwy, Dover, DE 19901-2276. Tel 302-857-6000; Tel 302-857-6290; Fax 302-739-5182; *Art Dept Chmn* Arturo Bassolos
Estab 1960; FT 4; pub; D & E; Scholarships; SC 13, LC 9; 50-60 maj
Ent Req: HS dipl or GED, SAT or ACT
Degrees: BS(Art Educ), BS(General Art) & BS(Art Business)

Courses: Art Appreciation, †Art Education, Art History, Ceramics, Commercial Art, Design, Drawing, Fibers, Independent Study, Interior Design, Jewelry, Lettering, Painting, Photography, Printmaking, Sculpture, Senior Exhibition (one man show & research), Teacher Training
Adult Hobby Classes: Courses—same as above
Summer School: Courses—same as above

NEWARK

UNIVERSITY OF DELAWARE, Dept of Art, 104 Recitation Hall, Newark, DE 19716; 210 S College Ave, Newark, DE 19716-5200. Tel 302-831-2244; Elec Mail artdepartment@udel.edu; Internet Home Page Address: www.udel.edu/art/; *Chair* Janet Hethorn
Estab 1833

REHOBOTH BEACH

REHOBOTH ART LEAGUE, INC, 12 Dodds Lane, Rehoboth Beach, DE 19971. Tel 302-227-8408; Fax 302-227-4121; Internet Home Page Address: www.rehobothartleague.org; *Exec Dir* Dr Sheila Bravo; *Educ Dir* Kim Klabe
Estab 1938; Maintain a non-profit art gallery; pvt; D & E; Scholarships; SC 7; D 400, others 400
Ent Req: interest in art
Courses: Calligraphy, Ceramics, Drawing, Painting, Photography
Adult Hobby Classes: Enrl 150. Courses—Ceramics, Drawing, Painting, Pottery
Children's Classes: Courses—Art Forms

WILMINGTON

CHASSIE MERIKS ACADEMY OF PERFORMANCE ART, 6 S Union St, #871 Wilmington, DE 19805-3828. *Chmn Bd* Voleen Chassie
Open Mon - Sat Noon- 9 PM; Average Annual Attendance: 2,000; Mem: individual $500 - $2500

DISTRICT OF COLUMBIA

WASHINGTON

CATHOLIC UNIVERSITY OF AMERICA, School of Architecture & Planning, 620 Michigan Ave NE, Washington, DC 20064. Tel 202-319-5188; Fax 202-319-5728; Elec Mail arch@cua.edu; Internet Home Page Address: architecture.cua.edu/; *Dean* Gregory K Hunt; *Prof* Stanley I Hallet FAIA; *Prof* Ernest Fredson Wilson PhD, MArchit; *Prof* W Dodd Ramberg, BArchit; *Assoc Prof* Julius S Levine, MCP; *Prof* George T Marcou, MArchit; *Prof* Theodore Naos, MArchit; *Assoc Prof* Thomas Walton, PhD; *Prof* John V Yanik, MArchit; *Asst Prof* Ann Cederna, MArchit; *Asst Prof* Jill St Clair Riley RA; *Asst Prof* J Ronald Kabriel, MArchit; *Asst Prof* Lavinia Pasquina; *Assoc Prof* Terrence Williams AIA; *Asst Dean/Asst Prof* Erik Jenkins; *Assoc Prof* Vytenis A Gureckas RA; *Assoc Prof* Barry D Yatt AIA, CSI
Estab 1887, dept estab 1930; den; D & E; SC 6, LC 4 per sem, GC 15 per sem; D 240, maj 240, grad 95
Ent Req: HS dipl and SAT for undergrad, BS or BA in Archit or equivalent plus GPA of 2.5 in undergrad studies for grad
Degrees: BArchit & BS(Archit) 4 yr, MArchit 4 yr
Tuition: $10,110 per sem
Courses: Architecture, Drafting, Graphics, History and Theory of Architecture, Landscape Architecture, Photography, Planning, Practice, Technology, Urban Design
Children's Classes: Session of 3 wks. Courses—High School Program
Summer School: Dir, Richard Loosle. Enrl 100, term of 5-9 wks May-Aug. Courses—Computers, Construction & Documents, Design Studio, Environmental Systems, Graphic, History & Theory of Architecture, Photography, Structures
—Dept of Art, 620 Michigan Ave NE, Salve Regina Hall Washington, DC 20064-0001. Tel 202-319-5282; Internet Home Page Address: arts-sciences.cua.edu/art/; *Prof* Thomas Nakashima; *Chmn Dept* John Winslow; *Asst Prof* Nora Heimann
Estab 1930; den; D & E; Scholarships; SC 19, LC 9, GC 4; D 412, E 101, non-maj 449, maj 32, grad 4
Ent Req: HS dipl and SAT for undergrad, BA-BFA; MAT, GRE for grad
Degrees: BA (Studio Art, Art History, Studio Art for Secondary Educ)
Tuition: FT $9550 per sem; PT $735 per cr hr
Courses: †Art Education, †Art History, †Ceramics, Design, †Digital Arts, †History of Art & Archeology, †Painting, Photography, Printmaking, †Sculpture
Summer School: Chmn, John Winslow. Term of 4-5 wks beginning June. Courses—Drawing, Ceramics, Painting, Special Independent Courses, Digital Arts

CORCORAN SCHOOL OF ART, 500 17th St NW, Washington, DC 20006-4899. Tel 202-639-1800; Fax 202-639-1768; Internet Home Page Address: www.corcoran.edu; *Dir Art & The Book* Kerry McAleer-Keeler MFA; *Assoc Chair* Lorraine Schmidt; *Interim Chair, Undergrad Design* Francheska Guerrero; *Chair Fine Art Photog* Muriel Hasbun; *Interim Chair, Arts & Humanities* Lisa Lipinski; *Interim Chair, Fine Art* Lynn Sures; *Chair, Foundation* Rick Wall
Estab 1890; pvt; D & E; Scholarships; SC 84, LC 42; D 300 maj, E 750 non-maj
Ent Req: HS dipl, SAT or ACT, portfolio & interview
Degrees: BFA 4 yrs
Tuition: $16,970 per yr
Courses: Animation, Art Appreciation, Art History, Business & Law for the Artist, Ceramics, Computer Art, Design, Drawing, Fine Arts, Furniture, History of Photography, Illustration, Interior Design, Painting, Philosophy, Photography, Printmaking, Sculpture, Typography, Video

Adult Hobby Classes: Enrl 1000 per sem; tuition $380-$1060 for 13-15 wks. Courses—Art History, Ceramics, Color & Design, Computer Graphics, Drawing, Furniture, Interior Design, Landscape Design, Painting, Photography, Printmaking, Sculpture

Children's Classes: Enrl 70, tuition $127 per 5 wk session, Saturday ages 6-10; $380 per 13 wk session, Saturday ages 10-15. Courses—General Studio ages 15-18. Courses—Ceramics, Computer Art, Drawing, Painting, Photography, Portfolio Prep Workshop, Screen printing

Summer School: Dean, Samuel Hoi. Enrl 400; Adult—tuition $350-$960 for 6 wks beginning June. Courses—Art History, Ceramics, Computer Graphics, Drawing, Illustration, Interior Design, Landscape Design, Painting, Photography, Printmaking, Sculpture, Watercolor. HS (ages 15-18)—tuition $390-$690 for 5 wks beginning June. Courses—Ceramics, Drawing, Painting, Photography, Portfolio Prep, Pre-College. Children's Workshops (ages 6-10)—tuition $10 for 5 day session beginning June

GEORGE WASHINGTON UNIVERSITY, Dept of Art of Fine Arts & Art History, 801 22nd St NW, Smith Hall of Art Rm 101 Washington, DC 20052-0058. Tel 202-994-6085; Fax 202-994-8657; Elec Mail art@gwu.edu; Internet Home Page Address: www.art.gwu.edu; *Prof* David Bjelajac PhD; *Prof* Barbara Von Barghahn PhD; *Prof* J Franklin Wright Jr, MFA; *Prof* Turker Ozdogan, MFA; *Assoc Prof* Philip Jacks, PhD; *Assoc Prof* Dean Kessmann, MFA; *Asst Prof* Alexander Dumbadze, PhD; *Asst Prof* Siobhan Rigg, MFA; *Asst Prof* Bibiana Obler, PhD; *Asst Prof* Julia Brown, MFA; *Asst Prof* James Sham, MFA; *Asst Prof* Mika Natif, PhD
Estab 1821, dept estab 1893; Maintains nonprofit art gallery located at Gallery 102 Smith Hall of Art, maintains art/architecture library; on-campus shop for purchase of supplies; pvt; D & E; Scholarships; SC 103, LC 74, GC 68; D 1350, GS 196
Ent Req: HS dipl, ent exam
Degrees: BA 4 yr, MA 2-2 1/2 yr, MFA 2 yr
Courses: American Art, †Art History, †Ceramics, Classical Art & Archaeology, Commercial Art, Contemporary Art, †Design, †Drawing, †Graphic Arts, History of Art & Architecture, Medieval Art, Mixed Media, †Painting, †Photography, †Printmaking, Renaissance & Baroque Art, Restoration & Conservation, †Sculpture, †Video, †Visual Communications
Summer School: Tuition $680 per cr hr for two 6 wk sessions. Courses—Art History, Ceramics, Drawing, Painting, Photography, Sculpture, Visual Communications

GEORGE WASHINGTON UNIVERSITY, School of Interior Design, 2100 Foxhall Rd NW, Washington, DC 20007-1150. Tel 202-242-6700; Elec Mail nblossom@gwu.edu; Internet Home Page Address: www.gwu.edu/; *Dept Chmn* Erin Speck
Estab 1875; maintains non profit art gallery, The Dimock Gallery, Lisner auditorium, 730 21st St NW, Washington DC; pvt; D & E; Scholarships; SC 16
Degrees: AA, BA & BFA
Courses: Aesthetics, Art History, Arts & Humanities, Ceramics, Design, Drafting, Drawing, Graphic Arts, †Graphic Design, Historical Preservation, †History of Decorative Art, †Interior Design, Painting, Photography, Printmaking, Sculpture, †Studio Art, Textile Design, Theatre Arts
Adult Hobby Classes: Graphic Design, History of Decorative Art, Interior Design, Studio Art
Summer School: Dir, Dr Sharon Fechter. Enrl 40, 8 wks, June-July. Courses—History of Decorative Art, Interior Design, Studio Arts

GEORGETOWN UNIVERSITY, Dept of Art & Art History, Walsh 102, Washington, DC 20057; Walsh Bldg Rm 102, 1221 36th St NW Washington, DC 20057-0001. Tel 202-687-7010; Fax 202-687-3048; Internet Home Page Address: www.georgetown.edu/departments/amth; *Prof* Elizabeth Prelinger PhD; *Chmn & Prof* Alison Hilton PhD; *Prof* Peter Charles, MFA; *Assoc Prof* B G Muhn, MFA; *Asst Prof* John Morrell, MFA; *Prof* Roberto Bocci; *Asst Prof* L Collier Hyams, MFA; *Asst Prof* Al Acres, PhD; *Dir Gallery* Evan Reed, MFA
Estab 1789, dept estab 1967; Maintain nonprofit art gallery, 1221 36th St, NW, Washington, DC 20057; FT 15; pvt; Jesuit/Catholic; D & E; SC 20, LC 15; D 1000 (includes non-maj), maj 20 studio & 15 art history per yr
Ent Req: HS dipl
Degrees: BA 4 yrs
Tuition: campus res available
Courses: †Art History, †Design, Digital Art, †Drawing, †Mixed Media, †Painting, †Photography, †Printmaking, †Sculpture
Adult Hobby Classes: Continuing Studies Dean Robert Manuel
Summer School: Assoc Dean, Ester Rider. Courses offered

TRINITY COLLEGE, Fine Arts Program, 125 Michigan Ave NE, Washington, DC 20017-1090. Tel 202-884-9280, 884-9000; Fax 202-884-9229; Elec Mail easbyr@trinitydc.edu; Internet Home Page Address: www.trinitydc.edu/academics/depts/finearts/index; *Chmn & Assoc Prof* Dr Rebecca Easby; *Lectr* Eugene D Markowski; *Prof* Dr Yvonne Dixon
Estab 1897; den; D & E; Scholarships; SC 8, LC 2-3; D 120, maj 12
Ent Req: HS dipl, SAT or ACT, recommendation
Degrees: BA 4 yr
Courses: Art History, Design, Documentary, Drawing, Film, Graphic Design, History of Art & Architecture, Lettering, Painting, Photography, Photojournalism, Printmaking, Sculpture
Summer School: Dir, Susan Ikerd. Courses—Vary

UNIVERSITY OF THE DISTRICT OF COLUMBIA, Dept of Mass Media, Visual & Performing Arts, 4200 Connecticut Ave NW, MB46 A03 Washington, DC 20008-1122. Tel 202-274-7402; Fax 202-274-5817; Internet Home Page Address: www.udc.edu; *Prof* Meredith Rode, PhD; *Prof* Manon Cleary, MFA; *Chairperson & Prof* Yvonne Pickering-Carter, MFA; *Asst Prof* George Smith, MS
Estab 1969; pub; D & E; SC 65, LC 21; D 616, E 99, non-maj 405, maj 112
Ent Req: HS dipl, GED
Degrees: AA(Advertising Design) 2 yrs, BA(Studio Art) and BA(Art Educ) 4 yrs
Tuition: Res—undergrad $360 per sem; non-res—undergrad $1320 per sem; no campus res

Courses: †Advertising Design, †Art Education, Art History, Ceramics, Conceptual Art, Drawing, Graphic Arts, Graphic Design, Handicrafts, Illustration, Lettering, Mixed Media, Museum Staff Training, †Painting, Photography, †Printmaking, Sculpture
Summer School: C A Young. Enrl 200. Courses—Art History, Ceramics, Drawings, Painting, Photography

FLORIDA

BOCA RATON

FLORIDA ATLANTIC UNIVERSITY, D F Schmidt College of Arts & Letters Dept of Visual Arts & Art History, 777 Glades Rd, AH52 Room 118 Boca Raton, FL 33431-6424. Tel 561-297-3870; Fax 561-297-3078; Elec Mail art@fau.edu; Internet Home Page Address: www.fau.edu/vaah; *Chair, Prof Art, Graphic Design* Linda Johnson; *Prof Art, Graphic Design* Stephanie Cunningham; *Instr Art, Ceramics* Bonnie Seeman; *Asst Prof Art & Photography* Sharon Hart; *Assoc Prof Art, Foundations, Drawing & Painting* Amy Broderick; *Asst Prof Art, Graphic Design* Eric Landes; *Asst Prof Art, Printmaking* Juana Valdes; *Prof Art, Ceramics* Angela DiCosola; *Asst Prof Art History* Karen Leader, Ph.D; *Asst Prof Art History* Paula Carabell; *Prof Art, Painting/Drawing* Walter Hnatysh; *Chair, Assoc Prof Art History & Classical Archaeology* Brian McConnell, Ph.D; *Asst Prof Art, Graphic Design* Jeane Cooper; *Assoc Prof Art, Graphic Design* Tammy Knipp; *Prof Art, Painting/Drawing* Carol Prusa; *Vis Instr Painting* Ariel Baron-Robbins; *Vis Instr Sculpture* Mark Oliver; *Vis Instr Ceramics* Chanda Glendinning; *Vis Instr Graphic Design* Annette Piskel; *Vix Instr Art History* Roger Hurlburt
Estab 1964; Maintains a non-profit art gallery; on-campus art supply shop.; pub; D & E; Scholarships, Fellowships; SC 36, LC 10, GC 12; D 1600, maj 600+, grad 7, gs 16, special students 7
Degrees: BFA & BA 4 yrs, MFA
Tuition: Res—$199.54 per cr hr; nonres—$718.09 per cr hr; grad res—$369.82 per cr hr; nonres—$1,024.81 per cr hr
Courses: Aesthetics, Art Appreciation, †Art Education, †Art History, Ceramics, Design, †Drawing, †Graphic Design, †History of Art & Architecture, Mixed Media, Museum Studies, Painting, Photography, Printmaking, Sculpture, Silkscreen & Etching, †Studio Arts, Web Design
Adult Hobby Classes: Courses offered through continuing education
Summer School: Courses offered

LYNN UNIVERSITY, Art & Design Dept, 3601 N Military Trail, Boca Raton, FL 33431-5507. Tel 561-237-7000; Internet Home Page Address: www.lynn.edu; *Prof* Tuscano
Estab 1962; Scholarships
Degrees: AA, BFA, BS & Design
Courses: Advertising Design, Art Appreciation, Art History, Corporate Identity Rendering Techniques, Design, Drawing, Environmental Design, Graphics, Painting, Photography, Portfolio & Exhibition, Textile Design

BRADENTON

STATE COLLEGE OF FLORIDA MANATEE - SARASOTA, (Manatee Community College) Art, Design, Humanities, PO Box 1849, Bradenton, FL 34206-7046. Tel 941-752-5251; Fax 941-727-6088; Internet Home Page Address: www.scf.edu; *Prof* Sherri Hill, MA; *Prof, Film* Del Jacobs, MA; *Prof, Photog* Drew Webster, MFA; *Prof* Sue Wyer, BA; *Prof* Jamie Tracy, MFA; *Prof* Katherine Beura, MA
Estab 1958; Maintain a non-profit art gallery, State College of Flroida Fine Art Gallery; FT 7, PT 5; pub; D, E, online; Scholarships; SC 30, LC 15; D 310, E 90, maj 75
Ent Req: HS dipl, SAT
Degrees: AA & AS 2 yrs
Courses: 2-D & 3-D Design, Art Appreciation, Art History, Ceramics, Color Fundamentals, Commercial Art, Costume Design & Construction, Design, Drawing, Figure Drawing, Film, Graphic Arts, Graphic Design, †Graphic Design Technology, History of Art & Architecture, Interior Design, Lettering, Mixed Media, Painting, Photography, Printmaking, Sculpture, Stage Design, Theatre Arts, Video

CLEARWATER

SAINT PETERSBURG COLLEGE, Fine & Applied Arts at Clearwater Campus, 2465 Drew St, Clearwater, FL 33765; PO Box 13489, Saint Petersburg, FL 33733-3489. Tel 727-341-3600, 341-4360, 791-2611; Fax 727-791-2605; Internet Home Page Address: www.spcollege.edu; Telex 727-791-2548; *Assoc Prof* Kevin Grass; *Asst Prof* Kim Kirchman; *Instr* Marjorie Greene; *Asst Prof* Barton Gilmore; *Dean* Dr Jonathan Steele; *Dept Chmn* Jonathan Barnes
Estab 1927. College has eight campuses; Maintain nonprofit art gallery; Muse Gallery, 2465 Drew St Clearwater FL 33765; art library; FT6; pub; D & E; Scholarships; SC 125 LC 5; D 160, E 400, maj 20-25
Ent Req: HS dipl
Degrees: AA & AS 2 yr, BS 4 yr
Courses: †2-D & 3-D, Architecture, Art Appreciation, Art History Survey, Ceramics, Costume Design & Construction, Design, Drawing, Graphic Arts, Painting, Photography, †Printmaking, Sculpture, Stage Design, †Studio Lighting, Theatre Arts
Summer School: Dept Chair, Jonathan Barnes. Courses—Same as regular session; 10 wk session.

CORAL GABLES

UNIVERSITY OF MIAMI, Dept of Art & Art History, PO Box 248106, Coral Gables, FL 33124-8106. Tel 305-284-2542; Fax 305-284-2115; Elec Mail art-arh@miami.edu; Internet Home Page Address: www.miami.edu/art; *Asst Prof*

Ivan Albrecht MFA; *Prof* Darby Bannard, BA; *Asst Prof* Carsten Meier, MFA; *Assoc Prof* Paula Harper PhD, MFA; *Prof* Perri Lee Roberts PhD, MFA; *Assoc Prof* Carlos Aquirre, MFA; *Prof* J Tomas Lopez, MFA; *Asst Prof* William Betsch PhD, MFA; *Chair, Assoc Prof* Lise Drost, MFA; *Assoc Prof* Brian Curtis, MFA; *Instr* Kyle Trowbridge, MFA; *Instr* Joel Hollander, PhD; *Asst Prof* Rebecca P Brienen, PhD; *Asst Prof* Billie G Lynn, MFA; *Instr* Mariah Hausman, MFA; *Prof* William D. Carlson, MFA
Estab 1925, dept estab 1960; On-campus shop where art supplies may be purchased; pvt; D&E; Scholarships; SC 71, LC 16, GC 50; D 1100, non-maj 870, maj 230, grad 20, other 5
Ent Req: HS dipl, SAT
Degrees: BA & BFA 4 yrs, MA(Art History) 2 yrs& MFA 3 yrs
Tuition: Res & nonres—undergrad $27,384 per yr, $13,692 per sem, $1,140 per cr hr
Courses: †Art History, †Ceramics, Design, Digital Imaging, Drawing, †Glassblowing, †Graphic Design, †Illustration, †Multimedia, †Painting, †Photography, †Printmaking, †Sculpture
Summer School: Tuition $790 per cr for two 6 wk terms. Courses—Limited regular courses, special workshops, travel

DAYTONA BEACH

DAYTONA BEACH COMMUNITY COLLEGE, Dept of Fine Arts & Visual Arts, PO Box 2811, Daytona Beach, FL 32120-2811. Tel 904-255-8131; Fax 904-947-3134; *Dean* Dr Frank Wetta; *Prof* Denis Deegan, MFA; *Prof* Pamela Griesinger, MFA; *Prof* Gary Monroe, MFA; *Prof* Eric Breitenbach, MS; *Prof* Patrick Van Duesen, BS; *Prof* Dan Biferie, MFA; *Prof* Bobbie Clementi, MFA; *Prof* Jacques A Dellavalle, MFA; *Prof* John Wilton, MFA; *Prof* Patricia Thompson, MA
Estab 1958; pub; D & E; Scholarships; SC 15, LC 3; D 250, E 50, maj 30
Ent Req: HS dipl or GED
Degrees: 2 year program offered
Tuition: Res—$45 per sem hr; nonres—$143.25 per sem hr
Courses: Advertising Design, Art Appreciation, †Art Education, Art History, Ceramics, Cinematography, Constructions, Design, Digital Imaging, Drafting, Drawing, Film, Fine Arts, Graphic Arts, †Graphic Design, History of Art & Architecture, Illustration, Interior Design, Museum Staff Training, Painting, †Photography, Printmaking, Sculpture, Teacher Training, †Theatre Arts, Video
Summer School: Enrl 15; tuition $35 per cr hr for 3 cr. Courses—Painting I & II

DELAND

STETSON UNIVERSITY, Department of Creative Arts, 421 N Woodland Blvd, Unit 8252 Deland, FL 32723-0001. Tel 386-822-7266; Elec Mail cnelson@stetson.edu; Internet Home Page Address: www.stetson.edu/departments/art; *Dept Chmn* Nathan Wolek; *Prof* Dan Gunderson; *Assoc Prof* Matt Roberts; *Asst Prof* Ekaterina Kudryavtseva; *Prof* Gary Bolding; *Prof* Joseph Witek; *Asst Prof* Julia Schmitt
Estab 1880; Maintains nonprofit art gallery: Hand Art Center, 139 E Michigan Ave, Deland, FL 32724; FT 6; pvt; D&E; Scholarships; SC 7, LC 3 per sem
Ent Req: col boards
Degrees: 4 yr
Courses: Art History, Ceramics, Design, Digital Art, Drawing, Mixed Media, Painting, Photography, Sculpture, Video

DUNEDIN

DUNEDIN FINE ART CENTER, 1143 Michigan Blvd, Dunedin, FL 34698-2712. Tel 727-298-3322; Fax 727-298-3326; Elec Mail gabissett@dfac.org; Internet Home Page Address: www.dfac.org; *CFRE Exec Dir* George Ann Bissett; *Dir of Youth* Todd Still; *Dir Adult Educ* Catherine Bergmann; *Admin Asst* Barbara Ferguson
Estab 1975; 501c3 org; continuing education classes; maintains 3 nonprofit art gallery, art library; FT & PT 54; pvt; D & E & weekends; Scholarships; SC 20-25, LC 5-10; approx 900 D, E, non-majors
Activities: gallery store sells art supplies
Ent Req: none
Degrees: none
Tuition: no campus res
Courses: Art Appreciation, Art Education, Art History, Arts for the Handicapped, Batik, Calligraphy, Ceramics, Children's Art, Clay, Collage, †Continuing Studio Arts Education, Design, Drawing, Fashion Arts, Film, Fine Crafts, Graphic Arts, Graphic Design, Handicrafts, Jewelry, Lettering, Mixed Media, Painting, Pastel, Photography, Pottery, Printmaking, Sculpture, Silversmithing, Studio Visual Arts, Textile Design, Video, Weaving
Children's Classes: Courses—Fine Arts, Drama
Summer School: Dir, Todd Still. Enrl 150 per wk for 10 wks

FORT LAUDERDALE

ART INSTITUTE OF FORT LAUDERDALE, 1799 SE 17th St, Fort Lauderdale, FL 33316-3000. Tel 954-527-1799; Fax 305-728-8637; Internet Home Page Address: www.aifl.edu; WATS 800-275-7603; *Dir Admis* Eileen Northrop; *Dir Educ* Steve Schwab; *Dir Visual Communs* Rosanne Giuel; *Dir Photo* Ed Williams; *Dir Interior Design* Bill Kobrynich, AA; *Asst Chmn Advertising Design* Lorna Hernandez, AA; *Dir Music & Video Bus* Ed Galizia, AA; *Dir Fashion Design* June Fisher, AA
Estab 1968; pvt; D & E; Scholarships; D 1900, maj 1900
Ent Req: HS dipl
Degrees: AS(technology), BA
Courses: Advertising Design, Art History, Computer Animation, Conceptual Art, Display, Drafting, Drawing, †Fashion Arts, Fashion Design, Graphic Arts, Graphic Design, Illustration, Industrial Design, †Interior Design, Lettering, Mixed Media, Multimedia, Painting, †Photography, Video

Summer School: Same as regular semester

FORT MYERS

EDISON COMMUNITY COLLEGE, Gallery of Fine Arts, 8099 College Pkwy SW, Fort Myers, FL 33919-5566. Tel 941-489-9313; Internet Home Page Address: www.edison.edu; *Instr of Art* Robert York; *Music Instr* Dr Dennis Hill; *Music Instr* Dr Glenn Cornish; *Music Instr* Dr T Defoor; *Theatre Arts Instr* Richard Westlake; *Head Dept Fine & Performing Arts* Edith Pendleton
Estab 1962; FT 1, PT 5; pub; D & E; Scholarships
Ent Req: HS dipl
Degrees: AA & AS 2 yrs
Courses: 3-D Design, Art Appreciation, Art History, Ceramics, Design, Drawing, Intro to Computer Imaging, Jewelry, Painting, Photography, Printmaking, Sculpture
Adult Hobby Classes: Enrl 20. Courses—any non-cr activity of interest for which a teacher is available

FORT PIERCE

INDIAN RIVER COMMUNITY COLLEGE, Fine Arts Dept, 3209 Virginia Ave, Fort Pierce, FL 34981-5596. Tel 772-462-7824; *Asst Dean Arts & Sciences* Raymond Considine; *Chmn Fine Arts* David Moberg; *Vis Arts Dir* Linda Waugaman; *Instr* Francis Sprout; *Instr* Cira Cosentino
Estab 1960; pub; D & E; Scholarships; SC 10, LC 4; D 45, E 18, Maj 25, Non-Maj 10. Other 10
Ent Req: HS dipl
Degrees: AA & AS 2 yrs
Tuition: Res—$48 per unit; nonres—$48 per unit
Courses: Acting, Advertising Design, Art History, Design, Drawing, General Art, Graphic Arts, Intro to Drama, Landscape, Music Theory, Painting, Portrait, Printmaking, Vocal Ensemble
Summer School: Dir, Linda Waugaman. Enrl 80. Courses—Theater & Music

GAINESVILLE

UNIVERSITY OF FLORIDA, School of Art & Art History, 101, FAC Complex, Gainesville, FL 32611-5800; PO Box 115801, Gainesville, FL 32611-5801. Tel 352-392-0201 (Dept); 273-3000 (Univ Galleries); 273-2805 (Libr); Fax 352-392-8453 (Dept); 846-0266 (Univ Galleries); 846-2747 (Libr); Elec Mail heipp@ufl.edu; Internet Home Page Address: www.arts.ufl.edu/art; *Prof* Anna Calluori Holcombe, MFA; *Assoc Prof* Sergio Vega, PhD; *Prof* Barbara Barletta PhD, MFA; *Prof & Dir* Richard Heipp, MFA; *Prof* Robin Poynor, PhD; *Prof* Nan Smith, MFA; *Assoc Prof* Craig Roland, PhD; *Assoc Prof* Robert Mueller, MFA; *Assoc Prof* Brian Slawson, MFA; *Prof* Celeste Rogerge, MFA; *Prof* Linda Arbuckle, MFA; *Assoc Prof* Maria Rogal, MFA; *Prof* Melissa Hyde, PhD; *Assoc Prof* Ron Janowich, MFA; *Prof* Glenn Willumson, PhD; *Assoc Prof* Jack Stenner, PhD; *Asst Prof* Michelle Tillander, PhD, MFA; *Assoc Prof* Guolong Lai, PhD; *Assoc Prof* Julia Morrisroe, MFA; *Assoc Prof* Katerie Gladdys, MFA; *Assoc Prof* Elizabeth Ross, PhD; *Assoc Prof* Victoria Rovine, PhD; *Assoc Prof* Ellen Knudson, MFA; *Asst Prof* Sean Miller, MFA; *Assoc Prof* Craig Smith, PhD, MFA; *Asst Prof* Maya Stanfield-Mazzi, Phd; *Asst Prof* Bethany Taylor, MFA; *Asst Prof* Joyce Tsai, PhD; *Assoc Instr* Amy Vigilante, Phd, MFA; *Vis Asst Prof* Amy Freeman, MFA
Estab 1925; Maintains nonprofit University Galleries, 400 SW 13th St, Fine Arts Bldg B, Gainesville, FL 32611; Architecture & Fine Arts Library, 201 Fine Arts Bldg A PO Box 117017, Univ FL, Gainesville, FL 32611; FT 36; pub; D & E; Scholarships; SC 40, LC 26, GC 11; maj 400 upper div, grad 160
Activities: Schols & fels offered
Ent Req: HS dipl, SAT, ACT, TOEFL, SCAT or AA degree (transfers must have 2.0 average) GRE
Degrees: BAA & BFA 4 yrs, MA 2 yrs, MFA 3 yrs, PhD
Tuition: Res—undergrad $5700, grad $11,950; nonres—undergrad $29,344, grad $17,150 per cr hr; undergrad room—$5250
Courses: †Art & Technology, †Art Education, †Art History, †Ceramics, †Creative Photography, †Drawing, †Graphic Design, †Museum Studies, †Painting, †Printmaking, †Sculpture
Summer School: Limited classes

JACKSONVILLE

FLORIDA COMMUNITY COLLEGE AT JACKSONVILLE, SOUTH CAMPUS, Art Dept, 11901 Beach Blvd, Jacksonville, FL 32246-6624. Tel 904-646-2031; Fax 904-646-2396; Internet Home Page Address: www.fccj.org; *Gallery Coordr* Elizabeth Louis; *Prof* Derby Ulloa; *Prof* Mary Joan Hinson; *Prof* Stephen Heywood; *Faculty Coordr Fine Arts* Larry Davis
Estab 1966; Maintain nonprofit art gallery; FT 5; pub; D & E; Scholarships; SC 14, LC 6; D 150, E 75
Ent Req: HS dipl
Degrees: AA & AS 2 yrs
Tuition: no campus res
Courses: Batik, Blockprinting, Ceramics, Computer Graphics, Drawing, Experimentations, Graphic Design, History of Art & Architecture, Painting, Photography, Sculpture, Serigraphy
Adult Hobby Classes: Enrl 75-80. Courses—Art Appreciation, Crafts, Drawing, Painting, Photography
Summer School: Courses—Ceramics, Design, Drawing, Painting, Printmaking, Sculpture

JACKSONVILLE UNIVERSITY, Dept of Art, Theater, Dance, 2800 University Blvd N, College of Fine Arts Jacksonville, FL 32211-3321. Tel 904-256-7374; Fax 904-256-7375; Elec Mail dchapma@ju.edu; Internet Home Page Address: www.ju.edu; *Div Chair Theater & Dance* Brian Palmer; *Dance* Cari Coble; *Div*

Chair Art Dana Chapman Tupa; *Dean* Bill Hill; *Vis Asst Prof of Glass* Brian Frus; *Assoc Prof Art Hist* Cheryl Sowder; *Asst Prof Photog* Ginger Sheridan; *Assoc Prof of Art* Jack Turnock; *Asst Prof of Animation* Eric Kunzendorf; *Vis Asst Prof Film* Carolina Conte; *Artist in Res* Jonathan Christie; *Asst Prof of Computer Art & Design* Selin Ozguzer; *Artist in Res* Kristi Johnson; *Vis Asst Prof* Mariah Malec; *Asst Prof of Theatre* Allison Steadman; *Prof of Theatre* Ben Wilson; *Asst Prof* Debbie Jordan
Estab 1932; Maintains nonprofit art gallery, Alexander Brest Museum; pvt; D & E; Scholarships; SC 47, LC 13; D 403, maj 80
Ent Req: HS dipl, ent exam
Degrees: BFA, BA, BS & BAEd, 4 yr; MAT
Courses: Advertising Design, Art Appreciation, Art Education, Art History, Commercial Art, †Computer Art & Design, Conceptual Art, Costume Design & Construction, Design, Drawing, †Film, †Graphic Arts, †Graphic Design, Hot Glass, Lettering, Mixed Media, Painting, Printmaking, Stage Design, †Studio Art, †Theatre Arts, Video, †Visual Communication

UNIVERSITY OF NORTH FLORIDA, Dept of Communications & Visual Arts, 4567 St Johns Bluff Rd S, Jacksonville, FL 32224. Tel 904-620-2650; Tel 904-620-2624 (admis); Internet Home Page Address: www.unf.edu; *Chmn* Oscar Patterson; *Prof* Louise Freshman Brown, MFA; *Assoc Prof* David S Porter, MFA; *Assoc Prof* Robert L Cocanougher, MFA; *Assoc Prof* Paul Ladnier, MFA; *Asst Prof* Debra E Murphy, MFA
Estab 1970; pub; D & E; Scholarships; maj 385
Ent Req: AA
Degrees: BA 2 yr, BFA
Courses: Advertising Design, Aesthetics, Art Appreciation, Art History, Broadcasting, †Ceramics, Commercial Art, Computer Images, Conceptual Art, Design, Digital Photography, †Drawing, Electronic Multi-Media, Graphic Arts, Graphic Design, †History of Art & Architecture, Illustration, Lettering, Mixed Media, †Painting, †Photography, Printmaking, †Sculpture, †Video
Summer School: Various courses offered on demand

KEY WEST

FLORIDA KEYS COMMUNITY COLLEGE, Fine Arts Div, 5901 College Rd, Key West, FL 33040-4397. Tel 305-296-9081, 296-1520 (Box Office); Fax 305-292-5155; *Chmn Fine Arts Div* G Gerald Cash
Scholarships
Degrees: AA, AS
Tuition: Res—$42 per cr hr; nonres—$158 per cr hr
Courses: Art Appreciation, Art History, Calligraphy, †Ceramics, Commercial Art, Costume Design & Construction, Design, Display, Drafting, Drawing, Film, †Fine Arts, Graphic Arts, Graphic Design, Handicrafts, Jewelry, Jewelry Making, Mixed Media, Painting, †Photography, Printmaking, Sculpture, Stage Design, †Theatre Arts, Voice
Adult Hobby Classes: Enrl 150; Sept-Apr. Courses—Acting, Costume Design, Theatre Production (Lighting, Stagecraft, Design)

LAKE CITY

FLORIDA GATEWAY COLLEGE, Liberal Art Dept, 149 SE College Place, Lake City, FL 32025-2006. Tel 386-752-1822; Fax 386-754-4594; Internet Home Page Address: www.fgc.edu
Estab 1962
Ent Req: HS dipl
Degrees: AA 2 yrs

LAKE WORTH

PALM BEACH COMMUNITY COLLEGE, Dept of Art, 4200 S Congress Ave, Lake Worth, FL 33461-4796. Tel 561-439-8142; Fax 561-439-8384; Elec Mail slateryp@pbcc.cc.fl.us; Cable FLASUNCOM; *Art Dept Chmn* W Patrick Slatery; *Architecture & Interior Design Chmn* Zenida Young; *Graphic Design Chmn* Timothy Eichner
Estab 1933; Maintain nonprofit art gallery; Pub; D & E; Scholarships; SC 20, LC 5; D 15,000 maj 400
Ent Req: HS dipl or over 25
Degrees: AA and AS 2 yr, cert
Courses: Advertising Design, Architectural Drawing, Architecture, Art Appreciation, Art History, †Basic Design, Ceramics, Commercial Art, Design, Drawing, Enameling, †Etching, Graphic Arts, Graphic Design, Handicrafts, History of Art & Architecture, Illustration, Interior Design, Intermedia, Jewelry, Lithography, Painting, Photography, Printmaking, Screen Printing, Stage Design, Technical Photo Courses, Theatre Arts, Typography, Weaving
Summer School: Assoc Dean Humanities, Richard Holcomb. Enrl 300; tuition $36.50 per cr hr. Courses—Art Appreciation, Ceramics, Crafts, Design, Drawing, History of Art, Photography

LAKELAND

FLORIDA SOUTHERN COLLEGE, Department of Art & Art History, 111 Lake Hollingsworth Dr, Lakeland, FL 33801-5698. Tel 863-680-4743, 680-4111; Fax 863-680-4147; Elec Mail art@flsouthern.edu; Internet Home Page Address: www.flsouthern.edu; *Div Fine & Performing Arts Chair, Prof Art History* James Rogers, PhD; *Assoc Prof Art, Dept Art & Art History Chair, Dir Studio Programming* William Otremsky, MFA; *Asst Prof Art & Dir Foundation Prog* Kelly Sturhahn, MFA; *Asst Prof Art & Dir Graphic Design Prog* Samuel Romero, MFA; *Adjunct Asst Prof Art History* Nadine Pantano, PhD; *Adjunct Prof Art* Joseph Mitchell, MFA; *Adjunct Instr Art* Eric Blackmore, BFA; *Adjunct Asst Prof Art Educ* Jacquelyn Hanson, MFA; *Prof Emerita* Beth Ford, MA; *Sec* Katie Imeson, BFA

Estab 1885; Maintains nonprofit art gallery, Melvin Art Gallery, art/architecture library & Roux Library (same address); campus store for purchasing art supplies; den; private; D & E; Scholarships; SC 34, LC 10, maj 34; enrl 100
Activities: Melvin Art Gallery
Ent Req: HS dipl
Degrees: BA/BFA Studio Art, Graphic Design, BA Art History; BA/BS Art Ed, BFA Graphic Design
Courses: †Art Education, †Art History, Ceramics, Conceptual Art, Design, †Drawing, Graphic Design, History of Art & Architecture, †Painting, Photography, Printmaking, †Restoration & Conservation, Sculpture, †Studio Art, †Teacher Training, Video
Summer School: Craig Story. Courses—see summer schedule

MADISON

NORTH FLORIDA COMMUNITY COLLEGE, Dept Humanities & Art, 325 NW Turner Davis Dr, Madison, FL 32340-1611. Tel 850-973-9481; *Chmn Dr* Barbara McCauley; *Instr Dr* William F Gardner Jr
Estab 1958; pub; Scholarships
Degrees: AA
Tuition: Res—$47 per sem hr; nonres—$169.15 per sem hr
Courses: Art History, Ceramics, Design, Drawing, Painting, Sculpture

MARIANNA

CHIPOLA COLLEGE, Dept of Fine & Performing Arts, 3094 Indian Circle, Marianna, FL 32446. Tel 850-718-2301; Fax 850-718-2206; Elec Mail stadsklevj@chipola.edu; Internet Home Page Address: www.chipola.edu; *VPres Instr* Sarah Clemmons; *Dir Fine & Performing Arts* Daniel Powell
Estab 1947; pub; D & E; Scholarships; SC 8, LC 2; D 60
Ent Req: HS dipl
Degrees: AA 2 yr
Tuition: Res—$59 per sem hr; nonres—$180 per sem hr
Courses: 2-D & 3-D Design, Art History, Ceramics, Color Picture Comp, Crafts, Drawing, Graphic Arts, Painting, Purpose of Arts, Sculpture, Stage Design, Theatre Arts
Summer School: Courses—varied

MIAMI

FLORIDA INTERNATIONAL UNIVERSITY, School of Art & Art History, University Park Campus Bldg VH 216, Miami, FL 33199. Tel 305-348-2897, 348-2000 (main); Fax 305-348-0513; Internet Home Page Address: www.fiu.edu/~viart/; *Prof* William Maguire; *Prof* William J Burke; *Prof* R F Buckley; *Prof* Manuel Torres; *Prof* Ed del Valle; *Prof* Mirta Gomez; *Assoc Prof* Barbara Watts; *Prof* Juan Martinez; *Prof* Carol Damian; *Assoc Prof* Dan Guernsey; *Assoc Prof* Pip Brant; *Grad Prof* Geoffrey Olsen; *Assoc Prof* Tori Arpad; *Asst Prof* Jacek Kolasinski; *Dir Museum Studies* Marta de la Torre
Estab 1972, dept estab 1972; pub; D & E; Scholarships; SC 170, LC 27, GC 14; D 900, E 150, non-maj 250, maj 265, grad 25
Ent Req: 1000 on SAT, 3.0 HS grade point average
Degrees: BFA, BA, MFA, Museum Studies Grad Cert
Courses: Art Appreciation, Art History, Ceramics, Drawing, †Electronic Art, Jewelry, Painting, Photography, Printmaking, Sculpture
Summer School: Dir, Clive King. Enrl 160; tuition $55 per sem hr for term of 6.5 wks beginning May 13 & June 28

INTERNATIONAL FINE ARTS COLLEGE, 1501 Biscayne Blvd (Ste 100) Miami, FL 33132-1459. Tel 305-373-4684; Fax 305-374-7936; *Pres College* Erika Fleming; *Dean Acad Affairs* Deborah Mas; *Pub Rels Media Contact* Kim Resnik
Estab 1965, dept estab 1966; Maintain nonprofit art gallery; pvt; D; SC 6; D 180, maj 110
Ent Req: HS dipl
Degrees: AA
Courses: Accessory Design, Computer Animation, Fashion Design and Merchandising, Film and Digital Production, Graphic Design, Interior Design, Motion Graphics, Visual Effects

MIAMI-DADE COMMUNITY COLLEGE, Arts & Philosophy Dept, 11011 SW 104th St, Miami, FL 33176-3393. Tel 305-237-2281; Fax 305-237-2871; *Chmn* Robert Huff; *Prof* Charles Dolgos; *Prof* Charles Fink; *Prof* Robert Krantzler; *Prof* Peter Kuentzel; *Prof* Alberto Meza; *Prof* Wade Semerena; *Prof* Wickie Whalen; *Prof* Richard Williams; *Instr* Jennifer Basile; *Assoc Prof Sr* Annette Wells
Estab 1960, dept estab 1967; Nonprofit - Kendall Campus Art Gallery, M123, 11011 SW 104th St, Miami, FL 33176; Pub; D & E; Scholarships; SC 14, LC 4; E 300, non-maj 150, maj 150
Ent Req: open door
Degrees: AA & AS 2 yr
Courses: Art Appreciation, Art History, Ceramics, Commercial Art, †Computer Art, Design, Drawing, Jewelry, Metals, Painting, Photography, Printmaking, Sculpture
Adult Hobby Classes: Courses by demand
Summer School: Dir, Robert Huff. Courses vary

NEW WORLD SCHOOL OF THE ARTS, 25 NE Second St, Miami, FL; 300 NE Second Ave, Miami, FL 33132-2297. Tel 305-237-3620; Fax 305-237-3794; Elec Mail hgershfe@mdcc.edu; Internet Home Page Address: www.mdcc.edu/nwsa/horizons; *Dean* Louise Romeo; *Asst Dean Visual Arts* Yelena Gershfeld
Estab 1987; A Cooperative venture of University of Florida & Miami-Dade Community College; pub; D; SC 43, LC 6; D 249, maj 249
Publications: Art in Ecological Perspective
Ent Req: HS dipl, entrance exam, portfolio review

Degrees: AA 2 yr, BFA 4 yr
Courses: Advertising Design, Art Education, Art History, †Ceramics, Collage, Conceptual Art, Cyberarts, Design, †Drawing, †Graphic Design, †Illustration, Intermedia, Mixed Media, †Painting, †Photography, †Printmaking, Restoration & Conservation, †Sculpture, Theatre Arts
Summer School: scholarships

MIAMI SHORES

BARRY UNIVERSITY, Dept of Fine Arts, 11300 NE Second Ave, Miami Shores, FL 33161. Tel 305-899-3421 (chair), 899-4923 (asst to chmn); Fax 305-899-2972; Internet Home Page Address: www.barry.edu/finearts; *Dean* Dr Karen Callaghan; *Chair Fine Arts Dept* Dr Silvia Lizama
Estab 1940; Maintain nonprofit art gallery, Andy Gato Gallery (same address); on-campus art shop where art supplies may be purchased; FT 8; pvt; D & E; Scholarships; SC 63, LC 15; D 300, E 60, maj 80
Activities: Schols offered
Ent Req: HS dipl
Degrees: BA, BFA, MA (Photo), MFA (Photo)
Tuition: Undergrad $14,080 per semester; grad $960 per cr hr
Courses: Art Appreciation, Art History, Ceramics, Collage, Commercial Art, Costume Design & Construction, Design, Drawing, Graphic Design, History of Art & Architecture, Mixed Media, Painting, †Photography, Sculpture
Summer School: Dr Karen Callaghan, Dean, Col of Arts & Sciences.
Courses—Ceramics, Drawing, Photography, Graphic Design, Art History

NICEVILLE

NORTHWEST FLORIDA STATE COLLEGE, (Okaloosa-Walton Community College) Mattie Kelly Arts Center Galleries, 100 College Blvd, Niceville, FL 32578. Tel 850-729-6044; Fax 850-729-5286; Elec Mail artgalleries@nwfsc.edu; *Dir* Jeanette Shires; *Gallery Dir* K. C. Williams
Estab 1964, dept estab 1964; Maintain nonprofit art gallery & library; Pub; D & E; Scholarships; SC 26, LC 3; D 2,000, E 1,000, maj 80
Ent Req: HS dipl
Degrees: AA 2 yrs
Courses: 2-D & 3-D Design, Acting, Art Appreciation, Art History, Ceramics, Costume Design & Construction, Design, Drafting, Drawing, Ethics, Graphic Arts, Graphic Design, Handicrafts, History of Art & Architecture, Humanities, Interior Design, Jewelry, Museum Staff Training, Painting, Philosophy, Photography, Printmaking, Religion, Sculpture, Silversmithing, Stage Design, Teacher Training, Theatre Arts, Weaving
Adult Hobby Classes: Enrl 15 per class. Courses—Antiques, Interior Decorating, Painting, Photography, Pottery, Vase Painting, others as needed

OCALA

CENTRAL FLORIDA COMMUNITY COLLEGE, Humanities Dept, 3001 SW College Rd, Ocala, FL 34474-4415. Tel 352-237-2111, Ext 293; Fax 352-231-0510; Internet Home Page Address: www.cfcc.cc.fl.us; *Prog Facilitator* Carolyn West
Estab 1957; pub; D & E; SC 5, LC 1; 3500, non-maj 85, maj 15
Ent Req: HS dipl
Degrees: AA & AS 2 yr
Courses: Art History, Ceramics, Design, Drawing, Painting, Printmaking, Sculpture
Adult Hobby Classes: Ceramics, Commercial Art; Design, Drawing, Painting
Summer School: Two 6 wk terms

ORLANDO

UNIVERSITY OF CENTRAL FLORIDA, Art Dept, 4000 Central Florida Blvd, Orlando, FL 32816-8005; PO Box 161342, Orlando, FL 32816-1342. Tel 407-823-2676; Fax 407-823-6470; Internet Home Page Address: www.pegasus.cc.ucs.edu/~art; *Dept Adv* Jagdish Chauda
Estab 1963; pub; Scholarships
Degrees: BA, BFA, cert
Courses: Art History, Ceramics, Design, Drawing, Fibers & Fabrics, Graphic Design, Painting, Photography, Printmaking, Sculpture
Summer School: Tuition same as above. Courses—vary

VALENCIA COMMUNITY COLLEGE - EAST CAMPUS, Art Dept, 701 N Econlochachee Trail, Room 3-112 Orlando, FL 32825; PO Box 3028, Orlando, FL 32802-3028. Tel 407-299-5000, Ext 2270; Fax 407-293-8839; Internet Home Page Address: www.valencia.cc.fl.us; *Chmn* Rickard Rietveld; *Dir* Jackie Otto-Miller
Estab 1967, dept estab 1974; pub; D & E; Scholarships; SC 16, LC 5; D 6858
Ent Req: HS dipl
Degrees: AA and AS 2 yrs
Courses: Ceramics, Drafting, Drawing, Film, †Graphic Design, History of Art & Architecture, Illustration, Intermedia, Lettering, Painting, Photography, Printmaking, Sculpture, Stage Design, †Theatre Arts, Visual Arts Today
Summer School: Same as for regular acad yr

PALATKA

FLORIDA SCHOOL OF THE ARTS, Visual Arts, 5001 Saint Johns Ave, Palatka, FL 32177-3807. Tel 386-312-4300, 312-4072 (Barrineau); Internet Home Page Address: www.sjrcc.cc.fl.us/floarts; *VPres Student Servs* Annette W Barrineau, MFA; *Coordr Graphic Design* Phil Parker, BFA; *Dir Galleries* David Ouellette, MFA
Estab 1974, dept estab 1974; pub; D; Scholarships; SC 35, LC 10; D 85, maj 85

Ent Req: HS dipl, recommendation, review, interview
Degrees: AA 2 yrs, AS 2 1/2 yrs
Courses: Advertising Design, Art History, Commercial Art, Display, Drafting, Drawing, Graphic Arts, †Graphic Design, Illustration, Lettering, Mixed Media, †Painting, Photography, †Printmaking, †Stage Design, †Theatre Arts

PANAMA CITY

GULF COAST COMMUNITY COLLEGE, Division of Visual & Performing Arts, 5230 W Hwy 98, Panama City, FL 32401-1058. Tel 850-769-1551, ext 3886; Fax 850-873-3520; Elec Mail robourke@gulfcoast.edu; Internet Home Page Address: www.gc.cc.fl.us; *Dir* Rosemarie O'Bourke, MS; *Assoc Prof* Sharron Barnes, MA; *Assoc Prof* Roland L Hockett, MS
Estab 1957; pub; D & E; SC 5, LC 2; D 300, E 70, non-maj 330, maj 40
Ent Req: HS dipl
Degrees: AA 2 yrs
Courses: Art History, Ceramics, Design, Drawing, Illustration, Lettering, Photography
Adult Hobby Classes: Macrame, Painting, Weaving
—Art Gallery, 5230 W Hwy 98, Panama City, FL 32401. Tel 850-872-3887; Fax 850-872-3836
Open Mon - Fri 8 AM - 4 PM; No admis fee
Collections: Paintings; sculpture; photographs

PENSACOLA

PENSACOLA STATE COLLEGE, Visual Arts Dept, 1000 College Blvd, Pensacola, FL 32504-8998. Tel 850-484-2550; Fax 850-484-2564; Elec Mail klien@pensacolastate.edu; Internet Home Page Address: www.pensacolastate.edu; *Head Dept* Krist Lien
Estab 1948; Maintains nonprofit Anna Lamar Switzer Center for Visual Arts; art supplies sold at on-campus store; FT 9, PT 11; pub; D & E; Scholarships; SC 43, LC 7, GC 7, Other 2; maj 446
Ent Req: HS dipl
Degrees: AS & AA 2 yrs, BAS 4 yrs
Tuition: no campus res
Courses: Advertising Design, †Art, Art History, †Art Studio, Ceramics, Crafts, Design, Drawing, †Graphic Design, Mixed Media, †Multimedia, Painting, †Photography, Pottery, Sculpture, Typography, Video
Adult Hobby Classes: Courses—Ceramics
Summer School: Dir, Krist Lien. Enrl 300. Courses—same as regular session

UNIVERSITY OF WEST FLORIDA, Dept of Art, 11000 University Pkwy, Pensacola, FL 32514-5732. Tel 850-474-2045; Fax 850-474-2043; Elec Mail art@uwf.edu; Internet Home Page Address: www.uwf.edu/art; *Assoc Prof* Suzette J Doyon PhD, MFA; *Assoc Prof* Jim Jipson, MFA; *Asst Prof* Joseph Herring, MFA; *Asst Prof* Valerie George, MFA; *Gallery Dir* Nicholas Croghan, MFA, MA; *Program Dir* John Markowitz, MFA; *Asst Prof* Thomas Asmuth, MFA; *Assoc Prof* Barbara Larson, PhD, MA; *Adj Instr* Amy Bowman; *Adj Instr* Dale Castellucci; *Adj Instr* Gina Cestaro; *Adj Instr* Sara Gevurtz; *Adj Instr* Donna Harper; *Adj Instr* Joy Holland; *Adj Instr* Sally Miller; *Adj Instr* Quintin Owens; *Adj Instr* Elizabeth Petersen; *Adj Instr* Rachael Pongetti; *Adj Instr* Marzia Ransom; *Adj Instr* Gregory Saumders; *Adj Instr* Lyda Toy; *Adj Instr* Suzanne Tuzzeo
Estab 1967; Maintain nonprofit art gallery; University Art Gallery, 1000 University Pkwy, Pensacola, FL 32514; Pub; D & E; Scholarships; SC 20, LC 10; non-maj 100, maj 350
Activities: Schls offered
Degrees: BA & BFA 4 yr
Courses: Aesthetics, †Art Education, †Art History, †BFA, Calligraphy, Ceramics, Design, Drawing, †Graphic Design, Handicrafts, †History of Art & Architecture, Illustration, Intermedia, †Jewelry, Mixed Media, Museum Staff Training, Painting, Photography, Printmaking, Sculpture, †Studio Art, Teacher Training, Video
Summer School: Dir, Jim Jipson. Enrl 400; 2 sessions. Courses—Ceramics, Drawing, Painting, Photography, Printmaking, Sculpture

SAINT AUGUSTINE

FLAGLER COLLEGE, Visual Arts Dept, 74 King St, Saint Augustine, FL 32084; PO Box 1027, Saint Augustine, FL 32085-1027. Tel 904-829-6481; Internet Home Page Address: www.flagler.edu; *Chmn* Don Martin; *Prof* Enzo Torcoletti, MFA; *Asst Prof* Kerry Tustin, MFA; *Instr* Maureen O'Neil, MFA
Estab 1968; pvt; D & E; Scholarships; SC 29, LC 7; 1000, maj 100
Ent Req: HS dipl
Degrees: BA 4 yr
Courses: Advertising Design, Air Brush, †Art Education, Art History, Drawing, †Graphic Design, Illustration, Painting, Photography, Sculpture, Visual Arts, Visual Communications
Summer School: Acad Affairs, William Abare. Tuition $180 per hr for terms of 7 wks beginning May. Courses—Airbrush, Ceramics, Computer Illustration, Painting

SAINT PETERSBURG

ECKERD COLLEGE, Art Dept, 4200 54th Ave S, Saint Petersburg, FL 33711-4700. Tel 727-864-8340; Fax 727-864-7890; *Prof* Kirk Wang; *Prof* Arthur Skinner; *Prof* Brian Ransom
Estab 1958; Pvt; Scholarships
Degrees: BA, BF
Courses: Art Education, Art History, Calligraphy, Ceramics, Design, Drawing, †Film, Painting, Photography, Printmaking, †Sculpture, †Theatre Arts, †Video
Adult Hobby Classes: Enrl 25. Courses—Ceramics, Drawing, Painting
Summer School: Dir, Cheryl Gold. Enrl 150

SARASOTA

ART CENTER SARASOTA, 707 N Tamiami Trail, Sarasota, FL 34236-4050.
Tel 941-365-2032; Fax 941-366-0585; Elec Mail visualartcenter@aol.com; Internet
Home Page Address: www.artsarasota.org; *Exec Dir* Lisa-Marie Confessore; *Educ
Coordr* Jill Kowal; *Pres* William van Osnabrugge; *Instr* Barbara Nechis; *Instr*
Peter Spataro; *Instr* Edward Minchin; *Instr* Charles Meyrick; *Instr* Win Jones;
Instr Frank Webb; *Instr* Bill Buchman; *Instr* Joseph Melancon; *Instr* Pat Deadman
Estab 1926; Maintain nonprofit art gallery & library; Art Ctr Sarasota, 707 N
Tamiami Trail, Sarasota, FL 34236-4050; Not-for-profit; D&E; SC 32, LC 6, other
5, workshops; D 200, E 10
Ent Req: Varied
Degrees: Cert of Completion
Courses: Art Appreciation, Art Education, Art History, Calligraphy, Ceramics,
Collage, Drawing, Mixed Media, Painting, Photography, Sculpture, Watercolor
Adult Hobby Classes: 200. Courses—Drawing, Painting
Children's Classes: 20 per class maximum
Summer School: Educ Coordr Jill Kowal. Enrl 80. Courses—Watercolor

NEW COLLEGE OF THE UNIVERSITY OF SOUTH FLORIDA, Fine Arts
Dept, Humanities Division, 5700 N Tamiami Trail, Sarasota, FL 34243. Tel
941-359-4360, 359-5605; Internet Home Page Address: www.newcollege.usf.edu
Estab 1963; FT 4; pub; D; SC 6, LC 5; D 150-200, maj 15
Ent Req: ent exam, SAT
Degrees: BA(Fine Arts) 3 yrs
Courses: †Aesthetics, †Art History, Ceramics, †Color Theory, Design, †Drawing,
Life Drawing, †Painting, †Printmaking, †Sculpture, Stained Glass

RINGLING SCHOOL OF ART & DESIGN, 2700 N Tamiami Trail, Sarasota,
FL 34234. Tel 941-351-5100; Fax 941-359-7517; *Pres* Thomas E Linehan; *Dean
Admis* Jim Dean
Estab 1931; 31; pvt; Scholarships; 830
Ent Req: HS dipl or equivalency, portfolio
Degrees: BFA, 4 yrs
Courses: †Computer Animation, †Fine Arts, †Graphic Design, †Illustration,
†Interior Design, Painting, †Photography, Sculpture
Adult Hobby Classes: Enrl 150

TALLAHASSEE

FLORIDA A & M UNIVERSITY, Dept of Visual Arts, Humanities & Theatre,
515 Orr Dr, 208 Tucker Hall Tallahassee, FL 32307. Tel 850-599-3831; Fax
850-599-8417; Internet Home Page Address: www.famu.edu; *Chmn* Luther D
Wells
Estab 1887; pub; D & E; Scholarships; D 5887, non-maj 5800, maj 87
Ent Req: HS dipl, ent exam
Degrees: BS & BA with Fine Arts Cert
Tuition: Res—$62.10 per sem hr; nonres $236.94 per sem hr
Courses: Art Education, Art History, Ceramics, Design, Drawing, Metals, Plastic,
Textile Design, Wood
Summer School: Enrl 125; tuition same as regular session for term of 9 & 7 wks
beginning June. Courses—Arts, Ceramics, Design, Drawing, Metal & Plastics,
Textile Design, Wood

FLORIDA STATE UNIVERSITY, Art Dept, 220 Fine Arts Bldg, Tallahassee,
FL 32306-1150. Tel 850-644-6474; Fax 850-644-8977; Elec Mail
hdstripl@mailer.fsu.edu; Internet Home Page Address: www.fsu.edu/~svad; *Chmn
Studio Art* Roald Nasgaard, PhD; *Prof* James Roche, MFA; *Prof Emeritus* Ed
Love, MFA; *Prof* George Blakely, MFA; *Prof* Robert Fichter, MFA; *Prof Emeritus*
Trevor Bell, MFA; *Prof Emeritus* William Walmsley, MFA; *Assoc Prof* George
Bocz, MEd; *Assoc Prof* Janice E Hartwell, MFA; *Assoc Prof* Charles E Hook,
MFA; *Assoc Prof* Gail Rubini, MFA; *Prof* Mark Messersmith, MFA; *Assoc Prof*
Paul Rutkovsky, MFA; *Assoc Prof* Terri Lindbloom, MFA; *Assoc Prof* Kasuya
Bowen, MFA; *Assoc Prof* Keith Roberson, MFA; *Prof & Assoc Chair* Ray
Burggraf; *Assoc Prof* Donald Odita; *Prof* Pat Ward Williams; *Assoc Prof* Lilian
Garcia-Roil; *Asst Prof* Scott Groeninger; *Asst Prof* Steve Jones
Estab 1857, dept estab 1911; maintains nonprofit gallery; Cate Wyatt-Magalian,
Daniel Kariko & John Raulerson; pub; D & E; Scholarships; SC 45, LC. 2, GC
22; non-maj 400, maj 488, grad 35
Ent Req: HS dipl, B average & test scores of at least 24 (composite) on the ACT
or 1100 (verbal plus math) on the SAT I
Degrees: BA, BFA, BS, MFA
Tuition: Res--undergrad $73.19 per cr hr, grad $146.01 per cr hr;
nonres--undergrad $306.14 per cr hr, grad $506.74 per cr hr
Courses: Ceramics, Drawing, Graphic Arts, Painting, Photography, Printmaking,
Sculpture
Summer School: Term of 13 wks; two terms of six & a half wks
—**Art Education Dept,** 028 WJB, Tallahassee, FL 32306-1232; 301 Francis
Eppes Bldg, Tallahassee, FL 32306. Tel 850-644-2926; 850-644-5473; Fax
850-644-5067; Elec Mail mrosal@fsu.edu; Internet Home Page Address:
www.fsu.edu/~are; *Prof* Tom Anderson PhD; *Chmn Art Educ Dept* David Gussak
PhD; *Assoc Prof* Pat Villeneuve PhD; *Prof* Marcia L Rosal PhD; *Prof* Anniina
Suominen Guyas
Estab 1857, dept estab 1948; Maintain an art/architecture library, Mary Mooty
Library, Florida State Univ, 028WJB, Tallahassee, FL 37306-1232; on-campus art
supplies shop; pub; D & E; Scholarships; LC, GC; 80 maj, 85 GS
Ent Req: HS dipl
Degrees: BA(Art Educ) 4 yr, MS(Art Edu & Art Therapy) & MA(Arts Admin).
1-2 yr, EDS degree, PhD
Tuition: Res-- $2,379; non res--$9, 716
Courses: †Art Education, Art Therapy, Arts Administration, Special Population,
Teacher Training
Summer School: Studio Art & Art History Emphasis
—**Art History Dept,** PO Box 3061151, Tallahassee, FL 32306-1151; 530 W Call

St, Tallahassee, FL 32306. Tel 850-644-1250; Fax 850-644-7065; Elec Mail
arh@www.fsu.edu; Internet Home Page Address: www.fsu.edu/~arh; *Dean School
Visual Arts* Jerry L Draper PhD; *Prof* Robert M Neuman PhD; *Prof* Jehnne
Teilhet-Fisk; *Prof* Cynthia J Hahn PhD; *Assoc Prof* Lauren Weingarden PhD;
Assoc Prof Karen Bearor PhD; *Asst Prof* Jack Freiberg PhD; *Asst Prof* Brenda
Jordan, PhD; *Chmn* Paula Gerson
Estab 1857, dept estab 1948; Maintain nonprofit art gallery, Fine Art Museum;
pub; D & E; Scholarships
Ent Req: HS dipl
Degrees: MA(Art History) 2 1/2 yr, PhD(Art History) 3 yr
Tuition: Res—$59.93 per cr hr; nonres—$223.34 per cr hr
Courses: Art Appreciation, †Art History, Arts Administration, History of Art &
Archeology

TALLAHASSEE COMMUNITY COLLEGE, Art Dept, 444 Appleyard Dr,
Tallahassee, FL 32304-2895. Tel 850-201-8713; Elec Mail baroodyj@tcc.fl.edu;
Internet Home Page Address: www.tcc.fl.edu; *Art Coordr* Julie Baroody; *Dean Dr*
Marge Banocy-Payne
Estab 1966; Maintain nonprofit art gallery; TC Art Gallery, 444 Appleyard Dr,
Tallahassee FL 32304; art supplies available on-campus; PT 4; pub; D & E;
Scholarships; SC 13, LC 3; D 350 per sem, E 150 per sem
Ent Req: HS dipl
Degrees: AA 2 yrs
Courses: Art Appreciation, Art History, Color Theory, Design, Drawing, †Graphic
Design, History & Appreciation of Cinema, Painting, Photography, Printmaking,
Silkscreen, Silversmithing, Watercolor
Summer School: Dean, Dr Marge Benocy-Payne. Courses—Basic Photo,
Methods/Concepts

TAMPA

HILLSBOROUGH COMMUNITY COLLEGE, Fine Arts Dept, 2112 N 15th
St, Tampa, FL 33605-3648. Tel 813-253-7000 ext 7674; Fax 813-259-6425;
Internet Home Page Address: www.hccfl.edu; Internet Home Page Address:
www.hccfl.edu/4c; *Dir* Suzanne Crosby; *Assoc Prof* Tracy Reller; *Assoc Prof*
Katherine Moyse; *Assoc Prof* Christopher W Weeks; *Gallery Dir* Carolyn Kossar
Estab 1967; Maintains ACC Ybor Campus Art Gallery; pub; D, E & weekends;
Scholarships; SC 10, LC 10
Degrees: AA, AS
Tuition: Res—$48.06 per cr hr; nonres—$177.61 per cr hr
Courses: Art Appreciation, Art History, Ceramics, Conceptual Art, Costume
Design & Construction, Design, Drawing, †Film, Graphic Arts, Graphic Design,
Mixed Media, Painting, Photography, Printmaking, Sculpture, Stage Design,
Theatre Arts
Summer School: Summer I & II sems

UNIVERSITY OF SOUTH FLORIDA, School The Arts, 4202 E Fowler Ave,
FAH 110, College of Visual & Performing Arts Tampa, FL 33620-7350. Tel
813-974-2360; Fax 813-974-9226; Elec Mail ddennis3@usf.edu; Internet Home
Page Address: www.art.usf.edu; *Dir* Wallace Wilson; *Prof* Louis Marcus; *Prof*
Elisabeth Fraser; *Assoc Prof* Wendy Babcox; *Assoc Prof* Neil Bender; *Assoc Prof*
John Byrd; *Assoc Prof* Elisabeth Condon; *Assoc Prof* Gregory Green; *Assoc Prof*
Robert Lawrence; *Assoc Prof* Riccardo Marchi; *Assoc Prof* Anat Pollack; *Assoc
Prof* Bradlee Shanks; *Assoc Prof* Helena Szepe; *Asst Prof* Cesar Cornejo; *Asst
Prof* McArthur Freeman; *Asst Prof* Ezra Johnson; *Asst Prof* Esra Akin-Kivanc;
Asst Prof Noelle Mason; *Asst Prof* Allison Moore
Estab 1956; Maintain nonprofit library, Visual Resource Library, same address;
maintain nonprofit art gallery, Oliver Gallery; FT 4; pub; D&E; online;
Scholarships, Fellowships; SC 100, LC 125, GC 20, other 50; D 625, E 50,
non-maj 400, maj 350, grad 50
Ent Req: HS grad, 14 units cert by HS, ent exam, portfolio for BFA
Degrees: BA (Art) minimum 120 sem hrs, BFA 120 sem hrs, MFA 60 sem hrs &
MA(Art History) 40 sem hrs
Tuition: Undergraduate in State:$211/cr; Out of state $575/cr; Graduate in State
$431/cr; Out of state $877/cr
Courses: †Art Appreciation, Art History, Ceramics, Collage, Drawing, Electronic
Media, Mixed Media, Museum Staff Training, Painting, Photography, Printmaking,
Sculpture, Video
Summer School: Dir Wallace Wilson. Enrol 150

UNIVERSITY OF TAMPA, College of Arts & Letters, 401 W Kennedy Blvd,
Tampa, FL 33606-1450. Tel 813-258-7495; Elec Mail lrothe@ut.edu; Internet
Home Page Address: www.utarts.com; *Prof* Lew Harris; *Prof* Catherine
Chastain-Elliott; *Dir Gallery* Dorothy Cowden; *Prof* Santiago Echevery; *Prof*
Doug Sutherland; *Prof* Kendra Frorup; *Prof* Jack King; *Prof* Ina Kaur; *Prof*
Brooke Scherer; *Prof* Chris Valle
Estab 1930; Maintains nonprofit art gallery, University of Tampa, Scarfone/Hartley
Gallery; 9; pvt; D & E; Scholarships; SC 17, LC 8; non-maj 100, maj 170
Ent Req: Admis to Univ of Tampa
Degrees: 4 yrs
Tuition: Info on website
Courses: †Animation, †Art Appreciation, Art Education, Art History, Arts
Management, Ceramics, Computer Graphics, Design, †Digital Arts, Drawing,
Graphic Design, Painting, Photography, Printmaking, Sculpture
Summer School: Art courses offered

TEMPLE TERRACE

FLORIDA COLLEGE, Division of Art, 119 N Glen Arven Ave, Temple Terrace,
FL 33617-5578. Tel 813-988-5131; Fax 813-899-6772; Internet Home Page
Address: www.flcoll.edu; *Faculty* Julia Gibson
Estab 1947; FT 1; pvt; D&E; Scholarships
Degrees: AA
Courses: †Design I, †Design II

WINTER HAVEN

POLK COMMUNITY COLLEGE, Art, Letters & Social Sciences, 999 Ave H NE, Winter Haven, FL 33881-4299. Tel 863-297-1025; Fax 863-297-1037; Internet Home Page Address: www.polk.cc.fl.us; *Prof* Gary Baker, MFA; *Prof* Bob Morrisey, MFA; *Dean of Arts* Hugh B Anderson, MFA
Estab 1964; pub; D & E; Scholarships; SC 10, LC 1; D 175, E 50
Ent Req: HS dipl
Degrees: AA & AS 2 yrs
Courses: Advertising Design, Art Appreciation, Ceramics, Design, Drawing, Film, Interior Design, Painting, Photography, Printmaking, Sculpture, Theatre Arts
Adult Hobby Classes: Enrl 60. Courses—Calligraphy, Ceramics, Christmas Crafts, Drawing, Interior Design, Jewelry, Painting

WINTER PARK

ROLLINS COLLEGE, Dept of Art, Main Campus, 1000 Holt Ave, Winter Park, FL 32789-4409. Tel 407-646-2498; Fax 407-628-6395; Internet Home Page Address: www.rollins.edu; *Chmn* Ron Larned
Estab 1885; pvt; D & E; Scholarships; SC 11, LC 10; D & E 250
Degrees: BA 4 yr
Courses: Aesthetics, Art History, Art History Survey, Design, Drawing, Humanities Foundation, Painting, Principles of Art, Sculpture
Adult Hobby Classes: Selected Studio & History courses
Summer School: Selected Art History & Appreciation courses

GEORGIA

AMERICUS

GEORGIA SOUTHWESTERN STATE UNIVERSITY, Dept of Fine Arts, 800 Gsw State University Dr, Americus, GA 31709-4376. Tel 912-931-2204; Fax 912-931-2927; *Chmn* Dr Duke Jackson
Scholarships
Degrees: BA, BSEd, BSA, cert
Tuition: Res—$1099 per sem; nonres—$2610 per sem
Courses: Ceramics, Drawing, Glassblowing, Graphic Design, Jewelry, Painting, Photography, Printmaking, Sculpture, Textile Design

ATHENS

UNIVERSITY OF GEORGIA, FRANKLIN COLLEGE OF ARTS & SCIENCES, Lamar Dodd School of Art, 270 River Rd, Athens, GA 30602-7676. Tel 706-542-1511; Fax 706-542-0226; Elec Mail artinfo@uga.edu; Internet Home Page Address: www.uga.edu; *Dean* Wyatt Anderson; *Dir* Carmon Colangelo; *Assoc Dir* Richard Johnson; *Grad Coordr* Andy Nasisse; *Assoc Dir* Shelley Zuraw; *Assoc Prof Ceramics* Ted Saupe; *Prof Drawing & Painting* Judy McWillie; *Prof Fabric Design* Glen Kaufman; *Dir Graphic Design* Lanny Webb; *Assoc Prof Interior Design* Thom Houser; *Asst Prof Jewelry & Metalwork* Robert Jackson; *Asst Prof Scientific Illustration* Gene Wright; *Prof Sculpture* Larry Millard; *Assoc Prof Printmaking* Melissa Harshman; *Assoc Prof Photog* Stephen Scheer; *Franklin Prof Art History* Andrew Ladis; *Wheatley Prof Drawing & Painting* Arthur Rosenbaum; *Distinguished Research Prof Drawing & Painting* James Herbert; *Gallery Coordr* Robin Dana; *Assoc Prof Art Educ* Dr Carole Henry; *Asst Prof Art Educ* Dr Pam Taylor; *Asst Prof Art Educ* Dr Richard Siegesmund; *Franklin Fellow Asst Prof* Dr Jessie Whitehead; *Prof Art History* Evan Firestone; *Asst Prof Art History* Asen Kirin; *Asst Prof Art History* Alisa Luxenberg; *Assoc Prof Art History* Tom Polk; *Assoc Prof Art History* Janice Simon; *Prof Art History* Francis Van Keuren; *Asst Prof Digital Media* Michael Oliveri; *Asst Prof Drawing & Painting* Radcliffe Bailey; *Asst Prof Drawing & Painting* Jim Barsness; *Assoc Prof Drawing & Painting* Scott Belville; *Assoc Prof Drawing & Painting* Diane Edison; *Assoc Prof Drawing & Painting* Stefanie Jackson; *Assoc Prof Drawing & Painting* Bill Marriott; *Assoc Prof Drawing & Painting* Joe Norman; *Prof Fabric Design* Ed Lambert; *Assoc Prof Foundations* Christopher Hocking; *Asst Prof Foundations* Gretchen Hupfel; *Prof Graphic Design* Ron Arnholm; *Acad Professional Graphic Design* Joey Hannaford; *Asst Prof Graphic Design* Alex Murawski; *Prof Graphic Design* Susan Roberts; *Prof Graphic Design* Ken Williams; *Asst Prof Interior Design* Jane Lily; *Asst Prof Interior Design* Welynda Wright; *Asst Prof Photog* Michael Marshall; *Lectr Photog* Mary Ruth Moore; *Acad Professional Photog* Ben Reynolds; *Assoc Prof Printmaking* Joe Sanders; *Assoc Prof Sculpture* Jim Buonaccorsi; *Assoc Prof Sculpture* Imi Hwangho; *Assoc Prof Sculpture* Rocky Sapp
Opened 1801, chartered 1875; Maintain art library & nonprofit art gallery; Pub; D; Scholarships, Fellowships, Assistantships; SC 145, LC 60, GC 99; non-maj 50, maj 950, grad 80
Ent Req: HS dipl, SAT
Degrees: BA, BFA, BSEd, MA, MFA, MAE, EdS, EdD, PhD
Tuition: Res—undergrad $1,517 per sem, grad $1,888 per sem; nonres—undergrad $5,138 per sem, grad $6,397 per sem
Courses: Art Appreciation, †Art Education, †Art History, †Ceramics, Digital Media, Drawing, †Graphic Arts, †Graphic Design, Illustration, †Interior Design, †Jewelry, Lettering, Mixed Media, †Painting, †Photography, †Printmaking, †Scientific Illustration, †Sculpture, Silversmithing, †Textile Design, Weaving
Summer School: Dir, Carmen Colangelo, Assoc Dir Rick Johnson; Enrl 600, 35 courses

ATLANTA

ART INSTITUTE OF ATLANTA, 6600 Peachtree-Dunwoody, 100 Embassy Row Atlanta, GA 30328-6773. Tel 770-394-8300; Fax 770-394-0008; Internet Home Page Address: www.aia.artinstitute.edu; *Pres* Janet Day; *Dean* Larry Stulpz

The Institute has the following departments: Graphic Design, Photography, Interior Design, Culinary Arts, Computer Animation, Multi Media Web Design; Scholarships
Degrees: AA
Courses: Advertising Design, Cartooning, Commercial Art, Design, Display, Drawing, Fashion, Graphic Arts, Interior Design, Lettering, Mixed Media, Painting, Photo Design, Photography, Portrait, Video

ATLANTA TECHNICAL INSTITUTE, Visual Communications Class, 1560 Metropolitan Pkwy, Atlanta, GA 30310. Tel 404-756-3700; Fax 404-756-0932; Internet Home Page Address: www.atlantatech.org; *Head Dept* Eric Jefferies
Estab 1967; pub; D; SC 13; D 25, E 25
Ent Req: HS dipl, ent exam
Degrees: AA in conjunction with the Atlanta Metro Col
Courses: Advertising Design, Commercial Art, Graphic Arts, Photography, Print Production Art, Video

CLARK-ATLANTA UNIVERSITY, School of Arts & Sciences, 223 James P Brawley Dr SW, Atlanta, GA 30314-4358. Tel 404-880-8000; Internet Home Page Address: www.cau.edu; *Assoc Prof* Christopher Hickey; *Chmn Dept* Belinda A Peters; *Prof* Emmanuel Asihene; *Asst Prof* Dorothy Batey; *Instr* Javier Tolbert; *Instr* Constance Boothe; *Instr* Norman Meyer
Estab 1869, dept estab 1964; pvt; D; Scholarships; SC 8, LC 8; D 198, non-maj 120, maj 85
Ent Req: HS dipl
Degrees: BA (Art, Fashion Design) 4 yrs, Honors Program
Courses: Art Education, Art History, Design, Drawing, Fashion Design, Graphic Design, Illustration, Painting, Photography, Printmaking, Sculpture
Summer School: Summer school program offered.

EMORY UNIVERSITY, Art History Dept, 571 Kilgo Cir, 133 Carlos Hall Atlanta, GA 30322-1120. Tel 404-727-6282; Fax 404-727-2358; Elec Mail grobins@emory.edu; Internet Home Page Address: arthistory.emory.edu/home/index.html; *Prof* C Jean Campbell PhD; *Asst Prof* Todd Cronan PhD; *Dir Undergrad Studies & Sr Lectr* Dorothy Fletcher MA; *Prof* Sidney L Kasfir PhD; *Prof* Sarah Collyer McPhee, PhD; *Assoc Prof* Judith C Rohrer, PhD; *Assoc Prof* Eric Varner, PhD; *Prof* Walter S Melion; *Assoc Prof* Elizabeth Carson Pastan; *Prof* Gay Robbins; *Assoc Prof* Rebecca R Stone; *Assoc Prof* Bonna Daix Westcoat
Estab 1847; pvt; D; Scholarships; SC 27, LC 26, GC 18; non-maj 240, maj 80, grad 41
Ent Req: HS dipl, ent exam, SAT
Degrees: BA(Art History) & PhD(Art History)
Courses: †Art History, Ceramics, Drawing, Film, History of Art & Architecture, Museum Staff Training, Painting, Photography, Sculpture, Video
Summer School: Dir, Elizabeth Pastan. Enrl 51; tuition $621 per cr hr, 2 six wk sessions. Courses—Drawing, History of Art Abroad, Photography, Video, Sculpture, Studio Art, Various seminars in Europe (variable 8 cr hr)

GEORGIA INSTITUTE OF TECHNOLOGY, College of Architecture, 247 Fourth St, Atlanta, GA 30332-0155. Tel 404-894-3880; Fax 404-894-2678; Elec Mail tom.galloway@coa.gatech.edu; Internet Home Page Address: arch.gatech.edu; *Dean* Thomas D Galloway PhD; *Assoc Dean* Douglas Allen; *Assoc Dean* Sabir Khan
Estab 1885, dept estab 1908; Maintain nonprofit art gallery, Atlanta Contemporary Art Center; pub; D & E; Scholarships; SC 31, LC 86, GC 109; D 639, maj 731, grad 275
Ent Req: HS dipl, SAT
Degrees: BS(Architecture), BS(Building Construction), BS(Industrial Design) & M (Architecture) 2 yr & 3 1/2 yrs (for students w/out degree in Architecture), PhD MCRP 2 yr, PhD MS (Building Construction & Integrated Facility Management) 2 yr, MS (undesignated) 1-2 yr, MS (Advanced Architectural Design) 1yr, MID 2yr & 3yr (for students w/out degree in Industrial Design), MS (Music Technology) 2 yr
Courses: Aesthetics, †Architecture, Art Appreciation, Art History, †Building Construction, †City & Regl Planning, Conceptual Art, Constructions, Design, Drafting, Drawing, †Facility Management, Graphic Arts, Graphic Design, History of Art & Architecture, †Industrial Design, Intermedia, Music, Painting, Photography, Printmaking, Teacher Training
Summer School: Dir, Ellen Dunham-Jones. Enrl 50; tuition same. Courses—vary

GEORGIA STATE UNIVERSITY, Ernest G Welch School of Art & Design, PO Box 4107, Atlanta, GA 30302-4107. Tel 404-413-5221; Fax 404-413-5261; Elec Mail artundergrad@gsu.edu; grad@gsu.edu; Internet Home Page Address: www.gsu.edu; *Dir* Michael White; *Assoc Dir* Maria Gindhart; *Grad Dir* John Decker
Estab 1913; Maintain non-profit art gallery, Ernest G Welch School of Art & Design Galleries, 10 Peachtree Ctr Ave, Atlanta, GA 30303; FT 35; pub; D & E; Scholarships; SC 80, LC 16; maj 450, others 300
Activities: Schols, fels offered
Ent Req: HS dipl, ent exam, college board, interview
Degrees: BFA, BA(Art) and BA(Art History) 4 yrs, MA(Art History), MAEd (Art Education), MFA (Studio), MFA
Courses: Art Education, Art History, Ceramics, Drawing, Graphic Design, Interior Design, Painting, Photography, Printmaking, Sculpture, Textile Design
Children's Classes: Enrl 10-15, 8-10 wk term
Summer School: Enrl 350-400. Courses—Art Education, Art History, Studio

AUGUSTA

AUGUSTA STATE UNIVERSITY, Dept of Art, 2500 Walton Way, Augusta, GA 30904-2200. Tel 706-667-4888; Fax 706-729-2429; Elec Mail cjunod@aug.edu; Internet Home Page Address: www.aug.edu; *Assoc Prof* Kristin Casaletto, MFA; *Prof* Janice Whiting, MFA; *Prof* Michael Schwartz, PhD; *Prof* Brian Rust, MFA; *Morris Eminent Scholar in Art* William Willis, MFA; *Prof* Priscilla Hollingsworth, MFA; *Prof* Jennifer Onofrio, MFA; *Prof* Raoul Pacheco; *Chair* Alan MacTaggart

Estab 1925, dept estab 1965; independent dept estab 2006; Maintains nonprofit art gallery: Mary S Byrd Gallery of Art, Washington Hall, Augusta State University, 2500 Walton Way, Augusta, GA 30904; art supplies may be purchased at bookstore; pub; D & E; Scholarships; SC 46, LC 4; D 300, E 45, non-maj 80, maj 100
Ent Req: HS dipl, SAT
Degrees: BA & BFA
Courses: Aesthetics, Art History, †Ceramics, Design, †Drawing, Mixed Media, †Painting, Photography, Printmaking, †Sculpture
Adult Hobby Classes: Contact Continuing Education Dept for info

BARNESVILLE

GORDON COLLEGE, Dept of Fine Arts, 419 College Dr, Barnesville, GA 30204-1762. Tel 770-358-5118; Fax 770-358-3031; *Instr* Marlin Adams; *Dir* Jason Horn
Scholarships
Degrees: AA
Tuition: Res—$627 per sem; nonres—$2694 per sem
Courses: Art Appreciation, Ceramics, Design, Drawing, Graphic Design, Illustration, Introduction to Art, Painting, Photography, Printmaking, Survey Art History

CARROLLTON

STATE UNIVERSITY OF WEST GEORGIA, Art Dept, 1601 Maple St, Carrollton, GA 30118-0002. Tel 770-836-6521; Fax 770-836-4392; Internet Home Page Address: www.westga.edu/~artdept; *Chmn* Bruce Bobick
Estab 1906; Maintain nonprofit art gallery - Department of Art Gallery, State U of West Georgia; Pub; D&E; Scholarships; SC 39, LC 16, GC 2, Other 9; maj 230, grad 15
Ent Req: HS dipl, ent exam
Degrees: BFA, AB(Studio, Pre-Medical Illustration, Art History), MEd 1 yr full-time
Courses: Art Appreciation, †Art Education, Art History, †Ceramics, Design, Drawing, †Graphic Design, †Interior Design, †Painting, Papermaking, †Photography, †Printmaking, †Sculpture
Summer School: Dir, B Bobick, 8 wk sem in Carrollton, summer study abroad program in Bayeux, France. Courses—Art Appreciation, Art Education, Art History, Ceramics, Design, Drawing, Painting, Printmaking, Sculpture, Photography

CLEVELAND

TRUETT-MCCONNELL COLLEGE, Fine Arts Dept & Arts Dept, 100 Alumni Dr, Cleveland, GA 30528-1264. Tel 706-865-2134; Fax 706-865-0975; Internet Home Page Address: www.truett.cc.ga.us; *Instr* Susan Chapman; *Prof* Dr David N George; *Chmn* Dr Edwin Calloway
Estab 1946; den; D & E; SC 10, LC 2; D 700, non-maj 98, maj 15
Ent Req: HS dipl, SAT
Degrees: AA and AS 2 yr
Courses: 3-D Design, Aesthetics, Art History, Ceramics, Drawing, Graphic Design, Handicrafts, Painting, Sculpture

COCHRAN

MIDDLE GEORGIA STATE COLLEGE, (Middle Georgia College) Humanities Division, Dept of Art - School of Liberal Arts, Dept of Media, Culture & the Arts, 1100 2nd St SE, Cochran, GA 31014-1564. Tel 478-934-3085; Fax 478-934-3517; Elec Mail cagnew@mgc.edu; Internet Home Page Address: www.mgc.edu; *Chmn* Dr Kevin Cantwell; *Assoc Prof of Art* Charlie Agnew; *Asst Prof Graphic Design* Steven Arnold; *Asst Chair* Dr Robert McTyre; *Asst Prof Art* Charles Ward
Estab as Junior College Unit of University of Georgia, now a 4 yr school as well; Maintains a nonprofit art gallery, Peacock Gallery, Cochran Campus same address; Campus bookstore; FT 2; Pub; D, E & online; Scholarships; SC 15, LC 3, online-Art Apprec; D 250, E 60, non-maj 180, maj 70
Activities: Schols offered
Ent Req: HS dipl, GED
Degrees: AA 2 yr, Graphic Design certificate
Tuition: Res—$1,514.24 instate tuition & fees for 12 hrs; $4,657.40 out of state tuition & fees
Courses: Art Appreciation, Art History, Ceramics, Design, Drawing, Fine Art, Graphic Arts, Graphic Design, Hands-on Art, Painting, Photography, Sculpture, Understanding Art
Summer School: Enrl 90-120, Art Apprec (multiple campuses); Dr. Martha Venn, VPres Academic Affairs

COLUMBUS

COLUMBUS STATE UNIVERSITY, Dept of Art, Fine Arts Hall, 4225 University Ave, Columbus, GA 31907-5679. Tel 706-568-2047; Fax 706-568-2093; Internet Home Page Address: www.colstate.edu; *Chmn* Jeff Burden
Estab 1958; pub; D & E; Scholarships; SC 30, LC 7, GC 28; D 300, E 50, maj 130, grad 20
Ent Req: HS dipl, ent exam
Degrees: BS(Art Educ), BFA(Art) & MEd(Art Educ) 4 yr
Courses: Art Appreciation, Art Education, Art History, Ceramics, Critical Analysis, Design, Drawing, Graphic Arts, Graphic Design, Painting, Photography, Printmaking, Sculpture, Textile Design
Summer School: Enrl 200; term of one quarter. Courses—various

DAHLONEGA

NORTH GEORGIA COLLEGE & STATE UNIVERSITY, Fine Arts Dept, 322 Georgia Cir Dahlonega, GA 30597. Tel 706-864-1423; Fax 706-864-1429; Internet Home Page Address: www.ngcsu.edu; *Dept Head* Dr Lee Barrow; *Assoc Prof* CM Chastain; *Asst Prof* Hank Margeson; *Asst Prof* Michael Marling de Cuellar
Estab 1873; pub; D & E; Scholarships
Degrees: BA, BS, MEd
Tuition: Res—undergrad $2954 per yr, grad $2918 per yr; nonres—undergrad $3991per sem, grad $3200 per sem; campus res available
Courses: Art Appreciation, †Art Education, Art History, †Ceramics, Computer Graphics, Design, †Drawing, Painting, †Photography, Printmaking, Scientific Illustration, †Sculpture, Textile Design, Weaving
Children's Classes: Enrl 10; tuition $30. Courses—Children's Art
Summer School: Dir, Lee Barrow. Courses—Art Appreciation, Drawing, Painting, Photography, Pottery

DECATUR

AGNES SCOTT COLLEGE, Dept of Art, 141 E College Ave, Decatur, GA 30030-3797. Tel 404-471-6000; Fax 404-638-5369; Internet Home Page Address: www.agnesscott.edu; *Chmn* Anne Beidler
Estab 1889; pvt; D; Scholarships; SC 13, LC 15; non-maj 200, maj 23
Degrees: BA 4 yr
Courses: Aesthetics, Art History, Drawing, Graphic Arts, Painting, Printmaking, Sculpture

DEMOREST

PIEDMONT COLLEGE, Art Dept, PO Box 10, Demorest, GA 30535-0010. Tel 706-778-3000; Fax 706-778-2811; Internet Home Page Address: www.piedmont.edu; *Dept Head* Cheryl Goldsleger
Estab 1897; Pvt; Scholarships
Degrees: BA
Courses: Art Appreciation, Art Education, Art History, Ceramics, Drawing, Graphic Design, Painting, Photography, Printmaking, Sculpture

GAINESVILLE

BRENAU UNIVERSITY, Art & Design Dept, One Centennial Circle, Gainesville, GA 30501. Tel 770-534-6240; Fax 770-538-4599; Elec Mail lmjones@lib.brenau.edu; Internet Home Page Address: www.brenau.edu; *Graphic Design Prog Dir* Mark A Taylor, MEd; *Art & Design Chair* Lynn M Jones, MHP; *Cur, Arts Management Prog Dir* Jean Westmacott, MFA; *Fashion Merchandising Prog Dir* Janet Morley; *Interior Design Prog Dir* Christopher R Sherry, ASID; *Instr* Jere Williams, MFA; *Studio Arts Prog Dir* Mary Beth Looney, MFA; *Instr* Sandra McGowen, FASID; *Instr* Michael Marling, MFA; *Asst Prof* Carol Platt, ASID; *Instr* Frank Saggus, MFA
Estab 1878; Maintain nonprofit gallery, Breneau University Galleries, One Central Circle, Gainesville, GA 30506; W; D & E; weekends; Scholarships; 100; D, 75; E, 25
Ent Req: HS dipl
Degrees: BFA, BA, BS 4 yr
Courses: Advertising Design, Aesthetics, †Art Appreciation, †Art Education, Art History, †Art Management, †Ceramics, †Commercial Art, †Design, Drafting, †Drawing, †Fashion Design, †Fashion Merchandising, Graphic Design, History of Art & Architecture, Interior Design, †Painting, Photography, †Sculpture, †Silversmithing
Summer School: Dir, Dr John Upchurch. Enrl 300. Courses—Dance, Music, Theatre, Art & Design

LAGRANGE

LAGRANGE COLLEGE, Lamar Dodd Art Center Museum, 601 Broad St, LaGrange, GA 30240-2999. Tel 706-812-7211; Fax 706-812-7212; Internet Home Page Address: www.lgc.peachnet.edu; *Dept Head* John D Lawrence
Estab 1831; FT 3, PT 1; pvt; D & E; Scholarships; SC 11, LC 2; maj 40
Ent Req: HS dipl, ent exam
Degrees: BA 4 yr
Courses: Art Education, Art History, Art History Survey, Batik, Ceramics, Drawing, Graphic Design, Painting, Photography, Printmaking, Sculpture, Textile Design
Summer School: Dir, Luke Gill. Enrl 200. Courses—Art History, Ceramics, Drawing, Photography

MACON

MERCER UNIVERSITY, Art Dept, 1400 Coleman Ave, Macon, GA 31207-0003. Tel 478-301-2591; Fax 478-301-2171; *Assoc Prof* Gary L Blackburn
Estab 1945; FT 4; den; D; SC 9, LC 7, GC 2; maj 25
Ent Req: HS dipl
Degrees: BA 4 yr
Courses: Art Education, Art History, Ceramics, Drawing, Photography, Printmaking, Sculpture
Adult Hobby Classes: Evening classes
Summer School: Dir, JoAnna Watson. 2 terms, 5 wks. Courses—Art Education, Ceramics, Crafts, Drawing, Painting, Photography, Sculpture

WESLEYAN COLLEGE, Art Dept, 4760 Forsyth Rd, Macon, GA 31210-4462. Tel 478-477-1110; Fax 478-757-2469; Internet Home Page Address: www.wesleyancollege.edu; *Asst Prof* Lebe Bailey, MFA; *Asst Prof* Francise deLarosa, MFA
Estab 1836; den; D & E; Scholarships; SC 38, LC 10; D 159, non-maj 13, maj 45, others 12
Ent Req: HS dipl, SAT, GPA
Degrees: BFA 4 yrs, BA
Courses: Advertising Design, Art Education, Art History, Ceramics, Commercial Art, Drawing, Elementary School Arts & Crafts, Graphic Arts, Graphic Design, Illustration, Painting, Photography, Printmaking, Sculpture, Special Topics in Art, Stage Design, Teacher Training, Theatre Arts, Visual Arts
Summer School: Art History Survey, Ceramics, Graphic Design, Illustration, Painting, Photography, Printmaking, Sculpture

MILLEDGEVILLE

GEORGIA COLLEGE & STATE UNIVERSITY, Art Dept, 231 W Hancock St, Milledgeville, GA 31061. Tel 478-445-4572; Fax 478-445-6088; Internet Home Page Address: www.gscu.edu; *Chmn* Dorothy D Brown
Scholarships
Courses: Art Appreciation, †Art Education, Art History, Ceramics, Design, Drawing, Handicrafts, Jewelry, Painting, Printmaking, Sculpture, Textile Design, Weaving
Adult Hobby Classes: Courses offered
Summer School: Courses offered

MOUNT BERRY

BERRY COLLEGE, Art Dept, 2277 Martha Berry Hwy NW, Mount Berry, GA 30149-9707. Tel 706-236-2219; Fax 706-238-7835; Elec Mail tmew@berry.edu; *Prof & Chmn* T J Mew PhD; *Asst Prof* Jere Lykins, MEd; *Asst Prof* V Troy PhD, MEd; *Asst Prof* Brad Adams, MFA
Estab dept estab 1942; Maintain nonprofit art gallery; Moon Gallery, Moon Bldg, Berry College Campus, Mt Berry, GA 30149; pvt; D & E; Scholarships; SC 24, LC 9; D 122, non-maj 38, maj 84, others 7
Ent Req: HS dipl, SAT, CEEB, ACT
Degrees: BA, BS 4 yrs
Courses: Aesthetics, †Art Appreciation, Art Education, Art History, Calligraphy, †Ceramics, Collage, Conceptual Art, Constructions, Design, Drawing, Ecological Art, Film, Graphic Arts, †Graphic Design, History of Art & Architecture, †Painting, †Photography, Printmaking, Sculpture, Teacher Training, Video
Summer School: Chair, Art Dept, Dr T J Mew III. Courses—Same as above

MOUNT VERNON

BREWTON-PARKER COLLEGE, Visual Arts, Hwy 280, Mount Vernon, GA 30445; PO Box 197, Mount Vernon, GA 30445-0197. Tel 912-583-2241, Ext 306; Fax 912-583-4498; Internet Home Page Address: www.bpc.edu; *Dir* E W Addison, MFA; *Pres* David Smith
Estab 1906, dept re-estab 1976; pvt, den; D & E; SC 10, LC 4; in dept D 19, non-maj 4, maj 15
Ent Req: HS dipl
Degrees: AA(Visual Arts) 2 yrs
Courses: 2-D & 3-D Design, Art History, Art Media & Theory, Art for Teachers, Drawing, Painting, Photography, Printmaking, Sculpture
Adult Hobby Classes: Same courses as above, on and off campus classes
Summer School: Same courses as above

ROME

SHORTER COLLEGE, Art Dept, 315 Shorter Ave, Rome, GA 30165-4267. Tel 706-291-2121; Fax 706-236-1515; Internet Home Page Address: www.shorter.edu; *Co-Chair* Brian Taylor; *Prof* Christine Colley
Estab 1873, dept estab 1900; pvt; D; Scholarships; SC 40, LC 7; non-maj 15, maj 20
Ent Req: HS dipl
Degrees: BA(Art) and BFA(Art Ed) 4 yr
Courses: Art Appreciation, Art Education, Art History, †Ceramics, Color Theory, Commercial Art, Design, †Drawing, Graphic Arts, Graphic Design, Illustration, †Mixed Media, †Painting, Photography, Printmaking, †Sculpture, Theatre Arts
Children's Classes: Enrl 20; tuition varies

SAVANNAH

ARMSTRONG ATLANTIC STATE UNIVERSITY, Department of Art, Music & Theatre, 11935 Abercorn St, Savannah, GA 31419-1997. Tel 912-344-2556; Fax 912-344-3419; Internet Home Page Address: www.finearts.armstrong.edu; *Chmn* Dr Tom Cato
Maintain nonprofit art gallery; FT 8, PT varies per sem; pub; D&E; Scholarships; SC 35, LC 12, GC 6; Maj 240
Ent Req: Admis to Univ
Degrees: BA, BFA, BS Art Educ
Tuition: $143 per cr hr in-state; $530 per cr hr out-of-state
Courses: †Advertising Design, Art Appreciation, Art Education, Art History, Ceramics, Design, Drawing, Handicrafts, Jewelry, †Mixed Media, Painting, Photography, Printmaking, Sculpture, †Visual Arts, Weaving
Children's Classes: Printing, Sculpture

SAVANNAH STATE UNIVERSITY, Dept of Fine Arts, PO Box 20512, Savannah, GA 31404-9708. Tel 912-358-3370; Fax 912-353-3159; *Dir* Dr Peggy Blood, MFA, MA, PhD; *Asst Prof* Nicholas Silberg; *Lectr* Brandon Williams

Estab 1880s, dept estab 1950s; Maintain nonprofit art gallery; pub; D & E; SC 13, LC 3
Ent Req: HS dipl
Degrees: BFA
Tuition: Res—$1700 per sem, nonres—$3800 per sem; campus res available
Courses: Advertising & Editorial Illustration, Art History, Basic Design, Calligraphy, Ceramics, Color Theory, Computer Design, Graphic Design, Interior Design, Painting, Photography, Sculpture, Textile Design, Weaving
Summer School: Dir, Dr Luetta Milledge. Enrl 60; tuition $180. Courses—on demand

STATESBORO

GEORGIA SOUTHERN UNIVERSITY, Dept of Art, PO Box 8032, Statesboro, GA 30460-1000. Tel 912-681-5918, 681-5358; *Prof* Thomas Steadman, MFA; *Assoc Prof* Jessica Hines, MFA; *Assoc Prof* Dr Jane R Hudak, MFA; *Assoc Prof* Henry Iler, MFA; *Assoc Prof* Dr Bruce Little, MFA; *Assoc Prof* Onyile B Onyile, MFA; *Assoc Prof* Elizabeth Peak, MFA; *Assoc Prof* Dr Roy B Sonnema, MFA; *Asst Prof* Patricia Walker, MFA; *Asst Prof* Marie Cochran, MFA; *Temp Asst Prof* Greg Carter, MFA; *Temp Asst Prof* Patricia Carter, MFA; *Temp Asst Prof* Micheal Obershan, MFA; *Temp Asst Prof* Iris Sandkulher, MFA; *Temp Instr* Julie McGuire, MFA; *Head Dept* Richard Tichich, MFA
pub; D & E; Scholarships; SC, LC
Ent Req: HS dipl
Degrees: BA & BSEd 4 yr
Courses: Art Education, Art History, Ceramics, Commercial Art, Constructions, Drawing, Graphic Arts, Graphic Design, Lettering, Mixed Media, Painting, Photography, Printmaking, Sculpture, Teacher Training
Adult Hobby Classes: Enrl 40; tuition $35 per 10 wks. Courses—Painting, Photography
Children's Classes: Offered in Laboratory School & Sat Program

THOMASVILLE

THOMAS UNIVERSITY, (Thomas College) Humanities Division, 1501 Mill Pond Rd, Thomasville, GA 31792. Tel 229-226-1621, Ext 142; Fax 229-226-1653; Internet Home Page Address: www.thomas.edu; *Asst Prof of Art* James Adams; *Div Chmn* Ann Landis
Scholarships
Degrees: AA
Tuition: $250 per cr hr
Courses: Art Appreciation, Art Education, Drawing, Painting
Adult Hobby Classes: Enrl 30; 2 terms (quarters) per yr. Courses—Art Structure
Children's Classes: Courses offered on demand
Summer School: Enrl 60; summer quarter. Courses—same as regular yr

TIFTON

ABRAHAM BALDWIN AGRICULTURAL COLLEGE, Art & Humanities Dept, 2802 Moore Hwy, ABAC Sta Tifton, GA 31794-5698. Tel 912-386-3236, 386-3250; Internet Home Page Address: www.abac.peachnet.edu; *Pres* Homer Day
Degrees: Cert AA
Tuition: Res $832 per sem; nonres $2572 per sem
Courses: Art Appreciation, Art History, Design, Drawing, Painting

VALDOSTA

VALDOSTA STATE UNIVERSITY, Dept of Art, 1500 N Patterson St, Valdosta, GA 31698-0001. Tel 229-333-5835; Fax 229-259-5121; Elec Mail apearce@valdosta.edu; *Dept Head* A Blake Pearce
Estab 1906; Maintains nonprofit gallery, Valdosta State University Art Gallery; FT 17; pub; D&E; Scholarships; SC 25, LC 10; maj 310, total 11,800
Ent Req: SAT or ACT
Degrees: BA, BFA (Int Des), BFA (Art Ed) & BFA (Art) 4 yr
Courses: Advertising Design, Aesthetics, Art Appreciation, †Art Education, Art History, Ceramics, Collage, Commercial Art, Computer Graphics, Constructions, Design, Drawing, Graphic Arts, Graphic Design, History of Art & Architecture, Illustration, †Interior Design, Intermedia, Lettering, Mixed Media, Painting, Photography, Portfolio Preparation, Printmaking, Sculpture, Teacher Training
Summer School: Tuition res—$155 per qtr hr for 4 or 8 wk term. Courses—Art Appreciation, Computer Graphics, Design, Studio

YOUNG HARRIS

YOUNG HARRIS COLLEGE, Dept of Art, 1 College St, Young Harris, GA 30582-4137; PO Box 68, Young Harris, GA 30582-0068. Tel 706-379-3111; Fax 706-379-4306; Internet Home Page Address: www.yhc.edu; *Chmn* Richard Aunspaugh
Estab 1886; Maintain nonprofit art gallery; Clegg Art Gallery, PO Box 236, Young Harris, GA 30582; FT 2; pvt; D; Scholarships; SC 5, LC 1; D 450, maj 25
Ent Req: HS dipl
Degrees: AFA 2 yr
Courses: Art Appreciation, Art History, Design, Drawing, Painting, Sculpture, Stage Design, Theatre Arts

HAWAII

HAIKU

THE ASHLAND ACADEMY OF ART, 222 Laniloa Way, Haiku, HI 96708-5381. Tel 541-482-3567; Fax 541-482-0994; Elec Mail info@ashlandacademyofart.com; Internet Home Page Address: www.ashlandacademyofart.com

Circ

HONOLULU

HONOLULU ACADEMY OF ARTS, The Art Center at Linekona, 900 S
Beretania St Honolulu, HI 96814. Tel 808-532-8700; Fax 808-532-8787; Elec Mail
webmaster@honoluluacadmey.org; Internet Home Page Address:
www.honoluluacademy.org; *Cur Art Ctr* Carol Khewhok; *Head Operational*
Robert White; *Librn* Ronald F Chapman; *Keeper Lending* Gwen Harada; *Cur
Textiles* Reiko Brandon; *Spec Events* Vicki Reisner; *Assoc Dir* David J de la Torre;
Pub Rels Dir Charlene Aldinger; *Dir Develop* Judy Dawson; *Cur Film* Ann
Brandman; *VChmn* Samuel A Cooke; *Registrar* Sanna Saks Deutsch; *Annual Fund
Coordr* Linda Grzywaca; *Mus Shop Mgr* Kathee Hoover; *Cur Educ* Daren
Thompson; *Cur Asian Art* Julia White; *Cur Western Art* Jennifer Saville; *Dir, CEO
& Pres* George R Ellis; *CFO* Eric Watanabe
Estab 1946; FT 3, PT 1; pvt
Ent Req: 16 yrs of age with talent
Degrees: no degrees granted
Tuition: varies
Courses: Ceramics, Drawing, Etching, Lithography, Painting, Printmaking
Adult Hobby Classes: Tuition $130 per sem. Courses—Ceramics, Drawing,
Jewelry, Painting, Printmaking, Watercolors, Weaving
Children's Classes: tuition $95 for 11 wks. Courses—Drawing, Exploring Art,
Painting

HONOLULU COMMUNITY COLLEGE, Commercial Art Dept, 874
Dillingham Blvd, Honolulu, HI 96817-4598. Tel 808-845-9211; Fax
808-845-9173; Internet Home Page Address: www.hcc.hawaii.edu; *Dept Head*
Sandra Sanpei; *Instr Commercial Art* Michel Kaiser; *Instr Graphic Arts* Romolo
Valencia, BA
College maintains three art departments: Commercial Art, Art & Graphic Arts;
pub; D & E; SC 20, LC 2; D 150 majors
Ent Req: 18 yrs of age, English & math requirements, motivation, interest in
learning, willingness to work
Degrees: AS 2 yr
Courses: Advertising Design, Commercial Art, Drafting, Drawing, Graphic Arts,
Graphic Design, Illustration, Lettering, Painting, Photography, Printmaking, Textile
Design

UNIVERSITY OF HAWAII, Kapiolani Community College, 4303 Diamond
Head Rd, Honolulu, HI 96816-4421. Tel 808-734-9282; Fax 808-734-9151; *Chmn*
Kauka de Silva
Estab 1965; FT 8, PT 7; pub; D & E; Scholarships; SC 11, LC 5; D 4800, E 500
Ent Req: ent exam
Degrees: AA and AS 1-2 yr
Tuition: No campus res
Courses: Art Appreciation, Art History, Ceramics, Computer Graphics, Conceptual
Art, Design, Drawing, History of Art & Architecture, Painting, Photography,
Sculpture
Adult Hobby Classes: Enrl 15 per class; tuition depends on number of units.
Courses—Art Appreciation, Art History, Ceramics, Color Theory, Computer
Graphics, Conceptual Art, Design

UNIVERSITY OF HAWAII AT MANOA, Dept of Art, 2535 McCarthy Mall,
Honolulu, HI 96822-2233. Tel 808-956-8251; Fax 808-956-9043; Elec Mail
uhart@hawaii.edu; Internet Home Page Address: www.hawaii.edu/art; *Dept Chair*
Gaye Chan; *Assoc Chair* Frank Beaver; *Dir Gallery* Tom Klobe
Estab 1907; FT 26, PT 25; pub; D; Scholarships; SC 64, LC 34; maj 450, grad 40
Ent Req: HS dipl or GED and SAT or ACT
Degrees: BA(Art History), BA(Studio), BFA 4 yr, MA & MFA
Courses: Aesthetics, Art Appreciation, †Art History, Calligraphy, †Ceramics,
Design, †Drawing, †Fiber Arts, †Glass, Graphic Arts, †Graphic Design,
†Intermedia, Mixed Media, Museum Staff Training, †Painting, †Photography,
†Printmaking, Sculpture, Textile Design, Video
Adult Hobby Classes: Drawing, Painting, Sculpture
Summer School: Dean, Victor Kobayashi. Tuition $123 per cr hr, non res $130
per cr hr, plus fees. Courses—Art History (Western, Asian & Pacific), Ceramics,
Drawing, Design, Fiber, Glass, Painting, Photography, Printmaking, Sculpture

KAHULUI

MAUI COMMUNITY COLLEGE, Art Program, 310 Kaahumanu Ave, Kahului,
HI 96732-1644. Tel 808-244-9181; Internet Home Page Address:
mauicc.hawaii.edu; *Div Chmn* Dorothy Pyle
Estab 1967; FT 1, PT 3; pub; D & E; Scholarships; SC 8, LC 2; 2600
Ent Req: ent exam
Degrees: AA, AAF, AS, 2 yr Cert (ACH)
Courses: Advertising Design, Architecture, †Batik, †Ceramics, Copper Enameling,
Display, †Drawing, Graphic Arts, Graphic Design, History of Architecture,
†History of Art & Architecture, Jewelry, †Painting, †Photography, Sculpture,
†Textile Design, †Weaving, Welding
Adult Hobby Classes: Enrl 200. Courses—Art, Art History, Ceramics, Drawing,
Intro to Visual Art, Painting

LAIE

BRIGHAM YOUNG UNIVERSITY, HAWAII CAMPUS, Division of Fine
Arts, 55-220 Kulanui St, Laie, HI 96762-1294. Tel 808-293-3211; Fax
808-293-3645, 293-3900; *Chmn* Dr Jeffrey Belnap
Scholarships
Degrees: BA
Tuition: Church mem $2035 per sem; non church mem $1837 per sem
Courses: †Ceramics, †Painting, Polynesian Handicrafts, †Printmaking, †Sculpture

Summer School: Dir, V Napua Tengaio. Tuition $60 per cr, 2 four wk blocks.
Courses—Ceramics, Polynesian Handicrafts

LIHUE

KAUAI COMMUNITY COLLEGE, Dept of Art, 3-1901 Kaumualii, Lihue, HI
96766. Tel 808-245-8284, 245-8226; Fax 808-245-8220; *Faculty* Wayne A Miyata,
MFA; *Faculty* Waihang Lai, MA
Estab 1965; FT 2, PT 1; pub; D & E; Scholarships; SC 6, LC 2; D 965, E 468
Ent Req: HS dipl
Degrees: AA and AS 2 yr
Courses: Art History, Ceramics, Drawing, Oriental Brush Painting, Painting,
Photography
Summer School: Term of 6 wk beginning June and July

PEARL CITY

LEEWARD COMMUNITY COLLEGE, Arts & Humanities Division, 96-045
Ala Ike, Pearl City, HI 96782. Tel 808-455-0228; Fax 808-455-0638; Internet
Home Page Address: www.lcc.hawaii.edu; *Dean* Dr Mark Silliman
Estab 1968; pub; D & E; Scholarships; SC 11, LC 3; D 400, E 100
Ent Req: over 18 yrs of age
Degrees: AA & AS 2 yrs
Tuition: Res—$32 per cr hr; nonres—$213 per cr hr
Courses: 2-D Design, 3-D Design, Art History, Aspects of Asian Art, Ceramics,
Costume Design & Construction, Drawing, Graphic Arts, Painting, Photography,
Printmaking, Sculpture, Theatre Arts
Summer School: Enrl 100; Term of 7 wks beginning June 12th. Courses—vary

IDAHO

BOISE

BOISE STATE UNIVERSITY, Art Dept, 1910 University Dr, Boise, ID
83725-0002. Tel 208-426-1230; Fax 208-426-1243; Internet Home Page Address:
www.boisestate.edu/art; *Chmn* Dr Gary Rosine
Estab 1932; pub; D & E; Scholarships; SC 51, LC 8, GC 4; D 2539, maj 550, GS
14
Ent Req: HS dipl
Degrees: BA, BFA, BA(Educ), BFA(Educ), BA(Graphic Design), BA (Art
History), BFA(Graphic Design) 4 yr, MA(Art Educ) 4 yr
Courses: Architecture, †Art Education, Art History, †Art Metals, Ceramics,
Design, Drawing, †Graphic Design, †Illustration, Painting, Photography,
Printmaking, Sculpture
Summer School: Dir, Gary Rosine. Enrl 200; tuition $112.80 per cr hr for 5 wks.
Courses—Art History, Basic Design, Elementary School Art Methods, Introduction
to Art, Special Topics, Watercolor

COEUR D'ALENE

NORTH IDAHO COLLEGE, Art Dept, 1000 W Garden Ave, Coeur D'Alene,
ID 83814-2199. Tel 208-769-3300; Fax 208-769-7880; Internet Home Page
Address: www.nic.edu; *Dept Chmn* Allie Vogt, MA; *Instr* Lisa Lynes, MA
Degrees: BA, AA
Tuition: Res—in county $564 per sem, $79 per cr hr, $69 each additional cr hr;
nonres—$1942 per sem, $251 per cr hr,$241 each additional cr hr
Courses: Art Appreciation, Art History, Ceramics, Design, Drawing, Graphic
Design, Illustration, Letter Form, Life Drawing, Painting, Photography, Portfolio,
Professional Advertising, Sculpture, Stage Design, Weaving

LEWISTON

LEWIS-CLARK STATE COLLEGE, Art Dept, 500 Eighth Ave, Lewiston, ID
83501-2691. Tel 208-746-2341; Internet Home Page Address: www.lcsc.edu; *Prof*
Lawrence Haapanen
Estab 1893; Maintains reference library; FT 1; pub; D & E; Scholarships; SC 10,
LC 1; D 89, E 43
Ent Req: HS dipl or GED, ACT
Degrees: BA and BS 4 yrs
Courses: Art Education, Composition, Drawing, Graphic Arts, Independent Study,
Painting, Stage Design, Teacher Training, Theatre Arts, Video
Adult Hobby Classes: Discipline Coordr, Robert Almquist, MFA

MOSCOW

UNIVERSITY OF IDAHO/COLLEGE OF ART & ARCHITECTURE, Dept
of Art & Design, 875 Perimeter Dr, Moscow, ID 83844-9803. Tel 208-885-6851;
Fax 208-885-9428; Elec Mail artdesign@uidaho.edu; Internet Home Page Address:
www.uidaho.edu/caa/artdesign/; *Prof* Lynne Haagenson; *Assoc Prof* Delphine
Keim-Campbell; *Dept Chair* Prof Sally Machlis; *Gallery Dir & Lectr* Roger
Rowley; *Sr Instr* Val Carter; *Assoc Prof* Gregory Turner-Rahman; *Asst Prof* Marco
Deyasi; *Asst Prof* J Casey Doyle; *Asst Prof* Stacy Isenbarger; *Asst Prof* Rachel
Fujita
Estab 1923; Supplies may be purchased on campus; Pub; D & E; Scholarships;
SC 35, LC 17, GC 14
Ent Req: HS dipl or equivalent
Degrees: BA, BS, BFA, MFA

Courses: †Art Appreciation, †Art Education, Art History, Ceramics, †Drawing, Graphic Design, Interaction Design, †Mixed Media, Painting, Photography, Printmaking, Sculpture, Visual Communication
Summer School: Courses—vary

NAMPA

NORTHWEST NAZARENE COLLEGE, Art Dept, 623 Holly St, Nampa, ID 83686-5855. Tel 208-467-8011; Internet Home Page Address: www.nnu.edu; Art Head Jim Willis
FT 3; Den; D & E; Scholarships; SC 12, LC 5; D 200, E 40, maj 24
Ent Req: HS dipl
Degrees: BA & BS 4 yr
Courses: Art Education, Ceramics, Crafts for Teachers, Drawing, Graphic Design, History of Art & Architecture, Illustration, Painting, Printmaking, Sculpture, Teacher Training
Adult Hobby Classes: Crafts, Painting
Summer School: Courses—Art Education

POCATELLO

IDAHO STATE UNIVERSITY, Dept of Art & Pre-Architecture, 921 S 8th Ave, Stop 800 Pocatello, ID 83201-5377. Tel 208-282-2361, 282-2488; Fax 208-282-4741; Elec Mail kovarudo@isu.edu; Internet Home Page Address: www.isu.edu; Chmn Rudy Kovacs, MFA; Faculty Doug Warnock, MFA; Faculty Scott Evans, MFA; Faculty Tony Martin, MFA; Instr Dr Linda Leeuwrik, PhD; Asst Lectr Amy Jo Popa, MFA; Instr Angie Ziellnski, MFA; Adjunct Wayne Rudd, MFA; Adjunct Ryan Babcock, MFA; Adjunct Juliet Feige, MFA; Adjunct Louis Pirro; Vis Asst Lectr Benjamin Hunt, MFA; Vis Asst Lectr Bryan Park, MFA
Estab 1901; Maintain nonprofit art gallery; on-campus shop sells art supplies; pub; D & E; Scholarships; SC 32, LC 6, GS 22; maj 75, GS 15, total 500
Ent Req: HS dipl, GED, ACT
Degrees: BA, BFA and MFA 4 yr
Courses: Art Education, Art History, Ceramics, Design, Drawing, Metals, Painting, Printmaking, Sculpture, Weaving
Adult Hobby Classes: Enrl 20; tuition $45 for 6 wk term. Courses—Drawing, Landscape Painting
Children's Classes: Enrl 20; tuition $40 for 8 wk term. Courses—Vary
Summer School: Dir/Chair, Rudy Kovacs. Enrl 75. Courses—Art History, Ceramics

REXBURG

RICKS COLLEGE, Dept of Art, 16 E Main St, Rexburg, ID 83460-9514. Tel 208-356-2913, 356-4871; Instr Scott Franson; Instr Vince Bodily; Instr Gerald Griffin; Instr Mathew Geddes; Instr Leon Parson; Instr Gary Pearson; Chmn Kelly Burgner
Estab 1888; pvt; D & E; Scholarships; SC 23, LC 1; D 123, maj 123
Ent Req: HS dipl
Degrees: AAS, AAdv Design and AFA 2 yrs
Courses: Art Appreciation, Art Education, Art History, Ceramics, Drawing, †Fine Art, †Graphic Design, Illustration, Painting, †Photography, Typography
Adult Hobby Classes: Enrl 150. Courses—Art History, Introduction to Visual Arts
Summer School: Dir, Jim Gee. Enrl 370; tuition $60 per cr hr. Courses—Art History, Ceramics, Drawing, Graphic Design, Illustration, Photography

SUN VALLEY

SUN VALLEY CENTER FOR THE ARTS, (Sun Valley Center for the Arts & Humanities) Dept of Fine Art, PO Box 656, Sun Valley, ID 83353-0656. Tel 208-726-9491; Fax 208-726-2344; Internet Home Page Address: www.sunvalleycenter.org; Artistic Dir Kristin Poole; Dir Educ Britt Udesen; Exec Dir Sam Gappmayer; Cur Visual Arts Courtney Gilbert
Estab 1971; Maintain a nonprofit art gallery; D, E & weekends; SC
Ent Req: Some dance require prior exp
Courses: †Calligraphy, †Ceramics, †Collage, †Drafting, †Lettering, †Mixed Media, †Painting, †Photography, †Printmaking, †Sculpture
Adult Hobby Classes: Calligraphy, Ceramics, UFE Drawing
Children's Classes: Enrl vary per sem. Courses—Ceramics
Summer School: Dir, Britt Udesen. Courses—Ceramics, Mixed Media, Painting from Nature, Photography, Watercolor

TWIN FALLS

COLLEGE OF SOUTHERN IDAHO, Art Dept, PO Box 1238, Twin Falls, ID 83303-1238. Tel 208-733-9554, Ext 344; Fax 208-736-3014; Internet Home Page Address: www.csi.cc.id.us; WATS 800-680-0274; Assoc Prof Russell Hepworth, MFA; Chmn Mike Green, MFA
Estab 1965; pub; D & E; Scholarships; SC 26, LC 2; D 3000, E 2000, non-maj 50, maj 45
Ent Req: HS dipl, ACT
Degrees: dipl or AA
Tuition: campus res—room & board
Courses: Art History, Ceramics, Design, Drawing, Lettering, Mixed Media, Painting, Papermaking, Photography, Printmaking, Sculpture, Theatre Arts
Children's Classes: Enrl 50; tuition $20 per class. Courses—Crafts, Drawing, Photography, Pottery
Summer School: Dir Jerry Beck. Courses—Art General, Crafts, Drawing, Papermaking, Pottery

ILLINOIS

AURORA

AURORA UNIVERSITY, Art Dept, 347 S Gladstone Ave, Aurora, IL 60506-4892. Tel 630-844-5519, 892-7431; Fax 630-844-7830; Elec Mail slowery@aurora.edu; Internet Home Page Address: www.aurora.edu; Prof Stephen Lowery, MFA
Estab 1893, dept estab 1979; Maintain nonprofit art gallery; Downstairs Dunham Gallery, Dunham Hall; pvt; D & E; SC 7, LC 1; D 102, E 96, non-maj 171
Ent Req: HS dipl
Degrees: BA 4 yrs
Courses: 2-D Design, 3-D Design, Art Appreciation, Drawing, Media Technology, Painting, Photography, Sculpture
Summer School: Courses—Photography, Media Technology

BELLEVILLE

SOUTHWESTERN ILLINOIS COLLEGE, (Belleville Area College) Art Dept, 2500 Carlyle Ave, Belleville, IL 62221-5899. Tel 618-235-2700; Internet Home Page Address: www.southwestern.cc.il.us; Dept Head Jerry Bolen
Estab 1948; pub; D & E; Scholarships; SC 36, LC 9; D 4000, E 3500, maj 200
Ent Req: HS dipl
Degrees: AA and AS 2 yrs
Courses: Advertising Design, Art Appreciation, Art Education, Art History, Calligraphy, Ceramics, Commercial Art, Design, Drawing, Film, Graphic Arts, Graphic Design, History of Art & Architecture, Jewelry, Lettering, Painting, Photography, Printmaking, Sculpture, Theatre Arts, Video
Summer School: Dept Head, Jerry Bolen. Tuition $30 per hr for 8 wks. Courses—Art History, Ceramics, Drawing, Photography

BLOOMINGTON

ILLINOIS WESLEYAN UNIVERSITY, School of Art, PO Box 2900, Bloomington, IL 61702-2900. Tel 309-556-1000 (information), 556-3077 (school of art), 556-3134 (Dir); Internet Home Page Address: www.iwu.edu; Instr Connie Wells, MFA; Instr Therese O'Halloran, MFA; Instr Timothy Garvey PhD, MFA; Instr Kevin Strandberg, MFA; Instr Sherri McElroy, MS; Dir Miles Bair, MA
Estab 1855, school estab 1946; pvt; D; Scholarships; non-maj 150, maj 60
Ent Req: HS dipl, SAT or ACT
Degrees: BA, BFA
Courses: Art History, Ceramics, Drawing, Graphic Design, Painting, Photography, Printmaking, Sculpture

BOURBONNAIS

OLIVET NAZARENE UNIVERSITY, Dept of Art, 1 University Ave, Bourbonnais, IL 60915-2345. Tel 815-939-5229, 939-5172; Fax 815-939-5112; Elec Mail bgreiner@olivet.edu; Internet Home Page Address: www.olivet.edu; Prof & Chair William Greiner
Estab 1907, dept estab 1953; Maintain a nonprofit art gallery: Brandenburg Gallery, Larsen Fine Arts Bldg; FT 3, PT 3; den; D & E; Scholarships; SC 14, LC 4; D 100, non-maj 80, maj 21
Ent Req: HS dipl
Degrees: MBA, BS & BA 4 yrs, MEd & MTheol 2 yrs
Courses: †Art Education, Art History, †Ceramics, Drawing, Film, Graphic Arts, Graphic Design, Lettering, †Painting, Photography, Printmaking, Sculpture, Teacher Training, Textile Design

CANTON

SPOON RIVER COLLEGE, Art Dept, 23235 N County Hwy 22, Canton, IL 61520. Tel 309-647-4645; Fax 309-647-6498; Internet Home Page Address: www.src.edu; Instr Tracy Snowman; Dir Dr Sue Spencer
College maintains three campuses; Scholarships
Degrees: AA
Tuition: $42 per cr hr
Courses: Ceramics, Design, Drawing, Painting, Sculpture

CARBONDALE

SOUTHERN ILLINOIS UNIVERSITY, School of Art & Design, 1100 S Normal Ave, Mail Code 4301 Carbondale, IL 62901-4301. Tel 618-453-4315; Fax 618-453-7710; Internet Home Page Address: www.artanddesign.siuc.edu; Prof Harris Deller, MFA; Undergrad Acad Adv Valerie Brooks, MS Ed; Prof, Head Grad Studies & Studio Area Head Jerry Monteith, MFA; Asst Dir & Prof Kay M Zivkovich, MFA; Assoc Prof Erin Palmer, MFA; Prof & Studio Area Head Richard E Smith, MFA; Assoc Prof & Acad Area Head Carma Gorman PhD; Dir & Prof Peter Chametzky, PhD; Assoc Prof Jiyong Lee, MFA; Assoc Prof & Head Undergrad Studies Najjar Abdul-Musawwir, MFA; Prof & Design Area Head Steve Belletire, BFA; Prof Xuhong Shang, MFA; Asst Prof Pattie Chalmers, MFA; Assoc Prof Stacey Sloboda, PhD; Asst Prof Alex Lopez, MFA; Assoc Prof Sally Gradle, PhD; Coordr Visual Resources/Facilitator Web Enhanced Curriculum Eric Peterson, BA; Asst Prof Barbara Bickel, PhD; Asst Prof Sun Kyoung Kim, MFA; Asst Prof Robert A Lopez, MFA; Asst Prof Aaron Scott, MFA; Asst Prof Mark Pease, MFA
Estab 1874; Maintain nonprofit art library - School of Art & Design Surplus Gallery at the Glove Factory, 432 S Washington, SIUC, Carbondale, IL 62901, School of Art Design, Vergette Gallery, located on the first floor of the Allyn Bldg, in room 107; art supplies available on-campus; pub; D & E; Scholarships; SC 100, LC 24, GC 28; D 1304, E 338, non-maj 400, maj 400, grad 60, others 400

Ent Req: HS dipl, upper 50 percent of class, ACT
Degrees: BA, BFA 4 yrs, MFA 3 yrs
Tuition: Res—undergrad $4,740, grad $5,826, undergrad $260 per cr hr, grad $351 per cr hr; nonres—undergrad $9,416, grad $12,137 per sem, undergrad $650 per cr hr, grad $877 per cr hr; campus res—available
Courses: Advertising Design, Aesthetics, †Art Education, †Art History, Art for Elementary Education, †Blacksmithing, †Ceramics, Collage, Commercial Art, †Communication Design, Conceptual Art, Constructions, †Design, Drafting, †Drawing, †Foundry, †Glassblowing, Goldsmithing, Graphic Arts, †Graphic Design, †History of Art & Architecture, †Industrial Design, †Jewelry, Lettering, Mixed Media, Museum Staff Training, †Painting, †Printmaking, †Sculpture, Silversmithing, †Teacher Training, Web Design
Adult Hobby Classes: Drawing, Jewelry, Painting
Children's Classes: Enrl 150; tuition $30 per 4-6 wk term. Courses—Ceramics, Drawing, Fibers, Jewelry, Mask-Making, Painting, Papermaking, Printing, Sculpture, 3-D Design
Summer School: 500; tuition undergrad res $243 per hr, grad res $328 for term of 2-8 wks beginning May. Courses—selection from regular courses
—**Applied Arts,** 1365 Douglas Dr, Mail Code 6604 Carbondale, IL 62901-2583. Tel 618-453-8863; *Prog Rep* David White
Art Dept estab 1960; 5; pub; D; D 65, maj 65
Ent Req: HS dipl, ent exam
Degrees: AAS 2 yr, BS 4 yr
Tuition: Res—undergrad $75.00 per cr hr; nonres—undergrad $225.00 per cr hr
Courses: Air Brush & Photo Retouching, Drawing, Graphic Design

CARLINVILLE

BLACKBURN COLLEGE, Dept of Art, 700 College Ave, Carlinville, IL 62626-1401. Tel 217-854-3231, Ext 235; Fax 217-854-3713; Internet Home Page Address: www.blackburn.edu/; *Prof* James M Clark, MFA; *Chmn* Melba Buxbaum
Estab 1837; FT 2, PT 2; pvt; D & E; Scholarships; SC 14, LC 7; maj 15
Ent Req: HS grad
Degrees: BA 4 yrs
Courses: †Art History, Ceramics, Drawing, Painting, Printmaking, Sculpture, Studio Art, †Teacher Training, Theatre Arts

CHAMPAIGN

UNIVERSITY OF ILLINOIS, URBANA-CHAMPAIGN, College of Fine & Applied Arts, 608 E Lorado Taft Dr, 100 Architecture Bldg Champaign, IL 61820-6922. Tel 217-333-1660; Elec Mail FAA@illinois.edu; Internet Home Page Address: faa.illinois.edu; *Dean* Robert Graves, PhD; *Exec Asst Dean* Mary Ellen O'Shaughnessey; *Assoc Dean* Gaines Hall
Estab 1931; FT 268, PT 150; pub; D; Fellowships; undergrad 2000, grad 750
Ent Req: HS grad, ent exam
Degrees: bachelors 4 yrs, Masters, Doctorate
Adult Hobby Classes: Scheduled through University Extension
Children's Classes: Sat; summer youth classes
Summer School: courses offered
—**School of Art & Design,** 408 E Peabody Dr, 143 Art & Design Bldg Champaign, IL 61820-6924. Tel 217-333-0855; Fax 217-244-7688; Internet Home Page Address: www.art.illinois.edu; *Dir, Prof* Nan Goggin, MFA; *Exec Assoc Dir, Prof* Alan T Mette, MFA; *Assoc Dir, Prof* Joseph Squier, MFA; *Asst Dir Grad Studies, Assoc Prof* Conrad Bakker, MFA
Estab 1867, dept estab 1877; pub; D & E; Scholarships; SC 119, LC 72, GC 77; maj 521, grad 100, others 10
Ent Req: HS dipl, ACT, SAT, CLEP
Degrees: BFA 4 yrs, MA 2 yrs, MFA 2-3 yrs, EdD & PhD 5 yrs
Tuition: Res—undergrad $8542 per yr, $4271 per sem; res—grad $8358 per yr, $4179 per sem; nonres—undergrad $22,628 per yr, $11,314 per sem, nonres—grad $21,168 per yr, $10,584 per sem; campus res—room & board $7716 for double
Courses: Art Education, Art History, Drawing, Graphic Design, Industrial Design, Metals, Mixed Media, Painting, Photography, Printmaking, Sculpture, †Video
Adult Hobby Classes: Enrl 150; tuition varies. Courses—Art History, Art Education, Studio
Children's Classes: 220; tuition $75 per sem. Courses—Creative Arts for Children
Summer School: Courses—foundation & lower division courses with some limited offerings & independent study at upper division & graduate levels

CHARLESTON

EASTERN ILLINOIS UNIVERSITY, Art Dept, 600 Lincoln Ave Charleston, IL 61920. Tel 217-581-3410; Fax 217-581-6199; Elec Mail artdept@eiu.edu; Internet Home Page Address: www.eiu.edu/~artdept; *Dept Chmn* Glenn Hild, MFA; *Prof* Denise Rehm-Mott, MFA; *Prof* Charles Nivens, MFA; *Prof* Janet Marquardt-Cherry, PhD; *Prof* Mary Leonard-Cravens, MFA; *Prof* Jeff Boshart, MFA; *Prof* David Griffin, MFA; *Prof* Eugene Harrison; *Prof* Dwain Naragon, MFA; *Prof* Stephen Eskilson, PhD; *Prof* Patricia Belleville; *Prof* Chris Kahler, MFA; *Assoc Prof* Ke-Hsin Chi, MFA; *Assoc Prof* Ann Coddington Rast, MFA; *Assoc Prof* Robert Petersen, PhD; *Asst Prof* Dave Richardson, MFA; *Asst Prof* Mary Simpson, PhD
Estab 1895, dept estab 1930; Maintain nonprofit art gallery, Tarble Arts Center, 600 Lincoln Ave, Charleston, IL 61920; FT 18, PT 1; pub; D & E; Scholarships; SC 60, LC 27, GC 25; non-maj 724, maj 219, grad 11
Ent Req: HS dipl, ACT
Degrees: BA 4 yrs, MA 1 yr, Specialist Educ 2 yrs
Tuition: AY13 for IL & bordering state residents $279 per credit hr
Courses: Art Appreciation, †Art Education, Art History, Ceramics, Drawing, †Graphic Design, Jewelry, Painting, Printmaking, Sculpture, Studio Art

Summer School: Enrl 95; tuition 2 studios varies depending on faculty teaching; AY13 for IL & bordering state residents $279 per credit hr Courses—Same as regular session

CHICAGO

AMERICAN ACADEMY OF ART, 332 S Michigan Ave, Chicago, IL 60604-4434. Tel 312-461-0600; Fax 312-294-9570; Elec Mail info@aaart.edu; Internet Home Page Address: www.aaart.edu; *Dir Educ* Duncan J Webb; *Pres* Richard H Otto
Estab 1923; Maintain nonprofit gallery, Bill L Parks Gallery, on-site; Art & Architecture Library: Irving Shapiro Library, on-site; FT 17, PT 22; pvt; D & E; Scholarships; SC 13, LC; D 396, E 3, Maj 394, Grad 5
Ent Req: HS dipl, portfolio
Degrees: BFA
Courses: †3-D Animation, †Advertising Design, Art History, Commercial Art, Design, †Drawing, †Electronic Design, Graphic Arts, †Graphic Design, History of Art & Architecture, †Illustration, †Multimedia/Web Design, †Painting, †Photography, †Sculpture, †Video

CITY COLLEGES OF CHICAGO, Daley College, 7500 S Pulaski Rd, Art & Architecture Dept Chicago, IL 60652-1369. Tel 773-838-7721; Internet Home Page Address: www.cc.edu/daley/; *Prof* A Lerner; *Prof* T Palazzolo; *Prof* C Grenda; *Prof* M Rosen; *Chmn* David Riter
Estab 1960; 5500
Degrees: AA
Tuition: In-county res— $47.50 per cr hr; out-of-county res—$140.36 per cr hr; out-of-state res—$210.45 per cr hr
Courses: Architecture, Art Appreciation, Art History, Ceramics, Design, Drawing, Handicrafts, Painting, Photography, Weaving
—**Kennedy-King College,** 6800 S Wentworth Ave, Art & Humanities Dept Chicago, IL 60621-3733. Tel 773-291-6518; Internet Home Page Address: www.ccc.edu/kennedyking/; *Chmn* Dr Thomas Roby
Estab 1935; Enrl 9010
Degrees: AA, AS
Tuition: In-county res—$47.50 per cr hr; out-of-county res—$92.86 per cr hr; out-of-state res—$162.85 per cr hr
Courses: Art Appreciation, Ceramics, Humanities, Painting, Photography
—**Harold Washington College,** 30 E Lake St, Art & Humanities Dept, Rm 406 Chicago, IL 60601-2408. Tel 773-553-6065; 5600; Internet Home Page Address: www.ccc.edu/hwashington/; *Chmn Humanities* Paul Urbanick
Estab 1962; Enrl 8000
Degrees: AA, AS
Tuition: In-county res—$47.50 per cr hr; out-of-county res—$145.48 per cr hr; out-of-state res—$204.34 per cr hr
Courses: Art Appreciation, Ceramics, Commercial Art, Humanities, Painting, Photography, Printmaking, Sculpture
—**Malcolm X College,** 1900 W Van Buren St, Art and Humanities Dept Chicago, IL 60612-3145. Tel 312-850-7324; Fax 773-850-3323; Internet Home Page Address: www.cc.edu/malcolmx/; *Asst Prof* Barbara J Hogu; *Chmn Humanities* Mark Schwertley
Estab 1911; Enrl 5000
Degrees: AA
Tuition: In-county res—$47.50 per cr hr; out-of-county res—$92.86 per cr hr
Courses: Art Appreciation, Drawing, Freehand Drawing, Individual Projects
—**Olive-Harvey College,** 10001 S Woodlawn Ave, Art and Humanities Dept Chicago, IL 60628-1645. Tel 773-291-6530; 6534; Internet Home Page Address: www.ccc.edu/oliveharvey/acaddep/humani/index; *Chmn Humanities* Richard Reed
Estab 1957; Enrl 4700
Degrees: AA, Liberal Arts
Tuition: In-county res—$47.50 per cr hr; out-of-county res—$98.86 per cr hr; out-of-state res—$162.85 per cr hr
Courses: Art Appreciation, Arts & Crafts, Ceramics, Color Photography, Painting, Photography, Visual Arts Photography
—**Truman College,** 1145 W Wilson Ave, Art & Humanities Dept Chicago, IL 60640-6063. Tel 773-907-4062; Fax 773-907-4464; Internet Home Page Address: www.ccc.edu/truman; *Chmn Humanities* Dr Michael Swisher
Estab 1956; Enrl 3800
Degrees: AA, AAS
Tuition: In-county res—$47.50 per cr hr; out-of-county res—$92.86 per cr hr; out-of-state res—$162.85 per cr hr
Courses: Ceramics, Painting, Photography
—**Wright College,** 3400 N Austin Ave, Art Dept Chicago, IL 60634-4229. Tel 773-481-8365; Internet Home Page Address: www.ccc.edu/wright/; *Chmn* James Mack
Estab 1934; FT 3; pub; D & E; SC 15, LC 8; D 3000, E 2500
Ent Req: HS dipl
Degrees: AA, AS
Tuition: In-county res— $47.50 per cr hr; out-of-county res—$92.86 per cr hr; out-of-state res—$162.85 per cr hr
Courses: Arts & Crafts, Ceramics, Drawing, Lettering, Painting, Photography, Sculpture, Visual Arts
Adult Hobby Classes: Enrl 400; tuition $15 per course for 6 or 7 wks. Courses—Drawing, Fashion, Painting, Watercolor
Summer School: Dir, Roy LeFevour. Enrl 24; 8 wk session. Courses—Vary

COLUMBIA COLLEGE, Art Dept, 600 S Michigan Ave, Chicago, IL 60605-1900. Tel 312-663-1600; Fax 312-987-9893; *Coordr Graphics* Marlene Lipinski, MFA; *Architectural-Grad Studies & Coordr Interior Design* Joclyn Oats, BFA; *Coordr Fine Arts* Tom Taylor, BFA; *Coordr Illustration* Fred Nelson, BFA; *Coordr Fashion Design* Dennis Brozynski, BFA; *Coordr Pkg Designs* Kevin Henry, BFA
Estab 1893; pvt; D & E; Scholarships; SC 43, LC 17
Ent Req: HS dipl
Degrees: BA 4 yrs, MFA

Tuition: Res—undergrad $5800 per sem, $396 per cr hr; no campus res
Courses: Advertising Design, Architecture, Art Education, Art History, Calligraphy, Ceramics, Commercial Art, Drafting, Drawing, Fashion Arts, Film, Graphic Arts, Graphic Design, Handicrafts, Illustration, Industrial Design, Interior Design, Jewelry, Mixed Media, Painting, Printmaking, Sculpture, Silk Screen, Typography

DEPAUL UNIVERSITY, Dept of Art, 1150 W Fullerton Ave, College of Liberal Arts & Sciences Chicago, IL 60614-8160. Tel 312-362-8194; Fax 312-362-5684; Internet Home Page Address: www.depaul.edu; *Gallery Dir* Robert Tavani, MFA; *Prof* Robert Donley, MFA; *Assoc Prof* Simone Zurawski PhD, MFA; *Assoc Prof* Elizabeth Lillehoj PhD, MFA; *Assoc Prof* Bibiana Swarez, MFA; *Asst Prof* Jenny Morlan, MFA; *Asst Prof* Paul Jaskot PhD, MFA; *Asst Prof* Mark Pohlad PhD, MFA; *Chmn Dept* Stephen Luecking, MFA
Estab 1897, dept estab 1965; pvt; D; Scholarships; SC 20, LC 12; D 150 art maj
Ent Req: HS dipl, SAT or ACT
Degrees: BA(Art) 4 yrs
Tuition: All tuition fees are subject to change, contact admissions office for current fees; campus res available
Courses: †Advertising Design, Aesthetics, Architecture, Art Appreciation, †Art History, Ceramics, Computer Graphics, Design, †Drawing, Film, Graphic Arts, †Graphic Design, Illustration, Intermedia, Mixed Media, †Painting, †Photography, †Printmaking, †Sculpture, Studio Art, †Video
Summer School: Chmn, Stephen Luecking

HARRINGTON INSTITUTE OF INTERIOR DESIGN, 200 W Madison St, Harrington Coll Design Fl 2 Chicago, IL 60606-3433. Tel 312-939-4975; Fax 312-939-8005; Internet Home Page Address: www.interiordesign.edu; *Dept Chair* Crandon Gustafson
Estab 1931; pvt; D & E; Scholarships; D 220, E 209
Ent Req: HS dipl, interview
Degrees: AA & BA(interior design)
Courses: Interior Design
Adult Hobby Classes: Courses—Interior Design

THE ILLINOIS INSTITUTE OF ART - CHICAGO, 350 N Orleans St, Ste 136-L Chicago, IL 60654-1510. Tel 312-280-3500; Fax 312-280-8562; Internet Home Page Address: www.ilic.artinstitutes.edu; *Pres* John Jenkins; *Dir Admis* Janis K Anton; *Dean Acad Affairs* Sandra Graham; *Dir Financial Services* Robert Smetak; *Dean Student Affairs* Betty Kourasis; *Dir Housing* Valerie Rand; *Librn* Juliet S Teipel; *Registrar* Luciana Stabila
Estab 1916; Maintain art & architecture libr; pvt; D & E, yr-round; Scholarships; SC 7, LC, GC; 2170 total
Ent Req: HS dipl, portfolio review
Degrees: BA, AAS, BFA
Courses: Advertising, Culinary Arts, Culinary Management, Digital Filmmaking & Video Production, Fashion Design, Fashion Marketing & Management, Fashion Merchandising, Fashion Production, Game Art & Design, General Education, Graphic Design, Interactive Media Design, Interactive Media Production, Interior Design, Media Arts & Animation, Visual Communications, Visual Effects of Motion Graphics

ILLINOIS INSTITUTE OF TECHNOLOGY, College of Architecture, 3360 S State St, S R Crown Hall Chicago, IL 60616-3850. Tel 312-567-3262; Fax 312-567-8871; Elec Mail arch@iit.edu; Internet Home Page Address: www.arch.iit.edu; *Assoc Prof* Peter Beltemacchi; *Studio Dir* Dirk Denison; *Dean* Donna Robertson; *Assoc Prof* Paul Thomas; *Prof* Mahjoub Elnimeiri; *Prof* Peter Land; *Assoc Prof* David Hovey; *Assoc Prof* George Schipporeit; *Assoc Prof* David Sharpe; *Assoc Prof* Arthur Takeuchi; *Asst Dean Student Affairs* Dr Lee W Waldrep
Estab 1895 as Armour Institute, consolidated with Lewis Institute of Arts & Sciences 1940; FT 23; pvt; 345
Degrees: BA 5 yr, MA 3 yr
Tuition: $15,000 per yr
Courses: Architecture
Summer School: Term June 15 through August 8
—Institute of Design, 350 N La Salle St, 4th Fl Chicago, IL 60654. Tel 312-595-4900; Fax 312-595-4901; Elec Mail whitney@id.iit.edu; Internet Home Page Address: www.id.iit.edu/; *Dir* Patrick Whitney
Estab 1937; FT 10, PT 29; pvt; D; Scholarships; D 150
Degrees: BS 4 yr, MD, PhD(Design)
Tuition: Undergrad $9300per sem, grad $11,315 per sem
Courses: Industrial Design, Photography, Visual Communications

LOYOLA UNIVERSITY OF CHICAGO, Fine Arts Dept, 6525 N Sheridan Rd, Chicago, IL 60626-5761. Tel 773-508-2820; Fax 773-508-2282; Internet Home Page Address: www.luc.edu; *Prof Emeritus* Ralph Arnold, MFA; *Prof Emeritus* Juliet Rago, MFA; *Assoc Prof* James Jensen, MFA; *Assoc Prof* Judith Dewell PhD, MFA; *Assoc Prof* Marilyn Dunn PhD, MFA; *Assoc Prof* Brian Fiorentino, MFA; *Assoc Prof* Patricia Hernes, MFA; *Assoc Prof* Eliza Kenney, MM; *Assoc Prof* Frank Voduarka, MFA; *Assoc Prof* Paula Wisotzki PhD, MFA; *Assoc Prof* Dorothy Dwight, MM; *Assoc Prof* Michel Balasis, MFA; *Assoc Prof* Nicole Ferentz, MFA; *Chmn Fine Arts Dept* Eugene Geimzer, MFA
Estab 1870, dept estab 1970; PT 25; den; D & E; Scholarships; SC 25, LC 17
Degrees: BA 4 yr
Courses: Advertising Design, Aesthetics, Art Appreciation, †Art History, †Ceramics, Commercial Art, Computer Graphics, †Design, †Drawing, Graphic Design, History of Art & Architecture, Jewelry, †Painting, †Photography, †Printmaking, Sculpture, †Visual Communications
Summer School: Dir, Dr Mark Wolff. Courses—Art Appreciation, Art History, Ceramics, Drawing, Painting, Photography

NORTH PARK UNIVERSITY, (North Park College) Art Dept, 3225 W Foster Ave, Campus Box 21 Chicago, IL 60625-4823. Tel 773-244-5637, 6200; Fax 773-583-0858; Elec Mail nmurray@northpark.edu; Internet Home Page Address: www.northpark.edu; *Chmn Dept* Neale Murray, MA; *Asst Prof* Kelly Vanderbrug; *Asst Prof* David Johanson

Estab 1957; PT2; den; D & E; Scholarships; SC 18, LC 5; D 40
Ent Req: HS dipl
Degrees: BA 4 yrs
Courses: Advertising Design, Aesthetics, Art Education, Art History, Calligraphy, Ceramics, Commercial Art, Drawing, Illustration, Painting, Photography, Printmaking, Sculpture, Teacher Training
Summer School: Enrl 25. Courses—Ceramics, Drawing, Painting, Sculpture

NORTHEASTERN ILLINOIS UNIVERSITY, Art Dept, 5500 N St Louis, Chicago, IL 60625. Tel 773-442-4910; Fax 773-442-4920; Internet Home Page Address: www.neiu.edu; *Chmn* Mark P McKernin
Estab 1969; Maintain nonprofit art gallery, Fine Arts Gallery, 550 N St Louis Ave, Chicago, IL 60625; Pub; D & E; Scholarships; SC 44, LC 22; total 10,200, maj 175, grad 1,583, others 798
Ent Req: HS dipl, GED, upper half high school class or higher ACT
Degrees: BA 4 yrs
Courses: Art Education, Art History, Ceramics, Commercial Art, Computer Graphics, Drawing, Graphic Arts, Jewelry, Painting, Photography, Printmaking, Sculpture

SAINT XAVIER UNIVERSITY, Dept of Art & Design, 3700 W 103rd St, Chicago, IL 60655-3199. Tel 773-779-3300; Fax 773-779-9061; Internet Home Page Address: www.sxu.edu; *Assoc Prof* Mary Ann Bergfeld, MFA; *Assoc Prof* Brent Wall, MFA; *Assoc Prof* Michael Rabe PhD, MFA; *Assoc Prof* Cathie Ruggie Saunders, MFA; *Assoc Prof* Monte Gerlach, MS; *Chmn* Jayne Hileman, MFA; *Instr* Nathan Peck
Estab 1847, dept estab 1917; Nonprofit gallery - Gallery/Art & Design, Saint Xavier Un, 3700 W 103rd St, Chicago, Il 60655; FT6; pvt; D & E; Scholarships; SC 35, LC 15; D 50, E 5, maj 75, others 250
Ent Req: HS dipl
Degrees: BA & BS 4 yrs
Courses: Art Business, Art Education, Art History, Ceramics, †Collage, Drawing, Film, Graphic Design, †History of Art & Architecture, Illustration, Painting, Photography, Printmaking, Sculpture, Teacher Training, Video
Adult Hobby Classes: Enrl 15-20; tuition $20-$40 per course. Courses—Drawing, Calligraphy, Painting, Photography
Summer School: Dir, Richard Venneri. Courses—Various studio courses

SCHOOL OF THE ART INSTITUTE OF CHICAGO, 112 S Michigan Ave, Chicago, IL 60603-6105. Tel 312-629-6100; Fax 312-629-6101; Internet Home Page Address: www.artic.edu; *Chmn Arts Admin* Nicholas Lowe; *Chmn Architecture - Interior Architecture & Designed Objects* Andy Hall; *Chmn Art Education* Drea Howenstein; *Chmn Art History, Theory & Criticism* David Raskin; *Chmn Ceramics* Xavier Toubes; *Chmn Fashion Design* Nick Cave; *Chmn Film, Video, New Media & Animation* Gregg Bordowitz; *Chmn Liberal Arts* Paul Ashley; *Chmn Painting & Drawing* Michelle Grabner; *Chmn Printmedia* Peter Power; *Chmn Sculpture* A Laurie Palmer; *Pres* Walter Massey
Estab 1866; FT 80, PT 160; pvt; D 1600; E 600; Scholarships; SC 280, LC 90, GC 50; maj 1400, non-maj 800
Income: $31,558,200
Purchases: $30,211,300
Ent Req: portfolio; recommendations
Degrees: BFA 4 yrs, MFA 2 yrs, Grad Cert(Art History) 1 yr, MA(Art Therapy) 1 yr, MA(Modern Art History, Theory & Criticism) 2 yr
Tuition: BFA $9600 per term, $604 per cr hr; MFA $9900 per term, $666 per cr hr
Courses: †Art Education, †Art History, Art Therapy, Book Arts, †Ceramics, †Drawing, †Fashion Arts, †Fiber, †Film, †Graphic Arts, Interior Architecture, †Painting, †Performance, †Photography, †Printmaking, †Sculpture, †Sound, †Textile Design, †Video, †Visual Communications, †Weaving
Adult Hobby Classes: Tuition $360 non cr course, $669 1 1/2 cr course. Courses—Varies, see summer session
Children's Classes: Tuition $240 non cr course. Courses—Drawing, Exploring the Arts Workshop, Multi-Media, Open Studio
Summer School: Dir, E W Ross. Enrl 200 (degree), 121 (non-degree); tuition undergrad $1338 per 3 cr hr for 4 & 8 wk term, grad $1455 for 8 wk seminar & courses. Courses—Art Education & Therapy, Art & Technique, Art History, Ceramics, Drawing, Fashion Design, Fiber, Filmmaking, Interior Architecture, Painting, Performance, Photo, Printmaking, Theory & Criticism, Sculpture, Sound, Video & Visual Communications

UNIVERSITY OF CHICAGO, Dept of Art History, 5540 S Greenwood, Chicago, IL 60637. Tel 773-702-0278; Fax 773-702-5901; Elec Mail arthistory@uchicago.edu; Internet Home Page Address: arthistory.uchicago.edu; *Chair* Christine Mehnng; *Dir Grad Studies* Aden Kumle
Estab 1892; Maintains Visual Resource Center; five yr duration fels open to all; art supplies sold at on-campus store; pvt; D; SC, LC and GC vary
Ent Req: Through Humanities Div of students office
Degrees: BA 4 yrs, PhD
Courses: Art History

UNIVERSITY OF ILLINOIS AT CHICAGO, College of Architecture, 929 W Harrison St, M/C 030, Rm 3100, Jefferson Hall Chicago, IL 60607-7076. Tel 312-996-3351, Art & Design 996-3337; Fax 312-996-5378; Internet Home Page Address: http://adweb.aa.uic.edu; *Dir School Archit* Katerina Ruedi; *Chmn Dept Art & Art History* David Sokol; *Dean* Judith Russi Kirshner
Estab 1946; FT 80, PT 28; pub; D; Scholarships; SC 79, LC 10, GC 3; D 579, non-maj 325, maj 579, grad 17
Ent Req: 3 units of English plus 13 additional units, rank in top one-half of HS class for beginning freshman, transfer students 3.25 GPA
Degrees: BA(Design), BA(Studio Arts), BA(Art Educ), BA(History of Archit & Art), BA(Music), BA(Theatre), BArchit, MFA(Studio Art or Design), MArch, MA(Theatre)
Courses: †Architecture, †Art Education, †Art History, Ceramics, †Communications Design, †Comprehensive Design, Drawing, †Film, †Industrial Design, †Painting, †Photography, †Printmaking, †Sculpture, †Studio Arts, †Urban Planning & Policy, †Video

Children's Classes: Enrl 50; tuition $5. Courses—Saturday school in connection with art education classes
Summer School: Dir, Morris Barazani. Tuition res undergrad $229, nonres undergrad $547 for term of 8 wks beginning June

UNIVERSITY OF ILLINOIS AT CHICAGO, Biomedical Visualization, 1919 W Taylor St, Rm 211, College of Health & Human Development Science Chicago, IL 60612-7246. Tel 312-996-7337; Elec Mail sbarrows@uic.edu; Internet Home Page Address: www.sbhis.uic.edu; *Clinical Asst Prof* Raymond Evenhouse; *Res Asst Prof* Mary Rasmussen; *Clinical Asst Prof* John Daugherty; *Prog Coordr* Scott Barrows CMI, FAMI; *Clin Asst Prof* Gregory Blew
Estab 1923; pub; D; Scholarships; SC, LC. GC; D 24, grad 24
Ent Req: Bachelors degree
Degrees: Master of Assoc Medical Sciences in Biomedical Visualization
Courses: 3-D Modeling, †Advertising Design, Computer Animation, †Conceptual Art, Design, Drawing, Graphic Design, Illustration, Instructional, Multimedia, Prosthetics, Sculpture, Surgical Illustration

CHICAGO HEIGHTS

PRAIRIE STATE COLLEGE, Art Dept, 202 S Halsted, Chicago Heights, IL 60411. Tel 708-709-3500, 709-3671; Fax 708-755-2587; Internet Home Page Address: www.prairie.cc.il.us; *Dept Chmn* Don Kouba
Estab 1958; FT 4, PT 30; pub; D & E; SC 24, LC 6; dept 600, maj 200
Ent Req: HS dipl, ACT
Degrees: AAF 2 yrs Cert 1 yr
Courses: Advertising Design, Airbrush, Art Appreciation, Art Education, Commercial Art, Computer Graphics, Design, †Drawing, †Graphic Design, Illustration, †Interior Design, Jewelry, Life Drawing, Materials Workshop, Package Design, Painting, †Photography, Production Processes, Sign Painting, Stained Glass, Typography, Video Graphics
Summer School: Dir, John Bowman. Tuition $48 per cr hr for term of 8 wks. Courses—Art History, Drawing, Graphic Design, Interior Design, Painting, Photography

DEKALB

NORTHERN ILLINOIS UNIVERSITY, School of Art, 1425 W Lincoln Hwy, DeKalb, IL 60115-2828. Tel 815-753-1473; Fax 815-753-7701; Elec Mail bbradford2@niv.edu; Internet Home Page Address: www.art.niv.edu; *Dir School of Art* Douglas Boughton, PhD; *Asst Dir* Lee Sido, MFA; *Grad Coordr* Michael Barnes, MFA; *Div Head FA Studio* Billie Giese, MFA; *Div Head Art History* Rebecca Houze PhD; *Div Head Art Educ* Kerry Freedman PhD; *Div Head Design* Kurt Schultz, MFA; *Foundations Coordr* Cynthia Hellyer-Heinz, MFA; *Recruiter* Blaine Bradford, MFA
Estab 1895; Maintain nonprofit art gallery; Jack Olson Memorial Gallery, Rm 200, School of Art; Pub; D & E; Scholarships, Fellowships; SC 127, LC 59, GC 98, other 15; D 2,200, maj 750, grad 130
Ent Req: HS dipl, ACT, SAT
Degrees: BA, BFA, BSEd 4 yrs, MA, MS 2 yrs, MFA 3 yrs, Phd 3 yrs
Tuition: Res—$8,893 per yr; nonres—$17,760 per yr; campus res available
Courses: Advertising Design, Art Appreciation, †Art Education - includes initial cert, †Art History, †Ceramics, †Computer Graphics/Design, †Drawing, Goldsmithing, †Graphic Design, History of Art & Architecture, †Illustration, †Intermedia, †Jewelry/Metalwork, Mixed Media, Museum Staff Training, †Painting, †Photography, †Printmaking, †Sculpture, Silversmithing, Teacher Training, Textile Design, Video, †Visual Communications, Weaving, Web Page Design
Summer School: Dir, Douglas Boughton, PhD. Tuition res—$115.48 per cr hr, nonres—$288.78 per cr hr. Courses—Vary

DECATUR

MILLIKIN UNIVERSITY, Art Dept, 1184 W Main St, Decatur, IL 62522-2084. Tel 217-424-6227; Fax 217-424-3993; Elec Mail webmaster@mail.millikin.edu; Internet Home Page Address: www.millikin.edu; *Chmn Art Dept* Edwin G Walker, MFA
Estab 1901, dept estab 1904; Maintain nonprofit art gallery; Perkinson Gallery, 1184 W Main St, Decatur IL 62522; FT 5, PT 4; pvt; D & E; Scholarships; SC 47, LC 3; D 1,700, non-maj 25, maj 110
Ent Req: HS dipl, ACT
Degrees: BA & BFA 4 yrs
Courses: Art Education, Art History, Ceramics, Commercial Art, Computer Graphics, Design, Graphic Arts, Graphic Design, Illustration, Painting, Photography, Printmaking, Sculpture, Teacher Training
Summer School: Dean of Arts & Sciences. Enrl 400; tuition $225 per cr hr for 7 wk term beginning June 13. Courses—Ceramics, Drawing, Painting, Photography

DES PLAINES

OAKTON COMMUNITY COLLEGE, Language Humanities & Art Divisions, 1600 E Golf Rd, Des Plaines, IL 60016-1256. Tel 847-635-1600; Fax 847-376-7094; Elec Mail jkrauss@oakton.edu; *Chmn & Prof* James A Krauss, MA; *Assoc Prof* Peter Hessemer, MFA; *Assoc Prof* Bernard K Krule, MS; *Asst Prof* Mark Palmeri, MFA; *Cur Gallery* Nathan Harpaz; *Asst Prof* Judy Langston; *Asst Prof* Kathryn Howard-Rogers
Estab 1970; Maintain nonprofit art gallery; Koehnline Art Gallery 1600 E Golf Rd, Des Plaines IL 60016; libr resources available as part of general college libr; art supplies sold at on-campus store; Pub; D & E, Weekends; Scholarships; SC 9, LC 4; Enrl 1,000
Degrees: AA, AFA

Courses: Architecture, Art Appreciation, Art History, Ceramics, Design, Drawing, Graphic Arts, Graphic Design, History of Art & Architecture, Museum Staff Training, Painting, Photography, Printmaking, Sculpture
Summer School: Dir, Prof Art James A Krauss. Enrl 90; tuition $91 cr for 8 wk term. Courses—Design I, Photography, Ceramics, Field Study, Painting, Drawing

EAST PEORIA

ILLINOIS CENTRAL COLLEGE, Arts & Communication Dept, One College Dr, East Peoria, IL 61635. Tel 309-694-5113; Fax 309-694-8095; Internet Home Page Address: www.icc.edu; *Assoc Dean* Chris Gray, MA; *Prof, Dept Chair & Cur* Jennifer Costa, MFA; *Prof* John Tuccillo, MFA; *Prof* Janet Newton, MFA; *Prof* Roger Bean, MA; *Assoc Prof* Eli Davis, MFA; *Assoc Prof* David Smit, BFA; *Asst Prof* Anita Tuccillo, MFA; *Asst Prof* Megan Foster-Campbell, PhD; *Asst Prof* Anastasia Samoylova, MFA
Estab 1967, dept estab 1967; Maintains nonprofit art gallery, Performing Art Center Gallery 305A; art supplies available on-campus; pub; D & E; SC 27, LC 3; D 1,000, E 500, maj 322
Ent Req: HS dipl
Degrees: Assoc(Arts & Sciences) 2 yrs, Assoc(Applied Science)
Tuition: $93 per sem hr; no campus res
Courses: Advertising Design, †Architecture, Art Education, Art History, Ceramics, Color, Commercial Art, Design, Drawing, Graphic Design, Illustration, Interior Design, Painting, Photography, Printmaking, Sculpture, Typography
Adult Hobby Classes: Tuition $75 per cr hr. Courses—Drawing, Painting, Ceramics
Summer School: See website

EDWARDSVILLE

SOUTHERN ILLINOIS UNIVERSITY AT EDWARDSVILLE, Dept of Art & Design, PO Box 1608, Edwardsville, IL 62026-0001. Tel 618-650-5044; Fax 618-650-5050; Elec Mail igausep@siue.edu; Internet Home Page Address: www.siue.edu/ART/; *Chmn Dept* Ivy Schroeder, PhD; *Head Art History* Pamela Decoteau; *Head Printmaking* Robert R Malone, MFA; *Head Drawing* Dennis L Ringering, MFA; *Head Fiber & Fabric* Laura Strand, MFA; *Head Ceramic* Daniel J Anderson, MFA; *Art Educ* Joseph A Weber PhD, MFA; *Photog & Graphic Design* Steven Brown, MFA; *Head Painting* Jane Barrow, MFA; *Head Sculpture* Thomas D Gipe, MFA
Estab 1869, dept estab 1959; pub; D & E; Scholarships; SC 65, LC 26, GC 45; D 250, E 75, maj 200, grad 50
Ent Req: HS dipl, ACT, portfolio req for BFA & MFA
Degrees: BA, BS & BFA 4 yrs NFA 3 yrs, MS 2 yrs
Courses: Aesthetics, †Art Education, Art History, †Ceramics, †Drawing, †Graphic Design, History of Art & Architecture, Jewelry, Metalsmithing, Mixed Media, †Painting, Photography, †Printmaking, †Sculpture, †Teacher Training, Textile Arts
Children's Classes: Enrl 250; Summer classes. Courses—Ceramics, Drawing, Painting, Photography
Summer School: Chmn, Joe Weber. Courses—Ceramics, Drawing, Painting, Photography

ELGIN

ELGIN COMMUNITY COLLEGE, Fine Arts Dept, 1700 Spartan Dr, Elgin, IL 60123-7193. Tel 847-697-1000; *Instr* Roger Gustafson; *Instr* John Grady; *Instr* Howard Russo; *Dean* Dr David Broad
Scholarships
Degrees: AA
Tuition: In district—$52.50 per cr hr; res—$230.26 per cr hr; nonres—$278.70 per cr hr
Courses: Art Appreciation, Art History, Ceramics, Design, Drawing, Jewelry, Painting, Photography, Printmaking, Sculpture

JUDSON UNIVERSITY, School of Art, Design & Architecture, 1151 N State St, Elgin, IL 60123-1498. Tel 847-628-2500, Ext 1030; Fax 847-628-1029; Internet Home Page Address: www.judsonu.edu; *Chmn Dept Art & Design* GE Colpitts; *Interim Chmn Dept Architecture* Stacie Burtleson; *Gallery Dir* Jeff Carl; *Asst Prof* Joseph Cory; *Asst Prof* Melanie Gibb; *Grad Coordr* Royce Earnest; *Dean Dr* Curtis Sartor; *Prof* Jhennifer A Amundson; *Asst Prof* David M Ogoli; *Assoc Prof Dr* Chris Miller; *Instr* Peter Sheesley; *Instr* Sarah Baranski; *Instr* David Amundson; *Instr* August Demel; *Instr* Craig Farnsworth; *Instr* Tom Joeger; *Instr* Robert Johnson; *Instr* Mark Taxgenson; *Instr* Jeremy Lindsey; *Instr* John Hriunak; *Instr* Ian Hukman; *Instr* Mark Van Donand; *Instr* Tony Yeboah; *Instr* Sean Gallagher
Maintains nonprofit gallery, Draewell Gallery Fine Arts Building Jackson College 1051 N State St, Elgin, IL 60123; maintains nonprofit library. On-campus shop sells art supplies; Pvt; D, E; Scholarships; SC 15, LC 10, GC 10 (Arch only); D 738, E 376, M 231 (incl arch), GS 63, O 59
Ent Req: HS dipl, ACT, or SAT
Degrees: BA 4 yrs, MArch 6 yrs
Courses: †Architecture, Art Appreciation, Art Education, Ceramics, Design, Design History, Drawing, †Fine Arts, Graphic Arts, Graphic Design, History of Art & Architecture, Mixed Media, Painting, Photography, Printmaking, Sculpture, †Teacher Training, †Visual Communications

ELMHURST

ELMHURST COLLEGE, Art Dept, 190 Prospect, Elmhurst, IL 60126. Tel 630-617-3542; Fax 630-279-4100; Internet Home Page Address: www.elmhurst.edu; *Chmn* Richard Paulsen, MFA; *Prof* John Weber, MFA; *Asst Prof* Lynn Hill, MFA; *Asst Prof* Mary Lou Stewart, MFA
Estab 1871; Pvt; D & E; Scholarships; SC 13, LC 8; D 1927, E 1500, maj 33
Ent Req: HS dipl, ACT or SAT

Degrees: BS, BA & BM 4 yrs
Courses: †Art Business, †Art Education, Design, †Electronic Imaging, †Painting, †Photography, †Printmaking, †Sculpture
Summer School: Dir, Dr Marie Baehr. Enrl 1379; tuition $375 per cr hr for courses of 4, 6 & 8 wks. Courses in selected programs

EVANSTON

NORTHWESTERN UNIVERSITY, EVANSTON, Dept of Art Theory & Practice, 1859 Sheridan Rd, Rm 244, Evanston, IL 60208-2207. Tel 847-491-7346; Fax 847-467-1487; Elec Mail art-theory@northwestern.edu; Internet Home Page Address: www.art.northwestern.edu; *Prof* William Conger; *Prof* Ed Paschke; *Prof* James Valerio; *Assoc Prof* Judy Ledgerwood; *Lectr* James Yood; *Lectr* Charlie Cho; *Assoc Prof* Jeanne Dunning; *Asst Prof* Lane Relyea; *Lectr* William Cass; *Lectr* Dan Devening; *Lectr* Pamela Bannos
Estab 1851; FT 11, PT 3; pvt; D & E; Scholarships, Fellowships; SC 40, LC 6, GC 6, seminars; D 800, E 40, non-maj 750, maj 50, grad 12
Ent Req: requirements set by university admissions; for MFA prog a distinctive record and portfolio is required
Degrees: AB 4 yrs, MFA 2+
Tuition: $27,000
Courses: Conceptual Art, Drawing, †Painting, Photography, †Practice of Art, †Printmaking, Sculpture
Summer School: Courses—Introductory
—Dept of Art History, 1880 Campus Dr, 3-400 Kresge Hall Evanston, IL 60208-0888. Tel 847-491-7077; Fax 847-467-1035; Elec Mail art-history@northwestern.edu; Internet Home Page Address: www.arthistory.northwestern.edu; *Prof* Stephen Eisenman, PhD; *Prof* Hollis Clayson, PhD; *Chmn, Assoc Prof* Claudia Swan, PhD; *Prof* David Van Zanten, PhD; *Chmn & Assoc Prof* Sarah E Fraser, PhD; *Assoc Prof* Huey Copeland, PhD; *Asst Prof* Hannah Feldman, PhD; *Asst Prof* Cecily J Hilsdale, PhD; *Assoc Prof* Christina Kiaer, PhD; *Asst Prof* Krista Thompson, PhD; *Adjunct Prof* Hamid Naficy, PhD; *Adjunct Prof* Marco Ruffini, PhD; *Adjunct Prof* James Cuno, PhD; *Adjunct Prof* Bernadette Fort, PhD; *Assoc Prof* Jesus Escobar; *Lectr* Christine Bell
Estab 1851; Maintains art library, Derring Library, Northwester U, Evanston Il, 60208; pvt; D & E; Scholarships; LC 36, GC 15; maj 60, grad 40
Ent Req: HS dipl, SAT or ACT
Degrees: PhD, MA, BA
Tuition: $5,468 per qtr
Courses: 20th Century Art, Architecture, Architecture of Ancient Rome, †Art History, †Handicrafts, History of Art & Architecture, Introduction to African Art, Medieval Art, Renaissance Art
Summer School: Courses—vary in Art History

FREEPORT

HIGHLAND COMMUNITY COLLEGE, Art Dept, 2998 W Pearl City Rd, Freeport, IL 61032-9341. Tel 815-235-6121; Fax 815-235-6130; Internet Home Page Address: www.highland.cc.il.us; *Dir* Thomas Brandt
Estab 1962; FT 1, PT 5; pub; D & E; Scholarships; SC 6, LC 1; 126
Ent Req: HS dipl, ent exam
Degrees: AS, AA, ABA, AAS 2 yrs
Courses: Art History, Art Materials & Processes, Design, Drawing, Fabrics, Graphic Design, History of Modern Art, Introduction to Art, Metals & Jewelry, Painting, Pottery, Printmaking, Sculpture
Adult Hobby Classes: Enrl 278. Courses—Basic Drawing, Oil, Charcoal, Printmaking, Sculpture, Pottery, Handweaving & Related Crafts, Rosemaking, Macrame, Needlepoint
Children's Classes: Occasional summer workshops for high school and elementary school students
Summer School: Courses same as above

GALESBURG

CARL SANDBURG COLLEGE, 2400 Tom L Wilson Blvd, Galesburg, IL 61401. Tel 309-344-2518; Fax 309-341-5471; Elec Mail lmohr@sandburg.edu; Internet Home Page Address: www.sandburg.edu; *Art Coordr & Instr* Lisa Mohr
Maintains nonprofit art gallery
Courses: Art Appreciation, Art History, Ceramics, Drawing, Graphic Design, Painting, Photography, Printmaking, Theatre Arts

KNOX COLLEGE, Dept of Art, 2 E South St, Galesburg, IL 61401-4999. Tel 309-341-7000, 341-7423 (Art Dept Chmn); *Asst Prof* Lynette Lombard; *Chmn* Frederick Ortner
Scholarships
Degrees: BA 4yrs
Tuition: $28,230 per yr, room & board $5630 per yr
Courses: Art History, Ceramics, Design, Drawing, History of Art & Architecture, Painting, Photography, Printmaking, Sculpture

GODFREY

LEWIS & CLARK COMMUNITY COLLEGE, Art Dept, 5800 Godfrey Rd, Godfrey, IL 62035-2466. Tel 618-466-3411, Ext 279; *Assoc Dean* Dr Linda Chapman
Estab 1970, formerly Monticello College; FT 2, PT 3; pub; D & E; Scholarships; SC 13, LC 2; D 1800, E 600, maj 40
Ent Req: HS dipl, ent exam, open door policy
Degrees: AA 2 yrs
Courses: Advanced Drawing, Art History, Basic Design, Ceramics, Drawing, Fibers, Painting, Printmaking, Sculpture, Weaving
Adult Hobby Classes: Enrl 30; tuition variable. Courses—Antiques, Interior

Design, Introduction to Drawing & Painting
Summer School: Enrl 15; tuition $17 per sem hr for 8 wks.
Courses—Introduction to Visual Arts

GRAYSLAKE

COLLEGE OF LAKE COUNTY, Art Dept, 19351 W Washington St, Grayslake, IL 60030-1198. Tel 847-543-2040; Fax 847-543-3040; Internet Home Page Address: www.clcillinois.edu; *VPres Educ Affairs* Rich Haney; *Ceramics* David Bolton; *Photog* Roland Miller; *Computer Art* Terry Dixon; *Drawing & Design* Hans Habeger; *Painting & Watercolor* Robert Lossmann
Estab 1969, dept estab 1969; Maintains nonprofit art gallery, Robert T. Wright Community Gallery of Art, 19351 W Washington St, Grayslake, IL, 60030; pub; D & E; SC 22, LC 5; D 250, E 250, non-maj 500, maj 100
Ent Req: HS dipl, SAT, GED
Degrees: AA & AS 2 yrs
Courses: 2-D & 3-D Design, Art Appreciation, Art Education, Art History, Ceramics, Drawing, Graphic Arts, Graphic Design, Jewelry, Mixed Media, Painting, Photography, Sculpture, Watercolor
Adult Hobby Classes: Advertising, Ceramics, Drawing, Lettering, Mixed Media, Portrait, Stained Glass
Summer School: Courses—same as above

GREENVILLE

GREENVILLE COLLEGE, Art Dept, 315 E College Ave, Dept of Art Greenville, IL 62246-1145. Tel 618-664-2800, 664-7119; Fax 618-664-1373; Elec Mail steve.heilmer@greenville.edu; Internet Home Page Address: www.greenville.edu/academics/departments/art; *Dept Head* Steve Heilmer, MFA; *Asst Prof* Jacob Amundson; *Asst Prof* Jessa Wilcoxen; *Dir* Dr Sharon Grimes
Estab 1892, dept estab 1965; Maintains a nonprofit art gallery - Rowland Art Gallery, Maves Art Center; John Hubbell, Adj; pvt; D & E; Scholarships; SC 20, LC 6; D 135, non-maj 105, maj 30
Activities: Schols offered
Ent Req: HS dipl
Degrees: BA 4 yrs, BS 4 1/2 yrs
Tuition: $15,000per yr; campus—room & board $7,000 per yr
Courses: Advertising Design, Art Education, Art History, †Ceramics, Design, Digital Media, †Drawing, Film, †Graphic Design, Handicrafts, †Graphic Design, History of Art & Architecture, Mixed Media, †Painting, Photography, †Sculpture, †Teacher Training, Video
Summer School: Intro to Fine Arts - Dr. Sharon Grimes, Dir

JACKSONVILLE

MACMURRAY COLLEGE, Art Dept, 447 E College Ave, Jacksonville, IL 62650-2590. Tel 217-479-7000; Fax 217-479-7086; Internet Home Page Address: www.mac.edu; *Chmn Art Dept* Raymond Yeager
Estab 1846; den; Scholarships; SC 29, LC 6
Degrees: BA 4 yr
Courses: Advertising Design, Ceramics, Drawing, Painting, Photography, Sculpture, Teacher Training

JOLIET

JOLIET JUNIOR COLLEGE, Fine Arts Dept, 1215 Houbolt Rd, Joliet, IL 60431-8800. Tel 815-729-9020, Ext 2232; Fax 815-744-5507; Internet Home Page Address: www.jjc.cc.il.us; *Chmn Dept* Jerry Lewis, MM; *Instr* James Dugdale, MA; *Instr* Joe Milosevich, MFA; *Instr* Steve Sherrell, MFA
Estab 1901, dept estab 1920; pub; D & E; Scholarships; SC 15, LC 4; D 10,000, maj 120
Ent Req: HS dipl, ent exam
Degrees: AA 2 yrs
Courses: 2-D & 3-D Design, Art Appreciation, Art History, Ceramics, Drawing, Graphic Arts, Interior Design, Jewelry, Painting, Silversmithing, Weaving
Summer School: Dir, Jerry Lewis, MM. Courses—Same as winter school

UNIVERSITY OF SAINT FRANCIS, (College of Saint Francis) Fine Arts Dept, 500 N Wilcox St, Division of Humanities & Fine Arts Joliet. IL 60435-6169. Tel 815-740-3360; Fax 815-740-4285; Internet Home Page Address: www.stfrancis.edu; *Dept Head* Dr Patrick Brannon
Estab 1950; Maintain nonprofit art gallery; Moser Performing Arts Gallery Center; Pvt; D & E; SC 6, LC 3; D 150, maj 25
Ent Req: HS grad, ent exam
Degrees: BA(Creative Arts with Art Specialization or Art Educ)
Courses: Advanced Drawing & Painting, Applied Studio, Basic Design, Ceramics, Fabrics, Photography, Silversmithing, Special Topics, Textiles
Children's Classes: Courses—Art in variety of media
Summer School: Term of 6 wks beginning June

LAKE FOREST

LAKE FOREST COLLEGE, Dept of Art, 555 N Sheridan Rd, Lake Forest, IL 60045-2399. Tel 847-234-3100; Fax 847-735-6291; Internet Home Page Address: www.lfc.edu; *Lectr* Mary Lawton PhD; *Chmn* Anne Roberts
Estab 1857; pvt; D & E; Scholarships; SC 8, LC 21; D 1050 (sch total), maj 38
Ent Req: HS dipl, SAT, CEEB or ACT
Degrees: BA 4 yrs
Courses: Aesthetics, Architecture, Art Appreciation, Art Education, Art History, Computer Assisted Design, Drawing, Film, Graphic Design, History of Art & Architecture, Painting, Photography

Adult Hobby Classes: Enrl 5-15. Courses—Photography
Summer School: Dir, Arthur Zilversmit. Enrl 200; tuition $990 per 4 sem hrs for 7 wks. Courses—Photography

LINCOLN

LINCOLN COLLEGE, Art Dept, 300 Keokuk St, Lincoln, IL 62656-1699. Tel 217-732-3155; Fax 217-732-8859; Internet Home Page Address: www.lincolncollege.com; *Assoc Prof* Bob Stefl; *Chmn* E J Miley; *Instr Painting & Design* Karen Miley
Estab 1865; pvt; D & E; Scholarships; SC 35, LC 5; maj 200
Ent Req: HS dipl
Degrees: AA
Courses: Art Appreciation, Art History, Ceramics, Design, Drawing, Graphic Design, Illustration, Mixed Media, Painting, Photography, Stage Design, Theatre Arts
Children's Classes: Courses offered through summer
Summer School: Dir, EJ Miley Jr. Courses—Art of France & Italy

LISLE

ILLINOIS BENEDICTINE UNIVERSITY, Department of Fine Arts, 5700 College Rd, Scholl #105 Lisle, IL 60532-2851. Tel 630-829-6320; Fax 630-960-4805; Elec Mail pseely@ben.edu; Internet Home Page Address: www.ben.edu/finearts; *Chair* Peter Seely, MA; *Cur* Teresa J Parker; *Prof* William Scarlato; *Instr* Jennifer Scavone; *Instr* David Marcet; *Instr* Vincent Lucarelli
Estab 1887, dept estab 1978; Maintains campus-wide display of permanent coll & 3 areas for rotating exhibs. Scholarships offered annually to all students for one yr; pvt & den & Benedictine Catholic; D & E; Scholarships; SC 10, LC 7; Full time 1150, grad 915
Library Holdings: Slides
Ent Req: HS dipl, ACT, SAT
Degrees: BA, BS, MS & MBA 4 yrs
Tuition: Undergrad $15,220 per yr; campus res available
Courses: Art Appreciation, Art History, Calligraphy, Design, Drawing, Graphic Arts, Lettering, Painting, Photography, Printmaking

MACOMB

WESTERN ILLINOIS UNIVERSITY, Department of Art, 1 University Cir, 32 Garwood Hall Macomb, IL 61455-1390. Tel 309-298-1549; Fax 309-298-2605; Elec Mail ca-wright@wiu.edu; Internet Home Page Address: www.wiu.edu/art/; *Interim Dean Fine Arts & Commun* Sharon Evans; *Prof* Julie Mahoney, MFA; *Asst Prof* Susan Czechowski, MFA; *Asst Prof* Dr Keith Holz, PhD; *Asst Prof* William Howard, MFA; *Prof* Jenny Knavel, MFA; *Asst Prof* Damon McArthur, MFA; *Asst Prof* Terry Rathje, MA; *Asst Prof* Tim Waldrop, MFA; *Prof* Bruce Walters, MFA; *Assoc Prof* Kat Myers, MFA; *Prof* Jan Clough, MFA; *Chair Dept of Art & Prof* Charles Wright, MFA; *Asst Prof Art* Maile Hutterer, PhD; *Asst Prof Art* Henry Charles Oursler, MFA; *Assoc Prof Art* Brett Eberhardt, MFA; *Asst Prof Art* Shawn Spangler, MFA
Estab 1900, dept estab 1968; Maintains a nonprofit art gallery, Univ Art Gallery, Western Illinois Univ, Macomb, IL, 61455. Tuition Wavers/Talent Grants $500-$2,000 open to all students, renewable 4 yrs; Pub; D & E; SC 49, LC 18, GC 9; non-maj 250, maj 130, gs 40
Ent Req: HS dipl
Degrees: BA 4 yrs, BFA, MA - Museum Studies
Tuition: Res—undergrad $7,200 per yr
Courses: Art Appreciation, Art Education, Art History, Ceramics, Conceptual Art, Design, Drawing, Foundry Casting, Goldsmithing, Graphic Arts, Graphic Design, History of Art & Architecture, Illustration, Jewelry, Metal Working, Mixed Media, Museum Staff Training, Museum Studies, Painting, Printmaking, Sculpture
Summer School: Chair, Charles Wright. Enrl 103; 8 wk session. Courses—Art Appreciation, Studio

MALTA

KISHWAUKEE COLLEGE, Art Dept, 21193 Malta Rd, Malta, IL 60150-9600. Tel 815-825-2086; Fax 815-825-2072; Elec Mail arr@kishwaukeecollege.edu; Internet Home Page Address: www.kishwaukeecollege.edu; *Pres* Thomas L Choice; *Dean, Arts, Communs & Social Sciences* Tara Y Carter
Courses: †Drawing, †Jewelry, †Metalsmithing, †Painting, †Printmaking

MOLINE

BLACK HAWK COLLEGE, Art Dept, 6600 34th Ave, Moline, IL 61265-5899. Tel 309-796-5469; Fax 309-792-3418; Elec Mail thorsonz@bhc.edu; Internet Home Page Address: www.bhc.edu; *Assoc Prof* David Murray; *Asst Prof & Co Chair Commun & Fine Arts* Zaiga Thorson; *Instr* Melissa Hebert
Estab 1962; maintain a nonprofit art gallery, Artspace; pub; D & E; Scholarships; SC 17, LC 4; D 300, E 100, non-maj 300, maj 60
Ent Req: HS dipl
Degrees: AA & AAS(Commercial Art) 2 yrs
Courses: Art Appreciation, Art History, Ceramics, Commercial Art, Computer Graphics, Design, Drawing, Graphic Design, Illustrator, Jewelry, Life Drawing, Painting, Photography, Photoshop
Adult Hobby Classes: Calligraphy, Drawing, Painting, Stained Glass, Photography
Summer School: Chmn, Jonathan Palumaki. Enrl 30; tuition $48 per cr hr for term of 6 wks beginning in June. Courses—Art Appreciation

MONMOUTH

MONMOUTH COLLEGE, Dept of Art, 700 E Broadway, McMichael Academic Hall Monmouth, IL 61462-1963. Tel 309-457-2311; Fax 309-734-7500; Internet Home Page Address: www.monm.edu; *Dept Chair & Assoc Prof Art* Stacy Lotz; *Prof Art* Cheryl Meeker; *Asst Prof Art* Brian Baugh; *Lectr* Tyler Hennings
College estab 1853; Maintains nonprofit art gallery, Len G. Everett Gallery; FT 3, PT 3; pvt; D&E; Scholarships, Grants; SC 16, LC 4
Ent Req: 15 units incl English, history, social science, foreign language, mathematics & science, SAT or ACT
Degrees: BA 4 yr
Courses: Advanced Special Topics, †Art Education, Art History, Ceramics, Contemporary Art, Drawing, †Graphic Design, Independent Study, Open Studio, Painting, Photography, Printmaking, Sculpture, Secondary Art Methods, Senior Art Seminar
Adult Hobby Classes: 10; ceramics

MOUNT CARROLL

CAMPBELL CENTER FOR HISTORIC PRESERVATION STUDIES, 203 E Seminary St, Mount Carroll, IL 61053-1361. Tel 815-244-1173; Fax 815-244-1619; Elec Mail registrations@campbellcenter.org; Internet Home Page Address: www.campbellcenter.org; *Exec Dir* Sharon Welton
Estab 1979; Maintains Campbell Memorial Research Library & Campbell Ctr for Historic Preservation Studies, 203 E Seminary, Mt Carroll, Ill; PT 45; pub; D May - mid-Oct; Scholarships
Tuition: $550-$1275 fee per course, 3-6 days; campus res available
Courses: Collections Care, Conservation, Historic Preservation, Museum Staff Training

NAPERVILLE

NORTH CENTRAL COLLEGE, Dept of Art, 30 N Brainard St, Naperville, IL 60566-4690. Tel 630-637-5542; Fax 630-637-5691; *Adjunct Prof* Joan Bredendick, MFA; *Adjunct Prof* Edward Herbeck, MFA; *Chair Art Dept, Assoc Prof* Barry Skurkis, MA; *Asst Prof* Gerard Ferrari, MA; *Adjunct Prof* John Slavik, MA; *Assoc Prof Art* Wendy Koenig, PhD; *Assoc Prof Art* Kelvin Mason, MFA; *Asst Prof Art* Christine Rabenold, MFA; *Vis Lectr Art* Lydia Hwang, MA; *Vis Lectr Art* Lora Kleviter, MFA; *Vis Lectr Art* Linda McElherne, MA; *Ceramic Studio Asst* Tom Goodell, BFA; *Dean, Grad & Continuing Educ* Peter Barger
Estab 1861; Maintains nonprofit art gallery & library; on-campus shop sells art supplies; pvt; D & E; Scholarships; SC 30, LC 15; non-maj 3000, maj 50
Ent Req: HS dipl, SAT or ACT
Degrees: BA 4 yrs
Tuition: Res & nonres—undergrad $23,115 per yr, $7705 per term, $570-$1,710 part time per term; non-degree—$135-$2394 per term; campus res—room & board $7440 per yr
Courses: Advanced Studio, Aesthetics, Art Education, Art History, Ceramics, Design, Drawing, Figure Drawing, Handicrafts, History of Art & Architecture, Painting, Photography, Printmaking, Sculpture, Teacher Training, Theatre Arts
Adult Hobby Classes: Enrl 3800. Tuition $50 for 6 wks. Courses offered through Continuing Education
Summer School: Dir, Peter Barger. Enrl 1000; tuition $1440 per course. Courses—Ceramics, Drawing, Painting

NORMAL

ILLINOIS STATE UNIVERSITY, College of Fine Arts, Campus Box 5600, Normal, IL 61790-5600. Tel 309-438-8321; Fax 309-438-8318; Elec Mail FineArts@IllinoisState.edu; Internet Home Page Address: www.cfa.ilstu.edu; *Dean* James Major
Estab 1857; FT 40; 6 vis profs per yr; pub; D & E; Scholarships, Fellowships; SC 50, LC 35, GC 40; D 20,000, non-maj 100, maj 500, grad 40
Ent Req: HS dipl, SAT or ACT
Degrees: BA & BS 4 yrs, BFA 5 yrs, MA, MS, MFA
Tuition: Res—undergrad & grad $2430 per yr, $1215 per sem, $75 per hr; nonres—undergrad $6030 per yr, $3015 per sem, $225 per hr, grad $2454 per yr, $1227 per sem
Courses: †Art Education, Art Foundations, †Art History, †Art Therapy, †Ceramics, †Drawing, †Fibers, †Glass, †Graphic Design, †Intaglio, Jewelry Design, †Lithography, †Metalwork, Mixed Media, †Painting, †Photography, †Sculpture, Video Art
Summer School: 8 wk term beginning in June

OGLESBY

ILLINOIS VALLEY COMMUNITY COLLEGE, Division of Humanities & Fine Arts, 815 N Orlando Smith Ave, Oglesby, IL 61348-9691. Tel 815-224-2720, Ext 491; *Instr* David Bergsieker, MFA; *Instr* Dana Collins, MFA
Estab 1924; pub; D & E; Scholarships; SC 14, LC 2; D 120, E 44, non-maj 156, maj 8
Degrees: AA 2 yrs
Tuition: $50 per sem hr
Courses: Art Education, Art History, Ceramics, Drawing, Graphic Design, Painting, Photography, Sculpture, Weaving
Summer School: Tuition $50 per sem

PEORIA

BRADLEY UNIVERSITY, Dept of Art, 1501 W Bradley Ave, Heuser Art Ctr Peoria, IL 61606-1048. Tel 309-677-2967; Fax 309-677-3642; Internet Home Page Address: www.bradley.edu; *Chair* Paul Krainak

FT 10, PT 4; Pvt; Scholarships, Assistantships; maj 121, others 500
Ent Req: HS grad
Degrees: BA, BS, BFA 4 yrs, MA, MFA 3 yrs
Tuition: $7990 per yr
Courses: Art History, †Art Metal, Ceramics, Drawing, Graphic Arts, Graphic Design, Illustration, Painting, Photography, Printmaking, Sculpture
Summer School: Chair, James Hansen. Enrl 39; tuition $281 per cr hr for courses June-Aug. Courses—Ceramics, Drawing, Graphic Design, Independent Study, Painting, Printmaking

QUINCY

QUINCY UNIVERSITY, Dept of Art, 1800 College Ave, Quincy, IL 62301-2699. Tel 217-228-5200, Ext 5371; Fax 217-228-5354; Internet Home Page Address: www.quincy.edu; *Prof Art* Robert Lee Mejer
Estab 1860, dept estab 1953; FT 3, PT 2; pub; D & E; SC 21, LC 13; maj 25, total enrl 1715, E 150
Ent Req: HS grad, ACT or SAT ent exam
Degrees: BA, BS & BFA 4 yrs
Courses: 2-D & 3-D Design, Aesthetics, Art Appreciation, Art Education, Art History, Art Seminars, Ceramics, Commercial Art, Design, Drawing, Illustration, Jewelry, Mixed Media, Modern Art, Non-Western Art, Painting, Photography, Printmaking, Sculpture, Teacher Training, Weaving
Summer School: Dir, Robert Lee Mejer. Tuition $190 per sem hr, optional jr yr abroad

RIVER GROVE

TRITON COLLEGE, School of Arts & Sciences, 2000 N Fifth Ave, River Grove, IL 60171. Tel 708-456-0300; Internet Home Page Address: www.triton.cc.il.us; *Chmn* Norman Weigo
Estab 1965; FT 5, PT 6; pub; D & E; SC 17, LC 3; D 650, E 150, maj 138, adults and non-cr courses
Ent Req: HS dipl, some adult students are admitted without HS dipl, but with test scores indicating promise
Degrees: AA 2 yrs
Courses: Advertising Design, Art History, Ceramics, Commercial Art, Drawing, Graphic Arts, Graphic Design, Illustration, Lettering, Painting, Printmaking, Recreational Arts & Crafts, Sculpture, Theatre Arts
Adult Hobby Classes: Enrl 550. Courses—Candle Making, Continuing Education Classes, Crafts, Drawing, Ceramics, Jewelry, Quilting, Painting, Plastics, Stained Glass, Sculpture, Theatre Arts
Summer School: Dir, Norm Wiegel. Enrl 100; tuition $27 per cr hr. Courses—Selection from regular classes offered

RIVERSIDE

RIVERSIDE ARTS CENTER, 32 E Quincy Rd, Riverside, IL 60546-2129. Tel 708-442-6400; Elec Mail rivarts@sbcglobal.net; Internet Home Page Address: riversideartscenter.com; *Financial Dir* Tami Gagne; *Gallery Cur* Garry Henderson
Average Annual Attendance:

ROCK ISLAND

AUGUSTANA COLLEGE, Art Dept, 639 38th St, Rock Island, IL 61201-2210. Tel 309-794-7729; Fax 309-794-7659; Elec Mail arschussheim@augustana.edu; Internet Home Page Address: www.augustana.edu; *Prof* Peter Xiao; *Prof* Megan Quinn; *Assoc Prof* Kelvin Mason; *Adj Prof* Christian Mortenson; *Adj Prof* Corrine Smith; *Chair* Rowen Schussheim-Anderson; *Asst Prof* Vickie Phipps
Estab 1860; Maintain nonprofit art gallery, Augustana Art Museum, same location; on-campus shop where art supplies may be purchased; FT 5, PT 1, Adj 2; pvt; D; Scholarships, Fellowships; SC 8, LC 9, LabC 3; Enrol 2200
Activities: Schols offered
Ent Req: HS grad plus exam
Degrees: BA 4 yr
Tuition: Undergrad $35,835
Courses: †Art Education, †Art History, Ceramics, Design, †Drawing, Graphic Arts, †Graphic Design, Painting, Photography, Printmaking, Sculpture, †Studio Art, Teacher Training, Textile Design, Weaving
Children's Classes: Enrl 175; tuition $38 for 4wk term. Courses—Calligraphy, Clay, Drawing, Mixed Media, Painting, Sculpture, Weaving
Summer School: Prof Darrin Good. Enrl 100; tuition $513 per sem hr for 5 wk term. Courses—Drawing, Fabric Design, Painting, Photography, Weaving

ROCKFORD

ROCK VALLEY COLLEGE, Humanities and Fine Arts Division, 3301 N Mulford Rd, Rockford, IL 61114-5699. Tel 815-654-4410; Fax 815-654-5359; Elec Mail faco1dr@rvc.cc.il.us; Internet Home Page Address: www.rvc.cc.il.us; *Prof* Cherri Rittenhouse; *Prof* Lester Salberg; *Prof* Lynn Fischer-Carlson; *Div Chmn* Dave Ross
Estab 1964, dept estab 1965; FT 2, PT 3; pub; D & E; SC 10, LC 4; D 158, non-maj 70, maj 27
Degrees: AA, AS & AAS 2 yrs
Courses: Art Education, Art History, Color Theory, Commercial Art, Design, Drawing, Painting, Printmaking

ROCKFORD COLLEGE, Dept of Fine Arts, 5050 E State St, Clark Arts Ctr Rockford, IL 61108-2311. Tel 815-226-4000; Fax 815-394-5167; Internet Home Page Address: www.rockford.edu; *Chmn Dept Fine Arts* Robert N McCauley

Estab 1847, dept estab 1848; FT 4, PT 2; pvt; D & E; Scholarships; SC 20, LC 3-4; D 750, E 700, non-maj 135, maj 45
Ent Req: HS dipl, SAT or ACT
Degrees: BA, BFA and BS 4 yrs, MAT 2 yrs
Courses: Art History, Ceramics, Drawing, Painting, Papermaking, Photography, Printmaking, Sculpture
Summer School: Dir, Dr Winston McKean. Courses—Art History, Fine Arts (Studio), Stage Design

SOUTH HOLLAND

SOUTH SUBURBAN COLLEGE, Art Dept, 15800 S State St, South Holland, IL 60473. Tel 708-596-2000; *Chmn* Joe Rejholec
Degrees: AA, AAS
Tuition: $53 per cr hr
Courses: †Advertising Design, Art Appreciation, Art History, Calligraphy, Ceramics, Design, Drawing, Illustration, Jewelry, Painting, Printmaking, Sculpture
Summer School: Dir, Dr Fred Hanzelin. Enrl 65. Courses - Art History, Ceramics, Design, Drawing, Nature of Art

SPRINGFIELD

SPRINGFIELD COLLEGE IN ILLINOIS, Dept of Art, 1500 N Fifth, Springfield, IL 62702. Tel 217-525-1420 ext 518; Elec Mail admissions@sci.edu; Internet Home Page Address: www.sci.edu; *Head Dept* Jeff Garland; *Instr* Marianne Stremsterfer, BA; *Instr* John Seiz, MA; *Instr* Jim Allen, MA; *Instr* Lisa Manuele, BA
Estab 1929, dept estab 1968; pvt; D & E; SC 12, LC 4; D 27, E 6, non-maj 11, maj 16
Ent Req: HS dipl, ACT
Degrees: AA 2 yrs
Courses: 2-D & 3-D Design, Art History, Ceramics, Design, Drawing, History of Art & Architecture, Painting, Photography, Printmaking, Weaving
Adult Hobby Classes: Enrl 125; tuition $125 per cr hr. Courses—Art History, Ceramics, Design, Drawing, Photography
Children's Classes: Enrl 20; tuition $30 for 2 wks in summer. Courses—Art for Children 6 - 9 yrs, 10 - 14 yrs
Summer School: Dir, Dorothy Shiffer. Tuition $125 per cr hr

UNIVERSITY OF ILLINOIS AT SPRINGFIELD, Visual Arts Program, 1 University Plaza, Springfield, IL 62703-5407. Tel 217-206-6790; Fax 217-206-7280; Elec Mail bdixo2@uis.edu; Internet Home Page Address: www.uis.edu; *Assoc Prof* Bob Dixon, MFA & MS; *Asst Prof* Barbara Bolser
Estab 1969, dept estab 1974; pub; D & E; Scholarships; SC 24, LC 10
Ent Req: 2 yrs col educ
Degrees: BA(Creative Arts) 2 yrs
Courses: Aesthetics, Art History, †Ceramics, Conceptual Art, Constructions, Design, Drawing, †Graphic Arts, Graphic Design, †Mixed Media, †Painting, †Photography, †Printmaking, †Sculpture, †Video

SUGAR GROVE

WAUBONSEE COMMUNITY COLLEGE, Art Dept, Rte 47 at Waubonsee Dr, Von Ohlen Hall (VON 209), Sugar Grove Campus Sugar Grove, IL 60554-9454. Tel 630-466-4811; Fax 630-466-9102; Internet Home Page Address: www.waubonsee.edu; *Chmn* Stephanie Decicco
Estab 1967; pub; D & E; Scholarships; SC 8, LC 3; D approx 275, E approx 200, maj 25
Ent Req: HS dipl, open door policy for adults without HS dipl
Degrees: AA, AS and AAS 2 yrs
Courses: Art Education, Art History, Ceramics, Drawing, Painting, Teacher Training, Theatre Arts
Adult Hobby Classes: Enrl 250; Courses—Ceramics, Interior Design, Painting, Graphic Arts
Children's Classes: Enrl 50. Courses—Dramatics, Experience in Art.
Summer School: Courses— as per regular session

UNIVERSITY PARK

GOVERNORS STATE UNIVERSITY, College of Arts & Science, Art Dept, 1 University Pkwy, University Park, IL 60466-0975. Tel 708-534-5000; Fax 708-534-7895; Internet Home Page Address: www.govst.edu; *Div Chmn* Dr Joyce Kennedy
Scholarships; 175
Degrees: BA, MA
Tuition: Undergrad $95 per cr hr, grad $101 per cr hr
Courses: Art History, Art Studio, Ceramics, Drawing, Electronic Arts, History of Art & Architecture, Jewelry, Mixed Media, Painting, Photography, Printmaking, Sculpture
Summer School: Dir, Mary Bookwalter. Enrl 150; tuition $79.25 per cr hr for May-Aug term. Courses—Art History, Art Studio

WHEATON

WHEATON COLLEGE, Dept of Art, 501 E College, Wheaton, IL 60187. Tel 630-752-5050, 752-5000; Internet Home Page Address: www.wheaton.edu/homeArt; *Chmn* Dr E John Walford
Estab 1861; FT 4; pvt; D & E; Scholarships; SC 32, LC 16; 2350, maj 38, grad 450
Ent Req: HS dipl
Degrees: BA 4 yrs

Courses: Aesthetics, Art Education, Ceramics, Creativity Practicum, Drawing, Film, Graphic Arts, Graphic Design, History of Art & Architecture, Painting, Philosophy of Art, Photography, Printmaking, Sculpture, Television Production, Theory & Techniques, Video

WINNETKA

NORTH SHORE ART LEAGUE, 620 Lincoln, Winnetka, IL 60093. Tel 847-446-2870; Fax 847-446-4306; Elec Mail nsal@sbcglobal.net; Internet Home Page Address: www.northshoreartleague.org; *Bd Pres* Cindy Fuller
Estab 1924; pvt; D & E; Scholarships; SC 20; D 200, E 150
Ent Req: adults must be art league mem
Degrees: continuing educ cr
Tuition: Classes meet once per week for a 12-14 week period; no campus res
Courses: Ceramics, Children's Film, Costume Design & Construction, Critique, Drawing, Fashion Arts, Graphic Arts, Mixed Media, Painting, Printmaking
Children's Classes: various classes
Summer School: Arts Educ Mgr, Josh Barney & Exec Dir, Linda Nelson; six week sessions; art camp

INDIANA

ANDERSON

ANDERSON UNIVERSITY, Art Dept, 1100 E Fifth St, Anderson, IN 46012-3462. Tel 765-641-4320; Fax 765-641-4328; *Chmn* M Jason Knapp
Estab 1928; pvt; D & E; Scholarships; SC 30, LC 3; non-maj 15, maj 60
Ent Req: HS dipl, ent exam plus recommendation
Degrees: BA 4 yrs
Courses: Advertising Design, Art Education, †Art History, Ceramics, Commercial Art, Drawing, Glass, †Graphic Arts, Graphic Design, History of Art & Architecture, Illustration, Jewelry, Lettering, Museum Staff Training, †Painting, †Photography, Printmaking, Sculpture, †Stage Design, Teacher Training
Summer School: Dir, Robert Smith

BLOOMINGTON

INDIANA UNIVERSITY, BLOOMINGTON, Henry Radford Hope School of Fine Arts, 1201 E 7th St, Rm 123 Bloomington, IN 47405-5501. Tel 812-855-7766; Fax 812-855-7498; Elec Mail faoffice@indiana.edu; Internet Home Page Address: www.indiana.edu/~finaweb; *Dir, Assoc Prof* Tim Mather; *Assoc Prof* Malcolm Smith; *Asst Prof* Christyl Boger
Estab 1911; pub; D; Scholarships; SC 55, LC 100, GC 110; maj undergrad 300, grad 135 (45 Art History, 90 Studio), others 5600
Ent Req: admis to the Univ
Degrees: BA, BFA, 4 yrs, MA, MFA, PhD
Tuition: Res—undergrad $4,412 per yr, grad $168.60 per cr hr; nonres—undergrad $13,416 per yr, grad $491.15 per cr hr, room & board avg $5,608 per yr
Courses: Art History, Ceramics, Graphic Design, Jewelry, Painting & Drawing, Photography, Printed Textiles, Printmaking, Sculpture, Woven Textiles
Summer School: Dir, John Goodheart. Tuition res—undergrad $71 per cr hr, grad $93 per cr hr; nonres—undergrad $222.15 per cr hr, grad $266.60 per cr hr. Courses—Art History, Ceramics, Drawing, Painting, Photography

CRAWFORDSVILLE

WABASH COLLEGE, Art Dept, 301 W Wabash Ave, Crawfordsville, IN 47933-2417. Tel 765-361-6386; Fax 765-361-6341; Elec Mail huebnerg@wabash.edu; Internet Home Page Address: www.wabash.edu; *Chmn* Gregory Huebner; *Prof* Doug Calisch; *Gallery Dir* Lali Hess; *Asst Prof Art History* Elizabeth Morton
Estab 1832, dept estab 1950; Maintain nonprofit art gallery; Eric Dean Gallery, Randolph Deer Art Wing, Fine Arts Ctr, Wabash College, 301 W Wabash Ave, Crawfordsville, IN 47933; Pvt, men only; D; Scholarships, Fellowships; SC 16, LC 7; D 100, non-maj 80, maj 20
Ent Req: HS dipl, SAT
Degrees: BA 4 yrs
Courses: 2-D & 3-D Design, Aesthetics, Architecture, Art History, †Ceramics, Design, †Drawing, †History of Art & Architecture, †Painting, †Photography, †Sculpture

DONALDSON

ANCILLA COLLEGE, Art Dept, PO Box 1, Donaldson, IN 46513-0001. Tel 574-936-8898; Tel 866-ANCILLA (toll free); Fax 574-935-1773; *Act Dept Head* Charles Duff
Estab 1936, dept estab 1965; pvt; D & E; SC 9-12, LC 2
Ent Req: HS dipl
Degrees: AA, AAA(Applied Arts) 2 yrs
Tuition: Undergrad $145 per cr hr
Courses: Aesthetics, Art Appreciation, Calligraphy, Ceramics, Design, Drawing, Enameling, Graphic Design, Lettering, Photography
Children's Classes: Enrl 12; tuition $40 for 6 sessions; Courses—Crafts for Children, Drawing and Painting for Children. Classes on Saturday

EVANSVILLE

UNIVERSITY OF EVANSVILLE, Art Dept, 1800 Lincoln Ave, Evansville, IN 47722-0001. Tel 812-488-2043; Fax 812-488-2101; Elec Mail bb32@evansville.edu; *Dept Head, Prof* William Brown, MFA; *Assoc Prof* Ralph

Larmann, MFA; *Assoc Prof* Stephanie Frasier, MFA; *Instr* Tracy Maurer, MA; *Instr* Mark Schoenbaum, MFA; *Instr* Evan Crowley, MFA; *Instr* Francis Cadora, BS; *Instr* Valerie Milholland, MA; *Instr* Jesika Ellis, MA
Estab 1854; Maintains nonprofit Mel Peterson Gallery & Krannert Gallery; Pvt; D & E; Scholarships; SC 20, LC 10; D 2,600, maj 70
Ent Req: HS dipl
Degrees: BA(Art History), BS(Art Educ, Art & Assoc Studies), BFA, BA(Art) 4 yrs, pre-BS(Art Theory)
Courses: †Art & Assoc Studies, Art Appreciation, †Art Education, †Art History, †Ceramics, Design, Drawing, †Graphic Design, Jewelry, Life (figure) Drawing, †Painting, Photography, Printmaking, †Sculpture, †Visual Communication
Summer School: Tuition $210 5 wk sessions. Courses—Art Appreciation, Ceramics, Photography

UNIVERSITY OF SOUTHERN INDIANA, Department of Art, 8600 University Blvd, Evansville, IN 47712-3590. Tel 812-465-7047; Fax 812-465-1263; Elec Mail vthomas@usi.edu; Internet Home Page Address: www.usi.edu; *Assoc Prof* Hilary Braysmith, PhD; *Prof Emeritus* Leonard Dowhie Jr, MFA; *Assoc Prof* Margaret Skoglund, PhD; *Prof* Kathryn Waters, MFA; *Prof Emeritus* John McNaughton, MFA; *Assoc Prof* Joseph Uduehi, Ed D; *Assoc Prof* Joan Kempf de Jong, MFA; *Prof* Michael Aakhus, MFA; *Contract Asst Prof Graphic Design* Chuck Armstrong, MFA; *Instr* Virginia Poston, MA; *Asst Prof* Xinran Hu, MFA; *Asst Prof* Robert Millard-Mendez, MFA; *Contract Asst Prof Art* Sarah Bielski, MFA; *Contract Asst Prof Art* Andrew Kosten, MFA; *Asst Prof Art* Alisa Holeu, MFA
Estab 1969; maintains nonprofit art galleries, Kenneth P McCutchan Art Center & Palmina F & Stephen S Pace Galleries; library; on-campus shop for purchase of art supplies; FT 15, PT 13; pub; D & E; Scholarships, Fellowships; SC 27, LC 4; D 220, E 32, maj 208, non maj 12
Ent Req: HS dipl
Degrees: BS (Art Educ), BA & BS (Art) 4 yrs
Tuition: Res—$184.67 per cr hr; nonres—$439.53 per cr hr
Courses: Art Appreciation, †Art Education, Art History, Ceramics, Contemporary Art, †Design, †Drawing, †Film, †Graphic Arts, †Graphic Design, Painting, Photography, Printmaking, Sculpture
Adult Hobby Classes: Enrl 25. Courses—Silkscreen
Children's Classes: Enrl 80, Sat am, 3 age groups
Summer School: Summer sessions offered

FORT WAYNE

INDIANA-PURDUE UNIVERSITY, Dept of Fine Arts, 2101 E Coliseum Blvd, Fort Wayne, IN 46805-1499. Tel 260-481-6705; Fax 260-481-6707; Elec Mail webers@ipfw.edu; Internet Home Page Address: new.ipfw.edu/fine-arts/; *Chmn* Dana Goodman; *Asst Prof* Kirsten Ataoguz; *Asst Prof* Laurel Campbell; *Assoc Prof* Christopher Ganz; *Prof* John Hrehov; *Assoc Prof* Nancy McCroskey; *Prof* Audrey Ushenko
Estab 1920, dept estab 1976; pub; D & E; Scholarships; SC 96, LC 5; non-maj 60, maj 235
Degrees: AB, AS, BFA 4 yrs
Tuition: Res—$122.75 per cr hr; nonres—$213.95 per cr hr; no campus res
Courses: Art History, †Ceramics, †Computer Design, †Crafts, †Drawing, †Graphic Arts, Illustration, †Metalsmithing, †Painting, †Photography, †Printmaking, †Sculpture
Children's Classes: Enrl 75; tuition $60 for 11 wks. Courses—Ceramics, Drawing, Painting, Sculpture

UNIVERSITY OF SAINT FRANCIS, School of Creative Arts, 2701 Spring St, Fort Wayne, IN 46808-3994. Tel 260-434-7591; Fax 260-434-7604; Elec Mail rcartwright@sf.edu; Internet Home Page Address: www.sf.edu/art; *Dean* Rick Cartwright, MFA; *Assoc Prof* Mary Klopfer, MFA; *Assoc Prof* Jane Martin, MFA; *Assoc Prof* Karen McArdle, MFA; *Instr* Tom Keesee, MFA; *Instr* Alan Nauts, BA; *Prof* Maurice A Papier, MS; *Asst Prof* Neal McDonald, MFA; *Asst Prof* Cara Wade, MFA; *Asst Prof* Esperanca Camara, PhD; *Asst Prof* Patricia Edwards, MA; *Asst Prof* Kristin Fedders, PhD; *Instr* Bob Mayer, MS
Estab 1890; Maintains a nonprofit art gallery, John P. Weatherhead Gallery, Rolland Art Center, 2701 Spring St, Fort Wayne, IN 46808; also maintains an art/architecture library, Lee & Jim Vann Library; Pvt; D, E, weekends & summer; Scholarships; SC 22, LC 6, GC 14, workshops; D 150, maj 150
Ent Req: HS dipl, class rank in HS, SAT
Degrees: MA (Studio Art), BA (Communication, Communication Arts & Graphic Design, Computer Art, Studio Art), BS (Education, Visual Art All Grade Major grades K-12; Education - Secondary Education Visual Arts grds 9-12); AA (Communication Arts & Graphic Design); Minors: Art, Art History, Communication, Speech
Courses: †2D Composition, †3D Composition, Advertising Design, Animation, †Art Education, Art History, Ceramics, †Commercial Art, Computer Graphics, †Design, †Desktop Publishing, Display, Drawing, Fashion Arts, Graphic Arts, Graphic Design, Painting, Photography, Printmaking, †Sculpture, †Teacher Training
Children's Classes: Enrl 60; tuition $75 per sem. Courses—General Art Instruction grades K - 8
Summer School: Dir, Dean Rick Cartwright; two 6 wk sessions. Courses—Art Appreciation, Computer Graphics, Drawing, Painting

FRANKLIN

FRANKLIN COLLEGE, Art Dept, 101 Branigin Blvd, Franklin, IN 46131-2598. Tel 317-738-8279; Fax 317-736-6030; Internet Home Page Address: www.franklincoll.edu; *Chmn Dept* Michael Swanson
Estab 1834; FT 2, PT 2; den; D; Scholarships; SC 9, LC 4; 900
Ent Req: HS grad
Degrees: BA 4 yrs
Courses: Art History, Basic Design, Design, Drawing, Painting, Sculpture

GOSHEN

GOSHEN COLLEGE, Art Dept, 1700 S Main St, Goshen, IN 46526-4794. Tel 219-535-7595; Fax 219-535-7660; Internet Home Page Address: www.goshen.edu; WATS 800-348-7422; *Prof* Abner Hershberger, MFA; *Asst Prof* John Mishler, MFA; *Chmn* John Blosser
Estab 1950; den; D & E; Scholarships; D 145, E 25, non-maj 60, maj 50
Ent Req: HS dipl, top half of class
Degrees: BA(Art) with Indiana Teaching Cert
Courses: Aesthetics, Architectural Drawing, Architecture, Art Appreciation, †Art Education, Art History, †Ceramics, Commercial Art, Design, Drafting, Drawing, Graphic Design, †Jewelry, †Painting, Photography, †Printmaking, Sculpture, Stage Design, †Teacher Training, †Theatre Arts, Video

GREENCASTLE

DEPAUW UNIVERSITY, Art Dept, PO Box 37, Greencastle, IN 46135-0037. Tel 765-658-4340, 4800; Fax 765-658-6552; Internet Home Page Address: www.depauwuniversity.edu; *Prof Chmn* Mitch Murback; *Prof* David Herrold
Estab 1837, dept estab 1877; pvt den; D; SC 14, LC 9, GC 18; D 300, E 20 (Art Dept), non-maj 25%, maj 75%, grad 20
Ent Req: HS dipl, upper half of high school graduating class
Degrees: BA & BM 4 yrs
Courses: Art Education, Art History, Ceramics, Drawing, Painting, Photography, Printmaking, Studio Arts

HAMMOND

PURDUE UNIVERSITY CALUMET, Dept of Communication & Creative Arts, 2200 169th St, Hammond, IN 46323-2094. Tel 219-989-2393; Fax 219-989-2008; Internet Home Page Address: www.calumet.purdue.edu; *Head* Yahya R Kamalipour
Estab 1946; pub; D & E; Scholarships; SC 1-4, LC 1-2, GC 1
Ent Req: HS dipl
Courses: Architecture, Art Education, Ceramics, Drawing, Film, Painting, Photography, Teacher Training, Theatre Arts, Video

HANOVER

HANOVER COLLEGE, Dept of Art, 359 LeGrange Rd, Hanover, IN 47243; PO Box 108, Hanover, IN 47243-0108. Tel 812-866-7000; Fax 812-866-7114; Internet Home Page Address: www.hanover.edu; *Interim Chmn Dept* Debbie Whistler
Estab 1827, dept estab 1967; pvt; D & E; Scholarships; SC 16, LC 4; D 1142
Ent Req: HS dipl
Degrees: BS and BA 4 yrs
Courses: Advertising Design, Aesthetics, Art Education, Art History, Ceramics, Collage, Commercial Art, Constructions, Drawing, Fiber, Film, Glass Blowing, Graphic Arts, Graphic Design, Jewelry, Painting, Photography, Printmaking, Sculpture, Stage Design, Stained Glass, Teacher Training, Theatre Arts, Video

HUNTINGTON

HUNTINGTON COLLEGE, Art Dept, 2303 College Ave, Huntington, IN 46750-1299. Tel 219-356-6000; Fax 219-356-9448; *Asst Prof* W Kenneth Hopper; *Asst Prof* Rebecca L Coffman; *Dean* Ron Webb
Estab 1897; den; D & E; SC 5, LC 3
Ent Req: HS dipl, SAT & two recommendations
Degrees: BA 4 yr
Courses: Art Appreciation, †Art Education, Art History, Arts & Crafts, Ceramics, Computer Graphics, Drawing, Fine Arts, †Graphic Design, Painting, Photography
Summer School: Dean, Ron Webb.

INDIANAPOLIS

INDIANA UNIVERSITY-PURDUE UNIVERSITY, INDIANAPOLIS, Herron School of Art & Design, 735 W New York St, Indianapolis, IN 46202-5222. Tel 317-278-9400; Fax 317-278-9471; Internet Home Page Address: herron.iupui.edu; *Dean* Valerie Eickmeier; *Asst Prof, Dir Foundation* Reagan Furqueron; *Assoc Prof, Chair Fine Arts* Cory Robinson; *Asst Prof, Dir Art Therapy* Juliet King; *Prof, Visual Communication Design* Eva Roberts; *Prof, Dir Grad Progs* Andrew Winship; *Gallery Dir* Paula Katz
Estab 1902; Non-profit art gallery - Herron Gallery, 735 W New York St, Indianapolis, IN 46202; Herron Library (see above); pub; D & E; Scholarships; SC 115, LC 14, GC 10; D 800, non-maj 400, grad 60
Degrees: BFA and BAE 4 yrs, MAE 5 yrs
Courses: †Art Education, †Art History, †Ceramics, Computer Graphics, Drawing, †Fine Arts, Furniture Design, Graphic Arts, Graphic Design, Illustration, Mixed Media, Painting, †Photography, †Printmaking, †Visual Communications
Adult Hobby Classes: Sat school $225.00
Children's Classes: Enrl 225; tuition $200 (partial scholarships) for 10 wk term, Saturday art classes for jr & sr HS students. Youth Art Day Camp $200 per wk
Summer School: 2 two-week sessions of Honors Art $400/ses

MARIAN UNIVERSITY, Visual Arts Dept, 3200 Cold Spring Rd, Indianapolis, IN 46222-1997. Tel 317-955-6000; Fax 317-955-0263; Internet Home Page Address: www.marian.edu; *Instr* Roberta Williams, MA; *Chmn* Jamie Higgs, PhD; *Assoc Prof Art* Megan Wright, MFA; *Asst Prof Art* Brian Crain, MFA; *Asst Prof Art* William Foley, BA; *Asst Prof Art History* Jenny Pauckner, MFA
Estab 1851, dept estab 1938; Maintains nonprofit Marian University Art Gallery (same address); schols open to fine arts students; Annie Loechle, PhD; Pvt; D & E; Scholarships; SC 36, LC 15; D 59, Maj 59
Special Subjects: Art History, Graphic Design

Ent Req: HS dipl, SAT
Degrees: AA 2 yrs, BA 4 yrs
Tuition: Res—undergrad incl room & board $21,172 per yr; nonres—$21,720, room & board incl
Courses: Art Appreciation, †Art Education, †Art History, Art Therapy, †Arts Administration, Ceramics, Crafts, Design, Drawing, †Graphic Design, History of Art & Architecture, Interior Design, Painting, †Photography, †Printmaking, Sculpture, Stage Design, Teacher Training, Theatre Arts

UNIVERSITY OF INDIANAPOLIS, Dept Art & Design, 1400 E Hanna Ave, Christel de Haan Fine Arts Ctr Indianapolis, IN 46227-3630. Tel 317-788-3253; Elec Mail dschaad@uindy.edu; Internet Home Page Address: www.uindy.edu; *Chair* Dee Schaad, MFA; *Assoc Prof* James Vuwigh; *Assoc Prof* Donna Adams; *Asst Prof* Julia Taugner; *Asst Prof* Christine Bently; *Instr* Carolyn Springer; *Instr* Marilyn McEiwan; *Asst Prof* Nelson Weitan
Estab 1902; Christel DeHaan Fine Arts Ctr Gallery; pvt, den; D & E; Scholarships; SC 40, LC 5, GC 8; D 400, E 160, maj 100, grad 20
Ent Req: HS dipl, SAT, upper half of HS class
Degrees: BA, BS 4 yrs & BFA
Courses: Advertising Design, Art Appreciation, Art Education, Art History, Ceramics, Commercial Art, Design, Drawing, Graphic Arts, History of Art & Architecture, Jewelry, Lettering, Occupational Therapy, Painting, Photography, †Pre-Art Therapy, †Pre-Medical Illustration, Printmaking, Sculpture, Teacher Training, †Visual Communications Design
Children's Classes: Enrl 20; free for 10 wk session. Courses—Drawing
Summer School: Dir, Dee Schaad. Enrl 60; $330 per cr hr. Courses—Art Appreciation, Ceramics, Computer, Photography, Printmaking

MARION

INDIANA WESLEYAN UNIVERSITY, School of Arts & Humanities, Division of Art, 4201 S Washington St, Marion, IN 46953-4974. Tel 765-677-2711; Fax 765-677-1042; Internet Home Page Address: www.indwes.edu; *Assoc Prof* Robert Curfman, MFA; *Asst Prof* Rodney Crossman, BS Ed; *Prof* Ron Mazellen, MFA; *Prof* Dallas Walters, MFA; *Asst Prof* Dan Pocock, MFA; *Asst Prof* Daniel Hall, MA; *Asst Prof* Kenton Stiles, PhD; *Prof* William Goodman, MFA; *Asst Prof* William Carpenter, MFA; *Asst Prof* Wendy Puffer, MA; *Art Instr* Carl Rudy, BS
Estab 1890, dept estab 1969; Maintains Beards Art Center Galleries, 4200 John Wesley Ct, Marion, IN, 46953. Art supplies sold at on-campus store; pvt, den; D & E; Scholarships; SC & LC; Maj 275
Ent Req: HS dipl
Degrees: BS: art educ, ceramics, computer graphics, fine art, illustration, interior design, media design, painting, photography, pre-art therapy, printmaking
Courses: †Animation, Art Appreciation, Art Education, Art History, Ceramics, Commercial Art, Drawing, Graphic Arts, Graphic Design, Illustration, Jewelry, Painting, Photography, Pre-Art Therapy, Printmaking, Sculpture, Silversmithing, Stained Glass, †Teacher Training, †Visual Arts Education, †Web Design
Summer School: Dir, Robert Curfman. Enrl 20

MUNCIE

BALL STATE UNIVERSITY, Dept of Art, 217 Riverside Ave, Muncie, IN 47306-0001. Tel 765-285-5838; Fax 765-285-5275; Internet Home Page Address: www.bsu.edu; *Chmn* Thomas Spoerner, EdD
Estab 1918; FT 21; pub; D & E; Scholarships; SC 82, LC 25, GC 30; non-maj 386, maj 341, grad 15
Ent Req: HS dipl
Degrees: BS & BFA 4 yrs, MA 1 yr
Courses: Art Appreciation, †Art Education, Art History, †Ceramics, †Drawing, †Graphic Design, Jewelry, †Metals, †Painting, †Photography, †Printmaking, †Sculpture, Silversmithing
Summer School: Enrl 5000; tuition $1090 for term of 5 wks beginning May

NEW ALBANY

INDIANA UNIVERSITY-SOUTHEAST, Fine Arts Dept, 4201 Grant Line Rd, New Albany, IN 47150-6405. Tel 812-941-2342; Fax 812-941-2529; Internet Home Page Address: www.ius.edu; *Coordr of Fine Arts* Anne Allen; *Assoc Prof* John R Guenthler, MFA; *Assoc Prof* Debra Clem, MFA; *Asst Prof* Marilyn Whitesell
Estab 1945, dept estab 1966; pub; D & E; SC 25, LC 2; D 150, E 35, non-maj 100, maj 50
Ent Req: HS dipl
Degrees: BA 4 yrs
Courses: Advertising Design, Art Appreciation, Art Education, Art History, Ceramics, Drawing, Painting, Printmaking
Adult Hobby Classes: Courses—Crafts, Watercolor
Summer School: Courses—Same as above

NORTH MANCHESTER

MANCHESTER COLLEGE, Dept of Art, 604 College Ave, North Manchester, IN 46962. Tel 260-982-5000, Ext 5327; Fax 260-982-5043; Internet Home Page Address: www.manchester.edu; *Chmn Dept* Thelma S Rohrer, MA; *Assoc Prof* Ejenobo Oke, MFA
Estab 1889; Maintains nonprofit Gallery G & Link Gallery on campus; campus store for purchase of art supplies; pvt, den; D & E; Scholarships; SC 15, LC 5; D 45, maj 15
Ent Req: HS dipl
Degrees: BA & BS 4 yrs

Courses: Art Appreciation, Art Education, †Art History, Camera Techniques, Ceramics, Drawing, Graphic Design, Handicrafts, History of Art & Architecture, Painting, Photography, Sculpture, Teacher Training, Textile Design

NOTRE DAME

SAINT MARY'S COLLEGE, Dept of Art, Moreau Center for the Arts, Notre Dame, IN 46556. Tel 574-284-4631; Fax 219-284-4716; Elec Mail jtourtil@saintmarys.edu; Internet Home Page Address: www3.saintmarys.edu; *Chmn* Julie Tourtillotte
Estab 1844; Maintains nonprofit gallery (same address); on-campus shop sells art supplies; Pvt, W; D & E; Scholarships, Fellowships; SC 21, LC 10; maj 50
Ent Req: CEEB, standing, recommendations, others
Degrees: BA and BFA 4 yrs
Tuition: $31,020 per yr
Courses: Art Appreciation, Art Education, Art History, Ceramics, Computer Media, †Costume Design & Construction, †Design, Drawing, Fibers, Holography, Mixed Media, Painting, Photo Silkscreen, Photography, Printmaking, Sculpture, Stage Design, †Video
Children's Classes: Summer fine art camps
Summer School: Dir Registrar. Courses vary. Enrollment up to 15.

UNIVERSITY OF NOTRE DAME, Dept of Art, Art History & Design, 132 O'Shaughnessy Hall, Notre Dame, IN 46556. Tel 219-631-7602; Fax 219-631-6312; Elec Mail art.art.1@nd.edu; *Chmn* Austin Collins, CSC; *Grad Dir* Richard Gray; *Office Coordr* Mary Foster
Estab 1855; FT 15, PT 8; pvt; D; Scholarships; SC 38, LC 8, GC 20; maj 100
Ent Req: upper third HS class, ent exam
Degrees: BA, BFA 4 yrs, MA, MFA
Courses: †Art History, †Ceramics, Drawing, Fibers, †Graphic Design, †Industrial Design, †Painting, †Photography, †Printmaking, †Sculpture
Summer School: Enrl 30-50; $93 per cr hr plus general fee for 7 wk term. Courses—Art History, Ceramics, Photography, Studio Workshops

OAKLAND CITY

OAKLAND CITY UNIVERSITY, Division of Fine Arts, 143 N Lucretia St, Oakland City, IN 47660-1037. Tel 812-749-4781, Ext 274; Elec Mail dhazelwo@oak.edu; Internet Home Page Address: www.oak.edu; *Prof* Donna Hazelwood, PhD; *Prof* Joseph E Smith, MFA; *Assoc Prof* Carol Spitler, MA; *Asst Prof* Brenda Graham, DME
Maintain nonprofit art gallery; J Michael Dunn Gallery; art supplies available on-campus; FT 4, PT 1; pvt; den; D & E; Scholarships; SC 15, LC 5; maj 35
Ent Req: HS dipl, SAT or ACT
Degrees: AA 2 yrs, BA & BS 4 yrs
Courses: Advertising Design, Art Appreciation, †Art Education, Art History, Ceramics, Commercial Art, Conceptual Art, Design, Drawing, Graphic Arts, †Graphic Design, History of Art & Architecture, Painting, Photography, Printmaking, Sculpture, Teacher Training
Summer School: Courses vary

RICHMOND

EARLHAM COLLEGE, Art Dept, 801 National Rd W, Drawer 48 Richmond, IN 47374-4021. Tel 765-983-1200, 983-1410; Fax 765-983-1247; Internet Home Page Address: www.earlham.edu; *Convener* Kristin Fedders
Estab 1847; den; D; Scholarships; SC 10, LC 7; maj 12-18
Ent Req: HS dipl
Degrees: BA 4 yrs
Courses: Art History, Ceramics, Drawing, Film, Painting, Photography, Printmaking, Theatre Arts

INDIANA UNIVERSITY-EAST, Humanities Dept, 2325 Chester Blvd, Richmond, IN 47374-1289. Tel 765-973-8200; Fax 765-973-8485; Internet Home Page Address: www.indiana.edu; *Chmn* Dr TJ Rivard
Tuition: Res—$108.40 per cr hr; nonres—$267.40 per cr hr
Courses: Art Appreciation, Art Education, Art History, Drawing, Handicrafts, Painting, Photography, Sculpture

SAINT MARY OF THE WOODS

SAINT MARY-OF-THE-WOODS COLLEGE, Art Dept, 1 Saint Mary-of-the-Woods College, Hulman Hall Saint Mary of the Woods, IN 47876. Tel 812-535-5151, 535-5141; Fax 812-535-4613; Internet Home Page Address: www.smwc.edu; *Area Coordr* Donna Dene English; *Gallery Dir* Sheila Genteman; *Assoc Prof* Thomas Swopes; *Asst Prof* Pat Jancosek
Estab 1840; FT 2, PT 1; den(W); D; Scholarships; SC 15, LC 4; maj 14
Ent Req: HS dipl, SAT or ACT
Degrees: BA & BS 4 yrs, MAAT
Courses: †Art Education, Art History, †Ceramics, Design, Drawing, †Graphic Design, †Painting, Photography, Teacher Training

SOUTH BEND

INDIANA UNIVERSITY SOUTH BEND, Fine Arts Dept, 1700 Mishawaka Ave, South Bend, IN 46615-1400. Tel 219-237-4134; Fax 219-237-4317; Internet Home Page Address: www.iusb.edu; *Chmn* Thomas Miller; *Prof* Alan Larkin, MFA; *Adjunct Asst Prof* Linda Crimson, MFA; *Adjunct Asst Prof* Anthony Droega, MFA
Estab 1964; pub; D & E; SC 18, LC 6; non-maj 380, maj 48
Ent Req: HS dipl
Degrees: AA(Fine Arts) 2 yr, BA & BFA(Fine Arts) 4 yr

Courses: Art Education, Art History, Drawing, Graphic Design, Painting, Printmaking, Sculpture
Summer School: Chmn, Anthony Droege. Tuition same as regular session; two 6 wk summer sessions. Courses—Art Appreciation, Drawing, Painting

TERRE HAUTE

INDIANA STATE UNIVERSITY, Dept of Art, Fine Arts 108, Terre Haute, IN 47809. Tel 812-237-3697; Fax 812-237-4369; Elec Mail artdept@indstate.edu; Internet Home Page Address: www.indstate.edu/art-dept/; *Chmn* Alden Cavanaugh
Estab 1870; Maintains nonprofit University Art Gallery, Center for Fine & Performing Arts, Terre Haute, IN 47809; art supplies sold at on-campus store; pub; D & E; Scholarships; SC 66, LC 45, GC 61; D 2432, E 311, maj 180, grad 40
Ent Req: HS dipl, top 50% of class with C average
Degrees: BA(Art History), BS(Studio Art), BSed(Art Education), BFA(Studio Art) 4 yr, MA(Studio Art) 1 yr & MFA(Studio Art) 2 yr
Tuition: Res—undergrad $262 per cr hr, (18 hr) grad $328 per cr hr; nonres—undergrad $558 per cr hr (9 hr), grad $645 per cr hr
Courses: Aesthetics, Art Appreciation, †Art Education, †Art History, †Ceramics, †Drawing, †Graphic Design, †Painting, Papermaking, †Photography, †Printmaking, †Sculpture, Studio Furniture, Teacher Training, Wood Sculpture
Summer School: Dir, Dr Louis Jensen. Tuition res—undergrad $262, grad $328 per cr hr; nonres—undergrad $558, grad $645 per cr hr for term of two 5 wks beginning June. Courses—variety of studio & lecture courses

UPLAND

TAYLOR UNIVERSITY, Visual Art Dept, 236 W Reade Ave, Upland, IN 46989-1002. Tel 765-998-2751, Ext 5322; Fax 765-998-4680; Elec Mail visualarts@taylor.edu; Internet Home Page Address: www.taylor.edu; *Assoc Prof, Gilkison Family Chair in Art History* Rachel Smith; *Asst Prof* Larry Blakely; *Assoc Prof* Craig Moore; *Asst Prof* Kathy Hermann; *Instr* Shawn Casbarro; *Asst Prof* Robert Alsobrook; *Assoc Prof* Jonathan Bouw
Estab 1846, dept estab 1968; Maintain nonprofit art gallery, Metcalf Gallery; art library, Zondervan Library, Taylor Univ, 236 W Reade Ave Upland IN 46989; FT 7, PT 4; pvt; D ; Scholarships; SC 18, LC 7; D 200, non-maj 250, maj 94
Ent Req: HS dipl, SAT, recommendations
Degrees: BA and BS 4 yrs
Courses: Art History, †Art Studio, Ceramics, †Design, Drawing, Graphic Arts, †Graphic Design, †History of Art & Architecture, Metals, Mixed Media, †New Media, Painting, Photography, Printmaking, Sculpture, †Silversmithing, †Video

VINCENNES

VINCENNES UNIVERSITY JUNIOR COLLEGE, Humanities Art Dept, 1002 N First St, Vincennes, IN 47591. Tel 812-888-5110; Fax 812-888-5531; Elec Mail ajendrzejewski@indian.vinu.edu; Internet Home Page Address: www.vinu.edu; *Prof* Amy DeLap; *Prof* Jim Pearson; *Assoc Prof* Steve Black; *Assoc Prof* Deborah Hagedorn; *Assoc Prof* John Puffer; *Assoc Prof* Bernard Hagedorn; *Chmn* Andrew Jendrzejewski
Estab 1971; Maintain a nonprofit art gallery: Shircliff Gallery of Art, 1002 1st St, Vincennes University, Vincennes, IN 47591; Pub; D&E; Scholarships; SC 14, LC 2, Other Course 2; non-maj 80, maj 80
Ent Req: HS dipl
Degrees: AA, AS
Courses: Art Appreciation, †Art Education, Art History, Ceramics, †Commercial Art, †Design, Drawing, Fine Art, Graphic Arts, †Graphic Design, †Occupational Therapy, Painting, Photography, Printmaking, Sculpture, †Teacher Training

WEST LAFAYETTE

PURDUE UNIVERSITY, WEST LAFAYETTE, Patti and Rusty Rueff School of Visual & Performing Arts, Art & Design Dept, 552 W Wood St, West Lafayette, IN 47907-2002. Tel 765-494-3058; Fax 765-496-2076; Elec Mail adinfo@purdue.edu; Internet Home Page Address: www.cla.purdue.edu/vpa/vpa; *Dept Chair (art & design)* Robert Sabol, PhD; *Head of School (upa)* Harry Bulow, PhD
Estab 1869; Maintain a nonprofit art gallery (same address); FT 32; pub; D & E; Scholarships; SC 39, LC 14, GC 16; Grad 26
Ent Req: (see Purdue's admis website)
Degrees: BA 4 yrs, MFA
Tuition: Res—$4,466 per sem; nonres—$13,550 per sem
Courses: †Advertising Design, Aesthetics, Art Appreciation, Art Education, Art History, Ceramics, †Conceptual Art, Costume Design & Construction, Design, †Drawing, †Graphic Arts, †Graphic Design, History of Art & Architecture, Illustration, †Industrial Design, †Interior Design, †Jewelry, †Metals, †New Media, †Painting, †Photography, †Printmaking, †Sculpture, †Silversmithing, Stage Design, Teacher Training, †Textile Design, †Textiles, Theatre Arts, †Video, †Visual Communications Design, †Weaving

WINONA LAKE

GRACE COLLEGE, Dept of Art, 200 Seminary Dr, Winona Lake, IN 46590-1224. Tel 574-372-6021; Fax 574-372-5152; Elec Mail davisaw@grace.edu; Internet Home Page Address: www.grace.edu; *Assoc Prof* Gary Nietcr, MA; *Assoc Prof* Timothy Young, MFA; *Head Dept* Art Davis, MA
Estab 1952, dept estab 1971; maintain nonprofit art gallery, Mount Memorial Art Gallery; pvt; D & E; Scholarships; SC 12, LC 3; maj 80, non-maj 200
Ent Req: HS dipl, SAT
Degrees: 4 yr Art Major, 4 yr Educ Major, 4 yr Graphic Art, 4 yr Illustration, 4 yr Drawing/Painting

Courses: 2-D Design, 3-D Design, Art Appreciation, †Art Education, Art History, Ceramics, †Drawing, †Graphic Design, †Illustration, Painting, Photography, Printmaking, Teacher Training, Typography
Children's Classes: Children's Art Encounters, 6th - 12th grade, $50

IOWA

AMES

IOWA STATE UNIVERSITY, Dept of Art & Design, 158 College of Design Bldg, Ames, IA 50011-3092. Tel 515-294-6724; Fax 515-294-2725; Internet Home Page Address: www.iastate.edu; *Coordr Graphic Design* Sung Yung Kang; *Coordr Graphic Design* Debra Satterfield; *Coordr Integrated Arts* Arthur Croyle; *Coordr Interior Design* Fred Malvern; *Coordr Core Prog* Ann Sobiech-Munson; *Assoc Chair* Steve Herrnstadt
Estab 1858, dept estab 1920; Maintain nonprofit art gallery, Gallery 181, 134 College of Design, Iowa State Univ, Ames IA 50011; pub; D ; Scholarships; SC 45, LC 15, GC 15; D 1,000, maj 960, grad 40
Ent Req: HS dipl
Degrees: BA, BFA(Graphic Design, Integrated Studio Arts, Interior Design), MFA(Graphic & Interior Design, Integrated Studio Arts); MA First Professional Degree Interior Design, Graphic Design; MA Environmental Graphic Design
Courses: Art History, †Graphic Design, Integrated Arts: Ceramics, Drawing, Illustration, Digital Design, Metals, Wood, Painting, Photography, Printmaking, Fibers, †Interior Design
Summer School: Dir, Chair Dept Roger Baer. Term of 8 wks. Courses—Art Education, Art History, Design, Drawing, Painting

BOONE

DES MOINES AREA COMMUNITY COLLEGE, Art Dept, 1125 Hancock Dr, Boone Campus Boone, IA 50036-5326. Tel 515-432-7203; Fax 515-432-6311; Internet Home Page Address: www.demac.cc.ia.us; *Chmn* Pete Conis
Estab 1927, dept estab 1970; pub; D & E; SC 3, LC 2; D 100, E 60
Ent Req: HS dipl
Degrees: AA, AS 2 yrs
Courses: Art Appreciation, Art History, Art in Elementary School, Drawing, Exploring Art Media, Landscaping, Life Drawing, Painting, Stage Design, Teacher Training, Theatre Arts

CEDAR FALLS

UNIVERSITY OF NORTHERN IOWA, Dept of Art, 104 Kamerick Art Bldg, Cedar Falls, IA 50614-0362. Tel 319-273-2077; Fax 319-273-7333; Elec Mail artdept@uni.edu; Internet Home Page Address: www.uni.edu/artdept/Home.html; *Asst Prof* Soo Hostetler, MFA; *Prof* Roy Behrens, MA; *Prof* Charles Adelman PhD; *Prof* JoAnn Schnabel, MFA; *Prof* Thomas Stancliffe, MFA; *Prof, Art Dept Head* Jeff Byrd, MFA; *Prof* Philip Fass, MFA; *Assoc Prof* Aaron Wilson, MFA; *Prof* Richard Colburn, MFA; *Assoc Prof* Tim Dooley, MFA; *Asst Prof* Elizabeth Sutton, PhD; *Secy* Angela Kroemer; *Prof* Mary Frisbee Johnson
Estab 1876, dept estab 1945; Maintain nonprofit art gallery; art library; pub; D & E; Scholarships; SC 65, LC 20, GC 31; 13,500, non-maj 515, maj 400, grad 5
Ent Req: HS dipl, ACT
Degrees: BA & BFA 4 yrs, MA 1 1/2 yr
Tuition: Res—undergrad $2058 per sem, grad $2406 per sem; nonres— $5212 per sem, grad $5618 per sem, campus res—room & board $4148 per yr
Courses: Art Appreciation, Art Education, Art History, Ceramics, Drawing, Graphic Design, Illustration, †Jewelry/Metals, †Painting, Performance Art, Printmaking, Sculpture
Summer School: Dir Mary Frisbee Johnson. Enrl 75

CEDAR RAPIDS

COE COLLEGE, Dept of Art, 1220 1st Ave NE, Cedar Rapids, IA 52402-5008. Tel 319-399-8559; Fax 319-399-8557; Elec Mail pthompso@coe.edu; Internet Home Page Address: www.coe.edu/academics/art; *Chmn* Peter Thompson, MFA; *Assoc Prof* Andrea Kann; *Asst Prof* Lucy Goodson, MFA; *Lectr* Kathleen Carracio, MFA; *Prof* John Beckelman, MFA; *Adjunct* Priscilla Steele; *Asst Prof* David Webber
Estab 1851; Maintain nonprofit gallery & library, Marvin Cone Gallery, Eaton-Buchan Gallery, 1220 1st Ave NE, Cedar Rapids IA; on-campus shop where supplies may be purchased; pvt; D & E; Scholarships; SC 15, LC 5; D 1200
Ent Req: HS dipl, SAT, ACT
Degrees: BA 4 yr
Courses: Advertising Design, Aesthetics, Architecture, Art Appreciation, †Art Education, †Art History, †Ceramics, Collage, Costume Design & Construction, Design, Digital Art, Drafting, †Drawing, Film, Graphic Arts, Graphic Design, Mixed Media, †Painting, †Photography, †Printmaking, †Sculpture, †Teacher Training, Video

KIRKWOOD COMMUNITY COLLEGE, Dept of Arts & Humanities, 6301 Kirkwood Blvd SW, 336 Cedar Hall Cedar Rapids, IA 52404-5260. Tel 319-398-4956; Fax 319-398-7135; Elec Mail abareis@kirkwood.edu; Internet Home Page Address: www.kcc.edu; *Dean* Jennifer Bradley; *Prof* Doug Hall, MFA; *Prof* Helen Gruenwald, MA; *Asst Prof* Tonua Kehoe; *Instr & Fine & Performing Arts Spec* Arbe Bareis; *Instr* Rahatbek Sodaev; *Instr* Ben Johnson; *Instr* Robert Naujoks; *Instr* Daniel Cox; *Instr* Jim Ellis
Estab 1966; maintains nonprofit art gallery. Campus shop where art supplies may be purchased; pub; D & E; Scholarships; SC 18, LC 6; D 180, E 50
Ent Req: HS dipl

Degrees: AA 2 yr
Courses: Art Appreciation, Art History, Ceramics, Design, Drawing, Glass, Graphic Arts, Photography, Printmaking, Sculpture
Adult Hobby Classes: Fundamentals of Photography $395
Summer School: Tuition $35 per cr hr. Courses—Art History, Art Appreciation, Ceramics, Design, Drawing, Lettering, Painting, Photography, Printmaking, Sculpture

MOUNT MERCY COLLEGE, Art Dept, 1330 Elmhurst Dr NE, Cedar Rapids, IA 52402-4797. Tel 319-363-8213; Fax 319-363-5270; Internet Home Page Address: www2.mtmercy.edu; *Prof* Charles Barth PhD, MFA; *Prof* Jane Gilmor, MFA; *Asst Prof* David VanAllen, MFA; *Instr* Robert Naujoks, MFA
Estab 1928, dept estab 1960; Maintain nonprofit art gallery; Janalyn Hanson White Gallery; art library; Pvt; D & E; Scholarships; SC 12, LC 5; D 1,100, E 300, non-maj 150, maj 45
Ent Req: HS dipl, ACT
Degrees: BA 4 yr
Courses: †Art Education, Art History, Calligraphy, Ceramics, Design, Drawing, Graphic Arts, Graphic Design, Jewelry, Painting, Photography, Sculpture, Textile Design, Travel Study
Summer School: Dir, Susan Pauly, VPres Acad Affairs. Enrl 500; tuition $1,215 per 3 hr course, two 5 wk sessions. Courses—Art Appreciation, Ceramics, Graphic Design, Photography

CENTERVILLE

INDIAN HILLS COMMUNITY COLLEGE, Dept of Art, 721 N 1st St, Centerville, IA 52544-1223. Tel 641-856-2143; Fax 641-856-5527; Internet Home Page Address: www.ihcc.cc.iowa.us; WATS 800-670-3641; *Head Dept* Mark McWhorter; *Instr* Enfys McMurrey, MA; *Instr* David Johnson
Estab 1932, dept estab 1967; pub; D & E; Scholarships; SC 10; D 70, E 30, non-maj 50, maj 14
Ent Req: HS dipl or equal, open door
Degrees: AA 2 yr
Courses: Art Appreciation, Art History, Arts & Crafts, Ceramics, Design, †Design, †Drafting, Drawing, †Occupational Therapy, Painting, †Photography, Raku Pottery, †Theatre Arts
Summer School: Chmn, Mark McWhorter. Courses—Art Appreciation, Ceramics, Design, European Art Tours, Painting

CLINTON

ASHFORD UNIVERSITY, (Mount Saint Clare College) Art Dept, 400 N Bluff, Clinton, IA 52732. Tel 563-242-4023; Fax 563-242-2003; Internet Home Page Address: www.ashford.edu; *Head Dept* Prof Anna Pagnucci
Estab 1928, dept estab 1940; Maintain non-profit art gallery, Clare Hall (same address); Pvt; D & E; Scholarships; SC 5, LC 1; non-maj 80, maj 8
Ent Req: HS dipl
Degrees: AA, BA, MA
Courses: 2-D & 3-D Design, †Animation, Art Appreciation, †Art Education, †Art History, Calligraphy, Ceramics, Computer Art, Computer Graphics, Design, Desktop Publishing, Drawing, Fiber Art, Fiber Sculpture, †Graphic Arts, †Graphic Design, †Painting, †Photography, †Printmaking, †Sculpture, †Teacher Training, †Video
Summer School: Art Appreciation, Calligraphy, Painting

EASTERN IOWA COMMUNITY COLLEGE, Clinton Community College, 1000 Lincoln Blvd, Clinton, IA 52732-6299. Tel 563-244-7001; Fax 319-244-7026; Internet Home Page Address: www.eicc.edu; *Instr* Carolyn Phillips
Estab 1946; Pub; D&E, distance educ; Scholarships
Ent Req: depends on specific scholarship
Degrees: AA
Tuition: Res—$65 fees included per sem; nonres—$97.50 fees included per sem
Courses: Art Appreciation, Art History, Design, Drawing, Painting, Photography, Printmaking

COUNCIL BLUFFS

IOWA WESTERN COMMUNITY COLLEGE, Art Dept, 2700 College Rd, Council Bluffs, IA 51503-1057; PO Box 4C, Council Bluffs, IA 51502-3004. Tel 712-325-3200; Fax 712-325-3424; *Chmn* Frances Parrott
2000
Degrees: BA 4 yr
Tuition: Res—undergrad $79 per cr hr; nonres—undergrad $114
Courses: Art Appreciation, Art History, Ceramics, Design, Drawing, Painting, Photography, Sculpture

CRESTON

SOUTHWESTERN COMMUNITY COLLEGE, Art Dept, 1501 W Townline St, Creston, IA 50801-1098. Tel 641-782-7081; Fax 641-782-3312; Internet Home Page Address: www.swcc.cc.ia.us; *Dir Art Dept* Linda Dainty
Estab 1966; pub; D & E; Scholarships; SC 6, LC 3; D 550, E 200, non-maj 40, maj 15, others 15
Ent Req: HS dipl
Degrees: AA 2 yrs
Courses: Art Appreciation, Art Education, Art History, Ceramics, Computer Graphics, Design, Drawing, Graphic Design, Painting, Photography, Teacher Training
Adult Hobby Classes: Enrl 10-30; tuition $30 per sem. Courses—Per regular session
Summer School: Workshops in arts science

DAVENPORT

SAINT AMBROSE UNIVERSITY, Art Dept, 518 W Locust St, Davenport, IA 52803-2898. Tel 563-333-6000; Fax 563-333-6243; Internet Home Page Address: www.sau.edu; web.sau.edu/art; *Chair Art Dept & Prof Art History* Dr Terri Switzer, PhD; *Prof Art* Leslie Bell, MFA; *Prof Art* Kristin Quinn, MFA; *Asst Prof Art* Renee Meyer Ernst, MFA; *Asst Prof Art* Joseph Lappie, MFA
Estab 1892; pvt; D & E; Scholarships; SC 33, LC 15; undergrad 2885, maj 140, grad 844
Ent Req: HS dipl
Degrees: BA 4 yrs
Courses: Art Education, Art History, Calligraphy, Drawing, Graphic Arts, Graphic Design, Illustration, Lettering, Painting, Photography, Printmaking, Teacher Training, Web Design
Summer School: Tuition $400 per sem hr. Courses—vary

DECORAH

LUTHER COLLEGE, Art Dept, 700 College Dr, Decorah, IA 52101-1041. Tel 563-387-2000, 387-1114; Fax 563-387-1391; Elec Mail martinka@luther.edu; Internet Home Page Address: www.luther.edu; *Head Dept* Kate Martinson
Estab 1861; FT 3, PT 2; den; D; Scholarships; SC 13, LC 5; D 160
Ent Req: HS dipl or ent exam
Degrees: BA 4 yr
Courses: †Aesthetics, †Art Education, Art Management, †Ceramics, Computer Art, †Drawing, Fibers, Graphic Arts, Hand Made Paper, †History of Art & Architecture, †Lettering, †Painting, †Printmaking, Spinning, †Stage Design, †Teacher Training, †Theatre Arts
Children's Classes: Enrl 50; Courses offered spring & fall
Summer School: Acad Dean, A Thomas Kraalsel. Enrl 200 June & July. Courses—Drawing, Invitation to Art

DES MOINES

DRAKE UNIVERSITY, Dept Art & Design, 2507 University Ave, Des Moines, IA 50311-4516. Tel 515-271-2863; Fax 515-271-2558; Elec Mail admissions@drake.edu; Internet Home Page Address: www.drake.edu/artsci/art; *Chmn & Prof Art* Robert Craig
Estab 1881; Maintains nonprofit Anderson Gallery at Harmon Fine Arts Center, 2505 Carpenter Ave, Des Moines, IA 50311; FT 10, PT 8; pvt; D & E; Scholarships; SC 64, LC 15, GC 33; D 140, maj 140
Ent Req: 2 pt average in HS or previous col
Degrees: BA, BFA
Courses: †Drawing, †Graphic Design, †History of Art & Architecture, †Painting, †Printmaking, †Sculpture

GRAND VIEW COLLEGE, Art Dept, 1200 Grandview Ave, Des Moines, IA 50316-1599. Tel 515-263-2800; Fax 515-263-2974; Internet Home Page Address: www.gvc.edu; *Dept Head* Dennis Kaven
Scholarships
Degrees: BA, cert
Tuition: Res—undergrad $6290 per sem
Courses: Art Therapy, Computer Graphics, Drawing, Jewelry, Painting, Photography, Printmaking, Textile Design, Theatre Arts

DUBUQUE

CLARKE COLLEGE, Dept of Art, 1550 Clarke Dr, Dubuque, IA 52001-3198. Tel 563-588-6300; Fax 563-588-6789; Elec Mail joan.lingen@clarke.edu; Internet Home Page Address: www.clarke.edu; *Chmn & Prof Art* Joan Lingen PhD; *Prof Art* Douglas Schlesier, MFA; *Prof Art* Louise Kamas, MFA; *Assoc Prof* Carmelle Zserdin, MA; *Assoc Prof* Al Grivetti, MFA
Estab 1843; Maintain nonprofit art gallery; Quigley Gallery; pvt, den; D & E; Scholarships; SC 15, LC 4; maj 60, others 1200
Ent Req: HS grad, 16 units and Col Ent Board
Degrees: BFA(studio), BA(studio & art history) & BFA(graphic design)
Courses: Aesthetics, Art Appreciation, †Art Education, Art History, Book Arts, Calligraphy, †Ceramics, Costume Design & Construction, Design, †Drawing, †Graphic Design, History of Art & Architecture, Lettering, Mixed Media, †Painting, Photography, †Printmaking, †Sculpture, Stage Design, †Teacher Training, †Theatre Arts
Adult Hobby Classes: Enrl varies; 3, 4, 7 & 15 wk terms
Children's Classes: Enrl 15 per camp; tuition $60 per wk, summers
Summer School: Dir, Karen Adams. 3-4 wk term. Courses—Varies from yr to yr

LORAS COLLEGE, Dept of Art, 1450 Alta Vista, Dubuque, IA 52001. Tel 563-588-7117; Fax 563-588-7292; Internet Home Page Address: www.loras.edu; *Chmn & Prof* Roy Haught; *Assoc Prof* Thomas Jewell Vitale; *Instr* Tom Gibbs
Degrees: MA (Art Educ & Studio Arts), BA
Tuition: Res & nonres—$13,645 per yr
Courses: Art Appreciation, †Art Education, †Art History, Design, Drawing, †Fibers, Painting, Printmaking, Sculpture, †Studio Art
Summer School: Dir, John Hess. Enrl $170 per course

ESTHERVILLE

IOWA LAKES COMMUNITY COLLEGE, Dept of Art, 300 S 18th St, Estherville, IA 51334-2721. Tel 712-362-2604; Fax 712-362-8363; Estab 1967; pub; D & E; Scholarships; SC 26, LC 1
Ent Req: HS dipl
Degrees: AA, AS(Commercial Art) 2 yrs
Tuition: Res—undergrad $917 per sem; nonres—undergrad $941 per sem

Courses: Advertising Design, Art History, Calligraphy, Ceramics, Commercial Art, Commercial Studio Portfolio Preparation, Computer Graphics, Drawing, Graphic Arts, Graphic Design, Illustration, Mixed Media, Painting, Photography
Summer School: Courses—Internships in Commercial Art

FOREST CITY

WALDORF COLLEGE, Art Dept, 106 S Sixth St Forest City, IA 50436. Tel 641-585-2450; Fax 641-582-8194; Internet Home Page Address: www.waldorf.edu; *Chair* Kristi Carlson; *Adjunct* Lori Hadacek
Estab 1903; FT 1, PT 2; den; D & E; Scholarships; SC 4, D 80, maj 15
Ent Req: HS dipl, ACT or SAT
Degrees: AA, 2 yr, BA, 3 yr
Courses: Art Appreciation, †Art History, Design, Drawing, Painting, Photography, Printmaking

FORT DODGE

IOWA CENTRAL COMMUNITY COLLEGE, Dept of Art, 330 Ave M, Fort Dodge, IA 50501. Tel 515-576-7201; Internet Home Page Address: www.iccc.cc.ia.us; *Chmn* Rusty Farrington
Estab 1966; Pub; D & E; Scholarships; SC 4, LC 2; D 120, E 15, non-maj 153, maj 20
Ent Req: HS dipl
Degrees: AA 2 yr
Courses: Art History, Painting, Studio Art
Summer School: Dir, Rusty Farrington. Enrl 45; tuition $53 per cr hr

GRINNELL

GRINNELL COLLEGE, Dept of Art, 1108 Park St, Grinnell, IA 50112. Tel 641-269-3064, 269-3085; Fax 515-269-4420; Internet Home Page Address: www.grinnell.edu; *Prof* Merle W Zirkle; *Interim Dir* Bobbie McKibbin; *Chmn* Tony Crowley
Estab 1846, dept estab 1930; Maintain nonprofit art gallery; Faueconer Art Gallery-Bucksbaum Center for Arts; pvt; D; Scholarships; SC 9, LC 9; D 150, non-maj 125, maj 25
Ent Req: HS dipl, SAT or ACT
Degrees: BA 4 yrs
Courses: Art Education, Art History, Ceramics, Design, Drawing, Jewelry, Painting, Printmaking, Sculpture

IOWA CITY

UNIVERSITY OF IOWA, School of Art & Art History, 150 Art Bldg W, Iowa City, IA 52242-1706. Tel 319-335-1771; Fax 319-335-1774; Internet Home Page Address: www.uiowa.edu; *Prof Foil Stamping* Virginia Myers; *Prof Metalsmithing & Jewelry* Chunghi Choo; *Dir* Dorothy Johnson
Estab 1847, school estab 1911; FT 38, PT 3; pub; D & E; Scholarships; SC 60, LC 55, GC 55; D 681, maj 508, grad 173
Ent Req: HS dipl, ACT or SAT, upper rank in HS
Degrees: BA and BFA 4 yr, MA, MFA, PhD
Courses: Aesthetics, †Art Education, †Art History, †Calligraphy, †Ceramics, Conceptual Art, †Design, †Drawing, †Graphic Design, Industrial Design, Interior Design, †Intermedia, †Jewelry, †Multimedia, †Painting, †Photography, †Printmaking, †Sculpture, †Silversmithing, Teacher Training, †Video
Summer School: Dir, Dorothy Johnson. Enrl undergrad 195, grad 115; tuition res—undergrad $1030, grad $1467; nonres—undergrad $3780, grad $4726 for term of 8 wks, beginning June 10. Courses—Full range of Art Education, Art History, Studio Courses

IOWA FALLS

ELLSWORTH COMMUNITY COLLEGE, Dept of Fine Arts, 1100 College Ave, Iowa Falls, IA 50126-1199. Tel 641-648-4611; Fax 641-648-3128; Internet Home Page Address: www.iavalley.cc.il.us/eco; *Chmn* Greg Metzen
Estab 1890; pub; D & E; SC 10, LC 1; in dept D 20-25
Ent Req: HS dipl, ACT
Degrees: AA 2 yrs
Courses: †Advertising Design, Art Appreciation, Art History, Ceramics, Commercial Art, Design, Drawing, Graphic Arts, Graphic Design, Illustration, Lettering, Mixed Media, Painting, Photography, Sculpture
Adult Hobby Classes: Enrl 12; tuition $20 per 20 hrs. Courses—Pottery
Summer School: Dir, Dr Del Shepard. Enrl 14; tuition $40 per sem hr for 4 weeks. Courses—Art Interpretation

LAMONI

GRACELAND UNIVERSITY, Fine Arts Div, One University Pl, Lamoni, IA 50140. Tel 641-784-5270; Fax 641-784-5487; Elec Mail finearts@graceland.edu; Internet Home Page Address: www.graceland.edu; *Dept Coordr & Assoc Prof* Julia Franklin; *Asst Prof* Kitty Miller; *Assoc Prof* Robert Stephens; *Asst Prof* John Stanko; *Instr* Chuck Manuel; *Instr* Amber McDole
Estab 1895, dept estab 1961; Maintain nonprofit art gallery, Constance Gallery, The Helene Center Art Gallery & The Shaw Center Art Gallery, 1 University Pl, Lamoni, IA; pvt den; D; Scholarships; SC 36, LC 10; D 250, E 15, non-maj 60, maj 85, others 4
Ent Req: HS dipl
Degrees: BA and BS 4 yrs

Courses: Art Appreciation, †Art Education, Art History, Ceramics, Color Theory, †Commercial Design, Computer Graphic Design, Design, Drawing, †Graphic Design, Illustration, †Painting, Photography, †Printmaking, †Sculpture
Children's Classes: 138 summer art camp attendance, one week $75
Summer School: Dir, Dr Velma Ruch

MASON CITY

NORTH IOWA AREA COMMUNITY COLLEGE, Dept of Art, 500 College Dr, Mason City, IA 50401-7213. Tel 641-423-1264, Ext 242; Tel 888-406-4222; Fax 641-423-1711; Elec Mail allisway@niacc.edu; Internet Home Page Address: www.niacc.cc.edu; *Instr* Melissa Lovingood, MFA; *Instr & Chair* Wayne Allison, MFA; *Adjunct* Ken Anderson; *Adjunct* Ted Bieth; *Adjunct Emer* Peggy Bang; *Adjunct* Dean Swenson; *Adjunct* Paula Haaus, MFA
Estab 1964; Maintains nonprofit NIACC Auditorium Gallery; schols open to art majors; on-campus shop where art supplies may be purchased; pub; D & E; Scholarships; SC 4, LC 2; D 240, E 100, maj 30
Ent Req: HS dipl
Degrees: AA 2 yr
Tuition: Res— $800 per 15 cr hrs; nonres—$1200 per 15 cr hr
Courses: 2-D Design, Art Appreciation, Art Education, Art History, Ceramics, Computer Graphic Design, †Design, Drawing, †Graphic Arts, †Graphic Design, †History of Art & Architecture, †Mixed Media, Painting, Photography

MOUNT PLEASANT

IOWA WESLEYAN COLLEGE, Art Dept, 601 N Main, Mount Pleasant, IA 52641. Tel 319-385-8021; Internet Home Page Address: www.iwc.edu; *Chmn* Don R Jones; *Chmn Fine Arts Div* Ann Kligensmith; *Design Ctr Adjunct* Mike Foley; *Ceramist Adjunct* Truly Ball; *Art Educ Adjunct* Don Kramer
Estab 1842; den; Scholarships; SC 10, LC 4; maj 32
Degrees: BA 4 yr
Courses: Art Education, Art History, Ceramics, Design, Drawing, Graphic Arts, Introduction to Art, Painting, Photography, Printmaking, Secondary Art, Special Problems, Twentieth Century Art History, †Visual Communication & Design

OTTUMWA

INDIAN HILLS COMMUNITY COLLEGE, OTTUMWA CAMPUS, Dept of Art, 525 Grandview, Ottumwa, IA 52501. Tel 641-683-5111 ext 1825; Fax 641-683-5206; Elec Mail mark.mcwhorter@indianhills.edu; Internet Home Page Address: www.indianhills.edu; WATS 800-726-2585; *Dean Arts & Sciences* Darlas Shockley; *Dept Head* Mark McWhorter; *Instr* Lisa Fritz
Estab 1965; Maintains nonprofit art gallery, Indian Hills Art Gallery 525 Grandview Ottumwa, IA 52501; schols open to art majors; on-campus shop where art supplies may be purchased; pub; D & E; Scholarships; SC 7, LC 2; D 150, E 70, maj 25
Ent Req: HS dipl, GED, ACT or SAT
Degrees: AA, AAS & AAA 2 yrs
Tuition: Res—$137 per sem cr hr; nonres—$160 per sem cr hr (res acquired after 90 days)
Courses: Advertising Design, Aesthetics, Art Appreciation, Art History, Ceramics, Crafts, Design, Drafting, Drawing, Film, †Graphic Design, Handicrafts, History of Art & Architecture, Lettering, Occupational Therapy, Painting, Photography, Sculpture
Adult Hobby Classes: Enrl 10-20; tuition $35 per sem cr hr. Courses—Ceramics, Painting, Watercolor
Summer School: Dean Arts & Sciences, Darlas Shockley. Enrl 120; 6 wk session. Courses—Liberal Arts, $137 per hr

PELLA

CENTRAL COLLEGE, (Central University of Iowa) Art Dept, 812 University, Pella, IA 50219. Tel 641-628-5261; Internet Home Page Address: www.central.edu; *Chmn* J Vruwink, MFA
Estab 1853; pvt; D & E; Scholarships; SC 20, LC 6; D 180, non-maj 140, maj 40
Ent Req: HS dipl, ACT
Degrees: BA 4 yrs
Courses: Art History, Ceramics, Drawing, Glassblowing, Modern Art, Painting, Primitive Art, Studio Art

SIOUX CITY

BRIAR CLIFF UNIVERSITY, Art Dept, 3303 Rebecca St, Sioux City, IA 51104-2324. Tel 712-279-5321 or 800-662-3303; Fax 712-279-1698; Elec Mail bill.welu@briarcliff.edu; Internet Home Page Address: www.sbc.edu/academic/arts; *Chairperson* William J Welu, MFA; *Assoc Prof* Dr Judith A Welu, MFA, EdD; *Lectr* Jeff Baldus, BA; *Lectr* Noreen Eskildsen, MA
Estab 1930; Maintain nonprofit art gallery; Clausen Art Gallery; pvt, den; D & E; Scholarships; SC 8, LC 5; D 250, non-maj 150, maj 30
Ent Req: HS dipl, ACT
Degrees: BA and BS 4 yr, MA in Educ
Courses: 2, 3 & 4 (major studio areas & independent study), Art 1, Art Appreciation, Art Education, Art History, Ceramics, Collage, Critical Seminar, Design, Drawing, Intermedia, †Mixed Media, †Painting, †Sculpture, †Teacher Training
Summer School: Dr Judith Welu. Enrl 30-40; tuition $210 per cr hr for 5 wk term. Courses—Contemporary Art History, Elementary Art Education, Pottery

MORNINGSIDE COLLEGE, Art Dept, 1501 Morningside Ave, Sioux City, IA 51106-1717. Tel 712-274-5212; Fax 712-274-5101; Elec Mail bowitz@morningside.edu; Internet Home Page Address: www.morningside.edu; *Chmn* John Bowitz; *Asst Prof* Terri McGaffin; *Instr* John Kolbo; *Instr* Shannon Sargent; *Instr* Jim Bisenius; *Instr* Amy Foltz; *Instr* Dolie Thompson

Estab 1894; Maintain nonprofit art gallery, Helen Levitt Gallery & Eppley Gallery 3625 Garretson Ave, Sioux City, IA 51106; on-campus shop for art supplies; FT 4; pvt; D & E; Scholarships; SC 17, LC 4; D 161, maj 90
Ent Req: HS dipl
Degrees: BA and BS (Art Educ) 4 yrs
Courses: Advertising Design, Art Education, Art History, Ceramics, Commercial Art, Conceptual Art, Costume Design & Construction, Design, Drawing, Film, Graphic Arts, Graphic Design, Illustration, Mixed Media, Painting, Photography, Printmaking, Sculpture, Stage Design, Studio, Teacher Training, Theatre Arts, Video
Summer School: Dir, John Bowitz. Enrl 50; tuition $270 per cr, May, June, July. Courses—Drawing, Photography

SIOUX CITY ART CENTER, 225 Nebraska St, Sioux City, IA 51101-1712. Tel 712-279-6272; Fax 712-255-2921; Elec Mail kwelch@sioux-city.org; Internet Home Page Address: www.siouxcityartcenter.org; *Dir* Al Harris-Fernandez; *Chair* Doug Palmer; *Cur* Todd Behrens; *Exhib & Coll Coordr* Shannon Sargent; *Pres* Jay Chesterman; *Sec* Kjersten Welch; *Studio Prog Coordr* Jenny Bye; *Educ Liaison* Alice Harley; *Develop Coordr* Regis Garvey; *Develop Assoc* Kari Kellen; *ArtSplash Coordr* Lisa Verschoor-Matney
Estab 1938; Maintains nonprofit art gallery, Atrium Gift Gallery, 225 Nebraska St, Sioux City IA 51101; Margaret Avery Heffernan Reference Library, non-circulating, vis by appt only; pvt & pub partnership; D & E; Scholarships; SC 14-20, LC 1-2, GC 15; D 100, E 400
Courses: Ceramics, Drawing, Mixed Media, Painting, Photography, Printmaking, Stained Glass
Adult Hobby Classes: Enrl 62, tuition $92-$125 (mem) & $100-$1567 (non-mem) for 8 wk quarterly terms; Courses—Drawing, Painting (Oil, Watercolor), Stained Glass, Mosaics, Printmaking, Digital Photography, Black & White Film Photography, Adobe Photoshop, Ceramics, Pottery from Wheel, Assemblage Art
Children's Classes: Enrl 252; tuition $5-$80 (mem) & $5 - $96 (non-mem) for 8 wk quarterly term; Courses—Clay, Drawing, Mixed Media, Painting
Summer School: Project SOAR: Dir, Alice Marley; open to HS students; Enrl 10 per workshop; Tuition $10 per student; Courses—Photography, Ceramics, Drawing, Painting. Art Camp: Dir, Jenny Bye; open to ages 6 - 12; Enrl 24 per AM & PM sessions; $100 half-day, $200 full day (mem) & $123 half-day, $246 full day (non-mem) for 6-day camp offered over 2 wks; 4 - 5 camps offered through summer with AM, PM or full-day options; Courses—Drawing, Painting, Clay, Mixed Media

WAVERLY

WARTBURG COLLEGE, Dept of Art, 100 Wartburg Blvd, Waverly, IA 50677-2200. Tel 319-352-8200; Internet Home Page Address: www.wartburg.edu/art; WATS 800-553-1797; *Dept Head* Thomas Payne, MFA; *Asst Prof* Barbara Fedeler, MFA
Estab 1852; Non-profit art gallery; den; D & E; Scholarships; SC 18, LC 4; D 135, non-maj 110, maj 25
Ent Req: HS dipl, PSAT, ACT & SAT, foreign students TOEFL and upper 50 percent of class
Degrees: BA(Art), BA(Art Educ) 4 yrs
Tuition: Res—undergrad $15,510 per yr, $5850 room & board
Courses: Advertising Design, Art Appreciation, Art Education, Art History, Computer Graphic Design, Design, Drawing, Graphic Design, Metal Design, Painting, Photography, Printmaking, Sculpture
Summer School: Courses—Drawing, Independent Study, Painting

KANSAS

ATCHISON

BENEDICTINE COLLEGE, Art Dept, 1020 N Second St, Atchison, KS 66002. Tel 913-367-5340; Fax 913-367-6102; Internet Home Page Address: www.benedictine.edu; *Chmn* Dan Carrell
Estab 1971; FT 1; den; D; SC 15, LC 3; D 145, non-maj 123, maj 22
Ent Req: HS dipl, ent exam
Degrees: BA 4 yr
Courses: Art Education, Art History, Calligraphy, Ceramics, Drawing, Graphic Arts, Painting, Photography, Printmaking, Sculpture, Teacher Training

BALDWIN CITY

BAKER UNIVERSITY, Dept of Mass Media & Visual Arts, 618 Eighth St, Baldwin City, KS 66006. Tel 785-594-4509; Fax 785-594-2522; Elec Mail bknappe@bakeru.edu; Internet Home Page Address: www.bakeru.edu/contact/directories/academic-departments/art; *Chair & Asst Prof Art History* Brett Knappe; *Prof Art* Inge Balch; *Instr Art* Jenn Jarnot
Estab 1858; Maintains nonprofit art gallery: Holt/Russell Gallery, Baker Univ, PO Box 65, Baldwin City, KS 66006; schols open to all incoming students; pvt; D & E; Scholarships; SC 14, LC 9; D 180, maj 25
Ent Req: HS dipl, provision made for entrance without HS dipl by interview & comt action
Degrees: BA (Art) 4 yrs
Tuition: $19,925 per yr
Courses: Art Education, †Art History, Ceramics, Drawing, Graphic Arts, History of Art & Architecture, Painting, †Photography, Printmaking, Sculpture, Teacher Training
Summer School: Available; enrl & courses offered vary

COFFEYVILLE

COFFEYVILLE COMMUNITY COLLEGE, Art Dept, 400 W 11th St, Coffeyville, KS 67337-5064. Tel 620-252-7020; Fax 620-252-7098; Elec Mail michaeld@coffeyville.edu; Internet Home Page Address: www.ccc.cc.ks.us; *Head Dept* Michael DeRosa
Estab 1923, dept estab 1969; pub; D & E; Scholarships; SC 8, LC 2; D 300, E 60, non-maj 300, maj 25
Ent Req: HS dipl
Degrees: AA
Courses: Art Appreciation, Art Education, Art History, Ceramics, Constructions, Design, Drawing, Film, Handicrafts, Mixed Media, Painting, Photography, Printmaking, Sculpture, Theatre Arts, Video
Adult Hobby Classes: Enrl 15-20; 3 month sem. Courses—Crafts
Children's Classes: Enrl 15; tuition $60 for 2 wks. Courses—Clay, Sculpture
Summer School: Dir, Michael DeRosa. Enrl 25; 2 month session.
Courses—Ceramics I, Drawing I

COLBY

COLBY COMMUNITY COLLEGE, Visual Arts Dept, 1255 S Range, Colby, KS 67701. Tel 785-462-3984; Fax 785-462-4600; Internet Home Page Address: www.colby.edu; *Dir* Kathy Gordon
Estab 1965, dept estab 1966; pub; D & E; Scholarships; SC 18, LC 8; D 141, E 210, maj 18
Activities: Bookstore
Ent Req: HS dipl
Degrees: AA 2 yrs
Courses: †Art Appreciation, †Art Education, †Art History, Color Structure & Design, †Drawing, †Graphic Design, Painting, †Printmaking
Adult Hobby Classes: Enrl 10-20; tuition $15 per hr

EL DORADO

BUTLER COUNTY COMMUNITY COLLEGE, Art Dept, 901 S Haverhill Rd, El Dorado, KS 67042-3225. Tel 316-321-2222; Fax 316-322-3318; Internet Home Page Address: www.butlercc.edu; *Dean* Larry Patton; *Instr* Valerie Haring
Estab 1927, dept estab 1964; Maintain nonprofit art gallery; Erman B White Gallery, 901 S Haverhill, El Dorado KS 67042; pub; D & E, online courses; Scholarships; SC 13, LC 1; D 168, E 57
Ent Req: HS dipl, ACT, EED
Degrees: AA 2 yr
Tuition: Res—$44 per cr hr; nonres—$89.50 per cr hr
Courses: Art History, Ceramics, Drawing, †Glasswork, Interior Design, Painting, Printmaking, Silversmithing

EMPORIA

EMPORIA STATE UNIVERSITY, Dept of Art, 1200 Commercial St, Emporia, KS 66801-5057. Tel 620-341-5246; Fax 620-341-6246; Internet Home Page Address: www.emporia.edu/art; *Chair* Elaine Henry; *Asst Prof* Matthew Derezinski; *Prof* Dan R Kirchhefer; *Asst Prof* Patrick Martin; *Asst Prof* Andre Piper; *Prof* Larry Schwarm; *Asst* Eric Conrad; *Asst* Roberta Eichenberg; *Lectr* Deborah Maxwell; *Lectr* Susan Nakao; *Lectr* John Hasegawa; *Lectr* Lily Liu; *Asst* Monica Kjellman-Chapin
Estab 1863, dept estab early 1900s; Maintain nonprofit art gallery; Norman R Eppink Art Gallery, Johnkins Hall, Emporia State Univ, Emporia, KS 66801; art supplies available on-campus; pub; D & E; Scholarships; SC 42, LC 15, GC 30; D 920, E 60, maj 182, grad 10
Ent Req: HS dipl, HS seniors may enroll in regular classes, ACT 21
Degrees: BFA, BSE, BS(Art Therapy) 4 yr, MS(Art Therapy)
Courses: Art Appreciation, †Art Education, Art History, †Ceramics, Design, Drawing, Engraving Arts, Fibers, Glass, †Graphic Design, Metals, Mixed Media, †Painting, †Photography, †Printmaking, †Sculpture, Teacher Training
Adult Hobby Classes: Metals, Ceramics & Photography
Summer School: Chair, Elaine Henry. Courses—most of the regular classes

GARDEN CITY

GARDEN CITY COMMUNITY COLLEGE, Art Dept, 801 Campus Dr, Garden City, KS 67846. Tel 316-276-7611; Fax 316-276-9630; *Chmn Human & Fine Arts* Kevin Brungardt
Degrees: AA
Tuition: Res—undergrad $44 per cr hr; nonres—$78 per cr hr
Courses: Art Appreciation, Art History, Ceramics, Design, Drawing, Handicrafts, Interior Design, Jewelry, Painting, Photography, Printmaking, Stage Design, Stained Glass

GREAT BEND

BARTON COUNTY COMMUNITY COLLEGE, Fine Arts Dept, 245 NE 30 Rd, Great Bend, KS 67530-9251. Tel 316-792-9260; Internet Home Page Address: www.barton.cc.ks.us/dudekswatercolors; *Dir* Steve Dudek, MFA; *Instr* Marcia Polenberg, MFA
Estab 1965, dept estab 1969; FT 4 PT 3; pub; D & E; Scholarships
Ent Req: HS dipl or GED
Degrees: AA
Courses: Advertising Design, Architecture, Art Appreciation, Art Education, Art History, Ceramics, Commercial Art, Computer Graphics, Constructions, Design, Drawing, Graphic Arts, Graphic Design, Illustration, Interior Design, Jewelry, Occupational Therapy, Painting, Photography, Sculpture, †Stained Glass, †Web Design

Adult Hobby Classes: Enrl 50-300; tuition $38 per cr hr. Courses—Ceramics, Computer Graphics, Design, Drawing, Graphic Design, Individual Art Projects, Jewelry, Painting, Photo
Summer School: Dir, Steve Dudek. Enrl 30-60; tuition $38 per hr for 8 wks. Courses—Art Education, Art Media, Ceramics, Drawing, Individual Art Projects, Painting, Photo

HAYS

FORT HAYS STATE UNIVERSITY, Dept of Art & Design, 600 Park St, Hays, KS 67601-4099. Tel 785-628-4247; Fax 785-628-4087; Elec Mail ctaylor@fhsu.edu; Internet Home Page Address: www.fhsu.edu/art/; *Chmn* Leland Powers, MFA; *Prof* Joel Dugan, MFA; *Prof* Chaiwat Thumsujarit, MFA; *Prof* Zoran Stevanov PhD, MFA; *Instr* Erica Bittel, MA; *Asst Prof* Linda Ganstrom, MFA; *Assoc Prof* Allen Craven, MFA; *Prof* Gordon Sherman, MFA; *Asst Prof* Tobias Flores, MFA; *Prof* Karrie Simpson Voth, MFA; *Assoc Prof* Amy Schmierbach, MFA; *Instr* Charmion Arthur, MA; *Instr* Joyce Jilg, MA
Estab 1902, dept estab 1930; maintains nonprofit gallery, Moss-Thorns Gallery of Art, 600 Park St Hays, KS 67601-4009; on-campus art supply shop; pub; D & E; Scholarships; SC 66, LC 19, GC 28; D 742, non-maj 555, maj 286, grad 36, others 7
Ent Req: HS dipl
Degrees: BA & BFA 4 yrs, MFA 2 - 3 yrs
Tuition: Res—undergrad $145.27 per cr hr, grad $200.67 per cr hr; non-res—undergrad $427.37 pr cr hr, grad $510.02 per cr hr; campus res vailable
Courses: Advertising Design, Art Appreciation, †Art Education, †Art History, †Ceramics, Commercial Art, Design, †Drawing, †Graphic Design, †Handicrafts, Illustration, †Interior Design, Intermedia, Lettering, Mixed Media, †Painting, †Photography, †Printmaking, †Sculpture, †Teacher Training, Textile Design

HESSTON

HESSTON COLLEGE, Art Dept, 325 S College Ave, Hesston, KS 67062-9112; PO Box 3000, Hesston, KS 67062-2093. Tel 316-327-8164; Internet Home Page Address: www.hesston.edu; *Head Dept* Lois Misegadis; *Faculty Emeritus* Paul Friesen
Estab 1915; pvt; D; Scholarships; SC 9, SC 1; non-maj 50, maj 5
Ent Req: HS dipl
Degrees: AA 2 yr
Tuition: $8100 annual tuition; campus res available
Courses: Art Appreciation, Art History, Ceramics, Design, Drawing, Graphic Design, Painting, Photography, Printmaking, Sculpture, Theatre Arts

HUTCHINSON

HUTCHINSON COMMUNITY COLLEGE, (Hutchinson Community Junior College) Visual Arts Dept, 600 E 11th St, Hutchinson, KS 67501-5800. Tel 620-665-3500; Fax 620-665-3310; Elec Mail brewerb@hutchcc.edu; Internet Home Page Address: www.hutchcc.edu; *Prof* Roy Swanson; *Color & Graphic Instr* Scott Brown; *Ceramics & Sculpture Instr* Jerri Griffin; *Art History Instr* Teresa Preston; *Chmn* William Brewer
Estab 1928; Maintains nonprofit art gallery, Stringer Fyer Gallery; maintains art/architecture library, Parker Library; pub; D & E, on-line; Scholarships; SC 20+; D 215, E 41, non-maj 180, maj 81
Ent Req: HS dipl
Degrees: AA 2 yrs
Courses: Advertising Design, Architecture, Art Appreciation, Art Education, Art History, Ceramics, Commercial Art, Computer Graphics Design, Design, Drafting, Drawing, Graphic Arts, Graphic Design, Jewelry, Painting, Printmaking, Sculpture, Silversmithing, Stage Design, Teacher Training, Theatre Arts, Video
Summer School: Dir, Jeff Adams; Tuition $27 per hr for 6 wk session.
Courses—Art Appreciation, Art Education

IOLA

ALLEN COUNTY COMMUNITY COLLEGE, Art Dept, 1801 N Cottonwood, Iola, KS 66749. Tel 316-365-5116; Internet Home Page Address: www.allencc.net; *Dept Head* Steven R Greenwall, MFA
Estab 1965; pub; D & E; Scholarships; SC 5, LC 2; D 700, E 1000, non-maj 40, maj 10
Ent Req: HS dipl or GED
Degrees: AA, AS & AAS 2 yr
Courses: 2-D & 3-D Design, Art Appreciation, Art Fundamentals, Ceramics, Commercial Art, Drawing, Painting, Photography, Sculpture
Summer School: Courses—all courses

LAWRENCE

HASKELL INDIAN NATIONS UNIVERSITY, Art Dept, 155 Indian Ave, Lawrence, KS 66046-4817. Tel 785-749-8431, Ext 252; Internet Home Page Address: www.haskell.com; *Instr* B J Wahnee, MA
Estab 1884, dept estab 1970; pub; D; SC 14, LC 1; in dept D, non-maj 90, maj 30
Ent Req: HS dipl or GED, at least 1/4 Indian, Eskimo or Aleut and receive agency approval
Degrees: AA & AAS 2 yrs, BA 4 yr
Tuition: Government funded for native Americans only; campus res available
Courses: Art Appreciation, Art History, Ceramics, Design, Drawing, Jewelry, Native American Architecture, Native American Art History, Native American Cultural/Tribal Art Forms, Native American Painting, Painting, Sculpture, Textile Design
Summer School: Enrl 150

UNIVERSITY OF KANSAS, The School of the Arts, Dept of Visual Art, 1467 Jayhawk Blvd, Lawrence, KS 66045-3140. Tel 785-864-4401; Fax 785-864-4404; Elec Mail visualart@ku.edu; Internet Home Page Address: art.ku.edu; *Assoc Prof* Norman Akers; *Assoc Prof* Jane Asbury; *Asst Prof* Shawn (Daina) Bitters; *Prof Emer* Phillip Blackhurst; *Assoc Prof & Undergrad Coordr* Ruth Bowman; *Asst Prof* David Brackett; *Asst Prof* Matt Burke; *Prof* Carol Ann Carter; *Asst Prof* John Derby; *Lectr* Stacey Fox; *Prof Emer* Norman Gee; *Prof* Dawn Guernsey; *Assoc Prof* John Hachmeister; *Assoc Prof & Grad Dir* Tanya Hartman; *Prof* Jon Havener; *Prof & Chair* Mary Anne Jordan; *Prof* Cima Katz; *Assoc Prof & Assoc Dean* Elizabeth Kowalchuk; *Assoc Prof* Michael Krueger; *Prof* Gerald Lubensky; *Asst Prof* Marshall Maude; *Prof* Judith McCrea; *Assoc Prof* Yoomi Nam; *Assoc Prof* So Yeon Park; *Prof* Lin Stanionis; *Assoc Prof* Denise Stone; *Prof* Jon Swindell; *Asst Prof* Maria Velasco; *Assoc Prof* David Vertacnik; *Assoc Prof* Gina Westergard
Estab 1864; Maintains nonprofit art gallery; art supplies sold at on-campus store; Pub; D & E; Scholarships, Fellowships; SC 70, GC 35; 260
Ent Req: Portfolio review, essays
Degrees: BA, BAE, BFA, MA, MFA 4-5 yr
Tuition: Res—undergrad $262.50, grad $295.50 per cr hr; nonres—undergrad $689.35, grad $691.25 per cr hr
Courses: Art Education, Art History, Ceramics, Drawing, Goldsmithing, Mixed Media, Painting, Printmaking, Sculpture, Silversmithing, Teacher Training, Textile Design, Weaving
Summer School: Dir, Mary Anne Jordon
—Dept of Art, 1467 Jayhawk Blvd, Art & Design Bldg Rm 300 Lawrence, KS 66045-7594. Tel 785-864-4401; Fax 785-864-4404; *Chmn* Judith McCrea
Estab 1885; FT 19; Scholarships; SC 50, GC 25; maj 160
Tuition: Res—undergrad $899 per sem, grad $1088 per sem; nonres— $2985 per sem
Courses: †Drawing, New Genres, †Painting, †Printmaking, †Sculpture
Summer School: Dir, Judith McCrea. Enrl 60; tuition $57 for 8 wks.
Courses—Life Drawing, Intro to Drawing I & II, Painting I-IV
—Dept of Design, 1467 Jayhawk Blvd, Art & Design Bldg Rm 300 Lawrence, KS 66045-7531. Tel 785-864-4401; *Chmn* Lois Greene
Estab 1921; FT 25, PT 5; SC 83, LC 32, GC 26; maj 550, grad 30
Tuition: Res—undergrad $2041.50 per yr, $68.05 per cr hr; nonres—undergrad $8460 per yr, $282 per cr hr
Courses: †Art Education, †Ceramics, Design, †Graphic Design, †Illustration, †Industrial Design, †Interior Design, †Jewelry, Photography, †Textile Design, Textile Printing & Dyeing, Visual Communications, †Weaving
Summer School: Term of 4-8 wks beginning June
—Kress Foundation Dept of Art History, Spencer Museum of Art, Rm 209, Lawrence, KS 66045. Tel 785-864-4713; Fax 785-864-5091; Elec Mail arthist@lark.cc.ukans.edu; *Dept Chair* Linda Stone-Ferrier; *Prof Emeritus* Chu-tsing Li PhD; *Prof* Charles Eldredge PhD; *Prof* Marilyn Stokstad PhD; *Prof* Stephen Goddard; *Prof & Asian Grad Adv* Marsha Weidner; *Assoc Prof* Edmund Eglinski PhD; *Assoc Prof* Amy McNair; *Assoc Prof* David Catetorts PhD; *Asst Prof* John Teramoto PhD; *Asst Prof* Patrick Frank; *Lectr* Roger Ward; *Dir Mus* Andrea Norris PhD; *Asst Prof* Patricia Darish PhD; *Assoc Prof* John Pultz
Estab 1866, dept estab 1953; pub; D & E; Scholarships; LC 30, GC 10; D 900, E 40, maj 50, grad 70
Ent Req: HS dipl
Degrees: BA, BFA, BGS, MA, PhD
Tuition: Res—undergrad $2041.50 per yr, $68.05 per cr hr; nonres—undergrad $8460 per yr, $282 per cr hr
Courses: African Art, American Art, Art History, Chinese Art, Japanese Art, Photography, Western European Art
Summer School: Enrl 80. Intro courses—Art History, Asian Art History & Modern Art History. Classes in Great Britain & Rome
—Dept of Art & Music Education & Music Therapy, 311 Bailey Hall, Lawrence, KS 66045-0001. Tel 785-864-4784; Fax 785-864-5076; *Chmn Dept* Lois Greene; *Assoc Prof* Denise Stone PhD; *Asst Prof* Elizabeth Kowalchek
Estab 1865, dept estab 1969; pub; D & E; Scholarships; GC 12; D 535, maj 123, grad 123, others 289
Ent Req: HS dipl, ent exam
Degrees: BAE 5 yrs, MA 1-6 yrs, PhD 3-6 yrs
Tuition: Res—undergrad $2041.50 per yr, $68.05 per cr hr; nonres—undergrad $8460 per yr, $282 per cr hr
Courses: Visual Arts Education
Summer School: Term of 8 wks beginning June

LEAVENWORTH

UNIVERSITY OF SAINT MARY, (Saint Mary College) Fine Arts Dept, 4100 S 4th St, Leavenworth, KS 66048-5082. Tel 913-682-5151 ext 6068; Fax 913-758-6140; Elec Mail prindaville0211@stmary.edu; Internet Home Page Address: www.stmary.edu; *Asst Prof & Prog Dir* Shelby Prindaville, MFA; *Assoc Prof* Susan Nelson, MFA
Estab 1923; Maintains a nonprofit art gallery, Goppert Gallery (same address); schols open to new students; Pvt, Catholic; D & E; Scholarships; SC 20, LC 3; non-maj 80, maj 25
Activities: Schols offered
Ent Req: HS dipl
Degrees: BA, BS 4 yr
Tuition: Res—$8,475 per sem
Courses: Advertising Design, Art Appreciation, Art History, Ceramics, Commercial Art, Computer Graphics, Design, Drawing, Graphic Arts, Graphic Design, Illustration, †Mixed Media, Painting, Photography, Printmaking

LIBERAL

SEWARD COUNTY COMMUNITY COLLEGE, Art Dept, 1801 N Kansas, Liberal, KS 67901-2054; PO Box 1137, Liberal, KS 67905-1137. Tel 620-417-1453; Elec Mail susan.copas@sccc.edu; Internet Home Page Address: www.sccc.edu; *Dept Chair* Susan Copas; *Art Instr* Dustin Farmer

Estab 1969; pub; D & E; online; Scholarships; SC 23, LC 5; D 1,000, E 700
Ent Req: HS dipl
Degrees: AA 2 yrs
Courses: Art Education, Art History, Ceramics, Design, Drawing, Graphic Design, Handicrafts, History of Art & Architecture, Painting, Photography, Sculpture, Silversmithing, Visual Communication

LINDSBORG

BETHANY COLLEGE, Art Dept, 421 N First St, Lindsborg, KS 67456. Tel 785-227-3311, Ext 8145; Fax 785-227-2860; Elec Mail kahlerc@bethanylb.edu; Internet Home Page Address: www.bethanylb.edu; *Prof* Mary Kay, MFA; *Asst Prof* Frank Shaw, MFA; *Head Art Dept* Caroline Kahler, MFA; *Asst Prof* Ed Pogue, MFA; *Dr* Bruce Kahler; *Instr* James Turner
Estab 1881; Maintain nonprofit art gallery, Mingenback Art Center Gallery, Corner of Olson & Second St, Lindsburg, KS 67456; Den, Private, Denominational, Coed, ELCA - Lutheran Church of America; D & E; Scholarships; SC 26, LC 4, GC 2; D 150, non-maj 120, maj 40
Ent Req: HS dipl
Degrees: BA 4 yr
Courses: †Art Administration, Art Appreciation, †Art Education, Art History, Art Therapy, †Basketry-textiles, †Ceramics, Design, †Drawing, Jewelry, †Painting, Photography, Printmaking, †Sculpture, Studio Concentration, †Teacher Training, †Webpage Design
Summer School: Acad Dean, Dr Gene Bales

MANHATTAN

KANSAS STATE UNIVERSITY, Art Dept, 322 Willard Hall, Manhattan, KS 66506. Tel 785-532-6605; Fax 785-532-0334; Elec Mail art@ksu.edu; Internet Home Page Address: www.ksu.edu/art; *Head Dept & Prof* Duane Noblett, MFA; *Prof* Yoshiro Ikeda, MFA; *Prof* Elliott Pujol, MFA; *Prof* Glen R Brown, PhD; *Prof* Anna Calluori Holcombe, MFA; *Assoc Prof* Daniel Hunt, MFA; *Assoc Prof* Kathleen King, MFA; *Asst Prof* Barri Lester, MFA; *Asst Prof* Rachel Melis, MFA; *Asst Prof* Nancy Morrow, MFA; *Prof* Lynda Andrus, MFA; *Asst Prof* Thomas Bookwalter, BFA; *Asst Prof* Jason Scuilla, MFA; *Asst Prof* Roger Rouston, MFA; *Prof* Teresa Tempero Schmidt, MFA
Estab 1863, dept estab 1965; Non-Profit art gallery, Chapman Gallery of Art, Kansas State Univ, 116 Willard Hall, Manhattan, KS 66506. Art supplies may be purchased on campus; pub; D & E; Scholarships, Fellowships; SC 45, LC 19, GC 7; D 1940, E 60, non-maj 1800, maj 400, grad 15
Ent Req: HS dipl
Degrees: BS(Art Educ) jointly with Col Educ, BA & BFA 4 yrs, MFA 60 sem cr
Courses: †Art Education, †Art History, †Ceramics, Design, †Drawing, Graphic Arts, †Graphic Design, †Illustration, †Jewelry, †Painting, †Printmaking, †Sculpture
Summer School: Dir, Duane Noblett. Courses—most of above, varies from summer to summer
—College of Architecture Planning & Design, 115 Seaton Hall, Manhattan, KS 66506-2900. Tel 785-532-5950; Fax 785-532-6722; Elec Mail dela@ksu.edu; Internet Home Page Address: aalto.arch.ksu.edu; *Assoc Dean* Ray Weisenburger; *Dean* Dennis Law
Estab 1904; FT 53; 800
Degrees: BA, MA(Archit, Regional Planning & Interior Archit)
Tuition: Res—$75.55 per cr hr; nonres--$301.15 per cr hr
Courses: Architectural Programming, Architecture, Art History, Building Construction, Landscape Architecture, Landscape Design
Adult Hobby Classes: Dean, Lane L Marshall. Courses—Graphic Delineation, Preservation
Children's Classes: Courses—Special Design Program in June
Summer School: Dean, Lane L Marshall. 8 wks of courses beginning June 4th. Courses—Design Discovery Program, Design Studio

MCPHERSON

MCPHERSON COLLEGE, Art Dept, 1600 E Euclid, McPherson, KS 67460-3847; PO Box 1402, McPherson, KS 67460-1402. Tel 316-241-0731; Internet Home Page Address: www.mcpherson.edu; *Asst Prof* Kelly Frigard; *Chmn* Wayne Conyers
Estab 1887; den; D & E; Scholarships; SC 14, LC 5; D 150, maj 10, others 140
Ent Req: HS dipl, ACT
Degrees: AB 4 yr
Courses: †Art Education, Art History, Ceramics, Drawing, †Interior Design, Lettering, Museum Staff Training, Painting, Printmaking, Teacher Training, Textile Design

NORTH NEWTON

BETHEL COLLEGE, Dept of Art, 300 E 27th St, North Newton, KS 67117-8061. Tel 316-283-2500; Fax 316-284-5286; Internet Home Page Address: www.bethelks.edu; *Chmn* Merrill Kraball; *Assoc Prof* Gail Lutsch, MFA
Estab 1888, dept estab 1959; den; D; Scholarships; SC 11, LC 3; D 240, non-maj 215, maj 25
Ent Req: HS, ACT
Degrees: BA(Art) 4 yrs
Courses: Art Education, Art History, Ceramics, Crafts, Drawing, Graphic Arts, Graphic Design, Painting, Photography, Printmaking, Sculpture
Adult Hobby Classes: Enrl 15; tuition $40 per 6 wk session. Courses—Ceramics, Drawing, Painting
Summer School: Courses—Drawing, Painting

OTTAWA

OTTAWA UNIVERSITY, Dept of Art, 1001 S Cedar St, Ottawa, KS 66067-3399. Tel 785-242-5200; Fax 785-242-7429; Internet Home Page Address: www.ottawa.edu; *Chmn* Frank J Lemp
Estab 1865; FT 1; pvt; D; Scholarships; SC 16, LC 5; D 35, maj 5
Ent Req: HS grad, SAT, ACT
Degrees: BA 4 yrs
Courses: Art Education, Art History, Arts Management, Ceramics, Drawing, Graphic Arts, Painting, Photography
Children's Classes: Outreach Progs
Summer School: Dir, Frank Lemp. Tuition $89 per cr hr for 8 wk session. Courses—Art Fundamentals

OVERLAND PARK

JOHNSON COUNTY COMMUNITY COLLEGE, Fine Arts Dept & Art History Dept, 12345 College Blvd, Overland Park, KS 66210-1299. Tel 913-469-8500; Fax 913-469-4409; Elec Mail lthomas@jccc.edu; Internet Home Page Address: www.jccc.edu; *Adjunct Prof Fine Art* Doug Baker, MFA; *Adjunct Prof Art History* Tracy Boswell, MA; *Adjunct Prof Fine Art* John Carroll, MFA; *Adjunct Assoc Prof Fine Art* Anthony Baab, MFA; *Asst Prof Fine Art & Sculpture Dept Coordr* Mark Cowardin, MFA; *Assoc Prof Fine Art & Ceramic Dept Coordr* Laura-Harris Gascogne, MFA; *Adjunct Prof Fine Art* Keiko Kira, MFA; *Adjunct Prof Photog* John Lamberton, MFA; *Adjunct Assoc Prof Art History/Architecture* Ted Meadows, MA; *Adjunct Assoc Prof Art History* Kathleen Mendenhall, MA; *Adjunct Prof Art History* Rajee Mohan, MA; *Adjunct Asst Prof Art History* Jennifer Newlands, MA; *Adjunct Prof Fine Art* Syndey Pener, MFA; *Adjunct Prof Fine Art* Zigmunds Priede, MA; *Adjunct Assoc Prof Fine Art* Ruthanne Robertson, MFA; *Adjunct Assoc Prof Fine Art* Angelica Sandoval, MFA; *Assoc Prof Art History & Chair Art History* Allison Smith, PhD; *Adjunct Assoc Prof Fine Art* Bridget Stewart, MFA; *Prof & Chair Fine Art* Larry Thomas, MFA; *Adjunct Prof Art History* Ann Wiklund, MFA; *Adjunct Asst Prof Art History* Valerie Zell, MA; *Adjunct Prof Photog* Mary Wessel, MFA; *Adjunct Asst Prof Art History* Marie Dolembo, MA; *Adjunct Assoc Prof Fine Art* Nick Haney, MA; *Adjunct Asst Prof Photog* Philip Heying, BFA; *Adjunct Asst Prof Art History* Brian Hogarth, MA; *Adjunct Asst Prof Art History* Heather Kauten; *Adjunct Assoc Prof Fine Art* Any Kephart, MFA; *Adjunct Asst Prof Fine Art* Misha Kligman, MFA; *Adjunct Asst Prof Photog* Doug Koch, MFA; *Adjunct Assoc Prof Photog* Adam Long, MFA; *Adjunct Prof Photog* Jeff Nichols, MFA; *Adjunct Prof Photog* Meghan Nichols, MFA; *Adjunct Asst Prof Photog* Craig Sands, BFA; *Adjunct Asst Prof Fine Art* Andrew Shell, MFA; *Adjunct Asst Prof Photog* Charles Stonewall, MA; *Prof Photog & Photog Dept Coordr* Tom Tarnowski, MFA
Estab 1969; Maintain 3 nonprofit art galleries, Nerman Museum of Contemp Art, Student Art Gallery, Faculty & Alumni Gallery, all JCCC address; on-campus shop sells art supplies; pub; D, E & weekends; Scholarships; SC 30, LC 4; Enrl in Fine Arts & Art History D 1272, E 219
Ent Req: HS dipl or equivalent
Degrees: AA 2 yr
Courses: 2-D & 3-D Design, †Architecture, Art History, Ceramics, †Design, †Digital Imaging for Artists, Drawing, Life Drawing, Painting, Photography, Sculpture, Silversmithing, Studio Workshop
Children's Classes: Accelerated fine arts for gifted children
Summer School: Dir, Larry Thomas, Prof & Chair Fine Arts Dept. Enrl 95; tuition $75 per cr hr for term of 8 wks. Courses—Ceramics, Design, Drawing, Painting, Photography, Sculpture, Silversmithing

PITTSBURG

PITTSBURG STATE UNIVERSITY, Art Dept, 1701 S Broadway St, Pittsburg, KS 66762-7500. Tel 620-235-4302; Fax 620-235-4303; Elec Mail art@pittstate.edu; Internet Home Page Address: www.pittstate.edu/art; *Chairperson* Larrie J Moody PhD; *Prof* Marjorie K Schick, MFA; *Assoc Prof* Malcolm E Kucharski, MFA; *Asst Prof* Andree Flageolle, PhD; *Asst Prof* Stephanie K Bowman, MFA; *Asst Prof* Jr James M Oliver, MFA; *Asst Prof* Rhona E Shand, MFA
Estab 1903, dept estab 1921; Maintain nonprofit art gallery, Pittsburg State University Art Gallery, Art Dept - Porter Hall, 1701 S Broadway, Pittsburg. KS 66762-7512; pub; D & E; Scholarships; SC 50, LC 24, GC 22; D 600, E 50, non-maj 300, maj 90, grad 10
Ent Req: HS dipl
Degrees: BFA & BSED 4 yr, MA 36 hr
Courses: Art Appreciation, †Art Education, Art History, †Ceramics, †Commercial Art, Crafts, Design, Drawing, †Jewelry, †Jewelry Design, †Painting, Photography, Printmaking, Sculpture, Teacher Training
Summer School: Dir, Larrie J Moody. Enrl 100; tuition res—undergrad $105 per cr hr; grad $141 per cr hr; nonres—undergrad $299 per cr hr, grad $349 per cr hr, for term of 2 4 wk sessions (June & July). Courses—Art Education, Ceramics, Crafts, Drawing, Painting

PRATT

PRATT COMMUNITY COLLEGE, Art Dept, 348 NE SR 61, Pratt, KS 67124. Tel 620-672-5641 Ext 228, 800-794-3091; Fax 620-672-5288; Elec Mail marshas@prattcc.edu; Internet Home Page Address: www.pcc.cc.ks.us; Internet Home Page Address: www.prattcc.edu; *Art Instr* Marsha Shrack, MFA
Maintain Delmar Riney Gallery, PCC 348 NE SR 61, Pratt. Art supplies sold at on campus store; 1; Pub; D & E; Scholarships; SC 6, LC; D 100, E 15, Maj 25
Ent Req: HS dipl
Degrees: AA and AS
Tuition: Res—$39 per cr hr; nonres—$68 per cr hr
Courses: Art Appreciation, Ceramics, Design, Drawing, Elementary School Arts, Graphic Design, Illustration, Introduction to Art, Painting, Photography, Printmaking

Summer School: Dir Marsha Shrack; Graphic Design, Illustration, Introduction to Art

SALINA

KANSAS WESLEYAN UNIVERSITY, Art Dept, 100 E Claflin, Salina, KS 67401. Tel 785-827-5541; Fax 785-827-0927; Elec Mail jill.wagner@kwu.edu; Internet Home Page Address: www.kwu.edu; *Asst Prof Graphic Design* Jill Wagner; *Asst Prof of Art Dept Chair* Lori Wright
Estab 1886; Maintains nonprofit art gallery - The Gallery at Kansas Wesleyan Univ; pvt; D & E; Scholarships; SC 15, LC 4; maj 15, others 500 for two sem
Degrees: AB 4 yr
Tuition: Res—undergrad $17,000; fees incl room & board
Courses: †Advertising Art, †Art Appreciation, †Art Education, †Art History, †Art Studio, †Ceramics, †Design, †Drawing, †Graphic Arts, †Graphic Design, †Painting, †Photography, †Printmaking, †Sculpture
Summer School: Enrl 125; for term of 8 wks beginning June

STERLING

STERLING COLLEGE, Art Dept, 125 W Cooper St, Sterling, KS 67579-1533; PO Box 98, Sterling, KS 67579-0098. Tel 620-278-2173; Fax 620-278-4375; Internet Home Page Address: www.sterling.edu; *Chmn* David Cook
Estab 1876; den; D & E; Scholarships; SC 16, LC 2; D 410
Ent Req: HS dipl
Degrees: BA & BS
Courses: 2-D Color Design, 3-D Design, Ceramics, Costume Design & Construction, Drawing, Fibers, Graphic Arts, Graphic Design, Painting
Adult Hobby Classes: Enrl 25; tuition $20. Courses—all areas
Children's Classes: Art Education

TOPEKA

WASHBURN UNIVERSITY OF TOPEKA, Dept of Art, 1700 SW College, Topeka, KS 66621. Tel 785-670-1125; Fax 785-670-1189; Elec Mail art@washburn.edu; Internet Home Page Address: www.washburn.edu/cas/art/; *Art Prof Chmn* Glenda Taylor; *Assoc Prof* Azyz Sharafy; *Assoc Prof* Marguerite Perret; *Asst Prof* Mary Dorsey Wanless; *Asst Prof* Ye Wang; *Catron Prof of Art* Jennifer Marsh; *Asst Prof* Michael Hager; *Lectr* Emily Rice; *Asst Prof* Kelly Watt
Estab 1868; Maintain nonprofit art gallery, Mulvane Art Museum, Washburn University, 1700 SW College, Topeka, KS 66621; on-campus art supplies shop; FT 9; pub; D&E; Scholarships; SC 23, LC 7, GC 1; non-maj 300, maj 100
Ent Req: HS dipl
Degrees: BA and BFA 4 yr
Tuition: Res—$225 per cr hr; nonres—$509 per cr hr
Courses: Art Appreciation, Art History, Art Introduction, Ceramics, Computer Graphic Design, Computer Publication, Computers, Design, Drawing, Etching, Lithography, Painting, Photography, Printmaking, Sculpture, Silkscreen, Watercolor
Children's Classes: Tuition $35 for ten 1 1/2 hr sessions
Summer School: VPres Acad Affairs, Dr Randy Pembrook. $225 per cr hr; courses—Art history, Art studio

WICHITA

FRIENDS UNIVERSITY, Art Dept, 2100 University Ave, Wichita, KS 67213. Tel 316-295-5100; Tel 316-295-5656; Fax 316-263-1092; Fax 316-295-5656; Elec Mail maber@friends.edu; Internet Home Page Address: www.friends.edu; *Chmn* Ted Krone
Estab 1898; den; D & E; Scholarships; SC 18, LC 4; D 329, E 37
Ent Req: HS dipl
Degrees: MA 6 yrs, BA & BS 4 yrs
Courses: †Aesthetics, †Art Education, †Art History, †Ceramics, †Computer Graphics, †Design, †Drawing, †Fine Arts 2 & 3-D, †Graphic Design, †Painting, Photography, Printmaking, Sculpture, Silversmithing, Teacher Training
Adult Hobby Classes: Courses—Drawing, Jewelry, Painting

WICHITA CENTER FOR THE ARTS, Mary R Koch School of Visual Arts, 9112 E Central, Wichita, KS 67206. Tel 316-634-2787; Fax 316-634-0593; Elec Mail arts@wcfta.com; Internet Home Page Address: www.wcfta.com; *Exec Dir* Howard W Ellington; *Dir Educ* Pam Bugler; *Dir Gallery* Brian Hinkle; *Dir Arts Based Pre-School* Wayna Buch; *Theatre Develop* John Boldenow; *Pub Rels* Kim Kufahl
Estab 1920; Maintain nonprofit art gallery; Hurst Sales Gallery; art library; 35; pvt; D&E; Scholarships; SC 40; D 450, E 150
Courses: 3-D Design, Art Education, Art History, Ceramics, Drawing, Enameling, Mixed Media, Painting, Photography, Pottery, Printmaking, Sculpture, Teacher Training, Weaving
Adult Hobby Classes: Enrl 300; tuition $130 for 12 wk term. Courses—Performing Arts, 2-D & 3-D Design
Children's Classes: Enrl 300; tuition $70. Courses—Performing Arts, 2-D & 3-D Design
Summer School: Dir Educ, Pam Bugler. Enrl 300; tuition $45-$55 for 6 wk term. Courses—same as regular sessions

WICHITA STATE UNIVERSITY, School of Art & Design, 1845 Fairmount St, Box 67 Wichita, KS 67260-0067. Tel 316-978-3555; Fax 316-978-5418; Internet Home Page Address: finearts.wichita.edu/design; *Grad Coordr* Ronald Christ; *Interim Dir* Barry Badgett
Estab 1895, dept estab 1901; pub; D & E; Scholarships; D 1149, E 194, non-maj 78, maj 285, grad 51, others 2
Ent Req: HS dipl
Degrees: BAE, BA & BFA 4 yr, MFA 2 yr, MA 1 yr

Courses: †Art Education, †Art History, †Ceramics, Drawing, †Graphic Design, Illustration, Lettering, †Painting, Photography, †Printmaking, †Sculpture, Teacher Training
Summer School: Tuition as above for term of 8 wks

WINFIELD

SOUTHWESTERN COLLEGE, Art Dept, 100 College St, Winfield, KS 67156-2499. Tel 620-229-6000; Internet Home Page Address: www.sckans.edu; Estab 1885; pvt & den; D & E; Scholarships; SC 12, LC 4
Ent Req: HS dipl
Degrees: BA 4 yr
Courses: Art Education
Adult Hobby Classes: Design, History of Art, Life Drawing, Painting
Summer School: Chmn, Michael Wilder. Courses—Art History, Design, Drawing, Painting, Sculpture

KENTUCKY

BARBOURVILLE

UNION COLLEGE, Music and Fine Arts Dept, 310 College St, Barbourville, KY 40906-1499. Tel 606-546-1334; Fax 606-546-1625; Internet Home Page Address: www.unionky.edu; *Chmn* Dr Thomas McFarland
Estab 1879; Den; D & E; Scholarships; LC
Ent Req: HS dipl
Degrees: BA, BS and MA (Educ) 4 yr
Courses: Art History

BEREA

BEREA COLLEGE, Art & Art History Program, CPO 2162, Berea, KY 40404-2342. Tel 859-985-9715; Fax 859-985-3541; Elec Mail lisa_kriner@berea.edu; Internet Home Page Address: www.berea.edu; *Prof* William Morningstar, MFA; *Dir & Asst Prof* Meghan C Doherty, PhD; *Asst Prof* Kevin N Gardner, MFA; *Asst Prof* Tina M Gebhart, MFA; *Assoc Prof* Eileen McKiernan Gonzalez, PhD; *Asst Prof* Sarah Gross, MFA; *Asst Prof* Julie A Hruby, PhD; *Chmn* Lisa L Kriner, MFA
Estab 1855, dept estab 1936; Maintains a nonprofit art gallery - Doris Ulmann Galleries; on-campus shop for purchase of art supplies; pvt; D; Scholarships; SC 31, LC 24; C 1670, E 1 (total); D 350, maj 50
Ent Req: HS dipl (preference given to students from Southern Appalachian region)
Degrees: BA 4 yr
Tuition: None; campus res—room and board $300-$1800 based on income
Courses: Archaeology, †Art History, †Ceramics, Design, †Drawing, †Fashion Arts, Fiber Arts, †Painting, †Printmaking, †Sculpture

BOWLING GREEN

WESTERN KENTUCKY UNIVERSITY, Art Dept, 1906 College Heights Blvd, Bowling Green, KY 42101-1000. Tel 270-745-3944; Fax 270-745-5932; Elec Mail art@wku.edu; Internet Home Page Address: www.wku.edu/dept/academic/ahss/art/art.html; *Dept Head* Kim Chalmers
Maintains on-campus art supply shop; FT 10, PT 9; Pub; D & E; SC 49, LC 21; maj 187
Ent Req: HS dipl
Degrees: BA & BFA 4 yrs, MA(Art Educ)
Courses: †Art Education, Art History, †Ceramics, Design, Drawing, Graphic Design, †Painting, Photography, †Printmaking, †Sculpture, †Weaving
Summer School: Dept Head Kim Chalmers. Enrl 100; tuition res $97 per cr hr, nonres $265 per cr hr. Courses—Lecture & Studio Art Courses

CAMPBELLSVILLE

CAMPBELLSVILLE UNIVERSITY, Department of Art, One University Dr, Campbellsville, KY 42718; UPO 863, 1 University Dr Campbellsville, KY 42718-2190. Tel 270-789-5268; Fax 270-789-5524; Elec Mail ljcundiff@campbellsville.edu; Internet Home Page Address: www.campbellsville.edu (click on Academics-College of Arts & Sciences); *Prof of Art* Linda Cundiff; *Instr* Myrtie Parsley; *Instr* Henrietta Scott; *Assoc Prof Art* Davie Reneav; *Instr* Jeffrey Walker; *Instr* Cora Renfro; *Asst Prof* Dejan Mraovic
Estab 1906; dept estab 1967; Non-profit art gallery - Pence Chowning Art Gallery; 1 University Dr, UPO 863 Campbellsville, KY 42718; Montgomery Library; Pvt; D & E; Scholarships; SC 26, LC 5; D 35, E 10, non-maj 12, maj 30, others 8 minors
Activities: Schols offered
Ent Req: HS dipl, ACT, portfolio
Degrees: BA, BS with/without teacher cert
Tuition: $9800 per yr
Courses: Art Appreciation, Art Education, Art History, Ceramics, Collage, Commercial Art, Constructions, Design, Drawing, Elementary School Art, †Graphic Arts, Graphic Design, Jewelry, †Jewelry Design, Mixed Media, Painting, Photography, Printmaking, Sculpture, Secondary School Art, Stage Design, Teacher Training, Theatre Arts
Adult Hobby Classes: Enrl 15; tuition $50 per audit hr. Courses—Understanding Art, courses above as auditors
Summer School: Term of 8 wks. Courses—Art Appreciation,

CRESTVIEW HILLS

THOMAS MORE COLLEGE, Art Dept, 333 Thomas More Pky, Crestview Hills, KY 41017. Tel 859-341-5800, Ext 3420; Fax 859-344-3345; Internet Home Page Address: www.thomasmoore.edu; *Chmn* Rebecca Bilbo; *Assoc Prof* Barbara Rauf, MFA
Estab 1921; pvt; D & E; SC 12, LC 4; D 12, E 5, maj 17
Ent Req: HS dipl
Degrees: BA, BES, BS, AA & AES
Courses: Aesthetics, Anatomy, Art Education, Art History, Arts Management, Ceramics, Color, Design, Drawing, Figure Drawing, Painting, Perspective, Photography, Printmaking, Sculpture, Teacher Training, Theatre Arts
Summer School: Dir, Dr Raymond Hebert. Courses—various

GEORGETOWN

GEORGETOWN COLLEGE, Art Dept, Anne Wright Wilson Fine Arts Bldg, Georgetown College Georgetown, KY 40324; 400 E College St, Wilson Art Bldg Rm 106 Georgetown, KY 40324. Tel 502-863-8106; Fax 502-868-8888; Elec Mail juilee_decker@georgetowncollege.edu; Internet Home Page Address: www.georgetowncollege.edu/art/; *Gallery Dir & Cur Coll* Laura Stewart; *Prof Art History & Dept Chair* Dr Juliee Decker
Estab 1829

HIGHLAND HEIGHTS

NORTHERN KENTUCKY UNIVERSITY, Dept of Visual Arts, Nunn Dr, Highland Heights, KY 41099-0001. Tel 859-572-5421; Fax 859-572-6501; Internet Home Page Address: www.nku/-art/; *Chmn* Thomas F McGovern
Estab 1968; Maintains nonprofit University Galleries, Dept of Visual Arts; art supplies sold at on-campus store; FT 20, PT 8; pub; D, E & Summer; Scholarships; SC 13; Enrl 510
Activities: Schols available
Ent Req: HS grad, ACT scores
Degrees: BA(Art Educ), BFA(Studio Art), BFA (Graphic Design), BA(Graphic Design), BA (Studio Art)
Courses: Aesthetics, Art Appreciation, †Art Education, †Art History, †Ceramics, Design, †Drawing, †Graphic Design, History of Art & Architecture, Mixed Media, New Media, †Painting, †Photography, †Printmaking, †Sculpture, Teacher Training, Video
Summer School: Chmn, Thomas McGovern. Enrl 170; tuition $47 per sem hr for sessions. Courses—Art Education, Drawing, Graphic Design, Printmaking, Ceramics

LEXINGTON

TRANSYLVANIA UNIVERSITY, Art Program, 300 N Broadway, Lexington, KY 40508-1776. Tel 859-233-8141, 233-8119; Internet Home Page Address: www.transy.edu; *Prof* Dr Nancy Wolsk, PhD; *Prof, Div Chair* Jack Girard, MFA; *Assoc Prof, Prog Dir* Kurt Gohde, MFA; *Prof of Art* Dan S Selter, MA; *Asst Prof* Kimberly Miller; *Gallery Dir* Andrea Fisher, BFA
Estab 1780; Maintain a nonprofit gallery, The Morlan Gallery, Transylvania Univ, 300 N Broadway, Lexington, KY 40508; pvt; D & E; Scholarships; SC 20, LC 3; D 105, E 14, maj 18
Ent Req: HS dipl
Degrees: BA
Courses: †Aesthetics, Art Appreciation, †Art Education, Art History, Ceramics, Collage, Costume Design & Construction, Design, Drawing, Film, †History of Art & Architecture, Mixed Media, Painting, Photography, †Printmaking, Sculpture, Stage Design, Teacher Training, Theatre Arts

UNIVERSITY OF KENTUCKY, Dept of Art, College of Fine Arts, Rm 207 Fine Arts Bldg Lexington, KY 40506-0001. Tel 859-257-8151; Fax 859-257-3042; Internet Home Page Address: www.edu/finearts; *Dean* Robert Shay; *Chmn* Jack Gron
Estab 1918; FT 22, PT 15; pub; D; Scholarships, Assistantships; SC 23, LC 19, GC 6; maj 200, others 1500
Degrees: BA, BFA, MA & MFA 3 yr
Courses: †Art Education, †Art History, Ceramics, Drawing, Fibers, Graphic Design, Painting, Photography, Printmaking, Sculpture, †Studio Art, Video
Summer School: Dir, Jack Gron. Tuition res—$118 per cr hr, nonres—$341 per cr hr. Courses—varied

LOUISVILLE

JEFFERSON COMMUNITY COLLEGE & TECHNICAL COLLEGE, Fine Arts, 109 E Broadway, Fine Arts Dept Louisville, KY 40202-2000. Tel 502-213-2518; *Fine Art Dept Head* Prof J Barry Motes; *Prof* Dr Amy Stewart; *Asst Prof* Lisa Simon
Estab 1968; Maintain nonprofit art gallery, Krantz Art Gallery, VTI 116, 110 E Chestnut; on-campus shop where art supplies may be purchased; PT 6; pub; D & E; Scholarships; SC 11, LC 6; D 4774, E 4172
Ent Req: HS dipl
Degrees: AA & Assoc in Photography 2 yrs
Tuition: $135/credit hrs
Courses: †Advertising Design, Aesthetics, Art Education, Art History, †Commercial Art, Drawing, Graphic Design, Painting, †Photography, Sculpture, †Theatre Arts
Summer School: Dean, Dr Robert Deger. Tuition $45 per cr hr. Courses—Art Appreciation, Drawing, Photography

UNIVERSITY OF LOUISVILLE, Allen R Hite Art Institute, Department of Fine Arts, Belkaap Campus Louisville, KY 40292-0001. Tel 502-852-6794; Fax 502-852-6791; Internet Home Page Address: www.art.louisville.edu; *Chmn Dept Fine Arts, Dir Hite Art Institute* James T Grubola, MFA; *Assoc Prof* Moon-he Balk, MFA; *Asst Prof* Todd Burns, MFA; *Assoc Prof* Tom Buser, PhD; *Assoc Prof* Mary Carothers, MFA; *Prof* Ying Kit Chan, MFA; *Assoc Prof* Stow Chapman, MS; *Prof* Robert Douglas, PhD; *Assoc Prof* Mitch Eckert, MFA; *Power Creative Designer-in-Residence* Leslie Friesen, BFA; *Assoc Prof* Christopher Fulton, PhD; *Assoc Prof* Linda Gigante, PhD; *Prof* Lida Gordon, MFA; *Assoc Prof* Barbara Hanger, MFA; *Assoc Prof* Ben Hufbauer, PhD; *Assoc Prof* Jay Kloner, PhD; *Asst Prof* Scott Massey, MFA; *Prof* Stephanie Maloney, PhD; *Assoc Prof* Mark Priest, MFA; *Prof* Steve Skaggs, MS; *Prof* John Whitesell, MFA; *Gallery Dir & Adjunct Assoc Prof* John Begley, MFA; *Adjunct Assoc Prof* Peter Morrin, MFA; *Prof Emeritus* Donald Anderson, MFA; *Prof Emeritus* Henry Chodkowski, MFA; *Prof Emeritus* Dario Cofi, PhD; *Prof Emeritus* Suzanne Mitchell, MFA; *Prof Emeritus* William Morgan, PhD; *Asst Prof* Che Rhodes, MFA; *Asst Prof* Susan Jarosi, PhD Estab 1846, dept estab 1935; Maintain nonprofit art galleries; Hite Art Institute Galleries, Schneider Hall, Univ of Louisville, Louisville, KY 40292. Library: Margaret Bridwell Art Library, Scheider Hall; FT 21, PT 18; pub; D & E; Scholarships; SC 60, LC 50, GC 38; D 1,200, E 200, non-maj 50, maj 500, grad 65
Ent Req: HS dipl, CEEB
Degrees: MA 1 to 2 yrs, PhD 3 yrs, BA 4 yrs, BFA 4 yrs
Courses: Aesthetics, †Art Education, †Art History, †Ceramics, †Design, †Drawing, †Fiber, †Glass, †Graphic Design, †History of Art & Architecture, Interior Architecture, †Interior Design, †Jewelry, †Museum Staff Training, †Painting, †Photography, †Printmaking, †Sculpture
Summer School: Dir, James T Grubola. Enrl 100 for May-Aug. Courses—Various Art & Art History Classes

MIDWAY

MIDWAY COLLEGE, Art Dept, 512 E Stephens St, Midway, KY 40347-1120. Tel 859-846-4421, Ext 5809; Fax 859-846-5349; Internet Home Page Address: www.midway.edu; *Instr Music & Choir* Wayne Gebb; *Chmn* Steve Davis-Rosenbaum; *Instr* Kate Davis-Rosenbaum
FT 2; Den, W; D; Scholarships; SC 7, LC 3; 55
Ent Req: HS dipl, ACT
Degrees: 2 yr
Courses: Art Education, Art in the Child's World, Basic Design, Ceramics, Drawing, Historical Furniture, Painting, Sculpture, Textile Design

MOREHEAD

MOREHEAD STATE UNIVERSITY, Art & Design Dept, Claypool-Young Art Bldg 211, Morehead, KY 40351; 265 University Blvd Morehead, KY 40351. Tel 606-783-2771, 783-2193; Fax 606-783-5048; Elec Mail b.whitt@morehead-st.edu; Internet Home Page Address: www.moreheadstate.edu/art; *Chmn* Robert Franzini; *Prof* David Bartlett; *Prof* Elisabeth Mesa-Gaido; *Assoc Prof* Deeno Golding; *Prof* Gary Mesa-Gaido; *Assoc Prof* Joy Gritton; *Asst Prof* Braden Frieder; *Asst Prof* Dougfeng Li; *Asst Prof* Jennifer Reis; *Art Instr* Seth Green; *Art Instr* Bethany Kalk; *Art Instr* Susan Hawkins
Estab 1922; Maintain nonprofit art gallery, Claypool-Young Art Gallery, 265 Univ Blvd, MSU, Morehead, KY 40351, Gal Dir Jennifer Reis; maintain on-campus art supplies shop; pub; D & E; Scholarships; SC 45, LC 14, GC 26; D 900, E 20, non-maj 800, maj 180, GS 55, others 145
Ent Req: HS dipl, ACT
Degrees: BA 4 yr, MA 1 - 2 yr
Courses: Art Education, Ceramics, Computer Art, Drawing, Graphic Design, Illustration, Mixed Media, Painting, Photography, Printmaking, †Sculpture
Summer School: Dept Chair Robert Franzini, Enrl 150, 2 - 4 week sessions, courses - Studio & Art History

MURRAY

MURRAY STATE UNIVERSITY, Dept of Art, 218 Wells Hall, Murray, KY 42071-3318. Tel 270-762-3741; Fax 270-762-3920; Internet Home Page Address: www.murraystate.edu; *Chmn* Richard Dougherty; *Prof* Dale Leys, MFA; *Prof* Paul Sasso, MFA; *Prof* Jerry Speight, MFA; *Assoc Prof* Michael Johnson, MFA; *Assoc Prof* Camille Sarre PhD, MFA; *Assoc Prof* Steve Bishop, MFA; *Asst Prof* Peggy Schrock PhD, MFA; *Gallery Dir* Albert Sperath, MFA; *Asst Prof* Jeanne Beaver; *Asst Prof* Sarah Guthworth; *Asst Prof* Alma Hale; *Asst Prof* Nicole Hard; *Asst Prof* Susan O'Brien; *Lectr* Zbynek Smetana
Estab 1925, dept estab 1931; pub; D & E; Scholarships; SC 117, LC 15, GS 48; non-maj 475, maj 200, grad 13
Ent Req: HS dipl, ACT, portfolio required for grad students
Degrees: BA, BS & BFA 4 yr, MA(Studio) 1 1/2 - 2 yrs
Courses: Art Appreciation, Art Education, Art History, Ceramics, Drawing, Graphic Design, History of Art & Architecture, Jewelry, †Painting, †Photography, †Printmaking, †Sculpture, Silversmithing, Surface Design, Teacher Training, Textile Design, †Weaving, Wood Design
Children's Classes: Summer art workshops for HS students
Summer School: Dir, Dale Leys. Enrl 40-80; tuition res—undergrad $67 per hr, grad $99 per hr; nonres—undergrad $193 per hr, grad $282 per hr for short sessions of 5 wk 7 1/2 wk or 10 wk terms

OWENSBORO

BRESCIA UNIVERSITY, (Brescia College) Art Dept, 717 Frederica St, Owensboro, KY 42301-3019. Tel 502-685-3131; Fax 502-686-4266; Elec Mail info@brescia.edu; Internet Home Page Address: www.brescia.edu; *Chmn* Sr Mary Diane Taylor; *Prof Fine Arts* David Stratton; *Asst Prof Art* Frank Krevens

Estab 1950; Maintain nonprofit art gallery; Anna Eaton Stout Memorial Art Gallery, 717 Frederica St, Owensboro, KY 42301; on-campus shop where art supplies may be purchased; FT 3; den; D&E; weekend; Scholarships; SC 32, LC 10; 960, maj 30
Ent Req: HS dipl, placement exam, ACT, GED
Degrees: BA 4 yr
Courses: 2-D & 3-D Design, Advertising Design, Art Appreciation, †Art Education, Art History, Calligraphy, †Ceramics, Design, Drawing, Film, †Graphic Design, Mixed Media, Painting, Photography, Printmaking, Stained Glass

KENTUCKY WESLEYAN COLLEGE, Dept Art, 3000 Frederica St, Owensboro, KY 42302-6055. Tel 270-926-3111, Ext 250; Fax 270-926-3196; Internet Home Page Address: www.kwc.edu; *Acting Chmn* Monte Hamm
Dept estab 1950; den; Scholarships; SC 11, LC 4; maj 40
Degrees: BA 4 yr
Courses: Arts & Crafts, Design, Painting
Summer School: Enrl 60. Courses—Art for the Elementary Schools, Art Survey

PIKEVILLE

PIKEVILLE COLLEGE, Humanities Division, 147 Sycamore St, Pikeville, KY 41501-9118. Tel 606-218-5250; Fax 606-218-5269; Elec Mail webmaster@pc.edu; Internet Home Page Address: www.pc.edu; *Gallery Dir* Janice Ford; *Chmn* Dr Brigitte LaTrespo
Estab 1889; Maintain nonprofit art gallery, Weber Art Gallery, 147 Sycamore St, Pikeville, KY 41501; pvt den; D & E; SC 16, LC 5
Ent Req: SAT, ACT
Degrees: BA & BS 4 yrs
Courses: †Art Education, Art History, Ceramics, Drawing, History of Art & Architecture, Painting, Printmaking, Sculpture, †Teacher Training
Summer School: Courses—vary

PIPPA PASSES

ALICE LLOYD COLLEGE, Art Dept, 100 Purpose Rd, Pippa Passes, KY 41844-8884. Tel 606-368-2101, Ext 6083; Fax 606-368-6496; Internet Home Page Address: www.alc.edu; *Instr* Mike Ware
Estab 1923; FT 1; pvt; D & E; Scholarships; SC 6, LC 1
Ent Req: HS dipl, ent exam
Degrees: BS & BA 4 yrs
Courses: Art Appreciation, Art History Survey No 2, †Art for Elementary Education, Pottery
Children's Classes: Enrl 10-20; tuition free. Courses—Drawing, Painting, Sculpture

RICHMOND

EASTERN KENTUCKY UNIVERSITY, Art Dept, Campbell 309, Richmond, KY 40475; 521 Lancaster Ave, Richmond, KY 40475-3102. Tel 859-622-1629; Fax 859-622-5904; Elec Mail artsmith@acs.eku.edu; Internet Home Page Address: www.art.eku.edu; *Chmn* Dr Gil R Smith
Estab 1906; Maintain nonprofit art gallery; Frederick Giles Gallery, Campbell Building 309, Eastern Kentucky University, Richmond, KY 40475-3102; pub; D&E; Scholarships; SC 40, LC 14, GC 12, other 5; non-maj 70, maj 251, grad 6
Ent Req: HS grad
Degrees: BA, BFA & MA(Educ) 4 yrs
Courses: Art Appreciation, †Art Education, Art History, †Ceramics, Drawing, †Graphic Design, †Interior Design, †Metals, †Painting, †Photography, †Sculpture
Adult Hobby Classes: Non-credit courses offered
Summer School: Enrl & courses vary; tuition same as regular sem

WILLIAMSBURG

CUMBERLAND COLLEGE, Dept of Art, 7523 College Station Dr, Williamsburg, KY 40769-1386. Tel 606-549-2200; Fax 606-539-4490; Internet Home Page Address: cumberlandcollege.edu; *Chmn* Kenneth R Weedman
Estab 1889; Maintains nonprofit art gallery on campus; den; D & E; Scholarships; SC 20, LC 10; D 1614, E 60, maj 30
Ent Req: HS dipl, ACT test
Degrees: BA and BS 4 yr
Courses: Aesthetics, Art Appreciation, Art Education, Art History, Computer Imaging, Design, Drawing, Film, Painting, Printmaking, Sculpture, Stage Design, Teacher Training, Theatre Arts, Video

WILMORE

ASBURY UNIVERSITY, Art Dept, 1 Macklem Dr, Wilmore, KY 40390-1152. Tel 859-858-3511, Ext 2250; Fax 859-858-3921; Internet Home Page Address: www.asbury.edu; *Instr Prof* Linda Stratford; *Art Dept Chair, Instr Prof* Keith Barker; *Instr* Chris Segre-Lewis; *Instr Prof* Margaret Park Smith; *Asst Prof* Josh Smith
Estab 1890; Maintain nonprofit art gallery, Asbury Art Galleries (same address as school); FT 5, PT 6; pvt; D & E; Scholarships; SC 24, LC 6; D 1350, maj 45, others 250
Ent Req: HS dipl
Degrees: AB & BS 4 yr
Courses: Aesthetics, Animation, Art Appreciation, Art Education, Art History, Ceramics, Design, Drawing, Graphic Arts, Graphic Design, History of Art & Architecture, Painting, Photography, Printmaking, Sculpture, Stained Glass, Teacher Training
Summer School: Courses - Photography, Painting, Seminar in France

LOUISIANA

ALEXANDRIA

LOUISIANA STATE UNIVERSITY AT ALEXANDRIA, Dept of Fine Arts & Design, 8100 Hwy 71 S, Coughlin 146 Alexandria, LA 71302-9119. Tel 318-445-3672; Internet Home Page Address: www.lsu.edu; *Prof Art* Roy V deVille, MA
Estab 1960; pub; D; Scholarships; D 200, E 50, non-maj 300, maj 15
Ent Req: HS dipl, entrance exam, state exam & ACT
Degrees: Fine Arts Assoc 2-3 yr
Children's Classes: Enrl 50; tuition $189 per course. Courses—Painting, Pottery
Summer School: Enrl 150; tuition $120 per cr. Courses—Art Appreciation, Art History, Painting, Pottery

BATON ROUGE

LOUISIANA STATE UNIVERSITY, School of Art, 123 Art Bldg, Baton Rouge, LA 70803. Tel 225-388-5411; Fax 225-578-5424; Internet Home Page Address: www.lsu.edu; *Prof* Richard Cox PhD, MFA; *Prof* Mark Zucker PhD, MFA; *Prof* Patricia Lawrence PhD, MFA; *Prof* Melody Guichet, MFA; *Prof* A J Meek, MFA; *Prof* Christopher Hentz, MFA; *Prof* Kimberly Arp, MFA; *Prof* Robert Hausey, MFA; *Prof* Gerald Bower, MFA; *Assoc Prof* Michael Book, MFA; *Asst Prof* Gregory Elliot, MFA; *Asst Prof* Paul Dean, MFA; *Asst Prof* Herb Goodman, MFA; *Asst* Larry Livaudais, MFA; *Asst* Lynne Baggett, MFA; *Asst* Susan Ryan, MFA; *Asst* Kirsten Noreen; *Dir* Michael Daugherty, MFA; *Asst* Edward Smith; *Asst Prof* Denyce Celentano; *Asst Prof* Cynthia Handel; *Asst Prof* Robert Silverman; *Asst Prof* Parrott Bacot
Estab 1874, dept estab 1935; pub; D & E; Scholarships
Ent Req: HS dipl, ACT scores
Degrees: BFA 4 yr, MFA 3
Courses: †Art History, †Ceramics, Drawing, †Graphic Design, †Painting, †Printmaking, †Sculpture
Summer School: Tuition res—$273, nonres—$653 for 8 wk course
—**Student Union Art Gallery,** 216 LSU Student Union Art Gallery, Louisana State University Baton Rouge, LA 70803. Tel 225-578-5162; Fax 225-578-4326; Elec Mail unionartgallery@lsu.edu; *Dir* Judy Stahl
Open Mon-Fri 10AM-6PM, Sun 1PM-5PM, cl on major holidays; No admis fee
Collections: paintings; drawings; lithographs; silkscreens; photographs; sculptures

SOUTHERN UNIVERSITY A & M COLLEGE, School of Architecture, PO Box 11947, Southern Branch Baton Rouge, LA 70813-1947. Tel 225-771-3015; Fax 225-771-4709; Internet Home Page Address: subr.edu/architecture/awotona; *Dean* Adenrele Awotona; *Instr* Jill Bambury; *Instr* John Delgado; *Instr* Charles Smith; *Instr* Randall Teal; *Instr* Archie Tiner; *Instr* Lonnie Wilkinson; *Instr* Annette Williams; *Instr* Kelley Roberts; *Instr* Henry Thurman
Estab 1956; pub; D & E; Scholarships; SC 14; D 250, non-maj 7, maj 162
Ent Req: HS dipl
Degrees: BA 5 yrs
Courses: Architecture, Art Education, Computer, Graphic Arts, Painting, Printmaking
Summer School: Dir, E D Van Purnell. Term of 8 wks beginning June. Courses—Architectural Design, Construction Materials & Systems, Graphic Presentation, Structures

GRAMBLING

GRAMBLING STATE UNIVERSITY, Art Dept, PO Box 1184, Grambling, LA 71245-1184. Tel 318-274-3811; Fax 318-274-3723; Internet Home Page Address: www.grambling.edu; *Chmn* Thomas O Smith
Degrees: BA 4 yr
Tuition: Res—$1044 per sem; nonres—$2019 per sem
Courses: Art Appreciation, †Art Education, Art History, Ceramics, Computer, Design, Drawing, Handicrafts, Illustration, Painting, Printmaking, Sculpture, Teacher Training

HAMMOND

SOUTHEASTERN LOUISIANA UNIVERSITY, Dept of Visual Arts, SLU 10765, Hammond, LA 70402. Tel 504-549-2193; Fax 985-549-5316; Internet Home Page Address: www.selu.edu; *Prof* Ronald Kennedy, MFA; *Assoc Prof* Gail Hood, MFA; *Asst Prof* Gary Keown, MFA; *Instr* Lynda Katz, MFA; *Prof* C Roy Blackwood, MFA; *Lectr* Susan Wingard; *Lectr* Rancy Boyd-Snee; *Asst Prof* Irene Nero; *Asst Prof* John Valentine; *Lectr* April Hammock; *Lectr* Malcolm McClay; *Interim Dept Head* David Everson; *Asst Prof* Kim Finley-Stansbury; *Asst Prof* Timothy Van Beke; *Lectr* Peggy Cogswell; *Lectr* Robert Labranche; *Lectr* Timothy Roper; *Lectr* Timothy Silva
Estab 1925; Maintain nonprofit art gallery; Clark Hall Gallery, SLU 10765, Hammond, N 70402; art supplies available on-campus; Pub; D & E; Scholarships; SC 25, LC 4, GC 2; D 121, E 75, maj 122
Ent Req: HS dipl, ACT
Degrees: BA(Educ), BA(Humanities), BA(Cultural Resource Management) 4 yrs
Courses: Art Education, Art History, Ceramics, Digital Design, Drawing, Painting, Photography, Printmaking, Sculpture, Teacher Training
Summer School: Dir, C Roy Blackwood. Enrl 150; 8 wk term. Courses—Art Education, Art Survey for Elementary Teachers

LAFAYETTE

UNIVERSITY OF LOUISIANA AT LAFAYETTE, Dept of Visual Arts, Ullafayette Box 43850, Lafayette, LA 70504. Tel 337-482-6056; Fax 337-482-5907; Internet Home Page Address: www.arts.louisiana.edu; *Dept Head* Brian Kelly

Estab 1900; FT 68, PT 7; pub; D&E; Scholarships; univ 18,000
Degrees: BFA 4-5 yrs
Courses: †Advertising Design, †Art Education, †Ceramics, †Choreographic Design, †Fine Arts, †Photography
Summer School: Dir, Gordon Brooks. Enrl 300; study aboard program in Paris, France & London, England. Courses—Ceramics, Computer Art, Design, Drawing, Film & Video Animation, Painting, Photography

LAKE CHARLES

MCNEESE STATE UNIVERSITY, Dept of Visual Arts, 4205 Ryan St, Lake Charles, LA 70605-4511. Tel 337-475-5060; Fax 337-475-5927; *Chmn* Lynn Reynolds
Estab 1950, dept estab 1953; Maintains nonprofit art gallery, Abercrombie Gallery; on-campus shop sells art supplies; FT 9; pub; D & E; Scholarships; SC 24, LC 4, GC 1; D 85, E 15, non-maj 215, maj 85
Ent Req: HS dipl
Degrees: BA (Art Educ) & BA (Studio Arts) 4 yrs
Courses: †Advertising Design, Art Appreciation, †Art Education, Art History, †Ceramics, †Drawing, Graphic Arts, Graphic Design, Mixed Media, †Painting, †Photography, †Printmaking, Survey crafts course
Adult Hobby Classes: Enrl 50; tuition $254 per sem (3 hrs). Courses—Art History & Ceramics
Summer School: Dir, Bill Iles. Enrl 100; tuition $343 per 3 hrs. Courses—Basic Design, Beginning Drawing, Ceramics, Printmaking, Photography

MONROE

UNIVERSITY OF LOUISIANA AT MONROE, (Northeast Louisiana University) Dept of Art, 700 University Ave, Stubbs 141 Monroe, LA 71203-3708. Tel 318-342-1375, 342-5252; Fax 318-342-1369; Internet Home Page Address: www.ulm.edu; *Instr* Brian Fassett, MFA; *Instr* Richard Hayes, MFA; *Instr* Gary Ratcliff, MFA; *Instr* Robert Ward, MFA; *Instr* Cynthia Kee, MFA; *Instr* James Norton, MFA; *Instr* Joni Noble, MFA; *Instr* Linda Ward, MFA; *Head Dept* Ronald J Alexander, MFA; *Asst Prof* Cliff Tresner
Estab 1931, dept estab 1956; pub; D & E; Scholarships; SC 28, LC 4, GC 9; non-maj 300, maj 125, GS 3
Ent Req: HS dipl
Degrees: BFA 4 yrs, MEd
Courses: 3-D Design, Advertising Design, Analytical Perspective, Art Appreciation, Block Printing, Ceramics, Drawing, Figure Drawing, Painting, Photography, Printmaking, Sculpture, Silkscreen, Survey Class
Adult Hobby Classes: Enrl 20. May 31 - July 2. Courses—Art 411
Summer School: Dir, Ronald J Alexander. Courses—Art Appreciation, Art Education, Drawing, Painting

NATCHITOCHES

NORTHWESTERN STATE UNIVERSITY OF LOUISIANA, School of Creative & Performing Arts - Dept of Fine & Graphic Arts, 140 Central Ave, Natchitoches, LA 71497-0001. Tel 318-357-5744; Fax 318-357-5906; Elec Mail barthelemys@nsula.edu; Internet Home Page Address: www.nsula.edu/art; *Prof* Michael Yankowski, MFA; *Assoc Prof* Roger A Chandler, MArch, PhD; *Prof* Clyde Downs, MFA; *Asst Prof* Robert Moreau, MFA; *Asst Prof* F Brooks DeFee, MA; *Asst Prof* W Anthony Watkins; *Asst Prof* Matt DeFord; *Asst Prof* Isaac Powell
Estab 1885; Maintains nonprofit gallery, Hanchey Gallery, AA Fredericks & Alice Dear Fine Art Building, NSU 71497; Watson Libr, NSU 71497; Orville J Hanchey Gallery, 140 Central Ave, Natchitoches, LA 71497. Art supplies may be purchased on campus; Pub; D, E & internet; Scholarships; SC 67, LC 17, GC 36; non-maj 60, maj 101, grad 16
Ent Req: Selective admis
Degrees: BFA 4 yrs, MA 2 yrs, special prog for advanced students MA in Art
Courses: †Advertising Design, Art Appreciation, †Art Education, Art History, Ceramics, Commercial Art, Design, Drawing, Graphic Arts, †Graphic Design, History of Art & Architecture, Painting, Printmaking, Professional Photography, Sculpture, Stained Glass, Stringed Instrument Construction
Adult Hobby Classes: Courses—most of above

NEW ORLEANS

DELGADO COLLEGE, Dept of Fine Arts, 501 City Park Ave, New Orleans, LA 70119-4324. Tel 504-483-4400, 483-4069; Fax 504-483-4954; Elec Mail lcoppi@dcc.edu; Internet Home Page Address: www.dcc.edu; *Chmn Fine Arts* Lisette Copping
Dept estab 1967. College has 2 campuses; pub; D & E; Scholarships; SC 12-20, LC 12-20; D 150, E 65, maj 60
Ent Req: HS dipl, 18 yr old
Degrees: AA and AS 2 yrs
Courses: Art Appreciation, Art History, Ceramics, Drawing, History of Art & Architecture, Jewelry, Painting, Sculpture

LOYOLA UNIVERSITY OF NEW ORLEANS, Dept of Visual Arts, 6363 Saint Charles Ave, New Orleans, LA 70118. Tel 504-865-2011, 861-5456; Fax 504-861-5457; Internet Home Page Address: www.loyno.edu; *Chmn* Carol Leak
Den; D & E; Scholarships; SC 9, LC 3; D 150, E 45, maj 28
Ent Req: HS dipl, ent exam
Degrees: BSA 4 yrs
Courses: Art History, Ceramics, Computer Graphics, Design, Drawing, Painting, Photography, Printmaking, Sculpture, Teacher Training
Summer School: Chmn, John Sears. Enrl 40; term of 6 wks beginning in June. Courses—Drawing, Painting, Printmaking, Sculpture

SOUTHERN UNIVERSITY IN NEW ORLEANS, Fine Arts & Philosophy Dept, 6400 Press Dr, New Orleans, LA 70126-0002. Tel 504-286-5000, 286-5267; Fax 504-286-5296; *Asst Prof* Gary Oaks, MFA; *Music* Roger Dickerson, MFA; *Music* Valeria King, MFA; *Chmn* Sara Hollis, MA; *Instr* Cynthia Ramirez; *Instr* Charlie Johnson; *Instr* Arthur Pindle; *Instr* Tommy Myrick; *Instr* Edward Jordan
Estab 1951, dept estab 1960; pub; D & E; D 21, E 26, non-maj 700, maj 47
Ent Req: HS dipl
Degrees: BA 4 yrs, BS(Art Educ) 4 yrs, BS(Music Educ) 4 yrs
Courses: African & American Art, African Art, Art Education, Art History, Ceramics, Commercial Art, Crafts, Drawing, Painting, Photography, Printmaking, Sculpture, Video
Adult Hobby Classes: Courses offered
Summer School: Courses offered

TULANE UNIVERSITY, School of Architecture, 6823 Saint Charles Ave, 304 Richardson Mem Bldg New Orleans, LA 70118-5665. Tel 504-865-5389; Fax 504-862-8798; Internet Home Page Address: www.tsaarch.edu; *Dean* Donald Gatzke
Estab 1907; FT 24, PT 12; pvt; 320
Degrees: BA, MA(Archit)
Tuition: $9380 per sem
Courses: Computer Graphics, Design, Frank Lloyd Wright's Architecture, History, Life Drawing, Structures, Technology, Theory
—Sophie H Newcomb Memorial College, 1229 Broadway, Woldenberg Art Ctr New Orleans, LA 70118-5210. Tel 504-865-5327; Fax 504-862-8710; Internet Home Page Address: www.2tulane.edu; *Assoc* Theresa Cole; *Prof* Gene H Koss; *Prof* Marilyn R Brown; *Assoc Prof* Ronna Harris; *Assoc Prof* Jeremy Jernegan; *Prof* Barry Bailey; *Prof* Elizabeth Boone; *Chmn* Arthur Okazaki; *Assoc Prof* Sandy Chism; *Asst Prof* Pamela Franco; *Assoc Prof* Michael Plante; *Prof* Bill Tronzo
Estab 1886; pvt; D & E; Scholarships; SC 33, LC 25, GC 29; D 817 per sem, E 37 per sem
Ent Req: HS dipl, CEEB, interview, review of work by chmn & or faculty (optional)
Degrees: BA, BFA, BA(Art Biology), MA, MFA
Tuition: $26,000 incl room & board per yr
Courses: American Art, Ceramics, Drawing, Glass Blowing, Painting, Photography, Pre-Columbian Art, Printmaking, Sculpture
Adult Hobby Classes: Art History, Ceramics, Drawing, Glass, Painting, Photography, Printmaking, Sculpture
Children's Classes: Offered through the Dept of Educ
Summer School: Dean, Richard Marksbury. Courses—Art History, Ceramics, Drawing, Glass, Painting, Photography, Sculpture

UNIVERSITY OF NEW ORLEANS-LAKE FRONT, Dept of Fine Arts, 2000 Lakeshore Dr, New Orleans, LA 70148-0001. Tel 504-280-6410; Fax 504-280-7346; Elec Mail cola@uno.edu; Internet Home Page Address: www.finearts.uno.edu; *Prof Emeritus* Doyle J Gertjejansen, MFA; *Prof* Richard A Johnson, MFA; *Chair & Assoc Prof* Cheryl A Hayes, MFA; *Vis Artist* Anya Martin, MFA; *Vis Artist* Tony Campbell, MFA; *Vis Artist* AAron McNamee, MFA; *Asst Prof* Dan Rule, MFA; *Asst Prof* Rebecca Reynolds, PhD; *Vis Lectr* Alexa Arroyo, MA; *Instr* Jeff Rinehart, MFA; *Instr* Kathy Rodriguez, MFA, MA
Estab 1958, dept estab 1968; Maintains 2 non-profit art galleries, Uno-St Claude Gallery, 2429 St. Claude Ave, New Orleans, LA 7017; Uno Fine Arts Gallery, Dept of Fine Arts, 2000 Lakeshore Dr, New Orleans LA 70117; on-campus supply shop; pub; D & E; Scholarships; SC 29, LC 24, GC 34; D 11,000 (university), non-maj 1900, maj 150, grad 20
Ent Req: HS dipl
Degrees: BA 4 yrs, MFA 60 hrs
Tuition: In-state $6,578; Out of state $19,068
Courses: †Art History, †Design, Digital Art, Drawing, Graphic Design, Hyper-Media, †Painting, †Photography, †Printmaking, †Sculpture, Video-Digital
Summer School: Tuition $913 for one credit of 8 wks beginning June. Courses—Art Fundamentals, Art History, Drawing, Painting, Photography, Sculpture, Printmaking

XAVIER UNIVERSITY OF LOUISIANA, Dept of Fine Arts, 1 Drexel Dr New Orleans, LA 70125. Tel 504-483-7556; Internet Home Page Address: www.xula.edu; *Chmn* Ron Bechet; *Prof* John T Scott, MFA; *Asst Prof* Mrs Nelson Marsalis, MFA
Estab 1926, dept estab 1935; den; D & E; Scholarships; SC 48, LC 10; D 50, E 12, non-maj 10, maj 52
Ent Req: HS dipl, SAT or ACT, health cert, C average at least
Degrees: BA, BA (Art Ed), BFA, BS & MA
Courses: Art Appreciation, Art History, Black & White Photography, Ceramics, Design, Graphic Ad Design, Painting, Photography, Printmaking
Adult Hobby Classes: Courses—Creative Crafts

PINEVILLE

LOUISIANA COLLEGE, Dept of Art, 1140 College Dr, Pineville, LA 71359; PO Box 561, Pineville, LA 71359-0001. Tel 318-487-7262; Fax 318-487-7337; Elec Mail reynoso@lacollege.edu; Internet Home Page Address: www.lacollege.edu; *Adjunct Prof* Preston Gilchrist; *Dept Coordr* Rondall Reynoso; *Asst Prof* Wang-Ling Chou; *Adjunct Prof* John Ammons; *Asst Prof* Tim Roper
Estab 1906; Maintains nonprofit gallery, Weathersby Fine Arts Building Gallery, 1140 College Dr, Box 561, Pineville, LA 71359; Den; D & E; Scholarships; SC 42, LC 9, Lab C; D 26
Ent Req: HS grad
Degrees: BA 50 hrs art, 127 total; BFA 78 hrs art, 134 total
Courses: †Art Education, †Ceramics, Commercial Art, Design, Drawing, †Graphic Design, †Painting, Sculpture, †Studio Arts, Teacher Training, †Web Design

RUSTON

LOUISIANA TECH, School of Art, 1 Mayfield St, Ruston, LA 71272; PO Box 3175W, Tech Sta Ruston, LA 71272-0001. Tel 318-257-3909; Fax 318-257-4890;

Elec Mail ddablow@latech.edu; Internet Home Page Address: www.art.latech.edu; *Dir* Dean Dablow
Estab 1894; maintain nonprofit art gallery, School of Art Gallery; art & architecture libr at same address; FT 11, PT 3; pub; D&E; Scholarships; SC 98, LC 8, GC 87; maj 380, Grad 17
Ent Req: HS dipl
Degrees: BID, BFA, MFA 3 yrs
Courses: †Advertising Design, Art Appreciation, Art Education, Art History, †Ceramics, †Commercial Art, Conceptual Art, Design, †Drawing, †Graphic Arts, †Graphic Design, Illustration, †Interior Design, †Painting, †Photography, †Printmaking, †Sculpture, †Studio Art
Summer School: varies

SHREVEPORT

CENTENARY COLLEGE OF LOUISIANA, Dept of Art, 2911 Centenary Blvd, Shreveport, LA 71104-3396. Tel 318-869-5261, 869-5011; Fax 318-869-5730; Elec Mail ballen@bata.centenary.edu; Internet Home Page Address: www.centenary.edu/department/art/; *Chmn Dept & Prof* Bruce Allen, MFA; *Lectr* Neil Johnson, BA; *Vis Asst Prof* Lisa Nicoletti, PhD; *Instr* Diane Dufilho, MA
Estab 1825, dept estab 1935; Maintain Turner Art Center Gallery; den; D & E; Scholarships; SC 22, LC 8; D 125 per sem
Ent Req: HS dipl, SAT or ACT
Degrees: BA 4 yrs
Courses: Aesthetics, Art Education, Art History, Ceramics, Drafting, Drawing, Graphic Arts, Painting, Printmaking, Sculpture, Teacher Training

THIBODAUX

NICHOLLS STATE UNIVERSITY, Dept of Art, 906 E 1st St, Thibodaux, LA 70310-6701. Tel 985-448-4597; Fax 985-448-4596; Internet Home Page Address: www.nicholls.edu; *Art Dept Head* Dennis Sipiorski
Estab 1948; FT 8; pub; D & E; Scholarships; SC 73, LC 6; D 100, non-maj 20, maj 80, others 20
Ent Req: HS dipl, ACT
Degrees: BA 4 yrs
Courses: Applied Design, Art Appreciation, Art Education, Art History, Ceramics, Design, Drawing, Graphic Design, Illustration, Painting, Papermaking, Photography, Printmaking, Rendering, Sculpture, Water Media

MAINE

AUGUSTA

UNIVERSITY OF MAINE AT AUGUSTA, College of Arts & Humanities, 46 University Dr, University Heights Augusta, ME 04330-9488. Tel 207-621-3000; Fax 207-621-3293; Internet Home Page Address: www.uma.maine.edu; *Prof* Philip Paratore, MFA; *Prof* Robert Katz, MFA; *Prof* Karen Gilg, MFA; *Prof* Tom Hoffman, MFA; *Prof* Lizabeth Libbey, MFA; *Prof* Bill Moseley, MFA; *Prof* Mark Polishook, MFA; *Prof* Roger Richman, MFA; *Prof* Donald Stratton, MFA; *Prof* Charles Winfield, MFA; *Assoc Prof* Brooks Stoddard, MFA; *Chmn* Joshua Nadel, MFA
Estab 1965, dept estab 1970; pub; D & E; SC 20, LC 8; D 50, E 40, non-maj 40, maj 60
Ent Req: HS dipl
Degrees: AA(Architectural Studies) 2 yrs
Courses: Advertising Design, Art History, Ceramics, Drawing, Graphic Arts, Mixed Media, Painting, Paper Making, Photography, Sculpture
Summer School: Provost, Richard Randall. Enrl 30-50; tuition $52 per cr hr for term of 7 wks beginning last wk in June. Courses - Drawing, Painting, Sculpture

BRUNSWICK

BOWDOIN COLLEGE, Art Dept, 9300 College Station, Visual Arts Ctr Brunswick, ME 04011-8493. Tel 207-725-3697; Fax 207-725-3996; Internet Home Page Address: www.bowdoin.edu; *Prof* Linda Docherty PhD; *Chair* Mark Wethli, MFA; *Dir Art History* Susan Wegner, PhD; *Prof* Thomas B Cornell, AB; *Lectr* John Bisbee, BFA; *Asst Prof* Stephen Perkinson, PhD; *Asst Prof* Pamela Fletcher, PhD; *Asst Prof* Michael Kolster, MFA; *Prof* Jim Mullen, MFA; *Vis Asst Prof* Anna Hepler, MFA; *Asst Prof* De-Nin Lee, MFA; *Prof* Clifton Olds, PhD; *Vis Asst Prof* Meghan Brady, MFA; *Vis Asst Prof* Wiebke Theodore, MArch; *Vis Asst Prof* Meggan Gould, MFA
Estab 1794; maintain a nonprofit art gallery: Bowdoin College Museum of Art, Walker Art Bldg, 9400 College Station Brunswick ME 04011; maintains an art/architecture library: Pierce Art Library, Visual Arts Center, 9300 College Station, Brunswick ME; on-campus shop where art supplies may be purchased; pvt; D & E; Scholarships; SC 12, LC 12; maj 54
Ent Req: HS dipl
Degrees: AB 4 yrs
Courses: Architecture, Art History, Digital Animation, Drawing, History of Art & Architecture, Painting, Photography, Printmaking, Sculpture, Stage Design, Visual Arts

DEER ISLE

HAYSTACK MOUNTAIN SCHOOL OF CRAFTS, PO Box 518, Deer Isle, ME 04627-0518. Tel 207-348-2306; Fax 207-348-2307; Internet Home Page Address: www.haystack-mtn.org; *Dir* Stuart J Kestenbaum

Estab 1950; Maintains nonprofit art gallery, Haystack's Ctr for Community Progs, 22 Church St, Deer Isle ME 04627; maintains art library; on-campus shop where art supplies may be purchased; FT 36; pvt; D, Summer school; Scholarships; SC; D 82
Courses: Basketry, Blacksmithing, Ceramics, Fabric, Glassblowing, Graphic Arts, Metalsmithing, Papermaking, Quiltmaking, Stained Glass, Weaving, Woodworking
Summer School: Dir, Stu Kestenbaum. Enrl 80; tuition $475 for 1 wk, $890 for 2 wks. Courses—Basketry, Blacksmith, Fabric Arts, Glassblowing, Graphics, Metalsmithing, Papermaking, Quiltmaking, Woodworking

GORHAM

UNIVERSITY OF SOUTHERN MAINE, Dept of Art, 37 College Ave, Gorham, ME 04038-1032. Tel 207-780-5460; Fax 207-780-5759; Internet Home Page Address: www.usm.maine.edu/artdepartment; *Internship Coordr* Patti Volland; *AA1/Outreach* Deborah Loughlin; *Dir Exhibs* Carolyn Eyler; *Environmental & Studio Tech* Stephen Walsh; *Assoc Prof Drawing & Painting* George Burk; *Prof Art Hist* Donna Cassidy; *Prof Sculpture* Duncan Hewitt; *Prof Photog* Rose Marasco; *Prof Sculpture* Michael Shaughnessy; *Asst Prof Art Educ* Kelly Hrenko; *Prof Digital & Foundation* Jan Piribeck
Estab 1878, dept estab 1956; Maintains nonprofit art gallery, USM Art Gallery; maintains art library, USM Libraries; pub; D & E & weekend; SC 33 LC 14; maj 162
Ent Req: HS dipl, portfolio
Degrees: BA, BFA
Tuition: Res—undergrad $253 per cr hr; nonres—undergrad $665 per cr hr
Courses: Art Education, Art History, Ceramics, Design, †Digital Art, Drawing, Mixed Media, Painting, Philosophy of Art; Problems in Art, Photography, Printmaking, Sculpture

LEWISTON

BATES COLLEGE, Art & Visual Culture, 2 Andrews Rd, Lewiston, ME 04240-6020; 75 Russell St, Lewiston, ME 04240. Tel 207-786-8212; Fax 207-786-8335; Elec Mail aodom@bates.edu; Internet Home Page Address: www.bates.edu; *Pres* Elaine Hansen; *Assoc Prof* Edward S Hardwood; *Prof* Erica Rand; *Asst Prof, Chmn* Trian Nguyen; *Assoc Prof* Pamela Johnson; *Lectr* Susan Denlsnap; *Senior Lectr* Robert Feintuch; *Senior Lectr* Elke Morris
Estab 1864, dept estab 1964; Maintain nonprofit art gallery, Bates College Mus of Art; on-campus shop where art supplies may be purchased; FT 5, PT 4; pvt; D & E; Scholarships; SC 26, LC 37; 1650 total
Degrees: BA 4 yr
Courses: Aesthetics, Art History, Ceramics, Drawing, History of Art & Architecture, Painting, Photography, Printmaking, Sculpture, †Studio Art

ORONO

UNIVERSITY OF MAINE, Dept of Art, 107 Lord, Orono, ME 04469-5712. Tel 207-581-3245; Fax 207-581-3276; Elec Mail um.art@umit.maine.edu; Internet Home Page Address: www.maine.edu/art; *Prof* Laurie E Hicks PhD; *Prof* Michael H Lewis, MFA; *Assoc Prof* Constant Albertson, PhD; *Assoc Prof & Chair* Michael Grillo, PhD, MA; *Assoc Prof* Andy Mavery, MFA; *Adjunct Assoc Prof* Nina Sutcliffe, MA; *Asst Prof* Ed Nadeau, MFA; *Adjunct Asst Prof* Karen Linehan, MA; *Adjunct Asst Prof* Wayne Hall, MFA; *Adjunct Asst Prof* Jorge Gonzalez, MFA; *Adjunct Asst Prof* Kerstin Engman, MFA; *Adjunct Asst Prof* Susan Camp, MFA; *Adjunct Prof* John Eden, MFA; *Prof* James Linehan, MFA; *Prof* Susan Groce, MFA; *Assoc Prof* Justin Wolff, PhD; *Instr* Matthew Smolinsky, MFA; *Adjunct Asst Prof* Greg Ondo, MFA
Estab 1862, dept estab 1946; Maintain nonprofit art gallery, Lord Hall, Dept of Art, Univ of Maine, Orono, ME 04469; on-campus art supply shop; pub; D & E; Scholarships; SC 57, LC 24, GC; maj 175-200; minors 80
Ent Req: HS dipl, 3 CEEB tests
Degrees: BA 4 yrs, BFA
Tuition: Res—undergrad $8480; nonres—undergrad $20,750; campus res—room & board $7484 per yr
Courses: Aesthetics, Art Appreciation, †Art Education, †Art History, Computer Art, Design, Digital Art, Drawing, Graphic Design, History of Art & Architecture, Mixed Media, †New Media, Painting, Photography, Printmaking, Sculpture, †Studio Art, Teacher Training
Children's Classes: Chair, Laurie E Hicks, PhD. Enrl 110-125; tuition $25 for 8 wks during the Fall sem. Courses—Art Education
Summer School: Dir, Robert White. Tuition $105 per cr hr, 3-8 wk courses. Courses—Art Education, Art History, Basic Drawing, Basic Painting, Computer Graphics, Photography, Printmaking

PORTLAND

MAINE COLLEGE OF ART, 522 Congress St # 4, Portland, ME 04101-3378. Tel 207-775-3052; Fax 207-775-5087; Elec Mail info@meca.edu; Internet Home Page Address: www.meca.edu; *Pres* Christine J Vincent; *Dean* Greg Murphy; *Instr* John Eide, MFA; *Instr* Mark Jamra, BFA; *Instr* John T Ventimiglia, MFA; *Instr* Mark Johnson, MFA; *Instr* George LaRou, MFA; *Instr* Gan Xu, PhD; *Instr* Joan Uraneck, MFA; *Instr* Honour Mack, MFA; *Instr* Paul Diamato, MFA
Estab 1882; pvt; D & E; Scholarships; SC 37, LC 9; D 330, E300, maj 330, others 170 HS, 75 children (4th-9th grades)
Ent Req: HS dipl, portfolio
Degrees: BFA 4 yr (under Maine law, & academically advanced HS Sr may take the freshman yr at Maine College of Art for both HS & Maine College of Art cr), MFA 2 yr
Courses: Art Education, Art History, Art in Service, †Ceramics, Computer Arts, Design, Drawing, †Graphic Design, Illustration, †Jewelry, †Metalsmithing, Mixed Media, New Media Illustration, †Painting, †Photography, †Printmaking, †Sculpture, †Self-Designed Media Arts, †Silversmithing, Video, Woodworking & Furniture Design

Adult Hobby Classes: 300; tuition 325 per 1 cr course plus lab fee $10-$25. Courses—Apparel Design, Cartooning, Ceramics, Design, Drawing, Electronic Imaging, Graphic Design, Illustration, Jewelry, Landscape Design, Metalsmithing, Painting, Photography, Printmaking, Sculpture, Textile Design
Children's Classes: $245; tuition $150 for 10 wk term. Courses—Ceramics, Computer Graphics, Drawing, Graphic Design, Metalsmithing, Photography, Printmaking, Sculpture
Summer School: Dir, Margo Halverson. Courses—Art History, Ceramics, Computer Imaging, Drawing, Graphic Design, Jewelry & Metalsmithing, Painting, Photography, Printmaking, Sculpture, Watercolor, 2 & 3-D Design

PORTLAND POTTERY INC, 118 Washington Ave, Portland, ME 04101-2631. Tel 207-772-3273; Fax 207-780-6451; Internet Home Page Address: www.portlandpottery.com
Courses: †Jewelry, †Pottery, †Sculpture

ROCKPORT

MAINE PHOTOGRAPHIC WORKSHOPS, THE INTERNATIONAL T.V. & FILM WORKSHOPS & ROCKPORT COLLEGE, 2 Central St, Rockport, ME 04856-5936; PO Box 200, Rockport, ME 04856-0200. Tel 207-236-8581; Fax 207-236-2558; Elec Mail info@theworkshops.com; Internet Home Page Address: www.theworkshops.com; *Founder & Dir* David H Lyman; *Registrar* Kerry Curren; *Student Svcs* Christy Smith
Estab 1973; Scholarships; 1200
Degrees: AA 2 yr, MFA
Courses: 3-D Art, Animation, Archaeology, Art History, Collage, Commercial Art, Conceptual Art, Digital Media, Drawing, Film, Graphic Arts, Graphic Design, History of Cinema, History of Photography, Illustration, Interactive Multimedia, Painting, Photography, Printmaking, Psychology of Symbols, Screen Dynamics, Teacher Training, Video
Adult Hobby Classes: Enrl 1000
Summer School: Dir, David H Lyman. Enrl 2000; tuition $250-$600 for 1 wk workshop. Courses—Directing, Editing, Film, Video, Writing

WATERVILLE

COLBY COLLEGE, Art Dept, 4000 Mayflower Hill, Waterville, ME 04901-8840. Tel 207-872-3233; Fax 207-872-3141; *Prof* Harriett Matthews, MFA; *Prof* David Simon, PhD; *Prof* Michael Marlais, PhD; *Assoc Prof* Scott Reed, MFA; *Asst Prof* Ankeney Weitz, PhD; *Assoc Prof* Berin Engman, MFA; *Assoc Prof* Veronique Plesch, PhD; *Asst Prof* Laura Saltz, PhD; *Vis Asst Prof* Dee Peppe, MFA
Estab 1813, dept estab 1944; Maintain nonprofit art gallery; pvt; D & E; Scholarships; SC 25, LC 25; D 500, non-maj 425, maj 75
Ent Req: HS dipl
Degrees: BA 4 yrs
Courses: Art History, †Art History, Ceramics, Drawing, History of Art & Architecture, Painting, †Painting, Photography, Printmaking, †Printmaking, Sculpture, †Sculpture

MARYLAND

BALTIMORE

BALTIMORE CITY COMMUNITY COLLEGE, Dept of Fine Arts, 2901 Liberty Heights Ave, Main Bldg, Rm 243 Baltimore, MD 21215-7807. Tel 410-462-7605; Internet Home Page Address: www.bccc.edu; *Chmn* Rose Monroe; *Assoc Prof* David Bahr, MFA; *Asst Prof* Sally De Marcos, MEd
Estab 1947; Harbor Campus address Lombard St & Market Place, Baltimore, MD 21202; FT 7, PT 20; pub; D & E; Scholarships; D & E 9800, non-maj 505, maj 388
Ent Req: HS dipl or HS equivalency, ent exam
Degrees: AA 2 yrs
Courses: Advertising Design, Art Education, Art History, Ceramics, Commercial Art, Drawing, †Fashion Design, Fashion Illustration, †Fashion Merchandising, Graphic Arts, †Graphic Design, Jewelry, Painting, †Photography, Printmaking, Sculpture, Textile Design
Adult Hobby Classes: Tuition res $56 per cr; nonres $168 per cr. Courses—same as above
Summer School: Dir, Dr Stephen Millman. Enrl 2655. Courses - Ceramics, Crafts, Design, Drawing, Fashion Design, Painting

COLLEGE OF NOTRE DAME OF MARYLAND, Art Dept, 4701 N Charles St, Baltimore, MD 21210-2404. Tel 410-532-5520; Fax 410-532-5795; Elec Mail dfirmani@ndm.edu; Internet Home Page Address: www.ndm.edu; WATS (Md) 800-435-0200; all other 800-435-0300; *Chmn Prof* Domenico Firmani PhD; *Prof* Kevin Raines, MFA; *Assoc Prof* Geoff Delanoy, MFA
Estab 1899; Maintains nonprofit gallery, Gormley Gallery, 4701 N Charles, Baltimore, MD 21210; den, W; wkend; M; D & E, wkend; Scholarships; SC 32, LC 20, GC 5; D 680, non-maj 480, maj 45
Ent Req: HS dipl, SAT
Degrees: BA 4 yrs
Courses: Advertising Design, Art Education, †Art History, Commercial Art, Design, Drawing, †Graphic Arts, Graphic Design, Illustration, †Museum Staff Training, Painting, †Photography, Printmaking, Sculpture, †Studio, Teacher Training
Adult Hobby Classes: Enrl 55; tuition $150 per cr (1-9 cr). Courses offered in Weekend College & Continuing Education Programs

Summer School: Enrl 35; tuition $95 per cr. Courses—Drawing, History of Art Surveys, Painting, Photography, Printmaking, Sculpture, Teacher Training

COPPIN STATE COLLEGE, Dept Fine & Communication Arts, 2500 W North Ave, Baltimore, MD 21216-3698. Tel 410-383-5400; Fax 410-383-9606; Internet Home Page Address: www.coppin.edu; *Chmn* Dr Judith Willner
FT 1, PT 2; Scholarships; SC 6, LC 7; D 350, E 45
Degrees: BS, MA & Doc in Art Education
Courses: Advertising Design, Art Education, Art History, Calligraphy, Ceramics, Drawing, Film, Graphic Design, Lettering, Painting, Photography, Printmaking, Sculpture, Teacher Training, Theatre Arts

GOUCHER COLLEGE, Art & Art History Dept, 1021 Dulaney Valley Rd, Baltimore, MD 21204-2780. Tel 410-337-6000, 337-6570; Internet Home Page Address: www.goucher.edu; *Prof, Chair* Allyn Massey; *Prof* Gail Husch; *Prof* Ed Worteck; *Prof* April Osttinger; *Prof* Matthew McConville
Estab 1885; Rosenberg Gallery & Silber Gallery; FT 5, PT 6-7; pvt; D & E; Scholarships; SC 23, LC 19; D 500, non-maj 450, maj (art) 40
Ent Req: HS dipl, SAT, achievement tests (CEEB), American College Testing Program
Degrees: BA 4 yrs (18 depts for undergrads)
Courses: †Aesthetics, †Art Education, †Art History, †Arts Administration, †Ceramics, †Communications, †Conceptual Art, †Constructions, †Mixed Media, †Painting, †Photography, †Printmaking, †Sculpture, †Video

JOHNS HOPKINS UNIVERSITY, Dept of the History of Art, 3400 N Charles St, Baltimore, MD 21218-2680. Tel 410-516-7117; Fax 410-516-5188; Elec Mail arthist@jhu.edu; Internet Home Page Address: www.jhu.edu; *Chmn* Dr Stephen Campbell
Estab 1947; FT 5, PT 3; pvt; D & E; Scholarships; LC; 10-20 in advanced courses, 80-100 in introductory courses
Tuition: $31,620 per yr
Courses: †Art History, History of Art & Archaeology
Summer School: Enrl 30
—School of Medicine, Dept of Art as Applied to Medicine, 1830 E Monument St, Ste 7000, Baltimore, MD 21205. Tel 410-955-3213; Fax 410-955-1085; Elec Mail dbalch1@jhmi.edu; Internet Home Page Address: www.hopkinsmedicine.org/medart; *Dir Dept* Gary P Lees, MS; *Assoc Prof* Timothy H Phelps, MS; *Assoc Prof* Howard C Bartner, MA; *Assoc Prof* David Rini, MA; *Asst Prof* Dale R Levitz, MS; *Assoc Prof* Corinne Sandone, MA; *Assoc Prof* Norman Barker, MS; *Asst Prof* Juan R Garcia, MA; *Asst Prof* Anne R Altemus, MA; *Lectr* Joseph Dieter Jr; *Asst Prof* Miguel A Schon, PhD; *Prof Pathology* Grover M Hutchins, MD; *Lectr* Joan A Freedman, MS; *Assoc Prof* Ian Suk; *Instr* Virginia Ferrante
Univ estab 1876, School Medicine estab 1893, dept estab 1911; Maintains an art library; pvt; D; Scholarships; SC 13, LC 5, GC 11
Ent Req: Baccalaureate degree
Degrees: MA
Tuition: $36,100 per yr
Courses: Illustration, Photography, Sculpture, Video

MARYLAND INSTITUTE, College of Art, 1300 W Mt Royal Ave, Baltimore, MD 21217. Tel 410-669-9200; *Pres* Fred Lazarus IV
Estab 1826; FT 45, PT 55; pvt; D & E; Scholarships; D 1107, E 554, Sat 280
Ent Req: HS grad, exam
Degrees: BFA & MFA 4 yrs
Tuition: $15,000 per yr; campus res—$4800
Courses: Ceramics, Computer Graphics, Drawing, Fibers & Wood, Graphic Design, Illustration, Interior Design, Painting, Photography, Printmaking, Sculpture
Adult Hobby Classes: Evenings & Saturdays, cr-non cr classes
Children's Classes: Saturdays & Summer classes
Summer School: Dir Continuing Studies, M A Marsalek. Enrl 1066; tuition $400 per sem per class for Continuing Studies
—Hoffberger School of Painting, 1300 W Mt Royal Ave, Baltimore, MD 21217. Tel 410-225-2255; Fax 410-225-2408; *Dir* Grace Hartigan
Fel awarded annually for study at the grad level; limited to 14
Tuition: $16,500
—Rinehart School of Sculpture, 1300 W Mt Royal Ave, Baltimore, MD 21217. Tel 410-225-2255; Fax 410-225-2408; *Dir* Maren Hassinger
Tuition: $16,500
Adult Hobby Classes: Enrl 748; tuition $200 per cr
Children's Classes: Enrl 174; tuition $170 per class
—Mount Royal School of Art, 1300 Mount Royal Ave, Baltimore, MD 21217. Tel 410-225-2255; *Faculty* Babe Shapiro; *Faculty* Salvatore Scarpitta 79
Degrees: MAT 2 yrs
Tuition: $16,750
Courses: Aesthetics, Art Education, Art History, Calligraphy, †Ceramics, †Drawing, History of Art & Archeology, Intermedia, †Mixed Media, Painting, Photography, †Sculpture, Studio Art, Teacher Training, Video
—Graduate Photography, 1300 W Mount Royal Ave, Baltimore, MD 21217. Tel 410-225-2306; *Dir* Will Larson
Degrees: MFA 2 yrs
Tuition: Res—grad $17,000 per yr
Courses: History of Photography
—Art Education Graduate Studies, 1300 W Mount Royal Ave, Baltimore, MD 21217. Tel 410-225-2306; *Dir* Dr Karen Carroll
Degrees: MFA 2 yrs
Tuition: Res—grad $17,000 per yr
Courses: Art Education, Teacher Training

MORGAN STATE UNIVERSITY, Dept of Art, 1700 E Coldspring Lane, Baltimore, MD 21251. Tel 443-885-3021, 885-3333 (Main); Internet Home Page Address: www.morgan.edu; *Fine Arts Dept Chmn* Dr Nathan Carter; *Coordr Art Dept* Kenneth Royster
Estab 1867, dept estab 1950; FT 7; pub; D & E; Scholarships; SC 28, LC 11, GC 17; D 340, E 50, non-maj 250, maj 140, GS 11

Ent Req: HS dipl
Degrees: BA(Art & Music Performance) & MA(Music)
Courses: 3-D Design, Architecture, Art Education, Art History, Ceramics, Design, Drawing, †Gallery, Graphic Arts, Graphic Design, Illustration, Painting, Photography, Sculpture, †Theatre Arts

SCHULER SCHOOL OF FINE ARTS, 5 E Lafayette Ave, Baltimore, MD 21202-2880; 7 E Lafayette Ave, Baltimore, MD 21202-2807. Tel 410-685-3568; Elec Mail schulerschool@gmail.com; Internet Home Page Address: www.schulerschool.com; *Dir* Francesca Schuler Guerin; *Asst Dir* Hans Schuler Guerin
Estab 1959; Maintain library; pvt; D & E, Sat workshops; SC 9, GC 3; D 50, E 30, grad 2
Degrees: 4 yrs; dipl, 5 yr scholarship
Tuition: $5,500 per yr, part-time students pay by schedule for sem
Courses: Drawing, Painting, Sculpture
Children's Classes: Tuition $750-$1200 (summer - ages 14 & over). Courses—Drawing, Painting, Sculpture
Summer School: Dir, Francis S. Guerin. Enrl 30; tuition $750 for term of 6 wks beginning June, $1,300 for 6 hrs per day, 6 wks. Courses—Drawing, Oil Painting, Sculpture, Watercolor

UNIVERSITY OF MARYLAND, BALTIMORE COUNTY, Imaging & Digital Arts (IMDA), Dept of Visual Arts, 5401 Wilkens Ave, Rm 111, Baltimore, MD 21250. Tel 410-455-2150; Fax 410-455-1053; Elec Mail sbradley@umbc.edu; Internet Home Page Address: art.umbc.edu; *Assoc Prof* Guenet Abraham; *Prof & Dir Imaging Research Ctr* Dan Bailey; *Affiliate Assoc Prof, Chief Cur AOK Libr & Dir CBSA* Tom Beck; *Asst Prof* Kelley Bell; *Undergrad Prog Dir* Melanie Berry; *Affiliate Assoc Prof & Assoc Dir Imaging Research Ctr* Lee Boot; *Assoc Prof & Grad Prog Dir* Steve Bradley; *Adjunct Faculty* Susan Campbell; *Assoc Chair & Assoc Prof* Lynn Cazabon; *Assoc Prof* Irene Chan; *Assoc Prof* Cathy Cook; *Prof* Mark Alice Durant; *Asst Prof* Eric Dyer; *Adjunct Faculty* Joan Feldman; *Affiliate Assoc Prof & Dir Ctr for Art Design & Visual Culture* Symmes Gardner; *Assoc Prof & Chair* Vin Grabill; *Prog Mgmt Specialist* Mary Hess; *Assoc Prof & Assoc Chair* Preminda Jacob; *Affiliate Assoc Prof* Harvey Kirstel; *Affiliate Assoc Prof* James Mahoney; *Asst Prof* Neal MacDonald; *Assoc Prof* Lisa Moren; *Asst Prof* Callie Neylan; *Assoc Prof* Timothy Nohe; *Assoc Prof & Assoc Dean Coll Arts, Humanities & Soc Sciences* Kathy O'Dell; *Adjunct Faculty* Bodil Ottesen; *Adjunct Faculty* John Penny; *Assoc Prof* Peggy Re; *Prof* James Smalls; *Prof* Ellen Handler Spitz; *Asst Prof* Dan Sturgeon; *Asst Prof* Calla Thompson; *Exhib & Tech Dir, Ctr for Art, Design & Visual Culture* William-John Tudor; *Assoc Prof* Fred Worden
Estab 1966; Maintains coll in Albin O Kuhn Library & Gallery; art supplies sold on campus; pub; D & E; SC 27, LC 12, GC 4; in dept D 485, non-maj 375, maj 110
Library Holdings: Book Volumes; Manuscripts; Maps; Other Holdings Archives; Artifacts; Special Collections; Photographs
Ent Req: HS dipl, SAT
Degrees: BA 4 yrs, MFA
Courses: Advertising Design, Aesthetics, †Art History, Calligraphy, Ceramics, Collage, Commercial Art, Conceptual Art, †Drawing, †Film, Graphic Arts, †Graphic Design, †History of Art & Architecture, Intermedia, Lettering, Mixed Media, †Painting, Photography, Printmaking, †Video
Summer School: Dir, David Yager. Six wk term. Courses—Drawing, Film, History, Photography, Video

BEL AIR

HARFORD COMMUNITY COLLEGE, Visual, Performing and Applied Arts Division, 401 Thomas Run Rd, Bel Air, MD 21015-1696. Tel 443-412-2000; Fax 443-412-2180; Elec Mail vpaa@harford.edu; Internet Home Page Address: www.harford.edu; *Dean* Paul Labe Jr; *Dir* James McFarland; *Assoc Prof Art* Kenneth Jones; *Assoc Prof Art* Heidi Neff; *Assoc Prof Art* Jeffrey Ball; *Assoc Prof Theatre* Dr Ben Fisler; *Asst Prof Photog* Chris Heard; *Assoc Prof Mass Communs* Wayne Hepler; *Interior Design Faculty* Betty Reeves; *Asst Prof Mass Communs* Claudia Brown; *Asst Prof Music* Dr Neil Anderson-Himmelspach
Estab 1957; Maintain Chesapeake Gallery, Harford Community College, 401 Thomas Run Rd, Bel Air, MD 21015. Art supplies sold at campus shop; FT 10, PT 40; pub; D & E; SC 105, LC 13; FT 6,000, PT 4,500
Ent Req: HS dipl
Degrees: AA 2 yrs
Tuition: Res—undergrad $87 per cr hr; nonres—undergrad $174 (out of county), $261 (out of state) per cr hr
Courses: Architecture, Art History, Ceramics, Costume Design & Construction, Design, Design & Technical Theatre, Digital Imaging, †Digital Media, Drawing, Film, †Fine Art, Graphic Arts, Graphic Design, History of Art & Architecture, Illustration, †Interior Design, Mixed Media, Painting, Performing Arts, †Photography, Printmaking, Sculpture, Stage Design, Theatre Arts, Video
Summer School: Div Chair, Paul Labe

BOWIE

BOWIE STATE UNIVERSITY, Fine & Performing Arts Dept, 14000 Jericho Park Rd, MLK Bldg, Rm 236 Bowie, MD 20715-3319. Tel 301-860-4000; Fax 301-860-3767; *Coordr Gallery Dir* Robert Ward; *Chmn* Clarence Knight
Estab 1865, dept estab 1968; FT 8; pub; D; SC 7, LC 3; D 1600, E 350, non-maj 180, maj 45
Ent Req: HS dipl
Degrees: BA(Art) 4 yrs
Courses: African & American History, Art History, Ceramics, Cinematography, Computer Graphics, Crafts, Design, Drawing, Graphics, Museum & Gallery Study, Painting, Photography, Sculpture
Summer School: Dir, Dr Ida Brandon. Courses—Ceramics, Media Workshop

CATONSVILLE

COMMUNITY COLLEGE OF BALTIMORE COUNTY, (Catonsville Community College) Art Dept, 800 S Rolling Rd, Catonsville, MD 21228-5317. Tel 410-455-4429; Fax 410-455-5134; Elec Mail pglasgow@ccbc.cc.md.us; *Chmn Dept* Paul Glasgow
Estab 1957; pub; D & E; Scholarships; SC 26, LC 6; D 600, E 400, non-maj 200, maj 300, applied arts maj 350
Ent Req: HS dipl
Degrees: cert & AA 2 yrs
Courses: †Advertising Design, Art Education, Art History, Ceramics, Commercial Art, Drawing, Graphic Design, Illustration, Interior Design, Painting, †Photography, Sculpture
Adult Hobby Classes: Chmn Dept, Dr Dian Fetter
Summer School: Same as above

COLLEGE PARK

UNIVERSITY OF MARYLAND, Dept of Art History & Archaeology, 1211-D Art-Sociology Bldg, College Park, MD 20742-1335. Tel 301-405-1479; 405-1494; Fax 301-314-9652; Elec Mail jh24@umail.umd.edu; Internet Home Page Address: www.inform.umd.edu/EdRes/colleges/ARHU/Depts/ArtHistory; *Chmn* June Hargrove
Estab 1944; FT 17, PT 2; pub; D; Scholarships; SC 39, LC 37, GC 22; 2000 per sem, maj 102, grad 77
Ent Req: 3.0 grade average
Degrees: BA, MA, PhD
Courses: Art History
Adult Hobby Classes: Enrl 500 per yr. Courses—Art History
Summer School: Dir, Dr Melvin Hall. Enrl 350; tuition res—$170; nonres—$280 per cr hr for term of 6 wks. Courses—Art History
—Department of Art, 1211-E Art-Sociology Bldg, College Park, MD 20742-1311. Tel 301-405-1442; Fax 301-314-9740; Elec Mail artdept@umail.umd.edu; Internet Home Page Address: www.inform.umd.edu/EdRes/colleges/ARHU/Depts/Art; *Chmn* John Ruppert
Estab 1944; FT 19, PT 5; pub; D; Scholarships; SC 39, LC 37, GC 22; 850 per sem, maj 170, grad 20
Ent Req: 3.0 grade average
Degrees: BA, MFA
Courses: 2-D & 3-D Drawing, Art Theory, Artist Survival, Design, Lithography, Mixed Media, Papermaking, Photography, Printmaking
Summer School: Dir, Dr Melvin Berstein. Two six-week sessions. Courses—Design, Drawing, Painting, Printmaking, Sculpture

CUMBERLAND

ALLEGANY COMMUNITY COLLEGE, Art Dept, 12401 Willow Brook Rd SE, Cumberland, MD 21502. Tel 301-724-7700; Fax 301-724-6892; Internet Home Page Address: www.ac.cc.md.us; *Chmn* James D Zamagias
Estab 1966; FT 1 PT 3; pub; D & E; Scholarships; SC 6, LC 1; Enrl D 30, E 9
Ent Req: HS dipl
Degrees: AA 2 yrs
Courses: 2-D & 3-D Design, Ceramics, Drawing, Painting, Survey of Art History
Adult Hobby Classes: Courses offered
Summer School: Dir, James D Zamagias. Term of 6 wks beginning July. Courses—Painting, 2-D Design

EMMITSBURG

MOUNT SAINT MARY'S UNIVERSITY, Visual & Performing Arts Dept, 16300 Old Emmitsburg Rd, Emmitsburg, MD 21727-7702. Tel 301-447-6122, Ext 5308; Fax 301-447-5755; Internet Home Page Address: www.msmary.edu; *Prof* Margaret Rahaim, MFA; *Art Faculty* Dr Kurt Blaugher; *Prof* Elizabeth Holtry, MFA; *Prof Dr* Andrew Rosenfeld; *Prof* Barry Long, MA
Estab 1808; pvt; D & E; Scholarships; SC 13, LC 3; D 1528, maj 20
Ent Req: HS dipl, SAT
Degrees: BA and BS 4 yrs
Courses: Art Education, †Art History, Ceramics, Design, †Drawing, Graphic Arts, Graphic Design, Mixed Media, †Painting, Photography, Printmaking, †Sculpture, †Theatre Arts

FREDERICK

HOOD COLLEGE, Dept of Art, 401 Rosemont Ave, Frederick, MD 21701-8575. Tel 301-663-3131; Fax 301-694-7653; Internet Home Page Address: www.hood.edu; *Assoc Prof* Fred Bohrer; *Chmn* Dr Anne Derbes
Estab 1893; Varies from PT to FT; pvt; W; D; SC 18, LC 16; D 700, maj 60
Ent Req: HS dipl
Degrees: BA 4 yrs
Courses: Art History, Three Areas of Concentration: Studio Arts, Visual Communications
Summer School: Dir, Dr Patricia Bartlett. Tuition by course for term of 6 wks, June-Aug. Courses—Internships and Independent Studies, Photography, Watercolor and Sketching, Woodcut

FROSTBURG

FROSTBURG STATE UNIVERSITY, Dept of Visual Arts, 101 Braddock Rd, Frostburg, MD 21532-2303. Tel 301-687-4797; Fax 301-689-4737; Elec Mail ddavis@frostburg.edu; WATS 800-687-8677; *Head Dept* Dustin P Davis
Estab 1898; FT 3; pub; D; Scholarships; SC 25, LC 5; D 230, maj 150, GS 13

Ent Req: HS dipl
Degrees: BFA(Art Educ Cert) 4 yr
Courses: 2-D & 3-D Design, Art Appreciation, Art Criticism, Art Education, Art History, Art Therapy, Ceramics, Crafts, Drawing, Graphic Design, Painting, Photography, Printmaking, Sculpture, Teacher Training, Visual Imagery

HAGERSTOWN

HAGERSTOWN JUNIOR COLLEGE, Art Dept, 11400 Robinwood Dr, Hagerstown, MD 21742-6514. Tel 301-790-2800, Ext 221; Fax 301-739-0737; *Coordr* Ben Culbertson; *Pres* Norman Shea
Estab 1946; pub; D & E; SC 10, LC 4; D 110, E 66
Degrees: AA, 2 yrs
Tuition: Washington County res—$70 per cr hr; out-of-county—$114 per cr hr; nonres—$143per cr hr
Courses: Art Appreciation, Art History, Art Methods, Basic Design, Ceramics, Drawing, Painting, Photography, Sculpture, Video
Summer School: Courses - Art & Culture, Basic Drawing, Painting, Photography, Special Studies in Ceramics, Parent & Child Art Studio

LARGO

PRINCE GEORGE'S COMMUNITY COLLEGE, Art Dept, 301 Largo Rd, English & Humanities Div Largo, MD 20774-2109. Tel 301-322-0966; Fax 301-808-0960; Internet Home Page Address: www.pg.cc.md.us; *Chmn* Gary Kirkeby
Estab 1958, dept estab 1967; 5 FT, 16 PT; pub; D & E; Scholarships; SC 18, LC 2; D 220, E 140, maj 11
Ent Req: HS dipl, CGP test
Degrees: AA
Courses: Art Appreciation, Art Survey, Ceramics, Commercial Advertising, Commercial Design, Computer Graphics, Design, Drawing, Graphic Arts, Graphic Design, Illustration, Lettering, Multimedia, Painting, Photography, Sculpture
Summer School: Dean, Dr Robert Barshay. Courses—Drawing, Intro to Art, Painting, Photography

PRINCESS ANNE

UNIVERSITY OF MARYLAND EASTERN SHORE, Art & Technology Dept, 11868 Academic Oval, Princess Anne, MD 21853-1299. Tel 410-651-6488, 651-2200; Fax 410-351-7959; *Coordr Art Educ* Ernest R Satchell
Degrees: BA 4 yr
Tuition: Res—$124 per cr hr incl room & board per sem; nonres—$265
Courses: Art Appreciation, Art Education, Art History, Calligraphy, Ceramics, Drawing, Handicrafts, Jewelry, Painting, Photography, Printmaking, Sculpture

ROCKVILLE

MONTGOMERY COLLEGE, Dept of Art, 51 Manakee St, Rockville, MD 20850. Tel 240-566-4083; Elec Mail artsinstitute@montgomerycollege.edu; Internet Home Page Address: artsinstitute.montgomerycollege.edu; *Dean Arts* Deborah Preston; *Art Chair Germantown* Ziki Findikoglu; *Art Chair Rockville* Kay McCrohan; *Art Chair Tacoma Park* Wilfred Brunner; *Acting Dir, School of Art + Design* Maggie Noss; *Chair Commun Art Technology* Ed Riggs
Estab 1946; Maintain nonprofit art galleries, Cafritz Art Center Gallery, Commun Art Technology Gallery, Globe Hall Atrium Gallery, Sarah Silberman Art Gallery; Pub; D & E & W; Scholarships; SC 65, LC 13; 2,800
Ent Req: HS dipl, SA+D portfolio review
Degrees: AA Studio Art, Art Ed, Art History; AFA Studio Art, Graphic Design; AAS Graphic Design
Tuition: County Res—$93; state res— $191; out-of-state—$257
Courses: †Architecture, Art Appreciation, †Art History, Ceramics, Color Crafts, †Commercial Art, Computer Graphics, Design, Drawing, Enameling, Film, Goldsmithing, Graphic Design, History of Art & Architecture, †Illustration, †Interior Design, Jewelry, Metalsmithing, Painting, †Photography, Printmaking, Sculpture, Stage Design, Theatre Arts, Video
Adult Hobby Classes: Tuition & classes vary
Children's Classes: Tuition & classes vary
Summer School: Chmn Prof James L Brown. Tuition $35 per sem hr. Courses—Ceramics, Color, Crafts, Design, Drawing, Painting, Printmaking, Sculpture, Art History

SAINT MARY'S CITY

SAINT MARY'S COLLEGE OF MARYLAND, Art & Art History Dept, 18952 East Fischer Rd Saint Mary's City, MD 20686. Tel 240-895-2000, 895-4250; Fax 240-895-4958; Elec Mail srjohnson@smcm.edu; Internet Home Page Address: www.smcm.edu; *Dept Chmn* Sue Johnson, MFA; *Prof* Jeffrey Carr, MFA; *Asst Prof* Joe Lucchesi, PhD; *Asst Prof* Rebecca Brown, PhD
Estab 1964; pub; D & E; Scholarships; SC 14, LC 16; D 155, E 43, non-maj 128, maj 70
Ent Req: HS dipl, SAT scores
Degrees: BA
Courses: Art History, Digital Imaging, Drawing, Graphic Arts, Mixed Media, Painting, Photography, Printmaking, Sculpture
Adult Hobby Classes: Art History, Drawing, Mixed Media, Painting, Photography, Printmaking, Sculpture
Summer School: Tuition $110 per cr

SALISBURY

SALISBURY STATE UNIVERSITY, Art Dept, 1101 Camden Ave, Salisbury, MD 21801-6860. Tel 410-543-6270; Fax 410-548-3002; Internet Home Page Address: www.ssu.edu; *Chmn* Paul Flexner, PhD; *Assoc Prof* John R Cleary, MFA; *Asst Prof* Ursula M Ehrhardt, MA; *Asst Prof* Dean A Peterson, MA; *Assoc Prof* Marie Cavallaro

Estab 1925, dept estab 1970; Maintain nonprofit art gallery; Atrium Gallery & Fueton Gallery; Pub; D & E; Scholarships; SC 26, LC 7, GC 1; non-maj 500, maj 111, grad 2
Ent Req: HS dipl, SAT verbal & math, ACT
Degrees: BA & BFA 4 yrs,
Courses: †Advertising Design, Art Appreciation, Art Education, Art History, Ceramics, Commercial Art, Design, †European Field Study, Glassblowing, History of Art & Architecture, †Independent Study, Painting, Photography, †Principles of Color, Sculpture, †Visual Communications

SILVER SPRING

MARYLAND COLLEGE OF ART & DESIGN, 7600 Takoma Ave CF 120, Silver Spring, MD 20912. Tel 240-567-4454; Fax 240-567-5820; Internet Home Page Address: www.mcadmd.org; *Pres* Wesley E Paulson; *Dean* Don Smith; *Asst Prof* Chris Medley, MFA
Estab 1955; pvt; D & E; Scholarships; Degree Prog 83, Enrichment & Special Students 175
Ent Req: HS dipl, SAT verbal scores, letter of recommendation, portfolio interview
Degrees: AFA 2 yrs
Courses: Advertising Design, Art History, Commercial Art, Computer Graphics, Design, Drawing, Graphic Arts, Graphic Design, Illustration, Intermedia, Lettering, Painting, Photography, Printmaking, Sculpture
Adult Hobby Classes: Enrl 1000; tuition $80-180 for 6-10 wks.
Courses—Computer, Design, Drawing, Painting, Photography, Printmaking, Sculpture, Watercolor
Children's Classes: Enrl 1200; tuition $80-100 for 1-8 wks.
Courses—Cartooning, Ceramics, Computer, Design, Drawing, Painting, Photography, Printmaking, Sculpture
Summer School: Dir, David Gracyalny. Enrl 1000; tuition $80-250 for 1-9 wks.
Courses—Cartooning, Ceramics, Computer, Design, Drawing, Painting, Photography, Printmaking, Sculpture, Watercolor

TOWSON

TOWSON STATE UNIVERSITY, Dept of Art, 8000 York Rd, Towson, MD 21252-0002. Tel 410-704-3682, 704-2808; Fax 410-704-2810; Elec Mail jflood@towson.edu; Internet Home Page Address: www.towson.edu/art; *Dept Chmn* James Flood
Estab 1866; FT 15, PT 9; pub; D & E
Ent Req: HS grad
Degrees: BA, BS, MEd(Art Educ) 4 yr & MFA; spring sem Florence, Italy, Feb-May
Courses: Art Education, Art History, Ceramics, Drawing, Enameling, Graphic Arts, Jewelry, Painting, Sculpture, Textile Design, Weaving, Wood & Metal
Adult Hobby Classes: Enrl 60
Summer School: Dir, Jim Flood. Enrl 25; 2 five wk sessions. Courses—Art History, Studio

WESTMINSTER

WESTERN MARYLAND COLLEGE, Dept of Art & Art History, 2 College Hill, Westminster, MD 21157-4390. Tel 410-848-8700; Internet Home Page Address: www.wmdc.edu; *Prof* Wasyl Palijczuk; *Assoc Prof* Michael Losch; *Dept Head* Sue Bloom
Estab 1867; FT 4, PT 2; independent; D & E; Scholarships; SC 15, LC 12, GC 6; D 1213, maj 40-60, grad 15
Ent Req: HS dipl, ent exam, SAT
Degrees: BA, BS & MEd 4 yrs
Courses: Ceramics, Computer Graphics, Design, Drawing, Graphic Design, †History of Art & Architecture, Jewelry, Lettering, Painting, Photography, Printmaking, Sculpture, †Teacher Training
Summer School: Two 5 wk terms beginning June 21. Courses—Art History, Ceramics, Painting, Printmaking, Sculpture, Weaving

MASSACHUSETTS

AMHERST

AMHERST COLLEGE, Dept of Art & the History of Art, 107 Fayerweather Hall, Amherst, MA 01002-5000; PO Box 5000, Amherst, MA 01002-5000. Tel 413-542-2365; Fax 413-542-7917; Elec Mail finearts@amherst.edu; Internet Home Page Address: www.amherst.edu/~finearts; *Prof* Natasha Staller; *Head of Studio, Wm R Mead Prof of Art* Robert T Sweeney; *John C Newton Prof of Art & History of Art & Black Studies* Rowland O Abiodun; *Chmn Wm McCall Vickery 1957 Prof History of Art & Amer Studies* Carol Clark; *Prof of Art & History of Art* Nicola M Courtright; *Prof, Resident Artist* Betsey Garand; *Prof, Resident Artist* David I Gloman; *Prof Art* Carol Keller; *Vis Asst Prof* Justin Kimball; *Prof of History of Art & Asian Languages/Civilizaitions* Samuel C Morse; *Prof Fine Arts* Joel M Upton
Estab 1822; Maintain nonprofit art gallery, The Eli Marsh Gallery, 105 Fayerweather Hall ; FT 11; pvt; D; Scholarships; SC 15, LC 15
Ent Req: HS dipl
Degrees: BA 4 yrs
Tuition: $32,400 comprehensive fee for yr + room & board
Courses: 3-D Design, Aesthetics, Anatomy, Art History, Drawing, Painting, Photography, Printmaking, Sculpture

UNIVERSITY OF MASSACHUSETTS, AMHERST, College of Arts & Sciences, Fine Arts Center, Department of Art, Amherst, MA 01003-2510; 151 Presidents Dr, OFC 1 Amherst, MA 01003-9311. Tel 413-545-3929; Internet Home Page Address: www.umass.edu; *Chmn Dept* Ronald Michaud
Estab 1958; FT 36; Pub; SC 50, LC 19, GC 20; maj undergrad 430, grad 85
Ent Req: HS grad, portfolio & SAT required, 16 units HS
Degrees: BA, BFA, MFA
Courses: Ceramics, Design, Drawing, Painting, Photography, Printmaking, Sculpture
Summer School: Dir, Angel Ramirez. Courses—Architectural Drawing, Design, Drawing, Painting, Photography
—**Art History Program,** 130 Hicks Way, 317 Bartlett Hall Amherst, MA 01003-9269. Tel 413-545-3595; Fax 413-545-3880; Internet Home Page Address: www.umass.edu; *Prof* Walter B Denny PhD; *Prof* Craig Harbison PhD; *Assoc Prof* Kristine Haney PhD; *Assoc Prof* Laetitia La Follette PhD; *Prof* Bill Odel; *Dir* Ronald Michaud
Estab 1947, prog estab 1958; pub; D & E; Scholarships, Fellowships; LC 36, GC 16; D 1735, non-maj 1369, maj 105, grad 40
Ent Req: HS dipl & transcript, SAT
Degrees: BA, MA
Courses: Aesthetics, American Art to 1860, Ancient Art, Architecture, †Art History, Greek & Roman Art & Architecture, History of Art & Archeology, Islamic Art, Museum Staff Training, Renaissance to Modern Art, Survey
Adult Hobby Classes: All courses available through Continuing Education
Summer School: Courses—Introduction to Art, Modern Art
—**Dept of Landscape Architecture & Regional Planning,** 111 Thatcher Rd Ofc1, 109 Hills Amherst, MA 01003-9361. Tel 413-545-2255; Fax 413-545-1772; Internet Home Page Address: www.umass.edu/larp; *Asst Dept Head* Merle Willman PhD; *Dept Head* Jack Ahern
Estab 1903; pub; D; SC 6, LC 5; 35
Degrees: MA(Archit, Regional Planning & Landscape Design)
Courses: Aspects of Design Environment, Drafting, Drawing, Drawing & Measuring, Environmental Policy & Planning, Landscape Architecture, Site Planning, Studio Landscape
Summer School: Planning & design short courses

BEVERLY

ENDICOTT COLLEGE, School of Visual & Performing Arts, 376 Hale St, Beverly, MA 01915-2098. Tel 978-232-2250; Fax 978-232-2231; Elec Mail htobin@endicott.edu; Internet Home Page Address: www.endicott.edu; *Dean* Mark Towner; *Chmn Performing Arts* Rebecca Kenneally; *Visual Arts Coordr* Kathleen Moore; *Chmn, Visual Communs* Sanford Farrier; *Assoc Dean Interior Design* Kevin Renz; *Chair, Interior Design* Rachelle McClure; *Chair, Fine Arts* Carol Pelletier
Estab 1939; Maintain non-profit art galleries: Heftler Gallery, Spencer Gallery, Grillo Gallery, Walter J Manninen Center for the Arts, Endicott Col, Beverly, MA; pvt, co-ed; D & E; Scholarships; SC 120, LC 25; 310, non-maj 40, maj 270
Ent Req: HS dipl
Degrees: BS 4 yr & BFA
Tuition: Res—$25,848 per yr, room & board $12,388
Courses: Advertising Design, Aesthetics, Art History, †Art Therapy, †Ceramics, †Commercial Art, Design, Drafting, Drawing, Graphic Arts, Graphic Design, History of Art & Architecture, Illustration, †Interior Design, †Interior Design, Painting, †Photography, Printmaking, Sculpture, †Studio Art, Theatre Arts

MONTSERRAT COLLEGE OF ART, 23 Essex St, Beverly, MA 01915; PO Box 26, Beverly, MA 01915-0026. Tel 978-921-4242; Fax 978-922-4268; Elec Mail admiss@montserrat.edu; Internet Home Page Address: www.montserrat.edu; *Dean* Laura Tonelli; *Painting* Rob Roy; *Printmaking* Stacy Thomas-Vickory; *Photog* Ron DiRito; *Illustration* Fred Lynch; *Graphic Design* John Colan; *Gallery Dir* Leonie Bradbury; *Art Educ* Diane Ayott; *Pres* Helena Sturnick; *Sculpture Chair* Meredith Davis; *Foundation Dept* Judy Brown; *Liberal Arts Chair* Marjorie Augenbraum
Estab 1970; Maintain nonprofit art gallery on campus, Montserrat Gallery, 301 Gallery, Carol Schlosberg Gallery; Paul Scott Library; art supplies available on-campus; Pvt; D & E weekend workshops; Scholarships; SC 150, LC 50, Cont Educ; D 270, E 150, Other 300
Ent Req: Personal interview and portfolio review
Degrees: BFA 4 yr dipl granted
Tuition: $20,500 per yr, $10,250 per sem; $600 reg fee per yr/$300 reg fee per sem
Courses: Advertising Design, Animation, Art Education, Art History, †Book Arts, Conceptual Art, Design, Drawing, Fashion Arts, Graphic Arts, †Graphic Design, †Illustration, Lettering, Mixed Media, †Painting, †Photography, †Printmaking, †Sculpture, Video
Adult Hobby Classes: Courses—Drawing, Graphic Design, Painting, Photography, Printmaking
Summer School: Dir of Cont Educ, Kathleen Burke Enrl 60; Pre-College Prog in July & Aug. Courses—Life Drawing, Painting, Illustration, Printmaking

BOSTON

BOSTON CENTER FOR ADULT EDUCATION, 122 Arlington St, Boston, MA 02116-5307. Tel 617-267-4430; Fax 617-247-3606; Internet Home Page Address: www.bcae.org; *Exec Dir* Mary McTique
Estab 1933; pvt; D & E; Scholarships; SC 26, LC 2; D 2300, E 20,000
Ent Req: Open to all over 17
Courses: Architecture, Art Appreciation, Art History, Calligraphy, Ceramics, Clay Sculpture, Crafts, Drawing, Interior Design, Painting, Photography, Sculpture, Studio Crafts, Theatre Arts, Video, Weaving
Summer School: Same as winter program

BOSTON UNIVERSITY, Graduate Program - Arts Administration, 808 Commonwealth Ave, Boston, MA 02215-1206. Tel 617-353-4064; Fax 617-358-1230; Elec Mail artsadmn@bu.edu; Internet Home Page Address: www.bu.edu/artsadmin; *Dir* Daniel Ranalli; *Prof* Richard Maloney Estab 1992; pvt; E; Assistantships; GC 25
Ent Req: BA dipl
Degrees: MS (Arts Administration), 2 yr
Tuition: Res—\$40,848 FT, \$740 per cr hr; campus res available
Courses: Art History, Museum Staff Training

BOSTON UNIVERSITY, School for the Arts, 855 Commonwealth Ave, Visual Arts Division Boston, MA 02215-1303. Tel 617-353-3371, 3350; Fax 617-353-7217; Elec Mail visuarts@bu.edu; Internet Home Page Address: www.bu.edu; *Dir School of Visual Arts* Lynne Allen; *Prof* Hugh O'Donnell; *Chmn Graphic Design* Alston Purvis; *Chmn Art Educ* Barry Shauck; *Prof* John Walker
Estab 1869, sch estab 1954; Pvt; D; Scholarships; SC 38, LC 12, GC 15; 395, non-maj 75, maj 260, grad 60
Ent Req: HS dipl, portfolio
Degrees: BFA 4 yrs, MFA 2 yrs
Tuition: \$35,000 per yr incl room & board
Courses: †Art Education, Design, Drawing, †Graphic Design, †Painting, Photography, Printmaking, †Sculpture, Studio Teaching (grad level), Teacher Training

EMMANUEL COLLEGE, Art Dept, 400 The Fenway, Boston, MA 02115. Tel 617-735-9807; Fax 617-735-9877; Internet Home Page Address: www.emmanuel.edu/; *Chmn Art Dept* Theresa Monaco MA; *Prof* Ellen Glavin, ShD; *Prof* C David Thomas, MFA; *Assoc Prof* Kathleen A Soles, MFA
Estab 1919, dept estab 1950; pvt; D & E; Scholarships; SC 30, LC 11; D 300, E 50, non-maj 200, maj 80
Ent Req: HS dipl, SAT
Degrees: BA & BFA 4 yrs
Courses: †Art Education, †Art History, Art Therapy, Ceramics, Drawing, Graphic Arts, †Graphic Design, Mixed Media, †Painting, †Printmaking, Sculpture, †Teacher Training
Adult Hobby Classes: Enrl 300; tuition \$193 per cr. Courses—Art Educ, Art History, Art Theory, In Studio Art
Summer School: Dir, Dr Jacquelyn Armitage. Enrl 230; tuition \$143 per cr hr for term of 6 wks in June-Aug

LESLEY UNIVERSITY, (The Art Institute of Boston at Lesley University) College of Art & Design, 700 Beacon St, Boston, MA 02215-2598. Tel 617-262-1223; Fax 617-437-1226; Elec Mail admissions@lesley.edu; Internet Home Page Address: www.lesley.edu/aib; *Dean* Stan Trecker; *Sr Assoc Dean Acad Affairs* Matthew Cherry; *Chair Animation* John Casey; *Chair Art History* Stuart Steck; *Chair Design* Kristina Lamour Sansone; *Chair Fine Arts* Michael David; *Chair Foundation* Arlene Grossman; *Chair Illustration* Susan LeVan; *Chair Photog* Andre Ruesch
Estab 1912; Maintains nonprofit art gallery, art library, Lesley Univ Col of Art & Design - main gallery; Lesley Univ Col of Art & Design Library (both at same address); pvt; D & E; Scholarships; SC 80, LC 20; D 535, E 200
Ent Req: HS dipl, portfolio and interview
Degrees: BFA, MFA
Courses: Animation, Art Education, Art History, Ceramics, Commercial Art, Computer Graphics, Conceptual Art, Design, Drawing, †Fine Arts, †Graphic Design, †Handicrafts, †History of Art & Architecture, Illustration, †Mixed Media, Painting, †Photography, Printmaking, Sculpture, Typography, Video
Adult Hobby Classes: Courses—Continuing education offers most of the above typically 2-3 cr each
Summer School: Dir, Diana Arcadipone, Assoc Dean Courses—most of above

MASSACHUSETTS COLLEGE OF ART, 621 Huntington Ave, Boston, MA 02115-5801. Tel 617-879-7000; Fax 617-879-7250; Internet Home Page Address: www.massart.edu; *Dean Grad & Continuing Educ* Richard Aronowitz; *Chmn Fine Arts 2D* Roger Tibbets; *Chmn Fine Arts 3D* Joe Wood; *Chmn Media* Barbara Bosworth; *Chmn Critical Studies* John Russell; *Pres* Katherine Sloan; *Chair Environmental Design* Paul Hajian; *Chair Commun Design* Elizabeth Resnick; *Chair Art Educ* John Crowe
Estab 1873; Maintain a nonprofit art gallery: Arnhein Gallery, Bakalar Gallery, Deren Gallery, 621 Huntington Ave, Boston, MA 02115; maintain an art/architecture library: Martan R Godine Library, 621 Huntington Ave, Boston, MA 02115; on-campus shop where art supplies may be purchased; Pub; D & E; SC 400, LC 250, GC 50; D 1,100, E 1,000, grad 100
Ent Req: HS transcript, college transcript, SAT, statement of purpose, portfolio
Degrees: BFA 4 yrs, MFA 2 yrs, MSAE 2 yrs
Courses: Architectural Design, Art Education, Art History, Ceramics, Fashion Design, Fibers, Film, Film Making, Freshman Artistic Seminars, Glass, Graphic Design, Illustration, Industrial Design, Intermedia, Metals, Painting, Photography, Printmaking, Sculpture, Video
Adult Hobby Classes: Courses—All areas
Children's Classes: Courses—All areas
Summer School: Assoc Dir Continuing Educ, Susan Gately. Courses—all areas

MOUNT IDA COLLEGE, Chamberlayne School of Design & Merchandising, 777 Dedham St, Boston, MA 02459-3310. *School Dir* Phyllis Misite; *Lectr* Rose Botti-Salitsky
Estab 1892, dept estab 1952; pvt; D & E; D 253, E 38, maj 253
Ent Req: HS dipl
Degrees: AA, BA
Courses: Drawing, Fashion Arts, Graphic Arts, Illustration, Interior Design, Jewelry, Merchandising, Painting, Sculpture, Textile Design
Summer School: Dir Susan Holton. Courses—same as regular acad yr

NORTHEASTERN UNIVERSITY, Dept of Art & Architecture, 360 Huntington Ave, Boston, MA 02115-5000. Tel 617-373-2347; Fax 617-373-8535; *Chmn* Elizabeth Cromley, PhD; *Prof* Mardges Bacon PhD; *Assoc Prof* T Neal Rantoul,

MFA; *Assoc Prof* Mira Cantor, MFA; *Assoc Prof* George Thrush, MArchit; *Assoc Prof* Julie Curtis, MFA; *Assoc Prof* Edwin Andrews, MFA; *Assoc Prof* Tom Starr, MFA; *Asst Prof* Peter Wiederspahn, MArchit; *Asst Prof* Ann McDonald, MFA
Estab 1898, dept estab 1952; pvt; D & E; Scholarships; D 1200, E 1200, non-maj 1500, maj 380
Ent Req: HS dipl
Degrees: BA & BS 4 yrs
Tuition: Freshmen \$4460 per acad qtr; upperclassmen \$5775 per acad qtr; campus res available
Courses: Animation, Architectural Design, Architecture, Art History, Computer Aided Design, Design, Drafting, Drawing, Graphic Arts, Graphic Design, History of Art & Architecture, Illustration, Media Design, Mixed Media, Multimedia, Painting, Photography, Video
Adult Hobby Classes: Enrl 180; tuition \$116 per 12 wk quarter cr. Courses—same as full-time program
Summer School: Chmn, Peter Serenyi. Enrl 240. Tuition & courses—same as above

SCHOOL OF FASHION DESIGN, 136 Newbury St, Boston, MA 02116-2904. Tel 617-536-9343; Elec Mail sfdboston@aol.com; Internet Home Page Address: www.schooloffashiondesign.org
Estab 1934; pvt; D, E & Sat; Scholarships; D approx 60, E approx 40
Ent Req: HS dipl
Degrees: No degrees, 2 yr cert or 3 yr dipl
Courses: Costume Design & Construction, Drafting, Drawing, Fashion Arts, Illustration, Textile Design, Theatre Arts
Adult Hobby Classes: 100; tuition \$1080 per 3 cr course. Courses—Fashion Design
Summer School: Dir, James Hannon. Enrl 100; tuition \$1080 per 3 cr course of 10 wks. Courses—Fashion Design

SCHOOL OF THE MUSEUM OF FINE ARTS, 230 The Fenway, Boston, MA 02115. Tel 617-267-6100, 369-3581; Fax 617-424-6271; Elec Mail ddluhy@mfa.org; Internet Home Page Address: www.smfa.edu; *Dean* Deborah H Dluhy PhD; *Provost* Daniel Poteel II; *Dean Faculty* Lorne Falk
Estab 1876; Grossman Gallery; pvt; D & E; Scholarships; SC 190 LC 30 GC 12 CE 78 per sem; D 678 E 646, grad 100
Ent Req: HS dipl, HS and col transcripts, portfolio
Degrees: Dipl, BFA, BFA plus BA or BS, MFA, MAT, BFA-E, Post BA all degrees in affiliation with Tufts University
Courses: Art Education, Art History, Ceramics, Drawing, Film, Graphic Arts, Graphic Design, Illustration, Jewelry, Mixed Media, Painting, Performance, Photography, Printmaking, Sculpture, Video
Adult Hobby Classes: E & Saturday classes; 1.5 cr or 3 cr per course. Courses—Artists' Books, Ceramics, Drawing, Electronic Arts, Film/Animation, Graphic Design, Jewelry, Mixed Media, Painting, Papermaking, Photography, Printmaking, Sculpture, Stained Glass, Video
Summer School: Dir Continuing Educ, Debra Samdperil

UNIVERSITY OF MASSACHUSETTS - BOSTON, Art Dept, 100 Morrissey Blvd, Harbor Campus Boston, MA 02125-3300. Tel 617-287-5730; Fax 617-287-5757; Internet Home Page Address: www.umb.edu; *Emeritus Prof* Ruth Butler PhD; *Emeritus Prof* Hal Thurman; *Prof* Paul Tucker PhD; *Assoc Prof* Ronald Polito PhD; *Prof* Wilfredo Chiesa; *Assoc Prof* Melissa Shook; *Asst Prof* Margaret Wagner, MFA; *Asst Prof* Victoria Weston PhD, MFA; *Chmn* Anne McCauley; *Assoc Prof* Ann Torke, PhD; *Assoc Prof* Pamela Jones; *Asst Prof* Elizabeth Marrin
Sch estab 1965, dept estab 1966; pub; D & E; SC 18, LC 32; D 900, E 100, maj 200
Ent Req: Entrance exam
Degrees: BA
Tuition: Res—\$1055 per sem; nonres—\$4421 per sem (plus fees)
Courses: Aesthetics, Art History, Drawing, Film, Graphic Arts, History of Art & Architecture, Intermedia, Painting, Photography, Printmaking, Sculpture, Video
Summer School: Enrl 150; tuition \$140 per cr, 2 sessions. Courses—American Art in Boston, Ancient to Medieval Art, Drawing, Photography

BRIDGEWATER

BRIDGEWATER STATE COLLEGE, Art Dept, School and Summer Sts, Bridgewater, MA 02325. Tel 508-531-1200; Fax 508-279-6128; Internet Home Page Address: www.bridgew.edu; *Prof* Roger Dunn PhD, PhD, MFA; *Prof* Mercedes Nunez, MFA; *Prof* Dorothy Pulsifer, MA; *Assoc Prof* Rob Lorenson, MFA; *Assoc Prof* Collin Asmus, MFA; *Asst Prof* Beatrice St Laurent, PhD; *Asst Prof* Preston Saunders, MFA; *Asst Prof* Ivana George, MFA; *Chmn* Brenda Molife, PhD; *Asst Prof* Shanshan Cui, MFA; *Asst Prof* Magaly Ponce, MFA; *Asst Prof* Mary Dondero, MFA; *Asst Prof* John Hooker, MFA; *Asst Prof* Leigh Craven, MFA; *Asst Prof* Donald Tarallo, MFA
Estab 1840; Maintain nonprofit art gallery; The Wallace Anderson Gallery, 40 School St, Bridgewater, MA 02325; Maintain Maxwell Library, Park Ave, Bridgewater, MA 02325; pub; D & E; SC 35, LC 10, GC 35; D 1000, E 400, non-maj 960, maj 280, grad 10
Ent Req: HS dipl, SAT
Degrees: BA 4 yrs
Courses: †Art Appreciation, Art Education, Art History, Ceramics, †Commercial Art, Drawing, Goldsmithing, Graphic Arts, Graphic Design, Handicrafts, †History of Art & Architecture, Jewelry, †Mixed Media, Painting, †Photography, Printmaking, Sculpture, Silversmithing, †Studio Art, †Teacher Training, †Textile Design, †Video, Watercolor, †Weaving
Adult Hobby Classes: Enrl 100. Courses—Same as day courses; rotational
Summer School: Dir, Brenda Molife, PhD. Enrl 40. Courses—Same as above

CAMBRIDGE

HARVARD UNIVERSITY, Dept of History of Art & Architecture, 485 Broadway, Cambridge, MA 02138-3845. Tel 617-495-2377; Fax 617-495-1769; Internet Home Page Address: www.fas.harvard.edu; *Chmn Dept* Ioli Kalavrezou

Estab 1874; FT 24; pvt; Scholarships; LC 26 incl GC 12; undergrad 88, grad 100
Courses: Art History

MASSACHUSETTS INSTITUTE OF TECHNOLOGY, School of Architecture and Planning, 77 Massachusetts Ave, Rm 7-231 Cambridge, MA 02139-4301.
Dean William J Mitchell; *Head Dept* Stanford Anderson; *Urban Studies & Planning* Bish Sanyal; Peggy Cain
Estab 1865; FT 62; pvt; Scholarships; SC, LC, GC; 600
Degrees: MA, PhD(Building Technol); Media Arts & Sciences
Tuition: $26,960 per yr
Courses: History of Art & Architecture
—**Center for Advanced Visual Studies,** 265 Massachusetts Ave, Fl 3 Cambridge, MA 02139-4301; 77 Massachusetts Ave # N52-390, Cambridge, MA 02139-4301.
Tel 617-253-4415; Fax 617-253-1660; Internet Home Page Address: cavs.mit.edu; *Dir* Steve Benton
Estab dept 1967; pvt; D & E; SC 9, LC 1, GC 5; D & E 250, non-maj 240, grad 10
Ent Req: BA degree
Degrees: MS(Visual Studies)
Tuition: $26,690 per yr
Courses: Art & Technology, Environmental Art, †Video
Summer School: Art Workshop

CHESTNUT HILL

BOSTON COLLEGE, Fine Arts Dept, 140 Commonwealth Ave, Devlin Hall #434 Chestnut Hill, MA 02467-3800. Tel 617-552-4295; Fax 617-552-0134; Internet Home Page Address: www.bostoncollege.com; *Chmn* John Michalczyk FT 11, PT 20
Degrees: BA offered
Courses: Art History, Ceramics, Drawing, Film, Painting, Photography, Sculpture, Studio Art

PINE MANOR COLLEGE, Visual Arts Dept, 400 Heath St, Chestnut Hill, MA 02467-2332. Tel 617-731-7157; Fax 617-731-7199; Internet Home Page Address: www.pmc.edu; *Div Chmn* Bob Owcvark; *Prog Coordr Photog Dept* Susan Butler
Estab 1911; pvt; D; SC 25, LC 25; D 80
Ent Req: HS dipl
Degrees: AA & AS 2 yrs, BA 4 yrs
Tuition: Res—undergrad $11,940 per acad yr; campus res—room & board $7450 per acad yr
Courses: Architecture, †Art History, Costume Design & Construction, Drafting, Drawing, Graphic Arts, Interior Design, Museum Staff Training, Painting, Printmaking, Sculpture, Stage Design, Theatre Arts, Visual Arts
Adult Hobby Classes: Studio courses 25, lecture courses 25
Summer School: Dir, Dr Eva I Kampits

CHICOPEE

OUR LADY OF ELMS COLLEGE, Dept of Fine Arts, 291 Springfield St, Chicopee, MA 01013-2839. Tel 413-594-2761; Fax 413-592-4871; *Chmn Dept* Nancy Costanzo
Estab 1928, dept estab 1950; pvt; D & E; Scholarships; SC 14, LC 6; D 210, non-maj 193, maj 17
Ent Req: HS dipl, Col Ent Exam (Verbal and Math)
Degrees: BA 4 yrs
Courses: Art Education, Art History, Calligraphy, Ceramics, Drawing, Painting, Photography, Printmaking, Sculpture

DOVER

CHARLES RIVER SCHOOL, Creative Arts Program, 56 Centre St, Dover, MA 02030-2207; PO Box 339, Dover, MA 02030-0339. Tel 508-785-0068, 785-8250; Fax 508-785-8291; Elec Mail crcap@charlesriverschool.edu; Internet Home Page Address: www.crcap.org; *Dir* Toby Dewey
Estab 1910, program estab 1970; pvt summer school; D; Scholarships
Ent Req: Open to ages 8-15 years (as of July 1)
Courses: Art, Computer, Dance, Drama, Media, Music, Photography, Textile Design, Writing
Summer School: Dir, Toby Dewy Jr. Enrl 235; tuition $1675 per session. Courses—Computer

FRAMINGHAM

DANFORTH MUSEUM OF ART SCHOOL, 123 Union Ave, Framingham, MA 01702-8291. Tel 508-620-0050; Fax 508-872-5542; Internet Home Page Address: www.danforthmuseum.org; *Dir* Patricia Walker
Estab 1975; Maintain nonprofit art museum, Danforth Museum of Art, 123 Union Ave, Framingham, MA 01702; pvt; D&E; Scholarships; SC
Ent Req: None
Tuition: Varies per course; museum members receive a tuition reduction
Courses: Art History, Ceramics, †Collage, Drawing, Graphic Arts, Jewelry, Painting, Photography, Printmaking, Sculpture, Weaving
Adult Hobby Classes: Enrl 200 - 400; tuition varies per 10 wk sessions. Courses—Arts, Crafts, Photography
Children's Classes: Enrl 200 - 400; tuition varies per 8 wk session. Courses—Art Multi-Media, Ceramics
Summer School: Enrl 200-300; tuition varies per 1 wk courses. Courses—Same as above

FRAMINGHAM STATE COLLEGE, Art Dept, 100 State St, Framingham, MA 01701; PO Box 9101, Framingham, MA 01701-9101. Tel 508-620-1220, 626-4831 (Cote); Fax 508-626-4022; Elec Mail mcote@fre.mass.edu; Internet Home Page Address: www.framingham.edu; *Assoc Prof* Elizabeth Perry; *Prof* Barbara Milot; *Chmn* Marc Cote; *Asst Prof* Erika Schneider; *Asst Prof* Timothy McDonald; *Asst Prof* Keri Straka; *Asst Prof* Brian Bishop; *Prof* John Anderson
Estab 1839, dept estab 1920; Maintain nonprofit art gallery, Mazmarian Gallery 100 State St Framingham MA 01701; Catherine Carter; pub; D & E; Scholarships; SC 20, LC 10, GC 10; D 3,000, E 2500, maj 105, grad 20
Special Subjects: Illustration
Ent Req: HS dipl, portfolio review
Degrees: BA 4 yrs
Courses: Art Appreciation, †Art Education, †Art History, †Ceramics, Collage, Commercial Art, †Fashion Arts, †Graphic Design, Museum Studies, †Printmaking, †Sculpture, †Studio Art
Adult Hobby Classes: Art History, Studio Art

GREAT BARRINGTON

SIMON'S ROCK COLLEGE OF BARD, Visual Arts Dept, 84 Alford Rd, Great Barrington, MA 01230-2499. Tel 413-528-0771; Fax 413-528-7365; Elec Mail admit@simons-rock.edu; Internet Home Page Address: www.simons-rock.edu; *Prof* William D Jackson; *Prof* Arthur Hillman, MFA; *Prof Ceramics* John Kingston, MFA
Estab 1966; PT 2; pvt; D & E; Scholarships; SC 14, LC 4
Ent Req: Personal interview
Degrees: AA 2-3 yrs, BA 4 yrs
Tuition: $21,740 per yr; campus res—room $3270, board $3430
Courses: 2-D Design, 3-D Design, Aesthetics, Art History, Artist & the Book, Ceramics, Drawing, Graphic Design, Illustration, Intermedia, Introduction to the Arts, Jewelry, Microcomputer Graphics, Painting, Photography, Printmaking, Sculpture

GREENFIELD

GREENFIELD COMMUNITY COLLEGE, Art Dept, One College Dr, Greenfield, MA 01301. Tel 413-775-1241; Internet Home Page Address: art.gcc.mass.edu; *Dept Chair* Paul Lindale, MFA; *Prof* John Bross, MFA; *Prof* Penne Krol, MFA; *Prof* Budge Hyde, MFA; *Prof* Tom Young, MFA; *Instr* Jennifer Simms, MFA; *Instr* Joan Qibgirne, MFA; *Instr* Elliott Mitchell, MFA; *Instr* Mikael Petriaccia, MFA; *Art Historian* Breta Yuars Petruccia, MFA
Estab 1962; maintains a small gallery & on campus store where art supplies may be purchased; pub; D & E; Scholarships; SC 16; in school D 1400, E 400, maj 110
Ent Req: HS dipl
Degrees: AA, AS 2 yrs
Courses: †Art History, Collage, Conceptual Art, †Drawing, Illustration, †Painting, †Photography, †Printmaking, Video
Summer School: Elizabeth Roop. Tuition $38 per cr for a 7 wk term. Courses—Color, Design, Drawing Workshop, Multi Media Design, Photography

HOLYOKE

HOLYOKE COMMUNITY COLLEGE, Dept of Art, 303 Homestead Ave, Holyoke, MA 01040-1099. Tel 413-538-7000; Fax 413-534-8975; Internet Home Page Address: www.hcc.mass.edu; *Dean of Humanities & Fine Arts* John Field
Estab 1946; FT2; pub; D & E; Scholarships; SC 7, LC 4; D 115, E 20, maj 50
Ent Req: HS dipl, portfolio
Degrees: AA 2 yrs
Courses: Art Education, Drawing, Graphic Arts, Graphic Design, History of Art & Architecture, Painting, Photography
Summer School: Dir, William Murphy. Courses—Per regular session, on demand

LEXINGTON

MUNROE CENTER FOR THE ARTS, (Lexington Friends of the Arts, Inc.) 1403 Massachusetts Ave, Lexington, MA 02420-3804. Tel 781-862-6040; Fax 781-674-2787; Internet Home Page Address: www.munroecenter.org; *Exec Dir* Christian Herold, MA; *Dir Educ* Hannah Hammond-Hagman
Estab 1994; Maintain nonprofit art gallery; PT 16; pub; D & E; Scholarships; SC 100, LC 20; D 700, E 300
Ent Req: Registration
Courses: Aesthetics, Art Education, Ceramics, †Costume Design & Construction, †Fashion Arts, Illustration, Mixed Media, Painting, Printmaking, Sculpture, Theatre Arts
Adult Hobby Classes: Enrl 300; tuition $150 per class. Courses—Ceramics, Faux Art, Painting, Printmaking, Quilt Making, Sculpture, Yoga
Children's Classes: Enrl 700; tuition $120 per class. Courses—Drama, Drawing, Ceramics, Mixed Media, Painting, Woodworking
Summer School: Enrl 360; tuition $250 per wk, Integrated Creative Arts Camp (ages 6-12)

LINCOLN

DECORDOVA MUSEUM SCHOOL, 51 Sandy Pond Rd, Lincoln, MA 01773-2600. Tel 781-259-0505; Fax 781-259-0507; Elec Mail info@decordova.org; Internet Home Page Address: www.decordova.org/school/; *Acting Dir Educ* Lynn Thompson; *School Dir* Emily Garner; *Educ Asst* Kate Legg; *Ceramic Studio Mgr* Bruce Barry; *Jewelry & Silversmithing Studio Mgr* Kimon Yannopoulos
Office open Mon - Fri 9 AM - 4 PM; Studio open Mon - Thurs 9:15 Am - 9:45 PM, Fri - Sun 9:15 AM - 4:45 PM; Gallery open Mon - Thurs 9:30 AM - 9 PM, Fri 9:30 AM - 4 PM, Sat & Sun 10 AM - 4 PM; No admis fee to gallery; tuition

for classes varies; Facility has 7 studios dedicated to Calligraphy, Ceramics, Drawing, Jewelry, Painting, Printmaking, Sculpture & Watercolor; also maintains School Gallery

Activities: 100 adult classes/workshops per term; 20 - 30 children's classes/workshops per term; children's progs in July; Professional Development Points available to teachers for all classes; schls available

Courses: Book Arts, Calligraphy, Ceramics, Collage, Color Design, Jewelry, Painting, Photography, Printmaking, Sculpture, Silversmithing, Watercolor

LONGMEADOW

BAY PATH COLLEGE, Dept of Art, 588 Longmeadow St, Longmeadow, MA 01106-2292. Tel 413-567-0621; Fax 413-567-9324; Internet Home Page Address: www.baypath.edu; *Dir* Dr John Jarvis
Estab 1947; pvt; W; D & E; SC 18, LC 2; D 660, E 400, maj 10
Ent Req: HS dipl
Degrees: AFA 2 yr
Courses: Ceramics, Drawing, Graphic Arts, Handicrafts, History of Art & Architecture, Painting
Adult Hobby Classes: Enrl 300; tuition $80 per 8 wk course. Courses - Drawing, Painting, Watercolor

LOWELL

UNIVERSITY OF MASSACHUSETTS LOWELL, Dept of Art, 71 Wilder St Ste 8, Lowell, MA 01854-3096. Tel 978-934-3494; Fax 978-934-4050; Internet Home Page Address: www.uml.edu; *Chmn Dept* James Coates; *Prof* Brenda Pinardi, MFA; *Prof* Arno Minkkinen, MFA; *Assoc Prof* James Veatch, EdM; *Prof* Fred Faudie; *Assoc Prof* John C Freeman
Estab 1975 (merger of Lowell State College and Lowell Technological Institute); Maintain nonprofit art gallery; Duggan Gallery & University Gallery; Pub; D & E; D 1,200, E 25, non-maj 450, maj 150
Ent Req: HS dipl, SAT
Degrees: BFA 4 yrs
Courses: Graphic Design, Photography, †Studio Art, Visual Communication Design
Adult Hobby Classes: Enrl 15 - 20 per course; tuition $135. Courses—Art Appreciation, Drawing, Painting, Survey of Art
Summer School: Enrl 10-15; tuition $135 per cr for 3 weeks. Courses—Art Appreciation, Drawing, Photography, Survey of Art I & II, Seminars in Italy, Greece, Finland, France

MEDFORD

TUFTS UNIVERSITY, Dept of Art & Art History, 11 Talbot Ave, Medford, MA 02155-5812. Tel 617-627-3567; Elec Mail amy.west@tufts.edu; Internet Home Page Address: ase.tufts.edu/art; *Prof* Andrew McClellan, PhD; *Assoc Prof & Chmn* Daniel Abramson, PhD; *Assoc Prof* Cristelle Baskins, PhD; *Asst Prof* Eva Hoffman, PhD; *Assoc Prof* Ikumi Kaminishi, PhD; *Assoc Prof* Christina Maranci, PhD; *Assoc Prof* Eric Rosenberg, PhD; *Prof* Peter Probst, PhD; *Asst Prof* Monica McTighe, PhD; *Asst Prof* Karen Overbey, PhD; *Assoc Prof* Adriana Zavala
Maintain nonprofit art gallery, Tufts University Art Gallery, 40R Talbot Ave, Medford, MA 02155; maintain art/architecture lib, Tisch Library, Tuft University; Pvt; D; Scholarships; maj 100; GS 24
Ent Req: HS dipl
Degrees: BA, BS, BFA, MA, MFA; cert in museum studies
Tuition: admissions.tufts.edu
Courses: †Architecture, †Art History, Calligraphy, Ceramics, Design, Drawing, Film, Graphic Arts, Graphic Design, History of Architecture, Illustration, Interdisciplinary Studio Art, Jewelry, Lettering, Metal Working, Mixed Media, Museum Staff Training, Museum Studies, Studio
Adult Hobby Classes: Courses offered
Summer School: Mgr, Sean Recroft. Enrl 100; tuition $1650 per cr for 6 wks. Courses—Boston Architecture, Modern Art, Survey, Museum History

NORTH DARTMOUTH

UNIVERSITY OF MASSACHUSETTS DARTMOUTH, College of Visual & Performing Arts, 285 Old Westport Rd, North Dartmouth, MA 02747-2300. Tel 508-999-8564; Fax 508-999-9126; Internet Home Page Address: www.umassd.edu; *Dean* John Laughton PhD; *Chmn Music Dept* Eleanor Carlson, DMA; *Chmn Art Educ* Arlene Mollo; *Chmn Fine Art* Anthony J Miraglia, MFA; *Chmn Design* Spencer Ladd; *Chmn Art History* Michael Taylor; *Coordr Gallery* Lasse Antonsen, MA
Estab 1895, col estab 1948; Maintain nonprofit art gallery; art supplies available on-campus; FT 46, PT 25; pub; D & E; Scholarships; SC 75, LC 41, GC 7; D 700
Ent Req: HS dipl, SAT, open admis to qualified freshmen
Degrees: BFA and BA 4 yr, MFA and MAE 2-5 yrs
Courses: Art Education, Art History, Ceramics, Design, Electronic Imaging, Illustration, Jewelry, Painting, Photography, Printmaking, Sculpture, Textile Design
Adult Hobby Classes: Enrl 175; tuition $365 for 14 wk session. Courses—13 including Art History, Ceramics, Jewelry
Children's Classes: Enrl 35; tuition $95 for 9 wk session. Courses—Children's Theater
Summer School: Dir, Dean R Waxler. Enrl 240; tuition $365 for 5 wk session. Courses—15 including Art History, Crafts

NORTHAMPTON

SMITH COLLEGE, Art Dept, 22 Elm St, Hillyer Hall Northampton, MA 01063-6304. Tel 413-584-2700, 585-3100; Fax 413-585-3119; Internet Home Page Address: www.smith.edu/art; *Prof* Marylin Rhie PhD; *Prof* John Davis, PhD; *Lectr*

Martin Antonetti; *Prof* Brigitte Buettner, PhD; *Prof* Barbara Kellum, PhD; *Prof* Dana Leibsohn, PhD; *Prof* John Moore, PhD; *Prof* Craig Felton Dr, PhD; *Assoc Prof* Frazer Ward, PhD; *Asst Prof* Laura Kalba, PhD
Estab 1875, dept estab 1877; maintains art library; on-campus shop for purchase of art supplies; FT 17; pvt, W; D & E; Scholarships; SC 24, LC 34; maj 170
Ent Req: HS dipl, col board exam
Degrees: BA 4 yrs
Courses: Architecture, Art History, Color, Design with Computer, Drafting, Drawing, Graphic Arts, Graphic Design, History of Art & Architecture, Landscape Architecture, Painting, Photography, Printmaking, Sculpture

NORTON

WHEATON COLLEGE, Art Dept, 26 E Main St, Norton, MA 02766-2322. Tel 508-285-7722; Fax 508-286-3565; *Chmn Dept* Andrew Howard
Estab 1834; Maintain nonprofit art gallery; Watson Fine Arts Center; FT 6, PT 3; pvt; Scholarships; SC 6, LC 18; 1,500
Degrees: BA (art history) 4 yr, BFA (Studio Art)
Courses: 2-D & 3-D Design, †Art History, Drawing, Painting, Photography, Printmaking, Sculpture

PAXTON

ANNA MARIA COLLEGE, Dept of Art, 50 Sunset Ln, Paxton, MA 01612-1106; PO Box 114, Paxton, MA 01612-0114. Tel 508-849-3441; Internet Home Page Address: www.annamaria.edu; *Chmn Dept* Alice Lambert
Estab 1948; FT 2, PT 4; pvt; D & E; Scholarships; SC 15, LC 12; D 397, maj 32
Ent Req: HS dipl, ent exam
Degrees: 4 yr
Courses: †Advertising Design, Aesthetics, †Art Education, Art History, †Art Therapy, Ceramics, Drawing, Enameling, Lettering, Macrame, Modeling, Painting, Photography, Rug Design, Sculpture, Silk Screen, Stitchery, †Studio Art, †Teacher Training, Weaving
Summer School: Dir, Ann McMorrow. Two sessions beginning May.

PITTSFIELD

BERKSHIRE COMMUNITY COLLEGE, Dept of Fine Arts, 1350 West St, Pittsfield, MA 01201-5786. Tel 413-499-4660; Fax 413-447-7840; *Instr* Benigna Chilla, MFA
Estab 1960, dept estab 1961; pub; D & E; Scholarships; SC 16, LC 4; D 72, E 75, non-maj 12, maj 72
Ent Req: HS dipl
Degrees: AA 2 yrs
Courses: 2-D Design, 20th Century Art, 3-D Design, Applied Graphics, Art History, Drawing, Mixed Media, Painting, Photography, Primitive Art, Printmaking
Adult Hobby Classes: Continuing education evening classes, some may be applied to degree program
Summer School: 7 wks beginning June. Courses—Design, Drawing, Painting, Photography

QUINCY

QUINCY COLLEGE, Art Dept, 1250 Hancock St, Ste 101N Quincy, MA 02169-4331. Tel 617-984-1600; Fax 617-984-1779; Internet Home Page Address: quincycollege.edu; *Chmn Humanities* Dr Kenneth Bindseil; *Pres* Sue Harris; *Adj Prof* Marylou Clark; *Adj Instruc* Brian Adgate; *Adj Instruc* Tracy Spadafora; *Adjunct Instr* David Tander; *Adj Instr* Robert Littlefield; *Asst Prof* Steve Dooner
In transition from city control to private control; D & E; SC, LC; 3800 (entire college)
Ent Req: Open
Degrees: AA, AS and Cert offered
Tuition: Res & non-res $1700 per sem
Courses: †Art History, †Collage, †Design, Development to American Film, Drawing, Painting, Photography, †Theatre Arts
Summer School: Same format as regular cr courses; Dean Bindseil, Dean of Liberal Arts & Sciences

SALEM

SALEM STATE UNIVERSITY, (Salem State College) Art & Design Department, 352 LaFayette St, Salem, MA 01970. Tel 978-542-6222; Fax 978-542-6597; Elec Mail bgross@salemstate.edu; Internet Home Page Address: www.salem.mass.edu; *Chmn Dept* Benjamin Gross, MFA; *Prof* Richard Lewis, MFA; *Prof* John Volpacchio, MFA; *Prof* Mark Malloy, MFA; *Prof* Patricia Johnston, PhD; *Prof* Mary Mellili, MFA; *Asst Prof* Caroline P. Murphy, PhD; *Asst Prof* Rebecca Plummer Rohloff, PhD; *Assoc Prof* Haig Demarjian, MFA; *Assoc Prof* Ken Reker, MFA
Estab 1854; Maintain nonprofit art gallery, Winfisky Gallery. Art supplies may be purchased on-site; Pub; D & E; Scholarships; SC 19, LC 8, GC 5; maj 210
Ent Req: HS dipl
Degrees: BA 4 yrs, MAT in Art
Tuition: Res—$910 per yr; nonres—$7,050 per yr; campus res available
Courses: 3-D Studio, †Art Education, †Art History, Ceramics, †Graphic Design, Illustration, †Metals, Mixed Media, Multimedia Design, †Painting, †Photography, †Printmaking, Sculpture
Summer School: Pres, Dr Patricia M. Meservey

SOUTH HADLEY

MOUNT HOLYOKE COLLEGE, Art Dept, 50 College St, South Hadley, MA 01075; Lower Lake Rd, South Hadley, MA 01075-1499. Tel 413-538-2200; Fax 413-538-2167; Internet Home Page Address: www.mtholyoke.edu/acad.art/; *Studio Chmn* Joseph Smith; *Interim Chmn* Michael P Davis; *Art History* Ajay Sinha

Estab 1837; Maintain nonprofit art gallery; Blanchaid Campus Center; Pvt, W; D & E; Scholarships; SC 13, LC 32; D 409, maj 52
Ent Req: SAT, college boards
Degrees: BA
Courses: †Architecture, †Art History, Drawing, †Film, †History of Art & Architecture, Painting, Photography, Printmaking, Sculpture
Adult Hobby Classes: Continuing education program leading to BA

SPRINGFIELD

SPRINGFIELD COLLEGE, Dept of Visual & Performing Arts, 263 Alden St, Springfield, MA 01109-3788. Tel 413-748-3540; Fax 413-748-3580; *Chmn* Ronald Maggio; *Asst Prof* Martin Shell, MFA; *Asst Prof* Chris Haynes, MFA; *Asst Prof* Simone Alter-Muri, Ed; *Asst Prof* Cynthia Noble, MA; *Asst Prof* Leslie Abrams, MA; *Instr* Charles Abel, MFA; *Instr* Holly Murray, MFA; *Instr* Ruth West, MFA; *Instr* John Moriarty, MFA; *Instr* Catherine Lydon, MFA; *Instr* Scott Redman; *Instr* Jorge Costa; *Instr* Monika Burzcyk
Estab 1885, dept estab 1971; Maintain nonprofit art gallery; Wieliam Blizard Gallery; Pvt; D & E; Scholarships; SC 30, LC 6; D 400, E 10, non-maj 300, maj 50
Ent Req: HS dipl, SAT, portfolio
Degrees: BA, BS 4 yr, MS(Art Therapy) 2 yr
Courses: Advertising Design, Aesthetics, Art Appreciation, Art Education, Art History, †Art Therapy, Arts Management, Ceramics, Collage, †Computer Graphics, Computer Graphics Animation, Conceptual Art, Constructions, Costume Design & Construction, Design, Drawing, Graphic Arts, Graphic Design, History of Art & Architecture, Illustration, Intermedia, Mixed Media, Museum Staff Training, Painting, Photography, Printmaking, Restoration & Conservation, Sculpture, Stage Design, Teacher Training, Theatre Arts, Video

TRURO

TRURO CENTER FOR THE ARTS AT CASTLE HILL, INC, 10 Meetinghouse Rd, Truro, MA 02666; PO Box 756, Truro, MA 02666-0756. Tel 508-349-7511; Fax 508-349-7513; Elec Mail info@castlehill.org; Internet Home Page Address: www.castlehill.org; *Pres* Kim Kettler; *Exec Dir* Cherie Mittenthal Estab 1972; Maintain nonprofit art gallery, Kohl Gallery; over 45 other nationally known instructors; pvt summer school; D & E; Scholarships; SC 50, LC 3; studio courses; lect courses; poetry readings; 730
Ent Req: None
Courses: Book Arts, Ceramics, Drawing, †Illustration, Jewelry, Literature, Painting, Photography, Printmaking, Sculpture, Wood, Writing
Children's Classes: Classes in painting, printmaking, sculpture, jewelry
Summer School: Exec Dir, Cherie Mittenthal. Enrl 700-730; tuition $180-$220 per workshop. Courses—Book, Clay, Drawing, Illustration, Jewelry, Painting, Paper Arts, Photography, Printmaking, Sculpture, Woodwork, Writing

WALTHAM

BRANDEIS UNIVERSITY, Dept of Fine Arts, 415 South St Waltham, MA 02454-9110. Tel 781-736-2655; Internet Home Page Address: www.brandeis.edu; *Chmn* Graham Campbell
Estab 1948; FT 12; pvt; D; Scholarships; SC 10, LC 28; 2800
Ent Req: HS dipl, college board ent exam
Degrees: BS 4 yr
Courses: Art History, Design, Drawing, Painting, Sculpture
Summer School: Dir, Sanford Lotlor. Enrl 10-12 per course; tuition $585 per course for 4 week term. Courses—Introduction to History of Art II, Survey of Western Architecture

WELLESLEY

WELLESLEY COLLEGE, Art Dept, 106 Central St, Wellesley, MA 02481-8203. Tel 781-283-2042; Fax 781-283-3647; *Chmn* Patricia Berman; *Prof* Peter J Fergusson PhD; *Prof* James W Rayen, MFA; *Prof* Richard W Wallace PhD; *Prof* Miranda Marvin PhD, MFA; *Prof* Margaret Carroll PhD; *Prof* Carlos Dorrien, MFA; *Prof* Lilian Armstrong, PhD, MA; *Prof* Bunny Harvey, MFA; *Prof* Alice T Friedman PhD; *Assoc Prof* Anne Higonnet, PhD; *Assoc Prof* Elaine Spatz-Rabinowitz, MFA; *Assoc Prof* Judy Block, MFA; *Assoc Prof* Phyllis McGibbon, MFA; *Asst Prof* Heping Liu, MA, PhD
Estab 1875, dept estab 1886; pvt; D; SC 19, LC 46; D 1233
Ent Req: HS dipl
Degrees: BA
Courses: †Architecture, †Art History, Drawing, Graphic Arts, Painting, Photography, Printmaking, Sculpture, †Studio Art

WEST BARNSTABLE

CAPE COD COMMUNITY COLLEGE, Art Dept, Humanities Division, Route 132 West Barnstable, MA; 2240 Iyanough Rd, West Barnstable, MA 02668-1532. Tel 508-362-2131; Fax 508-362-8638; Internet Home Page Address: www.capecod.mass.edu; *Prof* Sara Ringler, MFA; *Prof* Marie Canaves, MFA; *Coordr Art* Robert McDonald, MFA
Estab 1963, dept estab 1973; pub; D & E; SC 14, LC 7; in school D 2000, E 3000, maj 100
Ent Req: HS dipl
Degrees: AA and AS 2 yrs
Courses: Art History, †Digital Imaging, Drawing, †Film, Graphic Design, Illustration, Life Drawing, Mixed Media, Painting, †Papermaking/Book Arts, †Printmaking, †Quark Express, †Sculpture, Stage Design, Theatre Arts, Video, Visual Fundamentals, †Watercolor Advanced Projects

Adult Hobby Classes: Courses—Art History, Drawing, Graphic Design, Watercolor
Summer School: Assoc Dean, Humanities, Bruce Bell. Courses—Art History, Drawing, Graphic Design, Visual Fundamentals

WESTFIELD

WESTFIELD STATE COLLEGE, Art Dept, 577 Western Ave, Westfield, MA 01086-2501. Tel 413-572-5630; Fax 413-562-3613; *Chmn* Barbara Keim Estab 1972; Maintain nonprofit art gallery; Arno Maris Art Gallery; Pub; D & E; Scholarships
Ent Req: HS dipl & portfolio review
Degrees: BA (Fine Arts) 4 yrs
Courses: Anatomy, Art Appreciation, Art Education, Art History, Commercial Art, Computer Graphics, Design, Drawing, Illustration, Lettering, Mixed Media, Practicum, Printmaking, Sculpture, Teacher Training
Adult Hobby Classes: Enrl 100. Courses—Design Fundamentals, Studio Courses
Summer School: Dept Chmn, P Conant. Courses—Design Fundamentals, Studio Courses

WESTON

REGIS COLLEGE, Dept of Art, 235 Wellesley St, Weston, MA 02193-1545. Tel 781-768-7000; Fax 781-768-8339; Internet Home Page Address: www.regiscollege.edu; *Chmn* Sr Marie de Sales Dinneen
Estab 1927, dept estab 1944; den; D & E; Scholarships; SC 12, LC 12; D 250, non-maj 200, maj 50
Ent Req: HS dipl, SAT, various tests
Degrees: BA 4 yr
Courses: †Art History, Art Therapy, Ceramics, Computer Design, Coordinating Seminars, Drawing, Enameling, Etching, Graphic Techniques, Illustration, †Introduction to Art, Painting, Silk Screen, Stained Glass, Weaving, Woodcut

WILLIAMSTOWN

WILLIAMS COLLEGE, Dept of Art, Spencer Art Bldg, 35 Driscoll Hall Dr Williamstown, MA 01267. Tel 413-597-2377 (Art History Office), 3578 (Art Studio Office), 3131 (Main); Fax 413-597-3498 (Art History Office), 597-3693 (Art Studio Office); Internet Home Page Address: web.williams.edu/Art/; *Assoc Prof, Chair* Peter Low; *Dept Adminr Asst* Beverly Sylvester
Estab 1793, dept estab 1903; FT 12, PT 12; pvt; D; Scholarships; SC 14, LC 40, GC 10; 2000, maj 85, grad 29
Ent Req: HS dipl
Degrees: BA 4 yrs, MA(History of Art) 2 yrs
Tuition: $25,352 per yr; campus res—rm $3440, bd $3490
Courses: Architecture, Art History, Drawing, Painting, Photography, Printmaking, Sculpture, Video

WORCESTER

ASSUMPTION COLLEGE, Dept of Art, Music & Theatre, 500 Salisbury St, Worcester, MA 01609-1265; PO Box 15005, Worcester, MA 01615-0005. Tel 508-767-7000; Internet Home Page Address: www.assumption.edu; *Prof* Rev Donat Lamothe, PhD; *Assoc Prof* Barbara Beall-Fofana, PhD; *Asst Prof* Scott Glushien, MFA; *Vis Asst Prof* Edith Read, MFA; *Vis Asst Prof* Thomas Grady, MFA; *Vis Asst Prof* Jeremy Long, MFA
Estab 1904, dept estab 1976; Maintain a nonprofit art gallery & library at Emmanuel d'Alzen Library; den; D; Scholarships; D 600, E 25
Ent Req: HS dipl
Degrees: BA 4 yr
Tuition: $17,950 per yr; campus res available
Courses: †Advertising Design, Aesthetics, Architecture, Art Education, Art History, †Commercial Art, †Design, Drawing, Graphic Arts, †Graphic Design, History of Art & Architecture, Painting, †Photography, Printmaking, †Sculpture, †Stage Design, Theatre Arts

CLARK UNIVERSITY, Dept of Visual & Performing Arts, 950 Main St, Worcester, MA 01610-1477. Tel 508-793-7113; Fax 508-793-8844; Internet Home Page Address: www.clarku.edu; *Dir Studio Art Prog* Elli Crocker, MFA; *Dean Admissions* Harold Wingood; *Chmn* Rhys Townsend; *Prof* Sarah Bule; *Assoc Prof* Sarah Walker; *Instr* Stephen Dirado
Estab 1887; University gallery on campus; FT 4, PT 10; pvt; D & E; Scholarships; SC 50, LC 24; Maj 100, non-maj 450, other 20
Ent Req: HS dipl, CEEB, achievement tests, SAT & ACH
Degrees: BA
Courses: Aesthetics, Costume Design & Construction, Drawing, †Graphic Design, History of Art & Architecture, †Painting, †Photography, Printmaking, Screen Studies, Sculpture, Stage Design, Theatre Arts, Video, Video Production, Visual Design, Visual Studies
Adult Hobby Classes: Offered through Clark University College of Professional and Continuing Education
Summer School: Offered through Clark University College of Professional and Continuing Education

COLLEGE OF THE HOLY CROSS, Dept of Visual Arts, One College St, Worcester, MA 01610; 1 College St, Worcester, MA 01610-2322. Tel 508-793-2011; Internet Home Page Address: www.holycross.edu; *Prof* Virginia C Raguin PhD, SJ; *Assoc Prof* Susan S Schmidt, MFA; *Assoc Prof* Robert Parke-Harrison, MFA; *Assoc Prof* Father John Reboli PhD, SJ; *Assoc Prof* Michael Beatly, MFA; *Prof* Joanna Ziegler, PhD; *Asst Prof* Alison Fleming, PhD; *Asst Prof* Cristi Rinklin, MFA; *Instr* Naomi Ribner, MFA
Estab 1843, dept estab 1954; pvt; D; SC 12, LC 15; D 485, maj 25

Ent Req: HS dipl, SAT, ATS
Degrees: BA 4 yr
Courses: Aesthetics, Architecture, †Art History, †Digital Art, Drawing, Graphic Arts, Graphic Design, History of Art & Architecture, Painting, Photography, Printmaking, Sculpture, †Studio

WORCESTER CENTER FOR CRAFTS, 25 Sagamore Rd, Worcester, MA 01605-3914. Tel 508-753-8183; Fax 508-797-5626; Elec Mail wcc@worcestercraftcenter.org; Internet Home Page Address: www.worcestercraftcenter.org; *Exec Dir* Davie R Leach; *Gallery Store* Candace Casey; *Registrar* Bettie Carlson; *Weaving* Christine Folz; *Dept Head* Tom O'Malley; *Silversmith* Sarah Nelson; *Metals Dept Head* Linda Hansen; *Glass Dept Head* Alex Bernstein
Estab 1856; Maintain nonprofit art gallery, Krikorian Gallery; Pvt; D & E; Scholarships; varies; D & E 280
Ent Req: No req for adult educ
Courses: Art History, Ceramics, Design, Drawing, Enameling, †Fibre, Furniture Restoration, Glass Blowing, Goldsmithing, Handicrafts, Jewelry, Lampworking, Photography, Sculpture, Silversmithing, Stained Glass, Surface Design, †Wood Working
Adult Hobby Classes: Enrl 1,500; tuition $300 Sept-July. Courses—Ceramics, Enamel, Furniture Refinishing, Photography, Stained Glass, Textiles, Weaver & Fibre, Wood Working, Metal Working, Glass Blowing
Children's Classes: Enrl 500; tuition $300 per 12 wks. Courses—Ceramics, Metals, Photography, Surface Design, Weaving
Summer School: Enrl 100 adults & children, also children's summer camp. Courses—Ceramics, Furniture Refinishing, Glass, Metal, Photography, Textile, Wood

WORCESTER STATE COLLEGE, Visual & Performing Arts Dept, 486 Chandler St, Worcester, MA 01602-2861. Tel 508-929-8824, 929-8000; Elec Mail cnigro@worcester.edu; Internet Home Page Address: www.worcester.edu; *Chmn* Dr Christie Nigro; *Prof* Dr Ellen Kosmere; *Assoc Prof* Michael C Hachey; *Prof* Michel D Merle; *Asst Prof* Bryce Vinokurov
Estab 1874; pub; D & E; SC 18, LC 9; D & E 725
Ent Req: HS dipl, col board exams, completion of systems application form
Degrees: BA and BS 4 yrs
Courses: Art Education, Art History, Collage, Drafting, Drawing, Environmental Design, Graphic Design, Handicrafts, History of Urban Form, Intermedia, Mixed Media, Painting, Printmaking, Sculpture
Summer School: Usually 5-8 courses & workshops

MICHIGAN

ADRIAN

ADRIAN COLLEGE, Art & Design Dept, 110 S Madison St, Adrian, MI 49221-2575. Tel 517-265-5161; Fax 517-264-3153; Elec Mail croyer@adrian.edu; Internet Home Page Address: www.adrian.edu; *Prof* Pauleve Benio, MFA; *Chmn, Assoc Prof* Catherine M Royer, MFA; *Asst Prof* Garin Horner, MFA; *Asst Prof* Juliana Clendenin, MFA; *Coordr Art Educ* Sue Thompson, MAE; *Instr* Elijah Van Benscheten, MFA; *Instr* Gregory Jones, MFA; *Instr* Brian Pitman, MFA; *Instr* Deborah Campbell, MFA; *Instr* Debra Irvine-Stiver, MAE; *Instr* Robert Stranges, MAE
Estab 1859, dept estab 1962; Maintain nonprofit art gallery; Suptnitz Gallery, Adrian Col, 110 S Madison, Adrian MI 49221; art supplies available on-campus; pvt, den; D & E; Scholarships; SC 32, LC 18; in dept D 300, E 50, non-maj 220, maj 120
Ent Req: HS dipl, ACT, SAT
Degrees: BA, BS in Interior Design & BFA with teaching cert
Courses: Art Education, Art History, Arts Management, Ceramics, Design, Drafting, Drawing, Graphic Design, History of Art & Architecture, Interior Design, Mixed Media, Painting, Photography, Pre-Art Therapy, Printmaking, Sculpture, Textile Design
Children's Classes: youth art prog, 80 per term, $75
Summer School: Dir, Catherine Royer. Enrl 15; May term, summer term June-July. Courses—Advanced Study, Art Education, Design, Drawing

SIENA HEIGHTS UNIVERSITY, Studio Angelico-Art Dept, 1247 Siena Heights Dr, Adrian, MI 49221. Tel 517-264-7860; Fax 517-264-7739; Internet Home Page Address: www.sienaheights.edu; *Prof* Joseph Bergman, MFA; *Prof* John Wittershiem, MFA; *Prof & Chmn* Christine Reising, MFA; *Prof* Deborah Danielson, MFA; *Instr* Jamie Goode, MFA; *Instr* Lois DeMots, MA; *Asst Prof* Paul McMullen; *Assoc Prof Art History* Peter Barr, PhD; *Instr* Niki Havekost, MFA; *Instr* Jean Buescher, MFA; *Instr* Todd Marsee, MFA; *Instr* Robert Stranges, MArtEd; *Instr* Jean Lash, MArtEd
Estab 1919; Maintains nonprofit art gallery, Klemm Gallery, Studio Angelico; Pvt; D & E; Scholarships; SC 56; D 200, maj 96
Ent Req: HS dipl
Degrees: BA & BFA 4 yrs
Tuition: Undergrad $6,350 per sem
Courses: Aesthetics, Architecture, Art Appreciation, Art Education, Art History, †Ceramics, †Drawing, †Graphic Design, †Metalsmithing, †Painting, †Photography, †Printmaking, †Sculpture
Summer School: Courses—Bookmaking, Ceramics, Mixed Media, Portrait Painting, Watercolor

ALBION

ALBION COLLEGE, Dept of Visual Arts, 611 E Porter St, Albion, MI 49224-1887. Tel 517-629-0246; Elec Mail rkruger@albion.edu; Internet Home Page Address: www.albion.edu; *Chmn Dept Visual Arts* Lynne Chytilo; *Asst Prof* Billie Wicker, MA; *Prof* Douglas Goering, MFA

Estab 1835; den; D & E; Scholarships; SC 32, LC 8
Ent Req: HS dipl
Degrees: BA and BFA 4 yrs
Courses: Art History, Ceramics, Drawing, Film, Painting, Photography, Printmaking, Sculpture, Stage Design, Teacher Training, Theatre Arts
Summer School: Acad Dean, Dr Daniel Poteet.

ALLENDALE

GRAND VALLEY STATE UNIVERSITY, Art & Design Dept, 1 Campus Dr, Allendale, MI 49401-9401. Tel 616-331-3486; Fax 616-331-3240; Elec Mail jenkinsv@gvsu.edu; Internet Home Page Address: www.gvsu.edu; *Chmn* Virginia Jenkins MFA; *Prof* Ed Wong-Ligda; *Prof* Beverly Seley; *Prof* Lorelle Thomas; *Assoc Prof* Richard Weis; *Assoc Prof* Ann Keister; *Assoc Prof* Paul Wittenbraker; *Assoc Prof* Bill Hosterman; *Assoc Prof* Jill Eggers; *Asst Prof* Anna Campbell; *Asst Prof* Hsiao-ping Chen; *Asst Prof* Brett Colley; *Asst Prof* Sigrid Danielson; *Assoc Prof* Tim Fisher; *Asst Prof* Hoon Lee; *Assoc Prof* Kristen Strom; *Asst Prof* Norwood Viviano; *Asst Prof* Katalin Zaszlavik; *Assoc Prof* Renee Zettle-Sterling
Estab 1960; Mem: Maintains non-profit art gallery; on campus shop where supplies can be purchased; pub; D & E; Scholarships; SC 52, LC 12, GC 1; D 380, E 40, maj 1,400, non-maj 420
Ent Req: ACT, Entrance portfolio
Degrees: BA(Studio), BS(Studio), BFA 4 yrs, BA(Art Educ), BA (Art Hist), BA (Art Educ), BS (Art Educ)
Courses: Art Appreciation, †Art Education, Art History, †Ceramics, Drawing, †Goldsmithing, †Graphic Design, †Illustration, †Jewelry, †Painting, †Printmaking, †Sculpture, †Silversmithing, Visual Studies
Summer School: Courses—Introduction to Art, Art for the Classroom Teacher, Workshops, 2-D Design, Color & Design, Intro to Drawing

ALMA

ALMA COLLEGE, Clack Art Center, Dept of Art & Design, 614 W Superior, Alma, MI 48801. Tel 517-463-7220, 463-7111; Fax 517-463-7277; Internet Home Page Address: www.alma.edu; *Asst Prof* C Sandy Lopez-Isnardi; *Assoc Prof* Robert Rozier; *Prof, Chmn* Carrie Anne Parks-Kirby
Estab 1886; pvt; D & E; Scholarships; SC 10-20, LC 4-8; D 250, maj 45-50
Degrees: BA, BFA
Courses: Advertising Design, Aesthetics, Art Education, Art History, Ceramics, Computer Graphics, Drawing, Foreign Study, Graphic Design, History of Art & Architecture, Illustration, Jewelry, Mixed Media, Museum Staff Training, Painting, Photography, Printmaking, Scientific Illustration, Sculpture, Weaving

ANN ARBOR

UNIVERSITY OF MICHIGAN, ANN ARBOR, School of Art & Design, 2000 Bonisteel Blvd, Rm 2055, Ann Arbor, MI 48109-2069. Tel 734-764-0397; Fax 734-615-9753; Elec Mail a+d@umich.edu; Internet Home Page Address: www.art-design.umich.edu; *Prof* Vince Castagnacci; *Prof* James Cogswell; *Prof* Julie Ellison; *Prof* Daniel Herwitz; *Prof* Al Hinton; *Prof* Joanne Leonard; *Prof* Lou Marinaro; *Prof* Dwayne Overmyer; *Prof* Panos Papalambros; *Prof* Ted Ramsay; *Prof* Bryan Rogers; *Prof* Jon Rush; *Prof* Allen Samuels; *Prof* Sherri Smith; *Prof* James Steward; *Prof* Takeshi Takahara; *Assoc Prof* Edward West; *Assoc Prof* Larry Cressman; *Assoc Prof* Susan Crowell; *Assoc Prof* Holly Hughes; *Assoc Prof* Sadashi Inuzuka; *Assoc Prof* Shaun Jackson; *Assoc Prof* Carol Jacobsen; *Assoc Prof* Malcom McCullough; *Assoc Prof* Dennis Miller; *Assoc Prof* Marianetta Porter; *Assoc Prof* Michael Rodemer; *Assoc Prof* Brad Smith; *Assoc Prof* Joe Trumpey; *Asst Prof* Jan-Henrik Andersen; *Asst Prof* Phoebe Gloeckner; *Asst Prof* Andy Kirshner; *Asst Prof* Heidi Kumao; *Asst Prof* Patricia Olynyk; *Asst Prof* Cynthia Pachikara; *Asst Prof* Janie Paul; *Asst Prof* Dan Price; *Asst Prof* Stephanie Rowden; *Asst Prof* Hannah Smotrich; *Asst Prof* Satoru Takahashi; *Asst Prof* Nick Tobier; *Asst Prof* Alicyn Warren; *Vis Assoc Prof* David Chung; *Vis Assoc Prof* Rebekah Modrak; *Vis Assoc Prof* Elona Van Gent; *Vis Assoc Prof* Anne Mondro; *Vis Assoc Prof* Rich Pell; *FT Lectr* Doug Hesseltine; *FT Lectr* Mary Schmidt
Estab 1817, sch estab 1974; maintains nonprofit art galleries: Jean Paul Slusser Gallery & Warren M Robbins Gallery, both on-campus; Work Exhibition Space, 306 State St, Ann Arbor, MI 48104. Art library, University of Michigan Art, Architecture and Engineering Library, 2281 Bonisteel Blvd, Ann Arbor, MI 48109-2094; FT 40, PT 20; pub; D & E; Scholarships; non-maj 100, maj 500, grad 30
Ent Req: HS dipl, portfolio exam
Degrees: BFA, MFA
Courses: Art History, Ceramics, Collage, Conceptual Art, Constructions, Costume Design & Construction, Design, †Display, Drawing, Graphic Arts, Graphic Design, Lettering, Mixed Media, Painting, Photography, Printmaking, Sculpture, †Textiles, Video, Weaving
—Dept of History of Art, 519 S State St, Ann Arbor, MI 48109-1357. Tel 734-764-5400; Fax 734-647-4121; Elec Mail dianek@umich.edu; Internet Home Page Address: www.umich.edu/~hartspc/histart; *Interim Chmn* Diane Kirkpatrick; *Dir Kelsey Museum & Prof* Elaine K Gazda; *Dir Museum Art* James Steward; *Prof* R Ward Bissell; *Prof* Margaret Root; *Assoc Prof* Thelma Thomas; *Prof* Martin Powers; *Assoc Prof* Patricia Simons; *Prof* Celeste Brusati; *Asst Prof* Alka Patel; *Asst Prof* Qiang Wing; *Asst Prof* Robert Maxwell; *Asst Prof* Rebecca Zurier; *Asst Prof* Elizabeth Sears; *Asst Prof* Matthew Biro; *Asst Prof* Jacqueline Francis; *Asst Prof* Maria Gough; *Asst Prof* Howard Lay
Dept estab 1910; FT 16; pub; Scholarships, Fellowships; maj 75, grad 60
Degrees: BA, MA, PhD
Tuition: Res—undergrad $61,840 per yr, grad $11,654 per yr; nonres—undergrad $21,346 per yr, grad $23,132 per yr
Courses: †Art History, Museology
Summer School: Chmn, Diane Kirkpatrick. Enrl 77; tuition res $379 per cr, nonres $803 per cr

BATTLE CREEK

KELLOGG COMMUNITY COLLEGE, Arts & Communication Dept, 450 North Ave, Battle Creek, MI 49017-3397. Tel 269-965-3931; Fax 269-965-0280; Internet Home Page Address: www.kellogg.edu; *Art Instr* Ryan Flathu; *Art Instr* Peter Williams; *Chmn* Paula Puckett
Estab 1962; Maintains nonprofit art gallery, Davidson Gallery; FT 9, PT 18; pub; D & E; occupational cert; Scholarships; SC, LC; D 2,200, E 2,000, maj 60
Ent Req: None
Degrees: AA 2-4 yr
Courses: †Advertising Design, Animation, †Architecture, Art Appreciation, †Art Education, Art History, †Ceramics, Design, Drafting, †Drawing, †Graphic Design, †Industrial Design, †Mixed Media, †Painting, †Photography, †Sculpture, Stage Design, Teacher Training, Theatre Arts
Adult Hobby Classes: Courses—all areas
Summer School: Courses—Basic Art & Appreciation

BENTON HARBOR

LAKE MICHIGAN COLLEGE, Dept of Art & Science, 2755 E Napier Ave, Benton Harbor, MI 49022-1881. Tel 616-927-3571, Ext 5180; *Instr* Ken Schaber, MFA
Estab 1943; pub; D & E; Scholarships; SC 10, LC 5; 3377 total
Ent Req: Open door policy
Degrees: AA 2 yrs
Courses: 2-D & 3-D Design, Art Appreciation, Art Education, Art History, Ceramics, Design, Drawing, Occupational Therapy, Painting, Photography, Printmaking, Sculpture, Weaving

BERRIEN SPRINGS

ANDREWS UNIVERSITY, Dept of Art, Art History & Design, N US Rt 31, Berrien Springs, MI 49104-0001. Tel 616-471-7771; Fax 616-471-3949; Internet Home Page Address: www.andrews.edu; *Chmn* Gregory Constantine; *Prof* Steve Hansen; *Instr* Robert Mason
Estab 1952; FT 4; den; D & E; SC 18, LC 5; enrl 130, maj 20
Ent Req: HS grad
Degrees: BS(Art Educ), BA 4 yrs, BFA 4 yrs
Courses: Art Education, Art History, Ceramics, Drawing, European Study, Graphic Design, Painting, Photography, Printmaking, Sculpture

BIG RAPIDS

FERRIS STATE UNIVERSITY, Visual Communication Dept, 119 South St Bus 302, Big Rapids, MI 49307-2284. Tel 231-591-2442; *Dept Head* Kaaren Denyes 10; Scholarships
Degrees: AAS & BS
Tuition: Res—undergrad $2142 per sem; nonres—undergrad $4838 per sem
Courses: Advertising Design, Air Brush, Art History, Concept Development, Conceptual Art, Creative Writing, Design, Drawing, Figure Drawing, Film, †Graphic Arts, †Graphic Design, Illustration, Intermedia, Lettering, Mixed Media, Painting, Photography, Printmaking, Production Art, Rendering, Typography, Video
Adult Hobby Classes: Enrl 400; tuition $180 per cr hr
Summer School: Dir, Karl Walker. Tuition $180 per qtr

BIRMINGHAM

BIRMINGHAM BLOOMFIELD ART CENTER, 1516 S Cranbrook Rd, Birmingham, MI 48009-1855. Tel 248-644-0866; Fax 248-644-7904; Internet Home Page Address: www.bbartcenter.org (ULC); *Pres & Ceo* Annie Van Gelderen; *VPres Programs* Cynthia Mills; *Youth Prog Dir* Susan Owens; *VP Fin* Gwenn Rosseau; *Exec Asst* Diane Taylor
Estab 1957; Maintains Robinson Gallery, Kantgias/Desalle Gallery, LaBan Commons Gallery; maintains art/architecture libr; PT 100; pub; Community School of the Arts; D, E & weekends; Scholarships; SC & LC 500; 3600 total
Courses: Ceramics, Collage, Conceptual Art, Design, Drawing, Fashion Arts, Figure Drawing, Illustration, Jewelry, Jewelry & Metalsmithing, Mixed Media, Original Watercolor, Painting, Painting-Oil, Perspective Drawing, Photography, Printmaking, Sculpture, Still-Life & Landscape Drawing, Teen & Adult Portfolio Prep, Weaving
Adult Hobby Classes: Enrl 3000-3500; tuition $0-$300 for 3-39 hrs. Courses—Design, Drawing, Fibers, Jewelry, Painting, Pottery, Printmaking, Sculpture
Children's Classes: Enrl 500; tuition $75-$100.
Summer School: Youth Prog Dir, Susan Owens. Enrl 500; 2 wk term. Children's Summer Art Camp

BLOOMFIELD HILLS

CRANBROOK ACADEMY OF ART, 39221 Woodward Ave, Bloomfield Hills, MI 48304-5100; PO Box 801, Bloomfield Hills, MI 48303-0801. Tel 248-645-3300; Fax 248-645-3591; Elec Mail caaadmissions@cranbrook.edu; Internet Home Page Address: www.cranbrookart.edu; *Head 2-D Design Dept* Elliott Earls; *Head Fiber Dept* Mark Newport; *Head Metalsmithing Dept* Iris Eichenberg; *Head Painting Dept* Beverly Fishman; *Head Photo Dept* Liz Cohen; *Head Ceramics Dept* Anders Ruhwald; *Head Archit Dept* William Massie; *Head Dept Print Media* Randy Boltan; *Head Sculpture Dept* Heather McGill; *Head 3-D Design Dept* Scott Klinker; *Dir* Reed Kroloff
Estab 1932; Maintain nonprofit art gallery; Cranbrook Art Mus & Cranbrook Acad of Art Library; on-campus shop for art supplies; Pvt; D & E; Studio Prog minimum 30 hrs wk; Scholarships; SC, GC 2; GS 150
Ent Req: Portfolio

Degrees: MFA & MArchit 2 yrs
Tuition: $30,688 per yr; campus res—room & board $5,324 (single), $2,993 (double)
Courses: Architecture, Ceramics, Design, Fiber, Metalsmithing, Painting, Photography, Print Media, Sculpture
Summer School: Mgr, Chris Schneider. Summer Art Institute offers prog to high schoolers ages 13 - 18

DEARBORN

HENRY FORD COMMUNITY COLLEGE, McKenzie Fine Art Ctr, 5101 Evergreen Rd, Dearborn, MI 48128-1495. Tel 313-845-9634, 9600; Fax 313-845-6321; Internet Home Page Address: www.hfcc.net; *Div Dir* Rick Goward; *Mgr Performing Arts* Dale Van Dorp; *Dept Head* Martin Anderson; *Instr Interior Design* Pamela Banduric; *Mgr Enrichment* Robert Cadez; *Ceramics* Cathy Dambach; *Drawing* Kevin Donahue; *Graphic Design* Kirk McLendon; *Dance* Diane Mancinelli; *Music* Kevin Dewey; *Philosophy* John Azar; *Speech* Stanley Moore; *Radio* Jay Kornek; *Dir Theater* George Popovich
Estab 1938; FT 6, PT 40; pub; D & E; Scholarships; SC 25, LC 9; D 3500, E 7500, maj 600
Ent Req: HS dipl
Degrees: AA 2 yrs
Courses: 2-D Design, 3-D Design, Art Appreciation, Art History, †Ceramics, Drawing, †Graphic Design, †Interior Design, Jewelry, †Painting, Photography, Printmaking, Sculpture, Textile Design
Children's Classes: Ceramics, Jewelry, Painting/Drawing, Sculpture
Summer School: Dir, Martin W Anderson. Tuition res-$30 per cr hr, nonres $42. Courses—Art Appreciation, Art History, Ceramics, Color Photography, Directed Study, Drawing, Black & White Photography, 2-D Design

DETROIT

COLLEGE FOR CREATIVE STUDIES, 201 E Kirby, Detroit, MI 48202. Tel 313-664-7400; Internet Home Page Address: www.collegeforcreativestudies.edu; *Pres* Richard L Rogers; *Acad Dean* Imre Molnar; *Chmn Transportation Design* Mark West; *Chmn Crafts* Tom Madden; *Chmn Liberal Arts* Julie Longo; *Chmn Graphic Design* Doug Kisor; *Chmn Entertainment Arts* Scott Bogoniewski; *Chmn Photog* Bruce Feklman; *Chmn Fine Arts* Gilda Snowden; *Chmn Illustration* Gil Ashby; *Chair Advertising Design* Mark Zapico; *Chair Product Design* Vincenzo Iavicoli
Estab 1926; maintain nonprofit art gallery; pvt; D & E; Scholarships; SC, LC; D 950, E 250, others 200; 1307 students
Ent Req: HS dipl & portfolio
Degrees: BFA 4 yrs
Courses: †Advertising Design, †Art History, †Ceramics, †Commercial Art, †Conceptual Art, Crafts, †Design, †Drawing, †Film, Fine Arts, Glass, †Graphic Arts, †Graphic Design, †Illustration, Industrial Design, †Interior Design, †Jewelry, †Mixed Media, †Painting, †Photography, †Printmaking, †Sculpture, †Silversmithing, †Textile Design, †Video, †Weaving
Adult Hobby Classes: Enrl 281. Courses—Computer Technology, Crafts, Fine Arts, Graphic Commun, Industrial Design, Photography
Children's Classes: Enrl 59. Courses—Art, Music
Summer School: Dean Acad Affairs, Imre Molnar; Dir Continuing Educ, Carla Gonzalez; Enrl 230; tuition $476 per cr hr. Courses—Computer Technology, Crafts, Fine Arts, Industrial Design, Photography

MARYGROVE COLLEGE, Department of Art, 8425 W McNichols Rd, Detroit, MI 48221-2546. Tel 313-927-1370; Elec Mail nsmith@marygrove.edu; Internet Home Page Address: www.marygrove.edu; *Dean* Rose DeSloover, MFA; *Asst Prof* James Lutomski, MFA; *Asst Prof* Beverly Hall Smith; *Chmn & Asst Prof* Nelson Smith, MFA; *Asst Prof* Cindy Read; *Asst Prof* Diane Rieman, MFA; *Instr* Anita Ricks-Bates, MFA; *Instr* Christine Hagedorn, MFA
Estab 1910; maintains nonprofit art gallery, The Gallery Marygrove College, 8425 W McNichols, Detroit, MI 48221; pvt; D & E; SC 37, LC 20, GC 5; D 150, E 25, non-maj 60, maj 50, grad 5
Ent Req: Interview with portfolio
Degrees: BA & BFA 4 yrs
Courses: Advertising Design, Art Education, Art History, †Ceramics, Constructions, †Drawing, †Graphic Arts, Graphic Design, Mixed Media, †Painting, Photography, †Printmaking, Sculpture, †Teacher Training
Adult Hobby Classes: Enrl 65; tuition $35-$90 per course. Courses—Drawing, Painting, Photography
Children's Classes: Enrl 100; tuition $20-$50 per course. Courses—Ceramics, Painting, Photography
Summer School: Dean Continuing Educ, Sr Andrea Lee, PhD. Enrl 40, tuition $86 per cr hr for term of two 6 wk terms. Courses—Basic courses, graduate and undergraduate

UNIVERSITY OF DETROIT MERCY, School of Architecture, 4001 W McNichols Rd, Detroit, MI 48221-3038. Tel 313-993-1532; Fax 313-993-1512; Internet Home Page Address: www.architecture.udmercy.edu; *Dean* Stephan P Vogel; *Prof* John C Mueller; *Assoc Dean* Stephan J LaGrassa
Estab 1877, school estab 1964; pvt; D & E; Scholarships; SC 14, LC 36; D 200, maj 200
Ent Req: HS dipl, B average
Degrees: MArch 5 years
Tuition: Undergrad $8235 per 12-18 cr hrs per sem, $420 per 1-11 cr; grad $9075 per 12-18 cr hrs per sem, $605 per 1-11 cr
Courses: Architecture, Design

WAYNE STATE UNIVERSITY, Dept of Art & Art History, 4841 Cass Ave, 150 Arts Bldg Detroit, MI 48202-1203. Tel 313-577-2980; Fax 313-577-3491; *Chmn* Marian Jackson; *Interim Chmn* Robert Marten
FT 25, PT 20

Courses: Art History, Ceramics, Drawing, Fibers, Graphic Design, Industrial Design, Interdisciplinary Electronic Media, Interior Design, Metals, Painting, Photography, Printmaking, Sculpture
Summer School: Tuition same as regular sem for 7 wks. Courses—Art History, Ceramics, Drawing, Fibers, Painting, Photography, Sculpture

DOWAGIAC

SOUTHWESTERN MICHIGAN COLLEGE, Fine & Performing Arts Dept, 58900 Cherry Grove Rd, Dowagiac, MI 49047-9726. Tel 616-782-5113; Internet Home Page Address: www.swmich.edu; *Chmn & Instr* Dr John Korzon, DA; *Instr* David R Baker, MFA; *Instr* Patty Bunner, MFA
Estab 1964; pub; D & E; Scholarships; SC 13, LC 3; D 200, E 100, non-maj 200, maj 100
Ent Req: HS dipl
Degrees: AA & AS
Tuition: Res—undergrad $50 per cr hr; nonres—undergrad $85 per cr hr; foreign, in service & out of state $66 per cr hr
Courses: Advertising Design, Architecture, Ceramics, Commercial Art, Drafting, Drawing, Graphic Arts, Lettering, Painting, Photography, Printmaking
Adult Hobby Classes: Art Appreciation, Ceramics, Painting, Photography
Summer School: Dir, Marshall Bishop. Enrl 1000; 7 wk terms

EAST LANSING

MICHIGAN STATE UNIVERSITY, Dept of Art & Art History, 113 Kresge Art Ctr, East Lansing, MI 48824-1119. Tel 517-355-7610; Fax 517-432-3938; Elec Mail art@msu.edu; Internet Home Page Address: www.art.msu.edu; *Prog Head* Dr Kenneth Haltman; *Dir Grad Prog* Dr Janice Simpson
Estab 1855; FT 30; pub; D & E; Scholarships; SC 77, LC 45, GC 25; D 2500, non-maj 1500, maj 450, grad 60
Ent Req: HS dipl
Degrees: BA & BFA 4 yrs, MA 1 yr, MFA 2 yrs
Courses: Art Education, Art History, Ceramics, Collage, Conceptual Art, Constructions, Design, Drawing, Graphic Design, History of Art & Architecture, Mixed Media, †Museum Studies, Painting, Photography, Printmaking, Sculpture, Teacher Training, Video
Adult Hobby Classes: Tuition $10 per session. Courses—History of Art & Studio Art
Children's Classes: Enrl 150; tuition $50 for 10 wks. Courses—Computer, Drawing, Painting, Photography, Sculpture
Summer School: Dir, Jim Hopfensperger

ESCANABA

BAY DE NOC COMMUNITY COLLEGE, Art Dept, 2001 N Lincoln Rd, Escanaba, MI 49829-2511. Tel 906-786-5802; Fax 906-789-6913; *Instr Drawing & Design* Craig Seckinger; *Instr Art History* Joann Leffel; *Instr Pottery* Al Hansen
Maintain nonprofit art gallery; Scholarships; SC 6, LC 2; D 60, E 20
Degrees: AA, AS
Tuition: County res—$53.50 per cr hr; non-county res—$73.50 per cr hr; non-state res—$117.50 per cr hr
Courses: Art History, Ceramics, Design, Drawing, Painting, Sculpture

FARMINGTON HILLS

OAKLAND COMMUNITY COLLEGE, Art Dept, 27055 Orchard Lake Rd, Orchard Ridge Campus Farmington Hills, MI 48334-4556. Tel 248-522-3400; Fax 248-471-7544; Internet Home Page Address: www.oaklandcc.edu; *Chmn* Robert Piepenburg
Degrees: AA and ASA offered
Tuition: District res—$48-70 per cr hr; non-district—$82.40 per cr hr
Courses: Advertising Design, Art Appreciation, Art History, Calligraphy, Ceramics, Design, Drawing, Fashion Arts, Handicrafts, Photography, Sculpture

FLINT

MOTT COMMUNITY COLLEGE, (Charles Stewart Mott Community College) Fine Arts & Social Sciences Division, 1401 E Court St, Flint, MI 48503-2089. Tel 810-762-0332; Fax 810-762-5670; Elec Mail marycusack@mcc.edu; Internet Home Page Address: www.mcc.edu; *Dean* Mary Cusack; *Prof* Jessie Sirna, MA; *Prof* Thomas Bohnert, MAEd; *Prof* John Dempsey; *Prof* Mara Fulmer; *Asst Prof* James Shurter; *Instr* Dustin Price
Estab 1923; Maintain a non-profit art gallery; pub; D & E; SC 45, LC 7; D & E 250, maj 250
Ent Req: HS dipl or 19 yrs old
Degrees: AFA 2 yrs
Tuition: Fall 2012 $108.05 in district, $161.75 out of district, $215.86 out of state per contact hour
Courses: Art Appreciation, Art Education, Art History, Ceramics, Drawing, Film, Graphic Design, Jewelry, Painting, †Photography, Printmaking, Sculpture, Theatre Arts, Video
Adult Hobby Classes: Classes offered through cont education division
Summer School: Tuition same as above; 7.5 wk sessions

GRAND RAPIDS

AQUINAS COLLEGE, Art Dept, 1607 Robinson Rd SE, Grand Rapids, MI 49506-1799. Tel 616-459-8281, Ext 2413; Fax 616-459-2563; Elec Mail zimmekat@aquinas.edu; Internet Home Page Address: www.aquinas.edu; WATS 800-678-9593; *Chmn Dept & Prof* Ron Pederson, MFA; *Prof* Sr Marie Celeste Miller PhD, MFA; *Prof* Steve Schousen, MFA; *Assoc Prof & Dir Exhibs* Dana Freeman, MFA; *Assoc Prof* Kurt Kaiser, MFA; *Adjunct Assoc Prof Painting* Sharon Sandberg, MFA; *Prof* Joseph Becherer, PhD; *Prof Art History* Lena Meijer; *Adjunct Asst Prof Art Educ* HJ Slider, MA; *Adjunct Prof* Don Kerr, MFA; *Adjunct Assoc Prof* Chris LaPorte, MFA; *Adjunct Instr Ceramics* Madeline Kaczmarczyk
Estab 1940, dept estab 1965; maintains nonprofit art gallery, AMC Gallery, 1607 Robinson Rd SE, Grand Rapids, MI 49506; pvt; den; D & E; Scholarships; SC 30, LC 12; non-maj 80, maj 50
Ent Req: HS dipl
Degrees: BA and BFA 4 yrs
Courses: Art Appreciation, †Art Education, †Art History, †Ceramics, Conceptual Art, Constructions, Design, †History of Art & Architecture, Mixed Media, †Painting, †Photography, †Printmaking, †Sculpture, Stage Design, Theatre Arts

CALVIN COLLEGE, Art Dept, 3201 Burton SE, Grand Rapids, MI 49546. Tel 616-957-6271; Fax 616-957-8551; Internet Home Page Address: www.calvin.edu; *Prof* Helen Bonzelaar PhD, MFA; *Prof* Franklin Spevers, MS; *Assoc Prof* Anna Greidanus Probes, MFA; *Prof* Henry Luhikhuizen PhD, MFA; *Chmn Dept* Carl Huisman
Estab 1876, dept estab 1965; den; D & E; Scholarships; SC 16, LC 4, GC 5; maj 130, grad 4, others 4
Ent Req: HS dipl, SAT or ACT
Degrees: BA(Art, Art Educ, Art History) & BFA(Art), MAT
Courses: Advertising Design, Aesthetics, Architecture, Art Appreciation, Art Education, Art History, Art Therapy, Ceramics, Commercial Art, Conceptual Art, Constructions, Graphic Design, History of Art & Architecture, Jewelry, Painting, Photography, Printmaking, Sculpture, Silversmithing, Teacher Training
Summer School: Courses vary

GRAND RAPIDS COMMUNITY COLLEGE, Visual Art Dept, 143 Bostwick NE, Grand Rapids, MI 49503. Tel 616-234-3544; Fax 611-234-3368; Elec Mail nantonak@grcc.cc.edu; Internet Home Page Address: grcc.cc.edu; *Dept Head Visual Arts* Nick Antonakis; *Art Gallery Dir* Robin Van Rooyen
Estab 1914; Maintains nonprofit art gallery, Grand Rapids Community College Art Gallery; FT 7, PT 11; pub; D, E & W; Scholarships; SC 17, LC 2; D 250, E 75, maj 60
Ent Req: HS dipl or ent exam
Degrees: AA 2 yrs & AFA 2 yrs
Courses: 20th Century Art, Art Education, Art History, Ceramics, Color & Design, Drawing, Graphic Design, History of Art & Architecture, Life Drawing, Mixed Media, Painting, Photography, Teacher Training
Summer School: Term of 7 wks beginning May. Courses—Art History, Drawing, Photography, Pottery, Outdoor Painting, Drawing

KENDALL COLLEGE OF ART & DESIGN, 17 Fountain St NW, Grand Rapids, MI 49503-3194. Tel 616-451-2787; Internet Home Page Address: www.KendallCollArtDes.edu; *Pres* Oliver H Evans PhD; *Chmn Foundation Fine Arts* Tom Gondek, MFA; *Chmn Design Studies* Bruce Mulder, MEd; *Chmn Art History & Liberal Arts* Ruth O'Keefe, MA
Estab 1928; FT 27, PT 39; pvt; D & E; Scholarships; SC 64, LC 27, AH 9; 581
Ent Req: HS dipl, ACT, SAT
Degrees: BFA & BS 4 yrs
Courses: Advertising Design, †Art History, Design, Drafting, Drawing, †Fine Arts, †Furniture Design, Graphic Design, History of Art & Architecture, †Illustration, †Industrial Design, †Interior Design, Mixed Media, Painting, Photography, Printmaking, Sculpture, Video, †Visual Communications
Adult Hobby Classes: 524; tuition $150-$160 for 8 wk term. Courses—Ceramics, Computer Art, Drawing, Jewelry Design, Painting, Photography
Children's Classes: 826; tuition $65 & up for 6 wk term. Courses—Ceramics, Drawing, Painting, Photography, Sculpture
Summer School: Full semester, May - July; same program as regular session

HANCOCK

FINLANDIA UNIV, International School of Art and Design, 200 Michigan St, Hancock, MI 49930-1427. Tel 906-487-7225; Fax 906-487-7290; Elec Mail art&design@finlandia.edu; Internet Home Page Address: www.finlandia.edu; *Prof* Phyllis Fredenall, MFA; *Dean* Denise Vandeville, MFA; *Assoc Prof* Rick Loduha, MFA; *Assoc Prof* Robert Grame, MFA; *Vis Artist* Phillip Faulkner
Estab 1896, dept estab 1997; Maintains 2 galleries exhibiting student art for sale & sustainable Keweenaw Resource Center on campus; pvt; D & E; Scholarships; SC 38, LC 9; D 80, E 30, non-maj 6, maj 80
Ent Req: HS dipl, open door policy
Degrees: AA 2 yrs, BFA, BA 4 yrs
Tuition: $9,699 per sem; campus res available
Courses: Advertising Design, Aesthetics, Art Education, Art History, Art Therapy, †Ceramics, Design, Drawing, †Fashion Arts, Fiber, †Graphic Arts, †Graphic Design, History of Art & Architecture, †Integrated Design, †Painting, Photography, Printmaking, Product Design, Sculpture, †Sustainable Design, Teacher Training, †Textile Design, Visual Communications, Weaving

HILLSDALE

HILLSDALE COLLEGE, Art Dept, 33 E College St, Hillsdale, MI 49242-1298. Tel 517-437-7341, Ext 2371; Fax 517-437-3923; Internet Home Page Address: www.hillsdale.edu; *Dir* Samuel Knecht, MFA; *Asst Prof* Tony Frudakis, MFA; *Instr* Patrick Forshay; *Instr* Will Bippes
Estab 1844; pvt; Scholarships; SC 12, LC 5; D 1000, non-maj 150, maj 15
Ent Req: HS dipl, SAT
Degrees: BA & BS 4 yrs
Courses: Advertising Design, Art Education, Art History, Ceramics, Drawing, Film, Graphic Arts, History of Art & Architecture, Illustration, Lettering, Painting, Photography, Printmaking, Restoration & Conservation, Sculpture, Stage Design, Teacher Training, Video

Summer School: Dir, Rich Moeggenberg. Courses—Vary

HOLLAND

HOPE COLLEGE, Dept of Art & Art History, 275 Columbia Ave, Art Dept Holland, MI 49423; PO Box 9000, Holland, MI 49422-9000. Tel 616-395-7500; Fax 616-395-7499; Elec Mail nelson@hope.edu; Internet Home Page Address: www.hope.edu; *Prof* William Mayer, MFA; *Assoc Prof* Katherine Sullivan, MFA; *Prof* Bruce McCombs, MFA; *Assoc Prof & Chmn* Steve Nelson, MFA; *Asst Prof* Stephanie Milanowski, MFA; *Asst Prof* Anne Heath-Wiersma, PhD; *Gallery Dir* Heidi Kraus, PhD
Estab 1866, dept estab 1962; Maintain nonprofit art gallery; DePree Gallery, Hope College, 275 Columbia Ave, Holland, MI 49423; art supplies cam be purchased at college bookstore; den; D & E; Scholarships; SC 18, LC 12; D 185, E 61, non-maj 488, maj 26
Ent Req: HS dipl, CEEB-SAT or ACT
Degrees: BA and BM 4 yrs
Tuition: $13,430 per sem
Courses: 2-D & 3-D Design, †Art Education, †Art History, †Ceramics, Design, †Drawing, †Painting, †Photography, †Printmaking, †Sculpture
Summer School: Registrar, Carol DeJong. Tuition $250 per sem hr. Courses—Vary from yr to yr

INTERLOCHEN

INTERLOCHEN CENTER FOR THE ARTS, Interlochen Arts Academy, Dept of Visual Art, 4000 Hwy M-137, Interlochen, MI 49643-0199; PO Box 199, Interlochen, MI 49643-0199. Tel 231-276-7200; Internet Home Page Address: www.interlochen.org; *Dir Visual Arts* Melinda Zacher
Maintain a nonprofit art gallery & art/architecture library; Pvt; D; Scholarships; SC, LC; 440, non-maj 30, maj 50
Ent Req: portfolio, HS dipl, post grad certificate
Tuition: $46,500 per yr, includes room & board
Courses: Art History, Ceramics, Design, Drawing, Fiber Art, Jewelry, Mixed Media, Painting, Photography, Printmaking, Sculpture, Silversmithing, Textile Design, Weaving
Summer School: Dir Visual Arts, Melinda Zacher. Enrl 2,500. Interlochen Arts Camp, formerly National Music Camp Courses & same as above

IRONWOOD

GOGEBIC COMMUNITY COLLEGE, Fine Arts Dept, E 4946 Jackson Rd, Ironwood, MI 49938. Tel 906-932-4231, Ext 283; *Chmn* Jeannie Milakovich
Estab 1932; pub; D & E; Scholarships; SC 14, LC 3; D 37, E 32, non-maj 65, maj 4
Ent Req: HS dipl or equivalent
Degrees: AA 2 yrs
Adult Hobby Classes: Courses—Painting
Summer School: Dean Instruction, Dale Johnson. Courses—Ceramics, Ceramic Sculpture, Drawing, Painting

KALAMAZOO

KALAMAZOO COLLEGE, Art Dept, 1200 Academy St, Kalamazoo, MI 49006-3295. Tel 616-337-7047; Fax 616-337-7067; Elec Mail fischer@kzoo.edu; *Prof* Richard Koenig, MFA; *Chmn* Tom Rice, MFA
Estab 1833, dept estab approx 1940; pvt; D; Scholarships; SC 14, LC 10; (school) 1200, non-maj 250 (dept), maj 20, others 5
Ent Req: HS dipl, SAT, ACT, class rank
Degrees: BA 4 yrs
Courses: Aesthetics, Art History, Ceramics, Drawing, Painting, Photography, Printmaking, Sculpture, Teacher Training

KALAMAZOO INSTITUTE OF ARTS, KIA School, 314 S Park St, Kalamazoo, MI 49007-5102. Tel 269-349-7775; Fax 269-349-9313; Elec Mail denisel@kiarts.org; Internet Home Page Address: www.kiarts.org; *Dir KIA School* Denise Lisiecki, MA; *Head Children's Prog* Anne Forrest, MFA; *Head Weaving Dept* Gretchen Huggett, BS; *Head Jewelry Dept* Lauren Tripp; *Chair Ceramics* Brian Hirt, MFA; *Head Jewelry Dept* Kelli Jackson; *Chair Photog & Digital Media* Mary Whalen; *Head Printmaking* Alexa Karabin
Estab 1924; Maintains nonprofit art gallery & art library, Mary & Edwin Meader Fine Arts Library; PT 50; pvt, nonprofit; D & E; Scholarships; SC 85 LC 1; D 530, E 490
Tuition: $180-$290 depending upon membership; no campus res
Courses: Art Appreciation, Ceramics, Courses for the Handicapped, Design, Digital Media, Drawing, Glass, Home School, Jewelry, Mixed Media, Painting, Photography, Printmaking, Sculpture, Silversmithing, †Video, Weaving
Children's Classes: Enrl 400; tuition $108-$220 for one sem; Courses—Varied
Summer School: Dir, Denise Lisiecki. Enrl 900; tuition $108-$285 June - Aug. Courses—Full schedule

KALAMAZOO VALLEY COMMUNITY COLLEGE, Center for New Media, 100 E Michigan Ave, Kalamazoo, MI 49007; PO Box 4070, Kalamazoo, MI 49003-4070. Tel 616-372-5000; Elec Mail kmatson@kvcc.edu; Internet Home Page Address: www.kvcc.edu; *Dept Chair Humanities* Martin Obed; *Coordr Technical Communs* Karen Matson; *Dir Fine Art* Arleigh Smyrnios; *Coordr Ctr for New Media* Linda Rzoska; *Instr* David Baker; *Instr* Ravi Akoor
Estab 1968; pub; D, E, & Sun; Scholarships; SC 12, LC, Post Assoc Degree Cert; D 300, E 100
Ent Req: Open Door
Degrees: AA, AS and Cert (1 yr)

Courses: 2-D Design, Advertising Design, Aesthetics, Art Appreciation, Art Education, Calligraphy, Ceramics, Commercial Art, Design, Drafting, Drawing, Electronic Publishing, Graphic Design, Illustration, Illustration Media, Illustrator, Lettering, Pagemaker, Painting, Photography, Photoshop, Teacher Training
Adult Hobby Classes: Courses—Same as regular session
Children's Classes: Courses—Ceramics
Summer School: Instr, Arleigh Smyrnios; Enrl 1125; tuition $43.25 per cr hr for 8 wk term. Courses—Ceramics, Design, Drawing, Watercolor, Electronic Publishing

WESTERN MICHIGAN UNIVERSITY, Frostic School of Art, R2110 Richmond Center for Visual Arts, 1903 West Michigan Ave Kalamazoo, MI 49008-5213. Tel 269-387-2436; Fax 269-387-2477; Internet Home Page Address: www.wmich.edu/art; *Dir* Tricia Hennessy; *Foundation Area Coordr Sculpture* Karen Bondarchuk; *Art Educ Area Coordr* Bill Charland; *Digital Media Photog Area Coordr* William Davis; *Painting Area Coordr* Dick dePeaux; *Jewelry/Metals Area Coordr* Caroline Gore; *Ceramics Area Coordr* Ed Harkness; *Art History Area Coordr* Joyce Kubiski; *Art Appreciation* Al LaVergne; *Printing Area Coordr* Nichole Maury; *Art Edu* Christina Chin; *Art Appreciation* Cut Crotchett; *Art History* Ancrew Hennlich; *Foundation* Jim Hopfensperger; *Graphic Design* Nicholas Kwler; *Graphic Design* Ryan Lewis; *Photo/Intermedia* Adriane Little; *Photo/Intermedia* Ginger Owen; *Art Appreciation* Ginger Solomon; *Graphic Design* Leon Sun; *Painting* Vince Torano; *Art History* Mary-Louise Totton; *Printmaking* Patricia Villalelobos
Estab 1904, dept estab 1939; Maintains a nonprofit art gallery: Albertine Monroe-Brown Gallery, Rose Netzorg & James Wilfrid Kerr Gallery, Robert & Eleanor DeVries Gallery, Richmond Center for Visual Arts; FT 22; pub; D & E; Scholarships; SC 60, LC 9, GC 8; non-maj 400, maj 430, grad 22
Activities: Schls offered
Ent Req: HS dipl, ACT
Degrees: BA, BS & BFA 4 yrs, MA - Art Education
Tuition: Res—undergrad $353-385 per cr hr, grad $510 per cr hr; nonres—undergrad $793-858 per cr hr, grad $1,024 per cr hr; campus res—room & board $8,000
Courses: Art Appreciation, †Art Education, †Art History, †Ceramics, †Drawing, †Graphic Design, †Jewelry/Metals, †Painting, †Photography/Intermedia, †Printmaking, †Sculpture

LANSING

LANSING COMMUNITY COLLEGE, Visual Arts & Media Dept, PO Box 40010, Lansing, MI 48901-7210; 315 N Grand Ave, Lansing, MI 48933-1213. Tel 517-483-1476; Fax 517-483-1050; Internet Home Page Address: www.lcc.edu; *Prof* Constance Peterson, BS; *Prof* Sharon Wood, MFA; *Prof* Ike Lea; *Prof* Fred Clark, MFA; *Prof* Brian Bishop, MFA; *Prof* Susie Stanley, BA; *Prof* Jim Redding, MA
Estab 1957; FT & PT 40; pub; D & E, weekends - online; Scholarships; SC 80, LC 10; D 758, E 506, non-maj 400, maj 560, others 304
Ent Req: HS dipl
Degrees: AA 2 yrs
Courses: Advertising Design, Commercial Art, †Computer Graphics Animation, †Computer Graphics Web Design, †Conceptual Art, Design, †Digital Effects, Drawing, †Film, †Graphic Design, Illustration, †Multimedia, Painting, †Photography, Printmaking, †Sequential Art, Typography
Adult Hobby Classes: Enrl 60; duration 16 wks. Courses— Watercolor, Matting & Framing, Photography, Photoshop
Summer School: Dir, Mary Cusack. Enrl 250. Courses—Same as Fall & Spring sem

LIVONIA

MADONNA UNIVERSITY, College of Arts & Humanities, 36600 Schoolcraft Rd, Livonia, MI 48150-1176. Tel 734-432-5300; Elec Mail dsemivan@madonna.edu; Internet Home Page Address: www.madonna.edu; *Chmn Art Dept* Douglas Semivan, MFA; *Instr Visual Arts Educ* G Aseneth Andrews, MA; *Instr Art History* Ralph F Glenn, MA; *Instr Visual Arts Educ* Melissa Liford, MA; *Instr Art History* Jeanne Moore, MA; *Instr Studio Art* Mary Rousseaux, MFA; *Instr Graphic Design* Robin Ward, BFA
Estab 1947; Maintain a nonprofit art gallery; on-campus shop where art supplies may be purchased; pvt; D & E; Scholarships; SC 17, LC 3; D 43, E 22, maj 17
Ent Req: HS dipl, portfolio
Degrees: AA 2 yrs, AB 4 yrs
Courses: †Advertising Design, Architecture, Art Appreciation, Art Education, Art History, Calligraphy, Ceramics, Collage, †Commercial Art, Computer Art, Design, Display, †Drawing, †Film, †Fine Arts, †Graphic Arts, †Graphic Design, History of Art & Architecture, Illustration, Lettering, Mixed Media, Painting, Photography, Printmaking, Sculpture, Teacher Training, Video
Adult Hobby Classes: Enrl 25; tuition $70 per 10 wk course. Courses—Painting
Summer School: Dir, Prof R F Glenn. Enrl 25 for 6-8 wks. Courses—Art History, Printmaking, Teacher Art Education

SCHOOLCRAFT COLLEGE, Dept of Art & Design, 18600 Haggerty Rd, Livonia, MI 48152-2696. Tel 734-462-4400; Fax 734-462-4538; *Prof* Stephen Wroble, MA; *Dean Art Dept* Jean Bonner
Estab 1964; pub; D & E; Scholarships, Fellowships; SC 13, LC 4; D 300, E 150, maj 100
Ent Req: Ent exam
Degrees: AAS & AA 2 yrs
Courses: Ceramics, Computer Aided Art & Design, Design, Drawing, Film, Graphic Arts, History of Art & Design, Jewelry, Painting, Photography, Printmaking, Sculpture
Adult Hobby Classes: Acrylic Painting, Ceramics, Drawing, Jewelry, Macrame, Photography, Stained Glass

Children's Classes: Enrl 40; tuition same as above. Courses—Talented & Gifted Program
Summer School: Design, Drawing, Printmaking, Watercolor

MARQUETTE

NORTHERN MICHIGAN UNIVERSITY, Dept of Art & Design, 1401 Presque Isle, Marquette, MI 49855. Tel 906-227-2194, 227-2279; Fax 906-227-2276; Elec Mail art@num.edu/department/ad_career.html; Internet Home Page Address: www.nmu.edu; *Prof* Thomas Cappuccio; *Prof* John D Hubbard; *Prof* William C Leete; *Prof* Diane D Kordich; *Prof* Dennis Staffne; *Prof* Dale Wedig; *Asst Prof* Jane Milkie; *Asst Prof* Sam Chung; *Head Dept* Michael J Cinelli; *Asst Prof* Derrick Christen; *Asst Prof* Steve Leuthold; *Asst Prof* Stephan Larson
Estab 1899, dept estab 1964: pub; D & E; Scholarships; SC 30, LC 20, GC 18
Ent Req: HS dipl, ACT
Degrees: BS, BFA, BA 4 yrs, MAE
Courses: †Art Education, †Art History, †Ceramics, Computer Graphics, †Drawing, Electronic Imaging, †Film, Graphic Design, Illustration, Industrial Design, Jewelry, Painting, Photography, Printmaking, Sculpture, Silversmithing, Video
Summer School: Dir, Michael J Cinelli. Enrl 15-20; 6 wk terms

MIDLAND

ALDEN B. DOW MUSEUM OF SCIENCE & ART, (Arts Midland Galleries & School) Alden B. Dow Museum School, 1801 W St Andrews, Midland, MI 48640. Tel 517-631-3250; Fax 517-631-7890; Elec Mail winslow@mcfta.org; Internet Home Page Address: www.mcfta.org; *Dir* B B Winslow; *Mus School Mgr* Armin Mersmann
Estab 1971; Maintains a non-profit art gallery & on-campus art supplies shop.; pvt; D & E; Scholarships; SC 12-20, LC 2; D & E 250
Courses: Aesthetics, Art Appreciation, Art History, Calligraphy, Ceramics, Collage, Conceptual Art, Constructions, Design, Drawing, History of Art & Architecture, Metalsmithing, Mixed Media, Museum Staff Training, Painting, Papermaking, Photography, Printmaking, Sculpture, Stained Glass, Textile Design, Weaving
Adult Hobby Classes: Enrl 200; tuition $85-$120 per sem
Children's Classes: Enrl 50; tuition $50-$65 per sem
Summer School: School Coordr Armin Mersmann

NORTHWOOD UNIVERSITY, Alden B Dow Creativity Center, 4000 Whiting Dr, Midland, MI 48640-2398. Tel 989-837-4478; Fax 989-837-4468: Elec Mail creativity@northwood.edu; Internet Home Page Address: www.northwood.edu/abd; *Exec Dir* Dr Grover B Proctor Jr; *Asst Dir* Christianna Schartow
Estab 1978; Pvt; Scholarships, Fellowships

MONROE

MONROE COUNTY COMMUNITY COLLEGE, Humanities Division, 1555 S Raisinville Rd, Monroe, MI 48161-9746. Tel 734-384-4153; Fax 734-457-6023; Elec Mail pdorcey@monroeccc.edu; Internet Home Page Address: www.monroeccc.edu; *Secy* Penny Dorcey-Naber; *Asst Prof Art* Theodore Vassar; *Asst Prof Art* Gary Wilson; *Adjunct Prof Art* Dan Stewart
Maintains a nonprofit art gallery; on-campus shop for purchase of art supplies ; FT 2; pub; D & E; Scholarships; SC 16, LC 5
Degrees: AFA offered
Tuition: Res—$73 per cr hr; nonres—$121-134 per cr hr
Courses: Art Appreciation, Art History, †Art for Elementary Teachers, Ceramics, Design, Drawing, †Film, †Graphic Arts, †Graphic Design, Illustration, †Mixed Media, Painting, Printmaking, †Sculpture, †Theatre Arts

MOUNT PLEASANT

CENTRAL MICHIGAN UNIVERSITY, Dept of Art, 163 Wightman Hall, Rm 132 Mount Pleasant, MI 48859. Tel 989-774-3025; Fax 989-774-2278; Internet Home Page Address: www.art.cmich.edu; *Chmn Dept* Al Wildey
Estab 1892; Maintain a nonprofit art gallery, CMU Art Gallery, Preston & Franklin, Mt Pleasant, MI 48859; FT 17, PT 2; pub; D & E; Scholarships, Fellowships; SC 81, LC 27; for univ 19,800
Ent Req: HS dipl
Degrees: BA, BFA & BAA 4 yrs
Courses: Aesthetics, Art Appreciation, Art Criticism, Art Education, Art History, Ceramics, Drawing, Fiber Design, Graphic Design, Painting, Photography, Printmaking, Sculpture

MUSKEGON

MUSKEGON COMMUNITY COLLEGE, Dept of Creative & Performing Arts, 221 S Quarterline Rd, Muskegon, MI 49442-1493. Tel 231-773-9131, Ext 324; Fax 231-777-0255; Elec Mail tim.norris@muskegoncc.edu; erin.hoffman@muskegoncc.edu; Internet Home Page Address: www.muskegoncc.edu; *Dept Chmn* Sheila Wahamaki; *Prog Coordr* Tim Norris; *Prog Coordr* Erin Hoffman
Estab 1926; Maintain nonprofit art gallery, Overbrook Art Gallery; pub; D & E; Scholarships; SC 18, LC 6; D 280, E 60
Ent Req: HS dipl
Degrees: AA 2 yrs
Courses: †Art Appreciation, Art Education, Art History, Beginning Art, Ceramics, Design, Drawing, Painting, Printmaking, Sculpture

OLIVET

OLIVET COLLEGE, Art Dept, 320 S Main St, Olivet, MI 49076-9406. Tel 616-749-7000; *Chmn* Gary Wertheimer, MFA; *Prof* Donald Rowe; *Instr* Susan Rowe, MFA
Estab 1844, dept estab 1870; pvt; D & E; Scholarships; SC 17, LC 8, GC 10; D 610, non-maj 50, maj 20, grad 2
Ent Req: HS dipl
Degrees: BS and BM 4 yrs, MA 1 yr
Courses: Art History, †Commercial Art, †Design, †Drawing, †Painting, †Printmaking, †Sculpture

PETOSKEY

NORTH CENTRAL MICHIGAN COLLEGE, Art Dept, 1515 Howard St, Petoskey, MI 49770-8740. Tel 231-348-6651, 348-6600; Fax 231-348-6628; *Dept Contact* Shanna Robinson, MFA; *Instr* Andrea Gerring; *Instr* Rosemary Gould; *Instr* Richard Cunningham; *Instr* Dawn Swaim; *Instr* Joel Stoppel; *Instr* Bonnie Hill
Art supplies sold at on-campus store ; D & E ; SC & LC
Degrees: AA offered
Courses: Art Education, Art History, †Ceramics, Design, Drawing, †Graphic Arts, Graphic Design, Painting, Photography, Printmaking, Sculpture, †Silversmithing, Stained Glass, †Textile Design, †Weaving
Adult Hobby Classes: Courses offered
Summer School: Courses offered

PONTIAC

CREATIVE ART CENTER-NORTH OAKLAND COUNTY, 47 Williams St, Pontiac, MI 48341-1759. Tel 248-333-7849; Fax 248-333-7841; Elec Mail createpont@aol.com; Internet Home Page Address: www.pontiac.mi.us/cac; *Exec Dir* Angela Petroff
Open Tues - Sat 10 AM - 5 PM, cl holidays; No admis fee; Estab 1964 to present the best in exhibitions, educational activities & community art outreach; non-profit community arts center serving adults & children with ongoing exhibits; Average Annual Attendance: 10,000; Mem: 160; dues organizations $50, family $40, general $35, artists & seniors $20; ann meeting in Apr; pub; D, E & Weekends; Scholarships; SC 15; 200
Income: Financed by endowment, mem, city & state appropriation, trust funds, Mich Council for the Arts
Activities: Classes for adults & children; lects open to pub; 6 vis lectrs per year; concerts; exten prog to local schools
Ent Req: Open enrollment
Tuition: Varies; no campus res
Courses: Ceramics, Dance, Drawing, Painting, Photography, Sculpture, Theatre Arts
Adult Hobby Classes: Tuition $45-$150
Children's Classes: Courses—Dance, Drawing, Music, Painting, Sculpture
Summer School: Three wk session. Courses—Creative Writing, Dance, Drama, Visual Arts

PORT HURON

SAINT CLAIR COUNTY COMMUNITY COLLEGE, Jack R Hennesey Art Dept, 323 Erie St, Port Huron, MI 48060-3812; PO Box 5015, Port Huron, MI 48061-5015. Tel 810-984-3881; *VPres Acad Svcs* Anita Gliniecki; *Dept Chmn* David Korff; *Advertising Design Faculty* John Henry; *Theater* Nancy Osborn
Estab 1923; pub; D & E; Scholarships; SC 30, LC 5; D 60
Ent Req: HS dipl
Degrees: AA and AAS 2 yrs
Courses: †Advertising Design, Art Appreciation, Art Education, Art History, Calligraphy, †Commercial Art, Costume Design & Construction, †Drafting, Drawing, Mixed Media, Painting, Photography, †Pottery, Printmaking, Sculpture, Stage Design, †Theatre Arts, Weaving
Adult Hobby Classes: Courses—Drawing, Painting, Pottery

ROCHESTER

OAKLAND UNIVERSITY, Dept of Art & Art History, 2200 N Squirrel Rd, Rochester, MI 48309-4402; Oakland Univ College of Arts & Sciences, 310 Wilson Hall Rochester, MI 48309-4401. Tel 248-370-3375; Fax 248-370-3375; Elec Mail eis@oakland.edu; Internet Home Page Address: www2.oakland.edu/art-history/; *Chmn Dept & Spec Instr* Andrea Eis; *Prof* Susan Wood, PhD; *Prof* Janice Schimmelman, PhD; *Assoc Prof* Claude Baillargeon, PhD; *Assoc Prof* Vagner M Whitehead, MFA; *Asst Prof* John Corso, PhD; *Asst Prof* Susan Evans, MFA; *Asst Prof* Taylor Hokanson, MFA; *Asst Prof* Shuishan Yu, PhD; *Asst Prof* Cody VanderKaay, MFA; *Adjunct Asst Prof* Lynn G Fausone, MFA; *Spec Instr* Sally S Tardella; *Gallery Dir & Spec Instr* Stephen Goody, MFA; *Assoc Prof* Tamara Jhashi, PhD
Estab 1957, dept estab 1960; Maintains Oakland Univ Art Gallery & libr within dept; FT & PT 28; pub; D & E; Scholarships; SC 37, LC 43; Maj 228
Ent Req: HS dipl
Degrees: BA 4 yrs
Courses: †Art History, †Studio Art

SCOTTVILLE

WEST SHORE COMMUNITY COLLEGE, Division of Humanities & Fine Arts, 3000 N Stiles Rd, Scottville, MI 49454-9791. Tel 231-845-6211; Internet Home Page Address: www.westshore.cc.mi.us; *Chmn* Sharon Bloom; *Assoc Prof* Rebecca Mott, MA; *Instr* Teresa Soles, MA; *Instr* Judy Peters, BA

Estab 1965; PT 3, FT 7; Pub; D & E; Scholarships; SC 18, LC 10; non-maj 250, maj 10
Ent Req: HS dipl
Degrees: AA 2 yrs
Courses: †Art History, Ceramics, Drafting, Drawing, Graphic Design, Mixed Media, Painting, Photography, Printmaking, Sculpture, Stage Design, †Theatre Arts
Adult Hobby Classes: Art Workshops & Studio, Crafts, Photography
Summer School: Painting, Pottery

SOUTHFIELD

LAWRENCE TECHNOLOGICAL UNIVERSITY, College of Architecture, 21000 W Ten Mile Rd, Southfield, MI 48075-1051. Tel 248-204-2800; Fax 248-204-2900; Internet Home Page Address: www.ltu.edu; *Asst Dean* Betty Lee Seydler-Hepworth; *Dean* Neville H Clouten
Estab 1932; Pvt; D&E
Degrees: BArchit, BA(Archit Illustration), BS(Archit), BS(Interior Archit)
Courses: †Architecture, †Interior Architecture
Summer School: Dir, Harold Linton. Enrl 75; tuition $250. Courses—Pre-College Architecture

SPRING ARBOR

SPRING ARBOR COLLEGE, Art Dept, 106 E Main St, Sta 19 Spring Arbor, MI 49283-9701. Tel 517-750-1200, Ext 1364; Internet Home Page Address: www.arbor.edu; *Div Dir Music Arts* Bill Bippes, MFA; *Asst Prof* Roger Valand, MFA; *Dir* Paul Wolber, MA
Estab 1873, dept estab 1971; pvt den; D & E; Scholarships; SC 17, LC 6; D 200, E 20, non-maj 20, maj 32
Ent Req: HS dipl
Degrees: AA(Commercial) 2 yrs, BA 4 yrs
Courses: †Advertising Design, Commercial Art, †Drawing, †Graphic Arts, †Illustration, †Painting, †Printmaking, †Sculpture, †Teacher Training

TRAVERSE CITY

NORTHWESTERN MICHIGAN COLLEGE, Art Dept, 1701 E Front St, Traverse City, MI 49686-3016. Tel 231-922-1325; Fax 231-922-1696; Internet Home Page Address: www.nmc.edu; *Chmn Dept* Mike Torre, MA; *Instr* Jill Hinds, BFA; *Art Historian* Jackie Shinners, MFA
Estab 1951, dept estab 1957; FT 4, PT 12; pub; D & E; Scholarships; SC 40, LC 4; non-maj 400, maj 75
Ent Req: HS dipl
Degrees: AA 2 yrs, AAS
Courses: Advertising Design, Art Education, Art History, Commercial Art, Drawing, Goldsmithing, Graphic Arts, Graphic Design, Illustration, Jewelry, Lettering, Life Drawing, Painting, Perspective, Photography, Pottery, Printmaking, Publication Design, Reproduction Techniques, Silversmithing, Typography·
Adult Hobby Classes: Enrl 50; tuition $23. Courses - Drawing, Life Drawing, Painting, Pottery, Printmaking
Summer School: Dir, Stephen Ballance. Enrl 100 tuition $53 per billing hr in-district, $87.75 per billing hr other for 8 week terms. Courses—drawing, Photography, Pottery

TWIN LAKE

BLUE LAKE FINE ARTS CAMP, Art Dept, 300 E Crystal Lake Rd, Twin Lake, MI 49457-9499. Tel 231-894-1966; Fax 231-893-5120; Internet Home Page Address: www.bluelake.org; *Chmn* Carol Tice; *Exec Asst* Lisa Martin
Estab 1966; Pub; Scholarships
Courses: 2D-3D, Ceramics, Drawing, Fibre Arts, Illustration, Painting, Sculpture, Weaving, Wheel-Work
Adult Hobby Classes: Call for information
Summer School: Summer prog for middle and high school students

UNIVERSITY CENTER

DELTA COLLEGE, Art Dept, 1961 Delta Rd University Center, MI 48710. Tel 517-686-9000, Ext 9101; *Assoc Prof & Dept Chmn* Gina Dominique, MFA; *Prof* Randal Crawford, MFA; *Instr* Michael Glowacki; *Instr* Andrew Rieder
Estab 1960; Maintains a nonprofit gallery, Delta Galleria 1961 Delta Rd University Center MI 48710; art collection in main library; art supplies sold on campus bookstore; pub; D & E, Off Campus Centers; Scholarships; SC 21, LC 5; Non-maj 1000, Maj 150
Ent Req: open door policy
Degrees: AFA 2 yrs
Courses: Art Education, Art History, Ceramics, Design, Digital Imaging, Drawing, Graphic Arts, Graphic Design, Painting, Photography, Printmaking, Sculpture

SAGINAW VALLEY STATE UNIVERSITY, Dept of Art & Design, 7400 Bay Rd, University Center, MI 48710-0001. Tel 517-790-4390; Elec Mail mzivich@svsu.edu; *Prof* Matthew Zivich, MFA; *Prof* Barron Hirsch, MFA; *Chmn Dept, Prof* Hideki Kihata, MFA; *Adjunct Instr* Sara B Clark, MFA; *Assoc Prof* Rodney Nowosielski, MFA; *Asst Prof* Shaun Bangert; *Asst Prof* Mike Mosher; *Instr* David Littell; *Instr* Craig Prime; *Instr* Terry Basmadjian; *Instr* Marlene Pellcrito
Estab 1960, dept estab 1968; Maintain nonprofit art gallery; University Gallery & Marshall Fredericks Sculpture Gallery; Pub; D & E; Scholarships; SC approx 20, LC approx 15; D 200, E 50, maj 65
Ent Req: HS dipl
Degrees: BA(Art), BFA 4 yrs or less

Courses: Advertising Design, Art Education, Art History, Ceramics, Commercial Art, Design, Drafting, Drawing, Graphic Arts, Graphic Design, Handicrafts, Illustration, Lettering, Occupational Therapy, Painting, Photography, Printmaking, Sculpture, Teacher Training, Theatre Arts
Summer School: Courses vary

WARREN

MACOMB COMMUNITY COLLEGE, Art Dept, 14500 E 12 Mile Rd, Division of Humanities Warren, MI 48088-3870. Tel 810-445-7000, 445-7354; *Prof* James Pallas, MFA; *Prof* David Barr, MA
Estab 1960, dept estab 1965; pvt; D & E; Scholarships; SC 14, LC 6
Ent Req: HS dipl, ent exam
Degrees: AA 2 yrs
Courses: Art History, Ceramics, Design, Drawing, Painting, Photography, Sculpture

YPSILANTI

EASTERN MICHIGAN UNIVERSITY, Dept of Art, 114 Ford Hall, Ypsilanti, MI 48197-2251. Tel 734-487-1268, 487-0192; Fax 734-481-1095; Internet Home Page Address: www.art.acad.emich.edu; *Head Dept* Tom Venner
Estab 1849, dept estab 1901; pub; D & E; Scholarships; SC 55, LC 18; undergrad maj 420, non-maj 800, grad 100
Ent Req: HS dipl
Degrees: BA(Art History), BFA(Studio Art), BS & BA(Art Educ) 4 yrs, MA(Art Educ), MA(Studio) & MFA 2 yrs
Courses: Art Education, †Art History, †Ceramics, †Drawing, †Graphic Design, †Jewelry, †Painting, †Photography, †Printmaking, †Sculpture, †Textile Design
Children's Classes: Enrl 40; tuition $35 for 8-10 classes offered on Sat for Art talented & gifted
Summer School: Term of 7 1/2 wks, major & non-major courses

MINNESOTA

BEMIDJI

BEMIDJI STATE UNIVERSITY, Visual Arts Dept, 1500 Birchmont Dr, Bemidji, MN 56601. Tel 218-755-3735; Fax 218-755-4406; Internet Home Page Address: www.bemidjistate.edu; *Chmn* MaryAnn Papanek-Miller; *Prof* Kyle Crocker PhD; *Asst Prof* John Holden, MFA; *Asst Prof* Steve Sundahl, MFA; *Asst Prof* Jaineth Skinner, MFA; *Asst Prof* Carol Struve, MFA
Estab 1918; pub; D & E; Scholarships; SC 54, LC 17, GC individual study
Ent Req: HS dipl, ACT, SAT, PSAT, or SCAT
Degrees: BA, BS(Teaching) and BS(Tech Illustration, Commercial Design), BFA
Courses: Advertising Design, Art Appreciation, Art Education, Art History, Ceramics, Crafts, Design, Drawing, Graphic Arts, Graphic Design, Jewelry, Painting, Printmaking, Sculpture, Teacher Training
Adult Hobby Classes: Tuition res—$46.70 per qtr hr. Courses—Graphic Design, Elementary Art Concepts & Methods, Secondary Art Concepts & Methods
Summer School: Dir, M Kaul. Enrl 250; tuition res—undergrad $46.70 per qtr hr, nonres—undergrad $101.40 per qtr hr. Courses—Art, Ceramics, History, Metals, Painting, Printmaking, 3-D Design

BLOOMINGTON

NORMANDALE COMMUNITY COLLEGE, Art Dept, 9700 France Ave S, Bloomington, MN 55431-4399. Tel 952-487-8143; Fax 952-487-8230; Internet Home Page Address: www.normandale.mncu.edu; *Instr* D R Peterson, BFA; *Instr* Marilyn Wood, MFA; *Art Coordr* Martha Wittstruck
Estab 1969; Pub; D&E
Degrees: AA
Courses: Art Appreciation, Art History, Ceramics, Design, Drawing, Jewelry, Painting, Photography, Sculpture
Adult Hobby Classes: Courses offered
Summer School: Courses offered

BROOKLYN PARK

NORTH HENNEPIN COMMUNITY COLLEGE, Art Dept, 7411 85th Ave N, Brooklyn Park, MN 55445-2231. Tel 763-424-0702; Fax 763-493-0568; Elec Mail lance.kiland@nhcc.edu; Internet Home Page Address: www.nhcc.edu; *Instr* Lance Kiland; *Instr* Will Agar; *Instr* David Hebb; *Instr* Susan MacDonald; *Instr* Dan Mason; *Instr* Jane Bassuk; *Instr* Jerry Mathiason; *Instr* Steve Pauley
Estab 1964; Non-profit gallery: Joseph F Gazzuolo Gallery, North Hennepin Community College, 7411 85th Ave N Brooklyn, MN 55445; Art & Architecture Library: Learning Media Center.; FT 6; pub; D, E & Wknd; Scholarships; SC 15, LC 4; Total college enrollment: 8,751
Ent Req: HS dipl. ent exam
Degrees: AA, AS & AAS 2 yr
Courses: 2-D & 3-D Design, Art History, Contemporary Crafts, Digital Photography, Drawing, Graphic Design, Illustration, Introduction to Art, Jewelry, Metalsmithing, Painting, Photography, Printmaking, Typography, Video, Visual Communications
Adult Hobby Classes: Enrl 28. Courses—Drawing, Jewelry, Painting, Quilt Making
Children's Classes: Enrl 20. Courses—Art Theatre, Computer, Language, Photography, Sports

Summer School: Enrl 28; tuition $234. Courses—Drawing, Introduction of Art, Photography

COLLEGEVILLE

SAINT JOHN'S UNIVERSITY, Art Dept, Box 2000, Collegeville, MN 56321. Tel 320-363-2011, 363-5036; Internet Home Page Address: www.csbsju.edu/; *Assoc Prof* James Hendershot, MFA; *Assoc Prof* Bro Alan Reed, MFA; *Assoc Prof* Sr Baulu Kuan, MFA; *Asst Prof* Andrea Shaker, MFA; *Prof* Dennis Frandrup, MFA; *Lectr* Susan Hendershot, MFA; *Instr* Anne Salisbury, PhD; *Lectr* James Rolle, BFA; *Lectr* Robert Wilde, MA
Estab 1856, joint studies with College of Saint Benedict; pvt; Scholarships; SC 20, LC 15
Ent Req: HS dipl
Degrees: BA, BS
Courses: Art History, Ceramics, Drawing, Jewelry, Painting, Photography, Printmaking, Sculpture
Adult Hobby Classes: Occasional adult education classes

COON RAPIDS

ANOKA RAMSEY COMMUNITY COLLEGE, Art Dept, 11200 Mississippi Blvd NW, Coon Rapids, MN 55433-3499. Tel 763-427-2600; Fax 612-422-3341; Internet Home Page Address: www.an.cc.mm.us; *Dean* Brenda Robert; *Instr* Robert E Toensing, MFA
Estab 1970; Pub; D&E; Scholarships
Degrees: AA offered
Courses: Advertising Design, Art Appreciation, Art Education, Ceramics, Design, Drawing, Film, Glassblowing, Jewelry, Painting, Photography, Sculpture

DULUTH

UNIVERSITY OF MINNESOTA, DULUTH, Art Dept, 10 University Dr, 317 Humanities Bldg Duluth, MN 55812-2403. Tel 218-726-8225, 800-232-1339; Fax 218-726-6532; Elec Mail art@ub.d.umn.edu; Internet Home Page Address: www.d.umn.edu/art/; *Prof* Thomas F Hedin PhD, MFA; *Prof* Dean R Lettenstrom, MFA; *Assoc Prof* Robyn Roslak PhD, MA; *Prof* James Klueg, MFA; *Asst Prof* Robert Repinski, MFA; *Assoc Prof* Janice Kmetz, MFA; *Prof, Head Dept* Gloria D Brush, MFA; *Assoc Prof* Alyce Coker; *Assoc Prof* Sarah Bauer, MFA; *Asst Prof* Catherine Ishino, MFA; *Asst Prof* Alison Aune, PhD; *Asst Prof* Philip Choo; *Asst Prof* Eun-Kyung Suh
B; Pub; D & E; Scholarships, Fellowships; SC 30, LC 6, GC 10; D 200, E 50, maj 414, grad 3
Ent Req: HS dipl, HS rank & ACT req, col prep req
Degrees: BFA, BA 4 yrs, MFA in Graphic Design
Courses: †2D & 3D Digital Studios, Art Appreciation, Art Education, Art History, †Art in Technologies, Ceramics, Design, Drawing, Fibers, Graphic Design, †History of Art, †Interactive Design, Intermedia, Jewelry, Mixed Media, †Motion Graphics, Museum Staff Training, Painting, Photography, Printmaking, Sculpture, Silversmithing, †Studio Major, Teacher Training, †Typography, Weaving
Adult Hobby Classes: 10 wk courses. Courses—Studio Arts, Graphic Design
Summer School: Dir, Haren Heikel. 5 wk summer sessions. Courses—Art Appreciation, Art Education, Ceramics, Drawing, Graphic Design, Jewelry & Metals, Painting, Photography

ELY

VERMILION COMMUNITY COLLEGE, Art Dept, 1900 E Camp St, Ely, MN 55731-1996. Tel 218-365-7273; Internet Home Page Address: www.vcc.edu; WATS 800-657-3608; *Instr* Chris Koivisto
Estab 1922, dept estab 1964; pub; D & E; SC 13, LC 5; D 63, E 15, non-maj 65, maj 13
Ent Req: HS dipl
Degrees: AA 2 yr
Courses: Art Appreciation, Art History, Ceramics, Drawing, Painting, Sculpture
Adult Hobby Classes: $105 per cr. Courses—Drawing, Introduction, Painting, Ceramics

FERGUS FALLS

LUTHERAN BRETHREN SCHOOLS, Art Dept, 815 W Vernon Ave, Fergus Falls, MN 56537-2676. Tel 218-739-3371, 739-3376; *Head Dept* Gaylen Peterson
Estab 1900; den; D & E; SC 1, LC 1; D 20
Ent Req: HS dipl, questionnaire
Courses: Drawing

GRAND MARAIS

GRAND MARAIS ART COLONY, PO Box 626, Grand Marais, MN 55604-0626. Tel 218-387-1284; Fax 218-387-1395; Elec Mail arts@boreal.org; Internet Home Page Address: grandmaraisartcolony.org; *Faculty* Kelly Dupre; *Faculty* Hazel Belvo; *Faculty* Sharon Frykman; *Faculty* Steve Frykman; *Faculty* Naomi Hart; *Faculty* Karen Knutson; *Faculty* Susan Frame; *Instr* Joann Krause; *Instr* Jeanne Larson; *Faculty* Michaelin Otis
Estab 1947; D & E; Scholarships; SC 4; D 200
Ent Req: Open
Courses: Drawing, Painting, Pastels, Personal Creativity
Adult Hobby Classes: Enrl 200; tuition same as above; 15 wks of 1 - 2 wk workshops. Courses—Drawing, Painting
Children's Classes: Enrl 50; tuition $70 for 1 full wk. Courses—Drawing, Mixed Media, Painting

Summer School: Dir, Jay Andersen. Courses—Drawing, Painting, Watercolor

HIBBING

HIBBING COMMUNITY COLLEGE, Art Dept, 1515 E 25th St, Hibbing, MN 55746-3300. Tel 218-262-6700; Internet Home Page Address: www.hcc.mnscu.edu; *Instr* Theresa Chudzik; *Instr* Bill Goodman
Pub; D&E; Scholarships
Degrees: AA & AAS 2 yrs
Courses: Art Appreciation, Ceramics, Design, Drawing, Introduction to Theatre, Painting, Photography, Sculpture, Stage Craft

MANKATO

BETHANY LUTHERAN COLLEGE, Art Dept, 700 Luther Dr, Mankato, MN 56001-6163. Tel 507-344-7000; Fax 507-344-7376; Internet Home Page Address: www.blc.edu; *Head of Dept* William Bukowski
Estab 1927, dept estab 1960; FT 2, PT 3; den; D; Scholarships; SC 2, LC 2; D 36, non-maj 40, maj 18
Ent Req: HS dipl, ACT
Degrees: AA 2 yr, dipl
Courses: †3-D Design, Art Appreciation, Art History, Art Structure, Ceramics, †Computer Graphics, Design, Drawing, Painting, †Web Design
Summer School: Dir, William Bukowski. Enrl 20; tuition $130 for 2 wk - 1 1/2 days

MANKATO STATE UNIVERSITY, Art Dept, PO Box 8400, MSU Box 42 Mankato, MN 56002-8400. Tel 507-389-6412; Internet Home Page Address: www.mankato.ms.us.edu; WATS 507-389-5887; *Chmn* Roy Strassberg
Estab 1868, dept estab 1938; FT 15; pub; D & E; Scholarships; SC 42, LC 28, GC 54; D 3000 (total), E 500, non-maj 1000, maj 200, grad 25
Ent Req: HS dipl
Degrees: BA, BFA and BS 4 yr, MA and MS 1-1 1/2 yr
Courses: Art Education, Art History, Ceramics, Drawing, Fibers, Graphic Arts, Painting, Photography, Printmaking, Sculpture
Summer School: Tuition same as above

MINNEAPOLIS

ART INSTRUCTION SCHOOLS, Education Dept, 3400 Technology Dr., Minneapolis, MN 55418. Tel 612-362-5060; Elec Mail info@artists-ais.com; Internet Home Page Address: www.artists-ais.edu; *Dir* Judith Turner
Estab 1914; pvt
Courses: Fundamentals of Art and Specialized Art
Adult Hobby Classes: Enrl 5000; tuition $1495 - $2000. Courses—Fundamentals of Art, Specialized Art

AUGSBURG COLLEGE, Art Dept, 2211 Riverside Ave, Minneapolis, MN 55454-1351. Tel 612-330-1285; Fax 612-330-1649; Elec Mail anderso3@augsburg.edu; *Chmn* Kristin Anderson
Estab 1869, dept estab 1960; FT 3, PT 4; den; D & E; Scholarships; SC 15, LC 6; D 200, maj 60, others 1500
Ent Req: HS dipl
Degrees: BA 4 yrs
Tuition: $7235 per sem; campus res—room & board $4022
Courses: Art Education, Art History, Calligraphy, Ceramics, Communications Design, Drawing, Environmental Design, Handicrafts, History of Art & Architecture, Painting, Photography, Sculpture, Stage Design, Teacher Training, Theatre Arts
Adult Hobby Classes: Enrl 1200; tuition $780 per course. Courses—Art History, Calligraphy, Ceramics, Communications Design, Drawing, Environmental Design, Painting, Publication Design
Summer School: Enrl 350; term of six or four wks beginning end of May

MINNEAPOLIS COLLEGE OF ART & DESIGN, 2501 Stevens Ave S, Minneapolis, MN 55404-4347. Tel 612-874-3700, 874-3754; Fax 612-874-3701; Elec Mail admissions@mcad.edu; Internet Home Page Address: www.mcad.edu; *Chair Design Dept* Bernard Canniffe; *Prof Design Dept* Tom Garrett; *Prof* Jan Jancourt; *Prof* Elizabeth Erickson; *Prof* Rebecca Alm
Estab 1886; Maintains library; Morrison Bldg Rm 127, 2501 Stevens Ave S, Minneapolis, MN 55404; FT 32, PT 609; pvt; D; Scholarships; SC 82, LC 60, GC 3; D 650, E 325, maj 620, grad 40
Ent Req: HS dipl or GED
Degrees: BS & BFA 4 yr, MFA
Tuition: $21,300 annual tuition off campus, $25,000 annual tuition on campus
Courses: †Advertising Design, †Animation, †Comic Art, Computer Graphics, †Design Theory & Methods, †Drawing, †Film, †Furniture Design, †Graphic Arts, †Graphic Design, †Illustration, †Interactive Media, Liberal Arts, Packaging & Product Design, †Painting, †Photography, †Printmaking, Screen Printing, †Sculpture, Video, Web & Multimedia
Adult Hobby Classes: Continuing Studies
Children's Classes: Courses offered
Summer School: Dir of Continuing Studies, cost & enrollment varies. Professional, youth & enrichment courses.

UNIVERSITY OF MINNESOTA, MINNEAPOLIS, Art History, 271 19th Ave S, 338 Heller Hall Minneapolis, MN 55455-0121. Tel 612-624-4500; Fax 612-626-8679; Elec Mail arthist@umn.edu; Internet Home Page Address: www.arthist.umn.edu; *Prof* Frederick Asher, PhD; *Prof* Gabriel P Weisberg, PhD; *Prof* Frederick A Cooper; *Prof* Sheila J McNally, PhD; *Prof* Karal Ann Marling, PhD; *Prof* Robert Poor, PhD; *Assoc Prof* John Steyaert, PhD; *Prof* Robert Silberman, PhD; *Prof* Catherine Asher, PhD; *Assoc Prof* Jane Blocker, PhD; *Asst Prof* Michael Gaudio; *Chmn & Prof* Steven Ostrow, PhD

An on-campus shop where art supplies may be purchased; Pub; D & E; Scholarships, Fellowships; LC 28, GC 59; maj 68, grad 52
Ent Req: HS dipl, ent exam, GRE required for grad school
Degrees: BA 4 yrs, MA 2 yrs, PhD
Courses: †Art History, †Film, †History of Art & Archaeology
Adult Hobby Classes: Enrl 200; sem system. Courses—Ancient & Modern Art History, Asian Art History
Summer School: Dir, Steven Ostrow.
—Dept of Art, 405 21st Ave S, Minneapolis, MN 55455. Tel 612-625-8096; Fax 612-625-7881; Elec Mail artdept@umn.edu; Internet Home Page Address: artdept.umn.edu; *Chmn Dept* Clarence Morgan, MFA; *Prof* Karl Bethke, MFA; *Prof* Curtis Hoard, MFA; *Prof* Thomas Rose, MA; *Prof* Mary Diane Katsiaficas, MFA; *Assoc Prof* Thomas Cowette, BFA; *Assoc Prof* David Feinberg, MFA; *Assoc Prof* Gary Hallman, MFA; *Assoc Prof* Lynn Gray, MFA; *Assoc Prof* James Henkel, MFA; *Assoc Prof* Guy Baldwin, MFA; *Assoc Prof* Jerald Krepps, MFA; *Assoc Prof* Thomas Lane, MFA; *Assoc Prof* Susan Lucey, MFA; *Assoc Prof* Marjorie Franklin, MFA; *Assoc Prof* Joyce Lyon, MFA; *Assoc Prof* Alexis Kuhr, MFA; *Assoc Prof* Wayne Potratz, MA; *Asst Prof* Christine Arle Baumler, MFA; *Asst Prof* Margaret Bohls, MFA; *Asst Prof* Lynn Lukkas, MFA; *Asst Prof* Ryuta Wakajima, MFA
Estab 1851, fine arts estab 1939; pub; D & E; Scholarships; SC 39, LC 7; D 1000, E 560, maj 325, grad 55
Ent Req: HS dipl, PSAT, ACT
Degrees: BA, BFA, MFA
Courses: Ceramics, Critical Theory, Drawing, Electronic Art, Neon, Painting, Papermaking, Photography, Printmaking, Sculpture, Silkscreening
Adult Hobby Classes: Courses—same as above
Children's Classes: Summers Honors College for HS students
Summer School: Dir, Carol Ann Dickinson. Courses—same as above
—Split Rock Arts Program, 1420 Eckles Ave, 360 Coffey Hall St Paul, MN 55108-1030. Tel 612-624-4000; Fax 612-624-6210; Elec Mail splitrockarts@umn.edu; Internet Home Page Address: www.cce.umn.edu/splitrockarts; *Dir* Andrea Gilats; *Prog Assoc* Vivien Oja
Estab 1984; Scholarships; Enrl 550; Courses: Creativity Enhancement, Creative Writing, Fine Crafts, Visual Arts
Publications: Split Rock Arts Program catalog, annually
Tuition: $540 plus; campus res—$180-$516 per wk
Courses: Basketry, Beadworking, Bookmaking, †Ceramics, †Collage, Creativity Enhancement Fabric Art, †Design, †Drawing, †Fashion Arts, †Handicrafts, †Jewelry, †Mixed Media, †Painting, †Printmaking, Quiltmaking, †Sculpture, †Textile Design, †Weaving

MOORHEAD

CONCORDIA COLLEGE, Art Dept, 901 S Eighth, Moorhead, MN 56562. Tel 218-299-4623; Fax 218-299-4256, 299-3947; *Assoc Prof* David Boggs, MFA; *Asst Prof* Heidi Allen, MFA; *Asst Prof* Susan Pierson Ellingson PhD, MFA; *Instr* Barbara Anderson, MA; *Instr* John Borge, BA; *Prof* Duane Mickelson, MFA; *Asst Prof* Ross Hilgers; *Chair* Robert Meadows Rogers, PhD
Estab 1891; den; D&E; Scholarships; SC 10, LC 5; D 300, maj 80, total 2900
Ent Req: HS dipl, character references
Degrees: BA and BM 4 yrs, independent studio work, work-study prog and special studies
Courses: 2-D Foundations, 3-D Foundations, †Art Education, †Art History, Ceramics, Drawing, Figure Drawing, Graphic Design, Macintosh Computer Design Lab, Painting, Photography, Printmaking, Sculpture, Senior Project, †Studio Art
Summer School: Enrl 40; tuition $1200 for term of 4 wks beginning May 15 & June 12. Courses—Art Education, Art History, Drawing, Graphic Design, Painting, Printmaking, Travel Seminar, 2-D Foundation

MINNESOTA STATE UNIVERSITY-MOORHEAD, (Moorhead State University) Dept of Art & Design, 1104 7th Ave S, Dille Center for the Arts Moorhead, MN 56563-0001. Tel 218-477-2151; 477-2152; Fax 218-477-5039; Elec Mail artdept@mnstate.edu; Internet Home Page Address: www.mnstate.edu; *Prof* Allen Sheets, MFA; *Asst Prof* Anna Arnar, PhD; *Prof* Carl Oltvedt, MFA; *Asst Prof* Jim Park, MFA; *Assoc Prof* Donald Clark, MFA; *Assoc Prof* Zhimin Guan, MFA; *Asst Prof* Sherry Short, MFA; *Assoc Prof* Wil Shynkaruk, MFA; *Asst Prof* Bjorn Anderson, PhD; *Asst Prof* Brad Bachmeier, MFA; *Asst Prof* John Volk, MFA
Estab 1887; Maintains a nonprofit art gallery, Roland Dille Center for the Arts Gallery, MSUM Campus; Pub; D & E; Scholarships; SC 47, LC 20; D 7,500, maj 400
Ent Req: HS dipl
Degrees: BA, BS, BFA
Courses: †Art Appreciation, Art Education, Art History, Ceramics, †Design, Drawing, Graphic Design, †History of Art & Architecture, Illustration, Painting, Photography, Printmaking, Sculpture, Teacher Training

MORRIS

UNIVERSITY OF MINNESOTA, MORRIS, Humanities Division, 600 E 4th St, Morris, MN 56267. Tel 320-589-2211, 589-6251; Internet Home Page Address: www.morris.umn.edu; *Chmn* Frederick Peterson PhD
Estab 1960, dept estab 1963; pub; D; Scholarships; SC 16, LC 8; D 195, non-maj 150, maj 45
Ent Req: top 50% in HS, ACT or PSAT
Degrees: BA 4 yrs
Courses: †Art History, †Studio Art, Teacher Training

NORTH MANKATO

SOUTH CENTRAL TECHNICAL COLLEGE, Commercial & Technical Art Dept, 1920 Lee Blvd, North Mankato, MN 56003-2504. Tel 507-389-7200; Internet Home Page Address: www.sctc.mnscu.edu; *Instr* Kevin McLaughlin; *Instr* Robert Williams

Estab 1969; FT 2; pub; D; Scholarships; D 20
Ent Req: Portfolio
Degrees: AA 2 yr
Courses: Advertising Design, Calligraphy, Commercial Art, Conceptual Art, Desktop Publishing, Drafting, Drawing, Fashion Arts, Graphic Arts, Graphic Design, Illustration, Lettering, Mixed Media, Multi-Media, †Web Page Design

NORTHFIELD

CARLETON COLLEGE, Dept of Art & Art History, One N College St, Northfield, MN 55057. Tel 507-646-4341, 646-4000 (main); *Chmn* Alison Kettering
Estab 1921; pvt; Scholarships; SC 30, LC 20; maj 42, others 550
Degrees: 4 yr
Courses: †Art History, †Studio Art

SAINT OLAF COLLEGE, Art Dept, 1520 Saint Olaf Ave, Northfield, MN 55057-1574. Tel 507-646-3248, 646-3025; Fax 507-646-3332; Internet Home Page Address: www.stolaf.edu; *Chmn* Urve Dell; *Museum Dir* Jill Ewald; *Prof* Malcolm Gimse, MFA; *Assoc Prof* Jan Shoger, MFA; *Assoc Prof* Meg Ojala, MFA; *Assoc Prof* Ron Gallas, MFA; *Assoc Prof* Mary Griep, MFA; *Assoc Prof* Mathew Rohn, MFA; *Asst Prof* Steve Edwins, MFA; *Asst Prof* John Saurer, MFA; *Asst Prof* Judy Yourman, MFA; *Instr* Don Bratland, MFA
Estab 1875, dept estab 1932; den; D & E; Scholarships
Ent Req: HS dipl, SAT
Degrees: BA 4 yr
Courses: Advertising Design, Aesthetics, †Animation, †Architecture, Art Appreciation, †Art Education, †Art History, †Art Studio, Ceramics, Commercial Art, Conceptual Art, Design, Drafting, Drawing, Film, Graphic Arts, Graphic Design, History of Art & Architecture, Illustration, Interior Design, Intermedia, Landscape Architecture, Mixed Media, Painting, Photography, Printmaking, Sculpture, Stage Design, Teacher Training, Theatre Arts, Video
Adult Hobby Classes: Dir, Heidi Quiram, Academic Outreach. Enrl 300; two 5 wk sessions. Courses—Art History, Studio
Summer School: Dir, Susan Hammerski. Enrl 300; two 5 wk sessions. Courses—Art History, Studio

ROCHESTER

ROCHESTER COMMUNITY & TECHNICAL COLLEGE, Art Dept, 851 30th Ave SE, Rochester, MN 55904-4915. Tel 507-285-7215 (Pres), 285-7210 (main); Internet Home Page Address: www.roch.edu; *Instr* Terry Richardson, MS; *Instr* Pat Kraemer, MS; *Instr* Terry Dennis, MS
Estab 1920s; pub; D & E; Scholarships; SC 17, LC 4; D & E 4000, maj 50
Ent Req: state req
Degrees: AAS. AA
Courses: Advertising Design, Art Appreciation, Art History, †Ceramics, Craft Design Series, Design, †Drawing, Fibers, †Graphic Design, Interior Design, Jewelry, †Painting, Photography, Printmaking, Sculpture, Stage Design, Theatre Arts, Weaving
Adult Hobby Classes: All areas, cr & non cr for variable tuition. Courses—Cartooning, & others on less regular basis
Summer School: Dir, A Olson. Art workshops are offered for at least one session each summer

SAINT CLOUD

SAINT CLOUD STATE UNIVERSITY, Dept of Art, 720 4th Ave S, KVAC Rm 101 Saint Cloud, MN 56301-4442. Tel 320-308-4283; Fax 320-308-2232; Elec Mail art@stcloudstate.edu; Internet Home Page Address: www.stcloudstate.edu/~art; *Chair* David Sebberson
Estab 1869; FT 13, PT 6; Pub; D & E; SC 65, LC 15, GC 20; maj 400
Ent Req: HS dipl
Degrees: BA, BFA, BS, 4 yrs
Courses: †2-D Media, †3-D Media, Art History, Ceramics, Drawing, Graphic Design, †Integrated Media, Painting, Photography, Printmaking, Sculpture, Teacher Training
Summer School: Two terms

SAINT JOSEPH

COLLEGE OF SAINT BENEDICT, Art Dept, 37 S College Ave, Saint Joseph, MN 56374. Tel 320-363-5011; Internet Home Page Address: www.csbjsu.edu; *Assoc Prof* Sr Baulu Kuan, MA; *Assoc Prof* James Hendershot, MA; *Asst Prof* Andrea Shaker, MFA; *Instr* Robert Wilde, MFA; *Chmn* Sr Dennis Frandrup
Estab 1913; joint studies with St John's University, Collegeville, MN; pvt; D & E; Scholarships; SC 21, LC 15; D 1893, maj 70
Ent Req: HS dipl, SAT, PSAT, ACT
Degrees: BA(Art) & BA(Art History) 4 yr, internships & open studio
Courses: †Art History, †Ceramics, †Drawing, Jewelry, Mixed Media, †Painting, †Photography, †Printmaking, †Sculpture

SAINT PAUL

BETHEL COLLEGE, Dept of Art, 3900 Bethel Dr, Saint Paul, MN 55112-6999. Tel 651-638-6400; Fax 651-638-6001; Internet Home Page Address: www.bethelcollege.edu; *Prof* Wayne L Roosa PhD; *Prof* Ken Steinbach, MFA; *Prof* Kirk Freeman, MFA; *Assoc Prof* Jeffrey Wetzig, MFA; *Assoc Prof* Lex Thompson, MFA; *Asst Prof* Jessica Henderson, MFA; *Asst Prof* Michelle Westmark, MFA

Estab 1871; Maintains 2 non-profit art galleries, Olson Gallery & Johnson Gallery; FT 7; den; D; Scholarships; SC 29, LC 7; non-maj 100, maj 70
Ent Req: HS dipl, SAT, ACT, PSAT or NMSQT, evidence of a standard of faith & practice that is compatible to Bethel lifestyle
Degrees: BA(Art Educ), BA(Art History) & BA(Studio Arts) 4 yr, BFA
Tuition: $30,700
Courses: 2-D Design, 3-D Design, †Art Education, †Art History, †Ceramics, †Drawing, †Graphic Design, †Painting, †Photography, †Printmaking, †Sculpture

CONCORDIA UNIVERSITY, Art Dept, 275 Syndicate St N, Fine Arts Division Saint Paul, MN 55104-5436. Tel 651-641-8743; Fax 651-654-0207; Internet Home Page Address: www.csp.edu; *Prof* Karla Ness; *Chmn* Keith Williams
Estab 1897, dept estab 1967; den; D & E; Scholarships; SC 14, LC 3; D 84, E 20, others 35
Ent Req: HS dipl
Degrees: BS and BA 4 yrs
Courses: Aesthetics, Art Education, Art History, Ceramics, Drawing, Jewelry, Painting, Photography, Printmaking, Sculpture, Teacher Training, Theatre Arts
Summer School: Courses—Art Educ Methods, Art Fundamentals

HAMLINE UNIVERSITY, Dept of Studio Arts & Art History, 1536 Hewitt Ave, Saint Paul, MN 55104-1205. Tel 651-523-2296; Fax 651-523-3066; Internet Home Page Address: www.hamline.edu/depts/art/; *Artist-in-Residence* Leonardo Lasansky, MFA; *Assoc Prof* Andrew Wykes MFA; *Dept Chair, Assoc Prof* Aida Audeh, PhD; *Dir Soeffker Gallery & Permanent Coll, Lectr* John-Mark Schlink, MFA; *Vis Asst Prof* Bruce Thomas; *Vis Asst Prof* Ann Paulk, PhD; *Vis Asst Prof* Elizabeth Avery PhD; *Vis Asst Prof* Kate Fisher, MFA; *Vis Asst Prof* Steve Stenzel, MFA; *Vis Asst Prof* Krista Walsh, MFA; *Vis Asst Prof* Jessica Street, PhD
Estab 1854; maintain non-profit art gallery, Soeffker Gallery, Drew Fine Arts Bldg, same address; pvt; D & E; Scholarships; SC 18, LC 7; non-maj 70, maj 35
Activities: Schols offered
Ent Req: HS dipl
Degrees: BA 4 yrs
Courses: Art Education, †Art History, Drawing, †Painting, †Photography, †Printmaking, Sculpture
Summer School: Dean, John Matachek

MACALESTER COLLEGE, Art Dept, 1600 Grand Ave, Saint Paul, MN 55105-1899. Tel 651-696-6279; Fax 651-696-6266; Elec Mail godollei@macalester.edu; Internet Home Page Address: www.macalester.edu; *Prof, Chair* Donald Celender; *Prof* Ruthann Godollei; *Assoc Prof* Stanton Sears; *Asst Prof* Christine Willcox; *Instr* Amy DiGennaro; *Instr* Gary Erickson; *Instr* Mary Hark
Estab 1946; Maintain nonprofit art gallery on campus; pvt; D; Scholarships; SC 16, LC 13; Maj 20
Degrees: BA(Art) 4 yr
Courses: 20th Century Art, American Art, Art of the Last Ten Years, Ceramics, Classical Art, Design, Drawing, Far Eastern Art, Fibers, Mural Painting, Painting, Principles Art, Printmaking, Renaissance Art, Sculpture, Senior Seminar, Tribal Art, Women in Art

ST. CATHERINE UNIVERSITY, (College of Saint Catherine) Art & Art History Dept, 2004 Randolph, Saint Paul, MN 55105. Tel 651-690-6636, 690-6000; Internet Home Page Address: www.stkate.edu; *Chmn & Assoc Prof* Todd Deutsch; *Assoc Prof* Pat Olson; *Assoc Prof* Carol Lee Chase; *Asst Prof* Amy Hamlin; *Asst Prof* Tamsie Ringler
Dept estab 1915; Maintains a nonprofit art gallery - Catherine G. Murphy Gallery (same location); maintains an art/architecture library - Visual Resources Library.; FT 3, PT 5; Pvt, (Women only); D & E; Scholarships; SC, LC; Maj 65
Activities: Schols offered
Ent Req: HS dipl
Degrees: BA(Art) 4 yr
Tuition: $510 per cr hr, $21,000 per yr
Courses: Art & Technology, Art Appreciation, Art Education, †Art History, Ceramics, Drawing, Graphic Arts, Graphic Design, Illustration, Jewelry, Mixed Media, Museum Staff Training, Painting, Photography, Pottery, Printmaking, Publication Design, Sculpture, †Studio Art, Typography, Women in Art
Adult Hobby Classes: Special Workshops
Summer School: Enrl 30. Courses—Art Education, Art History, Art Studio

UNIVERSITY OF MINNESOTA, Dept of Design, Housing & Apparel, 1985 Buford Ave, 240 McNeal Hall Saint Paul, MN 55108-6136. Tel 612-624-9700; Fax 612-624-2750; Internet Home Page Address: www.dha.design.umn.edu; *Head Dept* Dr Elizabeth Bye
Dept estab 1851; Maintains an on-campus shop where art supplies may be purchased; Pub; D & E; SC 57, LC 54, GC 25; D 740 (spring quarter 92), grad 70
Ent Req: HS dipl; math requirement
Degrees: BS, BFA, MFA, MS, MA & PhD 4 yr
Tuition: Res—undergrad $448.08 per cr; grad $7,006, 6-14 cr; nonres—undergrad $640.39 per cr
Courses: †Applied Design, †Costume Design & Construction, Costume History, Decorative Arts, Design, Drawing, Graphic Arts, †Housing, †Interior Design, †Retail Merchandising, Textile Design, †Textiles Clothing
Summer School: Courses—vary each yr

UNIVERSITY OF SAINT THOMAS, Dept of Art History, 2115 Summit Ave, Mail 57P Saint Paul, MN 55105-1048. Tel 651-962-5560, 962-5000; Fax 651-962-5861; Elec Mail setocke@stthomas.edu; Internet Home Page Address: www.stthomas.edu; *Prof* Mark Stansbury O'Donnell; *Prof* Victoria Young; *Prof* Craig Ellason; *Prof* Shelly Nordtorp-Madson; *Prof* Elizabeth Kindall; *Prof* Wm Barnes; *Prof* Julie Risser; *Prof* Heather Shirey
Estab 1885, dept estab 1978; Maintains a nonprofit art gallery; FT 8 Adjuncts 4; Pvt; D & E; Scholarships; SC 25, LC 8; D 2847, E 275, maj 40
Ent Req: HS dipl
Degrees: BA 4 yr
Courses: Architecture, †Art History, Costume Design & Construction, Design, History of Art & Architecture, Museum Staff Training

Summer School: Dir, Dr Susan Webster

SAINT PETER

GUSTAVUS ADOLPHUS COLLEGE, Art & Art History Dept, 800 W College Ave, Schaefer Fine Arts Ctr Saint Peter, MN 56082-1485. Tel 507-933-8000, 933-7019; Internet Home Page Address: www.gustavus.edu; *Chmn* Linnea Wren
Estab 1876; FT 8, PT 2; den; D; Scholarships; SC 27; 2300 total, 750 art, maj 50
Ent Req: HS grad, ent exam
Degrees: BA 4 yr
Courses: Art Appreciation, †Art Education, †Art History, Basic Design, Bronze Casting, Ceramics, Design, Drawing, Painting, Photography, Printmaking, Sculpture, †Studio Art, Teacher Training
Summer School: Independent Study prog for three 4 wk periods during June, July or Aug

WHITE BEAR LAKE

CENTURY COLLEGE, Humanities Dept, 3300 Century Ave N, White Bear Lake, MN 55110-1842. Tel 651-779-3200; Fax 651-779-3417; Internet Home Page Address: www.cedntury.edu; *Instr* Mel Sundby; *Instr* Karin McGinness; *Chmn* Kenneth Maeckelbergh; *Instr* Dawn Saks; *Instr* Larry Vienneau; *Instr* Mary Aspness
Estab 1968; Maintains Century College Art Gallery on campus; pub; D, E & Sat; Scholarships; SC 20, LC 8; D 75, E 30
Degrees: AA
Tuition: Res—$95.76 per sem cr; nonres—$181.41 per sem cr
Courses: American Art, Art Appreciation, Art History, Art Therapy, Calligraphy, Ceramics, Design, Drawing, Film, Graphic Arts, Graphic Design, Interior Design, Lettering, Painting, Photography, Theatre Arts, Video
Adult Hobby Classes: Enrl 6000: tuition varies. 39 courses offered
Children's Classes: Enrl 500; tuition under $100 each course. 30 courses offered
Summer School: Dean Sue Ehlers. Tuition $181.41 per cr

WILLMAR

RIDGEWATER COLLEGE, Art Dept, 2101 15th Ave NW, Willmar, MN 56201-3096; PO Box 1097, Willmar, MN 56201-1097. Tel 320-231-5102, 231-5132; Fax 320-231-6602; Internet Home Page Address: www.ridgewater.mnscu.edu; *Chmn Art Dept & Coordr Art Gallery* Robert Mattson
Estab 1962-63; pub; D & E; SC 8, LC 3; D 50, maj 15
Ent Req: HS dipl
Degrees: AA & AS 2 yrs
Courses: Art Education, Ceramics, Display, Drawing, Graphic Arts, Graphic Design, History of Art & Architecture, Introduction to Studio Practices, Painting, Structure, Teacher Training
Adult Hobby Classes: Courses—Ceramics, Design, History of Art, Painting

WINONA

SAINT MARY'S UNIVERSITY OF MINNESOTA, Art & Design Dept, 700 Terrace Heights, Winona, MN 55987. Tel 507-457-1593; Fax 507-457-6967; Internet Home Page Address: www.smumn.edu; WATS 800-635-5987; *Prof* Margaret Mear, MFA; *Prof* Roderick Robertson, MFA; *Chair* Preston Lawing; *Prof* Robert McCall; *Instr* Michelle Cochran; *Instr* Charles Campbell; *Instr* John Whelan
Estab 1912, dept estab 1970; Nonprofit - Lillian Davis Hogan Galleries, 700 Terrace Heights, Winona, MN 55987; Den; D; Scholarships; SC 20, LC 6; in school D 1,390
Ent Req: HS dipl
Degrees: BA 4 yrs
Courses: Art Appreciation, Art History, Ceramics, Computer Design, Design, Drawing, †Electronic Publishing, †Graphic Design, Illustration, Painting, Photography, Printmaking, Sculpture, †Studio Arts, Theatre Arts

WINONA STATE UNIVERSITY, Dept of Art, PO Box 5838, Winona, MN 55987. Tel 507-457-5395; Fax 507-457-5086; Internet Home Page Address: www.winona.edu; *Prof* Judy Schlawin, MS; *Assoc Prof* Don Schmidlapp, MFA
Estab 1860; pub; D & E; Scholarships
Degrees: BA and BS
Courses: Art Education, Art History, Ceramics, Drawing, Graphic Design, Interior Design, Lettering, Painting, Printmaking, Sculpture, Weaving
Summer School: Courses offered

MISSISSIPPI

BLUE MOUNTAIN

BLUE MOUNTAIN COLLEGE, Art Dept, Box 296, Blue Mountain, MS 38610. Tel 662-685-4771, Ext 162; Internet Home Page Address: www.bmc.edu; *Chmn Dept* William Dowdy, MA
Estab 1873, dept estab 1875; FT 2; den; D & E; Scholarships; SC 16, LC 2; D 28, E 12, non-maj 20, maj 8, others 12
Ent Req: HS dipl
Degrees: BA & BS(Educ) 4 yr
Courses: Art History, Commercial Art, Drawing, Painting
Adult Hobby Classes: Enrl 12; tuition $42 per sem hr. Courses—Drawing, Painting
Summer School: Dir, William Dowdy. Enrl 20

BOONEVILLE

NORTHEAST MISSISSIPPI JUNIOR COLLEGE, Art Dept, 101 Cunningham, Booneville, MS 38829. Tel 662-728-7751, Ext 229; Internet Home Page Address: www.necc.cc.ms.us; *Instr* Terry Anderson; *Instr* Judy Tucci; *Chmn* Jerry Rains; *Chair Visual Arts* Marty McLendon
Estab 1948; Anderson Hall Art Gallery; FT 3, PT 1; pub; D & E; Scholarships; SC 6, LC 3; D 2800, maj 30
Ent Req: HS dipl, ent exam
Degrees: 2 yr Assoc degrees in art educ, fine arts and interior design
Courses: Advertising Design, Aesthetics, Art Education, Art History, Ceramics, Design, Drafting, Drawing, Painting, Teacher Training, Theatre Arts
Adult Hobby Classes: Watercolor

CLARKSDALE

COAHOMA COMMUNITY COLLEGE, Art Education & Fine Arts Dept, 3240 Friars Pt Rd, Clarksdale, MS 38614. Tel 662-627-2571, Ext 208; *Chmn* Henry Dorsey
Degrees: AA
Tuition: In district—$700 per yr; res—$2511.70 per yr; outside district $1100 per yr; outside state $2100 per yr; out of district boarding $2911.70 per yr, out of state boarding $3911.70 per yr
Courses: Art Appreciation, Art Education, Art History, Drawing, Handicrafts, Intro to Art
Adult Hobby Classes: Enrl 15-32; tuition $27.50 per sem hr. Courses—Art & Music Appreciation

CLEVELAND

DELTA STATE UNIVERSITY, Dept of Art, 1003 W Sunflower Rd, Cleveland, MS 38733-0001. Tel 662-846-4720; Internet Home Page Address: www.deltastate.edu; *Chmn* Ron Koehler; *Prof* William Carey Lester Jr; *Prof* Kim Rushing; *Prof* Patricia Brown; *Assoc Prof* Joseph Abide; *Asst Prof* M Duncan Baird; *Asst Prof* Benjamin Johnston; *Asst Prof* Allison Melton; *Asst Prof* Cetin Oguz; *Asst Prof* Robyn Moore; *Instr* Mollie Rollins Rushing; *Prof* Dr Cliff McMahon
Estab 1924; Maintain nonprofit art gallery; Wright Art Center Gallery; on-campus shop for art supplies; FT 10 PT 2; pub; D & E; Scholarships; SC 42, LC 10, GC 30; maj 160
Ent Req: HS dipl
Degrees: BA & BFA
Courses: †Advertising Design, †Art Appreciation, †Art Education, Art History, Ceramics, Computer Graphics, †Design, Drawing, Fibers, †Film, †Graphic Design, Illustration, †Painting, †Photography, Printmaking, †Sculpture, †Video, †Weaving
Summer School: Tuition & living expenses $488 per term, June 2 - July 3 or July 7 - Aug 8. Courses—Art for Elementary, Ceramics, Drawing, Internship in Commercial Design, Introduction to Art, Painting, Sculpture

CLINTON

MISSISSIPPI COLLEGE, Art Dept, PO Box 4020, Clinton, MS 39058-0001. Tel 601-925-3231; Fax 601-925-3926; Internet Home Page Address: www.mc.edu/campus/academics/arts; *Head Art Dept* Randy B Miley
Estab 1825, dept estab 1950; FT 5, PT 1; den; HS grad; Scholarships, Assistantships; SC 22, LC 3; maj 80, others 300
Ent Req: HS dipl, BA, BS, BE(Art), MA(Art) and ME(Art) 4 yr, Freshman Art merit
Courses: †Art Education, Art History, Ceramics, Drawing, Foundry Casting, †Graphic Design, †Interior Design, †Painting, †Sculpture
Adult Hobby Classes: Enrl 50; tuition $35 for 5 weeks. Courses—Calligraphy, Drawing, Flower Arranging, Painting
Summer School: Dir, Dr Miley. Tuition $1200 for two 6-wk terms. Courses—Ceramics, Drawing, Painting, Printmaking

COLUMBUS

MISSISSIPPI UNIVERSITY FOR WOMEN, Division of Fine & Performing Arts, 1100 College St, W 70, Columbus, MS 39701-5800. Tel 662-329-7341; Internet Home Page Address: www.muw.edu/fine_arts/; *Head Dept* Dr Michael Garrett; *Prof* David Frank; *Prof* Thomas Nawrocki, MFA; *Asst Prof* Robert Gibson, MFA; *Asst Prof* John Alford, MFA
Estab 1884; FT 8, PT 3; pub; D & E; Scholarships; SC 49, LC 8; D 263, E 39, non-maj 45, maj 72
Ent Req: HS dipl, ACT, SAT
Degrees: BA, BS and BFA 4 yrs
Courses: Architectural Construction & Materials, †Art Education, Art History, Calligraphy, Ceramics, Commercial Art, Conceptual Art, Graphic Design, Illustration, †Interior Design, Lettering, †Metal Art, Mixed Media, †Painting, Photography, †Printmaking, Sculpture, Stage Design, Teacher Training, †Theatre Arts, Weaving
Adult Hobby Classes: Courses—Drawing, Painting, Weaving
Summer School: Courses—Vary according to demand

DECATUR

EAST CENTRAL COMMUNITY COLLEGE, Art Dept, PO Box 129, Decatur, MS 39327-0129. Tel 601-635-2121; Elec Mail bguraedy@eccc.cc.ms.us; Internet Home Page Address: www.eccc.edu; *Head Dept* J Bruce Guraedy, MEd; *Art Instr* Todd Eldridge

Estab 1928, dept estab 1965; pub; D, E & Sat; Scholarships; SC 10, LC 8; D 175, E 70, non-maj 100, maj 10
Ent Req: HS dipl, GED
Degrees: AA and AS 2 yrs
Courses: Advertising Design, Art Appreciation, Art Education, Art History, Ceramics, Collage, Design, Drafting, Drawing, Fashion Arts, Handicrafts, Illustration, Industrial Design, Interior Design, Landscape Architecture, Mixed Media, Painting, Printmaking, Sculpture, Stage Design, Theatre Arts
Adult Hobby Classes: Enrl 15; tuition $100 per sem for 10 wks.
Courses—Beginning Painting, Drawing, Painting
Children's Classes: Kid's College & pvt lessons available
Summer School: Vice Pres of Continuing Educ, Gene Davis. Enrl 300 - 400; tuition $50 per sem hr for term of 10 wks. Courses—vary according to student demand

ELLISVILLE

JONES COUNTY JUNIOR COLLEGE, Art Dept, 900 S Court St, Ellisville, MS 39437-3999. Tel 601-477-4148, 477-4000; Fax 601-477-4017; *Chmn Fine Arts* Jeff Brown
Estab 1927; pub; D; Scholarships; SC 12, LC 4; D 100, E 12, maj 15, others 12
Ent Req: HS dipl
Degrees: AA 2 yrs
Adult Hobby Classes: Enrl 20. Courses—Painting
Summer School: Term of 4 wks beginning June. Courses—same as regular session

GAUTIER

MISSISSIPPI GULF COAST COMMUNITY COLLEGE-JACKSON COUNTY CAMPUS, Art Dept, PO Box 100, Gautier, MS 39553-0100. Tel 228-497-9602; *Chmn Fine Arts Dept* Johnnie Gray, MA; *Instr (2-D)* Mary Hardy, MA; *Instr (3-D)* Kevin Turner
Maintains nonprofit gallery, MGCCC/Jackson County Campus Fine Arts Gallery P.O. Box 100, Gautier MS 39553; Pub; D & E; Scholarships; SC 9, LC 2; D 90, E 8, non-maj 62, maj 28
Degrees: AA, 2 yrs
Tuition: Res—$65 per cr
Courses: †3-D Design, Art Appreciation, Art Education, †Art for Elementary Teachers, Ceramics, Design, Drawing, Painting, Sculpture

HATTIESBURG

UNIVERSITY OF SOUTHERN MISSISSIPPI, Dept of Art & Design, 118 College Dr (#5033), Hattiesburg, MS 39406-0002. Tel 601-266-4972; Fax 601-266-6379; Elec Mail johnhouse@usm.edu; Internet Home Page Address: www.vsm.edu/visualarts; *Prof* James Meade Jr, MFA; *Chair Prof* John House, MFA; *Prof* Janet Gorzegno, MFA; *Prof* Deanna Douglas, MFA; *Mus Dir* Mark Riesby; *Assoc Prof* Jennifer Torres
Estab 1910; Maintain a nonprofit art gallery, USM Museum of Art, also maintain an art/architecture library; on-campus shop where art supplies may be purchased and Barnes & Noble book store; FT 9, PT 6; pub; D & E; Scholarships; SC 64, LC 41, GC 20; non-maj 35, maj 120, grad 5
Ent Req: HS dipl
Degrees: BA, BS, BFA, MAE
Courses: Art History, †Ceramics, †Design, Drawing, †Graphic Design, †Mixed Media, Painting, Photography, Printmaking, Sculpture

ITTA BENA

MISSISSIPPI VALLEY STATE UNIVERSITY, Fine Arts Dept, 14000 Highway 82 W, Itta Bena, MS 38941-1401. Tel 662-254-3482; Fax 662-254-3485; Elec Mail lhorn@musu.edu; Internet Home Page Address: www.mvsu.edu.com; *Co-Gallery Dir* Dorothy Vaughn; *Co-Dir Gallery* Ronald Minks; *Acting Head* Lawrence Horn; *Assoc Prof Art* Frank Hardmon; *Asst Prof Art* Charles Davis
Estab 1952; SC 8, LC 2; pub; D & E
Ent Req: HS dipl
Degrees: BA & BS
Tuition: Res—undergrad $2094.50 per sem; out-of-state—$3074.50
Courses: 2 & 3-D Design, African American Art History, Art Appreciation, Art History, Arts & Crafts, Ceramics, Color Fundamentals, Commercial Art, Drawing, Graphic Arts, Illustration, Painting, Photography, Printmaking, Public School Art, Typography, Visual Communications
Summer School: Courses—Art Appreciation, Public School Art

JACKSON

BELHAVEN COLLEGE, Art Dept, 1500 Peachtree St, Jackson, MS 39202-1789. Tel 601-968-5950; Fax 601-968-9998; Elec Mail mhause@belhaven.edu; Internet Home Page Address: belhaven.edu; *Asst Prof Art* William Morse; *Asst Prof Art History* Melissa Hause; *Asst Prof of Art* Nate Theisen; *Instr* Gretchen Haien; *Instr* Sam Beibers
Estab 1883, dept estab 1889; Maintain nonprofit art gallery, Bessie Cary Lemly Gallery, Belhaven College, 1500 Peachtree St, Jackson, MS 39202; den; D & E; Scholarships; SC 6; D 650, E 200, maj 30
Ent Req: HS dipl
Degrees: BA
Courses: Aesthetics, Art Appreciation, Art Education, Art History, Design, Drawing, Graphic Design, Painting, Photography, Printmaking, Sculpture

JACKSON STATE UNIVERSITY, Dept of Art, 1400 John R Lynch St, Jackson, MS 39217-0001. Tel 601-979-2040; Fax 601-968-7010; Elec Mail liberalarts@jsums.edu; Internet Home Page Address: www.jsums.edu; *Chmn* John M Sullivan; *Assoc Prof* Hyun Chong Kim; *Assoc Prof* Charles W Carraway; *Assoc Prof* Lealan Swanson
Estab 1949; Maintain nonprofit art gallery; pub; D; Scholarships; SC 16, LC 7, GC 1; D 486, maj 57
Ent Req: HS dipl
Degrees: BA & BS(maj in Art) 4 yrs
Courses: Art History, Ceramics, Commercial Art, Drawing, Graphic Arts, Painting, Studio Crafts
Adult Hobby Classes: Athenian Art Club activities
Children's Classes: Enrl 75; tuition $100. Courses—General Art
Summer School: Dir, B Graves. Enrl 3000; tuition $100. Courses—Art Education, Painting

MILLSAPS COLLEGE, Dept of Art, 1701 N State St, Jackson, MS 39210-0001. Tel 601-974-1000, 974-1432; Internet Home Page Address: www.millsaps.edu; *Chmn* Elise Smith, MFA; *Asst Prof* Collin Asmus, MA; *Instr* Kay Holloway, MFA; *Instr* Sandra Smithson; *Instr* Steven Jones
Estab 1913, dept estab 1970; priv; D & E; Scholarships; LC 4; non maj 100, maj 20
Ent Req: HS dipl, SAT combined 1100 average
Degrees: BA 4 yr
Courses: Aesthetics, Architecture, Art History, Calligraphy, Ceramics, Design, Drawing, History of Art & Architecture, Lettering, Museum Staff Training, Painting, Photography, Printmaking, Sculpture, Stage Design, Teacher Training, Textile Design, Theatre Arts, Weaving
Adult Hobby Classes: Tuition $35 per class
Children's Classes: Limited courses

LORMAN

ALCORN STATE UNIVERSITY, Dept of Fine Arts, 1000 ASU Dr, No 29, Lorman, MS 39096-7500. Tel 601-877-6271, 877-6100; Fax 601-877-6262; *Instr* John Buchanan; *Chmn* Joyce Bolden PhD
Estab 1871, dept estab 1973; pub; D & E; SC 9, LC 3
Ent Req: HS dipl, ACT
Courses: Art Appreciation, Art Education, Ceramics, Drawing, Painting
Adult Hobby Classes: Drawing, Graduate Level Art Education, Painting
Summer School: Courses—Art Education, Fine Arts

MOORHEAD

MISSISSIPPI DELTA COMMUNITY COLLEGE, Dept of Fine Arts, Hwy 3 & Cherry St, Moorhead, MS 38761; PO Box 668, Moorhead, MS 38761-0668. Tel 662-246-6322; Fax 662-246-6321; Internet Home Page Address: www.mdcc.cc.ms.us; *Coordr* Wallace Mallette; *Coordr* Cindy Ray; *Chmn* Simone Strawbridge; *Instr* Nancy Stone-Street
Estab 1926; pub; D & E; Scholarships; SC 11, LC 2; D 68, E 29, maj 28
Ent Req: HS dipl, ent exam
Degrees: AA 2 yrs
Courses: Advertising Design, Art Appreciation, Art Education, Art History, Ceramics, Design, Drawing, Graphic Arts, Painting, Printmaking, Sculpture, Stage Design, Theatre Arts
Adult Hobby Classes: Enrl 29. Courses—Ceramics, Painting

POPLARVILLE

PEARL RIVER COMMUNITY COLLEGE, Visual Arts, Dept of Fine Arts & Communication, 101 Hwy 11 N, Poplarville, MS 39470-2216. Tel 601-403-1000; Elec Mail cnull@prcc.edu; Internet Home Page Address: www.prcc.edu; *Chmn* James A Rawls; *Instr* Charleen A Null; *Instr Art* Anna Holsten
Estab 1921; FT 1, PT 2; pub; D & E; Scholarships; SC 4, LC 2; D 85 - 100, non-maj 65 - 75, maj 20 - 25, E 20 - 40, non-maj 20 - 30, maj 10 - 20
Ent Req: HS dipl or ACT Score & GED
Degrees: AA
Courses: Art Appreciation, Art Education, Art History, Calligraphy, Design, Drafting, Drawing, Elementary Art Education, Handicrafts, Interior Design, Introduction to Art, Painting, Photography, Teacher Training

RAYMOND

HINDS COMMUNITY COLLEGE, Dept of Art, 501 E Main St, Raymond, MS 39154-9700; PO Box 1100, Raymond, MS 39154-9799. Tel 601-857-3275; 5261; Fax 601-857-3392; Elec Mail info@hindscc.edu; Internet Home Page Address: www.hindscc.edu; *Chmn* Melanie Atkinson; *Instr* Paula Duren; *Instr* Randy Minton; *Instr* Sarah Teasley
Estab 1917; Maintain nonprofit art gallery; Marie Hull Gallery, Art Department, Hinds Community College, Raymond, MS 39154-1100; FT 4; pub; D & E; Scholarships; SC 6, LC 2; D 400, E 75, maj 60
Activities: Schls offered
Degrees: AA 2 yr
Tuition: In-state $1,960
Courses: Art Appreciation, Art Education, Art History, Ceramics, Commercial Art, †Computer Art, Design, Drawing, Graphic Arts, Graphic Design, Landscape Architecture, Painting, Photography
Adult Hobby Classes: Courses offered
Summer School: Dir. Helanie Atkinson. Enrl 24; tuition $165 for 8 wk term. Courses—Art Appreciation

STARVILLE

MISSISSIPPI STATE UNIVERSITY, Dept of Art, Starville, MS; PO Box 5182, Mississippi State, MS 39762-5182. Tel 662-325-2970, 325-2224 (admis), 325-6900 (art dept); Fax 662-325-3850; Elec Mail da@ra.msstate.edu; Internet Home Page Address: www.caad.msstate.edu; *Head* Kay DeMarsche, MFA; *Prof* Brent Funderburk, MFA; *Prof* Marita Gootee, MFA; *Prof* Robert Long, MFA; *Prof* Jamie Mixon, MFA; *Prof* Linda Seckinger; *Assoc Prof* Tim McCourt, MFA; *Assoc Prof* Soon Ee Ngoh, MFA; *Assoc Prof* Jeffrey Haupt, MFA; *Assoc Prof* Patrick Miller, MFA; *Assoc Prof* Jamie Runnells, MFA; *Asst Prof* Angi Bourgeois, PhD; *Asst Prof* Ben Harvey, PhD; *Instr* Bill Andrews, MFA; *Asst Prof* Critz Campbell, MFA; *Asst Prof* James Davis, MFA; *Asst Prof* Rebecca Davis, MFA; *Asst Prof* Jason DeMarte, MFA; *Lectr* Chuck Galey, BFA; *Lectr* Jayson Triplett, MFA
Estab 1879, dept estab 1971; maintains nonprofit art gallery, Dept of Art Gallery, PO Box 5182, MS State, MS 39759; maintains art library, Giles Hall, MSU, MS 39759; on-campus shop where art supplies may be purchased; Pub; D&E; Scholarships; SC 80, LC 30; D 750, non-maj 650, maj 300
Ent Req: HS dipl
Degrees: BFA 4-5 yrs
Courses: †Art Appreciation, Art History, Ceramics, †Design, Drawing, †Fine Art, †Graphic Design, †Museum Staff Training, Painting, Photography, Printmaking, Sculpture
Adult Hobby Classes: Enrl 40; tuition $1,700 per yr. Courses—Drawing, Fundamentals, Painting

TOUGALOO

TOUGALOO COLLEGE, Art Dept, 500 W County Line Rd, Tougaloo College Div of Humanities Tougaloo, MS 39174-9700. Tel 601-977-4431; Fax 601-977-4425; Internet Home Page Address: www.tougaloo.edu; *Dean Humanities* Andrea Montgomery, PhD
Estab 1869, dept estab 1968

UNIVERSITY

UNIVERSITY OF MISSISSIPPI, Department of Art, 116 Meek Hall, University, MS 38677; PO Box 1848, University, MS 38677-1848. Tel 662-915-7193 (art dept); Fax 662-915-5013; Elec Mail art@olemiss.edu; Internet Home Page Address: www.olemiss.edu/depts/art; *Assoc Prof* Tom Dewey II, PhD, MA; *Prof* Paula Temple, MFA; *Assoc Prof* Betty Crowther PhD, MFA; *Prof* Aileen Ajootian PhD, MA; *Prof* Nancy Wicker, PhD; *Prof* Jan Murray, MFA; *Chair & Prof* Sheri Rieth, MFA; *Assoc Prof* Virginia Chavis; *Assoc Prof* Matt Long; *Assoc Prof* Brooke White; *Assoc Prof* Durant Thompson; *Asst Prof* Philip Jackson; *Asst Prof* Lou Haney
Dept estab 1949; Maintains a nonprofit art gallery & on-campus shop where art supplies may be purchased; FT 12, PT 13; pub; D, online; Scholarships, Financial aid; SC 64, LC 45, GC 25, other 9; non-maj 350, maj 265, grad 16
Ent Req: HS dipl
Degrees: BA 4 yr, BFA 4 yr, MFA 3 yr
Tuition: Res—undergrad $2,302 per sem; campus res—room $800-$966
Courses: †Art History, †Ceramics, Drawing, †Graphic Design, †Painting, †Photography, †Printmaking, †Sculpture
Summer School: Two 4 wk sessions beginning June. Courses—Art History, Drawing, Painting, Foundations

MISSOURI

BOLIVAR

SOUTHWEST BAPTIST UNIVERSITY, Art Dept, 1600 University Dr, Bolivar, MO 65613. Tel 417-326-1651, 328-1605; *Chmn* Wesley A Gott, MFA; *Adjunct Prof* Diane Callahan, BFA; *Asst Prof* John Gruber, MFA; *Adjunct Prof* Sandra Maupin, MA
Sch estab 1879, dept estab 1974; Maintains nonprofit gallery, Driskill Art Gallery, 1600 University Ave Bolivar, MO 65613; Den; D & E; Scholarships; SC 30, LC 3; D 150, E 20, maj 35
Ent Req: HS dipl
Degrees: BS, BA, MS, MBA & MPT
Tuition: Res & nonres—undergrad $5,000 per yr; campus res—room & board $3,100 per acad yr
Courses: †Art Education, Art History, †Ceramics, †Commercial Art, Costume Design & Construction, †Drawing, †Graphic Arts, Graphic Design, †Painting, †Photography, †Printmaking, †Sculpture, Stage Design, †Teacher Training, Theatre Arts
Adult Hobby Classes: Enrl 10; per hr for 15 weeks. Courses—Drawing, Painting, Photography
Summer School: Enrl 600; Dir Dr Bill Brown, Dean of Music, Arts & Letters, 4 wk term beginning in June, also a 4 wk term beginning in July. Courses—Internships

CANTON

CULVER-STOCKTON COLLEGE, Art Dept, 1 College Hill Canton, MO 63435-1299. Tel 217-231-6367, 231-6368; Fax 217-231-6611; Elec Mail croyer@culver.edu, jjorgen@culver.edu; Internet Home Page Address: www.culver.edu/; *Assoc Prof* Joseph Jorgensen; *Prof* Gary Thomas
Estab 1853; pvt; D; Scholarships; SC 16, LC 6; 1030, maj 40
Ent Req: HS dipl, ACT or Col Board Ent Exam
Degrees: BFA & BA(Visual Arts), BS(Art Educ) & BS(Arts Management) 4 yrs

Courses: †Art Education, Art History, †Ceramics, Design, Drawing, †Graphic Design, Illustration, †Painting, †Photography, Printmaking, †Sculpture, Teacher Training

Summer School: Reg, Barbara Conover. Tuition $150 per cr hr. Courses—Various studio workshops

CAPE GIRARDEAU

SOUTHEAST MISSOURI STATE UNIVERSITY, Dept of Art, 1 University Plz, Art Bldg 306, Mail Stop 4500 Cape Girardeau, MO 63701-4710. Tel 573-651-2143, 651-2000; Internet Home Page Address: www.smsu.edu; *Prof & Interim Chmn* Ron Clayton; *Assoc Prof* Lane Fabrick; *Assoc Prof* Pat Reagan; *Asst Prof* Louise Bodenheimer

Estab 1873, dept estab 1920; FT11; pub; D & E; Scholarships; SC 28, LC 10, GC 18; D 1300

Ent Req: HS dipl

Degrees: BS, BS(Educ) & BA 4 yrs, MAT

Courses: 3-D Design, Advertising Design, Art History, Ceramics, Color Composition, Commercial Art, Design Foundation, Drawing, Fiber, Graphic Design, Illustration, Lettering, Painting, Perceptive Art, Printmaking, Screen Printing, Sculpture, Silversmithing, Typography, Video Art Graphic

COLUMBIA

COLUMBIA COLLEGE, Art Dept, 1001 Rogers, Columbia, MO 65216-0001. Tel 573-875-8700; Fax 573-875-7209; Internet Home Page Address: www.ccis.edu; *Instr* Sidney Larson, MA; *Instr* Ben Cameron, MA; *Instr* Richard Baumann, MFA; *Instr* Michael Sledd, MFA; *Chmn* Tom Watson; *Instr Painting* Jodie Garrison; *Instr Photog & Ceramics* Ed Collings

Estab 1851; FT 5, PT 2; den; D; Scholarships; SC 55, LC 13; D 180, non-maj 80, maj 115

Ent Req: HS dipl or equivalent, ACT or SAT, also accept transfer students

Degrees: AA 2 yrs, BA, BS and BFA 4 yrs

Courses: Art History, Ceramics, Drawing, Fashion Arts, Graphic Arts, Graphic Design, Illustration, Painting, Photography

Adult Hobby Classes: Enrl 15; tuition $75 per cr. Courses—Arts & Crafts, Photography

Summer School: Evening Studies Dir, Dr John Hendricks. Enrl 20; tuition $75 per cr hr

STEPHENS COLLEGE, Art Dept, 1200 E Broadway, Columbia, MO 65215-0001. Tel 573-442-2211, Exten 4363; Elec Mail jterry@stephens.edu; Internet Home Page Address: www.stephens.edu; *Instr* Robert Friedman; *Chair* Dr James H Terry; *Instr* Lillian Sung

Estab 1833, dept estab 1850; Maintain nonprofit art gallery; Davis Art Gallery; art supplies available on-campus; Pvt; D & E; Scholarships; SC 20, LC 11; D 450, maj 5, others 10

Ent Req: SAT or ACT, recommendations, interview

Degrees: BA 3-4 yrs, BFA 3 1/2-4 yrs

Courses: Advertising Design, Art Education, Art History, Ceramics, Commercial Art, Costume Design & Construction, Drawing, †Fashion Arts, Film, Graphic Arts, †Graphic Design, History of Art & Architecture, Illustration, Occupational Therapy, †Painting, †Photography, †Printmaking, †Sculpture, †Stage Design, Teacher Training, †Theatre Arts, †Video

Children's Classes: Tuition $900 per yr; Stephens Child Study Center, grades K-3, preschool; includes special creative arts emphasis

UNIVERSITY OF MISSOURI - COLUMBIA, Dept of Art, A 126 Fine Arts, Columbia, MO 65211. Tel 573-882-3555; Fax 573-884-6807; Elec Mail plattm@missouri.edu; Internet Home Page Address: art.missouri.edu; *Dept Chmn & Prof* Melvin Platt; *Assoc Prof (Painting & Drawing)* William Hawk; *Prof, Dir Undergrad Studies (Graphic Design)* Deborah Huelsbergen; *Assoc Prof (Painting & Drawing)* Nathan P Boyer; *Asst Prof (Photog)* Joe Johnson; *Prof (Graphic Design)* Jean Brueggenhohann; *Asst Tchs Prof & Dir Florence Prog* Mark Langeneckert; *Assoc Prof (Sculpture)* James Calvin; *Assoc Prof (Environmental Sculpture, Video & Performance)* Bede Clarke; *Prof (Ceramics)* Cherie Sampson; *Prof (Fibers)* Jo Stealey; *Assoc Prof, Dir Grad Studies (Painting & Drawing)* J Brett Grill; *Assoc Prof (Graphic Design, Interactive Media)* Ric Wilson; *Prof (Painting & Drawing)* Lampo Leong; *Asst Prof* Chris Daniggelis; *Asst Prof* Joe Pintz; *Asst Tchg Prof* Matthew Ballou; *Asst Tchg Prof* Alexis Callender; *Asst Tchg Prof* Travis Shaffer; *Asst Prof* Jessica Thornton

Estab 1839, dept estab 1912; Maintains a nonprofit art gallery, George Caleb Bingham Gallery, A125 Fine Arts, Dept Art; maintains Ellis Library; schols open to continuing outstanding students; on-campus art supply shop; FT 19, PT 13; pub; D, E & wknd; Scholarships; SC 100 LC 3, GC 20; non-maj 1000 per sem, maj 270, grad 28

Activities: Schls offered

Ent Req: HS dipl

Degrees: BA, BFA, MFA

Tuition: Res—undergrad $261.60 per cr hr, grad $326.70 per cr hr; nonres—undergrad $688.10 per cr hr, grad $843.50 per cr hr plus fees

Courses: †Advertising Design, †Art Appreciation, †Art Education, †Art History, †Asian Brush Painting & Calligraphy, †Calligraphy, †Ceramics, Design, †Drawing, †Fibers, †Graphic Design, Introduction to Art, †Mixed Media, †Painting, †Photography, †Printmaking, †Sculpture, †Video

Summer School: Dept Chair, Melvin Platt, Courses—Ceramics, Drawing, Fibers, Painting, Photography, Printmaking, 2D & 3D

—Art History & Archaeology Dept, 109 Pickard Hall, Columbia, MO 65211-1420. Tel 573-882-6711; Fax 573-884-5269; Internet Home Page Address: www.missouri.edu; *Prof Emeritus* Osmund Overby PhD; *Prof* Norman Land PhD; *Prof Emeritus* William R Biers PhD; *Prof Emeritus* Patricia Crown PhD; *Chmn* Anne Rudloff Stanton PhD; *Prof* Marcus Rautman; *Prof Emeritus* Howard Marshall; *Prof* Kathleen Slane; *Assoc Prof* Keith Eggener; *Assoc Prof* Susan

Langdon; *Assoc Prof* Kristin Schwain; *Asst Prof* Michael Yonan; *Instr* Elizabeth Hornbeck, PhD

Estab 1839, dept estab 1892; pub; D & E; Scholarships; LC 42, GC 18; maj 48, grad 39

Ent Req: HS dipl, SAT, GRE for grad students

Degrees: BA 4 yrs, MA 2-3 yrs, PhD 4 yrs

Tuition: Res—undergrad $246 per cr hr; nonres—undergrad $370 per cr hr; campus res available

Courses: Art History, Classical Archaeology, Historic Preservation, History of Art & Archeology

Summer School: Courses offered

FERGUSON

SAINT LOUIS COMMUNITY COLLEGE AT FLORISSANT VALLEY, Liberal Arts Division, 3400 Pershall Rd, Ferguson, MO 63135-1408. Tel 314-513-4375; Fax 314-513-2086; *Acting Chmn Div* Carol Berger; *Prof* Kim Mosley; *Assoc Prof* Jim Gormley; *Assoc Prof* John Ortbals; *Assoc Prof* Larry Byers; *Assoc Prof* Chris Licata; *Assoc Prof* Bob Langnas; *Assoc Prof* Eric Shultis; *Instr II* Janice Nesser-Chu

Estab 1962; Maintains nonprofit gallery, St. Louis Community College at Florissant Valley, 3400 Pershall Rd, St Louis 63135; FT10; pub; D & E; Scholarships; SC 36, LC 4; maj 70

Activities: Art supplies available at on-campus store

Ent Req: HS dipl, ent exam

Degrees: AA, AFA 2 yr, AAS 2 yr

Courses: Advertising Design, Air Brush, Art Appreciation, Art History, Ceramics, Commercial Art, Design, Drawing, Electronic Cert, Graphic Design, Illustration, Lettering, Painting, Photography, Printmaking, Sculpture, Silversmithing, Transfer Art, Typography, Video

Adult Hobby Classes: variable - through continuing educ div

Summer School: Courses—Design, Drawing, Figure Drawing, Lettering, Painting

FULTON

WILLIAM WOODS-WESTMINSTER COLLEGES, Art Dept, 501 Westminster Ave, Fulton, MO 65251-1230. Tel 573-592-4367; Fax 573-592-1623; Internet Home Page Address: www.williamwoods.edu; *Chmn* Paul Clervi; *Instr* Terry Martin, MA; *Instr* Tina Mann, MA; *Instr* Bob Elliott, MA; *Instr* Ken Greene, BA; *Instr* Jane Mudd; *Instr* Greig Thompson; *Instr* Dr Aimee Sapp; *Instr* Joe Potter

Estab 1870; Maintain nonprofit art gallery; Mildred M Cox Gallery, One Univ Ave, Fulton, MO 65251; Pvt; D & E; Scholarships; SC 54, LC 6; maj 100

Ent Req: HS dipl, SAT or ACT

Degrees: BA, BS & BFA 4 yr

Courses: Advertising Design, Aesthetics, Art Appreciation, Art Education, Art History, Art Therapy, Ceramics, Collage, Commercial Art, Costume Design & Construction, Design, Drawing, Film, Goldsmithing, Graphic Arts, Graphic Design, Handicrafts, History of Art & Architecture, Illustration, Interior Design, Jewelry, Painting, Photography, Printmaking, Sculpture, Silversmithing, Stage Design, Teacher Training, Theatre Arts, Video, Weaving

HANNIBAL

HANNIBAL LA GRANGE COLLEGE, Art Dept, 2800 Palmyra, Hannibal, MO 63401. Tel 573-221-3675; *Instr* Bill Krehmeier; *Instr* Dorothy Hahn; *Chmn* Robin Stone

Scholarships

Degrees: AA, BA(Art)

Tuition: $4425 per sem (12-17 hrs)

Courses: Advertising Design, Art Appreciation, Art Education, Art History, Calligraphy, Cartooning, Ceramics, Commercial Art, Design, Drawing, Handicrafts, Lettering, Mixed Media, Painting, Photography, Printmaking, Sculpture, Textile Design

Summer School: Dean, Dr Woodrow Burt. Term 2-4 wk & one 8 wk. Courses—vary

HILLSBORO

JEFFERSON COLLEGE, Dept of Art, 1000 Viking Dr, Hillsboro, MO 63050-2440. Tel 636-797-3000; Internet Home Page Address: www.jeffco.edu

JEFFERSON CITY

LINCOLN UNIVERSITY, Dept Visual and Performing Arts, 820 Chestnut St, Jefferson City, MO 65102-3500. Tel 573-681-5195; Fax 573-681-5004; Elec Mail govangd@lincolnu.edu; Internet Home Page Address: www.lincolnu.edu/finearts; *Asst Prof* Cheryl Unterschulz; *Prof* James Tatum; *Asst Prof* Rebecca Stonesanders; *Asst Prof* Cynthia Byler; *Asst Prof* James Crow

Estab 1927; Fine arts gallery; Richardson Fine Arts Center; FT 3, PT 4; pub; D&E; Scholarships; SC 19, LC 6; maj 50, others 100

Ent Req: HS dipl

Degrees: BS(Art) & BS(Art Educ) 4 yr

Courses: Applied Art, †Art Appreciation, Art Education, Art History, †Ceramics, †Commercial Art, †Design, †Drawing, †Graphic Arts, Graphic Design, †Handicrafts, †History of Art & Architecture, †Mixed Media, †Painting, †Photography, †Printmaking, Studio Art, Teacher Training

Summer School: Courses—same as above

JOPLIN

MISSOURI SOUTHERN STATE UNIVERSITY, Dept of Art, 3950 Newman Rd, Joplin, MO 64801-1595. Tel 417-625-9563; Fax 417-625-3046; Elec Mail kyle-n@mail.mssu.edu; Internet Home Page Address: www.mssu.edu; *Prof* V A Christensen; *Prof* David Noblett; *Adjunct Prof* Alice Knepper; *Dept Head* Nick Kyle; *Prof* Josie Mai; *Prof* Burt Bucher; *Prof* Frank Pishkur; *Adjunct Prof* Peggy Beckham

Estab 1937; Maintains nonprofit art gallery; on-campus art supply shop; FT 7; pub; D & E; Scholarships; SC 24, LC 2, Non-credit 4; D 500, non-maj 15 maj 125, others 10
Ent Req: HS dipl
Degrees: BA & BSE 4 yrs
Courses: Aesthetics, Art Appreciation, Art Education, Art History, Ceramics, Commercial Art, Design, Drawing, †Graphic Communications, Graphic Design, Mixed Media, Painting, Photography, Printmaking, Sculpture, Silversmithing, †Studio, Studio Crafts, Teacher Training, Typography
Adult Hobby Classes: Enrl 60; Tuition varies. Courses—Clay, Jewelry, Photographic (Digital), Watercolor
Summer School: Dir, Nick Kyle. Art Appreciation, Studio Course

KANSAS CITY

AVILA COLLEGE, Art Division, Dept of Humanities, 11901 Wornall Rd, Kansas City, MO 64145-1698. Tel 816-942-8400, Ext 2289; Fax 816-501-2459; Internet Home Page Address: www.avila.edu; *Instr* Sharyl Wright; *Instr* Kelly Mills; *Instr* Lisa Sugimoto; *Chmn Humanities* Carol Coburn; *Chmn Art & Design* Susan Lawlor; *Instr* Marci Aylward
Estab 1948; 7 adjunct instrs; den; D & E; Scholarships; SC 35, LC 4; D 140, E 20, non-maj 120, maj 40
Ent Req: HS dipl, SAT and PSAT
Degrees: BA 4 yrs
Courses: Art Appreciation, Art Education, Art History, Ceramics, Commercial Art, Design, Drawing, Graphic Arts, Graphic Design, Illustration, Painting, Photography, Printmaking, Sculpture, Teacher Training
Adult Hobby Classes: Courses offered

KANSAS CITY ART INSTITUTE, 4415 Warwick Blvd, Kansas City, MO 64111-1820. Tel 800-522-5224; Fax 816-802-3309; Elec Mail info@kcai.edu; Internet Home Page Address: www.kcai.edu; *Pres* Kathleen Collins, MFA; *Prof* Chris Chapin; *Asst Prof* Michael Kidwell; *Asst Prof* Jamie Gray; *Asst Prof* Marty Maxwell Lane
Estab 1885; Maintain nonprofit art gallery; H & R Block Art Space, 16 E 43rd St, Kansas City, MO 64111; library Jannes Library & Learning Ctr, 4538 Warwick Blvd, Kansas City, MO 64111/ on-campus shop for purchase of art supplies; Pvt; D & E; Scholarships; maj areas 7, LC 104 in liberal arts; D 540, E 740
Activities: Book traveling exhibs; originate traveling exhibs
Ent Req: HS dipl, portfolio interview, recommendations, essay
Degrees: BFA 4 yrs
Tuition: $29,866 per yr, $14,933 per sem, $1,244 per cr hr; campus res—room $9,100 per yr (double occupancy)
Courses: †Animation, †Art History, †Ceramics, †Creative Writing, †Design, †Digital Film, Drawing, Fashion Arts, Film, Graphic Design, Painting, †Photography, †Printmaking, †Sculpture, †Textile, Weaving
Adult Hobby Classes: tuition varies

MAPLE WOODS COMMUNITY COLLEGE, Dept of Art & Art History, 2601 NE Barry Rd, Kansas City, MO 64156-1299. Tel 816-437-3000, Ext 3226; Internet Home Page Address: www.maplewoods.cc.mo.us; *Head Dept* Jennie Frederick
Estab 1969; PT 6; pub; D & E; Scholarships; SC 12, LC 2; D 125, E & Sat 80
Ent Req: HS dipl or GED
Degrees: AA 2 yrs
Courses: Art Education, Art Fundamentals, Art History, Ceramics, Commercial Art, †Computer, †Design, Drawing, †Fiber, Painting, Photography, Printmaking, Sculpture
Adult Hobby Classes: Courses same as above
Children's Classes: Summer classes.
Summer School: Dir, Helen Mary Turner. Courses—Ceramics, Drawing, Painting

METROPOLITAN COMMUNITY COLLEGE - PENN VALLEY, (Penn Valley Community College) Art Dept, 3201 SW Trafficway, Kansas City, MO 64111. Tel 816-604-4757; Fax 816-759-4606; Elec Mail darlene.town@mcckc.edu; Internet Home Page Address: www.mcckc.edu/pennvalley/humanities/art; *Div Chmn Humanities* Vicki Raine; *Art Instr/Gallery Dir* Bernadette Torres; *Art Instr* Mary Beth Moley
Maintain nonprofit art gallery, Carter Art Center (same address); schols open to all art majors; on-campus shop where art supplies may be purchased; Pub (Metropolitan Community Col - Kansas City); Scholarships
Degrees: AAS - Graphic Design
Tuition: District res—$87 per sem hr; non-district res—$156 per sem hr; non-state res—$210 per sem hr
Courses: Animation, Art Fundamentals, Art History, Cartooning, Ceramics, †Commercial Art, Computer Graphics, †Digital Prepness, Drawing, Fashion Arts, †Graphic Arts, †Graphic Design, Painting, Photography, Sculpture, †Web Design

ROCKHURST UNIVERSITY, Dept of Communication & Fine Arts, 1100 Rockhurst Rd, Kansas City, MO 64110-2508. Tel 816-501-4000; Tel 816-501-4407 (Gallery); Internet Home Page Address: www.rockhurst.edu; *Gallery Dir* Anne Pearce
Maintains Greenlease Art Gallery

UNIVERSITY OF MISSOURI-KANSAS CITY, Dept of Art & Art History, 5100 Rockhill Rd, 204 Fine Art Bldg Kansas City, MO 64110-2446. Tel 816-235-1501; Fax 816-235-5507; Elec Mail art@umkc.edu; Internet Home Page Address: www.umkc.edu/art; *Chmn* Kati Toivaner
Estab 1933; Average Annual Attendance: 11,000; FT 10, PT 7; pub; D & E; Scholarships; maj 138
Income: $15,000 (financed through city and state)
Ent Req: contact Admis Office
Degrees: BA (Art), (Studio Art) & (Art History)
Courses: Art Appreciation, †Art History, Computer Art, Drawing, Graphic Design, Intermedia, Painting, Photography, Printmaking

Summer School: Dir, B L Dunbar. Enrl 65; 8 wk term. Courses—Art History, Drawing, Painting, Photography, Printmaking

KIRKSVILLE

TRUMAN STATE UNIVERSITY, Art Dept, 100 E Normal St, Kirksville, MO 63501-4200. Tel 660-785-4417; *Head Div Fine Arts* Robert L Jones
Estab 1867; pub; D & E; Scholarships; SC 27, LC 8; D 220, non-maj 45, maj 155
Ent Req: HS dipl
Degrees: BFA(Visual Communications Studio) 4 yrs, BA(Liberal Arts) 4 yrs, BA(Art History) 4 yrs
Courses: †Art History, †Ceramics, Fibers, †Painting, †Photography, †Printmaking, †Sculpture, Visual Communications
Summer School: Enrl 80-100; term of two 5 wk sessions beginning June & July

LIBERTY

WILLIAM JEWELL COLLEGE, Art Dept, 500 College Hill, Liberty, MO 64068. Tel 816-781-7700, Ext 5415; Fax 816-415-5027; *Chmn* Nano Nore, MFA; *Instr* Rebecca Koop, BFA
Estab 1849, dept estab 1966; pvt (cooperates with the Missouri Baptist Convention); D & E; Scholarships; D 120, E 35-40, maj 30
Degrees: BA(Art) & BS 4 yrs
Courses: Art Appreciation, Art Education, Art History, Calligraphy, Ceramics, Computer Graphic, Design, Drawing, Fibers, Painting, Photography, Printmaking, Sculpture, Weaving
Adult Hobby Classes: Enrl 10 - 15; tuition $120 per 14 wk sem. Courses—Drawing, Illustration, Jewelry/Silversmithing, Painting, Photography
Children's Classes: Enrl 10 - 15; tuition $30 - $40 for a 6 wk session. Courses—Ceramics, Drawing, Painting, Photography
Summer School: Dir, Dr Steve Schwegler; Illustration Academy, Dirs John & Mark English

MARYVILLE

NORTHWEST MISSOURI STATE UNIVERSITY, Dept of Fine & Performing Arts, 800 University Dr, Maryville, MO 64468-6001. Tel 660-562-1326; Fax 660-562-1346; Elec Mail oehler@nwmissouri.edu; Internet Home Page Address: www.nwmissouri.edu/dept/art/index.htm; *Assoc Prof/Chair* Dr David Oehler, PhD; *Prof* Dr Kim Spradling, PhD; *Assoc Prof* Armin Muhsam, MFA; *Assoc Prof* Glen Williams, MFA; *Assoc Prof* Craig Warner, MFA; *Asst Prof* Dr Martha Breckenridge, PhD; *Asst Prof* Chris Graves, MFA; *Instr* Robert Schultz, MFA; *Instr* Veronica Watkins, MFA; *Prof* Phil Laber, MFA; *Instr* Kwok-Pong (Bobby) Tso, MFA
Estab 1905, dept estab 1915; Maintains nonprofit Olive De Luce Fine Art Gallery; art supplies sold at on-campus store; FT 10, PT 2; pub; D & E; Scholarships; SC 74, LC 19; D 475, E 25, non-maj 350, maj 172
Ent Req: HS dipl
Degrees: BA, BFA, BSE & BA 4 yrs
Tuition: In-state 25 cr hr $266; out of state $474.64
Courses: Advertising Design, Art Appreciation, †Art Education, Art History, †Ceramics, Commercial Art, Computer Graphics, Constructions, †Design, †Drawing, †Graphic Design, History of Art & Architecture, Interactive Digital Media, Intl Study in Art History, Intl Study in Studio, Jewelry, Metalsmithing, Mixed Media, †Painting, †Photography, †Printmaking, †Sculpture, Teacher Training, †Weaving
Children's Classes: Courses—Art Educ Club workshops $15
Summer School: Chmn Dept Art, Dave Oehler. Offerings vary yr to yr. Courses—Art Education, Ceramics, Jewelry, Painting, Photography, Watercolor

NEOSHO

CROWDER COLLEGE, Longwell Museum/Art Department, 601 Laclede, Neosho, MO 64850. Tel 417-455-5470; Tel 417-451-3223; Fax 417-451-4280; Internet Home Page Address: www.longwellmuseum.weebly.com; Internet Home Page Address: www.crowder.edu; *Art Instr* Casey Stueber; *Gallery Coordr* Jessica Lingenfelter; *Art Instr* Allen Bishop
Estab 1964; Maintain non-profit art gallery, Longwell Museum, same address as school; on-campus shop where art supplies may be purchased; FT 1, PT 1; Pub; D & E; Scholarships; D 1000, E 300, maj 20, others 250
Ent Req: HS grad or equivalent
Degrees: AA & AAS 2 yrs
Courses: †20-30 Design, Art Appreciation, Art History, Ceramic Design, †Ceramics, †Costume Design & Construction, Design, Drawing, Fibers Design, †Graphic Arts, †Graphic Design, Jewelry, Painting, †Photography, Sculpture, †Stage Design, †Theatre Arts, †Weaving
Summer School: Dean of Col, Jackie Vietti. Term of 8 wks beginning in June. Courses—Varied acad courses

NEVADA

COTTEY COLLEGE, Art Dept, 1000 W Austin, Nevada, MO 64772. Tel 417-667-8181; Elec Mail bfulton@cottey.edu; Internet Home Page Address: www.cottey.edu; *VPres* Cathryn Pridal, PhD; *Art Faculty* Brianne Fulton, MFA
Estab 1884; maintains nonprofit art gallery, PEO Foundation Gallery; on-campus shop where art supplies may be purchased; FT 3; pvt; W; D ; Scholarships; SC 15, LC 4; maj 12-15, total 369
Activities: Schols offered
Ent Req: HS grad, AC Board
Degrees: AA 2 yrs & AS 2 yrs, AFA visual arts, selective BA degrees

Courses: Art Appreciation, Art History, Ceramics, Design, Drawing, Graphic Arts, Handicrafts, Illustration, Jewelry, Metals, Painting, Photography, Printmaking, Weaving

PARKVILLE

PARK UNIVERSITY, Dept of Art & Design, 8700 NW River Park Dr, Box 42 Parkville, MO 64152-4358. Tel 816-741-2000, Ext 6457; Fax 816-741-4911; Elec Mail donnabach@mail.park.edu; *Chmn* Donna N Bachman; *Asst Prof* Thomas H Smith; *Asst Prof* Kay M Boehr
Estab 1875; Maintain nonprofit gallery; Campanella Gallery; Pvt; D & E; Scholarships; SC 13, LC 4; D 50, non-maj 40, maj 130
Ent Req: HS dipl, ACT
Degrees: BA, 4 yrs
Tuition: Res—undergrad $165 per cr hr; campus res—$2,425 room & board
Courses: 3-D Design, Advertising Design, Art Education, Art History, Ceramics, Drawing, †Fiber, Graphic Design, History of Art & Architecture, Interior Design, Painting, Photography, Sculpture, Teacher Training
Summer School: Tuition $165 per cr hr for 8 wk term. Courses—Ceramics, Printmaking, varied curriculum

POINT LOOKOUT

COLLEGE OF THE OZARKS, Dept of Art, PO Box 17, Art Dept Point Lookout, MO 65726-0017. Tel 417-334-6411, Ext 4255; Internet Home Page Address: www.cofo.edu; *Prof* Anne Allman PhD; *Prof* Jayme Burchett, MFA; *Prof* Jeff Johnston, MFA; *Assoc Prof* Richard Cummings
Estab 1906, dept estab 1962; Maintain nonprofit art gallery; Boger Art Gallery, Art Dept, PO Box 17, Point Lookout, MO 65726; pvt; D ; Scholarships; SC 22, LC 4; D 200, E 25, non-maj 180, maj 40
Ent Req: HS dipl, ACT
Degrees: BA & BS 4 yr
Tuition: No fees are charged; each student works 960 hrs in on-campus employment
Courses: †Art Education, †Ceramics, Computer Art, †Design, †Drawing, Fibers, Graphic Design, †Painting, †Photography, †Printmaking, †Sculpture

SAINT CHARLES

LINDENWOOD COLLEGE, Art Dept, 209 S Kingshighway St, Saint Charles, MO 63301-1693. Tel 636-949-4862, 949-2000; *Chmn Dept, Contact* Elaine Tillinger
Estab 1827; FT 4, PT 4; pvt; D & E; Scholarships; SC 24, LC 16; D 200, E 30, maj 40
Ent Req: HS dipl, ent exam
Degrees: BA, BS, BFA 4 yrs, MA, MFA
Courses: Art Education, Art History, Ceramics, Computer Art, Design, Drawing, Graphic Arts, Painting, Photography, Printmaking, Sculpture, Teacher Training

SAINT JOSEPH

MISSOURI WESTERN STATE UNIVERSITY, Art Dept, 4525 Downs Dr, Saint Joseph, MO 64507-2246. Tel 816-271-4200, Ext 4282; Fax 816-271-4181; Elec Mail sauls@missouriwestern.edu; Internet Home Page Address: www.missouriwestern.edu; *Chmn Dept* Dr Allison Sauls PhD; *Asst Prof* David Harris, MFA; *Asst Prof* Neil Lawley, MFA; *Prof* Geo Sipp, MFA; *Assoc Prof* Teresa Harris, MFA; *Assoc Prof* Peter Hriso; *Instr* Eric Fuson; *Adjunct Prof* Aubony Chalfont, MFA; *Adjunct Prof* Mikhail Kligman, MFA; *Adjunct Prof* Amy Lenharth, MFA; *Adjunct Prof* Terry Oldham, MA
Estab 1969; Maintains nonprofit gallery, Gallery 206; MWSU Library; art supplies sold at on-campus store; Pub; D & E; Scholarships; SC 25, LC 8; D 355, E 100, non-maj 120, maj 130, grad 10
Ent Req: HS dipl, GED, ACT
Degrees: BSE (Art Educ), BA & BFA (Graphic Design), BFA (Studio, Digital Animation)
Courses: Advertising Design, Aesthetics, Animation, Art Appreciation, Art Education, Art History, Ceramics, Commercial Art, Computer Art, Design, Drawing, Graphic Arts, Graphic Design, History of Art & Architecture, Illustration, Painting, Photography, Printmaking, Sculpture, Teacher Training, Tools & Techniques
Adult Hobby Classes: adult classes through western institute prog
Children's Classes: children's classes through western institute prog
Summer School: Chmn, Dr Allison Sauls. Tuition res—$130 for 5 or more cr hrs, nonres—$240 for 5 or more cr hrs; term of 8 wks beginning June 1. Courses—Art Education, Ceramics, Introduction to Art, Photomedia, Painting

SAINT LOUIS

FONTBONNE UNIVERSITY, Fine Art Dept, 6800 Wydown Blvd, Saint Louis, MO 63105-3043. Tel 314-889-1431; Fax 314-889-1451; Internet Home Page Address: www.fontbonne.edu; *Prof* Hank Knickmeyer, MFA; *Assoc Prof* Victor Wang, MFA; *Assoc Prof* Deanna Jent, MFA; *Assoc Prof* Tim Liddy, MFA; *Asst Prof* Michael Sullivan, MFA; *Assoc Prof* Catherine Connor-Talasek, MFA; *Asst Prof & Chair* Mark Douglas, MFA
Estab 1923; Maintains nonprofit gallery, Gallery of Art 6800 Wydown Blvd, St Louis, MO 63105; Fontbonne University Fine Arts Gallery; pvt; D & E; Scholarships; SC 10, LC 2, GC 6; non-maj 10, maj 46, grad 12, others 5
Ent Req: HS dipl, portfolio
Degrees: BA and BFA 4 yrs, MA 1 yr, MFA 2 yrs

Courses: Art Appreciation, Art Education, Art History, †Ceramics, Design, †Drawing, †Fibers, †Graphic Design, Illustration, †Painting, †Photography, †Sculpture, Teacher Training, Weaving
Adult Hobby Classes: Tuition $150 per cr. Courses—Art History
Summer School: Dir, Mark Douglas. Enrl 75; tuition subject to chg, see website. Courses—Ceramics, Drawing, Modern Art, Painting, Printmaking

MARYVILLE UNIVERSITY OF SAINT LOUIS, Art & Design Program, 650 Maryville University Dr, Saint Louis, MO 63141-7299. Tel 314-529-9300, 529-9381 (art div); Tel 800-627-9855; Fax 314-529-9940; Internet Home Page Address: www.maryville.edu; *Prof Art & Prog Dir Graphic Design* Cherie Fister, MFA; *Assoc Prof Art & Prog Dir Studio Art* John Baltrushunas, MFA; *Prof* Steven Teczar, MFA; *Asst Prof & Prog Dir, Interior Design* Darlene Davison, BFA; *Instr Interior Design* Martha Whitaker, BFA; *Instr Graphic Design* Laurie Eisenbach-Bush, BFA; *Asst Prof Art History* Todd Brenningmeyer, PhD; *Assoc Prof Interactive Design* Jon Fahnestock, MFA; *Asst Prof Art* Scott Angus, MFA
Estab 1872, dept estab 1961; Maintains nonprofit gallery, Morton J May Foundation Gallery; on-campus shop for purchase of art supplies; Pvt; D, E & W; Scholarships; SC 74, LC 6; D 200, E 30, non-maj 60, maj 180
Ent Req: HS dipl, ACT or SAT
Degrees: BA, BFA
Tuition: $10,192 per sem; $612 per cr hr; campus res—room & board $10,000 per yr
Courses: 2-D & 3-D Design, 3-D Modeling, Advertising Design, Animation, Art Education, †Art History, †Art Studio, †Auto CAD, †Ceramics, †Color Theory, Design, †Display, †Drafting, Drawing, Environmental Graphics, †Fibers & Soft Sculpture, †Furniture Design, †Graphic Arts, †Graphic Design, †Handmade Book, History of Art & Architecture, Identity Design, Illustration, †Interactive Design, †Interior Design, Mixed Media, Motion Graphics, Packaging, †Painting, †Painting the Figure, †Photography, †Printmaking, †Sculpture, †Silversmithing, †Teacher Training, Video, †Weaving, Web Design
Adult Hobby Classes: Enrl & tuition vary. Courses—Art & Architectural History, Art in St Louis, Drawing, Painting, Photography
Children's Classes: Enrl 115; tuition $150 (1 cr) & $100 (no cr) for 10 wk session. Courses—Ceramics, Cartooning, Drawing, Painting, Photography, Printmaking, Watercolor
Summer School: Enrl 60; tuition same as regular year. Courses—Photography, Art Appreciation, Art History, Auto CAD, Drawing, Painting

SAINT LOUIS COMMUNITY COLLEGE AT FOREST PARK, Art Dept, 5600 Oakland Ave, Saint Louis, MO 63110-1393. Tel 314-644-9350; Fax 314-644-9752; Internet Home Page Address: www.stlcc.cc.mo.us; *Asst Prof* Evann Richards, BA; *Instr* Joe C Angert, MA; *Instr* Allen Arpadi, BA
Estab 1962, dept estab 1963. College maintains three campuses; PT 14; pub; D & E; Scholarships; SC 36, LC 6; D 200, E 100, non-maj 75, maj 75
Ent Req: HS dipl
Degrees: AA & AAS 2 yrs
Courses: Advertising Design, Art Appreciation, Art Education, †Art History, Ceramics, Color, Commercial Art, Commercial Photography, Computer-Assisted Publishing, Design, Drawing, Film, †Graphic Design, Illustration, Lettering, †Painting, †Photography
Adult Hobby Classes: Courses—Drawing, Painting, Photography, Printmaking, Sculpture, Video
Summer School: Chmn, Leon Anderson. Enrl 100. Courses—Same as those above

SAINT LOUIS COMMUNITY COLLEGE AT MERAMEC, Art Dept, 11333 Big Bend Blvd, Saint Louis, MO 63122. Tel 314-984-7500, 984-7632; Internet Home Page Address: www.stlcc.edu/mc/dept/art; *Prof* Margaret Keller; *Prof* Chuck Groth; *Prof* Rene Behrend; *Prof* David Hanlon; *Prof* Betsy Morris; *Prof* James Ibur; *Prof* Joe Chesla; *Prof* Erin Leclerc; *Prof* Mary Huelsmann; *Prof* Michael Swoboda; *Prof* Virginia Heisler; *Prof* Ken Wood; *Prof* David Montgomery; *Prof* Bradley Fratello; *Prof* Michael Lorenz; *Prof* Timothy Linder
Estab 1964; Maintain nonprofit art gallery, Meramec Contemporary Art Gallery (on campus); Pub; D & E; Scholarships; SC 130, LC 10
Ent Req: HS dipl
Degrees: AFA 2 yr, AAS 2yr
Courses: Advertising Design, †Architecture, Art History, Ceramics, Commercial Art, Drawing, Illustration, Interior Design, Painting, Photography, Printmaking, Sculpture, †Video
Summer School: Chmn Dept, Tim Linder. Courses—Art Appreciation, Ceramics, Design, Drawing, Photography

SAINT LOUIS UNIVERSITY, Fine & Performing Arts Dept, 221 N Grand Blvd, Saint Louis, MO 63103-2097. Tel 314-977-3030; Fax 314-977-3447; *Chmn* Dr Cindy Stollhans
Maintains McNamee Gallery, St Louis; Scholarships
Degrees: BA
Tuition: Undergrad $6765 full-time per term, $468 part-time per hr
Courses: Approaching the Arts, Art History, Design, Drawing, Painting, Photography, Sculpture, †Studio Art
Summer School: Courses—Drawings, Painting, Studio Art

UNIVERSITY OF MISSOURI, SAINT LOUIS, Dept of Art & Art History, 8001 Natural Bridge Rd, Saint Louis, MO 63121-4499. Tel 314-516-5975; Fax 314-516-5003; Internet Home Page Address: www.umsl.edu/~art; *Chmn* Dan Younger MFA; *Prof* Ken Anderson, MFA; *Prof* Yael Even PhD, MFA; *Prof* Jeanne Morgan Zarucchi, PhD; *Asst Prof* Terry Suhre, MFA; *Assoc Prof* Gretchen Schisla, MFA; *Sr Lectr* Juliana Yuan, MA; *Des Lee Foundation Prof Art Educ* E Louis Lankford, PhD; *Assoc Prof* Marian Amies, MFA; *Asst Prof* Phillip Robinson, MFA; *Assoc Prof* Jeffrey Sippel, MFA; *Asst Prof* Jennifer McKnight, MFA; *Instr* Luci McMichael, MAT; *Assoc Prof* Ruth Bohan, PhD; *Assoc Prof* Susan Cahan, PhD; *Asst Prof* Susan Waller, PhD
Estab 1963; Maintain nonprofit art gallery; Gallery 210; Pub; D & E; Scholarships; SC 66, LC 52, GC 7; maj 270 (50 Art History, 220 Studio Art)

Ent Req: HS dipl
Degrees: BA(Art Hist), BFA
Courses: Art Education, †Art History, Design, †Drawing, †General Fine Arts, †Graphic Design, Illustration, †Painting, †Photography, †Printmaking

WASHINGTON UNIVERSITY, School of Art, 1 Brookings Dr, Campus Box 1031 Saint Louis, MO 63130-4862. Tel 314-935-6500; Fax 314-935-4862; Elec Mail jpike@art.wustl.edu; Internet Home Page Address: www.wustl.edu; *Dean School* Jeffrey C Pike; *Assoc Dean School* Georgia Binnington; *Assoc Dean* Michael Byron; *Dir Grad Studies* Eric Troffkin
Estab 1853; Maintain nonprofit art gallery, The Des Lee Gallery, 1627 Washington Ave, St. Louis, MO 63104; pvt; D; Scholarships, Fellowships; SC 62, LC 10, GC 31; maj 320, grad 20
Ent Req: HS dipl, SAT or ACT, portfolio
Degrees: BFA 4 yrs, MFA 2 yrs
Tuition: $26,900 per yr, $13,450 per sem, $1,120 per cr hr; campus res—room & board available
Courses: †Advertising Design, Aesthetics, Architecture, Art Appreciation, Art Education, Art History, †Ceramics, Costume Design & Construction, Design, Drawing, †Fashion Arts, †Fashion Design, †Glass Blowing, Graphic Arts, †Graphic Design, History of Art & Architecture, †Illustration, Mixed Media, Occupational Therapy, †Painting, †Photography, †Printmaking, †Sculpture, Stage Design, Theatre Arts, Video
Summer School: Enrl 50; tuition $$4565 HS program for term beginning June 12- Jul 16. Courses—Painting, Printmaking, Photography. Drawing, Computer Graphics, Fashion, Sculpture, Ceramics, Florence, Italy, enrl 40; tuition $2850, $750 room, June 1 - June 30. Courses—On-site Drawing, Photography, Book Arts & Painting
—School of Architecture, 1 Brookings Dr, Campus Box 1079 Saint Louis, MO 63130-4862. Tel 314-935-6200; Fax 314-935-7656; Internet Home Page Address: www.wustl.edu; *Dean School* Cynthia Weese, FAIA
Estab 1910; pvt; D; Scholarships; SC 28, LC 58, GC 42; 300, maj 200, grad 100
Degrees: BA(Arch), March, MA(UD)
Tuition: $18,350 per yr, $765 per cr hr
Courses: †Architecture, Design, Drawing, Interior Design, Landscape Architecture, Photography
Adult Hobby Classes: Enrl 43; tuition $175 per unit. Cert degree program, Bachelor of Technology in Architecture
Summer School: Tuition varies. Courses—Advanced Architectural Design, Fundamentals of Design, Structural Principles

SPRINGFIELD

DRURY COLLEGE, Art & Art History Dept, 900 N Benton Ave, Springfield, MO 65802-3791. Tel 417-873-7263, 873-7879; Fax 417-873-6921; Internet Home Page Address: www.drury.edu; *Chmn* Alkis Tsolakis
Estab 1873; FT 6, PT 9; den; D; Scholarships; SC 12, LC 5; 2246
Ent Req: HS dipl
Degrees: 4 yrs
Courses: Architecture, Art History, Ceramics, Commercial Art, Photography, Studio Arts, Teacher Training, Weaving
Adult Hobby Classes: Enrl 25-35; tuition $125 per cr hr. Courses—Studio Art & History of Art
Children's Classes: Summer Scape, gifted children. Courses—Architecture, Design, Photography
Summer School: Dir, Sue Rollins. Enrl 292; tuition $125 per cr hr June-Aug for 9 wk term. Courses—Art History, Ceramics, Drawing, Painting, Photography

EVANGEL UNIVERSITY, Humanities-Art Dept, 1111 N Glenstone Ave, Trask Hall 3rd Floor Springfield, MO 65802-2125. Tel 417-865-2815; Fax 417-865-9599; Internet Home Page Address: www.evangel.edu; *Dept Chair* Nathan Nelson
Maintains nonprofit Barnett Fine Art & Design Gallery
Activities: Schols & fels available
Courses: Advertising Design, Art Appreciation, Art Education, Art History, Ceramics, Collage, Commercial Art, Conceptual Art, Costume Design & Construction, Design, Drawing, Film, Graphic Arts, Graphic Design, History of Art & Architecture, Mixed Media, Painting, Photography, Printmaking, Sculpture, Stage Design, Teacher Training, Textile Design, Theatre Arts, Weaving

MISSOURI STATE UNIVERSITY, Dept of Art & Design, 901 S National Springfield, MO 65897-0001. Tel 417-836-5110; Fax 417-836-6055; Elec Mail artanddesign@missouristate.edu; Internet Home Page Address: www.art.missouristate.edu; *Head Dept* Prof Wade S. Thompson; *Assoc Dean Summer School* Dr. Roger Stoner
Estab 1901; Maintains nonprofit gallery, Brick City Gallery, 215 W Mill St, Springfield, MO 65806; on-campus art supplies shop; FT 28, PT 15; pub; D & E; Scholarships; SC 54, LC 19, GC; maj 556, others 18,930
Ent Req: HS dipl, ent exam
Degrees: BFA (Art, Design) BS (Education Comprehensive & Electronic Arts) & BA (Art History) 4 yrs
Courses: Art Appreciation, †Art Education, †Art History, †Ceramics, Computer Animation, †Digital Arts, †Drawing, †Electronic Arts, †Graphic Design, Illustration, †Metals/Jewelry, †Painting, †Photography, †Printmaking, †Sculpture
Adult Hobby Classes: Tuition $98 per cr hr for 1 & 2 wk sessions
Summer School: Dean, Dr. Carey Adams. Enrl 6,836; special workshops available during summer session; tuition $154 per cr hr & Student Services fee for 4, 5 & 8 week sessions. Courses—Selected from above curriculum

UNION

EAST CENTRAL COLLEGE, Art Dept, 1964 Prairie Dell Rd, Union, MO 63084-4344. Tel 636-583-5195, Ext 2258; Internet Home Page Address: www.ecc.cc.mo.us/enter.html; *Dir* John Anglin; *Instr* James Crow

Estab 1968; FT 2, PT 1; pub; D & E; Scholarships; SC 8, LC 8; D 370, E 120, maj 40
Ent Req: HS dipl, ent exam
Degrees: AA & AAS 2 yrs
Courses: Art Appreciation, Art Education, Art History, Business of Art, Design, Drawing, Figure Drawing, Handicrafts, History of Art & Architecture, Lettering, Painting, Photography, Printmaking, Sculpture, Teacher Training
Adult Hobby Classes: Enrl 121; tuition $21-$38 per semester. Courses—Painting
Children's Classes: Tuition $25 for 4 wk summer term. Courses—Art, Drawing, Sculpture, Painting
Summer School: Tuition $21 per cr hr for 8 wk term. Courses—Art Appreciation, Art History

WARRENSBURG

CENTRAL MISSOURI STATE UNIVERSITY, Dept Art & Design, PO Box 800, Art Ctr 120 Warrensburg, MO 64093-5299. Tel 660-543-4481; Fax 660-543-8006; Internet Home Page Address: www.ucmo.edu; *Chair Dept* Mick Luehrman, PhD; *Asst Prof* David Babcock, MFA; *Prof* Kathleen Desmond, EdD; *Prof* John Haydu, MFA; *Prof* Joyce Jablonski, MFA; *Prof* Andrew Katsourides, MFA; *Prof* John Louder, MFA; *Instr* Melanie Lowrance, MFA; *Assoc Prof* John Lynch, MFA; *Prof* LeRoy McDermott, PhD, EdD; *Assoc Prof* Clint Orr, MFA; *Assoc Prof* Susan Stevenson, PhD; *Asst Prof* Rahila Weed, PhD; *Prof* Christina Willey, MFA; *Prof* Neva Wood, MFA; *Prof* Matthew Zupnick, MFA
Estab 1871; Maintains a nonprofit art gallery, Art Center Gallery, Art Ctr 120, Warrensburg MO 64093; on-campus shop where art supplies may be purchased; pub; D & E; Scholarships; SC 52, LC 10, GC 7; D 472, maj 537, grad 4
Ent Req: HS dipl, Missouri School & Col Ability Test, ACT
Degrees: BSE & BFA 4 yrs
Courses: †Advertising Design, †Art Appreciation, †Art Education, Art History, †Ceramics, †Commercial Art, †Design, Drawing, †Graphic Design, †History of Art & Architecture, Illustration, †Interior Design, Painting, †Printmaking, Sculpture, †Studio Art, Teacher Training, †Textile Design, †Weaving
Summer School: Chair Dept, Mick Luehrman. Term of 12 wks beginning second wk in May. Courses—Ceramics, Drawing, Grad Studio Courses, Painting, Art Educ

WEBSTER GROVES

WEBSTER UNIVERSITY, Art Dept, 470 E Lockwood Blvd, Webster Groves, MO 63119-3194. Tel 314-968-7171 or 314-961-2660; Fax 314-968-7139; Internet Home Page Address: www.webster.edu; *Chmn* Tom Lang, MFA; *Asst Prof* Carol Hodson, MFA; *Asst Prof* Jeffrey Hughes PhD, MFA; *Asst Prof* Brad Loudenback, MFA; *Asst Prof* Jeri Au, MFA; *Asst Prof* Gary Passanise, MFA
Estab 1915; dept estab 1946; pvt; D & E; Scholarships; SC 60, LC 15; 1100, maj 100
Ent Req: HS dipl, SAT or ACT
Degrees: BA & BFA 4 yrs
Courses: †Art Education, †Art History, †Ceramics, Collage, Conceptual Art, †Drawing, Film, †Graphic Design, †Painting, †Papermaking, †Photography, †Printmaking, †Sculpture, †Teacher Training
Adult Hobby Classes: Tuition $175 per cr hr for 16 wk sem. Courses—Art, Photography, Watercolor
Summer School: Assoc Dean Fine Arts, Peter Sargent. Tuition $175 per cr hr for term of 6 or 8 wks beginning June. Courses—Introductory Photography, Sculpture Workshop: Bronze

MONTANA

BILLINGS

MONTANA STATE UNIVERSITY-BILLINGS, Art Dept, 1500 University Dr, Billings, MT 59101-0252. Tel 406-657-2324; Fax 406-657-2187; Elec Mail kpitman@msubillings.edu; Internet Home Page Address: www.msubilling.edu/art; *Chair* Connie M Landis
Estab 1927; Maintains non profit Northcutt Steele Gallery on campus; Art supplies may be purchased at on-campus shop; FT 6, PT 4; pub; D & E; Scholarships
Ent Req: HS dipl
Degrees: AA, BA(Lib Arts, Studio & Art Educ Option K-12)
Courses: †Art Education, Art History, Ceramics, †Collage, †Computer Graphics, †Design, Drawing, †Lithography, Painting, Photography, †Printmaking, Sculpture
Summer School: Tuition res—$415.55 per cr, nonres—$786.65 per cr for three sessions from May through Aug. Courses—various studio courses and workshops

ROCKY MOUNTAIN COLLEGE, Art Dept, 1511 Poly Dr, Billings, MT 59102-1796. Tel 406-657-1094, 657-1040 (main), 657-1000 (admis); Internet Home Page Address: www.rocky.edu; *Chmn* Mark Moak
Estab 1878; dept estab 1957; pvt; D; Scholarships; SC 12, LC 5; 112, non-maj 40, maj 30, others 5
Ent Req: HS dipl, ACT
Degrees: BA & BS 4 yrs
Courses: Art Education, Art History, Ceramics, Drawing, Graphic Design, Painting, Photography, Sculpture, Teacher Training
Adult Hobby Classes: Enrl 100; tuition $20 for 5 wks. Courses—Crafts, Painting, Picture Framing

BOZEMAN

MONTANA STATE UNIVERSITY, School of Art, 213 Haynes Hall, Bozeman, MT 59717. Tel 406-994-4501; Fax 406-994-3680; Elec Mail art@montana.edu; Internet Home Page Address: www.montana.edu/art; *Dir School of Art* Vaughan

Judge; *Adjunct Instr Metalsmithing* Bryan Peterson; *Prof Graphic Design* Jeffrey Conger; *Asst Prof Graphic Design* Meta Newhouse; *Prof Art History* Todd Larkin; *Prof Graphic Design* Stephanie Newman; *Asst Prof Ceramics* Josh DeWeese; *Asst Prof Printmaking* Gesine Janzen; *Asst Prof Painting* Sarah Mast; *Asst Prof - Painting & Drawing* Rollin Beamish; *Asst Prof - Art History* Regina Gee; *Asst Prof - Foundation* Dean Adams; *Assoc Prof Art History* Melissa Ragain; *Assoc Prof Ceramics* Jeremy Hatch; *Assoc Prof Sculpture* Jim Zimpel; *Adjunct Instr Foundations* Denise Reibe

Estab 1893; Maintain nonprofit art gallery; Helene E Copeland Gallery, Montana State Univ, Bozeman, MT 59717; creative arts library; art supplies available in bookstore; 14; pub; D & E; Scholarships, Fellowships; SC 43, LC 21, GC 14; maj 450, grad 15

Ent Req: HS dipl 2.5 GPA or ACT score of 20

Degrees: BFA, MFA, BA

Tuition: Res—$5,730 per yr, nonres—$15,580 per yr

Courses: †Art Education, †Art History, †Ceramics, Design, †Drawing, Goldsmithing, Graphic Arts, †Graphic Design, History of Art & Architecture, Illustration, Jewelry, Metals, Mixed Media, †Painting, †Printmaking, †Sculpture, †Silversmithing, †Studio Arts, Teacher Training

Summer School: Dir, Richard Helzer. Enrl 65; tuition res—$284.65 per cr, nonres—$695.05 per cr for 12 wk term. Courses—Art History, Ceramics, Drawing, Graphic Design, Metals, Painting, Printmaking, Sculpture, Special Workshops

—School of Architecture, Cheever Hall, Rm 160, Bozeman, MT 59717-3760; PO Box 173760, Bozeman, MT 59717-3760. Tel 406-994-4256; Fax 406-994-6696; Elec Mail architecture@montana.edu; Internet Home Page Address: www.arch.montana.edu/; *Interim Dir* Steven Juroszek; *Interim Assoc Dir* John Brittingham

FT 13, PT 1; Pub; D & E; Scholarships; LabC 31, LC 39; maj 400

Degrees: BA(Environmental Design), MArch

Tuition: Res—$3,079 per yr; nonres—$9,075 per yr

Courses: Architectural Graphics, Architecture, Computer Applications in Architecture, Construction Drawings & Specifications, Design Fundamentals, Environmental Controls, History, Professional Practice, Structures, Theory

Summer School: Res—$171.40 undergrad per cr, $190.35 per cr, nonres—$421.25 undergrad per cr, $440.20 grad per cr

DILLON

THE UNIVERSITY OF MONTANA WESTERN, (Western Montana College) Art Program, 710 S Atlantic, Dillon, MT 59725. Tel 406-683-7232; Fax 406-683-7493; Elec Mail r_horst@umwestern.edu; Internet Home Page Address: www.umwestern.edu/; *Chmn Dept* Randy Horst; *Prof* David Regan; *Prof* Eva Mastandrea

Estab 1897; Maintains nonprofit gallery, The University of Montana - Western Art Gallery & Museum, 710 S Atlantic, Dillon, MT 59725. Art supplies may be purchased on campus; FT 3; pub; 3 1/2 block sessions; Scholarships; SC 18, LC 2; maj 30

Ent Req: HS dipl

Degrees: BS & BA 4 yrs

Courses: Art Education, Art History, Ceramics, †Computer Art, Drawing, Glass Blowing, †Illustration, Painting, Photography, Printmaking, Sculpture

Summer School: Dir Anneliese Ripley. Courses—Ceramics, Glassblowing, Travel Study

GREAT FALLS

UNIVERSITY OF GREAT FALLS, (College of Great Falls) Art Dept, 1301 20th St S, Art Bldg Great Falls, MT 59405-4934. Tel 406-761-8210; 791-5375; Fax 406-791-5394; Elec Mail jbecker@ugf.edu; Internet Home Page Address: www.ugf.edu; *Prof Art* Julia Becker; *Prof Music* Dr John Cubbage; *Adjunct Prof Art* Susan Thomas; *Adjunct Prof Art* David Rothweiler; *Adjunct Prof Art* Sophia Sparklin; *Adjunct Prof Art* Leslie Fontana; *Adjunct Prof Art* Doug Wendt; *Adjunct Prof Art* Rebecca Scott

Estab 1933; Maintain library exhibit space on-campus; UGF Library, same address; on-campus shop where art supplies may be purchased; FT 1, PT 2; pvt; D & E; weekends & special sessions; Scholarships, Fellowships; SC 15, Lab C, LC9; approx 1,000, majs 38

Activities: Schols offered

Ent Req: high school grad, entry tests

Degrees: 4 yrs

Tuition: $10,000 per yr

Courses: †Art Appreciation, Art Education, †Art History, †Book Arts, †Calligraphy, Ceramics, †Collage, †Conceptual Art, Design, Drawing, †Film, †Graphic Design, †Handicrafts, †History of Art & Architecture, †Mixed Media, †Museum Staff Training, †Painting, †Photography, †Printmaking, †Restoration & Conservation, †Sculpture, †Stage Design, †Teacher Training, †Textile Design, †Theatre Arts, †Video

Children's Classes: Enrl 24; summer; pastel painting; drawing in nature; textile design; book arts; life drawing

Summer School: General art classes; Kerri Koteskey, Registrar

HAVRE

MONTANA STATE UNIVERSITY-NORTHERN, Humanities & Social Sciences, PO Box 7751, Havre, MT 59501-7751. Tel 406-265-3751, 265-3700; Fax 406-265-3777; Internet Home Page Address: www.montanastateuniv.edu; *Art Dept Chmn* Will Ron

Estab 1929; pub; D & E; Scholarships; SC 15, LC 5, GC 9; D 425, grad 7

Ent Req: HS dipl

Degrees: AA 2 yrs, BS(Educ) and BA 4 yrs, MSc(Educ)

Courses: Art Education, Ceramics, Commercial Art, Drafting, Drawing, Graphic Arts, Painting, Sculpture

Adult Hobby Classes: Enrl 60. Courses—Classroom and Recreational Art, Watercolor Workshop

Summer School: Dir, Dr Gus Korb. Enrl 1390; two 5 wk sessions. Courses—Art Education, Art Methods K-12, Art Therapy

MILES CITY

MILES COMMUNITY COLLEGE, Dept of Fine Arts & Humanities, 2715 Dickinson St, Miles City, MT 59301-4799. Tel 406-234-3031; Internet Home Page Address: www.milescc.edu; *Instr* Fred McKee, MFA

Estab 1937, dept estab 1967; pub; D & E; Scholarships; SC 17, LC 1; D 36, E 23, non-maj 55, maj 4

Ent Req: HS dipl, ACT

Degrees: AA 2 yrs, cert

Courses: Art Appreciation, Ceramics, Design, Graphic Arts, Graphic Design, Jewelry, Painting, Photography

Adult Hobby Classes: Enrl 39; tuition $58 per cr hr. Courses—Crafts, Jewelry Making, Painting, Photography, Pottery

Children's Classes: Kids Kamp-2 wks in summer

MISSOULA

UNIVERSITY OF MONTANA, Dept of Art, Campus Dr 32 Missoula, MT 59812. Tel 406-243-4181; Fax 406-243-4968; Elec Mail artdept@selway.umt.edu; Internet Home Page Address: www.umt.edu/art; *Prof* Steven Connell, MFA; *Prof* Marilyn Bruya, MFA; *Prof* Beth Lo, MFA; *Prof* David James, MFA; *Co-Chair* Barbara Tilton, MFA; *Assoc Prof* Rafael Chacon, PhD; *Assoc Prof* Mary Ann Bonjorni, MFA; *Assoc Prof* Martin Fromm, MFA; *Chmn, Assoc Prof* James Bailey, MFA; *Asst Prof* Elizabeth Dove, MFA; *Co-Chair* Cathryn Mallory

Pub; D & E; Scholarships; SC 107, LC 14, GC 38; non-maj 899, maj 1,542, grad 76

Ent Req: HS dipl

Degrees: BA & BFA 4 yrs, MA & MFA

Courses: Art Appreciation, Art Criticism and Social History of Art, Art Education, †Art History, †Ceramics, †Drawing, History of Art & Architecture, Mixed Media, †Painting, †Photography, †Printmaking, †Sculpture

Summer School: Co-Chairs Bobby Tilton & Cathryn Mallory. Enrl 25 per class; Courses—Various regular & experimental classes

NEBRASKA

BELLEVUE

BELLEVUE COLLEGE, Art Dept, 1000 Galvin Rd S, Bellevue, NE 68005-3058. Tel 402-291-8100; *Chmn* Dr Joyce Wilson PhD

Scholarships

Degrees: BA, BFA, BTS(Commercial Art)

Tuition: Undergrad—$135 per cr hr, grad $265 per cr hr

Courses: Advertising Design, Aesthetics, Art History, Art Management, Ceramics, Commercial Art, Design, Drawing, History of Art & Architecture, Life Drawing, Painting, Papermaking, Photography, Printmaking, Sculpture

Summer School: Tuition $132 per cr hr

BLAIR

DANA COLLEGE, Art Dept, 2848 College Dr, Blair, NE 68008-1041; PO Box 324, Blair, NE 68008-0324. Tel 402-426-7206, 426-9000; *Prof* Starla Stensaas; *Chmn* Dr Milton Heinrich

Scholarships

Degrees: BA, BS

Tuition: $6700 per sem

Courses: Advertising Design, Art Appreciation, Art Education, Art History, Ceramics, Commercial Art, Drawing, Jewelry, Painting, Photography, Printmaking, Sculpture, Teacher Training, Theatre Arts

CHADRON

CHADRON STATE COLLEGE, Dept of Art, 1000 Main St, Chadron, NE 69337-2690. Tel 308-432-6326; Fax 308-432-6464; Elec Mail rbird@asc.edu; Internet Home Page Address: www.csc.edu.art; *Chmn* Richard Bird, MFA; *Asst Prof* Mary Donahue, MFA; *Asst Prof* Laura Bentz, MFA; *Prof* Don Ruleaux, MFA; *Instr* Nancy Sharps, MA; *Instr* Daniel Binkard; *Instr* Dewayne Gimeson

Estab 1911, dept estab 1935; Maintain nonprofit art gallery, Gallery 239 & Main Art Gallery, 100 Main, Chadron, NE 69337; Library; on-campus shop where art supplies may be purchased; pub; D & E; Scholarships; SC 24, LC 4, GC 6; D 2000, off-campus 500, non-maj 40, maj 65

Ent Req: HS dipl

Degrees: BS & BA 4 yrs

Tuition: Res—undergrad $180 per hr, grad $220 per hr; nonres—undergrad $315 per hr, grad $388 per hr; campus res—room & board $2,400

Courses: Advertising Design, Art Appreciation, Art Education, Art History, Ceramics, Design, Drawing, Glass, Graphic Design, Jewelry, Painting, Photography, Printmaking, Sculpture

Adult Hobby Classes: Enrl 30. Tuition varies. Courses vary

Summer School: Dir, Dr Taylor. Enrl 30; tuition same as above. Courses—usually 2 - 4 courses on semi-rotation basis

COLUMBUS

CENTRAL COMMUNITY COLLEGE - COLUMBUS CAMPUS, Business & Arts Cluster, 4500 63rd St, Columbus, NE; PO Box 1027, Columbus, NE 68602-1027. Tel 402-564-7132; *Head Dept* Ellen Lake; *Instr* Richard Abraham, MA; *Instr* Kathleen Lohr, MA
Estab 1969, dept estab 1971; pub; D & E; Scholarships; SC 8, LC 1; D 100, E 20, non-maj 77, maj 43
Ent Req: HS dipl, GED
Degrees: AA 2 yrs
Courses: Air Brush, Art History, Ceramics, Color Theory, †Commercial Art, Design, Drafting, Drawing, Graphic Arts, Handicrafts, Interior Design, Life Drawing, Mixed Media, Painting, Photography, Printmaking, Stage Design, Textile Design, Theatre Arts
Summer School: Dir, Richard D Abraham. Enrl 25; tuition $41 per hr for term of 7 wks beginning June. Courses—Drawing, Painting

CRETE

DOANE COLLEGE, Dept of Art, 1014 Boswell Ave, Crete, NE 68333-2426. Tel 402-826-2161, 826-8273; Internet Home Page Address: www.doane.edu; *Head Dept* Richard Terrell
Estab 1872, dept estab 1958; FT 3; pvt; D; Scholarships; SC 6, LC 5; 150, non-maj 140, maj 10
Ent Req: HS dipl
Degrees: BA 4 yrs
Courses: Art Education, Art History, Ceramics, Drawing, Film, Graphic Design, Painting, Printmaking, Sculpture, Stage Design

HASTINGS

HASTINGS COLLEGE, Art Dept, 710 N Turner, Hastings, NE 68901-7621. Tel 402-461-7396; Fax 402-461-7480; Elec Mail tmcgehee@hastings.edu; Internet Home Page Address: www.hastings.edu; *Dir Pub Rels* Joyce Ore; *Chmn Dept* Turner McGehee; *Prof* Tom Kreager
Estab 1925; FT 3, PT 2; den; D & E; Scholarships; SC 16, LC 5; maj 50, others 350
Ent Req: HS grad
Degrees: BA 4 yrs
Courses: †Art Appreciation, Art Education, Art History, Ceramics, Color, †Commercial Art, Design, Drawing, Glass Blowing, †Graphic Design, Painting, †Photography, Printmaking, Sculpture

KEARNEY

UNIVERSITY OF NEBRASKA, KEARNEY, Dept of Art & Art History, 905 W 25th St, Kearney, NE 68849-0003. Tel 308-865-8353; Fax 308-865-8806; Internet Home Page Address: www.unk.edu; *Chmn & Prof* Doug Waterfield; *Assoc Prof* Jake Jacobson, MFA; *Assoc Prof* Tom Dennis, MFA; *Asst Prof* Richard Schuessler, MFA; *Asst Prof* John Stanko; *Asst Prof* Derrick Burbul; *Asst Prof* Chad Fonfara; *Asst Prof* Donna Alden, PhD; *Asst Prof* Victoria Goro-Rapoport; *Prof* Mark Hartman; *Prof* Lori Santos; *Lectr* John McKirahan; *Lectr* John Franczak
Estab 1905; Maintains nonprofit art gallery, Walker Art Gallery, 2506 12th Ave, Kearney, NE. Campus shop where art supplies may be purchased; FT 13, PT 11; pub; D & E; Scholarships; SC 20, LC 12, GC 18; D 870, E 22, non-maj 1400, maj 250, grad 25
Ent Req: HS dipl, SAT or ACT recommended
Degrees: BFA, BA, BA(Art History), BA(Educ), 4 yrs, MA(Educ-Art)
Courses: Aesthetics, Art Education, Art History, Ceramics, Computer Graphics, †Drawing, Glass Blowing, †Painting, Photography, †Printmaking, †Sculpture, †Teacher Training, Visual Communication & Design
Summer School: Chmn, Doug Waterfield. Enrl 250; Courses—Drawing

LINCOLN

NEBRASKA WESLEYAN UNIVERSITY, Art Dept, 5000 St Paul, Lincoln, NE 68504. Tel 402-465-2273; Fax 402-465-2179; Internet Home Page Address: www.nebrwesleyan.edu; *Assoc Prof* Lisa Lockman, MFA; *Adjunct Prof Art* Susan Horn, MFA; *Dept Chair, Prof Art History* Dr Donald Paoletta, PhD; *Asst Prof* David Gracie, MFA
Estab 1888, dept estab 1890; Maintains nonprofit gallery, Elder Gallery 50th & Huntington Sts, Lincoln, NE 68504; FT 3 PT 2; pvt; D & E; Scholarships; SC 22, LC 4; non-maj 300, maj 50
Ent Req: HS dipl, ent exam
Degrees: BA, BFA & BS 4 yrs
Courses: Art Education, Art History, Ceramics, Design, Drawing, Graphic Arts, Graphic Design, Jewelry, Painting, Photography, Printmaking, Sculpture, Silversmithing
Adult Hobby Classes: Enrl 30; tuition $152 per sem hr. Degree Program
Summer School: Enrl 30; tuition $152 per sem hr per 8 wks

UNIVERSITY OF NEBRASKA-LINCOLN, Dept of Art & Art History, Stadium Dr & T St, Richards Hall 120 Lincoln, NE 68588-0114. Tel 402-472-2631; Fax 402-472-9746; Elec Mail artdept@unl.edu; Internet Home Page Address: www.unl.edu/art; *Chmn Grad Comt* Gail Kendall, MFA; *Chmn Dept* Ed Forde, MFA
Estab 1869, dept 1912; Maintain nonprofit art gallery; Eisentrager/Howard Gallery, 1st Floor Richards Hall, Stadium Dr & T St, Univ Nebr, Lincoln 68588-0114; art supplies available on-campus; FT 20, PT 8; pub; D & E; Scholarships; SC 71, LC 27, GC 45; D 1950, E 175, non-maj 600, maj 400, grad 25
Ent Req: HS dipl
Degrees: BA, BFA, MFA 2-3 Yrs

Courses: †2-D & 3-D Design, Advertising Design, †Art History, Book Art, †Ceramics, †Commercial Art, †Drawing, †Graphic Arts, †Graphic Design, †Illustration, Mixed Media, †Painting, Papermaking, †Photography, †Printmaking, †Sculpture
Summer School: Dir, Nancy Stara. Enrl 250; two 5 wk sessions beginning June & Aug. Courses—Art History, Ceramics, Drawing, Painting, Photography, Printmaking, Special Problems & Topics

NORFOLK

NORTHEAST COMMUNITY COLLEGE, Dept of Liberal Arts, 801 E Benjamin Ave, Norfolk, NE 68701-6831; PO Box 469, Norfolk, NE 68702-0469. Tel 402-371-2020, Ext 480; Fax 402-644-0650; Internet Home Page Address: www.northeastcollege.com; *Instr* Julie Noyes, MA; *Instr* Harry Lindner, MA
Estab 1928; FT 3 PT 1; pub; D & E; Scholarships; SC 5, LC 5; D 150, E 50, non-maj 100, maj 50
Ent Req: HS dipl
Degrees: AA & AS 2 yrs
Courses: Art Education, Art History, Drawing, Graphic Design, Painting, Photography
Adult Hobby Classes: Oil Painting
Summer School: Chmn Dept, Patrick Keating. Tuition same as regular yr. Courses—Photography

OMAHA

COLLEGE OF SAINT MARY, Art Dept, 7000 Mercy Rd, Omaha, NE 68106-2632. Tel 402-399-2405; Internet Home Page Address: www.csm.edu; *Chmn Dept* Tom Schlosser
Estab 1923; pvt; W; D & E; Scholarships; SC 11, LC 5; D 620, maj 18, special 2
Ent Req: HS dipl
Degrees: BA and BS 4 yrs
Courses: Art History, Ceramics, Computer Graphics, Design, Painting, Photography, Sculpture, Teacher Training, Women in Art
Adult Hobby Classes: Enrl 587; tuition $133 per cr hr. Evening & weekend college offer full range of general education classes
Summer School: Dir, Dr Vernon Lestrud. Enrl 572; tuition $133 per cr hr. Full range of studio & history general education classes

CREIGHTON UNIVERSITY, Fine & Performing Arts Dept, 2500 California Plaza, Omaha, NE 68178. Tel 402-280-2509, 280-2700; Fax 402-280-2320; Internet Home Page Address: www.creighton.edu; *Assoc Chair* Fr Michael Flecky SJ, MFA; *Assoc Chair Performing Arts* Alan Klem, MFA; *Dance Coordr* Valerie Roche, ARAD; *Instr* John Thein, MFA; *Instr* Carole Seitz, MFA; *Instr* Bob Bosco, MFA; *Instr* Bill Hutson, MFA; *Instr* Jerry Horning, MFA; *Theater Coordr* Bill Vandest, MFA; *Instr* Don Doll SJ, MFA; *Instr Art History* Roger Aikin; *Instr Sculpture* Littleton Alston; *Gallery Dir* Fr Ted Bohr SJ; *Music Coordr* Dr Fredrick Henna; *Instr Music* Fr Charles Jurgensmeier; *Instr Arts Mgmt* Mike Markey; *Theater Instr* Michael McCandaless; *Instr Set Design* Mark Krejci
Estab 1878, dept estab 1966; den; D & E; Scholarships; SC 87, LC 16; 888, non-maj 850, maj 38, cert prog 24
Ent Req: HS dipl, regular col admis exam
Degrees: BA & BFA 4 yrs
Courses: 3-D Design, Advertising Design, Art Appreciation, Art Education, Art History, Ceramics, Color Theory, Design, Drawing, History of Art & Architecture, Intaglio, Lithography, Painting, Photography, Printmaking, Sculpture, Studio Fundamentals, Teacher Training, †Theatre Arts
Adult Hobby Classes: Advertising, Art History, Ceramics, Design, Life Drawing, Painting, Photography

UNIVERSITY OF NEBRASKA AT OMAHA, Dept of Art & Art History, 6001 Dodge St, Omaha, NE 68182-0002. Tel 402-554-2420, 554-2800; Internet Home Page Address: www.unomaha.edu; *Chmn* Dr Frances Thurber; *Prof* Donalyn Heise; *Prof* Mary Caroline Simpson; *Assoc Prof* Henry Serenco, MFA; *Assoc Prof* Gary Day, MFA; *Assoc Prof* James Czarnecki, MFA; *Asst Prof* Bonnie O'Connell, MFA; *Prof* Barbara Simcoe; *Prof* Larry Bradshaw; *Prof* David Helm
Estab 1908, dept estab 1910; FT 12 PT 8; pub; D & E; Scholarships; SC 32, LC 22, GC 10; D 550, E 100
Ent Req: HS dipl
Degrees: BA & BFA 4 yrs
Courses: †Art Education, †Art History, †Ceramics, †Drawing, †Painting, Paper Making, †Printmaking, †Sculpture
Summer School: Chmn Dept, Dr Martin Rosenberg. Tuition same as above for term of 5 wks. Courses—Vary

PERU

PERU STATE COLLEGE, Art Dept, PO Box 10, Peru, NE 68421-0010. Tel 402-872-2271, 872-3815; Elec Mail perry@nscs.peru.edu; *Prof* Kenneth Anderson Scholarships
Degrees: BA, BAEd, BS, MA
Tuition: Res—$65.75 per sem; nonres—$131.50 per sem
Courses: Art Appreciation, Art Education, Art History, Ceramics, Design, Drawing, Figure Drawing, Independent Art Study, Lettering, Painting, Photography, Printmaking, Sculpture, Stage Design
Summer School: $65.75 cr for 5 weeks

SCOTTSBLUFF

WESTERN NEBRASKA COMMUNITY COLLEGE, Division of Language & Arts, 1601 E 27th St, Scottsbluff, NE 69361-1899. Tel 308-635-3606; Internet Home Page Address: www.wncc.net; *Chmn Div Language* Paul Jacobson; *Chmn Art* Ziya Sever, MA

Estab 1926; FT 2; pub; D & E; Scholarships; SC 8, LC 3; D 60, E 150, non-maj 50, maj 10
Ent Req: HS dipl
Degrees: AA & AS 2 yrs
Courses: Art Education, Art History, Drawing, History of Film, Music Education, Painting, Photography, Theatre Arts
Adult Hobby Classes: Enrl 150; tuition $15 per course. Courses—Carving, Drawing, Macrame, Pottery, Sculpture, Stained Glass, Watercolor & Oil Painting, Weaving

SEWARD

CONCORDIA UNIVERSITY, Art Dept, 800 N Columbia, Seward, NE 68434. Tel 402-643-3651; Internet Home Page Address: www.cune.edu; *Prof* Richard Wiegmann, MFA; *Prof* Lynn Soloway, MFA; *Prof* Jim Bockelman, MFA; *Head Dept* William R Wolfram, MFA; *Prof* Kenneth Schmidt, PhD
Estab 1894; Maintain nonprofit art gallery; Marxhausen Art Gallery, 800 N Columbia Ave, Seward, NE 68434; den; D & E; Scholarships; SC 40, LC 7; non-maj 10, maj 95
Ent Req: HS dipl
Degrees: BS, BA 4 yr, BFA 4 yr
Courses: Advertising Design, †Art Education, Ceramics, Collage, †Commercial Art, Design, Drawing, Graphic Arts, Graphic Design, Illustration, Mixed Media, Painting, Photography, Printmaking, Sculpture, Teacher Training
Summer School: Tuition $210 per cr hr for term of 2 1/2 wks beginning early May

WAYNE

WAYNE STATE COLLEGE, Dept Art & Design, 1111 Main St, Wayne, NE 68787-1172. Tel 402-375-7359; Fax 402-375-7204; Internet Home Page Address: www.wsc.edu; *Prof* Steve Elliot; *Prof* Pearl Hansen; *Dept Chair* Wayne Anderson; *Prof* Marlene Mueller; *Prof* Vic Reynolds; *Lectr* Judith Berry
Estab 1910; Maintains nonprofit gallery, Norstrand Visual Arts Gallery, FA, 111 Main, Wayne NE 68787; 8 FT & PT; pub; D&E; Scholarships; SC 21, LC 8; maj 85, others 700, total 4,000
Ent Req: HS grad
Degrees: BA, BS, MA & MS
Courses: †Advertising Design, †Art Appreciation, Art History, †Ceramics, Commercial Art, Design, Drafting, Drawing, Graphic Arts, Handicrafts, Jewelry, Painting, †Printmaking, Sculpture, †Teacher Training
Summer School: Three sessions

YORK

YORK COLLEGE, Art Dept, 1125 E 8TH ST, York, NE 68467-3200. Tel 402-362-4441, Ext 218; *Asst Prof* Paul M Shields
Sch estab 1956, dept estab 1962; Pvt; D; Scholarships; SC 6, LC 1; D 26, non-maj 20, maj 10
Ent Req: HS dipl, ACT
Degrees: AA 2 yrs
Tuition: Res—undergrad $5,150 per sem
Courses: 2-D & 3-D Design, Art Appreciation, Art History, Commercial Design, Drawing, Painting

NEVADA

INCLINE VILLAGE

SIERRA NEVADA COLLEGE, Fine Arts Dept, 999 Tahoe Blvd, Incline Village, NV 89451-9500. Tel 775-831-1314; Elec Mail ashipley@sierranevada.edu; Internet Home Page Address: www.sierranevada.edu; *Dir Gallery* Russell Dudley; *Chmn* Anne Shipley; *Dir Summer Arts* Sheri Leigh; *Asst Prof* J Damron; *Asst Prof* Mary Kenny; *Asst Prof* Chris Lanier
Estab 1969; Maintains Tahoe Gallery, Abernathy Hall, 800 College Dr, Incline Village, Nev; art supplies available at on-campus shop; pvt; D & E; Scholarships; SC 75, LC 8; D 260, E 40, maj 30
Collections: Contemporary ceramics; Contemporary mixed media
Ent Req: HS dipl, 2.5 grade point avg
Degrees: BA, BFA 4 yr
Courses: Art Appreciation, Art Education, Art History, †Ceramics, Design, Digital Arts, †Drawing, †Film, Graphic Arts, Mixed Media, Music, †Painting, †Photography, Printmaking, Sculpture, Teacher Training, †Theatre Arts, †Video
Adult Hobby Classes: Enrl 80; tuition per cr. Courses—Ceramics
Summer School: Dir, Sheri Leigh. Enrl 200; tuition $420 per course non cr. Courses—Studio Arts

LAS VEGAS

UNIVERSITY OF NEVADA, LAS VEGAS, Dept of Art, 4505 S Maryland Pkwy, Las Vegas, NV 89154-9900; PO Box 455002, Las Vegas, NV 89154-5002. Tel 702-895-3237; Fax 702-895-4346; Internet Home Page Address: http://art.unlv.edu/MFA/; *Assoc Prof* Cathie Kelly; *Prof* Thomas J Holder; *Prof* Jeffrey Burden; *Assoc Prof* Pasha Rafat; *Assoc Prof* Mary Warner; *Prof & Chmn* Mark Burns; *Prof* Catherine Angel; *Asst Prof* Emily Kennerk; *Asst Prof* Louisa McDonald; *Asst Prof* Sang-Duok Seo; *Prof* Bob Tracy; *Asst Prof* Stephen Hendee; *Asst Prof* Helga Watkins; *Asst Prof* Kirsten Swenson

Estab 1955; Maintains Donna Beam Fine Art Gallery, 4505 Maryland Pkwy Box 5002, Las Vegas NV 89154; Pub; D & E; Scholarships; SC 32, LC 18; all courses 551, maj 95
Ent Req: HS dipl, ACT
Degrees: BA and BFA 5 yrs, MFA
Courses: Art Appreciation, Ceramics, Drawing, Graphic Design, Intermedia, Painting, Photography, Printmaking, Sculpture
Summer School: Dir, Thomas Holder. Enrl varies; 5 wk session. Courses—Ceramics, Drawing, Painting, Printmaking

RENO

UNIVERSITY OF NEVADA, RENO, Art Dept, Mail Stop 224, Reno, NV 89557-0001. Tel 775-784-1110, 784-6682; Internet Home Page Address: www.unr.edu; *Chmn Dept* Ed W Martinez
Estab 1940; FT 10; pub; D & E; Scholarships; SC 20, LC 6, GC 5; maj 120, others 800
Ent Req: HS grad and 16 units
Degrees: BA 4 yr
Courses: †Art Education, †Art History, †Ceramics, †Drawing, Graphic Design, †Painting, †Photography, †Printmaking, †Sculpture
Adult Hobby Classes: Evening division in all areas
Summer School: Courses in all studio areas

NEW HAMPSHIRE

DURHAM

UNIVERSITY OF NEW HAMPSHIRE, Dept of Arts & Art History, 30 College Rd, Paul Creative Arts Ctr Durham, NH 03824-2617. Tel 603-862-2190, 862-1234, 862-1360; Fax 603-862-2191; Internet Home Page Address: unhinfo.unh.edu; *Chmn* Scott Schneph; *Prof* David Andrew PhD; *Prof* Michael McConnell; *Assoc Prof* David Smith PhD; *Assoc Prof* Maryse Searls-McConnel, MFA; *Assoc Prof* Mara Witzling PhD, MFA; *Assoc Prof* Chris Enos, MFA; *Assoc Prof* Craig Hood, MFA; *Assoc Prof* Grant Drumheller, MFA; *Asst Prof* Jennifer Moses, MFA; *Asst Prof* Langdon Quin, MFA; *Asst Prof* Joy Stone; *Asst Prof* Brian Chu; *Assoc Prof* Eleanor Hight; *Assoc Prof* Patricia Emison
Estab 1928, dept estab 1941; pub; D & E; Scholarships; SC 60, LC 20; non-maj 1000, maj 175, grad 5, others 60
Ent Req: HS dipl, portfolio
Degrees: BFA & BA(Studio Arts & Art History) 4 yrs, MAT 5 yrs
Courses: Architecture, Art Education, Art History, Ceramics, Drawing, Painting, Photography, Printmaking, Sculpture

HANOVER

DARTMOUTH COLLEGE, Dept of Art History, 6033 Carpenter Hall, Hanover, NH 03755-3570. Tel 603-646-2306; Fax 603-646-3428; Elec Mail art.history@dartmouth.edu; Internet Home Page Address: www.dartmouth.edu/~arthist/; *Chair* Ada Cohen; *Admin* Elizabeth Alexander
Estab 1906; Maintain nonprofit art gallery; Hood Museum of Art, Hanover, NH 03755; FT 8; pvt; D; LC 25, other 6; in col 4000, maj 46
Degrees: AB 4 yr
Tuition: $36,915 per yr, room & board $10,930
Courses: †Art History

HENNIKER

NEW ENGLAND COLLEGE, Art & Art History, 98 Bridge St, Henniker, NH 03242-3292. Tel 603-428-2211; Fax 603-428-7230; Internet Home Page Address: www.nec.edu; *Prof* Marguerite Walsh, MFA; *Prof* Farid A Haddad, MFA; *Assoc Prof* Inez McDermott, MA; *Asst Prof* Darryl Furtkamp, MFA
Estab 1946; Maintain nonprofit art gallery; New England College Art Gallery, Preston Barn, Henniker, NH 03242; art supplies can be purchased on-campus; Pvt; D; Scholarships; non-maj 250; maj 65
Degrees: BA
Courses: †Art Appreciation, †Art History, Design, Drawing, Graphic Arts, Mixed Media, †Painting, †Photography, Printmaking, Sculpture

MANCHESTER

NEW HAMPSHIRE INSTITUTE OF ART, 148 Concord St, Manchester, NH 03104-4858. Tel 603-623-0313; Internet Home Page Address: www.nhia.edu; *Interim Pres* Dr Daniel Lyman
Estab 1898; pvt; cr and adult educ courses; D & E; Scholarships; SC 16; 1000
Ent Req: none
Degrees: BFA
Courses: Aesthetics, Art Appreciation, Art Education, Art History, Calligraphy, †Ceramics, Collage, Design, Fashion Arts, Handicrafts, History of Art & Architecture, Illustration, Jewelry, Mixed Media, †Painting, †Photography, Printmaking, Sculpture, Silversmithing, Theatre Arts, Weaving
Adult Hobby Classes: Enrl 400; tuition $150-$600 for 12-15 wks. Courses—Art History, Ceramics, Drawing, Fiber Arts, Painting, Photography, Printmaking, Sculpture
Children's Classes: Enrl 75; tuition $75-$125 for 6-12 wks. Courses—Artful Hands
Summer School: Courses—Same as in Fall & Spring

SAINT ANSELM COLLEGE, Dept of Fine Arts, 100 Saint Anselm Dr, Manchester, NH 03102-1308. Tel 603-641-7370; Fax 603-641-7116; Internet Home Page Address: www.anselm.edu; *Chmn* Katherine Hoffman
Estab 1889; FT 3; pvt; D & E; Scholarships; SC 2, LC 9; 1500
Ent Req: HS dipl, relative standing, SAT, interview
Degrees: BA 4 yr
Courses: Aesthetics, Architecture, †Art History, Design, Drawing, Film, †Fine Arts, Graphic Arts, Graphic Design, Mixed Media, Painting, Photography, Printmaking, Sculpture, Teacher Training, Theatre Arts
Summer School: Dir, Dennis Sweetland. Courses—Vary

NASHUA

RIVIER COLLEGE, Art Dept, 420 Main St, Nashua, NH 03060. Tel 603-888-1311, Ext 8276;
Estab 1933, dept estab 1940; pvt; D & E; Scholarships; SC 100, LC 25; D 50,E 40, non-maj 20, maj 70
Ent Req: HS dipl, SAT, certain HS equivalencies, preliminary evidence of artistic ability, slide portfolio
Degrees: AA 2 yrs, BA, and BFA 4 yrs
Courses: Aesthetics, Art Appreciation, Art Education, Art History, Calligraphy, Ceramics, Collage, Conceptual Art, Design, †Digital Imaging, Drawing, †Graphic Design, †Illustration, Mixed Media, †Painting, †Photography, Printmaking, Sculpture, Silversmithing, Teacher Training, Weaving
Adult Hobby Classes: Enrl 60; tuition $171 per cr for 15 wk term. Courses—Variety of fine arts & design studio courses
Children's Classes: Enrl 24. Courses—Pre-college summer art program
Summer School: Dir, Rose Arthur, PhD. Tuition $132 per cr for 6 wks. Courses—Master Workshops in Basic Design, Drawing, Etching, Graphic Design, Painting, Sculpture

NEW LONDON

COLBY-SAWYER COLLEGE, Dept of Fine & Performing Arts, 100 Main St, New London, NH 03257. Tel 603-526-3000, 526-3661, Ext 3666 (Chair); Fax 603-526-2135; Elec Mail colbyweb@colby-sawyer.edu; Internet Home Page Address: www.colby-sawyer.edu; *Prof* Loretta Barnett, MFA; *Prof* Jon Keenan, MFA; *Chair & Asst Prof* Brian Clancy, PhD; *Asst Prof* Nicholas Gaffney, MFA; *Asst Prof* Brandy Gibbs-Riley, MFA; *Assoc Prof* Bert Yarborough, MFA
Estab 1837; Maintains nonprofit Marian Graves Mugar Art Gallery & campus shop for purchase of art supplies; FT 6; pvt; D; Scholarships; SC 24, LC 25; 1150 univ; 60 dept
Ent Req: high school dipl
Degrees: BA (Art, Art History & Graphic Design), BFA (Art & Graphic Design)
Courses: Acting, Advertising Design, Aesthetics, American Art, Art Appreciation, †Art History, †Ceramics, Creative Expression, Dance, †Design, †Drawing, †Graphic Design, History of Art & Architecture, Life Drawing, Music, †Painting, †Photography, †Printmaking, †Sculpture, Stage Craft, Theatre Design, Theatre History, Typography

PLYMOUTH

PLYMOUTH STATE COLLEGE, Art Dept, 17 High St, Plymouth, NH 03264-1595. Tel 603-535-2201; Fax 603-535-3892; Elec Mail bhaust@mail.plymouth.edu; Internet Home Page Address: www.plymouth.edu; *Head Dept* Bill Haust
Estab 1871; FT 11; pub; D & E; Scholarships; SC 17, LC 8; D 3050, maj 90
Ent Req: HS grad, references, health record, transcript, SAT, CEEB, ACT
Degrees: BS, BFA & BA 4 yr
Courses: Architecture, Art Appreciation, †Art Education, †Art History, †Ceramics, Design, †Drawing, †Graphic Design, Illustration, Museum Staff Training, †Painting, †Photography, †Printmaking, †Sculpture, †Teacher Training
Adult Hobby Classes: Dir, Gail Carr. Enrl 50. Courses—Vary
Children's Classes: Courses available
Summer School: Courses vary

RINDGE

FRANKLIN PIERCE COLLEGE, Dept of Fine Arts & Graphic Communications, 40 University Dr, Rindge, NH 03461-5046. Tel 603-899-4000; Fax 603-899-4308; *Co-Chmn* Robert Diercks
Estab 1962; pvt; D & E; Scholarships; SC 20, LC 2
Ent Req: HS dipl
Degrees: BA(Fine Arts), BA(Graphic Design)
Courses: Art Education, Art History, Ceramics, Color Photography, Commercial Art, Design, Drawing, Graphic Design, Illustration, Painting, Photography, Printmaking, Sculpture, Stage Design, Teacher Training
Summer School: Color Photography, Landscape Painting

SHARON

SHARON ARTS CENTER, School Arts & Crafts, 457 NH Route 123, Sharon, NH 03458-7116. Tel 603-924-7256; Fax 603-924-6074; Elec Mail keri@sharonarts.org; Internet Home Page Address: www.sharonarts.org
Estab 1947; Maintains a nonprofit art gallery, Sharon Arts Gallery, 30 Grove St, Peterborough, NH 03458, 603-924-7676; PT 30; pvt; D & E; Scholarships; SC 75; classes yr round; D 700, E 100
Ent Req: none
Tuition: $180 members, $215 non-members
Courses: Basketry, Calligraphy, Ceramics, Drawing, †Glassmaking, Jewelry, Painting, Photography, Printmaking, Sculpture, Weaving, Woodcarving

Adult Hobby Classes: Enrl 900. Courses—Visual & Tactile Arts
Children's Classes: Enrl 100. Courses—Visual & Tactile Arts
Summer School: Dir, Deb DeCicco. Courses—Visual & Tactile Arts, Drawing, Painting, Jewelry, Ceramics, Weaving & others; July Art Week for Teens

NEW JERSEY

BLACKWOOD

CAMDEN COUNTY COLLEGE, Visual & Performing Arts Dept, 200 College Dr, Blackwood, NJ 08012-3228; PO Box 200, Blackwood, NJ 08012-0200. Tel 856-227-7200; Fax 856-374-4969; *Prof* L Dell'Olio; *Dean & Prof* J Rowlands
Estab 1966; Scholarships; SC 12, LC 10; 100
Ent Req: HS dipl or equivalent
Degrees: AA 2 yrs
Courses: Art History, Art Therapy, Ceramics, Computer Graphics, Design, Drawing, Painting, Sculpture
Adult Hobby Classes: Special sessions
Children's Classes: Special sessions
Summer School: Courses available

CALDWELL

CALDWELL COLLEGE, Dept of Fine Arts, 120 Bloomfield Ave, Caldwell, NJ 07006-5310. Tel 973-618-3238; Fax 973-618-3915; Elec Mail jcroce@caldwell.edu; Internet Home Page Address: www.caldwellcollege.edu; *Prof* Lawrence Szycher; *Chmn* Judith Croce; *Prof* Kendall Baker; *Asst Prof* Jennifer Noonan
Estab 1939; Maintain a nonprofit art gallery, Viscegia Art Gallery, same address; library; FT 3, PT 6; pvt; D & E; Scholarships; SC 45+, LC 10+, GC 5; D 1,535, E 1,000, maj 35, dept 90, GS 10
Activities: Schols offered
Ent Req: HS grad, art portfolio
Degrees: BA 3-4 yr, BFA 4-5 yr
Courses: †Advertising Design, †Aesthetics, †Art Appreciation, Art Education, Art History, Art Therapy, Ceramics, †Collage, †Commercial Art, †Conceptual Art, †Design, Drawing, †Graphic Arts, †Graphic Design, †History of Art & Architecture, †Mixed Media, †Museum Staff Training, Painting, Photography, †Printmaking, Sculpture, †Teacher Training, †Video

CAMDEN

RUTGERS UNIVERSITY, CAMDEN, Art Dept, 311 N 5th St, Fine Arts Ctr Camden, NJ 08102-1405. Tel 609-225-6176; Fax 609-225-6330; Internet Home Page Address: www.camden.rutgers.edu; *Chmn* John Giannotti
FT 5, PT 9; pub; D; SC 24, LC 13; art D 450, maj 75
Ent Req: HS dipl, must qualify for regular col admis, portfolio
Degrees: BA(Art) 4 yrs
Courses: Art History, Computer Animation, Computer Graphics, Drawing, Graphic Design, Museum Studies, Painting, Photography, Printmaking, Sculpture
Summer School: Chmn, John Giannotti. Courses—Varies

DEMAREST

THE ART SCHOOL AT OLD CHURCH, 561 Piermont Rd, Demarest, NJ 07627-1615. Tel 201-767-7160; Fax 201-767-0497; Elec Mail info@tasoc.org; Internet Home Page Address: www.tasoc.org; *Admin Dir* Karen Shalom; *Communs* Lorraine Zaloom; *Exec Dir* Maria Danziger; *Opers Dir* Peter Schmidt; *Dir Gallery* Rachael Faillace; *Exec Asst* Melissa Pazcoguin; *Ceramic Studio Mgr* David Shirey
Estab 1974; Maintain nonprofit art gallery; The Mikhail Zakin Gallery at Old Church, 561 Piermont Rd, Demarest, NJ 07627; on-campus shop with limited art supplies; Pub; D & E; Scholarships, Fellowships; SC 75; D 475, E 325
Publications: Centerling, semi-annual
Tuition: Varies per course
Courses: Art Appreciation, †Assemblage, Ceramics, †Collage, †Crocheting, Drawing, Fiber Art, Glass Bead Making, Jewelry, †Knitting, †Metalsmithing, Mixed Media, Painting, Photography, Printmaking, †Quiltmaking, Sculpture, Stained Glass
Adult Hobby Classes: Enrl 450. Courses—Ceramics, Drawing, Metals, Painting, Printmaking. Sculpture, Basketry, Glass
Children's Classes: Enrl 250. Courses—Ceramics, Drawing, Painting, Sculpture, Textiles

DOVER

JOE KUBERT SCHOOL OF CARTOON & GRAPHIC ART, INC, 37 Myrtle Ave, Dover, NJ 07801-4085. Tel 973-361-1327; Fax 973-361-1844; Internet Home Page Address: www.kubertsworld.com; *Instr* Hy Eisman; *Instr* Irwin Hasen; *Instr* Douglas Compton; *Instr* Michael Chen; *Instr* Jose Delbo; *Instr* Kim Demulder; *Instr* Jim McWeeney; *Instr* Judy Mates; *Instr* Greg Webb; *Instr* John Troy; *Pres* Joe Kubert
Estab 1976; pvt; D & E; Scholarships; SC all, LC all; D 200, E 100
Ent Req: HS dipl, interview, portfolio
Degrees: 3 yr dipl
Courses: Cartoon Graphics, Cinematic Animation, Commercial Art, Design, Graphic Arts, Illustration, Lettering, Painting, Video
Adult Hobby Classes: Enrl 100; tuition $200 per 12 wks. Courses—Basic & Advanced Paste-Ups & Mechanicals, Cartoon Workshop, Computer Graphic/Animation Workshop

Children's Classes: Enrl 20; tuition $15 per class. Courses—Saturday Cartoon Sketch Class
Summer School: Courses—same as regular session

EDISON

MIDDLESEX COUNTY COLLEGE, Visual Arts Dept, 155 Mill Rd, Edison, NJ 08837-3601; PO Box 3050, Edison, NJ 08818-3050. Tel 732-906-2589; Fax 732-906-2510; *Chmn* Jay Siegfried
Scholarships
Degrees: AA
Tuition: County $57.50 per cr hr; out-of-county $115; out-of-state $115 per cr hr
Courses: Art Appreciation, Art Education, Art Foundation, Art Fundamentals (2-D & 3-D Design), Art History, Art Industry & Communication, Ceramics, Drawing, Painting, Printmaking, Sculpture, Stage Design
Adult Hobby Classes: Courses offered
Summer School: Dir, Warren Kelerme. Courses—Art History, Ceramics, Drawing, Painting

EWING

THE COLLEGE OF NEW JERSEY, School of Arts & Sciences, 2000 Pennington Rd, Ewing, NJ 08628; PO Box 7718, Ewing, NJ 08628-0718. Tel 609-771-2652; Fax 609-637-5134; Internet Home Page Address: www.tcnj.edu; *Chmn Dept* Lois Fichner-Rathus; *Prof* Bruce Rigby, MFA; *Assoc Prof* Kenneth Kaplowitz, MFA; *Assoc Prof* Charles Kumnick, MFA; *Assoc Prof* Marcia Taylor, PhD, MAATR; *Assoc Prof* Wendell Brooks, MFA; *Assoc Prof* Elizabeth Mackie, MFA; *Asst Prof* Philip Sanders, MA; *Asst Prof* Charles McVicker, BPA; *Asst Prof* William Nyman, MFA; *Dept Chair* Anita Allyn; *Prof Art History* Lee-Ann Riccardi
Estab 1855; FT 17, PT 18; pub; D & E; Scholarships; SC 40, LC 10, GC 11; non-maj 5200, maj 300
Ent Req: HS dipl
Degrees: BA & BFA 4 yr
Courses: Advertising Design, Art Appreciation, †Art Education, Art History, Ceramics, Computer Animation, Computer Graphics, Design, Display, Drafting, Drawing, †Fine Arts, †Graphic Design, History of Art & Architecture, Illustration, †Interior Design, Intermedia, Jewelry, Lettering, Mixed Media, Painting, Photography, Printmaking, Sculpture, Silversmithing, Teacher Training
Summer School: June & July five wk sessions, Governor's School of the Arts (July)

GLASSBORO

ROWAN UNIVERSITY, Dept of Art, 201 Mullica Hill Rd, Glassboro, NJ 08028-1702. Tel 856-256-4000; Fax 856-256-4814; Internet Home Page Address: www.rowan.edu; *Chair* Fred Adelson, PhD; *Asst Chair* Keith Adams
Estab 1925; Maintain nonprofit art gallery, Westby Gallery, Westby Hall, Rowan Univ, Rt #322, Glassboro, NJ 08028; Pub; D & E; Scholarships; SC 80, LC15; D 6,100, E 5,000, maj 300
Ent Req: HS dipl, ent exam, portfolio and SAT
Degrees: BA 4 yrs, BFA 4 yrs, MA
Courses: Advertising Design, Art Appreciation, Art Education, Art History Survey, Batik, Ceramics, Computer Art, Drawing, Enameling, Fiber Arts, Illustration, Jewelry, Puppetry, Sculpture, Theatrical Design
Children's Classes: Enrl 30. Courses—Crafts, Drawing, Mixed Media, Painting
Summer School: Dir, Dean H Sosa. Enrl 100; Courses—Drawing, Painting, Printing

HACKETTSTOWN

CENTENARY COLLEGE, Humanities Dept, 400 Jefferson St, Hackettstown, NJ 07840-2184. Tel 908-852-1400; *Pres* Dr Barbara-Jayne Lewthwaite; *Assoc Prof* Richard Wood, MFA; *Asst Prof Interior Design* Elena Kays, MFA; *Instr* Elizabeth Desabritas, MFA; *Assoc Prof* Carol Yoshimine-Webster, MFA
Estab 1874; pvt; Scholarships; SC 11, LC 2; maj 70, others 367, total 678
Exhibitions: Gallery Exhibitions (BFA students) Architecture Site, Art/Design reviews, Interior Design students
Ent Req: high school dipl
Degrees: BFA(Art & Design), AA(Interior Design), BFA(Interior Design), BS(Communications)
Adult Hobby Classes: Tuition $98 per cr. Courses—Graphic Arts, Interior Design
Summer School: Dir, Larry Friedman. Tuition $98 per cr. Courses—Graphic Art, Interior Design

JERSEY CITY

NEW JERSEY CITY UNIVERSITY, Art Dept, 2039 Kennedy Blvd, Jersey City, NJ 07305. Tel 201-200-3214, Ext 3241; Fax 201-200-3224; Elec Mail rosenberg@njcu.edu; Internet Home Page Address: www.njcu.edu; *Prof* Ben Jones, MFA; *Prof* Mary Campbell, MFA; *Prof* Jose Rodeiro PhD, MFA; *Prof* Charles Plosky, MFA; *Prof* Herbert Rosenberg, MFA; *Assoc Prof* Raymond Statlander, MFA; *Asst Prof* Mauro Altamura, MFA; *Asst Prof* Winifred McNeill, MFA; *Asst Prof* Ellen Quinn, MFA; *Art History Prof* Midori Yoshimoto, PhD; *Prof* Dennis Raverty, PhD; *MFA* Dennis Dittrich; *MFA* Hugo Bastidas; *MFA* Brian Gustafson; *MFA* Deborah Jack; *Jewelry & Metals Prof* Ken MacBain, MFA; *Printmaking Prof* Martin Kruck, MFA
Estab 1927, dept estab 1961; Maintains 2 nonprofit art galleries, Lemmerman Gallery at Hepburn Hall, 2039 Kennedy Blvd and Visual Art Gallery, 100 Culver Ave; maintains architecture library, Art Dept 100 Culver Ave Jersey City NJ 07305; FT 13 PT 15; pub; D & E; Scholarships; SC 61, LC 19, GC 31; D 350, E 60, GS 60

Ent Req: HS dipl or equivalent
Degrees: BA & BFA 128 sem hrs, MA, MFA 60 sem hrs, grad assistantship
Courses: Advertising Design, Aesthetics, Art Appreciation, Art Education, Art History, Art Therapy, Ceramics, †Communication Design, Conceptual Art, †Crafts, Design, Digital Imaging, Drawing, †Fine Arts, Graphic Design, History of Art, Industrial Design, Intermedia, Jewelry, Lettering, Metalsmithing, Mixed Media, Painting, †Photography, Printmaking, Sculpture, †Teacher Certification

SAINT PETER'S COLLEGE, Fine Arts Dept, 2641 Kennedy Blvd, Jersey City, NJ 07306. Tel 201-915-9238; Fax 201-915-9240; Internet Home Page Address: www.spc.edu; *Chmn* Jon D Boshart PhD
Estab 1872, dept estab 1963; Maintain nonprofit art gallery; St Peter's College Art Gallery; Jesuit; D & E; Scholarships; SC 8, LC 20; D 2,000, E 900, maj 15
Ent Req: HS dipl
Degrees: BA, BA in Cursu Classico, BS 4 yrs
Courses: Advertising Design, Aesthetics, Architecture, Art Appreciation, Art Education, †Art History, Commercial Art, †Drawing, †Graphic Arts, History of Art & Architecture, Mixed Media, †Painting, Photography, Restoration & Conservation, †Sculpture, Teacher Training
Adult Hobby Classes: Tuition $508 per sem. Courses—Art History, Studio
Summer School: Dir, Dr Boshart. Tuition $1,524 per 3 cr, one 3 wk session & two 5 wk sessions. Courses—Art History, Electives, Drawing, Film History, Introduction to Visual Arts, Painting, Photography, Graphic Arts, Museum Courses

LAKEWOOD

GEORGIAN COURT UNIVERSITY, Dept of Art, 900 Lakewood Ave, Lakewood, NJ 08701-2697. Tel 732-987-2437; Internet Home Page Address: www.georgian.edu; *Prof* Geraldine Velasquez, EdD; *Assoc Prof* Sr Mary Phyllis Breimayer, PhD; *Assoc Prof* Suzanne Pilgram, MFA; *Asst Prof* Sr Joyce Jacobs, MA; *Lectr* Nicholas Caivano, MA; *Asst Prof* Lisa Festa, PhD
Estab 1908, dept estab 1924; Maintains nonprofit art gallery, Christina Geis Gallery Georgian Court Univ 900 Lakewood Ave Lakewood NJ 08701; pvt; D & E; Scholarships; SC 18, LC 11; 240, non-maj 150, maj 90
Ent Req: HS dipl, col board scores, portfolio
Degrees: BA 4 yr, BFA
Courses: †Art (studio & art history), †Art Education, †Art History, Calligraphy, Ceramics, Color & Design, Commercial Art, Computer Graphics, Drawing, Fashion Arts, Graphic Design, Illustration, Jewelry, Lettering, Painting, Photography, Printmaking, Sculpture, Teacher Training, Textile Design, Weaving
Summer School: Courses in Art History

LAWRENCEVILLE

RIDER UNIVERSITY, Dept of Fine Arts, 2083 Lawrenceville Rd, Lawrenceville, NJ 08648-3099. Tel 609-896-5168; *Chmn* Dr Jerry Rife
Estab 1966; FT 5; pvt; D & E; SC 9, LC 4; D 3500, E 5169, maj 35
Ent Req: HS dipl
Degrees: BA(Fine Arts) 4 yrs
Courses: Drawing, Graphic Arts, Graphic Design, Painting
Summer School: Courses—Drawing, Art & Society

LINCROFT

BROOKDALE COMMUNITY COLLEGE, Center for the Visual Arts, 765 Newman Springs Rd, Lincroft, NJ 07738-1599. Tel 732-224-2000; Fax 732-224-2060; Internet Home Page Address: www.brookdale.cc.nj.us; *Chmn* Ed O'Neill
Estab 1968; Pub; D & E
Ent Req: HS dipl
Degrees: AA
Tuition: County res—$90 per cr hr; non-county res—$165 per cr hr; non-state res—$341 per cr hr
Courses: Ceramics, Design, Drawing, Jewelry, Painting, Printmaking

LIVINGSTON

ART CENTRE OF NEW JERSEY, 284 Beaufort Ave Ste 3, Riker Hill Art Pk Bldg 501 Livingston, NJ 07039-1042. Tel 973-227-3488; Fax 973-227-3488; *Pres* Tim Maher; *First VPres* Elaine Denton; *Second VPres* Salomon Kadoche; *Treas* Louis de Smet
Estab 1924 as an art school & presently is a venue for workshops, art events, lects, critiques, exhibitions, etc; Two pub exhibs per yr; Mem: 250; dues $12.50; annual meeting in May; Pub; D (open studies with models, no classes) Mon & Fri 1-3:30, Sat 11-1:30; Scholarships; D 60
Income: Financed by mem & art sales
Publications: Membership newsletter
Courses: Painting
Adult Hobby Classes: Workshops

MADISON

DREW UNIVERSITY, Art Dept, 36 Madison Ave, College of Liberal Arts Madison, NJ 07940-1434. Tel 973-408-3553, 408-3000; Fax 973-408-3768; *Prof* Livio Saganic, MFA; *Dept Chmn* Michael Peglau, PhD; *Asst Prof* Margaret Kuntz, PhD; *Adjunct Asst Prof* William Mutter, MFA; *Adjunct Asst Prof* Raymond Stein; *Prof* Sara Henry-Corrington; *Adjunct Asst Prof* Lisa Solon, MBA; *Adjunct Asst Prof* Anne Gaines, MFA; *Adjunct Asst Prof* Tom Birkner, MFA; *Adjunct Asst Prof* Jim Jeffers, MFA
Estab 1928; Maintain nonprofit art gallery; Korn Gallery, Drew University, Madison, NJ 07940; pvt; D & E; Scholarships; SC 17, LC 10; D 275, E 12, maj 45, minors 15

Ent Req: HS dipl
Degrees: BA 4 yrs
Courses: Aesthetics, †Art History, Ceramics, Computer Graphics, Design, Drawing, History of Art & Architecture, Painting, Photography, Printmaking, Sculpture
Summer School: Dir, Catherine Messer. Enrl 300; tuition $1200 for 4, 5 or 6 wk term. Courses—Art History for the Blind, Ceramics, Computer Graphics, Photography

FAIRLEIGH DICKINSON UNIVERSITY, Fine Arts Dept, 285 Madison Ave, Madison, NJ 07940. Tel 973-443-8500; Internet Home Page Address: www.fdu.edu; *Faculty* Judy Moonelis; *Faculty* George Cochrane
Estab 1942, dept estab 1965; pvt; D & E; Scholarships; SC 37, LC 9
Ent Req: HS dipl, SAT
Degrees: degrees BA (Art & Fine Arts)
Tuition: Res—undergrad $367 per cr, room & board; nonres—undergrad $367 per cr hr; campus res available
Courses: Advertising Design, Art Appreciation, Art History, Bio & Wildlife Illustration, Calligraphy, Ceramics, Commercial Art, Computer Animation, Computer Graphics, Design, Desktop Publishing, Drawing, †Graphic Design, History of Art & Architecture, Illustration, Lettering, Mixed Media, Painting, Photography, Printmaking, Sculpture

MAHWAH

RAMAPO COLLEGE OF NEW JERSEY, School of Contemporary Arts, 505 Ramapo Valley Rd, Mahwah, NJ 07430-1680. Tel 201-529-7368; Fax 201-684-7481; Internet Home Page Address: www.ramapo.edu; *Dean* Steven Perry, MFA; *Prof* Judith Peck, EdD; *Prof Painting* W Wada, MFA; *Prof* Jay Wholley, MFA; *Asst Prof Photo* Yolanda del Amo, MFA; *Assoc Prof Art History* Meredith Davis, PhD; *Assoc Prof Art History* John Peffer, PhD; *Assoc Prof 3D Design & Animation* Ann LePore, MFA; *Asst Prof Drawing & Painting* Jackie Skrzynski, MFA
Estab 1968; Maintain non-profit art galleries, Kresge Foundation Gallery, Andre Z Pascal Gallery & Seldon Rodman Gallery of popular Arts, all on campus; Potter Library, campus; pub; SC 53, LC 15; majs 110
Ent Req: HS dipl, SAT
Degrees: BA
Courses: †Art & Technology, Art History, †Art Therapy, Drawing, †Film, †Graphic Design, †Installation Art, Painting, Photography, Sculpture, †Stage Design, †Theatre Arts, †Video Art
Summer School: Dir, Shalom Gorewitz. Tuition $71.50 cr hr, $91.50 out of state. Courses—Computer Graphics, Photography

MONTCLAIR

MONTCLAIR ART MUSEUM, Yard School of Art, 3 S Mountain Ave, Montclair, NJ 07042. Tel 973-746-5555; Fax 973-746-9118; Elec Mail mail@montclair-art.com; Internet Home Page Address: www.montclair-art.com; *Dir* Jacquelyn Roesch Sanchez
Art school estab 1924; FT 18; pvt; D & E; Scholarships; SC 17; D 300 per term, E 100 per term
Courses: Art Education, Chinese Print, Collage, Drawing, Mixed Media, Painting, Portraiture, Printmaking, Sculpture
Adult Hobby Classes: Enrl 300; tuition $135-$175, duration 8 wks.
Courses—Anatomy, Drawing, Painting, Pastels, Portraiture, Still Life, Watercolor
Children's Classes: Enrl 90; tuition $120-$140 per 8 wk sem. Courses—Mixed Media

MONTCLAIR STATE UNIVERSITY, Fine Arts Dept, 1 Normal Ave, College of the Arts Montclair, NJ 07043-1699. Tel 973-655-7295; Internet Home Page Address: www.montclair.edu; *Dean* Geoffrey Newman; *Chmn* John Czerkowicz
Estab 1908; FT 18, PT 4; pub; Scholarships; SC 35, LC 18; maj 250, grad maj 200
Ent Req: HS grad and exam, interview, portfolio
Degrees: BA 4 yr, BFA 4 yr, MA
Courses: Art Education, Art History, Ceramics, Drawing, Film, Graphic Design, Illustration, Jewelry, Metalwork, Painting, Photography, Printmaking, Sculpture, TV as Art, Textile Design
Summer School: Life Drawing, Painting, Photography, Sculpture

MORRISTOWN

COLLEGE OF SAINT ELIZABETH, Art Dept, 2 Convent Rd, Morristown, NJ 07960-6989. Tel 973-290-4315; Elec Mail vbutera@cse.edu; Internet Home Page Address: www.cse.edu; *Chmn Dept* Dr Virginia Fabbri Butera; *Assoc Prof* Sr Anne Haarer; *Adjunct Prof* Elaine Chong; *Adjunct Prof* Raul Villarreal; *Adjunct Prof* Todd Doney; *Adjunct Prof* Rocio Scary; *Adjunct Prof* Will Suarez
Estab 1899, dept 1956; Maintain a nonprofit art gallery, Terese F Maloney Art Gallery, College of St Elizabeth, 2 Convent Rd, Morristown, NJ 07960; www.maloneyartgallery.org; den, W, M & W continuing studies; D & E; Scholarships; SC 17, LC 4; D 250, maj 27
Ent Req: HS dipl, ent exam
Degrees: BA 4 yrs
Courses: Advertising Design, Aesthetics, Art Appreciation, Art History, Calligraphy, Ceramics, †Collage, Color and Design, Conceptual Art, Drawing, Graphic Arts, Graphic Design, Mixed Media, Painting, Photography, Printmaking, Sculpture, Silversmithing, Teacher Training

NEW BRUNSWICK

RUTGERS, THE STATE UNIVERSITY OF NEW JERSEY, Mason Gross School of the Arts, Visual Arts Dept, 33 Livingston Ave, New Brunswick, NJ 08901-1959. Tel 732-932-7711 (Grad Admissions), 445-3770 (Undergrad

Admissions); Fax 732-932-2217; Internet Home Page Address: www.gradstudy.rutgers.edu (Grad); www.mgsa.rutgers.edu/visual.htm; *Dean* George B Stauffer; *Dir Visual Arts* Patricia Mayar; *Assoc Dean* Dennis Benson; *Prof* Lauren Ewing; *Prof* Raphael Ortiz; *Prof* Gary Kuehn; *Prof* Diane Neumaier; *Prof* Martha Rosler; *Assoc Prof* Thomas Nozkowski; *Assoc Prof* Barbara Madsen; *Assoc Prof* John Yay; *Assoc Prof* Ardele Lister; *Assoc Prof* Toby MacLennan; *Asst Prof* Hanneline Rogeberg; *Asst Prof* Gerry Beegan; *Asst Prof* Jason Francisco; *Asst Prof* Stephen Westfall
Estab 1766, school estab 1976; maintains nonprofit art gallery, Mason Gross Art Gallery; pub; D; Scholarships; SC 50, LC 20, GC 28; MFA prog 60, BFA prog 450
Ent Req: HS dipl, portfolio
Degrees: BHA, BFA, MFA
—Graduate Program in Art History, 71 Hamilton St, Voorhees Hall New Brunswick, NJ 08901-1248. Tel 732-932-7041, 932-7819; Fax 732-932-1261; Internet Home Page Address: www.arthistory.rutgers.edu; *Prof* Matthew Baigell; *Prof* Sarah McHam; *Prof* Jack J Spector PhD; *Prof* Rona Goffen; *Prof* Tod Marder; *Prof* Jocelyn Small; *Assoc Prof* John F Kenfield PhD; *Assoc Prof* Archer Harvey; *Assoc Prof* Sarah Brett-Smith; *Assoc Prof* Angela Howard; *Dir Prog & Assoc Prof* Catherine Puglisi PhD
Estab 1766, grad prog estab 1971; pub; D; Scholarships, Fellowships; grad courses 15; grad students 97
Ent Req: BA
Degrees: MA 2 yrs, PhD 4 yrs
Tuition: Res—undergrad $191 per cr hr, grad $2315 per sem; nonres—$282 per cr hr, grad $3394 per sem
Courses: Architecture, Art History, History of Art & Archeology, Museum Staff Training
Summer School: Intro to Art Hist, 19th & 20th century Art

NEWARK

RUTGERS UNIVERSITY, NEWARK, Arts, Culture & Media, 110 Warren St, University Heights Bradley Hall Newark, NJ 07102-1809. Tel 973-353-5119; Fax 973-353-1392; Internet Home Page Address: www.rutgers.edu; WATS 800-648-5600; *Chair* Ian Watson; *Deputy Chair* Paul Sternberger
FT 20; Pub; D; Scholarships; D 486, maj 100
Ent Req: HS dipl, or as specified by col and univ
Degrees: BA 4 yr, BFA(Design)
Courses: Art Appreciation, Art Education, Art History, Ceramics, Computer Graphics, Design, Drawing, Graphic Design, History of Art & Architecture, Illustration, Painting, Photography, Printmaking, Sculpture, Stage Design, Teacher Training, Theatre Arts
Summer School: Dir, Annette Juliano. Enrl 100. Courses—Art History, Ceramics, Drawing, Painting, 2-D Design, 3-D Design

OCEAN CITY

OCEAN CITY ARTS CENTER, 1735 Simpson Ave, Ocean City, NJ 08226-3070. Tel 609-399-7628; Fax 609-399-7089; Elec Mail ocarts@pro-usa.net; Internet Home Page Address: www.oceancityartscenter.org; *Instr Guitar* Rob Gummel; *Instr Painting* Sue Rau; *Exec Dir* Lorraine Hansen; *Instr* Annie Arena; *Marketing & Pub Rels* Christine Harry; *Bookkeeper* Peg Castagna; *Instr* Lee Kuchler; *Instr* Susan Myers; *Instr* Patty Guckes; *Instr* Marie Natale; *Instr* Kim Weiland; *Instr* Sue Van Duyne
Estab 1966; Maintains nonprofit art gallery, Ocean City Arts Center Gallery; Pvt; D & E; weekends; Scholarships; SC 14, LC 1; D 1, E 8
Ent Req: none
Tuition: Varies
Courses: Ceramics, Collage, Dance, Drawing, Film, Handicrafts, Mixed Media, Painting, Photography, Pottery, Sculpture, Stained Glass, Theatre Arts, Video
Adult Hobby Classes: 50; $65 - $150
Children's Classes: 250; $65 - $350; art camp, performing arts camp, tv/media camp, guitar camp
Summer School: Exec Dir, Lorraine Hansen. Same classes offered during summer plus workshops & demonstrations

PARAMUS

BERGEN COMMUNITY COLLEGE, Visual Art Dept, 400 Paramus Rd, Rm A335, Paramus, NJ 07652. Tel 201-447-7100; Fax 201-612-8225; Internet Home Page Address: www.bergen.cc.nj.us; *Dean Art & Humanities* Michael Redmond pub; D&E; Scholarships
Degrees: AA
Tuition: In county—$57.60 per cr; nonres—$119.70 per cr hr
Courses: Animation, Art Anatomy, Art Appreciation, Art History, Ceramics, Color Theory, Commercial Illustration, Craft Design, Design, Drawing, Fundamentals Art, Graphic Design, Handicrafts, Interior Design, Lettering, Painting, Photography, Printmaking, Sculpture

PATERSON

PASSAIC COUNTY COMMUNITY COLLEGE, Division of Humanities, One College Blvd, Paterson, NJ 07505-1179. Tel 973-684-6555; Fax 973-523-6085; Elec Mail mgillan@pccc.cc.nj.us; Internet Home Page Address: www.pccc.cc.nj.us/poetry/index.htm; *Prof* Mark G Bialy; *Pres* Steve Rose; *Cur Gallery* Jane Havv; *Exec Dir Cultural Arts* Maria Mazziotti Gillan; *Asst Dir* Aline Papazian
Estab 1969; pub; D & E; SC 4, LC 3; D 100, E 25
Ent Req: HS dipl, New Jersey basic skills exam
Degrees: AA 2 yrs

Courses: Advertising Design, Aesthetics, Art Appreciation, Art History, Commercial Art, Design, Drawing

PEMBERTON

BURLINGTON COUNTY COLLEGE, Humanities & Fine Art Div, 601 Pemberton Browns Mills Rd, Pemberton, NJ 08068-1599. Tel 609-894-9311, Ext 7441; Internet Home Page Address: www.bcc.edu; *Art Lectr & Prog Coordr* Diane Spellman-Grimes
Estab 1969; pub; D & E; Scholarships
Ent Req: HS dipl, equivalent
Degrees: AA
Tuition: County res—$69.50 per cr hr; non-county res—$84.50 per cr hr; non-state res—$120.50 per cr hr
Courses: Art Appreciation, Art Education, Art History, Art Therapy, Calligraphy, Ceramics, Design, Drawing, Film, Handicrafts, Introduction To Teaching Art, Modernism, Painting, Photography, Sculpture, Theatre Arts, Video
Adult Hobby Classes: 10; tuition $150. Courses—Ceramics
Summer School: Dir, Diane Grimes. Courses—Ceramics, Drawing, Painting, Sculpture

PRINCETON

PRINCETON UNIVERSITY, Dept of Art & Archaeology, 105 McCormick Hall, Princeton, NJ 08544-1018. Tel 609-258-3782; Fax 609-258-0103; Internet Home Page Address: www.princeton.edu; *Chmn* Robert Bagley, MFA; *Dir Prog Chinese & Japanese Art & Archaeology* Yoshiaki Shimiza; *Chmn Prog in Classical Archaeology* William A P Childs, PhD; *Prof* T Leslie Shear Jr, PhD; *Prof* Thomas Leisten, PhD; *Prof* Anne-Marie Bouche; *Prof* Peter Bunnell, MFA; *Prof* Esther da Costa-Meyer, MFA; *Prof* Slobodan Curcic, MFA, PhD; *Prof* Hal Foster, MFA; *Prof* John Pinto, MFA, PhD; *Prof* Hugo Meyer, MFA, PhD; *Prof* Thomas Kaufmann, MFA, PhD; *Chmn* Patricia Fortini-Brown, MFA
Estab 1783; pvt; Scholarships; LC 16, GC 9; 761, maj 55, grad 50
Degrees: PhD
Tuition: $32,500 per yr
Courses: American Art, Archaeology, Early Chinese Art, Greek Archaeology, Islamic Art & Architecture, Italian Renaissance Art & Architecture, Later Japanese Art, Photography
—School of Architecture, Architecture Bldg Rm S-110, Princeton, NJ 08544. Tel 609-258-3741; Fax 609-258-4740; Elec Mail soa@princeton.edu; Internet Home Page Address: www.princeton.edu; *Dean* Stan Allen
Estab 1919; FT 16; pvt; D; Scholarships, Fellowships; SC 6, LC 13, GC 6, seminars 17; undergrad 120, grad 50
Ent Req: HS dipl
Degrees: BA, MA, PhD
Tuition: $32,500 per yr
Courses: Acoustics & Lighting, Building & Science Technology, Environmental Engineering, History of Architectural Theory, Modern Architecture, Urban Studies

RANDOLPH

COUNTY COLLEGE OF MORRIS, Art Dept, 214 Center Grove Rd, Randolph, NJ 07869-2086. Tel 973-328-5000; Fax 973-328-5445; *Chmn & Prof* James Gwynne
Estab 1970; pub; D & E; SC 15, LC 3; maj 263
Ent Req: HS dipl
Degrees: AA(Humanities/Art) 2 yrs, AAS(Photography Technology) 2 yrs
Courses: Advertising Design, Art History, Ceramics, Color & Design, Drawing, Major Styles & Historical Periods, Modern Art, Painting, Photography, Printmaking, Sculpture
Summer School: Two 5 week day sessions, one evening session

SEWELL

GLOUCESTER COUNTY COLLEGE, Liberal Arts Dept, 1400 Tanyard Rd, Sewell, NJ 08080-4249. Tel 856-468-5000; Fax 856-488-2018; Internet Home Page Address: www.gcc.nj.edu; *Head* John Henzy
Estab 1967; Special program offered for gifted students; art gallery on campus; 130 PT & FT; pub; D & E; Scholarships; SC 6, LC 6
Ent Req: HS dipl
Degrees: AA
Tuition: Res—$79 per cr hr; nonres—$80 per cr hr
Courses: Art History, Arts & Crafts for Handicapped, Ceramics, Drawing, General Design, Graphic Arts, Jewelry, Mixed Media, Painting, Sculpture
Summer School: Dir, Dr Mossman

SHREWSBURY

GUILD OF CREATIVE ART, 620 Broad St, Rte 35 Shrewsbury, NJ 07702-4117. Tel 732-741-1441; Elec Mail guildofcreativeart@verizon.net; Internet Home Page Address: www.guildofcreativeart.com; *Co-Pres* Deborah Redden; *Co-Pres* Vincent Matulewich
Estab 1960; Maintain nonprofit art gallery; Non-profit coop; D&E; Scholarships; SC; D & E
Ent Req: Membership adult $30 per yr
Tuition: $150 per 10 wks
Courses: †Drawing, Painting
Adult Hobby Classes: Courses—Design, Drawing, Painting
Children's Classes: Enrl $250; tuition $65 for 10 wk term. Courses—Design, Life Drawing, Painting
Summer School: Oil & Acrylic Painting, Watercolor

SOUTH ORANGE

SETON HALL UNIVERSITY, College of Arts & Sciences, 400 S Orange Ave, South Orange, NJ 07079-2697. Tel 973-761-9459; Fax 973-275-2368; Internet Home Page Address: www.shu.edu; *Chmn* Charlotte Nichols PhD; *Prof* Julius Zsako PhD; *Prof* Barbara Cate; *Prof* Jeanette Hile, MA; *Assoc Prof* Alison Dale, MA; *Asst Prof* Arthur Cook, MM; *Asst Prof* Arline Lowe, MM; *Asst Prof* Joel Friedman, DMA; *Asst Prof* Deborah Gilwood, MA; *Asst Prof* K D Knittel PhD, MA; *Asst Prof* Susan Leshnoff, EdD; *Asst Prof* Ira Greenberg, MFA
Estab dept 1968; FT 10, PT 9; pvt; D & E; Scholarships, Fellowships; SC 8
Degrees: BA 4 yr, MA
Courses: Advertising, Art Education, Art History, Chinese Brush Painting, Commercial Art, Drawing, Fine Art, Graphic Design, Illustration, Mixed Media, Music Art, Painting, Printmaking, Sculpture
Summer School: Dir, Petra Chu. Enrl 200; May - Aug. Courses—Art, Art History, Fine Arts

TOMS RIVER

OCEAN COUNTY COLLEGE, Humanities Dept, College Dr, Toms River, NJ 08754-2001; PO Box 2001, Toms River, NJ 08754-2001. Tel 732-255-0400; Fax 732-255-0444; Internet Home Page Address: www.ocean.edu; *Coordr* Joseph Conrey; *Prof* Patricia Kennedy, MS; *Prof* Lisa Horning, MS; *Prof* Howard Unger, EdD; *Prof* John R Gowen, EdD; *Prof* Arthur Waldman, EdD; *Pres* Stephen McCleary
Estab 1964; dept estab 1964; pub; D & E; Scholarships; SC 19, LC 3; D 1500, E 1500, maj 67
Ent Req: HS dipl
Degrees: AA in Liberal Arts with concentration in Fine Art & AAS(Visual Commun Technology) 2 yrs
Courses: Advertising Design, Aesthetics, Art History, Calligraphy, Ceramics, Commercial Art, Conceptual Art, Costume Design & Construction, Drawing, Film, Graphic Arts, Graphic Design, Handicrafts, Lettering, Painting, Photography, Printmaking, Sculpture, Stage Design, Theatre Arts
Summer School: Enrl 175; tuition $34 for term of 5 wks or 6 wks beginning June. Courses—Arts & Humanities, Basic Drawing, Ceramics, Computer Graphics, Crafts, Photography

TRENTON

JOHNSON ATELIER TECHNICAL INSTITUTE OF SCULPTURE, 60 Sculptors Way, Trenton, NJ 08619-3428. Tel 609-890-7777; Fax 609-890-1816; Elec Mail lrn2sculpt@aol.com; Internet Home Page Address: www.gotrain.com/schools; *Pres* James Barton, MFA; *Acad Dir* James E Ulry, MFA; *Dir* Dona Warner, BFA; *Acad Asst* E Gyuri Hollosy, MFA
Open by appointment; Estab 1974; pvt; D & E; Scholarships; SC 12; apprentices 20, interns 2
Ent Req: HS dipl, portfolio review
Degrees: The Atelier is a non degree granting institution with a two year apprenticeship program in sculpture
Tuition: $4800 per acad yr, $400 monthly
Courses: Ceramic Shell, Foundry, Metal Chasing, Modeling & Enlarging, Moldmaking, Patina, Restoration & Conservation, Sand Foundry, Sculpture, Structures, Wax Working & Casting

UNION

KEAN UNIVERSITY, Fine Arts Dept, 1000 Morris Ave, Union, NJ 07083-7133. Tel 908-527-2307; Fax 908-527-2804; *Dir Gallery* Alec Nicolescu; *Coordr Interior Design* Linda Fisher; *Coordr Art Educ* Michael DeSiano; *Coordr Art History* Louis Kachur; *Chmn* Jack Cornish
Estab 1855; FT 31; pub; D & E; Scholarships; SC 58, LC 37, GC 24; FT 383, PT 236, maj 656, grad 37
Ent Req: HS dipl, portfolio interview for art maj, SAT
Degrees: BA 4 yrs, BFA 4, MA(Art Educ)
Courses: Advertising Design, Aesthetics, †Art Education, †Art History, Ceramics, †Commercial Art, Display, Drafting, Drawing, Film, Furniture Making, Graphic Arts, Graphic Design, Illustration, †Interior Design, Jewelry, Lettering, Museum Staff Training, Occupational Therapy, Painting, Photography, Printmaking, Sculpture, Textile Design
Summer School: Asst Dir, George Sisko. Courses—Art History, Art in Education, Ceramics, Drawing, Introduction to Art, Introduction to Interior Design, Jewelry, Life Drawing, Painting, Printmaking, Sculpture, Watercolor

VINELAND

CUMBERLAND COUNTY COLLEGE, Humanities Div, PO Box 1500, College Drive, Vineland, NJ 08362-1500. Tel 609-691-8600; Fax 609-691-8813, Ext 314; Elec Mail art@cccnj.net; *Coordr, Asst Prof* Diane Spellman-Grimes
Maintain nonprofit gallery; pub; D&E; Scholarships; SC 24, LC 8; maj 88
Degrees: AS
Tuition: County res—$737 per sem; out-of-county res—$122.50 per cr hr; out-of-state res—$245 per cr hr
Courses: Art Appreciation, †Art Education, Art History, †Design, Drawing, †Graphic Arts, †Graphic Design, Multi-media, Painting, Photography, Video
Adult Hobby Classes: non-cr
Summer School: Computer Graphics

WAYNE

WILLIAM PATERSON UNIVERSITY, Dept Arts, 300 Pompton Rd, Power Art Wayne, NJ 07470-2103. Tel 973-720-2401; Fax 973-720-3805; Elec Mail lazarusa@wpunj.edu; Internet Home Page Address: www.wpunj.edu; *Art Dept*

Chmn Alejandro Anreus; *Assoc Prof* James Brown; *Assoc Prof* Zhiyuan Cong; *Asst Prof* Angela DeLaura; *Assoc Prof* Leslie Farber; *Prof* Ming Fay; *Assoc Prof* David Horton; *Asst Prof* Elaine Lorenz; *Prof* Charles Magistro; *Asst Prof* Lily Prince; *Asst Prof* Steve Rittler; *Prof* David Shapiro; *Asst Prof* Thomas Uhlein; *Asst Prof* He Zhang; *Asst Prof* Nisha Drinkard; *Asst Prof* Robin Schwartz; *Asst Prof* Deborah Frizzell; *Asst Prof* Lauren Razzore; *Asst Prof* Bruce Gionet; *Asst Prof* Maggie Williams; *Prof* Ofelia Garcia
Dept estab 1958; Maintain a nonprofit art gallery, Ben Shahn Galleries, 300 Pompton Rd, Wayne, NJ 07470; maintain art/architecture library, Askeyy Library, 300 Pompton Rd, Wayne, NJ 07470; FT 24, PT 8; pub; D; Scholarships; SC 135, LC 60, GC 50; maj 450, grad 30, E non-maj 170
Ent Req: SATs, portfolio
Degrees: BA 4 yr, BFA, MFA
Tuition: Res—undergrad $73, grad $131
Courses: Advertising Design, †Art Education, †Art History, Ceramics, †Commercial Art, Computer Animation, Computer Graphics, Computer Illustration, Conceptual Art, †Design, Film, †Furniture Design, †Graphic Arts, Graphic Design, History of Art & Architecture, †Illustration, Lettering, Museum Staff Training, †Painting, †Photography, †Printmaking, Stage Design, †Teacher Training, †Textile Design
Summer School: Dir, Alan Lazarus. Enrl 150; tuition $65 per cr, $90 out of state. Courses—Art History, Drawing, Painting, Photography

WEST LONG BRANCH

MONMOUTH UNIVERSITY, Dept of Art & Design, 400 Cedar Ave, 800 Bldg, Rm 822 West Long Branch, NJ 07764-1804. Tel 732-571-3428; Fax 732-263-5273; Internet Home Page Address: www.monmouth.edu; *Chmn* Vincent Dimattio, MFA; *Prof* Pat Cresson; *Assoc Prof* Ellen Garfield, MA; *Assoc Prof* Richard Davis, MFA; *Assoc Prof* Karen Bright, MFA; *Asst Prof* Edward Jankowski, MFA
Estab 1933; pvt; D & E; Scholarships; SC 25, LC 8; in dept D 108, E 6, non-maj 80, maj 108, audits 6
Ent Req: HS dipl, portfolio for transfer students
Degrees: BA(Art), BFA & BA(Art Educ) 4 yr
Courses: Appreciation of Art, †Art Education, Art History, †Ceramics, Drawing, Graphic Arts, Handicrafts, History of Art & Architecture, Metalsmithing, †Painting, Photography, Printmaking, †Sculpture, Teacher Training
Adult Hobby Classes: Courses—Painting
Summer School: Art Appreciation, Ceramics, Independent Study, Painting, Sculpture

WEST WINDSOR

MERCER COUNTY COMMUNITY COLLEGE, Arts, Communication & Engineering Technology, 1200 Old Trenton Rd, West Windsor, NJ 08550-3407. Tel 609-586-4800, Ext 3348; Fax 609-586-2318; Internet Home Page Address: www.mccc.edu; *Dean* Robert A Terrano, MFA; *Cur* Tricia Fagan; *Prof* Mel Leipzig, MFA; *Prof* Frank Rivera, MFA; *Instr* Michael Welliver, MFA
Estab 1902, dept estab 1967; FT 10, PT 13; pub; D & E; Scholarships; SC 44, LC 6; E 350, maj 261
Ent Req: HS dipl
Degrees: AA & AAS 2 yrs
Courses: †Advertising Design, †Architecture, Art Education, Art History, †Ceramics, Commercial Art, Design, Drawing, Film, Graphic Arts, Graphic Design, History of Art & Architecture, Illustration, †Painting, †Photography, Printmaking, †Sculpture, †Theatre Arts, Video
Adult Hobby Classes: Enrl 448. Tuition varies. Courses—Calligraphy, Ceramics, Drawing, Painting, Photography, Stained Glass
Children's Classes: Enrl 1000. Tuition varies. Courses—Drawing, Maskmaking, Painting, Printmaking, Soft Sculpture
Summer School: Dir, R Serofkin. Enrl 712 (camp college); 2 - 4 wk sessions. Dir, M Dietrich. Enrl 22; 4 wks. Courses—Architecture. Dir, M K Gitlick. Enrl 160; Arts Camp 2 - 4 wk sessions. Also regular cr courses

NEW MEXICO

ALBUQUERQUE

UNIVERSITY OF NEW MEXICO, College of Fine Arts, Fine Arts Ctr, Albuquerque, NM 87131-1396; 1 University of New Mexico, MSC04 2560 Albuquerque, NM 87131-0001. Tel 505-277-2111; Fax 505-277-0708; Internet Home Page Address: www.unm.edu
Estab 1935; pub
Degrees: BFA, MA, MAFA, PhD(Art)
Tuition: $78.50 per cr hr, $35.57 (12-15 hrs) per cr hr
Courses: †Architecture, Art Appreciation, Art Education, †Art History, Ceramics, Dance, Drawing, Electronic Arts, Film, History of Art & Architecture, Jewelry, Music, Painting, Photography, Printmaking, Sculpture, Theater
Adult Hobby Classes: Wide variety of courses offered
Summer School: Arts of the Americas Program, wide variety of courses offered
—**Dept of Art & Art History,** 1 University of New Mexico, MSC04 2560 Albuquerque, NM 87131-0001. Tel 505-277-5861; Fax 505-277-5955; Internet Home Page Address: www.unm.edu/~artdept2/; *Chmn* Joyce Szabo, PhD
Estab 1889; John Sommers Gallery; fine arts library; art supplies available at univ bookstore; pub; D & E; Scholarships, Fellowships; SC 190, LC 43, GC 73; E 511, non-maj 230, maj 227, grad 116
Ent Req: HS dipl
Degrees: BA, BAFA & BFA 4 yrs, MA 2 yrs, MFA 3 yrs, PhD 3+ yrs

Tuition: Per cr hr: res-undergrad $190.45; res-grad $209.30; nonres-undergrad $190.45-$622.60; nonres-grad $209.30-$637.97
Courses: Aesthetics, Architecture, Art Appreciation, Art History, Ceramics, Conceptual Art, Design, †Digital/Electronic Art, Drawing, Film, Graphic Arts, History of Art & Architecture, Metalwork, Mixed Media, Painting, Photography, Printmaking, Sculpture, Video
Children's Classes: Offered through Art Educ Dept
Summer School: Tuition res/nonres-undergrad $190.45; res/nonres-grad $209.30. Two 4 wk terms & one 8 wk term beginning June 9, 2008. Courses—same as above
—**Tamarind Institute,** 108-110 Cornell Dr SE, Albuquerque, NM 87106. Tel 505-277-3901; Fax 505-277-3920; Elec Mail tamarind@unm.edu; Internet Home Page Address: finearts.unm.edu/tamarind.htm; *Tamarind Master Printer & Studio Mgr* Bill Lagattuta; *Dir* Marjorie Devon; *Educ Dir* Rodney Hamon
Estab 1960; Maintains nonprofit art gallery; Pub; D; Fellowships; SC, LC; enrl 8
Ent Req: Extensive previous experience in lithography &/or undergrad degree in printmaking
Degrees: Cert as Tamarind Master Printer 2 yrs
Tuition: $160 per cr hr
Courses: †Lithography
Summer School: 4 wk prog; campus res available. Courses—Various lithographic techniques

VSA ARTS OF NEW MEXICO, (Very Special Arts of New Mexico) Enabled Arts Center, 4904 4th St NW, Albuquerque, NM 87107-3906. Tel 505-345-2872; Fax 505-345-2896; Elec Mail info@vsartsnm.org; Internet Home Page Address: vsartsnm.org; *Exec Dir* Beth Rudolph; *Dir* Deborah Malshibini; *Exhib Coordr* Wendy Zollinger
Estab 1992; Center is a studio program for individuals with disabilities focusing on pre-vocational, vocational & studio skills; maintain nonprofit art gallery, Very Special Arts Gallery, 4904 Fourth St, NW, Albuquerque, NM 87107; pvt; D; D 30-40
Ent Req: 14 years or older
Courses: Art Appreciation, Ceramics, Collage, Drawing, Mixed Media, Painting, Printmaking, Sculpture, †Theatre Arts

FARMINGTON

SAN JUAN COLLEGE, Art Dept, 4601 College Blvd, Farmington, NM 87402-4699. Tel 505-326-3311, Ext 281, 599-0281; Fax 505-599-0385; Internet Home Page Address: www.sjc.cc.nm.us; *Dept Chmn* Bill Hatch
Estab 1956; FT 1, PT 5; pub; D & E; Scholarships
Ent Req: HS dipl
Degrees: AA
Tuition: Res—$15 per cr hr; nonres—$25 per cr hr
Courses: Art Appreciation, Art Education, Art History, Calligraphy, Ceramics, Design, Drawing, Film, Graphic Design, Jewelry, Painting, Photography, Printmaking, Sculpture

HOBBS

NEW MEXICO JUNIOR COLLEGE, Arts & Sciences, 5317 Lovington Hwy, Hobbs, NM 88240. Tel 505-392-4510; Fax 505-392-1318; Internet Home Page Address: www.nmjc.cc.nm.us; *Dean* Mickey D Best, MFA; *Instr* Lawrence Wilcox, MFA; *Instr* George Biggs, MFA
Estab 1965; pub; D & E; Scholarships; SC 6, LC 1; D 100, E 30, non-maj 200, maj 20
Ent Req: HS dipl, GED or special approval
Degrees: AA 2 yrs
Courses: Advertising Design, †Animation, Ceramics, Collage, Color & Design, Drawing, Interior Design, Painting, Photography, Printmaking
Adult Hobby Classes: Drawing, Painting, Portraiture, Watercolor
Children's Classes: Drawing, Painting
Summer School: Dean, Steve McLeary. Courses—Ceramics, Printmaking

LAS CRUCES

NEW MEXICO STATE UNIVERSITY, Art Dept, PO Box 30001, Dept 3572 Las Cruces, NM 88003-8001. Tel 505-646-1705; Fax 505-646-8036; Elec Mail artdept@msu.edu; *Dept Head* Spencer Fidler, MFA; *Assoc Prof* William Green, MFA; *College Asst Prof* Jacklyn St Aubyn, MFA; *Assoc Prof* Julia Barello, MFA; *Assoc Prof* Rachel Stevens, MFA; *Assoc Prof* Elizabeth Zarur, PhD; *College Asst Prof* Julie Fitzsimmons, MFA; *Prof* Joshua Rose, MFA; *Dir Ceramics* Amanda Jaffe; *Photo Dir* David Taylor; *Asst Prof* Stephanie Taylor, PhD; *Asst Prof* Peter Fine
Estab 1975; Maintains nonprofit art gallery, NMSU Art Gallery, DW Williams Art Center, NMSU, Las Cruces, NM 88003; Pub; D & E; Scholarships, Fellowships; SC 52, LC 25, GC 53; maj 280, grad 31
Ent Req: HS dipl
Degrees: BA & BFA 4 yrs, MFA 3 yrs, MA(Studio) & MA(Art Hist) 2 yrs
Courses: Art Appreciation, Art History, Ceramics, Design, Drawing, Graphic Arts, Graphic Design, Illustration, Jewelry, †Metal Arts, Mixed Media, Painting, Photography, Printmaking, Restoration & Conservation, Sculpture, Silversmithing
Summer School: Prof, Spencer Fidler

LAS VEGAS

NEW MEXICO HIGHLANDS UNIVERSITY, Dept of Communications & Fine Arts, 901 University Ave, Las Vegas, NM 87701-4072. Tel 505-454-3238, 454-3573; Fax 505-454-3068; Internet Home Page Address: www.nmhu.edu/Department/commarts; *Asst Prof* Arthur Trujillo; *Chmn* Andre Garcia-Nuthmann

Estab 1898; pub; D & E; Scholarships; SC 24, LC 8, GC 12; non-maj 55, maj 51, grad 4
Ent Req: HS dipl, ACT, Early Admis Prog, GED
Degrees: BA 4 yrs, BFA, MA 1 yr
Courses: Art Education, Art History, Calligraphy, Ceramics, Drawing, Graphic Arts, Jewelry, Lettering, Painting, Photography, Printmaking, Sculpture, Silversmithing, Stage Design, Teacher Training, Theatre Arts
Adult Hobby Classes: Courses—Ceramics, Painting, Weaving
Summer School: Mainly studio plus core curriculum, depending upon staffing

PORTALES

EASTERN NEW MEXICO UNIVERSITY, Dept of Art, 1500 S Ave K, Sta 27 Portales, NM 88130-7400. Tel 505-562-2778; Internet Home Page Address: www.enmu.edu/; *Chmn* Jim Bryant; *Asst Prof* Mary Finneran, MFA; *Asst Prof* Greg Erf, MFA; *Asst Prof* Phil Geraci, MFA; *Asst Prof* Galina McGuire, MFA; *Asst Prof* Mic Muhlbauer, MFA
Estab 1932; pub; D & E; Scholarships; SC 44, LC 6, GC 25; D 507, E 150, maj 110
Ent Req: HS dipl, GED, ACT
Degrees: AA 2 yrs, BS, BA & BFA 4 yrs
Courses: †Advertising Design, Art Education, Art History, Calligraphy, †Ceramics, †Commercial Art, †Drawing, †Graphic Arts, Graphic Design, Illustration, †Jewelry, Lettering, †Painting, Photography, †Sculpture, †Teacher Training, Theatre Arts, Video
Summer School: Courses—Ceramics, Commercial Art, Crafts, Drawing, Lettering, Photography

SANTA FE

COLLEGE OF SANTA FE, Art Dept, 1600 Saint Michaels Dr, Santa Fe, NM 87505-7615. Tel 505-473-6500; Fax 505-473-6501; Elec Mail info@csf.edu; Internet Home Page Address: www.csf.edu; *Emeritus* Richard L Cook, MA; *Prof* Ronald Picco, MFA; *Asst Prof* Robert Sorrell, MFA; *Asst Prof* David Schienbaum, MFA; *Asst Prof* James Enyeart, MFA; *Asst Prof* Richard Fisher, MFA; *Asst Prof* Nancy Sutor, MFA; *Asst Prof* Khristaan Villela, PhD; *Asst Prof* Roxanne Malone, MFA; *Asst Prof* Don Messec, MA; *Adjunct Assoc* Steve Fitch, MFA; *Adjunct Assoc* Linda Swanson, MFA; *Dir Gallery* Lake McTighe, MFA; *Chmn* Gerry Snyder, MA
Estab 1947, dept estab 1986; pvt; D & E; Scholarships; SC 35, LC 10; D 350, non-maj 250, maj 95, non-degree 30
Ent Req: HS dipl or GED
Degrees: BA & BFA (Visual Arts)
Courses: Aesthetics, Art, Art Appreciation, Art Education, †Art History, †Art Studio, Art Therapy, Ceramics, Collage, Conceptual Art, Constructions, †Drawing, Film, Intermedia, Mixed Media, Museum Staff Training, †Painting, †Photography, †Printmaking, Psychology, †Sculpture, Theatre Arts, Video
Children's Classes: Enrl 20-25; tuition $500-$750 for 3 wk term.
Courses—General Studio Art
Summer School: Dir, Gerry Snyder. Courses—Art History, Drawing, Lifecasting, Painting, Photography, Printmaking, Sculpture

INSTITUTE OF AMERICAN INDIAN ARTS, Museum of Contemporary Native Arts, 108 Cathedral Pl, Santa Fe, NM 87501-2027. Tel 505-428-5900; Fax 505-983-1222; Elec Mail pphillips@iaia.edu; Internet Home Page Address: www.iaiamuseum.org; *Dir* Patsy Phillips; *Chief Cur* Ryan Rice; *Cur Coll* Tatiana Lomahaftew-Singer; *Registrar* Joy Farley; *Admin & Finance* Ramona Arnold; *Spec Proj & Community Relations* Larry Phillips; *Mus Educ Prog Coordr* Hayes A Locklear; *Mus Shop Mgr* Laura Ellerby; *Chief Security* Thomas Atencio; *Dep Security Office* Maria Favella; *Mus Studies Dept Faculty* Michelle McGeough; *Mus Studies Dept Chair* Jessie Ryker-Crawford; *Primitive Edge Gallery Coordr* Mary Deleary
Estab 1972; Maintain art gallery, Lloyd Kiva, 108 Cathedral Pl, Santa Fe, NM 87501; nonprofit art gallery, Primitive Edge Gallery, 83 Avan Nu Po Rd, Santa Fe, NM 87508, library, 89 Avan Nu Po Rd, Santa Fe, NM 87505; congressionally funded; D, E, Online; Scholarships; SC, LC; D 192
Ent Req: HS dipl
Degrees: AAS, AA, AFA, BFA, BA, Cert
Tuition: $100 per cr hr
Courses: †Ceramics, †Creative Writing, †Film, †Graphic Arts, †Graphic Design, †Indigenous Liberal Arts, †Museum Staff Training, †Museum Studies, †Native Studies, †New Media Arts, †Painting, †Photography, †Sculpture, †Silversmithing, †Studio Art, †Theatre Arts, †Video, †Weaving
Adult Hobby Classes: Beadwork, Dancing, Exhib Techniques, Traditional Clothing, Flute Making, Fiber Arts
Summer School: Dir, Hayes Lewis. Courses—Museum Studies, Summer Film & Television Workshop

SANTA FE ARTS INSTITUTE, 1600 Saint Michaels Dr, Santa Fe, NM 87505-7615; PO Box 24044, Santa Fe, NM 87502-0044. Tel 505-424-5050; Fax 505-424-5051; Internet Home Page Address: www.sfai.org; *Dir* Diane R Karp, Dr; *Res Dir* Sheilah Wilson
Estab 1985; ; pvt; D & E; Scholarships; SC 12; varies
Ent Req: Portfolio review
Courses: Collage, Installation, Mixed Media, Painting, Photography, Sculpture, Video, Video Art
Adult Hobby Classes: Installation & Video Art, Master classes in Printing, Mixed Media, Sculpture
Children's Classes: Summer youth workshops

SILVER CITY

WESTERN NEW MEXICO UNIVERSITY, Dept of Expressive Arts, 1000 W College Ave, Silver City, NM 88062; PO Box 680, Dept of Expressive Arts Silver City, NM 88062-0680. Tel 505-538-6149; Fax 505-538-6243; Elec Mail admissions@wnmu.edu; *Prof* Gloria Maya, MFA; *Prof* Claude Smith, MFA; *Prof* Michael Metcalf, MFA; *Co-Chmn Music* Ben Tucker; *Co-Chmn Theater* Jack Ellis

Estab 1893; Mem: Maintains non profit art gallery, McCray Gallery Expressive Arts Dept W NM Univ PO Box 680 Silver City NM 88061; on campus shop where art supplies are purchased; Pub; D & E; Scholarships; SC 10, LC 7; D 211, non-maj 196, maj 15
Ent Req: HS dipl
Degrees: BA, BS, BFA, & MA, 4 yrs
Courses: Advertising Design, Art Appreciation, Art Education, Art History, †Ceramics, Costume Design & Construction, Design, Drawing, Fiber Arts, Graphic Arts, Occupational Therapy, †Painting, Photography, †Printmaking, †Sculpture, Silversmithing, Stage Design, Teacher Training, Textile Design, Theatre Arts, †Video, Weaving
Adult Hobby Classes: Ceramics, Fiber, Lapidary
Summer School: Enrl 80-100. Courses—Art Appreciation, Ceramics, Clay Workshop, Elementary Art Methods, Painting & Drawing Workshop, Printmaking, Special Art Tours in New Mexico & Europe

NEW YORK

ALBANY

COLLEGE OF SAINT ROSE, The Center For Art and Design, 432 Western Ave, Albany, NY 12203-1490. Tel 518-485-3900; Fax 518-485-3920; Elec Mail maurenp@strose.edu; Internet Home Page Address: www.strose.edu; *Chmn* Paul Mauren, MFA; *Assoc Prof* Ann Breaznell, MFA; *Prof* Scott Brodie, MFA; *Asst Prof* Lucy Bowditch PhD, MFA; *Asst Prof* Jessica Loy, MFA; *Asst Prof* Thomas Santelli, MFA; *Asst Prof* Jennifer Childress, MFA; *Asst Prof* Robert O'Neil, MFA; *Asst Prof* Gina Occhiogrosso, MFA; *Asst Prof* Theresa Flanigan PhD; *Asst Prof* Kris Tolmie, MFA; *Asst Prof* Ben Schwab, MFA; *Assit Prof* Robert Shane, Ph.D; *Assoc Prof* Chris St. Cyr; *Assoc Prof* Susan Meyer
Estab 1920, dept estab 1970; Maintain nonprofit art gallery, Esther Massry Art Gallery, 1002 Madison Ave, Albany NY 12203. Scholarship $3,000-$14,000, 4 yr; anyone can apply, contact: Marian Chilson; pvt; D & E; Scholarships; SC 50, LC12, GC 20; non-maj 110, maj 225, GS 30
Ent Req: HS dipl, SAT or ACT, rank in top 2/5 of class
Degrees: BFA(Graphic Design, Studio Arts), BS(Art Educ, Studio Arts), MS(Art Educ), MA(Studio Art)
Tuition: $12,307 per sem undergrad (12-17 cr/sem), $815 per sem hr
Courses: Aesthetics, Art Education, Art History, Design, Drawing, Graphic Design, Painting, Photography, Printmaking, Sculpture, Studio Art, †Teacher Training, Typography
Adult Hobby Classes: Enrl 20; tuition $250 per cr hr. Courses—Some continuing education courses each sem
Summer School: Chmn Paul Mauren. Courses—Photoshop, Theories of Art Educ (grad course). Kris Tolmie, Dir Pre-College Summer Experience

THE SAGE COLLEGES, Dept Visual Arts, 140 New Scotland Ave, Albany, NY 12208-3425. Tel 518-292-1778; Fax 518-292-7758; Elec Mail bielic@sage.edu; Internet Home Page Address: www.sage.edu; *Interim Chair Visual Arts* Kevin Stoner; *Asst to the Chair* Cathleen Bieling
Estab 1957, dept estab 1970; Maintain a nonprofit art gallery - Opaika Gallery, The Sage Colleges, 140 W Scotland Ave, Albany, NY 12208; Pvt; D & E; Scholarships; SC 43, LC 16 (Art); D 700 (total), 200 (art), E 823 (total)
Ent Req: HS dipl, references, records, SAT, portfolio
Degrees: MA (Art Ed), AAS 2 yrs, BA (Theatre), AS-BFA (fine arts, graphic design, interior design)
Courses: Art Education, Art History, Ceramics, Collage, Design, Drafting, Drawing, Fine Arts, Fine Arts Illustration, Graphic Arts, Graphic Design, History of Art & Architecture, Illustration, Interior Design, Intermedia, Lettering, Mixed Media, Painting, Photography, Printmaking, Sculpture, Studio Studies, Teacher Training, Theatre Arts
Children's Classes: Summer courses for High School students
Summer School: Dir, Dierdra Zarrillo. Enrl 60.

STATE UNIVERSITY OF NEW YORK AT ALBANY, Art Dept, 1400 Washington Ave, Albany, NY 12222-1000. Tel 518-442-4020; Fax 518-442-4807; Elec Mail bh996@albany.edu; Internet Home Page Address: www.albany.edu; *Prof* Roberta Bernstein, PhD; *Prof* Edward Mayer, MFA; *Prof* Phyllis Galembo, MFA; *Assoc Prof* Mark Greenwold, MFA; *Assoc Prof* Marja Vallila, MFA; *Dept Chair & Prof* JoAnne Carson, MFA; *Assoc Prof* David Carbone, MFA; *Assoc Prof* Sarah Cohen, PhD; *Asst Prof* Rachel Dressler, PhD; *Asst Prof* Daniel Goodwin, MFA; *Technician* Roger Bisbing, MFA; *Asst Prof* Leona Christie, MFA; *Asst Prof* Yvette Mattern, MFA; *Assoc Prof* Michael Werner, PhD; *Prof* John Overbeck, PhD
Estab 1848; Art library; art supplies available on-campus; pub; D & E; Scholarships; SC 43, LC 20, GC 33; D 750, E 400, non-maj 600, maj 150, grad 45
Ent Req: HS dipl
Degrees: BA 4 yr, MA 1.5 yr, MFA 2 yr
Tuition: Res—undergrad $1700 per sem, $137 per cr hr, grad $2550 per sem, $213 per cr hr; nonres—undergrad $4150 per sem; $346 per cr hr, grad $4208 per sem, $351 per cr hr; campus res—room & board $3440.50 per sem
Courses: Aesthetics, †Art History, Design, Digital Imaging, †Drawing, Mixed Media, †Painting, †Photography, †Printmaking, †Sculpture, Video
Adult Hobby Classes: Courses in all studio areas
Summer School: Dir, Michael DeRensis. Enrl 350.

ALFRED

NEW YORK STATE COLLEGE OF CERAMICS AT ALFRED UNIVERSITY, School of Art & Design, 1 Saxon Dr, Alfred, NY 14802-1205. Tel 607-871-2441 or 800-541-9229; Fax 607-871-2198; Elec Mail admissions@alfred.edu; Internet Home Page Address: art.alfred.edu; *Dean* Leslie Bellavance; *Secy Grad Students* Billie Burns

Estab 1900; Maintains a nonprofit art gallery, Fosdick-Nelson Gallery, 1 Pine St, Alfred NY 14802, Robert Turner Student Gallery & Cohen Gallery; Scholes Library, 2 Pine St, Alfred NY 14802; on campus shop where art supplies may be purchased; FT 35; pvt; D & E; Scholarships; SC, LC, GC; maj undergrad 500, grad 37; 2 yrs of foundation study & 2 yrs of upper level study
Activities: Schols offered
Ent Req: Portfolio, GPA, SAT, HS dipl, essay, letter(s) of recommendation
Degrees: BFA, MFA 2 yrs, BS Art Hist
Tuition: Res—$23,474 out-of-state $17,818 in-state per yr
Courses: Art Education, †Art History, †Art Therapy †Ceramic Art, Ceramics, †Costume Design & Construction, Digital Imaging, †Dimensional Studies, †Display, Drawing, Electronic Integrated Arts, Glass Arts, Graphic Design, †Interactive Art, †Interactive Media, †Metals, †Mixed Media, Painting, Photography, Pre-Art Therapy, †Print Media, Printmaking, †Sculpture, †Sculpture/Dimensional studies, Sonic Arts, †Sonic Arts, †Stage Design, †Theatre Arts, Video, †Video Arts
Summer School: Cathy Johnson Admin Asst to Dean, Dean's Office, School Art & Design. Tuition 4 cr $1,976. Courses—Art History, Ceramics, Glass, Painting, Sculpture, Expanded Media, Sonic Arts, Video, Drawing, Painting, Photography

AMHERST

DAEMEN COLLEGE, Art Dept, 4380 Main St, Amherst, NY 14226-3592. Tel 716-839-8241; Fax 716-839-8516; Internet Home Page Address: www.daemen.edu; *Assoc Prof* Dennis Barraclough, MFA; *Asst Prof & Chmn* Joseph Kukella, MFA; *Instr* Jane Marinsky, BFA; *Instr* Joan Goldberg, BFA; *Instr* David Cinquino, MFA; *Instr* Dana Hatchett, MFA; *Prof* James Allen, MFA; *Asst Prof* Kevin Kegler, MAH
Estab 1947; pvt; D & E; Scholarships; SC 50; D 1800, non-maj 1740, maj 100
Ent Req: HS dipl, art portfolio
Degrees: BFA(Drawing, Graphic Design, Illustration, Painting, Printmaking, Sculpture), BS(Art), & BS(Art Educ) 4 yrs
Courses: †Advertising Design, Aesthetics, Art Appreciation, †Art Education, Art History, Ceramics, Computer Art, Design, Drawing, †Graphic Design, †Illustration, †Painting, Photography, †Printmaking, †Sculpture, Stage Design, Textile Design, Theatre Arts, Weaving, †Website Design
Summer School: Dean, Charles Reedy

ANNANDALE-ON-HUDSON

BARD COLLEGE, Center for Curatorial Studies Graduate Program, PO Box 5000, Annandale-on-Hudson, NY 12504-5000. Tel 845-758-7598; Fax 845-758-2442; Elec Mail ccs@bard.edu; Internet Home Page Address: www.bard.edu/ccs/; *Dir* Maria Lind; *Grad Comt* Johanna Burton; *Grad Comt* Ingrid Schaffner; *Grad Comt* Franklin Sirmons; *Dean of Grad Studies* Norton Batkin; *Grad Comt* Liam Gillick; *Grad Comt* Tirdad Zolghadr
Prog estab 1994; Maintains nonprofit art gallery, Hessel Mus of Art & CCS Galleries, Ctr for Curatorial Studies Mus, Bard Col, Annandale-on-Hudson, NY 12504-5000; Art library; on-campus shop where art supplies may be purchased; pvt; D; Scholarships, Fellowships; GC 20; grad 25
Ent Req: BA, BFA or equivalent
Degrees: Master's 2 yr
Courses: Aesthetics, Art History, †Museum Staff Training

BARD COLLEGE, Milton Avery Graduate School of the Arts, PO Box 5000, Annandale-on-Hudson, NY 12504-5000. Tel 845-758-7481; Fax 845-758-7507; Elec Mail mfa@bard.edu; Internet Home Page Address: www.bard.edu/mfa; *Dir* Arthur Gibbons; *Mng Dir* Susan Tveekrem
Estab 1981; Maintains a nonprofit art gallery, Bard Hessel Museum of Art, Bard College, Annandale-on-Hudson NY 12504; CCS Bard Library; art supplies sold at on-campus store; pvt; D, E & Summer; Scholarships; GC; GS 80
Degrees: MFA
Courses: Film, Music, Painting, Performance, Photography, Sculpture, Video, Writing
Summer School: Dir Arthur Gibbons. A student enrolls in 3 summer res terms & 2 winter independent study terms. 13 cred awarded each summer for conference, presentation & seminar. 6.5 cred awarded per independent study. 8 cred awarded for Master's proj, for a total of 60 cred.

AURORA

WELLS COLLEGE, Dept of Art, 170 Main St, Aurora, NY 13026-1101. Tel 315-364-3440, 364-3266; *Asst Prof* Rosemary Welsh; *Div Chmn* Susan Forbes
Estab 1868; pvt, W; D; Scholarships; SC 19, LC 20; D 500 (total), non-maj 122, maj 18
Ent Req: HS dipl, cr by exam programs
Degrees: BA 4 yrs
Courses: Aesthetics, †Art History, †Ceramics, †Drawing, †Painting, Photography, Printmaking, Teacher Training, †Theatre Arts

BAYSIDE HILLS

QUEENSBOROUGH COMMUNITY COLLEGE, Dept of Art & Photography, 222-05 56th Ave, Bayside Hills, NY 11364. Tel 718-631-6395; Fax 718-631-6612; Internet Home Page Address: www.qcc.cuny.edu; *Assoc Prof* Robert Rogers, MFA; *Asst Prof* Jules Allen, MFA; *Chmn Dr* JoAnn Wein; *Asst Prof* Javier Cambre; *Assoc Prof* Kenneth Golden; *Prof* Paul Tschinkel; *Asst Prof* Anissa Mack
Estab 1958, dept estab 1968; Maintains nonprofit art gallery, Queensborough Community College Art Gallery, Oakland Building, 222-05 56th Ave, Bayside, NY 11364; Pub; D & E; Scholarships; SC 21, LC 14; D 9,000, E 4,000
Ent Req: HS dipl, placement exams
Degrees: AA & AS

Courses: Advertising Design, Art History, Artist Apprenticeships, Arts Internships, Arts for Teachers of Children, Ceramics, Color Theory, Design, Digital Art & Design, Drawing, Graphic Design, Illustration, Painting, †Photography, Printmaking, Sculpture, Video
Summer School: Dir, Jo Ann Wein. Courses—Drawing, Photography, Sculpture, Art History, 2-D Design

BINGHAMTON

STATE UNIVERSITY OF NEW YORK AT BINGHAMTON, Dept of Art History, PO Box 6000, Binghamton, NY 13902-6000. Tel 607-777-2111; Fax 607-777-4466; Elec Mail arthist@binghamton.edu; Internet Home Page Address: www.arthist.binghamton.edu; *Chmn Dept* Barbara Abou-El-Haj; *Assoc Prof* John Tagg; *Assoc Prof* Karen Barzman; *Assoc Prof* Thomas McDonough; *Assoc Prof* Aruna D'Souza; *Assoc Prof* Nancy Um
Estab 1950; Pub; D&E; Scholarships; LC 32, GC 63; 679, non-maj 400, maj 40, grad 43
Ent Req: HS dipl, Regents Scholarship, ACT or SAT
Degrees: BA 4 yrs, MA 1-2 yrs, PhD varies
Courses: †Architecture, †Art History, †Cinema, Printmaking, †Studio Art, Video
Summer School: Tuition same as acad yr, 3 separate sessions during summer. Courses—Art History

BROCKPORT

STATE UNIVERSITY OF NEW YORK COLLEGE AT BROCKPORT, Dept of Art, Tower Fine Arts Bldg, Brockport, NY 14420-2985; 350 New Campus Dr, Brockport, NY 14420-2914. Tel 716-395-2209; Fax 716-395-2588; Internet Home Page Address: www.brockport.edu; *Chmn* Debra Fisher; *Prof* Jennifer Heuker; *Asst Prof* Alisia Chase; *Asst Prof* Tim Massey; *Assoc Prof* James Morris
Maintain nonprofit art gallery; FT 3, PT 6; Pub; D; Scholarships; SC 33, LC 29; 8188, maj 100, grad 2000, grad 30
Ent Req: HS dipl, ent exam
Degrees: BA, BS & BFA 4 yrs
Courses: Artists Books, †Ceramics, Design, Drawing, †Jewelry, †Painting, †Photography, †Printmaking, †Sculpture, Video
Adult Hobby Classes: Courses—Ceramics, Drawing, Methods, Museum & Gallery Studies, Painting, Photography, Sculpture, 2-D & 3-D Design
Summer School: Dir, Dr Kenneth O'Brien

BRONX

BRONX COMMUNITY COLLEGE, Music & Art Dept, 2155 University Ave, Bliss Hall 303 Bronx, NY 10453-2804. Tel 718-289-55351, 289-5252; Fax 718-289-6433; Internet Home Page Address: www.bcc.cuny.edu/artmusic/index.html; *Chmn Dr* Ruth Bass
Pub; AM, PM
Ent Req: HS dipl, equivalent
Degrees: Cert, AS, AAS
Tuition: Res—$1305 per sem; nonres—$1538 per sem
Courses: Art Appreciation, Art History, Ceramics, Commercial Art, Design, Drawing, Modern Art, Painting, Photography, Printmaking, †Sculpture
Adult Hobby Classes: Enrl 25; tuition $45 for 7 wks. Courses—Calligraphy, Drawing

HERBERT H LEHMAN COLLEGE, Art Dept, 250 Bedford Park Blvd W, Bronx, NY 10468-1527. Tel 718-960-8256; Fax 718-960-7203; *Chmn* Herbert R Broderick, MFA; *Assoc Prof* Arvn Bose; *Asst Prof* David Gillison, MFA
Estab 1968; pub; D & E; Scholarships; SC 18, LC 29, GC 31; non-maj 100, major 50, grad 15
Ent Req: HS dipl, ent exam
Degrees: BA & BFA 4 yrs, MA, MFA & MA 2 yrs
Courses: †Art History, †Graphic Arts, †Painting, †Sculpture
Summer School: Dean, Chester Robinson. Enrl 45; Courses—Art History, Drawing, Painting

MANHATTAN COLLEGE, School of Arts, 3900 Manhattan College Pkwy, Bronx, NY 10471-3927. Tel 718-862-7346; Fax 718-862-8444; Elec Mail mdonnel@manhattan.edu; Internet Home Page Address: www.manhattan.edu; *Dean of Art* Maryann O'Donnell; *Prof* Mark Pottunger; *Prof* Scott Grimaldi; *Prof* Hugh Berberich
Estab 1853; pvt den; D&E; Scholarships; LC 8, Art 4, Music 4; D 3000
Ent Req: HS dipl
Degrees: BA, BS
Courses: Art History, Ceramics, Drawing, Film, Graphic Arts, Graphic Design, History of Art & Architecture, Painting, Photography, Printmaking, Sculpture

BRONXVILLE

CONCORDIA COLLEGE, Art Dept, 171 White Plains Rd, Bronxville, NY 10708-1998. Tel 914-337-9300; Fax 914-395-4500;
Estab 1881; pvt; D; Scholarships; SC 4, LC 2
Ent Req: HS dipl, SAT or ACT
Degrees: BA and BS 4 yrs
Courses: Art Education, Art History, Ceramics, Computer Graphics, Drawing, Handicrafts, History of Art & Architecture, Painting, Photography, Sculpture, Teacher Training
Adult Hobby Classes: Courses—Painting

SARAH LAWRENCE COLLEGE, Dept of Art History, 1 Mead Way, Bronxville, NY 10708-5999. Tel 914-337-0700; Internet Home Page Address: www.slc.edu; *Dean* Jerrilynn Dodds; *Faculty* David Castriota; *Faculty* Joseph C Forte; *Faculty* Susan Kart; *Faculty* Judith Rodenbeck

Estab 1926; FT 1, PT 9; pvt; D; Scholarships
Ent Req: HS dipl
Degrees: BA 4 yrs
Tuition: $17,280 per yr
Courses: Art History, Drawing, Filmmaking, Painting, Photography, Printmaking, Sculpture, Visual Fundamentals
Summer School: Center for Continuing Education

BROOKHAVEN

INTERNATIONAL COUNCIL FOR CULTURAL EXCHANGE (ICCE), PO Box 361, Brookhaven, NY 11719-0361. Tel 800-690-4223; Fax 212-982-4017; Elec Mail info@ICCE-Travel.org; Internet Home Page Address: www.icce-travel.org; *Prog Coordr* Stanley I Gochman PhD; *International Planning Dir* Julie Gochman
Estab 1982; pvt, nonprofit; May-Nov International Prog (Europe 2-3 wks); SC, LC
Ent Req: Minimum age - 17
Degrees: college cr
Tuition: Depends on prog
Courses: Art Appreciation, Art History, Drawing, History of Art & Architecture, Mixed Media, Theatre Arts
Summer School: Tuition approx $3698 for 2-3 wk session abroad. Courses—Landscape, Painting

BROOKLYN

BROOKLYN COLLEGE, Art Dept, 2900 Bedford Ave, Brooklyn, NY 11210-2850. Tel 718-951-5181; Fax 718-951-5670; Internet Home Page Address: www.brooklyn.cuny.edu; *Chmn* Michael Mallory
Estab 1962; Pub; AM, PM; Scholarships
Degrees: BA, BFA, MA, MFA
Tuition: Res (in state)—undergrad $1,600 per sem, grad $160 per cr hr; non res—undergrad $3,400 per sem, grad $285 per cr hr
Courses: Aesthetics, Art History, Calligraphy, Ceramics, Collage, Computer Graphics, Design, Drawing, Graphic Arts, Graphic Design, History of Art & Architecture, Intermedia, Mixed Media, Museum Staff Training, Painting, Photography, Printmaking, Sculpture
Adult Hobby Classes: Enrl 50. Courses—Studio Art
Summer School: Enrl 100-150; two summer sessions. Courses—Art History, Computer Graphics, Studio Art

KINGSBOROUGH COMMUNITY COLLEGE, Dept of Art, 2001 Oriental Blvd, Brooklyn, NY 11235-2333. Tel 718-368-5000, 368-5718 (art); Fax 718-368-4872; Internet Home Page Address: www.kingsborough.edu; Estab 1965, dept estab 1972; Maintains nonprofit Art Gallery, in Arts & Sciences Bldg on campus; pub; D & E; SC 10, LC 8; maj 135
Ent Req: HS dipl
Degrees: AS 2 yrs
Courses: Art History, Ceramics, Design, Drawing, Graphic Design, Illustration, Painting, Photography, Sculpture
Adult Hobby Classes: Overseas travel courses
Summer School: Courses—Art

LONG ISLAND UNIVERSITY, BROOKLYN CAMPUS, Art Dept, 1 University Plz, Bldg 3 Brooklyn, NY 11201-5301. Tel 718-488-1051; *Prof* Liz Rudey; *Chmn* Bob Barry; *Prof* Nancy Grove; *Prof* Cynthia Dantzic; *Prof* Hilary Lorenz
Maintain nonprofit art gallery; The Salena Gallery, The Resnick Gallery & The Kumbie Gallery; FT 5, PT 15; Pvt; D & E; Scholarships; SC 20, LC 6; maj 35
Ent Req: HS dipl, ent exam
Degrees: BA, BFA in Art Educ & Studio Art
Courses: †Art Education, Art History, Arts Management, Calligraphy, Ceramics, †Color, †Computer Graphics, Drawing, Media Arts, Medical-Scientific Illustration, Painting, †Photography, Printmaking, Sculpture, †Teacher Training, Teaching Art to Children, †Video, Visual Experience
Adult Hobby Classes: Courses—Teaching Art to Children
Summer School: Dir, Liz Rudey. Term of two 6 wk sessions. Courses—Ceramics, Drawing, Painting, Art History, Calligraphy

NEW YORK CITY COLLEGE OF TECHNOLOGY OF THE CITY UNIVERSITY OF NEW YORK, Dept of Advertising Design & Graphic Arts, 300 Jay St, Brooklyn, NY 11201-1909. Tel 718-260-5175; Fax 718-254-8555; Elec Mail jmason@citytech.cuny.edu; Internet Home Page Address: www.citytech.cuny.edu; *Chmn* Joel Mason
Estab 1946; Maintain nonprofit art gallery, Grace Gallery, 300 Jay St, N1124, Brooklyn, NY 11201; pub; D & E; Scholarships; SC 16, LC 3; D 650, E 350
Ent Req: HS dipl
Degrees: AAS 2 yr, BTech 4 yr, BComm 2 yr, AAS Graphic Arts, BTech Graphic Arts 4 yr Cert, Desktop Pub
Courses: 3-D Animation, †Advertising Design, †Computer Graphics, †Digital Graphics, Digital Video, †Digital Video, †Digital Work Flow, Drawing, Graphic Arts, Graphic Design, Illustration, †Multi-Media, Packaging, Painting, Photography, †Photography Binding Finishing, Printmaking, Type Spacing, Video, Web Design
Summer School: Computer Graphics, Design, Illustration, Lettering, Life Drawing, Paste-up, Photography, Video Design

PRATT INSTITUTE, School of Art & Design, 200 Willoughby Ave, Brooklyn, NY 11205-3899. Tel 718-636-3600; Fax 718-636-3410; Internet Home Page Address: www.pratt.edu; *Dean* Frank Lind
Pub; 3700
Degrees: BFA & BID 4 yr, MA, MF, MFA & MPF 2 yr
Tuition: Undergrad $7200 per sem, grad $505 per cr hr

Courses: †Art Education, †Art History, †Ceramics, †Computer Graphics, †Drawing, †Film, †Graphic Design, †Illustration, †Industrial Design, †Interior Design, †Painting, †Photography, †Printmaking, †Sculpture, †Video
Adult Hobby Classes: Enrl 195. Various courses offered
Children's Classes: Morning classes
Summer School: Dean, Vieri Salvadori. Enrl for high school students only; tuition $400 per 4 cr. Courses—Computer Graphics, Fine Arts, Foundation Art
—School of Architecture, 200 Willoughby Ave, Brooklyn, NY 11205. Tel 718-636-3404; Fax 718-399-4332; Internet Home Page Address: www.pratt.edu; *Dean* Thomas Hanrahan
Degrees: BArch 5 yr, MArch
Tuition: $15,800 per yr
Courses: Architecture, Art History, Construction Documents In Professional Practice, Design, History of Architecture, Landscape Architecture, Materials, Structures

PROMOTE ART WORKS INC (PAWI), Job Readiness in the Arts-Media-Communication, 123 Smith St, Brooklyn, NY-6218. Tel 718-797-3116; Fax 718-855-1208; Elec Mail executive@micromuseum.com; Internet Home Page Address: www.micromuseum.com; *Technical Dir* William Laziza
Estab 1993; Internship; ongoing; Scholarships
Ent Req: interview process
Courses: †Conceptual Art, †Interactive Media, †Mixed Media, †Video
Adult Hobby Classes: Tuition $50 per hr. Courses—Video Editing
Children's Classes: Tuition $15 per class. Courses—Dance, Drama, Movement
Summer School: Tuition $15 per class. Courses—Art, Science

BROOKVILLE

C W POST CAMPUS OF LONG ISLAND UNIVERSITY, School of Visual & Performing Arts, 720 Northern Blvd, Brookville, NY 11548-1300. Tel 516-299-2000, 299-2395 (visual & performing arts); Internet Home Page Address: www.cwpost.liunet.edu; *Chmn & Prof* Jerome Zimmerman; *Prof* Marilyn Goldstein; *Prof* Howard LaMarcz; *Prof* Robert Yasuda; *Assoc Prof* David Henley; *Assoc Prof* Jacqueline Frank; *Assoc Prof* Frank Olt; *Assoc Prof* Joan Powers; *Asst Prof* John Fekner; *Asst Prof* Richard Mills; *Asst Prof* Carol Huebner-Venezia; *Asst Prof* Donna Tuman; *Asst Prof* Vincent Wright; *Dean Visual & Performing Arts* Lynn Croton
Dept estab 1957; pvt; D & E; Scholarships; SC 70, LC 15, GC 40; D 2000, E 450, non-maj 2000, maj 250, grad 150, others 50
Ent Req: HS dipl, portfolio
Degrees: BA(Art Educ), BA(Art Hist), BA(Studio), BS(Art Therapy) & BFA(Graphic Design) 4 yrs, MA(Photography), MA(Studio), MS(Art Educ) & MFA(Art, Design or Photography) 2 yrs
Courses: †Advertising Design, Aesthetics, †Art Education, †Art History, Ceramics, Collage, Commercial Art, Computer Graphics, Conceptual Art, Constructions, Drawing, Film, Fine Arts, Graphic Arts, Graphic Design, Handicrafts, Illustration, Intermedia, Jewelry, Lettering, Mixed Media, Painting, Photography, Printmaking, Sculpture, Stage Design, Teacher Training, Theatre Arts, Video, Weaving
Adult Hobby Classes: Courses—Varied
Summer School: Prof, Howard LaMarcz. Duration 3-5 wk sessions. Courses—varied

BUFFALO

LOCUST STREET NEIGHBORHOOD ART CLASSES, INC, 138 Locust St, Buffalo, NY 14204-1246. Tel 716-852-4562; Fax 716-852-4562; Elec Mail locuststt@verizon.net; *Dir & Painting Teacher* Molly Bethel; *Photog Instr* Ken Morgan; *Screen Printing Instr* Art Pepe; *Clay Instr* Dorothy Harold; *Instr* Garry Collins; *Instr* Sky Bethel
Open Tues - Thurs & Sat Noon - 5 PM; Estab 1959; Inc 1971; Maintains an informal on-site art/architecture library; Pvt; D & Weekend; SC 4, Other 1; Non-maj 300 per yr
Collections: Permanent collection of paintings by students
Exhibitions: Annual Art Show
Tuition: No tuition fees
Courses: Clay, †Drawing, †Painting, †Photography, Public Art Projects, Spoken Word Poetry
Adult Hobby Classes: Enrl 120. Courses—Clay, Drawing, Painting, Photography
Children's Classes: Enrl 200. Courses—Clay, Drawing, Painting
Summer School: Dir, Molly Bethel, Coordr, Sky Bethel -Enrl adults and children. Course—Drawing, Painting, Photog, children's summer day program

STATE UNIVERSITY OF NEW YORK COLLEGE AT BUFFALO, Fine Arts Dept, 1300 Elmwood Ave, Buffalo, NY 14222-1004. Tel 716-878-6014; Fax 716-878-6697; Internet Home Page Address: www.buffalostate.edu; *Chmn* Peter Sowiski
Estab 1875, dept estab 1969; FT 16; pub; D & E; SC 34, LC 17, GC 6; maj 300 (art) 50 (BFA) 12 (art history)
Ent Req: HS dipl
Degrees: BA(Art), BA(Art History) & BFA 4 yrs
Courses: †Art History, †Drawing, †Painting, †Papermaking, †Photography, †Printmaking, †Sculpture
Summer School: Dir, Gerald Accurso. Courses—Art History, Studio

UNIVERSITY AT BUFFALO, STATE UNIVERSITY OF NEW YORK, Dept of Visual Studies, 202 Center for the Arts, Buffalo, NY 14260-6010. Tel 716-645-6878 ext 1350; Fax 716-645-6970; Elec Mail uginfo@acsu.buffalo.edu; vs-gradinfo@acsu.buffalo.edu; Internet Home Page Address: www.visualstudies.buffalo.edu; *Chmn, Prof* David Schirm; *Distinguished Prof Emeritus* Harvey Breverman; *Prof* Tyrone Georgiou; *Assoc Prof* Tony Rozak; *Assoc Prof* Millie Chen; *Assoc Prof* Jolene Rickard; *Assoc Prof* Paul Vanouse; *Asst Prof* Gary Nickard; *Asst Prof* Reinhard Reitzenstein; *Assoc Prof* Steven Kurtz;

Asst Prof Sylvie Belanger; *Asst Prof* Joan Linder; *Distinguished Prof* John Quinan; *Prof* Adele Henderson; *Prof* Livingston Watrous; *Asst Prof* George Hughes; *Asst Prof* Nancy Anderson; *Asst Prof* Binggi Huang; *Asst Prof* Elizabeth Otto; *Asst Prof* Lori Johnson; *Assoc Prof* Charles Carman; *Asst Prof* Benjamin Van Dyke; *Asst Prof* Megan Michalak
Estab 1846; Maintain nonprofit art gallery, Dept of Visual Studies Gallery 202 Center For The Arts, Buffalo, NY 14260-6010; FT 14, PT 14; pub; D & E; Scholarships, Fellowships; SC 80, LC 35, GC 20, Other 30; D & E 350, non-maj 100, maj 325, grad 50
Ent Req: HS dipl
Degrees: BA, BFA & MFA, MA
Courses: Aesthetics, Art History, †Communications Design, †Computer Art, Conceptual Art, Criticism & Theory, Design, Drawing, Foundations, Graphic Design, Installation, Mixed Media, †Painting, †Photography, †Printmaking, Public Art Practice, †Sculpture, Typography, Video
Summer School: Enrl 104; tuition res $180 per cr hr, nonres $389 per cr hr for 3-6 wk term. Courses—Computer Art, Drawing, Painting, Photo, Printmaking

VILLA MARIA COLLEGE OF BUFFALO, Art Dept, 240 Pine Ridge Rd, Buffalo, NY 14225-3999. Tel 716-896-0700; Fax 716-896-0705; Internet Home Page Address: www.villa.edu; *Chmn* Brian R Duffy, MFA
Estab 1961; pvt; D & E; Scholarships; SC 27, LC 3; D 450, E 100, maj 170
Ent Req: HS dipl of equivalency
Degrees: AA, AAS & AS 2 yrs
Courses: 3-D Design, Advertising Design, Advertising Graphics, Art History, Color Photo, Commercial Design, Computer-aided Design, Design, Drafting, Drawing, Etching, Graphic Arts, Graphic Design, History of Interior Design, History of Photography, Interior Design, Lettering, Mechanical Systems & Building Materials, Painting, Photography, Printmaking, Rendering & Presentation, Sculpture, Serigraphy, Studio Lighting, Textile Design, View Camera Techniques
Adult Hobby Classes: Courses - Drawing, Painting, Photography
Summer School: Enrl 10-20. Courses—a variety of interest courses, including Drawing, Painting and Photography

CANANDAIGUA

FINGER LAKES COMMUNITY COLLEGE, Visual & Performing Arts Dept, 4355 Lake Shore Dr, Canandaigua, NY 14424. Tel 716-394-3500, Ext 257; Fax 716-394-5005; *Prof* Wayne Williams, MFA; *Asst Prof* John Fox, MFA; *Pres* Daniel T Hayes
Estab 1966; FT 5; pub; D & E; SC 14, LC 2; D 60, non-maj 700, maj 50
Ent Req: HS dipl
Degrees: AA & AAS 2 yrs
Courses: Advertising Design, Art History, Ceramics, Commercial Art, Drawing, Graphic Arts, Graphic Design, Illustration, Painting, Photography, Printmaking, Sculpture, Stage Design, Theatre Arts
Summer School: Courses—Per regular session

CANTON

ST LAWRENCE UNIVERSITY, Dept of Fine Arts, 23 Romoda Dr, Canton, NY 13617. Tel 315-229-5192; Internet Home Page Address: www.stlawu.edu; *Assoc Prof* Dorothy Limouze, PhD; *Assoc Prof* Faye Serio, MFA; *Assoc Prof* Chandreyi Basu, PhD; *Assoc Prof* Melissa Schulenberg, PhD; *Asst Prof* Amy Hauber, MFA; *Asst Prof* Mark Denaci, PhD; *Asst Prof* Kasarian Dane, MFA; *Prof* Obiora Udechukwu, MFA; *Instr* Linda Strauss
Estab 1856; Non-Profit art gallery, Richard F Brush Art Gallery. Art supplies may be purchased on campus; pvt; D&E; SC 16, LC 13; maj 80, non-maj 300
Ent Req: HS dipl
Degrees: BA
Courses: Art Education, Art History, Ceramics, Drawing, History of Art & Architecture, Painting, Photography, Printmaking, Sculpture, Video
Summer School: Dir, Donna Fish. Enrl 10-20. Courses—Art History, Studio

CAZENOVIA

CAZENOVIA COLLEGE, Center for Art & Design Studies, 22 Sullivan St, Studio Art Cazenovia, NY 13035-1085. Tel 800-654-3210; Fax 315-655-2190; Internet Home Page Address: www.cazenovia.edu; *Pres* Mark Tierno; *Prof* Lillian Ottaviano, MFA; *Prof* Jeanne King, MFA; *Prof* Jo Buffalo, MFA; *Prof & Chmn* Charles Goss, MFA; *Assoc Prof* Kim Waale, MFA; *Assoc Prof* Anita Welych, MFA; *Assoc Prof* Karen Steen, MFA; *Instr* Patricia Beglin, MA; *Asst Prof* Laurie Selleck, MFA; *Asst Prof* Allyn Stewart, MFA; *Asst Prof* Tod Guynn, MFA; *Asst Prof* Elizabeth Moore, MS; *Asst Prof* Josef Ritter, MFA
Estab 1824; pvt; D & E; Scholarships; SC 21, LC 3; D 660
Ent Req: HS dipl
Degrees: AS, AAS, BS, BFA, & BPS 2 yr & 4 yr progs
Courses: †Advanced Studio Art, †Advertising Design, Advertising Layout, Basic Design, Ceramics, Drafting, Drawing, Fashion Design, †Illustration, †Interior Design, Lettering, Office & Mercantile Interiors, Painting, Photography, Printmaking, Rendering, Residential Interiors, Typography
Adult Hobby Classes: Enrl 200; Courses—large variety
Summer School: Dir, Marge Pinet. Enrl 100; Courses—Variety

CHAUTAUQUA

CHAUTAUQUA INSTITUTION, School of Art, 1 Ames Ave, Chautauqua, NY 14722; PO Box 1098, Chautauqua, NY 14722-1098. Tel 716-357-6233; Fax 716-357-9014; Elec Mail art@ciweb.org; Internet Home Page Address: www.ciweb.org; *Dir Art School* Don Kimes

Estab 1874; maintain nonprofit art gallery, Strohl Art Center & Logan Galleries; pvt; D (summers only) & E; Scholarships; SC 40, LC 20; D 38, maj 38, GS 10, other 28
Ent Req: portfolio review, min 2 yrs previous univ level art studies, coll credit granted
Courses: Ceramics, Drawing, Painting, Printmaking, Sculpture
Summer School: Dir, Don Kimes.

CLAYTON

THOUSAND ISLANDS ARTS CENTER - HOME OF THE HANDWEAVING MUSEUM, (Handweaving Museum & Arts Center) 314 John St, Clayton, NY 13624-1017. Tel 315-686-4123; Elec Mail info@tiartscenter.org; Internet Home Page Address: www.tiartscenter.org; *Exec Dir* Leslie W Rowland; *Cur* Sonja Wahl
Estab 1964; maintain a nonprofit art gallery: Catherine C. Johnson Gallery, 314 John St, Clayton, NY 13624; maintain an art/architecture library: Berta Frey Memorial Library, 314 John St, Clayton, NY 13624; PT 33; brd of trustees, non-profit; D & E (weekdays & weekends); SC 35; D 210, E 10
Degrees: no degrees but transfer cr
Courses: Basketry, Bird Carving, Ceramics, Decoy Carving, Drawing, Fashion Arts, Fiber Arts, Handicrafts, Jewelry, Mixed Media, Painting, Pottery, Quilting, Sculpture, †Sewing, Spinning, Weaving
Children's Classes: Drawing, Painting, Pottery, Weaving
Summer School: Marcia Rogers, Educator - Courses—Country Painting, Decoy Carving, Painting on Silk, Pottery, Quilting, Sculpture, Watercolor Painting, Weaving

CLINTON

HAMILTON COLLEGE, Art Dept, 198 College Hill Rd, Clinton, NY 13323. Tel 315-859-4269; Elec Mail art@hamilton.edu; Internet Home Page Address: www.hamilton.edu; *Prof* William Salzillo, MFA; *Prof* Robert Muirhead, MFA; *Assoc Prof Art* Ella Gant, MFA; *Assoc Prof* Rebecca Murtaugh; *Vis Asst Prof* Christopher Russell; *Kevin Kennedy Assoc Prof Art* Katharine Kuharic
Maintains a nonprofit art gallery, Emerson Gallery 198 College Hill Rd, Clinton, NY 13325

COBLESKILL

STATE UNIVERSITY OF NEW YORK, COBLESKILL, Art Dept, State Rte 7, Cobleskill, NY 12043. Tel 518-255-5700; Internet Home Page Address: www.cobleskill.edu;
Estab 1950; pub; D & E; SC 2, LC 2; D 95
Ent Req: HS dipl
Degrees: AA & AS 2 yrs, BT 4 yrs
Courses: Art Education, Art History, Drawing, Painting, Sculpture, Teacher Training, Theatre Arts
Adult Hobby Classes: Enrl 4000 per yr; tuition $9 per course. Courses—large variety of mini-courses

CORNING

CORNING COMMUNITY COLLEGE, Division of Humanities, One Academic Dr, Corning, NY 14830. Tel 607-962-9456; *Prof* Margaret Brill, MA; *Assoc Prof* Fred Herbst; *Prof* David Higgins, MFA
Estab 1958, dept estab 1963; FT 3; pub; D & E; SC 8, LC 6
Ent Req: HS dipl, SAT
Degrees: AA, AS, AAS 2 yrs
Courses: Architecture, Art Appreciation, Art History, Ceramics, Design, Drawing, History of Art & Architecture, Jewelry, Painting, Photography, Silkscreen, Silversmithing
Adult Hobby Classes: Enrl 18
Summer School: Dir, Betsy Brune

CORTLAND

STATE UNIVERSITY OF NEW YORK, COLLEGE AT CORTLAND, Dept Art & Art History, PO Box 2000, Room 222 Dowd Cortland, NY 13045-0900. Tel 607-753-4316; Fax 607-753-5967; Elec Mail anne.mclorn@cortland.edu; Elec Mail lori.ellis@cortland.edu; Internet Home Page Address: www.cortland.edu/art/; *Chmn & Prof* Lori Ellis; *Prof* Jeremiah Donovan, MFA; *Prof* Barbara Wisch PhD, MAT; *Prof* Charles Heasley, MFA; *Assoc Prof* Kathryn Kramer PhD, MFA; *Asst Prof* Martine Barnaby, MFA; *Asst Prof* Jennifer McNamara, MFA; *Asst Prof* Vaughn Randall, MFA
Estab 1868, dept estab 1948; Maintains Dowd Art Gallery; pub; D & E; Scholarships; SC 40, LC 10; D 5600 (total), 1200 (art), maj 80
Ent Req: HS dipl, all college admissions standards based on high school average or scores from SAT, ACTP or Regent's tests
Degrees: BA 4 yrs, BFA 4 yrs
Courses: Art Appreciation, Art Education, †Art History, Ceramics, Computer Generated Prints, Computers in the Visual Arts, Contemporary Art, Design, Drawing, Fabric Design, †Graphic Design (New Media), †History of Art & Architecture, †Lettering Typography, Lithography, Modern Art, Painting, Photography, Printmaking, Sculpture, Silkscreen, Surrealism, Weaving
Summer School: Two terms of 5 wks beginning June 26. Courses—Art History, Studio

DIX HILLS

THE ART LEAGUE OF LONG ISLAND, Stevenson Academy Program, 107 E Deer Park Rd, Dix Hills, NY 11746-4818. Tel 631-462-5400; Elec Mail info@thestevensonacademy.com; Internet Home Page Address: www.thestevensonacademy.com

Average Annual Attendance:

ELMIRA

ELMIRA COLLEGE, Art Dept, One Park Pl, Elmira, NY 14901. Tel 607-735-1800, 735-1804 (Acad Affairs); Tel 607-735-1724 (Admis); Fax 607-735-1712; Internet Home Page Address: www.elmira.edu; *Chmn* Doug Holtgrewe; *Prof* James Cook; *Asst Prof* Leslie Kramer, MFA; *Asst Prof* Mac Dennis, MFA; *Asst* John Diamond-Nigh, MFA; *Asst* Jan Kather, MFA
Estab 1855; pvt; D & E; Scholarships; SC 26, LC 15, GC 8; D 250, E 125, maj 35, grad 6
Ent Req: HS dipl
Degrees: AA, AS, BA, BS & MEduc
Courses: †Art Education, †Art History, †Ceramics, †Drawing, †Painting, †Photography, †Printmaking, †Sculpture, †Video
Adult Hobby Classes: Tuition $180 - $265 per cr hr. Courses—Art History, Ceramics, Drawing, Landscape Painting & Drawing, Painting, Photography, Video
Summer School: Dir, Lois Webster. Tuition undergrad $180 cr hr, grad $265 per cr hr. Courses—Art History, Ceramics, Drawing, Landscape Painting & Drawing, Painting

FARMINGDALE

STATE UNIVERSITY OF NEW YORK AT FARMINGDALE, Visual Communications, 2350 Broadhollow Rd, Farmingdale, NY 11735-1006. Tel 631-420-2181; Fax 631-420-2034; Internet Home Page Address: www.farmingdale.edu/art; *Dept Chmn* Wayne Krush; *Asst Prof* George Fernandez; *Assoc Prof* Thomas Germano; *Assoc Prof* Paul Gustafson; *Assoc Prof* Mark Moscarillo; *Asst Prof* Donna Proper; *Assoc Prof* Allison Puff; *Assoc Prof* Bill Steedle
Estab 1912; 10 FT, 6 PT; pub; D&E
Ent Req: portfolio, drawing test
Degrees: BT
Tuition: Res—$3,700 per yr; nonres—$8,300 per yr
Courses: Calligraphy, Computer Art, Computer Graphics, Design, Drawing, Electronic Publishing, Illustration, Layout, Multi-Media, Painting, Pastels, Photography, Printmaking, Typography, Watercolors, Web Design
Adult Hobby Classes: Tuition $45 per credit hr. Courses same as above
Summer School: Dir, Francis N Pellegrini. Tuition $45 per cr; June-Aug. Courses—Advertising, Art History, Design, Drawing, Lettering, Mechanical Art, Production

FLUSHING

QUEENS COLLEGE, Art Dept, 65-30 Kissena Blvd, Flushing, NY 11367. Tel 718-997-5770, 997-5411; Internet Home Page Address: www.qc.edu; *Chmn* James Saslow
Nonprofit art gallery on 4th fl; also a museum; 13 FT instrs
Degrees: BA, BFA, MA, MFA, MSEd
Courses: Advertising Design, Architecture, Art Appreciation, Art Education, Art History, Calligraphy, Ceramics, Design, Drawing, Illustration, Painting, Photography, Printmaking, Sculpture
Summer School: Courses held at Caumsett State Park

FOREST HILLS

FOREST HILLS ADULT AND YOUTH CENTER, 6701 110th St, Forest Hills, NY 11375-2378. Tel 718-263-8066; *Prin HS* Elma Fleming
Degrees: Cert
Tuition: $70 plus materials for 7 wk course
Courses: Art Appreciation, Calligraphy, Drawing, Handicrafts, Painting, Quilting

FREDONIA

STATE UNIVERSITY OF NEW YORK AT FREDONIA, Dept of Art, 280 Central Ave, Rockefeller Art Center Rm 269 Fredonia, NY 14063-1127. Tel 716-673-3537; Elec Mail lundem@fredonia.edu; Internet Home Page Address: www.fredonia.edu; *Prof* Marvin Bjurlin; *Prof* Robert Booth; *Prof* Paul Bowers; *Prof* John Hughson; *Prof* Daniel Reiff, PhD; *Chmn* Mary Lee Lunde; *Prof* Alberto Rey; *Prof* Liz Lee; *Asst Prof* Jan Conradi
Estab 1867, dept estab 1948; pub; D & E; Scholarships; SC 30, LC 18; D 650, E 70, non-maj 610, major 140
Ent Req: ent req HS dipl, GRE, SAT, portfolio review all students
Degrees: BA 4 yrs, BFA 4 yrs
Courses: Art History, †Ceramics, Drawing, †Graphic Arts, †Illustration, †Painting, †Photography, Printmaking, †Sculpture, Video

GARDEN CITY

ADELPHI UNIVERSITY, Dept of Art & Art History, 1 South Ave, Garden City, NY 11530-4213; PO Box 701, Garden City, NY 11530-0701. Tel 516-877-4460; Fax 516-877-4459; Internet Home Page Address: www.adelphi.edu; *Prof* Richard Vaux; *Assoc Prof* Thomas MacNulty; *Asst Prof* Dale Flashner; *Chmn* Harry Davies; *Asst Prof* Geoffrey Grogan; *Asst Prof* Jacob Wisse
Estab 1896; Maintain nonprofit art gallery; FT 7, PT 18; pvt; D & E; Scholarships; SC 50, LC 10, GC 20; D 700, E 100, maj 130, grad 60
Ent Req: HS dipl; portfolio required for undergrad admis, portfolio required for grad admis
Degrees: BA 4 yrs, MA 1 1/2 yrs

Courses: †Advertising Design, Aesthetics, Art Education, Art History, Calligraphy, Ceramics, Design, Drawing, Graphic Arts, Graphic Design, History of Art & Architecture, Jewelry, Lettering, Mixed Media, Painting, Photography, Printmaking, Sculpture, Teacher Training
Summer School: Chmn, Harry Davies. Tuition—same as regular session; two 4 wk summer terms also 2 wk courses. Courses—Crafts, Drawing, Painting, Sculpture, Photography

NASSAU COMMUNITY COLLEGE, Art Dept, One Education Dr, Garden City, NY 11530. Tel 516-572-7162; Fax 516-572-9673; *Prof* Robert Lawn; *Prof* Edward Fox
Estab 1959, dept estab 1960; pub; D & E; Scholarships; SC 22, LC 5; D & E 20,000
Ent Req: HS dipl
Degrees: AA 2 yrs, cert in photography & advertising design 1 yr
Courses: Advertising Art, Art History, Arts & Crafts, Ceramics, Drawing, Fashion Arts, Painting, Photography, Printmaking, Sculpture
Summer School: Two 5 wk terms

GENESEO

STATE UNIVERSITY OF NEW YORK COLLEGE AT GENESEO, Dept of Art, One College Circle, Geneseo, NY 14454. Tel 716-245-5814, 245-5211 (main); Fax 716-245-5815; Internet Home Page Address: www.geneseo.edu; *Chmn* Carl Shanahan
Estab 1871; FT 8, PT 3; pub; D & E; Scholarships; SC 35, LC 7; D 1000, E 1150, maj 115
Ent Req: HS dipl, ent exam
Degrees: BA(Art) 3-4 yrs
Courses: 2-D & 3-D Design, Art History, Ceramics, Computer Art, Drawing, Graphic Arts, Jewelry, Painting, Photography, Photolithography, Sculpture, Textile Design, Wood Design
Summer School: Enrl 180; Courses vary

GENEVA

HOBART & WILLIAM SMITH COLLEGES, Art Dept, Houghton House Gallery, 1 Kings Lane Geneva, NY 14456; 300 Pulteney St, Geneva, NY 14456. Tel 315-781-3487; Fax 315-781-3689; Internet Home Page Address: www.hws.edu; *Chair* Nicholas Ruth
Estab 1822; FT 6; pvt; D; Scholarships; SC 15, LC 8; D 1,800
Ent Req: HS dipl, ent exam
Degrees: BA & BS 4 yrs
Courses: †Architecture, †Art History, Drawing, Mixed Media, Painting, Photography, Printmaking, Sculpture, †Studio Art

HAMILTON

COLGATE UNIVERSITY, Dept of Art & Art History, 13 Oak Dr, Hamilton, NY 13346-1386. Tel 315-228-7633, 228-1000; Fax 315-824-7787; Internet Home Page Address: www.colgate.edu; *Chmn* John Knecht, MFA; *Prof* Eric Van Schaack PhD, MFA; *Prof* Jim Loveless, MFA; *Assoc Prof* Judith Oliver PhD, MFA; *Assoc Prof* Robert McVaugh, PhD; *Assoc Prof* Lynn Schwarzer, MFA; *Asst Prof* Padma Kaimal, MA; *Asst Prof* Mary Ann Calo, MA; *Asst Prof* Daniella Dooling, MA; *Asst Prof* Carol Kinne, MA
Estab 1819, dept estab 1905; pvt; D; Scholarships; SC 22, LC 23; D 941, maj 50
Ent Req: HS dipl, CEEB or ACT
Degrees: BA 4 yrs
Courses: Art History, Combined Media, Drawing, Mixed Media, Motion Picture Productions, Painting, Photography, Printmaking, Sculpture

HEMPSTEAD

HOFSTRA UNIVERSITY, Department of Fine Arts, 118A Calkins Hall, Hempstead, NY 11549-1000. Tel 516-463-5475; Fax 516-463-6268; Elec Mail fadmh@hofstra.edu; Internet Home Page Address: www.hofstra.edu; *Chmn* Douglas Hilson
Estab 1935, dept estab 1945; Maintain nonprofit art gallery, Rosenberg, Calkins Hall, Hofstra Univ, Hempstead, NY 11550; FT 11; pvt; D & E; Scholarships; SC, LC 20, GC 16; D 1610, maj 100, grad 10
Ent Req: HS dipl
Degrees: BA, MA, BS
Tuition: Undergrad $7,140 per sem
Courses: Appraisal of Art and Antiques, Art History, Drawing, Graphic Arts, Jewelry, Painting, †Photography, †Sculpture
Summer School: Dean, Deanna Chitayat. Courses—Art History, Fine Arts

HERKIMER

HERKIMER COUNTY COMMUNITY COLLEGE, Humanities Social Services, 100 Reservoir Rd, Herkimer, NY 13350-1598. Tel 315-866-0300, Ext 200; Fax 315-866-7253; Internet Home Page Address: www.hccc.ntcnct.com; *Dean* Jennifer Boulanger, MFA; *Asst Dean* Pat Haag, MFA; *Assoc Prof* James Bruce Schwabach, MFA; *Assoc Prof* Mariann Wrinn, MFA; *Asst Prof* Gale Farley
Estab 1966; pub; D & E; SC 8, LC 4; D 329 (total), maj 16
Ent Req: HS dipl, SAT or ACT; open
Degrees: AA, AS & AAS 2 yrs
Courses: 2-D Design, †3-D Design, Art Appreciation, Art History, †Ceramics, Drawing, Painting, Photography, †Sculpture, Theatre Arts, Video
Adult Hobby Classes: Enrl 40 cr, 100 non-credit; Courses—Art Appreciation, Calligraphy, Pastels, Portraits, Photography

Children's Classes: Enrl 40; tuition varies. Courses—Cartooning Workshop, Introduction to Drawing
Summer School: Dir, John Ribnikac. Enrl 40. Courses—Same as regular session

HOUGHTON

HOUGHTON COLLEGE, Art Dept, One Willard Ave, Houghton, NY 14744. Tel 716-567-2211; *Head Art Dept* Gary Baxter
Estab 1883; den; D & E; Scholarships; SC 8, LC 6
Degrees: AA & AS 2 yrs, BA & BS 4 yrs
Courses: Ceramics, Drawing, Graphic Design, Painting, Photography, Printmaking, Sculpture

ITHACA

CORNELL UNIVERSITY, Dept of Art, College of Architecture, Art & Planning, 224 Tjaden Hall Ithaca, NY 14850-2432. Tel 607-255-3558; Fax 607-255-3462; Elec Mail artinfo@cornell.edu; Internet Home Page Address: www.aap.cornell.edu; *Assoc Prof* Michael Ashkin; *Assoc Prof* Roberto Bertoia; *Chair & Assoc Prof* Iftikhar Dadi; *Prof* Jean Locey; *Assoc Prof* Elisabeth Meyer; *Asst Prof* Carl Ostendarp; *Assoc Prof* Gregory Page; *Assoc Prof* Maria Park; *Assoc Dean, Assoc Prof* Barry Perlus; *Assoc Prof* Jolene Rickard; *Assoc Prof* Stan Taft
Estab 1868, dept estab 1921; Maintain nonprofit art gallery; Olive Tjaden Gallery, Rm 101; Fine Arts Library, Cornell Univ; art supplies available on-campus; Pvt; D; Scholarships; SC 25, LC 1, GC 4; maj 130, grad 12
Ent Req: HS dipl, HS transcript, SAT
Degrees: BFA, MFA
Tuition: $29,500 grad
Courses: Drawing, Painting, Photography, Printmaking, Sculpture, †Studio Art
Summer School: Dir, Charles Jermy; Tuition $1,210 per cr for term of 3 & 6 wks beginning May 28
—**Dept of the History of Art & Visual Studies,** GM08 Goldwin Smith Hall, Ithaca, NY 14853-0001. Tel 607-255-9861; Fax 607-255-0566; Elec Mail art_history-mailbox@cornell.edu; Internet Home Page Address: www.arts.cornell.edu/histart/index.htm; *Prof* Andrew Ramage PhD; *Assoc Prof* Judith E Bernstock PhD; *Assoc Prof* Peter I Kuniholm PhD; *Assoc Prof* Claudia Lazzaro PhD; *Assoc Prof* Laura L Meixner PhD
Estab 1939; pvt; D; Scholarships; LC 64, GC 12; D 1300, maj 40, grad 18, others 5
Ent Req: HS dipl, SAT, grad admis requires GRE
Degrees: BA, PhD
Tuition: $25,970 yr
Courses: 1940-1990 Art, Art History, Classical Art & Architecture, Gothic Art & Architecture
Summer School: Dean, Glenn Altschuler. Tuition $410 per cr hr. Courses—Introductory

ITHACA COLLEGE, Fine Art Dept, 101 Ceracche Ctr, Ithaca, NY 14850-7277. Tel 607-274-3330; Fax 607-274-1358; Internet Home Page Address: www.ithaca.edu; *Prof* Raymond Ghirardo, MFA; *Chmn* Susan Weisend, MFA; *Lectr* Pat Hunsinger; *Lectr* Bill Hastings; *Lectr* Linda Price; *Asst Prof* Jeremy Long; *Asst Prof* Carla Stetson
Estab 1892, dept estab 1968; Maintain nonprofit art gallery; Handwerker Gallery, 1170 Gannett Center, Ithaca, NY 14850; Pvt; D & E; Scholarships; SC 27; non-maj 300, maj 50
Ent Req: HS dipl, SAT scores
Degrees: BA and BFA 4 yrs & Teacher Education
Courses: 2-D Design, †Art Education, Art History, Computer Art, Drawing, Figure Drawing, Painting, Printmaking, Sculpture, Silkscreen
Summer School: Chmn, Susan Weisand. Enrl 10-20. Courses—Intro to Drawing, Computer Art, Intro to Ceramics

JAMAICA

SAINT JOHN'S UNIVERSITY, Dept of Fine Arts, 8000 Utopia Pkwy, Jamaica, NY 11439. Tel 718-990-6161; Fax 718-990-1907; *Gallery Dir* Mohammad Mohsin; *Chmn* Paul Fabozzi
Pvt; D; Scholarships; SC 24, LC 9; D 1300, maj 100
Ent Req: HS dipl, ent exam, portfolio review
Degrees: BFA & BS 4 yrs
Courses: Advertising Design, Aesthetics, Art Appreciation, Art Education, Art History, Ceramics, Collage, Commercial Art, Conceptual Art, Design, Drawing, Film, †Fine Arts, Graphic Arts, †Graphic Design, History of Art & Architecture, †Illustration, Industrial Design, Intermedia, Jewelry, Lettering, Mixed Media, †Painting, †Photography, †Printmaking, Saturday Scholarship Program, †Sculpture, Video
Adult Hobby Classes: Courses—Drawing, Figure, Painting, Sculpture
Summer School: Courses—Drawing, Painting

YORK COLLEGE OF THE CITY UNIVERSITY OF NEW YORK, Fine & Performing Arts, 94-20 Guy Brewer Blvd, Jamaica, NY 11451. Tel 718-262-2400; Fax 718-262-2998; *Prof* Jane Schuler PhD; *Coordr Fine Arts* Phillips Simkin; *Assoc Prof* Ernest Garthwaite, MA; *Assoc Prof* Arthur Anderson, MFA
Estab 1968; pub; D & E; 4303
Ent Req: HS dipl
Degrees: BA 4 yrs
Courses: Art Education, Art History, Computer Graphics, Drawing, Graphic Arts, Painting, Photography, Printmaking, Sculpture
Summer School: Dean, Wallace Schoenberg. Enrl $20 per course; tuition $47 per cr for term of 6 wks beginning late June. Courses—Art History, Drawing, Painting

JAMESTOWN

JAMESTOWN COMMUNITY COLLEGE, Arts, Humanities & Health Sciences Division, 525 Falconer St, Jamestown, NY 14701-1999. Tel 716-665-5220, Ext 394; Fax 716-665-9110; Elec Mail billdisbro@mail.sunyjcc.edu; Internet Home Page Address: www.sunyjcc.edu; *Art Coordr* Bill Disbro

Estab 1950, dept estab 1970; Maintain nonprofit art gallery; Week Gallery; FT 1, PT 7; pub; D & E; Scholarships; SC 11, LC 1; D 310, E 254
Ent Req: open
Degrees: AA 60 cr hrs; AS Fine Arts; Studio Art
Courses: Ceramics, Computer Graphics, Design, Drawing, Introduction to Visual Art, Painting, Photography, Survey of Visual Arts, Video
Summer School: Dir, Roslin Newton. Enrl 25-50; Courses—Ceramics, Drawing, Painting, Photography

LOCH SHELDRAKE

SULLIVAN COUNTY COMMUNITY COLLEGE, Division of Commercial Art & Photography, 112 College Rd, Loch Sheldrake, NY 12759-5721; PO Box 4002, Loch Sheldrake, NY 12759-4002. Tel 845-434-5750; Internet Home Page Address: www.sullivan.suny.edu; *Chmn Art Dept* Mike Fisher; *Prof* L Jack Agnew, MEd; *Prof* Thomas Ambrosino, BPS; *Instructional Asst* Charles Arice; *Assoc Prof* Mary Clare
Estab 1962, dept estab 1965; pub; D & E; SC 24; D 200, maj 180
Ent Req: HS dipl or equivalent
Degrees: AA, AS & AAS 2 yrs
Courses: Advertising Design, Commercial Art, Computer Graphics, Design, Drawing, Graphic Arts, Graphic Design, Photography
Summer School: Assoc Dean of Faculty for Community Services, Allan Dampman

LONG ISLAND CITY

SCULPTURE CENTER SCHOOL, STUDIOS & GALLERY, 44-19 Purves St, Long Island City, NY 11101. Tel 718-361-1750; Internet Home Page Address: www.sculpture-center.org; *Contact* John Emison
Estab 1933; Scholarships

LOUDONVILLE

SIENA COLLEGE, Dept of Creative Arts, 515 Loudon Rd, Loudonville, NY 12211-1459. Tel 578-783-2325 (Liberal Arts Office); Fax 518-783-4293; Internet Home Page Address: www.siena.edu; *Chair & Prof Art History* Patricia Trutty-Coohill; *Asst Prof Photog & Video* Amanda Green, MFA; *Asst Prof Journalism* Rebecca Taylor, JD; *Prof Theatre* Mahmood Karimi-Hakak, DSE; *Asst Prof Theatre Design* Denise Massman, MFA; *Asst Prof Painting & Drawing* Scott Foster, MFA; *Assoc Prof Music* Paul Koyne, PhD; *Asst Prof Music* Timothy Reno, PhD
Estab 1937; Maintain nonprofit art gallery; den; D & E; Scholarships; SC & LC; Enrl 3000, maj 60
Ent Req: HS dipl
Degrees: BA
Tuition: $26,185 per year without room & board
Courses: Aesthetics, †Chorus, †Costume Design & Construction, †Design, Drawing, †Film, Graphic Design, History of Art & Architecture, Mixed Media, †Museum Staff Training, Music, Painting, †Photography, Printmaking, †Stage Design, Theatre Arts, †Video, †Voice
Summer School: Enrl 35; tuition $315 per cr hr for 7 wk term. Courses—Intro to Visual Arts

MIDDLETOWN

ORANGE COUNTY COMMUNITY COLLEGE, Arts & Communication, 115 South St, Middletown, NY 10940-6404. Tel 845-341-4787; Fax 845-341-4775; Internet Home Page Address: www.sunyorange.edu; *Chair* Mark Strunsky; *Asst Prof Arts & Communs* Joseph Litow; *Asst Prof Arts & Communs* Susan Slater-Tanner
Estab 1950, dept estab 1950; Maintain a nonprofit art gallery, Harriman Student Gallery, 115 South St, Middletown, NY 10940; Pub; D & E; Scholarships; SC 16, LC 8; D 135, maj 60
Ent Req: HS dipl
Degrees: AA 2 yrs, AAS(Visual Comm Graphics)
Tuition: $1,550 per semester; no campus res
Courses: Art History, Color, Computer Graphic Design, Design, Drawing, Painting, Photography, Sculpture

NEW PALTZ

STATE UNIVERSITY OF NEW YORK AT NEW PALTZ, Art Education Program, 1 Hawk Dr, Smiley Art Bldg 108-A New Paltz, NY 12561-2447. Tel 845-257-3850; Internet Home Page Address: www.newpaltz.edu/arted; *Chmn Art Studio & Art Educ* Myra Mimlitsch-Gray; *Prog Dir Art Educ* Margaret Johnson; *Assoc Chair* David Cavallaro
Pub; D & E; SC, LC, GC; maj 600, grad 100
Degrees: BA, MS, MA
Tuition: res—$2,175 per person; nonres—$5,305 per person
Courses: Art Education, Ceramics, Graphic Design, Metal, Painting, Photography, Printmaking, Sculpture

NEW ROCHELLE

THE COLLEGE OF NEW ROCHELLE, School of Arts & Sciences Art Dept, 29 Castle Pl, New Rochelle, NY 10805-2330. Tel 914-654-5274; Elec Mail estern@cnr.edu; Internet Home Page Address: www.cnr.edu/artdept; *Chair* Emily Stern, MFA; *Prof* William C Maxwell, PhD; *Assoc Prof* Cristina deGennaro, MFA; *Assoc Prof* Margie Neuhaus, MFA; *Prof* Susan Canning, PhD

Estab 1904, dept estab 1929; Maintain nonprofit gallery, Castle Gallery, 29 Castle Pl, New Rochelle, NY 10805; Pvt, women only; D&E; Scholarships; SC 52, LC 14, GC 21; D 150, non-maj 45, maj 105, grad 98
Ent Req: HS dipl, SAT or ACT scores, college preparatory program in high school
Degrees: BA, BFA and BS 4 yrs
Tuition: $9950 per yr; campus res— room and board $4320 per yr
Courses: †Art Education, †Art History, †Art Therapy, Ceramics, Collage, Computer Graphics, Design, Drawing, Fiber Arts, Film, Graphic Design, Jewelry, Metalwork, Mixed Media, Painting, Photography, Printmaking, Sculpture, Teacher Training
Summer School: Painting for non-maj; pre-college prog, other courses available for college students

NEW YORK

AESTHETIC REALISM FOUNDATION, 141 Greene St, New York, NY 10012-3201. Tel 212-777-4490; Fax 212-777-4426; Internet Home Page Address: www.aestheticrealism.org; *Chmn Educ* Ellen Reiss; *Exec Dir* Margot Carpenter
Estab 1973, as a not for profit educational foundation to teach Aesthetic Realism, the philosophy founded in 1941 by American poet & critic Eli Siegel (1902-1978), based on his historic principle: "The world, art, and self explain each other: each is the aesthetic oneness of opposites."; Maintains nonprofit art gallery, Terrain Gallery, same location
Publications: The Right of Aesthetic Realism to Be Known, weekly periodical
Courses: Anthropology, Art Criticism, Art History, Drawing, Education, †Film, Marriage, Music, Poetry, Singing, Theatre Arts
Children's Classes: Learning to Like the World

AMERICAN ACADEMY IN ROME, 7 E 60th St, New York, NY 10022-1030. Tel 212-751-7200; Fax 212-751-7220; Internet Home Page Address: www.aarome.org; *Pres* Adele Chatfield Taylor; *Exec VPres* Wayne Linker; *Chmn* Michael I Sovern
Estab 1894, chartered by Congress 1905; consolidated with School of Classical Studies 1913; Dept of Musical Composition estab 1921; Fellowships for independent study in Rome at the Acad in the fields of architecture, landscape architecture, design, painting, sculpture, musical composition, classical and post-classical studies, history of art, Italian studies are open to citizens of the United States. Painters and sculptors receive a supplies allowance of $600 per year. Approx 30 fellowships are awarded each year Applicants' material is judged by independent juries of professionals in the field of award. Stipend and travel allowances total $6200, plus room, studio or study, and partial board. Application forms and information sheets are available from the New York office. Applications and supporting material and $25 application fee must be received at the Academy's New York office by November 15 of each year; Mem: Annual meeting Oct; Board in Feb; Scholarships
Summer School: 28 fellowships

AMERICAN UNIVERSITY, Dept of Art, 520 W 43rd St, Apt 21E New York, NY 10036-4352. Tel 202-885-1670; Fax 202-885-1132; Elec Mail dkimes@american.edu; *Chmn Dept & Prof* Don Kimes, MFA; *Prof* C Stanley Lewis, MFA; *Prof* Mary Garrard; *Prof* Norma Broude, PhD; *Prof* M Oxman, MFA; *Assoc Prof* Ron Haynie Oxman, MFA; *Assoc Prof* Deborah Kahn, MFA; *Assoc Prof* Michael Graham, MFA; *Asst Prof* Helen Langa, PhD; *Asst Prof* Luis Silva, MFA; *Prof* Barbara Rose, PhD; *Assoc Prof* Chemi Montes, MFA; *Instr* Glenn Goldberg, MFA; *Instr* Steven Cushner, MFA; *Instr* Susan Yanero, MFA; *Instr* Sharo Fischel, MFA; *Instr* Carol Goldberg, MFA; *Instr* Jo Weiss Le, MFA; *Instr* Jeneen Piccuirro, MFA; *Instr* Guy Zoller, MFA; *Instr* Rachel Simons, PhD; *Instr* Laurie Swindull, MFA
Estab 1893, dept estab 1945; Maintain nonprofit art gallery; Watkins Gallery, Dept of Art, 4400 Massachusetts Ave NW, Washington, DC; pvt; D&E; Scholarships, Fellowships; SC 26, LC 15, GC 19 and 6 Art History courses in Italy Program; D & E 1600, maj 191, grad 70
Ent Req: HS dipl
Degrees: BA, BFA(Studio Art), BA(Design), BA(Art History) 4 yrs, MA(Art History) 18 months, MFA(Painting, Sculpture, Printmaking) 2 yrs
Courses: Aesthetics, Art Appreciation, †Art History, Ceramics, Collage, Computer Graphics, Constructions, †Drawing, †Graphic Design, History of Art & Architecture, Lettering, Mixed Media, Multimedia, †Painting, †Printmaking, †Sculpture
Summer School: Dept Adminr, Glenna Haynie. Design, Studio & Art History

ART STUDENTS LEAGUE OF NEW YORK, 215 W 57th St, New York, NY 10019-2193. Tel 212-247-4510; Fax 212-541-7024; Internet Home Page Address: www.theartstudentleague.org;
Estab 1875; FT 65; pvt; Scholarships; LC; D 1200, E 800, Sat 500 (adults and children)
Ent Req: none
Courses: Drawing, Graphic Arts, Illustration, Painting, †Printmaking, Sculpture
Children's Classes: Classes on Saturday
Summer School: Enrl 800, beginning June

THE ART STUDIO NEW YORK, 145 W 96th St, New York, NY 10025-6403. Tel 212-932-8484; Elec Mail info@theartstudiony.com; Internet Home Page Address: www.rebeccarts.com; *Founder, Dir & Instr* Rebecca Schweiger
Average Annual Attendance:
Courses: †Drawing, †Mixed Media, †Painting

BERNARD M BARUCH COLLEGE OF THE CITY UNIVERSITY OF NEW YORK, Art Dept, 1 Bernard Baruch Way, 55 Lexington Ave at 24th St New York, NY 10010-5585. Tel 212-802-2287, 802-6590; Fax 212-802-6604; Internet Home Page Address: www.petersons.com; *Chmn* Virginia Smith; *Chair* Philip Lambert
Estab 1968; pub; D & E; SC 26, LC 16; D 2000, E 500
Ent Req: HS dipl
Degrees: BA, BBA & BSEd 4 yrs, MBA 5 yrs, PhD

Courses: Advertising Design, Art History, Ceramics, Computer Graphics, Drawing, History of Art & Architecture, Illustration, Painting, Photography, Sculpture
Summer School: Courses - Art History Survey, Ceramics, Crafts, Drawing, Painting, Photography

THE CHILDREN'S AID SOCIETY, Visual Arts Program of the Philip Coltoff Center at Green Arts and After School Program, 105 E 22nd St, New York, NY 10010-5413. Tel 212-254-3074; Fax 212-420-9153; Elec Mail antoniaa@childrensaidsociety.org; Internet Home Page Address: www.childrensaidsociety.org; *Dir* Steve Wobido; *Dir Arts Prog* Antonia Abram; *Asst Dir* Brendan Leach
Estab 1854, dept estab 1968; D & E; Scholarships; SC 18; D 200, E 175
Courses: †Architecture, Ceramics, Collage, Comic Book Art, Drawing, Enameling, Handicrafts, Jewelry, †Mixed Media, Painting, Photography, Pottery, †Printmaking, Puppet Making, Woodworking
Adult Hobby Classes: Enrl 95; Courses—Cabinetmaking, Ceramics, Drawing, Enameling, Painting, Photography, Pottery
Children's Classes: Enrl 325; Courses—Dance, Drawing, Enameling, Mixed Media, Painting, Photography, Puppet Making, Woodwork, Theatre & Mime
Summer School: Dir Antonia Abram

CITY COLLEGE OF NEW YORK, Art Dept, 160 Convent Ave, New York, NY 10031-9101. Tel 212-650-7420; Fax 212-650-7438; Elec Mail art@ccny.cuny.edu; Internet Home Page Address: www.ccny.cuny.edu; *Dir Mus Studies* Prof Harriet Senie, PhD; *Assoc Prof* Ellen Handy, PhD; *Dir* Annette Weintraub, BFA; *Assoc Prof* Colin Chase; *Prof* Sylvia Netzer; *Prof* Ina Saltz; *Asst Prof* Leo Fuentes; *Asst Prof* Molly Aitken; *Assoc Prof* Becca Albee; *Lectr* Patterson Beckwith; *Prog Dir Art Ed Asst Prof* Marit Dewhurst; *Dir, Lectr* Megan Foster, MFA; *Assoc Prof* Ethan Ham; *Lectr* Craig Houser; *Assoc Prof & Chair* Anna Indych-Lopez; *Lectr* Lise Kjaer; *Assoc Prof* Hajoe Moderegger; *Lectr* Tom Thayer; *Asst Prof* Mark Addison Smith; *Asst Prof* Abby Kornfeld; *Asst Prof* Joe Moore
Estab 1847; pub; D & E & Sat; Scholarships; SC 125, LC 25, GC 35; D 1600, E 133, maj 400, grad 60
Ent Req: HS dipl, entrance placement exams
Degrees: BA, MA, BFA, MFA
Tuition: Res—undergrad $2415 per sem, $205 per cr hr; nonres—undergrad $435 per cr hr
Courses: Art Education, Art History, Ceramics, Design, Drawing, Graphic Arts, Graphic Design, Intermedia, Mixed Media, Museum Staff Training, Painting, Photography, Printmaking, Sculpture
Adult Hobby Classes: Courses—Advertising & Design, Art History, Ceramics, Drawing, Graphics, Museum Studies, Painting, Photography, Sculpture

CITY UNIVERSITY OF NEW YORK, PhD Program in Art History, 365 5th Ave, The Graduate Center New York, NY 10016-4309. Tel 212-817-8035; Fax 212-817-1502; Elec Mail arthistory@gc.cuny.edu; Internet Home Page Address: web.gc.cuny.edu/dept/arthi; Internet Home Page Address: www.web.gc.cuny.edu/dept/arthi; *Prof Emeritus* Jack Flam; *Prof* Laurie Schneider Adams; *Prof Emerita* Rosemarie Haag Bletter; *Prof* Anna Chave; *Prof Emertus* George Corbin; *Prof* Mona Hadler; *Prof Emerita* Eloise Quinones-Keber; *Prof Emerita* Diane Kelder; *Prof* Gail Levin; *Prof Emerita* Patricia Mainardi; *Prof Emerita* Sally Webster; *Prof* Romy Golan; *Prof* Barbara Lane; *Prof Emeritus* Stuart Liebman; *Prof* Katherine Manthorne; *Prof* Kevin Murphy; *Prof* James M Saslow; *Prof* Harriet Senie; *Prof* Judy Sund; *Prof Emerita* Lisa Vergara; *Prof* Claire Bishop; *Prof* David Joselit; *Prof* Jennifer Ball; *Prof* Amanda Wunder; *Prof* M Antonella Pelizzari
Estab 1961, prog estab 1971; Maintain nonprofit art gallery (James Gallery)on campus; art libr within Mina Rees Libr; pub; D & E; Scholarships, Fellowships; LC 10, GC 6; D 200
Ent Req: BA or MA in Art History
Degrees: PhD
Tuition: Res—$2435 per sem, $275 per cr hr; nonres—$3800 per sem, $475 per cr hr
Courses: African, Art History, Modern and Contemporary Art & Architecture, Native American & Pre-Columbian Art & Architecture, Oceanic, Renaissance & Baroque Art & Architecture

COLUMBIA UNIVERSITY, Graduate School of Architecture, Planning & Preservation, 1172 Amsterdam Ave, 400 Avery Hall New York, NY 10027-7055. Tel 212-854-3414; Fax 212-864-0410; Internet Home Page Address: www.arch.columbia.edu; *Dean Architectural Planning* Bernard Tschumi; *Chmn Div Urban Design* Stan Allen; *Prof* Sig Guava
Estab 1881; FT 31, PT 32; pvt; Scholarships, Fellowships; 400
Ent Req: Bachelor's degree in appropriate area of study
Degrees: MPlanning & MPreservation 2 yr, MArchit 3 yr
Tuition: $25,800
Courses: Architecture, Architecture & Urban Design, Historic Preservation, Urban Planning
—**Dept of Art History & Archaeology,** 1190 Amsterdam Ave, 826 Schermerhorn Hall, Mail Code 5517 New York, NY 10027-7054. Tel 212-854-4505; Fax 212-854-7329; Internet Home Page Address: www.columbia.edu/cu/arthistory; Telex 749-0397; *Dir Grad Studies* Barry Bergboll; *Chmn* Joseph Connors
Pvt
Degrees: MA, MPhil, PhD
Tuition: $27,000 per yr
Courses: Aesthetics, Architecture, Art Appreciation, Art History, Classical Art & Archeology, Far Eastern Art & Archeology, History & Theory of Art History, History of Architecture, History of Art & Archeology, History of Western Art, Near Eastern Art & Archeology, Primitive & Pre-Columbian Art & Archeology
—**Columbia College,** 1130 Amsterdam Ave, 208 Hamilton Hall, Mail Code 2805 New York, NY 10027-7050. Tel 212-854-2522; Internet Home Page Address: www.college.columbia.edu/about; *Dean* Austin Quigley
Pvt, M; Scholarships, Fellowships
Degrees: BA & BS 4 yr
Tuition: $27,000 per yr

Courses: Art and Archaeology of South Eastern Asia, Asian Art and Archaeology, Classical Art and Archaeology, History of Western Art, Near Eastern Art and Archaeology, Primitive and Pre-Columbian Art and Archaeology
—**School of the Arts, Division of Visual Arts,** 2960 Broadway, 305 Dodge Hall, MC 1803 New York, NY 10027. Tel 212-854-2829, 854-4065; Fax 212-854-7708; Internet Home Page Address: www.columbia.edu/cu/arts/; *Prog Coordr* Liz Perlman; *Chmn* Ronald Jones
Estab 1754, div estab 1945; pvt; D & E; Scholarships
Ent Req: special students required to have studied at the college level in an institution of higher learning, non-degreed students are permitted to register for one or more courses in the division
Degrees: BA
Tuition: Undergrad $18,624 per yr, grad $19,000 per yr
Courses: Drawing, Graphic Arts, Mixed Media, Painting, Photography, Printmaking, Sculpture, Video
Summer School: Prof, Tomas Vu-Daniel. Tuition $2600 for 2-6 wk sessions, Courses—Digital Art, Drawing, Painting, Photography, Printmaking
—**Barnard College,** 3009 Broadway, New York, NY 10027-6909. Tel 212-854-2118; *Chmn* Benjamin Buchloh
Estab 1923; pvt, W; Scholarships; maj 29, total 1930
Degrees: AB 4 yrs
Tuition: $16,228 per yr; campus res available
Courses: Art History, Drawing, Painting
—**Teachers Col Program in Art & Art Educ,** 525 W 120th St, Teachers College New York, NY 10027-6610. Tel 212-678-3000; Fax 212-678-4048; Internet Home Page Address: www.columbia.edu; *Dir* Judith Burton; *Interim Dean* Edmund Gordon
Estab 1888; pvt; Scholarships, Fellowships, Assistantships; GC; 225
Ent Req: Bachelor's degree & Portfolio review
Degrees: EDD, EDDCT, EDM, MA
Tuition: $705 per cr hr
Courses: Art Appreciation, Art Education, Artistic-Aesthetic Development, Ceramics, Crafts, Curriculum Design, Design, Drawing, Historical Foundations, Museum Studies, Painting, Painting Crafts, Philosophy of Art, Photography, Printmaking, Sculpture, Teacher Education
Adult Hobby Classes: Enrl 35; tuition $150 per 10 wk session

COOPER UNION, School of Art, 30 Cooper Sq, New York, NY 10003-7120. Tel 212-353-4200; Elec Mail artschool@cooper.edu; Internet Home Page Address: cooper.edu; *Dean* Saskia Bos; *Assoc Dean* Steven Lam
Estab 1859; Nonprofit gallery - The Arthur J. Houghton Gallery, 7 E 7th St, New York, NY 10003; FT 10, PT 60; pvt; D & E; Scholarships
Ent Req: HS dipl, ent exam
Degrees: BFA 4 yr
Tuition: Free
Courses: †Calligraphy, †Conceptual Art, †Design, †Drawing, †Film, †Graphic Design, †Painting, †Photography, †Printmaking, †Sculpture, †Video
Adult Hobby Classes: Extended Studies Prog
Children's Classes: Enrl 200. Courses—Pre College Art & Architecture for HS students
Summer School: Dir, Stephanie Hightower. Enrl 100. Courses—Same as above

EDUCATION ALLIANCE, Art School & Gallery, 197 E Broadway, New York, NY 10002-5598. Tel 212-780-2300; Fax 212-979-1225; Internet Home Page Address: www.edalliance.org; *Dir* Walt O'Neill
Estab 1889; PT 26; priv; D & E; Scholarships
Ent Req: None
Degrees: Cert
Tuition: Varies per course
Courses: Ceramics, Drawing, Metal Sculpture, Mixed Media, Painting, Photography, Sculpture
Adult Hobby Classes: Enrl 150; 15 wk term; Courses—Painting, Drawing, Sculpture, Metal Sculpture, Ceramics, Photography, Photo Silk Screen
Children's Classes: Enrl 20; 30 wk term. Courses—Mixed Media
Summer School: Dir Clare J Kagel. Enrl 60; tuition by the course for 10 wk term. Courses—Painting, Sculpture

FASHION INSTITUTE OF TECHNOLOGY, Art & Design Division, 227 W 27th St, New York, NY 10001-5992. Tel 212-217-7999; Internet Home Page Address: www.fitnyc.edu; *Chmn Interior Design* Takashi Kamiya; *Chmn Fashion Design* Colette Wong; *Chmn Fashion Illustrations* Ed Soyka; *Chmn Jewelry Design* Michael Coan; *Chmn Fashion Merchandising Mgmt* Robin Litwinsky; *Chmn Foreign Languages* James Cascaito; *Chmn Fine Arts* Stephanie DeManuelle; *Chmn Commun Design* Suzanne E Anoushian; *Chmn Advertising & Mktg Communs* Richard Balestrino; *Chmn Technical Design* Deborah Beard; *Chmn Educational Skills* Charlotte Brown; *Chmn Interior Design* Grazyna W Pilatowicz; *Chmn International Trade* Christine Sala Pomeranz; *Chmn Photog* Brian E Emery; *Chmn Production Mgmt* Mario Federici; *Chmn Science & Math* Rene Mathez; *Chmn Science & Math* Geoffrey Rogers; *Chmn Social Science* Yasemin Celik Levine; *Chmn Textile Develop & Mktg* Jeffrey Silberman; *Chmn Textile/Surface Design* Karen A Gentile
Estab 1951; pub; D & E; Scholarships; SC 317, LC 26; D 4011, E 7004
Ent Req: HS dipl, ent exam
Degrees: AAS 2 yr, BFA 4 yr
Tuition: Res—undergrad $1200 per sem; nonres—undergrad $2825 per sem; campus res—room & board $4412 per yr
Courses: Accessories Design, †Advertising Design, Art History, †Display, History of Art & Architecture, †Illustration, †Interior Design, †Jewelry, Painting, †Photography, Printmaking, †Restoration & Conservation, Sculpture, Silversmithing, †Textile Design, Toy Design, Weaving
Adult Hobby Classes: Part-time Studies
Summer School: VPres Student Affairs, Stayton Wood. Enrl 4589; tuition $78-$200 per course for term of 3, 5 & 7 wks beginning June. Courses—Same as above

FORDHAM UNIVERSITY, Art Dept, 113 W 60th St, Arts Division, Lincoln Ctr New York, NY 10023-7414. Tel 212-636-6000; Internet Home Page Address: www.fordham.edu; *Div Chmn* William Conlon
Estab 1968; FT 7; pvt; D & E; Scholarships; SC 18, LC 25; D 900, E 1750, maj 56
Ent Req: HS dipl
Degrees: BA 4 yrs
Courses: Aesthetics, Costume Design & Construction, Drawing, Graphic Arts, History of Art & Architecture, Painting, Photography, Sculpture, Stage Design, Teacher Training, Theatre Arts
Summer School: Dir, Dr Levak. Four terms per summer for 5 wks each
—**Center Gallery,** 70 Lincoln Center Plz, Lincoln Center Campus New York, NY 10023-6594. Tel 212-636-6000
Call for hours
Collections: Photographs; paintings; sculpture; drawings
—**Push Pin Gallery,** 113 W 60th St, Visual Arts Complex New York, NY 10023. Tel 212-636-6000
Call for hours
Collections: Works by student artists including paintings, drawings, & sculpture

GREENWICH HOUSE INC, Greenwich House Pottery, 16 Jones St, New York, NY 10014-4132. Tel 212-242-4106; Fax 212-645-5486; Elec Mail pottery@greenwichhouse.org; Internet Home Page Address: www.greenwichhousepottery.org; *Asst Dir* Lynne Lerner; *Dir* Elizabeth Zawada; *Programs Coordr* Gail Heidel; *Studio Mgr* Josephine Burr
Estab 1909, parent organization estab 1902; Maintains nonprofit art gallery, Jane Hartsook Gallery, 16 Jones St, New York, NY 10014; 26; pvt; D & E; Scholarships; SC 32; D 200, E 94
Ent Req: none
Degrees: none
Tuition: No campus res
Courses: Art History, Ceramics, Glazing Chemistry, Sculpture
Adult Hobby Classes: Enrl 200. Courses—Pottery Wheel, Handbuilding, Sculpture
Children's Classes: Enrl 50. Creative technique instruction
Summer School: Dir, Elizabeth Zawada. Enrl 40;

HARRIET FEBLAND ART WORKSHOP, 245 E 63rd St, Ste 1803, New York, NY 10065. Tel 212-759-2215; Elec Mail harrietfebland@aol.com; Internet Home Page Address: www.harrietfebland.com; *Instr* John Close; *Dir & Instruc* Harriet FeBland
Estab 1962; Pvt; D; SC 6, LC 1, GC 2; D 90, others 30
Income: Financed by student tuition
Ent Req: Review of previous work, paintings or sculpture
Tuition: $1,600 per 15 wk class, $700 for 5 wk 1 hr critique session
Courses: Collage, †Constructions, Drawing, †Mixed Media, †Moku-Hanga woodcut block printing, †Painting
Adult Hobby Classes: 70; $2,000 per sem (15 wk each sem). Courses—Advanced Painting, Assemblage, Construction, Drawing
Summer School: Dir, Harriet FeBland. Workshops for 2 to 3 wks are given at various universities in US & England

HENRY STREET SETTLEMENT ARTS FOR LIVING CENTER, 466 Grand St, New York, NY 10002-4804. Tel 212-598-0400; Fax 212-505-8329; *Dir* Barbara Tate
Estab 1895; pvt; D; Scholarships; D 60, E 60
Ent Req: None
Courses: Calligraphy, Ceramics, Drawing, Graphic Arts, Mixed Media, Painting, Printmaking, Sculpture
Adult Hobby Classes: Courses—Crafts, Drawing, Painting, Pottery
Children's Classes: Courses—Arts & Crafts, Cartooning, Drawing, Experimental Art, Painting, Pottery, Printmaking

HUNTER COLLEGE, Art Dept, 695 Park Ave, New York, NY 10021-5085. Tel 212-772-4995; Fax 212-772-4458; Internet Home Page Address: reg.hunter.edu; *Chmn Art Dept* Sanford Wurmfeld; *Head MFA Prog* Joel Carreiro; *Head MA Prog* Ulko Bates
Estab 1890, dept estab 1935; Maintain nonprofit art gallery; Leubsdorf Gallery 68th St & Lexington Ave, NYC, NY 10004; Times Square Gallery, 450 W 41st St, NYC; FT 29; pub; D & E; SC 20-25, LC 10, GC 14-20; D 250 (including evening), maj 250, GS 250
Ent Req: HS dipl
Degrees: BA & BFA 4 yrs
Tuition: Res—$35 per cr hr; nonres—$285 per cr hr
Courses: Art History, Ceramics, Drawing, Painting, Photography, Printmaking, Sculpture

INTERNATIONAL CENTER OF PHOTOGRAPHY, School, 1114 Ave of the Americas at 43rd St, New York, NY 10036. Tel 212-857-0001; Fax 212-857-0091; Elec Mail education@icp.org; Internet Home Page Address: www.icp.org; *Facilities Supv* H Eugene Foster; *Digital Media Labs* Per Gylfe; *Chair Photog & Photojournalism Prog* Alison Morley
Educ Dept open Mon - Fri 9:30 AM - 7 PM, Sat 9 AM - 3 PM, cl Sun, July 4, Thanksgiving, Christmas & New Years Days; Maintains classrooms, Bard Studios, color & black-and-white labs, digital labs, professional shooting studio, research ctr w/ library & archives & Rita K Hillman Education Gallery; Average Annual Attendance: 5,000
Exhibitions: Rita K Hillman Gallery: displays work of students, faculty & staff
Activities: Teen Academy; 1-yr cert progs; 2-yr MFA progs; continuing educ progs; travel progs
Courses: Photography

JOHN JAY COLLEGE OF CRIMINAL JUSTICE, Dept of Art, Music & Philosophy, 899 Tenth Ave, New York, NY 10019-1029. Tel 212-237-8325; Internet Home Page Address: www.jjay.cuny.edu; *Chmn* John Pittman; *Prof* Laurie Schneider PhD; *Assoc Prof* Helen Ramsaran, MFA

Estab 1964, dept estab 1971; FT 4, PT 3; pub; D & E; SC 5, LC 6; D 180, E 180
Ent Req: HS dipl
Degrees: BA and BS 4 yr
Courses: Art History, Drawing, Painting, Sculpture

LOWER EAST SIDE PRINTSHOP INC, 306 W 37th St, 6th Fl, New York, NY 10018. Tel 212-673-5390; Fax 212-979-6493; Elec Mail info@printshop.org; Internet Home Page Address: http://printshop.org; *Exec Dir* Dusica Kirjakovic; *Studio Dir & Master Printer* James Miller; *Progs Dir* Sei Young Kim

MANHATTAN GRAPHICS CENTER, 250 W 40th St, New York, NY 10018. Tel 212-219-8783; Fax 212; Elec Mail manhattangraphicscenter@verizon.net; Internet Home Page Address: www.manhattangraphicscenter.org; *Pres* Ruth Moscovitch; *VPres* Bob Shore; *VPres* Jaz Graf; *Instr* Frederick Mershimer; *Instr* Vijay Kumar; *Instr* Margaret Nussbaum; *Instr* Arnold Brooks; *Instr* Takuji Hamanaka
Estab 1986; Center is a nonprofit printmaking school & workshops where artists may work in a variety of media, including etching, silkscreen, lithography, woodcut, monotype & other printmaking techniques; schols open to new mems demonstrating financial need; on-campus shop where art supplies may be purchased; Pub; D & E; Weekends; Scholarships; SC 25 LC 3
Tuition: $85-395
Courses: †Graphic Arts, Photography, Printmaking
Adult Hobby Classes: Enrl 10; tuition $30 per wk. Courses—Etching, Lithography, Monotype, Silkscreen, Woodcut

MARYMOUNT MANHATTAN COLLEGE, Fine & Performing Arts Div, 221 E 71st St, New York, NY 10021-4597. Tel 212-774-0760; Fax 212-774-0770; Elec Mail mfleischer@mmm.edu; Internet Home Page Address: www.marymount.mm.edu; *Prof Theatre* Barbara Adrian; *Asst Prof Theatre* John Basil; *Asst Prof Art History* Adrienne Bell; *Asst Prof Art Dir Hewitt Gallery* Millie Burns; *Assoc Prof Art & Chair Art Dept* Hallie Cohen; *Assoc Prof Theatre* Kevin Connell; *Assoc Prof Theatre* Robert Dutiel; *Assoc Prof Art* Millie Falcaro; *Assoc Prof Dance* Anthony Ferro; *Prof & Chair Theatre* Mary Fleischer; *Assoc Prof Dance* Jens Giersdorf; *Assoc Prof Art* James Holl; *Assoc Prof & Chair Dance* Katie Langan; *Artist in Res, Dance* Nancy Lushington; *Prof Theatre & Chair Fine & Performing Arts* David Mold; *Asst Prof Theatre* Jeff Morrison; *Prof Theatre* Richard Niles; *Assoc Prof Theatre* Ellen Orenstein; *Prof Theatre* Ray Recht; *Artist in Res, Musical Theatre* Christine Riley; *Prof Theatre* Mark Ringer; *Assoc Prof Art History* Jason Rosenfeld; *Asst Prof Art* Nicholas Schneider; *Assoc Prof Theatre* Patricia Simon; *Asst Prof Theatre* Jill Stevenson; *Assoc Prof Dance* Haila Strauss; *Asst Prof Dance* Tami Stronach; *Assoc Prof Dance & Music* Andrew Warshaw; *Asst Prof Theatre* Kirche Zeile
Estab 1936; Maintains nonprofit Hewitt Gallery of Art; FT 25; pvt; D & E ; Scholarships; SC & LC; maj 700
Ent Req: HS dipl
Degrees: BA & BFA
Tuition: $22,420 per yr
Courses: Aesthetics, Art Appreciation, Art Education, †Art History, Arts Management, Ceramics, Choreography, †Commercial Art, Conceptual Art, Costume Design & Construction, Dance, Design, Display, Drafting, Drawing, Film, Graphic Arts, Graphic Design, History of Art & Architecture, Illustration, Intermedia, Mixed Media, Musical Theatre, Painting, Photography, Printmaking, Sculpture, Stage Design, †Theatre Arts, Video

NATIONAL ACADEMY SCHOOL, (National Academy School of Fine Arts) 5 E 89th St, New York, NY 10128-0602. Tel 212-996-1908; Fax 212-426-1711; Elec Mail mpellegrin@nationalacademy.org; Internet Home Page Address: www.nationalacademy.org; *Dir School* Maurizio Pellegrin
Estab 1826; Maintain nonprofit art gallery 5 E 89th St, New York NY 10028; 45; pvt; D, E & weekends; Scholarships; SC 60, LC 4, GC 1; Enrl 600, Maj, Cont Educ
Activities: Schols offered
Ent Req: Portfolio required for the Studio Intensive
Degrees: cert; dipl
Tuition: varies
Courses: Anatomy, †Art History, Career Development Seminar, Collage, Composition-Portraiture, Drawing, Drawing the Classical Orders, Life Sketch Class, †Mixed Media, Painting, †Photography, Printmaking, Sculpture, †Theory and Criticism, †Video, Workshops
Adult Hobby Classes: Enrl 550; tuition varies per class. Courses—Drawing, Painting, Printmaking, Sculpture & related subjects
Children's Classes: Enrl 25; tuition varies per class. Courses ages 6-16 & older—Drawing & Painting
Summer School: Dir, Maurizio Pellegrin, Enrl 300. Courses—Drawing, Painting, Printmaking, Sculpture, Watercolor, Mixed Media & variety of workshops

NEW SCHOOL UNIVERSITY, Adult Education Division, 66 W 12th St, New York, NY 10011-8871. Tel 212-229-5600; Fax 212-929-2456; *Dean* Elissa Tenny
Estab 1919
Ent Req: HS dipl; 24 or older for BA program
Degrees: BA, MA
Tuition: Varies per course
Courses: Advertising Design, Art Appreciation, Art History, Calligraphy, Cartooning, Ceramics, Design, Drawing, Fashion Arts, Film, Fine Art, Glassblowing, Jewelry, Painting, Photography, Printmaking, Sculpture, Textile Design
Adult Hobby Classes: Enrl 1500; tuition $220 per course. Courses—All fine arts
Children's Classes: Summer Program for Young Adults
Summer School: Dir, Wallis Osterholz. Enrl 500; 6 wk term. Courses—All fine arts

NEW YORK ACADEMY OF ART, Graduate School of Figurative Art, 111 Franklin St, New York, NY 10013-2911. Tel 212-966-0300; Fax 212-966-3217; Elec Mail michael@nyaa.edu; Internet Home Page Address: www.nyaa.edu; *Instr* Randolph Melick; *Chmn* Harvey Citron; *Instr* Edward Schmidt; *Instr* Martha Mayer Erlebacher; *Instr* Vincent Desiderio; *Exec Dir* Stephen Farthing

Estab 1983; Maintain art library; NY Academy of Art Library; pvt; Scholarships
Degrees: MFA 2 yrs, part-time MFA 4 yrs
Courses: Anatomy, Art History, Drawing, †Figurative Art, History of Art & Architecture, Painting, Sculpture
Adult Hobby Classes: Enrl 250; tuition $350-$400 per course for 12 wk term. Courses—Anatomy, Drawing, Painting, Sculpture
Children's Classes: Enrl 60; tuition $0-350 for 8-12 weeks
Summer School: Dir, Jesse Penridge. Enrl 250; tuition $250 per course for 9 wk term. Courses—Anatomy, Drawing, Painting, Sculpture

NEW YORK INSTITUTE OF PHOTOGRAPHY, 211 E 43rd St, New York, NY 10017-4707. Tel 212-867-8260; Fax 212-867-8122; Elec Mail info@nyip.com; Internet Home Page Address: www.nyip.com; *Dir* Chuck DeLaney
Estab 1910; pvt; Flexible; distance learning; Correspondence course in photography approved by New York State and approved for veterans; Enrollment 10,000
Degrees: cert of graduation
Courses: Digital Photography, Photoshop, Still Photography

NEW YORK SCHOOL OF INTERIOR DESIGN, 170 E 70th St, New York, NY 10021-5167. Tel 212-472-1500; Fax 212-472-3800; Elec Mail admission@nysid.edu; Internet Home Page Address: nysid.edu; *Pres* Inge Heckel; *Dean* Scott Ageloff; *Assoc Dean* Ellen Fisher; *Area Coordr* Peter Brandt; *Area Coordr* Judith Gura; *Area Coordr* Veronica Whitlock
Estab 1916; Maintain nonprofit art gallery & library, 161 E 69 St, New York, NY 10021; art supplies may be purchased on campus; over 80; pvt; D & E & Wknds; Scholarships, Fellowships; SC, LC, GC; 750 maj & grad
Ent Req: HS dipl, application & interview
Degrees: AAS, BFA, MFA
Tuition: No campus res
Courses: Art History, Color, Design Materials, Drafting, Drawing, History of Art & Architecture, †Interior Design, Space Planning
Summer School: Dean, Scott Ageloff. Enrl 275

NEW YORK STUDIO SCHOOL OF DRAWING, PAINTING & SCULPTURE, 8 W Eighth St, New York, NY 10011. Tel 212-673-6466; Fax 212-777-0996; Internet Home Page Address: www.nyss.org; *Dean* Graham Nickson; *Dir Prog* Elisa Jensen
Estab 1964; pvt; D; Scholarships; SC 13, LC 2; D100
Ent Req: HS dipl, portfolio of recent work
Degrees: Cert, MFA
Tuition: $4700 per sem; campus res—available
Courses: Drawing, Drawing Marathon, Painting, Sculpture
Adult Hobby Classes: 40; tuition $375 per 13 wks. Courses—Drawing (from the model)
Summer School: Courses—Drawing, Painting, Sculpture

NEW YORK UNIVERSITY, Institute of Fine Arts, 1 E 78th St, New York, NY 10075-0119. Tel 212-992-5800; Elec Mail ifa.program@nyu.edu; Internet Home Page Address: www.nyu.edu/gsas/dept/fineart; *Judy & Michael Steinhardt Dir* Patricia Rubin; *Deputy Dir* David O'Connor; *Deputy Dir* Priscilla P Soucek; *Dir Masters Studies* Robert Lubar; *Sherman Fairchild Chmn* Michele Marincol
Pvt; D & E; Scholarships, Fellowships; grad 400
Tuition: $2988 per course
Courses: Conservation and Technology of Works of Art; Curatorial Staff Training, History of Art & Architecture
—Dept of Art & Art Professions, 34 Stuyvesant St, New York, NY 10003-7599. Tel 212-998-5700; Fax 212-995-4320; Internet Home Page Address: steinhardt.nyu.edu/art/; *Chmn* David Darts; *Prog Dir Art Therapy* Ikuko Acosta; *Prog Dir* Jesse Bransford; *MFA Prog Dir* Sue de Beer; *Prog Dir Costume Studies* Nancy Deihl; *Prog Dir Art Educ & PhD* Dipti Desai; *Prof* Carlo Lamagna; *Prog Dir Visual Arts Admin* Sandra Lang; *MFA Prog Co-Dir & BFA Proj* John Torreano
FT 10, PT 72; Pvt; D & E; Scholarships, Fellowships; undergrad SC 26, LC 13, grad SC 40, LC 25; maj undergrad 115, grad 230
Ent Req: col board ent exam, 85 HS average, portfolio, interview
Degrees: BS, MA, EdD, DA, PhD
Tuition: $3256 per cr
Courses: †Art Education, Art Therapy, Arts Administration, Ceramics, Collage, Computer Art, Costume Studies, Dealership & Collecting Folk Art, †Drawing, †Intermedia, Jewelry, Mixed Media, †Painting, †Photography, †Printmaking, †Sculpture, Studio Art, Teacher Training, Video

PACE UNIVERSITY, Theatre & Fine Arts Dept, 156 Williams St, Pace Plaza New York, NY 10038-5300. Tel 212-346-1352; Fax 212-346-1424; Internet Home Page Address: www.pace.edu/pace; *Chmn* Dr Lee Evans
Estab 1950; pvt; D & E; Scholarships; SC 4, LC 20; D 200, E 150, 700-800 per yr art only
Ent Req: HS dipl, ent exam
Degrees: 4 yr, Art History Major
Courses: Art History, Drawing, Graphic Design, Modern Art, Oriental Art, Studio Art
Adult Hobby Classes: Courses same as above
Summer School: Two summer sessions. Courses—Studio Art

PARSONS THE NEW SCHOOL FOR DESIGN, 66 Fifth Ave, New York, NY 10011-8802. Tel 212-229-8900; Internet Home Page Address: www.newschool.edu/parsons; *Exec Dean* Joel Towers; *Dean School of Art & Design* Sarah Lawrence; *Dean School of Art, Media & Tech* Sven Travis; *Dean School of Constructed Environments* William Morrish; *Dean School of Design Strategies* Miodrag Mitrasinovic; *Dean School of Fashion* Simon Collins
Estab 1896; pvt (see also Otis Art Institute of Parsons School of Design, Los Angeles, California); D & E; Scholarships; SC 200, LC 400, GC 25; D 1800, E 4000, GS 25, other 40
Ent Req: HS dipl, portfolio
Degrees: AAS, BFA, BBA, MA, MFA & MArch
Tuition: $22,000 per yr, $734 per cr

Courses: †Advertising Design, Aesthetics, Architecture, †Art Education, Art History, Calligraphy, †Ceramics, †Commercial Art, Fashion Arts, †Fine Arts, Graphic Design, History of Art & Architecture, †History of Decorative Arts, Illustration, Industrial Design, Interior Design, Jewelry, Lighting Design, Marketing & Fashion Merchandising, Painting, Photography, Product Design, Sculpture, †Textile Design
Adult Hobby Classes: Enrl 4200; tuition $374 per cr for term of 12 wks.
Courses—Advertising, Computer Graphics, Fashion Design, Fine Arts, Floral Design, Illustration, Interior Design, Lighting Design, Marketing & Merchandising, Product Design, Surface Decoration, Theatre Design
Summer School: Dir, Francine Goldenhar. Tuition $4000 for term of 4-6 wks.
Courses—Art, Art History, Design

PRATT INSTITUTE, Pratt Manhattan, 144 W. 14th St, New York, NY 10011. Tel 212-647-7775; Fax 212-461-6026; Internet Home Page Address: www.prattinst.edu; *Dir* David Marcincowski
Estab 1892; Maintain nonprofit art gallery, Pratt Manhattan Gallery, 144 W 14th St, 2nd Fl, New York, NY 10011; pvt; D; Scholarships
Ent Req: HS dipl, portfolio, interview
Degrees: AOS, 2 yrs
Tuition: $810 per cr; campus res available
Courses: Advertising Design, Art History, Commercial Art, Computer Graphics, Design, Graphic Design, Illustration

SCHOOL OF VISUAL ARTS, 209 E 23rd St, New York, NY 10010-3994. Tel 212-592-2000; Fax 212-725-3587; Elec Mail squidley@sva.edu; Internet Home Page Address: www.schoolofvisualarts.edu; *Chmn* Silas H Rhodes; *Pres* David Rhodes
Estab 1947; Maintains a nonprofit art gallery, Visual Arts Gallery, 601 W 26th St, NY, NY; maintains an art/architecture library, Visual Arts Library, 380 2nd Ave, NY, NY; on-campus shop for purchase of art supplies; 800 practicing artists, scholars, critics; pvt; D, E & W; Scholarships; FT 3363, PT 137
Publications: Art & Academe, semi-annual; Portfolio, annual; Words, semi-annual
Ent Req: HS transcript, portfolio review, SAT or ACT test results, interview, 2 letters of recommendation
Degrees: BFA, MFA, MAT (K-12) in Art Educ, MPS Art Therapy
Tuition: $22,080 plus fees per yr
Courses: †Advertising Design, †Animation, †Art Appreciation, †Art Education, Art History, †Cartooning, Ceramics, Commercial Art, †Computer Art, Conceptual Art, Design, Display, Drafting, Drawing, †Film, Graphic Arts, †Graphic Design, History of Art & Architecture, †Illustration, †Interior Design, Intermedia, Mixed Media, †Painting, †Photography, †Printmaking, †Sculpture, Silversmithing, Teacher Training, †Video
Adult Hobby Classes: Enrl 2446; tuition $175 per cr for 12 wks/sem.
Courses—Advertising & Graphic Design, Art Education, Art History, Art Therapy, Computer Art, Craft Arts, Film & Video, Fine Arts, Humanities Sciences, Illustration & Cartooning, Interior Design, Photography
Children's Classes: Enrl 200; tuition $200 course 8wks/sem.
Courses—Cartooning, Design, Drawing, Film, Interior Design, Painting, Photography, Portfolio Preparation, Sculpture
Summer School: Exec Dir, Joseph Cipri. Enrl 2471; tuition $175 per cr 10 wks.
Courses—Same as adult education classes, Archaeology in Greece, Painting in Barcelona

SKOWHEGAN SCHOOL OF PAINTING & SCULPTURE, 200 Park Ave, Ste 1116 New York, NY 10003-1503. Tel 212-529-0505; Fax 212-473-1342; Elec Mail mail@skowheganart.org; Internet Home Page Address: www.skowheganart.org; *Exec Dir Develop & Admin* Kate Haw; *Exec Dir Prog* Sarah Workneh
Estab 1946; Maintain art library; Robert Lehman Library; 10; pub, nine wk summer residency prog for independent work; Fellowships; 65
Ent Req: proficient in English, 21 years of age & slide portfolio or video
Degrees: cr recognized for transfer, no degrees
Tuition: $5200 includes room & board
Courses: No acad work; individual critiques only
Summer School: Enrl 65; 9 wk summer res prog in Maine for independent work. Contact admin office at 200 Park Ave S, No 1116, New York, NY 10003

WOOD TOBE-COBURN SCHOOL, 8 E 40th St, New York, NY 10016-0105. Tel 212-686-9040; Fax 212-686-9171; Internet Home Page Address: www.woodtobecoburn.com; *Pres* Sandi Gruninger
Estab 1937; FT 7, PT 10; pvt; D; Scholarships; 2 yr course, 16 months, for HS grad; 1 yr course, 9-12 months, for those with 15 or more transferable college sem cr, classroom study alternates with periods of work in stores or projects in fashion field; 250
Degrees: AOS(Occupational Studies)
Courses: Display, Fabrics, Fashion Arts, Fashion Design, Fashion Merchandising, Marketing & Management

NIAGARA FALLS

NIAGARA UNIVERSITY, Fine Arts Dept, PO Box 1913, Niagara Falls, NY 14109. Tel 716-285-1212; Internet Home Page Address: www.niagara.edu; *Chmn* Sharon Watkinson
Tuition: $3750 per sem
Courses: Art Appreciation, Art History, Ceramics, Drawing, Painting
Adult Hobby Classes: Enrl 150; tuition $85 per sem. Courses—Ceramics, Painting
Summer School: Dir, L Centofanti. Enrl 25; tuition $185 per sem hr.
Courses—Ceramics

OAKDALE

DOWLING COLLEGE, Dept of Visual Arts, 150 Idle Hour Blvd, Oakdale, NY 11769. Tel 631-244-3000; Fax 631-589-6644; Internet Home Page Address: www.dowling.edu; *Asst Prof Visual Arts* Dr Mary Abell; *Dept Chair, Coordr*

Visual Commus Prog & Asst Prof Visual Arts Elissa Iberti; *Assoc Prof Visual Arts* Kathy Levine; *Instr Visual Arts* Sorina Ivan; *Assoc Prof Visual Arts* Dr Stephen Lamia; *Asst Prof Visual Arts* Pam Brown; *Asst Prof Visual Arts* Betty Ann Derbentli; *Asst Prof Visual Arts* Kathy Reba; *Instr Visual Arts* Herb Reichert; *Asst Prof Visual Arts* Elvis Richardson; *Asst Prof Visual Arts* Tom Williams
maintain a nonprofit art gallery: The Anthony Giordano Gallery, Dir Pam Brown, Dowling College, Idle Hour Blvd, Oakdale, NY 11769; maintain an art/architecture library: Slide Collection-Betty Ann Derbentli, Cur, Dowling College, Fortunoff Hall 323, Idle Hour Blvd, Oakdale, NY 11769; Pvt; D & E; Scholarships; D 1100, E 500
Ent Req: HS dipl
Degrees: BA(Visual Art), BA(Visual Communications), BS and BBA 4 yrs
Courses: 2-D & 3-D Design, Advertising Design, Art Criticism, Art History, Calligraphy, Ceramics, Computer Graphics, Costume Design & Construction, Design, Drawing, Graphic Arts, Graphic Design, History of Art & Architecture, Illustration, Jewelry, Lettering, Life Drawing, Painting, Photography, Printmaking, Sculpture, †Stage Design, Textile Design
Adult Hobby Classes: Software Instruction
Children's Classes: Software Instruction
Summer School: Software Instruction

OLD WESTBURY

NEW YORK INSTITUTE OF TECHNOLOGY, Fine Arts Dept, PO Box 8000, Northern Blvd Old Westbury, NY 11568-8000. Tel 516-686-7516, 686-7542; Fax 516-686-7613; Elec Mail pvoci@nyit.edu; Internet Home Page Address: www.iris.edu/nyit.edu/finearts; *Chmn & Assoc Prof* Peter Voci; *Prof* Faye Fayerman, MFA; *Adjunct Prof* Albert Prohaska, MA; *Assoc Prof* Nieves Micas, MA; *Asst Prof* Lev Poliakov, MA; *Adjunct Asst Prof* Steven Woodburn, MFA; *Adjunct Instr* Martin Clements, MA; *Adjunct Asst Prof* Richard Shen; *Adjunct Asst Prof* Joanne Hartman; *Asst Prof* Jane Grundy; *Adjunct Asst Prof* Charles DiDiego; *Adjunct Instr* Blase Decelestino; *Adjunct Assoc Prof* Antonio DiSpigna; *Adjunct Asst Prof* Donna Voci
Estab 1910, dept estab 1963; pvt; D; Scholarships; SC 11, LC 85; D 427, non-maj 100, maj 327
Ent Req: HS dipl, portfolio review
Degrees: BFA 4 yr
Tuition: No campus res
Courses: †Advertising Design, Aesthetics, †Architecture, Art Appreciation, †Art Education, Art History, Calligraphy, Computer Graphics, Design, Drafting, Drawing, Film, Fine Arts, †Graphic Arts, †Graphic Design, Illustration, †Interior Design, Lettering, Mixed Media, Painting, Photography, Printmaking, Sculpture
Summer School: Courses—Drawing, Interior Design, Painting, Sculpture

STATE UNIVERSITY OF NEW YORK COLLEGE AT OLD WESTBURY, Visual Arts Dept, PO Box 210, Old Westbury, NY 11568-0210. Tel 516-876-3000, 876-3056, 876-3135 (acad affairs); Internet Home Page Address: www.oldwestbury.edu; *Prof* William McGowin; *Chmn* Mac Adains
Estab 1968. Dept estab 1969; pub; D & E; SC 10, LC 10; D & E 277
Ent Req: HS dipl, skills proficiency exam, GED, special exception - inquire through admissions
Degrees: BA & BS(Visual Arts) 4 yr
Courses: Collage, Conceptual Art, History of Art & Architecture, Mixed Media, Painting, Photography, Printmaking, Sculpture, TV Production/Editing, Video

ONEONTA

HARTWICK COLLEGE, Art Dept, 1 Hartwick Dr, Oneonta, NY 13820-4000. Tel 607-431-4825; Fax 607-431-4191; *Chmn* Gloria Escobar, MFA; *Prof* Phil Young, MFA; *Prof* Roberta Griffith, MFA; *Asst Prof* Dr Elizabeth Ayer, MFA; *Asst Prof* Terry Slade, MFA; *Assoc Prof* Dr Fiona Dejardin, MFA; *Assoc Prof* Leesa Rittelmann
Estab 1797; FT 7, PT 8; pvt; D; Scholarships; 1500, non-maj 1433, maj 67
Ent Req: HS dipl, SAT or ACT, recommendation from teacher or counselor & personal essay, $35 fee
Degrees: BA 4 yr
Courses: †Art History, Ceramics, Drawing, Graphic Design, Painting, Photography, Printmaking, Sculpture, †Studio, Teacher Training
Summer School: High sch arts workshop, 3 wks in July

STATE UNIVERSITY OF NEW YORK COLLEGE AT ONEONTA, Dept of Art, 222 Fine Arts Ctr, Oneonta, NY 13820. Tel 607-436-3717; Internet Home Page Address: www.oneonta.edu; *Prof* Sven Anderson; *Instr* Nancy Callahan; *Instr* Yolanda Sharpe; *Instr* Ellen Farber; *Instr* Thomas Sakoulas
Estab 1889; pub; D & E; SC 31, LC 22; D 660, E 35, maj 123, 25-30 at Cooperstown Center
Ent Req: ent req HS dipl, regents scholarship exam, SAT & ACT
Degrees: degrees BA(Studio Art, Art History) other programs include: one leading to MA(Museum History, Folk Art) in conjunction with the New York State Historical Assn at Cooperstown, NY 13326 (Daniel R Porter III, SUNY Dir); a 3-1 program in conjunction with the Fashion Institute of Technology in New York City, with 3 years at Oneonta as a Studio Art major leading to a BS degree and/or 1 year at FIT leading to an AAS, Advertising & Communications, Advertising Design, Apparel Production & Management, Fashion Buying & Merchandising, Fashion Design, Textile Design, and/or Textile Technology
Courses: 2-D Design, 3-D Design, Art History, Ceramics, Computer Art, Drawing, Images of Women in Western Art, Painting, Visual Arts
Adult Hobby Classes: Offered only on a subscription basis at normal tuition rates through the Office of Continuing Education
Summer School: Enrl 40-50. Tuition same as in regular session for two 4 & 5 wk terms beginning June and July. Courses—Studio

ORANGEBURG

DOMINICAN COLLEGE OF BLAUVELT, Art Dept, 470 Western Hwy, Orangeburg, NY 10962-1295. Tel 845-359-7800; Fax 845-359-2313; Internet Home Page Address: www.dc.edu; *Dir Dept Arts & Science* William Hurst

Estab 1952; Independent; D&E
Degrees: BS & BA 4 yr
Courses: Art Education, Art History, Drawing, Painting
Adult Hobby Classes: Enrl 40; tuition $117 per cr. Courses—Art History, Painting
Summer School: Dir, A M DiSiena. Enrl 35: tuition $117 per cr. Courses—History of Art, Watercolor

OSSINING

POLYADAM CONCRETE SYSTEM WORKSHOPS, 11-1 Woods Brooke Circle, Ossining, NY 10562-2070. Tel 914-941-1157; Internet Home Page Address: www.polyadam.com; *Dir* George E Adamy, MBA
Estab 1968; Art supplies available on-campus; FT 1, PT 1; pvt; D & E; SC 13, LC 2, GC 13; D 20, E 30
Courses: Collage, Constructions, Museum Staff Training, †Plastics, Polyadam Concrete Casting & Construction, Restoration & Conservation, Sculpture, Teacher Training
Adult Hobby Classes: Courses offered
Children's Classes: Courses offered
Summer School: Courses offered

PLATTSBURGH

CLINTON COMMUNITY COLLEGE, Art Dept, 136 Clinton Point Dr, Plattsburgh, NY 12901-5690. Tel 518-562-4200; Fax 518-561-8261; Internet Home Page Address: www.clintoncc.suny.edu; *Chmn* Mark Davison
Estab 1966
Ent Req: HS dipl
Degrees: AS & AA 2 yr
Tuition: Res—$94 per cr hr; nonres—$188 per cr hr
Courses: Art Appreciation, Design, Drawing, Painting, Photography, Sculpture, Theatre Arts

STATE UNIVERSITY OF NEW YORK AT PLATTSBURGH, Art Dept, 101 Broad St, Myers Fine Arts Bldg Plattsburgh, NY 12901-2637. Tel 518-564-2000; Fax 518-564-7827; Internet Home Page Address: www.plattsburgh.edu; *Chmn* Rick Mikkelson, MFA
Estab 1789, dept estab 1930; FT 9, PT 4; pub; D & E; Scholarships; SC 30, LC 10; D 700, maj 154
Ent Req: HS dipl, EOP
Degrees: BA & BS 4 yrs
Courses: †Art History, †Ceramics, †Computer Graphics, †Drawing, †Graphic Arts, †Graphic Design, Illustration, Lettering, Mixed Media, †Painting, †Photography, †Printmaking, †Sculpture
Summer School: Dir, J Worthington. Tuition $137 for 5 wks. Courses—Ceramics, Painting, Photography, Sculpture

PLEASANTVILLE

PACE UNIVERSITY, Dyson College of Arts & Sciences, 861 Bedford Rd, Fine Arts Dept Pleasantville, NY 10570-2799. Tel 914-773-3675; Internet Home Page Address: www.pace.edu; *Assoc Dean Arts & Science* Joseph Franko; *Chmn* John Mulgrew, MA; *Prof* Barbara Friedman, MFA; *Prof* Janetta Benton PhD, MFA; *Prof* Linda Gottesfeld, MFA; *Prof* Roger Sayre, MFA; *Prof* Jillian McDonald; *Prof* William Pappenheimer; *Prof* Charlotte Becket
FT 5, PT 12; Pvt; D & E; SC 4, LC 4
Ent Req: HS dipl
Degrees: AA & BS
Tuition: Campus res available
Courses: Advertising Design, Aesthetics, Architecture, Art Appreciation, Art Education, Ceramics, Commercial Art, †Conceptual Art, Design, Drawing, Graphic Arts, Graphic Design, History of Art & Architecture, Illustration, Interior Design, Painting, Photography, Printmaking, Sculpture, Typography
Summer School: Dir, Prof John Mulgrew. Courses—Art History, Ceramics, Drawing, Painting

POTSDAM

STATE UNIVERSITY OF NEW YORK COLLEGE AT POTSDAM, Dept of Fine Arts, 44 Pierrepont Ave, Brainerd Hall 219 Potsdam, NY 13676-2294. Tel 315-267-2251; Fax 315-267-4884; Internet Home Page Address: www.potsdam.edu; *Prof* James Sutter MFA; *Asst Prof* Mary Jo McNamara; *Asst Prof* Marc Leuthold; *Asst Prof* Tracy Watts PhD; *Chmn* Mark Huff
Estab 1948; pub; D & E
Ent Req: HS dipl, SAT, portfolio review recommended
Degrees: BA 4 yrs, special program Empire State studio sem in New York City
Courses: †Art History, †Ceramics, Drawing, †Painting, Photography, †Printmaking, †Sculpture
Adult Hobby Classes: Enrl 15; tuition $30 for 10 weeks. Courses—Pottery
Children's Classes: Enrl 30; tuition $20 for 6 weeks. Courses—General Art Workshop
Summer School: Dir, Joe Hildreth. Enrl 50-60; tuition $180 for 4 cr class of 5 weeks. Courses—Ceramic Survey, Intro to Studio Art

POUGHKEEPSIE

DUTCHESS COMMUNITY COLLEGE, Dept of Visual Arts, 53 Pendell Rd, Poughkeepsie, NY 12601-1595. Tel 845-431-8000; Fax 845-431-8991; *Dir* Eric Somers
Estab 1957; pub; D & E; Scholarships; SC 24, LC 22; D 660, E 340, maj 100

Ent Req: HS dipl
Degrees: AAS (Commercial Art)
Courses: Glass, Leather, Metal, Painting, Photography, Plastic, Weaving, Wood

VASSAR COLLEGE, Art Dept, 124 Raymond Ave, Poughkeepsie, NY 12604-0001. Tel 845-437-5220; Fax 845-437-7707; Elec Mail liaguis@vassar.edu; Internet Home Page Address: www.art.vassar.edu; *Prof* Nicholas Adams; *Prof* Susan D Kuretsky; *Assoc Prof* Peter Charlap; *Prof* Karen Lucic; *Assoc Prof* Brian Lukacher; *Prof* Molly Nesbit; *Prof* Eve D'Ambra; *Prof* Lisa Collins; *Prof* Harry Roseman; *Assoc Prof* Laura Newman; *Asst Prof* Tobias Armborst; *Asst Prof* Andrew Tallon; *Asst Prof* Yvonne Elet; *Asst Prof* Karen Hwang
Estab 1861; Maintain non-profit art gallery, Frances Lehman Loeb Art Ctr; Vassar College Art Library; FT 10, PT 7; pvt; D & E; Scholarships; SC 8, LC; maj 90, others 2400
Activities: Schols offered
Ent Req: HS grad, ent exam
Degrees: BA(Art History) 4 yr
Courses: Architecture, Art History, †Design, Drafting, Drawing, †History of Art & Architecture, Painting, Printmaking, Sculpture

PURCHASE

MANHATTANVILLE COLLEGE, Art Dept, 2900 Purchase St, Purchase, NY 10577-2132. Tel 914-323-5331; Fax 914-323-5311; *Head Dept* Ann Bavar
Estab 1841; pvt; D & E; Scholarships; SC 25, LC 10, GC 7; D 180, non-maj 90, maj 90, grad 10
Ent Req: HS dipl, portfolio, interview
Degrees: BA and BFA 4 yrs, MAT 1 yr, special prog MATA (Masters of Art in Teaching Art)
Courses: Advertising Design, Art Education, Art History, Book Design, Ceramics, Commercial Art, Conceptual Art, Constructions, Design, Drawing, Graphic Arts, Graphic Design, Illustration, Lettering, Metal Sculpture, Painting, Photography, Printmaking, Sculpture, Teacher Training
Summer School: Dir, Don Richards. Two sessions June & July. Courses—Art History, Ceramics, Computer Graphics, Drawing, Painting, Sculpture

PURCHASE COLLEGE, STATE UNIVERSITY OF NEW YORK, School of Art+Design, 735 Anderson Hill Rd, Purchase, NY 10577-1499. Tel 914-251-6750; Fax 914-251-6793; Elec Mail art+design@purchase.edu; Internet Home Page Address: www.purchase.edu/art+design; *Dir* Ravi Rajan; *Prof* Donna Dennis; *Prof* Murray Zimiles; *Prof Emeritus* Antonio Frasconi; *Assoc Prof* Sharon Horvath; *Asst Prof* Kate Gilmore; *Prof* Warren Lehner; *Assoc Prof* Carol Bankerd; *Assoc Prof* Bill Deere; *Assoc Prof* Robin Lynch; *Vis Asst Prof* YuJune Gina Park; *Asst Prof* Jessica Wexler; *Prof Emeritus* Philip Zimmermann; *Asst Prof* Julian Kreimer; *Vis Asst Prof* Christopher Ulivo; *Vis Assoc Prof* Cynthia Lin; *Prof Emeritus* Robert Berlind; *Assoc Prof Emeritus* Judith Bernstein; *Prof Emerita* Nancy Davidson; *Prof Emeritus* Irving Sandler; *Asst Prof* John Lehr; *Assoc Prof* Jo Ann Walters; *Prof Emeritus* John Cohen; *Asst Prof* Stella Ebner; *Assoc Prof* Cassandra Hooper; *Prof Emerita* Margot Lovejoy; *Assoc Prof* Nancy Bowen; *Asst Prof* Christopher Robbins; *Assoc Prof Emeritus* Ken Strickland; *Prof Emeritus* Abe Ajay
Estab 1967; Maintain nonprofit art gallery, Richard & Dolly Maass Gallery & Purchase College library; On-campus shop where art supplies may be purchased; Average Annual Attendance: 50,000; Mem: 900; FT 18, PT 40; pub; D & E; Scholarships, Fellowships; SC, LC, GC; 3600, maj 500
Ent Req: HS Dipl/GED, bachelors for MFA, recommendations & test scores required
Degrees: BFA 4 yr, MFA 2 yr, MA/MFA 3 yr
Tuition: Res—undergrad $5,271 per yr; nonres—$14,320 per yr; res—grad $8,870 per yr; nonres—grad $15,160 per yr
Adult Hobby Classes: Enrl 450-500
Children's Classes: Enrl 100; summer session art program
Summer School: Kelly Jackson; Enrl 400; 6 wk sessions

RIVERDALE

COLLEGE OF MOUNT SAINT VINCENT, Fine Arts Dept, 6301 Riverdale Ave, Riverdale, NY 10471-1093. Tel 718-405-3200; Fax 718-601-6392; *Prof* Richard Barnett, BFA; *Chmn & Prof* Enrico Giordana, BFA
Estab 1911; pvt; D & E; Scholarships; SC 22, LC 10; D 950, E 50
Ent Req: HS dipl and SAT
Degrees: BA, BS and BS(Art Educ) 4 yrs
Courses: Art History, Ceramics, Design, Drawing, Painting, Photography
Summer School: Dir Continuing Education, Dr Marjorie Connelly. Courses—vary each summer

RIVERHEAD

SOUTHAMPTON COLLEGE OF LONG ISLAND UNIVERSITY, Arts & Media Division, 121 Speonk-Riverhead Rd - LIU Bldg, Long Island University at Riverhead Riverhead, NY 11901-3499. Tel 631-287-8010; Fax 631-287-8253; Internet Home Page Address: www2.southampton.liu.edu
Estab 1963

ROCHESTER

MONROE COMMUNITY COLLEGE, Art Dept, 1000 E Henrietta Rd, Rochester, NY 14623-5780. Tel 716-292-2000; Fax 716-427-2749; Internet Home Page Address: www.monroe.cc.edu; *Assoc Prof* Joe Hendrick, MFA; *Prof* Bruce Brown, MFA
Estab 1961; Monthly art exhibitions in school library; 3 FT, PT varies; pub; D & E; SC 16, LC 4
Ent Req: HS dipl

Degrees: Assoc in Arts 2 yrs, Assoc in Science 2 yrs, Assoc in Applied Science 2 yrs
Tuition: $1525 per nine months
Courses: Art History, Ceramics, †Commercial Art, Drafting, Drawing, Graphic Arts, Graphic Design, Handicrafts, Illustration, Jewelry, Lettering, Painting, Printmaking, Sculpture, Textile Design, Theatre Arts, Video, Weaving
Adult Hobby Classes: Tuition $36 per hr. Courses—Batik, Ceramics, Jewelry, Leatherwork, Macrame, Rugmaking, Soft Sculpture, Weaving
Summer School: Dir, George C McDade

NAZARETH COLLEGE OF ROCHESTER, Art Dept, 4245 East Ave, Rochester, NY 14618-3790. Tel 716-389-2525; Fax 716-586-2452; *Head Dept* Ron Netsky; *Assoc Prof* Kathy Calderwood, BFA; *Prof* Karen Trickey, MSEd; *Assoc Prof* Maureen Brilla, MFA; *Prof* Lynn Duggan, MFA; *Assoc Prof* Mitchell Messina, MFA; *Asst Prof* Catherine Kirby, MFA; *Assoc Prof* Ellen Horovitz, PhD; *Dir* Dorothy Bokelman, PhD
Estab 1926, dept estab 1936; pvt; D & E; Scholarships; SC 40, LC 15, GC 6; D 180, E 74, non-maj 50, maj 200, grad 48
Ent Req: HS dipl
Degrees: BA and BS 4 yrs
Courses: †Art Education, †Art History, Art Therapy, Ceramics, Computer Graphics, Drawing, †Graphic Arts, Jewelry, Painting, Photography, Printmaking, Sculpture, Textile Design
Summer School: 6 wks beginning July 5th. Courses—Grad & undergrad

ROBERTS WESLEYAN COLLEGE, Art Dept, 2301 Westside Dr, Rochester, NY 14624-1997. Tel 716-594-9471; Internet Home Page Address: www.roberts.edu; *Dir Art* Loren Baker; *Assoc Prof* Douglas Giebel; *Chmn Fine Arts & Music* Noel Magee
Estab 1866; pvt; D; Scholarships
Ent Req: HS dipl
Degrees: BA(Fine Art), BA(Studio Art), BS(Studio Art), BS(Art Education)
Tuition: $14,366 per yr
Courses: Art Appreciation, Art Education, Art History, Ceramics, Design, Drawing, Graphic Design, Jewelry, Lettering, Painting, Photography, Printmaking, Sculpture, Weaving

ROCHESTER INSTITUTE OF TECHNOLOGY, College of Imaging Arts & Sciences, 55 Lomb Memorial Dr, Rochester, NY 14623. Tel 716-475-2646; Fax 716-475-6447; *Design Chair* Patti LaChance; *Assoc Dean* Frank Cost; *Dean Col* Dr Joan Stone; *Art Chair* Don Arday; *School for American Crafts Chair* Julia Galloway; *Foundations Chair* Joyce Hertzson
Degrees: BFA, MFA
Tuition: Undergrad $9,208 per qtr, grad $10,058 per qtr
Courses: †Art Education, †Ceramics, Computer Graphics, Design, Drawing, †Film, Fine Art Studio, Graphic Arts, †Graphic Design, History of Art & Architecture, Illustration, Industrial Design, Interior Design, Jewelry, Metals, Painting, †Photography, Printmaking, Sculpture, Silversmithing, Teacher Training, Video, Wood
Adult Hobby Classes: Courses offered
Children's Classes: One wk summer workshop for juniors in HS
Summer School: 5 wk sessions, 2 1/2 wk sessions, & special one wk workshops
—**School of Design,** 73 Lomb Memorial Dr, College of Fine & Applied Arts Rochester, NY 14623-5602. Tel 716-475-2668; Fax 716-475-6447; *Chmn Graphic Design* Mary Anne Begland; *Chmn Industrial, Interior & Packaging Design* Toby Thompson; *Chmn Foundation Studies* Joyce Hertzson; *Chmn Crafts* Michael White; *Prof* Kener E Bond Jr, BEd; *Prof* Frederick Lipp, MFA; *Prof* R Roger Remington, MS; *Prof* Joanne Szabla PhD, MS; *Prof* James E Thomas, MFA; *Prof* Lawrence Williams, MFA; *Prof* Philip W Bornarth, MFA; *Prof* Barbara Hodik PhD, MFA; *Prof* James Ver Hague, MFA; *Prof* Robert A Cole, MS; *Prof* Robert Heischman, UCFA; *Prof* Craig McArt, MFA; *Prof* William Keyser, MFA; *Prof* Doug Sigler, MFA; *Prof* Robert Schmitz, MFA; *Prof* Richard Hirsch, MFA; *Prof* Richard Tanner, MS; *Prof* Michael Taylor, MFA; *Prof* Mark Stanitz, MA; *Prof* Len Urso, MFA; *Prof* Max Lenderman, MFA; *Prof* Albert Paley, MFA; *Prof* Wendell Castle, MFA; *Prof* Robert C Morgan PhD, MFA; *Prof* James H Sias, MA; *Prof* Robert Wabnitz, Dipl & Cert; *Assoc Prof* Edward C Miller, MFA; *Assoc Prof* Bruce Sodervick, MFA; *Assoc Prof* Joseph A Watson, MFA; *Assoc Prof* Robert M Kahute, MFA; *Assoc Prof* Steve Loar, MFA; *Asst Prof* Heinz Klinkon, BFA; *Asst Prof* Doug Cleminshaw, MFA; *Asst Prof* Elizabeth Fomin, MFA; *Asst Prof* Glen Hintz, MFA; *Asst Prof* Thomas Lightfoot PhD, MFA
Estab 1829; FT 47, PT 19; pvt; 1000
Ent Req: HS grad, ent exam, portfolio
Degrees: BFA, MFA
Tuition: Undergrad $333 per cr, grad $425 per cr
Courses: Computer Graphics, Drawing, Glass Blowing, History of Art & Archeology, Illustration, †Industrial Design, †Interior Design, Jewelry, Sculpture, †Silversmithing, Stained Glass, †Textile Design, †Weaving
Adult Hobby Classes: Crafts, Design, Painting
Summer School: Enrl 250; tuition undergrad $260 per cr, grad $330 per cr for 8 wk term beginning June. Courses—Ceramics, Computer Graphics, Glass, Graphic Design, Metal, Painting, Printmaking, Textiles, Wood, Industrial, Interior, Packaging Design, Art History, 2-D and 3-D Design
—**School of Photographic Arts & Sciences,** 70 Lomb Memorial Dr, Rochester, NY 14623-5604. Tel 716-475-2716; Fax 716-475-5804; *Assoc Dir* Nancy Stuart, AB; *Chmn Imaging & Photographic Technology* Andrew Davidhazy, MEd; *Chmn Fine Arts Photo* Ken White, MEd; *Chmn Film/Video* Howard Lester, MEd; *Chmn Biomedical Photo Communs* Michael Peres, MEd; *Chmn American Video Institute* John Ciampa, JD; *Chmn Photographic Processing & Finishing Management* James Rice, BS; *Prof* John E Karpen, MFA; *Prof* Weston D Kemp, MFA; *Prof* Lothar K Engelmann PhD, MFA; *Prof* Russell C Kraus, EdD; *Prof* David J Robertson, BFA; *Assoc Prof* Owen Butler, BFA; *Assoc Prof* Kerry Coppin, BFA; *Assoc Prof* Jeff Weiss, BFA; *Assoc Prof* Patti Ambroge, BFA; *Assoc Prof* Bradley T Hindson, BA; *Assoc Prof* Alan Vogel, BA; *Assoc Prof* Robert Kayser, BA; *Assoc Prof* James Reilly, MA; *Assoc Prof* Guenther Cartwright, BA; *Assoc Prof* Howard LeVant, BS; *Assoc Prof* Elliott Rubenstein, MA; *Assoc Prof* Erik Timmerman, BS; *Assoc Prof* Douglas F Rea, MFA; *Assoc Prof* Steve Diehl, BS; *Assoc Prof* Mark

Haven, BA; *Assoc Prof* John Retallack, BA; *Asst Prof* Tom Lopez, MS; *Asst Prof* Stephanie Maxwell, MS; *Asst Prof* Bruce Lane, MS; *Asst Prof* Adrianne Carrageorge, MS; *Asst Prof* Lorett Falkner, MS; *Asst Prof* Deni Defenbaugh, MS; *Asst Prof* Sabrine Susstrink, MS; *Asst Prof* Kaleen Moriority, MS; *Asst Prof* Jack Holm, MS; *Asst Prof* Glen Miller, MS; *Asst Prof* William Osterman, MFA; *Asst Prof* Martha Leinroth, MFA; *Lectr* Dan Larken, MFA; *Dir* William DuBois, MS 900
Degrees: AA, BA, MA
Tuition: Undergrad $333 per cr, grad $425 per cr
Courses: Advertising, Biomedical Photography, Film, Film Studies, Photographic Communications, Photographic Technology, Photography, Processing & Finishing, Video
Summer School: Courses—Photography, Film/Video, Motion Picture Workshops, Narrative/Documentary/Editorial workshop, Nature Photography
—**School of Printing Management & Sciences,** 69 Lomb Memorial Dr, College of Imaging Arts & Sciences Rochester, NY 14623-5602. Tel 716-475-2728; Fax 716-475-7029; *Dir* Harold Gaffin; *Dean* Joan Stone; *Chmn Design Composition Division* Emery E Schneider, BS & MEd; *Coordr Grad Prog* Joseph L Noga, MS; *Paul & Louise Miller Prof* Robert G Hacker, BS; *Prof* Barbara Birkett, BS; *Prof* Miles F Southworth, BS; *Assoc Prof* William H Birkett, BS; *Assoc Prof* Clifton T Frazier, BS; *Assoc Prof* Herbert H Johnson, BS; *Assoc Prof* Archibald D Provan, BS; *Assoc Prof* Werner Rebsamen, dipl; *Asst Prof* Robert Y Chung, BA; *Asst Prof* Hugh R Fox, AB & JD; *Asst Prof* David P Pankow, BA & MA
School has 25 laboratories, occupying 125,000 sq ft. More than 70 courses are offered; 700
Degrees: BS, MS
Tuition: Undergrad $333 per cr, grad $425 per cr
Courses: Color Separation, Flexography, Gravure, Ink & Color, Introduction to Book Production, Newspaper Design, Printmaking, Systems Planning, Typography & Design
Summer School: Graphic Arts, Layout & Printing, Reproduction Photography, Ink & Color, Newspaper & Magazine Design, Hand Papermaking, Web Offset, Gravure, Lithography, Printing Plates, Typography, Bookbinding
—**School for American Craft,** 73 Lomb Memorial Dr, Rochester, NY 14623-5602. Tel 716-475-5778; *Dean* Dr Joan Stone; *Dir* Thomas Morin; *Chmn* Richard Pannen
Degrees: BS, BFA, MS, MST
Tuition: Undergrad $333 per cr, grad $425 per cr
Courses: Ceramics, Furniture & Wood Working, Glass, Metals, Textiles
Adult Hobby Classes: Extensive seminar schedule
Summer School: scholarships

UNIVERSITY OF ROCHESTER, Dept of Art & Art History, PO Box 270038, 424 Morey Hall Rochester, NY 14627-0038. Tel 585-275-9249; Fax 585-442-1692; Elec Mail aah_vcs@mail.rochester.edu; Internet Home Page Address: www.rochester.edu/college/aah; *Chmn* Allen C Topolski
Estab 1902; Maintain nonprofit art gallery; Hartnett Art Gallery, Rochester NY; FT 11, PT 5; pvt; D; Scholarships; SC 25, LC 25; maj 15, others 600
Degrees: BA, MA, PhD(Visual & Cultural Studies)
Courses: Art History, Drawing, History of Art & Architecture, Painting, Photography, Sculpture, †Video
Summer School: Enrl 40; tuition & duration vary

VISUAL STUDIES WORKSHOP, 31 Prince St, Rochester, NY 14607-1499. Tel 585-442-8676; Fax 585-442-1992; Elec Mail info@vsw.org; Internet Home Page Address: www.vsw.org; *Dir* Tate Shaw; *Fiscal Officer* Laraine Gallagher; *Ed Afterimage* Karen vanMeenen; *Exhibs Coordr* Rick Hock; *Assoc Ed Afterimage* Lucia Sommer
Open by appt; Gallery open Thurs 3-7 PM, Fri 3-5 PM, Sat - Sun 2-6 PM; Estab 1969 to establish a center for the transmission & study of the visual image; Visual Studies Workshops produce & or present approx 20 exhibitions per yr encompassing contemporary & historical issues; subjects vary from photography, film, video, artists' book works & related media; maintains Siskind Gallery and Bookstore ; Mem: Dues artist $35, researcher $75, friend $250, advocate $750; Pub; E, weekend & summer
Library Holdings: Original Documents; Other Holdings; Pamphlets; Periodical Subscriptions; Photographs; Prints; Reels; Slides; Video Tapes
Special Subjects: Mixed Media, Photography
Collections: 19th & 20th century photographs, mechanical prints & artists' books
Exhibitions: Rotating exhibits
Publications: Afterimage, bi-monthly
Activities: Classes for adults; Summer Institute prog with intensive short term workshops for artists & mus professionals; lects open to pub, 15 vis lectrs per yr; gallery talks; tours (by appointment); schols offered; original objects of art lent to institutions with proper exhibs facilities; lending collection contains 27,000 photographs of original artwork; originates traveling exhibs to mus, colleges & universities; mus shop sells books, magazines, original art & prints
Degrees: MFA
Courses: †Artist's Books, †Display, Photography
—**Research Center,** 31 Prince St, Rochester, NY 14607-1499. Tel 716-442-8676; Fax 716-442-1992; Elec Mail library@vsw.org; Internet Home Page Address: www.vsw.org; *Cur Colls* Jessica McDonald
Open by appt; Estab 1971 to maintain a permanent collection for the study of the function & effect of the visual image; For reference only
Library Holdings: Audio Tapes; Book Volumes 19,000; Cassettes; Clipping Files; Exhibition Catalogs; Kodachrome Transparencies; Lantern Slides; Motion Pictures; Original Art Works; Other Holdings Posters; Pamphlets; Periodical Subscriptions 160; Photographs; Prints; Reproductions; Slides; Video Tapes
Collections: Illustrated book coll; photographic print coll

SANBORN

NIAGARA COUNTY COMMUNITY COLLEGE, Fine Arts Division, 3111 Saunders Settlement Rd, Sanborn, NY 14132-9460. Tel 716-614-6222; Fax 716-614-6700; Internet Home Page Address: www.sunyniagara.cc.ny.us; *Dept Coordr MFA* Barbara Buckman; *Prof* Bud Jacobs; *Prof* Nancy Knechtel

Estab 1965; FT 15, PT 14; pub; D & E; Scholarships; SC 12, LC 4; D 400, E 120, maj 140
Ent Req: HS dipl
Degrees: AS(Fine Arts) 2 yrs
Courses: Advertising Design, Aesthetics, Art Appreciation, Art History, Art Therapy, Ceramics, Commercial Art, Conceptual Art, Constructions, Design, Drafting, †Drawing, Film, Graphic Arts, †Graphic Design, Handicrafts, Illustration, Lettering, Mixed Media, Museum Staff Training, †Painting, Photography, Sculpture, Stage Design, Theatre Arts, Visual Art

SARATOGA SPRINGS

SKIDMORE COLLEGE, Dept of Art & Art History, 815 N Broadway, Saratoga Springs, NY 12866-1632. Tel 518-580-5000, 580-5030 (Dept Art & Art History); Fax 518-580-5029; Internet Home Page Address: www.skidmore.edu; *Chmn* Peter Stake
Estab 1911; FT 20; pvt; Scholarships; SC 32, LC 18; maj 350, 2000 total
Ent Req: HS grad, 16 cr, ent exam, portfolio
Degrees: BA & BS 4 yrs
Courses: Art History, Ceramics, Computer Imaging, Design, Drawing, Graphic Design, Jewelry/Metalsmithing, Painting, Photography, Printmaking, Sculpture, Weaving
Summer School: Dir, Regis Brodie. Enrl 194 for two 6 wk sessions.
Courses—Advanced Studio & Independent Study, Art History, Ceramics, Drawing, Etching, Jewelry, Lettering, Painting, Photography, Sculpture, 2-D Design, Video, Watercolor, Weaving

SCHENECTADY

UNION COLLEGE, Dept of Visual Arts, 807 Union St, Arts Bldg Schenectady, NY 12308-3103. Tel 518-388-6714; Fax 518-388-6567; Internet Home Page Address: www.union.edu; *Chmn Visual Arts* Chris Duncan
Estab 1795; FT 7; pvt; D; Scholarships; SC 14, LC 4; maj 35
Ent Req: HS dipl, ent exam
Degrees: BA with emphasis in music, art or theatre arts 4 yr
Courses: 3-D, Art History, Drawing, Painting, Photography, Printmaking, Sculpture, Stage Design, Theatre Arts, †Visual Arts
Adult Hobby Classes: Enrl 30; Courses—Drawing, Photography
Children's Classes: Enrl 15
Summer School: Dean, Jane Zacek. Enrl 30; Courses—Art History, Drawing, 3-D, Painting, Photography, Printmaking

SELDEN

SUFFOLK COUNTY COMMUNITY COLLEGE, Art Dept, 533 College Rd, Selden, NY 11784-2899. Tel 631-451-4110; Internet Home Page Address: www.sunysuffolk.edu; *Dept Head* Arthur Kleinfelder
FT 6, PT 6
Ent Req: HS dipl, equivalent
Degrees: AFA
Tuition: Res $98.50 per cr hr; nonres (out of state) $198 per cr hr
Courses: Art Appreciation, Art History, Ceramics, Design, Drawing, Painting, Printmaking
Adult Hobby Classes: Enrl 200; tuition $15 per hr. Courses—Photography, Interior Design
Summer School: Dir, Maurice Flecker. Tuition res $60 per cr for 6-8 wk sessions. Courses—Painting, Sculpture, 2-D Design, Life Drawing, Printmaking & Ceramics

SPARKILL

SAINT THOMAS AQUINAS COLLEGE, Art Dept, 125 Rte 340, Sparkill, NY 10976. Tel 845-398-4000, Ext 4136; Fax 845-398-4071; *Prof* Carl Rattner, MFA, DA; *Assoc Prof* Barbara Yonz, MA, MFA; *Asst Prof* Nina Bellisio, MFA; *Asst Prof* Matthew Finn, MFA; *Asst Prof* Carol Lagsteid, MFD, MSW; *Adj Prof* Annie Sheih, MFA; *Adj Prof* Jane Marcy; *Adj Asst Prof* Rene Smith
Estab 1952, dept estab 1969; Maintain nonprofit art gallery; art supplies furnished for all studio classes; schols vary; Pvt; D & E; Scholarships; SC, LC; D 1,100, maj 50
Ent Req: HS dipl
Degrees: BA and BS 4 yrs
Tuition: $21,140 per yr, incl room & board
Courses: Advertising Design, Art Appreciation, Art History, Art Therapy, Ceramics, Commercial Art, Conceptual Art, Display, Drawing, Graphic Design, Jewelry, Mixed Media, Painting, Photography, Printmaking, Sculpture, Video
Summer School: Dir, Dr Joseph Keane. Tuition $210 for 3 cr course. Courses—Varies 3-6 art courses including Ceramics, Painting, Photography

STATEN ISLAND

COLLEGE OF STATEN ISLAND, Performing & Creative Arts Dept, 2800 Victory Blvd, Bldg IP-203 Staten Island, NY 10314-6609. Tel 718-982-2520; Fax 718-982-2537; Elec Mail jonest@mail.csi.cuny.edu; Internet Home Page Address: www.csi.cuny.edu; *Coordr Art Prog* Prof Pat Passlof; *Prof* Ralph Martel; *Asst Prof* Tracey Jones; *Adj Assoc Prof* Mor Pipman; *Adj Assoc Prof* Geoffrey Dorfman; *Asst Prof* Beatrix Reinhardt; *Asst Prof* Siona Wilson; *Prof* Nanette Salomon; *Adj Asst Prof* Robert Ludwig; *Adj Asst Prof* Howard Smith; *Adj Asst Prof* Faustino Quintanilla; *Adj Assoc Prof* Janine Coyne; *Adj Asst Prof* Nicole Frocheur; *Adj Asst Prof* Craig Manister; *Adjunct Asst Prof* Robert Morgan Taylor
Maintains nonprofit galleries, The College of Staten Island Art Gallery & The CSI Student Art Gallery; Pub; D, E & W; SC, LC, GC 1
Degrees: BS(Art), BS(Photography), BA(Art), BA(photography)

Tuition: Res—undergrad $170 per cr hr, grad $185 per cr hr
Courses: †Art Appreciation, †Art History, †Design, †Drawing, †History of Art & Architecture, †Museum Staff Training, †Painting, †Photography, †Printmaking, Sculpture
Summer School: Courses offered

INSTITUTE FOR ARTS & HUMANITIES EDUCATION, New Jersey Summer Arts Institute, 270 Lawrence Ave, Staten Island, NY 10310-3026. Tel 732-220-1600; Fax 732-220-1515; Elec Mail ihe@ihenj.org; *Exec Dir* Maureen Heckerman
Estab 1980; Students earn HS cr; 4 FT; pvt; D & E; Scholarships; 130
Publications: Quarterly newsletter
Ent Req: audition, master class, portfolio, interview
Courses: Advertising Design, Aesthetics, Architecture, Art Appreciation, Art Education, Art History, Ceramics, Collage, Conceptual Art, Costume Design & Construction, Design, Display, Drawing, Fashion Arts, Film, Graphic Arts, Graphic Design, History of Art & Architecture, Illustration, Intermedia, Jewelry, Mixed Media, Painting, Photography, Printmaking, Sculpture, Stage Design, Teacher Training, Textile Design, Theatre Arts, Video, Weaving

WAGNER COLLEGE, Arts Administration Dept, One Campus Rd, Staten Island, NY 10301. Tel 718-390-3271, 390-3100; Fax 718-390-3223; Elec Mail gpsull@wagner.edu; Internet Home Page Address: www.wagner.edu; *Chmn* Gary Sullivan; *Instr* Lillian Stausland; *Instr* Robert Williams
Estab 1948; Maintain nonprofit art gallery; pvt; D & E; SC 20, LC 6; maj 35, others 2000
Ent Req: HS grad
Degrees: BA(Art), BS(Art Admin)
Courses: 2-D Design, 3-D Design, Advertising Design, Art History, Arts Administration, Ceramics, Crafts Design, Drawing, Graphic Arts, Mixed Media, Painting, Photography, Printmaking, Sculpture
Summer School: Two sessions of 4 wks, Dir Extensions & Summer Prog, Maureen Connolly

STONE RIDGE

ULSTER COUNTY COMMUNITY COLLEGE/SUNY ULSTER, Dept of Art, Design, Music, Theatre & Communication, 491 Cottekill Rd, Stone Ridge, NY 12484. Tel 845-687-5066 (Art Dept); Fax 845-687-5083; Elec Mail machelli@sunyulster.edu; Internet Home Page Address: www.sunyulster.edu; *Chmn* Iain Machell, MFA; *Prof* Sean Nixon, MFA
Estab 1963; Maintain nonprofit art gallery, Muroff-Kotler Gallery, Stone Ridge Campus, Stone Ridge, NY 12484; Maintain Library, Macdonald Dewitt Library; PT 7; pub; D & E; Scholarships; SC 17, LC 6; D 500, E 190, non-maj 590, maj 100
Activities: Schols offered
Ent Req: HS dipl
Degrees: AA 2 yrs, AS 2 yrs
Tuition: Full-time NY res $3,820 per yr; full-time other $7,640 per yr; no campus res
Courses: 2-D Design, 3-D Design, Art Appreciation, Art History, Computer Art, Computer Assisted Graphic Design, Desk-Top Publishing, Drawing, Fashion Arts, †Graphic Design, Life Drawing, Painting, Photography, Web Page Design
Summer School: Visual Arts Coordr, Iain Machell. Enrl 30 - 50; tuition $285 per 3 sem hrs for 6 wks. Courses—Computer Art, Drawing, Painting, Photography

STONY BROOK

STONY BROOK UNIVERSITY, (State University of New York at Stony Brook) College of Arts & Sciences, Dept of Art, Staller Center for the Arts, State University of NY at Stony Brook Stony Brook, NY 11794-5400. Tel 631-632-7250; Fax 631-632-7261; Elec Mail jvotolo@notes.cc.sunysb.edu; Internet Home Page Address: www.art.sunysb.edu; *Prof* Melvin H Pekarsky, MA; *Prof* Donald B Kuspit PhD; *Prof* Howardena Pindell, MFA; *Prof* Toby Buonagurio, MA; *Prof* Michele H Bogart, PhD; *Chair & Prof* Anita Moskowitz, PhD; *Prof* Barbara Frank, PhD; *Asst Prof* Grady Gerbracht, MFA; *Asst Prof* Martin Levine, MFA; *Assoc Prof* Stephanie Dinkins, MFA; *Assoc Prof* Christa Erickson, MFA; *Assoc Prof* Nobuho Nagasawa, MFA; *Lectr* Shoki Goodarzi, PhD; *Vis Assoc Prof* Richard Leslie, PhD; *Artist in Res* Gary Schneider, MFA; *Asst Prof* Andrew Uroskie, PhD; *Asst Prof* Zabet Patterson, PhD; *Lectr* Helen Harrison, MA
Estab 1957; Maintains nonprofit gallery, Staller Center for The Arts, Stony Brook University, Stony Brook, NY, 11797-5400; maintains an art library, Frank Melville Jr, Memorial Library; art supplies can be purchased at on-campus shop; FT 7; pub; D, E, winter & summer sessions; SC 41, LC 49, GC 47; D 13,733, E 1,116, non-maj 2,890, maj 12,276, GS 7,675
Ent Req: HS dipl, SAT
Degrees: BA(Art History) & BA(Studio Art), MA(Art History & Criticism), MFA(Studio Art), PhD(Art History & Criticism)
Tuition: Undergrad $4,350 per yr, grad $6,900 per yr
Courses: †Aesthetics, †Art Criticism, †Art History, Ceramics, †Collage, Conceptual Art, †Constructions, †Costume Design & Construction, Drawing, †Electronic Media, History of Art & Architecture, †Mixed Media, Painting, †Performance Art, Photography, Printmaking, Sculpture, †Stage Design, †Studio Art, †Video
Summer School: Tuition res—undergrad $18 per cr hr, grad $288 per cr hr; nonres—undergrad $442 per cr hr, grad $455 per cr hr for term of 6 wks (two sessions). Courses vary in areas of Art Education, Art History & Criticism, Studio Art

SUFFERN

ROCKLAND COMMUNITY COLLEGE, Graphic Arts & Advertising Tech Dept, 145 College Rd, Suffern, NY 10901-3699. Tel 845-574-4251; Fax 845-356-1529; *Discipline Coordr* Emily Harvey

Estab 1965; pub; D & E; SC plus apprenticeships; D 900, E 300, maj 200
Ent Req: open
Degrees: AAS 2 yrs
Courses: Advertising Design, Alternative Processes in Photography, Art Appreciation, Art History, Art Therapy, Color Production, Drawing, Electric Art, Graphic Arts, Graphic Design, Lettering, Lithography, Painting, Photography, Portfolio Workshop, Sculpture, Serigraphy Printing
Adult Hobby Classes: Enrl 528; tuition varies. Courses—Ceramics, Crafts
Summer School: Dir, Emily Harvey. Enrl 180; June - Aug. Courses—Computer Graphics, Drawing, Overseas Program, Painting, Sculpture

SYRACUSE

LE MOYNE COLLEGE, Fine Arts Dept, Le Moyne Heights, Syracuse, NY 13214-1399; 1419 Salt Springs Rd, Syracuse, NY 13214. Tel 315-445-4100, 445-4147; Elec Mail belfortj@mail.lemoyne.edu; Internet Home Page Address: www.lemoyne.edu; *Chmn & Prof* Jacqueline Belfort-Chalat; *Adjunct Asst Prof* Barry Darling; *Adjunct Asst Prof* Charles Wollowitz; *Adjunct Prof* J Exline, MA; *Adjunct Asst Prof* William West, MA; *Adjunct Asst Prof* David G Moore
Estab 1946; Maintain nonprofit art gallery: Wilson Art Gallery, Lemoyne College, Syracuse, NY 13214; Pvt; D&E; SC 6, LC 5; non-maj 350
Ent Req: HS dipl, SAT or ACT
Degrees: BS & BA 4 yrs
Courses: †Art Appreciation, Art History, Drawing, Graphic Arts, Painting, †Photography, †Printmaking, Sculpture

SYRACUSE UNIVERSITY, College of Visual & Performing Arts, 102 Shaffer Art Bldg, School of Art & Design Syracuse, NY 13244-1010. Tel 315-443-2507; Fax 315-443-1303; *Interim Dir* Barbara Walter, MFA; *Dean* Carole Brzozowski, MS
Estab 1873; Maintain nonprofit art gallery; Lowe Art Gallery, 102 Shaffer Art Bldg, Syracuse Univ, Syracuse, NY 13244; FT 60, PT 52; pvt; D & E; Scholarships; SC 200, LC 25, GC 100; D 1,200
Ent Req: HS dipl, portfolio review
Degrees: BID 5 yrs, BFA 4 yrs, MFA & MA(Museum Studies) 2 yrs
Tuition: Undergrad $13,480 per yr; grad $406 per cr; campus res available
Courses: †Advertising Design, †Art Education, †Art History, †Art Photography, †Ceramics, †Communications Design, †Computer Graphics, Drawing, Environmental Design, †Fashion Arts, Fibers, Film, †Illustration, †Industrial Design, †Interior Design, †Metalsmithing, †Museum Studies Program, †Painting, Papermaking, †Printmaking, †Sculpture, †Surface Pattern Design, †Textile Design, †Video, Weaving
Adult Hobby Classes: Enrl 155; tuition undergrad $276 per cr. Courses—same as above
Children's Classes: Enrl 80; tuition $50 per sem. Courses—general art
Summer School: Tuition undergrad $408 per cr, grad $456 per cr. Courses—same as above
—**Dept of Fine Arts (Art History),** 308 Bowne Hall, Syracuse, NY 13244-1200. Tel 315-443-4184; Fax 315-443-4186; Elec Mail ljstraub@syr.edu; Internet Home Page Address: http://finearts.syr.edu/; *Prof* Gary Radke PhD; *Prof* Meredith Lillich PhD; *Prof* Laurinda Dixon PhD; *Prof* Mary Marien PhD; *Prof* Barbara Larson PhD; *Prof* Alan Braddock
Estab 1870. dept estab 1948; Pvt; D & E; Scholarships; LC 25, GC 15; non-maj 900, maj 71, grad 46
Ent Req: HS dipl, SAT
Degrees: BA, MA
Tuition: Undergrad $15,800 per yr
Courses: American Art, Art & Music History, Art Appreciation, Art History, Arts & Ideas, Baroque, History of Art & Archeology, Italian Medieval Art, Photography

TROY

EMMA WILLARD SCHOOL, Dept of Visual & Performing Arts, 285 Pawling Ave, Troy, NY 12180-5294. Tel 518-833-1300; Internet Home Page Address: http//www.emmawillard.org; *Dept Chmn* Debra Spiro-Allen
Estab 1814, dept estab 1969; See website for full listing; pvt Women only; D; Scholarships
Ent Req: Grades 9-12 & Post Graduate
Tuition: $19,600 incl room & board
Courses: Advanced Studio Art, Art Appreciation, Art History, Ceramics, Dance, Drawing, Jewelry, Music, Photography, Printmaking, Theatre Arts, Visual Arts Foundation, Weaving

RENSSELAER POLYTECHNIC INSTITUTE, School of Architecture, 110 Eighth St, Troy, NY 12180-3590. Tel 518-276-6466; Fax 518-276-3034; Internet Home Page Address: www.arch.rpi.edu; *Dean* Alan Balfour
Estab 1929; FT 18, PT 18; pvt; D; Scholarships; 275
Degrees: BA(Archit), MA(Archit), MS(Lighting)
Tuition: Undergrad $23,525 per yr
Courses: Design, History, Practice, Structure, Studio
Summer School: Architectural Design
—**Eye Ear Studio Dept of Art,** 110 8th St, School of Humanities, Art & Social Sciences Troy, NY 12180-3522. Tel 518-276-4778; Internet Home Page Address: www.arts.rpi.edu; *Chmn* Neil Rolnick PhD; *Asst Dir* Laura Garrison; *Prof* Larry Keegan; *Clerk Specialist* Amy Horowitz
Scholarships, Fellowships
Degrees: MFA (Electronic Arts) 2 1/2 - 3 yrs
Tuition: $15,880 annual tuition
Courses: Animation, Computer Graphics, Computer Music, Drawing, Installation, Painting, Performance, Sculpture, Video

RUSSELL SAGE COLLEGE, Visual & Performing Arts Dept, 65 1st St, Schacht Fine Arts Ctr Troy, NY 12180-4013. Tel 518-244-2000; Fax 518-271-4545; Internet Home Page Address: www.sage.edu/rsc; *Chmn & Dir Creative Arts* Leigh Davies

Pvt, W; 20-40 per class
Ent Req: HS grad
Degrees: fine arts and divisional maj in Music, Art and Drama 4 yrs
Courses: 2-D Design, †Arts Management, †Creative Arts Therapy

UTICA

MOHAWK VALLEY COMMUNITY COLLEGE, 1101 Sherman Dr, Utica, NY 13510-5394. Tel 315-792-5446; Fax 315-792-5666; Elec Mail lmigliori@mucc.edu; Internet Home Page Address: www.mvcc.edu; *Pres* Michael I Schafer PhD; *Prof* Ronald Labuz PhD; *Assoc Prof* Henry Godlewski, BS; *Head Dept* Larry Migliori, MS; *Assoc Prof* E Duane Isenberg, MA; *Assoc Prof* Jerome Lalonde, MA; *Assoc Prof* Robert Clarke, BFA; *Instr* Thomas Maneen, BFA; *Asst Prof* Alex Piejko, BFA; *Instr* James Vitale; *Assoc Prof* Christine Miller; *Instr* Scott Selden; *Assoc Prof* Wayne Freed; *Instr* Christi Harrington; *Instr* Aaron Board; *Instr* Kathleen Partridge; *Instr* David Yahnke; *Instr* Scot Connor; *Instr* Sara Demas
Estab 1947, dept estab 1955; Maintain a nonprofit art gallery: Small Works, an art/architecture library: James O'Looney and on-campus shop where art supplies may be purchased; FT 16, ADJ 14; pub; D & E; Scholarships; SC 42 (over 2 yr period), LC 10 (over 2 yr period); D 450, E varies, maj 450
Ent Req: HS dipl, GED
Degrees: AAS 2 yrs
Tuition: Campus res—available
Courses: †Advertising Design, Aesthetics, Art Appreciation, Art History, Computer Graphics, †Design, Drawing, Graphic Arts, Graphic Design, †Handicrafts, History of Art & Architecture, Illustration, Lettering, Painting, †Photography, Textile Design, Weaving
Adult Hobby Classes: Enrl 440. Courses—Air Brush, Design, Illustration, Painting, Photography, Sketching, Watercolor
Children's Classes: Coll for child
Summer School: Dir, Larry Migliori. Enrl 40. Courses—Drawing, Design, Photography

MUNSON-WILLIAMS-PROCTOR ARTS INSTITUTE, Pratt MWP College of Art, 310 Genesee St, Utica, NY 13502-4799. Tel 315-797-0000; Fax 315-797-9349; Elec Mail admissions@mwpai.edu; Internet Home Page Address: www.mwpai.org; *Prof* Steve Arnison; *Prof* Daniel Buckingham; *Prof* Chris Irick; *Prof* Nancy Long; *Prof* Ken Marchione; *Prof* Bryan McGrath; *Prof* Keith Sandman; *Asst Prof* Sandra Stephens; *Prof* Lisa Gregg Wightman; *Assoc Prof* Cynthia Koren; *Prof* Greg Lawler
Estab 1941; Maintains nonprofit gallery & library. Art supply store on campus; pvt; d, e; Scholarships; adults 1900, children 533, pratt at mwp 160
Activities: On-campus shop sells art supplies
Tuition: $12,400/sem
Courses: 2-D & 3-D Design, Advertising Design, Art Education, Ceramics, Color Theory, Dance, Drawing, Goldsmithing, Graphic Arts, Graphic Design, Humanities, Illustration, Metal Arts, Painting, Photography, Pottery, Printmaking, Sculpture, Silversmithing, †Video
Adult Hobby Classes: Enrl 805. Courses—Dance, Design, Drawing, Jewelry, Painting, Photography, Pottery, Printmaking, Sculpture
Children's Classes: Enrl 423. Courses - Dance, Drawing, Painting,
Summer School: Dir, Dean Ken Marchione. Enrl 413, tuition $65 - $110 for 4 wk term. Courses—Dance Drawing, Jewelry Making, Painting, Photography, Pottery

UTICA COLLEGE OF SYRACUSE UNIVERSITY, Division of Art & Science, 1600 Burrstone Rd, Utica, NY 13502-4892. Tel 315-792-3092; Fax 315-792-3831; Internet Home Page Address: www.utica.edu; *Dean Arts & Sciences* Lawrence R Aaronson
Estab 1946, school of art estab 1973; pvt; D; Scholarships; SC 20, LC 7; School of Art D 94, Utica College maj 14
Degrees: BS(Fine Arts) 4 yrs
Courses: Art History, †Ceramics, Design, Drafting, Drawing, Film, Graphic Arts, Occupational Therapy, †Painting, Photography, †Sculpture, Stage Design, Theatre Arts, Video

WATERTOWN

JEFFERSON COMMUNITY COLLEGE, Art Dept, 1220 Coffeen St, Watertown, NY 13601-1822. Tel 315-786-2404; Fax 315-788-0716; Elec Mail johndeans@ccmgate.sunyjefferson.edu; Internet Home Page Address: www.sunyjefferson.edu; *Pres* John Deans
Estab 1963; FT 1; pub; D & E; Scholarships; SC 2, LC 1; 850
Ent Req: HS dipl, GED
Degrees: AA, AS & AAS 2 yr
Courses: 2-D Studio, Art Appreciation, Art History, Ceramics, Computer-Aided Art & Design, Film Appreciation, Photography, Sculpture, Snow Sculpture
Summer School: Pres, John T Henderson

WEST NYACK

ROCKLAND CENTER FOR THE ARTS, 27 S Greenbush Rd, West Nyack, NY 10021-2700. Tel 845-358-0877; Fax 845-358-0971; Elec Mail info@rocklandartcenter.org; Internet Home Page Address: www.rocklandartcenter.org; *Dir School* Daly Flanagan, MS; *Exec Dir* Julianne Ramos, MFA; *Artistic Dir* Lynn Stein
Estab 1947; Maintain nonprofit galleries: Emerson Gallery (same address), Catherine Konner Sculpture Park, Gallery One; schols open to children, adults, need based; on-campus art shop sells ceramic supplies only; Pvt; D & E, Weekends; Scholarships; SC 100; D 900, E 400
Collections: Contemporary painting & drawing coll
Publications: Artline newsletter; art school catalogues; exhibition catalogues
Degrees: Non-degree
Tuition: Varies per course

Courses: Ceramics, Creative Writing, Drawing, †Fashion Arts, †Glass, Handicrafts, †Jewelry, †Mixed Media, Painting, †Photography, Printmaking, †Silversmithing, †Teacher Training
Adult Hobby Classes: Enrl 300; tuition $170 - $350 for twelve 3 hr sessions. Courses—Ceramics, Fine Arts & Crafts, Writing
Children's Classes: Enrl 300; tuition $155-$200 for ten 1 1/2 hr sessions. Courses—same as above
Summer School: Dir, Daly Flanagan. Enrl 100 children & 200 adults; tuition average $120 per 6 wks. Courses—same as above

WHITE PLAINS

WESTCHESTER COMMUNITY COLLEGE, Westchester Art Workshop, 196 Central Ave, County Ctr White Plains, NY 10606-1102. Tel 914-684-0094; Fax 914-684-0608; *Prog Dir* Abre Chen
Estab 1926; 75; pub; D & E; Scholarships; SC 90 per sem, 5 sem per yr; D 650, E 550, others 700 (cr given for most courses)
Ent Req: no special req
Degrees: AA, AS & AAS
Tuition: No campus res
Courses: Art Appreciation, Art Foundation, Art Therapy, Calligraphy, Ceramics, Commercial Art, Computer Art Animation, Design, Drawing, Faux Finishes, Goldsmithing, Graphic Arts, Graphic Design, Illustration, Jewelry, Lost Wax Casting, Mixed Media, Painting, Photography, Portrait Painting, Printmaking, Quilting, Sculpture, Silversmithing, Stained Glass, Video, Weaving
Adult Hobby Classes: 100
Children's Classes: Enrl 150. Courses—Cartooning, Ceramics, Drawing, Jewelry, Mixed Media, Painting
Summer School: 700. Courses—same as above

WOODSTOCK

WOODSTOCK SCHOOL OF ART, INC, PO Box 338, Woodstock, NY 12498-0338. Tel 845-679-2388; Fax 845-679-3802; Elec Mail wsart@earthlink.net; Internet Home Page Address: www.woodstockschoolofart.com; *Pres* Kate O'Neil; *Instr* Kate McGloughlin; *Instr* Eric Angeloch; *Instr* Richard Segalman; *Instr* Hong Nian Zhang; *Instr* Staats Fasoldt; *Instr* Lois Woolley; *Instr* Pia Oste-Alexander; *Instr* Tricia Cline; *Instr* Mariella Bisson; *Instr* Christina Debarry; *Instr* Jon deMartin; *Instr* Steve Dininno; *Instr* Ron Netsky; *Instr* Michael Peery; *Instr* Paul Abrams; *Instr* Christie Scheele; *Instr* Mary Anna Goetz; *Instr* Alex Kveton; *Instr* Donald Elder; *Instr* F Tor Gudmundsen; *Instr* Keith Gunderson
Estab 1968, dept estab 1981; Maintains nonprofit gallery, Woodstock School of Art Gallery; maintains art/architecture libr; Chris Gallego, Janet Walsh, Vince Natale, Robert Otinigian, Judith Reeve; pvt nonprofit; D & E; Scholarships; SC 19, LC 8; D 400
Courses: Collage, Drawing, Painting, Printmaking, Sculpture
Summer School: Tuition $400 per wk. Courses—Collage, Drawing, Etching, Landscape, Lithography, Monotype, Painting, Pastel, Portrait, Sculpture, Watercolor, Figure

NORTH CAROLINA

ASHEVILLE

UNIVERSITY OF NORTH CAROLINA AT ASHEVILLE, Dept of Art, One University Heights, Asheville, NC 28804. Tel 828-251-6600, 257-6559 (Art Dept); Elec Mail tcooke@enca.edu; Internet Home Page Address: www.unca.edu/art/; *Chmn* S Tucker Cooke, MFA
Estab 1927, dept estab 1965; pub; D & E; Scholarships; SC 20, LC 5; 3277, maj 69
Ent Req: HS dipl, ent exam
Degrees: BA, BFA 4-5 yrs
Courses: 2-D & 3-D Design, Art Education, Art History, Ceramics, Drawing, Intermedia, Life Drawing, Mixed Media, Painting, Photography, Printmaking, Sculpture
Adult Hobby Classes: Contact Educ Dept 704-251-6420
Summer School: Dir, S Tucker Cooke. Courses vary

BOONE

APPALACHIAN STATE UNIVERSITY, Dept of Art, Herbert Wey Hall, Rm 232, Boone, NC 28608. Tel 828-262-2000; Fax 828-262-6312; Internet Home Page Address: www.appstate.edu; *Prof* Marianne Suggs; *Prof* Glenn Phifer; *Asst Prof* Eli Bentor; *Asst Prof* Joan Durden; *Prof* Judy Humphrey; *Asst Prof* L Kathleen Campbell; *Chmn* Laura Ives; *Prof* Robin Martindale; *Instr* Lilith Eberle-Nielander; *Instr* Tim Ford; *Instr* Henry T Foreman; *Instr* Kyle Van Lusk; *Instr* Margaret Carter Martine; *Instr* Dr Janet Montgomery; *Instr* Mary Perry; *Instr* Mary Prather; *Instr* Nancy Sokolove; *Instr* Sonny Struss; *Instr* Vicki Clift; *Instr* Susie Winters; *Instr* Ann Thompson; *Asst Prof* Christopher Curtin; *Assoc Prof* Ed Midgett; *Assoc Prof* Gary Nemcosky; *Prof* William G Phifer; *Assoc Prof* Eric Purves; *Prof* Marilyn Smith; *Asst Prof* Lisa Stinson; *Assoc Prof* Jim Toub; *Assoc Prof* Gayle Weitz; *Assoc Prof* Barbara Yale-Read; *Asst Prof* Margaret Yaukey
Estab 1960; pub; D; Scholarships; SC 52, LC 14; D 1000, maj 350, grad 45
Ent Req: HS dipl, ent exam
Degrees: BA, BS & BFA (graphic design, art educ, studio art, art marketing & production) 4 yrs
Courses: Art Appreciation, Art History, Fibers, Graphic Arts
Children's Classes: After sch art program enrl 40, $250 per sem
Summer School: Chmn, Laura Ives. Enrl 60; $75 per hr res, $239 per hr non-res. Courses—per regular session

BREVARD

BREVARD COLLEGE, Department of Art, One Brevard College Dr, Brevard, NC 28712. Tel 828-883-8292; Fax 828-884-3790; Internet Home Page Address: www.brevard.edu; *Chair Div Fine Arts* Laura L Franklin, DMA; *Coordr Fine Arts* Anne Chapin, PhD; *Prof* Bill Byers, MFA; *Prof* M Jo Pumphrey, MFA; *Assoc Prof* Kyle Lusk, MFA
Estab 1853; Maintains nonprofit art gallery: Spiers Gallery on campus & an on-campus art supplies shop; FT 4, PT 4; pvt, den; D & E; Scholarships; SC 12, LC 2; non-maj 20, maj 60
Ent Req: HS dipl
Degrees: BA
Tuition: $22,100
Courses: †Art Appreciation, Art History, Ceramics, Drawing, Film, Graphic Arts, Graphic Design, †History of Art & Architecture, †Mixed Media, Painting, Photography, Printmaking, Sculpture
Summer School: Courses vary

CHAPEL HILL

UNIVERSITY OF NORTH CAROLINA AT CHAPEL HILL, Art Dept, Hanes Art Ctr, CB#3405 Chapel Hill, NC 27599-3405. Tel 919-962-2015; Fax 919-962-0722; Internet Home Page Address: www.unc.edu/depts/art; *Prof* Mary C Sturgeon PhD; *Chm & Prof* Mary Sheriff PhD; *Prof* Jaroslav Folda PhD; *Asst Chm & Prof* Beth Grabowski, MFA; *Prof* Dennis Zaborowski, MFA; *Prof* Jim Hirschfield, MFA; *Prof* Elin O Slavick, MFA; *Assoc Prof* Dorothy Verkerk, MFA; *Prof* Yun-Dong Nam, MFA; *Assoc Prof* Pika Ghosh, PhD; *Asst Prof* Carol Magee, PhD; *Asst Prof* Lyneise Williams, PhD; *Asst Prof* Jeff Whetstone, MFA; *Assoc Prof* Juan Logan, MFA; *Asst Prof* Kimowan McLain, MFA; *Assoc Prof* Mary Pardo, PhD; *Asst Prof* Glaire Anderson, PhD; *Instr* Susan Harbage-Page, MFA; *Asst Prof* Mario Marzan; *Asst Prof* Cary Levine; *Instr* Michael Sonnichsen; *Instr* David Tinapple
Estab 1793, dept estab 1936; Maintain nonprofit art gallery; John & June Allcott Gallery, UNC-CH, Dept of Art, Chapel Hill, NC 27599; on-campus shop where art supplies may be purchased; Pub; D; Scholarships; SC 30, LC 30, GC 10; D 100 undergrad, 55 grad
Ent Req: HS dipl, SAT
Degrees: BA & BFA 4 yr, MFA & MA(Art History) 2 yr, PhD(Art History) to 6 yr
Tuition: Res—undergrad $693 per sem, grad $693 per sem; nonres—undergrad $4,959 per sem, grad $4,959; campus res—available
Courses: Architecture, †Art History, Ceramics, †Drawing, History of Art & Architecture, †Mixed Media, †Painting, Photography, Printmaking, Sculpture
Summer School: Assoc Prof Dorothy Verkerk. Courses—Various Art History & Studio Courses

CHARLOTTE

CENTRAL PIEDMONT COMMUNITY COLLEGE, Visual & Performing Arts, PO Box 35009, Charlotte, NC 28235-5009. Tel 704-330-2722; Internet Home Page Address: www.cpcc.cc.nc.us; *Chmn* Mary Lou Paschal
Estab 1963; Scholarships
Ent Req: HS dipl, equivalent
Degrees: AS, AA & AAS 2 yrs
Tuition: Res undergrad $27.50 per cr hr; nonres $169.75 per cr hr
Courses: Advertising Design, Architecture, Art Appreciation, Art History, Artists Books (special topic), Bronze Casting, Ceramics, Computer Aided Design, Design, Drawing, Interior Design, Jewelry, Painting, Photography, Printmaking, Sculpture, Weaving

QUEENS COLLEGE, Fine Arts Dept, 1900 Selwyn Ave, Charlotte, NC 28207-2450. Tel 704-334-2212; Tel 800-849-0202; Elec Mail cas@queens.edu; Internet Home Page Address: www.queens.edu; *Fine Arts Chmn* Robert F Porter
Estab 1857; Den; Scholarships; SC 19, LC 7
Degrees: BA
Courses: Art History, Ceramics, Commercial Art

UNIVERSITY OF NORTH CAROLINA AT CHARLOTTE, Dept Art, 9201 University City Blvd, Rowe 173 Charlotte, NC 28223-0001. Tel 704-687-2473; Fax 704-687-2591; Internet Home Page Address: www.art.uncc.edu; *Prof & Chair* Roy Strassberg; *Gallery Mgr* Dean Butckovitz; *Assoc Prof* Winston Tite; *Asst Prof* Joan Tweedy; *Assoc Prof* Eldred Hudson; *Prof Emeritus* Lili Corbus; *Assoc Prof* Susan Brenner; *Prof Emeritus* Heather Hoover; *Asst Prof* David Brodeur; *Lectr* Keith Bryant; *Assoc Prof* Jamie Franki; *Lectr* Frances Hawthorne; *Lectr* Ann Kluttz; *Assoc Prof* Jeff Murphy; *Asst Prof* Bonnie Noble; *Assoc Prof* Mary Tuma; *Prof* David Edgar; *Asst Prof* Jim Frakes; *Asst Prof* Maja Godlewska; *Lectr* Kristin Rothrock; *Coordr Undergrad Educ* Malena Bergmann; *Asst Prof* John Ford; *Asst Prof* Heather Freeman; *Asst Prof* Pamela Lawton; *Lectr* Michael Simpson; *Lectr* Deborah Wall; *Lectr* Jason Tselentis; *Asst Prof* Angela Herren
Estab 1965, dept estab 1971; Maintain nonprofit art gallery, Rowe Gallery & Cone Center Gallery, Art Dept, UNC Charlotte, NC 28223; pub; D & E; SC 96, LC 32, Other 16; maj 500
Ent Req: HS dipl, SAT, Col Boards, Portfolio Review for studio degrees
Degrees: BA (Art & Art History) & BFA 4 yrs, K - 12 Art Educ Cert 4 yrs
Courses: Art Education, Art History, Ceramics, Design, Drawing, Electronic Media, Fibers, Graphic Design, Illustration, Jewelry, Painting, Photography, Printmaking, Sculpture
Summer School: Prof Roy Strassberg. Enrl 120; tuition res—$413.90, nonres—$1487.90; two 5 wk sessions, one 3 wk session. Courses—Art Appreciation, Ceramics, Design, Drawing, Painting, Photography

CULLOWHEE

WESTERN CAROLINA UNIVERSITY, Dept of Art/College of Arts & Science, 25 University Dr, 340 Stillwell Bldg Cullowhee, NC 28723-9646. Tel 828-227-7210; Fax 828-227-7505; Elec Mail wcrawford@wcu.edu; Internet Home

Page Address: www.wcu.edu/as/arts/; *Head Dept* Robert Godfrey, MFA; *Prof* James Thompson, PhD; *Prof* Jon Jicha, MFA; *Prof* James E Smythe, MFA; *Prof* Joan Byrd, MFA; *Assoc Prof* Louis Petrovich-Mwaniki, PhD; *Assoc Prof* Cathryn Griffin, MFA; *Assoc Prof* Lee P Budahl, PhD; *Asst Prof* Marya Roland, MFA; *Asst Prof* Matt Liddle, MFA
Estab 1889, dept estab 1968; pub; D & E; Scholarships; SC 51, LC 12; non-maj 1200 per sem, maj 150
Ent Req: HS dipl, SAT & C average in HS
Degrees: BFA, BA & BSE 4 yrs, MA, art honors studio
Courses: Art Appreciation, Art Education, Art History, Book Arts, Ceramics, Conceptual Art, Drawing, Graphic Design, Intermedia, Jewelry, Painting, Photography, Printmaking, Sculpture, Silversmithing, Weaving
Summer School: Dir, Dr Oakley Winters. Course—Art History, Studio Courses in Ceramics, Design, Drawing, Experimental Studio, Fibers, Metalsmithing, Painting, Sculpture

DALLAS

GASTON COLLEGE, Art Dept, 201 Hwy 321 S, Dallas, NC 28034. Tel 704-922-6343, 922-6344; *Dept Chmn* Gary Freeman
Estab 1965; pub; D & E; Scholarships; SC 22, LC 3; D 286, E 70, maj 50
Ent Req: HS dipl
Degrees: AA & AFA 2 yrs, cert 1 yr
Courses: 2-D & 3D Design, Ceramics, Commercial Art Fundamentals, Computer Graphics, Drawing, Jewelry, Painting, Photography, Pottery, Printmaking, Sculpture, Wood Design
Summer School: Dir, Gary Freeman. Enrl 20; term of 11 wks beginning June. Courses—Design, Drawing, Painting, Pottery, Sculpture

DAVIDSON

DAVIDSON COLLEGE, Art Dept, 315 N Main St, Belk Visual Arts Center Davidson, NC 28036-9404; PO Box 7117, Davidson, NC 28035-7117. Tel 704-894-2344; Fax 704-894-2691; Elec Mail brking@davidson.edu; Internet Home Page Address: www.davidson.edu; *Prof* Larry L Ligo PhD, MFA; *Prof* Nina Serebrennikov, MFA, PhD; *Chmn* C Shaw Smith Jr, MFA, PhD; *Emeritus Prof* W Herbert Jackson; *Prof* Cort Savage; *Prof* Tyler Starr; *Prof* Hagit Barkai
Estab 1837, dept estab 1950; Maintains nonprofit art gallery - Van Euery/Smith Galleries, Art Dept, PO Box 7117, Davidson, NC 28035; pvt ; D; Scholarships
Ent Req: Col Boards, HS transcripts
Degrees: BA & BS 4 yrs
Tuition: $49,723 total per yr (comprehensive fee); campus res—room & board fee included in tuition
Courses: Aesthetics, Art History, Collage, Conceptual Art, †Digital Art, Drawing, Graphic Design, History of Art & Architecture, Painting, Printmaking, Sculpture, Theatre Arts

DOBSON

SURRY COMMUNITY COLLEGE, Art Dept, 630 South Main St, Dobson, NC 27017. Tel 336-386-8121; Fax 336-386-8951; Internet Home Page Address: www.surry.edu; *Instr* William Sanders; *Dean* John Collins
Estab 1966; Varies
Ent Req: HS dipl, equivalent
Degrees: AA
Tuition: Res $27.50 per cr hr; nonres $169.75 per cr hr
Courses: Art Appreciation, Art History, Commercial Art, Design, Drawing, Handicrafts, Painting, Printmaking, Sculpture

DURHAM

DUKE UNIVERSITY, Dept of Art, Art History & Visual Studies, PO Box 90764, Durham, NC 27708-0764. Tel 919-684-2224; Fax 919-684-4398; Elec Mail deptaah@duke.edu; Internet Home Page Address: www.duke.edu/web/art; *Chair & Prof* Hans J Van Miegroet, PhD; *Assoc Prof & Dir Grad Studies* Gennifer Weisenfeld, PhD; *Assoc Prof & Dir Undergrad Studies* Sheila Dillon, PhD
Pvt; D; Scholarships; SC 36, LC 84, GC 28, Seminars 32; D 1850, maj 134
Ent Req: HS dipl & ent exam for BA
Degrees: BA, PhD in Art History, JD/MA in Law & the History of Art
Tuition: Campus res—available
Courses: Aesthetics, Architecture, Art History, Conceptual Art, Design, Drawing, Film, Graphic Design, History of Art & Architecture, Mixed Media, Museum Staff Training, Painting, Photography, Printmaking, Sculpture, Visual Studies & Culture
Summer School: Dir, Paula E Gilbert. Two 6 wk sessions offered

NORTH CAROLINA CENTRAL UNIVERSITY, Art Dept, 1801 Fayetteville St, Durham, NC 27707-3129; PO Box 19555, Durham, NC 27707-0021. Tel 919-560-6100; Fax 919-560-6391; Internet Home Page Address: www.nccu.edu; *Chmn* Dr Melvin Carver, MPD; *Prof* Achameleh Debela, PhD; *Prof* Rosie Thompson, PhD; *Prof* Isabell Chicquor, MFA; *Prof, Dir Art Museum* Kenneth Rodgers, MFA; *Prof* John Hughley, EDD; *Prof* Michelle Patterson, EDD
Estab 1910, dept estab 1944; pub; D & E; SC 30, LC 11; D 120, E 30, non-maj 1678, maj 120
Ent Req: HS dipl, SAT
Degrees: in Art Educ, Visual Communications & Studio Art 4 yrs
Courses: †Advertising Design, †Art Education, Art History, Calligraphy, Ceramics, Commercial Art, Drawing, Engineering Graphics, Graphic Arts, Handicrafts, Illustration, Jewelry, Lettering, Painting, Printmaking, Sculpture, Stained Glass, Studio Arts, Teacher Training
Children's Classes: Saturday school

ELIZABETH CITY

ELIZABETH CITY STATE UNIVERSITY, School of Arts & Humanities, Dept of Art, 1704 Weeksville Rd, 125 Fine Arts Bldg, Campus Box 912 Elizabeth City, NC 27909-7977. Tel 252-335-3345; Fax 252-335-3482; Elec Mail arjoyner@mail.ecsu.edu; Internet Home Page Address: www.ecsu.edu; *Chair* Alexis Joyner, MFA; *Prof* Drusiano Scerbo, MFA; *Assoc Prof* William Drescher, MFA; *Asst Prof* Frederick Pellum, MFA; *Asst Prof* Jeff Whelan, MFA; *Asst Prof Art Educ* Dr Phyllis Hill
Estab 1891, dept estab 1961; Maintains nonprofit University Gallery; pub; D & E; Scholarships; SC 27, LC 18, advance courses in Studio and History of Art; D 2003, E 455, non-maj 1928, maj 75
Ent Req: HS dipl, portfolio
Degrees: BA & BS, 4 yrs
Courses: Art Appreciation, Art History, Art Studio general, Ceramics, Drawing, Graphic Design, Painting, Photography, Printmaking, Sculpture, Teacher Training
Summer School: Dir, Warren Poole. Enrl 950. Courses—Same as regular session

FAYETTEVILLE

FAYETTEVILLE STATE UNIVERSITY, Performing & Fine Arts, 1200 Murchison Rd, Fayetteville, NC 28301-4298. Tel 910-672-1457, 672-1571; Fax 910-672-1572; *Head Div of Fine Arts & Humanities* Dr Robert G Owens
Estab 1877; pub; D & E; D 60, E 20
Ent Req: HS dipl, ent exam
Degrees: BA & BFA 4 yr
Courses: Advertising Design, Aesthetics, Art Education, Ceramics, Drawing, Graphic Arts, Handicrafts, History of Art & Architecture, Leather Craft, Lettering, Painting, Photography, Sculpture, Weaving
Summer School: Dir, Dr Beeman C Patterson. Courses—Art in Childhood Education, Arts & Crafts, Drawing, Photography, Survey of Art

METHODIST COLLEGE, Art Dept, 5400 Ramsey St, Fayetteville, NC 28311-1498. Tel 910-630-7107; Fax 910-630-2123; Internet Home Page Address: www.methodist.edu/; *Chmn* Silvana Foti, MFA; *Prof* Peggy S Hinson
Estab 1960; FT 2, PT 1; den; D & E; Scholarships; SC 6, LC 4; D 650, maj 22
Ent Req: HS dipl, SAT
Degrees: BA & BS 4 yrs
Courses: Art Education, Art History, Design, Drawing, Painting, Papermaking, Photography, Printmaking, Sculpture
Summer School: 3 terms, 3 wk early session, 5 wk main session, 6 wk directed study. Courses—Art Appreciation, Painting, Sculpture, others as needed

GOLDSBORO

THE ARTS COUNCIL OF WAYNE COUNTY, (Goldsboro Art Center) 102 N John St, Goldsboro, NC 27530-3633. Tel 919-736-3300; Fax 919-736-3335; Elec Mail artscouncil@artsinwayne.org; Internet Home Page Address: www.artsinwayne.org; *Exec Dir* Sarah Merritt; *Gallery Dir* Becca Scott Reynolds; *Admin Asst* Jo Fleischmann
Estab 1963; Maintains nonprofit art gallery; pub; D & E; Scholarships; SC 25; D 150, E 60, others 210
Courses: Drawing, Painting, Pottery, Spinning
Adult Hobby Classes: Enrl 75; tuition $19 for 11 wk term. Courses—Calligraphy, Oil Painting, Pottery, Watercolors

WAYNE COMMUNITY COLLEGE, Liberal Arts Dept, Caller Box 8002, Goldsboro, NC 27533. Tel 919-735-5151; Fax 919-736-3204; Internet Home Page Address: www.wayne.cc.nc.us; *Instr* Patricia Turlington; *Chmn* Ann Spicer
Estab 1957; 4 FT, PT varies
Degrees: AA, AS, AAS & AFA 2 yr
Tuition: Res $27.50 per cr hour; nonres $159.75 per cr hr
Courses: Art Appreciation, Art History, Design, Drawing
Adult Hobby Classes: Courses offered

GREENSBORO

GREENSBORO COLLEGE, Dept of Art, Division of Fine Arts, 815 W Market St, Greensboro, NC 27401-1875. Tel 336-272-7102, Ext 301; Fax 336-271-6634; Internet Home Page Address: www.gborocollege.edu; *Assoc Prof* Ray Martin, MFA; *Prof* Robert Kowski, MFA; *Instr* James V Langer; *Instr* Ginger Williamson
Estab 1838; Maintain nonprofit art gallery; Irene Cullis Gallery, Greensboro Col; pvt den; D & E, weekends; Scholarships; SC 15, LC 4; D 200, non-maj 50, maj 20
Ent Req: HS dipl
Degrees: BA 4 yrs
Courses: Art Appreciation, †Art Education, Art History, Ceramics, Design, Drawing, †Painting, Photography, Printmaking, †Sculpture, Stage Design, †Theatre Arts
Adult Hobby Classes: Enrl 40; tuition $225 per cr hr. Courses—Art History
Summer School: Dir, Dr John Drayer. Tuition $138 per cr hr for two 5 wk sessions. Courses—Art Appreciation, Art History

GUILFORD COLLEGE, Art Dept, 5800 W Friendly Ave, Greensboro, NC 27410-4173. Tel 336-316-2000; Fax 336-316-2299; Elec Mail glorio@guilford.edu; Internet Home Page Address: www.guilford.edu; *Prof of Art* David Newton; *Prof of Art* Roy Nydorf; *Prof of Art, Dept Chair* Adele Wayman
Estab 1837, dept estab 1970; Maintain nonprofit art gallery, Hege Library Art Gallery; private; D & E; Scholarships; studio, lectrs; 40 maj
Ent Req: HS dipl, entrance examination
Degrees: BA 4 yr, BFA 4 yr
Courses: Art History, Ceramics, Design, Drawing, History of Art & Architecture, Painting, Photography, Printmaking, Sculpture

NORTH CAROLINA AGRICULTURAL & TECHNICAL STATE UNIVERSITY, Visual Arts Dept, 312 N Dudley St, Greensboro, NC 27411-0001. Tel 336-334-7993; *Chmn* Stephanie Santmyers
Estab 1930; FT 4, PT 1; pub; SC 29, LC 7; maj 50
Courses: 2-D Design, 3-D Design, Advertising Design, Aesthetics, Art Appreciation, †Art Design, †Art Education, Art History, Ceramics, Crafts, Design, Drawing, Graphic Arts, Graphic Design, Handicrafts, Illustration, †Painting, Printmaking, Sculpture, Teacher Training, Textile Design
Summer School: Dir, Dr Ronald Smith. Courses—Crafts, Public School Art, Art History, Art Appreciation

UNIVERSITY OF NORTH CAROLINA AT GREENSBORO, Art Dept, 527 Highland Ave, Greensboro, NC 27412-5015; PO Box 26170, Greensboro, NC 27402-6170. Tel 336-334-5248; Fax 336-334-5270; Elec Mail e_kane@uncg.edu; Internet Home Page Address: www.uncg.edu/art; *Prof* Michael Ananian; *Prof* George Dimock; *Prof* Andrew Dunnill; *Prof* Patricia Wasserboehr; *Prof* Billy Lee; *Prof* John Maggio; *Prof* Carl Goldstein; *Lectr* Richard Gantt; *Prof* Amy Lixi Purcell; *Prof* Mariam Stephan; *Prof* Heather Holian; *Prof* Nikki Blair; *Prof* Barbara Campbell; *Lectr* Christopher Cassidy; *Lectr* Bryan Ellis; *Prof* Sarah Martin; *Lectr* Leah Sobsey; *Lectr* Susanne Thomas; *Lectr* Christopher Thomas; *Prof* Lee Walton; *Prof* Eun-Hee Lim; *Prof* Elizabeth Perrill; *Prof* Jennifer Meanley; *Head* Lawrence Jenkens; *Prof* Sheryl Oring; *Lectr* Corey Dzenko; *Prof* Sunny Spillane
Dept estab 1935; maintains nonprofit gallery, The Gallery at the Gatewood, UNCG, 527 Highland Ave, Greensboro, NC 27412; art library, UNCG Visual Resources Library, 105 The Weatherspoon Art Museum, PO Box 26170, Greensboro, NC 27402-6170. Campus shop where art supplies may be purchased; FT 26; pub; D&E; Scholarships, Fellowships; SC 78, LC 43, GC 46, other 15; D 450, grad 13
Ent Req: HS grad, ent exam
Degrees: BA, BFA & MFA 2 yrs
Tuition: In-state undergrad $3,779 per yr; out-of-state $17,577 per yr
Courses: †Art Education, †Art History, Ceramics, Conceptual Art, †Design, Digital Design, Drawing, Graphic Design, Mixed Media, Museum Studies, †Painting, Photography, Printmaking, †Sculpture, Teacher Training, Video
Summer School: Head of dept. Lawrence Jenkens. Enrl 351; beginning May - June and July - Aug. Courses—Art Educ, Art History, Design, Drawing, Etching, Painting, Photography, Sculpture

GREENVILLE

EAST CAROLINA UNIVERSITY, School of Art & Design, 2000 Leo Jenkins Fine Arts Ctr, Mail Stop 502 Greenville, NC 27858-2502. Tel 252-328-6665; Fax 252-328-6441; Internet Home Page Address: www.ecu.edu; *Dir* Michael H Drought; *Asst Dir* Scott Eagle; *Asst Dir* Dr Kate LaMere
Estab 1907; Maintain nonprofit gallery; Wellington B Gray Art Gallery, Greenville SC; on-campus shop sells art supplies; FT 49, PT 11; pub; D&E; Scholarships, Fellowships; SC 215, LC 25, GC 85; non-maj 1,400, maj 500, grad 50
Activities: Schols offered
Ent Req: HS dipl, 20 units, Col Board Exam
Degrees: BA, BFA, MFA, MAEd
Tuition: Campus res—available
Courses: Animation, Art Appreciation, †Art Education, †Art History, †Ceramics, Color & Design, Drawing, †Fabric Design, Goldsmithing, Graphic Design, History of Art & Architecture, †Illustration, Independent Study, Interactive Design, Interdisciplinary 3-D Design, †Metal Design, †Painting, †Photography, †Printmaking, †Sculpture, Silversmithing, †Teacher Training, †Textile Design, Video, †Weaving, †Wood Design, Work Experience in the Visual Arts & Design
Children's Classes: Children's afterschool art classes
Summer School: Dir, Michael H Drought. Enrl 200; two 5 wk terms. Courses—Foundation & Survey

HICKORY

LENOIR RHYNE COLLEGE, Dept of Art, PO Box 7471, Visual Arts Ctr Hickory, NC 28603-7471. Tel 828-328-1741; Fax 828-328-7338; Internet Home Page Address: www.lrc.edu; *Chmn Dept* Robert Winter PhD; *Asst Prof* Douglas Burton, MA; *Instr* Tom Perryman, MA
Estab 1892, dept estab 1976; den; D & E; Scholarships; SC 5; D 1200, E 350
Ent Req: HS dipl
Degrees: AB & BS 4 yrs
Courses: Aesthetics, Art Appreciation, Art Education, Art History, Ceramics, Drawing, Painting, Photography, Printmaking, Sculpture
Adult Hobby Classes: Courses on Tues & Thurs evenings
Children's Classes: Summer courses for gifted & talented
Summer School: Dir, Dr James Lichtenstein. Enrl 900; tuition $175 per sem hr for 2-5 wk terms beginning June. Courses—Art Appreciation, Art Education, Ceramics, Painting

HIGH POINT

HIGH POINT UNIVERSITY, Fine Arts Dept, 932 Montlieu Ave, University Sta High Point, NC 27260; 833 Montlieu Ave, Campus Box 25 High Point, NC 27262-4221. Tel 336-841-9282; Fax 336-841-5123; Elec Mail awheless@highpoint.edu; *Asst Prof* Alexa Schlimmer; *Chmn* Andrea Wheless
Estab 1924, dept estab 1956; pvt den; D & E; Scholarships; SC 16, LC 6; non-maj 950, maj 10
Ent Req: HS dipl, SAT
Degrees: AB & BS 4 yrs
Courses: Advertising Design, Aesthetics, †Art Education, Art History, Ceramics, Crafts, Drawing, History of Art & Architecture, Interior Design, Painting, Printmaking, Sculpture, Stage Design, Teacher Training, †Theatre Arts

Summer School: Enrl 200; two 5 wk sessions. Courses—Art Education, Crafts, Design, Interior Design

JAMESTOWN

GUILFORD TECHNICAL COMMUNITY COLLEGE, Commercial Art Dept, PO Box 309, Jamestown, NC 27282-0309. Tel 336-454-1126, Ext 2230; Fax 336-819-2022; Elec Mail reidm@gtcc.cc.nc.us; Internet Home Page Address: www.technet.gtcc.cc.nc.us/; *Instr* Awilda Feliciano, BFA; *Instr* Frederick N Jones, MFA; *Instr* Scott Burnette, BA; *Head* Margaret Reid, MFA; *Instr* Michael Swing; *Instr* Alex Forsyth; *Instr* Julie Evans
Estab 1964; pub; D & E; Scholarships; SC 20, LC 4; D 130, E 60
Ent Req: HS dipl, English & math placement
Degrees: AAS 2 yrs
Courses: †Advertising Design, Art History, Commercial Art, Computer Graphics, Drafting, Drawing, Graphic Arts, Illustration, Lettering, Photography
Adult Hobby Classes: Courses—Variety of subjects
Summer School: 9 wk term. Courses—Various

KINSTON

LENOIR COMMUNITY COLLEGE, Dept of Visual Art, PO Box 188, Kinston, NC 28502-0188. Tel 252-527-6223, Ext 923; *Prof* Henry Stindt
Pub; D&E
Degrees: AA, AS & AFA
Tuition: Res—$27.50 per cr hr; nonres—$169.75 per cr hr
Courses: Ceramics, Commercial Art, Design, Drawing, Illustration, Introduction to Art, Painting, Photography, Printmaking
Summer School: Dir, Gerald A Elliott. Enrl 32; tuition $51 for 12 cr hrs. Courses—Lecture & Studio Art

LAURINBURG

SAINT ANDREWS PRESBYTERIAN COLLEGE, Art Program, 1700 Dogwood Mile, Laurinburg, NC 28352. Tel 910-277-5240, Ext 5264, 277-5264; Fax 910-277-5020; Elec Mail mcdavids@sapc.edu; Internet Home Page Address: www.sapc.edu/art; *Chmn Art Dept & Instr* Stephanie McDavid
Estab 1960; FT 2; den; D; Scholarships; SC 14, LC 2; D 852, maj 20 - 30
Ent Req: HS dipl, SAT, 2.6 grade point average, 12 acad units
Degrees: BA, MS & BM 4 yrs or 32 courses
Courses: Art Appreciation, Art Education, Art History, Computer Graphics, Design, Drawing, Painting, Photography, Printmaking, Sculpture, Video
Summer School: Studio courses offered

ST. ANDREWS PRESBYTERIAN COLLEGE, Art Gallery, 1700 Dogwood Mile, Laurinburg, NC 28352. Tel 910-277-5264; Fax 910-277-5020
Open Mon - Fri 9 AM - 4:30 PM; No admis fee
Collections: Paintings; photographs; sculpture

LEXINGTON

DAVIDSON COUNTY COMMUNITY COLLEGE, Humanities Div, PO Box 1287, 2997 DCCC Rd Lexington, NC 27293-1287. Tel 336-249-8186, Ext 253 or 314; Fax 336-249-0379; Internet Home Page Address: www.davidson.cc.nc.us/; Estab 1963, dept estab 1966; FT 2, PT 3; pub; D & E; Scholarships; SC 14, LC 4; D 100, E 30, non-maj 195, maj 30
Ent Req: HS dipl
Degrees: AFA, AS & AA 2 yrs
Courses: Art Education, Art History, Design, Drafting, Handicrafts, Independent Studio, Painting, Photography, Printmaking, Sculpture
Adult Hobby Classes: Courses—Variety taught through continuing educ

MARS HILL

MARS HILL COLLEGE, Art Dept, 100 Athletic St, Mars Hill, NC 28754-9134; PO Box 370, Mars Hill, NC 28754-0370. Tel 828-689-1396; Elec Mail rcary@mhc.edu; Internet Home Page Address: www.mhc.edu; *Chmn* Scott Lowley
Estab 1856, dept estab 1932; pvt and den; D & E; Scholarships; SC 9, LC 6; D 120, non-maj 100, maj 20
Ent Req: HS dipl, ent exam
Degrees: BA 4 yrs
Courses: †Advertising Design, Aesthetics, †Art Education, †Art History, Ceramics, †Graphic Arts, †Painting, Photography, †Printmaking, Sculpture, †Teacher Training, †Theatre Arts
Summer School: Enrl 450; tuition $65 per cr hr for 5 wk term. Courses—Introduction to the Arts & Photography

MISENHEIMER

PFEIFFER UNIVERSITY, Art Program, PO Box 960, Misenheimer, NC 28109-0960. Tel 704-463-1360, Ext 2667; Fax 704-463-1363; Internet Home Page Address: www.pfeiffer.edu/; *Dir* James Haymaker
Estab 1965; FT 1; den; D; Scholarships; SC 4, LC 4; D 100
Ent Req: HS dipl
Degrees: BA
Courses: Art Education, Art History, Ceramics, Drawing, Painting, Sculpture

MOUNT OLIVE

MOUNT OLIVE COLLEGE, Dept of Art, 634 Henderson St, Mount Olive, NC 28365-1263. Tel 919-658-2502, 658-7181; Fax 919-658-7180; *Chmn* Larry Lean

Estab 1951; den; D & E; Scholarships; SC 5, LC 3
Degrees: BA & BS
Courses: American Art, Art Appreciation, Art History, Design, Drawing, Painting
Summer School: Courses—Art Appreciation

MURFREESBORO

CHOWAN COLLEGE, Division of Art, 200 Jones Dr, Murfreesboro, NC 27855. Tel 252-398-6500, Ext 267; Fax 252-398-6500; Internet Home Page Address: www.chowan.edu; *Head Div* Haig David-West
Estab 1848, dept estab 1970; den; Scholarships; SC 18, LC 3; maj 64
Ent Req: HS dipl, SAT recommended
Degrees: AA 2 yrs
Courses: Advertising Design, Art Appreciation, Art Education, Art History, Ceramics, Commercial Art, Drawing, Figure Drawing, Illustration, Lettering, Painting
Summer School: Dir, Doug Eubank. Courses—Art Appreciation, Ceramics, Drawing, Painting

PEMBROKE

UNIVERSITY OF NORTH CAROLINA AT PEMBROKE, Art Dept, PO Box 1510, Pembroke, NC 28372-1510. Tel 910-521-6216; Fax 910-521-6639; Elec Mail art@uncp.edu; Internet Home Page Address: www.uncp.edu; *Chair* Dr Richard Gay; *Prof* Dr John Antoine Labadie; *Assoc Prof & Dir Grad Art Educ* Dr Ann Horton-Lopez; *Prof & Coordr Undergrad Art Educ* Dr Tulla Lightfoot; *Asst Prof* Brandon Sanderson; *Asst Prof & Gallery Dir* Carla Rokes; *Asst Prof* Adam Walls; *Asst Prof* David Hicks; *Asst Prof* Dr Nancy Palm; *Assoc Prof* Joseph Begnaud
Estab 1887; Maintains nonprofit art galleries: Locklear Hall Art Gallery & A D Gallery; art supplies sold on campus store; FT 10, PT 3; pub; D & E; Scholarships; SC 46, LC 25, GC 7; non-maj 6,130, maj 115
Ent Req: CEEB scores, HS record, scholastic standing in HS grad class
Degrees: BA 4 yrs, MA(Art Ed) 2 yrs, MAT(Art Ed)
Courses: Art Appreciation, †Art Education, Art History, Ceramics, Computer Graphics, Design, Drawing, History of Art & Architecture, Mixed Media, Painting, Printmaking, Sculpture, Teacher Training
Summer School: Variety of courses

PENLAND

PENLAND SCHOOL OF CRAFTS, Penland Rd, Penland, NC 28765-8000; PO Box 37, Penland, NC 28765-0037. Tel 828-765-2359; Fax 828-765-7389; Internet Home Page Address: www.penland.org
Estab 1929; Maintain nonprofit art gallery; Penland Gallery; Nonprofit org; D (summer, spring & fall classes); Scholarships; SC 112; D approx 1,200
Ent Req: age 19 and above, special fall and spring sessions require portfolio and resume
Degrees: none granted but cr may be obtained through agreement with East Tennessee State Univ & Western Carolina Univ
Courses: Basketry, Blacksmithing, Book Arts, Ceramics, †Drawing, Fibers, Glass, Jewelry, Metalsmithing, †Painting, Papermaking, Photography, Printmaking, Sculpture, †Surface Design, †Textiles, Weaving, Woodworking
Summer School: Dir, Jean McLaughlin. Tuition varies for 1, 2 & 2-1/2 wk courses between June & Sept; 8 wk concentrations-spring & fall.
Courses—Basketry, Book Arts, Clay, Drawing, Fibers, Glass, Iron, Metal, Paper, Photography, Printmaking, Sculpture, Surface Design, Wood

RALEIGH

MEREDITH COLLEGE, Art Dept, 3800 Hillsborough St, Gaddy-Hamrick Art Ctr Raleigh, NC 27607-5237. Tel 919-760-8332; Fax 919-760-2347; *Chmn* Rebecca Bailey
Estab 1898; den; W; D & E; Scholarships; SC 15, LC 5; D 490, E 130, maj 85, others 30
Ent Req: HS dipl
Degrees: AB 4 yrs
Courses: Advertising Design, Art Appreciation, Art Education, Art History, Calligraphy, Ceramics, Computer Graphics, Costume Design & Construction, Design, Drawing, Graphic Design, Handicrafts
Adult Hobby Classes: Courses—Art History, Ceramics, Drawing, Fibers, Graphic Design, Painting, Photography, Sculpture
Summer School: Dir, John Hiott. Courses—vary

NORTH CAROLINA STATE UNIVERSITY AT RALEIGH, School of Design, PO Box 7701, Raleigh, NC 27695-7701. Tel 919-515-8310, 515-8317 (School Design); Fax 919-515-7330; Internet Home Page Address: www.ncsu.edu/; *Head Design & Technology Dept* Haig Khachatoorian; *Prof* Percy Hooper; *Assoc Prof* Bryan Lafitte; *Prof* Vincent M Foote; *Prof* Glen Lewis; *Dept Secy, Grad Prog Asst* Cheryl Eatmon
Estab 1948; FT 38, PT 5; pub; Architecture 251, Art & Design 60, Graphic Design 118, Industrial Design 135, Landscape Architecture 94
Ent Req: col board, ent exam
Degrees: BEnv(Design in Architecture, Design, Graphic & Industrial Design, Landscape Architecture, March), MGraphic Design, MLandscape Arch, 4-6 yrs
Courses: Architecture, Design, Graphic Design, Industrial Design, Landscape Architecture, Product Design, Visual Design
Summer School: Courses—Undergrad: Architecture, Graphic Design, Industrial Design, Landscape Architecture

PEACE COLLEGE, Art Dept, 15 E Peace St, Raleigh, NC 27604-1194. Tel 919-508-2000; Fax 919-508-2326; Internet Home Page Address: www.peace.edu; *Head Dept* Carolyn Parker

Estab 1857; pvt; D & E; SC 8, LC 2; D 600
Ent Req: HS dipl, SAT
Degrees: AA & AFA 2 yrs & 4 yrs
Courses: †Liberal Arts

ROCKY MOUNT

NORTH CAROLINA WESLEYAN COLLEGE, Dept of Visual & Performing Arts, 3400 N Wesleyan Blvd, Rocky Mount, NC 27804-9906. Tel 252-985-5100, 985-5167 (Dept Visual & Art); Fax 252-977-3701; Internet Home Page Address: www.ncwc.edu; *Instr* Everett Mayo Adelman; *Instr* Michele A Cruz; *Dir Theater Dept* David Blakely
Founded 1956; opened 1960; Scholarships
Ent Req: HS dipl
Degrees: BA
Tuition: Res—$9,758 per year
Courses: Advertising Design, Architecture, Art Appreciation, Art Education, Visual Communication
Adult Hobby Classes: Enrl 1055; tuition $125 per sem hr. Courses—Art Appreciation, American Architecture

STATESVILLE

MITCHELL COMMUNITY COLLEGE, Visual Art Dept, 500 W Broad St, Statesville, NC 28677-5293. Tel 704-878-3200; Internet Home Page Address: www.mitchell.cc.nc.us; *Chmn* Donald Everett Moore, MA; *Instr* James Messer
Estab 1852, dept estab 1974; FT 2, PT 1; pub; D & E; Scholarships; SC 12-15, LC 5; D 85, E 40, non-maj 100, maj 25
Ent Req: HS dipl, HS transcripts, placement test
Degrees: AA & AFA 2 yrs
Courses: Art History, †Ceramics, Color Theory, Drawing, Intermedia, †Painting, Printmaking, †Sculpture
Adult Hobby Classes: Enrl 100; tuition $130 per 10 wks. Courses—Continuing education courses in art & crafts available

SYLVA

SOUTHWESTERN COMMUNITY COLLEGE, Advertising & Graphic Design, 447 College Dr, Sylva, NC 28779-8581. Tel 828-586-4091, Ext 233; Fax 828-586-3129; Internet Home Page Address: www.southwest.cc.nc.us/; *Instr* Bob Clark, MS; *Instr* Bob Keeling, BFA; *Photog Instr* Matthew Turlington
Estab 1964, dept estab 1967; Maintains a nonprofit art gallery; FT 2, PT 2; pub; D; Scholarships; SC 19, LC 14; D 36, maj 50
Ent Req: HS dipl
Degrees: AAS
Courses: Advertising Design, †Airbrush, Art Appreciation, Computer Graphics, Conceptual Art, Design, Drafting, Drawing, Graphic Arts, Graphic Design, Illustration, †Painting, †Penstriping, Photography, Screenprinting, Technical Illustration, Typography
Adult Hobby Classes: Enrl 30, tuition $35 per class hr

WHITEVILLE

SOUTHEASTERN COMMUNITY COLLEGE, Dept of Art, PO Box 151, Whiteville, NC 28472-0151. Tel 910-642-7141, Ext 237; Fax 910-642-5658; Internet Home Page Address: www.sccnc.edu; *Instr, Chair* September Krueger
Estab 1965; FT 1 PT 1; pub; D & E; SC 18, LC 7
Ent Req: HS dipl or 18 yrs old
Degrees: AFA 2 yrs
Tuition: Res—$27.50 per cr hour; non-res—$169.75
Courses: Art History, Ceramics, Drawing, Painting, Pottery, Printmaking, Sculpture
Adult Hobby Classes: Tuition res—$25 per course
Summer School: Dir, Christa Balogh

WILKESBORO

WILKES COMMUNITY COLLEGE, Arts & Science Division, PO Box 120, Wilkesboro, NC 28697-0120. Tel 336-838-6100; Fax 336-838-6277; Internet Home Page Address: www.wilkes.cc.mc.us; *Instr* Dewey Mayes; *Dir* Blair Hancock
Estab 1965, dept estab 1967; pub; D & E; Scholarships; SC 2, LC 2; D 1600, E 800
Ent Req: HS dipl
Degrees: AA, AFA
Courses: Art History, Art Travel Courses, Costume Design & Construction, Drafting, Drawing, Painting, Photography, Sculpture, Theatre Arts
Summer School: Dir, Bud Mayes

WILMINGTON

UNIVERSITY OF NORTH CAROLINA AT WILMINGTON, Dept of Fine Arts - Division of Art, 601 S College Rd, Wilmington, NC 28403-3201. Tel 910-962-3415 (Dept of Art); *Prof* Ann Conner, MFA; *Prof* Donald Furst, MFA; *Prof, Chmn* Kemille Moore, PhD
Estab 1789, dept estab 1952; pub; D & E
Ent Req: HS dipl, ent exam
Degrees: BCA 4 yrs
Courses: Art Appreciation, Art History, Ceramics, Design, Drawing, Painting, Printmaking, Sculpture
Adult Hobby Classes: Courses—Drawing, Painting

Summer School: Dir, David Miller. Two 5 wk sessions. Courses—Varied

WILSON

BARTON COLLEGE, Art & Design Dept, PO Box 5000, Wilson, NC 27893-7000. Tel 252-399-6477; Fax 252-399-6572; Elec Mail sfecho@barton.edu; Internet Home Page Address: www.barton.edu; *Asst Prof* Gerard Lange, MFA; *Chmn* Susan C Fecho, MFA; *Assoc Prof* Mark Gordon, MFA; *Assoc Prof* Ben Bridgers
Estab 1903, dept estab 1950; Maintains a nonprofit art gallery, Barton Art Galleries, PO Box 5000, 704A College St, Wilson NC 27893; art library; on-campus shop where art supplies may be purchased; Pvt; D, E, weekend; Scholarships; SC 15, LC 8; D 100, non-maj 70, maj 50, others 15 (PT)
Ent Req: HS dipl, ent exam
Degrees: BS, BA & BFA 4 yrs
Tuition: Undergrad—$17,500 per yr; $2173 campus res—room & board $3785 per yr
Courses: †Art Appreciation, †Art Education, †Art History, †Ceramics, †Collage, †Commercial Art, †Design, †Drawing, Graphic Arts, †Graphic Design, †Illustration, †Mixed Media, Museum Staff Training, †Painting, †Photography, †Printmaking, †Sculpture, †Teacher Training, †Video, †Visual Communication, †Visual Design

WINGATE

WINGATE UNIVERSITY, Art Department, PO Box 3015, Wingate, NC 28174-0159. Tel 704-233-8000; WATS 800-755-5550; *Chmn Div* Louise Napier
Estab 1896, dept estab 1958; den; D & E; Scholarships; D & E 1500
Ent Req: HS grad
Degrees: BA(Art), BA(Art Education) 4 yrs
Courses: 3-D Design, Art Appreciation, Art History, Art Methods, Ceramics, Composition, Drawing, Film, Gallery Tours, Metalsmithing, Painting, Photography, Printmaking, Sculpture, Sketching
Summer School: Pres, Dr Jerry McGee. Term of 4 wks beginning first wk in June. Courses—all regular class work available if demand warrants

WINSTON SALEM

SALEM ACADEMY & COLLEGE, Art Dept, 601 S Church St, Winston Salem, NC 27101-5376. Tel 336-721-2600, 721-2683; Fax 336-721-2683; *Asst Prof* Penny Griffin; *Prof* John Hutton; *Assoc Prof* Kimberly Varnadoe
Non-profit art gallery: Salem Fine Arts Center Gallery; Den, W; D & E; Scholarships; D 642, maj 44
Ent Req: HS Dipl
Degrees: BA 4 yrs
Courses: Art History, Design, Drawing, Graphic Design, Painting, Printmaking, Sculpture

WINSTON-SALEM

SAWTOOTH CENTER FOR VISUAL ART, 251 N Spruce St, Winston-Salem, NC 27101-2735. Tel 336-723-7395; Fax 336-773-0132; Elec Mail info@sawtooth.org; Internet Home Page Address: sawtooth.org; *Exec Dir* Sherri Nielson; *Youth Coordr* Katie Longinotti; *Registrar* Julie Morgan
Estab 1945 as Community School of Craft & Art; PT 75; D, E & weekends; Scholarships; SC
Degrees: non-degree
Tuition: $25-$250 per 10 wk course
Courses: Basketry, Book Arts, Calligraphy, Ceramics, Computer Graphics, Drawing, Jewelry, Lampwork, Mixed Media, Painting, Papermaking, Photography, Printmaking, Silversmithing, Stained Glass, Teacher Training, Textile Design, Weaving, Wood Carving
Adult Hobby Classes: Enrl 2000; tuition $100-$250 for 5-10 wk term. Courses—All visual arts & craft mediums
Children's Classes: Enrl 1000; tuition $60-$100 for 5 wks. Courses—35 different media oriented courses
Summer School: Enrl 600; tuition $250 for 4 wks

WAKE FOREST UNIVERSITY, Dept of Art, 1834 Wake Forest Rd, Winston-Salem, NC 27106; Box 7232, Art Dept, Reynolda Sta Winston Salem, NC 27109. Tel 336-758-5310; Fax 336-758-6014; Internet Home Page Address: www.wfu.edu/art; *Prof* Page Laughlin; *Prof* Harry B Titus Jr; *Prof* Bernadine Barnes; *Prof* David Finn; *Assoc Prof* David Faber; *Assoc Prof* John Pickel; *Instr* Alix Hitchcock; *Charlotte C Weber Prof Art* David M Lubin; *Asst Prof* John J Curley; *Asst Prof* Morna O'Neill; *Gallery Dir* Paul Bright; *Asst Prof* Joel Tanber
Estab 1834, dept estab 1968; Maintains nonprofit Charlotte & Phillip Hanes Art Gallery & art libr on campus; art supplies sold at on-campus store; Pvt; D; Scholarships; SC 14, LC 28
Ent Req: HS dipl, SAT
Degrees: BA 4 yrs
Courses: Art History, Collage (Summer I), Drawing, Film, Painting, Photography, Printmaking, Restoration & Conservation, Sculpture, †Studio Art
Summer School: Assoc Dean & Dean of Summer Session Toby Hale. Enrl 25; tuition $235 per cr. Courses—Independent Study, Intro to Visual Arts, Practicum, Printmaking Workshop

WINSTON-SALEM STATE UNIVERSITY, Art Dept, Fine Arts Bldg, FA 112, Winston-Salem, NC 27110. Tel 336-750-2520; Fax 336-750-2522; Elec Mail legettel@wssu.adp.wssu.edu; Internet Home Page Address: www.wssu.edu/academic/arts-sci/finearts.usp; *Prof* Arcenia Davis; *Asst Prof* Marvette Aldrich; *Interim Chmn* Lee David Legette

Estab, 1892, dept estab 1970; pub; D & E; SC 10, LC 7; D 65, nonmaj 275, maj 65
Ent Req: HS Dipl
Degrees: BA 4 yr
Courses: Art Education, Art History, Drawing, Graphic Arts, Painting, Sculpture
Summer School: Courses offered

NORTH DAKOTA

BISMARCK

BISMARCK STATE COLLEGE, Fine Arts Dept, 1500 Edwards Ave, Bismarck, ND 58501-1299. Tel 701-224-5471; Internet Home Page Address: www.bsc.edu; *Assoc Prof* Richard Sammons; *Instr* Tom Porter; *Instr* Marietta Turner; *Instr* Michelle Lindblom; *Instr* Dan Rogers; *Instr* Carol Cashman; *Instr* Barbara Cichy; *Chmn* Jonelle Masters
Estab 1961; FT 3 PT 9; pub; D & E
Degrees: AA 2 yrs
Tuition: Res—undergrad $904.32 per sem; nonres—undergrad $2200.08 per sem
Courses: Art Appreciation, Ceramics, Design, Drawing, Elementary Art, Gallery Management, Handicrafts, Introduction to Understanding Art, Jewelry, Lettering, Painting, Photography, Printmaking, Sculpture
—The Else Forde Gallery, 1500 Edwards Ave, Schafer Hall Bismarck, ND 58501-1276. Tel 701-224-5601; Elec Mail barbara.jirges@bsc.nodak.edu; Internet Home Page Address: www.ndga.org/galleries/bscg.html; *Dir* Barbara Jirges
Open Mon - Thurs 7 AM - 9 PM, Fri 7 AM - 4 PM, Sun 6 PM - 9 PM
Collections: Student artwork; works by local, regional & national artists

DICKINSON

DICKINSON STATE UNIVERSITY, Dept of Art, 291 Campus Dr, Div of Fine Arts and Humanities Dickinson, ND 58601-4853. Tel 701-483-2312; Tel 701-483-2060; Elec Mail ronald.gingerich@dickinsonstate.edu; *Chmn* Ron Gingerich, MFA; *Gallery Dir & Assoc Prof Art* Carol Eacret-Simmons, MFA; *Assoc Prof* Marilyn Lee, MFA
Estab 1918, dept estab 1959; Maintains nonprofit art gallery, Dickinson State Univ Art Gallery (same address); art supplies may be purchased on-campus; pub; D & E; Scholarships; SC 36, LC 8; D approx 150 per quarter, non-maj 130, maj 20
Ent Req: HS dipl, out-of-state, ACT, minimum score 18 or upper-half of class
Degrees: BA, BS and BCS 4 yr
Courses: †Art Education, Art History, †Ceramics, Color, Costume Design & Construction, Display, Drawing, Graphic Arts, †Graphic Arts Minor, Graphic Design, Handicrafts, Intermedia, Jewelry, Lettering, Painting, Photography, Printmaking, Sculpture, Stage Design, Teacher Training, Theatre Arts
Adult Hobby Classes: Enrl varies; courses - Photography; watercolor; ceramics
Children's Classes: Varies

FARGO

NORTH DAKOTA STATE UNIVERSITY, Division of Fine Arts, PO Box 6050, Dept 2330 Fargo, ND 58108-6050. Tel 701-231-8011; Internet Home Page Address: www.ndsu.edu; *Asst Prof* Kimble Bromley, MFA; *Lectr* David Swenson, MFA; *Lectr* Jaime Penuel, BFA; *Lectr* Kent Kapplinger, BFA
Estab 1889, dept estab 1964; Maintain Memorial Union Art Gallery at the University; FT 5; pub; D & E; Scholarships; SC 21; D 225, E 60, non-maj 250, maj 30
Ent Req: HS dipl
Degrees: BA & BS 4 yr
Courses: Architecture, Art Appreciation, Art History, Ceramics, Design, Drafting, Drawing, Fashion Arts, History of Art & Architecture, Interior Design, Landscape Architecture, Painting, Photography, Printmaking, Sculpture, Textile Design, Theatre Arts

GRAND FORKS

UNIVERSITY OF NORTH DAKOTA, Art Department, 3350 Campus Rd, Stop 7099 Grand Forks, ND 58202-7099. Tel 701-777-2257; Fax 701-777-2903; Elec Mail patrick_luber@und.nodak.edu; Internet Home Page Address: www.und.edu/dept/arts2000/; *Chmn* Patrick Luber
Estab 1883; D FT 11; pub; Scholarships; SC 30, LC 4, GC 14; maj 90, others 1000
Degrees: BFA, BA, BSEd, MFA
Tuition: Campus res—available
Courses: Aesthetics, Art Appreciation, †Art Education, Art History, †Ceramics, Design, †Digital Media, Drawing, †Fibers, Goldsmithing, History of Art & Architecture, †Jewelry, Lettering, †Metalsmithing, †Painting, †Photography, †Printmaking, †Sculpture, Silversmithing, †Teacher Training, †Weaving
Adult Hobby Classes: Enrl 800-1000; tuition $2428 per yr. Courses—Various studio art & art history
Summer School: Dir, J McElroy-Edwards. Enrl 100; tuition one half cash of regular sem. Courses—Varies every summer

JAMESTOWN

JAMESTOWN COLLEGE, Art Dept, PO Box 1559, Jamestown, ND 58402-1559. Tel 701-252-3467; Fax 701-253-4318; Internet Home Page Address: www.jc.edu; *Chmn* Sharon Cox

Maintain nonprofit art gallery, Reiland Fine Art Center 6003 College Lane c/o Sharon Cox, Dir Jamestown College, ND 58405; Raugust Library; art supplies available on-campus; FT 21; Pvt, den; D & E; Scholarships; SC 13, LC 4; 146, maj 14
Ent Req: HS dipl
Degrees: BA and BS 4 yr, directed study and individual study in advanced studio areas, private studios
Courses: †2-D Design; Art Business; Fine Arts, Advertising Design, Art Appreciation, Art Education, Art History, Ceramics, Design, Drawing, Eastern Art History, Graphic Design, History of Art & Architecture, Museum Staff Training, Painting, Photography, Printmaking, Sculpture, Stage Design, Teacher Training, Textile Design, Theatre Arts, Weaving
Summer School: Enrl 20-25, 3 sessions of 6 wks beginning in May

MINOT

MINOT STATE UNIVERSITY, Dept of Art, Division of Humanities, 500 University Ave W, Minot, ND 58701-0002. Tel 701-858-3000, 858-3171, 858-3109; Fax 701-839-6933; Elec Mail davidsoc@misu.nodak.edu; Internet Home Page Address: www.warp6.cs.misu.nodak.edu; *Chmn Div Humanities* Conrad Davidson; *Art Dept Coordr* Walter Piehl
Estab 1913; FT 4; pub; Scholarships; SC 30; per quarter 200, maj 40
Degrees: BA & BS 4 yr
Courses: Advertising Design, Art History, Ceramics, Design, Drawing, Handicrafts, Jewelry, Painting, Photography, Printmaking, Sculpture, Silk Screen, Weaving
Summer School: Courses—same as above

VALLEY CITY

VALLEY CITY STATE COLLEGE, Art Dept, 101 College St SW, Valley City, ND 58072-4098. Tel 701-845-7598, 845-0701; Internet Home Page Address: www.vcsu.edu; *Div Chair* Diana P Skroch; *Instr* Richard Nickel; *Dept Chair* Linda Whitney
Estab 1890, dept estab 1921; pub; D & E; Scholarships; SC 20, LC 3; D 1300, E 200, non-maj 120, maj 30
Ent Req: HS dipl, ACT
Degrees: AA 2 yr, BS & BA 4 yr
Courses: †Art Appreciation, †Art Education, Art History, Ceramics, Computer Graphics, Design, Drawing, Mixed Media, Painting, Printmaking, Theatre Arts

WAHPETON

NORTH DAKOTA STATE COLLEGE OF SCIENCE, Dept of Graphic Arts, 800 N Sixth St, Wahpeton, ND 58076-0002. Tel 440-671-2401; Elec Mail wad_king@ndscs.nodak.edu; Internet Home Page Address: www.ndscs.nodak.edu; *Dept Head* Wade King
Estab 1903; dept estab 1970; pub; D & E
Degrees: AA 2 yr
Courses: Drafting, Graphic Design, Layout Design & Image Assembly, Lettering, Painting
Adult Hobby Classes: Enrl 15; tuition $30. Courses—Calligraphy, Drawing, Painting
Summer School: varies

OHIO

ADA

OHIO NORTHERN UNIVERSITY, Dept of Art & Design, 525 S Main St, Ada, OH 45810-6000. Tel 419-772-2160; Fax 419-772-2164; Elec Mail art@onu.edu; Internet Home Page Address: www.onu.edu/a&s/art; *Chmn* William Brit Rowe; *Assoc Prof Art* Melissa Eddings; *Asst Prof Art* William Mancuso; *Instr* Linda Lehman; *Instr* Rhonda Grubbs; *Asst Prof Art* Luke Sheets
Estab 1871; Maintain nonprofit art gallery; Elzay Art Gallery 525 Main St Ada OH 45810; Stambaugh Theatre Gallery; Pvt; D; Scholarships; SC 30, LC 8; non-maj 20, maj 40
Ent Req: HS dipl, ent exam, portfolio
Degrees: BA and BFA 4 yrs
Tuition: Freshman $17,000 per sem
Courses: †Advertising Design, †Art Appreciation, Art Education, Ceramics, Drawing, Graphic Design, History of Art & Architecture, Jewelry, Museum Studies, Painting, Photography, Printmaking, Sculpture, Teacher Training

AKRON

UNIVERSITY OF AKRON, Myers School of Art, 150 E Exchange St, Akron, OH 44325-7801. Tel 330-972-6030; Fax 330-972-5960; Internet Home Page Address: http://art.uakron.edu; *Dept Head* Del Rey Loven
Estab 1870; Maintains nonprofit gallery, Emily Davis Gallery, & art / architecture library; Pub; D & E; Scholarships; SC 25, LC 7, GC 8; D 943, E 129, non-maj 493, maj 450
Ent Req: HS dipl
Degrees: BA, BFA 4 yr
Courses: †Advertising Design, Art Appreciation, Art Education, †Art History, †Art Studio, †Ceramics, Computer, †Drawing, †Graphic Design, History of Art & Architecture, Illustration, †Jewelry, †Metalsmithing, Museum Staff Training, †New Media, †Painting, †Photography, †Printmaking, †Sculpture, †Silversmithing, Teacher Training, Video

ALLIANCE

MOUNT UNION COLLEGE, Dept of Art, 1972 Clark Ave, Alliance, OH 44601-3993. Tel 330-823-2590, 823-2083 (Chmn), 823-3860 (Secy of Dept); *Chmn* Joel Collins, MFA
Estab 1846; D; pvt; Scholarships; SC 27, LC 6; D 150, non-maj 125, maj 25
Ent Req: HS dipl, SAT
Degrees: BA
Courses: Aesthetics, Art Education, Art History, Drawing, Painting, Printmaking, Sculpture, Teacher Training

ASHLAND

ASHLAND UNIVERSITY, Art Dept, 401 College Ave, Ashland, OH 44805-3799. Tel 419-289-4142; Internet Home Page Address: www.ashland.edu; *Chmn* David Edgar, MFA; *Prof* Carl M Allen, MA; *Assoc Prof* Charles D Caldemeyer, MFA; *Asst Prof* Keith A Dull, MA; *Asst Prof* Robert A Stanley, EdD
Estab 1878; FT 4; den; D & E; Scholarships; D 1460, maj 32, minors 12
Ent Req: HS dipl
Degrees: BA, BS 4 yr
Courses: †Advertising Design, Art Appreciation, Art Education, †Ceramics, †Commercial Art, Computer Art, Constructions, Costume Design & Construction, Design, Drawing, Fashion Arts, Interior Design, Photography/Multi Media, Visual Communication, available through affiliation with the Art Institute of Pittsburgh: Fashion Illustration

ATHENS

OHIO UNIVERSITY, School of Art, 1 Ohio University, School of Art Athens, OH 45701-2942. Tel 740-593-4288, 593-0497; Elec Mail boothe@ohio.edu; Internet Home Page Address: www.ohiou.edu/art/index; *Dir* Power Boothe
Estab 1936; 39; pub; D & E; Scholarships, Fellowships; SC 88, LC 30, LGC 29, SGC 50; maj 573, others 1718
Ent Req: secondary school dipl, portfolio
Degrees: BFA, MA & MFA 4-5 yrs
Courses: †Art Education, †Art History, †Art Therapy, †Ceramics, Drawing, Fibers, Glass, †Graphic Design, †Illustration, †Painting, †Photography, †Printmaking, †Sculpture, †Studio Arts, †Visual Communication
Summer School: Two 5 wk sessions June-July & July-Aug; 8 qtr hr maximum per session; SC, LC, GC

BEREA

BALDWIN-WALLACE COLLEGE, Dept of Art, 275 Eastland Rd, Berea, OH 44017-2088. Tel 440-826-2900; Internet Home Page Address: www.bw.edu; *Prof Art History* Harold D Cole; *Chmn Div* Dr Marc Vincent
Estab 1845; den; D & E; SC 23, LC 12; 1900, maj 65
Degrees: AB 4 yrs
Courses: Art Education, Art History, Ceramics, Design & Color, Drawing, Painting, Photography, Printmaking, Sculpture

BLUFFTON

BLUFFTON UNIVERSITY, Art Dept, 1 University Dr, Bluffton, OH 45817-2104. Tel 419-358-3000; Elec Mail luginbuhlg@bluffton.edu; Internet Home Page Address: www.bluffton.edu; *Chair* Gregg Luginbuhl
Average Annual Attendance:
Courses: †Art Education, Graphic Design

BOWLING GREEN

BOWLING GREEN STATE UNIVERSITY, School of Art, 1000 Fine Arts Bldg, Bowling Green, OH 43403. Tel 419-372-2786; Fax 419-372-2544; *Dir Grad Studies* Charlie Kanwischer; *Chmn Design Studies* Mark Zust; *Chmn 3-D Studies* Kathy Hagan; *Chmn 2-D Studies* Lynn Whitney; *Chmn Art Educ* Dr Karen Kakas; *Chmn Art History* John Lavezzi PhD; *Dir Gallery* Jacqueline Nathan; *Dir* Tomas Hilty
Estab 1910, dept estab 1946; pub; D & E; Scholarships, Fellowships; SC 53, LC 14, GC 33; D 2460, E 150, non-maj 350, maj 750, grad 25, others 15
Ent Req: ACT (undergrad), GRE (grad)
Degrees: BA, BS & BFA 4 yrs, MA 1 yr, MFA 2 yrs
Courses: Advertising Design, †Art Education, †Art History, †Ceramics, †Computer Art, Design, †Drawing, †Fibers, †Glass, †Graphic Design, Jewelry, †Jewelry/Metals, †Painting, †Photography, †Printmaking, †Sculpture, †Silversmithing, Weaving
Children's Classes: Enrl 100; tuition $40 per 10 wk sem of Sat mornings
Summer School: Dir, Lou Krueger. Enrl 300; tuition $1224 for 8 wk & 6 wk session. Undergrad Courses—Drawing, Photography, Printmaking, Sculpture, Special Workshops

CANTON

CANTON MUSEUM OF ART, 1001 Market Ave N, Canton, OH 44702-1075. Tel 330-453-7666; Fax 330-453-1034; Internet Home Page Address: www.cantonart.org; *Exec Dir* Manuel J Albacete; *Cur Exhibits & Registrar* Lynnda Arrasmith; *Bus Mgr* Kay McAllister; *Cur Educ* Lauren Kuntzman
Maintain a nonprofit art gallery & an art/architecture library; Pub; D & E; Scholarships; SC 28; D 322, E 984, others 1306
Tuition: Call office for tuition & class schedules
Courses: †Painting, †Pottery, †Sculpture

MALONE UNIVERSITY, (Malone College) Dept of Art, 2600 Cleveland Ave NW, Canton, OH 44709-3308. Tel 330-471-8231; Fax 330-471-8477; Elec Mail mhaines@malone.edu; Internet Home Page Address: www.malone.edu/art; *Prof* Claire Murray Adams; *Prof* Barbara Drennen; *Chmn Visual Arts* Gary Spangler
Estab 1956; Maintains 2 nonprofit art galleries, Gerald & Mary Ellen McFadden Gallery & Fountain Gallery, Malone Univ, Johnson Ctr, 2600 Cleveland Ave NW, Canton, OH 44709; also maintains 2 art libraries, Art-in-a-Case, Malone Univ, Cattell Library, 2600 Cleveland Ave NW, Canton, OH 44709 & Mary Ellen McFadden Art Library, Malone Univ, 2600 Cleveland Ave NW, Canton, OH 44709.; den; D & E; Scholarships; SC 2, LC 2; D 75, maj 50
Ent Req: HS dipl, ent exam
Degrees: BA & BS(Educ) 4 yr
Courses: Applied Design, Art Appreciation, †Art Education, Art History, Ceramics, †Drawing, Graphic Design, History and Criticism of Art, †Painting, Photography, Printmaking, Sculpture, Teacher Training, Textile Design
Summer School: Professional Develop Coord, Dr. Nancy Varian; Graduate teacher workshops available during summer session: jewelry, bookmaking, photography, watercolors, fibers & ceramics.

CHILLICOTHE

OHIO UNIVERSITY-CHILLICOTHE CAMPUS, Fine Arts & Humanities Division, 571 W Fifth St, Chillicothe, OH 45601-2209; PO Box 629, Chillicothe, OH 45601-0629. Tel 740-774-7200; Fax 740-774-7214; Elec Mail mcadamsm@ohio.edu; Internet Home Page Address: www.ohiou.edu; *Assoc Prof* Margaret McAdams, MFA; *Assoc Prof* Dennis Deane, MFA
Estab 1946; FT 2 PT 1; pub; D & E; Scholarships
Ent Req: HS dipl, ACT or SAT
Degrees: campus for freshman & sophomores only
Courses: Art Appreciation, Art Education, Ceramics, Design, Drawing, Film, Graphic Design, History of Art & Architecture, Painting, Photography, Teacher Training

CINCINNATI

ANTONELLI COLLEGE, 124 E Seventh St, Cincinnati, OH 45202. Tel 513-241-4338; Fax 513-241-9396; Internet Home Page Address: www.antonellic.com; *Dept Head Commercial Arts* James Slouffman; *Dept Head Photog* Chas E Martin; *Dept Head Interior Design* Kristen Courtney Altenau; *Dept Head Bus Office Tech* Pam Bingham
Estab 1947; FT 5, PT 12; pvt; D & E; D 200
Ent Req: HS dipl, review of portfolio
Degrees: AAS
Courses: †Commercial Art, †Interior Design, †Photography
Adult Hobby Classes: Courses offered
Summer School: Courses offered

ART ACADEMY OF CINCINNATI, 1212 Jackson St, Cincinnati, OH 45202-7106. Tel 513-562-6262; Fax 513-562-8778; Internet Home Page Address: www.artacademy.edu; *Prof* Anthony Batchelor; *Pres* Gregory A Smith, BFA; *Prof* Mark Thomas, MFA; *Instr* Kenn Knowlton, MFA; *Instr* Calvin Kowal, MS; *Instr* Larry May, MFA; *Chmn Acad Studies Dept* Diane Smith, MA; *Instr* Jay Zumeta, MA; *Instr* April Foster, MFA; *Instr* Rebecca Seeman, MFA; *Instr* Paige Williams; *Chmn Foundation Dept* Claire Darley, MFA; *Instr* Gary Gaffney, MFA; *Instr* Kim Krause, MFA
Estab 1887; pvt; D & E; Scholarships; 220
Ent Req: HS grad, SAT
Degrees: degrees cert offered at the Academy, 4-5 yr
Courses: Advertising Design, Aesthetics, Art Education, Art History, Commercial Art, †Communication Design, Conceptual Art, Constructions, Design, Drawing, Graphic Arts, Graphic Design, Illustration, Museum Staff Training, Painting, Photography, Printmaking, Sculpture
Adult Hobby Classes: Enrl 2000. Courses—Design, Drawing, Illustration, Painting, Photography, Sculpture
Children's Classes: Enrl 500; tuition $100 per class. Courses—Drawing, Painting, 3-D Design

THE ART INSTITUTE OF CINCINNATI, AIC College of Design, 1171 E Kemper Rd, Cincinnati, OH 43246-3322. Tel 513-751-1206; Fax 513-751-1209; Elec Mail aic@aic-arts.edu; Internet Home Page Address: aic-arts.edu; *Instr Foundation Art* Cyndi Mendell; *CEO* Marion Allman; *Instr Illustration & Design* Frederic Bonin Pissarro; *Instr Computer Graphics* Dan Bittman; *Instr Computer Graphics* Randy Zimmerman; *Pres* Sean M Mendell; *Gen Educ* Marlene Shmalo; *Instr* Kay Somone; *Interactive Instr* Dave Solno
Estab 1976; On-campus shop sells art supplies; 5 FT, 4 PT; priv; D, E; Scholarships; D 80
Ent Req: HS dipl, portfolio, interview
Degrees: Design & Computer Graphics AD 2 yr
Tuition: $17,760 yr (3 semesters)
Courses: Advertising Design, †Art History, Commercial Art, Computer Graphics, Design, †Display, †Drawing, †Graphic Arts, Graphic Design, †History of Art & Architecture, Illustration, Interactive Media, †Lettering, †Mixed Media, Packaging, †Photography, Print, †Textile Design, †Video, Web
Summer School: Sean Mendell, Dir

COLLEGE OF MOUNT SAINT JOSEPH, Art Dept, 5701 Delhi Pike, Cincinnati, OH 45233-1670. Tel 513-244-4420; Fax 513-244-4222; Elec Mail dan mader@mail.msj.edu; Internet Home Page Address: www.msj.edu; WATS 800-654-9314; *Assoc* Beth Belknap, MDES; *Asst Prof* John Griffith, MFA; *Asst Prof* Gerry Bellas, MFA; *Chmn* Daniel Mader, MA; *Asst Prof* Robert Voight, BA; *Assoc Prof* Walter Loyola, MFA; *Prof* Sharon Kesterson-Bullen, EdD; *Asst Prof* Craig Lloyd
Estab 1920; den; D & E; Scholarships; SC 35, LC 4; 203 maj
Ent Req: HS dipl, national testing scores

Degrees: AA 2 yr, BA and BFA 4 yr
Courses: †Art Education, Art History, †Ceramics, †Drawing, †Fabrics Design, †Graphic Design, †Interior Design, †Jewelry, Lettering, †Painting, †Photography, †Pre-Art Therapy, †Printmaking, †Sculpture

UNIVERSITY OF CINCINNATI, School of Art, 6431 Aronoff Bldg, Cincinnati, OH 45221; PO Box 210016, Cincinnati, OH 45221-0016. Tel 513-556-2962; Fax 513-556-2887; Elec Mail jonathan.riess@uc.edu; Internet Home Page Address: www.daap.uc.edu/art/default; *Dir, School of Art & Prof Fine Arts* Mark Harris MA; *Dir MFA Prog, Chair & Prof Fine Arts* Kimberly Burleigh, MFA; *Dir Art Hist Prog & Asst Prof Art Educ* Theresa Leininger-Miller, PhD; *Dir Art Educ Prog & Asst Prof Art Educ* Flavia Bastos, PhD; *Foundations Coordr, Undergrad Adv & Assoc Prof Fine Arts* Denise Burge, MFA; *Assoc Prof Fine Arts* Benjamin Britton, MFA; *Prof Fine Arts* Roy Cartwright, MFA; *Assoc Prof Fine Arts* Tarrence Corbin, MFA; *Assoc Prof Fine Arts* Linda Einfalt, MFA; *Prof Fine Arts* Wayne Enstice, MA; *Prof Fine Arts* Frank Herrmann, MFA; *Asst Prof Art History* Mikiko Hirayama, PhD; *Prof Fine Arts* Don Kelley, MFA; *Assoc Prof Fine Arts* Diane Mankin, MFA; *Asst Prof Fine Arts* Matthew Lynch, MFA; *Prof Art History* Kristi Nelson, PhD; *Asst Prof Art History* Kimberly Paice, PhD; *Asst Prof Art Educ* Nancy Parks, EdD; *Prof Art History* Jonathan Riess, PhD; *Chmn & Assoc Prof Art Educ* Robert Russell, PhD; *Prof Fine Arts* Jane Alden Stevens, MFA; *Prof Fine Arts* John Stewart, MFA; *Prof Fine Arts* Jim Williams, MFA; *Assoc Prof Fine Arts* Charles Woodman, MFA
Estab 1819, dept estab 1946; Maintain nonprofit gallery; library; art supplies available for purchase on-site; Pub; D & E; Scholarships
Ent Req: HS dipl - top 3rd class rank, transfers to Fine Arts, portfolio optional & MFA, portfolio required
Degrees: BA(Art History) 4 yr, 5 yr with teaching certification, BFA(Fine Arts) 4 yr, 5 yr with teaching certification, MA(Art History) 2 yr, MA(Art Educ) 2 yr, MFA 2 yr
Courses: Art Education, Art History, Ceramics, Conceptual Art, Contemporary Art & Theory, Digital Art, Drawing, Electronic Arts, Museum Staff Training, Painting, Photography, Printmaking, Sculpture, Teacher Training, Video
Adult Hobby Classes: Art Education, Art History
Children's Classes: Enrl 25; tuition $60 for 10 wks. Courses—Intro to Life Drawing
Summer School: Dir, Wayne Enstice. Enrl 200. Courses—Art Education, Art History, Fine Arts

XAVIER UNIVERSITY, Dept of Art, 1658 Herald Ave, Room 190A Cincinnati, OH 45207-7311; 3800 Victory Pkwy, Cincinnati, OH 45207-1035. Tel 513-745-3811; Fax 513-745-1098; Elec Mail chouteau@xavier.edu; Internet Home Page Address: www.xavier.edu/art; *Prof* Marsha Karagheusian-Murphy, MFA; *Chair & Prof* Suzanne Chouteau, MFA; *Assoc Prof* Kelly Phelps, MFA; *Assoc Prof* Bruce Erikson, MFA; *Assoc Prof* Jonathan Gibson, MFA
Estab 1831, dept estab 1935; Maintain nonprofit Xavier University Art Gallery, A.B. Cohen Ctr, 1658 Herald Ave., Cincinnati, OH 45207-7311; Xu McDonald Library, 3800 Victory Pkwy, Cincinnati OH 45207; pvt; D & E & weekend degree; Scholarships; SC 17, LC 20; D 403, E 349, non-maj 349, maj 54
Ent Req: HS dipl, SAT or ACT
Degrees: BA 4 yr, BFA 4 yr
Tuition: Undergrad $15,115 per semester
Courses: Advertising Design, Aesthetics, Art Appreciation, Art Education, Art History, Art Therapy, Ceramics, Collage, Commercial Art, Constructions, Design, Display, Drawing, Graphic Arts, Graphic Design, History of Art, Intermedia, Mixed Media, Painting, Photography, Printmaking, Sculpture, Teacher Training, Textile Design, Weaving
Summer School: Krista Warner, Coordr; School Art, Graphic Design, Web Design, Fiber Arts, Drawing

CLEVELAND

CASE WESTERN RESERVE UNIVERSITY, Dept of Art History & Art, 11201 Euclid Ave, Mather House Cleveland, OH 44106-7110. Tel 216-368-4118; Fax 216-368-4681; Elec Mail dxt6@case.edu; Internet Home Page Address: cwru.edu/artsci/arth/arth.html; *Prof* Henry Adams; *Assoc Prof, Dept Chmn* Catherine Scallen; *Assoc Prof* Anne Helmreich; *Asst Prof* Noelle Giuffrida; *Asst Prof* Elina Gertsman; *Prof* Jenifer Neils; *Asst Prof* Erin Banay; *Asst Prof* Maggie Popkin; *Asst Prof* Andrea Rager; *Assoc Vis Prof* Jose Teixeira
Estab 1875; pvt; D & E; Scholarships; SC 24, LC 55, GC 73; D 644, grad 75
Exhibitions: Annual faculty exhibition & MA student shows
Activities: Schols offered
Ent Req: HS transcript, SAT or ACT, TOEFL for foreign students
Degrees: BA, BS, MA and PhD
Tuition: $20,710 per sem—undergrad; campus res available; $14,472 per sum—grad
Courses: Architecture, †Art Education, †Art History, Ceramics, Costume Design & Construction, Enameling, †History of Art & Architecture, Jewelry, Medical Illustration, †Museum Staff Training, Painting, Photography, †Teacher Training, Textile Design, Weaving
Summer School: June & July. Courses—Art Education, Art History, Art Studio, Museum Studies

CLEVELAND INSTITUTE OF ART, 11141 E Blvd, Cleveland, OH 44106-1710. Tel 216-421-7000; Fax 216-421-7438; Internet Home Page Address: www.cia.edu; *Dept Head Biomedical Art* Amanda Almon; *Dept Head Ceramics* William Brouillard; *Dept Head Jewelry & Metals* Kathy Buszkiewicz; *Dept Head Illustration* John Chuldenko; *Dept Head Industrial Design* Daniel Cuffaro; *Dept Head Printmaking* Margaret Denk-Leigh; *Dept Head TIME Digital Arts* Megan Ehrhart; *Interim Environment Chmn, Dept Head Interior Design* Michael Gollini; *Head Drawing* Sarah Kabot; *Dept Head Illustration* Dominic Scibilia; *Dept Head Photog* Barry Underwood; *Dept Head Glass* Brent Young; *Pres* Grafton Nunes
Estab 1882; pvt; D & E; Scholarships; SC 90, LC 38; D 483, E 266, non-maj 169, maj 300, others 23
Ent Req: HS dipl SAT, ACT and transcript, portfolio

Degrees: BFA 4 yrs, BS & MEd (educ with Case Western Reserve Univ) 4 yrs
Tuition: Res $25,624 per yr, incl rm & board; non-res $23,768 per yr
Courses: Aesthetics, Art Education, Art History, †Ceramics, †Drawing, †Enameling, †Fiber, †Film, †Glass, †Graphic Arts, †Illustration, †Industrial Design, †Interior Design, †Jewelry, †Medical Illustration, †Painting, †Photography, †Printmaking, †Sculpture, †Silversmithing
Adult Hobby Classes: Enrl 266; tuition varies per course. Course—Calligraphy, Ceramic, Crafts, Design, Drawing, Fiber & Surface Design, Graphic Design, Painting, Printmaking, Sculpture, Silversmithing, Watercolor
Children's Classes: Enrl 210; tuition varies per course. Courses—Art Basics, Ceramic Sculpture, Crafts, Design, Drawing, Painting, Portfolio Preparation, Printmaking, Photography
Summer School: Dir, Lisa Reichel. Courses—Ceramics, Design, Drawing, Jewelry & Metalsmithing, Photography, Printmaking, Sculpture, Watercolor

CLEVELAND STATE UNIVERSITY, Art Dept, 2121 Euclid Ave, AB106 Cleveland, OH 44115-2214. Tel 216-687-2040; Fax 216-687-2275; Internet Home Page Address: www.csuohio.edu; *Chmn & Assoc Prof* George Mauersberger, MFA; *Prof* Thomas E Donaldson PhD; *Prof* Walter Leedy Jr PhD; *Prof* Marvin H Jones, MA; *Prof* Kenneth Nevadomi, MFA; *Prof* Masumi Hayashi, MFA; *Assoc Prof* Kathy Curnow PhD, MFA; *Assoc Prof* Laurel Lampela PhD, MFA; *Assoc Prof* Richard Schneider, MA; *Chmn* John Hunter PhD, MA; *Asst Prof* Claudia Mesch, PhD
Estab 1972; pub; D & E; Scholarships; SC 26, LC 32
Ent Req: HS dipl
Degrees: BA 4 yr
Courses: †Art Education, †Art History, †Ceramics, Computer Graphics, †Drawing, Introduction to Studio Art, †Painting, †Photography, †Printmaking, †Sculpture
Summer School: Chmn, John Hunter. Tuition & courses same as regular schedule

CUYAHOGA COMMUNITY COLLEGE, Dept of Art, 2900 Community College Ave, Cleveland, OH 44115-3196. Tel 216-987-4248, 4600; Elec Mail Gerald-Kramer@tri-C.cc.oh.us; Internet Home Page Address: www.tri-c.cc.oh.us; *Coordr Fine Art Prog* Gerald Kramer, MFA; *Assoc Prof* Richard Karberg; *Assoc Prof* Jacqueline Freedman
Estab 1963. College maintains four campuses; PT 6; pub; D & E; Scholarships; SC 15, LC 4; D 1,000, E 1,000, maj 1,000
Ent Req: HS dipl/GED
Degrees: AA, AS
Courses: Art Appreciation, Art Education, Art History, Calligraphy, Ceramics, Graphic Design, Occupational Therapy, Painting, Photography, Printmaking, Sculpture, Stage Design, Teacher Training, Theatre Arts, Video
Summer School: Courses—various

COLUMBUS

CAPITAL UNIVERSITY, Fine Arts Dept, 2199 E Main St, Huber Hall Columbus, OH 43209-3913. Tel 614-236-6201; Fax 614-236-6169; *Chmn* Gary Ross, MA; *Asst Prof* Donald Duncan, MS; *Instr* Gretchen Crawford, MA, ATR, LPC
FT 3
Degrees: BA, BFA
Tuition: $15,260 per yr, grad $508 per cr hr, room & board $4400 per yr
Courses: Advertising Design, Art Education, Art History, Ceramics, Design, Drawing, Jewelry, Painting, Photography, Sculpture, Stained Glass, Theatre Arts, Weaving

COLUMBUS COLLEGE OF ART & DESIGN, Fine Arts Dept, 107 N Ninth St, Columbus, OH 43215. Tel 614-224-9101; Internet Home Page Address: www.ccad.edu; *Dean* Lowell Tolstedt
Estab 1879; 68; pvt; approved for Veterans; D & E; Scholarships
Ent Req: HS grad, art portfolio
Degrees: BFA 4 yr
Courses: Advertising Design, Fashion Arts, Fine Arts, Graphic Arts, Illustration, Industrial Design, Interior Design, Packaging Design, Painting, Retail Advertising, Sculpture
Children's Classes: Saturday sessions 9 - 11:30 AM

OHIO DOMINICAN COLLEGE, Art Dept, 1216 Sunbury Rd, Columbus, OH 43219-2099. Tel 614-253-2741, 251-4580; Fax 614-252-0776; *Dept Chmn* William Vensel
Estab 1911; den; D & E; Scholarships; SC and LC 709 per sem; D 139, E 105, maj 17
Ent Req: HS dipl
Degrees: BA 4 yrs, also secondary educ cert or special training cert, K-12
Courses: Ceramics, Color & Materials, History of Art, Painting, Sculpture, Studio Humanities

OHIO STATE UNIVERSITY, School of Architecture, 190 W 17th Ave, 109 Brown Columbus, OH 43210. Tel 614-292-1012; Fax 614-292-7106; Internet Home Page Address: www.osu.edu; *Dir* Robert Livesey
Estab 1899; FT 43, PT 23; pub; Scholarships; Archit 450, Landscape Archit 170, City & Regional Planning 65
Degrees: BS(Archit), MA, PhD
Tuition: Res—$5000 per yr
Courses: City Planning, Design, History of Architecture, Landscape Architecture
Adult Hobby Classes: Enrl limited; Tuition $170-$469.
Summer School: Dir, Robert Liveson. Enrl 50-70; tuition $170-$469 for 10 wks.
—**College of the Arts,** 146 Hopkins Hall, 128 N Oval Mall Columbus, OH 43210-1318. Tel 614-292-5171; Fax 614-292-5218; Internet Home Page Address: www.arts.osu.edu; *Dean Col* Judith Koroscik
Univ estab 1870, col estab 1968; pub; D & E; Scholarships; SC 106, LC 192, GC 208; D 3678, E varies, non-maj 2300, maj 893, grad 150

Ent Req: HS dipl
Degrees: BA, MA, PhD
Tuition: Res—$1200 per qtr; nonres—$3000 per qtr
Courses: Art, Art History, Dance, Music, †Stage Design, †Teacher Training, †Theatre Arts, †Weaving
Adult Hobby Classes: Courses—art experiences in all media for local adults
Children's Classes: Enrl 300 per quarter; fees $36 per quarter; Saturday School. Courses—art experiences in all media for local children
Summer School: Same as regular session
—**Dept of Art,** 146 Hopkins Hall, 128 N Oval Mall Columbus, OH 43210-1318. Tel 614-292-5072; Fax 614-292-1674; Elec Mail art_advisor@osu.edu; Internet Home Page Address: www.art.osu.edu; *Chmn* Sergio Soave
Maintain nonprofit art gallery, OSU Urban Arts Space So W Town St, Columbus OH; maintain art/architecture library, maintains OSU Fine Arts Library, Wexner Center; on campus shop where art supplies may be purchased; FT 21, PT 34; Pub; D & E; Scholarships; SC 56, LC 6, GC 30
Degrees: BA, BFA, MFA
Tuition: Res—undergrad $8667 per yr, grad $9592 per year; nonres—undergrad $20,562 per year, grad $22,950 per year
Courses: Art & Technology, †Ceramics, †Drawing, †Glass, †Painting, †Photography, †Printmaking, †Sculpture
Adult Hobby Classes: Offered through CAP (Creative Art Program) & CED (Continuing Education)
—**Dept of Art Education,** 258 Hopkins Hall, 128 N Oval Mall Columbus, OH 43210-1318. Tel 614-292-7183; Fax 614-688-4483; Internet Home Page Address: www.art.ohio-state.edu/ArtEducation; *Chmn Dept* James Hutchens PhD; *Prof* Robert Arnold PhD; *Prof* Terry Barrett PhD; *Prof* Judith Koroscik PhD; *Prof* Michael Parsons PhD; *Prof* Margaret Wyszomirski PhD; *Prof Emeritus* Arthur Efland PhD; *Prof Emeritus* Kenneth Marantz EdD; *Assoc Prof* Don Krug PhD; *Assoc Prof* Sydney Walker PhD; *Prof* Patricia Stuhr PhD; *Assoc Prof* Vesta Daniel EdD; *Asst Prof* Christine Ballangee-Morris PhD; *Asst Prof* Georgianna Short PhD
Estab 1907; pub; D & E; Scholarships, Fellowships; SC 2, LC 42, GC 48, other 14; maj 65, grad 110
Ent Req: HS dipl
Degrees: BAE, MA, PhD
Tuition: Res—$1500 per qtr; nonres—$4300 per qtr
Courses: Art Appreciation, †Art Education, †Art History, †Arts Administration, †Arts Policy, Computer Graphics, Ethnic Art, History of Art, †Industrial Design, †Teacher Training
Summer School: Chmn Dept, James Hutchens, PhD. Courses—Art Educ
—**Dept of Industrial Interior & Visual Communication Design,** 280 Hopkins Hall, 128 N Oval Mall Columbus, OH 43210. Tel 614-292-6746; Fax 614-292-0217; Elec Mail design@osu.edu; Internet Home Page Address: www.arts.ohio-state.edu/design; *Chmn* Wayne E Carlson
FT 11, PT 5; Public ; Day & Evening classes; Scholarships; SC 35, LC 10, GC 10
Degrees: BS, MA, MFA
Tuition: Res—$1461 per quarter; nonres—$4244 per quarter
Courses: 3-D Computer Modeling, †Architecture, †Design, †Design Development, †Design Education, †Design Management, †Graphic Design, Manufacturing Materials & Processes, Research Problems & Design, Visual Thinking Design Methodology
Summer School: Advanced Typography
—**Dept of the History of Art,** 215 Pomerene Hall, 1760 Neil Ave Columbus, OH 43210-1221. Tel 614-292-7481; Fax 614-292-4401; Internet Home Page Address: www.history-of-art.ohio-state.edu;
Estab 1871, dept estab 1968; pub; D & E; Scholarships, Fellowships; LC 56, GC 29; D 854, non-maj 700, maj 71, grad 73
Ent Req: HS dipl
Degrees: BA, MA 2 yrs, PhD 4-6 yrs
Courses: †Art History, History of Art & Archeology
Summer School: Enrl 250; tuition same as regular session for term of ten wks beginning June. Courses—vary each yr

CUYAHOGA FALLS

CUYAHOGA VALLEY ART CENTER, 2131 Front St, Cuyahoga Falls, OH 44221-3219. Tel 330-928-8092; Fax 330-928-8092; Elec Mail cvartcenter@sbcglobal.net; Internet Home Page Address: http://cvartcenter.org/; *Instr* Robert Putka; *Instr* Dino Massaroni; *Instr* Jack Liberman; *Instr* Beth Lindenberger; *Instr* Tony Cross; *Instr* Dave Everson; *Instr* Carolyn Lewis; *Instr* Mary Sanders; *Pres* Larry Kerr; *Instr* Jack Mulhollen; *Dir* Linda Nye; *Instr* Sally Heston; *Instr* Susan Mencini; *Instr* Tom Jones; *Instr* Linda Hutchinson; *Instr* Monalea Hutchins; *Instr* Elinore Korow
Estab 1934; maintains a nonprofit art gallery, 2131 Front St, Cuyahoga Falls, OH, 44221; Nonprofit; D & E; SC 23; 300 D&E
Exhibitions: Regional Painting; Whiskey Painters of America; Summer Painting Show; Members Show; Cuyahoga Falls High School Showing; Small Painting Show; Student Show; Akron Soc Artists; Abstract Show; Akron Camera Club
Ent Req: none, interest in art
Degrees: none
Courses: Ceramics, Collage, †Design, Drawing, †Mixed Media, Painting, †Pottery, †Printmaking, Special Workshops, †Textile Design, †Weaving
Adult Hobby Classes: 200; tuition $85 for members, $100 for nonmembers per 10 wks. Courses—Drawing, Painting, Pottery
Children's Classes: 100; tuition $50 for members, $60 for nonmembers per 10 wks
Summer School: Dir, Linda Nye. Enrl 20. Courses—Same as regular session, Young People's art

STUDIOS OF JACK RICHARD CREATIVE SCHOOL OF DESIGN, Professional School of Painting & Design, 2250 Front St, Cuyahoga Falls, OH 44221-2510. Tel 330-929-1575; Fax 330-929-2285; Elec Mail jackprichard@aol.com; *Dir* Jack Richard
Estab 1960; pvt; D & E; Scholarships; SC 20, LC 10; D 50-60, E 50-60

Degrees: cert of accomplishment
Courses: Aesthetics, †Art Appreciation, Art Education, Color, Design, Drawing, Illustration, Mural, Occupational Therapy, Painting, Photography, †Restoration & Conservation, Sculpture
Adult Hobby Classes: Enrl 200-300 per session; tuition $11 per class.
Courses—Design, Drawing, Painting
Children's Classes: Tues morning & evening
Summer School: Dir, Jane Williams. Enrl 90; tuition $10 - $12 per class
Courses—Design, Drawing, Painting

DAYTON

SINCLAIR COMMUNITY COLLEGE, Division of Fine & Performing Arts, 444 W Third St, Dayton, OH 45402. Tel 937-512-5313; Fax 937-512-2130; Elec Mail kelly.joslin@sinclair.edu; Internet Home Page Address: www.sinclair.edu; *Chair Arts & Asst Prof* Kelly Joslin; *Assoc Prof* Kevin Harris; *Prof Reach Coordr* Tess Little; *Prof* George Hageman; *Prof* Mark Echtner; *Prof* Richard Jurus; *Instr* Nancy Mitchell; *Asst Prof* Robert Coates; *Instr* Bridgett Bogle; *Asst Prof* Kay Koeninger
Estab 1973; Maintain nonprofit art gallery on-campus; Pub; D & E, wkend & web; Scholarships; SC 80, LC 8; 1,500 per qtr
Exhibitions: Rotating three week exhibitions of nationally known artists in four different galleries
Ent Req: HS dipl, ent exam
Degrees: AA 2 yrs
Courses: Advertising Design, †Art Appreciation, †Art History, Ceramics, Commercial Art, Digital Photography, Drawing, Graphic Arts, Painting, Photography, Sculpture, Theatre Arts
Adult Hobby Classes: Drawing for seniors - free to those over 60
Summer School: Chair of Art, Kelly Joslin. Enrl 1,200. Courses—Art Appreciation, Ceramics, Computer Photography, Drawing, Printing, Studio Art

UNIVERSITY OF DAYTON, Visual Arts Dept, 300 College Park, Dayton, OH 45469-1690. Tel 937-229-3237; Fax 937-229-3943; Internet Home Page Address: www.as.dayton.edu/visualarts; *Prof, Chmn Dept* Fred Niles, MFA; *Assoc Prof* Mary Zahner PhD, MFA; *Assoc Prof* Tim Wilbers, MFA; *Assoc Prof* Peter Gooch, MFA; *Assoc Prof* Roger Crum PhD, MFA; *Assoc Prof* Gary Marcinowski, MFA; *Asst Prof* Jayne Whitaker, MFA; *Asst Prof* Lari Gibbons, MFA; *Asst Prof* Joel Whitaker, MFA; *Prof* Sean Wilkinson, MFA; *Asst Prof* Judith Huacuja-Person; *Asst Prof* Matt Rappaport
Estab 1850; pvt; D & E; Scholarships; SC 15, LC 8; D 275, E 75-100, non-maj 100, maj 250
Ent Req: HS dipl
Degrees: BA, BFA
Courses: Animation, †Art Education, †Art History, Ceramics, Computer Modeling, Digital Imaging, Drawing, Illustration, Mixed Media, †Painting, †Photography, †Printmaking, †Sculpture, †Visual Communication Design
Summer School: Tuition $456 per cr hr

WRIGHT STATE UNIVERSITY, Dept of Art & Art History, 3640 Colonel Glenn Hwy, Dayton, OH 45435-0002. Tel 937-775-2896; Fax 937-775-3049; Elec Mail glen.cebulash@wright.edu; Internet Home Page Address: www.wright.edu/cola/Dept/art; *Prof* Kimberly Vito, MFA; *Chair & Prof* Glen Cebulash, MFA; *Assoc Prof* Penny Park, MFA; *Assoc Prof* Benjamin Montague, MFA; *Assoc Prof* Stefan Chinov, MFA; *Asst Prof* Tracy Longley-Cook, MFA; *Asst Prof* Karla Huebner, PhD; *Asst Prof* Danielle Rante, MFA; *Asst Prof* Caroline Hillard, PhD; *Asst Prof* Jeremy Long, MFA; *Asst Prof* John Dickinson, MFA
Estab 1964; dept estab 1965; Maintain nonprofit art gallery; University Art Galleries, 3640 Col Glenn Hwy, Dayton, OH 45435; Pub; D & E; Scholarships; SC 67, LC 16, GC 8; D 516, E 43, non-maj 80, maj 150
Ent Req: HS dipl
Degrees: BA(Studio Art), BA(Art History), BFA 4 yr
Tuition: Res—undergrad $4,271 per semester; nonres—undergrad $8,273 per semester
Courses: Art Education, Art History, Drawing, Painting, Photography, Printmaking, Sculpture
Summer School: Chair & Prof, Glen Cebulash. Enrl 65; tuition res $219 per cr hr, nonres $425 per cr hr. Courses—Drawing, Photography, Printmaking, Sculpture

DELAWARE

OHIO WESLEYAN UNIVERSITY, Fine Arts Dept, 61 S Sandusky St, Delaware, OH 43015. Tel 740-368-3600; Fax 740-368-3299; Internet Home Page Address: www.owu.edu; *Prof* Carol Neuman de Vegvar, PhD; *Chmn* James Krehbiel, MFA; *Prof* Cynthia Cetlin, MFA; *Asst Prof* Jonathan Quick, MFA; *Asst Prof* Frank Hobbs, MFA; *Asst Prof* Kristina Bogdanov, MFA; *Asst Prof* Jeffrey Nilan, MFA
Estab 1842; dept estab 1864; Maintains nonprofit Richard M Ross Art Museum, 60 S Sandusky St, Delaware, OH 43015; art supplies sold at on campus store; pvt; D & E; Scholarships, Fellowships; D 1950, non-maj 1850, maj 100
Ent Req: HS dipl, SAT or ACT
Degrees: BA and BFA 4 yrs
Courses: Aesthetics, Art Education, Art History, Ceramics, Computer Imaging, Drawing, Graphic Design, Jewelry, Painting, Photography, Printmaking, Sculpture, Teacher Training
Summer School: Dean, Charles Stinemetz. Tuition $2,160 per unit for 6 wks. Courses—Varies

ELYRIA

LORAIN COUNTY COMMUNITY COLLEGE, Art Dept, 1005 N Abbe Rd, Elyria, OH 44035. Tel 440-366-4032; Fax 440-365-6519; Internet Home Page Address: www.lorainccc.edu; *Chmn* Dr Robert Beckstrom

Estab 1966; FT 2 PT varies by sem
Ent Req: HS dipl or equiv
Degrees: AA
Tuition: County res—$72.50 per cr hr; out-of-county res—$87.50 per cr hr; out-of-state res—$178 per cr hr
Courses: Art Appreciation, Ceramics, Design, Drawing, Painting, Photography, Printmaking, Sculpture, Textile Design

FINDLAY

UNIVERSITY OF FINDLAY, Art Program, 1000 N Main St, Findlay, OH 45840-3653. Tel 419-434-4445; Fax 419-434-4531; Internet Home Page Address: www.findlay.edu; *Dean College Liberal Arts* Dr Dennis Stevens; *Prof* Douglas Salveson; *Assoc Prof* Jack (Ed) Corle; *Asst Prof* Lansford Holness; *Asst Prof* Diane Kontar
Estab 1882; Maintain a nonprofit art gallery; Dudley & Mary Marks Lea Gallery, The Univ of Findlay; FT 4, PT 4; pvt; D & E; Scholarships; SC 21, LC 8; maj 60
Ent Req: HS dipl
Degrees: AA 2yr, BA & BS 4 yr
Courses: Advertising Design, Aesthetics, Art Education, Art History, Ceramics, Collage, Drawing, Graphic Design, Painting, Photography, Printmaking, Sculpture, Teacher Training
Adult Hobby Classes: Enrl 10-20. Courses—Ceramics
Children's Classes: Courses—Ceramics, Drawing

GAMBIER

KENYON COLLEGE, Art Dept, 106 College Dr, Horvitz Hall Gambier, OH 43022. Tel 740-427-5459; Fax 740-427-5230; Internet Home Page Address: www.kenyon.edu; *Prof* Barry Gunderson, MFA; *Prof* Eugene J Dwyer PhD, MFA; *Prof* Gregory P Spaid, MFA; *Prof* Claudia Esslinger, MFA; *Prof* Melissa Dabakis, MFA; *Assoc Prof* K Read Baldwin; *Prof* Sarah Blick; *Vis Assoc Prof Art* Karen M Garhart; *Assoc Prof* Marcella M Hackbardt; *Prof* Karen F Snouffer; *Assoc Prof* Kristen Van Ausdall; *Vis Asst Prof* Craig Hill, MFA; *Vis Asst Prof* Austin Porter; *Vis Asst Prof* Emily Zeller, MFA; *Adjunct Asst Prof* Yan Zhou; *Instr* Ellen Sheffield; *Instr* Monica Fullerton
Estab 1824, dept estab 1965; Maintain nonprofit art gallery; Olin Art Gallery, Kenyon College, Gambier, OH 43022; pvt; D; Scholarships; SC 15, LC 10; D 450, non-maj 250, maj 60
Ent Req: HS dipl
Degrees: BA
Courses: †Art History, †Studio Art

GRANVILLE

DENISON UNIVERSITY, Studio Art Program, Bryant Arts Center, 201 W College St (Rm 401) Granville, OH 43023. Tel 740-587-6596; Fax 614-587-6417; Elec Mail coudend@denison.edu; Internet Home Page Address: www.denison.edu; *Assoc Prof* Michaela Vivero, MFA; *Assoc Prof* Ronald Abram, MFA; *Assoc Prof & Chair* Carrie Olson, MFA; *Asst Prof* Sheila Wilson, MFA; *Asst Prof* Tommy White, MFA
Estab 1831, dept estab 1931; Maintains nonprofit gallery; Denison Mus, Granville, OH 43023; maintains art/ architecture libr; pvt; D; Scholarships; SC 24, LC 16; D 800, maj 65, double maj 35
Ent Req: HS
Degrees: BA, BFA, BS 4 yr
Courses: †Art History, †Ceramics, †Drawing, Mixed Media, †Painting, †Photography, †Printmaking, †Sculpture

HAMILTON

FITTON CENTER FOR CREATIVE ARTS, 101 S Monument Ave, Hamilton, OH 45041-2833. Tel 513-863-8873; Fax 513-863-8865; Elec Mail rjatfitton@aol.com; Internet Home Page Address: www.fittoncenter.org; *Arts in Common Dir* Henry Cepluch; *Exhib* Cathy Mayhugh; *Exec Dir* Rick H Jones
Estab 1992; pub; D & E; Scholarships; SC 50, LC 2; D & E 400
Ent Req: varies by program
Degrees: MFA
Courses: Aesthetics, Art Appreciation, Art Education, Art History, Drawing, Fashion Arts, Film, Graphic Arts, Graphic Design, Handicrafts, Illustration, Industrial Design, Intermedia, Painting, Photography

MIAMI UNIVERSITY, Dept Fine Arts, 1601 Peck Blvd, Hamilton, OH 45011. Tel 513-529-2900, 785-3000; Fax 513-785-3145; Internet Home Page Address: www.ham.muohio.edu; *Prof* Edward Montgomery; *Art Coordr* Phil Joseph
Date estab 1809; Pub; D; Scholarships
Ent Req: HS dipl
Degrees: BA
Tuition: Full-time $1524.45 per sem; part-time $125.85 per cr hr
Courses: Advertising Design, Art Education, Art History, Drawing, Painting, Printmaking
Summer School: Courses—Drawing, Painting

HIRAM

HIRAM COLLEGE, Art Dept, PO Box 67, Hiram, OH 44234-0067. Tel 330-569-5304; Fax 330-569-5309; Elec Mail SaffordLB@Hiram.edu; Internet Home Page Address: www.hiram.edu; *Assoc Prof, Dept Chair* Chris Ryan; *Prof* George Schroeder Emeriti; *Prof* Linda Bourassa; *Prof* Lisa Stafford
Estab 1850; Maintain nonprofit art gallery; Frohring Art Gallery; FT 3, PT 2; pvt; E & Weekend; Scholarships; SC 21, LC 19; D 400
Ent Req: HS dipl

Degrees: AB 4 yr, MAIS (master arts in interdisciplinary studies)
Tuition: $19,650 per acad yr
Courses: Aesthetics, Art Education, †Art History, Ceramics, Drawing, Painting, Photography, Printmaking, Sculpture, †Studio Art, Teacher Training
Summer School: Enrl 15-20 per course; 6-7 wks. Courses—Art History, Ceramics, Film Studies, Photography

HURON

BOWLING GREEN STATE UNIVERSITY, FIRELANDS COLLEGE, Humanities Dept, One University Dr, Huron, OH 44839. Tel 419-433-5560; Fax 419-433-9696; Internet Home Page Address: www.firelands.bgsu.edu/~dsapp; *Prof Art* David Sapp
Estab 1907, col estab 1966; Maintain nonprofit art gallery, Little Gallery; BGSU Firelands, One University Dr, Huron, OH 44839. Art supplies sold at on-campus store; FT 1, PT 3; pub; D & E Sat; Scholarships; SC 12, LC 3; D 2000
Ent Req: HS dipl, SAT
Degrees: AA 2 yr
Courses: Art Appreciation, Art Education, Art History, Drawing, Graphic Design, Mixed Media, Painting, Printmaking, Studio Foundations
Summer School: Term of 5 wks beginning July. Courses—Studio Courses

KENT

KENT STATE UNIVERSITY, School of Art, 400 Janik Dr, Kent, OH 44242; PO Box 5190, Kent, OH 44242-0001. Tel 330-672-9292; Fax 330-672-4729; Elec Mail chavice@kent.edu; Internet Home Page Address: www.kent.edu/; *Dir* Christine Havice; *Dir Galleries* Anderson Turner
Estab 1910; Maintain nonprofit art gallery: Downtown Gallery, 141 E Main St, Kent; School Gallery, 201 Art Bldg, 400 Janik Dr., Kent. Scholarships to undergrads; Fellowships & Teaching Assistantships to grads for 1 yr given annually & semi-annually; FT 43, PT 6; pub; D & E; Scholarships, Grants; SC 105, LC 35, GC 50; non-maj 600, maj 600, grad 100
Ent Req: HS dipl, ACT
Degrees: BFA, BA 4 yrs, MA 1 - 2 yrs, MFA 2 - 3 yrs
Tuition: Res—undergrad $4673 per sem; grad $4971 per sem; nonres—undergrad $8653 per sem, grad $8729 per sem, campus res—room starts at $2720, board starts at $1555 per sem
Courses: Advertising Design, Art Appreciation, †Art Education, †Art History, Calligraphy, †Ceramics, Collage, Commercial Art, Conceptual Art, Constructions, Design, Display, †Drawing, Goldsmithing, Graphic Arts, †Graphic Design, †History of Art & Architecture, Hot Glass, †Illustration, Intermedia, †Jewelry, Lettering, Mixed Media, Museum Staff Training, †Painting, †Printmaking, †Sculpture, Silversmithing, Teacher Training, †Textile Design, †Weaving
Adult Hobby Classes: Tuition free to adults 50 yr & retired or 60 yr old (non-credit basis)
Children's Classes: Enrl 100; tuition $15 per 10 wk session, two 5 wk sessions, fall & spring
Summer School: Dir, Christine Havice, Enrl 500; tuition $425 per cr hr, 8 wk term. Courses—Art Education, Art History, Blossom Art Crafts

KIRTLAND

LAKELAND COMMUNITY COLLEGE, Fine Arts Department, 7700 Clock Tower Dr, Kirtland, OH 44094. Tel 440-525-7459 (Dept), 525-7000 (main); Internet Home Page Address: www.lakelandcc.edu; *Prof* Teresa Hess, MFA; *Assoc Prof* Christopher Berry, MFA; *Instr* Derek O'Brien, MFA
Estab 1967, dept estab 1968; Maintains a nonprofit art gallery, 7700 Clocktower Dr, Kirtland, OH, 44094; FT 3 PT varies; pub; D & E, weekends; Scholarships; D & E 350
Ent Req: HS dipl
Degrees: AA with concentration in Art 2 yrs, AA Technology degree in Graphic Design
Tuition: In-county res—$89.90 per cr hr; out-of-county res—$110.15 per cr hr; out-of-state—$235 per cr hr
Courses: Art Appreciation, Art History, Ceramics, Drawing, Jewelry, Painting, Sculpture
Summer School: Courses—Ceramics, Drawing, Jewelry, Painting, Sculpture

MARIETTA

MARIETTA COLLEGE, Art Dept, 215 Fifth St Marietta, OH 45750. Tel 740-376-4643; Fax 740-376-4529; Elec Mail garoza@marietta.edu; Internet Home Page Address: www.mcnet.marietta.edu; *Prof* Ron Wright; *Chmn* Valdis Garoza
Estab 1835; 4; pvt; Grants, Loans; SC 20, LC 7; maj 75, total col 1600
Degrees: BA(Studio, Art History, Art Education & Graphic Design), BFA
Courses: Advertising Design, Art Appreciation, Art Education, Art History, Calligraphy, Carving in Wood & Stone, Ceramics, Commercial Art, Computer Graphic, Design, Drawing, Jewelry Making, Life Drawing, Lithography & Silkscreen, Modeling & Casting, Painting, Printmaking, Stained Glass

MOUNT VERNON

MOUNT VERNON NAZARENE UNIVERSITY, (Mount Vernon Nazarene College) Art Dept, 800 Martinsburg Rd, Mount Vernon, OH 43050-9500. Tel 740-397-9000 x 3040; Internet Home Page Address: www.mvnc.edu; *Instr* John Donnelly; *Chmn* Jim Hendrickx
Estab 1968, dept estab 1970; Maintain a nonprofit gallery & library; on-campus bookstore sells art supplies; Den; D & E; Scholarships; SC 20, LC 5; D 1,052, non-maj 1,032, maj 20
Ent Req: HS dipl & grad of upper 2/3, ACT

Degrees: BA; Sr project required for graduation
Courses: Aesthetics, Art Education, Art History, Art in the Western World, Ceramics, Design Fundamentals, Drafting, Drawing, Graphic Communication, Graphic Design, Painting, Photography, Printmaking, Sculpture, Selected Topics, Senior Project

NEW CONCORD

MUSKINGUM COLLEGE, Art Department, 163 Stormont St, Johnson Hall New Concord, OH 43762-1118. Tel 740-826-8211, 826-8310; Internet Home Page Address: www.muskingum.edu/; *Asst Prof* Ken McCollum; *Chmn* Yan John Sun; *Instr* Rhoda Van Tassel; *Instr* Amy Kennedy
Estab 1837; FT 3; pvt; D; Scholarships; SC 13, LC 6; D 300, maj 15
Ent Req: HS dipl, ent exam, specific school standards
Degrees: BA and BS 4 yr
Courses: †Art Education, Art History, Ceramics, Design, Drawing, Graphic Arts, Painting, Photography, Sculpture, Teacher Training
Adult Hobby Classes: Enrl 60. Courses—Art Educ
Children's Classes: Enrl 10. Courses—Ceramics

OBERLIN

OBERLIN COLLEGE, Dept of Art, 101 N Professor St, Oberlin, OH 44074-1056. Tel 440-775-8411; Fax 440-775-6905; Elec Mail college.admissions@oberlin.edu; Internet Home Page Address: www.oberlin.edu; *Chmn* Daniel Goulding PhD; *Prof* John Pearson, MFA; *Assoc Prof* Susan Kane PhD, MFA; *Assoc Prof* Patricia Mathews PhD, MFA; *Assoc Prof* Sarah Schuster, MFA; *Assoc Prof* Johnny Coleman, MFA; *Assoc Prof* Nanette Yannuzzi Macias, MFA; *Asst Prof* Paul Yanto; *Asst Prof* Pipo Nguien-Ouy; *Asst Prof* Doug Sanderson; *Asst Prof* Andy Shaken; *Asst Prof* Will Wilson; *Asst Prof* Rian Brown-Urso; *Asst Prof* Julie Davis; *Asst Prof* Erik Inglis; *Dean Admissions* Debra Chermonte
Estab 1833, dept estab 1917; pvt; D & E; Scholarships; SC 28, LC 38, advanced undergrad & grad courses 13; D approx 1200, non-maj 500, maj 100, grad 5
Ent Req: HS dipl, SAT
Degrees: BA 4 yr
Courses: Art History, Drawing, History of Art & Architecture, Interactive Media, Painting, Photography, Sculpture, Silkscreening

OXFORD

MIAMI UNIVERSITY, Art Dept, 501 E High St, New Art Bldg Oxford, OH 45056-1846. Tel 513-529-2900; Fax 513-529-1532; Internet Home Page Address: www.miami.muohio.edu; *Dean School Fine Arts* Pamela Fox; *Chmn* Jerry W Morris
Estab 1809, dept estab 1929; pub; D & E; Scholarships; SC 49, LC 35, GC 20; D 2309, non-maj 1890, maj 419, grad 32
Ent Req: HS dipl, class rank, ACT or SAT
Degrees: BFA & BS(Art) 4 yrs, MFA 2 yrs, MA(Art or Art Educ)
Courses: †Advertising Design, Architecture, †Art Education, †Art History, Calligraphy, †Ceramics, Collage, Commercial Art, Display, †Drawing, Graphic Arts, †Graphic Design, †History of Art & Architecture, †Jewelry, Lettering, Museum Staff Training, †Painting, †Photography, †Printmaking, †Sculpture, †Silversmithing, Stitchery, †Teacher Training, Weaving
Children's Classes: Enrl 70; tuition $30 per sem. Courses—General Art
Summer School: Dir, Geoff Eacker. Courses—Crafts

PAINESVILLE

LAKE ERIE COLLEGE, Fine Arts Dept, 391 W Washington St, Painesville, OH 44077-3389. Tel 440-375-7455; Fax 440-375-7454; Internet Home Page Address: www.lakeerie.edu; *Prof* Paul Gothard; *Assoc Prof Theater* John Huston; *Asst Prof Visual Art* Nancy Prudic; *Asst Prof Dance* Lisa DeCat
Estab 1856; maintains nonprofit gallery, BK Smith Gallery; FT 4, PT 2; pvt; D & E; SC 20, LC 7; 800 total
Ent Req: col board exam
Degrees: BA & BFA 4 yrs
Courses: Art Education, †Art History, †Ceramics, Design, Drawing, Introductory Art, †Painting, †Photography, †Printmaking, Sculpture
Summer School: Courses vary

SAINT CLAIRSVILLE

OHIO UNIVERSITY-EASTERN CAMPUS, Dept Comparative Arts, 45425 National Rd, Saint Clairsville, OH 43950. Tel 740-695-1720; Internet Home Page Address: www.eastern.ohiou.edu; *Prof* David Miles
Pub; D & E; Scholarships
Degrees: BA & BS 4 yrs
Tuition: Res—undergrad $92 pr cr hr, grad $100 per cr hr; nonres—undergrad $102 per cr hr, grad $110 per cr hr
Courses: Art Appreciation, Art Education, Design, Drawing, Photography

SPRINGFIELD

SPRINGFIELD MUSEUM OF ART, 107 Cliff Park Rd, Springfield, OH 45501-2501. Tel 937-325-4673; Fax 937-325-4674; Elec Mail ktrout@springfield.net; Elec Mail afortescue@springfieldart.net; Internet Home Page Address: www.springfieldart.museum; *Dir* Ann Fortescue; *Admin Asst* Katherine Trout; *Cur* Charlotte Gordon; *Bookkeeper* Julie Griffin, CPA

Estab 1951; Maintain nonprofit art gallery & library (same address); PT 15; pvt (art school will be a co-op with Clark State Community Col & mus; D & E; Scholarships; D 600
Tuition: $15-$150 for 9 wks sessions
Courses: Ceramics, Drawing, Glass Blowing, Jewelry, Painting, Photography, Sculpture
Adult Hobby Classes: Enrl 287; tuition varies
Children's Classes: Enrl 286; tuition $39 per qtr. Courses—vary

WITTENBERG UNIVERSITY, Art Dept, N Wittenberg Ave Koch Hall, Springfield, OH 45501; PO Box 720, Springfield, OH 45501-0720. Tel 937-327-6231; Fax 937-327-6349; Elec Mail jmann@wittenberg.edu; Internet Home Page Address: www.wittenberg.edu; *Prof* Jack Mann, MFA; *Asst Prof* Kevin Salzman, MFA; *Assoc Prof* Ed Charney, MFA; *Asst Prof* Scott Douley, MFA; *Instr* Amy Morris, MA
Estab 1842; maintains nonprofit gallery, Ann Miller Gallery in Koch Hall Art Dept; pvt den; D & E; Scholarships; SC 30, LC 17; D 350, non-maj 270, maj 80
Ent Req: HS dipl, class rank, transcript, SAT or ACT test results, recommendations & if possible, a personal interview
Degrees: BA & BFA 4 yr
Courses: †Art Education, †Art History, †Ceramics, †Computer Imaging, Drawing, †Illustration, Jewelry, †Painting, Photography, †Printmaking, †Sculpture, †Teacher Training
Summer School: Provost, William Wiebenga. Courses—Art in the Elementary School, Fundamentals of Art, Painting

SYLVANIA

LOURDES UNIVERSITY, Art Dept, 6832 Convent Blvd, Sylvania, OH 43560-4805. Tel 419-885-3211; Fax 419-882-3987; Elec Mail tmatteson@lourdes.edu; Internet Home Page Address: www.lourdes.edu; *Chmn Fine Arts* Todd A Matteson; *Assoc Prof* Erin Palmer Szavuly; *Instr* Charlene Taylor, MA; *Instr* Tamara Monk-Hilty, MFA; *Instr* Thomas Hilty, MFA; *Instr* Peggy Halbig Martinez, M.Ed; *Instr* Julia Chytil Hayes, MA; *Instr* Lynn Brinkman, MA; *Instr* Patrick Dubrevil, MFA; *Instr* Sr Sharon Havelak, O.S.F., MA
Estab 1958; pvt, den; D & E; Scholarships; SC 12, LC 9; D 70, E 30, non-maj 60, maj 35
Ent Req: HS dipl, ACT or SAT
Degrees: AA, BA, BIS, MA
Courses: Aesthetics, Art Appreciation, Art Education, Art History, Art Therapy, Calligraphy, Ceramics, Copper Enameling, Design, Drawing, Fiber Arts, Painting, Printmaking, Sculpture, Weaving
Children's Classes: Summer art prog for children
Summer School: Dir, Todd Matteson. Enrl 30; tuition $274 per cr for 10 wk & 5 wk term. Courses—Art History, Studio Courses

TIFFIN

HEIDELBERG COLLEGE, Dept of Art, 310 E Market St, Tiffin, OH 44883-2462. Tel 419-448-2186; *Chmn* Jim Hagemeyer
Estab 1850; FT 2, PT 3; pvt; D; Scholarships; SC 22, LC 9; 200, maj 24
Ent Req: HS dipl, each applicant's qualifications are considered individually
Degrees: AB 4 yrs, independent study, honors work available
Courses: Advertising Design, Aesthetics, Art Education, Ceramics, Chip Carving, Commercial Art, Copper Enameling, Display, Drawing, Graphic Arts, Graphic Design, History of Art & Architecture, Illustration, Jewelry, Lettering, Metal Tooling, Mosaic, Museum Staff Training, Painting, Sculpture, Stage Design, Teacher Training, Textile Design
Summer School: Term of 6 wks beginning June. Courses—Materials & Methods in Teaching, Practical Arts

TOLEDO

UNIVERSITY OF TOLEDO, Dept of Art, 620 Grove Pl, University Art Bldg Toledo, OH 43620-1515. Tel 419-530-8300; Fax 419-530-8337; Internet Home Page Address: www.ut.edu; *Chmn* David Guip PhD; *Prof* Diana Attie, MS; *Prof* Linda Ames-Bell, MFA; *Prof* Peter Elloian, MFA; *Assoc Prof* Carolyn Autry, MFA; *Assoc Prof* Marc Gerstein, MFA; *Assoc Prof* Rex Fogt, MFA
Estab 1919; FT 13, PT 12; D & E; Scholarships
Ent Req: HS dipl
Degrees: BA, BFA, BEd 4 yr; MEd (Art Educ) 2 yr
Courses: Advertising Design, Art Education, †Art History, †Ceramics, Design, †Drawing, †Metalsmithing, †Painting, †Photography, †Printmaking, †Sculpture
Summer School: Courses offered from those above

UNIVERSITY HEIGHTS

JOHN CARROLL UNIVERSITY, Dept of Art History & Humanities, 20700 N Park Blvd, University Heights, OH 44118-4520. Tel 216-397-4388 (art dept); 397-1886 (main); Internet Home Page Address: www.jcu.edu; *Chmn* Dr Gerald Guest
Estab 1886, dept estab 1965; pvt; D & E; SC 3, LC 30; D 400, non-maj 350, maj-humanities 30, art hist 14
Ent Req: HS dipl, SAT
Degrees: BA Art History 4 yrs, BA Humanities 4 yrs
Courses: Art History, Drawing, Film, History of Art & Architecture, Modern History

WESTERVILLE

OTTERBEIN COLLEGE, Art Dept, 1 Otterbein College, Westerville, OH 43081-2006. Tel 614-823-1258, 823-1556 (General); Fax 614-823-1118; Internet Home Page Address: www.otterbein.edu; *Chmn* Nicholas Hill

Maintains a nonprofit art gallery, Dunlap Gallery, Batelle Fine Art Center; OC Fisher Gallery, Roush Hall, O C, Westerville, OH 43081; Pvt; D & E; Scholarships; SC 11, LC 4; maj 100
Ent Req: HS dipl
Degrees: BA 4 yrs
Courses: Art Education, Art History, Ceramics, Computer Art, Drawing, Graphic Design, Painting, Photography, Printmaking, Sculpture

WILBERFORCE

CENTRAL STATE UNIVERSITY, Dept of Art, P.O. Box 1004, Wilberforce, OH 45384-1004. Tel 513-376-6011; Elec Mail info@csu.edu; Internet Home Page Address: www.centralstate.edu/; *Assoc Prof* Abner Cope; *Assoc Prof* Larry Porter; *Assoc Prof* Ronald Claxton; *Asst Prof* Dwayne Daniel
Estab 1856; FT 6; D; SC 20, LC 8; D 175, maj 50, others 130
Ent Req: HS dipl
Degrees: BA and BS 4 yr
Courses: Advertising Design, Art Education, Art History, Ceramics, Drawing, Graphic Arts, Lettering, Painting, Sculpture, Studio, Teacher Training

WILBERFORCE UNIVERSITY, Art Dept, P.O. Box 1001, Wilberforce, OH 45384. Tel 937-376-2911; *Adv* James Padgett, MFA
Estab 1856, dept estab 1973; pvt; D; Scholarships; SC 22, LC 5
Ent Req: HS dipl
Degrees: BA, BS & BA(Educ) 4 yrs
Courses: Commercial Art, Fine Arts, Printmaking, Sculpture, Teacher Training
Summer School: Courses offered

WILLOUGHBY

WILLOUGHBY SCHOOL OF FINE ARTS, Visual Arts Dept, 38660 Mentor Ave, Willoughby, OH 44094-7797. Tel 440-951-7500; Fax 440-975-4592; Elec Mail info@fineartsassociation.org; Internet Home Page Address: www.fineartsassociation.org/; *Dept Chair* Mary Sarns; *Dir* Charles Lawrence
Estab 1957; pvt; D & E; Scholarships; D 85, E 195
Courses: Ceramics, Drawing, Intermedia, Mixed Media, Painting, Photography

WILMINGTON

WILMINGTON COLLEGE, Art Dept, 1870 Quaker Way, Wilmington, OH 45177-2473. Tel 937-382-6661, Ext 474; Internet Home Page Address: www.wchome.wilmington.edu; *Chmn* Hal Shunk; *Prof* Terry Inlow
Scholarships
Degrees: BA
Tuition: $12,790 per yr
Courses: Art Education, Art History, Ceramics, Design, Drawing, Handicrafts, Painting, Photography, Printmaking, Sculpture, Stage Design

WOOSTER

THE COLLEGE OF WOOSTER, Dept of Art and Art History, 1220 Beall Ave, Ebert Art Ctr Wooster, OH 44691. Tel 330-263-2388; Fax 330-263-2633; Elec Mail rseling@wooster.edu; Internet Home Page Address: www.wooster.edu/en/Academics/Areas-of-Study/Art-and-Art-History.aspx; WATS 800-321-9885; *Asst Prof* Kara Morrow, PhD; *Prof* Walter Zurko, MFA; *Chmn* John Siewert, PhD; *Assoc Prof* Marina Mangubi, MFA; *Assoc Prof* Bridget Murphy Milligan, MFA; *Asst Prof* Diana Presciutti, PhD; *Admin Coordr* Rose Seling
Estab 1866; Maintain non-profit art gallery, The Col of Wooster Art Mus, same address; pvt; D & E; SC 13, LC 19; D 1800, maj 40
Ent Req: HS dipl
Degrees: BA 4 yr
Courses: Architecture, Art Education, †Art History, Ceramics, Drawing, History of Art & Architecture, Mixed Media, Painting, Photography, Printmaking, Sculpture, Studio Art
Adult Hobby Classes: Available through student activities board. Enrl 12-20; tuition varies
Summer School: Dir, Dr Charles Hampton

YELLOW SPRINGS

ANTIOCH COLLEGE, Visual Arts Dept, 1 Morgan Pl, Yellow Springs, OH 45387-1683. Tel 937-581-8201; Internet Home Page Address: www.antioch-college.edu; *Prof* Christopher Garcia, MFA; *Prof* Nevin Mercede, MFA; *Prof* David Lapalombara, MFA
Estab 1853; pvt; D & E; SC 48, LC 10; D 665 per sem, non-maj 100, maj 50
Ent Req: HS dipl
Degrees: BA
Courses: Ceramics, Drawing, Painting, Printmaking, Sculpture

YOUNGSTOWN

YOUNGSTOWN STATE UNIVERSITY, Dept of Art, One University Plaza, Youngstown, OH 44555. Tel 330-742-3000 (Main), 742-3627 (Dept); Fax 330-742-7183; Internet Home Page Address: www.ysu.edu; *Chmn* Susan Russo
Estab 1908, dept estab 1952; FT 15, PT 13; pub; D & E; SC 44, LC 26, GC 8; D & E 1250, maj 300, grad 15
Ent Req: HS dipl
Degrees: AB, BFA & BS 4 yrs

Courses: Art & Technology, †Art Education, †Art History, †Ceramics, †Commercial Art, Drawing, Graphic Arts, †Graphic Design, Illustration, Jewelry, Museum Staff Training, †Painting, Photography, †Printmaking, †Sculpture, †Teacher Training
Adult Hobby Classes: Courses—Calligraphy, Ceramics, Drawing, Painting, Photography, Weaving
Summer School: Two 5 wk sessions beginning June. Courses—same as above

OKLAHOMA

ADA

EAST CENTRAL UNIVERSITY, School of Fine Arts, 1100 E 14th St, Box L-3 ECU Ada, OK 74820-6915. Tel 580-559-5353; Fax 580-436-4042; Elec Mail bjessop@mailclerk.ecok.edu; Internet Home Page Address: www.ecok.edu; *Chair* F Bradley Jessop, EdD; *Asst Prof* Alexandra Knox, MFA; *Asst Prof* Katy Seals, MFA; *Asst Prof* Tayrn Chubb, PhD; *Instr* Wayneath Weddle, MEd; *Instr* John Green, BFA; *Instr* Angela Church, MFA
Estab 1909; Maintains nonprofit art gallery; Pogue Art Gallery, Attn: Dr. Taryn Chubb, Dir PMB 0-6 ECU, 1100 E 14th St, Ada, OK 74820; on-campus art supply shop; schols open to majors; pub; D, E & online; Scholarships; SC 33, LC 10, GC 4; D 400, E 40, non-maj 320, maj 90, grad 4
Ent Req: HS dipl, ACT
Degrees: BFA (Studio, Graphic Arts, Art Educ) 4 yr, MEd 33 hrs, post grad work, pub service prog
Tuition: Res—undergrad $107.43, grad $139.05; nonres—undergrad $317.95, grad $391.05
Courses: Aesthetics, Art Appreciation, †Art Education, Art History, Ceramics, †Commercial Art, Design, Drawing, †Graphic Arts, Graphic Design, Handicrafts, History of Art & Architecture, Painting, Photography, Printmaking, Sculpture, †Silversmithing
Adult Hobby Classes: Enrl 25 average. Courses—Drawing, Painting
Children's Classes: Drawing, painting
Summer School: Chair, Dr Bradley Jessop. Tuition undergrad $120.26, grad $155.30. Courses—Art Education, Drawing, Painting, Sculpture

ALTUS

WESTERN OKLAHOMA STATE COLLEGE, Art Dept, 2801 N Main, Altus, OK 73521. Tel 580-477-2000; Fax 580-521-6154; Internet Home Page Address: www.western.cc.uk.us; *Chmn* Jerry Bryan
Pub; D&E; Scholarships
Degrees: AA, AS, AT
Tuition: Res—undergrad $45 per hr; nonres—undergrad $67.50 per hr
Courses: Advertising Design, Art Appreciation, Art History, Ceramics, Design, Drawing, Handicrafts, Jewelry, Painting, Photography, Printmaking, Sculpture, Stage Design, Video, Weaving

BETHANY

SOUTHERN NAZARENE UNIVERSITY, Art & Design Department, 6729 NW 39th Expressway, Bethany, OK 73008. Tel 405-789-6400; 491-6631; Fax 405-491-6381; Elec Mail mfeisal@snu.edu; Internet Home Page Address: www.snu.edu; *Dean Arts & Sciences* Martha Banz; *Dept Chair* Prof Marcia M Feisal; *Assoc Professional Specialist* Prof Whitney Porch; *Adjunct Prof* Prof Brian Mays
Schols open to art & design majors declared for at least one yr with grade point over 3.0. On-campus shop where art supplies may be purchased; pvt; D & E; Scholarships; SC 16, LC 1; D 51, E 6, non-maj 38, maj 13
Ent Req: HS dipl, ACT
Degrees: BA
Courses: Aesthetics, Art Education, Art History, †B&W Digital, Commercial Art, Crafts, †Design, Drawing, †Graphic Design, Painting, Pottery, Printmaking, Sculpture, †Teacher Training
Children's Classes: Enrl 55; tuition $115 one wk summer art camp (grades 3 - 12). Courses—Drawing, Pottery, Watercolor & various crafts
Summer School: Dir, Nila Murrow. Same as children's classes

CHICKASHA

UNIVERSITY OF SCIENCE & ARTS OF OKLAHOMA, Arts Dept, 1727 W Alabama, Chickasha, OK 73018. Tel 405-574-1302; Fax 405-574-1220; Elec Mail facknappj@usao.edu; Internet Home Page Address: www.usao.edu/usao.art; *Chmn, Assoc Prof Art* Jacquelyn Knapp, MFA; *Prof* Steven Brown, MFA; *Asst Prof* Layne Thrift, MFA; *Asst Prof* Blake Morgan; *Asst Prof* Jordan Vinyard; *Adjunct Instr* Taylor Preston
Estab 1909; pub; D; Scholarships; SC 26, LC 3; maj 95, others 180
Activities: Schols offered
Ent Req: ACT: 24
Degrees: BA, BFA
Courses: †Art Education, Art History, Ceramics, Computer Graphics, Design, Drawing, Graphic Arts, Graphic Design, Jewelry, Mixed Media, Painting, Photography, Pottery, Printmaking, Sculpture, Teacher Training
Summer School: Enrl 60; Courses—Ceramics, Jewelry, Painting, Photography, Sculpture, digital photo

CLAREMORE

ROGERS STATE COLLEGE, Art Dept, 1701 W Will Rogers Blvd, Claremore, OK 74017-3252. Tel 918-341-7510, 343-7744; *Dir* Gary E Moeller, MFA

Estab 1971; pub; D & E; Scholarships; SC 22, LC 3; D 126, E 60, non-maj 146, maj 82
Ent Req: HS dipl, ACT
Degrees: AA & AS 2 yr
Courses: Art History, Ceramics, Drawing, †Fine Arts, †Graphic Technology, Lettering, Painting, Photography, Printmaking, Sculpture
Children's Classes: Tuition $42 per hr. Courses—Children's Art
Summer School: Tuition $42 per hr for term of 8 wks beginning June 5th. Courses—Advanced Ceramics, Art Appreciation, Drawing, Graphic Technology, Painting

DURANT

SOUTHEASTERN OKLAHOMA STATE UNIVERSITY, Dept of Art, Communication & Theatre, 1405 N 4th, Durant, OK 74701. Tel 580-745-2352; Fax 580-745-7477; Elec Mail gbeach@sosu.edu; Internet Home Page Address: www.se.edu; *Chmn* Dell McLain; *Dir Art* Gleny Beach; *Instr* Jack Ousey
Estab 1909; Maintains nonprofit Centre Gallery, Visual & Performing Arts Ctr, 1614 N 1st Ave, Durant, OK 74701; pub; D, E & Online; Scholarships; SC 18, LC 8
Ent Req: HS dipl, col exam
Degrees: BA & BAEduc 4-5 yrs, BS Graphic Design & Visual Commun
Courses: †Aesthetics, Applied Design, Art Appreciation, Art Education, Art History, Ceramics, †Commercial Art, Crafts, Design, Drawing, Graphic Arts, †Graphic Design, Jewelry, †Non-Western Art & Culture, Painting, †Photography, Printmaking, Sculpture
Adult Hobby Classes: Enrl 20; 12 wk term. Courses—Ceramics, Drawing, Jewelry, Painting
Summer School: Dir, Susan H Allen. Enrl 130; tuition same as above. Courses—Art Appreciation, Ceramics

EDMOND

UNIVERSITY OF CENTRAL OKLAHOMA, Dept of Art & Design, 100 N University Dr, Edmond, OK 73034-5207. Tel 405-974-5201; Fax 405-341-4964; *Chmn* Dr Bob E Palmer
Estab 1890; pub; D & E; Scholarships; maj 280, grad 20, dept 1168, school 13,086
Ent Req: HS dipl, health exams, IQ test, scholarship tests
Degrees: BA, BS and MEduc 3-4 yrs
Courses: Advertising Design, African Art, Art Appreciation, †Art Education, Art History, Art in America, Arts & Crafts, Ceramics, Commercial Art, Drawing, Etching & Lithography, Figure Drawing, †Graphic Arts, †Graphic Design, Illustration, Jewelry, Metal Design, Mixed Media, Museum Staff Training, Painting, †Photography, Printmaking, Sculpture, Studio Art, Teacher Training, Weaving
Summer School: Chmn, Dr Bob E Palmer. Enrl 276; tuition $60.20 per cr hr lower div, $61.20 per cr hr upper div. Courses—Art Appreciation, Art History, Ceramics, Computer Graphics, Design, Drawing, European Study Tour, Fibers, Figure Drawing, Jewelry, Painting, Sculpture

LAWTON

CAMERON UNIVERSITY, Art Dept, 2800 W Gore Blvd, Lawton, OK 73505-6320. Tel 580-581-2450; Fax 580-581-2453; Elec Mail tammyj@cameron.edu; Internet Home Page Address: www.cameron.edu; *Chmn* Edna McMillan; *Prof* Benson Warren; *Assoc Prof* Kathy Liontas-Warren; *Asst Prof* Monika Linehan; *Asst Prof* Elizabeth Tilak
Estab 1970; uT 5; pub; D & E; Scholarships; SC 22, LC 5; D 417, E 90, maj 60
Ent Req: HS dipl
Degrees: BA & BFA 4 yrs
Courses: Art Appreciation, Art Education, †Art History, Ceramics, Color, Crafts, Design, Drawing, Graphic Arts, Graphic Design, †Mixed Media, Painting, Photography, †Printmaking, †Sculpture
Summer School: Courses—Art Education, Ceramics, Drawing, Graphics, Mixed Media, Painting, Photography, Printmaking

MIAMI

NORTHEASTERN OKLAHOMA A & M COLLEGE, Art Dept, 200 I St NE Miami, OK 74354. Tel 918-542-8441, 540-6354; Fax 918-542-9759; Internet Home Page Address: www.neoam.cc.ok.us/; *Instr* Kirsten Couch; *Chmn* David Froman
Estab 1919; pub; D & E; Scholarships; SC 12, LC 3
Ent Req: HS dipl
Degrees: AA 2 yr
Courses: Advertising Design, Art Appreciation, Art Education, Calligraphy, Ceramics, Commercial Art, Costume Design & Construction, Design, Display, Drawing, Fashion Arts, Graphic Arts, Lettering, Painting, Photography, Sculpture, Stage Design, Theatre Arts, Video

NORMAN

UNIVERSITY OF OKLAHOMA, School of Art, 520 Parrington Oval, Rm 202, Norman, OK 73019. Tel 405-325-2691; Fax 405-325-1668; Internet Home Page Address: www.ou.edu/finearts/art; *Dir* Dr Andrew Phelan; *Asst Dir Undergrad* Karen Hayes-Thumann; *Asst Dir Grad* Andrew Stout
Estab 1911; pub; D&E; Scholarships; SC 65, LC 25, GC 15; maj 400, others 1200
Degrees: BFA, BA(Art History), MA(Art History) & MFA

Courses: Art Appreciation, Art Education, †Art History, †Ceramics, †Drawing, Figurative Sculpture, †Film, †Graphic Design, Jewelry, Metal Design, Museum Staff Training, †Painting, †Photography, Printmaking, Sculpture, Video

OKLAHOMA CITY

OKLAHOMA CHRISTIAN UNIVERSITY OF SCIENCE & ARTS, Dept of Art & Design, PO Box 11000, Oklahoma City, OK 73136-1100. Tel 405-425-5556; Fax 405-425-5547; Internet Home Page Address: www.ocusa.edu; *Assoc Prof* Cherry Tredway PhD, MFA; *Asst Prof* David Crismon, MFA; *Med Adjunct Prof* Annette Pate, MEd; *Adjunct Prof* Skip McKinstry, MEd; *Adjunct Prof* Donna Watson PhD, MEd; *Chmn* Michael J O'Keefe, MFA
Estab 1949; FT 2 PT 15; D; Scholarships
Ent Req: Check with admissions
Degrees: BFA
Tuition: $2125 per trimester (12-16 hrs)
Courses: †Advertising Design, Art Appreciation, †Art Education, Art History, Computer Graphics, Design, Drawing, Graphic Design, Illustration, †Interior Design, Painting, Photography, Printmaking, Stage Design

OKLAHOMA CITY UNIVERSITY, Norick Art Center, 2501 N Blackwelder, Oklahoma City, OK 73106. Tel 405-521-5226; Fax 405-557-6029; Internet Home Page Address: www.okcu.edu; *Chmn* Jack R Davis; *Prof* Bruce Macella
Estab 1904; FT 2, PT 8; D & E; Scholarships; SC 36, LC 6; maj 45
Ent Req: HS dipl or equivalent
Degrees: 4 yr
Courses: Airbrush, Art History, Ceramics, Computer Graphics, Design, Drawing, †Graphic Design, History of Art & Architecture, Illustration, Mixed Media, Painting, Photography, Printmaking, Sculpture, †Studio Art, Teacher Training
Adult Hobby Classes: Summer workshops
Summer School: Chmn, Jack Davis. Enrl 15; tuition $335 per cr hr for two 6 wk sessions May to July, July to Aug. Courses—Ceramics, Drawing, Painting, Sculpture

OKMULGEE

OKLAHOMA STATE UNIVERSITY, Graphic Arts Dept, Visual Communications, 1801 E Fourth, Okmulgee, OK 74447. Tel 918-293-5050; Fax 918-293-4625; Elec Mail braithw@osu-okmulgee.edu; Internet Home Page Address: www.osu.okmulgee.edu; *Instr* Mark Moore; *Instr* Kurt Stenstrom; *Instr* James McCullough; *Instr* Mary Trammell; *Instr* Dennis Crouch; *Instr* Mary Dickson; *Instr* Pam Wedel; *Instr* Gary Jobe; *Instr* Becky Mounger; *Instr* Jerry Poppenhouse
Estab 1946, dept estab 1970; Maintain nonprofit art gallery, Conoco Art Gallery, Student Union, OSU-Okmulgee; FT 10, PT 1; pub; D & E; Scholarships; SC 12, LC 1; D 130, E 18
Ent Req: HS dipl or 18 yrs of age
Degrees: 2 yr Assoc, degree granting technical school
Courses: Advertising Design, †Art History, Commercial Art, Drafting, Drawing, Graphic Arts, †Graphic Design, Illustration, Lettering, †Multimedia, Photography, †Studio

SHAWNEE

OKLAHOMA BAPTIST UNIVERSITY, Art Dept, 500 W University, Shawnee, OK 74801. Tel 800-654-3285; Fax 405-878-2069; Internet Home Page Address: www.okbu.edu; *Part-Time Instr* Delaynna Trim, MA; *Asst Prof* Julie Blackstone, MA; *Part-Time Instr* Chris Owens, MFA; *Chmn Prof* Steve Hicks, MFA; *Asst Prof* Corey Fuller, MFA
Estab 1910; Maintain nonprofit art gallery; Den; D & E; Scholarships; SC 23, LC 8, grad 1; D 250, E 15, non-maj 92, maj 70
Activities: Schols offered
Ent Req: HS dipl, SAT-ACT
Degrees: BA & BFA 4 yrs
Tuition: Res—undergrad $9,915 per sem, $661 per hr; nonres—undergrad; campus res—room & board $3,360 per acad yr
Courses: †Advertising Design, Art Appreciation, †Art Education, Art History, Calligraphy, Ceramics, Design, †Drawing, Fibers, Graphic Arts, Graphic Design, History of Art & Architecture, Museum Staff Training, †Painting, Photography, †Printmaking, Teacher Training, Theatre Arts, Weaving

SAINT GREGORY'S UNIVERSITY, Dept of Art, 1900 W MacArthur Dr, Shawnee, OK 74804. Tel 405-878-5100; Fax 405-878-5198; Elec Mail info@stgregorys.edu; *Chmn & Prof Emerita* Shirlie Bowers Wilcoxson, BFA; *Instr* Stephen L Mauldin, MFA
Estab 1898, dept estab 1960; den; D & E; Scholarships; SC 8, LC 4; D 750
Ent Req: HS dipl, ACT or SAT
Degrees: AA 2 yrs, 4 yrs
Courses: †Art Appreciation, Art History, Ceramics, Commercial Art, Drawing, Mixed Media, †Museum Staff Training, †Painting, †Photography, Sculpture

STILLWATER

OKLAHOMA STATE UNIVERSITY, Department of Art, Graphic Design and Art History, 108 Bartlett Ctr for the Visual Arts, Stillwater, OK 74078. Tel 405-744-6016; Fax 405-744-5767; Elec Mail artdepartment@okstate.edu; Internet Home Page Address: www.art.okstate.edu; *Assoc Prof* Carey Hissey; *Prof* Chris Ramsay; *Assoc Prof* Brandon Reese; *Prof* Mark Sisson; *Prof* Jack Titus; *Assoc Prof* Jennifer Borland; *Assoc Prof* Phil Choo; *Assoc Prof* Cristina Gonzalez; *Lectr* Teresa Holder; *Lectr* Jo Lynch; *Assoc Prof* Angela Piehl; *Lectr* Priscilla Swarz; *Asst Prof* Louise Siddons; *Asst Prof* Shaoqian Zhang; *Asst Prof* Justen Reyner; *Assoc Prof* Liz Roth; *Asst Prof* Irene Backus; *Dept Head Art & Art History* Rebecca Brienen; *Asst Prof* Patrick Finley

Estab 1890, dept estab 1928; Maintain nonprofit art gallery, Gardiner Art Gallery, 108 Bartlett Ctr for the Visual Arts, Okla State U, Stillwater, OK 74078-4085; art library, Visual Resource Library, 106 Bartlett Ctr Art Dept, Stillwater, OK 74078; Pub; D & E; Scholarships; SC 51, LC 17, GC 4; D 850, E 60, non-maj 810, maj 210
Activities: Schols & fels offered
Ent Req: HS dipl
Degrees: BA, BA, MA (Art Hist), BFA, 4 yr
Courses: Advertising Design, Art Appreciation, Art Education, Art History, Ceramics, Commercial Art, Computer Graphics, Constructions, Design, Drawing, Goldsmithing, Graphic Arts, Graphic Design, History of Art & Architecture, Illustration, Jewelry, Museum Staff Training, Painting, Printmaking, Sculpture, Silversmithing, Typography
Adult Hobby Classes: Enrl 169; tuition $950 per sem. Courses—Lecture, Studio

TAHLEQUAH

NORTHEASTERN STATE UNIVERSITY, College of Arts & Letters, 600 N Grand, Tahlequah, OK 74464. Tel 918-456-5511, Ext 2705; Fax 918-458-2348; Internet Home Page Address: www.nsuok.edu; *Instr* Jerry Choate, MFA; *Instr* R C Coones, MFA; *Chmn* James Terrell, EdD; *Instr* Bobby Martin; *Instr* Dawn Ward; *Instr Art History* Andrew Vassar; *Asst Dean* Paul Westbrook
Estab 1889; pub; D & E; Scholarships; non-maj 50, maj 30, grad 10
Ent Req: HS dipl
Degrees: BA & BA(Educ) 4 yr
Courses: Art Education, Art History, Ceramics, Commercial Art, Costume Design & Construction, Drafting, Drawing, Graphic Arts, Lettering, Painting, Photography, Printmaking, Sculpture, Stage Design, Teacher Training, Theatre Arts
Adult Hobby Classes: Enrl 20; tuition $20.85 per cr hr for 1 sem. Courses—Indian Art
Summer School: Dir, Tom Cottrill. Courses—Art Education, Fundamentals of Art

TULSA

ORAL ROBERTS UNIVERSITY, Art Dept, 7777 S Lewis Ave, Tulsa, OK 74171-0001. Tel 918-495-6611; Fax 918-495-6033; Elec Mail sbranston@oru.edu; Internet Home Page Address: www.oru.edu; *Chmn* Stuart Branston, MFA; *Asst Prof* Jason Howell, MFA; *Instr* Nathan Opp, MA; *Adj Prof* Darlene Gaskil
Estab 1965; pvt; D & E; Scholarships; SC 22, LC 3; D 287, maj 100, others 87
Ent Req: HS dipl, SAT
Degrees: BA(Art Educ), BA & BS(Graphic Design Print), BA(Studio Art) & BS(Graphic Design Video) 4 yrs
Courses: Advertising Design, Art Appreciation, †Art Education, Art History, Calligraphy, Ceramics, Constructions, Design, Drawing, Graphic Arts, †Graphic Design, Handicrafts, Illustration, Interior Design, Intermedia, Jewelry, Lettering, Mixed Media, Painting, Photography, Printmaking, Sculpture, †Studio Art, Teacher Training

TULSA COMMUNITY COLLEGE, Art Dept, 909 S Boston Ave, Tulsa, OK 74119-2095. Tel 918-595-7000; Fax 918-595-7295; Internet Home Page Address: www.tulsa.cc.okay.us; *Instr* Dwayne Pass, MFA; *Instr* William Derrevere, MA; *Instr* Lucas Greco, MFA
Estab 1970; Maintain nonprofit art gallery, TCC Student Art Gallery; PT 8; pub; D & E; Scholarships; SC 16, LC 7; non-maj 40, maj 160
Ent Req: HS dipl
Degrees: AA 2 yrs
Tuition: Campus residency available
Courses: Art Appreciation, Art History, †Ceramics, Commercial Art, Design, Drawing, Glass Blowing, Goldsmithing, Graphic Arts, †Graphic Design, Jewelry, Painting, Photography, Printmaking, Professional Practices, Sculpture, Silversmithing
Adult Hobby Classes: Special prog of art courses & crafts courses
Summer School: Art Appreciation, Color & Design, Drawing, Painting

UNIVERSITY OF TULSA, School of Art, 600 S College Ave, Tulsa, OK 74104. Tel 918-631-2202; Fax 918-631-3423; Internet Home Page Address: www.utulsa.edu; *Asst Prof, Art Hist & Visual Cult* Michaela Merryday; *Asst Prof, Photog* Glenn Herbert Davis; *Asst Prof, Art Hist* Susan M Dixon
Estab 1898; Maintain nonprofit art gallery, Alexandre Hogue Gallery, financed by University (annual attendance 1,000); pvt; D & E; Scholarships; SC 20, LC 13, GC 22, Continuing Educ; maj 110, others 400
Degrees: BA, BFA, MA, MFA and MTA 4 yrs
Courses: Advertising Design, Architecture, Art Appreciation, †Art Education, Ceramics, Graphic Design, †Painting, Photography, †Printmaking, †Sculpture
Adult Hobby Classes: Courses offered through Continuing Educ
Summer School: H Teresa Valero, Summer School Dir

WEATHERFORD

SOUTHWESTERN OKLAHOMA STATE UNIVERSITY, Art Dept, 100 Campus Dr, Weatherford, OK 73096-3001. Tel 405-772-6611, Ext 3756, 774-3757; Fax 405-772-5447; Internet Home Page Address: www.swosu.edu/depts/art/index; *Chmn* Joe London; *Asst Prof* Jan Bradfield; *Asst Prof* Bob Durlac; *Assoc Prof Pharmacy Practice* Norman Taber, MFA
Estab 1901, dept estab 1941; pub; D & E; Scholarships; SC 35, LC 8, GC 43; D 5000
Ent Req: HS dipl
Degrees: BA(Art), BA(Art Educ) and BA(Commercial Art) 4 yr
Courses: Advertising Design, Art Education, Art History, Ceramics, Commercial Art, Drawing, Graphic Arts, Graphic Design, Illustration, Jewelry, Lettering, Mixed Media, Painting, Sculpture, Teacher Training
Adult Hobby Classes: Varies
Summer School: Varies

OREGON

ALBANY

LINN BENTON COMMUNITY COLLEGE, Fine & Applied Art Dept, 6500 SW Pacific Blvd, Albany, OR 97321. Tel 541-917-4999; Fax 541-967-6550; *Instr* John Aikman; *Instr* Rich Bergeman; *Instr* Jason Widmer; *Chmn* Doris Litzer
Estab 1968; pub; D & E; SC 14, LC 2; D 2000, E 4000
Ent Req: open entry
Degrees: AA, AS & AAS 2 yrs
Courses: †Advertising Design, Art History, Ceramics, Display, Drafting, Drawing, †Graphic Arts, †Graphic Design, Handicrafts, Illustration, Lettering, Painting, Photography, Sculpture, Textile Design, Theatre Arts
Adult Hobby Classes: Painting, Tole Painting, Watercolor

ASHLAND

SOUTHERN OREGON UNIVERSITY, Art & Art History Dept, 1250 Siskiyou Blvd, Ashland, OR 97520-5001. Tel 541-552-6386; Fax 541-552-6564; Internet Home Page Address: www.sou.edu/art; *Dept Chmn* Margaret Sjogren; *Prof* Marlene Alt; *Asst Prof Art* David Bithell; *Admin Prog Asst* Zoey Boyles; *Prof* Cody A Bustamante; *Asst Prof* Melissa Geppert; *Adjunct Faculty* Damon Harris; *Prof Art/Applied Multimedia* Donald Kay; *Adjunct Faculty* Steven LaRose; *Assoc Prof* Erika Leppmann; *Instr* Jennifer Longshore; *Adjunct Instr* Kathleen Murney; *Asst Prof* Robin Strangfeld; *Asst Prof* Tracy Templeton; *Adjunct Faculty* Robin Wyshak
Estab 1926; Galleries at the center for visual arts, 1250 Siskiyou Blvd Ashland OR 97520; pub; D & E; Scholarships; SC 53, LC 17, GC 18; D 120, E 30, non-maj 700, maj 100
Ent Req: HS dipl, SAT or ACT
Degrees: BFA, BA or BS(Art) 4 yrs
Courses: Art Appreciation, Art Education, †Art History, Ceramics, Commercial Art, Computer Art, Conceptual Art, Design, Drawing, Graphic Arts, Graphic Design, Illustration, Intermedia, Mixed Media, Museum Staff Training, Painting, Photography, Printmaking, Sculpture
Adult Hobby Classes: Various courses
Children's Classes: Summer classes
Summer School: Enrl 210; 4 - 8 wk term. Courses—various

BEND

CENTRAL OREGON COMMUNITY COLLEGE, Dept of Art, 2600 NW College Way, Bend, OR 97701-5933. Tel 541-382-6112, 383-7510; Fax 541-385-5978; Elec Mail jhamblin@cocc.edu; Internet Home Page Address: www.cocc.edu/finearts/; *Prof* Sara Krempel, MA
Estab 1949; pub; D & E; Scholarships; in col D 2025, E 2000
Ent Req: HS dipl
Degrees: AA, AS, Cert
Courses: Calligraphy, Ceramics, Drawing, Painting, Photography, Printmaking, Stage Design, Theatre Arts
Adult Hobby Classes: Enrl 1500-2000; tuition, duration & courses offered vary
Summer School: Dir, John Weber. Courses—General courses

COOS BAY

COOS ART MUSEUM, 235 Anderson Ave, Coos Bay, OR 97420-1610. Tel 541-267-3901, 267-4877 (art education); Fax 541-267-4877; Elec Mail info@coosart.org; Internet Home Page Address: www.coosart.org; *Exec Dir* Steven Broocks; *Dir Art Educ* Karen Hammer
Open Tues - Fri 10 AM - 4 PM, Sat 1 - 4 PM; Estab 1966; 5 separate galleries with the Art Mus, one rental/sales gallery; pvt; D & E, Weekends; SC 30, LC 10; D 25, E 15
Tuition: Varies
Courses: Art Appreciation, Art History, Ceramics, Collage, Design, Drawing, Glass Fusing, Painting, Paste Papers, Printmaking
Adult Hobby Classes: Enrl 100; tuition for 10 wks, mem $40/$45, non-mem $48/$53
Children's Classes: Tuition varies depending on courses & membership status
Summer School: Tuition same as above

SOUTHWESTERN OREGON COMMUNITY COLLEGE, Visual Arts Dept, 1988 Newmark, Coos Bay, OR 97420. Tel 541-888-7322, 888-7321; Fax 541-888-7801; Internet Home Page Address: www.socc.edu/; *Div Dir* Bob Bower; *Prof* Melanie Schwartz, MFA; *Prof* James Fritz
Estab 1962, dept estab 1964; pub; D & E; Scholarships; SC 11, LC 1; D 420, E 300, non-maj 250, maj 170
Degrees: AA 2 yrs
Courses: Art History, Calligraphy, Ceramics, Computer Art, Design, Drawing, Handmade Paper, Painting, Printmaking, Sculpture
Adult Hobby Classes: Tuition $396 per qtr. Courses—Art History, Calligraphy, Ceramics, Drawing, Glassworking, Handmade Paper & Prints, Painting
Children's Classes: Only as occasional workshops
Summer School: Dean Instruction, Phill Anderson. Tuition varies. Courses—Ceramics, Painting & Composition, Watercolor

CORVALLIS

OREGON STATE UNIVERSITY, Dept of Art, 106 Fairbanks Hall, Corvallis, OR 97331-8540. Tel 541-737-4745; Fax 541-737-8686; Internet Home Page Address: www.oregonstate.edu/dept/arts/; Internet Home Page Address: www.oregonstate.edu/dept/arts/gallery/index.htnl; *Chmn* James Folts, MS; *Prof*

Harrison Branch, MFA; *Prof* Clinton Brown, MFA; *Prof* Thomas Morandi, MFA; *Prof* Henry Sayre PhD, MFA; *Assoc Prof* Shelley Jordon, MFA; *Assoc Prof* Barbara Loeb PhD, MFA; *Asst Prof* Andrea Marks, MFA; *Asst Prof* Yuji Hiratsuka, MFA; *Asst Prof* John Bowers, MFA; *Asst Prof* John Maul, MFA; *Sr Research Assoc* Douglas Russell, BA; *Prof* Elizabeth Pillod, MFA; *Assoc Prof* Kay Campbell; *Asst Prof* Julie Green; *Asst Prof* John Nettleton; *Asst Prof* Muneera U Spence
Estab 1868, dept estab 1908; Maintains nonprofit art gallery, 100 Fairbanks Hall, Corvallis, OR 97331; pub; D & E; Scholarships; SC 63, LC 16, GC 271; non-maj 2000, maj 525
Ent Req: HS dipl
Degrees: BA, BS, BFA & MAIS
Tuition: Res—undergrad $1360 per quarter; res—grad $2542 per quarter; nonres—undergrad $4780 per quarter; nonres—grad $4270 per quarter; campus res available
Courses: 2-D & 3-D Design, Art History, Drawing, Graphic Design, Painting, Photography, Printmaking, Sculpture, Visual Appreciation
Summer School: Dir, John Maul. Enrl 75; 3 wk session beginning 3rd wk in June. Jumpstart-Preschool Visual Arts Workshop for HS students

EUGENE

LANE COMMUNITY COLLEGE, Art & Applied Design Dept, 4000 E 30th Ave, Eugene, OR 97405-0640. Tel 541-463-5409; Fax 541-463-4185; *Art Div* Mary Jo Workman
Estab 1964, dept estab 1967; LCC Art Gallery, 4000 E 30th Ave, Eugene OR 97405; FT 10; pub; D & E; Scholarships; SC 42, LC 4; D 300, E 75, non-maj 240, maj 60
Ent Req: HS dipl
Degrees: AA, AAS 2 yrs
Courses: 2-D & 3-D Design, Advertising Design, Art Appreciation, Art Education, Art History, Ceramics, Commercial Art, Design, Drawing, †Fiber, Film, †Graphic Design, History of Art & Architecture, Illustration, Intermedia, Jewelry, Lettering, Metal Casting, Painting, Photography, Printmaking, Sculpture, Silversmithing, Textile Design, †Video
Adult Hobby Classes: 250; tuition $39 for 30 hrs & fees. Courses—Art Appreciation, Calligraphy, Ceramics, Chinese Brush Painting, Doll Making, Drawing, Jewelry, Oil Painting, Papermaking, Sculpture, Stained Glass, Watercolor
Summer School: Dean, Rick Williams. Enrl 205; tuition $75.50 per cr hr; Courses—Art Appreciation, Drawing, Sculpture, Watercolor, Design

MAUDE KERNS ART CENTER, 1910 E 15th Ave, Eugene, OR 97403-2094. Tel 541-345-1571; Fax 541-345-6248; Elec Mail mkac@efn.org; Internet Home Page Address: www.mkartcenter.org; *Exec Dir* Karen Marie Pavelec
Estab 1950; pvt; D & E; Scholarships; SC 45; D & E 450
Courses: Calligraphy, Ceramics, Design, Drawing, Glass Blowing, Graphic Design, Handicrafts, Jewelry, Lampworking, Leaded Glass, †Mixed Media, †Painting, Photography, Printmaking, Sculpture, Textile Design, Weaving
Adult Hobby Classes: Enrl 100. Courses—Per regular session
Children's Classes: Enrl 200; tuition $75. Courses—Ceramics, Drawing & other special workshops
Summer School: Courses varied

UNIVERSITY OF OREGON, Dept of Fine & Applied Arts, 5232 University of Oregon, Eugene, OR 97403-5295. Tel 541-346-3610; Fax 541-346-3626; Internet Home Page Address: http://art-uo.uoregon.edu; *Assoc Prof* L Alpert
FT 20, PT 10; Pub; D; Scholarships; D 1475, non-maj 350, maj 1050
Degrees: BA, BS 4 yrs, BFA 5 yrs, MFA 2 yrs minimum after BFA or equivalent
Courses: Ceramics, Drawing, Fibers, Jewelry, Metalsmithing, Painting, Photography, Printmaking, Sculpture, Visual Design
Summer School: Dir, Ron Trebon. 8 wks beginning June. Courses—Ceramics, Computer Graphics, Drawing, Fibers, Jewelry, Metalsmithing, Painting, Photography, Printmaking, Sculpture, Visual Design

GRESHAM

MOUNT HOOD COMMUNITY COLLEGE, Visual Arts Center, 26000 SE Stark St, Gresham, OR 97030-3300. Tel 503-491-7309; Fax 503-491-7389; *Assoc Dean* Chris Bruya
Scholarships
Degrees: AA
Courses: Art Education, Art History, Calligraphy, Ceramics, Design, Drawing, Film, Graphic Design, Illustration, Jewelry, Painting, Printmaking, Sculpture
Adult Hobby Classes: Tuition $30 per cr. Courses—All studio courses
Summer School: Dir, Eric Sankey. Enrl 60 - 90; two 5 wk sessions. Courses—Calligraphy, Ceramics, Drawing, Watercolor

LA GRANDE

EASTERN OREGON UNIVERSITY, School of Arts & Science, 1 University Blvd, Division of Arts & Letters La Grande, OR 97850-2807. Tel 541-962-3672; Fax 503-962-3596; Elec Mail dimondt@eou.edu; Internet Home Page Address: www.eou.edu; *Prof Art* Thomas Dimond, MFA; *Assoc Prof* Terry Gloeckler, MFA; *Dean Arts & Sciences* Denny Swonger; *Prof Art* Kat Galloway, MFA; *Prof Art* Doug Kaigler, MFA; *Assoc Prof* Jason Brown, MFA; *Instr Photog* Mel Buffington; *Instr Art Educ* Lisa Brown
Estab 1929; pub; D & E; SC 35, LC 15; Non-maj 30, maj 65
Ent Req: HS dipl
Degrees: degrees BA & BS in Art, Endorsement in Art
Courses: Aesthetics, †Art Appreciation, Art Education, Art History, †Calligraphy, Ceramics, †Conceptual Art, †Constructions, †Costume Design & Construction, Design, Drawing, †Film, Glass, †Graphic Arts, †Graphic Design, †Handicrafts,

†History of Art & Architecture, Jewelry, Life Drawings, †Mixed Media, Painting, Photography, †Printmaking, Sculpture, †Silversmithing, †Stage Design, †Teacher Training, †Textile Design, †Theatre Arts, †Video
Summer School: Dir, Dr Doyle Slater. Enrl 400. Term of 4-8 wks. Courses—Two or three per summer, beginning & advanced level

MARYLHURST

MARYLHURST UNIVERSITY, Art Dept, 17600 Pacific Hwy, Marylhurst, OR 97036; PO Box 261, Marylhurst, OR 97036-0261. Tel 503-636-8141; Fax 503-636-9526; Elec Mail studentinfo@marylhurst.edu; Internet Home Page Address: www.marylhurst.edu; *Dir* Kelcey Beardsley; *Instr* Kristin Collins; *Instr* Dennis Cunningham; *Instr* Margaret Shirley; *Instr* Rich Rollins; *Instr* Terri Hopkins; *Instr* Martha Pfanschmidt; *Instr* Denise Roy; *Dir* Paul Sutinen; *Instr* Nancy Hiss; *Instr* Trude Parkinson; *Instr* Peggy Suzio; *Instr* Marlene Bauer; *Instr* Libby Farr; *Instr* Louise Farrar-Wegener; *Instr* Carole Hermanson; *Instr* Kathleen Huun; *Instr* Michele Kremers; *Instr* Paul Pavlock; *Instr* Cheryl Schneidermann; *Instr* Elizabeth Spurgeon; *Instr* William Washburn; *Instr* Nancy Wilkins; *Instr* Stephanie Robison Baggs
Estab 1980; Maintain nonprofit art gallery; The Art Gym, Marylhurst University, PO Box 261, Marylhurst, OR 97036; pvt; D&E; Scholarships; SC 35, LC 16, other 4; non-maj 50, maj 140
Ent Req: HS dipl or equivalent
Degrees: BA, BFA, MA (Art Therapy)
Courses: Art History, Art Therapy Program, Design, Drawing, History of Photography, Interior Design, Lighting, Mixed Media, Museum Staff Training, Painting, Photography, Printmaking, Sculpture, Textiles
Summer School: Dir, Paul Sutinen. Enrl 100; tuition $293 per cr for 10 wk term. Courses—Drawing, Interior Design, Painting, Photography, Printmaking, Sculpture

MCMINNVILLE

LINFIELD COLLEGE, Department of Art & Visual Culture, 900 SE Baker, ADD-Ste A466 McMinnville, OR 97128-6808. Tel 503-883-2804; Elec Mail mills@linfield.edu; Internet Home Page Address: www.linfield.edu/art/; *Chmn Dept* Ph.D. Brian Winkenweder; *Prof* Ron Mills; *Prof* Nils Lou; *Assoc Prof* Liz Obert; *Gallery Dir* Cris Moss; *Instr* Totem Shriver; *Instr* Adrianne Santina; *Instr* Luke Zimmerman
Estab 1849, dept estab 1964; Mem: Maintains non-profit gallery, Linfield Fine Arts Gallery 900 SE Bater St Suite A466, McMinnville OR 97128; On-campus shop where art supplies may be purchased; pvt; D; Scholarships; SC 20, LC 6; non-maj 250, maj 35
Activities: Art supplies available at on-campus shop
Ent Req: HS dipl
Degrees: BA 4 yr
Tuition: $30,604 per yr
Courses: †Aesthetics, Art Education, Art History, Ceramics, †Conceptual Art, †Design, Drawing, †Graphic Arts, †Graphic Design, Mixed Media, Painting, Photography, Printmaking, Sculpture, Teacher Training

MONMOUTH

WESTERN OREGON STATE COLLEGE, Creative Arts Division, Visual Arts, 345 N Monmouth Ave, Monmouth, OR 97361. Tel 503-838-8000; Fax 503-838-8995; Internet Home Page Address: www.wou.edu; *Prof* Kim Hoffman; *Chmn Creative Arts* Dr Tom Bergeron
Estab 1856; FT 8, PT 2; pub; D & E; Scholarships; SC 72, LC 21, GC 27; total 3600
Degrees: BA and BS 4 yr
Courses: Art Education, Art History, Art Theory, Ceramics, Design, Drawing, Graphic Design, Individual Studies, Painting, Printmaking, Sculpture

ONTARIO

TREASURE VALLEY COMMUNITY COLLEGE, Art Dept, 650 College Blvd, Ontario, OR 97914-3423. Tel 541-881-8822; Internet Home Page Address: www.tvcc.cc.or.us; *Chmn* Robin Jackson
Estab 1961; PT 4; pub; D & E; Scholarships; SC 14, LC 1; D 50, E 35, non-maj 10, maj 15
Ent Req: Placement testing
Degrees: AS & AA 2 yrs
Tuition: Res—$40 per cr; nonres—$54 per cr; out of state—$56; international—$100; campus res available
Courses: Art History, †Ceramics, Drawing, Painting, Sculpture
Summer School: Chmn, Robert M Jackson. Tuition $190 for term of 8 wks beginning June 22. Courses—Ceramics, Drawing, Painting

OREGON CITY

CLACKAMAS COMMUNITY COLLEGE, Art Dept, 19600 S Molalla Ave, Oregon City, OR 97045. Tel 503-657-8400, Ext 2540; Internet Home Page Address: www.clackamas.cc.or.us; *Chmn* Rich True
Estab 1969; Pub; D&E
Ent Req: HS dipl
Degrees: AA
Tuition: Res—$37 per cr hr, nonres—$131 per cr hr
Courses: Advertising Design, Art History, Calligraphy, Ceramics, Design, Drawing, Jewelry, Painting, Sculpture

PENDLETON

BLUE MOUNTAIN COMMUNITY COLLEGE, Fine Arts Dept, 2411 NW Carden Ave, Pendleton, OR 97801-1655; PO Box 100, Pendleton, OR 97801-1000. Tel 541-276-1260; Fax 541-276-6119; Internet Home Page Address: www.bmcc.or.us; *Chmn* Michael Booth; *Chmn* Doug Radke

Estab 1962, dept estab 1964; Maintain nonprofit art gallery; Betty Fevis Memorial Art Gallery; art library; art supplies available at bookstore; pub; D & E; SC 8, LC 2 per qtr; D 255, E 72
Ent Req: HS dipl or equivalent
Degrees: AA, 2 yrs
Tuition: Res—undergrad $50 per cr hr; nonres—undergrad $100
Courses: Art History, Ceramics, Drawing, Jewelry, Lettering, Painting, Sculpture

PORTLAND

LEWIS & CLARK COLLEGE, Dept of Art, 0615 SW Palatine Hill Rd, Portland, OR 97219-7879. Tel 503-768-7390, 768-7000; Fax 503-768-7401; Elec Mail buether@lclark.edu; Internet Home Page Address: www.lclark.edu/~art/; *Prof* Phyllis Yes; *Assoc Prof* Michael Taylor; *Asst Prof* Sherry Fowler; *Asst Prof* Theodore Vogel; *Vis Lect* Robert B Miller; *Vis Lect* Bruce West; *Instr* Debra Beers
Dept estab 1946; pvt; D; Scholarships; SC 10, LC 2
Ent Req: HS dipl
Degrees: BS and BA 4 yr
Courses: Art History, Ceramics, Drawing, Graphic Arts, History of Art & Architecture, Jewelry, Painting, Printmaking, Sculpture, Weaving

OREGON COLLEGE OF ART & CRAFT, (Oregon College of Fine Arts) 8245 SW Barnes Rd, Portland, OR 97225-6349. Tel 503-297-5544; Fax 503-297-3155; Elec Mail admissions@ocac.edu; Internet Home Page Address: www.ocac.edu; *Chief Enrol Officer* Anne Boerner; *Pres* Denise Mullen; *Chair, MFA* Karl Burkheimer; *Book Arts* Barb Tetenbaum; *Painting* Michelle Ross; *Metals* Christine Clark; *Ceramics* Dylan Beck; *Fibers* Emily Nachison; *Photo* Mark Rupert
Estab 1907; Maintains nonprofit gallery, Hoffman Gallery & OCAC library (same location); Ft 10, PT 13; pvt; non-profit; D & E; Scholarships; SC 52, LC 17, GC 3, other 28; D 65, E 1000, Non-Maj 5, Maj 300, Grad 55, other 5
Activities: Schols offered
Ent Req: portfolio review
Degrees: BFA 4 yrs, MFA 2 yrs, Cert prog 3 yrs, arbitrary prog 2 yrs
Tuition: $914.20 per cr hr for 1-11 cr; $10,469 per semester (12+ cr hrs); no campus res
Courses: †Art History, Book Arts, †Ceramics, †Drawing, †Jewelry, †Mixed Media, Painting, Photography, Printmaking, †Restoration & Conservation, †Sculpture, Silversmithing, Textile Design, Weaving, Wood
Adult Hobby Classes: Enrl 1300; tuition $200-$450 noncr hr $700 per cr hrs for 10 wk term. Courses—Book Arts, Ceramics, Painting, Drawing, Fibers, Metals, Photography, Wood
Children's Classes: Enr 1,100; $300, $325, $375 - camp
Summer School: Community Prog Coordr Kathy Baker. Enrl 300; tuition $250 for 1 wk workshop. Courses—same as above

PACIFIC NORTHWEST COLLEGE OF ART, 1241 NW Johnson, Portland, OR 97209. Tel 800-818-PNCA; Fax 503-226-3587; Elec Mail pncainfo@pnca.edu; *Pres* Sally Lawrence; *Instr* William Moore; *Instr* Paul Missal; *Instr* Betsy Lindsay; *Instr* Robert Hanson; *Instr* Frank Irby; *Instr* Anne Johnson; *Instr* Chris Gander; *Instr* Tom Fawkes; *Dir Enrol* Jennifer Satalino; *Instr* David Ritchie; *Instr* Cynthia Pachikara; *Instr* Horatio Law; *Instr* Robert Selby
Estab 1909; FT 19, PT 24; pvt; D & E; Scholarships; SC 54, LC 15; D 258, PT 47, E 249
Ent Req: HS dipl, portfolio, essay
Degrees: BFA 4 yr
Courses: Art History, †Ceramics, †Drawing, †Graphic Design, †Illustration, †Intermedia, †Painting, †Photography, †Printmaking, †Sculpture
Adult Hobby Classes: Enrl 546; tuition $250 per 12 wk term. Courses—Ceramics, Graphic Design, Illustration, Life Drawing, Painting, Photography, Printmaking, Sculpture & other art-related courses
Children's Classes: Enrl 132; tuition $125 per 12 wk term. Courses—Ceramics, Drawing, Painting, Printmaking, Sculpture
Summer School: Dean, Continuing Educ, Lennie Pitkin. Enrl 500; tuition $210 per 12 wk term. Courses—Wide range of Visual Arts

PORTLAND COMMUNITY COLLEGE, Visual & Performing Arts Division, PO Box 19000, Portland, OR 97280-0990. Tel 503-977-4264, Ext 4263; Fax 503-977-4874; *Div Dean* Steve Ward
Estab 1961, dept estab 1963; pub; D & E, Sat; SC 40, LC 5; D 864, E 282, total 1212
Ent Req: none
Degrees: AA 2 yrs
Courses: Art History, Calligraphy, Ceramics, Drawing, Graphic Design, Painting, Photography, Printing Tech, Sculpture, Stage Design, Theatre Arts
Adult Hobby Classes: Tuition varies per quarter. Courses—various
Children's Classes: Courses offered
Summer School: Dept Chmn, Mary Stupp-Greer. Enrl 400; Term of 8 wks beginning June. Courses—same as regular session

PORTLAND STATE UNIVERSITY, Dept of Art, PO Box 751, Portland, OR 97207-0751. Tel 503-725-3515; Fax 503-725-4541; Internet Home Page Address: www.art.pdx.edu; *Dept Chmn, Prof* Michihiro Kosuge, MFA; *Prof* William Fosque, MFA; *Asst Prof* William LePore, MA; *Assoc Prof* Elizabeth Mead, MFA; *Assoc Prof* Sue Taylor, PhD; *Assoc Prof* Daniel Pirosky, BA; *Assoc Prof* Jane Kristof, PhD; *Assoc Prof* Susan Agre-Kippenhan, MFA; *Assoc Prof* Eleanor Erskins, MFA; *Assoc Prof* Susan Harlan, MFA; *Assoc Prof* Junghee Lee, MA; *Asst Prof* Lee Charmin, MFA; *Asst Prof* Charles Colbert, PhD; *Asst Prof* Anne McClanan, PhD
Estab 1955; pub; D & E; Scholarships; E 2000, non-maj 1300, maj 600, grad 12, others 70
Ent Req: HS dipl, SAT
Degrees: BS & BA(Art) 4 yr, MFA (Painting, Printmaking, Sculpture) 2 yr
Courses: Art History, †Drawing, †Graphic Design, †Painting, Printmaking, †Sculpture

Summer School: Enrl 4-500; term of 8-12 wks beginning June 28.
Courses—vary. Two centers, one in Portland and one at Cannon Beach: The
Haystack Program

REED COLLEGE, Dept of Art, 3203 S E Woodstock Blvd, Portland, OR
97202-8199. Tel 503-771-1112; Fax 503-788-6691; Internet Home Page Address:
www.reed.edu; *Chmn Art History & Humanities* William J Diebold; *Prof Art*
Michael Knutson; *Asst Prof Art* Geraldine Ondrizek
Estab 1911; FT 5; pvt; D; Scholarships; SC 7, LC 5; D 1150, E 15
Degrees: BA 3-5 yr
Courses: Aesthetics, Architecture, †Art History, Ceramics, †Conceptual Art,
†Drawing, Graphic Arts, History of Art & Architecture, †History of Art &
Architecture, Humanities, †Painting, Photography, Printmaking, Restoration &
Conservation, †Sculpture, Theory
Adult Hobby Classes: Courses offered & MA degree
Summer School: Courses offered

ROSEBURG

UMPQUA COMMUNITY COLLEGE, Fine & Performing Arts Dept, PO Box
967, Roseburg, OR 97470-0226. Tel 541-440-4600, Ext 691; Elec Mail
rochess@umpqua.edu; Internet Home Page Address: www.umpqua.edu; *Dir Fine
Arts* Susan Rochester
Estab 1964; Maintain nonprofit art gallery, Umpqua Community College, 1140
College Rd, Roseburg, OR 97470; pub; D & E; Scholarships; SC 21, LC 3; D
190, E 90, maj 30
Ent Req: HS dipl
Degrees: AA 2 yr
Courses: Art History, Basic Design, Ceramics, Drawing, Painting, Photography,
Sculpture, Theatre Arts
Adult Hobby Classes: Enrl 195; tuition $45 & lab fee for 10 weeks.
Courses—Ceramics, Drawing, Painting, Photography, Sculpture

SALEM

CHEMEKETA COMMUNITY COLLEGE, Dept of Humanities &
Communications, Art Program, 4000 Lancaster Dr NE, Salem, OR 97305-1453;
PO Box 14007, Salem, OR 97309-7070. Tel 503-399-5184; Fax 503-399-5214;
Elec Mail donb@chemeketa.edu; Internet Home Page Address: art.chemeketa.edu,
artgallery.chemeketa.edu; *Dir* Don Brase; *Instr* Lee Jacobson, MFA; *Instr* Kay
Bunnenberg-Boehmer, MFA; *Instr* Carol Bibler, MFA; *Adjunct* Gary Rawlins,
BFA; *Adjunct* Deanne Beausoleil, MA; *Instr* Deborah Trousdale, MFA; *Adjunct*
Cynthia Herron, MFA; *Instr* Laurce Mack, MFA; *Adjunct* Jane Lieber Mays, BA
Estab 1969, dept estab 1975; Maintain nonprofit art gallery; Chemeketa
Community College Art Gallery; art supplies available in bookstore; Pub; D, E &
Weekend; Scholarships; SC 40, LC 6; D 175, E 175
Ent Req: none
Degrees: AA 2 yr
Courses: Art Appreciation, †Art Glass, Art History, Art as a Profession, Ceramics,
Design, †Drafting, Drawing, Film, Graphic Design, Painting, Photography,
Printmaking, Sculpture, †Theatre Arts
Adult Hobby Classes: Enrl 150-200; tuition $56 per cr hr
Summer School: Tuition varies, 8 wk term

PENNSYLVANIA

ALLENTOWN

CEDAR CREST COLLEGE, Art Dept, 100 College Dr, Allentown, PA
18104-6196. Tel 610-606-4666; Internet Home Page Address:
www.cedarcrest.edu/; *Prof* Nelson Maniscalco, MFA; *Prof* Pat Badt, MFA; *Asst
Prof* William Clark, MFA; *Asst Prof* Jill Odegaard; *Asst Prof* Kim Sloane
Estab 1867; Maintain nonprofit art gallery, Tempkins Gallery; FT 3, PT 2; pvt,
women only; D & E; Scholarships; SC 10, LC 6; 1000
Ent Req: HS dipl, CEEB
Degrees: BA, BS, Interdisciplinary Fine Arts Maj (art, theatre, music, dance,
creative writing), 4 yr
Courses: Aesthetics, Art Education, Art History, Ceramics, Comparative Study of
Art, Drawing, Jewelry, Metal Forming, Painting, †Printmaking, Sculpture, Theatre
Arts
Summer School: Courses—Ceramics, Jewelry-Metalsmithing, Sculpture, Painting

MUHLENBERG COLLEGE, Dept of Art, 2400 Chew St, Allentown, PA
18104-5586. Tel 484-664-3100; Internet Home Page Address:
www.muhlenbergcollege/artdept; Internet Home Page Address:
www.muhlenberg.edu; *Chmn* Jadviga Da Costa Nunes PhD; *Assoc Prof* Scott
Sherk, MFA; *Asst Prof* Raymond S Barnes, MFA; *Asst Prof* Joseph Elliott, MFA;
Instr Kevin Tuttle; *Instr* David Haas; *Instr* Carol Heft
Estab 1848; FT 4, PT 6; pvt, pub; D & E; SC 16, LC 17; D 2000, non-maj 284,
maj 60
Ent Req: HS dipl, 3 achievement tests & English Composition Achievement
required
Degrees: BA 4 yrs
Tuition: Res—$26,700 per yr with room & board
Courses: Art Education, †Art History, Ceramics, †Design, Drawing, Graphic Arts,
History of Art & Architecture, Painting, Photography,
Printmaking, Sculpture, †Studio Arts, †Teacher Training, †Theatre Arts
Adult Hobby Classes: Courses—Art History, Drawing, Painting, Photography,
Photo-Journalism

Summer School: Dean of Evening Coll, S Laposata; Courses—same as adult
educ courses

BETHLEHEM

LEHIGH UNIVERSITY, Dept of Art, Architecture & Design, 17 Memorial Dr
E, Bethlehem, PA 18015-3029. Tel 610-758-3610; Internet Home Page Address:
www.lehigh.edu; *Assoc Prof* Bruce Thomas PhD; *Prof* Ricardo Viera, MFA; *Prof* Lucy
Gans, MFA; *Prof* Anthony Viscardi, MArch; *Assoc Prof* Berrisford Boothe, MFA;
Prof Practice Christine Ussler, MArch; *Assoc Prof* Anna Chupa, MFA; *Assoc Prof*
Amy Forsyth, MArch; *Lectr* Jason Travers, MFA; *Asst Prof* Wesley Heiss, M
Arch; *Asst Prof* Marilyn Jones, MFA; *Asst Prof* Hyun Tae Jung, PhD; *Asst Prof*
Nikolai Nikolov, M Arch; *Asst Prof* Nicholas Sawicki, PhD; *Asst Prof* Susan Kart,
PhD
Estab 1925; Maintains Art Galleries, Zoellner Art Center, 420 E Packer Ave,
Bethlehem, PA 18015; FT 9, PT 1; pvt; D & E; SC 22, LC 16; D & E 100
Ent Req: HS dipl, SAT, CEEB
Degrees: BA 4 yrs
Courses: †Architecture, †Art, †Art History, †Design, Drawing, Graphic Design,
Museum Studies, Painting, Photography, Product Design, Sculpture
Summer School: Courses—Architectural Design, Art History, Graphic Design
Workshop, Color

MORAVIAN COLLEGE, Dept of Art, 1200 Main St, Church Street Campus
Bethlehem, PA 18018-6614. Tel 610-861-1680; Fax 610-861-1682; Elec Mail
jciganick@moravian.edu; Internet Home Page Address: www.moravian.edu; *Chmn*
Angela Fraleigh, MFA; *Dir of Payne Gallery* Diane Radycki, PhD; *Prof* Kristin
Baxter, EdD; *Instr* Jeffrey Hurwitz; *Instr* Renzo Faggioli; *Vis Artists* Kirsli Spinks,
MA; *Instr* Aron Johnston; *Instr* Matthew Shelley; *Instr* Doug Zucco; *Instr* Martha
Kearns; *Instr* Elizabeth Krenos; *Instr* Ted Colegrove; *Instr* Kristine Kotsch; *Instr*
Jan Ciganick
Estab 1742, dept estab 1963; Maintains Payne Gallery of Moravian College
located at same address; pvt; D & E; Scholarships; SC 15, LC 8; D 1200, E 500,
non-maj 1200, maj 140
Ent Req: HS dipl
Degrees: BA and BS 4 yrs
Courses: †Advertising Design, †Art Education, †Art History, †Ceramics, Design,
Digital Video, †Drawing, Graphic Arts, Graphic Design, Handicrafts, History of
Art & Architecture, Jewelry, Museum Staff Training, Painting, Photography,
Printmaking, Sculpture, †Teacher Training & Certification
Children's Classes: Summer camp $100 per wk per student
Summer School: Dir Continuing Studies, Donna Smith. Enrl 110. Courses—Same
as above

NORTHAMPTON COMMUNITY COLLEGE, Art Dept, 3835 Green Pond Rd,
Bethlehem, PA 18020-7599. Tel 610-861-5300, Ext 5485; Fax 610-861-5373;
Internet Home Page Address: www.northampton.edu; *Asst Prof* Andrew Szoke;
Prog Coordr Gerald Rowan
Estab 1967; pub; D & E; Scholarships; SC 12, LC 8; D 100, E 350
Ent Req: HS dipl, portfolio
Degrees: AAS(Advertising), cert in photography
Courses: 3-D Materials, Advertising Design, Architecture, Art History, Ceramics,
Color & Spatial Concepts, Computer Graphics, Drafting, Drawing, Fashion Arts,
Graphic Arts, Graphic Design, Handicrafts, History of Art & Architecture,
Illustration, Interior Design, Lettering, Painting, Photography, Pottery, Printmaking,
Sculpture
Adult Hobby Classes: Courses—Art, Photography

BLOOMSBURG

BLOOMSBURG UNIVERSITY, Dept of Art & Art History, 400 E 2nd St,
Bloomsburg, PA 17815-1399. Tel 570-389-4646; Fax 570-389-4459; Internet
Home Page Address: www.bloomu.edu; *Chmn* Dr Christine Sperling; *Prof* Vera
Viditz-Ward, MFA; *Assoc Prof* Charles Thomas Walter PhD, MA; *Asst Prof*
Meredith Grimsley, MFA; *Assoc Prof* Vincent Hron, MFA; *Assoc Prof* Jason
Godeke, MFA; *Asst Prof* Marilee Salvator, MFA; *Asst Prof* Sue O'Donnell, MFA;
Asst Prof Dr Nogin Chung, PhD
Estab 1839, dept estab 1940; Maintains nonprofit Haas Gallery of Art, 2nd Fl
Mitrani Hall, 400 E 2nd St, Bloomsburg PA 17815; art supplies sold at on-campus
store; pub; D & E; Scholarships; SC 24, LC 9; D 1000, E 30, maj 100, non-maj
930
Ent Req: HS dipl
Degrees: BA(Art Studio) & BA(Art History)
Courses: Art History, Computer Graphics, Crafts, General Design, Painting,
Photography, Printmaking, Sculpture, †Textile Design
Summer School: Dean, Michael Vavrek. Enrl 200. Courses—Art History, General
Studio

BLUE BELL

MONTGOMERY COUNTY COMMUNITY COLLEGE, Art Center, 340 De
Kalb Pike, Blue Bell, PA 19422. Tel 215-641-6328; Elec Mail fshort@mc3.edu;
Internet Home Page Address: www.mc3.edu; *Coordr* Frank Short; *Assoc Prof*
Roger Cairns, MFA; *Asst Prof* Cheryl Gelover, MFA; *Asst Prof* Michael Connelly;
Assoc Prof Patrick Winston
Estab 1967; Maintains Fine Art Center Gallery & campus shop for limited
purchase of art supplies; FT 5, PT 31; Pub; D, E & online; Scholarships; SC 39,
LC 6; D 250
Ent Req: HS dipl
Degrees: AA & AFA Fine Arts, AAS Commercial Art & Digital Design
Tuition: Count res—undergrad $96 per cr hr; nonres—$192 per cr hr
Courses: Art History, Ceramics, †Digital Art, †Digital Design*, †Digital
Photography, Drawing, †Fine Art, Graphic Design, Illustration, Painting,
Photography, Printmaking, Sculpture, Typography, †Woodworking

Summer School: Coord, Frank Short. Enrl 66; tuition $35 per cr.
Courses—Ceramics, Drawing, Painting, Photography

BRYN MAWR

BRYN MAWR COLLEGE, Dept of the History of Art, 101 N Merion Ave, Bryn Mawr, PA 19010-2899. Tel 610-526-5210; Elec Mail info@brynmawr.edu; Internet Home Page Address: www.brynmawr.edu/arts; *Dept Admin* Adrienne Clarke
Estab 1913; maintains library, Rhys Carpenter Library; pvt, W (men in grad school); D; Scholarships, Fellowships; LC 10, GC 8; maj 15, grad 30, others 250
Degrees: BA 4 yr, MA, PhD
Tuition: $21,860 per yr; campus res—room & board $7870
Courses: †Architecture, Art History, †Graphic Arts, †History of Art & Architecture

HARCUM COLLEGE, Fashion Design, 750 Montgomery Ave, Bryn Mawr, PA 19010-3405. Tel 610-526-6050; Internet Home Page Address: www.harcum.edu; *Dir* Winifred Curtis
Estab 1915; FT 1, PT 5; pvt, W; D & E; Scholarships; SC 7, LC 1; D 40, E 8, maj 10
Ent Req: HS dipl
Degrees: AA 2 yr
Courses: Commercial Art, Drawing, Fashion Arts, Graphic Design, History of Art & Architecture, Lettering, Painting, Sculpture

CALIFORNIA

CALIFORNIA UNIVERSITY OF PENNSYLVANIA, Dept of Art, 250 University, California, PA 15419. Tel 724-938-4000, 938-4182; Fax 724-938-4256; Internet Home Page Address: www.cup.edu; *Chmn Dept* Richard Mieczinkowski
Estab 1852, dept estab 1968; pub; D & E; SC 20, LC 5; maj 137
Ent Req: SAT
Degrees: Cert(Art Educ), BA 4 yrs
Courses: Advertising Design, Aesthetics, Art Appreciation, Art Education, Art History, Ceramics, Commercial Art, Costume Design & Construction, Design, Drawing, Fashion Arts, Graphic Arts, Handicrafts, Illustration, Interior Design, Jewelry, Mixed Media, Painting, Printmaking, Sculpture, Stage Design, Stained Glass, Textile Design, Weaving
Adult Hobby Classes: Enrl 25 per class. Courses—Pottery, Stained Glass
Summer School: Chmn, Richard Grinstead. Term of 5 or 10 wks beginning June

CARLISLE

DICKINSON COLLEGE, Dept of Art & Art History, PO Box 1773, Weiss Ctr for the Arts Carlisle, PA 17013-2896. Tel 717-245-1053; Fax 717-245-1937; Elec Mail millejoa@dickinson.edu; Internet Home Page Address: www.dickinson.edu/departments/arts/; *Assoc Prof* Ward Davenny; *Prof* Melinda Schlitt, PhD; *Asst Prof* Elizabeth Lee, PhD; *Asst Prof* Anthony Cervino; *Adjunct Faculty* Andrew Bale; *Asst Prof* Todd Arsenault; *Adjunct Faculty* Lisa Dorrill, PhD; *Assoc Prof* Crispin Sartwell
Estab 1773, dept estab 1940; Maintains nonprofit art gallery, The Trout Gallery, Weiss Center for the Arts, PO Box 1773, Carlisle, PA 17013. Campus shop where art supplies may be purchased; pvt; D; SC 10, LC 15; D 2400, non-maj 550, Maj 80
Ent Req: HS dipl, SAT
Degrees: BA and BS 4 yrs
Courses: Art History, Ceramics, †Contemporary Art, Drawing, History of Art & Architecture, Italian Renaissance, Painting, Photography, Printmaking, Sculpture, †Studio Major, †Video
Summer School: Dir, Diane Fleming. Term of 6 wks beginning May. Courses—per regular session

CHELTENHAM

CHELTENHAM CENTER FOR THE ARTS, 439 Ashbourne Rd, Cheltenham, PA 19012-1705. Tel 215-379-4660; Fax 215-663-1946; Elec Mail info@cheltenhamarts.org; Internet Home Page Address: www.cheltenhamarts.org; *Events & Publicity Coordr* Traci Nelson; *Educ Dir* Joan Phillips
Estab 1940; maintain nonprofit art gallery at same address; community; D & E; 6-wk terms, 6 per yr; Scholarships; SC 50; D 875, E 200, Other 250
Ent Req: children, teens & adults; open to the public
Tuition: Course prices vary
Courses: Ceramics, Drawing, Jewelry, Painting, Pottery, Printmaking, Sculpture, Stained Glass, Theater Classes, Theatre Arts, Video

CHEYNEY

CHEYNEY UNIVERSITY OF PENNSYLVANIA, Dept of Art, 1837 University Cir, Cheyney, PA 19319-0200. Tel 610-399-2000; Internet Home Page Address: www.cheyney.edu; *Fine Arts Dept Chmn* J Hank Hamilton Jr
Estab 1937; pub; D & E; Scholarships; SC 16, LC 4
Ent Req: HS dipl, ent exam
Degrees: BA 4 yrs
Courses: Drawing, Handicrafts, Painting, Sculpture

CLARION

CLARION UNIVERSITY OF PENNSYLVANIA, Dept of Art, 840 Wood St, Clarion, PA 16214-1240. Tel 814-393-2000, ext 2291; Fax 814-393-2168; Elec Mail ggreenberg@clarion.edu; Internet Home Page Address: www.clarion.edu/art;

Prof Catherine Joslyn; *Asst Prof* James Rose; *Asst Prof & Chmn* Gary Greenberg; *Asst Prof* Kaersten Colvin; *Assoc Prof* Dr Joe Thomas; *Asst Prof* Melissa Kuntz; *Asst Prof* Mark Franchino; *Instr* Scott Turri
Estab 1867; Maintains nonprofit University Gallery; Pub; D & E; Scholarships; SC 13, LC 10; D & E 925 per sem, day 450, eve 50, non-maj 150, maj 85
Ent Req: HS dipl
Degrees: BFA(Art), BA(Art), BA(Art History)
Courses: 3-D Design, Art Appreciation, †Art History, †Ceramics, Commercial Design, Design, †Drawing, †Fabric, †Fiber, †Graphic Arts, Graphic Design, Handicrafts, History of Art & Architecture, Jewelry, †Printmaking, †Sculpture, Textile Design, Weaving
Adult Hobby Classes: Enrl 20; tuition $50 - $90 for 9-12 wk course. Courses—Calligraphy, Ceramics, Drawing, Painting
Summer School: Tuition $210 per cr hr for 2-5 wk sessions. Courses—Various

EAST STROUDSBURG

EAST STROUDSBURG UNIVERSITY, Fine Arts Center, 200 Prospect St, Fine Arts Bldg East Stroudsburg, PA 18301-2999. Tel 570-422-3759; Fax 570-422-3777; Internet Home Page Address: www.esu.edu; *Chmn* Dr Herbert Weigand
Estab 1894; FT 3, PT 2; pub; D & E; Scholarships; SC 17, LC 6, grad 1; D 45
Ent Req: HS dipl, HS equivalency
Degrees: BA in Fine Arts
Tuition: Res—undergrad $1192 per sem, grad $1845 per sem; nonres—undergrad $4301 per sem, grad $3074 per sem; campus res available
Courses: Aesthetics, American Art Communication Graphics, Art Education, Art History, Calligraphy, Ceramics, Design, Drawing, Graphics, Handicrafts, Lettering, Painting, Printmaking, Sculpture
Summer School: Tuition res—grad $89 per cr hr

EASTON

LAFAYETTE COLLEGE, Dept of Art, 317 Hamilton St, Williams Ctr for the Arts Easton, PA 18042. Tel 610-330-5355; Fax 610-330-5355; Elec Mail ahldiane@lafayette.edu; *Prof Art* Ed Kerns; *Dept Head* Diane Cole Ahl
Estab 1827; FT 4, PT 4; pvt; D & E; SC 8, LC 12; D 300, E 250, non-maj 1, maj 17
Ent Req: HS dipl, ent exam, selective admis
Degrees: BS and AB 4 yr
Courses: 2-D & 3-D Design, Art History, Drawing, Graphic Design, History of Architecture, Painting, Photography, Printmaking, Sculpture
Summer School: Graphic Design, Painting, Photography

EDINBORO

EDINBORO UNIVERSITY OF PENNSYLVANIA, Art Dept, 219 Meadville St, Doucette Hall Edinboro, PA 16444-0001. Tel 814-732-2406; Internet Home Page Address: www.edinboro.edu; *Chmn Crafts* Bernard Maas; *Fine Arts Representative* Ben Gibson; *Dir Gallery* William Mathie; *Chairperson* Dr Connie Mullineaux; *Asst Chmn of Art* Franz Stohn
Estab 1857; FT 34, PT 2; pub; D & E; Scholarships; SC 86, LC 30, GC 20; D 400 art maj, non-maj 6000, grad 30
Ent Req: HS dipl, SAT
Degrees: BSEd, BFA and BA 4 yrs, MA 1 yr, MFA 2 yrs
Courses: Advertising Design, Art Education, Art History, Ceramics, †Communications Graphics, Film, Goldsmithing, Handicrafts, History of Art & Architecture, Jewelry, Mixed Media, †Painting, †Photography, †Printmaking, †Sculpture, †Silversmithing, †Teacher Training, †Textile Design, Video, Weaving
Summer School: Chmn, Ian Short. Tuition $129 per cr for two 5 wk sessions

ERDENHEIM

ANTONELLI INSTITUTE, Professional Photography & Commercial Art, 300 Montgomery Ave, Erdenheim, PA 19038-8242. Tel 215-836-2222; Fax 215-836-2794; Elec Mail admissions@antonelli.org; Internet Home Page Address: www.antonelli.org; *Pres* John Hayden; *Instr* Joseph Wilk; *Dir Educ* Tricia Fleming; *Placement, Faculty* Andrew Simcox; *Graphic Design* Chris Patchell; *Graphic Design* Ed Zaworn; *Photog* Vladmir Hartman; *Photog* Mimi Janosy; *Photog* Todd Murray; *Photog* Robert Wood
Estab 1938; Maintain art library; pvt; D; SC, LC; D 205, Maj 205
Ent Req: HS dipl
Degrees: A (Specialized Technology)
Courses: Advertising Design, Art History, †Commercial Art, Design, Drawing, Film, Graphic Arts, †Graphic Design, History of Art & Architecture, Illustration, †Photography, Typography
Adult Hobby Classes: Workshops as scheduled
Summer School: Workshops

ERIE

MERCYHURST COLLEGE, Dept of Art, 501 E 38th St, Erie, PA 16546-0002. Tel 814-824-2000; Fax 814-825-2188; Elec Mail thubert@mercyhurst.edu; Internet Home Page Address: www.mercyhurst.edu; *Chair, Prof* Daniel Burke; *Asst Prof* Gary Cardot; *Asst Prof* Jodi Staniunas Hopper; *Assoc Prof* Thomas Hubert; *Asst Prof* Robert Tavani
Estab 1926, dept estab1926; Maintain nonprofit art gallery, Cummings Art Gallery, 501 E 38th St, Erie PA 16546; FT 6, PT 4; pvt; D & E; Scholarships; SC 45, LC 12; D 80, E 20, maj 100
Ent Req: HS dipl, col boards
Degrees: BA 4 yr

Courses: 3-D Design, †Advertising Design, Aesthetics, Airbrush Painting, †Art Appreciation, Art Education, Art Foundations, Art History, Art Therapy, Ceramics, †Design, Drawing, †Graphic Arts, Graphic Design, †History of Art & Architecture, Independent Study, Individualized Studio, Internship, Painting, Photography, Printmaking, Sculpture, Senior Seminar, Teaching Internship, †Weaving

FARMINGTON

TOUCHSTONE CENTER FOR CRAFTS, 1049 Wharton Furnace Rd, Farmington, PA 15437-1195. Tel 724-329-1370; Fax 724-329-1371; Internet Home Page Address: www.touchstonecrafts.com; *Registrar* Laura Peters
Estab 1983; 90 PT; pvt; D; Scholarships; D 500
Courses: Ceramics, Design, Fashion Arts, Handicrafts, Illustration, Jewelry, Painting, Photography, Printmaking, Sculpture, Silversmithing, Textile Design, Video, Weaving
Adult Hobby Classes: Enrl 400; tuition $100-$250 per wk.
Courses—Blacksmithing, Clay, Fibre, Glass, Metal, Painting, Photography, Printmaking, Wood
Children's Classes: Enrl 100. Courses—Art

GETTYSBURG

GETTYSBURG COLLEGE, Dept of Visual Arts, 300 N Washington St, Gettysburg, PA 17325. Tel 717-337-6121; Elec Mail atrevely@gettysburg.edu; Internet Home Page Address: www.gettysburg.edu; *Prof* Alan Paulson; *Assoc Prof* James Agard; *Asst Prof* Carol Small; *Instr* Lisa Dorrill; *Instr* Jim Ramos; *Instr* Brent Blair; *Instr* John Winship; *Chmn* Mark Warwick
Estab 1832, dept estab 1956; pvt; D; SC 10, LC 15; D 300
Ent Req: HS dipl, ent exam
Degrees: BA 4 yrs
Courses: 2-D & 3-D Design, American Indian Art, Architecture, †Art History, Art of Cinema, Ceramics, Design, Drawing, Film, Gallery Training, History of Art & Architecture, Museum Staff Training, Painting, Printmaking, Sculpture

GLENSIDE

ARCADIA UNIVERSITY, (Beaver College) Dept of Fine Arts, 450 Easton Rd, Glenside, PA 19038. Tel 215-572-2900; Internet Home Page Address: www.arcadia.edu; *Asst Prof* Bonnie Hayes, MA, ABD; *Assoc Prof* Betsey Batchelor, MFA; *Asst Prof* Judith Taylor, MFA; *Asst Prof* W Scott Rawlins, MFA; *Chmn* Robert Mauro, MFA
Estab 1853; PT 7; pvt; D & E; Scholarships; SC 43, LC 14; in Col D FT 625, PT 115, maj in dept 30, maj in dept 140
Ent Req: HS dipl, SAT, ACT, optional portfolio review
Degrees: BA and BFA 4 yrs, MA(Educ) 1 yr
Courses: Art Education, Art History, †Art Therapy, Ceramics, Design, Drawing, Goldsmithing, Graphic Design, History of Art & Architecture, Interior Design, Jewelry, Painting, Photography, Printmaking, Silversmithing
Summer School: Chmn, Robert Mauro. Enrl approx 30; tuition $1040 per cr hr for term of 7 wks. Courses—Drawing, Painting, Visual Fundamentals

GREENSBURG

SETON HILL UNIVERSITY, Art Program, 1 Seton Hill Dr Greensburg, PA 15601. Tel 724-834-2200, Ext 4255; Fax 724-830-1294; Elec Mail admit@setonhill.edu; Internet Home Page Address: setonhill.edu; *Asst Prof* Maureen Vissat, MA; *Dir Gallery & Asst Prof* Carol Brode, MA; *Prog Dir & Assoc Prof* Mary Kay Neff; *Dir Grad Adult Studies* Christine Schaeffer; *Assoc Prof* Patricia Beachley, MFA; *Assoc Prof* Philip Rostek, MFA; *Assoc Prof* Nina Denninger, MA; *Instr* Richard Stoner; *Instr* Jim Andrews; *Instr* Brian Ferrell; *Instr* Nora Thompson; *Instr* Sandy Trimble; *Asst* Dana Elmendorf; *Instr* David Stanger
Estab 1918, dept estab 1950; Maintains nonprofit art gallery, Harlan Gallery & library, Reeves Library (same address) ; Pvt, den; D & E & Sat; Scholarships; SC 40, LC 8, GC 11; D 1,875, maj 111, minor 15, pt 10, grad 35
Ent Req: HS dipl, review portfolio
Degrees: BA, BFA 4 yr
Courses: 3-D Design, Advanced 2-D Media, Advanced 3-D Media, †Art Education, †Art History, †Art Therapy, †Ceramics, Design, Digital Imaging, †Drawing, Fabrics, †Graphic Design, Jewelry, Metalsmithing, †Painting, Photography, †Printmaking, Professional Practice, †Restoration & Conservation, †Sculpture, †Studio Art, †Theatre Arts, Typography, †Weaving, †Web Design
Adult Hobby Classes: Enrl 25; tuition $425 per cr for 14 wk sem. Courses—Art History, Photography, Design
Summer School: Dir, Christine Schaffer. Enrl 529. 19 art maj, Courses—Art in Elementary Educ, Digital Imaging

GREENVILLE

THIEL COLLEGE, Dept of Art, 75 College Ave, Greenville, PA 16125-2181. Tel 724-589-2094, 589-2000; Internet Home Page Address: www.thiel.edu; *Chmn Dept* Ronald A Pivovar, MFA
Estab 1866, dept estab 1965; pvt; D & E; Scholarships; SC 14, LC 11; D 105, non-maj 65, maj 40
Ent Req: HS dipl, interviews
Degrees: BA 4 yrs
Courses: Art History, Ceramics, Drawing, Graphic Arts, Jewelry, Painting, Printmaking, Sculpture, Stage Design, Theatre Arts
Adult Hobby Classes: Classes offered

Summer School: Asst Acad Dean, Richard Houpt. Term of 4 wks beginning June 3. Courses—Art History, Extended Studies, Drawing

HARRISBURG

HARRISBURG AREA COMMUNITY COLLEGE, Division of Communications, Humanities & the Arts, One HACC Dr, Harrisburg, PA 17110. Tel 717-780-2423; 780-2426; Fax 717-780-3281; Internet Home Page Address: www.hacc.edu; *Chmn Art Dept* Sara F Meng PhD; *Chmn Theatre* Marnie Brennan, MA; *Instr* Brenda Eppley, MFA; *Instr* Jim Lard, MFA; *Instr* Ronald Talbott, MFA; *Instr* Marjaneh Talebi, MFA; *Instr* Robert Trovell, MFA, PhD; *Instr* Monica Smith-Talbott, MFA
Estab 1964; Maintains Rose Lehrman Art Gallery; pub; D & E; SC 15, LC 5
Ent Req: HS dipl
Degrees: AA 2 yrs
Courses: Art History, Ceramics, Crafts Marketing, Drawing, Graphic Design, Jewelry, Painting, Photography, Printmaking, Sculpture, Theatre Arts
Adult Hobby Classes: Courses—Calligraphy, Drawing, Painting, Photography, Pottery
Children's Classes: Courses—Calligraphy, Creative Dramatics
Summer School: Dir, Michael Dockery. Courses vary

HAVERFORD

HAVERFORD COLLEGE, Fine Arts Dept, 370 Lancaster Ave, Haverford, PA 19041-1392. Tel 610-896-1267 (Art Dept); Fax 610-896-1495; *Prof* R Christopher Cairns, MFA
Estab 1833, dept estab 1969; pvt; D, M; Scholarships; maj 12
Ent Req: HS dipl, programs in cooperation with Bryn Mawr College, Fine Arts Program
Degrees: BA 4 yrs
Courses: Drawing, Graphic Arts, History of Art & Architecture, Painting, Photography, Sculpture

Cantor Fitzgerald Gallery, Whitehead Campus Ctr, 370 Lancaster Ave Haverford, PA 19041. Tel 610-896-1287; Elec Mail hcexhibits@gmail.com; Internet Home Page Address: www.haverford.edu/HHC/exhibits; *Campus Exhibit Coordr* Matthew Seamus Callinan
Open Mon-Tues & Thurs-Fri 11AM-5PM, Wed 11AM-8PM, Sat-Sun 12PM-5PM; No admis fee
Collections: paintings; sculpture

MAIN LINE ART CENTER, 746 Panmure Rd, Haverford, PA 19041-1218. Tel 610-525-0272; Fax 610-525-5036; Internet Home Page Address: www.mainlineart.org; *Admin Exec Dir* Judy S Herman; *Instr* Carol Cole, BA; *Instr* Liz Goldberg, MFA; *Instr* Robert Finch, BFA; *Instr* Ginny Kendall, BFA; *Instr* Carol Kardon, BFA; *Instr* Bonnie Mettler, BFA; *Instr* Francine Shore, BFA; *Instr* Carson Fox, BFA; *Instr* Sallee Rush, BFA; *Instr* Moe Brooker, MFA; *Instr* Mimi Oritsky, MFA; *Instr* Val Rossman, MFA; *Instr* Scott Wheelock, MFA; *Instr* Martha Kent Martin, BFA; *Instr* Patrick Arnold, BFA; *Instr* Carol Stirton-Broad, BFA; *Instr* Lydia Lehr, MFA; *Instr* Ann Simon, MFA; *Instr* Kathie Regan-Dalzell, BA; *Instr* Nury Vicens, MFA; *Instr* Susanna T Saunders, BA
Estab 1937; pvt; D & E; Scholarships; SC 45; D 300, E 250
Courses: Art History, Batik, Calligraphy, Ceramics, Collage, Drawing, Faux Painting, Jewelry, Mixed Media, Painting, Photography, Printmaking, Sculpture, Silversmithing, Textile Design, Tie-dyeing
Children's Classes: Enrl 1500, Courses—General Arts, Pottery
Summer School: Admin Dir, Judy S Herman. Tuition varies, classes begin mid-June. Courses—same as above

HUNTINGDON

JUNIATA COLLEGE, Dept of Art, 1700 Moore St, Huntingdon, PA 16652. Tel 814-643-4310, Ext 3683; Internet Home Page Address: www.juniata.edu; *Chmn Dept* Karen Rosell
Estab 1876; FT 3, PT 1; pvt; D; Scholarships; SC 12, LC 3; 1100, maj 40
Ent Req: HS dipl
Degrees: BA 4 yrs
Tuition: Campus res
Courses: Aesthetics, Arts Management, Ceramics, Computer Graphics, Drawing, History of Art & Architecture, Museum Studies, Painting, Photography, Theatre Arts
Summer School: Dir, Jill Pfrogner, Courses —Art History, Ceramics, Studio Art

INDIANA

INDIANA UNIVERSITY OF PENNSYLVANIA, College of Fine Arts, 470 S 11th St, Sprowls Hall Rm 110 Indiana, PA 15705-1044. Tel 724-357-2530; Fax 724-357-3296; Elec Mail jlstrong@grove.iup.edu; Internet Home Page Address: www.arts.iup.edu; *Assoc Prof* Andrew Gillham; *Asst Prof* Lynda LaRoche; *Assoc Prof* Dr Marjorie Mambo; *Assoc Prof* Dr Brenda Mitchell; *Assoc Prof* Dr Irene Kabala; *Asst Prof* Ivan Fortushniak; *Assoc Prof* Fuyuko Matsubara; *Prof* Susan Palmisano; *Assoc Prof* Penny Rode; *Assoc Prof* Kevin Turner; *Dir, Turning & Furniture Design Ctr* Steve Loar
Estab 1875, dept estab 1875; on-campus shop for purchase of art supplies; pub; D & E; Scholarships, Assistantships; SC 26, LC 21, GC 30; D 250, non-maj 1700, maj 270, grad 30
Ent Req: HS dipl, SAT, portfolio review, ACT
Degrees: BS(Art Educ), BA(Art History & Humanities with Art Concentration), BFA(Studio Art Concentration) 4 yr, MA 2 yr & MFA
Courses: Art Education, †Art History, †Art Studio, Ceramics, Computer Graphics, Design, Drawing, Fiber Arts, Goldsmithing, Graphic Design, Jewelry, Painting, Papermaking, Printmaking, Sculpture, Silversmithing, Weaving, Woodworking

Adult Hobby Classes: Enrl 60; Courses—Ceramics, Drawing
Summer School: Dir, Andrew Gillham. Enrl 140; tuition regular acad sem cr cost. Courses—Art Appreciation, Art History, Special Workshops, Studios

JOHNSTOWN

UNIVERSITY OF PITTSBURGH AT JOHNSTOWN, Dept of Fine Arts, 450 Schoolhouse Rd, Johnstown, PA 15904-2990. Tel 814-269-7000 (Main); Fax 814-269-2096; Elec Mail vgrash@pitt.edu; Internet Home Page Address: www.upj.pitt.edu; *Dept Head* Dr Valerie Grash
Estab 1968; Art supplies sold at on campus store ; pub, pvt; D & E; LC 15; D 160, maj 3
Ent Req: HS dipl, SAT
Degrees: BA 4 yrs
Courses: †Art History, Film, History of Art & Architecture, Photography, Stage Design, †Theatre Arts

KUTZTOWN

KUTZTOWN UNIVERSITY, College of Visual & Performing Arts, PO Box 730, Kutztown, PA 19530-0730. Tel 610-683-4500; Fax 610-683-4547; *Dean* William Mowder
Institution estab 1860, art dept estab 1929; pub; D & E; Scholarships; SC 284, LC 40, GC 8; D 943, maj 10
Ent Req: HS dipl
Degrees: BFA 4 yr, BS(Art Educ) 4 yr, MA(Educ)
Courses: Advertising Design, Art Education, Ceramics, Drawing, Fine Metals, Graphic Design, Illustration, Jewelry, Painting, Photography, Printmaking, Sculpture, Weaving, Woodworking
Children's Classes: Young at Art
Summer School: Regular sessions 5 wks. Courses—Art Ed, Studio

LAPLUME

KEYSTONE COLLEGE, Fine Arts Dept, One College Green, LaPlume, PA 18440-1000; PO Box 50, LaPlume, PA 18440-0200. Tel 570-945-5141, Ext 3300, 3301; Fax 570-945-6767; Elec Mail cliff.prokop@keystone.edu; Internet Home Page Address: www.keystone.edu; *Prof* William Tersteeg, MFA; *Art Dept Coordr* Stacey Donahue-Semenza, BFA; *Prof* Ward V Roe, MFA; *Assoc Prof* Sally Tosti, MFA; *Instr* Nikki Moser, BFA; *Chmn Fine Arts* Clifton Prokop, MFA; *Assoc Prof* Drake Gomez, MFA; *Assoc Prof* Dave Potter, MA; *Instr* Trevor Herceg, MFA; *Instr* Jodi Dunn, PhD; *Instr* Kevin O'Neil, MFA; *Instr* Elizabeth Burkhauser; *Instr* Frank Groyl
Estab 1868, dept estab 1965; Maintains Linder Gallery at the College; pvt; D & E, weekends; Scholarships; SC 15, LC 2; D 100
Ent Req: HS dipl, SAT
Degrees: AFA 2 yrs, BS (Art Educ), BA (Fine Art)
Tuition: Res—$9848 per yr, incl rm & board
Courses: 2-D Design, 3-D Design, Advertising Design, †Art Appreciation, Art History, Ceramics, Color, Commercial Art, †Costume Design & Construction, Design, Drawing, Film, Graphic Design, †History of Art & Architecture, Intro to Commercial Design, Life Drawing, Mixed Media, Painting, Photography, Printmaking, Sculpture, Silversmithing, †Stage Design, †Teacher Training, †Theatre Arts

LANCASTER

FRANKLIN & MARSHALL COLLEGE, Art & Art History Dept, PO Box 3003, Lancaster, PA 17604-3003. Tel 717-291-4199; Fax 717-358-4599; Internet Home Page Address: www.fandm.edu/art; *Dept Chair* Virginia A Maksymowicz; *Prof* Richard K Kent; *Assoc Prof* Linda Aleci; *Assoc Prof* Michael Clapper; *Assoc Prof* Jun-Cheng Liu; *Assoc Prof* James C Paterson; *Assoc Prof* Amelia Rauser; *Asst Prof* John C Holmgren; *Asst Prof* Kostis Kourelis
Estab 1966; pvt; D & E; Scholarships; SC 10, LC 17; in col D 1900, E 580
Ent Req: HS dipl, SAT
Degrees: BA 4 yr
Tuition: Res—$90,810 per yr
Courses: Architecture, Art History, Basic Design, Drawing, History of Art & Architecture, Painting, Printmaking, Sculpture

PENNSYLVANIA SCHOOL OF ART & DESIGN, 204 N Prince St, Lancaster, PA 17603-3528. Tel 717-396-7833; Fax 717-396-1339; Internet Home Page Address: www.psad.edu; *Pres* Mary Colleen Heil
Estab 1982; Maintain nonprofit art gallery on-campus; art library; 40 FT & PT; pvt; D & E; Scholarships; SC 160, LC 9; D 200, E 150, non-maj 60, maj 140
Ent Req: HS dipl
Degrees: BFA (Fine Art, Graphic Design, Illustration) 4 yr
Courses: Aesthetics, Art History, †Drawing, †Fine Art, †Graphic Design, †Illustration, Interior Design, †Photography
Adult Hobby Classes: Enrl 800; tuition $380 per cr. Cert Programs in Desktop Publishing, Interior Design. Studio cr & non-credit courses for youths & adults; web site design cert
Children's Classes: Enrl 250; tuition $160 per cr, 20 contact hrs. Courses—Figure Drawing, Studio
Summer School: Dir, Tracy Beyl. Enrl 220; tuition youth $160 for 20 contact hrs, adult $380 per cr for 30 hrs. Courses—Computer, Interior Design, Photography, Studio

LEWISBURG

BUCKNELL UNIVERSITY, Dept of Art, 701 Moore Ave, Lewisburg, PA 17837-2010. Tel 570-524-1307; Internet Home Page Address: www.bucknell.edu; *Prof* Janice Mann PhD, MFA; *Prof* Neil Anderson, MFA; *Prof* James Turnure PhD, MFA; *Prof* Christiane Andersson PhD, MFA; *Prof* Jody Blake PhD, MFA; *Head Dept* Rosalyn Richards, MFA

Estab 1846; pvt; D; Scholarships; SC 19, LC 20, GC 30; D 500, non-maj 450, maj 50, grad 2
Ent Req: HS dipl
Degrees: BA 4 yrs
Courses: Art History, Drawing, Graphic Arts, History of Art & Architecture, Painting, Photography, Printmaking, Sculpture
Summer School: Dir, Lois Huffines. Courses—Lectures, Studio

LOCK HAVEN

LOCK HAVEN UNIVERSITY, Dept of Fine Arts, 401 N Fairview St, Lock Haven, PA 17745-2342. Tel 570-893-2151, 893-2011, 893-2143; Fax 570-893-2432; Internet Home Page Address: www.lhup.edu; *Chmn* Bridgett Glenn
FT 4; pvt; D; Scholarships
Degrees: BA
Tuition: Res—$3468 per 2 sem, $144 per cr hr; nonres—$6824 per 2 sem, $284 per cr hr
Courses: 2-D Design, 3-D design, Art Appreciation, Art Education, Art History, Arts & Crafts, Ceramics, Drawing, Jewelry, Painting, Photography, Printmaking, Sculpture, Stage Design, Textile Design, Weaving
Summer School: Courses offered

LORETTO

ST FRANCIS COLLEGE, Fine Arts Dept, 110 Franciscan Way, Loretto, PA 15940-9709. Tel 814-472-3216; Fax 814-472-3044, 472-3000 (main); Elec Mail colson@sfcpa.edu; Internet Home Page Address: www.sfcpa.edu; *Chmn* Charles Olsen, MFA
Scholarships
Degrees: minor in fine arts
Tuition: $463 per cr hr; campus res—room & board available
Courses: Art Appreciation, Art History, Culture & Values, Design, Drawing, Exploration of Arts, Independent Study, Modern Art, Museum Staff Training, Painting, Photography, Weaving

MANSFIELD

MANSFIELD UNIVERSITY, Art Dept, 135 Stadium Dr, 118 Allen Hall Mansfield, PA 16933-1611. Tel 570-662-4500; Fax 570-662-4114; *Assoc Prof* Tom Loomis, MA; *Asst Prof & Chmn Dept* Dr Bonnie Kutbay, MA
Estab 1857; pub; D; Scholarships; SC 26, LC 18; D 700, maj 90
Ent Req: HS dipl, SAT, portfolio & interview
Degrees: BA & BS(Studio Art), BA(Art History) & BSE(Art Educ) 4 yr, MEd(Art Educ)
Courses: Advertising Design, Aesthetics, Art Education, Art History, Ceramics, Color & Design, Computer Art, Drawing, Fibers, History of Art & Architecture, Jewelry, Lettering, Painting, Printmaking, Sculpture, Studio Crafts, Visual Studies in Aesthetic Experiences, Weaving
Adult Hobby Classes: Enrl 10. Courses—Art History, Studio Art, Graduate Level Art Education
Children's Classes: Enrl 100, tuition $20 for 10 wks, fall sem. Courses—Elementary Art Education
Summer School: Courses—Ceramics, Drawing, Fibers, Graduate Courses, Painting, Printmaking, Sculpture, Studio Courses

MEADVILLE

ALLEGHENY COLLEGE, Art Dept, 520 N Main St, Meadville, PA 16335-3902. Tel 814-332-4365; Elec Mail name@allegheny.edu; Internet Home Page Address: www.allegheny.edu; *Chair Art Dept* Amara Geffen
Estab 1815, dept estab 1930; pvt; D; Scholarships; SC 10 per sem, LC 6 per sem; 550, maj 30, non-maj 250
Ent Req: HS dipl, ent exam
Degrees: BA and BS 4 yr
Courses: Art History, Ceramics, Costume Design & Construction, †Drawing, Film, Mixed Media, †Painting, †Photography, †Printmaking, †Sculpture, Stage Design, Theatre Arts, †Video

MEDIA

DELAWARE COUNTY COMMUNITY COLLEGE, Communications, Art & Humanities, 901 S Media Line Rd, Media, PA 19063-5382. Tel 610-359-5000, Ext 5398; Fax 610-359-7331; Elec Mail craport@dccc.edu; Internet Home Page Address: www.dccc.edu; *Prof* Bertha Gutman, MFA; *Prof* Jaime Treadwell, MFA; *Prof* Bob Jones, MFA; *Prof* David Yox, MFA; *Dean* Clayton A Railey III, PhD
Estab 1967; Maintains The Art Gallery at DCCC; pub; D & E; Studio & lecture courses
Degrees: AFA
Courses: 2-D & 3-D Design, Advertising, Advertising Design, Aesthetics, Art Education, Art History, Commercial Art, Computer Graphics, Design, Desk Top Publishing, Drawing, Graphic Arts, Graphic Design, History of Art & Architecture, Illustration, Lettering, Mixed Media, Painting, Photography, Production Techniques, Sculpture, Teacher Training, Theatre Arts, Typography
Adult Hobby Classes: Enrl varies; tuition varies. Courses—Calligraphy, Crafts, Drawing, Graphic Design, Interior Design, Needlepoint, Photography, Stained Glass, Sketching, Woodcarving
Summer School: Tuition res $27 per cr hr, nonres $81 per cr hr for term of 6 wks. Courses—Drawing, Painting

MIDDLETOWN

PENN STATE HARRISBURG, School of Humanities, 777 W Harrisburg Pike, Middletown, PA 17057-4898. Tel 717-948-6189; Fax 717-948-6724; Internet Home Page Address: www.hbg.psu.edu/; *Prof* Irwin Richman PhD; *Assoc Prof* Troy Thomas PhD; *Dir Humanities* Simon J Bronner; *Dir Humanities* Linda Ross
Estab 1965; Maintain nonprofit art gallery; Morrison Gallery, Gallery Lounge; PT 10; pub; D & E; Scholarships; SC 7, LC 15; D & E 60, grad 40
Degrees: BHumanities, MA
Courses: Aesthetics, Architecture, Art Education, Art History, Drawing, Folk Art & Architecture, Graphic Design, †History of Art & Architecture, Mixed Media, Museum Staff Training, Painting, Photography, Theatre Arts, Video, Visual Studies

MILLERSVILLE

MILLERSVILLE UNIVERSITY, Dept of Art & Design, PO Box 1002, Millersville, PA 17551-0302. Tel 717-872-3298; Fax 717-871-2004; Elec Mail wanda.doyle@millersville.edu; Internet Home Page Address: www.millersville.edu; *Prof Drawing, 2D & Graphic Design* Jeri L Robinson; *Prof Drawing, Painting & Watercolor* Robert Andriulli; *Assoc Prof Art Educ* Dr Barbara J Bensur; *Instr Drawing* Leslie E Brown; *Asst Prof 2D & 3D Design, Drawing & Sculpture* Line Bruntse; *Asst Prof 2D Design & Drawing* Ben J Cunningham; *Asst Prof Art History* Dr Christine Filippone; *Assoc Prof Photog* Shauna L Frischkorn; *Assoc Prof Graphic Design* Nancy R Mata; *Asst Prof Fine Arts Metals* Allyssa Gold; *Asst Prof Graphic & Interactive Design* James Pannafino; *Chair & Assoc Prof Printmaking* Brant D Schuller; *Assoc Prof Ceramics* Deborah S Sigel; *Interim Dept Sec* Wanda Doyle; *Asst Prof Art History* William W Wolfe; *Asst Grad Prof Art Educ* Dr Victoria Weaver
Estab 1855, dept estab 1930; Maintains nonprofit art gallery, library, & campus store for art supply purchase; pub; D & E; SC 65, LC 10, GC 64; maj 330, grad 20
Ent Req: HS dipl
Degrees: BA(Art), BS(Art Educ), BFA 4 yr, MEd(Art Educ) 1 yr
Tuition: Res—$2902 undergrad, $4397.75 - $4663.25 grad per sem; nonres—$7255 undergrad, $6546.75 - $6812.25 grad per sem
Courses: Art Appreciation, Art Education, Art History, Ceramics, Computer Art, Conceptual Art, Design, Drawing, Graphic Arts, Graphic Design, Handicrafts, History of Art & Architecture, Illustration, Jewelry, Mixed Media, Painting, Photography, Printmaking, Sculpture, Silversmithing, Teacher Training, †Visual Communication
Summer School: Chair, Jeri Robinson. Enrl 200; term of 5 wks, two sessions beginning June & July. Courses—Art, Art Education, Art History

MONROEVILLE

COMMUNITY COLLEGE OF ALLEGHENY COUNTY, BOYCE CAMPUS, Art Dept, 595 Beatty Rd, Monroeville, PA 15146-1348. Tel 724-327-1327; *Adjunct Prof* Kathy Gilbert; *Adjunct Prof* Jesse Almasi; *Adjunct Prof* Jamie Boyd
Pub; D & E; SC 13, LC 1; D 200, E 40, non-maj 140, maj 60
Ent Req: HS dipl
Degrees: AS 2 yrs
Tuition: $58 per cr
Courses: Art History, Ceramics, Collage, Color & Design, Constructions, Drawing, Graphic Arts, Mixed Media, Painting, Photography, Printmaking, Sculpture
Adult Hobby Classes: Ceramics, Color & Design, Drawing, History of Art, Mixed Media, Painting, Photography, Printmaking
Children's Classes: Enrl varies. Courses—Drawing, Painting
Summer School: Courses—Vary

NANTICOKE

LUZERNE COUNTY COMMUNITY COLLEGE, Commercial Art Dept, 1333 S Prospect St, Nanticoke, PA 18634-3814. Tel 570-740-0364; Internet Home Page Address: www.luzerne.cc.pa.usa; WATS 800-377-5222; *Instr* Mike Molnar, BFA; *Instr & Coordr* Sam Cramer, BFA; *Instr* William Karlotski, BFA; *Coordr* Susan Sponenberg, BFA; *Instr* Chris Veda
Estab 1967; pub; D & E; SC 20, LC 7; D 140, E 60, non-maj 5, maj 60
Ent Req: HS dipl
Degrees: 2 year programs offered
Courses: Advertising Design, Airbrush, Art Education, Art History, Color & Design, Color Photography, †Computer Graphics, Conceptual Art, Design, Drawing, †Graphic Design, Illustration, Life Drawing, Mixed Media, Painting, Photography, Typography
Adult Hobby Classes: Enrl 350 per yr. Courses—Drawing, Graphic Design, Painting, Photography, Printmaking
Children's Classes: Enrl 500 per yr; summer sessions. Courses—Drawing, Painting
Summer School: Dir, Doug Williams, Enrl 20; Pre College Prog in July & Aug. Courses—Illustration, Life Drawing, Painting, Printmaking

NEW WILMINGTON

WESTMINSTER COLLEGE, Art Dept, 319 S Market St, Charles Freeman Hall - Rm 213 New Wilmington, PA 16172-0001; PO Box 162, New Wilmington, PA 16142-0162. Tel 724-946-7239, 946-6260; Fax 724-946-7070; Elec Mail barnerdl@westminster.edu; *Chmn* Dr David L Barner
Estab 1852; 3; den; D; Scholarships; maj 30, total 1100
Degrees: BS & BA(Fine Arts, Educ) 4 yrs
Courses: 2-D Design, 3-D Design, Art History, Ceramics, Computer Graphics, Drawing, Oil Painting, Photography, Printmaking, Sculpture
Children's Classes: Enrl 20

NEWTOWN

BUCKS COUNTY COMMUNITY COLLEGE, Fine Arts Dept, 275 Swamp Rd, Newtown, PA 18940-9677. Tel 215-504-8531; Fax 215-504-8530; Elec Mail orlando@bucks.edu; Internet Home Page Address: www.bucks.edu/gallery; *Instr* Jon Alley; *Instr* Robert Dodge; *Instr* Jack Gevins; *Instr* Alan Goldstein; *Instr* Catherine Jansen; *Instr* Diane Lindenheim; *Instr* Marlene Miller; *Instr* Charlotte Schatz; *Instr* Helen Weisz; *Instr* Mark Sfirri; *Instr* Milt Sigel; *Instr* Gwen Kerber; *Instr* John Mathews; *Chmn Dept* Frank Dominguez
Estab 1965; pub; D & E; D & E 9200 (school)
Ent Req: HS dipl
Degrees: AA
Courses: Art History, Ceramics, Design, Drawing, Glass, Graphic Design, Jewelry, Painting, Photography, Printmaking, Sculpture, Woodworking

PHILADELPHIA

ART INSTITUTE OF PHILADELPHIA, 1622 Chestnut St, Philadelphia, PA 19103-5119. Tel 215-567-7080; Tel 800-275-2474; Elec Mail magomez@aii.edu; Internet Home Page Address: www.artinstitutes.edu/philadelphia; *Pres* Michael DePrisco
Estab 1966; FT 40, PT 65; pvt; D & E; Scholarships; SC 30, LC 8; D 1125, E 72
Ent Req: HS dipl, portfolio
Degrees: AST 2 yr
Tuition: $4635 per qtr
Courses: Advertising Design, Art History, Computer Graphics, Design, †Fashion Illustration, †Fashion Merchandising, Graphic Design, Illustration, †Interior Design, Lettering, Mixed Media, †Photography, Weaving

HUSSIAN SCHOOL OF ART, Commercial Art Dept, 111 S Independence Mall E Ste 300, Philadelphia, PA 19106-2521. Tel 215-574-9600; Fax 215-574-9800; Elec Mail info@hussianart.edu; Internet Home Page Address: www.hussianart.edu; *Pres* Bruce Wartman; *Adminr* Maureen Flanagan; *Admis Dir* Lynne Wactman; *Dean Acad Affairs* Melissa Morgan
Estab 1946; Maintain library for students & faculty only; on-campus art supplies shop for students only; FT 1, PT 25; pvt; D; Scholarships; SC & LC; D 140
Ent Req: HS dipl, portfolio interview
Degrees: AST
Tuition: No campus res
Courses: †Advertising Design, Airbrush, Art History, Commercial Art, Computer Graphics, †Digital Media, Drawing, Fine Art, Graphic Arts, Graphic Design, †Illustration, Mixed Media, Painting, Photography, Printmaking
Adult Hobby Classes: Courses offered
Summer School: Dir, Wilbur Crawford. Summer workshop in Advertising Design, Drawing, Illustration & Fantasy Illusion

LA SALLE UNIVERSITY, Dept of Art, 1900 W Olney Ave, Philadelphia, PA 19141-1108. Tel 215-951-1126; Internet Home Page Address: www.lasalle.edu/; *Chmn Dept Fine Arts* Dr Charles White
Estab 1865, dept estab 1972; den; D & E; SC 2; D 4, maj 2
Ent Req: HS dipl
Degrees: BA 4 yr
Courses: Art History, Painting, Printmaking
Summer School: Selected courses offered

MOORE COLLEGE OF ART & DESIGN, 1920 Race St, 20th St Philadelphia, PA 19103-1108. Tel 215-568-4515; Fax 215-568-8017; Elec Mail info@moore.edu; Internet Home Page Address: www.moore.edu; *Acad Dean* Dona Lantz; *Chmn Fine Arts* Paul Hubbard; *Chmn Fashion Design* Janice Lewis; *Chmn Liberal Arts* Jonathan Wallis; *Chmn Illustration* Bill Brown; *Chmn Interior Design* Margaret Leahy; *Chmn Textile Design* Deborah Warner; *Chmn Basic Arts* Moe Brooker; *Pres* Happy Craven Fernandez; *Chmn Graphic Design* Gigi McGee; *Chmn Art Educ* Lynne Horoschak; *Chmn Photog & Digital Arts* James Johnson
Estab 1848; Maintains nonprofit art galleries: The Goldie Paley Gallery and the Levy Gallery for the Arts in Philadelphia, 20th St & The Parkway, Philadelphia, PA 19103; also maintains an art/architecture library on site; Pvt, women only; D & E; Scholarships, Fellowships; SC 217, LC 47; D 525, non-maj 1
Ent Req: HS dipl, portfolio, SAT
Degrees: BFA 4 yr
Courses: †2-D & 3-D Design, †Art Education, †Art History, Ceramics, †Curatorial Studies, Design, Display, †Drafting, Drawing, Fashion Arts, Film, Graphic Arts, †Graphic Design, History of Art & Architecture, †Illustration, †Interior Design, Jewelry, Mixed Media, †Painting, †Photography, Photography & Digital Arts, †Printmaking, Sculpture, Teacher Training, †Textile Design, Weaving
Adult Hobby Classes: Tuition—$970 per design & media classes, 2 cr each; $685 per design & media classes, audit; $565 per art & design fundamentals & fine art classes, 2 cr each; $395 per art & design fundamentals & fine art classes audit; personal enrichment & career development classes: art & design fundamentals, fine arts, digital media for print & web, digital photography, fashion studies, interior designing. Enrl 800 annually
Children's Classes: Enrl 1200 annually; tuition—$310 per class; registration $40 per student; fine art & design classes K-12
Summer School: Dir Continuing Educ, Neil di Sabato

PENNSYLVANIA ACADEMY OF THE FINE ARTS, Office of Admission, 128 N Broad St, Philadelphia, PA 19102-1424. Tel 215-972-7600; Fax 215-972-0839; Elec Mail admissions@pafa.edu; Internet Home Page Address: www.pafa.edu; *CEO* David R Brigham; *Painting Dept Chair* Al Gury; *Sculpture Dept Chair* Rob Roesch; *Printmaking Dept Chair* Tony Rosati; *Liberal Arts Dept Chair* Dr Kevin Richards
Estab 1805; Maintain a nonprofit art gallery & art/architecture library - Gallery 118 N Broad St, Philadelphia, PA 19102; Library 128 N Broad St. On-campus shop where art supplies may be purchased; Pvt; D & E; Scholarships; SC 15, LC 4, GC

Publications: Newsletter/Calendar, quarterly
Ent Req: HS dipl, portfolio & recommendations
Degrees: Cert, 4 yrs; Academy BFA, BFA Coordinated prog with Univ Pennsylvania, MFA 2 yrs, Post-Baccalaureate prog 1 yr
Tuition: Nonres—undergrad $13,185 per sem, MFA $16,330 per sem, Post-Baccalaureate $14,040 per sem; no campus res
Courses: Anatomy, Drawing, Mixed Media, Painting, Perspective, Printmaking, Sculpture
Adult Hobby Classes: Enrl 310; tuition varies per class; Courses—Drawing, Painting, Printmaking, Sculpture
Children's Classes: Enrl 700; tuition varies; Courses—Theme Camps
Summer School: Dir, Michael Kowbuz. Enrl 500-600; tuition varies; Courses—Drawing, Painting, Printmaking, Sculpture

PHILADELPHIA COMMUNITY COLLEGE, Dept of Art, 1700 Spring Garden St, Philadelphia, PA 19130-3936. Tel 215-751-8771; *Assoc Prof* Karen Aumann, BFA; *Asst Prof & Head Art Dept* Christopher Feiro
Estab 1967; Pub; D & E; SC 10, LC 6; D 80 art maj
Ent Req: HS dipl, portfolio
Degrees: AA 2 yr
Courses: 2-D Design, 3-D Design, Art History, Ceramics, Computer Graphics, Design, Drawing, Graphic Design, Painting, Photography, Transfer Foundation Program
Summer School: Dir, Bob Paige. Tuition $61 per cr Courses—Art History, Ceramics, Design, Drawing, Painting

PHILADELPHIA UNIVERSITY, 4201 Henry Ave, Philadelphia, PA 19144-5497. Tel 215-951-2700; Fax 215-951-2651; Fax 215-951-2651; Internet Home Page Address: www.philau.edu; *Exec Dean* Dr Ronald C Kender; *Pres* Dr Stephen Spinell Jr; *Assoc Provost* Lloyd Russolo; *Exec Dean College & Architecture* Dr Louis Padulo
Estab 1884; On-campus shop where art supplies may be purchased; FT 23; pvt; D&E; Scholarships; GC 2700, UG 486
Degrees: BS 4 yrs, MBA, MS Fashion Apparel Studies, MS Interactive Media & Design, MS Industrial Design, MS Textile Design, MS Textile Engineering, Ms Interior Architecture, MS Sustain Design, MS Construction Mgmt
Tuition: $30,356 per yr
Courses: Aesthetics, Architecture, Art History, Chemistry & Dyeing, Constructions, Design, Drawing, Fashion Apparel Management, Fashion Design, Fashion Merchandising, Graphic Design, History of Art & Architecture, Interior Design, Knitted Design, Occupational Therapy, Photography, Print Design, Restoration & Conservation, Textile Design, Textile Engineering, Textile Quality Control & Testing, Weaving Design
Summer School: Dir, Maxine Lentz

SAINT JOSEPH'S UNIVERSITY, Art Dept, 5600 City Ave, Philadelphia, PA 19131-1376. Tel 610-660-1000, 660-1840; Fax 610-660-2278; Elec Mail dmcnally@sju.edu; Internet Home Page Address: www.sju.edu/int/academics/cas/art/index.htm/; *Chmn/Prof Painting* Dennis McNally, PhD; *Prof Painting* Steve Cope, MFA; *Prof Ceramics* Jury Smith, MFA; *Prof Art History* Emily Hage, PhD; *Photog* Susan Fenton, MFA; *Prof Sculpture/3D* Ron Klein, MFA; *Adj Prof* Peter Bonner, MFA; *Adj Prof* Jeanne Brody, PhD; *Adj Prof* Sabrina DeTurk, PhD; *Adj Prof* Marie Eldin, MED; *Adj Prof* Roberta Fallon, PhD; *Adj Prof* Beverly Fisher, MFA; *Adj Prof* David Freese, BS; *Adj Prof* Marta Sanchez-Dallam, MFA; *Adj Prof* Alison Stigora, MFA; *Adj Prof* Kathleen Vaccaro, MFA
Estab 1851, prog estab 1975; Maintains a non-profit art gallery, Boland Hall, 5600 City Ave, Phila, PA, www.sju.edu/int/resources/gallery; Pvt, den; D & E; Scholarships; SC 58, LC 31; D 4400, maj 55, grad 1500
Ent Req: HS dipl
Degrees: BA
Courses: Architecture, †Art, Art Appreciation, †Art Education, Art History, Ceramics, Digital Photography, Drawing, History of Art & Architecture, †Mixed Media, Mosaics, Painting, Photography, Sculpture

SAMUEL S FLEISHER ART MEMORIAL, 719 Catharine St, Philadelphia, PA 19147-2811. Tel 215-922-3456; Fax 215-922-5327; Elec Mail info@fleisher.org; Internet Home Page Address: www.fleisher.org; *Instr* Cathy Hopkins; *Instr* Frank Gasparro; *Instr* Louise Clement; *Dir* Thora E Jacobson
Estab 1898; administered by the Philadelphia Museum of Art; maintains nonprofit gallery, Dene M Louchheim Galleries, 719 Catharine St; Matilda Rosenbaum Memorial Library (children) 719 Catharine St; pvt; E; Scholarships; SC 80, LC 1; E 2000
Ent Req: none
Degrees: none
Courses: †Calligraphy, Ceramics, Drawing, Painting, Photography, Printmaking, Sculpture
Adult Hobby Classes: Enrl 850; tuition free Sept-May. Courses—Ceramics, Drawing, Painting, Photography, Printmaking, Sculpture
Children's Classes: Enrl 425; tuition free Sept-May. Courses—Drawing, Painting, Papermaking, Sculpture
Summer School: Ceramics, Drawing, Landscape Painting, Painting, Photography, Printmaking, Sculpture

TEMPLE UNIVERSITY, Tyler School of Art, 2001 N 13th St, Philadelphia, PA 19122-6016. Tel 215-777-9000; Elec Mail tyler@temple.edu; Internet Home Page Address: www.temple.edu/tyler; *Chmn Painting, Drawing, & Sculpture* Margo Margolis, MFA; *Chmn Graphic Arts & Design* Stephanie Knopp, MFA; *Chmn Crafts* Nick Kripal, MFA; *Chmn Art History* Gerald Silk, PhD; *Chmn Univ Art & Art Educ* Jo-Anna Moore, MFA; *Chmn Foundation Prog* Gerard Brown, MFA; *Prog Dir Architecture* Kate Wingert-Playdon, BArch; *Sr Assoc Dean* Brigitte Knowles; *Interim Dean* Robert Stroker; *Vice Dean* Hester Stinnett, MFA; *Exec Asst to Dean* Doris Izes
Dept estab 1935; Maintains nonprofit art gallery: Temple Gallery; Pub; D & E; Scholarships, Fellowships; maj 1,200

Ent Req: HS dipl, SAT, portfolio
Degrees: BA(Art History & Studio Art), BS(Art Educ), BFA, MA(Art History), MEd(Art Educ), MFA & PhD(Art History)
Tuition: Res—undergrad $9,194 per yr, grad $12,480 per yr; nonres—undergrad $16,442 per yr, grad $18,210 per yr
Courses: Animation, †Architecture, †Art Education, †Art History, †Ceramics, Computers, Drawing, †Fibers Fabric Design, Film, Foundry, †Glass, †Graphic Design, Handmade Cameras, †History of Art & Architecture, Illustration, Metals, †Painting, Papermaking, Performance Art, †Photography, †Printmaking, Sculpture, Video, Weaving
Children's Classes: Courses—Computer & Studio, also programs for HS students

UNIVERSITY OF PENNSYLVANIA, Graduate School of Fine Arts, 210 S 34th St, 102 Meyerson Hall Philadelphia, PA 19104. Tel 215-898-3425; Elec Mail admission@design.upenn.edu; Internet Home Page Address: www.design.upenn.edu/fine-arts; *Grad Prog Coordr* Jane Irish; *Dir Admis & Financial Aid* Joan Wetson; *Registrar* Andrea Porter
Estab 1874; pvt; Scholarships, Fellowships; GC; 47
Ent Req: ent exam, portfolio
Degrees: MFA
Tuition: Grad $26,234 per yr, $13,612 per sem; campus res available
Courses: Architectural Design, Fine Arts, Landscape Architecture
Summer School: Dir, Adele Santos. Tuition $2500 per 6 wks. Studio courses in Paris, Venice & India
—Dept of Architecture, 210 S 34th St, 102 Meyerson Hall Philadelphia, PA 19104-3899. Tel 215-898-5728; Fax 215-573-2192; Internet Home Page Address: www.design.upenn.edu/architecture; *Chmn Grad Group* David Leatherbarrow; *Interim Chmn* Richard Wesley
FT 7, PT 25; 180
Degrees: MA 3 yrs, PhD 4 - 5 yrs
Tuition: Grad $24,200 per yr, $12,100 per sem; campus res available
Courses: Architectural Design and Construction
Summer School: Chmn, Adele Santos. Enrl 70; tuition $1200 per 3 cr course (4-6 wks duration). Courses—Summer studios (only upper level students)
—Dept of Landscape Architecture & Regional Planning, Meyerson, Rm 119, Philadelphia, PA 19104-6311; 210 S 34th St, 102 Meyerson Hall Philadelphia, PA 19104-3899. Tel 215-898-6591; Fax 215-573-3770; Internet Home Page Address: www.design.upenn.edu/landscape-architecture; *Chmn* John Dixon Hunt
FT 6, PT 5; Scholarships; LC 7, Design Courses 4; 68
Degrees: MLA 2 - 3 yrs, MRP 2 yrs, Cert & joint degrees available
Tuition: Grad $24,200 per yr, $12,100 per sem; campus res available
Courses: Computation - GIS & CAD, Design Studio, Field Ecology, History & Theory, Regional Planning Studio, Workshop Series

UNIVERSITY OF THE ARTS, Philadelphia Colleges of Art & Design, Performing Arts & Media & Communication, 320 S Broad St, Philadelphia, PA 19102-4901. Tel 215-717-6030 (Univ), 875-1100 (PCAD), 800-616-2787 (Admissions); Fax 215-875-1100 (PCAD); Internet Home Page Address: www.uarts.edu; *Pres* Sean T Buffington; *Interim Dean, College of Art & Design* Alida Fish; *Dean, College of Performing Arts* Richard J Lawn; *Dean, Div Liberal Arts* Peter Stambler; *Provost* Kirk E Pillow
Estab 1876; pvt; D & E; Scholarships; undergrad 760, grad 120
Ent Req: ent req HS dipl, portfolio & audition SAT
Degrees: degrees BFA 4 yrs, BS, BM, MA, MFA, MM, Mid, Mat cert
Tuition: $17,250 per yr
Courses: Acting, Aesthetics, Animation Business of the Arts, Art Education, Art History, Calligraphy, †Ceramics, Collage, Conceptual Art, Constructions, Dance Education, Digital Storytelling, Drawing, †Film, Goldsmithing, †Graphic Design, †Illustration, †Industrial Design, Interactive Narrative, Interface Design, Intermedia, Jazz Dance Performance, Jazz Music Theory, Jewelry, Lettering, Media Technology, Mixed Media, Multimedia, Museum Exhibition Design, †Museum Staff Training, Music Education, Music Industry: Modern Ballet, Musical Theater, †Painting, Performance & Composition, †Photography, †Printmaking, †Sculpture, Silversmithing, †Teacher Training, †Textile Design, Weaving
Adult Hobby Classes: Courses—Ceramics, Computer Graphics, Creative Writing, Design, Fine Arts, Illustration, Jewelry & Metalsmithing, Photography, Printmaking, Sculpture, Woodworking
Children's Classes: Courses—Acting, Animation, Bookmaking, Ceramics, Comix, Creative Writing, Dance, Drama, Drawing, Figure Drawing, Graphic Design, Illustration, Jewelry, Musical Theater, Painting, Photography, Sculpture
Summer School: Courses—Acting, Crafts, Design, Fine Arts, Jazz Performing, Media Arts, Musical Theater

PITTSBURGH

ART INSTITUTE OF PITTSBURGH, 420 Blvd of the Allies Pittsburgh, PA 15219. Tel 412-263-6600, 291-6200; Fax 412-263-6667; Elec Mail admissions-aip@aii.edu; Internet Home Page Address: www.aip.aii.edu; *Pres* George Pry; *Technology* Allan Agamedia, BS; *Media Arts & Animation* James Allen, AST; *Digital Media Production/Video Production* Cy Anderson, BS; *Gen Educ* Douglas Anke, BS; *Photog* Karen Antonelli, BA; *Industrial Design Technology* Alan Assad, MEd; *Industrial Design Technology* Cyril Assad, BFA; *Media Arts & Animation* Michele Bamburak, BA; *Multimedia & Web Design* David Barton, BA; *Graphic Design* Mark Bender, BFA; *Media Arts & Animation* Sean Benedict, BA; *Dir Gen Educ* Heather A Bigley, MS; *Gen Educ* Maria Boada, MS; *Gen Educ* Diane Bowser, MA; *Media Arts & Animation/Gen Educ* J Nicholas Brockmann, MFA; *Gen Educ* Chad Brown, BA; *Graphic Design* Stephen M Butler, BS; *Multimedia & Web Design* Michael Cantella, BA; *Media Arts & Animation* Richard Catizone; *Gen Educ* Alberta Patella Certo, MEd; *Industrial Design Technology* Dan-Horia Chinda, MArch; *Gen Educ, Graphic Design* Angelo L Ciotti, MA; *Digital Design* Bob Clements, BS; *Photog* Brian Colkitt, AST; *Computer Animation* Ruth Comley, BA; *Graphic Design* Jeff Davis, MFA; *Graphic Design* Frank J DeGennaro, BS; *Gen Educ* Maura Doern-Danko, MFA;

Photog Thomas Donley, AST; *Gen Educ* Elizabeth C Dunn, MAT; *Graphic Design* Earl Easter, BS; *Photog* Anderson B English, MFA; *Industrial Design Technology* William Farrell; *Gen Educ* John C Franke, BA; *Video Production* Donald Gabany, BA; *Graphic Design* Deborah Giancola, MPA; *Interior Design* Jordene Gates, BS; *VPres, Dean Educ* Edward A Gill, MEd; *Graphic Design* David S Giuliani, BS; *Graphic Design* Albert Gotlieb, MFA; *Foundations* Maurice Graves, MA; *Gen Educ* Kathy Griffin, MEd; *Industrial Design Technology* Eric Hahn, BFA; *Graphic Design* John L Hassinger; *Gen Educ* Janna L Haubach, MEd; *Prog Chmn Digital Media Production* Douglas N Heaps, BS; *Photog* Bruce Henderson, BS; *Media Arts & Animation* Joseph Herron, BFA; *Interior Design* Margaret Herron, BA; *Video Production* James Hudson, BS; *Multimedia & Web Design* Patricia Adamcik-Huettel, AST; *Gen Educ* Jason Joy, MA; *Video Production* Douglas R Kennedy; *Graphic Design* Amy Kern, MFA; *Graphic Design* Michael W LaMark, MS; *Prof Foundations Studies* Una Charlene Langer-Holt; *Photog* Barry Lavery, MDiv; *Interior Design* Pamela A Lisak; *Graphic Design* Leslie B Lockerman, BFA; *Gen Educ* Frederick Lorini, MFA; *Media Arts & Animation* Angela Love, BS; *Video Production* Andrew Maietta, MLS; *Graphic Design* Michael Malle; *Gen Educ* Edward M Matus, MA; *Gen Educ* Richard Matvey, MEd; *Chair Multimedia & Design* Sharon McGuire, BA; *Photog* G Chris Miller, BS; *Graphic Design* Linda Miller; *Graphic Design* Ronald A Miller, BA; *Graphic Design & Digital Design* Joseph W Milne, BA; *Industrial Design Technology* William R Mitas, BS; *Graphic Design* Connie Moore, MAT; *Gen Educ* Linda Musto, BS; *Industrial Design* Lars Nyquist, BA; *Culinary Arts & Management* Shawn Oddo, AOS; *Digital Design* Shawn O'Mara, BS; *Graphic Design* Michael N Opalko, BFA; *Gen Educ* Robert Peluso, PhD; *Industrial Design Technology* David Pence, BS; *Gen Educ* Stephanie Perry, MBA; *Multimedia & Web Design* Dante Piombino, BA; *Media Arts & Animation* Francis A Pionati, MFA; *Gen Educ* Linda Rathburn, MEd; *Industrial Design Technology* Scott Ritiger, BA; *Industrial Design Technology* Arturo Rivero; *Multimedia & Web Design* Leon L Salvayon, MEd; *Media Arts & Animation* Michael C Schwab, BFA; *Media Arts & Animation* John Simpson Jr, BA; *Interior Design* James J Smelko, BS; *Interior Design* Kelly JK Spewock, MFA; *Multimedia & Web Design* Jay W Speyerer, BS; *Graphic Design* Mary Jean Stabile, BS; *Media Arts & Animation* Jeffrey Styers, BS; *Gen Educ* Rebecca Suhoza, MA; *Graphic Design, Media Arts & Animation* Andrew Sujdak, BS; *Gen Educ* Michele M Thomas, MS; *Interior Design* John Michael Toth, BA; *Media Arts & Animation* Edward A Urian, BS; *Media Arts & Animation* David M Walters, BA; *Graphic Design, Media Arts & Animation* Helen Webster, BFA; *Media Arts & Animation* Greg Weider, BFA; *Media Arts & Animation* Hans Westman, BA; *Gen Educ* Jialu Wu, PhD; *Industrial Design* James Yedinak, BA; *Graphic Design* Shirley Yee, MFA; *Media Arts & Animation* Jeffrey Zehner, BS; *Graphic Design, Media Arts & Animation* Flavia Zortea, BFA; *Dir Entertainment Technology Center* Douglas Henderson
Estab 1921; Maintain nonprofit art gallery & art library; pvt; D & E; Scholarships; 2300
Ent Req: HS grad
Degrees: AA 2 yrs, dipl
Tuition: $334 per cr hr, AS prog 105 cr, BS prog 180 cr
Courses: Culinary Arts, Digital Design, Digital Media Production, Game Art & Design, Graphic Design, Industrial Design, Interior Design, Media Arts & Animation, Multimedia, Photography, Video, Web Site Administration
Summer School: Dir, Melinda Trempus.

CARLOW COLLEGE, Art Dept, 3333 Fifth Ave, Pittsburgh, PA 15213. Tel 412-578-6000, 578-6003; Internet Home Page Address: www.carlow.edu; *Assoc Chmn* Suzanne Steiner; *Chmn Dept of Art* Dale Hussman
Estab 1945; FT 1, PT 3; den; D & E; Scholarships; SC 17, LC 6; 800, maj 35
Ent Req: HS dipl and transcript, col boards
Degrees: BA, Cert Art Education
Tuition: $13,468 per yr; campus res—room & board $5490
Courses: 2-D Design, American Art, Art Education, Art Therapy, Ceramics, Drawing, Fiber Arts, Painting, Printmaking, Sculpture, Survey of Art, Teacher Training, Twentieth Century Art

CARNEGIE MELLON UNIVERSITY, College of Fine Arts, 5000 Forbes Ave, Rm 100, Pittsburgh, PA 15213-3815. Tel 412-268-2000, Ext 2349 (dean's office), Ext 2409 (art); Elec Mail djmartin@andrew.cmu.edu; Internet Home Page Address: www.cmu.edu/cfa; *Interim Dean* Dan Martin; *Assoc Dean* Barbara Anderson
Estab 1905; Maintain a nonprofit art gallery, Regina Gouger Miller Gallery, 5000 Forbes Ave Pornell Center for the Arts, Pittsburgh, PA 15213; maintain an art library, Hunt Library, 4th flr, Carnegie Mellon Univ, 5000 Forbes Ave, Pittsburgh, PA 15213. Art supplies may be purchased on campus; pvt; D & E; Scholarships, Fellowships; SC, LC, GC
Ent Req: col board ent exam plus auditions or portfolio
Degrees: 4-5 yr, MFA in Stage Design available in Dept of Drama
Tuition: Undergrad $19,400 per yr; campus res available
Courses: Architecture, Conceptual Art, Constructions, Costume Design & Construction, Design, Graphic Arts, Graphic Design, Mixed Media, Painting, Photography, Printmaking, Restoration & Conservation, Sculpture, Stage Design, Theatre Arts, Video
Summer School: Term of 6 wks. Courses—includes some pre-college courses
—School Architecture, 201 College of Fine Arts, Pittsburgh, PA 15213-3890. Tel 412-268-2354; Fax 412-268-7819; Internet Home Page Address: www.cmu.edu/architecture; *Head* Stephen Lee
FT 22, PT 20; 295
Degrees: BArch, MS, PhD
Tuition: Undergrad $19,400 per yr
Courses: Architecture
Summer School: Dir, John Papinchak. Tuition $2094 per 6 wks
—School of Design, MMCH 110, Pittsburgh, PA 15213; 5000 Forbes Ave, Pittsburgh, PA 15213-3890. Tel 412-268-2828; Fax 412-268-7838; Elec Mail info@design.cmu.edu; Internet Home Page Address: www.cmu.edu/enrollment/admission/finearts/design.html; *Dept Chmn* Wayne Chung; *Head* Terry Irwin
FT 14, PT 4; 200
Degrees: BFA 4 yrs
Tuition: Res—undergrad $19,400 per yr

Courses: Graphic Design, Industrial Design
Adult Hobby Classes: Calligraphy
Summer School: Design Studio
—School of Art, 5000 Forbes Ave, Pittsburgh, PA 15213-3890. Tel 412-268-2409; Elec Mail artscool@andrew.cmu.edu; Internet Home Page Address: www.cmu.edu/art; *Head* John Carson; *Assoc Head* Bob Bingham
FT 28, PT 2-6; Scholarships; 215
Degrees: BFA & MFA
Tuition: Undergrad & grad $21,275 per yr
Courses: †Art, Art History, Ceramic Sculpture, Computer, Conceptual Art, Constructions, Drawing, Mixed Media, Painting, Printmaking, Sculpture, Video
Children's Classes: Enrl 100: tuition $575 for 9 months. Courses—same as undergrad prog
Summer School: Dir, Janice Hart. Enrl 50; tuition $3200 for 6 wks. Courses—same as undergrad prog

CHATHAM COLLEGE, Fine & Performing Arts, Woodland Rd, Pittsburgh, PA 15232-2826. Tel 412-365-1100; Internet Home Page Address: www.chatham.edu; *Dir* Margaret Ross; *Asst Prof* Michael Pestel; *Chmn* Pat Montley
Estab 1869; FT 2, PT 2; pvt; W; SC 17, LC 7
Ent Req: HS grad
Degrees: BA 4 yrs
Courses: Aesthetics, Art Appreciation, Art Education, †Art History, Conceptual Art, Constructions, Design, Drawing, Film, History of Art & Architecture, Independent Study, Introduction to Art, Mixed Media, †Painting, Photography, Printmaking, †Sculpture

LA ROCHE COLLEGE, Division of Design, 9000 Babcock Blvd, Pittsburgh, PA 15237-5898. Tel 412-367-9300; Fax 412-536-1527; Elec Mail maria.ripepi@laroche.edu; Internet Home Page Address: www.laroche.edu; *Asst Prof* Neha Agarwal, MFA; *Assoc Prof* Thomas Bates, MA, MPA; *Asst Prof* Patrick Connolly, MA; *Asst Prof* Richard Helfrich, MA; *Prof* Lauren Lampe, MFA; *Vis Prof* RJ Thompson, BS; *Asst Prof & Dept Chair Interior Design* Nicole Bieak Kreidler, MS; *Prof* Devvrat Nagar, MEd, GD Arch; *Asst Prof* Maria Ripepi, MFA; *Asst Prof* Lisa Kamphaus, BFA
Estab 1963, dept estab 1965; PT 15; pvt; D & E; SC 25, LC 15; D & E 220, non-maj 50, maj 170
Ent Req: HS dipl
Degrees: BA and BS 4 yr
Courses: 3-D Design, Advertising Design, Aesthetics, Airbrush Illustration, Art History, Building Technology, Buyer Behavior, Ceramics, Commercial Art, Communication, Computer Graphics, Contract Documents, Directed & Independent Studies, Display, Drawing, Fashion Design, Foundation Design, †Graphic Arts, †Graphic Design, Illustration, Industrial Design, †Interior Design, Lettering, Marketing Strategy, †Multimedia Design, Package Design, Painting, Photography, Portfolio Preparation, Sculpture, Sr Design Seminar, Textile Design
Summer School: Dir Admis, David McFarland.

POINT PARK COLLEGE, Performing Arts Dept, 201 Wood St, Pittsburgh, PA 15222-1984. Tel 412-392-3450; Fax 412-391-1980; *Chmn* Ronald Allan Lindblom
Degrees: BA & BFA
Tuition: $4300 per sem
Courses: Architecture, Art Appreciation, Art History, †Fashion Illustration, †Film, †Interior Design, †Photography, †Stage Design, Theatre Design, †Visual Arts

UNIVERSITY OF PITTSBURGH, Henry Clay Frick Dept History of Art & Architecture, 104 Frick Fine Arts Bldg, Pittsburgh, PA 15260. Tel 412-648-2400; Fax 412-648-2792; Internet Home Page Address: www.haa.pitt.edu; *Chmn* Kirk Savage; *Mellon Prof* Terence Smith, PhD; *Prof Emeritus* David Wilkins, PhD; *Asst Prof* Christopher Drew Armstrong, PhD; *Asst Prof* Josh Ellenbogen, PhD; *Assoc Prof* Gao Minglu, PhD; *Assoc Prof* Barbara McCloskey, PhD; *Prof* Franklin Toker, PhD
Estab 1787; dept estab 1927; Maintain nonprofit, University Art Gallery; Fine Arts Library; on-campus shop sells art supplies; Pvt; D & E; Scholarships, Fellowships; LC 35, GC 10; D 750, E 250, grad 30
Ent Req: HS dipl, BA, GRE for grad work
Degrees: BA 4 yrs, MA 2 yrs, PhD
Tuition: Res—grad $6,142 per sem; nonres—grad $11,725 per sem
Courses: †Architectural Studies, †Architecture, Art History, History of Art & Architecture
Summer School: Dir, Kirk Savage. Enrl 150; 6 wks, 2 sessions 3-4 wks, 3 sessions
—Dept of Studio Arts, 118 Frick Fine Arts Bldg, Pittsburgh, PA 15260. Tel 412-648-2430; Fax 412-648-3660; Internet Home Page Address: www.pitt.edu/~studio; *Assoc Prof* Michael Morrill; *Assoc Prof* Kenneth Batista; *Prof* Paul Glabicki; *Assoc Prof* Delanie Jenkins; *Asst Prof* Bovey Lee; *Assoc Prof* Edward Powell
Estab 1968; FT 6, PT 4-7; pub; D & E; SC 29; 1,000 non-majors; 75 majors
Degrees: BA
Tuition: Res—$11,000 per yr
Courses: Design, Drawing, Graphic Design, Painting, Print Etching, Sculpture

RADNOR

CABRINI COLLEGE, Dept of Fine Arts, 610 King of Prussia Rd, Radnor, PA 19087-3698. Tel 610-902-8380; Fax 610-902-8539; *Chmn Dept* Adeline Bethany, EdD
Estab 1957; FT 2, PT 3; den; D & E; Scholarships; SC 11, LC 4
Ent Req: HS dipl, satisfactory average & rank in secondary school class, SAT, recommendations
Degrees: BA(Arts Administration, Fine Arts & Graphic Design), BS & BSED
Courses: Art Education, Ceramics, Computer Publication Design, Design & Composition, Drawing, Graphic Design, History of Art & Architecture, Painting, Teacher Training
Adult Hobby Classes: Courses offered

Summer School: Dir, Dr Midge Leahy. Term of 6 wks beginning May & July. Courses—Color Theory, Drawing, Elem Art Methods, Mixed Media, Painting

READING

ALBRIGHT COLLEGE, Dept of Art, 13th & Bern Sts, Reading, PA 19604; PO Box 15234, Reading, PA 19612-5234. Tel 610-921-7715; Fax 610-921-7530; Internet Home Page Address: www.alb.edu; *Prof* Tom Watcke; *Chmn* Kristen Woodward; *Asst Prof* Dr Richard Hamwi; *Assoc Prof* Gary Adlestein; *Lectr* Christopher Youngs
Estab 1856, dept estab 1964; maintains nonprofit gallery, Freedman Gallery 13th & Bern St, PO Box 15234, Reading, PA 19612-5234; Pvt; D & E; Scholarships; SC 14, LC 7; D 322, E 41, non-maj 340, maj 14, others 20
Ent Req: HS dipl, SAT
Degrees: BA 4 yrs
Courses: †Art Education, Art History, Ceramics, †Commercial Art, Constructions, †Design, Drawing, Fashion Arts, Film, †Graphic Arts, History of Art & Architecture, Interior Design, Mixed Media, †Painting, Photography, Printmaking, †Sculpture, †Teacher Training, †Textile Design, Theatre Arts
Adult Hobby Classes: Enrl 40; tuition $110 per cr. Courses—Drawing, Photography
Children's Classes: Enrl 25-35; tuition $35-$50 per course. Courses—Crafts, Drawing
Summer School: Enrl 30 - 50; 2 terms of 4 wks beginning in June & July. Courses—Art History, Drawing, Painting

ROSEMONT

ROSEMONT COLLEGE, Art Program, 1400 Montgomery Ave, Rosemont, PA 19010-1699. Tel 610-527-0200; Fax 610-526-2984; Elec Mail admissions@rosemont.edu; Internet Home Page Address: www.rosemont.edu; *Chmn Div* Tina Walduier Bizzarro, PhD; *Assoc Prof & Dir Gallery* Patricia Nugent, MFA; *Assoc Prof* Michael Willse, MFA; *Asst Prof* Amy Orr, MFA
Estab 1921; FT 6, PT 4; pvt; W (exchange with Villanova Univ, Cabrini College, Eastern College, The Design Schools); D; Scholarships; total col 600, art 200, grad approx 17
Ent Req: HS dipl, SAT
Degrees: BFA (Studio Art), BA (Art History, Studio Art), Teacher cert in Art K-12
Courses: Aesthetics, American Indian Art, Art Criticism, Art Education, Ceramics, Creativity & the Marketplace, Drawing, Fiber History, Graphic Arts, Painting, Photography, Printmaking, Sculpture, Studio Art, Teacher Training
Summer School: Dir, Tina Walduier Bizzarro

SCRANTON

LACKAWANNA COLLEGE, Fine Arts Dept, 501 Vine St, Scranton, PA 18509-3251. Tel 570-961-7827; Internet Home Page Address: www.lacka.ljc.edu; *Chmn* John De Nunzio
Estab 1885
Ent Req: HS dipl or equivalent
Degrees: AA
Tuition: $795 per cr, $585 per 3 cr
Courses: Fine Arts, Survey Class

MARYWOOD UNIVERSITY, Art Dept, 2300 Adams Ave, Scranton, PA 18509-1598. Tel 570-348-6211, 348-6278; Fax 570-Fax: 340-6023; Internet Home Page Address: www.marywood.edu; *Chmn* Matt Povse
Estab 1915; Maintains 3 nonprofit art galleries, Mahady Gallery, Suraci Gallery, The Maslow Collection Study Gallery for Contemporary Art - all on campus; on-campus shop where art supplies may be purchased; FT 13, PT 36; pvt; D & E; Scholarships; SC 56, LC 14, GC 58; maj 275, grad 100
Ent Req: HS dipl, portfolio & interview
Degrees: BA(Art Educ), BA (Art Therapy, Arts Admin), BFA (Painting, Illustration, Graphic Design, Photography, Ceramics, Sculpture), MA(Studio Art, Art Educ, Art Therapy), MFA (Visual Arts with concentration in Ceramics, Graphic Design, Illustration, Sculpture, Painting, Printmaking, Photography)
Courses: Advertising Design, Aesthetics, †Art Education, Art History, †Art Therapy, †Ceramics, Drawing, Graphic Arts, †Graphic Design, †Illustration, Jewelry, †Painting, †Photography, †Printmaking, †Sculpture, Serigraphy, †Weaving

PENN FOSTER COLLEGE, (Harcourt Learning Direct) School of Interior Design, 925 Oak St, Scranton, PA 18515. Tel 570-342-7701, Ext 341; Fax 570-343-0560; Elec Mail russell.day@pennfoster.edu; *Chief Certification Officer* Connie Dempsey; *Dept Chair* Russell Day
Estab 1890, dept estab 1969; FT 1; pvt; distance educ; 4200
Ent Req: completion of high school
Degrees: career diploma, mem CID International, AS Interior Design, AS Graphic Design
Courses: Art Appreciation, †Graphic Design, Interior Decorating
Adult Hobby Classes: Interior Decorating
Summer School: Dept Chair, Russell Day
—**Art/Graphic Design,** 14300 N Northsight Blvd, Scottsdale, AZ 85260. Tel 480-947-6644; Fax 480-951-6030; Internet Home Page Address: www.pennfostercollege.edu; *Sr Instr* Sharon Hopkins
Estab 1890; FT 1, PT 2; pvt; open enrollment; Distance Learning
Ent Req: HS dipl
Degrees: Assoc of Science
Courses: Art Appreciation, Drafting, †Graphic Design
Adult Hobby Classes: Drawing, Painting

SHIPPENSBURG

SHIPPENSBURG UNIVERSITY, Art Dept, 1871 Old Main Dr, Huber Art Ctr Shippensburg, PA 17257-2200. Tel 717-477-1530; Fax 717-477-4049; Internet Home Page Address: www.shippensburg.edu; *Chmn Art Dept* William Hynes, MFA; *Assoc Prof* Janet Ruby; *Asst Prof* Bill Davis, MFA; *Asst Prof* Dr Stephen Hirshon, MFA; *Asst Prof* Michael Campbell, MFA; *Asst Prof* Steven Dolbin

Estab 1871, dept estab 1920; pub; D & E; Scholarships; SC 17, LC 6; D 400, E 100, non-maj 600, grad 15, continuing educ 20
Ent Req: HS dipl, Portfolio review
Degrees: BA(Art)
Courses: Art History, Arts & Crafts, Ceramics, Drawing, Enamelling, Painting, Printmaking, Sculpture
Adult Hobby Classes: Sr citizen tuition waived in regular classes if space is available
Summer School: Dir, William Hynes. Lectr & Studio courses

SLIPPERY ROCK

SLIPPERY ROCK UNIVERSITY OF PENNSYLVANIA, Dept of Art, 1 Morrow Way, Slippery Rock, PA 16057-1313. Tel 724-738-2020; Fax 724-738-4485; *Prof, Chmn* Thomas Como; *Prof* Heather Hertel; *Prof* Sean MacMillan; *Asst Prof* John Shumway, MFA; *Prof* Dr Kurt Pitluga; *Prof* Katherine Mickle, MFA; *Prof* June Edwards, MFA; *Prof* Barbara Westman
Maintain nonprofit art gallery, gaultgallery@maltbycenter; FT 9; Pub; D & E; SC 27, LC 3; maj 70
Ent Req: HS dipl
Degrees: BA(Art), BFA(Art) 4 yr
Courses: Art History, Art Synthesis, Ceramics, Drawing, Graphic Design, Metalsmithing, Mixed Media, Painting, Photography, Printmaking, Sculpture, Teacher Training, Textile Design
Summer School: Tuition $129 per cr hr

SWARTHMORE

SWARTHMORE COLLEGE, Dept of Art & Art History, 500 College Ave, Swarthmore, PA 19081-1390. Tel 610-328-8116, 328-8000; Fax 610-328-7793; Elec Mail jcianfrl@swarthmore.edu; Internet Home Page Address: www.swarthmore.edu; *Assoc Provost & Assoc Prof* Patricia L Reilly, PhD; *Prof* Constance Cain Hungerford PhD, MFA; *Chmn & Prof* Michael Cothren PhD, MFA; *Prof* Brian A Meunier, MFA; *Assoc Prof* Janine Mileaf, PhD; *Prof* Syd Carpenter, MFA; *Prof* Randall L Exxon, MFA
Estab 1864, dept estab 1925; pvt; D; Scholarships; SC 14, LC 33; non-maj 500, maj 25
Ent Req: HS dipl, SAT, CEEB
Degrees: BA 4 yrs
Tuition: $23,020 per yr, campus res—room & board $7500 per yr
Courses: Aesthetics, Architecture, Art, Art History, Ceramics, Drawing, History, History of Architecture, History of Art & Architecture, History of Cinema, Landscape Architecture, Mixed Media, Painting, Philosophy, Photography, Printmaking, Sculpture, Stage Design, Theatre Arts, Theatre Program, Urban History

UNIVERSITY PARK

PENNSYLVANIA STATE UNIVERSITY, UNIVERSITY PARK, Penn State School of Visual Arts, 210 Patterson Bldg, University Park, PA 16802. Tel 814-865-0444; Fax 814-865-1158; Internet Home Page Address: www.sova.psu.edu; *Asst Prof Art* Janet Hartranft; *Prof Art & Women's Studies (Drawing/Painting)* Micaela Amato; *Assoc Prof Art Educ* Patricia Amburgy; *Asst Prof Women's Studies & Art (Art Criticism)* Irina Aristarkhova; *Assoc Prof Art (Drawing/Painting)* John Bowman; *Assoc Prof Art (Core Prog & Drawing/Painting)* Paul Chidester; *Assoc Prof Art (Fayette Campus)* David DiPietro; *Prof Art Educ* Yvonne Gaudelius; *Assoc Prof Art (Printmaking)* Robin Gibson; *Asst Prof Art (Photog)* Lonnie Graham; *Prof Art Educ & Women's Studies* Karen Keifer-Boyd; *Asst Prof Art (New Media)* Matthew Kenyon; *Assoc Prof Art Educ* Wanda Knight; *Prof Art (Gen Educ)* Jerrold Maddox; *Asst Prof Art (Sculpture)* Cristin Millet; *Prof Art (Drawing/Painting)* Helen O'Leary; *Assoc Prof Art (Art Criticism)* Simone Osthoff; *Asst Prof Art Educ & Curriculum & Instruction* Kimberly Powell; *Assoc Prof Art (Ceramics)* Elizabeth Quackenbush; *Assoc Prof Art (New Media)* Carlos Rosas; *Assoc Prof Art (Printmaking & New Media)* Jean Sanders; *Asst Prof Integrative Art & Art (Photog)* Keith Shapiro; *Asst Prof Art Educ & Women's Studies* Stephanie Springgay; *Prof Art (Ceramics)* Christopher Staley; *Prof Art Educ* Mary Ann Stankiewicz; *Prof Art Educ* Christine Thompson; *Asst Prof Art (Metal Art & Technology)* James Thurman; *Dir & Prof Art Educ* Charles Garoian; *Distinguished Prof Art (Drawing/Painting)* Robert Yarber; *Assoc Prof Art & Art Educ* David Ebitz; *Instr Art Educ* Jody Guy; *Asst Prof Art (Photog)* Stephen Rubin; *Asst Prof Art (Sculpture)* Bonnie Collura; *Asst Prof Art (Ceramics)* Del Harrow
Estab 1855, col estab 1963; Maintains nonprofit art gallery, Edwin Zoller Gallery, 210 Patterson Bldg, Penn State Univ, University Park, PA 16802; maintains art library, Pattee Library. Art supplies may be purchased on campus ; pub; D & E; SC 282, LC 99, GC 104
Ent Req: HS dipl and GPA, SAT, successful portfolio review
Degrees: PhD, MEd, MFA, MS, BA, BFA, BDES, IDS
Tuition: Res—$6,082 per sem; nonres—$11,097 per sem
Courses: †Art Appreciation, Art Education, †Art History, Ceramics, †Collage, Drawing, †Interdisciplinary Digital Studios, Metals, †Mixed Media, †Museum Staff Training, †New Media, Painting, Photography, Printmaking, Sculpture, †Teacher Training, †Video
Summer School: Courses— limited
—**Dept of Art History,** 229 Arts Bldg, University Park, PA 16802-1920. Tel 814-865-6326; Fax 814-865-1242; Elec Mail cxz3@psu.edu; Internet Home Page Address: www.arthistory.psu.edu; *Evan Pugh Prof Emeritus* Hellmut Hager, PhD; *Prof Emeritus* Roland E Fleischer, PhD; *Evan Pugh Prof* Anthony Cutler, PhD; *Assoc Prof Emeritus* Jeanne Chenault Porter PhD; *Assoc Prof* Elizabeth B Smith PhD; *Assoc Prof* Elizabeth J Walters PhD; *Assoc Prof* Brian Curran, PhD; *Assoc Prof & Dept Head* Craig Zabel, PhD; *Assoc Prof* Charlotte Houghton, PhD; *Assoc Prof* Nancy Locke, PhD; *Asst Prof* Chika Okeke-Agulu, PhD; *Assoc Prof* Sarah Rich, PhD; *Asst Prof* Madhuri Desai, PhD

Estab 1855, dept estab 1963; pub; D & E; Scholarships, Fellowships, Assistantships; LC 50, GC 36; maj 50, grad 35
Ent Req: HS dipl
Degrees: BA, MA, PhD
Tuition: Res—$3273 per sem; nonres—$7044 per sem
Courses: 19th & 20th century European Art & Architecture, Aesthetics, American Art & Architecture, Ancient Egyptian, †Art History, Contemporary Art, Criticism, Early Christian & Byzantine Art, German Baroque & Rococo Architecture, Greek & Roman Art & Architecture, Historiography, History of Art & Archeology, History of Photography, Iconology, Italian Renaissance & Baroque Art & Architecture, Late Antique, Museum Studies, Northern Renaissance & Baroque Art, Spanish & French Baroque & Rococo Art, Western Medieval Art & Architecture
Adult Hobby Classes: Classes offered through Continuing Education
Summer School: Courses same as regular session, but limited

UPPER BURRELL

PENNSYLVANIA STATE UNIVERSITY AT NEW KENSINGTON, Depts of Art & Architecture, 3550 Seventh St Rd, Upper Burrell, PA 15068. Tel 724-339-5466, 339-5456; Internet Home Page Address: www.psu.edu/dept/arts/schools/schools; *Assoc Prof Art* Bud Gibbons
Estab 1968; pub; D; Scholarships; SC 3-4, LC 1 per sem
Ent Req: col boards
Degrees: 2 yr (option for 4 yr at main campus at University Park)
Courses: Art Education, Art History, Ceramics, Design, Drawing, Music, Painting, Theatre Arts
Adult Hobby Classes: Courses—Ceramics, Painting, Theater for Children
Children's Classes: Courses—Art, Drama, Music Workshops
Summer School: Dir, Joseph Ferrino. Enrl 100; 8 wk term. Courses—Art, Drama, Music, Workshops

VILLANOVA

VILLANOVA UNIVERSITY, Dept of Theater, 800 Lancaster Ave, Villanova, PA 19085. Tel 610-519-4610, 519-4660 (History); Internet Home Page Address: www.villanova.edu; *Prof* George Radan; *Asst Prof* Dr Mark Sullivan; *Chmn* Bro Richard Cannuli
Estab 1842, dept estab 1971; pvt; D & E; SC 25, LC 6; D 35, maj 35
Ent Req: HS dipl, SAT
Degrees: BFA 4 yrs; courses taught in conjunction with Rosemont College
Courses: †Aesthetics, Archaeology, Art Education, Art History, Conservation, Drawing, Painting, Theatre Arts
Adult Hobby Classes: Enrl 20-30; tuition $585 per course in 14 wk sem. Courses—Calligraphy, Drawing
Summer School: Held in Siena, Italy. Courses—Art History, Language, Studio Art

WASHINGTON

WASHINGTON & JEFFERSON COLLEGE, Art Dept, 50 S Lincoln St, Olin Art Ctr Washington, PA 15301-4812. Tel 724-222-4400, 223-6110; Internet Home Page Address: www.wj.edu; *Chmn Art Dept & Assoc Prof* John Lambertson; *Asst Prof* Patrick T Schmidt, MFA; *Adjunct Prof* James McNutt, MA
Estab 1787, dept estab 1959; Maintain nonprofit art gallery; pvt; D & E; Scholarships; SC 14, LC 8; D 162, E 18, non-maj 139, maj 23, others 15
Ent Req: HS dipl, SAT, achievement tests
Degrees: BA 4 yr
Courses: Art Appreciation, Art Education, Art History, Ceramics, Design, Drawing, Framing & Matting, Gallery Management, Lettering, Painting, Photography, Printmaking, Restoration & Conservation, Sculpture, Teacher Training
Summer School: Dir, Dean Dlugos. Enrl 250, two 4 wk sessions, June-Aug. Courses—Drawing, Framing, Matting, Photography

WAYNE

WAYNE ART CENTER, 413 Maplewood Ave, Wayne, PA 19087-4792. Tel 610-688-3553; Fax 610-995-0478; Elec Mail wayheart@worldnet.att.net; Internet Home Page Address: www.wayneart.com/reginfo; *Instr* Carolyn Howard; *Instr* Regina Allen, MFA; *Instr* Maevernon Varnum; *Instr* Deena Ball, BA; *Instr* Candace Stringer; *Instr* Nancy Barch; *Instr* Susan Branco; *Instr* Maggie DeBaecke, BA; *Instr* Paul DuSold; *Pres* Leslie Ehrin, BA; *Instr* Karen Carlin Fogerty; *Instr* Frances Galante, BA; *Instr* Margaret Gardner, BA; *Instr* Virginia Garwood; *Instr* Denise Gonzalez; *Instr* Mimi Green; *Instr* Mark Gruener; *Instr* Ann Howes; *Instr* Patricia Jordan; *Instr* Pat Kerr; *Instr* Andi Lieberman; *Instr* James Lloyd; *Instr* Charlotte Martin; *Instr* Cornelia Maxion; *Instr* James McFarlane; *Instr* Kathy Miller; *Instr* Lyn Mueller
Estab 1930; pvt; D & E; SC 25, others 40
Ent Req: none; free program for senior citizens
Courses: Mixed Media, Painting, Pottery, Sculpture, Woodcarving
Children's Classes: Tuition $35 for 10 wk sem, yearly dues $6. Courses—Drawing, Painting, Sculpture
Summer School: Exec Dir, Meg Miller. Courses—same as above plus Landscape Painting

WAYNESBURG

WAYNESBURG COLLEGE, Dept of Fine Arts, 51 W College St, Waynesburg, PA 15370-1258. Tel 724-627-8191, 852-3296; Fax 724-627-6416; Internet Home Page Address: www.waynesburg.edu/~art; *Prof* Susan Phillips, MFA; *Instr* Nathan Sims

Estab 1849, dept estab 1971; pvt; D & E; Scholarships; SC 25, LC 6; D 131, E 3, maj 17
Ent Req: HS dipl
Degrees: BA (Visual Commun) 4 yrs, MBA
Courses: Art Education, Art History, Ceramics, Computer Applications for Visual Communication, Computer Graphics, Design, Desk Top Publishing, Drawing, Graphic Arts, Layout & Photography for Media, Media Presentation, Painting, Photo-Journalism, Photography, Printmaking, Sculpture, Television, Theatre Arts, Typography, †Visual Art, †Visual Communication, †Visual Communication-Print Media
Adult Hobby Classes: Courses—Art History, Graphic Design, Photography
Summer School: Dept Chmn, Daniel Morris.

WEST MIFFLIN

COMMUNITY COLLEGE OF ALLEGHENY COUNTY, Fine Arts Dept, 1750 Clairton Rd, South Campus West Mifflin, PA 15122-3029. Tel 412-469-1100; Fax 412-469-6370; Internet Home Page Address: www.ccac.edu; *Chmn* George Jaber
Estab 1968; FT 2; pub; D&E
Ent Req: HS dipl
Degrees: AA, AS
Tuition: County res—$920 per yr, $68 per cr hr
Courses: Advertising Design, Art Appreciation, Calligraphy, Ceramics, Commercial Art, Computer Graphics, Design, Drawing, Handicrafts, Painting, Photography

WILKES-BARRE

WILKES UNIVERSITY, Dept of Art, Bedford Hall, Wilkes-Barre, PA 18766. Tel 570-826-1135; Internet Home Page Address: www.wilkes.edu; *Chmn* Terry Zipay, PhD; *Assoc Prof* Sharon Bowar; *Adjunct Prof* Sedor Sieboda PhD; *Adjunct Prof* Jan Conway, MFA; *Adjunct Prof* Jean Adams, BA
Estab 1947; pvt; D & E; Scholarships; SC 20, LC 7; D 170, E 23, non-maj 120, maj 35
Ent Req: HS dipl, SAT
Degrees: BA 4 yr
Courses: †Art Education, †Art History, †Ceramics, †Communication Design, Drawing, Painting, †Photography, †Printmaking, †Sculpture, Surface Design, Teacher Training, Textile Design
Adult Hobby Classes: Courses variable
Summer School: Dir, Henry Steuben. Tuition $350 per cr for 5 wk day, 8 wk evening or 3 wk pre-session. Courses—Art Studio, Ceramics, Photography, Surface Design

WILLIAMSPORT

LYCOMING COLLEGE, Art Dept, 700 College Pl, Williamsport, PA 17701-5192. Tel 570-321-4000, 321-4002; Elec Mail estomin@lycoming.edu; Internet Home Page Address: www.lycoming.edu/; *Chmn* B Lynn Estomin, MFA; *Prof* Amy Golahny PhD, MFA; *Asst Prof* Gustavo Plascencia, MFA; *Prof* Seth Goodman, MFA; *Instr* Katherine Sterngold, MFA; *Asst Prof* Howard Tran, MFA; *Instr* Kim Rhone, MFA
Estab 1812; Maintain nonprofit art gallery; Lycoming Col Art Gallery; art supplies available on-campus; pvt; D & E; Scholarships; SC 18, LC 8; College 1,500, Dept 500, maj 70
Ent Req: HS dipl, ACT or SAT
Degrees: BA 4 yr
Courses: Advertising Design, †Art Education, †Art History, Ceramics, †Commercial Art, Computer Design & Animation, Computer Graphics, †Conceptual Art, Costume Design & Construction, Design, Drawing, †Film History, Graphic Arts, Graphic Design, †History of Art & Architecture, †Painting, †Photography, †Printmaking, †Sculpture, Stage Design, Teacher Training, Theatre Arts

PENNSYLVANIA COLLEGE OF TECHNOLOGY, The Gallery at Penn College, 1 College Ave, Williamsport, PA 17701-5799. Tel 570-320-2445; Elec Mail gallery@pct.edu; Internet Home Page Address: www.pct.edu/gallery; *Gallery Dir* Lenore Penfield; *Gallery Asst* Penny Lutz
Parent school est 1914; gallery est 2001; On-campus art supplies shop; Maintain a nonprofit art gallery; pub; D & E; Scholarships; SC
Ent Req: HS dipl, placement test
Degrees: AA 2 yr, BGD 4 yr, SD 2 yr
Courses: †Advertising Design, Art History, Ceramics, Drawing, Graphic Arts, Graphic Design, History of Art & Architecture, Illustration, Painting, Photography, Technical Illustration

YORK

YORK COLLEGE OF PENNSYLVANIA, Dept of Music, Art & Speech Communications, 441 Country Club Rd, York, PA 17405-3651. Tel 717-846-7788; Fax 717-849-1602; Internet Home Page Address: www.ycp.edu; *Coordr Div Arts* Pamela Hemzik; *Coordr, Graphic Design* Paul Saikai, BA; *Asst Prof* Otto Tomasch, MFA; *Adjunct* Mary Todenhoff, MFA; *Adjunct* Penelope Grumbine-Hornock, MFA; *Adjunct* Marian Lorence, MPA; *Adjunct* Laure Drogoul, MA
Estab 1941; pvt; D & E; SC 17, LC 7
Ent Req: HS dipl, SAT or ACT
Degrees: BA 4 yrs & AA 2 yrs
Courses: Art Appreciation, Art Education, Art History, Ceramics, Commercial Art, Computer Graphics, Drawing, Graphic Design, Painting, Photography, Sculpture
Adult Hobby Classes: Enrl 40; Courses—per regular session
Summer School: Dir, Thomas Michalski.

PUERTO RICO

MAYAGUEZ

UNIVERSITY OF PUERTO RICO, MAYAGUEZ, Dept of Humanities, College of Fine Arts & Theory of Art Programs, PO Box 9000, Mayaguez, PR 00681-9000. Tel 787-832-4040, Ext 3160, 265-3846; Fax 809-265-1225; *Dir* Rafael Jackson PhD; *Prof* Yvette Cabrera, MFA; *Prof* Sandra Aponte, MFA; *Prof* Alfredo Ortiz, MFA; *Prof* Carlos Fajardo, MFA; *Prof* Felix Zapata, MFA; *Prof* Edwin Cordero, MFA; *Prof* Ramon Lopez, MFA
Estab 1970; Maintains nonprofit Art Gallery, Chardon Bldg, UPR - Mayaguez, Mayaguez, PR 00680; FT 40; pub; D; SC 20, LC 15; 402, maj 115
Ent Req: HS dipl
Degrees: BA(Art Theory) and BA(Plastic Arts) 4 yrs
Courses: Aesthetics, Art Appreciation, †Art Criticism, Art Education, Art History, †Art Theary, Calligraphy, Ceramics, Commercial Art, Design, Drawing, Graphic Arts, Illustration, Painting, Photography, Printmaking, Restoration & Conservation, Sculpture, Stage Design, Teacher Training, Theatre Arts
Adult Hobby Classes: Enrl 40

PONCE

PONTIFICAL CATHOLIC UNIVERSITY OF PUERTO RICO, Dept of Fine Arts, 2250 Las Americas Ave, Ste 508 Ponce, PR 00717-9997. Tel 787-841-2000; Elec Mail bellas_artes@email.pucpr.edu; Internet Home Page Address: www.pucpr.edu; *Head Dept* Edwin J Mattei, MA; *Auxiliary Prof* Beverly Zapata, MA
Estab 1948, dept estab 1964; Maintain nonprofit art gallery, Galeria Diego J Alcala Laboy; den, Pvt; D & E; Scholarships; SC 36, LC 4, GC 10; 66 maj
Ent Req: HS dipl
Degrees: BA 4 yrs, MA 2 yrs
Tuition: Res—undergrad $150 per cr hr, grad $200 per cr hr
Courses: Advertising Design, Aesthetics, Art Appreciation, Art Education, Art History, Ceramics, Conceptual Art, Constructions, Contemporary Form, Design, Drawing, †Graphic Arts, Graphic Design, History in Art in Puerto Rico, †Mixed Media, Painting, Photography, Printmaking, Sculpture

RIO PIEDRAS

UNIVERSITY OF PUERTO RICO, Dept of Fine Arts, Ponce de Leon Ave, Rio Piedras, PR; UPR Sta, PO Box 21849 San Juan, PR 00931-1849. Tel 787-764-0000 Ext 3611; Fax 787-773-1721; Elec Mail departmentodebellasartes@yahoo.com; *Dir* Guy Paizy; *Prof* Arturo Davila PhD, MA; *Prof* Susana Herrero, MA; *Prof* Pablo Rubio, MA; *Prof* Jaime Romano, MA; *Prof* Nelson Millan, MFA; *Prof* Maria Del Pilar Gonzalez, PhD; *Assoc Prof* Alejandro Quinteros, MFA; *Auxiliary Prof* Roberto Barrera, MFA; *Prof* Teresa Tio, PhD; *Assoc Prof* Martin Garcia, MFA; *Prof* Brenda Alejandro, PhD; *Assoc Prof* Ingrid Jimenez PhD, MFA; *Auxiliary Prof* Nilsevady Fussa PhD; *Instr* Nathan Budoff, MFA
Estab 1902, dept estab 1950; pub; D & E & Sat; Scholarships; SC 25, LC 15; D 200, maj 45
Ent Req: HS dipl
Degrees: BA 4 yrs
Courses: Art Appreciation, Art History, †Art Theory, Art in Puerto Rico, Color Theory, †Conceptual Art, Design, †Digital Images, Drawing, †Graphic Arts, †History of Art & Architecture, †Mixed Media, †Museum Staff Training, Painting, Photography, Pre-Hispanic Art of Antilles, Printmaking, Sculpture, Video

SAN GERMAN

INTER AMERICAN UNIVERSITY OF PUERTO RICO, Dept of Art, Call Box 5100, San German, PR 00683. Tel 787-264-1912, Ext 7552; *Auxiliary Prof* Fernando Santiago, MA; *Auxiliary Prof* Maria Garcia Vera, MFA; *Instr* Jose B Alvarez, BA
Estab 1912, dept estab 1947; pvt; D; SC 20, LC 12; D 135, maj 135
Ent Req: HS dipl, college board, presentation of portfolio
Degrees: BA 4 yrs
Tuition: Res—undergrad $98 per cr, grad $145 per cr; campus res available
Courses: †Art Education, Art History, Calligraphy, †Ceramics, Drawing, Experimental Design in Native Media, †Graphic Arts, Handicrafts, Leather, Macrame, Metals, †Painting, †Photography, †Sculpture
Summer School: Dir, Jaime Carrero. Enrl 10; tuition $75 per cr hr for 5 wk term. Courses—Art Appreciation

SAN JUAN

ESCUELA DE ARTES PLASTICAS DE PUERTO RICO, El Morro Grounds, School of Fine Arts San Juan, PR 00901; Escuela de Artes Plasticas de Puerto Rico, PO Box 9021112 San Juan, PR 00902-1112. Tel 787-725-8120; Fax 787-725-8111; Elec Mail info@eap.edu; Internet Home Page Address: eap.edu; *Chancellor* Aro Ivonne Maria Marcial Vega; *Student Aid Coordr* Alfred Diaz; *Acting Dean Acad/Study Affairs* Teresa Lopez; *Institutional Researcher* Shirley A Tavares, EdD
Estab 1966; Maintains nonprofit art gallery on campus (same address); schols open to sophomore, junior & senior students with 3.00 or above GPA; Francisco Oller Learning Resource Center Library; FT 17, PT 48; Pub; D&E; Scholarships; SC 82, LC 47; D 456, E 95
Ent Req: HS dipl, ent exam, portfolio or admis seminar, interview & essay
Degrees: BA 4 yrs
Tuition: In-state $4,404 per yr, $90 per cr; out-of-state $7,644 per yr, $180 per cr

Courses: †Art Education, Design & Visual Computer, †Fashion Design, †Industrial Design, †Painting, †Sculpture
Adult Hobby Classes: Enrl 244; tuition $144 per cr. Courses—Graphic, Painting, Sculpture, Photography

RHODE ISLAND

BRISTOL

ROGER WILLIAMS UNIVERSITY, Visual Art Dept, One Old Ferry Rd, Bristol, RI 02809-2921. Tel 401-254-3617; Internet Home Page Address: www.rwuonline.cc/; *Prof* Ronald Wilczek; *Assoc Prof* Sharon Delucca; *Asst Prof* Rebecca Leuchak; *Asst Prof* Kathleen Hancock
Estab 1948, dept estab 1967; pvt; D & E; Scholarships; SC 18, LC 8; D 1800, E 1500, maj 42
Ent Req: HS dipl
Degrees: AA 2 yr, BA 4 yr, apprenticeship and senior teaching
Courses: †Graphic Design, †Painting, †Photography, †Printmaking, Sculpture

KINGSTON

UNIVERSITY OF RHODE ISLAND, Dept of Art & Art History, Fine Arts Ctr, 105 Upper College Rd Ste 1 Kingston, RI 02881-0820. Tel 401-874-2131, 874-5821; Fax 401-874-2729; Elec Mail artdept@etal.uri.edu; *Chair* Wendy W Roworth, PhD; *Prof* William Klenk PhD; *Prof* Robert Dilworth, MFA; *Prof* Richard Calabro, MFA; *Prof* Gary Richman, MFA; *Prof* Barbara Pagh, MFA; *Assoc Prof* Mary Hollinshead, PhD; *Assoc Prof* Ronald Onorato PhD; *Assoc Prof* Sherri Wills, MFA, MA; *Asst Prof* Annu Palakunnathu Matthew, MFA; *Asst Prof* Ron Hutt, MFA
Estab 1892; Maintain nonprofit art gallery, URI Fine Arts Center Galleries, Fine Arts Center URI, Kingston, RI 02881; Ft 12, PT 6; pub; D & E; Scholarships; SC 21, studio seminars 24, LC 23; D 900, E 30, non-maj 725, maj 200, other 10 - 20
Ent Req: same as required for Col of Arts & Sciences
Degrees: BA(Studio), BA(Art History) & BFA(Art Studio) 4 yrs
Courses: Aesthetics, Architecture, †Art Appreciation, Art History, Collage, Conceptual Art, Digital Art, Digital Design, Drawing, Film, Graphic Arts, †Graphic Design, History of Art & Architecture, Painting, Photography, †Printmaking, Sculpture, Studio Art, †Video
Adult Hobby Classes: Art History, Drawing, Painting, Sculpture
Summer School: Courses— Art History, Drawing, Photography

NEWPORT

NEWPORT ART MUSEUM, Coleman Center for Creative Studies, 76 Bellevue Ave, Newport, RI 02840-7411. Tel 401-848-8200; Fax 401-848-8205; Elec Mail info@newportartmuseum.com; Internet Home Page Address: www.newportartmuseum.com; *Exec Dir* Elizabeth Goddard; *Dir Educ* Maggie Anderson
Estab 1912; D & E; Scholarships; SC 25, LC 3; D 300 (total)
Ent Req: none
Degrees: none
Tuition: Varies by course
Courses: Art History, Ceramics, Collage, Design, Drawing, Etching, Graphic Arts, Graphic Design, Handicrafts, History of Art & Architecture, Jewelry, Multimedia, Painting, Pastels, Photography, Printmaking, Sculpture
Adult Hobby Classes: Enrl 200; tuition varies; 6, 8 or 10 wk courses
Children's Classes: Enrl 100 per term; tuition varies per 6, 8, or 10 wk session
Summer School: Summer school dir - Maggie Amderson, Dir Educ; Enrl 160; tuition varies. Courses—Painting, Drawing, Workshops, Children's Multimedia

SALVE REGINA UNIVERSITY, Art Dept, 100 Ochre Point Ave, Newport, RI 02840-4149. Tel 401-847-6650; *Chmn* Barbara Shamblin, MFA; *Assoc Prof* Daniel Ludwig, MFA; *Asst Prof* Bert Emerson, MAT
Estab 1947; den; D & E; Scholarships; SC 28, LC 8; D 270 per sem (dept), non-maj 95, maj 72
Ent Req: HS dipl, ent exam
Degrees: BA 4 yr
Courses: 2 & 3-D Design, Aesthetics, Anatomy, Art History, Ceramics, Commercial Art, Design, Drawing, Environmental Design, Film, Graphic Arts, Graphic Design, History of Art & Architecture, Illustration, Painting, Photography, Sculpture, Theatre Arts
Summer School: Dir, Jay Lacouture

PROVIDENCE

BROWN UNIVERSITY, Dept History of Art & Architecture, 64 College St, Providence, RI 02912; PO Box 1855, Providence, RI 02912-1855. Tel 401-863-1174; Fax 401-863-7790; Internet Home Page Address: www.brown.edu/Departments/Art_Architecture; *Prof* Maggie Bickford; *Prof* Sheila Bonde; *Chmn, Prof* K Dian Kriz, PhD; *Prof* Jeffrey Muller; *Prof* Dietrich Neumann; *Andrea V Rosenthal Prof Modern Art* Douglas Nickel; *Prof* Catherine Zerner
Pvt; D; Scholarships; LC 13-15, GC 10-12; maj 59, grad 47
Degrees: BA, MA, PhD
Tuition: $33,888 per yr
Courses: 19th & 20th Century Architecture & Painting, †Art History, Chinese Art, Greek, History of Art & Archaeology, Introduction to Art, Italian & Roman Art & Architecture
Summer School: Dean, Karen Sibley. Courses—limited
—**Dept of Visual Art,** 64 College St, Providence, RI 02912; PO Box 1861,

Providence, RI 02912-1861. Tel 401-863-2423; Fax 401-863-1680; Elec Mail
sheila_haggerty@brown.edu; Internet Home Page Address:
www.brown.edu/Departments/Visual_Art; *Chmn* Wendy Edwards; *Assoc Prof*
Leslie Bostrom, MFA; *Prof* Richard Fishman; *Asst Prof* Paul Myoda
Pvt; D; SC 19-21, LC 13-15, GC 10-12; maj 140
Degrees: BA
Tuition: $19,528 per yr
Courses: Art of the Book, Computer Art, Drawing, Painting, Printmaking,
Sculpture

PROVIDENCE COLLEGE, Art & Art History Dept, 549 River Ave, Providence,
RI 02918-0001. Tel 401-865-2401, 865-2707; Fax 401-865-2410; *Chmn* Dr Ann
Wood Norton; *Prof* Joan Branham; *Prof* James Baker; *Assoc Prof* Adrian G
Dabash, MFA; *Assoc Prof* Richard A McAlister, MFA; *Assoc Prof* Alice Beckwith
PhD, MFA; *Asst Prof* James Janecek, MFA; *Asst Prof* Richard Elkington, MFA;
Asst Prof Deborah Johnson PhD, MFA; *Slide Librn* John DiCicco, MFA
Estab 1917, dept estab 1969; Maintain Hunt - Cavanaogh Gallery in Hunt -
Cavanaogh Hall of Providence College; pvt; D & E; SC 49, LC 8; D 254, E 250,
non-maj 209, maj 45
Ent Req: HS dipl, portfolio needed for transfer students
Degrees: BA 4 yr
Courses: †Art History, †Ceramics, †Drawing, †Painting, †Photography,
†Printmaking, †Sculpture
Adult Hobby Classes: Dean, Dr O'Hara. Courses—History of Architecture, Art
History, Calligraphy, Ceramics, Drafting, Drawing, Painting, Photography,
Sculpture, Studio Art, Watercolor
Summer School: Dir, James M Murphy. Tuition $180 & $50 lab fee for three cr
courses beginning mid-June through July. Courses—Art History, Calligraphy,
Ceramics, Drawing, Painting, Photography, Printmaking, Soft and Hard Crafts. A
summer program is offered at Pietrasanta, Italy: Dir, Richard A McAlister, MFA.
Courses—Art History, Languages, Literature, Religious Studies, Studio Art,
Drawing, Painting, Sculpture

RHODE ISLAND COLLEGE, Art Dept, 600 Mt Pleasant, Providence, RI
02908. Tel 401-456-8054; Fax 401-456-4755; Elec Mail nbockbrader@ric.edu;
Internet Home Page Address: www.ric.edu/art; *Prof* Krisjohn O Horvat, MFA; *Prof*
Mary Ball Howkins PhD, MFA; *Assoc Prof* Donna Kelly PhD, MFA; *Prof*
William Martin, MFA; *Prof* Heemong Kim, MFA; *Prof* Stephen Fisher, MFA;
Assoc Prof Lisa Russell, MFA; *Assoc Prof* Bryan E Steinberg, MFA; *Prof,
Chairperson* Nancy Bockbrader, MFA; *Assoc Prof, Found Coordr* Doug Bosch,
MFA; *Asst Prof* Richard Whitten, MFA; *Asst Prof* Amy Montali, MFA
Estab 1854, dept estab 1969; Maintain nonprofit gallery, Bannister Gallery,
Roberts Hall, 600 Mt Pleasant Ave, Providence, RI 02908; Pub; D & E;
Scholarships; SC 48, LC 10, GC 15; D 450, E approx 50, non-maj approx 100,
maj 350, grad 25
Ent Req: HS dipl, CEEB and SAT
Degrees: BA(Art History), BA, BS(Art Educ) & BFA(Studio Art) 4 yr, MAT 1 yr
Courses: Aesthetics, Art Appreciation, †Art Education, †Art History, †Ceramics,
Design, Drawing, Fibers, †Graphic Design, History of Art & Architecture,
†Jewelry, Metals, †Metalsmithing/Jewelry Design, †Painting, †Photography,
†Printmaking, †Sculpture, Teacher Training
Adult Hobby Classes: Visual Arts in Society, Drawing, Design, Photography
Summer School: Courses—Ceramics, Drawing, Painting, Photography, Relief
Printing

RHODE ISLAND SCHOOL OF DESIGN, 2 College St, Providence, RI
02903-2784. Tel 401-454-6100; Fax 401-454-6309; Elec Mail
admissions@risd.edu; Internet Home Page Address: www.risd.edu; *Pres* John
Maeda; *Interim Provost* Rosanne Somerson; *Interim Assoc Provost* Patricia
Phillips
Estab 1877; Maintain nonprofit art gallery, Mus of Art, RI School of Design, 224
Benefit St, Providence, RI 02903; Fleet Library, 15 Westminster St; on-campus art
supplies shop; Pvt; endowed; D & E; Scholarships, Fellowships, Grants, Loans;
SC, LC, GC; under grad 1,975, grad 431
Publications: RISD Views, bimonthly; Catalogue of Degree Programs (annually);
Annual Report; Continuing Ed Catalogues, 5 times a year
Ent Req: HS grad, SAT, visual work
Degrees: BFA, BArch, MFA, MID, MLA, MAT, MArch, MA, MDes
Tuition: $39,482
Courses: †Apparel Design, †Architecture, †Art History, †Ceramics, †Digital
Media, †Film/Animation/Video, †Furniture Design, †Glass, †Graphic Design,
†Illustration, †Industrial Design, †Interior Architecture, †Jewelry & Metalsmithing,
†Landscape Architecture, †Liberal Arts, †Painting, †Photography, †Printmaking,
†Sculpture, †Teaching & Learning in Art/Design, †Textile Design
Adult Hobby Classes: Enrl 4500; tuition varies. Courses—Advertising & Print
Design, Apparel Design, Ceramics, Computer Graphics, Culinary Arts, Glass,
Illustration, Interior Design, Jewelry, Natural Science Illustration, New Media,
Painting, Photography, Printmaking, Sculpture, Textile, Video
Summer School: Art & Design, Graphic Design

WARWICK

COMMUNITY COLLEGE OF RHODE ISLAND, Dept of Art, 400 East Ave,
Warwick, RI 02886-1807. Tel 401-825-2220; Fax 401-825-2282; Internet Home
Page Address: www.ccri.edu/art; *Prof* M Kelman; *Prof* C Smith; *Prof* T Morrissey;
Prof Natalie Coletta; *Prof* Nancy Wyllie; *Asst Prof* Yvonne Leonard; *Asst Prof*
Mazih Adam; *Dept Chmn & Asst Prof* Mark Zellers; *Asst Prof* Mark Hartshorn
Estab 1964; On-campus art supplies shop; FT 10, PT 15; pub; D & E;
Scholarships; SC 16, LC 3, seminar 1; D 4600
Ent Req: HS dipl, ent exam, equivalency exam
Degrees: AA, AFA, AS & AAS 2 yr
Tuition: Res—$832 per sem, $77 per cr hr
Courses: Art Appreciation, Art Education, Art History, Ceramics, Commercial Art,
Drawing, Graphic Arts, Graphic Design, History of Modern Art, Interior Design,
Life Drawing, Mixed Media, Painting, Photography, Sculpture, Survey of Ancient
Art

Summer School: Chmn, Rebecca Clark. Enrl 200; 7 wk term.
Courses—Ceramics, Crafts History of Modern Art, Drawing

SOUTH CAROLINA

AIKEN

UNIVERSITY OF SOUTH CAROLINA AT AIKEN, Dept of Visual &
Performing Arts, 471 University Pkwy, Aiken, SC 29801. Tel 803-641-3305;
Chmn Jack Benjamin; *Prof* Albin Beyer; *Asst Prof* John Elliot; *Instr* Robert
McCreary, BS; *Instr* Michael Southworth, BS
Estab 1961, dept estab 1985; pub; D & E; SC 31, LC 6; D 180, E 60
Ent Req: HS dipl, GED, SAT
Degrees: BA & MFA
Courses: Advertising Design, Art History, Ceramics, Commercial Art, Drawing,
Graphic Design, Illustration, Painting, Photography, Printmaking, Sculpture,
Theatre Arts
Adult Hobby Classes: Tuition $1060 per sem. Courses—Vary
Summer School: Dir, A Beyer. Courses—Vary

CHARLESTON

CHARLESTON SOUTHERN UNIVERSITY, Dept of Language & Visual Art,
PO Box 118087, Charleston, SC 29411-8087. Tel 843-863-7000; *Chmn* Dr Pamela
Peak
Estab 1960; den; D & E; Scholarships; SC 14, LC 2; D 80, E 71, maj 15
Ent Req: GED or HS dipl
Degrees: BA and BS 4 yrs
Courses: Art Education, Ceramics, Drawing, Graphic Arts, History of Art &
Architecture, Painting, Sculpture, Teacher Training
Summer School: Enrl 1500; tui $45 per sem hr; campus res—room and board
$240 per sem; two 5 wk sessions beginning June. Courses—same as regular
session

COLLEGE OF CHARLESTON, School of the Arts, 44 Saint Philip St,
Charleston, SC 29424. Tel 843-953-7766; Fax 843-953-4988; *Chmn Music Dept*
Steve Rosenberg; *Chmn Theatre Dept* Mark Landis; *Chmn Studio Art* Michael
Tyzack; *Chmn Art History* Diane Johnson; *Dir, Arts Management* Karen Chandler;
Dir, Historic Preservation Robert Russell; *Dir, Historic Preservation* Ralph
Muldrow; *Dean* Valerie B Morris
Estab 1966; Maintain nonprofit art gallery; Halsey Gallery, College of Charleston
School of Arts, Charleston, SC 29424; pub; D & E; Scholarships; SC 36, LC 24
Ent Req: HS dipl
Degrees: BA(Fine Arts) 4 yrs
Courses: Art History, Arts Management, Drawing, Historic Preservation, History
of Art & Architecture, Painting, Photography, Printmaking, Sculpture, Stage
Design, Theatre Arts

GIBBES MUSEUM OF ART, 135 Meeting St, Charleston, SC 29401-2217. Tel
843-722-2706; Fax 843-720-1682; Elec Mail mloftus@gibbesmuseum.com;
Internet Home Page Address: www.gibbesmuseum.com; *Exec Dir* Angela D Mack;
Dir Fin & Admin Janet Scarborough; *Dir Coll Admin* Zinnia Willits; *Dir Mus Rels*
Marla Loftus; *Dir Opers* Greg Jenkins; *Cur Coll* Sara Arnold; *Cur Exhibs* Pam
Wall; *Assoc Cur Educ* Rebecca Sailor; *Mem Mgr* Wendi Ammons; *Prog & Events
Mgr* Lasley Steever; *Sales & Rental Coordr* Shari Knight-Gillum
Estab 1905; D & E; Scholarships; SC, LC; varies
Ent Req: none
Tuition: varies
Courses: †Art Appreciation, †Art Education, †Art History, †Children's Drawing
Workshops, †Paints & Drawings, †Photography, †Teacher Training
Children's Classes: Enrl, tuition & courses vary
Summer School: Dir, Rebecca Sailor

CLEMSON

**CLEMSON UNIVERSITY, COLLEGE OF ARCHITECTURE, ARTS &
HUMANITIES,** Art Dept, 2-121 Lee Hall, Clemson, SC 29634-0509. Tel
864-656-3881; Internet Home Page Address: http://www.clemson.edu/caah/art;
Pres James Barker; *Dean, CAAH* Richard E (Rick) Goodstein; *Chair, Art Dept*
Greg Shelnutt; *Grad Coordr* David Detrich
Estab 1967; Maintain non-profit art gallery Lee Gallery, Denise
Woodward-Detrich, Dir; Gunnin Art & Architecture Library (26,000 vols);
on-campus shop where art supplies may be purchased; pub; D; GC 24, SC 40, LC
29 (undergrad courses for service to pre-architecture and other Univ requirements);
approx 1500 annually, grad maj 10
Ent Req: available on request
Degrees: BA, BS, BFA-Art 120 hrs, MFA-Art 60 hrs
Tuition: Res—$3592 per sem; nonres—$5890 per sem
Courses: Architecture, Art History, Ceramics, Drawing, Painting, Photography,
Printmaking, Sculpture

CLINTON

PRESBYTERIAN COLLEGE, Visual & Theater Arts, PO Box 975, Harper Ctr
Clinton, SC 29325-0975. Tel 864-833-2820, 833-8316; Fax 864-833-8600; Internet
Home Page Address: www.presby.edu; *Asst Prof* Lesley Preston; *Chmn* Mark R
Anderson
Estab 1880, Dept estab 1966; den; D & E; Scholarships; SC 8, LC 5; D 200,
non-maj 190, maj 10
Ent Req: HS dipl with C average, SAT

Degrees: BA & BS 4 yr
Courses: 2-D & 3-D Design, Art Appreciation, Art Education, Art History, Drawing, Painting
Summer School: Dean, J W Moncrief. Enrl 150; tuition $120 per sem. Courses—Art Appreciation, Painting

COLUMBIA

BENEDICT COLLEGE, School of Humanities, Arts & Social Sciences, 1600 Harden St, Columbia, SC 29204-1058. Tel 803-705-4711; Fax 803-705-6599; Elec Mail brooksc@benedict.edu; Internet Home Page Address: www.benedict.edu; *Prof Art & Dir Ponder Gallery* Tyrone Geter; *Chmn Fine Arts Dept* Charles Brooks; *Prof* Gina Moore; *Asst Prof* Wendell Brown; *Assoc Prof* Alexander Wilds; *Assoc Prof* Jasmin Cyril
Estab 1870; Maintains a nonprofit Gallery - The Ponder Gallery; maintains an art/architecture library - Fine Arts Dept (art area); on-campus shop where art supplies may be purchased; schols open to art majors vary; pvt; D, E & CE; Scholarships; SC 11, LC 6; D 20
Ent Req: HS dipl
Degrees: BA(Teaching of Art), BA (Studio Art)
Tuition: $13800 per yr (room & board incl)
Courses: Art Appreciation, Art Education, Art History, Ceramics, Drawing, Graphic Design, Painting, Sculpture, Teacher Training
Summer School: Term of two 5 wk sessions beginning June. Courses—Art Appreciation

COLUMBIA COLLEGE, Dept of Art, 1301 Columbia College Dr, Columbia, SC 29203-5998. Tel 803-786-3012; Fax 803-786-3893; Internet Home Page Address: www.columbiacollegesc.edu; *Chmn* Stephen Nevitt
Estab 1854; FT 4, PT 1; pvt; D&E; Scholarships
Degrees: BA (Studio Art), BA (Studio Art with Art Educ Certification)
Tuition: $15,570 per yr; campus res—room & board $5240 per yr; additional fee $300
Courses: 3-D Design, Advertising Design, Art Appreciation, Art History, Ceramics, Design, Drawing, Life Drawing, Painting, Photography, Printmaking, †Sculpture
Adult Hobby Classes: Enrl 20 per class. Courses—Art Appreciation, Art History, Drawing, Photography
Summer School: Dir, Becky Hulion. Enrl 20 per class. Courses—Art Appreciation, Art History, Art Education, Drawing, Photography, Printmaking

UNIVERSITY OF SOUTH CAROLINA, Dept of Art, McMaster College, Columbia, SC 29208-0001. Tel 803-777-4236, 777-0535, 777-7480; Fax 803-777-0535; Internet Home Page Address: www.cal.sc.edu/Art/index.html; *Chmn* Robert F Lyon; *Chmn Studio* Richard Rose; *Chmn Art Educ* Cynthia Colbert, EdD; *Chmn Art History* John Bryan, EdD; *Chmn Media Arts* Sandra Wertz PhD, EdD; *Asst Chmn* Harry Hansen
Estab 1801, dept estab 1924; pub; D & E; Scholarships; SC 89, LC 57, GC 73; D 1620, E 174, non-maj 1000, maj 520, grad 82
Ent Req: HS dipl
Degrees: BA, BFA & BS 4 yrs, MA & MAT 2 yr, MFA 3 yrs
Courses: †3-D Studies, †Advertising Design, †Art Education, †Art History, †Ceramics, †Commercial Art, †Drawing, †Graphic Arts, †Graphic Design, Illustration, Jewelry, Museum Staff Training, Painting, Photography, Printmaking, Restoration & Conservation
Adult Hobby Classes: Enrl 125; tuition $127 per hr for 16 wk term. Courses—Art for Elementary School, Basic Drawing, Ceramics, Fiber Arts, Fundamentals of Art, Interior Design, Intro to Art
Children's Classes: Enrl 100; tuition $30 for 9 wk term. Courses—Children's Art
Summer School: Enrl 400; tuition undergrad $127 per hr, grad $141 per hr. Courses—Same as acad yr

FLORENCE

FRANCIS MARION UNIVERSITY, Fine Arts Dept, PO Box 100547, Florence, SC 29502-0547. Tel 843-661-1385; Fax 843-661-1529; Internet Home Page Address: www.departments.fmarion.edu/finearts; *Prof & Chmn* Lawrence P Anderson
Estab 1969; Maintains nonprofit art gallery: Hyman Fine Arts Center Gallery; Pub; D&E; Scholarships
Degrees: BA
Courses: Art Appreciation, †Art Education, Art History, †Ceramics, Costume Design & Construction, Design, Drafting, Drawing, Film, Graphic Design, †Painting, †Photography, Sculpture, †Stage Design, †Theatre Arts, Video

GAFFNEY

LIMESTONE COLLEGE, Art Dept, 1115 College Dr, Gaffney, SC 29340-3799. Tel 864-489-7151, Ext 513; *Chmn* Andy Cox
Estab 1845; pvt; D & E; Scholarships; SC 19, LC 9; D 112, maj 42, others 3
Ent Req: HS dipl, ent exam
Degrees: BS(Educ, Studio) 4 yrs
Courses: 2-D & 3-D Design, Ceramics, Painting, Printmaking, Silk-Screen, Wood-Block

GREENVILLE

BOB JONES UNIVERSITY, School of Fine Arts, Div of Art & Design, 1700 Wade Hampton Blvd, Greenville, SC 29614-1000. Tel 864-242-5100, Ext 2720; Fax 864-233-9829; Internet Home Page Address: www.bju.edu; *Dean* Darren Lawson, PhD; *Chmn* Jay Bopp, MFA; *Design Dept Head* Jonathan Andrews, MA;

Instr Kevin Isgett, MFA; *Instr* Ross Shoe, MFA; *Studio Dept Head* Michael Slattery, MA; *Instr* Michelle Berg Radford, MFA; *Instr* Jared Stanley, MA; *Instr* Diane Mattox, MA; *Instr* Karen Flora, MA; *Instr* Pam Adams, MA; *Instr* Laurilyn Hall
Estab 1927, dept estab 1945; Maintain nonprofit art gallery, BJU Museum & Gallery, at univ & JS Mack Library. Campus shop where art supplies may be purchased; pvt; D; Scholarships; SC 29, LC 12, GC 10; M 59, W 57
Ent Req: HS dipl, letters of recommendation
Degrees: BFA & BS 4 yrs
Tuition: $4980 per yr, $2490 per sem; campus res—room & board $3900 per yr
Courses: Aesthetics, †Apparel, Art Appreciation, †Art Education, Art History, Bronze Casting, Calligraphy, †Ceramics, Costume Design & Construction, †Design, Drawing, Goldsmithing, Graphic Arts, †Graphic Design, Handicrafts, History of Art & Architecture, Illustration, †Interior Design, Jewelry, Lettering, Mixed Media, †Occupational Therapy, †Painting, Photography, Printmaking, Sculpture, Silversmithing, †Teacher Training, †Textile Design, Weaving
Summer School: Dir Jay Bopp, enrol 20; Painting: basic painting, adv painting, watercolor

FURMAN UNIVERSITY, Art Dept, 3300 Poinsett Hwy, Greenville, SC 29613-1000. Tel 864-294-2074; Internet Home Page Address: http://www2.furman.edu/academics/arts/pages/default.aspx
Estab 1826; maintains a nonprofit art gallery, Thompson Art Gallery, ROE Art Bldg; pvt; D & E; Scholarships; SC 21, LC 8; D 245, non-maj 205, maj 60
Ent Req: HS dipl, SAT
Degrees: BA 4 yr
Courses: Advertising Design, Art Appreciation, Art Criticism, Art Education, Art History, Ceramics, Crafts, Drawing, Graphic Design, †History of Art, Painting, Photography, Printmaking, Sculpture, Typography, Web Design

GREENVILLE COUNTY MUSEUM OF ART CENTER FOR MUSEUM EDUCATION, (Greenville County Museum School of Art) 420 College St, Greenville, SC 29601-2099. Tel 864-271-7570, ext 12; Fax 864-271-7579; Elec Mail abarr@greenvillemuseum.org; Internet Home Page Address: www.greenvillemuseum.org; *Coordr* Anne Q Barr
Estab 1960; Museum collections incl Andrew Wyeth, Jasper Johns, William H Johnson & an extensive collection of American art; PT 35; pub; D & E; Scholarships; SC 12, LC 2, GC 6; D 250, E 170
Tuition: Call for brochure
Courses: Art History, Drawing, Painting, Photography, †Pottery, †Printmaking

GREENVILLE TECHNICAL COLLEGE, Visual Arts Dept, PO Box 5616, Greenville, SC 29606-5616. Tel 864-848-2024, 848-2000; Fax 864-848-2003; Internet Home Page Address: www.greenvilletech.com; *Campus Dir* Nancy Welch; *Dept Head* Blake Praytor
Degrees: AA (Fine Art, Graphic Design) Cert Program
Tuition: In-county res—$71 per cr hr, out of county $78 per cr hr, out of state $157 per cr hr
Courses: Art Appreciation, Art History, Film, Graphic Design, Photography
Adult Hobby Classes: Courses offered
Summer School: Dir, Dr David S Trask. Enrl 35. Courses—Art Appreciation

GREENWOOD

LANDER UNIVERSITY, College of Arts & Humanities, 320 Stanley Ave, Greenwood, SC 29649-2056. Tel 864-388-8323; Fax 864-388-8144; Elec Mail amactagg@lander.edu; Internet Home Page Address: www.lauder.edu; *Prof Art* Alan C MacTaggart; *Prof Art* Roger A Wohlford; *Assoc Prof Art* Robert H Poe; *Assoc Prof Art History* Dr Tom R Pitts; *Asst Prof Art Educ* Dr Linda Neely; *Instr Graphics* Briles Lever
Estab 1872; Maintains a nonprofit art gallery, Monsanto Art Gallery, Cultural Center, Greenwood, SC 29649; FT 6, PT 4; pub; D & E; Scholarships; SC 28, LC 7, GC 7, Study Tours 2; D 330, E 150, non-maj 250, maj 80, grad 11
Ent Req: HS dipl
Degrees: BS (Art) 4 yrs, BS (K-12 certification), MAT (Art) 14 months
Courses: Advertising Design, Art Appreciation, Art Education, Art History, Ceramics, Commercial Art, Costume Design & Construction, Display, Drafting, Drawing, Film, Graphic Arts, Graphic Design, Handicrafts, Mixed Media, Painting, Photography, Printmaking, Sculpture, Stage Design, Study Tour to Europe, †Teacher Training, Theatre Arts, Video
Summer School: Dir, Dr L Lundquist. Enrl 300; tuition $173 per sem hr for 4 wks. Courses—Art Appreciation, Ceramics, Grad Art Education, Mass Media, Music Appreciation, Photography; Speech Fundamentals, Theatre & Film Appreciation, TV Production, Undergrad Art Education

HARTSVILLE

COKER COLLEGE, Art Dept, 300 E College Ave, Hartsville, SC 29550-3797. Tel 843-383-8150; Elec Mail jgrosser@coker.edu; Internet Home Page Address: www.coker.edu/art/; *Prof Art, Chair* Jean Grosser; *Assoc Prof Design* Ken Maginnis; *Prof Painting & Drawing* Jim Boden; *Asst Prof & Gallery Dir* Larry Merriman
Estab 1908; Maintain nonprofit art gallery; Cecelia Coker Bell Gallery, 300 E College Ave, Hartsville, SC 29550; FT 3; pvt; D & E; Scholarships; SC 24, LC 12; 1000, maj 50
Ent Req: HS dipl, ent exam
Degrees: BA and BS 4 yrs
Courses: Art Appreciation, †Art Education, Art History, Ceramics, Conceptual Art, Design, Drawing, †Fine Arts, †Graphic Design, Illustration, Painting, †Photography, Sculpture, Teacher Training, Web Design

NEWBERRY

NEWBERRY COLLEGE, Dept of Art, 2100 College St, Newberry, SC 29108-2197. Tel 803-276-5010; Fax 803-321-5627; *Asst Prof* Elizabeth Ruff; *Head Dept* Bruce Nell-Smith

Estab 1856, dept estab 1973; den; D & E; SC 35, LC 2; D 114, non-maj 106, maj 15
Ent Req: HS dipl, SAT
Degrees: BA (Art Studio) 4 yrs, BA (Arts Mgt), two courses in independent study, financial aid available
Courses: Art History, Drawing, Mixed Media, Painting, Printmaking, Stage Design, Theatre Arts

ORANGEBURG

CLAFLIN COLLEGE, Dept of Art, 400 Magnolia St, Orangeburg, SC 29115-6815. Tel 803-535-5335 (Art Dept); Internet Home Page Address: www.claflincollege.edu; *Assoc Prof* Dr Kod Igwe; *Instr* Cecil Williams; *Chmn* Herman Keith
School estab 1869, dept estab 1888; pvt; D; Scholarships; SC 10, LC 2; D 20
Ent Req: HS dipl, SAT
Degrees: BA 4 years, BA Teacher Educ 4 years
Courses: Advanced Studio, †Advertising Design, Afro-American Art History, †Art Education, Art History, Ceramics, Drawing, Film, Graphic Arts, Lettering, Painting, Photography, Printmaking, Sculpture, Theatre Arts, Video
Summer School: Dir, Karen Woodfaulk. Enrl 10-12, 6 wk term beginning June. Courses—Art Appreciation, Art-Elem School Crafts, Advertising Art, Textile Design

SOUTH CAROLINA STATE UNIVERSITY, Dept of Visual & Performing Arts, 300 College St NE, Orangeburg, SC 29117-0001. Tel 803-536-7101; Fax 803-536-7192; Elec Mail jwalsh@scsu.edu; Internet Home Page Address: www.scsu.edu/; *Asst Prof* Johnathon Walsh; *Asst Prof* Kimberly Ledee; *Asst Prof* Leslie Rech; *Asst Prof* Steven Crall; *Instr* Frank Martin II
Dept estab 1972; Maintains nonprofit gallery; music & fine arts libr; pub, state; D & E; SC 15, LC 7; D 73, nonmaj 8, maj 73
Ent Req: HS dipl
Degrees: BA & BS 4 yrs, MS approx 2 yrs
Courses: †Art Education, †Design, †Printmaking, †Sculpture
Adult Hobby Classes: Ceramics, Sculpture, Drawing, Painting
Summer School: Dir, Dr Leroy Davis. Tuition $90 per cr hr. Courses—Art Appreciation, Arts & Crafts for Children

ROCK HILL

WINTHROP UNIVERSITY, Dept of Art & Design, 701 Oakland Ave, Rock Hill, SC 29733. Tel 803-323-2653; Elec Mail waldenr@winthrop.edu; Internet Home Page Address: www.winthrop.edu; *Prof* Mary Mintich; *Prof* John Olvera; *Prof* David Freeman; *Prof* Alf Ward; *Assoc Prof* Dr Seymour Simmons; *Assoc Prof* Alan Huston; *Assoc Prof* Paul Martyka; *Assoc Prof* Jim Connell; *Assoc Prof* Laura Dufresne; *Assoc Prof* Phil Moody; *Assoc Prof* Margaret Johnson; *Assoc Prof* David Stokes; *Assoc Prof* Dr Peg DeLamater; *Asst Prof* Chad Dresbach; *Asst Prof* Marge Moody; *Asst Prof* Dr Alice Burmeister; *Chmn* Jerry Walden
Estab 1886; pub; D & E; SC 42, LC 10; in college D 5300, non-maj 300, maj 345, grad 10
Ent Req: HS dipl, SAT, CEEB
Degrees: BA and BFA 4 yrs
Courses: Advertising Design, Art Appreciation, †Art Education, †Art History, Calligraphy, †Ceramics, Color, Commercial Art, Design, Display, Drafting, †Drawing, Fashion Arts, Graphic Arts, †Graphic Design, Handicrafts, History of Art & Architecture, Illustration, Industrial Design, †Interior Design, †Jewelry, Lettering, Mixed Media, Museum Staff Training, †Painting, †Photography, †Printmaking, †Sculpture, Silversmithing, Teacher Training, Textile Design, Weaving

SPARTANBURG

CONVERSE COLLEGE, School of the Arts, Dept of Art & Design, 580 E Main St, Spartanburg, SC 29302-1931. Tel 864-596-9000, 596-9181, 596-9178; Fax 864-596-9606; Elec Mail art.design@converse.edu; Internet Home Page Address: www.converse.edu; *Prof & Dept Chmn* Teresa Prater; *Prof Studio Art* Mayo MacBoggs, MFA; *Asst Prof & Coordr Educ* Dianne R Bagnal, MA; *Assoc Prof & Coordr Interior Design* Ruth Beals; *Assoc Prof Studio Art* Andrew Blanchard; *Asst Prof Interior Design* Michael Fornaro, PhD; *Assoc Prof & Coordr Art History* Suzanne Schuweiler, PhD; *Assoc Prof & Coordr Studio Art* David Zacharias
Estab 1889; Maintains nonprofit Milliken Gallery, 580 E Main St, Spartanburg, SC 29302; art/architecture library not for public use; pvt, women only; D & E; Scholarships; SC 40, LC 17; In dept: non-maj 30, maj 100, grad 30
Ent Req: HS dipl, SAT, CEEB, ACT, Advanced placement in Art & Art History
Degrees: BA & BFA 4 yrs, M.Ed, M.AT
Courses: Art Appreciation, †Art Education, †Art History, †Art Therapy, Ceramics, Design, Drafting, Drawing, Graphic Design, †History of Art & Architecture, †Interior Design, Jewelry, Museum Staff Training, Occupational Therapy, Painting, Photography, Printmaking, Restoration & Conservation, Sculpture, Silversmithing, †Studio Art, Teacher Training
Summer School: Dir, Joe Dunn

SPARTANBURG COUNTY MUSEUM OF ART, The Art School, 200 E St John St, Spartanburg, SC 29306. Tel 864-582-7616; Fax 864-948-5353; Elec Mail artschool@spartanburgartmuseum.org; Internet Home Page Address: www.spartanburgartmuseum.org; *Dir* Bob LoGrippo
Estab 1962; Maintain nonprofit art gallery; schols offered ann; Pvt; D & E; Loans; SC 25; 300-400
Ent Req: none
Tuition: $110-$185 for 8-12 wk classes & weekend workshops
Courses: Calligraphy, Cartooning, Drawing, Figure Drawing, Mixed Media, Painting, Portraiture, Pottery & Ceramic Design, †Printmaking, Sculpture, Stained Glass

Adult Hobby Classes: $110-$185 for Art Appreciation, Fine Arts
Children's Classes: $70-$100 for 4-8 wk classes & weekend workshops
Summer School: Dir, Robert LoGrippo. Enrl 200. Art Camp, 1-6 wk sessions

SOUTH DAKOTA

ABERDEEN

NORTHERN STATE UNIVERSITY, Art Dept, 1200 S Jay St, Aberdeen, SD 57401-7198. Tel 605-626-2514; Fax 605-626-2263; Elec Mail kilianp@northern.edu; Internet Home Page Address: www.northern.edu/artdept/index.html; *Prof* Mark McGinnis, MFA; *Prof* Bill Hoar PhD, MFA; *Prof & Coordr* Peter Kilian, MFA; *Asst Prof* Ruth McKinney; *Prof* Mark Shekore, MFA; *Asst Prof & Adjunct* Joel McKinney; *Adjunct Instr* Troy McQuillen; *Adjunct Instr* Roxanne Hinze
Maintain nonprofit art gallery, Northern Galleries, 1200 S Jay St, Aberdeen, SD 57401; Estab 1901, dept estab 1920; pub; D & E; Scholarships; SC 40, LC 14, GC 6; D 385, non-maj 300, maj 85
Ent Req: HS dipl
Degrees: AA 2 yrs, BA, BSEd 4 yrs
Courses: †Advertising Design, Aesthetics, Art Appreciation, Art Education, Art History, Ceramics, Commercial Art, †Computer Graphics, Design, Drawing, Fiber Arts, Graphic Arts, History of Art & Architecture, Mixed Media, Painting, Photography, Printmaking, Sculpture, Teacher Training, Theatre Arts, Video
Adult Hobby Classes: Enrl 30; tuition $74.10 per cr
Summer School: Prof, Peter Kilian, Dir

BROOKINGS

SOUTH DAKOTA STATE UNIVERSITY, Dept of Visual Arts, PO Box 2802, Brookings, SD 57007-0001. Tel 605-688-4103; Fax 605-688-6769; Elec Mail SDSU_ArtDept@sdstate.edu; Internet Home Page Address: http://sdstate.edu/academic/programs/index.cfm; *Prof Head Dept* Michael Steele, MFA; *Prof* Leda Cempellin, PhD; *Prof* Jeannie French, MFA; *Prof* Scott Wallace, MFA; *Asst Prof* Cable Hardin; *Assoc Prof* Randy Clark; *Asst Prof* Diana Behl, MFA; *Instr* Mark Stemwedel, MFA; *Instr* Shannon Frewaldt, MFA; *Instr* Larry Taylor, MFA; *Instr* Elizabeth Bashore Heeren; *Instr* Marian Melkumyan; *Instr* Peter Reichardt; *Instr* Molly Wilks; *Instr* Elijah Van Benschoten
Estab 1881; Maintain nonprofit art gallery; Ritz Gallery, Box 2802, 111 Grove Hall, SDSU Brookings SD 57007; art supplies available on-campus; Pub; D & E; Scholarships; SC 33, LC 8, online Art History; Enrl non-maj 20, maj 230
Ent Req: HS dipl, ent ACT
Degrees: BA & BS 128 sem cr; Cert
Courses: †Animation, Art Appreciation, †Art Education, Art History, †Ceramics, Design, Drawing, General Art, †Graphic Design, †History of Art & Architecture, History of Art & Design, Intermedia, Mixed Media, †Painting, †Printmaking, †Sculpture

MADISON

DAKOTA STATE UNIVERSITY, College of Liberal Arts, 820 N Washington Ave, 114 Beadle Hall Madison, SD 57042-1735. Tel 605-256-5270; Fax 605-256-5021; Internet Home Page Address: www.dsu.edu; *Prof* John Laflin; *Prof* Roger Reed; *Assoc Prof* Alan Fisher; *Assoc Prof* James Janke; *Assoc Prof* Nancy Moose; *Assoc Prof* Louise Pope; *Assoc Prof* James Swanson; *Dean* Eric Johnson
Estab 1881; FT 1, PT 1; pub; D; Scholarships; SC 16, LC 5; D 120, maj 20
Ent Req: HS dipl, ACT
Degrees: BS 4 yrs
Tuition: Res—undergrad $1620 per yr; nonres—$5152 per yr
Courses: Art Education, Art History, Ceramics, Drawing, Jewelry, Painting, Sculpture, Teacher Training
Summer School: Term of 8 wks beginning June

MITCHELL

DAKOTA WESLEYAN UNIVERSITY, Art Dept, 1200 W University Ave, Mitchell, SD 57391-4358. Tel 800-333-8506; Internet Home Page Address: www.dwu.edu/art/index.htm
Courses: †Art Appreciation, †Art History, †Ceramics, †Design, †Drawing, †Painting

SIOUX FALLS

AUGUSTANA COLLEGE, Art Dept, 2001 S Summit Ave, Sioux Falls, SD 57197-0002. Tel 605-336-5428; WATS 800-727-2844; *Chmn* Carl A Grupp, MFA; *Asst Prof* Tom Shields, MFA; *Instr* John Peters, MFA; *Instr* Gerry Punt, BA
Estab 1860; den; D & E; Scholarships; SC 14, LC 3; total 1861
Ent Req: HS dipl, ent exam
Degrees: BA & MAT
Tuition: $13,960 annual tuition; campus res—room & board $4058
Courses: †Art Education, †Drawing, Etching, †Graphic Design, History of Art & Architecture, Lithography, Painting, Printmaking, Sculpture, Teacher Training
Children's Classes: Enrl 15; tuition $600 fall & spring. Courses—Ceramics, Drawing
Summer School: Dir, Dr Gary D Olson. Term of 7 wks beginning June. Courses—Arts, Crafts, Drawing

UNIVERSITY OF SIOUX FALLS, Dept of Art, 1101 W 22nd St, Division of Fine Arts/Music Sioux Falls, SD 57105-1600. Tel 605-331-5000; Internet Home Page Address: www.usiouxfalls.edu; *Chmn* Nancy Olive; *Pres* Mark Benedetto

Estab 1883; pub; Scholarships; SC, LC; 1000
Degrees: BA with maj in Art or Art Educ 4 yrs
Courses: Art Education, Art History, Ceramics, Drawing, Graphic Design, Handicrafts, Painting, Photography, Sculpture
Summer School: Terms one 3 wk session, two 4 wk sessions. Courses—Crafts, Design, Drawing, Education

SPEARFISH

BLACK HILLS STATE UNIVERSITY, Art Dept, University Sta, Box 9003, Spearfish, SD 57799-9003. Tel 605-642-6011, 642-6420; *Prof* Steve Babbitt; *Prof* James Knutson; *Prof* Susan Hore-Pabst; *Prof* Janeen Larson; *Prof* Stephen Parker; *Prof* Randall Royer; *Instr* Abdollah Farrokhi; *Chmn* Jim Cargill
Estab 1883; FT 13; pub; D; Scholarships; SC 15, LC 4; maj 50
Ent Req: HS dipl, transcripts, ACT, physical exam
Degrees: BA 4 yrs
Courses: Art Education, Calligraphy, Ceramics, Commercial Art, Drafting, Drawing, Painting, Photography, Sculpture
Summer School: Art in our Lives, Ceramics, Drawing, Painting, School Arts & Crafts

VERMILLION

UNIVERSITY OF SOUTH DAKOTA, Department of Art, College of Fine Arts, 414 E Clark St, Vermillion, SD 57069-2307. Tel 605-677-5636; 677-5011; Elec Mail jday@usd.edu; Internet Home Page Address: www.usd.edu/; *Chmn & Dean* John Day, MFA; *Prof* Lloyd Menard, MFA; *Prof* Jeff Freeman, MFA; *Prof* John Banasiak, MFA; *Assoc Prof* Martin Wanserski, MFA; *Assoc Prof* Ann Balakier PhD, MFA; *Prof* Dennis Wavrat, MFA; *Instr* Michael Hill
Estab 1862, dept estab 1887; pub; D & E; Scholarships; SC 32, LC 9, GC 9; non-maj 300, maj 80, grad 17
Ent Req: HS dipl, ACT
Degrees: BFA, BFA with Teacher Cert, MFA
Courses: Advertising Design, Aesthetics, Art Appreciation, Art History, †Ceramics, Commercial Art, Design, Drawing, †Graphic Design, Graphics, History of Art & Architecture, Lettering, Mixed Media, Museum Staff Training, †Painting, †Photography, †Printmaking, †Sculpture, Teacher Training
Summer School: Chmn, Lawrence Anderson. Tuition per cr hr for terms of 4 wks to 15 wks. Courses—variable offerings in summer-not all disciplines are offered each summer

YANKTON

MOUNT MARTY COLLEGE, Art Dept, 1105 W Eighth St, Yankton, SD 57078. Tel 605-668-1011, 668-1574; Fax 605-668-1607; Internet Home Page Address: www.mtmc.edu; *Dept Head* David Kahle, MA
Estab 1936; den; D; SC 17, LC 5; 9
Ent Req: HS dipl
Degrees: BA 4 yrs, MA(Anesthesia)
Courses: 2-D & 3-D Design, Art Appreciation, Calligraphy, Ceramics, Collage, Design, Drawing, Handicrafts, Mixed Media, Printmaking, Teacher Training
Adult Hobby Classes: Enrl 100-150; tuition $283 per 11 cr hrs, $3390 full time. Courses—Art Appreciation, Calligraphy, Ceramics, Crafts, Design, Painting & Drawing, Photography, Printmaking
Summer School: Dir, Sr Pierre Roberts. Tuition $100 per cr hr for term of wks beginning June & July

TENNESSEE

CHATTANOOGA

CHATTANOOGA STATE TECHNICAL COMMUNITY COLLEGE, Advertising Arts Dept, 4501 Amnicola Hwy, Chattanooga, TN 37406-1018. Tel 423-697-4400, 697-4441; Fax 423-697-2539; Internet Home Page Address: www.cstcc.cc.tn.us; *Dir Fine Arts* Denise Frank; *Asst Prof* Alan Wallace
FT 2; pub; D & E; Scholarships; SC 30, LC 5; D 3000, E 2000
Ent Req: HS dipl
Degrees: Cert, AA(Advertising Art)
Tuition: Res—$56 per cr hr; nonres—$168 per cr hr
Courses: Advertising Concepts, Advertising Design, Air Brush, Art Education, Art History, Ceramics, Commercial Art, Drafting, Drawing, Graphic Arts, Graphic Design, Illustration, Internships, Painting, Photography, Production Art, Teacher Training, Typography
Adult Hobby Classes: Tuition $45 per course. Courses—Painting, Photography
Children's Classes: Tuition $20 per course. Courses—Arts & Crafts, Ceramics & Sculpture
Summer School: Tuition $140 per term of 10 wks

UNIVERSITY OF TENNESSEE AT CHATTANOOGA, Dept of Art, 615 McCallie Ave, Chattanooga, TN 37403-2504. Tel 423-755-4178; Fax 423-785-2101; Internet Home Page Address: www.utc.edu; *Head & Prof* Matt Greenwell, MFA; *Prof* Anne Lindsey PhD; *Prof* Maggie McMahon, MFA; *Prof* Gavin Townsend PhD, MFA; *Prof* E Alan White, MFA; *Prof* Ron Buffington, MFA; *Asst Prof* David Young, MFA; *Clinical Prof* Nandini Makrandi; *Lectr* Robert Cox; *Lectr* Dan Bething; *Lectr* Leslie Jensen-Inman
Estab 1928; Maintains a nonprofit art gallery, Cress Gallery of Art, 615 McCallie Ave, Chattanooga TN 37403; pub; D & E; Scholarships; SC 45, LC 11, other 6; D 501, E 15, non-maj 320, maj 196, grad 1
Ent Req: HS dipl, ACT or SAT, health exam
Degrees: BA, BS, BFA 4 yrs

Courses: †3D, †Art Appreciation, Art Education, Art History, Ceramics, Drawing, Graphic Design, †History of Art & Architecture, †Mixed Media, Painting, †Photography, Printmaking, Sculpture, †Web Media
Summer School: Same as reg semester

CLARKSVILLE

AUSTIN PEAY STATE UNIVERSITY, Dept of Art, 601 College St, Clarksville, TN 37044; PO Box 4677, Clarksville, TN 37044-0001. Tel 931-648-7333; Elec Mail marsh@apsu02.apsu.edu; Internet Home Page Address: www.apsu.edu/; *Assoc Prof* Gregg Schlanger, MFA; *Assoc Prof* Kell Black, MFA; *Chair* Cindy Marsh, MFA
Estab 1927, dept estab 1930; pub; D & E; Scholarships; GC 3; D 740, E 75, non-maj 590, maj 150
Ent Req: HS dipl
Degrees: BFA, BA & BS 4 yrs
Courses: †Art Education, Art History, †Ceramics, Drawing, †Graphic Design, Illustration, Lettering, †Painting, †Photography, †Printmaking, †Sculpture
Summer School: tuition $192 per cr

CLEVELAND

CLEVELAND STATE COMMUNITY COLLEGE, Dept of Art, 3535 Adkisson Dr, Cleveland, TN 37312-2813; PO Box 3570, Cleveland, TN 37320-3570. Tel 423-472-7141; Fax 423-478-6255; WATS 800-604-2722; *Head* Jere Chumley, MA
Estab 1967; pub; D & E; Scholarships; SC 6, LC 5; D 95, E 20, non-maj 60, maj 35
Ent Req: HS dipl or GED
Degrees: AA and AS 2 yrs
Tuition: Res—$647 per sem; nonres—$2585 per sem
Courses: Architecture, Art Appreciation, Art Education, Art History, Calligraphy, Ceramics, Design, Drafting, Drawing, History of Art & Architecture, Painting, Photography, Sculpture
Adult Hobby Classes: Drawing, Painting

LEE UNIVERSITY, Dept of Communication & the Arts, 1120 N Ocoee St, Cleveland, TN 37311-4475. Tel 423-614-8240; Fax 423-614-8242; Internet Home Page Address: www.leeuniversity.edu; *Chmn* Dr Matthew Melton
Estab 1918; Pvt
Ent Req: HS dipl
Degrees: BA, BS
Tuition: Res—$5500 on campus per sem
Courses: Art Appreciation, Art History, Drawing, Film, Painting, Photography

COLLEGEDALE

SOUTHERN ADVENTIST UNIVERSITY, Art Dept, PO Box 370, Collegedale, TN 37315-0370. Tel 423-238-2732, 237-2111; *Chmn* Wayne Hazen
Estab 1969; den; D & E; Scholarships; LC 4; maj 50
Ent Req: HS dipl, ent exam
Degrees: BA(Art), BA(Art & Educ) & BA(Computer Graphic Design) 4 yr
Courses: Animation, Art, Art Appreciation, Art Education, Art History, Ceramics, Computer Graphic Design, Design, Drawing, Fine Art, Graphic Arts, Graphic Design, Painting, Printmaking, Sculpture

COLUMBIA

COLUMBIA STATE COMMUNITY COLLEGE, Dept of Art, 1665 Hampshire Pike, Columbia, TN 38401-5653. Tel 931-540-2722; Internet Home Page Address: www.coscc.cc.tn.us; *Prof* Fred Behrens, MFA; *Div Chm* Marvin Austin PhD
Estab 1966; pub; D & E; Scholarships; SC 17, LC 4; D 230, non-maj 215, maj 12-15
Ent Req: open door institution
Degrees: AA & AS 2 yrs
Courses: Art History, †Art Studio, Design, Drawing, Film, Painting, Photography, Printmaking, Visual Arts
Children's Classes: Enrl 18-20, tuition $30 per session

GATLINBURG

ARROWMONT SCHOOL OF ARTS & CRAFTS, Arrowmont School of Arts & Crafts, 556 Parkway, Gatlinburg, TN 37738-3202; PO Box 567, Gatlinburg, TN 37738-0567. Tel 865-436-5860; Fax 865-430-4101; Elec Mail info@arrowmont.org; Internet Home Page Address: www.arrowmont.org; *Dir* Bill May; *Prog Dir* Bill Griffith
Estab 1945; Maintains nonprofit gallery, Sandra J Blain Galleries, Arrowmont School of Arts & Crafts 556 Parkway, Gatlinburg, TN 37738; maintains art library; on-campus shop for purchase of art supplies; Pvt; D & E (operate mostly in spring & summer with special programs for fall & winter); Scholarships, Fellowships; SC 44-50, GC 30; D 2000
Ent Req: Must be 18 yrs & older
Degrees: none granted, though cr is offered with approval
Tuition: Tuition varies
Courses: Basketry, Bookbinding, Ceramics, Drawing, Enamel, Fused Glass, Jewelry, Mixed Media, Painting, Papermaking, Photography, Printmaking, Quilting, Sculpture, Silversmithing, Stained Glass, Textile Design, Weaving, Woodturning, Woodworking
Adult Hobby Classes: Winter (evenings) $150-$200
Children's Classes: Winter/Summer $95

GREENEVILLE

TUSCULUM COLLEGE, Fine Arts Dept, Division of Arts & Humanities, 2299 Tusculum, Greeneville, TN 37743; PO Box 5084, Greeneville, TN 37743-0001. Tel 423-636-7300; Internet Home Page Address: www.tusculum.edu; *Asst Prof Art* Tom Silva
Estab 1794; den; D; Scholarships; SC 25, LC 3; D 445, maj 18
Ent Req: HS dipl
Degrees: BA & BS 4 yrs
Courses: Art Education, Ceramics, Drawing, History of Art & Architecture, Painting, Printmaking, Sculpture
Adult Hobby Classes: Enrl 14. Courses—Painting

HARROGATE

LINCOLN MEMORIAL UNIVERSITY, Division of Humanities, 6965 Cumberland Gap Pkwy, Harrogate, TN 37752. Tel 423-869-3611; Internet Home Page Address: www.lmunet.edu; *Assoc Prof Art* Betty DeBord; *Instr* Alex Buckland; *Chmn Humanities* Colun Leckey
Estab 1897, dept estab 1974; pvt; D & E; SC 30, LC 3; D 120, E 75, non-maj 97, maj 98
Ent Req: HS dipl
Degrees: BA 4 yrs
Courses: Aesthetics, Art Education, Art History, Ceramics, Commercial Art, Drawing, Film, Goldsmithing, †Graphic Arts, Jewelry, Lettering, Museum Staff Training, †Painting, †Photography, †Sculpture, Silversmithing, †Teacher Training, †Textile Design, †Theatre Arts, Weaving

JACKSON

LAMBUTH UNIVERSITY, Dept of Human Ecology & Visual Arts, 705 Lambuth Blvd, Jackson, TN 38301-5280. Tel 731-427-4725 (Jackson); Tel 901-678-5087 (Memphis); Elec Mail lambuth@memphis.edu; Internet Home Page Address: www.lambuth.edu; *Chmn* Lawrence A Ray PhD; *Asst Prof* June Creasy, MS; *Asst Prof* Lendon H Noe, MS; *Lectr* Susan Haubold, MEd; *Lectr* Belinda A Patterson, BS; *Lectr* Glynn Weatherley, BS; *Lectr* Rosemary Carroway, BA
Estab 1843, dept estab 1950; Methodist; D & E; Scholarships; SC 21, LC 10
Ent Req: HS dipl
Degrees: BA, BS, B(Mus) & B(Bus Ad) 4 yrs
Courses: Advertising Design, Aesthetics, †Art Education, †Art History, †Commercial Art, Crafts, †Drawing, Fiber Crafts, †Graphic Design, Human Ecology, †Interior Design, †Painting, †Photography, †Printmaking, †Sculpture, Stage Design, †Stained Glass, Visual Art
Adult Hobby Classes: Adult Evening Prog. $1800 per term
Children's Classes: Enrl 45-50; tuition $50 for 5 wk term. Courses—Elementary art classes
Summer School: Dir, William Shutowski. Courses—Art Appreciation, Art Education, Basic ID, Painting, Printmaking

UNION UNIVERSITY, Dept of Art, 1050 Union University Dr, Jackson, TN 38305-3697. Tel 901-668-1818; Fax 901-661-5175; Elec Mail lbenson@uu.edu; Internet Home Page Address: www.uu.edu; *Prof* Chris Nadaskay; *Chmn* Aaron Lee Benson; *Instr* Jonathan Gillette; *Instr* Lori Nolen
Estab 1824, dept estab 1958; Maintain nonprofit art gallery; Union Univ Gallery of Art, Jackson TN; Pvt; D & E; Scholarships; SC 20, LC 5; D 200, E 40, maj 28
Ent Req: HS dipl, portfolio, ACT
Degrees: BA and BS 4 yrs
Courses: Art Appreciation, Art Education, Ceramics, Design, †Drafting, Drawing, Graphic Design, Painting, Photography, Printmaking, Sculpture, Teacher Training
Children's Classes: Enrl 6-8 $185
Summer School: Dir Debra Tayloe

JEFFERSON CITY

CARSON-NEWMAN COLLEGE, Art Dept, 1646 S. Russell Ave, Art Dept Jefferson City, TN 37760-2204. Tel 865-475-9061; Fax 865-471-3502; Elec Mail sgray@cn.edu; Internet Home Page Address: www.cn.edu; *Assoc Prof & Second Dept Chmn* David Underwood; *Artist-in-Residence* William Houston; *Chmn Dept* H T Niceley; *Asst Prof* Julie Rabun; *Assoc Prof* John Alford
Col estab 1851; maintain a nonprofit art gallery: The Omega Gallery, Warren Art Bldg, 2130 Branner Ave, Jefferson City, TN 37760; FT 3; pvt; D & E; Scholarships; SC 32, LC 16; maj 85
Ent Req: HS dipl
Degrees: BA(Art & Photography) 4 yrs
Courses: Aesthetics, Art Education, Art History, Computer Graphics, Drawing, Graphic Design, Painting, Photography, Printmaking, Senior Seminar, Support Systems

JOHNSON CITY

EAST TENNESSEE STATE UNIVERSITY, College of Arts and Sciences, Dept of Art & Design, PO Box 70708, Johnson City, TN 37614-1710. Tel 423-439-4247; Fax 423-439-4393; Internet Home Page Address: etsu.edu/cas.art; *Prof* M Wayne Dyer; *Prof* Michael Smith, MFA; *Prof* Vida Hull, PhD; *Prof* Ralph Slatton, MFA; *Assoc Prof* David Dixon, MFA; *Assoc Prof* Don Davis, MFA; *Assoc Prof* Mira Gerard, MFA; *Prof* Anita DeAngelis, MFA; *Assoc Prof* Peter Pawlowicz, PhD; *Prof, Interim Chair* Catherine Murray, MFA; *Assoc Prof* Scott Koterbay, PhD; *Assoc Prof* Pat Mink; *Asst Prof* Travis Graves; *Gallery Dir* Karlota Contreras-Koterbay; *Visual Resource Cur* Lisa Jones
Estab 1911, dept estab 1949; Maintain nonprofit gallery, Slocumb Galleries, Carroll Reece Museum & slide and visual resource library on ETSU campus. On-campus shop sells art supplies; Pub; D & E; Scholarships; SC 102, LC 30, GC 46; maj 400

Ent Req: HS dipl, ACT or SAT
Degrees: BA & BFA 4 yrs, MA, MFA
Courses: †Aesthetics, †Art History, †Ceramics, Commercial Art, Conceptual Art, Design, Drawing, Film, Goldsmithing, †Graphic Design, History of Art & Architecture, Illustration, †Jewelry, †Metalsmithing, Mixed Media, †Painting, †Photography, Printmaking, †Sculpture, Silversmithing, Teacher Training, Video, Weaving, †Weaving/Fibers
Adult Hobby Classes: Cr/no cr classes at night. Courses—Art History, Drawing, Photography, painting
Summer School: Dir, M Wayne Dyer. Term for 2-5 wks. Courses—Book Arts, Ceramics, Computer Art, Stone Carving

KNOXVILLE

UNIVERSITY OF TENNESSEE, KNOXVILLE, School of Art, 1715 Volunteer Blvd, Ste. 213, Knoxville, TN 37996-2410. Tel 865-974-3407; Fax 865-974-3198; Internet Home Page Address: www.web.utk.edu/~art; *Dir School of Art* Paul Lee; *Assoc Dir* Tim Hiles
Estab 1794, dept estab 1951; Maintain nonprofit art gallery; Ewing Gallery; art supplies available on campus; FT 27, PT 15; pub; D & E; Scholarships; SC 51, LC 23, GC 50; D 1,600, E 250, non-maj 300, maj 400, grad 40
Ent Req: HS dipl
Degrees: BA & BFA, MFA; both undergraduate & graduate cr may be earned through the affiliated program at Arrowmont School of Arts & Crafts, Gatlinburg, TN
Tuition: Res—undergraduate $1,302 per sem, grad $1,653 per sem; nonres—undergrad $3,034 per sem, campus res—room & board $3,166 per yr
Courses: †Art History, †Ceramics, †Drawing, †Graphic Design, Media Arts, †Painting, †Printmaking, †Sculpture, †Watercolors
Summer School: Dir, Norman Magden. Enrl 400; term of 2 sessions beginning June & Aug. Courses—Art History, Design, Drawing, Media Arts

MARYVILLE

MARYVILLE COLLEGE, Dept of Fine Arts, 502 East Lamar Alexander Pkwy, Maryville, TN 37804. Tel 865-981-8000; Internet Home Page Address: www.maryvillecollege.edu; *Asst Prof* Carl Gombert; *Asst Prof* Jeff Turner; *Chmn* Dan Taddie
Estab 1937; FT 2, PT 1; den; D&E; Scholarships; SC 10, LC 6
Degrees: 4 yr
Courses: Art Education, Art History, Ceramics, Computer Graphics, Drawing, Fabric Design, Graphic Design, Painting, Photography, Printmaking, Visual Theory & Design, Weaving
Adult Hobby Classes: Courses offered
Children's Classes: Art Education, Crafts

MEMPHIS

MEMPHIS COLLEGE OF ART, 1930 Poplar Ave, Overton Park Memphis, TN 38104-2756. Tel 901-272-5100; Fax 901-272-5158; Elec Mail info@mca.edu; Internet Home Page Address: www.mca.edu; *Pres* Dr Ron Jones; *Acad Dean & Div Chair Foundation* Remy Miller, MFA; *Div Chair Fine Arts* Howard Paine, MFA; *Div Chair Design Arts* David Chioffi, MFA; *Div Chair Foundations* Remy Miller, MFA; *Cur Galleries* Cat Blackwell Pence; *Dir Grad Studies* Haley Morris-Cafiero, MFA; *Dir Grad Studies* Dr Cathy Wilson, MA
Estab 1936; maintain art libr & nonprofit art gallery on campus; art supplies available for purchase on campus; FT 22, PT 22; pvt; D & E; Scholarships; SC 132, LC 73, GC 20; D 300, E 300, GS 19
Ent Req: HS dipl
Degrees: BFA 4 yrs, MFA 2 yrs, MA 1 yr
Tuition: $25,600
Courses: †Advertising Design, Aesthetics, Architecture, †Art Education, Art History, †Book Arts, †Ceramics, Collage, †Commercial Art, †Computer Arts, Conceptual Art, †Design, Digital Media Animation, †Drawing, Goldsmithing, †Graphic Arts, †Graphic Design, History of Art & Architecture, †Illustration, Intermedia, †Jewelry, Lettering, Mixed Media, †Painting, †Papermaking, †Photography, †Printmaking, †Sculpture, †Silversmithing, Video
Adult Hobby Classes: Classes vary
Children's Classes: Classes vary
Summer School: Dir, Mary Beth Haas, Cece Palazola, Dir Community Educ

RHODES COLLEGE, Dept of Art, 2000 N Pkwy, Memphis, TN 38112. Tel 901-843-3000, 3442; Fax 901-843-3727; Internet Home Page Address: www.rhodes.edu; *Chmn, Asst Prof* Victor Coonin, MFA; *Assoc Prof* David McCarthy; *Assoc Prof* Diane Hoffman, MFA; *Instr* Hallie Charney, MFA; *Asst Prof* Val Vaigardson; *Prof* Jim Lutz; *Asst Prof* Margaret Woodhull
Estab 1848, dept estab 1940; pvt; D & E; SC 17, LC 12; D 250, non-maj 240, maj 10
Ent Req: SAT or ACT, 13 acad cr, 16 overall
Degrees: BA 4 yrs
Tuition: campus res—room & board
Courses: Aesthetics, Architecture, Art History, Drawing, History of Art & Architecture, Museum Staff Training, Painting, Photography, Printmaking, Sculpture

UNIVERSITY OF MEMPHIS, Art Dept, 108 Jones Hall, Memphis, TN 38152-3305. Tel 901-678-2216; Fax 901-678-2735; *Chmn Asst* Wayne Simpkins; *Chmn Asst* Brenda Landman; *Acting Chmn* Sandy Lowrance
Estab 1912; pub; D & E; Scholarships; SC 100, LC 40, GC 30; D 2200, maj 467, grad 80
Ent Req: HS dipl, SAT
Degrees: BA & BFA 4 yrs, MA 1 yr, MFA 2 yrs
Tuition: Campus residence available

Courses: Art Education, Ceramics, Drawing, Graphic Design, History of Art & Architecture, Illustration, Interior Design, Museum Staff Training, Painting, Photography, Printmaking, Sculpture, Teacher Training
Adult Hobby Classes: Courses offered
Summer School: Dir, Robert E Lewis

MURFREESBORO

MIDDLE TENNESSEE STATE UNIVERSITY, Art Dept, 1301 E Main St, Murfreesboro, TN 37132-0001. Tel 615-898-2300; 898-5653 (Gallery); Fax 615-898-2254; Internet Home Page Address: www.mtsu.edu; *Instr* Jean Nagy; *Instr* Barry Buxkamper; *Instr* Ollie Fancher; *Instr* Pati Beachley; *Instr* Klaus Kallenberger; *Instr* Janet Higgins; *Instr* Christie Nuell; *Instr* Lon Nuell; *Instr* Marissa Recchia; *Instr* Charles Jansen; *Instr* Tanya Tewell; *Instr* Nancy Kelker; *Instr* John O'Connell; *Instr* Doug Schatz; *Instr* David Shaul; *Instr* Shirley Yokley; *Chmn Art Dept* Mark Price; *Instr* Carlyle Johnson
Estab 1911, dept estab 1952; Maintains Todd Gallery; pub; D & E; Scholarships; SC 62, LC 10, GC 35; non-maj 900, maj 200, grad 5
Ent Req: HS dipl
Degrees: BS(Art Educ), & BFA 4 yrs
Courses: †Art Education, †Ceramics, †Commercial Art, Drawing, Goldsmithing, Graphic Design, †Jewelry, †Painting, †Printmaking, †Sculpture, †Silversmithing, Textile Design
Adult Hobby Classes: Courses Offered
Children's Classes: Creative Art Clinic for Children; enrl 45; tuition $25 per term
Summer School: Courses Offered

NASHVILLE

CHEEKWOOD NASHVILLE'S HOME OF ART & GARDENS, Education Dept, 1200 Forrest Park Dr, Nashville, TN 37205-4242. Tel 615-353-9827; Fax 615-353-2162; *Pres* Jane Jerry; *Dir Museum* John Wentenhall; *Cur Coll* Celia Walker; *Dir Botanical Gardens* Bob Brackman; *Dir Educ* Mary Grissim
Estab 1960; pvt; D & E; Scholarships; SC 10-15, LC 5-10
Courses: Art Appreciation, Art History, Ceramics, Drawing, Jewelry, Landscape Design, Painting, Papermaking, Sculpture, Weaving
Adult Hobby Classes: Enrl 750; tuition $110-$137. Courses—Clay on Wheel, Drawing, Horticulture, Landscape Design, Painting, Photography, Sculpture
Children's Classes: Enrl 200; tuition $90-$110. Courses—Clay Jewelry, Drawing, Environmental Science, Film Making, Gardening, Painting, Photography, Sculpture
Summer School: Enrl 900; tuition $90-$110. Courses—Clay Jewelry, Drawing, Environmental Science, Film Making, Gardening, Painting, Photography, Sculpture

FISK UNIVERSITY, Art Dept, 1000 17th Ave N, Nashville, TN 37208-3045. Tel 615-329-8674, 329-8500; Fax 615-329-8551; Internet Home Page Address: www.fisk.edu; *Asst Prof* Alicia Henry, MA; *Chmn & Instr* Lifran Fort, MA
Estab 1867, dept estab 1937; pvt; D; Scholarships; SC 10, LC 3; 65, non-maj 40, maj 15
Ent Req: HS dipl, SAT
Degrees: BS & BA 4 yrs
Courses: Aesthetics, African Art, African-American Art, Art History, Drawing, Painting, Sculpture

NOSSI COLLEGE OF ART, 590 Cheron Rd, Nashville, TN 37115. Tel 615-514-2787; Fax 615-514-2788; Elec Mail admissions@nossi.com; Internet Home Page Address: www.nossi.edu; *Exec VPres* Cyrus Vatandoost, BA; *Graphic Design Coordr* Bruce Stanley, BFA; *Illustration Coordr* Arden von Haeger, AS; *Founder, CEO & Pres* Nossi Vatandoost, BFA; *VPres Acad Affairs* Dr Byron Edwards, PhD
Estab 1973; pvt; D, E & online; Scholarships; SC 37, LC 15. Other 25
Activities: Mus shop sells art supplies
Ent Req: HS dipl or GED
Degrees: AOS degree; 2 yr Graphic Art, BA Graphic Art & Design, AOS 2 yr Photography, BA Commercial Illustration; BA Digital Photog and Video
Tuition: $4,700 per sem
Courses: Advertising Design, Architecture, Art Appreciation, Art Education, Art History, †Commercial Art, Conceptual Art, Design, Display, Drawing, Graphic Arts, †Graphic Design, Illustration, Lettering, Mixed Media, Painting, †Photography, Video

VANDERBILT UNIVERSITY, Dept of Art, 2301 Vanderbilt Pl, Box 351660-B Nashville, TN 37235-1660. Tel 615-343-7241; Fax 615-322-3467; Internet Home Page Address: www.vanderbilt.edu; *Prof Emeritus* Donald H Evans, MFA; *Prof* Michael Aurbach, MFA; *Sr Lectr* Susan DeMay, MFA; *Sr Lectr* Carlton Wilkinson, MFA; *Chair* Marilyn Murphy, MFA; *Sr Lectr* Ron Porter, MFA; *Sr Lectr* Libby Rowe; *Lectr* Robert Durham
Estab 1873, dept estab 1944; Maintain nonprofit gallery; Fine Arts Gallery, Nashville, TN; maintain arts section in gen library; Jean & Alexander Heard Library. Art supplies may be purchased on campus; Pvt; D; Scholarships, Fellowships; SC 19, LC 29, GC 2; D, non-maj 367, maj 9
Ent Req: HS dipl, ent exam
Degrees: BA 4 yrs
Courses: Art Appreciation, Art History, Ceramics, Drawing, Multimedia Design, Painting, Photography, Printmaking, Sculpture, Video
Summer School: Dean, Richard McCarty. Tuition $840 per cr hr for two 4 wk terms beginning early June. Courses—Vary

WATKINS COLLEGE OF ART, DESIGN & FILM, (Watkins Institute) 2298 Rosa L Parks Blvd, Nashville, TN 37228-1573. Tel 615-383-4848; Fax 615-383-4849; Elec Mail ewood@watkins.edu; Internet Home Page Address: www.watkins.edu; *Pres* Ellen L Meyer; *Dean, VPres Acad Affairs* John M Sullivan; *Prof & Chair Film School* Steven Womack; *Prof* Valorie Stover Quarles; *Assoc Prof Film & Instr Community Educ* Robert Gordon; *Assoc Prof Film* Charles Kanganis; *Asst Prof Film* Sean Miller; *Prof Fine Art* Terry Thacker;

Asst Prof & Chair of Fine Art Kristi Hargrove; *Asst Prof Fine Art & Studio Facilities Mgr* Brady Haston; *Asst Prof Fine Art & Adjunct Instruc Phtog* Ron Lambert; *Asst Prof Fine Art* Derek Cote; *Asst Prof & Coordr Graphic Design* Dan Brawner; *Asst Prof Graphic Design* Judith Sweeney O'Bryan; *Asst Prof & Chair Interior Design* Jennifer Overstreet; *Assoc Prof Interior Design* Cheryl Gulley; *Asst Prof Interior Design* Jenny Myers; *Assoc Prof & Chair Photog* Robin Paris; *Prof Photog* Joy McKenzie; *Instr & Dir Gen Educ & BA Prog* Cary Miller; *Vis Instr Art History* Lillian Fish
Estab 1885; FT 19, PT 61; pvt; D; Scholarships; SC 71, LC 27; D 403; non-maj 2, maj 393, other 8
Ent Req: HS graduate ACT 21, college trans 2.6 or better, portfolio req for BFA progs
Degrees: Approved by Tennessee Higher Education Commission, BFA in Fine Art; BFA in Film; BFA in Photography; BFA in Int Design; BFA in Graphic Design; BA in Art; certificate in film
Tuition: All programs $18,900 per yr; $630 per cr hr
Courses: †Advertising Design, Aesthetics, Art History, †Ceramics, †Conceptual Art, †Design, Drafting, †Drawing, †Film, †Fine Art, †Graphic Design, †History of Art & Architecture, Illustration, †Interior Design, †Mixed Media, †Painting, †Photography, †Printmaking, †Production Design, †Sculpture, Stage Design, Theatre Arts, †Video, †Weaving, †Web Design
Adult Hobby Classes: Enrl 605; tuition $150-$200; various courses
Children's Classes: Enrl 541; tuition $150-$200; various courses
Summer School: Enrl 226; tuition $150-$200; various courses

SEWANEE

UNIVERSITY OF THE SOUTH, Dept of Fine Arts, Carnegie Hall, Sewanee, TN 37383-0001. Tel 913-598-1201; Elec Mail pmalde@seraph1.sewaner.edu; Internet Home Page Address: www.sewanee.edu; *Chmn Dept* Gregory Clark
FT 6; Pvt, den; D; SC 20, LC 20; D 250; non-maj 225, maj 30
Degrees: BS & BA, MDiv
Courses: Art History, Drawing, Painting, Photography, Printmaking, Sculpture, Video
Summer School: Dir, Dr John Reishman. Enrl 150 for term of 6 wks beginning June; tuition $400 per cr. Courses—History of Western Art II, Painting, Photography

SMITHVILLE

TENNESSEE TECH UNIVERSITY, Appalachian Center for Craft, 1560 Craft Center Dr, Smithville, TN 37166-7352. Tel 931-372-3051; Fax 615-597-6803; Elec Mail craftcenter@tntech.edu; Internet Home Page Address: www.tntech.edu/craftcenter
Average Annual Attendance:

TULLAHOMA

MOTLOW STATE COMMUNITY COLLEGE, Art Dept, 6015 Ledford Mill Rd, Dept 245 Tullahoma, TN 37388-7972. Tel 931-455-3804; Fax 931-393-1681; Internet Home Page Address: www.mscc.edu; *Art Teacher* Ann Smotherman; *Dean* Dr Mary McLemore; *Art Teacher* Brian Robinson
Estab 1969; Pub; D & E; Scholarships
Ent Req: HS dipl or equivalent
Tuition: In state—$2199 per yr; out of state—$4022.50 per yr
Courses: Art Appreciation, Arts & Crafts, Ceramics, Commercial Art, Design, Drawing, Painting, Photography
Adult Hobby Classes: Enrl 200
Children's Classes: Enrl 40

TEXAS

ABILENE

ABILENE CHRISTIAN UNIVERSITY, Dept of Art & Design, 1 ACU, Abilene, TX 79699-0002. Tel 915-674-2085; Fax 915-674-2051; Elec Mail maxwellj@acu.edu; Internet Home Page Address: www.acu.edu/academics/cas/art.html; *Head Dept & Chmn* Jack Maxwell; *Prof* Robert Green; *Prof* Ginna Sadler; *Prof* Nil Santana; *Prof* Geoff Broderick; *Prof* Dan McGregor; *Prof* Ronnie Rama; *Prof* Kitty Wasemiller; *Prof* Mike Wiggins
Estab 1906; Maintain nonprofit art gallery, Clover Virginia Shore Art Gallery, 142 Don Morris Center, Box 27987, Abilene, TX 79699-7987; FT 8, PT 2; pvt; D & E; Scholarships; SC 31, LC 8; maj 130
Ent Req: upper 3/4 HS grad class or at 19 standard score ACT composite
Degrees: BA, BA(Educ) & BFA 4 yrs
Courses: Advertising Design, Architecture, Art Appreciation, Art Education, Art History, Ceramics, Design, Drawing, Graphic Design, History of Art & Architecture, †Illustration, Jewelry, Painting, Photography, Pottery, Printmaking, Sculpture
Summer School: Chmn, Jack Maxwell, Enrl 10; tuition $347 per sem hour. Courses— Drawing, Introduction to Art History, Sculpture, Graphic Design

HARDIN-SIMMONS UNIVERSITY, Art Dept, 2200 Hickory St, Abilene, TX 79601-2345; Box 16085, Abilene, TX 79698. Tel 325-671-2223; Elec Mail mjones@hsutx.edu; Internet Home Page Address: www.hsutx.edu/academics/music_art/art; *Prof* Martha Kiel, MEd; *Prof & Chmn* Mike Jones, MFA; *Assoc Prof* Steve Neves, MFA
Univ estab 1891; Maintains nonprofit Ira Taylor Gallery; den; D & E; Scholarships; SC 27, LC 5; D 110, E 60, non-maj 35, maj 75
Ent Req: HS dipl, SAT, ACT

Degrees: BA, BBS, BFA 4 yrs
Courses: Art Appreciation, Art Education, Art History, †Ceramics, †Drawing, †Graphic Design, †Painting, †Photography, †Printmaking, Sculpture, †Teacher Training
Summer School: Prof & Chair, Mike Jones. Courses—Art Appreciation, Ceramics, Drawing, History of Graphic Design Online, Photography

MCMURRY UNIVERSITY, Art Dept, 1401 Sayles Blvd, McMurray Station Box 278 Abilene, TX 79605-4207. Tel 915-793-4888; Fax 915-793-4662; Internet Home Page Address: www.mcm.edu; *Head Dept* Kathy Walker-Millar, BS; *Prof* J Robert Miller, BS; *Asst Prof* Linda Stricklin, BS; *Instr* Judy Deaton
Estab 1923; pvt; D & E; Scholarships; SC 19, LC 1; D 80, E 8, non-maj 18, maj 15
Ent Req: HS dipl
Degrees: BA, BFA & BS 4 yrs
Courses: Art Education, Art History, Assemblage Sculpture, Ceramics, Design, Drawing, Jewelry, Painting, Teacher Training
Adult Hobby Classes: Enrl 24; tuition $360 fall, spring & summer terms. Courses—Art Education I & II
Summer School: Dir, Bob Maniss. Two summer terms. Courses—Art Education I, Exploring the Visual Arts

ALPINE

SUL ROSS STATE UNIVERSITY, Dept of Fine Arts & Communications, C-43, Alpine, TX 79832-0001. Tel 915-837-8130; Fax 915-837-8046; *Prof* Charles R Hext, MFA; *Asst Prof* Carol Fairlie, MFA; *Asst Prof* Jim Bob Salazar, MFA
Estab 1920, dept estab 1922; pub; D & E; Scholarships; SC 21, LC 3, GC 19; D 183, E 32, non-maj 170, maj 25-30, GS 15
Ent Req: HS dipl, ACT or SAT
Degrees: BFA 4 yrs, MEd(Art) 1 1/2 yrs
Courses: Advertising Art, †Advertising Design, †Art Appreciation, †Art Education, †Art History, †Ceramics, Collage, †Commercial Art, Conceptual Art, Constructions, Costume Design & Construction, Design, Drafting, Drawing, †Graphic Arts, †Graphic Design, Handicrafts, †History of Art & Architecture, Illustration, Industrial Design, Interior Design, Jewelry, Landscape Architecture, †Mixed Media, †Painting, Photography, †Printmaking, Restoration & Conservation, †Sculpture, Stage Design, †Teacher Training

ALVIN

ALVIN COMMUNITY COLLEGE, Art Dept, 3110 Mustang Rd, Alvin, TX 77511-4807. Tel 281-756-3752; Fax 281-388-4903; Elec Mail dlavalley@alvin.cc.tx.us; *Chmn* Dennis LaValley
Estab 1949; D & E
Ent Req: HS dipl
Degrees: AA 2 yrs
Courses: Art Appreciation, Art History, †Art Metals, Ceramics, Design Communication, Drawing, Graphic Design, Graphic Media, Painting, †Photography, Sculpture
Summer School: Dir, Bruce Turner. 6-12 wk term. Courses—Vary

AMARILLO

AMARILLO COLLEGE, Visual Art Dept, PO Box 447, Amarillo, TX 79178-0001. Tel 806-371-5000, Ext 5084; Internet Home Page Address: www.actx.edu/~visual_arts/; *Prof* William Burrell, MFA; *Assoc Prof* Dennis Olson, MFA; *Asst Prof* Steven Cost, MFA; *Instr* Pedro Gonzalez, MFA; *Assoc Prof* Joseph Walsh, MA; *Instr* Alix Christian; *Instr* Victoria Taylor-Gore; *Dept Head* Kenneth Pirtle, BFA
Estab 1926; pub; D & E; Scholarships; SC 18, LC 2; D 142, E 60
Ent Req: HS dipl, CEEB
Degrees: AA 2 yrs
Courses: Art History, Ceramics, Drawing, †Fine Art, †Graphic Design, Illustration, Jewelry, Layout, †Painting, †Sculpture, Typographics

ARLINGTON

UNIVERSITY OF TEXAS AT ARLINGTON, Art & Art History Department, 335 Fine Arts Bldg, Arlington, TX 76019; 502 S Cooper St, Box 19089 Arlington, TX 76019. Tel 817-272-2891; Fax 817-272-2805; Elec Mail art@uta.edu; Internet Home Page Address: www.uta.edu; *Chmn* Robert Hower; *Asst Prof* Melia Belli; *Sr Lectr* Mark Clive; *Sr Lectr* Bryan Florentin; *Assoc Prof* Lisa Graham; *Assoc Prof* Benito Huerta; *Vis Asst Prof* Kelly Ingelright; *Assoc Prof* Marilyn Jolly; *Prof* David Keens; *Assoc Prof* Leighton McWilliams; *Vis Asst Prof* Fred Miller; *Prof* Kenda North; *Assoc Prof* Andrew Ortiz; *Assoc Prof* Nancy Palmeri; *Prof Emeritus* Jack Plummer; *Adjunct Prof* Erik Tosten; *Assoc Prof* Dr Mary Vaccaro; *Assoc Prof* Barton Weiss; *Assoc Prof* Nicholas Wood; *Prof* Beth Wright; *Adjunct Prof* Paul Benero; *Vis Asst Prof* Stephen Lapthisophon; *Asst Prof* Darryl Lauster; *Adjunct Prof* David Pinkston; *Adjunct Prof* Fred Spaulding; *Adj Asst Prof* Stephanie Clark; *Adj Asst Prof* Debra Dewitte; *Adj Asst Prof* Carlos Donjuan; *Vis Asst Prof* Sedrick Huckaby; *Asst Prof* Seiji Ikeda; *Asst Prof* Benjamin Lima; *Adj Asst Prof* Chaitra Linehan; *Adj Asst Prof* Mark Mueller; *Asst Prof* Ya'Ke Smith; *Asst Prof* Tore Terrasi
Estab 1895, dept estab 1937; Maintain nonprofit art gallery, The Gallery at UTA; maintain art/architecture library, 601 W Nedderman, Architecture Building Rm 104, Arlington, TX 76019; on-campus shop where art supplies may be purchased; pub; D & E; Scholarships; SC 115, LC 51, GC 40; D 764, E 108, non-maj 20, maj 800, grad 27
Ent Req: HS dipl, SAT of ACT
Degrees: BA(Art, Art History), MFA, BFA, Cert Teaching
Tuition: Res—$13,670 per yr; nonres—$21,935 per yr

Courses: Advertising Design, Art Appreciation, Art Education, †Art History, Clay, Conceptual Art, Constructions, Design, Display, †Drawing, Film, Glass, Glass Blowing, †Graphic Design, History of Art & Architecture, Illustration, Intermedia, Mixed Media, Museum Staff Training, †Painting, †Photography, †Printmaking, †Sculpture, Teacher Training, †Video

AUSTIN

AUSTIN COMMUNITY COLLEGE, Dept of Commercial Art, North Ridge Campus, 11928 Stonehollow Dr, Austin, TX 78758-3190. Tel 512-223-7000 (Main), 223-4830 (Dept); Fax 512-223-4444; Internet Home Page Address: www.austin.cc.tx.us/; *Head Dept South Campus* Steve Kramer
Estab 1974; FT 3, PT 30; pub; D & E; 386 per sem
Ent Req: HS dipl or GED
Degrees: AAS 2 yr, Multi Media Cert
Courses: Advertising, Animation, Art History, Calligraphy, Ceramics, Commercial Art, Commercial Art History, Computer Layout & Design, Desktop Publishing, Drawing, Environmental Graphics, Figure Drawing, Graphic Arts, Graphic Design, Graphics Practicum, Illustration, Illustrative Techniques, Metalsmithing, Painting, Photography, †Printmaking, Production Art, †Sculpture, Silkscreening, Typography Design, †Video

CONCORDIA UNIVERSITY, Dept of Fine Arts, 11400 Concordia University Dr, Austin, TX 78726-1887. Tel 512-452-7661; Fax 512-459-8517; Internet Home Page Address: www.concordia.edu; *Chmn* Dr David Kroft
Estab 1925; FT 1; den; D; Scholarships; SC 1, LC 1; D 350
Ent Req: HS dipl
Degrees: AA 2 yrs
Courses: Art Fundamentals, Ceramics, Design, Drawing, Drawing Media, Relief Printing

UNIVERSITY OF TEXAS, School of Architecture, I University Station, B7500 Austin, TX 78712-0803. Tel 512-471-1922; Fax 512-471-0716; Elec Mail lwspeck@mail.utexas.edu; Internet Home Page Address: www.utexas.edu; *Dean* Lawrence Speck
Estab 1909; FT 38, PT 9; pub; Scholarships; undergrad 450, grad 210
Ent Req: reasonable HS scholastic achievement, SAT, ACT
Degrees: BA, MA, PhD
Tuition: Res—$80 per cr hr, grad $120 per cr hr; nonres—$295 per cr hr, grad $335 per cr hr
Courses: †Architecture, Community & Regional Planning
Adult Hobby Classes: Courses through Division of Continuing Education
Children's Classes: Six week summer program for high school
Summer School: Dir, Harold Box
—Dept of Art & Art History, Austin, TX 78712; 1 University Station # D1300, Austin, TX 78712. Tel 512-471-3382; Fax 512-471-7801; Elec Mail shanesullivan@mail.utexas.edu; Internet Home Page Address: www.finearts.utexas.edu/aah/; *Chair* John Yancey; *Assoc Chair* Lee Chesney; *Asst Dir Develop* Carolyn Porter; *Asst Chair - Art History* Susan Rather; *Asst Chair - Design* Kate Catterall; *Asst Chair - Studio Art* Daniel Sutherland; *Asst Chair - Visual Art Studies* Christopher Adejumo; *Foundations Dir* Robert Anderson; *Undergrad Coordr* Shane Sullivan; *Grad Coordr-Art History* Maureen Howell; *Grad Coordr-Art Educ, Design, Studio Art* Judy Clark
Estab 1938; Maintain nonprofit art gallery; Creative Research Laboratory, 2832 E Martin Luther King Jr Blvd, Austin, TX 78705; art library; art supplies may be purchased at university coop; FT & PT 80; pub; D & E; Scholarships, Fellowships; SC 20, LC 15, GC 20; enrl grad 150, 700 undergrad maj
Ent Req: acad & portfolio application
Degrees: BA 4yrs, BFA 4 yrs, MA 2 yrs, MFA 2 yrs, PhD & MFA 3yrs
Tuition: Res—undergrad $4,154 & fees per sem, grad $3,642 & fees per sem; nonres—undergrad $13,293 & fees per sem, grad $7,361 & fees per sem
Courses: Art Appreciation, Art Education, Art History, Ceramics, Design, Digital-Time Arts, Drawing, Metals, Painting, Performance Art, Photography, Printmaking, Sculpture, Teacher Training, †Video Art
Summer School: Two 6 wk terms

BEAUMONT

LAMAR UNIVERSITY, Art Dept, PO Box 10027, LU Sta, Beaumont, TX 77710. Tel 409-880-8141; Fax 409-880-1799; Elec Mail donna.meeks@lamar.edu; Internet Home Page Address: www.lamar.edu; *Prof* Lynne Lokensgard, PhD; *Prof* Meredith M Jack, MFA; *Prof* Keith Carter, BS; *Assoc Prof* Prince Thomas, MFA; *Chmn & Prof* Donna M Meeks, MFA; *Assoc Prof* Kurt Dyrhaug, MFA; *Assoc Prof* Ann Matlock, MFA; *Asst Prof* Xenia Fedorchenko, MFA; *Instr* Linnis Blanton, BFA; *Instr* Rose Matthis, MFA; *Asst Prof* Fu-Chia-Wen Lien, PhD; *Instr* Jamie Paul Kessler, MFA; *Instr* Ray Daniels, MFA; *Instr* Greg Busceme, MFA
Estab 1923, dept estab 1951; Maintains nonprofit art gallery, Dishman Art Museum, Lamar Univ, PO Box 10027, Beaumont, TX, 77710; pub; D & E; Scholarships; SC 60, LC 76; D 547, E 111, non-maj 300, maj 190
Ent Req: HS dipl, SAT/ACT
Degrees: BFA, BS & MA, 4 yr
Courses: Advertising Design, Aesthetics, Art Appreciation, †Art Education, †Art History, †Ceramics, †Commercial Art, †Computer Graphics, Design, †Drawing, †Graphic Arts, †Graphic Design, †Illustration, Jewelry, Museum Staff Training, †Painting, †Photography, †Printmaking, †Sculpture, †Teacher Training, Textile Design, Weaving
Summer School: Dir, Donna M Meeks. Enrl 125; tuition res $360, nonres $1185 per 3 sem hrs for 5 wk sessions. Courses—Art Appreciation, Computers in Art, Drawing, Watercolor & Illustration

BELTON

UNIVERSITY OF MARY HARDIN-BAYLOR, College of Visual & Performing Arts, 900 College St, UMHB Box 8012 Belton, TX 76513-2578. Tel 254-295-4678; Fax 254-295-4675; Elec Mail hseals@umhb.edu; Internet Home

Page Address: www.umhb.edu; *Chmn* Hershall Seals; *Dean* Ted Barnes; *Prof* John Hancock; *Prof* Helen Kwiatkowski; *Prof* Barbar Fontaine-White; *Asst Prof* Yvonne Cao; *Asst Pro* David Hill
Estab 1845; Maintain a nonprofit art gallery Baugh Center for the Visual Arts Art Gallery, 700 College St, UMHB Box 8012, Belton, TX 76513; PT 3; pvt; D & E; Scholarships; SC 29, LC 4, six independent learning course per sem; D 300, E 50, non-maj 250, maj 55
Ent Req: upper half of HS grad class
Degrees: BA, BFA 4 yrs
Tuition: $690 per cr hr
Courses: Advertising Design, Art Appreciation, Art Education, Art History, Ceramics, †Collage, Drawing, Graphic Design, Jewelry, Painting, Photography, Printmaking, Sculpture, Silversmithing, †Studio Art, Teacher Training
Children's Classes: Summer Art

BIG SPRING

HOWARD COLLEGE, Art Dept, 1001 Birdwell Ln, Division of Fine Arts Big Spring, TX 79720-5015. Tel 915-264-5000; Fax 915-264-5082; *Prof* Mary Dudley; *Dept Chair* Liz Lowery
Estab 1948, dept estab 1972; pub; D & E; Scholarships; SC 5, LC 1; D 70, E 20, non-maj 60, maj 10
Ent Req: HS dipl, ACT
Degrees: AA
Courses: Art Appreciation, Art Education, Art History, Ceramics, Drawing, Painting, Watercolors

BROWNSVILLE

UNIVERSITY OF TEXAS AT BROWNSVILLE & TEXAS SOUTHMOST COLLEGE, Fine Arts Dept, 80 Fort Brown, Brownsville, TX 78520. Tel 956-544-8200; *Chmn Fine Arts* Terry Tomlin
Estab 1973; pub; D & E; Scholarships; SC 10, LC 10; D 300, E 100
Ent Req: HS dipl
Degrees: AA (Fine Arts) 2-3 yrs, BA 4 yr
Courses: Art Education, Ceramics, Design I and II, Drawing, Graphic Design, History of Art & Architecture, Painting, Photography, Sculpture
Adult Hobby Classes: Courses—Ceramics, Drawing
Summer School: Dir, Terry Tomlin. Courses—Art Appreciation, Art History

BROWNWOOD

HOWARD PAYNE UNIVERSITY, Dept of Art, 1000 Fisk St, Brownwood, TX 76801-2715. Tel 915-646-2502; Internet Home Page Address: www.hputx.edu; *Dean* Donal Bird PhD; *Chmn Dept Art* Ann Smith, MA
Estab 1889; FT 2, PT 2; den; D & E; Scholarships; SC 18, LC 8; D 120, E 25, maj 2
Ent Req: HS dipl, ent exam
Degrees: BA & BS 4 yrs
Courses: Art Appreciation, Art Education, Art History, Ceramics, Computer Graphics, Design, Drawing, Graphic Arts, Graphic Design, Handicrafts, Painting, Photography
Adult Hobby Classes: Enrl 30; tuition $50 per course. Courses—Travel Seminars
Summer School: Enrl 75; tuition term of 4 wks beginning June. Courses—Art Educ, Crafts, Drawing, Painting

CANYON

WEST TEXAS A&M UNIVERSITY, Art, Theatre & Dance Dept, PO Box 60747, Canyon, TX 79016-0001. Tel 806-651-2799; Fax 806-651-2818; Elec Mail rbrantley@mail.wtamu.edu; Internet Home Page Address: www.wtamu.edu; *Head Dept* Royal Brantley, MFA; *Prof* Robert Caruthers, MFA; *Prof* Darold Smith, MFA; *Assoc Prof* David Rindlisbacher, MFA; *Asst Prof* Scott Frish, MFA; *Instr* Barbara Lines, MA; *Asst Prof* Harold Lenfestey PhD
Estab 1910; Maintain nonprofit art gallery, Northern Hall Art Gallery, same address; maintains an art library at WTAMU; Pub; D & E; Scholarships; SC 70, LC 23, GC 50; maj 62, non-maj 15, grad 21
Ent Req: HS dipl
Degrees: BA, BS, BFA, MA & MFA
Courses: Aesthetics, †Art Education, Art History, †Ceramics, Computer Art, †Drawing, †Glassblowing, Graphic Arts, †Graphic Design, Illustration, †Jewelry, †Painting, †Printmaking, †Sculpture, †Silversmithing, Teacher Training

COLLEGE STATION

TEXAS A&M UNIVERSITY, College of Architecture, 3137 TAMU, College Station, TX 77843-3137. Tel 979-845-1221; Fax 979-845-4491; Elec Mail reganjt@archone.tamu.edu; Internet Home Page Address: www.tamu.edu; *Dean* Tom Regan
Estab 1905; FT 92; pub; D; Scholarships; maj Ed 800, total 1750
Ent Req: SAT; Achievement, HS rank
Degrees: BEnviron Design, BS(Building Construction), BLandscape Arch, March, MLandscape, MUrban Planning, PhD(Urban Science) 4 yr, MS(Construction Mgmt), MS(Land Development), MS(Architecture), PhD(Architecture), MS(Visualization) (Computer Animation)
Courses: Architecture, Art History, Computer Animation, Constructions, Design, Drafting, Drawing, History of Art & Architecture, Illustration, Landscape Architecture, Photography, Restoration & Conservation, Video
Summer School: Dir, Rodney Hill. Enrl 1000; Courses—Arch Design, Arch History, Construction Science, Drawing, Planning

COMMERCE

TEXAS A&M UNIVERSITY COMMERCE, Dept of Art, PO Box 3011, Commerce, TX 75429-3011. Tel 903-886-5208; Fax 903-886-5987; Internet Home Page Address: www.tamu-commerce.edu; *Head* William Wadley; *Instr Ceramics* Barbara Frey, MFA; *Instr Printmaking* Lee Baxter Davis, MFA; *Instr Sculpture* Jerry Dodd, MFA; *Coordr Grad Progs & Instr Painting* Michael Miller, MFA; *Instr Art History* Ivana Spalatin, MFA; *Asst Prof* Stan Godwin, MFA; *Prof Photog* Bill McDowell; *Coordr New Media* Lee Whitmarsh; *Gallery Coordr* Brenda Feher-Simonelli
Pub; D & E; Scholarships; SC 64, LC 29, GC 19; maj 300, GS 30
Ent Req: HS dipl, ACT or SAT
Degrees: BA, BS & BFA 4 yr, MFA 2 yr, MA & MS 1 1/2 yr. There is a special prog called the Post Masters-MFA which is worked out on an individual basis
Courses: †Advertising Design, Aesthetics, †Art Education, Art History, †Ceramics, Collage, †Commercial Art, Constructions, Drafting, †Drawing, †Graphic Arts, †Graphic Design, History of Art & Architecture, †Illustration, Industrial Design, †Intermedia, †Jewelry, Lettering, Lithography, †Mixed Media, †Painting, Papermaking & Casting, †Photography, †Printmaking, †Sculpture, Silversmithing, †Teacher Training, Video
Adult Hobby Classes: Enrl 15; tuition $77 per sem. Courses—Bonzai, Ceramics, Drawing, Painting, Watercolor
Summer School: Enrl 15; tuition res—$64.75-$393; nonres—$134.75-$2121, for 2 terms of 2 to 6 wks beginning June. Courses—Art Education, Ceramics, Design, Drawing, Painting, Printmaking

CORPUS CHRISTI

DEL MAR COLLEGE, Art Dept, 101 Baldwin Blvd, Corpus Christi, TX 78404-3894. Tel 361-698-1216; Fax 361-698-1511; Elec Mail krosier@delmar.edu; Internet Home Page Address: www.delmar.edu; *Chair & Prof* Ken Rosier, MFA; *Prof* Randolph Flowers, MS; *Prof* Kitty Dudics, MFA; *Assoc Prof* Cynthia Perkins, MA; *Assoc Prof* Amorette Garza, MFA; *Asst Prof* Gerardo Cobarruvias, MA
Estab 1941, dept estab 1965; Maintains nonprofit Joseph A Cain Memorial Gallery; pub; D & E; Scholarships; SC 21, LC 3; D 500, E 100, non-maj 400, maj 139
Ent Req: HS dipl, SAT score or any accepted test including GED
Degrees: AA 2 yr in studio, art educ
Tuition: Res—$330 per 3 sem hrs; nonres—$480+ per 3 sem hrs
Courses: Art Appreciation, †Art Education, Art History, Ceramics, Design, Drawing, Graphic Design, †Life Drawing, Painting, Photography, Printmaking, Sculpture, †Watercolor
Adult Hobby Classes: Tuition varies according to classes. Courses—same as above

CORSICANA

NAVARRO COLLEGE, Art Dept, 3200 W Seventh Ave, Corsicana, TX 75110. Tel 903-874-6501; Fax 903-874-4636; Elec Mail tsale@nav.cc.tx.us; WATS 800-NAVARRO; *Dir* Tom Sale
Estab 1946; FT2, PT2; pub; D & E; Scholarships; SC 6, LC 2; D 300, maj 30
Ent Req: HS dipl, ent exam, special permission
Degrees: AA, AS, A Gen Educ & A Appl Sci 60 sem hr
Courses: 2-D & 3-D Design, Advertising Design, Art Appreciation, Ceramics, Commercial Art, †Computer Art, Design, Drafting, Drawing, Graphic Arts, Illustration, Multi-Media, Painting, Photography, Sculpture, Video
Adult Hobby Classes: Enrl 200; tuition $30-$150 for sem of 6-12 wks. Courses—Art Appreciation, Crafts, Design, Drawing, Painting, Photography, Sculpture
Summer School: Enrl 30; Courses—Art Appreciation

DALLAS

THE ART INSTITUTE OF DALLAS, 8080 Park Lane (Ste 100), Dallas, TX 75231-5900. Tel 214-692-8080; Fax 214-692-6541; Internet Home Page Address: www.aid.edu; WATS 800-275-4243; *Registrar* Tom Chauvin; *Pres* Thomas W Newsom
Estab 1998; Maintains nonprofit art gallery: Pegasus Art Gallery; Mildred Kellez Library; on-campus shop for purchasing art supplies; pvt; D & E; Scholarships
Ent Req: HS dipl, equivalent
Degrees: AA & BA
Courses: Computer Animation Multimedia, †Culinary & Restaurant Management, Fashion Design, †Film, †Graphic Design, Interior Design, †Management, Photography, Visual Communication
Adult Hobby Classes: Enrl 850; tuition $2050 per quarter. Courses—Commercial Art, Culinary Arts, Fashion Merchandising, Interior Design, Photography, Video

DALLAS BAPTIST UNIVERSITY, Dept of Art, 3000 Mountain Creek Pkwy, Dallas, TX 75211-9299. Tel 214-333-5316, 333-5300; Fax 214-333-8857; Elec Mail dawna@dbu.edu; Internet Home Page Address: www.dbu.edu; *Head Art Dept* Dawna Hamm Walsh PhD; *Asst Prof* Jim Hutchinson, MFA; *Dean Fine Arts* Dr Ron Bowles; *Instr* Nancy Cole, MFA; *Instr* Dana Hamrick Ferrara, MFA; *Instr* Lee Bowman, MA; *Instr* Tempy Berg-Gilbert, MA; *Instr* Angela Pitts, MFA; *Instr* Mary Morgan, MFA; *Instr* Ron Bland, MA; *Instr* Dawn Gold; *Instr* Tamra Sawyer; *Instr* Spray Gleaves
Estab 1965; Maintains Learning Center Gallery, Dept of Art, Dallas Baptist Univer, 3000 Creek Pkwy, Dallas, TX 75244-9299; FT 3, PT 18; pvt den; D, E, wknds, online; Scholarships; SC 20, LC 6, GC 15, online classes; D 175, E 90, non-maj 50, maj 75, grad 10
Activities: Schols offered
Ent Req: HS dipl
Degrees: BA & BS 4 yrs, Grad Art Degree: MLA

Tuition: $800 per cr hr
Courses: Advertising Design, Aesthetics, Art Appreciation, Art Education, Art History, Commercial Art, Crafts, Design, Drawing, Fine Arts, Graphic Arts, Graphic Design, History of Art & Architecture, †Mixed Media, †Museum Studies, Painting, Photography, Religious & Christian Art, Sculpture, Theatre Arts
Summer School: Dir, Dr Dawna Walsh, PhD. Tuition $800 per cr hr.
Courses—Sculpture, Drawing, Painting. Art Travel Program for cr available

SOUTHERN METHODIST UNIVERSITY, Division of Art, PO Box 750356, Dallas, TX 75275-0356. Tel 214-768-2489; Fax 214-768-4257; Elec Mail jsulliva@mail.smu.edu; Internet Home Page Address: www.smu.edu/~art; *Dir* Philip VanKeuren; *Prof* Laurence Scholder; *Prof* Bill Komodore; *Asst Prof* Peter Beasecker; *Asst Prof* Charles DeBus; *Prof* Barnaby Fitzgerald; *Asst Prof* Debora Hunter; *Asst Prof* Cynthia Lin; *Asst Prof* Mary Vernon; *Chair* Jay Sullivan; *Asst Prof* Karen Kittelson; *Assoc Prof* Arthur Koch
Estab 1911, Meadows School of Arts estab 1964; pvt; D & E; Scholarships; SC 43; maj 40, grad 9
Ent Req: selective admis
Degrees: BFA(Art), BFA(Art History), BA(Art History) 4 yr, MFA(Art) 2 yr, MA(Art History) 1 1/2 yr
Courses: †Art History, †Ceramics, †Color and Composition, Bronze Casting, †Drawing, †Painting, †Photography, †Printmaking, †Sculpture
Adult Hobby Classes: Ceramics, Color and Composition
Summer School: Selected courses in art & art history at Taos, NM

DENISON

GRAYSON COUNTY COLLEGE, Art Dept, 6101 Grayson Dr, Denison, TX 75020-8238. Tel 903-463-8662; Fax 903-463-5284; Internet Home Page Address: www.gcc.edu; *Inst* Evette Moorman; *Instr* Terri Blair; *Dept Head* Steve O Black
Estab 1965; PT 2; pub; D & E; Scholarships; LC 3; D 63, E 35
Ent Req: HS dipl
Degrees: AA 2 yrs
Courses: 3-D Design, Art Appreciation, Art Education, Art History, Color & Design, Drawing, Foundations of Art, Painting
Adult Hobby Classes: Ceramics, Drawing, Painting
Summer School: Dir, Steve O Black. Courses—Art Appreciation, Foundations of Art, Drawing, Painting

DENTON

TEXAS WOMAN'S UNIVERSITY, School of the Arts, Dept of Visual Arts, PO Box 425469, Denton, TX 76204-5469. Tel 940-898-2530; Fax 940-898-2496; Elec Mail visualarts@twu.edu; Internet Home Page Address: www.twu.edu/as/va; *Dir School of the Arts* John Weinkein, MFA; *Prof* Linda Stuckenbruck, MFA; *Prof Dr* John A Calabrese PhD, MFA; *Prof* Susan Kae Grant, MFA; *Adjunct Assoc Prof* Don Radke, MFA; *Adjunct Prof* Laurie Weller, MFA; *Asst Prof* Colby Parsons-O'Keefe, MFA; *Instr* David Bieloh, MA
Estab 1901; pub; D & E; Scholarships; SC 21, LC 34, GC 17; non-maj 400, maj 110, undergrad 150, total 750
Ent Req: HS dipl, MA and MFA portfolio review required
Degrees: BA and BFA 4 yrs, MA 1 yr, MFA 2 yrs
Courses: Art Education, Art History, Bookmaking-Topography, Clay, †Graphic Design, Handmade Paper, Painting, Photography, Sculpture
Summer School: tuition same as above for 2 5-wk sessions. Courses—Art Design, Art Education, Art History, Clay, Drawing, Fibers, Painting, Photography

UNIVERSITY OF NORTH TEXAS, College of Visual Arts & Design, 1201 W Mulberry St, Denton, TX 16201; 1155 Union Cir, #305100 Denton, TX 76203-5017. Tel 940-565-2855; Fax 940-565-4717; Elec Mail cvad@unt.edu; Internet Home Page Address: art.unt.edu; *Assoc Dean* Eric Ligon, MFA; *Chair, Dept Art Educ* Denise Baxter, PhD; *Chair, Dept Studio* Annette Lawrence, MFA; *Assoc Prof Interior Design* Bruce Nacke, MFA; *Assoc Prof Interior Design* Johnnie Stark, MFA; *Assoc Prof Fashion Design* Marian O'Rourke-Kaplan, MA; *Chair, Dept Design* Cynthia Mohr, MFA; *Regents Prof Metals* Harlan Butt, MFA; *Prof Drawing & Painting* Vincent Falsetta; *Prof Drawing & Painting* Robert Jessup; *Prof Art Educ* Terry Barrett; *Regents Prof* Elmer Taylor, MFA; *Prof Fashion Design* Myra Walker; *Assoc Prof Art History* Nada Shabout, PhD; *Assoc Prof Art History* Jennifer Way, PhD; *Assoc Prof Comm Design* Michael Gibson; *Assoc Dean & Distinguished Teaching Prof* Eric Ligan, MFA; *Prof Photog* Dornith Doherty, MFA; *Assoc Prof Design* Jane Stidham, MFA; *Assoc Prof Printmaking* Larry Gibbons; *Assoc Prof Art History* Kelly Donahue-Wallace, PhD; *Assoc Prof Drawing & Painting* Matthew Bourbon, MFA; *Prof Sculpture* Richard Davis, MFA; *Assoc Prof Metals* Ana Lopez, MFA; *Asst Prof Art History* Lisa Owen, PhD; *Assoc Prof Art History* Mickey Abel, PhD; *Assoc Prof Commun Design* Keith Owens, MFA; *Assoc Dean* Jerry Austin, MFA; *Assoc Prof Fashion Design* Li Fen Chang, MFA
Estab 1890, dept estab 1901; Maintain nonprofit art gallery, University Art Gallery, 1201 W Mulberry, Denton, TX 76201; Willis Library; on-campus shop for purchase of art supplies; art library; pub; D & E; Scholarships, Fellowships; SC 212, LC 43, GC 29; maj 2,100, grad 150
Ent Req: HS dipl, SAT, GRE, portfolio for MFA, letters of recommendation for PhD
Degrees: BA 4 yrs, BFA 4 yrs, MFA, MA, PhD
Courses: Art Appreciation, †Art Education, †Art History, †Arts, †Ceramics, †Communication Design, Conceptual Art, Design, Drawing, †Electronic Media Art, †Fashion Arts, †Innovation Studies, †Interior Design, †Jewelry, †Leadership, †Mixed Media, †Photography, †Printmaking, †Sculpture, Teacher Training, Textile Design, †Weaving
Adult Hobby Classes: Tuition determined by class. Courses—Mini-classes in arts and craft related areas. Offered by Mini Course Office.
Children's Classes: Courses—Mini-classes in arts and crafts related areas; special prog for advanced students. Offered by Mini-Course Office

Summer School: Dean, Robert Milues. Enrl 700-900 per session; tuition res—undergrad & grad $99 per sem hr for term of 5 wks; nonres—undergrad $335 per sem hr, grad $531.90 per sem hr for term of 5 wks; 2 summer sessions.
Courses—Art Appreciation, Art Education, Art History, Design, Drawing, Fashion, Interior Design, Painting, Photography

EDINBURG

UNIVERSITY OF TEXAS PAN AMERICAN, Art Dept, 1201 W University Dr, Edinburg, TX 78539-2970. Tel 956-381-2011; Fax 210-384-5072; Elec Mail nmoyer@panam.edu; Internet Home Page Address: www.panam.edu/dept/art/; *Prof Sculpture* Richard P Hyslin; *Prof Painting* Philip S Field; *Prof Printmaking & Drawing* Wilbert R Martin; *Chmn Dept* Nancy Moyer PhD; *Asst Prof Ceramics* Charles Wissinger; *Asst Prof Painting & Printmaking* Lenard Brown; *Asst Prof Art History* Richard Phillips; *Gallery Dir* Dindy Reich; *Art Educ* James Dutremaine
Estab 1927, dept estab 1972; maintain nonprofit art gallery, Charles and Dorothy Clark Gallery, FIAB, Art Dept. UT-PA, Edinburg, TX 78539; University Gallery, CAS, Art Dept. UT-PA, Edinburg, TX 78539; pub; D & E; Scholarships; SC 43, LC 14; D 1200, E 150, non-maj 650, maj 209
Ent Req: immunization, top 50%, GED
Degrees: BA and BFA 4 yrs
Courses: Advertising Design, Aesthetics, Art Appreciation, †Art Education, Art History, †Ceramics, Collage, Computer Graphic, Design, Drawing, †Graphic Design, Illustration, †Jewelry, Lettering, †Painting, Photography, †Printmaking, †Sculpture, Silversmithing
Summer School: Dir, Nancy Moyer. Enrl 20 per class; tuition $31-$78 for term of 5 wks beginning June 2 & July 9. Courses—Art Appreciation, Art Education, Basic Design, Beginning & Advanced Painting, Ceramics, Drawing, Elementary Art Educ, Printing

EL PASO

UNIVERSITY OF TEXAS AT EL PASO, Dept of Art, 500 W University, Fox Fine Arts Bldg El Paso, TX 79902-5816. Tel 915-747-5181, 747-5000; Fax 915-747-6749; Elec Mail artdept@utep.edu; Internet Home Page Address: www.utep.edu/arts; *Head Dept* Albert Wong
Estab 1939; FT 12, PT 9; pub; D & E; Scholarships; SC 24, GC 8; 200
Degrees: BA & BFA 4 yrs, MA (Studio & Art Ed)
Courses: Art Education, Art History, Ceramics, Design, Drawing, Graphic Design, Metals, Painting, Printmaking, Sculpture
Adult Hobby Classes: Enrl 9; tuition varies from class to class. Courses—offered through Extension Division
Children's Classes: Enrl 25; tuition $25 for 6 week class. Courses—Kidzart

FORT WORTH

SAGER STUDIOS, 320 N Bailey Ave, Fort Worth, TX 76107-1003. Tel 817-626-3105; *Owner* Judy Sager
Estab 1964; pvt; D & E; D 8, E 16
Ent Req: entrance exam, portfolio preparation stressed
Degrees: BFA 4 yr
Tuition: $35 per month
Courses: Ceramics, Collage, Design, Drawing, Lettering, Mixed Media, Painting, Photography, Printmaking, Sculpture, Teacher Training
Children's Classes: Special classes for gifted students ages 10-24

TEXAS CHRISTIAN UNIVERSITY, School of Art, PO Box 298000, Fort Worth, TX 76129. Tel 817-257-7643; Fax 817-257-7399; Elec Mail art@tcu.edu; Internet Home Page Address: www.art.tcu.edu; *Dean of Fine Arts* Scott Sullivan; *Dir School of Art* Sally Packard; *Prof* Babette Bohn PhD, MFA; *Prof* Lewis Glaser, MFA; *Prof* Susan Harrington, MFA; *Prof* Mark Thistlethwaite PhD, MFA; *Prof* Luther Smith, MFA; *Prof* Lori Diel, PhD; *Prof* Frances Colpitt, PhD; *Prof* Dusty Crocker, MA; *Prof* Chris Powell, MFA; *Prof* Cameron Schoepp, MFA; *Prof* Adam Fung, MFA; *Prof* Nick Bontrager, MFA
Estab 1909; Maintain 2 nonprofit art gallery, Fort Worth Contemporary Arts 2900 W Berry St, Fort Worth TX 76129 & Mondy Gallery 2805 S. University Dr, Fort Worth TX 76129; Pvt; D & E; Scholarships, Fellowships; SC 35, LC 10, GC; maj 170, others 450
Degrees: BA, BFA & BFA Art Ed, MFA, MA
Courses: Advertising Design, †Art Education, †Art History, Ceramics, Drawing, †Graphic Design, †Painting, †Photography, †Printmaking, †Sculpture, Teacher Training
Summer School: Dir, Amanda Allison. Enrl 200; tuition $200 per sem hr. Courses-ARA Camp

TEXAS WESLEYAN UNIVERSITY, Dept of Art, 1201 Wesleyan St, Fort Worth, TX 76105-1536. Tel 817-531-4444; Fax 817-531-4814; *Dean, Theater Arts* Joe Brown; *Dean Art Dept* Kit Hall; *Dir Art Dept* Bob Pevitts
Den; D & E; Scholarships; SC, LC
Ent Req: HS dipl
Degrees: BA 4 yrs
Courses: Art Education, Ceramics, Drawing, History of Art & Architecture, Painting, Printmaking, Teacher Training

GAINESVILLE

NORTH CENTRAL TEXAS COLLEGE, Division of Communications & Fine Arts, 1525 W California St, Gainesville, TX 76240-4636. Tel 940-668-7731; Fax 940-668-6049; Internet Home Page Address: www.nctc.cc.tx.us; *Chmn* Mary Dell Heathington; *Prof* Scott Robinson
Estab 1924; pub; D & E; Scholarships; SC 14, LC 1; D 50
Ent Req: HS dipl, SAT or ACT, individual approval

Degrees: AA and AFA 2 yrs
Courses: Art Appreciation, Art History, Ceramics, Drawing, Figure Drawing, Jewelry, Painting, Sculpture
Adult Hobby Classes: Enrl 120; tuition in county $28 per cr hr, out of county $40 per cr hr, out of state $64 per cr hr; Courses—Basketry, Country Art, Drawing, Flower Arrangement, Painting, Weaving
Children's Classes: Enrl 20; tuition $15. Courses - Art

GEORGETOWN

SOUTHWESTERN UNIVERSITY, Sarofim School of Fine Art, Dept of Art & Art History, PO Box 770, Georgetown, TX 78627-0770. Tel 512-863-1504; Fax 512-863-1422; Elec Mail vainl@southwestern.edu; Internet Home Page Address: www.southwestern.edu; *Co-Chmn Prof* Thomas Howe PhD; *Prof* Patrick Veerkamp, MFA; *Prof* Mary Visser, MFA; *Co-Chmn Prof* Victoria Star Varner, MFA; *Assoc Prof* Kimberly Smith, PhD; *Prof* Patrick Hojonsky, PhD; *Prof* Allison Miller, PhD
Estab 1840, dept estab 1940; Maintains nonprofit art gallery, Sarofim School of Fine Art, Fine Art Gallery & Smith Library Center, 1001 E University Ave, Georgetown, TX 78626; art supplies may be purchased on- campus; Jonathon Faber, Mat Rebholz, Kimberly Jones, Rowena Dasch Houuhton; pvt; D; Scholarships; SC 28, LC 9; D 160, maj 46
Ent Req: HS dipl, SAT, portfolio
Degrees: BA 4 yrs, BFA 4 yrs
Courses: Architecture, Art Education, Art History, Ceramics, †Computer Imaging, Design, Drawing, Painting, Photography, Printmaking, Sculpture
Summer School: Courses—various

HILLSBORO

HILL COLLEGE, Fine Arts Dept, 112 Lamar Dr, Hillsboro, TX 76645-2799. Tel 254-582-2555, ext 224 (Visual Arts) or ext 270 (Performing Arts); Fax 254-582-5791; Elec Mail ccason@hillcollege.edu; Internet Home Page Address: www.hillcollege.edu; *Coordr Fine Arts* Phillip Lowe; *Visual Fine Arts Coordr* Christine Cason
Estab 1921; Maintain nonprofit art gallery, Regent's Gallery, Admin Bldg, 112 Lamar Dr, Hillsboro, TX; Pub; D & E; Scholarships; SC & LC
Degrees: AA, cert
Tuition: In district—$73 per sem hr; res—$90.33 per sem hr; nonres—$157 per sem hr
Courses: Art Appreciation, Art History, Costume Design & Construction, Design, Digital Imaging, Drawing, †Graphic Design, Mixed Media, Painting, Photography, Sculpture, Stage Design, Theatre Arts

HOUSTON

ART INSTITUTE OF HOUSTON, 4140 Southwest Fwy Ste 100, Houston, TX 77027-7319. Tel 713-623-2040; Fax 713-966-2700; Internet Home Page Address: www.aih.aii.edu; WATS 800-275-4244; *School of Design* John Luukkonen; *Dir Educ* Joe Orlando
Estab 1964; FT 25, PT 15; pvt; D & E; Scholarships; D 800, E 145
Ent Req: ent req HS transcripts & graduation or GED, interview
Degrees: AA
Courses: Fashion Merchandising, Graphic Design, Illustration, Interior Design, Photography
Adult Hobby Classes: Applied Photography, Interior Planning, Layout & Production

HOUSTON BAPTIST UNIVERSITY, Dept of Art, 7502 Fondren Rd, Houston, TX 77074-3298. Tel 281-649-3000; *Chmn* James Busby
Estab 1963; den; D & E; Scholarships; SC 7, LC 9; D 2500, maj 35
Ent Req: HS dipl, ent exam
Degrees: BA & BS
Courses: Art Appreciation, Art Education, Ceramics, Design, Drawing, Elementary Art with Teacher Certification, History of Art & Architecture, Painting, Printmaking, Sculpture

MUSEUM OF FINE ARTS, HOUSTON, Glassell School of Art, 5101 Montrose Blvd, Houston, TX 77005-1803; PO Box 6826, Houston, TX 77256. Tel 713-639-7500; Fax 713-639-7709; Elec Mail glassell@mfah.org; Internet Home Page Address: www.mfah.org/visit/glassell-school; *Dir* Joseph Havel; *Assoc Dir* Jennifer Cronin; *Faculty Chair & Studio School Dean* Patrick Palmer; *Admin Dean, Junior School* Pamela Perez; *Assoc Dir Core Residency Prog* Mary Leclere
Estab 1979. under the auspices of the Museum of Fine Arts, Houston; Maintains nonprofit art gallery, Laura Lee Blanton Gallery. Affiliate of Museum of Fine Arts, Houston; pvt; D & E; Fellowships; SC 34, LC 5; studio 1087, Jr 3407
Activities: Schols offered
Ent Req: ent req portfolio review, transfer students
Degrees: 4 yr cert
Tuition: Junior school: $150-300; studio school: $600 SC, $400 art history
Courses: Art History, Ceramics, †Design, Digital Media, †Drawing, Enamel, †Jewelry, Painting, Photography, †Printmaking, †Sculpture
Summer School: Jujio school $150 per course, 2984 enrollment

RICE UNIVERSITY, Visual & Dramatic Arts, 6100 Main St, MS 549 Houston, TX 77005-1892; PO Box 1892, MS 549 Houston, TX 77251-1892. Tel 713-348-4882; Fax 713-348-5910; Elec Mail arts@rice.edu; Internet Home Page Address: arts.rice.edu; *Prof Emeritus* Basilios N Poulos, MA; *Prof* Karin Broker, MFA; *Prof Emeritus* George Smith, MFA; *Prof* Geoffrey Winningham, MFA; *Assoc Prof* Brian Huberman, MFA; *Prof* John Sparagana, MFA; *Assoc Prof* Darra Keeton, MFA; *Assoc Prof* Christopher Sperandio; *Sr Admin* Gaylon Denney
Estab 1912, dept estab 1966-67; Maintains nonprofit art gallery; Rice University Art Gallery, PO Box 1892, MS-55, Houston, TX 77251-1892; Pvt; D & E; Scholarships, Fellowships; D 125, non-maj 75, maj 50, grad 2 (BFA)

Ent Req: HS dipl, CEEB, evaluations of HS counselors and teachers, interview
Degrees: BA 4 yrs, BFA 5 yrs
Tuition: $12,800 per yr, $6,400 per sem, grad $13,300 per yr, $6,650 per sem; PT $740 per yr, $370 per sem; campus res—room & board $6,000 per yr
Courses: †Art History, Design, Drawing, Film, Painting, Photography, Printmaking, Sculpture, Video
Adult Hobby Classes: Classes offered for adults & children at university

SAN JACINTO COLLEGE-NORTH, Art Dept, 5800 Uvalde, Houston, TX 77049. Tel 281-459-7119; Internet Home Page Address: www.sjcd.cc.tx.us; *Instr* Ken Luce; *Chmn Fine Arts Dept* Randy Snyder
Estab 1972; pub; D & E; Scholarships; SC 16, LC 3; D 56, E 21, non-maj 50, maj 27
Ent Req: HS dipl
Degrees: AA 2 yrs
Courses: Art Appreciation, Art History, Drawing, Painting, Sculpture
Adult Hobby Classes: Enrl 50; tuition $15 - $40 per 6-18 hrs. Courses—Calligraphy, Ceramics, Origami, Pastel Art, Photography, Stained Glass
Children's Classes: Enrl 15, tuition $30 per 6 wks. Courses—Pastel Art
Summer School: Dir, Kenneth A Luce. Enrl 10 - 25; tuition $78 - $96. Courses—vary beginning May

TEXAS SOUTHERN UNIVERSITY, College of Liberal Arts & Behavioral Sciences, 3100 Cleburne Ave, Houston, TX 77004. Tel 713-313-7337; Fax 713-313-1869; *Assoc Prof* Alvia Wardlaw; *Art Coordr & Assoc Prof* Harvey Johnson; *Chmn* Dianne Jemmson-Pollard; *Assoc Prof Dr* Sarah Trotty; *Assoc Prof* Leamon Green; *Instr* Maya Watson
Estab 1949; Maintains nonprofit art gallery: University Museum & Lobby of Biggers Center; Pub; D & E; Scholarships; SC 31, LC 12, GC 4; maj 50, other 100
Ent Req: HS dipl
Degrees: BA in Art
Courses: Art Education, Ceramics, Design, Drawing, Hot Print Making, Painting, Sculpture, Silk Screen Painting, Weaving

UNIVERSITY OF HOUSTON, Dept of Art, 4800 Calhoun Rd, Houston, TX 77004-2693. Tel 713-743-3001; Fax 713-743-2823; *Chmn* Dr W Jackson Rushing
Estab 1927; FT 29, PT 7; pub; D & E; Scholarships; D 600 maj
Ent Req: HS dipl, SAT
Degrees: BA, BFA, MFA
Courses: Art History, Ceramics, †Graphic Communications, Interior Design, Jewelry/Metals, †Paint/Drawing, Painting, Photography, †Photography/Video, Printmaking, †Sculpture, Silversmithing, Video

UNIVERSITY OF SAINT THOMAS, Fine and Performing Arts Dept, 3800 Montrose Blvd, Houston, TX 77006-4626. Tel 713-522-7911; Fax 713-942-5015; Elec Mail stewarca@stthom.edu; Internet Home Page Address: www.stthom.edu; *Dept Chmn* Claire McDonald; *Chmn Art History* Bernard Bonario, PhD; *Chmn Studio Arts* Suzanne Manns; *Asst Prof* Charles Anthony Stewart
Estab 1947; Den; D & E; Scholarships; SC 50, LC 22, GC 18; D 220, E 100, non-maj 265, maj 30, GS 25
Ent Req: HS dipl
Degrees: BA (Liberal Arts, Art History emphasis), BA (Studio Arts), BFA (Studio Arts), MLA (Art History)
Courses: Art History, †Ceramics, †Collage, †Costume Design & Construction, †Drawing, †Mixed Media, †Painting, †Photography, †Printmaking, †Sculpture, †Silversmithing, †Stage Design, †Studio Arts, †Teacher Training, †Theatre Arts

HUNTSVILLE

SAM HOUSTON STATE UNIVERSITY, Art Dept, Box 2089, Huntsville, TX 77341. Tel 936-294-1315; Fax 936-294-1251; Internet Home Page Address: www.shsu.edu; *Prof* Jimmy Barker, MFA; *Assoc Prof* Kenneth L Zonker, MFA; *Asst Prof* Patrick Lawler, MFA; *Asst Prof* Kate Borcherbing, MFA; *Dept Head* Martin Amorous, MFA; *Prof* Sharon King; *Ceramics* Matt Wilt; *Prof* Tony Shipp; *Asst Prof* Charlotte Drumm
Estab 1879, dept estab 1936; pub; D; SC 26, LC 7, GC 12; D 844, non-maj 100, maj 170, grad 15
Ent Req: HS dipl, ACT or SAT
Degrees: BA, BFA 4 yrs, MFA 2 yrs, MA 1 1/2 yrs
Courses: 2-D & 3-D Design, Advertising Design, Art History, Ceramics, Drawing, Illustration, Jewelry, Life Drawing, Painting, Printmaking, Sculpture, Studio Art
Summer School: Chmn, Jimmy H Barker. Courses—Art History, Crafts, Drawing, Watercolor, 2-D Design

HURST

TARRANT COUNTY COLLEGE NORTHEAST CAMPUS, Art Dept, 828 Harwood Rd, Northeast Campus Hurst, TX 76054-3219. Tel 817-515-6571; Fax 817-515-6256; Elec Mail martha.gordon@tccd.edu; Internet Home Page Address: www.tccd.net; *Chair & Assoc Prof* Martha Gordon, MFA; *Assoc Prof* Karmien Bowman, MA; *Assoc Prof* Anitra Blayton, MFA; *Assoc Prof & Coordr Graphic Commun* Lynn Dally, MFA; *Assoc Prof* Cynthia Hurt, MFA; *Assoc Prof* Richard (Scott) Parker, MFA; *Instr* Suzanne Perez, MA; *Assoc Prof* Andrew Stalder, MFA; *Assoc Prof Photog* Richard Doherty, MFA; *Assoc Prof Photog* Patricia Richards, MFA; *Instr Graphic Commun* Christopher Flynn, BA; *Instr Graphic Commun* Sean Foushee, BA
Estab 1967, dept estab 1968; Art supplies sold on-campus store; pub; D, E & weekends; SC 19, LC 3; D 200, E 150, non-maj 150, maj 200
Ent Req: HS dipl, GED, admis by individual approval
Degrees: AA and AAS 2 yrs
Tuition: Res—$50 per sem hr, minimum; nonres—of county $73, others $165 per sem hr with $200 minimum fee, aliens $120 per sem hr with $200 minimum fee; no campus res

Courses: Advertising Design, Art Appreciation, Art Education, Art History, Ceramics, Collage, Constructions, †Design, Drawing, Jewelry, Mixed Media, Painting, Photography, Printmaking, Sculpture
Adult Hobby Classes: Enrl 50; for 7 wks. Courses—Drawing, Oil-Acrylic, Tole Painting, Ceramics enrl 14, $200
Children's Classes: Enrl 100; 7 wks. Courses—Cartooning, Ceramics, College for Kids, Drawing, Painting
Summer School: Dir, Dr Jane Harper. Enrl 100; tuition as above for term of 6 wks beginning June. Courses—Art Appreciation

KILGORE

KILGORE COLLEGE, Visual Arts Dept, 1100 Broadway, Fine Arts Kilgore, TX 75662-3204. Tel 903-984-8531; Fax 903-983-8600; Internet Home Page Address: www.kilgore.edu; *Instr* Larry Kitchen; *Instr* O Rufus Lovett; *Chmn* John Hillier
Estab 1935; D & E; Scholarships: SC 11, LC 3; D 75, E 25, non-maj 25, maj 50
Ent Req: HS dipl
Degrees: AAAS & AA
Tuition: District res—$31 per sem hr; non-district res—$53 per sem hr; non-state res—$239 per sem hr
Courses: †Art Education, †Art History, Commercial Art, †Drawing, Painting, Photography, Printmaking, Sculpture

KINGSVILLE

TEXAS A&M UNIVERSITY-KINGSVILLE, Art Dept, 700 University Blvd, MSC 157 Kingsville, TX 78363-8202. Tel 361-593-2619; Fax 361-593-2662; Internet Home Page Address: www.tamuk.edu; *Prof* William Renfro; *Prof* Richard Scherpereel; *Prof* Maurice Schmidt; *Lectr* Peggy Wilkes; *Chmn* Santa Barraza
Estab 1925, dept estab 1930; pub; D & E; SC 21, LC 5, GC 2; D 700, non-maj 300, maj 400, art maj 150, grad 20
Ent Req: HS dipl
Degrees: BFA & BA 4 yr
Courses: Advertising Design, Art Education, Art History, Ceramics, Design, Drawing, Graphic Arts, History of Art & Architecture, Painting, Principles of Art, Printmaking, Sculpture, Teacher Training
Adult Hobby Classes: Courses offered
Summer School: Courses—full schedule

LAKE JACKSON

BRAZOSPORT COLLEGE, Art Dept, 500 College Dr, Lake Jackson, TX 77566-3199. Tel 979-230-3000; Fax 979-230-3465; Elec Mail kfunkhou@brazosport.edu; Internet Home Page Address: www.brazosport.edu; *Fine Arts Dept Chmn* Kate Funkhouser; *Instr* Eric Schnell
Estab 1968; Maintains Brazosport Col Art Gallery, 500 Col Dr, Lake Jackson; pub; D & E; Scholarships; SC 10, LC 4; D 220 Maj 30
Ent Req: HS dipl or GED
Degrees: AA 2 yrs
Courses: Art Appreciation, Art History, Ceramics, Design, Drawing, Mixed Media, Painting, Sculpture, Theatre Arts
Adult Hobby Classes: Ceramics, China Painting, Painting

LEVELLAND

SOUTH PLAINS COLLEGE, Fine Arts Dept, 1401 S College Ave, FA-133 Levelland, TX 79336-6503. Tel 806-894-9611, Ext 2261; Elec Mail dgomez@spc.cc.tx.us; Internet Home Page Address: www.spc.cc.tx.us; *Chmn* Dr Bruce Keeling; *Asst Prof* Lynette Watkins; *Asst Prof* Kara Donatelli; *Asst Prof* Leslie Lewis; *Assoc Prof* Allison Black; *Assoc Prof* Ippy Greer; *Assoc Prof* Angela Heath
Estab 1958; Maintains a non-profit art gallery; on-campus shop to purchase art supplies; FT 5, PT 2; pub; D & E; Scholarships; SC 13, LC 3; D 252, E 76, maj 52
Ent Req: HS dipl
Degrees: AA 2 yrs
Courses: 2-D Design, Art Appreciation, Art Education, Art History, Ceramics, Design, Design I, Drawing, Painting, Photography, Silversmithing, Teacher Training
Adult Hobby Classes: Enrl 62; tuition & duration vary. Courses—Drawing, Painting, Photography, Crafts
Children's Classes: Enrl 116; tuition & duration vary. Courses—Crafts, Drawing, Painting
Summer School: Dr Yancy Nunez. Enrl 66; tuition same as regular sem for 6 wk term. Courses—Art History, Life Drawing, Photography

LUBBOCK

LUBBOCK CHRISTIAN UNIVERSITY, Dept of Communication & Fine Art, 5601 19th St, Lubbock, TX 79407-2099. Tel 806-796-8800; Fax 806-796-8917; Internet Home Page Address: www.lcu.edu; *Chmn & Instr* Dr Michelle Kraft, MA; *Prof* Karen Randolph, MFA
Estab 1956; Scholarships
Degrees: BA & BSID
Tuition: $3200 annual tuition
Courses: Advertising Design, †Animation, Art Appreciation, Art Education, Art History, Design, †Digital Imaging, Drawing, Fine Arts, Graphic Arts, Graphic Design, Handicrafts, Painting, Sculpture
Summer School: Dir, K Randolph. Tuition $310 per course for 3-4 wk session. Courses—Art, Art & Children, Art History, Desktop Publishing, 2-D Design

TEXAS TECH UNIVERSITY, Dept of Art, P.O. Box 42081 Lubbock, TX 79409-2081. Tel 806-742-3825; Fax 806-742-1971; Internet Home Page Address: www.depts.ttu.edu/art; *Dir & Prof* Tina Fuentes, MFA; *Assoc Dir & Assoc Prof* Nancy Slagle, MFA; *Assoc Dir & Assoc Prof* Andrew Martin, MFA
Estab 1925, dept estab 1967; Maintain a nonprofit art gallery Landmark Arts & art library Visual Resource Center; on-campus shop for purchase of art supplies; pub; D & E; Scholarships; SC 60 undergrad, 20 grad, LC 20 undergrad, 15 grad; D 1400, non-maj 950, maj 400, grad 50
Ent Req: HS dipl, SAT or ACT test
Degrees: BFA & BA(Art History), MAE 36 hrs, MFA 60 hrs minimum, PhD 54 hrs beyond MA minimum
Tuition: Variable for res and nonres; campus residence available
Courses: Advertising Design, Aesthetics, Art Appreciation, †Art Education, †Art History, Ceramics, Computer-Aided Design, Design, †Design Communication, Digital Imaging, Drawing, Graphic Design, Illustration, Installation, Intermedia, Jewelry, Lettering, Mixed Media, Painting, Photography, Printmaking, Sculpture, Silversmithing, †Studio Art, Teacher Training, Weaving
Adult Hobby Classes: Computer-Aided Design, Photography, Studio Art
Children's Classes: Art Project for talented high school students, Artery; classes in art for elementary & middle school students
Summer School: Dir, Future Akins-Tillett, Assoc Prof. Courses—Art Education, Ceramics, Drawing, Glassblowing, Jewelry & Metalsmithing, Painting, Papermaking, Photography, Printmaking, Sculpture, Textile Design, Weaving

MESQUITE

EASTFIELD COLLEGE, Humanities Division, Art Dept, 3737 Motley Dr, Mesquite, TX 75150-2099. Tel 972-860-7100; Internet Home Page Address: www.efc.dccd.edu; *Dean* Rachel Wolf
Degrees: AA
Tuition: $79 per 3 cr hr
Courses: Art Appreciation, Art History, Ceramics, Design, Drawing, Jewelry, Painting, Sculpture

MIDLAND

MIDLAND COLLEGE, Art Dept, 3600 N Garfield, Midland, TX 79705. Tel 432-685-4624 (fine arts & communs div); Fax 432-685-4769; Elec Mail kmoss@midland.edu; Internet Home Page Address: www.midland.edu; *Instr* Carol Bailey, MA; *Prof* Kent Moss, MFA; *Dean* William Feeler; *Instr* Susan Randall; *Instr* Michael Hubbard, MFA; *Instr* Dagan Sherman, MFA
Estab 1972; Non-profit art gallery & Library; schols open to financial aid applicants; on-campus art supplies shop; pub; D & E; Scholarships; SC 15, LC 3; D 80, E 75, non-maj 125, maj 25
Ent Req: HS dipl
Degrees: AA and AAA 2 yrs
Tuition: Res—undergrad $327 per 12 hrs plus $40 fee; nonres—undergrad $351 per 12 hrs plus $40 fee; no campus res
Courses: †Art Appreciation, Art History, †Ceramics, Collage, †Design, Drawing, †Graphic Design, Illustration, †Jewelry, Mixed Media, †Painting, †Photography, †Printmaking, †Sculpture, Teacher Training
Adult Hobby Classes: Ceramics, Painting, Photography
Children's Classes: Kid's College
Summer School: Dir, William Feeler, Dean; Enrl 40. Courses—varied

NACOGDOCHES

STEPHEN F AUSTIN STATE UNIVERSITY, Art Dept, PO Box 13001, Nacogdoches, TX 75962-0001. Tel 409-468-4804, 2011; Fax 409-468-4041; Internet Home Page Address: www.sfasu.edu; *Chmn* Jon D Wink, MFA
Estab 1923; pub; D & E; Scholarships; SC 28, LC 11, GC 11; D 461, non-maj 150, maj 200, grad 20
Ent Req: HS dipl, ACT score 18
Degrees: BA & BFA 4 yrs, MFA 2 yrs, MA 1 yr
Courses: †Advertising Design, Art Appreciation, †Art Education, Art History, †Ceramics, Cinematography, Design, †Drawing, Film, Illustration, †Interior Design, †Jewelry, †Painting, †Photography, †Printmaking, †Sculpture, Silversmithing, Stage Design, Teacher Training, Theatre Arts, Video
Summer School: Dir, Jon D Wink. Beginning & advanced art classes. Courses—Varies summer to summer

ODESSA

UNIVERSITY OF TEXAS OF PERMIAN BASIN, Dept of Art, 4901 E University Blvd, Odessa, TX 79762-0001. Tel 432-552-2286; Fax 432-552-3285; Elec Mail price_p@utpb.edu; Internet Home Page Address: utpb.edu; *Chmn* Pam Price, MFA; *Assoc Prof* Chris Stanley, MFA; *Asst Prof* Marianne Berger Woods, PhD; *Asst Prof* David Poindexter, MFA; *Lectr* Dan Askew, MFA
Estab 1972; Maintain nonprofit art gallery, Nancy Fyfe Cardozier Art Gallery, Art Dept, UTPB, 4901 E. University, Odessa, TX 79762; art supplies available on-campus; pub; D & E; Scholarships; SC 48, LC 13; non-maj 10, maj 83
Degrees: BA, BFA
Tuition: Campus residency available
Courses: Art Education, Ceramics, Commercial Art, Drawing, Graphic Design, Painting, Photography, Printmaking, Sculpture
Summer School: Courses—varied

PARIS

PARIS JUNIOR COLLEGE, Visual Art Dept, 2400 Clarksville St, Paris, TX 75460-6298. Tel 903-784-0438, 800-441-1398 (TX), 800-232-5804 (US); Fax 903-784-9370; Elec Mail smoore@parisjc.edu; Internet Home Page Address: www.parisjc.edu; *Instr & Exhib Dir* Susan Moore, MFA

Estab 1924; Maintain nonprofit art gallery, art dept-Foyer Gallery, Attn Susan Moore, Paris Junior College, 2400 Clarksville, Paris, TX 75460; pub; D & E; Scholarships; SC 11, LC 2; D 30-60, E 50-70, non-maj 60-65, maj 15-20
Ent Req: none
Degrees: AA & AS in Art 2 yrs
Courses: Art Appreciation, Art History, †Art Metals (General Art Preparatory Program), Ceramics, Design, Digital Art, Drawing, Life Drawing, Painting, Photography, Sculpture
Adult Hobby Classes: Enrl 20. Courses—Art Appreciation, Art Metals, Ceramics, Design, Drawing, Graphic Art, Painting, Photography, Sculpture
Summer School: Dir, Cathie Tyler. 2-5 wk sessions June-Aug. Courses—Art Appreciation

PASADENA

SAN JACINTO JUNIOR COLLEGE, Division of Fine Arts, 8060 Spencer Hwy, Pasadena, TX 77501-5998. Tel 281-476-1501; Fax 281-478-2711; Internet Home Page Address: www.sjcd.cc.tx.us; *Acting Div Chmn & Dean Fine Arts* Dr Jerry Ivins
Estab 1961; pub; D & E; SC 5, LC 1; D 230, E 45, non-maj 120, maj 155
Ent Req: HS dipl, GED or individual approval
Degrees: AA and AS 2 yrs
Courses: Advertising Art, Advertising Design, Art Appreciation, Art History, Ceramics, Commercial Art, Design, Drawing, Free Illustration, Lettering, Painting, Photography, Sculpture
Summer School: Courses—Design, Painting Workshop

PLAINVIEW

WAYLAND BAPTIST UNIVERSITY, Dept of Art, School of Fine Art, School of Fine Arts, Art Dept, Plainview, TX 79072; 1900 West Seventh, WBU #249 Plainview, TX 79072-6900. Tel 806-291-1083; Fax 806-291-1980; Elec Mail kellerc@wbu.edu; Internet Home Page Address: www.wbu.edu; *Prof* Candace Keller, PhD; *Asst Prof* Mark Hilliard, MFA; *Prof* Harold Temple, PhD; *Asst Prof* Trey Shirley
Estab 1908; Maintains nonprofit art gallery; Abraham Art Gallery 1900 W 7th WBU 249 Plainview Tx 79072; Maintains art/architecture libr, Learning Resource Center 1900 W 7th Plainview Tx 79072. Art supplies may be purchased on campus; 3; Pvt & Den; D & E; Scholarships; SC 15, LC 2; D 150, E 50, non-maj 160, maj 45, grad 5
Ent Req: HS dipl, ent exam
Degrees: BA and BS 4 yrs
Tuition: $395 per sem hr
Courses: Advertising Design, †Art Appreciation, Art Education, Art History, Ceramics, Commercial Art, †Costume Design & Construction, Design, †Drawing, Film, Graphic Arts, †Graphic Design, †History of Art & Architecture, Painting, Photography, Printmaking, Sculpture, †Silversmithing, Stage Design, †Theatre Arts, Watercolor Studio
Adult Hobby Classes: Enrl 90 - 100; 16 wk term. Courses—Art Appreciation, Ceramics, Design, Drawing, Painting, Sculpture, Watercolor
Children's Classes: Enrl 25-35; tuition $60 for 2 wk term. Courses offered through Academy of fine Art on Campus
Summer School: Art Cur, Candace Keller. Enrl 30-40; 3 wk term. Courses—Ceramics, Teacher Art Education, Watercolor

ROCKPORT

SIMON MICHAEL SCHOOL OF FINE ARTS, 510 E King St, Rockport, TX 78382-3951; PO Box 1283, Rockport, TX 78381-1283. Tel 361-729-6233; *Head Dept* Simon Michael
Estab 1947; FT 1; pvt; professionals & intermediates
Courses: Drawing, Landscape Architecture, Mixed Media, Painting, Sculpture
Summer School: Enrl varies; tuition varies for each 1 wk workshop.
Courses—Travel Art Workshop in USA and Europe

SAN ANGELO

ANGELO STATE UNIVERSITY, Art & Music Dept, 2601 W Ave N San Angelo, TX 76909. Tel 325-942-2085; Fax 325-942-2152; Elec Mail david.scott@angelo.edu; Internet Home Page Address: www.angelo.edu/; *Interim Head* David Scott, PhD
Estab 1963, dept estab 1976; Scholarships open to art majors for one year annually; for further info contact David Scott, Dept Head; pub; D & E; Scholarships; SC 20, LC 9; D 400 (art), E 50, non-maj 320, maj 80
Ent Req: HS dipl
Degrees: BA(Art) &Teaching Certification, BFA
Courses: Art Education, Art History, Ceramics, Creative Design, Drawing, Etchings, †Graphic Illustration, Greek & Roman Art, History of Contemporary Art, History of Italian Renaissance, Intaglio Processes, Introduction to Art, Jewelry, Painting, Primary Art Theory, †Printmaking, †Sculpture
Summer School: Courses—Art Education, Art History, Ceramics, Introduction to Art, Sculpture, Studio Courses incl Design & Drawing

SAN ANTONIO

OUR LADY OF THE LAKE UNIVERSITY, Dept of Art, 411 SW 24 St, San Antonio, TX 78207-4689. Tel 210-434-6711, Ext 435; Internet Home Page Address: www.ollusa.edu/; *Chmn* Alfredo Cruz; *Assoc Prof* Sr Jule Adele Espey PhD; *Assoc Prof* Jody Cariolano; *Dean* Sr Isabel Ball PhD
Estab 1911, dept estab 1920; FT 2, PT 1; den; D & E; Scholarships; SC 12, LC 3; non-maj 62, maj 8

Ent Req: HS dipl, completion of GED tests, 35 on each test or average of 45 on tests
Degrees: BA(Art)
Courses: Art Appreciation, Art Education, Art History, Ceramics, Computer Design, Design, Drawing, Graphic Arts, Painting, Photography, Printmaking, Sculpture
Adult Hobby Classes: Courses offered

SAINT MARY'S UNIVERSITY, Dept of Fine Arts, One Camino Santa Maria, San Antonio, TX 78228. Tel 210-436-3797, 436-3011; *Chmn* Sharon McMahon
Estab 1852; FT 8, PT 12; pvt; D & E; SC 10, LC 20; D 60, maj 58
Ent Req: HS dipl or GED, ent exam
Degrees: BA 4-5 yrs
Tuition: Res $4548, incl rm & board; $365 per cr hr
Courses: 3-D Design, Art Education, Drawing, Graphic Design, History of Art & Architecture, Painting, Photography, Printmaking, Sculpture, Teacher Training, Theatre Arts
Adult Hobby Classes: Enrl 75-100; tuition $25. Courses—vary
Summer School: Courses—vary

SAN ANTONIO COLLEGE, Visual Arts & Technology, 1300 San Pedro Ave, San Antonio, TX 78212-4299. Tel 210-733-2894, 733-2000; Fax 210-733-2338; Internet Home Page Address: www.accd.edu/sac; *Chmn* Richard Arredondo; *Fine Arts Program Dir* Mark Pritchett
Estab 1955; FT 17, PT 20; pub; D & E; SC 75, LC 4; D 1000-1300, E 250-450
Ent Req: Ent req HS dipl, GED, TASP, ent exam
Degrees: AA & AS 2 yrs
Courses: Art Appreciation, Art History, Art Metals, Ceramics, Design, Drawing, Electronic Graphics, †Graphic Arts, Graphic Design, Illustration, Painting, Photography, Printmaking, Sculpture
Summer School: Dir, Richard Arredondo. Enrl 500; Courses—Same as for regular school yr

TRINITY UNIVERSITY, Dept of Art, 715 Stadium Dr, San Antonio, TX 78212-7201. Tel 210-736-7216, 736-7011; Internet Home Page Address: www.trinity.edu; *Chmn & Prof* Kate Ritson, MFA; *Asst Prof* Elizabeth Ward, MFA
Estab 1869; pvt; D & E; SC 39, LC 20; D 144, E 30, non-maj 50, maj 90
Ent Req: HS dipl, CEEB, SAT, 3 achievement tests
Degrees: BA 4 yrs
Courses: Art Education, Drawing, Graphic Arts, Painting, Photography, Printmaking, Sculpture, †Studio Art
Adult Hobby Classes: Courses offered by Department of Continuing Educ
Summer School: Dir, Dept of Continuing Educ. Courses vary

UNIVERSITY OF TEXAS AT SAN ANTONIO, Dept of Art & Art History, One USTA Cir, San Antonio, TX 78249-0642. Tel 210-458-4352; Fax 210-458-4356; *Prof Emeritus* James Broderick, MA; *Prof* Ronald Binks, MFA; *Prof Emeritus* Charles Field, MFA; *Prof* Judith Sobre PhD; *Prof* Ken Little, MFA; *Dept Chair* Gregory Elliott, MFA; *Prof* Dennis Olsen, MA; *Prof* Constance Lowe, MFA; *Assoc Prof* Richard Armendariz; *Assoc Prof* Ovidio Giberga; *Prof* Kent Rush, MFA; *Assoc Prof* Scott Sherer, PhD; *Assoc Prof* Libby Rowe, MFA; *Asst Prof* Teresa Eckmann, PhD; *Asst Prof* Juliet Wiersema, PhD; *Asst Prof* Julie Johnson, PhD; *Asst Prof* Christine Blizard; *Asst Prof* Mark Mccoin
Estab 1974; Maintain non-profit art gallelry, main gallery same location; UTSA Satellite space, 1518 S Alamo St, San Antonio TX 78204; 14; Pub; D & E; Scholarships; SC 31, LC 25, GC 17; non-maj 180, maj 500, grad 46
Ent Req: HS dipl, ACT, grad
Degrees: BFA 4 yrs, MFA 2 yrs, MA 1 yr
Courses: Art Appreciation, Art History, Ceramics, Conceptual Art, Design, Drawing, History of Art & Architecture, New Media/Video, Painting, Photography, Printmaking, Sculpture
Summer School: Chmn Gregory Elliott - Tuition $264 per sem. Courses—Art History, Ceramics, Drawing, Painting, Photography, Printmaking, Sculpture

UNIVERSITY OF THE INCARNATE WORD, Art Dept, 4301 Broadway, San Antonio, TX 78209. Tel 210-829-6000; Internet Home Page Address: www.uiw.edu; *Prof* E Stoker, MA; *Lectr* Don Ewers, MA; *Chmn* Kathy Vargas, MFA; *Asst Prof* Miguel Cortinas, MFA; *Asst Prof* John Dawes, MFA
Estab 1881, dept estab 1948; Maintains nonprofit gallery, Semmes Gallery, 4301 Broadway, San Antonio, TX 78209; Den; D & E; Scholarships; SC 14, LC 9; D 195, non-maj 120, maj 30
Ent Req: HS dipl, ent exam
Degrees: BA 4 yrs
Courses: Advertising Design, Art Education, Art History, Ceramics, Costume Design & Construction, Design, Drawing, Fashion Arts, Graphic Arts, Graphic Design, Museum Staff Training, Painting, Photography, Printmaking, Sculpture, Stage Design, Textile Design, Theatre Arts, Weaving

SAN MARCOS

TEXAS STATE UNIVERSITY - SAN MARCOS, (Southwest Texas State University) Dept of Art and Design, 601 University Dr, San Marcos, TX 78666-4684. Tel 512-245-2611; Fax 512-245-7969; Elec Mail en04@tx.state.edu; Internet Home Page Address: www.swt.edu; *Chmn* Dr Erik Nielsen; *Prof* Mark Todd; *Prof* Jean Laman, MFA; *Prof* Neal Wilson; *Prof* Roger Bruce Colombik; *Prof* David Shields; *Prof* Beverley Penn; *Prof* Michel Conroy; *Prof* Brian Row; *Prof* Eric Weller; *Prof* Randal Reid; *Prof* William Meek; *Assoc Prof* Jeff Davis; *Assoc Prof* Jeff Dell; *Assoc Prof* James Housefield; *Assoc Prof* Holly Shields; *Assoc Prof* Tom Beono; *Asst Prof* Ivanrele Blanco; *Asst Prof* Erica Duguane; *Asst Prof* Teri Evans Palmer; *Asst Prof* Michelle Hays; *Asst Prof* Alan Pizer
Estab 1903, dept estab 1916; Maintains a nonprofit art gallery; pub; D & E; Scholarships; SC 11, LC 7, GC 6; D 1600, E 150, non-maj 1350, maj 1100
Ent Req: HS dipl, ACT, SAT
Degrees: BFA (Commun Design & Studio), BFA Art Ed all-level & BA(Art History), BA 4 yr, MFA Commun Design

Courses: Advertising Design, Art Appreciation, Art Education, Art History, Communication Design, Computer Graphics, Design, Digital Images, Drawing, Fibers, Graphic Arts, Graphic Design, Illustration, Metals, Multi-Media, Painting, Photography, Printmaking, Sculpture, Teacher Training, Watercolor
Children's Classes: summers only; one week; $15
Summer School: Chmn, Erik Nielson. Two 6 week terms

SEGUIN

TEXAS LUTHERAN UNIVERSITY, Dept of Visual Arts, 1000 W Court St, Seguin, TX 78155-9996. Tel 830-372-8000, Ext 6017; Internet Home Page Address: www.tlu.edu; *Chmn* J Nellermoe, MA; *Assoc Prof* T Paul Hernandez; *Asst Prof* Landa King
Estab 1923; FT 2; D; SC 18, LC 3; 1000, maj 10
Ent Req: HS dipl
Degrees: BA(Art) 4 yrs
Courses: Advertising Design, Art Appreciation, Art Concepts, Art Education, Art History, Ceramics, Design, Drawing, Independent Study, Painting, Printmaking, Sculpture
Adult Hobby Classes: Enrl 12; tuition $72 for 6 wk term. Courses—Art Appreciation, Sketching
Summer School: Instr, John Nellermoe. Enrl 12; tuition $75 for 6 wk term. Courses—Ceramics, Painting

SHERMAN

AUSTIN COLLEGE, Art Dept, 900 N Grande, Ste 61587, Sherman, TX 75090-4440. Tel 903-813-2000; Elec Mail mmonroe@austinc.edu; Internet Home Page Address: www.austinc.edu/; *Prof* Mark Smith; *Chmn* Tim Tracz; *Prof* Mark Monroe, MFA; *Prof* Jeffrey Fontana; *Studio Mgr* Joseph Allison
Estab 1848; Maintains a nonprofit art gallery, Ida Green Gallery, Austin College, 900 N Grand Ave Sherman, TX 75090-4440; pvt; D; Scholarships; SC 9, LC 5, GC 8; D 350, maj 55, grad 2
Ent Req: ent exam plus acceptance by admis comt
Degrees: BA 4 yrs, MA 5 yrs
Courses: Art History, Ceramics, Drawing, History of Art & Architecture, Painting, Photography, Printmaking, Sculpture, Silversmithing, Theatre Arts, Video

TEMPLE

TEMPLE COLLEGE, Art Dept, 2600 S First St, Temple, TX 76504. Tel 254-298-8282; Internet Home Page Address: www.templejc.edu; *Chmn* Michael Donahue, MFA
Estab 1926; 43; pub; D & E; Scholarships; SC 4, LC 2; D 100, E 15, non-maj 85, maj 15
Ent Req: HS dipl, ACT or SAT
Degrees: AA 2 yrs
Courses: Art Appreciation, Art History, Ceramics, Communications, Design, Drawing, Figure Drawing, Painting, Printmaking, Sculpture
Adult Hobby Classes: Enrl 15 per class; tuition $19 per 8 sessions. Courses—Arts & Crafts, Calligraphy, Drawing

TEXARKANA

TEXARKANA COLLEGE, Art Dept, 2500 N Robison Rd, Texarkana, TX 75599-0001. Tel 903-838-4541; Fax 903-832-5030; *Prof* Valerie Owens
Estab 1927; D & E; Scholarships
Ent Req: HS dipl
Tuition: District res—$375 for 15 cr hrs; out of district res—$570 for 15 cr hrs
Courses: Art Appreciation, Ceramics, Drawing, Painting, Sculpture, Weaving
Summer School: Enrl 20; tuition $300. Courses—Drawing & Ceramics

TYLER

TYLER JUNIOR COLLEGE, Art Program, PO Box 9020, Tyler, TX 75711-9020. Tel 903-510-2200, 510-2234; Internet Home Page Address: www.tyler.cc.tx.us; Internet Home Page Address: www.tjc.edu; *Dept Dir* Chris Stewart; *Art Instr* CJ Cavanaugh; *Art Instr* Barbara Holland; *Art Instr* Derrick White
Estab 1925; Maintain nonprofit art gallery; art supplies available on-campus; Pub; D & E; Scholarships; SC 13, LC 3; 600+
Degrees: AA
Tuition: Res—undergrad $578 per yr
Courses: Art Appreciation, Art Education, Art History, Ceramics, Design, Drawing, Painting, Sculpture, Weaving
Adult Hobby Classes: Courses—Offered
Children's Classes: Courses—Offered for ages 5-8 & 9-12
Summer School: Courses—Offered

UNIVERSITY OF TEXAS AT TYLER, Department of Art, School of Visual & Performing Arts, 3900 University Blvd, Tyler, TX 75799-0001. Tel 903-566-7250; Fax 903-566-7062; Internet Home Page Address: uttyler.edu/arts/studioarts; *Assoc Prof & Chmn* Gary C Hatcher, MFA; *Prof* James R Pace, MFA; *Asst Prof* Jill Blondin, PhD; *Asst Prof* Alexis Serio; *Asst Prof* Dewane Hughes; *Asst Prof* Dr Barbara Airulla; *Asst Prof* Sally Campbell
Estab 1973; Maintain nonprofit art gallery, The Meadowlands Gallery, 3900 University Blvd., Tyler, TX 75799; pub; D & E; Scholarships; SC 32, LC 18, GC 12
Ent Req: AA degree or 60 hrs of college study
Degrees: BA, BFA, MAT, MAIS, MFA
Tuition: Res—$432 per sem; nonres—$2988 per sem

Courses: Aesthetics, †Art Education, †Art History, Ceramics, Drawing, Graphic Arts, Graphic Design, History of Art & Architecture, Interior Design, Mixed Media, Painting, Photography, Printmaking, Sculpture, †Silversmithing, †Studio Art, Teacher Training
Summer School: Dir, Gary C. Hatcher, Courses—vary

VICTORIA

VICTORIA COLLEGE, Fine Arts Dept, 2200 E Red River, Victoria, TX 77901. Tel 361-573-3291; Fax 361-572-3850; Internet Home Page Address: www.vc.cc.tx.us/; *Prof* Fred Spaulding; *Head Dept* Dr Marylynn Fletcher
Estab 1925; pub; D & E; SC 9, LC 3; D 100, E 40, non-maj 40, maj 100
Ent Req: HS dipl
Degrees: AA
Courses: Art Appreciation, Art Education, Art Fundamentals, Art History, Ceramics, Design, Drafting, Drawing, Graphic Arts, Graphic Design, †Occupational Therapy, Painting, Sculpture, Stage Design, †Teacher Training, Theatre Arts
Summer School: Courses—as above

WACO

BAYLOR UNIVERSITY - COLLEGE OF ARTS AND SCIENCES, Dept of Art, Waco, TX 76798-7263; 1 Bear Pl, #97344 Waco, TX 76798-7344. Tel 254-710-1867; Fax 254-710-1566; Elec Mail Arts_Sciences_Webmaster@baylor.edu; Internet Home Page Address: www.baylor.edu; *Chmn* Mark W Anderson, MFA; *Prof & Artist in Res* Karl Umlauf, MFA; *Prof* Berry J Klingman, MFA; *Prof & Ceramic in Res* Paul A McCoy, MFA; *Prof* Heidi J Hornik PhD, MA; *Assoc Prof* Robbie Barber, MFA; *Prof* Mary Ruth Smith PhD, MFA; *Assoc Prof* Julia Hitchcock, MFA; *Sr Lectr* Karen Pope, PhD; *Asst Prof* Virginia Green, MFA; *Asst Prof* Susan Mullally, MFA; *Lectr* Leah Force, MFA; *Asst Prof* Mack Gingles; *Asst Prof* Nathan Elkins; *Asst Prof* Benny Fountain
Estab 1845, dept estab 1870; Maintains non-profic art gallery: Martin Mus. 1401 S Univ Parks Dr, Waco TX 78706, Karin Gilliam, Dir; maintains Crouch Fine Arts Libr; on-campus art supplies shop; den; D & E; Scholarships; SC 65, LC 24, GC 12; D 1600, E60, non-maj 1300, maj 200
Ent Req: HS dipl, ent exam, SAT/ACT tests
Degrees: BA & BFA(Studio) 4 yrs
Courses: 2-D Design, 3-D Design, †Art History, †Ceramics, Drawing, †Fibers, †Graphic Design, †Painting, †Photography, †Printmaking, †Sculpture
Summer School: Prof, Mark W Anderson

MCLENNAN COMMUNITY COLLEGE, Visual Arts Dept, 1400 College Dr, Waco, TX 76708-1499. Tel 254-299-8000, 299-8791 (art dept); Fax 254-299-8778; Elec Mail amurad@mclennan.edu; Internet Home Page Address: www.mclennan.edu; *Dir* Donald C Blamos; *Coordr* Andrew Murad
Estab 1965; Maintain nonprofit art gallery; 3 located on campus; Pub; D & E; SC 8, LC 3; D 35, non-maj 20, maj 40
Ent Req: HS dipl
Degrees: AA 2 yrs
Tuition: Res—$34 per sem hr; nonres—$39 per sem hr, out-of-state & international $94; no campus res
Courses: Art Appreciation, Art History, Ceramics, Design, Design Communication, Drafting, Oil Painting, Painting, Photography, Problems in Contemporary Art, Sculpture, Watercolor
Adult Hobby Classes: Tuition depends on the class. Courses—Ceramics, Drawing, Jewelry, Painting, Sculpture, Stained Glass
Summer School: Dir, Andrew Murad. Tuition $55. Courses—Design, Drawing, Watercolor, Art Appreciation

WEATHERFORD

WEATHERFORD COLLEGE, Dept of Speech Fine Arts, 225 College Park Dr, Weatherford, TX 76086-5699. Tel 817-594-5471, Ext 211; Elec Mail endy@wc.edu; Internet Home Page Address: www.wc.edu/; *Head Visual Arts & Instr* Myrlan Coleman; *Head Speech & Fine Arts* Cal Lewiston; *Instr* Daniel Birdsong; *Instr* Cassie Hannah
Estab 1856, dept estab 1959; Maintains nonprofit art gallery on campus; pub; D & E ; Scholarships; SC 12, LC 4; D 58, non-maj 30, maj 16, others 12
Ent Req: HS dipl
Degrees: AA
Courses: Art Appreciation, Art History, Design, Drawing, Intermedia, Mixed Media, Painting, Photography
Summer School: Dir Cal Lewiston.

WHARTON

WHARTON COUNTY JUNIOR COLLEGE, Art Dept, 911 Boling Hwy, Wharton, TX 77488. Tel 979-532-4560; Internet Home Page Address: www.wcjc.cc.tx.us
Maintain nonprofit art gallery; pub; D & E; Scholarships; SC 8, LC 2; D 140, E 100
Ent Req: HS dipl, GED
Degrees: 2 yrs
Courses: Art Education, Art Fundamentals, Art History, Calligraphy, Ceramics, Design, Drawing, History of Art & Architecture, Painting, Sculpture, Teacher Training
Summer School: Dir Jess Coleman. Enrl 36; 6 wk term. Courses—Foundation of Art, Drawing

WICHITA FALLS

MIDWESTERN STATE UNIVERSITY, Lamar D. Fain College of Fine Arts, 3410 Taft Blvd, Dept of Art Wichita Falls, TX 76308-2036. Tel 940-397-4264; Fax 940-397-4369; Elec Mail art@mwsu.edu; Internet Home Page Address: finearts.mwsu.edu/art/; *Chair* Nancy Steele-Hamme; *Dean College of Fine Arts* Dr Ron Fischli
Estab 1926; Maintain a nonprofit art gallery, Midwestern State Univ Art Gallery, 3140 Taft Blvd, Wichita Falls, TX 76308; Pub; D & E; Scholarships
Ent Req: HS dipl, ACT, SAT
Degrees: BA, BFA & BFA with Teacher Cert 4 yrs
Tuition: refer to website
Courses: Art Appreciation, Art Education, Art History, †Ceramics, †Commercial Art, Design, Drawing, †Metals, †Painting, †Photography, †Printmaking, †Sculpture, †Teacher Training
Summer School: Dir, Dr. Nancy Steele-Hamme. Courses—Commercial Art

UTAH

CEDAR CITY

SOUTHERN UTAH STATE UNIVERSITY, Dept of Art, 351 W Center, Cedar City, UT 84720. Tel 435-586-7962, 586-5426; Elec Mail felstead@suu.edu; Internet Home Page Address: www.suu.edu; *Chmn* Brian P Hoover
Estab 1897; FT 4, PT 2; pub; D & E; Scholarships; SC 29, LC 6; D 300, E 80, maj 60, minors 45
Ent Req: HS dipl ent exam
Degrees: BA and BS 4 yrs
Courses: Ceramics, Commercial Art, Drawing, Graphic Arts, Graphic Design, History of Art & Architecture, Illustration, Painting, Sculpture, Teacher Training
Summer School: Dir, Arlene Braithwaite. Tuition same as regular school. Courses—Drawing, Ceramics, Art Methods for Elementary School, Art Appreciation

EPHRAIM

SNOW COLLEGE, Art Dept, 150 E College Ave, Ephraim, UT 84627. Tel 435-283-7039, 283,7414; Internet Home Page Address: www.snow.edu; *Chmn* Carl Purcell
Estab 1888; Pub; D&E; Scholarships
Ent Req: HS dipl
Degrees: AA, AAS
Tuition: Res—$707 per yr; nonres— $2942 per yr
Courses: Art Appreciation, Ceramics, Design, Drawing, Interior Design, Jewelry, Painting, Photography, Printmaking, Sculpture

LOGAN

UTAH STATE UNIVERSITY, Dept of Landscape Architecture Environmental Planning, College of Humanities, Arts & Social Science, Logan, UT 84322-4005. Tel 435-797-0500; Fax 435-797-0503; Elec Mail cjohnson@hass.usu.edu; Internet Home Page Address: www.usu.edu/~laep/; *Acting Head* Craig Johnson
FT 6, PT 3
Degrees: BA, BLA & MLA 4 yr
Tuition: Res—$309 per cr hr; nonres—$736 per cr hr
Courses: †Landscape Architecture, †Town & Regional Planning
—Dept of Art, UMC 4000, Logan, UT 84322. Tel 435-797-3460 3; Fax 435-797-3412; *Prof* Glen Edwards; *Prof* Craig Law; *Prof* Jon Anderson; *Prof* Adrian Van Suchtelen; *Assoc Prof* Thomas Toone; *Assoc Prof* John Neely; *Assoc Prof* Marion Hyde; *Assoc Prof* Christopher Terry; *Assoc Prof* Sara Northerner; *Assoc Prof* Greg Schulte; *Assoc Prof* Janet Shapero; *Asst Prof* Jane Catlin; *Asst Prof* Lauren Schiller; *Asst Prof* Alan Hashimoto; *Asst Prof* Julie Johnson; *Asst Prof* Koichi Yamamoto
Estab 1890; D & E; D 500, maj 500, grad 37
Ent Req: HS dipl, HS transcript, ACT
Degrees: BA, BS & BFA 4 yr, MA 2 yr, MFA 3 yr
Tuition: Res—undergrad $1060, grad $935; nonres—undergrad $3182, grad $2751
Courses: †Art Education, †Art History, †Ceramics, †Drawing, †Graphic Arts, †Illustration, †Painting, †Photography, †Printmaking, †Sculpture
Summer School: Head, Prof Craig Shaw. 4 wk session. Courses—Basic Drawing, Ceramics, Exploring Art, Individual Projects, Photography, 3-D Design, 2-D Design, Various Summer Workshops

OGDEN

WEBER STATE UNIVERSITY, Dept of Visual Arts, 2001 University Circle, Ogden, UT 84408-2001. Tel 801-626-6762, 6000; Fax 801-626-6976; Internet Home Page Address: www.weber.edu/; *Chair & Assoc Prof* Matthew Choberka, MFA; *Prof* Mark Biddle, MFA; *Prof* Susan Makov, MFA; *Assoc Prof* Angelika Pagel PhD, MFA; *Asst Prof* Naseem Banerji PhD, MFA; *Asst Prof* Stephen Wolochowicz, MFA; *Asst Prof* Liese Zahabl, MFA; *Asst Prof* Jason Manley, MFA; *Prof* Kathleen (K) Stevenson, MFA; *Asst Prof* Larry Clarkson, MFA; *Asst Prof* Joshua Winegar, MFA; *Asst Prof* Paul Crow, MFA
Estab 1933, dept estab 1937; Maintains non-profit art gallery, Mary Elizabeth Dee Shaw Gallery, 2001 University Cr, Katie Lee, Dir; on-campus art supplies shop; pub; D & E; Scholarships; SC 66, LC 17; D 2464, E 694, non-maj 700, maj 200
Ent Req: HS dipl, ACT
Degrees: BA, BFA, 4 yr

Courses: †2-D, †3-D, Advertising Design, Art Appreciation, Art Education, Art History, Ceramics, Commercial Art, Conceptual Art, Design, Drawing, Graphic Arts, History of Art & Architecture, Illustration, Painting, Photography, Printmaking, †Sculpture, Silversmithing, Textile Design, Video, Weaving

PROVO

BRIGHAM YOUNG UNIVERSITY, Dept of Visual Arts, 1 BYU, Provo, UT 84602-0002. Tel 801-422-4266; Fax 801-422-0695; Elec Mail aliesha_cook@byu.edu; Internet Home Page Address: cfac.byu.edu/va/; *Chmn* John Telford; *Assoc Chmn* Gary Barton
Estab 1875, dept estab 1893; Gallery 303, F-303 HFAC, Provo, UT 84602; FT 33, PT 50; den; D & E; Scholarships; SC 50, LC 40, Grad 15; E 1975, maj 908, pre-maj 335, grad 45
Ent Req: HS dipl or ACT
Degrees: BA and BFA 4 yrs, MFA 2 yrs and MA 1 1/2 yrs
Courses: †Art Education, †Art History, Calligraphy, †Ceramics, †Drawing, Graphic Design, Illustration, †Painting, Photography, †Printmaking, †Sculpture, †Teacher Training
Summer School: Courses same as regular session

SAINT GEORGE

DIXIE COLLEGE, Art Dept, 225 S 700 E, Saint George, UT 84770-3875. Tel 435-652-7700, 652-7792; Elec Mail hanson@dixie.edu; Internet Home Page Address: www.dixie.edu; *Prof* Glen Blakely; *Asst Prof* Del Parson; *Chmn* Brent Hanson; *Asst Prof* Dennis Martinez
Estab 1911; pub; D & E; Scholarships; SC 24, LC 7, GC 1; D 400, maj 30
Ent Req: HS dipl, ACT
Degrees: AA and AS 2 yrs
Courses: 3-D Design, Advertising Design, Art Education, Art History, Ceramics, Commercial Art, Costume Design & Construction, Drafting, Drawing, Film, Illustration, Interior Design, Life Drawing, Painting, Photography, Portrait Drawing, Printmaking, Sculpture, Teacher Training, Textile Design, Theatre Arts, Video, Weaving
Adult Hobby Classes: Weaving
Children's Classes: 10 wk session
Summer School: Varies

SALT LAKE CITY

SALT LAKE COMMUNITY COLLEGE, Graphic Design Dept, 4600 S Redwood Rd, Salt Lake City, UT 84123-3145; PO Box 30808, Salt Lake City, UT 84130-0808. Tel 801-957-4630, 957-4072; Internet Home Page Address: www.slcc.edu; *Div & Dept Chair* Steve Mansfield, BA; *Dean* Elwood Zaugg; *Prof* Rob Adamson; *Prof* Rodayne Esmaye; *Prof* Neal Reiland; *Prof* Fred VanDyke, BA; *Prof* Sheila Chambers, BA; *Instr* Richard Graham, BA; *Instr* Terry Martin, BA; *Instr* Lana Gruendell, BA
FT 3, PT 3; Pub; D & E; Scholarships; SC 44, LC 7; D 123, E 10, non-maj 81, maj 42
Ent Req: HS dipl or equivalent, aptitude test
Degrees: Dipl, AAS(Design), AAS(Animation), AAS(Illustration), AAS (Photography), AAS (Multimedia)
Courses: Advertising Design, Art Principles, Computer Graphics, Drawing, †Graphic Design, Illustration, †Lettering, Photography
Summer School: Dean, James Schnirel. Enrl 30; tuition $145 for term of 10 wks beginning June. Courses—Aesthetics, Drawing, Lettering, Media & Techniques

UNIVERSITY OF UTAH, Dept of Art & Art History, 375 South 1530 East, Rm 161, Salt Lake City, UT 84112-0380. Tel 801-581-7200 (Main), 581-8677 (Dept); Fax 801-585-6171; Elec Mail info@art.utah.edu; Internet Home Page Address: www.art.utah.edu; *Dean* Raymond Tymas-Jones; *Prof* Joseph Marotta, MFA; *Asst Prof Lectr* Laurel Caryn, MFA; *Prof* Sheila Muller, PhD; *Prof* David Pendell, MFA; *Prof* Raymond Morales, BA; *Prof* Roger D (Sam) Wilson, MA; *Chair & Assoc Prof* Elizabeth Peterson, PhD; *Assoc Prof* Kaiti Slater, MFA; *Assoc Prof* Justin Diggle, MFA; *Asst Prof Lectr* Dave Eddy, MFA; *Assoc Prof* Paul Stout, MFA; *Asst Prof Lectr* John Erickson, MFA; *Asst Prof* Beth Krensky, PhD; *Asst Prof* Edward Bateman; *Assoc Prof* Kim Martinez, MFA; *Asst Prof* John O'Connell, MFA; *Asst Prof Lectr* Maureen O'Hara Ure, MFA; *Asst Prof* Paul Paret, PhD; *Assoc Prof* Brian Snapp, MFA; *Assoc Prof* Carol Sogard, MFA; *Instr* Sandy Brunvand, MFA; *Instr* Elizabeth DeWitte, MFA; *Instr* Tom Hoffman; *Instr* Kristina Lenzi; *Instr* Maryann Webster; *Asst Prof* Lela Graybill, PhD; *Asst Prof* Alison Denyer, MFA; *Instr* Diana Gardiner; *Asst Prof* Elena Shtromberg; *Instr* Nolan Baumgartner, MFA; *Instr* Michael Dooley, MA; *Instr* Martin Novak, MFA
Estab 1850, dept estab 1888; Maintain nonprofit art gallery, Alvin Gittens Gallery, 375 S, 1530 E, Rm. 161, Salt Lake City, UT 84112-0380; on-campus shop sells art supplies; pub; D & E; Scholarships; SC 148, LC 47, GC 38/semester; D 1736, E 403, non-maj 1043, maj 1428, grad 51
Ent Req: HS dipl
Degrees: degrees BA (Art History) & BFA 4 yrs (Art), MA (Art History) and MFA (Art) 2 yrs
Courses: Art Appreciation, †Art Education, †Art History, †Ceramics, †Drawing, †Graphic Design, Illustration, Lettering, †Mixed Media, †Painting/Drawing, †Photography/Digital Imaging, †Printmaking, †Sculpture/Intermedia, Silversmithing, Teacher Training, †Transmedia, Video

WESTMINSTER COLLEGE OF SALT LAKE CITY, Dept of Arts, 1840 S 1300 E, Salt Lake City, UT 84105-3697. Tel 801-484-7651; Fax 801-484-5579; Internet Home Page Address: www.wcslc.edu; *Chmn Fine Arts Prog* Craig Glidden
Estab 1875; FT 2, PT 5; pvt; D; Scholarships; SC 25, LC 2; D 900-1000, maj 25
Ent Req: HS dipl, ent exam acceptable, HS grade point average
Degrees: BA & BS 4 yrs

Courses: Art Education, Art History, Ceramics, Drawing, Painting, Photography, Sculpture, Teacher Training, Weaving

VERMONT

BENNINGTON

BENNINGTON COLLEGE, Visual Arts Division, 1 College Dr, Bennington, VT 05201-6003. Tel 802-442-5401; Fax 802-440-4350; Elec Mail feedback@bennington.edu; Internet Home Page Address: www.bennington.edu/Home.aspx; *Pres* Elizabeth Coleman; *Dean Admissions & Fin Aid* Ken Himmelman; *Dir Admissions* Lauren Magrath
Estab 1932; FT E 70; pvt; Scholarships
Degrees: AB 4 yrs & MA 2 yrs
Tuition: $28,150 per yr; campus res
Courses: 3-D Modeling, Animation Lithography, Architecture, Art History, CAD, Ceramics, Cultural Studies, Drawing, Etching Studio, Graphics, Painting, Photography, Printmaking, Sculpture, Visual Arts

BURLINGTON

UNIVERSITY OF VERMONT, Dept of Art, 304 Williams Hall, Burlington, VT 05405-0001. Tel 802-656-2014; Fax 802-656-8429; Internet Home Page Address: www.uvm.edu; *Chmn* William E Mierse
24; Pub; D & E; D 25
Degrees: BA 4 yrs
Courses: Art Education, Art History, Ceramics, Clay Silkscreen, Computer Art, Design, Drawing, Fine Metals, Lithography, Painting, Photography, Printmaking, Sculpture, Teacher Training, Video, Visual Art
Adult Hobby Classes: College of Continuing Education
Summer School: Dir, Lynne Ballard. Two 9 wk sessions beginning in May

CASTLETON

CASTLETON STATE COLLEGE, Art Dept, 45 Alumni Dr, Fine Arts Ctr Castleton, VT 05735-4454. Tel 802-468-5611; Fax 802-468-5237; Elec Mail information@castleton.edu; Internet Home Page Address: www.csc.vsc.edu; *Head Dept* Jonathon Scott; *Prof* William Ramage; *Coordr* Mariko Hancock
Estab 1787; Pub; D & E; Scholarships; SC 31, LC 3, GC varies; D 1900, E 1000, non-maj 300, maj 52, grad 5
Ent Req: HS dipl, ACT, SAT, CEEB
Degrees: BA(Art) & BA Art(2nd major Education) 4 yrs
Courses: Advertising Design, Art History, Calligraphy, Computer Graphics, Drawing, Education, Graphic Design, Lettering, Painting, Photography, Printmaking, Professional Studio Arts, Sculpture, Typography, Video
Summer School: Enrl 24. Courses—Introduction to Art History, Introduction to Studio Art

COLCHESTER

ST MICHAEL'S COLLEGE, Fine Arts Dept, Winooski Park, Colchester, VT 05439-0001. Tel 802-654-2000; Internet Home Page Address: www.smcvt.edu; *Chmn* Paul LeClair, MFA; *Assoc Prof* Lance Richbourg, MFA; *Asst Prof* Gregg Blasdel, MFA; *Asst Prof* Amy Werbel, MFA
Estab 1903, dept estab 1965; den; D & E; SC 8, LC 3
Ent Req: HS dipl
Degrees: BA 4 yrs
Tuition: Res—undergrad $18,615 per yr, campus res—available
Courses: Art Education, Art History, Art Theory, Calligraphy, Costume Design & Construction, Drawing, Graphic Arts, History of Art & Architecture, Painting, Photography, Printmaking, Sculpture, Stage Design, Teacher Training, Theatre Arts
Summer School: Dir, Dr Art Hessler. Session 1, 5 wks beginning mid May, session 2, 6 wks beginning last wk in June. Courses—Calligraphy, Drawing, Painting

JOHNSON

JOHNSON STATE COLLEGE, Dept Fine & Performing Arts, Dibden Center for the Arts, 337 College Hill, Johnson, VT 05656. Tel 802-635-1310; Fax 802-635-1248; Elec Mail parizom@badger.jsc.vsc.edu; Internet Home Page Address: www.jsc.vsc.edu; *Gallery Dir* Suzanne Ritger; *Photog Dept Head* John M Miller; *Assoc Prof* Lisa Jablow; *Prof Sculpture* Susan Calza; *Dept Painting* Ken Leslie; *Asst Prof Art History* Mary Martin; *Asst Prof Music-Jazz* Steve Blair
Estab 1828; Maintain nonprofit art gallery; Julian Scott Memorial Gallery, Johnson State Col, Johnson VT 05656; art library; art supplies available at Vt Studio Ctr; pub; D & E; Scholarships; SC 30, LC 10, GC 20; D 325, non-maj 200, maj 140
Ent Req: HS dipl
Degrees: BA & BFA 4 yrs, MFA 3 yrs
Tuition: Res—undergrad $177 per cr; nonres—undergrad $400 per cr; campus res—room & board $5,000 per yr
Courses: Art Education, Art History, Ceramics, Design, Drawing, Painting, Photography, Printmaking, Sculpture, Studio Art
Children's Classes: Gifted & talented prog for high school students
Summer School: Dir, Mary Pariyo. Courses—Mixed Media, Painting, Sculpture

MIDDLEBURY

MIDDLEBURY COLLEGE, History of Art & Architecture Dept, 78 Chateau Rd, Johnson Memorial Bldg Middlebury, VT 05753-6133. Tel 802-443-5234; Fax 802-443-2250; Elec Mail midd@middlebury.edu; Internet Home Page Address: www.middlebury.edu; *Chmn* Peter Broucke; *Coordr* Mary Lousplain; *Prof* John Hunisak; *Prof* Kristen Hovins; *Prof* Glenn Andres; *Vis Asst Prof* Katherine Smith-Abbott; *Prof* Cynthia Atheron; *Vis Asst Prof* Parker Croft; *Robert P Youngman Cur Asian Art* Colin Mackenzie; *Dir College Museum* Richard Saunders
Estab 1800; pvt; D; SC 7, LC 30; maj 77, others 500 per term
Ent Req: exam and cert
Degrees: BA
Courses: Art History, Design, Drawing, Painting, Photography, Printmaking, Sculpture

NORTHFIELD

NORWICH UNIVERSITY, Dept of Architecture and Art, 158 Harmon Dr, Northfield, VT 05663-1000. Tel 802-485-2000; Fax 802-485-2580; Elec Mail ddoz@norwich.edu; Internet Home Page Address: www.norwich.edu/acad; *Div Head & Assoc Prof* Michael Hoffman, MFA; *Prof* Earl Fechter, MFA; *Asst Prof* Arthur Schaller; *Asst Prof* Kirsten van Aalst; *Prof* Robert Schmidd, MFA; *Assoc Prof* David Woolf, MFA; *Prof* Arnold Aho, MFA; *Architectural History* Dr Lisa Shrenk
Maintains Kreitzberg Library; art supplies can be purchased at on-campus shop; Pvt; D; SC, LC; D 65 (studio art), E 8, non-maj 126
Ent Req: HS dipl
Degrees: BA
Tuition: Campus residency available
Courses: Architecture, Art History, Design, Drawing, Painting, Photography, Printmaking

PLAINFIELD

GODDARD COLLEGE, Dept of Art, 123 Pitkin Rd Plainfield, VT 05667. Tel 802-454-8311; Internet Home Page Address: www.goddard.edu; *Instr* Cynthia Ross; *Instr* David Hale; *Head* Jon Batdorff
Estab 1938; pvt; D & E
Degrees: BA 4 yr, MA 1-2 yr
Tuition: Res—undergrad $16,528 (comprehensive) per sem, $8,920 (tuition only) per sem; nonres—undergrad $9,163 per sem, grad $5,105 per sem; campus res available
Courses: Art Education, Art History, Ceramics, Drawing, Holography, Painting, Photography, Printmaking, Sculpture, Video, Weaving

POULTNEY

GREEN MOUNTAIN COLLEGE, Dept of Art, 1 College Circle Poultney, VT 05764. Tel 802-287-8000; Fax 802-287-8099; *Chmn* Susan Smith-Hunter; *Prof* Dick Weis; *Prof* Richard Weinstein
Estab 1834; maj 60
Ent Req: scholarships
Degrees: BFA 4 yrs
Tuition: Res and non-res $17000 per sem
Courses: Art History, Ceramics, Design, Drawing, Fine Art Studio, Graphic Design, Graphic Design Studio, Illustration, Painting, Photography, Printmaking, Sculpture

VIRGINIA

ANNANDALE

NORTHERN VIRGINIA COMMUNITY COLLEGE, Art Dept, 8333 Little River Tpke, Annandale, VA 22003-3796. Tel 703-323-3107; Fax 703-323-4248; Internet Home Page Address: www.nv.cc.va.us; *Chmn* Duncan Tebow; *Admin & Prog Specialist* Nancy Minogue; *Prof* Elizabeth Tebon; *Asst Prof* Theresa McFadden; *Asst Prof* Giogio Porta
Estab 1960s; Maintains nonprofit Verizon Gallery, in Campus Community Ctr; Pub; D, E & weekends; Scholarships; SC; D 650, E 200
Ent Req: open admis
Degrees: degrees AA(Art Educ), AA(Art History) AAS(Commercial Art), AA(Fine Arts) & AA(Photography) 2 yrs, AAA(Fine Art)
Courses: Art History, Ceramics, Computer Graphics, Design, Drawing, †Fine Arts, Painting, Sculpture
Summer School: Chmn Humanities Div, Dr Duncan Tebow. Tuition same as regular session; 2 five wk D sessions and 1 ten wk E session during Summer. Courses—varied, incl study abroad

ARLINGTON

MARYMOUNT UNIVERSITY, School of Arts & Sciences Div, 2807 N Glebe Rd, Arlington, VA 22207-4299. Tel 703-522-5600; Fax 703-284-3859; Internet Home Page Address: www.marymount.edu; *Prof* Christine Haggerty, MFA; *Prof* Judy Bass, MFA; *Assoc Prof* Bridget Murphy; *Assoc Prof* Mark Trubridge
Estab 1950; Maintain nonprofit art gallery; Barry Gallery; art supplies sold at on-campus shop; pvt; D & E; SC 20, LC 12
Ent Req: HS dipl, SAT results, letter of recommendation
Degrees: BA 4 yrs
Tuition: Res—undergrad $11,580 per sem, grad $750 per cr hr; campus res available
Courses: Advertising Design, †Art Education, Art History, Art of the Book, Clothing Design & Construction, Design, Drawing, Fashion Arts, Figure Drawing, †Graphic Design, Interior Design, Jewelry Design, Painting, Performance Media, Photography, Printmaking, Sculpture, †Studio Arts, Textile Design, Video

Adult Hobby Classes: Courses—any course in fine arts
Summer School: See website

ASHLAND

RANDOLPH-MACON COLLEGE, Dept of the Arts, 204 Henry St, Ashland, VA 23005-1634. Tel 804-798-8375, 798-8372; Fax 804-752-7231; Internet Home Page Address: www.rmc.edu; *Prof* R D Ward; *Assoc Prof* Joe Mattys; *Lectr* Evie Terrono; *Chmn* E Raymond Berry; *Instr Music* James Doering; *Dir Coral Act* Dave Greennagle
Estab 1830, dept estab 1953; FT 5, PT 2; pvt; D; SC 4, LC 4; D 200, non-maj 200
Degrees: BA & BS 4 yrs
Tuition: Res—undergrad $9905 per yr; campus res available
Courses: †Art History, †Art Management, †Drama, Drawing, †Music, Painting, †Studio Art

BLACKSBURG

VIRGINIA POLYTECHNIC INSTITUTE & STATE UNIVERSITY, Dept of Art & Art History, 201 Draper Rd, Blacksburg, VA 24061-0001. Tel 540-231-5547; Fax 540-231-5761; Elec Mail dmyers@vt.edu; Internet Home Page Address: www.art.vt.edu; *Prof Emerita* Jane Aiken PhD; *Prof* Steve Bickley, MFA; *Prof* Derek Myers, MFA; *Prof* Ann-Marie Knoblauch, PhD; *Prof* Robert Fields, MFA; *Prof* Alison Slein, MFA; *Prof* Gregg Bryson, MFA; *Prof* Robert Graham, MFA; *Prof* Ray Kass, MFA; *Prof* Janet Niewald, MFA; *Head Dept* L Bailey Van Hook PhD; *Prof* David Crane, MFA; *Prof* Truman Capone, MFA; *Prof* Sally Cornelius, PhD
Estab 1969; FT 13; pub; D&E; Scholarships; SC 25, LC 12; Maj 300
Degrees: BA 4 yrs, BFA 5 yrs
Tuition: In state N/A; out of state N/A
Courses: Advertising Design, Art Appreciation, Art History, Ceramics, Commercial Art, Computer Art, Design, Drawing, Graphic Arts, Graphic Design, Illustration, Mixed Media, Painting, Sculpture
Summer School: Dir, Derek Myers. Enrl 150; tuition proportional to acad yr for two 5 wk sessions. Courses—Advertising Design, Art History, Ceramics, Computer Art, Design, Drawing, Graphic Design, Illustration, Painting, Sculpture, Watercolor

BRIDGEWATER

BRIDGEWATER COLLEGE, Art Dept, 402 E College St, Bridgewater, VA 22812-1599. Tel 540-828-5396; Fax 540-828-2160; Internet Home Page Address: www.bridgewater.edu; *Dept Head* Nan Covert, MFA
FT 2; Scholarships
Ent Req: HS dipl, sophomore review portfolio
Degrees: BA 4 yr
Tuition: $20,000 per yr undergrad
Courses: Art History, †Computer Graphics, Design, Drawing, Painting, Photography, Printmaking, Sculpture

BRISTOL

VIRGINIA INTERMONT COLLEGE, Fine Arts Div, 1013 Moore St, Bristol, VA 24201-4225. Tel 540-669-6101; Fax 540-669-5763; *Chmn* Dr Jon Mehlferber; *Instr* Tedd Blevins, MFA
Estab 1884; den; D & E; Scholarships; SC 15, LC 4; D 35, non-maj 110
Ent Req: HS dipl, review of work
Degrees: BA(Art) & BA(Art Educ) 4 yrs, AA 2 yrs
Tuition: $17510 per yr (incl board)

BUENA VISTA

SOUTHERN VIRGINIA COLLEGE, Division of Arts and Humanities, One College Hill Dr, Buena Vista, VA 24416. Tel 540-261-8471; Fax 540-261-8451; Elec Mail bcrawford@southvirginia.edu; Internet Home Page Address: www.southernvirginia.edu; *Head Dept* Barbara Crawford
Estab 1867; pvt; D; SC 10, LC 5; D 185, non-maj 175, maj 2
Ent Req: HS dipl, SAT or ACT
Degrees: AA & BA 2 yrs
Courses: Art Education, Art History, Design, Italian Renaissance, Painting, Photography, Study Abroad, Teacher Training

CHARLOTTESVILLE

UNIVERSITY OF VIRGINIA, McIntire Dept of Art, Fayerweather Hall, Charlottesville, VA 22904; PO Box 400130, Charlottesville, VA 22904-4130. Tel 434-924-6123; Fax 434-924-3647; Elec Mail mwd2f@virginia.edu; Internet Home Page Address: www.virginia.edu/art/; *Art History Instr* Lawrence Goedde; *Art History Instr* Daniel Ehnbom; *Prof* Paul Barolsky; *Prof* Malcolm Bell; *Prof* John Dobbins; *Assoc Prof & Chair* Francesca Fiorani; *Prof* Maurie McInnis; *Prof* David Summers; *Assoc Prof* Dorothy Wong; *Studio Faculty* William Bennett; *Studio Faculty* Richard Crozier; *Studio Faculty* Dean Dass; *Studio Faculty* Kevin Everson; *Studio Faculty* Philip Geiger; *Studio Faculty* Sanda Iliescu; *Studio Faculty* Megan Marlatt; *Studio Faculty* Akemi Ohira-Rollando; *Studio Faculty* Elizabeth Schoyer; *Studio Faculty* William Wylie; *Assoc Prof Art History* Sarah Betzer; *Assoc Prof Art History* Douglas Fordham; *Assoc Prof* Carmenita Higginbotham; *Lectr Arts Admin* George Sampson; *Asst Prof, Art History* Eric Ramirez-Weaver; *Assoc Prof Art History* Tyler Jo-Smith; *Univ Prof* Elizabeth Turner; *Asst Prof Studio Art* Lydia Moyer; *Asst Prof Studio Art* Pamela Pecchio
Estab 1819, dept estab 1951; Maintain nonprofit art gallery, Fralin Mus of Art, 155 Rugby Rd, PO Box 400119, Charlottesville, Va 22904; Fiske Kimball Fine Arts Library; Has on campus shop where art supplies can be purchased; FT 21; pub; D; Scholarships; SC 38, LC 20, GC 10; D 1600, maj 140, grad 45,
Activities: Schols offered
Ent Req: HS dipl
Degrees: BA(Studio and Art History), MA(Art History & Architectural) and PhD(Art History & Architectural)
Courses: Art History, Computer Graphics, Drawing, †Film, †New Media, Painting, Photography, Printmaking, Sculpture
Summer School: Enrl 15; tuition varies. Courses—Art History, Studio Art

DANVILLE

AVERETT COLLEGE, Art Dept, 420 W Main St, Danville, VA 24541-3692. Tel 804-791-5600, 791-5797; Fax 804-791-5647; *Coordr* Diane Kendrick, MFA; *Prof* Robert Marsh, MFA
Estab 1859, dept estab 1930; pvt; D & E; Scholarships; SC 13, LC 5; D 1000, non-maj 250, maj 25
Ent Req: HS dipl
Degrees: AB
Tuition: $10128 per yr
Courses: Advertising Design, Art Education, Art History, Ceramics, Commercial Art, Drawing, Fashion Arts, History of Art & Architecture, Illustration, Jewelry, Lettering, Painting, Printmaking, Sculpture, Teacher Training, Textile Design
Summer School: Two 4 wk sessions

FAIRFAX

GEORGE MASON UNIVERSITY, College of Humanities & Social Sciences, Dept of Art & Art History, 4400 University Dr, Fairfax, VA 22030-4444. Tel 703-993-1010; Fax 703-323-3849; Internet Home Page Address: www.gmu.edu/; *Prof* M Kravitz; *Dir Institute of the Arts* Betsy Brininger
Estab 1948, dept estab 1981; pub; D & E; SC 16, LC 15; non-maj 200, maj 130
Ent Req: HS dipl, SAT or CEEB
Degrees: BA
Courses: †Art History, Computer Graphics, Drawing, Graphic Arts, Painting, Photography, Printmaking, Sculpture, †Studio Art
Summer School: Courses—Art Appreciation, Art Education, Studio Arts
   —**College of Visual & Performing Arts, Fine Arts Gallery,** Johnson Ctr Rm 123, Fairfax, VA 22030. Tel 703-993-8888; Elec Mail ekravitz@gmu.edu; Internet Home Page Address: www.gmu.edu/depts/gallery/; *Dir* Walter Kravitz
Open Mon - Fri 9 AM - 9 PM; Gallery 123

FARMVILLE

LONGWOOD UNIVERSITY, Dept of Art, 201 High St Farmville, VA 23909. Tel 434-395-2284; Fax 434-395-2775; Elec Mail mcqueenjg@longwood.edu; Internet Home Page Address: www.lwc.edu/; *Assoc Prof* Christopher M Register; *Prof* Randall W Edmonson; *Prof* John SJ Burke; *Asst Prof* Claire B McCoy; *Prof* Mark Baldridge; *Asst Prof* Kelly Nelson; *Asst Prof* Martin Brief; *Asst Prof* Johnson Bowles; *Asst Prof* Anna Cox; *Lectr* John Williams
Estab 1839, dept estab 1932; Maintains nonprofit gallery, Longwood Center for the Visual Arts, Main Street, Farmville, VA 23901; pub; D & E; Scholarships; SC 59, LC 15; non-maj 450 per sem maj 225 per sem
Ent Req: HS dipl
Degrees: BFA (Art Educ, Art History, Studio) 4 yr
Courses: 3-D Design, Art Appreciation, Art Education, Art History, Basic Design, Ceramics, Crafts, Design, Drawing, Fibers, Graphic Design, Illustration, Jewelry, Metalsmithing, Painting, Photography, Printmaking, Sculpture, Stained Glass, Teacher Training, Typography, Wood Design
Summer School: Dir, Randall W Edmonson. Tuition varies for one 3-wk & two 4-wk sessions. Courses—Varied

FREDERICKSBURG

UNIVERSITY OF MARY WASHINGTON, Dept of Art & Art History, 1301 College Ave, Fredericksburg, VA 22401-5300. Tel 540-654-2088; Fax 540-654-1952; Internet Home Page Address: www.mwc.edu; Others TTY 540-654-1104; *Chair & Assoc Prof* Jean Ann Dabb; *Prof* Joseph Dreiss; *Prof* Lorene Nickel; *Assoc Prof* Steve Griffin; *Asst Prof* Marjorie Och; *Sr Lectr* Carole Garmon
Estab 1904; pub; D & E; Scholarships; SC 18, LC 20; Maj 100
Ent Req: HS dipl, ent exam
Degrees: BA, BS & BLS 4 yrs
Courses: Art History, Ceramics, Drawing, Painting, Photography, Printmaking, Sculpture, †Studio Art

HAMPDEN SYDNEY

HAMPDEN-SYDNEY COLLEGE, Fine Arts Dept, PO Box 34, Winston Studio Hampden Sydney, VA 23943-0034. Tel 434-223-6205; Elec Mail dlewis@hsc.edu; Internet Home Page Address: www.hsc.edu/academics/finearts; *Chair* David Lewis
Average Annual Attendance:

HAMPTON

HAMPTON UNIVERSITY, Dept of Fine & Performing Arts, 1 Hampton University, Armstrong Hall Rm 144 Hampton, VA 23668-0100. Tel 757-727-5416, 727-5402; Internet Home Page Address: www.hamptonu.edu/academics; *Chmn* Dr Karen Ward
Estab 1869; pvt; D; Scholarships; SC 22, LC 7, GC 9; maj 80, others 300, grad 7
Ent Req: HS grad

Degrees: BA, BS
Courses: Ceramics, Interior Design, Painting, Photography
Summer School: Dir, Sheila May. Courses—Advanced Workshop in Ceramics, Art Educ Methods, Art Methods for the Elementary School, Basic Design, Ceramics, Commercial Art, Design, Drawing & Composition, Graphics, Metalwork & Jewelry, Painting, Understanding the Arts

HARRISONBURG

EASTERN MENNONITE UNIVERSITY, Art Dept, 1200 Park Rd, Harrisonburg, VA 22802-2462. Tel 540-432-4000; Fax 540-432-4444; Elec Mail cyndi.gusler@emu.edu; Internet Home Page Address: www.emu.edu; *Chair* Cyndi Gusler
Income:
Courses: †Art Education, †Digital Media, †Photography, †Studio Art

JAMES MADISON UNIVERSITY, School of Art & Art History, 800 S Main St, Harrisonburg, VA 22807-0001. Tel 540-568-6216; Fax 540-568-6598; *Dir* Dr Cole H Welter; *Prof* James Crable, MFA; *Prof* Steve Zapton, MFA; *Prof* Barbara Lewis, MFA; *Prof* Kathleen Arthur PhD, MFA; *Prof* Gary Chatelain, MFA; *Prof* Jack McCaslin, MFA; *Prof* Masako Miyata, MFA; *Prof* Kenneth Szmagaj, MFA; *Assoc Prof* Sang Yoon, MFA; *Assoc Prof* Trudy Cole-Zielanski, MFA; *Asst Prof* William Tate, MArch; *Asst Prof* Peter Ratner, MFA; *Asst Prof* Corinne Diope, MFA; *Instr* Stuart Downs, MA
Estab 1908; pub; D & E; Scholarships; SC 31, LC 21, GC 22; D & E 1254, maj 184, GS 12
Ent Req: HS dipl, grads must submit portfolio, undergrads selected on portfolio & acad merit
Degrees: BA(Art History), BS & BFA(Studio) 4 yrs, MA(Studio, Art History, Art Educ) 1 1/2 to 2 yrs, MFA 60 cr hrs
Tuition: Res—undergrad $56 per cr; undergrad $252 per cr; room & board available
Courses: Advertising Design, Aesthetics, †Art Education, †Art History, Art Therapy, †Ceramics, Computer Graphics, Drafting, †Drawing, Goldsmithing, †Graphic Design, Interior Design, †Jewelry, Museum Staff Training, Painting, Papermaking, Photography, Printmaking, Sculpture, Silversmithing, Stained Glass, Textile Design, Typography, Weaving
Adult Hobby Classes: Tuition res—$250, nonres—$658 for 1-3 cr hr.
Courses—Summer workshop, all beginning courses
Children's Classes: Enrl 260; tuition $40 for 8 sessions

LEXINGTON

WASHINGTON AND LEE UNIVERSITY, Div of Art, 204 W Washington St, Lexington, VA 24450-2116. Tel 540-458-8857, 463-8861 (Art Dept); Fax 540-458-8104; Elec Mail psimpson@wlu.edu; *Prof* Pamela H Simpson PhD, MFA; *Prof* Larry M Stene, MFA; *Assoc Prof* Kathleen Olson-Janjic, MFA; *Assoc Prof* Joan O'Mara Bent, MFA; *Head* George Bent, MFA, PhD
Estab 1749, dept 1949; pvt; D; Scholarships; SC 14, LC 26; D 1700 (in col) non-maj 200, maj 20
Ent Req: HS dipl, SAT, 3 CEEB, one English CEEB plus essay on skills in English, English composition test; entrance requirements most rigorous in English; required of all, including art majors
Degrees: BA 4 yrs
Courses: Art History, Drawing, Graphic Arts, Greece), History of Art & Architecture, Museum Staff Training, Painting, Printmaking, Sculpture, Stage Design, Study Art Abroad (Italy, Theatre Arts

LYNCHBURG

LYNCHBURG COLLEGE, Art Dept, 1501 Lakeside Dr, Lynchburg, VA 24501-3113. Tel 804-544-8349; Fax 804-544-8277; Internet Home Page Address: www.lynchburg.edu/academic/art; *Prof* Richard Pumphrey, MFA; *Prof* Beverly Rhoads, MFA; *Lectr* Barbara Rothermel, MLA
Estab 1903, dept estab 1948; Maintains nonprofit art gallery, The Davra Gallery, Dillard Fine Arts Building, 1501 Lakeside Dr, Lynchburg, VA 24501; pvt; D & E; SC 26, LC 16, GC 2; D 400, E 50, non-maj 410, maj 45
Ent Req: HS dipl
Degrees: BA & BS 4 yrs
Courses: Art Appreciation, Art History, Ceramics, Design, Drawing, Figure Drawing, Graphic Arts, Graphic Design, Painting, Photography, Sculpture
Summer School: Art Education, Art History & Studio

RANDOLPH-MACON WOMAN'S COLLEGE, Dept of Art, 2500 Rivermont Ave, Lynchburg, VA 24503-1526. Tel 804-947-8486; Fax 804-947-8138; Internet Home Page Address: www.rmwc.edu; *Acting Chmn* Kathy Muehlemann
Estab 1891; FT 4; pvt, W; D; Scholarships; SC 18, LC 15; maj 35, others 305
Degrees: BA 4 yrs
Courses: American Art, Art History, Art Survey, Ceramics, Drawing, Painting, Printmaking, Sculpture
Summer School: Dir, Dr John Justice. Enrl 30; 4 wk term. Courses—various

NEWPORT NEWS

CHRISTOPHER NEWPORT UNIVERSITY, Dept of Fine Performing Arts, 1 University Pl, Newport News, VA 23606-2949. Tel 757-594-7089, 594-7000; Fax 757-594-7389; Internet Home Page Address: cnu.edu; *Chmn* Lawrence Wood, MA; *Asst Prof* B Anglin, BA; *Prof* David Alexick PhD, MA; *Prof* Belle Pendleton, MA, PhD; *Assoc Prof* Greg Henry, BFA, MFA
Estab 1974; Maintain nonprofit art gallery; pub; D & E; Scholarships; SC 18, LC 9; D 250, E 60, non-maj 200, maj 100
Ent Req: HS dipl, admis comt approval

Degrees: BA & BS 4 yrs
Courses: †Art, †Art Appreciation, Art Education, Art History, Ceramics, Collage, Costume Design & Construction, Drawing, Graphic Arts, †Music (BM), Painting, Photography, †Printmaking, Sculpture, Stage Design, Theatre Arts
Adult Hobby Classes: 100 variable
Summer School: Dir, Dr Barry Woods. Enrl 25; tuition $300. Courses—Ceramics, Drawing, Painting

NORFOLK

NORFOLK STATE UNIVERSITY, Fine Arts Dept, 700 Park Ave Norfolk, VA 23504. Tel 757-823-8844; Elec Mail webmaster@nsu.edu; Internet Home Page Address: www.nsu.edu/; *Head Dept* Rod A Taylor PhD
Estab 1935; pub; D & E; SC 50, LC 7; D 355, E 18, non-maj 200, maj 155
Ent Req: HS dipl
Degrees: BA(Art Educ), BA(Fine Arts) and BA(Graphic Design) 4 yrs, MA and MFA in Visual Studies
Courses: Advertising Design, Aesthetics, Art Appreciation, †Art Education, Art History, Calligraphy, Ceramics, Commercial Art, †Costume Design & Construction, Design, Drawing, †Fashion Arts, Graphic Arts, †Graphic Design, †Handicrafts, Illustration, Lettering, Mixed Media, Painting, Photography, Printmaking, Sculpture, †Teacher Training
Adult Hobby Classes: Enrl 30. Courses—Ceramics, Crafts
Children's Classes: Enrl 45; tuition none. Courses—all areas

OLD DOMINION UNIVERSITY, Art Dept, Visual Arts Bldg, Rm 203, Norfolk, VA 23529. Tel 757-683-4047, 683-3000; Fax 757-683-5923; Elec Mail rrlove@odu.edu; Internet Home Page Address: www.odu.edu/al/art; *Grad Prog Dir & Assoc Prof* Kenneth Fitzgerald; *Dir Gallery* Frederick Bayersdorfer; *Prof* Ken Daley; *Prof* Linda McGreevy; *Assoc Prof* Elliott Jones; *Prof* Robert Wojtowicz; *Assoc Prof* Richard Nickel; *Assoc Prof* John Roth; *Assoc Prof* Dianne deBeixedon; *Lect* Patricia Edwards; *Assoc Prof* Peter Eudenbach; *Instr* Agnieszka Whelan; *Asst Prof* Ivanete Blanco; *Asst Prof* Jiwon Lee; *Asst Prof* Greta Pratt; *Asst Prof* Anne Muraoka
Estab 1962; Maintain a nonprofit art gallery, Baron & Ellin Gordon Art Galleries, 4509 Monarch Way, Norfolk, VA 23529; maintain an art library, Elise N. Hofheimer Art Libr, Diehn Fine & Performing Arts Ctr, Rm 109, Norfolk, VA 23529; Pub, Commonwealth of Virginia; D, E, weekend (Sat); Scholarships, Fellowships, Assistantships; SC, LC, GC; 1,244 day; 296 evening; 500 majors; 3 grad stud
Ent Req: HS, dipl, SAT
Degrees: BA(Art History, Art Education or Studio Art), BFA
Tuition: Res—$263 per cr hr; nonres—$741 per cr hr
Courses: Aesthetics, Art Appreciation, †Art Education, †Art History, Ceramics, Clay, Computer Imaging, Crafts, Design, †Drawing, †Goldsmithing, Graphic Arts, †Graphic Design, History of Art & Architecture, Illustration, †Jewelry, Metals, Mixed Media, Museum Staff Training, †Painting, †Photography, †Printmaking, †Sculpture, †Silversmithing, †Studio Art, Teacher Training, Textile Design, Weaving
Adult Hobby Classes: Enrl 18; tuition $60-$90 per 8 wk course. Courses—Painting
Children's Classes: Enrl 25. Courses—2 semesters, Governor's Magnet School classes
Summer School: Chair, Prof Dianne deBeixedon. Enrl 125; tuition res $263 per cr hr; nonres $741 per cr hr

VIRGINIA WESLEYAN COLLEGE, Art Dept of the Humanities Div, 1584 Wesleyan Dr, Norfolk, VA 23502-5599. Tel 757-455-3200; Fax 757-461-5025; *Assoc Prof* Barclay Sheaks; *Assoc Prof* Joyce B Howell PhD, MFA; *Adjunct Instr* Ken Bowen, MA
Pvt, den; D & E; Scholarships; SC 21, LC 8; E 20
Ent Req: HS dipl, SAT
Degrees: BA(Liberal Arts) 4 yrs
Tuition: $16,500 per yr; campus res available
Courses: Aesthetics, Art Appreciation, Art Education, Art History, Ceramics, Computer Art, Drawing, Fabric Enrichment, Graphic Arts, Graphic Design, Handicrafts, History of Art & Architecture, Jewelry, Mixed Media, Painting, Photography, Printmaking, Sculpture, Silversmithing, Stage Design, Teacher Training, Theatre Arts, Weaving
Adult Hobby Classes: Enrl 20

PETERSBURG

RICHARD BLAND COLLEGE, Art Dept, 11301 Johnson Rd, Petersburg, VA 23805-7100. Tel 804-862-6272, 862-6100; *Pres* James B McNeer; *Chmn* David Majewski
Estab 1960, dept estab 1963; pub; D & E; SC 3, LC 3; D 73
Ent Req: HS dipl, SAT, recommendation of HS counselor
Degrees: AA(Fine Arts) 2 yrs
Tuition: Res—undergrad $1140 per sem; nonres—$3125 per sem
Courses: Art Appreciation, Art History, Basic Design, Drawing, Painting, Sculpture
Adult Hobby Classes: Courses—Interior Design, Yoga

VIRGINIA STATE UNIVERSITY, Department of Art & Design, PO Box 9026, Petersburg, VA 23806-0001. Tel 804-524-5944; Fax 804-524-5472; Elec Mail sbernard@vsu.edu; Elec Mail tlarose@vsu.edu; Internet Home Page Address: www.vsu.edu; *Chmn & Dir* Thomas Larose, PhD; *Asst Prof* Ann Ford; *Asst Prof* Meena Khalili Clifford
Estab 1882, dept estab 1935; Maintains nonprofit art gallery, Meredith Art Gallery, 216 Harris Hall, Petersburg, VA 23806; on-campus art supplies shop; Pub; D & E; SC 16, LC 6; D 400, E 60, non-maj 302, maj 130
Ent Req: HS dipl

Degrees: BFA (Visual Arts) 4 yrs
Tuition: Res—undergrad $1,614 per sem, res grad—$4,600 room & board; nonres undergrad—$1,996 per sem, nonres grad—$4,967
Courses: Animation, Art Appreciation, Art History, Ceramics, Computer Graphics, Drawing, Graphic Design, Illustration, Internship, Lettering, Painting, Photography, Printmaking, Sculpture, Senior Thesis, Silkscreen, †Studio, Typography
Summer School: Dir, Dr V Thota, Art Appreciation. Courses—Drawing, Art Crafts

PORTSMOUTH

TIDEWATER COMMUNITY COLLEGE, Visual Arts Center, 340 High St, Portsmouth, VA 23704-3795. Tel 757-822-6999; Fax 757-822-6800; Internet Home Page Address: www.tcc.edu; *Dir* Ed Gibbs; *Prof* Rob Hawkes; *Prof* Craig Nilson; *Asst Prof* Corinne Lilyard-Mitchell; *Asst Prof* Ed Francis; *Asst Prof* Rhonda Todoroff; *Asst Prof* Tom Siefmund; *Assoc Prof* Rosemary Hill; *Instr* Lisa Finley; *Pub Rels Specialist* Janet Sydenstricker
Estab 1968; pub; D & E; SC 12, LC 3; D 120, E 180, non-maj 190, maj 110
Ent Req: HS dipl
Degrees: AA(Fine Arts), AAS(Graphic Arts) 2 yrs
Courses: †Advertising Design, Art Appreciation, Art History, Ceramics, Computer Graphics, Design, Drawing, Illustration, Lettering, Painting, Photography, Sculpture
Adult Hobby Classes: Offered through Continuing Educ Div
Summer School: Dir Anne Iott. Enrl 15 per course; tuition per course beginning May. Courses—Art History, Ceramics, Design, Drawing, Painting

RADFORD

RADFORD UNIVERSITY, Art Dept, 801 E. Main St., Radford, VA 24142-0001; PO Box 6965, Radford, VA 24142-6965. Tel 540-831-5754; Elec Mail sarbury@radford.edu; Internet Home Page Address: www.radford.edu; *Chmn* Dr Steve Arbury, PhD; *Prof* Halide Salam; *Asst Prof* Ed LeShock, MFA; *Assoc Prof* Jennifer Spoon, MFA; *Prof* Charles Brouwer, MFA; *Asst Prof* Dr Eloise Philpot, PhD; *Asst Prof* Matthew Johnston, PhD; *MFA* ZL Feng; *Asst Prof* Richard Bay, EdD; *Asst Prof* Drew Dodson, MFA; *Asst Prof* John O'Connor, MA
Estab 1910, dept estab 1936; Maintains nonprofit art gallery, Radford University Art Museum; Pub; D & E; Scholarships; D 1,250, E 80, non-maj 1,086, maj 202, grad 32
Activities: Limited art supplies sold in campus bookstore
Ent Req: HS dipl, SAT
Degrees: BA, BFA, BS & BS (teaching) 4 yrs, MFA 2 yrs, MS 1 yr
Courses: Animation, Art Appreciation, Art Education, Art Foundations, Art History, Baroque & Rococo Art, Ceramics, Contemporary Art, Drawing, Graphic Design, Jewelry, Lettering, †Museum Staff Training, Painting, Photography, Sculpture, Teacher Training, Visual Arts

RICHMOND

J SARGEANT REYNOLDS COMMUNITY COLLEGE, Humanities & Social Science Division, PO Box 85622, Richmond, VA 23285-5622. Tel 804-371-3263; Internet Home Page Address: www.jsr.cc.va.us; *Assoc Div Chmn* Patricia Johnson; *Head Art Prog* Barbara Glenn
Estab 1972
Ent Req: HS dipl or equivalent
Degrees: AA
Tuition: Res—$4.52 per cr hr; nonres—$175.40 per cr hr
Courses: Art Appreciation, Art History, Design, Drawing, Graphic Design, Handicrafts, Interior Design, Painting, Photography, Sculpture

UNIVERSITY OF RICHMOND, Dept of Art and Art History, Modlin Center for the Arts, Richmond, VA 23173. Tel 804-289-8272, 289-8276; Fax 804-287-6006; *Chmn* Charles W Johnson Jr PhD; *Prof* Stephen Addiss, PhD; *Assoc Prof* Margaret Denton, PhD; *Assoc Prof* Mark Rhodes; *Assoc Prof* Tanja Softie; *Asst Prof* Erling Sjovold; *Exec Dir Univ Mus* Richard Waller
Estab 1840; Maintains nonprofit art gallery; Pvt; D & E; Scholarships; SC 29, LC 15
Ent Req: HS dipl, CEEB
Degrees: BA and BS 4 yrs
Tuition: Res—&14,000 per yr
Courses: †Architecture, †Art History, Ceramics, Color & Design, Design, Drawing, History of Art & Architecture, †Mixed Media, Museum Staff Training, Museum Studies, Painting, Photography, Printmaking, Sculpture, †Studio Art

VIRGINIA COMMONWEALTH UNIVERSITY, Art History Dept, PO Box 843046, Richmond, VA 23284-3046. Tel 804-828-2784; Fax 804-828-7468; Internet Home Page Address: www.vcu.edu; *Prof* Dr Baba Tunde Lawal; *Prof* Robert Hobbs; *Prof* Howard Risatti; *Assoc Prof* Dr Charles Brownell; *Assoc Prof* Fredrika H Jacobs; *Asst Prof* Dr Ann G Crowe; *Asst Prof* Dr James Farmer; *Chmn* Bruce M Koplin
Degrees: BA, MA, PhD
Courses: Motion Pictures Western Survey, Pre-Columbian Art & Architectures
—**School of the Arts,** 325 N Harrison St, Richmond, VA 23284-9057; PO Box 842519, Richmond, VA 23284-2519. Tel 804-828-2787; Fax 804-828-6469; Elec Mail arts@vcu.edu; Internet Home Page Address: www.vcu.edu/arts; *Dean* Richard Toscan
Estab 1838; Maintains a nonprofit gallery, Anderson Gallery, 907 1/2 West Franklin St, Richmond, VA 23284. Arts supplies may be purchased on campus; FT 155, PT 153; pub; D & E; Scholarships, Fellowships, Assistantships; 2,984
Ent Req: ent req portfolio or audition
Degrees: BA, BFA, MFA, MAE, BM
Courses: 2-D Art, Art Education, Art Experience, Art History, Ceramics, Costume Design & Construction, Design, Exceptional Art, Fashion Arts, †Film, Fine Art, Graphic Arts, Graphic Design, Interior Design, Jewelry, Painting, Photography, Print, Printmaking, Sculpture, Theatre Arts

Summer School: Dir, Sue F Munro. Courses 3 - 8 wks, most art disciplines

ROANOKE

HOLLINS UNIVERSITY, Art Dept, PO Box 9583, Roanoke, VA 24020-9583. Tel 540-362-6323; Elec Mail huadm@hollins.edu; rsulkin@hollins.edu; Internet Home Page Address: www.hollins.edu/academics/art/; *Prof & Chair* Robert Sulkin
Estab 1842; Maintains nonprofit gallery, Eleanor Wilson Museum, 8009 Fishburn Dr, Roanoke VA 24020
Courses: Art History, †Studio

VIRGINIA WESTERN COMMUNITY COLLEGE, Communication Design, Fine Art & Photography, 3095 Colonial Ave SW, Roanoke, VA 24015-4705; PO Box 14007, Roanoke, VA 24038-4007. Tel 540-857-7385, 857-7255 (Dept Head); Fax 540-857-6096; Elec Mail dcurtis@vw.cc.va.us; Internet Home Page Address: www.vw.cc.va.us; *Interim Chmn Div Human* Dr John Capps, EdD; *Dept Head* Elizabeth Bailey
PT 10; Pub; D & E; Scholarships; SC 11, LC 2
Ent Req: HS dipl
Degrees: AA(Fine Art), AAS (Commun Design)
Adult Hobby Classes: Oil Painting, Papermaking, Watercolor

SALEM

ROANOKE COLLEGE, Fine Arts Dept-Art, 221 College Ln, Olin Hall Salem, VA 24153-3747. Tel 540-375-2374; Fax 540-375-2559; Elec Mail partin@roanoke.edu; Internet Home Page Address: www.roanoke.edu; *Chmn* Bruce Partin, PhD; *Prof* Scott Hardwig, MFA; *Assoc Prof* Elizabeth Heil, MFA; *Assoc Prof* Dr Jane Long, MFA; *Asst Prof* Katherine Shortridge; *Asst Prof* James Hargrove
Estab 1842, dept estab 1930; Maintain nonprofit art gallery, Olin Galleries; pvt; D&E; Scholarships; SC 16, LC 8; D 130, non-maj 120, maj 40
Ent Req: HS dipl, SAT or ACT, 13 acad cr - 2 English, 2 Social Sciences, 5 Arts & Humanities, 2 Math, 2 Science
Degrees: BA 4 yrs
Courses: Advertising Design, Art Education, †Art History, Ceramics, Drawing, Graphic Design, Painting, Photography, Printmaking, Sculpture, Stage Design, †Studio Arts
Children's Classes: Ceramics
Summer School: Dir, Ms Leah Russell. Courses—Art History, Studio

STAUNTON

MARY BALDWIN COLLEGE, Dept of Art & Art History, 318 Prospect St, Staunton, VA 24401. Tel 540-887-7196; Fax 540-887-7139; Internet Home Page Address: www.mbc.edu; *Assoc Prof* Paul Ryan; *Assoc Prof* Dr Sara N James; *Asst Prof* Jim Sconyers; *Instr* Nancy Ross; *Vis Artist* Anne Hanger; *Adjunct Instr* Beth Young
Estab 1842; Maintain nonprofit gallery, Hunt Gallery at Mary Baldwin College, Staunton, VA 24401; pvt; D & E; Scholarships; SC 40, LC 30; D 173, E 32, non-maj 172, maj 45, others 4 non-credit
Ent Req: HS dipl
Degrees: BA & BS 4 yrs
Courses: Art Appreciation, Art Criticism, Art History, Ceramics, Drawing, Film, Graphic Design, Historical Preservation, Interior Design, Museum Staff Training, Painting, Photography, Printmaking, Teacher Training, Typography, Video

STERLING

MAGNUM OPUS, 20963 Sandstone Sq Sterling, VA 20163-7209. Tel 703-790-0861; *Head Dept* John Fettes
Estab 1955; pvt; D & E; SC 1; D 63, E 12
Courses: Drawing, Painting
Summer School: Dir, John Fettes.

SWEET BRIAR

SWEET BRIAR COLLEGE, Art History Dept, 134 Chapel Rd, Sweet Briar, VA 24595-5001. Tel 804-381-6125 (Art History Dept), 381-6100; Fax 804-381-6152; Elec Mail witcombe@sbc.edu; Internet Home Page Address: www.sbc.edu/academics/arth/; *Prof* Aileen H Laing PhD; *Chmn* Christopher Witcombe; *Prof* Diane D Moran, PhD
Estab 1901, dept estab 1930; pvt; D; Scholarships; SC 19, LC 19; D 375 per term, maj 32
Ent Req: HS dipl, col boards
Degrees: BA 4 yrs
Courses: †Art History, Drawing, Graphic Arts, History of Art & Architecture
Adult Hobby Classes: Fibre Art History, Graphic Design, Modern Art

WILLIAMSBURG

COLLEGE OF WILLIAM & MARY, Dept of Fine Arts, PO Box 8795, Williamsburg, VA 23187-8795. Tel 757-221-2530 (Dept of Arts); *Ralph H Wark Prof Art & Art History* Dr Alan Wallach, MFA; *Assoc Prof* Marlene Jack, MFA; *Assoc Prof* William Barnes, MFA; *Asst Prof* Lewis Choen, MFA; *Lectr* Joseph Dye, MFA
Estab 1693, dept estab 1936; pub; D; SC 20, LC 22; D 5000, non-maj 825, maj 64
Ent Req: HS dipl
Degrees: BA 4 yrs
Tuition: Res—$1560 per sem; nonres—$4500 per sem; campus res available

Courses: †Architecture, †Art History, †Ceramics, †Drawing, †Painting, †Printmaking, †Sculpture
Summer School: Dir, Nell Jones. Courses—Art History, Design, Painting, Drawing

WISE

CLINCH VALLEY COLLEGE OF THE UNIVERSITY OF VIRGINIA, Visual & Performing Arts Dept, One College Ave, Wise, VA 24293. Tel 540-328-0100; Fax 540-328-0115; *Chmn* Susan Adams Ramsey
Estab 1954, dept estab 1980; pub; D & E; Scholarships; SC 9, LC 4
Ent Req: HS dipl, SAT or ACT
Degrees: BA & BS 4 yrs
Tuition: Res/non-res—$77 per cr; res/non-res—12-18 cr $1,735
Courses: Applied Music, Art Education, Art History, Ceramics, Costume Design & Construction, Drawing, Film, History of Art & Architecture, Music History & Literature, Music Theory, Painting, Performance, Sculpture, Stage Design, Teacher Training, Theatre Arts
Adult Hobby Classes: Dir, Dr Winston Ely
Summer School: Courses—Same as above

WASHINGTON

AUBURN

GREEN RIVER COMMUNITY COLLEGE, Art Dept, 12401 SE 320th St, Auburn, WA 98092-3699. Tel 253-833-9111; Fax 253-288-3465; Internet Home Page Address: www.greenriver.edu; *Faculty* Heather McGeachy; *Faculty* Cindy Small
Estab 1965; pub; D & E; SC 31, LC 4; D 330, E 120
Ent Req: HS dipl or 18 yrs old
Degrees: AA 2 yr
Tuition: Living with parents $7380, other housing $11,052
Courses: Art History, Ceramics, Computer Enhanced Design, Craft, Design, Drawing, Painting, Papermaking, Photography, Weaving
Summer School: Dir, Bruce Haulman. Tuition $193.66. Courses—Ceramics, Drawing, Painting, Photography

BELLEVUE

BELLEVUE COMMUNITY COLLEGE, Art Dept, 3000 Landerholm Circle SE, Bellevue, WA 98007-6484. Tel 206-641-2341; Fax 425-643-2690; *Dept Chmn* Carolyn Luark; *Photo Instr* John Wesley; *Art History Instr* Vicki Artimovich
Estab 1966; pub; D & E; SC 15, LC 5; 600, maj 50
Ent Req: no ent req
Degrees: AA 2 yrs
Tuition: Varies according to courses taken
Courses: Art History, Design, Drawing, Interior Design, Painting, Photography, Sculpture, Textile Design
Adult Hobby Classes: Enrl 600. Courses—Ceramics, Design, Drawing, Jewelry, Painting, Photography, Sculpture

BELLINGHAM

WESTERN WASHINGTON UNIVERSITY, Art Dept, 516 High St, Fine Arts Complex, Rm 116 Bellingham, WA 98225-5946. Tel 360-650-3660; Fax 360-647-6878; Internet Home Page Address: www.wwu.edu; *Chmn Dept Art* Thomas Johnston
Estab 1899; FT 15, PT 6; pub; D & E; Scholarships; D 1500, E 200
Ent Req: HS dipl, ent exam
Degrees: BA 4 yr, BA(Educ) 4 yr, BFA 5 yr, MEd 6 yr
Courses: †Art History, †Ceramics, †Drawing, †Fibers, †Graphic Design, †Metals, †Painting, †Sculpture
Adult Hobby Classes: Enrl 200; tuition $43 per cr continuing educ; Courses—Ceramics, Drawing, Fibers, Paintings, Sculpture
Children's Classes: Enrl 100; tuition $125 one wk session; Courses—Adventures in Science/Arts
Summer School: Dir, Shirley Ennons. Tuition $404, six & nine week sessions; Courses—Art Education, Art History, Ceramics, Drawing, Fibers, Painting, Sculpture

BREMERTON

OLYMPIC COLLEGE, Social Sciences & Humanities Div, 1600 Chester Ave, Bremerton, WA 98337-1699. Tel 360-792-6050, 7767; Fax 360-792-7689; Elec Mail rlawrence@oc.ctc.edu; Internet Home Page Address: www.oc.ctc.edu/; *Dir* Randy Lawrence; *Instr* Ina Wu, MFA
Estab 1946; Olympic College Art Gallery; pub; D & E; Scholarships; LC 3; D 125, E 75
Ent Req: HS dipl
Degrees: AA, AS & ATA 2 yrs, cert
Courses: Art Appreciation, Art History, Ceramics, Drawing, Jewelry, Life Drawing, Native American Art History, Painting, Papermaking, Photography, Printmaking, Sculpture, Stained Glass
Adult Hobby Classes: Calligraphy, Painting

CHENEY

EASTERN WASHINGTON UNIVERSITY, Dept of Art, 526 Fifth St, Art 1400 Cheney, WA 99004-1619. Tel 509-359-2493; Fax 509-359-7028; Internet Home Page Address: www.ewu.edu; Internet Home Page Address: www.visual.arts.ewu.edu; *Chmn* Lanny Devono; *Prof Art History* Dr Barbara Miller

Estab 1886; pub; D; Scholarships; SC 58, LC 21, GC 18; D 600, non-maj 200, maj 200, GS 20
Degrees: BA, BEd and BFA 4 yrs, MA and MEd 1 to 2 yrs
Tuition: Res—undergrad $81 per cr hr, grad $130 per cr hr; nonres—undergrad $287 per cr hr, grad $394 per cr hr
Courses: Aesthetics, Art Appreciation, Art Education, Art History, Ceramics, Design, Drawing, Graphic Design, Mixed Media, Painting, Photography, Printmaking, Sculpture, Teacher Training
Summer School: Dir, Richard L Twedt. Enrl 200; tuition $120 per cr undergrad, $190 per cr grad for 8 wk term. Courses—Art History, Art in Humanities, Drawing, Painting, Photography

ELLENSBURG

CENTRAL WASHINGTON UNIVERSITY, Dept of Art, 400 E University Way, Ellensburg, WA 98926-7564. Tel 509-963-2665; Elec Mail chinm@cwu.edu; Internet Home Page Address: www.cwu.edu/~art; *Chmn* William Folkestad
Estab 1891; Maintains nonprofit gallery, Sarah Spurgeon Gallery, Dept Art, 400 E University Way MS 7564 Ellensburg WA 98926; 12; pub; D; maj 150, others 7134
Ent Req: GPA 2
Degrees: BA, BFA, MA & MFA 4-5 yrs
Courses: Art Appreciation, †Art Education, Art History, †Ceramics, †Computer Art, Design, †Drawing, †Graphic Design, Illustration, †Jewelry, †Painting, Papermaking, †Photography, Printmaking, †Sculpture, †Wood Design
Adult Hobby Classes: Art in Elementary School, Art in Secondary School
Summer School: Dir, Dr William Folkestad. Tuition $80 per cr for 4, 6, 8 wk sessions. Courses—Art Appreciation, Ceramics, Computer Art, Drawing, Painting

EVERETT

EVERETT COMMUNITY COLLEGE, Art Dept, 2000 Tower St, Everett, WA 98201-1390. Tel 425-388-9439; Fax 425-388-9129; Elec Mail gkammer@everettcc.edu; Internet Home Page Address: www.evcc.ctc.edu; *Instr Art* Lowell Hanson; *Instr Art* Thom Lee; *Instr Art* Sandra Lepper; *Dir* Greg Kammer
Maintain nonprofit art gallery, Russell Day Gallery; on-campus shop where art supplies may be purchased; Pub; D&E; Scholarships; SC, LC, Online/Distance Learning
Degrees: AA, AFA & ATA 2 yr
Tuition: $56 per cr hr
Courses: Advertising Design, †Aesthetics, Art Appreciation, Art Education, Art History, Ceramics, Commercial Art, Design, Drawing, Graphic Arts, Graphic Design, Industrial Design, Media Production, Multimedia, Painting, Photography, Printmaking, †Studio Arts, Theatre Arts, †Written Arts

LACEY

ST MARTINS COLLEGE, Humanities Dept, 5300 Pacific Ave SE, Lacey, WA 98503-1297. Tel 360-491-4700; Fax 360-459-4124; Internet Home Page Address: www.stmartin.edu; *Pres* David R Spangler, PhD
Dept estab 1895; pvt; D & E
Ent Req: HS dipl
Degrees: BA
Tuition: FT $7780 per sem
Courses: Art Appreciation, Art History, Ceramics, Design, Drawing, Painting, Printmaking

LAKEWOOD

FORT STEILACOOM COMMUNITY COLLEGE, Fine Arts Dept, 9401 Farwest Dr SW, Lakewood, WA 98498-1919. Tel 253-964-6500, 964-6655; Fax 253-964-6318; Elec Mail mpederse@pierce.ctc.edu; Internet Home Page Address: www.pierce.ctc.edu/; *Chmn* Morrie Pedersen
Estab 1966, dept estab 1972; FT 2, PT 2; pub; D & E; SC 20, LC 5; D 3500
Ent Req: ent exam
Degrees: AA 2yrs
Courses: Drawing, Figure Drawing, Painting, Photography, Printmaking
Adult Hobby Classes: Courses vary
Summer School: Dir, Walt Boyden. Tuition $19 per cr hr. Courses—Ceramics, Drawing, Painting.

LONGVIEW

LOWER COLUMBIA COLLEGE, Art Dept, 1600 Maple St, Longview, WA 98632-3907; PO Box 3010, Longview, WA 98632-0310. Tel 360-577-2300, Ext 3414 (Art Dept); Fax 360-577-3400; Internet Home Page Address: lcc.ctc.edu/; *Instr* Yvette O'Neill, MA; *Chmn* Rosemary Powelson, MFA
Estab 1934; pub; D & E; Scholarships; SC 36, LC 8; D 200, E 100
Ent Req: open admis
Degrees: AAS 2 yrs
Courses: Art History, Calligraphy, Ceramics, Design, Drawing, Graphic Arts, Painting, Photography, Printmaking, Sculpture
Adult Hobby Classes: Courses—Matting & Framing, Relief Woodcuts, Recreational Photography

MOSES LAKE

BIG BEND COMMUNITY COLLEGE, Art Dept, 7662 Chanute St, Moses Lake, WA 98837. Tel 509-762-5351 ext 269; Internet Home Page Address: www.bbcc.ctc.edu; *Dir* Rie Palkovic; *Art Instr* Francis Palkovic; *Art Instr* Betty Johanssen

Estab 1962; Art supplies can be purchased at on-campus shop; pub; D & E; SC 8, LC 2; D 325, E 60, maj 10-15
Ent Req: HS dipl
Degrees: AA 2 yrs
Courses: Art Appreciation, Basic Design, Ceramics, Drawing, History of Art & Architecture, Lettering, Painting, Photography, Poster Art, Pottery, Sculpture
Adult Hobby Classes: Enrl 15. Courses—Drawing

MOUNT VERNON

SKAGIT VALLEY COLLEGE, Dept of Art, 2405 E College Way, Mount Vernon, WA 98273-5899. Tel 360-416-7724 (Dept Art), 428-1261; Fax 360-416-7690; *Chmn* Ann Chadwick-Reid
Estab 1926; FT 2, PT 6; pub; D & E; Scholarships; SC 32, LC 1; D 2500, E 3500
Ent Req: open
Courses: Art Appreciation, Art History, Ceramics, Design, Drawing, Figure Drawing, Jewelry, Painting, Photography, Printmaking, Sculpture
Adult Hobby Classes: Four nights a week
Summer School: Dir, Bert Williamson

PASCO

COLUMBIA BASIN COLLEGE, Esvelt Gallery, 2600 N 20th Ave, Pasco, WA 99301-4108. Tel 509-547-0511 ext 2374; Fax 509-546-0401; Elec Mail mdryburgh@columbiabasin.edu; Internet Home Page Address: www.cbc2.org/arts/arts_center; *Art Dept Lead & Instr* James Craig, MFA; *Dean Arts & Humanities* Bill McKay; *Dir Gallery & Instr* Mary Dryburgh; *Instr* Tracy Petre; *Instr* Greg Pierce
Estab 1955; Maintains a non-profit art gallery & on-campus art supplies shop.; FT 3, PT 5; pub; D & E, wkends; Scholarships; SC 12, LC 3
Degrees: AA & AS
Tuition: Res—$178.50; nonres—$684.50
Courses: Art Appreciation, Art History, Ceramics, Design, Drawing, Graphic Design, Metal Casting & Foundry, Photography, Sculpture, Stage Design
Adult Hobby Classes: Enrl 5000; tuition $400 per qtr. Courses—Art Appreciation, Fine Arts, Graphic Design
Summer School: Dir, Bill McKay. Enrl 1500; tuition $400 for 8 wks. Courses—Ceramics, Drawing, Illustration, Introduction to Art

PULLMAN

WASHINGTON STATE UNIVERSITY, Fine Arts Dept, PO Box 647450, Pullman, WA 99164-7450. Tel 509-335-8686; Fax 509-335-7742; *Chmn* Paul Lee
Estab 1890, dept estab 1925; FT 12; pub; D & E; Scholarships; SC 29, LC 13, GC 25; D 1593, E 131, maj 220, GS 25
Ent Req: HS dipl
Degrees: BA(Fine Arts) 4 yrs, BFA 4 yrs, MFA 2 yrs
Tuition: Res—$1829; nonres—$5272
Courses: Ceramics, Drawing, Electronic Imaging, Painting, Photography, Printmaking, Sculpture

SEATTLE

THE ART INSTITUTES, The Art Institute of Seattle, 2323 Elliott Ave, Seattle, WA 98121-1642. Tel 206-448-6600; Fax 206-448-2501; Elec Mail aisadm@aii.edu; Internet Home Page Address: www.ais.edu; *Pres* Elden Monday; *Dir Interior Design, Industrial Design Tech* William R Edgar; *Dir Graphic Design, Web Design & Interactive Media, Digital Design* Douglas Heinlein
Estab 1946; pvt; D&E; Scholarships; SC 60%, LC 40%; D 2000, E 350
Ent Req: HS dipl, portfolio approval recommended but not required
Degrees: prof dipl, AA 2 yr
Tuition: $13,365 per yr for 3 qtrs
Courses: Advertising Design, †Audio Production, Animation, Culinary Arts, Multimedia, Fashion Marketing, Industrial Design, Commercial Art, Commercial Art Technician, †Costume Design & Construction, †Design, Fashion Arts, Fashion Merchandising, Film, Graphic Arts, Graphic Design, Illustration, Interior Design, Layout & Production, Lettering, Photography, †Textile Design, Video

CITY ART WORKS, Pratt Fine Arts Center, 1902 S Main St, Seattle, WA 98144-2206. Tel 206-328-2200; Fax 206-328-1260; Elec Mail info@pratt.org; Internet Home Page Address: www.pratt.org; *Exec Dir* Michelle Bufano; *Dir Progs* Brandi Clark
Open daily 9 AM - 9 PM; Estab 1979; pvt; D & E; Scholarships, Fellowships; SC 300; D 1000, E 1000
Ent Req: open enrollment
Degrees: no degree prog
Courses: Collage, Drawing, Glass blowing & casting, Goldsmithing, Illustration, Jewelry, Mixed Media, Painting, Printmaking, Sculpture, Silversmithing
Adult Hobby Classes: Enrl 2000; tuition $100-$500 for 8 wk class. Classes—Drawing, Glass, Jewelry, Painting, Printmaking, Sculpture
Children's Classes: Drawing, Glass, Printmaking, Sculpture
Summer School: Educ Dir, Janet Berkow. Enrl 50; tuition $400-$650 per wk-long class. Classes—Glassblowing, Jewelry, Printmaking, Sculpture

CORNISH COLLEGE OF THE ARTS, Art Dept, 1000 Lenora St, Seattle, WA 98121-2707. Tel 206-726-5151; Fax 206-720-1011; Elec Mail admission@cornish.edu; Internet Home Page Address: www.cornish.edu; *Pres* Sergei Tschernisch; *Provost* Lois Harris PhD; *Art Dept Chair* David Ulrich; *Design Dept Chair* Grant Donesky
Estab 1914; 18; pvt; D ; Scholarships, Fellowships; SC 80, LC 12; D 330, non-maj 10, maj 168 (art), 162 (dos)
Ent Req: HS dipl, application for admission, portfolio review

Degrees: BFA 4 yr, BM 4 yr
Courses: †Animation, Art History, Drawing, Furniture Design, †Gaming Design, Graphic Design, †Illustration, †Interior Design, †Media Art, †Motion Design, †Package Design, Painting, Photography, Printmaking, Sculpture, Video, †Visual Communications, †Web Design

NORTH SEATTLE COMMUNITY COLLEGE, Art Dept, 9600 College Way N, Humanities Division Seattle, WA 98103-3514. Tel 206-934-3709; Fax 206-527-3784; Elec Mail lhull@sccd.ctc.edu; Internet Home Page Address: www.northseattle.edu; *Instr Drawing & Painting* Michelle Kelly, MFA; *Jewelry & Metal Design* Lynne Hull, MFA; *Instr Comp Art* Mark Meyer, MFA; *Ceramics* Liza Halvorson, MFA; *Digital Photog* Erin Burns, MFA; *Gallery Cur* Brenda Anderson, MFA; *Printmaking & Drawing* Amanda Knowles, MFA
Estab 1970; Maintains North Seattle Community College Art Gallery, Library, & on-campus store for art supply purchase; pub; D & E; Scholarships; SC 27, LC 7; D 150, E 65
Income: State funded, foundation endowments, grants
Ent Req: HS dipl
Degrees: AA 2 yr, AFA, CFA 2 yr, CJD
Tuition: Res—undergrad $657.75 per quarter, $62.752 per cr, nonres—$2,393.75 per quarter; no campus res
Courses: Art Appreciation, Art History, Ceramics, Conceptual Art, Design, Drawing, Goldsmithing, History of Art & Architecture, Jewelry, Painting, Photography, Printmaking, Sculpture, Silversmithing
Adult Hobby Classes: Enrl 6600; tuition $657.75 per quarter for res, $2,393.75 per quarter for nonres. Courses—Art History, Basic Drawing, Ceramics, 2-D & 3-D Design, Intro to Art, Jewelry Design, Painting, Sculptures, Water Solvable Media

SEATTLE CENTRAL COMMUNITY COLLEGE, Humanities - Social Sciences Division, 1701 Broadway, Seattle, WA 98122-2400. Tel 206-587-3800; Fax 206-344-4390; Internet Home Page Address: www.seattlecentral.org; *Prof* Ileana Leavens; *Chmn* Audrey Wright; *Prof* Tatiana Garmendia; *Asst Prof* Don Barrie; *Asst Prof* Don Tanze; *Instr* Royal Alley-Bavaes
Estab 1970; pub; D & E; Scholarships; SC 15, LC 5; D 70, E 50
Ent Req: HS dipl, ent exam
Degrees: AA 2 yrs
Tuition: Res—$426 per qtr; nonres—$1692 per qtr; no campus res
Courses: †Aesthetics, †Art Appreciation, Art History, †Design, †Drawing, †History of Art & Architecture, †Mixed Media, Painting, †Printmaking
Summer School: Dir, Ileana Leavens. Courses—Art History, Painting, Sculpture

SEATTLE PACIFIC UNIVERSITY, Art Dept, 3307 Third Ave W, Seattle, WA 98119. Tel 206-281-2079; Fax 206-281-2500; *Prof* Michael Caldwell; *Dean Col Arts & Sciences* Joyce Erickson
Scholarships, Fellowships
Tuition: $4223 per qtr for 12-17 cr; campus res—$1620 room, board & meals
Courses: Art Appreciation, †Art Education, Ceramics, Design, Drawing, Fashion Arts, Handicrafts, Industrial Design, Interior Design, Jewelry, Painting, Printmaking, Sculpture, Textile Design, Weaving
Children's Classes: Tuition $23 for 8 wk session. Courses - General Art for Children
Summer School: Dir, Larry Metcalf. Two 4 wk sessions. Courses - Elementary Art Education Workshops, Fabrics, Monoprinting, Painting, Papermaking, Silkscreening

SEATTLE UNIVERSITY, Dept of Fine Arts, Visual Art Division, 901 12th Ave, Seattle, WA 98122-4411; PO Box 222000, Seattle, WA 98122-1090. Tel 206-296-5356 (Fine Arts Dept), 296-6000; Fax 206-296-5433; Elec Mail venker@seattleu.edu; Internet Home Page Address: www.seattleu.edu/artsci; *Chmn* Josef Venker, SJ, MFA; *Assoc Prof* Francisco Guerrero, MFA; *Assoc Prof* Naomi Kasumi, MFA; *Asst Prof* Claire Garoutte, MFA; *Asst Prof* Ken Allan, PhD; *Asst Prof* Naomi Hume, PhD; *Asst Prof* Alexander Mouton, MFA; *Lectr* Danila Rumold, MFA
1891; Maintain a nonprofit art gallery - Kinsey Gallery, Hedreen Gallery & Vachon Gallery; on-campus art supplies shop; Jesuit/Catholic; D; Scholarships; SC 25, LC 15; D 160, maj 160
Ent Req: HS dipl and entrance exam
Degrees: BA prog offered
Tuition: $685 per cr hr; FT $30,825 per yr
Courses: †Art History, Calligraphy, †Ceramic Sculpture, Ceramics, Costume Design & Construction, †Design, Drawing, Film, Graphic Design, History of Art & Architecture, Painting, †Photography, Printmaking, Stage Design, Studio Art, Theatre Arts, Video
Summer School: Courses—same as regular session

SHORELINE COMMUNITY COLLEGE, Humanities Division, 16101 Greenwood Ave N, Seattle, WA 98133-5696. Tel 206-546-4741; Fax 206-546-5869; Elec Mail mbonar@shoreline.edu; Internet Home Page Address: www.shoreline.edu; *Dean* Norma Goldstein, PhD; *Prof* Chris Simons, MFA; *Prof* Bruce Armstutz, MFA; *Prof* K Takechi; *Prof* Christine Shefner; *Prof* Jim Reddin
Estab 1964; On-campus shop sells art supplies; pub; D & E; Scholarships; SC 9, LC Art History Survey; D 5500
Publications: EBBTIDE, biweekly; Spindrift, annual art & literary publication
Ent Req: HS dipl, col ent exam
Degrees: AA & AFA
Courses: †Advertising Design, Aesthetics, Art Appreciation, Art History, Ceramics, †Commercial Art, Conceptual Art, Constructions, †Costume Design & Construction, Design, †Drafting, Drawing, †Fashion Arts, Film, †Graphic Arts, †Graphic Design, History of Art & Architecture, Mixed Media, Multimedia, Painting, †Photography, Sculpture, Stage Design, †Textile Design, †Video
Summer School: Dir, Marie Rosenwasser. Enrl 45 maximum; two 4 wk terms. Courses—Ceramics, Design, Design Appreciation, Drawing, Electronic Design, Graphic Design, Painting, Photography, Sculpture

UNIVERSITY OF WASHINGTON, School of Art, PO Box 353440, Seattle, WA 98195-3440. Tel 206-543-0970 (Admin), 543-0646 (Advising); Fax 206-685-1657; Internet Home Page Address: www.art.washington.edu; *Dir* Christopher Ozubko

Estab 1878; Maintain a nonprofit art gallery Jacob Lawrence Gallery, Rm 132, Art Bldg; Art Library, Art Bldg Rm 101; pub; D & E; Scholarships; SC 113, LC 84, GC 30; Maj 1100, grad 125
Ent Req: must meet university admis req, must be matriculated to enroll in art classes in acad yr
Degrees: BFA 4 yrs, BA 4 yrs, MA, PhD and MFA, BDes, MDes
Courses: †Art History, †Ceramics, Drawing, Fibers, †Graphic Design, †Industrial Design, †Interaction Design, Interdisciplinary Visual Arts, †Painting, †Photography, †Printmaking, †Sculpture, Textile Design, Video, Weaving
Summer School: Dir, C Ozubko. Enrl 830; 2-month term. Various courses offered through UW Extension, open to community

SPOKANE

GONZAGA UNIVERSITY, Dept of Art, 502 E Boone, College of Arts & Sciences Spokane, WA 99258-1774. Tel 509-328-4220, Ext 6686; *Prof* J Scott Patnode; *Prof* R Gilmore; *Prof* Mary Farrell; *Chmn* Terry Gieber; *Asst Prof* Shalon Parker
Estab 1962; Maintain art/architecture library; FT 4, PT 2; pvt; D & E; SC 20, LC 5, GC 12; D 250 incl maj 40, others 80
Ent Req: HS dipl
Degrees: BA 4 yrs
Tuition: $10,000 per sem; campus res available
Courses: 2-D Design, Art Education, Ceramics, Drawing, †History of Art, Painting, Printmaking, Teacher Training
Summer School: Dean Arts & Sciences, Marc Manganaro. Term of 8 wks beginning June. Courses— Drawing, Painting, Printmaking

SPOKANE FALLS COMMUNITY COLLEGE, Fine Arts Dept, 3410 W Fort George Wright Dr, Spokane, WA 99204-5288. Tel 509-533-3500; 533-3710 (Art Dept); Fax 509-533-3484; Elec Mail jof@sfcc.spokane.cc.wa.us; Elec Mail finearts@spokanefalls.edu; Internet Home Page Address: www.spokanefalls.edu; *Dean* Bonnie Brunt; *Asst Prof* Tom O'Day; *Dept Chmn* Carolyn Stephens; *Asst Prof* Patty Haag; *Asst Prof* Carl Richardson; *Asst Prof* Mardis Nenno; *Adjunct Asst Prof* Peter Jagoda; *Adjunct Asst Prof* Lee Ayars; *Adjunct Asst Prof* Cindy Wilson; *Adjunct Asst Prof* Kurt Madison; *Adjunct Asst Prof* Margot Casstevens; *Adjunct Asst Prof* Tobe Harvey; *Adjunct asst Prof* Bradd Skubinna; *Adjunct Asst Prof* Leona Lopez Schindler; *Asst Prof* Megan Martens-Haworth; *Asst Prof* Garric Simonsen; *Asst Prof* Bernadette Vielbig
Estab 1963; pub; D & E & Sat; Scholarships; SC 41, LC 5, workshops; D 600, E 200
Ent Req: HS dipl, GED
Degrees: AAA 3 yr, AA, AFA & CFA 2 yr
Tuition: Res—$467 per quarter; nonres—$1837 per quarter; no campus res
Courses: Art Education, Art History, †Bronze Casting, Ceramics, Computer Arts, Design 2D & 3D Advanced, Digital Paint, Drawing, Exhibit, Fiber Arts, Handicrafts, Health/Safety in Art, Illustration, Intro to Art, Jewelry, Lettering, Mat/Frame, Mixed Media, †Mold Making, Non-Western Art, Painting, Photography, Portfolio, Printmaking, Sculpture
Adult Hobby Classes: Enrl 10-20; tuition $25.60 for 6 week term. Courses—Art History, Ceramics, Drawing, Watercolor
Children's Classes: Enrl 20-22; tuition $30 for 4 wks. Art Experiences, Courses—Ceramics, Drawing
Summer School: Enrl 100; tuition $50.30 per cr or $503 per 10-18 cr; 6-8 wk term. Courses—Art Workshops, Ceramics, Color & Design, Drawing, Intro to Art, Watercolor

WHITWORTH COLLEGE, Art Dept, 300 W Hawthorne Ave, Spokane, WA 99251-0001. Tel 509-777-1000, 777-3258 (Art Dept); Fax 509-466-3781; Internet Home Page Address: www.whitworth.edu; *Fine Arts Dept Chmn & Asst Prof* Barbara Filo, MA & MFA; *Assoc Prof* Gordon Wilson, MFA; *Instr* Jeff Harris, MFA; *Instr* Carl Stejer; *Assoc Prof* Scott Kolbo, MFA
Pvt; D & E; Scholarships; SC 18, LC 6
Ent Req: HS dipl
Degrees: BA 4 yrs, MA, MAT & MEd 2 yrs
Courses: Art Administration, Art Education, Art History, Ceramics, Drawing, Graphic Design, Leaded Glass, Mixed Media, Painting, Printmaking

STANWOOD

PILCHUCK GLASS SCHOOL, 1201-316th St NW, Stanwood, WA 98292. Tel 360-445-3111; Fax 360-445-5515; Elec Mail info@pilchuck.com; Internet Home Page Address: www.pilchuck.com; *Exec Dir* James Baker
Estab 1971; summer location: 1201 316th St NW, Stanwood, WA 98292-9600, Tel: 206-445-3111, Fax: 206-445-5515; FT & PT 50; pvt; D & E; Scholarships; SC 25; D & E 250
Ent Req: 18 years or older
Courses: Constructions, Glass, Sculpture
Summer School: Exec Dir, Marjorie Levy. Enrl 250; tuition approx $2200 for 2 1/2 wk course. Courses—Casting, Cold Working, Flamework, Fusing, Glassblowing, Mosaic, Stained Glass

TACOMA

PACIFIC LUTHERAN UNIVERSITY, Dept of Art, 12180 Park Ave, Dept Art Tacoma, WA 98447-0001. Tel 253-535-7573; Fax 253-536-5063; Internet Home Page Address: www.plu.eduartd; *Chmn* John Hallam PhD; *Prof* David Keyes, Ma; *Assoc Prof* Dennis Cox, MFA; *Assoc Prof* Beatrice Geller, MFA; *Assoc Prof* Lawrence Gold, MFA; *Assoc Prof* Walt Tomsic, MFA
Estab 1890, dept estab 1960; Maintain nonprofit art gallery on-campus; Den; D & E; Scholarships; SC 29, LC 8; D 800, E 75, maj 60
Ent Req: HS dipl, SAT
Degrees: BA, BAEd & BFA 4 yrs

Tuition: $19,000 per yr
Courses: Art Appreciation, Art Education, Art History, †Ceramics, †Drawing, Electronic Imaging, †Graphic Arts, †Graphic Design, Illustration, †Mixed Media, †Painting, †Photography, †Printmaking, †Sculpture

TACOMA COMMUNITY COLLEGE, Art Dept, 6501 S 19th St, Tacoma, WA 98466-6100. Tel 253-566-5000, 566-5260 (Art Dept); Fax 253-566-6070; Internet Home Page Address: www.tacoma.ctc.edu; *Art Dept Chmn* Richard Mahaffey
Estab 1965; FT 5; pub; D & E; Scholarships; SC 35, LC 1; D & E 1500
Degrees: AAS & Assoc in Liberal Arts 2 yrs
Courses: 2-D & 3-D Design, Art History, Figure Drawing, Jewelry, Painting, Photography, Pottery, Printmaking, Sculpture

UNIVERSITY OF PUGET SOUND, Art Dept, 1500 N Warner St #1072, Tacoma, WA 98416-1072. Tel 253-879-2806; Fax 253-879-3500; Elec Mail ledgar@pugetsound.edu; Internet Home Page Address: www.pugetsound.edu; *Chmn* Linda Williams
Estab 1935; maintains nonprofit gallery, Kittredge Gallery, same location; FT 7; pvt; D; Scholarships; SC 17, LC 15; maj 119, undergrad 455
Ent Req: HS grad
Degrees: BA 4 yrs
Courses: Art History, Ceramics, Design, Drawing, Oriental Art, Painting, Photography, Printmaking, Sculpture, Studio Art, Studio Design
Summer School: Courses—Art Education, Art History, Ceramics, Drawing, Painting, Watercolor

VANCOUVER

CLARK COLLEGE, Art Dept, 1800 E McLoughlin Blvd, Vancouver, WA 98663-3598. Tel 360-694-6521; Fax 360-992-2828; Internet Home Page Address: www.clark.edu; *Coordr* Chuck Ramsey
Estab 1933, dept estab 1947; pub; D & E; Scholarships; SC 87, LC 3; D 400, E 500
Ent Req: open door
Degrees: Assoc of Arts & Science, Assoc of Applied Science, & Assoc of General Studies 2 yrs
Courses: Art History, Calligraphy, Ceramics, Drawing, Graphic Design, Handicrafts, Jewelry, Lettering, Painting, Photography
Summer School: Dir Chuck Ramsey. Enrl 40 FTE; tuition $27.50 per cr. Courses—Art Appreciation, Art History, Calligraphy, Ceramics, Drawing, Photography, Watercolor

WALLA WALLA

WALLA WALLA COMMUNITY COLLEGE, Fine Arts Dept, 500 Tausick Way, Walla Walla, WA 99362-9267. Tel 509-527-1873; Elec Mail lisa.rasmussen@wwcc.edu; Internet Home Page Address: www.wwcc.edu; *Coordr & Instr* Lisa Anne Rasmussen; *Instr* Elizabeth Harris; *Instr* Margaret Jamison; *Instr* Warren Rood; *Instr* Sara Wyman
Estab 1967; Maintains a non-profit art gallery; on-campus art supply shop; pub; D, E, online; Scholarships; SC 8, LC 2; D115, E 15, non-maj 100, maj 15
Ent Req: HS dipl, equivalent
Degrees: AA 2 yr
Tuition: $476.16 ea studio class (4) Cr; 5 Cr classes $595.20
Courses: Art Appreciation, Art History, Ceramics, Commercial Art, Design, Drawing, Handicrafts, Photography, Pottery, Printmaking, Sculpture
Adult Hobby Classes: Watercolors, Woodworking 2 Cr
Children's Classes: Kids college $200
Summer School: Tuition same as regular quarter

WHITMAN COLLEGE, Art Dept, 345 Boyer Ave, Olin Hall Walla Walla, WA 99362-2067. Tel 509-527-5204; Fax 509-527-5039; *Chmn* Charles Timm-Ballard; *Instr* Charly Bloomquist; *Vis Asst Prof Art* Mare Bolker; *Asst Prof Art* Michelle Acuff; *Asst Prof Art* Justin Lincoln; *Vis Asst Prof Art* Joe Page; *Instr* Malunda Povlsen-Jones; *Instr* Dawn Forbes
Estab 1883; Maintains nonprofit gallery, Sheehan Gallery & Bleesway Student Gallery; Pvt; D & E; Scholarships; SC 31, LC 3; D 320, E 30, non-maj 200, maj 150
Ent Req: HS dipl, ent exam
Degrees: BA 4 yrs
Tuition: $26,870 per yr
Courses: Aesthetics, Art History, Book Arts, Ceramics, Drawing, History of Art & Architecture, Painting, Photography, Printmaking, Sculpture

WENATCHEE

WENATCHEE VALLEY COLLEGE, Art Dept, 1300 Fifth St, Wenatchee, WA 98801. Tel 509-682-6780; Fax 504-664-2538; Elec Mail sbailey@wvc.edu; *Prof* Scott Bailey
Estab 1939; Maintain nonprofit art gallery, Robert Graves Gallery, 1300 Fifth St, Wenatchee, WA 98801; pub; D & E; Scholarships; SC, LC; D 550, E 200, maj 45
Ent Req: HS dipl, open door policy
Degrees: AA 2 yrs
Courses: Aesthetics, Art Appreciation, Art History, Ceramics, Color Theory, Design, Drawing, Graphic Arts, Graphic Design, Illustration, Painting, Printmaking, Sculpture
Summer School: Dir, Dr Joann Schoen

YAKIMA

YAKIMA VALLEY COMMUNITY COLLEGE, Dept of Visual Arts, S 16th Ave & Nob Hill Blvd, Yakima, WA 98907; PO Box 22520, Yakima, WA 98907-2520. Tel 509-574-4846 (Chair), 574-4844 (R Dorn), 574-4845 (Assoc

faculty), 574-4600 (Main); Elec Mail rfisher@yvcc.edu; Elec Mail rdorn@yucc.edu; Internet Home Page Address: www.yvcc.edu; *Dir* Robert A Fisher; *Faculty* Herb Blisard; *Faculty* Rachel Dorn
Estab 1928; Maintain nonprofit art gallery affiliated with Larson Gallery at Yakima Valley Col, PO Box 22520, Yakima, WA 98907; art supplies available on-campus; PT 5; pub; D&E; Scholarships; SC 9, LC 2; D 250, E 100, non-maj 320, maj 30
Ent Req: HS dipl
Degrees: AA & AS offered
Tuition: Res—$66.55 per cr hr; nonres—$79.74 per cr hr with waiver; international $238.25
Courses: Art Appreciation, Art History, Ceramics, Design, Drawing, Graphic Design, Jewelry, Painting, Photography, Sculpture, Silversmithing
Summer School: Dir, Robert A Fisher. Tuition $530 per quarter, FT

WEST VIRGINIA

ATHENS

CONCORD COLLEGE, Fine Art Division, PO Box 1000, Athens, WV 24712-1000. Tel 304-384-3115; Fax 304-384-9044; *Prof* Gerald C Arrington, MFA; *Asst Prof* Sheila M Chipley, EdD; *Asst Prof* Steve Glazer, EdD
Estab 1872, dept estab 1925; pub; D & E; Scholarships; SC 32, LC 3; non-maj 200, maj 75, D 75
Ent Req: HS dipl
Degrees: BA & BS 4 yrs
Tuition: Res—$1223 per sem; nonres—$2488 per sem; campus res—room & board available
Courses: †Advertising, Advertising Design, Art Education, Art History, Ceramics, Collage, Commercial Art, Drawing, Graphic Arts, Graphic Design, Handicrafts, Illustration, Painting, Printmaking, Sculpture, Teacher Training
Adult Hobby Classes: Enrl varies; tuition based on part-time rates. Courses—Vary
Children's Classes: Enrl varies; tuition none for 4 wk sessions. Courses vary
Summer School: Term of 5 wks beginning June. Courses—varied

BETHANY

BETHANY COLLEGE, Dept of Fine Arts, 1 Main St, Bethany, WV 26032. Tel 304-829-7000; Fax 304-829-7312; Internet Home Page Address: www.bethanywv.edu; *Assoc Prof Studio Art* Kenneth Morgan; *Head Dept* Herb Weaver
Estab 1840, dept estab 1958; den; D; Scholarships; SC 27, LC 7; D 136, non-maj 106, maj 30
Ent Req: HS dipl
Degrees: BA & BS 4 yrs
Tuition: $14,752 per yr; campus res available
Courses: Art History, Calligraphy, Ceramics, Drawing, Graphic Design, Illustration, Painting, Photography, Sculpture

BLUEFIELD

BLUEFIELD STATE COLLEGE, Division of Arts & Sciences, 219 Rock St, Bluefield, WV 24701-2198. Tel 304-327-4000; Fax 304-325-7747; Internet Home Page Address: www.bluefieldstate.edu; *Prof* Joyce Shamro; *Head Dept* Jim Voelker
Estab 1895; pub; D & E; Scholarships, Fellowships; SC 14, LC 4; D 125, E 40, non-maj 150, minor 10, other 5
Ent Req: HS dipl, 18 yrs old
Degrees: BA, BA(Humanities), BS, BS(Educ) & BS(Engineering Technology) 4 yrs
Courses: Art Education, Art History, Ceramics, Computer Art, Drawing, Painting, Photography, Printmaking, Sculpture
Adult Hobby Classes: Enrl 10-15. Courses—Art in Western World, Photography, Television, Woodcarving
Children's Classes: Enrl varies. Courses—Ceramics, Drawing
Summer School: Dir, Dwight Moore. Enrl 15-20; term of 5 wks beginning June/July. Courses—Art Educ & Appreciation (workshops on occasion)

BUCKHANNON

WEST VIRGINIA WESLEYAN COLLEGE, Art Dept, 59 College Ave, Buckhannon, WV 26201-2699. Tel 304-473-8000, 473-8433; Elec Mail mason_k@wvwc.edu; Internet Home Page Address: www.wvwc.edu/aca/art/artfront; *Assoc* Margo Davis; *Chmn & Assoc Prof* Kelvin Mason; *Assoc Prof* Carol Pelletier; *Asst Prof* Brent Patterson
Estab 1890; Maintains nonprofit art gallery; art supplies available for purchase on campus; Den; D & E; SC 16, LC 6; non-maj 120, maj 20, grad 2
Ent Req: HS dipl, ent exam
Degrees: BA
Courses: Art Education, Art History, Ceramics, Computer Graphics, Computer Illustration, Design, Drawing, Graphic Design, Painting, Printmaking, Sculpture, Theatre Arts

CHARLESTON

UNIVERSITY OF CHARLESTON, Carleton Varney Dept of Art & Design, 2300 MacCorkle Ave SE, Charleston, WV 25304. Tel 304-357-4725; Fax 304-357-4175; Elec Mail swatts@ucwv.edu; *Coordr* Steve Watts; *Dir* Joellen Kerr; *Instr* Tracy Wasinger, BS
Estab 1888; FT 3, PT 3; pvt; D & E; Scholarships; maj 55

Ent Req: usual col req
Degrees: 4 yr
Courses: Advanced Studio, Art Administration, Art Appreciation, †Art Education, Art History, Color Theory, Design, Drafting, Drawing, †Interior Design, Painting, Photography, Printmaking, Teacher Training
Children's Classes: Enrl 30; tuition by the wk. Courses—Summer Art Camp Program
Summer School: Dir, Joellen Kerr. Tuition $60 per wk. Courses—Summer Colors

ELKINS

DAVIS & ELKINS COLLEGE, Dept of Art, 100 Campus Dr, Elkins, WV 26241-3996. Tel 304-637-1212; Fax 304-637-1287; Elec Mail larosem@DnE.edu; *Head, Assoc Prof* Matthew LaRose; *Adjunct Instr* Holly Adams; *Adjunct Instr* Mary Rayme; *Adjunct Instr* Donna Morgan
Estab 1904; FT 1, PT 3; pvt, den; D & E; Scholarships; SC 18, LC 4; non-maj 30, maj 10
Ent Req: HS dipl
Degrees: BA, BS
Tuition: $5290 per sem; campus res available
Courses: †Art Education, Art History, Ceramics, Costume Design & Construction, Drawing, Graphic Arts, Painting, Pottery, †Printmaking, Sculpture, Stage Design, †Theatre Arts, Weaving
Adult Hobby Classes: Enrl 90
Summer School: Dir Margo Blevin. Augusta Heritage Arts Workshop. Courses—Appalachian Crafts, Basketry, Bushcraft, Calligraphy, Chair Bottoming, Dance, Folkcarving, Folklore Musical Instrument Construction & Repair, Papermaking, Pottery, Stained Glass, Woodworking

FAIRMONT

FAIRMONT STATE COLLEGE, Div of Fine Arts, 1201 Locust Ave, Fairmont, WV 26554-2451. Tel 304-367-4000; Internet Home Page Address: www.fscwv.edu; *Prof* John Clovis, MFA; *Prof Dr* Stephen Smigocki PhD, MFA; *Prof* Barry Snyder, MFA; *Prof* Lynn Boggess, MFA
Pub; D & E; Scholarships; D maj 35, non-maj 15
Ent Req: HS dipl
Degrees: BA(Art Educ) and BS(Graphics, Fine Arts) 4 yrs
Courses: †Art Education, Art History, Ceramics, Commercial Design, Design, Drawing, Graphic Arts, Painting, Photography, Printmaking, Sculpture
Adult Hobby Classes: Two - three times a wk for 16 wks. Courses—same as above
Children's Classes: Enrl 20; tuition $25 per 6 wk term. Courses—Art for children ages 5 - 12, 2 - D & 3 - D Design
Summer School: Dir Dr S Snyder. Enrl 50; 4 wks per sessions. Courses—Art Education, Drawing, Design, Painting, Art Appreciation

GLENVILLE

GLENVILLE STATE COLLEGE, Dept of Fine Arts, 200 High St, Glenville, WV 26351-1200. Tel 304-462-6340; Fax 304-462-4049; Elec Mail liza.brenner@glenville.edu; Internet Home Page Address: www.glenville.edu; *Chmn* Lloyd E Bone Jr; *Assoc Prof* Liza Brenner, MFA; *Assoc Prof* Chris Cosner, MFA; *Assoc Prof* Duane Chapman, MFA
Estab 1872, dept estab 1952; Maintains a non-profit art gallery & on-campus supplies shop; pub; D & E; Scholarships; SC 25, LC 3; D 128, E 42, non-maj 14, maj 55
Ent Req: HS dipl
Degrees: BA 4 yrs
Courses: Art Appreciation, †Art Education, Art History, †Ceramics, Drawing, Graphic Arts, Jewelry, Lettering, †Painting, Photography, Printmaking, Sculpture, †Studio Art, Textile Design, Weaving

HUNTINGTON

MARSHALL UNIVERSITY, Dept of Art & Design, 1 John Marshall Dr, Huntington, WV 25755-0003. Tel 304-696-6760; 696-2296 (Gallery); Fax 304-696-6505; Elec Mail clercx@marshall.edu; Internet Home Page Address: www.marshall.edu; *Chmn* Byron Clercx
Estab 1903; Maintains Birke Art Gallery; FT 10; pub; maj incl grad 108
Ent Req: HS grad
Degrees: BFA & MA in art educ & studio 4 yrs
Courses: Art Education, Ceramics, Graphic Design, Painting, Photography, Printmaking, Sculpture, Weaving
Summer School: Tuition $427.10 for 6 sem hrs, nonres $1247.10 for 5 wk terms

INSTITUTE

WEST VIRGINIA STATE UNIVERSITY, Art Dept, PO Box 1000, Campus Box 4 Institute, WV 25112-1000. Tel 304-766-3196, 766-3198; Fax 304-768-9842; Internet Home Page Address: www.wvstateu.edu; *Chair* Reidun Ovrebo PhD; *Asst Prof* Molly Erlandson; *Asst Prof* Paula Clendenin
D & E; Scholarships; SC 26, LC 11
Ent Req: HS dipl
Degrees: AB(Art) and BSEd(Art) 4 yrs
Tuition: Res—$1282 per sem; nonres—$2946 per sem
Courses: Appalachian Art & Crafts, Art Education, Art History, Ceramics, Computer Graphics, Design, Drawing, Figure Drawing, Graphic Design, Painting, Photography, Printmaking, Sculpture, Teacher Training
Summer School: Dir, R Ovrebo. Enrl 75.; 3 or 6 wk session. Courses—Art Appreciation, Basic Studio

KEYSER

POTOMAC STATE COLLEGE, Dept of Art, 101 Fort Ave, Keyser, WV 26726-2600. Tel 304-788-6800; Internet Home Page Address: www.wvu.edu; *Pres* Anthony Whitmore, MA; *Chmn* Richard Davis
College estab 1953, dept estab 1974; FT 2; pub; D & E; SC 8, LC 2; D 160, non-maj 150, others 10
Ent Req: HS dipl
Degrees: AA 2 yrs, AAS 2 yrs
Courses: Drawing, Painting, Sculpture, Visual Foundation
Summer School: Dir, Edward Wade. Courses—Art Appreciation, Drawing, Painting

MONTGOMERY

WEST VIRGINIA INSTITUTE OF TECHNOLOGY, Creative Arts Dept, 405 Fayette Pike, Montgomery, WV 25136-2436. Tel 304-442-3192 (Dept), 442-3071; Elec Mail rsimile@wvutech.edu; Internet Home Page Address: www.wvutech.edu; *Head Dept* Robert Simile
Estab 1896; pub; Scholarships; 3500 (total)
Ent Req: HS grad
Degrees: AS, BA and BS 2-4 yrs
Courses: Art Appreciation, Ceramics, Design, Graphic Design, Painting

MORGANTOWN

WEST VIRGINIA UNIVERSITY, College of Creative Arts, School of Art & Design, PO Box 6111, School of Art & Design Morgantown, WV 26506-6111. Tel 304-293-4077/2552; Fax 304-293-5731; Elec Mail alison.helm@mail.wvu.edu; Internet Home Page Address: www.wvu.edu; *Prof* Robert Anderson, MFA; *Prof* Janet Snyder, PhD; *Prof* Victoria Fergus PhD, MFA; *Prof* Naijun Zhang, MFA; *Prof* Kristina Olson, MA; *Prof* Eve Faulkes, MFA; *Prof & Dir of Art* Alison Helm, MFA; *Prof* Joseph Lupo, MFA; *Visiting Asst Prof* Dylan Collins, MFA; *Asst Prof* Joseph Galbreath, MFA; *Assoc Prof* Gerald Habarth, MFA; *Assoc Prof* Jason Lee, MFA; *Assoc Prof* Rhonda Reymond, PhD; *Assoc Prof* Shoji Satake, MFA; *Assoc Prof* Michael Sherwin, MFA; *Asst Prof* Robert Moore, MFA; *Asst Prof* kofi Opoku, MFA; *Assoc Prof, Dir* Alison Helm
Estab 1867, div estab 1897; Maintain nonprofit art gallery; Mesaros Gallery; Evansdale Library; on-campus shop where art supplies may be purchased; 16; Pub; D & E; Scholarships; SC, LC, GC; D 250, non-maj 5, maj 323, grad 20, others 87
Ent Req: HS dipl
Degrees: BFA & certification (Art Educ) and BFA 4 yrs, MA (Art) and MFA (Art) 3 yrs; grad degrees
Courses: Art Appreciation, †Art Education, †Art History, Basic Design, †Ceramics, †Conceptual Art, †Design, Drawing, Electronic Media, †Graphic Arts, †Graphic Design, †History of Art & Architecture, †Mixed Media, †Museum Staff Training, †Occupational Therapy, †Painting, Photography, †Printmaking, †Sculpture, Video

PARKERSBURG

WEST VIRGINIA UNIVERSITY AT PARKERSBURG, Art Dept, 300 Campus Dr, Parkersburg, WV 26101-8656. Tel 304-424-8000; Fax 304-424-8354; Internet Home Page Address: www.wvup.wvnet.edu; *Chmn* Dr Nancy Nanney; *Asst Prof* Henry Aglio, MFA; *Instr* Sarah Beth Cox
Estab 1961, dept estab 1973; pub; D & E; Scholarships; SC 25, LC 5; D 120, E 80, non-maj 125, maj 8
Ent Req: HS dipl plus diagnostic tests in Reading, Math & English
Degrees: AA 2 yrs, BA
Courses: Art History, Bronze Castings, Ceramics, Drawing, Painting, Photography, Printmaking, Wood Carvings
Summer School: Chmn, Dr Nancy Nanney. Tuition $49.50 per cr hr

SHEPHERDSTOWN

SHEPHERD UNIVERSITY, Dept of Contemporary Art & Theater, Ctr for Contemporary Art, 92 W Campus Dr Shepherdstown, WV 25443; P.O. Box 5000, Shepherdstown, WV 25443-5000. Tel 304-876-5254; Fax 304-876-5766; Elec Mail rsmith@shepherd.edu; Internet Home Page Address: www.shepherd.edu/artweb/; WATS 800-826-6807; *Dean* Dow Benedict; *Coordr Photog* Rich Bruner; *Coordr Design* Kristin Kaineg; *Chair & Coordr Non-Toxic Printmaking* Rhonda Smith; *Dir Exhib* Mike Mendez; *Coordr Painting* Sonya Evanisko; *Co-Coordr Photog* Stephanie Robbins; *Coordr Theater* Ed Herendeen; *Coordr Sculpture* Christian Benefiel; *Coordr Art History* Chris Coltrin; *Coordr Art Educ* David Modler; *Coordr Computer Labs* Melissa Scotton
Estab 1872; Maintain a nonprofit art gallery - Frank Center Gallery, Frank Center for Creative Arts, Shepherd Univ, Shepherdstown, WV 25443; on-campus shop where art supplies may be purchased; FT 11, PT 15; pub; D & E; Scholarships; SC 58, LC 12, GC 4; maj 250; grad stu 2-5
Ent Req: HS dipl, portfolio
Degrees: AA and BFA, BA(Educ)
Tuition: $2,282/sem full-time
Courses: Advertising Design, Aesthetic Criticism, Aesthetics, Art Appreciation, †Art Education, Art History, Art Therapy, Conceptual Art, Constructions, Design, Drawing, †Graphic Design, History of Art & Architecture, Intermedia, Mixed Media, †Painting, †Photography, †Printmaking, †Sculpture, Teacher Training, Theatre Arts, Video
Summer School: Chair, Rhonda Smith. Enrl 60; courses—Art Appreciation, Studio, Photo

WEST LIBERTY

WEST LIBERTY STATE COLLEGE, Div Art, PO Box 295, 125 Campus Service Center West Liberty, WV 26074-0295. Tel 304-336-8096; Fax 304-336-8056; Elec Mail dejaager@wlsc.edu; Internet Home Page Address: www.wlsc.edu; *Chmn* Mark Williams, MFA; *Assoc Prof* Robert Villmagna; *Asst Prof* Brian Fencl; *Assoc Prof* Jim Haizlett; *Instr* Brad Johnson; *Instr* Paula Lucas
Estab 1836; pub; D & E; Scholarships; SC 40, LC 6; D 855, E 140, non-maj 900, maj 90, others 12
Ent Req: HS dipl, score of 17 or higher on ACT test or cumulative HS GPA of at least 2.0 or a combined verbal/math score of 680 on the SAT
Degrees: BA and BS 4 yrs
Courses: Advertising Design, Art Appreciation, †Art Education, Art History, Ceramics, Computer Graphics, Costume Design & Construction, Drawing, Film, Graphic Arts, †Graphic Design, History of Art & Architecture, Illustration, Jewelry, Lettering, Painting, Photography, Printmaking, Sculpture, Stage Design, Studio Crafts, Theatre Arts, Weaving
Summer School: Dir, David T Jauersak. Tuition res $100 per sem hr, nonres $190 per sem hr. Courses—Art Education, Special Education

WISCONSIN

APPLETON

LAWRENCE UNIVERSITY, Dept of Art & Art History, Wriston Art Ctr, 613 E College Ave Appleton, WI 54911; 711 E Boldt Way Appleton, WI 54911. Tel 920-832-6621; Fax 920-832-7362; Internet Home Page Address: www.lawrence.edu/dept/art; *Chmn* Carol Lawton; *Assoc Prof* Robert Neilson; *Assoc Prof* J Lindemann; *Assoc Prof* J Shimon; *Assoc Prof* Elizabeth Carlson; *Assoc Prof* Benjamin Rhinehart
Estab 1847; Maintain nonprofit art gallery; FT 6; pvt; D; Scholarships; SC 21, LC 21
Ent Req: HS performance, CEEB scores, recommendation
Degrees: BA 4 yrs
Tuition: $40,200 includes room & board per 3 term yr
Courses: 3-D Design, Art Education, †Art History, Ceramics, Drawing, Painting, Photography, Printmaking, Sculpture, †Studio Art, Studio Ceramics

DE PERE

SAINT NORBERT COLLEGE, Div of Humanities & Fine Arts, 100 Grant St, De Pere, WI 54115-2099. Tel 920-403-3119 (Dir of Humanities); Fax 920-403-4086; Internet Home Page Address: www.snc.edu/; *Dir* Dr Howard Ebert
Estab 1898; FT 6; pvt den; D; SC 19, LC 5; D 60, maj 60
Ent Req: HS dipl, ent exam
Degrees: BA 4 yrs
Courses: Aesthetics, Art Education, Art History, Ceramics, Drawing, Graphic Arts, Graphic Design, Illustration, Jewelry, Painting, Photography, Sculpture, Teacher Training
Summer School: Terms of 3 or 5 wks beginning June. Courses—Art Education, Ceramics, Drawing, History of Art, Painting, Sculpture

EAU CLAIRE

UNIVERSITY OF WISCONSIN-EAU CLAIRE, Dept of Art & Design, 105 Garfield Ave, Eau Claire, WI 54701-4811; PO Box 4004, Eau Claire, WI 54702-4004. Tel 715-836-3277; Fax 715-836-4882; Internet Home Page Address: www.uwec.edu/; *Chmn* Christos Theo; *Prof Art & Design* Li-ying Bao; *Prof* Eugene Hood; *Prof* D Scott Robertson; *Dir Foster Gallery Woodshop Supv* Tom Wagener; *Assoc Prof* Lia Johnson; *Asst Prof* Jyl Kelley; *Asst Prof* Jason Lanka; *Assoc Prof* Jian Luo; *Assoc Prof* Susan O'Brien; *Assoc Prof* Karen O'Day; *Asst Prof* Gill Olon; *Assoc Prof* Sandra Starck; *Asst Prof* Wanrudee Buranakorn; *Asst Prof* Sooyun Im
Estab 1916; Maintains a nonprofit art gallery: Foster Gallery, Univ WI-Eau Claire, 121 Water St. Eau Claire, WI; pub; D & E; Scholarships; SC, LC varies; maj 325
Ent Req: HS dipl
Degrees: BA, BS & BFA 4 yrs
Tuition: Res—$8,148 per yr; nonres—$16,176 per yr
Courses: †Art Education, †Art History, †Ceramics, †Drawing, †Graphic Design, †Illustration, †Painting, †Photography, †Printmaking, †Sculpture

FOND DU LAC

MARIAN UNIVERSITY, Art Dept, 45 S National Ave, Fond Du Lac, WI 54935-4621. Tel 920-923-7612; Fax 920-923-7154; Elec Mail mmerline@marianuniversity.edu; Internet Home Page Address: www.mariancoll.edu/; *Dean Arts, Humanities & Letters* James van Dyke, PhD; *Chair Art Dept* Mark Merline, MFA; *Assoc Prof* Tom Wallestad; *Instr* Hillary Quella; *Instr* Leah Klapperich; *Instr* Deborah Bartelt; *Instr* Shane McAdams; *Instr* Evelyn McLean-Cowan
Estab 1936; Four yr schols open to all; pvt; D & E; Scholarships; SC 10, LC 10; D 1,200, E 200, maj 50
Ent Req: HS dipl, ACT or SAT
Degrees: BA and BS 4 yrs
Tuition: $19,590 per yr, $300 per cr; campus res available
Courses: †Advertising Design, Aesthetics, Art Appreciation, †Art Education, Art History, †Art Therapy, Ceramics, †Commercial Art, †Conceptual Art, †Constructions, Design, †Display, Drawing, Fiber Arts, †Graphic Arts, Illustration, Jewelry, Mixed Media, Painting, Photography, Printmaking, Puppetry, Sculpture, Teacher Training

Adult Hobby Classes: Workshops, summer sessions, continuing education
Children's Classes: In Relationship with Art Education
Summer School: Workshops, cr art courses

GREEN BAY

UNIVERSITY OF WISCONSIN-GREEN BAY, Arts Dept, 2420 Nicolet, Green Bay, WI 54311-7001. Tel 920-465-2348, 465-2310; Fax 920-465-2890; Internet Home Page Address: www.uwgb.edu; *Assoc Prof* Ronald Baba; *Prof* David Damkoehler; *Chmn* Curt Heuer; *Assoc Prof* Jeff Benzow; *Assoc Prof* Christine Style; *Asst Prof* Jan Bradfield; *Asst Prof* Jennifer Mokren; *Asst Prof* Elizabeth Ament; *Prof* Jery Dell; *Prof* Carol Emmons; *Prof* Karon Winzenz
Estab 1970; FT 3; pub; D & E; SC 29, LC 3; D 5500
Ent Req: HS dipl, ent exam
Degrees: BA and BS 4 yrs
Courses: Acting & Directing, Aesthetics, Art Education, Ceramics, Costume & Makeup Design, Drawing, Environmental Design, Graphic Communications, Graphic Design, Intermedia, Jewelry, Mixed Media, Painting, Photography, Printmaking, Sculpture, Stage Design, Styles, Textile Design, Theatre Arts
Children's Classes: Varies
Summer School: Courses—vary

KENOSHA

CARTHAGE COLLEGE, Art Dept, 2001 Alford Park Dr, Kenosha, WI 53140-1929. Tel 262-551-5859; Fax 262-551-6208; Internet Home Page Address: www.carthage.edu; *Chmn* Ed Kalke
Estab 1963; Priv, den; D & E; Scholarships
Degrees: BA
Tuition: Res—$18,205 per term; campus res—room & board $5465
Courses: Advertising Design, Art Education, Art History, Basic Photography, Ceramics, Design, Drawing, Graphic Design

UNIVERSITY OF WISCONSIN-PARKSIDE, Art Dept, 400 Wood Rd, Kenosha, WI 53144; PO Box 2000, Kenosha, WI 53141-2000. Tel 414-595-2581; Fax 414-595-2271; *Prof* Douglas DeVinny, MFA; *Assoc Prof* Dennis Bayuzick, MFA; *Assoc Prof* Alan Goldsmith, MFA; *Prof* David Holmes, MFA; *Asst Prof* Trenton Baylor, MFA; *Asst Prof* Susan Funkenstein, PhD; *Lectr* Rob Miller, MA; *Asst Prof* Lisa Barber; *Asst Prof* Tao Chen
Estab 1965; Maintain nonprofit art gallery; Commun Arts Gallery, Kenosha, WI; art supplies available on-campus; Pub; D & E; Scholarships; SC 25, LC 6
Ent Req: ent req HS dipl, upper 50%
Degrees: BA and BS 4 yrs
Courses: Advertising Design, Aesthetics, †Animation, Art Appreciation, †Art Education, Art History, Art Metals, †Ceramics, †Design, †Drawing, †Graphic Arts, †Graphic Design, History of Art & Architecture, Illustration, †Illustration, Jewelry, Life Drawing, †Painting, †Printmaking, †Sculpture, Silversmithing, Teacher Training, Textile Design, Weaving, †Web Design
Summer School: Tuition $210 res hr for term of 8 wks beginning mid June. Courses—Vary from summer to summer

LA CROSSE

UNIVERSITY OF WISCONSIN-LA CROSSE, Center for the Arts, 1725 State St, La Crosse, WI 54601-3788. Tel 608-785-8230; Fax 608-785-8840; Internet Home Page Address: www.uwlax.edu/art; *Chmn* Jennifer Williams Terpstra; *Gallery Dir* John Ready
Estab 1905; University maintains a nonprofit art gallery; on-campus shop for purchase of art supplies; FT 8; pub; D & E; Scholarships; SC 25, LC 5; (univ) 7600
Ent Req: HS dipl
Degrees: BA and BS 4 yrs
Tuition: Res—$155.90 per cr hr; nonres—$468.90 per cr hr
Courses: 2-D & 3-D Design, Aesthetics in Art Criticism in the Visual Arts, Ancient Art of the Western World, Art Appreciation, Art Education, Art Metals, Blacksmithing, Ceramics, Computer Art, Drawing, Figure Drawing, Graphic Arts, History of American Art, Medieval Art of the Western World, Modern Art of the Western World, Multi-Cultural Art Survey, Painting, Printmaking, Renaissance Art of the Western World, Sculpture
Adult Hobby Classes: Courses—Blacksmithing, Ceramics, Outreach Jewelry
Summer School: Courses—vary

VITERBO COLLEGE, Art Dept, 815 S Ninth, La Crosse, WI 54601. Tel 608-796-3000, 796-3755; Fax 608-791-0367; Elec Mail lschoenfielder@viterbo.edu; Internet Home Page Address: www.viterbo.edu/; *Asst Prof* Edward Rushton; *Instr* Diane Crane; *Chmn* Lisa Schoenfielder; *Prof* Peter Fletcher; *Asst Prof* Tom Bartel
Estab 1890; pvt; D & E; Scholarships; SC 10-12, LC 6; D 55, maj 55
Degrees: BA, BAEd & BS 4 yrs
Courses: Advertising Design, Art Education, Art History, Ceramics, Commercial Art, Drawing, Fibers, Graphic Arts, Illustration, Painting, Photography, Printmaking, Sculpture, Teacher Training, Weaving

WESTERN WISCONSIN TECHNICAL COLLEGE, Graphics Division, 400 7th St N, La Crosse, WI 54601-3368. Tel 608-785-9200; Fax 608-785-9473; Elec Mail west@fahlr.wwtc.edu; Internet Home Page Address: wwtc.edu; *Chmn* Richard Westpfahl; *Program Head* Philip Brochhauren; *Instr* Barb Fischer; *Instr* Craig Kunce; *Instr* Lane Butz; *Instr* Eddie Hale; *Instr* Ken Hey; *Instr* Chris Bucheit; *Visual Com Instr* Mark Davini; *Visual Com Instr* Jacob Griggs; *Electronic Imaging & Print Instr* Janet Oglesby; *Electronic Imag & Print Instr* Eugene Van Roy
Estab 1911, dept estab 1964; pub; D & E; Scholarships; SC & LC 16; D 130, E 145, non-maj 132, maj 143

Ent Req: HS dipl or GED
Degrees: AAS 2 yrs
Courses: Advertising Design, †Commercial Art, Computer Graphics, Display, Film, †Graphic Arts, Graphic Design, Illustration, Lettering, Media, Mixed Media, Painting, Photography, Printing & Publishing, Stage Design, Video, Visual Communications
Adult Hobby Classes: Enrl 264. Courses—Color Photo Printing, Painting, Photography, Computer Graphics
Summer School: Dir, Richard Westpfahl. Courses—varied

MADISON

EDGEWOOD COLLEGE, Art Dept, 1000 Edgewood College Dr, Madison, WI 53711-1997. Tel 608-663-2307; Fax 608-663-3291; Elec Mail rtarrell@edgewood.edu; Internet Home Page Address: www.edgewood.edu/; *Assoc Prof* David Smith; *Assoc Prof* Melanie Herzog; *Instr* Ellen Meyer; *Instr* Mary Lybarger; *Asst Prof* Randy Feig; *Asst Prof* Janice M Havlena; *Prof* Robert Tarrell; *Asst Prof* Alan Luft; *Instr* Tracy Dietzel; *Instr* Jane Fasse
Estab 1941; Maintain nonprofit art gallery; DeRicci Gallery; den; D & E; Grants
Ent Req: HS dipl, ACT
Degrees: BA or BS 4 yrs
Tuition: $7100 per sem; campus res available
Courses: †Art Education, Art Therapy, Calligraphy, Ceramics, Design, Drawing, Graphic Design, Painting, Photography, †Printmaking, Sculpture, †Teacher Training, Textile Design, Video
Summer School: Dir, Dr Joseph Schmiedicke. Tuition $110 per cr. Courses—vary

MADISON AREA TECHNICAL COLLEGE, Art Dept, 1701 Wright St, Madison, WI 53704-2599. Tel 608-246-6058, 246-6100, 246-6002; Fax 608-246-6880; *Chmn* Jerry E Butler PhD
Estab 1911; Pub; D & E; Scholarships; SC 45, LC 12; D 5,300, E 23,000 (part-time)
Ent Req: HS dipl
Degrees: AA 2 yrs (Commercial Art, Interior Designing, Photography & Visual Communications)
Tuition: $64 per cr
Courses: Advertising Design, Art History, Calligraphy, Ceramics, †Commercial Art, Design, Display, Drawing, Handicrafts, Illustration, Jewelry, Lettering, Painting, †Photography, Printmaking, Visual Communications
Adult Hobby Classes: Enrl 1,000. Courses—same as regular session

UNIVERSITY OF WISCONSIN, MADISON, Dept of Art, 455 N Park St, 6241 Humanities Bldg Madison, WI 53706-1483. Tel 608-262-1660; Fax 608-265-4593; Internet Home Page Address: www.art.wisc.edu; *Prof* Jim Escalante; *Prof* Jack Damer; *Prof* Leslee Nelson; *Emer Prof* Bruce Breckenridge; *Emer Prof* Cavaliere Ketchum; *Emer Prof* Richard Long; *Emer Prof* Truman Lowe; *Emer Prof* George Cramer; *Prof* Doug Marschalek; *Prof* Frances Myers; *Prof* Carol Pylant; *Prof* Steve Feren; *Prof* David Becker; *Prof* Elaine Scheer; *Prof* John Rieben; *Prof* Tom Loeser; *Prof* Derrick Buisch; *Prof* Michael Connors; *Assoc Prof* Theresa Marche; *Prof* T L Solien; *Prof* Laurie Beth Clark; *Emer Prof* Patricia Fennell; *Emer Prof* Fred Fenster; *Prof* Aristotle Georgiades; *Assoc Prof* Nancy Mladenoff; *Assoc Prof* Gail Simpson; *Prof* Lisa Gralnick; *Assoc Prof* John Hitchcock; *Assoc Prof* Stephen Hilyard; *Asst Prof* Steven Driscoll Hixson; *Asst Prof* Fred Stonehouse; *Assoc Prof* Paul Sacaridz; *Asst Prof* Kim Cridler; *Asst Prof* Tom Jones; *Asst Prof* Michael J McClure
Estab 1911; Maintains nonprofit art gallery; FT 32; pub; D & E; Scholarships, Fellowships; SC 68, LC 2, GC 19; maj 500, grad 100
Degrees: BS, BFA, MA, MFA
Tuition: Res—undergrad $2,930 per sem, grad $4,160 per sem; nonres—undergrad $9,930 per sem, grad $11,795 per sem
Courses: Art Education, Book Making, Ceramics, Design, Drawing, Etching, Glass, Graphic Design, Illustration, Intermedia, Jewelry, Lettering, Lithography, Mixed Media, Painting, Papermaking, Performance, Photography, Printmaking, Sculpture, Serigraphy, Stage Design & Lighting, Typography, Video, Wood, Woodworking
Summer School: Three wk early session, 8 wk session, 4 wk session
—**Dept of Art History,** 800 University Ave, 232 Conrad A Elvehjem Building Madison, WI 53706-1414. Tel 608-263-2340; Fax 608-265-4593; Elec Mail arthistory@ls.wisc.edu; Internet Home Page Address: arthistory.wisc.edu/; *Prof Art History* Barbara C Buenger; *Prof* Henry J Drewal; *Prof* Narcisco G Menocal; *Prof, Dept Chmn* Gail L Geiger; *Prof* Jane C Hutchison; *Prof* Julia K Murray; *Prof* Quitman E Phillips; *Dept Adminr* Sandra Russell; *Prof* Nicholas D Cahill; *Prof* Thomas E A Dale; *Asst Prof* Anna V Andrzejewski; *Asst Prof* Jill H Casid; *Assoc Prof* Nancy R Marshall; *Assoc Prof* Ann Smart Martin; *Instr* Dan Fuller; *Instr* Gautama Vajracharya
Estab 1848, dept estab 1925; Art supplies available at univ bookstore; Pub; D & E; Scholarships, Fellowships; LC 15, GC 18-20; D 1,200, maj 250, non-maj 1,100, grad 150, continuing educ 100
Ent Req: BA, BS, BFMA
Degrees: MA, PhD
Tuition: Res—$4,160 per sem; nonres—$11,796 per sem
Courses: 20th Century Photography, African Art, American Art, †Art History, Asian Art, Ceramics, Dutch Painting, Greek Art & Society, Material Culture, Modern Art, Printmaking, Sculpture, Venetian Painting, Visual Culture, Western Architecture, Women's Art
—**Graduate School of Business, Bolz Center for Arts Administration,** 975 University Ave, Madison, WI 53706-1324. Tel 608-263-4161; Fax 608-265-2739; Elec Mail ataylor@bus.wisc.edu; Internet Home Page Address: www.bolzcenter.org/; *Dir* Andrew Taylor
Estab 1969
Degrees: MA
Tuition: Res bus MA $1,777.35 per sem, non-res $4,985.35 per sem
Courses: Arts Administration Seminars, Colloquium in Arts Administration

MANITOWOC

SILVER LAKE COLLEGE, Art Dept, 2406 S Alverno Rd, Manitowoc, WI 54220-9319. Tel 920-684-6691, 686-6181; Fax 920-684-7082; Elec Mail merdmann@silver.sl.edu; Internet Home Page Address: www.sl.edu/art; *Prof, Chmn* Sr Mariella Erdmann, MFA; *Assoc Prof* Dionne Landgraff, PhD; *Assoc Prof* Tracey Richardson, MFA
Estab 1936, dept estab 1959; pvt; D & E, wkends; SC 21, LC 6; D 50, E 10, non-maj 25, maj 25
Ent Req: HS dipl, ACT or SAT
Degrees: BA(Studio Art) or BA(Art Educ) 4 yrs
Courses: †Art Education, Art History, Calligraphy, Ceramics, †Commercial Art, Computer Graphics, Drawing, Graphic Arts, Graphic Design, Jewelry, Lettering, Mixed Media, Painting, Photography, Printmaking, Sculpture, †Studio Art, Teacher Training, Textile Design
Adult Hobby Classes: Courses—Vary
Children's Classes: Courses—Clay, Drawing, Fibers, Graphics, Painting, Sculpture
Summer School: Dir, Sr Lorita Gaffney. Courses—Vary

MARINETTE

UNIVERSITY OF WISCONSIN COLLEGE - MARINETTE, Art Dept, 750 W Bay Shore St, Marinette, WI 54143-4253. Tel 715-735-4322; Fax 715-735-4307; Elec Mail ssinfo@uwc.edu; Internet Home Page Address: www.uwc.edu; *Prof* Judith Baker; *Prof* Frank Zetzman; *Prof* Heidi Jensen; *Prof* Diana Budde; *Prof* Tom Fleming; *Prof & Chmn* Kitty Kingston; *Prof* Stephanie Coupolos-Selle; *Prof* James LaMalfa
Estab 1850, dept estab 1946; Maintains nonprofit Fini art Gallery; Theater on the Bay; Library, Lonnie Schofield, Dir; Campus shop where art supplies may be purchased; Pub; D, E & weekend; Scholarships; SC 7, LC 3, live video; D non-maj 100, maj 10
Ent Req: HS dipl or GED
Degrees: AAS 2 yrs
Tuition: Res—undergrad $2,300 per sem; nonres—undergrad $4,203 per sem
Courses: 2-D Design, Art History, †Digital Cinema, †Digital Design, Drawing, Painting, Photography, Sculpture, Survey of Art
Summer School: Dir, Sidney Bremer. Tuition $70 per cr. Courses—Art Appreciation, Art History

MENOMONIE

UNIVERSITY OF WISCONSIN-STOUT, Dept of Art & Design, 324 Applied Art Bldg, Menomonie, WI 54751; PO Box 790, Art & Design Dept Menomonie, WI 54751-0790. Tel 715-232-1141; Fax 715-232-1669; Elec Mail jacksonm@uwstout.edu; Internet Home Page Address: www.uwstout.edu/cas/; *Head Dept* Ron Verdon, MFA; *Prof* Todd Boppel, MFA; *Prof* Doug Cumming, MFA; *Prof* Eddie Wong, MFA; *Prof* Dr Claudia Smith PhD, MFA; *Prof* Susan Hunt, MFA; *Prof* Rob Price, MFA; *Prof* Paul De Long, MFA; *Asst Prof* William De Hoff, MFA; *Asst Prof* Mark Kallsen, MFA; *Asst Prof* Kate Maury, MFA; *Asst Prof* Maureen Mitton, MFA; *Asst Prof* Timothy O'Keeffe, MFA; *Asst Prof* Benjamin Pratt, MFA; *Asst Prof* David Gariff, MFA; *Asst Prof* David Morgan, MFA; *Lectr* Nancy Blum-Cumming, MFA
Estab 1893, dept estab 1965; pub; E; SC 60, LC 6; D 24, non-maj 1200, maj 630
Ent Req: HS dipl
Degrees: BS(Art), BFA(Art) 4 yrs
Courses: †Art Education, Art History, Art Metals, Art Period Courses, Blacksmithing, Ceramics, Design, Drawing, Fashion Illustration, †Graphic Design, †Industrial Design, †Interior Design, Painting, Printmaking, Sculpture, Silversmithing
Children's Classes: Sat classes in Art Design, Art History, Fine Arts, Graphic Arts
Summer School: Dir, Gene Bloedorn. Courses—Advanced Graphic Design, Ceramics, Drawing, Design, Life Drawing, Painting, Printmaking

MEQUON

CONCORDIA UNIVERSITY, Division of Performing & Visual Arts, 12800 N Lake Shore Dr, Mequon, WI 53097-2418. Tel 262-243-5700; Fax 262-243-4351; Elec Mail gayland.store@con.edu; Internet Home Page Address: www.cuw.edu; *Dir* Dr Gene Edward Veith; *Prof* Maaji Bell; *Prof* Jeff Shaarhan; *Prof* Terry Valentine; *Prof* Dean Graf
Estab 1881, dept estab 1971; Maintain nonprofit art gallery, Concordia University Art Gallery; den; D & E; SC 25, LC 4; non-maj 100, maj 60
Ent Req: HS dipl
Degrees: BA
Courses: †Aesthetics, †Art Education, †Art History, †Calligraphy, †Ceramics, Design, †Design, †Drawing, †Graphic Arts, †Graphic Design, †History of Art & Architecture, †Mixed Media, †Painting, †Photography, †Printmaking, †Sculpture, †Teacher Training, †Weaving
Summer School: Dr. William Cario, Asst VPres of Acad, Terms of 6 wks. Courses—Drawing & Painting (outdoors)

MILWAUKEE

ALVERNO COLLEGE, Art Dept, 3400 S 43rd St, Milwaukee, WI 53219-4844; PO Box 343922, Milwaukee, WI 53234-3922. Tel 414-382-6000, 382-6148; Fax 414-382-6354; *Chmn* Nancy Lamers
Estab 1948; pvt, W only in degree program; D & E; Scholarships; SC 20, LC 5; D 2300, E 2300, maj 60
Ent Req: GPA, class rank and ACT or SAT
Degrees: BA 4 yrs (or 128 cr)

Tuition: $6000 per sem; campus res—room & board available, $1900 per sem
Courses: Art Education, Art History, Art Therapy, Ceramics, Computer Graphics, Drawing, Enameling (Cloisonne), Fibers, General Crafts, Introduction to Visual Art, Metal Working, Painting, Printmaking, Sculpture, Teacher Training
Summer School: Term June to Aug. Courses—Art Education, Studio Art

CARDINAL STRITCH UNIVERSITY, Art Dept, 6801 N Yates Rd, Milwaukee, WI 53217-3985. Tel 414-410-4100; Fax 414-351-7516; Elec Mail tbernie@stritch.edu; Internet Home Page Address: www.stritch.edu/; *Asst Prof* Peter Galante; *Asst Prof* Teri Wagner; *Instr* Michal Ann Carley; *Asst Prof* Steven Sellars; *Asst Prof* Timothy Abler; *Dean Arts & Scis* Dr Dickson K Smith
Estab 1937; den; D & E; Scholarships; SC 29, LC 17; maj 98
Ent Req: HS dipl, ent exam
Degrees: AA, BA, BFA
Courses: †Art Education, †Art History, †Ceramics, Computer Graphics, †Drawing, †Fibers, †Film, †Graphic Design, Illustration, †Jewelry, †Metalsmithing, †Painting, †Photography, †Printmaking, †Sculpture, †Textile Design, †Video
Adult Hobby Classes: Enrl 200; tuition $40-$100 per 8-12 wk sessions. Courses—Basic, Ceramics, Drawing, Mixed Media, Painting, Watercolor
Children's Classes: Enrl 100; tuition $60 per child per 12 classes. Courses—traditional media plus various crafts

MILWAUKEE AREA TECHNICAL COLLEGE, School of Media & Creative Arts, 700 W State St, Milwaukee, WI 53233-1419. Tel 414-297-6433; Fax 414-297-7689; Elec Mail carlsobd@matc.edu; Internet Home Page Address: www.matc.edu; *Assoc Dean* Brian Carlson, BA & MS; *Instr* Howard Austin, MS; *Instr* Edward Adams, MFA; *Instr* Corrine Kraus, BFA; *Instr* Mark Saxon, AAS; *Instr* Robert Stocki, BFA; *Dean* Mohammad Dakwar, BS
Estab 1912, dept estab 1958; pub; D & E & Online; Scholarships, Financial aid; D 240, E 150
Ent Req: HS dipl
Degrees: AA 2 yrs & 1 yr Technical
Courses: 3-D Modeling & Animation, Advertising Design, Audio Production, Commercial Art, Computer Graphics, Computer Simulation & Gaming, Design, Display, Drawing, Graphic Arts, Graphic Design, Illustration, †Mixed Media, Mobile App Design, Multimedia, Music, Photography, Video, Visual Communications, eProduction
Adult Hobby Classes: Tuition $46.10 per cr

MILWAUKEE INSTITUTE OF ART & DESIGN, 273 E Erie St, Milwaukee, WI 53202-6003. Tel 414-847-3200; Fax 414-291-8077; Internet Home Page Address: www.miad.edu; *Provost* David Martin; *Pres* Neil Hoffman; *Chmn 2D/4D Design* Phil Belair; *Chmn 3D Design* Robert Lynch; *Chmn Art History & Sciences* Debra Ripley; *Chmn Fine Arts* Robert Smith; *Chmn Foundations* Jason Yi; *Chmn Writing & Humanities* Courtney Maloney
Estab 1974; FT 100, PT 60; pvt; D&E; Scholarships; SC, LC; D 400, maj 472
Ent Req: HS dipl, portfolio
Degrees: BFA 4 yrs
Tuition: $21,000 per yr
Courses: Advertising Design, Aesthetics, Art History, Conceptual Art, Constructions, Design, Display, Drafting, Drawing, Graphic Design, History of Art & Architecture, Illustration, Industrial Design, Interior Design, Painting, Photography, Printmaking, Sculpture

MOUNT MARY COLLEGE, Art & Design Division, 2900 N Menomonee River Pky, Milwaukee, WI 53222. Tel 414-258-4810; Fax 414-256-1224; Elec Mail huebner@mtmary.edu; Internet Home Page Address: www.mtmary.edu; *Prof* Angelee Fuchs, MA; *Prof* Joseph Rozman, MFA; *Assoc Prof* Sandra Keiser, MA; *Assoc Prof* Sr Aloyse Hessburg, MA; *Assoc Prof* Pamela Steffen, MBS; *Chmn* Lynn Kapitan, PhD; *Assoc Prof* Sr Carla Huebner, MS, MA; *Assoc Prof* Dennis Klopfer, MS; *Asst Prof* Melody Todd, MS; *Asst Prof* Greg Miller, MS; *Asst Prof* Karen McCormick, MA; *Asst Prof* Troy Gerth, MFA; *Instr* Patty Rass, MA; *Instr* Sue Loesl, MA; *Asst Prof* Nancy Lohmiller, BA; *Prof* Sr Rosemarita Huebner, MFA; *Instr* Janice Stewart, MA; *Instr* Dianne Atkinson, MA; *Instr* Mary Bartling, BA; *Prof* Bruce Moon, PhD; *Asst Prof* Leona Nelson, MA; *Asst Prof* Elizabeth Gaston, PhD; *Instr* Barbara Chappell, MA; *Instr* Sandra Tonz; *Instr* Joan Kadow; *Instr* Marie Perloneo; *Asst Prof* Debra Heermans, MA; *Instr* Jackie Halverson, MA; *Instr* Carol Powers, PhD
Estab 1913, dept estab 1929; Maintains Marian Gallery, 2900 Menomonee River Pky, Milwaukee, WI 53222; art supplies available at on-campus shop; pvt, W only; D & E; Scholarships; SC 22, LC 12, GC12; D 200, E 30, non-maj 50, maj 300, grad 50
Ent Req: HS dipl
Degrees: BA 4 yrs, MA(Art Therapy)
Tuition: $11,380 per yr, $5660 per sem; campus res—available; board $750 - $1000 per sem
Courses: †Advertising Design, Aesthetics, Architecture, Art Appreciation, †Art Education, Art History, †Art Therapy, Calligraphy, Ceramics, †Commercial Art, Constructions, †Costume Design & Construction, Design, Display, Drawing, †Fashion Arts, †Graphic Arts, †Graphic Design, Handicrafts, †History of Art & Architecture, †Interior Design, †Lettering, †Mixed Media, †Occupational Therapy, †Painting, †Photography, †Printmaking, †Sculpture, Silversmithing, †Teacher Training, †Textile Design, Video
Adult Hobby Classes: Enrl 1300; tuition variable, on going year round. Courses—Varied, self-interest
Children's Classes: Enrl 125; tuition $65 for 1-6 wk term, summer only. Courses—Arts & Crafts
Summer School: Dir, Toni Wulff

UNIVERSITY OF WISCONSIN-MILWAUKEE, Peck School of the Arts, Dept of Art & Design, 3203 N Downer Ave (MIT371), Milwaukee, WI 53211; PO Box 413, Milwaukee, WI 53201-0413. Tel 414-229-4200; Fax 414-229-2973; Elec Mail art-info@uwm.edu; Internet Home Page Address: www.arts.uwm.edu; *Chair* Lee Ann Garrison; *Dir Grad Studies* Denis Sargent; *Dir Foundations* Josie Osborne

Dept of Art & Design estab 1919; Peck School of the Arts estab 1962; Maintain a nonprofit art gallery, INOVA Institute of Visual Art, PO Box 413, Milwaukee, WI 53201; maintains Golda Meier Library; scholarships of $55,000 open to all art students for 1 yr annually; art supplies sold at on-campus store; FT 23, PT 33; pub; D & E; Scholarships; SC 60, LC 6, GC; non maj 600, maj 1100, grad 25
Ent Req: Portfolio review/application
Degrees: BFA(Art), BFA with teachers cert, BA(Art), MA(Art), MS(Art Educ), MFA(Art)
Tuition: www.bfs.uwm.edu/fees
Courses: Art Appreciation, Art Education, Ceramics, Design, Digital Studio Practice, Drawing, Fibers, Graphic Design, Interarts, Metals, Painting, Photography, Printmaking, Sculpture, Teacher Training, Textile Design
Adult Hobby Classes: jewelry & metalsmithing $140 per workshop
Summer School: Lee Ann Garrison, Chair

OSHKOSH

UNIVERSITY OF WISCONSIN OSHKOSH, Dept of Art, 800 Algoma Blvd, Oshkosh, WI 54901-8651. Tel 920-424-2222; Fax 920-424-1738; Internet Home Page Address: www.uwosh.edu/art; *Chmn* Edwin Jager; *Asst Prof* Jaehan Bae; *Asst Prof* Michael Beitz; *Asst Prof* Jessica Calderwood; *Assoc Prof* Karina Cutler-Lake; *Asst Prof* Mary Hoefferie; *Prof* Li Hu; *Prof* Jeff Lipschutz; *Prof* Richard Masters; *Assoc Prof* Susan Maxwell; *Prof* Gail Panske; *Prof* Arthur Pontynen; *Assoc Prof* Andrew Redington; *FT* Barbara Rosenthal; *Asst Prof* Emmet Sandberg; *Assoc Prof* Wendy Strauch-Nelson
Estab 1871; Maintain nonprofit art gallery, Priebe Gallery, Dept. of Art, University of Wisconsin, Oshkosh, WI 54901; schols open to art majors; on-campus art supplies shop; FT 18; pub; D & E; Scholarships; SC 56, LC 14, GC 31; D 10,5000, E 2500, maj 300, minors 70
Ent Req: HS dipl
Degrees: BA, BS(Art) 4 yrs, BFA 82 cr
Tuition: Res—$2606.90; non-res—$8548.90; campus res—room & board $2658
Courses: Advertising Design, †Art Appreciation, Art History, †Art Metals, Ceramics, Commercial Art, †Design, Drawing, †Functional Design, Graphic Arts, Graphic Design, Jewelry, Lettering, Painting, Photography, Printmaking, Sculpture, Teacher Training, Textile Design, Woodcraft

PLATTEVILLE

UNIVERSITY OF WISCONSIN-PLATTEVILLE, Dept of Fine Art, 1 University Plz, Art Bldg 212B Platteville, WI 53818-3099. Tel 608-342-1781; Fax 608-342-1491; Internet Home Page Address: www.uwplatt.edu; *Instr* Steve Vance; *Instr* Kaye Winder; *Chmn* David Van Buren
Estab 1866; FT 8; pub; D & E; SC 30, LC 5, GC 3; maj 105
Ent Req: HS dipl, ent exam
Degrees: BA and BS 4 yrs
Tuition: Res—undergrad $3520; nonres—undergrad $12,300; campus res—room & board $1295 per sem
Courses: Art Survey, Art in Elementary Education, Ceramics, Drawing, Ethnic Art, Fiber & Fabrics, Graphic Design, Illustration, Lettering & Typographic, Painting, Photography, Printmaking
Summer School: Enrl 2200; term of 8 wks beginning June. Courses—same as regular session

RICE LAKE

UNIVERSITY OF WISCONSIN, Center-Barron County, Dept of Art, 1800 College Dr, Rice Lake, WI 54868-2414. Tel 715-234-8176, Ext 5408; Fax 715-234-1975; Internet Home Page Address: www.uwc.edu; *Prof* Don Ruedy, MFA
Estab 1968; FT 1 PT 1; pub; D & E; Scholarships; SC 8, LC 2; D 63, E 10, non-maj 57, maj 16
Ent Req: HS dipl
Degrees: AA
Tuition: In-state—$1280
Courses: Art History, Calligraphy, Design, Drawing, Jewelry, Lettering, Painting, Printmaking, Theatre Arts
Children's Classes: Enrl 30; tuition $40 for 2 wks in summer. Courses—Art

RIPON

RIPON COLLEGE, Art Dept, 300 Seward St, PO Box 248 Ripon, WI 54971-0248. Tel 920-748-8110; Elec Mail kainee@ripon.edu; Internet Home Page Address: www.ripon.edu/academics/; *Chmn* Rafael Salas; *Prof* Evelyn Kain; *Asst Prof* Travis Nygard; *Asst Prof* Mollie Oblinger
Estab 1851; Pvt; D; Scholarships, Financial aid; SC 13, LC 8; maj 20
Ent Req: grad from accredited secondary school, SAT or ACT is recommended, but not required
Degrees: BA
Tuition: $18,000 per yr
Courses: †Art History, Design, Drawing, Mixed Media, Painting

RIVER FALLS

UNIVERSITY OF WISCONSIN-RIVER FALLS, Art Dept, 410 S Third St River Falls, WI 54022-5001. Tel 715-425-3266; Fax 715-425-0657; Elec Mail michael.a.padgett@uwrf.edu; Internet Home Page Address: www.uwrf.edu/art/welcome; *Chmn* Michael Padgett
Estab 1874, major estab 1958; pub; D; Scholarships; SC 26, LC 18; non-maj 400, maj 170
Ent Req: HS dipl
Degrees: BA, BS(Educ), BFA and BS(Liberal Arts) 4 yrs

Courses: Aesthetics, †Art Education, Art History, Ceramics, Costume Design & Construction, Drawing, Fibers, Film, Glass Blowing, Graphic Design, History of Art & Architecture, Jewelry, Painting, Photography, Printmaking, Silversmithing, Stained Glass, Textile Design
Summer School: Dir, Dr Lynn Jermal. Enrl 1600; 4 wk sessions. Courses—Clay, Fibers, Glass, Painting, Printmaking, Sculpture

STEVENS POINT

UNIVERSITY OF WISCONSIN-STEVENS POINT, Dept of Art & Design, 1800 Portage St, College of Fine Arts Stevens Point, WI 54481-1925. Tel 715-346-2669, 346-4066; Fax 715-346-4072; Elec Mail rstolzer@uwsp.edu; Internet Home Page Address: www.uwsp.edu/acad/cofa/index.htm; Internet Home Page Address: www.uwsp.edu/art-design/; *Prof* Rex Dorethy, MFA; *Prof* Robert Stowers, MFA; *Prof* Diane Bywaters, MFA; *Prof* Anne-Bridget Gary, MFA; *Prof* Robert Erickson, MFA; *Prof* Larry Ball, MFA; *Prof* Rob Stolzer, MFA; *Prof* Guillermo Penafiel, MFA; *Prof* John O Smith, MFA; *Lect* Mark Pohlkamp, MFA; *Prof* Susan Morrison, MFA; *Assoc Lectr* Sheila Sullivan; *Acad Dept Assoc* Mimi Johnson; *Dir Gallery* Caren Heft; *Sr Lectr* Mark Brueggeman; *Assoc Lectr* William McKee; *Asst Prof* Diana Black; *Asst Prof* Stuart Morris; *Asst Prof* Kristin Theilking; *Assoc Lect* Mary Rosek; *Assoc Lect* Keven Brunett; *Art Hist Librn* Matthew Sackel; *Prof* Cortney Chaffin, MFA; *Prof* Jillian Noble, MFA
Estab 1894; Maintain a nonprofit art gallery, Edna Carlsten Art Gallery; Pub; D & E; Scholarships; SC 47, LC 8, GC 7; D 866, non-maj 666, maj 325
Ent Req: HS dipl
Degrees: BA(Fine Arts) & BFA(Art-Professional)
Courses: †Advertising Design, †Art Appreciation, †Art Education, †Art History, Ceramics, †Commercial Art, Computer Graphics, †Design, Drawing, †Graphic Arts, Graphic Design, †History of Art & Architecture, †Landscape Architecture, Painting, Photography, Printmaking, Sculpture, †Studio Art
Children's Classes: Art Workshop

SUPERIOR

UNIVERSITY OF WISCONSIN-SUPERIOR, Programs in the Visual Arts, PO Box 2000, Holden Fine Arts Ctr 3101 Belknap & Catlin Superior, WI 54880-4500. Tel 715-394-8391, 394-8101; Elec Mail lgrittne@staff.uwsuper.edu; Internet Home Page Address: www.uwsuper.edu; *Prof* Mel Olsen, MFA; *Prof* William Morgan, MFA; *Assoc Prof* Laurel Scott PhD, MFA; *Assoc Prof* Susan Loonsk, MFA; *Lectr* Kim Borst, MFA; *Lectr* Pope Wright, MA; *Chmn* James Grittner, MFA; *Lectr* Tim Cleary
Estab 1896, dept estab 1930; Maintain nonprofit art gallery; Pub; D & E; Scholarships; SC 7, LC 3, GC 8; D 250, E 100-125, non-maj 250, maj 100, grad 30
Ent Req: HS dipl
Degrees: BS, BS(Photography), BS(Art Therapy), BFA & BFA(Photography) 4 yrs, BFA with cert 5 yrs, MA 5 - 6 yrs
Courses: †Art Education, †Art History, †Art Therapy, †Ceramics, Collage, Design, Drawing, †Jewelry, †Painting, †Photography, †Printmaking, †Sculpture, †Silversmithing, †Teacher Training, †Weaving
Adult Hobby Classes: Ceramics, Crafts, Drawing, Fibers, Metalwork, Painting, Photography
Children's Classes: Summer session only
Summer School: Dir, Mel Olsen. Courses—Art History, Ceramics, Drawing, Painting, Photography

WAUKESHA

CARROLL COLLEGE, Art Dept, 100 N East Ave, Waukesha, WI 53186-5593. Tel 262-547-1211, 524-7191; Internet Home Page Address: www.cc.edu; *Co-Chmn* Thomas Selle; *Assoc Prof* Philip Krejcarek, MFA
Estab 1846; pvt; D & E; Scholarships; SC 21, LC 4; D 1100, E 350
Ent Req: HS dipl, SAT or ACT
Degrees: BA
Courses: Museum Staff Training, †Pre-Architecture; Commercial Art; Weaving, Sculpture, †Stage Design, †Teacher Training, Textile Design, †Theatre Arts, †Video
Adult Hobby Classes: Enrl 20 per session. Courses—Photographing Your Own Work
Children's Classes: New program
Summer School: Asst Prof, Thomas Selle. Enrl varies; tuition varies for term of 6 wks. Courses—Drawing, Graphics, Photography

WHITEWATER

UNIVERSITY OF WISCONSIN-WHITEWATER, Art Dept, 800 W Main St, Ctr of the Arts 2073 Whitewater, WI 53190-1790. Tel 262-472-1324; Fax 262-472-2808; Elec Mail art@uww.edu; Internet Home Page Address: www.uww.edu; *Chmn* Chris Henige
Estab 1868; maintain nonprofit art gallery, Crossman Gallery, 800 W Main St, CA1030; FT 16, PT 1; pub; D & E; Scholarships; SC 41, LC 18; D 270, maj 200
Ent Req: HS dipl
Degrees: BA & BS(Art, Art Educ, Art History, Graphic Design), BFA 4 yrs
Courses: Advertising Design, Art Appreciation, Art Education, †Art History, Ceramics, Commercial Art, Drawing, †Graphic Design, Illustration, Jewelry, Painting, Photography, Printmaking, Sculpture, Teacher Training
Adult Hobby Classes: Enrl 240; tuition non res—undergrad $296.40 per cr, res undergrad—$96.90 per cr
Summer School: Dir, Richard Lee. Enrl 80; 3 & 6 wk terms, May-Aug. Courses—Art History, Ceramics, Drawing

WYOMING

CASPER

CASPER COLLEGE, Dept of Visual Arts, 125 College Dr, Casper, WY 82601-4699. Tel 307-268-2060; Fax 307-268-2224; Elec Mail lmunns@acad.cc.whecn.edu; *Instr* Justin Hayward; *Prog Dir* Linda Lee Ryan, MFA; *Instr* Nancy Madura, MFA; *Instr* Valerie Innella; *Instr* Michael Keogh, MFA; *Instr* Michael Olson; *Instr* Wendy Riley
Pub; D & E; Scholarships; LC 2; D 3870
Ent Req: HS dipl
Degrees: AA 2 yrs
Courses: Advertising Design, Art History, Ceramics, Collage, Commercial Art, Drafting, Drawing, Handicrafts, Illustration, Jewelry, Painting, Photography, Sculpture, Silversmithing, Textile Design, Theatre Arts
Summer School: Tuition $624 for summer sem or $52 per hr. Courses—Air Brush, Ceramics, Drawing, Jewelry, Painting, Photography

CHEYENNE

LARAMIE COUNTY COMMUNITY COLLEGE, Division of Arts & Humanities, 1400 E College Dr, Cheyenne, WY 82007-3295. Tel 307-778-1158; Fax 307-778-1399; Elec Mail kerryhart@lccc.wy.edu; *Dean* Kerry Hart, MA; *Instr* Matt West, MFA; *Instr* Ron Medina, MFA
Estab 1969; maintains nonprofit gallery; pub; D & E; Scholarships; SC 19, LC 3; D 125, E 100, non-maj 150, maj 20
Ent Req: HS dipl
Degrees: AA
Courses: Ceramics, Computer Graphics, Designs & Welded Sculpture, Drawing, Metals, Painting, Photography, Sculpture, Theatre Arts
Summer School: Dean, Chuck Thompson. Enrl 40; tuition $50 per cr hr for 8 wk term. Courses—Ceramics, Computer Graphics, Drawing, Metals, Watercolor

LARAMIE

UNIVERSITY OF WYOMING, Dept of Art, 1000 E University Ave, Dept 3138 Laramie, WY 82071-2000. Tel 307-766-3269; Fax 307-766-5468; Elec Mail kwold@uwyo.edu; rlk@uwyo.edu; *Head Dept* Ricki Klages
Estab 1886, dept estab 1946; FT 9; pub; D; Scholarships; SC 23, LC 6, GC 13; D 80, non-maj 600, maj 120, grad 16
Ent Req: HS dipl
Degrees: BA, BS and BFA 4 yrs
Courses: Art Appreciation, †Art Education, Art History, †Ceramics, †Design, †Drawing, †Graphic Design, †Painting, †Printmaking, †Sculpture
Adult Hobby Classes: Courses offered through University of Wyoming Art Museum
Summer School: Dir, Ricki Klages. Enrl 140; tuition res—undergrad $94 per cr hr 1-12, grad $164 per cr hr 1-12; non res—undergrad $322 per cr hr 1-12, grad $470 per cr hr 1-12, 4 & 8 wk sessions. Courses—Art Appreciation, Art History, Ceramics, Drawing, Graphic Design, Painting, Printmaking, Sculpture

POWELL

NORTHWEST COMMUNITY COLLEGE, Dept of Art, 231 W Sixth St, Powell, WY 82435. Tel 307-754-6111, 754-6201; Elec Mail mastersm@nwc.cc.wy.us; *Instr & Asst Prof* Lynn Thorpe; *Assoc Prof* John Giarrizzo; *Asst Prof* Morgan Tyree; *Chmn* Mike Masterson; *Asst Prof* Peder Gjovick; *Assoc Prof* Craig Satterlee
Estab 1946, dept estab 1952; pub; D & E; Scholarships; SC 12, LC 4; D 130, E 222, non-maj 317, maj 35
Ent Req: HS dipl, nonres ACT
Degrees: AA 2 yrs
Courses: Advertising Design, Art Education, Ceramics, Commercial Art, Drawing, Graphic Arts, Graphic Design, Handicrafts, History of Graphic Design, Lettering, Painting, Photography, Printmaking
Adult Hobby Classes: Enrl 100. Courses—Vary each sem

RIVERTON

CENTRAL WYOMING COLLEGE, Art Center, 2660 Peck Ave, Riverton, WY 82501-2273. Tel 307-855-2216, 855-2211; Fax 307-855-2090; Elec Mail nkehoe@cwc.edu; Internet Home Page Address: www.cwc.edu; *Chair Dept* Nita Kehoe; *Prof Photog* Lonnie Slorck; *Ceramics* Markus Urbanik; *Prof 2-D* Matt Flint
Estab 1966; Maintain nonprofit art gallery; Robert A Peck Gallery; pub; D & E; Scholarships; SC 30, LC 2; D 1500, E 500, non-maj 200, maj 100, others 20
Ent Req: HS dipl, GED
Degrees: AA 2 yrs
Courses: Art Appreciation, Art Education, Art History, Bronze Casting, Ceramics, Design, Drawing, Fiber Arts, Graphic Design, Mixed Media, Moldmaking, Painting, Photography, Printmaking, Sculpture, Textile Design, Video
Adult Hobby Classes: Enrl 30 plus; tuition $15-$50. Courses—Varied Art & General Curriculum
Children's Classes: Enrl 200; classes for a day, wk or sem. Courses—varied
Summer School: Dir, Nita Kehoe; Limited Art offerings

ROCK SPRINGS

WESTERN WYOMING COMMUNITY COLLEGE, Art Dept, 2500 College Dr, Rock Springs, WY 82901-5802. Tel 307-382-1600, Ext 723; Elec Mail fmcewin@uucc.cc.uy.us; *Head Dept* Dr Florence McEwin
Estab 1969; Maintain nonprofit gallery & library, Hay Library; on-campus shop where art supplies may be purchased; pub; D & E; Scholarships; SC 12, LC 1; D 675, E 600, maj 20
Ent Req: HS dipl
Degrees: AA 2 yrs
Tuition: $1,200 ann
Courses: Advertising Design, Art Appreciation, Art History, Ceramics, Collage, Design, Drafting, Drawing, Film, Graphic Design, History of Art & Architecture, Life Drawing, Mixed Media, Museum Staff Training, Painting, Photography, Printmaking, Sculpture, Stage Design, Theatre Arts, Video
Adult Hobby Classes: Enrl 100. Courses—Crafts, Drawing, Painting, Pottery
Children's Classes: Dance
Summer School: Dir, Florence McEwin. Courses—Ceramics, Photography

SHERIDAN

SHERIDAN COLLEGE, Art Dept, 3059 Coffeen Ave, Sheridan, WY 82801-9133; PO Box 1500, Sheridan, WY 82801-1500. Tel 307-674-6446, ext 3008; Fax 307-674-4293; Elec Mail rdugal@sheridan.edu; Internet Home Page Address: www.sheridan.edu; *Prog Chair* Rod Dugal; *Prof* Ryan Muldowney
Estab 1951; Maintains on-campus store for art supply sale; PT 3; pub; D & E; Scholarships; SC 28, LC 3; maj 10
Ent Req: HS grad
Degrees: AFA 2 yrs
Courses: Art Appreciation, Ceramics, Design, Drawing, Etching, Graphic Design, Jewelry, Lithography, Painting, Photography, Pottery, Sculpture, Silk Screen
Adult Hobby Classes: Enrl 40-60; tuition varies. Courses—Drawing, Painting, Pottery, Stained Glass
Children's Classes: Enrl 10-15; tuition varies. Courses—Pottery
Summer School: Enrl 10-15; tuition varies. Courses—Painting, Pottery

TORRINGTON

EASTERN WYOMING COLLEGE, Art Dept, 3200 W C St, Torrington, WY 82240-1699. Tel 307-532-8291; Fax 307-532-8225; Elec Mail cphillip@ewc.wy.edu; Internet Home Page Address: ewc.wy.edu; *Head Dept* Daniel Fielder
Estab 1948; Maintains FA Lobby Art Gallery; art supplies sold at on-campus store; PT 2; pub; D & E; Scholarships; SC 9, LC 1; D 50, maj 4, non-maj 46
Ent Req: varied
Degrees: AA and AAS 2 yrs
Courses: Ceramics, Commercial Art, Design I, Drawing, General Art, Graphic Arts, History of Art & Architecture, Painting, Photography, Sculpture
Adult Hobby Classes: Painting Workshops
Summer School: Head, Daniel Fielder

Canadian Art Schools

ALBERTA

BANFF

BANFF CENTRE, PO Box 1020 Office of the Registrar, 107 Tunnel Mountain Dr Banff, AB T1L 1H5 Canada. Tel 403-762-6180; Fax 403-762-6345; Elec Mail arts_info@banffcentre.ca; Internet Home Page Address: www.banffcentre.ca; Cable ARTSBANFF
Estab 1933 for summer study, winter cycle prog began 1979; Pub; Day - Mostly Independent Study; Scholarships
Ent Req: Resume, slides of work, post-secondary art training at a university or art school and/or professional experience in field
Tuition: Tuition depends on Prog
Courses: Art Studio, Ceramics, Media Arts, Photography, †Theatre Arts, †Video
Adult Hobby Classes: Courses - Art Studio, Ceramics Studio, Photography Studio, Visual Community
Summer School: Courses - Art Studio, Ceramics Studio, Photography Studio, Visual Community

CALGARY

ALBERTA COLLEGE OF ART & DESIGN, 1407-14 14th Ave NW, Calgary, AB T2N 4R3 Canada. Tel 403-284-7600; Fax 403-289-6682; Elec Mail admissions@acad.ab.ca; Internet Home Page Address: www.acad.ab.ca; *Painting Dept* Jim Ulrich; *Pres* Desmond Rochfort; *VPres External Affairs & Develop* Colleen Evans; *VPres Finance* Eric Fecter; *Acad Head Media Arts* Alan Dunning; *Acad Head Design* Eugene Ouchi; *Acad Head Fine Arts* Stuart Parker; *Acad Head Liberal Studies* Mireille Perron
Estab 1926; Maintain nonprofit art gallery; The Illingworth Kerr Gallery; pub; D & E; Scholarships; SC 250, LC 14; D 1000, E 500, non-maj 60, maj 850, others 60
Ent Req: HS dipl, portfolio
Degrees: BFA; BDes
Tuition: $9108 per yr plus course costs (Canadian funds)
Courses: Ceramics, Drawing, †Fibre, Glass, †Interdisciplinary, Jewelry, †Media & Digital Technology, Painting, Photographic Arts, Photography, Printmaking, Sculpture, Visual Communications
Adult Hobby Classes: Enrl 1500; tuition varies per course. Courses—Ceramics, Art Fundamentals, Drawing, Jewelry, Painting, Printmaking, Sculpture, Glass, Textiles, Watercolor, Photography
Children's Classes: Enrl 560; tuition $110 per course; Pre-College Studio $135 for 18 hrs. Courses—Ceramics, Jewelry, Mixed Media, Painting, Painting for Teenagers, Puppetry, Sculpture
Summer School: Dir Continuing Educ, David Casey, Enrl varies 100 approx

MOUNT ROYAL COLLEGE, Dept of Interior Design, 4825 Richard Rd SW, Calgary, AB T3E 6K6 Canada. Tel 403-240-6100; Fax 403-240-6939; Elec Mail fharks@mtroyal.ab.ca; Internet Home Page Address: www.mtroyal.ab.ca; *Chmn* Frank Harks; *Admin Support* Sarah Block
Estab 1910; FT 5, PT 10; pub; D & E; Scholarships; SC 12, LC 17
Ent Req: HS dipl
Degrees: 2 yr dipl
Tuition: $3857 per sem
Courses: Business Principles & Practices, Design, Graphic Presentation, History of Art & Architecture, History of Furniture, †Interior Design, Sculpture, Stage Design, Technical Design & Drafting
Adult Hobby Classes: Enrl 50. Courses—Interior Design Program

UNIVERSITY OF CALGARY, Dept of Art, 2500 University Dr NW, Calgary, AB T2N 1N4 Canada. Tel 403-220-5110; Fax 403-289-7333; Internet Home Page Address: www.ucalgary.ca; *Dean, Faculty Fine Arts* Dr Ann Calvert
Estab 1965; FT 21, PT 6; pub; D & E; SC 56, LC 19, GC 8; D 263, E 31, all maj
Ent Req: HS dipl
Degrees: BA(Art History), BFA(School Art, Art), MFA(Studio)
Tuition: $2513 per session
Courses: †Architecture, †Art Education, Art Fundamentals, †Art History, Art Theory, Conceptual Art, Costume Design & Construction, Drawing, Film, Graphic Arts, History of Art & Architecture, Intermedia, Mixed Media, Museum Staff Training, †Painting, †Photography, †Printmaking, †Sculpture, Stage Design, †Theatre Arts, Video
Summer School: Two terms of 6 wks, May-July. Courses—Art History, Drawing, Printmaking, Painting, Art Fundamentals, Art Education, Sculpture

EDMONTON

UNIVERSITY OF ALBERTA, Dept of Art & Design, 398 Fine Arts Bldg, Edmonton, AB T6G 2C9 Canada. Tel 780-492-3261; Fax 780-492-7870; Elec Mail artdes@gpu.srv.ualberta.ca; Internet Home Page Address: www.ualberta.ca/ARTDESIGN; *Chair* Czary Gajewski; *Asst Chair* Stan Szynkowski; *Grad Adv* Dawn McLean; *Undergrad Adv* Caitlin Wells; *Exec Asst* Kathleen Berto; *Prof, Grad Programs* Steven Harris; *Coordr Industrial Design* Prof. Robert Lederer; *Coordr Visual Commus Design* Prof Bonnie Sadler Takach; *Coordr History of Art, Design & Visual Culture* Dr Lianne McTavish; *Coordr Printmaking & Drawing* Prof Sean Caulfield; *Prof & Coordr Painting* Allen Ball
Estab 1908, dept estab 1946; Maintains a nonprofit art gallery, FAB Gallery & Design Gallery, Fine Arts Bldg; Maintains an art/architecture library. Art supplies may be purchased on campus; Pub; D & E; Scholarships; SC 51, LC 42, grad 23; Maj 748, grad 54
Ent Req: HS dipl, portfolio
Degrees: BFA 4 yrs, BDES 4 yrs, MFA, MA, M Des 2 yrs, PhD
Tuition: Undergrad $6,596-52 per yr, grad $5,252-39 per yr; international $8,021.86
Courses: †Advertising Design, †Art History, †Commercial Art, †Conceptual Art, †Design, Design & Visual Culture, Drawing, †Graphic Arts, †Graphic Design, History of Art, †History of Art & Architecture, †Industrial Design, †Painting, †Printmaking, †Sculpture, †Visual Communication Design
Summer School: Dir, Dr. E Boone Enrl 150; tuition $420 per course. Courses—Art History, Drawing, Painting, Printmaking, Sculpture, Visual Commun Design

LETHBRIDGE

UNIVERSITY OF LETHBRIDGE, Div of Art, 4401 University Dr, Lethbridge, AB T1K 3M4 Canada. Tel 403-329-2691; Fax 403-382-7127; Elec Mail inquiries@uleth.ca; Internet Home Page Address: www.uleth.ca; *Assoc Prof* Carl Granzow, MFA; *Asst Prof* Leslie Dawn, MFA; *Asst Dean* Jennifer Gordon
Estab 1967; pub; D & E; Scholarships; SC 26, LC 9
Ent Req: HS dipl
Degrees: BA & BFA 4 yrs
Tuition: Res—undergrad $5184 per sem; nonres—undergrad $10,320 per sem
Courses: Aesthetics, Art Appreciation, Art Education, Art History, Conceptual Art, Costume Design & Construction, Design, Drawing, History of Art & Architecture, Intermedia, Mixed Media, Museum Staff Training, Painting, Photography, Printmaking, Sculpture, Stage Design, Teacher Training, Theatre Arts, Video

RED DEER

RED DEER COLLEGE, Dept of Visual Arts, 100 College Blvd, PO Box 5005 Red Deer, AB T4N 5H5 Canada. Tel 403-342-3300; Fax 403-340-8940; Internet Home Page Address: www.rdc.ab.ca; *Chmn Visual Arts* Graham Page
Estab 1973; FT 6, PT 2; pub; D & E; Scholarships; max 50 first yr students, 30 second yr
Ent Req: HS dipl, portfolio
Degrees: dipl, BFA 2 yrs
Tuition: undergrad—$77-80 per cr
Courses: Art History, Ceramics, Drawing, Fundamentals of Visual Communication, Painting, Printmaking, Sculpture
Adult Hobby Classes: Enrl 300; tuition $74 - $100 per course. Courses—Ceramics, Drawing, Glass Blowing
Children's Classes: Enrl 80; tuition $350 per wk. Courses—Drawing, Painting, Sculpture
Summer School: Dir, Ann Brodie. Enrl 500; tuition $200 per wk. Courses—Applied Arts, Drawing, Glass Blowing, Painting, Printmaking

BRITISH COLUMBIA

KELOWNA

UNIVERSITY OF BRITISH COLUMBIA OKANAGAN, (Okanagan University College) Dept of Creative Studies, 3333 University Way, Kelowna, BC V1V 1V7 Canada. Tel 250-807-9761; Fax 250-807-8027; Elec Mail neil.cadger@ubc.ca; Internet Home Page Address: www.ubc.ca/okanagan/creative/welcome.html; *Assoc Prof Visual Art* Briar Craig; *Dept Head & Assoc Prof (Performance - Theater)* Neil Cadger; *Asst Prof (Visual Art)* Renay Egami; *Assoc Prof (Visual Art)* Johann Feught; *Assoc Prof (Creative Writing)* Anne Fleming; *Assoc Prof (Visual Art)* Stephen Foster; *Assoc Prof (Visual Art)* Fern Helfand; *Assoc Prof (Creative Writing)* Nancy Holmes; *Assoc Prof (Visual Art)* Byron Johnston; *Asst Prof (Performance - Theater)* Virginie Magnat; *Assoc Prof (Visual Art)* Gary Pearson; *Assoc Prof (Visual Art)* Bryan Ryley; *Assoc*

Prof (Visual Art) Jim Tanner; *Assoc Prof (Creative Writing)* Sharon Thesen; *Asst Prof (Performance Theatre)* Denise Kenney; *Asst Prof (Visual Art)* Aleksandra Dulic; *Asst Prof (creative writing)* Michael V Smith
Estab 2005; Maintains a nonprofit art gallery, Fina Gallery, UBC Okanagan, 333 University Way, Kelowna, BC V1V 1V7; 17; pub; D & E; Scholarships; SC 75, LC 18, GC 4; D 200, E 20
Ent Req: HS dipl
Degrees: BFA 4 yr, BA Creative Writing, MFA Interdisciplinary graduate studies
Tuition: Res—undergrad $4,600 per year
Courses: Aesthetics, †Art History, Collage, Conceptual Art, Constructions, †Creative Writing, †Drawing, Film, Graphic Arts, †Intermedia, Mixed Media, †Painting, †Photography, †Printmaking, †Sculpture, Theater Arts, †Video
Summer School: 40 $300 per course, painting, drawing, aramids

VANCOUVER

EMILY CARR UNIVERSITY OF ART + DESIGN, 1399 Johnston St, Vancouver, BC V6H 3R9 Canada. Tel 604-844-3800; Fax 604-844-3801; Elec Mail jdedominicis@ecuad.ca; Internet Home Page Address: www.ecuad.ca; *VP Enrol & Student Servs Registrar* Jennifer DeDominicis; *Pres & Vice Chancellor* Dr Ronald Burnett; *VPres Acad & Provost* Dr David Bogen; *Dean Faculty of Design & Dynamic Media* Bonne Zabalotney; *Dean Faculty of Culture & Community* Susan Stewart; *Dean Faculty of Grad Studies* Cameron Cartiere; *Dean Faculty of Visual Art & Material Practice* Aoife MacNamara; *VP Finance & Admin* Michael Clifford; *VP New Campus Proj* Cindy Brooks
Estab 1925; Maintains nonprofit Charles H Scott Gallery, Concourse Gallery, & Media Gallery; art/architecture library; pub; D & E; SC 653, LC 188, GC 24; D 1884, E 300, Grad 41
Activities: Schols offered
Ent Req: HS dipl plus presentation of folio of art work
Degrees: 2 yr masters, 4 yr degree
Tuition: res—$4100 per yr; non-res—$13,000 per yr
Courses: Animation, Art History, Ceramics, Conceptual Art, Design, Drawing, Film, Graphic Arts, Graphic Design, Illustration, Intermedia Studies, Mixed Media, Painting, Photography, Printmaking, Sculpture, Video
Adult Hobby Classes: Enrl 2000; tuition $250 per course. Courses—Design, Fine Arts
Summer School: Dir, Sadira Rodriques Enrl 700; tuition $250. Courses—Design, Fine Arts

LANGARA COLLEGE, Department of Design: Design Formation, 100 W 49th Ave, Vancouver, BC V5Y 2Z6 Canada. Tel 604-323-5306; Fax 604-323-5555; Elec Mail shancoc k@langara.bc.ca; Internet Home Page Address: www.langara.bc.ca/design-formation/index.html; *Dept Chmn* Sherry Hancock; *Instr* Scott Geib; *Instr* Jake Hill; *Instr* Kevin Smith; *Instr* Marcela Noriega
Estab 1970; pub; D; Scholarships; SC 7, LC 1; D 160
Ent Req: HS dipl, portfolio
Degrees: Design Formation dipl
Courses: Art History, Ceramics, Commercial Art, Conceptual Art, Design, Drawing, Graphic Arts, Graphic Design, History of Art & Architecture, Painting, Photography, Printmaking, Sculpture, Typography

UNIVERSITY OF BRITISH COLUMBIA, Dept of Art History, Visual Art & Theory, 400-6333 Memorial Rd., Vancouver, BC V6T 122 Canada. Tel 604-822-2757; Fax 604-822-9003; Elec Mail ahva.dept@ubc.ca; Internet Home Page Address: www.ahva.ubc.ca; *Head* Scott Watson PhD; *Prof* Rhodri Windsor-Liscombe PhD; *Prof* Richard Prince, BA; *Assoc Prof* Marvin Cohodas PhD, BA; *Asst Prof* Dana Claxton; *Prof* Xiong Gu; *Asst Prof* Katherine Hacker; *Assoc Prof* Gareth James; *Asst Prof* Carol Knicely; *Asst Prof* Jaleh Mansoor; *Assoc Prof* Joseph Monteyne; *Prof* John O'Brian; *Asst Prof* Manuel Pina; *Assoc Prof* Marina Roy; *Assoc Prof* Maureen Ryan; *Asst Prof* T'Ai Smith; *Prof* Catherine Soussloff; *Prof* Charlotte Townsend-Gault; *Assoc Prof* Barbara Zeigler; *Asst Prof* Hsingyuan Tsao
Maintain the Irving K Barber Learning Centre, 1961 East Mall, Vancouver, BC V6T 121; there is an on-campus art supply shop.; D & E; Scholarships, Fellowships
Degrees: BA, BFA, MA, MFA, PhD
Courses: Art History, †Asian, Graphic Arts, History of Art & Architecture, †Indigenous Arts of the America, Mixed Media, Painting, Photography, Printmaking, Sculpture, †Western
—**School of Architecture,** 6333 Memorial Rd, Vancouver, BC V6T 1Z2 Canada. Tel 604-822-2779; Fax 604-822-3808; Internet Home Page Address: www.arch.ubc.ca; *Dir* Christopher Macdonald
Estab 1946; For reference only; maintain nonprofit art gallery, Downtown Gallery & Studio, UBC School of Architecture, 319 West Hastings, Vancouver, BC; FT 14; pub; Scholarships, Fellowships
Library Holdings: Book Volumes 3500; Clipping Files; Other Holdings Architectural plans; Pamphlets; Periodical Subscriptions 17; Slides
Degrees: MArch & MASA
Tuition: $2,500 per yr for Canadian students; MArch $10,000 per yr for International students, MASA $7,200 per yr for International students
Courses: Architectural History, Architecture, Computational Design, Design Studios, Environmental Design, Structures, Urban Design
Adult Hobby Classes: Enrl 170; tuition $2,448 per yr for 3 yr program
Summer School: Dir, Christopher Macdonald. Courses—vary

VICTORIA

UNIVERSITY OF VICTORIA, Dept of Visual Arts, MS 8011, Victoria, BC V8W 2Y2 Canada. Tel 250-721-8011; Fax 250-721-6595; Elec Mail ntrembla@finearts.uvic.ca; *Chmn & Assoc Prof* Lynda Gammon; *Assoc Prof* Vikky Alexander, BFA; *Prof* Robert Youds, MFA; *Asst Prof* Steve Gibson PhD; *Asst Prof* Daniel Naskarin, MFA
Estab 1963; pub; D & E; Scholarships, Fellowships; 50

Ent Req: HS dipl
Degrees: BFA, MFA
Tuition: Undergrad $2000 per yr
Courses: Digital Multimedia, Drawing, Painting, Photography. Printmaking, Sculpture
Summer School: Drawing, Painting, Printmaking
—**Dept of History in Art,** PO Box 1700, Victoria, BC V8W 2Y2 Canada. Tel 250-721-7942; Fax 250-721-7941; Elec Mail cgibson@finearts.uvic.ca; Internet Home Page Address: www.finearts.uvic.ca/historyinart/; *Dean* G Hogya PhD; *Prof* John L Osborne PhD; *Prof* S Anthony Welch PhD; *Assoc Prof* Kathlyn Liscomb PhD; *Assoc Prof* Victoria Wyatt PhD; *Assoc Prof* Astri Wright PhD; *Assoc Prof* Lianne McLarty PhD; *Asst Prof* Catherine Harding PhD; *Asst Prof* Christopher Thomas PhD; *Chair* Carol Gibson-Wood; *Prof* Nancy Micklewright, PhD LC 52, grad 20
Degrees: BA, MA, PhD
Tuition: $2,265 per yr, rm & board $4,600-$5,224
Courses: Asian, Canadian, European, Islamic & Native American Art
Summer School: May-Aug

MANITOBA

WINNIPEG

UNIVERSITY OF MANITOBA, School of Art, 203 Fitzgerald Bldg, Winnipeg, MB R3T 2N2 Canada. Tel 204-474-9303; Fax 204-275-3148; *Dir* Dale Amundson, MFA; *Prof* Sharon Alward, MFA; *Prof* Marilyn Baker, PhD; *Assoc Prof* Oliver Botar, PhD; *Assoc Dir & Assoc Prof* James Bugslag, PhD; *Faculty* Cliff Eyland, MFA; *Prof* Jeff Funnell, MFA; *Lectr* Ted Howorth, MFA; *Prof* David McMillan, MFA; *Assoc Prof* Alexander Poruchnyk, MFA; *Prof* Bill Pura, MFA; *Prof* Gordon Reeve, MFA; *Prof* Mary Ann Steggles, MFA; *Faculty* Charlotte Werner, PhD
Estab 1950; Maintain nonprofit art gallery; Pub; D&E; Scholarships; SC 35, LC 16; D 440
Ent Req: HS dipl and portfolio
Degrees: BFA
Tuition: $4,200 per yr
Courses: †Art History, †Ceramics, †Drawing, †Foundations, †Graphic Design, †Painting, †Photography, †Printmaking, †Sculpture
Summer School: Courses—Studio & Art History
—**Faculty of Architecture,** 201 Russell Bldg, Winnipeg, MB R3T 2N2 Canada. Tel 800-432-1960; Fax 204-474-7532; Internet Home Page Address: www.umanitoba.ca; *Dean* Michael Cox; *Assoc Dean, Head Environmental Design* Charles Thomsen; *Head Landscape Archit* Alan Tate; *Acting Head Dept City Planning* Ian Whight; *Head Dept Architecture* Ian MacDonald; *Head Dept Interior Design* Lynn Chalmers
Estab 1913; Pub; Scholarships; Environmental Studies 218, Archit 110, Interior Design 284, City Planning 72, Landscape 60
Ent Req: Senior matriculation or Bachelor for particular subject
Degrees: BED, BID, MArchit, MCP, MID, M(Land Arch)
Tuition: $1,900 per yr
Courses: Architecture, Environmental Design, Interior Design, Landscape, Landscape Architecture

NEW BRUNSWICK

EDMUNDSTON

UNIVERSITE DE MONCTON, CAMPUS D'EDMUNDSTON, Dept of Visual Arts Arts & Lettres, 165 Blvd Hebert, Edmundston, NB E3V 2S8 Canada. Tel 506-737-5050; *Chief* Roger Jurvais
Estab 1946, dept estab 1968; pub; D & E; Scholarships; SC 12, LC 1; D 20, E 11, non-maj 25, maj 6
Ent Req: HS dipl
Degrees: BA(Fine Arts) 4 yrs
Tuition: $2430; campus res—room & board $1545 per yr
Courses: Art History, Drawing, Painting, Sculpture

FREDERICTON

NEW BRUNSWICK COLLEGE OF CRAFT & DESIGN, 457 Queen St, Fredericton, NB E3B 5H1 Canada; PO Box 6000, Fredericton, NB E3B 5H1 Canada. Tel 506-453-2305; Fax 506-457-7352; *Dir Craft School* Luc Paulin
Estab 1946; pub; D& E; Workshops; 70 plus PT
Ent Req: HS dipl, transcript, questionnaire and interview
Degrees: 3 yr dipl
Courses: Advertising Design, Art History, Ceramics, †Clothing Design & Construction, Colour, †Creative Graphics, Design, Drawing, Fashion Arts, Graphic Arts, Illustration, Jewelry, †Native Arts Studies, Photography, Silversmithing, Textile Design, Weaving
Adult Hobby Classes: Courses—Weekend workshops

UNIVERSITY OF NEW BRUNSWICK, Art Education Section, 3 Bailey Dr, Fredericton, NB E3B 5H5 Canada; PO Box 4400, Faculty of Education Fredericton, NB E3B 5A3 Canada. Tel 506-453-4666; Fax 506-453-3569; *Science Librn* Francesca Holyoke
Tuition: Res—$1975 per yr
Courses: Art Education for Elementary Teachers, Art History, Art Media for Schools, Art Seminar, Children's Art for Teachers
Children's Classes: 70; tuition $15 for 6 weeks, one afternoon per wk

MONCTON

UNIVERSITE DE MONCTON, Dept of Visual Arts, 18 Ave Antonine-Maillet, Moncton, NB E1A 3E9 Canada. Tel 506-858-4033; Fax 506-858-4166; Elec Mail janice.comeau@umoncton.ca; Internet Home Page Address: www.umoncton.ca/umcm-fass-artsvisuels/; *Chmn Sculpture Dept* Andre LaPointe; *Prof Printmaking* Jacques Arseneault; *Prof Painting* Gisele Ouellette; *Prof Ceramics* Gerry Collins; *Prof Art History* Hermengilde Chiasson
Estab 1967; Maintain nonprofit art gallery; Galarie d'art Louiseet Reuben Colten, 405 Ave de L'Universite Moncton, NB, Canada, E1A 3E9; Bibliotheione Champlain ; 6; pub; D & E; Scholarships; SC 7, LC 3; D 45, E 75,
Ent Req: HS dipl
Degrees: BA(Fine Arts) 4 yrs; BA (Fine Arts Educ) 6 yrs
Tuition: $4,920
Courses: Art Education, Art History, †Ceramics, Drawing, †Painting, †Photography, †Printmaking, †Sculpture, †Teacher Training

SACKVILLE

MOUNT ALLISON UNIVERSITY, Dept of Fine Arts, 53 York St, Mrs Lesley Bonang, Sec Sackville, NB E4L 1C9 Canada. Tel 506-364-2490; Fax 506-364-2606; Elec Mail finearts@mta.ca; Internet Home Page Address: www.mta.ca/finearts; *Head Prof* Thaddeus Holownia, BA; *Assoc Prof* Erik Edson, MFA; *Assoc Prof* Dr Anne Koval, BA, MA, PhD; *Adjunct Prof* Gemey Kelly, BFA; *Lectr* Dan Steeves, BFA; *Asst Prof* Leah Garnett, MFA; *Lectr* Karen Stentaford, MFA, BFA, BEd; *Asst Prof* Chris Down, BFA, MFA; *Asst Prof* Adriana Kuiper, BFA, MFA; *Asst Prof* Jerry Ropson, BFA, MFA; *Lectr* Paula Cowan, BFA, MFA
Estab 1854; On campus shop where art supplies may be purchased; Pub; D & E 20; Scholarships; SC 34, LC 19; Maj140, non Maj 59
Ent Req: HS dipl
Degrees: BFA 4 yrs
Tuition: Tuition $6,720 (Canadian), $13,440 (non-Canadian) plus meals Various plans from $3,098 to $3,370, residence single $4,204, supersingle $4,501, double $3,636
Courses: †Art History, †Drawing, Open Media, †Painting, †Photography, †Printmaking, †Sculpture

NEWFOUNDLAND

CORNER BROOK

MEMORIAL UNIVERSITY OF NEWFOUNDLAND, Division of Fine Arts, Visual Arts Program, Visual Arts Program Division of Fine Arts, PO Box 2000 Grenfell Campus Corner Brook, NF A2H 6P9 Canada. Tel 709-637-6200; Fax 709-637-6203; Elec Mail vachair@grenfell.mun.ca; Internet Home Page Address: www2.swgc.mun.ca/visual/; *Head Fine Arts* Todd Hennessey; *Prof & Chair Visual Arts* Kent Jones; *Prof* Marlene MacCallum; *Prof* David Morrish; *Prof* Michael Coyne; *Asst Prof* Maggie Atkinson; *Assoc Prof* Don Foulds; *Assoc Prof* Gerard Curtis; *Prof* Barb Hunt; *Assoc Prof* Pierre LeBlanc; *Asst Prof* Ingrid Percy
Estab 1975, dept estab 1988; Maintain nonprofit art gallery; Sir Wilfred Grenfell College, Corner Brook, NF A2H6P9; maintain art/architecture library, Ferris Hodgett Library, Grenfell Campus, Memorial Univ of New England Corner Brook, NL A2H6P9; pub; D & E; Scholarships; Studio & lect courses; D 50, Maj 80
Degrees: BFA
Courses: Aesthetics, Art Appreciation, Art History, Design, Digital Imaging, History of Art & Architecture, Mixed Media, Painting, Photography, Printmaking, Sculpture, †Theatre Arts
Adult Hobby Classes: Drawing, Studio Areas
Children's Classes: Art

NOVA SCOTIA

ANTIGONISH

ST FRANCIS XAVIER UNIVERSITY, Fine Arts Dept, PO Box 5000, Antigonish, NS B2G 2W5 Canada. Tel 902-867-2417, 863-3300; Fax 902-867-5153; Elec Mail iroach@stfx.ca; Internet Home Page Address: www.stfx.ca; *Chmn* Iris Delgado
PT 4; Scholarships
Degrees: BA
Tuition: undergrad—$4370, room & board—$5190-$6270
Courses: Art History, Design, Drawing, Painting, Printmaking, Stained Glass
Adult Hobby Classes: Courses - Drawing, General Studio, Painting
Children's Classes: Courses - Drawing, Painting, Printmaking
Summer School: Dir, Angus Braid. Enrl 15; 5 wk sem beginning July-Aug. Courses—General Studio

HALIFAX

DALHOUSIE UNIVERSITY, Faculty of Architecture, Halifax, NS B3H 3J5 Canada. Tel 902-494--2211; Fax 902-423-6672; Elec Mail arch.office@dal.ca; Internet Home Page Address: www.dal.ca/~arch/architecture/index; *Dean* T Emodi; *Prof* J Grant Wanzel; *Prof* D Procos; *Prof* Michael Poulton; *Assoc Prof* S Parcell; *Assoc Prof* T Cavanagh; *Prof* B MacKay-Lyons; *Asst Prof* Susan Guppy; *Assoc Prof* Richard Kroeker; *Assoc Prof* Christine Macy; *Asst Prof* Steven Mannell; *Dir* Jacques Rousseau; *Prof* Essy Baniassad; *Prof* Frank Palermo; *Asst Prof* Austin Parsons

Estab 1911, faculty estab 1961; pvt; D; Scholarships; approx 200, maj 200, grad 2
Ent Req: previous 2 yrs at univ
Degrees: MArchit 4 yrs, Post-professional MArchit 1 yr minimum
Tuition: $2200 per acad term; differential for foreign students
Courses: Architecture, Art History, Constructions, Drafting, Environmental Studies, Photography, Urban & Rural Planning
Summer School: Three terms per yr

NOVA SCOTIA COLLEGE OF ART & DESIGN, 5163 Duke St, Halifax, NS B3J 3J6 Canada. Tel 902-444-9600; Fax 902-425-2420; Internet Home Page Address: www.nscad.ns.ca; *Acting Dean* Dr Christina Holzer-Hunt; *Pres Prof* David J B Smith; *VPres & Provost* James Moy; *Dir MFA Program* Jan Peacock; *Dir MDes Prog* Rudi Meyer
Estab 1887; Maintains nonprofit Anna Leonowens Gallery; NSCAD Library; art supplies sold at on campus store; pvt; D & E; Scholarships, Fellowships; SC 67, LC 31, GC 8 each sem; FT 810, PT 183, grad 14
Ent Req: HS dipl, portfolio or project
Degrees: BFA, BD(Graphic Design), BA, MFA & MA(Art Educ), MDes
Tuition: Canadian—$2750.40 FT; International—$6062.40
Courses: Art Education, Art History, Ceramics, Computer Art, Design, Drawing, Fashion Arts, Film, Graphic Arts, Graphic Design, Jewelry, Mixed Media, Painting, Photography, Printmaking, Sculpture, Textile Design, Video

WOLFVILLE

ACADIA UNIVERSITY, Art Dept, Wolfville, NS B4P 2R6 Canada. Tel 902-542-2200; Fax 902-542-4727; Elec Mail ask.acadia@acadiau.ca; Internet Home Page Address: http://www.acadiau.ca/index.html; *Chmn & Prof* Wayne Staples; *Dean of Arts* Thomas Regan; *Asst Dean of Arts* Maurice Tugwell; *Admin Secy* Audrey Dorey
Scholarships
Degrees: BA, BAM, BM, MA
Tuition: $3850 per yr
Courses: Art History, Drawing, Painting
Summer School: Dir, Prof Wayne Stapler. Enrl 30

ONTARIO

DUNDAS

DUNDAS VALLEY SCHOOL OF ART, DVSA Gallery, 21 Ogilvie St, Dundas, ON L9H 2S1 Canada. Tel 905-628-6357; Fax 905-628-1087; Elec Mail dvsa@cogeco.net; Internet Home Page Address: www.dvsa.ca; *Registrar* Bonnie Wheeler; *Dir* Arthur Greenblatt
Estab 1964; Maintain nonprofit art gallery & art/architecture library, DVSA Gallery & Library. Art supplies may be purchased on campus; pvt; D & E; Scholarships; SC 65, LC 2; GC 1; D 2,000, E 2,000
Ent Req: part time no-req, special programs -interview with portfolio
Courses: Art Appreciation, Art History, Ceramics, Collage, Conceptual Art, Constructions, Design, Drawing, Mixed Media, Painting, Photography, Printmaking, Sculpture
Adult Hobby Classes: Enrl 1500; tuition $225 for 10 wk term. Courses—Ceramics, Drawing, Painting, Photography, Printmaking, Sculpture
Children's Classes: Enrl 1200; tuition $180 for 10 wk term. Courses—Drawing, Painting, Pottery
Summer School: Enrl 1800; tuition starting from $115 per 1/2 day session

GUELPH

UNIVERSITY OF GUELPH, School of Fine Art & Music (SOFAM), University of Guelph School of Fine Arts and Music, Zavitz Hall Room 201 Guelph, ON N1G 2W1 Canada. Tel 519-824-4120, Ext 53988; Fax 519-821-5482; Elec Mail rmcginni@uoguelph.ca; Internet Home Page Address: www.uoguelph.ca/sofam/index.html; *Dir* John D Kissick
Estab 1966; Contact for schols information: Robin McGinnis, Admin; FT 23, PT 20; pub; D; Scholarships; SC 30, LC 30 Grad 9; 959, maj 300
Ent Req: HS dipl
Degrees: BA 3 yrs, BA (Hons) 4 yrs
Tuition: Res—undergrad $2014.50 per sem; part-time $403 per course; campus res available
Courses: Aesthetics, Alternative Media, †Art History, Collage, †Conceptual Art, †Drawing, History of Art & Architecture, †Intermedia, †Painting, †Photography, †Printmaking, †Sculpture, Video
Summer School: Chair, Thomas Tritschler. Courses—Vary

HAMILTON

MCMASTER UNIVERSITY, School of Art, Drama & Music, 1280 Main St W, 4M1 Commons Bldg Rm 105 Hamilton, ON L8S 4M2 Canada. Tel 905-525-9140, Ext 24655; Fax 905-527-3731; Elec Mail ryank@mcmaster.ca; *Prog Dir* Dr G Warner; *Prog Coordr* Kathy Ryan
Estab 1934; FT 21; SC 12, LC 29; 85
Degrees: BA(Art History), Hons BA(Studio & Art History) 3-4 yrs
Tuition: $127.69 per unit; international $415 per unit; campus res available
Courses: †Art History, Music Drama, †Studio Art Program

KINGSTON

QUEEN'S UNIVERSITY, Dept of Art, 67 University Ave. Department of Art-Ontario Hall Kingston, ON K7L 3N6 Canada. Tel 613-533-6166, 2448, 2446; Elec Mail art@queensu.ca; Internet Home Page Address: www.queensuca/artsci; *Dean* Robert Silverman

Estab 1932; pub; D & E; SC 16, LC 25
Ent Req: Grade XIII
Degrees: BA 3 yrs, BA(hons) & BFA 4 yrs, MA(Conservation), MA(Art History), PhD(Art History)
Tuition: $4430 per year, campus res available; non-res—$11,220 per year
Courses: Art Conservation, Art History, Drawing, Painting, Printmaking, Restoration & Conservation, Sculpture
Summer School: Drawing, Painting, Sculpture

ST LAWRENCE COLLEGE, Dept of Graphic Design, 100 Portsmouth Ave, Kingston, ON K7L 5A6 Canada. Tel 613-545-3910, 544-5400 ext 1140; Fax 613-545-3923; Elec Mail liaison@sl.on.ca; Internet Home Page Address: www.sl.on.ca; *Chmn* Don Niven
Estab 1967, dept estab 1969; pub; D & E
Ent Req: Hs dipl & portfolio
Degrees: Dipl (Visual & Graphic Design) 3 yrs, Cert (Basic Photography, Cert Graphic Design)
Courses: Art History, Commercial Art, Communications, Computer Graphics, Drawing, †Graphic Design, Illustration, Marketing, Mixed Media, Painting, Photography, Printmaking

LONDON

UNIVERSITY OF WESTERN ONTARIO, John Labatt Visual Arts Centre, 1151 Richmond St, Ste 2 London, ON N6A 3K7 Canada. Tel 519-661-3440; Fax 519-661-2020; Elec Mail mlennon@uwo.ca; Internet Home Page Address: www.uwo.ca/visarts/; *Chmn* Madeline Lennon
Estab 1967; pub; D & E; SC 23, LC 31; maj 235
Ent Req: HS dipl, portfolio and/or interview
Degrees: BA 3 yrs, BA(Hons) and BFA 4 yrs
Tuition: res—$4701.01 per year; non-res—$10,483.79 per year
Courses: Drawing, †History of Art & Architecture, Museum Staff Training, †Painting, †Photography, †Printmaking, †Sculpture
Summer School: Enrl limited; term of 6 wks beginning July. Courses—Visual Arts

OAKVILLE

SHERIDAN COLLEGE, Faculty of Animation, Arts & Design, 1430 Trafalgar Rd, Oakville, ON L6H 2L1 Canada. Tel 905-845-9430; Fax 905-815-4041; Internet Home Page Address: www.sheridancollege.ca; *Dean* Ronni Rosenberg, MFA, MArch, RGD; *Assoc Dean Design Illustration & Photography* Donna Braggins, MA, RGD; *Assoc Dean Material, Art & Design* Heather Whitton, BFA, MEd; *Assoc Dean Animation & Game Design* Angela Stukator, PhD; *Assoc Dean Film Television & Journalism* Sandy McKean, BA; *Assoc Dean Visual & Performing Arts* Michael Rubinoff, BA, LL.B
Estab 1967; Maintains nonprofit art gallery, The Gallery (same address); schols open to qualified students; FT 109; pub; D & E; Scholarships; SC 80%, LC 20%; D 4500
Income: Financed by Ontario Government
Ent Req: HS dipl
Degrees: BAA 4 yr
Tuition: $4.288 to $12,883 per yr (dom); $14,802 to $28,815 (int'l)
Courses: Advanced Special Effects Makeup, Prosthetics & Props, †Advanced Television & Film, †Art & Art History (Bachelor of Arts), †Art Fundamentals, †Bachelor of Animation, †Bachelor of Design (Honours), †Bachelor of Game Design, †Bachelor of Illustration, †Bachelor of Interaction Design, †Bachelor of Interior Design, †Bachelor of Music Theatre Performance, †Bachelor of Photography, †Communication, Culture & Information Technology, †Computer Animation, †Computer Animation - Digital Character Animation, †Corporate Communications, †Crafts & Design - Ceramics, †Crafts & Design - Furniture, †Crafts & Design - Glass, †Crafts & Design - Textiles, †Game Level Design, †Interior Decorating, †Journalism - Broadcast, †Journalism - New Media, †Journalism - Print, †Makeup for Media & Creative Arts, †Media Arts, †Media Fundamentals, †Performing Arts - Preparation, †Technical Production for Theatre & Live Events, †Theatre & Drama Studies (Bachelor of Arts), †Visual & Creative Arts, †Visual Effects, †Visual Merchandising Arts, †Web Design
Adult Hobby Classes: Enrl 2800; tuition varies
Summer School: Enrl 600. Programs-various Visual & Performing Arts

OTTAWA

CARLETON UNIVERSITY, Dept of Art History, 1125 Colonel Bay Dr, Ottawa, ON K1S 5B6 Canada. Tel 613-520-7400; Fax 613-520-3575; Internet Home Page Address: http://www2.carleton.ca/about/; *Dir* Michael Bell
Estab 1964; FT 8, PT 2; D & E; Scholarships; SC 2, LC 25, GC 3; D over 700, maj 135
Ent Req: HS dipl
Degrees: BA 6 Hons 3-4 yrs
Tuition: Res—$1353.19 per sem
Courses: Art History

SOUTHAMPTON

SOUTHAMPTON ART SOCIETY, Southampton Art School, 20 Albert St Highway 21, Box 115 Southampton, ON N0H 2L0 Canada. Tel 519-797-5068; Fax 519-797-2486; Elec Mail info@theartsschool.org; Internet Home Page Address: www.theartsschool.org; *Dir* Carole Cleary
Estab 1958 as a summer school; pub; D, July and Aug; Scholarships
Tuition: Adults $180 per wk; students (14-18) $85 per wk; children (10-13) $70 per wk, half days only; no campus res

Courses: Art Appreciation, Art History, Calligraphy, Collage, Design, Drawing, Handicrafts, Jewelry, Mixed Media, Painting, Photography, Printmaking, Sculpture, Textile Design
Adult Hobby Classes: Enrl 100; tuition varies. Courses—Culinary, Ferro-Cement Sculpture, Knitting, Photography, Quilting, Rug Hooking
Children's Classes: Enrl 175; tuition $60 per wk. Courses—Crafts, Drawing, Painting, Sculpture
Summer School: Dir, Carole Cleary. Enrl 250; tuition $70-$180 per wk. Courses—Acrylic, Collage, Drawing, Figures, Mixed Media, Oil, Printmaking, Portraits, Watercolor

THUNDER BAY

LAKEHEAD UNIVERSITY, Dept of Visual Arts, 955 Oliver Rd, Thunder Bay, ON P7B 5E1 Canada. Tel 807-343-8110; Fax 807-345-8023; Elec Mail mark.wisenholt@lakeheadu.ca; Internet Home Page Address: www.lakeheadu.ca/~vartswww/visualarts; *Chmn Visual Arts Dept* Mark Nissenhold, MFA; *Prof* Patricia Vervoort, MA; *Prof* Ann Clarke, MFA; *Instr* Janet Clark; *Instr* Roly Martin; *Instr* Alison Kendall; *Instr* Sarah Link; *Instr* Mavourneen Trainor-Bruzzese
Div estab 1976, dept estab 1988; pub; D & E; Scholarships
Ent Req: HS dipl, portfolio
Degrees: HBFA, Dipl in Arts Admin
Courses: Art History, †Ceramics, Drawing, †Painting, †Printmaking, †Sculpture
Adult Hobby Classes: Studio and art history courses
Summer School: Dir, Dan Pakulak. Tuition $390 per course for 6 wks

TORONTO

GEORGE BROWN COLLEGE OF APPLIED ARTS & TECHNOLOGY, Dept of Graphics, PO Box 1015, Sta B, Toronto, ON M5T 2T9 Canada. Tel 416-415-2000, 415-2165; Fax 416-415-2600; Elec Mail mmaynard@gbrown.on.ca; Internet Home Page Address: http://www.georgebrown.ca/; *Chmn* Michael Maynard
Estab 1970; FT 30, PT 60; D & E; D 900, E 2000
Ent Req: HS grade 12 dipl, entr exam
Degrees: 3 yr dipl, 1 yr cert
Courses: †Advertising Design, Air Brush Techniques, Calligraphy, Cartooning, †Commercial Art, Computer Graphics, Graphic Arts, Graphic Design, Illustration, †Lettering, Marker Rendering Techniques, Painting, Photography, Video

HUMBER COLLEGE OF APPLIED ARTS & TECHNOLOGY, The School of Media Studies, 205 Humber College Blvd, Toronto, ON M5T 2T9 Canada. Tel 416-675-3111, Ext 4111; Fax 416-675-9730; Elec Mail enquiry@humber.ca; Internet Home Page Address: www.sms.humberc.on.ca; *Dean* William Hanna
Estab 1967; pub; D & E; SC 300, LC 75, GC 6; grad 50, PT 25
Ent Req: HS dipl, mature student status, one yr of employment plus 19 yrs of age
Degrees: none, 2 & 3 yr dipl courses
Tuition: Canadian res—$1703 per yr; international—$10,200 per year
Courses: Art History, Drafting, Drawing, Film, Furniture Design, Graphic Arts, †Graphic Design, †Industrial Design, †Interior Design, †Landscape Technology, †Packaging Design, Photography, TV Production
Adult Hobby Classes: Enrl 4042; tuition & duration vary. Beginning classes in most regular courses
Children's Classes: Nature studies

KOFFLER CENTER OF THE ARTS, School of Visual Art, 4588 Bathurst St, Toronto, ON M2R 1W6 Canada. Tel 416-636-1880, Ext 270; Fax 416-636-5813; Internet Home Page Address: www.kofflerarts.org/Home-Page/; *Dir Cultural Programming, Mktg & Develop* Diane Uslaner
Estab 1977; Gallery estab 1975; pub; D & E; Scholarships; D 400, E 98; SC 35
Courses: Ceramics, Clay, Drawing, Mixed Media, Painting, Sculpture, Stone Sculpture, †Theater Arts
Adult Hobby Classes: Enrl 350-400. Courses—Drawing, Painting, Sculpture
Children's Classes: 50 Drawing, Painting, Ceramics

OCAD UNIVERSITY, (Ontario College of Art & Design) 100 McCaul St, Toronto, ON M5T 1W1 Canada. Tel 416-977-6000; Fax 416-977-6006; Internet Home Page Address: www.ocad.ca; *Pres* Sara Diamond; *VPres Admin* Peter Caldwell; *Dir Library Servs* Jill Patrick; *VPres Acad* Sarah McKinnon; *Dean Art* Vladimir Spicanovic; *Dean Design* Doreen Balabanoff; *Dean Liberal Studies* Kathryn Shailer; *Registrar* Elisabeth Paradis; *Media & Communs Officer Mktg & Communs* Sarah Mulholland
Estab 1876; Maintain art/architecture library: Dorothy H Hoover Library, 113 McCaul St, Toronto; maintain an on-site not for profit art gallery; on-campus shop for purchase of art supplies; pub; D & E; Scholarships; SC 296 LC 53; D 2144, E 2000, grad summer 900
Ent Req: HS dipl, English requirement, interview
Degrees: BFA, BDes, MFA, MDes, MA, EMDes
Tuition: $1,095.90 per cr; $547.95 per half-cr; international students $3,115.90 per cr, $1,557.95 per half-cr; no campus res
Courses: Aboriginal Visual Culture, †Advertising Design, Anthropology, Art History, Arts of Latin American & Asia, †Calligraphy, †Ceramics, Collage, †Commercial Art, Communication Design, Communication studies, Conceptual Art, Contemporary Theory & Criticism, Creative Writing, †Criticism & Curatorial Practice, Cultural Studies, †Design, Digital &n Media Studies, Display, †Drawing, Drawing & Painting, English, English Literature & Composition, Expanded Animation, †Fashion Arts, Film, Film Studies, Furniture Design, †Graphic Arts, †Graphic Design, History of Art & Architecture, Humanities, †Illustration, Industrial Ceramics, †Industrial Design, †Integrated Media, †Jewelry, Linguistics, †Material Art & Design, Fiber, Mixed Media, Native Studies, †On-Screen Media, †Painting, Philosophy, †Photography, †Printmaking,

Science/Technology/Mathematics, †Sculpture, †Sculpture/Installation, Silversmithing, Social Sciences, Sociology, Stage Design, Sustainability in Design, Video, Visual Culture, Wearable Technology, †Weaving, Women's Studies
Summer School: Registrar, Elisabeth Paradis. Summer courses run for three, six or twelve week periods. Classes take place form one to four days per week and may be scheduled mornings, afternoons and/or evenings. summer domestic 1st yr tuition $1,073.90 CAD per cr ($536.95 per half cr); Summer International 1st yr tuition $3,099.90 CAD per cr ($1,549.95 per half cr). Courses—Drawing & Painting, General Art, Photography, Printmaking, General Design, Material Art & Design (Fibre, Jewelry/Metalsmithing, Ceramics) English, History & Theory of Visual Culture, Humanities, Social Sciences, Science/Technology/Mathematics

TORONTO ART THERAPY INSTITUTE, 66 Portland St Ste 103, Toronto, ON M5V 2M6 Canada. Tel 416-924-6221; Fax 416-924-0156; Elec Mail torontoarttherapy@bellnet.ca; Internet Home Page Address: www.tati.on.ca; *Dir Acad Prog & Internships* Gilda S Grossman, MSW & EdD; *Psychiatric Consultant to Training Prog* Dr Jodi Lofchy, MD; *Supv* Nell Bateman, MA; *Instr & Supv* Jacqueline Fehlner, BA; *Instr & Supvr* Kathryn Hubner Kozman, BA; *Instr & Supv* Barbara Merkur, MA; *Instr* Ellen Bateman, BA; *Instr* Helen Burt, BA; *Instr* Mercedes Chacin De Fuchs, MEd; *Instr* Temmi Ungerman, MA; *Instr* Lyn Westwood, BA; *Instr* Val Zoulalian, BA; *Thesis Adv* O Robert Bosso PhD, BA; *Thesis Adv* Ruth Epstein, EdD; *Thesis Adv* Vince Murphy PhD, EdD; *Thesis Adv* Ken Morrison PhD, EdD
Estab 1968; D & E
Degrees: Dipl, BA and MA(Art Therapy) through affiliation with other US colleges; graduate level cert program in art therapy
Adult Hobby Classes: Enrl 6-12; fee $40 per session. Courses—workshops
Children's Classes: Enrl 6-12; fee $20 per session. Courses—workshops

TORONTO SCHOOL OF ART, 980 Dufferin St, 2nd Floor Toronto, ON M6H 4B4 Canada. Tel 416-504-7910; Fax 416-504-8171; Elec Mail info@tsa-art.com; Internet Home Page Address: tsa-art.com; *Instr* Susan Beniston; *Instr & Dir* Brian Burnett; *Instr* Moira Clark; *Instr* Denis Cliff; *Instr* Andy Fabo; *Instr* Simon Glass; *Instr* Megan Williams; *Instr* Tobi Asmoucha; *Instr* Tom Campbell; *Instr* Trish Delaney; *Instr* Sharon Epstein; *Instr* Eric Glavin; *Instr* Sandra Gregson; *Instr* Janice Gurney; *Instr* Catherine Heard; *Instr* Thomas Hendry; *Instr* Maria Hlady; *Instr* Marie Lehman; *Instr* John Leonard; *Instr* Tina Poplawski; *Instr* Gretchen Sankey; *Instr* Donnely Smallwood; *Instr* Erica Shuttleworth; *Instr* Janet Morton; *Instr* Andy Patton; *Instr* Joe Fleming; *Instr* Kate Brown; *Admin Mgr* Sharon Shields
Estab 1969; pvt; D & E; Scholarships; D 300 E 200 Majs 10 Grads 5
Ent Req: portfolio
Degrees: 3 yr dipl, 1 yr portfolio develop, 1 yr independent studio program
Tuition: $3,100 full-time, $5.500 foreign students; no campus res
Courses: Drawing, Mixed Media, Painting, Photography, Printmaking, Sculpture
Summer School: Dir Brian Burnett

UNIVERSITY OF TORONTO, Dept of Fine Art, 27 King's College Circle, Toronto, ON M5S 1A1 Canada. Tel 416-946-7624; Fax 416-946-7627; Elec Mail chairfa@chass.utoronto.ca; Internet Home Page Address: www.library.utoronto.ca/fineart; *Chmn* Marc Gotlieb; *Assoc Chmn Grad Studies* Mark Cheetham; *Assoc Chmn Visual Studies* Lisa Steele; *Undergrad Coordr Art History* Alexander Nagel; *Undergrad Coordr Visual Studies* George Hawken
Estab 1934; FT 21, PT 13; pub; Scholarships, Fellowships; LC, GC
Degrees: BA 4 yrs, MA 2 yrs, PhD 5 yrs
Tuition: Nonres—undergrad $12,024; campus res available
Courses: Aesthetics, Architecture, Art History, Art Studio, Conceptual Art, Drawing, Graphic Arts, History of Art & Architecture, Painting, Photography, Printmaking, Sculpture, Video
Adult Hobby Classes: Enrl 250
—Faculty of Architecture, Landscape & Design, 230 College St, Toronto, ON M5T 1R2 Canada. Tel 416-978-5038; Fax 416-971-2094; Internet Home Page Address: www.ald.utoronto.ca; *Dean* George Baird; *Coordr, Eric Arthur Gallery* Larry Richards; *Dir Master of Archit* An Te Liu, BA, MArch; *Master Urban Design* Robert Levit, BA, MArch
Estab 1895; pub; D; Scholarships; SC 5, LC 33, GC 11; 299, non-maj 6, maj 293, grad 13
Ent Req: previous BA or BS degree; portfolio of work & reference letters
Degrees: MA Archit; MA Landscape Archit; MA Urban Design
Tuition: Domestic students $2970 per sem; foreign students $14,250 per sem
Courses: Construction Management, Design, History & Theory Building Science, Professional Practice, Structural Design
—Programme in Landscape Architecture, 230 College St, Toronto, ON M5T 1R2 Canada. Tel 416-978-2011; Fax 416-971-2094; Internet Home Page Address: www.ald.toronto.ca; *Assoc Prof* John Danahy, BLA; *Assoc Dean, Dir Prog in Landscape Architecture* Robert Wright
Estab 1827, dept estab 1965; pub; D; Scholarships; maj 100
Ent Req: grad 13 dipl
Degrees: MA(Land Archit)
Tuition: Canadian Students $2970 per sem; foreign students $14,250 per sem
Courses: Computer Art, Computer Modeling, Design, Drawing, Environment, Research & Writing Studio
Summer School: Contact, Prof Gerald Englar. Enrl 20; tuition $1200 for 4 wks non-degree. Courses—Career initiation program for Architecture & Landscape Architture

YORK UNIVERSITY, Dept of Visual Arts, 4700 Keele St, Ctr for Fine Arts, Rm 232 Toronto, ON M3J 1P3 Canada. Tel 416-736-5187; Fax 416-736-5875; Elec Mail gfwhiten@yorku.ca; Internet Home Page Address: www.yorku.ca/finearts.visa; *Chmn Prof* Tim Whiten
Estab 1969; FT 26, PT 8; pub; D & E; Scholarships; SC 53, LC 17; D over 400, maj 400, others 120
Ent Req: HS dipl, interview and portfolio evaluation for studio statement for art history
Degrees: BA(Hons), BFA(Hons) 4 yrs, MA in Art History, MFA in Visual Arts
Tuition: Res—$3951 per year; nonres—$10,381 per year (prices quoted are Canadian dollars)

Courses: Art History, Criticism, Design, Drawing, Graphic Arts, Interdisciplinary Studio, Painting, Photography, Sculpture, Theory

WATERLOO

UNIVERSITY OF WATERLOO, Fine Arts Dept, 200 University Ave W, Waterloo, ON N2L 3G1 Canada. Tel 519-885-1211, ext 2442; Fax 519-888-4521; Internet Home Page Address: www.finearts.waterloo.ca; *Prof* Jan Uhde PhD, BFA; *Prof* Art Green, BFA; *Prof* Jane Buyers, BA; *Prof & Chmn* Bruce Taylor, MFA; *Assoc Prof* Joan Coutu, PhD, MA; *Asst Prof* Doug Kirton, MFA, BFA; *Asst Prof* Cora Cluett, MFA, BFA; *Asst Prof* Lois Andison; *Dean* Ken Coates; *Instr* Eva McCavley; *Instr* Paul Dignan
Estab 1958, dept estab 1968; Maintains nonprofit gallery, University of Waterloo Art Gallery 200 University Ave W, Waterloo Ont N2L3G1, Maintains art/architecture library; Eva McCavley, Paul Dignan; Pub; D & E; Scholarships; SC 25, LC 27, GC; maj 150; Day 150
Ent Req: HS dipl
Degrees: BA 3 yrs, BA(Hons) 4 yrs
Tuition: $4,476 per yr; $3,510-$4,150 room & board; campus res available
Courses: †Art History, Ceramic Sculpture, Ceramics, Computer Animation, Computer Imaging, †Drawing, †Film Theory & History, Illustration, †Painting, Photography, †Printmaking, †Sculpture
Summer School: Enrl 30. Courses—Drawing

WINDSOR

UNIVERSITY OF WINDSOR, Visual Arts, School of Visual Arts, Windsor, ON N9B 3P4 Canada. Tel 519-253-3000, Ext 2829; Fax 519-971-3647; Elec Mail art@uwindsor.ca; Internet Home Page Address: www.cronus.ca/unit/visualarts/visualartsasf; *Prof* Brian E Brown; *Prof* Dr Veronica Mogyorody; *Prof* Michael J Farrell; *Prof* Susan Gold-Smith; *Prof* William C Law; *Prof* Cyndra MacDowall; *Instr* Rod Strickland; *Prof* Sigi Torinus; *Asst Prof Art History & Visual Culture* Dr Lee Rodney; *Prof* Dr Jennifer Willet; *Dir & Prof* Brenda Francis Pelkey
Estab 1960; Maintains nonprofit art galleries: LeBel Gallery, School of Visual Arts, Univ of Windsor, Windsor, Ontario N9B 3P4; SoVA Projects Art Gallery, School of Visual Arts, Univ Windsor, LeBel Bldg. Art Supplies may be purchased on campus; FT 8, PT 3; pub; D & E; Scholarships, Assistantships; SC 32, LC 10, GC 6; D 250, maj 300, G students 10
Ent Req: Ontario Secondary School Graduation Dipl (OSSD) plus 6 Ontario Acad Courses (OAC) or equivalent
Degrees: BA in Visual Arts or Art History 3 yrs, BA (Hons) in Visual Arts or Art History, Combined honors degree program and BFA 4 yrs, MFA 2 yrs
Tuition: Undergrad $2,620 per sem, grad $1,704 per sem
Courses: †Art History, Built Environment, †Drawing, Green Corridor, †Integrated Media, Multi Media, †Painting, Photography, †Printmaking, †Sculpture

PRINCE EDWARD ISLAND

CHARLOTTETOWN

HOLLAND COLLEGE, Photography & Digital Imaging, 140 Weymouth St, Charlottetown, PE C1A 4Z1 Canada. Tel 902-566-9551; Fax 902-629-4239; Elec Mail info@hollandc.pe.ca; Internet Home Page Address: www.hollandc.pe.ca/index.htm; *Instr* Alex Murchinson
Estab 1977; Schols open to all; Alex Murchinson, Jean Duchesne; Pub; D; Scholarships; SC, LC; D 25
Ent Req: Grad 12, portfolio, questionnaire
Degrees: Dipl
Tuition: $3250 per yr
Courses: †Graphic Design, Photography, Woodworking
Adult Hobby Classes: $285

QUEBEC

MONTREAL

CONCORDIA UNIVERSITY, Faculty of Fine Arts, 1455 Maisonneuve Blvd West, Montreal, PQ H3C 1M8 Canada. Tel 514-848-2424; Fax 514-848-4599; Internet Home Page Address: www.concordia.ca/; *Dean* Christopher Jackson
D & E; Scholarships
Ent Req: HS dipl, CEGEP dipl Prov of Quebec
Degrees: BFA, post-BFA Dipl in Art Educ & Art Therapy, full-time leading to teaching cert, MA(Art Educ), MA(Art History), MA(Art Therapy), PhD(Art Educ)
Courses: †Art Education, †Art History, †Art Therapy, †Ceramics, Cinema, †Contemporary Dance, †Design Art, †Drawing, †Fibres, Interdisciplinary Studies, †Music, †Painting, †Photography, †Printmaking, †Sculpture, †Theatre Arts, Women & the Fine Arts
Adult Hobby Classes: Courses offered
Children's Classes: Enrl 75; tuition $75 for 8 wk term, $125 for 2 terms
Summer School: Courses offered

MCGILL UNIVERSITY, Dept of Art History, 853 Sherbrooke St W, 2nd Floor Dawson Hall Montreal, PQ H3A 2T6 Canada. Tel 514-398-6541; Fax 514-398-7247; *Chmn* Christine Ross, PhD; *Assoc Prof* T Glenn, PhD; *Faculty Lectr* R Meyer, PhD; *Asst Prof* C Solomon-Kiefer, PhD
Pvt; D; Assistantships; SC 2, LC 7, GC 12
Ent Req: HS dipl or CEGEP Dipl

Degrees: BA(Art History), 3 & 4 yr, MA(Art History) 2 yr, PhD(Art History)
Tuition: Res—$1,500 per yr, nonres—$7,000 per yr
Courses: Ancient Greek Art, Baroque Art, †History of Art & Archaeology, Medieval Art, Modern Art, Renaissance Art
—**School of Architecture**, 815 Sherbrooke St W, Montreal, PQ H3A 2K6 Canada. Tel 514-398-6704; Fax 514-398-7372; Internet Home Page Address: www.mcgill.ca/architecture; *Prof* Ricardo Castro; *Prof* David Covo; *Prof* Annmarie Adams; *Prof* Vikram Bhatt; *Prof* Martin Bressani; *Prof (Emeritus)* Derek Drummond; *Prof* Avi Friedman; *Prof* Robert Mellin; *Prof* Alberto Perez-Gomez; *Prof* Adrian Sheppard; *Prof* Pieter Sijpkes; *Prof (Emeritus)* Radoslav Zuk; *Prof* Nik Luka
Estab 1896; Maintains a nonprofit art gallery (exhib room); Art supplies may be purchased on campus; FT 10, PT 36, FTE 18; Semi-Public; D; Scholarships; SC 10, LC 35, GC 45; D 200; GS 110
Ent Req: ent exam
Degrees: B.Sc.(Arch); MArch I (Professional); MArch II (Post-Professional); PhD
Tuition: Res—$1,700 per yr; nonres—$4,900 per yr; Quebec res—$1,700; Canadian res—$4,900; International res—$14,000
Courses: Architectural Design, Architecture, History of Architecture

UNIVERSITE DE MONTREAL, Dept of Art History, PO Box 6128, Downtown Station Montreal, PQ H3C 3J7 Canada. Tel 514-343-6111; Fax 514-343-2393; Elec Mail larouchm@ere.umontreal.ca; Internet Home Page Address: www.umontreal.ca; *Instr* Yves Deschamps; *Instr* Nicole Dubreuil; *Instr* Francois Marc Gagnon; *Instr* Chantal Hardy; *Instr* Alain Laframboise; *Instr* Lise Lamarche; *Instr* Johanne Lamoureux; *Instr* Luis de Moura Sobral; *Instr* Gilles Marsolais; *Instr* Constance Naubert-Riser; *Instr* Serge Tousignant; *Instr* Jean Trudel; *Instr* Peter Krausz; *Instr* David W Booth; *Instr* Andre Gaudreault; *Dir* Michel Larouche
Dept estab 1961; pvt; D & E; SC 20, LC 70, GC 10; D 270, non-maj 113, maj 106, grad 80, others 151
Ent Req: HS dipl
Degrees: BA & MA
Tuition: Campus res available
Courses: Art History, Film, Fine Arts

UNIVERSITE DU QUEBEC A MONTREAL, Famille des Arts, CP 8888, Succursale Center Ville, Montreal, PQ H3C 3P8 Canada. Tel 514-987-4545; Tel 514-987-3000, ext 3956; *Dept Head* Louise Dusseault Letocha; *Head Art History* Nycole Paquin
Estab 1969
Ent Req: 2 yrs after HS
Degrees: Baccalaureat specialize 3 yrs; Master Degrees in Visual Arts; programs in Environmental Design, Graphic Design, History of Art, Visual Arts (engraving, sculpture, painting); MA(Musicology)
Tuition: $166.50 per cr
Courses: Architectural Drafting, Ceramic Sculpture, Design, Drawing, Etching and Engraving, Graphic Techniques, Modeling, Mural Painting, Museum Staff Training, Painting, Scenography, Teacher Training
Adult Hobby Classes: Cert in visual arts available

QUEBEC

UNIVERSITE QUEBEC CITE UNIVERSITAIRE, School of Visual Arts, Laval University, Edifice La Fabrique, Quebec, PQ G1K 7P4 Canada. Tel 418-656-3333; Fax 418-656-7678; Elec Mail arv@arv.ulaval.ca; *Faculty Dean Arts, Architecture & Amenagement* Takashi Nakajima; *Dir Visual Arts* Marie Andree Doran
Estab 1970; pub; D; 550
Ent Req: 2 yrs col
Degrees: BA(Arts Plastiques, Commun, Graphique, Enseignement des Arts Plastiques); cert(arts plastiques); MA(Visual Arts)
Tuition: Res—undergrad $1952 per yr, $558 per qtr
Courses: Computer Graphic, Drawing, Engraving, Graphic Arts, Graphic Design, Illustration, Lithography, Painting, Photography, Sculpture, Silk Screen, Video

TROIS RIVIERES

UNIVERSITY OF QUEBEC, TROIS RIVIERES, Fine Arts Section, PO Box 500, Department des arts, 3351 boul des Forges Trois Rivieres, PQ G9A 5H7 Canada. Tel 819-376-5136, 5011; Fax 819-376-5226; Elec Mail Peirre-Simon_Doyon@utqr.uquebec.ca; Internet Home Page Address: www.uqtr.uquebec.ca/arts; *Prof* Graham Cantieni; *Dir Dept Arts* Pierre-Simon Doyon, PhD

Estab 1969; pub; D & E; SC 12, LC 8, GC 28; D 150, E 100
Activities: r3 Galerie d'art
Ent Req: ent exam or DEC
Degrees: BA(Fine Arts) & BA(Art Education)
Tuition: $50 per course
Courses: Art Education, Art History, †Drawing, †Glass, †Painting, †Paper, †Printmaking, †Sculpture
Adult Hobby Classes: Enrl 100. Courses—Art History, Painting, Printmaking

SASKATCHEWAN

REGINA

UNIVERSITY OF REGINA ARTS EDUCATION PROGRAM, Visual Arts Dept, Regina, SK S4S 0A2 Canada. Tel 306-585-5872; Fax 306-779-4744; *Acting Head* Ruth Chambers; *Head* Leesa Streifler
Maintain nonprofit art gallery; FT 9; pub; D&E; Scholarships, Fellowships; SC, LC, GC; 650
Ent Req: HS grad
Degrees: 2 yr cert, BA 3 yrs, BA 4 yrs, BFA 4 yrs, MFA 2 yrs
Tuition: $284 per class
Courses: †Art Appreciation, †Art History, †Ceramics, †Drawing, Intermedia, Painting, †Printmaking, †Sculpture
Summer School: Introductory courses offered
—**Art Education Program,** Faculty of Education, Regina, SK S4S 0A2 Canada. Tel 306-585-4546; Fax 306-585-4880; Elec Mail norm.yakel@uregina.ca; Internet Home Page Address: www.uregina.ca/arts; *Dean Faculty Fine Arts* Katherine Laurin; *Dean Educ* Margaret McKinnon; *Chair Arts Educ Prog* Norm Yakel
Estab 1965; FT 9; pub; D & E; Scholarships; LC 6; D 160, E 20, maj 10
Ent Req: HS dipl, matriculation or degree for maj in art
Degrees: BA 3 & 4 yr, BEduc 3 yr
Tuition: Res—$2,490 per sem, visa students $4,110 per sem
Courses: Aesthetics, Art Education, †Dept offers courses in all the arts including performing arts
Children's Classes: Sat
Summer School: Exten Courses, H Kindred; Dean Educ, Dr Toombs. Term of 3 to 6 wks beginning May

SASKATOON

UNIVERSITY OF SASKATCHEWAN, Dept of Art & Art History, 3 Campus Dr, Murray Bldg 181 Saskatoon, SK S7N 5A5 Canada. Tel 306-966-4196; Fax 306-966-4266; Elec Mail mcleanj@abyss.usask.ca; Internet Home Page Address: www.usask.ca/art/index; *Head* Lynne Bell
Estab 1936; FT 13, PT 4; pub; D; Scholarships; SC, LC, GC; approx 880, BFA prog 130, grad 9
Ent Req: HS grad
Degrees: BA 3 yrs, BAHons(Art History), BA(Advanced) 4 yrs, BFA 4 yrs, MFA(Studio Art), BEd(Art)
Tuition: $117.20 per cr unit; $351.60 per 3 cr units; $703.20 per 6 cr units
Courses: Art Education, Art History, Drawing, History of Art & Architecture, Mixed Media, Painting, Photography, Printmaking, Sculpture
Summer School: Dir, Bob Cram, Extension Cr Studies. Enrl 200; tuition $366 per 6 wk term. Courses—Art Educ, Art History, Drawing, Painting, Photography, Printmaking, Sculpture

III ART INFORMATION

Major Museums Abroad

Major Art Schools Abroad

State Arts Councils

State Directors and Supervisors of Art Education

Art Magazines

Newspaper Art Editors and Critics

ALBANIA

TIRANA

M **MEZURAJ MUSEUM,** Sun Business Center, Kavaja Ave 1st Fl Tirana, Albania. Tel 355 42 67196; Fax 355 42 67199; Elec Mail info@mezuraj.museum; Internet Home Page Address: mezuraj.museum/index.html; *Dir* Moikom Zeqo; *Pres* Eduart Mezuraj; *VPres* Leonard Mezuraj; *Cur* Maksim Naci; *Archivist Asst* Mariola Naci
Open Mon - Sat 9 AM - 18 PM; cl Sun & holidays; Admis foreigners 3 euro, adults 300 lek, students 50 lek; exhib opening, for the protection & admin of mus objects, memory preservation, archaeological searching, enterprise etc; 680m, 2 exhib rooms, 1 hall of exhibs, 2 offices; Average Annual Attendance: 200,000
Income: Private mus financed by the mus pres, Eduart Mezuraj (according to the legal statute of the mus)
Purchases: Purchases are made for enriching archaeological collections & that of contemporary & traditional art
Library Holdings: CD-ROMs; Cassettes; Compact Disks; DVDs; Exhibition Catalogs; Original Art Works; Original Documents; Photographs; Prints; Reproductions; Sculpture; Video Tapes
Special Subjects: Archaeology, Historical Material, History of Art & Archaeology, Art History, Bronzes, African Art, Ceramics, Jewelry, Coins & Medals
Collections: Archeological objects, pre-historic, antique & middle-aged, iconographic art, many other works of Albanian artists; Traditional painters' & contemporary Albanian painters' collections
Publications: Mezuraj Album; Mezuraj Collection of Helidon Haliti; Mezuraj Collection of Artur Muharremi
Activities: Lectrs open to the public; gallery talks; schols; book traveling exhibs; mus shop sells books, original art, reproductions, prints

ALGERIA

ALGIERS

M **MUSEE NATIONAL DES ANTIQUITES,** Parc de la Liberte, Algiers, Algeria. Tel 74-66-86; Fax 74-74-71; *Dir* Drias Lakhdar; *Cur* Mohammed Temmam
Collections: Algerian antiquities & Islamic art

M **MUSEE NATIONAL DES BEAUX ARTS D'ALGER,** National Museum of Algiers, Place Dar-el Salem, El Hamma, Algiers, Algeria. Tel 664916; Fax 662054; *Dir* Dalila Orfali
Open Sat - Thurs 9 AM - 12 PM & 1 PM - 5 PM; Admis 20 DA (Algerian dinars); 1930; art gallery; Ground floor & two floors & two major entrances
Purchases: Annual commission of acquisitions
Collections: Contemporary Algerian art; paintings; drawings; bronze reliefs; ancient paintings 14th - 19th century (European)
Publications: Guides; exhibition catalogues; collections catalogues
Activities: Exhibitions; commemorations; conferences; concerts; tours

ARGENTINA

BUENOS AIRES

M **FUNDACION FEDERICO JORGE KLEMM,** Marcelo T de Alvear 626, Buenos Aires, Argentina. Tel 4312-3334/4443; Elec Mail admin@fundacionfjklemm.org; Internet Home Page Address: www.fundacionfjklemm.org/home/home.asp
Income:

M **FUNDACION PROA,** Av. Pedro de Mendoza 1929, La Boca, Caminito Buenos Aires, C1169AAD Argentina. Tel 54-11-4104-1000; Elec Mail info@proa.org; Internet Home Page Address: www.proa.org
Income:

M **MUSEO DE ARTE HISPANOAMERICANO ISAAC FERNANDEZ BLANCO,** Suipacha 1422, Buenos Aires, CP 1011 Argentina. Tel 5411-4327-0272; Tel 5411-4327-0228; *Dir* Jorge Cometti
Open Tues - Sun 2 PM - 7 PM; Admis $1, free Thurs
Collections: Personal collection of Don Isaac White Fernandez, Dona Celina Gonzalez Garano & others; paintings, furniture, silverware, and other decorative arts

M **MUSEO DE ARTE LATINOAMERICANO DE BUENOS AIRES,** Avenida Figueroa Alcorat 3415, Buenos Aires, C1425CLA Argentina. Tel 54 11 4808 6500; Elec Mail info@malba.org.ar; Internet Home Page Address: www.malba.org.ar/web; *Cur* Marcelo E Pacheco; *Gen Mgr* Emilio Xarrier
Open Mon noon - 8 PM, Wed - Fri noon - 8 PM, Sat - Sun 10 AM - 7 PM; No admis fee
Collections: History of Spanish American art; Avant-garde movement from beginning to present; Costantini Collection

M **MUSEO DE ARTE MODERNO,** Museum of Modern Art, Avenida San Juan 350, Buenos Aires, 1147 Argentina. Tel (11) 4361-1121; Elec Mail mambamail@gmail.com; Internet Home Page Address: www.aamamba.org.ar; *Dir* Raul Santana
Open Tues - Fri 10 AM - 8 PM, Sun & holidays 11 AM - 8 PM
Collections: Latin American paintings, especially Argentine, and contemporary schools

M **MUSEO DE BELLAS ARTES DE LA BOCA,** Fine Arts Museum, Avenida Pedro de Mendoza 1835, Buenos Aires, 1169 Argentina. Tel (11) 4301-1080; Fax (11) 4301-1080; Elec Mail museoquinquela@yahoo.com.ar; *Dir* Dr Guillermo C De La Canal
Open Tues - Fri 10 AM - 5 PM, Sat & Sun 11 AM - 5 PM; Admis 3 pesos
Collections: Paintings, sculptures, engravings & maritime museum

M **MUSEO MUNICIPAL DE ARTE ESPANOL ENRIQUE LARRETA,** Municipal Museum of Spanish Art, Juramento 2291 y Obligado 2139, Buenos Aires, 1428 Argentina. Tel (11) 4784-4040; Fax (11) 4783-2640; *Dir* Mercedes di Paola de Picot
Collections: 13th - 16th century wood carvings, gilt objects and painted panels, paintings of Spanish School of 16th and 17th centuries, tapestries, furniture

M **MUSEO NACIONAL DE ARTE DECORATIVO,** National Museum of Decorative Art, Avda del Libertador 1902, Buenos Aires, 1425 Argentina. Tel 11-4801-8248; Fax 11-4802-6606; Elec Mail museo@mnad.org; Internet Home Page Address: www.mnad.org; *Dir* Alberto Guillermo Bellucci
Open 2 PM to 7 PM; Admis general 50 pesos
Collections: European works; furniture, sculptures and tapestries; glasses, porcelains, hardstones, Oriental lacquers

M **MUSEO NACIONAL DE BELLAS ARTES,** National Museum of Fine Arts, Avda del Libertador 1473, Buenos Aires, 1425 Argentina. Tel 11-4803-0802; Fax 11-4803-4062; Elec Mail museo@mnba.org.ar; Internet Home Page Address: www.mnba.org.ar/index.php; *Dir* Alberto G Bellucci
Open hrs Museum: Tues - Fri 12:30 PM - 7:30 PM, Sat & Sun 9:30 AM - 7:30 PM; Library: Tues - Fri 12:30 PM - 7:30 PM, Sat 10:30 AM - 7:30 PM; Opened in 1896, the Nat Mus of Fine Arts has 32 exhibit halls with state of the art technology for both traditional & multimedia shows.
Collections: Argentine, American and European art, both modern and classical

CORDOBA

M **MUSEO PROVINCIAL DE BELLAS ARTES EMILIO A CARAFFA,** Provincial Museum of Fine Arts, Avenida Hipolito Irigoyen 651, Cordoba, 5000 Argentina. Tel (351) 469-0786; *Dir Lic* Graciela Elizabeth Palella
Collections: Provincial art center, including art library and archives; Argentine and foreign paintings, sculptures, drawings and engravings

CORDOVA

M **MUSEO MUNICIPAL DE BELLAS ARTES DR GENARO PEREZ,** Av Gral Peace 33, Cordova, 5000 Argentina. Tel 0351 433-1512; Fax 0351 433-2720; Elec Mail museogp@agora.com.ar; Internet Home Page Address: www.agora.com.ar/museogp; *Dir* Jorge Gonzalez
Open Mon - Fri 9:30 AM - 1:30 PM & 4:30 PM - 8:30 PM, Sat - Sun 10 AM - 8 PM
Collections: Permanent collection of Argentine and Cordovan painting from 1868 to the present; 19th century pieces; generation of the 1930s; nonfigurative avant-garde of the 1950s; movements from 1960 to the present

LA PLATA

M **MUSEO DE ARTE CONTEMPORANEO LATINOAMERICANO,** Calle 50 entre 6 y 7, La Plata, CP 1900 Argentina. Tel 0221 427-1843; Elec Mail maclamlp@infovia.com.ar; Internet Home Page Address: www.macla.laplata.gov.ar; *Dir Gen* Cesar Lopez Osornio
Autumn - Winter Tues - Fri 10 AM - 8 PM, Sat - Sun 2 PM - 9 PM; Spring - Summer Tues - Fri 10 AM - 8 PM, Sat - Sun 4 PM - 10 PM; cl Mon; No admis fee

Collections: Exhibitions of contemporary Latin American art

ROSARIO

M **MUSEO MUNICIPAL DE ARTE DECORATIVO FIRMA Y ODILO ESTEVEZ,** Municipal Decorative Arts Museum, Santa Fe 748, Rosario, 2000 Argentina. Tel (031) 480-2547; Elec Mail museoestevez@rosario.gov.ar; Internet Home Page Address: www.rosario.gov.ar/museoestevez; *Cur* P A Sinopoli
Collections: Antique glass; paintings by Van Utrecht, Antolinez, De Hondecoeter, Gerard, Lucas; 16th - 18th centuries furniture & silver; ceramics; antique glass; ivories; silver

M **MUSEO MUNICIPAL DE BELLAS ARTES JUAN B CASTAGNINO,** Municipal Museum of Fine Arts, Pellegrini 2202, Rosario, 2000 Argentina. Tel 341-421-7310; Fax 341-421-7310; *Dir* Prof Miguel Ballesteros
Library with 3000 vols
Collections: Works by Jose de Ribera, Goya, Valdes Leal & a complete collection of Argentine art from 19th century to present

SANTA FE

M **MUSEO DE BELLAS ARTES ROSA GALISTEO DE RODRIGUEZ,** Museum of Fine Arts, 4 de Enero 1510, Santa Fe, 3000 Argentina. Tel (342) 459-6142; Fax (342) 459-6142; *Dir* Nydia Pereyra Salva de Impini
Library with 4000 vols
Collections: Contemporary Argentine & modern art

TANDIL

M **MUSEO MUNICIPAL DE BELLAS ARTES DE TANDIL,** Municipal Museum of Fine Arts, Chacabuco 357, Tandil, 7000 Argentina. Tel 2293-42000; *Dir* E Valor
Collections: Paintings of classical, impressionist, cubist and modern schools

ARMENIA

YEREVAN

M **NATIONAL GALLERY OF ARMENIA,** 1 Arami St, Republic Sq Yerevan, 375010 Armenia. Tel 374-10 58-08-12; 58-21-61; Fax 374-10 58-08-12; Elec Mail galleryarmenia@yahoo.com; Internet Home Page Address: www.gallery.am; *Dir* Dr Shahen Khachatryan
Open Tues - Sun 10:30 AM - 6 PM; cl Mon & holidays; No admis fee
Collections: Collection of more than 19,000 Russian, Armenian and western European paintings, sculptures, & graphic and applied arts

AUSTRALIA

ADELAIDE

M **ART GALLERY OF SOUTH AUSTRALIA,** North Terrace, Adelaide, SA 5000 Australia. Tel (+61 8) 8207-7000; Fax (+61 8) 8207-7070; Elec Mail agsa.info@artgallery.sa.gov.au; Internet Home Page Address: www.artgallery.sa.gov.au; *Dir* Nick Mitzevich; *Cur of European Art* Jane Messenger; *Cur of Australian Art* Tracy Lock-Weir; *Sr Cur of Prints, Drawings & Photographs* Julie Robinson; *Assoc Cur of Prints, Drawings & Photographs* Maria Zagala; *Cur of Asian Art* James Bennett; *Cur of European & Australian Decorative Arts* Robert Reason; *Assoc Dir* Mark Horton
Open 10 AM - 5 PM daily, cl Dec 25; No admis fee; charges for some exhibs; Estab 1881; Main art gallery of the state of South Australia; Average Annual Attendance: 600,000
Income: Financed by South Australian state government
Purchases: Continually adding to the permanent collection
Library Holdings: Auction Catalogs; Book Volumes; CD-ROMs; Cards; Clipping Files; Exhibition Catalogs; Fiche; Original Documents; Pamphlets; Periodical Subscriptions; Records
Special Subjects: Decorative Arts, Drawings, Etchings & Engravings, Ceramics, Glass, Furniture, Painting-British, Painting-European, Photography, Prints, Sculpture, Watercolors, Textiles, Pottery, Woodcuts, Jewelry, Porcelain, Asian Art, Silver, Laces, Islamic Art, Painting-Australian
Collections: Representative selection of Australian, British and European paintings, prints, drawings and sculpture; large coll of ceramics, glass and silver; extensive Australian Colonial Coll; Asian Arts; SE Asian ceramics; furniture; photography
Exhibitions: Several temporary exhibitions per year
Publications: Exhibition catalogues, collection catalogues, newsletter, ann report
Activities: Classes for children; docent training; lects open to pub, lectrs for mems only; concerts; gallery talks; tours; traveling exhibs to Australian & New Zealand galleries; mus shop sells books, magazines, reproductions; prints, gifts, postcards & posters

BALLARAT

M **ART GALLERY OF BALLARAT,** 40 Lydiard St N, Ballarat, 3350 Australia. Tel 03-5320-5858; Fax 03-5320-5791; Elec Mail artgal@ballarat.vic.gov.au; Internet Home Page Address: www.balgal.com
Income:

BENALLA

M **BENALLA ART GALLERY,** Bridge St, Benalla, 3672 Australia; PO Box 227, Benalla, 3671 Australia. Tel 03-5762-3027; Fax 03-5762-5640; Elec Mail gallery@benalla.vic.gov.au; Internet Home Page Address: www.benallaartgallery.com
Circ

BRISBANE

M **INSTITUTE OF MODERN ART,** 420 Brunswick St, Fortitude Valley Brisbane, Australia; PO Box 2176, Fortitude Valley Brisbane, 4006 Australia. Tel 61 7 3252 5750; Fax 61 7 3252 5072; Elec Mail ima@ima.org.au; Internet Home Page Address: www.ima.org.au; *Dir* Robert Leonard; *Prog Mgr* Anna Zammit; *Exhib Officer* Ross Manning; *Gallery Mgr* Dhana Merritt; *Communications* Karike Ashworth; *Bookkeeper* Jewel MacKenzie; *Ed* Evie Franzidis; *Designer* Ngaio Parr
Open Tues - Sat 11 AM - 5 PM; Thurs 11 AM - 8 PM; No admis fee; Estab 1975; Second oldest contemporary art space; progs of exhibs & events featuring emerging & established local, nat, & international artists; Mem: 300; dues family $75, individual $50, concession $25
Collections: Modern and contemporary art in various media; Rotating exhibitions; See website for details
Activities: Lects open to pub; 72 vis lectrs per yr; concerts; gallery talks; tours; organize traveling exhibs; mus shop sells books, magazines

BULLEEN VIC

M **HEIDE MUSEUM OF MODERN ART,** 7 Templestowe Rd, Bulleen VIC, 3105 Australia. Tel 61-3-9850-1500; Fax 61-3-9852-0154; Elec Mail info@heide.com.au; Internet Home Page Address: www.heide.com.au
Open Tues - Sun 10 AM - 5 PM; Admis $14, seniors $12, conc $10, mems free; Estab 1981, to continue the legacy of founders, John & Sunday Reed; Three separate gallery spaces showing modern & contemporary Australian art; Average Annual Attendance: 40,000; Mem: 1,500
Collections: Over 2,000 works of art & a unique body of cultural material that documents the social & artistic history of Heide
Activities: Classes for adults & children; lects open to pub; lects for mems only; gallery talks; tours; mus shop sells books, magazines, Australian designed gifts, accessories & exhib catalogues

BUNBURY

M **BUNBURY REGIONAL ART GALLERIES,** 64 Wittenoom St, Bunbury, 6230 Australia. Tel 08-9721-8616; Internet Home Page Address: www.brag.org.au
Circ

CANBERRA

M **NATIONAL GALLERY OF AUSTRALIA,** Parkes Pl, Parkes Canberra, ACT 2600 Australia; PO Box 1150, Canberra, ACT 2601 Australia. Tel (02) 6240 6411; Fax (02) 6240 6529; Elec Mail information@nga.gov.au; Internet Home Page Address: www.nga.gov.au; *Dir* Ron Radford; *Asst Dir* Simon Elliott; *Asst Dir* Adam Worrall; *Asst Dir* David Perceval
Open daily 10 AM - 5 PM, cl Christmas; No admis fee
Library Holdings: Auction Catalogs; Audio Tapes; Book Volumes; Clipping Files; Exhibition Catalogs; Manuscripts; Memorabilia; Original Documents; Pamphlets; Periodical Subscriptions
Collections: Australian coll includes fine and decorative arts, folk art, commercial art, architecture and design; International coll contains arts from Asia, Southeast Asia, Oceania, Africa, Pre-Columbian America and Europe
Activities: Classes for adults & children; lectrs open to the pub; lectrs for mems only; concerts; gallery talks; tours; galley shop sells books, magazines, reproductions, prints; children's gallery

L **Research Library,** PO Box 1150, Canberra, ACT 2601 Australia. Tel 612 6240 6530; Fax 612 6273 2155; Elec Mail joye.volker@nga.gov.au; Internet Home Page Address: www.nga.gov.au/research; *Chief Librn* Joye Volker; *Bib Serv Librn* Helen Hyland; *Acquisitions Librn* Gillian Currie
Open Mon - Fri 10 AM - 4:45 PM; estab 1975; Natl Gallery of Australia
Library Holdings: Auction Catalogs 54,000; Book Volumes 140,000; Clipping Files 75,000; DVDs 500; Exhibition Catalogs 15,000; Fiche 35,000; Manuscripts 70; Other Holdings Serials 2,000; Periodical Subscriptions 800; Video Tapes 300
Special Subjects: Collages, Folk Art, Decorative Arts, Illustration, Mixed Media, Photography, Drawings, Etchings & Engravings, Graphic Arts, Graphic Design, Islamic Art, Manuscripts, Painting-American, Painting-British, Painting-French, Painting-German, Painting-Italian, Painting-Japanese, Posters, Prints, Sculpture, Painting-European, Portraits, Watercolors, Ceramics, Conceptual Art, Crafts, Printmaking, Fashion Arts, Asian Art, Video, Furniture, Costume Design & Constr, Glass, Bookplates & Bindings, Handicrafts, Jewelry, Oriental Art, Restoration & Conservation, Tapestries, Textiles, Woodcarvings, Woodcuts, Landscapes, Painting-Scandinavian, Painting-Australian, Painting-New Zealand, Display
Activities: Docent training; concerts; gallery talks; tours; sponsoring of competitions; lectrs for mem only; mus shop sells books, magazines, original art, reproductions & prints

CASTLEMAINE

M **CASTLEMAINE ART GALLERY AND HISTORICAL MUSEUM,** 12 Lyttleton St, Castlemaine, 3450 Australia. Tel 03-5472-2292; Fax 03-5472-2292; Internet Home Page Address: archive.amol.org.au/art_trails/castlemaine
Circ

HAMILTON

M **HAMILTON ART GALLERY,** 107 Brown St, Hamilton, 3300 Australia. Tel 03-5573-0460; Fax 03-5571-1017; Elec Mail info@hamiltongallery.org; Internet Home Page Address: www.hamiltongallery.org

HOBART

M **TASMANIAN MUSEUM AND ART GALLERY,** 40 Macquarie St, Hobart, 7001 Australia; GPO Box 1164, Hobart, 7001 Australia. Tel (03) 62114177; Fax (03) 62114112; Elec Mail emagmail@tmag.tas.gov.au; Internet Home Page Address: www.tmag.tas.gov.au; *Dir* Bill Bleathman; *Deputy Dir Coll & Res* Dr Andrew Rozefelds; *Deputy Dir Pub Progs* Peta Dowell-Hentall
Open 10AM-5PM; No admis fee; Estab 1840 by Royal Society of Tasmania; Gallery contains art, science, humanities
Library Holdings: Auction Catalogs; Book Volumes; Clipping Files; Exhibition Catalogs; Kodachrome Transparencies; Pamphlets; Periodical Subscriptions
Collections: Australian and Tasmanian art
Activities: Classes & holiday programs for children; lects open to pub; concerts; gallery talks; tours; lending of original art to galleries & museums; mus shop sells books, magazines, reproductions, prints

HORSHAM

M **HORSHAM ART GALLERY,** 80 Wilson St, Horsham, 3400 Australia. Tel 03-5362-2888; Fax 03-5382-5407; Elec Mail hrag@hrcc.vic.gov.au; Internet Home Page Address: www.horshamartgallery.com.au
Average Annual Attendance:

LAUNCESTON

M **LAUNCESTON CITY COUNCIL,** Queen Victoria Museum and Art Gallery, 2 Invermay Rd, Launceston, 7248 Australia; PO Box 403, Launceston, 7250 Australia. Tel (03) 6323-3777; Fax (03) 6323-3776; Elec Mail enquiries@gvmag.tas.gov.au; Internet Home Page Address: www.gvmag.tas.gov.au; *Dir* Mr Richard Mulvaney
Open daily 10 AM - 4 PM, cl Good Friday & Christmas day; No admis fee; Estab 1891; Museum & art gallery on two separate sites; Average Annual Attendance: 100,000
Library Holdings: Auction Catalogs; Audio Tapes; Book Volumes; CD-ROMs; Clipping Files; Compact Disks; DVDs; Exhibition Catalogs; Manuscripts; Maps; Memorabilia; Pamphlets; Periodical Subscriptions; Photographs; Records
Special Subjects: Decorative Arts, Etchings & Engravings, Ceramics, Glass, Metalwork, Porcelain, Portraits, Pottery, Prints, Textiles, Sculpture, Drawings, Photography, Watercolors, Ethnology, Costumes, Crafts, Woodcuts, Furniture, Silver, Scrimshaw, Laces, Painting-Australian
Collections: Pure & applied art; Tasmanian history: Tasmanian & general anthropology; Tasmanian botany, geology, paleontology & zoology
Activities: Classes for children & children; lects open to pub; lects for mems only; concerts; gallery talks; tours; schols; mus shops & art gallery sells books, reproductions, prints & giftware

LISMORE

M **LISMORE REGIONAL GALLERY,** 131 Molesworth St, Lismore, 2480 Australia. Tel +61-2-6622-2209; Fax +61-2-6622-2228; Elec Mail artgallery@lismore.nsw.gov.au; Internet Home Page Address: www.lismoregallery.org
Open Tues - Wed & Fr i - Sat 10 AM - 4 PM, Thurs 10 AM - 6 PM

MELBOURNE

M **MONASH UNIVERSITY MUSEUM OF ART,** 900 Dandenong Rd, Ground Fl, Bldg F, Caulfield Campus Melbourne, VIC 3145 Australia. Tel 61-3-9905-4217; Fax 61-3-9905-4345; Elec Mail muma@monash.edu; Internet Home Page Address: www.monash.edu.au/muma; *Dir* Max Delany; *Sr Cur & Coll Mgr* Geraldine Barlow; *Cur Colls* Kirrily Hammond; *Cur Exhib* Francis Parker
Open Tues - Fri 10 AM - 5 PM, Sat noon - 5 PM; No admis fee; Estab 1961; University art museum, found on contemporary art; Average Annual Attendance: 30,000
Collections: Monash Univ Coll
Publications: Please refer to www.monash.edu.au/muma/publications
Activities: Lects open to the pub; gallery talks; tours; lending of original objects of art to college mus & galleries; mus shop sells books & magazines

M **NATIONAL GALLERY OF VICTORIA,** 180 St Kilda Rd, Melbourne, VIC 3004 Australia. Tel (03) 92080222; Fax (03) 9 2080245; *Dir* Dr Gerard Vaughan; *Deputy Dir* Frances Lindsay
Open 10 AM - 5 PM, Thurs 10 AM - 9 PM, cl Mon; Library with 20,000 vols
Collections: Asian art; Australian art; pre-Columbian art; modern European art; antiquities, costumes, textiles, old master and modern drawings, paintings, photography, prints and sculpture

MILDURA

M **MILDURA ARTS CENTRE,** 199 Cureton Ave, Mildura, 3500 Australia; PO Box 105, Mildura, 3502 Australia. Tel 03-5018 8330; Fax 03-5021 1462; Elec Mail arts_centre@mildura.vic.gov.au; Internet Home Page Address: www.milduraarts.net.au
Open daily 10 AM - 5 PM

PERTH

M **ART GALLERY OF WESTERN AUSTRALIA,** Perth Cultural Centre, Perth, WA Australia; PO Box 8363, Perth Business Centre Perth, WA 6849 Australia. Tel (08) 94926682; 61894926682; Fax (08) 94926655; Elec Mail admin@artgallery.wa.gov.au; Internet Home Page Address: www.artgallery.wa.gov.au; *Dir* Stefano Carboni, PhD
Open Wed - Mon 10 AM - 5 PM, cl Tues, Good Friday & Christmas Day, Anzac Day
Collections: Australian Aboriginal Artifacts; British, European & Australian paintings, prints, drawings, sculptures & crafts
Activities: Docent training; lects open to pub; 500 vis lectrs per yr; gallery talks; tours; Western Australian Indigenous Art Award; mus shop sells books, magazines, reproductions, prints & giftware

SOUTH BRISBANE

M **QUEENSLAND ART GALLERY,** Gallery of Modern Art, PO Box 3686, South Brisbane, QLD 4101 Australia. Tel (07) 3840 7303; Fax (07) 3844 8865; Elec Mail gallery@gag.qld.gov.au; Internet Home Page Address: www.qag.qld.gov.au; *Dir* Tony Ellwood; *Deputy Dir Prog & Corp Serv* Andrew Clark; *Deputy Dir Curatorial & Coll Devel* Suhanya Raffel; *Mgr Mktg & Bus Develop* Celestine Doyle; *Curatorial Mgr, Australian Art* Julie Ewington; *Curatorial Mgr Asian & Pacific Art* Russell Storer; *Curatorial Mgr Nat Art & Australian Cinematheque* Kathryn Weir
Open Mon - Fri 10 AM - 5 PM, Sat & Sun 9 AM - 5 PM; Admis free, except special exhibs; Estab 1895; pub art mus for the state of Queensland
Collections: Predominantly Australian art, ceramics, decorative arts, paintings and drawings; British and European paintings and sculpture; historical & contemporary Asian & Pacific art
Publications: see www.australianartbooks.com
Activities: Classes for children; lects open to the pub; lects for mems only; gallery talks; tours; extension prog serves regional Queensland; lending of original objects of art; organize traveling exhibs; mus shop sells books, magazines, & collectibles

SYDNEY

M **ART GALLERY OF NEW SOUTH WALES,** Art Gallery Rd, The Domain Sydney, 2000 Australia. Tel 02-9225-1700; Fax 02-9221-6226; Elec Mail artmail@ag.nsw.gov.au; Internet Home Page Address: www.artgallery.nsw.gov.au; *Dir* Edmund Capon
Open Mon - Tues & Thurs - Sun 10 AM - 5 PM, Wed 10 AM - 9 PM; No admis fee (fees may apply for special exhibits); Average Annual Attendance: 1,200,000
Collections: Australian Aboriginal and Melanesian art; Australian art; collections of British and European painting and sculpture; Asian art, including Japanese ceramics and painting and Chinese ceramics; contemporary art; photography; prints & drawings
Activities: Classes for children; lects open to public; lects for members only; concerts; gallery talks; tours; films; scholarships offered; mus shop sells books, magazines, original art & reproductions

M **MUSEUM OF APPLIED ARTS & SCIENCES,** 500 Harris St, Ultimo, Sydney, 2007 Australia. Tel 612-9217-0111; Internet Home Page Address: www.powerhousemuseum.com; *Dir* Dr Kevin Fewster AM
Open daily 10 AM - 5 PM; Admis adults $10, child/conc $3, family $25; additional fees apply for temporary exhibitions; Estab 1879; Library with 20,000 vols; Average Annual Attendance: 600,000; Mem: 30,000
Collections: Scientific Instruments; Numismatics; Philately; Astronomy; Technology; Design; Decorative Arts; History
Activities: Classes for adults & children; lects open to public & mems only; 5-10; books, magazines, reproductions, prints, gifts

M **MUSEUM OF CONTEMPORARY ART,** 140 George St, The Rocks Sydney, 2000 Australia; PO Box R1286, Royal Exchange Sydney, 1223 Australia. Tel 612-9245-2400; Fax 612-9252-4361; Elec Mail mail@mca.com.au; Internet Home Page Address: www.mca.com.au; *Dir* Elizabeth Ann Macgregor
Open daily 10 AM - 5 PM, cl holidays; No admis fee
Collections: Contemporary art archives; J W Power Collection; Loti & Victor Smorgon Collection of Contemporary Australian Art; Maningrida Collection of Aboriginal Art; Ramingining Collection of Aboriginal Art; Arnotts Biscuits Collection of Aboriginal bark painting

M **POWERHOUSE MUSEUM,** 500 Harris St Ultimo, Haymarket Sydney, 1238 Australia; PO Box K346, Haymarket Sydney, 1238 Australia. Tel 02-9217-0111; Internet Home Page Address: www.powerhousemuseum.com
Income:

M **THE UNIVERSITY OF SYDNEY,** The Nicholson Museum, University of Sydney, Sydney, 2006 Australia. Tel +61-2 93512812; Fax +61-2 93517305; Elec Mail michael.turner@arts.usyd.edu.au; Internet Home Page Address: www.usyd.edu.au/museums/; *Sr Cur* Michael C Turner; *Pub Programs Mgr* Craig Barker; *Conservator* Ms Jo Atkinson; *Coll Mgr* Maree Darrell; *Curatorial Asst* Elizabeth Bollen
Open Mon - Fri 10 AM - 4:30 PM, Sun noon - 4 PM, cl public holidays; No admis fee; Estab 1860; Antiquities from the Mediterranean; Average Annual Attendance: 45,000; Mem: 450 Mems Friends Nicholson Museum Dues $50 Aus yr
Income: Financed through university grant
Collections: Antiquities of Egypt, Near East, Europe, Greece, Italy
Activities: Classes for adults & children; school educ prog; lects for members only, 6 vis lectrs per yr; gallery talks, tours; sales shop sells books, reproductions, greeting cards, mugs, cards, bookmats, mousemats, key rings

AUSTRIA

BREGENZ

M **KUNSTHAUS BREGENZ,** Karl Tizian Platz, Bregenz, A-6900 Austria. Tel 43-5574 48594-0; Fax 43-5574 48594-408; Elec Mail kub@kunsthaus-bregenz.at; Internet Home Page Address: www.kunsthaus-bregenz.at; *Dir* Dr Yilmaz Dziewio; *Cur* Dr Rudolf Sagmeister; *Cur Kub Arena* Eva Birkenstock; *Publs* Dr Katrin Wiethege; *Communs* Birgit Albers; *Educ* Lisa Hann
Open Tues - Sun 10 AM - 6 PM, Thurs 10 AM - 9 PM; Admis adults 9, euro, students 6 euro
Collections: Collection of contemporary Austrian art; Paintings, sculpture, object and conceptual art, video art, mixed-media and photography; International works in art and architecture
Activities: Classes for adults & children; lects open to the pub; mus shop sells books

M **VORARLBERG MUSEUM,** (Vorarlberg Provincial Museum) Kornmarkt1, Bregenz, 6900 Austria. Tel 43 0 5574 460 50; Elec Mail info@vorarlbergmuseum.at; Internet Home Page Address: www.vorarlbergmuseum.at; *Dir* Dr Andreas Rudigier
Open daily 10 AM - 20 PM; Admis adults 9 euro, student 6.50 euro
Library Holdings: Auction Catalogs; Book Volumes; DVDs; Exhibition Catalogs; Maps; Original Documents
Special Subjects: Decorative Arts, Drawings, Portraits, Textiles, Painting-European, Graphics, Archaeology, Religious Art, Crafts, Antiquities-Roman
Collections: Visual art, history & archaeological artifacts
Activities: Classes for adults & children; lects open to pub; lects for mems only; tours; lending of original objects of art to other mus

EISENSTADT

M **BURGENLAND PROVINCIAL MUSEUM,** Museumgasse 1-5, Eisenstadt, 7000 Austria. Tel 02682 600 1234; Fax 02682 600 1277; Elec Mail landesmuseum@bgld.gv.at; Internet Home Page Address: www.burgenland.at/landesmuseum
Open Tues - Sat 9 AM - 5 PM, Sun & holidays 10 AM - 5 PM
Collections: art, folklore & historic artifacts

GRAZ

M **KUNSTHAUS GRAZ AM UNIVERSAL JOANNEUM,** (Kunsthaus Graz am Landesmuseum Joanneum) Lendkai 1, Graz, A-8020 Austria. Tel 43-316/8017-9200; Fax 43-316/8017-9212; Elec Mail kunsthaus@museum-joanneum.at; Internet Home Page Address: www.museum-joanneum.at/kunsthaus; *Dir* Peter Pakesch; *Cur* Katrin Bucher Trantow; *Cur* Adam Budak
Open Tues - Sun 10 AM - 6 PM; Admis adults 7 euro, seniors 5.50 euro, students up to 27 yrs 3 euro, students in school groups 1.50 euro, families 14 euro, children 6 and under free; Estab 2003; international contemporary art of the last five decades; Average Annual Attendance: 80,000
Collections: Multi-disciplinary contemporary art

M **UNIVERSALMUSEUM JOANNEUM GMBH,** MariahilferstraBe 2-4, Graz, 8020 Austria. Tel 43-316/8017-0; Fax 43-316/8017-9699; Elec Mail welcome@museum-joanneum.at; Internet Home Page Address: www.museum-joanneum.at; *Dir* Dr Wolfgang Muchitsch; *Intendant* Peter Pakesch
See website for hours; See website; Estab 1811
Library Holdings: Audio Tapes; Book Volumes; CD-ROMs; Cards; Compact Disks; DVDs; Exhibition Catalogs; Framed Reproductions
Special Subjects: Archaeology, Historical Material, Glass, Metalwork, Photography, Textiles, Sculpture, Drawings, Graphics, Ethnology, Religious Art, Folk Art, Painting-European, Portraits, Coins & Medals, Baroque Art, Renaissance Art, Period Rooms, Painting-German, Military Art
Activities: Educ prog; classes for adults & children; lects open to pub; gallery talks; tours; sponsoring of competitions; The Council of Europe Museum Prize, 1983; fels available; sa;es shop sells books, magazines & souvenirs

INNSBRUCK

M **TIROLER LANDESMUSEUM FERDINANDEUM,** Tyrolese Provincial Museum, MuseumstraBe 15, Innsbruck, A-6020 Austria. Tel 0512/59489-110; Internet Home Page Address: www.tiroler-landesmuseum.at; *Dir* Dr Wolfgang Heighorner
Open Tues - Sun 10 AM - 6 PM

KLAGENFURT

M **CARINTHIAN PROVINCIAL MUSEUM,** Landesmuseum Karnten, Museumgasse 2, Klagenfurt, 9021 Austria. Elec Mail info@landesmuseum-ktn.at
Open Tues - Fri 9 AM - 4 PM, Sat 10 AM - 1 PM
Collections: Art and cultural artifacts of Carinthia

LINZ

M **LENTOS ART MUSEUM,** Ernst-Koref-Promenade 1, LENTOS Kunstmuseum Linz Linz, 4020 Austria. Tel +43-732-7070-3600; Tel +43-732-7070-3614; Fax +43-732-7070-3604; Elec Mail info@lentos.at; Internet Home Page Address: www.lentos.at; *Dir* Stella Rollig
Open daily 10 AM - 9 PM, cl Christmas; Admis adults 6.50 Euro, students under 26, seniors & military 4.50 Euro, student groups free; family rates, combination & annual tickets available; Estab 2003 as successor to the New Gallery of the City of Linz

Collections: Wolfgang Gurlitt Collection

M **MUSEUM OF MODERN ART - LINZ,** Ernst-Koref-Promenade 1, Linz, A-4020 Austria. Tel 43 0 732-7070-3600; Fax 43 0 732-7070-3604; Elec Mail info@lentos.at; Internet Home Page Address: www.lentos.at/en/index.asp; *Dir* Stella Rolling; *Dir* Dr Gernot Barounig
Open Mon - Fri 10 AM - 6 PM, Thurs 10 AM - 9 PM, cl holidays; Admis adults 6.50 euro, under 26 & seniors 4.50 euro, families 13 euro, children under 7 free, school group 2 euro per student
Collections: Comprises 1500 works in painting, sculpture and object art; over 10,000 works on paper; 850 photographs, including photographic history and development

MIESENBACH

M **GAUERMANN MUSEUM,** Scheuchenstein 127, Miesenbach, A-2761 Austria. Tel 43-2632-8267; Fax 43-2632-8267; Elec Mail kulturvereingauermann@utanet.at; Internet Home Page Address: www.miesenbach.at/KKV
Average Annual Attendance:

SALZBURG

M **MUSEUM DER MODERNE SALZBURG MONCHSBERG,** Monchsberg 32, Salzburg, 5020 Austria. Tel 43-662-84-22-20-401; Fax 43*662-842220701; Elec Mail info@museumdermoderne.at; Internet Home Page Address: www.museumdermoderne.at
Open Tues - Sun 10 AM - 6 PM, Wed 10 AM - 9 PM, cl Mon; Admis adults 8 euro, seniors 6 euro, children over six 6 euro

M **Museum der Moderne Salzburg Rupertinum,** Wiener-Philharmoniker-Gasse 9, Salzburg, 5020 Austria. Tel 43-662-84-22-20-451; *Dir* Toni Stoos; *Cur* Dr Eleonora Louis; *Cur* Dr Margit Zuckriegl
Admis adults 6 euro, seniors 4 euro, children over six 4 euro
Collections: 20th century paintings, sculpture, graphics and photography; Art in between the war periods; Contemporary Austrian and international art

M **RESIDENZGALERIE SALZBURG,** Residenzplatz 1, Salzburg, A-5010 Austria. Tel (0662) 84 04 51; Fax (0662) 84 04 51-16; Elec Mail residenzgalerie@salzburg.gv.at; Internet Home Page Address: www.residenzgalerie.at; *Dir* Dr Roswitha Juffinger; *Educ Cur* Dr Gabriele Groschner; *Pub Rels* Dr Erika Mayr-Oehring; *Archiving/Internet* Dr Thomas Habersatter
Open 10 AM - 5 PM, cl Mon; Admis 7 euro (reduced 6); European paintings of the 16th - 19th centuries; Average Annual Attendance: 60,000
Income: Income from public collection of the govt of Salzburg
Collections: European paintings, 16th - 19th centuries
Publications: Exhibition catalogues
Activities: Classes for adults & children; lects open to pub; 200 vis lectrs per yr; concerts; gallery talks; tours; literature, cinema, modern art lent to mus, official collections; mus shops sells books, magazines, reproductions, postcards, souvenirs

M **SALZBURG MUSEUM,** (Salzburger Museum) Mozartplatz 1, Salzburg, A-5010 Austria. Tel 0043(0)662/620808-0; Fax 0043(0)662/620808-720; Elec Mail office@salzburgmuseum.at; Internet Home Page Address: www.salzburgmuseum.at; *Dir* Dr Erich Marx
Open Tues - Sun 9 AM - 5 PM, Thurs 9 AM - 8 PM; July, Aug, Dec Mon 9 AM - 5 PM; Admis 7 euros; Estab 1834; Library with 100,000 vols including 7 mus; Mem: 5,000
Income: 50% city of Salzburg, 50% country of Salzburg
Collections: Art, coins, musical instruments, costumes, peasant art; Prehistoric & Roman archaeology; Toy, fortress, folk and excavation museums
Exhibitions: 18 different exhibs per yr
Activities: Classes for adults & children; lects open to pub; 2,500 vis lectrs per yr; concerts; gallery talks; tours; sponsoring of competitions; Mus of the Year Award 2009; lending of original art to mus around the world; originate traveling exhibs; mus shop sells books; reproductions; prints; jr mus Kinderwell (children's world)

TULLN

M **EGON SCHIELE MUSEUM TULLN,** A-3430 Tulln an der Donau, Donaulande 28, Tulln, Austria. Tel 43-2272-64570; Fax 43-2272-64116; Elec Mail stadtamt@tulln.at; Internet Home Page Address: egonschiele.museum.com
Average Annual Attendance:

VIENNA

M **AKADEMIE DER BILDENDEN KUNSTE WIEN,** Gemaldegalerie der Akademie der bildenden Kunst Wien, Schillerplatz 3, Vienna, 1010 Austria. Tel 58816-2222; Fax 586 3346; Elec Mail gemgal@akbild.ac.at; Internet Home Page Address: akademiegalerie.at; *Dir* Dr Renate Trnek; *Asst* Dr Martina Fleischer; *Mag* Andrea Domanig; *Mag Dipl Rest* Astrid Lehner
Open Tues - Sun 10 AM - 4 PM, cl Mon; Admis 7 euro; Estab 1822; old masters 15 - 19th century
Income: Financed by government
Special Subjects: Painting-European, Painting-Dutch, Painting-French, Painting-Flemish, Painting-Spanish, Painting-Italian, Painting-German
Collections: European Paintings of the 14th - 20th centuries - Hieronymus Bosch, Hans Baldung Grien; 17th century Dutch (Rembrandt, Ruisdael, van Goyen, Jan Both & others); Flemish, (Rubens, Jordaens, van Dyck), Guardi, Magnasco, Tiepolo, bequests by Count Lamberg, Prince Liechtenstein, Wolfgang von Wurzbach; Glyptotheque (Coll 19th-century sculpture)
Activities: Lects open to public; gallery talks; books, slides, postcards

M **ALBERTINA MUSEUM,** Albertinaplatz 1, Vienna, 1010 Austria. Tel 43-1-534-830; Fax 43-1-533-7697; Elec Mail info@albertina.at; Elec Mail membership@albertina.at; Internet Home Page Address: www.albertina.at; *Dir* Klaus Albrecht Schroder; *Deputy Dir* Marlies Sternath
Open daily 10 AM - 8 PM, Wed 10 AM - 9 PM; Admis adults 9.50 euro, seniors 8 euro, students up to 26 yrs 7 euro, students up to 19 yrs 3.50 euro, children under 6 yrs no charge; Estab 1796; Average Annual Attendance: 600,000
Library Holdings: Auction Catalogs; Book Volumes; Exhibition Catalogs; Periodical Subscriptions
Special Subjects: Drawings, Prints, Watercolors, Posters, Miniatures
Collections: Drawings 44,000; sketchbooks, miniatures & posters; The Batlinger Collection; Masterwork of Modern Art from the Albertina
Exhibitions: 5-6 exhibs per year
Activities: Classes for adults & children; lects open to pub; mus shop sells books, magazines, reproductions, prints

M **BELVEDERE MUSEUM,** (Osterreichische Galerie) Osterreichische Galerie Belvedere, Prinz Eugen Stra Be 27, Vienna, 1030 Austria. Tel 43 (01) 79 557 134; Tel 43 (01) 79 557 108/109; Fax 43 (01) 79 557 121; Elec Mail info@belvedere.at; Internet Home Page Address: www.belvedere.at; *Dir* Dr Agnes Husslein-Arco; *Deputy Dir & COO* Alfred Weidinger
Open daily 10 AM - 6 PM, Wed 10 AM - 9 PM; Admis adult 12.50 euro; combined ticket upper & lower Belvedere 22.50 euro; Mus incls two palaces, Upper & Lower Belvedere with extensive gardens in the Baroque style & the modernistic 21er Haus, winter palace of Prince Eugene of Savoy; Average Annual Attendance: 1,100,000
Library Holdings: Auction Catalogs; Audio Tapes; Book Volumes; CD-ROMs; Cards; Compact Disks; DVDs; Exhibition Catalogs; Kodachrome Transparencies; Lantern Slides; Manuscripts; Memorabilia; Original Art Works; Original Documents; Other Holdings; Pamphlets; Periodical Subscriptions; Photographs; Prints; Records; Reproductions; Slides; Video Tapes
Special Subjects: Period Rooms, Bronzes, Sculpture, Watercolors, Religious Art, Landscapes, Portraits, Painting-French, Restorations, Baroque Art, Medieval Art
Collections: Upper Belvedere incls permanent collections; Austrian Art from Medieval Art to Contemporary Art
Exhibitions: Lower Belvedere stages temporary exhibs with artwork from around the world; The 21er Haus stages temporary exhibs with art from 1930 to Contemporary Art
Publications: Exhibition Catalogues, Catalogues Raisonnes, Collection Guides
Activities: Classes for adults & children; docent training; lects open to pub; 2-3 vis lectrs per yr; concerts; gallery talks; tours; fellowships; BC21 Art Award; extension progs directed to schools & sr citizens; artmobile; mus shop sells books, reproductions & prints

M **Research Center,** Belvedere Museum Research Ctr, Rennweg 4 Vienna, 1030 Austria; Prinz Eugen-STR 27, Vienna, 1030 Austria. Tel 43 (01) 79 557 232; Fax 43 (01) 79 557 235; Elec Mail research@belvedere.at; Internet Home Page Address: www.belvedere.at; *Dir* Dr Agnes Husslein-Arco
Open daily 10 AM - 7 PM; Admis ann ticket 15 euro, monthly season ticket 5 euro, day ticket 2 euro
Library Holdings: Auction Catalogs; Book Volumes; CD-ROMs; Clipping Files; DVDs; Exhibition Catalogs; Kodachrome Transparencies; Lantern Slides; Manuscripts; Original Documents; Periodical Subscriptions; Photographs; Slides; Video Tapes

M **Osterreichisches Barockmuseum,** Unteres Belvedere, Rennweg 6A Vienna, Austria.
Collections: Austrian Baroque art (paintings and sculptures)

M **Augarten Contemporary,** Scherzergasse 1a, Vienna, 1020 Austria. Tel 43 (01) 21 686 16 21; Fax 43 (01) 216 40 22; Elec Mail info@belvedere.at; Internet Home Page Address: www.belvedere.at; *Dir* Dr Agnes Husslein-Arco
Open Thurs - Sun 11 AM - 7 PM; Admis adults 5 euro; Laboratory of all the movements & genres of contemporary art offering young artists opportunities in the institutional sector
Activities: Classes for adults; artist in residence prog; gallery talks; tours; BC21-Boston Consulting & Belvedere Contemporary Art Award; sales shop sells books

M **Gustinus Ambrosi-Museum,** Scherzergasse 1A, Vienna, 1020 Austria. Tel 0043 (01) 21 686 16-21; Fax 0043 (01) 216 4022; Elec Mail info@belvedere.at
Open Thurs - Sun 11 AM - 7 PM; Admis adult 5 euro; Estab 1978; mus houses bronze & stone sculptures by the Austrian sculptor Gustinus Ambrosi
Collections: Sculpture by G Ambrosi (1893-1975)

M **Expositur der Osterreichischen Galerie auf Schloss Halbturn,** Burgenland, Halbturn, A-7131 Austria. Tel (02172) 3307
Collections: 20th century Austrian paintings & sculptures

M **Osterreichische Galerie und Internationale Kunst des XX - Jahrhunderts,** Vienna 3rd, Prinz-Eugen-Strasse 27, Vienna, Austria. Tel +43 1 795 57-0; Elec Mail public@belvedere.at; Internet Home Page Address: www.belvedere.at;Agnes Husslein-Arco; *Cur* Bettina Steinbrügge; *Cur* Cosima Rainer
Admis. adults 19 e, seniors (over 60), students (under 27) & reduced admis with Vienna-Card 15 e
Collections: International painting & sculpture; Austrian art dating from the Middle Ages to the present; Prominent works of French Impressionists; Viennese Biedermeier paintings

M **ESSL MUSEUM,** An der Donau-Au 1, Vienna, 3400 Austria. Tel 43-0-2243/370-50; Fax 43-0-2243/370-50; Elec Mail anmeldunq@essl.museum; Internet Home Page Address: www.sammlung-essl.at
Average Annual Attendance:

M **KUNST HAUS WIEN, MUSEUM HUNDERTWASSER,** Untere Weibgerberstrabe 13, Vienna, 1030 Austria. Tel +43-1-712-04-95; Fax +43-1-712-04-96; Elec Mail info@kunsthauswien.com; Internet Home Page Address: www.kunsthauswien.com; *Dir* Dr Franz Patay
Open daily 10 AM - 7 PM; Admis adults 10 euro, combined ticket 12 euro; Estab 1991; Average Annual Attendance: 160,000
Activities: Mus shop sells books, reproductions & prints

M **KUNSTHISTORISCHES MUSEUM VIENNA,** (Kunsthistorisches Museum) Museum of Fine Arts, Burgring 5, Vienna, 1010 Austria. Tel 43 1-525240; Fax (43) 1-52524-4099; Elec Mail info@khm.at; Internet Home Page Address: www.khm.at; *Chief Dir* Dr Sabine Haag
Open Tues - Wed, Fri - Sun 10 AM - 6 PM, Thurs 10 AM - 9 PM; Admis fee ann ticket 34 euro, adults 14 euro, concessions; 11 euro, children & teens under 19 no admis fee; Average Annual Attendance: 1.3 million
Special Subjects: Decorative Arts, Glass, Antiquities-Assyrian, Gold, Portraits, Pottery, Bronzes, Manuscripts, Painting-European, Sculpture, Tapestries, Textiles, Costumes, Religious Art, Woodcuts, Jewelry, Silver, Antiquities-Byzantine, Painting-Dutch, Painting-French, Ivory, Coins & Medals, Baroque Art, Painting-Flemish, Renaissance Art, Embroidery, Medieval Art, Antiquities-Oriental, Painting-Spanish, Painting-Italian, Antiquities-Persian, Antiquities-Egyptian, Antiquities-Greek, Antiquities-Roman, Painting-German, Antiquities-Etruscan, Enamels
Collections: Egyptian coll; antiquities, ceramics, historical carriages & costumes, jewelry, old musical instruments, paintings, tapestries, weapons; coll of secular & ecclesiastical treasures of Holy Roman Empire & Hapsburg Dynasty
Exhibitions: (07/10/2013-06/01/2014) Lucian Freud; (10/20/2014-01/01/2015) Diego Velazquez
Activities: Classes for adults & children; lects open to pub; concerts; gallery talks; mus shop sells books, reproductions, prints & jewelry

MUMOK MUSEUM MODERNER KUNST STIFTUNG LUDWIG WIEN Tel 43-1-52500; Fax 43-1-52500-1300; Elec Mail info@mumok.at; Internet Home Page Address: www.mumok.at; *Dir* Karola Kraus
Open Mon 2 PM - 7 PM, Tues - Sun 10 AM -7 PM, Thurs 10 AM - 9 PM; Admis 10 euro, reduced fee 8 - 17 euro; Estab 1962; Museum modern & contemporary art
Library Holdings: Book Volumes; Exhibition Catalogs; Filmstrips; Pamphlets
Collections: Works of the 20th century; artists represented include: Archipenko, Arp, Bartach, Beckman, Boeckl, Bonnard, Delaunay, Ernst, Gleizes, Hofer, Hoflehner, Jawlensky, Kandinsky, Kirchner, Klee, Kokoschka, Laurens, Leger, Marc, Matisse, Miro, Moore, Munch, Nolde, Picasso, Rodin, Rosso, Wotruba & others; Classical Modernism, NouveauRealisme, Fluxus Pop Art; concept art; sand art; vienna Actionism
Exhibitions: (02/21/2014-05/18/2014) Memory Ware, discours Works and Documents of the Herbert Foundation; (02/21/2014-06/01/2014) Moyra Davey; (03/14/2014-02/08/2015) Vienna Actiionism and Its Context; (06/06/2014-09/14/2014) Classical Modernism; (06/06/2014-09/14/2014) Henkel Art Award 2013; (10/04/2014-01/18/2015) Cosima von Bonin; (10/04/2014-01/25/2015) Jenni Tischer - Baloise Art Prize
Publications: Catalogues
Activities: Classes for adults & children; lects open to pub; lects for mems only; gallery talks; tours; school progs; schls & fels offered; organize traveling exhibs; mus shop sells books, magazines, catalogues, design, editins, posters

AZERBAIJAN

BAKU

M **AZERBAIJAN STATE MUSEUM OF ART,** 31 Istiglaliyat St, Baku, 370001 Azerbaijan. Tel 99-412 92-51-17; 92-10-85
Open Tues - Sun 10 AM - 6 PM, cl Mon; Admis foreigners 10,000 manats, residents 5,000 manats, students free
Collections: Works by various European artists from the 16th to the 19th centuries; Ceramics, metalwork, utensils, miniatures, needlework, national clothing and jewelry, carpets, arms & armaments, sculptures

BAHAMAS

NASSAU

M **NATIONAL ART GALLERY OF THE BAHAMAS,** West and West Hill St, PO Box SS-6341 Nassau, Bahamas. Tel 242-328-5800; Fax 242-322-1180; Elec Mail info@nagb.org.bs; Internet Home Page Address: www.nagb.org.bs/nagb.html; *Dir & Cur* Erica Moiah James
Open Tues - Sat 10 AM - 4 PM; Admis adults $5, seniors & students $3, children under 12 free
Collections: Contemporary Bahamian and international art in various media

BANGLADESH

DHAKA

M **MINISTRY OF CULTURAL AFFAIRS,** (Bangladesh National Museum) Bangladesh National Museum, GPO Box No 355, Shahbag Dhaka, 1000 Bangladesh. Tel 88-02-8619396-9, 8619400; Fax 88-02-8615585; Elec Mail dgmuseum@yahoo.com; Internet Home Page Address: www.bangladeshmuseum.gov.bd; *Contact* Shahidur Rahman Khan; *Deputy Keeper Pub Educ Dept* Dr Niru Shamsun Nahar
Open Apr - Sept, Sat - Wed 10:30 AM - 5:30 PM, Oct - Mar, Sat - Wed 9:30 AM - 4:30 PM, Fri 3 - 8 PM (summer); 2:30 - 7:30 PM (winter); Admis foreigners 7 bdt, adult 10 bdt, children 2 bdt; 1913, coll, preservation & display of antiquities; 44 galleries & 4 curatorial depts; Average Annual Attendance: 0.53 million
Income: 5 million bdt (2012-2013)

Library Holdings: Book Volumes; Cards; DVDs; Exhibition Catalogs; Memorabilia; Photographs; Sculpture
Special Subjects: Archaeology, Drawings, Historical Material, Interior Design, Art Education, Art History, Ceramics, Collages, Metalwork, Photography, Pottery, Pre-Columbian Art, Painting-American, Prints, Silver, Textiles, Manuscripts, Maps, Painting-British, Painting-European, Painting-French, Painting-Japanese, Architecture, Graphics, Sculpture, Watercolors, American Indian Art, American Western Art, Bronzes, African Art, Anthropology, Archaeology, Ethnology, Southwestern Art, Costumes, Religious Art, Crafts, Folk Art, Primitive art, Woodcarvings, Woodcuts, Decorative Arts, Portraits, Posters, Painting-Canadian, Dolls, Furniture, Glass, Jade, Jewelry, Oriental Art, Asian Art, Painting-Dutch, Carpets & Rugs, Ivory, Scrimshaw, Coins & Medals, Restorations, Tapestries, Calligraphy, Miniatures, Painting-Flemish, Renaissance Art, Dioramas, Embroidery, Antiquities-Oriental, Painting-Spanish, Painting-Italian, Antiquities-Persian, Islamic Art, Antiquities-Egyptian, Antiquities-Greek, Antiquities-Roman, Mosaics, Cartoons, Painting-German, Leather, Reproductions, Painting-Russian, Enamels, Painting-Scandinavian
Collections: 44 galleries; Buddhist & Brahminical stone sculptures, architectural pieces; Arabic and Persian inscriptions, calligraphy, coin cabinet; Sanskrit & Bengali manuscripts, plaques, figures, stamped and inscribed slabs, votive seals, moulded and decorated brick; Paintings, arms & armament, porcelain, metal work, embroidered quilts, ivory works; Furniture, tribal and folk arts and crafts; Objects related to Liberation War
Exhibitions: Nakshi Kantha, Ornament, Rare Book Coin Exhib Etc
Publications: Research Oriented Books, magazines, catalogues, booklets, view-card and many more
Activities: Classes for adults & children; publish & sale of publ; guide to school students & general pub (visitor); concerts; gallery talks; sponsoring of competitions; awards, occasional prog to minimum of 128 students; mus shop sells books, magazines, reproductions, prints, slides, pens, t-shirts, paper weights, research oriented publs & other items; junior mus incl: Ahsasn Manzil Mus, Dhake; Osmany Mus, Sylhet; Zia Memorial Mus, Chittagong; Shilpacharya Zaninul, Abedin; Sangrahashala, Mymensingh; Palli Kavi JasImuddin, Sangrahashala

SHANMONDI, DHAKA

M **BENGAL GALLERY OF FINE ARTS,** House 42, Road 26 (new), Shelkh Kamal Saranl Shanmondi, Dhaka, 1209 Bangladesh. Tel +8802-9128942; Fax +8802-9146111; Elec Mail gallery@bengalfoundation.org; Internet Home Page Address: www.bengalfoundation.org; *Mgr Dir* Luva Nahid Choudhury; *Dir* Subir Choudhury
Open 12 PM - 8 PM; Estab 2000; first modern art gallery in Bangladesh; Display area 76M, spread over 188 Sq M; Average Annual Attendance: 20,000; Mem: Private limited company
Income: Sponsored by Bengal Foundation Trust
Publications: Over 250 catalogues, brochures & flyers
Activities: Host art exhibs; lects open to pub; book launches; 10 vis lects per yr; gallery talks; mus shop sells books, magazines, original art, reproductions, prints, CDs & DVDs

BELARUS

MINSK

M **NATIONAL ART MUSEUM OF THE REPUBLIC OF BELARUS,** 20 Lenin St, Minsk, 220030 Belarus. Tel 375-17-227-71-63; Fax 375-172-27-56-72; Elec Mail nmmrb@tut.by; Internet Home Page Address: www.artmuseum.by; *Dir* Vladimir Prokoptsov
Open Mon & Wed - Sun 11 AM - 7 PM, cl Tues
Collections: More than 25,600 exhibits; modern Belarusian art, painting, sculpture, drawing, applied art; national Belarusian art, 17th-20th century; ancient Belarusian art, paintings, icons, ceramics, porcelain, arts and crafts; manuscripts and books, 16th-19th century; West European art, 16th-20th century; Russian art, 18-20th century; Eastern Art, 15th - 20th century

BELGIUM

ANTWERP

M **CITY OF ANTWERP,** Kunsthistorische Musea, Museum Mayer van den Bergh, Lange Gasthuisstraat 19 Antwerp, 2000 Belgium. Tel (0) 3-338-81-88; Fax (0) 3-338-81-99; Elec Mail museum.mayervandenbergh@stad.antwerpen.be; Internet Home Page Address: www.museummayervandenbergh.be; *Dir* Claire Baisier; *Cur* Rita Van Dooren
Open Tues - Sun 10 AM - 5 PM, cl Mon except Easter Mon & Whit Mon, cl Jan 1 & May 1, Ascension Day, Nov 1 & Dec 25; Admis individual 8 euro & 6 euro, mems, groups of 12+, ages 19 - 25 1 euro, natl mus assoc mems, school groups & youth under 12 free; Estab 1904
Collections: Painting 13th-18th century; sculpture 14th-16th century; all decorative arts, mainly late medieval
M **Rubenshuis,** Wapper 9-11, Antwerp, 2000 Belgium. Tel (03) 201-15-55; Fax (03) 227-36-92; Elec Mail rubenshuis@stad.antwerpen.be; Internet Home Page Address: www.rubenshuis.be; *Dir* Ben Van Beneden
Open Tues - Sun 10 AM - 5 PM, cl Mon; Admis E 8, 19 - 26 yrs old E 1, groups E 6; 18 or under, 65 or over, disabled and companion, ICOM mem free
Library Holdings: Auction Catalogs; Book Volumes; Exhibition Catalogs; Manuscripts; Original Documents; Periodical Subscriptions; Photographs; Reproductions
Special Subjects: Baroque Art, Painting-Flemish

Collections: Reconstruction of Rubens' house & studio; paintings by P P Rubens, his collaborators & pupils
Activities: Lending of original objects of art to other museums; mus shop sells books, magazines, reproductions, prints, merchandizing
L **Rubenianum,** Kolveniersstraat 20, Antwerp, 2000 Belgium. Tel (03) 201-15-77; Fax (03) 201-15-87; Elec Mail rubenianum@stad.antwerp.be; Internet Home Page Address: www.rubenianum.be; *Cur* Veronique Van de Kerckhof; *Librn* Ute Staes
Open Mon - Fri 8:30 AM - Noon; 1 PM - 4:30 PM; No admis fee; Center for the study of 16th & 17th century Flemish art; library & photo archives
Library Holdings: Auction Catalogs 18,500; Book Volumes 40,000; Exhibition Catalogs; Periodical Subscriptions 127; Photographs 110,000
Special Subjects: Art History, Drawings, Etchings & Engravings, Painting-Dutch, Painting-Flemish, Prints, Portraits, Religious Art, Antiquities-Greek, Antiquities-Roman
Publications: Corpus Rubenianum Ludwig Burchard
M **Middleheim Openluchtmuseum voor Beeldhouwkunst,** Middelheimlaan 61, Antwerp, 2020 Belgium. Tel 32 (0) 3 288-33-60; Fax 32 (0) 3 288-33-99; Elec Mail middelheimmuseum@stad.antwerpen.be; Internet Home Page Address: www.middelheimmuseum.be; *Dir* Sara Weyns
Open Oct - Mar 10 AM - 5 PM, Apr & Sept 10 AM - 7 PM, May & Aug 10 AM - 8 PM, June - July 10 AM - 9 PM; No admis fee
Library Holdings: Auction Catalogs; Book Volumes; DVDs; Exhibition Catalogs; Photographs
Special Subjects: Art History, Sculpture, Painting-European
Collections: Modern & contemporary sculpture of Rodin, Maillol, Zadkine, Marini, Manzu, Giaconetti, Gargallo, Moore, Antony Gormly, Erwin Wurm, Chris Burden, exhibitions of contemporary sculpture
Publications: Collection Catalogue, Exhibition Catalogues
Activities: Classes for adults & Children; mus shop sells books, prints
M **Museum Smidt van Gelder,** Belgielei 91, Antwerp, 2000 Belgium. Tel (03) 239-06-52; Fax (03) 230-22-81; *Asst Keeper* Clara Vanderhenst
Collections: Collections of Chinese & European porcelains, 17th century Dutch paintings, 18th century French furniture
M **Museum Mayer van den Bergh,** Lange Gasthuisstraat 19, Antwerp, 2000 Belgium. Tel (03) 232-42-37; *Cur* Hans Nieuwdorp
Collections: Collection of paintings, including Breughel, Metsys, Aertsen, Mostaert, Bronzino, Heda, de Vos, & medieval sculpture

M **EUGEEN VAN MIEGHEM MUSEUM,** Beatrijslaan 8, Antwerp, 2050 Belgium. Internet Home Page Address: www.vanmieghemmuseum.com

M **INTERNATIONAAL CULTUREEL CENTTRUM,** International Cultural Centre, Meir 50, Antwerp, 2000 Belgium. Tel 03-226-03-06; *Dir* Willy Juwet

M **KONINKLIJK MUSEUM VOOR SCHONE KUNSTEN ANTWERPEN,** Royal Museum of Fine Arts, Leopold de Waelplaats, Antwerp, 2000 Belgium; Plaatsnydersstraat 2, Antwerp, 2000 Belgium. Tel (03) 238-78-09; Fax (03) 248-08-10; Elec Mail info@kmska.be; Internet Home Page Address: www.kmska.be; *Dir* Paul Huvenne
Open Tues - Sat 10 AM - 5 PM, Sun 10 AM - 6 PM, cl Mon; temporarily closing May 2011 for major overhaul, reopening autumn 2014; Admis 6euros/4euros/free; Estab 1890; Library with 35,000 vols; Average Annual Attendance: 100,000+
Library Holdings: Auction Catalogs; Book Volumes; CD-ROMs; Exhibition Catalogs; Fiche; Periodical Subscriptions
Special Subjects: Drawings, Sculpture, Painting-European
Collections: Five Centuries of Flemish Painting: Flemish Primitives, early foreign schools, 16th-17th century Antwerp School, 17th century Dutch School, 19th and 20th century Belgian artists; works of De Braekeleer, Ensor, Leys, Permeke, Smits and Wouters
Publications: Yearbook
Activities: Classes for adults & children; dramatic progs; docent training; lects open to pub; concerts; gallery talks; tours; lending of original objects of art; mus shop sells books, magazines & reproductions

M **MUSEUM PLANTIN-MORETUS/PRENTENKABINET,** Vrijdagmarkt 22, Antwerp, 2000 Belgium. Tel 32 3 221 14 50; Fax 32 3 221 1471; Elec Mail museum.plantin.moretus@stad.antwerpen.be; Internet Home Page Address: www.museumplantinmoretus.be; *Dept Educ, Interpretation & Commun* Odette Peterink; *Dir* Iris Kockelbergh; *Cur Print Cabinet* Marijke Hellemans; *Cur Library* Dirk Imhof; *Cur Historical House* Werner Van Hoof
Museum open Tues - Sun 10 AM - 5 PM, open on Easter Mon and Whit Mon; Reading Room Mon - Fri 10 AM - 4 PM; cl Mon, New Year's Eve & Day, May 1, Ascension Day, Nov 1 & 2, Christmas Day & Day after; Admis fee adults 8 euros, groups & seniors 65 & over 6 euros, (12-26 yr old 1 euro, school groups with card, handicapped persons and their companions & reading room, 1-12 yr old no admis fee; House built 16th c., Mus estab 1877; Library of 30,000 books of 15th - 18th centuries; printcabinet 80,000 drawing & print from 1500 to 21st century; Average Annual Attendance: 80,000
Library Holdings: Auction Catalogs; Book Volumes; Exhibition Catalogs; Manuscripts; Original Documents; Periodical Subscriptions
Special Subjects: Decorative Arts, Drawings, Etchings & Engravings, Historical Material, Ceramics, Furniture, Porcelain, Portraits, Prints, Period Rooms, Woodcuts, Manuscripts, Maps, Sculpture, Tapestries, Watercolors, Religious Art, Woodcarvings, Carpets & Rugs, Restorations, Baroque Art, Calligraphy, Painting-Flemish, Renaissance Art, Leather, Reproductions, Bookplates & Bindings
Collections: Designs, copper and wood engravings, printing presses, typography; Coll of Antwerp Iconographics; modern drawings: Jensor, F Jespers, H leys, W Vaes, Rik Wovters; modern engravings: Cantre, Ensor, Masereel, J Minne, W Vaes; old drawings: Jordaens, E and A Quellin, Rubens, Schut, Van Dyck; old engravings: Galle, Goltzius, Hogenborch, W Hollar, Yegher, Wiericx, etc; typographical coll
Activities: Classes for children; lects open to pub; gallery talks; tours; lending coll incl printing & books, & serves museums & exhibitions; mus shop sells books, original art, prints, reproductions, gifts, objects about colls

ANTWERPEN

M **ROCKOX HOUSE,** Keizerstraat 10-12, Antwerpen, 2000 Belgium. Tel 32-0-3-201-92-50; Fax 32-0-3-201-92-51; Elec Mail hildegard.vandevelde@kbc.be; Internet Home Page Address: www.rockoxhuis.be/html/rockox_e1.html
Average Annual Attendance:

M **THE RUBENS HOUSE,** Wapper 9-11, Antwerpen, 2000 Belgium. Tel +32-3-201-15-55; Fax +32-3-227-36-92; Elec Mail info.rubenshuis@stad.antwerpen.be; Internet Home Page Address: www.rubenshuis.be
Average Annual Attendance:

BRUGES

M **MUSEA BRUGGE,** (Hospitaalmuseum) Sint-Janshospitaal, Mariastraat 38, Bruges, 8000 Belgium; Dijver 12, Bruges, 8000 Belgium. Tel 32-50-44-87-11; Fax 32-50-44-87-78; Elec Mail musea@brugge.be; Internet Home Page Address: www.museabrugge.be; *Cur (in chief)* Manfred Sellink
Open Tues - Sun 9:30 AM - 5 PM, Pharmacy cl between 11:45 AM - 2 PM, cl Mon, Dec 25, Jan 1 & Ascension Day (afternoon); Admis individual 8 Euros, reduced 6 Euros, children under 12 free; Preserved hospital building, chapel, attic displaying monumental roof-truss system, apothecary chamber & herb garden, masterpieces by Hans Memling
Special Subjects: Furniture, Silver, Painting-European, Sculpture, Pewter
Collections: Works by Hans Memling
Activities: Mus shop sells books, prints & other items

M **MUSEA BRUGGE,** Volkskunde Museum, Balstraat 43, Bruges, 8000 Belgium; Dijver 12, Bruges, 8000 Belgium. Tel 050-44-87-11; Fax 050-44-87-78; Elec Mail musea@brugge.be; Internet Home Page Address: www.museabrugge.be; *Cur* Aleid Hemeryck
Open Tues - Sun 9:30 AM - 5 PM, cl Mon, Dec 25, Jan 1 & Ascension Day (afternoon); Admis individual 4 Euros, reduced 3 Euro, children under 12 free; 8 almshouses from 17th c with modern architectural extension, incl classroom, cobbler's workshop, hatter's workshop, Flemish living room, confectioner's bakery, pharmacy, inn, tailor's workshop, bedroom
Special Subjects: Folk Art, Period Rooms, Laces
Collections: Old objects in different decors
Publications: Brief guide

M **OLV-ter-Potterie, Our Lady of the Potterie,** Potterierei 79 b, Brugge, 8000 Belgium; Dijver 12, Bruges, 8000 Belgium. Tel 32-50-44-87-11; Fax 32-50-44-87-78; Elec Mail musea@brugge.be; Internet Home Page Address: www.museabrugge.be; *Cur (in chief)* Manfred Sellink
Open Tues - Sun 9:30 AM - 12:30 PM, & 1:30 PM - 5 PM, cl Mon, Dec 25, Jan 1 & Ascension Day (afternoon); Admis individual 4 Euros, reduced 3 Euro, children under 12 free; Has existed since the 13th c; Baroque church & historic hospital served by monks & nuns in the 13th c. The wards have become a museum
Collections: Works of art, incl objects related to healthcare, worship & the monastery

M **Gruuthuse Museum,** Dijver 17, Brugge, 8000 Belgium; Dijver 12, Bruges, 8000 Belgium. Tel 32-50-44-87-11; Fax 32-50-44-87-78; Elec Mail musea@brugge.be; Internet Home Page Address: www.museabrugge.be; *Cur* Aleid Hemeryck
Open Tues - Sun 9:30 AM - 5 PM, cl Mon, Dec 25, Jan 1 & Ascension Day (afternoon); Admis individual 8 Euros, reduced 6 Euro, children under 12 free; City palace
Special Subjects: Pottery, Silver, Tapestries
Collections: Room of Honor: tapestries, fireplace, decorated timber
Exhibitions: History of Bruges & its inhabitants; Room of Honor
Activities: Mus shop sells books, prints

M **Sound Factory - Lantaarntoren,** Concertgebouw, T Zand 34 Bruges, 8000 Belgium; Dijver 12, Bruges, 8000 Belgium. Tel 32-50-44-87-11; Fax 32-50-44-87-78; Elec Mail musea@brugge.be; Internet Home Page Address: www.museabrugge.be; *Cur* Aleid Hemeryck
Open Tues - Sun 9:30 AM - 5 PM, cl Mon, Dec 25, Jan 1 & Ascension Day (afternoon); Admis individual 6 Euros, reduced 5 Euros, children 12 & under free; Sound factory in the Lantern Tower of the contemporary concertgebouw, to create yourself the sounds of the city through interactive sound art. Location also offers an excellent view over the old town & its towers

M **Stadhuis - Town Hall,** Burg 12, Bruges, 8000 Belgium; Dijver 12, Bruges, 8000 Belgium. Tel 32-50-44-87-11; Fax 32-50-44-87-78; Elec Mail musea@brugge.be; Internet Home Page Address: www.museabrugge.be; *Cur* Aleid Hemeryck
Open daily 9:30 AM - 5 PM, cl Dec 25, Jan 1 & Ascension Day (afternoon); Admis individual 4 Euro, reduced 3 Euro, admis to Brugse Vrije incl, children under 12 free; Bruges Town Hall, dating from 1376, with Gothic Chamber
Special Subjects: Period Rooms
Collections: Gothic Chamber: 19th c wall paintings, polychrome ceiling; painted figures
Exhibitions: Governors & Governed

M **Groeningemuseum,** Dijver 12, Bruges, 8000 Belgium. Tel 32-50-44-87-11; Fax 32-50-44-87-78; Elec Mail musea@brugge.be; Internet Home Page Address: www.museabrugge.be; *Cur* Till Holger Borchert
Open Tues - Sun 9:30 AM - 5 PM, cl Mon, Dec 25, Jan 1 & Ascension Day (afternoon); Admis individual 8 Euros, reduced 6 Euros, youngsters (6-25) 1 Euro; A rich & fascinating array of artworks from the southern Netherlands (Belgium) over a period of six centuries (15th-21st)
Collections: The Flemish primitives & various Renaissance & Baroque masters; Pieces from the Neo-classical & Realistic periods & milestones from the Symbolist & Modernist movement; Masterpieces by the Flemish Expressionists & a selection of post 1345 modern art

M **Gentpoort,** Gentpoortvest, Bruges, 8000 Belgium; Dijver 12, Bruges, 8000 Belgium. Tel 32-50-44-87-11; Fax 32-50-44-87-78; Elec Mail musea@brugge.be; Internet Home Page Address: www.museabrugge.be; *Cur* Aleid Hemeryck
Open Thurs - Sun 9:30 AM - 12:30 PM & 1:30 PM - 5 PM, cl Mon, Tues, Wed, Dec 25, Jan 1 & Ascension Day (afternoon); Admis individual 4 Euros, reduced 3 Euro, children under 12 free; Ghent Gate, 1 of 4 medieval Bruges city gates which have survived to contemporary times

M **Arentshuis - Arents House,** Dijver 16, Brugge, 8000 Belgium; Dijver 12, Bruges, 8000 Belgium. Tel 32-50-44-87-11; Fax 32-50-44-87-78; Elec Mail musea@brugge.be; Internet Home Page Address: www.museabrugge.be; *Cur* Till Holger Borchert
Open Tues - Sun 9:30 AM - 5 PM, cl Mon, Dec 25, Jan 1 & Ascension Day (afternoon); Admis individual 4 Euros, reduced 3 Euro, youngsters (6-25) 1 Euro; 18th century mansion with drawing colls of the Steinmet-Kabinet & permanent presentation around the British-Bruges artist Frank Brangwyn
Collections: Works of British-Bruges artist Frank Brangwyn (1867-1956); paintings, watercolors, engravings, furniture & carpet designs
Exhibitions: Located on ground floor ever changing exhibs of expressive art, usually in association with the Groeninge mus

M **SINT-Janshuismolen & Koeleweimolen,** Kruisvest, Bruges, 8000 Belgium; Dijver 12, Bruges, 8000 Belgium. Tel 32-50-44-87-11; Fax 32-50-44-87-78; Elec Mail musea@brugge.be; Internet Home Page Address: www.museabrugge.be; *Cur* Aleid Hemeryck
Open Tues - Sun 9:30 AM - 12:30 PM & 1:30 PM - 5 PM, cl Mon & Ascension Day (afternoon); Sint Janshuis Mill: May 1 - Aug 31; Koelewei Mill: July 1 - Aug 31; Admis individual 3 Euros, reduced 2 Euro, children under 12 free; Sint-Janshuis Mill circa 1770, historic active grain mill located at its original site; Koelewei Mill circa 1765, historic active grain mill transplanted near Dampoort (Dam Gate) in 1996

M **Belfort - Belfry,** Markt 7, Bruges, 8000 Belgium; Dijver 12, Bruges, 8000 Belgium. Tel 32-50-44-87-11; Fax 32-50-44-87-78; Elec Mail musea@brugge.be; Internet Home Page Address: www.museabrugge.be; *Cur* Aleid Hemeryck
Open daily 9:30 AM - 5 PM, cl Dec 25, Jan 1 & Ascension Day (afternoon); Admis individual 8 Euros, reduced 6 Euros, children under 6 free; Historic Belfry tower, 83 meters high with 366 steps, contains treasury room, clock mechanism & carillon with 47 bells
Activities: Mus shop sells books, magazines, reproductions, prints

M **Brugse Vrije - Liberty of Bruges,** Burg 11a, Bruges, 8000 Belgium; Dijver 12, Bruges, 8000 Belgium. Tel 32-50-44-87-11; Fax 32-50-44-87-78; Elec Mail musea@brugge.be; Internet Home Page Address: www.museabrugge.be; *Cur* Aleid Hemeryck
Open daily 9:30 AM - 12:30 PM & 1:30 PM - 5PM, cl Dec 25, Jan 1 & Ascension Day (afternoon); Admis individual 4 Euros, reduced 3 Euro, admis to Stadhuis incl, children under 12 free; Former location of city courts, now houses Municipal Archives; contains Court of Justice & Renaissance Chamber
Collections: Renaissance Chamber: contains monumental 16th c fireplace with wood, marble & alabaster mantle designed by Lanceloot Blondeel

M **Archeologiemuseum - Archaeology Museum,** Mariastraat 36a, Bruges, 8000 Belgium; Dijver 12, Bruges, 8000 Belgium. Tel 32-50-44-87-11; Fax 32-50-44-87-78; Elec Mail musea@brugge.be; Internet Home Page Address: www.museabrugge.be; *Cur* Aleid Hemeryck
Open Tues - Sun 9:30 AM - 12:30 PM & 1:30 PM - 5 PM, cl Mon, Dec 25, Jan 1 & Ascension Day (afternoon); Admis individual 4 Euros, reduced 3 Euro, children under 12 free; Mus confronts aspects of life from prehistory, the roman period & the middle ages (early & late) through a series of do & search tasks
Collections: Archaeological finds

M **Onze-Lieve-Vrouwekerk/Church of Our Lady,** Mariastraat, Bruges, 8000 Belgium; Dijver 12, Bruges, 8000 Belgium. Tel 32-50-44-87-11; Fax 32-50-44-87-78; Elec Mail musea@brugge.be; Internet Home Page Address: www.museabrugge.be; *Cur* Aleid Hemeryck
Open Mon - Sat 9:30 AM - 12:30 PM & 1:30 PM - 5 PM, catholic holidays, Sun 1:30 PM - 5 PM, cl Dec 25, Jan 1 & Ascension Day (afternoon); Admis individual 6 Euros, reduced 5 Euros, children under 12 free; Church with 122 meter high brick steeple
Special Subjects: Woodcarvings, Renaissance Art
Collections: Madonna & Child, by Michaelangelo; 16th c ceremonial tombs of Mary of Bergundy & Charles the Bold; painted tombs from 13th & 14th c; choir aisle: paintings & woodcarvings

M **Gezellemuseum,** Rolweg 64, Bruges, 8000 Belgium; Dijver 12, Bruges, 8000 Belgium. Tel 32-50-44-87-11; Fax 32-50-44-87-78; Elec Mail musea@brugge.be; Internet Home Page Address: www.museabrugge.be; *Cur* Aleid Hemeryck
Open Tues - Sun 9:30 AM - 12:30 PM & 1:30 PM - 5 PM, cl Mon, Dec 25, Jan 1 & Ascension Day (afternoon); Admis individual 4 Euros, reduced 3 Euro, children under 12 free; Birthplace of Flemish writer Guido Gezelle, with garden & biological kitchen garden
Collections: The Man Who Gives Fire by Jan Fabre
Exhibitions: Displays on the art of the written word

BRUSSELS

L **BIBLIOTHEQUE ROYALE DE BELIQUE/KONINKLIJKE BIBLIOTHEEK VAN BELGIE,** (Bibliotheque Royale Albert I) The Belgian National Library, 4 blvd de l'Empereur, Brussels, 1000 Belgium. Tel (02) 519-53-11; Internet Home Page Address: www.kbr.be; *Dir* Pierre Cockshaw
Collections: Coins, medals, maps, manuscripts, prints, rare printed books housed in Belgian National Library

M **BOZAR CENTRE FOR FINE ARTS, BRUSSELS,** Ravensteinstraat 23, Brussels, 1000 Belgium. Tel 02-507-82-00; Fax 02-507-85-15; Elec Mail info@bozar.be; Internet Home Page Address: www.bozar.be; *CEO* Paul Dujarain
Income:

M **ERASMUS HOUSE MUSEUM,** (Museum Erasmus) 31 Rue du Chapitre, Brussels, 1070 Belgium. Tel 2-521-13-83 + 32-2-521-13-83; Fax 2-527-12-69 + 32-2-522-12-69; Elec Mail info@erasmushouse.museum; Internet Home Page Address: www.erasmushouse.museum
Open Tues - Sun 10 AM - 6 PM; Admis 1.25 euro; Mus dedicated to Erasmus of Rotterdam, 16th century house, printings & furniture; library iwth 4000 vols.
Collections: Documents, paintings, manuscripts relating to Erasmus & other humanists of the 16th century

M **MUSEE HORTA,** 25 rue Americaine, Brussels, 1060 Belgium. Tel 02-5430490; Fax 02-5387631; Elec Mail info@hortamuseum.be; Internet Home Page Address: www.hortamuseum.be; *Dir* Francoise Aubry
Open Tues - Sun 2 PM - 5:30 PM, cl Mon, Jan 1, Easter, May 1, Ascension Day, Jul 21, Aug 15, Nov 1 & 11, Dec 25; open to tour groups in the morning; Admis 7 E 3.50 E (student, sr under 18) 2.50 E; Library with 4000 vols
Library Holdings: Exhibition Catalogs; Manuscripts; Original Documents; Photographs; Slides
Collections: Works of art by V Horta; architecture & furniture
Activities: Mus shop sells books, prints, jewelry, postcards, calendars

M **MUSEES ROYAUX D'ART ET D'HISTOIRE,** Royal Museums of Art and History, 10 Parc du Cinquantenaire, Brussels, 1000 Belgium. Tel 02-741-72-11; Fax 02-733-77-35; Elec Mail info@mrah; Internet Home Page Address: www.rmah.be; *Interim Dir* Michel Draguet; *Head Commun* Bart Suys; *Head Exhibs* Karin Theunis
Open Tues - Fri 9:30 AM - 5 PM, Sat - Sun 10 AM - 5 PM, cl Mon; Admis 5 euro, 4 euro & 1.50 euro; Archeology, antiquities, European decorative arts, non-European; Average Annual Attendance: 165,000
Income: Financed by federal state
Library Holdings: Auction Catalogs; Book Volumes; Exhibition Catalogs
Special Subjects: Anthropology, Archaeology, Decorative Arts, Folk Art, Historical Material, Ceramics, Glass, Metalwork, Antiquities-Assyrian, Flasks & Bottles, Furniture, Gold, Photography, Porcelain, Pottery, Pre-Columbian Art, Prints, Silver, Textiles, Tapestries, Graphics, American Indian Art, Ethnology, Costumes, Crafts, Primitive Art, Eskimo Art, Jade, Jewelry, Oriental Art, Asian Art, Antiquities-Byzantine, Carpets & Rugs, Ivory, Coins & Medals, Baroque Art, Miniatures, Renaissance Art, Embroidery, Laces, Medieval Art, Antiquities-Oriental, Antiquities-Persian, Islamic Art, Antiquities-Egyptian, Antiquities-Greek, Antiquities-Roman, Mosaics, Stained Glass, Antiquities-Etruscan, Enamels
Collections: Pre-Columbian art; Belgian, Egyptian, Greek, Roman and classical art; Medieval, Renaissance and modern art - ceramics, furniture, glass, lace, silver, tapestries, textiles; ethnography; folklore; Oceanic, South-East Asia; American Indian; India; Merovingians; stone; instruments; Islamic Art
Activities: Classes for adults & children; lects open to pub; tours; award: Prix Des Musees 2007; mus shop sells books, magazines, original art, reproductions

M **ROYAL MUSEUMS OF ART & HISTORY,** (Musical Instruments Museum) Musical Instruments Museum, rue Montagne de la Cour 2, Rue Villa Hermosa 1 Brussels, B-1000 Belgium. Tel 32 02 545 01 30; Fax 32 02 545 01 77; Elec Mail info@mim.be; Internet Home Page Address: www.mim.be
Open Tues - Fri 9:30 AM - 5 PM, Sat - Sun 10 AM - 5 PM; Admis adults 8E, students, seniors, foreign teachers & groups 6E, unemployed, disabled, school & youth groups 2E, Belgian teachers, children under 12, friends of MIM, lCOM & first Wed of the month (afternoon) no charge; Average Annual Attendance: 135,000
Income: Government Org
Library Holdings: Auction Catalogs; Audio Tapes; Book Volumes; CD-ROMs; Cassettes; Compact Disks; DVDs; Exhibition Catalogs; Periodical Subscriptions
Collections: Modern & historical musical instruments
Activities: Classes for adults & children; lects open to pub; concerts; mus shop sells books, reproductions & other library items

M **ROYAL MUSEUMS OF FINE ARTS OF BELGIUM,** 3 Rue De La Regence, Brussels, 1000 Belgium; 9 Rue Du Musee, Brussels, 1000 Belgium. Tel 32.2.508.32.11; Fax 32.2.508.32.32; Elec Mail info@fine-arts-museum.be; Internet Home Page Address: www.fine-arts-museum.be; *Dir* Michel Draguet
Open 10 AM - 5 PM; Admis 5 euro
Special Subjects: Photography, Period Rooms, Painting-British, Painting-European, Sculpture, Painting-Dutch, Painting-French, Painting-Flemish, Renaissance Art
Collections: Ancient art & Modern art
Activities: Classes for adults & children; lects open to public, gallery talks, tours; scholarships, fellowships; mus shop sells books, magazines, reproductions, prints, slides
M **Musee d'Art Ancien,** 3 rue de la Regence, Brussels, 1000 Belgium; 9 Rue de Musée, Brussels, 1000 Belgium. Tel 32.2.508.32.11; Fax 32.2.508.32.32; Elec Mail info@fine.arts.museum.be; Internet Home Page Address: www.fine-arts-museum.be; *Dept Head* Helena Bussers
Collections: Paintings & drawings (15th - 19th centuries) & old & 19th century sculptures
M **Musee d'Art Moderne,** 9 Rue de Musée, Brussels, 1000 Belgium. Tel 32.2.508.32.11; Fax 32.2.508.32.32; Elec Mail info@fine-arts-museum.be; Internet Home Page Address: www.fine-arts-museum.be; *Dept Head* Frederik Leen; *Dir* Eliane De Wilde
Collections: Temporary exhibitions; 20th & 19th century paintings, drawings & sculptures
Activities: Classes for adults & children; lects open to public, gallery talks, tours; scholarships, fellowships; books, magazines, reproductions, prints & slides
M **Musee Constantin Meunier,** Rue de Musée 9, Brussels, B-1000 Belgium. Tel 02-648-44-49; Internet Home Page Address: www.fine-arts-museum.be
No admis fee
Collections: Paintings, drawings and sculptures by Constantin Meunier, the artist's house and studio
M **Musee Wiertz,** 62 rue Vautier, Brussels, 1050 Belgium. Tel 32 (0) 2 508 32 11; Fax 32 (0) 2 508 32 32; Elec Mail info@fine-arts-museum.be; Internet Home Page Address: www.fine-arts-museum.be; *Head Cur* Philippe Roberts-Jones
Open Tues - Sun 10 AM - 5 PM; cl Mon, Jan 1, 2nd Thurs Jan, May 1, Nov 11, Dec 24, 25, & 31; Admis 8 euro, seniors & students under 26 5 euro; comb with Musee Magritte Mus 13 euro
Collections: Paintings by Antoine Wiertz

GHENT

M **THE GHENT MUSEUM OF FINE ARTS,** Citadelpark, Ghent, B-9000 Belgium; Hofbouwlaan 28, Ghent, B-9000 Belgium. Tel 0032-09-240-07-00; Fax 0032-09-240-07-90; Elec Mail museum.msk@gent.be; Internet Home Page Address: www.mskgent.be; *Dir* Robert Hoozee
Open Tues - Sun 10 AM - 6 PM; Admis adults 6 euro, under 25 & over 55 3.75 euro, citizens & children under 12 free
Special Subjects: Drawings, Etchings & Engravings, Landscapes, Marine Painting, Portraits, Woodcuts, Painting-European, Painting-French, Sculpture, Watercolors, Religious Art, Painting-Dutch, Baroque Art, Painting-Flemish, Renaissance Art, Medieval Art, Painting-Italian
Collections: Developments in visual arts from the middle ages to the first half of the 20th century; Painting of the Southern Netherlands; Sculpture and other European paintings

LIEGE

M **LE GRAND CURTIUS,** (Musees D'Archeologie Et Des Arts Decoratifs) Musée d'Ansembourg, 13 Quai de Maestricht, Liege, 4000 Belgium. Tel 32-4-221.68.12; Fax 32-4-221.68.09; Elec Mail infograndcurtius@liege.be; Internet Home Page Address: www.grandcurtiusliege.be; *Dir - Mus City of Liege* Jean-Marc Gay; *Cur Glass* Jean-Paul Philippart; *Cur Archaeology* Jean-Luc Schutz; *Cur American & Religious Art* Philippe Joris; *Cur Decorative Arts* Soo Yang Geuzaine
Open Mon - Sun 10 AM - 6 PM; cl Tues; Admis 5 euro, free first Sun of month except when temporary exhibs; Estab 2003; Ancient (16th-18th c) bldg connected by contemporary spaces; Average Annual Attendance: 85,000
Income: Municipal Mus
Special Subjects: Decorative Arts, Glass, Metalwork, Furniture, Silver, Sculpture, Religious Art, Crafts, Painting-European, Coins & Medals, Baroque Art, Renaissance Art, Medieval Art, Antiquities-Roman, Stained Glass, Enamels
Collections: 18th century decorative arts of Liege, housed in a mansion of the same period; Archaeology, decorative arts, religious art, glass, arms & weapons, ancient clocks
Publications: Catalogue of coll & temporary exhib
Activities: Classes for children; lects open to pub; 5 vis lectrs per yr; mus shop sells books, postcards, small gifts; Le Petit Curtius

M **MUSE DES BEAUX-ARTS DE LIEGE (BAL),** (Museum of Art Wallon) Fine Arts Museum, Feronstree 86, Liege, 4000 Belgium. Tel (0032) 4 221 9231; Fax (0032) 4 221 9232; Elec Mail bal@liege.be; Internet Home Page Address: www.beauxartsliege.be; *Cur* Regine Remon; *Cur* Gregory Desauvage; *Cur* Carmen Genten
Open Tues - Sun 10 AM -18 PM, cl Mon; Admis adults 5E, children 12 - 18 & senior citizens 3E, children 11 & under no charge; Fine Arts Mus; Temporary & permanent exhibs
Collections: Paintings & sculptures from the 16th - 21st century
Exhibitions: Jeunes Artistes
Activities: Classes for adults & children; visits; mus shop sells books, magazines & reproductions

MORLANWELZ

M **MUSEE ROYAL ET DOMAINE DE MARIEMONT,** Chaussee de Mariemont 100, Morlanwelz, 7140 Belgium. Tel (64) 21-21-93; Fax (64) 26-29-24; Elec Mail info@musee-mariemont.be; Internet Home Page Address: www.musee-mariemont.be; *Cur* Daniel Courbe; *Scientific Cur* Marie-Cecile Bruwier; *Librn* Bertrand Federinov
Open Apr. - Sept Tues - Sun 10 AM - 6 PM Oct - Mar Tues - Sun 10 AM - 5 PM, cl Mon; Admis temporary exhibs with reduction 4 euro, permanent coll 1 euro; Maintains library with 150,000 volumes; Mem: Friends of Mariemont 10 or 15 euro
Library Holdings: Auction Catalogs; Book Volumes; Cards; Exhibition Catalogs; Manuscripts; Maps; Original Art Works; Original Documents; Pamphlets; Periodical Subscriptions; Photographs; Prints; Reproductions; Sculpture
Special Subjects: Archaeology, Decorative Arts, Drawings, Etchings & Engravings, Ceramics, Glass, Metalwork, Furniture, Gold, Porcelain, Pottery, Textiles, Bronzes, Manuscripts, Maps, Sculpture, Graphics, Jade, Jewelry, Oriental Art, Asian Art, Historical Material, Ivory, Coins & Medals, Calligraphy, Miniatures, Embroidery, Islamic Art, Antiquities-Egyptian, Antiquities-Greek, Antiquities-Roman, Mosaics, Cartoons, Pewter, Antiquities-Etruscan, Enamels, Bookplates & Bindings
Collections: Belgian archaeology; porcelain from Tournai; Egyptian, Grecian, Roman, Chinese & Japanese antiquities; rare books & manuscripts
Publications: catalogues of exhibitions; monographic, scientific review: Les Cahiers de Mariemont
Activities: Classes for children & children; lects open to public; lects for mems only; concerts; tours; competitions; award: Prix des musees-wallonie, 2007, Prix de bonne pratique-reflexions sur le musee et L'integration sociale, 2009, Prix des enfants-wallonne, 2012, Tripadvisor-Certificat d'excellence, 2013; mus shop sells books, reproductions & prints

NAMUR

M **FELICIEN ROPS MUSEUM,** Rue Fumal 12 B, Namur, 5000 Belgium. Tel 32-81-77-67-25; Fax 32-81-77-69-25; Elec Mail info@museerops.be; Internet Home Page Address: www.museerops.be/museum; *Dir* Veronique Carpiaux
Open Tues - Sun 10:00 AM - 18:00 PM; cl Jan 1st, Dec 24, 25, & 31; Admis 5 euro, 3 euro; mus is situated in Old Namur in a 19th century residence
Income: provincial institution of Namur
Purchases: bookshop with postcards, posters
Library Holdings: Auction Catalogs; Book Volumes; Exhibition Catalogs; Original Documents; Periodical Subscriptions
Special Subjects: Drawings, Art History, Painting-European, Prints, Embroidery

Collections: Coll of Rop's prints, drawings & paintings
Exhibitions: Three exhibs per yr
Publications: 3 publ per yr
Activities: Classes for children; lects open to the pub; 2 vis lectrs per yr; concerts; gallery talks; schols; traveling exhibs to other mus worldwide; mus shop sells books, reproductions

M   **THE NAMUR PROVINCIAL MUSEUM OF ANCIENT ARTS,** Rue de Fer 24, Namur, 5000 Belgium. Tel 32 0 81 77 67 54; Fax 32 0 81 77 69 24; Elec Mail musee.arts.anciens@province.namur.be; *Cur* Toussaint Jacques
Open Tues - Sun 10 AM - 6 PM; Admis adult 3E, students, senior citizens & groups 1.5E, children under 12 no charge
Library Holdings: Book Volumes; Exhibition Catalogs; Manuscripts; Maps; Periodical Subscriptions
Special Subjects: History of Art & Archaeology, Art History, Glass, Metalwork, Gold, Silver, Manuscripts, Maps, Painting-European, Sculpture, Drawings, Archaeology, Textiles, Religious Art, Painting-European, Ivory, Coins & Medals, Miniatures, Renaissance Art, Embroidery, Medieval Art, Enamels
Collections: Medieval & Renaissance collection of sculptures, paintings, silver and other artifacts; Treasure of Hugo d'Oignies
Exhibitions: (11/15/2013-02/16/2014) Fabulous Stories of Animals & Men
Publications: Catalog of Exhib
Activities: Educ prog; classes for children; lects open to pub; mus shop sells books, reproductions, prints, DVDs

VERVIERS

M   **MUSEES COMMUNAUX DE VERVIERS: BEAUX-ARTS,** Community Museum of Fine Arts, Rue Renier 17, Verviers, 4800 Belgium. Tel 087-33-16-95; Internet Home Page Address: www.verviers.be; *Cur* Marie-Paule Deblanc
Collections: European & Asian painting and sculpture, ceramics, & folk arts

BERMUDA

HAMILTON

M   **BERMUDA NATIONAL GALLERY,** City Hall Arts Centre, Church St Hamilton, Bermuda; Ste # 191, 48 Par-la-Ville Rd Hamilton, HM 11 Bermuda. Tel 441-295-9428; Fax 441-295-2055; Elec Mail director@bng.bm; Internet Home Page Address: www.bermudanationalgallery.com; *Dir* Laura T Gorham
Open Mon - Sat 10 AM - 4 PM; No admis fee
Collections: Diverse masks, paintings, photographs, prints, sculptures, decorative arts and more; African coll; Bermuda Coll; Contemporary coll; European Watlington coll; Photography & Print coll

BHUTAN

PARO

M   **NATIONAL MUSEUM OF BHUTAN,** Paro, Bhutan. Tel +975-8-271257; Fax +975-8-271470; Elec Mail nmb@druknet.bt; Internet Home Page Address: www.nationalmuseum.gov.bt/visitor-information.html
Average Annual Attendance:

BOLIVIA

CASILLA

M   **MINISTERIO DE EDUCACION, CULTURA Y DEPORTES,** Museo Nacional de Arte, Calle Comercio, esq Socabaya, Casilla, 11390 Bolivia. Tel 591-2-408600; Fax 591-2-408542; Elec Mail mma@mma.org.bo; Internet Home Page Address: www.mma.org.bo; *Dir* Teresa Villegas de Aneiva; *Coordr* Teresa Adriázola; *Documentation, Archivist & Bibliologist* Reynaldo Gutierrez; *Prensa* Oscar R Mattos
Open 9 AM - 12:30 PM & 3 PM - 7 PM; Bs 10 (Extranjeros); Circ 150 pers/mes; Colonial, Contemporary and Escultura y Huebles Galleries; Average Annual Attendance: 65,000
Library Holdings: Audio Tapes; Book Volumes; CD-ROMs; Cards; Cassettes; Clipping Files; Compact Disks; Exhibition Catalogs; Fiche; Framed Reproductions; Memorabilia; Original Art Works; Original Documents; Other Holdings; Pamphlets; Periodical Subscriptions; Photographs; Prints; Records; Reels; Sculpture; Slides; Video Tapes
Collections: Colonial & local modern art; pictura Latinoamericana
Publications: Hemoria 1990-2002. Postales, Catalogs
Activities: Lect open to public, concerts, gallery talks, tours; lending original objects of art; books, magazines

LA PAZ

M   **MUSEO NACIONAL DE ARQUEOLOGIA,** National Museum, Calle Tihuanaco 93, Casilla Oficial 64 La Paz, Bolivia. Tel 29624; *Dir* Max Portugal Ortiz
Collections: Anthropology, archaeology, ethnology, folklore, Lake Titicaca district exhibitions, traditional native arts and crafts

BOTSWANA

GABORONE

M   **NATIONAL MUSEUM, MONUMENTS AND ART GALLERY,** (National Museum and Art Gallery) 331 Independence Ave, Private Bag 00114 Gaborone, Botswana. Tel 697-4616; Fax 390-2797; Elec Mail national.museum@gov.bw; Internet Home Page Address: www.botswana-museum.gov.bw; *Dir* Ms Tickey Pule; *Head of Art Division* Lesiga Phillip Segola; *Head of Archeology* Phillip Segadika; *Head of Educ* Ms Phodiso Tube; *Head Tech Support* Stephen Mogotsi; *Head of Ethnology* Rudolf Mojalemotho; *Head of Natural History* Bruce Hargreaves; *Head of IT* Keletso Setlhabi; *Head of Admin* Rosinah Setshwaelo
Open 9 AM - 5 PM; No admis fee; Estab 1968
Income: Financed by govt
Library Holdings: Auction Catalogs; Book Volumes; Cards; Periodical Subscriptions; Slides; Video Tapes
Special Subjects: Decorative Arts, Photography, Pottery, Textiles, Drawings, Graphics, Sculpture, Watercolors, Bronzes, African Art, Anthropology, Archaeology, Ethnology, Costumes, Ceramics, Crafts, Folk Art, Primitive art, Portraits, Posters, Porcelain, Coins & Medals, Tapestries, Dioramas, Reproductions
Collections: Art of all races of Africa south of the Sahara; scientific colls relating to Botswana
Exhibitions: Artists in Botswana (annual); HIV/AIDS (annual); Basket & Craft Exhibition (annual); Photographic (annual)
Publications: Zebra's Voice (quarterly); annual report; exhib catalogue
Activities: Classes for children; tours; sponsoring of competition; annual visual arts awards; lending of objects of art to other ministries; originate traveling exhibs to other countries; mus shop sells books, magazines, original art

BRAZIL

OURO PRETO

M   **MUSEU DA INCONFIDENCIA,** History of Democratic Ideals and Culture, Praca Tiradentes, 139, Ouro Preto, 35400 Brazil. Tel 031-3551-1121; 031-3551-5233; Elec Mail inconfidencia@veloxmail.com.br; ruimourao@veloxmail.com.br; *Dir* Rui Mourao
Average Annual Attendance: 150,000-200,000
Collections: Objects & documents related to the 1789 Revolutionaries of Minas Gerais (the Inconfidentes); Antonio Francisco Lisboa's coll of works; Religious art; Furniture from the 18th & 19th century; Religious music from the 18th century in Minas Gerais; Objects related to the Empire period (19th century); Objects related to the Vila Rica (the old Ouro Preto)
Publications: Oficina do Inconfidencis, Revista de Trabalho (annual issue) and Isto e Inconfidencia (bulletin published four times a year), Museu da Inconfidencia (institutional book of the museum)
Activities: Educ prog; activities for adults & children; guided tours; student training; ext prog offers film exhibs; mus shop sells books, magazines, reproductions, slides, postal cards, CD-ROMs, compact disks, DVDs, exhibs catalogs

RIO DE JANEIRO

M   **MUSEU DE ARTE MODERNA DE RIO DE JANIERO,** Museum of Modern Art, Av Infante Dom Henrique 85, CP 44 Rio de Janeiro, 20021 Brazil. Tel 021-240-6351; *Pres* M F Nascimento Brito; *Exec Dir* Gustavo A Capanema
Collections: Collections representing different countries

M   **MUSEU NACIONAL DE BELAS ARTES,** National Museum of Fine Arts, Ave Rio Branco 199, Rio de Janeiro, 20040 Brazil. Tel 240-9869; *Dir* Prof Heloisa A Lustosa
Open Tues - Fri 10 AM - 6 PM, Sat - Sun 2 PM - 6 PM; Library with 12,000 vols
Collections: 19th & 20th century Brazilian art, works by outstanding painters; European paintings & sculptures - works by Dutch, English, French, German, Italian, Portuguese & Spanish masters; masterpieces of foreign coll: Dutch school - eight Brazilian landscapes by Frans Post; French school - 20 Paintings by Eugene Boudin; Ventania (Storm) by Alfred Sisley; Italian School Portrait of the Cardinal Amadei by Giovanni Battista Gaulli, Baciccia; Sao Caetano (c 1730) by Giambattista Tiepolo. Graphic art department; Prints & drawings by Annibale Carracci, Chagall, Daumier, Durer, Toulouse Lautrec, Picasso, Guido Reni, Renoir, Tiepolo, etc

SALVADOR

M   **FUNDACAO INSTITUTO FEMININO DA BAHIA,** Early Art Museum: Bahia Women's College, Rua Monsenhor Flaviano 2, Salvador, Brazil. Tel (071) 321 7522; Fax (071) 3329 5681; Elec Mail museu@institutofeminino.org.br; Internet Home Page Address: www.institutofeminino.org.br; *Dir* Ana Uchoa Peixotu
Open Tues - Fri 10 AM - Noon, 1 PM - 6 PM, Sat 2 PM - 6 PM; Admis fee adults R$5, students & seniors R$3; Estab 1923; Circ 20,000; Average Annual Attendance: 4000
Income: Property investments & rent
Collections: Religious art; Brazilian art; women's apparel, jewelry, gold, silver; Costumes & Textiles
Publications: Catalogue, Costume and Textile Museum
Activities: Classes for children; concerts; gallery talks; mus shop sells books

SAO PAULO

M **MUSEU DE ARTE CONTEMPORANEA DA UNIVERSIDADE DE SAO PAULO,** Contemporary Art Museum of Sao Paulo University, Rua de Reitoria 160, Sao Paulo, 05508-900 Brazil. Tel (011) 3091 3039; Fax (011) 3812 0218; Elec Mail infomac@edu.usp.br; Internet Home Page Address: www.mac.usp.br; *Dir* Dr Elza Ajzenberg
Open Tues - Fri 10 AM - 7 PM, Sat & Sun 10 AM - 4 PM
Collections: Painting, sculptures, prints & drawings by masters of the international school & Brazilian Art

M **MUSEU DE ARTE DE SAO PAULO,** Sao Paulo Art Museum, Ave Paulista 1578, Sao Paulo, 01310-200 Brazil. Tel 251-5644; Fax 284-0574; *Dir* Julio Neves
Collections: Representative works by Portinari & Lasar Segall; ancient & modern paintings & sculptures: American, 19th - 20th Centuries; Brazilian, 17th - 20th Centuries; British, 18th - 20th Centuries; Dutch, Flemish & German, 15th - 20th Centuries; French, 16th - 20th Centuries; Italian, 13th - 20th Centuries; Spanish & Portuguese, 16th - 19th Centuries

M **MUSEU DE ARTE MODERNA SAO PAULO,** Parque do Ibirapuera, Gate 3 - s/n Sao Paulo, 04094-000 Brazil. Tel 55 11 5085-1300; Fax 55 11 5085-2342; Internet Home Page Address: www.mam.org.br; *Cur* Felipe Chaimovich
Open Tues - Sun 10 AM - 6 PM; Admis R $5.50, under 10 & over 60 free, Sun free
Collections: Multidisciplinary modern art from the 1950's to the present

BRUNEI DARUSSALAM

BANDAR SERI BAGAWAN

M **BRUNEI MUSEUM,** Jalan Kota Batu, Brunei Museums Department Bandar Seri Bagawan, BD1510 Brunei Darussalam. Tel 2244545; Internet Home Page Address: www.museums.gov.bn
Average Annual Attendance:

BULGARIA

PAZARDZHIK

M **STANISLAV DOSPEVSKY MUSEUM,** Maria-Luisa 54, Pazardzhik, 4400 Bulgaria. Tel 2-71-52; *Dir* Ganka Radulova
Collections: House where the painter lived & worked; exhibition of paintings, icons, personal effects & documents

PLOVDIV

M **REGIONAL MUSEUM OF ARCHAEOLOGY,** Regional Archaeological Museum-Plovdiv, Pl Saedinenie 1, Plovdiv, 4000 Bulgaria. Tel 032 633106; Fax 032 633106; Elec Mail ram.plovdiv@gmail.com; Internet Home Page Address: archaeologicalmuseumplovdiv.og; *Dir* Dr Kostadin Kissiov
Open winter: Tues - Sat 9:30 AM - 17 PM; summer: Tues - Sun 10 AM - 18 PM; Admis 5 leva; Estab 2010; Library with 15,000 vols; Average Annual Attendance: 9,000
Income: Municipal budget
Library Holdings: Book Volumes; CD-ROMs; Compact Disks; DVDs; Exhibition Catalogs; Maps; Other Holdings; Photographs; Reels; Slides
Collections: Prehistory; classical & medieval archaeology; epigraphic monuments, jewelry, numismatics, toreutics & vessels
Activities: Excavations; mus shop sells books, original art, reproductions, prints & other items

SOFIA

M **NATIONAL GALLERY FOR FOREIGN ART,** 1 Alexander Nevsky Sq, Sofia, Bulgaria. Tel 988-49-22; Fax 980-60-81; *Dir* Georgi Lipovanski
Open Mon & Wed - Sun 11 AM - 6 PM, cl Tues; Admis 10Lv, Mon free
Collections: Ancient and contemporary art, emphasis on European, Indian, Japanese, Buddhist, and African work; Engravings

M **NATSIONALNA HUDOZHESTVENA GALERIJA,** National Art Gallery, Moskovska 6, Sofia, 1000 Bulgaria; 1 Prince Alexander Battenberg Sq, Sofia, 1000 Bulgaria. Tel 00359-2-9800071; Fax 00359-2-9803320; Elec Mail europiabg@hotmail.com; Internet Home Page Address: www.nationalartgallery-bg.org; *Dir* Mr Boris Danailov; *Deputy Dir* B Yossitova; *Deputy Dir* B Klimentiev
Open Tues - Sun 10 AM - 6 PM, cl Mon; Admis fee adults 4 BGN leva, students 2 BGN leva; National Museum for Bulgarian Visual Arts
Income: Ministry of Culture
Library Holdings: Auction Catalogs; CD-ROMs; Compact Disks; DVDs; Exhibition Catalogs; Framed Reproductions; Kodachrome Transparencies; Original Art Works; Original Documents; Photographs; Prints; Reproductions; Sculpture; Slides
Collections: National & foreign art; Permanent expositions of paintings & sculpture
Exhibitions: Temporary exhibitions of Bulgarian & foreign art
Activities: Classes for children; concerts, gallery talks, tours; lending of original art objects to galleries within the country; originates traveling exhibs to

municipality & private galleries; mus shop sells books, magazines, original art, reproductions & prints

CAMBODIA

PHNOM PENH

M **CAMBODIAN NATIONAL MUSEUM,** Ang Eng St 13, Corner St 184 Phnom Penh, Cambodia. Tel 023-211-753; Elec Mail museum_cam@camnet.com.kh; *Dir* Khun Samen
Open daily 8 AM - 11:30 AM & 2 PM - 5:30 PM; Admis $2
Collections: Over 5000 objects on display; Khmer artifacts, statues, pre-Angkorian pottery & Brahmanist lingas; coins

CHILE

SANTIAGO

M **MUSEO CHILENO DE ARTE PRECOLOMBINO,** Banderas 361, Corner of Compania Santiago, Chile. Tel 56-02-688-7348; Fax 56-02-697-2779; Elec Mail mmarin@museoprecolombino.cl; Internet Home Page Address: www.precolombino.cl; *Dir* Carlos del Solar Aldunate
Open Tues - Sun 10 AM - 6 PM, cl Mon; Admis adults $4, students & children free
Collections: Permanent exhibition of items predating Spanish conquest; 3000 specimens of ceramics, textiles, sculptures and others

M **MUSEO DE ARTE CONTEMPORANEO,** Parque Forestal s/n, Mosqueto St, Univ of Chile Santiago, Chile. Tel 56-02 977-1741, 1746, 1755; Elec Mail mac@uchile.cl; Internet Home Page Address: www.mac.uchile.cl/index.html; *Dir* Francisco Brugnoli
Open Tues - Fri 11 AM - 7 PM, Sat 11 AM - 6 PM, Sun 11 AM - 2 PM; Admis 600, students 400
Collections: Over 2000 pieces of art produced in Chile since the late 19th century to the present; 600 paintings, 130 drawings, 80 sculptures; contemporary and modern work by local and international artists

M **MUSEO DE ARTE POPULAR AMERICANO,** Museum of American Folk Art, Parque Forestal S/N, Casilla 2100, Univ of Chile Santiago, Chile. Tel 2-682-1450; Fax 2-682-1481; *Dir* Sylvia Rios Montero
Open Tues - Fri 9 AM - 5 PM
Collections: Araucanian silver; American folk arts of pottery, basketware, metal & wood

M **MUSEO NACIONAL DE BELLAS ARTES,** National Museum of Fine Arts, Parque Forestal S/N, Casilla 3209 Santiago, Chile. Tel (2) 6330655; Fax (2) 6393297; Elec Mail milan.ivelic@mnba.cl; Internet Home Page Address: www.mnba.cl; *Dir* Milan Ivelic; *Contemporary Art Cur* Ramon Castillo; *Art Cur* Angelica Perez
Open Tues - Sun 10 AM - 18:50 PM; Admis adults $600 Chilean pesos; Estab 1880; maintain Chilean artistic heritage; Chilean & foreign painting, sculpture, engraving etc; Average Annual Attendance: 253,000
Library Holdings: Book Volumes; CD-ROMs; Clipping Files; Compact Disks; DVDs; Exhibition Catalogs; Manuscripts; Original Documents; Photographs; Prints; Records; Reproductions; Slides; Video Tapes
Special Subjects: Etchings & Engravings, Landscapes, Marine Painting, Photography, Portraits, Sculpture, Latin American Art, Religious Art, Painting-Dutch, Painting-French, Painting-Flemish, Painting-Spanish, Painting-Italian
Collections: Baroque, Chilean & Spanish paintings; sculpture; engravings; contemporary art
Activities: Classes for children; docent training; lects open to the public; opening events; gallery talks; guided tours; Museo Sin Muros, Salas MNBA Mall Plaza; lending of original objects of art to mus & cultural ctrs; organize traveling exhibs to Chilean regions; mus shop sells books, magazines, original art, reproductions, prints & memorabilia

M **ORDEN FRANCISCANA DE CHILE,** Museo Colonial de San Francisco, PO Box 1220, Alameda Bernardo O'Higgins 834 Santiago, Chile. Tel (2) 639 8737; Fax (02) 639 8737; Internet Home Page Address: www.sanfrancisco.cl; *Dir* Rosa Puga
Open 10 AM to 1 PM and 3 PM - 6 PM; Admis $750 niños $250
Income: Income from pvt support
Collections: 16th - 19th century art; collection of 17th century paintings in Chile; the life of St Francis depicted in 53 pictures; other religious works of art, furniture
Exhibitions: Arte religioso de la Escuela quiteña
Publications: Pinturas de la Serie de San Francisco Edic Morgan Antártica; Catýlogo del Museo de San Francisco
Activities: Mus shop sells books, original art, reproductions, prints, handicrafts, ceramics, oil paintings & religious articles

CHINA

BEIJING

M **BEIJING ART MUSEUM,** Wanshou Temple, North of West 3rd Ring Rd Beijing, 100081 China. Tel 8610-68479391, 68413380; Fax 8610-68472390
Open Tues - Sun 9 AM - 4 PM, cl Mon; Admis 20 yuan

Collections: 50,000 pieces; Bronze and jade articles of Shang and Zhou dynasties, pottery, porcelains, enamels, carved lacquer ware, ivory & wood carving; Chinese paintings and calligraphy of Ming and Qing dynasties; Textiles, coins; Modern Chinese and Japanese arts and crafts

M **BEIJING ARTS AND CRAFTS MUSEUM,** 4th Fl No 200, Wangfujing St, Dongcheng Dist Beijing, 100005 China. Tel 8610-65289326; 65288866; Fax 8610-65289326; Elec Mail bwg@gongmeigroup.com.cn; Internet Home Page Address: www.gongmeigroup.com.cn/doce/bwg.htm; *Pres* Zeng Jian-zhong
Open Mon - Fri 9 AM - 5 PM, Sat - Sun 10 AM - 5 PM; Admis 10 yuan
Collections - 3,000 pieces of fine arts & crafts; Traditional Chinese arts & crafts, jade & ivory carvings, lacquer; Handicrafts of gold inlaid ware, antique porcelain, ancient bronze, embroidery; Paintings and calligraphy

M **NAITONAL ARTS AND CRAFTS MUSEUM,** Fuxing Men Nei Dajie 101, Xi Cheng Qu Beijing, China. Tel 8610-66053476
Open Tues - Sun 9:30 AM - 4 PM; Admis 8 yuan
Collections: Clay figurines from Jiangsu, cloisonne from Beijing, lacquerware from Fujian, and ceramics from Jingdezhen; Arts & crafts, traditional and modern national folk art

M **NATIONAL ART MUSEUM OF CHINA,** 1 Wusi Dajie, East Dist Beijing, 100010 China. Tel 84033500; Elec Mail spanr@namoc.org; Elec Mail bgs@namoc.org; Internet Home Page Address: www.namoc.org/namoc/about; *Dir* Fan Di'an
Open Tues - Sun 9 AM - 5 PM, cl Mon; Admis 20 RMB
Collections: More than 60,000 fine art works; Chinese paintings, prints, sculptures, sketches, iconography; folk and traditional arts and crafts, puppets, toys, kites, textiles, embroidery; decorative arts

GUANGZHOU

M **GUANDONG MUSEUM OF ART,** 38 Yanyu Rd, Guangzhou, 510105 China.

KAOHSIUNG CITY

M **KAOHSIUNG MUSEUM OF FINE ARTS,** 80 Meishuguan Rd, Gushan Dist Kaohsiung City, China. Tel 07-5550331; Fax 07-5550307; Elec Mail servicemail@kmfa.gov.tw; Internet Home Page Address: www.kmfa.gov.tw; *Dir* Lee Jiun-Shyan
Open Tues - Sun 9 AM - 5 PM, cl Mon
Collections: Collection of 2,698 works in 18 categories; 583 works of calligraphy; 211 sculptures; 466 oil paintings; 337 watercolors; 245 sketches

SHANGHAI

M **MUSEUM OF CONTEMPORARY ART SHANGHAI,** People's Park, 231 Nanjing West Rd Shanghai, 200003 China. Tel 86 21 63279900; Fax 86 21 63271257; Elec Mail info@mocashanghai.org; Internet Home Page Address: www.mocashanghai.org; *Chm & Dir* Samuel Kung
Open Wed 10 AM - 9:30 PM, Thurs - Tues 10 AM - 6 PM; Admis adults 30 RMB (after 6 PM 20 RMB), students, senior citizens, military & handicapped 15 RMB, children under 1.3 m in height & members no charge; Estab 2005
Collections: Chinese and international contemporary art

TAICHUNG

M **NATIONAL TAIWAN MUSEUM OF FINE ARTS,** 2 sec 1 Wu Chuan W Rd, Taichung, 403 China. Tel 886 04 2372-3552; Fax 886-04-2375-9105; Elec Mail artnet@art.ntmofa.gov.tw; Internet Home Page Address: www.ntmofa.gov.tw; *Dir* Tsai-Lang Huang
Open Tues - Fri 9 AM - 5 PM, Sat - Sun 9 AM - 6 PM, cl Mon; No admis fee
Collections: Over 10,000 items created over various centuries from the Ming & Qing dynasties to the present

TAIPEI

M **MUSEUM OF CONTEMPORARY ART - TAIPEI,** 39 ChangAn W Rd, Taipei, 103 China. Tel 886-2-2552-3721; Fax 886-2-2559-3874; Elec Mail services@mocataipei.org.tw; Internet Home Page Address: www.mocataipei.org.tw/_english/index.asp; *Dir* Jui-Jen Shih; *Deputy Dir* Yu-Chieh Lin
Open Tues - Sun 10 AM - 6 PM, cl Mon; Admis 50 NT, under 6 & over 65 free
Library Holdings: Exhibition Catalogs; Kodachrome Transparencies
Special Subjects: Archaeology
Collections: International and local contemporary art in various media
Activities: Classes for adults & children; gallery talks; serving Zhong Shan Book Street; mus shop sells books

TAIWAN, R.O.C.

M **NATIONAL PALACE MUSEUM,** 221 Chi-Shan Rd Sec 2, Wai-shuang-hsi Taiwan, R.O.C., Taipei 11143 China. Tel 886-2-2881-2021; Fax 886-2-2882-1440; Elec Mail service@npm.gov.tw; Internet Home Page Address: www.npm.gov.tw; *Dir* Chou Kung-Shin; *Dep Dir* Fung Ming-Chu; *Dep Dir* Huang Yong-Tai
Open daily 9 AM - 5 PM, Sat evening 5 - 8:30 PM no charge; Admis fee NT$160 adults, NT$80 students (with ID), NT$120 group; Estab 1925 in Peking, 1965 in Wai-Shuang-hsi, Taipei; Circ non-circ
Income: Income: NT$125,001,000

Purchases: 91 pieces of Vietnamese under glaze blue doyce lain, 16 pieces of Southeast Asian textile, 1 Gandharan standing bodhisattva sculpture, and 1 Kashmiri seated Buddha sculpture
Library Holdings: Auction Catalogs; Audio Tapes; Book Volumes; CD-ROMs; Cassettes; Clipping Files; Compact Disks; DVDs; Exhibition Catalogs; Fiche; Maps; Original Documents; Periodical Subscriptions; Photographs; Slides; Video Tapes
Special Subjects: Ceramics, Pottery, Manuscripts, Bronzes, Religious Art, Crafts, Woodcarvings, Portraits, Jade, Jewelry, Porcelain, Oriental Art, Ivory, Tapestries, Calligraphy, Miniatures, Embroidery, Enamels
Collections: Bronzes, calligraphy, carved lacquer, embroidery, enamelware, jades, miniature crafts, oracle bones, paintings, porcelain, pottery, rare and old books & documents from Shang Dynasty to Ch'ing Dynasty, tapestry, writing implements
Exhibitions: Compassion and Wisdom: Religious Sculptural Arts; Orientation Gallery; Gems in the Rare Books Collection; Heaven-Sent Conveyances: Highlights of Ch'ing Historical Documents; Arts from Ch'Ing Imperial Collection; Splendors of Ch'ing Furniture (1800-1911); Transitions and Convergences (221-960); Oversized Hanging and Hand Scrolls Selections; Prototypes of Modern Styles (960-1350); The Ancient Art of Writing: Selections from the History of Chinese Calligraphy; The New Era of Ornamentation (1350-1521); The Contest of Craft: Ming Dynasty's Chia-Ching to Ch'ung-chen (1522-1644); Painting and Calligraphy Donated and Entrusted to the National Palace Museum; Treasures from an Age of Prosperity: The Reigns of Emperors K'ang-hsi, Yung-cheng and Ch'ien-Jung (1662-1795); Toward Modernity: Late Ch'ing Dynasty (1796-1911); NPM Outdoor Public Art: Intertia/Exertion; The Mystery of Bronzes; The Neolithic Age: The Beginning of Civilization (6200-1600 B.C.E); Classical Civilization: The Bronze Age (1600-221 B.C.E.); From Classic to Tradition (221 B.C.E.-220 C.E.); Dazzling Gems of the Collection: Famous Pieces from the Ch'ing Dynasty Palaces
Publications: The National Palace Museum Monthly of Chinese Art; The National Palace Museum Research Quarterly; Exploring Asia: Episode One of the NPM Southern Branch; The Tradition of Re-Presenting Art; Diagrams Showing the Reconstruction of Various Structures in the Prefecture of Taiwan; Illustrated Catalog of Painting and Calligraphy in the National Palace Mus; The Heavenly Collection: Treasures from the Emperor Ch'ien-lung Library; Kanjur Manuscript: Tibetan-language edition, hand-copied in gold ink K'ang-hsi reign, Ch'ing dynasty-Illuminations I&III; Exquisite Beauty-Islamic Jades; New Visions at the Ch'ing Court: Giuseppe Castiglione and Western-Style Trends; Lasting Impressions: Seals from the Museum Collection (in Chinese); Treasures of the Forbidden City: Palace Imprints of the Ch'ing Dynasty (in Chinese); The Old is New NPM Guidebook: Splendors of the New National Palace Museum; Treasures of the National Palace Museum (Painting and Calligraphy & Books and Documents); Treasures from the Working of Nature: Eight Thousand Years of Antiquities; Marvelous Sparks of the Brush: Painting & Calligraphy, Books & Documents
Activities: Docent training, classes for children, teenagers & adults; teacher training workshops; dramatic progs; lects open to pub; 150 per yr; concerts, tours, sponsoring of competitions; teacher's workshops & reproduction exhibs throughout Taiwan; originate traveling exhibs on education upon invitation; shop sells books, reproductions, prints; children's gallery within mus's main building

L **Library,** Wai-shuang-hsi, Shih-Lin, Taipei, China, Republic of. Tel 886-2-2881-2021; Fax 886-2-2882-1440; Elec Mail service@npm.gov.tw; Internet Home Page Address: www.npm.gov.tw; *Dep Dir* Shih Shou-Chien; *Dep Dir* Lin Po-Ting
Library Holdings: Book Volumes 48,000; Other Holdings Documents 395,000; Rare books 191,000; Periodical Subscriptions 683

COLOMBIA

BOGOTA

M **BANCO DE LA REPUBLICA MUSEO DEL ORO,** Museo del Oro, Calle 16 No 5-41, Bogota, 1 Colombia. Tel 571-3432222; Fax 571-2847450; Elec Mail wmuseo@banrep.gov.co; Internet Home Page Address: www.banrep.gov.co/museo/eng/home4.htm; *Dir* Ms Maria Alicia Uribe; *Chief Visitors' Serv* Ms Diana Vargas
Open Tues - Sat 9 AM - 6 PM, Sun 10 AM - 4 PM, cl Mon; Admis adults 3000, under 12 and over 65 free, Sun free
Special Subjects: Anthropology, Archaeology, Metalwork, Gold, Pottery, Pre-Columbian Art, Textiles, Restorations
Collections: Pre-Hispanic Goldwork Collection; Pottery, stone, shell, wood & textile archaeological objects
Activities: International exhibs displayed in recognized mus & cultural institutions around the world; mus shop sells books, reproductions & other items

M **MUSEO COLONIAL,** Museum of the Colonial Period, Carrera 6, No 9-77, Bogota, Colombia. Tel (1) 6352418-2866768.3416017; Elec Mail teramo@cable.net.co; *Dir* Teresa Morales de Gomez
Open Mon - Fri 9 AM - 5 PM, Sat - Sun 10 AM - 4 PM; Admis $.50; Estab Aug 6, 1942
Collections: Spanish colonial period art work: paintings, sculpture, furniture, gold and silver work, drawing

M **NATIONAL MUSEUM OF COLOMBIA,** Carrera 7, Calles 28 y 29 Bogota, Colombia. Tel 57 1 334 8366; Fax 57 1 337 4134; Elec Mail info@museonacional.gov.co; Internet Home Page Address: www.museonacional.gov.co
Open Tues - Sat 10 AM - 6 PM, Sun 10 AM - 5 PM; Admis adults $3, students $2, children over 5 $1, children under 5, senior citizens, ICOM and members no charge
Collections: Colombian art and artifacts from the earliest inhabitants to present

COSTA RICA

SAN JOSE

M **MUSEO DE ARTE COSTARRICENSE,** Apdo 378, Fecosa, San Jose, 1009 Costa Rica. Tel 2256-1281; Fax 2296-4533; Elec Mail macprensa@musarco.go.cr; Internet Home Page Address: www.musarco.go.cr; *Dir* Ricardo Alfieri; *Pub Relations* Marissia L Obando Razak
Open 9 AM - PM; No admis fee; Estab 1978; Average Annual Attendance: 60,000
Collections: Representative Costa Rican art
Activities: Classes for adults & children; docent training

M **MUSEO NACIONAL DE COSTA RICA,** Calle 17, Avda Central y 2, Apdo 749 San Jose, 1000 Costa Rica. Tel 221-44-29; Fax 233-74-27; *Dir* Melania Ortiz Volio
Collections: Pre-Columbian & colonial religious art; natural history

COTE D'IVOIRE

ABIDJAN

M **MUSEE DE LA COTE D'IVOIRE,** BP 1600, Abidjan, Cote d'Ivoire. Tel 22-20-56; *Dir* Dr B Holas
Collections: Art, ethnographic, scientific & sociological exhibits

CROATIA

RIJEKA

M **MUZEJ MODERNE I SUVREMENE UMJETNOSTI,** (Moderna Galerija) Museum of Modern and Contemporary Art, Dolac 1/II, Rijeka, 51000 Croatia. Tel 334280; Fax 330-982; Elec Mail mmsu@mmsu.rihr; Internet Home Page Address: www.mmsu.hr; *Dir* Dr Jerica Ziherl
Open Tues - Sun 10 AM - 1 PM & 5 PM - 8 PM, cl Mon; Admis 7.50 euro; Estab 1948; Modern & contemporary art
Library Holdings: Audio Tapes; Book Volumes; CD-ROMs; DVDs; Exhibition Catalogs; Filmstrips; Video Tapes
Special Subjects: Drawings, Photography, Graphics, Prints, Sculpture, Posters
Collections: Paintings, sculptures & graphics, drawings, photographs, mixed media, video
Publications: Catalogues of temporary exhibitions
Activities: Classes for adults & children; Lects open to pub; gallery talks; tours

SPLIT

M **ARCHEOLOSKI MUZEJ U SPLITU,** Archaeological Museum, Zrinjsko-Frankopanska 25, Split, 21000 Croatia. Tel (21) 44 574; Fax (21) 44 685; *Dir* Emilio Marin
Library with 30,000 vols
Collections: Relics from the Greek colonies; prehistoric & numismatic coll; medieval monuments from the 9th to the 13th century

M **GALERIJA UMJETNINA,** Art Gallery, Lovretska 11, Split, 21000 Croatia. *Dir* Milan Ivanisevic
Open Mon - Wed 6 PM - 9 PM, Thurs - Sat 10 AM - 1 PM & 6 PM - 9 PM, cl Sun; Admis adults 10kn, students & seniors 5kn; Library with 10,000 vols
Collections: Paintings & sculptures; ancient & modern art

VELIKA GORICA

M **MUZEJ TUROPOLJA,** Trg kralja Tomislava 1, Velika Gorica, HR 10410 Croatia. Tel 1-721-325; Fax 1-725-077; Elec Mail muzej-turopolja@muzej-turopolja.hr
Circ

ZAGREB

M **ARHEOLOSKI MUZEJ,** Archaeological Museum, Zrinski trg 19, Zagreb, 10000 Croatia. Tel 1-421-420; Fax 1-427-724; Elec Mail amz@amz.hr; Internet Home Page Address: www.amz.hr; *Dir* Ante Rendic-Miocevic; *Deputy Dir* I Van Mirnik
Open Tues, Wed, Fri 10 AM - 5 PM, Thurs 10 AM - 8 PM, Sat - Sun 10 AM - 1 PM; Admis family 30 kn, adults 20 kn, children, students & seniors 10 kn; Estab 1846
Income: funded by the city of Zagreb
Library Holdings: Book Volumes
Collections: Neolithic 13th century
Publications: Vjesnik AM2; catalogues & monographs of the archaeological mus in Zagreb
Activities: Mus shop sells books, reproductions, & other items

M **CROATIAN ACADEMY OF SCIENCES AND ARTS,** (Strossmayerova Galerija Starih Majstora) Strossmayer Gallery of Old Masters, Trg Nikole Subica Zrinskog 11, Zagreb, 10000 Croatia. Tel 385 (0) 1 4895-115/116-119; Fax 385 (0) 1-4819-979; Elec Mail sgallery@hazu.hr; Internet Home Page Address: www.hazu.hr/strossmayeroug-galerija-starih-m.html; Internet Home Page Address: www.mdc.hr/strossmayer; *Dir* Prof Borivoj Popovcak; *Cur* Ljerka Dulibic; *Cur* Iva Pasini Trzec; *Librn* Indira Samec Flaschar
Open Tues 10 AM - 7 PM, Wed - Fri 10 AM - 4 PM, Sat-Sun 10 AM - 1 PM; Admis students 10 kn, other 30 kn; Estab 1884; Gallery of old masters from 14th - 19th century; Average Annual Attendance: 9,000

Income: Ministry of science; ministry of culture
Library Holdings: Book Volumes 10,000; Exhibition Catalogs 2,000
Collections: Dutch 15th-18th century; French coll mostly 18th & 19th century; Italian coll, Fra Angelico - Piazzetta, nine rooms, paintings & sculpture, 13th to 19th century
Activities: Classes for children; gallery talks, 50 vis lects per yr; mus shop sells books & reproductions

M **MODERNA GALERIJA,** Gallery of Modern Art, Andrije Hebranga 1, Zagreb, 10000 Croatia. Tel 00 385 1 60 410 40; Tel 00 385 1 60 410 55; Fax 00385 1 60 410 45; Elec Mail moderna-galerija@zg.t-com.hr; Internet Home Page Address: www.moderna-galerija.hr; *Dir* Biserka Rauter Plancic
Open Tues - Fri 11 AM - 7 PM, Sun 11 AM - 2 PM, cl Mon & holidays; Admis 40 kn, groups 30 kn, students 20 kn; Estab 1905; Circ 1,500; Library with 4000 vols; Average Annual Attendance: 50,000
Income: $1,300,000 kn (financed by state treasury)
Library Holdings: Cards 2,000; Exhibition Catalogs 1,500; Video Tapes 200
Special Subjects: Drawings, Marine Painting, Photography, Woodcuts, Painting-French, Sculpture, Tapestries, Graphics, Prints, Watercolors, Primitive art, Woodcarvings, Landscapes, Painting-European, Portraits, Coins & Medals, Painting-German
Collections: Collection of sculptures, graphic arts & paintings; medals; video & new media
Exhibitions: Studio Josip Racic young artists exhibitions (10 per yr); 13 temporary exhibs per yr in Moderna Galerija
Publications: Dossier
Activities: Classes for children; lects open to pub; 4 vis lectrs per yr; original objects of art lent to other museums & galleries in & around Croatia; mus shop sells reproductions, books, magazines

M **MUNZEJ SUVREMENE UMJETNOSTI,** Habdeliceva 2, Zagreb, 10000 Croatia. Tel 1-431-343; Fax 1-431-404; *Dir* Snjezanda Pintaric
Collections: Five galleries exhibiting contemporary art, antique & Renaissance works, primitive art, Ivan Mestrovic's sculpture & photography

M **Galerija Benko Horvat,** Habdeliceva 2, Zagreb, 10000 Croatia. *Cur* Zelimir Koscevic; *Chief Cur* Mladen Lucic
Collections: Antique & Renaissance art

M **Galerija Primitivne Umjetnosti, Gallery of Naive Art,** Cirilometodska 3, Zagreb, 41000 Croatia. Tel 041 423 669; *Cur* Mrzljak Franjo

M **Galerija Suvremene Umjetnosti, Gallery of Contemporary Art,** Katarinin trg 2, Zagreb, 10000 Croatia. Tel 1 425-227; Fax 1-273-469; *Cur* Marijan Susovski

M **MUZEJ ZA UMJETNOST I OBRT,** Museum of Arts & Crafts, Trg Marsala Tita 10, Zagreb, 10000 Croatia. Tel 385 1 4882 118, 4882 111; Fax 385 1 4828 088; Elec Mail muo@muo.hr; Internet Home Page Address: www.muo.hr; *Dir* Miroslav Gasparovic; *Asst Dir* Vesna Juric Bulatovic; *Chief Librn* Andelka Galic
Open Tues, Wed, Fri & Sat 10 AM - 7 PM, Thurs 10 AM - 10 PM, Sun 10 AM - 2 PM; Admis adults 30 kn ($6), students & retired 20 kn ($3), groups 15 kn ($2.50); Estab 1880, collecting art and decorative arts from 13th - 20th century; Library with 70,000 vols; Average Annual Attendance: 100,000; Mem: 100,000
Income: 2.500000 euro
Library Holdings: Auction Catalogs; Book Volumes; CD-ROMs; Exhibition Catalogs; Fiche; Framed Reproductions; Manuscripts; Maps; Original Art Works; Original Documents; Pamphlets; Periodical Subscriptions; Photographs; Prints; Reproductions
Special Subjects: Etchings & Engravings, Architecture, Flasks & Bottles, Portraits, Pottery, Bronzes, Manuscripts, Painting-British, Tapestries, Drawings, Graphics, Photography, Sculpture, Watercolors, Textiles, Costumes, Religious Art, Ceramics, Crafts, Landscapes, Decorative Arts, Judaica, Painting-European, Posters, Dolls, Furniture, Glass, Jewelry, Porcelain, Silver, Metalwork, Painting-French, Carpets & Rugs, Ivory, Coins & Medals, Restorations, Baroque Art, Miniatures, Painting-Flemish, Renaissance Art, Embroidery, Laces, Painting-Spanish, Painting-Italian, Gold, Stained Glass, Painting-German, Pewter, Leather, Bookplates & Bindings
Collections: Applied arts from the 14th to the 20th century; ceramics, glass, tapestries, textiles, paintings & sculptures, furniture, clocks & watches, metal, photography, design architecture; Anka Gvozdanovic Coll
Activities: Classes for adults & children; children's workshops; lects open to pub; 10 vis lectrs per yr; concerts; gallery talks; tours; lending of original objects of art to other mus & galleries in Croatia; organize traveling exhibs throughout Europe; mus shop sells books, original art, reproductions, prints & other items

ZAGREBA

M **STROSSMAYER'S OLD MASTERS GALLERY,** Trg Nikole Subica Zrinskog 11, Zagreba, 10000 Croatia. Tel 385-1-481-33-44; Fax 385-1-481-99-79; Elec Mail sgallery@hazu.hazu.hr; Internet Home Page Address: http://www.mdc.hr/strossmayer/eng/index.html
Open Tues 10 AM - 1 PM, 5 PM - 7 PM, Wed - Sun 10 AM - 1 PM

CUBA

HAVANA

M **MUSEO DE ARTES DECORATIVAS,** Calle 17, No 502 Vedado, Havana, 10100 Cuba. Tel 320924; Fax 613857; *Dir* Maria Heidy Lopez Moyael Castillo
Open Tues - Sat 11 AM - 7 PM, cl Mon & Sun; Library with 2500 vols
Collections: Porcelain, bronzes, gold & silver work & tapestries

M **MUSEO NACIONAL DE BELLAS ARTES,** National Museum, Animas entre Zulueta y Monserate, Havana, CP 10200 Cuba. Tel (537) 639 042; *Dir* Pilar Fernandez Priesto
Open Tues - Sat 10 AM - 6 PM, Sun 10 AM - 2 PM, cl Mon

Collections: Renaissance and other European art; Cuban art from colonial times to the present

CYPRUS

LEFKOSIA

M **ARCHBISHOP MAKARIOS III FOUNDATION ART GALLERIES,** Plateia Archiepiskopou Kyprianou Lefkosia, Lefkosia, Cyprus.
Open Mon - Tues & Thurs - Fri 8:30 AM - 1 PM, Thurs & Sat 8:30 AM - 1 PM & 3 - 5:30 PM
Collections: Greek & European paintings & icons

NICOSIA

M **DEPARTMENT OF ANTIQUITIES,** Cyprus Museum, PO Box 22024, Nicosia, 1516 Cyprus. Tel 0035722865848/0035722865888; Fax 0035722303148; Elec Mail antiquitiesdept@da.mcw.gov.cy; Internet Home Page Address: www.mcw.gov.cy/da; *Acting Dir (Aug-Oct)* Dr Marina Ieronymidou; *Acting Dir* Dr Despo Pilides; *Librn* Maria Economidou
Open Wed 8 AM - 4 PM, Thurs - Fri 8 AM - 4 PM, Sat 9 AM - 4 PM, Sun 10 AM - 1 PM, cl Mon, New Year's Day, Greek Orthodox Easter, Christmas Day; Admis 3.40 euro; Estab 1910; 14 exhibition galleries from the Neolithic to the Roman period, early Christian period; Average Annual Attendance: 150,000; Mem: ICOM
Income: Through government budget
Library Holdings: Auction Catalogs; Book Volumes; CD-ROMs; Compact Disks; DVDs; Exhibition Catalogs; Fiche; Filmstrips; Framed Reproductions; Manuscripts; Maps; Memorabilia; Motion Pictures; Original Art Works; Original Documents; Pamphlets; Periodical Subscriptions; Photographs; Prints; Reproductions; Sculpture; Slides; Video Tapes
Special Subjects: Afro-American Art, Archaeology, Etchings & Engravings, Ceramics, Glass, Metalwork, Antiquities-Assyrian, Furniture, Gold, Bronzes, Jewelry, Antiquities-Byzantine, Ivory, Coins & Medals, Antiquities-Oriental, Antiquities-Greek, Antiquities-Roman, Mosaics, Military Art, Enamels
Collections: Bronze cauldron from Salamis; middle and late Bronze-age Geometric, Archaic, Classical, Hellenistic and Graeco-Roman pottery; Mycenaean vases; Neolithic stone tools and vessels; sculpture from Archaic to Greco-Roman Age, including the Fine Arsos Head, the Aphrodite of Soli, and the bronze statue of Septimus Severus; silver trays from Lambousa
Exhibitions: (05/13/2013-02/16/2014) Fragments: Ceramic finds from Byzantine & Medieval Nicosia
Publications: ARDAC, Monographs; RDAC (Report of the Department of Antiquities)
Activities: Classes for children; lects open to pub; concerts; lending of original objects of art to mus & academies in Europe & USA; organize traveling exhibs to mus & academies; originate traveling exhibs to Europe and America; sales shop sells books, reproductions, slides, postcards

CZECH REPUBLIC

BRNO

M **MORAVSKA GALERIE V BRNE,** Moravian Gallery in Brno, Husova 18, Brno, 662 26 Czech Republic. Tel ++420 532 169 131; Fax ++420 532 169 181; Elec Mail info@moravska-galerie.cz; Internet Home Page Address: www.moravska-galerie.cz; *Dir* Jan Press; *Gen Secy* Katerina Tlachova
Open Wed & Fri - Sun 10 AM - 6 PM, Thurs 10 AM - 7 PM, cl Mon & Tues; Admis 1-4 Euros; Estab 1873; Library with 120,000 vols; Average Annual Attendance: 100,000
Income: National Institution, main source of financing is the state budget
Library Holdings: Auction Catalogs; Book Volumes; CD-ROMs; Compact Disks; DVDs; Exhibition Catalogs; Manuscripts
Special Subjects: Decorative Arts, Etchings & Engravings, Landscapes, Ceramics, Glass, Metalwork, Photography, Porcelain, Textiles, Woodcuts, Manuscripts, Painting-European, Sculpture, Tapestries, Drawings, Graphics, Prints, Watercolors, Costumes, Religious Art, Pottery, Woodcarvings, Portraits, Posters, Furniture, Jewelry, Oriental Art, Painting-Dutch, Restorations, Baroque Art, Painting-Flemish, Renaissance Art, Medieval Art, Antiquities-Oriental, Painting-Italian, Gold, Painting-German, Painting-Russian, Bookplates & Bindings
Collections: European Art Collection - ceramics, furniture, glass, graphic design, jewelry, photography, textiles; Fine Art Collection - graphic art, painting, sculpture, 14th century to present; Oriental Art Collection; Design, architecture
Exhibitions: Ca 20 per yr
Publications: Ca 6 per yr
Activities: Classes for adults & children; art workshops; lects open to pub; 20 vis lects per yr; concerts; gallery talks; tours; awards, Michal Ranny Prize; lending of original objects of art to other mus; mus shop sells books, magazines, reproductions, prints, gifts, jewelry & accessories

JABLONEC NAD NISOU

M **MUZEUM SKLA A BIZUTERIE,** Museum of Glass & Jewelry, Jiraskova 4, Jablonec nad Nisou, 46600 Czech Republic. Tel 31 16 81; Fax 31 17 04; *Dir* Jaroslava Slaba
Library with 11,500 vols
Collections: Bohemian glass making & jewelry; exhibitions

LIBEREC V

M **OBLASTNI GALERIE V LIBERCI,** U Tiskarny 81/1, Liberec V, 460 01 Czech Republic. Tel 420-485-106-325; Fax 420-485-106-321; Elec Mail oblgal@ogl.cz; Internet Home Page Address: www.ogl.cz
Circ

LITOMERICE

M **SEVEROCESKA GALERIE VYTVARNEHO UMENI V LITOMERICICH,** North Bohemian Gallery of Fine Arts in Litomerice, Mirove Nam 24, Litomerice, 412-01 Czech Republic. Tel 416-73-23-82; Fax 416-73-23-83; Elec Mail info@galerie-ltm.cz; Internet Home Page Address: galerie-ltm.cz; *Dir* Dr Jan Stibr, PhD; *Cur Coll Early Art* Dr Lubomir Turcan, PhD; *Cur Coll Modern & Contemporary Art* Jaroslava Pichova, BSc; *Registrar & Cur Coll Naiv Art* Alena Berankova; *Restorer & Conservator* Eva Votockova, MFA; *Educ & Prog Officer* Dr Olga Kubelkova, PhD; *Graphic Designer & Photographer* Jan Brodsky, MA
Open May - Sep Sun 9 AM - noon & 1 PM - 6 PM; Oct - Apr Tues - Sun 9 AM - noon & 1 PM - 5 PM; Admis adults 32 K, students & seniors 16 K, children 6 - 12 8 K; Estab 1956; Early art colls from the 13th-16th centuries, Baroque art colls & art of the 19th-21st centuries, Naiv art, works from the Litomerice area & Northwest Bohemia, works of leading artists in Czech fine art; Average Annual Attendance: 17,000
Special Subjects: Drawings, Etchings & Engravings, Landscapes, Sculpture, Graphics, Prints, Religious Art, Painting-European, Baroque Art, Renaissance Art, Medieval Art
Collections: Gothic Art Coll; Renaissance Art coll; Baroque Art coll; art of the 19th, 20th & 21st centuries; Naiv Art coll
Publications: Exhib catalogs
Activities: Classes for adults & children; lects open to the pub; 218 vis lectrs per yr; concerts; tours; lending of original objects of art to mus & art galleries in Czech Republic & abroad; mus shop sells exhib catalogs

PRAGUE

M **CESKE MUZEUM VYTVARNYCH UMENI V PRAZE,** 19-21 Husova St, Old Town Prague, 110 00 Czech Republic. Tel 420-222-220-218; Fax 420-222-221-190; Elec Mail muzeum@cmvu.cz; Internet Home Page Address: www.cmvu.cz/en; *Dir* Ivan Neumann
Open Tues - Sun 10 AM - 6 PM, cl Mon; Admis adults 50 K, children over 6 20 K, under 6 free
Collections: Series of work acquired at the beginning of the 1960s; 19th century art and the turn of the 20th century; realist trends

M **GALERIE HLAVNIHO MESTA PRAHY,** City Gallery Prague, Marianske namesti 98/1, 110 00 Prague, 1 16000 Czech Republic. Tel +420 222 314 259; Fax +420 222 327 683; Elec Mail office@citygalleryprague.cz; Internet Home Page Address: www.citygalleryprague.cz;Christine Kocova
Open Tues - Sun 10.00 - 20.00, cl Mon; Admis 20 - 120 K
Collections: Pragensia work; 19th & 20th centuries Czech artists
Activities: Classes for children; lects open to pub; concerts; tours; Museum shop sells books & magazines

M **GALERIE RUDOLFINUM,** Alsovo Nabrezi 12, Prague, 110 01 Czech Republic. Tel 420-227-059-205; Fax 420-222-319-293; Elec Mail galerie@rudolfinum.org; Internet Home Page Address: www.galerierudolfinum.cz
Average Annual Attendance:

M **MUCHA MUSEUM,** Kaunicky palac, Panska 7 Prague, 110 00 Czech Republic. Tel 420 224 216 415; Fax 420 224 216 415; Elec Mail info@mucha.cz; Internet Home Page Address: www.mucha.cz; *Mng Dir* Sebastian Pawlowski; *Deputy Dir* Hana Lastovickova
Open daily 10 AM - 6 PM
Collections: Works of Alphonse Mucha

M **MUSEUM OF DECORATIVE ARTS IN PRAGUE,** Ulice 17 listopadu 2, Prague, 110 00 Czech Republic. Tel 420 251 093 111; Fax 420 251 093296; Elec Mail info@upm.cz; Internet Home Page Address: www.upm.cz; *Dir* Dr Helena Koenigsmarkova; *Chief Cur* Radim Vondracek; *Project Mgr Exhib* Dusan Seidl
Open Tues 10 AM - 7 PM, Wed - Sun 10 AM - 6 PM; Library open Mon noon - 6 PM, Tues 10 AM- 8 PM, Wed - Fri 10 AM - 6 PM, Sat 10 AM - 2 PM; cl July & Aug; Admis concessions 40K - 70K, combined 120K, family 200K; Estab 1885; Circ 5,000; Art Library with 150,000 vols; permanent coll; stories of materials; Average Annual Attendance: 80,000; Mem: The Society of Friends of the Museum of Decorative Arts in Prague
Income: Financed by the Ministry of Culture of the Czech Republic
Library Holdings: Auction Catalogs; Book Volumes; CD-ROMs; DVDs; Exhibition Catalogs; Original Documents; Pamphlets; Periodical Subscriptions; Slides
Special Subjects: Decorative Arts, Historical Material, Glass, Metalwork, Flasks & Bottles, Painting-American, Textiles, Woodcuts, Painting-British, Painting-European, Painting-French, Painting-Japanese, Tapestries, Graphics, Photography, Prints, Costumes, Religious Art, Ceramics, Posters, Painting-Canadian, Furniture, Jewelry, Porcelain, Oriental Art, Silver, Painting-Dutch, Painting-Flemish, Painting-Polish, Renaissance Art, Painting-Spanish, Painting-Italian, Mosaics, Painting-Australian, Painting-German, Painting-Russian, Painting-Israeli, Painting-Scandinavian, Painting-New Zealand
Collections: European applied art from 12th to 21st century; collections of glass, ceramics, china, furniture, textiles, tapestries, gold & silver work, iron, ivory, clocks, prints, posters, photography, contemporary design, fashion, toys, porcelain, jewelry, watches; UPM holdings Mus of Textile in Ceska Skalice, 20th century furniture, Kamenice nad Lipou

Activities: Classes for adults & children; lects open to pub; tours; gallery talks; awards, Gloria Musbaus (2008, 2009,2010), Gloria Musealis (2012); schols offered; lends original objects of art to museums worldwide; originates traveling exhibs to museums worldwide; mus shop sells books, magazines, original art, reproductions, prints & other items; Josef Sudek Gallery, The Chateau at Kamenice nad Lipou

M **NARODNI GALERIE V PRAZE,** National Gallery in Prague, Staromestske nam, Prague, 110 00 Czech Republic. Tel (02) 534457; *Dir* Dr Milan Knizak
Open Tues - Sun 10 AM - 6 PM; Admis from 20K to 250 K; Estab 1796; Library with 75,000 vols
Collections: Architecture; Czech sculpture of the 19th and 20th century; French and European art of the 19th and 20th century; Old Czech art; Old European Art; graphic art, modern art; Oriental art; European Old Masters; Bohemian Art from the Era of Emperor Rudolf II to the Close of the Baroque; Medieval Art in Bohemia and Central Europe (1200 - 1550); 19th and 20th Century Art; Asian Art
Activities: Classes for adults & children; lectrs open to pub; lects for mems only; 85 vis lectrs per yr; concerts; gallery talks; fellowships offered; mus shop sells books, prints, reproductions, slides

M **ZIDOVSKE MUZEUM,** Jewish Museum, U Stare skoly 1, Prague, 110 01 Czech Republic. Tel 420 221 749 211; Fax 420 222 749 300; Elec Mail office@jewishmuseum.ct; Internet Home Page Address: www.jewishmuseum.ct; *Dir* Dr Leo Pavlat; *Deputy Dir* Michal Frankl
Open Mon - Fri & Sun winter 9 AM - 4:30 PM, summer 9 AM - 6 PM, cl Sat & Jewish holidays; Admis fee adults 300 K, under 15 yrs & students 200 K, under 6 yrs free; Library with 100,000 vols
Special Subjects: Judaica
Collections: Historical archival materials of Bohemian & Moravian Jewish religious communities; library of ancient books with a coll of Hebrew manuscripts; children's drawings & works of painters from the Terezin concentration camp; silver from Czech synagogues; textiles from synagogues of historic interest; Holocaust memorial
Activities: Classes for children; vis lectrs per yr cca 50; concerts; gallery talks

DENMARK

AALBORG

M **KUNSTEN MUSEUM OF MODERN ART AALBORG,** (Nordjylands Kunstmuseum) Kong Christians Alle 50, Aalborg, DK-9000 Denmark. Tel (+45) 99 82 41 00; Elec Mail kunsten@aalborg.dk; Internet Home Page Address: www.kunsten.dk; *Dir* Gitte Orskou; *Cur* Stinna Toft; *Cur* Dakob Vengberg Sevel
Open museum open Tues - Sun 10 AM - 5 PM, cl Mon; Admis museum adults 75 DKK, discounts for students, seniors, groups, children free; Estab 1879, building inaugurated 1972; Museum contains 3,700 art works; Average Annual Attendance: 70,000
Income: Self-governing institution with state, county & municipal funding
Purchases: Modern & contemporary art
Collections: Collection of graphics, painting & sculpture from 1900 to the present, Danish and international
Exhibitions: 8-10 spec exhibitions annually
Publications: Approx 4 exhibition catalogs annually
Activities: Concerts; gallery talks; tours; exten prog to school district of Nordjylland County; traveling exhibition within school district of Nordjylland County; sales shop sells books, reproductions, scarves, T-shirts, magazines, prints; occasional exhibitions for children; occasional workshops for children

AARHUS C

M **AARHUS KUNSTMUSEUM,** Aros Aarus Kunstmuseum, Aros Alle 2, Aarhus C, 8000 Denmark. Tel 86-13-52-55, 87-30-6600; Fax 86-13-3351, 87-30-6601; Elec Mail info@aros.dk; Internet Home Page Address: www.aarhuskunstmuseum.dk, www.aros.dk; *Dir* Jens Erik Sorensen
Open Tues - Sun 10 AM - 5 PM, Wed 10 AM - 10 PM, cl Mon; Admis adults 90 Kr, seniors & students 75 Kr; groups of 20+ Kr 75 per head; children under 18 free admis; Library with 1000 vols
Collections: Danish & European art, Danish Golden ages, Danish modernism-Asger Jorn, Richard Mortensen, contemp Danish & international, Jeff Koons, Gilbert & George

CHARLOTTENLUND

M **ORDRUPGAARDSAMLINGEN,** Ordrupgaard, Vilvordevej 110, Charlottenlund, 2920 Denmark. Tel 39-64-11-83; Fax 39-64-10-05; Elec Mail ordrupgaard@ordrupgaard.dk; Internet Home Page Address: www.ordrupgaard.dk; *Dir* Anne-Birgitte Fonsmark
Open Tues - Fri 1 PM - 5 PM, Sat & Sun 11 AM - 5 PM; Finn Juhl's House: Sat & Sun & Nat holidays 11 AM - 4:45 PM, cl Mon; Admis 95 Dkr adults, children under18 free; special fees & hours during temporary exhibitions; Masterpieces by French impressionists; Danish art from the 19th and 20th centuries; art museum set in a large, lovely park; new extension by 2aha Hadid; the famous Danish architect Finn Fuhl's house
Library Holdings: Auction Catalogs; Book Volumes; Exhibition Catalogs; Kodachrome Transparencies; Manuscripts; Memorabilia; Photographs; Video Tapes
Special Subjects: Painting-French, Architecture, Period Rooms, Painting-Scandinavian
Collections: Wilhelm Hansen Collection; paintings by Cezanne, Corot, Courbet, Degas, Delacroix, Gauguin, Manet, Pissarro, Renoir, Sisley & other French & Danish artists from the 19th century & the beginning of the century
Activities: Classes for children; Lects open to pub; lects for mems only; gallery talks; mus shop sells books, magazines, reproductions, prints & Souvenirs

COPENHAGEN

L **DANMARKS KUNSTBIBLIOTEK,** (Kunstakademiets Bibliotek) Danish National Art Library, One Kongens Nytorv, Copenhagen, 1053 K Denmark. Tel 45 3374 4800; Fax 45 3374 4888; Elec Mail dkb@kunstbib.dk; Internet Home Page Address: www.kunstbib.dk; *Dir* Patrick Kragelund, PhD
No admis fee; Estab 1754 (National Research Library); Circ 80,000
Income: Government financed palannum c 12,000,000 Kr, per annum c 1,000,000 (not including donations
Library Holdings: Book Volumes 175,000; Other Holdings Architectural Drawings 350,000; Photographs 350,000; Slides 170,000
Activities: Classes adults; docent training; lects open to pub, 3 vis lectrs per yr; lending of original objects of art of exhib on architecture

M **DESIGNMUSEUM DANMARK,** (Kunstindustrimuseet) Bredgade 68, 1260 Copenhagen K, Copenhagen, Denmark. Tel 33-18-5656; Fax 33-18-5666; Elec Mail info@designmuseum.dk; Internet Home Page Address: www.designmuseum.dk; *Dir* Anne-Louise Sommer; *Chief Librn* Lars Dybdahl; *Cur* Ulla Houkjaer; *Cur* Christian H Olesen; *Cur* Kirsten Toftegaard
Open Tues - Sun 11 AM - 5 PM, Wed 11 AM - 9 PM; cl Mon; Admis Adults 75 Kr, under 18 free; Library with 100,000 vols
Library Holdings: Auction Catalogs; Book Volumes; Exhibition Catalogs; Periodical Subscriptions
Special Subjects: Interior Design, Architecture, Art Education, Art History, Ceramics, Glass, Silver, Textiles, Tapestries, Graphics, Costumes, Pottery, Decorative Arts, Posters, Furniture, Porcelain, Oriental Art, Asian Art, Carpets & Rugs, Baroque Art, Renaissance Art, Embroidery, Laces
Collections: Chinese and Japanese art and handicrafts; European decorative and applied art from the Middle Ages to present - bookbindings, carpets and tapestries, furniture, jewelry, porcelain and pottery, silverware, glass and textiles

M **KOEBENHAVNS MUSEUM,** Museum at Copenhagen, Vesterbrogade 59, DK - 1620 Copenhagen, Denmark; Absalonsgade 3, DK - 1658 Copenhagen, Denmark. Tel 45-33-21-07-72; Fax 45-33-25-07-72; Elec Mail sekr@kbhbymuseum.dk; Internet Home Page Address: www.copenhagen.dk; *Dir* Jette Sandahl
Open daily 10 AM - 5 PM; Admis adults 20 Kr, seniors 10 Kr, children 14 & under & Fri free; Estab 1901; Copenhagen's more than 800 yrs long history, The Soeren Kierleegaard room
Collections: Objects, paintings and models from the history of Copenhagen

M **NATIONALMUSEET,** The National Museum of Denmark, Prinsens Palae, Ny Vestergade 10 Copenhagen, 1220 Denmark; Frederiksholms Kanal 12, Copenhagen, DK 1220 Denmark. Tel 3313 4411; Fax 3251 4800; Internet Home Page Address: www.natmus.dk; *Dir* Per Kristian Madsen
Open Tues - Sun 10 AM - 5 PM, cl Mon; No admis fee; Museum of Cultural History; Average Annual Attendance: 1 million
Collections: Museum has 5 divisions, including Danish historical collection, folk museum, ethnographic collection, classical antiquities collection, royal coin & medal collection; Danish Prehistory (13000 BC - 1050 AD); Middle Ages & Renaissance Denmark (1050-1660); 18th Century Denmark; Stories of Denmark: 1660-2000; The Royal Collection of Coins & Medals; The Collection of Egyptian and Classical Antiquities; Ethnographic Collection; The Children's Museum; The National Museum's Victorian Home
Exhibitions: (06/22/2013-11/17/2013) Viking
Activities: Classes for children; mus shop sells books, reproductions, prints; The Childrens Mus, Ny Vestergade 10,14711 Denmark

M **NY CARLSBERG GLYPTOTEK,** Ny Carlsberg Glyptotek, Dantes Plads 7, Copenhagen, 1556 Denmark. Tel 33-41-81-41; Fax 33-91-20-58; Elec Mail info@glyptoteket.dk; Internet Home Page Address: www.glyptoteket.dk; *Dir* Flemming Friborg; *Pres* Hans Edvard Norregard-Nielsen
Open Tues - Sun 11 AM - 5 PM, cl Mon; Admis 75 Kr, children under 18 & Sun free; Art museum; Average Annual Attendance: 350,000
Collections: Danish & French paintings & sculptures from 19th & 20th centuries; Egyptian, Etruscan, Greek & Roman sculpture
Activities: Mus shop sells books, magazines, reproductions

M **ROSENBORG SLOT,** The Danish Royal Collections, Oster Voldgade 4A, Copenhagen, 1350K Denmark. Tel (+45) 33 15 32 86; Elec Mail museum@dkks.dk; Internet Home Page Address: www.rosenborgslot.dk; *Mus Dir* Jorgen Selmer; *Dir Chamberlain* Henning Fode; *Senior Cur* Jorgen Hein; *Asst Cur* Peter Kristiansen; *Cur* Alex Harms
Open Jan - Apr & Nov - mid-Dec 11 AM - 2 PM, cl Mon; May 10 AM - 4 PM, June - Aug 10 AM - 5 PM, Sept - Oct 10 AM - 4 PM; Admis adults 80 Kr, students & seniors 55 Kr, children 17 & under free; Estab 1833; Museum of Danish royal history from 1600-1850, home of the crown jewels & regalia; Average Annual Attendance: 250,000
Income: DKK 35,000,000 (30% state financed & 70% own income)
Library Holdings: Auction Catalogs; Book Volumes; CD-ROMs; Exhibition Catalogs; Kodachrome Transparencies; Original Documents; Pamphlets; Periodical Subscriptions; Photographs; Prints
Special Subjects: Historical Material
Collections: Crown Jewels; arms, apparel, jewelry & furniture from period 1470-1863
Publications: Guidebooks
Activities: Concerts; lending of original art to other mus; Mus shop sells books, prints & souvenirs

M **STATENS MUSEUM FOR KUNST,** Royal Museum of Fine Arts, Solvgade 48-50, Copenhagen, DK 1307 Denmark. Tel 33-74-84-94; Fax 33-74-84-04; Elec Mail smk@smk.dk; Internet Home Page Address: www.smk.dk; *Dir* Allis Helleland; *Press Coordr* Jacob Fibiger Andersen; *Const Chief Mktg & Communs* Katja Marcuslund
Open Tues - Sun 10 AM - 5 PM, Wed 10 AM - 8 PM, cl Mon; Admis to exhib: individual 75 KR; no admis fee for collections; Estab 1896/National Gallery; The Danish National Gallery; Average Annual Attendance: 350,000

Collections: Danish paintings and sculpture; various other works by 19th and 20th century Scandinavian artists; old masters of Italian, Flemish, Dutch and German Schools; modern French art; 700 years of art history, from 1300-today
Exhibitions: LA Ring on the Edge of the World; Andre Derain
Publications: Publications for each exhib
Activities: Classes for adults & children; lects open to pub; concerts; gallery talks; tours; lending of original objects of art to domestic & foreign museums; book traveling exhibs; originates traveling exhibs; mus shop sells books, magazines & prints; junior mus

M **THORVALDSENS MUSEUM,** BertelThorvaldsens Plads 2, 1213 Copenhagen, Denmark. Tel 33-32-15-32; Elec Mail thm@thorvaldsensmuseum.dk; Internet Home Page Address: www.thorvaldsensmuseum.dk; *Dir* Stig Miss; *Cur* William Gelius; *Cur* Margrethe Floryan; *Cur* Kristine Boggild Johannsen; *Head of Communs* Bettina Weiland; *Head of Educ* Line Esbjorn
Open Tues 10 AM - 5 PM; Admis adults 40 Kr, seniors 30 Kr, children ages 17 & under and Wed free; Estab 1848; Sculptures, paintings, antiquities
Special Subjects: Drawings, Sculpture
Collections: Sculpture & drawings by Bertel Thorvaldsen (1770 - 1844) & his collections of contemporary paintings, drawings & prints; Painting coll containing works by leading European & Scandinavian painters from Thorvaldsen's own time; Thorvaldsen's Collections of ancient artifacts, gems & coins
Activities: Classes for adults & children; lects open to pub; concerts; gallery talks; tours; mus shop sells books, prints, slides, plaster casts

EBELTOFT

M **GLASMUSEET EBELTOFT,** Strandvejen 8, Ebeltoft, 8400 Denmark. Tel 8634-1799; Elec Mail glasmuseet@glasmuseet.dk; Internet Home Page Address: www.glasmuseet.dle; *Exec Dir* Dagmar Brendstrup; *Exhib Coordr* Sandra F Blach; *Head Pub Rels & Communs* Pia S Bittner
Open Tues - Sun Jan - Mar & Nov - Dec 10 AM - 4 PM; cl Mon; Apr - June & Sept - Oct daily 10 AM - 5 PM, July - Aug 10 AM - 6 PM; Admis adults 85 Kr, children 13-17 20 Kr, children 0-12 free; Estab 1986; Contemporary art in glass; Average Annual Attendance: 50,000
Library Holdings: Auction Catalogs; Book Volumes; Exhibition Catalogs; Periodical Subscriptions
Special Subjects: Decorative Arts, Historical Material, Glass, Crafts
Collections: More than 1500 glass objects from over 700 Danish & international artists
Exhibitions: Solo & group exhibs throughout the yr
Publications: Exhib catalogs
Activities: Classes for children; lects open to pub, 4-6 vis lectrs per yr; concerts; gallery talks; tours; originate traveling exhibs worldwide; mus shop sells books, magazines & original art, works of glass

FAABORG

M **FAABORG MUSEUM,** Gronnegade 75, Faaborg, 5600 Denmark. Tel 62-61-06-45; Fax 62-61-06-65; Elec Mail info@faaborgmuseum.dk; Internet Home Page Address: www.faaborgmuseum.dk
Income:

HORSENS

M **HORSENS KUNSTMUSEUM,** Carolinelundsvej 2, Horsens, 8700 Denmark. Tel 76-29-23-70; Elec Mail kunstmuseum@horsens.dk; Internet Home Page Address: www.horsenskunstmuseum.dk
Average Annual Attendance:

HUMLEBAEK

M **LOUISIANA MUSEUM OF MODERN ART,** Gammel Strandvej 13, Humlebaek, 3050 Denmark. Tel +45 49190719; Fax +45 49193505; Elec Mail curatorial@louisiana.dk; Internet Home Page Address: www.louisiana.dk; *Dir* Poul Erik Toejner; *Cur* Kjeld Kjeldsen; *Cur* Anders Kold; *Cur* Helle Crenzien; *Cur* Mette Marcus; *Cur* Kirsten Degel; *Publ* Michael Juul Holm
Open Tues - Fri 11 AM - 10 PM, Sat - Sun - 11 AM - 6 PM, cl Mon; Admis 95 Kr; Estab 1958; Average Annual Attendance: 500,000
Collections: Danish, International & Modern art from 1950, including sculpture & paintings
Activities: Classes for children; concerts; cinema; theatre; lect for members only

ISHOJ

M **ARKEN MUSEUM FOR MODERNE KUNST,** Skovvej 100, Ishoj, 2635 Denmark. Tel 43-54 -02-22; Internet Home Page Address: www.arken.dk/composite-1.htm
Circ

KOLDING

M **TRAPHOLT MUSEUM OF MODERN ART AND DESIGN,** Trapholt, Aeblehaven 23, Kolding, 6000 Denmark. Tel 45-76-30-05-30; Fax 45-76-30-05-33; Elec Mail kunstmuseum@trapholt.dk; Internet Home Page Address: www.trapholt.dk; *Dir* Karen Gron; *Cur* Vera Westergaard; *Cur* Kirk Denson
Open Tues & Thurs - Sun 10 AM - 5 PM, Wed 10 AM - 8 PM, cl Mon; Admis adults 75 Kr, seniors 60 Kr; under 18 free; Estab 1988; Modern art & design; Average Annual Attendance: 65,000

Collections: Collection features Danish visual art; Sculpture, furniture design, applied art and design produced after 1900; National and international artists

RODOVRE

M **HEERUP MUSEUM,** Kirkesvinget 1, Rodovre, 2610 Denmark. Tel 363 78700; Elec Mail heerupmuseum@rk.dk; Internet Home Page Address: www.heerup.dk
Open Tues - Sun 11 AM - 4 PM; Admis adults 35 Kr, students, groups & senior citizens 20 Kr, children under 16, school groups & members no charge
Collections: Works of Henry Heerup

SILKEBORG

M **SILKEBORG KUNSTMUSEUM,** Museum Jorn, Silkeborg, Gudenavej 7-9, DK Silkeborg, 8600 Denmark. Tel 45 86 82 53 88; Fax 45 86 81 51 31; Elec Mail info@silkeborgkunstmuseum.dk; Elec Mail info@museumjorn.dk; Internet Home Page Address: www.silkeborgkunstmuseum.dk; Internet Home Page Address: www.museumjorn.dk; *Dir* Jacob Thage
Open Apr 1 - Oct 31 Tues - Sun 10 AM - 5 PM; Nov 1 - Mar 31 Tues - Fri 12 - 4 PM, Sat - Sun 10 AM - 5 PM; Admis adults 70 DKK, children under 18 no charge
Collections: Danish and European works
Activities: Mus shop sells books, magazines, reproductions, souvenirs, toys, & prints

DOMINICAN REPUBLIC

SANTO DOMINGO

M **GALERIA NACIONAL DE BELLAS ARTES,** National Fine Arts Gallery, Avenida Independencia esq Maximo Gomez, Santo Domingo, Dominican Republic. Tel 687-3300; *Dir* Dr Jose de J Alvarez Valverde
Collections: Paintings and sculptures previously exhibited in the Museo Nacional

M **MUSEO DE ARTE MODERNO,** Av Cesar Nicolas Penson esquina Av Maximo Gomez, Plaza de la Cultura Juan Pablo Duarte Santo Domingo, Dominican Republic. Tel 809-685-2153; Fax 809-682-8280; Elec Mail museo_de_arte_moderno@yahoo.com; Elec Mail museo.moderno@codetel.net.do; Internet Home Page Address: www.museodeartemoderno.org.do; *Dir* Pedro Henriquez Urena
Open Tue - Sun 10 AM - 6 PM; Admis adults 50 peso, students 20 peso
Collections: More than 1000 pieces; paintings, drawings, sculptures, videos, architecture, models, engravings, photographs; Dominican, Caribbean and Latin American art

ECUADOR

QUITO

M **MUSEO MUNICIPAL DE ARTE E HISTORIA ALBERTO MENA CAAMANO,** Civic Museum of Arts and History, Calle Espejo 1147 y Benalcazar, Apdo 17-01-3346 Quito, Ecuador. Tel 584-326; Fax 584 362; *Dir* Alfonso Ortiz Crespo
Collections: Sculptures; paintings; documents

M **MUSEO NACIONAL DE ARTE COLONIAL,** Cuenca St & Mejia St, Quito, Apdo 2555 Ecuador. Tel 212-297; *Dir* Carlos A Rodriguez
Collections: Art from the Escuela Quitena of the Colonial epoch - 17th, 18th and 19th century art and some contemporary art

EGYPT

ALEXANDRIA

M **GRECO-ROMAN MUSEUM,** 51 Museum St, Alexandria, Egypt. Tel (3) 4825820; *Dir* Doreya Said
Library with 15,000 vols
Collections: Exhibits from the Byzantine, Greek and Roman eras

ASWAN

M **NUBIA MUSEUM,** el Fanadek St, Aswan, 81111 Egypt. Tel 20 97 319333; Fax 20 97 317998; Elec Mail nubiamuseum@numibia.net; Internet Home Page Address: www.numibia.net/nubia; *Dir* Ossama Meguid
Admis adults 20LE, children 10LE
Collections: Egyptian artifacts

CAIRO

M **COPTIC MUSEUM,** Old Cairo, Cairo, Egypt. Tel (2) 775-133; *Dir* Mahar Salib
Open daily 9 AM - 5 PM; Library with 6500 vols
Collections: Architecture, bone, ebony, frescos, glass, icons, ivory, manuscripts, metalwork, pottery, sculpture, textiles, woodcarvings

M **EGYPTIAN NATIONAL MUSEUM,** Midan-el-Tahrir Kasr El-Nil, Cairo, Egypt. Tel (2) 775-133; *Dir* Mohammed Saleh
Library with 39,000 vols
Collections: Ancient Egyptian art from prehistoric times through 6th century AD (excluding Coptic & Islamic periods); houses the Department of Antiquities

M **MUSEUM OF ISLAMIC ART,** Ahmed Maher Sq, Bab al-Khalq Cairo, 11638 Egypt. Tel 90-19-30-3901520; *Dir-Gen* Farouk S Asker
Open 9 AM - 4 PM, except Fri 9:30 AM - 11:30 AM & 1:30 PM - 4 PM; Estab 1881; Museum maintains library with 14,000 volumes; Average Annual Attendance: 31,000
Income: government
Collections: Works of art showing evolution of Islamic art up to 1879
Publications: Islamic Archaeological studies, 5 vols

GIZA

M **MOHAMED MAHMOUD KHALIL & HIS WIFE MUSEUM,** 1 Kafour St, Giza, Egypt. Tel +202 33 6 23 78; Fax +202 33 6 23 76
Average Annual Attendance:

EL SALVADOR

SAN SALVADOR

M **MUSEO DE ARTE DE EL SALVADOR,** Final Avenida la Revolucion, Colonia San Benito San Salvador, El Salvador. Tel 503-2243-6099; Fax 503-2243-1726; Elec Mail info.marte@marte.com.sv; Internet Home Page Address: www.marte.org.sv; *Exec Dir* Roberto Galicia; *Prog Dir* Rafael Alas; *Educ Prog Dir* Violeta Renderos; *Mktg Dir* Melida Porras
Open Tues - Sun 10 AM - 6 PM, cl Mon; Admis adults 1.50, students 0.50, under 8 and seniors free, Sun free; Estab 2003; Average Annual Attendance: 50,000
Collections: Three exhibit halls dedicated to temporal national and international work; Great Hall filled with Salvadoran paintings; MARTE's collection mainly formed of Salvadoran works (265)
Exhibitions: Artist of the month from collection
Publications: One pub per yr
Activities: Classes for adults & children; docent training; lects open to pub; 6 vis lectrs per yr; concerts; tours; mus shop sells prints, jewelry, textiles & accessories of local & international

ENGLAND

BATH

M **AMERICAN MUSEUM IN BRITAIN,** Claverton Manor, Bath, BA2 7BD England. Tel (1225) 460503; Fax (1225) 469160; Elec Mail info@americanmuseum.org; Internet Home Page Address: www.americanmuseum.org; *Cur* Laura Beresford; *Librn & Mktg* Cathryn Spence; *Deputy Dir* Julian Blades; *Educ & Visitor Svcs* Laura Brown; *Mem & Friends* Lynne Erskine; *Colls Mgr* Katherine Hebert; *Dir* Richard Wendorf
Open Tues - Sun noon - 5 PM, cl Mon, Aug daily noon - 5 PM; Admis fee adults 8 pounds, seniors 7 pounds, children 5-6 yrs 4.50 pounds, family (2 adults, 2 children) 21.50 pounds; Estab 1961; Regency Manor House built in 1820 ; Average Annual Attendance: 40,000
Library Holdings: Auction Catalogs 400; Audio Tapes 60; Book Volumes approx 10,000; CD-ROMs; Compact Disks; DVDs; Exhibition Catalogs; Manuscripts; Photographs 500; Records 80; Slides 400; Video Tapes 20
Collections: American decorative arts from 17th to 19th centuries; Early printed maps
Publications: America in Britain jour yearly; newsletter biannually
Activities: Classes for adults & children; docent training; lects open to pub, 4 vis lectrs per yr; concerts; gallery talks; tours; original objects of art lent to other mus; mus shop sells books, original art

M **HOLBURNE MUSEUM OF ART,** Great Pulteney St, Bath, BA2 4DB England. Tel (1225) 466669; Fax (1225) 333121; Elec Mail holburne@bath.ac.uk; Internet Home Page Address: www.bath.ac.uk/Holburne; *Dir* Dr Alexander Sturgis; *Cur* Amina Wright; *Educ Officer* Cleo Witt; *Cur Decorative Art* Matthew Winterbottom
Open Tues-Sat 10 AM-5 PM, Sun 2:30 PM-5:30 PM, cl mid Dec-mid Feb; Admis varies; Estab 1916
Collections: Paintings by 17th & 18th century masters, including Gainsborough, Turner, British & Continental; fine art, porcelain & silver
Activities: Educ prog; classes for adults & children; docent training; lects open to pub; 30 vis lectrs per yr; gallery talks; tours; concerts; originates traveling exhibs; mus shop sells books, reproductions, prints

M **VICTORIA ART GALLERY,** Bridge St, Bath, BA2 4AT England. Tel (1225) 477233; Fax (1225) 477231; Elec Mail victoria_enquiries@bathnes.gov.uk; Internet Home Page Address: www.victoriagal.org.uk; *Mgr* Joe Benington; *Colls Mgr* Katherine Wall
Open Tues-Sat 10 AM - 5 PM, Sun 1:30 PM - 5 PM, cl Mon; No admis fee; Estab 1900; a purpose-built facility with permanent collection & temporary exhibs; Average Annual Attendance: 105,000
Purchases: Howard Hodgkin: Silence 1997-2004, Oil on Wood; William Brooker: Pink Chair 1953, Oil on Canvas
Collections: British & European paintings from 17th to 20th century; English pottery, porcelain, antique glass

BIRMINGHAM

M **BIRMINGHAM MUSEUMS TRUST,** (Birmingham Museums and Art Gallery) Birmingham Museums and Art Gallery, Chamberlain Sq, Birmingham, B3 3DH England. Tel (121) 303-2834; Fax (121) 303 1394; Elec Mail bmag.enquiries@birmingham.gov.uk; Internet Home Page Address: www.bmag.org.uk; *Dir Mus Opers* Ann Sumner; *Head Heritage* Chris Rice; *Head Interpretation & Exhib* Toby Watley
Open Mon - Thurs & Sat 10 AM - 5 PM, Fri 10:30 AM - 5 PM, Sun 12:30 - 5 PM; No admis fee, except for some temp exhibs; Estab 1867 Museum & Art Gallery; Average Annual Attendance: 682,000
Income: Birmingham City Council 6M pa, Arts Council England, plus Trusts & charities
Purchases: Purchases made according to published collecting policy
Collections: Fine and applied art, including English works since 17th century, foreign schools from Renaissance, Pre-Raphaelite works; silver, ceramics, coin, textile colls; Old and New World archeology, ethnography and local history colls; branch museums house furniture, machinery and applied arts; Pinto Collection of Treen; Staffordshire Hoard
Exhibitions: ongoing prog of temporary exhibs
Publications: world Art from Birmingham Museums & Art Gallery
Activities: Classes for children in school parties; family activities; lects open to pub; gallery talks; tours; mus shop sells books, reproductions, prints, jewelry & gifts

BRIGHTON

M **ROYAL PAVILION & MUSEUMS,** (Royal Pavilion, Art Gallery and Museums) Brighton Museum & Art Gallery, Royal Pavilion Gardens, Brighton, BN1 1EE England. Tel (03000) 290900; Fax 01273 292871; Elec Mail visitor.services@brighton-hove.gov.uk; Internet Home Page Address: www.brighton-hove-museums.org.uk; *Cur Fine Art* Jenny Lund
Open Tues - Sun & bank holidays 10 AM - 5 PM; cl Mon, Dec 24, Dec 25 & 26, cl for essential maintenance Jan 1 - Apr 22 - 26 2013; No admis fee; Estab 1873 - mus, art gallery, library
Income: Brighton & City Council; owned by local authority, grants & funding
Special Subjects: Drawings, Ceramics, Furniture, Ethnology, Costumes, Crafts, Decorative Arts, Glass
Collections: Fashion & Style, World Art, 20th Century Art & Design; Mr Willett's Popular Pottery & Local History, Fine Art
Exhibitions: Ongoing temporary exhib programming
Activities: Classes for adults & children; lects open to public; Gallery talks; mus shop sells books, reproductions, prints, gen gifts & souvenirs

BRISTOL

M **BRISTOL MUSEUMS AND ART GALLERY,** Queen's Rd, Bristol, BS8 1RL England. Tel (0117) 922 3571; Fax (0117) 922 2047; Elec Mail general_museum@bristol-city.gov.uk; Internet Home Page Address: www.bristol-city.gov.uk/museums; *Divisional Dir, Museums & Heritage* Hilary McGowan
Collections: Fine and applied arts of Great Britain; archaeological and ethnological collection; Oriental Art

CAMBRIDGE

M **UNIVERSITY OF CAMBRIDGE,** The Fitzwilliam Museum, Trumpington St, Cambridge, CB2 1RB England. Tel (01223) 332900; Fax (01223) 332923; Elec Mail fitzmuseum-enquiries@lists.cam.ac.uk; Internet Home Page Address: www.fitzmuseum.cam.ac.uk; *Dir* Dr Timothy Potts; *Keeper of Applied Art* Dr Victoria Avery; *Sr Asst Keeper, Applied Art* Dr James Lin; *Keeper of Antiquities* Dr Lucilla Burn; *Sr Asst Keeper Antiquities* Julie Dawson; *Keeper of Coins and Medals* Dr Mark Blackburn; *Asst Keeper Coins and Medals* Dr Adrian Popescu; *Asst Dir & Keeper of Paintings, Drawings & Prints* David Scrase; *Sr Asst Keeper Paintings, Drawings & Prints* Jane Munro; *Sr Asst Keeper Prints* Craig Hartley; *Keeper of Manuscripts & Printed Books* Dr Stella Panayotova; *Asst Dir Central Serv* Kate Carreno; *Sr Asst Keeper Admin* Thyrza Smith; *Head of Educ* Julia Tozer; *Sr Asst Keeper Antiquities* Dr Sally Ann Ashton; *Asst Keeper Coins & Medals* Dr Martin Allen; *Asst Dir Conservation* Rupert Featherstone
Open Tues - Sat 10 AM - 5 PM, Sun - Mon & Bank Holidays Noon - 5 PM, cl Dec 24 - Dec 26 & Dec 31 - Jan 1; No admis fee; Estab 1848; Mus & gallery; library with 300,000 vols; Average Annual Attendance: 300,000
Collections: European ceramics; Greek, Roman, western Asiatic & Egyptian antiquities; arms & armor, coins, drawings, furniture, illuminated manuscripts, manuscripts, paintings, prints, sculpture, textiles
Activities: Classes for adults & children; dramatic prog; lects open to pub; concerts; gallery talks; tours; lending of original objects of art; mus shop sells books, reproductions, stationery goods & jewelry

DONCASTER

M **DONCASTER MUSEUM AND ART GALLERY,** Chequer Rd, Doncaster, DN1 2AE England. Tel 1302-734293; Fax 1302 73 5409; Elec Mail museum@doncaster.gov.uk; Internet Home Page Address: www.doncaster.gov.uk/museums; *Mus Mgr* C Dalton; *Mus Officer Art & Exhibs* Neil McGregor
Open Mon - Sat 10 AM - 5 PM, Sun 2 PM - 5 PM; No admis fee; Estab 1909; 7 gallery areas with permanent and temporary exhibs; Average Annual Attendance: 78,000
Income: By local authority
Special Subjects: Archaeology, Drawings, Etchings & Engravings, Landscapes, Ceramics, Photography, Porcelain, Portraits, Pottery, Prints, Maps, Painting-British, Painting-French, Sculpture, Prints, Watercolors, African Art, Textiles, Costumes,

Religious Art, Woodcarvings, Woodcuts, Decorative Arts, Posters, Glass, Jewelry, Silver, Marine Painting, Coins & Medals, Tapestries, Painting-Flemish, Laces, Painting-Italian, Antiquities-Roman, Pewter, Reproductions, Painting-Russian
Collections: European painting, ceramics and glass, silver and jewelry; The King's Own Yorkshire Light Infantry Regimental Collection; Archaeology & Natural History
Publications: The Don Pottery, 1801-1893 (March 2001)
Activities: Classes for adults & children; lects open to pub; 20 vis lectrs per yr; concerts; gallery talks; books traveling exhibs 5 per yr; mus shop sells books, prints

EAST MOLESEY

M **HISTORIC ROYAL PALACES,** Hampton Court Palace, East Molesey, KT8 9AU England. Tel (081) 7819500; *Palace Dir* Hugh Player; *Supt Royal Coll* Chris Stevens
Open mid Oct - mid Mar: Mon 10:15 AM - 4:30 PM, Tues - Sun 9:30 AM - 4:30 PM; mid Mar - mid Oct: Mon 10:15 AM - 6 PM, Tues - Sun 9:30 AM - 6 PM; Admis 10.80 pounds; OAP, student 8.20 pounds, child 7.20 pounds; Represents art, architecture & gardens from the Tudor Period to Georgian Period
Special Subjects: Woodcarvings
Collections: Paintings & tapestries, including Andrea Mantegna's 9 paintings of The Triumphs of Caesar
Activities: Classes for adults & children; dramatic progs; lects open to pub; tours; sales of books

KENDAL

M **ABBOT HALL ART GALLERY & MUSEUM OF LAKELAND LIFE & INDUSTRY,** Kendal, LA9 5AL England. Tel (01539) 722464; Fax (01539) 722494; Elec Mail info@abbothall.org.uk; Internet Home Page Address: www.abbothall.org.uk; *Dir* Edward King; *Deputy Dir* Cherrie Trelogan; *Head of Publicity & Mktg* Sandy Kitching; *Head of Finance & Admin* Beryl Tulley
Open Jan 18 - Dec 20 Mon - Sat 10:30 AM - 5 PM 18; Admis adults 4.75 pounds, children & students 3.52 pounds, concessions; Estab 1962; 18th house beside the river bank, 18 rooms plus active modern and contemporary exhib prog; Average Annual Attendance: 35,000
Library Holdings: Cards; Exhibition Catalogs; Pamphlets; Photographs; Sculpture
Collections: Gallery provides changing exhibitions of local and international interest; houses permanent colls of 18th century furniture, paintings and objects d'art; modern paintings; sculpture; drawings; museum features working and social life of the area; 18th century portraits, Esp Romney; watercolors & drawings, including Ruskin, Constable, Turner; lake district landscapes; modern British art; Post-Lucian Freud, Bridget Riley; Paula Rego; Bridget Riley
Publications: Exhibition Catalogues
Activities: Classes for children; lects open to public; books

LEEDS

M **LEEDS MUSEUMS & GALLERIES,** Temple Newsam Rd, Off Selby Rd Leeds, LS15 0AE England. Tel (113) 264 7321; Elec Mail temple.newman.house@leeds.gov.uk; Internet Home Page Address: www.leeds.gov.uk/templenewmanhouse; *Dir* Miss Bobbie Robertson; *Cur* James Lomax; *Asst Cur* Polly Putnam; *Property Mgr* Philip Miles
Open all year 10:30 AM - 5 PM, cl Mon except Bank Holidays; last admis 45 mins before closing; Admis adults 3.70 euro, children 2.70 euro; Estab 1922; mus of decorative art, furniture & paintings; Tudor-Jacobean Mansion; Average Annual Attendance: 40,000
Income: Local Government
Library Holdings: Auction Catalogs; Photographs; Prints; Sculpture
Special Subjects: Decorative Arts, Drawings, Historical Material, Landscapes, Architecture, Art Education, Art History, Ceramics, Glass, Furniture, Gold, Pottery, Painting-American, Prints, Period Rooms, Silver, Textiles, Manuscripts, Painting-British, Painting-European, Painting-French, Tapestries, Sculpture, Watercolors, Costumes, Religious Art, Crafts, Dolls, Jade, Jewelry, Porcelain, Oriental Art, Asian Art, Painting-Dutch, Carpets & Rugs, Ivory, Restorations, Baroque Art, Renaissance Art, Embroidery, Antiquities-Oriental, Painting-Spanish, Painting-Italian, Antiquities-Greek, Cartoons, Pewter
Collections: Old Master and Ingram family paintings; Chippendale furniture, silver, wallpapers
Activities: Classes for adults & children; concerts; gallery talks; tours; mus shop sells books, reproductions, prints
M **Leeds Art Gallery,** The Headrow, Leeds, LS1 3AA England. Tel (113) 247-8256; Fax (113) 244 9689; Elec Mail city.art.gallery@leeds.gov.uk; Internet Home Page Address: leeds.gov.uk/artgallery; *Cur* Nigel Walsh; *Educ Officer* Amanda Phillips; *Acting Prin Keeper* Catherine Hall; *Cur Exhibs* Sarah Brown
Open Mon & Tues, Thurs - Sat 10 AM - 5 PM, Wed Noon - 5 PM, Sun 1 - 5 PM; No admis fee; Estab 1888; Gallery with outstanding collections of British 19th & 20th centuries & changing exhib progs; Average Annual Attendance: 500,000
Collections: English Watercolors; English & European paintings of 19th century; modern British paintings & sculpture
Exhibitions: Temporary exhibition programme
Activities: Educ prog; classes for adults & children; Artspace interactive family zone; lects open to pub; gallery talks; tours; Exten prog Picture Lending Scheme; original objects of art lent to individual & corporate subscribers; originate traveling exhibs; mus shop sells book, reproductions, prints, postcards, souvenirs & other items
M **Lotherton Hall,** Leeds, LS253EB, Aberford, England. Tel (113) 281-3259; Fax (113) 281-2100; Elec Mail michael.thaw@leeds.gov.uk; Internet Home Page Address: www.leeds.gov.uk; *Cur* Adam White; *Keeper* Michael Thaw
Open Mar - Oct daily 10 AM - 5 PM, Nov - Feb daily 10 AM - 4 PM; last admission 45 minutes before cl; Admis 5, concessions 4; Historic house open as mus with gardens; Gascoigne family coll; special costume ; Average Annual Attendance: 30,000
Income: Leeds City Council (owned)

Collections: Gascoigne Collection of 17th to 20th century paintings, ceramics, silver, furniture, jewelry costumes; British historic furniture; silver; ceramics
Activities: Classes for adults & children; dramatic progs; six lectrs per yr; concerts; gallery talks; tours; mus shop sells books, reproductions, prints

LEICESTER

M **LEICESTERSHIRE HERITAGE SERVICES,** Environment & Heritage Services, Leicestershire County Council, County Hall, Glenfield Leicester, LE3 8TD England. Tel (0116) 265-6781; Fax (0116) 265-6844; Elec Mail museums@leics.gov.uk; Internet Home Page Address: www.leics.gov.uk/index/community/museums.htm; *Head, Heritage Svcs* Heather Broughton
Open Mon - Sat 10 AM - 4:40, Sun 2 PM - 5 PM
Collections: Major special collections include 18th, 19th and 20th century British Art, German Expressionists (largest public collection in Britain); European Art from Renaissance to present; contemporary art

LINCOLN

M **LINCOLNSHIRE COUNTY COUNCIL,** (Lincolnshire City Council) Library & Heritage Services, City Hall, Beaumont Fee Lincoln, LN1 1DF England. Tel 01522-550586; Fax 01522-516720; Elec Mail customer_services@lincolnshire.gov.uk; Internet Home Page Address: www.lincolnshire.gov.uk; *Head of Libraries & Heritage* Jonathan Platt
Oversees 3 museums & Lincolnshire Archives, 49 libraries, 10 mobile libraries, 3 hospital libraries, 2 prison libraries, 1 Immigration & Repatriation Centre Library; Average Annual Attendance: 350,000
Income: Euro 8.8m net cost to Lincolnshire County Council
Library Holdings: Book Volumes; CD-ROMs; Cards; Clipping Files; Compact Disks; DVDs; Manuscripts; Maps; Memorabilia; Original Art Works; Original Documents; Other Holdings; Pamphlets; Periodical Subscriptions; Photographs; Prints; Records; Reels; Reproductions; Sculpture; Slides; Video Tapes
Special Subjects: Archaeology, Ceramics, Glass, Metalwork, Furniture, Photography, Porcelain, Portraits, Pottery, Period Rooms, Manuscripts, Maps, Painting-British, Sculpture, Watercolors, Ethnology, Costumes, Crafts, Decorative Arts, Dolls, Coins & Medals, Medieval Art, Leather, Military Art
Collections: Over 3 million items of historical interest relating to Lincolnshire
Activities: Classes for adults & children; lects open to pub; concerts; gallery talks; tours; lending of original objects of art to pub & pvt bodies & individuals; mus shop sells books, magazines, original art, reproductions, & prints
M **Museum of Lincolnshire Life,** Burton Rd, Lincoln, LN1 3LY England. Tel (1522) 528448; *Prin Keeper* J Finch; *Keeper Collections Mgmt* A Martin; *Keeper Visitor & Community Serv* K Howard
Collections: Displays illustrating the social, agricultural & industrial history of Lincolnshire over the last three centuries
M **The Collection: Art & Archaeology in Lincolnshire,** Danes Terr, Lincoln, LN2ILP England. Tel (1522) 550990; Elec Mail thecollection@lincolnshire.gov.uk; Internet Home Page Address: www.thecollectionmuseum.com; *District Mgr* William Mason; *Keeper of Art* Dawn Heywood; *Keeper of Archaeology* Antony Lee
Open 10 AM - 4 PM; No admis fee; Art gallery estab 1927, Museum estab 1906 (new bldg opened 2005); Collection brings together award winning Archaeology Mus & region's premier art gallery, The Usher; Average Annual Attendance: 120,000
Special Subjects: Archaeology, Decorative Arts, Drawings, Etchings & Engravings, Landscapes, Ceramics, Glass, Metalwork, Furniture, Gold, Prints, Sculpture, Watercolors, Ethnology, Costumes, Pottery, Portraits, Silver, Coins & Medals, Miniatures, Antiquities-Egyptian, Antiquities-Greek, Antiquities-Roman, Mosaics, Enamels
Collections: Exhibits the Usher coll of watches, miniatures, porcelain; special coll of works by Peter De Wint; a general coll of paintings, sculpture & decorative art; coll of coins & tokens from Lincolnshire; archaeological coll spanning 300,000 yrs from stone age to later medieval period; geology, ethnography, arms & armour
Activities: Classes for adults & children; lectrs open to pub; tours; mus shop sells books, magazines & prints

LIVERPOOL

M **WALKER ART GALLERY,** William Brown St, Liverpool, L3 8EL England. Tel (151) 478-4199; Fax (151) 478-4190; Elec Mail thewalker@liverpoolmuseums.org.uk; Internet Home Page Address: www.liverpoolmuseums.org.uk; *Dir Art Galleries* Sandra Penketh; *Head Fine Art* Ann Bukantas; *Cur Fine Art* Xanthe Brooke; *Cur Brit Art* Laura MacCulloch; *Cur Metal Work & Glass* Alyson Pollard; *Cur Costume & Textiles* Pauline Rushton; *Asst Cur (DEC Art)* David Moffat
Open 10 AM - 5 PM daily; 1878; Historic, modern, & contemporary fine & applied arts from 12th - 21st century; Average Annual Attendance: 250,000
Income: (funded direct from UK government)
Special Subjects: Afro-American Art, Decorative Arts, Drawings, Etchings & Engravings, Landscapes, Ceramics, Glass, Furniture, Porcelain, Pottery, Prints, Silver, Manuscripts, Painting-British, Painting-European, Sculpture, Tapestries, Graphics, Hispanic Art, Watercolors, Bronzes, Costumes, Religious Art, Woodcuts, Portraits, Metalwork, Painting-Dutch, Ivory, Baroque Art, Miniatures, Painting-Flemish, Painting-Polish, Renaissance Art, Medieval Art, Painting-Spanish, Painting-Italian, Stained Glass, Painting-German, Painting-Scandinavian
Collections: English & European drawings, paintings, prints, sculpture, watercolors, incl colls of Italian & Netherlandish primitives; pop art; 17th - 19th century European
Exhibitions: 3 major shows per yr
Activities: Classes for adults & children; concerts; gallery talks; tours; lending of original art to Northwest England region; originates traveling exhibs; mus shop sells books, reproductions, prints, postcards, jewelry & ceramics; big art for little children

LONDON

M **BRITISH MUSEUM,** Great Russell St, London, WC1B 3DG England. Tel 020 7323 8000; Elec Mail info@thebritishmuseum.ac.uk; Internet Home Page Address: www.britishmuseum.org; *Dir* Neil MacGregor
Open Mon - Sun10 AM - 5:30 PM, Fri selected galleries open to 8 PM; No admis fee; fee for spec exhibitions; Estab 1753
Collections: Ancient Egypt & The Sudan; Ancient Near East; Greek & Roman; Prehistory & Europe; Asia; Africa, Oceania & the Americas; coins & medals, prints & drawings
Activities: Educ prog; lects open to pub; mus shop

M **THE COURTAULD INSTITUTE OF ART,** The Courtauld Gallery, Somerset House, Strand London, WC2R 0RN England. Tel (020) 78482526; Fax (020) 7848 2589; Elec Mail galleryinfo@courtauld.ac.uk; Internet Home Page Address: www.courtauld.ac.uk; *Dir* Deborah Swallow; *Head of Gallery* Ernst Vegelin; *Cur Drawings* Stephanie Buck; *Asst Cur Works on Paper* Rachel Sloan; *Cur Decorative Arts* Alexandra Gerstein; *Cur 20th Century Art* Barnaby Wright; *Registrar* Julia Blanks; *Paper Conservator* Kate Edmondson; *Paintings Conservator* Graeme Barraclough
Open Mon - Sun 10 AM - 6 PM; Admis 6 pounds, concessions 4.50 euro; Estab 1932; Collection of paintings, prints, drawings & decorative arts 14th - 20th century; Average Annual Attendance: 250,000
Special Subjects: Decorative Arts, Drawings, Ceramics, Portraits, Prints, Painting-European, Painting-French, Sculpture, Bronzes, Landscapes, Silver, Painting-British, Baroque Art, Painting-Flemish, Renaissance Art, Medieval Art, Painting-Italian, Islamic Art, Painting-German
Collections: Samuel Courtauld Collection of Impressionist & Post-Impressionist Art; other colls include old masters, early 20th century French and English paintings, modern British art, English landscape paintings and drawings; 550 paintings, ranging from 1300-1950; 500 items of sculpture, furniture & decorative art; 7000 drawings; 20,000 prints
Exhibitions: 3 exhibs per yr
Activities: Classes for adults & children; lect open to public; gallery talks; tours; junction outreach to schools & hospitals; originates traveling exhibs; mus shop sells books

M **DALI UNIVERSE,** County Hall Gallery, Riverside Bldg, County Hall London, SE1 7PB England. Tel 0870 744 7485; Fax 020 7620 3120; Elec Mail operations@countyhallgallery.com; Internet Home Page Address: www.daliuniverse.com;
Open 10 AM - 6:30 PM; Admis adults £12, senior citizens, students and children 12& over £10, children under 12 no charge
Collections: Works by Dali

M **THE DESIGN MUSEUM,** 28 Shad Thames, London, SE1 2YD England. Tel 020-7403-6933; Fax 0870-909-1909; Elec Mail info@designmuseum.org; Internet Home Page Address: www.designmuseum.org; *Dir* Deyan Sudjic
Open daily 10 AM - 5:45 PM; Admis adults 11 pounds, concessions 10 pounds, students 7 pounds, under 12 free; Estab 1989; International design mus; Average Annual Attendance: 250,000; Mem: 2,000
Collections: Devoted to contemporary design in every format; furniture, graphics, architecture and industrial design
Activities: Classes for adults & children; lects open to pub; gallery talks; tours; Design of the Year award; organize traveling exhibs; mus shop sells books, magazines, original art, reproductions, prints & slides

M **DULWICH PICTURE GALLERY,** A/B, Gallery Rd, London, SE21 7AD England. Tel (0208) 693-5254; Fax (0208) 299-8700; Elec Mail enquiries@dulwichpicturegallery.org.uk; *Dir* Ian DeJardin; *Dir Learning & Pub Affairs* Gillian Wolfe; *Head of Communications* Ellie Manwell; *Dir Develop & Communs* Lily Harriss; *Dir Finance* Paula Dimond; *Chief Cur* Xavier Bray
Open Tues - Fri 10 AM - 5 PM, Sat & Sun, bank holidays & Good Friday 11 AM - 5 PM, cl Mon except bank holiday Mondays; Admis Exhib: adult 11 euro, senior 10 euro; Permanent Coll: adult 6 euro, senior 5 euro, Srs, concessions fee; Estab 1811; 17th & 18th century European Old Master paintings in oldest public gallery in England; Average Annual Attendance: 150,000; Mem: Friends of Dulwich Picture Gallery
Library Holdings: Book Volumes; Clipping Files; Exhibition Catalogs; Original Documents; Pamphlets; Photographs; Prints; Slides
Collections: Collections of Old Masters from 1626 onwards, including Claude, Cuyp, Gainsborough, Murillo, Poussin, Raphael, Rembrandt, Rubens, Teniers, Tiepolo, Van Dyck, Watteau & others
Exhibitions: (10/16/2013-12/01/2014) An American in London: Whistler & the Thames
Publications: catalogues
Activities: Classes for adults & children; lects open to pub; concerts; gallery talks; tours; small vis attraction of the yr 2005; Sandford Award for Heritage Educ 2006; extension prog in London; book traveling exhibs vary; organize traveling exhibs; mus shop sells books, magazines, reproductions, prints, gift items, exhib posters, merchandise, jewelry, cards & Christmas gifts

M **ENGLISH HERITAGE,** (Victoria and Albert Museum) Cromwell Rd, South Kensington London, SW7 2RL England. Tel 207942-2000; Fax 207942-2266; Elec Mail vanda@vam.ac.uk; Internet Home Page Address: www.vam.ac.uk; *Dir* Dr Martin Roth
Open daily 10 AM - 5:45 PM; No admis fee to the mus, some exhib & events carry a separate charge; Estab 1857, to enable everyone to enjoy its coll & explore the cultures that created them, and to inspire those who shape contemporary design; Average Annual Attendance: 2,700,000
Income: Grant-in-aid from government plus fundraising
Special Subjects: Drawings, Glass, Furniture, Textiles, Sculpture, Prints, Ceramics, Woodcarvings, Metalwork
Collections: Fine and applied arts of all countries, periods and styles, including Oriental art. European colls are mostly post-classical, architectural details, art of the book, bronzes, calligraphy, carpets, ceramics, clocks, costumes, cutlery,

drawings, embroidery, enamels, engravings, fabrics, furniture, glass, gold and silversmiths' work, ironwork, ivories, jewelry, lace, lithographs, manuscripts, metalwork, miniatures, musical instruments, oil paintings, posters, pottery and porcelain, prints, sculpture, stained glass, tapestries, theatre art, vestments, watches, watercolors, woodwork
Activities: Classes for adults & children; lects open to pub; concerts; gallery talks; tours; fellowships; originates traveling exhibs to mus & galleries in UK & internationally; mus shop sells books, magazines, original art; reproductions & prints

M **Apsley House (Wellington Collection),** Hyde Park Corner, London, W1J 7NT England. Tel 011-44-207-4995676; Fax 011-44-207-4936576; Internet Home Page Address: www.english-heritage.eng.uk; *Keeper of the Wellington Coll* Dr Josephine Oxley
Open please see website; Admis please see website; Opened to the public 1952; Old Masters, silver, sculpture & porcelain; Average Annual Attendance: 50,000
Income: Income from govt grants
Special Subjects: Architecture, Ceramics, Furniture, Porcelain, Portraits, Period Rooms, Silver, Painting-British, Painting-European, Painting-French, Sculpture, Decorative Arts, Metalwork, Painting-Dutch, Coins & Medals, Painting-Flemish, Painting-Spanish, Gold
Collections: Paintings, silver, porcelain, sculpture, orders and decorations, and personal relics of the first Duke of Wellington
Activities: Classes for children; lects open to pub; lects for mems only; concerts; gallery talks; shop sells books, reproductions, slides

M **V&A Museum of Childhood,** Cambridge Heath Rd, London, E2 9PA England. Tel 0208 983 5200; Fax 020-8983-5225; Elec Mail moc@vam.ac.uk; Internet Home Page Address: www.museumofchildhood.org.uk; *Cur, Dir* Rhian Harris
Open 10 AM - 5:45 PM; No admis fee; Estab 1972; National Museum of Childhood; Average Annual Attendance: 390,000
Income: Government funded
Library Holdings: Auction Catalogs; Memorabilia; Original Documents; Periodical Subscriptions
Special Subjects: Drawings, Photography, Costumes, Crafts, Dolls, Furniture, Jewelry, Embroidery
Collections: Dolls, ceramics, costumes, textiles, furniture & toys; articles related to childhood; British Toy Making Archive
Activities: Classes for adults & children, art activities, inset envelopes for address and spec events on school holidays & weekends; drop in activities & workshops for families & children; lects open to pub; gallery talks; tours; lending of original objects of art; organize traveling exhibs; mus shop sells books, magazines

M **INSTITUTE OF CONTEMPORARY ARTS,** 12 Carlton House Terrace, London, SW1Y 5AH England. Tel 44-0-20-7930-0493; Internet Home Page Address: www.ica.org.uk; *Dir* Ekow Eshun
Open Mon Noon - 11 PM, Tues - Sat Noon - 1 AM, Sun Noon - 10:30 PM; Admis Mon - Fri 2 pounds, Sat - Sun 3 pounds
Collections: Changing exhibits of contemporary art in various media; painting, graphic art, video, photography, film

M **NATIONAL GALLERY,** Trafalgar Sq, London, WC2N 5DN England. Tel (02) 7747-2885; Fax (02) 7930-4764; Elec Mail information@ng.london.org.uk; Internet Home Page Address: www.nationalgallery.org.uk; *Dir* Nicholas Penny; *Chair* Mark Getty
Open daily 10 AM - 6 PM, Fri until 9 PM; No admis fee, some charging exhibs (temp shows); Estab 1824; Houses one of the great collections of Western European painting in the world; Average Annual Attendance: 4,300,000
Collections: Principal schools, British, Dutch, Early Netherlandish, French, German, Italian; Western European painting up to early 20th century
Activities: Classes for adults & children; concerts; gallery talks; tours; sales shop sells books, magazines, prints

M **NATIONAL PORTRAIT GALLERY,** 2 St Martin's Place, London, WC2H 0HE England. Tel 207-306-0055; Fax 207-306-0056; Internet Home Page Address: www.npg.org.uk; *Chmn Trustees* Sir William Proby Bt, CBE, DL; *Dir* Sandy Nairne; *Deputy Dir* Pim Baxter
Open daily 10 AM - 6 PM, Thurs & Fri 10 AM - 9 PM; No admis fee; ticket prices for special exhibs vary; Estab 1856; home to the largest Collection of portraiture in the world, featuring men & women who have made a significant contribution to British history & culture from the Middle Ages until the present day; Average Annual Attendance: 2 million; Mem: Membership & patrons scheme
Library Holdings: Clipping Files; Exhibition Catalogs; Manuscripts; Original Documents; Photographs; Prints; Reproductions
Special Subjects: Drawings, Portraits, Prints, Photography, Sculpture, Painting-British
Collections: National Collection of portraits spanning last 500 years, including sculpture, photographs & digital media
Publications: Vanity Fair Portraits; Beatles to Bowie: The 60s Exposed; Twiggy: A Life in Photographs; Lucian Freud Portraits; Man Ray Portraits
Activities: Educ prog; classes for adults & children; school groups/workshops; lects open to pub; concerts; gallery talks; tours; competitions; annual BP Portrait Award; annual Taylor Wessing Photographic Portrait Prize; lending of original objects of art to touring exhibs; originate traveling exhibs to UK mus & galleries & international orgs; mus shop sells book, magazines, reproductions, prints, slides & other gift items

M **QUEEN'S GALLERY,** Buckingham Palace Rd, London, SW1A 1AA England. Tel (20) 7839-1377; Internet Home Page Address: www.royal.gov.uk

M **ROYAL ACADEMY OF ARTS,** Burlington House, Piccadilly London, W1J 0BD England. Tel 20-7300-8000; Fax 20-7300-8001; Elec Mail webmaster@royalacademy.org.uk; Internet Home Page Address: www.royalacademy.org.uk; *Pres* Christopher Le Brun; *Chief Exec & Secy* Charles Saumarez Smith, CBE
Open Sat - Thurs 10 AM - 6 PM, Fri 10 AM - 10 PM; Admis Varied; Estab 1768; Average Annual Attendance: 750,000
Income: Exhib ticket sales & pvt corporate sponsors
Library Holdings: Book Volumes; Exhibition Catalogs; Original Documents

Collections: Paintings, prints, architectural collection
Exhibitions: Six exhibs per yr
Publications: Exhib Catalogues for exhib listed
Activities: Educ prog; classes for adults & children; 3 yr post-grad arts course (full time); lects open to the pub; gallery talks; lend original objects of art to other galleries for exhibs; sales shop sells books, magazines, cards, jewelry & clothing

L **Library,** Burlington House, Piccadilly London, W1J 0BD England. Tel 020-7300-5737; Fax 020-7300-5650; Elec Mail library@royalacademy.org.uk; Internet Home Page Address: www.royalacademy.org.uk; *Libr* Adam Waterton; *Asst Librn* Miranda Stead
Open Tues - Fri 10 AM - 1 PM & 2 PM - 5 PM; No admis fee; Estab 1768
Library Holdings: Book Volumes 40,000; Clipping Files 500; Exhibition Catalogs 8,000; Manuscripts; Other Holdings Engravings; Fine arts books 20,000; Manuscripts; Original drawings

M **SOUTH LONDON GALLERY,** 65 Peckham Rd, London, SE5 8UH England. Tel +44(0) 20 7703 6120; Fax +44(0) 20 7252 4730; Elec Mail mail@southlondongallery.org; Internet Home Page Address: www.southlondongallery.org; *Gallery Dir* Margot Heller; *Mktg & Communs* Sangeeta Sathe; *Prog Mgr* Simon Parris; *Educ & Outreach Mgr* Frances Williams; *Assoc Cur* Anne-Sophie Dinant
Open Tues - Sun noon - 6 PM, cl Mon; No admis fee; Estab 1891; Since 1993 the gallery has staged ground-breaking solo & group exhibitions of works by artists such as Gilbert & George, Tracey Emin, Gavin Turk, Mona Hatoum, Bill Viola, Barbara Kruger, Tom Friedman; Average Annual Attendance: 30,000
Collections: Contemporary British art; 20th century original prints; paintings of the Victorian period; topographical paintings & drawings of local subjects permanent coll exhibited periodically
Exhibitions: Exhibitions from permanent collection
Activities: Educ prog; classes for adults & children; lects open to pub; concerts; gallery talks; tours; shop sells books & postcards

M **TATE GALLERY,** Millbank, London, SW1P 4RG England. Tel (207) 887-8000; *Dir* Nicholas Serota
Open daily 10 AM - 5:50 PM, Fri 10 AM - 10 PM; No admis fee
Collections: Works of Blake, Constable, Hogarth, Turner and the Pre-Raphaelites; British painting from the 16th century to present; modern foreign painting from Impressionism onward; modern sculpture; collection totals 12,000, including 5500 prints

M **THE WALLACE COLLECTION,** Hertford House, Manchester Sq London, W1U 3BN England. Tel (20) 7563-9500; Fax (20) 7224-2155; Elec Mail collections@wallacecollection.org; Internet Home Page Address: www.wallacecollection.org; *Dir* Dr Christopher Martin Vogtherr
Open daily 10 AM - 5 PM; No admis fee; Estab 1900; Circ Reference library; Average Annual Attendance: 380,000
Income: Government of UK plus 30% generated income
Purchases: Cl coll, purchases not permitted
Library Holdings: Auction Catalogs; Book Volumes; Exhibition Catalogs; Fiche; Periodical Subscriptions; Reels
Special Subjects: Decorative Arts, Art History, Ceramics, Glass, Portraits, Silver, Bronzes, Manuscripts, Painting-British, Painting-European, Painting-French, Sculpture, Watercolors, Porcelain, Painting-Dutch, Ivory, Miniatures, Painting-Flemish, Painting-Italian, Painting-German, Enamels
Collections: Arms & Armour; French Furniture; Sevres Porcelain; paintings & works of art of all European schools; miniatures; sculpture; maiolica, renaissance glass & enamels
Publications: The Noble Art of the Sword: Fashion & Fencing in Renaissance Europe; Catalogue of European Arms & Armour; Catalogue of Glass & Limoges Painted Enamels
Activities: Classes for adults & children; docent training; lects open to pub; concerts; gallery talks; mus shop sells books, reproductions & other items

M **WHITECHAPEL ART GALLERY,** 80-82 Whitechapel High St, London, E1 7QX England. Tel (020) 7522 7888; Fax (020) 7377 1685; Elec Mail info@whitechapel.org; Internet Home Page Address: www.whitechapel.org; *Dir* Iwona Blazwick; *Press Officer* David Gleeson; *Head Admin* Alison Digance; *Finance Officer* Raksha Patel
Open Tues - Sun 11 AM - 6 PM; Thurs till 9 PM; No admis fee except one spec exhib per year; Estab 1901; Established & emerging contemporary artists; Mem: Membership fees start at £ 40
Collections: Changing exhibitions, primarily of modern & contemporary art
Activities: Classes for adults, classes for children; lects for members only, gallery talks, tours; mus shop sells books, magazines, prints

M **WILLIAM MORRIS GALLERY,** Lloyd Park, Forest Rd London, E17 4PP England. Tel 0208 496 4390; Elec Mail wmg.enquires@walthamforest.gov.uk; Internet Home Page Address: www.wmgallery.org.uk; *Mus, Gallery & Archives Mgr* Anna Mason; *Exhib & Coll Officer* Carien Kremer; *Activities & Events Officer* Rebecca Jacobs; *Learning & Outreach Officer* Sharon Trotter; *Operations Support Officer* Linda Weston
Open Wed - Sun 10 AM - 5 PM, Tues pre-booked groups & school visits 10 AM - 5 PM; No admis fee; Estab 1950; Promotes the life, work & continuing influence of William Morris through its internationally renowned coll; Average Annual Attendance: 130,000; Mem: Friends of the William Morris Gallery
Income: Local government
Library Holdings: Auction Catalogs; Book Volumes; CD-ROMs; Exhibition Catalogs; Manuscripts; Memorabilia; Original Art Works; Original Documents; Pamphlets; Periodical Subscriptions; Photographs; Prints; Records
Special Subjects: Ceramics, Furniture, Textiles, Architecture, Drawings, Crafts, Woodcuts, Decorative Arts, Carpets & Rugs, Tapestries, Embroidery, Stained Glass
Collections: Morris's original designs, textiles, wallpapers, furniture, stained glass, ceramics, metalwork, books, archival materials, personal items (coffee cup & satchel); Works by Edward Burne-Jones, Dante Gabriel Rossetti & Philip Webb also represented; Wide range coll of arts & crafts material (includes works by Arthur Heygate Mackmurdo & the Century Guild, William De Morgan, Walter Crane, May Morris, George Jack, Frank Brangwyn & Christopher Whall & others)

Exhibitions: (10/12/2013-12/15/2013) Giles Deacon; (01/18/2014-03/30/2014) English Magic - We sit starving amidst our gold, Jeremy Deller: British Pavilion, Venice Bienalle
Publications: William Morris in 50 Objects, by Anna Mason & Carien Kremer
Activities: Classes for adults & children; dramatic progs; docent training; lects opent to pub; 9 vis lectrs per yr; concerts; gallery talks; tours; awards, ArtFund: Mus of the Year 2013, Mus & Heritage Awards: Best Permanent Exhib; mus shop sells books, magazines, original art by local artists, prints, postcards, stationery, accessories & clothing, branded items, household, tiles & ceramics, jewellery, exhib merchandise

MANCHESTER

M **MANCHESTER CITY GALLERIES,** (Wythenshawe Hall, City Art Galleries) Manchester Art Gallery, Mosley St, Manchester, M23 JL England. Tel 0161 235 8888; Fax 0161 274 7145; Internet Home Page Address: www.manchestergalleries.org; *Head of Galleries* Moira Stevenson
Open Tues - Sun 10 AM - 5 PM; No admis fee; Estab1882; reopened following major refurbishment in 2002
Income: owned & managed by Manchester city council
Special Subjects: Decorative Arts, Painting-British, Crafts, Painting-European, Silver
Collections: British art; English costume, enamels, silver and decorative arts; Old Master and Dutch 17th century painting; pre-Raphaelite painting
Activities: Classes for adults & children; lectrs open to the public; lectrs for mems only; gallery talks; tours; mus shop sells books, reproductions, prints

M **UNIVERSITY OF MANCHESTER,** Whitworth Art Gallery, Oxford Rd, Manchester, M15 6ER England. Tel 0161-275-7450; Fax 0161-275-7451; Elec Mail whitworth@manchester.ac.uk; Internet Home Page Address: www.manchester.ac.uk/whitworth; *Dir* Dr Maria Balshaw
Open Mon - Sat 10 AM - 5 PM; Sun 12 noon - 4 PM; No admis fee; Estab 1889; Collections of fine art & design; Average Annual Attendance: 87,000
Income: 130,000
Library Holdings: Exhibition Catalogs
Special Subjects: Portraits, Prints, Textiles, Painting-British, Drawings, Watercolors, Etchings & Engravings, Embroidery
Collections: British drawings and watercolors; contemporary British paintings and sculpture; Old Master and modern prints; textiles, wallpapers
Exhibitions: Programs change regularly, see website for latest info
Activities: Classes for adults & children; family workshops; lects open to pub; 10-20 vis lectrs per yr; concerts; gallery talks; tours; mus shop sells books, magazines, reproductions, prints, gifts, postcards

NEWCASTLE-UPON-TYNE

M **TYNE AND WEAR ARCHIVES & MUSEUMS,** Laing Art Gallery, Newcastle Discovery, New Bridge St Newcastle-upon-Tyne, NE1 8AG England. Tel (0191) 2327734; Fax (0191) 222 0952; Elec Mail laing@twmuseums.org.uk; Internet Home Page Address: www.twmuseums.org.uk; *Dir Tyne & Wear Museums* Alec Coles; *Cur Laing Art Gallery* Julie Milne
Open Mon - Sat 10 AM - 5 PM, Sun 2 - 5 PM; No admis fee; Estab 1904; The Laing Art Gallery is the premier art gallery in Newcastle. Show exhibitions of contemporary and historical art; Average Annual Attendance: 295,000
Collections: British oil paintings since 1700 (with works by Burne-Jones, Gainsborough, Landsear, Reynolds, Turner); British prints & watercolors; British (especially local) ceramics, costume, glass, pewter, silver of all periods; modern works by Ben Nicholson, Henry Moore & Stanley Spencer
Activities: Educ prog; classes for adults & children; 40 vis lectrs per yr; tours; lending of original objects of art to various galleries; mus shop sells books, magazines, original art, reproductions, prints, original craft & design

M **Sunderland Museum & Winter Gardens,** Burdon Rd, Sunderland, SR1 1PP England. Tel 191-5532323; Tel 180010191553 (text phone); Fax 191-5537828; Elec Mail info@sunderlandmuseum.org.uk; Internet Home Page Address: www.sunderlandmuseum.org.uk; *Mgr* Jo Cunningham; *Learning Officer* Jennie Lambert; *Keeper of Art* Shaura Gregg; *Keeper of Art History* Martin Rovtledge
Open Mon - Sat 10 AM - 5 PM, Sun 2 - 5 PM; No admis fee; Estab 1846; mus, art gallery, winter gardens; Average Annual Attendance: 300,000; Mem: Friends of Sunderland Museums (FOSUMS)
Income: local authority
Special Subjects: Archaeology, Decorative Arts, Drawings, Etchings & Engravings, Landscapes, Marine Painting, Ceramics, Glass, Photography, Portraits, Pottery, Prints, Silver, Textiles, Woodcuts, Painting-British, Watercolors, Ethnology, Porcelain, Historical Material, Embroidery
Collections: Local history, pottery, fine art, natural history & archaeology
Activities: Classes for adults & children; lects open to pub; awards; mus shop sells books, magazines, reproductions, prints, unique gifts

M **Shipley Art Gallery,** Prince Consort Rd, Newcastle, England. Tel 191-477-1495
Collections: Contemporary craft & paintings from the old masters

M **South Shields Museum & Art Gallery,** Ocean Rd, Newcastle, England. Tel 191-456-8740
Collections: Local art history

NEWPORT

M **BOROUGH OF NEWPORT MUSEUM AND ART GALLERY,** John Frost Sq, Newport, NP9 1HZ England. Tel (1633) 840064; Fax (1633) 222615; *Cur* Robert Trett
Open Mon - Thur 9:30 AM - 2 PM, Fri 9:30 AM - 4:30 PM, Sat 9:30 AM - 4 PM; No admis fee
Collections: Early English watercolors; oil paintings by British artists; local archeology (especially Roman); natural & social history

OXFORD

M **MODERN ART OXFORD,** 30 Pembroke St, Oxford, OX1 1BP England. Tel
(01865) 722733; Fax (01865) 722573; Elec Mail info@modernartoxford.org.uk;
Internet Home Page Address: www.modernartoxford.org.uk; *Dir* Andrew Nairne;
Cur Suzanne Cotter; *Head Educ* Sarah Mosop; *Head Develop* Katie Harding;
Head Mktg Kirsty Kelso
Open Tues - Sat 10 AM - 5 PM, Sun 12 - 5 PM, cl Mon; No admis fee; Purpose
to pioneer progs of contemp art; Library with 15,000 vols; Average Annual
Attendance: 200,000; Mem: 300 mems; 20 pounds, (30 pounds concessions)
Income: Uk charity reg; public funding
Library Holdings: Exhibition Catalogs; Periodical Subscriptions
Exhibitions: Features changing international exhibitions of 20th century painting,
photography, prints, sculpture, drawing, film & video
Activities: Classes for adults & children; lects open to pub; 10 vis lectrs per yr;
concerts; gallery talks; tours; mus shop sells books, magazines, prints

M **OXFORD UNIVERSITY,** Ashmolean Museum, Beaumont St, Oxford, OX1 2PH
England. Tel (01865) 278000; Fax (01865) 278018; Internet Home Page Address:
www.ashmol.ox.ac.uk; *Dir* Dr Christopher Brown
Open Tues - Sat 10 AM - 5 PM, Sun noon - 5 PM, bank holidays 10 AM - 5 PM,
cl Mon; No admis fee; Estab 1683
Collections: British, European, Egyptian, Mediterranean & Near Eastern
archaeology; Chinese Bronzes; Chinese & Japanese porcelain, painting & lacquer;
Dutch, English, Flemish, French & Italian oil paintings; Indian sculpture &
painting; Hope Collection of engraved portraits; Tibetan, Indian and Islamic art
objects; collection of coins from various countries and times; Old Master and
modern drawings, prints and watercolors

PLYMOUTH

M **PLYMOUTH CITY MUSEUM AND ART GALLERY,** Drake Circus,
Plymouth, PL4 8AJ England. Tel (01752) 304774; Fax (01752) 304775; Elec Mail
plymouth.museum@plymouth.gov.uk; Internet Home Page Address:
www.plymouthmuseum.gov.uk; *Cur* Nicola Moyle
Open Tues - Fri 10 AM - 5:30 PM, Sat & Bank Holiday Mon 10 AM - 5 PM; No
admis fee; Estab 1838 to illustrate arts of the West Country; Average Annual
Attendance: 70,000
Collections: The Clarendon Collection of Portraits of 16th & 17th Century
English worthies; Collection of Cookworthy's Plymouth & Bristol Porcelain; The
Cottonian Collection of early printed & illuminated books
Activities: Classes for adults & children, dramatic progs, concerts & gallery talks;
lects open to pub; books, magazines, reproductions, prints, gifts & souvenirs

SHEFFIELD

M **FRIENDS OF BISHOPS HOUSE,** (Weston Park Museum) Weston Park,
Sheffield, S10 2TP England. Tel (114) 2768588; Fax 114-275-0957; Elec Mail
info@sheffieldgalleries.co.uk; *Dir* K Streets; *Sr Prin* Janet Barnes
Estab 1875
Collections: Sheffield silver, Old Sheffield Plate, British and European cutlery,
coins and medals, ceramics
M **Abbeydale Hamlet,** Abbeydale Rd S, Sheffield, S7 2QW England. Tel (114)
2367731; *Dir* K Streets
Collections: An 18th century scytheworks with Huntsman type crucible steel
furnace, tilt-hammers, grinding-shop and hand forges
M **Bishop's House,** Meersbrook Park, Sheffield, S8 9BE England. Tel (114)
2557701; Elec Mail enquiries@bishophouse.org.uk; Internet Home Page Address:
www.friendsofbishopshouse.org.uk; *Dir (Museums Sheffield)* K Streets
Open Sat & Sun 10 AM - 4 PM; Admis free, donations welcome; Estab 1974;
Former Yedman Farmer's house; Average Annual Attendance: 1500
Income: (financed by donations & shop sales)
Collections: A late 15th century timber-framed domestic building with 16th - 17th
century additions; Artifacts from Sheffield Castle
Activities: Classes for children; dramatic progs; tours; mus shop sells books,
reproductions, prints crafts & souvenirs

SOUTHAMPTON

M **SOUTHAMPTON CITY ART GALLERY,** Civic Centre, Southampton, S014
7LP England. Tel 023-8083-2277; Fax 023-8083-2153; Elec Mail
art.gallery@southampton.gov.uk; *Cur* Adrian B Rance; *Prin Officer Arts* Elizabeth
Goodall; *Head* Margaret Heller
Open Tues - Sat 10 AM - 5 PM, Sun 1 PM - 4 PM, cl Mon; No admis fee
Collections: Continental Old Masters; French 19th & 20th centuries schools;
British painting from the 18th century to present; contemporary sculpture &
painting

SOUTHPORT

M **ATKINSON ART GALLERY,** Lord St, Southport, PR8 No 1DH England. Tel
(1704) 0151934 Ext 2110; Fax (151) 934-2109; *Arts & Cultural Svcs Mgr (Mus &
Galleries)* Joanna Jones
Open Tues - Thurs & Sat 10 AM - 5 PM, Fri noon - 5 PM, Sun 2 PM - 5 PM, cl
Mon & bank holidays; No admis fee; Estab 1878; Average Annual Attendance:
25,000
Collections: British art - local, contemporary & historic; British 18th, 19th & 20th
centuries oils; drawings, prints, sculptures & watercolors
Activities: Gallery talks; sales shop sells books, postcards & cards

STOKE ON TRENT

M **THE POTTERIES MUSEUM & ART GALLERY,** Bethesda St, Stoke On
Trent, ST1 3DW England. Tel 01782-232323; Fax 01782-232500; Elec Mail
museums@stoke.gov.uk; Internet Home Page Address:
www.stoke.gov.uk/museums; *Mgr* Pamela Mallalieu; *Head of Mus* Ian Lawley
Open Sun - Thurs 1 PM - 5 PM; Admis adults 2.50 pounds, concessions 1.50
pounds, family 5.95 pounds, children under 5 yrs & wheelchair users free;
Average Annual Attendance: 170,000
Collections: English ceramics coll incl Staffordshire ware; fine & decorative arts;
20th Century British Art
Activities: Educ prog; classes for adults; drop-in art craft for children; lects open
to pub; gallery talks; tours; concerts; sponsoring of competitions; 2 book traveling
exhibs; originate traveling exhibs; mus shop sells books, magazines

WOLVERHAMPTON

M **WOLVERHAMPTON ARTS & HERITAGE,** (Wolverhampton Art Gallery and
Museum) Wolverton Art Gallery, Lichfield St, Wolverhampton, WV1 1DU
England. Tel 44 (0) 1902 552055; Fax 44 (0) 1902 552053; Elec Mail
artgallery@wolverhampton.gov.uk; Internet Home Page Address:
www.wolverhamptonart.org.uk; *Art Galleries & Museums Officer* Corinne Miller;
Head Mktg & Opers Zoe Papiernik
Open Mon - Sat 10 AM - 5 PM; No admis fee; Estab 1884, giving Wulfrunians
their permanent art display; Average Annual Attendance: 150,000
Special Subjects: Painting-British, Asian Art, Enamels
Collections: Contemporary British art; 18th century British paintings; 19th & 20th
centuries British painting & watercolors; branch museums have English enamels,
japanning & porcelain; Victorian & Georgian; over 12,000 items in coll
Activities: Classes for adults & children; lects open to pub; gallery talks; tours;
mus shop sells books, reproductions, prints, general arts & crafts products

YORK

M **YORK CITY ART GALLERY,** Exhibition Sq, York, Y01 7EW England. Tel 01
904 687687; Fax (01904) 551866; Internet Home Page Address:
www.yorkartgallery.org.uk; *Mgr* Lorna Sergeant; *Asst Cur Decorative Art* Helen
Walsh; *Asst Cur Fine Arts* Jennifer Alexander; *Cur Fine Arts* Laura Turner
Open daily 10 AM - 5 PM, Dec 24th & 31st 10 AM - 2:30 PM with last admis at
2:15 PM, cl Dec 25, 26 & Jan 1; No admis fee; Estab 2000; Displays of fine
paintings & ceramics
Collections: British and European paintings, including the Lycett Green Collection
of Old Masters; modern stoneware pottery; paintings and drawings by York artists,
notably William Etty; watercolors, drawings and prints, mostly local topography
Activities: Classes for adults & children; lects open to pub; gallery talks; mus
shop sells books, original art, prints, slides, cards

ESTONIA

TALLINN

M **EESTI KUNSTIMUUSEUM,** Kumu Art Museum, Weizenbergi 34, Valge 1
Tallinn, 10127 Estonia. Tel 372-602-6001; Fax 372-602-6002; Elec Mail
muuseum@ekm.ee; Internet Home Page Address: www.ekm.ee; *Dir Gen* Sirje
Helme; *Dir* Anu Liivak; *Communs Mgr* Marika Parn
Open May - Sept Tue - Sun 11 AM - 6 PM, cl Mon, Oct - Apr Wed - Sun 11 AM
- 6 PM, cl Mon & Tues; Admis adults 85 eek, students & seniors 50 eek, families
155 eek; 5,500 sq ft exhib space; Average Annual Attendance: 186,000
Library Holdings: Auction Catalogs; Book Volumes; CD-ROMs; Cards;
Cassettes; DVDs; Exhibition Catalogs; Manuscripts; Periodical Subscriptions;
Reproductions
Collections: Classics of Estonian art from the 18th century to World War II;
Estonian art from 1945-1991 and contemp art
Exhibitions: 15 exhibs per year
Activities: Classes for adults & children; dramatic progs; docent training; lectrs
for mems only; concerts; gallery talks; tours; schols; fels; awarded European Mus
Award 2008; extension prog in art; mus shop sells books, magazines
M **Adamson-Eric Museum,** Luhike Jalg 3, Tallinn, 10130 Estonia. Tel
372-644-5838; Fax 372-644-5837; Elec Mail adamson-eric@ekm.ee; *Dir* Ulle
Kruus; *Cur* Kersti Koll
Open Wed - Sun 11 AM - 6 PM, cl Mon - Tue; Admis adults 20 eek, children &
seniors 10 eek, families 30 eek
Collections: Art of Estonian painter Adamson-Eric
M **Kadriorg Kunstimuuseum,** Weizenbergie 37-28, Tallinn, 10127 Estonia. Tel
372-606-6400, 606-6403 (Palace), 601-5844 (Museum); Fax 372-606-6401; Elec
Mail kadriorg@ekm.ee; *Dir* Kadi Polli; *Cur* Aleksandra Murre; *Cur* Juri
Kuuskemaa
Open Palace May - Sept Tue - Sun 10 AM - 5 PM, cl Mon; Oct - Apr Wed - Sun
10 AM - 5 PM; Mus daily Wed - Sun 10 AM - 5 PM, cl Mon & Tues; Admis
adults 65 eek, children & seniors 35 eek, families 115 eek; Palace adults 55 eek,
children & seniors 30 eek, families 100 eek; Museum adults 20 eek, children &
seniors 10 eek, families 35 eek
Collections: Palace; European and Russian art between 16th and 20th century;
Museum; 16th to 20th century Western European, Russian and Chinese art
M **Niguliste Museum,** Niguliste 3, Tallinn, 10146 Estonia. Tel 372-631-4330; Fax
372-631-4327; Elec Mail niguliste@ekm.ee; Internet Home Page Address:
www.ekm.ee/niguliste; *Dir* Tarmo Saaret; *Cur* Krista Anderson; *Cur* Merike
Koppel; *Asst Cur* Triin Hallas
Open Wed - Sun 10 AM - 5 PM, cl Mon & Tues; Admis adults 50 eek, children
& seniors 30 eek, families 70 eek; Estab 1984 to collect & wxhib ecclesiastical
art; Late-Gothic architecture

Collections: Ecclesiastical Medieval and Baroque art between the 13th and 18th centuries; Silverware of guilds, crafts, Brotherhood of the Black Heads and church
Publications: Mand, Ann. Bernt Notke: Between Innovation & Tradition; Tallin: Art Museum of Estonia, 2010 (exhib catalog)
Activities: Educ prog; classes for adults & children; lects open to pub; concerts; gallery talks; mus shop sells books, magazines, reproductions

M **Kristjan Raud House Museum,** K Raula 8, Tallinn, 11614 Estonia. Tel 372-670-0023; Fax 372-602-6002; Elec Mail kristjan.raud@ekm.ee; *Cur* Maire Toom
Open Thurs - Sat 10 AM - 5 PM, cl July; No admis fee
Collections: National romanticism in former home of Estonian artist

TARTU

M **ESTONIA NATIONAL MUSEUM,** Veski 32, Tartu, Estonia. Tel 372 7350 400; Internet Home Page Address: www.erm.ee
Open Mon - Fri 8 AM - 5 PM
Collections: Estonian artifacts, drawings, photographs & films

ETHIOPIA

ADDIS ABABA

M **MUSEUM OF THE INSTITUTE OF ETHIOPIAN STUDIES,** University of Addis Ababa, PO Box 1176 Addis Ababa, Ethiopia. Tel 550844; Fax 552-688; *Head* Ahmed Zekaria
Collections: Ethiopian cultural artifacts, ethnology colls, cultural history documents; religious art from 14th century to present

FIJI

SUVA

M **FIJI MUSEUM,** PO Box 2023, Govt Bldgs Suva, Fiji. Tel 679-331-5944, 331-5043; Fax 679-330-5143; Elec Mail information@fijimuseum.org.fj; fijimuseum@connect.com.fj; Internet Home Page Address: www.fijimuseum.org.fj; *Dir* Sagale Buadromo
Open Mon - Thurs 9:30 AM - 4:30 PM, Fri 9:30 AM - 4 PM, Sat 9:30 AM - 4:30 PM; Admis adults $7.00, children & students $5.00
Collections: Five main galleries of pre-history, Indo-Fijian work, Fiji history, Masi & art; Historical, ethnographical, sculptures, textiles, fine arts

FINLAND

ESPOO

M **ESPOO MUSEUM OF MODERN ART (EMMA),** WeeGee House, Ahertajantie 5, Tapiola Espoo, Finland; PO Box 6661, Espoon Kaupunki, F1-02070 Finland. Tel 358 0 9 8165 7512; Fax 358 0 9 8165 7510; Elec Mail info@emma.museum; Internet Home Page Address: www.emma.museum/eng; *Dir* Markku Valkonen; *Chief Cur* Paivi Talasmaa
Open Tues, Thurs, Fri 11 AM - 6 PM, Wed 11 AM - 8 PM, Sat & Sun 11 AM - 5 PM; Admis 10 or 8 euros; Estab 2006
Collections: Primarily post-war Finnish art (Saastamoinen Foundation Art Collection
Activities: Lects open to pub; Emmarrize Award 2010 & 2013; mus shop

M **GALLEN-KALLELAN MUSEO,** Gallen-Kallelan tie 27, Espoo, 02600 Finland. Tel 09-849-2340; Fax 09-541-6426; Internet Home Page Address: www.gallen-kallela.fi
Income:

HELSINKI

M **DESIGNMUSEO - DESIGN MUSEUM,** Korkeavuorenkatu 23, Helsinki, 00130 Finland. Tel 3589-622-0540; Fax 3589-6200-5455; Elec Mail info@designmuseum.fi; Internet Home Page Address: www.designmuseum.fi; *Dir* Marianne Aav; *Cur* Jukka Savolainen; *Cur* Harri Kivilinna; *Cur* Ebba Brannback
Open Tues 11 AM - 8 PM, Wed - Sun 11 AM - 6 PM, cl Mon; June 1 - Aug 31 Mon - Sun 11 AM - 6 PM; Admis adults 7 euro, seniors 6 euro, students 3 euro, children free
Collections: History and development of Finnish design with over 35,000 objects, 40,000 drawings and 100,000 images

M **DIDRICHSEN ART MUSEUM,** Kuusilahdenkuja 1, Helsinki, 00340 Finland. Tel 358-09-4778-330; Elec Mail office@didrichsenmuseum.fi; Internet Home Page Address: www.didrichsenmuseum.fi/eng

M **HELSINGIN TAIDEMUSEO - HELSINKI ART MUSEUM,** (Helsingin Kaupungin Taidemuseo - Helsinki City Art Museum) Yrjonkatu 21 B, PO Box 5400 Helsinki, 00099 Finland. Tel 358-9-310-87-041; Fax 358-9-310-87-040; Internet Home Page Address: www.taidemuseo.hel.fi; *Dir* Janne Gallen-Kallela-Siren; *Cur* Erja Pusa; *Cur* Elina Leskela; *Cur* Teija Mononen
Collections: All works of art acquired by the city of Helsinki since the 19th century; 7,500 works; Various other donated small collections; contemporary art; Katarina & Leonard Backsckara Collection; Gosta Becker Collection

M **Taidemuseo Tennispalatsi - Tennis Palace Art Museum,** Tennis Palace, 2nd Fl, Salomonkatu 15 Helsinki, Finland; PO Box 5400, Helskini, 00099 Finland. Tel 358-9-310-87001; Fax 358-9-310-87000; Internet Home Page Address: www.taidemuseo.fi; *Dir* Mr Janne Gallen-Kallela-Siren; *Chief Cur Exhibs* Ms Erja Pusa; *Chief Cur Colls* Ms Elina Leskela; *Chief of Educ* Ms Kaisa Kettunen
Open Tues - Sun 11 AM - 7 PM, cl Mon; Admis 7 euro, discount 5 euro, under 18 free, ticket sales close at 6 PM
Collections: Emphasis of the colls is on 20th and 21st century Finnish art; donated colls; accessioned colls; public art
Publications: Catalogs: The Backsbacka Collectiion - The Halt of the Helsinki Art Museum & Katriina Salmela-Hasanin in David Hasanin taide kokoelma

M **Taidemuseo Meilahti - Meilahti Art Museum,** Tamminiementie 6, Helsinki, 00250 Finland; PO Box 5400, Helsinki, 00099 Finland. Tel 358-9-310-87031; Fax 358-9-310-87030
Open Tues - Sun 11 AM - 6:30 PM, cl Mon; Admis 6 euro, discount 5 euro, under 18 free

M **Kluuvin Galleria - Kluuvi Gallery,** Unioninkatu 28 B, Helsinki, 00100 Finland; PO Box 5400, Helsinki, 00099 Finland. *Mgr* Tuija Kuchka
Open Tues - Sat 11 AM - 5 PM, Sun 12 PM - 4 PM, cl Mon; No admis fee
Collections: Experimental and non-commercial Finnish art

M **SUOMEN KANSALLISMUSEO,** National Museum of Finland, Mannerheimintie 34, Helsinki, 00100 Finland; PO Box 913, Helsinki, FI-00101 Finland. Tel (09) 40501 358 401286469 (museum hours); 358 401286454 (office hours); Fax (09) 40509400; Elec Mail kansallismuseo@nba.fi; Internet Home Page Address: www.kansallismuseo.fi; *Dir Gen* Helena Edgren, PhD
Open Tues - Sun 11 AM - 6 PM, cl Mon; Admis adults 8 euro, under 18 yrs old free; Estab 1893; Numerous branch galleries throughout Finland; Average Annual Attendance: 100,000
Special Subjects: American Indian Art, Anthropology, Decorative Arts, Drawings, Folk Art, Historical Material, Ceramics, Glass, Metalwork, Flasks & Bottles, Gold, Photography, Porcelain, Portraits, Pottery, Prints, Period Rooms, Silver, Textiles, Graphics, Archaeology, Ethnology, Costumes, Religious Art, Crafts, Primitive art, Judaica, Eskimo Art, Dolls, Furniture, Jade, Jewelry, Oriental Art, Asian Art, Carpets & Rugs, Ivory, Scrimshaw, Coins & Medals, Baroque Art, Miniatures, Renaissance Art, Embroidery, Laces, Medieval Art, Islamic Art, Stained Glass, Pewter, Leather, Painting-Scandinavian
Collections: Ethnographical Colls with Finnish, Finno-Ugrian & Comparative Ethnographical Colls; Finnish Historical Colls with a coll of coins & medals; Archaeological Colls with Finnish & Comparative Colls
Activities: Classes for children; dramatic progs; lects open to pub; ten vis lectrs per yr; concerts; tours; gallery talks; mus shop sells books, reproductions & prints; Workshop Vintti

M **SUOMEN RAKENNUSTAITEEN MUSEO,** Museum of Finnish Architecture, Kasarmikatu 24, Helsinki, 00130 Finland. Tel +358-9-85675101; Fax +358-9-85675100; Elec Mail mfa@mfa.fi; Internet Home Page Address: www.mfa.fi; *Dir* Juulia Kauste
Open Tues, Thurs, Fri 10 AM - 4 PM, Wed 10 AM - 8 PM, Sat, Sun 11 Am - 4 PM; Admis adults 5 euro, students 2.50 euro, children under 18 free, Fri free; Estab 1956; Library with 30,000 vols
Special Subjects: Decorative Arts, History of Art & Archaeology, Interior Design, Landscape Architecture, Architecture, Art Education, Art History, Furniture, Landscapes
Collections: Finnish architecture coll (mainly on post 1900 architecture) includes 85,000 photographs, 32,000 slides, 500,000 original drawings
Exhibitions: Changing exhibs on Finnish & international architecture; Permanent Exhibition: Decades of Finnish Architecture 1900-1970
Activities: Classes for children; lects open to pub; gallery talks; tours; originates traveling exhibs; mus shop sells books & magazines

M **VALTION TAIDEMUSEO - FINNISH NATIONAL ART GALLERY,** Ateneumin Taidemuseo - Ateneum Art Museum, Kaivokatu 2, Helsinki, FI-00100 Finland. Tel 358-09-1733-6401; Fax 358-09-1733-6403; Elec Mail ainfo@ateneum.fi; Internet Home Page Address: www.ateneum.fi; *Dir Gen* Risto Ruohonen; *Dir* Maija Tanninen-Mattila; *Cur* Leena Ahtola-Moorhouse; *Cur* Timo Huusko; *Cur* Heikki Malme
Open Tue - Fri 9 AM - 6 PM, Wed - Thurs 9 AM - 8 PM, Sat - Sun 11 AM - 5 PM, cl Mon; Admis adults 8/6.50 euro, under 18 free
Collections: Governs over 20,000 works of Finnish and International art; 4300 paintings and 750 sculptures from 18th century to the early 60s; 650 works from international artists; Prints from the late 19th century to the present; Nordic and European prints; Japanese woodcuts

M **Nykytaiteen Museo Kiasma - Museum of Contemporary Art Kiasma,** Mannerheiminaukio 2, Helsinki, FIN-00100 Finland. Tel 358-09-1733-6501; Fax 358-09-1733-6503; Elec Mail info@kiasma.fi; Internet Home Page Address: www.kiasma.fi; *Dir* Pirkko Siitari; *Chief Cur* Marja Sakavi
Open Tue 10 AM - 5 PM, Wed - Fri 10 AM - 8:30 PM, Sat 10 AM - 6 PM, Sun 10 AM - 5 PM, cl Mon; Admis adults 10 euro, students & seniors 8 euro
Collections: More than 9000 works of art; International and national contemporary art; Painting, photography, graphics, prints
Exhibitions: (02/07/2014-04/20/2014) Ars Fennica; (04/11/2014-09/07/2014) Alfredo Jaar
Activities: Classes for adults & children; lects open to pub; concerts; gallery talks; tours; mus shop sells books, prints & other items

M **Sinebrychoffin Taidemuseo - Sinebrychoff Art Museum,** Bulevardi 40, Helsinki, 00120 Finland. Tel 358-09-1733-6462; Fax 358-09-1733-6476; Elec Mail ulla.huhtanaki@fng.fi; Internet Home Page Address: www.sinebrychoffintaidemuseo.fi; *Dir* Ulla Huhtamaki; *Cur* Reetta Kuojarvi-Narhi; *Cur* Ulla Aartomaa; *Chief Cur* Minerva Keltanen
Open Tue & Fri 10 AM - 6 PM, Wed - Thurs 10 AM - 8 PM, Sat - Sun 11 AM - 5 PM; Admis adults 7.5 euro, students & seniors 6 euro, under 18 free
Library Holdings: Auction Catalogs; Exhibition Catalogs; Prints
Collections: European art from the 14th to the 19th century; Swedish portraits, icons, graphics and miniatures; Glassware, porcelain, silverware, statues, clocks, and furniture; Paul & Fanny Sinebrychoff Collection
Activities: Lects open to pub; concerts; tours; mus shop sells reproductions, prints, postcards

KUOPIO

M **KUOPIO ART MUSEUM,** Kauppakatu 35, Kuopio, 70100 Finland. Internet Home Page Address: taidemuseo.kuopio.fi
Admis general 4 euro, other 2 euro

PORI

M **PORI ART MUSEUM,** Etelaranta, Pori, 28100 Finland. Tel 358-2- 621-1080; Fax 358-2-621-1091; Elec Mail taidemuseo@pori.fi; Internet Home Page Address: www.poriartmuseum.fi
Circ

TAMPERE

M **SARA HILDEN ART MUSEUM,** Sarkanniemi, Tampere, FI-33230 Finland. Tel +03-5654-3500; Fax +03-5654 3510; Elec Mail sara.hilden@tampere.fi; Internet Home Page Address: www.tampere.fi/sarahilden; *Dir* Riitta Valorinta; *Cur Colls* Paivi Loimaala; *Cur Exhibs* Virpi Nikkari
Open May 1 - Aug 30 Mon - Sun noon - 7 PM, Sep 7 - Apr 30 Tues - Sun 11 AM - 6 PM; Admis adult 5 Euro, children (7-16) 3 Euro, under 7 free; Estab 1979
Library Holdings: Auction Catalogs; Audio Tapes; Cassettes; Compact Disks; DVDs; Exhibition Catalogs; Original Documents; Periodical Subscriptions; Slides; Video Tapes
Collections: Sara Hilden Foundation Collection: 4600 works of art
Activities: Classes for children; senior art educ; lectrs open to the pub; gallery talks; tours; mus shop sells books, cards & posters

TURKU

M **TURKU ART MUSEUM,** Aurakatu 26, Turku, 20100 Finland. Tel 358-2-2627-100; Fax 358-2-26-27-090; Internet Home Page Address: www.turuntaidemuseo.fi; *Dir* Kari Immonen; *Cur* Christian Hoffmann; *Cur* Mia Haltia; *Cur* Jenny Nybom
Open Tues - Fri 11 AM - 7 PM, Sat - Sun 11 AM - 5 PM, cl Mon; Admis adults 7.50 euro, students, seniors & unemployed 5 euro, groups 10 or more 5 euro/person, children under 16 yrs free, Fri 4 PM - 7 PM free; Estab 1904; Average Annual Attendance: 35,000
Library Holdings: Auction Catalogs; Exhibition Catalogs; Periodical Subscriptions; Slides; Video Tapes
Collections: 19th & 20th centuries Finnish & Scandinavian art, drawings, paintings, prints & sculpture; 19th & 20th centuries international print coll
Activities: Lects open to pub; concerts; gallery talks; tours; mus shop sells books, magazines, original art, reproductions, prints, slides

FRANCE

AIX-EN-PROVENCE

M **MUSEE GRANET,** 18 rue Roux-Alpheran, Aix-en-Provence, 13100 France. Tel 33 04 42 52 87 84; Fax 33 (0) 442 52 87 82; Elec Mail administrationgranet@agglo-fraysdaix.fr; Internet Home Page Address: www.museegranet-aixenprovence.fr/www/index1.html; *Dir Conservateur, en chef du patimoine* Bruno Ely; *Conservateur Adjoint* Ludmila Virassamy Naiken
Collections: European paintings, sculpture & artifacts

ALENCON

M **MUSEE DES BEAUX-ARTS ET DE LA DENTELLE,** rue Charles Aveline, Alencon, 61000 France. Tel 2-33-32-40-07; Fax 2-33-26-51-66; *Dir* Aude Pessey-Lux
Open Sept 1 - June 30 10 AM - noon & 2 PM - 6 PM, cl Mon, July 1 - Aug 31 Mon - Sun 7 AM - 7 PM; Admis fee adults 2.80 euros, group 10 or more & students 2.30 euros, children 14 & under & journalists free
Collections: 17th - 19th century French, Dutch & Flemish paintings; 16th - 19th century French, Italian & Dutch drawings; 16th - 20th century Alencon, Flemish, Italian & Eastern European lace

ANGERS

M **MUSEE DES BEAUX-ARTS,** Museum of Fine Arts, 10 rue du Musee, Angers, 49100 France. Tel 02-41-18-24-40; Fax 02-41-18-24-41; Elec Mail musees@ville.angers.fr; Internet Home Page Address: www.ville.angers.fr; *Conservateur en Chief Dir* Ariane James-Sarazin; *Conservateur en Chief Interim Dir Cur* Christine Besson; *Cur* Catherine Lesoeur
Open daily 10 AM - 6:30 PM; Admis 4 euro; Average Annual Attendance: 109,367 visitors
Income: Municipal budget
Library Holdings: Auction Catalogs; Book Volumes; CD-ROMs; Cards; Exhibition Catalogs; Framed Reproductions; Kodachrome Transparencies; Manuscripts; Original Documents; Periodical Subscriptions; Photographs; Slides
Collections: Paintings of the 17th & 18th centuries; Dutch, Flemish & French schools; sculpture, including busts by Houdon
Activities: Classes for adults & children; 3-4 book traveling exhibs per yr; mus shop sells books, magazines, reproductions, prints, slides, jewelry

ANGOULEME

M **MUSEE D'ANGOULEME,** 1 rue de Friedland, Angouleme, 16000 France. Tel 05-45-95-79-88; Internet Home Page Address: www.angouleme.fr/museeba
Average Annual Attendance:

ANTIBES

M **MUSEE PICASSO,** Chateau Grimaldi, Antibes, 06600 France. Tel 04-92-90-54-20-26; Fax 04-92-90-54-21; Elec Mail musee.picasso@ville-antibes.fr; Internet Home Page Address: www.antibes-juanlespins.com; *Conservateur & Chief Dir* Jean-Louis Andral
Open yr round 16/09 - 14/06: 10 12 & 14 - 18; 15/06 -15/09: 10 - 18, late-night opening in July & Aug, Wed & Fri until 20, cl Mon & pub holidays (Jan 1, May 1, Nov1, Dec 25); Admis 6 euro, concession 3 euro (proof of status required), combined ticket: 10 euro, no admis fee to mus & temporary exhibs from 1st Tues in Nov - Sun, 1st Tues in Feb - Sun; accessible to people of limited mobility
Income: Income from Assn des Amis du musee Picasso
Collections: Modern and contemporary art; works by Picasso; Nicholas de Stael; Germaine Richier; Hans Hartung; Anna-Eva Bergman
Activities: Classes for adults & children; lects open to pub; 6 lectrs per yr; mus shop sells books, magazines, reproductions, prints cards, cosmetics, DVDs

AVIGNON

M **COLLECTION LAMBERT EN AVIGNON,** 5 rue Violette, Avignon, 84000 France. Tel 04-90-16-56-20; Internet Home Page Address: www.collectionlambert.com

M **MUSEE DU PETIT PALAIS,** Place du Palais des Papes, Avignon, 84000 France. Tel 4-90-86-44-58; Fax 4-90-82-18-72; Elec Mail musee.petitpalais@wamadgo.fr; Internet Home Page Address: www.fondation-calvet.org; www.avignon.fr; *Dir* Dominique Vingtain
Open 10AM-1PM and 2PM-6PM, cl Tues, Jan1, May 1, & Dec 25; Admis 6 euro, students 3 euro, children 12 & under free
Library Holdings: Cards; Exhibition Catalogs; Reproductions
Collections: Italian paintings covering the period from 14th - 16th century; Medieval sculpture from Avignon from 12th - 15th century; paintings of the Avignon School of 14th - 15th centuries
Publications: Peinture Italienne, musee de Petit Palais Avignon RMN, 2005
Activities: Classes for adults & children; concerts, gallery tours; mus shop sells books, reproductions, & prints

BORDEAUX

M **LA MAIRIE DE BORDEAUX,** Place Pey Berland, Hotel de ville Bordeaux, 33000 France; Bordeaux Cedex, Place Pey Berland, Bordeaux, 33077 France. Tel 05-56-10-20-30

M **MUSEE GOUPIL BORDEAUX,** cours du Medoc 40, Bordeaux, 33300 France. Tel +33-56-69-10-83; Fax +33-56-43-21-68; Internet Home Page Address: http://www.culture.gouv.fr/GOUPIL/FILES/accueil_musee.html
Open Tues - Sat 14 - 18

BOURGES

M **MUSEE ESTEVE,** 13 rue Edouard Branly, Bourges, France. Tel 02-48-24-75-38; Fax 02-48-24-29-48; Elec Mail musee-esteve@ville-bourges.fr; Internet Home Page Address: www.ville-bourges.fr

BREST

M **LE MUSEE DES BEAUX-ARTS,** 24 rue Traverse, Brest, 29200 France. Tel 02-98-00-87-96; Fax 02-98-00-87-78; Elec Mail musee-beaux-arts@brest-metropole-oceane.fr; Internet Home Page Address: www.musee.brest.fr; *Dir* Francoise Daniel
Open 10 AM - noon, 1 - 18 PM; Admis 4 euro, 2.50 euro
Library Holdings: Cards; Exhibition Catalogs
Special Subjects: Landscapes, Ceramics, Painting-European, Asian Art, Painting-French, Baroque Art, Painting-Italian
Collections: Paintings; Pont-Aven School
Exhibitions: Autour de Charles Estienne
Publications: Catalogues d'exposition
Activities: Classes for children; concerts; lects open to pub; mus shop sells books

CERET

M **MUSEE D'ART MODERNE DE CERET,** 8, Bd Marechal Joffre, Ceret, 66400 France; BP 60413, Ceret cedex, 66403 France. Tel 33-04-68-87-27-76; Fax 33-04-68-87-31-92; Elec Mail contact@musee-ceret.com; Internet Home Page Address: www.musee-ceret.com; *Dir & Cur* Nathalie Gallissot
Open year round: May 2 - Sept 30 open daily, Oct - Apr open Wed - Mon & cl Tues; hrs Jul 1 - Sep 15 10 AM - 7 PM; Modern & contemporary art school of Paris - catalamish art
Special Subjects: Drawings, Landscapes, Ceramics, Prints, Painting-French, Sculpture, Painting-Spanish
Collections: Modern Art; European Art; Works by: Picasso, Gris, Chagall, Soutine, Herbin, Nasson, Nanolo, Tapies, Grano, Brossa
Activities: Classes for children; concerts; mus shop sells books, reproductions, prints & other items

CHANTILLY

M MUSEE ET CHATEAU DE CHANTILLY (MUSEE CONDE), Cedex 60500
Chantilly, France. Tel 03 44 6273180; Fax 03 44 563073; Elec Mail
reservations@chateaudechantilly.com; Internet Home Page Address:
www.chateaudechantilly.com; *Cur* Nicole Garnier; *Cur Libr* Olivier Bosc; *Cur*
Grange Ashred
Open Mar - Oct 10 AM - 6 PM; Nov - Feb 10:30 AM - 5 PM, cl Tues; Admis
Adults 14 Euro; visite du parc et du Mus Conde; painting galleries, grand
apartments, private apartments of the Duke Aumale, the libr, the chapel; Average
Annual Attendance: 265,000
Library Holdings: Book Volumes; Exhibition Catalogs; Manuscripts; Maps;
Original Documents; Periodical Subscriptions; Photographs; Prints
Special Subjects: Decorative Arts, Drawings, Art History, Painting-European,
Graphics, Sculpture, Archaeology, Religious Art, Woodcarvings, Manuscripts,
Asian Art, Painting-French, Tapestries, Baroque Art, Painting-Flemish,
Renaissance Art, Painting-Italian, Antiquities-Egyptian, Antiquities-Greek,
Antiquities-Roman
Collections: Ceramics, manuscripts & paintings
Exhibitions: (09/2014-01/2015) To Fra Angelico from Bottticelli
Publications: Exhibition Catalogue, Fra Angelico
Activities: Classes for children; lects open to the public; 5 vis lectrs per yr;
concerts; gallery talks; tours; mus shop sells books, magazines, original art,
reproductions, prints, slides, porcelain, tapestries, etc

DIJON

M MUSEE DES BEAUX-ARTS DE DIJON, Museum of Fine Arts, Palais des
Etats Cour de Bour, Dijon, 21000 France. Tel 3-80-74-52-70; Fax 3-80-74-53-44;
Chief Cur Emmanuel Starcky
Collections: Furniture, objects of art, paintings of French & foreign schools,
sculpture; Granville Collection

FONTAINEBLEAU

M ETABLISSEMENT PUBLIC DU CHATEAU DE FONTAINEBLEAU,
National Museum of Fontainebleau, Chateau de Fontainebleau, Fontainebleau,
77300 France. Tel (01) 60715070; Fax (01) 60-71-50-71; Elec Mail
resa.chateau-de-fontainebleau@culture.gour; Internet Home Page Address:
www.chateaudefontainebleau.fr; *Pres* Jean-François Hebert; *Cur* Vincent Cochet;
Cur Valerie Carpentior; *Cur* Isabelle Tamisier-Vetois; *Cur* Vincent Droguet; *Cur*
Christopher Beyeler; *Dir du pateimoire et des Coll* Xavier Salmon
Open 9:30 AM - 6 PM Apr - Sept, 9:30 AM - 5 PM Oct - Mar,; Admis 10 Euros,
8 Euros discount price, children under 18 free; Estab to show 8 centuries of
history; State apartments, small apartments, Chinese Museum, Napoleon I's
Museum
Collections: Paintings, furniture and interiors of 1st Empire and 17th, 18th and
19th centuries
Publications: Visitor's guide (French, English, German, Russian, Italian, Spanish,
Japanese, Chinese edits); many other publs of the cur of the castle
Activities: Educ prog; classes for children; lect open to public; 20-30 vis lectrs
per yr; concerts; theater

GRENOBLE

M MUSEE DES BEAUX-ARTS, 5 Place de Lavalette, Grenoble, 38000 France. Tel
76-54-09-82; *Chief Cur* Serge Lemoine
Open Mon & Wed - Sun 10 AM - 18:30 PM, cl Tues & May 1; Admis. 8 e, no
charge under 26 & jobseekers on presentation of proof of less than three months
& for all, the first Sunday of the month.
Collections: 16th, 17th and 18th century paintings; French, Italian, Spanish,
Flemish schools; modern coll; Egyptology coll

LILLE

M MUSEE DES BEAUX-ARTS DE LILLE, Museum of Fine Arts, 18 bis rue de
Valmy, Lille, 59800 France. Tel 3-20-06-78-00; Fax 3-20-06-78-15; Elec Mail
atopic@maurie-lille.fr; Internet Home Page Address: www.pba_lille.fr; *Chief Cur*
Alain Topic; *Conservateur* Annie de Wambrechies; *Conservateur* Damian Berne;
Conservateur Fluce Mozjoisu Puenault
Open Mon 2 PM - 6 PM, Wed - Sun 10 AM - 6 PM
Library Holdings: Auction Catalogs; Book Volumes; Exhibition Catalogs;
Original Documents; Periodical Subscriptions; Photographs; Prints; Slides
Collections: Western European paintings from 15th - 20th centuries; collection of
ceramics, objects of art and sculptures; collection of plans en relief
Publications: Catalogue de Ceramiques; Catalogue de Sculpture
Activities: Classes for adults & children; mus shop sells books, reproductions,
prints

LYON

M MUSEE DES BEAUX-ARTS, Museum of Fine Arts, 20 Place des Terreaux,
Lyon, 69001 France. Tel 04 72 101740; Fax 04 78 281245; Elec Mail
conservation@mba_lyon.fr; Internet Home Page Address: www.mba-lyon.fr; *Chief
Cur* Sylvie Ranond
Open Wed - Mon 10 AM - 6 PM, Fri 10:30 AM - 6 PM, cl Tues; Admis general 6
euro, reduced 4 euro
Library Holdings: Cards; Exhibition Catalogs
Collections: Ancient, Medieval & Modern sculpture; Egyptian, Greek & Roman
antiquities; French art since the Middle Ages; French, Hispano-Moorish, Italian &
Oriental ceramics; Gothic & Renaissance art; Islamic art; modern art & murals by
Puvis de Chavannes; painting of the French, Flemish, Dutch, Italian & Spanish
schools
Activities: Classes for adults & children; lect open to public; concerts; gallery
talks; mus shop sells books

M MUSEE DES TISSUS, MUSEE DES ARTS DECORATIFS DE LYON, 34 rue
de la Charite, Lyon, 69002 France. Tel 04-78-3842-00; Fax 0472402512; Elec
Mail info@museedestissus.com; Internet Home Page Address:
www.museedestissus.com; *Dir* Maximilien Durand; *Librn* Pascale Le Cacheux;
Registrar Isabel Bretones; *Textile Analysis* Marie-Helene Guefton; *Conservator
Textiles* Marie Schoefer; *Educ Dept* Cecile Demoncept; *Conservator Textiles*
Catherine Petit de Bantel; *Accounting Serv* Marie-Claire Noyerie; *Coll
Management* Claire Berthommier
Open 10 AM - 5:30 PM; Admis adults 10 euro, students 7.50 euro, 12 and under
free; Estab 1856 by the Chamber of Commerce of Lyon; Displays textile history
from the Coptic antiquity to the 20th century & decorative arts from the 16th -
20th century; Average Annual Attendance: 90,000
Library Holdings: Auction Catalogs; Book Volumes; Cards; Exhibition Catalogs;
Manuscripts; Original Art Works; Original Documents; Periodical Subscriptions;
Photographs; Prints
Special Subjects: Decorative Arts, Textiles, Costumes
Collections: Re-created French 18th century salons with furniture, objects d'art &
decorative pieces; 15th & 16th centuries Italian majolicas; tapestries of Middle
Ages & Renaissance; European drawings from 16th to 19th century; History of
textiles, embroidery & lace from the coptic antiquity to modern
Publications: Museum of Decorative Arts, handbook of the colls; exhibs catalogs
Activities: Classed for adults & children; lects open to pub; concerts; scholarships
offered; mus shop sells books, magazines, reproductions, prints

MARSEILLES

M MUSEE DES BEAUX-ARTS, Centre de la Vieille Charite, 2 rue de la Charite
Marseilles, 13002 France. Tel 4 91 14 59 30; Fax 4 91 14 59 31; *Cur* Marie-Paule
Vial
Collections: Prints, drawings, paintings, sculpture, photography, textile &
decorative arts

ORLEANS

M MUSEE DES BEAUX-ARTS D'ORLEANS, Museum of Fine Arts, 1 Rue
Fernand Rabier, Orleans, 45000 France. Tel 02 38 79 2155; Fax 02 38 79 2008;
Elec Mail musee-ba@ville-orleans.fr; Internet Home Page Address:
www.ville-orleans.fr/Sports/Expositions02.cfm; Internet Home Page Address:
www.musees.regioncentre.fr; *Cur Adjoint* Benedicte De Donker; *Cur* Galliot
Rateau Veronique
Open Tues - Sun 10 AM - 6 PM; Admis 3 euro, exhib & mus 4 euro; Estab 1797;
The mus ranks among France's richest and oldest museums; artwork from
European artistic creation from the 16th to the 20th century; Average Annual
Attendance: 60,000; Mem: 800
Library Holdings: Auction Catalogs; Book Volumes; CD-ROMs; Cards; DVDs;
Exhibition Catalogs; Fiche; Framed Reproductions; Manuscripts; Memorabilia;
Original Documents; Other Holdings; Periodical Subscriptions; Photographs;
Reproductions; Slides
Special Subjects: Decorative Arts, Drawings, Etchings & Engravings, Landscapes,
Furniture, Portraits, Prints, Silver, Painting-European, Painting-French, Sculpture,
Watercolors, Religious Art, Woodcuts, Painting-Dutch, Ivory, Miniatures,
Painting-Flemish, Renaissance Art, Medieval Art, Painting-Spanish,
Painting-Italian, Painting-German, Enamels
Collections: Dutch, French, Flemish, German, Italian & Spanish paintings, prints,
& drawings, primarily from 17th & 18th centuries; sculpture; 19th & 20th century
art works
Exhibitions: (10/2013-01/2014) Andre Roboillard et Iart Torut; (10/2013-01/2014)
Joseph Nnodj dessins et photographies; (04/2014-06/2014) Records nu Orleans:
archeologie et histoire de la ville
Publications: Quick book, exhibition catalogue
Activities: Classes for children; visits for adults in groups; lects open to the pub;
lects for mems only; 190 vis lectrs per yr; concerts; gallery talks; lending original
object of art to French & international mus & institutions; mus shop sells books,
magazines, reproductions; prints, slides & other items

M Historical & Archaeological Museum of Orleans, Hotel Cabu, Sq Abbe
Desnoyers Orleans, 45000 France. Tel 02 38 79 2155; Fax 02 38 79 2008; Elec
Mail Musee-mh@ville-orleans.fr; Internet Home Page Address:
www.ville-orleans.fr/Sports/Expositions02.cfm; *Cur* I Kinka-Ballesteros; *Asst*
Catherine Gorget-Letellier; *Cur* B de Donker
Open yr round; Admis 5 euro; Estab 1862; The museum preserves the treasures of
Gallic & Gallo-Roman bronzes of international reputation in Renaissance hotel,
middle-age sculptures, Renaissance paintings, local industries, evolution of the
Orleans harbor & works of arts related to Joan of Arc; Average Annual
Attendance: 5,000
Library Holdings: Book Volumes; Cards; Exhibition Catalogs; Framed
Reproductions
Special Subjects: Archaeology, Decorative Arts, Architecture, Furniture, Period
Rooms, Painting-French, Sculpture, Bronzes, Textiles, Crafts, Woodcarvings,
Portraits, Porcelain, Coins & Medals, Tapestries, Renaissance Art, Medieval Art,
Antiquities-Roman
Collections: Treasure of bronzes & archaeological pieces, local & regional craft
works, earthenware, porcelain, pewter, spun glass, religious statuary & Joan of Arc
iconography
Publications: Catalogues francais
Activities: Classes for children; visits for adults in groups; mus shop sells books,
magazines, postcards

PARIS

M CENTRE NATIONAL D'ART ET DE CULTURE GEORGES POMPIDOU,
Musee National d'Art Moderne, 19 Rue Beaubourg, Cedex 04 Paris, 75191
France. Tel 00 33 (0) 1 44 78 12 33; Fax 00 33 (0) 1 44 78 12 07; Elec Mail
info@centrepompidou.fr; Internet Home Page Address: www.centrepompidou.fr;
Pres Alain Seban; *Dir* Agnes Saal; *Nat Mus Dir* Alfred Pacquement; *Communs
Dir* Francoise Pams
Open 11 AM - 10 PM, cl Tues & May 1; Galleries 1 & 2 Thurs 11 PM; Admis
adult E 13 - E 11 (depending on period), concessions E 10 or E 9 (depending on
period); Circ 1.5 million (2011); Centre composed of mus; library, Bibliotheque
Publique d'Information; research centre, Institut de Recherche et Coordination
Acoustique/Musique; The Atelier Brancusi; 2 cinemas; 2 theatres; Average Annual
Attendance: 3.6 million (2011); Mem: 46,700; meet 2-3 times a week
Income: Mem & mus friends
Library Holdings: Auction Catalogs; Audio Tapes; Book Volumes; CD-ROMs;
Cards; Cassettes; Clipping Files; Compact Disks; DVDs; Exhibition Catalogs;
Framed Reproductions; Manuscripts; Original Documents 380,000; Periodical
Subscriptions; Photographs; Reproductions; Slides; Video Tapes
Collections: 20th century paintings, prints, drawings & sculpture; art films &
photographs; designs & architecture
Publications: Catalogues & numerous other publs
Activities: Classes for adults & children; docent training; lects open to the pub;
33,600 vis lectrs per yr; concerts; gallery talks; tours; award, Price Marcel
Duchamp; schols; fels; lending original objects of art to Centre Pompidou mobile;
20 book traveling exhibs per yr; originates traveling exhibs to co-productions with
main mus & art centers around the world; mus shop sells books, magazines,
reproductions, prints, slides; jr gallery

L ECOLE NATIONALE SUPERIEURE DES BEAUX-ARTS, Le Service de
Collections, 14 rue Bonaparte, Paris, 75272 France. Tel (1) 47-03-50-82; Fax (1)
47-03-52-98; Elec Mail consultation-collections@ensba.fr; Internet Home Page
Address: http:www.ensba.fr; *Dir of School* Nicolas Bourriaud; *Dir Coll* Kathy
Alliou
Open Mon - Fri (Meditheque) 1 PM - 7 PM; (Mon - Fri Collections 1:30 - 6 PM);
No admis fee; Estab 1819; 120,000 vol library for school with 600 students & 75
instructors, 500,000 works of art
Income: Ministere de la Culture
Library Holdings: Auction Catalogs; Audio Tapes; Book Volumes; CD-ROMs;
Cassettes; DVDs; Exhibition Catalogs; Manuscripts; Original Art Works; Original
Documents; Periodical Subscriptions; Photographs; Prints; Sculpture; Video Tapes
Special Subjects: Art History, Constructions, Landscape Architecture, Decorative
Arts, Illustration, Photography, Calligraphy, Drawings, Etchings & Engravings,
Graphic Arts, Manuscripts, Painting-French, Prints, Sculpture, Painting-European,
Archaeology, Art Education, Bookplates & Bindings, Miniatures,
Antiquities-Greek, Antiquities-Roman, Coins & Medals, Reproductions,
Architecture
Collections: paintings; sculptures; plaster casts; prints; photographs; manuscripts
Activities: Classes for adults; lects open to pub; 50 vis lectrs per yr; traveling
exhibs varies, Princeton Art Mus, Dahesh Mus (NY); mus shop sells books

M LES ARTS DECORATIFS, 107 rue de Rivoli, Paris, 75001 France. Tel 01
44-55-57-50; Fax 01 44555785; Elec Mail webmaster@lesartsdecoratifs.fr; Internet
Home Page Address: www.lesartsdecoratifs.fr; *Pres* Héléne David Weill; *Mus Dir*
Béatrice Salmon; *Dir gen* Marie-Liesse Baudrez
Open Tues - Sun 11 AM - 6 PM, Thurs 11 AM - 9 PM, cl Mon
Library Holdings: Auction Catalogs; Book Volumes; Exhibition Catalogs;
Original Art Works
Collections: Exhibs of textiles & costumes, exhibs of publicity; decorative arts
coll from Middle Ages to present; library with 100,000 vols; Musee Nissim de
Camondo - unique 18th century objects bequeathed by Count Moise de Camondo;
Exhibs of decorative arts, design, textiles & costumes, graphism, exhibs of
publicity; decorative arts coll from Middle Ages to present; toys & jewels
Activities: Classes for adults and children; lects open to public; organize traveling
exhibs; mus shop sells original art, reproductions, design and decorative arts

M MAISON EUROPEENNE DE LA PHOTOGRAPHIE, 5/7 rue de Fourcy, Paris,
75004 France. Tel 33 144 78 75 00; Fax 33 144 78 75 15; Internet Home Page
Address: www.mep-fr.org; *Pres* Henry Chapier; *Dir* Jean-Luc Monterosso
Open Wed -Sun 11 AM - 8 PM; Admis adults 6E, children 8 & over, senior
citizens, students & teachers 3E, children under 8, journalists with press card &
handicapped no charge
Collections: Photographs

M MUSEE CARNAVALET-HISTOIRE DE PARIS, 23 rue de Sevigne, Paris,
75003 France. Tel (1) 01 44 59 58 58; Fax 01 44 59 58 11; Internet Home Page
Address: www.paris-france.org/musee; *Head* Bernard de Montgolfier
Open Tues - Sun 10 AM - 6 PM; Admis free; Estab 1880; Average Annual
Attendance: 250,000
Special Subjects: Drawings, Architecture, Ceramics, Photography, Period Rooms,
Sculpture, Graphics, Prints, Archaeology, Decorative Arts, Portraits,
Painting-French
Collections: History and archaeology of Paris; prints and drawings; photography,
sculpture
Activities: Classes for adults & children; lects open to pub; concerts; mus shop
sells books, magazines, reproductions, slides

M MUSEE COGNACQ-JAY, Cognacq-Jay Museum, 8 rue Elzevir, Paris, 75003
France. Tel 01 40 27 07 21; Fax 01 40 27 89 44; Elec Mail
reservation.cognay-jay@paris.fr; Internet Home Page Address:
www.cogney-jay.paris.fr; *Conservateur Gen* Jose de Los Llanos; *Svcs* Nathalie
Flom; *Cur* Benjamin Couilleaux; *Documentalist* Clair Suamarni
Open 10AM - 6 PM; No admis fee, except for temp exhibs; Estab 1929; Gallery
contains European art of the XVIIIth Century
Special Subjects: Drawings, Painting-British, Painting-French, Sculpture,
Watercolors, Decorative Arts, Portraits, Furniture, Jewelry, Porcelain, Tapestries,
Miniatures, Painting-Italian

Collections: 18th century works of art; English and French furniture, pastels,
paintings, porcelain, sculpture; miniatures, drawings
Publications: Catalogue of miniatures; Catalogue of miniatures; Catalogue of
paintings; Catalogue of drawings & pastels
Activities: Classes for children; lects open to pub; gallery talks; tours; mus shop
sells books, reproductions; catalogues & mus collections

M MUSEE D'ART MODERNE DE LA VILLE DE PARIS, 11 ave du President
Wilson, Post 9 rue Gaston de St Paul Paris, 75116 France. Tel 1-53-67-40-00; Fax
1-47-23-35-98; *Cur* Suzanne Page
Collections: Modern painting and sculpture

M MUSEE D'ORSAY, 62 rue de Lille, Paris, 75343 France. Tel 33-01-40-49-48-14;
Fax 33-01-45-48-21-23; Internet Home Page Address: www.musee-orsay.fr; *Dir*
Guy Cogeval; *Gen Adminr* Thierry Gausseron; *Sponsorship & International
Relations* Olivier Simmat
Open Tues - Wed & Fri - Sun 9:30 AM - 6 PM, Thurs 9:30 AM - 9:45 PM, cl
Mon; Admis 8 euro, discount 5.50 euro, under18 free; Estab 1986; 17,000 sq ft;
Average Annual Attendance: 3,000,000 (est); Mem: 20,000
Library Holdings: Book Volumes; CD-ROMs; Cards; Compact Disks; DVDs;
Exhibition Catalogs; Framed Reproductions; Reproductions; Sculpture
Collections: French art from 1848 - 1914; Paintings, sculptures, furniture,
photography, decorative arts, graphic arts, architecture; collection of impressionist
masterpieces; Louvre Museum Collection; Musee du Jeu de Paume Collection
Activities: Educ progs; concerts; mus shop sells books, magazines, reproductions,
cards, exhib catalogs, CD Roms, DVD's, sculptures & stationary

M Musee de Orangerie, Jardin des Tuileries, Paris, 75001 France. Tel
33-01-44-50-43-00; Elec Mail information@musee-orangerie.fr; Internet Home
Page Address: www.musee-orangerie.fr; *Dir* Marie-Paule Vial
Open Mon - Sun 9 AM - 6 PM, cl Tues; Admis 7.5 euro, discount 5 euro, under
26 living in the European union no charge
Collections: coll of Jean Walter & Paul Guillaume; Les Nympheas; Hebert:
paintings by Ernest Hebert
Exhibitions: (10/19/2013-01/13/2014) Frida Kahlo/Diego Rivera L'art enfusion

M MUSEE DU JEU DE PAUME, (Musee du Louvre) Louvre Museum, Paris
Cedex 01, Paris, 75058 France. Tel +33 1-40-20-50-50; Fax +33 1-40-20-54-42;
Elec Mail info@louvre.fr; Internet Home Page Address: www.louvre.fr; Telex
21-4670; *Pres & Dir* Henri Loyrette; *Admin Gen* Didier Selles
Open Mon, Thurs, Sat - Sun 9 AM - 6 PM, Wed & Fri 9 AM - 10 PM, cl Tues;
Admis general 9E, reduced 6E; Average Annual Attendance: 8,300,000
Collections: Art of Islam; The Edmond de Rothschild Collection; Oriental, Greek,
Roman Etruscan and Egyptian antiquities; objets d'art, drawings, paintings;
Medieval & Renaissance sculpture; History of the Louvre
Activities: Classes for adults & children; lects open to public; concerts, gallery
talks, tours; mus shop sells books, magazines, reproductions, prints, slides, jewels,
post cards

MPlace de la Concorde, Paris, 7-5008 France. Tel 01 4703 1250; Fax 01 4703 1251;
Elec Mail info@jeudepaume; Internet Home Page Address: www.jeudepaume; *Dir*
Marta Gili
Open Tues - Wed 11 AM - 9 PM; Admis 8.50 euro, 5.50 euro concessions; Tues 5
- 9 PM no charge to students & visitors under 26; Average Annual Attendance:
300,000
Income: Subsidised by the ministry of culture & commun
Library Holdings: Book Volumes; Cards; DVDs; Exhibition Catalogs
Activities: Classes for adults & children; lects open to pub; 14 vis lectrs per yr;
organize traveling exhibs, Europe, USA, Canada; mus shop sells books, magazines

M MUSEE DU PETIT PALAIS, Municipal Museum, Ave Winston Churchill, Paris,
75008 France; 5 Ave Dutuit, Paris, 75008 France. Tel 0153434000; Fax
0153434052; Internet Home Page Address: www.petitpalais.paris.fr; *Cur* Gilles
Chazel
Open Tues - Sun 10 AM - 6 PM, Thurs 10 AM - 8 PM temporary exhibs, cl Mon
& pub holidays; No admis fee to permanent coll & interior garden; Estab 1900
Collections: Egyptian, Etruscan and Greek antiquities; paintings, sculpture and
other works of art to 19th century
Activities: Classes for children; lects open to pub; concerts; originate traveling
exhibs; mus shop sells books & magazines

M MUSEE GUIMET, 6 place d'Ilena, 19 Ave d'Iena Paris, 75116 France. Tel 1-56
52 53 39; Fax 1 56 52 53 54; Elec Mail resa@museeguimet.fr; Internet Home
Page Address: www.museeguimet.fr; *Pres* Olivier de Bernon; *Dir* Frederic Sallet
Open Mon & Wed - Sun 10 AM - 6 PM, cl Tues; Admis 7.50 euros, reduced 5.50
euros; temp exhibs: 8 euros, reduced 6 euros; Estab 1889; Maintains library with
100,000 vols. Main exhib contains 4,000+ works on 5,500 Sq m; Average Annual
Attendance: 300,000
Income: Admis fees & state funds
Library Holdings: Auction Catalogs; Book Volumes; CD-ROMs; Compact Disks;
Exhibition Catalogs; Filmstrips; Manuscripts; Maps; Micro Print; Original Art
Works; Original Documents; Photographs; Prints; Records; Reproductions
Special Subjects: Archaeology, Drawings, Ceramics, Glass, Furniture, Gold,
Pottery, Textiles, Bronzes, Manuscripts, Sculpture, Photography, Costumes, Jade,
Jewelry, Porcelain, Asian Art, Carpets & Rugs, Ivory, Calligraphy,
Antiquities-Oriental
Collections: Art, archaeology, religions, history of India, Afghanistan, Central
Asia, China, Korea, Japan, Khmer, Tibet, Thailand and Indonesia
Exhibitions: (10/2013-02/2014) Louis Delaporte & Cambodia: the birth of a myth
Activities: Classes for adults & children; lects open to pub; concerts; mus shop
sells books, reproductions, prints

M MUSEE GUSTAVE-MOREAU, 14 rue de La Rochefoucauld, Paris, F-75009
France. Tel 0033-1-48-74-38-50; Fax 0033-1-48-74-18-71; Elec Mail
info@musee-moreau.fr; Internet Home Page Address: www.musee-moreau.fr; *Dir*
Genevieve Lacambre
Open Wed - Sun 10 AM - 12:45 PM & 2 PM - 5:15 PM, cl Tues

Collections: Several of Gustave Moreau's masterpieces with preparatory work; Over 4,800 drawings and 450 watercolors; Collection of personal artifacts and souvenirs in former apartment

M **MUSEE MARMOTTAN MONET,** 2 rue Louis Boilly, Paris, 75016 France. Tel 1-44-96-50-33; Fax 1-40-50-65-84; Elec Mail marmottan@marmottan.com; Internet Home Page Address: www.marmottan.com; *Dir* Jacques Taddei; *Conservateur* Marianne Delaford; *Admin* Caroline Genet-Bondeville
Open Wed - Sun 11 AM - 6 PM, Tues 11 AM - 9 PM, cl Mon, New Year's, May 1, Christmas; Admis 9 euros, reduced price 5.50 euros, children under 8 free
Collections: Coll of Primitives, Renaissance, Empire and Impressionist works; medieval miniatures in Wildenstein coll
Activities: Educ prog; classes for children; mus shop sells books, magazines, original art, reproductions, prints

M **MUSEE NATIONAL DES MONUMENTS FRANCAIS,** Palais de Chaillot, Place du Trocadero Paris, 75116 France. Tel (01) 4405 3910; Fax (01) 4755 4013; *Cur* Guy Cogeual
Open 10 AM - 6 PM, cl Mon; Library with 10,000 works on art history
Collections: Full scale casts of the principal French monuments and sculpture from the beginning of Christianity to the 19th century; full scale reproductions of Medieval murals

M **MUSEE NATIONAL DU MOYEN AGE,** (Musee National Du Moyen Age Thermes & Hotel De Cluny) 6 Place Paul Painleve, Paris, 75005 France. Tel 0153737800; Fax 0153737835; Elec Mail contact.musee-moyenage@culture.gouv.fr; Internet Home Page Address: www.musee-moyenage.fr; *Dir, Conservateur* Elisabeth Taburet Delahaye; *Cur* Isabelle Bardies-Fronty; *Cur* Damien Berne; *Cur* Christine Descatoire; *Cur* Michel Huynh; *Cur* Sophie Lagabrielle; *Coll Mgr* Alain Decouche; *Commun & Sponsorship* Natacha Provensal; *Cultural Action Dept* Elisabeth Clave; *Documentation Dept* Jean Christophe Ton-That
Open 9:15 AM to 5:45 PM, cl Tues, Jan 1, May 1, Dec 25; Admis 8.50 euros, 18-25 with residence in EC 6.50 euros, no admis fee for European Union residents under 26 yrs of age & teachers working in French schools with card pass & every 1st Sun for everybody; Estab 1843 (first pub opening 1844); Two joined bldgs: 1st century Roman Bath & Cluny Abbots 15 century residence; Average Annual Attendance: 300,000; Mem: 600
Collections: Enamels, furniture, goldsmithery, ivories, paintings, sculptures & tapestries of the Middle Ages-from the 10th to the beginning of the 16th centuries; Gallo-Roman antiquities
Publications: Catalogues; guidebooks
Activities: Classes for adults & children; concerts; gallery talks; tours; mus shop sells books, reproductions

M **MUSEE RODIN,** Rue de Varenne 79, Paris, 75007 France; 19 boulevard des Invalides, Paris, 75007 France. Tel 00-33-0-1-44-18-61-10; Fax 00-33-0-1-44-18-61-30; Elec Mail goldberger@musee-rodin.fr; Internet Home Page Address: www.musee-rodin.fr; *Dir* Catherine Chevillot; *Cur Colls* Mrs Aline Magnien; *Vice-Dir* Philippe Andre-Bernavon; *Head Library Research* Mrs Helene Pinet
Open yr round 10 AM - 5 PM, cl Mon; Admis adult 9 euro, 18-25 5 euro, under 18 free; Estab 1919
Library Holdings: Auction Catalogs; Audio Tapes; CD-ROMs; Exhibition Catalogs; Manuscripts; Maps; Original Documents; Periodical Subscriptions; Video Tapes
Special Subjects: Sculpture
Collections: 6,600 sculptures by Rodin; Drawings, paintings, engravings, photographs, archives and personal coll
Exhibitions: Prog on website
Activities: Mus shop sells books, magazines, reproductions

M **MUSEO NATIONAL PICASSO,** Hotel Sale 5, Thorigny St Paris, 75003 France. Tel 01-42-71-25-21; Fax 01-48-04-75-46; Internet Home Page Address: www.musee-picasso.fr; *Dir* Jean Clair
Open Apr 1 - Sept 30 Wed - Sun 9:30 AM - 6:30 PM, Oct 1 - Mar 31 Mon - Sun 9:30 AM - 5:30 PM; Admis adult 7.70 euro, 18-25 5.70 euro, under 18 free
Collections: Works of Pablo Picasso from 1848 to 1972 following chronological stylistic changes; 200 paintings, 3000 drawings, sculptures, collages, illustrated books and manuscripts; Picasso personal collection and collection of friends

RENNES

M **MUSEE DES BEAUX-ARTS,** 20, quai Emile Zola, Rennes, 35000 France. Tel 02-23-62-17-45; Fax 02-23-62-17-49; Elec Mail museebeauxarts@ville-rennes.fr; Internet Home Page Address: www.mbar.org; *Cur* Guillaume Kazerouni; *Dir* Anne Dary; *Cur* Francois Coulon; *Cur* Lawreno Imbernon
Open Tues 10 AM - 6 PM, Wed - Sun 10 AM - noon & 2 - 6 PM, cl Mon; Mem: fee 100 FF
Library Holdings: Cards; Exhibition Catalogs
Collections: Egyptian, Greek and Roman archeology; drawings, paintings and sculptures from 15th - 21st centuries; cabinet de curiosites
Exhibitions: Objects of the 18th century
Activities: Classes for children & children; lects for mems only; 6 vis lectrs per yr; concerts; gallery talks; fels; lending of original art to other mus; mus shop sells books

STRASBOURG

M **MUSEE DES BEAUX-ARTS,** Museum of Fine Arts, Chateau des Rohan, 2 Place du Chateau Strasbourg, Cedex 67076 France. Tel 88-52-50-00; Internet Home Page Address: www.musees-strasbourg.org; *Cur* Dominique Jacquot
Collections: Old Masters; 17th to 19th century French schools; Italian schools

TOULOUSE

M **MUSEE DES AUGUSTINS,** 21 rue de Metz, Toulouse, 31000 France. Tel 33 (0) 5 61 22 21 82; Fax 33 (0) 5 61 22 34 69; Elec Mail augustins@mairie-toulouse.fr; Elec Mail courrier.augustins@mairie-toulouse.fr; Internet Home Page Address: www.augustins.org; *Dir* Axel Hemery; *Cur* Charlotte Riou; *Registrar* Berne Caroline
Open daily 10 AM -6 PM, Wed 10 AM-9 PM, cl Jan 1, Dec 25, May 1; Admis 4 euro, no admis fee to organ concert; Estab 1795; Average Annual Attendance: 120,000
Library Holdings: Book Volumes; Cards; Exhibition Catalogs; Kodachrome Transparencies; Periodical Subscriptions; Photographs; Slides
Special Subjects: Painting-French, Sculpture, Religious Art, Painting-European, Painting-Flemish, Medieval Art, Painting-Italian
Collections: The museum houses a collection of paintings and sculptures dating from the early Middle Ages to the beginning of the 20th Century
Publications: Guides to collection
Activities: Classes for children; lects open to pub, 6 vis lectrs per year, concerts, gallery talks, tours; mus shop sells books

TOURS

M **MUSEE DES BEAUX-ARTS/PALAIS DES ARCHEVEQUES,** Museum of Fine Arts, 18 Place Francois Sicard, Tours, 37000 France. Tel 02-47-05-68-73; Fax 02-47-05-38-31; Elec Mail musee-beauxarts@ville-tours.fr; Internet Home Page Address: www.tours.fr; *Conservateur En Chef* Sophie Join-Lambert; *Communs* Eric Garin
Open 9 AM - 12:45 PM & 2 PM - 6 PM; Admis 4 E; reduced rate 2 E, free 1st Sun of month; Estab 1801
Library Holdings: Auction Catalogs; CD-ROMs; Cards; DVDs; Exhibition Catalogs; Framed Reproductions; Kodachrome Transparencies; Lantern Slides
Special Subjects: Decorative Arts, Drawings, Historical Material, Landscapes, Marine Painting, Collages, Glass, Gold, Photography, Painting-American, Textiles, Bronzes, Manuscripts, Maps, Painting-European, Painting-French, Painting-Japanese, Sculpture, Tapestries, Graphics, Hispanic Art, Prints, Watercolors, Costumes, Religious Art, Ceramics, Crafts, Pottery, Woodcarvings, Portraits, Furniture, Jewelry, Porcelain, Asian Art, Silver, Metalwork, Painting-Dutch, Carpets & Rugs, Ivory, Coins & Medals, Baroque Art, Calligraphy, Miniatures, Painting-Flemish, Renaissance Art, Embroidery, Medieval Art, Painting-Spanish, Painting-Italian, Islamic Art, Antiquities-Greek, Antiquities-Roman, Cartoons, Painting-German, Leather, Military Art, Antiquities-Etruscan, Enamels, Painting-Scandinavian
Collections: Ancient and Modern Tapestries; Furniture; French School of 18th Century, including Boucher and Lancret; Italian Paintings of 13th to 16th Century, including Mantegna and primitives; 17th Century Paintings, including Rembrandt and Rubens; 19th Century Paintings, including Degas, Delacroix and Monet; Sculptures: Bourdelle, Houdon, Lemoyne, Rodin, Davidson, Calder
Activities: Classes for adults & children; lects open to pub; 4 vis lectrs per yr; concerts; mus shop sells books, reproductions & prints

VERSAILLES

M **ESTABLISHMENT PUBLIC DU CHATEAU DU RUSEE,** (Musee National du Chateau de Versailles) Et du Dophine national de versailles, Chateau de Versailles, R P 834 Versailles, Cedex 78000 France. Tel 01 30 83 7600; Fax 01 30 83 7607; Elec Mail bibliotheque.conservatoire@chateauversailles.fr (mus library); Elec Mail documentation@chateauversailles.fr; Internet Home Page Address: www.chateauversailles.fr; *Pres* Catherine Pegard; *Chief Cur* Beatrix Saule
Open Apr 2 - Oct 31, 9 AM - 6:30 PM (last admis 6) Nov 1 - Apr 1, 9 AM - 5:30 PM (last admis 5); Admis 15 E; reduced rate: 13 E - free admis under 18; palace & garden free; Average Annual Attendance: 4,500,000; Mem: Dues 50 euro - 80 euro per yr
Library Holdings: Auction Catalogs; Book Volumes; Clipping Files; Exhibition Catalogs; Periodical Subscriptions
Special Subjects: Decorative Arts, Landscape Architecture, Landscapes, Portraits, Painting-French, Sculpture, Tapestries, Architecture, Drawings, Woodcarvings, Painting-European, Furniture, Porcelain, Restorations, Tapestries
Collections: paintings, sculptures & carriages from 17th to 19th centuries; decorative arts from 17th-19th century, drawings & prints; decorative arts from 17th-19th century, drawings & prints
Exhibitions: (10/22/2013-02/23/2014) Andre Le Notre
Activities: Classes for children; lects open to pub; lects for mems only; concerts; tours; mus shop sells books, reproductions, prints, souvenirs & spin-offs

GABON

LIBREVILLE

M **MUSEE NATIONAL DES ARTS ET TRADITIONS DU GABON,** Ave du General de Gaulle, BP 3115 Libreville, Gabon. Tel 241-76-14-56; Elec Mail museegabon@numibia.net; Internet Home Page Address: www.numibia.net/gabon; *Dir* Ludovic Obiang
Open Mon - Fri 8:30 AM - 6 PM; No admis fee
Collections: 2,500 objects of Gabon ethnography, history and art

GAMBIA

BANJUL

M **GAMBIAN NATIONAL CENTRE FOR ARTS AND CULTURE MUSEUM,**
Independence Dr, PMB 151 Banjul, Gambia. Tel 220-422-6244; Fax
220-422-7461; Elec Mail baba_baba_c.@yahoo.com; Elec Mail
hceesay@gmail.com; Internet Home Page Address: www.ncac.gm; *Exec Dir* Bala
S K Saho; *Dir Cultural Heritage* Baba Ceesay; *Dir Copyright* Hassoum Ceesay
Open Mon - Thurs 9 AM - 6 PM, Fri - Sun, 9 AM - 5 PM; Admis museum D50,
monuments D100; Estb 1989; History & ethnography
Library Holdings: CD-ROMs; Cassettes
Collections: Permanent collection of cultural objects; Artifacts, works of art,
books, historical documents and photographs relating to the ethnographic and
historical culture of the region
Activities: Classes for children; sales shop sells books, reproductions, prints,
slides & attire; Wassu Museum, Wassu

GEORGIA

TBILISI

M **SHALVA AMIRANASHVILI MUSEUM OF FINE ARTS,** 1 Lado Gudiashvili
str, Tbilisi, 0105 Georgia. Tel 995-32-99-99-09; Fax 995-32-99-66-35; Elec Mail
info@museum.ge; Internet Home Page Address: www.museum.ge; *Gen Dir* David
Lordkipanidze
Open, daily 11 AM - 6 PM, cl Mon; Admis adult 3 gel, students 1.5 gel, under 6
free
Collections: Best-known samples of Georgian artwork; 60,00 objects; gold pieces,
icons, crosses, cut-enamel, jewelry, textiles; Collections of Russian, Western
European and Asian artwork

GERMANY

AACHEN

M **SUERMONDT-LUDWIG-MUSEUM,** Wilhelmstrasse 18, Aachen, 52070
Germany. Tel (0241) 47980-0; Fax (0241) 37075; Telex 2-9166; *Dir* Dr Ulrich
Schneider
Open Tues - Sun 12 noon - 6 PM, Wed 12 noon - 9 PM, cl Mon; Admis 3 euro,
groups 7 or more 1.50 euro ea
Collections: Paintings from the Middle Ages to the Baroque; portraits from
Middle Ages to present; sculpture from the Middle Ages; graphic art (ceramics,
textiles)

BERLIN

M **BRUCKE MUSEUM,** Bussardsteig 9, Berlin, 14195 Germany. Tel
49-30-831-20-29; Fax 49-30-831-5961; Elec Mail Bruecke-Museum@t-online.de;
Internet Home Page Address: www.Bruecke-Museum.de; *Dir & Prof* Dr
Magdalena Moeller
Open Sun, Mon, Wed-Sat 11:00 AM - 5: 00 PM, cl Tues; Estab 1967 upon the
donation of Karl Schmidt-Rottluff; Dedicated to the works of the mems of the
artist's group Brucke.; Mem: 850; dues 25 Euro; meetings throughout yr
Library Holdings: Other Holdings publs on the Brucke group, Expressionism &
Collections: German expressionism, paintings, sculptures & graphic art of the
Brucke group
Publications: Brucke Archiv-Meft, appears at irregular intervals
Activities: Tours; originate traveling exhibs; mus shop sells catalogues
accompanying exhibs

M **DEUTSCHE KUNSTHALLE,** (Deutsche Guggenheim) Unter den Linden 13/15,
Berlin, 10117 Germany. Tel +49 (0)30-20 20 93-0; Fax +49 (0)30-20 20 93-20;
Elec Mail db.kunsthalle@db.com; Internet Home Page Address:
www.deutsche-guggenheim.com; Internet Home Page Address:
deutsche-bank-kunsthalle.com
Open daily 10 AM - 8 PM; Admis adults 4E, reduced 3E, children under 12 &
Mon free.
Activities: Classes for children; lects open to pub; gallery talks; tours; sales shop
sells books, magazines & prints

M **STAATLICHE MUSEEN ZU BERLIN STIFTUNG PREUSSISCHER
KULTURBESITZ,** National Museums in Berlin, Prussian Cultural Heritage
Foundation, Stauffenbergstrasse 41, Berlin, 10785 Germany. Tel 0049
30-266-423401; Fax 0049 30-266-423410; Elec Mail
kommunikation@smb.spk-berlin.de; Internet Home Page Address:
www.smb.museum; *Gen Dir* Prof Dr Michael Eissenhauer; *Head Dept Presse
Kommunikation Sponsoring* Mechtild Kronenberg
Special Subjects: Archaeology, Drawings, Etchings & Engravings, Folk Art,
Landscapes, Ceramics, Collages, Glass, Antiquities-Assyrian, Flasks & Bottles,
Furniture, Porcelain, Portraits, Pottery, Pre-Columbian Art, Painting-American,
Prints, Silver, Textiles, Woodcuts, Manuscripts, Painting-British, Painting-Japanese,
Sculpture, Tapestries, Graphics, Photography, Watercolors, Bronzes, African Art,
Ethnology, Costumes, Religious Art, Crafts, Painting-European, Posters, Jewelry,
Oriental Art, Asian Art, Antiquities-Byzantine, Painting-Dutch, Painting-French,
Carpets & Rugs, Coins & Medals, Restorations, Baroque Art, Calligraphy,
Miniatures, Renaissance Art, Period Rooms, Embroidery, Laces, Medieval Art,
Antiquities-Oriental, Painting-Spanish, Painting-Italian, Antiquities-Persian, Islamic
Art, Antiquities-Greek, Antiquities-Roman, Cartoons, Painting-German, Leather,
Reproductions, Antiquities-Etruscan, Enamels
Collections: Supervises 19 museums and departments, in addition to an art library
and a museum library & research laboratory
Activities: Classes for adults & children; lects open to pub; tours; mus shop sells
books, magazines, reproductions, prints & merchandising products; Junior mus:
Kindergaline in Bode-Museum, Am Kupfergraben1, 10778 Berlin
—**Agyptisches Museum and Papyrussammlung, Egyptian Museum,** Bodestrabe
1-3, Berlin, 10178 Germany. Tel 0049 30 2090 5544; Fax 0049 30 2090 5109;
Elec Mail aemp@smb.spk-berlin.de; Internet Home Page Address:
www.smb.museum/aemp; *Dir* Prof Dr Dietrich Wildung
Open Fri - Wed 10 AM - 6 PM, Thurs 10 AM - 10 PM; Library with 15,000 vols
Collections: Art & cultural history of ancient Egypt
—**Antikensammlung, Collection of Classical Antiquities,** Bodestrabe 1-3,
Berlin, 10178 Germany. Tel 0049 30 2090 5577; Fax 0049 30 2090 5202; Elec
Mail ant@amb.spk-berlin.de; Internet Home Page Address: www.smb.museum/ant;
Dir Dr Andreas Scholl; *Deputy Dir* Dr Gertrud Platz
Open Fri - Wed 10 AM - 6 PM, Thurs 10 AM - 10 PM
Collections: Greek & Roman antiquities
—**Gemaldegalerie,** Stauffenbergstrasse 40, Berlin, 10785 Germany. Tel 0049 30
266 2951; Fax 0049 30 266 2103; Elec Mail gg@smb.spk-berlin.de; Internet
Home Page Address: www.smb.museum/gg; *Dir* Dr Bernd Lindemann; *Deputy Dir*
Dr Rainald Grosshans
Open Fri - Wed 10 AM - 6 PM, Thurs 10 AM - 10 PM
—**Kunstgewerbemuseum, Museum of Decorative Arts,** Tiergartenstrasse 6,
Berlin, 10785 Germany. Tel 0049 30 266 2951; Fax 0049 30 266 2947; Elec Mail
kgm@smb.spk-berlin.de; Internet Home Page Address: www.smb.museum/kgm;
Dir Dr Angela Schonberger; *Deputy Dir* Lothar Lambacher
Open Tues - Fri 10 AM - 6 PM, Sat - Sun 11 AM - 6 PM
Collections: Arts & crafts
—**Kupferstichkabinett-Sammlung der Zeichnungen und Druckgraphik,
Museum of Prints and Drawings,** Matthaikirchplatz 8, Berlin, 10785 Germany.
Tel 0049 30 266 2951; Fax 0049 30 266 2959; Elec Mail kk@smb.spk-berlin.de;
Internet Home Page Address: www.smb.museum/kk; *Dir* Dr Hein-Th Schulze
Altcappenberg; *Deputy Dir* Dr Holm Bevers
Open Tues-Wed & Fri 10 AM - 6 PM, Thurs 10 AM - 10 PM, Sat-Sun 11 AM - 6
PM; study room Tues - Fri 9 AM - 4 PM; Library with 40,000 vols
Collections: Drawings, prints & illustrated books of all European art
—**Museum fur Indische Kunst, Museum of Indian Art,** Takustrabe 40, Berlin,
14195 Germany. Tel 0049 30 8301 361; Fax 0049 30 8301 502; Elec Mail
mik@smb.spk-berlin.de; Internet Home Page Address: www.smb.museum/mik; *Dir*
Prof Dr Marianne Yaldiz; *Deputy Dir* Raffael Gadebusch
—**Museum fur Islamische Kunst, Museum of Islamic Art,** Bodestrabe 1-3,
Berlin, 10178 Germany. Tel 0049 30 2090 5401; Fax 0049 30 2090 5402; Elec
Mail isl@smb.spk-berlin.de; Internet Home Page Address: www.smb.museum/isl;
Dir Prof Dr Claus-Peter Haase; *Deputy Dir* Dr Jens Kroger
Open Fri-Wed 10 AM - 6 PM, Thurs 10 AM - 10 PM; Library with 25,000 vols
—**Museum fur Ostasiatische Kunst, Museum of East Asian Art,** Takustrabe 40,
Berlin, 14195 Germany. Tel 0049 30 8301 382; Fax 0049 30 8301 501; Elec Mail
oak@smb.spk-berlin.de; Internet Home Page Address: www.smb.museum/oak; *Dir*
Prof Dr Willibald Veit; *Deputy Dir* Dr Herbert Butz
Open Tues 10 AM - 6 PM, Sat-Sun 11 AM - 6 PM
Collections: Paintings & ceramics of China & Japan
—**Ethnologisches Museum-Ethnological Museum,** Arnimallee 27, Berlin, 14195
Germany. Tel 0049 30 80 30 14 38; Fax 0049 30 8301 500; Elec Mail
md@smb.spk-berlin.de; Internet Home Page Address: www.smb.museum/em; *Dir*
Prof Dr Viola Konig; *Deputy Dir* Dr Richard Haas
Open Tues-Fri 10 AM - 6 PM, Sat-Sun 11 AM - 6 PM
Collections: Items of different cultures: Africa, East Asia (China & Tibet), Europe
& North America
—**Museum fur Volkskunde, Museum of German Ethnology,** Im Winkel 6/8,
Berlin, D-14195 Germany. Tel 83901-01; Fax 030/83901283; *Dir* Dr Erika
Karasek
Library with 25,000 vols
Collections: Folklore objects from German-speaking population in Europe
—**Museum fur Vor- und Fruhgeschichte, Museum of Pre- & Early History,**
Schloss Charlottenburg, Langhansbau Berlin, 14059 Germany. Tel 0049 30 3267
4811; Fax 0049 30 3267 4812; Elec Mail mvf@smb.spk-berlin.de; Internet Home
Page Address: www.smb.museum/mvf; *Dir* Prof Wilfried Menghin; *Deputy Dir* Dr
Alix Hansel
Open Fri-Wed 9 AM - 5 PM, Sat-Sun 10 AM - 5 PM
—**Alte Nationalgalerie, Old National Gallery,** Bodestrabe 1-3, Berlin, 10178
Germany. Tel 0049 30 2090 5801; Fax 0049 30 2090 5802; Elec Mail
ang@smb.spk-berlin.de; Internet Home Page Address: www.smb.museum/ang; *Dir*
Prof Dr Peter-Klaus Schuster; *Leiter der Alten* Dr Bernhard Maaz
Open Fri-Wed 10 AM - 6 PM, Thurs 10 AM - 10 PM
Collections: 19th & 20th century works
—**Skulpturensammlung und Museum fur Byzantinische Kunst-Sculpture
Collection and Museum of Byzantine Art,** Bodestrabe 1-3, Berlin, 10178
Germany. Tel 0049 30 2090 5601; Fax 0049 30 2090 5602; Elec Mail
sbm@smb.spk-berlin.de; Internet Home Page Address: www.smb.museum/sbm;
Dir Prof Dr Arne Effenberger
Open Fri-Wed 10 AM - 6 PM, Thurs 10 AM - 10 PM

M **STIFTUNG DEUTSCHES HISTORISCHES MUSEUM,** Unter den Linden 2,
Berlin, 10117 Germany. Tel +49 30 203040; Fax 20304543; Elec Mail
info@dhm.de; Internet Home Page Address: www.dhm.de; *Pres* Prof Dr Alexander
Koch; *Cur* Dr Dieter Vorsteher-Seiler
Open daily 10 AM - 6 PM; Admis adults 6 Euros, children under 18 free; Estab
1987
Library Holdings: Auction Catalogs; CD-ROMs; Exhibition Catalogs
Special Subjects: Drawings, Historical Material, Photography, Textiles,
Manuscripts, Posters, Coins & Medals, Medieval Art, Painting-German, Military
Art
Collections: Objects documenting everyday life; Historical documents, maps,
house archive; contemporary documents after 1914; arts & posters; paintings
before 1900; paintings, 20th century sculpture, photographs, numismatics; applied
arts & plastic; everyday life culture: medical equipment, household supplies,

textiles, badges, toys, postcards; militaria: weapons, harnesses, military devices, medals, uniforms, flags
Exhibitions: Permanent Exhib: German History in Images & Artifacts from Two Millenia; German history in pictures & documents
Activities: Educ progs for adults & children; lectrs open to the pub; lending of original objects of art to mus; mus shop sells books, magazines

BIELEFELD

M **KUNSTHALLE BIELEFELD,** Artur-Ladebeck-Strasse 5, Bielefeld, 33602 Germany. Tel + 49 (0) 521329 99 50-10; Fax +49 (0)521 32 999 50-50; Elec Mail info@kunsthalle-bielefeld.de; Internet Home Page Address: www.kunsthalle-bielefeld.de; *Dir* Dr Friedrich Meschede; *Pres, Officer* Christiane Heuwinkel; *Deputy Dir* Dr Jutta Hulsewig-Johnen
Open Tues, Thurs, Fri & Sun 11 AM - 6 PM, Wed 11 AM - 9 PM, Sat 10 AM - 6 PM, cl Mon; Admis adults 7 Euro; discounts 4 Euro - 2 Euro, family 14 Euro; 1968; art mus, 20th & 21st century; Museum & exhib space
Library Holdings: Auction Catalogs; Book Volumes; CD-ROMs; Compact Disks; DVDs; Exhibition Catalogs; Maps; Prints; Video Tapes
Collections: Expressionist painting, Bauhaus art, American painting after 1945, Cubistic sculpture, graphics-library, children's atelier
Publications: Catalogues
Activities: Classes for adults & children; docent training; classes for the blind; lects open to pub; 5 vis lectrs per yr; concerts; gallery talks; tours; mus shop sells books

BONN

M **KUNSTMUSEUM BONN,** Art Museum of Bonn, Friedrich-Ebert-Allee 2, Bonn, 53113 Germany. Tel (0228) 776260; Fax (0228) 776220; Elec Mail kunstmuseum@bonn.de; Internet Home Page Address: www.kunstmuseum-bonn.de; *Dir* Prof Dr Stephen Berg; *Deputy Dir* Dr Christoph Schreier; *Cur & Head Exhib* Dr Volker Adolphs; *Cur Graphic Dept* Dr Stefan Gronert
Open Tues - Sun 11 AM - 6 PM, Wed 11 AM - 9 PM, cl Mon; Admis 7 Euro for adults, 3.50 Euro for students; Estab 1948; Average Annual Attendance: 100,000
Library Holdings: Auction Catalogs; Book Volumes; Exhibition Catalogs
Collections: Art of the 20th century, especially August Macke & the Rhenish expressionists; German Art since 1945; contemporary international graphic arts
Activities: Classes for adults & children; lects open to pub; concerts; gallery talks; tours; originates traveling exhib to art mus in Europe & USA; Kunstladen sells books, original art, reproductions, prints & t-shirts, wine-bottles, etc

M **LANDSCHAFTSVERBAND RHEINLAND,** Rheinisches Landesmuseum Bonn, Colmanstr 14-16, Bonn, 53115 Germany; Bachstr 5-9, Bonn, 53115 Germany. Tel +49 228 2070 0; Fax +49 228 2070 289; Elec Mail info@landesmuseum.lvr.de; Internet Home Page Address: www.landesmuseum.lvr.de; *Dir* Dr Gabriele Uelsberg; *Press Officer* Dr Brigitte Beyer-Rotthoff
Open Tues - Sun 11 - 1800; Admis 8 -5, children under 18 no charge; Estab 1820; archeologie/art; Average Annual Attendance: 120,000
Library Holdings: Auction Catalogs; Book Volumes; Exhibition Catalogs; Fiche; Maps; Pamphlets; Periodical Subscriptions; Photographs; Prints; Slides
Collections: Rhenish sculpture, painting & applied arts from the Middle Ages up to the present; finds from the Stone Age, Roman times till the Middle Ages; Renaissance, modern art, photographic coll
Publications: Das Rhein Landemuseum Bonn, Bonner Jahrbucher; Jule im Museum; several series of research reports & catalogs
Activities: Educ prog; classes for children; docent training; holiday activities for children; concerts, tours; lects open to pub; gallery talks; Ceram-Preis fur das archaol. Sachbuch (every 5 yrs), Leo Breur-Förderpreis (every 2 yrs); organize traveling exhibs; mus shop sells books

BREMEN

M **KUNSTHALLE BREMEN,** Bremen Art Gallery, Am Wall 207, Bremen, 28195 Germany. Tel 49 (0) 421-32-90-80; Fax 49 (0) 421-32-90-8470; Elec Mail info@kunsthalle-bremen.de; Internet Home Page Address: www.kunsthalle-bremen.de; *Dir* Dr Christoph Grunenberg; *Cur* Dr Dorothee Hansen; *Cur* Dr Anne Buschhoff; *Pub Rels* Rebekka Maiwald; *Pub Rels* Jasmin Nickein
Open Spring 2013 Wed - Sun 10 AM - 5 PM, Tues 10 AM - 9 PM, cl Mon; Admis family 12 euro, adults 6/3 Euro, children 6 - 21: 3 Euro, groups 5 Euro per person, mems free; Estab 1823; Art museum; Mem: 8,000
Library Holdings: Auction Catalogs; Book Volumes; Exhibition Catalogs
Special Subjects: Painting-European, Sculpture, Drawings, Graphics, Painting-French, Painting-German
Collections: Japanese drawings and prints; European paintings, Middle Ages to modern, especially French and German Art of the 19th century; 17th - 21st century sculpture; illustrated books
Activities: Educ prog; classes for adults & children; lectrs open to the public; lectrs for mems only; 20 vis lectrs per year; concerts; Kunstpreis der Boettcherstrasse in Bremen; tours; mus shop sells books, magazines, gifts, reproductions

BRUNSWICK

M **HERZOG ANTON ULRICH-MUSEUM,** (Herzog Anton Ulrich-Museum-Kunstmuseum des Landes Niedersachsen) Kunstmuseum des Landes Niedersachsen, Museumstrasse 1, Brunswick, 38100 Germany. Tel 0531-1225-0; Fax 0531-1225-2408; Elec Mail info@museum-braunschweig.de; Internet Home Page Address: www.museum-braunschweig.de; *Dir* Dr J Luckhardt; *Paintings* Dr Silke Gatenbroeker; *Sculptures* Dr Regine Marth; *Decorative Arts* Dr Alfred Walz; *Prints & Drawings* Dr Thomas Doring; *Educ* Dr Sven Nommensen
Open Tues, Thurs - Sun 10 AM - 5 PM, Wed 1 PM - 8 PM, cl Mon; Admis 5 Euros, reduced 2.50 Euros; Estab 1754; Library with 60,000 vols, 170,000 objects

of art in the collection; Average Annual Attendance: 60,000; Mem: Freundeskris dci Herzog Anton Ulrich Museum, 470 mems
Library Holdings: Auction Catalogs; Book Volumes; Exhibition Catalogs
Collections: European Paintings - Renaissance & Baroque; European Renaissance & Baroque decorative art, including bronzes, clocks, French 16th century enamels, Italian maiolika, furniture, glass, ivory & wood carvings, laces; Medieval art; prints & drawings from the 15th century to present; East Asian decorative art; Coll of graphic works; print room
Exhibitions: Epochal Masterpieces of the Herzog Anton Ulrich-Museum from Antiquity to Present
Publications: Exhibition catalogue; inventory catalogue
Activities: Educ prog; classes for adults & children; docent training; lects open to pub; lects for members only; 20 vis lectrs per year; concerts; gallery talks; tours; lending of original objects of art to other museums; mus shop sells books, prints, postcards, reproductions

COLOGNE

M **MUSEEN DER STADT KOLN,** Museums of the City of Cologne, Zeughausstr 1-3, Cologne, 50667 Germany. Tel 0221-22125789; Fax 0221-22124154; Elec Mail ksm@museenkoeln.de; Internet Home Page Address: www.museenkoeln.de; *Acting Dir* Dr Michael Euler Schmidt; *Dir* Rita Wagner; *Dir* Bettina Mosler
Open Tues 10 AM - 8 PM, Wed 10 AM - 5 PM, Thurs 10 AM - 10 PM; Admis 4.20 euro, students & children under 6 no charge; 1888; History of Cologne; Average Annual Attendance: 70,000
Library Holdings: Auction Catalogs; CD-ROMs; Exhibition Catalogs; Manuscripts; Periodical Subscriptions
Activities: Classes for children; tours; mus shop sells books, reproductions & prints

M **Josef-Haubrich-Kunsthalle,** Josef-Haubrich-Hof, Cologne, 50676 Germany. Tel 221-221-23-35; Fax 221-221-4552

M **Koelnisches Stadtmuseum,** Zeughausstrasse 1-3, Cologne, 50667 Germany. Tel 221-221-25789; Fax 221-221-24154; Elec Mail ksm@museenkoeln.de; Internet Home Page Address: www.museenkoeln.de/ksm; *Dir* Dr H Mario Kramp; *Acting Dir* Dr Michael Euler-Schmidt; Dr Bettina Mosler; Rita Wagner, MA
Open Tues 10 AM - 8 PM, Wed-Sun 10 AM - 5 PM, cl Mon; Admis general 5 Euro, reduced 3.50 Euro, free audio-guides; Estab 1888 Historical Mus Cologne; Average Annual Attendance: 80,000
Income: Municipal Mus, City of Cologne subsidized
Library Holdings: Auction Catalogs; Book Volumes; CD-ROMs; Cassettes; Compact Disks; DVDs; Exhibition Catalogs; Manuscripts; Maps; Memorabilia; Original Documents; Pamphlets; Periodical Subscriptions; Records; Video Tapes
Collections: Graphic Arts of Cologne and the Rhineland; photograph coll of the Rhineland; industrial arts of Cologne; religious and rural art and culture; Paintings - local art; Local history; Ceramics; Musical instruments
Activities: Classes for adults & children; docent training; lects open to pub, 5-10 vis lectrs per yr; mus shop sells books, magazines, reproductions, prints, ceramics, replicas of original art

M **Museum fuer Ostasiatische Kunst,** Universitaetsstr.100, Cologne, 50674 Germany. Tel 49 221 221-28601; Fax 49 221 221-28610; Elec Mail mok@museenkoeln.de; Internet Home Page Address: www.museenkoeln.de; *Dir* Dr Adele Schlombs; *Vice Dir* Dr Petra Rosch
Open Tues - Sun 11 AM - 5 PM, Thurs 11 AM - 8 PM; Admis 6 Euro, 3.50 Euro reduced; special exhib fees: 10 Euro, 7 Euro; Estab 1909, museum focused on East Asian Art; Library with 18,000 vols; Average Annual Attendance: 30,000 - 45,000
Income: Financed by Friends of the Museum of East Asian Art, annual fee 550,000 euros
Purchases: Objects for the museum
Library Holdings: Auction Catalogs; Book Volumes 11,000; Exhibition Catalogs
Collections: Art of China, Korea and Japan
Publications: Exhib catalogue, bilingual (German & English); Exhibition guide (German)
Activities: Classes for adults & children; docent training; mus shop sells books, magazines, original art

M **Museum Ludwig,** Heinrich Boll Platz, Cologne, 50667 Germany. Tel 0049-221-221-26165; Fax 221-221-24114; Elec Mail info@museum-ludwig.de; Internet Home Page Address: www.museum-ludwig.de; *Dir* Dr Philipp Kaiser; *Deputy Dir* Katia Baudin; *Communs* Anne Niermann; *Communs* Leonie Pfenning; *Communs* Judith Schlereth
Open Tues - Sun 10 AM - 6 PM, 1st Thurs of the month: 10AM-10PM; Admis 10 euro, reduced 7 euro; Museum for 20th century art and contemporary art; Average Annual Attendance: 350,000
Income: Mus of the city of Cologne
Library Holdings: Auction Catalogs; Exhibition Catalogs; Fiche; Periodical Subscriptions
Special Subjects: Drawings, Photography, Prints, Sculpture, Graphics
Collections: Painting & sculpture from 1900 to present; 20th century art/contemporary art/ expressionism/Picasso; Russian avant-garde; Pop art; Media art, photography from the beginnings to present
Exhibitions: (10/11/2013-01/26/2014) Not Yet Titled: Now & Forever at Museum Ludwig; (10/11/2013-01/26/2014) Louise Lawler: Adjusted
Publications: Regular exhibition catalogues
Activities: Classes for adults & children, docent training; lects open to public, gallery talks; concerts; tours, Wolfgang Hahn Prize of Gesellschaft for Modern Artist at Museum Ludwig; lendig of original art to patron's clubs; mus shop sells books, magazines, & prints

M **Rautenstrauch-Joest-Museum,** Cacilien Str 29-33, Cologne, 50667 Germany; Leonhard-Tietz Str 10, Cologne, 50667 Germany. Tel 49-0221-221-31356; Fax 49-0221-221-31333; Elec Mail ursula.metz@stadt-koeln.de; Internet Home Page Address: www.museenkoeln.de/rjm; *Dir* Prof Dr Klaus Schneider; *Deputy Dir Indonesia* Dr Jutta Engelhard; *Cur South Pacific* Dr Burkhard Fenner; *Cur Africa* Dr Clara Himmelheber; *Cur Textile Collection* Brigitte Majlis; *Cur America* Dr Stephanie Teufel; *Cur Historical Ethnographic Photographs* Dr Margit Zara Krpata; *Event Mgr* Oliver Leub
Open Tues - Sun 10 AM - 6 PM, Thurs until 8 PM; Admis varies depending on exhib; Estab 1901

Library Holdings: Book Volumes; Exhibition Catalogs; Periodical Subscriptions
Collections: Ethnological museum; folk culture (non European)
Activities: Classes for adults & children; mus shop sells books, magazines, catalogs, ethnographic art

M **Romisch-Germanisches Museum,** Roncalliplatz 4, Cologne, D-50667 Germany. Tel 221-22305; Fax 221 24030; Elec Mail rgm@stadt-koeln.de; Internet Home Page Address: museenkoeln.de/roemisch-germanisches-museum; *Dir (provisional)* Dr Marcus Trier; *Dep Dir* Dr Friederike Naumann-Steckner
Open Tues - Sun 10 AM - 5 PM; Admis adults 5-7 Euros, (dependent on special exhibs), students 3.50 Euro; Estab 1946; archaeological collections; Roman art, migration period collection; Average Annual Attendance: 300,000; Mem: 750; Archaeological Society
Special Subjects: Archaeology, Crafts, Jewelry, Metalwork, Medieval Art, Antiquities-Roman, Mosaics, Gold
Collections: Early and pre-historic discoveries; Roman art; inscriptions; sculptures; gold ornaments; glass and industrial arts
Publications: Koelner Jahrbuch
Activities: Classes for adults & children; dramatic progs, docent training; lects open to pub & mem; 5 vis lectrs per yr; gallery talks; tours; shop sells books, magazines, reproductions, prints, slides

L **Roemisch-Germanisches Museum,** Roncalliplatz 4, Cologne, 50667 Germany. Tel 221-22122304; Fax 221-22124030; Elec Mail barbara.schauer@stadt.koeln.de; Internet Home Page Address: www.museenkoeln.de/roemisch-germanisches-museum; *Dir (provisional)* Dr Marcus Trier
Open Tues - Sun 10 AM - 5 PM; Admis depending on additional special exhibs; Estab 1946; Roman and early art from Cologne and Europe
Library Holdings: Book Volumes 11,000; Exhibition Catalogs
Collections: Roman and Early Medieval Art; Jewelry from the migration period
Publications: Kolner Jahrbuch
Activities: Guided tours; classes for adults & children; lectrs open to the public; 6 vis lectrs per yr; mus shop sells books, reproductions & prints

M **Museum Schnutgen,** Cacilienstrasse 29-33, Cologne, 50667 Germany; Leonhard-Tietz-Str 10, Cologne, 50676 Germany. Tel 221 221-23620; Fax 221 221-28489; Elec Mail museum.schnuetgen@stadt-koeln.de; Internet Home Page Address: www.museenkoeln.de; *Dir* Dr Moritz Woelk
Open Tues - Sun 10 AM - 6 PM, Thurs 10 AM - 8 PM, cl Mon; Admis 6 euro, reduced 3.50 euro; Estab 1910 & 1956; Art of the Middle Ages, sculpture, textiles, stained glass & Baroque
Library Holdings: Auction Catalogs; Exhibition Catalogs; Fiche; Periodical Subscriptions; Slides
Special Subjects: Glass, Furniture, Silver, Textiles, Manuscripts, Sculpture, Religious Art, Woodcarvings, Ivory, Baroque Art, Renaissance Art, Medieval Art, Stained Glass, Enamels
Collections: Art of the early Middle Ages to Baroque
Activities: Classes for adults & children; concerts

M **Wallraf-Richartz-Museum,** Obenmarspforten, at the Cologne City Hall Cologne, 50677 Germany. Tel 0221-221-21119; Fax 0221-221-22629; Elec Mail wallraf@museenkoeln.de; Internet Home Page Address: www.museenkoeln.de; *Dir* Dr Andreas Bluhm
Open Tues 10 AM - 8 PM, Wed-Fri 10 AM - 6 PM, Sat - Sun 11 AM - 6 PM; cl Mon; Admis adults 5.80 euro, others 3.30 euro; Picture gallery
Special Subjects: Drawings, Portraits, Sculpture, Graphics, Watercolors, Religious Art, Etchings & Engravings, Painting-European, Painting-Dutch, Painting-French, Baroque Art, Painting-Flemish, Renaissance Art, Medieval Art, Painting-Spanish, Painting-Italian, Painting-German
Collections: Paintings from 13th century to 1900; 19th century sculpture
Activities: Shop sells books, reproductions, slides

DUSSELDORF

L **KUNSTAKADEMIE DUSSELDORF, HOCHSCHULE FUR BILDENDE KUNST - BIBLIOTHEK,** State Academy of Art - Library, Eiskellerstrasse 1, Dusseldorf, 40213 Germany, Tel (0211) 1396-461; Fax (0211) 1396-225; Elec Mail brigitte.blockhaus@kunstakademie-duesseldorf.de; Internet Home Page Address: www.kunstakademie-duesseldorf.de; *Librn* Brigitte Blockhaus, MA; *Librn Asst* Klaus Schumann
Open Mon - Wed 9 AM - 5 PM, Thurs 9 AM - 7 PM, Fri 10 AM - 2 PM, holidays 10 AM - 1 PM & 2 PM - 5 PM; Estab 1774; Library with 130,000 vols
Purchases: E 40 000 p a
Library Holdings: Auction Catalogs; Book Volumes; CD-ROMs; DVDs; Exhibition Catalogs; Fiche; Manuscripts 13; Periodical Subscriptions 110; Slides 50,000

M **KUNSTHALLE DUSSELDORF,** (Stadtische Kunsthalle Dusseldorf) Grabbeplatz 4, Dusseldorf, 40213 Germany. Tel (0211) 899-6243; Fax (0211) 892-9168; Elec Mail mail@kunsthalle-duesseldorf.de; Internet Home Page Address: www.kunsthalle-duesseldorf.de; *Dir* Dr Gregor Jansen; *Cur* Dr Magdalena Holzhey; *Secy* Claudia Paulus; *Press & Commun* Dirk Schewe; *Cur* Elodie Evers; *Mng Dir* Ariane Berger
Open Tues - Sun 11 AM - 6 PM; Admis Euro 5, 50, / 3, 50; Estab 1967; Modern & contemporary art
Exhibitions: Contemporary art exhibitions
Activities: Classes for adults & children; docent training; dramatic progs; lects open to pub; concerts; gallery talks; originate traveling exhibs to museums in Europe; sales shops sell books, magazines, reproductions, prints, Kit Kurstin Tunnel

M **MUSEUM KUNSTPALAST,** (Kunstmuseum Dusseldorf) Ehrenhof 4-5, Dusseldorf, 40479 Germany. Tel (0211) 899-0200; Fax (0211) 892-9307; Elec Mail info@smkp.de; Internet Home Page Address: www.smkp.de; *Gen Dir* Beat Wismer; *Commercial Dir* Carl Grouwet; *Head of Mktg* Barbara Wiench; *Head of Comm* Marina Schuster; *Head of Educ* Dr Sylvia Neysters; *Head of Glass Coll* Dedo von Kerssenbrock-Krosigk; *Head of Modern Art* Kay Heymer; *Head of Dept Painting* Dr Bettina Baumgartel; *Head of Dept Prints & Drawings* Dr Gunda Luyken; *Head Sculpture & Applied Art* Dr Barbara Til
Open Tues, Wed, Fri - Sun 11 AM - 6 PM, Thurs 11 AM - 9 PM, cl Mon; Admis Collection: 7 Euro, concessions 5.50 Euro

Collections: Collections of European & applied art from middle ages to 1800, prints, drawings & contemporary art at 5 museum locations
Activities: Classes for adults & children

FRANKFURT

M **FOTOGRAFIE FORUM FRANKFURT,** (Fotografie Forum International) Braubachstrasse 30-32, Frankfurt, D-60311 Germany. Tel +49 (0) 69.291726; Fax +49 (0) 69.28639; Elec Mail contact@fffrankfurt.de; Internet Home Page Address: www.fffrankfurt.org; *Artistic Dir* Celina Lunsford; *Mng Dir* Sabine Seitz
Open Tues - Fri 11 AM - 6 PM, Sat - Sun 11 AM - 5 PM, cl Mon.; Admis adults 4E, seniors & students 3E, groups of 10 or more 2E, members free; Estab 1984
Library Holdings: Book Volumes; Exhibition Catalogs
Special Subjects: Photography
Collections: Photographs
Activities: Classes for Adults; lects open to pub; gallery talks

M **LIEBIEGHAUS, SKULPTURENSAMMLUNG,** Museum of Sculpture, Schaumainkai 71, Frankfurt, 60596 Germany. Tel 6500490; Fax 650049150; Elec Mail info@liebieghaus.de; Internet Home Page Address: www.liebieghaus.de; *Dir* Max Hollein
Open Tues & Fri - Sun 10 AM - 6 PM, Wed - Thurs 10 AM - 9 PM, cl Mon; Admis 7 euro, reduced 5 euro; 9 euro, reduced 7 euro (special exhib); Sculpture from antiquities to neo-classicism
Library Holdings: Book Volumes; Cards; Exhibition Catalogs; Lantern Slides
Collections: Sculpture of Egypt, Greece, Rome Medieval period, East Asia, Rococo style, Baroque period & neo-classicism
Activities: Classes for adults & children; dramatic prog; docent training; lects open to pub; lects for members only; concerts; tours; mus shop sells books, slides & other items

M **MUSEUM FUR ANGEWANDTE KUNST FRANKFURT,** Museum of Applied Arts, Schaumainkai 17, Frankfurt, 60594 Germany. Tel (069) 2123-40-37; Fax (069) 212-30703; Elec Mail info.angewandte-kunst@stadt-frankfurt.de; Internet Home Page Address: www.angewandtekunst-frankfurt.de; *Dir* Matthias K Wagner
Open Tues & Thurs - Sun 10 AM - 5 PM, Wed 10 AM - 9 PM; cl Mon; Admis regular 8 euro, reduced 4 euro; Estab 1877; European art 12th-21st century, Asian art, Design, Book Art, Graphics, Islamic Art, International Product Design; Average Annual Attendance: 120,000
Library Holdings: Auction Catalogs; Audio Tapes; Book Volumes; Compact Disks; DVDs; Exhibition Catalogs; Kodachrome Transparencies; Lantern Slides; Manuscripts; Photographs; Slides
Special Subjects: Ceramics, Glass, Gold, Costumes, Crafts, Furniture, Jewelry, Asian Art, Carpets & Rugs, Baroque Art, Calligraphy, Islamic Art
Collections: European applied art from Gothic to art nouveau; Far Eastern & Islamic works of art; Industrial Product Design, historical villa with nine epoche halls
Activities: Classes for adults & children; lects open to pub; lects for members only, 10 vis lectrs per yr; concerts; gallery talks; tours; originate traveling exhibs; mus shop sells contemporary jewelry; jr mus Museum with the Suitcase

M **STADELSCHES KUNSTINSTITUT UND STADTISCHE GALERIE,** Staedel Museum, Schaumainkai 63, Frankfurt, 60596 Germany; Durerstrasse 2, Frankfurt, 60596 Germany. Tel (069) 605098-0; Fax (069) 605098111; Elec Mail info@staedelmuseum.de; Internet Home Page Address: www.staedelmuseum.de; *Dir* Max Hollein; *Deputy Dir & Cur Italian Painting, Dutch Painting & German Painting until 1800* Dr. Jochen Sander; *Cur Spec Proj* Dr Eva Mongi-Vollmer; *Cur Prints & Drawings from 1750* Dr Jutta Schuett; *Cur 19th & 20th Cent Painting* Dr Felix Kraemer; *Cur Prints & Drawings until 1750* Dr Martin Sonnabend; *Cur Contemporary Art* Dr Martin Engler
Open Tues - Wed & Sat - Sun 10 AM - 6 PM, Thurs & Fri 10 AM - 9 PM; Admis 12 euro, reduced 10 euro, Sat & Sun 14 euro, reduced 12 euro, children under 12 free; Family card (every day (except Mon) 24 euro; Library with 100,000 vols
Library Holdings: Auction Catalogs; Audio Tapes; Book Volumes; Cards; Exhibition Catalogs; Reproductions; Slides
Collections: Paintings, sculptures, prints, drawings
Publications: Exhibition catalog
Activities: Classes for adults & children; dramatic progs; lects for mems only; concerts; gallery talks; tours; mus shop sells books; magazines; reproductions; prints; slide posters; toys

HAMBURG

M **HAMBURGER KUNSTHALLE,** Glockengiesserwall, Hamburg, 20095 Germany. Tel (040) 428131200; Fax (040) 428543409; Elec Mail info@hamburger-kunsthalle.de; Internet Home Page Address: www.hamburger-kunsthalle.de; *Dir* Prof Dr Hubertus Gassner; *Bus Mgr* Roman Passarge; *Prints & Drawings* Andreas Stolzenburg; *Old Masters Paintings* Martina Sitt; *19th Century Paintings* Jenns Howoldt; *Early 20th Century Painting* Ulrich Luckhardt
Open Tues - Wed & Fri - Sun 10 AM - 6 PM, Thurs 10 AM - 9 PM; Admis Euro 8.50, Concessions Euro 5; Estab 1869; Library with 70,000 vols; Average Annual Attendance: 300,000; Mem: 13,000
Library Holdings: Auction Catalogs; Book Volumes; Exhibition Catalogs; Maps; Original Documents; Pamphlets; Periodical Subscriptions; Sculpture
Collections: Drawings, engravings & masterworks of painting from 14th century to present; sculpture from 19th and 20th centuries
Publications: Catalogues
Activities: Classes for adults & children; docent training; lects open to pub; 15 vis lectrs per year; concerts; gallery talks; tours; sponsoring of competitions; mus shop sells books, magazines & prints

M MUSEUM FUR KUNST UND GEWERBE HAMBURG, Steintorplatz, Hamburg, D 20099 Germany. Tel (040) 428134 880; Fax (040) 4 28134 999; Elec Mail service@mkg-hamburg.de; Internet Home Page Address: www.mkg-hamburg.de; *Dir* Prof Sabine Schulze; *Mng Dir* Udo Goerke; *Secy Gen* Dennis Conrad; *Press Dept* Michaela Hille; *Ancient World* Dr Frank Hildebrandt; *Oriental & Far Eastern Art* Dr Nora von Achenbach; *European Sculpture, Decorative Arts & Applied Art* Dr Christine Kitzlinger; *Graphic Art* Dr Juergen Doering; *Textiles* Angelika Riley; *Registrar* Annika Pohl-Ozawa; *Mktg* Silke Oldenburg; *Art Nouveau & 20th Century* Dr Claudia Banz; *Cooperation Dept* Dennis Conrad; *Asian Art* Dr Nora von Achenbach; *Photography* Dr Esther Ruelfs
Open Tues, Wed & Fri - Sun 10 AM - 6 PM, Thurs 10 AM - 9 PM, cl Mon; Admis 10 Euro, concessions 7 Euro; Estab 1877; Average Annual Attendance: 250,000; Mem: Justus Brinckmann Gesellschaft 60 Euro
Income: 8,000,000 Euro
Library Holdings: Auction Catalogs; Book Volumes; Exhibition Catalogs; Maps; Original Art Works; Original Documents; Periodical Subscriptions; Photographs; Sculpture
Special Subjects: Archaeology, Decorative Arts, Drawings, Historical Material, History of Art & Archaeology, Illustration, Interior Design, Landscape Architecture, Architecture, Art Education, Art History, Ceramics, Glass, Metalwork, Gold, Photography, Pottery, Prints, Silver, Bronzes, Silversmithing, Woodcuts, Manuscripts, Maps, Sculpture, Graphics, Textiles, Costumes, Religious Art, Crafts, Primitive art, Etchings & Engravings, Judaica, Posters, Furniture, Jade, Jewelry, Porcelain, Oriental Art, Asian Art, Antiquities-Byzantine, Carpets & Rugs, Ivory, Coins & Medals, Restorations, Tapestries, Baroque Art, Calligraphy, Miniatures, Renaissance Art, Period Rooms, Medieval Art, Antiquities-Oriental, Antiquities-Persian, Islamic Art, Antiquities-Egyptian, Antiquities-Greek, Antiquities-Roman, Mosaics, Cartoons, Painting-German, Leather, Reproductions, Antiquities-Etruscan, Enamels, Bookplates & Bindings
Collections: European art & sculpture from Middle Ages to present; Near & Far East art; European applied art; Art Nouveau; Modern Applied Art & Industrial Design; East Asia & The Islamic World; Graphic Design; Photography; Musical Instruments; Fashion & Textiles; Posters; Rare books
Activities: Classes for adults & children; Lects open to pub; concerts; gallery talks; tours; awards; mus shop sells books, magazines, prints, original art; Hubertus Wald Kinderreich

HANOVER

M MUSEUM AUGUST KESTNER, (Kestner-Museum) Trammplatz 3, Hanover, 30159 Germany. Tel (0511) 1682120; Fax 16846530; Elec Mail museum-august-kestner@hanover-stadt.de; Internet Home Page Address: www.museum-august-kestner.de; *Contact* Dr Wolfgang Schepers; *Prof* Dr Christian E Joebcu
Open Tues & Thurs - Sun 11 AM - 6 PM, Wed 11 AM - 8 PM; Admis 5 Euro; Estab 1889; Neo-Renaissance building/enlarged 1960; Mem: Membership 60 euro per year
Library Holdings: Auction Catalogs; Book Volumes; Exhibition Catalogs; Kodachrome Transparencies; Periodical Subscriptions; Photographs; Prints
Collections: Ancient, medieval & modern coins & medals; Egyptian, Greek, Etruscan & Roman art objects & medieval art; illustrated manuscripts & incunabula of the 15th - 20th centuries; product design 1900-2000
Activities: Classes for adults & children; lects open to pub; 2-3 traveling exhibs per yr; originate traveling exhibs; mus shop sells books, reproductions, prints, slides

KARLSRUHE

M BADISCHES LANDESMUSEUM, Schlossplatz 1, Karlsruhe, 76131 Germany. Tel 0721-926-6514; Fax 721-926-6537; Elec Mail info@landesmuseum.de; Internet Home Page Address: www.landesmuseum.de; *Dir & Prof* Dr Harald Siebenmorgen
Open Tues - Thurs 10 AM - 5 PM, Fri - Sun 10 AM - 6 PM; Admis 4, reduced 3; Estab 1921; Maintains library with 70,000 vols; Average Annual Attendance: 300,000
Library Holdings: Auction Catalogs; Book Volumes; Exhibition Catalogs; Periodical Subscriptions
Special Subjects: Archaeology, Decorative Arts, Ceramics, Glass, Furniture, Porcelain, Pottery, Bronzes, Sculpture, Costumes, Religious Art, Crafts, Jewelry, Oriental Art, Antiquities-Byzantine, Carpets & Rugs, Ivory, Coins & Medals, Baroque Art, Renaissance Art, Medieval Art, Antiquities-Oriental, Islamic Art, Antiquities-Egyptian, Antiquities-Greek, Antiquities-Roman
Collections: Antiquities of Egypt, Greece & Rome; art from middle ages to present; medieval, Renaissance & baroque sculpture; coins, weapons & folklore
Activities: Classes for adults & children; lects open to pub; concerts; tours; originate diverse traveling exhibs; mus shop sells books, magazines, original art, reproductions & prints

M STAATLICHE KUNSTHALLE - STATE ART GALLERY, (Staatliche Kunsthalle) Hans-Thoma-Strasse 2-6, Karlsruhe, 76133 Germany; Postfach 11 12 53, Karlsruhe, 76062 Germany. Tel ++49-721-926-3359; Fax ++49-721-926-6788; Elec Mail info@kunsthalle-karlsruhe.de; Internet Home Page Address: www.kunsthalle-karlsruhe.de; *Head* Prof Dr Pia Muller-Tamm; *Deputy Dir* Otmar Bohmes; *Cur* Dr Holger Jacob-Friesen; *Cur Prints & Drawings* Dr Dorit Schafer; *Cur Prints & Drawings* Dr Astrid Reuter; *Head Mus Educ Svcs* Dr Sibylle Brosi; *Head Pub Rels* Alexandra Hahn; *Bus Adminr Mgr* Priska Wessbecher
Open Tues - Sun & pub holidays 10 AM - 6 PM; Admis 6 Euros; Estab 1846; Coll spanning eight hundred years of art - 800 works permanently on display; Average Annual Attendance: 125,000
Library Holdings: Auction Catalogs; Book Volumes; CD-ROMs; Exhibition Catalogs; Fiche; Periodical Subscriptions
Collections: 15th - 20th century German painting & graphics; 16th - 20th century Dutch, Flemish & French paintings & graphics; approx 90,000 prints & drawings, sculptures, 19th - 20th century

Publications: Staatliche Kunsthalle (mus guide in German, English & French)
Activities: Classes for adults & children; docent training; training for adults; lects open to pub; gallery talks; concerts; tours; mus shop sells books, reproductions, prints, Junge Kunsthalle

KASSEL

M STAATLICHE MUSEEN KASSEL, State Museums of Kassel, Schloss Wilhelmshohe, Kassel, 34131 Germany; Post Box 410420, Kassel, 34066 Germany. Tel (0561) 31680-0; Fax (0561) 31680-111; Elec Mail info@museum-kassel.de; Internet Home Page Address: www.museum-kassel.de; *Dir* Dr Michael Eissenhauer
Open Thurs - Sun 10 AM - 5 PM; Admis 3.50 Euros; Library with 60,000 vols; collection of paintings, antiquities, graphics
Library Holdings: Auction Catalogs; Exhibition Catalogs
Collections: Department of classical antiquities gallery of 15th - 18th century old master paintings, coll of drawings & engravings
Activities: Educ prog; classes for adults & children; concerts; mus shop sells books

MUNICH

A BAYERISCHE STAATSGEMALDESAMMLUNGEN/BAVARIAN STATE ART GALLERIES, Pinakothek der Moderne, Barerstrasse 29, Munich, 80799 Germany. Tel (089) 23805 360; Fax (089) 23805251; Elec Mail info@pinakothek.de; Internet Home Page Address: www.pinakothek.de; *Head* Prof Dr Klaus Schrenk
Open Tues - Wed & Fri - Sun 10 AM - 6 PM, Thurs 10 AM - 8PM; cl Mon, New Year's Eve, Shrove Tues, May 1, Christmas Eve & Day & Boxing Day; Admis general 10 euro, reduced 7 euro, Sun 1 euro; Estab 2002; consists of 4 galleries; Average Annual Attendance: 387,000
Library Holdings: Book Volumes; CD-ROMs; Cards; Cassettes; Compact Disks; DVDs; Exhibition Catalogs; Maps; Memorabilia; Photographs; Reproductions; Video Tapes
Special Subjects: Architecture, Drawings, Graphics, Painting-German, Painting-Israeli, Photography, Sculpture, Watercolors, Painting-American, American Western Art, Asian Art, Collages, Crafts, Portraits, Furniture, Glass, Jewelry, Period Rooms, Painting-European, Painting-Dutch, Flasks & Bottles, Painting-Japanese, Painting-Russian, Painting-Scandinavian, Painting-British, Painting-Italian
Collections: works of classical modernists; works by Bacon, Baselitz, Beuys, Judd, de Kooning, Polke, Twombley & Warhol; contemporary art; 20th & 21st century applied art; National collection of works on paper
Activities: Classes for adults & children, docent training, progs for disadvantaged persons; concerts; seminars; tours; mus shop sells books, magazines, slides, gifts, postcards, reproductions, prints & design objects

M Neue Pinakothek, Barerstrasse 29, Munich, 80799 Germany. Tel (089) 238050195; Fax (089) 23805251; Elec Mail info@pinakothek.de; Internet Home Page Address: www.pinakothek.de; *Head* Dr Reinhold Baumstark
Open Mon & Fri - Sun 10 AM - 6 PM, Wed 10 AM - 10 PM; cl Tues, Thurs, New Year's Eve, May 1, Christmas Eve & Day; Admis general 5.50 euro, reduced 6 euro, Sun 1 euro, children under 18 free
Library Holdings: Book Volumes; CD-ROMs; Cards; Cassettes; Compact Disks; DVDs; Exhibition Catalogs; Maps; Memorabilia; Photographs; Reproductions; Video Tapes
Special Subjects: Landscapes, Painting-British, Painting-European, Painting-French, Sculpture, Portraits, Painting-Dutch, Painting-Flemish, Painting-Polish, Painting-Spanish, Painting-Italian, Painting-German, Painting-Russian, Painting-Scandinavian
Collections: 18th century sculpture; international art
Activities: Classes for adults & children; lects open to pub, seminars, concerts, gallery talks, tours; mus shop sells books, reproductions, prints, slides, gifts, postcards

M Alte Pinakothek, Barerstrasse 27, Munich, 80799 Germany. Tel (089) 23805 216; Fax (089) 23805251; Elec Mail info@pinakothek.de; Internet Home Page Address: www.pinakothek.de; *Head* Prof Dr Reinhold Baumstark
Open Tues 10 AM - 10 PM, Wed - Sun 10 AM - 6 PM; cl Mon, New Year's Eve, Shrove Tues, May 1, Christmas Eve & Day & Boxing Day; Admis general 5.50 euro, reduced 6 euro, Sun 1 euro; children under 18 free; Average Annual Attendance: 237,000
Library Holdings: Book Volumes; CD-ROMs; Cards; Cassettes; Compact Disks; DVDs; Exhibition Catalogs; Maps; Memorabilia; Photographs; Reproductions; Video Tapes
Special Subjects: Landscapes, Marine Painting, Portraits, Painting-European, Religious Art, Baroque Art, Painting-Flemish, Renaissance Art, Medieval Art, Painting-Spanish, Painting-Italian, Painting-German
Collections: 14th - 18th century Flemish, Spanish, Italian, German & other European paintings
Activities: Classes for adults & children; lects open to pub; seminars; tours; concerts; gallery talks; mus shop sells books, reproductions, prints, slides, gifts, postcards

M Schack-Galerie, Prinzregentenstrabe 9, Munich, 80538 Germany. Tel +49 89 23805 224; Fax +49 89 23805 251; Elec Mail info@pinakothek.de; Internet Home Page Address: www.schack-galerie.de; *Head* Dr Reinhold Baumstark
Open Wed - Sun 10 AM - 6 PM; cl Mon & Tues, New Year's Eve, May 1, Ascension Day, Feast of Corpus Christi, Assumption Day, German Unification Day, Christmas Eve & Day; Admis general 3 euro, reduced 2.50 euro, Sun 1 euro, children under 18 free; Estab 1939
Library Holdings: Book Volumes; CD-ROMs; Cards; Cassettes; Compact Disks; DVDs; Exhibition Catalogs; Maps; Memorabilia; Photographs; Reproductions; Video Tapes
Special Subjects: Painting-German
Collections: 19th century German paintings
Activities: Classes for adults & children; lects open to pub; concerts; gallery talks; tours; mus shop sells books, reproductions, prints, slides, postcards, gifts

M **BAYERISCHES NATIONALMUSEUM,** Bavarian National Museum, Prinzregentenstrasse 3, Munich, 80538 Germany; Postfach 221424, Munich, 80504 Germany. Tel (089) 2112401; Fax (089) 21124201; Elec Mail bay.nationalmuseum@bnm.mwn.de; Internet Home Page Address: www.bayerisches-nationalmuseum.de; *Gen Dir* Dr Renate Eikelmann
Open Tues - Wed & Fri - Sun 10 AM - 5 PM, Thurs 10 AM - 8 PM, cl Mon; Admis adults 5 Euro, reduced 4 Euro; 1855 (founded), 1862 (opened), 1900 (opening of the present building); One of Europe's major art and cultural history museums
Special Subjects: Decorative Arts, Ceramics, Metalwork, Flasks & Bottles, Furniture, Gold, Silver, Bronzes, Tapestries, Costumes, Folk Art, Dolls, Glass, Jewelry, Ivory, Baroque Art, Miniatures, Medieval Art, Enamels
Collections: European fine arts: decorative arts, paintings, folk art, sculpture; most valuable and extensive crib coll in the world; ceramic art; furniture; textiles
Activities: Educ prog; classes for children, classes for adults; docent training; workshops; lects open to public; concerts; gallery talks; tours; Mus shop sells books, magazines, reproductions, prints, ceramics, glass, paper

M **HAUSDERKUNST,** Prinzregentenstrabe 1, Munich, 80538 Germany. Tel +49 (0)89 21127-113; Fax +49 (0)89 21127-157; Elec Mail mail@hausderkunst.de; Internet Home Page Address: www.hausderkunst.de
Open Fri - Wed 10 AM - 8 PM, Thurs 10 AM - 10 PM; Admis 5-10 euro; Non-collecting museum
Collections: German art
Activities: Classes for adults & children; lects open to pub; gallery talks; tours; mus shop sells books & magazines

M **LENBACHHAUS,** Stadtische Galerie im Lenbachhaus and Kunstbau Munchen, Luisenstr 33 Munich, 80333 Germany. Tel 49 89 23 33 20 00; Fax 49 89 23 38 26 93; Elec Mail lenbachhaus@muenchen.de; Internet Home Page Address: www.lenbachhaus.de
Open Wed - Sun 10 AM - 6 PM, Tues 10 AM - 9 PM; From Mar 2009 to Summer 2012 the Lenbachhaus will be cl for renovation. The Kunstbau will be open. There will be lower admission fees for the Kunstbau during this time; Admis regular 10 euro, reduced 5 euro; Estab 1929 as an art museum; Works by artists of the "Blue Rider" group, Munich School, 3 international contempory art
Collections: Collection of 19th- & 20th-century paintings especially by Blauer Reiter artists

M **STAATLICHE GRAPHISCHE SAMMLUNG MUNCHEN,** Katharina von Bora Str 10, Munich, D-80333 Germany. Tel (089) 289 27650; Fax (089) 289 27653; Elec Mail direkton@graphische-sammlung.mwn.de; Elec Mail info@sgsm.eu; Internet Home Page Address: www.sgsm.eu; *Dir* Dr Michael Semff; *Cur* Dr Achim Riether; *Cur* Dr Andreas Strobl; *Cur* Dr Kurt Zeitler; *Cur* Dr Susanne Wagini
Study Hall open Tues - Wed 10 AM - 1 PM, 2 PM - 5 PM, Thurs 10 AM - 1 PM, 2 PM - 6 PM, Fri 10 AM - 12:30 PM; exhibs: see Pinakothek der Moderne; No admis fee for study hall; for exhibs see Pinakothek der Moderne; Estab 1758; Library with 50,000 vols; Average Annual Attendance: 1000 (Study Hall)
Special Subjects: Graphics
Collections: French, 15th to 20th century German, Italian & Dutch prints & drawings; international prints & drawings; Portraits (prints); views of different places (prints)
Exhibitions: Three to four exhibs per yr
Activities: Lects for members & different unions only; 350 vis lectrs per year; originates traveling exhibs to other graphic departments

M **STAATLICHE MUNZSAMMLUNG,** State Coin Collection, Residenzstrasse 1, Munich, 80333 Germany. Tel (089) 227221; Fax 089-2998859; Elec Mail info@staatliche-muenzsammlung.de; Internet Home Page Address: www.staatliche-muenzsammlung.de; *Dir* Dr Dietrich Klose; *Cur* Dr Kay Ehling; *Spec Tasks & Coin Finds* Dr Annette Krane; *Cur* Dr Martin Hirsch
Open Tues - Sun 10 AM - 5 PM; Admis adults 2.50 Euro, seniors & students 2 Euro & Sun 1 Euro, children free; Estab 1565; Library with 14,000 vols; Average Annual Attendance: 8,000; Mem: 50 Euro (friends of the mus)
Income: Mostly by state
Library Holdings: Auction Catalogs; Book Volumes; Exhibition Catalogs
Special Subjects: Metalwork, Coins & Medals
Collections: Coins from different countries & centuries; medals; precious stones from antiquity, Middle Ages & Renaissance; Banknotes, shares; 17th century Japanese lacquer cabinets
Exhibitions: Special exhibs every year
Publications: Sylloge Nummorum Graecorum, exhibition catalogues
Activities: Lects open to pub; 15 vis lectrs per yr; originates traveling exhibs to museums, banks, universities, schools; mus shop sells books & reproductions

M **STAATLICHE SAMMLUNG AEGYPTISCHER KUNST,** State Museum of Egyptian Art, Hofgartenstrasse 1, Meiserstraße 10 Munich, 80333 Germany. Tel (089) 4989 29 8546; Fax (089) 289 27 638; Elec Mail poststelle@stmukwk.bayern.de; Internet Home Page Address: www.aegyptisches-museum-muenchen.de/de/index.htm; *Dir* Dr Sylvia Schoske
Open Tues - Fri 9 AM - 4 PM, Tues 7 PM - 9 PM, Sat - Sun 10 AM - 5 PM, cl Mon; Estab 1970; Average Annual Attendance: 80,000
Collections: Permanent Exhibitions
Activities: Classes for children; lects open to pub; gallery talks; mus & exhibs halls; books & various items

M **STADTISCHE GALERIE IM LENBACHHAUS,** Luisenstrasse 33, Munich, 80333 Germany. Tel (089) 233-32000; Fax (089) 233-32003; Elec Mail lenbachhaus@muenchen.de; Internet Home Page Address: www.lenbachhaus.de; *Dir* Dr Helmut Friedel
Open Tues - Sun 10 AM - 6 PM; Admis 6 Euro, reduced 3 Euro, family 9 Euro
Collections: Art Nouveau; The Blue Rider and Kandinsky and Klee; paintings by Munich artists; contemporary art
Activities: Classes for children; gallery talks; tours; mus shop sells books, magazines, original art, reproductions, prints & slides

NUREMBERG

M **GERMANISCHES NATIONALMUSEUM,** Kartausergasse 1, Postf 11 95 80 Nuremberg, D 90402 Germany. Tel ++49-(0)911-1331-0; Fax ++49-(0)911-1331-200; Elec Mail info@gnm.de; Internet Home Page Address: www.gnm.de; *Head* Prof Dr. G Ulrich Grossmann; *Dir Prints & Drawings* Dr Daniel Hess; *Dir Folk toys* Dr Claudia Selheim; *Dir Archives* Dr Birgit Jooss; *Dir Mgmt* Stefan Rosenberger; *Dir Mktg & Commun* Dr Andrea Langer; *Dir Library* Dr Johannes Pommeranz
Open Tue - Sun 10 AM - 6 PM, Wed 10 AM - 9 PM; Admis Wed 6-9 PM free, 6 Euro and reduced rate 4 Euro, small group/family rate 9 Euro; Estab 1852; mus archive, library for art and culture of the German speaking world; Library with 500,000 vols. Mus of German art & culture from the stone age to present; Average Annual Attendance: 350,000; Mem: 4.000/E 40
Income: 14.5 mio Euro; state 30%, land 60%, town 10%
Purchases: 400.000 Euro
Library Holdings: Auction Catalogs; Book Volumes; CD-ROMs; Exhibition Catalogs; Fiche; Manuscripts; Maps; Original Art Works; Original Documents; Pamphlets; Periodical Subscriptions; Photographs; Prints
Special Subjects: Archaeology, Drawings, Etchings & Engravings, Historical Material, Glass, Furniture, Gold, Porcelain, Pottery, Silver, Textiles, Maps, Painting-European, Sculpture, Tapestries, Graphics, Watercolors, Folk Art, Woodcarvings, Woodcuts, Landscapes, Decorative Arts, Manuscripts, Dolls, Metalwork, Carpets & Rugs, Ivory, Coins & Medals, Baroque Art, Renaissance Art, Medieval Art, Stained Glass, Painting-German, Military Art
Collections: Ancient historical objects, archives, books, folk art, furniture, manuscripts, musical instruments, paintings, sculpture, textiles, toys, weapons
Exhibitions: Traveling Companions; Witnesses to Mobility; The Fruit of Promise; Citrus Fruits in Art & Culture
Publications: Museum yearbook, catalogues of exhibitions and permanent collections, museum guides, popular books on the museum's collections
Activities: Classes for adults & children in Art Educ Center; docent training; lects open to pub & mem; concerts; gallery talks; tours; lending of original object of art to scientifically relevant exhibs & museums for special exhibs; book traveling exhibs, 1 per year; originates traveling exhibs, 1-2 per yr; mus shop sells books, magazines, reproductions, prints, postcards, souvenirs

RECKLINGHAUSEN

M **MUSEEN DER STADT RECKLINGHAUSEN,** Recklinghausen City Museums, Grosse Perdekamp Str 25-27, Recklinghausen, 45657 Germany. Tel (02361) 501935; Fax (02361) 501932; Elec Mail info@kunst-re.de; Internet Home Page Address: www.kunst-re.de; *Dir* Dr Ferdinand Ullrich; *Dir* Dr Hans-Jurgen Schwalm; *Custodian Mus Icons* Dr Eva Haustein-Bartsch
Open Tues - Sun 10 AM - 6 PM; Admis C 75 - 2.50 Euro; Estab 1950-1988; contemporary art, outsider art, icons; Average Annual Attendance: 20,000
Library Holdings: Auction Catalogs; Book Volumes; Exhibition Catalogs
Collections: Paintings, sculpture, drawings & prints by contemporary artists; outsider art; icons
Activities: Award, Kunstpreis: Junger westen; since 1948 for artists younger than 35; lending of original objects of art to Artothek; mus shop sells books, original art, reproductions & slides

STUTTGART

M **STAATSGALERIE STUTTGART,** Konrad-Adenauer-Strasse 30-32, Stuttgart, 70173 Germany; PO Box 104342, Stuttgart, 70038 Germany. Tel +49-711-47040-0; Fax +49-711-236 9983 (Dept Painting & Sculpture); +49-711-470-40333 (Dept Prints & Drawings); Elec Mail info@staatsgalerie.de; Internet Home Page Address; Others +49-711-47040-249; *Dir* Dr Christiane Lange; *Head Communs* Dr Beate Wolf; *Cur Early German Art* Dr Elsbeth Wiemann; *Cur Italian Art* Dr August Bernhard Rave; *Cur Art 1800-1900* Dr Christofer Conrad; *Cur Art 1900-1980* Dr Ina Conzen; *Cur Contemporary Art & Photography* Alice Koegel; *Cur Prints & Drawings* Dr Hans-Martin Kaulbach; *Cur Prints & Drawings* Dr Corinna Hoper; *Archives* Dr Werner Esser; *Provenance Research* Dr Anja Heuss; *Deputy Dir* Dr Ina Conzen; *Archives* Dr Wolf Eiermann
Open Wed & Fri 10 AM - 6 PM, Tues & Thurs 10 AM - 8 PM, Sat & Sun 10AM-6PM, cl Mon; Admis (coll) E 5.50/ E 4(reduced); Wed & Sat free; (spl exhib) E 12/E 9 (reduced); Built between 1838-1843; Neue Staatsgalerie built 1984, extension 2002; Old German Masters 14th - 16th century, Dutch paintings 16th - 18th century, Italian paintings 14th - 18th century, Baroque paintings, 19th century paintings & 21st century paintings & sculptures, Contemporary Art, Photography; Average Annual Attendance: 200,000; Mem: 12,500
Library Holdings: Auction Catalogs; Book Volumes; Clipping Files; Exhibition Catalogs
Special Subjects: Drawings, Etchings & Engravings, Photography, Painting-European, Sculpture, Graphics, Prints, Painting-Dutch, Period Rooms, Medieval Art, Painting-Italian, Painting-German
Collections: European art, 14th - 21st century; international art of the 20th century; graphic art
Exhibitions: (For future exhibs please use website)
Publications: exhib catalogs
Activities: Classes for adults & children; docent training; lects open to pub; tours for children & handicapped persons; concerts; gallery talks; mus shop sells books, reproductions, prints

WITTEN

M **MARKISCHES MUSEUM DER STADT WITTEN,** Husemannstrasse 12, Witten, 58452 Germany. Tel (02302) 5812550; *Dir* Dr Wolfgang Zemter
Collections: 20th century German paintings, drawings & graphics

GHANA

ACCRA

M **GHANA NATIONAL MUSEUM,** Barnes Rd, PO Box 3343 Accra, Ghana. Tel 00233 021 221633; Fax 00233 021 221635; Elec Mail gmmb-acc@africaonline.com.gh; *Head* E A Asante
Open daily 9 AM - 5 PM
Collections: Art, archeological and ethnological colls for Ghana and West Africa

GREECE

ANDROS

M **MUSEUM OF CONTEMPORARY ART, BASIL AND ELISE GOULANDRIS FOUNDATION,** Hora, Andros, 84500 Greece. Tel 30-22820-22444; Fax 30-22820-22490; Elec Mail info@goulandris.gr; info@moca-andros.gr; Internet Home Page Address: www.goulandris.gr/en; www.moca-andros.gr; *Dir* Dr Kyriakos Koutsomallis; *Art Historian* Eleana Margariti; *Press Commun* Eleni Galani; *Admin of Scholarships* Alexandra Papakostopoulou
Open during temporary exhib Mon, Wed - Sat 10 AM - 2 PM & 6 PM - 8 PM, Sun 10 AM - 2 PM, cl Tues; Admis adults 6 euros, students 3 euros; Estab 1979; 3 levels, 8 rooms; Average Annual Attendance: 30,000
Income: Self-financed
Library Holdings: Auction Catalogs; Book Volumes; Cards; Exhibition Catalogs; Pamphlets
Collections: The Basil & Elise Goulandris Collection
Publications: Isamu Noguchi: Between East & West (exhib catalogs)
Activities: Classes for children; lects open to pub; gallery talks; tours; schols available; lending original object of art to other mus; mus shop sells books, original art, reproductions, prints, decorative artistic items, jewelry

ATHENS

M **ARCHAEOLOGICAL MUSEUM OF CORINTH,** c/o Am Sch of Classical Studies, 54 Souideas Athens, Greece. Tel 0741 31207; *Dir* Phani Pachiyanni
Open Mon - Fri 8 AM - 5 PM, Sat - Sun 8:30 AM - 5 PM

M **BENAKI MUSEUM,** Odos Koumbari 1, Athens, 10674 Greece. Tel 36 11 617; Fax 36 22 547; *Dir* Dr Angelos Delivorrias
Library, historical archives and photographic archives are maintained
Collections: Ancient Greek art, chiefly jewelry; Byzantine and post-Byzantine art, icons and crafts; collections of Islamic art and Chinese porcelain; Greek popular art and historical relics; textiles from Far East and Western Europe

M **BYZANTINE & CHRISTIAN MUSEUM, ATHENS,** (Byzantine Museum) 22 Vasilissis Sophias Ave, Athens, 10675 Greece. Tel 213 213 9500-1; Fax 7231883; Elec Mail bma@byzantinemuseum.gr; Internet Home Page Address: www.byzantinemuseum.gr; *Dir* Eugenia Chalkia; *Deputy Dir* Anastasia Lazaridou; *Deputy Dir* K Ph Kalafatis
Open Apr - Oct: Tues - Sun 8 AM - 19:30 PM, Nov - Mar Tues -Sun 8:30 AM - 15:00 PM; cl Mon, Jan 1, Mar 25, Good Friday (open 12:00-17:00), Easter Sunday, May1, Dec 25-26; Admis full: 4E, reduced: 2E; Founded 1914; Library & photo archives are maintained; Average Annual Attendance: 80,00; Mem: 250; dues 40 E once a month
Purchases: Publication (diaries & other) ; works of art
Library Holdings: Fiche; Periodical Subscriptions; Reproductions
Special Subjects: Archaeology, Decorative Arts, Architecture, Ceramics, Metalwork, Textiles, Manuscripts, Painting-European, Tapestries, Costumes, Religious Art, Jewelry, Antiquities-Byzantine, Coins & Medals, Embroidery, Medieval Art, Islamic Art, Antiquities-Greek, Mosaics, Painting-Russian
Collections: Byzantine & Post-Byzantine icons, ceramics, marbles, metalwork; Christian & Byzantine sculpture & pottery; liturgical items; Greek manuscripts; historic photographs
Exhibitions: Permanent exhib (Byzantine coll)
Publications: European & Hellenic Ceramic of 18th century
Activities: Classes for adults & children; disabled group; lects open to pub; concerts; gallery talks; 5 vis lectrs per year; artmobile; lending of original objects of art to museums & institutions in Europe & America; book 1 traveling exhib per yer; mus shop sells books, cards, posters, video cassettes, CDs, CD-ROMs, reproductions, prints, slides, replicas, engravings, wall-paintings & accessories

M **FRISSIRAS MUSEUM,** 3 Monis Asteriou, Plaka Athens, Greece. Tel +30-2103234678; Fax +30-2103316027; Elec Mail frissiras@lawfrissiras.gr; Internet Home Page Address: www.frissirasmuseum.com
Average Annual Attendance:

M **MUSEUM OF CYCLADIC ART,** 4 Neophytou Douka St, Athens, 106 74 Greece. Tel 30 210 7228321 3; Fax 30 7239382; Elec Mail museum@cycladic.gr; Internet Home Page Address: www.cycladic.gr; *Pres* Sandra Marinopoulos; *Dir* Nicholas Stampolidis
Open Mon & Wed - Fr - Sati 10 AM - 5 PM, Sun 11 AM - 5 PM; Admis adults 7E, students, senior citizens & Mon 3.5E, children under 18, archeologists, ICOM & Eurocard holders journalists, visitors with disabilities no charge; Estab 1986, study & promotion of art culture of the Aegean & Cyprus; Mem: Dues doner 500 euro; supporter 250 euro; member 80 euro
Special Subjects: Archaeology, Antiquities-Greek, Antiquities-Roman
Collections: Greek art & artifacts of the Cycladic era
Publications: Catalogue of the colls; catalogue of the temporary exhibs; Timelines; educational booklets

Activities: Classes for adults & children; lects open to the pub; gallery talks; tours; mus shop sells books, original art, reproductions

M **NATIONAL ARCHAEOLOGICAL MUSEUM,** Patission Ave, Athens, 10682 Greece. Tel 8217717; Fax 8213573; 8230800; Elec Mail earn@culture.gr; Internet Home Page Address: www.namuseum.gr; *Dir* Dr Nikolaos Kaltsas; *Head of Sculpture* Eleni Kourinou, Dr; *Head of Bronze* Dr Rosa Proskynitopoulou; *Head of Pub Rels, Educ* Dr Alexandra Christopoulou; *Architect, Head of Technical Support* Mrs Vasiliki Drouga; *Head of Prehistoric Coll* Dr Eleni Papazoglou; *Vase & Minor Art Coll* Dr Anastasta Goidolou; *Vase & Minor Art Coll* Dr George Kavvadias
Open summer: Mon 13:30 PM - 20:00 PM, Tues - Sun 8 AM - 20:00 PM, winter: Mon 13:30 PM - 20:00 PM, Tues, Wed, Fri-Sun 8:30 AM - 15:00 PM; Admis 7 Euro, reduced 3 Euro, students free; Estab 1889; 9.000 sq meters of exhib galleries; Average Annual Attendance: 312,000; Mem: Soc of Friends of the Nat Arch Mus
Income: Financed by the state
Library Holdings: Auction Catalogs; Book Volumes; CD-ROMs; DVDs; Exhibition Catalogs; Periodical Subscriptions; Photographs; Prints; Reproductions; Slides; Video Tapes
Special Subjects: Archaeology, History of Art & Archaeology, Art History, Ceramics, Glass, Gold, Silver, Bronzes, Sculpture, Jewelry, Ivory, Miniatures, Antiquities-Egyptian, Antiquities-Greek, Antiquities-Roman, Antiquities-Etruscan
Collections: Original Greek sculptures; Roman period sculptures; Bronze Age relics; Mycenaean treasures; Greek vases, terracottas; jewels; Egyptian antiquities; neolithic coll, cyclodic collection, Stathetes jewelry collection; coll of Cypriot Antiquities, vases & minor arts collection (terracotta figurines), Vlastos-Serpieris, glass vessels, gold jewelry & silver vessels; Hellenistic pottery Coll
Publications: Worshiping Women (catalogue); Eretria (catalogue); Myth & Colnage (catalogue)
Activities: Classes for deaf children & elderly people; fire educ progs every yr for school-classes; musical & theatrical performances; lectrs for mems only; 12 vis lectrs per year; concerts; lending of original objects of art to scientific archaeological exhibitions; European & US mus; sales shop sells books, reproductions, prints, slides, jewelry, painting art, toys (puzzles), accessories, bags, cravates, mantilla

M **NATIONAL GALLERY - ALEXANDROS SOUTZOS MUSEUM,** Hellnic Army Park, Athens, 11525 Greece; PO Box 18009, Athens, 11601 Greece. Tel 210-721-6560, 723-5857; Fax 210-722-4889; Elec Mail secretary@nationalgallery.ge; Internet Home Page Address: www.nationalgallery.ge; *Dir* Marina Lambraki-Plaka; *Western European Painting Cur* Efi Agathonikou; *Conservation Chief* Michael Doulgeridis; *Admin Chief* Marina Laurbraki-Platea; *19th century Greek Painting* Maria Katsanaki; *Early 20thc-1940* Zina Kaloudi; *Early 20thc-1940* Annie Malama; *After 1945 & New Media* Lina Tsikouta; *Printmaking & Drawings* Marilena Cassimatis; *Sculpture* Tonia Giannoudaki; *Sculpture* Artemis Zezvou; *European Projects* Katerina Tavantzi; *Photographic & Historical Archivist* Georgia Mataxa
Open Mon & Wed 10 - 1800, Thurs - Sat & Sun 9 -1500, cl Tues; Admis 5 euros, 3 euros (discounted admis); Mus of modern Greek art (1500-2000); Average Annual Attendance: 100,000
Income: State/sponsoring
Library Holdings: Book Volumes; CD-ROMs; Cards; Cassettes; Exhibition Catalogs; Framed Reproductions; Memorabilia; Reproductions
Collections: Engravings; 14th - 21st century European painting; 17th - 20th century Greek engravings, paintings & sculpture; impressionist, post-impressionist & contemporary drawings
Activities: Classes for children; concerts; gallery talks; tours; extension prog serves other Mus; organize traveling exhibs to other mus in Greece & abroad; sales shop sells books, original art, reproductions, prints

M **Coumantaros Art Gallery,** 123 Konstantinou Paloiologou & Thermopylon St, Sparta, 23100 Greece. Tel 30 27310 81822, 81557
Open Mon - Sat 9 - 15, Sun 10 - 14, cl Tues

M **NATIONAL MUSEUM OF CONTEMPORARY ART,** Amv Frantzi 14, Athens, 11743 Greece; 17-19 Vas. Georgiou B' & Rigillis, Athens, 10675 Greece. Tel 210-9242111-3; Fax 210-9245200; Elec Mail protocol@emst.gr; Internet Home Page Address: www.emst.gr; *Dir* Anna Kafetsi
Admis adults 3 euro, students 1.5 euro, mems, children under 12, seniors, disabled & attendants free, Thurs 5-10 PM free to all; Estab 2000; Mus of contemporary art
Library Holdings: Auction Catalogs; Audio Tapes; CD-ROMs; Compact Disks; DVDs; Exhibition Catalogs; Original Documents; Pamphlets; Periodical Subscriptions; Photographs; Records; Slides; Video Tapes
Collections: Painting and three-dimensional work; historical and contemporary; photography, new media, architecture and design
Publications: Catalogues (included with all art exhibs)
Activities: Classes for adults & children; gallery talks; tours; organize traveling exhibs to other cities in Greece; sales shop sells books, magazines

ATTICA

M **VORRES MUSEUM OF CONTEMPORARY GREEK ART AND FOLK ART,** Paiania, Attica, GR 190 02 Greece. Tel (210) 664-2520/664-4771; Fax 66 45 77 5; Elec Mail mvorres@otrnet.gr; Internet Home Page Address: www.vorresmuseum.gr; *Pres* Ian Vorres; *Dir* George Vorres
Open Mon - Fri for groups by appointment only, Sat -Sun 10 AM - 2 PM; Admis group 10 Euros, adults 5 Euros, children 3 Euros; Estab 1983; New 2000 sq meter wing to the Museum of Contemporary Greek Art; Average Annual Attendance: 70,000 - 80,000; Mem: Friends; 500 euro ann
Income: Sale of tickets & catalogues, rental of space for receptions
Library Holdings: Book Volumes; Exhibition Catalogs; Reproductions
Special Subjects: Folk Art, Ceramics, Glass, Furniture, Coins & Medals, Antiquities-Greek
Collections: Contemporary Greek art; Greek Folk art

Publications: Catalogues & volumes for each part of the museum in Greek & English
Activities: Classes for children; special guided tours

DELPHI

M **DELPHI ARCHAEOLOGICAL MUSEUM,** Delphi, 33054 Greece. Tel 30-22650-82312; Fax 30-22650-82966; Elec Mail iepka@culture.gr; *Dir* Athanasia Psalti
Open daily 7:30 AM - 7 PM; Admis adult 6 euro, reduced 3 euro, under 18 free; Museum and site 9 euro; Estab 1902; Average Annual Attendance: 350,000
Collections: Sculptures, artifacts & architecture from the Oracle of Delphi and surrounding excavation site; Athenian treasury, stoa, theatre, Temple of Apollo, stadium, Temple of Athena, Roman Agora and more
Activities: Classes for adults & children; tours; 5 vis lectrs per yr

M **MINISTRY OF CULTURE & TOURISM,** (The Delphi Museum) The Delphi Museum, 10th Ephorate of Prehistoric & Classical Antiquities, Delphi, 33054 Greece. Tel 3022650 82313 / 82346; Fax 3022650 82966; Elec Mail iepka@culture.gr; *Dir & Archaeologist* Nansy Psalti; *Archaeologist* Dr Sotiris Raptopoulos; *Archaeologist* Dr Elena C Partida, MA, PhD; *Archaeologist* Anthoula Tsaroucha
Open daily 8:30 AM - 3 PM (Winter schedule), Tues - Sun 8 AM - 8 PM, Mon 1:30 PM - 8 PM (Summer); Admis 6 Euros, concessionary 3 Euros; Estab 1903; Library with 4800 vols; Average Annual Attendance: 350,000
Library Holdings: Book Volumes; CD-ROMs; Cards; Exhibition Catalogs; Maps; Periodical Subscriptions; Photographs; Slides
Special Subjects: History of Art & Archaeology, Architecture, Ceramics, Metalwork, Silver, Sculpture, Bronzes, Archaeology, Crafts, Landscapes, Glass, Jewelry, Asian Art, Historical Material, Ivory, Coins & Medals, Antiquities-Egyptian, Antiquities-Greek, Antiquities-Roman, Mosaics, Gold
Collections: Permanent exhibition of ancient sculpture, vases, inscriptions, statuettes, bronze weapons, tools of different periods
Activities: Mus shop sells books, reproductions, prints, slides, corporate gifts, office & paper products, accessories, games

HERAKLION

M **HERAKLION ARCHAEOLOGICAL MUSEUM,** 2 Xanthoudidou St, Heraklion, 71202 Greece. Tel 2810-279000; Fax 2810-279071; Elec Mail amh@culture.gr; Internet Home Page Address: www.culture.gr; *Dir* Dr George Rethemiotakis
Open Summer: 8 AM - 8 PM, Winter: 8 AM - 3 PM; Mon 1 - 8 PM; Admis 4 euros; Temporary exhibs including highlights from the permanent colls
Income: Pub sector
Library Holdings: Book Volumes; CD-ROMs; Exhibition Catalogs; Other Holdings; Pamphlets; Periodical Subscriptions
Collections: Development of Cretan & Minoan art; Classical & late antiquity exhibits
Publications: N Dimopoulou - Rethemiotaki; The Meraklion Archaeological Museum; Latsis Foundation; Athens, 2005
Activities: Classes for children; lending of original objects of art to Greece & other countries; mus shop sells books, prints & slides

OLYMPIA

M **ARCHAEOLOGICAL MUSEUM OF OLYMPIA,** Olympia, 27065 Greece. Tel 2624022529; Fax 2624022529; Elec Mail zepka@culture.gr; Internet Home Page Address: www.culture.gr; *Head* Georgia Chatzi-Spiliopoulou; *Archaeologist* Matzanas Christos; *Archaeologist* Liaggouras Christos; *Archaeologist* Leventour Roula; *Archaeologist* Loumiot Gourlomat Kalliopi; *Archaeologist* Antonopoulos Konstantinos; *Archaeologist-Museologist* Alexandra Seleli
Open Winter 8 AM - 3 PM, Summer 8 AM - 8 PM; Admis adults 19 - 65 yrs mus or site 6 euro, site & museum (joint) 9 euro, over 65 mus or site 3 euro, joint 5 euro; children free; Estab 1982 as an archaeological mus; Prehistoric, classical and Roman antiquities; Average Annual Attendance: 440,000
Library Holdings: Book Volumes; CD-ROMs; Cards; DVDs; Exhibition Catalogs; Maps; Pamphlets; Periodical Subscriptions
Special Subjects: Bronzes, Archaeology, Ceramics, Antiquities-Greek, Antiquities-Roman
Collections: Ancient Greek sculpture, bronzes, ceramics & glass
Publications: Arapoyanni Xeni, Olympia; Vikatou Olympia, olympia archaeological site and museums; Chatzi Spiliopoulou Georgia, Archaeological Museum of Olympia
Activities: Classes for children; docent training; educational material for school classes; family trail for the Bronzes Gallery of the mus; mus shop sells books, reproductions, slides, cards

RETHYMNON

M **L. KANAKAKIS MUNICIPAL GALLERY,** 5 Chimaras St., Rethymnon, 74100 Greece. Tel +30-2831-55847/52530; Fax +30-2831-52689; Elec Mail rca@ret.forthnet.gr; Internet Home Page Address: www.rca.gr
Average Annual Attendance:

THESSALONIKI

M **GREEK MINISTRY OF CULTURE,** Archaeological Museum of Thessaloniki, 6 Manolis Andronikou St, Thessaloniki, 54621 Greece; 6 Manolis Andronikou St, PO Box 506 19, P C 54013 Thessaloniki, 54621 Greece. Tel 00302310-830538; Fax 00302310-831037; Elec Mail info.amth@culture.gr; Internet Home Page Address: www.amth.gr; *Dir* Dr Polyxeni Adam-Veleni
Open Summer: Mon 13:30 PM - 20.00 PM, Tues - Sun 8 AM - 20.00 PM; Winter: Mon 10:30 PM - 17.00 PM, Tues -Sun 8:30 PM - 15.00 PM; Admis

adults 6E, seniors 3E; Estab 10-27-1962; Archaeological collections displayed in one building gallery; Average Annual Attendance: 100,000
Income: Financed by state
Library Holdings: Auction Catalogs; Book Volumes; Exhibition Catalogs; Filmstrips; Photographs; Slides
Special Subjects: Archaeology, Architecture, Ceramics, Glass, Metalwork, Bronzes, Jewelry, Ivory, Coins & Medals, Antiquities-Greek, Antiquities-Roman, Mosaics, Gold
Collections: Macedonian archaeology, mainly from Thessaloniki, Chalkidiki, Kilkis & Pieria (from the prehistoric times to late antiquity)
Exhibitions: 5,000, 15,000, 200,000 yrs ago An exhibition about life; Prehistoric Macedonia; Towards the Birth of Cities; In Macedonia from the 7th CBE until late antiquity; Thessaloniki the Metropolis of Macedonia; The gold of Macedon; Kalindou: An Ancient City in Macedonia: Alexander the Great; Field-House-Garden-Grave (open ground exhib) Macedonia: from fragments to pixels
Publications: Lithos: Acts of a Day Conference on the Conservation of the Store Object; Archaeology Behind Battle Lines. In Thessaloniki of the turbulent years 1912-1922
Activities: Nat progs for children, hands-on activities; periodic exhibs inspired by themes both from ancient & modern culture; lects open to public, 12 vis lects per yr; concerts; tours; gallery talks; workshops; lending original objects of art to museums in Europe and elsewhere; Originates traveling exhibitions on Alexander the Great that circulate to other regions in Macedonia supports archaeology research; mus shop sells books, reproductions, prints, slides, puzzles, scarves, ties, t-shirts, bags

M **STATE MUSEUM OF CONTEMPORARY ART,** (Thessaloniki State Museum of Contemporary Art) 21 Kolokotroni St, Stavroupoli Thessaloniki, 56430 Greece. Tel 30-2310-589-149; Fax 30-2310-600123; Elec Mail info@greekstatemuseum.com; Elec Mail library@greekstatemuseum.com; Internet Home Page Address: www.greekstatemuseum.com; *Dir* Dr Maria Tsantsanoglou; *Pub Rels Officer* Chrysa Zarkali; *Press Office* Yiota Sotiropoulou; *International Relations* Atwina Ioaunou; *Library Contact* Alexandros Daniel
Open Mon - Fri 10 AM - 2 PM & 5 PM - 9 PM, Sat - Sun 10 AM - 9 PM; Admis adults 3 euro, students 1.5 euro; Estab 1997; Average Annual Attendance: 45,000
Income: State funded
Library Holdings: Book Volumes; Exhibition Catalogs; Fiche
Collections: George Costakis Collection; Russian avant-garde art, 1,275 oil paintings, constructions, and drawings; 100 works of art, 200 paintings and sculptures; Contemporary art by Greek artists
Exhibitions: Variety of exhibs throughout yr
Publications: List of publs accompanying the exhibs
Activities: Classes for adults & children, access prog for visual impaired people; concerts, gallery talks & tours; originates traveling exhibs to all visitors; sales shop sells books & promotional objects

GREENLAND

NUUK

M **GREENLAND NATIONAL MUSEUM & ARCHIVES,** Hans Egedevej 8, PO Box 145 Nuuk, 3900 Greenland. Tel 299-32-26-11; Fax 299-32-26-22; Elec Mail nka@natmus.gl; Internet Home Page Address: www.natmus.gl; *Dir* Daniel Thorleifsen
Open June 1 - Sept 30 Tues - Sun 10 AM - 4 PM; Oct 1 - May 31 Tues - Sun 1 PM - 4 PM, cl Mon
Special Subjects: Archaeology, Watercolors, Ethnology, Crafts, Eskimo Art, Scrimshaw
Collections: Inuit Archaeological colls; Gustav Holm Collection of Ammassalik in the 1880s; Inughuit-Polareskimos around 1900, kayaks, art and handicrafts, early Inuit art of the 19th century; Modern and contemporary Inuit art; Photography coll; Norse Coll

GUATEMALA

GUATEMALA CITY

M **MUSEO NACIONAL DE ARQUEOLOGIA Y ETNOLOGIA,** Archaeological & Ethnographical Museum, Edif No 5, La Aurora Guatemala City, Zona 13 Guatemala. Tel 472-0489; Fax 472-0489; *Dir* Patricia del Aguila Flores
Open Tues - Fri 9 AM - 4 PM, Sat - Sun 9 AM - noon & 1:30 PM - 4 PM; Admis Guatemalans Q3.00, foreigners Q30.00; Estab 1931; Average Annual Attendance: 85,000
Collections: Mayan art
Publications: Simposio de Investigaciones Arqueologicas en Guatemala
Activities: Sales shop sells books, magazines, slides

M **MUSEO NACIONAL DE ARTE MODERNO,** Edificio No 6, Finca La Aurora Guatemala City, Zona 13 Guatemala. Tel 310-403; *Dir* J Oscar Barrientos
Open Tues - Fri 9 AM - 4 PM, Sat & Sun 9 AM - 12 noon & 1:30 PM - 4 PM; Admis Q10
Collections: Paintings, sculpture, engravings, drawings

M **UNIVERSIDAD FRANCISCO MARROQUIN,** 6 Calle Final, Zona 10 Guatemala, 01010 Guatemala. Tel 502-2338-7700; Fax 502-2334-6896; Elec Mail inf@ufm.edu.gt; Internet Home Page Address: www.ufm.edu
M **Popol Vuh Archaeological Museum,** Universidad Francisco Marroquin, 6 calle final zona 10 Guatemala City, 01010 Guatemala. Tel 502-2338-7896; Tel

502-2361-2301; 2311; 2321; Elec Mail popolvuh@ufm.edu.gt; Internet Home Page Address: www.popolvuh.ufm.edu.gt; *Cur* Oswaldo Chinchilla
Open Mon - Fri 9 AM - 5 PM, Sat 9 AM - 1 PM, cl Sun; Admis adults Q35, students Q15, children 2-12 Q10
Collections: Collection of pre-Hispanic art, stone sculptures and ceramics; Pre-classic, classic and post-classic Maya eras, colonial art, folk art; Textiles, clothing, masks and decorative arts

M **Museo Ixchel de Traje Indigena,** Universidad Francisco Marroquin, 6 calle final zona 10 Guatemala City, 01010 Guatemala. Tel 502-2331-3739, 331-3622; Elec Mail info@museoixchel.org; Internet Home Page Address: museoixchel.org; *Admin* Rosa Amparo Lopez de Enriquez; *Head Photogr, Photo Archive* Anne Girard De Marroquin; *Exhibits Dir* Pilar Cruz de Morales; *Dir Pub Rels* Annabella Pellegrini Macal; *Dir Mus Shop* Silvia Bauer Estrada; *Dir Educ* Fabiana Flores de Saenz
Open Mon - Fri 9 AM - 5 PM, Sat 9 AM - 1 PM; Admis adults $5, students $2, children $1.50; Estab 1977; Two large spaces to collect, conserve, document, recover and exhibit the Maya textiles of Guatemala, with emphasis on the cultural, technical and artistic significance of the Maya weavings; Average Annual Attendance: 8,850; Mem: 125; dues $40, corporate $135
Income: Financed by admissions, donations, activities, conferences, workshops
Library Holdings: Kodachrome Transparencies; Photographs
Collections: Indigenous clothing and handwoven fabrics from 120 highland communities; Sculptures, photographs, paintings, ceramics, jewelry and more; Pre-Hispanic Maya clothing, Maya-Hispanic clothing, Historic Maya clothing, Contemporary Maya clothing; Embroidery: Stitches that Unite Cultures
Publications: Exhibit & collection catalogs; Books, calendars
Activities: Classes for adults & children; docent training; workshops; tours; mus shop sells books, reproductions, handicrafts, Mayan weavings & dress

GUINEA

CONAKRY

M **NATIONAL MUSEUM OF GUINEA,** 1ere Ave, Conakry BP 139 Conakry, Guinea. Tel 224-415-060; Fax 224-451-066; *Dir Gen* M Sory Kaba
Open Tues - Sun 9 AM - 6 PM, cl Mon; Admis nationals 500 FG, students 100 FG, foreigners 1000 FG
Collections: Ethnographic coll of masques, statues, musical instruments and archaeological artifacts

HAITI

PORT AU PRINCE

M **CENTRE D'ART,** 58 rue Roy, Port au Prince, Haiti. Tel 2-2018; *Dir* Francine Murat
Collections: Haitian art

HONDURAS

COMAYAGUA

M **MUSEO ARQUEOLOGIA DE COMAYAGUA,** Ciudad de Comayagua, Plaza San Francisco Comayagua, Honduras. Tel 72-03-86; *Dir* Salvador Turcios
Open Tues - Fri & Sun 8:30 AM - 4 PM, Sat 8:30 AM - 1 PM, cl Mon
Collections: Archaeology dating back to 1000 BC; colonial collections

HONG KONG

KOWLOON

M **HONG KONG MUSEUM OF ART,** 10 Salisbury Rd, Tsimshatsui Kowloon, Hong Kong. Tel 852 2721 0116; Fax 852 2723 7666; Elec Mail museumofart@lcsd.gov.hk; Internet Home Page Address: hk.art.museum; *Chief Cur* Tang Hoi-Chiu
Open daily 10 AM - 6 PM, Sat 10 AM - 8 PM, cl Thurs except pub holidays, cl 5 PM on Christmas Eve; Admis standard HK$10, concessionary HK$ 5, Wed no admis fee
Collections: Chinese antiquities; Chinese paintings & calligraphy with a specialization of Cantonese artists; historical collection of paintings, prints & drawings of Hong Kong, Macau & China; local & contemporary art

POKFULAM

M **HONG KONG UNIVERSITY,** (Hong Kong University Museum and Art Gallery) University Museum and Art Gallery, 90 Bonham Rd, Pokfulam, Hong Kong. Tel 852-2241-5500; Fax 852-2546-9659; Elec Mail museum@hkusua.hku.hk; Internet Home Page Address: www.hku.hk/hkumag/main.html; *Acting Dir* Anita Wong Yia-fong; *Cur* Tina Pang Yee-wan
Open Mon - Sat 9:30 AM - 6 PM, Sun 1 PM - 6 PM; No admis fee
Special Subjects: Decorative Arts, Folk Art, Religious Art, Crafts, Woodcarvings, Asian Art, Calligraphy, Antiquities-Oriental

Collections: Houses over 2,000 items of Chinese antiquities; Ceramics, bronze, paintings; examples dating from Neolithic period to Qing dynasty; Bronze from Shang to Tang dynasties and coll of Yuan dynasty Nestorian crosses; Jade, wood, and stone carvings; Chinese oil paintings; Old Hong Kong photographs
Activities: Workshops; Lects open to the pub; gallery talks; mus shop sells books, reproductions, souvenirs

HUNGARY

BUDAPEST

M **LUDWIG MUSEUM - MUSEUM OF CONTEMPORARY ART,** Komor Marcell u 1, Budapest, H-1095 Hungary. Tel 361-555-3444; Fax 361-555-3458; Elec Mail info@ludwigmuseum.hu; Internet Home Page Address: www.ludwigmuseum.hu; *Dir* Barnabas Bencsik; *Chief Cur* Kati Simon; *Head of Colls* Krisztina Szipocs
Open Tues - Sun 10 AM - 8 PM; cl Mon; Admis adults HUF 2200, students & senior citizens, HUF 1100; Estab 1989; Contemporary Art; Average Annual Attendance: 90,000
Library Holdings: Book Volumes; Exhibition Catalogs; Periodical Subscriptions
Special Subjects: Photography, Painting-American, Prints, Painting-French, Sculpture, Painting-Polish, Painting-German, Painting-Russian
Collections: Museum of contemporary art in Hungary to collecting international art; Collection from end of 1960s to present; Pieces of American Pop art and hyperrealism; Eastern-European avant-garde from the 1960's and 70's; geometric, minimalist work; international New painting from 1980s; Conceptual and Action art; International Contemporary Art
Publications: Collection of Ludwig Museum - Museum of Contemporary Art Budapest
Activities: Classes for children; film clubs; screenings; concerts; gallery talks; auxiliary family progs; museum educ; conferences; sales shop sells books; magazines

M **MAGYAR NEMZETI GALERIA,** Hungarian National Gallery, Buda Palace, Buildings A, B, C, D, Szent Gyorgy ter 2 Budapest, H-1014 Hungary; PO Box 31, Budapest, H-1250 Hungary. Tel 361 11 201 9032; Fax 212 7356; Elec Mail info@mng.hu; Internet Home Page Address: www.mng.hu; *Gen Dir* Dr Laszlo Baan; *Deputy Dir* Gyorgy Szucs
Open 10 AM - 6 PM; cl Mon; Admis permanent exhibs 1400 HUF, temporary exhibs 3200 HUF; Estab 1957; collects Hungarian art from the 11th century to date; Average Annual Attendance: 600,000
Income: Financed by the state
Library Holdings: Auction Catalogs; Book Volumes; Exhibition Catalogs
Collections: Ancient & modern Hungarian paintings & sculpture; medal cabinet; panel paintings
Activities: Classes for children; docent training; lects open to pub; 2,000 vis lectrs per yr; concerts; gallery talks; tours; mus shop sells books, reproductions, slides, magazines, prints

M **MAGYAR NEMZETI MUZEUM - HUNGARIAN NATIONAL MUSEUM,** Muzeum Krt 14-16, Budapest, 1088 Hungary; PF 364, Budapest, H-1370 Hungary. Tel 361-327-77-00, 327-77-68; Fax 361-317-78-06; Elec Mail hnm@hnm.hu; Internet Home Page Address: www.hnm.edu; *Dir* Dr Tibor Kovacs
Open Tues - Sun 10 AM - 6 PM, cl Mon; Admis Adult 1,000 HUF, students (6-26) & seniors (62-70) 500 HUF, under 6 free
Special Subjects: Anthropology, Decorative Arts, Drawings, Folk Art, Landscapes, Architecture, Ceramics, Glass, Metalwork, Furniture, Gold, Photography, Portraits, Prints, Silver, Textiles, Bronzes, Woodcuts, Manuscripts, Maps, Painting-European, Sculpture, Graphics, Archaeology, Ethnology, Costumes, Religious Art, Woodcarvings, Jewelry, Antiquities-Byzantine, Carpets & Rugs, Coins & Medals, Restorations, Miniatures, Renaissance Art, Embroidery, Medieval Art, Antiquities-Oriental, Antiquities-Egyptian, Antiquities-Greek, Antiquities-Roman, Leather, Military Art, Antiquities-Etruscan, Enamels
Collections: Archaeological coll from Paleolithic to present; Posters, decorative arts, silverware, arts and crafts, textiles, household items, ceramics, glassware, seals, stamps, weapons, musical instruments, toys, pewter, metalwork; Photography coll; Coin coll
Activities: Concerts; tours; lending of art objects to var museums; mus shop sells books & reproductions

M **MUCSARNOK,** Palace of Art, Dozsa Gyorgy, UT 37 Budapest, 1146 Hungary. Tel 1 343 7401; Fax 1 343 5202; Elec Mail info@mucsarnok.hu; Internet Home Page Address: www.mucsarnok.hu; *Dir* Zsolt Petránye
Open Tues, Wed, Fri - Sun 10 AM - 6 PM, Thurs 12 AM - 8 PM, cl Mon; Library: Mon & Wed 2 PM - 5 PM, Tues & Thurs 10 AM - 2 PM; Library with 15,000 vols
Collections: Hungarian & foreign art

M **SZEPMUVESZETI MUZEUM,** Museum of Fine Arts Budapest, Dozsa Gyorgy ut 41, Budapest, 1146 Hungary. Tel +36-1 469 7100; Fax +36-1 469 7171; Elec Mail info@szepmuveszeti.hu; Internet Home Page Address: www.szepmuveszeti.hu; *Gen Dir* Dr Laszlo Baan; *Deputy Gen Dir* Maria Mihaly; *Deputy Dir ResearcH* Dr Andrea Czere
Open Tues - Sun 10 AM - 5:30 PM, cl Mon; Admis 1,600 HUF; Estab 1896; Museum's coll is made up of international art, including all periods of European art & comprises more than 100,000 pieces; Average Annual Attendance: 550,000; Mem: Ministry for human resources
Income: State supported
Library Holdings: Auction Catalogs; Book Volumes; CD-ROMs; Compact Disks; Exhibition Catalogs; Fiche; Kodachrome Transparencies; Manuscripts; Original Documents; Other Holdings; Periodical Subscriptions; Photographs; Prints; Reproductions; Sculpture
Special Subjects: Etchings & Engravings, Landscapes, Marine Painting, Painting-British, Painting-European, Painting-French, Sculpture, Drawings,

Graphics, Painting-Dutch, Baroque Art, Painting-Flemish, Medieval Art, Painting-Spanish, Antiquities-Egyptian, Antiquities-Greek, Antiquities-Roman
Collections: Old Master, paintings Egyptian, 19th century art, 20th century art, old sculpture collection; Vasarely Collections; Classical antiquities, prints & drawings after 1800
Exhibitions: Permanent Exhibs of the collections; 6-8 temporary exhibs per yr
Publications: Bulletin, exhib catalogues, monographics, educ materials; catalogues of certain parts of colls
Activities: Classes for adults, children & mentally disabled; dramatic progs; docent training; exhibs; lects open to pub & lects for mems only; 5,000 vis lectrs per yr; concerts; gallery talks; tours; sponsoring of competitions; awards, 2011 mus magazine (Museum Cafe) Bronze Medal; artmobile; lending of original objects of art to national & international art institutions; mus shop sells books, magazines, original art, reproductions, prints slides & other items

ESZTERGOM

M **KERESZTENY MUZEUM,** Christian Museum, Mindszenty ter 2, Esztergom, H-2500 Hungary; PF 25, Esztergom, H-2500 Hungary. Tel +36 33 413880; Fax +36 33 413880; Elec Mail keresztenymuzeum@vnet.hu; Internet Home Page Address: www.christianmuseum.hu; *Pres* Pal Csefalvay
Open Wed-Sun, Mar 15 - Apr 30 11 AM - 3 PM; May 1 - Oct 31 10 AM - 6 PM; Nov 1 - Jan 1 11 AM - 3 PM, cl Mon & Tues; Admis individual 600 Huf; Estab 1875; Old Hungarian and European Painting; Applied Arts; Average Annual Attendance: 20,000
Library Holdings: Book Volumes; Exhibition Catalogs; Periodical Subscriptions
Special Subjects: Decorative Arts, Drawings, Etchings & Engravings, Folk Art, Ceramics, Glass, Flasks & Bottles, Furniture, Portraits, Pottery, Prints, Silver, Textiles, Woodcuts, Painting-European, Sculpture, Tapestries, Watercolors, Ethnology, Religious Art, Crafts, Woodcarvings, Jewelry, Porcelain, Metalwork, Painting-Dutch, Carpets & Rugs, Ivory, Coins & Medals, Baroque Art, Painting-Flemish, Renaissance Art, Embroidery, Medieval Art, Painting-Spanish, Painting-Italian, Stained Glass, Painting-German, Painting-Russian, Enamels
Collections: Hungarian, Austrian, Dutch, French, German & Italian medieval paintings and silver artwork, miniatures, porcelain, statues & tapestries
Publications: Catalogues of temporary exhib
Activities: Lects open to public; 4 vis lectrs per year; concerts; gallery talks; mus shop sells books, reproductions, prints & CD-ROMs

KECSKEMET

M **MAGYAR FOTOGRAFIAI MUZEUM - HUNGARIAN MUSEUM OF PHOTOGRAPHY,** Katona Jozsef ter 12, Kecskemet, H-6000 Hungary; Pf 446, Kecskemet, H-6001 Hungary. Tel 36-76-483-221; Fax 36-76-508-259; Elec Mail info@fotomuzeum.hu; Internet Home Page Address: www.fotomuzeum.hu; *Dir & Cur* Peter Baki
Open Apr - Oct Wed - Sun 10 AM - 5 PM, Nov - March Wed - Sun 10 AM - 4 PM, cl Mon - Tues; Admis adults HUF 150, students & seniors HUF100
Collections: Collection of over 500,000 photographs from 1840s onward; Original negatives, cameras, photographic history, artifacts, relics, medals, awards; Andre Kertesz coll; Pal Rosti album; Rudolf Baloghs WWII negative collection; Laszlo Moholy-Nagy Collection

M **MAGYAR NAIV MUVESZEK MUZEUMA,** Museum of Hungarian Native Art, Gaspar A U 11, Kecskemet, 6000 Hungary. Tel (076) 324767; *Dir* Dr Pal Banszky
Collections: Works of Hungarian primitive painters and sculptors

PECS

M **JANUS PANNONIUS MUZEUM,** Pf 158, Pecs, 7601 Hungary. Tel (072) 514-040; Fax (072) 514-042; Elec Mail jpm@jpm.hu; Internet Home Page Address: www.jpm.hu; *Head* Mrs Julia Fabeny; *Head Art History Dept* Mr Jozsef Sarkany; *Cur* Mrs Orsolya Kovacs; *Mus Educ* Mr Gabor Tillai; *Art Historian* Mr George Varkony; *Art Historian* Andras Nagy
Open Tues - Sun 10 AM - 6 PM, cl Mon; Admis 1200 HUF adults; 600 HUF seniors/students; Estab 1904; Library with 20,000 vols
Library Holdings: Auction Catalogs; Book Volumes; Cassettes; Exhibition Catalogs; Manuscripts; Memorabilia; Periodical Subscriptions
Special Subjects: Watercolors, Antiquities-Byzantine, Antiquities-Roman
Collections: Modern Hungarian art, 1880-2003; archaeology, ethnology, local history
Exhibitions: Zsolnay Ceramics (1955); Vasarely (1973); Csontvary (1983)
Publications: Catalogs of exhibs
Activities: Classes for adults & children; lects open to pub; 10 vis lectrs per year; concerts; gallery talks; tours; lending of original art objects; originate traveling exhibs; mus shop sells books, prints & reproductions

SOPRON

M **SOPRONI MUZEUM,** Foter 8, Sopron, 9400 Hungary. Tel 99 311-327; Fax 99 311 347; *Dir* Dr Attila Kornyei
Library with 20,000 vols
Collections: Folk & local Baroque art

SZENTENDRE

M **FERENCZY MUZEUM,** Foter 6, PF 49 Szentendre, 2000 Hungary. Tel (26) 310244; Fax (26) 310790; Elec Mail kozmuvelodes@pmmi.hu; Internet Home Page Address: www.pmmi.hu; *Dir* Laszlo Simon, PhD; *Deputy Dir* Feno Darko, PhD; *Dir* Audras Czeyk; *Deputy Dir* Judit Kovacs
Open daily 9 AM - 5 PM; Admis fee 400 HUF; Estab 1951; Library with 22,000 vols; Average Annual Attendance: 1700

Income: Supported by county govt
Library Holdings: Book Volumes; Exhibition Catalogs
Special Subjects: Archaeology, Drawings, Folk Art, Ceramics, Pottery, Sculpture, Tapestries, Graphics, Dolls, Carpets & Rugs
Collections: Paintings, sculptures, drawings; archaeological, ethnographic & local history collections; Gobelin tapestries; Kmetty-Kerenyi Collection; Kovoes Margil Ceramic Collection; Barcsay Collection; Vajda Collection; Anna-Ames Collection; Kovacs Margit Ceramic Coll
Exhibitions: Roman lapidarium, dolls & toy soldiers exhibition
Activities: Classes for adults & children; excavations in Pest County, scientific researches, temporary exhibs; concerts; lending of original art objects to fellow institutions & other museums; mus shop sells books, reproductions, stamps & DVDs & other gift items

ZALAEGERSZEG

M **GOCSEJI MUZEUM,** Batthyany U2, PO Box 176 Zalaegerszeg, 8900 Hungary. Tel 36-92-311-455; Fax 36-92-511-972; Elec Mail muzeum@zmmi.hu; Internet Home Page Address: www.zmmi.hu; *Art Historian & Deputy Dir* Dr Laszlo Kostyal; *Historian* Uatalin Beres Kissne; *Ethnographer* Maria Marx
Library with 12,000 vols
Special Subjects: Archaeology, Folk Art, Historical Material, Furniture, Photography, Sculpture, Hispanic Art
Collections: Regional paintings & sculptures
Exhibitions: Constant exhibs: Zsigmond Kisfaludi Strobl, sculptor; Janos Neineth, ceramics

ICELAND

REYKJAVIK

M **LISTASAFAN REYKJAVIKUR - REYKJAVIK ART MUSEUM,** Halfnarhus - Harbour House, Tryggvagata 17, Postbox 110 Reykjavik, 110 Iceland. Tel 354-590-1200; Fax 354-590-1201; Elec Mail listasafn@reykjavik.is; Internet Home Page Address: www.artmuseum.is; *Dir* Hafthor Yngvason
Open daily 10 AM - 5 PM; Admis for all 3 museums; adults kr 500, seniors kr 250, under 18 free, Thurs free
Collections: Three colls of work by individual Icelandic artists; In charge of general art coll and outdoor sculpture coll for city of Reykjavik; Housed in three locations, Halfnarhus, Kjarvalsstadir & Asmundarsafn; Diverse exhibitions of contemporary and experimental art both Icelandic and international; Erro Coll

M **Kjarvalsstadir,** Flokagata 105, Reykjavik, Iceland. Tel 354-517-1290
Open daily 10 AM - 5 PM
Collections: Icelandic and international modern art; Johannes S Kjarval Collection

M **Asmundarsafn - Asmundur Sveinsson Sculpture Museum,** Sigtun 105, Reykjavik, Iceland. Tel 354-553-2155
Open May - Sept 10 AM - 4 PM, Oct - Apr 1 PM - 4 PM
Collections: Asmundur Sveinsson Sculpture Collection

M **LISTASAFN EINARS JONSSONAR,** National Einar Jonsson Art Gallery, PO Box 1051, Reykjavik, IS T2T Iceland. Tel (55) 13797; Fax 562 3909; Elec Mail lej@lej.is; Internet Home Page Address: www.lej.is; *Dir* Julianna Gottskalksdottir
Open Mon - Wed, Fri - Sun 14:00 - 17:00; Admis 600 ISK, 400 ISK 67+; Estab 1923; Sculpture
Income: Run by the Icelandic state
Collections: Sculpture and paintings by Einar Jonsson
Activities: Classes for adults & children; mus shop sells books, reproductions

M **LJOSMYNDASAFN REYKJAVIKUR - REYKJAVIK MUSEUM OF PHOTOGRAPHY,** Grofarhus, Tryggvagotu 15 Reykjavik, 101 Iceland. Tel 354-411-6390; Fax 354-411-6399; Elec Mail photomuseum@reykjavik.is; Internet Home Page Address: www.ljosmyndasafnreykjavikur.is; *Dir* Maria Karen Siguraadottir
Open Mon - Fri 12 PM - 7 PM, Sat - Sun 1 PM - 5 PM; No admis fee
Collections: Collection includes 1.5 million photographs and items related to photography and photographic history; Professional and amateur work by Reykjavik photographers
Activities: Mus shop sells books, magazines & reproductions

M **NATIONAL GALLERY OF ICELAND,** Frikirkjuvegi 7, Reykjavik, 101 Iceland. Tel 354-515-9600; Fax 354-515-9601; Elec Mail info@listasafn.is; Internet Home Page Address: www.listasafn.is; *Dir* Dr Halldor Bjorn Runolfsson; *Cur* Dagny Heoidal
Open Tues - Sun 10 AM - 5 PM, cl Mon; No admis fee
Collections: Collection of international and national Icelandic art covering the 19th and 20th centuries

M **NATIONAL MUSEUM OF ICELAND,** Library, Sudurgata 41, Reykjavik, 101 Iceland. Tel 354-530-2200; Fax 354-530-2201; Elec Mail nationalmuseum@nationalmuseum.is; Internet Home Page Address: www.nationalmuseum.is; *Dir* Margret Hallgrimsdottir; *Head Librn* Groa Finnsdottir
Open Mon - Fri 1 PM - 4 PM, cl Sat & Sun; No admis fee; 1863 mus & library; Library with 20,000 vols
Library Holdings: Book Volumes 20,000
Collections: Archaeological & ethnological artifacts, Icelandic antiquities, portraits, folk art

INDIA

BARODA

M **BARODA MUSEUM AND PICTURE GALLERY,** Sayaji Park, Baroda, 390005 India. Tel 0265-2793801, 2793589; Fax 0265-2791959; *Dir* R D Parmar; *Cur* V M Patel
Open 10:30 AM - 5:30 PM; Estab 1894; Library with 23,000 books
Income: financed by government of Gujarat
Special Subjects: Decorative Arts, Historical Material, History of Art & Archaeology, Interior Design, Landscapes, Architecture, Art Education, Art History, Glass, Flasks & Bottles, Photography, Porcelain, Portraits, Pottery, Prints, Silver, Textiles, Bronzes, Manuscripts, Maps, Painting-European, Painting-French, Sculpture, Graphics, Watercolors, Archaeology, Ethnology, Costumes, Ceramics, Crafts, Folk Art, Woodcarvings, Etchings & Engravings, Painting-Japanese, Dolls, Furniture, Jade, Jewelry, Oriental Art, Asian Art, Antiquities-Byzantine, Metalwork, Painting-British, Painting-Dutch, Carpets & Rugs, Ivory, Scrimshaw, Coins & Medals, Restorations, Tapestries, Baroque Art, Calligraphy, Miniatures, Painting-Flemish, Renaissance Art, Embroidery, Medieval Art, Antiquities-Oriental, Painting-Spanish, Painting-Italian, Antiquities-Persian, Islamic Art, Antiquities-Egyptian, Antiquities-Greek, Antiquities-Roman, Mosaics, Stained Glass, Leather, Antiquities-Etruscan, Painting-Russian, Enamels, Antiquities-Assyrian
Collections: Indian archeology & art, numismatic colls; Asiatic & Egyptian Colls; Greek, Roman, European civilizations & art; European paintings

CALCUTTA

M **INDIAN MUSEUM,** 27 Jawaharlal Nehru Rd, Calcutta, 700016 India. Tel 33 249 5699; Fax 33 249 5696; *Dir* Dr Sakti Kali Basu
Collections: Bronzes and bronze figures, ceramics, coins, copper and stone implements of prehistoric and proto-historic origin; geology, botany and zoology collections

CHENNAI

M **GOVERNMENT MUSEUM & NATIONAL ART GALLERY,** 406 Pantheon Rd, Egmore Chennai, 600008 India. Tel 91-44-28193238; Fax 91-44-28193035; Elec Mail govtmuse@tngov.in; Internet Home Page Address: www.chennaimuseum.org; Internet Home Page Address: www.governmentmuseumchennai.org; *Dir* S S Jawahar IAS
Open Sat - Thurs 9:30 AM - 5 PM, cl Fri; Admis Indians: adults Rs 15, children Rs 10, students Rs 5; foreigners: adults Rs 250, children Rs 125, students Rs 75; Estab 1851; 47 galleries (Archaeology, Anthropology & Botany, Zoology, Geology, Numismatics & children's Mus); Rock & Cave Art Gallery; Average Annual Attendance: 10,000,000
Library Holdings: Book Volumes; Pamphlets
Collections: Ancient & modern Indian art; Buddhist sculptures; bronzes; archaeology; natural sciences coll
Publications: 164 books & publications issued;
Activities: Classes for children; dramatic progs; docent training as well as training in handcrafts; plant preservation; & chemical conservation; extension progs to schools & other countries; mus shop sells books, prints, slides & postcards

JUNAGADH

M **JUNAGADH MUSEUM,** Sakkar Bag, Junagadh, 362001 India. Tel 21685; *Dir* P V Dholakia
Collections: Archaeology, miniature paintings, manuscripts, sculptures, decorative & applied arts

MUMBAI

M **CHHATRAPATI SHIVAJI MAHARAJ VASTU SANGRAHALAYA,** (Prince of Wales Museum of Western India) 159-61 Mahatma Gandhi Rd, Fort Mumbai, 400023 India. Tel 2284484; 22844519; Fax 22045430; Elec Mail csmus@hathway.com; Elec Mail csmusmumbai@crmail.com; *Dir* Sabyasachi Mukherjee; *Dir, Galleries* Usha Toraskar; *Asst Dir, Admin* Ajay Kochle; *Admin Officer* V K V Nair; *Registrar* Gajanan A Shetti; *Cur, European Painting* Dilip Ranade Sr; *Cur, Coll Management & Art Section* Manisha Nene Sr; *Cur, Miniature Painting & Numismatics* Vandana Prapanna; *Asst Cur, Art Section* Renu Jathar; *Asst Cur, Educ* Dr Prasanna Mangrulkar; *Asst Cur* Dr Mrinalini Jamkhedkar; *Sr Curatorial Asst* Aparna Bhogal; *Sr Curatorial Asst* Manoj Chowdhary; *Chief Conservator* Anupam Sah; *Conservation Asst* Omkar Kadu; *Conservation Asst* Dilip Mistry
Open Tues - Sun 10:15 AM - 6 PM, cl Mon; Admis international visitors over 12 yrs Rs 300, visitors over 12 yrs Rs 25, college students with ID Rs 15, children 12 yrs & under Rs 05; Estab 1922; Library with 20,000 books & 9,000 journals; Average Annual Attendance: 5 million
Income: financed by charitable institutions
Library Holdings: Auction Catalogs; Book Volumes; Exhibition Catalogs; Periodical Subscriptions
Special Subjects: Anthropology, Archaeology, Decorative Arts, History of Art & Archaeology, Architecture, Ceramics, Photography, Porcelain, Portraits, Pottery, Textiles, Bronzes, Painting-British, Painting-European, Painting-French, Sculpture, Watercolors, Ethnology, Religious Art, Crafts, Primitive art, Woodcuts, Manuscripts, Jade, Jewelry, Oriental Art, Ivory, Calligraphy, Miniatures, Painting-Flemish, Renaissance Art, Antiquities-Oriental, Islamic Art, Painting-German, Reproductions
Collections: Paintings; archaeology; natural history; arms & armour; Textiles; sculpture; numismatics

Publications: Indian Life & Landscape by Western Artists; The Tata Collection of Chinese Antiquities in the CSMVS; The Dream of an Inhabitant of Mogul; A Centennial Bouquet; Jewels on the Crescent; Indian Coinage; The Museum Mumbai Guidebook; Tibet through the Eyes of Li Gotami; Gita Govinda Love Poems of Krishna - The Blue God
Activities: Classes for adults & children; lects for mems only; concerts; gallery talks; tours; schols; fels; Sant Ghadge Maharaj Brihanmumbai Municipal Corp Cleanliness Award, 2008; renovation of children's creativity centre; Arms Gallery, pre & proto history complex; mus shop sells books, magazines, reproductions, prints, CDs, DVDs, bags, greeting cards, artificial jewelry, & other gift items

M **HERAS INSTITUTE OF INDIAN HISTORY AND CULTURE,** Heras Institute Museum, St Xavier's College Campus, 5, Mahapalika Marg Mumbai, 400001 India. Tel 91-22-226220665, ext 320/321; Elec Mail herasinstitute@xaviers.edu; Internet Home Page Address: herasinstitute.museum.com; *Head* Dr Joan Dias
By advance invitation; No admis fee; Estab 1926; Library with 30,000 vols; Average Annual Attendance: 500
Library Holdings: Book Volumes; CD-ROMs; Maps; Sculpture
Special Subjects: Archaeology, Portraits, Bronzes, Religious Art, Coins & Medals
Collections: Indian stone sculptures, woodwork, paintings; old rare maps, books, metal artifacts, coins, ivories
Exhibitions: Heras week, last week in July
Activities: Research methodology; workshops; seminars; lects open to pub; scholarships offered

NEW DELHI

M **CRAFTS MUSEUM,** Ministry of Textiles, Department of Handlooms Crafts Museum, Bhairon Marg, Pragati Maidan New Delhi, 110001 India. Tel 2337-1641; Fax 2337 1515; Elec Mail rgcraftsmuseum@gmail.com; *chmn* Dr Ruchira Ghose; *Deputy Dir* Nidhi; *Consultant* Mushtak Khan
Open 10 AM - 5 PM, cl Mon; Admis free; Estab 1956
Income: Government funding
Library Holdings: Book Volumes; DVDs; Exhibition Catalogs; Memorabilia; Original Documents; Photographs
Collections: Indian traditional crafts, folk & tribal arts; folk crafts
Activities: Educ progs; lects open to pub; mus shop sells books, magazines, original art, reproductions, prints, slides & large variety of crafts

M **NATIONAL GALLERY OF MODERN ART,** Jaipur House India Gate, Sher Shah Rd New Delhi, 110003 India. Tel 23384560; *Dir* Dr Anis Farooqi
Open 10 AM - 5 PM, cl Mon
Collections: Indian contemporary paintings, sculptures, graphics, drawings, architecture, industrial design, prints and minor arts

M **NATIONAL MUSEUM OF INDIA,** Janpath, New Delhi, 110011 India. Tel 301 8159; Fax 301 9821; *Dir Gen* Dr R C Sharma
Open 10 AM - 5 PM, cl Mon; Library with 30,000 vols
Collections: Arabic, Indian, Persian, Sanskrit language manuscripts; Central Asian antiquities and murals; decorative arts

M **RABINDRA BHAVAN ART GALLERY,** Lalit Kala Akademi (National Academy of Art), 35 Ferozeshah Rd, New Delhi, India. Tel 91-11-23009200; Fax 91-11-23009292; Elec Mail lka@lalitkala.gov.in; Internet Home Page Address: www.lalitkala.gov.in; *Chmn* Dr K K Chakravarty; *Secy* Mr Ramaprishnar Vedala; *Deputy Secy* Vikram Mehra; *Deputy Secy* Dr Tyotish Joshi
Open 9:30 AM - 6 PM; Estab 1954 to provide reference to art patrons; 9 galleries under one roof; bldg 144 running ft ea gallery
Income: Govt of India funding
Purchases: Books, periodicals, DVDs, newspaper, etc
Library Holdings: Book Volumes; CD-ROMs; Clipping Files; Compact Disks; DVDs; Exhibition Catalogs; Manuscripts; Original Art Works; Pamphlets; Periodical Subscriptions; Photographs; Reels; Reproductions; Sculpture; Slides; Video Tapes
Special Subjects: Afro-American Art, American Indian Art, Decorative Arts, Drawings, History of Art & Archaeology, Landscape Architecture, Art Education, Art History, Conceptual Art, Glass, Mixed Media, American Western Art, Textiles, Manuscripts, Sculpture, Architecture, Hispanic Art, Latin American Art, Mexican Art, Photography, Bronzes, Archaeology, Southwestern Art, Religious Art, Ceramics, Crafts, Folk Art, Pottery, Woodcarvings, Woodcuts, Jade, Porcelain, Oriental Art, Asian Art, Metalwork, Ivory, Coins & Medals, Restorations, Calligraphy, Miniatures, Mosaics
Collections: Permanent collection of graphics, paintings, sculpture, graphics & mix media work
Exhibitions: Triennale India; National Exhibition of Art; Internal & external exhibs
Activities: Camps & workshops for artists; gallery talks; National Academy award; Triennial award; fels; schols; NEA Award; scholarships and fels offered; sales shop sells books, magazines, reproductions, slides, prints

INDONESIA

EAST JAVA

M **NATIONAL MUSEUM OF EAST JAVA,** Jl. Lebak Rejo 7 Surabaya, East Java, 60134 Indonesia. Tel 62-31-3894679; Elec Mail anon@sby.centrin.net.id; Internet Home Page Address: mputantular.tripod.com

JAKARTA

M **GALERI NASIONAL INDONESIA,** Indonesia National Gallery, Jl Medan Merdeka Timur No 14, Jakarta, 10110 Indonesia. Tel 62-21-34833954/5; Fax 62-21-3813021; Elec Mail galnas@indosat.net.id; Internet Home Page Address: www.galeri-nasional.or.id; *Dir* Tubagus Sukmana; *Drs* Sumarmin; *Drs* Eddy Susilo
Open 10 AM - 4 PM for permanent exhibs, 10 AM - 2 PM for temporary exhibs; 1998

Library Holdings: Audio Tapes; Cassettes; Clipping Files; Exhibition Catalogs; Pamphlets; Photographs; Slides
Collections: Modern and contemporary art in paintings, drawings, prints, statues, photography and installation; 1700 works by Indonesian and international artists; Painting, Drawing, Installations
Publications: Newspaper, E-Mail, Pamphlets
Activities: Socialization; Books traveling exhibits twice a year; Originates exhibs that circulate based on purpose; Mus shop sells books, magazines

JAKARTA PUSAT

M **MUSEUM NASIONAL INDONESIA,** Jl Medan Merdeka Barat 12, Jakarta Pusat, Indonesia. Tel 021-3811551; Fax 62-21-3447778; Elec Mail museumnasional_ina@yahoo.co.id; Internet Home Page Address: www.museumnasional.org; *Dir* Dr Retno Sulristianingsih, MM
Open Tues - Thurs 8:30 AM - 4 PM, Fri 8:30 AM - 4 PM (cl 11:30 AM - 1 PM), Sat & Sun 8:30 AM - 5 PM; cl Mon; Admis adults IDR 750, under 17 & students IDR 250; Apr 24, 1778, the purpose is to promote research in the field of arts & science, especially in history, archaeology, ethnography & physics
Collections: Over 141,000 cultural objects relating to Indonesian culture and history; Bronze, ceramics, textiles, numismatics, relics, sculpture; Chinese ceramics of the Han, Tang and Ming dynasties; Bronze and gold coll from Indonesian classical period
Exhibitions: Museum Volkenkunde
Publications: Catalogues, magazines, newspapers, brochures, leaflets, posters
Activities: Classes for adults & children; lectrs open to the public; 400 vis lectrs per yr; tours; sponsoring of competitions; fels; lending of original objects of art to Museum Volkenkunde, Leiden; 2 book traveling exhibs per yr; originates traveling exhibs to Province mus; mus shop sells books, magazines, original art, prints

UBUD

M **AGUNG RAI MUSEUM OF ART,** Jl. Pengosekan, Gianyar Ubud, 80571 Indonesia. Tel 62-0361-975748; Fax 62-0361-975332; Elec Mail info@armamuseum.com; Internet Home Page Address: www.armamuseum.com

IRAN

ISFAHAN

M **ARMENIAN ALL SAVIOUR'S CATHEDRAL MUSEUM,** Julfa, PO Box 81735-115 Isfahan, Iran. Tel 243471; *Dir* Levon Minassian
Collections: 450 paintings, miniatures & tomb portraits; 700 ancient books

TEHRAN

M **TEHRAN MUSEUM OF CONTEMPORARY ART,** (Teheran Museum of Modern Art) N. Karegar Ave, Laleh Park, PO Box 41-3669 Tehran, Iran. *Dir* Ali Reza Semiazar
Museum maintains library
Collections: Modern Western art works

IRAQ

BAGHDAD

M **DIRECTORATE - GENERAL OF ANTIQUITIES AND HERITAGE,** Sahat Al-Risafi, Baghdad, Iraq. Tel 4165317; *Dir* Alae Al-Shibli
M **Babylon Museum,** Sahat Al-Risafi, Babylon, Iraq. Tel 4165317; *Dir* Alae Al-Shibli
Collections: Models, pictures & paintings of the remains at Babylon

M **IRAQI MUSEUM,** Salhiya Quarter, Baghdad, Iraq. Tel 36121-5; *Dir* Dr Hana' Abdul Khaleq
Collections: Antiquities from the Stone Age to the 17th century, including Islamic objects

IRELAND

CORK

M **CRAWFORD ART GALLERY,** Emmet Pl, Cork, Ireland. Tel 353-0-21-4907855; Fax 353-0-21-4805043; Elec Mail info@crawfordartgallery.ie; Internet Home Page Address: www.crawfordartgallery.ie
Open Mon - Wed & Fri - Sat 10 AM - 5 PM, Thurs 10 AM - 8 PM; No admis fee

DUBLIN

M **DUBLIN CITY GALLERY THE HUGH LANE,** Charlemont House, Parnell Sq N Dublin, 1 Ireland. Tel (01) 2225-550; Fax (01) 8722 182; Elec Mail info.hughlane@dublincity.ie; Internet Home Page Address: www.hughlane.ie; *Dir* Barbara Dawson
Open Tues - Thurs 10 AM - 6 PM, Fri & Sat 10 AM - 5 PM, Sun 11 AM - 5 PM, cl Mon; No admis fee; Estab 1908

Special Subjects: Sculpture
Collections: Works of Irish, English & European artists; Sir Hugh Lane Collection; Francis Bacon studio
Activities: Educ prog; classes for adults & children; lects open to pub; concerts; gallery talks; tours; mus shop sells books, magazines & prints

M **GALLERY OF PHOTOGRAPHY,** Meeting House Sq, Temple Bar Dublin, 2 Ireland. Tel 353-1-671-4654; Fax 353-1-670-9293; Elec Mail info@galleryofphotography.ie; Internet Home Page Address: www.galleryofphotography.ie; *Dir* Tanya Kiang; *Projects Mgr* Trish Lambe
Open Tue - Sat 11 AM - 6 PM, Sun 1 PM - 6 PM; No admis fee
Collections: contemporary photography

M **IRISH MUSEUM OF MODERN ART,** Royal Hospital, Military Rd, Kilmainham Dublin, 8 Ireland. Tel 353-1-6129900; Fax 353-1-6129999; Elec Mail info@imma.ie; Internet Home Page Address: www.imma.ie; *Dir* Enrique Joncosa; *Sr Cur* Rachael Thomas; *Sr Cur* Helen O'Donoghue; *Sr Cur* Christina Kennedy; *Cur* Sean Kissane; *Cur* Lisa Moran
Open Tues - Sat 10 AM - 5:30 PM, Wed 10:30 AM - 5:30 PM, Sun & bank holidays Noon - 5:30 PM, cl Mon, Apr 6, Dec 24 -26; No admis fee except for occasional special exhibs; 1991; coll & presentation of modern & contemporary art; Average Annual Attendance: 450,000; Mem: Dues patron 4,000 euro, benefactor 350 euro, supporter 150 euro, family 70 euro, concession 30 euro, individual 50 euro
Income: Financed by the government of Ireland
Collections: Comprises 4,500 works; permanent coll of 1,650 works by Irish & international artists; Madden Arnholz Collection of 2,000 old master prints
Exhibitions: Temporary exhibs which run throughout the yr;
Publications: IMMA publishes catalogues for all exhibs
Activities: Artists' residency prog; workshops etc; lectrs open to the public; concerts; gallery talks; guided tours; Mus shop sells books, magazines

M **NATIONAL GALLERY OF IRELAND,** Merrion Sq W & Clare St, Dublin, 2 Ireland. Tel 6615133; Fax 6615372; Elec Mail info@ngi.ie; Internet Home Page Address: nationalgallery.ie; *Dir* Raymond Keaveney; *Keeper & Head Colls* Fionnuala Croke; *Cur Irish Art* Dr Brendan Rooney; *Cur Northern European Art* Dr Adriaan E Waiboer; *Cur European Art 1850-1950* Janet McLean; *Cur British Paintings* Adrian Le Harivel; *Cur Prints & Drawings* Anne Hodge; *Librn* Andrea Lydon; *Head Conservation* Simone Mancini; *Keeper & Head Educ* Dr Marie Bourke
Open Mon - Sat 9:30 AM - 5:30 PM, Thurs 8:30 AM - 5:30 PM, Sun Noon - 5:30 PM; No admis fee; Estab 1854; Fine art mus housing Irish & European paintings; library with 30,000 vols, painting, sculpture, and the fine arts in Dublin; Average Annual Attendance: 800,000; Mem: The Friends of the NGI
Income: State funded
Library Holdings: Auction Catalogs; Book Volumes; Exhibition Catalogs; Original Art Works; Original Documents; Other Holdings; Pamphlets
Special Subjects: Historical Material, Art History, Portraits, Painting-American, Prints, Painting-British, Etchings & Engravings, Painting-French, Painting-European, Painting-Dutch, Miniatures, Painting-Flemish, Painting-Spanish, Painting-Italian, Painting-German, Bookplates & Bindings
Collections: British, Dutch, Flemish, French, German, Italian, Irish, Russian & Spanish masters since 1250; drawings, prints, oil paintings, sculptures, watercolors; The Yeats Museum (works by Jack B. Yeats (1871 - 1957); National Portrait Collection (16th-21st century); Fine arts library archival material relates to study of Irish Art & NGI
Publications: National Gallery of Ireland: Essential Guide (revised edition 2008); National Gallery of Ireland Companion Guide (publ Oct 2009); Thomas Roberts: Landscape & Patronage in Eighteenth-Century Ireland by William Laffan & Brendan Rooney (2009); Gabriel Metsu by Adrian Waiboer (2010)
Activities: Classes for adults & children; family progs; workshops; outreach progs; lects open to pub; 10 vis lectrs per year; gallery talks; tours; concerts; NGI awarded full accreditation (2007) under the mus standards prog for Ireland; fels available; lend original objects of art to sister institutions & accredited international museums; mus shop sells books, magazines, reproductions, prints, slides & other items

M **NATIONAL MUSEUM OF IRELAND,** Kildare St, Dublin, 2 Ireland. Tel 6 777 444; Fax 6 766 116; Internet Home Page Address: www.museum.ie; *Dir* Patrick F Wallace
Open Tues - Sat 10 AM - 5 PM, Sun 2 - 5 PM; No admis fee
Special Subjects: Archaeology
Collections: Art and Industrial Division; Irish Antiquities Division; Irish Folklife Division; Natural History Division

M **NATIONAL PRINT MUSEUM,** Old Garrison Chapel Beggars Bush, Haddington Rd Dublin, 4 Ireland. Tel 353 1 660 3770; Fax 353 1 667 3545; Elec Mail npmuseum@iol.ie; Internet Home Page Address: www.nationalprintmuseum.ie; *Chm* Sean Sills; *Mgr & Proj Coordr* Mairead White
Open Mon - Fri 9 AM - 5 PM, Sat - Sun 2 - 5 PM; Admis 3.5E
Collections: Artifacts related to print history

KILKENNY

M **BUTLER GALLERY,** The Castle Kilkenny, Ireland. Tel 353-0-56-776-1106; Fax 353-0-56-777-0031; Elec Mail info@butlergallery.com; Internet Home Page Address: www.butlergallery.com
Circ

LIMERICK

M **THE HUNT MUSEUM,** Rutland St, Limerick, Ireland. Tel 353-61-312833; Fax 353-61-312834; Elec Mail info@huntmuseum.com; Internet Home Page Address: www.huntmuseum.com
Circ

M **LIMERICK CITY GALLERY OF ART,** Pery Sq, Carnegie Bldg Limerick, Ireland. Tel 061-310633; Fax 061-310228; Elec Mail artgallery@limerickcity.ie; Internet Home Page Address: gallery.limerick.ie
Average Annual Attendance:

SLIGO

M **THE MODEL,** (The Model Arts and Niland Gallery) The Niland Collection, The Mall, Sligo, Ireland. Tel 353-071-914-1405; Fax 353-071-914-3694; Elec Mail info@themodel.ie; Internet Home Page Address: www.themodel.ie
Open Tues - Sat 10 AM - 5:30 PM, Sun noon - 5 PM, cl Mon; No admis fee; Estab 2001; multi-disciplinary art center; Suite of contemporary galleries & galleries specifically designed for coll purposes; Average Annual Attendance: 90,000
Income: public funding
Collections: The Niland Collection
Exhibitions: Changing schedule of exhibs
Publications: Books, 3 published per yr
Activities: Classes for adults & children; ten vis lectrs per yr; concerts; gallery talks; tours; lending of original objects of art; mus shop sells books & magazines

ISRAEL

HAIFA

M **HAIFA MUSEUM OF MODERN ART,** 26 Shabbetai Levi St, Haifa, Israel. Tel (04) 855 3255; Fax (04) 855 2714; *Cur* Tal Nissim
Open Mon, Wed & Thurs 10 AM - 4 PM, Tues 4 PM - 8 PM, Fri 10 AM - 1 PM, Sat 10 AM- 3 PM, cl Sun; Library with 10,000 vols
Collections: Israeli paintings, sculpture, drawings & prints; modern American, French, German & English paintings; art posters

M **HAIFA MUSEUMS NATIONAL MARITIME MUSEUM,** 198 Allenby St, Haifa, Israel. Tel (04) 8536622; Fax (04) 8539286; Elec Mail nautic@netvision.net.il; *Chief Cur* Zemer Avshalom; *Cur* Merav Bonai; *Asst Cur* Orit Rotgaizer; *Sec* Rachel Tapiro; *Librn* Rena Mirkoff
Open Mon & Wed - Thurs 10 AM - 5 PM, Tues 10 AM - 2 PM, 5 PM - 8 PM, Fri & holidays 10 AM - 1 PM, Sat 10 AM - 2 PM; Admis Adults NIS 22, children/students/soldiers NIS 16, concessions NIS 4.00; Estab 1953; Includes Archaeological collection; Circ Reference only
Library Holdings: Book Volumes approx 5,000; Exhibition Catalogs; Maps; Original Art Works; Periodical Subscriptions 35
Collections: Ancient Haifa; ancient coins from Israel; antiquities from the excavations of Shikmona from the Bronze Age to Byzantine period; Biblical, Cypriot and Greek pottery and sculpture; Near Eastern figurines; Ship models; Maps; Maritime artifacts and gear
Exhibitions: Pirates - the Skull & Crossbones; Maritime paintings by Moshe Rosenthalis
Publications: Exhib catalogues; postcards
Activities: Classes for adults, classes for children; prog school classes; lects open to public, gallery talks, tours

M **HAIFA MUSEUMS TIKOTIN MUSEUM OF JAPANESE ART,** 89 Hanassi Ave, Haifa, 34-642 Israel. Tel (04) 8383554; Fax (04) 8383557; Elec Mail curator@tmja.org.il; Internet Home Page Address: www.haifamuseums.org.il; *Chief Cur* Dr Ilana Singer; *Youth Activity Organizer* Sophia Berezansky; *Librn* Rena Minkoff
Open Mon - Thurs 10 AM - 4 PM, Fri 10 AM - 1 PM, Sat 10 AM - 3 PM; Estab May 1960
Library Holdings: Auction Catalogs; Book Volumes; Exhibition Catalogs; Periodical Subscriptions
Collections: Ceramics, folk art, drawings, metalwork, netsuke, prints, paintings
Publications: Catalogs
Activities: Classes for adults & children; lects open to public, concerts, gallery talks, tours; mus shop sells books, reproductions, slides, posters & Japanese handicrafts

M **HECHT MUSEUM,** Univ of Haifa, Mt Carmel Haifa, 31905 Israel. Tel 04-8257773, 04-8240308; Fax 04-8240724; Elec Mail mshunit@univ.haifa.ac.il; Internet Home Page Address: mushecht.haifa.ac.il; *Dir & Cur* Ofra Rimon; *Asst to Dir* Shunit Marmelstein
Open Sun - Mon & Wed - Thurs 10 AM - 4 PM, Tue 10 AM - 7 PM, Fri 10 AM - 1 PM, Sat 10 AM - 2 PM; No admis fee; Archaeology of Israel; Art; Barlizon School; Impressionists; School of Paris & more
Special Subjects: Drawings, Etchings & Engravings, Historical Material, History of Art & Archaeology, Landscapes, Art Education, Art History, Glass, Metalwork, Manuscripts, Sculpture, Watercolors, Bronzes, Archaeology, Ceramics, Crafts, Pottery, Woodcarvings, Judaica, Painting-European, Jewelry, Silver, Antiquities-Byzantine, Painting-Dutch, Painting-French, Ivory, Coins & Medals, Restorations, Painting-Polish, Antiquities-Oriental, Painting-Italian, Antiquities-Persian, Antiquities-Egyptian, Antiquities-Greek, Antiquities-Roman, Mosaics, Gold, Painting-German, Antiquities-Etruscan, Painting-Israeli, Antiquities-Assyrian
Collections: Archaeological period beginning with the Chalcolithic period and ending in the Byzantine period; Art gallery with works from Hecht Family Collection; French painting of the Barbizon School, Impressionism, Post-Impressionism, School of Paris and Jewish art of the 19th and 20th century; Coins, seals, weights, jewelry, toys, oil lamps, metalwork, woodwork, glass, mosaics and stone
Exhibitions: The Ma'agan Mikhael Ancient Ship; The Great Revolt in the Galilee; Ancient Crafts and Industries; Phoenicians at the Northern Coast of Israel in the Biblical Period; Hoards & Genizot as Chapters in History; The Great Revolt in the Galilee

Publications: Exhib catalog
Activities: Classes for adults and children; concerts, gallery talks, tours; schols available; mus shop sells books, reproductions & other items

HERZLIYA

M **HERZLIYA MUSEUM OF CONTEMPORARY ART,** 4 Ha'banim St, Herzliya, 46379 Israel. Tel 972 9 9551011; Fax 972 9 9500043; Elec Mail info@herzliyamuseum.co.il; Internet Home Page Address: www.herzliyamuseum.co.il; *Dir* Dalia Levin; *Admin* Tammy Zilbert; *Cur & Registrar* Maya Shimony
Open Mon, Wed & Fri- Sat 10 AM - 2 PM, Tues & Thurs 4 - 8 PM
Collections: Contemporary art

JERUSALEM

M **BEIT HA'OMANIM,** The Jerusalem Artists' House, 12 Shmuel Hanagid St, Jerusalem, 94592 Israel. Tel (972-2) 6253653; Fax (972-2) 6258594; Elec Mail artists@zahav.net.il; Internet Home Page Address: www.art.org.il; *Dir* Ruth Zadka; *Asst Dir* Idit Helman; *Asst T* Keller; *Gallery Mgr* Shulamith Efrat
Open Sun - Thurs 10 AM - 1 PM, 4 PM - 7 PM, Fri 10 AM - 1 PM, Sat 11 AM - 2 PM; No admis fee; Estab 1965
Library Holdings: Exhibition Catalogs
Collections: Artwork of Israeli & Jerusalemite artists
Exhibitions: International Exhibitions
Publications: Research catalogues following exhibitions
Activities: Lects open to pub, gallery talks, tours; mus shop sells original art, reproductions, prints

M **THE ISRAEL MUSEUM, JERUSALEM,** The Rockefeller Museum, Rockefeller Bldg, Sultan St, c/o Israel Mus PO Box 71117 Jerusalem, 91710 Israel. Tel (2) 6282251; Fax (2) 6271926; Elec Mail fawziib@imj.org.il; Internet Home Page Address: www.imj.org.il; *Cur* Fawzi Ibrahim
Open Sun, Mon, Wed -& Thurs 10 AM - 3 PM, Sat 10 AM - 2 PM, cl Tues & Fri; No admis fee; Estab 1938; Archaeological finds from Prehistory to Ottoman Empire
Collections: Archaeology of the Land of Israel; Islamic period; Prehistory to Ottoman periods - all periods covering 2 million years
Exhibitions: Image and Artifact: Treasures of the Rockefeller Museum and Aerial Photographs
Publications: Image and Artifact: Treasures of the Rockefeller Museum with Aerial Photographs by Duby Tal and Mata Haramari, 2000

M **THE ISRAEL MUSEUM, JERUSALEM,** PO Box 71117, Jerusalem, 91710 Israel. Tel (02) 670-8811; Fax 972-2-6708080; Internet Home Page Address: www.imj.org.il; *Dir* Mr James Snyder; *Chief Cur Fine Arts* Mira Lapidot; *Spokesperson* Rachel Schechter; *Head of Mktg* Shai Yamin; *Deputy Dir* Dor Lin
Open Sun, Mon, Wed, Thurs, Sat 10 AM - 5 PM, Tues 4 PM - 9 PM, Fri 10 AM - 4 PM; Admis fee 42 nis, students 30 nis, children 5-17 yrs 21 nis, family 120 nis; Estab 1965; Average Annual Attendance: 400,000+
Library Holdings: Auction Catalogs; Book Volumes; Exhibition Catalogs; Periodical Subscriptions
Special Subjects: American Indian Art, Anthropology, Archaeology, Decorative Arts, Drawings, Etchings & Engravings, Landscapes, Collages, Glass, Antiquities-Assyrian, Flasks & Bottles, Photography, Portraits, Pottery, Pre-Columbian Art, Painting-American, Prints, Manuscripts, Maps, Sculpture, Architecture, Graphics, Latin American Art, Watercolors, African Art, Ethnology, Costumes, Ceramics, Crafts, Woodcarvings, Woodcuts, Judaica, Painting-European, Painting-Japanese, Posters, Furniture, Jewelry, Porcelain, Asian Art, Antiquities-Byzantine, Painting-Dutch, Painting-French, Carpets & Rugs, Coins & Medals, Baroque Art, Calligraphy, Miniatures, Painting-Flemish, Renaissance Art, Period Rooms, Embroidery, Medieval Art, Antiquities-Oriental, Painting-Italian, Antiquities-Persian, Islamic Art, Antiquities-Egyptian, Antiquities-Greek, Antiquities-Roman, Mosaics, Gold, Antiquities-Etruscan, Painting-Israeli, Enamels
Collections: Judaica & Jewish ethnography; Fine arts comprising separate department for Israeli art, European art, modern art, contemporary art; prints, drawings, photography design & architecture; Asian art, arts of Africa, Oceania & the Americas
Exhibitions: Approx 20 per yr & permanent collections
Publications: Catalogues, IM Journal in archaeology; IM Magazine; IM Studies
Activities: Classes for adults & children; summer camps; family activities; concerts; gallery talks; tours; sponsoring of competitions; lending of original objects of art to museums worldwide; originates traveling exhibs to museums worldwide; mus shop sells books, reproductions, prints & gift items
M **Billy Rose Art Garden,** PO Box 71117, Jerusalem, 91710 Israel. Tel 2-670881; Fax 2-5631833; Elec Mail info@imj.org.il; Internet Home Page Address: www.imj.org.il; *Dir* James S Snyder; *Chief Cur Fine Arts* Mira Lapidot; *Deputy Dir* Dor Lin
Open Sun, Mon, Wed, Thurs, Sat 10 AM - 5 PM, Tues 4 - 9 PM, Fri 10 AM - 2 PM; Admis nis adult 36, nis student 26, nis child 18; 1965 as encyclopedic mus of the state of Israel; Average Annual Attendance: 500,000; Mem: 10,000, family nis 360, senior nis 95
Special Subjects: American Indian Art, Anthropology, Drawings, Historical Material, Landscapes, Mexican Art, Antiquities-Assyrian, Flasks & Bottles, Furniture, Photography, Porcelain, Portraits, Pottery, Pre-Columbian Art, Painting-American, Period Rooms, Silver, Textiles, Bronzes, Woodcuts, Manuscripts, Maps, Painting-British, Painting-French, Painting-Japanese, Graphics, Hispanic Art, Latin American Art, Sculpture, Watercolors, African Art, Archaeology, Ethnology, Southwestern Art, Costumes, Religious Art, Primitive art, Woodcarvings, Etchings & Engravings, Judaica, Posters, Eskimo Art, Painting-Canadian, Jewelry, Oriental Art, Asian Art, Antiquities-Byzantine, Painting-Dutch, Ivory, Scrimshaw, Restorations, Tapestries, Baroque Art, Calligraphy, Miniatures, Painting-Flemish, Painting-Polish, Medieval Art, Antiquities-Oriental, Painting-Spanish, Painting-Italian, Antiquities-Persian, Islamic Art, Antiquities-Egyptian, Antiquities-Roman, Mosaics, Gold, Painting-German,

Antiquities-Etruscan, Painting-Russian, Painting-Israeli, Enamels, Painting-Scandinavian
Collections: Modern European, American & Israeli sculpture & Reuven Lipchitz collection of Jacques Lipchitz's bronze sketches

M **Samuel & Saidye Bronfman Archaeology Wing,** PO Box 71117, Jerusalem, 91 710 Israel. Tel 972-2-6708812; Fax 972-2-6708906; Elec Mail alisonas@imj.org.il; Internet Home Page Address: www.imj.org.il; Telex 972-26708906; *Chief Cur Archaeology* Dr Haim Gitler
Open Sat - Mon & Wed - Thurs 10 AM - 5 PM, Tues 4-9 PM, Fri & holidays 10 AM - 2 PM; Admis adult 48 skekel, child 24 shekel; Estab 1965; Average Annual Attendance: 90,000; Mem: 10,900 local mems and patrons
Special Subjects: Drawings, Glass, Metalwork, Furniture, Gold, Photography, Pre-Columbian Art, Painting-American, Prints, Manuscripts, Maps, Painting-French, Tapestries, Graphics, Latin American Art, Sculpture, Watercolors, African Art, Anthropology, Archaeology, Ethnology, Ceramics, Folk Art, Woodcarvings, Etchings & Engravings, Calligraphy, Miniatures, Painting-Flemish, Painting-European, Jade, Jewelry, Oriental Art, Asian Art, Silver, Antiquities-Byzantine, Painting-Dutch, Carpets & Rugs, Historical Material, Ivory, Coins & Medals, Baroque Art, Calligraphy, Miniatures, Painting-Flemish, Renaissance Art, Medieval Art, Antiquities-Oriental, Painting-Spanish, Painting-Italian, Antiquities-Persian, Islamic Art, Antiquities-Egyptian, Antiquities-Greek, Antiquities-Roman, Mosaics, Painting-German, Antiquities-Etruscan, Painting-Russian, Painting-Israeli, Antiquities-Assyrian
Collections: Collection of archaeology of Israel from Prehistoric times to Islamic & Crusader periods; material found in excavations since 1948; Collections of Picasso
Exhibitions: (02/13/2013-01/04/2014) Herod the Great: The King's Final Journey; (05/01/2013-01/04/2014) I Am Gabriel - A Scroll in Stone from the Time of Herod
Publications: Herod th Great: The Kings Fnal Journey
Activities: Classes for children

L **Shrine of the Book,** PO Box 71117, Jerusalem, 91 710 Israel. Tel 26708811; Fax 25631833; *Cur* Dr Adolfo Roitman
D Samuel & Jeanne H Gottesman Center for Biblical MSS
Collections: Houses the Dead Sea Scrolls (discovered in Qumran) & manuscripts from adjacent sites on western shore of the Dead Sea, Masada & Nahal Hever

M **MUSEUM ON THE SEAM,** 4 Chel Handasa St, Jerusalem, 91016 Israel; PO Box 1649, Jerusalem, 91016 Israel. Tel 972-2-6281278; Fax 972-2-6277061; Elec Mail info@mots.org.il; Internet Home Page Address: http://www.mots.org.il/eng/Index.asp
Average Annual Attendance:

POST KEFAR-MENAHEM

M **SHEPHELA MUSEUM,** Kibbutz Kefar-Menahem, Post Kefar-Menahem, 79875 Israel. Tel (08) 850 1827; Fax 08 8508486; Elec Mail museum_hash@kfar-menachem.org.11; Internet Home Page Address: www.touryoav.org.11/museums; *Dir* Ora Dvir; *Cur* Lea Fait; *Cur* Moshe Saidi
Open Mon - Fri & Sun 8:30 AM - 12:30 PM; Sat 11 AM - 4 PM; Admis $2.50; Estab 1975; archaeology; Average Annual Attendance: 10,000
Income: $100,000
Special Subjects: Historical Material, Painting-Israeli
Collections: Collection of fine arts, children's art & antiquities; New Hebrew Settlement (1930s)
Exhibitions: 4 art exhibitions per year of Israeli contemporary art
Activities: Educ progs for classes and kindergartens in the various exhibs

TEL AVIV

M **ERETZ-ISRAEL MUSEUM,** 2 Chaim Levanon St, Tel Aviv, 61 170 Israel; PO Box 17068, Ramat Aviv Tel Aviv, 61 170 Israel. Tel (972) 3 6415244; Fax (972) 36412408; Internet Home Page Address: www.eimuseun.co.il
Open Sun - Wed 10 AM - 4 PM, Thurs 10 AM - 8 PM, Fri & Sat 10 AM - 2 PM; Consists of 15 museums & their collections
Collections: ancient glass; historical documents of Tel Aviv-Yafo; Jewish ritual & secular art objects; ceramics, coins, prehistoric finds, scientific & technical apparatus, traditional work tools & methods

M **Ceramics Museum,** PO Box 17068, Ramat Aviv Tel Aviv, 61 170 Israel. Tel 6415244; Fax 6412408; *Cur* Dr Ir It Ziffer
Open Sun - Thurs 9 AM - 3 PM; Admis adults 33, students 25, retired seniors 17; Estab 1958
Collections: Pottery throughout history; Reconstruction of a Biblical Dwelling from the Time of the Monarchy
Activities: Educ prog; classes for children; mus shop sells books, original art

M **Museum of Antiquities of Tel-Aviv-Jaffa,** 10 Mifratz Shlomo St, Jaffa, 680 38 Israel; PO Box 8406, Jaffa, 61083 Israel. Tel 972 3 6825375; Fax 972 3 6813624; Internet Home Page Address: www.eimuseum.co.il; *Dir* Dr Tzvi Shacham
Open Sun - Thurs 9 AM - 1 PM; Admis fee Adults 10 NIS, students 5 NIS
Special Subjects: Archaeology, Glass, Ceramics, Coins & Medals
Collections: Archaeological findings from Tel Aviv-Yafo area, covering Neolithic to Byzantine periods

M **Museum of Ethnography and Folklore,** PO Box 17068, Ramat Aviv Tel Aviv, 61 170 Israel. *Dir* D Davidowitz
Collections: Jewish popular art & costumes

M **TEL AVIV MUSEUM OF ART,** 27 Shaul Hamelech Blvd, POB 33288 Tel Aviv, 61332 Israel. Tel (03) 607 7020; Fax (03) 6958099; Internet Home Page Address: www.tamuseum.com; *Head* Prof Mordechai Omer
Open Mon & Wed 10 AM - 4 PM, Tues & Thurs 10 AM - 10 PM; Fri 10 AM - 2 PM; Sat 10 AM - 4 PM; cl Sun; Library with 50,000 vols
Collections: Works from 17th century to present; Israeli art
Activities: Classes for adults & children; lects open to pub, concerts, gallery talks, tours; mus shop sells books, magazines & reproductions

ITALY

ARDEA

M **RACCOLTA MANZU,** Via Laurentina km. 32, Ardea, 0040 Italy. Tel +39-06-9135022; Internet Home Page Address: www.museomanzu.beniculturali.it
Circ

BARI

M **PINACOTECA PROVINCIALE,** Via Spalato 19, Bari, 70121 Italy. Tel (080) 5412421/22/25; Fax 080/5583401; Elec Mail pinacotecaprov.bari@tin.it; *Dir* Dr Clara Gelao; *Acad Dipl in Fine Arts* Anna Martucci
Open Tues - Sat 9:30 AM - 7 PM, Sun 9 AM - 1 PM, cl Mon; Estab 1928; The gallery is located in the Palazzo della Province, a building constructed in the 1930s
Special Subjects: Drawings, Etchings & Engravings, Landscapes, Photography, Sculpture, Watercolors, Bronzes, Religious Art, Ceramics, Folk Art, Pottery, Painting-European, Portraits, Furniture, Baroque Art, Renaissance Art, Medieval Art, Painting-Italian
Collections: Apulian, Venetian & Neapolitan paintings & sculptures from 11th - 19th century; Grieco coll: 50 paintings from Fattom to Morandi; 23 paintings from the Banco di Napoli coll
Publications: Catalogues of all the collections
Activities: Classes for adults & children; concerts; gallery talks; mus shop sells books, reproductions

BERGAMO

M **GALLERIA DELL' ACCADEMIA CARRARA,** Piazza Giacomo Carrara 82/A, Bergamo, 24100 Italy. Tel (035) 399643; Fax (035) 224510; *Dir* Dr F Rossi
Collections: Paintings by: Bellini, Raffaello, Pisanello, Mantegna, Botticelli, Beato Angelico, Previtali, Tiepolo, Durer, Brueghel, Van Dyck

M **MUSEO ADRIANO BERNAREGGI,** Bergamo via Pignolo 76, Bergamo, Italy. Tel 035-248772; Fax 035-215517; Elec Mail info@museobernareggi.it; Internet Home Page Address: www.museobernareggi.it

BOLOGNA

M **INSTITUZIONE GALLERIA D'ARTE MODERNA DI BOLOGNA,** Museo d'Arte Moderna di Bologna, Via Don Minzoni 14, Bologna, 40121 Italy. Tel 39-051-6496611; Fax 39-051-6496600; Elec Mail info@mambo-bologna.org; Internet Home Page Address: www.mambo-bologna.org; *Dir* Gianfranco Maraniello; *Cur* Andrea Viliani; *Asst Dir* Eva Fuchs; *Educ Dept* Veronica Ceruti; *Educ Dept* Cristina Francucci; *Commun & Mktg* Lara Facco; *Commun & Mktg* Ellsa Maria Cerra
Open Tues - Wed & Fri - Sun 10 AM - 6 PM, Thurs 10 AM - 10 PM, cl Mon; Admis (temp exhibs) 6 euro, under 18 over 65 4 euro, under 6 free; permanent coll free; Ground floor permanent collection, first floor temporary exhibs of contemporary art; Average Annual Attendance: 100,000; Mem: Dues prestige 100 euro, family 75 euro, individual 21 - 50 euro
Collections: Collection of modern art from the late 18th century to the present
Activities: Classes for adults & children; lects open to pub; concerts; gallery talks; tours

M **Museo Morandi,** Piazza Maggiore 6, Bologna, 40121 Italy. Tel 39-051-203332; Elec Mail mmorandi@comune.bologna.it; Internet Home Page Address: www.museomorandi.it; *Contact* Lorenza Selleri
Open Tues - Fri 9 AM - 6:30 PM, Sat - Sun 10 AM - 6:30 PM; No admis fee
Collections: Giorgio Morandi Collection; 62 oil paintings, 18 watercolors, 92 drawings, 78 etchings, sculptures and engravings
Exhibitions: Casa Morandi in Ula Fondazia Has
Activities: Classes for adults & children; mus shop sells books, reproductions, prints

M **Villa delle Rosa,** Via Saragozza 228, Bologna, 40135 Italy. Tel 39-051-436818; Elec Mail mamboedu@comune.bologna.it; *Contact* Giulia Pezzoli
Open only during exhibitions 3 PM - 7 PM; No admis fee
Collections: Temporary exhibitions of Italian and international artists

M **MUSEO MORANDI,** Piazza Maggiore 6, Palazzo d'Accursio Bologna, Italy. Elec Mail mmorandi@comune.bologna.it; Internet Home Page Address: www.museomorandi.it
Average Annual Attendance:

M **PINACOTECA NAZIONALE,** Via Belle Arti 56, Bologna, 40126 Italy. Tel (051) 243222; Fax 051 251368; Elec Mail sbas-bo@iperbolt.bologna.it; *Dir* Dr Marzia Faictti; *Consultant to Pub* Carla Pirani; *Consultant to Pub* Luigi Chieppa
Open Mon - Fri 9 AM - 1:30 PM; Estab 1882; Gallery contains dept of prints and drawings; Average Annual Attendance: 150,000
Library Holdings: Book Volumes; CD-ROMs; Cards; Exhibition Catalogs; Photographs; Slides
Collections: 14th - 18th century Bolognese paintings; German & Italian engravings
Activities: Classes for adults & children; concerts; gallery talks; tours; lending of original objects of art to museums in different countries; mus shop sells books, reproductions

BOLZANO

M **MUSEUM OF MODERN AND CONTEMPORARY ART-BOLZANO,** Via Dante 6, Bolzano, 39100 Italy. Tel +39-0471-22-34-11; Fax +39-0471-22-34-12; Elec Mail info@muselon.it
Average Annual Attendance:

FLORENCE

M FONDAZIONE CASA BUONARROTI, (Museo della Casa Buonarroti) Via Ghibellina 70, Florence, 50122 Italy. Tel (055) 241-752; Fax (055) 241-698; Elec Mail fond@casabuonarroti.it; Internet Home Page Address: www.casabuonarroti.it; *Dir* Pina Ragionieri; *Pres* Antonio Paolucci
Open Mon, Wed - Sun 9:30 AM - 2 PM, cl Tues, New Year's day, Easter Sun, May 1, Aug 15 & Christmas day; Admis intero 6.50 Euros, ridotes 4 Euros
Collections: Works by Michelangelo & others; items from the Buonarroti Family colls
Activities: Mus shop sells books, magazines, reproductions, prints, slides

M GALLERIA D'ARTE MODERNA DI PALAZZO PITTI, Piazza Pitti 1, Florence, 50125 Italy. Tel 055 238 8601/616; Fax 055 2654520; Elec Mail gam@polomuseale.firenze.it; Internet Home Page Address: www.polomuseale.firenze.it/musei/artemoderna; *Dir* Annamaria Giusti
Open Tues - Sun 8:15 AM - 6:50 PM, cl Mon, New Year's Day, May 1, Christmas Day; Admis 8.50 euro full price, 4.25 reduced price, free for citizens of EU under 18 and over 65; tickets also valid for the Palatina Gallery; Collection of paintings and sculpture mostly Italian that date from 18th century to World War I
Collections: Paintings and sculptures of the 19th and 20th century; Artists of Makchiaioli movement

M GALLERIA DEGLI UFFIZI, Uffizi Gallery, Piazzale degli Uffizi, Florence, 50122 Italy. Tel (055) 238 85; Fax (055) 238 8694; Elec Mail direzion.uffizi@polomuseale.it; Internet Home Page Address: www.polomuseale.firenze.it; *Dir* Antonio Natali; *Dir Dept Dal Duecento Al Primo Cinsciemento* Angelo Tartuferi; *Dir Dept Dal Secondo Rinas Al Seicento & l'arte Contemporanca* Francesco de Luca; *Dir Dip dal Settecento* Valentina Conticelli; *Dir Dip Anyichita Classica* Giovanni Giusti; *Dir Architettura Eprogettazion* Antonio Godoci
Open Tues - Sun 8:15 AM - 7 PM; Admis fee 6.50 euro, except European citizens 3.50 euro, Italian citizens under 18 or over 65 free; Vedi depliant; Mem: Aruice degli Uffici
Library Holdings: Auction Catalogs; Audio Tapes; Book Volumes; CD-ROMs; Cards; Compact Disks; DVDs; Exhibition Catalogs; Maps; Photographs; Prints; Records; Reproductions; Slides; Video Tapes
Collections: Florentine Renaissance paintings
Activities: Classes for children; mus shop sells books, magazines, reproductions, prints & slides

M GALLERIA DELL' ACCADEMIA, Via Ricasoli 58-60, Florence, 50122 Italy. Tel (055) 2388609; Fax (055) 2388764; Elec Mail GalleriaAccademia@polomuseale.firenze.it; Internet Home Page Address: www.uffizi.firenze.it; *Dir* Angelo Tartuferi; *Vice Dir* Lia Brunori
Open Tues - Sun 8:15 AM - 6:50 PM, cl Mon; Admis 6.50 euro; Estab 1784; Gallery includes 2 floors, 2 bookshops; Average Annual Attendance: 1,000,000
Collections: Michelangelo's statues in Florence & works of art of 13th - 19th century masters, mostly Tuscan; 19th century plaster models, 18th-19th century Russian icons, ancient musical instruments
Activities: Classes for children; concerts; Mus shop sells books, reproductions, prints, slides

M GALLERIA PALATINA, Palazzo Pitti, Piazza Pitti Florence, 50125 Italy. Tel (055) 238-8611; *Dir* Dr Marco Chiarini
Collections: Paintings from 16th and 17th century

M MUSEO DEGLI ARGENTI E MUSEO DELLE PORCELLANE, Palazzo Pitti, 50125 Italy. Tel 055/23-88-709; 055/23-88-761; Fax 055/23-88-710; Elec Mail argenti@sbas.firenze.it; Internet Home Page Address: www.sbas.firenze.it; *Dir* Marilena Mosco; *Vice Dir* Ornella Casazza
Open Jan, Feb, Nov & Dec 8:15 AM - 4:30, Mar 8:15 AM - 5:30 PM, Apr - Oct 8:15 AM - 7:30 PM; Admis adults 4 Euro, children under 18 & seniors over 65 free; Gallery is a treasury of rare quality that houses a collection belonging to the Medici, Lorena and Savoia. It is located in the historical Palazzo Pimi in Florence Sec XVI
Library Holdings: Auction Catalogs; Book Volumes; CD-ROMs; Cards; Cassettes; Kodachrome Transparencies; Maps
Collections: Summer state apartments of the Medici Grand Dukes; gold, silver, enamel, objects d'art, hardstones, ivory, amber, cameos and jewels, principally from the 15th to the 18th century; period costumes exhibited in Galleria del Costume on premises
Activities: Mus shop sells books, reproductions, prints, slides

M MUSEO DI SAN MARCO, Piazza San Marco 3, Florence, 50121 Italy; Via La Pira 1, Florence, 50121 Italy. Tel 39-055-23-88-608; Fax 39-055-23-88-704; Elec Mail museosanmarco@polomuseale.firenze.it; *Dir* Magnolia Scudieri; *Vice Dir* Dr Liia Brunori
Open Mon - Fri 8:15 AM - 1:50 PM, Sat & Sun 8:15 AM - 16:50 (4.50) PM; Admis 4 Euro, 2 Euro (reduced) ; Estab 1869
Special Subjects: Renaissance Art
Collections: Fra Angelico frescoes, paintings & panels; qui lasciarono traccia di se pittori come Domenico Chirlandaio e Giovanni Antonio Sogliani, che affrescaronoi due Refettori, e Fra' Bartolomeo, l'altro grande artista che visse nel convento all'inizio del Cinquecento; mentre nel'area un tempo destinata a Foresteria sono collocati i reperti architettonici e decorativi provenienti dagli edifici dell'antico Centro di Firenze demolito alla fine del' Ottocento; Al primo piano del Museo, insieme alle celle del Dormitorio, si trova la Biblioteca Monumentale, opera di Michelozzo, che ospita un' esposizione di corali miniati che fanno parte della ricca collezione appartenente al Museo

GENOA

M COMUNE DI GENOVA - DIREZIONE CULTURA SETTORE MUSEI, Via Garibaldi 18, Genoa, 16124 Italy. Tel 010-2476368; *Dir* Laura Tagliaferro
M Galleria di Arte Moderna con Opere Della Collezione Wolfson, Villa Serra, Via

Capolungo 3, Nervi, Genoa, 16167 Italy; Largo Pertini 4, Genova, I - 16121 Italy. Tel (010) 3726025; Tel (010) 5574739; Fax (010) 5574701; Elec Mail gam@comune.genova.it; Internet Home Page Address: www.gamgenova.it; *Cur* Maria Flora Giubilei
Open Tues - Sun 10 AM - 7 PM, cl Mon; A coll of modern art
Library Holdings: Book Volumes; Cards; Exhibition Catalogs; Memorabilia
Collections: 19th & 20th century paintings
Publications: General Catalogue & a Little Guide both in Italian & English
Activities: Classes for adults & children; docent training; lects for mem only; concerts; gallery talks; conferences; musical events; theatrical events; lending of original objects of art to other museums & pub scientific institutions for temporary exhib; originates traveling exhib to other museums; mus shop sells books

M Museo d'Arte Orientale Edoardo Chiossone, Viletta di Negro, Piazzale Mazzini 4N Genoa, 16122 Italy. Tel (010) 542285; Fax 010 580526; Elec Mail museochiossone@comune.genova.it; Internet Home Page Address: www.museosanmarco.it; *Cur* Dr Donatella Failla
Open to pub Tues - Fri 9 AM - 7 PM, Sat & Sun 10 AM - 7 PM, cl Mon; Admis E 4.00; Estab 1971
Collections: Japanese works of art from 11th to 19th century (about 20,000 pieces) collected in Japan during the Meiji period by Edoardo Chissone
Exhibitions: Kodomono Hi; Tanabata Matsuri; Hina Matsuri
Activities: Concerts, gallery talks, tours; mus shop sells books

M Museo di Strada Nuova Palazzo Rosso, Via Garibaldi 18, Genoa, 16124 Italy. Tel (0039) 010 5574972; Fax (0039) 010 5574973; Elec Mail museidistradanuova@comune.genova.it; Internet Home Page Address: www.museopalazzorosso.it; *Cur, Mus Dir* Dr Piero Boccardo; *Municipal Servant* Raffaella Besta
Open Tues - Fri 9.00 AM - 19.00 PM, Sat - Sun 10.00 AM - 19.00, cl Mon; Admis 8.00 Euro (for 3 mus); 1874 when Duchess of Galliera Maria Brignole-Sale donated the palace & its collections to the Municipality of Genoa; Average Annual Attendance: 110,000
Special Subjects: Drawings, Portraits, Painting-French, Sculpture, Baroque Art, Painting-Flemish, Renaissance Art, Period Rooms, Painting-Italian
Collections: Paintings by Van Dyck, Durer, Guercino, Veronese, Reni, Preti, Strozzi; Drawings & prints by Guercino, Carracci, Cambiaso, Reni & Genoese Artists of XVII & XVIII centuries
Publications: Exhib catalogs
Activities: Classes for adults & children, docent training; Lectrs open to pub, concerts, guided tours; Mus shop, books, reproductions, prints

M Museo Giannettino Luxoro, Via Aurelia 29, Nervi, Genoa, 16167 Italy. Tel 322673
Collections: Flemish & Genoese 17th & 18th centuries paintings, ceramics

M Raccolte Frugone in Villa Grimaldi, Villa Grimaldi, Via Capolungo 9, Nervi, Genoa, 16167 Italy. Tel (010) 322 396; Fax 010 5574701; Elec Mail raccoltefrugone@comune.genova.it; Internet Home Page Address: www.comune.genova.it/tarismo/musei/frugone/welcome.htm; Internet Home Page Address: www.raccoltefrugone.it; *Cur* Dr Maria Flora Giubilei
Open Tues - Fri 9 AM - 7 PM, Sat & Sun 10 AM - 7 PM, cl Mon
Collections: 19th & 20th century Italian artists; Sculpture and paintings by 19th & 20th century Italian artists

LIVORNO

M MUSEO CIVICO GIOVANNI FATTORI, Via S. Jacopo in, Acquaviva, 65 Livorno, 57127 Italy. Tel +39-0586-808001-804847; Fax +39-0586-806118; Elec Mail museofattori@comune.livorno.it; Internet Home Page Address: pegaso.comune.livorno.it/index; *Mgr* Dr Francesca Giampaolo; *Asst Mgr* Francesco Luschi
Open 10 - 13 AM & 16 - 19 PM, cl Mon; Admis 4 euro, 2.50 euro; Fine art mus; Average Annual Attendance: 12,000
Library Holdings: Book Volumes; Exhibition Catalogs; Original Documents
Special Subjects: Archaeology, Art History, Prints, Graphics, Sculpture, Antiquities-Byzantine, Coins & Medals, Painting-Italian, Antiquities-Roman, Antiquities-Etruscan
Collections: Giovanni Fattori & Macchiaioli paintings; 19th & 20th Tuscan & Italian paintings; Byzantine icons; numismatics; archeology
Publications: Exhib catalogs
Activities: Educ activities for children & students; temporary exhibs; lects open to pub; gallery talks; tours; schols; fels; extension prog serves town & province of Livorno; lending of original art to mus & institutions; mus shop sells books, reproductions, prints, postcards & posters

LUCCA

M MUSEO E PINACOTECA NAZIONALE DI PALAZZO MANSI, National Museum and Picture Gallery of the Palazzo Mansi, Via Galli Tassi 43, Lucca, 55100 Italy. Tel (0583) 55570; Fax (0583) 312221; Elec Mail sbdpsae_lu.museilucchesi@beniculturali.it; Internet Home Page Address: www.luccamuseinazionali.it; *Dir* Dr Antonia d'Aniello; *Sezione Architettonica* Glauco Borella; *Opers* Dr Ilaria Pergola
Open Tue - Sat 8:30 AM - 7:30 PM, Sun 8:30 AM - 1:30 PM, cl Mon, New Year's, May 1, & Christmas; Admis general 4 euro, with Musco Nazionale di Villa Guinigi 6.50 euro; Est 1977; Paintings, sculptures, frescos, furniture, tapestries; Average Annual Attendance: 15,000
Income: Ministero Beni Culturali
Collections: Works of Tuscan, Venetian, French & Flemish Schools; paintings by such masters as Titian & Tintoretto; Paintings and sculptures XVIII-XX
Activities: Classes for adults & children; concerts, gallery talks; tours; scholarships

M SOPRINTENDENZA DI LUCCA MASSA CARRARA, (Soprinteudeuza Di Pisa e Massa Carrara) Museo Nazionale Di Villa Guinigi, Villa Guinigi, Via della Quarquonia Lucca, 55100 Italy. Tel (0583) 496033; Fax (0583) 312221; Elec Mail sbapsae-lu.museinazionali@beniculturali.it; Internet Home Page Address: www.luccamuseinazionali.it; *Dir* Dr Antonia d'Aniello; *Dir Sezione Architectomica* Glauco Borella
Open Tues - Sat 8:30 AM - 7:30 PM, Sun 8:30 AM - 1:30 PM; Admis 4 euro; with Museo Nazionale di Palazzo Meusi 6.50 Euro; Estab 1924; 15th century historical bldg; Average Annual Attendance: 10,000

Income: Ministero Culturali
Collections: Roman and late Roman sculptures and mosaics; Romanesque, Gothic and Renaissance Sculpture; paintings from 12th to 18th century; Ancient coins, medals, Italian ceramics, & silverware
Publications: Matteo Civitali
Activities: Classes for adults & children; docent training; lects open to pub; 350 vis lectrs per year; concerts, gallery talks, tours

MANTUA

M **SOPRINTENDENZA PER I BENI STORICI ARTISTICI ED ETNOANTROPOLOGICI PER LE PROVINCE DI MANTOVA BRESCIA E CREMONA,**(Museo Ducale Soprintendenza per I beni storici artistici ed etnoantropologici per le province di Mantova Brescia e Cremona)Museo di Palazzo Ducale, Piazza Sordello 40, Mantua, 46100 Italy. Tel (0376) 352100 (Museum), 352111 (Soprintendenza); Tel 352104 (Segreteria Soprintendenza); Fax (0376) 366274; Elec Mail sbsae-mn@beniculturali.it; Internet Home Page Address: www.mantovaducale.beniculturali.it; *Conservatore* Dr Giovanna Paolozzi Strozzi; *Conservatore* Dr Stefano L'occaso; *Vice Dir* Dr Renata Casarin; *Cur* Dr Stefano L'Occaso
Open 8:15 - 19:15; Admis 6.50 euro, 3.25 euro, free; Estab 1882; Huge monumental architecture (XIII-XIX centuries) with paintings by Andrea Mantegna, Pisanello, Peter Paul Rubens, tapestries by Raphael; Average Annual Attendance: 200,000
Income: State museum
Library Holdings: Book Volumes; CD-ROMs; DVDs; Exhibition Catalogs; Framed Reproductions; Maps; Micro Print; Motion Pictures; Video Tapes
Special Subjects: Archaeology, Etchings & Engravings, Ceramics, Glass, Photography, Porcelain, Prints, Maps, Painting-European, Painting-French, Tapestries, Architecture, Drawings, Sculpture, Watercolors, Ethnology, Religious Art, Crafts, Woodcarvings, Landscapes, Decorative Arts, Collages, Portraits, Dolls, Silver, Marine Painting, Painting-Dutch, Carpets & Rugs, Ivory, Coins & Medals, Baroque Art, Painting-Flemish, Renaissance Art, Medieval Art, Painting-Italian, Antiquities-Egyptian, Antiquities-Greek, Antiquities-Roman, Mosaics, Cartoons, Painting-German
Collections: Classical Antiquities & Sculpture; picture gallery; modern sculptures, tapestries; prints, drawings
Publications: S L'occaso, The Ducal Palace - Mantua, Milano 2009; G Algeri; Palazzo Ducale di Mantova, Montova 2003
Activities: Classes for adults & children; lects open to pub; 4-5 vis lectrs per yr; concerts; gallery talks; tours; lending of original objects of art to exhibs worldwide; artmobil; mus shop sells books, magazines, reproductions, prints & other items

MILAN

M **MUSEO POLDI PEZZOLI,** Via A Manzoni 12, Milan, 20121 Italy. Elec Mail info@museopoldipezzoli.it; Internet Home Page Address: www.museopoldipezzoli.it; *Dir* Dr Annalisa Zanni; *Cur* Lavinia Galli; *Cur* Andrea Di Lorenzo; *Registrar* Federica Manoli
Admis 9 euro full price, 6 euro reduced; Estab 1881
Library Holdings: Exhibition Catalogs; Manuscripts; Photographs; Prints; Sculpture
Collections: Paintings from 14th - 18th century; armor, tapestries, rugs, jewelry, porcelain, glass, textiles, furniture, clocks and watches; Netsuke and Okimono
Publications: The Poldi Pezzoli Visitors' Guide; Masterpieces of Painting
Activities: Classes for adults & children; docent training; concerts; gallery talks; tours; schols; mus shop sells books, original art, reproductions, prints, slides & cards

M **PINACOTECA AMBROSIANA,** Piazza Pio XI, 2, Milan, 20123 Italy. Tel (02) 806-921; Fax (02) 806-92210; Elec Mail info@ambrosiana.eu; Internet Home Page Address: www.ambrosiana.eu; *Dir* Dr Franco Buzzi
Open Tues - Sun 10 AM - 5 PM; Admis adults 15 euro, children 10 euro
Collections: Leonardo da Vinci, Botticelli, Caravaggio, Luini, Raphael, Titian; drawings, miniatures, ceramics and enamels

M **PINACOTECA DI BRERA,** Via Brera 28, Milan, 20121 Italy. Tel 722631; Fax 72001140; *Dir* Dr Luisa Arrigoni
Open Tues - Sun 8:30 AM - 7:30 PM, cl Mon; The gallery is located in the 17th century Palazza di Brera
Collections: Pictures of all schools, especially Lombard and Venetian; paintings by Mantegna, Bellini, Crivelli, Lotto, Titian, Veronese, Tintoretto, Tiepolo, Foppa, Bergognone, Luini, Piero della Francesca, Bramante, Raphael, Caravaggio, Rembrandt, Van Dyck, Rubens; also Italian 20th century works
Activities: Mus shop sells books, original art, slides

M **RACCOLTE ARTISTICHE DEL CASTELLO SFORZESCO,** (Civiche Raccolte Artistiche) Museo DeGli Strumenti Musicali, Castello Sforzesco, Milan, 20121 Italy. Tel 02-884 63730, 63742; Fax 02-884-63650; Elec Mail c.craaiapplicata@comune.milano.it; Internet Home Page Address: www.comune.milano.it/craai; Internet Home Page Address: www.milanocastello.it; Internet Home Page Address: www.turismo.milano.it; *Conservatore Responsabile* Francesca Tasso
Open Tues - Sun 9 AM - 1 PM & 2 - 5:30 PM; Admis 3 euro, reduced 1,50 euro; Musical instruments
Library Holdings: Book Volumes; Exhibition Catalogs; Photographs
Collections: Musical instruments from XVI-XX century
Activities: Classes for adults & children; guided tours; lects open to pub; 2 vis lectrs per yr; concerts; mus shop sells books, reproductions

M **Raccolta delle Stampe Achille Bertarelli,** Castello Sforzesco, Milan, 20121 Italy. Tel 0039 02 884-63835; Fax 0039-02-884-63812; Elec Mail craai.bertarelli@comune.milano.it; Internet Home Page Address: www.comune.milano.it/craai; *Dir* Dr Claudio Salsi; *Cur* Giovanna Mori

Open Mon - Fri 9 AM - 2 PM; No admis fee; Di Stampe collection by appointment
Activities: Conferences; Mus shop sells books

M **Civiche Raccolte Archeologiche e Numismatiche,** Via B Luini 2, Milan, 20123 Italy. Tel 02 805-3972; Fax 02 86452796; *Dir* Dr Ermanno Arslan
Collections: Ancient Egyptian, antique & modern coins; Etruscan, Greek & Roman Collections

M **Museo d'Arte Applicata,** Castello Sforzesco, Milan, 20121 Italy. Tel 02-884-63730, 63742; Fax 02-884-63650; Elec Mail c.craaiapplicata@comune.milano.it; Internet Home Page Address: www.comune.milano.it/craai; *Conservatore Responsabile* Dr Francesca Tasso
Open Tues - Sun 9 AM - 5:30 PM; Admis fee 3 euro, reduced 1,50 euro
Library Holdings: Book Volumes; Exhibition Catalogs; Photographs
Collections: Furniture, sculpture, glasses, porcelain, bronzes, ivory, irons, decorative arts, tapestries, metalworks
Activities: Classes for adults & children; conferences; gallery talks; mus shop sells books, prints & reproductions

M **Galleria d'Arte Moderna,** Villa Reale, Via Palestro 16 Milan, 20121 Italy. Tel 02-86463054; Fax 02 864-63054; *Dir* Dr Maria Teresa Fiorio
Collections: Painting & sculpture from Neo-Classical period to present day; includes the Grassi Collection & Museo Marino Marini (approx 200 sculptures, portraits, paintings, drawings & etchings by Marini)

MODENA

M **GALLERIA, MEDAGLIERE E LAPIDARIO ESTENSE,** Soprintendensa Per Ibeni Storici Artistici Ed Etnoantropologici Di Modena e Reggio Emilis, Palazzo dei Musei, Piazza S Agostino 337 Modena, 41100 Italy. Tel 059-39-57-11; Fax 059-23-01-96; Fax 059-23-01-96; Elec Mail sbsae-mo@beniculturali.it; Internet Home Page Address: www.spsae-mo.beniculturali.it; *Dir* Stefano Casciu; *Cur Dipinti-Disegni* Giovanna Paolozri Strozei; *Cur Scultura* Daniela Ferriani
Open Tues - Sun 9 AM - 7 PM, cl Mon; There are two galleries: Galleria, Museo e Medagliere Estense & Museo Lapidario Estense
Collections: Bronzes, coins, drawings, medals, minor arts, paintings, prints & sculptures, most from the Este family; Xilografie
Publications: See web site

NAPLES

M **MUSEO CIVICO GAETANO FILANGIERI,** Via Duomo 288, Naples, 80138 Italy. Tel (081) 203175; *Dir* Antonio Buccino Grimaldi
Open Mon - Sat 9:30 AM - 2 PM & 3:30 PM - 7 PM, Sun & holidays 9:30 AM - 1:30 PM
Collections: Paintings, furniture, archives, photographs

M **MUSEO DI CAPODIMONTE,** Palazzo di Capodimonte, Naples, 80131 Italy. Tel (081) 7499154; Fax (081) 7445032; Elec Mail sspsae-na.capodimonte@beniculturali.it; Internet Home Page Address: www.polomusealenapoli.beniculturali.it; *Dir* Dr Fabrizio Vona
Open 9:30 AM - 7 PM, cl Wed; Admis 7.50 Euro, children under 18 & seniors over 65 yrs no charge; Painting, sculpture, objects XII-XXSEC
Special Subjects: Decorative Arts, Ceramics, Glass, Metalwork, Portraits, Painting-French, Tapestries, Sculpture, Porcelain, Oriental Art, Painting-Dutch, Ivory, Coins & Medals, Painting-Flemish, Medieval Art, Painting-Spanish, Painting-Italian, Islamic Art
Collections: Paintings from 13th to 18th century; paintings and sculptures of 19th century; arms and armor; medals and bronzes of the Renaissance; porcelain; contemporary art, 20th century
Activities: Classes for adults & children; concerts; mus shop sells books, reproductions

M **MUSEO NAZIONALE DI SAN MARTINO,** National Museum of San Martino, Largo San Martino 5, Naples, 80129 Italy. Tel 081-578 1769; *Dir* Dr Ossa Rossana Muzii
Collections: 16th - 18th century pictures & paintings; 13th - 19th century sculpture, majolicas & porcelains; section of modern prints, paintings & engravings; Neapolitan historical collection

PADUA

M **MUSEI CIVICI DI PADOVA - CAPPELLA DEGLI SCROVENGNI,** Musei Civici Agli Eremitani (Civic Museum) - Scrovegni Chapel, Piazza Eremitani 8, Padua, 35121 Italy. Tel 049-82045/51; Fax 049-8204566; Elec Mail musei@comune.padova.it; Internet Home Page Address: http://padovacultura.padovanet.it; *Dir* Davide Banzato; *Funzionario Archeological M* Francesca Verdvese; *Funzionario Art Mus* Elisabetta Gastaldi; *Funzionario Numismatic Mus* Valeria Vettorato; *Librn* Dr Gilda Mantovani; *Management Musei* Marilena Varotto
Open year round 9 AM - 7 PM; Admis full price 12 euro, reduced for groups of 10 or more $8 euro, children 6-17 yrs 8 euro, students 5 euro, children 5 yrs & under free (prices include 1 euro reservation fee); Estab 1825
Library Holdings: Book Volumes; Exhibition Catalogs
Special Subjects: Archaeology, Decorative Arts, Drawings, History of Art & Archaeology, Landscapes, Art History, Ceramics, Furniture, Gold, Porcelain, Portraits, Bronzes, Painting-European, Sculpture, Graphics, Glass, Jewelry, Antiquities-Byzantine, Painting-Dutch, Ivory, Coins & Medals, Restorations, Painting-Flemish, Renaissance Art, Medieval Art, Painting-Italian, Antiquities-Egyptian, Antiquities-Greek, Antiquities-Roman, Mosaics, Painting-German, Pewter, Antiquities-Etruscan
Collections: Archaeological Museum; Art Gallery - bronzes, ceramics, industrial arts, painting, sculpture; Bottacin Museum - Greco-Roman, Italian, Paduan, Venetian, Napoleonic coins and medals; Renaissance gallery; Medieval and

Modern Art; Archeological Collection; Numismatic Collection; Stone Tablets, multi media room for the Scrovegni; Chapel & multi media point in Egyptian room
Publications: Bollettino del Museo Civico
Activities: Classes for children; concerts; Mus shop sells books, reproductions, prints, slides

PARMA

M GALLERIA NAZIONALE, Palazzo Pilotta 15, Parma, 43100 Italy. Tel (0521) 233309; Fax (0521) 206336; *Dir* Lucia Fornari Schianchi
Collections: Paintings from 13th to 19th century, including works by Correggio, Parmigianino, Cima, El Greco, Piazzetta, Tiepolo, Holbein, Van Dyck, Mor, Nattier & several painters of the school of Parma; modern art

PERGOLA

M THE GILDED BRONZES, L. go S. Giacomo, Pergola, 61045 Italy. Tel 0721-734090/7373271; Elec Mail museo@bronzidorati.com; Internet Home Page Address: www.bronzidorati.com
Circ

PERUGIA

M GALLERIA NAZIONALE DELL'UMBRIA, Umbrian National Gallery, Corso Vannucci 19, Palazzo dei Priori Perugia, 06121 Italy. Tel 39 075 5741410; Fax 39 075 5741400; Elec Mail gallerianazionaleumbria@beniculturali.it; Internet Home Page Address: www.gallerianazionaleumbria.it; *Dir* Fabio De Chirico; *Cur* Federica Zalarra; *Educ Prog* Maria Brucato; *Maintenance* Gianluca Delogu
Open 8:30 AM - 7:30 PM, cl Mon; Admis fee 6.50 euro, EU citizens 18-25 yrs 3.50 euro; 1863, civic museum; Average Annual Attendance: 80,000
Special Subjects: Drawings, Ceramics, Furniture, Gold, Textiles, Bronzes, Sculpture, Jewelry, Ivory, Baroque Art, Renaissance Art, Medieval Art, Painting-Italian, Stained Glass
Collections: Jewels; paintings from the Umbrian School from the 13th - 18th century; 13th-15th century sculptures; Umbrian clothes from 13th century
Activities: Classes for adults & children; docent training; concerts & gallery talks; museum sells books, magazines, original art, reproductions, prints, slides

PISA

M MUSEO NAZIONALE DI SAN MATTEO, Convento di San Matteo, Lungarno Mediceo Pisa, 56100 Italy. Tel (050) 23750; *Dir* Dr Mariagiulia Burresi
Open Tues - Sat 9 AM - 7 PM, Sun 9 AM - 2 PM, cl Mon; Admis 4 euro, concessions 2 euro
Collections: Sculptures by the Pisanos and their school; collection of the Pisan school of the 13th and 14th centuries, and paintings of the 15th, 16th, and 17th centuries; ceramics; collection of coins and medals

POSSAGNO

M MUSEO GIPSOTECA ANTONIO CANOVA POSSAGNO, Via Canova 74, 31054th Possagno, 31054 Italy. Tel +39-0423-544323; Fax +39-0423-922007; Elec Mail posta@museocanova.it; Internet Home Page Address: www.museocanova.it; *Pres* Giancarlo Galan; *Sec* Orazio Scardellato; *Dir* Mario Guderzo
Open 9:30 AM - 6 PM; Admis 8 euro, 6 euro; Average Annual Attendance: 30,000
Library Holdings: Book Volumes; CD-ROMs; Exhibition Catalogs; Prints; Sculpture
Collections: Plaster cast models; paintings; drawings
Activities: Guided tours; concerts; schols; mus shop sells books, original art, reproductions, prints, postcards, gadgets, slides

ROME

M GALLERIA BORGHESE, Galleria Borghese, Piazzale Scipione Borghese 5, Rome, 00197 Italy. Tel 06-8413979; Fax 06 8840756; *Chief Cur* Kristine Herrmann Fiore; *Dir* Anna Coliva; *Chief Cur* Marina Minozzi; *Supt* Rosella Vodret
Open Tues - Sun 9 AM - 19 PM, cl Mon, Christmas & New Year's Day, ticket reservation needed; Admis 8.50 Euro; if exhib in course 13.50 Euro; Greek, Roman & ancient art, Fifteenth & Twentieth century sculpture & Painting
Income: Pub & private
Collections: Baroque & Classical; 580 paintings about XV-XVII-XVIII, 450 sculptures
Exhibitions: One or two exhibs ann
Publications: Catalogues
Activities: Classes for adults & children; concerts; Mus shop, books, reproductions, prints

M GALLERIA DORIA PAMPHILJ, Piazza del Collegio Romano 2, Rome, 00186 Italy; Piazza Grazioli 5, Rome, 00186 Italy. Tel (06) 679-73-23; Fax (06) 6780939; Elec Mail arti.rm@doriapamphilj.it; Internet Home Page Address: www.doriapomphilj.it; *Dir* Jonathan Doria Pamphilj; *Scientific Cur* Andrea G de Marchi
Open Fri - Wed 10 AM - 5 PM, cl Thurs; Admis 8 euro, seniors over 65, students & groups 5.70 euro
Special Subjects: Porcelain, Pottery, Bronzes, Painting-European, Painting-Flemish, Painting-Italian, Antiquities-Roman, Bookplates & Bindings
Collections: Paintings by Caravaggio, Carracci, Correggio, Filippo Lippi, Lorrain, del Piombo, Titian, Velazquez
Activities: Mus shop sells books, prints, slides, jewelry & other items

M GALLERIA NAZIONALE PALAZZO BARBERNI, National Gallery of Rome, Via Quattro Fontane 13, Rome, 00184 Italy. Tel (06) 4824184; 4814591; Fax (06) 4880560; Elec Mail sspsae-rni.gnaa@beniculturali.it; *Dir* Dr Anna Lo Bianco; *Registrar* Giuliano Forti; *Dir Art History* Dr Michele Di Monte; *Supt* Rossella Vodret; *Registrar* Michela Ulivi; *Pub Relations* Simona Baldi
Open Tues - Sun 8:30 AM - 7 PM; Admis full price 7 euro, reduced price 3.50 euro; Paintings from XIII to XVIII Century, Raphael Caravage, etc., 34 rooms 3 floors; Average Annual Attendance: 240,000
Library Holdings: Audio Tapes; Book Volumes; Cards; Exhibition Catalogs; Maps; Photographs; Reproductions
Collections: Italian & European paintings from 12th - 18th century; Baroque architecture; Sculptures by Bernini, Algardi & others
Activities: Classes for adults & children; lectrs open to pub; 10-12 vis lectrs per yr; concerts; sponsored competitions; museum shop sells books, magazines, reproductions, slides & gadgets

M ISTITUTO NAZIONALE PER LA GRAFICA, National Institute for Graphic Arts, Calcografia, Via della Stamperia 6 Rome, 00187 Italy. Tel (06) 699 801; Fax (06) 699 21454; Internet Home Page Address: www.grafica.arti.beniculturali.it; *Dir* Doff Serenita Papaldo
Collections: Italian & foreign prints; drawings from the 14th century to the present

M MUSEI CAPITOLINI, Piazza del Campidoglio 1, Rome, 00186 Italy. Tel (06) 6710 2475; Fax (06) 67 85844; Elec Mail musei.orteoutica@couruue.coua.it; Internet Home Page Address: www.atac.roma.it; *Dir* Anna Mura Sommella
Open Tues - Sun 9 AM - 8 PM.; Admis ordinary 6.50 euro, reduced 4.50 euro
Library Holdings: Auction Catalogs; Book Volumes; CD-ROMs; Cards; Exhibition Catalogs; Reproductions
Special Subjects: Ceramics, Furniture, Sculpture, Bronzes, Archaeology, Decorative Arts, Painting-European, Porcelain, Carpets & Rugs, Coins & Medals, Tapestries, Baroque Art, Medieval Art, Painting-Italian, Antiquities-Egyptian, Antiquities-Greek, Mosaics, Antiquities-Etruscan
Collections: Ancient sculptures, Art History
Publications: Musei Capitolini, Guida, Electa 2005 (rist. 2011)
Activities: Visiteguidate per adulti E nagazu; 5 vis lectrs per yr; concerts; lending of original objects of art to international exhibs; mus shop sells books, postcards, reproductions

M MUSEO D'ARTE CONTEMPORANEA ROMA, via Reggio Emilia 54, Rome, 00198 Italy. Tel 39-06-6710-70400; Fax 39-06-855-4090; Elec Mail macro@comune.roma.it; Internet Home Page Address: www.macro.roma.museum; *Dir* Danilo Eccher
Open Tues - Sun 9 AM - 7 PM, cl Mon, holidays 10 AM - 2 PM; Admis 1 euro
Collections: Permanent collection of significant contemporary Italian art since the 1960s

M MUSEO NAZIONALE ROMANO, National Museum of Rome, Piazza dei Cinquecento 79, Rome, 00185 Italy. Tel 06-48 3617; Fax 06-48 14125; *Dir* Prof Adriano La Regina
Collections: Archaeological coll; Roman bronzes and sculpture; numismatics

ROVIGO

M PINACOTECA DELL'ACADEMIA DEI CONCORDI-PALAZZO ROVERELLA, Via Laurenti, 8/10, Rovigo, 45100 Italy. Tel (0425) 21654; Fax (0425) 27 993; Elec Mail piuocotcco@concordi.it; Internet Home Page Address: www.concordi.it
Open Tues - Sun 9:30 Am - 12:30 PM, Mon 15.00 PM - 19.00 PM ; Admis 5 Euros, reduced 4 Euro
Collections: Venetian paintings from the 14th to 18th century; Flemish paintings, contemporary art
Activities: Classes for children, schools' progs; concerts; gallery talks; guided tours; museum shop sells books, reproductions, prints

SASSARI

M MUSEO NAZIONALE G A SANNA, Museo Archeologico Nazionale G A Sanna, Via Roma 64, Sassari, 07100 Italy. Tel 272-203; Fax 079-27-1524; Elec Mail museosanna@beniculturali.it; Internet Home Page Address: www.archeossnu.beniculturali.it; *Dir* Dr Gabriella Gasperetti
Open Tues - Sun 9 AM - 8 PM; Admis 4 euro, 2 euro reduced; Estab 1931
Collections: Archeological Collections; Collection of Sardinian Ethnography

TURIN

M ARMERIA REALE, Royal Armory, Piazza Castello 191, Turin, 10122 Italy. Tel (011) 543889; Fax (011) 5087799; Elec Mail armeriareale@artito.arti.beniculturali.it; Internet Home Page Address: www.artito.arti.beniculturali.it; *Dir* Alessandra Guerrini; *Conservatore* Massimiliano Caldera; *Ref Didattica & Secy* M Giuseppina Romagnoli
Open Tues - Sun 8:30 AM - 6:20 PM; cl Mon; Admis 12 euro (plus Palazzo Reale, Galleria Sabauda & Museo di Antichita), 6 euro reduced, under 18 & seniors 65 no charge
Collections: Archaeological Arms; Arms and Armours from 13th - 18th century; Arms of the 19th and 20th century; Oriental Arms; equestrian arms; engravings of Munich School; coins & metals, decorative arts, prints, textiles & sculpture
Publications: La Loggia di Carlo Alberto
Activities: Classes for adults & children; docent training; lects open to pub; tours; schols; fels

M **FONDAZIONE TORINO MUSEI,** (Musei Civici di torino) Galleria Civica d'Arte Moderna e Contemporanea, Via Magenta 31, Turin, 10128 Italy. Tel (011) 4429518; Fax (011) 4429550; Elec Mail gam@fondazionetorinomusei.it; Internet Home Page Address: www.gamtori; *Dir* Danilo Eccher; *Pres* Patrizia Asproni; *Vice Dir* Riccardo Passoni; *Conservatore* Virginia Bertone; *Conservatore* Elena Volpato
Open 10 AM - 6 PM, cl Mon; Admis 10 Euro, 8 Euro reduction, free 1st Tues each month; Estab 1863; Coll with more than 47,000 art works; Mem: Amici Fondazione Torino Musei
Library Holdings: Auction Catalogs; Book Volumes; CD-ROMs; Exhibition Catalogs; Kodachrome Transparencies; Original Documents; Pamphlets; Periodical Subscriptions; Prints; Reproductions; Sculpture; Slides; Video Tapes
Collections: modern art; paintings; sculpture; installations from 1800 - 1900 & contemporary art; video coll; graphic art; photography
Publications: Catalogs for each exhibition
Activities: Classes for adults & children; lects open to pub; concerts; gallery talks; mus shop sells books, magazines, reproductions; photographic archive

M **GALLERIA SABAUDA,** Via XX Setiembre 86, Turin, 10122 Italy; Via Accademia delle Scienze 5, Soprintendenza Beni Storici Artistici ed Etnoantropologici del Piemonte Turin, 10123 Italy. Tel 011-5641729-731; Fax 54 95 47; Elec Mail galleriasabauda@artito.arti.beniculturali.it; Internet Home Page Address: www.artito.arti.beniculturali.it; *Dir* Dr Annamaria Bava; *Conervatore* Dr Giorgio Careddu; *Conservatore* Dr Giorgia Corso; *Secy* Daniela Ferrero e Carla Mastella
Open Tues - Sun 9 AM - 6:30 - PM; cl Mon; Admis full 8 euro, reduced 3 euro, children under 7 yrs no charge; Art Museum
Library Holdings: Auction Catalogs; Exhibition Catalogs; Kodachrome Transparencies; Lantern Slides; Periodical Subscriptions; Photographs; Reproductions; Slides
Collections: Flemish Masters; French Masters; Italian Masters; Dutch & early Italian colls; Piedmontese Masters; furniture, sculpture, jewelry; (galleria moved to Manica Nuova, Palazzo Reale of Turin, where selection of 100 masterpieces from the museum's colls is currently on view. The new Galleria Sabauda is scheduled to open in 2014)
Publications: on-line: www.sabaudaeducational.com
Activities: Classes for children

VATICAN CITY

M **MONUMENTI, MUSEI E GALLERIE PONTIFICIE,** Vatican Museums and Galleries, Musei Vaticani, v-120 Vatican City, 00120 Italy. Tel 39-0669883041; Fax 39-0669885236; Elec Mail direzione.musei@scv.va; Internet Home Page Address: www.vatican.va; *Acting Dir Gen* Dr Francesco Buranelli; *Secy* Dr Edith Cicerchia; *Adminr* Dr Franceso Riccardi; *Head of Scientific Research Cabinet* Dr Nazzareno Gabrielli; *Chief Paintings Restorer* Maurizio De Luca; *Cur Photographic Archive* Dr Guido Comini; *Press Ofc* Dr Lucina Vattuone; *Press Ofc* Dr Cristina Gennaccari
Open Mon-Sat 9AM-6PM, Last Sun of each month except holidays 9AM-2PM; cl Sun; cl Vatican holidays Jan 1, 6; Feb 11; Mar 19; Apr 12, 13; Ma 1, 21; June 11, 29; Aug 15, 16; Nov 1; Dec 8, 25, 26; Admis reg 14 euro; reduced to 8 euro, children under 18, students under 26 with valid id, pilgrimages, school groups; special reduced for school groups 4 euro from Nov to Feb; free entrance on last Sunday of each month and on Sept 27; Estab 1506 by Pope Julius II
Collections: Twelve museum sections with Byzantine, medieval & modern art; classical sculpture; liturgical art; minor arts
Publications: For all except Missionary Museum: Bollettino dei Monumenti, Musei, Gallerie Pontificie

—**Museo Pio Clementino,** Citta del Vaticano, Vatican City, 00120 Vatican City. Tel (06) 6988-3333; Fax (06) 6988-5061; *Cur* Paolo Liverani
Founded by Pope Clement XIV (1770-74) & enlarged by his successor, Pius VI; exhibits include the Apollo of Belvedere, the Apoxyomenos by Lysippus, the Laocoon Group, the Meleager of Skopas, the Apollo Sauroktonous by Praxiteles

—**Museo Sacro,** Citta del Vaticano, Vatican City, 00120 Vatican City. Tel (06) 6988-3333; Fax (06) 6988-5061; *Cur* Dr Giovanni Morello
Founded in 1756 by Pope Benedict XIV; administered by the Apostolic Vatican Library
Collections: Objects of liturgical art, historical relics & curios from the Lateran, objects of Paleolithic, medieval & Renaissance minor arts, paintings of the Roman era

—**Museo Profano,** Citta del Vaticano, Vatican City, 00120 Vatican City. Tel 06-6988-3333; Fax 06-6988-5061; *Cur* Dr Giovanni Morello
Founded in 1767 by Pope Clement XIII; administered by the Vatican Apostolic Library
Collections: Bronze sculpture & minor art of the classical era

—**Museo Chiaramonti e Braccio Nuovo,** Citta del Vaticano, Vatican City, 00120 Vatican City. Tel 06-6988-3333; Fax 06-6988-5061; *Cur* Paolo Liverani
Founded by Pope Pius VII at the beginning of the 19th century, to house the many new findings excavated in that period
Collections: Statues of the Nile, of Demosthenes & of the Augustus of Prima Porta

—**Museo Gregoriano Etrusco,** Citta del Vaticano, Vatican City, 00120 Vatican City. Tel 06-6988-3333; Fax 06-6988-5061; *Cur* Maurizio Sannibale
Founded by Pope Gregory XVI in 1837
Collections: Objects from the Tomba Regolini Galassi of Cerveteri, the bronzes, terracottas & jewelry, & Greek vases from Etruscan tombs

—**Museo Gregoriano Egizio,** Citta del Vaticano, Vatican City, 00120 Vatican City. Tel 06-6988-3333; Fax 06-6988-5061; *Consultant* Prof Jean-Claude Grenier
Inaugurated by Pope Gregory XVI in 1839
Collections: Egyptian papyri, mummies, sarcophagi & statues, including statue of Queen Tuia (1300 BC)

—**Museo Gregoriano Profano,** Citta del Vaticano, Vatican City, 00120 Vatican City. Tel 06-6988-3333; Fax 06-6988-5061; *Cur* Paolo Liverani
Founded by Gregory XVI in 1844 & housed in the Lateran Palace, it was transferred to a new building in the Vatican & opened to the public in 1970
Collections: Roman sculptures from the Pontifical States; Portrait-statue of Sophocles, the Marsyas of the Myronian group of Athena & Marsyas, the Flavian reliefs from the Palace of the Apostolic Chancery

—**Museo Pio Cristiano,** Citta del Vaticano, Vatican City, 00120 Vatican City. Tel 06-6988-3333; Fax 06-6988-5061; *Cur* Giandomenico Spinola
Founded by Pius IX in 1854 & housed in the Lateran Palace; transferred to a new building in the Vatican & opened to the public in 1970
Collections: Sarcophagi; Latin & Greek inscriptions from Christian cemeteries & basilicas; the Good Shepherd

—**Museo Missionario Etnologico,** Citta del Vaticano, Vatican City, 00120 Vatican City. Tel 06-6988-3333; Fax 06-6988-5061; *Cur* Rev Roberto Zagnoli
Founded by Pius XI in 1926 & housed in the Lateran Palace; transferred to a new building in the Vatican & opened to the public in 1973
Collections: Ethnographical colls from all over the world
Publications: Annali

—**Pinacoteca Vaticana,** Citta del Vaticano, Vatican City, 00120 Vatican City. Tel 06-6988-3333; Fax 06-6988-5061; *Cur* Arnold Nesselrath
Inaugurated by Pope Pius XI in 1932
Collections: Paintings by Fra Angelico, Raphael, Leonardo da Vinci, Titian & Caravaggio, & the Raphael Tapestries

—**Collezione d'Arte Religiosa Moderna,** Citta del Vaticano, Vatican City, 00120 Vatican City. Tel 06-6988-3333; Fax 06-6988-5061; *Cur* Dr Mario Ferrazza
Founded in 1973 by Pope Paul VI; paintings, sculptures & drawings offered to the Pope by artists & donors

—**Vatican Palaces,** Citta del Vaticano, Vatican City, 00120 Vatican City. Tel 06-6988-3333; Fax 06-6988-5061; *Cur* Dr Arnold Nesserath
Chapel of Beato Angelico (or Niccolo V, 1448-1450); Sistine Chapel constructed for Sixtus IV (1471-1484); Borgia Apartment decorated by Pinturicchio; Chapel of Urbano VIII (1631-1635); rooms & loggias decorated by Raphael; Gallery of the Maps (1580-83)

VENICE

M **BIENNALE DI VENEZIA,** S Marco, Ca' Giustinian Venice, 30124 Italy. Tel 5218711; Fax 52 36 374; *Pres* Gian Luigi Rondi
Collections: Visual arts, architecture, cinema, theatre, music. Owns historical archives of contemporary art

M **FONDAZIONE MUSEI CIVICI DI VENEZIA,** (Musei Civici Veneziani) San Marco 52, Venice, 30124 Italy. Tel 39041 5225625; Fax 39041 5200935; *Dir* Prof Giandomenico Romanelli

M **Museo Correr,** San Marco 52, Venice, 30124 Italy. Tel 39041 2405211; Fax 39041 5200935; Elec Mail mkt.musei@comune.venezia.it; Internet Home Page Address: www.museicivicivenezian.it; *Dir* Giandomenico Romanelli
Open Mar 22 - Nov 2: 9 AM - 7 PM, Nov 3 - Mar 21: 9 AM - 5 PM, (ticket office closes an hour before) cl Jan 1 & Dec 25; Admis general12 euro, reduced 6.50 euro (incl Doge's Palace, Archeological Mus, Biblioteca Marcian Monumental Rms); 13 euro, reduced 7.50 euro (also incl one other Civic Mus)
Library Holdings: Auction Catalogs; Book Volumes; CD-ROMs; Cards; Cassettes; DVDs; Exhibition Catalogs; Micro Print; Photographs; Prints; Reproductions
Special Subjects: Decorative Arts, Etchings & Engravings, Landscapes, Architecture, Ceramics, Glass, Furniture, Portraits, Prints, Period Rooms, Silver, Textiles, Bronzes, Manuscripts, Maps, Painting-British, Painting-European, Sculpture, Tapestries, Graphics, Religious Art, Porcelain, Coins & Medals, Miniatures, Painting-Flemish, Renaissance Art, Medieval Art, Painting-German, Military Art
Collections: Coll comprises various area of interest: neoclassical rooms, historical colls throwing light on city's institutions, urban affairs & everyday life; Picture gallery colls of Venetian painting from early 16th century
Publications: Museum Guide
Activities: Classes for adults & children; docent training; lects open to pub; conferences; concerts; gallery talks; tours; schols & fels; lending original object of art for international exhibs; originates traveling exhibs; mus shop sells books, magazines, original art, reproductions, prints, slides & merchandising

M **Ca'Rezzonico, Museo del Settecento Veneziano,** Dorsoduro 3136, Venice, 30123 Italy. Tel 39041 241 0100; Fax 39041 241 0100; Elec Mail info@fmcvenezia.it; Internet Home Page Address: www.visitmuve.it; *Dir* Filippo Pedrocco; *Cur* Alberto Craievich
Open Mar 22 - Nov 2: 10 AM- 6 PM, Nov 3 - Mar 21: 10 AM - 5 PM; The ticket office closes an hour before; cl Tues & Jan 1, Dec 25 & May 1 ; Admis general 8 euro, reduced: 5.50 euro; Mus contains important 18th century Venetian paintings amid furnishings of the age; Average Annual Attendance: 100,000
Library Holdings: Auction Catalogs; Book Volumes; CD-ROMs; Cards; Cassettes; DVDs; Exhibition Catalogs; Micro Print; Photographs; Prints; Reproductions
Special Subjects: Drawings, Etchings & Engravings, Ceramics, Glass, Furniture, Portraits, Textiles, Bronzes, Tapestries, Architecture, Porcelain, Baroque Art, Painting-Italian
Collections: 18th century Venetian art, sculpture, etc; Egidio Martini Picture Gallery; Mestrovich Collection
Publications: Museum Guide; Martini's Collection Guide; Mestrovich's Collection Guide
Activities: Classes for adults & children; docent training; lects open to pub; concerts; gallery talks; tours; conferences; theatre lects; schols & fels; lend original art objects for international exhibs; mus sells books, magazines, original art, reproductions, prints, slides & merchandising

M **Museo Vetario di Murano,** Fondamenta Giustiniani 8, Murano, 30121 Italy.
Collections: Venetian glass from middle ages to the present

M **Palazzo Mocenigo,** Santa Croce 1992, Venice, 30125 Italy. Tel 39041 721798; Fax 39041 5241614; Elec Mail mkt.musei@comune.venezia.it; Internet Home Page Address: www.museicivicivenezian.it; *Dir* Giandomenico Romanelli; *Cur* Paola Chiapperino
Open Mar 22 - Nov 2: 10 AM - 5 PM, Nov 3 - Mar 21: 10 AM - 4 PM, cl Mon, New Year's Day, Christmas Day & May 1; Admis general 4 euro, reduced 2.50 euro
Library Holdings: Auction Catalogs; Book Volumes; CD-ROMs; Cards; Cassettes; DVDs; Exhibition Catalogs; Micro Print; Photographs; Prints; Reproductions

Special Subjects: Flasks & Bottles

Collections: Palace of the Doges; coll of fabrics & costumes; library on history of fashion

Publications: Museum Guide

Activities: Classes for schools & families; docent training; conferences; concerts; theatrical lects

M **Galleria Internazionale d'Arte Moderna di Ca'Pesaro,** Santa Croce 2076, Venice, 30135 Italy. Tel 39 041721127; Fax 39 0415241075; Elec Mail pesaro@fmcvenezia.it; Internet Home Page Address: www.visitmuve.it; *Dir* Gabriella Belli; *Cur* Silvio Fuso

Open Apr 1 - Oct 31 10 AM - 6 PM, Nov 1 - Mar 31 10 AM - 5 PM; cl Mon, New Year's Day, Christmas Day, May 1; Admis general 8 euro, reduced 5.50 euro

Library Holdings: Auction Catalogs; Book Volumes; CD-ROMs; Cards; Cassettes; DVDs; Exhibition Catalogs; Micro Print; Photographs; Prints; Reproductions

Special Subjects: Drawings, Etchings & Engravings, Art History, Conceptual Art, Photography, Painting-American, Painting-European, Sculpture, Decorative Arts, Glass, Restorations, Painting-Italian

Collections: 19th & 20th centuries works of art

Publications: Museum Guide

Activities: Educ prog for schools & families; docent training; conferences; mus shop

M **Doge's Palace,** San Marco 1, Venice, 30124 Italy. Tel 39 0412715911; Fax 39 0415285028; Elec Mail mkt.musei@comune.venezia.it; Internet Home Page Address: www.museicivicivenezia.it; *Dir* Giandomenico Romanelli

Open Mar 22 - Nov 2: 9 AM - 7 PM, Mar 21: 9 AM - 5 PM, cl New Year's Day, Christmas Day; Admis Museum Correr, Archeological Mus, Nazionale and Monumental Rooms of Biblioteca Marciana, & one other Civic Mus, 13 euro full price, 7.50 euro reduced price; Mus Correr, Archeological Mus, Monumental rooms of Biblioteca Marciana, 12 euro full price, 6.50 euro reduced price; Formerly the Doge's residence & seat of Venetian government, the Palace is Gothic architecture. The bldg & its sculptural decoration date from various periods. Along the facades of the Palace run loggias that overlook St. Mar's Square & the lagoon.

Collections: Works by Titian, Veronese, Tintoretto, Vittoria & Tiepolo comprises vast council chambers, delicately-decorated residential apartments & austere prison-cells

Publications: Museum Guide

Activities: Educ progs for schools & families; docent training; conferences; conventions

M **Clock Tower,** San Marco, Venice, 30124 Italy. Tel 39041 5209070; Elec Mail mkt.musei@comune.venezia.it; Internet Home Page Address: www.museicivicivenezia.it

Open to visits with specialized guide, only upon prior booking; Admis general 12 euro, reduced 7 euro, holders of the ticket for the Clock Tower get free admis to the Museo Correr & a reduction on the museums of St. Mark's Square ticket which gives access to Doge's Palace

M **Carlo Goldoni's House,** San Polo 2794, Venice, 30125 Italy. Tel 39041 2759325; Fax 39041 2440081; Elec Mail mkt.musei@comune.venezia.it; Internet Home Page Address: www.museicivicivenezia.it; *Dir* Giandomenico Romanelli; *Cur* Paola Chiapperino

Open Mar 22 - Nov 2: 10 AM - 5 PM, Nov 3 - Mar 21: 10 AM - 4 PM, cl Wed, New Year's Day, Christmas Day, May 1; Admis general 2.50 euro, reduced 1.50 euro; The archive & library have over 30,000 works with theatrical texts, studies & original manuscripts.

Library Holdings: Auction Catalogs; Book Volumes; CD-ROMs; Cards; Cassettes; DVDs; Exhibition Catalogs; Micro Print; Photographs; Prints; Reproductions

Collections: Puppet theatre from Cá Grimani ai Servi, formerly part of the Cá Rezzonico collection

Activities: Educ prog for schools & families; docent training; conferences; conventions

M **Museo Fortuny,** San Marco 3780, Venice, 30124 Italy. Tel 39041 5200995; Fax 39041 5223088; Elec Mail mkt.musei@comune.venezia.it; Internet Home Page Address: www.museicivicivenezia.it; *Dir* Giandomenico Romanelli; *Cur* Daniela Ferretti

Open Wed - Mon 10 AM - 6 PM, ticket office open 10 AM - 5 PM, cl Tues, Dec 25 & Jan 1; Admis general 8 euro, reduced 5 euro; Once owned by the Pesaro family, this large Gothic palazzo in Campo San Beneto was transformed by Mariano Fortuny into his own atelier of photography, stage-design, textile-design & painting. The piano nobile & ground floor spaces are used for special exhibs.

Collections: Fortuny tapestries & colls

Publications: Museum Guide

Activities: Educ prog for schools & families; docent training; conferences; conventions

M **Glass Museum,** Fondamenta Giustinian 8, Murano, 30121 Italy. Tel 39041 739586; Fax 39041 739586; Elec Mail mkt.musei@comune.venezia.it; Internet Home Page Address: www.museicivicivenezia.it; *Dir* Giandomenico Romanelli; *Cur* Silvio Fuso

Open Mar 22 - Nov 2: 10 AM - 6 PM, Nov 3 - Mar 21: 10 AM - 5 PM, cl Wed, New Year's Day, Christmas Day, May 1; Admis general 5.50 euro, reduced 3 euro

Collections: Venetian glass from Roman ages to present

Publications: Museum Guide

Activities: Educ prog for adults & children; docent training; lects open to pub; concerts; gallery talks, tours; conferences; theatre lect; schols & fels; lend original art object for international exhibs; mus sells books, magazines, original art, reproductions, prints, slides & merchandising

M **Lace Museum,** Piazza Galuppi 187, Burano, 30012 Italy. Tel 39041 730034; Fax 39041 735471; Elec Mail mkt.musei@comune.venezia.it; Internet Home Page Address: www.museicivicivenezia.it; *Dir* Giandomenico Romanelli; *Cur* Paola Chiapperino

Open Mar 22 - Nov 2: 10 AM - 5 PM, Nov 3 - Mar 21: 10 AM - 54PM, cl Tues, New Year's Day, Christmas Day, May 1; Admis general 4 euro full, reduced 2.50 euro; Mus houses archives of Andriana Marcello Lace School founded in 1872. It played an important role in the city's cultural & economic life for over a century

Collections: Two hundred rare & precious examples of Venetian lace from the 16th to 20th century

Activities: Educ prog for adults & children; docent training; lects open to pub; lend original art objects for international exhibs; mus sells books, original art, reproductions, prints, slides & merchandising

M **Museum of Natural History,** Santa Croce 1730, Venice, 30135 Italy. Tel 39041 2750206; Fax 39041 721000; Elec Mail mkt.musei@comune.venezia.it; Internet Home Page Address: www.museicivicivenezia.it; *Dir* Giandomenico Romanelli; *Cur* Mauro Bon; *Cur* Luca Mizzan

Open Tues - Fri 9 AM - 1 PM, Sat & Sun 10 AM - 4 PM, Ligabue Expedition Room & Tegnue Aquarium, cl Mon, New Year's Day, Christmas Day, May 1; No admis fee; An important scientific institution, this contains various collections & an important library. It is also a centre for research & surveys regarding the Venetian lagoon & its fauna

Library Holdings: Auction Catalogs; Book Volumes; CD-ROMs; Cards; Cassettes; DVDs; Exhibition Catalogs; Micro Print; Photographs; Prints; Reproductions

Collections: Atmospheric account of the Ligabue Expedition in the discovery of the Ouranosaurus nigeriensis dinosaur; aquarium reproduction of the tegnue, a formation of seabed rocks of the Venetian coast

Publications: Scientific reviews

Activities: Educ prog for schools & families; docent training

M **FONDAZIONE SCIENTIFICA QUERINI STAMPALIA,** (Museodella Fondazione Querini) Palazzo Querini-Stampalia, Castello 5252 Venice, 30122 Italy. Tel 041 2711411; Fax 041 2711445; Elec Mail fondazione@querinistampalia; Internet Home Page Address: www.querinistampalia.it; *Dir* Marigusta Lazzari; *Pres* Dr Marino Cortese; *Mus Organizer* Dr Babet Trevisan; *Librn* Cristina Celegon; *Admin Organizer* Federico Acerboni; *Exhibs & Special Events Organizer* Dora De Diana

Open Mus: Tues - Sun 10 AM - 7 PM, cl Mon; Library: Tues - Sat 10 AM - 10 PM, Sun 10 AM - 6 PM, Admis 10 euro, 8 euro (reduced); 1869; 18th Century Patrician Residence; Average Annual Attendance: 150,000; Mem: From 40 euro amici@querinistampalia.org

Income: 3,500,000 euro

Library Holdings: Book Volumes; CD-ROMs; DVDs; Manuscripts; Maps; Original Art Works; Original Documents; Pamphlets; Periodical Subscriptions; Photographs; Prints

Special Subjects: Decorative Arts, Furniture, Porcelain, Portraits, Painting-European, Architecture, Ceramics, Painting-Italian

Collections: 14th - 19th century Italian paintings; Contemporary art colls; Manuscripts, drawings

Exhibitions: Contemporary art exhibs during the year

Publications: Various publications

Activities: Classes for adults & children; lectrs open to the public; concerts, gallery talks; tours; lending of original objects of art to mus & art exhibs; organize traveling exhibs to other mus; mus shop sells books, design objects, jewelry & other items

M **GALLERIA DELL'ACCADEMIA,** Campo della Carita 1059A, Venice, 30100 Italy. Tel (041) 5222247; *Dir* Giovanna Scire Nepi

Open Tues - Sun 8:15 AM - 7:15 PM, Mon 8:15 AM - 2 PM

Collections: Venetian painting, 1310-1700

M **GALLERIA G FRANCHETTI,** Calle Ca d'Oro, Canal Grande Venice, 30100 Italy. Tel (041) 522349; Fax (041) 5238790; *Dir* Dr Adriana Augusti; *Cur* Claudia Cremonini

Open Mon 8:15 AM - 2 PM, Tues - Sat 8:15 AM - 7:15 PM; Admis 5 euro, students & seniors 2.50 euro

Collections: Sculpture & paintings

M **MUSEO ARCHEOLOGICO,** Piazza S Marco 17, Venice, 30124 Italy. Tel (041) 5225978; *Dir* Dr Giovanna Luisa Ravagnan

Open Mon - Fri 9 AM - 5 PM; Admis fee 4 euro, reduced fee 2 euro

Collections: Greek & Roman sculpture, jewels, coins

M **MUSEO D'ARTE ORIENTALE,** Ca' Pesaro, Canal Grande Venice, 30100 Italy. Tel 27681; *Dir* Dr Adriana Ruggeri

M **PEGGY GUGGENHEIM COLLECTION MUSEUM,** Palazzo Venier dei Leoni, Dorsoduro 701 Venice, I-30123 Italy. Tel 39-041-2405-411; Fax 39-041-520-6885; Elec Mail info@guggenheim-venice.it; Internet Home Page Address: www.guggenheim-venice.it; *Dir* Philip Rylands

Open Wed - Mon 10 AM - 6 PM, cl Tues & Christmas Day; Admis adults 12 euro, over 65 10 euro, students under 26 7 euro, under 10 free

Library Holdings: Exhibition Catalogs; Photographs

Collections: European and American art of the first half of the 20th century; Personal art collection of Peggy Guggenheim in former home; Gianni Mattioli Collection; Nasher Sculpture Garden Collection; Temporary exhibitions

Activities: Classes for children; docent training; lects mems only; concerts; tours; mus shop sells books magazines & reproductions

M **SEMINARIO PATRIARCALE DI VENEZIA,** Pinacoteca Manfrediniana, Dorsoduro 1, Venice, 30123 Italy. Tel 041 241 1018; Fax 041 274 3998; Elec Mail segreteria@seminarionenetia.it; *Don* Lucio Cilia

Open to pub upon request

Collections: Paintings & sculptures of the Roman, Gothic, Renaissance & Neo-classical period

VERONA

M **MUSEI CIVICI D' ARTE DI VERONA,** Museo di Castelvecchio, Castelvecchio 2, Verona, 37121 Italy. Tel (045) 8062611; Fax 0039 045 8010729; Elec Mail castelvecchio@comune.verona.it; Internet Home Page Address: www.comune.verona.it/castelvecchio/cvsito; *Dir* Dr Paola Marini; *Architetto* Alba Di Lieto; *Conservator* Ettorc Napione; *Conservator Medgglier* Antonella Arzone; *Dirigente Unita Archeologica Didattica* Margherita Bolla

Open Tues - Sun 9 AM - 7 PM, cl Mon; Admis general 6 Euro, groups of 15+, seniors & students 4.50 Euro, children 8-14 w/adult 1 Euro; Paintings and sculptures XIII-XVIII C mainly from Northern Italy; Average Annual Attendance: 150,000

—**Galleria Comunale d' Arte Moderna e Contemporanea,** Vla Forti 1, Verona, 37121 Italy. Tel (045) 8001903; *Sr Dir Dotl* Grossi Cortenova
—**Museo Archaeologico al Teatro Romano,** Regaste Redentore, Verona, 37129 Italy. Tel (045) 8000360; *S Dir Dssa* Margherita Bolla
—**Museo di Castelvecchio,** Corso Castelvecchio 2, Verona, 37121 Italy. Tel 0039-45-8062611; Fax 0039-45-8010729; Elec Mail castelveccio@commune.verona.it; Internet Home Page Address: www.commune.verona.it; *S Dir Dssa* Paola Marini
—**Museo Lapidario Maffeiano,** Piazza Bra, Verona, 37121 Italy. Tel (045) 590087
—**Museo degli Affreschi e Tomba di Giulietta,** Via del Pontiere, Verona, 37122 Italy. Tel (045) 8000361

JAMAICA

KINGSTON

M **INSTITUTE OF JAMAICA,** (National Art Gallery of Jamaica) National Art Gallery of Jamaica, 12 Ocean Blvd, Kingston Mall Kingston, Jamaica. Tel 876-922-1561, 8540; Fax 876-922-8544; Elec Mail veerle.poupeye@natgalja.org; Internet Home Page Address: www.galleryjamaica.org; *Exec Dir* Veerle Poupeye; *Chief Cur* Dr David Boxer
Open Tue - Thurs 10 AM - 4:30 PM, Fri 10 AM - 4 PM, Sat 10 AM - 3 PM, cl Sun & Mon; Admis adults J$200, students and children free; Estab 1974; Pub art gallery; Average Annual Attendance: 16,000
Collections: Permanent coll includes overview of 20th century Jamaican art since 1922 in ten galleries; Pre-twentieth century collection of Taino artifacts, Jamaican & West Indian art of the Spanish and English colonial periods; International coll of pre and post 1950 trends; Larry Wirth Collection of paintings and sculptures by Mallica Reynolds; Cecil Baugh coll of ceramics; Edna Manley Memorial Collection; A D Scott Collection; Matalon Collection
Activities: Classes for children; lectrs open to the pub; 5 vis lectrs per yr; gallery talks; tours; Aaron Matalon Award (Nat Biennial); lending of original art to Jamaican government offices & foreign missions; mus shop sells books, magazines, reproductions & other gift items

JAPAN

AOMORI

M **AOMORI CONTEMPORARY ART CENTRE,** 152-6 Yamazaki Goshizawa, Aomori, 030-0134 Japan. Tel +81-17-764-5200; Fax +81-17-764-5201; Elec Mail acac-1@acac-aomori.jp; Internet Home Page Address: www.acac-aomori.jp
Open 10 AM - 6 PM; No admis fee; Estab 2001; to provide opportunities to appreciate various art productions & to create a new art culture unique to Aomori City; Made up of three main halls: the linear Creative Hall & Residential Hall both designed with the image of bridges & the horseshoe-shaped Exhib Hall equipped with a gallery & circular rooftop stage
Library Holdings: Book Volumes
Activities: Classes for adults & children; lects open to pub; concerts; gallery talks; tours; fels

ASHIYA CITY

M **ASHIYA CITY MUSEUM OF ART & HISTORY,** 12-25 Ise-cho, Ashiya City, 659-0052 Japan. Tel +81-797-38-5432; Fax +81-797-38-5434; Internet Home Page Address: www.ashiya-museum.jp/
Open 10 AM - 5 PM; Admis fee changes with exhibs; Estab 1991; art & history mus
Activities: Lects open to pub; gallery talks; mus shop sells books

ATAMI CITY

M **MOA MUSEUM OF ART,** (MOA Bijutsukan) MOA Foundation, 26-2 Momoyama-Cho, Atami City, Shizuoka 413-8511 Japan. Tel 84-2511; Fax 84-2570; *Dir* Itsuka Okada
Open daily 9:30 AM - 4:30 PM, cl Thurs; Admis adults 1600 Yen, high school & col students 800 yen; Mus overlooks the ocean
Collections: Paintings, calligraphies & crafts from the East

FUKUOKA

M **FUKUOKA ART MUSEUM,** 1-6 Ohori-Koen Park, Chuo-ku Fukuoka, 810-0051 Japan. Tel 092-714-6051; Internet Home Page Address: www.fukuoka-art-museum.jp
Open Tues - Sat 9:30 AM - 5:30 PM, July - Aug 9:30 AM - 7:30 PM, cl Sun & Mon; Admis adults 200 yen, students 150 yen
Collections: Modern art gallery of 20th century Japanese and international art; Small works of print and drawings, Japanese paintings; Crafts galleries; Matsunaga Collection of tea ceremony utensils and Buddhist art from Tokoin Temple; Buddhist sculptures; Pre-modern gallery; Honda Collection of Southeast Asian Ceramics; Kusuma Collection of textiles

M **FUKUOKA ASIAN ART MUSEUM,** Riverain Center Bldg 7th-8th Fl, 3-1 Shimokawabata-machi, Hakata-ku Fukuoka, Japan. Tel 092 263 1100; Fax 092 263 1105; Elec Mail faam_e@faam.ajibi.jp; Internet Home Page Address: faam.city.fukuoka.lg.jp/home.html
Open Thurs -Tues 10 AM - 8 PM; Admis adults 200 yen, high school & college students 150 yen, junior high and under no charge; Estab 1999; Average Annual Attendance: 250,000

Library Holdings: Auction Catalogs; Book Volumes; DVDs; Exhibition Catalogs; Pamphlets; Periodical Subscriptions; Photographs; Prints
Collections: Modern & contemporary Asian art; Asia Collection 70: From the Collection of the Fukuoka Asian Art Mus
Activities: Classes for children; residency progs; workshops for adults & children; lects open to pub; 6 vis lectrs per yr; concerts; gallery talks; tours; artist researcher in residence; mus shop sells books, reproductions

HIROSHIMA

M **HIROSHIMA MUSEUM OF ART,** 3-2 Motomachi, Naka-ku Hiroshima, 730-0011 Japan. Tel 082 223 2530; Fax 082 223 2519; Elec Mail info@hiroshima-museum.jp; Internet Home Page Address: www.hiroshima-museum.jp; *Dir* Makoto Uda; *Chief Cur* Yoshiyuki Furutani
Open daily 9 AM - 5 PM; Admis adults 1000 yen, high school students 500 yen, junior high & elementary students 200 yen; Estab 1978; art mus; Modern art
Collections: Modern European & Japanese Western-Style paintings
Activities: 3-4 book traveling exhibs per yr; Mus shop sells books, original art, reproductions, prints & other items

IBARAKI

M **ART TOWER MITO, CONTEMPORARY ART CENTER,** (Mito Arts Foundation) 1-6-8 Goken-cho, Mito-shi Ibaraki, 310-0063 Japan. Tel +81-0-29-227-8111; Fax +81-0-29-227-8110; Elec Mail webstaff@arttowermito.or.jp; Internet Home Page Address: http://arttowermito.or.jp

M **MUSEUM OF MODERN ART, IBARAKI,** 666-1, Higashi Kubo Senba, Mito, Ibaraki, 310-0851 Japan. Tel 029-243-5111; Fax 029-243-9992; Elec Mail info@modernart.museum.ibk.ed.jp; Internet Home Page Address: www.modernart.museum.ibk.ed.jp
Open Tues - Sun 9:30 AM - 5 PM, cl Mon; Admis varies depending on exhib; Estab 1988 as a center of Ibaraki's art & culture; 2 galleries of special exhibs & 2 galleries of mus coll; Average Annual Attendance: 150,000
Special Subjects: Prints, Bronzes, Woodcuts, Painting-French, Sculpture, Watercolors
Collections: 3,400 works of modern & contemporary art

IKARUGA

M **HORYUJI,** Horyuji Temple, Aza Horyuji, Ikaruga-cho, Ikoma-gun Ikaruga, Japan.
Collections: Buddhist images and paintings; the buildings date from the Asuka, Nara, Heian, Kamakura, Ashikaga, Tokugawa periods

ITSUKUSHIMA

M **ITSUKUSHIMA JINJA HOMOTSUKAN,** Treasure Hall of the Isukushima Shinto Shrine, Miyajima-cho, Saeki-gun Itsukushima, Japan; Miyajima-cho, Hotsukaichi-City Hiroshima, Japan. Tel 0829-44-2020; Fax 0829-44-0517; *Cur & Chief Priest* Motoyoshi Nozaka
Open 8 AM - 5 PM; Admis 300 yen, high school students 200 yen, elementary students 100 yen
Collections: Paintings, calligraphy, sutras, swords, and other ancient weapons

KAGAWA

M **NAOSHIMA FUKUTAKE ART MUSEUM FOUNDATION,** (Chichu Art Museum) Chichu Art Museum, 3449-1 Naoshima, Kagawa, 761-3110 Japan. Tel +81-(0) 87-892-3755; Fax +81-(0) 87-840-8285; Elec Mail info@chichu.jp; Internet Home Page Address: www.chichu.jp; *Dir* Soichiro Fukutake; *Acting Dir* Fram Kitagawa
Open Mar - Sep: 10 AM - 6 PM; Oct - Feb: 10 AM - 5 PM; Admis adult 2000 yen, children under 15 free; Estab 2004, as a site to rethink the relationship between nature & people; Average Annual Attendance: 120,000
Collections: Artworks of Claude Monet, Walter De Maria & James Turrell
Activities: Classes for adults & children; lects open to the pub; tours; mus shop sells books, original art, prints

KOMAKI CITY

M **MENARD ART MUSEUM,** 5-250 Komaki, Komaki City, 485-0041 Japan. Tel +81-568-75-5785; Fax +81-568-77-0626; Elec Mail museum@menard.co.jp; Internet Home Page Address: http://museum.menard.co.jp
Open 10 - 17 (last entry 16:30); Admis gen 800 yen, high school & univ students 600 yen, elementary & jr high school students 300 yen; (prices for special exhibs may vary); Estab 1987

KURASHIKI

M **OHARA MUSEUM OF ART,** 1-1-15 Chuo, Kurashiki, 710-8575 Japan. Tel 86-422-0005; Fax 86-427-3677; Elec Mail info@ohara.or.jp; Internet Home Page Address: www.ohara.or.jp; *Dir* Shuji Takashina
Open Tues - Sun 9 AM - 5 PM, cl Mon; Admis general 1.300 yen; Estab 11-6-1930; 4 bldgs; Main Gallery with Western Art, Annex with Japanese Art, & Craft Art & Asian Art Gallery; Kojima Torajiro Memorial Hall with Kojima's works - Ancient Egypt & Orient artifacts
Special Subjects: Pottery, Painting-American, Prints, Textiles, Painting-European, Painting-French, Asian Art, Antiquities-Oriental, Antiquities-Persian, Antiquities-Egyptian

Collections: Ancient Egyptian, Persian & Turkish ceramics & sculpture; 19th & 20th century European paintings & sculpture; modern Japanese oil paintings, pottery, sculpture & textiles; Asiatic Art; Contemporary Japanese Art
Activities: Classes for adults; classes for children; lects open to public; gallery talks; mus shop sells books, reproductions, prints, accessories, stationery

KYOTO

M **KYOTO KOKURITSU HAKUBUTSUKAN,** Kyoto National Museum, 527 Chayacho, Higashiyama-ku Kyoto, 605-0931 Japan. Tel (075) 541-1151; Internet Home Page Address: http://www.kyohaku.go.jp; *Dir* Johei Sasaki
Estab 1897; Permanent coll gallery now under construction, renewal open expected 2013
Collections: Fine art; handicrafts & historical collections of Asia, chiefly Japan; over 65,000 research photographs

M **KYOTO KOKURITSU KINDAI BIJUTSUKAN,** The National Museum of Modern Art, Kyoto, Okazaki Enshoji-cho, Sakyo-ku, Kyoto, 606 - 8344 Japan. Tel (81) 75-761-4111; Fax (81) 75-771-5792; Elec Mail info@ma7.momak.go.jp; Internet Home Page Address: www.momak.go.jp; *Dir* Masaaki Ozaki; *Chief Cur* Hidetsugu Yamano; *Cur* Ryuichi Matsubara; *Cur* Yuko Ikeda; *Cur* Jitsuko Ogura; *Asst Cur* Chinatsu Makiguchi; *Asst Cur* Yui Nakao; *Cur Advisor* Shinji Kohmoto
Open Tues - Sun 9:30 AM - 5 PM, cl Mon & cl Tues if Mon is a national holiday; Admis adults 420 yen, 210 yen for groups of 20 or more, Univ students 130 yen, 70 yen for groups of 20 or more, high school students & children under 18 free; Estab 1963; modern and contemporary art of Japan & the world; Mem: 335; 3,000 yen, students 2,000 yen, special membership 20,000 yen, corporate membership 100, 000 yen
Collections: Painting (Japanese style, oil, watercolor), drawing, print, photography, sculpture, craft, and new Modern Contemporary media; Drawings, prints, photography, sculpture, crafts (ceramics, textiles, metalworks, wood and bamboo works, lacquers, jewelry); New Modern/Contemporary Media
Publications: Book on the complete collection of Japanese paintings, collection of oil on canvas, collection of prints, & collection of photography; collection catalog of photography, Nojima Yasuzo, Hasegawa Kiyoshi, Japanese-style painting, western-style painting, Kawai Kanjiro, Ikeda Masuo, W. Eugene Smith; exhibition catalogues; annual reports; Cross Sections (bulletins), Miru newsletter
Activities: Classes for adults & children; docent training; lects open to public, approx 20 per yr; concerts; gallery talks; lending of original objects of art to pub museums in Japan; Japanese painting, oil painting; approx 3 book traveling exhibs per yr; originates traveling exhibs to the National Museum of Modern Art, Tokyo & to museums in Japan; mus shop sells books, magazines, reproductions, postcards, calendars, designer goods, accessories & tableware

M **KYOTO-SHI BIJUTSUKAN,** Kyoto Municipal Museum of Art, Okazaki Park, Sakyo-ku Kyoto, Japan. Tel (075) 771-4107; Fax (075) 761-0444; Internet Home Page Address: www.city.kyoto.jp/bunshi/kmma; *Dir* Yashuhiko Murai
Open Tues - Sun 9 AM - 5 PM. cl Mon; Admis fee depends on exhib; Estab 1933; Colls & exhibs feature modern & contemporary Kyoto
Collections: Contemporary fine art objects, including Japanese pictures, sculptures, decorative art exhibits and prints

MARUGAME

M **MARUGAME GENICHIRO-INOKUMA MUSEUM OF CONTEMPORARY ART,** 80-1 Hamamachi, Marugame, 763-0022 Japan. Tel 0877-24-7755; Fax 0877-24-7766; Elec Mail mimoca_info@mimoca.org; Internet Home Page Address: www.mimoca.org
Circ

MATSUMOTO

M **THE JAPAN UKIYO-E MUSEUM,** 2206-1 Koshiba, Shimadachi, Matsumoto, 390-0852 Japan. Internet Home Page Address: www.ukiyo-e.co.jp/jum-e/index.html

M **MATSUMOTO CITY MUSEUM OF ART,** 4-2-22 chuo, Matsumoto, 390-0811 Japan. Tel 0263-39-7400; Elec Mail museum @city.matsumoto.nagano.jp

NAGOYA

M **AICHI PREFECTURAL MUSEUM OF ART,** 1-13-2 Higashisakura, Higashi-ku Nagoya, 461-8525 Japan. Tel 052 971 5511; Fax 052 971 5604; Elec Mail apma-webmaster@aac.pref.aichi.jp; Internet Home Page Address: www.art.aac.pref.aichi.jp
Open Tues - Thurs & Sat - Sun 10 AM - 6 PM, Fri 10 AM - 8 PM; Admis adults 500 yen, high school & college students 300 yen, children under 13 & handicapped no charge; Estab 1992; 3 exhib galleries & 5 coll galleries; Average Annual Attendance: 200,000
Collections: 20th-century fine arts; Kimura Teizo Collection

M **THE TOKUGAWA REIMEIKAI FOUNDATION,** The Tokugawa Art Museum, 1017 Tokugawa-cho, Higashi-ku Nagoya, 461-0023 Japan. Tel (052) 935-6262; Elec Mail info@tokugawa.or.jp; Internet Home Page Address: www.tokugawa-art-museum.jp/; *Dir* Yoshitaka Tokugawa
Open daily 10 AM - 5 PM; Admis 1,200 yen (discount prices for students & groups; Estab 10/11/1935; Mem: approx 1,000 people, 3,150-26,250 yen
Special Subjects: Ceramics, Textiles, Maps, Painting-Japanese, Costumes, Calligraphy, Antiquities-Oriental
Collections: Tokugawa Family Collection of 12,000 treasures, including scrolls, swords, calligraphy & pottery
Publications: Kinko Sosho Bulletin of The Tokugawa Reimeikai foundation The Tokugawa Institute for The History of Forestry

NARA

M **NARA KOKURITSU HAKUBUTSU-KAN,** Nara National Museum, 50 Nobori-oji-Cho, Nara, 630-8213 Japan. Tel (0742) 22-7771; Fax (0742) 26-7218; Internet Home Page Address: www.narahaku.go.jp (Japanese); Internet Home Page Address: www.narahaku.go.jp/english/indsx_e.htm (English); *Dir* Ken'ichi Yuyama
Open daily 9:30 AM - 5 PM except Fri (from end Apr to end Oct) & 4th Sat in Jan, Feb 3, Mar 12, Aug 15 & Dec 17 9:30 AM - 7 PM, cl Mon & New Year's day; Admis adults 500, univ students 250, elementary, jr high school & high school free; group admis (20+) adults 400 yen, univ students 200 yen, elementary, jr high school & high school free; Incls a conservation ctr consisting of 3 laboratories working on restoration of National Treasures & Important Cultural Properties; also incls a tea house for tea ceremony built in 18th century
Library Holdings: Auction Catalogs; Audio Tapes; Book Volumes; CD-ROMs; Cards; Clipping Files; Compact Disks; DVDs; Exhibition Catalogs; Filmstrips; Framed Reproductions; Kodachrome Transparencies; Maps; Original Art Works; Pamphlets; Periodical Subscriptions; Photographs
Special Subjects: Decorative Arts, Historical Material, Manuscripts, Painting-Japanese, Sculpture, Hispanic Art, Religious Art, Crafts, Asian Art, Restorations, Calligraphy
Collections: Art objects of Buddhist art, mainly of Japan, including decorative arts and archaeological relics, calligraphy, paintings, sculptures; Ancient Chinese Bronzes (Sakamoto coll)
Exhibitions: The 65th Annual Exhibition of Shoso-in Treasures; See website for additional exhibs
Publications: See website
Activities: Classes for adults & children; lects open to pub; 3,000 vis lectrs per yr; guided tours available to general public, schools & company groups; concerts; gallery talks; mus store sells books, magazines, reproductions, prints, post cards& souvenirs

L **Buddhist Art Library,**
Estab 1980
Library Holdings: Auction Catalogs; Exhibition Catalogs; Periodical Subscriptions; Photographs
Special Subjects: Art History, Historical Material, History of Art & Archaeology, Asian Art, Religious Art

NIIGATA

M **NIIGATA PREFECTURAL MUSEUM OF MODERN ART,** 3-278-14 Senshu, Nagaoka-Shi, Niigata, 940-2083 Japan. Tel 0258-28-4111; Fax 0258-28-4115; Elec Mail kinbi@coral.ocn.ne.jp; Internet Home Page Address: www.lalanet.gr.jp/kinbi/english/index.html; *Dir* Kenichi Tokunaga
Open 9:00-17:00; Admis 420 yen for permanent coll; Estab 1993
Special Subjects: Drawings, Photography, Painting-French, Painting-Japanese, Sculpture, Prints, Crafts, Pottery, Woodcuts, Posters, Porcelain, Calligraphy, Painting-German
Collections: 6,000 works
Exhibitions: 4-5 exhibs of various art genres per yr
Publications: Exhib catalogs; coll catalogs
Activities: Classes for adults & children; lects open to pub; concerts; gallery talks; exten prog serves schools & community ctrs in Niigata; originates traveling exhibs; mus shop sells books, reproductions, art goods

OSAKA

M **FUJITA BIJUTSUKAN,** Fujita Museum of Art, 10-32 Amijima-cho, Miyakojima-ku Osaka, Japan. Tel (06) 6351-0582; Fax 6351-0583; *Dir* Chikako Fujita
Open Tues - Sun 10 AM - 4:30 PM; Admis adults 800 yen, student/high school student 500 yen; Estab 1951
Collections: Scroll paintings; Ceramics, Japanese Paintings, Calligraphy, Buddhist Art
Activities: Mus shop sells books & prints

M **NATIONAL MUSEUM OF ART - OSAKA,** 4-2-55 Nakanoshima, Kita-ku Osaka, 530-0005 Japan. Tel 81-06-6447-4680; Fax 81-06-6447-4699; Internet Home Page Address: www.nmao.go.jp; *Dir* Akira Tatehata
Open Tues - Sun 10 AM - 5 PM, cl Mon (cl Tues when falls on national holiday); Admis adults 420 yen, students 130 yen, high school students 70 yen, children and seniors free
Library Holdings: Book Volumes; CD-ROMs; Compact Disks; DVDs; Exhibition Catalogs; Periodical Subscriptions; Photographs; Slides; Video Tapes
Collections: Japanese and international modern art in various media
Activities: Classes for children; Lects open to the public, concerts, gallery talks

M **OSAKA-SHIRITSU HAKUBUTSUKAN,** Osaka Municipal Museum of Art, 1-82 Chausuyama-Cho, Tennoji-ku Osaka, 543-0063 Japan. Tel (06) 6771-4874; Fax (06) 6771-4856; *Dir* Yutaka Mino
Open Tues - Sun 9:30 AM - 5 PM, cl Mon; Admis fee adults 300 yen, high school students 200 yen, junior high students & under free
Collections: Art of China, Korea & Japan

OTSU CITY

M **THE MUSEUM OF MODERN ART, SHIGA,** 1740-1 Seta-Minamiogaya-Cho, Otsu City, 520 2122 Japan. Elec Mail info@shiga-kinbi.jp; Internet Home Page Address: http://www.shiga-kinbi.jp
Open Tues - Sun 9:30 AM - 5 PM, (last admis 4:30 - PM), cl Mon; Admis adults 450 yen, high school & univ students 250 yen
Collections: Contemporary art, modern Japanese style painting & crafts

TOKYO

M **BRIDGESTONE BIJUTSUKAN,** Bridgestone Museum of Art, 10-1, Kyobashi 1-chome, Chuo-ku Tokyo, 104 Japan. Tel (03) 3563-0241; *Exec Dir* Kazuo Ishi Kure
Open Tues - Sat 10 AM - 8 PM, Sun & holidays 10 AM - 6 PM, cl Mon; Admis fee adults 800 yen, seniors 600 yen, students 500 yen, children 15 yrs & under free
Collections: Foreign paintings, mainly Impressionism and after; western style paintings late 19th century to present

M **IDEMITSU MUSEUM OF ARTS,** 3-1-1 Marunouchi, Chiyoda-ku Tokyo, 100-0005 Japan. Tel 03-3213-9402; Fax 03-3213-8473; Internet Home Page Address: www.idemitsu.co.jp/museum; *Dir* Shosuke Idemitsu; *Deputy Dir* Hiroyasu Yamato; *GM, Curatorial Dept* Taizou Kuroda
Open Tues - Thurs & Sat - Sun 10 AM - 5 PM, Fri 10 AM - 7 PM, cl Mon; Admis adults 1000 yen, student (over 15 yrs old) 700 yen; Estab 1966; Average Annual Attendance: 150,000; Mem: 700 mems; ann dues 8,000 yen
Income: Financed by donations
Special Subjects: Painting-American, Painting-Japanese, Asian Art, Painting-French
Collections: Oriental art & ceramics; Japanese paintings; calligraphy; Chinese bronzes; lacquer wares & paintings by Georges Rouault, Sam Francis
Activities: Lects open to pub; lects for members only; mus shop sells books & reproductions

M **INDEPENDENT ADMINISTRATIVE INSTITUTION NATIONAL INSTITUTES FOR CULTURAL HERITAGE,** Tokyo National Museum, 13-9 Ueno Park, Taito-ku Tokyo, 110-8712 Japan. Tel (03) 3822-1111; Fax (03) 3822-1113; Internet Home Page Address: www.tnm.jp; *Dir Gen* Masami Zeniya
Open Oct - Mar: Tues - Sun 9:30 AM - 5 PM, Apr - Sept: Sat - Sun 9:30 AM - 6 PM; Admis fee adults 600 yen, univ students 400 yen, seniors & children under 18 free; Estab 1872; Average Annual Attendance: 2,416,281; Mem: 2,085; dues 10,000 yen
Special Subjects: Archaeology, Decorative Arts, Drawings, Etchings & Engravings, Folk Art, Historical Material, Ceramics, Glass, Metalwork, Furniture, Gold, Photography, Porcelain, Pottery, Prints, Silver, Textiles, Bronzes, Manuscripts, Maps, Sculpture, Tapestries, Graphics, Ethnology, Costumes, Crafts, Primitive art, Woodcarvings, Painting-Japanese, Dolls, Jade, Jewelry, Oriental Art, Asian Art, Carpets & Rugs, Ivory, Coins & Medals, Calligraphy, Miniatures, Embroidery, Laces, Antiquities-Oriental, Pewter, Leather
Collections: Eastern fine arts, including paintings, calligraphy, sculpture, metal work, ceramic art, textiles, lacquer ware, archaeological exhibits
Exhibitions: Exhibs throughout the yr; 6-5 special exhibs annually
Activities: Classes for adults & children; lects open to pub; concerts; gallery talks; tours; mus shop sells books, magazines, original art, reproductions

M **INDEPENDENT ADMINISTRATIVE INSTITUTION NATIONAL MUSEUM OF ART NATIONAL MUSEUM OF WESTERN ART,** (The National Museum of Western Art, Tokyo) The National Museum of Western Art, 7-7 Ueno-Koen Taito-ku, Tokyo, 110-0007 Japan. Tel 81-3-3828-5131; Fax 81-3-3828-5135; Elec Mail wwwadmin@nmwa.go.jp; Internet Home Page Address: www.nmwa.go.jp; *Dir* Akiko Mabuchi
Open Mon - Thurs & Sat - Sun 9:30 AM - 5:30 PM, winter months (mid Dec - early Mar) 9:30 AM - 5 PM, Fri 9:30 AM - 8 PM; Admis 420 yen Adults, 130 yen college student, under 18 & over 65 free; Estab 4/1/1959; Average Annual Attendance: 989,344
Library Holdings: Auction Catalogs; Book Volumes; Clipping Files; Exhibition Catalogs; Fiche; Pamphlets; Periodical Subscriptions; Reproductions
Special Subjects: Decorative Arts, Drawings, Etchings & Engravings, Landscapes, Portraits, Prints, Painting-European, Sculpture, Tapestries, Watercolors, Bronzes, Religious Art, Jewelry, Painting-British, Painting-Dutch, Painting-French, Baroque Art, Painting-Flemish, Renaissance Art, Medieval Art, Painting-Spanish, Painting-Italian, Painting-German, Painting-Scandinavian
Collections: Western paintings from late medieval period through the early 20th century; French modern sculpture
Activities: Classes for adults & children; lects open to pub, concerts, gallery talks; mus shop sells books, magazines, reproductions, prints, others

M **THE NATIONAL MUSEUM OF MODERN ART, TOKYO,** (Independent Administrative Institution National Museum of Art) 3-1 Kitanomaru Koen, Chiyoda-ku Tokyo, 102-8322 Japan. Tel (03) 3214-2561; Fax (03) 3214-2577; Internet Home Page Address: www.momat.go.jp; *Dir* Kamogawa Sachio; *Deputy Dir* Matsumoto Tohru; *Chief Cur* Nakabayashi Kazuo; *Chief Cur* Kuraya Mika
Open Tues - Thurs & Sat - Sun 10 AM - 5 PM, Fri 10 AM - 8 PM, cl Mon (except when Mon is a holiday, the mus is open a & cl on Tues) yr-end of New Year holidays and during change of exhib; Admis adults 420 yen (coll & exhibs), col students 130 yen, high school students, seniors over 65 & children under 18 free; Estab 1952; Circ 151,930; Average Annual Attendance: 662,800
Income: 195,920,315 yen
Library Holdings: Auction Catalogs; Book Volumes; CD-ROMs; Clipping Files; Compact Disks; DVDs; Exhibition Catalogs; Fiche; Micro Print; Other Holdings; Pamphlets; Periodical Subscriptions; Photographs; Reels; Video Tapes
Special Subjects: Drawings, Ceramics, Collages, Glass, Gold, Porcelain, Prints, Painting-Japanese, Drawings, Graphics, Photography, Prints, Sculpture, Watercolors, Bronzes, Crafts, Etchings & Engravings, Landscapes, Manuscripts, Portraits, Posters, Dolls, Calligraphy
Collections: Drawings, paintings, photographs, prints, sculptures, watercolors
Publications: Mus Newsletter, Gendai no Me (Japanese); Catalogue (Bilingual); Annual Report (Bilingual); Bulletin (Bilingual)
Activities: Classes for adults & children offered in Japanese only; docent training; lects open to pub; concerts; gallery talks; tours; lending of original objects of art to museums (world); originates traveling exhib to museums mainly in Japan; mus shop sells books, magazines, original art, reproductions & prints; jr mus located at Crafts Gallery, 1-1 Kitanomaru-Koen, Chiyoda-Ku, Tokyo 102-0091; Nat Film Ctr, 3-7-6 Kyobashi, Chao-Ku, Tokyo 104-0031

M **Crafts Gallery,** Japan; 1 Kitanomaru Koen, Chiyoda-ku Tokyo, Japan. *Chief Cur* Mitsuhiki Hasebe
Average Annual Attendance: 163,592
Collections: Ceramics, lacquer ware, metalworks; Works by Living National Treasures

M **NEZU BIJUSUKAN,** Nezu Museum, 6-5-1 Minami-Aoyama, Minato-ku Tokyo, 107-0062 Japan. Tel (3) 3400 2536; Fax (3) 3400 2436; Internet Home Page Address: www.nezu-muse.or.jp; *Dir* Mr Nezu Koichi; *Deputy Dir* Dr Nishida Hiroko
Open Tues - Sun 10 AM - 5 PM, cl Mon; Admis special exhib 1200 yen, mus coll exhib 1000 yen; Estab 1940, opened 1941, to preserve & exhib East Asian arts; 6 galleries for exhib different types of Japanese & East Asian arts; Mem: Nezu Club: 3,000 yen per yr
Collections: Nezu Kaichiro, Sr's private collection & donations, incl about 7,000 items of calligraphy, sculpture, paintings, sword fittings, ceramics, lacquer-ware, archeological exhibits; 7 items designated as national treasures; 87 items designated as Important Cultural Properties
Exhibitions: 8 exhibs per yr
Publications: Coll catalog; exhib catalog; annual bulletin
Activities: Classes for adults; lects open to pub; gallery talks; tea ceremonies (limited for guests & mems); exten dept serves other mus; mus shop sells books, magazines, original art

M **NIHON MINGEIKAN,** Japan Folk Crafts Museum, 4-3-33 Komaba, Meguro-ku, Tokyo, 153-0041 Japan. Tel (03) 34674527; Fax (03) 3467-4537; Elec Mail intl@mingeikan.or.jp; Internet Home Page Address: www.mingeikan.or.jp; *Hon Dir* Sori Yanagi; *Pres* Yotaro Kobayashi; *Dir International Progs* Shigenao Ishimaru; *Asst* Mayumi Furuya
Open 10 AM - 5 PM, cl Mon; Admis 1000 yen, students 500 yen, elementary & jr high students 200 yen; Estab 1936; to introduce Mingei (the arts of the people); 4 large exhibits per yr; two-story building of stone and stucco with black tile roof, designed after traditional Japanese architecture by Soetsu Yanagi (1889-1961) founder of the museum; Average Annual Attendance: 50,000; monthly magazine Mingei; Mem: Dues 5,000 yen
Income: Nonprofit organization
Purchases: Budget 10,000 yen
Library Holdings: Book Volumes; CD-ROMs; Cassettes; Clipping Files; Compact Disks; DVDs; Kodachrome Transparencies; Manuscripts; Maps; Micro Print; Original Art Works; Original Documents; Pamphlets; Periodical Subscriptions; Photographs; Prints; Records; Slides; Video Tapes
Special Subjects: Watercolors, African Art
Collections: Folk-craft art objects from all parts of the world; works by Shoji Hamada, Kanjiro Kawai, Shiko Munakota, Keisuke, Serizawa, Bernard Leach, other Mingei Movement advocators
Activities: Educ prog; weaving; dyeing; letter painting; lacquerware; Lects open to pub; 5-6 vis lectrs per year; lects open to the pub; 4 lectrs per yr; annual New Works competition awards every fall; Japan Folk Crafts Mus Encouragement prizes; gallery talks; tours; lending of original objects of art to other high quality mus worldwide; book traveling exhibs, 1-2 per yr worldwide; mus shop sells books, prints, pottery, textiles, lacquered woodwork; original art; magazines, porcelain, ceramics, weaving, paper

M **TOKYO UNIVERSITY OF THE ARTS,** (Tokyo National University of Fine Arts & Music Art) The University Art Museum, 12-8 Ueno Park, Taito-ku Tokyo, 110-8714 Japan. Tel 81-3-5685-7755; Fax +81-3-5685-7805; Internet Home Page Address: www.geidai.ac.jp; *Mgr* Katsuyuki Matsui
Open 10 AM - 5 PM; Admis varies with exhibs; Estab 1970
Special Subjects: Ceramics, Metalwork, Pottery, Painting-Japanese, Architecture, Drawings, Sculpture, Bronzes, Archaeology, Textiles, Crafts, Woodcuts, Porcelain, Asian Art, Calligraphy
Collections: Paintings, sculptures & crafts of Japan, China & Korea
Publications: Tokyo Geijutsu Daigaku Daigaku Bijutsukan Nenpo
Activities: Mus shop sells books

M **TOKYO-TO BIJUTSUKAN,** Tokyo Metropolitan Art Museum, Ueno Koen 8-36, Taito-Ku Tokyo, 110-007 Japan. Tel (03) 3823-6921; Fax (03) 3823-6920; Internet Home Page Address: www.tob.kan.jp/eng; *Dir* Yoshitake Mamuro
Open daily 9 AM - 5 PM; cl 3rd Mon of ea month; Estab 1926
Collections: Sculptures

WAKAYAMA

M **KOYASAN REIHOKAN,** Museum of Buddhist Art on Mount Koya, Koyasan, Koya-cho, Ito-gun Wakayama, Japan. Tel 0736 562254; Fax 0736 562806; Internet Home Page Address: www.reihokan.or.jp (Japanese only)
Admis fee - adults 600 yen, jr students 350 yen, children 250 yen
Collections: Buddhist paintings and images, sutras and old documents, some of them registered National Treasures and Important Cultural Properties

YOKOHAMA

M **YOKOHAMA MUSEUM OF ART,** 3-4-1 Minatomirai, Nishi-ku Yokohama, 220-0012 Japan. Tel +81-(0) 45-221-0300; Fax +81-(0) 45-221-0317; Internet Home Page Address: www.yaf.or.jp/yma/en/index.html; *Chief Cur* Taro Amano; *Dir* Eriko Osaka; *Chief Cur* Tomoo Kashiwagi; *Cur* Naoaki Nakamura; *Cur* Hideko Numata
Open, Mon - Wed & Fri - Sun 10 AM - 6 PM, cl Thurs; Admis adults 500 yen, students 300 yen, middle school students 100 yen, elementary students free; permanent coll fees for special exhibs differ for each; Estab 1989; Average Annual Attendance: 700,000
Income: 100 million yen
Library Holdings: Auction Catalogs; Book Volumes; DVDs; Periodical Subscriptions; Video Tapes

Special Subjects: Drawings, Etchings & Engravings, Landscapes, Architecture, Art Education, Ceramics, Collages, Glass, Photography, Porcelain, Portraits, Pottery, Painting-American, Prints, Bronzes, Woodcuts, Painting-British, Painting-French, Painting-Japanese, Sculpture, Tapestries, Graphics, Latin American Art, Photography, Watercolors, Crafts, Woodcarvings, Asian Art, Painting-Spanish, Painting-German, Reproductions, Painting-Russian
Collections: Works of European & Japanese modern art; contemporary decorative arts, graphic design, architecture & film
Activities: Classes for adults & children; lects open to pub; 1,500 vis lectrs per year; concerts; gallery talks; tours; mus shop sells books, magazines, original art, reproductions, prints

JORDAN

AMMAN

M **DARAT AL FUNUN,** The Khalid Shoman Foundation, P O Box 5223, Amman, 11183 Jordan. Tel 962 6 4643251; Fax 962 6 4643253; Elec Mail darat@daratalfununorg; Internet Home Page Address: www.daratalfunun.org; *Founder & Pres* Suha Shoman; *Dir* Laura Srouji Khoury
Open Sat - Wed 10 AM - 7 PM; Ramadan 10 AM - 3 PM; Spreading awareness in the fields of the arts, architecture & archeology.
Collections: Paintings, prints, sculptures, drawings, photographs & illustrations by 69 Arab artists

M **JORDAN NATIONAL GALLERY OF FINE ARTS,** PO Box 9068, Amman, 11191 Jordan. Tel 00-962-6-463-0128; Fax 00-962-6-465-1119; Elec Mail info@nationalgallery.org; Internet Home Page Address: www.nationalgallery.org/Intro.html; *Dir* Dr Khalid Khreis; *Asst Dir for Artistic Affairs* Bana Fanous; *Asst Dir for Artistic Affairs* Nesleen Suboh
Open summer Mon, Wed - Thurs & Sat - Sun 9 AM - 7 PM, winter Mon, Wed - Thurs & Sat - Sun 9 AM - 5 PM, cl Tues & Fri; Admis $7; Estab 1980; Contemporary art from the developing world
Library Holdings: CD-ROMs; Cards; DVDs; Exhibition Catalogs
Special Subjects: Drawings, Etchings & Engravings, History of Art & Archaeology, Illustration, Landscape Architecture, Landscapes, Art Education, Art History, Ceramics, Collages, Mixed Media, Furniture, Painting-American, Prints, Textiles, Manuscripts, Painting-British, Painting-French, Sculpture, Architecture, Graphics, Photography, Watercolors, African Art, Woodcarvings, Woodcuts, Painting-Japanese, Portraits, Asian Art, Tapestries, Calligraphy, Miniatures, Painting-Spanish, Painting-Italian, Islamic Art, Painting-Russian
Collections: Over 2000 permanent works including paintings, prints, sculptures, photographs, installations, weavings, and ceramics by more than 900 artists from 60 countries; Neo Orientalist Coll
Activities: Classes for adults & children in graphic art; lects open to the pub; concerts, gallery talks; tours; sponsoring of competitions; touring mus to the pub living in distant areas; organize traveling exhibs worldwide; mus shop sells books, magazines, reproductions, prints & other mus items; jr mus

KAZAKHSTAN

ALMATY

M **A KASTEYEV STATE MUSEUM OF FINE ARTS,** 30a Satpaev St, Almaty, 480070 Kazakhstan. Tel 7-3272-478-356, 478-249, 476-195
Collections: Over 20,000 pieces of painting, graphics, sculpture, and decorative art from local and international artists

KOREA, REPUBLIC OF

GYEONGGI-DO

M **NATIONAL MUSEUM OF CONTEMPORARY ART, KOREA,** (National Museum of Contemporary Art) San 58-4 Gwangmyeong-gil 209, Makgye-dong Gwacheon-si Gyeonggi-do, 427-701 Korea, Republic of; 213 Gwangmyeong-ro, Gwacheon-si Gyeonggi-do, 427-701 Korea, Republic of. Tel 82-2-2188-6114; Fax 82-2-2188-6124; Elec Mail soleh@korea.kr; Internet Home Page Address: www.moca.go.kr; *Dir* Yung-Min Chung
Open Mar - Oct Tues - Thur 10 AM - 6 PM, Fri - Sun 10 AM - 7 PM; Nov - Feb Tues - Thur 10 AM - 5 PM, Fri - Sun 10 AM - 6 PM; Admis adults 8 won, under 18, over 65 free; Estab 1969; Only nat art mus in korea
Income: Government
Library Holdings: Auction Catalogs; Audio Tapes; Book Volumes; CD-ROMs; Clipping Files; Compact Disks; Exhibition Catalogs; Fiche; Memorabilia; Pamphlets; Periodical Subscriptions; Photographs; Prints; Slides; Video Tapes
Collections: Collection of contemporary Korean painting from 1910 to the present; Sculptures, craft, and decorative art; media art, installation art
Activities: Classes for adults & children; docent training; 10-15 vis lectrs per yr; concerts; gallery talks; tours; extension prog in Seoul & Gwacheon; mus shop sells books, magazines; National Museum of Art, Deoksugung, 99 Sejongdae-ro, Jung-gu Seoul

SEOUL

M **NATIONAL MUSEUM OF KOREA,** Sejong-ro, Chongno-gu, Seoul, Korea, Republic of. Tel (02) 720-2714; Fax (02) 734-7255; *Dir Gen* Yang-Mo Chung
Open Tues - Sun 9 AM - 6 PM, Sat, Sun & holidays 9 AM - 7 PM, cl Mon; Admis adults 2000 won, youth 7-18 yrs 1000 won, children under 6 yrs & adults over 65 yrs free; free 4th Sat each month; Seven branch museums & library with 20,000 vols

Collections: Korean archaeology, culture & folklore

M **SEOUL MUSEUM OF ART,** 30 Misulgwan-gil, Jung-Gu Seoul, 100-813 Korea, Republic of. Tel 82-02-2124-8800; Elec Mail smoa@seoul.go.kr; Internet Home Page Address: seoulmoa.seoul.go.kr; *Dir* Ha Johnghyeon; *Cur* Yoo Hee Young
Admis adults 700 won, military & police 300 won, over 65 and under 12 free; Open Mar - Oct 10 AM - 10 PM, Sat - Sun 10 AM - 7 PM, Nov - Feb 10 AM - 9 PM, Sat - Sun 10 AM - 6 PM
Collections: Currently holds 344 pieces of Korean painting, Western painting, print, sculpture, craft, calligraphy, media art, and photography

KUWAIT

HAWELLI

M **TAREQ RAJAB MUSEUM,** Tareq Rajab Museum, PO Box 6156, Hawelli, 32036 Kuwait. Tel 965-531-7358; Fax 965-533-9063; Elec Mail museum@trmkt.com; Internet Home Page Address: www.trmkt.com; *Co-Dir* Jehan Rajab
Open daily 9 AM - noon & 4 PM - 7 PM, Fri 9 AM - noon; Admis KD 2/-
Collections: Calligraphy, manuscripts, miniatures, ceramics, metalwork, glass, carvings; Artifacts from the Islamic world of the past 250 years; costumes, textiles, jewelry, and musical instruments; 30,000 items collected over last 50 years

M **Dar El Cid Exhibition Halls,** Bldg 24-26, St 1 Area 12 Jabriya, Kuwait; PO Box 6156, Hawelli, 32036 Kuwait. Tel 965-533-9063

M **Dar Jehan - Museum of Islamic Calligraphy,** Block 12, St 1 Jabriya, Kuwait. Open daily 9 AM - noon & 4 PM - 7 PM, Fri 9 AM - noon; No admis fee
Collections: Traces development of Islamic script from the 7th century to the present

KYRGYZSTAN

BISHKEK

M **G. AITIEV KYRGYZ NATIONAL MUSEUM OF FINE ARTS,** 196 Sovietskaya St, Bishkek, Kyrgyzstan; Abdrakhmanov St 196, Bishkek, 720000 Kyrgyzstan. Tel 996-312-661623, 664959; Fax 996-312-620548; Elec Mail knmii@mail.ru; Internet Home Page Address: www.knmii.lg.kg; *Dir* Shygaev Yuristanbek Abdievich
Open Tues - Sun 9 AM - 5 PM; Admis 100 KGS (= 2-3 US $); Estab 1935
Income: Government institution
Collections: 18,000 works of art; paintings, drawings, sculptures and traditional decorative and applied art; Several galleries of paintings from Soviet period; Replica Egyptian, Greek and classical Western sculptures; Collection of linocuts based on Manas epic
Activities: Classes for adults & children; mus shop sells books, magazines, prints, souvenirs

LATVIA

RIGA

M **LATVIJAS NACIONALAIS MAKSLAS MUZEJS,** Latvian National Museum of Art, 10a K Valdemara St, Riga, LV-1010 Latvia. Tel 371-67-325-051; Fax 371-67-357-408; Elec Mail lnmm@lnmm.lv; Internet Home Page Address: www.lnmm.lv; *Dir* Mara Lace; *Dir's Asst* Lveta Derkusova; *Dept Head* Ginta Gerharde-Upeniece; *Deputy Dir Coll Servs* Luta Lapina
Open ann Mon & Wed - Sun 11 AM - 5 PM, Fri 11 AM - 8 PM, cl Tues; Admis adults 3 Ls, children, students & seniors 1.50 Ls; Estab 1905; National art mus of Latvia; Average Annual Attendance: 100,000
Income: 150,000 euro per yr; including self-generated income; financed by government of Latvia
Special Subjects: Sculpture
Collections: More than 52,000 works of art reflecting the development of art in the Baltic area and Latvia from 18th century to present; Russian art from the 19th century to early 20th century; Latvian art of 2nd half of 20th century
Exhibitions: Permanent & special exhibs
Publications: Catalogues; research publs; mus writings, ann
Activities: Classes for adults & children; creative workshops; exhib hall arsenals showing contemporary exhibs; lects open to pub; 1,000 vis lectrs per yr; gallery talks; tours; organize traveling exhibs to other mus; mus shop sells books, reproductions, prints & souvenirs

M **Arsenals Exhibition Hall,** 1 Torna St, Riga, LV-1050 Latvia. Tel 371-67-357527; Fax 371-67-357520; Elec Mail pr.service@lnmm.lv; Internet Home Page Address: www.lnmm.lv; *Adminr* Velga Pule; *Head of Colls* Elita Ansone; *Cur Press, Information & Publicity* Natalie Suyunshalieva
Open Tues, Wed, Fri 12:00 - 18:00, Thurs 12:00 - 20:00, Sat, Sun 12:00 - 17:00; cl Mon; Admis adults 2.50 Ls, students children & seniors 1.50 Ls; Estab 1989; Exhib hall; Average Annual Attendance: 50,000
Library Holdings: Book Volumes; Compact Disks; Exhibition Catalogs; Original Documents; Periodical Subscriptions; Photographs
Special Subjects: Drawings, Etchings & Engravings, Landscapes, Glass, Photography, Portraits, Prints, Graphics, Sculpture, Watercolors, Woodcarvings, Woodcuts, Collages, Posters, Porcelain, Coins & Medals, Restorations, Miniatures, Painting-Russian
Collections: Latvian art of the late 20th century to the present

Activities: Classes for adults & children; lects open to the pub; concerts; gallery talks; tours; extension prog; lending of original art on request; organize traveling exhibs on request; mus shop sells books & magazines

LEBANON

BEIRUT

M **ARCHAEOLOGICAL MUSEUM OF THE AMERICAN UNIVERSITY OF BEIRUT,** Bliss St, Beirut, Lebanon; PO Box 11-0236, Beirut, Lebanon. Tel (961) 340549; Fax 961-1-363235; Elec Mail museum@aub.edu.lb; Internet Home Page Address: www.aub.edu.1b/museum_archeo/; *Dir* Dr Leila Badre; *Admin Asst* Amale Feghali; *Mus Asst* Lorine Mouawad; *Research Asst* Riva Daniel; *Research Asst* Reine Mady
Open Mon - Fri 9 AM - 5 PM; No admis fee; Estab 1868; Average Annual Attendance: 3700; Mem: 330; dues Fellows $500; Contributors $200; Family $150; Members $100; Students $10
Library Holdings: Audio Tapes; Cards; Maps; Pamphlets; Photographs
Special Subjects: Archaeology, Ceramics, Glass, Gold, Bronzes, Jewelry, Ivory, Coins & Medals, Islamic Art, Mosaics
Collections: Bronze and Iron Age Near Eastern pottery colls; bronze figurines, weapons and implements of the Bronze Age Near East; Greco-Roman imports of pottery from Near East sites; Paleolithic-Neolithic flint coll; Phoenician glass coll; pottery coll of Islamic periods; substantial coin coll
Activities: Classes for children; lects for members & pub; 875 vis lectrs per yr; gallery talks & tours; mus shop sells books, original art & reproductions, prints, pottery & jewelry

M **DAHESHITE MUSEUM AND LIBRARY,** PO Box 202, Beirut, Lebanon. *Dir* Dr A S M Dahesh
Library with 30,000 vols
Collections: Aquarelles, gouaches, original paintings, engravings, sculptures in marble, bronze, ivory and wood carvings

M **MUSEE NATIONAL,** National Museum of Lebanon, Rue de Damas, Beirut, Lebanon. Tel 4-01-00/4-40; *Dir* Dr Camille Asmar
Collections: Anthropological sarcophagi of the Greco-Persian period; Byzantine mosaics; royal arms, jewels and statues of the Phoenician epoch; Dr C Ford Collection of 25 sarcophagi of the Greek and Hellenistic epoch; goblets, mosaics, relief and sarcophagi of the Greco-Roman period; Arabic woods and ceramics

M **NICOLAS SURSOCK MUSEUM,** Sursock St, Achrafieh Beirut, Lebanon. Tel 961-1-334-133; *Pres* Ghassan Tueni; *Cur* Dr Loutfalla Melki
Open daily 10 AM - 1 PM & 4 PM - 7 PM
Collections: Permanent collection contains Japanese engravings and numerous works of Islamic art; Exhibitions of contemporary Lebanese and international artists

LIBERIA

MONROVIA

M **NATIONAL MUSEUM OF LIBERIA,** (National Museum) Broad & Buchanan Sts, PO Box 3223 Monrovia, Liberia. *Dir* Burdie Urey-Weeks
Collections: Liberian history & art

LIBYA

TRIPOLI

M **ARCHAEOLOGICAL, NATURAL HISTORY, EPIGRAPHY, PREHISTORY AND ETHNOGRAPHY MUSEUMS,** Assarai al-Hamra, Tripoli, Libya. Tel 38116/7; *Pres* Dr Abdullah Shaiboub
Administered by Department of Antiquities
Collections: Archaeology from Libyan sites

LIECHTENSTEIN

VADUZ

M **KUNSTMUSEUM LIECHTENSTEIN,** Stadtle 32 Vaduz, 9490 Liechtenstein. Tel (+423) 235 03 00; Fax (+423) 235 03 29; Elec Mail mail@kunstmuseum.li; Internet Home Page Address: www.kunstmuseum.li; *Dir* Dr Friedemann Malsch; *Cur* Christiane Meyer-Stoll; *Press Officer* Rene Schierscher
Open Tues, Wed, Fri - Sun 10 AM - 5 PM, Thurs 10 AM - 8 PM; Admis 8 Euros; Estab 2000; Mus of modern & contemporary art
Activities: Educ prog; lects open to pub; mus shop sells books

LITHUANIA

KAUNAS

M **M K CIURLIONIS STATE MUSEUM OF ART,** Vlado Putvinskio 55, Kaunas, LT-3000 Lithuania. Tel 370 37 229475; Fax 370 37 222606; *Dir* Osvaldas Daugelis
Open Sept - May Tues - Sun 11 AM - 5 PM, June - Aug Tues - Sun 10 AM - 5 PM

Collections: Lithuanian, European & Oriental art; 5 related galleries & museums in Kaunas & Druskininkai

VILNIUS

M **CONTEMPORARY ART CENTRE,** Vokieciu 2, Vilnius, LT-01130 Lithuania. Tel 370-5-2121945; Fax 370-5-2623954; Elec Mail info@cac.lt; Internet Home Page Address: www.cac.lt

M **LITHUANIAN ART MUSEUM,** Boksto 5, Vilnius, LT-011126 Lithuania. Tel +37052628030; Fax +37052126006; Elec Mail muziejus@ldm.pt; Internet Home Page Address: www.ldm.lt; *Dir* Romualdas Budrys; *Deputy Dir for Collections* Loreta Meskeleviciene
Open Tues - Sat noon - 6 PM, Sun & before national holiday noon - 5 PM, cl Mon & national holidays; Admis Lt 6, students Lt 3, children under 7 yrs, disabled & ICOM mem free; Estab 1907; Average Annual Attendance: 170500; Mem: ICOM, ICOM-Lietuva, Assn of Lithuanian Museums
Income: State budget funding provided
Purchases: Avg 17% of annual budget amount
Library Holdings: Book Volumes; CD-ROMs; Cards; Cassettes; Compact Disks; DVDs; Exhibition Catalogs; Lantern Slides; Manuscripts; Maps; Memorabilia; Original Art Works; Original Documents; Pamphlets; Periodical Subscriptions; Photographs; Prints; Reproductions; Video Tapes
Collections: Folk Art; Lithuanian & foreign fine and decorative arts from 14th century to present
Activities: Classes for adults & children; dramatic progs; docent training; family & specialized progs; Lects for members only; concerts, tours; originate traveling exhibs countrywide, worldwide, & to Europe; mus shop sells books, magazines, reproductions

LUXEMBOURG

LUXEMBOURG CITY

M **MUSEE NATIONAL D'HISTOIRE ET D'ART LUXEMBOURG,** Marche-aux-Poissons, Luxembourg City, L-2345 Luxembourg. Tel 47-93-30-1; Fax 47-93-30-271; Elec Mail musee@mnha.etat.lu; Internet Home Page Address: www.mnha.lu; *Prof Dir* Michel Polfer; *Chief Cur Fine Arts* Dr Malgorzata Nowara; *Chief Cur Numismatics* Francois Reinert; *Chief Cur Applied Arts* Jean-Luc Mousset
Open Tues - Wed & Fri - Sun 10 AM - 6 PM, Thurs 10 AM - 8 PM, cl Mon; Admis adults 5 euro, over 60 3 euro, Thurs & children under 13 free; Estab 1939, new bldg 2002; National collection of archaeology, history, fine & applied arts; Average Annual Attendance: 60,000
Library Holdings: Auction Catalogs; Book Volumes; CD-ROMs; DVDs; Exhibition Catalogs; Kodachrome Transparencies; Manuscripts; Maps; Original Documents; Other Holdings; Periodical Subscriptions; Photographs; Prints; Slides
Special Subjects: Archaeology, Decorative Arts, Drawings, Etchings & Engravings, Folk Art, Historical Material, Ceramics, Glass, Metalwork, Gold, Photography, Porcelain, Portraits, Pottery, Prints, Silver, Maps, Painting-French, Sculpture, Graphics, Watercolors, Textiles, Religious Art, Crafts, Collages, Painting-European, Furniture, Painting-Dutch, Coins & Medals, Restorations, Baroque Art, Painting-Flemish, Renaissance Art, Medieval Art, Painting-Italian, Antiquities-Roman, Mosaics, Stained Glass, Painting-German
Collections: Archaeological and ethnographic items from Luxembourg from pre-history through the 9th century; Decorative arts, medals, and weapons; Old Master paintings (4th century - 9th century); Modern & contemporary art
Activities: Classes for children; lectrs open to the public; 6 vis lectrs per year; gallery talks; tours; original objects of art lent to national & foreign institutions; mus shop sells books, magazines, reproductions, prints, slides, & games etc

MACAU

NAPE

M **CIVIC AND MUNICIPAL AFFAIRS BUREAU OF MACAU,** Macau Museum of Art, Macau Cultural Centre, Avenida Xian Xing Hai s/n Nape, Macau. Tel 853-87919-814, 800, 802; Fax 853-28751317; Elec Mail artmuseum@iacm.gov.mo; Internet Home Page Address: www.artmuseum.gov.mo; *Chmn Admin Comt* Tam Vai Man; *Dir* Chan Hou Seng
Open Mus 10 AM - 7 PM, no admis after 6:30 PM, cl Mon; Libr Tues - Fri 2 PM - 7 PM, Sat & Sun 11 AM - 7 PM, cl Mon & pub holidays; Admis adults 5 MOP, student 2 MOP, under 12 & over 65 free, free on Sun; Est March 3 1999; Average Annual Attendance: 90,000; Mem: MOP $30 per year, MOP $50 per year
Library Holdings: Book Volumes; DVDs; Exhibition Catalogs; Maps; Photographs; Prints
Special Subjects: Ceramics, Photography, Watercolors, Primitive art, Asian Art, Calligraphy
Collections: Chinese calligraphy and paintings, seals, ceramics, copperwares, Western paintings, contemporary art, photography and more; Performance Art, Furniture
Exhibitions: A Glimpse of the Past: Old Macau Photos; Historical Paintings of Macaio in the 19th Century
Publications: Exhibition Catalogs
Activities: Courses for children, adults, teenagers, & the handicapped, art seminars and courses; lects open to pub; Mus shop sells books, reproductions

MACEDONIA

SKOPJE

M **MUSEUM OF CONTEMPORARY ART - SKOPJE,** Samoilova bb, PO Box 482 Skopje, 1000 Macedonia. Tel 389-2-311-77-34; Fax 389-2-311-01-23; Elec Mail msu-info@msuskopje.org.mk; Internet Home Page Address: www.msuskopje.org.mk; *Dir* Emil Aleksiev
Open Tues - Sat 10 AM - 5 PM, Sun 9 AM - 2 PM, cl Mon; No admis fee
Collections: 4630 exhibits of international and national contemporary art; Art movements through 50s, 60s and 70s

MALAYSIA

KUALA LUMPUR

M **DEPARTMENT OF MUSEUMS MALAYSIA,** National Museum, Jalan Damansara, Kuala Lumpur, 50566 Malaysia. Tel (03) 2267 1111; Fax (02) 2267 1011; Elec Mail prmuziumnegara@jmm.gov.my; Internet Home Page Address: www.jmm.gov.my; Internet Home Page Address: www.muziumnegara.gov.my; *Dir Gen* Dato Ibrahim bin Ismail; *Deputy Dir Gen* Wan Jamaluddin bin Yusoff; *Dir Nat Mus* Kamarul Baharin bin A Kasim
Open 9 AM - 6 PM; Admis adults & children over 12; children in school uniform free; Estab 1963; Average Annual Attendance: 330,000
Income: Financed by govt
Special Subjects: Archaeology, Historical Material, Ceramics, Metalwork, Bronzes, Ethnology, Costumes, Asian Art, Antiquities-Oriental
Collections: Oriental & Islamic arts, ethnographical, archaeological & historical collections
Activities: Docent training; young volunteer classes; lects open to pub; gallery talks; tours; originates traveling exhibs to state mus; mus shop sells books, original art, reproductions, crafts

M **NATIONAL ART GALLERY OF MALAYSIA,** Balai Seni Lukis Negara 2, Jalan Temerloh Kuala Lumpur, 53200 Malaysia. Tel 603-4025-4990; Fax 603-4025-4987; Elec Mail info@artgallery.gov.my; Internet Home Page Address: www.artgallery.gov.my; *Dir Gen* Dr Saharudin Haji Ismail; *Cur* Faridah Hanim Abdul Wahab
Open Tues - Sun 10 AM - 6 PM; No admis fee
Collections: Permanent collection of more than 2500 pieces; Ceramics, Chinese ink painting, drawing, watercolors, installation, photography, prints, sculpture, textiles

MALDIVES

MALE

M **NATIONAL ART GALLERY OF MALDIVES,** 131 Majeedhee Magu, Male, 20131 Maldives. Tel 00-960-3337724; Fax 00-960-3337728; Elec Mail gallery@dhivehinet.net.mv; Internet Home Page Address: www.artgallery.gov.mv
Collections: Exhibitions of Maldivian and international contemporary art

MALTA

VALLETTA

M **HERITAGE MALTA,** (National Museum of Fine Arts) National Museum of Fine Arts, South St Valletta, Malta. Tel 356 21233034; Elec Mail theresa.m.vella@gov.nt; Internet Home Page Address: www.heritagemalta.org; *Senior Cur Fine Arts* Theresa Vella, MA; *Cur Modern Art* Dennis Vella, MA
Open daily 9 AM - 5 PM, cl Dec 24, 25, 31 & Jan 1; Admis 1LM, seniors over 65 & children under 18 .50; Estab 1975; Contains fine arts from the 14th century to present day
Library Holdings: Cards; Exhibition Catalogs; Original Documents; Pamphlets; Photographs
Special Subjects: Drawings, Etchings & Engravings, Ceramics, Furniture, Bronzes, Painting-European, Painting-French, Prints, Sculpture, Watercolors, Religious Art, Silver, Painting-Dutch, Baroque Art, Painting-Flemish, Medieval Art, Painting-Spanish, Painting-Italian
Collections: Fine arts; maiolica & pharmacy jars of 16th-19th century
Exhibitions: Changing exhibitions of contemporary art & historical themes
Publications: Exhibitions catalogues & postcards

MEXICO

COYOACAN

M **MUSEO FRIDA KAHLO CASA AZUL,** Londres 247, Col Del Carmen Coyoacan, 04000 Mexico. Tel 55-54-59-99; Fax 56-58-57-78; Elec Mail patrocinios@museoanahuacalli.org.mx; Elec Mail investigacion@museofridakahlo.org.mx; Internet Home Page Address: www.museofridakhalo.org; *Mus Coordr* Alejandra Lopez Estrada; *Organization Develop* Ximena Gomez Gonzalez Cosio
Open Tues - Sun 10 AM - 6 PM; Admis 45 ps, students 20 ps, guided tours 250 ps; The Blue House opened to pub in 1958; mission is to preserve & maintain the collection & the house by itself & to exhibit the works of art & the personal objects that belongs to Frida Kahlo & Diego Rivera; The Blue House is the house Frida Kahlo lived in, a place where things tell a story & invites to walk along its rooms, corridors, patios that show the intimate world of this artist.; Average Annual Attendance: 250,000
Library Holdings: Book Volumes; Cards
Special Subjects: Archaeology, Architecture, Mexican Art, Photography, Portraits, Sculpture, Folk Art
Collections: Former residence of Frida Kahlo; Household and personal items and artifacts, decorative arts, paintings, textiles; Private collection of work by other Mexican artists
Activities: Tours; Mus shop sells books, magazines, prints, jewelry, textiles, decorative art & catalogues

GUADALAJARA

M **MUSEO DEL ESTADO DE JALISCO,** Liceo 60 S H, Guadalajara, 44100 Mexico. Tel (3) 613-27-03; Fax (3) 614-52-57; *Dir* Dr Carlos R Beltran Briseno
Collections: Archaeological discoveries; early Mexican objects; folk art & costumes

M **MUSEO-TALLER JOSE CLEMENTE OROZCO,** Calle Aurelio Aceves 27, Sector Juarez Guadalajara, 44100 Mexico. *Mgr* Gutierre Aceves Piña
Open Mon - Fri 10 AM - 5 PM; No admis fee; The last studio J Corozco that shows contemporary art; Average Annual Attendance: 20,000
Collections: Paintings and sketches by the artist

MEXICO CITY

M **MUSEO DE ARTE CARRILLO GIL,** Carrillo Gil Museum of Contemporary Art, Av Revolucion 1608, San Angel Mexico City, DF 01000 Mexico. Tel 555-550-3983; Fax 525-550-4232; Internet Home Page Address: www.macg.inba.gob.mx; *Dir* Itala Schmelz; *Cur* Graciela Kasap; *Cur* Alberto Torres
Open Tues - Sun 10 AM - 6 PM; Admis 1.50 (85 pc), Sun free
Collections: Jose Clemente Orozco Collection; Work by Siqueiros, Rivera and many other 20th century Mexican artists

M **MUSEO DE ARTE MODERNO,** Museum of Modern Art, Bosque de Chapultepec, Paseo de la Reforma y Gandhi Mexico City, 11560 Mexico. Tel (5) 553-62-33; Fax (5) 553-62-11; Elec Mail maczavala@mam.org.mx; Internet Home Page Address: www.mam.org.mx; *Dir* Magalena Zavala Bonachea
Open Tues - Sun 10 AM - 5:30 PM; Admis $2 (1.10 euro), Sun free, discounts for teachers & students
Collections: International and Mexican coll of modern art
Activities: Classes for adults & children; lects open to pub; organize traveling exhibs Nat & International; mus shop sells books, magazines, prints, slides

M **MUSEO FRANZ MAYER,** Hidalgo 45, Centro Historico Mexico City, DF 06300 Mexico. Tel 5518-2266; Elec Mail fmayer@data.net.mx; Internet Home Page Address: www.franzmayer.org.mx; *Dir* Hector Rivero Borrell Miranda
Open Tues - Sun 10 AM - 5 PM, Wed 10 AM - 7 PM; Admis adults 35 ps, students 17 ps, children & seniors free
Collections: Collection of decorative arts in Mexico from 16th - 19th centuries; Temporary exhibits of photography & design; International & national origins; Silverwork, ceramics, furniture, textiles, sculpture, paintings, feather art, lacquer, ivory, tortoise shell, glass and enamel

M **MUSEO NACIONAL DE SAN CARLOS,** (Museo de San Carlos) Puente de Alvarado 50, Col Tabacalera Mexico City, 06030 Mexico. Tel 55-5566-8085; Fax 5-535-12-56; Internet Home Page Address: www.mnsancarlos.com; *Dir* Roxana Velasquez; *Dir* Maria Fernanda Matos Moctezuma; *Bibliotecaria* Ana Alvarado Ferandez
Open Mon - Fri 10:00 AM - 5:00 PM; Admis $2.50 (1.40 euro), Sun free; Estab 1986; European Art, Old Masters; Average Annual Attendance: 1,000
Library Holdings: Book Volumes; Cassettes; Exhibition Catalogs; Prints; Records
Collections: English, Flemish, French, German, Hungarian, Italian, Polish, Netherlandish and Spanish paintings from 14th - 19th centuries; Mexican Art
Activities: Lects open to the pub; 1,000 vis lectrs per yr; concerts; gallery talks; mus shop sells books
L **Eric Larsen,** Puente de Alvarado No 50, Col Tabacalera Mexico City, 06030 Mexico. Tel 5-592-37-21; Fax 5-535-12-56; Elec Mail s_biblios@yahoo.com; Internet Home Page Address: www.mnsancarlos.com; *Dir* Maria Fernanda Matos Moctezuma; *Bibliotecaria* Ana Alvardo Ferandez
Open Mon - Fri 10:00 AM - 5:00 PM; Circ 5,000; Average Annual Attendance: 1,000
Library Holdings: Book Volumes 2000; Cassettes; Exhibition Catalogs; Prints; Records
Activities: Lects open to the pub; 1,000 vis lectrs per yr; concerts; gallery talks

M **MUSEO NACIONAL DE ANTROPOLOGIA,** National Museum of Anthropology, Paseo de la Reforma y Calz, Gandhi Mexico City, 11560 Mexico. Tel (5) 553-19-02; Fax (5) 286-17-91; Internet Home Page Address: www.mna.inah.gob.mx; *Dir* Mari Carmen Serra Puche
Open Tues - Sun 9 AM - 7 PM; Admis 45 pesos Tues-Sat 9AM - 5PM, 150 pesos 5PM - 7 PM, free Sun 9AM - 5PM
Collections: Anthropological, archaeological & ethnographical colls

M **MUSEO NACIONAL DE ARTES E INDUSTRIAS POPULARES DEL INSTITUTO NACIONAL INDIGENISTA,** National Museum of Popular Arts and Crafts, Avda Juarez 44, Mexico City, 06050 Mexico. Tel 510-34-04; *Dir* Maria Teresa Pomar
Collections: Major permanent collections of Mexican popular arts and crafts

M **MUSEO NACIONAL DE HISTORIA,** National Historical Museum, Castillo de Chapultepec, Mexico City, 5 Mexico. Tel 553-62-02; *Dir* Lara T Amelia Tamburrino
Open Tues - Sun 9AM - 5 PM
Collections: The history of Mexico from the Spanish Conquest to the 1917 Constitution, through collections of ceramics, costumes, documents, flags and banners, furniture, jewelry & personal objects

M **PINACOTECA VIRREINAL DE SAN DIEGO,** Laboratorio Arte Alameda, Dr Mora 7, Alameda Central Mexico City, 06050 Mexico. Tel 5-10-27-93; Fax 5-12-20-79; Elec Mail info.artealameda@gmail.com; Internet Home Page Address: www.artealameda.bellasartes.gob.mx; *Dir* Tania Aedo Arankowsky; *Sub Dir* Karla Jasso; *Commun Dept* Gabriela Romero; *Adminr* Jose Antonio Hernandez; *Educ* Ana Sol Gonzalez
Open Tues - Sun 9 AM - 5 PM; Admis general entrance $15; students, teachers & seniors $7.50; Estab 2000, dedicated to the exhib, documentation, production & research on artistic practices that explore & setup a dialogue on the art technology relationship
Special Subjects: Intermedia
Collections: Under auspices of Instituto Nacional de Bellas Artes; paintings of the ·colonial era in Mexico
Activities: Classes for adults & children; concerts & gallery talks

PUEBLA

M **MUSEO DE ARTE JOSE LUIS BELLO Y GONZALEZ,** Poninento No 302, Puebla, Mexico. Tel 32-94-75; *Dir* Alicia Torres de Araujo
Collections: Ivories; porcelain; wrought iron; furniture; clocks; watches; musical instruments; Mexican, Chinese and European paintings, sculptures, pottery, vestments, tapestries, ceramics, miniatures

TOLUCA

M **MUSEO DE LAS BELLAS ARTES,** Museum of Fine Arts, Calle de Santos Degollado 102, Toluca, Mexico. Tel 52-722-2155329; *Dir* Prof Jose M Caballero-Barnard
Collections: Paintings; sculptures; Mexican colonial art

MOLDOVA

CHISINAU

M **NATIONAL MUSEUM OF FINE ARTS OF MOLDOVA,** 31 August 1989 str, Chisinau, 115 Moldova. Tel 373-2-24-17-30; Fax 373-2-24-53-32; Elec Mail art.museum@mail.md; Internet Home Page Address: www.artmuseum.md; *Dir* Tudor Zbarnea; *Deputy Dir* Svetlana Pociumban
Open Tues - Sun 10 AM - 5 PM, cl Mon; Admis adult 6 Leu, student 3 Leu; Estab 1939 to exhibit, conserve & restore art works; Display permanent and temporary exhibitions; Average Annual Attendance: 14,000
Income: $240,000 (financed by state)
Special Subjects: Decorative Arts, Drawings, Landscapes, Marine Painting, Ceramics, Collages, Glass, Flasks & Bottles, Gold, Photography, Porcelain, Portraits, Pottery, Silver, Textiles, Painting-European, Painting-French, Painting-Japanese, Sculpture, Tapestries, Graphics, Watercolors, Bronzes, Religious Art, Crafts, Woodcarvings, Oriental Art, Ivory, Juvenile Art, Coins & Medals, Restorations, Miniatures, Painting-Polish, Renaissance Art, Embroidery, Laces, Medieval Art, Painting-Spanish, Painting-Italian, Antiquities-Persian, Antiquities-Greek, Antiquities-Roman, Cartoons, Painting-German, Painting-Russian
Collections: Over 30 thousand pieces of Moldavian fine and decorative arts from the middle ages to the present; Painting, drawing, sculpture, crafts; Iconography, books, manuscripts; Permanent exhibitions of Russian, European and Asian art
Activities: Classes for adults & children; lects open to public; concerts; tours

MONGOLIA

ULAANBAATAR

M **A & D MUSEUM OF MONGOLIAN ART,** Tourist St 13/1, Chingeltei Dist Ulaanbaatar, Mongolia. Tel 976-11-317837; Tel 976-11-328948; Elec Mail asianart@magicnet.mn; Internet Home Page Address: www.mongolianantique.com; *Dir* Altangerel Ayurzana
Collections: Early bronzes, statues, thangkas, applique, embroidered work and textiles, iconography, ritual artifacts, furniture, household items and decorative arts

M **ZANABAZAR NATIONAL FINE ARTS MUSEUM,** Khudaldaany St, Barilgachdiin Sq Ulaanbaatar, Mongolia. Tel 976-11-326060, 326061; Fax 976-11-326060; Internet Home Page Address: www.zanabazarmuseum.org; *Dir* Batdorj Damndinsuren
Open Summer - Autumn daily 9 AM - 6 PM, Winter - Spring daily 10 AM - 5 PM; Admis adults 2500 tug, students 1000 tug, children 200 tug
Collections: Collection incl 10,000+ objects; Prehistoric art, work by Zanabazar, painted thangkas, silk appliques, Buddhist artifacts, traditional arts and crafts of Mongolia; Paintings by B Sharav

MONTENEGRO

CETINJE

M **NARODNI MUZEJ CRNE GORE,** National Museum of Montenegro, Novice Cerovica bb, Cetinje, 81250 Montenegro. Tel 382-41-230-310; Fax 382-41-230-310; Elec Mail nmcg@t-com.me; Internet Home Page Address: www.mnmuseum.org; *Dir* Pavle Pejovic
Open 9 AM - 17 PM
Special Subjects: Archaeology, Drawings, Historical Material, Ceramics, Photography, Portraits, Manuscripts, Sculpture, Graphics, Ethnology, Southwestern Art, Costumes, Religious Art, Coins & Medals
M **Historical Museum,**
Collections: General development of Montenegrin people and history through various periods; 1500 museum pieces, 300 archived items, 1500 photographs, maps, graphs, architecture & art
M **Ethnographic Museum,**
Collections: Ethnographic history of Montenegro through various traditional arts and crafts; Textiles, embroidery, musical instruments, material culture
M **Modern Art Gallery,**
Collections: Five colls; Arts of Yugoslav nations and ethnic groups, icons, Montenegrin fine art, Milica Saric-Vukmanovic Memorial Coll and a coll of frescoes
M **Biljarda - Peter II Petrovic Njegos Museum,**
Collections: Former residence of bishop and poet Peter II Petrovic Njegos; Personal artifacts, decorative arts, furniture, architecture, armaments
M **King Nikola's Museum,**
Collections: Montenegrin history and artifacts in former residence of royal family; Decorations, photographs, weapons, jewelry

MOROCCO

MARRAKECH

M **DAR SI SAID MUSEUM,** Riad Ez-Zaitoun El Jadid, Marrakech, Morocco. Tel 212-4-44-24-64
Open June 1 - Aug 31 Wed - Mon 9 AM - noon & 4 PM - 7 PM; Sept 1 - May 31 Wed - Mon 9 AM - noon & 2:30 PM - 6 PM, cl Tues; Admis 10 dirham
Collections: Berber silver jewelry, oil lamps, embroidered leather, rustic pottery and marble, furniture, carpets and other decorative and architectural arts

TANGIER

M **MUSEUM OF MOROCCAN ARTS,** Dar el Makhzen, Place de la Kasbah Tangier, Morocco. Tel 212-9-93-20-97; Internet Home Page Address: www.maroc.net/museums
Open June 1 - Aug 31 Wed - Mon 9 AM - 3:30 PM; Sept 1 - May 31 Wed - Mon 9 AM - noon & 3 PM - 6 PM; Admis 10 dirham
Collections: Ethnographic and artistic history of Morocco housed in former Governor's palace; Armaments, fabrics and textiles, costumes, glass, porcelain, pottery, architecture, ceramics
M **Museum of Antiquities,**
Open Wed - Mon 9:30 AM - noon & 1 PM - 5:30 PM, cl Tues
Collections: Bronzes and mosaics from Roman sites of Lixus, Cotta, Banasa and Volubilis; Ethnographic history of Tangier; Carthaginian tomb model with other related artifacts

MYANMAR

YANGON

M **NATIONAL MUSEUM OF ART AND ARCHAEOLOGY,** Jubilee Hall, 66/74 Pyay Road Yangon, Myanmar. Tel (01) 73706; *Chief Cur* U Kyaw Win
Collections: Regalia of King Thibaw of Mandalay

NAMIBIA

WINDHOEK

M **NATIONAL ART GALLERY OF NAMIBIA,** c/o John Meinert St & Robert Mugabe Ave, PO Box 994 Windhoek, Namibia. Tel 264-61-231160; Fax 264-61-240930; Elec Mail nagn@mweb.com.na; Internet Home Page Address: www.nagn.org.na/index.html; *Dir* Joe Madisia
Open Mon 10 AM - 5 PM, Tues - Fri 8 AM - 5 PM, Sat 9 AM - 2 PM, Sun 11 AM - 4 PM
Collections: Namibian art past and present, African and South African contemporary art; traditional crafts and decorative arts, textiles

NEPAL

BHAKTAPUR

M **NATIONAL ART GALLERY OF NEPAL,** Singhadhoka Bldg Bhaktapur Palace, Durbar Sq Bhaktapur, Nepal. Tel 01-610004
Open Tues - Sat 9:30 AM - 4:30 PM, cl Sun - Mon; Admis nationals 10 Rs, visitors Rs 20

Collections: Rare Nepalese paintings; Paubha scroll paintings, bronze, brass, stone and wooden artifacts

KATHMANDU

M NATIONAL MUSEUM OF NEPAL, Museum Rd, Chhauni Kathmandu, Nepal. Tel 211504; *Chief* Sanu Nani Kansakar
Open Mon, Wed - Sun 10:30 AM - 3 PM, Fri 10:30 AM - 2 PM, cl Tues & govt holidays
Collections: Art, history, culture, ethnology & natural history colls

M NEPAL ASSOCIATION OF FINE ARTS, Birendra Art Museum, Sitabhawan, Naxal Kathmandu, Nepal. Tel 4411729, 4421206; Fax 4221175, 4414665; Elec Mail nafa@wlink.com.np; Internet Home Page Address: www.nafa.org.np
Open Mon - Fri 9 AM - 5 PM, cl Sat - Sun; Admis nationals Rs 25, international visitors Rs 75
Collections: 189 pieces of contemporary and historical art by over 60 prominent Nepalese artists

NETHERLANDS

ALKMAAR

M STEDELIJK MUSEUM ALKMAAR, Alkmaar Municipal Museum, Canadaplein 1 Alkmaar, 1811 KE Netherlands. Tel 072-5489789; Elec Mail museum@alkmaar.nl; Internet Home Page Address: www.stedelijkmuseumalkmaar.nl; *Dir* Lidewij de Koekkoek; *Cur* Christi Klinkert; *Mktg Mgr* Hans Duncker; *Educator* Aafje Moonen
Open Tues - Sun 10 AM - 5 PM, cl Mondays during the year, Jan 1, Apr 30, and Dec 25; Admis new prices 1/14, see website; Average Annual Attendance: 40,000
Income: Financed by city
Special Subjects: Decorative Arts, Historical Material, Landscapes, Furniture, Porcelain, Portraits, Silver, Sculpture, Painting-European, Dolls, Painting-Dutch
Collections: Collection from Alkmaar region, including archaeological items, dolls and other toys, modern sculpture, paintings, silver, tiles; works by Gerard van Honthorst, Caesar van Everdingen, William van de Velde the Elder, Pieter Saenredam Maerten van Heemskerck
Activities: mus shop sells books, reproductions, prints & gifts

AMSTELVEEN

M MUSEUM JAN VAN DER TOGT, Dorpsstraat 50, Amstelveen, 1182 JE Netherlands. Tel +31-206415754; Fax +31-206415754; Elec Mail jvdtogt@xs4all.nl; Internet Home Page Address: www.jvdtogt.nl/en/contact.htm

AMSTERDAM

M HERMITAGE AMSTERDAM, Amstel 51, Amsterdam, Netherlands; PO Box 11675, 1001 GR Amsterdam, Netherlands. Tel 31 (0) 20 530 87 55; Fax 31 (0) 20 620 01 05; Internet Home Page Address: www.hermitage.nl
Open Thurs - Tues 10 AM - 5 PM; Wed 10 AM - 8 PM, cl Apr 30, Christmas & New Years; Admis adults 15 Euro; children under 17 & Amsterdam City Card holders no admis fee

M MUSEUM HET REMBRANDTHUIS, The Rembrandt House Museum, Jodenbreestraat 4, Amsterdam, 1011 NK Netherlands. Tel 020-5200400; Fax 020-5200401; Elec Mail museum@rembrandthuis.nl; Internet Home Page Address: www.rembrandthuis.nl; *Dir* E de Heer
Open daily 10 AM - 5 PM; Admis 8 euro; The house where Rembrandt lived for nearly 20 years; Average Annual Attendance: 250,000
Collections: Rembrandt's etchings and drawings; drawings and paintings by Rembrandt's pupils; contemporary artists influenced by Rembrandt
Activities: Educ prog; classes for children; tours; originate traveling exhibs; mus shop sells books, prints, & reproductions

M RIJKSMUSEUM, State Museum, Stadhouderskade 42, PO Box 74888 Amsterdam, 1071 DN Netherlands. Tel 003120 6747 000; Fax 003120 6747 001; Elec Mail info@rijksmuseum.nl; Internet Home Page Address: www.rijksmuseum.nl; *Gen Dir* W M J Pijbes; *Dir Colls* T D W Dibbits; *Managing Dir* K E Van Ginkel
Open daily 9 AM - 6 PM, Fri 9 AM - 8:30 PM; Admis 10 euro, 18 yrs & under free; Library with 200,000 vols
Library Holdings: Exhibition Catalogs; Framed Reproductions; Memorabilia; Photographs; Reproductions
Collections: Asiatic art; Dutch history & paintings; prints & drawings from all parts of the world; sculpture & applied art
Activities: Classes for adults & children; lects open to pub; tours; mus shop sells books, reproductions, prints & slides

M STEDELIJK MUSEUM AMSTERDAM, (Stedlijk Museum) Municipal Museum, Museumplein 10, Amsterdam, Netherlands; PO Box 75082, Amsterdam, 1070 AB Netherlands. Tel 31 (020) 573 29 11; Fax 31 (020) 675 2716; Elec Mail info@stedelijk.nl; Internet Home Page Address: www.stedelijk.nl; *Artistic Dir* Ann Dee Goldstein; *Mng Dir* Karin van Gilsk
Open Mon - Wed 10 AM - 6PM, Thurs 10 AM - 10 PM, Fri - Sun 10 AM - 6 PM; Admis family (6 persons or less) 30 E, adult 15 E, children 12 & under no admis fee; Estab 1895; municipal mus, now modern & contemporary art; Library with 180,000 vols; Average Annual Attendance: 500,000; Mem: Urban friends
Library Holdings: Book Volumes; CD-ROMs; Clipping Files; Compact Disks; DVDs; Periodical Subscriptions

Collections: Applied art & design; European & American trends after 1960 in paintings & sculptures
Activities: Classes for adults & children; lects open to pub; concerts; gallery talks; tours; lending of original objects of art to mus; mus shop sells books, magazines, reproductions & designer gifts

M VAN GOGH MUSEUM, Paulus Potterstraat 7, PO Box 75366 Amsterdam, 1070 AJ Netherlands. Tel +31 (0)20 570 52 00; Fax +31 (0)20 570 52 22; Elec Mail info@vangoghmuseum.nl; Internet Home Page Address: www.vangoghmuseum.nl; *Dir* Axel Ruger
Open daily 10 AM - 6 PM, Fri 10 AM- 10 PM; Admis adults 12.50, euro, children 13-17 2.50 euro, 12 & under free; Estab 1973; fine arts; Average Annual Attendance: 1,300,000
Library Holdings: Auction Catalogs; Audio Tapes; Book Volumes; CD-ROMs; Cassettes; Clipping Files; Exhibition Catalogs; Fiche; Filmstrips; Memorabilia; Motion Pictures; Original Art Works; Original Documents; Periodical Subscriptions; Photographs; Prints; Reproductions; Slides; Video Tapes
Special Subjects: Prints, Woodcuts, Sculpture, Watercolors, Manuscripts, Painting-Dutch
Collections: Some 550 drawings, 200 paintings & 700 letters by Vincent Van Gogh; Van Gogh's personal collection of English & French prints & Japanese woodcuts; Varied collection of 19th century art by contemporaries
Activities: Classes for children; lects open to pub; vis lectrs 8-10 per yr; guided tours; audio tours; group visits; originate traveling exhibs to Art Institute of Chicago; mus shop sells books, magazines, reproductions, prints & slides

APELDOORN

M NATIONAAL MUSEUM PALEIS HET LOO, Koninklijk Park 1, Apeldoorn, 7315 JA Netherlands. Tel +31-55-577-24-00; Fax +31-55-577-24-08; Elec Mail info@paleishetloo.nl; Internet Home Page Address: www.paleishetloo.nl
Average Annual Attendance:

ARNHEM

M MUSEUM VOOR MODERNE KUNST ARNHEM, Municipal Museum of Arnhem, Utrechtseweg 87, Arnhem, 6812 AA Netherlands. Tel (026) 3775300; Fax (026) 3775353; Elec Mail mmka@arnhem.nl; Internet Home Page Address: www.mmkarnhem.nl; *Dir* Hedwig Saam; *Head of Coll* Miriam Windhausen; *Press Officer* Peter de Kok; *Operational Mgr* Bart Weggemans
Open Tues - Sun 11 AM - 5 PM, cl Mon; Admis 7.5 euro; Average Annual Attendance: 50,000
Income: 3 million euro (financed by the city of Arnhem), 200.000 euro (additional funding)
Library Holdings: Auction Catalogs; Book Volumes; Exhibition Catalogs; Kodachrome Transparencies; Manuscripts; Original Documents; Periodical Subscriptions; Slides; Video Tapes
Collections: Design; Dutch and international paintings, drawings and prints; Dutch contemporary applied art; sculpture gardens; video; on design; realism; contemporary art
Activities: Classes for adults & children; docent training; four visiting lectrs per year; concerts; tours; lending of original objects of art to other art institutions; sales shop sells books, reproductions & bric-a-brac

DELFT

M MUSEUM HET PRINSENHOF, St Agathaplein 1, Delft, 2611 HR Netherlands; Postbus 78, Delft, 2600 ME Netherlands. Tel (015) 260 2358; Fax (015) 213 8744; Elec Mail erfgoeddelft@delft.nl; Internet Home Page Address: www.prinsenhof-delft.nl
Open Tues - Sun 11 - 17; Library with 6000 vols
Special Subjects: Historical Material, Ceramics, Pottery, Silver, Textiles, Maps, Painting-European, Tapestries, Archaeology, Religious Art, Portraits, Painting-Dutch, Restorations
Collections: Delft silver, tapestries and ware; paintings of the Delft School; modern art, Delftware, ceramics
Activities: Classes for adults & children; mus shop sells books & prints

DORDRECHT

M DORDRECHTS MUSEUM, Museumstraat 40, Dordrecht, 3311 XP Netherlands. Tel 078 6482148; Fax 078-6141766; Elec Mail museum@dordt.nl; Internet Home Page Address: www.dordt.nl; *Dir* Dr S J M De Groot
Open Tues - Sun 11 AM - 5 PM, cl Mon
Collections: Dutch paintings, prints, drawings & sculpture, 17th to 20th century drawings, paintings & prints

EINDHOVEN

M VAN ABBEMUSEUM, Eindhoven Municipal Museum, Bilderdijklaan 10, Eindhoven, 5611 NH Netherlands; PO Box 235, Eindhoven, 5600 AE Netherlands. Tel 0031-40-2381000; Fax 0031-40-2460680; Elec Mail info@vanabbemuseum.nl; Internet Home Page Address: www.vanabbemuseum.nl; *Dir* C Esche
Open Tues - Wed & Fri - Sun 11 AM - 5 PM, Thurs 11 AM - 9 PM; Admis adults 9 euro, groups & over 65 yrs 7 euro, students 4 euro, children under 12 yrs free; Average Annual Attendance: 110,000
Library Holdings: Audio Tapes; Book Volumes; CD-ROMs; Clipping Files; Compact Disks; DVDs; Exhibition Catalogs; Kodachrome Transparencies; Original Documents; Pamphlets; Photographs; Slides; Video Tapes
Collections: Modern and contemporary art; Lissitzky Collection
Activities: Classes for adults & children; lects open to pub; concerts; tours; mus shop sells books, magazines, & other design items

ENSCHEDE

M **RIJKSMUSEUM TWENTHE,** Rijksmuseum Twenthe, Lasondersingel 129, Enschede, 7514 BP Netherlands. Tel 31 53 4358675; Elec Mail info@rijksmuseumtwenthe.nl; Internet Home Page Address: www.rijksmuseumtwenthe.nl; *Dir* Drs Arnoud Odding
Open Tues - Sun 11 AM - 5 PM; Admis adults 7 euro, students 5 euro, children up to 18 free; Estab 1930; wide & varied collection of art & applied art from the Middle Ages to present day. The museum wants to provide a space in which the visitor can walk through the history of art.; Library with 24,000 vols; mus with ca. 8600 objects; Average Annual Attendance: 45,000
Library Holdings: Auction Catalogs; Compact Disks; DVDs; Exhibition Catalogs; Manuscripts; Original Art Works
Special Subjects: Decorative Arts, Drawings, Etchings & Engravings, Landscape Architecture, Art Education, Art History, Conceptual Art, Glass, Metalwork, Mixed Media, Flasks & Bottles, Furniture, Porcelain, Pottery, Painting-American, Prints, Silver, Bronzes, Manuscripts, Sculpture, Watercolors, American Western Art, Religious Art, Ceramics, Crafts, Woodcarvings, Woodcuts, Collages, Painting-European, Portraits, Painting-Dutch, Ivory, Tapestries, Miniatures, Pewter, Bookplates & Bindings
Collections: Coll of paintings & sculptures from middle ages to present
Activities: Classes for adults & children; film programme; lects open to pub; lects for mems only; gallery talks; tours; mus shop sells books, magazines, original art, reproductions

GRONINGEN

M **GRONINGER MUSEUM,** Museumeiland 1, Groningen, 9711ME Netherlands; PO Box 90, Groningen, 9700ME Netherlands. Tel (050) 366 6555; Fax (050) 312 0815; Elec Mail info@groningermuseum.nl; Internet Home Page Address: www.groningermuseum.nl; *Dir* Dr Andreas Bluhm
Open Tues - Sun 10 AM - 5PM, Fri 10 AM - 10 PM, cl Mon; No admis fee; Estab 1894; Library with 35,000 vols; Average Annual Attendance: 200,000
Library Holdings: Auction Catalogs; Audio Tapes; Book Volumes; CD-ROMs; DVDs; Exhibition Catalogs; Periodical Subscriptions
Collections: Paintings & drawings from the 16th - 20th century, mainly Dutch, including Averkamp, Cuyp, Fabritius, Jordaens, Rembrandt, Rubens, Teniers; Oriental ceramics; local archaeology & history; contemporary photography, design, fashion
Activities: Classes for adults & children; lects open to pub; tours; mus shop sells books, original art

HAARLEM

M **FRANS HALS MUSEUM,** Groot Heiligland 62, Haarlem, 2011 ES Netherlands; PO Box 3365, Haarlem, 2001 DJ Netherlands. Tel 5115775; Fax 5115776; Elec Mail office@franshalsmuseum.nl; Internet Home Page Address: www.franshalsmuseum.nl; *Dir* K Schampers
Open Tues - Sat 11 AM - 5 PM, Sun & public holidays noon - 5 PM, cl Dec 25 & Jan 1; Admis adults 10 euro, groups 7 euro per person; 16th & 17th century art, that focused on Haarlem painters from that period; Average Annual Attendance: 100,000
Collections: Works by Frans Hals & Haarlem school; antique furniture; modern & contemporary art coll
Activities: Mus shop

M **TEYLERS MUSEUM,** Spaarne 16, Haarlem, 2011 CH Netherlands. Tel (023) 5160960; Fax (023) 531 2004; Elec Mail info@teylersmuseum.nl; Internet Home Page Address: www.teylersmuseum.nl
Open Tues - Sun, cl Mon; Admis see website; Library with 150,000 vols
Collections: Coins, drawings, fossils, historical physical instruments, medals, minerals & paintings
Exhibitions: For current exhibs check website
Activities: Classes for adults & children; lects open to pub; tours; mus shop sells books, magazines, reproductions & fossils

HERTOGENBOSCH

M **NOORDBRABANTS MUSEUM,** Verwersstraat 41, PO Box 1004 Hertogenbosch, 5200 BA Netherlands. Tel (73) 6877877; Fax (73) 877 899; Elec Mail info@noordbrabantsmuseum.nl; Internet Home Page Address: www.noordbrabantsmuseum.nl; *Dir* Ch de Moog
Open Tues - Fri 10 AM - 7 PM, Sat & Sun Noon - 7 PM; Average Annual Attendance: 85,000
Library Holdings: Auction Catalogs; Book Volumes; Compact Disks; DVDs; Exhibition Catalogs; Fiche; Pamphlets; Periodical Subscriptions; Photographs; Slides; Video Tapes
Special Subjects: Archaeology, Drawings, Architecture, Art Education, Art History, Glass, Photography, Silver, Tapestries, Sculpture, Religious Art, Crafts, Woodcarvings, Painting-Dutch, Coins & Medals, Baroque Art, Painting-Flemish, Renaissance Art
Collections: All colls have an emphasis on local history: archaeology, arts & crafts, coins & medals, painting & sculpture
Activities: Classes for adults & children; lects for members only; 4 vis lectrs per yr; gallery talks; tours; originate to other museums; sales of books, magazines, reproductions, prints & slides

HOORN

M **WESTFRIES MUSEUM,** Rode Steen 1, Achterom 2-4 Hoorn, 1621 KV Netherlands. Tel (229) 280028; Fax (229) 280029; Elec Mail info@wfm.nl; Internet Home Page Address: www.wfm.nl; *Dir* Ath Geerdink
Open Mon - Fri 11 AM - 5 PM, Sat & Sun 1 PM - 5 PM; Estab 1880; Historical museum

Special Subjects: Archaeology, Historical Material, Porcelain, Portraits, Silver, Glass, Painting-Dutch, Period Rooms, Pewter
Collections: 17th & 18th century paintings, prints, oak panelling, glass, pottery, furniture, costumes, interiors; folk art; historical objects from Hoorn & West Friesland; West Friesland native painting; prehistoric finds
Activities: Classes for children; lects open to pub; mus shop sells books, magazines, reproductions

LEERDAM

M **STICHTING NATIONAAL GLASMUSEUM,** National Glass Museum, Lingedijk 28, Leerdam, 4142 LD Netherlands. Tel (03451) 13662; Fax (03451) 13662; *Cur* Dr T G Te Dhits
Open Apr 1 - Oct 31: Tues - Sun 10 AM - 5 PM, cl Mon; Nov 1 - Mar 31: Tues - Fri 10 AM - 5 PM, cl Mon, Sat & Sun; Admis Adults 4.50 euro, children 3 euro
Collections: Antique, machine-made & packaging glass; art glass; unique pieces; contemporary Dutch collection & works from America & Europe

LEEUWARDEN

M **FRIES MUSEUM,** Turfmarkt 11, Leeuwarden, 8900 CE Netherlands. Tel 58 212 3001; Fax 58 213 2271
Open Tues - Sun 11 AM - 5 PM, cl Mon; Admis adults 5 euro, 18 & under 2 euro, children 13 & under free
Collections: Archaeology, ceramics, costumes, folk art, historical items, painting, prints and drawings, sculpture

LEIDEN

M **MUSEUM DE LAKENHAL,** (Municipal Museum De Lakenhal) Oude Singel 28-32, PO Box 2044 Leiden, 2301 CA Netherlands. Tel 31-0-71-5165360; Fax 31-0-71-5134489; Elec Mail postbus@lakenhal.nl; Internet Home Page Address: www.lakenhal.nl; *Dir* M Knol; *Pub Rels Officer* M Schat; *Cur Old Master Paintings* Dr C Y Y Vogelaar; *Cur Modern Art* Dr R Wolthoorn; *Cur Modern Art* Dr D Wintgenshotte; *Cur History Dept* Dr J Zijlmans
Open Tues - Fri 10 AM - 5 PM, Sat - Sun & holidays noon - 5 PM; Admis 18 - 65 yrs 7.50 euro, CJP & 65+ 4.50 euro, museum card holds & up to age 18 free; History & Art of Leiden from the Middle Ages to the present; Average Annual Attendance: 40,000
Special Subjects: Decorative Arts, Landscapes, Glass, Furniture, Gold, Photography, Portraits, Pottery, Silver, Textiles, Maps, Painting-European, Tapestries, Drawings, Graphics, Sculpture, Religious Art, Ceramics, Crafts, Portraits, Porcelain, Painting-Dutch, Carpets & Rugs, Coins & Medals, Renaissance Art, Period Rooms, Medieval Art, Stained Glass, Pewter
Collections: Altar pieces by Lucas van Leyden; paintings by Rembrandt, Steen, van Goyen; pictures of Leiden School & modern Leiden School; arms, ceramics, furniture, glass, period rooms, pewter, silver
Activities: Classes for children; lects open to pub; 4 vis lectrs per yr; concerts; tours; mus shop sells books, magazines, original art, reproductions & slides

M **RIJKSMUSEUM VAN OUDHEDEN,** National Museum of Antiques, Rapenburg 28, Leiden, 2311 EW Netherlands; PO Box 11114, Leiden, 2301 EC Netherlands. Tel 31-0-71-5163-163; Fax 31-0-71-5149-941; Elec Mail info@rmo.nl; Internet Home Page Address: www.rmo.nl; *Dir* W Weijland
Open Tues - Fri 10 AM - 5 PM, Sat - Sun noon - 5 PM, cl Mon; Admis adults 8.50 euro, children 4 -17 5.50 euro, seniors 7.50 euro
Collections: Consists of more than 80,000 objects; statues of Roman emperors, prehistoric gold jewelry, Egyptian mummy cases and Etruscan masterpieces in bronze

MUIDEN

M **MUIDERSLOT RIJKSMUSEUM,** State Museum at Muiden, Muiden, 1398 AA Netherlands. Tel (0294) 256262; Fax (0294) 261056; Elec Mail info@muiderslot.nl; Internet Home Page Address: www.muiderslot.nl; *Dir* Hilgers Michiels van Kesrenich; *Cur* Dr Y Molenaar
Open Apr - Nov: Mon - Sat 10 AM - 5 PM, Sun 1 PM - 5 PM; Nov - Apr: Sat - Sun 1 PM - 4 PM only guided tours; Admis adults 7 euro, children 4-12 5 euro
Collections: 13th century castle furnished in early Dutch Renaissance 17th century style; paintings, tapestries, furniture & armory; sculptures, modern; reconstructed Dutch herb & vegetable gardens
Activities: Classes for adults & children; historical flower arrangements; educ prog; concerts; mus shop sells books

NIJMEGEN

M **NIJMEEGS MUSEUM COMMANDERIE VAN ST JAN,** Franse Plaats 3, Nijmegen, 6511 VS Netherlands. Tel 080-22-91-93; *Dir* Dr G T M Lemmens
Collections: Art and history of Nijmegen and region: Middle Ages - 20th Century; modern international art

OTTERLO

M **KROLLER-MULLER MUSEUM,** (Rijksmuseum Kroller-Muller Museum) Nationale Park de Hoge Veluwe, Houtkampweg 6 Otterlo, Netherlands; Box nr 1, Otterlo, 6730 AA Netherlands. Tel (0318) 591241; Fax 591515; Elec Mail info@kmm.nl; Internet Home Page Address: www.kmm.nl; *Dir* Dr Evert J van Straaten; *Deputy Dir* M J Vonhof; *Head of Collections & Presentations* Drs L Kreyn; *Cur* Drs T van Kooten; *Mktg Drs* L Boelryk; *Press* Drs W Vermeulen; *Educ Drs* H Tibosch
Open Tues - Sun 10 AM - 5 PM, cl Mon & Jan 1; Admis adults: park 8 euro & museum 8 euro, children 6-12 yrs: park 4 euro & museum 4 euro, children 6 &

under free, combined tickets available; Estab 1938; Library with 35,000 vols/no pub library; Average Annual Attendance: 275,000

Special Subjects: Drawings, Painting-European, Sculpture, Painting-Dutch, Painting-Flemish

Collections: Van Gogh Collection; 19th and 20th century art - drawings, paintings, sculpture garden, ceramics, graphic arts, sculpture and sculpture drawings; Contemporary Art

Publications: Sculpture Garden - Van Gogh Drawings & Paintings

Activities: Educ prog; printed tax children 4+; lects open to pub; concerts; mus shop sells books, magazines, original art, reproductions, prints & gifts

ROTTERDAM

M **MUSEUM BOIJMANS VAN BEUNINGEN,** Museum Park 18-20, Rotterdam, 3015 CX Netherlands; POB 2277, Rotterdam, 3000 CG Netherlands. Tel 010-441-9400; Fax 31(0) 10 43 60 500; Elec Mail info@boijmans.nl; Internet Home Page Address: www.boijmans.nl; *Mng Dir* Mrs I Klaassen; *Presentations* Mrs C Jacob; *Publicity & Mktg* Mrs S van Dongen; *Collections* Mrs P Wageman; *Dir* Sjarel Ex
Open Tues - Sun 11 AM - 5 PM, cl Mon, Jan 1, Apr 27, Dec 25; Admis adults 12.50 euro, students 6.25 euro, children under 18, ICOM card holders free; Average Annual Attendance: 200,000

Collections: Dutch school paintings including Bosch, Hals, Rembrandt, Van Eyck; 15th-20th century Dutch, Flemish, French, German, Italian & Spanish works; Baroque School; Impressionists; old, modern & contemporary sculpture; Dutch, Italian, Persian & Spanish pottery & tiles; Dutch design

Activities: Classes for children and adults; lects open to pub; concerts, gallery talks, tours, scholarships; mus shop sells books, reproductions, prints; Museumpark 18-20 POB 2277 3000 CG Rotterdam

THE HAGUE

M **HAAGS GEMEENTEMUSEUM,** Municipal Museum of The Hague, Stadhouderslaan 41, The Hague, 2517 HV Netherlands. Tel (070) 338 1111; Fax (070) 355 7360; Telex 3-6990; *Dir* Dr J L Locher
Open Tues - Sun 11 AM - 5 PM; Admis adults 9 euro, seniors 65+ 7 euro, students 5.50 euro, children up to 18 yrs free, groups 15 or more 7 euro, Ooievaarspas 4.50 euro, Fri free

Collections: Decorative Arts Collection includes ceramics, furniture, glass, silver; modern art of 19th & 20th century; musical instruments; history of The Hague

M **KONINKLIJK KABINET VAN SCHILDERIJEN MAURITSHUIS,** Royal Picture Gallery Mauritshuis, Korte Vijverberg 8, The Hague, 2513 AB Netherlands; PO Box 536, The Hague, 2501 CM Netherlands. Tel (070) 3023456; Fax (070) 3653819; Elec Mail secretariaat@Mauritshuis.nl; Internet Home Page Address: www.mauritshuis.nl; *Dir* Dr E E S Gordenker
Open Tues - Sat 10 AM - 5 PM, Sun 11 AM - 5 PM. Due to expansion & renovation the mus will be cl from Apr 2012 - Apr 2016. A selection of the coll will be on display at the Gemeentemuseum, The Hague (www.mauritshuisbuilds.com); Admis adults 10.50 Euro (until Nov 11), children free; Estab 1822; Picture gallery; Average Annual Attendance: 200,000

Library Holdings: Auction Catalogs; Book Volumes; Exhibition Catalogs; Kodachrome Transparencies; Periodical Subscriptions; Photographs; Reproductions

Collections: Paintings of the Dutch and Flemish Masters of the 15th, 16th, mainly 17th and 18th centuries, including G David, Holbein, Hals, Rembrandt, Van Dyck, Vermeer, Steen, Rubens

Publications: Made in Holland; Jan Steen In the Mauritshuis

Activities: Classes & progs for children; docent training; lects for mems; 12 vis lectrs per yr; guided tours; Frits Duparc Prize; mus shop sells books, magazines, reproductions, prints, slides & other gift items

NEW ZEALAND

AUCKLAND

M **AUCKLAND CITY ART GALLERY,** 5 Kitchener St, Auckland, 1 New Zealand; PO Box 5449, Auckland, 1 New Zealand. Tel (09) 307-7700; Fax (09) 302-1096; *Dir* Chris Saines
Open daily 10 AM - 5 PM, cl Christmas & Easter Fri; Admis adults $7, concession $5, Friends of Gallery $4, children 5 & under free, multi-pass available; Library with 33,000 vols

Collections: American & Australian paintings; general collection of European paintings & sculpture from 12th century on; historical & contemporary New Zealand painting, sculpture & prints

M **LOPDELL HOUSE GALLERY,** Titirangi & South Titirangi Roads, Auckland, 0604 New Zealand; PO Box 60109, Titirangi Auckland, 0604 New Zealand. Tel +64-9-817-8087; Fax +64-9 817 3340; Elec Mail info@lopdell.org.nz; Internet Home Page Address: www.lopdell.org.nz
Open daily 10AM-4:30PM; No admis fee; Estab 1990 as art gallery; Waitakere City Regional Art Gallery; Average Annual Attendance: 30,000

Publications: Len Castle: Making the Molecules Dance; Blast! Pat Hanley - the Painter & his Protests by Trish Cribben; To the Harbour by Stanley Palmer

Activities: Classes for adults & children; lects open to pub; concerts; gallery talks; tours; Secondary School Art Awards; Portage Ceramic Awards; exten dept lends original objects of art to schools; originates traveling exhibs to New Zealand Art Galleries; sales shop sells books, magazines, original art, reproductions, prints

L **UNIVERSITY OF AUCKLAND,** Elam School of Fine Arts Library, School of Fine Arts, Pvt Bag 92019 Auckland, 1142 New Zealand. Tel 0064 09 373 7599; Fax 0064 09 308 2302; Elec Mail elam-enquiries@auckland.ac.nz; Internet Home Page Address: www.auckland.ac.nz; *Dean of Elam School of Fine Arts* Jolyon D Saunders
Library with 30,000 vols

CHRISTCHURCH

M **CHRISTCHURCH ART GALLERY,** Cnr Worcester Blvd & Montreal St, PO Box 2626 Christchurch, 8140 New Zealand. Tel 64-3-941-7300; Fax 64-3-941-7301; Elec Mail art.gallery@ccc.govt.nz; Internet Home Page Address: www.christchurchartgallery.org.nz; *Dir* Jenny Harper
Open Mon - Tues & Thurs - Sun 10 AM - 5 PM, Wed 10 AM - 9 PM; No admis fee

Collections: Permanent collection of historical, 20th century and contemporary art; Collections of works on paper, glass, and traditional craft

DUNEDIN

M **DUNEDIN PUBLIC ART GALLERY,** The Octagon, Dunedin, New Zealand; PO Box 566, Dunedin, New Zealand. Tel (+643) 474 3240; Fax (+643) 474 3250; Elec Mail dpagmail@dcc.govt.nz; Internet Home Page Address: dunedin.art.museum
Open daily 9 AM - 5 PM, cl Christmas Day; No admis fee, except for special exhibs; Estab 1884; Average Annual Attendance: 180,000

Income: Local authority supplemented with grants, sponsorship, retail, hire of commercial spaces

Collections: 15th - 19th century European paintings; New Zealand paintings since 1876; Australian paintings 1900-60; British watercolors, portraits and landscapes; ancillary colls of furniture, ceramics, glass, silver, oriental rugs; De Beer coll of Old Masters, including Monet; Contemporary New Zealand Art

Activities: Classes for children; lects open to pub; concerts; gallery talks; tours; film screenings; 3 - 4 book traveling exhibs; originate traveling exhibs throughout New Zealand; mus shop sells books, magazines & reproductions

HAMILTON

M **WAIKATO MUSEUM,** 1 Grantham St, Hamilton, New Zealand; Private Bag 3010, Hamilton, 2020 New Zealand. Tel 07-838-6606; Elec Mail museum@hcc.govt.nz; Internet Home Page Address: www.waikatomuseum.co.nz; *Contact* Pauline Farquhar
Open daily 10 AM - 4:30 PM, cl Christmas Day; No admis fee; Maintains 8 galleries with various collections

Collections: Art coll is made up of 2500 pieces; Early years of European settlement; Images and artists of the Waikato region; Wood and stone carvings, flax weaving, adzes, waka, korowai, taiaha, ritual and archaeological materials, photographs

INVERCARGILL

M **ANDERSON PARK ART GALLERY INC,** Art Gallery, 91 McIvor Rd, Invercargill, New Zealand; PO Box 5095, Invercargill, 9843 New Zealand. Tel 03-215-7432; Fax 03-215-7472; Elec Mail andersonparkgallery@xtra.co.nz; Internet Home Page Address: www.andersonparkgallery.co.nz; *Mgr* Helen Nicoll; *Asst Mgr* Sarah Brown
Open daily 10:30 AM - 5 PM; cl Good Friday & Christmas Day; Admis by donation; Estab 1951; Historic house & pub gallery; Average Annual Attendance: Under 20,000; Mem: 254 mems, $30 double

Income: Grant from Invercargill City Council

Special Subjects: Bronzes, Painting-British, Ceramics, Painting-New Zealand

Collections: Contemporary New Zealand art

Exhibitions: Annual spring Exhib (Oct)

Publications: 50th Anniversary Book Release; How MacGoun Saw Southland, A Selection of Early Watercolors; How MacGoun Saw Southland, Booklet

Activities: Gallery talks; Tours; award given at annual exhib; exten prog to other galleries; mus shop sells prints, 50th Jubilee booklet - How Mac Goun Saw Southland

NAPIER

M **HAWKES BAY ART GALLERY AND MUSEUM,** 9 Herschell St, PO Box 248 Napier, New Zealand. Tel (6) 835-7781; Fax (6) 835-3984; Elec Mail info@hbmdg.co.nz; Internet Home Page Address: www.hbmdg.co.nz; *Dir* Douglas Lloyd Jenkins
Open Mon - Wed & Fri - Sun 10AM-6PM, Thurs 10AM-8PM; Admis adults $10, $9 students, children under 5 free; Average Annual Attendance: 220,000; Mem: 1200; Friends of the Heart

Library Holdings: Audio Tapes; Book Volumes; Cassettes; Clipping Files; Exhibition Catalogs; Kodachrome Transparencies; Lantern Slides; Manuscripts; Maps; Memorabilia; Original Art Works; Original Documents; Pamphlets; Periodical Subscriptions; Photographs; Prints; Records; Sculpture; Slides; Video Tapes

Special Subjects: Decorative Arts, Drawings, Historical Material, Landscapes, Art History, Ceramics, Glass, Pottery, Prints, Manuscripts, Tapestries, Architecture, Photography, Sculpture, Textiles, Costumes, Crafts, Primitive art, Etchings & Engravings, Portraits, Furniture, Jewelry, Maps, Embroidery

Collections: Antiques; Maori & Pacific artifacts; New Zealand painting & sculpture

Activities: Classes for children; Lects open to pub & members only; vis lectrs every year; Mus shop sells books, magazines, reproductions, prints, cards, and other items

PORIRUA CITY

M **PATAKA MUSEUM AND GALLERY,** Cnr Norrie and Parumoana St, PO Box 50218 Porirua City, New Zealand. Tel 64-4-237-1511; Fax 64-4-237-4527; Elec Mail pataka@pcc.govt.nz; Internet Home Page Address: www.pataka.org.nz; *Cur* Helen Kedgley; *Cur* Bob Maysmor; *Gen Mgr* Darcy Nicholas
Open Mon - Sat 10 AM - 4:30 PM, Sun 11 AM - 4:30 PM

Collections: Contemporary Maori, Pacific Island and New Zealand art; historical & ethnographic artifacts

WANGANUI

M **SARJEANT GALLERY,** PO Box 998, Queen's Park Wanganui, 4500 New Zealand. Tel (06) 349 0506; Fax (06) 349 0507; Elec Mail info@sarjeant.queenspark.org.nz; Internet Home Page Address: www.sarjeant.org.nz; *Sr Cur* Greg Anderson; *Cur/Pub Prog Mgr* Greg Donson; *Events & Communs Officer* Raewyne Johnson; *Educ Officer* Sietske Jansma; *Educ Officer* Andrea Cardner; *Technician* Garry George; *Technical Servs Coordr* Richard Wotton; *Opers Mgr* Paula Allen; *Asst Cur* Sarah McClintock; *Admin Officer* Teresa Wakefield
Open Mon - Sun & public holidays 10:30 AM - 4:30 PM, Anzac Day 1 PM - 4:30 PM, cl Good Fri & Christmas Day; No admis fee, donations welcome; Estab 1919; built as Art Gallery
Income: Financed by Wanganie Dist Council
Library Holdings: Auction Catalogs; Book Volumes; Clipping Files; Exhibition Catalogs; Periodical Subscriptions
Collections: New Zealand art with a strong photographic focus & regional art; First World War cartoons & posters; 19th & early 20th Century British & European art
Exhibitions: Approx 22 per year
Activities: Classes for children; artist in residence prog; shop specializes in glass & jewelry; gallery talks; events; venue for private functions

WELLINGTON

M **MUSEUM OF NEW ZEALAND TE PAPA TONGAREWA,** (National Art Gallery of New Zealand) Museum of New Zealand Te Papa Tongarewa, Cable St, Wellington, New Zealand. Tel 64 (4) 381 7000; Fax 64 (4) 381 7070; Elec Mail mail@tepapa.govt.nz; Internet Home Page Address: www.tepapa.govt.nz; *CEO & Dir* Dr Michael Houlihan; *Head Arts & Visual Culture* Jonathan Mane-Wheoki
Open Mon - Wed & Fri - Sun 10 AM - 6 PM, Thurs 10 AM - 9 PM; No admis fee; Estab Feb 1998; Library with 20,000 vols; Average Annual Attendance: 1,300,000
Collections: Australian, British, European & New Zealand art; Sir Harold Beauchamp Collection of early English drawings, illustrations & watercolors; Sir John Ilott Collection of prints; Nan Kivell Collection of British original prints; Monrad Collection of early European graphics; collection of Old Master drawings
Activities: Classes for children; lects open to pub; concerts; gallery talks; tours; mus shop sells books, magazines, original art, reproductions & prints

NICARAGUA

MANAGUA

M **EL MUSEO NACIONAL DE NICARAGUA DIOCLESIANO CHAVEZ,** National Museum of Nicaragua, National Palace, Plaza de la Republica Managua, Nicaragua. *Dir* Edgar Espinoza
Open Mon - Fri 8 AM - 5 PM, Sat - Sun 9 AM - 4 PM; Admis adults C$12, foreigners C$2, primary school C$3, college and high school C$5
Collections: National archaeological and ethnographic history artifacts; Pre-Columbian ceramics & traditional art; Latin American paintings, metate stone artifacts, Gueguense room; Rodrigo Penalba Collection

NORWAY

BERGEN

M **BERGEN MUSEUM OF ART,** Rasmus Meyers alle 9, Bergen, 5015 Norway. Tel +47-55-56-80-00; Fax +47-55-56-80-11; Elec Mail post@kunstmuseene.no; Internet Home Page Address: www.bergenartmuseum.no
Circ

M **VESTLANDSKE KUNSTINDUSTRIMUSEUM,** West Norway Museum of Decorative Art, Nordahl Brunsgate 9, Bergen, 5014 Norway. Tel (55) 33-66-33; Fax (55) 33-66-30; Elec Mail bibliotek@vk.museum.no; Internet Home Page Address: www.vk.museum.no; www.vk.museum.no/english/index.php; *Mus Dir* Jorunn Haakestad
Library with 20,000 vols
Library Holdings: Book Volumes; Exhibition Catalogs
Collections: Contemporary Norwegian and European ceramics, furniture, textiles; The General Munthe Collection of Chinese Art; collections of old European arts and crafts; The Anna B and William H Singer Collection of art and antiquities
Activities: Classes for children; tours; mus shop sells books & magazines

HAUGESUND

M **HAUGESUND BILLEDGALLERI,** Erling Skjalgssonsgt 4, Haugesund, 5501 Norway; Postboks 147, Haugesund, 5501 Norway. Tel 52-72-34-71; Fax 52-72-94-42; Elec Mail postmottak.billedgalleriet@haugesund.kommune.no; Internet Home Page Address: www.haugesund-billedgalleri.net
Open Tues - Wed & Fri - Sat noon - 3 PM, Thurs noon - 7 PM, Sun noon - 5 PM, cl Mon.

HORTEN

M **NORSK MUSEUM OF FOTOGRAFI,** P B 254 Horten, NO-3192 Norway. Tel 47 33 03 16 30; Elec Mail post@foto.museum.no
Collections: Photography

M **PREUS MUSEUM,** Kulturparken Karliohansvern, Horten, 3183 Norway; PO Box 254, Horten, 3192 Norway. Tel +47-330-31630; Elec Mail post@preusmuseum.no; Internet Home Page Address: www.preusmuseum.no/english/index.php

LILLEHAMMER

M **LILLEHAMMER KUNSTMUSEUM,** Lillehammer Municipal Art Gallery, PO Box 264, Stortorget 2 Lillehammer, 2601 Norway. Tel 61269444; Fax 61251944; *Exec Dir* Svein Olav Hoff
Collections: Norwegian paintings, sculpture and graphic art from 19th and 20th centuries

OSLO

M **KUNSTINDUSTRIMUSEET I OSLO,** Museum of Decorative Arts & Design, Oslo, St Olavs Gate 1, Oslo, 0165 Norway. Tel 22 203578; Fax 22 11 39 71; Elec Mail museum@kunstindustrimuseet.no; Internet Home Page Address: http://www.kunstindustrimuseet.no
Open Tues - Sun 11 AM - 3 PM, cl Mon; Estab 1876; Library with 52,000 vols
Collections: Collection from the 600s to the present of applied arts, fashion & design with ceramics, furniture, glass, silver, textiles from Norway, Europe & Far East

M **NASJONALGALLERIET,** Post Box 7014, St. Olavs plass, Universitetsgaten 13 Oslo, 0130 Norway. Tel (47) 22200404; Fax (47) 22261132; Elec Mail nga@nasjonalgalleriet.ho; Internet Home Page Address: www.nasjonalgalleriet.no; *Dir* Annichen Thue; *Chief Rest* Françoise Hanssen-Bauer; *Deputy Dir* Sitsel Hethedser; *Chief Cur Painting & Sculpture* Marit J Lange; *Cur of Prints & Drawings* Nils Hessel
Open Mon, Wed & Fri 10 AM - 6 PM, Thurs 10 AM - 8 PM, Sat 10 AM - 3 PM, Sun 11 AM - 3 PM, cl Tues; No admis fee; Library with 80,000 vols; Average Annual Attendance: 350,000
Income: Government grant; NSK 43,878,000
Library Holdings: Auction Catalogs; Book Volumes; Exhibition Catalogs; Pamphlets; Periodical Subscriptions; Slides
Collections: Norwegian paintings & sculpture; Old European paintings; icon coll; especially of modern French, Danish & Swedish art; a coll of prints & drawings; a small coll of Greek & Roman sculptures; the colls of paintings & sculpture up to 1945
Activities: Educ prog; lects open to pub; concerts; gallery talks

M **NORSK FOLKEMUSEUM,** Norwegian Folk Museum, Bygdoy, Museum Veien 10 Oslo, 0287 Norway; PO Box 720 Skoyen, Oslo, N-0214 Norway. Tel 22123700; Fax 22 12 37 77; Elec Mail post@norskfolkemuseum.no; Internet Home Page Address: www.norskfolkemuseum.no; *Dir* Olav Aavaas
Open summer: 10 - 18; winter: 11 - 15; Estab 1894; Mus of cultural history; Average Annual Attendance: 250,000
Collections: The Sami section provides an insight into the ancient culture of the Sami people. The Open Air Museum totals about 160 old buildings, all original. Among them are the 13th century Gol stave church; farmsteads from different districts of the country; single buildings of particular interest; The Old Town: 17th, 18th, 19th & 20th centuries town houses; Urban Colls; other colls include folk art & church history
Activities: Classes for adults & children; dramatic progs; lects open to pub; concerts; tours; mus shop sells books, replicas, gift items & souvenirs

M **NORSK SJØFARTSMUSEUM,** Norwegian Maritime Museum, Bygdoynesveien 37, Oslo, N-0286 Norway. Tel 4724114150; Fax 4724114151; Elec Mail fellespost@norsk-sjofartsmuseum.no; Internet Home Page Address: www.norsk-sjofartsmuseum.no; *Dir* Petter C Omtvedt; *Librn* Lisa Benson; *Research Cur* Per G Norseng
Open May 15 - Aug 31, 10 AM - 6 PM, Sept 1 - May 14, 10:30 AM - 4 PM; library cl in July; Admis adults NOK 40, students & seniors NOK 25, children free; Estab 1914; Library with 30,000 vols; Mem: Friends of Norsk Sjofartsmuseum
Library Holdings: Clipping Files; Manuscripts; Maps; Original Documents; Pamphlets; Periodical Subscriptions; Photographs; Prints
Special Subjects: Historical Material, Photography, Sculpture, Drawings, Prints, Archaeology, Marine Painting, Miniatures, Dioramas, Painting-Scandinavian
Collections: Amundsen's Gjoa; archives pertaining to maritime history; instruments, paintings, photographs of ships, ship models, tools & other items pertaining to maritime colls, shop and boat plans
Publications: Yearbook
Activities: Classes for adults; panoramic movies of the Coast of Norway and Oslo; lects open to pub; mus shop sells books, reproductions, prints, maritime objects

M **OSLO MUSEUM,** (Internasjonalt Kutlursenter & Museum IKM) Gallery IKM, Toyenbekken 5, Oslo, NO-0188 Norway. Tel 47 22 05 28 30; Elec Mail post@oslomuseum.no; Internet Home Page Address: www.oslomuseum.no
Open Tues - Sun 11 AM - 4 PM; Admis free
Collections: Documentation on immigration history & cultural changes in Norwegian society.; visual arts

L **STATENS KUNSTAKADEMI BIBLIOTEKET,** National Academy of Fine Arts Library, St Olavs Gate 32, Oslo, 0166 Norway. Tel 22-99-55-30; Fax 22-99-55-33; *Rector of Academy* Jan Ake Petterson
Library with 6000 volumes to support training by 14 teachers of 130 students

M **UNIVERSITETETS OLDSAKSAMLING,** University Museum of National Antiquities, Frederiksgate 2, Oslo, 0164 Norway. Tel 22416300; *Dir* Egil Mikkelsen
Collections: Archaeological finds from Norwegian Stone, Bronze & Iron Ages, also Medieval age, including religious art, 70,000 exhibits from prehistoric & Viking times, including Middle Ages

M **VIGELAND MUSEUM,** Nobelsgt 32, Oslo, 0268 Norway; City of Oslo Agency for Cultural Affairs and Sports Facilities, Postboks 1453 VIka Oslo, 0116 Norway. Tel 23-49-37-00; Fax 23-49-37-01; Internet Home Page Address: www.museumsnett.no/vigelandmuseet/eindex.htm; *Cur* Jarle Stromodden
Open Sept 1 - May 30 Tue - Sun 12 PM - 4 PM; June 1 - Aug 31 Tue - Sun 10 AM - 5 PM, cl Mon; Admis adults NOK 45, children 7-16 students & seniors NOK 25
Collections: Entire production of work by Gustav Vigeland; Sculptures in plaster, granite, bronze, marble, wrought iron; Thousands of drawings, woodcuts, woodcarvings; Original casts of sculpture work

OMAN

MUSCAT

M **MUSEUM OF OMANI HERITAGE,** Al Alam St, Way 1566 Muscat, Oman. Tel 96824600946; *Dir Gen* Hassan bin Mohammad bin Al Aliluwati
Open Sat - Wed 8 AM - 1:30 PM, Thurs 4 PM - 6 PM; Admis adults 500 bzs, children 200 bzs, under 6 100 bzs
Collections: Detailed archaeological and ethnographic items of Omani history and culture; Minerals, architecture, dhows, armaments, traditional arts and crafts

RUWI

M **NATIONAL MUSEUM OF OMAN,** Way 3123, A'Noor St Ruwi, Oman. Tel 96824701289
Open Sat - Thurs 9:30 AM - 1:30 PM; Admis adults 500 bzs, children 200 bzs, under 6 100 bzs
Collections: Costumes, jewelry, Omani silverwork, photographs, paintings and household items; Artifacts from the lives of five Sultans under the Al Said dynasty

PAKISTAN

KARACHI

M **NATIONAL MUSEUM OF PAKISTAN,** Burns Garden, Karachi, 74200 Pakistan. Tel (021)-2633881-2628280-2639930; *Supt* Mohammad Arif
Open daily 10 AM - 5 PM, cl Wed; Admis PK.RS. 4, students free; Estab 1971 as archaeological & history mus for preservation of cultural heritage & educ; Average Annual Attendance: 150,000
Collections: Antiquities dating from 7000 BC to modern times, large coll of coins and miniature paintings spreading from 6th century BC to present; ethnological material from the various regions of Pakistan; Buddhist and Hindu sculptures; paleolithic implements; handicrafts and manuscripts of the Muslim period; collection of defunct Victoria Museum
Activities: Originates traveling exhibs to USA, Germany, Japan, Korea & various other countries

LAHORE

M **LAHORE MUSEUM,** Shahrah-e-Quaid-e-Azam, Lahore, Pakistan. Tel 042-9210804-5; Fax 042-9210810; Elec Mail ihrmuseum@hot-mail.com; *Dir* Ms. Humera Alam; *Deputy Dir & Cur* Ms Naushaba Anjum; *Sr Librn* Mr Bashir Ahmed Bhatti; *Keeper Coins* Ms Naushaba Anjum; *Deputy Dir Admin* Mr Khuaja Khurshid Anwar
Open 9 AM - 5 PM; Admis foreigner Rs 100, adults Rs 10, children Rs 2; Estab 1864 to showcase cultural heritage; Average Annual Attendance: 282,213
Income: Punjals (Provincial Government) Pakistan
Purchases: Through acquisition committee/purchase committee
Library Holdings: Audio Tapes; Book Volumes 30,000; CD-ROMs; Cards; Cassettes; Clipping Files; Compact Disks; DVDs; Exhibition Catalogs; Fiche; Filmstrips; Framed Reproductions; Kodachrome Transparencies; Lantern Slides; Manuscripts; Maps; Memorabilia; Micro Print; Motion Pictures; Original Art Works; Original Documents; Pamphlets; Periodical Subscriptions; Photographs; Prints; Records; Reels; Reproductions; Sculpture; Slides; Video Tapes
Special Subjects: Archaeology, Decorative Arts, Historical Material, Architecture, Ceramics, Furniture, Textiles, Bronzes, Manuscripts, Watercolors, Costumes, Crafts, Asian Art, Carpets & Rugs, Coins & Medals, Restorations, Baroque Art, Miniatures, Renaissance Art, Embroidery, Antiquities-Persian, Islamic Art, Leather, Reproductions
Collections: Greco-Buddhist sculpture; Indo-Pakistan coins; miniature paintings; local arts; armor; stamps; Oriental porcelain & manuscripts; Islamic calligraphy; Stone Age material, pre and pro historic antiquities
Publications: Guides, catalogues on collection, research journal (Lahore Museum Bulletin)
Activities: Classes for adults & children; dramatic prog; internships; lects open to pub; 6 vis lectrs per yr; concerts; tours; lending original objects of art to world mus on governmental basis and to museums within the country; mus shop sells books, magazines, reproductions, prints, slides & other replicas of mus objects; Lahore City Heritage Museum as part of Lahore Museum

PALAU

KOROR

M **BELAU NATIONAL MUSEUM,** PO Box 666, Koror, 96940 Palau. Tel 680-488-2265; Fax 680-488-3183; Elec Mail info@belaunationalmuseum.com; Internet Home Page Address: www.belaunationalmuseum.com/index.html; *Dir & Cur* Faustina K Rehuher-Marugg
Collections: Five major colls including cultural objects, media, traditional and contemporary art, natural history and a research library; 4000 items relating to anthropology, art, and history; Over 20,000 photographic slides, 6000 prints, negatives, films, videos and recordings; Photos of Palau and Micronesia from the 18th century to the present; Ethnographic history of Palau people and culture

PANAMA

PANAMA CITY

M **MUSEO DE ARTE CONTEMPORANEO,** Av de los Martires, Calle San Blas Panama City, Panama. Tel 262-8012, 3380; Fax 262-3376; Internet Home Page Address: www.macpanama.org; *Exec Dir* Maria Fabrega de Arosemena; *Cur* Nuria Madrid
Open Tues - Sun 9 AM - 5 PM, Thurs 9 AM - 9 PM, cl Mon; Admis adults $2, children & seniors $1, students 0.50
Collections: Permanent coll of watercolor and oil paintings by contemporary Panamanian artists

PAPUA NEW GUINEA

BOROKO

M **PAPUA NEW GUINEA NATIONAL MUSEUM & ART GALLERY,** PO Box 5560, Boroko, Papua New Guinea. Tel 252405; Fax 259 447; *Dir* Soroi Marepo Eoe
Library with 4500 vols

PARAGUAY

ASUNCION

M **CENTRO DE ARTES VISUALES,** Museo Del Baro, Calle Grabadores del Cabichui, Canada y Emeterio Miranda Asuncion, Paraguay. Tel 595-21-601-996; Elec Mail museodelbarro@hotmail.com; Internet Home Page Address: www.museodelbarro.org; *Dir* Ticio Escobar
Open Thurs - Sat 3:30 PM - 8 PM; Admis Thurs & Sat adults 7gs, students 3gs; Fri no admis fee
Collections: Popular art by professional and amateur artists in Paraguay
M **Museo De Arte Indigena,**
Collections: Indigenous and traditional art and craft of Paraguay
M **Museo Paraguayo de Arte Contemporaneo,**
Collections: Contemporary and modern art from international and local artists; 300 engravings of Jose Guadalupe Posada; Guerra Grande photographic coll; Ignacio Nunez Soler Photography Coll; Miguel Acevedo drawing coll; Dora Guimaraes coll of 1175 drawings and engravings; Oscar Manesi Spanish and Latin American coll

M **MUSEO NACIONAL DE BELLAS ARTES,** Mariscal Estigarribia y Iturbe, Asuncion, Paraguay. *Dir* Jose Laterza Parodi
Collections: Paintings and sculptures

PERU

LIMA

M **MUSEO DE ARTE DE LIMA,** Lima Museum of Art, Paseo Colon 125, Lima, Peru. Tel (51-1) 42 34 732; Fax (51-1) 42 36 332; *Dir* Pedro Pablo Alayza
Collections: Peruvian art throughout history; Colonial painting; carvings, ceramics, furniture, metals, modern paintings, religious art, sculpture, textiles

M **MUSEO NACIONAL DE LA CULTURA PERUANA,** National Museum of Peruvian Culture, Avenida Alfonso Ugarte 650, Apdo 3048 Lima, 100 Peru. Tel 4235892; *Dir* Sara Acevedo Basurto
Collections: Ethnology, folklore, popular art

PHILIPPINES

MAKATI CITY

M **AYALA MUSEUM,** Makati Ave cnr De La Rosa St, Greenbelt Park Ayala Center Makati City, 1224 Philippines. Tel 632-757-7117; Fax 632-757-2787; Elec Mail museum_inquiry@ayalamuseum.org; Internet Home Page Address: www.ayalamuseum.org; *Dir* Florina Baker
Open Tues - Fri 9 AM - 6 PM, Sat - Sun 10 AM - 7 PM, cl Mon; Admis non-resident: adults PHP 350, children, students & seniors PHP 250; resident: adults PHP 150, children, students & seniors PHP 75

Collections: Dioramas of Philippine history, boat gallery, 19th century paintings, work by Fernando Amorsolo, Fernando Zoebel de Ayala y Montojo; Ethnographic coll of artifacts from Philippine history

MANILA

M **METROPOLITAN MUSEUM OF MANILA,** Bangko Sentral, ng Pilipinas Complex/Roxas Blvd Manila, Philippines. Tel (632) 536-1566; Fax (632) 528-0613; Elec Mail art4all@info.com.ph; *Pres, CEO* Corazón S Alvina
Open Mon - Sat 10 AM to 6 PM; Admis P50.00/P30.00; Estab 1976; initially to show foreign art; Average Annual Attendance: 240,000
Income: Financed from foundation
Library Holdings: Audio Tapes; Book Volumes; Cassettes; Exhibition Catalogs; Kodachrome Transparencies; Manuscripts; Pamphlets; Periodical Subscriptions; Photographs; Prints; Slides
Special Subjects: Pottery, Asian Art
Collections: Fine arts museum; paintings, graphic arts, sculptures & decorative arts
Publications: Catalogues, books on Filipino art & artists
Activities: Classes for adults & children; docent training; lects open to pub; 4 vis lectrs per year; gallery talks; provincial capitals; originate non-traditional rural traveling exhibs; sales of books

M **NATIONAL MUSEUM OF THE PHILIPPINES,** POB 2659, Padre Burgos St Manila, 1000 Philippines. Tel (632) 5271215; Fax 632-527-0306; Elec Mail directornmph@yahoo.com; Internet Home Page Address: www.nationalmuseum.gov.ph; *Dir* Corazon S Alvina; *Asst Dir* Cecilio G Salcedo; *Cur II, Med* Elenita D V Alba; *Cur II, Arch* Wilfredo Ronquillo; *Asst Dir* Maharlika A Cuevas; *Cur II, Conservation* Orlando Abinion; *Cur II, Sites & Branches* Angelita Fucanan; *Cur II, Geology* Roberto de Ocampo; *Cur II, Botany* Domingo Madulid PhD; *Cur II, Anthropology* Artemio Barbosa; *Cur II Zoology* Virgilio Pal Pal-Latoc; *Cur I Cultural Properties* Angel Bautista; *Cur II Restoration* Arnulfo F Dado
Open 10 AM - 4:30 PM; Admis adults 100.00 each, students 30.00 each upon presentation of ID; Estab October 29, 1901 - to protect, preserve & disseminate the heritage of the Filipino people; Arts/Anthropological/Archaeological/Zoological/Botanical & Geological; Average Annual Attendance: 201,383
Income: Varies yearly/financed by Philippine gov
Purchases: Paintings, specimens
Library Holdings: Audio Tapes; Book Volumes; CD-ROMs; Cassettes; Clipping Files; Compact Disks; DVDs; Exhibition Catalogs; Kodachrome Transparencies; Manuscripts; Original Art Works; Original Documents; Pamphlets; Periodical Subscriptions; Photographs; Prints; Reproductions; Sculpture; Slides; Video Tapes
Special Subjects: Anthropology, Archaeology, Decorative Arts, Drawings, Folk Art, Ceramics, Textiles, Sculpture, Ethnology, Costumes, Crafts, Landscapes, Asian Art, Ivory, Dioramas, Embroidery, Islamic Art
Collections: Fine arts, cultural, archaeological, sciences colls; Textile, arts & crafts, paintings, photographs, drawings
Exhibitions: Best of Philippine Art; San Diego Exhibits; Cloth Traditions; Juan Luna Exhibs; 5 Centuries of Maritime Trade before the Coming of the West; National Art Gallery permanent exhib
Publications: Nat Museum Papers; Ann Reports; A Voyage of 100 Years; Art-i-facts (newsletter)
Activities: Docent training; gallery talks; tours; sponsoring of competitions; lects for staff only; lectrs minimum one per month, concerts; metro Manila & suburbs; schools, universities & other institutions; nationwide; 19 Branches countrywide; Branches, schools, universities, local government units & other institutions; mus shop sells books, slides, magazines, crafts, prints & contemporary productions

PASIG CITY

M **LOPEZ MEMORIAL MUSEUM,** G/F Benpres Bldg, Exchange Rd & Meralco Ave, Ortigas Ctr Pasig City, Philippines. Tel 632-631-2417; Elec Mail pezseum@skyinet.net; Internet Home Page Address: www.lopezmuseum.org.ph/index.html; *Dir* Mercedes Lopez Vargas
Open Mon - Fri 8 AM - 5 PM, Sat 7:30 AM - 4 PM; Admis adults PHP 60, college students PHP 40, high school students PHP 30
Collections: 600 years of Filipino art and artistic history; 14th-15th century artifacts; Maps, rare books, manuscripts; Ming Dynasty porcelain

POLAND

BARANOW SANDOMIERSKI

M **CASTLE IN BARANOW,** Museum of Interiors, Zamkowa St 20, 39-450, Baranow Sandomierski, Poland. Tel 48 15 811 80 39; Fax 48 15 811 80 40; Elec Mail hotel.zamkowy@baranow.arp.com.pl; Internet Home Page Address: www.baranow.com.pl
Open Apr 1 - Oct 30 Tues - Sun 9 AM - 7 PM; Admis adults 10PLN; seniors, students & children 7 & over 6PLN; children 6 & under no charge; 16th-century castle
Collections: Period furnishings

GNIEZNO

M **MUZEUM POCZATKOW PANSTWA POLSKIEGO,** ul. Kostrzewskiego 1, Gniezno, 62-200 Poland. Tel 61-426-46-41; Fax 61-426-48-41; Elec Mail info@mppp.pl; Internet Home Page Address: www.mppp.pl/muzeum.htm
Circ

KIELCE

M **MUZEUM NARODOWE W KIELCACH,** National Museum in Kielce, Pl Zamkowy 1, Kielce, 25-010 Poland. Tel (041)3446764, 3442559; Fax (041)3448261; Elec Mail poczta@muzeumkielce.net; Internet Home Page Address: www.muzeumkielce.net; *Deputy Dir* Ryszard De Latour; *Dept Archaeology* Yolanta Gagorowska, PhD
Open Tues 10 AM - 6 PM, Wed -Sun 9 AM - 4 PM, cl Mon; Admis adults 10 PLN, children 5 PLN; Estab 1908; Circ Circulation: 1100; Library with 31,500 vols; Average Annual Attendance: 92,970
Library Holdings: Book Volumes 33,300; Exhibition Catalogs 2760; Periodical Subscriptions 3315
Special Subjects: Decorative Arts, Folk Art, Glass, Gold, Portraits, Textiles, Sculpture, Graphics, Photography, Landscapes, Painting-European, Furniture, Porcelain, Oriental Art, Silver, Tapestries, Baroque Art, Painting-Polish, Military Art
Collections: Polish paintings from 17th to 20th century; Polish baroque interiors; European-paintings, graphics, glass, pottery, gold, silver, furniture, arms & armour, coins, medals; historical and biographical materials, archaeology, natural history, folk art, car models; Polish archaeology, Polish folk art
Exhibitions: Historic interiors of 17th and 18th century; Gallery of Polish Painting and Decorative Arts; Old European and Oriental Arms and Armour; Sanctuary of Marshal Jozef Pilsudski; Paintings by Piotr Michatowski, Henryk Czarnecki, Jozef Deskur, Jozef Czapski; Polish archaeology; Polish folk art; natural history
Publications: The Ann of Nat Mus in Kielce; Corpus Inscriptionum Poloniae, vol 1-5; exhibit catalogs
Activities: Classes for adults & children; lects open to pub; 2000 vis lectrs per year; concerts; gallery talks; sponsoring of competitions; mus shop sells books & reproductions

KRAKOW

L **BIBLIOTEKA GLOWNA AKADEMII SZTUK PIEKNYCH,** Central Library of the Academy of Fine Arts, ul Smolensk 9, Krakow, 31-108 Poland. Tel 422-15-46 w 54; Fax (012)431-15-73; Elec Mail zewarcha@cyf-kr.edu.pl; *Dir* Elzbieta Warchalowska; *Cur* Janusz Antos; *Cur* Anna Szpor-Weglarska
Open Mon & Fri 9 AM - 2:30 PM, Tues, Wed & Thurs 9 AM - 7 PM, Sat 9 AM - 1 PM; Admis for our professors & students is free; Estab 1869, mus of Technology and Industry; Average Annual Attendance: 39,500
Library Holdings: Auction Catalogs; Book Volumes; CD-ROMs; Cards; Cassettes; Compact Disks; Exhibition Catalogs; Manuscripts; Maps; Original Art Works; Periodical Subscriptions; Photographs; Prints; Reproductions; Sculpture; Slides
Collections: Over 75,000 vols, 30,000 other items in collection; poster room, print room

M **MUZEUM NARODOWE W KRAKOWIE,** National Museum in Cracow, 3 Maja 1, Krakow, 30-062 Poland. Tel (012) 335331; *Dir* Tadeusz Chruscicki
Collections: National Museum in Krakow consists of several departments with various colls: 3 galleries exhibit Polish painting and sculpture from 14th to 20th century; Emeryk Hutten-Czapski Dept has graphic, numismatic and old book coll; Jan Matejko's House exhibits relics and paintings of the eminent Polish painter; Czartoryski Coll contains national relics, armory, Polish and foreign crafts and paintings, archaeology; Czartoryski Library and Archives holds colls of documents, codices, books and incunabula; Stanislaw Wyspianski Museum exhibits works by the Polish Modernist artist, handicrafts, architecture and town planning; Karol Szymanowski Museum contains exhibits relating to the life of the eminent composer

M **ZAMEK KROLEWSKI NA WAWELU,** Wawel Royal Castle, Wawel 5, Krakow, 31-001 Poland. Tel 48 12 422 1950; Fax 48 012 422 1950; Elec Mail zamek@wawel.edu.pl; Internet Home Page Address: www.wawel.krakow.pl; *Dir* Prof Jan Ostrowski; *Dir Mgr* Jerzy T Petrus; *Dir Prof* Marcin Fabianski; *Head Dept of Painting & Sculpture* Prof Kazimierz Kuczman
Open 9 AM - 3 PM; Admis varies with different exhibs; Estab 1930; Library with 17,500 vols; Average Annual Attendance: 1,050,000
Collections: Italian Renaissance furniture; King Sigismund Augustus 16th Century Collection of Flemish Tapestries; Oriental art objects; Polish, Western-European Oriental weapons; Western-European & Oriental pottery; Western European painting; royal treasury of crown jewels, gold objects, historical relics; Western European furniture; Western European Oriental textiles
Publications: Sudia Wawellana (annual); coll catalogs; source editions
Activities: Classes for children; docent training; lects open to pub, 2000 vis lectrs per yr; concerts; mus shop sells books, prints, slides, magazines, reproductions, prints

M **ZAMEK KROLEWSKI NA WAWELU-PANSTWOWE ZBIORY SZTU,** (Panstwowe Zbiory Sztuki na Wawelu) Wawel Royal Castle - State Art Collections, Wawel 5, Krakow, 31001 Poland. Tel +48-12-422-51-55; Fax +48-12-422-51-50; *Prof, Dir* Jan Ostrowski; *Deputy Dir* Jerzy T Petrus; *Asst Prof* Zbigniew Pianowski; *Deputy Dir* Prof Marcin Fabianski
Open Sun 10 AM - 3 PM, Fri 9:30 AM - 4 PM, Wed, Thurs, Sat 9:30 AM - 3 PM, cl Mon; Admis fees vary with exhibs, reductions for children, students & seniors; Estab 1930; Library with 20,912 vols; Average Annual Attendance: 1,000,000
Income: Financed by Ministry of Culture & Nat Heritage
Purchases: Polish regalia & items linked with the castle & royal ct
Library Holdings: Auction Catalogs; Book Volumes; CD-ROMs; Exhibition Catalogs; Original Documents; Periodical Subscriptions; Photographs
Collections: Colls of art in the royal castle; 16th century coll of Flemish tapestries; Italian & Dutch paintings; Oriental objects of art
Publications: Studia Waweliana; Acta Archaeologica Waweliana; catalogues of collections & temporary exhibitions

Activities: Classes for children; docent training; lects open to pub; 3,000 vis lectrs per yr; works lent to Polish & foreign mus; mus shop sells books, magazines, reproductions, prints & slides

LODZ

M **MUZEUM SZTUKI W LODZI,** Art Museum, Ul Wieckowskiego 36, Lodz, 90-734 Poland. Tel (42) 633-97-90; Fax (42) 632-99-41; Elec Mail muzeum@muzeumsztuki.lodz.pl; Internet Home Page Address: www.muzeumsztuki.lodz.pl; *Dir* Jaroslaw Suchan
Open Tues 10 AM - 5 PM, Wed & Fri 11 AM - 5 PM, Thurs noon - 6 PM, Sat - Sun 10 AM - 4 PM; No admis fee on Thurs; Estab 1931; 20th Century Art (International)
Library Holdings: Auction Catalogs; Book Volumes; Exhibition Catalogs; Original Documents; Pamphlets; Periodical Subscriptions; Prints
Collections: Gothic art; 15th to 19th century foreign paintings; 18th to 20th century Polish paintings; international modern art; Polish photography and multimedia collections
Publications: 111 Works from the Collection of Museum Sztuki in Lodzi
Activities: Classes for adults and children; music progs; lects open to pub; concerts; gallery talks; tours; schols and fellowships offered; mus shop sells books, reproductions, prints, slides

POZNAN

M **MUZEUM NARODOWE,** National Museum in Poznan, Al Marcinkowskiego 9, Poznan, 61-745 Poland. Tel 0048 61 852 5969; Tel 0048 61 85 68 000; Fax 0048 61 851 5898; Elec Mail mnoffice@man.poznan.pl; Elec Mail mnp@mnp.art.pl; Internet Home Page Address: www.mnp.art.pl; *Dir* Wojciech Suchocki; *Vice Dir* Dr Adam Socko
Open Tues - Thurs 9 AM - 3 PM, Fri noon - 9 PM, Sat - Mon noon - 6 PM; Admis 10 zl, 6 zl (reduced); Library has 85,000 vols; 8 branch museums; Average Annual Attendance: 191,329
Library Holdings: Auction Catalogs; Book Volumes; Cards; Exhibition Catalogs; Periodical Subscriptions; Photographs; Slides
Special Subjects: Decorative Arts, Drawings, Folk Art, Ceramics, Glass, Photography, Portraits, Prints, Silver, Painting-British, Graphics, Sculpture, Bronzes, Ethnology, Costumes, Religious Art, Crafts, Pottery, Landscapes, Collages, Painting-European, Posters, Furniture, Jewelry, Painting-Dutch, Painting-French, Coins & Medals, Restorations, Baroque Art, Miniatures, Painting-Flemish, Painting-Polish, Renaissance Art, Medieval Art, Painting-Spanish, Painting-Italian, Antiquities-Greek, Gold, Painting-German, Military Art, Reproductions
Collections: Polish paintings from 15th to 20th century; prints, drawings, sculpture; medieval art; European paintings from 14th to 19th century; modern art
Activities: Classes for adults & children; lects open to pub; concerts; gallery talks; original art lent to other mus; mus shop sells books, magazines, reproductions, prints, slides, posters & other gadgets

WARSAW

L **BIBLIOTEKA UNIWERSYTECKA W WARSZAWIE,** Library of the University of Warsaw, Ul Krakowskie Przedmiescie 32, Warsaw, 00-927 Poland. Tel 826-41-55; *Dir* Dr Henryk Hollender
Collections: Prints & drawings from 15th - 20th century; various memorial colls

M **CENTRUM SZTUKI WSPOLCZESNEJ,** Centre for Contemporary Art Ujazdowski Castle, Ujazdowski 2 Warsaw, 00-467 Poland. Tel 48-22-628-12-71-3, 48-22-628-76-83; Fax 48-22-628-95-50; Elec Mail csw@csw.art.pl; Internet Home Page Address: csw.art.pl; *Cur* Milada Slizinska; *Dir* Wojciech Keukowski; *Deputy Dir* Malgorzata Winter; *Cur* Stach Szablowski; *Cur* Ewa Gorzadek; *Cur* Adam Mazur; *Laboratory* Ika Sienkiewicz-Nowacka; *Film/Cinema Kino Lab* Ursula Sniegowska; *Experimental Film Archive* Lukasz Ronduda
Open Tues - Sat 11 AM - 7 PM, Fri 11 AM - 9 PM, cl Mon; Admis 12 zl, students seniors & children 6 zl
Library Holdings: CD-ROMs; DVDs; Exhibition Catalogs; Kodachrome Transparencies; Video Tapes
Collections: Exhibitions of contemporary art in various media
Activities: Classes for adults & children; lects open to public, concerts, gallery tours

M **MUZEUM NARODOWE W WARSZAWIE,** National Museum in Warsaw, Al Jerozolimskie 3, Warsaw, 00495 Poland. Tel +48 (022) 6211031or +48 (022) 6225665; Fax (22) 6228559; Elec Mail muzeum@mnw.art.pl; Internet Home Page Address: www.mnw.art.pl; *Dir* Agnieszka Morawinska; *Deputy Dir Communs & Develop* Mateusz Labuda; *Deputy Dir Research* Piotr Rypson
Open Tues, Wed, Fri, Sat & Sun 10 AM -6 PM, Thurs 10 AM - 9 PM, cl Mon; No admis fee on Tues; Estab 1862
Library Holdings: Auction Catalogs; Audio Tapes; Book Volumes; CD-ROMs; Exhibition Catalogs; Fiche; Manuscripts; Maps; Memorabilia; Original Documents; Periodical Subscriptions; Prints
Collections: Paintings, sculptures & drawings; Medieval & modern Polish 12th century art; Ancient Art Coll; Eastern Christian Art Coll; Oriental Art Coll; Decorative Art Coll; Miniature Room; European painting coll; Gallery of European Old Masters; Gallery of 18th century art; gallery of 20th & 21st century art; Dept of coins & medals; gallery of old Polish & European Portrait
Publications: Bulletin du Musee National de Varsouie, quarterly
Activities: Educ prog; classes for children; lects open to pub; concerts; gallery talks; tours; lending of original objects of art to mus and galleries all over the world; originate traveling exhibs to mus in Europe and US; mus shop sells books, magazines, reproductions, prints

M **ZACHETA - NATIONAL GALLERY OF ART,** (Narodowe Centrum Kultury) Pl Malachowskiego 3, Warsaw, 00-916 Poland. Tel 48-22-556-96-00; Fax 48-22-827-78-86; Elec Mail office@zacheta.art.pl; Internet Home Page Address: www.zacheta.art.pl; *Dir* Hanna Wroblewska; *Press Officer* Olga Gawerska
Open Tues - Sun noon - 8 PM; Admis 15 zl, concession 10 zl; Built in 1860-1900 for the presentation and promotion of contemporary art; Popularize & promote contemporary art; Average Annual Attendance: 35,000
Library Holdings: Audio Tapes; Book Volumes; CD-ROMs; Cassettes; Clipping Files; DVDs; Exhibition Catalogs; Original Documents; Photographs; Slides; Video Tapes
Collections: Oldest exhibition site in Warsaw; Contemporary and modern art in various media from Polish and international artists; Contemporary Polish Art in various media; Extensive permanent coll
Exhibitions: Organize only temporary exhibs
Activities: Classes for adults, children & artists; lects open to public; concerts; gallery talks and tours; lending of original art to other cultural institutions; Culture to go project; mus shop sells books, magazines, prints, reproductions, DVDs & gadgets

M **Kordegarda Gallery,** ul Krakowskie Przedmiescie 15/17, Warsaw, Poland. Tel 22-42-10-125; Elec Mail Kordegarda@nck.pl; Internet Home Page Address: www.kordegarda.org; *Cur* Marta Czyz
Open Tues - Sun 11 AM - 7 PM; No admis fee; Estab 2011; Kordegarda works as a place of presentation of contemporary Polish culture
Income: Financed from the budget of Ministry & Culture
Special Subjects: Prints, Graphics, Sculpture, Woodcuts, Portraits, Posters, Jewelry, Painting-Polish
Activities: Lects open to pub; concerts; gallery talks; tours; mus shop sells books, DVD's

WROCLAW

M **MUZEUM ARCHITEKTURY,** Museum of Architecture, Ul Bernardynska 5, Wroclaw, 50-156 Poland. Tel (+48) (071) 343-36-75; Fax (071) 344-65-77; Elec Mail muzeum@ma.wroc.pl; Internet Home Page Address: www.ma.wroc.pl; *Dir* Jerzy Ilkosz, MA; *Deputy Mgr* Ewa Jasienko
Open Tues - Wed & Fri - Sat 10 AM - 4 PM, Thurs noon - 6 PM, Sun 11 AM - 5 PM; Admis adults 2 euro, children 1 euro; Estab 1965; Museum housed in beautiful former Bernardine 14th Century Cloister Complex
Income: State budget, City of Wroclaw, Sponsors
Purchases: Architectural books and catalogues from other museums and institutions
Library Holdings: Audio Tapes; Book Volumes; CD-ROMs; Cassettes; Compact Disks; Exhibition Catalogs; Maps; Original Documents; Photographs; Reproductions; Sculpture; Slides; Video Tapes
Collections: Polish & other architecture; modern art; individual architecture, documents, photographs, projects
Publications: Books about architecture, art - Polish and foreign
Activities: Classes for adults & children; seminars for students; research conferences; lects open to public, concerts, gallery talks; awards: SYBILLA 2005, 2006, 2007; lending original objects of art to other museums; co-operation with traveling exhibs; mus shop sells books

M **MUZEUM NARODOWE WE WROCLAWIU,** National Museum in Wroclaw, Pl Powstancow Warszawy 5, Wroclaw, 50-153 Poland. Tel (71) 372-51-50; Fax (71) 343-56-43; Elec Mail muzeumnarodowe@wr.onet.pl; Internet Home Page Address: www.mnwr.art.pl; *Dir* Mariusz Hermansdorfer
Open 10 AM - 4 PM; Estab 1947; Library with 91,000 vols; 102,000 mus objects
Collections: Medieval art; Polish paintings from 17th - 20th century, European paintings; decorative arts, prints, ethnography & history relating to Silesia; numismatics
Publications: Exhibition catalogs
Activities: Classes for adults & children; books & magazines

ZAGAN

M **PALACE IN ZAGAN,** Szprotawska 4, Zagan, 68-100 Poland. Tel 48 684776461; Fax 48 684776462; Elec Mail marketing@palac.zagan.pl; Internet Home Page Address: www.palac.zagan.pl
Open Mon - Fri 7 AM - 4 PM; Admis 3 - 5 PLN
Collections: Period furnishings

PORTUGAL

EVORA

M **MUSEU DE EVORA,** Largo do Conde de Vila Flor, Evora, 7000-804 Portugal. Tel 266702604; Fax 266708094; Elec Mail mevora@imc.ip.pt; Internet Home Page Address: www.museudevora.imc-ip.pt; *Dir* Antonio Camaes Gouveia
Open Tues - Sun 10 AM - 6 PM, cl Mon; Admis 4 euros; Average Annual Attendance: 30,000; Mem: Amigos do Museu de Evora: 140; dues junior 12 euros, standard 24 euros, family 48 euros, enterprise 120 euros, benefactor 240 euros, contrib enterprise 1200 euros; mem req 120 hrs vol work
Special Subjects: Archaeology, Decorative Arts, Drawings, Landscape Architecture, Architecture, Ceramics, Glass, Metalwork, Furniture, Pottery, Silver, Textiles, Painting-European, Painting-French, Sculpture, Tapestries, Watercolors, Bronzes, Ethnology, Costumes, Religious Art, Portraits, Jewelry, Painting-Dutch, Carpets & Rugs, Coins & Medals, Baroque Art, Painting-Flemish, Renaissance Art, Embroidery, Medieval Art, Painting-Spanish, Painting-Italian, Islamic Art, Antiquities-Roman
Collections: Paintings: 16th century Flemish & Portuguese works; local prehistoric tools & Roman art & archaeology; sculpture from middle ages to the

19th century; 18th century Portuguese furniture & silver; textiles & paramonts from 16ty - 19th century
Publications: Exhib catalogs
Activities: Lects open to pub; gallery talks; mus shop sells books, magazines, reproductions, prints

LAMEGO

M **MUSEU DE LAMEGO,** Lamego, 5100 Portugal. Tel (054) 612008; Fax (054) 655264; *Dir* Dr Agostinho Ribeiro
Collections: 16th century Brussels tapestries; Portuguese painting of 16th and 18th centuries; sculpture; religious ornaments

LISBON

M **CASA MUSEU - DR ANASTACIO GONCALVES,** Ave 5 de Outubro, 6-8, Lisbon, 1050-055 Portugal. Fax 351 21 354 87 54; Elec Mail cmag@ipmuseus.pt; Internet Home Page Address: www.cmag-ipmuseus.pt; TWX 351 21 354 08 23
Open Tues 10 AM - 6 PM
Collections: Chinese porcelain

M **CENTRO DE ARTE MODERNA,** CAM - Calouste Gulbenkian Foundation, Rua Dr Nicolau de Bettencourt, Lisbon, 1050-078 Portugal. Tel 351 217823474; Fax 351 217 823037; Elec Mail cam@gulbenkian.pt; Internet Home Page Address: www.cam.gulbenkian.pt; *Dir* Isabel Carlos
Open Tues - Sun 10 AM - 6 PM; Admis 5 euros
Library Holdings: Book Volumes; Exhibition Catalogs
Special Subjects: Etchings & Engravings, Landscapes, Ceramics, Collages, Photography, Sculpture, Tapestries, Drawings, Graphics, Prints, Watercolors, Woodcuts
Collections: Portuguese & foreign art from the 20th & 21st century
Exhibitions: Temporary exhibs programmed permanently
Publications: Catalogues of the exhibs & guide to the coll
Activities: Classes for adults, children & families; docent training; gallery talks; lending of original objects of art to several mus & institutions on contemporary art; mus shop sells books, magazines

M **MUSEU CALOUSTE GULBENKIAN,** Av de Berne 45 A, Lisbon, 1067-001 Portugal. Tel 7935131; Fax 7955249; Elec Mail info@gulbenkian.pt; Internet Home Page Address: www.bulbenkian.pt; *Dir* Joao Castel-Branco Pereira
Collections: Gulbenkian art collection covering the period 2800 BC to present; classical, Oriental, European art; manuscripts, furniture, gold and silver; medals; tapestries

M **MUSEU NACIONAL DE ARTE ANTIGA,** National Museum of Ancient Art, Rua das Janelas Verdes, Lisbon, 1293 Portugal; Rua das Janelas Verdes, Lisbon, 1249-017 Portugal. Tel 21.3912800; Fax 213973703; Elec Mail mnarteantiga@ipmuseus.pt; Internet Home Page Address: www.mnarteantiga-ipmuseus.pt; *Dir* Dr Paulo Henriques; *Cur* Teresa Schneider, ARG; *Cur* Dr Leonor d'Orey, Dra; *Cur* Maria da Conceicao Borges de Sousa, Dra; *Cur* Dr José Alberto Seabra; *Cur* Dra Maria Antónia Pinto de Matos; *Cur* Dra Alexandra Markl
Open Tues 2 PM - 6 PM, Wed - Sun 10 AM - 6 PM; Admis general 3 Euros; Estab 1884; Library with 36,000 vols; Average Annual Attendance: 150,000; Mem: 650; 25 euros
Library Holdings: Auction Catalogs; Book Volumes; Exhibition Catalogs; Periodical Subscriptions
Collections: Portuguese and foreign plastic and ornamental art from 12th-19th century
Activities: Educ prog; docent training; lects open to pub; vis lectrs; gallery talks; mus shop has books, reproductions, original art, slides & prints

M **MUSEU NACIONAL DE ARTE CONTEMPORANEA,** National Museum of Contemporary Art, Museu Do Chiado, Rua de Serpa Pinto 4, Lisbon, Portugal. Tel 213432148; Fax 213432151; *Dir* Pedro Lapa
Open Tues 2 PM - 6 PM, Wed - Sun 10 AM - 6 PM, cl Mon; Admis 600 (PTE); Estab 1911, Nat Museum of Contemporary Art; Gallery includes 5 rooms with total area of 1200M
Special Subjects: Drawings, Period Rooms, Sculpture, Portraits
Collections: Contemporary painting and sculpture
Activities: Classes & workshops for children; originate traveling exhibs to Spain

PORTO

M **MUSEU NACIONAL DE SOARES DOS REIS,** National Museum of Soares Dos Reis, Palacio dos Carrancas, Rua de D Manuel II Porto, 4000 Portugal. Tel (02) 2081956; Fax (02) 2082851; *Dir* Dr Monica Baldaque
Collections: Furniture, glass, jewelry, old and modern paintings, porcelain, pottery, sculpture

M **MUSEU SERRALVES DE ARTE CONTEMPORANEA,** Serralves Foundation Museum of Contemporary Art, Rua D Joao de Castro 210, Porto, 4150-417 Portugal. Tel 351-22-615-6500, 351-808-200-543; Internet Home Page Address: www.serralves.com; *Dir* Joao Fernandes
Open Oct - Mar Tues - Sun 10 AM - 7 PM, Apr - Sept Tues - Fri 10 AM - 7 PM; Admis Museum & Park 5 euro, Park 2.5 euro, Fri - Sat Museum 3 euro, under 18 & Sun free
Collections: National and international contemporary art from the 1960s to the present

VISEU

M **MUSEU DE GRAO VASCO,** Adro d SE, Viseu, Portugal. Tel 422049; Fax 232 421241; Elec Mail mgv@ip.museu.pt; Internet Home Page Address: www.ipmuseus.pt; *Dir* Ana Paula Abrantes
Open Tues 2 PM - 6 PM, Wed - Sun 10 AM - 6 PM, cl Mon; Admis adults 3 euro, seniors 1.50 euro, children under 14 free; Circ 446; Average Annual Attendance: 45.597

Library Holdings: Book Volumes; Exhibition Catalogs; Manuscripts; Pamphlets; Periodical Subscriptions
Special Subjects: Ceramics, Furniture, Porcelain, Silver, Textiles, Sculpture, Religious Art, Pottery, Decorative Arts, Portraits, Carpets & Rugs, Coins & Medals, Painting-Flemish, Renaissance Art, Medieval Art
Collections: Flemish & Portuguese paintings; furniture, tapestries, ceramics & glassware; drawings, paintings
Activities: Thematic visits; lending of original objects of art to other museums; mus shop sells books & reproductions

ROMANIA

ARAD

M **COMPLEXUL MUZEAL ARAD,** Arad Museum Complex, Piata George Enescu 1, Arad, 310131 Romania. Tel 0257 281847; Fax 0257 280114; Elec Mail office@museumarad.ro; Internet Home Page Address: www.museumarad.ro; *Dir* Peter Hugel
Admis adults 2 RON, children, military, students & seniors 1 RON; Estab 1893
Collections: Archeological artifacts; Romanian & European art

BUCHAREST

L **BIBLIOTECA ACADEMIEI ROMANE,** Library of the Romanian Academy, Calea Victoriei 125, Bucharest, 71102 Romania. Tel (1) 650-30-43; Fax (1) 650-74-78; *Dir* Gabriel Strempel
Library Holdings: Other Holdings Items over 9 million
Collections: National depository for Romanian & United Nations publications; Romania, Latin, Greek, Oriental & Slavonic manuscripts, engravings, documents, maps, medals & coins

M **MUZEUL NATIONAL DE ARTA AL ROMANIEI,** National Museum of Art of Romania, Calea Victoriei 49-53, Bucharest, 70101 Romania. Tel 4021 315 51 93; Fax 4021 312 43 27; Elec Mail art@art.museum.ro; Internet Home Page Address: mnar.arts.ro; *Deputy Dir* Liviu Constantinescu; *Head Universal Gallery* Mrs Octav Boicescu; *Head Educ & Commun* Mrs Cristina Toma; *Gen Dir* Roxana Theodorescu
Open May - Sept 11 AM - 7 PM, Oct - Apr Wed - Sun 10 AM - 6 PM; Admis fee National Gallery 10.00 lei, European Art Gallery 8.00 lei, combined tickets National Gallery & European Art Gallery 15.00 lei; Estab 1948; Average Annual Attendance: 120,000
Income: The National Museum of Art of Romania is a public nonprofit cultural institution. Finance sources include visiting fees, subsidy of Ministry of Culture and from the Friends of The National Museum of Art Assn
Library Holdings: Exhibition Catalogs; Kodachrome Transparencies; Lantern Slides
Special Subjects: Archaeology, Decorative Arts, Drawings, Etchings & Engravings, Folk Art, Landscapes, Marine Painting, Architecture, Ceramics, Glass, Flasks & Bottles, Furniture, Gold, Photography, Porcelain, Portraits, Pottery, Period Rooms, Silver, Textiles, Bronzes, Manuscripts, Painting-British, Painting-European, Painting-French, Painting-Japanese, Graphics, Hispanic Art, Sculpture, Watercolors, Ethnology, Costumes, Religious Art, Crafts, Woodcarvings, Woodcuts, Judaica, Posters, Jade, Jewelry, Oriental Art, Asian Art, Antiquities-Byzantine, Metalwork, Painting-Dutch, Carpets & Rugs, Historical Material, Ivory, Restorations, Tapestries, Baroque Art, Calligraphy, Miniatures, Painting-Flemish, Painting-Polish, Renaissance Art, Embroidery, Laces, Medieval Art, Antiquities-Oriental, Painting-Spanish, Painting-Italian, Antiquities-Persian, Islamic Art, Antiquities-Egyptian, Antiquities-Roman, Painting-German, Pewter, Leather, Military Art, Reproductions, Painting-Russian, Enamels, Bookplates & Bindings
Collections: Romanian Medieval Art - 14th to early 19th century; Romanian Modern Art - 19th to first half of the 20th century; European Art - 14th to early 20th century
Publications: Exhibition catalogs
Activities: Classes for adults, children & teachers; workshops; concerts; gallery talks; tours; lending of original objects of art; books, magazines, reproductions, prints, puzzles, promotional objects
M **Ansamblul Brincovenesc Mogosoaia,** Str Donca Simo 18, Mogosoaia, 78911 Romania. Tel 667-02-40; *Dir* Alexandru Cebuc
Collections: Old Romanian art
M **The Art Collections Museum,** Calea Victoriei 111, Bucharest, 71102 Romania. Tel 4021 2129641; 4021 2121749
Open May - Sep: Wed - Sat 11 AM - 7 PM; Oct - Apr: Wed - Sat 10 AM - 6 PM
Collections: Romanian folk art; decorative arts; paintings, sculpture, graphic arts
M **K. H. Zambaccian Museum,** 21A Muzeul Zambaccian St, Bucharest, Romania. Tel 4021 2301920; Fax 4021 3129327; Elec Mail national.art@art.museum.ro; Internet Home Page Address: www.mnar.arts.ro
Open May - Sep: Wed - Sat 11 AM - 7 PM; Oct - Apr: Wed - Sun 10 AM - 6 PM
Collections: Romanian & European 19th & 20th century art
Publications: Museum's brochure
M **Theodor Pallady Museum,** 22 Spatarului St, Bucharest, Romania. Tel 4021 2114979
Open May - Sep: Wed - Sat 11 AM - 7 PM; Oct - Apr: Wed - Sat 10 AM - 6 PM

M **MUZEUL NATIONAL DE ARTA CONTEMPORANA,** National Museum of Contemporary Art, Izvor St 2-4, Wing E-4 Bucharest, Romania. Tel 0040-21-3189137, 3139115, 3125147; Fax 0040-21-319138, 3121502; Elec Mail info@mnac.ro; Internet Home Page Address: www.mnac.ro; *Gen Dir* Mihai Oroveanu; *Artistic Dir* Ruxandra Balaci; *Head Curatorial Dept* Raluca Velisar
Open Wed - Sun 10 AM - 6 PM; Estab 2004
Collections: Contemporary national and international art in various media

CLUJ-NAPOCA

M **MUZEUL DE ARTA CLUJ-NAPOCA,** Museum of Art Cluj-Napoca, Piata Libertatii 30, Cluj-Napoca, 400098 Romania. Tel 40/0264/596952; 596953; Fax 40/0264/596952; 596953; Elec Mail macn@cluj.astral.ro; Internet Home Page Address: www.macluj.ro; *Dir* Dr Livia Dragoi; *Chief, Cur Dept* Calin Stegerean
Open Wed - Sun 9 AM - 5 PM; cl Mon & Tues; Admis 3.06 LEI (permanent exhibs), 1.53 LEI (temporary exhibs)
Collections: Romanian & universal art, including graphics, paintings, sculpture and decorative arts from 16th - 20th century
Activities: mus shop sells books, magazines, reproductions & prints

CONSTANTA

M **MUZEUL DE ARTA CONSTANTA,** Str Muzeelor 12, Constanta, 8700 Romania. Tel (41) 61-70-12; *Dir* Doina Pauleanu
Collections: Modern & contemporary Romanian art

M **MUZEUL DE ISTORIE NATIONALA SI ARHEOLOGIE CONSTANTA,** National History & Archaeology Museum, Piata Ovidiu 12, Constanta, 900745 Romania. Tel (041) 0040-241-618763; Fax 0040-241-618763; Elec Mail archmus@minac.ro; Internet Home Page Address: www.minac.ro; *Dir* Dr Constantin Chera; *Dir* Dr Gabriel Custurea; *Dir* Dr Livia Buzoianu; *Dir* Dr Virgil Lungu; *Dir* Dr Constantin Bajenaru; *Dir* Dr Gabriel Talmatchi
Open 1.10 - 30.04 Tues - Sun 9 AM - 5 PM; 1.05 - 30.09 daily 8 AM - 8 PM; Admis 3 euro; Estab 1878; Library with 40,000 vols; Average Annual Attendance: 80,000
Income: 10,000,000 LEI or 3,000,000 euro
Library Holdings: Book Volumes; CD-ROMs; Compact Disks; DVDs; Maps; Photographs
Special Subjects: Archaeology, Historical Material, History of Art & Archaeology, Architecture, Art Education, Art History, Ceramics, Glass, Furniture, Gold, Photography, Silver, Manuscripts, Maps, Sculpture, Graphics, Anthropology, Archaeology, Ethnology, Costumes, Religious Art, Crafts, Pottery, Primitive art, Posters, Glass, Jewelry, Silver, Scrimshaw, Coins & Medals, Restorations, Dioramas, Medieval Art, Antiquities-Oriental, Islamic Art, Antiquities-Egyptian, Antiquities-Greek, Antiquities-Roman, Mosaics, Gold, Antiquities-Etruscan
Collections: Prehistory, history & archaeology of the region; statues, coins, Neolithic vessels; Smoking pipes collection
Exhibitions: Temporary exhibitions in summer
Publications: Pontica
Activities: Classes for children; mus shop sells books, magazines, reproductions, CDs & prints; Edificiu Roman cu Mozaic

PLOIESTI

M **ART MUSEUM PLOIESTI,** Blvd Independentei, Ploiesti, nr1 Romania. Tel 40 244 522264; Fax 40 244 511375; Elec Mail office@artmuseum.ro; Internet Home Page Address: www.artmuseum.ro; *Mgr* Florin Sicoie; *Deputy Mgr* Alice Neculea
Open Tues - Sun 9 AM - 7 PM
Collections: Modern & contemporary Romanian painting, graphics, sculpture & decorative arts

SIBIU

M **MUZEUL NATIONAL BRUKENTHAL,** Brukenthal Palace & European Art Gallery, Piata Mare 4-5, Sibiu, 550163 Romania. Tel 40-269-217691; Fax 40-269-211545; Elec Mail info@brukenthalmuseum.ro; Internet Home Page Address: www.brukenthalmuseum.ro/; *Dir Art Galleries* Dr Alexandru Sonoc; *Head of European Art Gallery* Dr Daniela Damboiu; *Gen Dir* Dr Sabin Adrian Luca; *Head of Contemporary Art Gallery* Liviana Dan; *Head of Library* Dr Constantin Ittu
Open Summer: Tues - Sun 10 AM - 6 PM, cl Mon & first Tues of month; Winter: Wed - Sun 10 AM - 6 PM, cl Mon & Tues; Admis adults 12 lei, groups of ten or more 8 lei, seniors & students 3 lei; Estab 1817; pub mus; European, Romanian & Contemporary Art from the 15th-21st century; Average Annual Attendance: 366,410; Mem: CODART, ICOM
Income: Governmental funding
Purchases: through donations
Library Holdings: Book Volumes; DVDs; Exhibition Catalogs; Fiche; Framed Reproductions; Manuscripts; Maps; Memorabilia; Original Documents; Pamphlets; Periodical Subscriptions; Reproductions
Special Subjects: Archaeology, Decorative Arts, Drawings, Etchings & Engravings, Historical Material, History of Art & Archaeology, Landscapes, Marine Painting, Art History, Ceramics, Glass, Metalwork, Mexican Art, Flasks & Bottles, Furniture, Photography, Pottery, Prints, Period Rooms, Silver, Bronzes, Manuscripts, Maps, Sculpture, Graphics, Hispanic Art, Watercolors, Textiles, Costumes, Religious Art, Crafts, Primitive art, Woodcarvings, Painting-European, Portraits, Jewelry, Porcelain, Oriental Art, Asian Art, Painting-Dutch, Painting-French, Carpets & Rugs, Coins & Medals, Restorations, Baroque Art, Miniatures, Painting-Flemish, Renaissance Art, Embroidery, Medieval Art, Painting-Spanish, Painting-Italian, Islamic Art, Antiquities-Egyptian, Antiquities-Greek, Antiquities-Roman, Painting-German, Pewter, Painting-Russian
Collections: Personal collections of Samuel von Brukenthal, German & Austrian painting; Flemish, Dutch, Italian painting, Transylvanian Sculpture in Stone, Plaster-cast copies of famous sculptures, cartography cabinet, print works & drawings cabinet, reception rooms (the Baroque Salons with original wallpaper), Anatolian Rug Coll, Romanian Art paintings (from 18th-20th century; Liturgical vestments from 14th-16th c); Transylvanian Altars (15th & 16th c)
Exhibitions: Permanent & temporary exhibs
Publications: Brukenthal Acta Musei; Bibliotheca Brukenthal Book Series; guides; albums; exhib catalogues; booklets
Activities: Classes for adults & children; docent training; workshops; lects for mems only; concerts, gallery talks; tours; sponsoring of competitions; schols;

awards to Prof Sabin Adrian Luca, Dr Elena Popescu & Dr Maria Ordeanu; European Union Prize for Cultural Heritage; lending original objects of art to mus from abroad for special exhibs; mus shop sells books, magazines, reproductions, prints, slides, DVD's, chocolate, personalized products & souvenirs

M **Altemberger House: The Museum of History,** Mitropoliei 2, Sibiu, 550179 Romania. Tel 40-269-218-143; *Dept Head* Adrian Georgescu
Collections: Material & ethnographic history of Sibiu and Southern Transylvania

M **Blue House & Romanian Art Gallery,** Piata Mare Nr 5, Sibiu, 550163 Romania. Tel 40 369 101 780; 40 269 217 691; Fax 40 269 211 545; Elec Mail info@brukenthalmuseum.md; Internet Home Page Address: www.brukenthalmuseum.md; *Head of Romanian Art Gallery* Dr Iulia Mesea; *Cur* Alexandra Ratiu, MA; *Cur* Adrian Luca, MA; *Conservator* Dorina Tiplic
Open Summer: Tues - Sun 10 AM - 6 PM, cl Mon & first Tues of month; Winter: Wed - Sun 10 AM - 6 PM, cl Mon & Tues; Admis adults 8 lei, 10 or more adults 4 lei, seniors 4 lei, students 2 lei; European, Romanian & Contemporary Art from the 17th-20th century; Average Annual Attendance: 366,410
Income: Government financial support & donations
Library Holdings: Book Volumes; CD-ROMs; Compact Disks; DVDs; Exhibition Catalogs
Special Subjects: Decorative Arts, Drawings, Etchings & Engravings, Ceramics, Glass, Furniture, Painting-American, Bronzes, Woodcuts, Sculpture, Graphics, Watercolors, Textiles, Religious Art, Woodcarvings, Carpets & Rugs, Baroque Art, Renaissance Art, Medieval Art, Islamic Art, Stained Glass
Collections: Romanian painting, sculpture, decorative arts, graphics
Exhibitions: Permanent: Romanian painting 17th - 20th century
Publications: Bruckenthal Acta Musei Guide; exhib catalogues; Eurographics
Activities: Classes for children; docent training; tours; loaning for temporary exhibs; organize traveling exhibs to country & abroad; mus shop sells books, magazines, reproductions, prints, post cards & personalized objects

L **The Brukenthal Library,** Piata Mare Nr 4, Sibiu, 550163 Romania. Tel 40 269 211 699; *Head of Brukenthal Library* Dr Constantin Ittu
Open only for research
Library Holdings: Book Volumes; Exhibition Catalogs; Manuscripts; Maps; Original Documents; Periodical Subscriptions; Photographs; Prints

M **Contemporary Art Gallery,** Tribunei St 6, Sibiu, 550176 Romania. Tel 40 0369 101783; *Head Contemporary Art Gallery* Liviana Dan
Open Summer: Tues - Sun 10 AM - 6 PM, cl Mon & first Tues of month; Winter: Wed - Sun 10 AM - 6 PM, cl Mon & Tues; Admis adults 5 lei, groups of 10 or more adults 4 lei, seniors 3 lei, students 1.25 lei; European, Romanian & Contemporary Art from the 15th-21st century

RUSSIA

KAZAN

M **THE STATE MUSEUM OF FINE ARTS OF TATARSTAN REPUBLIC,** (Tatar State Museum of Fine Arts) UI K Marska 64, Kazan, 420015 Russia. Tel +7 (843) 236-69-31; Elec Mail kazfineartmus@mail.ru; Internet Home Page Address: www.izo-museum.ru; *Dir* Rozaliva Nurgaleeva; *Science Deputy Dir* Dina Khisamova; *Storage Deputy Dir* Marina Kutnova
Open 10 AM - 17 PM; Admis 50 - 130 rubles; Estab 1967; Library with 10,000 exhibits; Average Annual Attendance: 160,000
Special Subjects: Decorative Arts, Drawings, Etchings & Engravings, Landscapes, Glass, Flasks & Bottles, Furniture, Gold, Porcelain, Portraits, Textiles, Maps, Painting-French, Graphics, Sculpture, Watercolors, Costumes, Religious Art, Ceramics, Folk Art, Primitive art, Woodcarvings, Painting-European, Asian Art, Silver, Painting-Dutch, Carpets & Rugs, Restorations, Baroque Art, Calligraphy, Embroidery, Laces, Medieval Art, Antiquities-Oriental, Painting-Italian, Islamic Art, Stained Glass, Painting-German, Leather, Military Art, Painting-Russian, Enamels
Collections: West European & Soviet paintings; Russian & National Art
Exhibitions: Permanent exhibs: Russian 16th-20th century; West-European 16th-19th century; Shishkin Feshin
Publications: Catalogues, monographies
Activities: Classes for children; lects for mems only; concerts; gallery talks; tours; schols; organize traveling exhibs to Europe & Russia; mus shop sells books, magazines, prints, monographies & booklets

National Art Gallery, UI K Marska 64, Kazan, 420015 Russia.

Modern Art Gallery, UI K Marska 64, Kazan, 420015 Russia.

Centre for Children's Creative Development, UI K Marska 64, Kazan, 420015 Russia.

MOSCOW

M **KREMLIN MUSEUMS,** Lebyazhiy per 4, Moscow, 125009 Russia. Tel 928-44-56; *Dir* I A Rodimtseva
Collections: Collections housed in Armoury & various Kremlin cathedrals

M **Kremlin Cathedrals,** Lebyazhir per 4, Moscow, 125009 Russia.
Collections: Icons, tombs & applied arts found in Cathedral of the Assumption, Cathedral of the Annunciation, Archangel Cathedral, Rizpolozhensky Cathedral & Cathedral of the Twelve Apostles

M **MOSCOW MUSEUM OF OUTSIDER ART,** Izmailovski Blvd 30, Moscow, 105043 Russia. Tel 095-465-6304; Fax 095-164-3738; Elec Mail outsider@izmaylovo.ru; Internet Home Page Address: www.museum.ru/outsider; *Dir* Vladimir Abakumov
Collections: Collection of national outsider art, neuve invention, and naive art

M **THE STATE MUSEUM OF ORIENTAL ART,** Nikitskij Blvd 12a., Moscow, 119019 Russia. Tel 7 (495) 691-0212; Fax 7 (495) 695-4846; Elec Mail info@orientmuseum.ru; Internet Home Page Address: www.orientmuseum.ru; *Dir* Alekeaudr V Sedov; *Deputy Dir Exhibs* Anna Kovalets; *Deputy Dir Develop* Nikolay Roginskij
Open daily 11 AM - 8 PM, cl Mon; Admis adults 150 rbls, students & pensioners

50 rbls, foreigners 300 rbls; Estab 1918; storage, study & poplarization of art & material culture of the East; Average Annual Attendance: 72,400
Income: Federal budget from the revenues in the main & auxiliary scientific funds
Library Holdings: Auction Catalogs; Book Volumes; Exhibition Catalogs; Manuscripts; Periodical Subscriptions; Photographs
Special Subjects: Archaeology, Etchings & Engravings, Ceramics, Antiquities-Assyrian, Bronzes, Painting-French, Textiles, Painting-Japanese, Oriental Art, Asian Art, Painting-Dutch, Carpets & Rugs, Calligraphy, Miniatures, Antiquities-Oriental, Antiquities-Persian, Islamic Art, Antiquities-Egyptian, Painting-Russian, Painting-Israeli, Enamels
Collections: Art of the Republics of Soviet Central Asia; Chinese art; monuments of art of Japan, India, Vietnam, Korea, Mongolia, Iran and other countries of the Middle and Far East
Activities: Classes for children; lects open to pub; concerts; gallery talks; tours; 4 book traveling exhibs per yr; organize traveling exhibs for the museums of Russia; mus shop sells books, magazines, original art, reporductions, prints, slides, oriental souvenirs

M **STATE TRETYAKOV GALLERY,** Krymskii val 10-14, Moscow, 117049 Russia. Tel 095-230-77-88; *Dir* P I Lebedev
Collections: 40,000 Russian icons; Russian & Soviet paintings, sculpture & graphic arts from 11th century to present

SAINT PETERSBURG

M **STATE HERMITAGE MUSEUM,** M Dvortsovaya naberezhnaya 34, Saint Petersburg, Russia. Tel (812) 1103420; Internet Home Page Address: www.hermitagemuseum.org; *Dir* Dr Mikhail Borisovich Piotrovski
Collections: Collection of the arts of prehistoric, ancient Eastern, Greco - Roman and medieval times; preserves over 2,600,000 objects d'art, including 40,000 drawings, 500,000 engravings; works by Leonardo da Vinci, Raphael, Titian, Rubens and Rembrandt; coins; weapons; applied art

M **STATE MUSEUM OF CERAMICS,** Inzhenernaya str 4, Saint Petersburg, 191186 Russia. Tel 370-01-60; Elec Mail info@rusmuseum.ru; *Dir* E S Eritsan
Open Wed - Sun 10 AM - 6 PM, Mon 10 AM - 5 PM; cl Tues
Collections: Russian art; paintings, pottery, porcelain & tapestries

M **STATE RUSSIAN MUSEUM,** Inzhenernaya Str 4, Saint Petersburg, 191011 Russia. Tel (812) 595-42-48; Elec Mail info@rusmuseum.ru; Internet Home Page Address: www.rusmuseum.ru/eng/; *Dir* V A Gusev
Open Mon 10 AM - 4 PM, Wed - Sun 10 AM - 5 PM, cl Tues
Collections: Collection of Russian icons; paintings, sculptures & drawings from the 11th to the 19th centuries

M **SUMMER GARDEN AND MUSEUM PALACE OF PETER THE GREAT,** Saint Petersburg, 191186 Russia. Tel 812-312-96-66; *Dir* T D Kozlova
Collections: 18th century sculpture & architecture

SARATOV

M **SARATOV A N RADISHCHEV ART MUSEUM,** Ul Radishcheva 39, Saratov, 410600 Russia. Tel 241918, 734726; Elec Mail radmuseum@renet.ru; *Dir* T V Grodskova
Open Tues - Fri & Sun 10 AM - 6 PM; Admis adults 5 roubles, seniors 3 roubles, students 2 roubles, children 1 rouble; library admis free; Estab 1885; Circ Library circulation: 8,400; Library with 34,000 vols & 20,000 exhibitions; Average Annual Attendance: Library attendance: 2,500
Library Holdings: Book Volumes 34,000; Manuscripts 7; Periodical Subscriptions 26
Collections: The Books from Bogolyubov A.P.; Russian Books XVIII-XXc; Foreign Books XVIII-XXc; Miniature Books; The History of Library
Publications: Russian Books XVIIIc

TVER

M **TVER ART GALLERY,** Sovetskaya 3, Tver, 170 Russia. Tel 34-25-61; Internet Home Page Address: www.gallery.tversu.ru; *Dir* Tatyana S Kuyukina; *Asst Dir* L G Margos; *Asst Dir* V A Bushljkova; *Asst Dir* V G Tkalich
Open 11 AM - 5 PM; Admis adults 50 roubles, children 10 roubles; Estab 1937; Library with 28,000 vols; 36,000 exhibits; Average Annual Attendance: 57,400; circ (art libraries) 1,500
Income: 31,716,300 roubles
Purchases: 31,440,300 roubles
Library Holdings: Auction Catalogs; Book Volumes; Compact Disks; Periodical Subscriptions
Special Subjects: Archaeology, Decorative Arts, Drawings, Etchings & Engravings, Folk Art, Historical Material, Landscapes, Marine Painting, Ceramics, Collages, Glass, Metalwork, Flasks & Bottles, Furniture, Gold, Photography, Portraits, Painting-American, Prints, Silver, Textiles, Bronzes, Manuscripts, Maps, Painting-British, Painting-European, Sculpture, Architecture, Graphics, Watercolors, Costumes, Religious Art, Pottery, Primitive art, Woodcarvings, Woodcuts, Judaica, Painting-Japanese, Posters, Jewelry, Porcelain, Oriental Art, Asian Art, Painting-Dutch, Painting-French, Carpets & Rugs, Ivory, Coins & Medals, Restorations, Tapestries, Baroque Art, Miniatures, Painting-Flemish, Painting-Polish, Renaissance Art, Embroidery, Laces, Medieval Art, Painting-Spanish, Painting-Italian, Islamic Art, Mosaics, Stained Glass, Painting-German, Pewter, Leather, Reproductions, Painting-Russian, Enamels, Painting-Scandinavian, Bookplates & Bindings
Collections: Paintings, graphics, sculptures, decorative arts
Exhibitions: 58 exhibs & 6 additional
Publications: 96 publs
Activities: Classes for children; dramatic progs; lects open to pub; 4,746 vis lectrs per yr; concerts; gallery talks; tours; schols; awards; lending of original art to

Russian Mus, Tretjakov Gallery; mus shop sells books, original art, reproductions, prints; junior mus Vladimir Serov's mus, Tver region Emmaus; Valentine Serov's Mus, Tver region Do-motkanovo

YAKUTSK

M **YAKUTSK MUSEUM OF FINE ARTS,** Ul Khabarova 27, Yakutsk, 677000 Russia. Tel 27798; *Dir* N M Vasileva
Collections: 17th to 20th century folk art

RWANDA

BUTARE

M **MUSEE NATIONAL DU RWANDA,** National Museum of Rwanda, PO Box 630, Butare, Rwanda. Tel 250-530-586; Fax 250-530-211; Elec Mail museum@nur.ac.rw; Internet Home Page Address: www.museum.gov.rw; *Dir* Dr Misago Kanimba
Collections: Ethnographic and artistic artifacts of Rwandan history and region

M **Rwesero Art Museum,** Nyanza, Rwanda.
Collections: Contemporary and historical visual arts, sculpture, decorative art, and traditional crafts

SAN MARINO

SAN MARINO CITY

M **MUSEO DI STATO REPUBLICA DI SAN MARINO,** State Museum, Palazzo Pergami Belluzzi, Piazzetta del Titano 1 San Marino City, San Marino. Tel 0549-882670, 0549-883835; Fax 0549-882679; Elec Mail info@museidistato.sm, museodistato@omniway.sm; Internet Home Page Address: www.museidistato.sm
Open Mar 20 - Sept 20 8 AM - 8 PM, Sept 21 - Mar 19 8:50 AM - 5 PM; Admis 3 euro
Collections: Over 5,000 artifacts of San Marino ethnographic and artistic history; Archaeological finds from Neolithic to the early Middle Ages; Architectural remains of the ancient Basilica; Paintings from 17th century convent; Fine art and sculpture by San Marino artists; Coins and medals

M **St Francis Museum,** Via Basilicius, San Marino, 47890 San Marino. Tel 0549-885132
Collections: Sacred arts and gallery housed in 14th century loggias Franciscian Monastery; Panel paintings, frescoes, canvases, furnishings, paraments; Emilio Ambron Collection

M **Museum of Ancient Arms,** Via Salita alla Cesta, San Marino, San Marino. Tel 0549-991295
Collections: History and development of ancient arms and armors of the San Marino region

M **Contemporary and Modern Art Gallery,** Galleria di via Eugippo, Via Eugippo San Marino, San Marino. Tel 0549-883002, 885414; Fax 0549-883003; Elec Mail galleria@museidistato.sm
Collections: 750 works from the early 20th century to the present in various media

SAUDI ARABIA

RIYADH

M **NATIONAL MUSEUM OF SAUDI ARABIA,** Al Muraba, PO Box 3734 Riyadh, 11481 Saudi Arabia. Tel 966-1-402-9500; Elec Mail info@saudimuseum.com; *Dir* Dr Ali S al-Moghanam
Open Mon - Wed & Sat - Sun 9 AM - noon & 4 PM - 6 PM, cl Thurs - Fri
Collections: History of Islam and the Saudi region in 10 galleries; Manuscripts, documents, antiques, decorative arts, traditional crafts

SCOTLAND

ABERDEEN

M **ABERDEEN ART GALLERY & MUSEUMS,** Schoolhill, Aberdeen, AB10 1FQ Scotland. Tel 01224 523700; Fax 01224 632133; Elec Mail info@aagm.co.uk; Internet Home Page Address: www.aagm.co.uk; Telex 7-3366; *Art Gallery & Mus Mgr* Christine Rew; *Keeper Fine Art* Jennifer Melville; *Keeper Applied Art* Allison Fraser; *Exhibs & Promotions Mgr* Deirdre Grant
Open Tues - Sat 10 AM - 5 PM, Sun 2 PM - 5 PM; No admis fee
Collections: 20th century British art; fine & decorative arts; James McBey print room
Activities: Classes for children; lects open to public; concerts; gallery talks; sales shop sells books, magazines

DUNDEE

M **DUNDEE CITY COUNCIL LEISURE & COMMUNITIES DEPARTMENT,** (Dundee Arts & Heritage) The McManus: Dundee's Art Gallery & Museum, Albert Sq, Dundee, DD1 1DA Scotland. Tel 01382307200; Fax 01382-432369; Internet Home Page Address: www.themcmanus-dundee.gov.uk; Internet Home Page Address: www.mcmanus.co.uk; *Sr Heritage Cur* Fiona Sinclair; *Sr Creative Learning Officer* Christine Miller; *Sr Cur Art* Anna Robertson
Open Mon - Sat 10 AM - 5 PM, Sun 12:30 - 4 PM; No admis fee; Estab 1872; Large regl mus with colls of art, history & natural history; Average Annual Attendance: 250,000

Income: Funded by Dundee City Council (E 1.6 m)
Special Subjects: Archaeology, Decorative Arts, Drawings, Etchings & Engravings, Historical Material, Landscapes, Marine Painting, Ceramics, Glass, Photography, Portraits, Prints, Silver, Textiles, Painting-British, Painting-European, Sculpture, Watercolors, Ethnology, Costumes, Woodcarvings, Scrimshaw, Coins & Medals, Renaissance Art, Antiquities-Greek, Antiquities-Roman, Stained Glass
Collections: 18th, 19th and 20th Century Scottish and English paintings; 17th Century Venetian and Flemish works; varied selection of watercolors and prints from the 18th - 20th Century; regional archaeology; Whaling history
Activities: Classes for adults & children; outreach program; lectrs open to the public; gallery talks; tours; Dundee Visual Arts Awards; lending of original objects of art to various institutions; mus shop sells prints & other merchandise

EDINBURGH

M **NATIONAL GALLERIES OF SCOTLAND,** Scottish National Gallery, The Mound, Edinburgh, EH2 2EL Scotland. Tel (0131) 624-6200; Fax (0131) 220-0917; Elec Mail enquiries@nationalgalleries.org; Internet Home Page Address: www.nationalgalleries.org; *Dir* Michael Clarke; *Deputy Dir & Chief Cur* Dr Patricia Allerston
Open 10 AM - 5 PM; No admis fee; Estab 1850; Average Annual Attendance: 897,014
Library Holdings: Auction Catalogs; Book Volumes; Exhibition Catalogs; Fiche; Pamphlets; Periodical Subscriptions; Reproductions; Slides
Special Subjects: Drawings, Etchings & Engravings, Landscapes, Painting-British, Painting-French, Painting-American, Watercolors, Religious Art, Painting-European, Furniture, Painting-Dutch, Coins & Medals, Tapestries, Renaissance Art, Painting-Spanish, Painting-Italian, Painting-German
Collections: European & Scottish drawings, paintings, prints & sculpture, 14th - 19th centuries
Activities: Classes for adults & children; lects open to pub; concerts; gallery talks; mus shop sells books, magazines, reproductions & other gift items

M **Scottish National Gallery of Modern Art,** Belford Rd, Edinburgh, EH4 3DR Scotland. Tel (0131) 6246200; Fax 0131 343 2802; Elec Mail enquiries@nationalgalleries.org; Internet Home Page Address: www.nationalgalleries.org; *Dir-Gen* John Leighton; *Chief Cur* Keith Hartley; *Dir* Simon Groom
Open Mon - Sun 10 AM - 5 PM; No admis fee to permanent coll; admis fee to some exhibs; Estab 1959; Two separate gallery bldgs set in extensive grounds and holding a coll of 20th & 21st century art; Average Annual Attendance: 300,000
Library Holdings: Auction Catalogs; Audio Tapes; Book Volumes; CD-ROMs; Cards; Cassettes; Clipping Files; Compact Disks; DVDs; Exhibition Catalogs; Manuscripts; Original Documents; Pamphlets; Periodical Subscriptions; Photographs; Prints; Records; Reels; Slides; Video Tapes
Collections: Western art from 20th & 21st centuries including painting, sculpture and graphic art; incl Matisse, Picasso, Dali & Scottish Art from Peploe to Douglas Gordon; Surrealism
Activities: Classes for adults & children; art clubs; lects open to public; gallery talks; tours; traveling exhibs circulated within the UK & internationally; mus shop sells books, magazines, reproductions, prints, slides & gifts

M **NATIONAL MUSEUMS SCOTLAND,** National Museum of Scotland, Chambers St, Edinburgh, EH1 1JF Scotland. Tel 0300 123 6789; Elec Mail info@nms.ac.uk; Internet Home Page Address: www.nms.ac.uk; *Dir* Dr Gordon Rintoul
Open daily 10 AM - 5 PM; No admis fee, except for special exhibs; Four museums including National Museum of Scotland, National War Museum, National Museum of Rural Life, National Museum of Flight; Average Annual Attendance: 2,500,000
Library Holdings: Auction Catalogs; Book Volumes; Exhibition Catalogs; Maps; Pamphlets; Periodical Subscriptions
Special Subjects: Decorative Arts, Ceramics, Glass, Metalwork, Antiquities-Assyrian, Photography, Porcelain, Silver, Textiles, Sculpture, American Indian Art, Archaeology, Costumes, Pottery, Eskimo Art, Furniture, Jade, Jewelry, Carpets & Rugs, Ivory, Scrimshaw, Coins & Medals, Miniatures, Islamic Art, Antiquities-Egyptian, Antiquities-Roman, Military Art
Collections: Collections of international applied arts; archaeology; natural sciences; science & tech; Scotland & Europe; world cultures
Activities: Classes for adults & children; dramatic prog; lect open to public; lect for mems only; gallery talks; tours; sponsoring of competitions; awards; TripAdvisor's Travelers Choice Award-Best Mus UK 2013; original works of art are lent to museums and cultural institutions; book traveling exhibs; originates traveling exhibs; mus shop sells books, magazines, reproductions, prints, toys, cards & jewelry

GLASGOW

M **GLASGOW MUSEUMS AND ART GALLERIES,** Kelvingrove, Glasgow, G3 8AG Scotland. Tel (141) 287-2000; Fax (141) 287-2690; *Dir* Julian Spalding
Library with 50,000 vols
Collections: Archaeology; British and Scottish art; Decorative Art Collection of ceramics, glass, jewelry, silver (especially Scottish); ethnography; Fine Art Collection representing the Dutch, Flemish, French and Italian schools; history; natural history

M **GLASGOW UNIVERSITY,** The Hunterian, University Ave, Glasgow, G12 8QQ Scotland. Tel (0141) 330 2139; Fax (0141) 330 3617; Elec Mail hunterian-enquiries@glasgow.ac.uk; Internet Home Page Address: www.glasgow.ac.uk/hunterian; *Cur Palaeontology* Dr N Clark; *Cur Mineralogy* Dr J Faithull; *Cur Archaeology* Dr S Coupar; *Cur Numismatics* Dr D Bateson; *Dir* Dr David Gaimster; *Cur Zoology* Maggie Reilly; *Senior Cur Art* Prof Pamela Robertson; *Cur Art* Peter Black; *Cur Art* Anne Dulau; *Deputy Dir* Mungo Campbell; *Head Mktg & Communications* Susan Ferguson; *Head Colls Management* Malcolm Chapman
Open Tues - Sat 10 AM - 5 PM, Sun 11 AM - 4 PM; All permanent galleries are free; Estab 1807 to serve the university and public; Three main sites on Univ Campus; Average Annual Attendance: 120,000

Income: Income from the university
Purchases: Purchases in areas of expertise of current colls
Special Subjects: Anthropology, Archaeology, Drawings, Historical Material, Ceramics, Porcelain, Pottery, Prints, Ethnology, Costumes, Furniture, Jade, Silver, Antiquities-Byzantine, Painting-Dutch, Ivory, Coins & Medals, Painting-Flemish, Antiquities-Egyptian, Antiquities-Greek, Antiquities-Roman, Gold
Collections: Prehistoric, Roman, ethnographical & coin colls; Paleontology, rocks & minerals; art, archaeology, medicine & anatomy, scientific instruments, zoology
Activities: Classes for adults & children; lect open to pub; gallery talks; exten prog serves scientific community, public, students, mus; shop sells books, reproductions, slides, toys

SENEGAL

DAKAR

M **MUSEES DEL'INSTITUT FONDAMENTAL D'AFRIQUE NOIRE,** Musee D'art Africain de Dakar, BP 6167, Dakar, Senegal. *Cur* Amadou Tahirou Diaw
Collections: African art; ethnography

SERBIA

BEOGRAD

M **MUZEJ GRADA BEOGRADA,** Zmaj Jovina 1, Beograd, 11000 Serbia. Tel 381-11-2638744; Fax 381-11-3283504; Elec Mail office@mgb.org.yu; Internet Home Page Address: www.mgb.org.yu/srp/sadrzaj/sadrz.htm
Average Annual Attendance:

M **NATIONAL MUSEUM OF SERBIA,** National Museum in Belgrade, Trg Republike 1a, Beograd, Serbia. Tel 381-11-33-060-00; Fax 381-11-2627-721; Elec Mail pr@narodnimuzej.rs; Internet Home Page Address: www.narodnimuzej.rs; *Dir* Dr Tatjana Cvjeticanin
Open Tues & Wed 10 AM - 5 PM, Thurs 11 AM - 8 PM, Sat noon - 8 PM, Sun 10 AM - 2 PM
Library Holdings: Book Volumes 36,000; CD-ROMs 120; Manuscripts 10; Other Holdings 132; Periodical Subscriptions 22 titles
Special Subjects: Archaeology
Collections: Ethnographic and material history of Serbian culture and region; Over 400,000 archaeological artifacts, pieces of medieval art, post-medieval art, modern and contemporary art and more; European Art coll
Publications: Exhibition catalogues; catalogues of collections, monographies; periodicals
Activities: Classes for adults & children; concerts; gallery talks; tours

M **Gallery of Frescoes,** Cara Urosa 20, Beograd, 11000 Serbia. Tel 381-11-2621-491; Fax 381-11-2183-655; Elec Mail gfres@narodnimuzej.rs; *Contact* Bojan Popovic
Open Mon - Wed & Sat 10 AM - 5 PM, Thurs noon - 8 PM, Sun 10 AM - 7 PM; No admis fee; Estab 1953; Average Annual Attendance: 6000
Special Subjects: Medieval Art
Collections: Copies of Frescoes; icons; miniatures; sculptures
Exhibitions: Five temporary exhibits per yr
Activities: Concerts; tours

M **Museum of Vuk and Dositej,** Gospodar Jevremova 21, Beograd, 11000 Serbia. Tel 381-11-2625-161; Elec Mail mvd@narodnimuzej.org.yu; *Contact* Ljiljana Cubric

M **Memorial Museum of Nadezda and Rastko Petrovic,** Ljube Stojanovica 25, Beograd, 11000 Serbia.

M **Lepenski Vir Museum,** Boljetin Village, Donji Milanovac, 19220 Serbia. Tel 381-63-206-271; *Contact* Vasoje Vasic

NOVI SAD

M **RAJKO MAMUZIC GALLERY OF FINE ARTS,** Vase Stajica br 1, Novi Sad, 21000 Serbia. Tel 381-21-520-223, 381-21-520-467; Fax 381-21-520-223; Elec Mail glurm@open.telekom.rs; Internet Home Page Address: www.galerijamamuzic.org.rs; *Graphic Arts Dir* Lazar Markovic, MA; *Art History* Nada Stanic, BA; *Art History* Jovanka Stolic, BA; *Art History* Ana Jovanov, BA
Open Wed - Sun 9 AM - 5 PM; No admis fee; Estab 1974; Anthology of Serbian fine arts from second half of the 20th century; Average Annual Attendance: 15,000
Income: Financed by the state
Library Holdings: Audio Tapes; Book Volumes; Cards; Clipping Files; Compact Disks; DVDs; Exhibition Catalogs; Manuscripts; Motion Pictures; Original Documents; Pamphlets; Photographs
Special Subjects: Art Education, Art History
Collections: Anthology of Serbian fine arts from second half of the 20th century; 800 works by 35 artists; paintings, sculptures, drawings; Serbian painting from second half 20th cen collected by Rajko Mamuzic
Activities: Classes for adults; concerts; gallery talks; tours; lend original object of art to various mus researching the same period & making exhibs; mus shop sells postcards

SINGAPORE, REPUBLIC OF

SINGAPORE

M **NATIONAL UNIVERSITY OF SINGAPORE CENTER FOR THE ARTS,**
University Cultural Centre, 50 Kent Ridge Crescent Singapore, 119279 Singapore, Republic of. Tel 65-6516-8817; Fax 65-6778-3738; Elec Mail museum@nus.edu.sg; Internet Home Page Address: www.nus.edu.sg/weblkc; *Sr Asst Dir* Ahmad Bin Mashadi; *Asst Cur* Qinyi Lim; *Asst Dir* Lim Nam Leng; *Mgr* Cindy Wong; *Marcom Asst Dir* Mathilda de Boer-Lim
Open Tue - Sat 10 AM - 7:30 PM, Sat 10 AM - 6 PM, cl Mon; No admis fee
Collections: Lee Kong Chian Collection of Chinese art spanning 7000 years; Ng Eng Teng Collection of sculpture; South and Southeast Asian collection of ceramics, textiles, sculptures, paintings and more; Straights Chinese collection
Activities: Classes for adults & children; docent training; mus shop sells exhibit catalogs

M **SINGAPORE ART MUSEUM,** 71 Bras Basah Rd, Singapore, 189555 Singapore, Republic of; 61 Stamford Rd #02-02, Singapore, 178892 Singapore, Republic of. Tel 65-6332-3222; Fax 65-6336-5361; Internet Home Page Address: www.singaporeartmuseum.sg; *Dir* Susie Lingham
Open Mon - Sun 10 AM - 7 PM, Fri 10 AM - 9 PM; Admis adults 10, students & seniors 5, Open House Days & Fri 6 PM - 9 PM free; Estab 1996
Special Subjects: Photography, Asian Art
Collections: Permanent collection of over 7,500 pieces of modern and contemporary Southeast Asian art
Exhibitions: (10/26/2013-02/16/2014) Singapore Biennale 2013: If The World Changed; (07/20/2013-04/27/2014) Not Against Interpretation: Untitled
Publications: Exhib catalogs; contemporary artists from Singapore
Activities: Classes for adults & children; dramatic progs; docent training; lectrs open to the public; gallery talks; tours; exten prog lends original objects of art to corp & pvt institutions; organize traveling exhibs internationally; mus shop sells books, magazines, reproductions, prints, merchandise, jewelry

SLOVAKIA

BANSKA BYSTRICA

M **CENTRAL SLOVAKIAN GALLERY,** Dolna 8, Banska Bystrica, 975-50 Slovakia. Tel 421-48-412-41-67; Elec Mail sgbb@isternet.sk; Internet Home Page Address: www.isternet.sk/sgbb; *Dir* Stefan Kocka
Open Tues - Fri 10 AM - 5 PM, Sat - Sun 10 AM - 4 PM, cl Mon
Collections: 8,250 works of modern and contemporary Slovakian art

BRATISLAVA

M **DANUBIANA MEULENSTEEN ART MUSEUM,** PO Box 9, Bratislava, 810 00 Slovakia. Tel 02-6252-8501; Fax 02-6252-8502; Elec Mail danubiana@danubiana.sk; Internet Home Page Address: www.danubiana.sk/eng/index.html

M **GALERIA MESTA BRATISLAVY,** Bratislava City Gallery, Mirbach Palace, Frantiskanske Nam 11 Bratislava, 81535 Slovakia. Tel 00421-7-54431556-8; Fax 00421-2-54432611; Elec Mail gmb@gmb.sk; Internet Home Page Address: www.gmb.bratislava.sk; *Dir* Dr Ivan Jancar; *Mgr* Zuzana Jakabova
Open Tues - Sun 11 AM - 6 PM, cl Mon; Admis general 4 Euro, children, students, seniors, disabled, natl mus assoc mems 2 Euro; Estab 1961; Public, owned by Town of Bratislava; Average Annual Attendance: 35,000
Income: Financed partially by town
Library Holdings: Auction Catalogs; Book Volumes; Exhibition Catalogs; Video Tapes
Special Subjects: Art History, Restorations
Collections: 18th-20th century art; Gothic painting & sculpture; permanent Baroque art exhibition (central Europe's)
Activities: Classes for children; lects open to pub; concerts; gallery talks; 2007, 2010, 2012 gallery of the year award (for Slovak Republic only); lending original objects of art to sister institutions; mus shop sells books, reproductions & prints

M **SLOVENSKA NARODNA GALERIA,** Slovak National Gallery, Riecna 1, Bratislava, 815 13 Slovakia. Tel +421 2 20476111; Fax +421 2 20476971; Elec Mail sng@sng.sk; Elec Mail sng@chello.sk; Internet Home Page Address: www.sng.sk; *Dir Gen* Alexandra Kusa, PhD; *Dir of Art Collections, Deputy Dir* Alexandra Homolova
Open Tues - Wed & Fri - Sun 10 AM - 6 PM, Thurs noon - 8 PM; cl Mon; Admis 3.50 euro; Estab 1948; Circ Circulation 5,500; Gallery contains art history, art collections, scientific research, culture & educ; Average Annual Attendance: 110,000; Mem: friends of SNG, 150
Library Holdings: Auction Catalogs; Book Volumes; CD-ROMs; Clipping Files; Compact Disks; Exhibition Catalogs; Fiche; Filmstrips; Manuscripts; Maps; Memorabilia; Micro Print; Original Documents; Periodical Subscriptions; Photographs; Reproductions; Slides; Video Tapes
Special Subjects: Archaeology, Drawings, Folk Art, History of Art & Archaeology, Illustration, Interior Design, Landscape Architecture, Architecture, Art Education, Ceramics, Collages, Conceptual Art, Mixed Media, Portraits, Prints, Silver, Textiles, Bronzes, Painting-British, Painting-French, Sculpture, Graphics, Hispanic Art, Photography, Watercolors, Costumes, Religious Art, Crafts, Painting-European, Posters, Jewelry, Porcelain, Oriental Art, Painting-Dutch, Restorations, Baroque Art, Calligraphy, Miniatures, Painting-Flemish, Renaissance Art, Medieval Art, Painting-Spanish, Painting-Italian, Antiquities-Roman, Mosaics
Collections: Applied arts; European & Slovak paintings; Dutch, Flemish and Italian works of art; graphics and drawings; sculpture

Publications: Renaissance (exhib & publ)
Activities: Classes for adults; classes for children; dramatic progs & other art of Slovakia; lects open to pub; 6-8 vis lectrs per yr; concerts; gallery talks; tours; schols; mus shop sells books, magazines, original art, reproductions, prints

DOLNY KUBIN

M **ORAVSKA GALERIA,** County House Dolny Kubin, Hviezdoslavovo Sq 11, Dolny Kubin, 02601 Slovakia. Tel 421-43-58-631-12; Fax 421-43-586-43-95; Elec Mail orgaldk@vuczilina.sk; ogaleria@nextra.sk; Internet Home Page Address: www.oravskagaleria.sk; *Dir* Eva Luptakova
Open Tues - Sun 10 AM - 5 PM; Admis adults to permanent exhibs 2 euro, temp exhibs 1 euro, seniors 1 euro, children & students 0.50 euro, res students 0.25 euro, disabled & children under 6 free
Collections: 7,472 works in 8 disciplines; craft of the 15th - 19th centuries, icons, Slovak artworks of the 20th century, traditional folk art

M **Gallery Mary Gregor,** Medvedzie, Tvrdosin, 02744 Slovakia. Tel 421-043-5322793; Internet Home Page Address: www.oravskagaleria.sk
Open Apr 1 - Sept 30 Tues - Sun 10 AM - 4 PM; Admis to permanent exhibs: adults 1 euro, children, disabled & seniors 0.50 euro; admis to exhib hall: adults 0.50 euro, children, disabled & seniors 0.25 euro, children under 6 free; family cardholder pass rates apply
Collections: Permanent collection of Slovakian artist Maria Medvecka

MEZILABORCE

M **WARHOL FAMILY MUSEUM OF MODERN ART,** A Warhol St, Mezilaborce, 06801 Slovakia. Tel 421-939-31207; Elec Mail pro@region.sk; Internet Home Page Address: www.region.sk/warhol/museum.html

SLOVENIA

KOBARID

M **KOBARID MUSEUM,** Gregorciceva 10 5222, Kobarid, Slovenia. Tel 00386 05 3890000; Fax 00386 05 3890000; Elec Mail info@kobariski-muzej.si; Internet Home Page Address: www.kobariski-muzej.si
Open Apr - Sept Mon - Fri 9 AM - 6 PM, Sat - Sun & holidays 9 AM - 7 PM; Oct - Mar Mon - Fri 10 AM - 5 PM, Sat - Sun & holidays 9 AM - 6 PM; Admis adults 4E, seniors, high school & university students 3E, children 2.5E
Collections: WWI history on the Isonzo front

LJUBLJANA

M **ARHITEKTURNI MUZEJ IN GALERIJE MESTA LJUBLJANA,**
Architecture Museum of Ljubljana, Grad Fuzine, Pot na Fuzine 2 Ljubljana, SI-1000 Slovenia. Tel 386-0-1-540-9798, 386-0-540-0346; Fax 386-0-1-540-0344; Elec Mail info@mgml.si; Internet Home Page Address: www.mgml.si; *Dir* Dr Peter Krecic
Open Mon - Fri 9 AM - 3 PM, Sat 10 AM - 6 PM, Sun 10 AM - 3 PM; Admis adults 3 euro, students children & seniors 1.5 euro
Collections: Central Slovenian museum for architecture, physical planning, industrial and graphic design and photography

M **Plecnik Collection,** Karunova 4, Ljubljana, 1000 Slovenia. Tel 386-0-1-280-16-00; Fax 386-0-1-280-16-05; Elec Mail info@mgml.si; Internet Home Page Address: www.mgml.si; *Cur* Ana Porok
Open for appointed groups only, guided visits on the hour; Mon & Fri 10 AM - 3 PM, Tues - Thurs 10 AM - 2 PM, Sat 9 AM - 3 PM, cl Sun & holidays; Admis adults 4 euro, students seniors & children 2 euro
Collections: Former residence and coll of artist Joze Plecnik
Activities: Classes for adults & children; lects open to the public; 15 vis lectrs per yr; gallery talks; tours; mus shop sells books, magazines, reproductions & prints

M **Jakopic Gallery,** Slovenska 9a, Ljubljana, 1000 Slovenia. Tel 386-0-1-425-23-93
Collections: Temporary exhibitions of international and national Slovakian artwork in various media

M **MODERNA GALERIJA & MUZEJ SODOBNE UMETNOSTI METELKOVA,** Museum of Modern Art & Museum of Contemporary Art Metelkova, Tomsiceva 14, Ljubljana, 1000 Slovenia. Tel 00386 12416 800; Fax 00386 12514 120; Elec Mail info@mg-lj.si; Internet Home Page Address: www.mg-lj-si; *Dir* Zdenka Badovinac
Open 10 AM - 6 PM, cl Mon; Admis adults 5 euro, students & pensioners 2.5 euro, groups (adults) 3.5 euro; Estab 1948; Library with 45,000 vols; Average Annual Attendance: 50,000
Income: Public funds
Library Holdings: Book Volumes; Exhibition Catalogs
Collections: Slovene art from Impressionists to present; international coll containing works of major artists of contemporary world art; Arteast 2000 (in Museum of Contemporary Art Metelkova)
Exhibitions: 20th Centure Continuities & Ruptures (in Museum of Modern Art); The Present and Presence (in Museum of Contemport Art Metelkova)
Activities: Classes for children; gallery talks; mus sells books & reproductions

M **NARODNA GALERIJA,** National Gallery of Slovenia, Puharjeva 9, Ljubljana, 1000 Slovenia. Tel 00386-(0) 1 24 15 400; Fax 00386-(0) 1-24 15 403; Elec Mail info@ng-slo.si; Internet Home Page Address: www.ng-slo.si; *Dir* Barbara Jaki, PhD; *Head Cur* Matcja Brescak, MA; *Head Conservation* Andrej Hrci, MA; *Head Educ* Kristina Preininger; *Head Librn* Mateja Krapez; *Cur* Andrej Smrekar, PhD; *Cur* Ferdinand Serbelj, PhD; *Head Documentation* Alenka Simoncic
Open Tues - Sun 10 AM - 6 PM; Admis general 7E, reduced 5E; Estab 1918 for the purpose of collection of art in Slovenia; Library with 37,000 vols; 15,000 works of art (paintings, sculptures, works on paper); Average Annual Attendance: 250,000

Income: Government
Library Holdings: Auction Catalogs; CD-ROMs; Clipping Files; DVDs; Exhibition Catalogs; Framed Reproductions; Manuscripts; Maps; Original Documents; Pamphlets; Periodical Subscriptions; Records; Reproductions; Video Tapes
Special Subjects: Drawings, Etchings & Engravings, Portraits, Prints, Manuscripts, Painting-French, Sculpture, Graphics, Photography, Sculpture, Watercolors, Religious Art, Woodcarvings, Woodcuts, Landscapes, Painting-European, Painting-Dutch, Coins & Medals, Restorations, Baroque Art, Painting-Flemish, Painting-Polish, Renaissance Art, Medieval Art, Painting-Spanish, Painting-Italian, Painting-German
Collections: Copies of medieval frescoes; European Masters from the 14th century to the beginning of the 20th century; Slovenian sculptures and paintings from the 13th to the 20th century; Slovenian graphic arts; Coll of posters; Archival-documentary coll; Photo-Library
Publications: Exhib Catalogues
Activities: Classes for adults & children, dramatic progs, docent training, workshops; lects open to the pub; 6 vis lectrs per yr, concerts, gallery talks, tours; lending of original objects of art to European galleries & mus; originate traveling exhibs to Slovenian mus; mus shop sells books, magazines, reproductions, prints & slides

SOUTH AFRICA

CAPE TOWN

M **IZIKO MUSEUMS OF SOUTH AFRICA,** (Iziko Michaelis Collection) Michaelis Collection, Iziko Old Town House, Greenmarket Sq Cape Town, South Africa; PO Box 61, Cape Town, 8000 South Africa. Tel (021) 481-3965/481-3970; Fax (021) 467-4680; Elec Mail hproud@iziko.org.za; Internet Home Page Address: www.iziko.org.za; *Cur* Hayden Proud
Open Mon - Sat 10 AM - 5 PM, cl Sun; Admis R 10.00 (ten rands); Estab 1914; Old Master Collection; Mem: 150 mems; friends of the Michaelis Coll R75.00; ann meeting Sep
Income: state funded
Library Holdings: Book Volumes
Collections: Dutch and Flemish graphic art and paintings of the 16th - 18th centuries; historical colls of the Iziko SA National Gallery
Exhibitions: Vis Artist's Residency Program
Activities: Classes for adults & children; lects open to pub; 2-3 vis lectrs per yr; concerts; gallery talks; lending of original objects of art to Haus der Kunst, Munich, schools from disadvantaged areas; progs for blind & disabled pupils; occasional travel exhibs to Sanlam Art Gallery, Bellville; mus shop sells books, postcards, brochures, current exhibs catalogues

M **SOUTH AFRICAN NATIONAL GALLERY,** Government Ave, Gardens, PO Box 2420 Cape Town, 8000 South Africa. Tel (021) 45-1628; Fax (021) 461-0045; *Dir* M Martin
Collections: 19th and 20th century South African art; 15th - 20th century, European art, including drawings, paintings, prints, sculptures and watercolors; traditional African art; 20th century American Art

DURBAN

M **DURBAN MUSEUMS,** City Hall, Smith St, Durban, 4000 South Africa; PO Box 4085, Durban, 4000 South Africa. Tel (031) 311 2264; Fax (031) 311 2273; Internet Home Page Address: www.durban.gov.za/museums; *Dir* C Brown; *Dir* R Omar
Open 8:30 AM - 4:00 PM; No admis fee; Estab 1910/Educ
Library Holdings: Auction Catalogs; Audio Tapes; CD-ROMs; Cassettes; Clipping Files; Compact Disks; Exhibition Catalogs; Slides; Video Tapes
Collections: Archaeology, paintings, graphic art, porcelain, sculptures, local history
Activities: Classes for adults & children; lects open to public

JOHANNESBURG

M **CITY OF JOHANNESBURG ART GALLERY,** Johannesburg Art Gallery, Cnr Klein & King George Sts, Joubert Park Johannesburg, 2044 South Africa. Tel (011) 725-3130; Fax (011) 720 6000; Elec Mail job@joburg.org.za; *Dir* R Keene
Open Tues - Sun 10 AM - 7 PM; No admis fee; Estab 1910; Art
Library Holdings: Auction Catalogs; Book Volumes; CD-ROMs; Clipping Files; Compact Disks; Exhibition Catalogs; Original Documents; Other Holdings Archives; Pamphlets; Periodical Subscriptions; Slides; Video Tapes
Collections: South African & international painting & sculpture; print coll; small coll of ceramics, textiles & fans
Activities: Classes for adults & children; lects open to pub; mus shop sells books

KIMBERLEY

M **WILLIAM HUMPHREYS ART GALLERY,** PO Box 885, Civic Centre Kimberley, 8300 South Africa. Tel (053) 83 11 7245; Fax (053) 83 22 221; Elec Mail whag@eject.co.za; Internet Home Page Address: www.whag.co.za; *Dir* Mrs Ann Pretorius; *Libr* Mrs Hesta Maree; *Project Leader* Ms Rika Stockenstrom; *Project Leader* Ms Liz Bozman
Open Mon - Fri 8 AM - 4:45 PM, Sat 10 AM - 4:45, Sun & holidays 9 AM - noon; Admis R 5.00 adults, R 2.00 children; Estab 1952; Circ 100; Art Mus; Average Annual Attendance: 22,000
Income: Central State: Dept Arts & Culture
Library Holdings: Auction Catalogs; Audio Tapes; Book Volumes; Cassettes; DVDs; Pamphlets; Periodical Subscriptions; Video Tapes

Collections: collection of Old Masters; collection of South African works of art; traditional and contemp SA ceramics; traditional SA artifacts; European & Cape furniture
Exhibitions: Traveling temporary exhibs
Publications: Newsletter; Carter, ACR The Work of War Artists in S.A. (reprints of the London Art Jour 1900)
Activities: Classes for adults & children; lects open to public; 10 vis lectrs per year; concerts; gallery talks; tours; sponsoring of competitions; Heritage; lending of original objects of art; mus shop sells books, original art, reproductions, prints

PIETERMARITZBURG

M **TATHAM ART GALLERY,** Chief Albert Luthuli (Commerical Rd) opposite City Hall, PO Box 321 Pietermaritzburg, 3200 South Africa. Tel 27 033 392 2800/1; Fax 27 033 394 9831; Internet Home Page Address: www.tatham.org.za; *Dir* Brendan Bell; *Asst Dir* Bryony Clark; *Educ Officer* Thulani Makhaye; *Technical Officer* Phumlani Ntshangase; *Admin Officer* Vimla Moodley
Open Mon - Fri 8 AM - 5 PM (Gallery Office), call for appt
Collections: 18th centuriy English & French paintings & sculpture; 19th & 20th century English graphics; modern European graphics; South African painting & sculpture

PORT ELIZABETH

M **NELSON MANDELA BAY MUNICIPALITY,** (The Nelson Mandela Metropolitan Art Museum) Nelson Mandela Metropolitan Art Museum, One Park Dr, Port Elizabeth, 6001 South Africa. Tel 27 (041) 506 2000; Fax 27 (041) 5863234; Elec Mail artmuseum@mandelametro.gov.za; Internet Home Page Address: www.artmuseum.co.za; *Dir* Dr Melanie Hillebrand
Open Mon & Wed - Fri 9 AM - 5 PM, Tues Noon - 5 PM, Sat, Sun 1 - 5 PM, pub holidays 2 - 5 PM, 1st Sun of month 9 AM - 2 PM; No admis fee
Library Holdings: Auction Catalogs; Audio Tapes; Book Volumes; CD-ROMs; Cassettes; DVDs; Exhibition Catalogs; Original Documents; Pamphlets; Periodical Subscriptions
Special Subjects: Decorative Arts, Drawings, Etchings & Engravings, History of Art & Archaeology, Landscapes, Marine Painting, Art Education, Art History, Ceramics, Collages, Conceptual Art, Portraits, Pottery, Prints, Textiles, Bronzes, Painting-European, Sculpture, Graphics, Photography, Watercolors, Anthropology, Ethnology, Costumes, Crafts, Woodcarvings, Woodcuts, Posters, Eskimo Art, Jewelry, Porcelain, Oriental Art, Asian Art, Painting-British, Carpets & Rugs, Restorations, Miniatures, Embroidery, Mosaics, Cartoons, Stained Glass
Collections: South African art (Eastern Cape), British art, international printmaking & Oriental art (including Indian miniatures & Chinese textiles)
Exhibitions: Active prog of temporary exhibs
Activities: Classes for adults & children; teacher training; lects open to pub; 5 vis lectrs per yr; concerts; gallery talks; tours; sponsoring of competitions; biennial exhib & award; extension prog serves Eastern Cape Province; artmobile; lending of original objects of art to other mus; organize traveling exhibs to other mus; mus shop sells books, reproductions, prints, gifts & other items

PRETORIA

M **PRETORIA ART MUSEUM,** Municipal Art Gallery, Arcadia Park, Pretoria, 0083 South Africa; PO Box 40925, Arcadia, 0007 South Africa. Tel (012) 344-1807; Fax (012) 344-1809; Elec Mail art.museum@tshwane.gov.za; Internet Home Page Address: www.pretoriaartmuseum.co.za; *Dir* D Oegema
Open Tues - Sun 10 AM - 5 PM; Estab 1964
Library Holdings: Auction Catalogs; Book Volumes; Clipping Files; Exhibition Catalogs; Pamphlets; Periodical Subscriptions
Special Subjects: Etchings & Engravings, Ceramics, Textiles, Tapestries, Drawings, Graphics, Photography, Prints, Sculpture, African Art, Crafts, Pottery, Woodcarvings, Painting-Dutch, Painting-Flemish
Collections: European graphics; 17th century Dutch art; 19th & 20th centuries South African art

SPAIN

ALZUZA

M **OTEIZA MUSEUM,** C/de la Cuesta 7, Alzuza, Navarra 31486 Spain. Tel 948332074; Fax 948332066; Elec Mail info@museooteiza.org; Internet Home Page Address: www.museooteiza.org; *Dir* Gregorio Diaz Ereno; *Deputy Dir* Juan Pablo Huercanos; *Cur* Elena Martin; *Head Finance Dept* Laura Escudero; *Head Didactic Dept* Aitziber Urtasun; *Head Documentation Dept* Borja Gonzalez Riera
Open June 1-Sept 30 Tues-Sun 11AM-7PM; Oct1-May 31 Tues-Fri 10AM-3PM, Sat-Sun & pub holidays 11AM-7PM; cl Mon; Admis adults 4 Euro, students & seniors over 65 2 Euro; children under 12 free
Collections: 1,690 sculptures; 800 drawings; 2,000 chalk laboratory studies

BARCELONA

M **INSTITUT DE CULTURA AJUNTAMENT DE BARCELONA,** Museo de Ceramica, Palacio de Pedralbes-Diagonal, N 686 Barcelona, 08034 Spain. Tel 00 34 93 256 3465; Fax (93) 2054518; Elec Mail macasanovas@bcn.cat; Internet Home Page Address: www.museoceramica.bcn.es/; *Chief Cur* Maria Antonia Casanovas
Open Tues - Sat 10 AM - 6 PM, Sun 10 AM - 3 PM; Admis 4.50 euro, children under 16, ICOM members, press & others free; Estab 1966; Library with 4,700 vols, rooms dedicated to Spanish & contemporary ceramics; Average Annual Attendance: 65,000

Income: financed by the municipality
Library Holdings: Auction Catalogs; Kodachrome Transparencies; Manuscripts; Periodical Subscriptions; Photographs; Slides
Collections: Spanish ceramics, 11th to 21st century; European, Oriental & North American Colls
Exhibitions: Mexican Colonial Pottery, Margit Denz; Between East and West, Pere Noguera, Lusterware, Picasso, Miro, Barcelo
Publications: Exhib catalogues
Activities: Classes for adults & children; conservation courses; lects open to pub; 3 vis lectrs per yr; concerts; gallery talks; tours; awards: Critic Assn 1982 & 2003; lending of original objects of art to temporary exhibs in mus all over the world; originate traveling exhibs to Spanish mus; sales shop sells books, original art, reproductions, postcards, catalogues

M **MUSEO DE LA FUNDACION ANTONI TAPIES,** Calle Arago 255, Barcelona, 08007 Spain. Tel 34 934870315; Fax 34 934870009
Collections: Anoni Tapies paintings

M **MUSEU D'ART CONTEMPORANI DE BARCELONA,** Placa dels Angels 1, Barcelona, 08001 Spain. Tel 34-93-412-08-10; Fax 34-93-412-46-02; Elec Mail coleccio@macba.cat; Internet Home Page Address: www.macba.es; *Dir* Bartomeu Mari; *Cur* Carles Guerra
Open Sep 25 - June 26 Mon - Fri 11 AM - 7:30 PM, Sat 10 AM - 8 PM, Sun 10 AM - 3 PM; June 27 - Sept 24 Fri 11 AM - 8 PM, Sat 10 AM - 8 PM, cl Tues; Admis Collection 7.5 euro, students 6 euro; Museum 7.5 euro, students 6 euro, under 14 & over 65 free
Collections: Many works from Catalonian, Spanish & international artists ranging from the 1950s to the present

M **MUSEU D'ART MODERN DE BARCELONA,** Museum of Modern Art, Parc de la Ciutadella, Barcelona, 08003 Spain. Tel 93-319-5728; *Dir* Cristina Mendoza Garriga
Library with 50,000 vols
Collections: Modern art

M **MUSEU NACIONAL D'ART DE CATALUNYA,** National Art Museum, Parc de Montjuic, Palau Nacional Barcelona, 08038 Spain. Tel (00 34) 93 622 03 60 (office); 93 622 03 76 (information); Fax (00 34) 93 622 03 74; Elec Mail mnac@mnac.cat; Internet Home Page Address: www.mnac.cat; *Dir* M Theresa Ocana Goma; *Head of Dept of Cur* M Cristina Hendoza Garriga
Open Tues - Sat 10 AM - 7 PM, Sun & holidays 10 AM - 2:30 PM, cl Jan 1, May 1 & Dec 25; Admis permanent coll 8.50 Euros, temporary exhib 5 Euros, permanent and temporary exhibs 8.50 Euros; Medieval, Romanesque, Gothic, Renaissance & Baroque modern art collections; Average Annual Attendance: 1,000,000
Library Holdings: Book Volumes; Cards; Compact Disks; DVDs; Exhibition Catalogs; Lantern Slides; Manuscripts; Original Documents; Pamphlets; Photographs; Prints; Reproductions; Slides; Video Tapes
Special Subjects: Drawings, Photography, Sculpture, Religious Art, Woodcarvings, Etchings & Engravings, Decorative Arts, Painting-European, Jewelry, Coins & Medals, Baroque Art, Renaissance Art, Medieval Art, Painting-Spanish, Enamels
Collections: Baroque & Renaissance paintings & sculpture; Catalan Gothic & Romanesque paintings & sculpture; modern paintings, sculpture & arts and crafts; photography; drawings & prints; numismatics
Publications: Publications on temporary and permanent collections
Activities: Classes for adults & children; docent training; dramatic progs; lects open to pub; concerts; gallery talks; tours; schols & fels offered; lending of original objects of art; mus shop sells books, magazines, original art; prints; reproductions, slides, gifts

M **MUSEU PICASSO,** Calle Montcada 15-23, Barcelona, 08003 Spain. Tel 93 256 30 00; Fax 93256 3001; Elec Mail museupicasso@bcn.cat; Internet Home Page Address: www.museupicasso.bcn.cat; *Dir* Bernardo Laniado-Romero; *Institutional Relations* Lluis Bagunya; *Head Conservation* Reyes Jimenez; *Cur* Malen Gual
Open Tues - Sun (including pub holidays) 10 AM - 8 PM; Admis 11 euros; Estab 1963; Average Annual Attendance: 950,000
Collections: Pablo Picasso, 1890-1972: 4,000 paintings, sculpture, drawings, ceramics and prints, including the series Las Meninas; photography on Picasso
Exhibitions: Yo Picasso: Selfportraits (2013); La Vida (2013)
Publications: Cartoons on the Front Line; Picasso in Paris: 1900-1907; Picasso 1936: Traces of an exhib (2011); Xavier Vilato: 1921-2000 The Road to Freedom; Economy; Picasso; Ceramica (2012)
Activities: Classes for adults & children; docent training; lects open to pub; concerts; gallery talks; tours; lending of original objects of art; organize traveling exhibs; mus shop sells books, magazines, prints, slides, reproductions

M **REAL ACADEMIA CATALANA DE BELLAS ARTES DE SAN JORGE ROYAL ACADEMY OF FINE ARTS (MUSEUM),** Royal Academy of Fine Arts, Casa Lonja, Paseo de Isabel II, n 1, 2 Barcelona, 08003 Spain. Tel (93) 319-24-32; Fax (93) 319-02-16; Elec Mail secretaria@racba.org; Internet Home Page Address: www.racba.org; *Pres & Exec Sr Dir* Joan Antoni Solans Huguet; *Sec Gen & Exec Sr Dir* Leopoldo Gil Nebot; *Conservador Mus & Ilmo Sr* Josep Bracons Clapes; *Treas & II Liu Sr Dir* Joan Uriach Marsal; *Librn* IIma Sra Dra Pilar Velez Vicente
Open Mon - Fri 10 AM - 2 PM, cl Aug; No admis fee; Estab 1849; Private collection
Library Holdings: Book Volumes; Exhibition Catalogs; Periodical Subscriptions
Activities: Lects open to pub; concerts; Mus shop sells books

BILBAO

M **GUGGENHEIM MUSEUM BILBAO,** Abandoibarra Et 2, Bilbao, 48001 Spain. *Dir Gen* Juan Ignacio Vidarte
Open Tues - Sun 10 AM - 8 PM, July - Aug Mon - Sun 10 AM - 8 PM, cl Mon; Admis adult 10.50 euro, senior 6.50 euro, under 12 free

M **MUSEO DE BELLAS ARTES DE BILBAO,** Museum of Fine Arts, Museo Plaza, 2, Bilbao, 48009 Spain. Tel (94) 4396060; Fax (94) 439-61-45; Elec Mail info@museobilbao.com; Internet Home Page Address: www.museobilbao.com; *Dir* Javier Viar Olloqui
Open Tues - Sun 10 AM - 8 PM; Admis general 6 euro, reduced 4.50 euro; Wed no admis fee
Library Holdings: Auction Catalogs; Audio Tapes; Book Volumes; CD-ROMs; Cards; Cassettes; Clipping Files; Compact Disks; DVDs; Exhibition Catalogs; Fiche; Filmstrips; Original Documents; Pamphlets; Periodical Subscriptions; Photographs; Prints
Collections: Paintings, sculpture; famous works by El Greco, Goya, Gauguin, Velazquez; general contemporary art; early Spanish paintings
Activities: Classes for adults & children; dramatic progs; docent training; lectrs open to the pub; lectrs for mems only; vis lectrs; schols; gallery talks; tours; mus shop sells books, original art, reproductions, prints & other items

CADIZ

M **FUNDACION MONTENMEDIO ARTE CONTEMPORANEO,** Cadiz, Spain. Tel 34-956-455-134; Elec Mail nmac@fundacionnmac.org; Internet Home Page Address: www.fundacionnmac.org/english/home.php

FIGUERES

M **GALA-SALVADOR DALI FOUNDATION MUSEUMS,** Salvador Dali Foundation, Torre Galatea, Pujada del Castell 28 Figueres, E-17600 Spain. Tel 34-972-677-505; Fax 34-972-501-666; Internet Home Page Address: www.salvador-dali.org; *Dir* Atoni Pixot
Special Subjects: Drawings, Etchings & Engravings, Photography, Sculpture, Jewelry
Collections: Permanent Collection: thousands of objects dating from all the various periods of Dali's life; 4000+ works of art in various media

M **Teatre Museu-Dali,** Gala Dali Sq 5, Figueres, E-17600 Spain. Tel 34-972-677-500;Jovdi Artigas-Cadena
Open Nov 1 - Feb 28 10:30 AM - 6 PM, Mar 1 - June 30 9:30 AM - 6 PM, July 1 - Sept 30 9 AM - 8 PM, Oct 1 - Oct 30 9:30 AM - 6 PM; Admis 10 euro, students & seniors 7 euro
Collections: Dali designed architectural piece

M **Dali Jewels Museum,** Ma Angels Vayreda St, Pujada del Castell St Figueres, E-17600 Spain. Tel 34-972-677-500;Jovdi Artigas-Cadena
Open Nov 1 - Feb 28 10:30 AM - 6 PM, Mar 1 - June 30 9:30 AM - 6 PM, July 1 - Sept 30 9 AM - 8 PM, Oct 1 - Oct 30 9:30 AM - 6 PM; Admis 6 euro, students & seniors 4 euro, under 9 free
Collections: Collection of 37 jewels in gold and precious stones; Drawings and paintings made during design of jewels from 1940-1970

M **Casa Museu Salvador Dali,** Torre Galatea, Pujada del Castell 28 Figueres, E-17600 Spain. Tel 34-972-251-015; Fax 34-972-251-083; Elec Mail pllgrups@fundaciodali.org; Internet Home Page Address: www.salvador-dali.org;Jovdi Artigas-Cadena
Open Mar 15 - June 14 & Sept 16 - Jan 6 10:30 AM - 6 PM, June 15 - Sept 15 9:30 AM - 9 PM; Admis adults 11 euro, students & seniors 8 euro, under 9 free; Average Annual Attendance: 99,717
Special Subjects: Decorative Arts, Furniture
Collections: Dali's only fixed residence from 1930-1982
Activities: Mus shop sells books & reproductions

M **Casa Museu Castell Gala Dali,** Torre Galatea, Pujada del Castell, 28 Figueres, E-17600 Spain. Tel 34-972-677-507; Fax 34-972-501-666; Elec Mail jac@fundaciodali.org; Elec Mail pbgrups@fundaciodali.org; Internet Home Page Address: www.salvador-dali.org; *Coordr Projects* Jovdi Artigas-Cadena
Open Mar 15 - June 14 /Sept 16 - Nov 1 10 AM - 8 PM, Nov 2 - Dec 31 10 AM - 5 PM; Admis adults 8 euro, students & seniors 6, under 9 free; 1996; Average Annual Attendance: 104,081
Special Subjects: Decorative Arts, Architecture, Glass, Furniture, Sculpture, Tapestries, Drawings, Watercolors, Costumes, Crafts, Painting-Spanish
Collections: Castle with interior designed and decorated with Dali artifacts and pieces; 2nd floor - clothes created by Dalí and dresses belonging to Gala by the world's leading fashion designers
Publications: Guide book of castle & catalog of temporary exhib
Activities: Prog of guided visits for school groups; concerts; tours; mus shop sells books, reproductions, & souvenirs

HERNANI

M **MUSEO CHILLIDA-LEKU,** B Jauregui 66, Hernani, E-20120 Spain. Tel 34-943-336006; Elec Mail anahornos@museochillidaleku.com; Internet Home Page Address: www.eduardo-chillida.com

LEON

M **MUSEO DE ARTE CONTEMPORANEO DE CASTILLA Y LEON,** Avenida de los Reyes Leoneses 24, Leon, 24008 Spain. Tel 34-987-09-00-00; Fax 34-987-09-11-11; Elec Mail musac@musac.es; Internet Home Page Address: musac.es/
Open to pub Tues - Fri 11 AM - 2 PM, 5 PM - 8 PM, Sat, Sun & holidays 11 AM - 3 PM, 5 PM - 9 PM; Admis 5 euro, reduced 2 euro; Estab 2005, mus for the present; 6 main galleries, 1 project room, 1 showcase; Average Annual Attendance: 100,000
Income: Financed through regional government
Library Holdings: Audio Tapes; Book Volumes; CD-ROMs; Cards; Clipping Files; Compact Disks; DVDs; Exhibition Catalogs; Filmstrips; Kodachrome Transparencies; Lantern Slides; Manuscripts; Memorabilia; Micro Print; Motion Pictures; Original Art Works; Original Documents; Other Holdings; Pamphlets; Periodical Subscriptions; Photographs; Prints; Records; Reels; Reproductions; Slides; Video Tapes

LLEIDA

M MUSEU D'ART JAUME MORERA, Calle Mayor 31, Casino Bldg Lleida, 25007 Spain. Tel 0034-973-700-419; Fax 0034-973-700-487; Elec Mail mmorera@paeria.cat; Internet Home Page Address: www.paeria.es/mmorera Open Tues-Sat 11AM-2PM & 5PM-8PM, Sun & holidays 11AM-2PM; No admis fee
Collections: paintings by Jaume Morera

MADRID

M LÁZARO GALDIANO FUNDACIÓN, (Museo Lazaro Galdiano) Calle Serrano 122, Madrid, 28006 Spain. Tel (91) 561 6084; Fax (91) 561 7793; Elec Mail secretaria.fundoucion@flg.es; Internet Home Page Address: www.flg.es; *Dir* Jesusa Vega; *Gerente Adjunto* Carlos Pantor; *Secretono Palromato* Juan Antonio Yeve Museum: open Mon, Wed - Sun 10 AM - 4:30 PM, cl Tues; Library: open Mon - Fri 9 AM - 2 PM, cl Sat & Sun; Admis Fee museum: 4 euro, Sun free; library: free
Collections: Ivories, enamels, furniture, manuscripts, tapestries, prints, coins, textiles, drawings, bindings, rare books; European paintings & sculpture XV-XIX; medals, pottery, antiquities
Activities: Docent training; concerts; mus shop sells books, magazines & reproductions

M MUSEO CERRALBO, Ventura Rodriguez 17, Madrid, 28008 Spain. Tel (91) 547 36 46; Fax (91) 559 11 71; Elec Mail museo.cerralbo@mcu.es; Internet Home Page Address: museocerralbo.mcu.es; *Dir* Lurdes Vaquero Arguelles; *Cur* M Angeles Granados Ortega; *Cur* Retela Rcio Martin Open Tues - Sat 9:30 AM - 15:00 PM, Sun & pub holidays 10 AM - 15:00 PM; Admis 3 euro, reduced 1.50 euro, free admis proof required at website; Estab 1924; pub institution; Mus House; Average Annual Attendance: 80,000
Library Holdings: Auction Catalogs; Book Volumes; CD-ROMs; DVDs; Exhibition Catalogs; Memorabilia; Original Documents; Periodical Subscriptions
Special Subjects: Archaeology, Drawings, Etchings & Engravings, Architecture, Ceramics, Glass, Metalwork, Furniture, Gold, Portraits, Pottery, Silver, Textiles, Bronzes, Manuscripts, Maps, Painting-British, Painting-European, Painting-French, Tapestries, Graphics, Hispanic Art, Photography, Sculpture, Watercolors, Archaeology, Ethnology, Costumes, Religious Art, Woodcarvings, Woodcuts, Decorative Arts, Judaica, Jewelry, Porcelain, Oriental Art, Asian Art, Painting-Dutch, Carpets & Rugs, Ivory, Coins & Medals, Restorations, Baroque Art, Miniatures, Painting-Flemish, Renaissance Art, Embroidery, Laces, Medieval Art, Painting-Spanish, Painting-Italian, Antiquities-Egyptian, Antiquities-Greek, Antiquities-Roman, Stained Glass, Painting-German, Pewter, Military Art, Antiquities-Etruscan, Enamels
Collections: Paintings; drawings; engravings; porcelain arms; carpets; coins; furniture; photographs; clocks; tapestries; books; sculptures; wood carvings; includes paintings by: El Greco, Ribera, Titian, Van Dyck & Tintoretto; library with 15,000 vols (historical library); archive (historical)
Publications: check website
Activities: Classes for children; educ progs include conferences; courses; families & children workshops; school activities; concerts; schols; awards, Europa Nostra; lending of original art to other mus; mus shop sells reproductions, books, slides, office objects & other items

M MUSEO DEL ROMANTICISMO, (Museo Romantico) Museum of the Romantic Period, Calle de San Mateo 13, Madrid, 28004 Spain. Tel 448-10-45; Fax 594-28-93; Elec Mail information.romanticismo@mcu.es; Internet Home Page Address: museoromanticismo.mcu.es; *Dir* Asuncion Cardona Suanzes Open winter: Tues - Sat 9:30 AM - 18:30 PM, Sun 10 AM - 15 PM, cl Mon; summer: Tues - Sat 9:30 AM - 20:30 PM, cl Mon; Admis 3 euros
Special Subjects: Decorative Arts, Drawings, Ceramics, Furniture, Gold, Photography, Portraits, Graphics, Dolls, Glass, Jewelry, Porcelain, Miniatures, Period Rooms, Painting-Spanish
Collections: Books, decorations, furniture and paintings of the Spanish Romantic period

M MUSEO NACIONAL CENTRO DE ARTE REINA SOFIA, Calle Santa Isabel 52, Madrid, 28012 Spain. Tel 34-91-744-10-00; Fax 34-91-774-10-56; Elec Mail info@museoreinasofia.es; Internet Home Page Address: www.museoreinasofia.es; *Dir* Manuel Borja-Viuel; *Dept Div & Chief Cur* Joao Fernandes; *Head of Exhibs* Teresa Velazquez; *Head of Colls* Rosario Peiro; *Dir Pub Progs* Berta Sureda; *Management* Michaux Miranda Open Mon & Wed - Sat 10 AM - 9 PM, Sun 10 AM - 7 PM, cl Tues; Admis 6 euro, children under 18 & sr citizens over 65 free; The primary aim of the Museo Nacional Centro de Arte Reina Sofia is to encourage public access to various manifestations in modern & contemporary art in order to broaden knowledge, promote education & foster social communication of the arts.; Average Annual Attendance: 2,705,529
Collections: Works produced between the end of the 19th century up to the present; 16,200 works of art in various media; 4000 paintings, 1400 sculptures, 3000 drawings, more than 5000 prints, more than 2600 photographs, 80 videos & 30 installations; 100 decorative art pieces and 30 pieces of architecture
Exhibitions: Please visit: www.museoreinasofia.es/exposiciones/actuales-en.html
Publications: Please visit: www.museoreinasofia.es/publicaciones/presentacion-en.html
Activities: Classes for adults & children; dramatic progs; decent training; lects open to pub; concerts; gallery talks; tours; schols; fels; fels; 2 book traveling exhibs per yr; organize 5-7 traveling exhibs to Serpentine Gallery, London; Tate Modern, London; Museum of Modern Art (MoMA), New York, Whitney Museum,

New York; Centre Georges Pompidou, Paris; Pinacoteca de Sao Paul, Brasil; Museu de Arte Contemporanea de Serralves, Oporto, Portugal; Stedelijk Van Abbemuseum Eidenhaven, Netherlands; Museum fur Neve Kunst ZKM, Karlsruhe, Germany; Sammlung Falckenberg, Hamburg, Germany; mus shop sells books, mags, reproductions, prints & slides

M MUSEO NACIONAL DEL PRADO, Ruiz de Alarcon 23, Madrid, 28014 Spain. Tel 34 91 330 2800; Internet Home Page Address: www.museodelprado.es; *Dir* Miguel Zugaza; *Assoc Dir* Gabriele Finaldi
Collections: Paintings by: Botticelli, Rembrandt, Velazquez, El Greco, Goya, Murillo, Raphael, Bosch, Van der Weyden, Zurbaran, Van Dyck, Tiepolo, Ribalta, Rubens, Titian, Veronese, Tintoretto, Moro, Juanes, Menendez, Poussin, Ribera; classical and Renaissance sculpture; jewels and medals; drawings & prints

M MUSEO SOROLLA, General Martinez Campos 37, Madrid, 28010 Spain. Tel 0034-91-3101584; Fax 0034-91-3085925; Elec Mail museo@msorolla.mcu.es; Internet Home Page Address: museosorolla.mcu.es

M MUSEO THYSSEN-BORNEMISZA, Paseo del Prado 8, Madrid, 28014 Spain. Tel 34 913690151; Fax 34 914202780; Elec Mail mtb@museothyssen.org; Internet Home Page Address: www.museothyssen.org/thyssen; *Chief Cur* Guillermo Solano; *Cur, Head Dept of Modern Art* Paloma Alarco; *Cur, Head Dept of Old Masters* Mar Borobia Open Tues - Sun 10 AM - 7 PM; Admis adults 6E, students with ID & seniors over 65 4E, children 12 & under no charge
Collections: 14th- to 20th-century fine art

M PATRIMONIO NACIONAL, Calle de Bailen s/n, Madrid, 28071 Spain. Tel 91-542-87-00; Fax 91-542-69-47; Internet Home Page Address: www.patrimonionacional.es; *Dir* Miguel Angel Recio Crespo Visit web site for admis fee & hours; Estab 1940 to administer former Crown property; responsible for all the museums situated in Royal Palaces & properties; governed by an admin council; Average Annual Attendance: 829,604
Income: 3,855,768.23 Euros
Library Holdings: Book Volumes; Cards; Exhibition Catalogs; Maps; Reels; Reproductions
Publications: Guides to all the Museums
Activities: Concerts; mus shop sells books, reproductions
M Palacio Real de Madrid, Calle Bailen s/n, Madrid, 28071 Spain. Tel (91) 542-00-59 Also maintains armoury and coach museum; Library with 350,000 vols
Collections: Special room devoted to 16th-18th century tapestries, clocks, paintings & porcelain from the Royal Palaces & Pharmacy
M Palacio Real de Aranjuez, Aranjuez, 28300 Spain. Tel 91-891-13-44
Collections: Royal Palace of 18th century art
M Monasterio de San Lorenzo de El Escorial, R Monasterio de San Lorenzo de El Escorial, Patrimonio Nacional Av D Juan de Borbon y Battenberg s/n Madrid, 28200 Spain. Tel (91) 8905903; Fax (91) 8907818; Elec Mail secretaria.escorial@patrimonionacional.es; Internet Home Page Address: www.patrimonionacional.es; *Consejero Gerente* O Jose Antonio Bordallo Huidobro; *Head Delegation in Saint Lawrence* D Manuel Terron Bermudez; *Cur* Almudena Perez de Tudela Open Apr - Sept 10 AM - 5 PM, Oct - Mar 10 AM - 6 PM; Please visit the website; Built by Juan B de Toledo & Juan de Herrera & contains many famous works by international artists of the 16th & 18th centuries from royal residences; Pictures mus; Average Annual Attendance: 635,062
Income: 2.891.904, 52 Euro
Library Holdings: Book Volumes; Cards; Exhibition Catalogs; Reproductions
Collections: Royal Collection of famous international work by artists of 16th & 18th centuries; paintings, sculptures, tapestries, mobiliary, clocks, lamps, porcelains, maps & prints
Activities: Concerts; mus shop sells books, reproductions
M Real Monasterio de las Huelgas, Calle Campas de Adentro s/n, Burgos, 09001 Spain. Tel (947) 20-16-30; Fax (947) 27-9729; Internet Home Page Address: www.patrimonionacional.es Founded by Alfonso VIII in the ninth century
M Real Monasterio de Santa Clara, 47100, Tordesillas (Valla dolid), Spain. Tel 983-77-00-71
Collections: 14th century art
M Museo de la Encarnacion, Plaza de la Encarnacion 1, Madrid, 28013 Spain. Tel 91-542-00-59
Collections: Monastic life in the 16th & 17th centuries
M Museo de las Descalzas Reales, Plaza de las Descalzas s/n, Madrid, 28013 Spain. Tel 91-542-00-59
Collections: Showing monastic life in the 16th & 17th centuries
M Palacios de la Granja y Riofrio, Bosque de Riofrio, 40420 Navas de Riofrio Segovia,; Plaza de Espana 17, La Granja de San Ildefonso Segovia, 40100 Spain. Tel 921-47-0019, 921-47-0020; Fax 921-47-1895; Elec Mail info@patrimonionacional.es; Internet Home Page Address: www.patrimonionacional.es; *Head Delegation* D Nilo Fernandez Ortiz Open Oct - Mar Tues - Sun 10 AM - 6 PM; Apr - Sept Tues - Sun 10 AM - 8 PM, cl Mon; 9 E, concessions 4E
Library Holdings: Book Volumes; Cards; Exhibition Catalogs; Reproductions
Special Subjects: Decorative Arts, Etchings & Engravings, Architecture, Ceramics, Painting-French, Sculpture, Tapestries, Drawings, Bronzes, Furniture, Porcelain, Carpets & Rugs, Dioramas, Painting-Spanish
Collections: Gardens & fountains in imitation of Versailles, tapestry museum
M Palacio de la Almudaina, Calle Palau Reial S/N, Palma de Mallorca Balearic Is, 07001 Spain. Tel (971) 72-71-45 Arab-Gothic palace

MALAGA

M **MUSEO PICASSO MALAGA,** Palacio de Buenavista San Augustin 8, Malaga, 29015 Spain. Internet Home Page Address: www2.museopicassomalaga.org/i_home.cfm

MALPARTIDA DE CACERES

M **MUSEO VOSTELL MARPARTIDA,** Apartado de correos 20, Malpartida de Caceres, Spain. Tel 927-01-08-12; Fax 927-01-08-14; Elec Mail museo@museovostell.org; Internet Home Page Address: www.museovostell.org

MARBELLA

M **MUSEO DEL GRABADO ESPANOL CONTEMPORANEO,** C/ Hospital Bazan s/n, Marbella, 29601 Spain. Tel 952-76-57-41; Fax 952-76-45-91; Elec Mail info@mgec.es; Internet Home Page Address: www.mgec.es; *Mgr* Jose Maria Wna Aquilar; *Dir* Maria Jose Montanes Garnica; *Admin* Pepro Fernandez Querra Open Summer Mon & Sat 9 AM-2 PM, Tues-Fri 9 AM-2 PM & 6:30 PM-11 PM; Winter Mon & Sat 9 AM - 2 PM, Tues-Fri 9 AM-9 PM; Admis adults 3 Euro, students 1.50 Euro, retired & children free; Estab 1992; preservation, promotion & exhib of 20th & 21st century engravings & Spanish artwork; Gallery located in the restored rooms of the former 16th century Hospital de la Encarnacion; Average Annual Attendance: 5725; Mem: 65; annual dues 60 Euro
Income: 100,000 euro (own resources; 300,000 euro (public admin)
Purchases: 400.000 euro
Library Holdings: Book Volumes; CD-ROMs; Compact Disks; DVDs; Exhibition Catalogs; Pamphlets; Periodical Subscriptions
Collections: prints & graphic works from the 19th century to the present; 15th - 18th century
Exhibitions: Collection of works by Goya, Fortuny, Baroja, Picasso, Miro, Dali, Chillida, Saura, Tapies, Barcelo & Plensa
Publications: Exhib catalogs (10 per yr)
Activities: Classes for adults & children; Techniques engraving courses; lects open to pub; concerts; 2 fellowships; Premios Nacionales De Grabado award; lending original objects of art to different institutions & organizations; organize traveling exhibs to different institutions & organizations; mus shop sells books, prints, slides, T-shirts & mugs

PAMPLONA

M **MUSEO DE NAVARRA,** Santo Domingo 47, Pamplona, E-31001 Spain. Tel 848-426-492; Elec Mail museo@navarra.es; Internet Home Page Address: www.cfnavarra.es/cultura/museo/eng/index.html; Internet Home Page Address: www.museodenavarra.navarra.es Open Tues - Sat 10 AM - 2 PM & 5 PM - 7 PM; Sun & holidays 11 AM - 2 PM; Admis adults 2 Euro; Sat afternoon, Sun, children under 18 & seniors over 65 free; Mem: Icom free
Special Subjects: Drawings, Portraits, Silver, Painting-European, Hispanic Art, Photography, Sculpture, Religious Art, Ivory, Coins & Medals, Renaissance Art, Embroidery, Medieval Art, Islamic Art, Mosaics
Collections: documentation on Navarre artists
Activities: Classes for children; dramatic progs; docent training; lects open to pub; concerts; mus shop sells books, reproductions, slides

SEGOVIA

M **MUSEO DE ARTE CONTEMPORANEO ESTEBAN VICENTE,** Plazuela de las Bellas Artes, Segovia, 40001 Spain. Tel 34-921-46-20-10; Fax 34-921-46-22-77; Elec Mail museo@museoestebanvicente.es; Internet Home Page Address: www.museoestebanvicente.es

SEVILLA

M **CENTRO ANDALUZ DE ARTE CONTEMPORANEO,** Avda Americo Vespucio 2, Sevilla, 41092 Spain. Tel 34-955-03-70-70; Fax 34-955-03-70-52; Elec Mail prensa.caac@juntadeandalucia.es; Internet Home Page Address: www.caac.es; *Dir* Juan Antonio Alvarel Reyes Open Tues - Sat 10 AM - 20 PM, Sun 10 AM - 15 PM, cl Mon; Admis 3.01 euros; Estab 1997
Income: Public, Andalucia's Government
Special Subjects: Photography
Activities: Educ progs; lects open to pub; concerts; organize traveling exhibs

M **MUSEO DE BELLAS ARTES DE SEVILLA,** Plaza del Museo 9, Sevilla, 41001 Spain. Tel 0034-954-78-65-00; Fax 0034-954-78-64-90; Elec Mail museobellasartessevilla.ccul@juntadeandalucia.es; Internet Home Page Address: www.juntadeandalucia.es/cultura/museos/MBASE/?; *Dir* Maria del Valme Munoz Rubio Open Tues - Sat 9 AM - 20:30 PM, Sun & pub holidays 9 AM - 14:30 PM, cl Mon; Admis 1.50 euro, no admis fee European Union Citizens with corresponding proof, Mems of ICOM; Estab 1835
Library Holdings: Exhibition Catalogs
Collections: Painting & sculpture XV - XX century; Sevillian mainly
Publications: Exhib catalogues
Activities: Exhibs; painters prog; lects open to pub; mus shop sells books, & other merchandise

TOLEDO

M **CASA Y MUSEO DEL GRECO: FUNDACIONES VEGA INCLAN,** El Greco's House, Calle Samuel Levi, Toledo, Spain. Tel (925) 22-40-46; *Dir* Ma Elena Gomez-Moreno
Collections: Artist's paintings and those of his followers; 16th century furniture
M **Museo del Greco,** Calle Samuel Levi, Toledo, Spain.
Collections: El Greco's paintings, including portraits of Christ and the apostles and other 16th and 17th century paintings

VALENCIA

M **MUSEO DE BELLAS ARTES DE VALENCIA,** C/ San Pio V, No 9, Valencia, 46010 Spain. Tel 96 387 03 00; Elec Mail museobellasartesvalencia@gva.es; Internet Home Page Address: museobellasartesvalencia.gva.es; *Dir* Fernando Benito Domenech
Open Tues-Sun 10AM-8PM; No admis fee
Collections: paintings; photographs & sculptures

VALLADOLID

M **MUSEO NACIONAL DE ESCULTURA,** C Cadenas de San Gregorio, 1, 2 y 3 Valladolid, 47011 Spain. Tel 983-25-03-75; Fax 00-34-983-25-93-00; Elec Mail museoescultura@mecd.es; Internet Home Page Address: museoescultura.mcu.es/; *Dir* Maria Bolanos Atienza; *Subdir* Manuel Arias Open Tues - Sat 10 AM - 2 PM & 4 - 7:30 PM, Sun & holidays 10 AM - 2 PM; Admis 3 euro, students 1.50 euro, under 18 & over 65 free
Special Subjects: Sculpture, Religious Art
Collections: Sculptures from the Middle Ages to the 19th century in various media; Collection de Repadaucciones Artisticas
Activities: Classes for adults & children; docent training; concerts; gallery talks; tours; mus shop sells books

M **MUSEO PATIO HERRERIANO DE VALLADOLID,** Calle Jorge Guillen 6, Valladolid, 47003 Spain. Tel 34-983-362-771; Fax 34-983-375-295; Elec Mail patioherreriano@museoph.org; Internet Home Page Address: www.museopatioherreriano.org

SRI LANKA

ANURADHAPURA

M **ARCHAEOLOGICAL MUSEUM,** Anuradhapura, Sri Lanka. Tel 411; *Keeper* J S A Uduwara
Collections: Stone sculptures, mural paintings & frescoes, coins, bronzes, pottery

COLOMBO

M **NATIONAL MUSEUMS OF SRI LANKA,** Sir Marcus Fernando Mawatha, PO Box 845 Colombo, 7 Sri Lanka. Tel 94-11-2694767; Fax 94-11-2692092; Elec Mail nmdep@slt.lk; Internet Home Page Address: www.museum.gov.lk; *Dir* Nanda Wickramasinghe
Open 9 AM - 6:30 PM, cl public holidays; Admis adults Rs 500, children Rs 300; Est 1877; Cultural objects; Average Annual Attendance: 1.5 million
Income: government financed & donations
Library Holdings: Book Volumes; CD-ROMs; Cards; Cassettes; Clipping Files; Compact Disks; Exhibition Catalogs; Manuscripts; Maps; Micro Print; Original Art Works; Original Documents; Other Holdings; Pamphlets; Periodical Subscriptions; Photographs; Prints; Records
Collections: Art, folk culture and antiquities of Sri Lanka
Publications: Spolia Zeylanica
Activities: Classes for children; lects open to the pub, gallery talks; books traveling exhibs; originates traveling exhibs; mus shop sells books, magazines, original art

SWEDEN

GOTEBORG

M **GOTEBORGS KONSTMUSEUM,** Goteborg Art Gallery, Gotaplatsen, Goteborg, 41256 Sweden. Tel (031) 612980; Fax (031) 18-41-19; *Dir* Bjorn Fredlund
Collections: French art from 1820 to present; Old Masters, especially Dutch and Flemish; Scandinavian art

HELSINGBORG

M **DUNKERS MUSEUM,** Kungsgatan 11, Helsingborg, 252 21 Sweden. Tel 042-10-74-00; Fax 042-10-74-10; Internet Home Page Address: www.dunkerskulturhus.se; *Dir* Elisabeth Alsheimer; *Dir, Young Culture* Marianne Westholm; *Asst to Dir* Ingrid Forsberg Open Tues-Wed & Fri-Sun 10AM-5PM, Thurs 10AM-8PM; cl Mon; Admis to exhib adults 70 SEK, seniors 50 SEK, students 35 SEK, children under 18 free
Collections: artwork

LANDSKRONA

M **LANDSKRONA MUSEUM,** Slottsgatan, Landskrona, 26131 Sweden. Tel 0418-470569; Fax 0148-473110; Elec Mail birthe.wibrand@kn.landskrona.de; Internet Home Page Address: www.landskrona.se/kommun/kultlur; *Dir* Christin Nielsen; *Art Secy* Birthe Wibrand
Open noon - 5 PM; No admis fee
Collections: Swedish paintings since 1900; modern Swiss art; Nell Walden collection of paintings & ethnology; Local history
Exhibitions: Temporary exhibs
Activities: Classes for children; lects open to public; concerts; mus shop sells books, reproductions, crafts

MORA

M **ZORNMUSEET,** Vasagatan 36, Mora, 792 21 Sweden; Box 32, Mora, 792 21 Sweden. Tel 46-0-250-592310; Fax 46-0-250-18460; Elec Mail info@zorn.se; Internet Home Page Address: www.zorn.se; *Mus Dir* Johan Cederlund
Open Sept 15-May 14 daily noon-4PM, May 15-Sept 14 Mon-Sat 9AM-5PM, Sun & pub holidays 11AM-5PM; Admis adults SEK 60; children under 15 free ; Estab 1939; Art by Anders Zorn & his art coll
Collections: Anders Zorn Collection
Activities: Mus shop sells books, reproductions, postcards, gifts

NORRKOPING

M **NORRKOPING ART MUSEUM,** Kristinaplatsen, Norrkoping, SE-602-34 Sweden. Tel 46-0-11-15-26-00; Fax 46-0-11-13-58-97; Elec Mail konstmuseet@norrkoping.se; Internet Home Page Address: www.norrkoping.se/konstmuseet; *Dir* Helena Persson
Open Sept - May Tues - Sun 11 AM - 5 PM, Tues & Thurs 11 AM - 8 PM; June - Aug Tues - Sun Noon - 4 PM, Wed Noon - 8 PM, cl Mon; No admis fee
Collections: Collection of Swedish art from the 1600s to the present, incl Modernism & graphic art
Activities: Classes for adults & children; dramatic programs; lects open to pub, 4 -6 vis lectrs per yr; concerts; gallery talks; tours; serves Ostergutland, Sweden, Abroad; originates traveling exhibs to mus in Sweden & abroad; mus shop sells books, magazines, reproductions, prints

SKARHAMN

M **NORDIC WATERCOLOUR MUSEUM,** Sodra hamnen 6, Skarhamn, 471 32 Sweden. Tel 46-304-60-00-80; Internet Home Page Address: www.akvarellmuseet.org; *Dir* Bera Nordal; *Mktg Dir* Benita Nilsson; *Mgr Educ* Lena Eriksson; *Economy* Kerstin Reinli; *Pub Rels* Max Sjalander
Open in summer daily 11 AM - 6 PM; Winter Tues - Sun Noon - 5 PM; Admis Summer adults 75 SEK; Winter adults 45 SEK; children under 25 free
Collections: artwork by contemporary international watercolorists

STOCKHOLM

M **ARKITEKTURMUSEET,** (Arkitektur Museet) The Swedish Museum of Architecture, Skeppsholmen, Stockholm, SE-11149 Sweden. Tel 468 587 270 00; Fax 46-8-587-270-70; Elec Mail info@arkitekturmuseet.se; Internet Home Page Address: www.arkitekturmuseet.se; *Dir* Lena Rahoult
Open Tues 10 AM - 8 PM, Wed - Sun 10 AM - 6 PM; Admis adults 50 sek, under 19 free, Fri 4 - 6 PM free; Estab 1978
Collections: Some 2 million drawings and sketches, 600,000 photographs and more than 2000 models assoc with the history of Swedish buildings and national and international architects; books & periodicals
Publications: Yearly book, exhib catalogues occasionally; Swedish modernism

M **MODERNA MUSEET,** Skeppsholmen, Box 16382 Stockholm, SE-10327 Sweden. Tel 46-8-5195-5289; Fax 46-8-5195-5210; Elec Mail info@modernamuseet.se; Internet Home Page Address: www.modernamuseet.se; *Dir* Lars Nittve
Open Tues 10 AM - 8 PM, Wed - Sun 10 AM - 6 PM, cl Mon; Admis adults 80 sek & 60 sek, under 18 free
Collections: Art spanning from 1900 to the present, includes key works by artists such as Duchamp, Picasso, Dali, Matisse and Rauschenberg as well as contemporary art; Photographic collection of work from the 1840s to the present

M **NATIONALMUSEUM,** Sodra Blasieholmshamnen, Stockholm, Sweden; PO Box 16176, Stockholm, 103 24 Sweden. Tel (08) 51954300; Fax (08) 51954450; Elec Mail info@nationalmuseum.se; Internet Home Page Address: www.nationalmuseum.se; *Dir Prof* Solfrid Soderlind
Open Jun - Aug, Tues 11 AM - 8 PM, Wed - Sun 11 AM - 5 PM, cl Mon; Open Sept - May, Tues & Thurs 11 AM - 8 PM, Wed & Fri - Sun 11 AM - 5 PM, cl Mon; Admis fee 100 SEK full price, 80 SEK reduced price; Estab 1792; Florentine and Venetian Renaissance building, 1866; Average Annual Attendance: 500,000; Mem: 5,900 mems of friends of The National Museum
Library Holdings: Book Volumes; Exhibition Catalogs; Original Documents
Special Subjects: Decorative Arts, Drawings, Etchings & Engravings, Glass, Porcelain, Portraits, Prints, Textiles, Painting-European, Painting-French, Sculpture, Crafts, Furniture, Glass, Painting-Dutch, Painting-Flemish, Painting-Spanish, Painting-Italian, Painting-German, Painting-Scandinavian
Collections: 16,000 works of paintings, icons & miniatures; sculptures, including antiquities; 500,000 drawings & prints; 30,000 items of applied art; collections of several royal castles with 7500 works of art from the middle ages to early 20th century applied arts also contemporary
Activities: Educ prog; classes for adults & children; lects open to pub; lectrs for mems only; gallery talks; tours; traveling exhibs to regl Swedish museums; mus shop sells books, reproductions, prints, jewelry, applied arts, glass & furniture

M **NORDISKA MUSEET,** Djurgardsvagen 6-16, Box 27820, Stockholm, S-115 93 Sweden. Tel (8) 519 54600; Fax (8) 51-95-45-80; Elec Mail nordiska@nordiskamuseet.se; Internet Home Page Address: www.nordiskamuseet.se; *Dir* Christina Mattsson
Collections: Costumes, industrial art, handcrafts, period furnishings; over one million exhibits

M **OSTASIATISKA MUSEET,** Museum of Far Eastern Antiquities, PO Box 16176, Skeppsholmen Stockholm, S-10324 Sweden. Tel (08) 51955750; Fax (08) 51955755; Elec Mail info@ostasiatiska.se; Internet Home Page Address: www.ostasiatiska.se; *Cable* Far Eastern; *Dir* Dr Magnus Fiskesjo
Open Tues noon- 8 PM, Wed - Sun noon-5 PM; Estab 1926
Collections: Chinese archaeology, Buddhist sculpture, bronzes, painting & porcelain, Stone-age pottery; Indian, Japanese & Korean art; Southeast Asian art and archaeology
Publications: Bulletin of Museum of Far Eastern Antiquities; Exhib catalogues; Monographs
Activities: Lects open to pub; concerts; gallery talks; tours; originate traveling exhibs; mus shop sells books, magazines, reproductions, prints, slides, ikebana tools, and souvenirs

M **STOCKHOLMS STADSMUSEUM,** City Museum, Ryssgarden Slussen Box 15025, Stockholm, 10465 Sweden. Tel (08) 50831600; Fax (08) 50831699; Elec Mail stadsmuseum@smf.stockholm.se; Internet Home Page Address: www.smf.stockholm.se; *Dir* Berit Svedberg
Collections: The Lohe Treasure, naive 19th century paintings of Josabeth Sjoberg & armed 15th century vessel; photographs; paintings; drawings, sketches & engravings
Activities: Classes for children; lects open to public, tours; mus shop sells books

SWITZERLAND

AARAU

M **AARGAUER KUNSTHAUS,** Aargauerplatz, PO Box Aarau, CH-5001 Switzerland. Tel 0041 (062) 8352330; Fax 0041 (062) 8352329; Elec Mail kunsthaus@ag.ch; Internet Home Page Address: www.aargauerkunsthaus.ch; *Dir* Madeleine Schuppli
Open Tues - Sun 10 AM - 5 PM; Thurs 10 AM - 8 PM; Admis adults SFr 15, students SFr 10, 16 and under free; Mus for contemporary art
Collections: Swiss painting and sculpture from 1750 to the present day; Caspar Wolf paintings (1735-1783) - art of the first painter of the Alps; landscape painter Adolf Staebli and Auberjonois, Bruhlmann, Amiet, G Giacometti, Hodler, Meyer-Amden, Louis Soutter, Vallotton
Activities: Classes for children; concerts; gallery talks; tours; mus shop sells books

BASEL

M **ANTIKENMUSEUM BASEL UND SAMMLUNG LUDWIG,** Basel Museum of Ancient Art & Ludwig Collection. St Albangraben 5, Basel, CH-4010 Switzerland. Tel 41-0-61-201-12-12; Fax 41-0-61-201-12-10; Elec Mail office@antikenmuseumbasel.ch; Internet Home Page Address: www.antikenmuseumbasel.ch; *Dir* Andrea Biguasca
Open Tues - Sun 10 AM - 5 PM, cl Mon; Admis CHF 10, CHF 5; Estab 1961
Collections: Only Swiss museum devoted to the art and culture of the Mediterranean area; Collection dates mainly from Greek, Italian, Etruscan, Roman and Egyptian periods; Sculptures, pottery, gold jewelry, bronze statues, clay figures
Activities: Classes for adults & children; lects open to pub; concerts; lending of original objects of art to other mus; mus shop sells books, magazines & reproductions

M **HISTORISCHES MUSEUM BASEL,** Verwaltung, Steinenberg 4 Basel, 4051 Switzerland. Tel (061) 205 86 00; Fax (061) 205 86 01; Elec Mail historisches.museum@bs.ch; Internet Home Page Address: www.hmb.ch; *Dir* Marie-Paule Jungblut
Open Tues - Sun 10 AM - 5 PM; Admis Adults 12 swiss francs, children under 13 free; Estab 1894; Historical mus with special exhib
Library Holdings: Auction Catalogs; Book Volumes; Exhibition Catalogs
Collections: Collection of objects from prehistory to 20th century contained in 4 branches; history, music, horsepower, domestic culture
Activities: Educ prog; classes for adults & children; gallery talks; tours; mus shop sells books, reproductions, prints, postcards, original art, gifts, toys for children

M **KUNSTMUSEUM BASEL,** (Oeffentliche Kunstsammlung Basel Kunstmuseum) St Alban-Graben 16, Basel, 4010 Switzerland. Tel (061) 206 62 62; Fax (061) 206 62 52; Elec Mail pressoffice@kunstmuseumbasel.ch; Internet Home Page Address: www.kunstmuseumbasel.ch; *Dir* Dr Bernhard Mendes Bürgi
Open Tues - Sun 10 AM - 5 PM; Admis 10-/8 - CHT; Library with 100,000 vols
Library Holdings: Auction Catalogs; Book Volumes; CD-ROMs; Exhibition Catalogs; Manuscripts; Original Documents; Periodical Subscriptions
Collections: Pictures from 15th century to present day, notably by Witz, Holbein & contemporary painters; coll includes Grunewald, Cranach the Elder, Rembrandt; 16th - 17th century Netherlandish painting, Cezanne, Gauguin & Van Gogh Impressionists; large coll of cubist art; sculptures by Rodin & 20th century artists; American art since 1945; German & Swiss masters, Klee, Matisse; contemporary art; important Beuys group
Activities: Educ prog; classes for adults & children; lects open to pub; 20 vis lectrs per yr; concerts; gallery talks; tours; originates traveling exhibs to partner mus; mus shop sells books, magazines, reproductions, prints & slides

M NATURHISTORISCHES MUSEUM BASEL, Natural History Museum of Basel, PO Box 1048, Augustinergasse 2 Basel, 4001 Switzerland. Tel (061) 266-55-00; Fax (061) 266-55-46; Elec Mail nmb@bs.ch; Internet Home Page Address: www.nmb.bs.ch; *Dir* Dr Christian A Neyer
Open 10 AM - 5 PM; cl Mon; Admis 7 - CHF, reduced; 5 - CHF; Estab 1821; Library with 58,000 vols
Collections: Anthropology, Entomology, mineralogy, fossils, animals, zoology, Western European Center for Ocean Drulling Prog, micropaleontological reference coll
Activities: Classes for adults; classes for children; docent training; mus shop sells books, magazines, other objects

M SWISS ARCHITECTURE MUSEUM, Steinenberg 7, PO Box 911 Basel, CH-4001 Switzerland. Tel 41-(0) 61- 261-14-13; Fax 41-(0) 61-261-14-28; Elec Mail info@sam-basel.org; Internet Home Page Address: www.sam-basel.org; *Dir* Hubertus Adam
Open Tues, Wed, Fri 11 - 18, Thurs 11 - 20:30, Sat & Sun 11 - 17; cl Mon; Admis 10 CHF; Estab 1984; Architecture mus; Average Annual Attendance: 22,000; Mem: 350
Income: Mems, fundraising, sponsoring & other
Special Subjects: Architecture
Activities: Classes for adults & children; lects open to pub; tours; book traveling exhibs, 0-1; organize traveling exhibs to mus; mus shop sells books, magazines, original art & reproductions

BERN

M KUNSTMUSEUM BERN, Musee des Beaux-Arts de Berne, Hodlerstrasse 8-12, Bern, CH-3000 Bern 7 Switzerland. Tel 0041 313280944; Fax 0041 313280955; Elec Mail info@kunstmuseumbern.ch; Internet Home Page Address: www.kunstmuseumbern.ch; *Dir* Dr Matthias Frehner
Open Tues 10 AM - 9 PM, Wed - Sun 10 AM - 5 PM, cl Mon; Admis Coll Sat - Fri 7.00, Exhibs Sat - Fri 8.00-18.00
Special Subjects: Drawings, Landscapes, Photography, Painting-European, Painting-French, Sculpture, Graphics, Painting-Spanish, Painting-Italian, Painting-German, Painting-Russian
Collections: Dutch & contemporary artists; French & other European Masters of the 19th & 20th centuries; Italian Masters; collection of Paul Klee works of 46 items; Niklaus Manuel; Hermann & Margrit Rupf Foundation, Adolf Wolfli Foundation; Swiss Baroque Masters; Swiss 19th & 20th Century Masters; 38,000 drawings & engravings; illustrations; works by Sophie Taeuber-Arp
Exhibitions: See website
Activities: Classes for adults and children; pvt & pub guided tours; mus shop or sales shop sells books, magazines, reproductions, prints & cards

M ZENTRUM PAUL KLEE, Monument im Fruchtland 3, Bern, 3006 Switzerland; Monument im Fruchtland 3, Postfach, Bern, 31 3000 Switzerland. Tel +41-031-359-01-01; Fax +41-031-359-01-02; Elec Mail kontakt@zpk.org; Internet Home Page Address: www.zpk.org; *CEO* Peter Fischer; *Chief Cur* Dr Michael Baumgatner
Open Tues - Sun 10 AM - 5 PM; Admis adults CHF 18, senior citizens, concessions, students & apprentices & groups of 10 or more CHF 16, kulturlegi CHF 9, Children 6-16 CHF 8
Special Subjects: Watercolors, Painting-German
Collections: over 10,000 pieces of artwork by Paul Klee
Activities: Concerts; tours

CHUR

M BUENDNER KUNSTMUSEUM, Postplatz, Postfach Chur, CH-7000 Switzerland. Tel (081) 2572868; Fax (081) 257 21 72; Elec Mail info@bkm.gr.ch; Internet Home Page Address: www.buendner-kunstmuseum.ch; *Dir* Stephan Kunz; *Conservator* Dr Katharina Ammann
Open 10 AM - 7 PM, cl Mon; Admis adults 12 Fr, seniors, apprentices, students & groups 10 Fr; 7,000 objects; Mem: 1,200
Library Holdings: Auction Catalogs; Book Volumes; CD-ROMs; Exhibition Catalogs; Photographs; Video Tapes
Collections: Alberto, Augusto & Giovanni Giacometti, Angelika Kauffmann, E L Kirchner; Swiss painting; Contemporary Swiss Art
Activities: Classes for adults & children; lects for mems only; concerts; gallery talks; tours; awards given, Manor-Kunstpreis, Suedostschweiz Medien; lending of original art to employees of cantou Graubunden; mus shop sells books, prints, postcards, reproductions

DAVOS

M KIRCHNER MUSEUM DAVOS, Ernst Ludwig Kirchner Platz, Davos, CH-7270 Switzerland. Tel +41-81-410-63-00; Fax +41-81-410-63-01; Elec Mail info@kirchnermuseum.ch; Internet Home Page Address: www.kirchnermuseum.ch; *Dir* Dr Karin Schick
Open 10 AM - 6 PM, 2 - 6 PM (seasonal); Admis adults CHF 12.00, seniors CHF 10.00, children & students CHF 5.00; 1982; Average Annual Attendance: 25,000
Special Subjects: Drawings, Etchings & Engravings, Furniture, Photography, Portraits, Textiles, Painting-European, Tapestries, Prints, Sculpture, Watercolors, Woodcuts
Collections: Works by Ernst Ludwig Kirchner & his contemporaries
Exhibitions: 2 exhibs per yr
Publications: Exhibs catalogues
Activities: Classes for adults & children; concerts; gallery talks; tours; extension prog includes research; mus shop sells books, reproductions, prints

GENEVA

M MUSEE D'ART MODERNE ET CONTEMPORAIN, 10 rue das Vieux-Grenadiers, Geneva, CH-1205 Switzerland. Tel 41-22-320-61-22; Fax 41-22-781-56-81; Internet Home Page Address: www.mamco.ch; *Dir* Christian Bernard
Open Tues - Fri Noon - 6 PM, Sat - Sun 11 AM - 6 PM, cl Mon; Admis 8 CHF, 5.50 euro, under 18 free, first Sun & Wed evening free

Collections: More than 3000 works of art and 300 photgraphs; largest museum in Switzerland for contemporary and modern international and national art

M MUSEES D'ART ET D'HISTOIRE, 2 rue Charles-Galland, CH-1206 Geneva, Switzerland. Tel 41 (0) 22 418 26 00; Fax 41 (0) 22 418 26 01; Elec Mail mah@ville-ge.ch; Internet Home Page Address: www.ville-ge.ch/mah; *Dir* Jean-Yves Marin; *Cur Archaeology* Jean-Luc Chappaz; *Cur Applied Art & Textile* Marielle Martiniani-Reber; *Cur Numismatic Coll* Matteo Campagnolo; *Cur Fine Art* Laurence Madeline; *Cur Graphic Arts* Christian Rumelin
Open Tues - Sun 11 AM - 6 PM, cl Mon; Between 5 & 10 CHF 5 to all temporary exhibitions, CHF 3, children under 18 free; Estab 1970; an encyclopedic museum, it houses colls in such diverse fields as archaeology, the fine arts and applied arts; largest Swiss coll of Egyptian antiques; also Near-East, Greek, Etruscan and Roman colls; Average Annual Attendance: 350,000 for the 5 museums
Library Holdings: Book Volumes; Cards; Exhibition Catalogs
Collections: Swiss art works; primitive Italian, French, German & Flemish art; modern art; archaeology; European sculpture & decorative arts; six attached museums
Exhibitions: See website
Activities: Classes for children; concerts; tours; Mus shop sells books, magazines & reproductions

GRUYERES

M MUSEUM HR GIGER, Chateau St Germain, Gruyeres, 1663 Switzerland. Tel 41-26-921-22-00; Fax 41-26-921-22-11; Elec Mail info@hrgigermuseum.com; Internet Home Page Address: www.hrgigermuseum.com
Open Apr-Oct daily 10AM-6PM, Nov-Mar Tues-Fri 1PM-5PM, Sat-Sun 10AM-6PM, cl Mon; Admis adults CHF 12.50 (EUR 8,20), students, seniors & military CHF 8.50 (EUR 5,60), children CHF 5.50 (EUR 3,60)
Collections: artwork by HR Giger

LIGORNETTO

M FEDERAL OFFICE OF CULTURE, Museo Vincenzo Vela, Ligornetto, 6853 Switzerland. Tel 41 (0)91 640 70 44 / 40; Fax 41 (0)91 647 32 41; Elec Mail museo.vela@bak.admin.ch; Internet Home Page Address: www.museo-vela.ch; *Cur* Dr Gianna A Mina
Open Mar to Dec
Library Holdings: Auction Catalogs; Book Volumes; Exhibition Catalogs; Periodical Subscriptions
Collections: Works of art by Vela family; paintings from eighteenth & nineteenth centuries Italian schools; original monument plasters by Vinceno Vela (1820-1891); plasters by Lorenzo Vela (1812-1897); Pictures by Spartaco; Lombard & Piemontese paintings from the eighteenth & nineteenth centuries
Activities: Classes for children; concerts; gallery talks; Mus shop sells books

LUCERNE

M KUNSTMUSEUM LUCERNE, Museum of Art Lucerne, Europaplatz 1, Lucerne, CH-6002 Switzerland. Tel (041) 226 78 00; Fax (041) 226 78 01; Elec Mail info@kunstmuseumluzern.ch; Internet Home Page Address: www.kunstmuseumluzern.ch; *Dir* Peter Fischer
Open Thurs - Sun 10 AM - 5 PM, Tues - Wed 10 AM - 8 PM, cl Mon; Admis adults CHF 12, groups of 10 or more CHF 10; Average Annual Attendance: 50,000
Library Holdings: Book Volumes; Cards; Exhibition Catalogs
Collections: Swiss art from ancient times to 20th century; European expressionism and contemporary works
Activities: Classes for adults & children; lects open to pub; 2-4 vis lectrs per yr; gallery talks; tours; mus shop sells books, magazines, original art, reproductions, prints & various shop articles

SCHAFFHAUSEN

M MUSEUM ZU ALLERHEILIGEN, Baumgartenstrasse 6, Schaffhausen, CH-8200 Switzerland. Tel +41 (0) 52 633 07 77; Fax +41 (0) 52 633 07 88; Elec Mail admin.allerheiligen@stsh.ch; Internet Home Page Address: www.allerheiligen.ch; *Dir* Dr h c Peter Jezler; *Cur* Dr Hortensia von Roda; *Cur* Dr Urs Weibel; *Cur* Daniel Gruetter, Lic Phil; *Cur* Dr Markus Honeisen; *Cur* Werner Rutishauser, Lic Phil; *Cur* Dr Matthias Fischer; *Cur* Lynn Kost
Open Tues - Sun 11 AM - 5 PM; Admis 2 SFr, 9 SFr (reduced), children 25 & under free
Library Holdings: Auction Catalogs; Book Volumes; Exhibition Catalogs
Special Subjects: Archaeology, Drawings, Historical Material, Ceramics, Collages, Glass, Metalwork, Antiquities-Assyrian, Furniture, Gold, Photography, Porcelain, Portraits, Pottery, Pre-Columbian Art, Silver, Textiles, Bronzes, Woodcuts, Manuscripts, Maps, Sculpture, Graphics, Latin American Art, Prints, Watercolors, Ethnology, Costumes, Religious Art, Crafts, Woodcarvings, Etchings & Engravings, Painting-European, Posters, Dolls, Jade, Jewelry, Oriental Art, Asian Art, Carpets & Rugs, Ivory, Coins & Medals, Restorations, Tapestries, Baroque Art, Miniatures, Renaissance Art, Dioramas, Period Rooms, Embroidery, Medieval Art, Antiquities-Persian, Antiquities-Greek, Antiquities-Roman, Mosaics, Stained Glass, Pewter, Leather, Military Art, Antiquities-Etruscan, Enamels
Collections: Prehistory, natural history and art, graphics, numismatics, playing cards; Sturzenegger Collection; Stemmler Collection; Ebnother Collection
Exhibitions: Permanent exhibs of the colls & changing exhibs
Publications: Interdisciplinary editions of the mus
Activities: Classes for children & families; workshops; lectrs; gallery talks; guided tours; lending of original objects of art to mems of kunstverein schaffhausen; mus shop sells books, original art, reproductions, prints & other items

SOLOTHURN

M **KUNSTMUSEUM SOLOTHURN,** Solothurn Art Museum, Werkhofstrasse 30, Solothurn, 4500 Switzerland. Tel (032) 6244000; Fax (032) 6225001; Elec Mail kunstmuseum@solothurn.ch; Internet Home Page Address: www.kunstmuseum-so.ch; *Cur* Dr Christoph Vogele; *Asst* Patricia Bieder; *Registrar* Christian Muller
Open Tues - Fri 11 AM - 5 PM, Sat - Sun 10 AM - 5 PM; No admis fee; Estab 1902; Art mus, mainly Swiss art; Average Annual Attendance: 20,000
Income: Financed mainly by city of Solothurn
Special Subjects: Portraits, Painting-European, Painting-French, Drawings, Sculpture, Watercolors, Religious Art, Landscapes, Baroque Art, Renaissance Art, Painting-German
Collections: Swiss art from 1850 to present, including Amiet, Hodler, Giacometti, Oppenheim, Raetz, Signer; small old master coll; small international coll includes Van Gogh, Matisse, Klimt, Leger
Exhibitions: 8 exhibs per yr
Publications: Broad selection of own exhib catalogues
Activities: Classes for adults & children; concerts; gallery talks; tours; mus shop sells books, prints, reproductions, postcards

ST GALLEN

M **HISTORISCHES UND VOLKERKUNDEMUSEUM,** (Historisches Museum) Historical Museum, Museumstrasse 50, St Gallen, CH-9000 Switzerland. Tel (071) 242-06-42; Fax (071) 242-06-44; Elec Mail info@hmsg.ch; Internet Home Page Address: www.hmsg.ch; *Cur* Dr Daniel Studer
Open Tues - Sun 10 AM - 5 PM
Special Subjects: American Indian Art, Glass, Pre-Columbian Art, Prints, Textiles, Graphics, Sculpture, African Art, Archaeology, Costumes, Religious Art, Ceramics, Eskimo Art, Porcelain, Asian Art, Period Rooms, Embroidery
Collections: Furniture, glass & glass painting, graphics, period rooms, pewter, porcelain, stoves, weapons; archeology; artifacts of different people from Egypt, Africa, N & S America & Asia
Activities: Mus shop sells books, magazines & original art

M **KUNSTMUSEUM ST. GALLEN,** Museumstrasse 32, St Gallen, CH-9000 Switzerland. Tel 41-71-242-06-71; Fax 41-71-242-06-72; Elec Mail info@kunstmuseumsg.ch; Internet Home Page Address: www.kunstmuseumsg.ch; *Dir* Roland Waspe; *Cur* Konrad B Herli
Open Tues - Sun 10 AM - 5 PM, Wed 10 AM - 8 PM, cl Mon
Collections: Paintings and sculptures from the late Middle Ages; Significant prints by Durer, Rembrandt and Callot; 17th century Dutch and Flemish painting; 19th century Swiss, German and French painting from Romanticism to Impressionism; Turn of the century modern and contemporary art

THUN

M **KUNSTMUSEUM THUN,** Hofstettenstrasse 14, Thun, CH-3602 Switzerland. Tel 41-0-33-225-84-20; Fax 41-0-33-225-89-06; Elec Mail kunstmuseum@thun.ch; Internet Home Page Address: www.kunstmuseumthun.ch; *Dir* Helen Hirsch
Open Tues - Sun 10 AM - 5 PM, Wed 10 AM - 7 PM, cl Mon; Admis CHF 10, CHF 8, CHF 4 12-16, 12 and under free; Estab 1948; Mus with mainly contemporary art exhibs & coll of Swiss art
Income: City of Thun & Kanton Bern
Purchases: Swiss Art
Library Holdings: Auction Catalogs; Book Volumes; CD-ROMs; DVDs; Exhibition Catalogs
Special Subjects: Drawings, Historical Material, Collages, Photography, Prints, Sculpture, Watercolors, Woodcuts, Portraits, Posters, Restorations, Reproductions
Collections: More than 7000 works; paintings, videos, sculpture, graphic arts, drawings; Minor and major Swiss artists both past and present; (see website)
Exhibitions: (see website)
Activities: Classes for adults & children; docent training; lects open to pub; concerts; gallery talks; tours; organize traveling exhibs; mus shop sells books, original art

WINTERTHUR

M **FOTOMUSEUM WINTERTHUR,** Gruzenstrasse 44 & 45, CH-8400 Winterthur, Switzerland. Tel 41-52-234-10-60; Fax 41-52-233-60-97; Elec Mail fotomuseum@fotomuseum.ch; Internet Home Page Address: www.fotomuseum.ch; *Dir* Duncan Forbes; *Dir* Thomas Seelig; *Sponsoring* Eleonore Gruffel-Sauter
Open Tues - Sun 11 AM - 6 PM, Wed 11 AM - 8 PM, cl Mon; Admis Museum Fr 10, reduction Fr 8, Collection Fr 9, reduction Fr 7; Estab 1993; contemporary as well as traditional for masters of 19th & 20th century; cultural-historical, sociological mus of applied photography; Average Annual Attendance: 54,550; Mem: 2,050 mems; dues 50 - 5,000
Income: 75% privately financed
Special Subjects: Porcelain, Photography
Collections: Contemporary photography in some 4000 photographs; rotating exhibitions
Activities: Classes for adults & children; lects open to pub; mus shop sells books, magazines & postcards

M **KUNSTMUSEUM WINTERTHUR,** PO Box 235, Museumstrasse 52 Winterthur, 8402 Switzerland. Tel (052) 2675162; Fax (052) 2675317; Elec Mail info@kmw.ch; Internet Home Page Address: www.kmw.ch; *Cur* Dr Dieter Schwarz
Open daily 10 AM - 5 PM, except Tues 10 AM - 8 PM; Estab 1848; Mem: Open to everyone
Collections: French, Italian, German and Swiss painting and sculpture of 19th and 20th centuries, including Monet, Degas, Picasso, Gris, Leger, Klee, Schlemmer, Schwitters, Arp, Kandinsky, Renoir, Bonnard, Maillol, Van Gogh, Rodin, Brancusi,

Morandi, Giacometti, de Stael; drawings and prints; European and American painting and sculpture after 1960: Agnes M Martin, Kelly, Marden, Mangold, Guston
Activities: Classes for children; lects open to pub; concerts; gallery talks, tours

M **MUSEUM OSKAR REINHART AM STADTGARTEN,** Stadthausstrasse 6, Winterthur, 8400 Switzerland. Tel (052) 267-51-72; Fax (052) 267 6228; Elec Mail museum.oskarreinhart@win.ch; Internet Home Page Address: www.museumoskarreinhart.ch; *Cur* Dr Peter Wegmann
Open Tues 10 AM - 10 PM, Wed 10 AM - 5 PM; Admis CHF 8, 6 reduced
Collections: Pictures & drawings by German, Swiss & Austrian Masters of the 18th to 20th centuries; Collections of drawings & prints
Publications: Catalogues of paintings on permanent display
Activities: Classes for children; concerts; mus shop sells books, reproductions & slides

ZURICH

M **MUSEUM RIETBERG ZURICH,** Gablerstrasse 15, Zurich, 8002 Switzerland. Tel (01) 206-31-31; Fax (01) 206-31-32; Elec Mail museum.rietberg@zurich.ch; Internet Home Page Address: www.rietberg.ch; *Dir* Dr Albert Lutz; *Deputy Dir* Dr Katharina Epprecht; *Cur* Judith Rickenbach; *Cur* Dr Johannes Beltz; *Cur* Lorenz Homberger; *Cur* Axel Langer; *Cur* Jorrit Britschgi; *Cur* Alexandra von Przychowski
Open Tues - Sun 10 AM - 5 PM, Wed & Thurs 10 AM - 8 PM; Admis sfr 16.00; Estab 1952; mus for non-European art; Gallery contains art from India, China, Japan, Africa, Ancient Americas; Average Annual Attendance: 80,000; Mem: 4,000
Library Holdings: Auction Catalogs; Book Volumes; Exhibition Catalogs
Collections: Asian, Oceanic and African art; Chinese bronzes; Baron von der Heydt Collection; The Berti Aschmann Foundation of Tibetan bronzes
Activities: Classes for adults & children; lects open to pub, 75 vis lectrs per yr; concerts; gallery talks; tours; 3 book traveling exhibs per yr; mus shop sells books, magazines, original art, reproductions, prints, posters, jewelry, stationery

M **SAMMLUNG E G BUHRLE,** Foundation E.G. Buhrle Collection, Zollikerstrasse 172, Zurich, CH-8008 Switzerland. Tel 41-44-422-00-86; Elec Mail info@buehrle.ch; Internet Home Page Address: www.buehrle.ch; *Dir & Cur* Dr Lukas Gloor
Only group visits by appointment
Collections: private coll of Emil Georg Buhrle; French Impressionism and Post-Impressionism; 19th century French art; French avant-garde after 1900; Dutch painting of the 17th century and Italian painting of the 16th - 18th centuries; Gothic wood sculptures

M **SCHWEIZERISCHES LANDESMUSEUM,** Museum of Cultural History of Switzerland, Museumstrasse 2, Zurich, CH-8021 Switzerland. Tel (044) 218 65 11; Fax (044) 211 29 49; Elec Mail kanzlei@sim.admin.ch; Internet Home Page Address: www.landesmuseum.ch; *Dir* Dr Andres Fuger
Open Tues - Sun 10:30 AM - 5 PM; Library with 85,000 vols
Collections: History & cultural development of Switzerland since prehistoric times
Activities: Sales of books, prints, souvenirs

M **ZUERCHER KUNSTGESELLSCHAFT,** Kunsthaus Zurich, Heimplatz 1, Zurich, 8001 Switzerland; Winkelwiese 4, Zurich, CH-8001 Switzerland. Tel +41(0)44 253 84 84; Fax +41(0)44 253 84 33; Elec Mail info@kunsthaus.ch; Internet Home Page Address: www.kunsthaus.ch; *Dir* Dr Christoph Becker; *Cur* Dr Philippe Buettner; *Cur* Dr Tobia Bezzola; *Cur* Bice Curiger; *Cur* Mirjam Varadinis; *Cur* Bernhard Von Waldkirch
Open Wed - Fri 10 AM - 8 PM, Sat, Sun & Tues 10 AM - 6 PM; Admis CHF 14 - 22; Estab 1910 for exhibs; Average Annual Attendance: 300,000; Mem: 18,000
Income: CHF 15 million budget
Library Holdings: Auction Catalogs; Book Volumes; CD-ROMs; DVDs; Exhibition Catalogs; Original Documents; Pamphlets; Periodical Subscriptions; Photographs; Prints; Sculpture; Video Tapes
Collections: Alberto Giacometti works; medieval and modern sculptures; paintings; graphic arts, 16th - 20th centuries, mainly 19th and 20th; photo and video coll
Activities: Educ prog; classes for adults & children; docent training; 4500 vis lectrs per yr; concerts; gallery talks; mus shop sells books, magazines, reproductions, prints & gifts

M **ZURICH UNIVERSITY OF THE ARTS (ZHDK),** (Museum Fur Gestaltung Zurich) Museum Fuer Gestaltung Zurich (Museum of Design Zurich), Ausstellungsstrasse 60, Zurich, CH-8005 Switzerland; PO Box, Zurich, CH-8031 Switzerland. Tel 41-(0)-43-446-67-67; Fax 41-(0)-43-446-45-67; Elec Mail welcome@museum-gestaltung.ch; Internet Home Page Address: www.museum-gestaltung.ch; Internet Home Page Address: www.museum-bellerive.ch; Internet Home Page Address: www.emuseum.ch; Internet Home Page Address: www.museum-gestaltung.ch/freundeskreis (Membership); *Dir* Christian Brandle; *Cur* Andres Janser; *Cur* Angeli Sachs; *Cur* Karin Gimmi
Open Tues - Sun 10 AM - 5 PM, Wed 10 AM - 8 PM, cl Mon; Admis Main Hall CHF 9, Gallery CHF 7, double exhibs CHF 12, annual pass CHF 50; Estab 1875; Mem: See www.museum-gestaltung.ch
Library Holdings: Audio Tapes; Book Volumes; CD-ROMs; Clipping Files; Compact Disks; DVDs; Exhibition Catalogs; Maps; Motion Pictures; Original Documents; Periodical Subscriptions; Photographs; Prints; Records; Video Tapes
Special Subjects: Decorative Arts, Drawings, Architecture, Glass, Photography, Prints, Textiles, Graphics, Ceramics, Crafts, Posters, Furniture, Cartoons
Collections: Posters, graphic arts, design objects, illustrations of 20th century cultural production & applied art; Book covers, textiles, ceramics, glass, works in metal and wood, puppets, industrial design
Exhibitions: Please see website
Publications: Please see website

Activities: Workshops for children/students; lects open to pub; galley talks & tours; traveling exhibs organized; mus shop sells books, magazines & design objects

SYRIA

DAMASCUS

M **AZEM PALACE - MUSEUM OF POPULAR ARTS AND TRADITIONS,** Old Town, Suq al-Buzuriyya Damascus, Syria. Tel 963-11-221-0122, 222-1737; Elec Mail min-tourism@mail.sy
Open Wed - Mon 8 AM - 1 PM & 4 PM - 7 PM, cl Tues; Admis 150 SP, students 15 SP
Collections: Former palace divided into quarters; examines Syria's past through domestic artifacts and decorative arts; Textiles, household items, traditional craft; brass, Damascene procar material, wood mosaics

M **NATIONAL MUSEUM OF DAMASCUS,** National Museum, Syrian University St. Damascus, 4 Syria. Tel 214-854; *Gen Dir* Dr Jawdat Chahade
Collections: Ancient, Byzantine, Greek, Islamic, Modern, Oriental, Prehistoric and Roman art

TANZANIA

DAR ES SALAAM

M **DAR-ES-SALAAM NATIONAL MUSEUM,** PO Box 511, Dar es Salaam, Tanzania. Tel (51) 22030; *Dir* M L Mbago
Collections: Archaeology from Stone Age sites; ethnography & history collections

THAILAND

BANGKOK

M **NATIONAL MUSEUM,** Na Phra-that Rd, Amphoe Phda Nakhon Bangkok, 10200 Thailand. Tel 2241396; *Dir* Mrs Chira Chongkol
Collections: Bronze & stone sculptures, prehistoric artifacts, textiles, weapons, wood-carvings, royal regalia, theatrical masks, marionettes, shadow-play figures

M **SUAN PAKKAD PALACE MUSEUM,** 352-354 Sri Ayudhya Rd, Phyathai Bangkok, Thailand. Tel 662-245-4934, 662-246-1775; Fax (662) 2472079; Elec Mail public@suanpakkad.com; Internet Home Page Address: www.suanpakkad.com/main_eng.php
Open daily 9 AM - 4 PM; Admis local 50 baht, visitor 100 baht; Estab 1944-1945; Art & archaeology; Average Annual Attendance: 20,000
Library Holdings: Cards; Photographs
Special Subjects: Drawings, Ceramics, Glass, Metalwork, Furniture, Gold, Photography, Porcelain, Pottery, Silver, Bronzes, Manuscripts, Painting-French, Sculpture, Crafts, Woodcarvings, Dolls, Jade, Jewelry, Ivory, Coins & Medals, Stained Glass
Collections: Combination of fine arts and ancient artifacts from private coll; Reconstructed traditional houses; pottery, jewelry, bronze objects, architecture; The Lacquer Pavilion; Buddha images
Publications: The Suan Pakkad Palace Coll; The Lacquer Pavilion
Activities: Tours; sales shop sells books & CDs

M **THAI NATIONAL GALLERY,** Chao Fa Rd, Ko Rattanakosin Dist Bangkok, 10200 Thailand. Tel 66-02-282-2639, 66-2281-2224; Elec Mail prdiv3@tat.or.th; Internet Home Page Address: www.tat.or.th; *Dir* Sakchai Pojnunvanich
Open Wed - Sun 9 AM - 4 PM
Collections: Traditional and contemporary Thai art by Thai artists from the 17th century onward

TONGA

NUKU'ALOFA

M **TONGAN NATIONAL CENTRE,** Taufa'ahau Rd, PO Box 2598 Nuku'alofa, Tonga. Tel 676-23-022; Fax 676-23-520
Open Mon - Fri 9 AM - 4 PM; No admis fee
Collections: Local historical and ethnographic artifacts, contemporary art and cultural handicrafts; Wood carvings, canoe making, jewelry, textiles, basket weaving

TRINIDAD AND TOBAGO

PORT OF SPAIN

M **MINISTRY OF THE ARTS & MULTICULTURALISM,** National Museum & Art Gallery, 117 Frederick St, Port of Spain, Trinidad and Tobago. Tel 62-35941; Fax 62-37116; Elec Mail nationalmuseum117@gmail.com; *Cur* Vel A Lewis; *Asst Cur* Nimah Muwakil-Zakuri; *Accounts Officer* Alicia Narad; *Sec* Rowena Ramnath
Open Tues - Sat 10 AM - 6 PM, Sun 2 PM - 6 PM; Estab 1892 to preserve the heritage of Trinidad & Tobago; 12,000 sq ft exhibit space; Average Annual Attendance: 60,000

Library Holdings: Book Volumes; Exhibition Catalogs; Original Documents; Pamphlets; Periodical Subscriptions; Photographs; Slides
Special Subjects: Archaeology, Drawings, Historical Material, Landscapes, Ceramics, Collages, Flasks & Bottles, Photography, Portraits, Pottery, Pre-Columbian Art, Prints, Woodcuts, Maps, Sculpture, Watercolors, Costumes, Woodcarvings, Coins & Medals, Restorations, Dioramas, Cartoons, Military Art, Reproductions
Collections: Fine art, archaeology, history & natural history colls
Exhibitions: August-Annual Independence Art Exhibition
Publications: Art catalogues
Activities: Museum theatre; children art & heritage workshop; lects open to pub; 6 vis lectrs per yr; concerts; gallery talks; tours; competitions; The Master Artist Award; lending of original objects of art to diplomatic missions abroad; originate traveling exhibs to governmental organizations; sales shop sells books, reproductions & prints

TUNISIA

KAIROUAN

M **RAQQADA NATIONAL MUSEUM OF ISLAMIC ART,** Sfax Rd, Kairouan, Tunisia. Tel 216-71-782-264; Fax 216-71-781-993; Elec Mail dg.amvppc@email.ati.tn
Open Sept 1 - June 30 9 AM - 4 PM; July 1 - Aug 31 8 AM - 2 PM; Admis 2 dt
Collections: Archaeological finds from Kairouan; Art & crafts from the Aghlabid residences at Reqqada and Al Abbasiya; Houses coll of Islamic art in Tunisia; ceramics, medals, bronze & glass, calligraphy & manuscripts

SOUSSE

M **SOUSSE MUSEUM,** Khalef al Fata Tower, Sousse, Tunisia. Tel 216-71-782-264; Fax 216-71-781-993
Open Tues - Sun 9 AM - noon & 2 PM - 6 PM, cl Mon; Admis 3 dt
Collections: Vast collection of mosaics; vases, masks, statues, burial tombs; Punic, Roman and early Christian period items and artifacts

TUNIS

M **MUSEE NATIONAL DU BARDO,** Bardo National Museum, 2000 Le Bardo, Tunis, Tunisia. Tel 513650; Fax 514050; *Dir* Habib Ben Younes
Collections: Ancient & modern Islamic art; Greek & Roman antiquities; Roman mosaics

TURKEY

ANKARA

M **ANADOLU MEDENIYETLERI MUZESI,** Museum of Anatolian Civilizations, Gozcu Sokak No 2, Ulus Ankara, Turkey. Tel 90-312-324-31-60, 61, 65; Fax 90-312-311-28-39; Elec Mail anmedmuz@ttnet.net.tr; Internet Home Page Address: www.anadolumedeniyetlerimuzesi.gov.tr; *Dir* Melih Arslan
Open daily 8:30 AM - 17 PM; Admis 15 TL; Estab 1921
Collections: Vast archaeological and ethnographic coll detailing Turkish history throughout every civilization in the region; Gold, silver, marble, bronze, coin colls, jewelry and more
Activities: Classes for children; lects open to pub; 10-15 vis lectrs per yr; concerts; schols; awards, European Mus of the Year Award (1997); sales shop sells books, reproductions, & prints; junior mus, Gordion Museum, Yassihoyuk Village, Polatli-Ankara

ISTANBUL

M **ISTANBUL ARKEOLOJI MUZELERI,** The Library of Archaeological Museums of Istanbul, Gulhane, Istanbul, 34400 Turkey. Tel 0 212 520 77 40; 520 77 41 - 42; Fax 0 212 527 43 00; Elec Mail info@istanbularkeoloji.gov.tr; Internet Home Page Address: www.istanbularkeoloji.gov.tr; *Act Dir* Zeynep S Kiziltan; *Librn* Havva KOC
Open 9 AM - 7 PM, cl Mon; No admis fee with permission from Dir of Museum; Estab 1902; Library with 80,000 plus vols; Average Annual Attendance: 400-500
Purchases: Donation library
Library Holdings: Auction Catalogs; Book Volumes; Exhibition Catalogs; Manuscripts; Maps; Original Documents; Pamphlets; Periodical Subscriptions; Photographs
Special Subjects: Archaeology, American Western Art
Collections: Architectural pieces; Turkish tiles; Akkadian, Assyrian, Byzantine, Egyptian, Greek, Hittite, Roman, Sumerian and Urartu works of art
Publications: The Annual of the Istanbul Archaeological Museum
Activities: Concerts, shows & painting exhibitions; lectrs in all topics (archaeology, philology & numismatics)

M **ISTANBUL MUSEUM OF MODERN ART,** Meclis-i Mebusan Ave, Liman Isletmeleri, Sahasi Antrepo No:4 Karakoy Istanbul, Turkey. Tel 0-212-334-73-00; Fax 212-243-43-19; Elec Mail info@istanbulmodern.org; Internet Home Page Address: www.istanbulmodern.org/en/f_index.html; *Nat Exhibitions Chief Cur* Levent Calikoglu; *Photog Exhib Cur* Engin Ozendes; *Design Cur* R Paul McMillen
Open Tues-Wed & Fri-Sun 10AM-6PM, Thurs 10AM-8PM, cl New Year's Day & first day of religious holidays; Admis adults 7TL, students, groups of 20 or more & seniors 65 & over 3TL; mus members, children under 12 & Thurs free

Collections: modern & contemporary art

M **TOPKAPI PALACE MUSEUM,** Sultanahmed, Istanbul, Turkey. Tel 28-35-47; *Dir* Turkoglu Sabahattin
Library with 18,000 manuscripts and 23,000 archival documents
Collections: Chinese & Japanese porcelains; miniatures & portraits of Sultans; private colls of Kenan Ozbel; Sami Ozgiritli's collection of furniture; Islamic relics; Sultan's costumes; Turkish embroideries; armor; tiles; applied arts; paintings

M **TURK VE ISLAM ESERLERI MUZESI,** Museum of Turkish and Islamic Art, Ibrahim Pasa Sarayi, Sultanhmet Istanbul, Turkey. Tel 5181805-06; Fax 5181807-06; Elec Mail tiemist@superonline.com; Internet Home Page Address: www.tiem.org; *Dir* Nazan Olcer; *Vice Dir* Cavit Avol; *Cur* Sula Ahboy
Open 9 AM - 4:30 PM; Admis general 1.250.000 Turkish Lira
Special Subjects: Woodcuts, Antiquities-Oriental
Collections: Illuminated manuscripts; monuments of Islamic art; metalwork and ceramics; Turkish and Islamic carpets; sculpture in stone and stucco; wood carvings; traditional crafts gathered from Turkish mosques and tombs
Activities: Mus shop sells books, magazines, original art, reproductions, prints, slides

MASLAK

M **ELGIZ MUSEUM OF CONTEMPORARY ART,** Meydan Sokak Beybi Giz Plaza B Blok, Maslak, 34398 Turkey. Tel 90-212-290-25-25; Fax 90-212-290-25-26; Elec Mail info@proje4l.org; Internet Home Page Address: www.elgizmuseum.org/EN/index.html
Open Tues by appointment, Wed-Fri 10AM-5PM, Sat 10AM-4PM, cl Sun, Mon & nat holidays
Collections: artworks by Turkish & international artists

TURKMENISTAN

BERZENGI

M **NATIONAL MUSEUM OF TURKMENISTAN,** Novo Firuzinskoye Chausse, Berzengi, Turkmenistan. *Dir* Mammetnurov Ovez
Open daily 10 AM - 5 PM, cl Tue; Admis $10
Collections: Household objects, national costumes, Turkmen crafts, books, ethnography

UGANDA

KAMPALA

M **NATIONAL MUSEUM OF UGANDA,** Plot 5 Kiira Rd, PO Box 365 Kampala, Uganda. Tel 256-41-423-2707; Fax 256-41-245-580; Elec Mail mumod@mtti.go.ug; Internet Home Page Address: www.mtti.go.ug; *Dir* Rose Nkaale Mwanga
Open Mon - Sat 10 AM - 6 PM, Sun 3 PM - 7 PM
Collections: Ethnographic collections from various regions of Uganda

UKRAINE

KYIV

M **KYIV MUSEUM OF RUSSIAN ART,** Tereshchenkovska vul 9, Kyiv, 01004 Ukraine. Tel (044) 234-82-88, 234-62-18, 287-73-24; Fax (044) 224-61-07; Fax (044) 451-40-27; Elec Mail museumru@ukr.net; Internet Home Page Address: www.museumru.kiev.ua; *Dir* Iurii Vakulenko; *Deputy Dir* Kateryna Ladyzenska; *Head Cur* Alla Iling; *Science Secy* Tatiana Kochubinska
Open Tues & Fri 11 AM - 6 PM, Wed, Sat & Sun 10 AM - 5 PM; Admis fl; Estab 1922; Average Annual Attendance: 70,000; Mem: 15 comt mems
Special Subjects: Decorative Arts, Drawings, Etchings & Engravings, Landscapes, Ceramics, Glass, Furniture, Porcelain, Portraits, Bronzes, Sculpture, Graphics, Watercolors, Religious Art, Folk Art, Marine Painting, Metalwork, Coins & Medals, Baroque Art, Miniatures, Medieval Art, Painting-Russian
Collections: 12,000 art objects
Activities: Classes for adults & children; workshops; lects open to pub, 720 vis lectrs per yr; concerts; tours; mus shop sells reproductions, magazines, prints; Children Picture Gallery

M **KYIV MUSEUM OF WESTERN & ORIENTAL ART,** The Bohdan and Vervara Khanenko Museum of Arts, Tereshchenkivska 15-17, Kyiv, Ukraine. Tel (+38044) 2350225; Fax (+38044) 2350206; Elec Mail khanenkomuseum@ukr.net; Internet Home Page Address: www.khanenkomuseum.kiev.ua; *Dir* E N Roslavets
Open Wed - Sun 10:30 AM - 5:30 PM, cl Mon & Tues; Admis 10 Ukrainian hryunas; Estab 1919; European art (14-19 cent) Byzantine icons, Asian art; Average Annual Attendance: 45,000
Income: State-run
Collections: 20,000 items
Exhibitions: 5 - 8 temporary exhib per yr
Publications: Oriental Collection
Activities: Mus shop sells books, reproductions, prints, souvenirs, cards & bookmarks

M **NATIONAL ART MUSEUM OF UKRAINE,** (Kyiv State Museum of Ukrainian Art) Ul Kirova 6, Kyiv, 252004 Ukraine; Hrushevskogo St 6, Kyiv, 01001 Ukraine. Tel 278-13-57; Fax 230-97-17; Elec Mail namu@i.com.ua; *Dir* Anatoly Melnyk; *Develop Dir* Mary Zadorozhnaya; *Head of Information Dept* Anya Groh
Open Wed - Thurs & Sun 10 AM - 6 PM, Fri noon - 8 PM, Sat 11 AM - 7 PM; Admis adults $2, student $1, children $.20; Average Annual Attendance: 120,000
Income: Financed by state budget
Collections: Portraits, icons, wood carvings & paintings from the Middle Ages; exhibits covering 8 centuries; modern art, Soviet art, Avant-Garde; Japanese calligraphy
Publications: Ukrainian Painting; Ukrainian Portrait XVI-XVIII; Monographies
Activities: Classes for adults & children; concerts; gallery talks; original objects of art lent to state museums in other countries; originates traveling exhibs to Tretiakov Gallery, Guggenheim Mus, Winnipeg Art Gallery, Chicago Cultural Ctr, New Church of Amsterdam, New York Ukrainian Mus; mus shop sells books, magazines, reproductions, almanacs

M **STATE MUSEUM OF UKRAINIAN DECORATIVE FOLK ART,** Ul Yanvarskogo Vosstaniya 21, Kyiv, Ukraine. *Dir* V G Nagai
Collections: Wood carvings, ceramics, weaving & applied arts from 16th century to present

ODESSA

M **ODESSA STATE MUSEUM OF EUROPEAN AND ORIENTAL ART,** Ul Pushkinshaya 9, Odessa, 270026 Ukraine. Tel 22-48-15; *Dir* N G Lutzkevich
Collections: Over 8000 art objects

UNITED ARAB EMIRATES

AL AIN

M **AL AIN NATIONAL MUSEUM,** Historic Environment Dept, PO Box 15715 Al Ain, United Arab Emirates. Tel 0097137641595; Fax 0097137658311; Elec Mail antiqan@emirates.net.ae; Elec Mail info.museum@adach.ae; Internet Home Page Address: www.aam.gov.ae/; *Dir* Mohammad Amer Mur Al Nayadi
Open Tues - Thurs & Sat-Sun 8 AM - 7:30 PM, Fri 2:30 - 7:30 PM; Admis adults $3, children under 10 $1; Estab 1969
Special Subjects: Archaeology, Ceramics, Glass, Gold, Bronzes, Ethnology, Jewelry, Coins & Medals
Collections: Archaeology and ethnography of UAE region; artifacts, ceramics, coins, weapons, jewelry, textiles, costumes, and decorative arts
Activities: Classes for children

SHARJAH

M **SHARJAH ART MUSEUM,** PO Box 19989, Sharjah, United Arab Emirates. Tel 971-6-6588222; Fax 971-6-568-6229; Internet Home Page Address: www.sdci.gov.ae/english/artmus.html; *Dir* Hoor Al Qasimi
Open Tues - Thurs 9 AM - 1 PM & 5 PM - 8 PM, Fri 5 PM - 8 PM, cl Mon; No admis fee
Collections: Various works by European painters depicting the Far and Near East; 8 sets of colls donated by H H Saikah Dr Sultan bin Mohammad Al Qasimi

URUGUAY

MALDONADO

M **MUSEO DE ARTE AMERICANO DE MALDONADO,** Treinta y Tres 823, Maldonado, Uruguay; Alfonso Espinola 1920, Montevideo, 11500 Uruguay. Tel 59842-22-22-76, 5982-600-1965; Fax 5982-600-7854; Elec Mail fundmaam@adinet.com.uy; Internet Home Page Address: www.fundmaam.org; *Dir* Jorge Paez Algorta
Open summer 6 PM - 11 PM; All other times by appointment; No admis fee
Collections: Foundation, museum and cultural center founded by Jorge Paez Vilaro; Pre-Columbian art, art of the colonial period, contemporary art, traditional & folk art, and art from Africa and Oceania

MONTEVIDEO

M **MUSEO DE ARTES DECORATIVAS,** 25 de Mayo 376, Montevideo, CP-11100 Uruguay. Tel 598-2-915-1101; Elec Mail webmaster@mec.gub.uy
Open Tues - Sat 12:15 PM - 6 PM, Sun 2 PM - 6 PM
Collections: European painting and decorative arts; ancient Greek and Roman art; Islamic ceramics of the 10th - 18th century

M **MUSEO MUNICIPAL DE BELLAS ARTES,** Avda Millan 4015, Montevideo, Uruguay. Tel 38-54-20; *Dir* Mario C Tempone
Collections: Paintings, sculptures, drawings, wood-carvings

M **MUSEO NACIONAL DE BELLAS ARTES,** National Museum of Fine Arts, Tomas Giribaldi 2283, Parque Rodo Montevideo, Uruguay. Tel 438-00; *Dir* Angel Kalenberg
Collections: 4217 ceramics, drawings, engravings, paintings & sculptures

UZBEKISTAN

NUKUS

M **SAVITSKY KARAKALPAKSTAN STATE ART MUSEUM,** K Rzaev St, Nukus, 230100 Uzbekistan. Tel 998-61-222-25-56; Fax 998-61-222-25-56; Elec Mail museum_savitsky@mail.ru; Internet Home Page Address: www.savitskycollection.org; www.museum.kr.uz; *Contact* Marinika Maratovna Babanazarova; *Cur* Valentina Egorovna Sycheva
Open Mon - Fri 9 AM - 5 PM, Sat - Sun 10 AM - 4 PM; Admis local adults: 3500 soums, students 2500 soums, children 1000 soums; visitor: adults 15000 soums, students 10000 soums, children 7000 soums; 1966; Russian Uzbek avant-garde artists, Karakalpak artists, folk applied art, art of ancient Khorezm; Average Annual Attendance: 70,000
Library Holdings: Auction Catalogs; Audio Tapes; Book Volumes; CD-ROMs; Cassettes; DVDs; Exhibition Catalogs; Lantern Slides; Manuscripts; Memorabilia; Motion Pictures; Pamphlets; Periodical Subscriptions; Photographs; Slides; Video Tapes
Special Subjects: Archaeology, Decorative Arts, History of Art & Archaeology, Architecture, Art History, Painting-American, Textiles, Painting-British, Painting-French, Drawings, Graphics, Sculpture, Watercolors, Costumes, Oriental Art, Carpets & Rugs, Coins & Medals, Restorations
Collections: Uzbek avant-garde of the 1920's and 1930s; Russian avant-garde of the 20th century and contemporary art of Karakalpakstan; Unique medieval ceramics, silver, jewelry and traditional textiles and ethnographic material
Activities: Classes for adults & children; dramatic progs; lects open to pub; gallery talks; tours; sponsoring of competitions; awards; ext prog serving rural areas; lending of original objects of art; mus shop sells books; magazines, reproductions, souvenirs

TASHKENT

M **FINE ART GALLERY OF UZBEKISTAN,** 2 Buyuk Turon St, Tashkent, 700078 Uzbekistan. Tel 998-71-133-56-74; Fax 998-71-133-77-65
Open Tues - Sat 11 AM - 5 PM, cl Sun & Mon
Collections: Works of fine arts by Uzbekistan artists from the early 20th century to the present; Numismatics of Central Asia

M **MUSEUM OF APPLIED ART,** 15 Rakatboshi St, Tashkent, Uzbekistan. Tel 998712-56-3943, 56-4042
Open daily 9 AM - 6 PM
Collections: More than 7000 pieces of traditional folk art from the 19th century to the present; Ceramics, glass and porcelain plates, hand-made and machine embroidery, national fabrics and textiles, carpets, works of wood engraving, miniatures, jewelry

M **STATE MUSEUM OF ARTS OF UZBEKISTAN,** 16 Movarounnahr St, Tashkent, Uzbekistan. Tel 99871-136-7436, 136-7740
Open Mon 10 AM - 1:30 PM, Wed - Sun 10 AM - 5 PM, cl Tues
Collections: Consists of more than 50,000 exhibits presenting decorative folk art and fine arts of Uzbekistan, Russia, Western Europea, and Asian artists; Engraving, ceramics, wood engravings, painting, textiles, embroidery, carpets and decorative metal works

VANUATU

PORT VILA

M **VANUATU CULTURAL CENTRE & NATIONAL MUSEUM,** Rue d'Artois St, Port Vila, Vanuatu. Tel 22129; Internet Home Page Address: www.vanuatuculture.org; *Cur* Takaronga Kuautonga
Open Mon - Fri 9 AM - 4:30 PM, Sat 9 AM - noon
Collections: Over 3500 artifacts relating to Vanuatu ethnographic history; Masks, gongs, mats, scale models, canoes; traditional and contemporary art, headdresses and examples of Lapita and Wusi pottery

VENEZUELA

CARACAS

M **GALERIA DE ARTE NACIONAL,** Plaza Morelos-Los Caobos, Apartado 6729 Caracas, 1010 Venezuela. Tel 578-18-18; Fax 578-16-61; *Dir* Rafael A Romero Diaz
Collections: Visual arts of Venezuela throughout history

M **MUSEO ALEJANDRO OTERO,** Complejo Cultural la Rinconada, Caracas, Venezuela. Tel 58-212-682-0102, 58-212-682-0941; Elec Mail fmaotero@cantv.net; *Dir* Nelson Oyarzabal
Open Tues - Fri 9 AM - 4 PM, Sat - Sun 10 AM - 4 PM; No admis fee
Collections: Contemporary art including major works by Alejandro Otero and other Venezuelan artists

M **MUSEO DE ARTE CONTEMPORANEO SOFIA IMBER,** Zona Cultural de Parque Central, Bellas Artes Caracas, Venezuela. Tel 58-212-573-82-89; Elec Mail maccsi@cantv.net; Internet Home Page Address: www.maccsi.org; *Dir* Luis Angel Duque
Open Tues - Sun 10 AM - 6 PM; No admis fee

Collections: Temporary exhibitions of national and international contemporary arts; painting, sculpture, drawing, cinema, video and photography

M **MUSEO DE BELLAS ARTES DE CARACAS,** Museum of Fine Arts, Plaza Morelos, Los Caobos Caracas, 1010 Venezuela. Tel (2) 571-01-69; Fax 058212-571 0169; Elec Mail fmba@reacciun.ve; Internet Home Page Address: www.museodebellasartes.org; *Dir* Maria Elena Huizi; *Exec Dir* Marisela Montes; *Chief Cur* Michaelle Ascencio
Open Mon - Fri 9 AM - 5 PM, weekends and holidays 10 AM - 5 PM; No admis fee; Estab 1917; museum of fine arts and study of the arts; Average Annual Attendance: 40,000
Income: Private and public funds
Purchases: Installation by Bernardi Roig
Library Holdings: Auction Catalogs; Audio Tapes; Book Volumes; CD-ROMs; Clipping Files; Exhibition Catalogs; Pamphlets
Special Subjects: Watercolors, Antiquities-Egyptian
Collections: Latin American & foreign paintings & sculpture; Cubism (old masters); Egyptian coll; Chinese ceramics; prints, drawings and photographs cabinet
Exhibitions: Gego: 1955-1990; Perú Milenario: 3,000 years of ancestral art; IV Bienal del Barro de América Roberto Guevara; Chema Madoz: Objetos 1990-1999; Sobre la Marcha: Dibujos de Pablo Benavides; Del Cuerpo a la Imagen; 150 Años de Fotografía en España; Chinese ceramics, Egyptian art, Cubism, drawings, prints and photographs cabinet, sculpture garden
Publications: Exhibition catalogs
Activities: Classes for children; dramatic progs; docent training; lects open to pub; concerts; gallery talks; tours; Daniela Chappard juried exhib; Josune Dorronsoro contest; originate traveling exhibs to mus internationally; mus shop sells books, magazines, original art, reproductions, prints, slides, cartisan crafts from Venezuela

SAN BERNARDINO

M **MUSEO DE ARTE COLONIAL QUINTA DE ANAUCO,** Ave Panteon, Sector the Erasos San Bernardino, Venezuela. Tel 58-212-551-86-50; Fax 58-212-551-85-17; Elec Mail artecolonialanauco@cantv.net; Internet Home Page Address: www.quintadeanauco.org.ve; *Dir* Carlos F Duarte
Open Tues - Fri 9 AM - 11:30 AM & 2 PM - 4:30 PM, Sat - Sun 10 AM - 4 PM; Admis adults Bs 4.000, students and children Bs 2.000; Estab 1942; paintings, sculpture, furnishings, dec arts; Mem: 500 mems
Income: financed by private funds
Collections: works of Venezuelan colonial period art; furniture, sculpture, ceramics, glass, silver, paintings, metalwork, textiles, glass and more
Activities: Classes for children; lects open to pub; 6 vis lectrs per yr; concerts; tours; conferences

VIETNAM

HANOI

M **VIETNAM FINE ARTS MUSEUM,** (Vietnam Museum of Fine Arts) 66 Nguyen Thai Hoc St, Hanoi, Vietnam. Tel (84-4) 3-8233084; Fax (84-4) 3-7341437; Elec Mail btmtvn@gmail.com; Internet Home Page Address: vnfam.vn; *Dir* Phan Van Tien; *Deputy Dir* Nguyen Anh Nguyet
Open daily 8:30 AM - 5 PM; Admis adults 20,000 VND, children 7,000 VND; Estab 26 June 1966; preserving and highlighting the nation's characteristic aesthetic values, the essence of Vietnamese plastic art from ancient times up to now
Purchases: Artwork and art books
Library Holdings: Book Volumes; Clipping Files; Fiche; Filmstrips; Manuscripts; Original Documents; Photographs; Records
Special Subjects: Decorative Arts, Drawings, Etchings & Engravings, Folk Art, Collages, Prints, Textiles, Sculpture, Graphics, Watercolors, Bronzes, Costumes, Ceramics, Crafts, Primitive art, Woodcarvings, Woodcuts, Restorations, Embroidery, Enamels
Collections: Ancient & modern ceramics, fine arts & handicrafts; Vietnamese cultural heritage; specialized library of over 1100 vols; Folk fine arts; Traditional Applied fine arts
Exhibitions: Ceramics & porcelain, excavations from wrecks in Vietnamese waters; Vietnamese fine arts from the doi moi (renewal) period up to present
Publications: Nguyen Phan Chanh's silk paintings, Vietnam Fine Arts Museum Guidebook of Vietnam Fine Arts Museum, VCD on Vietnamese Fine Arts Museum
Activities: Classes for children; exten program includes lending of original objects of art to art museums of Finland, Japan, Belgium; 5-7 book traveling exhibs per yr; organize traveling exhibs to local cities in Vietnam & abroad; mus shop sells books, magazines, original art, prints, reproductions, CD's, handcrafts & ceramics

HO CHI MINH

M **HO CHI MINH CITY FINE ARTS MUSEUM,** 97A Pho Duc Chinh St, Dist 1 Ho Chi Minh, Vietnam. Tel 08-829-4441; *Dir* Nguyen Toan Thi
Open Tues - Sun 9 AM - 4:45 PM; Admis 10,000 dong
Collections: Changing exhibits of contemporary art by local and international artists; Permanent collection of sketches, paintings, statues; works from the 1st century to the early 20th century

WALES

CARDIFF

M **AMGUEDDFA CYMRU - NATIONAL MUSEUM WALES,** (National Museum and Gallery of Wales) National Museum Cardiff, Cathays Park, Cardiff, CF10 3NP Wales. Tel 029 2057 3000, 0300 111 2 333; Fax 029 20 573321; Elec Mail post@museumwales.ac.uk; Internet Home Page Address: www.museumwales.ac.uk; *Dir Learning & Programmes* Janice Lane; *Keeper of Art* Oliver Fairclough; *Pres* Elizabeth Elias; *Dir Gen* David Anderson; *Dir Operations* Mark Richards; *Dir Research & Colls* John Williams-Davies
Open Tues - Sun 10 AM - 5 PM; No admis fee; Estab 1907; Natural sciences & art galleries; Average Annual Attendance: 350,000
Income: Sponsored by the Nat Assembly for Wales
Purchases: Include Thomas Girtin, Near Beddgelet, Leon Kossott From Wilksden Gieln, Autumn
Collections: Art, natural sciences, archaeology & industry of Wales; British and European fine and applied art; coll of Impressionist Art
Publications: Things of Beauty; National Museum of Wales - celebrating the first 100 years
Activities: Classes for adults & children, dramatic progs; lects open to pub, 30 vis lectrs per yr; concerts; gallery talks; tours; originate traveling exhibs; UK mus & galleries world-wide; mus shop sells books, reproductions, prints, slides

ZAMBIA

MBALA

M **MOTO MOTO MUSEUM,** PO Box 420230, Mbala, Zambia. Tel 450098; Elec Mail motomoto@zamnet.zm; Internet Home Page Address: www.zambiatourism.com/motomoto/index.htm; *Sr Keeper* Liyrsali Mushokabanji; *Asst Keeper* Mary Mberse; *Dir* Victoria Chrunau Pttiri; *Sr Keeper* Liwali Musttokabanji
Open 9 AM - 4:30 PM; Admis adults $3, children $1; Estab 1974; Educ & entertainment; mus of hist & ethnography

Income: government grants
Library Holdings: Book Volumes; Original Documents; Pamphlets; Periodical Subscriptions; Photographs
Special Subjects: Archaeology, Decorative Arts, Etchings & Engravings, Historical Material, History of Art & Archaeology, Art History, Maps, African Art, Anthropology, Ethnology, Crafts, Woodcarvings, Dioramas, Bookplates & Bindings
Collections: Ethnography, pre-history, history and natural history of Zambian region; Collection of artifacts, tools, traditional craft and ritual objects, masks, costumes, textiles, statues; Modern and Makonde art
Publications: Moto Moto Mus News letter
Activities: Classes for adults & children; outreach progs; gallery tours; sponsoring of competitions; traveling exhibs to other mus; organize traveling exhibs to surrounding villages & towns; mus shop sells books, magazines, original art, crafts & souvenirs

ZIMBABWE

HARARE

M **NATIONAL GALLERY OF ZIMBABWE,** 20 Julius Nyerere Way, Harare, Zimbabwe; PO Box CY 848 Causeway, Harare, Zimbabwe. Tel 704 666; Fax 704 668; Elec Mail ngallery@harare.africa.com; *Dir* George P Kahari; *Cur* Mrs Pip Curling; *Librn* Mrs Luness Mpunwa; *Conservation officer* Mrs Lilian Chaonwa
Open 9 AM - 5 PM; Admis adults 20 zimdollar, student 5 zimdollar; Estab 1957; Mem: 400
Income: Commission on sales & government grant
Collections: African traditional & local contemporary sculpture & paintings; ancient & modern European paintings & sculpture, including works by Bellini, Caracciolo, Gainsborough, Murillo, Reynolds, Rodin; Showa sculpture
Activities: Classes for adults & children, dramatic progs; lects open to pub; mus shop sells books, magazines & original art

ARGENTINA

BUENOS AIRES

UNIVERSIDAD DEL MUSEO SOCIAL ARGENTINO, Dept of Visual Arts,
Av Corrientes 1723, Buenos Aires, C1042AAD Argentina. Tel 54 11 4375 4601;
Fax 54 11 4375 4600; Elec Mail informes@umsa.edu.ar; Internet Home Page
Address: www.umsa.edu.ar; *Dean Organizer* Henry Vaccaro; *Dir Curating &
History of Art* Edward Colonna Tenconi
Courses: †Art History, †Drawing, †Painting, †Sculpture

AUSTRALIA

BARTON

ROYAL AUSTRALIAN INSTITUTE OF ARCHITECTS, 7 National Circuit,
Barton, ACT 2600 Australia; Level 2, National Circuit, PO Box 3373 Barton, ACT
2608 Australia. Tel 61 2 6121 2000; Fax 61 2 6121 2001; Elec Mail
national@raia.com.au; Internet Home Page Address: www.architecture.com.au;
Chief Exec David Parken LFRAIA
Estab 1930; Maintains architecture library, RAIA Chap, 2A Mugga Way, Red Hill,
ACT, Australia 2603

DARLINGHURST

NATIONAL ART SCHOOL, (School of Art and Design) Forbes St,
Darlinghurst, NSW 2010 Australia. Tel 02 9339 8744; Fax 02 9339 8740; Elec
Mail nas@det.nsw.edu.au; Internet Home Page Address: www.nas.edu.au; *Dir*
Bernard Ollis; *Head of Studies* Geoff Ireland; *Bus & Corp Svcs Mgr* Malcolm Bell
Approx 1850; Maintains a nonprofit art gallery, National Art School Gallery,
Forbes St, Darlinghurst, NSW 2010 Australia; maintains art/architecture library,
National Art School Library. Art supplies may be purchased on campus ; Pub,
NSN Dept of Education & Training; D & E; Scholarships, Fellowships; SC 6, LC
1, GC 2; enrl D 900, GS 50, other 1200
Ent Req: Portfolio of usual artwork & interview
Degrees: Bachelor of Fine Art, BFA (Honours); Master of Fine Art
Courses: Aesthetics, Art History, Ceramics, Drawing, History of Art &
Architecture, Painting, Photography, Printmaking, Sculpture
Adult Hobby Classes: Pub Programs
Summer School: Dir Jayne Dyer

FITZROY

AUSTRALIAN CATHOLIC UNIVERSITY, 115 Victoria Parade, Fitzroy, VIC
3065 Australia; Locked Bag 4115 DC, Fitzroy, VIC 3065 Australia. Tel 03 9953
3000; Elec Mail studentcentre@patrick.acu.edu.au
Courses: †Advertising Design, †Design, †Graphic Design, †Illustration, †Museum
Staff Training, †Painting, †Photography, †Printmaking, †Sculpture

HOBART

UNIVERSITY OF TASMANIA, Tasmanian School of Art, Locked Bag 57,
Hobart, 7001 Australia. Tel 61 3 6226 4300; Fax 61 3 6226 4308; Elec Mail
Lucia.Usmiani@utas.edu.au; Internet Home Page Address:
www.utas.edu.au/artschool; *Faculty of Arts* Prof J Pakulski; *Head* Prof Noel
Frankham; *Dep Head & Postgrad Coordr* Prof Jonathan Holmes; *Honours Coordr*
P Zika

LILYFIELD

UNIVERSITY OF SYDNEY, College of the Arts, Balman Rd, Lilyfield, 2040
Australia; Locked Bag 15, Rozelle, NSW, 2039 Australia. Tel 61-(2) 9351-1002;
Fax 61-(2) 9351-1101; Elec Mail enquiries@sca.usyd.edu.au; Internet Home Page
Address: www.usyd.edu.au/sca; *Dean* Prof Colin Rhodes; *Lect Theories of Art
Practice* Eril Baily; *Assoc Prof Painting* Brad Buckley; *Sr Lectr Photomedia*
Steven Lojewski; *Sr Lectr Printmedia* Justin Trendall; *Senior Lectr Sculpture*
Michael Goldberg; *Sr Lectr Theories of Art Practice* Ann Elias; *Lectr Ceramics* Jan
Guy; *Assoc Dean Research* Merilyn Fairskye; *Assoc Dean Learning & Teaching*
Jane Gavan; *Lectr Intermedia* Ryzard Dabek; *Lectr Photomedia* Tanya Peterson;
Lectr Theories of Art Practice Danie Mellor; *Sr Lectr Painting* Dr Debra Dawes;

Sr Lectr Painting Lindy Lee; *Lectr Painting* Mikala Dwyer; *Lectr Sculpture* Dr
Adam Geczy; *Lectr Silver & Jewelry* Joyce Hinterding; *Lectr Silver & Jewelry*
Oliver Smith; *Assoc Lectr Glass* Andrew Lavery; *Lectr Film* Josephine Starrs;
Lectr Film Geoff Weary
Estab 1976; Maintains non profit art gallery, SCA Galleries, Locked Bag 15,
Rozelle NSW, 2039 Australia; maintains art library, SCA LIbrary; Pub; D
Degrees: BVA, MVA, PhD
Courses: †Ceramics, Conceptual Art, Design, Drawing, †Film, †Glass,
Handicrafts, †Jewelry, Mixed Media, †Painting, †Photography. †Printmaking,
†Sculpture, Theories of Art Practice, Video

MELBOURNE

VICTORIAN COLLEGE OF THE ARTS, School of Art, 234 St Kilda Rd,
Melbourne, 3004 Australia. Tel (03) 9616 9300; *Dir* Andrea Hull

PADDINGTON

UNIVERSITY OF NEW SOUTH WALES, College of Fine Arts, PO Box 259,
Paddington, NSW 2021 Australia. Tel 612 9385 0684; Fax 612 9385 0706; Elec
Mail cofa@unsw.edu.au; Internet Home Page Address:
www.cofa.unsw.edu.au/home; *Dean* Ian Howard
Courses: †Art Education, †Ceramics, †Design, †Drawing, †Film, †Graphic
Design, †Jewelry, †Painting, †Printmaking, †Sculpture, †Textile Design, †Video

SYDNEY

JULIAN ASHTON ART SCHOOL, PO Box N676, Grosvenor Pl Sydney, NSW
1220 Australia. Tel 61 2 9241 1641; Internet Home Page Address:
www.julianashtonartschool.com/au; *Prin* Paul Ashton Delprat
Estab 1890
Courses: †Drawing, †Sculpture

UNIVERSITY OF SYDNEY, School of Philosophical and Historical Inquiry,
Sydney, NSW 2006 Australia. Tel 61-2-9351-2222; Fax 61-2-9351-3918; Internet
Home Page Address: www.usyd.edu.au.; *Prof* Dan Potts; *Prof* Margaret C Miller;
Assoc Prof Alison Betts
Estab 1850; Maintains a nonprofit art gallery, Nicholson Museum, Main
Quadrance A-14, Univ Sydney; 4; pub; D; LC, GC, LAB

AUSTRIA

SALZBURG

**INTERNATIONALE SOMMERAKADEMIE FUR BILDENDE KUNST
SALZBURG,** Salzburg International Summer Academy of Fine Arts,
Franziskanergasse 5a, Salzburg, 5010 Austria. Tel 84-21-13, 84-37-27; Fax
84-96-38; Elec Mail office@summeracademy.at; Internet Home Page Address:
www.summeracademy.at/en; *Dir* Hildegund Amanshauser; *Admin* Gabriele Winter;
Asst Baerbel Hartje
Estab 1953; pub; D; Scholarships; SC 20
Activities: Schols available
Ent Req: Over 17 yrs of age
Courses: †Architecture, †Conceptual Art, Curatorial Practice, †Display, †Drawing,
†Fashion Arts, †Film, †Goldsmithing, †Graphic Arts, †Mixed Media, †Painting,
†Photography, Printmaking, †Sculpture, †Silversmithing, †Textile Design, †Video
Summer School: Dir Hildegund Amanshauser

VIENNA

UNIVERSITAT FUR ANGEWANDTE KUNST WIEN, Oskar Kokoschka Platz
2, Vienna, A-1010 Austria. Tel (01) 71133-0; Fax (01) 71133-2089; Elec Mail
pr@uni.ak.ac.at; Internet Home Page Address: www.dieangewandte.at; *Chm Univ
Council* Robert Schachter; *Rector* Dr Gerald Blast; *Chm Senate* O Univ Prof Mag
art Sigbert Schenk; *Dean Studies* Prof Mag art Josef Kaiser; *Univ Dir* HR Mag iur
Dr Heinz Adamek; *Head Library* HR Mag iur Dr Gabriele Jurjevec-Koller
Estab 1868; Maintains art library, Universitatsibibliothek, Oskar Kokoschka-Platz
2, A-1010 Wien Austria; Pub; D; GC 12; 1700 total, GS 1300, other 400
Ent Req: Austrian Maturazeugnis or equivalent; entrance exam; for foreigners
proof of admis to a univ in home country
Degrees: MArch, MA, PhD, ScD, DScTech, MID
Tuition: 363 for EU mems, 726 for fgn students

Courses: †Advertising Design, †Aesthetics, †Architecture, †Art Appreciation, †Art Education, †Art History, †Calligraphy, †Ceramics, †Collage, †Commercial Art, †Conceptual Art, †Constructions, †Costume Design & Construction, †Crafts, †Design, †Drawing, †Fashion Arts, †Film, †Fine Arts, †Graphic Arts, †Graphic Design, †History of Art & Architecture, †Industrial Design, †Landscape Design, †Lettering, †Mixed Media, †Painting, †Photography, Printmaking, †Restoration & Conservation, †Sculpture, †Stage Design, Teacher Training, †Textile Design, †Theatre Arts, †Video, †Weaving

BARBADOS

BRIDGETOWN

UNIVERSITY OF THE WEST INDIES CAVE HILL CAMPUS, Errol Barrow Centre for Creative Imagination, P O Box 64 Bridgetown, BB11000 Barbados. Tel 246 417 4776; Fax 246 417 8903; Elec Mail ebcci@uwichill.edu.bb; Internet Home Page Address: www.cavehill.uwi.edu/ebcci

BELARUS

MINSK

BELARUSIAN STATE ACADEMY OF ARTS, Independence Ave 81, Minsk, 220012 Belarus. Tel 375 17 232 1542; Elec Mail info@belam.by; Internet Home Page Address: www.belan.by.com
Estab 1945
Courses: †Applied Arts, †Design, †Theatre Arts

BELGIUM

ANTWERP

KONINKLIJKE ACADEMIE VOOR SCHONE KUNSTEN, Royal Academy of Fine Arts Antwerp, 31 Mutsaertstraat, Antwerp, 2000 Belgium. Tel 03-213-71-00; Fax 03-213-71-19; *Dir* Prof Eric Ubben; *Prof* Nedda El-Asmar; *Prof* Walter Van Beirendonck; *Prof* Johan Pas
Estab 1663; Nadia Naveau, Vaast Colson, Tina Gillen; pub; D; SC 20, LC 10, ; D 650, grad 100
Ent Req: artistic entrance exam plus high school diploma
Degrees: BA (hons), MA (visual arts, conservation studies), PhD
Courses: †Art History, †Costume Design & Construction, †Design, †Drawing, †Fashion Arts, †Graphic Arts, †Graphic Design, †History of Art & Architecture, †Museum Staff Training, †Painting, †Photography, †Printmaking, †Restoration & Conservation, †Sculpture, †Silversmithing, †Stage Design, †Teacher Training, †Theatre Arts

BRUSSELS

ECOLE NATIONALE SUPERIEURE DES ARTS VISUELS DE LA CAMBRE, 21 Abbaye de la Cambre, Brussels, 1050 Belgium. Tel 00 32 2 626 17 80; Fax 00 32 2 640 96 93; Elec Mail lacambre@lacambre.be; Internet Home Page Address: www.lacambre.be; *Dir* Caroline Mierop
Estab 1926

BOLIVIA

CASILLA

UNIVERSIDAD NUR, Dept Arts, Av Cristo Redentor 100 Casilla, Santa Cruz de la Sie, Santa Cruz Casilla, 3273 Bolivia. Tel 591 3 333 7432; Internet Home Page Address: www.nur.edu; *Coordr Career Teaching* Jorge Braulio

BOSNIA AND HERZEGOVINA

SAVAJEVO

UNIVERSITY OF SARAJEVO, Academy of Fine Arts, Obala Maka Dizdara 3, Savajevo, 71000 Bosnia and Herzegovina. Tel 387 33 21 03 69; Fax 387 33 66 48 83; Elec Mail info@alu.unsa.ba; Internet Home Page Address: www.unsa.ba; *Dean* Nusret Pasic

BRAZIL

BELO HORIZONTE

UNIVERSIDADE FEDERAL DE MINAS GERAIS (UFMG), Escola de Belas Artes, Av Antonio Carlos, 6627 Pampulha Belo Horizonte, MG CEP 31270-901 Brazil. Tel 3409-5262; Fax 3409-5270; Elec Mail dir@eba.ufmg.br; Internet Home Page Address: www.eba.ufmg.br; *Dir* Evandro Jose Lemos da Cunha; *Vice Dir* Luiz Antonio Cruz Souza

RIO DE JANEIRO

ESCOLA DE ARTES VISUAIS, School of Visual Arts, 414 Rua Jardim Botanico, Parque Lage Rio de Janeiro, 22461-000 Brazil. Tel 55-21-2538-1091; 1879; Fax 55-21-2537-7878; Elec Mail eav@eavparquelage.org.br; Internet Home Page Address: www.eavparquelage.org.br; *Dir* Luiza Interlenghi
Estab 1975; maintain nonprofit art gallery, Cavalaricas; maintain art/architecture library; pub; D & E, Mon - Sat; SC 39, LC 19; 457
Ent Req: Free courses
Tuition: $70-$110
Courses: Aesthetics, Art Appreciation, Art Education, Art History, Drawing, Film, Graphic Arts, Mixed Media, Painting, Photography, Sculpture, Video
Summer School: Dir, Reynaldo Roels, Jr

BULGARIA

SOFIA

NIKOLAJ PAVLOVIC HIGHER INSTITUTE OF FINE ARTS, National Academy of Arts, Shipka 1, Sofia, 1000 Bulgaria. Tel 988-17-01; Fax 987-33-28; Elec Mail eduoffice@nha-bg.org; Internet Home Page Address: www.nha.bg; *Rector Prof* Svetoslav Kokalov
Estab 1896; Maintains nonprofit Acadmia Gallery & art/architecture library; Pub; D
Ent Req: Entrance exams
Degrees: BA, MA, DA
Courses: †Art Education, †Art History, †Book & Graphic Design, †Ceramics, †Digital Arts, †Graphic Arts, †Industrial Design, †Metalworking, †Painting, †Photography, †Poster & Visual Communication, †Sculpture, †Stage Design, †Textile Design, †Woodcarving

CAMBODIA

PHNOM PENH

ROYAL UNIVERSITY OF FINE ARTS (RUFA), 72 St 19 (Preah Ang Yukunthor), Sangkat Chey Chumneas Khan Daun Penh Phnom Penh, Cambodia. Tel 855 0 23 986 417; Elec Mail rufa@camnet.com.kh; Internet Home Page Address: www.rufa.edu.kh; *Rector* His Excellency Tuy Koeun; *Vice Rector* Mao Ngyhong; *Vice Rector* Proeung Chheang

CHILE

SANTIAGO DE CHILE

UNIVERSIDAD DE CHILE, Faculty of Arts, Libertador Bernardo O'Higgins 1058, Santiago de Chile, Chile. Tel 56 2 978 2000; Elec Mail mazola@uchile.cl; Internet Home Page Address: www.uchile.cl; *Rector* Victor Perez Vera
Courses: †Painting, †Photography, †Pottery, †Sculpture, †Silversmithing, †Textile Design

CHINA

JINAN

SHANDONG UNIVERSITY OF ART & DESIGN, 23 Qianfoshan East Rd, Jinan, 250014 China. Tel 86 531 2619385; Fax 86 531 2619550; Elec Mail kangwang59@sdada.edu.cn; Internet Home Page Address: www.sdada.edu.cn/english; *Pres* Pan Lusheng; *Dir International Exchange & Cooperation* Jackie Kang
Courses: †Architecture, †Digital Arts, †Drafting, †Fashion Arts, †Handicrafts, †Landscape Architecture

CHINA, REPUBLIC OF

TAIPEI

NATIONAL TAIWAN ACADEMY OF ARTS, Pan-chiao Park, Taipei, 22055 China, Republic of. Tel 967-6414; *Pres* S L Ling

COLOMBIA

BOGOTA

PONTIFICIA UNIVERSIDAD JAVERIANA, Carrera 7, No 40-62, Apdo Aereo 56710 Bogota, 11001000 Colombia. Tel 320 8320; Fax 571-288-23-35; Elec Mail Puj@javercol.javeriana.edu.co; Internet Home Page Address: www.javeriana.edu.co; *Dean Faculty of Architecture* Andres Gaviria; *Rector* Padre Joaquin Sanchez Garcia

Estab 1622

UNIVERSIDAD NACIONAL DE COLOMBIA, School of Visual Arts, Ciudad Universitaria - Bogota, Ave Carrera 30' 45-03, Bldg 303 Bogota, 111321 Colombia. Tel 57 1 3165538; Elec Mail ogutierrezr@unal.edu.co; Internet Home Page Address: www.facartes.unal.edu.co; *Dir* Oscar Gutierrez Rodriguez; *Dir* Jose David Lozano Moreno; *Contact* Stella Rivers

CROATIA

ZAGREB

AKADEMIJA IIKOVNIH UMJETNOSTI, Academy of Fine Arts of the University of Zagreb, LICA 85, Zagreb, 10000 Croatia. Tel 137 77300; Fax 137 73401; Elec Mail alu@alu.hr; Internet Home Page Address: www.alu.hr; *Dean* Dubravka/Babiae; *Assoc Prof* Slavomir Drinkovic
Estab 1907; Maintain nonprofit gallery; maintain art/architecture library; Pub; D; SC 100, LC 60, GC 40; Enrl D 400, maj 400, grad students 50
Ent Req: High school dipl
Degrees: BA, MA, PhD
Courses: Advertising Design, Aesthetics, Animation, †Art Education, Art History, Calligraphy, Collage, Costume Design & Construction, Drawing, Film, Graphic Arts, Graphic Design, History of Art & Architecture, Mixed Media, †Painting, Photography, †Printmaking, Restoration & Conservation, Sculpture, Stage Design, Teacher Training, Video

CZECH REPUBLIC

PRAGUE

AKADEMIE VYTVARNYCH UMENI, Academy of Fine Arts in Prague, U Akademie 4, Prague 7 Prague, 17022 Czech Republic. Tel 420 220 408 200; Fax 420 233 381 662; Elec Mail Kratka@avu.cz; petra.placakova@avu.cz; Internet Home Page Address: www.avu.cz; *Rector* Dr Jiri T Kotalik, PhD
Estab 1799; Maintains nonprofit art gallery, art/architecture library; art supplies sold at campus store; pub; D
Ent Req: Passing entrance exam
Degrees: HS educ
Courses: Architecture, Art History, Conceptual Art, Drawing, Graphic Arts, History of Art & Architecture, Mixed Media, Painting, Printmaking, Restoration & Conservation, Sculpture, Video
Adult Hobby Classes: Courses—Drawing (E)
Summer School: Dir Dr Roman Franta. Courses—Drawing, Painting

VYSOKA SKOLA UMELECKO-PRUMYSLOVA V PRAZE, Academy of Arts, Architecture & Design, Nam Jana Palacha 80, Prague, 116 93 Czech Republic. Tel 420-251-098-111; Fax 420-251-098-289; Elec Mail pr@vsup.cz; Internet Home Page Address: www.vsup.cz; *Pres* Pavel Liska, PhD; *Visual Arts Coordr* Hana Daredevil
Estab 1885; Maintains nonprofit art gallery & library; Pub; D; Scholarships; 450 D
Degrees: MgA
Courses: Aesthetics, Animation, Architecture, Art History, Calligraphy, Ceramics, Conceptual Art, Design, Drawing, Fashion Arts, Goldsmithing, Graphic Arts, Graphic Design, History of Art & Architecture, Lettering, Mixed Media, Museum Staff Training, Painting, Photography, Printmaking, Sculpture, Silversmithing, Textile Design

DENMARK

AARHUS

ARKITEKTSKOLEN AARHUS, Aarhus School of Architecture, Norreport 20, Aarhus, C 8000 Denmark. Tel 89-36-00-00; Fax 86 13 0645; Elec Mail a@aarch.dk; Internet Home Page Address: www.aarch.dk; *Rector* Staffan Henricksson
1965; Maintain an art/architecture library, Norreport 20, DK-8000 Aarhus C; on-campus shop where art supplies can be purchased; pub; D
Degrees: BA (Architecture), MA (Architecture)
Courses: †Architecture, †Design

COPENHAGEN

KONGELIGE DANSKE KUNSTAKADEMI, The Royal Danish Academy of Fine Arts, Kongens Nytorv 1, Copenhagen, DK-1050 Denmark. Tel 0045-33-74-46-00; Elec Mail bks@kunstakademiet.dk; Internet Home Page Address: www.kunstakademiet.dk; *Rector* Mikkel Bogh, PhD; *Prof, Time-Based Media* Gerard Byrne; *Prof, Painting* Anette Abrahamsson; *Prof, Sculpture* Martin Erik Andersen; *Prof, Language, Space & Scale* Katya Sander; *Prof, Graphic Arts* Thomas Locher; *Prof, Wall & Space* Nils Norman; *Prof, Media Arts* Angela Melitopoulos
Estab 1754; Maintains nonprofit art gallery Q gallery, Peder Skrams Gade 2, Copenhagen DK-1054; maintains art library; Pub; D; SC, LC, other; 200
Ent Req: Competitive
Degrees: MFA, MA

Courses: †Art Theory, Film, Graphic Arts, Mixed Media, Painting, Sculpture, Video, †Visual Art

DOMINICAN REPUBLIC

SANTO DOMINGO

DIRECCION GENERAL DE BELLAS ARTES, Fine Arts Council, Maximo Gomez, Av Independence Santo Domingo, Dominican Republic. Tel 809-682-1325; Fax 809-689-2643; Elec Mail dgba@bellasartes.gov.do; Internet Home Page Address: www.bellasartes.gov.do; *Dir* George Bernard

ENGLAND

BIRMINGHAM

BIRMINGHAM CITY UNIVERSITY, Faculty of Art & Design, Perry Barr, Birmingham, B42 2SU England. Tel (44 121) 331 6714; Fax (44 121) 331 6314; Elec Mail bcuinternational@enquiries.uk.com; Internet Home Page Address: www.bcu.ac.uk; *Dean Art & Design* J E C Price; *Prof* Mick Durman

BRIGHTON

UNIVERSITY OF BRIGHTON, Faculty of Arts, Grand Parade, Brighton, BN2 0JY England. Tel (1273) 643005; Elec Mail a.boddington@brighton.ac.uk; Internet Home Page Address: www.brighton.ac.uk/arts; *Dean, Faculty of Arts* Anne Boddington; *Dir Centre for Research & Develop* Prof Jonathan Woodham; *Head Humanities* Dr Patrick Maguire; *Head Art, Design, Media & Architecture* Karen Norqay
Estab 1859; Maintains a nonprofit art gallery as main bldg; maintains art/architecture library, St Peters House, University of Brighton. Scholarships offered to international students, see university website for details; Art supplies may be purchased on campus; Pub; D & E & summer schools classes; Scholarships; SC, LC, GC; Maj 3250, GS 450, PhD 80
Ent Req: Various as applicable
Degrees: PhD, MPhil, MA, MDes, MFA, BA, FDA
Tuition: See website
Courses: Aesthetics, Architecture, Art Education, Art History, Ceramics, Commercial Art, Conceptual Art, Costume Design & Construction, Design, Fashion Arts, Film, Graphic Arts, Graphic Design, Handicrafts, History of Art & Architecture, Mixed Media, Museum Staff Training, Painting, Photography, Printmaking, Sculpture, †Silversmithing, Teacher Training, Textile Design, Theatre Arts, Weaving
Adult Hobby Classes: See website
Summer School: Anne Asha, Dir; courses: Humanities, Arts & Design

GLOUCESTER

GLOUCESTERSHIRE COLLEGE OF ARTS & TECHNOLOGY, Llanthony Rd, Gloucester, GL525JQ England. Tel 44-1452 532000; Elec Mail info@gloscal.ac.uk; Internet Home Page Address: www.gloscal.ac.uk; *Prin* Greg Smith

IPSWICH

SUFFOLK COLLEGE, Department of Art & Design, Suffolk, Ipswich, IP4 1LT England. Tel 01473-255885; Fax 1473 230054; Elec Mail info@suffolk.ac.uk; Internet Home Page Address: www.suffolk.ac.uk; *Prin* Dave Muller

LEICESTER

DE MONTFORT UNIVERSITY, Faculty of Art and Design, The Gateway, Leicester, LE1 9BH England. Tel 116-255-7513; Fax 116 257 7353; Elec Mail enquiry@dmu.ac.uk; Internet Home Page Address: www.dmu.ac.uk; *Dean Art & Design* Gerard Moran

LIVERPOOL

LIVERPOOL JOHN MOORES UNIVERSITY, Aldham Robarts Learning Resource Centre, 70 Mount Pleasant, Liverpool, L3 5UX England. Tel (151) 231 21 21; Fax 151 231 3194; Internet Home Page Address: www.livjm.ac.uk

LONDON

CAMBERWELL COLLEGE OF ARTS, Peckham Rd, London, SE5 8UF England. Tel (020) 7514-6302; Fax (020) 7514-6310; Internet Home Page Address: www.camb.linst.ac.uk; *Head Prof* Roger Breakwell
Degrees: BA, MA
Courses: †Ceramics, †Drawing, †Graphic Design, †Illustration, †Metalwork, †Painting, †Photography, †Restoration & Conservation, †Sculpture, †Silversmithing

CHELSEA COLLEGE OF ART & DESIGN, Milbank, London, SW1P4JU England. Tel 207 514 7751; Fax (0171) 514 7777; *Prin* Bridget Jackson

CITY AND GUILDS OF LONDON ART SCHOOL, 124 Kennington Park Rd, London, SE11 4DJ England. Tel 020 7735 2306; Fax 020 7582 5361; Elec Mail admin@cityandguildsartschool.ac.uk; Internet Home Page Address: www.cityandguildsartschool.ac.uk; *Prin & Head of Fine Art* Tony Carter; *Admis Officer* Ed Budge; *Admin Asst* Emilia Yamamoto; *Admin Asst* Mari Shiba; *Deputy Dir* Magnus von Wistinghausen; *Develop Mgr* Lucrezia Serristori; *Acad Registrar* Susan Magee
Estab 1879; Maintains art library same location; art supplies available on campus; Independent; D & E; Scholarships; Degree & Grad Courses, Other
Activities: Schols available
Degrees: BA Hons & MA
Courses: †Art Appreciation, Art Education, Art History, †Drawing, Historical Stone carving, †History of Art & Architecture, †Lettering, Ornamental Wood carving, Painting, Printmaking, †Restoration & Conservation, †Sculpture

LONDON INSTITUTE, Lethaby Gallery, Central Saint Martins College of Art & Design, London Institute Gallery, 65 Davies St, London, W1Y 2DA England. Tel (071) 514 6000; Elec Mail info@arts.ac.uk; *Rector* Sir William Stubbs

ROYAL ACADEMY SCHOOLS, Fine Art, Burlington House, Piccadilly, London, W1J OBD England. Tel 020 7300 5650; Fax 020 7300 5856; Elec Mail schools@royalacademy.org.uk; Internet Home Page Address: www.royalacademy.org.uk; *Keeper Prof* Eileen Cooper RA; *Schools Admnr* Irina Zaraisky
Estab 1768; Maintains a nonprofit art gallery. Schols open annually to American residents with an MA degree in Fine Arts. Art supplies may be purchased on campus; Independent Royal Instn, pvt; D; Scholarships; Grad Course in Fine Arts, 3 yr Post Grad Course in Fine Art
Activities: Schols available
Ent Req: University Honours Degree, Bachelor's Degree in Fine Art
Degrees: Postgrad Dipl
Courses: Fine Arts, Painting, Printmaking, Sculpture

ROYAL COLLEGE OF ART, Kensington Gore, London, SW7 2EU England. Tel 0207 590 4444; Fax 0207 590 4500; Elec Mail rectorate@rca.ac.uk; Internet Home Page Address: www.rca.ac.uk; *Rector* Dr Paul Thompson
Estab 1837; Maintain library, same address; on-campus shop where art supplies may be purchased; Pub; D; SC 19
Ent Req: Undergrad degree
Degrees: MA, MPM, PhD
Courses: †Architecture, †Ceramics, Critical Writing in Art & Design, †Design, †Drawing, †Fashion Arts, †Goldsmithing, †Graphic Arts, †Graphic Design, †History of Art & Architecture, †Painting, †Photography, †Printmaking, †Sculpture, †Silversmithing, †Textile Design

SAINT MARTIN'S SCHOOL OF ART, 107 Charing Cross Rd, London, WC2H 0DU England. Tel 44-020-7514-7022; Fax 44-020-7514-7254; *Prin* Ian Simpson

SLADE SCHOOL OF FINE ART, University College, Gower St London, WC1E 6BT England. Tel 20-7679-2313; Fax 20-7679-7801; Elec Mail b.cohen@ucl.ac.uk; Internet Home Page Address: www.ucl.ac.uk; *Dir* Bernard Cohen
Estab 1871

UNIVERSITY OF LONDON, Goldsmiths' University of London, Lewisham Way, London, SE14 6NW England. Tel +44 (0) 207 919 7171; Fax +44 (0) 207 919 7509; Elec Mail international-office@gold.ac.uk; Internet Home Page Address: www.goldstr.ths.wc.uk; *Warden* Patrick Loughrey
On-campus shop where art supplies may be purchased; British Univ; D
Activities: Schols offered
Degrees: Yes
Courses: †Advertising Design, †Art Education, †Art History, †Ceramics, †Collage, †Conceptual Art, †Constructions, †Costume Design & Construction, †Design, †Drawing, †Fashion Arts, †Film, †Graphic Arts, †Graphic Design, †Mixed Media, †Museum Staff Training, †Occupational Therapy, †Painting, †Photography, †Printmaking, †Sculpture, †Stage Design, †Textile Design, †Theatre Arts, †Video

WIMBLEDON SCHOOL OF ART, Merton Hall Rd, London, SW19 3QA England. Tel 181-540-0231; Fax 181-543-1750; Elec Mail hinsley@wimbledon.ac.uk; Internet Home Page Address: www.wimbledon.ac.uk; *Prin* Colin Painter
—Dept of Foundation Studies, Palmerston Rd, London, SW19 1PB England. Tel 181-540-0231; Student Tel 181-540-7504; Fax 181-543-1750; *Dept Head* Yvonne Crossley
—Dept of Theatre, London, SW19 3QA England. Tel 181-540-0231; Fax 181-543-1750; *Dept Head* Malcolm Pride
—Dept of Fine Arts, London, SW19 3QA England. Tel 181-540-0231; Fax 181-543-1750; *Dept Head* Michael Ginsborg
—Department of History of Art & Contextual Studies, London, SW19 3QA England. Tel 181-540-0231; Fax 181-543-1750; *Dept Head* Dr Melissa McQuillan

MANCHESTER

MANCHESTER METROPOLITAN UNIVERSITY, Faculty of Art and Design, All Saints Bldg, Manchester, M15 6BH England. Tel (161) 247-2000; Fax (161) 247-6390; Elec Mail enquiries@mmu.ac.uk; Internet Home Page Address: www.mmu.ac.uk; *Dean Art & Design* R Wilson

NOTTINGHAM

NOTTINGHAM TRENT UNIVERSITY, School of Art and Design, Burton St, Nottingham, NG1 4BU England. Tel 115-941-8418; Internet Home Page Address: www.ntu.ac.uk; Telex 37-7534; *Dean* J P Lesquereux

OXFORD

UNIVERSITY OF OXFORD, Ruskin School of Drawing and Fine Art, 74 High St, Oxford, OX1 4BG England. Tel +44 (0) 1865 276 940; Fax +44 (0) 1865 276 949; Elec Mail info@ruskin-sch.ox.ac.uk; Internet Home Page Address: www.ruskin-sch.ox.ac.uk; *Head School* Dr Jason Gaiger; *Univ Lectr* Malcolm Bull, MA; *Prof, Univ Lectr* Maria Chevska, MA; *Prof, Univ Lectr* Brian Catling, MA; *Sr Res Fellow in Fin Art* Paul Bonaventura, MA; *Univ Lectr* Daria Martin; *Tutor* Jon Roome; *Tutor* Sarah Simblet; *Univ Lectr* Dr Elizabeth Price; *Univ Lectr* Corin Sworn; *Univ Lectr* Dr Anthony Gardner
Maintain library
Degrees: BFA, DPhil in Fine Art

PLYMOUTH

EXETER COLLEGE OF ART & DESIGN, Roland Levinsky Building, Plymouth, PL48AA England. Tel 845-111 6000; Fax 01392 210282; Elec Mail arts.admissions@plymouth.ac.uk; *Head* Prof M Newby; *Dean* David Coslett

SURREY

UNIVERSITY FOR THE CREATIVE ARTS, Falkner Rd. Farnham Surrey, GU9 7DS England. Tel 44 (0) 1252-722441; Fax 44 (0) 1252-892616; Internet Home Page Address: www.ucreative.ac.uk; *Vice-Chancellor* Simon Ofield-Kerr
Estab 2008, (founder col 1866); UCA campuses also at Canterbury, Epsom, Maidstone & Rochester; Art supplies available on-campus; pub; D; SC, LC, GC; Enrl 6,500
Degrees: BA (Hons); MA
Courses: Advertising Design, †Architecture, †Ceramics, Costume Design & Construction, Design, †Fashion Arts, †Film, Goldsmithing, Graphic Arts, Graphic Design, Mixed Media, Painting, Photography, Printmaking, Sculpture, Silversmithing, Textile Design, Video

ESTONIA

TALLINN

ESTONIAN ACADEMY OF ARTS, Tartu Maantee 1, Tallinn, 10145 Estonia. Tel (372) 626 7301; Fax (372) 626 7350); Elec Mail artrun@artrun.ee; Internet Home Page Address: www.artun.ee; *Rector* Ando Keskküla; *Prof Fine Arts* Kaisa Puustak; *Prof Applied Arts* Vilve Unt; *Prof Architecture* Veljo Kaasik; *Prof Institute of Design* Molit Summatavet; *Prof Institute of Art History* Mowt Kalm
Estab 1914; Pub; D & E; SC 20, LC 2, Postgrad 10; D 800, E 80, GS 140
Ent Req: Secondary educ, passing of entry exam
Degrees: Bachelor, Master, Doctor, dipl
Tuition: BA (general) 2051 Eur, Masters 2051 Eur in a study yr
Courses: †Architecture, †Art History, †Ceramics, †Design, †Fashion Arts, †Glass Art, †Goldsmithing, †Graphic Arts, †Graphic Design, †Interior Architecture, †Mixed Media, †Photography, †Restoration & Conservation, †Sculpture, †Stage Design, †Textile Design
Adult Hobby Classes: Open acad, diploma level educ

FINLAND

HELSINKI

KUVATAIDEAKATEMIA, Finnish Academy of Fine Arts, Kaikukatu 4, Helsinki, 00530 Finland. Tel 358-(9)-680 3320; Fax 358-(9)-680 33260; Elec Mail office@kuva.fi; Internet Home Page Address: www.kuva.fi/; *Rector* Mr Markus Konttiinen
Academy estab 1848; Maintains nonprofit art gallery, Gallery of the Finnish Academy of Fine Arts, Kasarmikah 44, Finland; FAFA Gallery, Lonnrotinkatu 35, 00180 Helsinki, Finland; maintains art library, Kasarmikah 36, 00130, Helsinki, Finland; Pub; D; please see www.kuva.fi/
Ent Req: Please see www.kuva.fi/
Degrees: BFA, MFA, DFA
Tuition: No tuition fee for degree students
Courses: Painting, Printmaking, Sculpture, Time and Space Arts

FRANCE

PARIS

ECOLE DU LOUVRE, School of the Louvre, 34 quai du Louvre, Paris, 75001 France. Tel 40-20-56-14; Fax 42-60-40-36; *Prin* D Ponnau

ECOLE NATIONALE SUPERIEURE DES ARTS DECORATIFS, National College of Decorative Arts, 31 rue d'Ulm, Paris, 75240 France. Tel 1-42-34-97-00; Fax 1-42-34-87-95; *Dir* Richard Peduzzi

ECOLE NATIONALE SUPERIEURE DES BEAUX-ARTS, National College of Fine Arts, 14 rue Bonaparte, Cedex 06 Paris, 75272 France. Tel (1)47-03-50-00; Fax (1)47-03-50-80; Elec Mail info@beauxartsparis.fr; Internet Home Page Address: www.ensba.fr; *Dir* Henry-Claude Cousseau
Estab 1648; Maintains temp exhibs of contemporary art or heritage coll; cabinet of drawings with 3 exhibs per yr; Mediatheque open access libr for students &

Servile de Collections, research libr for art historians, both on site; pub; D, E & Summer; SC, LC & GC
Ent Req: BA
Degrees: Dipl
Courses: Aesthetics, Art History, Conceptual Art, Drawing, Graphic Arts, Mixed Media, Painting, Photography, Printmaking, Sculpture, Video
Adult Hobby Classes: Summer courses only

ECOLE SPECIALE D'ARCHITECTURE, 254 blvd Raspail, Paris, 75014 France. Tel 33 (0)-1-40-47-40-47; Fax 33 (0)-1-43-22-81-16; Elec Mail info@esa-paris.fr; Internet Home Page Address: www.esa-paris.fr; *Dir* Odile Decq; *Head Acad* Marie-Helene Fabre; *Gen Sec* Armelle Cocheveeou
Estab 1865; Maintains a nonprofit Gallerie Speciale & art/architecture library; Pvt; D; Scholarships; SC 10, LC, GC
Activities: Schols available
Ent Req: HS dipl
Degrees: DESA
Tuition: 4,000 euros per sem
Courses: Aesthetics, Architecture, Art Education, Art History, Constructions, Design, Drawing, History of Art & Architecture, Mixed Media, Photography, Restoration & Conservation

UNIVERSITE DE PARIS I, PANTHEON-SORBONNE, UFR d'Art et d'Archeologie, 12 Place du Pantheon, Paris, 75231 France. Tel 1-46-34-97-00; *Actg Dir Art & Archaeology* L Pressouyre
Estab 1971

VILLENEUVE D'ASCQ

ECOLE D'ARCHITECTURE DE LILLE ET DES REGIONS NORD, 2 Green St, Villeneuve d'Ascq, 59650 France. Tel 20 61 95 50; Fax 20 61 95 51; Internet Home Page Address: www.lille.archi.fr; *Dir* Bernard Welcomme

GERMANY

BERLIN

UNIVERSITAT DER KUNSTE BERLIN, Postfach 12 05 44, Berlin, 10595 Germany; Einsteinufer 43-53, Berlin, 10587 Germany. Tel 030-31-85-0; Fax 0301 3185 2635; Elec Mail presse@udk-berlin.de; Internet Home Page Address: www.udk-berlin.de; *Pres & Dir* Prof Lothar Romain; *First VPres & Permanent Rep of Pres* Prof Peter Bayerer; *Dean Sch of Fine Art* Prof Burkhard Hold; *Dean Sch of Architecture & Design* Prof Kirsten Langkilde; *Dean Sch of Music* Dr Patrick Dinslage; *Dean Sch of Performing Arts* Dr Andreas Wirth; *Chancellor* Jürgen Schleicher; *Commun & Mktg Press & Publicity* Dr Jorg Kirchhoff; *Events and Alumni* Susanne S Reich; *Mktg* Christine Faber; *Internat Relations* Angelika Theuss; *Rep for Women's Affairs* Dr Sigrid Haase; *Mktg* Regina Dehning
Estab 1975
Exhibitions: Design Transfers
Activities: Classes held days; studio course, lect courses, grad courses; schols available

BRUNSWICK

HOCHSCHULE FUR BILDENDE KUNSTE/BRAUNSCHWEIG UNIVERSITY OF ART, Johannes-Selenka-Platz 1, Brunswick, 38118 Germany. Tel 391-9122; Fax 391 9292; Elec Mail hbk@hbk-bs.de; Internet Home Page Address: www.hbk-bs.de; *Rector* Prof Hubetus von Amelunxen
Estab 1963; Maintains nonprofit art gallery; maintains art library; Schols offered semi-annually; Pub; bd of trustees; D; Scholarships; SC, LC, GC; enrl 1,200
Ent Req: High school dipl, display of art & design work
Degrees: BA, MA
Tuition: 500 euro per semester
Courses: Advertising Design, Aesthetics, Art Appreciation, Art History, Art Mediation, Communication Arts, Communication Design, Conceptual Art, Constructions, Design, Display, Drawing, †Fashion Arts, Film, Fine Arts, †Goldsmithing, Graphic Arts, Graphic Design, †Industrial Design, Lettering, Mixed Media, Painting, Photography, Sculpture, Theatre Arts, Transportation Design, Video
Adult Hobby Classes: Classes for senior citizens

DRESDEN

HOCHSCHULE FUR BILDENDE KUNSTE DRESDEN, Bruhlsche Terrasse 1, Dresden, 01067 Germany; Postfach 160153, Dresden, 01287 Germany. Tel (351) 4402-0; Fax (351) 4402 250; Elec Mail presse@serv1.hfbk.dresden.de; Internet Home Page Address: www.hfbk-dresden.de; *Rector* Prof Christian Sery; *Dean* Prof Hans Peter Adamski; *Dean* Prof Heinz Leitner
Maintains nonprofit gallery & art/architecture library; Pub; D; Scholarships; SC, LC, GC; enrl 609
Ent Req: Abitur or equivalent, portfolio and entry exam
Degrees: Dipl after 5 years
Courses: Art History, †Conceptual Art, †Costume Design & Construction, †Drawing, †Graphic Arts, †Mixed Media, †Painting, †Restoration & Conservation, †Sculpture, †Stage Design, Theatre Arts, Video

DUSSELDORF

KUNSTAKADEMIE DUSSELDORF, Hochschule fur Bildende Kunste, State Academy of Art, Eiskellerstrasse 1, Dusseldorf, 40213 Germany. Tel (0211) 1396-0; Fax 0211 1396 225; *Dir* Markus Lupertz

FRANKFURT

STAATLICHE HOCHSCHULE FUR BILDENDE KUENSTE - STAEDELSCHULE, Academy of Fine Arts, Durerstrasse 10, Frankfurt, D 60596 Germany. Tel 069-605-008-0; Fax 069 605 008 66; Internet Home Page Address: www.staedelschule.de; *Rector* Prof Dr Daniel Birnbaum; *Fine Art* Simon Starling; *Fine Art* Wolfgang Tillmans; *Fine Art* Martha Rosler; *Fine Art* Michael Krebber; *Archit* Ben van Beskel
Estab 1817; pub; D; SC, LC; enrl 168
Ent Req: application with portfolio
Courses: Art History, Painting, Photography, Printmaking, Sculpture, Video

HAMBURG

HOCHSCHULE FUR BILDENDE KUNSTE, University of Fine Arts of Hamburg, Lerchenfeld 2, Hamburg, 22081 Germany. Tel 49-40 428989-207; Fax 49-40 428989-271; Elec Mail andrea.klier@hfbk-hamburg.de; Internet Home Page Address: www.hfbk-hamburg.de; *Pres* Martin Kottering
Estab 1767; Maintains HFBK gallery & library; art supplies sold at campus store; pub; D & E ; Scholarships; SC, LC & GC
Activities: Schols available
Ent Req: Higher educ entrance qualification, outstanding artistic ability, portfolio
Degrees: BA & MA (Fine Arts), PhD
Tuition: 375 euro per sem
Courses: Art Appreciation, Art Education, Art History, Ceramics, Commercial Art, Conceptual Art, Design, Drawing, Film, Goldsmithing, Graphic Arts, Graphic Design, Handicrafts, History of Art & Architecture, Mixed Media, Painting, Photography, Printmaking, Sculpture, Silversmithing, Stage Design, Teacher Training, Textile Design, Video

KARLSRUHE

STAATLICHE AKADEMIE DER BILDENDEN KUNSTE KARLSRUHE STATE ACADEMY OF FINE ARTS KARLSRUHE, State Academy of Fine Arts, Reinhold-Frank-Strasse 67, Karlsruhe, 76133 Germany. Tel 0721-926-5205; Fax 0721-926-5206; Elec Mail mail@kunstakademie.karlsruhe.de; Internet Home Page Address: www.kunstakademie.karlsruhe.de; *Rector* Prof Erwin Gross
Estab 1854; Maintains art library; pub; D; SC, LC
Courses: Drawing, Painting, Sculpture

LEIPZIG

HOCHSCHULE FUR GRAFIK UND BUCHKUNST, Academy of Visual Arts, Wachterstrasse 11, Leipzig, 04107 Germany. Tel (341) 2135-0; Fax 341 2135-166; Elec Mail hgb@hgb-leipzig.de; Internet Home Page Address: www.hgb-leipzig.de; *Rector* Prof Joachim Brohm
Maintains nonprofit art gallery; Pub; other

MUNICH

AKADEMIE DER BILDENDEN KUNSTE MUNCHEN, Academy of Fine Arts, Akademiestr 2-4, Munich, 80799 Germany. Tel 89-3852-0; Fax 89-3852-206; Elec Mail post@adbk.mhn.de; Internet Home Page Address: www.adbk.de; *Pres* Dr Otto Steidle
Estab 1770

NUREMBERG

AKADEMIE DER BILDENDEN KUNSTE IN NURNBERG, Academy of Fine Arts in Nuremberg, Bingstrasse 60, Nuremberg, 90480 Germany. Tel 0911-94040; Fax 0911 940 4150; Elec Mail info@adbk-nuernberg.de; Internet Home Page Address: www.adbk-nuernberg.de; *Prof* Peter Angermann; *Prof* Arno Brandlhuber; *Prof* Claus Bury; *Prof* Dr Christian Demand; *Prof* Rolf-Gunter Dienst; *Prof* Holger Felton; *Prof* Ralph Fleck; *Prof* Friederike Girst; *Prof* Thomas Hartmann; *Prof* Ottmar Horl; *Prof* Marko Lehanka; *Prof* Ulla Mayer; *Prof* Michael Munding; *Prof* Eva von Platen; *Prof* Hans Peter Reuter; *Prof* Georg Winter
Estab 1662; Pub; D
Ent Req: Qualifying examination, aptitude test
Degrees: State exam, dipl, cert, master schiler, dipl postgrad, master of architecture
Courses: Advertising Design, Architecture, Art Education, Art History, Conceptual Art, Design, Goldsmithing, Graphic Arts, Graphic Design, History of Art & Architecture, Mixed Media, Painting, Photography, Printmaking, Sculpture, Silversmithing, Teacher Training, Video

STUTTGART

STAATLICHE AKADEMIE DER BILDENDEN KUNSTE, Stuttgart State Academy of Art and Design, Am Weissenhof 1, Stuttgart, 70191 Germany. Tel 49 (0) 711-28440-0; Fax 49 (0) 711-28440-225; Elec Mail info@abk-stuttgart.de; Internet Home Page Address: www.abk-stuttgart.de; *Rector* Prof Dr Ludger Hunnekens

GREECE

ATHENS

ECOLE FRANCAISE D'ATHENES, French School of Athens, 6 Rue Didotou Athens, 10680 Greece. Tel (0030) 210 36 79 900; Fax (0030) 210 36 32 101; Elec Mail efa@efa.gr; Internet Home Page Address: www.efa.gr; *Dir* Prof D Mulliez

Estab 1846; Pub

HUNGARY

BUDAPEST

MAGYAR KEPZOMUVESZETI EGYETEM, Hungarian Academy of Fine Arts, Magyar Kepzomuveszeti Egyetem, 1062 Andrassy ut 69-71 Budapest, 1062 Hungary. Tel 3421-738; Fax +361 3427563; Elec Mail foreign@voyager.arts7.hu; Internet Home Page Address: www.arts7.hu; *Rector* Szabados Arpad
Estab 1871; Pub; D; SC, LC, GC, Postgrad
Ent Req: Final exam at secondary sch, entrance exam
Degrees: MA
Courses: †Art Education, †Art History, †Costume Design & Construction, †Drawing, †Graphic Arts, †Graphic Design, †Mixed Media, †Painting, †Photography, †Printmaking, †Restoration & Conservation, †Sculpture, †Stage Design, †Teacher Training, †Video

INDIA

BARODA

MAHARAJA SAYAJIRAO UNIVERSITY OF BARODA, Faculty of Fine Arts, University Rd, Baroda, 390002 India. Tel 795 600; Internet Home Page Address: www.msubaroda.ac.in; *Dean Faculty Fine Arts* P D Dhuhal
Estab 1949

LUCKNOW

UNIVERSITY OF LUCKNOW, College of Arts and Crafts, Faculty of Fine Arts, Badshah Bagh, Lucknow, UP 226007 India. Tel 43138; Fax 522 330065; *Dean* B N Arya

MUMBAI

RACHANA SANBAD, Academy of Architecture, Plot 278, Shankar Ghaneker Marg, Prabhadevi Mumbai, 400025 India. Tel (022) 2430 1024; Fax (022) 2430 1724; Elec Mail contact@aoamumbai.in; Internet Home Page Address: www.aoamumbai.in; *Prin* Suresh M Singh; *Prof* Milind B Amle; *Assoc Prof* Swati R Chokshi; *Asst Prof* Arun Narwekar; *Asst Prof* Aparna Herlekar
Estab 1955; Maintains a nonprofit art gallery, Rachana Sansad's Art Gallery, 278, Shankar Ghaneker Marg, Prabhadevi, Mumbai, 400 025, India. Art supplies may be purchased on campus; Pvt; D; Scholarships; SC, LC, GC; 300 students
Ent Req: 10+2 course
Degrees: B Architecture of Univ of Mumbai
Tuition: As per government norms
Courses: Architecture

IRELAND

BALLYVAUGHAN

BURREN COLLEGE OF ART, Newtown Castle, Ballyvaughan, Ireland. Tel 353-65-7077200; Fax 353-65-7077201; Elec Mail anna@burrencollege.ie; Internet Home Page Address: www.burrencollege.ie; *Pres* Mary Hawkes-Greene; *Dean & Head Painting* Conor McGrady; *Head Photography & Instr History Art* Martina Cleary; *Head Sculpture* Aine Phillips; *Head of Irish Studies* Gordon D'Arey
Estab 1993; Maintains nonprofit art gallery, BCA Gallery, Newtown Castle, Ballyvaughan, Co Clare; maintains art & architecture libr, maintains on-campus shop where art supplies can be purchased ; Pvt; D Acad yr and summer; SC, LC, GC 8
Activities: Schols offered
Ent Req: GPA 3 on Scale 4 per sem or yr (undergrad) BFA degree for MFA
Degrees: MFA, Post-Bac, PhD, JYA transfer cr for undergraduate, MA, postgraduate diploma
Courses: †Art & Ecology, Art History, Drawing, Painting, Photography, Sculpture
Adult Hobby Classes: Enrl 10-20 Summer Costs Vary
Summer School: Director Martina Cleary Head of Photography; max enrollment 12, tuition 3500 euro

DUBLIN

COLAISTE NAISIUNTA EALAINE IS DEARTHA, National College of Art & Design, 100 Thomas St, Dublin, 8 Ireland. Tel 353 1 6364 207; Fax 353 1 6364 200; Elec Mail fios@ncad.ie; Internet Home Page Address: www.ncad.ie; *Dir* Prof Declan McGonagle; *Head Design* Prof Angela Woods; *Head Educ* Prof Gary Granville; *Head Fine Art* Prof Philip Napier; *Head Visual Culture* Prof Niamh O'Sullivan; *Head Research & Acad Affairs* Prof Siun Hanrahan
Estab 1746; Art supplies may be purchased on campus; Pub; D, E & Easter & Summer periods; SC 12, LC 2 GC 5, Art, Design & Teacher Educ
Degrees: BA, BDes, MA, MFA, MLitt, PhD

Courses: Aesthetics, †Art Education, Art History, †Ceramics, Conceptual Art, †Design, Drawing, †Fashion Arts, †Goldsmithing, Graphic Design, Handicrafts, †Mixed Media, †Painting, Photography, †Printmaking, †Sculpture, Silversmithing, †Textile Design, Video, Weaving

ISRAEL

JERUSALEM

BEZALEL ACADEMY OF ARTS & DESIGN, PO Box 24046, Mount Scopus Jerusalem, 91240 Israel. Tel (2) 5893333; Fax (2) 582-3094; Elec Mail mail@bezalel.ac.il; Internet Home Page Address: www.bezalel.ac.il
Estab 1906; Maintains art & architecture lib, Bezalel Lib, Bezalel Acad, 7 Bezalel St, Mt Scopes Jerusalem 91260; maintains gift shop; 2,000
Degrees: BArch, B.DES, BFA, MFA, M.DES, M. Urban Des.
Courses: Advertising Design, †Architecture, Art History, Calligraphy, †Ceramics, †Design, Drawing, †Film, †Glass Design, †Goldsmithing, †Graphic Arts, †Graphic Design, †Industrial Design, †Painting, †Photography, †Printmaking, †Sculpture, †Video

ITALY

BOLOGNA

ACCADEMIA DI BELLE ARTI, Academy of Fine Arts, Via delle di Belle Arti 54, Bologna, 40126 Italy. Tel 39-051-4226411; Fax 39-051-253032; Elec Mail info@accademiabelleartibologna.it; Internet Home Page Address: www.accademiabelleartibologna.it; *Dir* A Baccilieri

FLORENCE

ACCADEMIA DI BELLE ARTI, Academy of Fine Arts, via Ricasoli 66, Florence, 50122 Italy. Tel 055-215-449; *Dir* D Viggiano

MILAN

ACCADEMIA DI BELLE ARTI DI BRERA, Academy of Fine Arts, Palazzo di Brera, via Brera 28 Milan, 20121 Italy; Via Fiori Oscuri 7, Milan, 20121 Italy. Tel 02-86-95-52-94; Fax 02-86-40-36-43; Elec Mail relazionigstone@accademiadibrera.milano.it; Internet Home Page Address: www.accademiadibrera.milano.it; *Pres* Gabriele Mazzotta
Estab 1776; Maintains art/architecture library; Ministero Univ & Research, pub; D; Scholarships; GC 28
Activities: Schols available
Ent Req: Secondary level school
Degrees: 1o Level, 3 yrs; 2o Level, 2 yrs
Tuition: See website for tuition

PERUGIA

ACCADEMIA DI BELLE ARTI PIETRO VANNUCCI, Academy of Fine Arts, Piazza San Francesco al Prato 5, Perugia, 06123 Italy. Tel 075-5730631; *Dir* Edgardo Abbozzo

ROME

ACCADEMIA DI BELLE ARTI DI ROMA, Academy of Fine Arts, via di Ripetta 222, Rome, 00186 Italy. Tel 06-322-70-25; Fax 06 3218007; Elec Mail Direzione@accademiabelleartiroma.it; Internet Home Page Address: www.accademiabelleartiroma.it; *Dir* Prof Gerardo LoRusso; *Instr* Prof Tiziana D'Achille
Estab 1873; pub; D; D 365
Activities: Schols
Tuition: from 500,00 to1500,00 euro
Courses: Decoratioin, Fashion Arts, Graphic Arts, Graphic Design, Painting, Scenography, Sculpture

AMERICAN ACADEMY IN ROME, Via Angelo Masina 5, Rome, 00153 Italy. Tel 06-58461; Fax 06 581 0788; Elec Mail info@aarome.org; Internet Home Page Address: www.aarome.org; *Dir* Caroline Bruzelius

BRITISH SCHOOL AT ROME, via Gramsci 61, Rome, 00197 Italy. Tel +39 06 326 4939; Fax +39 06 322 1201; Elec Mail info@brrome.it; Internet Home Page Address: www.bsr.ac.uk; *Dir* Christopher Smith; *Asst Dir* Susan Russell; *Asst Dir* Jacopo Benci; *Registrar & Publs Mgr* Gillian Clark; *Librn* Valerie Scott; *Bursar* Alvise Di Giulio; *Dir's Asst* Eleanor Murkett; *Hostel Supv* Geraldine Wellington; *School Sec* Maria Pia Malvezzi; *Subscriptions Sec* Jo Wallace-Hadrill; *Accounts Clerk* Isabella Gelosia; *Domestic Bursar* Renato Parente; *Archaeology Research Prof* Simon Keay
Estab 1901

ISTITUTO CENTRALE DEL RESTAURO, Central Institute for the Restoration of Works of Art, Piazza San Francesco di Paola 9, Rome, 00184 Italy. Tel 6488961; Fax 6 481 57 04; *Dir* Dott M d'Elia
Estab 1939

TURIN

ACCADEMIA ALBERTINA DI BELLE ARTI, via Accademia Albertina 6, Turin, 10123 Italy. Tel 011-889020; Fax 011 812 5688; Elec Mail info@accademiabertina.torino.it; *Pres* P Delle Roncole

VENICE

ACCADEMIA DI BELLE ARTI, Academy of Fine Arts, Campo della Carita 1050, Venice, 30123 Italy. Tel (041) 5225396; Fax (041) 5230 129; *Dir* Antonio Toniato

JAMAICA

KINGSTON

EDNA MANLEY COLLEGE OF VISUAL & PERFORMING ARTS, School of Visual Arts, One Arthur Wint Dr, Kingston 5 Kingston, Jamaica. Tel 876-929-2530; Fax 876-968-6171; Elec Mail info@emc.edu.jm; Internet Home Page Address: www.emc.edu.jm; *Dean* Hope Brooks; *Dir Studies-Degree* Annie Hamilton; *Dir Studies-Dipl* Hope Wheeler; *Libr Asst* Pamela James
Estab 1950; SC, LC
Ent Req: 5 CXC, portfolio review, drawing exam
Degrees: UWI/EMCUDA, BA, Dipl Studio Art, JBTE
Courses: †Advertising Design, †Aesthetics, †Art Education, †Art History, †Ceramics, †Design, †Display, †Drawing, †Goldsmithing, †Graphic Arts, †Graphic Design, †History of Art & Architecture, †Painting, †Photography, †Printmaking, †Sculpture, †Silversmithing, †Stage Design, †Teacher Training, †Textile Design, †Theatre Arts, †Weaving

JAPAN

KANAZAWA CITY

KANAZAWA COLLEGE OF ART, 5-11-1 Kodatsuno, Kanazawa-shi, Ishikawa 920 Kanazawa City, 920 Japan. Tel (81) 76-262-3531; Fax (81) 76-262-6594; Elec Mail admin@kanazawa-bidai.ac.jp; Internet Home Page Address: www.kanazawa-bidai.ac.jp; *Pres* Kenji Kuze
Estab 1946; Pub; D
Degrees: BA 4 yrs, MFA, PhD
Tuition: 535,800 yeb
Courses: Craft, Design, Fine Art, Liberal Arts

KYOTO

KYOTO CITY UNIVERSITY OF ARTS, 13-6 Kutsukake-Cho, Oheda, Nishikyo-Ku Kyoto, 610-11 Japan. Tel 075-332-0701; Fax 078-332-0709; Elec Mail admin@kcua.ac.jp; Internet Home Page Address: www.kcua.ac.jp; *Pres* Shumpei Ueyama

TOKYO

TAMA ART UNIVERSITY, 3-15-34 Kaminoge, Setagaya-Ku Tokyo, 158 8558 Japan. Tel (03) 3702-1141; Elec Mail pro@tamabi.ac.jp; Internet Home Page Address: www.tamabi.ac.jp; *Pres* Nobuo Tsuji
Pvt; D & E; D 3159, E 849, GS 206
Courses: †Art Science, †Ceramics, †Design, †Environmental Design, †Glass, †Graphic Arts, †Graphic Design, †Information Design, †Japanese Painting, †Metal Design, †Oil Painting, †Painting, †Printmaking, †Product Design, †Sculpture, †Teacher Training, †Textile Design, †Theatre Arts

TOKYO GEIJUTSU DAIGAKU TOSHOKAN, Tokyo National University of Fine Arts & Music, 12-8 Ueno Park, Taito-Ku, Tokyo, 110 8714 Japan. Tel 3828-7745; *Pres* Masao Yamamoto

KOREA, REPUBLIC OF

SEOUL

SEOUL NATIONAL UNIVERSITY, College of Fine Arts, 599 Gwanak-ro, Gwanak-gu Seoul, 151-742 Korea, Republic of. Tel 82-2-880-4447; *Dean* Se-ok Suh
Estab 1946

LATVIA

RIGA

VALST MAKSLAS AKADEMIJA, Latvian Academy of Arts, Kalpaka blvd 13, Riga, LV 186 Latvia. Tel 33-22-02; *Rector* Janis Andris Osis

LEBANON

BEIRUT

ACADEMIE LIBANAISE DES BEAUX-ARTS, PO Box 55251, Sin-El-Fil Beirut, Lebanon. Tel 961-1-480056; Fax 961-1-500779; Elec Mail alba@alba.edu; Internet Home Page Address: www.alba.edu/contact.html; *Chair* Georges Khodr

MEXICO

MEXICO CITY

ESCUELA NACIONAL DE ARTES PLASTICAS, National School of Plastic Arts, Ave Constitution 600, BO La Concha, Xochimilco, DF Mexico City, Mexico. Tel 54894921; Internet Home Page Address: www.enap.unam.mx; *Dir* Dr Jose Daniel Manzano Aquila
Estab 1781; Maintains nonprofit art galleries: Luis Nishizawa Gallery, Antonio Ramirez Gallery, & three more in San Carlos Academy; maintains an art/architecture library: Jose Maria Natividad Correa Toca (same address). Schols offered annually to internal students. On campus shop where art supplies may be purchased; Pub (Nat Autonomous Univ of MX); D & E; Scholarships; E, NM, M, Grad C; 3,500 students
Ent Req: High school dipl
Courses: †Advertising Design, †Aesthetics, †Art Appreciation, †Art Education, †Art History, †Calligraphy, †Ceramics, †Collage, †Commercial Art, †Conceptual Art, †Design, †Drawing, Engraving, †Film, †Graphic Arts, †Graphic Design, †Mixed Media, †Painting, †Photography, †Printmaking, †Restoration & Conservation, †Sculpture, †Silversmithing, †Stage Design, †Teacher Training, †Video
Adult Hobby Classes: Several courses
Children's Classes: Courses for children 6-12 yrs
Summer School: Courses of continuing educ. Dir, Rosa Marquez Rangel

INSTITUTO NACIONAL DE BELLAS ARTES, Instituto Nacional de Bellas Artes y Literatura, Paseo Reforma y Campo Marte, Mexico City, Mexico; Paseo de la Reforma y Campo, Marte s/n, Modula A, Piso 1, Col Chapultepec Polanco Mexico City, 11560 Mexico. Tel (55) 52 80 77 27; Fax (55) 52 80 47 39; Elec Mail amaldo@correo.inba.gob.mx; lvelarde@correo.inba.gob.mx; Internet Home Page Address: www.bellasartes.gob.mx; *Dir* Vicgor Sandoval de Leon

PUEBLA

UNIVERSIDAD DE LAS AMERICAS, Artes Graficas y Diseno, Santa Catarina Martir Puebla, 72820 Mexico. Tel 29 20 00; *Rector* Dr Enrique Cardenas Sanchez

NETHERLANDS

AMSTERDAM

ACADEMIE VAN BOUWKUNST, Academy of Architecture, Waterlooplein 211, Amsterdam, 1011 PG Netherlands. Tel 020-531-8218; Fax 020-623-2519; Elec Mail info@bwk.ank.nl; *Dir* A Oxenaar

RIJKSAKADEMIE VAN BEELDENDE KUNSTEN, State Academy of Fine Arts, Sarphatistraat 470, Amsterdam, 1018 GM Netherlands. Tel (20) 5270300; Fax (20) 5270301; Elec Mail info@rijksakademie.nl; Internet Home Page Address: www.rijksakademie.nl; *Dir* Dr Mevr Els van Odijk
Estab 1970 for research in visual arts
Activities: Open to young artists from all over the world

BREDA

AVANS HOGE SCHOOL, Academy of Art and Design/St Joost, Breda, POB 90116 Netherlands. Tel (76) 5250302; Fax (76) 5250305; Elec Mail info.akvstjoost@avans.nl; Internet Home Page Address: www.akv.stjoost.nl; *Dir* J H J M Van De Vijver
Maintains art/architecture library

THE HAGUE

KONINKLIJKE ACADEMIE VAN BEELDENDE KUNSTEN, Royal Academy of Fine and Applied Arts, Prinsessegracht 4, The Hague, 2514 AN Netherlands. Tel 070-315-47-77; Fax 070-315-47-78; Elec Mail post@kabk.nl; *Dir* C M Rehorst
Estab 1682

STICHTING DE VRIJE ACADEMIE VOOR BEELDENDE KUNSTEN, Paviljoensgracht 20-24, The Hague, Netherlands; Postbus 36, The Hague, 2501 CA Netherlands. Tel 70-363 8968; Fax 70-3638968; Elec Mail info@vrijeacademie.org; Internet Home Page Address: www.vrijeacademie.org; *Dir* Frans A M Zwartjes

NORWAY

OSLO

KUNSTHOGSKOLEN I OSLO, (Statens Kunstakademi) Oslo National Academy of the Arts, Fossveien 24, Oslo, 0551 Norway; PO Box 6853 St. Olavs plass, Oslo, 0130 Norway. Tel 22 99 55 00; Fax 22 99 55 02; Elec Mail khio@khio.no;

Internet Home Page Address: www.khio.no; *Fac of Visual Arts Dean* Stale Stenslie; *Fac of Design Dean* Halldor Gislason; *Fac of Performing Arts Dean* Harry Guttormsen
Estab Aug 1996; Maintains a nonprofit art gallery; Pub; D & E; D 550
Ent Req: General univ admis cert & entrance examination
Degrees: BA, MA
Courses: Advertising Design, Ceramics, Costume Design & Construction, Fashion Arts, Goldsmithing, Graphic Arts, Graphic Design, Opera, Painting, Printmaking, Sculpture, Silversmithing

PERU

LIMA

ESCUELA NACIONAL SUPERIOR DE BELLAS ARTES, National School of Fine Arts, 681 Jiron Ancash, Lima, Peru. Tel 427-2200; Fax 427-0799; Elec Mail ccbellasartes@yahoo.es; Internet Home Page Address: www.ensabap.edu.pe; *Dir Gen* Leslie Lee Crosby; *Dir Acad* Luis Tokuda Fujita
D, E & N
Ent Req: Seundaria completa, examen de admision, documentas personales (test)
Degrees: Titulo de artista plastico y docente anombre de la nacion
Adult Hobby Classes: Enrl 600; courses—painting & drawing
Children's Classes: Enrl 600; courses—painting & drawing
Summer School: Enrl 1200; courses— painting, drawing & graphic design; Dir Luis Tokuda

POLAND

CRACOW

AKADEMIA SZTUK PIEKNYCH IM JANA MATEJKI W KRAKOWIE, Academy of Fine Arts in Cracow, Pl Matekji 13, Cracow, 31-157 Poland. Tel 0048 12 422 24 50; Fax 0048 12 422 65 66; Elec Mail zebulano@cyf-kr.edu.pl; *Rector* Prof Stanislaw Rodzinski
Estab 1818; Pub; D & E
Degrees: BA, MA

LODZ

PANSTWOWA WYZSZA SZKOLA SZTUK PLASTYCZNYCH, Strzeminski Academy of Fine Arts & Design, Ul Wojska Polskiego 121, Lodz, 91-726 Poland. Tel 42-2547-598; Fax 42-2547-560; *Rector* Jerzy Trelinski

WARSAW

AKADEMIA SZTUK PIEKNYCH, Academy of Fine Arts, Ul Krakowskie Przedmiescie 5, Warsaw, 00-068 Poland. Tel 26-19-72; Fax 26 21 14
Estab 1904

WROCLAW

AKADEMIA SZTUK PIEKNYCH, (Panstwowa Wyzsza Szkola Sztuk Plastyczynch) Academy of Fine Arts, Pl Polski 3/4, Wroclaw, 50-156 Poland. Tel 315-58; *Rector* Konrad Jarodzki

PORTUGAL

LISBON

ESCOLA SUPERIOR DE BELAS ARTES, Faculdade De Belas Artes Da Universidade De Lisboa, Largo da Academia Nacional de Belas-Artes 2, Lisbon, 1249-058 Portugal. Tel 213 252 164; Fax 213 487 635; Elec Mail biblioteca@fba.ul.pt; Internet Home Page Address: www.fba.ul.pt; *Pres* Miguel Arruda; *Secy* Ana Paula Carreira
Art supplies may be purchased on campus; Pub; D; Scholarships; SC 5, LC, GC 4
Degrees: Licenciatura, Mestrado, Douturamento
Courses: Advertising Design, Art Education, Art History, Ceramics, Design, Drawing, Graphic Arts, Graphic Design, Museum Staff Training, Painting, Photography, Sculpture

OPORTO

ESCOLA SUPERIOR DE BELAS ARTES, School of Fine Arts, Av Rodrigues de Freitas 265, Oporto, Portugal. Tel 228-77; *Dir* Carlos Ramos

RUSSIA

MOSCOW

MOSCOW V I SURIKOV STATE ART INSTITUTE, 30 Tovarishcheskii Pereulok, Moscow, 109004 Russia. Tel (095)912-39-32; Fax (095)912-18-75; Elec Mail artinst@mail.ru; *Dir* L V Shepelev

SAINT PETERSBURG

ST PETERSBURG REPIN INSTITUTE OF PAINTING, SCULPTURE & ARCHITECTURE, Universitetskaya Nab 17, Saint Petersburg, 199034 Russia. Tel 812-323 6496; *Rector* O A Yeremeyev

SCOTLAND

DUNDEE

UNIVERSITY OF DUNDEE, Faculty of Duncan of Jordanstone College of Art & Design, 13 Perth Rd, Dundee, DD1 4HN Scotland. Tel 1382-345212; Fax 1382-227304; Elec Mail jordanstone@dundee.ac.uk; Internet Home Page Address: www.dundee.ac.uk; *Prin of the Univ* Sir Alan Langlands; *Dean of Faculty* Prof G Follett; *Head Sch of Fine Art* Tracy MacKenna; *Head Sch of TV & Imaging* S R Flack; *Sch of Design* Prof Mike Press
Art supplies may be purchased on campus; Pub; D & E; Scholarships; S 14, GC 5; D 1426, Maj 1426, GS 52
Ent Req: 3 Scottish Highers (including Art & English) or 2 A Levels plus portfolio or equivalent
Degrees: BDesign, BA Fine Art, BSc Architecture, BA in Art, Philosophy, Contemporary Studies, BSci Interactive Media Design, Innovative Product Design MArch, MSc Electronic Imaging, MFA, M Design, MPhil, PhD
Courses: †Animation & Electronic Imaging, †Architecture, †Art History, †Design, †Drawing, †Goldsmithing, †Graphic Design, †History of Art & Architecture, †Illustration, Innovative Product Design, †Interactive Media Design, †Interior Design, †Jewelry & Metalwork, †Painting, †Printmaking, †Sculpture, †Textile Design, †Video, †Weaving
Adult Hobby Classes: Embroidery, Pressmaking, Making Soft Furnishings, Printing for Pleasure & Life Drawing
Children's Classes: Children's Creative Textile Design, Young Adults Creative Textile Design
Summer School: Dir Dr John Blicharski, Various subjects available

EDINBURGH

EDINBURGH COLLEGE OF ART, Lauriston Pl, Edinburgh, EH3 9DF Scotland. Tel 131-221 6000; Fax 131-221 6001; Internet Home Page Address: www.eca.ac.uk; *Prin* Alistair Rowan

GLASGOW

THE GLASGOW SCHOOL OF ART, 167 Renfrew St, Glasgow, G3 6RQ Scotland. Tel 0141-353-4500; Fax 0141-353-4408; Elec Mail info@gsa.ac.uk; Internet Home Page Address: www.gsa.ac.uk; *Dir* Prof Seona Reid, CBE, BA, DLITT, DART, FRSA; *Deputy Dir & Dir Acad Develop* Prof Allan Walker, MA (Oxon) DipLI; *Dir Finance & Bus* Eliot Leviten, BSc (Hons) FCA; *Head Mackintosh School of Arch* Prof David Porter, BSc (Hons) Dip Arch ARIAS RIBA; *Head of School Design* Prof Irene McAra McWilliam, MA, FRSA; *Head of School of Fine Art* Prof Klaus Jung; *Dir Digital Design Studio* Prof Paul Anderson, MDes; *Head Research & Postgraduate* Naren Barfield, CertAD, DipFA, BA (Hons), MA, PhD, PGCert, ILTM
Estab 1845; Pub; D & E; Scholarships; SC 10, GC 5
Ent Req: portfolio
Degrees: BA, BDes, MEDes, BEng, MEng, MFA, MA, MLitt, MPhill, PhD
Courses: †Architecture, †Art Education, †Conceptual Art, †Design, †Graphic Arts, †Graphic Design, †Painting, †Photography, †Printmaking, †Textile Design

SLOVAKIA

BRATISLAVA

VYSOKA SKOLA VYTVARNYCH UMENI, Academy of Fine Arts & Design Bratislava, Hviezdoslavovo 18, Bratislava, 814 37 Slovakia. Tel 121 594 28 500; Fax (7) 54 43 23 40; (2) 59 42 85 03; Elec Mail rector@vsvu.sk; Internet Home Page Address: www.afad.sk; *Rector* Stanislav Stanoeci; *Vice Rector* Ivan Csudai; *Vice Rector* Silvia Sanesi-Lutrova; *Vice Rector* Josef Kovalcik; *Vice Rector* Lucia Okolicanyova
Estab 1949; Maintain non-profit gallery & non-profit library at same address; on-campus shop where art supplies may be purchased; pub; d; SC, LC, GC
Ent Req: admis exam
Degrees: BC (Bachelor), Mgr art (master), Art D, PhD (Doct oral)
Courses: Architecture, Design, Graphic Arts, Graphic Design, Handicrafts, Painting, Photography, Printmaking, Restoration & Conservation, Sculpture, Textile Design, Video

SOUTH AFRICA

CAPE TOWN

UNIVERSITY OF CAPE TOWN, Michaelis School of Fine Art, Private Bag x3, Rondebosch 7701 Cape Town, South Africa. Tel (21) 650911; Fax 21 650 213814 040; Elec Mail webmaster@uct.ac.za; Internet Home Page Address: www.uct.ac.za; *Dean* J W Rabie

DOORNFONTEIN

UNIVERSITY OF JOHANNESBURG, Faculty of Art, Design & Architecture, PO Box 17011, Doornfontein, 2028 South Africa. Tel (11) 406-2911; Fax (11) 402-0475; Elec Mail eugeneh@mail.twr.ac.za; Internet Home Page Address: www.twr.ac.za; www.twr.ac.za/fada; *Fine Art* M Edwards; *Industrial Design* P Oosthuizen; *Architecture* E Landzaad; *Graphic Design* E Blake
Estab 1930; pub; D; 950
Degrees: B Tech, M Tech, D Tech
Courses: Architecture, Art Appreciation, Art History, Ceramics, Design, Drawing, Fashion Arts, Goldsmithing, History of Art & Architecture, Painting, Printmaking, Sculpture, Silversmithing, Teacher Training

SPAIN

SEVILLA

REAL ACADEMIA DE BELLAS ARTES DE SANTA ISABEL DE HUNGRIA DE SEVILLE, Abades 14, Casa de los Pinos Sevilla, 41004 Spain. Tel 22-11-98; Elec Mail rabashih@insacan.org; *Pres* Antona dela Banda y Vargas

SWEDEN

STOCKHOLM

KONSTHOGSKOLAN, College of Fine Arts, Flaggmansvagen 1, PO Box 163 15 Stockholm, 103 26 Sweden. Tel (08) 6144000; Fax (08) 6798626; Elec Mail info@kxh.se; Internet Home Page Address: www.kkh.se; *Prin* Olle Kaks; *Rector* Marie-Louise Ekman; *Prof* Fredric Bedoire; *Prof* Peter Cornell; *Prof* Erik Dietman; *Prof* Peter Hagdahl; *Prof* Eberhard Holl; *Prof* Jan Lisinski; *Prof* Mari Rantanen; *Prof* Johan Scott; *Prof* Annette Senneby; *Prof* Johan Widen; *Prof* Anders Wilhelmsson

SWITZERLAND

GENEVA

ECOLES D'ART DE GENEVE, Geneva Schools of Art, 9 blvd Helvetique, Geneva, 1205 Switzerland. Tel 22-311-05-10; Fax 22-310-13-63; *Dir* Bernard Zumthor
—Ecole des Arts Decoratifs, School of Decorative Arts, rue Jacques-Necker 2 Geneva, 1201 Switzerland. Tel 22-732-04-39; Fax 22-731-87-34; *Dir* Roger Fallet

LAUSANNE

ECOLE CANTONALE D'ART DE LAUSANNE, Lausanne College of Art, 5 ave du Temple, Renens VD, PO Box 555 Lausanne, CH1001 Switzerland. Tel 021-316-99-33; Fax 021-316-92-66; Elec Mail ecal@ecal.ch; Internet Home Page Address: www.ecal.ch; *Dir* Alexis Georgacopoulos

NATIONAL ENDOWMENT FOR THE ARTS

Joan Shigekawa, Acting Chair
1100 Pennsylvania Ave NW
Washington, DC 20506-0001
Tel 202-682-5414
E-mail: chairman@arts.gov
Web Site: www.nea.gov

REGIONAL ORGANIZATIONS

Arts Midwest

David Fraher, Exec Dir
2908 Hennepin Ave, Ste 200
Minneapolis, MN 55408-1954
Tel 612-341-0755 ext 8024; Fax 612-341-0902
TDD: 612-822-2956
(IA, IL, IN, MI, MN, OH, ND, SD, WI)
E-mail: general@artsmidwest.org, david@artsmidwest.org
Web Site: www.artsmidwest.org

Mid-America Arts Alliance/ExhibitsUSA

Mary Kennedy McCabe, CEO
2018 Baltimore Ave
Kansas City, MO 64108
Tel 816-421-1388; Fax 816-421-3918
TDD: 800-735-2966
(AR, KS, MO, NE, OK, TX)
E-mail: info@maaa.org, mary@maaa.org
Web Site: www.maaa.org

Mid-Atlantic Arts Foundation

Alan W Cooper, Exec Dir
201 North Charles St, #401
Baltimore, MD 21201
Tel 410-539-6656; Fax 410-837-5517
TDD: 410-779-1593
(DC, DE, MD, NJ, NY, PA, VA, VI, WV)
E-mail: info@midatlanticarts.org, alan@midatlantic.org
Web Site: www.midatlanticarts.org

New England Foundation for the Arts

Rebecca Blunk, Exec Dir
145 Tremont St, 7th floor
Boston, MA 02111
Tel 617-951-0010; Fax 617-951-0016
(CT, MA, ME, NH, RI, VT)
E-mail: info@nefa.org
Web Site: www.nefa.org

Southern Arts Federation

Suzette M Surkamer, Exec Dir
1800 Peachtree St NW, Ste 808
Atlanta, GA 30309
Tel 404-874-7244; Fax 404-873-2148
TTD: 404-876-6240
(AL, FL, GA, KY, LA, MS, NC, SC, TN)
E-mail: saf@southarts.org, ssurkamer@southarts.org
Web Site: www.southarts.org

Western States Arts Federation

Anthony Radich, Exec Dir
1743 Wazee St, Ste 300
Denver, CO 80202
Tel 303-629-1166; Fax 303-629-9717

(AK, AZ, CA, CO, ID, MT, NV, NM, OR, UT, WA, WY)
E-mail: staff@westaf.org, anthony.radich@westaf.org
Web Site: www.westaf.org

STATE ART AGENCIES

Alabama State Council on the Arts

Jim Harrison, Chair
Albert B Head, Exec Dir
201 Monroe St
Montgomery, AL 36130-1800
Tel 334-242-4076; Fax 334-240-3269
E-mail: staff@arts.alabama.gov, al.head@arts.alabama.gov
Web Site: www.arts.state.al.us

Alaska State Council on the Arts

Benjamin Brown, Chair
Shannon Daut, Exec Dir
161 S Klevin St, Ste 102
Anchorage, AK 99508-1506
Tel 907-269-6610, 907-269-6607; Fax 907-269-6601
E-mail: aksca_info@alaska.gov, daut@alaska.gov
Web Site: www.eed.state.ak.us/aksca

Arizona Commission on the Arts

Mark Feldman, Chair
Robert C Booker, Exec Dir
417 W Roosevelt St
Phoenix, AZ 85003-1326
Tel 602-771-6501; Fax 602-256-0282
E-mail: info@azarts.gov, rbooker@azarts.gov
Web Site: www.azarts.gov

Arkansas Arts Council

Mildred J Franco, Chair
Joy Pennington, Exec Dir
323 Center St, Ste 1500
Little Rock, AR 72201
Tel 501-324-9766, 501-324-9770; Fax 501-324-9207
E-mail: info@arkansasarts.com, joy@arkansasheritage.org
Web Site: www.arkansasarts.com

California Arts Council

Wylie Aitken, Chmn
Craig Watson, Dir
1300 I St, Ste 930
Sacramento, CA 95814
Tel 916-322-6555; Fax 916-322-6575
E-mail: info@caartscouncil.com, cwatson@cac.ca.gov
Web Site: www.cac.ca.gov

Colorado Creative Industries

Robert B Clasen, Chmn
Margaret Hunt, Dir
1625 Broadway, Ste 2700
Denver, CO 80202
Tel 303-892-3802; Fax 303-892-3848
E-mail: coloarts@state.co.us, margaret.hunt@state.co.us
Web Site: www.coloarts.state.co.us

Connecticut Office of the Arts

Fitz Jellinghaus, Chmn
Christopher Bergston, Dep Commissioner
One Constitution Plaza, Second Fl

Hartford, CT 06103
Tel 860-256-2800; Fax 860-256-2811
E-mail: artsinfo@ctarts.org, kip.bergstrom@ct.gov
Web Site: www.cultureandtourism.org

Delaware Division of the Arts

Lisa Monty, Chair
Paul Weagraff, Dir
Carvel State Office Bldg, 4th floor
820 N French St
Wilmington, DE 19801
Tel 302-577-8278; Fax 302-577-6561
E-mail: paul.weagraff@state.de.us
Web Site: www.artsdel.org

DC Commission on the Arts and Humanities

Judith Terra, Chair
Lionell Thomas, Exec Dir
200 I St SE, Ste 1400
Washington, DC 20009
Tel 202-724-5613; Fax 202-727-4135
TTY: 202-724-4493
E-mail: lionell.thomas@dc.gov
Web Site: dcarts.dc.gov

Florida Division of Cultural Affairs

Glenn Lochrie, Chair
Sandy Shaughnessy, Div Dir
R A Gray Bldg, 3rd Fl, 500 S Bronough St
Tallahassee, FL 32399-0250
Tel 850-245-6470; Fax 850-245-6497
E-mail: sandy.shaughnessy@dos.myflorida.com
Web Site: www.florida-arts.org

Georgia Council for the Arts

Kathleen G Williams, Chmn Bd
Karen L Pary, Dir
75 5th St NW, Ste 1200
Atlanta, GA 30308
Fax 404-962-4839
E-mail: gaarts@gaarts.org
Web Site: gca.georgia.gov

Hawaii State Foundation on Culture and the Arts

Barbara Saronmines-Ganne, Chair
Eva Laird Smith, Exec Dir
250 South Hotel St, 2nd Fl
Honolulu, HI 96813
Tel 808-586-0300; Fax 808-586-0308
E-mail: eva.laird.smith@hawaii.gov
Web Site: www.state.hi.us/sfca

Idaho Commission on the Arts

Mark Hofflund, Chmn
Michael Faison, Exec Dir
2410 North Old Penitentiary Rd
Boise, ID 83712
Mailing Address: PO Box 83720
Boise, ID 83720-0008
Tel 208-334-2119; 800-278-3863; Fax 208-334-2488
E-mail: michael.faison@arts.idaho.gov
Web Site: www.arts.idaho.gov

Illinois Arts Council

Shirley Madigan, Chmn
Tatiana Gant, Exec Dir
100 W Randolph, Ste 10-500
Chicago, IL 60601-3298
Tel 312-814-6750; Fax 312-814-1471
E-mail: tatiana.gant@illinois.gov
Web Site: www.state.il.us/agency/iac

Indiana Arts Commission

Jon Ford, Chair
Lewis Ricci, Exec Dir
100 N Senate Ave, Rm N505
Indianapolis, IN 46204

Tel 317-232-1268; Fax 317-232-5595
E-mail: lricci@iac.in.gov
Web Site: www.in.gov/arts

Iowa Arts Council

Steve Hansen, Chmn
Mary Cownie, Exec Dir
Capitol Complex, 600 E Locust
Des Moines, IA 50319-0290
Tel 515-281-6412; Fax 515-242-6498
E-mail: mary.cownie@iowa.gov
Web Site: www.iowaartscouncil.org

Kansas Creative Arts Industries

Peter Jasso, Dir
1000 SW Jackson St, Ste 100
Topeka, KS 66612-1354
Tel 785-296-2178; Fax 785-296-3490
E-mail: pjasso@kansascommerce.com
Web Site: arts.state.ks.us

Kentucky Arts Council

Mary Michael Corbett, Chmn
Lori Meadows, Exec Dir
21st Fl, Capital Tower Plaza, 500 Mero St
Frankfort, KY 40601-1974
Tel 502-564-3757; Fax 502-564-2839
E-mail: lori.meadows@ky.gov
Web Site: www.artscouncil.ky.gov

Louisiana Division of the Arts

Gerri Hobdy, Chmn
Cathy Hernandez, Exec Dir
Louisiana Division of the Arts
PO Box 44247
Baton Rouge, LA 70804-4247
Tel 225-342-8180; Fax 225-342-8173
E-mail: arts@crt.state.la.us
Web Site: www.crt.state.la.us/arts

Maine Arts Commission

Charles V Stanhope, Chmn
Julie Richard, Dir
25 State House Station, 193 State St
Augusta, ME 04333-0025
Tel 207-287-2724; Fax 207-287-2725
E-mail: julie.richard@maine.gov
Web Site: mainearts.com

Maryland State Arts Council

Barbara Bershon, Chair
Theresa Colvin, Exec Dir
175 W Ostend St, Ste E
Baltimore, MD 21230
Tel 410-767-6555; Fax 410-333-1062
E-mail: tcolvin@msac.org
Web Site: www.msac.org

Massachusetts Cultural Council

Dr Ira Lapidus, Chair
Anita Walker, Exec Dir
10 St James Ave, 3rd Fl
Boston, MA 02116-3803
Tel 617-727-3668; Fax: 617-727-0044
E-mail: anita.walker@art.state.ma.us
Web Site: www.massculturalcouncil.org

Michigan Council for Arts and Cultural Affairs

Andrew Buchholz, Chmn
John Bracey, Exec Dir
Michigan Economic Development Corporation
300 N Washington Sq, 4th Fl
Lansing, MI 48913
Tel 517-241-4011; Fax 517-241-3979
E-mail: braceyj@michigan.org/arts/
Web Site: www.michiganadvantage.org/arts

Minnesota State Arts Board
Ellen McInnis, Chair
Sue Gens, Exec Dir
Park Square Ct
400 Sibley St, Ste 200
Saint Paul, MN 55101-1928
Tel 651-215-1600; Fax 651-215-1602
E-mail: sue.gens@state.mn.us
Web Site: www.arts.state.mn.us

Mississippi Arts Commission
Myrna Colley-Lee, Chair
Sallye Killebrew, Interim Exec Dir
501 N West St, Ste 1101A, Woolfork Bldg
Jackson, MS 39201
Tel 601-359-6030; Fax 601-359-6008
E-mail: skillebrew@arts.state.ms.us
Web Site: www.arts.ms.us

Missouri Arts Council
Nola Ruth, Chmn
Beverly Strohmeyer, Exec Dir
815 Olive St, Ste 16
Saint Louis, MO 63101-1503
Tel 314-340-6845; 866-407-4752 (toll free); TTD: 800-735-2966
Fax 314-340-7215
E-mail: bev.strohmeyer@ded.mo.gov
Web Site: www.missouriartscouncil.org

Montana Arts Council
Arlynn Fishbaugh, Exec Dir
830 N Warren St, Floor One, PO Box 202201
Helena, MT 59620
Tel 406-444-6430; Fax 406-444-6548
E-mail: afishbaugh@mt.gov
Web Site: art.mt.gov

Nebraska Arts Council
Robert Nefsky, Acting Chair
Suzanne T Wise, Exec Dir
1004 Farnam St, Plaza Level
Omaha, NE 68102
Tel 402-595-2122; 800-341-4067 (toll free); Fax 402-595-2334
E-mail: suzanne.wise@nebraska.gov
Web Site: www.nebraskaartscouncil.org

Nevada Arts Council
Tim Jones, Chmn
Susan Boskoff, Exec Dir
716 N Carson St, Ste A
Carson City, NV 89701
Tel 775-687-6680; Fax 775-687-6688
E-mail: sboskoff@nevadaculture.org
Web Site: nevadaculture.org/nac

New Hampshire State Council on the Arts
Dr Roger C Brooks, Chair
Lynn Graton, Acting Dir
19 Pillsbury St, 1st Fl
Concord, NH 03301-3570
Tel 603-271-2789; TTY/TTD: 800-735-2964; Fax 603-271-3584
E-mail: lynn.j.graton@dcr.nh.gov
Web Site: www.state.nh.us/nharts

New Jersey State Council on the Arts
Elizabeth A Mattson, Chmn
Nicholas Paleologos, Exec Dir
225 W State St, 4th Fl
PO Box 306
Trenton, NJ 08625-0306
Tel 609-292-6130; Fax 609-989-1440
Email: nicholas.paleologos@sos.state.nj.us
Web Site: www.artscouncil.nj.gov

New Mexico Arts Division
Sherry Davis, Chair
Loie Fecteau, Exec Dir
407 Galisteo St, 2nd Fl, Ste 270, Bataan Memorial Bldg
Santa Fe, NM 87501
Tel 505-827-6490; Fax 505-827-6043
E-mail: loie.fecteau@state.nm.us
Web Site: www.nmarts.org

New York State Council on the Arts
Aby Rosen, Chmn
Lisa Robb, Exec Dir
300 Park Ave S, 10th Fl
New York, NY 10010
Tel 212-627-4455; Fax
E-mail: lisa.robb@artsny.gov
Web Site: www.nysca.org

North Carolina Arts Council
Bobby Kadis, Chmn
Waynbe Martin, Exec Dir
MSC 4632 Dept of Cultural Resources
Raleigh, NC 27699-4632
Tel 919-807-6500; Fax 919-807-6532
E-mail: wayne.martin@ncdcr.gov
Web Site: www.ncarts.org

North Dakota Council on the Arts
David Trottier, Chmn
Jan Webb, Exec Dir
1600 E Century Ave, Ste 6
Bismarck, ND 58503
Tel 701-328-7590; Fax 701-328-7595
E-mail: jwebb@nd.gov
Web Site: www.nd.gov/arts/index.html

Ohio Arts Council
Jeffrey A Rich, Chair
Julie S Henahan, Exec Dir
30 E Broad St, 33rd Fl
Columbus, OH 43215-3414
Tel 614-466-2613; Fax 614-466-4494
E-mail: julie.henahan@oac.state.oh.us
Web Site: www.oac.state.oh.us

Oklahoma Arts Council
James Pickel, Chair
Amber Sharples, Exec Dir
2101 N Lincoln Blvd, Rm 640
Jim Thorpe Bldg
PO Box 52001-2001
Oklahoma City, OK 73152-2001
Tel 405-521-2931; Fax 405-521-6418
E-mail: amber.sharples@arts.ok.gov
Web Site: www.arts.ok.gov/

Oregon Arts Commission
Jean B Boyer Cowling, Chmn
Christine T D'Arcy, Exec Dir
775 Summer St NE, Ste 200
Salem, OR 97301-1284
Tel 503-986-0082; Fax 503-986-0260
E-mail: oregon.artscomm@state.or.us
Web Site: www.oregonartscommission.org

Pennsylvania Council on the Arts
Susan Corbett, Chair
Philip Horn, Exec Dir
216 Finance Bldg
Harrisburg, PA 17120
Tel 717-787-6883; Fax 717-783-2538
Email: phorn@pa.gov
Web Site: www.pacouncilonthearts.org

Rhode Island State Council on the Arts
Jean Rondeau, Chair
Randall Rosenbaum, Exec Dir
One Capitol Hill, 3rd Fl
Providence, RI 02908
Tel 401-222-3883; Fax 401-222-3018
E-mail: randall.rosenbaum@arts.ri.gov
Web Site: www.risca.state.ri.us

South Carolina Arts Commission

Dr Sarah Lynn Hayes, Chmn
Ken May, Exec Dir
1026 Sumter St, Ste 200
Columbia, SC 29201-3746
Tel 803-734-8696; Fax 803-734-8526
E-mail: info@arts.sc.gov
Web Site: www.southcarolinaarts.com

South Dakota Arts Council

Paul Higbee, Chair
Michael Pangburn, Dir
711 E Wells Ave
Pierre, SD 57501-3369
Tel 605-773-3301; 800-952-3625 (toll free); Fax 605-773-5657
E-mail: michaelpangburn@state.sd.us
Web Site: www.artscouncil.sd.gov

Tennessee Arts Commission

Bob Wormsley, Chmn
Anne Pope, Exec Dir
Citizens Plaza, 401 Charlotte Ave
Nashville, TN 37243-0780
Tel 615-741-1701; TDD 615-532-5940; Fax 615-741-8559
E-mail: anne.b.pope@tn.gov
Web Site: www.tn.gov/arts

Texas Commission on the Arts

Patty A Bryant, Chmn
Gary Gibbs, Exec Dir
E O Thompson Office Bldg
920 Colorado, Ste 501
PO Box 13406
Austin, TX 78701
Tel 512-463-5535; 800-252-9415 (toll free)
Fax 512-475-2699
E-mail: ggibbs@arts.texas.gov
Web Site: www.arts.state.tx.us

Utah Division of Arts and Museums

John T Nielsen, Chair
Lynnette Hiskey, Dir
617 E South Temple St
Salt Lake City, UT 84102-1177
Tel 801-236-7555; Fax 801-236-7556
E-mail: lhiskey@utah.gov
Web Site: artsandmuseums.utah.gov

Vermont Arts Council

Barbara Morrow, Chair
Alexander L Aldrich, Exec Dir
136 State St, Drawer 33
Montpelier, VT 05633-6001
Tel 802-828-3291; Fax 802-828-3363
E-mail: aaldrich@vermontartscouncil.org
Web Site: www.vermontartscouncil.org

Virginia Commission for the Arts

Deborah H Wyld, Chair
Foster Billingsley, Exec Dir
Lewis House, 2nd Fl
1001 E Broad St, Ste 330
Richmond, VA 23219
Tel 804-225-3132; Fax 804-225-4327
E-mail: foster.billingsley@arts.virginia.gov
Web Site: www.arts.virginia.gov

Washington State Arts Commission

Cindy Hill Finnie, Chair
Kristin Tucker, Exec Dir
711 Capitol Way S, Ste 600
PO Box 42675
Olympia, WA 98504-2675
Tel 360-753-3860; Fax 360-586-5351
E-mail: kris.tucker@arts.wa.gov
Web Site: www.arts.wa.gov

West Virginia Division of Culture & History-Commission on the Arts

Susan S Landis, Chmn
Arts & Humanities Section
West Virginia Div of Culture & History
1900 Kanawha Blvd E
Charleston, WV 25305-0300
Tel 304-558-0240; Fax 304-558-3560
Web Site: www.wvculture.org/arts

Wisconsin Arts Board

Bruce Bernberg, Chairperson
George Tzougros, Exec Dir
101 E Wilson St, First Fl
PO Box 8690
Madison, WI 53703
Tel 608-266-0190; Fax 608-267-0380
E-mail: artsboard@wisconsin.gov
Web Site: artsboard.wisconsin.gov

Wyoming Arts Council

Karen Stewart, Chmn
Rita Basom, Arts Council Mgr
2320 Capitol Ave
Cheyenne, WY 82002
Tel 307-777-7742; TDD 307-777-5964; Fax 307-777-5499
E-mail: rita.basom@wyo.gov
Web Site: wyoarts.state.wy.us

American Samoa Council on Culture, Arts and Humanities

Paogofie Fiaigoa, Chmn
Le'ala E Pili, Exec Dir
Territory of American Samoa
PO Box 1540
Pago Pago, AS 96799
Tel 684-633-4347; Fax 684-633-2059
E-mail: ascach07@gmail.com

Guam Council on the Arts and Humanities Agency

Monica Guzman, Chmn
Joseph Artero-Cameron, Dir
PO Box 2950
Hagatna, GU 96932
Tel 671-300-1204; Fax 671-300-1209
E-mail: joseph.cameron@caha.guam.gov
Web Site: www.guamcaha.org

Commonwealth Council for Arts and Culture (Northern Mariana Islands)

Joseph M Diaz, Chmn
Angel Hocog, Exec Dir
Dept of Community & Cultural Affairs
PO Box 5553, CHRB
Saipan, MP 96950
Tel 670-322-9982; Fax 670-322-9028
E-mail: angelshocog@yahoo.com

Institute of Puerto Rican Culture

Rafael Colon Oliviery, Chair
Mercedes Gomez, Exec Dir
PO Box 902-4184
San Juan, PR 00902-4184
Tel 787-724-3210; Fax 787-724-8393
E-mail: mgomez@icp.gobierno.pr
Web Site: www.icp.gobierno.pr

Virgin Islands Council on the Arts

Jose Raul Carrillo, Chmn
Betty L Mahoney, Exec Dir
5070 Norre Gade
Saint Thomas, VI 00802
Tel 340-774-5984; Fax 340-774-6206
E-mail: betty.mahoney@dpnr.gov.vi
Web Site: www.vicouncilonarts.org

State Directors and Supervisors of Art Education

ALABAMA

Martha Lockett, Arts & Character Specialist
State Department of Education
50 N Ripley St
Montgomery, AL 36104
Tel 334-242-9700; Fax 334-353-5714
E-mail: mlockett@alsde.edu

ALASKA

Andrea Noble-Pelant, Visual & Literary Arts Program Dir
Alaska Department of Education
411 W 4th Ave, Ste 1E
Anchorage, AK 99501-2343
Tel 907-269-6605
E-mail: andrea.noble-pelant@alaska.gov

ARIZONA

Lynn Tuttle, Dir Arts Educ
1535 W Jefferson
Phoenix, AZ 85007
Tel 602-364-1534
E-Mail: lynn.tuttle@azed.gov

ARKANSAS

Dr Tracy Tucker, Dir Curriculum & Instruction
Arkansas Department of Education
4 Capital Mall, Rm 301-B
Little Rock, AR 77201
Tel 501-682-1991
E-mail: tracy.tucker@arkansas.gov

CALIFORNIA

Tom Adams, Dir
California Department of Education
Curriculum Frameworks & Instructional Resources Division
1430 N St
Sacramento, CA 95814-5901
Tel 916-319-0881; Fax 916-319-0172
E-mail: tadams@cde.ca.gov

Nancy Carr, Visual & Performing Arts Consultant
California Department of Education
1430 N St, Ste 4309
Sacramento, CA 95814
Tel 916-445-5669; Fax 916-324-4848
E-mail: ncarr@cde.ca.gov

COLORADO

Karol Gates, Content Specialist
Colorado Department of Education
201 E Colfax Ave, Rm 408E
Denver, CO 80203-1799
Tel 720-202-9268
E-mail: gates_k@cde.state.co.us

CONNECTICUT

Dr Scott C Shuler, Arts Education Specialist
Connecticut State Department of Education
165 Capitol Ave, PO Box 2219
Hartford, CT 06106-1630
Tel 860-713-6543; Fax 860-713-7018
E-mail: scott.shuler@ct.gov

DELAWARE

Debora Hansen, Education Associate Visual & Performing Arts
Department of Education
401 Federal St, Ste 2
Dover, DE 19901
Tel 302-735-4000 ext 4190; Fax 302-739-4654
E-mail: dhansen@doe.k12.de.us

DISTRICT OF COLUMBIA

Jacquelyn Zimmermann, Dir Student Art Exhib Prog
Division of Academic Services
District of Columbia Public Schools
1200 First St NE
Washington, DC 20002
Tel 202-442-5885; Fax 202-442-5026
E-mail: jacquelyn.zimmermann@ed.gov

FLORIDA

Linda T Lovins, PhD, Arts Education Specialist
Office of the Humanities
Bureau of Curriculum, Instruction & Assessment
Florida Department of Education
Turlington Bldg, 325 Gaines St, Rm 432
Tallahassee, FL 32399-0400
Tel 850-245-0762; Fax 850-921-0367
E-mail: linda.lovins@fldoe.org

GEORGIA

Raymond Veon, Interim Dir Fine & Performing Arts
Georgia Department of Education
130 Trinity Ave
Atlanta, GA 30303
Tel 404-802-2698
E-mail: rveon@atlantapublicschools.us

HAWAII

Evan Tottori, Educational Specialist
Hawaii State Department of Education
PO Box 2360

Honolulu, HI 96804
Tel 808-586-3230
E-mail: evan_tottori/cib/hidoe@notes.k12.hi.us

IDAHO

Dr Peggy Wenner, Fine Arts & Humanities Coordinator
State Department of Education
Bureau of Curriculum & Accountability
PO Box 83720
Boise, ID 83720-0027
Tel 208-332-6949; Fax 208-334-4664
E-mail: pjwenner@sde.idaho.gov

ILLINOIS

Cornelia Powell, Education Consultant of Fine Arts
Professional Preparation & Certification (Arts Consultant)
Illinois State Board of Education
100 N First St
Springfield, IL 62777-0001
Tel 217-557-7323; Fax 217-782-7937
E-mail: cpowell@isbe.net

INDIANA

Courtney Cabrera, Fine Arts Specialist
Office of Program Development
Indiana Department of Education
South Tower, Ste 600
115 Washington St
Indianapolis, IN 46204
Tel 317-232-6610; Fax 317-232-8004
E-mail: ccabrera@doe.in.gov

IOWA

Roseanne Malek, Fine Arts Consultant
Department of Education Grimes State Office Bldg
400 E 14th St
Des Moines, IA 50319-0146
Tel 515-281-3199
E-mail: rosanne.malek@ed.state.ia.us

KANSAS

Joyce Huser, Education Program Consultant-Fine Arts
State Department of Education
120 SE 10th Ave
Topeka, KS 66612-1182
Tel 785-296-3201; Fax 913-296-7933
E-mail: jhuser@ksde.org

KENTUCKY

Robert Duncan, Arts & Humanities Consultant
Kentucky Department of Education
Capital Plaza Tower
500 Mero St, 18th Fl
Frankfort, KY 40601
Tel 502-564-4770; Fax 502-564-9848
E-mail: robert.duncan@education.ky.gov

LOUISIANA

Richard Baker, Fine Arts Coordinator
Louisiana Department of Education
1201 N 3rd St
Baton Rouge, LA 70802-5243
Tel 877-453-2721; Fax 225-342-0193
E-mail: richard.baker@la.gov

MAINE

Stephen L Bowen, Commissioner
Maine Department of Education
23 State House Station
Augusta, ME 04333-0023
Tel 207-624-6600; Fax 207-624-6700
E-mail: commish.doe@maine.gov

MARYLAND

Mary Gable, Asst State Superintendent
Maryland State Department of Education
Division of Instruction
200 W Baltimore St
Baltimore, MD 21201
Tel 410-767-0473
Fax 410-333-1146
E-mail: mgable@msde.state.md.us

MASSACHUSETTS

Dr. Lurline Munoz-Bennett, Arts & Equity Coordinator
Massachusetts Department of Education
Office of Humanities
75 Pleasant St
Malden, MA 02148-4906
Tel 781-338-6602
Fax 781-338-3395
E-mail: lmunoz-bennett@doe.mass.edu

MICHIGAN

Mary Head, Interim Art Consultant
Michigan Department of Education
Curriculum Development Department
608 W Allegan St, Box 30008
Lansing, MI 48909
Tel 517-335-3442
E-mail: headm1@michigan.gov

MINNESOTA

Beth Aune, Dir Academic Standards
1500 Hwy 36 W
Roseville, MN 55113
Tel 651-582-8795
E-mail: beth.aune@state.mn.us

MISSISSIPPI

Limeul Eubanks, Visual & Performing Arts Specialist
Mississippi Department of Education, Central High School
359 North West St
PO Box 771
Jackson, MS 39201-0771
Tel 601-359-2586; Fax 601-359-2040
E-mail: leubanks@mde.k12.ms.us

MISSOURI

Steve Williams, Consultant, Fine Arts
Missouri State Department of Elementary & Secondary Education
PO Box 480
Jefferson City, MO 65102-0480
Tel 573-751-2857
E-mail: steve.williams@dese.mo.gov

MONTANA

Jan Clinard, Dir Academic Initiatives
Office of the Commissioner of Higher Education
2500 Broadway St
PO Box 203201
Helena, MT 59620-3201
Tel 406-444-0652; Fax 406-444-1469
E-mail: jclinard@montana.edu

NEBRASKA

Scott Swisher, Dep Commissioner
Department of Education
301 Centennial Mall South, PO Box 94987
Lincoln, NE 68509-4987
Tel 402-471-2295; Fax 402-471-0117
E-mail: scott.swisher@nebraska.gov

NEVADA

James W Guthrie, Superintendent Public Instruction
Nevada Department of Education
700 E Fifth St
Carson City, NV 89701-9101
Tel 775-687-9217; Fax 775-687-9101
E-mail: krheault@doe.nv.gov

NEW HAMPSHIRE

Marcia McCaffrey, Arts Consultant
New Hampshire Department of Education
101 Pleasant St
Concord, NH 03301-3860
Tel 603-271-3193; Fax 603-271-1953
E-mail: mmccaffrey@doe.nh.us

NEW JERSEY

Dale Schmid, Visual & Performing Arts Coordinator
New Jersey Department of Education, Office of Standards
100 River View Plaza, PO Box 500
Trenton, NJ 08625-0500
Tel 609-984-6308; Fax 609-292-7276
Web Site: www.state.nj.us/education

NEW MEXICO

Loie Fecteau, Exec Dir State Arts Agency
Public Education Department
300 Don Gaspar Ave
Santa Fe, NM 87501
Tel 505-827-6490; Fax 505-827-6043
E-mail: loie.fecteau@state.nm.us
Web Site: www.ped.state.nm.us

NEW YORK

Leslie Yolen, Visual Arts Associate
Associate in Arts Education
New York State Department of Education
89 Washington Ave, Rm 320EB
Albany, NY 12234
Tel 518-474-5922; Fax 518-473-4884
E-mail: lyolen@mail.nysed.gov

NORTH CAROLINA

Bryar Cougle, Consultant, Theatre & Visual Arts K-12
North Carolina Department of Public Education
301 N Wilmington St

Raleigh, NC 27601-28215
Tel 919-807-3855
E-mail: tcougle@dpi.state.nc.uc

NORTH DAKOTA

Jan Webb, Exec Dir
North Dakota Council on the Arts
1600 E Century Ave, Ste 6
Bismarck, ND 58503-0649
Tel 701-328-7592; Fax 701-328-7595
E-Mail: jwebb@nd.gov

OHIO

Thomas D Rutan, Assoc Dir
Office of Curriculum & Instruction
Ohio Department of Education
25 S Front St, MS 509
Columbus, OH 43215-4104
Tel 614-728-1997
E-mail: tom.rutan@ode.state.oh.us

OKLAHOMA

Glen Henry, Dir
Arts in Education Program
State Department of Education
2500 N Lincoln Blvd
Oklahoma City, OK 73105-4599
Tel 405-521-3034; Fax 405-521-2971
E-mail: glen_henry@sde.state.ok.us

OREGON

Michael Fridley, Arts & Communications Specialist
Oregon Department of Education
255 Capitol St NE
Salem, OR 97310-0203
Tel 503-947-5660
E-mail: Michael.fridley@state.or.us

PENNSYLVANIA

William E Harner, Sec of Educ
PA Dept of Educ
333 Market St, 10th Fl
Harrisburg, PA 17126-0333
Tel 717-783-6788
Email: ra-educationsecretary@pa.gov

RHODE ISLAND

Deborah Gist, Commissioner
Rhode Island Department of Education
255 Westminster St
Providence, RI 02903
Tel 401-222-4600
E-mail: deborah.gist@ride.ri.gov

SOUTH CAROLINA

Scot Hockman, Visual & Performing Arts Education Associate
Office of Curriculum & Standards
State Department of Education

1429 Senate St, Ste 802-A
Columbia, SC 29201
Tel 803-734-0323; Fax 803-734-5359
E-mail: shockman@ed.sc.gov

SOUTH DAKOTA

Michael Pangburn, Exec Dir
South Dakota Arts Council
711 E Wells Ave
Pierre, SD 57501
Tel 605-773-3301; Fax 605-773-5657
E-mail: sdac@state.sd.us; michael.pangburn@state.sd.us
Web Site: artscouncil.sd.gov

TENNESSEE

Kim Leavitt, Dir, Arts Education
Tennessee Department of Education
401 Charlotte Ave
Nashville, TN 37243-0780
Tel 615-532-5934; Fax 615-741-8559
E-mail: kim.leavitt@tn.gov

TEXAS

Tom Waggoner, Dir of Fine Arts Programs
Curriculum and Professional Development
Texas Education Agency
Travis Bldg, #3-121
1701 N Congress Ave
Austin, TX 78701-1494
Tel 512-825-7230
E-mail: thomas.waggoner@tea.state.tx.us

UTAH

Cathy Jensen, State Specialist in Fine Arts Educ
Utah State Office of Education
250 East 500 S, PO Box 144200
Salt Lake City, UT 84114-4200
Tel 801-538-7793; Fax 801-538-7769
E-mail: cathy.jensen@schools.utah.gov

VERMONT

Ed Haggett, Dir Federal Programs
Department of Education
120 State St
Montpelier, VT 05620

Tel 802-828-5400; Fax 802-828-0573
E-Mail ed.haggett@state.vt.us

VIRGINIA

Cheryle C Gardner, Principal Specialist of Fine Arts
Virginia Department of Education
PO Box 2120
Richmond, VA 23218-2120
Tel 804-225-2881; Fax 804-786-5466
E-mail: cgardner@pen.k12.va.us, Cherry.Gardner@doe.virginia.gov

WASHINGTON

Randy Dorn, Supt
Old Capitol Bldg
Office of Supt Pub Information
PO Box 47200
Olympia, WA 98504-7200
Tel 360-725-6115; 360-753-6712
Email: randy.dorn@k12.wa.us

WEST VIRGINIA

John A Deskins, Arts Coordr
Office of Instruction
West Virginia Department of Education
Capitol Complex, Bldg 6, Rm 608
1900 Kanawha Blvd E
Charleston, WV 25305
Tel 304-558-5325; Fax 304-558-1834
E-mail: jdeskins@access.k12.wv.us

WISCONSIN

Rebecca Vail, Dir Art & Design
Wisconsin Department of Public Instruction
125 S Webster St, PO Box 7841
Madison, WI 53707-7841
Tel 608-266-2364
E-mail: rebecca.vail@dpi.wi.gov

WYOMING

Cindy Hill, Superintendent, Public Instruction
Department of Education
Hathaway Bldg, 2300 Capitol, 2nd Fl
Cheyenne, WY 82002
Tel 307-777-7675; Fax 307-777-6234
Web Site www.k12.wy.us
E-mail: supt@educ.state.wy.us

Art Magazines

A for Annuals; Bi-M for Bimonthlies; Bi-W for Biweeklies;
M for Monthlies; Q for Quarterlies; Semi-A for Semiannually; W for Weeklies

African Arts (Q)—Leslie Ellen Jones, Exec Ed & Art Dir; James S Coleman African Studies Center, University of California, 10244 Bunche Hall, 405 Hilgard Ave, PO Box 951310-1310, Los Angeles, CA 90095. Tel 310-825-3686; Fax 310-206-2250; E-mail afriartsedit@ international.ucla.edu; Website www.mitpressjournals.org/aa. Yearly $86.00

Afterimage (Bi-M)—Karen vanMeenen, Ed; Visual Studies Workshop Inc, 31 Prince St, Rochester, NY 14607. Tel 585-442-8676 ext 26; E-mail afterimage@vsw.org; Website www.vsw.org/ai. Yearly $33.00

American Art (3 times per year)—Emily Shapiro, Exec Ed; Smithsonian American Art Museum, 750 9th St NW, Ste 3100, Washington, DC 20001-4505. Tel 202-633-7970; E-mail AmericanArtJournal@si.edu; Website www.journals.uchicago.edu/AmArt. Yearly $49.00 individuals; $35.00 students

American Artist (11 issues)—Brian Riley, Mng Ed; 29 W 46th St, Third Floor, New York, NY 10036. Tel 866-917-2676; E-Mail americanartist@pcspublink.com; Website www.artistdaily.com. Yearly $34.95

American Craft (Bi-M)—Monica Moses, Ed in Chf; American Craft Council, 1224 Marshall St, NE, Ste 200, Minneapolis, MN 55413. Tel 612-206-3100; E-mail council@craftcouncil.org; Website www.americancraftmag.org. Yearly $25.00 US; $40.00 Canada & international

American Indian Art Magazine (Q)—Roanne Goldfien, Editorial Dir; American Indian Art Inc, 7314 E Osborn Dr, Scottsdale, AZ 5251. Tel 480-994-5445; Fax 480-945-9533; E-mail editorial@aiamagazine.com; Website www.aiamagazine.com. Yearly $20.00

American Journal of Archaeology (Q)—Sheila Dillon, Ed in Chf; Dept of Art, Art History and Visual Studies, Duke University, E Duke 116A, PO Box 90764, Durham, NC, 27708-0764. Tel 919-684-6082; Fax 919-684-4398; E-mail: sdillon@aia.bu.edu; Website www.ajaonline.org. Yearly $80.00 individuals; $50.00 students; $295.00 institutions

American Watercolor Society Newsletter (2 Issues)—American Watercolor Society, 47 Fifth Ave, New York, NY 10003. Tel 212-206-8986; Fax 212-206-1960; E-mail info@americanwatercolor-society.org; Website www.americanwatercolorsociety.org. Assoc. Membership yearly $50

Aperture (Q)—Melissa Harris; Ed in Chf; Aperture Foundation, 547 W 27th St, 4th Fl, New York, NY 10001. Tel 212-505-5555; Fax 212-971-7759; E-mail info@aperture.org; Website www.aperture.org. Yearly $75.00 US; $95.00 Canada; $105.00 international

Archaeology (Bi-M)—Claudia Valentino, Ed in Chf; Archaeological Institute of America, 36-36 33rd St, Long Island City, NY 11106. Tel 718-472-3050; Fax 718-472-3051; E-mail general@archaeology.org; Website www.archaeology.org. Yearly $29.94

Architectural Digest (M)—Margaret Russell, Ed in Chf; Architectural Digest, 4 Times Sq, 18th Fl, New York, NY 10036. Tel 800-365-8032; E-mail contact@archdigest.com; Website www.architecturaldigest.com. Yearly $24.99 US; $70.00 international

Archives of American Art Journal (Semi-A)—Darcy Tell, Ed; Victor Bldg Ste 2200, PO Box 37012, MRC 937, Washington DC 20013-7012. Tel 202-633-7971; Fax 212-399-6890; Website www.aaa.si.edu/publications/journal. $75 institutional

Art & Antiques (10 Issues)—John Dorfman, NY Sr Ed; 1319-cc Military Cutoff Rd #192, Wilmington, NC 28405. Tel 910-679-4402; Fax 919-869-1864; E-mail info@artandantiquesmag.com; Website www.artandantiquesmag.com. Yearly $29.50

Art + Auction (11 Issues)—Benjamin Genocchio, Ed in Chf; Louis Blouin Media (US), 601 W 26th St, Ste 410, New York, NY 10001. Tel 212-447-9555; Fax 212-447-5221; E-mail generalinfo@artinfo.com; Website www.artinfo.com/artandauction. Yearly $59.00 digital; $100.00 print

Art & Understanding—David Waggoner, Ed in Chf & Publr; Art & Understanding Inc, 25 Monroe St, Ste 205, Albany, NY 12210. Tel 518-426-9010; Fax 518-436-5354; E-mail mailbox@aumag.org; Website www.aumag.org. Yearly $24.95

Art Bulletin (Q)—Karen Lang, Ed in Chf; College Art Association of America Inc, 50 Broadway, 21st Fl, New York, NY 10004. Tel 212-691-1051; Fax 212-627-2381; E-mail nyoffice@collegeart.org; Website www.collegeart.org. Individual membership based on income

Art Business News—(Bi-M) Kathryn Peck, Ed; PO Box 91447, Long Beach, CA 90809. Tel 888-881-5861; E-mail abnsubs@pfsmag.com; Website artbusinessnews.com. Yearly $20.00 US; $25.00 Canada; $75.00 international

Art Documentation (Semi-A)—Judy Dyky, Content Ed; ARLIS/NA Publications, 7044 S 13th St, Oak Creek, WI 53154. Tel 800-817-0621 ext 450; Fax 414-768-2001; E-mail customercare@arlisna.org; Website www.arlisna.org. Free to members

Artforum International Magazine (10 Issues)—Michelle Kuo, Ed in Chf; Artforum International Magazine, 350 7th Ave, New York, NY 10001. Tel 212-475-4000; Fax 212-529-1257; E-mail generalinfo@artforum.com; Website www.artforum.com. Yearly $46.00 US; $65.00 Canada; $132.00 international

Art in America (M)—Lindsay Pollack, Ed in Chf; Brant Publications, 575 Broadway, 5th Fl, New York, NY 10012. Tel 212-941-2800; Fax 212-941-2844; E-mail aiaonline@brantpub.com; Website www.artinamericamagazine.com. Yearly $34.95 US; $79.95 Canada; $96.00 international

Artist's Magazine (10 Issues)—Maureen Bloomfield, Ed; F + W Media, 10151 Carver Rd, Ste 200, Blue Ash, OH 45242. Tel 513-531-2222; Fax 513-891-7153; E-mail tamedit@fwmedia.com; Website www.artistsmagazine.com. Yearly $20.96 US/Canada; $31.96 international

Art Journal (Q)—Katy Siegel, Ed in Chf; College Art Association of America Inc, 50 Broadway, 21st Fl, New York, NY 10004. Tel 212-691-1051; Fax 212-627-2381; E-mail nyoffice@collegeart.org Website www.collegeart.org. Free for members.

Art New England (6 Issues)—Judith Tolnick Champa, Ed in Chf; 332 Congress St, Ste 2, Boston, MA 02210. Tel 617-259-1040; Fax 617-259-1039; E-mail: editorial@artnewengland.com; Website www.artnewengland.com. Yearly $28.00

Artnews (11 Issues)—Milton Esterow, Ed & Publr; 48 W 38th St, New York, NY 10018. Tel 212-398-1690; Fax 212-819-0394; E-mail info@artnews.com; Website www.artnews.com. Yearly $24.95

Art of the West (7 Issues)—Vicki Stavig, Ed; 15612 Hwy 7, Ste 235, Minnetonka, MN 55345. Tel 952-935-5850; Fax 952-935-6546; E-mail: aotw@aotw.com; Website www.aotw.com. Yearly $25.00; $43.00 international

Art Papers (Bi-M)—1083 Austin Ave, NE, Ste 206, Atlanta, GA 30307. Tel 404-588-1837; Fax 404-588-1836; E-mail info@artpapers.org; Website www.artpapers.org. Yearly $35.00 US; $45.00 Canada & Mexico; $75.00 international

Arts (Q)—Kaywin Feldman, Pres & Dir; Minneapolis Institute of Arts, 2400 Third Ave S, Minneapolis, MN 55404. Tel 612-870-6314; Fax 612-870-3004; Website www.artsmia.org. Free for members

Artslink Newsletter (Q)—Kirsten Hilgeford, Mng Ed; Americans for the Arts 1000 Vermont Ave, NW 6th Fl, Washington, DC 20005. Tel 202-371-2830; Fax 203-271-0424; Website www.americansforthearts.org. Free for members

Arts Quarterly (Q)—Taylor Murrow, Ed; New Orleans Museum of Art, 1 Collins C Diboll Cir, City Park, New Orleans, LA 70124. Tel 504-658-4100; Fax 504-658-4199; E-mail info@noma.org; Website www.noma.org. Free for members

Art Therapy (Q)—Lynn Kapitan, Ed; American Art Therapy Association Inc, 4875 Eisenhower Ave, Ste 240, Alexandria, VA 22304. Tel 888-290-0878; Fax 703-783-8468; E-mail info@arttherapy.org; Website www.arttherapy.org. Yearly $190 (individuals, print); $261.00 (institutions, online); $298.00 (institutions, print & online)

Art Times (Bi-M)—Raymond J Steiner, Ed; PO Box 730, Mount Marion, NY 12456. Tel 845-246-6944; Fax 845-246-6944; E-mail info@arttimesjournal.com; Website www.arttimesjournal.com. Yearly $18.00 US; $35 international

Aviso (M)— John Strand, Publr; American Alliance of Museums, 1575 Eye St, NW, Ste 400, Washington, DC 20005. Tel 202-289-1818; Fax 202-289-6578; E-mail aviso@aam-us.org; Website www.aam-us.org. Free for members

Bomb (4 Issues)—Monica de la Torre Sr Ed; 80 Hanson Pl, Ste 703, Brooklyn, NY 11217. Tel 718-636-9100; Email generalinquiries@bombsite.com; Website www.bombsite.com. Yearly $22.00 US; $42.00 international

Bulletin of the Detroit Institute of Arts—Susan Higman, Dir; 5200 Woodward Ave, Detroit, MI 48202. Tel 313-833-7960; Fax 313-833-6409; E-Mail operator@dia.org; Website www.dia.org. Yearly $15.00

Canadian Art (Q)—Richard Rhodes, Ed; Canadian Art Foundation, 215 Spadina Ave, Ste 320, Toronto, ON M5T 2C7, Canada. Tel 416-368-8854; Fax 416-368-6135; E-Mail info@canadianart.ca; Website www.canadianart.ca. Yearly $34.00 US; $24.00 Canada; $42.00 international

Ceramics Monthly (M)—Sherman Hall, Ed; Ceramics Monthly, 600 N Cleveland Ave, Ste 210 Westerville, OH 43081. Tel 614-794-5843; Fax 614-794-5842; E-mail: editor@ceramicartsdaily.org; Website ceramicartsdaily.org/ceramics-monthly. Yearly $34.95

C Magazine (Q)—Amish Morell, Ed; PO Box 5 Sta B, Toronto, ON M5T 2T2, Canada. Tel 416-539-9495; Fax 416-539-9903; E-mail info@cmagazine.com; Website www.cmagazine.com. Yearly $29.00 US; $24.00 Canada; $34.00 international

City Arts Magazine (M)—Leah Baltus, Ed in Chf; Encore Media Group, 425 N 85th St, Seattle, WA 98103. Tel 206-443-0445; Fax 206-443-1246; E-mail info@cityartsmagazine.com; Website www.cityartsonline.com. Yearly $24.00

Cleveland Museum of Art Members Magazine—Barbara Bradley, Gregory Donley & Kathleen Mills, Eds; Publications Dept, 11150 East Blvd, Cleveland, OH 44106. Tel 216-421-7350; E-mail magazine@clevelandart.org; Website www.clevelandart.org. Free for members

Columbia Journal of Law & the Arts (Q)—Jack M Brownfield, Ed in Chf; Columbia University School of Law, 435 W 116th St, New York, NY 10027. Tel 212-854-1607; E-mail columbiajla@gmail.com; Website www.lawandarts.org. Yearly $60.00 domestic; $75.00 international

Communication Arts (6 Issues)—Patrick Coyne, Ed; 110 Constitution Dr, Menlo Park, CA 94025. Tel 650-326-6040; Fax 650-326-1648; E-mail editorial@commarts.com; Website www.commarts.com. Yearly $53.00 US; $99.00 international

Gesta (2 Issues)—Linda Safran & Adam S Cohen, Eds; International Center of Medieval Art, The Cloisters, Fort Tryon Park, New York, NY 10040. Tel 212-928-1146; Fax 212-428-9946; E-mail gesta@medievalart.org; Website www.medievalart.org. Free for ICMA members

IFAR Journal (Q)—Sharon Flescher, Ed in Chf; International Foundation for Art Research, 500 Fifth Ave, Ste 935, New York, NY 10110. Tel 212-391-6234; Fax 212-391-8794; E-mail kferg@ifar.org; Website www.ifar.org. Yearly $75.00; free with membership minimum of $250.00

IMA Magazine (Q)—Meg Liffick, Mng Ed; Indianapolis Museum of Art 4000 Michigan Rd, Indianapolis, IN 46208-3326. Tel 317-920-2660; Fax 317-931-1978; E-mail ima@imamuseum.org; Website www.imamuseum.org. Free for members

International Directory of Corporate Art Collections (Bi-A)—Shirley R Howarth, Ed; International Art Alliance, 2840 W Bay Dr #250, Belleair Bluffs, FL 33770. Tel 514-935-1228; Fax 514-935-1299; E-mail corporate.directory@earthlink.net; Website www.internationalartalliance.org. Yearly $115

Journal of Aesthetics & Art Criticism (Q)—Robert Stecker & Theodore Gracyk, Eds; American Society for Aesthetics, PO Box 915 Pooler, GA, 31322; Website www.aesthetics-online.org. Individuals $70.00; Student $35.00

Journal of Canadian Art History (A)—Martha Langford, Ed in Chf; Concordia University, 1455 blvd de Maissoneuve West, Montreal, QC H3G 1M8, Canada. Tel 514-848-2424, ext 4699; Fax 514-848-4584; E-mail jcah@concordia.ca; Website jcah-ahac.concordia.ca. Yearly $75.00 US, $60.00 Canada

Leonardo: Art, Science & Technology (5 Issues)—Roger F Malina, Exec Ed; MIT Press Journals, 55 Hayward St, Cambridge, MA 02142-1315. Tel 617-253-2889; Fax 617-577-1545; E-mail isast@leonardo.info; Website www.leonardo.info. Yearly (print and electronic access) $87.00 individuals; $698.00 institutions

Letter Arts Review (Q)—Christopher Calderhead, Ed; 1833 Spring Garden St, Greensboro, NC 27403. Tel 800-369-9598; Fax 336-272-9015; E-mail letter-arts-review@johnnealbooks.com; Website www.johnnealbooks.com. Yearly $48.00 US; $56.00 Canada; $70.00 international

Linea (3 times per year)—Stephanie Cassidy, Ed; The Art Students League of New York 215 W 57th St, New York, NY 10019. Tel 212-247-4510; Fax 212-541-7024; E-mail linea@artstudentsleague.org; Website www.asllinea.org. Free for members

Master Drawings (Q)—Jane Turner, Ed; Master Drawings Association Inc, 225 Madison Ave, New York, NY 10016. Tel 212-590-0369; Fax 212-685-4740; E-mail administrator@masterdrawings.org; Website www.masterdrawings.org. Yearly $125.00 domestic; $160.00 international

Metropolitan Museum of Art Bulletin (Q)—Thomas P Campbell Exec Dir; 1000 Fifth Ave, New York, NY 10028. Tel 212-535-7710; Website www.metmuseum.org. Free for members

Monthly Aspectarian (M)—Jeanne Spiro, Ed; 47 W Polk St, Ste 153 Chicago, IL 60605. Tel 847-966-1110; E-mail themonthlyaspectarian@gmail.com; Website www.monthlyaspectarian.com. Yearly $36.00

Museum (Bi-M)—John Strand, Publr; American Alliance of Museums, 1575 Eye St, NW, Ste 400, Washington, DC 20005. Tel 202-289-1818; Fax 202-289-6578; Website www.aam-us.org. Yearly $38.00 US; $56.00 Canada & Mexico; $80.00 international

October (Q)—Adam Lehner, Mng Ed; MIT Press Journals, 350 Fifth Ave, #7401, New York, NY 10118. Tel 212-253-7012; E-mail octobermagazine@gmail.com; Website www.mitpressjournals.org Yearly (print and electronic access) $55.00

Ornament (5 issues)—Robert Liu & Carolyn Benesh, Eds; Ornament Inc, PO Box 2349, San Marcos, CA 92079-2349. Tel 760-599-0222; Fax 760-599-0228; E-mail editorial@ornamentmagazine.com; Website www.ornamentmagazine.com. Yearly $29.99

Print (Bi-M)—Sarah Whitman, Ed; 10151 Carver Rd, Ste 200, Blue Ash, OH; Tel 513-531-2690; E-mail info@printmag.com; Website www.printmag.com. Yearly $40.00 US; $55.00 Canada; $81.00 international

Professional Artist (B-M)—Terry Sullivan, Ed; 1500 Park Center Dr, Orlando, FL 32835. Tel 407-563-7000; Fax 407-563-7099; Website www.professionalartistmag.com. Yearly $37.00

SchoolArts (9 Issues)—Nancy Walkup, Ed; Davis Publications Inc, 50 Portland St, Worcester, MA 01608. Tel 508-754-7201; Fax 508-753-3834; Website www.davisart.com. Yearly $24.95

Sculpture (10 Issues)—Glenn Harper, Ed; International Sculpture Center, 1633 Connecticut Ave, NW, 4th Fl, Washington, DC 20009. Tel 202-234-0555; Fax 202-234-2663; E-mail editor@sculpture.org; Website www.sculpture.org. Yearly $50.00

Sculpture Review (Q)—Giancarlo Biagi, Ed in Chf; National Sculpture Society, 75 Varick St, 11th Fl, New York, NY 10013. Tel 212-764-5645 ext 10; Fax 212-764-5651; Website www.sculpturereview.com. Yearly $25.00 US; $35.00 Canada; $50.00 international

Society of Architectural Historians Newsletter (Bi-M)—Helena Karabatsos, Ed; Society of Architectural Historians, 1365 N Astor St, Chicago IL, 60610. Tel 312-573-1365; E-Mail info@sah.org; Website www.sah.org.

Southwest Art (M)—Kristin Hoerth, Ed in Chf; 10901 W 120th Ave, Ste 350, Broomfield, CO 80021. Tel 303-442-0427; Fax 303-449-0279; E-mail southwestart@fwmedia.com; Website www.southwestart. com. Yearly $36.95 US; 46.95 Canada; $58.95 international

Stained Glass (Q)—Richard Gross, Ed; Stained Glass Association of America, 9313 E 63rd St, Raytown, MO 64133. Tel 800-438-9581; Fax 816-737-2801; Email webmaster@sgaaonline.com; Website stainedglassquarterly.com. Yearly $29.00 US; $47.00 Canada & Mexico; $59.00 international

Studies in Art Education (Q)—Laurie Hicks, Sr Ed; National Art Education Association, 1806 Robert Fulton Dr, Ste 300, Reston, VA 20191. Tel 703-860-8000; Fax 703-860-2960; E-mail info@arteducators.org; Website www.arteducators.org. Yearly $30.00 US; $45.00 Canada & international

Studio Potter (Semi-A)—Mary Barringer, Ed; PO Box 257, Shelburne Falls, MA 03107. Tel 413-625-9200; E-mail editor@studiopotter.org; Website www.studiopotter.org. Membership Yearly $70.00 US; $80.00 Canada; $85.00 international

Sunshine Artist (M)—Nate Shelton, Ed; Palm House Publishing, 4075 LB McLeod Rd, Ste E, Orlando, FL 32811. Tel 407-648-7479; E-mail business@sunshineartist.com; Website www.sunshineartist.com. Yearly $34.95

Vie des Arts (Q)—Bernard Levy, Ed in Chf; 5605 Ave de Gaspe, Local 603, Montreal, QC H2T 2A4, Canada. Tel 514-282-0205; Fax 514-282-0235; E-mail: admin@viedesarts.com Website www.viedesarts.com. Yearly $52.00 US; $28.00 Canada; $72.00 international

Walters Magazine (Q)—Julia Marciari-Alexander, Exec Dir; The Walters Art Museum, 600 N Charles St, Baltimore, MD 21201. Tel 410-547-9000; E-Mail info@thewalters.org; Website thewalters.org. Free to Members

Woman's Art Journal (2 Issues)—Joan Marter, Ed; Rutgers University, Dept of Art History, Voorhees Hall, 71 Hamilton St, New Brunswick, NJ 08901. Tel 732-932-7041, ext 20l; Fax 732-932-1261; E-mail waj@womansartjournal.org; Website womansartjournal.org. Yearly $39.00

Newspaper Art Editors and Critics

Cities for newspapers that do not start with city name
will have city name in parentheses as part of the listing

ALABAMA

Birmingham News—Michael Huebner (Arts Columnist)
Gadsden Times—Cyndi Nelson (Associate Editor)
Huntsville Times—Pat Ammons (Arts Reporter)
Press-Register—Tamara Ikenberg (Entertainment Reporter)
Times Daily—Teri Thornton (Lifestyle Editor)
The Valley Times-News—Cy Wood (Publr & Editor)

ALASKA

Anchorage Daily News—Mike Dunham (Arts & Entertainment Editor)

ARIZONA

(Flagstaff) Arizona Daily Sun—Laura Clymer (City Editor)
The Sierra Vista Herald—Janet LaValley (Features Editor)
East Valley Tribune—Terry Horne (Publr & Editor)
(Phoenix) Arizona Republic—Deb Van Tassel (Lifestyle Editor)
(Tucson) Arizona Daily Star—Cathy Burch (Sr Entertainment Reporter)

ARKANSAS

(Fort Smith) Southwest Times Record—Tina Dale (Features Editor)
(Little Rock) Arkansas Democrat Gazette—Jack Schnedler (Features Editor)
Paragould Daily Press—Steve Gillespie (Editor)
(Springdale) Northwest Arkansas Morning News—Rusty Turner (Publr & Editor)

CALIFORNIA

(Bakersfield) Californian—Jennifer Self (Lifestyles Editor)
Chico News & Review—Jason Cassidy (Arts & Culture Columnist)
Contra Costa Times—Randy McMullen (Arts & Entertainment Editor)
(Covina) San Gabriel Valley Tribune—Catherine Gaugh (Features Editor)
Davis Enterprise—Debbie Davis (Asst Publr & Editor)
(El Centro) Imperial Valley Press—Peggy Dale (Editor)
Fairfield Daily Republic—Amy Maginnis-Honey (Arts & Entertainment Writer)
Fresno Bee—Kathy Mahan (Features Editor)
(Long Beach) Press-Telegram—Leo Smith (Features Editor)
Los Angeles Daily News—Leo Smith (Features Editor)
(Los Angeles) La Opinion—Monica Lozano (Publr & CEO)
Los Angeles Times—Christopher Knight (Art Critic)
Madera Tribune—Tami Jo Nix (Sr Staff Writer)
Modesto Bee—Lisa Millegan Renner (Arts Reporter)
(Monterey) Herald—Mac McDonald (Entertainment Editor)
Napa Valley Register—Sasha Paulsen (Features Editor)
Oakland Tribune—Randy McMullen (Arts & Entertainment Editor)
(Palm Springs) The Desert Sun—Michael Felci (Lifestyles & Entertainment Editor)
Porterville Recorder—Rick Elkins (Publr & Editor)
(Riverside) Press-Enterprise—Fielding Buck (Guide Editor)
Sacramento Bee—Edward Ortiz (Arts & Entertainment Reporter)
San Bernardino County Sun—John Weeks (Features Editor)
San Diego Daily Transcript—Jennifer Chung-Klam (Special Sections Editor)
San Diego Union Tribune—Keli Dailey (Content Producer, Arts & Recreation)

San Francisco Chronicle—Leba Hertz (Arts & Entertainment Editor)
San Francisco Examiner—Leslie Katz (Arts & Entertainment Editor)
(San Jose) Mercury News—Charlie McCollum (Arts & Entertainment Editor)
San Mateo County Times—Lisa Wrenn (Features Editor)
(Santa Ana) Orange County Register—Jeff Miller (Arts Editor)
Santa Barbara News-Press—Marilyn McMahon (Features Writer)
(Torrance) The Daily Breeze—Leo Smith (Features Editor)
(Santa Rosa) Press Democrat—Joanne Derbort (Features Editor)
Turlock Journal—Kristina Hacker (Editor)
Vallejo Times-Herald—Richard Freedman (Community Editor)
Ventura County Star—Mark Wyckoff (Entertainment Editor)

COLORADO

Boulder Daily Camera—Kevin Huhn (Features & Entertainment Editor)
(Colorado Springs) The Gazette—Tracy Mobley-Martinez (Entertainment Editor)
Denver Post—Ray Rinaldi (Entertainment Editor)
Pueblo Chieftain—Scott Smith (Lifestyle Editor)

CONNECTICUT

(Bridgeport) Connecticut Post—Patrick Quinn (Arts & Entertainment Editor)
Danbury News-Times—Linda Tuccio-Koonz (Features Editor)
Greenwich Time—Patrick Quinn (Arts & Entertainment Editor)
Hartford Courant—Donna Larcen (Arts Editor)
New Haven Register—Rick Sandella (Features Editor)
(Stamford) The Advocate—Rebecca Haynes (Arts & Features)
(Waterbury) Republican-American—Rich Gray (Features Editor)

DELAWARE

Wilmington News-Journal—Betsy Price (Features Editor)

DISTRICT OF COLUMBIA

Washington Post—Christine Ledbetter (Arts Editor)
Washington Times—Daniel Wattenberg (Arts & Features Editor)

FLORIDA

Daytona Beach News Journal—Dave Wersinger (Accent Editor)
(Fort Myers) News-Press—Tammy Ayer (Lifestyles Editor)
(Fort Walton) Northwest Florida Daily News—Brenda Shoffner (Entertainment Editor)
Gainesville Sun—Bill Dean (Entertainment Editor)
(Jacksonville) Florida Times-Union—Tom Szaroleta (Asst Lifestyle Editor)
Lakeland Ledger—Jennifer Audette (Features Editor)
(Melbourne) Florida Today—Suzy Fleming Leonard (Features Editor)
Miami Herald—Aminda Marques (Exec Editor)
Ocala Star Banner—Dave Schlenker (Entertainment Editor)
Orlando Sentinel—Anne Dunlap (Arts & Entertainment Content Editor)
Palatka Daily News—Al Krombach (Editor)
Palm Beach Daily News—Jan Sjostrom (Arts Editor)
Palm Beach Post—Laura Lordi (Art Columnist)
Pensacola News-Journal—Teresa Zwierzchowski (Features Editor)
Saint Augustine Record—Anne Heymen (Features Editor)
Saint Petersburg Times—Lennie Bennett (Art Critic)
South Florida Sun-Sentinel—Gretchen Day Bryant (Features Editor)

Tallahassee Democrat—Mark Hinson (Sr Features Reporter)
The Tampa Tribune—Kim Franke-Folstad (Features Editor)

GEORGIA

Albany Herald—Jim Hendricks (Editor)
Atlanta Journal-Constitution—Kevin Riley (Editor)
The Augusta Chronicle—John Gogick (Exec Editor)
(Columbus) Ledger-Enquirer—Dawn Minty (Features Editor)
Macon Telegraph—Renee Corwine (Features Editor)
Savannah Morning News—Linda Sickler (Features & Entertainment Reporter)

HAWAII

Honolulu Star-Advertiser—Elizabeth Kieszkowski (Arts & Entertainment Editor)

IDAHO

(Boise) Idaho Statesman—Dana Oland (Arts Reporter)
Coeur d'Alene Press—Mike Patrick (Editor)
(Idaho Falls) Post-Register—Roger Plothow (Publr & Editor)
Lewiston Tribune—Jennifer K Bauer (Arts & Entertainment Reporter)
(Pocatello) Idaho State Journal—Jodeane Albright (Community Editor)

ILLINOIS

(Arlington Heights) Daily Herald—Diane Dungey (Deputy Mng Editor)
Belleville News-Democrat—Patrick Kuhl (Features Editor)
Bloomington Daily Pantagraph—Dan Craft (Entertainment Editor)
(Centralia) Morning Sentinel—Michelle Pennington (Lifestyles Editor)
(Champaign) News-Gazette—Tony Mancuso (Features Editor)
Chicago Sun-Times—Linda Bergstrom (Assoc Editor Features & Innovation)
Chicago Tribune—Howard Reich (Arts Critic)
Decatur Herald & Review—Tim Cain (Entertainment Editor)
DeKalb Daily Chronicle—Inger Koch (Features Editor)
Dixon Telegraph—Jeff Rogers (Mng Editor)
(Galesburg) Register-Mail—Tom Martin (Editor)
(Moline) Dispatch/Rock Island Argus—John Marx (Life Columnist)
Peoria Journal-Star—Danielle Hatch (Entertainment Editor)
(Rockford) Register-Star—Georgette Braun (Entertainment Columnist)
(Springfield) State Journal-Register—Brien Murphy (Features Editor)
(Watseka) Times-Republic—Carla Waters (Mng Editor)

INDIANA

(Bedford) Times-Mail—Mike Lewis (Mng Editor)
Connersville News-Examiner—Connie Gribbins (Lifestyles Editor)
(Crawfordsville) Journal-Review—Tina McGrady (Editor)
Evansville Courier and Press—Roger McBain (Arts & Entertainment Reporter)
(Fort Wayne) News Sentinel—Kevin Kilbane (Features Editor)
(Gary) Post-Tribune—Jon Gard (News Editor)
(Huntington) The Herald-Press—David Penticuff (Editor)
Indianapolis Star—Neal Taflinger (Free Time & Arts Editor)
(Muncie) The Star Press—Deb Sorrell (Lifestyles Editor)
Shelbyville News—Andrea Smithson (Editor)
South Bend Tribune—Andrew S Hughes (Arts & Entertainment Editor)
(Spencer) Evening World—Travis Curry (Editor)
Washington Times-Herald—Pat Morrison (News Editor)

IOWA

(Burlington) Hawk Eye—Craig Neises (Features Editor)
Cedar Rapids Gazette—Diana Nollen (Arts & Entertainment Writer)
Des Moines Register—Michael Morain (Arts Reporter)
(Iowa City) The Daily Iowan—Emma McClatchey (Arts Editor)
Muscatine Journal—Steve Jameson (Publr & Editor)
Newton Daily News—Bob Eschliman (City Editor)
Oelwein Daily Register—Deb Kunkle (City Editor)

Sioux City Journal—Bruce Miller (Mng Editor Entertainment & Living)
Washington Evening Journal—Linda Wenger (Lifestyles Editor)
Waterloo Courier—Meta Hemenway-Forbes (Features Editor)

KANSAS

Concordia Blade-Empire—Sharon Coy (Social Editor)
The Hays Daily News—Ron Fields (Mng Editor)
The Hutchinson News—Jason Probst (News Editor)
Lawrence Journal World—Sarah Henning (Features Reporter)
The Newton Kansan—Cristina Janney (News Editor)
The Norton Telegram—Michael Stephens (Society Editor)
Pratt Tribune—Conrad Easterday (Editor)
Salina Journal—Sharon Montague (Deputy Editor)
Topeka Capital-Journal—Bill Blankenship (Arts & Entertainment Editor)
Wichita Eagle—Denise Neil (Features Reporter)

KENTUCKY

(Ashland) Daily Independent—Lee Ward (Lifestyles Editor)
(Covington) Kentucky Post—Kerry Duke (Mng Editor)
(Elizabethtown) The News-Enterprise—Ben Sheroan (Editor)
(Hopkinsville) Kentucky New Era—Dennis O'Neil (Features Editor)
Lexington Herald-Leader—Sally Scherer (Lifestyles Editor)
Louisville Courier-Journal—Elizabeth Kramer (Visual Arts Critic & Writer)
Paducah Sun—Ron Clark (News Editor)
Winchester Sun—Rachel Gilliam (Community Editor)

LOUISIANA

(Alexandria) The Town Talk—LeCrete Robinson (Features Editor)
Bastrop Daily Enterprise—Mark Rainwater (Editor)
Crowley Post-Signal—Angela Becnel (Lifestyles Reporter)
(Hammond) The Daily Star—Lil Mirando (Exec Editor)
Minden Press-Herald—Jeri Bloxom (Community Editor)
(New Orleans) Times Picayune—Jim Amoss (Editor)
Shreveport Times—Derick Jones (Entertainment Editor)

MAINE

Bangor Daily News—Michael J Dowd (Metro & Standards Editor)
(Lewiston) Sun-Journal—Ursula Albert (Art Editor)
Portland Press Herald—Karen Beaudoin (Deputy Features Editor)

MARYLAND

(Annapolis) Capital—Brian Henley (Entertainment Editor)
Baltimore Sun—Tim Smith (Fine Arts Critic)
Columbia Flier—Stan Rappaport (News & Arts Editor)
(Hagerstown) The Herald-Mail—Jake Womer (Exec Editor)
Salisbury Daily Times—Cindy Robinson (Community Editor)

MASSACHUSETTS

(Boston) Christian Science Monitor—John Yemma (Editor)
Boston Globe—Rebecca Ostriker (Arts Editor)
Boston Herald—Sandra Kent (Arts & Lifestyle Editor)
(Brockton) Enterprise—Chazy Dowaliby (Editor)
The Sun Chronicle—Ken Ross (Features Editor)
(East Boston) Post-Gazette—Hilda Morrill (Features Writer)
(Framingham) MetroWest Daily News—Nancy Olesin (Arts Editor)
Haverhill Gazette—Al Getler (Publr & Editor)
Lowell Sun—Joanne Deegan (Lifestyle Copy Editor)
(North Andover) Eagle Tribune—Tracey Rauh (Mng Editor, Features)
(Pittsfield) Berkshire Eagle—Jeffrey Borak (Entertainment Editor)
(Quincy) Patriot Ledger—Chazy Dowaliby (Editor)
The Republican—Ray Kelly (Asst Mng Editor Arts & Entertainment)
Taunton Daily Gazette—Leeanne Hubbard (Lifestyles Editor)
Worcester Telegram & Gazette—Nancy Campbell (Features Editor)

MICHIGAN

Alpena News—Diane Speer (Lifestyles Editor)
Battle Creek Enquirer—Annie J Kelley (Features Editor)
Bay City Times—Carol Zedaker (Features Topic Editor)
(Benson Harbor-St Joseph) Herald-Palladium—Katie Krawczak (Features Editor)
(Big Rapids) Pioneer—Dave Clark (Editor)
Detroit Free Press—Steve Byrne (Arts & Entertainment Editor)
Detroit News—Leslie Green (Arts & Entertainment Editor)
Flint Journal—William Ketchum (Entertainment Reporter)
Grand Rapids Press—Jeffrey Kaczmarczyk (Arts & Entertainment Reporter)
Jackson Citizen Patriot—Zeke Jennings (Entertainment Reporter)
Kalamazoo Gazette—John Liberty (Entertainment Editor Reporter)
Lansing State Journal—Michael Hirten (Exec Editor)
Ludington Daily News—Melissa McGuire (Entertainment Editor)
(Mount Clemens) Macomb Daily—Debbie Komar (Features Editor)
Muskegon Chronicle—Lisha Arino (Entertainment Reporter)
(Pontiac) Oakland Press—Nicole Robertson (Arts & Entertainment Editor)
Saginaw News—Yfat Yossifor (Entertainment Reporter)

MINNESOTA

Austin Daily Herald—Adam Harringa (Editor)
Duluth News Tribune—Robin Washington (Editor)
Minneapolis Star Tribune—Claude Peck (Fine Arts & Features Editor)
(Red Wing) Republican Eagle—Anne Jacobson (Editor)
(Rochester) Post-Bulletin—Jay Furst (Mng Editor)
Saint Cloud Times—Stephanie Dickrell (Arts & Entertainment Reporter)
Saint Paul Pioneer Press—Kathy Berdan (Arts & Entertainment Team Leader)
(Willmar) West Central Tribune—Sharon Bomstad (Features Editor)
Worthington Daily Globe—Beth Rickers (Features Editor)

MISSISSIPPI

(Biloxi) Sun Herald—Scott Hawkins (Features & Sports Editor)
(Greenville) Delta Democrat-Times—Laura Smith (Mng Editor)
(Jackson) Clarion-Ledger—Annie Oeth (Features Editor)
(McComb) Enterprise-Journal—Jack Ryan (Publr & Editor)
Meridian Star—Michael Stewart (Exec Editor)
(Pascagoula) Mississippi Press—Gareth Clary (Exec Editor)
(Tupelo) Northeast Mississippi Daily Journal—Leslie Criss (Features & Special Sections Editor)

MISSOURI

(Independence) The Examiner—Karl Zinke (Mng Editor)
(Jefferson City) News Tribune—Gary Castor (Mng Editor)
Kansas City Star—Alice Thorson (Art Critic)
Neosho Daily News—John Ford (Mng Editor)
Saint Joseph News-Press—Jessica DeHaven (Lifestyles Editor)
Saint Louis Post-Dispatch—Jody Mitori (Arts & Entertainment Editor)
Springfield News-Leader—Sony Hocklander (Features Editor)
West Plains Daily Quill—Carol Bruce (City Editor)

MONTANA

Billings Gazette—Kristi Angel (Mng Editor)
(Butte) Montana Standard—Carmen Winslow (Mng Editor)
(Missoula) Missoulian—Sherry Devlin (Editor)

NEBRASKA

Kearney Hub—Mike Konz (Mng Editor)
The Lincoln Journal Star—Dave Bundy (Editor)
McCook Daily Gazette—Bruce Crobsy (Editor)
Omaha World-Herald—Betsie Freeman (Features Editor)

NEVADA

(Carson City) Nevada Appeal—Brian Sandford (Editor)
Las Vegas Review-Journal—Mark Whittington (Dep Editor Sports, Features & Entertainment)
Las Vegas Sun—Don Chareunsy (Sr Editor Arts & Entertainment)
Reno Gazette-Journal—Mimi Beck Knudsen (Features & Niche Publications Editor)

NEW HAMPSHIRE

New Hampshire Union Leader—Vin Sylvia (Dep Mng Editor Sports, Photos & Features)

NEW JERSEY

Press of Atlantic City—Gail Wilson (Asst Features Editor)
The News of Cumberland County—Matt Gray (Editor)
(Bridgewater) Courier News—Paul Grzella (Editor)
(Cherry Hill) Courier-Post—Tammy Paolino (Features Editor)
The (Bergen) Record—Martin Gottlieb (Editor)
(Jersey City) Jersey Journal—Judy Locorriere (Editor)
(Morristown) Daily Record—Joe Ungaro (Editor)
(Neptune) Asbury Park Press—Kathy Dzielak (Entertainment Editor)
Newark Star Ledger—Jay Lustig (Arts & Entertainment Editor)
(East Brunswick) Home News Tribune—Paul Grzella (Editor)
(Passaic) Herald News—Douglas Clancy (Exec Editor)
(Trenton) Trentonian—Paul Mickle (City Editor)
(Woodbury) Gloucester County Times—Joe Owens (General Mgr)

NEW MEXICO

Albuquerque Journal—Helen Taylor (Features Editor)
Carlsbad Current-Argus—Tom Schneider (City Editor)
Clovis News-Journal—David Stevens (Editor)
(Farmington) Daily Times—Hanna Grover (Special Sections Editor)
(Grants) Cibola Beacon—Donald Jaramillo (Mng Editor)
Hobbs News-Sun—Daniel Russell (Editor)
Roswell Daily Record—Andrew Poertner (Editor)
(Santa Fe) New Mexican—Kristina Melcher (Editor, Pasatiempo)

NEW YORK

Albany Times Union—Michael Janairo (Arts & Entertainment Editor)
Art Times—Raymond J Steiner (Co-Founder & Editor)
Batavia Daily News—Mark A Graczyk (Mng Editor)
(Binghamton) Press & Sun-Bulletin—Chris Kocher (Good Times Editor)
Buffalo News—Jeff Simon (Arts Editor)
Corning Leader—Stella Dupree (News Editor)
(Hornell) The Evening Tribune—John Anderson (Regional Editor)
(Melville) Newsday—Deborah Henley (Editor)
Middletown Times Herald-Record—Brenda Gilhooly (Custom Publishing Editor)
New York Daily News—Raakhee Mirchandani (Mng Editor Features)
New York Post—Margi Conklin (Mng Editor Features)
New York Times—Jan Benzel (Weekend Arts Section Editor)
(New York) Wall Street Journal—Eric Gibson (Leisure & Arts Editor)
(Nyack) The Journal News—Mary Dolan (Features Editor)
Poughkeepsie Journal—Kevin Lenihan (Local News Editor)
Rochester Democrat & Chronicle—Catherine Roberts (Features Editor)
(Saratoga Springs) Saratogian—Jill Wing (Features Editor)
(Schenectady) The Daily Gazette—Karen Bjornland (Life & Arts Writer)
Staten Island Advance—Sandra Zummo (Features Editor)
Syracuse Post-Standard—Kate Collins (Mng Producer Entertainment)
(Troy) Record—Bob Goepfert (Entertainment Coordr)
(Yorktown Heights) North County News—Kathleen Maffetone (Mng Editor)

NORTH CAROLINA

(Asheville) Citizen Times—Tony Kiss (Entertainment Editor & Blogger)
Charlotte Observer—Mike Weinstein (Sr Features Editor)
(Durham) The Herald Sun—Cliff Bellamy (Arts & Books Writer)

(Elizabeth City) The Daily Advance—Robert Kelly-Goss (Life Editor)
Goldsboro News-Argus—Becky Barclay (Lifestyles Editor)
(Greensboro) News & Record—Cindy Loman (Features Editor)
Greenville Daily Reflector—Steve Cagle (Assoc Features Editor)
Hendersonville Times-News—Lou Parris (Lifestyles Columnist)
(Lumberton) Robesonian—Jolisa Canty (Features Editor)
(Raleigh) News & Observer—Carole Tanzer Miller (Features Editor)
(Shelby) The Star—Matthew Tessnear (City Editor)
Washington Daily News—Mike Voss (Contributing Editor)
Wilmington Star-News—John Staton (Features Editor)
Wilson Times—Lisa Batts (Life Editor)

NORTH DAKOTA

Bismarck Tribune—Steve Wallick (City Editor)
Dickinson Press—Linda Sailer (Lifestyles Editor)
(Fargo) Inforum—Heidi Shaffer (Features Editor)
Minot Daily News—Dave Caldwell (Lifestyles Editor)

OHIO

Akron Beacon Journal—Lynne Sherwin (Features Editor)
Athens Messenger—Kathy Kerr (Community Editor)
Canton Repository—Dan Kane (Entertainment Editor)
Cincinnati Enquirer—Julie Engebrecht (Features Editor)
(Cleveland) The Plain Dealer—Karl Turner (News Editor)
Columbus Dispatch—Nancy Gilson (Arts Editor)
Dayton Daily News—Ron Rollins (Assoc Editor)
(Mansfield) News-Journal—Gere Goble (Features Editor)
Portsmouth Daily Times—Bob Strickley (Content Mgr & Editor)
Sandusky Register—Kathy Lilje (Features Editor)
Sidney Daily News—Patti Speelman (Localife Editor)
(Toledo) The Blade—Rod Lockwood (Features Editor)
(Willoughby) News Herald—Mark Meszoros (Asst Mng Editor, Features)
(Youngstown) Vindicator—Barb Shaffer (Society/Features Editor)

OKLAHOMA

Blackwell Journal-Tribune—Nixie Goff (News Editor)
Claremore Daily Progress—Randy Cowling (Mng Editor)
Elk City Daily News—Cheryl Overstreet (Community Editor)
Lawton Constitution—Elijah Morlett (Arts & Entertainment Reporter)
Muskogee Phoenix—Elizabeth Ridenour (City Editor)
(Oklahoma City) The Oklahoman—Rick Rogers (Fine Arts Editor)
(Pryor) Daily Times—Kathy Parker (Mng Editor)
Seminole Producer—Cheryl Phillips (Mng Editor)
Tulsa World—Ziva Branstetter (Enterprise Editor)

OREGON

(Coos Bay) World—Ryan Haas (City Editor)
(Eugene) Register-Guard—Chris Frisella (News Editor)
(Grants Pass) Daily Courier—Edith Decker (Features Editor)
(Medford) Mail Tribune—David Smigelski (Features Editor)
(Ontario) Argus Observer—Lindsey Parker (Lifestyle Reporter)
(Portland) Oregonian—Jolene Krawczak (Mng Editor, Features)
(Salem) Statesman-Journal—Carlee Wright (Entertainment Reporter)

PENNSYLVANIA

Allentown Morning Call—Jodi Duckett (Content Editor, Entertainment & Life)
Bradford Era—Marty Wilder (Editor)
(Doylestown) Intelligencer—Patricia Walker (Exec Editor)
(DuBois) Courier-Express—Jaime Hynds (Lifestyles Editor)
(Harrisburg) Patriot-News—Julie Hatmaker (Entertainment Reporter)
(Huntingdon) Daily News—Becky Weikert (Mng Editor)
(Johnstown) The Tribune Democrat—Renee Carthew (Features Editor)
(Lancaster) Sunday News—Margaret Gates (Features Editor)
(Levittown) Bucks County Courier Times—Patricia Walker (Exec Editor)
(Lewistown) Sentinel—Frank Jost (Mng Editor)
(Lock Haven) Express—Scott Johnson (City Editor)

(New Kensington-Tarentum) Valley News-Dispatch—Jeff Domenick (Editor)
Philadelphia Daily News—Michael Days (Editor)
Philadelphia Inquirer—Sandy Clark (Dep Mng Editor Arts, Features & Entertainment)
Pittsburgh Post-Gazette—Virginia Linn (Asst Mng Editor, Features & Enterprise)
Pittsburgh Tribune-Review—Kurt Shaw (Art Critic)
Reading Eagle—George L Hatza (Entertainment Editor)
(Scranton) Times-Tribune—Larry Holeva (Exec Editor)
(Towanda) Daily Review—Kelly Andrus (Editor)
(Wilkes-Barre) Times Leader—Christopher J. Hughes (Features Reporter)

RHODE ISLAND

Providence Journal—Alan Rosenberg (Mng Editor Features)
(South Kingstown) Narragansett Times—Matt Wunsch (Editor)

SOUTH CAROLINA

Aiken Standard—Mike Gibbons (Mng Editor)
Anderson Independent Mail—David Williams (City Editor)
Beaufort Gazette—Tom Robinette (Features Editor)
Charleston Post & Courier—Teresa Taylor (Features Editor)
(Columbia) Black News—Wendy Brinker Taylor (Exec Editor)
(Columbia) The State—Betsey Guzior (Features, Arts & Entertainment Editor)
(Florence) Morning News—Tucker Mitchell (Regional Editor)
Greenville News—Melissa Blanton (Entertainment Editor)
Myrtle Beach Sun News—Caroline Evans (Features Editor)
Orangeburg Times & Democrat—Wendy Crider (Features Editor)
(Spartanburg) Herald-Journal—Jose Franco (Life & Entertainment Editor)

SOUTH DAKOTA

(Mitchell) The Daily Republic—Candy DenOuden (Life Reporter)
(Sioux Falls) Argus Leader—Jay Kirschenmann (Arts & Music Reporter)

TENNESSEE

Chattanooga Times-Free Press—Shawn Ryan (Features Editor)
(Clarksville) Leaf Chronicle—Stacy Leiser (Arts & Entertainment Reporter)
(Columbia) Daily Herald—Marvine Sugg (Lifestyles Editor)
Elizabethton Star—Bryan Stevens (Lifestyles Editor)
Jackson Sun—Steve Coffman (Exec Editor)
Johnson City Press—John Molley (Mng Editor)
Kingsport Times-News—Becky Whitlock (Features Editor)
Knoxville News-Sentinel—Chuck Campbell (Entertainment Editor)
Lebanon Democrat—Amelia Hipps (Mng Editor)
(Memphis) Commercial Appeal—Bruce VanWyngarden (Editor)
(Morristown) Citizen Tribune—John Gullion (Mng Editor)
(Murfreesboro) Daily News Journal—Nancy DeGennaro (Lifestyles Reporter)
(Nashville) Tennessean—Linda Zettler (Lifestyles & Entertainment Editor)
(Oak Ridge) Oak Ridger—Darrell Richardson (Publr & Editor)

TEXAS

Abilene Reporter-News—Janet Van Vleet (Arts & Entertainment Reporter)
Amarillo Globe News—Chip Chandler (Features Editor)
Austin American-Statesman—Sharon Chapman (Entertainment Editor)
Beaumont Enterprise—Monique Batson (Web Editor)
(Corpus Christi) Caller-Times—Elizabeth Reese (Arts Columnist)
Dallas Morning News—Michael Merschel (Asst Arts & Features Editor)
Fort Worth Star-Telegram—Stephanie Allmon (Asst Mng Editor, Features)
Houston Chronicle—Melissa Aguilar (Sr Editor, Features)
(Lubbock) Avalanche Journal—William Kerns (Entertainment Editor)
Midland Reporter-Telegram—Megan Lea Buck (Features Editor)
(Nacogdoches) Daily Sentinel—Paul Bryant (City Editor)
Odessa American—Laura Dennis (Exec Editor)
Orange Leader—Gabriel Pruett (Editor)
Pecos Enterprise—Rosie Flores (Lifestyles Editor)
Plainview Daily Herald—Nicki Logan (Lifestyles Editor)

Port Arthur News—Roger Cowles (Editor)
San Antonio Express-News—Jim Kiest (Arts & Entertainment Editor)
(Tyler) Morning Telegraph—Stewart Smith (Arts & Entertainment Writer)
Waco Tribune-Herald—Carl Hoover (Entertainment Editor)
Waxahachie Daily Light—Neal White (Editor)
Wichita Falls Times Record News—Lana Sweeten-Shults (Arts & Entertainment Editor)

UTAH

(Logan) Herald Journal—Lance Frazier (Features Editor)
(Ogden) Standard-Examiner—Becky Wright (Features Writer)
(Provo) Daily Herald—Doug Fox (Asst Features Editor)
(Salt Lake City) Deseret News—Aaron Shill (Features Editor)
Salt Lake Tribune—David Burger (Arts, Entertainment & Culture Writer)

VERMONT

Burlington Free Press—Nicole Haley (Arts & Entertainment Editor)

VIRGINIA

(Arlington) USA Today—David Callaway (Editor-in-Chief)
Bristol Herald Courier—Phil Fernandez (Editor)
(Charlottesville) Daily Progress—Jane Dunlap Norris (Features Editor)
(Fredericksburg) Free Lance-Star—Katherine Shapleigh (Local News Editor)
Hopewell News—Elizabeth Farina (Editor)
(Lynchburg) News & Advance—Caroline Glickman (City Editor)
Newport News Daily Press—Karen Morgan (Features Editor)
(Norfolk) Virginian-Pilot—Mal Vincent (Entertainment Writer)
Richmond Times-Dispatch—Cindy Creasy (Features Editor)
Roanoke Times—Kathy Lu (Features Editor)
(Waynesboro) News Virginian—Gina Farthing (Features Editor)

WASHINGTON

(Aberdeen) The Daily World—David Haerle (Arts & Entertainment Editor)
Ellensburg Daily Record—Barb Owens (Design Editor)
(Everett) Herald—Melanie Munk (Features Editor)
(Moses Lake) Columbia Basin Herald—Joel Martin (Special Sections Editor)
Seattle Times—Lynn Jacobson (Features Editor)
(Spokane) Spokesman-Review—Addy Hatch (City Editor)
(Tacoma) News Tribune—Rosemary Ponnekanti (Arts Reporter)
(Vancouver) Columbian—Sue Vorenberg (Features Reporter)
Wenatchee World—Marco Martinez (Features Editor)

WEST VIRGINIA

Bluefield Daily Telegraph—Samantha Perry (Mng Editor)
Charleston Daily Mail—Monica Orosz (Features Editor)
Charleston Gazette—James A Haught (Editor)
Huntington Herald-Dispatch—Robyn Rison (Features Editor)
(Martinsburg) Journal—Paul Long (City Editor)
(Wheeling) News-Register—Linda Comins (Life Editor)

WISCONSIN

(Appleton) Post-Crescent—Ed Berthiaume (Features Editor)
(Eau Claire) Leader-Telegram—Rob Hanson (Entertainment Editor)
Green Bay Press-Gazette—Kendra Meinert (Entertainment & Weekend Editor)
Kenosha News—Kathy Troher (Features Editor)
(Madison) Capital Times—Paul Fanlund (Editor)
(Madison) Wisconsin State Journal—Gayle Worland (Arts Reporter)
Milwaukee Journal Sentinel—Mary Louise Schumacher (Art & Architecture Critic)
(Racine) Journal Times—Ann Walter (Features Editor)
Wausau Daily Herald—Mark Treinen (Exec Editor)

WYOMING

(Casper) Star-Tribune—Carol Seavey (Special Sections Editor)
(Cheyenne) Wyoming Tribune Eagle—Jodi Rogstad (Asst Mng Editor, Features)
(Riverton) The Ranger—Steve Peck (Publr & Editor)

PUERTO RICO

(San Juan) El Nuevo Dia—Luis A Ferre Rangel (Editor)
(San Juan) El Vocero de Puerto Rico—Jorge Rodriguez (Entertainment Reporter)

CANADA

ALBERTA

Calgary Herald—Tome Babin (Features Editor)
Calgary Sun—Kevin Williamson (Entertainment Columnist)
Edmonton Journal—Keri Sweetman (Arts & Life Editor)
Edmonton Sun—Nicole Bergot (City Editor)

BRITISH COLUMBIA

(Vancouver) The Province—Dharm Makwana (Entertainment Editor)
Vancouver Sun—Francois Marchand (Arts & Music Editor)
Victoria Times Colonist—Dave Paulson (Features Editor)

MANITOBA

Winnipeg Free Press—Alan Small (Arts & Life Editor)

NOVA SCOTIA

Halifax Chronicle Herald—Brian Ward (Assignment Editor)

ONTARIO

Hamilton Spectator—Jeff Day (Arts & Entertainment Editor)
(Kitchener) The Record—Neil Ballantyne (Life/Arts Editor)
London Free Press—James Reaney (Entertainment Columnist)
Ottawa Citizen—Jordan Timm (City Editor)
(Toronto) Globe & Mail—Gabe Gonda (Arts & Life Editor)
(Toronto) The Star—Alison Uncles (Assoc Editor, Features)
Windsor Star—Ted Shaw (Entertainment Editor)

QUEBEC

Montreal Gazette—Basem Boshra (Arts & Books Editor)
(Montreal) La Presse Ltee—Andre Pratt (Editor)
(Montreal) Le Journal de Montreal—Sophie Durocher (Culture Columnist)
(Quebec) Le Journal de Quebec—Sebastien Menard (Editor-in-Chief)
(Quebec) Le Soleil—Pierre-Paul Noreau (Editor-in-Chief)

SASKATCHEWAN

Regina Leader-Post—Irene Seiberling (Lifestyles Editor)
(Saskatoon) StarPhoenix—Cam Fuller (Entertainment Writer)

IV INDEXES

Subject

Personnel

Organizational

Subject Index

Major Subjects are listed first, followed by named collections.

AFRICAN ART

Academy of the New Church, Glencairn Museum, Bryn Athyn PA
African American Museum of Iowa, Cedar Rapids IA
African American Atelier, Greensboro NC
African Art Museum of Maryland, Columbia MD
Albany Museum of Art, Albany GA
Albion College, Bobbitt Visual Arts Center, Albion MI
Anacostia Community Museum, Smithsonian Institution, Washington DC
Art & Culture Center of Hollywood, Art Gallery/Multidisciplinary Cultural Center, Hollywood FL
Art Gallery of Ontario, Toronto ON
The Art Museum at the University of Kentucky, Lexington KY
The Art Museum of Eastern Idaho, Idaho Falls ID
Arts Council of Fayetteville-Cumberland County, The Arts Center, Fayetteville NC
Augustana College, Augustana College Art Museum, Rock Island IL
Ball State University, Museum of Art, Muncie IN
The Baltimore Museum of Art, Baltimore MD
Barnes Foundation, Merion PA
Baylor University, Martin Museum of Art, Waco TX
Beck Cultural Exchange Center, Inc, Knoxville TN
Berea College, Ulmann Doris Galleries, Berea KY
Birmingham Museum of Art, Birmingham AL
Blanden Memorial Art Museum, Fort Dodge IA
Blauvelt Demarest Foundation, Hiram Blauvelt Art Museum, Oradell NJ
Bowers Museum, Santa Ana CA
Brown University, Haffenreffer Museum of Anthropology, Providence RI
Bucknell University, Edward & Marthann Samek Art Gallery, Lewisburg PA
The Buffalo Fine Arts Academy, Albright-Knox Art Gallery, Buffalo NY
C W Post Campus of Long Island University, Hillwood Art Museum, Brookville NY
California African-American Museum, Los Angeles CA
California State University Stanislaus, University Art Gallery, Turlock CA
California State University, East Bay, C E Smith Museum of Anthropology, Hayward CA
California State University, Northridge, Art Galleries, Northridge CA
Capital University, Schumacher Gallery, Columbus OH
Center for Puppetry Arts, Atlanta GA
Cincinnati Art Museum, Cincinnati Art Museum, Cincinnati OH
City of Fayette, Alabama, Fayette Art Museum, Fayette AL
The College of Wooster, The College of Wooster Art Museum, Wooster OH
Columbus Museum, Columbus GA
Concordia Historical Institute, Saint Louis MO
Cornell Museum of Art and American Culture, Delray Beach FL
Cornell University, Herbert F Johnson Museum of Art, Ithaca NY
Craft and Folk Art Museum (CAFAM), Los Angeles CA
Crocker Art Museum, Sacramento CA
The Currier Museum of Art, Manchester NH
Dallas Museum of Art, Dallas TX
Dartmouth College, Hood Museum of Art, Hanover NH
Denver Art Museum, Denver CO
Detroit Institute of Arts, Detroit MI

Detroit Zoological Institute, Wildlife Interpretive Gallery, Royal Oak MI
Dickinson College, The Trout Gallery, Carlisle PA
Doncaster Museum and Art Gallery, Doncaster
Duke University, Nasher Museum of Art at Duke University, Durham NC
East Carolina University, Wellington B Gray Gallery, Greenville NC
East Los Angeles College, Vincent Price Art Museum, Monterey Park CA
East Tennessee State University, The Reece Museum, Johnson City TN
Edmundson Art Foundation, Inc, Des Moines Art Center, Des Moines IA
Emory University, Michael C Carlos Museum, Atlanta GA
En Foco, Inc, Bronx NY
Evansville Museum of Arts, History & Science, Evansville IN
Everhart Museum, Scranton PA
Everson Museum of Art, Syracuse NY
Fairbanks Museum & Planetarium, Saint Johnsbury VT
Fine Arts Museums of San Francisco, Legion of Honor, San Francisco CA
Fisk University, Aaron Douglas Gallery, Nashville TN
Fisk University, Carl Van Vechten Gallery, Nashville TN
Fitton Center for Creative Arts, Hamilton OH
Flint Institute of Arts, Flint MI
Florida State University and Central Florida Community College, The Appleton Museum of Art, Ocala FL
Fuller Craft Museum, Brockton MA
General Board of Discipleship, The United Methodist Church, The Upper Room Chapel & Museum, Nashville TN
Grand Rapids Art Museum, Grand Rapids MI
Grinnell College, Faulconer Gallery, Grinnell IA
Guilford College, Art Gallery, Greensboro NC
Hammonds House Museum, Atlanta GA
Hampton University, University Museum, Hampton VA
Heard Museum, Phoenix AZ
Higgins Armory Museum, Worcester MA
Historisches und Volkerkundemuseum, Historical Museum, St Gallen
Hofstra University, Hofstra University Museum, Hempstead NY
Howard University, Gallery of Art, Washington DC
Illinois State Museum, ISM Lockport Gallery, Chicago Gallery & Southern Illinois Art Gallery, Springfield IL
Indiana University, Art Museum, Bloomington IN
The Interchurch Center, Galleries at the Interchurch Center, New York NY
The Israel Museum, Jerusalem, Billy Rose Art Garden, Jerusalem
The Israel Museum, Jerusalem, Samuel & Saidye Bronfman Archaeology Wing, Jerusalem
The Israel Museum, Jerusalem, Jerusalem
Jacksonville University, Alexander Brest Museum & Gallery, Jacksonville FL
Jamestown-Yorktown Foundation, Jamestown Settlement, Williamsburg VA
Johns Hopkins University, Homewood Museum, Baltimore MD
Jordan National Gallery of Fine Arts, Amman
Joslyn Art Museum, Omaha NE
Kalamazoo Institute of Arts, Kalamazoo MI
Keene State College, Thorne-Sagendorph Art Gallery, Keene NH
Kenosha Public Museums, Kenosha WI

Kimbell Art Foundation, Kimbell Art Museum, Fort Worth TX
La Salle University Art Museum, Philadelphia PA
Lakeview Museum of Arts & Sciences, Peoria IL
Lamar University, Dishman Art Museum, Beaumont TX
Langston University, Melvin B Tolson Black Heritage Center, Langston OK
Las Vegas Natural History Museum, Las Vegas NV
Lehigh University Art Galleries, Museum Operation, Bethlehem PA
Lightner Museum, Saint Augustine FL
Louisiana Arts & Science Museum, Baton Rouge LA
Mabee-Gerrer Museum of Art, Shawnee OK
Macalester College, Macalester College Art Gallery, Saint Paul MN
Madison Museum of Fine Art, Madison GA
Maine College of Art, The Institute of Contemporary Art, Portland ME
Manchester Bidwell Corporation, Manchester Craftsmen's Guild Youth & Arts Program, Pittsburgh PA
Marietta College, Grover M Hermann Fine Arts Center, Marietta OH
Marquette University, Haggerty Museum of Art, Milwaukee WI
McPherson Museum and Arts Foundation, McPherson KS
Menil Foundation, Inc, The Menil Collection, Houston TX
Meredith College, Frankie G Weems Gallery & Rotunda Gallery, Raleigh NC
Mezuraj Museum, Tirana
Miami-Dade College, Kendal Campus, Art Gallery, Miami FL
Michelson Museum of Art, Marshall TX
Mingei International, Inc, Mingei International Museum - Balboa Park & Mingei International Museum - Escondido, San Diego CA
Ministry of Cultural Affairs, Bangladesh National Museum, Dhaka
Minneapolis Institute of Arts, Minneapolis MN
The Mint Museum, Mint Museum of Craft & Design, Charlotte NC
The Mint Museum, Charlotte NC
Missoula Art Museum, Missoula MT
Mobile Museum of Art, Mobile AL
Modern Art Museum, Fort Worth TX
Montreal Museum of Fine Arts, Montreal PQ
Morris Museum, Morristown NJ
Moto Moto Museum, Mbala
The Museum, Greenwood SC
Museum for African Art, New York NY
Museum of African American Art, Los Angeles CA
The Museum of Arts & Sciences Inc, Daytona Beach FL
Museum of Contemporary Art, North Miami FL
Museum of Fine Arts, Houston, Houston TX
Museum of Fine Arts, Saint Petersburg, Florida, Inc, Saint Petersburg FL
Museum of Vancouver, Vancouver BC
Museum of York County, Rock Hill SC
National Art Museum of Sport, Indianapolis IN
National Conference of Artists, Michigan Chapter Gallery, Detroit MI
National Museum of African Art, Smithsonian Institution, Washington DC
National Museum, Monuments and Art Gallery, Gaborone
The Nelson-Atkins Museum of Art, Kansas City MO
New Brunswick Museum, Saint John NB
New Orleans Museum of Art, New Orleans LA
New Visions Gallery, Inc, Marshfield WI

New World Art Center, T F Chen Cultural Center, New York NY
Nihon Mingeikan, Japan Folk Crafts Museum, Tokyo
North Carolina Central University, NCCU Art Museum, Durham NC
North Carolina State University, Gregg Museum of Art & Design, Raleigh NC
North Country Museum of Arts, Park Rapids MN
Norwich Free Academy, Slater Memorial Museum, Norwich CT
Oakland University, Oakland University Art Gallery, Rochester MI
Ohio University, Kennedy Museum of Art, Athens OH
Okanagan Heritage Museum, Kelowna BC
Okefenokee Heritage Center, Inc, Waycross GA
Omniplex Science Museum, Oklahoma City OK
Orlando Museum of Art, Orlando FL
Owensboro Museum of Fine Art, Owensboro KY
Page-Walker Arts & History Center, Cary NC
William Paterson University, Ben Shahn Art Galleries, Wayne NJ
The Pennsylvania State University, Palmer Museum of Art, University Park PA
Pensacola Museum of Art, Pensacola FL
Philbrook Museum of Art, Tulsa OK
Piedmont Arts Association, Martinsville VA
Plains Art Museum, Fargo ND
Polk Museum of Art, Lakeland FL
The Pomona College, Claremont CA
Portland Art Museum, Portland OR
Pretoria Art Museum, Municipal Art Gallery, Pretoria
Princeton University, Princeton University Art Museum, Princeton NJ
Purchase College, Neuberger Museum of Art, Purchase NY
Queens College, City University of New York, Godwin-Ternbach Museum, Flushing NY
Queensborough Community College, Art Gallery, Bayside NY
Reading Public Museum, Reading PA
Royal Ontario Museum, Toronto ON
Saint Joseph's Oratory, Museum, Montreal PQ
Saint Mary's College of California, Hearst Art Gallery, Moraga CA
St Mary's College of Maryland, The Dwight Frederick Boyden Gallery, St Mary's City MD
Saint Olaf College, Flaten Art Museum, Northfield MN
Saint Peter's College, Art Gallery, Jersey City NJ
Santa Barbara Museum of Art, Santa Barbara CA
Santa Clara University, de Saisset Museum, Santa Clara CA
Santa Monica Museum of Art, Santa Monica CA
Scripps College, Ruth Chandler Williamson Gallery, Claremont CA
Smithsonian Institution, Washington DC
Southern Connecticut State University, Art Dept, New Haven CT
Southern Illinois University Carbondale, University Museum, Carbondale IL
Southern Oregon University, Schneider Museum of Art, Ashland OR
The Speed Art Museum, Louisville KY
Springfield Museums, Springfield Science Museum, Springfield MA
Stanford University, Cantor Arts Center at Stanford University, Stanford CA
State University of New York at Binghamton, Binghamton University Art Museum, Binghamton NY
State University of New York at New Paltz, Samuel Dorsky Museum of Art, New Paltz NY
State University of New York at Oswego, Tyler Art Gallery, Oswego NY
State University of New York at Plattsburgh, Art Museum, Plattsburgh NY
Staten Island Museum, Staten Island NY
Stauth Foundation & Museum, Stauth Memorial Museum, Montezuma KS
Sweet Briar College, Art Collection & Galleries, Sweet Briar VA
Syracuse University, Art Collection, Syracuse NY
Syracuse University, SUArt Galleries, Syracuse NY
Lillian & Coleman Taube Museum of Art, Minot ND
Texas Tech University, Museum of Texas Tech University, Lubbock TX
Topeka & Shawnee County Public Library, Alice C Sabatini Gallery, Topeka KS
Towson University, Center for the Arts Gallery, Towson MD
Ukrainian Institute of Modern Art, Chicago IL
University of Alabama at Birmingham, Visual Arts Gallery, Birmingham AL

University of California, Berkeley, Berkeley Art Museum & Pacific Film Archive, Berkeley CA
University of California, Los Angeles, Fowler Museum at UCLA, Los Angeles CA
University of Colorado, CU Art Museum, Boulder CO
University of Delaware, University Museums, Newark DE
University of Georgia, Georgia Museum of Art, Athens GA
University of Illinois at Urbana-Champaign, Krannert Art Museum and Kinkead Pavilion, Champaign IL
University of Illinois at Urbana-Champaign, Spurlock Museum, Champaign IL
University of Kansas, Spencer Museum of Art, Lawrence KS
University of Maryland, College Park, The Art Gallery, College Park MD
University of Miami, Lowe Art Museum, Coral Gables FL
University of Michigan, Museum of Art, Ann Arbor MI
University of Missouri, Museum of Art & Archaeology, Columbia MO
University of North Carolina at Chapel Hill, Ackland Art Museum, Chapel Hill NC
University of Notre Dame, Snite Museum of Art, Notre Dame IN
University of Oklahoma, Fred Jones Jr Museum of Art, Norman OK
University of Pennsylvania, Arthur Ross Gallery, Philadelphia PA
University of Pennsylvania, Museum of Archaeology & Anthropology, Philadelphia PA
University of Richmond, University Museums, Richmond VA
University of Rochester, Memorial Art Gallery, Rochester NY
University of South Florida, Contemporary Art Museum, Tampa FL
University of Utah, Utah Museum of Fine Arts, Salt Lake City UT
University of Virginia, The Fralin Museum of Art at the University of Virginia, Charlottesville VA
University of Wisconsin-Madison, Chazen Museum of Art, Madison WI
University of Wisconsin-Stout, J Furlong Gallery, Menomonie WI
Valdosta State University, Art Gallery, Valdosta GA
Wadsworth Atheneum Museum of Art, Hartford CT
Wake Forest University, Museum of Anthropology, Winston Salem NC
The Walker African American Museum & Research Center, Las Vegas NV
Wayne Center for the Arts, Wooster OH
Wellesley College, Davis Museum & Cultural Center, Wellesley MA
Wheaton College, Beard and Weil Galleries, Norton MA
Williams College, Museum of Art, Williamstown MA
Winston-Salem State University, Diggs Gallery, Winston Salem NC

AFRO-AMERICAN ART

African American Museum of Iowa, Cedar Rapids IA
African American Atelier, Greensboro NC
African American Museum in Philadelphia, Philadelphia PA
Albany Museum of Art, Albany GA
Alton Museum of History & Art, Inc, Alton IL
American Art Museum, Smithsonian Institution, Washington DC
American Folk Art Museum, New York NY
American Sport Art Museum and Archives, Daphne AL
Amon Carter Museum of American Art, Fort Worth TX
Anacostia Community Museum, Smithsonian Institution, Washington DC
The Art Museum at the University of Kentucky, Lexington KY
Art Museum of Greater Lafayette, Lafayette IN
Art Museum of the University of Houston, Blaffer Gallery, Houston TX
Art Without Walls Inc, New York NY
Arts Council of Fayetteville-Cumberland County, The Arts Center, Fayetteville NC
ArtSpace/Lima, Lima OH
Asheville Art Museum, Asheville NC
Autry National Center, Southwest Museum of the American Indian, Mt. Washington Campus, Los Angeles CA
The Baltimore Museum of Art, Baltimore MD
Baruch College of the City University of New York, Sidney Mishkin Gallery, New York NY

Bates College, Museum of Art, Lewiston ME
Baton Rouge Gallery, Center For Contemporary Art, Baton Rouge LA
Beck Cultural Exchange Center, Inc, Knoxville TN
Birmingham Museum of Art, Birmingham AL
Eubie Blake, Baltimore MD
Booth Western Art Museum, Cartersville GA
California African-American Museum, Los Angeles CA
California State University, Northridge, Art Galleries, Northridge CA
Carteret County Historical Society, The History Place, Morehead City NC
Cartoon Art Museum, San Francisco CA
Center for Puppetry Arts, Atlanta GA
Central United Methodist Church, Swords Into Plowshares Peace Center & Gallery, Detroit MI
City of El Paso, El Paso TX
City of Fayette, Alabama, Fayette Art Museum, Fayette AL
City of Mason City, Charles H MacNider Museum, Mason City IA
Colgate University, Picker Art Gallery, Hamilton NY
College of William & Mary, Muscarelle Museum of Art, Williamsburg VA
Columbus Museum, Columbus GA
The Contemporary Austin, Austin TX
Cooper-Hewitt National Design Museum, Smithsonian Institution, New York NY
County of Henrico, Meadow Farm Museum, Glen Allen VA
Craft and Folk Art Museum (CAFAM), Los Angeles CA
Craftsmen's Guild of Mississippi, Inc, Agriculture & Forestry Museum, Ridgeland MS
Craftsmen's Guild of Mississippi, Inc, Mississippi Crafts Center, Ridgeland MS
Crocker Art Museum, Sacramento CA
Dallas Museum of Art, Dallas TX
Dartmouth College, Hood Museum of Art, Hanover NH
Davidson College, William H Van Every Jr & Edward M Smith Galleries, Davidson NC
Delaware Art Museum, Wilmington DE
Delta Blues Museum, Clarksdale MS
Department of Antiquities, Cyprus Museum, Nicosia
Detroit Institute of Arts, Detroit MI
Detroit Repertory Theatre Gallery, Detroit MI
DuSable Museum of African American History, Chicago IL
East Carolina University, Wellington B Gray Gallery, Greenville NC
Elmhurst Art Museum, Elmhurst IL
En Foco, Inc, Bronx NY
Fairfield University, Thomas J Walsh Art Gallery, Fairfield CT
Fine Arts Museums of San Francisco, Legion of Honor, San Francisco CA
Fisk University, Aaron Douglas Gallery, Nashville TN
Fisk University, Carl Van Vechten Gallery, Nashville TN
Fitton Center for Creative Arts, Hamilton OH
Flint Institute of Arts, Flint MI
Florence Museum, Florence SC
Folk Art Society of America, Richmond VA
General Board of Discipleship, The United Methodist Church, The Upper Room Chapel & Museum, Nashville TN
Gonzaga University, Art Gallery, Spokane WA
Grand Rapids Art Museum, Grand Rapids MI
Greenville County Museum of Art, Greenville SC
Hammonds House Museum, Atlanta GA
Hampton University, University Museum, Hampton VA
High Museum of Art, Atlanta GA
Howard University, Gallery of Art, Washington DC
Huntington Museum of Art, Huntington WV
Illinois State Museum, ISM Lockport Gallery, Chicago Gallery & Southern Illinois Art Gallery, Springfield IL
INTAR Gallery, New York NY
The Interchurch Center, Galleries at the Interchurch Center, New York NY
Iredell Museums, Statesville NC
Thomas Jefferson, Monticello, Charlottesville VA
Kentucky Museum of Art and Craft, Louisville KY
Knoxville Museum of Art, Knoxville TN
Lafayette Science Museum & Planetarium, Lafayette LA
LaGrange Art Museum, LaGrange GA
Langston University, Melvin B Tolson Black Heritage Center, Langston OK
Lehigh University Art Galleries, Museum Operation, Bethlehem PA
Lehman College Art Gallery, Bronx NY

LeMoyne Art Foundation, Center for the Visual Arts, Tallahassee FL
Longview Museum of Fine Art, Longview TX
Louisiana Department of Culture, Recreation & Tourism, Louisiana State Museum, New Orleans LA
Manchester Bidwell Corporation, Manchester Craftsmen's Guild Youth & Arts Program, Pittsburgh PA
Maryland Hall for the Creative Arts, Chaney Gallery, Annapolis MD
Menil Foundation, Inc, The Menil Collection, Houston TX
Mennello Museum of American Art, Orlando FL
Meredith College, Frankie G Weems Gallery & Rotunda Gallery, Raleigh NC
Metropolitan State University of Denver, Center for Visual Art, Denver CO
Miami-Dade College, Kendal Campus, Art Gallery, Miami FL
Mingei International, Inc, Mingei International Museum - Balboa Park & Mingei International Museum - Escondido, San Diego CA
The Mint Museum, Charlotte NC
Mississippi River Museum at Mud-Island River Park, Memphis TN
Missoula Art Museum, Missoula MT
Mobile Museum of Art, Mobile AL
Modern Art Museum, Fort Worth TX
Montclair Art Museum, Montclair NJ
Morehead State University, Kentucky Folk Art Center, Morehead KY
Morris Museum of Art, Augusta GA
Mount Vernon Hotel Museum & Garden, New York NY
Museum of African American Art, Los Angeles CA
The Museum of Arts & Sciences Inc, Daytona Beach FL
Museum of Contemporary Art, Chicago IL
Museum of Contemporary Art, North Miami FL
Museum of the National Center of Afro-American Artists, Boston MA
National Conference of Artists, Michigan Chapter Gallery, Detroit MI
National Museum of Women in the Arts, Washington DC
Nebraska Game and Parks Commission, Arbor Lodge State Historical Park & Morton Mansion, Nebraska City NE
The Nelson-Atkins Museum of Art, Kansas City MO
The New Jersey State Museum, Fine Art Bureau, Trenton NJ
New Orleans Museum of Art, New Orleans LA
New World Art Center, T F Chen Cultural Center, New York NY
Niagara University, Castellani Art Museum, Niagara NY
North Carolina State University, Gregg Museum of Art & Design, Raleigh NC
The Ogden Museum of Southern Art, University of New Orleans, New Orleans LA
Ohio Historical Society, National Afro-American Museum & Cultural Center, Wilberforce OH
Okefenokee Heritage Center, Inc, Waycross GA
Opelousas Museum of Art, Inc (OMA), Opelousas LA
Orlando Museum of Art, Orlando FL
Owensboro Museum of Fine Art, Owensboro KY
Page-Walker Arts & History Center, Cary NC
Panhandle-Plains Historical Museum, Canyon TX
The Pennsylvania State University, Palmer Museum of Art, University Park PA
Piedmont Arts Association, Martinsville VA
Polk Museum of Art, Lakeland FL
Portsmouth Historical Society, John Paul Jones House & Discover Portsmouth, Portsmouth NH
Pump House Center for the Arts, Chillicothe OH
Rabindra Bhavan Art Gallery, Lalit Kala Akademi (National Academy of Art), New Delhi
Rollins College, George D & Harriet W Cornell Fine Arts Museum, Winter Park FL
St Mary's College of Maryland, The Dwight Frederick Boyden Gallery, St Mary's City MD
Saint Peter's College, Art Gallery, Jersey City NJ
Santa Monica Museum of Art, Santa Monica CA
Scripps College, Clark Humanities Museum, Claremont CA
Scripps College, Ruth Chandler Williamson Gallery, Claremont CA
South Carolina Artisans Center, Walterboro SC
South Carolina State Museum, Columbia SC

South Dakota State University, South Dakota Art Museum, Brookings SD
Southeastern Center for Contemporary Art, Winston Salem NC
Southern Illinois University Carbondale, University Museum, Carbondale IL
The Speed Art Museum, Louisville KY
Springfield Art Museum, Springfield MO
Stanford University, Cantor Arts Center at Stanford University, Stanford CA
State University of New York at Binghamton, Binghamton University Art Museum, Binghamton NY
State University of New York at Geneseo, Bertha V B Lederer Gallery, Geneseo NY
State University of New York at Geneseo, Lockhart Gallery, Geneseo NY
State University of New York College at Buffalo, Buffalo NY
Stone Quarry Hill Art Park, Winner Gallery, Cazenovia NY
The Studio Museum in Harlem, New York NY
Sweet Briar College, Art Collection & Galleries, Sweet Briar VA
Taft Museum of Art, Cincinnati OH
Lillian & Coleman Taube Museum of Art, Minot ND
University of Alabama at Birmingham, Visual Arts Gallery, Birmingham AL
University of California, Berkeley, Berkeley Art Museum & Pacific Film Archive, Berkeley CA
University of California, Berkeley, Phoebe Apperson Hearst Museum of Anthropology, Berkeley CA
University of Colorado at Colorado Springs, Gallery of Contemporary Art, Colorado Springs CO
University of Georgia, Georgia Museum of Art, Athens GA
University of Illinois at Urbana-Champaign, Krannert Art Museum and Kinkead Pavilion, Champaign IL
University of Louisiana at Lafayette, Paul and Lulu Hilliard University Art Museum, Lafayette LA
University of Miami, Lowe Art Museum, Coral Gables FL
University of Michigan, Museum of Art, Ann Arbor MI
University of Missouri, Museum of Art & Archaeology, Columbia MO
University of North Carolina at Greensboro, Weatherspoon Art Museum, Greensboro NC
University of Pennsylvania, Arthur Ross Gallery, Philadelphia PA
University of Rhode Island, Fine Arts Center Galleries, Kingston RI
University of Richmond, University Museums, Richmond VA
University of Rochester, Memorial Art Gallery, Rochester NY
University of Texas at Austin, Blanton Museum of Art, Austin TX
The University of Texas at San Antonio, Institute of Texan Cultures, San Antonio TX
University of Wisconsin-Madison, Chazen Museum of Art, Madison WI
Viridian Artists Inc, New York NY
Wadsworth Atheneum Museum of Art, Hartford CT
The Walker African American Museum & Research Center, Las Vegas NV
Walker Art Gallery, Liverpool
Waterloo Center of the Arts, Waterloo IA
Waterworks Visual Arts Center, Salisbury NC
Wichita State University, Ulrich Museum of Art, Wichita KS
Williams College, Museum of Art, Williamstown MA
Winston-Salem State University, Diggs Gallery, Winston Salem NC
Wiregrass Museum of Art, Dothan AL
World Erotic Art Museum, Miami Beach FL
Yerba Buena Center for the Arts, San Francisco CA
Zigler Art Museum, Jennings LA

AMERICAN INDIAN ART

Academy of the New Church, Glencairn Museum, Bryn Athyn PA
Adams County Historical Society, Gettysburg PA
Alabama Department of Archives & History, Museum of Alabama, Montgomery AL
Alaska Department of Education, Division of Libraries, Archives & Museums, Sheldon Jackson Museum, Sitka AK
Alaska Heritage Museum at Wells Fargo, Anchorage AK
Albany Institute of History & Art, Albany NY

American Art Museum, Smithsonian Institution, Washington DC
American Folk Art Museum, New York NY
American Sport Art Museum and Archives, Daphne AL
Amon Carter Museum of American Art, Fort Worth TX
Anchorage Museum at Rasmuson Center, Anchorage AK
Appaloosa Museum and Heritage Center, Moscow ID
Archaeological Society of Ohio, Indian Museum of Lake County, Ohio, Willoughby OH
Arizona State University, Deer Valley Rock Art Center, Phoenix AZ
Arnot Art Museum, Elmira NY
The Art Museum at the University of Kentucky, Lexington KY
Art Museum of Greater Lafayette, Lafayette IN
Art Without Walls Inc, New York NY
Arts Council of Fayetteville-Cumberland County, The Arts Center, Fayetteville NC
ArtSpace/Lima, Lima OH
Asheville Art Museum, Asheville NC
Ataloa Lodge Museum, Muskogee OK
Augustana College, Augustana College Art Museum, Rock Island IL
Aurora University, Schingoethe Center for Native American Cultures & The Schingoethe Art Gallery, Aurora IL
Autry National Center, Museum of the American West, Griffith Park, Los Angeles CA
Ball State University, Museum of Art, Muncie IN
The Baltimore Museum of Art, Baltimore MD
Bay County Historical Society, Historical Museum of Bay County, Bay City MI
Bent Museum & Gallery, Taos NM
Berkshire Museum, Pittsfield MA
Berman Museum, Anniston AL
Besser Museum for Northeast Michigan, Alpena MI
Birmingham Museum of Art, Birmingham AL
Bone Creek Museum of Agrarian Art, David City NE
Bowers Museum, Santa Ana CA
Brandeis University, Rose Art Museum, Waltham MA
Brigham City Corporation, Brigham City Museum & Gallery, Brigham City UT
L D Brinkman, Kerrville TX
Brown University, Haffenreffer Museum of Anthropology, Providence RI
Bruce Museum, Inc, Greenwich CT
The Butler Institute of American Art, Art Museum, Youngstown OH
C W Post Campus of Long Island University, Hillwood Art Museum, Brookville NY
Cabot's Old Indian Pueblo Museum, Desert Hot Springs CA
California State Parks, State Indian Museum, Sacramento CA
California State University, Northridge, Art Galleries, Northridge CA
Cambridge Museum, Cambridge NE
Capital University, Schumacher Gallery, Columbus OH
Carlsbad Museum & Art Center, Carlsbad NM
Carson County Square House Museum, Panhandle TX
Cayuga Museum of History & Art, Auburn NY
Central United Methodist Church, Swords Into Plowshares Peace Center & Gallery, Detroit MI
Chelan County Public Utility District, Rocky Reach Dam, Wenatchee WA
Chief Plenty Coups Museum State Park, Pryor MT
Church of Jesus Christ of Latter-Day Saints, Museum of Church History & Art, Salt Lake City UT
Cincinnati Art Museum, Cincinnati Art Museum, Cincinnati OH
City of El Paso, El Paso Museum of Archaeology, El Paso TX
City of Mason City, Charles H MacNider Museum, Mason City IA
City of Springdale, Shiloh Museum of Ozark History, Springdale AR
City of Ukiah, Grace Hudson Museum & The Sun House, Ukiah CA
Clark County Historical Society, Pioneer - Krier Museum, Ashland KS
Colgate University, Picker Art Gallery, Hamilton NY
College of William & Mary, Muscarelle Museum of Art, Williamsburg VA
The College of Wooster, The College of Wooster Art Museum, Wooster OH
Colorado Historical Society, Colorado History Museum, Denver CO
Columbus Museum, Columbus GA
Cornell College, Peter Paul Luce Gallery, Mount Vernon IA

Rollins College, George D & Harriet W Cornell Fine Arts Museum, Winter Park FL
Roswell Museum & Art Center, Roswell NM
C M Russell, Great Falls MT
Ryerss Victorian Museum & Library, Philadelphia PA
Safety Harbor Museum of Regional History, Safety Harbor FL
Saginaw Art Museum, Saginaw MI
Saint Augustine Historical Society, Oldest House Museum Complex, Saint Augustine FL
Saint Joseph Museum, Saint Joseph MO
Saint Louis County Historical Society, St. Louis County Historical Society, Duluth MN
Saint Peter's College, Art Gallery, Jersey City NJ
Salisbury House Foundation, Salisbury House and Garden, Des Moines IA
San Bernardino County Museum, Fine Arts Institute, Redlands CA
School for Advanced Research (SAR), Indian Arts Research Center, Santa Fe NM
Seneca-Iroquois National Museum, Salamanca NY
Sheldon Museum & Cultural Center, Inc, Sheldon Museum & Cultural Center, Haines AK
Shoshone Bannock Tribes, Shoshone Bannock Tribal Museum, Fort Hall ID
Smithsonian Institution, Washington DC
Sooke Region Museum & Art Gallery, Sooke BC
South Carolina Artisans Center, Walterboro SC
South Dakota State University, South Dakota Art Museum, Brookings SD
Southern Plains Indian Museum, Anadarko OK
The Speed Art Museum, Louisville KY
Springfield Art Museum, Springfield MO
Springfield Museums, Springfield Science Museum, Springfield MA
Stamford Museum & Nature Center, Stamford CT
Stanford University, Cantor Arts Center at Stanford University, Stanford CA
Nelda C & H J Lutcher Stark, Stark Museum of Art, Orange TX
State Capital Museum, Olympia WA
State University of New York at Geneseo, Bertha V B Lederer Gallery, Geneseo NY
State University of New York at Geneseo, Lockhart Gallery, Geneseo NY
Ste Genevieve Museum, Sainte Genevieve MO
Stratford Historical Society, Catharine B Mitchell Museum, Stratford CT
Suomen Kansallismuseo, National Museum of Finland, Helsinki
Switzerland County Historical Society Inc, Switzerland County Historical Museum, Vevay IN
Tacoma Art Museum, Tacoma WA
Lillian & Coleman Taube Museum of Art, Minot ND
Texas Ranger Hall of Fame & Museum, Waco TX
Tohono Chul Park, Tucson AZ
Topeka & Shawnee County Public Library, Alice C Sabatini Gallery, Topeka KS
Trust Authority, Museum of the Great Plains, Lawton OK
Tubac Center of the Arts, Santa Cruz Valley Art Association, Tubac AZ
Turtle Bay Exploration Park, Redding CA
United States Coast Guard Museum, New London CT
United States Department of the Interior, Interior Museum, Washington DC
United States Military Academy, West Point Museum, West Point NY
University of Alabama at Birmingham, Visual Arts Gallery, Birmingham AL
University of Alaska, Museum of the North, Fairbanks AK
University of British Columbia, Museum of Anthropology, Vancouver BC
University of California, Berkeley, Phoebe Apperson Hearst Museum of Anthropology, Berkeley CA
University of California, Los Angeles, Fowler Museum at UCLA, Los Angeles CA
University of Colorado at Colorado Springs, Gallery of Contemporary Art, Colorado Springs CO
University of Illinois at Urbana-Champaign, Krannert Art Museum and Kinkead Pavilion, Champaign IL
University of Miami, Lowe Art Museum, Coral Gables FL
University of Minnesota Duluth, Tweed Museum of Art, Duluth MN
University of Nebraska-Lincoln, Great Plains Art Museum, Lincoln NE
University of Notre Dame, Snite Museum of Art, Notre Dame IN
University of Pennsylvania, Museum of Archaeology & Anthropology, Philadelphia PA

University of Rhode Island, Fine Arts Center Galleries, Kingston RI
University of Rochester, Memorial Art Gallery, Rochester NY
University of South Dakota, University Art Galleries, Vermillion SD
University of Southern Colorado, College of Liberal & Fine Arts, Pueblo CO
University of Tennessee, McClung Museum of Natural History & Culture, Knoxville TN
University of Utah, Utah Museum of Fine Arts, Salt Lake City UT
University of Victoria, The Legacy Art Gallery, Victoria BC
University of Virginia, The Fralin Museum of Art at the University of Virginia, Charlottesville VA
University of Wisconsin-Madison, Chazen Museum of Art, Madison WI
University of Wyoming, University of Wyoming Art Museum, Laramie WY
Utah State University, Nora Eccles Harrison Museum of Art, Logan UT
Vermilion County Museum Society, Danville IL
Wadsworth Atheneum Museum of Art, Hartford CT
Wake Forest University, Museum of Anthropology, Winston Salem NC
Washington University, Mildred Lane Kemper Art Museum, Saint Louis MO
Wayne County Historical Society, Museum, Honesdale PA
Wheaton College, Beard and Weil Galleries, Norton MA
Wichita State University, Ulrich Museum of Art, Wichita KS
Wildling Art Museum, Solvang CA
Wisconsin Historical Society, Wisconsin Historical Museum, Madison WI
Witte Museum, San Antonio TX
World Erotic Art Museum, Miami Beach FL
Wounded Knee Museum, Wall SD
Wyoming State Museum, Cheyenne WY
Yosemite Museum, Yosemite National Park CA
Yuma Fine Arts Association, Yuma Art Center, Yuma AZ
Zigler Art Museum, Jennings LA

AMERICAN WESTERN ART

Albuquerque Museum of Art & History, Albuquerque * NM
American Art Museum, Smithsonian Institution, Washington DC
Amon Carter Museum of American Art, Fort Worth TX
Appaloosa Museum and Heritage Center, Moscow ID
Arnot Art Museum, Elmira NY
Art Gallery of Hamilton, Hamilton ON
The Art Museum of Eastern Idaho, Idaho Falls ID
Art Without Walls Inc, New York NY
Artesia Historical Museum & Art Center, Artesia NM
ArtSpace/Lima, Lima OH
Autry National Center, Museum of the American West, Griffith Park, Los Angeles CA
Ball State University, Museum of Art, Muncie IN
The Baltimore Museum of Art, Baltimore MD
Berkshire Museum, Pittsfield MA
Berman Museum, Anniston AL
Birmingham Museum of Art, Birmingham AL
Blauvelt Demarest Foundation, Hiram Blauvelt Art Museum, Oradell NJ
Bone Creek Museum of Agrarian Art, David City NE
Booth Western Art Museum, Cartersville GA
Brigham City Corporation, Brigham City Museum & Gallery, Brigham City UT
Brigham Young University, B F Larsen Gallery, Provo UT
Brigham Young University, Museum of Art, Provo UT
L D Brinkman, Kerrville TX
Bradford Brinton, Big Horn WY
Brookgreen Gardens, Murrells Inlet SC
Cabot's Old Indian Pueblo Museum, Desert Hot Springs CA
California State University, Northridge, Art Galleries, Northridge CA
Cambridge Museum, Cambridge NE
Canajoharie Library & Art Gallery, Arkell Museum of Canajoharie, Canajoharie NY
Cape Ann Historical Association, Cape Ann Museum, Gloucester MA
Carlsbad Museum & Art Center, Carlsbad NM
Cartoon Art Museum, San Francisco CA
Cheekwood-Tennessee Botanical Garden & Museum of Art, Nashville TN

Church of Jesus Christ of Latter-Day Saints, Museum of Church History & Art, Salt Lake City UT
City of El Paso, El Paso TX
City of Mason City, Charles H MacNider Museum, Mason City IA
City of Ukiah, Grace Hudson Museum & The Sun House, Ukiah CA
Colorado Historical Society, Colorado History Museum, Denver CO
Columbus Museum of Art, Columbus OH
Coutts Museum of Art, Inc, El Dorado KS
Cripple Creek District Museum, Cripple Creek CO
Crocker Art Museum, Sacramento CA
Crook County Museum & Art Gallery, Sundance WY
Culberson County Historical Museum, Van Horn TX
The Currier Museum of Art, Manchester NH
Dallas Museum of Art, Dallas TX
Dartmouth College, Hood Museum of Art, Hanover NH
Denver Art Museum, Denver CO
Dixie State College, Robert N & Peggy Sears Gallery, Saint George UT
East Carolina University, Wellington B Gray Gallery, Greenville NC
Eiteljorg Museum of American Indians & Western Art, Indianapolis IN
Ellen Noel Art Museum of the Permian Basin, Odessa TX
Elmhurst Art Museum, Elmhurst IL
Favell Museum of Western Art & Indian Artifacts, Klamath Falls OR
Forest Lawn Museum, Glendale CA
Freer Gallery of Art & Arthur M Sackler Gallery, Freer Gallery of Art, Washington DC
Frontier Times Museum, Bandera TX
Gloridale Partnership, National Museum of Woodcarving, Custer SD
Grand Rapids Art Museum, Grand Rapids MI
Heard Museum, Phoenix AZ
Hidalgo County Historical Museum, Edinburg TX
High Desert Museum, Bend OR
High Museum of Art, Atlanta GA
The Historic New Orleans Collection, Royal Street Galleries, New Orleans LA
Historical Museum at Fort Missoula, Missoula MT
Hoyt Center for the Arts, New Castle PA
Huntington Museum of Art, Huntington WV
Illinois State Museum, ISM Lockport Gallery, Chicago Gallery & Southern Illinois Art Gallery, Springfield IL
Independence Historical Museum & Art Center, Independence KS
Indiana University, Art Museum, Bloomington IN
Istanbul Arkeoloji Muzeleri, The Library of Archaeological Museums of Istanbul, Istanbul
J.M.W. Turner Museum, Sarasota FL
James Dick Foundation, Festival - Institute, Round Top TX
Jefferson County Open Space, Hiwan Homestead Museum, Evergreen CO
Joe Gish's Old West Museum, Fredericksburg TX
The John L. Clarke Western Art Gallery & Memorial Museum, East Glacier Park MT
Johns Hopkins University, Evergreen Museum & Library, Baltimore MD
Joslyn Art Museum, Omaha NE
Keystone Gallery, Scott City KS
Klein Museum, Mobridge SD
Knoxville Museum of Art, Knoxville TN
Koshare Indian Museum, Inc, La Junta CO
Leanin' Tree Museum & Sculpture Garden of Western Art, Boulder CO
Lincoln County Historical Association, Inc, 1811 Old Lincoln County Jail & Lincoln County Museum, Wiscasset ME
Louisiana State Exhibit Museum, Shreveport LA
Loveland Museum/Gallery, Loveland CO
Luther College, Fine Arts Collection, Decorah IA
Marietta College, Grover M Hermann Fine Arts Center, Marietta OH
Maslak McLeod Gallery, Toronto ON
Mattatuck Historical Society, Mattatuck Museum, Waterbury CT
Mennello Museum of American Art, Orlando FL
Mexican Museum, San Francisco CA
Middle Border Museum & Oscar Howe Art Center, Mitchell SD
Middlebury College, Museum of Art, Middlebury VT
Ministry of Cultural Affairs, Bangladesh National Museum, Dhaka
Minot State University, Northwest Art Center, Minot ND
Missoula Art Museum, Missoula MT

ANTHROPOLOGY

Maysville, Kentucky Gateway Museum Center,
Maysville KY
McLean County Historical Society, McLean County
Museum of History, Bloomington IL
McPherson Museum and Arts Foundation, McPherson
KS
Milwaukee Public Museum, Milwaukee WI
Ministry of Cultural Affairs, Bangladesh National
Museum, Dhaka
Mississippi River Museum at Mud-Island River Park,
Memphis TN
Missouri Department of Natural Resources, Missouri
State Museum, Jefferson City MO
Mohave Museum of History & Arts, Kingman AZ
Montana State University, Museum of the Rockies,
Bozeman MT
Montclair Art Museum, Montclair NJ
Morris Museum, Morristown NJ
Moto Moto Museum, Mbala
Musees Royaux d'Art et d'Histoire, Royal Museums of
Art and History, Brussels
Museo De Las Americas, Denver CO
The Museum, Greenwood SC
The Museum of Arts & Sciences Inc, Daytona Beach
FL
Museum of Chinese in America, New York NY
Museum of New Mexico, Laboratory of Anthropology
Library, Santa Fe NM
Museum of Northern Arizona, Flagstaff AZ
Museum of Northern British Columbia, Ruth Harvey
Art Gallery, Prince Rupert BC
Museum of the City of New York, Museum, New York
NY
Museum of Vancouver, Vancouver BC
Museum of York County, Rock Hill SC
Muzeul de Istorie Nationala Si Arheologie Constanta,
National History & Archaeology Museum,
Constanta
National Museum of the American Indian, George
Gustav Heye Center, New York NY
National Museum of the American Indian, Smithsonian
Institution, Washington DC
National Museum of the Philippines, Manila
National Museum of Wildlife Art of the Unites States,
Jackson WY
National Museum, Monuments and Art Gallery,
Gaborone
National Park Service, Hubbell Trading Post National
Historic Site, Ganado AZ
Natural History Museum of Los Angeles County, Los
Angeles CA
Navajo Nation, Navajo Nation Museum, Window Rock
AZ
Nelson Mandela Bay Municipality, Nelson Mandela
Metropolitan Art Museum, Port Elizabeth
New Jersey State Museum, Fine Art Bureau, Trenton
NJ
No Man's Land Historical Society, No Man's Land
Museum, Goodwell OK
Northern Maine Museum of Science, Presque Isle ME
Oklahoma Historical Society, State Museum of History,
Oklahoma City OK
Panhandle-Plains Historical Museum, Canyon TX
Pennsylvania Historical & Museum Commission, The
State Museum of Pennsylvania, Harrisburg PA
Phelps County Historical Society, Nebraska Prairie
Museum, Holdrege NE
The Frank Phillips, Woolaroc Museum, Bartlesville OK
Plumas County Museum, Quincy CA
Port Huron Museum, Port Huron MI
Reading Public Museum, Reading PA
Riverside Metropolitan Museum, Riverside CA
Roberts County Museum, Miami TX
Rollins College, George D & Harriet W Cornell Fine
Arts Museum, Winter Park FL
Roswell Museum & Art Center, Roswell NM
Royal Ontario Museum, Toronto ON
C M Russell, Great Falls MT
Saint Augustine Historical Society, Oldest House
Museum Complex, Saint Augustine FL
Saint Joseph Museum, Saint Joseph MO
Saint Peter's College, Art Gallery, Jersey City NJ
Shirley Plantation Foundation, Charles City VA
Southern Illinois University Carbondale, University
Museum, Carbondale IL
Stanford University, Cantor Arts Center at Stanford
University, Stanford CA
State University of New York at Binghamton,
Binghamton University Art Museum, Binghamton
NY
Suomen Kansallismuseo, National Museum of Finland,
Helsinki

Texas Tech University, Museum of Texas Tech
University, Lubbock TX
Trust Authority, Museum of the Great Plains, Lawton
OK
University of British Columbia, Museum of
Anthropology, Vancouver BC
University of California, Berkeley, Phoebe Apperson
Hearst Museum of Anthropology, Berkeley CA
University of California, Los Angeles, Fowler Museum
at UCLA, Los Angeles CA
University of Illinois at Urbana-Champaign, Spurlock
Museum, Champaign IL
University of Memphis, Art Museum, Memphis TN
University of Miami, Lowe Art Museum, Coral Gables
FL
University of Pennsylvania, Museum of Archaeology &
Anthropology, Philadelphia PA
University of Tennessee, McClung Museum of Natural
History & Culture, Knoxville TN
The University of Texas at San Antonio, Institute of
Texan Cultures, San Antonio TX
University of Victoria, The Legacy Art Gallery, Victoria
BC
Wake Forest University, Museum of Anthropology,
Winston Salem NC
Whalers Village Museum, Lahaina HI
Wisconsin Historical Society, Wisconsin Historical
Museum, Madison WI
Witte Museum, San Antonio TX
Xavier University, Art Gallery, Cincinnati OH

ANTIQUITIES-ASSYRIAN

Academy of the New Church, Glencairn Museum, Bryn
Athyn PA
Baroda Museum and Picture Gallery, Baroda
Cincinnati Art Museum, Cincinnati Art Museum,
Cincinnati OH
Crocker Art Museum, Sacramento CA
Dallas Museum of Art, Dallas TX
Dartmouth College, Hood Museum of Art, Hanover NH
Department of Antiquities, Cyprus Museum, Nicosia
Detroit Institute of Arts, Detroit MI
Fetherston Foundation, Packwood House Museum,
Lewisburg PA
Fine Arts Museums of San Francisco, Legion of Honor,
San Francisco CA
Freer Gallery of Art & Arthur M Sackler Gallery,
Arthur M Sackler Gallery, Washington DC
Hecht Museum, Haifa
Hermitage Foundation Museum, Norfolk VA
Huntington Museum of Art, Huntington WV
Indiana University, Art Museum, Bloomington IN
The Israel Museum, Jerusalem, Billy Rose Art Garden,
Jerusalem
The Israel Museum, Jerusalem, Samuel & Saidye
Bronfman Archaeology Wing, Jerusalem
The Israel Museum, Jerusalem, Jerusalem
Bob Jones University Museum & Gallery Inc,
Greenville SC
Kimbell Art Foundation, Kimbell Art Museum, Fort
Worth TX
Kunsthistorisches Museum Vienna, Museum of Fine
Arts, Vienna
Loyola University Chicago, Loyola University Museum
of Art, Chicago IL
McLean County Historical Society, McLean County
Museum of History, Bloomington IL
Menil Foundation, Inc, The Menil Collection, Houston
TX
The Metropolitan Museum of Art, New York NY
Middlebury College, Museum of Art, Middlebury VT
The Mint Museum, Charlotte NC
Montreal Museum of Fine Arts, Montreal PQ
Musees Royaux d'Art et d'Histoire, Royal Museums of
Art and History, Brussels
Museum of Fine Arts, Saint Petersburg, Florida, Inc,
Saint Petersburg FL
Museum zu Allerheiligen, Schaffhausen
National Museums Scotland, National Museum of
Scotland, Edinburgh
The Nelson-Atkins Museum of Art, Kansas City MO
Polk Museum of Art, Lakeland FL
Princeton University, Princeton University Art Museum,
Princeton NJ
Rosicrucian Egyptian Museum & Planetarium,
Rosicrucian Order, A.M.O.R.C., San Jose CA
Saint Peter's College, Art Gallery, Jersey City NJ
Southern Baptist Theological Seminary, Joseph A
Callaway Archaeological Museum, Louisville KY
Stanford University, Cantor Arts Center at Stanford
University, Stanford CA

The State Museum of Oriental Art, Moscow
Toledo Museum of Art, Toledo OH
University of California, Berkeley, Phoebe Apperson
Hearst Museum of Anthropology, Berkeley CA
University of Chicago, Oriental Institute, Chicago IL
University of Illinois at Urbana-Champaign, Krannert
Art Museum and Kinkead Pavilion, Champaign IL
University of Missouri, Museum of Art & Archaeology,
Columbia MO
University of Rochester, Memorial Art Gallery,
Rochester NY
World Erotic Art Museum, Miami Beach FL

ANTIQUITIES-BYZANTINE

Art & Culture Center of Hollywood, Art
Gallery/Multidisciplinary Cultural Center,
Hollywood FL
Badisches Landesmuseum, Karlsruhe
Baroda Museum and Picture Gallery, Baroda
The Buffalo Fine Arts Academy, Albright-Knox Art
Gallery, Buffalo NY
Byzantine & Christian Museum, Athens, Athens
Cincinnati Art Museum, Cincinnati Art Museum,
Cincinnati OH
Dallas Museum of Art, Dallas TX
Department of Antiquities, Cyprus Museum, Nicosia
Detroit Institute of Arts, Detroit MI
Fetherston Foundation, Packwood House Museum,
Lewisburg PA
Fine Arts Museums of San Francisco, Legion of Honor,
San Francisco CA
Florence Museum, Florence SC
Freer Gallery of Art & Arthur M Sackler Gallery,
Arthur M Sackler Gallery, Washington DC
General Board of Discipleship, The United Methodist
Church, The Upper Room Chapel & Museum,
Nashville TN
Harvard University, Semitic Museum, Cambridge MA
Harvard University, Museum & Garden, Washington
DC
Hecht Museum, Haifa
Hermitage Foundation Museum, Norfolk VA
Huntington Museum of Art, Huntington WV
Indiana University, Art Museum, Bloomington IN
The Israel Museum, Jerusalem, Billy Rose Art Garden,
Jerusalem
The Israel Museum, Jerusalem, Samuel & Saidye
Bronfman Archaeology Wing, Jerusalem
The Israel Museum, Jerusalem, Jerusalem
Janus Pannonius Muzeum, Pecs
Kunsthistorisches Museum Vienna, Museum of Fine
Arts, Vienna
Lehigh University Art Galleries, Museum Operation,
Bethlehem PA
Magyar Nemzeti Muzeum - Hungarian National
Museum, Budapest
Menil Foundation, Inc, The Menil Collection, Houston
TX
The Metropolitan Museum of Art, New York NY
The Mint Museum, Charlotte NC
Mobile Museum of Art, Mobile AL
Montreal Museum of Fine Arts, Montreal PQ
Musees Royaux d'Art et d'Histoire, Royal Museums of
Art and History, Brussels
Musei Civici di Padova - Cappella Degli Scrovengni,
Musei Civici Agli Eremitani (Civic Museum) -
Scrovegni Chapel, Padua
Museo Civico Giovanni Fattori, Livorno
Museum fur Kunst und Gewerbe Hamburg, Hamburg
Museum of Fine Arts, Saint Petersburg, Florida, Inc,
Saint Petersburg FL
Princeton University, Princeton University Art Museum,
Princeton NJ
Pyramid Hill Sculpture Park & Museum, Hamilton OH
Queens College, City University of New York,
Godwin-Ternbach Museum, Flushing NY
Royal Arts Foundation, Belcourt Castle, Newport RI
Saint Peter's College, Art Gallery, Jersey City NJ
Southern Baptist Theological Seminary, Joseph A
Callaway Archaeological Museum, Louisville KY
Stanford University, Cantor Arts Center at Stanford
University, Stanford CA
State University of New York at New Paltz, Samuel
Dorsky Museum of Art, New Paltz NY
University of Delaware, University Museums, Newark
DE
University of Illinois at Urbana-Champaign, Krannert
Art Museum and Kinkead Pavilion, Champaign IL
University of Missouri, Museum of Art & Archaeology,
Columbia MO

University of North Carolina at Chapel Hill, Ackland Art Museum, Chapel Hill NC
University of Richmond, University Museums, Richmond VA
University of Toronto, University of Toronto Art Centre, Toronto ON
University of Virginia, The Fralin Museum of Art at the University of Virginia, Charlottesville VA
University of Wisconsin-Madison, Chazen Museum of Art, Madison WI
Wheaton College, Beard and Weil Galleries, Norton MA
World Erotic Art Museum, Miami Beach FL

ANTIQUITIES-EGYPTIAN

Academy of the New Church, Glencairn Museum, Bryn Athyn PA
African Art Museum of Maryland, Columbia MD
Albany Institute of History & Art, Albany NY
Albany Museum of Art, Albany GA
Arnot Art Museum, Elmira NY
Art & Culture Center of Hollywood, Art Gallery/Multidisciplinary Cultural Center, Hollywood FL
Art Without Walls Inc, New York NY
Badisches Landesmuseum, Karlsruhe
Ball State University, Museum of Art, Muncie IN
The Baltimore Museum of Art, Baltimore MD
Barnes Foundation, Merion PA
Baroda Museum and Picture Gallery, Baroda
Beloit College, Wright Museum of Art, Beloit WI
Berkshire Museum, Pittsfield MA
Blanden Memorial Art Museum, Fort Dodge IA
Brown University, Haffenreffer Museum of Anthropology, Providence RI
Bucknell University, Edward & Marthann Samek Art Gallery, Lewisburg PA
The Buffalo Fine Arts Academy, Albright-Knox Art Gallery, Buffalo NY
C W Post Campus of Long Island University, Hillwood Art Museum, Brookville NY
Cincinnati Art Museum, Cincinnati Art Museum, Cincinnati OH
The Cleveland Museum of Art, Cleveland OH
The College of Wooster, The College of Wooster Art Museum, Wooster OH
Crocker Art Museum, Sacramento CA
Dallas Museum of Art, Dallas TX
Dartmouth College, Hood Museum of Art, Hanover NH
Detroit Institute of Arts, Detroit MI
Detroit Zoological Institute, Wildlife Interpretive Gallery, Royal Oak MI
Dickinson College, The Trout Gallery, Carlisle PA
Emory University, Michael C Carlos Museum, Atlanta GA
Evansville Museum of Arts, History & Science, Evansville IN
Everhart Museum, Scranton PA
Fairbanks Museum & Planetarium, Saint Johnsbury VT
Fetherston Foundation, Packwood House Museum, Lewisburg PA
Fine Arts Museums of San Francisco, Legion of Honor, San Francisco CA
Florence Museum, Florence SC
Florida State University and Central Florida Community College, The Appleton Museum of Art, Ocala FL
Freer Gallery of Art & Arthur M Sackler Gallery, Arthur M Sackler Gallery, Washington DC
Grand Rapids Art Museum, Grand Rapids MI
Grand Rapids Public Museum, Public Museum of Grand Rapids, Grand Rapids MI
Hamilton College, Emerson Gallery, Clinton NY
Harvard University, Semitic Museum, Cambridge MA
Hebrew Union College - Jewish Institute of Religion, Skirball Museum Cincinnati, Cincinnati OH
Hecht Museum, Haifa
Hermitage Foundation Museum, Norfolk VA
Indiana University, Art Museum, Bloomington IN
Iredell Museums, Statesville NC
The Israel Museum, Jerusalem, Billy Rose Art Garden, Jerusalem
The Israel Museum, Jerusalem, Samuel & Saidye Bronfman Archaeology Wing, Jerusalem
The Israel Museum, Jerusalem, Jerusalem
Johns Hopkins University, Archaeological Collection, Baltimore MD
Johns Hopkins University, Evergreen Museum & Library, Baltimore MD
Bob Jones University Museum & Gallery Inc, Greenville SC

Joslyn Art Museum, Omaha NE
Kimbell Art Foundation, Kimbell Art Museum, Fort Worth TX
Kunsthistorisches Museum Vienna, Museum of Fine Arts, Vienna
Lightner Museum, Saint Augustine FL
Lincolnshire County Council, The Collection: Art & Archaeology in Lincolnshire, Lincoln
Louisiana Arts & Science Museum, Baton Rouge LA
Mabee-Gerrer Museum of Art, Shawnee OK
Magyar Nemzeti Muzeum - Hungarian National Museum, Budapest
McMaster University, McMaster Museum of Art, Hamilton ON
Menil Foundation, Inc, The Menil Collection, Houston TX
The Metropolitan Museum of Art, New York NY
Milwaukee Art Museum, Milwaukee WI
Ministry of Cultural Affairs, Bangladesh National Museum, Dhaka
Ministry of Culture & Tourism, The Delphi Museum, 10th Ephorate of Prehistoric & Classical Antiquities, Delphi
Montreal Museum of Fine Arts, Montreal PQ
Mount Holyoke College, Art Museum, South Hadley MA
Musee et Chateau de Chantilly (MUSEE CONDE), Chantilly
Musee Royal Et Domaine De Mariemont, Morlanwelz
Musees Royaux d'Art et d'Histoire, Royal Museums of Art and History, Brussels
Musei Capitolini, Rome
Musei Civici di Padova - Cappella Degli Scrovegni, Musei Civici Agli Eremitani (Civic Museum) - Scrovegni Chapel, Padua
Museo Cerralbo, Madrid
Museo De Bellas Artes de Caracas, Museum of Fine Arts, Caracas
The Museum, Greenwood SC
Museum fur Kunst und Gewerbe Hamburg, Hamburg
Museum of Fine Arts, Boston MA
Museum of Fine Arts, Saint Petersburg, Florida, Inc, Saint Petersburg FL
Museum of Vancouver, Vancouver BC
Muzeul de Istorie Nationala Si Arheologie Constanta, National History & Archaeology Museum, Constanta
Muzeul National Brukenthal, Brukenthal Palace & European Art Gallery, Sibiu
National Archaeological Museum, Athens
National Museums Scotland, National Museum of Scotland, Edinburgh
The Nelson-Atkins Museum of Art, Kansas City MO
Norwich Free Academy, Slater Memorial Museum, Norwich CT
Ohara Museum of Art, Kurashiki
Okanagan Heritage Museum, Kelowna BC
Panhandle-Plains Historical Museum, Canyon TX
Princeton University, Princeton University Art Museum, Princeton NJ
Putnam Museum of History and Natural Science, Davenport IA
Pyramid Hill Sculpture Park & Museum, Hamilton OH
Queens College, City University of New York, Godwin-Ternbach Museum, Flushing NY
Reading Public Museum, Reading PA
Rollins College, George D & Harriet W Cornell Fine Arts Museum, Winter Park FL
Rosemount Museum, Inc, Pueblo CO
The Rosenbach Museum & Library, Philadelphia PA
Rosicrucian Egyptian Museum & Planetarium, Rosicrucian Order, A.M.O.R.C., San Jose CA
Royal Arts Foundation, Belcourt Castle, Newport RI
Saint Peter's College, Art Gallery, Jersey City NJ
San Antonio Museum of Art, San Antonio TX
Scripps College, Ruth Chandler Williamson Gallery, Claremont CA
Soprintendenza per I beni storici artistici ed etnoantropologici per le province di Mantova Brescia e Cremona, Museo di Palazzo Ducale, Mantua
Southern Baptist Theological Seminary, Joseph A Callaway Archaeological Museum, Louisville KY
The Speed Art Museum, Louisville KY
Stanford University, Cantor Arts Center at Stanford University, Stanford CA
The State Museum of Oriental Art, Moscow
State University of New York at New Paltz, Samuel Dorsky Museum of Art, New Paltz NY
Szepmuveszeti Muzeum, Museum of Fine Arts Budapest, Budapest
Toledo Museum of Art, Toledo OH

Tufts University, Tufts University Art Gallery, Medford MA
University of Chicago, Oriental Institute, Chicago IL
University of Delaware, University Museums, Newark DE
University of Illinois at Urbana-Champaign, Krannert Art Museum and Kinkead Pavilion, Champaign IL
University of Illinois at Urbana-Champaign, Spurlock Museum, Champaign IL
University of Louisiana at Lafayette, Paul and Lulu Hilliard University Art Museum, Lafayette LA
University of Memphis, Art Museum, Memphis TN
University of Miami, Lowe Art Museum, Coral Gables FL
University of Michigan, Kelsey Museum of Archaeology, Ann Arbor MI
University of Missouri, Museum of Art & Archaeology, Columbia MO
University of Pennsylvania, Museum of Archaeology & Anthropology, Philadelphia PA
University of Puerto Rico, Museum of Anthropology, History & Art, Rio Piedras PR
University of Richmond, University Museums, Richmond VA
University of Rochester, Memorial Art Gallery, Rochester NY
University of Tennessee, McClung Museum of Natural History & Culture, Knoxville TN
University of Toronto, University of Toronto Art Centre, Toronto ON
University of Utah, Utah Museum of Fine Arts, Salt Lake City UT
Vassar College, The Frances Lehman Loeb Art Center, Poughkeepsie NY
Virginia Museum of Fine Arts, Richmond VA
Washington University, Mildred Lane Kemper Art Museum, Saint Louis MO
Worcester Art Museum, Worcester MA
World Erotic Art Museum, Miami Beach FL

ANTIQUITIES-ETRUSCAN

Academy of the New Church, Glencairn Museum, Bryn Athyn PA
Arnot Art Museum, Elmira NY
Art & Culture Center of Hollywood, Art Gallery/Multidisciplinary Cultural Center, Hollywood FL
Ball State University, Museum of Art, Muncie IN
Baroda Museum and Picture Gallery, Baroda
Berkshire Museum, Pittsfield MA
Brown University, Haffenreffer Museum of Anthropology, Providence RI
Bucknell University, Edward & Marthann Samek Art Gallery, Lewisburg PA
The Buffalo Fine Arts Academy, Albright-Knox Art Gallery, Buffalo NY
Cincinnati Art Museum, Cincinnati Art Museum, Cincinnati OH
Cornell Museum of Art and American Culture, Delray Beach FL
Crocker Art Museum, Sacramento CA
Dallas Museum of Art, Dallas TX
Dartmouth College, Hood Museum of Art, Hanover NH
Detroit Institute of Arts, Detroit MI
Emory University, Michael C Carlos Museum, Atlanta GA
Fetherston Foundation, Packwood House Museum, Lewisburg PA
Fine Arts Museums of San Francisco, Legion of Honor, San Francisco CA
Florence Museum, Florence SC
Florida State University and Central Florida Community College, The Appleton Museum of Art, Ocala FL
Hecht Museum, Haifa
Indiana University, Art Museum, Bloomington IN
The Israel Museum, Jerusalem, Billy Rose Art Garden, Jerusalem
The Israel Museum, Jerusalem, Samuel & Saidye Bronfman Archaeology Wing, Jerusalem
The Israel Museum, Jerusalem, Jerusalem
Kunsthistorisches Museum Vienna, Museum of Fine Arts, Vienna
Lehigh University Art Galleries, Museum Operation, Bethlehem PA
Magyar Nemzeti Muzeum - Hungarian National Museum, Budapest
Menil Foundation, Inc, The Menil Collection, Houston TX
The Metropolitan Museum of Art, New York NY
Montreal Museum of Fine Arts, Montreal PQ

Musee des Beaux-Arts/Palais des Archeveques,
  Museum of Fine Arts, Tours
Musee Royal Et Domaine De Mariemont, Morlanwelz
Musees Royaux d'Art et d'Histoire, Royal Museums of
  Art and History, Brussels
Musei Capitolini, Rome
Musei Civici di Padova - Cappella Degli Scrovengni,
  Musei Civici Agli Eremitani (Civic Museum) -
  Scrovegni Chapel, Padua
Museo Cerralbo, Madrid
Museo Civico Giovanni Fattori, Livorno
Museum fur Kunst und Gewerbe Hamburg, Hamburg
Museum of Fine Arts, Saint Petersburg, Florida, Inc,
  Saint Petersburg FL
Museum zu Allerheiligen, Schaffhausen
Muzeul de Istorie Nationala Si Arheologie Constanta,
  National History & Archaeology Museum,
  Constanta
National Archaeological Museum, Athens
Norwich Free Academy, Slater Memorial Museum,
  Norwich CT
Princeton University, Princeton University Art Museum,
  Princeton NJ
Putnam Museum of History and Natural Science,
  Davenport IA
Pyramid Hill Sculpture Park & Museum, Hamilton OH
Queens College, City University of New York,
  Godwin-Ternbach Museum, Flushing NY
Reading Public Museum, Reading PA
Rollins College, George D & Harriet W Cornell Fine
  Arts Museum, Winter Park FL
Saginaw Art Museum, Saginaw MI
Saint Peter's College, Art Gallery, Jersey City NJ
The Speed Art Museum, Louisville KY
Stanford University, Cantor Arts Center at Stanford
  University, Stanford CA
Tampa Museum of Art, Tampa FL
University of British Columbia, Museum of
  Anthropology, Vancouver BC
University of Missouri, Museum of Art & Archaeology,
  Columbia MO
University of Pennsylvania, Museum of Archaeology &
  Anthropology, Philadelphia PA
University of Virginia, The Fralin Museum of Art at
  the University of Virginia, Charlottesville VA
University of Wisconsin-Madison, Chazen Museum of
  Art, Madison WI
Vassar College, The Frances Lehman Loeb Art Center,
  Poughkeepsie NY
Wheaton College, Beard and Weil Galleries, Norton
  MA
World Erotic Art Museum, Miami Beach FL

ANTIQUITIES-GREEK

Academy of the New Church, Glencairn Museum, Bryn
  Athyn PA
Albany Museum of Art, Albany GA
Archaeological Museum of Olympia, Olympia
Arnot Art Museum, Elmira NY
Art & Culture Center of Hollywood, Art
  Gallery/Multidisciplinary Cultural Center,
  Hollywood FL
Art Without Walls Inc, New York NY
Badisches Landesmuseum, Karlsruhe
Ball State University, Museum of Art, Muncie IN
Baroda Museum and Picture Gallery, Baroda
Beloit College, Wright Museum of Art, Beloit WI
Berkshire Museum, Pittsfield MA
Blanden Memorial Art Museum, Fort Dodge IA
Brown University, Haffenreffer Museum of
  Anthropology, Providence RI
Bucknell University, Edward & Marthann Samek Art
  Gallery, Lewisburg PA
The Buffalo Fine Arts Academy, Albright-Knox Art
  Gallery, Buffalo NY
Byzantine & Christian Museum, Athens, Athens
C W Post Campus of Long Island University, Hillwood
  Art Museum, Brookville NY
Carleton College, Art Gallery, Northfield MN
Chrysler Art Museum, Art, Norfolk VA
Cincinnati Art Museum, Cincinnati Art Museum,
  Cincinnati OH
The Cleveland Museum of Art, Cleveland OH
The College of Wooster, The College of Wooster Art
  Museum, Wooster OH
Corcoran Gallery of Art, Washington DC
Crocker Art Museum, Sacramento CA
Dallas Museum of Art, Dallas TX
Dartmouth College, Hood Museum of Art, Hanover NH
Department of Antiquities, Cyprus Museum, Nicosia
Detroit Institute of Arts, Detroit MI

Dundee City Council Leisure & Communities
  Department, The McManus: Dundee's Art Gallery
  & Museum, Dundee
Emory University, Michael C Carlos Museum, Atlanta
  GA
Everhart Museum, Scranton PA
Fetherston Foundation, Packwood House Museum,
  Lewisburg PA
Fine Arts Museums of San Francisco, Legion of Honor,
  San Francisco CA
Florence Museum, Florence SC
Florida State University and Central Florida
  Community College, The Appleton Museum of Art,
  Ocala FL
Forest Lawn Museum, Glendale CA
Isabella Stewart Gardner, Boston MA
Greek Ministry of Culture, Archaeological Museum of
  Thessaloniki, Thessaloniki
Hamilton College, Emerson Gallery, Clinton NY
Harvard University, Semitic Museum, Cambridge MA
Hecht Museum, Haifa
Henry County Museum & Cultural Arts Center, Clinton
  MO
Hill-Stead Museum, Farmington CT
The Hispanic Society of America, Museum & Library,
  New York NY
Indiana University, Art Museum, Bloomington IN
The Israel Museum, Jerusalem, Samuel & Saidye
  Bronfman Archaeology Wing, Jerusalem
The Israel Museum, Jerusalem, Jerusalem
James Madison University, Sawhill Gallery,
  Harrisonburg VA
Johns Hopkins University, Evergreen Museum &
  Library, Baltimore MD
Bob Jones University Museum & Gallery Inc,
  Greenville SC
Joslyn Art Museum, Omaha NE
Kenosha Public Museums, Kenosha WI
Kimbell Art Foundation, Kimbell Art Museum, Fort
  Worth TX
Kunsthistorisches Museum Vienna, Museum of Fine
  Arts, Vienna
La Salle University Art Museum, Philadelphia PA
Leeds Museums & Galleries, Leeds
Lightner Museum, Saint Augustine FL
Lincolnshire County Council, The Collection: Art &
  Archaeology in Lincolnshire, Lincoln
Louisiana Arts & Science Museum, Baton Rouge LA
Luther College, Fine Arts Collection, Decorah IA
Mabee-Gerrer Museum of Art, Shawnee OK
Magyar Nemzeti Muzeum - Hungarian National
  Museum, Budapest
Maryhill Museum of Art, Goldendale WA
Menil Foundation, Inc, The Menil Collection, Houston
  TX
The Metropolitan Museum of Art, New York NY
Middlebury College, Museum of Art, Middlebury VT
Milwaukee Art Museum, Milwaukee WI
Ministry of Cultural Affairs, Bangladesh National
  Museum, Dhaka
Ministry of Culture & Tourism, The Delphi Museum,
  10th Ephorate of Prehistoric & Classical
  Antiquities, Delphi
Minneapolis Institute of Arts, Minneapolis MN
Montreal Museum of Fine Arts, Montreal PQ
Mount Holyoke College, Art Museum, South Hadley
  MA
Musee des Beaux-Arts/Palais des Archeveques,
  Museum of Fine Arts, Tours
Musee et Chateau de Chantilly (MUSEE CONDE),
  Chantilly
Musee Royal Et Domaine De Mariemont, Morlanwelz
Musees Royaux d'Art et d'Histoire, Royal Museums of
  Art and History, Brussels
Musei Capitolini, Rome
Musei Civici di Padova - Cappella Degli Scrovengni,
  Musei Civici Agli Eremitani (Civic Museum) -
  Scrovegni Chapel, Padua
Museo Cerralbo, Madrid
The Museum, Greenwood SC
Museum fur Kunst und Gewerbe Hamburg, Hamburg
The Museum of Arts & Sciences Inc, Daytona Beach
  FL
Museum of Cycladic Art, Athens
Museum of Fine Arts, Boston MA
Museum of Fine Arts, Saint Petersburg, Florida, Inc,
  Saint Petersburg FL
Museum of Vancouver, Vancouver BC
Museum zu Allerheiligen, Schaffhausen
Muzeul de Istorie Nationala Si Arheologie Constanta,
  National History & Archaeology Museum,
  Constanta

Muzeul National Brukenthal, Brukenthal Palace &
  European Art Gallery, Sibiu
Muzeum Narodowe, National Museum in Poznan,
  Poznan
National Archaeological Museum, Athens
National Museum of Fine Arts of Moldova, Chisinau
The Nelson-Atkins Museum of Art, Kansas City MO
New Brunswick Museum, Saint John NB
Norwich Free Academy, Slater Memorial Museum,
  Norwich CT
Okanagan Heritage Museum, Kelowna BC
Portland Art Museum, Portland OR
Princeton University, Princeton University Art Museum,
  Princeton NJ
Putnam Museum of History and Natural Science,
  Davenport IA
Pyramid Hill Sculpture Park & Museum, Hamilton OH
Queen's University, Agnes Etherington Art Centre,
  Kingston ON
Queens College, City University of New York,
  Godwin-Ternbach Museum, Flushing NY
Reading Public Museum, Reading PA
Rutgers, The State University of New Jersey, Zimmerli
  Art Museum, Rutgers University, New Brunswick
  NJ
Saint Bonaventure University, Regina A Quick Center
  for the Arts, Saint Bonaventure NY
St Mary's College of Maryland, The Dwight Frederick
  Boyden Gallery, St Mary's City MD
Saint Peter's College, Art Gallery, Jersey City NJ
San Antonio Museum of Art, San Antonio TX
Santa Barbara Museum of Art, Santa Barbara CA
Scripps College, Ruth Chandler Williamson Gallery,
  Claremont CA
Seattle Art Museum, Downtown, Seattle WA
Soprintendenza per I beni storici artistici ed
  etnoantropologici per le province di Mantova
  Brescia e Cremona, Museo di Palazzo Ducale,
  Mantua
The Speed Art Museum, Louisville KY
Spertus Institute of Jewish Studies, Chicago IL
Stanford University, Cantor Arts Center at Stanford
  University, Stanford CA
Staten Island Museum, Staten Island NY
Sweet Briar College, Art Collection & Galleries, Sweet
  Briar VA
Szepmuveszeti Muzeum, Museum of Fine Arts
  Budapest, Budapest
Tampa Museum of Art, Tampa FL
Toledo Museum of Art, Toledo OH
Tufts University, Tufts University Art Gallery, Medford
  MA
University of British Columbia, Museum of
  Anthropology, Vancouver BC
University of Chicago, Smart Museum of Art, Chicago
  IL
University of Cincinnati, DAAP Galleries-College of
  Design Architecture, Art & Planning, Cincinnati OH
University of Colorado, CU Art Museum, Boulder CO
University of Delaware, University Museums, Newark
  DE
University of Illinois at Urbana-Champaign, Krannert
  Art Museum and Kinkead Pavilion, Champaign IL
University of Illinois at Urbana-Champaign, Spurlock
  Museum, Champaign IL
University of Manitoba, Faculty of Architecture
  Exhibition Centre, Winnipeg MB
University of Miami, Lowe Art Museum, Coral Gables
  FL
University of Michigan, Kelsey Museum of
  Archaeology, Ann Arbor MI
University of Missouri, Museum of Art & Archaeology,
  Columbia MO
University of North Carolina at Chapel Hill, Ackland
  Art Museum, Chapel Hill NC
University of Pennsylvania, Museum of Archaeology &
  Anthropology, Philadelphia PA
University of Richmond, University Museums,
  Richmond VA
University of Texas at Austin, Blanton Museum of Art,
  Austin TX
University of Toronto, University of Toronto Art
  Centre, Toronto ON
University of Utah, Utah Museum of Fine Arts, Salt
  Lake City UT
University of Vermont, Robert Hull Fleming Museum,
  Burlington VT
University of Virginia, The Fralin Museum of Art at
  the University of Virginia, Charlottesville VA
University of Wisconsin-Madison, Chazen Museum of
  Art, Madison WI

Vassar College, The Frances Lehman Loeb Art Center, Poughkeepsie NY
Virginia Museum of Fine Arts, Richmond VA
Vorres Museum of Contemporary Greek Art and Folk Art, Attica
Washington University, Mildred Lane Kemper Art Museum, Saint Louis MO
Wellesley College, Davis Museum & Cultural Center, Wellesley MA
Wheaton College, Beard and Weil Galleries, Norton MA
World Erotic Art Museum, Miami Beach FL
Yale University, Yale University Art Gallery, New Haven CT

ANTIQUITIES-ORIENTAL

Academy of the New Church, Glencairn Museum, Bryn Athyn PA
Arnot Art Museum, Elmira NY
Art & Culture Center of Hollywood, Art Gallery/Multidisciplinary Cultural Center, Hollywood FL
The Art Museum at the University of Kentucky, Lexington KY
Art Without Walls Inc, New York NY
Asian Art Museum of San Francisco, Chong-Moon Lee Ctr for Asian Art and Culture, San Francisco CA
Badisches Landesmuseum, Karlsruhe
Ball State University, Museum of Art, Muncie IN
Barnes Foundation, Merion PA
Baroda Museum and Picture Gallery, Baroda
Bass Museum of Art, Miami Beach FL
Beloit College, Wright Museum of Art, Beloit WI
Berman Museum, Anniston AL
Bucknell University, Edward & Marthann Samek Art Gallery, Lewisburg PA
The Buffalo Fine Arts Academy, Albright-Knox Art Gallery, Buffalo NY
Billie Trimble Chandler, Texas State Museum of Asian Cultures, Corpus Christi TX
Chhatrapati Shivaji Maharaj Vastu Sangrahalaya, Mumbai
Cincinnati Art Museum, Cincinnati Art Museum, Cincinnati OH
The College of Wooster, The College of Wooster Art Museum, Wooster OH
Dallas Museum of Art, Dallas TX
Denver Art Museum, Denver CO
Department of Antiquities, Cyprus Museum, Nicosia
Department of Museums Malaysia, National Museum, Kuala Lumpur
Detroit Institute of Arts, Detroit MI
Erie Art Museum, Erie PA
Fetherston Foundation, Packwood House Museum, Lewisburg PA
Florence Museum, Florence SC
Freer Gallery of Art & Arthur M Sackler Gallery, Arthur M Sackler Gallery, Washington DC
Hecht Museum, Haifa
Henry County Museum & Cultural Arts Center, Clinton MO
Hermitage Foundation Museum, Norfolk VA
Hofstra University, Hofstra University Museum, Hempstead NY
Hong Kong University, University Museum and Art Gallery, Pokfulam
Independent Administrative Institution National Institutes for Cultural Heritage, Tokyo National Museum, Tokyo
Indiana University, Art Museum, Bloomington IN
The Israel Museum, Jerusalem, Billy Rose Art Garden, Jerusalem
The Israel Museum, Jerusalem, Samuel & Saidye Bronfman Archaeology Wing, Jerusalem
The Israel Museum, Jerusalem, Jerusalem
Joslyn Art Museum, Omaha NE
Kelly-Griggs House Museum, Red Bluff CA
Kunsthistorisches Museum Vienna, Museum of Fine Arts, Vienna
Leeds Museums & Galleries, Leeds
Lehigh University Art Galleries, Museum Operation, Bethlehem PA
Lightner Museum, Saint Augustine FL
Mabee-Gerrer Museum of Art, Shawnee OK
Madison Museum of Fine Art, Madison GA
Magyar Nemzeti Muzeum - Hungarian National Museum, Budapest
McPherson Museum and Arts Foundation, McPherson KS
Menil Foundation, Inc, The Menil Collection, Houston TX

Middlebury College, Museum of Art, Middlebury VT
Ministry of Cultural Affairs, Bangladesh National Museum, Dhaka
The Mint Museum, Charlotte NC
Montreal Museum of Fine Arts, Montreal PQ
Moravska Galerie v Brne, Moravian Gallery in Brno, Brno
Musee Guimet, Paris
Musees Royaux d'Art et d'Histoire, Royal Museums of Art and History, Brussels
The Museum, Greenwood SC
Museum fur Kunst und Gewerbe Hamburg, Hamburg
The Museum of Arts & Sciences Inc, Daytona Beach FL
Museum of Fine Arts, Saint Petersburg, Florida, Inc, Saint Petersburg FL
Museum of Vancouver, Vancouver BC
Muzeul de Istorie Nationala Si Arheologie Constanta, National History & Archaeology Museum, Constanta
New World Art Center, T F Chen Cultural Center, New York NY
Norwich Free Academy, Slater Memorial Museum, Norwich CT
Ohara Museum of Art, Kurashiki
The Old Jail Art Center, Albany TX
Portland Art Museum, Portland OR
Princeton University, Princeton University Art Museum, Princeton NJ
Putnam Museum of History and Natural Science, Davenport IA
Queens College, City University of New York, Godwin-Ternbach Museum, Flushing NY
Reading Public Museum, Reading PA
Jack Richard Gallery, Almond Tea Museum & Jane Williams Galleries, Divisions of Studios of Jack Richard, Cuyahoga Falls OH
Rosicrucian Egyptian Museum & Planetarium, Rosicrucian Order, A.M.O.R.C., San Jose CA
Royal Arts Foundation, Belcourt Castle, Newport RI
Saginaw Art Museum, Saginaw MI
Saint Peter's College, Art Gallery, Jersey City NJ
San Antonio Museum of Art, San Antonio TX
Shirley Plantation Foundation, Charles City VA
Spertus Institute of Jewish Studies, Chicago IL
Stanford University, Cantor Arts Center at Stanford University, Stanford CA
The State Museum of Fine Arts of Tatarstan Republic, Kazan
The State Museum of Oriental Art, Moscow
Staten Island Museum, Staten Island NY
The Tokugawa Reimeikai Foundation, The Tokugawa Art Museum, Nagoya
Toledo Museum of Art, Toledo OH
Towson University, Asian Arts & Culture Center, Towson MD
Turk ve Islam Eserleri Muzesi, Museum of Turkish and Islamic Art, Istanbul
University of British Columbia, Museum of Anthropology, Vancouver BC
University of Illinois at Urbana-Champaign, Krannert Art Museum and Kinkead Pavilion, Champaign IL
University of Missouri, Museum of Art & Archaeology, Columbia MO
University of North Carolina at Chapel Hill, Ackland Art Museum, Chapel Hill NC
University of Pennsylvania, Museum of Archaeology & Anthropology, Philadelphia PA
University of Pittsburgh, University Art Gallery, Pittsburgh PA
University of Richmond, University Museums, Richmond VA
University of Toronto, University of Toronto Art Centre, Toronto ON
University of Virginia, The Fralin Museum of Art at the University of Virginia, Charlottesville VA
University of Wisconsin-Madison, Chazen Museum of Art, Madison WI
Vizcaya Museum & Gardens, Miami FL
Woodmere Art Museum Inc, Philadelphia PA
Worcester Art Museum, Worcester MA
World Erotic Art Museum, Miami Beach FL

ANTIQUITIES-PERSIAN

Art & Culture Center of Hollywood, Art Gallery/Multidisciplinary Cultural Center, Hollywood FL
The Art Museum at the University of Kentucky, Lexington KY
Asian Art Museum of San Francisco, Chong-Moon Lee Ctr for Asian Art and Culture, San Francisco CA

Baroda Museum and Picture Gallery, Baroda
Bucknell University, Edward & Marthann Samek Art Gallery, Lewisburg PA
The Buffalo Fine Arts Academy, Albright-Knox Art Gallery, Buffalo NY
C W Post Campus of Long Island University, Hillwood Art Museum, Brookville NY
Cincinnati Art Museum, Cincinnati Art Museum, Cincinnati OH
Dallas Museum of Art, Dallas TX
Detroit Institute of Arts, Detroit MI
Detroit Zoological Institute, Wildlife Interpretive Gallery, Royal Oak MI
Fetherston Foundation, Packwood House Museum, Lewisburg PA
Florence Museum, Florence SC
Florida State University and Central Florida Community College, The Appleton Museum of Art, Ocala FL
Edsel & Eleanor Ford, Grosse Pointe Shores MI
Freer Gallery of Art & Arthur M Sackler Gallery, Arthur M Sackler Gallery, Washington DC
Harvard University, Semitic Museum, Cambridge MA
Hecht Museum, Haifa
Henry County Museum & Cultural Arts Center, Clinton MO
Hermitage Foundation Museum, Norfolk VA
Hofstra University, Hofstra University Museum, Hempstead NY
Huntington Museum of Art, Huntington WV
Indiana University, Art Museum, Bloomington IN
The Israel Museum, Jerusalem, Billy Rose Art Garden, Jerusalem
The Israel Museum, Jerusalem, Samuel & Saidye Bronfman Archaeology Wing, Jerusalem
The Israel Museum, Jerusalem, Jerusalem
Jacksonville University, Alexander Brest Museum & Gallery, Jacksonville FL
Johns Hopkins University, Evergreen Museum & Library, Baltimore MD
Bob Jones University Museum & Gallery Inc, Greenville SC
Kunsthistorisches Museum Vienna, Museum of Fine Arts, Vienna
Lahore Museum, Lahore
Mabee-Gerrer Museum of Art, Shawnee OK
Menil Foundation, Inc, The Menil Collection, Houston TX
The Metropolitan Museum of Art, New York NY
Ministry of Cultural Affairs, Bangladesh National Museum, Dhaka
The Mint Museum, Charlotte NC
Montreal Museum of Fine Arts, Montreal PQ
Musees Royaux d'Art et d'Histoire, Royal Museums of Art and History, Brussels
Museum fur Kunst und Gewerbe Hamburg, Hamburg
The Museum of Arts & Sciences Inc, Daytona Beach FL
Museum of Fine Arts, Saint Petersburg, Florida, Inc, Saint Petersburg FL
Museum zu Allerheiligen, Schaffhausen
National Museum of Fine Arts of Moldova, Chisinau
Norwich Free Academy, Slater Memorial Museum, Norwich CT
Ohara Museum of Art, Kurashiki
Princeton University, Princeton University Art Museum, Princeton NJ
Putnam Museum of History and Natural Science, Davenport IA
Reading Public Museum, Reading PA
Royal Arts Foundation, Belcourt Castle, Newport RI
Saint Peter's College, Art Gallery, Jersey City NJ
The Speed Art Museum, Louisville KY
Stanford University, Cantor Arts Center at Stanford University, Stanford CA
The State Museum of Oriental Art, Moscow
University of Chicago, Oriental Institute, Chicago IL
University of Missouri, Museum of Art & Archaeology, Columbia MO
Woodmere Art Museum Inc, Philadelphia PA
World Erotic Art Museum, Miami Beach FL

ANTIQUITIES-ROMAN

Academy of the New Church, Glencairn Museum, Bryn Athyn PA
Albany Museum of Art, Albany GA
Archaeological Museum of Olympia, Olympia
Art & Culture Center of Hollywood, Art Gallery/Multidisciplinary Cultural Center, Hollywood FL

The Art Museum at the University of Kentucky, Lexington KY
Art Without Walls Inc, New York NY
Badisches Landesmuseum, Karlsruhe
Ball State University, Museum of Art, Muncie IN
Baroda Museum and Picture Gallery, Baroda
Beloit College, Wright Museum of Art, Beloit WI
Blanden Memorial Art Museum, Fort Dodge IA
Bucknell University, Edward & Marthann Samek Art Gallery, Lewisburg PA
The Buffalo Fine Arts Academy, Albright-Knox Art Gallery, Buffalo NY
C W Post Campus of Long Island University, Hillwood Art Museum, Brookville NY
Carleton College, Art Gallery, Northfield MN
Cedar Rapids Museum of Art, Cedar Rapids IA
Chrysler Museum of Art, Norfolk VA
Cincinnati Art Museum, Cincinnati Art Museum, Cincinnati OH
The Cleveland Museum of Art, Cleveland OH
Crocker Art Museum, Sacramento CA
Dallas Museum of Art, Dallas TX
Department of Antiquities, Cyprus Museum, Nicosia
Detroit Institute of Arts, Detroit MI
Dickinson College, The Trout Gallery, Carlisle PA
Doncaster Museum and Art Gallery, Doncaster
Dundee City Council Leisure & Communities Department, The McManus: Dundee's Art Gallery & Museum, Dundee
Emory University, Michael C Carlos Museum, Atlanta GA
Everhart Museum, Scranton PA
Fetherston Foundation, Packwood House Museum, Lewisburg PA
Fine Arts Museums of San Francisco, Legion of Honor, San Francisco CA
Florence Museum, Florence SC
Florida State University and Central Florida Community College, The Appleton Museum of Art, Ocala FL
Forest Lawn Museum, Glendale CA
Freer Gallery of Art & Arthur M Sackler Gallery, Arthur M Sackler Gallery, Washington DC
Galleria Doria Pamphilj, Rome
Isabella Stewart Gardner, Boston MA
Greek Ministry of Culture, Archaeological Museum of Thessaloniki, Thessaloniki
Harvard University, Semitic Museum, Cambridge MA
Hebrew Union College - Jewish Institute of Religion, Skirball Museum Cincinnati, Cincinnati OH
Hecht Museum, Haifa
Hermitage Foundation Museum, Norfolk VA
Indiana University, Art Museum, Bloomington IN
Iredell Museums, Statesville NC
The Israel Museum, Jerusalem, Billy Rose Art Garden, Jerusalem
The Israel Museum, Jerusalem, Samuel & Saidye Bronfman Archaeology Wing, Jerusalem
The Israel Museum, Jerusalem, Jerusalem
James Madison University, Sawhill Gallery, Harrisonburg VA
Janus Pannonius Muzeum, Pecs
Johns Hopkins University, Archaeological Collection, Baltimore MD
Johns Hopkins University, Evergreen Museum & Library, Baltimore MD
Bob Jones University Museum & Gallery Inc, Greenville SC
Joslyn Art Museum, Omaha NE
Kenosha Public Museums, Kenosha WI
Kimbell Art Foundation, Kimbell Art Museum, Fort Worth TX
Kunsthistorisches Museum Vienna, Museum of Fine Arts, Vienna
Le Grand Curtius, Musée d'Ansembourg, Liege
Lehigh University Art Galleries, Museum Operation, Bethlehem PA
Lightner Museum, Saint Augustine FL
Lincolnshire County Council, The Collection: Art & Archaeology in Lincolnshire, Lincoln
Louisiana Arts & Science Museum, Baton Rouge LA
Luther College, Fine Arts Collection, Decorah IA
Mabee-Gerrer Museum of Art, Shawnee OK
Magyar Nemzeti Muzeum - Hungarian National Museum, Budapest
Massillon Museum, Massillon OH
McMaster University, McMaster Museum of Art, Hamilton ON
Menil Foundation, Inc, The Menil Collection, Houston TX
The Metropolitan Museum of Art, New York NY
Middlebury College, Museum of Art, Middlebury VT

Milwaukee Art Museum, Milwaukee WI
Ministry of Cultural Affairs, Bangladesh National Museum, Dhaka
Ministry of Culture & Tourism, The Delphi Museum, 10th Ephorate of Prehistoric & Classical Antiquities, Delphi
Minneapolis Institute of Arts, Minneapolis MN
The Mint Museum, Charlotte NC
Mobile Museum of Art, Mobile AL
Montreal Museum of Fine Arts, Montreal PQ
Mount Holyoke College, Art Museum, South Hadley MA
Musee des Beaux-Arts d'Orleans, Historical & Archaeological Museum of Orleans, Orleans
Musee des Beaux-Arts/Palais des Archeveques, Museum of Fine Arts, Tours
Musee et Chateau de Chantilly (MUSEE CONDE), Chantilly
Musee National d'Histoire et d'Art Luxembourg, Luxembourg City
Musee Royal Et Domaine De Mariemont, Morlanwelz
Museen der Stadt Koln, Romisch-Germanisches Museum, Cologne
Musees Royaux d'Art et d'Histoire, Royal Museums of Art and History, Brussels
Musei Civici di Padova - Cappella Degli Scrovengni, Musei Civici Agli Eremitani (Civic Museum) - Scrovegni Chapel, Padua
Museo Cerralbo, Madrid
Museo Civico Giovanni Fattori, Livorno
Museu de Evora, Evora
The Museum, Greenwood SC
Museum fur Kunst und Gewerbe Hamburg, Hamburg
Museum of Cycladic Art, Athens
Museum of Fine Arts, Boston MA
Museum of Fine Arts, Saint Petersburg, Florida, Inc, Saint Petersburg FL
Museum of Vancouver, Vancouver BC
Museum zu Allerheiligen, Schaffhausen
Muzeul de Istorie Nationala Si Arheologie Constanta, National History & Archaeology Museum, Constanta
Muzeul National Brukenthal, Brukenthal Palace & European Art Gallery, Sibiu
National Archaeological Museum, Athens
National Museum of Fine Arts of Moldova, Chisinau
National Museums Scotland, National Museum of Scotland, Edinburgh
The Nelson-Atkins Museum of Art, Kansas City MO
New Brunswick Museum, Saint John NB
Norwich Free Academy, Slater Memorial Museum, Norwich CT
Okanagan Heritage Museum, Kelowna BC
Panhandle-Plains Historical Museum, Canyon TX
Putnam Museum of History and Natural Science, Davenport IA
Pyramid Hill Sculpture Park & Museum, Hamilton OH
Queen's University, Agnes Etherington Art Centre, Kingston ON
Queens College, City University of New York, Godwin-Ternbach Museum, Flushing NY
Reading Public Museum, Reading PA
Rollins College, George D & Harriet W Cornell Fine Arts Museum, Winter Park FL
Rutgers, The State University of New Jersey, Zimmerli Art Museum, Rutgers University, New Brunswick NJ
St Mary's College of Maryland, The Dwight Frederick Boyden Gallery, St Mary's City MD
Saint Peter's College, Art Gallery, Jersey City NJ
Santa Barbara Museum of Art, Santa Barbara CA
Scripps College, Ruth Chandler Williamson Gallery, Claremont CA
Seattle Art Museum, Downtown, Seattle WA
Slovenska Narodna Galeria, Slovak National Gallery, Bratislava
The Society of the Cincinnati at Anderson House, Washington DC
Soprintendenza per I beni storici artistici ed etnoantropologici per le province di Mantova Brescia e Cremona, Museo di Palazzo Ducale, Mantua
The Speed Art Museum, Louisville KY
Spertus Institute of Jewish Studies, Chicago IL
Stanford University, Cantor Arts Center at Stanford University, Stanford CA
Staten Island Museum, Staten Island NY
Sweet Briar College, Art Collection & Galleries, Sweet Briar VA
Szepmuveszeti Muzeum, Museum of Fine Arts Budapest, Budapest
Tampa Museum of Art, Tampa FL

Toledo Museum of Art, Toledo OH
Tufts University, Tufts University Art Gallery, Medford MA
University of Chicago, Smart Museum of Art, Chicago IL
University of Colorado, CU Art Museum, Boulder CO
University of Delaware, University Museums, Newark DE
University of Illinois at Urbana-Champaign, Krannert Art Museum and Kinkead Pavilion, Champaign IL
University of Illinois at Urbana-Champaign, Spurlock Museum, Champaign IL
University of Manitoba, Faculty of Architecture Exhibition Centre, Winnipeg MB
University of Miami, Lowe Art Museum, Coral Gables FL
University of Michigan, Kelsey Museum of Archaeology, Ann Arbor MI
University of Missouri, Museum of Art & Archaeology, Columbia MO
University of Pennsylvania, Museum of Archaeology & Anthropology, Philadelphia PA
University of Pittsburgh, University Art Gallery, Pittsburgh PA
University of Toronto, University of Toronto Art Centre, Toronto ON
University of Vermont, Robert Hull Fleming Museum, Burlington VT
University of Virginia, The Fralin Museum of Art at the University of Virginia, Charlottesville VA
University of Wisconsin-Madison, Chazen Museum of Art, Madison WI
Vassar College, The Frances Lehman Loeb Art Center, Poughkeepsie NY
Village of Potsdam, Potsdam Public Museum, Potsdam NY
Vizcaya Museum & Gardens, Miami FL
Vorarlberg Museum, Bregenz
Wellesley College, Davis Museum & Cultural Center, Wellesley MA
Wheaton College, Beard and Weil Galleries, Norton MA
Worcester Art Museum, Worcester MA
World Erotic Art Museum, Miami Beach FL
Yale University, Yale University Art Gallery, New Haven CT

ARCHAEOLOGY

Academy of the New Church, Glencairn Museum, Bryn Athyn PA
African American Museum in Philadelphia, Philadelphia PA
African Art Museum of Maryland, Columbia MD
Al Ain National Museum, Al Ain
Alabama Department of Archives & History, Museum of Alabama, Montgomery AL
Alaska Heritage Museum at Wells Fargo, Anchorage AK
Alaska Museum of Natural History, Anchorage AK
American Architectural Foundation, Museum, Washington DC
Anchorage Museum at Rasmuson Center, Anchorage AK
Archaeological Museum of Olympia, Olympia
Archaeological Museum of the American University of Beirut, Beirut
Archaeological Society of Ohio, Indian Museum of Lake County, Ohio, Willoughby OH
Arizona Museum For Youth, Mesa AZ
Arizona State University, Deer Valley Rock Art Center, Phoenix AZ
Art Without Walls Inc, New York NY
ArtSpace/Lima, Lima OH
Aurora University, Schingoethe Center for Native American Cultures & The Schingoethe Art Gallery, Aurora IL
Autry National Center, Southwest Museum of the American Indian, Mt. Washington Campus, Los Angeles CA
Badisches Landesmuseum, Karlsruhe
Balzekas Museum of Lithuanian Culture, Chicago IL
Banco de la Republica Museo del Oro, Museo del Oro, Bogota
Baroda Museum and Picture Gallery, Baroda
Bay County Historical Society, Historical Museum of Bay County, Bay City MI
Beloit College, Wright Museum of Art, Beloit WI
Berea College, Ulmann Doris Galleries, Berea KY
Berman Museum, Anniston AL
Besser Museum for Northeast Michigan, Alpena MI

Beverly Historical Society, Cabot, Hale & Balch House Museums, Beverly MA
Bronx Community College (CUNY), Hall of Fame for Great Americans, Bronx NY
Brown University, Haffenreffer Museum of Anthropology, Providence RI
Bruce Museum, Inc, Greenwich CT
Byzantine & Christian Museum, Athens, Athens
California State University, East Bay, C E Smith Museum of Anthropology, Hayward CA
Cambridge Museum, Cambridge NE
Canadian Museum of Civilization, Gatineau PQ
Carlsbad Museum & Art Center, Carlsbad NM
Carson County Square House Museum, Panhandle TX
Carteret County Historical Society, The History Place, Morehead City NC
Chelan County Public Utility District, Rocky Reach Dam, Wenatchee WA
Chhatrapati Shivaji Maharaj Vastu Sangrahalaya, Mumbai
City of El Paso, El Paso Museum of Archaeology, El Paso TX
City of Nome Alaska, Carrie M McLain Memorial Museum, Nome AK
The City of Petersburg Museums, Petersburg VA
City of Providence Parks Department, Roger Williams Park Museum of Natural History, Providence RI
Clark County Historical Society, Heritage Center of Clark County, Springfield OH
Clark County Historical Society, Pioneer - Krier Museum, Ashland KS
Colorado Historical Society, Colorado History Museum, Denver CO
Columbus Museum, Columbus GA
Concord Museum, Concord MA
County of Henrico, Meadow Farm Museum, Glen Allen VA
Crook County Museum & Art Gallery, Sundance WY
Crow Wing County Historical Society, Brainerd MN
Culberson County Historical Museum, Van Horn TX
Dallas Museum of Art, Dallas TX
Delaware Archaeology Museum, Dover DE
Delaware Division of Historical & Cultural Affairs, Dover DE
Denison University, Art Gallery, Granville OH
Department of Antiquities, Cyprus Museum, Nicosia
Department of Economic & Community Development, Eric Sloane Museum, Kent CT
Department of Museums Malaysia, National Museum, Kuala Lumpur
Detroit Institute of Arts, Detroit MI
Doncaster Museum and Art Gallery, Doncaster
Dundee City Council Leisure & Communities Department, The McManus: Dundee's Art Gallery & Museum, Dundee
Dundurn Castle, Hamilton ON
East Tennessee State University, The Reece Museum, Johnson City TN
Edgecombe County Cultural Arts Council, Inc, Blount-Bridgers House, Hobson Pittman Memorial Gallery, Tarboro NC
Emory University, Michael C Carlos Museum, Atlanta GA
Everhart Museum, Scranton PA
Essex Historical Society and Shipbuilding Museum, Essex MA
Fairbanks Museum & Planetarium, Saint Johnsbury VT
Fairfield University, Thomas J Walsh Art Gallery, Fairfield CT
Farmington Village Green & Library Association, Stanley-Whitman House, Farmington CT
Ferenczy Muzeum, Szentendre
Fetherston Foundation, Packwood House Museum, Lewisburg PA
Fishkill Historical Society, Van Wyck Homestead Museum, Fishkill NY
Florence Museum, Florence SC
Florida State University, John & Mable Ringling Museum of Art, Sarasota FL
Forges du Saint-Maurice National Historic Site, Trois Rivieres PQ
Fort Morgan Heritage Foundation, Fort Morgan CO
Fort Ticonderoga Association, Ticonderoga NY
Freer Gallery of Art & Arthur M Sackler Gallery, Arthur M Sackler Gallery, Washington DC
Gem County Historical Society and Museum, Gem County Historical Village Museum, Emmett ID
Germanisches Nationalmuseum, Nuremberg
Gocseji Muzeum, Zalaegerszeg
Grand Rapids Public Museum, Public Museum of Grand Rapids, Grand Rapids MI

Greek Ministry of Culture, Archaeological Museum of Thessaloniki, Thessaloniki
Greenland National Museum & Archives, Nuuk
Hancock Shaker Village, Inc, Pittsfield MA
Hartwick College, The Yager Museum, Oneonta NY
Harvard University, Semitic Museum, Cambridge MA
Heard Museum, Phoenix AZ
Heart of West Texas Museum, Colorado City TX
Hebrew Union College, Skirball Cultural Center, Los Angeles CA
Hebrew Union College - Jewish Institute of Religion, Skirball Museum Cincinnati, Cincinnati OH
Hebrew Union College Museum, Jewish Institute of Religion Museum, New York NY
Hecht Museum, Haifa
Henry County Museum & Cultural Arts Center, Clinton MO
Heras Institute of Indian History and Culture, Heras Institute Museum, Mumbai
Heritage Museum Association, Inc, The Heritage Museum of Northwest Florida, Valparaiso FL
Herrett Center for Arts & Sciences, Jean B King Art Gallery, Twin Falls ID
Edna Hibel, Hibel Museum of Art, Jupiter FL
Higgins Armory Museum, Worcester MA
High Desert Museum, Bend OR
The Hispanic Society of America, Museum & Library, New York NY
Historic Arkansas Museum, Little Rock AR
Historic Newton, Newton MA
Historical Museum at Fort Missoula, Missoula MT
Historical Society of Martin County, Elliott Museum, Stuart FL
Historical Society of Palm Beach County, The Richard and Pat Johnson Palm Beach County History Museum, West Palm Beach FL
Historical Society of Rockland County, New City NY
Historisches und Volkerkundemuseum, Historical Museum, St Gallen
The History Center in Tompkins County, Ithaca NY
History Museum of Mobile, Mobile AL
Huguenot Historical Society of New Paltz Galleries, New Paltz NY
Huronia Museum, Gallery of Historic Huronia, Midland ON
Idaho Historical Museum, Boise ID
Illinois Historic Preservation Agency, Bishop Hill State Historic Site, Bishop Hill IL
Illinois State Museum, ISM Lockport Gallery, Chicago Gallery & Southern Illinois Art Gallery, Springfield IL
Independence Historical Museum & Art Center, Independence KS
Independence National Historical Park, Philadelphia PA
Independence Seaport Museum, Philadelphia PA
Independent Administrative Institution National Institutes for Cultural Heritage, Tokyo National Museum, Tokyo
Indian Pueblo Cultural Center, Albuquerque NM
Indiana State Museum, Indianapolis IN
Institute of Puerto Rican Culture, Museo Fuerte Conde de Mirasol, Vieques PR
Institute of Puerto Rican Culture, Museo y Parque Historico Ruinas de Caparra, San Juan PR
Iroquois County Historical Society Museum, Old Courthouse Museum, Watseka IL
Iroquois Indian Museum, Howes Cave NY
The Israel Museum, Jerusalem, Billy Rose Art Garden, Jerusalem
The Israel Museum, Jerusalem, Samuel & Saidye Bronfman Archaeology Wing, Jerusalem
The Israel Museum, Jerusalem, Jerusalem
Istanbul Arkeoloji Muzeleri, The Library of Archaeological Museums of Istanbul, Istanbul
Jamestown-Yorktown Foundation, Jamestown Settlement, Williamsburg VA
Thomas Jefferson, Monticello, Charlottesville VA
The Jewish Museum, New York NY
Johns Hopkins University, Homewood Museum, Baltimore MD
Bob Jones University Museum & Gallery Inc, Greenville SC
Kelly-Griggs House Museum, Red Bluff CA
Kenosha Public Museum, Kenosha WI
Klein Museum, Mobridge SD
Koshare Indian Museum, Inc, La Junta CO
Lac du Flambeau Band of Lake Superior Chippewa Indians, George W Brown Jr Ojibwe Museum & Cultural Center, Lac Du Flambeau WI
Lafayette Science Museum & Planetarium, Lafayette LA
Lahore Museum, Lahore

Lakeview Museum of Arts & Sciences, Peoria IL
Lehigh Valley Heritage Center, Allentown PA
Lincoln County Historical Association, Inc, 1811 Old Lincoln County Jail & Lincoln County Museum, Wiscasset ME
Lincolnshire County Council, Library & Heritage Services, Lincoln
Lincolnshire County Council, The Collection: Art & Archaeology in Lincolnshire, Lincoln
Livingston County Historical Society, Museum, Geneseo NY
Louisiana State Exhibit Museum, Shreveport LA
Loveland Museum/Gallery, Loveland CO
Magyar Nemzeti Muzeum - Hungarian National Museum, Budapest
Maine Historical Society, MHS Museum, Portland ME
Massillon Museum, Massillon OH
Maui Historical Society, Bailey House, Wailuku HI
Maysville, Kentucky Gateway Museum Center, Maysville KY
McLean County Historical Society, McLean County Museum of History, Bloomington IL
McPherson Museum and Arts Foundation, McPherson KS
Mezuraj Museum, Tirana
Ministry of Alberta Culture, Royal Alberta Museum, Edmonton AB
Ministry of Cultural Affairs, Bangladesh National Museum, Dhaka
Ministry of Culture & Tourism, The Delphi Museum, 10th Ephorate of Prehistoric & Classical Antiquities, Delphi
Ministry of the Arts & Multiculturalism, National Museum & Art Gallery, Port of Spain
Mission San Luis Rey de Francia, Mission San Luis Rey Museum, Oceanside CA
Mission San Miguel Museum, San Miguel CA
Mississippi River Museum at Mud-Island River Park, Memphis TN
Mohave Museum of History & Arts, Kingman AZ
Moncur Gallery, Boissevain MB
Montana State University, Museum of the Rockies, Bozeman MT
Montclair Art Museum, Montclair NJ
Montreal Museum of Fine Arts, Montreal PQ
Morris Museum, Morristown NJ
Morris Museum of Art, Augusta GA
Moto Moto Museum, Mbala
Mount Vernon Hotel Museum & Garden, New York NY
Musee Carnavalet-Histoire de Paris, Paris
Musee des Beaux-Arts d'Orleans, Historical & Archaeological Museum of Orleans, Orleans
Musee et Chateau de Chantilly (MUSEE CONDE), Chantilly
Musee Guimet, Paris
Musee National d'Histoire et d'Art Luxembourg, Luxembourg City
Musee Regional de lu Cote-Nord, Sept-Iles PQ
Musee Royal Et Domaine De Mariemont, Morlanwelz
Museen der Stadt Koln, Romisch-Germanisches Museum, Cologne
Musees Royaux d'Art et d'Histoire, Royal Museums of Art and History, Brussels
Musei Capitolini, Rome
Musei Civici di Padova - Cappella Degli Scrovengni, Musei Civici Agli Eremitani (Civic Museum) - Scrovegni Chapel, Padua
Museo Cerralbo, Madrid
Museo Civico Giovanni Fattori, Livorno
Museo de Arte de Ponce, The Luis A Ferre Foundation Inc, Ponce PR
Museo De Las Americas, Denver CO
Museo Frida Kahlo Casa Azul, Coyoacan
Museu de Evora, Evora
The Museum, Greenwood SC
Museum fur Kunst und Gewerbe Hamburg, Hamburg
Museum Het Prinsenhof, Delft
The Museum of Arts & Sciences Inc, Daytona Beach FL
Museum of Arts & Sciences, Inc, Macon GA
Museum of Contemporary Art - Taipei, Taipei
Museum of Cycladic Art, Athens
Museum of New Mexico, Laboratory of Anthropology Library, Santa Fe NM
Museum of Northern Arizona, Flagstaff AZ
Museum of Northern British Columbia, Ruth Harvey Art Gallery, Prince Rupert BC
Museum of the City of New York, Museum, New York NY
Museum of Vancouver, Vancouver BC
Museum of West Louisiana, Leesville LA

Museum of York County, Rock Hill SC

Museum zu Allerheiligen, Schaffhausen

Muzeul de Istorie Nationala Si Arheologie Constanta, National History & Archaeology Museum, Constanta

Muzeul National Brukenthal, Brukenthal Palace & European Art Gallery, Sibiu

The Namur Provincial Museum of Ancient Arts, Namur

Narodni Muzej Crne Gore, National Museum of Montenegro, Cetinje

National Archaeological Museum, Athens

National Museum of Ireland, Dublin

National Museum of Serbia, National Museum in Belgrade, Beograd

National Museum of the American Indian, George Gustav Heye Center, New York NY

National Museum of the American Indian, Smithsonian Institution, Washington DC

National Museum of the Philippines, Manila

National Museum, Monuments and Art Gallery, Gaborone

National Museums Scotland, National Museum of Scotland, Edinburgh

National Park Service, Hubbell Trading Post National Historic Site, Ganado AZ

The National Park Service, United States Department of the Interior, Statue of Liberty National Monument & The Ellis Island Immigration Museum, Washington DC

Natural History Museum of Los Angeles County, Los Angeles CA

Naval Historical Center, The Navy Museum, Washington DC

New Hampshire Antiquarian Society, Hopkinton Historical Society, Hopkinton NH

New Jersey Historical Society, Newark NJ

New Jersey State Museum, Fine Art Bureau, Trenton NJ

No Man's Land Historical Society, No Man's Land Museum, Goodwell OK

Noordbrabants Museum, Hertogenbosch

Norsk Sjøfartsmuseum, Norwegian Maritime Museum, Oslo

Northern Maine Museum of Science, Presque Isle ME

The Ohio Historical Society, Inc, Campus Martius Museum & Ohio River Museum, Marietta OH

Okanagan Heritage Museum, Kelowna BC

Oklahoma Historical Society, State Museum of History, Oklahoma City OK

Oshkosh Public Museum, Oshkosh WI

Panhandle-Plains Historical Museum, Canyon TX

Pennsylvania Historical & Museum Commission, The State Museum of Pennsylvania, Harrisburg PA

The Frank Phillips, Woolaroc Museum, Bartlesville OK

Ponca City Cultural Center & Museum, Ponca City OK

Port Huron Museum, Port Huron MI

Princeton University, Princeton University Art Museum, Princeton NJ

Putnam Museum of History and Natural Science, Davenport IA

Queensborough Community College, Art Gallery, Bayside NY

Rabindra Bhavan Art Gallery, Lalit Kala Akademi (National Academy of Art), New Delhi

Riverside Metropolitan Museum, Riverside CA

Roberson Museum & Science Center, Binghamton NY

Roberts County Museum, Miami TX

Rollins College, George D & Harriet W Cornell Fine Arts Museum, Winter Park FL

Rome Historical Society, Museum & Archives, Rome NY

The Rooms Corporation of Newfoundland & Labrador, Saint John's NF

Roswell Museum & Art Center, Roswell NM

Royal Ontario Museum, Toronto ON

C M Russell, Great Falls MT

Saco Museum, Saco ME

Safety Harbor Museum of Regional History, Safety Harbor FL

Saint Augustine Historical Society, Oldest House Museum Complex, Saint Augustine FL

Saint Joseph Museum, Saint Joseph MO

Saint Peter's College, Art Gallery, Jersey City NJ

San Bernardino County Museum, Fine Arts Institute, Redlands CA

Savitsky Karakalpakstan State Art Museum, Nukus

Scripps College, Ruth Chandler Williamson Gallery, Claremont CA

Seneca-Iroquois National Museum, Salamanca NY

Shaker Village of Pleasant Hill, Harrodsburg KY

Shirley Plantation Foundation, Charles City VA

Slater Mill, Old Slater Mill Association, Pawtucket RI

Slovenska Narodna Galeria, Slovak National Gallery, Bratislava

Sooke Region Museum & Art Gallery, Sooke BC

Soprintendenza per I beni storici artistici ed etnoantropologici per le province di Mantova Brescia e Cremona, Museo di Palazzo Ducale, Mantua

South Street Seaport Museum, New York NY

Southern Baptist Theological Seminary, Joseph A Callaway Archaeological Museum, Louisville KY

Spertus Institute of Jewish Studies, Chicago IL

The State Museum of Oriental Art, Moscow

Ste Genevieve Museum, Sainte Genevieve MO

Stone Quarry Hill Art Park, Winner Gallery, Cazenovia NY

Suomen Kansallismuseo, National Museum of Finland, Helsinki

Switzerland County Historical Society Inc, Switzerland County Historical Museum, Vevay IN

Tallahassee Museum of History & Natural Science, Tallahassee FL

The Temple-Tifereth Israel, The Temple Museum of Religious Art, Beachwood OH

Texas Tech University, Museum of Texas Tech University, Lubbock TX

Tokyo University of the Arts, The University Art Museum, Tokyo

Trust Authority, Museum of the Great Plains, Lawton OK

Tryon Palace Historic Sites & Gardens, New Bern NC

Turtle Bay Exploration Park, Redding CA

Turtle Mountain Chippewa Historical Society, Turtle Mountain Heritage Center, Belcourt ND

Tver Art Gallery, Tver

Tyne and Wear Archives & Museums, Sunderland Museum & Winter Gardens, Newcastle-upon-Tyne

United States Department of the Interior, Interior Museum, Washington DC

Universalmuseum Joanneum GmbH, Graz

University of Alaska, Museum of the North, Fairbanks AK

University of British Columbia, Museum of Anthropology, Vancouver BC

University of California, Los Angeles, Fowler Museum at UCLA, Los Angeles CA

University of Chicago, Oriental Institute, Chicago IL

University of Illinois at Urbana-Champaign, Spurlock Museum, Champaign IL

University of Manitoba, Faculty of Architecture Exhibition Centre, Winnipeg MB

University of Memphis, Art Museum, Memphis TN

University of Missouri, Museum of Art & Archaeology, Columbia MO

University of Pennsylvania, Museum of Archaeology & Anthropology, Philadelphia PA

University of Pittsburgh, University Art Gallery, Pittsburgh PA

University of Puerto Rico, Museum of Anthropology, History & Art, Rio Piedras PR

University of Tennessee, McClung Museum of Natural History & Culture, Knoxville TN

University of Victoria, The Legacy Art Gallery, Victoria BC

University of Wisconsin-Madison, Chazen Museum of Art, Madison WI

Vassar College, The Frances Lehman Loeb Art Center, Poughkeepsie NY

Vorarlberg Museum, Bregenz

Wade House Historic Site-Wisconsin Historical Society, Wesley W. Jung Carriage Museum, Greenbush WI

Wadsworth Atheneum Museum of Art, Hartford CT

Wake Forest University, Museum of Anthropology, Winston Salem NC

Wayne County Historical Society, Museum, Honesdale PA

West Florida Historic Preservation, Inc/University of West Florida, T T Wentworth, Jr Florida State Museum; Historic Pensacola Village; Pensacola Historical Society & Resource Center, Pensacola FL

Westfries Museum, Hoorn

Wethersfield Historical Society Inc, Museum, Wethersfield CT

Whalers Village Museum, Lahaina HI

Wisconsin Historical Society, Wisconsin Historical Museum, Madison WI

Woodlawn/The Pope-Leighey, Mount Vernon VA

ARCHITECTURE

Academy of the New Church, Glencairn Museum, Bryn Athyn PA

African Art Museum of Maryland, Columbia MD

Allentown Art Museum, Allentown PA

Alton Museum of History & Art, Inc, Alton IL

American Swedish Historical Foundation & Museum, American Swedish Historical Museum, Philadelphia PA

American Swedish Institute, Minneapolis MN

Arnot Art Museum, Elmira NY

Art & Culture Center of Hollywood, Art Gallery/Multidisciplinary Cultural Center, Hollywood FL

Art Gallery of Calgary, Calgary AB

Art Without Walls Inc, New York NY

Artesia Historical Museum & Art Center, Artesia NM

Arts Council of Fayetteville-Cumberland County, The Arts Center, Fayetteville NC

ArtSpace/Lima, Lima OH

Asheville Art Museum, Asheville NC

Asian Art Museum of San Francisco, Chong-Moon Lee Ctr for Asian Art and Culture, San Francisco CA

Athenaeum of Philadelphia, Philadelphia PA

Atlanta Historical Society Inc, Atlanta History Center, Atlanta GA

Atlanta International Museum of Art & Design, Museum of Design Atlanta, Atlanta GA

Ball State University, Museum of Art, Muncie IN

The Baltimore Museum of Art, Baltimore MD

Baroda Museum and Picture Gallery, Baroda

The Bartlett Museum, Amesbury MA

Belle Grove Inc., Belle Grove Plantation, Middletown VA

Beloit College, Wright Museum of Art, Beloit WI

Blanden Memorial Art Museum, Fort Dodge IA

Board of Parks & Recreation, The Parthenon, Nashville TN

Boston Public Library, Albert H Wiggin Gallery & Print Department, Boston MA

Brick Store Museum, Kennebunk ME

Bronx Community College (CUNY), Hall of Fame for Great Americans, Bronx NY

Bush-Holley Historic Site & Storehouse Gallery, Greenwich Historical Society/ Bush-Holley House, Cos Cob CT

Byzantine & Christian Museum, Athens, Athens

Cabot's Old Indian Pueblo Museum, Desert Hot Springs CA

Canadian Clay and Glass Gallery, Waterloo ON

Central United Methodist Church, Swords Into Plowshares Peace Center & Gallery, Detroit MI

Charleston Museum, Joseph Manigault House, Charleston SC

Chatham Historical Society, The Atwood House Museum, Chatham MA

Chatillon-DeMenil House Foundation, Chatillon-DeMenil House, Saint Louis MO

Chhatrapati Shivaji Maharaj Vastu Sangrahalaya, Mumbai

Chicago Architecture Foundation, Chicago IL

Chicago Athenaeum, Museum of Architecture & Design, Galena IL

Chinati Foundation, Marfa TX

Church of Jesus Christ of Latter-Day Saints, Museum of Church History & Art, Salt Lake City UT

The City of Petersburg Museums, Petersburg VA

City of San Antonio, San Antonio TX

Clemson University, Rudolph E Lee Gallery, Clemson SC

Columbia County Historical Society, Columbia County Museum and Library, Kinderhook NY

Columbia County Historical Society, Luykas Van Alen House, Kinderhook NY

Columbus Museum, Columbus GA

Cooper-Hewitt National Design Museum, Smithsonian Institution, New York NY

County of Henrico, Meadow Farm Museum, Glen Allen VA

Craigdarroch Castle Historical Museum Society, Victoria BC

Cranbrook Art Museum, Bloomfield Hills MI

Crocker Art Museum, Sacramento CA

Crow Wing County Historical Society, Brainerd MN

The Currier Museum of Art, Manchester NH

Dallas Museum of Art, Dallas TX

Danville Museum of Fine Arts & History, Danville VA

Davidson College, William H Van Every Jr & Edward M Smith Galleries, Davidson NC

Delaware Division of Historical & Cultural Affairs, Dover DE

Delaware Historical Society, Read House and Gardens, Wilmington DE

DeLeon White Gallery, Toronto ON

Delta Blues Museum, Clarksdale MS

Denver Art Museum, Denver CO

Piatt Castles, West Liberty OH
Pioneer Town, Pioneer Museum of Western Art,
    Wimberley TX
Plumas County Museum, Quincy CA
Pope County Historical Society, Pope County Museum,
    Glenwood MN
Porter-Phelps-Huntington Foundation, Inc, Historic
    House Museum, Hadley MA
Portsmouth Athenaeum, Joseph Copley Research
    Library, Portsmouth NH
PS1 Contemporary Art Center, Long Island City NY
Pyramid Hill Sculpture Park & Museum, Hamilton OH
Queensborough Community College, Art Gallery,
    Bayside NY
Rabindra Bhavan Art Gallery, Lalit Kala Akademi
    (National Academy of Art), New Delhi
Reynolda House Museum of American Art,
    Winston-Salem NC
Riley County Historical Society & Museum, Riley
    County Historical Museum, Manhattan KS
Riverside Metropolitan Museum, Riverside CA
Ross Memorial Museum, Saint Andrews NB
Royal Arts Foundation, Belcourt Castle, Newport RI
Royal Ontario Museum, Toronto ON
Ryerss Victorian Museum & Library, Philadelphia PA
Saco Museum, Saco ME
Saginaw Art Museum, Saginaw MI
Saint Augustine Historical Society, Oldest House
    Museum Complex, Saint Augustine FL
Saint Johnsbury Athenaeum, Saint Johnsbury VT
Saint Peter's College, Art Gallery, Jersey City NJ
San Francisco Museum of Modern Art, San Francisco
    CA
Santa Monica Museum of Art, Santa Monica CA
Santarella Museum & Gardens, Tyringham MA
Savitsky Karakalpakstan State Art Museum, Nukus
Scottsdale Cultural Council, Scottsdale Museum of
    Contemporary Art, Scottsdale AZ
Seneca Falls Historical Society Museum, Seneca Falls
    NY
Shaker Village of Pleasant Hill, Harrodsburg KY
Shirley Plantation Foundation, Charles City VA
Slovenska Narodna Galeria, Slovak National Gallery,
    Bratislava
Soprintendenza per I beni storici artistici ed
    etnoantropologici per le province di Mantova
    Brescia e Cremona, Museo di Palazzo Ducale,
    Mantua
South Street Seaport Museum, New York NY
The Speed Art Museum, Louisville KY
Spertus Institute of Jewish Studies, Chicago IL
Stanley Museum, Inc, Kingfield ME
State University of New York College at Buffalo,
    Buffalo NY
State University of New York College at Fredonia,
    Cathy and Jesse Marion Art Gallery, Fredonia NY
Stone Quarry Hill Art Park, Winner Gallery, Cazenovia
    NY
Stratford Historical Society, Catharine B Mitchell
    Museum, Stratford CT
Sturdivant Museum Association, Sturdivant Museum,
    Selma AL
The Summit County Historical Society of Akron, OH,
    Akron OH
Suomen rakennustaiteen museo, Museum of Finnish
    Architecture, Helsinki
Swiss Architecture Museum, Basel
Switzerland County Historical Society Inc, Switzerland
    County Historical Museum, Vevay IN
Tacoma Art Museum, Tacoma WA
Taft Museum of Art, Cincinnati OH
Tallahassee Museum of History & Natural Science,
    Tallahassee FL
Taos, Ernest Blumenschein Home & Studio, Taos NM
Tokyo University of the Arts, The University Art
    Museum, Tokyo
Topeka & Shawnee County Public Library, Alice C
    Sabatini Gallery, Topeka KS
Trust Authority, Museum of the Great Plains, Lawton
    OK
Tryon Palace Historic Sites & Gardens, New Bern NC
Turtle Mountain Chippewa Historical Society, Turtle
    Mountain Heritage Center, Belcourt ND
Tver Art Gallery, Tver
United Society of Shakers, Shaker Museum, New
    Gloucester ME
United States Capitol, Architect of the Capitol,
    Washington DC
University of Alabama at Birmingham, Visual Arts
    Gallery, Birmingham AL
University of British Columbia, Museum of
    Anthropology, Vancouver BC

University of California, California Museum of
    Photography, Riverside CA
University of California, Berkeley, Berkeley Art
    Museum & Pacific Film Archive, Berkeley CA
University of California, San Diego, Stuart Collection,
    La Jolla CA
University of California, Santa Barbara, University Art
    Museum, Santa Barbara CA
University of Chicago, Oriental Institute, Chicago IL
University of Louisiana at Lafayette, Paul and Lulu
    Hilliard University Art Museum, Lafayette LA
University of Manitoba, Faculty of Architecture
    Exhibition Centre, Winnipeg MB
University of Memphis, Art Museum, Memphis TN
University of New Mexico, The Harwood Museum of
    Art, Taos NM
University of Pittsburgh, University Art Gallery,
    Pittsburgh PA
University of Rhode Island, Fine Arts Center Galleries,
    Kingston RI
University of Victoria, The Legacy Art Gallery, Victoria
    BC
University of Wisconsin-Madison, Chazen Museum of
    Art, Madison WI
Vancouver Art Gallery, Vancouver BC
Vassar College, The Frances Lehman Loeb Art Center,
    Poughkeepsie NY
Vesterheim Norwegian-American Museum, Decorah IA
Victoria Mansion - Morse Libby House, Portland ME
Wade House Historic Site-Wisconsin Historical Society,
    Wesley W. Jung Carriage Museum, Greenbush WI
Wadsworth Atheneum Museum of Art, Hartford CT
Warner House Association, MacPheadris-Warner House,
    Portsmouth NH
West Baton Rouge Parish, West Baton Rouge Museum,
    Port Allen LA
West Florida Historic Preservation, Inc/University of
    West Florida, T T Wentworth, Jr Florida State
    Museum; Historic Pensacola Village; Pensacola
    Historical Society & Resource Center, Pensacola FL
Western Pennsylvania Conservancy, Fallingwater, Mill
    Run PA
Westover Plantation, Charles City VA
White House, Washington DC
Willard House & Clock Museum, Inc, North Grafton
    MA
William Morris Gallery, London
Woodrow Wilson, Washington DC
Wisconsin Historical Society, Wisconsin Historical
    Museum, Madison WI
Wistariahurst Museum, Holyoke MA
Woodlawn/The Pope-Leighey, Mount Vernon VA
Woodmere Art Museum Inc, Philadelphia PA
Workman & Temple Family Homestead Museum, City
    of Industry CA
Frank Lloyd Wright, Mount Vernon VA
Yale University, Yale Center for British Art, New
    Haven CT
Yokohama Museum of Art, Yokohama
Zurich University of the Arts (ZHdK), Museum Fuer
    Gestaltung Zurich (Museum of Design Zurich),
    Zurich

ART EDUCATION

African Art Museum of Maryland, Columbia MD
Walter Anderson, Ocean Springs MS
Art & Culture Center of Hollywood, Art
    Gallery/Multidisciplinary Cultural Center,
    Hollywood FL
Arts Midland Galleries & School, Alden B. Dow
    Museum of Science & Art, Midland MI
Baroda Museum and Picture Gallery, Baroda
Burke Arts Council, Jailhouse Galleries, Morganton NC
Bush-Holley Historic Site & Storehouse Gallery,
    Greenwich Historical Society/ Bush-Holley House,
    Cos Cob CT
Cape Ann Historical Association, Cape Ann Museum,
    Gloucester MA
Craft and Folk Art Museum (CAFAM), Los Angeles
    CA
Designmuseum Danmark, Copenhagen
Elverhoj Museum of History and Art, Solvang CA
Fisher Art Gallery, Marshalltown IA
Genesee Country Village & Museum, John L Wehle Art
    Gallery, Mumford NY
Hecht Museum, Haifa
High Museum of Art, Atlanta GA
International Museum of Art & Science, McAllen TX
J.M.W. Turner Museum, Sarasota FL
Jordan National Gallery of Fine Arts, Amman

LACE (Los Angeles Contemporary Exhibitions), Los
    Angeles CA
Latino Art Museum, Pomona CA
Leeds Museums & Galleries, Leeds
Ministry of Cultural Affairs, Bangladesh National
    Museum, Dhaka
Morris Museum of Art, Augusta GA
The Museum, Greenwood SC
Museum fur Kunst und Gewerbe Hamburg, Hamburg
Muzeul de Istorie Nationala Si Arheologie Constanta,
    National History & Archaeology Museum,
    Constanta
National Museum of Ceramic Art & Glass, Baltimore
    MD
Nelson Mandela Bay Municipality, Nelson Mandela
    Metropolitan Art Museum, Port Elizabeth
Noordbrabants Museum, Hertogenbosch
Palm Springs Art Museum, Palm Springs CA
George Phippen, Phippen Museum - Art of the
    American West, Prescott AZ
Rabindra Bhavan Art Gallery, Lalit Kala Akademi
    (National Academy of Art), New Delhi
Rajko Mamuzic Gallery of Fine Arts, Novi Sad
Jack Richard Gallery, Almond Tea Museum & Jane
    Williams Galleries, Divisions of Studios of Jack
    Richard, Cuyahoga Falls OH
Rijksmuseum Twenthe, Rijksmuseum Twenthe,
    Enschede
Saint Augustine Historical Society, Oldest House
    Museum Complex, Saint Augustine FL
Saint Peter's College, Art Gallery, Jersey City NJ
Slovenska Narodna Galeria, Slovak National Gallery,
    Bratislava
South Dakota State University, South Dakota Art
    Museum, Brookings SD
Stone Quarry Hill Art Park, Winner Gallery, Cazenovia
    NY
Suomen rakennustaiteen museo, Museum of Finnish
    Architecture, Helsinki
Texas A&M University, J Wayne Stark University
    Center Galleries, College Station TX
Yokohama Museum of Art, Yokohama

ART HISTORY

Akron Art Museum, Akron OH
Amon Carter Museum of American Art, Fort Worth TX
Walter Anderson, Ocean Springs MS
Art & Culture Center of Hollywood, Art
    Gallery/Multidisciplinary Cultural Center,
    Hollywood FL
Art Complex Museum, Carl A. Weyerhaeuser Library,
    Duxbury MA
Baroda Museum and Picture Gallery, Baroda
Belskie Museum, Closter NJ
Berea College, Ulmann Doris Galleries, Berea KY
Birger Sandzen Memorial Gallery, Lindsborg KS
Bush-Holley Historic Site & Storehouse Gallery,
    Greenwich Historical Society/ Bush-Holley House,
    Cos Cob CT
Cape Ann Historical Association, Cape Ann Museum,
    Gloucester MA
City of Antwerp, Middleheim Openluchtmuseum voor
    Beeldhouwkunst, Antwerp
Crocker Art Museum, Sacramento CA
Designmuseum Danmark, Copenhagen
Elverhoj Museum of History and Art, Solvang CA
Felicien Rops Museum, Namur
Fetherston Foundation, Packwood House Museum,
    Lewisburg PA
Fisher Art Gallery, Marshalltown IA
Fondazione Musei Civici Di Venezia, Galleria
    Internazionale d'Arte Moderna di Ca'Pesaro, Venice
Galeria Mesta Bratislavy, Bratislava City Gallery,
    Bratislava
General Board of Discipleship, The United Methodist
    Church, The Upper Room Chapel & Museum,
    Nashville TN
Genesee Country Village & Museum, John L Wehle Art
    Gallery, Mumford NY
Hawkes Bay Art Gallery and Museum, Napier
Hecht Museum, Haifa
High Museum of Art, Atlanta GA
Illinois State Museum, ISM Lockport Gallery, Chicago
    Gallery & Southern Illinois Art Gallery, Springfield
    IL
Indian Pueblo Cultural Center, Albuquerque NM
International Museum of Art & Science, McAllen TX
J.M.W. Turner Museum, Sarasota FL
James Dick Foundation, Festival - Institute, Round Top
    TX

ASIAN ART

Musees Royaux d'Art et d'Histoire, Royal Museums of Art and History, Brussels
Museo Cerralbo, Madrid
The Museum, Greenwood SC
Museum fur Angewandte Kunst Frankfurt, Museum of Applied Arts, Frankfurt
Museum fur Kunst und Gewerbe Hamburg, Hamburg
The Museum of Arts & Sciences Inc, Daytona Beach FL
Museum of Chinese in America, New York NY
Museum of Contemporary Art, Chicago IL
Museum of Fine Arts, Houston, Houston TX
Museum of Fine Arts, Saint Petersburg, Florida, Inc, Saint Petersburg FL
Museum of Vancouver, Vancouver BC
Museum zu Allerheiligen, Schaffhausen
Muskegon Museum of Art, Muskegon MI
Muzeul National Brukenthal, Brukenthal Palace & European Art Gallery, Sibiu
Nara Kokuritsu Hakubutsu-Kan, Nara National Museum, Nara
National Gallery of Canada, Ottawa ON
National Museum of the Philippines, Manila
National Museum of Women in the Arts, Washington DC
Naval Historical Center, The Navy Museum, Washington DC
Nelson Mandela Bay Municipality, Nelson Mandela Metropolitan Art Museum, Port Elizabeth
The Nelson-Atkins Museum of Art, Kansas City MO
New Orleans Museum of Art, New Orleans LA
New Visions Gallery, Inc, Marshfield WI
New World Art Center, T F Chen Cultural Center, New York NY
New York University, Grey Art Gallery, New York NY
Northern Illinois University, NIU Art Museum, DeKalb IL
Norwich Free Academy, Slater Memorial Museum, Norwich CT
Noyes Art Gallery, Lincoln NE
Oakland University, Oakland University Art Gallery, Rochester MI
Oberlin College, Allen Memorial Art Museum, Oberlin OH
Ohara Museum of Art, Kurashiki
Okanagan Heritage Museum, Kelowna BC
Owensboro Museum of Fine Art, Owensboro KY
Pacific - Asia Museum, Pasadena CA
Panhandle-Plains Historical Museum, Canyon TX
The Pennsylvania State University, Palmer Museum of Art, University Park PA
Philadelphia Museum of Art, Main Building, Philadelphia PA
Philbrook Museum of Art, Tulsa OK
Phoenix Art Museum, Phoenix AZ
Polk Museum of Art, Lakeland FL
The Pomona College, Claremont CA
Portland Art Museum, Portland OR
Princeton University, Princeton University Art Museum, Princeton NJ
Principia College, School of Nations Museum, Elsah IL
Putnam Museum of History and Natural Science, Davenport IA
Queens College, City University of New York, Godwin-Ternbach Museum, Flushing NY
Rabindra Bhavan Art Gallery, Lalit Kala Akademi (National Academy of Art), New Delhi
Reading Public Museum, Reading PA
Jack Richard Gallery, Almond Tea Museum & Jane Williams Galleries, Divisions of Studios of Jack Richard, Cuyahoga Falls OH
Rollins College, George D & Harriet W Cornell Fine Arts Museum, Winter Park FL
Royal Arts Foundation, Belcourt Castle, Newport RI
Royal Ontario Museum, Toronto ON
Rubin Museum of Art, New York NY
Ryerss Victorian Museum & Library, Philadelphia PA
Saginaw Art Museum, Saginaw MI
St Mary's College of Maryland, The Dwight Frederick Boyden Gallery, St Mary's City MD
Saint Olaf College, Flaten Art Museum, Northfield MN
Saint Peter's College, Art Gallery, Jersey City NJ
Salisbury House Foundation, Salisbury House and Garden, Des Moines IA
San Antonio Museum of Art, San Antonio TX
Santa Barbara Museum of Art, Santa Barbara CA
Santa Monica Museum of Art, Santa Monica CA
Scripps College, Ruth Chandler Williamson Gallery, Claremont CA
Seattle Art Museum, Downtown, Seattle WA
Seattle Art Museum, Seattle Asian Art Museum, Seattle WA

Norton Simon, Pasadena CA
Singapore Art Museum, Singapore
Smithsonian Institution, Washington DC
The Society of the Cincinnati at Anderson House, Washington DC
The Speed Art Museum, Louisville KY
Springfield Art Museum, Springfield MO
Stanford University, Cantor Arts Center at Stanford University, Stanford CA
The State Museum of Fine Arts of Tatarstan Republic, Kazan
The State Museum of Oriental Art, Moscow
State University of New York at Binghamton, Binghamton University Art Museum, Binghamton NY
State University of New York at New Paltz, Samuel Dorsky Museum of Art, New Paltz NY
State University of New York at Plattsburgh, Art Museum, Plattsburgh NY
Stauth Foundation & Museum, Stauth Memorial Museum, Montezuma KS
Stone Quarry Hill Art Park, Winner Gallery, Cazenovia NY
Suomen Kansallismuseo, National Museum of Finland, Helsinki
Sweet Briar College, Art Collection & Galleries, Sweet Briar VA
Tacoma Art Museum, Tacoma WA
Taft Museum of Art, Cincinnati OH
Lillian & Coleman Taube Museum of Art, Minot ND
Tokyo University of the Arts, The University Art Museum, Tokyo
Topeka & Shawnee County Public Library, Alice C Sabatini Gallery, Topeka KS
Towson University, Asian Arts & Culture Center, Towson MD
Towson University, Center for the Arts Gallery, Towson MD
Tulane University, Newcomb Art Gallery, New Orleans LA
Tver Art Gallery, Tver
Tyler Museum of Art, Tyler TX
University of Alabama at Birmingham, Visual Arts Gallery, Birmingham AL
University of British Columbia, Museum of Anthropology, Vancouver BC
University of California, Richard L Nelson Gallery & Fine Arts Collection, Davis CA
University of California, Berkeley, Berkeley Art Museum & Pacific Film Archive, Berkeley CA
University of California, Los Angeles, Fowler Museum at UCLA, Los Angeles CA
University of Chicago, Smart Museum of Art, Chicago IL
University of Cincinnati, DAAP Galleries-College of Design Architecture, Art & Planning, Cincinnati OH
University of Colorado, CU Art Museum, Boulder CO
University of Colorado at Colorado Springs, Gallery of Contemporary Art, Colorado Springs CO
University of Georgia, Georgia Museum of Art, Athens GA
University of Illinois at Urbana-Champaign, Krannert Art Museum and Kinkead Pavilion, Champaign IL
University of Illinois at Urbana-Champaign, Spurlock Museum, Champaign IL
University of Kansas, Spencer Museum of Art, Lawrence KS
University of Mary Washington, University of Mary Washington Galleries, Fredericksburg VA
University of Miami, Lowe Art Museum, Coral Gables FL
University of Michigan, Museum of Art, Ann Arbor MI
University of Missouri, Museum of Art & Archaeology, Columbia MO
University of Nevada, Reno, Sheppard Contemporary & University Galleries, Reno NV
University of North Carolina at Chapel Hill, Ackland Art Museum, Chapel Hill NC
University of North Carolina at Greensboro, Weatherspoon Art Museum, Greensboro NC
University of Oregon, Jordan Schnitzer Museum of Art, Eugene OR
University of Pennsylvania, Museum of Archaeology & Anthropology, Philadelphia PA
University of Pittsburgh, University Art Gallery, Pittsburgh PA
University of Richmond, University Museums, Richmond VA
University of San Diego, Founders' Gallery, San Diego CA
University of Tennessee, McClung Museum of Natural History & Culture, Knoxville TN

University of Toronto, University of Toronto Art Centre, Toronto ON
University of Utah, Utah Museum of Fine Arts, Salt Lake City UT
University of Victoria, The Legacy Art Gallery, Victoria BC
University of Virginia, The Fralin Museum of Art at the University of Virginia, Charlottesville VA
University of Wisconsin-Madison, Chazen Museum of Art, Madison WI
Vancouver Art Gallery, Vancouver BC
Vassar College, The Frances Lehman Loeb Art Center, Poughkeepsie NY
Village of Potsdam, Potsdam Public Museum, Potsdam NY
Virginia Museum of Fine Arts, Richmond VA
Wake Forest University, Museum of Anthropology, Winston Salem NC
Washburn University, Mulvane Art Museum, Topeka KS
Washington University, Mildred Lane Kemper Art Museum, Saint Louis MO
Wheaton College, Beard and Weil Galleries, Norton MA
Williams College, Museum of Art, Williamstown MA
Wolverhampton Arts & Heritage, Wolverton Art Gallery, Wolverhampton
Woodmere Art Museum Inc, Philadelphia PA
Worcester Art Museum, Worcester MA
World Erotic Art Museum, Miami Beach FL
Yokohama Museum of Art, Yokohama
Zigler Art Museum, Jennings LA

BAROQUE ART

Allentown Art Museum, Allentown PA
Arnot Art Museum, Elmira NY
Art Gallery of Hamilton, Hamilton ON
The Art Museum at the University of Kentucky, Lexington KY
Art Without Walls Inc, New York NY
Badisches Landesmuseum, Karlsruhe
Ball State University, Museum of Art, Muncie IN
Baroda Museum and Picture Gallery, Baroda
Bass Museum of Art, Miami Beach FL
Bayerische Staatsgemaldesammlungen/Bavarian State Art Galleries, Alte Pinakothek, Munich
Bayerisches Nationalmuseum, Bavarian National Museum, Munich
Beloit College, Wright Museum of Art, Beloit WI
Belvedere Museum, Osterreichische Galerie Belvedere, Vienna
Birmingham Museum of Art, Birmingham AL
Blanden Memorial Art Museum, Fort Dodge IA
Bruce Museum, Inc, Greenwich CT
Bucknell University, Edward & Marthann Samek Art Gallery, Lewisburg PA
The Buffalo Fine Arts Academy, Albright-Knox Art Gallery, Buffalo NY
Canadian Clay and Glass Gallery, Waterloo ON
Cincinnati Art Museum, Cincinnati Art Museum, Cincinnati OH
City of Antwerp, Rubenshuis, Antwerp
City of El Paso, El Paso TX
College of William & Mary, Muscarelle Museum of Art, Williamsburg VA
Comune di Genova - Direzione Cultura Settore Musei, Museo di Strada Nuova Palazzo Rosso, Genoa
Cornell College, Peter Paul Luce Gallery, Mount Vernon IA
The Courtauld Institute of Art, The Courtauld Gallery, London
Crocker Art Museum, Sacramento CA
Cummer Museum of Art & Gardens, Museum & Library, Jacksonville FL
The Currier Museum of Art, Manchester NH
Dallas Museum of Art, Dallas TX
Dartmouth College, Hood Museum of Art, Hanover NH
Denison University, Art Gallery, Granville OH
Denver Art Museum, Denver CO
Designmuseum Danmark, Copenhagen
Detroit Institute of Arts, Detroit MI
Dickinson College, The Trout Gallery, Carlisle PA
Fairfield University, Thomas J Walsh Art Gallery, Fairfield CT
Fine Arts Center for the New River Valley, Pulaski VA
Flint Institute of Arts, Flint MI
Florida State University, John & Mable Ringling Museum of Art, Sarasota FL
Fondazione Musei Civici Di Venezia, Ca'Rezzonico, Museo del Settecento Veneziano, Venice

BOOKPLATES & BINDINGS

BRONZES

Asian Art Museum of San Francisco, Chong-Moon Lee Ctr for Asian Art and Culture, San Francisco CA

Auburn University, Julie Collins Smith Museum, Auburn AL

Badisches Landesmuseum, Karlsruhe

Baroda Museum and Picture Gallery, Baroda

Bayerisches Nationalmuseum, Bavarian National Museum, Munich

Belvedere Museum, Osterreichische Galerie Belvedere, Vienna

Berman Museum, Anniston AL

Blanden Memorial Art Museum, Fort Dodge IA

Blauvelt Demarest Foundation, Hiram Blauvelt Art Museum, Oradell NJ

Boise Art Museum, Boise ID

Booth Western Art Museum, Cartersville GA

Roy Boyd, Chicago IL

Brigham Young University, Museum of Art, Provo UT

L D Brinkman, Kerrville TX

Bronx Community College (CUNY), Hall of Fame for Great Americans, Bronx NY

Brookgreen Gardens, Murrells Inlet SC

Bucknell University, Edward & Marthann Samek Art Gallery, Lewisburg PA

Canadian Clay and Glass Gallery, Waterloo ON

Canadian Museum of Civilization, Gatineau PQ

Canajoharie Library & Art Gallery, Arkell Museum of Canajoharie, Canajoharie NY

Cape Ann Historical Association, Cape Ann Museum, Gloucester MA

Cape Cod Museum of Art Inc, Dennis MA

Caramoor Center for Music & the Arts, Inc, Rosen House at Caramoor, Katonah NY

Carlsbad Museum & Art Center, Carlsbad NM

Carson County Square House Museum, Panhandle TX

Billie Trimble Chandler, Texas State Museum of Asian Cultures, Corpus Christi TX

Chhatrapati Shivaji Maharaj Vastu Sangrahalaya, Mumbai

Church of Jesus Christ of Latter-Day Saints, Museum of Church History & Art, Salt Lake City UT

Cincinnati Art Museum, Cincinnati Art Museum, Cincinnati OH

Colgate University, Picker Art Gallery, Hamilton NY

College of William & Mary, Muscarelle Museum of Art, Williamsburg VA

The College of Wooster, The College of Wooster Art Museum, Wooster OH

Concordia University Wisconsin, Fine Art Gallery, Mequon WI

Corcoran Gallery of Art, Washington DC

Cornell Museum of Art and American Culture, Delray Beach FL

The Courtauld Institute of Art, The Courtauld Gallery, London

Crocker Art Museum, Sacramento CA

Crook County Museum & Art Gallery, Sundance WY

Dahesh Museum of Art, Greenwich CT

Dallas Museum of Art, Dallas TX

Dartmouth College, Hood Museum of Art, Hanover NH

DeLeon White Gallery, Toronto ON

Denison University, Art Gallery, Granville OH

Denver Art Museum, Denver CO

Department of Antiquities, Cyprus Museum, Nicosia

Department of Museums Malaysia, National Museum, Kuala Lumpur

Detroit Institute of Arts, Detroit MI

Dixie State College, Robert N & Peggy Sears Gallery, Saint George UT

Eiteljorg Museum of American Indians & Western Art, Indianapolis IN

Ellen Noel Art Museum of the Permian Basin, Odessa TX

Erie Art Museum, Erie PA

Erie County Historical Society, Erie PA

Favell Museum of Western Art & Indian Artifacts, Klamath Falls OR

Fetherston Foundation, Packwood House Museum, Lewisburg PA

Fine Arts Museums of San Francisco, Legion of Honor, San Francisco CA

Five Civilized Tribes Museum, Muskogee OK

Flint Institute of Arts, Flint MI

Florida State University and Central Florida Community College, The Appleton Museum of Art, Ocala FL

Fondazione Musei Civici Di Venezia, Ca'Rezzonico, Museo del Settecento Veneziano, Venice

Fondazione Musei Civici Di Venezia, Museo Correr, Venice

Forest Lawn Museum, Glendale CA

Frankfort Community Public Library, Anna & Harlan Hubbard Gallery, Frankfort IN

Freer Gallery of Art & Arthur M Sackler Gallery, Arthur M Sackler Gallery, Washington DC

The Frick Art & Historical Center, Inc, Frick Art Museum, Pittsburgh PA

Frick Collection, New York NY

Galerie Montcalm, Gatineau PQ

Galleria Doria Pamphilj, Rome

Galleria Nazionale dell'Umbria, Umbrian National Gallery, Perugia

Gallery One Visual Arts Center, Ellensburg WA

General Board of Discipleship, The United Methodist Church, The Upper Room Chapel & Museum, Nashville TN

Glanmore National Historic Site of Canada, Belleville ON

Glessner House Museum, Chicago IL

Gonzaga University, Art Gallery, Spokane WA

Greek Ministry of Culture, Archaeological Museum of Thessaloniki, Thessaloniki

Headley-Whitney Museum, Lexington KY

Heard Museum, Phoenix AZ

Hebrew Union College - Jewish Institute of Religion, Skirball Museum Cincinnati, Cincinnati OH

Hebrew Union College Museum, Jewish Institute of Religion Museum, New York NY

Hecht Museum, Haifa

Henry County Museum & Cultural Arts Center, Clinton MO

Heras Institute of Indian History and Culture, Heras Institute Museum, Mumbai

Heritage Malta, National Museum of Fine Arts, Valletta

Hermitage Foundation Museum, Norfolk VA

Hill-Stead Museum, Farmington CT

Hillwood Museum & Gardens Foundation, Hillwood Estate Museum & Gardens, Washington DC

Hofstra University, Hofstra University Museum, Hempstead NY

The Huntington Library, Art Collections & Botanical Gardens, San Marino CA

Independent Administrative Institution National Institutes for Cultural Heritage, Tokyo National Museum, Tokyo

Independent Administrative Institution National Museum of Art, The National Museum of Western Art, Tokyo

Indiana University, Art Museum, Bloomington IN

Indianapolis Museum of Art, Indianapolis IN

The Israel Museum, Jerusalem, Billy Rose Art Garden, Jerusalem

Jacksonville University, Alexander Brest Museum & Gallery, Jacksonville FL

The John L. Clarke Western Art Gallery & Memorial Museum, East Glacier Park MT

John Weaver Sculpture Collection, Hope BC

Johns Hopkins University, Evergreen Museum & Library, Baltimore MD

Bob Jones University Museum & Gallery Inc, Greenville SC

Joslyn Art Museum, Omaha NE

Kalamazoo Institute of Arts, Kalamazoo MI

Kenosha Public Museums, Kenosha WI

Kentucky Derby Museum, Louisville KY

Kirkland Museum of Fine & Decorative Art, Denver CO

Knights of Columbus Supreme Council, Knights of Columbus Museum, New Haven CT

Knoxville Museum of Art, Knoxville TN

Koshare Indian Museum, Inc, La Junta CO

Kunsthistorisches Museum Vienna, Museum of Fine Arts, Vienna

Kyiv Museum of Russian Art, Kyiv

Lahore Museum, Lahore

League of New Hampshire Craftsmen, Grodin Permanent Collection Museum, Concord NH

Leanin' Tree Museum & Sculpture Garden of Western Art, Boulder CO

Lehigh University Art Galleries, Museum Operation, Bethlehem PA

Lightner Museum, Saint Augustine FL

Los Angeles County Museum of Natural History, William S Hart Museum, Newhall CA

Louisiana Arts & Science Museum, Baton Rouge LA

Louisiana Department of Culture, Recreation & Tourism, Louisiana State Museum, New Orleans LA

Louisiana State Exhibit Museum, Shreveport LA

Loveland Museum/Gallery, Loveland CO

Loyola University Chicago, Loyola University Museum of Art, Chicago IL

Luther College, Fine Arts Collection, Decorah IA

Magyar Nemzeti Muzeum - Hungarian National Museum, Budapest

Jacques Marchais, Staten Island NY

McMaster University, McMaster Museum of Art, Hamilton ON

Mennello Museum of American Art, Orlando FL

Mezuraj Museum, Tirana

Middle Border Museum & Oscar Howe Art Center, Mitchell SD

Middlebury College, Museum of Art, Middlebury VT

Midwest Museum of American Art, Elkhart IN

Milwaukee County War Memorial Inc., Villa Terrace Decorative Arts Museum, Milwaukee WI

Mingei International, Inc, Mingei International Museum - Balboa Park & Mingei International Museum - Escondido, San Diego CA

Ministry of Cultural Affairs, Bangladesh National Museum, Dhaka

Ministry of Culture & Tourism, The Delphi Museum, 10th Ephorate of Prehistoric & Classical Antiquities, Delphi

Minnesota Museum of American Art, Saint Paul MN

Missoula Art Museum, Missoula MT

Mobile Museum of Art, Mobile AL

Mohawk Valley Heritage Association, Inc, Walter Elwood Museum, Amsterdam NY

Montana State University, Museum of the Rockies, Bozeman MT

Montreal Museum of Fine Arts, Montreal PQ

Morris Museum, Morristown NJ

Musee des Beaux-Arts d'Orleans, Historical & Archaeological Museum of Orleans, Orleans

Musee des Beaux-Arts/Palais des Archeveques, Museum of Fine Arts, Tours

Musee Guimet, Paris

Musee National des Beaux Arts du Quebec, Quebec PQ

Musee Royal Et Domaine De Mariemont, Morlanwelz

Musei Capitolini, Rome

Musei Civici di Padova - Cappella Degli Scrovengni, Musei Civici Agli Eremitani (Civic Museum) - Scrovegni Chapel, Padua

Museo Cerralbo, Madrid

Museo De Las Americas, Denver CO

Museu de Evora, Evora

Museum fur Kunst und Gewerbe Hamburg, Hamburg

The Museum of Arts & Sciences Inc, Daytona Beach FL

Museum of Fine Arts, Saint Petersburg, Florida, Inc, Saint Petersburg FL

Museum of Latin American Art, Long Beach CA

Museum of Modern Art, Ibaraki, Ibaraki

Museum of the Plains Indian & Crafts Center, Browning MT

Museum zu Allerheiligen, Schaffhausen

Muskegon Museum of Art, Muskegon MI

Muzej za Umjetnost i Obrt, Museum of Arts & Crafts, Zagreb

Muzeul National Brukenthal, Blue House & Romanian Art Gallery, Sibiu

Muzeul National Brukenthal, Brukenthal Palace & European Art Gallery, Sibiu

Muzeum Narodowe, National Museum in Poznan, Poznan

Napoleonic Society of America, Museum & Library, Saint Helena CA

National Archaeological Museum, Athens

National Art Museum of Sport, Indianapolis IN

National Baseball Hall of Fame & Museum, Inc, Art Collection, Cooperstown NY

National Gallery of Canada, Ottawa ON

National Hall of Fame for Famous American Indians, Anadarko OK

National Museum of American Illustration, Newport RI

National Museum of Fine Arts of Moldova, Chisinau

The National Museum of Modern Art, Tokyo, Tokyo

National Museum of Racing, National Museum of Racing & Hall of Fame, Saratoga Springs NY

National Museum of Wildlife Art of the Unites States, Jackson WY

National Museum, Monuments and Art Gallery, Gaborone

National Palace Museum, Taiwan, R.O.C.

National Portrait Gallery, Smithsonian Institution, Washington DC

National Trust for Historic Preservation, Chesterwood, Stockbridge MA

Naval Historical Center, The Navy Museum, Washington DC

Nebraska Game and Parks Commission, Arbor Lodge State Historical Park & Morton Mansion, Nebraska City NE

CALLIGRAPHY

Panhandle-Plains Historical Museum, Canyon TX
Phoenix Art Museum, Phoenix AZ
Portland Art Museum, Portland OR
Princeton University, Princeton University Art Museum, Princeton NJ
Rabindra Bhavan Art Gallery, Lalit Kala Akademi (National Academy of Art), New Delhi
Saint John's University, Dr. M.T. Geoffrey Yeh Art Gallery, Queens NY
Saint Peter's College, Art Gallery, Jersey City NJ
Scripps College, Ruth Chandler Williamson Gallery, Claremont CA
Slovenska Narodna Galeria, Slovak National Gallery, Bratislava
Stanford University, Cantor Arts Center at Stanford University, Stanford CA
The State Museum of Fine Arts of Tatarstan Republic, Kazan
The State Museum of Oriental Art, Moscow
State University of New York at New Paltz, Samuel Dorsky Museum of Art, New Paltz NY
The Tokugawa Reimeikai Foundation, The Tokugawa Art Museum, Nagoya
Tokyo University of the Arts, The University Art Museum, Tokyo
Ukrainian Institute of Modern Art, Chicago IL
University of California, Berkeley, The Magnes Collection of Jewish Art & Life, Berkeley CA
University of Illinois at Urbana-Champaign, Krannert Art Museum and Kinkead Pavilion, Champaign IL
University of Indianapolis, Christel DeHaan Fine Arts Gallery, Indianapolis IN
University of Kansas, Spencer Museum of Art, Lawrence KS
University of North Dakota, Hughes Fine Arts Center-Col Eugene Myers Art Gallery, Grand Forks ND
University of Pittsburgh, University Art Gallery, Pittsburgh PA
University of Richmond, University Museums, Richmond VA
University of Wisconsin-Madison, Chazen Museum of Art, Madison WI
Willard House & Clock Museum, Inc, North Grafton MA

CARPETS & RUGS

Academy of the New Church, Glencairn Museum, Bryn Athyn PA
Albion College, Bobbitt Visual Arts Center, Albion MI
Amherst Museum, Amherst NY
Anchorage Museum at Rasmuson Center, Anchorage AK
Art Gallery of Calgary, Calgary AB
The Art Museum at the University of Kentucky, Lexington KY
Asian Art Museum of San Francisco, Chong-Moon Lee Ctr for Asian Art and Culture, San Francisco CA
Badisches Landesmuseum, Karlsruhe
Barnes Foundation, Merion PA
Baroda Museum and Picture Gallery, Baroda
Brick Store Museum, Kennebunk ME
Brigham Young University, Museum of Art, Provo UT
Bruce Museum, Inc, Greenwich CT
Bucknell University, Edward & Marthann Samek Art Gallery, Lewisburg PA
Canadian Museum of Civilization, Gatineau PQ
Caramoor Center for Music & the Arts, Inc, Rosen House at Caramoor, Katonah NY
Carson County Square House Museum, Panhandle TX
Chatham Historical Society, The Atwood House Museum, Chatham MA
Cincinnati Art Museum, Cincinnati Art Museum, Cincinnati OH
Clark County Historical Society, Pioneer - Krier Museum, Ashland KS
The College of Wooster, The College of Wooster Art Museum, Wooster OH
Colorado Historical Society, Colorado History Museum, Denver CO
Columbus Museum of Art, Columbus OH
Cooper-Hewitt National Design Museum, Smithsonian Institution, New York NY
Cornell College, Peter Paul Luce Gallery, Mount Vernon IA
County of Henrico, Meadow Farm Museum, Glen Allen VA
Coutts Museum of Art, Inc, El Dorado KS
Craft and Folk Art Museum (CAFAM), Los Angeles CA

Craigdarroch Castle Historical Museum Society, Victoria BC
Crocker Art Museum, Sacramento CA
Crow Wing County Historical Society, Brainerd MN
Dallas Museum of Art, Dallas TX
DAR Museum, National Society Daughters of the American Revolution, Washington DC
Designmuseum Danmark, Copenhagen
Detroit Institute of Arts, Detroit MI
Dixie State College, Robert N & Peggy Sears Gallery, Saint George UT
Dundurn Castle, Hamilton ON
Erie County Historical Society, Erie PA
Evanston Historical Society, Charles Gates Dawes House, Evanston IL
Ferenczy Muzeum, Szentendre
Fetherston Foundation, Packwood House Museum, Lewisburg PA
Fine Arts Museums of San Francisco, Legion of Honor, San Francisco CA
Florence Museum, Florence SC
Florida State University and Central Florida Community College, The Appleton Museum of Art, Ocala FL
Edsel & Eleanor Ford, Grosse Pointe Shores MI
Fuller Craft Museum, Brockton MA
General Board of Discipleship, The United Methodist Church, The Upper Room Chapel & Museum, Nashville TN
Germanisches Nationalmuseum, Nuremberg
Glanmore National Historic Site of Canada, Belleville ON
Glessner House Museum, Chicago IL
Grand Rapids Public Museum, Public Museum of Grand Rapids, Grand Rapids MI
Greene County Historical Society, Bronck Museum, Coxsackie NY
Hancock County Trustees of Public Reservations, Woodlawn: Museum, Gardens & Park, Ellsworth ME
Hebrew Union College - Jewish Institute of Religion, Skirball Museum Cincinnati, Cincinnati OH
Henry County Museum & Cultural Arts Center, Clinton MO
Henry Morrison Flagler Museum, Palm Beach FL
Hermitage Foundation Museum, Norfolk VA
Higgins Armory Museum, Worcester MA
Hill-Stead Museum, Farmington CT
Hillwood Museum & Gardens Foundation, Hillwood Estate Museum & Gardens, Washington DC
The Hispanic Society of America, Museum & Library, New York NY
Historic Arkansas Museum, Little Rock AR
The History Center in Tompkins County, Ithaca NY
Hoyt Center for the Arts, New Castle PA
Huguenot Historical Society of New Paltz Galleries, New Paltz NY
The Huntington Library, Art Collections & Botanical Gardens, San Marino CA
Huntington Museum of Art, Huntington WV
Illinois Historic Preservation Agency, Bishop Hill State Historic Site, Bishop Hill IL
Imperial Calcasieu Museum, Gibson-Barham Gallery, Lake Charles LA
Independent Administrative Institution National Institutes for Cultural Heritage, Tokyo National Museum, Tokyo
Indiana Landmarks, Morris-Butler House, Indianapolis IN
Indiana University, Art Museum, Bloomington IN
Institute of American Indian Arts, Museum of Contemporary Native Arts, Santa Fe NM
Iredell Museums, Statesville NC
The Israel Museum, Jerusalem, Samuel & Saidye Bronfman Archaeology Wing, Jerusalem
The Israel Museum, Jerusalem, Jerusalem
J.M.W. Turner Museum, Sarasota FL
Jacksonville University, Alexander Brest Museum & Gallery, Jacksonville FL
James Dick Foundation, Festival - Institute, Round Top TX
The Jewish Museum, New York NY
Johns Hopkins University, Evergreen Museum & Library, Baltimore MD
Kenosha Public Museums, Kenosha WI
Kereszteny Muzeum, Christian Museum, Esztergom
Kings County Historical Society & Museum, Hampton NB
Kirkland Museum of Fine & Decorative Art, Denver CO
Koshare Indian Museum, Inc, La Junta CO

Lac du Flambeau Band of Lake Superior Chippewa Indians, George W Brown Jr Ojibwe Museum & Cultural Center, Lac Du Flambeau WI
LaGrange Art Museum, LaGrange GA
Lahore Museum, Lahore
Lamar University, Dishman Art Museum, Beaumont TX
League of New Hampshire Craftsmen, Grodin Permanent Collection Museum, Concord NH
Leeds Museums & Galleries, Leeds
LeSueur County Historical Society, Chapter One, Elysian MN
Lightner Museum, Saint Augustine FL
The Long Island Museum of American Art, History & Carriages, Stony Brook NY
Longue Vue House & Gardens, New Orleans LA
Lós Angeles County Museum of Natural History, William S Hart Museum, Newhall CA
Luther College, Fine Arts Collection, Decorah IA
Magyar Nemzeti Muzeum - Hungarian National Museum, Budapest
Manitoba Historical Society, Dalnavert Museum, Winnipeg MB
Marblehead Museum & Historical Society, Jeremiah Lee Mansion, Marblehead MA
Marblehead Museum & Historical Society, Marblehead MA
Jacques Marchais, Staten Island NY
Marquette University, Haggerty Museum of Art, Milwaukee WI
Massillon Museum, Massillon OH
McDowell House & Apothecary Shop, Danville KY
McLean County Historical Society, McLean County Museum of History, Bloomington IL
Meredith College, Frankie G Weems Gallery & Rotunda Gallery, Raleigh NC
Mingei International, Inc, Mingei International Museum - Balboa Park & Mingei International Museum - Escondido, San Diego CA
Ministry of Cultural Affairs, Bangladesh National Museum, Dhaka
Mississippi River Museum at Mud-Island River Park, Memphis TN
Mississippi Valley Conservation Authority, R Tait McKenzie Memorial Museum, Almonte ON
Arthur Roy Mitchell, A.R. Mitchell Museum, Trinidad CO
Mohawk Valley Heritage Association, Inc, Walter Elwood Museum, Amsterdam NY
Montana State University, Museum of the Rockies, Bozeman MT
Montreal Museum of Fine Arts, Montreal PQ
Moody County Historical Society, Moody County Museum, Pierre SD
Morris Museum, Morristown NJ
Mount Vernon Hotel Museum & Garden, New York NY
Munson-Williams-Proctor Arts Institute, Museum of Art, Utica NY
Muscatine Art Center, Museum, Muscatine IA
Muscatine Art Center, Muscatine IA
Musee des Beaux-Arts/Palais des Archeveques, Museum of Fine Arts, Tours
Musee Guimet, Paris
Musees Royaux d'Art et d'Histoire, Royal Museums of Art and History, Brussels
Musei Capitolini, Rome
Museo Cerralbo, Madrid
Museu de Evora, Evora
Museu de Grao Vasco, Viseu
The Museum, Greenwood SC
Museum De Lakenhal, Leiden
Museum fur Angewandte Kunst Frankfurt, Museum of Applied Arts, Frankfurt
Museum fur Kunst und Gewerbe Hamburg, Hamburg
The Museum of Arts & Sciences Inc, Daytona Beach FL
Museum of Fine Arts Houston, Bayou Bend Collection & Gardens, Houston TX
Museum of Northern Arizona, Flagstaff AZ
Museum Plantin-Moretus/Prentenkabinet, Antwerp
Museum zu Allerheiligen, Schaffhausen
Muzej za Umjetnost i Obrt, Museum of Arts & Crafts, Zagreb
Muzeul National Brukenthal, Blue House & Romanian Art Gallery, Sibiu
Muzeul National Brukenthal, Brukenthal Palace & European Art Gallery, Sibiu
National Museum of American Illustration, Newport RI
National Museums Scotland, National Museum of Scotland, Edinburgh

Nebraska Game and Parks Commission, Arbor Lodge State Historical Park & Morton Mansion, Nebraska City NE
Nelson Mandela Bay Municipality, Nelson Mandela Metropolitan Art Museum, Port Elizabeth
The Nelson-Atkins Museum of Art, Kansas City MO
The Nemours Foundatioin, Nemours Mansion & Gardens, Wilmington DE
New Brunswick Museum, Saint John NB
New Visions Gallery, Inc, Marshfield WI
Nichols House Museum, Inc, Boston MA
North Carolina State University, Gregg Museum of Art & Design, Raleigh NC
Norwich Free Academy, Slater Memorial Museum, Norwich CT
Ohio University, Kennedy Museum of Art, Athens OH
The Old Jail Art Center, Albany TX
Owensboro Museum of Fine Art, Owensboro KY
Panhandle-Plains Historical Museum, Canyon TX
Pasadena Museum of History, Pasadena CA
Patrimonio Nacional, Palacios de la Granja y Riofrio, Madrid
Phelps County Historical Society, Nebraska Prairie Museum, Holdrege NE
Plumas County Museum, Quincy CA
Polk Museum of Art, Lakeland FL
Port Huron Museum, Port Huron MI
Portland Art Museum, Portland OR
Putnam Museum of History and Natural Science, Davenport IA
Queens College, City University of New York, Godwin-Ternbach Museum, Flushing NY
Riley County Historical Society & Museum, Riley County Historical Museum, Manhattan KS
Riverside Metropolitan Museum, Riverside CA
The Rockwell Museum of Western Art, Corning NY
The Rosenbach Museum & Library, Philadelphia PA
Ross Memorial Museum, Saint Andrews NB
Rubin Museum of Art, New York NY
Saginaw Art Museum, Saginaw MI
Saint Olaf College, Flaten Art Museum, Northfield MN
Saint Peter's College, Art Gallery, Jersey City NJ
Salisbury House Foundation, Salisbury House and Garden, Des Moines IA
Savitsky Karakalpakstan State Art Museum, Nukus
Schweinfurth Art Center, Auburn NY
The Society of the Cincinnati at Anderson House, Washington DC
Soprintendenza per I beni storici artistici ed etnoantropologici per le province di Mantova Brescia e Cremona, Museo di Palazzo Ducale, Mantua
South Carolina Artisans Center, Walterboro SC
South Dakota State University, South Dakota Art Museum, Brookings SD
The Speed Art Museum, Louisville KY
Spertus Institute of Jewish Studies, Chicago IL
Springville Museum of Art, Springville UT
Nelda C & H J Lutcher Stark, Stark Museum of Art, Orange TX
The State Museum of Fine Arts of Tatarstan Republic, Kazan
The State Museum of Oriental Art, Moscow
State University of New York at Binghamton, Binghamton University Art Museum, Binghamton NY
The Summit County Historical Society of Akron, OH, Akron OH
Suomen Kansallismuseo, National Museum of Finland, Helsinki
Swedish American Museum Association of Chicago, Chicago IL
Taos, Ernest Blumenschein Home & Studio, Taos NM
The Textile Museum, Washington DC
Textile Museum of Canada, Toronto ON
Tohono Chul Park, Tucson AZ
Topeka & Shawnee County Public Library, Alice C Sabatini Gallery, Topeka KS
Tryon Palace Historic Sites & Gardens, New Bern NC
Tver Art Gallery, Tver
Ukrainian Canadian Archives & Museum of Alberta, Edmonton AB
United States Department of State, Diplomatic Reception Rooms, Washington DC
University of California, Berkeley, The Magnes Collection of Jewish Art & Life, Berkeley CA
University of Georgia, Georgia Museum of Art, Athens GA
University of Kansas, Spencer Museum of Art, Lawrence KS
University of Pennsylvania, Arthur Ross Gallery, Philadelphia PA

University of Toronto, University of Toronto Art Centre, Toronto ON
University of Utah, Utah Museum of Fine Arts, Salt Lake City UT
University of Washington, Henry Art Gallery, Seattle WA
Vesterheim Norwegian-American Museum, Decorah IA
Victoria Mansion - Morse Libby House, Portland ME
Village of Potsdam, Potsdam Public Museum, Potsdam NY
Vizcaya Museum & Gardens, Miami FL
Wake Forest University, Museum of Anthropology, Winston Salem NC
Willard House & Clock Museum, Inc, North Grafton MA
William Morris Gallery, London
Wisconsin Historical Society, Wisconsin Historical Museum, Madison WI
Woodlawn/The Pope-Leighey, Mount Vernon VA
Woodmere Art Museum Inc, Philadelphia PA

CARTOONS

American Museum of Cartoon Art, Inc, Sunland CA
American Museum of the Moving Image, Astoria NY
Art & Culture Center of Hollywood, Art Gallery/Multidisciplinary Cultural Center, Hollywood FL
The Art Museum at the University of Kentucky, Lexington KY
Art Without Walls Inc, New York NY
ArtSpace/Lima, Lima OH
Barker Character, Comic and Cartoon Museum, Cheshire CT
Beck Cultural Exchange Center, Inc, Knoxville TN
Brigham Young University, Museum of Art, Provo UT
Bruce Museum, Inc, Greenwich CT
California State University, Northridge, Art Galleries, Northridge CA
Cartoon Art Museum, San Francisco CA
Central United Methodist Church, Swords Into Plowshares Peace Center & Gallery, Detroit MI
City of Mason City, Charles H MacNider Museum, Mason City IA
Colgate University, Picker Art Gallery, Hamilton NY
Cooper-Hewitt National Design Museum, Smithsonian Institution, New York NY
Coutts Museum of Art, Inc, El Dorado KS
Cripple Creek District Museum, Cripple Creek CO
Crocker Art Museum, Sacramento CA
Denison University, Art Gallery, Granville OH
East Tennessee State University, The Reece Museum, Johnson City TN
Erie Art Museum, Erie PA
Fort George G Meade Museum, Fort Meade MD
Galerie Montcalm, Gatineau PQ
Hartwick College, Foreman Gallery, Oneonta NY
Hartwick College, The Yager Museum, Oneonta NY
Headquarters Fort Monroe, Dept of Army, Casemate Museum, Hampton VA
The Jewish Museum, New York NY
Kansas State Historical Society, Kansas Museum of History, Topeka KS
Kelly-Griggs House Museum, Red Bluff CA
Lafayette College, Lafayette College Art Galleries, Easton PA
Leeds Museums & Galleries, Leeds
Longue Vue House & Gardens, New Orleans LA
Manchester Bidwell Corporation, Manchester Craftsmen's Guild Youth & Arts Program, Pittsburgh PA
Marylhurst University, The Art Gym, Marylhurst OR
McCord Museum of Canadian History, Montreal PQ
Ministry of Cultural Affairs, Bangladesh National Museum, Dhaka
Ministry of the Arts & Multiculturalism, National Museum & Art Gallery, Port of Spain
Montana State University, Museum of the Rockies, Bozeman MT
Musee des Beaux-Arts/Palais des Archeveques, Museum of Fine Arts, Tours
Musee Royal Et Domaine De Mariemont, Morlanwelz
Museum fur Kunst und Gewerbe Hamburg, Hamburg
Museum of Chinese in America, New York NY
Museum of the City of New York, Museum, New York NY
Muskegon Museum of Art, Muskegon MI
National Art Museum of Sport, Indianapolis IN
National Baseball Hall of Fame & Museum, Inc, Art Collection, Cooperstown NY
National Museum of American Illustration, Newport RI
National Museum of Fine Arts of Moldova, Chisinau

The National Park Service, United States Department of the Interior, Statue of Liberty National Monument & The Ellis Island Immigration Museum, Washington DC
National Portrait Gallery, Smithsonian Institution, Washington DC
Naval Historical Center, The Navy Museum, Washington DC
Nelson Mandela Bay Municipality, Nelson Mandela Metropolitan Art Museum, Port Elizabeth
New Britain Museum of American Art, New Britain CT
Norwich Free Academy, Slater Memorial Museum, Norwich CT
Panhandle-Plains Historical Museum, Canyon TX
Port Huron Museum, Port Huron MI
Prairie Art Gallery, Grande Prairie AB
Queens College, City University of New York, Godwin-Ternbach Museum, Flushing NY
Jack Richard Gallery, Almond Tea Museum & Jane Williams Galleries, Divisions of Studios of Jack Richard, Cuyahoga Falls OH
Rollins College, George D & Harriet W Cornell Fine Arts Museum, Winter Park FL
C M Russell, Great Falls MT
School of Visual Arts, Visual Arts Museum, New York NY
Sonoma State University, University Art Gallery, Rohnert Park CA
Soprintendenza per I beni storici artistici ed etnoantropologici per le province di Mantova Brescia e Cremona, Museo di Palazzo Ducale, Mantua
The Speed Art Museum, Louisville KY
Spertus Institute of Jewish Studies, Chicago IL
State University of New York College at Buffalo, Buffalo NY
Syracuse University, Art Collection, Syracuse NY
Syracuse University, SUArt Galleries, Syracuse NY
United States Military Academy, West Point Museum, West Point NY
United States Navy, Art Gallery, Washington DC
Wisconsin Historical Society, Wisconsin Historical Museum, Madison WI
World Erotic Art Museum, Miami Beach FL
Zurich University of the Arts (ZHdK), Museum Fuer Gestaltung Zurich (Museum of Design Zurich), Zurich

CERAMICS

A.E. Backus Museum of Art, Fort Pierce FL
Academy of the New Church, Glencairn Museum, Bryn Athyn PA
Adams National Historic Park, Quincy MA
African Art Museum of Maryland, Columbia MD
Al Ain National Museum, Al Ain
Albany Institute of History & Art, Albany NY
Alberta College of Art & Design, Illingworth Kerr Gallery, Calgary AB
Albion College, Bobbitt Visual Arts Center, Albion MI
Albuquerque Museum of Art & History, Albuquerque NM
Allentown Art Museum, Allentown PA
American Museum of Ceramic Art, Pomona CA
American Swedish Institute, Minneapolis MN
Anderson Park Art Gallery Inc, Art Gallery, Invercargill
Arab American National Museum, Dearborn MI
Archaeological Museum of Olympia, Olympia
Archaeological Museum of the American University of Beirut, Beirut
Arizona Museum For Youth, Mesa AZ
Arizona State University, ASU Art Museum, Tempe AZ
Arnot Art Museum, Elmira NY
Art & Culture Center of Hollywood, Art Gallery/Multidisciplinary Cultural Center, Hollywood FL
Art Community Center, Art Center of Corpus Christi, Corpus Christi TX
Art Complex Museum, Carl A. Weyerhaeuser Library, Duxbury MA
Art Gallery of Calgary, Calgary AB
Art Gallery of Nova Scotia, Halifax NS
Art Gallery of South Australia, Adelaide
The Art Museum at the University of Kentucky, Lexington KY
Art Museum of Greater Lafayette, Lafayette IN
ArtSpace/Lima, Lima OH
Asbury College, Student Center Gallery, Wilmore KY
Asheville Art Museum, Asheville NC
Asian Art Museum of San Francisco, Chong-Moon Lee Ctr for Asian Art and Culture, San Francisco CA

Augustana College, Augustana College Art Museum, Rock Island IL
Badisches Landesmuseum, Karlsruhe
Baldwin Historical Society Museum, Baldwin NY
Ball State University, Museum of Art, Muncie IN
The Baltimore Museum of Art, Baltimore MD
Balzekas Museum of Lithuanian Culture, Chicago IL
Barnes Foundation, Merion PA
Baroda Museum and Picture Gallery, Baroda
Bass Museum of Art, Miami Beach FL
Bates College, Museum of Art, Lewiston ME
Baton Rouge Gallery, Center For Contemporary Art, Baton Rouge LA
Bayerisches Nationalmuseum, Bavarian National Museum, Munich
Bellevue Arts Museum, Bellevue WA
Bemis Center for Contemporary Arts, Omaha NE
Bennington Museum, Bennington VT
Berea College, Ulmann Doris Galleries, Berea KY
Berkshire Museum, Pittsfield MA
Berman Museum, Anniston AL
Besser Museum for Northeast Michigan, Alpena MI
Bethany College, Mingenback Art Center, Lindsborg KS
Beverly Historical Society, Cabot, Hale & Balch House Museums, Beverly MA
Biggs Museum of American Art, Dover DE
Birger Sandzen Memorial Gallery, Lindsborg KS
Birmingham Museum of Art, Birmingham AL
Blanden Memorial Art Museum, Fort Dodge IA
Bone Creek Museum of Agrarian Art, David City NE
Brigham City Corporation, Brigham City Museum & Gallery, Brigham City UT
Brigham Young University, Museum of Art, Provo UT
Bradford Brinton, Big Horn WY
Brown University, Haffenreffer Museum of Anthropology, Providence RI
Bruce Museum, Inc, Greenwich CT
Bucknell University, Edward & Marthann Samek Art Gallery, Lewisburg PA
Burke Arts Council, Jailhouse Galleries, Morganton NC
The Butler Institute of American Art, Art Museum, Youngstown OH
Byzantine & Christian Museum, Athens, Athens
California State University, Northridge, Art Galleries, Northridge CA
Calvin College, Center Art Gallery, Grand Rapids MI
Cameron Art Museum, Wilmington NC
Canadian Clay and Glass Gallery, Waterloo ON
Canadian Museum of Civilization, Gatineau PQ
Canadian Museum of Nature, Musee Canadien de la Nature, Ottawa ON
Canton Museum of Art, Canton OH
Cape Cod Museum of Art Inc, Dennis MA
Caramoor Center for Music & the Arts, Inc, Rosen House at Caramoor, Katonah NY
Carlsbad Museum & Art Center, Carlsbad NM
Cedar Rapids Museum of Art, Cedar Rapids IA
Central United Methodist Church, Swords Into Plowshares Peace Center & Gallery, Detroit MI
Centro de Arte Moderna, CAM - Calouste Gulbenkian Foundation, Lisbon
Billie Trimble Chandler, Texas State Museum of Asian Cultures, Corpus Christi TX
Charles Allis Art Museum, Milwaukee WI
Charleston Museum, Charleston SC
Chatham Historical Society, The Atwood House Museum, Chatham MA
Chhatrapati Shivaji Maharaj Vastu Sangrahalaya, Mumbai
Cincinnati Art Museum, Cincinnati Art Museum, Cincinnati OH
City of Brea, Art Gallery, Brea CA
City of Cedar Falls, Iowa, James & Meryl Hearst Center for the Arts & Sculpture Garden, Cedar Falls IA
City of Mason City, Charles H MacNider Museum, Mason City IA
The City of Petersburg Museums, Petersburg VA
City of Port Angeles, Port Angeles Fine Arts Center & Webster Woods Art Park, Port Angeles WA
City of Springdale, Shiloh Museum of Ozark History, Springdale AR
Civic and Municipal Affairs Bureau of Macau, Macau Museum of Art, Nape
Sterling & Francine Clark, Williamstown MA
Clay Studio, Philadelphia PA
The Cleveland Museum of Art, Cleveland OH
Coastal Arts League Museum, Half Moon Bay CA
Cohasset Historical Society, Pratt Building (Society Headquarters), Cohasset MA
Colgate University, Picker Art Gallery, Hamilton NY

College of Saint Benedict, Gorecki Gallery & Gallery Lounge, Saint Joseph MN
College of William & Mary, Muscarelle Museum of Art, Williamsburg VA
The College of Wooster, The College of Wooster Art Museum, Wooster OH
Colorado Historical Society, Colorado History Museum, Denver CO
Columbia County Historical Society, Columbia County Museum and Library, Kinderhook NY
Columbus Museum, Columbus GA
Concord Museum, Concord MA
Concordia University, Marxhausen Art Gallery, Seward NE
Cooper-Hewitt National Design Museum, Smithsonian Institution, New York NY
Cornwall Gallery Society, Cornwall Regional Art Gallery, Cornwall ON
County of Henrico, Meadow Farm Museum, Glen Allen VA
The Courtauld Institute of Art, The Courtauld Gallery, London
Coutts Museum of Art, Inc, El Dorado KS
Craft and Folk Art Museum (CAFAM), Los Angeles CA
Craigdarroch Castle Historical Museum Society, Victoria BC
Cranbrook Art Museum, Bloomfield Hills MI
Creighton University, Lied Art Gallery, Omaha NE
Cripple Creek District Museum, Cripple Creek CO
Crocker Art Museum, Sacramento CA
Cummer Museum of Art & Gardens, Museum & Library, Jacksonville FL
The Currier Museum of Art, Manchester NH
Dallas Museum of Art, Dallas TX
Danforth Museum of Art, Danforth Museum of Art, Framingham MA
DAR Museum, National Society Daughters of the American Revolution, Washington DC
Dartmouth College, Hood Museum of Art, Hanover NH
Dartmouth Heritage Museum, Dartmouth NS
Daum Museum of Contemporary Art, Sedalia MO
Davidson College, William H Van Every Jr & Edward M Smith Galleries, Davidson NC
Deines Cultural Center, Russell KS
Delaware Archaeology Museum, Dover DE
Delaware Division of Historical & Cultural Affairs, Dover DE
Denison University, Art Gallery, Granville OH
Denver Art Museum, Denver CO
Department of Antiquities, Cyprus Museum, Nicosia
Department of Museums Malaysia, National Museum, Kuala Lumpur
Designmuseum Danmark, Copenhagen
Detroit Institute of Arts, Detroit MI
Detroit Zoological Institute, Wildlife Interpretive Gallery, Royal Oak MI
Dickinson College, The Trout Gallery, Carlisle PA
Dickinson State University, Art Gallery, Dickinson ND
Dixie State College, Robert N & Peggy Sears Gallery, Saint George UT
The Dixon Gallery & Gardens, Memphis TN
Doncaster Museum and Art Gallery, Doncaster
Drexel University, Drexel Collection, Philadelphia PA
Dundee City Council Leisure & Communities Department, The McManus: Dundee's Art Gallery & Museum, Dundee
East Tennessee State University, The Reece Museum, Johnson City TN
Edgecombe County Cultural Arts Council, Inc, Blount-Bridgers House, Hobson Pittman Memorial Gallery, Tarboro NC
Ellen Noel Art Museum of the Permian Basin, Odessa TX
Elmhurst Art Museum, Elmhurst IL
Emory University, Michael C Carlos Museum, Atlanta GA
Erie Art Museum, Erie PA
Erie County Historical Society, Erie PA
Wharton Esherick, Paoli PA
Evanston Historical Society, Charles Gates Dawes House, Evanston IL
Evergreen State College, Evergreen Gallery, Olympia WA
Everhart Museum, Scranton PA
Everson Museum of Art, Syracuse NY
Farmington Village Green & Library Association, Stanley-Whitman House, Farmington CT
Ferenczy Muzeum, Szentendre
Fetherston Foundation, Packwood House Museum, Lewisburg PA
Fine Arts Center for the New River Valley, Pulaski VA

Fine Arts Museums of San Francisco, Legion of Honor, San Francisco CA
Fisher Art Gallery, Marshalltown IA
Flint Institute of Arts, Flint MI
Florence Museum, Florence SC
Fondazione Musei Civici Di Venezia, Ca'Rezzonico, Museo del Settecento Veneziano, Venice
Fondazione Musei Civici Di Venezia, Museo Correr, Venice
Fondazione Scientifica Querini Stampalia, Venice
Fondo del Sol, Visual Art & Media Center, Washington DC
Edsel & Eleanor Ford, Grosse Pointe Shores MI
Forest Lawn Museum, Glendale CA
Fort Collins Museum of Art, Inc, Fort Collins CO
Freer Gallery of Art & Arthur M Sackler Gallery, Freer Gallery of Art, Washington DC
Freer Gallery of Art & Arthur M Sackler Gallery, Arthur M Sackler Gallery, Washington DC
The Frick Art & Historical Center, Inc, Frick Art Museum, Pittsburgh PA
Friends of Historic Kingston, Fred J Johnston House Museum, Kingston NY
Fuller Craft Museum, Brockton MA
Galleria Nazionale dell'Umbria, Umbrian National Gallery, Perugia
Gallery One Visual Arts Center, Ellensburg WA
George R Gardiner, Toronto ON
General Board of Discipleship, The United Methodist Church, The Upper Room Chapel & Museum, Nashville TN
Genesee Country Village & Museum, John L Wehle Art Gallery, Mumford NY
Georgian Court University, M Christina Geis Gallery, Lakewood NJ
Glanmore National Historic Site of Canada, Belleville ON
Glessner House Museum, Chicago IL
Gonzaga University, Art Gallery, Spokane WA
Grand Rapids Art Museum, Grand Rapids MI
Grand Rapids Public Museum, Public Museum of Grand Rapids, Grand Rapids MI
Greek Ministry of Culture, Archaeological Museum of Thessaloniki, Thessaloniki
Guilford College, Art Gallery, Greensboro NC
Halifax Historical Society, Inc, Halifax Historical Museum, Daytona Beach FL
Hammond-Harwood House Association, Inc, Hammond-Harwood House, Annapolis MD
Hancock County Trustees of Public Reservations, Woodlawn: Museum, Gardens & Park, Ellsworth ME
Harrison County Historical Museum, Marshall TX
Hawkes Bay Art Gallery and Museum, Napier
Haystack Mountain School of Crafts, Deer Isle ME
Headley-Whitney Museum, Lexington KY
Headquarters Fort Monroe, Dept of Army, Casemate Museum, Hampton VA
Heard Museum, Phoenix AZ
Hebrew Union College Museum, Jewish Institute of Religion Museum, New York NY
Hecht Museum, Haifa
Henry Gallery Association, Henry Art Gallery, Seattle WA
Henry Sheldon Museum of Vermont History and Research Center, Middlebury VT
Heritage Center, Inc, Pine Ridge SD
Heritage Malta, National Museum of Fine Arts, Valletta
Hermitage Foundation Museum, Norfolk VA
Hershey Museum, Hershey PA
Higgins Armory Museum, Worcester MA
High Museum of Art, Atlanta GA
Hill-Stead Museum, Farmington CT
Hillwood Museum & Gardens Foundation, Hillwood Estate Museum & Gardens, Washington DC
The Hispanic Society of America, Museum & Library, New York NY
Historic Arkansas Museum, Little Rock AR
Historic Cherry Hill, Albany NY
Historic Deerfield, Inc, Deerfield MA
Historic Hudson Valley, Pocantico Hills NY
Historic Newton, Newton MA
Historical Society of Bloomfield, Bloomfield NJ
Historical Society of Cheshire County, Keene NH
Historisches und Volkerkundemuseum, Historical Museum, St Gallen
History Museum of Mobile, Mobile AL
Hofstra University, Hofstra University Museum, Hempstead NY
Holter Museum of Art, Helena MT
Hoyt Center for the Arts, New Castle PA

Huguenot Historical Society of New Paltz Galleries, New Paltz NY

Hui No'eau Visual Arts Center, Gallery and Gift Shop, Makawao Maui HI

The Huntington Library, Art Collections & Botanical Gardens, San Marino CA

Huntington Museum of Art, Huntington WV

Huronia Museum, Gallery of Historic Huronia, Midland ON

Hyde Park Art Center, Chicago IL

Illinois State Museum, ISM Lockport Gallery, Chicago Gallery & Southern Illinois Art Gallery, Springfield IL

Illinois State University, University Galleries, Normal IL

Imperial Calcasieu Museum, Gibson-Barham Gallery, Lake Charles LA

Independence Seaport Museum, Philadelphia PA

Independent Administrative Institution National Institutes for Cultural Heritage, Tokyo National Museum, Tokyo

Indiana Landmarks, Morris-Butler House, Indianapolis IN

Indiana State Museum, Indianapolis IN

Indiana University, Art Museum, Bloomington IN

Indianapolis Museum of Art, Indianapolis IN

Institute of American Indian Arts, Museum of Contemporary Native Arts, Santa Fe NM

Institute of Puerto Rican Culture, Museo Fuerte Conde de Mirasol, Vieques PR

The Interchurch Center, Galleries at the Interchurch Center, New York NY

Iowa State University, Brunnier Art Museum, Ames IA

Iredell Museums, Statesville NC

Iroquois Indian Museum, Howes Cave NY

The Israel Museum, Jerusalem, Samuel & Saidye Bronfman Archaeology Wing, Jerusalem

The Israel Museum, Jerusalem, Jerusalem

Jacksonville University, Alexander Brest Museum & Gallery, Jacksonville FL

James Dick Foundation, Festival - Institute, Round Top TX

Jamestown-Yorktown Foundation, Jamestown Settlement, Williamsburg VA

Thomas Jefferson, Monticello, Charlottesville VA

Jersey City Museum, Jersey City NJ

The Jewish Museum, New York NY

Johns Hopkins University, Evergreen Museum & Library, Baltimore MD

Johns Hopkins University, Homewood Museum, Baltimore MD

Bob Jones University Museum & Gallery Inc, Greenville SC

Jordan National Gallery of Fine Arts, Amman

Kalamazoo Institute of Arts, Kalamazoo MI

Kelly-Griggs House Museum, Red Bluff CA

Kenosha Public Museums, Kenosha WI

Kentucky Museum of Art and Craft, Louisville KY

Kereszteny Muzeum, Christian Museum, Esztergom

Kings County Historical Society & Museum, Hampton NB

Kirkland Museum of Fine & Decorative Art, Denver CO

Knights of Columbus Supreme Council, Knights of Columbus Museum, New Haven CT

Kyiv Museum of Russian Art, Kyiv

La Salle University Art Museum, Philadelphia PA

Lafayette College, Lafayette College Art Galleries, Easton PA

LaGrange Art Museum, LaGrange GA

Lahore Museum, Lahore

Lamar University, Dishman Art Museum, Beaumont TX

Latino Art Museum, Pomona CA

Launceston City Council, Queen Victoria Museum and Art Gallery, Launceston

Le Musee des Beaux-Arts, Brest

League of New Hampshire Craftsmen, Grodin Permanent Collection Museum, Concord NH

Leeds Museums & Galleries, Leeds

LeMoyne Art Foundation, Center for the Visual Arts, Tallahassee FL

LeSueur County Historical Society, Chapter One, Elysian MN

Lightner Museum, Saint Augustine FL

Lincoln County Historical Association, Inc, 1811 Old Lincoln County Jail & Lincoln County Museum, Wiscasset ME

Lincolnshire County Council, Library & Heritage Services, Lincoln

Lincolnshire County Council, The Collection: Art & Archaeology in Lincolnshire, Lincoln

Livingston County Historical Society, Museum, Geneseo NY

Long Beach Museum of Art Foundation., Long Beach CA

The Long Island Museum of American Art, History & Carriages, Stony Brook NY

Longfellow-Evangeline State Commemorative Area, Saint Martinville LA

Longue Vue House & Gardens, New Orleans LA

Longview Museum of Fine Art, Longview TX

Louisiana Arts & Science Museum, Baton Rouge LA

Louisiana Department of Culture, Recreation & Tourism, Louisiana State Museum, New Orleans LA

Louisiana State University, Museum of Art, Baton Rouge LA

Loyola Marymount University, Laband Art Gallery, Los Angeles CA

Loyola University Chicago, Loyola University Museum of Art, Chicago IL

Luther College, Fine Arts Collection, Decorah IA

Mabee-Gerrer Museum of Art, Shawnee OK

Macalester College, Macalester College Art Gallery, Saint Paul MN

Madison Museum of Fine Art, Madison GA

Magyar Nemzeti Muzeum - Hungarian National Museum, Budapest

Maine Historical Society, Wadsworth-Longfellow House, Portland ME

Manchester Bidwell Corporation, Manchester Craftsmen's Guild Youth & Arts Program, Pittsburgh PA

Manitoba Historical Society, Dalnavert Museum, Winnipeg MB

Marblehead Museum & Historical Society, Jeremiah Lee Mansion, Marblehead MA

Marblehead Museum & Historical Society, Marblehead MA

The Mariners' Museum, Newport News VA

Maryland Art Place, Baltimore MD

Marylhurst University, The Art Gym, Marylhurst OR

Massillon Museum, Massillon OH

Mattatuck Historical Society, Mattatuck Museum, Waterbury CT

Maude Kerns Art Center, Eugene OR

Maysville, Kentucky Gateway Museum Center, Maysville KY

McCord Museum of Canadian History, Montreal PQ

McLean County Historical Society, McLean County Museum of History, Bloomington IL

Mennello Museum of American Art, Orlando FL

Mercer County Community College, The Gallery, West Windsor NJ

Meredith College, Frankie G Weems Gallery & Rotunda Gallery, Raleigh NC

Mesa Arts Center, Mesa Contemporary Arts Museum, Mesa AZ

Mexican Museum, San Francisco CA

Mezuraj Museum, Tirana

Midwest Museum of American Art, Elkhart IN

Milwaukee County War Memorial Inc., Villa Terrace Decorative Arts Museum, Milwaukee WI

Mingei International, Inc, Mingei International Museum - Balboa Park & Mingei International Museum - Escondido, San Diego CA

Ministry of Cultural Affairs, Bangladesh National Museum, Dhaka

Ministry of Culture & Tourism, The Delphi Museum, 10th Ephorate of Prehistoric & Classical Antiquities, Delphi

Ministry of the Arts & Multiculturalism, National Museum & Art Gallery, Port of Spain

Minnesota Museum of American Art, Saint Paul MN

Minot State University, Northwest Art Center, Minot ND

The Mint Museum, Mint Museum of Craft & Design, Charlotte NC

The Mint Museum, Charlotte NC

Missoula Art Museum, Missoula MT

Arthur Roy Mitchell, A.R. Mitchell Museum, Trinidad CO

Mobile Museum of Art, Mobile AL

Modern Art Museum, Fort Worth TX

James Monroe, Fredericksburg VA

Montana State University, Museum of the Rockies, Bozeman MT

Montclair Art Museum, Montclair NJ

Montreal Museum of Fine Arts, Montreal PQ

Moore College of Art & Design, The Galleries at Moore, Philadelphia PA

Moravska Galerie v Brne, Moravian Gallery in Brno, Brno

Morris Museum, Morristown NJ

Morris-Jumel Mansion, Inc, New York NY

Mount Saint Vincent University, MSVU Art Gallery, Halifax NS

Mount Vernon Hotel Museum & Garden, New York NY

Muscatine Art Center, Museum, Muscatine IA

Musee Carnavalet-Histoire de Paris, Paris

Musee d'art moderne de Ceret, Ceret

Musee des Beaux-Arts/Palais des Archeveques, Museum of Fine Arts, Tours

Musee des Maitres et Artisans du Quebec, Montreal PQ

Musee Guimet, Paris

Musee National d'Histoire et d'Art Luxembourg, Luxembourg City

Musee Regional de lu Cote-Nord, Sept-Iles PQ

Musee Royal Et Domaine De Mariemont, Morlanwelz

Musees Royaux d'Art et d'Histoire, Royal Museums of Art and History, Brussels

Musei Capitolini, Rome

Musei Civici di Padova - Cappella Degli Scrovengni, Musei Civici Agli Eremitani (Civic Museum) - Scrovegni Chapel, Padua

Museo Cerralbo, Madrid

Museo De Las Americas, Denver CO

Museo Del Romanticismo, Museum of the Romantic Period, Madrid

Museo di Capodimonte, Naples

Museu de Evora, Evora

Museu de Grao Vasco, Viseu

The Museum, Greenwood SC

Museum De Lakenhal, Leiden

Museum fur Angewandte Kunst Frankfurt, Museum of Applied Arts, Frankfurt

Museum fur Kunst und Gewerbe Hamburg, Hamburg

Museum Het Prinsenhof, Delft

Museum of Art & History, Santa Cruz, Santa Cruz CA

Museum of Art, Fort Lauderdale, Fort Lauderdale FL

Museum of Arts & Design, New York NY

The Museum of Arts & Sciences Inc, Daytona Beach FL

Museum of Arts & Sciences, Inc, Macon GA

Museum of Contemporary Art, North Miami FL

Museum of Contemporary Craft, Portland OR

Museum of Decorative Arts in Prague, Prague

Museum of Fine Arts Houston, Bayou Bend Collection & Gardens, Houston TX

Museum of Fine Arts, Houston, Rienzi Center for European Decorative Arts, Houston TX

Museum of Fine Arts, Saint Petersburg, Florida, Inc, Saint Petersburg FL

Museum of Florida Art, Deland FL

Museum of Latin American Art, Long Beach CA

Museum of New Mexico, New Mexico Museum of Art, Unit of NM Dept of Cultural Affairs, Santa Fe NM

Museum of Northern Arizona, Flagstaff AZ

Museum of Northern British Columbia, Ruth Harvey Art Gallery, Prince Rupert BC

Museum of Northwest Art, La Conner WA

Museum of the City of New York, Museum, New York NY

Museum of the Plains Indian & Crafts Center, Browning MT

Museum of Vancouver, Vancouver BC

Museum of York County, Rock Hill SC

Museum Plantin-Moretus/Prentenkabinet, Antwerp

Museum zu Allerheiligen, Schaffhausen

Muskegon Museum of Art, Muskegon MI

Muzej za Umjetnost i Obrt, Museum of Arts & Crafts, Zagreb

Muzeul de Istorie Nationala Si Arheologie Constanta, National History & Archaeology Museum, Constanta

Muzeul National Brukenthal, Blue House & Romanian Art Gallery, Sibiu

Muzeul National Brukenthal, Brukenthal Palace & European Art Gallery, Sibiu

Muzeum Narodowe, National Museum in Poznan, Poznan

Narodni Muzej Crne Gore, National Museum of Montenegro, Cetinje

National Archaeological Museum, Athens

National Baseball Hall of Fame & Museum, Inc, Art Collection, Cooperstown NY

National Museum of Ceramic Art & Glass, Baltimore MD

National Museum of Fine Arts of Moldova, Chisinau

The National Museum of Modern Art, Tokyo, Tokyo

National Museum of the American Indian, George Gustav Heye Center, New York NY

National Museum of the American Indian, Smithsonian Institution, Washington DC

National Museum of the Philippines, Manila
National Museum of Women in the Arts, Washington DC
National Museum, Monuments and Art Gallery, Gaborone
National Museums Scotland, National Museum of Scotland, Edinburgh
National Palace Museum, Taiwan, R.O.C.
The National Park Service, United States Department of the Interior, Statue of Liberty National Monument & The Ellis Island Immigration Museum, Washington DC
National Society of Colonial Dames of America in the State of Maryland, Mount Clare Museum House, Baltimore MD
National Society of the Colonial Dames of America in The Commonwealth of Virginia, Wilton House Museum, Richmond VA
Naval Historical Center, The Navy Museum, Washington DC
Nelson Mandela Bay Municipality, Nelson Mandela Metropolitan Art Museum, Port Elizabeth
The Nelson-Atkins Museum of Art, Kansas City MO
The Nemours Foundatioin, Nemours Mansion & Gardens, Wilmington DE
New Britain Museum of American Art, New Britain CT
New Brunswick Museum, Saint John NB
New England Maple Museum, Pittsford VT
New Hampshire Antiquarian Society, Hopkinton Historical Society, Hopkinton NH
New Jersey State Museum, Fine Art Bureau, Trenton NJ
New Mexico State University, Art Gallery, Las Cruces NM
New Visions Gallery, Inc, Marshfield WI
New World Art Center, T F Chen Cultural Center, New York NY
New York State Office of Parks Recreation & Historic Preservation, John Jay Homestead State Historic Site, Katonah NY
North Carolina State University, Gregg Museum of Art & Design, Raleigh NC
North Central Washington Museum, Wenatchee Valley Museum & Cultural Center, Wenatchee WA
North Dakota State University, Memorial Union Gallery, Fargo ND
Norwich Free Academy, Slater Memorial Museum, Norwich CT
Nova Scotia College of Art and Design, Anna Leonowens Gallery, Halifax NS
Noyes Art Gallery, Lincoln NE
The Ogden Museum of Southern Art, University of New Orleans, New Orleans LA
Ohio Historical Society, National Road-Zane Grey Museum, Columbus OH
Ohio University, Kennedy Museum of Art, Athens OH
Okanagan Heritage Museum, Kelowna BC
Olana State Historic Site, Hudson NY
Old Island Restoration Foundation Inc, Oldest House in Key West, Key West FL
The Old Jail Art Center, Albany TX
Old Salem Museums & Gardens, Museum of Early Southern Decorative Arts, Winston Salem NC
Orange County Museum of Art, Newport Beach CA
Owensboro Museum of Fine Art, Owensboro KY
Pacific - Asia Museum, Pasadena CA
Panhandle-Plains Historical Museum, Canyon TX
Paris Gibson Square, Museum of Art, Great Falls MT
Pasadena Museum of History, Pasadena CA
Patrimonio Nacional, Palacios de la Granja y Riofrio, Madrid
The Pennsylvania State University, Palmer Museum of Art, University Park PA
Pewabic Society Inc, Pewabic Pottery, Detroit MI
Phelps County Historical Society, Nebraska Prairie Museum, Holdrege NE
Philadelphia History Museum, Philadelphia PA
Philbrook Museum of Art, Tulsa OK
Phillips County Museum, Holyoke CO
Pilgrim Society, Pilgrim Hall Museum, Plymouth MA
Pinacoteca Provincial, Bari
Plains Art Museum, Fargo ND
Plumas County Museum, Quincy CA
Polk Museum of Art, Lakeland FL
Portland Art Museum, Portland OR
Portsmouth Historical Society, John Paul Jones House & Discover Portsmouth, Portsmouth NH
Pretoria Art Museum, Municipal Art Gallery, Pretoria
Princeton University, Princeton University Art Museum, Princeton NJ
Principia College, School of Nations Museum, Elsah IL

Purdue University Galleries, West Lafayette IN
Putnam Museum of History and Natural Science, Davenport IA
Queens College, City University of New York, Godwin-Ternbach Museum, Flushing NY
Queensborough Community College, Art Gallery, Bayside NY
Rabindra Bhavan Art Gallery, Lalit Kala Akademi (National Academy of Art), New Delhi
Randall Junior Museum, San Francisco CA
Randolph College, Maier Museum of Art, Lynchburg VA
Reading Public Museum, Reading PA
Rijksmuseum Twenthe, Rijksmuseum Twenthe, Enschede
Rollins College, George D & Harriet W Cornell Fine Arts Museum, Winter Park FL
The Rooms Corporation of Newfoundland & Labrador, Saint John's NF
Rose Lehrman Art Gallery, Harrisburg PA
Ross Memorial Museum, Saint Andrews NB
Roswell Artist-in-Residence Foundation, Anderson Museum of Contemporary Art, Roswell NM
Roswell Museum & Art Center, Roswell NM
Royal Arts Foundation, Belcourt Castle, Newport RI
Royal Pavilion & Museums, Brighton Museum & Art Gallery, Brighton
Ryerss Victorian Museum & Library, Philadelphia PA
Saco Museum, Saco ME
Saginaw Art Museum, Saginaw MI
Saint Augustine Historical Society, Oldest House Museum Complex, Saint Augustine FL
Saint Bonaventure University, Regina A Quick Center for the Arts, Saint Bonaventure NY
Saint Louis County Historical Society, St. Louis County Historical Society, Duluth MN
St Mary's College of Maryland, The Dwight Frederick Boyden Gallery, St Mary's City MD
Saint Olaf College, Flaten Art Museum, Northfield MN
Saint Peter's College, Art Gallery, Jersey City NJ
Salisbury House Foundation, Salisbury House and Garden, Des Moines IA
San Angelo Museum of Fine Arts, San Angelo TX
The Sandwich Historical Society, Inc & Sandwich Glass Museum, Sandwich Glass Museum, Sandwich MA
Santa Clara University, de Saisset Museum, Santa Clara CA
Santa Monica Museum of Art, Santa Monica CA
Scottsdale Cultural Council, Scottsdale Museum of Contemporary Art, Scottsdale AZ
Scripps College, Ruth Chandler Williamson Gallery, Claremont CA
Seneca-Iroquois National Museum, Salamanca NY
Ella Sharp, Jackson MI
Shelburne Museum, Museum, Shelburne VT
Shirley Plantation Foundation, Charles City VA
Slovenska Narodna Galeria, Slovak National Gallery, Bratislava
Smithsonian Institution, Washington DC
Society for Contemporary Craft, Pittsburgh PA
The Society of the Cincinnati at Anderson House, Washington DC
Sonoma State University, University Art Gallery, Rohnert Park CA
Soprintendenza per I beni storici artistici ed etnoantropologici per le province di Mantova Brescia e Cremona, Museo di Palazzo Ducale, Mantua
South Carolina Artisans Center, Walterboro SC
South Dakota State University, South Dakota Art Museum, Brookings SD
Southeastern Center for Contemporary Art, Winston Salem NC
Southern Illinois University Carbondale, University Museum, Carbondale IL
Southern Ohio Museum Corporation, Southern Ohio Museum, Portsmouth OH
Spartanburg Art Museum, Spartanburg SC
The Speed Art Museum, Louisville KY
Spertus Institute of Jewish Studies, Chicago IL
Springfield Art Museum, Springfield MO
Stanford University, Cantor Arts Center at Stanford University, Stanford CA
The State Museum of Fine Arts of Tatarstan Republic, Kazan
The State Museum of Oriental Art, Moscow
State University of New York at Binghamton, Binghamton University Art Museum, Binghamton NY
State University of New York at Geneseo, Bertha V B Lederer Gallery, Geneseo NY

State University of New York at New Paltz, Samuel Dorsky Museum of Art, New Paltz NY
State University of New York College at Buffalo, Buffalo NY
State University of New York College at Cortland, Dowd Fine Arts Gallery, Cortland NY
Staten Island Museum, Staten Island NY
Stauth Foundation & Museum, Stauth Memorial Museum, Montezuma KS
T C Steele, Nashville IN
Stone Quarry Hill Art Park, Winner Gallery, Cazenovia NY
Stratford Historical Society, Catharine B Mitchell Museum, Stratford CT
Suan Pakkad Palace Museum, Bangkok
The Summit County Historical Society of Akron, OH, Akron OH
Suomen Kansallismuseo, National Museum of Finland, Helsinki
Swedish American Museum Association of Chicago, Chicago IL
Switzerland County Historical Society Inc, Switzerland County Historical Museum, Vevay IN
Syracuse University, Art Collection, Syracuse NY
Syracuse University, SUArt Galleries, Syracuse NY
Tacoma Art Museum, Tacoma WA
Taft Museum of Art, Cincinnati OH
Tallahassee Museum of History & Natural Science, Tallahassee FL
Tampa Museum of Art, Tampa FL
Taos, Ernest Blumenschein Home & Studio, Taos NM
Lillian & Coleman Taube Museum of Art, Minot ND
Temiskaming Art Gallery, Haileybury ON
Texas Tech University, Museum of Texas Tech University, Lubbock TX
Thomas More College, Eva G Farris Art Gallery, Crestview KY
Tohono Chul Park, Tucson AZ
The Tokugawa Reimeikai Foundation, The Tokugawa Art Museum, Nagoya
Tokyo University of the Arts, The University Art Museum, Tokyo
Toledo Museum of Art, Toledo OH
Topeka & Shawnee County Public Library, Alice C Sabatini Gallery, Topeka KS
Towson University, Asian Arts & Culture Center, Towson MD
Trenton City Museum, Trenton NJ
Triton Museum of Art, Santa Clara CA
Tryon Palace Historic Sites & Gardens, New Bern NC
Tubac Center of the Arts, Santa Cruz Valley Art Association, Tubac AZ
Tulane University, Newcomb Art Gallery, New Orleans LA
Tver Art Gallery, Tver
Mark Twain, Hartford CT
Tyne and Wear Archives & Museums, Sunderland Museum & Winter Gardens, Newcastle-upon-Tyne
Ukrainian Institute of Modern Art, Chicago IL
Ukrainian Canadian Archives & Museum of Alberta, Edmonton AB
The Ukrainian Museum, New York NY
UMLAUF Sculpture Garden & Museum, Austin TX
United Society of Shakers, Shaker Museum, New Gloucester ME
United States Coast Guard Museum, New London CT
United States Figure Skating Association, World Figure Skating Museum & Hall of Fame, Colorado Springs CO
United States Naval Academy, USNA Museum, Annapolis MD
University of Alabama at Birmingham, Visual Arts Gallery, Birmingham AL
University of British Columbia, Museum of Anthropology, Vancouver BC
University of California, Richard L Nelson Gallery & Fine Arts Collection, Davis CA
University of California, Berkeley, The Magnes Collection of Jewish Art & Life, Berkeley CA
University of Chicago, Oriental Institute, Chicago IL
University of Colorado, CU Art Museum, Boulder CO
University of Georgia, Georgia Museum of Art, Athens GA
University of Illinois at Urbana-Champaign, Krannert Art Museum and Kinkead Pavilion, Champaign IL
University of Illinois at Urbana-Champaign, Spurlock Museum, Champaign IL
University of Indianapolis, Christel DeHaan Fine Arts Gallery, Indianapolis IN
University of Louisiana at Lafayette, Paul and Lulu Hilliard University Art Museum, Lafayette LA

University of Manitoba, Faculty of Architecture Exhibition Centre, Winnipeg MB
University of Miami, Lowe Art Museum, Coral Gables FL
University of Minnesota, Katherine E Nash Gallery, Minneapolis MN
University of Missouri, Museum of Art & Archaeology, Columbia MO
University of Montana, Montana Museum of Art & Culture, Missoula MT
University of Nebraska, Lincoln, Sheldon Memorial Art Gallery & Sculpture Garden, Lincoln NE
University of Nevada, Reno, Sheppard Contemporary & University Galleries, Reno NV
University of New Mexico, The Harwood Museum of Art, Taos NM
University of North Carolina at Chapel Hill, Ackland Art Museum, Chapel Hill NC
University of North Dakota, Hughes Fine Arts Center-Col Eugene Myers Art Gallery, Grand Forks ND
University of Pennsylvania, Museum of Archaeology & Anthropology, Philadelphia PA
University of Pittsburgh, University Art Gallery, Pittsburgh PA
University of Richmond, University Museums, Richmond VA
University of Rochester, Memorial Art Gallery, Rochester NY
University of Texas Pan American, Charles & Dorothy Clark Gallery; University Gallery, Edinburg TX
University of Texas Pan American, UTPA Art Galleries, Edinburg TX
University of Toronto, University of Toronto Art Centre, Toronto ON
University of Utah, Utah Museum of Fine Arts, Salt Lake City UT
University of Victoria, The Legacy Art Gallery, Victoria BC
University of Virginia, The Fralin Museum of Art at the University of Virginia, Charlottesville VA
University of Washington, Henry Art Gallery, Seattle WA
University of Wisconsin-Eau Claire, Foster Gallery, Eau Claire WI
University of Wisconsin-Madison, Chazen Museum of Art, Madison WI
University of Wisconsin-Madison, Wisconsin Union Galleries, Madison WI
USS Constitution Museum, Boston MA
Utah Department of Natural Resources, Division of Parks & Recreation, Territorial Statehouse State Park Museum, Fillmore UT
Utah State University, Nora Eccles Harrison Museum of Art, Logan UT
Valentine Richmond History Center, Richmond VA
Vassar College, The Frances Lehman Loeb Art Center, Poughkeepsie NY
Vesterheim Norwegian-American Museum, Decorah IA
Victoria Mansion - Morse Libby House, Portland ME
Vietnam Fine Arts Museum, Hanoi
Vizcaya Museum & Gardens, Miami FL
Vorres Museum of Contemporary Greek Art and Folk Art, Attica
VSA Arts of New Mexico, Very Special Arts Gallery, Albuquerque NM
Wade House Historic Site-Wisconsin Historical Society, Wesley W. Jung Carriage Museum, Greenbush WI
Wadsworth Atheneum Museum of Art, Hartford CT
Wake Forest University, Museum of Anthropology, Winston Salem NC
The Walker African American Museum & Research Center, Las Vegas NV
Walker Art Gallery, Liverpool
The Wallace Collection, London
Wallace State Community College, Evelyn Burrow Museum, Hanceville AL
Warner House Association, MacPheadris-Warner House, Portsmouth NH
Washburn University, Mulvane Art Museum, Topeka KS
Washington University, Mildred Lane Kemper Art Museum, Saint Louis MO
Waterloo Center of the Arts, Waterloo IA
Waterworks Visual Arts Center, Salisbury NC
Wayne Center for the Arts, Wooster OH
West Florida Historic Preservation, Inc/University of West Florida, T T Wentworth, Jr Florida State Museum; Historic Pensacola Village; Pensacola Historical Society & Resource Center, Pensacola FL
Western Illinois University, Western Illinois University Art Gallery, Macomb IL

Wheaton College, Beard and Weil Galleries, Norton MA
Willard House & Clock Museum, Inc, North Grafton MA
William Morris Gallery, London
Wiregrass Museum of Art, Dothan AL
Wisconsin Historical Society, Wisconsin Historical Museum, Madison WI
Woodlawn/The Pope-Leighey, Mount Vernon VA
Woodmere Art Museum Inc, Philadelphia PA
Worcester Art Museum, Worcester MA
World Erotic Art Museum, Miami Beach FL
Xavier University, Art Gallery, Cincinnati OH
Yokohama Museum of Art, Yokohama
Yuma Fine Arts Association, Yuma Art Center, Yuma AZ
Zigler Art Museum, Jennings LA
Zurich University of the Arts (ZHdK), Museum Fuer Gestaltung Zurich (Museum of Design Zurich), Zurich

COINS & MEDALS

Academy of the New Church, Glencairn Museum, Bryn Athyn PA
Adams County Historical Society, Gettysburg PA
African American Museum in Philadelphia, Philadelphia PA
Al Ain National Museum, Al Ain
Alaska Heritage Museum at Wells Fargo, Anchorage AK
Albany Institute of History & Art, Albany NY
Albuquerque Museum of Art & History, Albuquerque NM
Alton Museum of History & Art, Inc, Alton IL
American Swedish Historical Foundation & Museum, American Swedish Historical Museum, Philadelphia PA
Archaeological Museum of the American University of Beirut, Beirut
Art & Culture Center of Hollywood, Art Gallery/Multidisciplinary Cultural Center, Hollywood FL
The Art Museum at the University of Kentucky, Lexington KY
ArtSpace/Lima, Lima OH
Badisches Landesmuseum, Karlsruhe
Ball State University, Museum of Art, Muncie IN
Balzekas Museum of Lithuanian Culture, Chicago IL
Baroda Museum and Picture Gallery, Baroda
Bennington Museum, Bennington VT
Berkshire Museum, Pittsfield MA
Brick Store Museum, Kennebunk ME
Bronx Community College (CUNY), Hall of Fame for Great Americans, Bronx NY
Brookgreen Gardens, Murrells Inlet SC
Byzantine & Christian Museum, Athens, Athens
Cambridge Museum, Cambridge NE
Canadian Museum of Civilization, Gatineau PQ
Canadian War Museum, Ottawa ON
Cape Ann Historical Association, Cape Ann Museum, Gloucester MA
Cedar Rapids Museum of Art, Cedar Rapids IA
Cincinnati Art Museum, Cincinnati Art Museum, Cincinnati OH
City of High Point, High Point Museum, High Point NC
Clark County Historical Society, Pioneer - Krier Museum, Ashland KS
College of William & Mary, Muscarelle Museum of Art, Williamsburg VA
The College of Wooster, The College of Wooster Art Museum, Wooster OH
Colorado Historical Society, Colorado History Museum, Denver CO
Concordia Historical Institute, Saint Louis MO
Cornell University, Herbert F Johnson Museum of Art, Ithaca NY
Craft and Folk Art Museum (CAFAM), Los Angeles CA
Cripple Creek District Museum, Cripple Creek CO
Crocker Art Museum, Sacramento CA
Crook County Museum & Art Gallery, Sundance WY
Dallas Museum of Art, Dallas TX
DAR Museum, National Society Daughters of the American Revolution, Washington DC
Dartmouth College, Hood Museum of Art, Hanover NH
Dawson City Museum & Historical Society, Dawson City YT
Department of Antiquities, Cyprus Museum, Nicosia
Detroit Institute of Arts, Detroit MI
Doncaster Museum and Art Gallery, Doncaster

Dundee City Council Leisure & Communities Department, The McManus: Dundee's Art Gallery & Museum, Dundee
Dundurn Castle, Hamilton ON
Everhart Museum, Scranton PA
Fairbanks Museum & Planetarium, Saint Johnsbury VT
Farmington Village Green & Library Association, Stanley-Whitman House, Farmington CT
Favell Museum of Western Art & Indian Artifacts, Klamath Falls OR
Fetherston Foundation, Packwood House Museum, Lewisburg PA
Florence Museum, Florence SC
Florida State University, John & Mable Ringling Museum of Art, Sarasota FL
Fondazione Musei Civici Di Venezia, Museo Correr, Venice
Forest Lawn Museum, Glendale CA
Freer Gallery of Art & Arthur M Sackler Gallery, Arthur M Sackler Gallery, Washington DC
Frontier Times Museum, Bandera TX
Fulton County Historical Society Inc, Fulton County Museum (Tetzlaff Reference Room), Rochester IN
General Board of Discipleship, The United Methodist Church, The Upper Room Chapel & Museum, Nashville TN
Germanisches Nationalmuseum, Nuremberg
Glanmore National Historic Site of Canada, Belleville ON
Grand Rapids Art Museum, Grand Rapids MI
Grand Rapids Public Museum, Public Museum of Grand Rapids, Grand Rapids MI
Greek Ministry of Culture, Archaeological Museum of Thessaloniki, Thessaloniki
Guilford College, Art Gallery, Greensboro NC
Halifax Historical Society, Inc, Halifax Historical Museum, Daytona Beach FL
Harvard University, Semitic Museum, Cambridge MA
Hastings Museum of Natural & Cultural History, Hastings NE
Headquarters Fort Monroe, Dept of Army, Casemate Museum, Hampton VA
Hebrew Union College, Skirball Cultural Center, Los Angeles CA
Hecht Museum, Haifa
Heras Institute of Indian History and Culture, Heras Institute Museum, Mumbai
Heritage Glass Museum, Glassboro NJ
Heritage Museum & Cultural Center, Baker LA
Hermitage Foundation Museum, Norfolk VA
Hillwood Museum & Gardens Foundation, Hillwood Estate Museum & Gardens, Washington DC
The Hispanic Society of America, Museum & Library, New York NY
Historic Hudson Valley, Pocantico Hills NY
Historical Society of Cheshire County, Keene NH
History Museum of Mobile, Mobile AL
Huguenot Historical Society of New Paltz Galleries, New Paltz NY
Huntington Museum of Art, Huntington WV
Huronia Museum, Gallery of Historic Huronia, Midland ON
Imperial Calcasieu Museum, Gibson-Barham Gallery, Lake Charles LA
Independence Historical Museum & Art Center, Independence KS
Independence Seaport Museum, Philadelphia PA
Independent Administrative Institution National Institutes for Cultural Heritage, Tokyo National Museum, Tokyo
Indiana University, Art Museum, Bloomington IN
Institute of Puerto Rican Culture, Museo Fuerte Conde de Mirasol, Vieques PR
Iroquois County Historical Society Museum, Old Courthouse Museum, Watseka IL
Iroquois Indian Museum, Howes Cave NY
The Israel Museum, Jerusalem, Samuel & Saidye Bronfman Archaeology Wing, Jerusalem
The Israel Museum, Jerusalem, Jerusalem
Jacksonville University, Alexander Brest Museum & Gallery, Jacksonville FL
James Dick Foundation, Festival - Institute, Round Top TX
Jamestown-Yorktown Foundation, Jamestown Settlement, Williamsburg VA
Jersey City Museum, Jersey City NJ
The Jewish Museum, New York NY
Johns Hopkins University, Evergreen Museum & Library, Baltimore MD
Bob Jones University Museum & Gallery Inc, Greenville SC
Joslyn Art Museum, Omaha NE

Kenosha Public Museums, Kenosha WI

Kereszteny Muzeum, Christian Museum, Esztergom

Kings County Historical Society & Museum, Hampton NB

Knights of Columbus Supreme Council, Knights of Columbus Museum, New Haven CT

Koochiching Museums, International Falls MN

Kunsthistorisches Museum Vienna, Museum of Fine Arts, Vienna

Kyiv Museum of Russian Art, Kyiv

Lahore Museum, Lahore

Latvijas Nacionalais Makslas Muzejs, Arsenals Exhibition Hall, Riga

Le Grand Curtius, Musée d'Ansembourg, Liege

Lehigh University Art Galleries, Museum Operation, Bethlehem PA

Liberty Memorial Museum & Archives, The National Museum of World War I, Kansas City MO

Lightner Museum, Saint Augustine FL

Lincolnshire County Council, Library & Heritage Services, Lincoln

Lincolnshire County Council, The Collection: Art & Archaeology in Lincolnshire, Lincoln

The Long Island Museum of American Art, History & Carriages, Stony Brook NY

Longfellow-Evangeline State Commemorative Area, Saint Martinville LA

Magyar Nemzeti Muzeum - Hungarian National Museum, Budapest

Manitoba Historical Society, Dalnavert Museum, Winnipeg MB

Marblehead Museum & Historical Society, Jeremiah Lee Mansion, Marblehead MA

Marblehead Museum & Historical Society, Marblehead MA

The Mariners' Museum, Newport News VA

Maysville, Kentucky Gateway Museum Center, Maysville KY

McDowell House & Apothecary Shop, Danville KY

McLean County Historical Society, McLean County Museum of History, Bloomington IL

McMaster University, McMaster Museum of Art, Hamilton ON

Medina Railroad Museum, Medina NY

Mezuraj Museum, Tirana

Middlebury College, Museum of Art, Middlebury VT

Ministry of Alberta Culture, Royal Alberta Museum, Edmonton AB

Ministry of Cultural Affairs, Bangladesh National Museum, Dhaka

Ministry of Culture & Tourism, The Delphi Museum, 10th Ephorate of Prehistoric & Classical Antiquities, Delphi

Ministry of the Arts & Multiculturalism, National Museum & Art Gallery, Port of Spain

Mississippi River Museum at Mud-Island River Park, Memphis TN

Moderna Galerija, Gallery of Modern Art, Zagreb

Musee des Beaux-Arts d'Orleans, Historical & Archaeological Museum of Orleans, Orleans

Musee des Beaux-Arts/Palais des Archeveques, Museum of Fine Arts, Tours

Musee National d'Histoire et d'Art Luxembourg, Luxembourg City

Musee Royal Et Domaine De Mariemont, Morlanwelz

Musees Royaux d'Art et d'Histoire, Royal Museums of Art and History, Brussels

Musei Capitolini, Rome

Musei Civici di Padova - Cappella Degli Scrovengni, Musei Civici Agli Eremitani (Civic Museum) - Scrovegni Chapel, Padua

Museo Cerralbo, Madrid

Museo Civico Giovanni Fattori, Livorno

Museo De Las Americas, Denver CO

Museo de Navarra, Pamplona

Museo di Capodimonte, Naples

Museu de Evora, Evora

Museu de Grao Vasco, Viseu

Museu Nacional D'Art De Catalunya, National Art Museum, Barcelona

The Museum, Greenwood SC

Museum De Lakenhal, Leiden

Museum fur Kunst und Gewerbe Hamburg, Hamburg

The Museum of Arts & Sciences Inc, Daytona Beach FL

Museum of Northern British Columbia, Ruth Harvey Art Gallery, Prince Rupert BC

Museum of the City of New York, Museum, New York NY

Museum of Vancouver, Vancouver BC

Museum zu Allerheiligen, Schaffhausen

Muzej za Umjetnost i Obrt, Museum of Arts & Crafts, Zagreb

Muzeul de Istorie Nationala Si Arheologie Constanta, National History & Archaeology Museum, Constanta

Muzeul National Brukenthal, Brukenthal Palace & European Art Gallery, Sibiu

Muzeum Narodowe, National Museum in Poznan, Poznan

The Namur Provincial Museum of Ancient Arts, Namur

Narodna Galerija, National Gallery of Slovenia, Ljubljana

Narodni Muzej Crne Gore, National Museum of Montenegro, Cetinje

National Baseball Hall of Fame & Museum, Inc, Art Collection, Cooperstown NY

National Galleries of Scotland, Scottish National Gallery, Edinburgh

National Museum of Fine Arts of Moldova, Chisinau

National Museum of the American Indian, George Gustav Heye Center, New York NY

National Museum, Monuments and Art Gallery, Gaborone

National Museums Scotland, National Museum of Scotland, Edinburgh

The National Park Service, United States Department of the Interior, Statue of Liberty National Monument & The Ellis Island Immigration Museum, Washington DC

Naval Historical Center, The Navy Museum, Washington DC

New Brunswick Museum, Saint John NB

New Hampshire Antiquarian Society, Hopkinton Historical Society, Hopkinton NH

New Jersey Historical Society, Newark NJ

Noordbrabants Museum, Hertogenbosch

Northern Arizona University, Art Museum & Galleries, Flagstaff AZ

Norwich Free Academy, Slater Memorial Museum, Norwich CT

Ohio Historical Society, National Afro-American Museum & Cultural Center, Wilberforce OH

Order Sons of Italy in America, Garibaldi & Meucci Museum, Staten Island NY

Pacific - Asia Museum, Pasadena CA

Panhandle-Plains Historical Museum, Canyon TX

The Pennsylvania State University, Palmer Museum of Art, University Park PA

Phelps County Historical Society, Nebraska Prairie Museum, Holdrege NE

Philadelphia History Museum, Philadelphia PA

Plainsman Museum, Aurora NE

Plumas County Museum, Quincy CA

Polish Museum of America, Chicago IL

Portland Art Museum, Portland OR

Putnam Museum of History and Natural Science, Davenport IA

Queens College, City University of New York, Godwin-Ternbach Museum, Flushing NY

Rabindra Bhavan Art Gallery, Lalit Kala Akademi (National Academy of Art), New Delhi

Reading Public Museum, Reading PA

Riley County Historical Society & Museum, Riley County Historical Museum, Manhattan KS

Rollins College, George D & Harriet W Cornell Fine Arts Museum, Winter Park FL

The Rooms Corporation of Newfoundland & Labrador, Saint John's NF

Royal Ontario Museum, Dept of Western Art & Culture, Toronto ON

Saco Museum, Saco ME

Saint Augustine Historical Society, Oldest House Museum Complex, Saint Augustine FL

Saint Joseph's Oratory, Museum, Montreal PQ

Saint Louis County Historical Society, St. Louis County Historical Society, Duluth MN

Saint Mary's College of California, Hearst Art Gallery, Moraga CA

Saint Peter's College, Art Gallery, Jersey City NJ

Savitsky Karakalpakstan State Art Museum, Nukus

Schweinfurth Art Center, Auburn NY

Shirley Plantation Foundation, Charles City VA

The Society of the Cincinnati at Anderson House, Washington DC

Soprintendenza per I beni storici artistici ed etnoantropologici per le province di Mantova Brescia e Cremona, Museo di Palazzo Ducale, Mantua

The Speed Art Museum, Louisville KY

Spertus Institute of Jewish Studies, Chicago IL

Staatliche Munzsammlung, State Coin Collection, Munich

Stanford University, Cantor Arts Center at Stanford University, Stanford CA

Staten Island Museum, Staten Island NY

Stauth Foundation & Museum, Stauth Memorial Museum, Montezuma KS

Ste Genevieve Museum, Sainte Genevieve MO

Stiftung Deutsches Historisches Museum, Berlin

Suan Pakkad Palace Museum, Bangkok

Suomen Kansallismuseo, National Museum of Finland, Helsinki

Swedish American Museum Association of Chicago, Chicago IL

Syracuse University, SUArt Galleries, Syracuse NY

Tampa Museum of Art, Tampa FL

Tver Art Gallery, Tver

The Ukrainian Museum, New York NY

United Society of Shakers, Shaker Museum, New Gloucester ME

United States Coast Guard Museum, New London CT

United States Military Academy, West Point Museum, West Point NY

United States Naval Academy, USNA Museum, Annapolis MD

Universalmuseum Joanneum GmbH, Graz

University of British Columbia, Museum of Anthropology, Vancouver BC

University of California, Berkeley, The Magnes Collection of Jewish Art & Life, Berkeley CA

University of California, Santa Barbara, University Art Museum, Santa Barbara CA

University of Colorado, CU Art Museum, Boulder CO

University of Georgia, Georgia Museum of Art, Athens GA

University of Illinois at Urbana-Champaign, Spurlock Museum, Champaign IL

University of Indianapolis, Christel DeHaan Fine Arts Gallery, Indianapolis IN

University of Louisiana at Lafayette, Paul and Lulu Hilliard University Art Museum, Lafayette LA

University of Pennsylvania, Museum of Archaeology & Anthropology, Philadelphia PA

University of Richmond, University Museums, Richmond VA

University of Saskatchewan, Diefenbaker Canada Centre, Saskatoon SK

University of Virginia, The Fralin Museum of Art at the University of Virginia, Charlottesville VA

University of Wisconsin-Madison, Chazen Museum of Art, Madison WI

USS Constitution Museum, Boston MA

Vesterheim Norwegian-American Museum, Decorah IA

Vorres Museum of Contemporary Greek Art and Folk Art, Attica

The Walker African American Museum & Research Center, Las Vegas NV

George Washington, Alexandria VA

Washington University, Mildred Lane Kemper Art Museum, Saint Louis MO

West Florida Historic Preservation, Inc/University of West Florida, T T Wentworth, Jr Florida State Museum; Historic Pensacola Village; Pensacola Historical Society & Resource Center, Pensacola FL

Wheaton College, Beard and Weil Galleries, Norton MA

Willard House & Clock Museum, Inc, North Grafton MA

Wisconsin Historical Society, Wisconsin Historical Museum, Madison WI

Woodlawn/The Pope-Leighey, Mount Vernon VA

Worcester Art Museum, Worcester MA

World Erotic Art Museum, Miami Beach FL

Yarmouth County Historical Society, Yarmouth County Museum & Archives, Yarmouth NS

COLLAGES

African American Museum in Philadelphia, Philadelphia PA

Albuquerque Museum of Art & History, Albuquerque NM

American Sport Art Museum and Archives, Daphne AL

Arizona Museum For Youth, Mesa AZ

Arnot Art Museum, Elmira NY

Art & Culture Center of Hollywood, Art Gallery/Multidisciplinary Cultural Center, Hollywood FL

Art Gallery of Calgary, Calgary AB

The Art Museum at the University of Kentucky, Lexington KY

Art Without Walls Inc, New York NY

Arts Council of Fayetteville-Cumberland County, The Arts Center, Fayetteville NC

CONCEPTUAL ART

COSTUMES

Abington Art Center, Jenkintown PA
Academy of the New Church, Glencairn Museum, Bryn Athyn PA
Adams County Historical Society, Gettysburg PA
African American Museum in Philadelphia, Philadelphia PA
African Art Museum of Maryland, Columbia MD
Albuquerque Museum of Art & History, Albuquerque NM
American Museum of the Moving Image, Astoria NY
American Swedish Historical Foundation & Museum, American Swedish Historical Museum, Philadelphia PA
Amherst Museum, Amherst NY
Anchorage Museum at Rasmuson Center, Anchorage AK
The Andy Warhol Museum, Museum, Pittsburgh PA
Appaloosa Museum and Heritage Center, Moscow ID
Arab American National Museum, Dearborn MI
Arapahoe Community College, Colorado Gallery of the Arts, Littleton CO
Arizona Historical Society-Yuma, Sanguinetti House Museum & Garden, Yuma AZ
Arizona Museum For Youth, Mesa AZ
Art Center of Battle Creek, Battle Creek MI
Art Metropole, Toronto ON
The Art Museum at the University of Kentucky, Lexington KY
Art Without Walls Inc, New York NY
ArtSpace/Lima, Lima OH
Atlanta Historical Society Inc, Atlanta History Center, Atlanta GA
Badisches Landesmuseum, Karlsruhe
Baldwin Historical Society Museum, Baldwin NY
Balzekas Museum of Lithuanian Culture, Chicago IL
Barker Character, Comic and Cartoon Museum, Cheshire CT
Baroda Museum and Picture Gallery, Baroda
The Bartlett Museum, Amesbury MA
Bayerisches Nationalmuseum, Bavarian National Museum, Munich
Bennington Museum, Bennington VT
Berkshire Museum, Pittsfield MA
Besser Museum for Northeast Michigan, Alpena MI
Birmingham Museum of Art, Birmingham AL
Brick Store Museum, Kennebunk ME
Brown University, Haffenreffer Museum of Anthropology, Providence RI
Bruce Museum, Inc, Greenwich CT
Byzantine & Christian Museum, Athens, Athens
Cabot's Old Indian Pueblo Museum, Desert Hot Springs CA
Cambridge Museum, Cambridge NE
Canadian Museum of Civilization, Gatineau PQ
Canadian Museum of Nature, Musee Canadien de la Nature, Ottawa ON
Canton Museum of Art, Canton OH
Caramoor Center for Music & the Arts, Inc, Rosen House at Caramoor, Katonah NY
Carson County Square House Museum, Panhandle TX
Carteret County Historical Society, The History Place, Morehead City NC
Center for Puppetry Arts, Atlanta GA
Billie Trimble Chandler, Texas State Museum of Asian Cultures, Corpus Christi TX
Chatham Historical Society, The Atwood House Museum, Chatham MA
Church of Jesus Christ of Latter-Day Saints, Museum of Church History & Art, Salt Lake City UT
Cincinnati Art Museum, Cincinnati Art Museum, Cincinnati OH
City of Atlanta, Atlanta Cyclorama & Civil War Museum, Atlanta GA
City of High Point, High Point Museum, High Point NC
The City of Petersburg Museums, Petersburg VA
Clark County Historical Society, Heritage Center of Clark County, Springfield OH
Cohasset Historical Society, Pratt Building (Society Headquarters), Cohasset MA
Colorado Historical Society, Colorado History Museum, Denver CO
Columbia County Historical Society, Columbia County Museum and Library, Kinderhook NY
Columbus Museum, Columbus GA
Concord Museum, Concord MA
Concordia Historical Institute, Saint Louis MO
Craft and Folk Art Museum (CAFAM), Los Angeles CA
Cranford Historical Society, Cranford NJ
Cripple Creek District Museum, Cripple Creek CO

Crocker Art Museum, Sacramento CA
Crow Wing County Historical Society, Brainerd MN
Culberson County Historical Museum, Van Horn TX
Danville Museum of Fine Arts & History, Danville VA
DAR Museum, National Society Daughters of the American Revolution, Washington DC
Dartmouth College, Hood Museum of Art, Hanover NH
Dartmouth Heritage Museum, Dartmouth NS
Delta Blues Museum, Clarksdale MS
Denison University, Art Gallery, Granville OH
Department of Museums Malaysia, National Museum, Kuala Lumpur
Designmuseum Danmark, Copenhagen
Detroit Institute of Arts, Detroit MI
Doncaster Museum and Art Gallery, Doncaster
Dundee City Council Leisure & Communities Department, The McManus: Dundee's Art Gallery & Museum, Dundee
Erie County Historical Society, Erie PA
Evanston Historical Society, Charles Gates Dawes House, Evanston IL
Fairbanks Museum & Planetarium, Saint Johnsbury VT
Fall River Historical Society, Fall River MA
Farmington Village Green & Library Association, Stanley-Whitman House, Farmington CT
Fashion Institute of Technology, The Museum at FIT, New York NY
Fetherston Foundation, Packwood House Museum, Lewisburg PA
Fine Arts Museums of San Francisco, Legion of Honor, San Francisco CA
Fishkill Historical Society, Van Wyck Homestead Museum, Fishkill NY
Edsel & Eleanor Ford, Grosse Pointe Shores MI
Fort George G Meade Museum, Fort Meade MD
Fort Morgan Heritage Foundation, Fort Morgan CO
Fort Ticonderoga Association, Ticonderoga NY
Freer Gallery of Art & Arthur M Sackler Gallery, Arthur M Sackler Gallery, Washington DC
Fulton County Historical Society Inc, Fulton County Museum (Tetzlaff Reference Room), Rochester IN
Gala-Salvador Dali Foundation Museums, Casa Museu Castell Gala Dali, Figueres
Gem County Historical Society and Museum, Gem County Historical Village Museum, Emmett ID
Genesee Country Village & Museum, John L Wehle Art Gallery, Mumford NY
Germantown Historical Society, Philadelphia PA
Glessner House Museum, Chicago IL
Grand Rapids Art Museum, Grand Rapids MI
Grand Rapids Public Museum, Public Museum of Grand Rapids, Grand Rapids MI
Greene County Historical Society, Bronck Museum, Coxsackie NY
Halifax Historical Society, Inc, Halifax Historical Museum, Daytona Beach FL
Hammond Museum & Japanese Stroll Garden, Cross-Cultural Center, North Salem NY
Harvard University, Semitic Museum, Cambridge MA
Hawkes Bay Art Gallery and Museum, Napier
Hebrew Union College, Skirball Cultural Center, Los Angeles CA
Henry County Museum & Cultural Arts Center, Clinton MO
Henry Gallery Association, Henry Art Gallery, Seattle WA
Henry Sheldon Museum of Vermont History and Research Center, Middlebury VT
Heritage Glass Museum, Glassboro NJ
Heritage Museum & Cultural Center, Baker LA
Hermitage Foundation Museum, Norfolk VA
Hillwood Museum & Gardens Foundation, Hillwood Estate Museum & Gardens, Washington DC
The Hispanic Society of America, Museum & Library, New York NY
Historic Arkansas Museum, Little Rock AR
Historic Cherry Hill, Albany NY
Historic Deerfield, Inc, Deerfield MA
Historic Hudson Valley, Pocantico Hills NY
Historic Newton, Newton MA
Historic Northampton Museum & Education Center, Northampton MA
Historic Paris - Bourbon County, Inc, Hopewell Museum, Paris KY
Historical Society of Bloomfield, Bloomfield NJ
Historisches und Volkerkundemuseum, Historical Museum, St Gallen
The History Center in Tompkins County, Ithaca NY
Hoyt Center for the Arts, New Castle PA
Huguenot Historical Society of New Paltz Galleries, New Paltz NY

Huronia Museum, Gallery of Historic Huronia, Midland ON
Idaho Historical Museum, Boise ID
Imperial Calcasieu Museum, Gibson-Barham Gallery, Lake Charles LA
Independence Seaport Museum, Philadelphia PA
Independent Administrative Institution National Institutes for Cultural Heritage, Tokyo National Museum, Tokyo
Indiana State Museum, Indianapolis IN
International Clown Hall of Fame & Research Center, Inc, West Allis WI
Iredell Museums, Statesville NC
Iroquois County Historical Society Museum, Old Courthouse Museum, Watseka IL
Iroquois Indian Museum, Howes Cave NY
The Israel Museum, Jerusalem, Billy Rose Art Garden, Jerusalem
The Israel Museum, Jerusalem, Jerusalem
James Dick Foundation, Festival - Institute, Round Top TX
Jefferson County Historical Society, Watertown NY
Jefferson County Open Space, Hiwan Homestead Museum, Evergreen CO
Jersey City Museum, Jersey City NJ
Joe Gish's Old West Museum, Fredericksburg TX
Kelly-Griggs House Museum, Red Bluff CA
Kenosha Public Museums, Kenosha WI
Kentucky Derby Museum, Louisville KY
Kentucky Museum of Art and Craft, Louisville KY
Kings County Historical Society & Museum, Hampton NB
Knights of Columbus Supreme Council, Knights of Columbus Museum, New Haven CT
Kunsthistorisches Museum Vienna, Museum of Fine Arts, Vienna
LA County Museum of Art, Los Angeles CA
Lac du Flambeau Band of Lake Superior Chippewa Indians, George W Brown Jr Ojibwe Museum & Cultural Center, Lac Du Flambeau WI
Lafayette Museum Association, Lafayette Museum-Alexandre Mouton House, Lafayette LA
Lafayette Science Museum & Planetarium, Lafayette LA
Lahore Museum, Lahore
Launceston City Council, Queen Victoria Museum and Art Gallery, Launceston
Leeds Museums & Galleries, Leeds
Lehigh Valley Heritage Center, Allentown PA
LeSueur County Historical Society, Chapter One, Elysian MN
Liberty Hall Historic Site, Liberty Hall Museum, Frankfort KY
Liberty Memorial Museum & Archives, The National Museum of World War I, Kansas City MO
Lightner Museum, Saint Augustine FL
Lincoln County Historical Association, Inc, 1811 Old Lincoln County Jail & Lincoln County Museum, Wiscasset ME
Lincolnshire County Council, Library & Heritage Services, Lincoln
Lincolnshire County Council, The Collection: Art & Archaeology in Lincolnshire, Lincoln
Lockwood-Mathews Mansion Museum, Norwalk CT
The Long Island Museum of American Art, History & Carriages, Stony Brook NY
Longue Vue House & Gardens, New Orleans LA
Los Angeles County Museum of Art, Los Angeles CA
Louisiana Arts & Science Museum, Baton Rouge LA
Louisiana Department of Culture, Recreation & Tourism, Louisiana State Museum, New Orleans LA
Louisiana State Exhibit Museum, Shreveport LA
Loveland Museum/Gallery, Loveland CO
Magyar Nemzeti Muzeum - Hungarian National Museum, Budapest
Maine Historical Society, MHS Museum, Portland ME
Maine Historical Society, Wadsworth-Longfellow House, Portland ME
Manitoba Historical Society, Dalnavert Museum, Winnipeg MB
Marblehead Museum & Historical Society, Jeremiah Lee Mansion, Marblehead MA
Marblehead Museum & Historical Society, Marblehead MA
Massillon Museum, Massillon OH
Maysville, Kentucky Gateway Museum Center, Maysville KY
McCord Museum of Canadian History, Montreal PQ
McLean County Historical Society, McLean County Museum of History, Bloomington IL

Museum; Historic Pensacola Village; Pensacola Historical Society & Resource Center, Pensacola FL
Western Kentucky University, Kentucky Library & Museum, Bowling Green KY
Wethersfield Historical Society Inc, Museum, Wethersfield CT
Willard House & Clock Museum, Inc, North Grafton MA
Wiregrass Museum of Art, Dothan AL
Wisconsin Historical Society, Wisconsin Historical Museum, Madison WI
Wistariahurst Museum, Holyoke MA
Witte Museum, San Antonio TX
Woodlawn/The Pope-Leighey, Mount Vernon VA
Yarmouth County Historical Society, Yarmouth County Museum & Archives, Yarmouth NS

CRAFTS

African American Museum in Philadelphia, Philadelphia PA
African Art Museum of Maryland, Columbia MD
Albany Institute of History & Art, Albany NY
Albuquerque Museum of Art & History, Albuquerque NM
American Art Museum, Renwick Gallery, Washington DC
American Folk Art Museum, New York NY
American Swedish Historical Foundation & Museum, American Swedish Historical Museum, Philadelphia PA
American Swedish Institute, Minneapolis MN
Anchorage Museum at Rasmuson Center, Anchorage AK
Appaloosa Museum and Heritage Center, Moscow ID
Arizona Museum For Youth, Mesa AZ
Arizona State University, ASU Art Museum, Tempe AZ
Art & Culture Center of Hollywood, Art Gallery/Multidisciplinary Cultural Center, Hollywood FL
Art Gallery of Nova Scotia, Halifax NS
The Art Museum at the University of Kentucky, Lexington KY
Art Museum of Greater Lafayette, Lafayette IN
Arts Council of Fayetteville-Cumberland County, The Arts Center, Fayetteville NC
ArtSpace/Lima, Lima OH
Asheville Art Museum, Asheville NC
Associates for Community Development, The Arts Center, Inc, Martinsburg WV
Badisches Landesmuseum, Karlsruhe
Balzekas Museum of Lithuanian Culture, Chicago IL
Baroda Museum and Picture Gallery, Baroda
Bay County Historical Society, Historical Museum of Bay County, Bay City MI
Bellevue Arts Museum, Bellevue WA
Besser Museum for Northeast Michigan, Alpena MI
Bradford Brinton, Big Horn WY
Bucks County Historical Society, Mercer Museum, Doylestown PA
Bush-Holley Historic Site & Storehouse Gallery, Greenwich Historical Society/ Bush-Holley House, Cos Cob CT
Cameron Art Museum, Wilmington NC
Canadian Clay and Glass Gallery, Waterloo ON
Canadian Museum of Nature, Musee Canadien de la Nature, Ottawa ON
Carson County Square House Museum, Panhandle TX
Chhatrapati Shivaji Maharaj Vastu Sangrahalaya, Mumbai
City of Pittsfield, Berkshire Artisans, Pittsfield MA
City of Springdale, Shiloh Museum of Ozark History, Springdale AR
Clark County Historical Society, Heritage Center of Clark County, Springfield OH
Columbus Museum, Columbus GA
Concordia Historical Institute, Saint Louis MO
Confederation Centre Art Gallery and Museum, Charlottetown PE
Cooper-Hewitt National Design Museum, Smithsonian Institution, New York NY
Cornwall Gallery Society, Cornwall Regional Art Gallery, Cornwall ON
County of Henrico, Meadow Farm Museum, Glen Allen VA
Craft and Folk Art Museum (CAFAM), Los Angeles CA
Craftsmen's Guild of Mississippi, Inc, Agriculture & Forestry Museum, Ridgeland MS
Craftsmen's Guild of Mississippi, Inc, Mississippi Crafts Center, Ridgeland MS
Cranbrook Art Museum, Bloomfield Hills MI

Cripple Creek District Museum, Cripple Creek CO
Crocker Art Museum, Sacramento CA
Crook County Museum & Art Gallery, Sundance WY
Dallas Museum of Art, Dallas TX
Danforth Museum of Art, Danforth Museum of Art, Framingham MA
Davistown Museum, Liberty Location, Liberty ME
Delta Blues Museum, Clarksdale MS
Detroit Institute of Arts, Detroit MI
Durham Art Guild, Durham NC
East Tennessee State University, The Reece Museum, Johnson City TN
Erie Art Museum, Erie PA
Erie County Historical Society, Erie PA
Wharton Esherick, Paoli PA
Essex Historical Society and Shipbuilding Museum, Essex MA
Evanston Historical Society, Charles Gates Dawes House, Evanston IL
Farmington Village Green & Library Association, Stanley-Whitman House, Farmington CT
Fetherston Foundation, Packwood House Museum, Lewisburg PA
Fine Arts Center for the New River Valley, Pulaski VA
Fine Arts Museums of San Francisco, Legion of Honor, San Francisco CA
Fort Collins Museum of Art, Inc., Fort Collins CO
Freer Gallery of Art & Arthur M Sackler Gallery, Arthur M Sackler Gallery, Washington DC
Fuller Craft Museum, Brockton MA
Gala-Salvador Dali Foundation Museums, Casa Museu Castell Gala Dali, Figueres
Galerie Montcalm, Gatineau PQ
Gallery One Visual Arts Center, Ellensburg WA
Genesee Country Village & Museum, John L Wehle Art Gallery, Mumford NY
Georgetown College Gallery, Georgetown KY
Glasmuseet Ebeltoft, Ebeltoft
Grand Rapids Art Museum, Grand Rapids MI
Greenland National Museum & Archives, Nuuk
Hambidge Center for Creative Arts & Sciences, Rabun Gap GA
Hancock Shaker Village, Inc, Pittsfield MA
Hawkes Bay Art Gallery and Museum, Napier
Haystack Mountain School of Crafts, Deer Isle ME
Hebrew Union College, Skirball Cultural Center, Los Angeles CA
Hebrew Union College Museum, Jewish Institute of Religion Museum, New York NY
Hecht Museum, Haifa
Heritage Museum & Cultural Center, Baker LA
Heritage Museum Association, Inc, The Heritage Museum of Northwest Florida, Valparaiso FL
Hermitage Foundation Museum, Norfolk VA
Hershey Museum, Hershey PA
High Museum of Art, Atlanta GA
Hillwood Museum & Gardens Foundation, Hillwood Estate Museum & Gardens, Washington DC
The Hispanic Society of America, Museum & Library, New York NY
Historic Arkansas Museum, Little Rock AR
Historic Paris - Bourbon County, Inc, Hopewell Museum, Paris KY
The History Center in Tompkins County, Ithaca NY
Hong Kong University, University Museum and Art Gallery, Pokfulam
Hoyt Center for the Arts, New Castle PA
Huntington Museum of Art, Huntington WV
Huronia Museum, Gallery of Historic Huronia, Midland ON
Hyde Park Art Center, Chicago IL
Illinois Historic Preservation Agency, Bishop Hill State Historic Site, Bishop Hill IL
Illinois State Museum, ISM Lockport Gallery, Chicago Gallery & Southern Illinois Art Gallery, Springfield IL
Imperial Calcasieu Museum, Gibson-Barham Gallery, Lake Charles LA
Independence Seaport Museum, Philadelphia PA
Independent Administrative Institution National Institutes for Cultural Heritage, Tokyo National Museum, Tokyo
Indian Arts & Crafts Board, US Dept of the Interior, Sioux Indian Museum, Rapid City SD
Institute of Puerto Rican Culture, Museo Fuerte Conde de Mirasol, Vieques PR
The Interchurch Center, Galleries at the Interchurch Center, New York NY
International Clown Hall of Fame & Research Center, Inc, West Allis WI
Iroquois County Historical Society Museum, Old Courthouse Museum, Watseka IL

Iroquois Indian Museum, Howes Cave NY
The Israel Museum, Jerusalem, Jerusalem
James Dick Foundation, Festival - Institute, Round Top TX
Jersey City Museum, Jersey City NJ
Kenosha Public Museums, Kenosha WI
Kentucky Museum of Art and Craft, Louisville KY
Kereszteny Muzeum, Christian Museum, Esztergom
Koochiching Museums, International Falls MN
Koshare Indian Museum, Inc, La Junta CO
LA County Museum of Art, Los Angeles CA
Lac du Flambeau Band of Lake Superior Chippewa Indians, George W Brown Jr Ojibwe Museum & Cultural Center, Lac Du Flambeau WI
Lafayette Science Museum & Planetarium, Lafayette LA
Lahore Museum, Lahore
Landis Valley Village and Farm Museum, PA Historical & Museum Commission, Lancaster PA
Launceston City Council, Queen Victoria Museum and Art Gallery, Launceston
Le Grand Curtius, Musée d'Ansembourg, Liege
League of New Hampshire Craftsmen, Grodin Permanent Collection Museum, Concord NH
Leeds Museums & Galleries, Leeds
Leelanau Historical Museum, Leland MI
Lehigh Valley Heritage Center, Allentown PA
LeMoyne Art Foundation, Center for the Visual Arts, Tallahassee FL
Lincoln County Historical Association, Inc, 1811 Old Lincoln County Jail & Lincoln County Museum, Wiscasset ME
Lincolnshire County Council, Library & Heritage Services, Lincoln
Livingston County Historical Society, Museum, Geneseo NY
Long Beach Museum of Art Foundation, Long Beach CA
The Long Island Museum of American Art, History & Carriages, Stony Brook NY
Longfellow-Evangeline State Commemorative Area, Saint Martinville LA
Louisiana State Exhibit Museum, Shreveport LA
Loyola University Chicago, Loyola University Museum of Art, Chicago IL
Maison Saint-Gabriel Museum, Montreal PQ
Maitland Art Center, Maitland FL
Manchester Bidwell Corporation, Manchester Craftsmen's Guild Youth & Arts Program, Pittsburgh PA
Manchester City Galleries, Manchester Art Gallery, Manchester
Manitoba Historical Society, Dalnavert Museum, Winnipeg MB
Marietta College, Grover M Hermann Fine Arts Center, Marietta OH
The Mariners' Museum, Newport News VA
Maude Kerns Art Center, Eugene OR
McLean County Historical Society, McLean County Museum of History, Bloomington IL
Meredith College, Frankie G Weems Gallery & Rotunda Gallery, Raleigh NC
Mesa Arts Center, Mesa Contemporary Arts Museum, Mesa AZ
Mexican Museum, San Francisco CA
Mingei International, Inc, Mingei International Museum - Balboa Park & Mingei International Museum - Escondido, San Diego CA
Ministry of Cultural Affairs, Bangladesh National Museum, Dhaka
Ministry of Culture & Tourism, The Delphi Museum, 10th Ephorate of Prehistoric & Classical Antiquities, Delphi
Minnesota Museum of American Art, Saint Paul MN
Minnesota State University, Mankato, Mankato MN
The Mint Museum, Mint Museum of Craft & Design, Charlotte NC
The Mint Museum, Charlotte NC
Missoula Art Museum, Missoula MT
Mobile Museum of Art, Mobile AL
Moody County Historical Society, Moody County Museum, Pierre SD
Moore College of Art & Design, The Galleries at Moore, Philadelphia PA
Morris Museum, Morristown NJ
Morris Museum of Art, Augusta GA
Moto Moto Museum, Mbala
Musee des Beaux-Arts d'Orleans, Historical & Archaeological Museum of Orleans, Orleans
Musee des Beaux-Arts/Palais des Archeveques, Museum of Fine Arts, Tours
Musee des Maitres et Artisans du Quebec, Montreal PQ

Musee National d'Histoire et d'Art Luxembourg, Luxembourg City
Museen der Stadt Koln, Romisch-Germanisches Museum, Cologne
Musees Royaux d'Art et d'Histoire, Royal Museums of Art and History, Brussels
Museo De Las Americas, Denver CO
The Museum, Greenwood SC
Museum De Lakenhal, Leiden
Museum fur Angewandte Kunst Frankfurt, Museum of Applied Arts, Frankfurt
Museum fur Kunst und Gewerbe Hamburg, Hamburg
Museum of Arts & Design, New York NY
Museum of Chinese in America, New York NY
Museum of Contemporary Craft, Portland OR
Museum of Northern Arizona, Flagstaff AZ
Museum of Northern British Columbia, Ruth Harvey Art Gallery, Prince Rupert BC
Museum of the City of New York, Museum, New York NY
Museum of the Plains Indian & Crafts Center, Browning MT
Museum zu Allerheiligen, Schaffhausen
Muskegon Museum of Art, Muskegon MI
Muzej za Umjetnost i Obrt, Museum of Arts & Crafts, Zagreb
Muzeul de Istorie Nationala Si Arheologie Constanta, National History & Archaeology Museum, Constanta
Muzeul National Brukenthal, Brukenthal Palace & European Art Gallery, Sibiu
Muzeum Narodowe, National Museum in Poznan, Poznan
Nara Kokuritsu Hakubutsu-Kan, Nara National Museum, Nara
National Museum of Ceramic Art & Glass, Baltimore MD
National Museum of Fine Arts of Moldova, Chisinau
The National Museum of Modern Art, Tokyo, Tokyo
National Museum of the Philippines, Manila
National Museum of Women in the Arts, Washington DC
National Museum, Monuments and Art Gallery, Gaborone
National Palace Museum, Taiwan, R.O.C.
The National Quilt Museum, Paducah KY
Nationalmuseum, Stockholm
Nelson Mandela Bay Municipality, Nelson Mandela Metropolitan Art Museum, Port Elizabeth
New Brunswick Museum, Saint John NB
New England Maple Museum, Pittsford VT
New Hampshire Antiquarian Society, Hopkinton Historical Society, Hopkinton NH
New Jersey State Museum, Fine Art Bureau, Trenton NJ
New Mexico State University, Art Gallery, Las Cruces NM
New Visions Gallery, Inc, Marshfield WI
Niigata Prefectural Museum of Modern Art, Niigata
The Nippon Gallery at the Nippon Club, New York NY
Noordbrabants Museum, Hertogenbosch
North Carolina State University, Gregg Museum of Art & Design, Raleigh NC
Norwich Free Academy, Slater Memorial Museum, Norwich CT
Nova Scotia College of Art and Design, Anna Leonowens Gallery, Halifax NS
Nova Scotia Museum, Maritime Museum of the Atlantic, Halifax NS
Noyes Art Gallery, Lincoln NE
The Noyes Museum of Art, Oceanville NJ
Oakland Museum of California, Art Dept, Oakland CA
The Ogden Museum of Southern Art, University of New Orleans, New Orleans LA
Ohio Historical Society, National Afro-American Museum & Cultural Center, Wilberforce OH
The Ohio Historical Society, Inc, Campus Martius Museum & Ohio River Museum, Marietta OH
Okanagan Heritage Museum, Kelowna BC
Okefenokee Heritage Center, Inc, Waycross GA
Old Dartmouth Historical Society, New Bedford Whaling Museum, New Bedford MA
Oshkosh Public Museum, Oshkosh WI
Owensboro Museum of Fine Art, Owensboro KY
Panhandle-Plains Historical Museum, Canyon TX
Pasadena Museum of History, Pasadena CA
Phelps County Historical Society, Nebraska Prairie Museum, Holdrege NE
Pioneer Town, Pioneer Museum of Western Art, Wimberley TX
Please Touch Museum, Philadelphia PA
Plumas County Museum, Quincy CA

Pope County Historical Society, Pope County Museum, Glenwood MN
Pretoria Art Museum, Municipal Art Gallery, Pretoria
Principia College, School of Nations Museum, Elsah IL
Rabindra Bhavan Art Gallery, Lalit Kala Akademi (National Academy of Art), New Delhi
Randall Junior Museum, San Francisco CA
Rawls Museum Arts, Courtland VA
Rijksmuseum Twenthe, Rijksmuseum Twenthe, Enschede
Roberson Museum & Science Center, Binghamton NY
Rollins College, George D & Harriet W Cornell Fine Arts Museum, Winter Park FL
Rome Historical Society, Museum & Archives, Rome NY
The Rooms Corporation of Newfoundland & Labrador, Saint John's NF
Rose Lehrman Art Gallery, Harrisburg PA
Roswell Museum & Art Center, Roswell NM
Royal Pavilion & Museums, Brighton Museum & Art Gallery, Brighton
Saginaw Art Museum, Saginaw MI
Saint Anselm College, Alva de Mars Megan Chapel Art Center, Manchester NH
St Mary's College of Maryland, The Dwight Frederick Boyden Gallery, St Mary's City MD
San Diego State University, University Art Gallery, San Diego CA
San Francisco Maritime National Historical Park, Maritime Museum, San Francisco CA
Schweinfurth Art Center, Auburn NY
Seneca-Iroquois National Museum, Salamanca NY
Shaker Village of Pleasant Hill, Harrodsburg KY
Shoshone Bannock Tribes, Shoshone Bannock Tribal Museum, Fort Hall ID
Slovenska Narodna Galeria, Slovak National Gallery, Bratislava
Smithsonian Institution, Washington DC
Society for Contemporary Craft, Pittsburgh PA
Sooke Region Museum & Art Gallery, Sooke BC
Soprintendenza per I beni storici artistici ed etnoantropologici per le province di Mantova Brescia e Cremona, Museo di Palazzo Ducale, Mantua
South Carolina Artisans Center, Walterboro SC
South Carolina State Museum, Columbia SC
Southeastern Center for Contemporary Art, Winston Salem NC
Southern Plains Indian Museum, Anadarko OK
The Speed Art Museum, Louisville KY
Spertus Institute of Jewish Studies, Chicago IL
Stamford Museum & Nature Center, Stamford CT
State University of New York College at Buffalo, Buffalo NY
Staten Island Museum, Staten Island NY
Suan Pakkad Palace Museum, Bangkok
Suomen Kansallismuseo, National Museum of Finland, Helsinki
Swedish American Museum Association of Chicago, Chicago IL
Tallahassee Museum of History & Natural Science, Tallahassee FL
Tampa Museum of Art, Tampa FL
Texas Tech University, Museum of Texas Tech University, Lubbock TX
Tohono Chul Park, Tucson AZ
Tokyo University of the Arts, The University Art Museum, Tokyo
Trust Authority, Museum of the Great Plains, Lawton OK
Tubac Center of the Arts, Santa Cruz Valley Art Association, Tubac AZ
Tulane University, Newcomb Art Gallery, New Orleans LA
Ukrainian Canadian Archives & Museum of Alberta, Edmonton AB
The Ukrainian Museum, New York NY
United Society of Shakers, Shaker Museum, New Gloucester ME
University of British Columbia, Museum of Anthropology, Vancouver BC
University of California, Berkeley, The Magnes Collection of Jewish Art & Life, Berkeley CA
University of Colorado at Colorado Springs, Gallery of Contemporary Art, Colorado Springs CO
University of Georgia, Georgia Museum of Art, Athens GA
University of Pennsylvania, Museum of Archaeology & Anthropology, Philadelphia PA
University of Rochester, Memorial Art Gallery, Rochester NY

University of Saskatchewan, Diefenbaker Canada Centre, Saskatoon SK
University of Texas at El Paso, Stanlee & Gerald Rubin Center for the Visual Arts, El Paso TX
University of Victoria, The Legacy Art Gallery, Victoria BC
University of Washington, Henry Art Gallery, Seattle WA
Utah Arts Council, Chase Home Museum of Utah Folk Arts, Salt Lake City UT
Vermont State Craft Center at Frog Hollow, Burlington VT
Vesterheim Norwegian-American Museum, Decorah IA
Vietnam Fine Arts Museum, Hanoi
Vorarlberg Museum, Bregenz
VSA Arts of New Mexico, Very Special Arts Gallery, Albuquerque NM
Wade House Historic Site-Wisconsin Historical Society, Wesley W. Jung Carriage Museum, Greenbush WI
Wadsworth Atheneum Museum of Art, Hartford CT
The Walker African American Museum & Research Center, Las Vegas NV
Waterworks Visual Arts Center, Salisbury NC
West Baton Rouge Parish, West Baton Rouge Museum, Port Allen LA
West Florida Historic Preservation, Inc/University of West Florida, T T Wentworth, Jr Florida State Museum; Historic Pensacola Village; Pensacola Historical Society & Resource Center, Pensacola FL
Whatcom Museum, Bellingham WA
William Morris Gallery, London
Wisconsin Historical Society, Wisconsin Historical Museum, Madison WI
Worcester Center for Crafts, Krikorian Gallery, Worcester MA
Xavier University, Art Gallery, Cincinnati OH
Yarmouth County Historical Society, Yarmouth County Museum & Archives, Yarmouth NS
Yokohama Museum of Art, Yokohama
Zurich University of the Arts (ZHdK), Museum Fuer Gestaltung Zurich (Museum of Design Zurich), Zurich

DECORATIVE ARTS

Abington Art Center, Jenkintown PA
Academy of the New Church, Glencairn Museum, Bryn Athyn PA
Adams National Historic Park, Quincy MA
African Art Museum of Maryland, Columbia MD
Akron Art Museum, Akron OH
Alabama Department of Archives & History, Museum of Alabama, Montgomery AL
Albany Institute of History & Art, Albany NY
Albion College, Bobbitt Visual Arts Center, Albion MI
Albuquerque Museum of Art & History, Albuquerque NM
Allentown Art Museum, Allentown PA
American Architectural Foundation, Museum, Washington DC
American Art Museum, Renwick Gallery, Washington DC
American Art Museum, Smithsonian Institution, Washington DC
American Folk Art Museum, New York NY
American Museum of Ceramic Art, Pomona CA
American Swedish Historical Foundation & Museum, American Swedish Historical Museum, Philadelphia PA
Americas Society Art Gallery, New York NY
Amherst Museum, Amherst NY
Arab American National Museum, Dearborn MI
Arizona Museum For Youth, Mesa AZ
Arnot Art Museum, Elmira NY
Art & Culture Center of Hollywood, Art Gallery/Multidisciplinary Cultural Center, Hollywood FL
Art Center of Battle Creek, Battle Creek MI
Art Gallery of Greater Victoria, Victoria BC
Art Gallery of Nova Scotia, Halifax NS
Art Gallery of South Australia, Adelaide
The Art Museum at the University of Kentucky, Lexington KY
Art Museum of Greater Lafayette, Lafayette IN
Art Museum of Southeast Texas, Beaumont TX
Art Museum of the University of Houston, Blaffer Gallery, Houston TX
Arts Council of Fayetteville-Cumberland County, The Arts Center, Fayetteville NC
ArtSpace/Lima, Lima OH
Asian Art Museum of San Francisco, Chong-Moon Lee Ctr for Asian Art and Culture, San Francisco CA

Athenaeum of Philadelphia, Philadelphia PA
Atlanta Historical Society Inc, Atlanta History Center, Atlanta GA
Augustana College, Augustana College Art Museum, Rock Island IL
Avampato Discovery Museum, The Clay Center for Arts & Sciences, Charleston WV
Badisches Landesmuseum, Karlsruhe
Ball State University, Museum of Art, Muncie IN
The Baltimore Museum of Art, Baltimore MD
Balzekas Museum of Lithuanian Culture, Chicago IL
Barnes Foundation, Merion PA
Baroda Museum and Picture Gallery, Baroda
Bass Museum of Art, Miami Beach FL
Bay County Historical Society, Historical Museum of Bay County, Bay City MI
Bayerisches Nationalmuseum, Bavarian National Museum, Munich
Beaverbrook Art Gallery, Fredericton NB
Belle Grove Inc., Belle Grove Plantation, Middletown VA
Bellevue Arts Museum, Bellevue WA
Beloit College, Wright Museum of Art, Beloit WI
Bemis Center for Contemporary Arts, Omaha NE
Bennington Museum, Bennington VT
Berkshire Museum, Pittsfield MA
Besser Museum for Northeast Michigan, Alpena MI
Beverly Historical Society, Cabot, Hale & Balch House Museums, Beverly MA
Biggs Museum of American Art, Dover DE
Birmingham Museum of Art, Birmingham AL
Brick Store Museum, Kennebunk ME
Brigham City Corporation, Brigham City Museum & Gallery, Brigham City UT
Bradford Brinton, Big Horn WY
Bruce Museum, Inc, Greenwich CT
Bucknell University, Edward & Marthann Samek Art Gallery, Lewisburg PA
Thornton W Burgess, Museum, Sandwich MA
Bush-Holley Historic Site & Storehouse Gallery, Greenwich Historical Society/ Bush-Holley House, Cos Cob CT
Byzantine & Christian Museum, Athens, Athens
Cameron Art Museum, Wilmington NC
Canadian Clay and Glass Gallery, Waterloo ON
Canadian Museum of Civilization, Gatineau PQ
Canton Museum of Art, Canton OH
Cape Ann Historical Association, Cape Ann Museum, Gloucester MA
Captain Forbes House Museum, Milton MA
Caramoor Center for Music & the Arts, Inc, Rosen House at Caramoor, Katonah NY
Carnegie Museums of Pittsburgh, Carnegie Museum of Art, Pittsburgh PA
Carson County Square House Museum, Panhandle TX
Carteret County Historical Society, The History Place, Morehead City NC
Cedar Rapids Museum of Art, Cedar Rapids IA
Charleston Museum, Joseph Manigault House, Charleston SC
Charleston Museum, Charleston SC
Chatham Historical Society, The Atwood House Museum, Chatham MA
Chatillon-DeMenil House Foundation, Chatillon-DeMenil House, Saint Louis MO
Cheekwood-Tennessee Botanical Garden & Museum of Art, Nashville TN
Chhatrapati Shivaji Maharaj Vastu Sangrahalaya, Mumbai
Chicago Athenaeum, Museum of Architecture & Design, Galena IL
Chinese Culture Foundation, Center Gallery, San Francisco CA
Chrysler Museum of Art, Norfolk VA
Church of Jesus Christ of Latter-Day Saints, Museum of Church History & Art, Salt Lake City UT
Cincinnati Art Museum, Cincinnati Art Museum, Cincinnati OH
City of Austin Parks & Recreation, O. Henry Museum, Austin TX
City of High Point, High Point Museum, High Point NC
The City of Petersburg Museums, Petersburg VA
Clark County Historical Society, Heritage Center of Clark County, Springfield OH
Sterling & Francine Clark, Williamstown MA
Clemson University, Fort Hill Plantation, Clemson SC
The Cleveland Museum of Art, Cleveland OH
Clinton County Historical Association, Clinton County Historical Museum, Plattsburgh NY
Cohasset Historical Society, Pratt Building (Society Headquarters), Cohasset MA

The College of Wooster, The College of Wooster Art Museum, Wooster OH
Colorado Historical Society, Colorado History Museum, Denver CO
Columbia County Historical Society, Columbia County Museum and Library, Kinderhook NY
Columbia County Historical Society, Luykas Van Alen House, Kinderhook NY
Columbia Museum of Art, Columbia SC
Columbus Museum, Columbus GA
Columbus Museum of Art, Columbus OH
Concord Museum, Concord MA
Confederation Centre Art Gallery and Museum, Charlottetown PE
Cooper-Hewitt National Design Museum, Smithsonian Institution, New York NY
Corcoran Gallery of Art, Washington DC
Cornwall Gallery Society, Cornwall Regional Art Gallery, Cornwall ON
County of Henrico, Meadow Farm Museum, Glen Allen VA
The Courtauld Institute of Art, The Courtauld Gallery, London
Coutts Museum of Art, Inc, El Dorado KS
Craft and Folk Art Museum (CAFAM), Los Angeles CA
Cranbrook Art Museum, Bloomfield Hills MI
Cripple Creek District Museum, Cripple Creek CO
Crocker Art Museum, Sacramento CA
Cummer Museum of Art & Gardens, Museum & Library, Jacksonville FL
Cuneo Foundation, Museum & Gardens, Vernon Hills IL
Dallas Museum of Art, Dallas TX
Danville Museum of Fine Arts & History, Danville VA
DAR Museum, National Society Daughters of the American Revolution, Washington DC
Dartmouth College, Hood Museum of Art, Hanover NH
Delaware Art Museum, Wilmington DE
Delaware Historical Society, Read House and Gardens, Wilmington DE
Deming-Luna Mimbres Museum, Deming NM
Denison University, Art Gallery, Granville OH
Denver Art Museum, Denver CO
Designmuseum Danmark, Copenhagen
Detroit Institute of Arts, Detroit MI
Detroit Repertory Theatre Gallery, Detroit MI
Dickinson College, The Trout Gallery, Carlisle PA
The Dixon Gallery & Gardens, Memphis TN
Doncaster Museum and Art Gallery, Doncaster
Drexel University, Drexel Collection, Philadelphia PA
Duke University, Nasher Museum of Art at Duke University, Durham NC
Dundee City Council Leisure & Communities Department, The McManus: Dundee's Art Gallery & Museum, Dundee
Edgecombe County Cultural Arts Council, Inc, Blount-Bridgers House, Hobson Pittman Memorial Gallery, Tarboro NC
Egan Institute of Maritime Studies, Nantucket MA
Eiteljorg Museum of American Indians & Western Art, Indianapolis IN
Ellis County Museum Inc, Waxahachie TX
Elverhoj Museum of History and Art, Solvang CA
Environment Canada - Parks Canada, Laurier House, National Historic Site, Ottawa ON
Erie Art Museum, Erie PA
Erie County Historical Society, Erie PA
Wharton Esherick, Paoli PA
Essex Historical Society and Shipbuilding Museum, Essex MA
Establishment Public du Chateau du Rusee, Et du Dophine national de versailles, Versailles
The Ethel Wright Mohamed Stitchery Museum, Belzoni MS
Evanston Historical Society, Charles Gates Dawes House, Evanston IL
Evansville Museum of Arts, History & Science, Evansville IN
Everhart Museum, Scranton PA
Everson Museum of Art, Syracuse NY
Fall River Historical Society, Fall River MA
Farmington Village Green & Library Association, Stanley-Whitman House, Farmington CT
William A Farnsworth, Museum, Rockland ME
Fetherston Foundation, Packwood House Museum, Lewisburg PA
Fine Arts Museums of San Francisco, Legion of Honor, San Francisco CA
Fishkill Historical Society, Van Wyck Homestead Museum, Fishkill NY
Fitton Center for Creative Arts, Hamilton OH

Flint Institute of Arts, Flint MI
Florence Museum, Florence SC
Florida State University, John & Mable Ringling Museum of Art, Sarasota FL
Florida State University and Central Florida Community College, The Appleton Museum of Art, Ocala FL
Fondazione Musei Civici Di Venezia, Galleria Internazionale d'Arte Moderna di Ca'Pesaro, Venice
Fondazione Musei Civici Di Venezia, Museo Correr, Venice
Fondazione Scientifica Querini Stampalia, Venice
Edsel & Eleanor Ford, Grosse Pointe Shores MI
Forest Lawn Museum, Glendale CA
Fort Ticonderoga Association, Ticonderoga NY
Freer Gallery of Art & Arthur M Sackler Gallery, Arthur M Sackler Gallery, Washington DC
The Frick Art & Historical Center, Inc, Frick Art Museum, Pittsburgh PA
Friends of Historic Kingston, Fred J Johnston House Museum, Kingston NY
Frontier Times Museum, Bandera TX
Fuller Craft Museum, Brockton MA
Gala-Salvador Dali Foundation Museums, Casa Museu Castell Gala Dali, Figueres
Gala-Salvador Dali Foundation Museums, Casa Museu Salvador Dali, Figueres
Galerie Montcalm, Gatineau PQ
Gallery One Visual Arts Center, Ellensburg WA
General Board of Discipleship, The United Methodist Church, The Upper Room Chapel & Museum, Nashville TN
Genesee Country Village & Museum, John L Wehle Art Gallery, Mumford NY
Germanisches Nationalmuseum, Nuremberg
Germantown Historical Society, Philadelphia PA
Girard College, Stephen Girard Collection, Philadelphia PA
Glanmore National Historic Site of Canada, Belleville ON
Glasmuseet Ebeltoft, Ebeltoft
Glessner House Museum, Chicago IL
Grand Rapids Public Museum, Public Museum of Grand Rapids, Grand Rapids MI
Gunston Hall Plantation, Mason Neck VA
Hammond Museum & Japanese Stroll Garden, Cross-Cultural Center, North Salem NY
Hammond-Harwood House Association, Inc, Hammond-Harwood House, Annapolis MD
Hammonds House Museum, Atlanta GA
Hancock County Trustees of Public Reservations, Woodlawn: Museum, Gardens & Park, Ellsworth ME
Hancock Shaker Village, Inc, Pittsfield MA
Harvard University, Museum & Garden, Washington DC
Hawkes Bay Art Gallery and Museum, Napier
Haystack Mountain School of Crafts, Deer Isle ME
Headley-Whitney Museum, Lexington KY
Headquarters Fort Monroe, Dept of Army, Casemate Museum, Hampton VA
Heard Museum, Phoenix AZ
Hebrew Union College, Skirball Cultural Center, Los Angeles CA
Henry County Museum & Cultural Arts Center, Clinton MO
Henry Gallery Association, Henry Art Gallery, Seattle WA
Henry Morrison Flagler Museum, Palm Beach FL
Henry Sheldon Museum of Vermont History and Research Center, Middlebury VT
Heritage Center, Inc, Pine Ridge SD
Hermitage Foundation Museum, Norfolk VA
Herrett Center for Arts & Sciences, Jean B King Art Gallery, Twin Falls ID
Hershey Museum, Hershey PA
Higgins Armory Museum, Worcester MA
High Museum of Art, Atlanta GA
Hill-Stead Museum, Farmington CT
Hillwood Museum & Gardens Foundation, Hillwood Estate Museum & Gardens, Washington DC
The Hispanic Society of America, Museum & Library, New York NY
Historic Arkansas Museum, Little Rock AR
Historic Cherry Hill, Albany NY
Historic Columbian Theatre Foundation, Columbian Theatre Museum & Art Center, Wamego KS
Historic Deerfield, Inc, Deerfield MA
Historic Hudson Valley, Pocantico Hills NY
The Historic New Orleans Collection, Royal Street Galleries, New Orleans LA

Museum of Fine Arts, Saint Petersburg, Florida, Inc, Saint Petersburg FL

Museum of Southern History, Houston TX

Museum of the City of New York, Museum, New York NY

Museum of Vancouver, Vancouver BC

Museum of West Louisiana, Leesville LA

Museum of Wisconsin Art, West Bend WI

Museum of York County, Rock Hill SC

Museum Plantin-Moretus/Prentenkabinet, Antwerp

Muskegon Museum of Art, Muskegon MI

Muzej za Umjetnost i Obrt, Museum of Arts & Crafts, Zagreb

Muzeul National Brukenthal, Blue House & Romanian Art Gallery, Sibiu

Muzeul National Brukenthal, Brukenthal Palace & European Art Gallery, Sibiu

Muzeum Narodowe, National Museum in Poznan, Poznan

Muzeum Narodowe W Kielcach, National Museum in Kielce, Kielce

Nara Kokuritsu Hakubutsu-Kan, Nara National Museum, Nara

National Baseball Hall of Fame & Museum, Inc, Art Collection, Cooperstown NY

National Gallery of Canada, Ottawa ON

National Heritage Museum, Lexington MA

National Museum of American Illustration, Newport RI

National Museum of Fine Arts of Moldova, Chisinau

National Museum of the American Indian, George Gustav Heye Center, New York NY

National Museum of the American Indian, Smithsonian Institution, Washington DC

National Museum of the Philippines, Manila

National Museum of Women in the Arts, Washington DC

National Museum, Monuments and Art Gallery, Gaborone

National Museums Scotland, National Museum of Scotland, Edinburgh

National Park Service, Weir Farm National Historic Site, Wilton CT

The National Park Service, United States Department of the Interior, Statue of Liberty National Monument & The Ellis Island Immigration Museum, Washington DC

The National Quilt Museum, Paducah KY

The National Shrine of the North American Martyrs, Fultonville NY

National Silk Art Museum, Weston MO

National Society of Colonial Dames of America in the State of Maryland, Mount Clare Museum House, Baltimore MD

National Society of the Colonial Dames of America in The Commonwealth of Virginia, Wilton House Museum, Richmond VA

National Trust for Historic Preservation, Chesterwood, Stockbridge MA

National Trust for Historic Preservation, Shadows-on-the-Teche, New Iberia LA

National Trust for Historic Preservation, Washington DC

Nationalmuseum, Stockholm

Naval Historical Center, The Navy Museum, Washington DC

Nebraska State Capitol, Lincoln NE

Nelson Mandela Bay Municipality, Nelson Mandela Metropolitan Art Museum, Port Elizabeth

The Nelson-Atkins Museum of Art, Kansas City MO

The Nemours Foundatioin, Nemours Mansion & Gardens, Wilmington DE

Neustadt Collection of Tiffany Glass, Long Island City NY

New Brunswick Museum, Saint John NB

New Hampshire Antiquarian Society, Hopkinton Historical Society, Hopkinton NH

New Jersey State Museum, Fine Art Bureau, Trenton NJ

New Orleans Artworks at New Orleans Glassworks & Printmaking Studio, New Orleans LA

New Orleans Museum of Art, New Orleans LA

New Visions Gallery, Inc, Marshfield WI

New World Art Center, T F Chen Cultural Center, New York NY

New York State Historical Association, Fenimore Art Museum, Cooperstown NY

New York State Museum, Albany NY

New York State Office of Parks Recreation & Historic Preservation, John Jay Homestead State Historic Site, Katonah NY

New York State Office of Parks: Recreation and Historic Preservation, Senate House State Historic Site, Kingston NY

Newburyport Maritime Society, Inc, Custom House Maritime Museum, Newburyport MA

Nichols House Museum, Inc, Boston MA

The Noble Maritime Collection, Staten Island NY

North Carolina State University, Gregg Museum of Art & Design, Raleigh NC

Norwich Free Academy, Slater Memorial Museum, Norwich CT

Noyes Art Gallery, Lincoln NE

The Ogden Museum of Southern Art, University of New Orleans, New Orleans LA

The Ohio Historical Society, Inc, Campus Martius Museum & Ohio River Museum, Marietta OH

Okanagan Heritage Museum, Kelowna BC

Oklahoma Historical Society, State Museum of History, Oklahoma City OK

Olana State Historic Site, Hudson NY

Old Barracks Museum, Trenton NJ

Old Dartmouth Historical Society, New Bedford Whaling Museum, New Bedford MA

Old Salem Museums & Gardens, Museum of Early Southern Decorative Arts, Winston Salem NC

Opelousas Museum of Art, Inc (OMA), Opelousas LA

Order Sons of Italy in America, Garibaldi & Meucci Museum, Staten Island NY

Oshkosh Public Museum, Oshkosh WI

Owensboro Museum of Fine Art, Owensboro KY

Oysterponds Historical Society, Museum, Orient NY

Pacific - Asia Museum, Pasadena CA

Panhandle-Plains Historical Museum, Canyon TX

Paris Gibson Square, Museum of Art, Great Falls MT

Pasadena Museum of History, Pasadena CA

Passaic County Historical Society, Lambert Castle Museum & Library, Paterson NJ

Patrimonio Nacional, Palacios de la Granja y Riofrio, Madrid

Pennsylvania Historical & Museum Commission, The State Museum of Pennsylvania, Harrisburg PA

The Pennsylvania State University, Palmer Museum of Art, University Park PA

Pensacola Museum of Art, Pensacola FL

Philadelphia History Museum, Philadelphia PA

Phillips Academy, Addison Gallery of American Art, Andover MA

Phoenix Art Museum, Phoenix AZ

Piatt Castles, West Liberty OH

Pilgrim Society, Pilgrim Hall Museum, Plymouth MA

Pioneer Town, Pioneer Museum of Western Art, Wimberley TX

Plumas County Museum, Quincy CA

Polish Museum of America, Chicago IL

Polk Museum of Art, Lakeland FL

The Pomona College, Claremont CA

Pope County Historical Society, Pope County Museum, Glenwood MN

Port Huron Museum, Port Huron MI

Porter-Phelps-Huntington Foundation, Inc, Historic House Museum, Hadley MA

Portland Art Museum, Portland OR

Portland Museum of Art, Portland ME

Portsmouth Historical Society, John Paul Jones House & Discover Portsmouth, Portsmouth NH

Prairie Art Gallery, Grande Prairie AB

Princeton University, Princeton University Art Museum, Princeton NJ

Principia College, School of Nations Museum, Elsah IL

Putnam County Historical Society, Foundry School Museum, Cold Spring NY

Putnam Museum of History and Natural Science, Davenport IA

Quapaw Quarter Association, Inc, Villa Marre, Little Rock AR

Queens College, City University of New York, Godwin-Ternbach Museum, Flushing NY

Rabindra Bhavan Art Gallery, Lalit Kala Akademi (National Academy of Art), New Delhi

Reading Public Museum, Reading PA

Reynolda House Museum of American Art, Winston-Salem NC

Rijksmuseum Twenthe, Rijksmuseum Twenthe, Enschede

Riley County Historical Society & Museum, Riley County Historical Museum, Manhattan KS

Ringwood Manor House Museum, Ringwood NJ

Riverside County Museum, Edward-Dean Museum & Gardens, Cherry Valley CA

Roberson Museum & Science Center, Binghamton NY

Rock Ford Foundation, Inc, Rock Ford Plantation, Lancaster PA

Rollins College, George D & Harriet W Cornell Fine Arts Museum, Winter Park FL

Rome Historical Society, Museum & Archives, Rome NY

Roosevelt-Vanderbilt National Historic Sites, Hyde Park NY

Ross Memorial Museum, Saint Andrews NB

Roswell Museum & Art Center, Roswell NM

Royal Ontario Museum, Dept of Western Art & Culture, Toronto ON

Royal Pavilion & Museums, Brighton Museum & Art Gallery, Brighton

C M Russell, Great Falls MT

Ryerss Victorian Museum & Library, Philadelphia PA

Saco Museum, Saco ME

Saginaw Art Museum, Saginaw MI

Saint Anselm College, Alva de Mars Megan Chapel Art Center, Manchester NH

Saint Augustine Historical Society, Oldest House Museum Complex, Saint Augustine FL

Saint Bonaventure University, Regina A Quick Center for the Arts, Saint Bonaventure NY

Saint Joseph's Oratory, Museum, Montreal PQ

St Mary Landmarks, Grevemberg House Museum, Franklin LA

St Mary's College of Maryland, The Dwight Frederick Boyden Gallery, St Mary's City MD

Saint Peter's College, Art Gallery, Jersey City NJ

Salisbury House Foundation, Salisbury House and Garden, Des Moines IA

Salisbury University, Ward Museum of Wildfowl Art, Salisbury MD

San Diego Museum of Art, San Diego CA

The Sandwich Historical Society, Inc & Sandwich Glass Museum, Sandwich Glass Museum, Sandwich MA

Santarella Museum & Gardens, Tyringham MA

Savitsky Karakalpakstan State Art Museum, Nukus

Schuyler-Hamilton House, Morristown NJ

Schweinfurth Art Center, Auburn NY

Seneca-Iroquois National Museum, Salamanca NY

Shaker Museum & Library, Old Chatham NY

Shaker Village of Pleasant Hill, Harrodsburg KY

Ella Sharp, Jackson MI

Shelburne Museum, Museum, Shelburne VT

Shirley Plantation Foundation, Charles City VA

Slater Mill, Old Slater Mill Association, Pawtucket RI

Smith College, Museum of Art, Northampton MA

Smithsonian Institution, Washington DC

The Society of the Cincinnati at Anderson House, Washington DC

Soprintendenza per I beni storici artistici ed etnoantropologici per le province di Mantova Brescia e Cremona, Museo di Palazzo Ducale, Mantua

South Carolina Artisans Center, Walterboro SC

South Carolina State Museum, Columbia SC

South Dakota State University, South Dakota Art Museum, Brookings SD

The Speed Art Museum, Louisville KY

Spertus Institute of Jewish Studies, Chicago IL

Springfield Art Museum, Springfield MO

Springfield Museums, Connecticut Valley Historical Society, Springfield MA

Stanford University, Cantor Arts Center at Stanford University, Stanford CA

Nelda C & H J Lutcher Stark, Stark Museum of Art, Orange TX

The State Museum of Fine Arts of Tatarstan Republic, Kazan

State University of New York at Binghamton, Binghamton University Art Museum, Binghamton NY

State University of New York College at Buffalo, Buffalo NY

Staten Island Museum, Staten Island NY

Stauth Foundation & Museum, Stauth Memorial Museum, Montezuma KS

Stedelijk Museum Alkmaar, Alkmaar Municipal Museum, Alkmaar

T C Steele, Nashville IN

The Stewart Museum, Montreal PQ

Stone Quarry Hill Art Park, Winner Gallery, Cazenovia NY

The Summit County Historical Society of Akron, OH, Akron OH

Suomen Kansallismuseo, National Museum of Finland, Helsinki

Suomen rakennustaiteen museo, Museum of Finnish Architecture, Helsinki

Susquehanna University, Lore Degenstein Gallery, Selinsgrove PA

DIORAMAS

Scripps College, Ruth Chandler Williamson Gallery, Claremont CA
Seneca-Iroquois National Museum, Salamanca NY
Shoshone Bannock Tribes, Shoshone Bannock Tribal Museum, Fort Hall ID
The Society of the Cincinnati at Anderson House, Washington DC
Southern Illinois University Carbondale, University Museum, Carbondale IL
Southern Ohio Museum Corporation, Southern Ohio Museum, Portsmouth OH
Tinkertown Museum, Sandia Park NM
Tohono Chul Park, Tucson AZ
United States Department of the Interior, Interior Museum, Washington DC
United States Military Academy, West Point Museum, West Point NY
University of Chicago, Oriental Institute, Chicago IL
University of Minnesota, The Bell Museum of Natural History, Minneapolis MN
University of Saskatchewan, Diefenbaker Canada Centre, Saskatoon SK
The Walker African American Museum & Research Center, Las Vegas NV
George Washington, Alexandria VA
Whatcom Museum, Bellingham WA
Zigler Art Museum, Jennings LA

DOLLS

Adams County Historical Society, Gettysburg PA
African American Museum in Philadelphia, Philadelphia PA
Alaska Heritage Museum at Wells Fargo, Anchorage AK
Alton Museum of History & Art, Inc, Alton IL
Anchorage Museum at Rasmuson Center, Anchorage AK
Arizona Historical Society-Yuma, Sanguinetti House Museum & Garden, Yuma AZ
Art Without Walls Inc, New York NY
Arts Council of Fayetteville-Cumberland County, The Arts Center, Fayetteville NC
ArtSpace/Lima, Lima OH
Atlanta Historical Society Inc, Atlanta History Center, Atlanta GA
Barker Character, Comic and Cartoon Museum, Cheshire CT
Baroda Museum and Picture Gallery, Baroda
Bayerisches Nationalmuseum, Bavarian National Museum, Munich
Bennington Museum, Bennington VT
Berkshire Museum, Pittsfield MA
Besser Museum for Northeast Michigan, Alpena MI
Brick Store Museum, Kennebunk ME
Brooklyn Historical Society, Brooklyn OH
Thornton W Burgess, Museum, Sandwich MA
Cambria Historical Society, New Providence NJ
Cambridge Museum, Cambridge NE
Canadian Museum of Civilization, Gatineau PQ
Cape Ann Historical Association, Cape Ann Museum, Gloucester MA
Carnegie Museums of Pittsburgh, Carnegie Museum of Art, Pittsburgh PA
Carson County Square House Museum, Panhandle TX
Carteret County Historical Society, The History Place, Morehead City NC
Billie Trimble Chandler, Texas State Museum of Asian Cultures, Corpus Christi TX
Chatham Historical Society, The Atwood House Museum, Chatham MA
City of High Point, High Point Museum, High Point NC
City of Nome Alaska, Carrie M McLain Memorial Museum, Nome AK
Clark County Historical Society, Heritage Center of Clark County, Springfield OH
Clark County Historical Society, Pioneer - Krier Museum, Ashland KS
Cohasset Historical Society, Pratt Building (Society Headquarters), Cohasset MA
Colorado Historical Society, Colorado History Museum, Denver CO
Columbus Museum, Columbus GA
Craigdarroch Castle Historical Museum Society, Victoria BC
Cripple Creek District Museum, Cripple Creek CO
Crook County Museum & Art Gallery, Sundance WY
Crow Wing County Historical Society, Brainerd MN
Culberson County Historical Museum, Van Horn TX
DAR Museum, National Society Daughters of the American Revolution, Washington DC

Dartmouth Heritage Museum, Dartmouth NS
Deines Cultural Center, Russell KS
Deming-Luna Mimbres Museum, Deming NM
Erie Art Museum, Erie PA
Erie County Historical Society, Erie PA
Evanston Historical Society, Charles Gates Dawes House, Evanston IL
Evansville Museum of Arts, History & Science, Evansville IN
Everhart Museum, Scranton PA
Fairbanks Museum & Planetarium, Saint Johnsbury VT
Farmington Village Green & Library Association, Stanley-Whitman House, Farmington CT
Ferenczy Muzeum, Szentendre
Fetherston Foundation, Packwood House Museum, Lewisburg PA
Fishkill Historical Society, Van Wyck Homestead Museum, Fishkill NY
Frontier Times Museum, Bandera TX
Fruitlands Museum, Inc, Harvard MA
Fulton County Historical Society Inc, Fulton County Museum (Tetzlaff Reference Room), Rochester IN
Gadsden Museum, Mesilla NM
Gallery One Visual Arts Center, Ellensburg WA
Gem County Historical Society and Museum, Gem County Historical Village Museum, Emmett ID
Germanisches Nationalmuseum, Nuremberg
Germantown Historical Society, Philadelphia PA
Glanmore National Historic Site of Canada, Belleville ON
Grand Rapids Public Museum, Public Museum of Grand Rapids, Grand Rapids MI
Grassroots Art Center, Lucas KS
Halifax Historical Society, Inc, Halifax Historical Museum, Daytona Beach FL
Hammond-Harwood House Association, Inc, Hammond-Harwood House, Annapolis MD
Hancock Shaker Village, Inc, Pittsfield MA
Heard Museum, Phoenix AZ
Heart of West Texas Museum, Colorado City TX
Hebrew Union College, Skirball Cultural Center, Los Angeles CA
Henry County Museum & Cultural Arts Center, Clinton MO
Heritage Center, Inc, Pine Ridge SD
Heritage Museum Association, Inc, The Heritage Museum of Northwest Florida, Valparaiso FL
Edna Hibel, Hibel Museum of Art, Jupiter FL
Historic Cherry Hill, Albany NY
Historic Newton, Newton MA
Historical Society of Martin County, Elliott Museum, Stuart FL
Houston Baptist University, Museum of American Architecture and Decorative Arts, Houston TX
Houston Museum of Decorative Arts, Chattanooga TN
Hoyt Center for the Arts, New Castle PA
Huguenot Historical Society of New Paltz Galleries, New Paltz NY
Huronia Museum, Gallery of Historic Huronia, Midland ON
Illinois State Museum, ISM Lockport Gallery, Chicago Gallery & Southern Illinois Art Gallery, Springfield IL
Imperial Calcasieu Museum, Gibson-Barham Gallery, Lake Charles LA
Independence Historical Museum & Art Center, Independence KS
Independent Administrative Institution National Institutes for Cultural Heritage, Tokyo National Museum, Tokyo
Indiana State Museum, Indianapolis IN
The Interchurch Center, Galleries at the Interchurch Center, New York NY
International Clown Hall of Fame & Research Center, Inc, West Allis WI
Iowa State University, Brunnier Art Museum, Ames IA
Iredell Museums, Statesville NC
Iroquois County Historical Society Museum, Old Courthouse Museum, Watseka IL
Iroquois Indian Museum, Howes Cave NY
Jefferson County Open Space, Hiwan Homestead Museum, Evergreen CO
Jersey City Museum, Jersey City NJ
Kelly-Griggs House Museum, Red Bluff CA
Kenosha Public Museums, Kenosha WI
Kings County Historical Society & Museum, Hampton NB
Klein Museum, Mobridge SD
Koochiching Museums, International Falls MN
LA County Museum of Art, Los Angeles CA

Lac du Flambeau Band of Lake Superior Chippewa Indians, George W Brown Jr Ojibwe Museum & Cultural Center, Lac Du Flambeau WI
League of New Hampshire Craftsmen, Grodin Permanent Collection Museum, Concord NH
Leeds Museums & Galleries, Leeds
LeSueur County Historical Society, Chapter One, Elysian MN
Lightner Museum, Saint Augustine FL
Lincolnshire County Council, Library & Heritage Services, Lincoln
Livingston County Historical Society, Museum, Geneseo NY
The Long Island Museum of American Art, History & Carriages, Stony Brook NY
Longfellow-Evangeline State Commemorative Area, Saint Martinville LA
Longue Vue House & Gardens, New Orleans LA
Louisiana Arts & Science Museum, Baton Rouge LA
Louisiana Department of Culture, Recreation & Tourism, Louisiana State Museum, New Orleans LA
Louisiana State Exhibit Museum, Shreveport LA
Loveland Museum/Gallery, Loveland CO
Lyman Allyn Art Museum, New London CT
Manitoba Historical Society, Dalnavert Museum, Winnipeg MB
Marblehead Museum & Historical Society, Jeremiah Lee Mansion, Marblehead MA
Marblehead Museum & Historical Society, Marblehead MA
Marquette University, Haggerty Museum of Art, Milwaukee WI
Massillon Museum, Massillon OH
Maysville, Kentucky Gateway Museum Center, Maysville KY
McCord Museum of Canadian History, Montreal PQ
McDowell House & Apothecary Shop, Danville KY
McLean County Historical Society, McLean County Museum of History, Bloomington IL
McPherson Museum and Arts Foundation, McPherson KS
Meredith College, Frankie G Weems Gallery & Rotunda Gallery, Raleigh NC
Mexican Museum, San Francisco CA
Middle Border Museum & Oscar Howe Art Center, Mitchell SD
Mingei International, Inc, Mingei International Museum - Balboa Park & Mingei International Museum - Escondido, San Diego CA
Ministry of Alberta Culture, Royal Alberta Museum, Edmonton AB
Ministry of Cultural Affairs, Bangladesh National Museum, Dhaka
MonDak Heritage Center, History Library, Sidney MT
Montana State University, Museum of the Rockies, Bozeman MT
Moody County Historical Society, Moody County Museum, Pierre SD
Museo Del Romanticismo, Museum of the Romantic Period, Madrid
The Museum, Greenwood SC
Museum of Art & History, Santa Cruz, Santa Cruz CA
Museum of the City of New York, Museum, New York NY
Museum of the Plains Indian & Crafts Center, Browning MT
Museum of Vancouver, Vancouver BC
Museum of West Louisiana, Leesville LA
Museum zu Allerheiligen, Schaffhausen
Muzej za Umjetnost i Obrt, Museum of Arts & Crafts, Zagreb
The National Museum of Modern Art, Tokyo, Tokyo
National Society of Colonial Dames of America in the State of Maryland, Mount Clare Museum House, Baltimore MD
Nebraska Game and Parks Commission, Arbor Lodge State Historical Park & Morton Mansion, Nebraska City NE
Neville Public Museum of Brown County, Green Bay WI
New Brunswick Museum, Saint John NB
New Canaan Historical Society, New Canaan CT
New Hampshire Antiquarian Society, Hopkinton Historical Society, Hopkinton NH
New Jersey Historical Society, Newark NJ
No Man's Land Historical Society, No Man's Land Museum, Goodwell OK
North Carolina State University, Gregg Museum of Art & Design, Raleigh NC
Norwich Free Academy, Slater Memorial Museum, Norwich CT

Ohio Historical Society, National Afro-American Museum & Cultural Center, Wilberforce OH

The Ohio Historical Society, Inc, Campus Martius Museum & Ohio River Museum, Marietta OH

Old Dartmouth Historical Society, New Bedford Whaling Museum, New Bedford MA

Old Island Restoration Foundation Inc, Oldest House in Key West, Key West FL

Panhandle-Plains Historical Museum, Canyon TX

Pasadena Museum of History, Pasadena CA

Phelps County Historical Society, Nebraska Prairie Museum, Holdrege NE

Philadelphia History Museum, Philadelphia PA

The Frank Phillips, Woolaroc Museum, Bartlesville OK

Pine Bluff/Jefferson County Historical Museum, Pine Bluff AR

Plainsman Museum, Aurora NE

Please Touch Museum, Philadelphia PA

Pope County Historical Society, Pope County Museum, Glenwood MN

Port Huron Museum, Port Huron MI

Presidential Museum & Leadership Library, Odessa TX

Principia College, School of Nations Museum, Elsah IL

Putnam Museum of History and Natural Science, Davenport IA

Reading Public Museum, Reading PA

Red River Valley Museum, Vernon TX

Riley County Historical Society & Museum, Riley County Historical Museum, Manhattan KS

Riverside Metropolitan Museum, Riverside CA

The Rooms Corporation of Newfoundland & Labrador, Saint John's NF

Roswell Museum & Art Center, Roswell NM

Saco Museum, Saco ME

Saint Augustine Historical Society, Oldest House Museum Complex, Saint Augustine FL

Saint Joseph Museum, Saint Joseph MO

Saint Louis County Historical Society, St. Louis County Historical Society, Duluth MN

St Mary Landmarks, Grevemberg House Museum, Franklin LA

Saint Peter's College, Art Gallery, Jersey City NJ

Sea Cliff Village Museum, Sea Cliff NY

Seneca-Iroquois National Museum, Salamanca NY

Shaker Museum & Library, Old Chatham NY

Shelburne Museum, Museum, Shelburne VT

Shores Memorial Museum, Lyndon Center VT

Sooke Region Museum & Art Gallery, Sooke BC

Soprintendenza per i beni storici artistici ed etnoantropologici per le province di Mantova Brescia e Cremona, Museo di Palazzo Ducale, Mantua

South Carolina Artisans Center, Walterboro SC

Southern Illinois University Carbondale, University Museum, Carbondale IL

Southern Ohio Museum Corporation, Southern Ohio Museum, Portsmouth OH

The Speed Art Museum, Louisville KY

Stauth Foundation & Museum, Stauth Memorial Museum, Montezuma KS

Ste Genevieve Museum, Sainte Genevieve MO

Stedelijk Museum Alkmaar, Alkmaar Municipal Museum, Alkmaar

Stratford Historical Society, Catharine B Mitchell Museum, Stratford CT

Sturdivant Museum Association, Sturdivant Museum, Selma AL

Suan Pakkad Palace Museum, Bangkok

The Summit County Historical Society of Akron, OH, Akron OH

Suomen Kansallismuseo, National Museum of Finland, Helsinki

Tallahassee Museum of History & Natural Science, Tallahassee FL

Texas Tech University, Museum of Texas Tech University, Lubbock TX

Three Forks Area Historical Society, Headwaters Heritage Museum, Three Forks MT

Tinkertown Museum, Sandia Park NM

Tohono Chul Park, Tucson AZ

Ukrainian Canadian Archives & Museum of Alberta, Edmonton AB

United Society of Shakers, Shaker Museum, New Gloucester ME

University of Chicago, Oriental Institute, Chicago IL

University of Saskatchewan, Diefenbaker Canada Centre, Saskatoon SK

Vesterheim Norwegian-American Museum, Decorah IA

Village of Potsdam, Potsdam Public Museum, Potsdam NY

Wake Forest University, Museum of Anthropology, Winston Salem NC

The Walker African American Museum & Research Center, Las Vegas NV

Waterville Historical Society, Redington Museum, Waterville ME

Wellfleet Historical Society & Museum, Inc, Wellfleet MA

West Florida Historic Preservation, Inc/University of West Florida, T T Wentworth, Jr Florida State Museum; Historic Pensacola Village; Pensacola Historical Society & Resource Center, Pensacola FL

Whatcom Museum, Bellingham WA

Willard House & Clock Museum, Inc, North Grafton MA

Witte Museum, San Antonio TX

World Erotic Art Museum, Miami Beach FL

Yankton County Historical Society, Dakota Territorial Museum, Yankton SD

Yarmouth County Historical Society, Yarmouth County Museum & Archives, Yarmouth NS

DRAWINGS

A.E. Backus Museum of Art, Fort Pierce FL

Abington Art Center, Jenkintown PA

Academy Art Museum, Easton MD

Academy of the New Church, Glencairn Museum, Bryn Athyn PA

African American Museum in Philadelphia, Philadelphia PA

Alaska Heritage Museum at Wells Fargo, Anchorage AK

Albany Institute of History & Art, Albany NY

Albertina Museum, Vienna

Albuquerque Museum of Art & History, Albuquerque NM

Allentown Art Museum, Allentown PA

Alton Museum of History & Art, Inc, Alton IL

American Art Museum, Smithsonian Institution, Washington DC

American Swedish Historical Foundation & Museum, American Swedish Historical Museum, Philadelphia PA

American University, Katzen Art Center Gallery, New York NY

Amon Carter Museum of American Art, Fort Worth TX

Anchorage Museum at Rasmuson Center, Anchorage AK

Walter Anderson, Ocean Springs MS

Appaloosa Museum and Heritage Center, Moscow ID

Arab American National Museum, Dearborn MI

Arizona Historical Society-Yuma, Sanguinetti House Museum & Garden, Yuma AZ

Arizona Museum For Youth, Mesa AZ

Arnot Art Museum, Elmira NY

Art & Culture Center of Hollywood, Art Gallery/Multidisciplinary Cultural Center, Hollywood FL

Art Center of Battle Creek, Battle Creek MI

Art Community Center, Art Center of Corpus Christi, Corpus Christi TX

Art Gallery of Calgary, Calgary AB

Art Gallery of Nova Scotia, Halifax NS

Art Gallery of South Australia, Adelaide

The Art Museum at the University of Kentucky, Lexington KY

The Art Museum of Eastern Idaho, Idaho Falls ID

Art Museum of Greater Lafayette, Lafayette IN

Art Museum of Southeast Texas, Beaumont TX

Art Without Walls Inc, New York NY

Artesia Historical Museum & Art Center, Artesia NM

Arts Council of Fayetteville-Cumberland County, The Arts Center, Fayetteville NC

Artspace, Richmond VA

ArtSpace/Lima, Lima OH

Asbury College, Student Center Gallery, Wilmore KY

Baldwin-Wallace College, Fawick Art Gallery, Berea OH

Ball State University, Museum of Art, Muncie IN

The Baltimore Museum of Art, Baltimore MD

Balzekas Museum of Lithuanian Culture, Chicago IL

Bard College, Center for Curatorial Studies and the Hessel Museum of Art, Annandale-on-Hudson NY

Barnes Foundation, Merion PA

Baruch College of the City University of New York, Sidney Mishkin Gallery, New York NY

Bates College, Museum of Art, Lewiston ME

Baylor University, Martin Museum of Art, Waco TX

Bellevue Arts Museum, Bellevue WA

Bennington Museum, Bennington VT

Berkshire Museum, Pittsfield MA

Bertha V B Lederer Fine Arts Gallery-Suny Geneseo, Bertha V B Lederer Fine Arts Gallery, Geneseo NY

Besser Museum for Northeast Michigan, Alpena MI

Biggs Museum of American Art, Dover DE

Birmingham Museum of Art, Birmingham AL

Blauvelt Demarest Foundation, Hiram Blauvelt Art Museum, Oradell NJ

Bone Creek Museum of Agrarian Art, David City NE

Booth Western Art Museum, Cartersville GA

Boston Public Library, Albert H Wiggin Gallery & Print Department, Boston MA

Roy Boyd, Chicago IL

Brandywine Conservancy, Brandywine River Museum, Chadds Ford PA

Brigham City Corporation, Brigham City Museum & Gallery, Brigham City UT

Brigham Young University, B F Larsen Gallery, Provo UT

Brigham Young University, Museum of Art, Provo UT

Bruce Museum, Inc, Greenwich CT

Bucknell University, Edward & Marthann Samek Art Gallery, Lewisburg PA

Burke Arts Council, Jailhouse Galleries, Morganton NC

Bush-Holley Historic Site & Storehouse Gallery, Greenwich Historical Society/ Bush-Holley House, Cos Cob CT

The Butler Institute of American Art, Art Museum, Youngstown OH

C W Post Campus of Long Island University, Hillwood Art Museum, Brookville NY

Cabot's Old Indian Pueblo Museum, Desert Hot Springs CA

The California Historical Society, San Francisco CA

California State University Stanislaus, University Art Gallery, Turlock CA

California State University, Long Beach, University Art Museum, Long Beach CA

California State University, Northridge, Art Galleries, Northridge CA

Calvin College, Center Art Gallery, Grand Rapids MI

Cameron Art Museum, Wilmington NC

Canadian Clay and Glass Gallery, Waterloo ON

Canadian Museum of Civilization, Gatineau PQ

Canadian Museum of Nature, Musee Canadien de la Nature, Ottawa ON

Cape Ann Historical Association, Cape Ann Museum, Gloucester MA

Carnegie Mellon University, Hunt Institute for Botanical Documentation, Pittsburgh PA

Carnegie Museums of Pittsburgh, Carnegie Museum of Art, Pittsburgh PA

Carson County Square House Museum, Panhandle TX

Carteret County Historical Society, The History Place, Morehead City NC

Cartoon Art Museum, San Francisco CA

Cedar Rapids Museum of Art, Cedar Rapids IA

Centro de Arte Moderna, CAM - Calouste Gulbenkian Foundation, Lisbon

Chatham Historical Society, The Atwood House Museum, Chatham MA

City of Brea, Art Gallery, Brea CA

City of Cedar Falls, Iowa, James & Meryl Hearst Center for the Arts & Sculpture Garden, Cedar Falls IA

City of Fayette, Alabama, Fayette Art Museum, Fayette AL

City of Fremont, Olive Hyde Art Gallery, Fremont CA

City of Mason City, Charles H MacNider Museum, Mason City IA

City of Nome Alaska, Carrie M McLain Memorial Museum, Nome AK

City of Pittsfield, Berkshire Artisans, Pittsfield MA

City of Port Angeles, Port Angeles Fine Arts Center & Webster Woods Art Park, Port Angeles WA

City of Springdale, Shiloh Museum of Ozark History, Springdale AR

Clark County Historical Society, Heritage Center of Clark County, Springfield OH

Sterling & Francine Clark, Williamstown MA

Colgate University, Picker Art Gallery, Hamilton NY

College of New Jersey, Art Gallery, Ewing NJ

College of Saint Benedict, Gorecki Gallery & Gallery Lounge, Saint Joseph MN

College of William & Mary, Muscarelle Museum of Art, Williamsburg VA

Columbus Museum, Columbus GA

Columbus Museum of Art, Columbus OH

Comune di Genova - Direzione Cultura Settore Musei, Museo di Strada Nuova Palazzo Rosso, Genoa

Concordia University, Leonard & Bina Ellen Art Gallery, Montreal PQ

Confederation Centre Art Gallery and Museum, Charlottetown PE

Cooper-Hewitt National Design Museum, Smithsonian Institution, New York NY
Corcoran Gallery of Art, Washington DC
Cornell College, Peter Paul Luce Gallery, Mount Vernon IA
Cornell Museum of Art and American Culture, Delray Beach FL
Cornell University, Herbert F Johnson Museum of Art, Ithaca NY
Cornwall Gallery Society, Cornwall Regional Art Gallery, Cornwall ON
The Courtauld Institute of Art, The Courtauld Gallery, London
Coutts Museum of Art, Inc, El Dorado KS
Craft and Folk Art Museum (CAFAM), Los Angeles CA
Cranbrook Art Museum, Bloomfield Hills MI
Creighton University, Lied Art Gallery, Omaha NE
Cripple Creek District Museum, Cripple Creek CO
Crocker Art Museum, Sacramento CA
Crook County Museum & Art Gallery, Sundance WY
Crow Wing County Historical Society, Brainerd MN
Culberson County Historical Museum, Van Horn TX
The Currier Museum of Art, Manchester NH
Dahesh Museum of Art, Greenwich CT
Dallas Museum of Art, Dallas TX
Danforth Museum of Art, Danforth Museum of Art, Framingham MA
Danville Museum of Fine Arts & History, Danville VA
Dartmouth College, Hood Museum of Art, Hanover NH
Daum Museum of Contemporary Art, Sedalia MO
Davidson College, William H Van Every Jr & Edward M Smith Galleries, Davidson NC
Del Mar College, Joseph A Cain Memorial Art Gallery, Corpus Christi TX
DeLeon White Gallery, Toronto ON
Denver Art Museum, Denver CO
Detroit Institute of Arts, Detroit MI
Detroit Repertory Theatre Gallery, Detroit MI
Dickinson College, The Trout Gallery, Carlisle PA
Dixie State College, Robert N & Peggy Sears Gallery, Saint George UT
Doncaster Museum and Art Gallery, Doncaster
Dundee City Council Leisure & Communities Department, The McManus: Dundee's Art Gallery & Museum, Dundee
Eastern Illinois University, Tarble Arts Center, Charleston IL
Eiteljorg Museum of American Indians & Western Art, Indianapolis IN
Ellen Noel Art Museum of the Permian Basin, Odessa TX
Elmhurst Art Museum, Elmhurst IL
eMediaLoft.org, New York NY
Environment Canada - Parks Canada, Laurier House, National Historic Site, Ottawa ON
Erie Art Museum, Erie PA
Erie County Historical Society, Erie PA
Essex Historical Society and Shipbuilding Museum, Essex MA
Establishment Public du Chateau du Rusee, Et du Dophine national de versailles, Versailles
Evergreen State College, Evergreen Gallery, Olympia WA
Everhart Museum, Scranton PA
Farmington Village Green & Library Association, Stanley-Whitman House, Farmington CT
Federal Reserve Board, Art Gallery, Washington DC
Felicien Rops Museum, Namur
Ferenczy Muzeum, Szentendre
Fine Arts Museums of San Francisco, Legion of Honor, San Francisco CA
Fishkill Historical Society, Van Wyck Homestead Museum, Fishkill NY
Fisk University, Aaron Douglas Gallery, Nashville TN
Fisk University, Carl Van Vechten Gallery, Nashville TN
Fitchburg Art Museum, Fitchburg MA
Flint Institute of Arts, Flint MI
Florence Museum, Florence SC
Florida Southern College, Melvin Art Gallery, Lakeland FL
Florida State University, John & Mable Ringling Museum of Art, Sarasota FL
Fondazione Musei Civici Di Venezia, Ca'Rezzonico, Museo del Settecento Veneziano, Venice
Fondazione Musei Civici Di Venezia, Galleria Internazionale d'Arte Moderna di Ca'Pesaro, Venice
Edsel & Eleanor Ford, Grosse Pointe Shores MI
Forest Lawn Museum, Glendale CA
Fort Collins Museum of Art, Inc., Fort Collins CO

Fort Hays State University, Moss-Thorns Gallery of Arts, Hays KS
Fort Smith Regional Art Museum, Fort Smith AR
Freer Gallery of Art & Arthur M Sackler Gallery, Arthur M Sackler Gallery, Washington DC
The Frick Art & Historical Center, Inc, Frick Art Museum, Pittsburgh PA
Frick Collection, New York NY
Friends of Historic Kingston, Fred J Johnston House Museum, Kingston NY
Frontier Times Museum, Bandera TX
Fruitlands Museum, Inc, Harvard MA
Fuller Craft Museum, Brockton MA
Gala-Salvador Dali Foundation Museums, Casa Museu Castell Gala Dali, Figueres
Gala-Salvador Dali Foundation Museums, Salvador Dali Foundation, Figueres
Galerie Montcalm, Gatineau PQ
Galleria Nazionale dell'Umbria, Umbrian National Gallery, Perugia
Gallery One Visual Arts Center, Ellensburg WA
Georgian Court University, M Christina Geis Gallery, Lakewood NJ
Germanisches Nationalmuseum, Nuremberg
Germantown Historical Society, Philadelphia PA
The Ghent Museum of Fine Arts, Ghent
Glanmore National Historic Site of Canada, Belleville ON
Gonzaga University, Art Gallery, Spokane WA
Grand Rapids Public Museum, Public Museum of Grand Rapids, Grand Rapids MI
Great Lakes Historical Society, Inland Seas Maritime Museum, Vermilion OH
Greene County Historical Society, Bronck Museum, Coxsackie NY
Greenville College, Richard W Bock Sculpture Collection, Almira College House, Greenville IL
Grinnell College, Faulconer Gallery, Grinnell IA
Guggenheim Museum Soho, New York NY
Solomon R Guggenheim, New York NY
Guilford College, Art Gallery, Greensboro NC
Halifax Historical Society, Inc, Halifax Historical Museum, Daytona Beach FL
Hamilton College, Emerson Gallery, Clinton NY
Hammond-Harwood House Association, Inc, Hammond-Harwood House, Annapolis MD
Hancock Shaker Village, Inc, Pittsfield MA
Hartwick College, Foreman Gallery, Oneonta NY
Hartwick College, The Yager Museum, Oneonta NY
Hawkes Bay Art Gallery and Museum, Napier
Headquarters Fort Monroe, Dept of Army, Casemate Museum, Hampton VA
Heard Museum, Phoenix AZ
Hebrew Union College, Skirball Cultural Center, Los Angeles CA
Hebrew Union College - Jewish Institute of Religion, Skirball Museum Cincinnati, Cincinnati OH
Hecht Museum, Haifa
The Heckscher Museum of Art, Huntington NY
Henry County Museum & Cultural Arts Center, Clinton MO
Henry Gallery Association, Henry Art Gallery, Seattle WA
Gertrude Herbert, Augusta GA
Heritage Center, Inc, Pine Ridge SD
Heritage Malta, National Museum of Fine Arts, Valletta
Hermitage Foundation Museum, Norfolk VA
Edna Hibel, Hibel Museum of Art, Jupiter FL
Hickory Museum of Art, Inc, Hickory NC
Higgins Armory Museum, Worcester MA
High Desert Museum, Bend OR
High Museum of Art, Atlanta GA
Hill-Stead Museum, Farmington CT
Hillwood Museum & Gardens Foundation, Hillwood Estate Museum & Gardens, Washington DC
The Hispanic Society of America, Museum & Library, New York NY
Historic Arkansas Museum, Little Rock AR
The Historic New Orleans Collection, Royal Street Galleries, New Orleans LA
Historic Newton, Newton MA
The History Center in Tompkins County, Ithaca NY
Hofstra University, Hofstra University Museum, Hempstead NY
Housatonic Community College, Housatonic Museum of Art, Bridgeport CT
Hoyt Center for the Arts, New Castle PA
Huguenot Historical Society of New Paltz Galleries, New Paltz NY
Hui No'eau Visual Arts Center, Gallery and Gift Shop, Makawao Maui HI

The Huntington Library, Art Collections & Botanical Gardens, San Marino CA
Huronia Museum, Gallery of Historic Huronia, Midland ON
Hyde Park Art Center, Chicago IL
Illinois State Museum, ISM Lockport Gallery, Chicago Gallery & Southern Illinois Art Gallery, Springfield IL
Illinois State University, University Galleries, Normal IL
Illinois Wesleyan University, Merwin & Wakeley Galleries, Bloomington IL
Imperial Calcasieu Museum, Gibson-Barham Gallery, Lake Charles LA
Independence Seaport Museum, Philadelphia PA
Independent Administrative Institution National Institutes for Cultural Heritage, Tokyo National Museum, Tokyo
Independent Administrative Institution National Museum of Art, The National Museum of Western Art, Tokyo
Indiana University, Art Museum, Bloomington IN
Indianapolis Museum of Art, Indianapolis IN
The Interchurch Center, Galleries at the Interchurch Center, New York NY
Iredell Museums, Statesville NC
Iroquois Indian Museum, Howes Cave NY
The Israel Museum, Jerusalem, Billy Rose Art Garden, Jerusalem
The Israel Museum, Jerusalem, Samuel & Saidye Bronfman Archaeology Wing, Jerusalem
The Israel Museum, Jerusalem, Jerusalem
J.M.W. Turner Museum, Sarasota FL
Jacksonville University, Alexander Brest Museum & Gallery, Jacksonville FL
Thomas Jefferson, Monticello, Charlottesville VA
Jersey City Museum, Jersey City NJ
The Jewish Museum, New York NY
John Weaver Sculpture Collection, Hope BC
Johns Hopkins University, Evergreen Museum & Library, Baltimore MD
Jordan National Gallery of Fine Arts, Amman
Joslyn Art Museum, Omaha NE
Juniata College Museum of Art, Huntingdon PA
Kalamazoo Institute of Arts, Kalamazoo MI
Kamloops Art Gallery, Kamloops BC
Kenosha Public Museums, Kenosha WI
Kentucky Museum of Art and Craft, Louisville KY
Kereszteny Muzeum, Christian Museum, Esztergom
Kirchner Museum Davos, Davos
Kirkland Museum of Fine & Decorative Art, Denver CO
Kitchener-Waterloo Art Gallery, Kitchener ON
Klein Museum, Mobridge SD
Knoxville Museum of Art, Knoxville TN
Koninklijk Museum voor Schone Kunsten Antwerpen, Royal Museum of Fine Arts, Antwerp
Kroller-Muller Museum, Otterlo
Kunsthalle Bremen, Bremen Art Gallery, Bremen
Kunstmuseum Bern, Musee des Beaux-Arts de Berne, Bern
Kunstmuseum Solothurn, Solothurn Art Museum, Solothurn
Kunstmuseum Thun, Thun
Kyiv Museum of Russian Art, Kyiv
La Salle University Art Museum, Philadelphia PA
Lac du Flambeau Band of Lake Superior Chippewa Indians, George W Brown Jr Ojibwe Museum & Cultural Center, Lac Du Flambeau WI
LACE (Los Angeles Contemporary Exhibitions), Los Angeles CA
Lafayette College, Lafayette College Art Galleries, Easton PA
Lafayette Science Museum & Planetarium, Lafayette LA
LaGrange Art Museum, LaGrange GA
Latino Art Museum, Pomona CA
Latvijas Nacionalais Makslas Muzejs, Arsenals Exhibition Hall, Riga
Launceston City Council, Queen Victoria Museum and Art Gallery, Launceston
Lawrence University, Wriston Art Center Galleries, Appleton WI
Leeds Museums & Galleries, Leeds
Lehigh Valley Heritage Center, Allentown PA
LeMoyne Art Foundation, Center for the Visual Arts, Tallahassee FL
LeSueur County Historical Society, Chapter One, Elysian MN
Liberty Memorial Museum & Archives, The National Museum of World War I, Kansas City MO
Lightner Museum, Saint Augustine FL

Opelousas Museum of Art, Inc (OMA), Opelousas LA
Orange County Museum of Art, Newport Beach CA
Otis College of Art & Design, Ben Maltz Gallery, Los Angeles CA
Owensboro Museum of Fine Art, Owensboro KY
Panhandle-Plains Historical Museum, Canyon TX
Paris Gibson Square, Museum of Art, Great Falls MT
Parrish Art Museum, Water Mill NY
Pasadena Museum of California Art, Pasadena CA
Patrimonio Nacional, Palacios de la Granja y Riofrio, Madrid
The Pennsylvania State University, Palmer Museum of Art, University Park PA
Philadelphia History Museum, Philadelphia PA
Phillips Academy, Addison Gallery of American Art, Andover MA
The Frank Phillips, Woolaroc Museum, Bartlesville OK
George Phippen, Phippen Museum - Art of the American West, Prescott AZ
Pinacoteca Provinciale, Bari
Plains Art Museum, Fargo ND
Polk Museum of Art, Lakeland FL
The Pomona College, Claremont CA
Pope County Historical Society, Pope County Museum, Glenwood MN
Porter-Phelps-Huntington Foundation, Inc, Historic House Museum, Hadley MA
Portland Art Museum, Portland OR
Pretoria Art Museum, Municipal Art Gallery, Pretoria
Princeton University, Princeton University Art Museum, Princeton NJ
PS1 Contemporary Art Center, Long Island City NY
Purchase College, Neuberger Museum of Art, Purchase NY
Purdue University Galleries, West Lafayette IN
Putnam Museum of History and Natural Science, Davenport IA
Queens College, City University of New York, Godwin-Ternbach Museum, Flushing NY
Queensborough Community College, Art Gallery, Bayside NY
Quincy University, The Gray Gallery, Quincy IL
Rabindra Bhavan Art Gallery, Lalit Kala Akademi (National Academy of Art), New Delhi
Rahr-West Art Museum, Manitowoc WI
Randall Junior Museum, San Francisco CA
Randolph College, Maier Museum of Art, Lynchburg VA
Rawls Museum Arts, Courtland VA
Reading Public Museum, Reading PA
Jack Richard Gallery, Almond Tea Museum & Jane Williams Galleries, Divisions of Studios of Jack Richard, Cuyahoga Falls OH
Rider University, Art Gallery, Lawrenceville NJ
Rijksmuseum Twenthe, Rijksmuseum Twenthe, Enschede
Roberson Museum & Science Center, Binghamton NY
Rose Lehrman Art Gallery, Harrisburg PA
The Rosenbach Museum & Library, Philadelphia PA
Roswell Artist-in-Residence Foundation, Anderson Museum of Contemporary Art, Roswell NM
Roswell Museum & Art Center, Roswell NM
Royal Pavilion & Museums, Brighton Museum & Art Gallery, Brighton
C M Russell, Great Falls MT
Saginaw Art Museum, Saginaw MI
Saint Anselm College, Alva de Mars Megan Chapel Art Center, Manchester NH
Saint Bonaventure University, Regina A Quick Center for the Arts, Saint Bonaventure NY
Saint Joseph College, Art Gallery, University of Saint Joseph, West Hartford CT
Saint Joseph's Oratory, Museum, Montreal PQ
Saint Mary's College of California, Hearst Art Gallery, Moraga CA
St Mary's College of Maryland, The Dwight Frederick Boyden Gallery, St Mary's City MD
Saint Olaf College, Flaten Art Museum, Northfield MN
Saint Peter's College, Art Gallery, Jersey City NJ
San Francisco Maritime National Historical Park, Maritime Museum, San Francisco CA
San Francisco Museum of Modern Art, Artist Gallery, San Francisco CA
San Jose Museum of Art, San Jose CA
Santa Barbara Museum of Art, Santa Barbara CA
Santa Monica Museum of Art, Santa Monica CA
Savitsky Karakalpakstan State Art Museum, Nukus
School of Visual Arts, Visual Arts Museum, New York NY
Scottsdale Cultural Council, Scottsdale Museum of Contemporary Art, Scottsdale AZ

Scripps College, Ruth Chandler Williamson Gallery, Claremont CA
Seneca-Iroquois National Museum, Salamanca NY
1708 Gallery, Richmond VA
Severoceska Galerie Vytvarneho Umeni v Litomericich, North Bohemian Gallery of Fine Arts in Litomerice, Litomerice
Shaker Museum & Library, Old Chatham NY
Shirley Plantation Foundation, Charles City VA
R L S Silverado Museum, Saint Helena CA
Slovenska Narodna Galeria, Slovak National Gallery, Bratislava
Smith College, Museum of Art, Northampton MA
The Society of the Cincinnati at Anderson House, Washington DC
Sonoma State University, University Art Gallery, Rohnert Park CA
Soprintendenza per I beni storici artistici ed etnoantropologici per le province di Mantova Brescia e Cremona, Museo di Palazzo Ducale, Mantua
South Carolina Artisans Center, Walterboro SC
South Dakota State University, South Dakota Art Museum, Brookings SD
South Street Seaport Museum, New York NY
Southeastern Center for Contemporary Art, Winston Salem NC
Southern Oregon University, Schneider Museum of Art, Ashland OR
The Speed Art Museum, Louisville KY
Spertus Institute of Jewish Studies, Chicago IL
Springfield Art Museum, Springfield MO
Staatsgalerie Stuttgart, Stuttgart
Stamford Museum & Nature Center, Stamford CT
Stanford University, Cantor Arts Center at Stanford University, Stanford CA
Stanley Museum, Inc, Kingfield ME
Nelda C & H J Lutcher Stark, Stark Museum of Art, Orange TX
The State Museum of Fine Arts of Tatarstan Republic, Kazan
State University of New York at Binghamton, Binghamton University Art Museum, Binghamton NY
State University of New York at Geneseo, Bertha V B Lederer Gallery, Geneseo NY
State University of New York at Geneseo, Lockhart Gallery, Geneseo NY
The State University of New York at Potsdam, Roland Gibson Gallery, Potsdam NY
State University of New York at Ulster, Muroff-Kotler Visual Arts Gallery, Stone Ridge NY
State University of New York College at Buffalo, Buffalo NY
State University of New York College at Cortland, Dowd Fine Arts Gallery, Cortland NY
The Stewart Museum, Montreal PQ
Stiftung Deutsches Historisches Museum, Berlin
Stone Quarry Hill Art Park, Winner Gallery, Cazenovia NY
Stratford Historical Society, Catharine B Mitchell Museum, Stratford CT
Sturdivant Museum Association, Sturdivant Museum, Selma AL
Suan Pakkad Palace Museum, Bangkok
Suomen Kansallismuseo, National Museum of Finland, Helsinki
Susquehanna University, Lore Degenstein Gallery, Selinsgrove PA
Sweet Briar College, Art Collection & Galleries, Sweet Briar VA
Swetcharnik Art Studio, Mount Airy MD
Syracuse University, Art Collection, Syracuse NY
Syracuse University, SUArt Galleries, Syracuse NY
Szepmuveszeti Muzeum, Museum of Fine Arts Budapest, Budapest
Taft Museum of Art, Cincinnati OH
Tampa Museum of Art, Tampa FL
Taos, Ernest Blumenschein Home & Studio, Taos NM
Temiskaming Art Gallery, Haileybury ON
Texas Tech University, Museum of Texas Tech University, Lubbock TX
Thomas More College, Eva G Farris Art Gallery, Crestview KY
Thorvaldsens Museum, Copenhagen
Tinkertown Museum, Sandia Park NM
Tohono Chul Park, Tucson AZ
Tokyo University of the Arts, The University Art Museum, Tokyo
Topeka & Shawnee County Public Library, Alice C Sabatini Gallery, Topeka KS

Tulane University, Newcomb Art Gallery, New Orleans LA
Tulane University, University Art Collection, New Orleans LA
Tver Art Gallery, Tver
Tyne and Wear Archives & Museums, Sunderland Museum & Winter Gardens, Newcastle-upon-Tyne
Ukrainian Institute of Modern Art, Chicago IL
The Ukrainian Museum, New York NY
UMLAUF Sculpture Garden & Museum, Austin TX
United Society of Shakers, Shaker Museum, New Gloucester ME
United States Coast Guard Museum, New London CT
United States Figure Skating Association, World Figure Skating Museum & Hall of Fame, Colorado Springs CO
United States Military Academy, West Point Museum, West Point NY
United States Naval Academy, USNA Museum, Annapolis MD
Universalmuseum Joanneum GmbH, Graz
University at Albany, State University of New York, University Art Museum, Albany NY
University of Alabama at Birmingham, Visual Arts Gallery, Birmingham AL
University of Alabama at Huntsville, Union Grove Gallery & University Center Gallery, Huntsville AL
University of California, California Museum of Photography, Riverside CA
University of California, Richard L Nelson Gallery & Fine Arts Collection, Davis CA
University of California, Berkeley, Berkeley Art Museum & Pacific Film Archive, Berkeley CA
University of California, Berkeley, The Magnes Collection of Jewish Art & Life, Berkeley CA
University of California, San Diego, Stuart Collection, La Jolla CA
University of California, Santa Barbara, University Art Museum, Santa Barbara CA
University of Chicago, Smart Museum of Art, Chicago IL
University of Cincinnati, DAAP Galleries-College of Design Architecture, Art & Planning, Cincinnati OH
University of Colorado, CU Art Museum, Boulder CO
University of Colorado at Colorado Springs, Gallery of Contemporary Art, Colorado Springs CO
University of Delaware, University Museums, Newark DE
University of Georgia, Georgia Museum of Art, Athens GA
University of Illinois at Urbana-Champaign, Krannert Art Museum and Kinkead Pavilion, Champaign IL
University of Indianapolis, Christel DeHaan Fine Arts Gallery, Indianapolis IN
University of Kansas, Spencer Museum of Art, Lawrence KS
University of Louisiana at Lafayette, Paul and Lulu Hilliard University Art Museum, Lafayette LA
University of Louisville, Hite Art Institute, Louisville KY
University of Maine, Museum of Art, Bangor ME
University of Manchester, Whitworth Art Gallery, Manchester
University of Manitoba, Faculty of Architecture Exhibition Centre, Winnipeg MB
University of Mary Washington, Gari Melchers Home and Studio, Fredericksburg VA
University of Mary Washington, University of Mary Washington Galleries, Fredericksburg VA
University of Maryland, College Park, The Art Gallery, College Park MD
University of Massachusetts, Amherst, University Gallery, Amherst MA
University of Memphis, Art Museum, Memphis TN
University of Miami, Lowe Art Museum, Coral Gables FL
University of Minnesota, The Bell Museum of Natural History, Minneapolis MN
University of Minnesota, Frederick R Weisman Art Museum, Minneapolis MN
University of Minnesota Duluth, Tweed Museum of Art, Duluth MN
University of Missouri, Museum of Art & Archaeology, Columbia MO
University of Nebraska, Lincoln, Sheldon Memorial Art Gallery & Sculpture Garden, Lincoln NE
University of Nebraska-Lincoln, Great Plains Art Museum, Lincoln NE
University of Nevada, Reno, Sheppard Contemporary & University Galleries, Reno NV
University of New Hampshire, Museum of Art, Durham NH

EMBROIDERY

Kings County Historical Society & Museum, Hampton NB

Klein Museum, Mobridge SD

Knights of Columbus Supreme Council, Knights of Columbus Museum, New Haven CT

Koochiching Museums, International Falls MN

Kunsthistorisches Museum Vienna, Museum of Fine Arts, Vienna

LA County Museum of Art, Los Angeles CA

Lac du Flambeau Band of Lake Superior Chippewa Indians, George W Brown Jr Ojibwe Museum & Cultural Center, Lac Du Flambeau WI

Lafayette Science Museum & Planetarium, Lafayette LA

Lahore Museum, Lahore

League of New Hampshire Craftsmen, Grodin Permanent Collection Museum, Concord NH

Leeds Museums & Galleries, Leeds

Lehigh Valley Heritage Center, Allentown PA

Lightner Museum, Saint Augustine FL

Lincoln County Historical Association, Inc, 1811 Old Lincoln County Jail & Lincoln County Museum, Wiscasset ME

Livingston County Historical Society, Museum, Geneseo NY

The Long Island Museum of American Art, History & Carriages, Stony Brook NY

Longfellow-Evangeline State Commemorative Area, Saint Martinville LA

Longue Vue House & Gardens, New Orleans LA

Loveland Museum/Gallery, Loveland CO

Magyar Nemzeti Muzeum - Hungarian National Museum, Budapest

Maine Historical Society, Wadsworth-Longfellow House, Portland ME

Maison Saint-Gabriel Museum, Montreal PQ

Manitoba Historical Society, Dalnavert Museum, Winnipeg MB

Marblehead Museum & Historical Society, Jeremiah Lee Mansion, Marblehead MA

Marblehead Museum & Historical Society, Marblehead MA

Maysville, Kentucky Gateway Museum Center, Maysville KY

McCord Museum of Canadian History, Montreal PQ

McDowell House & Apothecary Shop, Danville KY

McLean County Historical Society, McLean County Museum of History, Bloomington IL

Mexican Museum, San Francisco CA

Middle Border Museum & Oscar Howe Art Center, Mitchell SD

Mingei International, Inc, Mingei International Museum - Balboa Park & Mingei International Museum - Escondido, San Diego CA

Ministry of Alberta Culture, Royal Alberta Museum, Edmonton AB

Ministry of Cultural Affairs, Bangladesh National Museum, Dhaka

Missoula Art Museum, Missoula MT

Monroe County Historical Association, Elizabeth D Walters Library, Stroudsburg PA

Montana State University, Museum of the Rockies, Bozeman MT

Montreal Museum of Fine Arts, Montreal PQ

Mount Saint Vincent University, MSVU Art Gallery, Halifax NS

Musee des Beaux-Arts/Palais des Archeveques, Museum of Fine Arts, Tours

Musee Royal Et Domaine De Mariemont, Morlanwelz

Musees Royaux d'Art et d'Histoire, Royal Museums of Art and History, Brussels

Museo Cerralbo, Madrid

Museo De Las Americas, Denver CO

Museo de Navarra, Pamplona

Museu de Evora, Evora

The Museum, Greenwood SC

Museum of Art & History, Santa Cruz, Santa Cruz CA

Museum of Arts & Design, New York NY

Museum of Contemporary Craft, Portland OR

Museum of Fine Arts Houston, Bayou Bend Collection & Gardens, Houston TX

Museum of Fine Arts, Houston, Houston TX

Museum of the City of New York, Museum, New York NY

Museum zu Allerheiligen, Schaffhausen

Muzej za Umjetnost i Obrt, Museum of Arts & Crafts, Zagreb

Muzeul National Brukenthal, Brukenthal Palace & European Art Gallery, Sibiu

The Namur Provincial Museum of Ancient Arts, Namur

National Museum of Fine Arts of Moldova, Chisinau

National Museum of the American Indian, Smithsonian Institution, Washington DC

National Museum of the Philippines, Manila

National Palace Museum, Taiwan, R.O.C.

The National Park Service, United States Department of the Interior, Statue of Liberty National Monument & The Ellis Island Immigration Museum, Washington DC

The National Quilt Museum, Paducah KY

National Silk Art Museum, Weston MO

National Society of Colonial Dames of America in the State of Maryland, Mount Clare Museum House, Baltimore MD

Naval Historical Center, The Navy Museum, Washington DC

Nelson Mandela Bay Municipality, Nelson Mandela Metropolitan Art Museum, Port Elizabeth

Neville Public Museum of Brown County, Green Bay WI

New Brunswick Museum, Saint John NB

New Hampshire Antiquarian Society, Hopkinton Historical Society, Hopkinton NH

New Jersey Historical Society, Newark NJ

New Jersey State Museum, Fine Art Bureau, Trenton NJ

No Man's Land Historical Society, No Man's Land Museum, Goodwell OK

North Carolina State University, Gregg Museum of Art & Design, Raleigh NC

Norwich Free Academy, Slater Memorial Museum, Norwich CT

The Ogden Museum of Southern Art, University of New Orleans, New Orleans LA

Old Dartmouth Historical Society, New Bedford Whaling Museum, New Bedford MA

Oshkosh Public Museum, Oshkosh WI

Panhandle-Plains Historical Museum, Canyon TX

Pasadena Museum of History, Pasadena CA

Phelps County Historical Society, Nebraska Prairie Museum, Holdrege NE

Philadelphia History Museum, Philadelphia PA

Pilgrim Society, Pilgrim Hall Museum, Plymouth MA

Plainsman Museum, Aurora NE

Plumas County Museum, Quincy CA

Pope County Historical Society, Pope County Museum, Glenwood MN

Port Huron Museum, Port Huron MI

Portsmouth Historical Society, John Paul Jones House & Discover Portsmouth, Portsmouth NH

Putnam Museum of History and Natural Science, Davenport IA

Queens College, City University of New York, Godwin-Ternbach Museum, Flushing NY

The Rooms Corporation of Newfoundland & Labrador, Saint John's NF

Royal Arts Foundation, Belcourt Castle, Newport RI

Rubin Museum of Art, New York NY

Saginaw Art Museum, Saginaw MI

Saint Joseph's Oratory, Museum, Montreal PQ

Saint Louis County Historical Society, St. Louis County Historical Society, Duluth MN

Saint Peter's College, Art Gallery, Jersey City NJ

The Sandwich Historical Society, Inc & Sandwich Glass Museum, Sandwich Glass Museum, Sandwich MA

Schweinfurth Art Center, Auburn NY

Shaker Museum & Library, Old Chatham NY

South Dakota State University, South Dakota Art Museum, Brookings SD

The Speed Art Museum, Louisville KY

Springfield Museums, Connecticut Valley Historical Society, Springfield MA

The State Museum of Fine Arts of Tatarstan Republic, Kazan

State University of New York at Binghamton, Binghamton University Art Museum, Binghamton NY

Staten Island Museum, Staten Island NY

Stauth Foundation & Museum, Stauth Memorial Museum, Montezuma KS

Ste Genevieve Museum, Sainte Genevieve MO

Stratford Historical Society, Catharine B Mitchell Museum, Stratford CT

Sturdivant Museum Association, Sturdivant Museum, Selma AL

The Summit County Historical Society of Akron, OH, Akron OH

Suomen Kansallismuseo, National Museum of Finland, Helsinki

Swedish American Museum Association of Chicago, Chicago IL

Tallahassee Museum of History & Natural Science, Tallahassee FL

Taos, La Hacienda de Los Martinez, Taos NM

The Temple-Tifereth Israel, The Temple Museum of Religious Art, Beachwood OH

Texas Tech University, Museum of Texas Tech University, Lubbock TX

Tohono Chul Park, Tucson AZ

Tver Art Gallery, Tver

Tyne and Wear Archives & Museums, Sunderland Museum & Winter Gardens, Newcastle-upon-Tyne

Ukrainian Institute of Modern Art, Chicago IL

Ukrainian Canadian Archives & Museum of Alberta, Edmonton AB

The Ukrainian Museum, New York NY

United Society of Shakers, Shaker Museum, New Gloucester ME

University of California, Berkeley, The Magnes Collection of Jewish Art & Life, Berkeley CA

University of Georgia, Georgia Museum of Art, Athens GA

University of Illinois at Urbana-Champaign, Krannert Art Museum and Kinkead Pavilion, Champaign IL

University of Kansas, Spencer Museum of Art, Lawrence KS

University of Manchester, Whitworth Art Gallery, Manchester

University of Richmond, University Museums, Richmond VA

University of Toronto, University of Toronto Art Centre, Toronto ON

University of Utah, Utah Museum of Fine Arts, Salt Lake City UT

University of Washington, Henry Art Gallery, Seattle WA

Vesterheim Norwegian-American Museum, Decorah IA

Vietnam Fine Arts Museum, Hanoi

Wadsworth Atheneum Museum of Art, Hartford CT

West Florida Historic Preservation, Inc/University of West Florida, T T Wentworth, Jr Florida State Museum; Historic Pensacola Village; Pensacola Historical Society & Resource Center, Pensacola FL

Wheaton College, Beard and Weil Galleries, Norton MA

Willard House & Clock Museum, Inc, North Grafton MA

William Morris Gallery, London

Wistariahurst Museum, Holyoke MA

Witte Museum, San Antonio TX

Woodlawn/The Pope-Leighey, Mount Vernon VA

Woodmere Art Museum Inc, Philadelphia PA

Xavier University, Art Gallery, Cincinnati OH

Yarmouth County Historical Society, Yarmouth County Museum & Archives, Yarmouth NS

ENAMELS

Academy of the New Church, Glencairn Museum, Bryn Athyn PA

Arnot Art Museum, Elmira NY

Art & Culture Center of Hollywood, Art Gallery/Multidisciplinary Cultural Center, Hollywood FL

The Art Museum at the University of Kentucky, Lexington KY

ArtSpace/Lima, Lima OH

Baroda Museum and Picture Gallery, Baroda

Bayerisches Nationalmuseum, Bavarian National Museum, Munich

Bellevue Arts Museum, Bellevue WA

Birmingham Museum of Art, Birmingham AL

Canadian Clay and Glass Gallery, Waterloo ON

Canadian Museum of Civilization, Gatineau PQ

Caramoor Center for Music & the Arts, Inc, Rosen House at Caramoor, Katonah NY

College of William & Mary, Muscarelle Museum of Art, Williamsburg VA

The Currier Museum of Art, Manchester NH

Department of Antiquities, Cyprus Museum, Nicosia

Detroit Institute of Arts, Detroit MI

Fine Arts Museums of San Francisco, Legion of Honor, San Francisco CA

Forest Lawn Museum, Glendale CA

Freer Gallery of Art & Arthur M Sackler Gallery, Arthur M Sackler Gallery, Washington DC

Fuller Craft Museum, Brockton MA

Gallery One Visual Arts Center, Ellensburg WA

Glanmore National Historic Site of Canada, Belleville ON

Hermitage Foundation Museum, Norfolk VA

Hillwood Museum & Gardens Foundation, Hillwood Estate Museum & Gardens, Washington DC

ESKIMO ART

ETCHINGS & ENGRAVINGS

African American Museum in Philadelphia, Philadelphia PA

Albion College, Bobbitt Visual Arts Center, Albion MI

Albuquerque Museum of Art & History, Albuquerque NM

Allentown Art Museum, Allentown PA

American Art Museum, Smithsonian Institution, Washington DC

American Swedish Historical Foundation & Museum, American Swedish Historical Museum, Philadelphia PA

American University, Katzen Art Center Gallery, New York NY

Amon Carter Museum of American Art, Fort Worth TX

Anchorage Museum at Rasmuson Center, Anchorage AK

Arizona Museum For Youth, Mesa AZ

Arnot Art Museum, Elmira NY

Art & Culture Center of Hollywood, Art Gallery/Multidisciplinary Cultural Center, Hollywood FL

Art Community Center, Art Center of Corpus Christi, Corpus Christi TX

Art Gallery of Calgary, Calgary AB

Art Gallery of Hamilton, Hamilton ON

Art Gallery of Nova Scotia, Halifax NS

Art Gallery of South Australia, Adelaide

The Art Museum at the University of Kentucky, Lexington KY

The Art Museum of Eastern Idaho, Idaho Falls ID

Art Museum of Greater Lafayette, Lafayette IN

Art Museum of Southeast Texas, Beaumont TX

Artspace, Richmond VA

ArtSpace/Lima, Lima OH

Asbury College, Student Center Gallery, Wilmore KY

Asheville Art Museum, Asheville NC

Augustana College, Augustana College Art Museum, Rock Island IL

Baldwin Historical Society Museum, Baldwin NY

Ball State University, Museum of Art, Muncie IN

Baroda Museum and Picture Gallery, Baroda

Baruch College of the City University of New York, Sidney Mishkin Gallery, New York NY

Bates College, Museum of Art, Lewiston ME

Baton Rouge Gallery, Center For Contemporary Art, Baton Rouge LA

Berkshire Museum, Pittsfield MA

Bertha V B Lederer Fine Arts Gallery-Suny Geneseo, Bertha V B Lederer Fine Arts Gallery, Geneseo NY

Besser Museum for Northeast Michigan, Alpena MI

Birmingham Museum of Art, Birmingham AL

Blanden Memorial Art Museum, Fort Dodge IA

Bone Creek Museum of Agrarian Art, David City NE

Boston Public Library, Albert H Wiggin Gallery & Print Department, Boston MA

Brandywine Conservancy, Brandywine River Museum, Chadds Ford PA

Brigham Young University, Museum of Art, Provo UT

Bruce Museum, Inc, Greenwich CT

Bucknell University, Edward & Marthann Samek Art Gallery, Lewisburg PA

The Buffalo Fine Arts Academy, Albright-Knox Art Gallery, Buffalo NY

Bush-Holley Historic Site & Storehouse Gallery, Greenwich Historical Society/ Bush-Holley House, Cos Cob CT

Cabot's Old Indian Pueblo Museum, Desert Hot Springs CA

California State University, Northridge, Art Galleries, Northridge CA

Calvin College, Center Art Gallery, Grand Rapids MI

Cameron Art Museum, Wilmington NC

Canadian Clay and Glass Gallery, Waterloo ON

Canadian Museum of Civilization, Gatineau PQ

Cape Ann Historical Association, Cape Ann Museum, Gloucester MA

Cape Cod Museum of Art Inc, Dennis MA

Carnegie Mellon University, Hunt Institute for Botanical Documentation, Pittsburgh PA

Carson County Square House Museum, Panhandle TX

Carteret County Historical Society, The History Place, Morehead City NC

Cartoon Art Museum, San Francisco CA

Center for Book Arts, New York NY

Central United Methodist Church, Swords Into Plowshares Peace Center & Gallery, Detroit MI

Centro de Arte Moderna, CAM - Calouste Gulbenkian Foundation, Lisbon

Channel Islands Maritime Museum, Oxnard CA

City of Cedar Falls, Iowa, James & Meryl Hearst Center for the Arts & Sculpture Garden, Cedar Falls IA

City of Mason City, Charles H MacNider Museum, Mason City IA

Clark County Historical Society, Heritage Center of Clark County, Springfield OH

Clark County Historical Society, Pioneer - Krier Museum, Ashland KS

Sterling & Francine Clark, Williamstown MA

Clinton Art Association, River Arts Center, Clinton IA

Colgate University, Picker Art Gallery, Hamilton NY

College of William & Mary, Muscarelle Museum of Art, Williamsburg VA

Columbus Museum, Columbus GA

Columbus Museum of Art, Columbus OH

Concordia Historical Institute, Saint Louis MO

Concordia University, Leonard & Bina Ellen Art Gallery, Montreal PQ

Cooper-Hewitt National Design Museum, Smithsonian Institution, New York NY

Cornell Museum of Art and American Culture, Delray Beach FL

Coutts Museum of Art, Inc, El Dorado KS

Craft and Folk Art Museum (CAFAM), Los Angeles CA

Cranbrook Art Museum, Bloomfield Hills MI

Cripple Creek District Museum, Cripple Creek CO

Crocker Art Museum, Sacramento CA

Crow Wing County Historical Society, Brainerd MN

Cummer Museum of Art & Gardens, Museum & Library, Jacksonville FL

The Currier Museum of Art, Manchester NH

Dahesh Museum of Art, Greenwich CT

Danville Museum of Fine Arts & History, Danville VA

Dartmouth College, Hood Museum of Art, Hanover NH

Daum Museum of Contemporary Art, Sedalia MO

Davidson College, William H Van Every Jr & Edward M Smith Galleries, Davidson NC

Deines Cultural Center, Russell KS

Delaware Art Museum, Wilmington DE

Denison University, Art Gallery, Granville OH

Department of Antiquities, Cyprus Museum, Nicosia

Detroit Institute of Arts, Detroit MI

Detroit Repertory Theatre Gallery, Detroit MI

Dickinson College, The Trout Gallery, Carlisle PA

Dixie State College, Robert N & Peggy Sears Gallery, Saint George UT

Doncaster Museum and Art Gallery, Doncaster

Duke University, Nasher Museum of Art at Duke University, Durham NC

Dundee City Council Leisure & Communities Department, The McManus: Dundee's Art Gallery & Museum, Dundee

Dundurn Castle, Hamilton ON

Durham Art Guild, Durham NC

Eastern Illinois University, Tarble Arts Center, Charleston IL

Egan Institute of Maritime Studies, Nantucket MA

Eiteljorg Museum of American Indians & Western Art, Indianapolis IN

Ellen Noel Art Museum of the Permian Basin, Odessa TX

Elmhurst Art Museum, Elmhurst IL

Emory University, Michael C Carlos Museum, Atlanta GA

Erie Art Museum, Erie PA

Evansville Museum of Arts, History & Science, Evansville IN

Evergreen State College, Evergreen Gallery, Olympia WA

Farmington Village Green & Library Association, Stanley-Whitman House, Farmington CT

Federal Reserve Board, Art Gallery, Washington DC

Fetherston Foundation, Packwood House Museum, Lewisburg PA

Fine Arts Center for the New River Valley, Pulaski VA

Fine Arts Museums of San Francisco, Legion of Honor, San Francisco CA

Flint Institute of Arts, Flint MI

Florence Museum, Florence SC

Florida Southern College, Melvin Art Gallery, Lakeland FL

Fondazione Musei Civici Di Venezia, Ca'Rezzonico, Museo del Settecento Veneziano, Venice

Fondazione Musei Civici Di Venezia, Galleria Internazionale d'Arte Moderna di Ca'Pesaro, Venice

Fondazione Musei Civici Di Venezia, Museo Correr, Venice

Fort Ticonderoga Association, Ticonderoga NY

Freer Gallery of Art & Arthur M Sackler Gallery, Arthur M Sackler Gallery, Washington DC

Frontier Times Museum, Bandera TX

Fruitlands Museum, Inc, Harvard MA

Frye Art Museum, Seattle WA

Fuller Craft Museum, Brockton MA

Gala-Salvador Dali Foundation Museums, Salvador Dali Foundation, Figueres

Gallery One Visual Arts Center, Ellensburg WA

Germanisches Nationalmuseum, Nuremberg

The Ghent Museum of Fine Arts, Ghent

Glanmore National Historic Site of Canada, Belleville ON

Glessner House Museum, Chicago IL

Gonzaga University, Art Gallery, Spokane WA

Grand Rapids Art Museum, Grand Rapids MI

Grand Rapids Public Museum, Public Museum of Grand Rapids, Grand Rapids MI

Grinnell College, Faulconer Gallery, Grinnell IA

Guilford College, Art Gallery, Greensboro NC

Hamilton College, Emerson Gallery, Clinton NY

Hancock County Trustees of Public Reservations, Woodlawn: Museum, Gardens & Park, Ellsworth ME

Hartwick College, The Yager Museum, Oneonta NY

Hawkes Bay Art Gallery and Museum, Napier

Headquarters Fort Monroe, Dept of Army, Casemate Museum, Hampton VA

Hebrew Union College, Skirball Cultural Center, Los Angeles CA

Hebrew Union College Museum, Jewish Institute of Religion Museum, New York NY

Hecht Museum, Haifa

Henry Gallery Association, Henry Art Gallery, Seattle WA

Heritage Center, Inc, Pine Ridge SD

Heritage Malta, National Museum of Fine Arts, Valletta

Edna Hibel, Hibel Museum of Art, Jupiter FL

Hickory Museum of Art, Inc, Hickory NC

High Museum of Art, Atlanta GA

Hill-Stead Museum, Farmington CT

Hillwood Museum & Gardens Foundation, Hillwood Estate Museum & Gardens, Washington DC

The Hispanic Society of America, Museum & Library, New York NY

Historic Arkansas Museum, Little Rock AR

The Historic New Orleans Collection, Royal Street Galleries, New Orleans LA

Hofstra University, Hofstra University Museum, Hempstead NY

Hoyt Center for the Arts, New Castle PA

Hui No'eau Visual Arts Center, Gallery and Gift Shop, Makawao Maui HI

The Huntington Library, Art Collections & Botanical Gardens, San Marino CA

Huronia Museum, Gallery of Historic Huronia, Midland ON

Hyde Park Art Center, Chicago IL

Illinois State Museum, ISM Lockport Gallery, Chicago Gallery & Southern Illinois Art Gallery, Springfield IL

Imperial Calcasieu Museum, Gibson-Barham Gallery, Lake Charles LA

Independence Seaport Museum, Philadelphia PA

Independent Administrative Institution National Institutes for Cultural Heritage, Tokyo National Museum, Tokyo

Independent Administrative Institution National Museum of Art, The National Museum of Western Art, Tokyo

Indiana University, Art Museum, Bloomington IN

The Interchurch Center, Galleries at the Interchurch Center, New York NY

Iredell Museums, Statesville NC

The Israel Museum, Jerusalem, Billy Rose Art Garden, Jerusalem

The Israel Museum, Jerusalem, Samuel & Saidye Bronfman Archaeology Wing, Jerusalem

The Israel Museum, Jerusalem, Jerusalem

J.M.W. Turner Museum, Sarasota FL

Jacksonville University, Alexander Brest Museum & Gallery, Jacksonville FL

Jamestown-Yorktown Foundation, Jamestown Settlement, Williamsburg VA

Thomas Jefferson, Monticello, Charlottesville VA

Jersey City Museum, Jersey City NJ

The Jewish Museum, New York NY

Johns Hopkins University, Evergreen Museum & Library, Baltimore MD

Bob Jones University Museum & Gallery Inc, Greenville SC

Jordan National Gallery of Fine Arts, Amman

Joslyn Art Museum, Omaha NE

Juniata College Museum of Art, Huntingdon PA

Kalamazoo Institute of Arts, Kalamazoo MI

Kamloops Art Gallery, Kamloops BC

Kenosha Public Museums, Kenosha WI

R L S Silverado Museum, Saint Helena CA
The Society of the Cincinnati at Anderson House, Washington DC
Sonoma State University, University Art Gallery, Rohnert Park CA
Soprintendenza per I beni storici artistici ed etnoantropologici per le province di Mantova Brescia e Cremona, Museo di Palazzo Ducale, Mantua
Southern Illinois University Carbondale, University Museum, Carbondale IL
Southern Methodist University, Meadows Museum, Dallas TX
The Speed Art Museum, Louisville KY
Spertus Institute of Jewish Studies, Chicago IL
Springfield Art Museum, Springfield MO
Staatsgalerie Stuttgart, Stuttgart
Stanford University, Cantor Arts Center at Stanford University, Stanford CA
Nelda C & H J Lutcher Stark, Stark Museum of Art, Orange TX
State Capital Museum, Olympia WA
The State Museum of Fine Arts of Tatarstan Republic, Kazan
The State Museum of Oriental Art, Moscow
State University of New York at Binghamton, Binghamton University Art Museum, Binghamton NY
State University of New York at Geneseo, Bertha V B Lederer Gallery, Geneseo NY
State University of New York at Geneseo, Lockhart Gallery, Geneseo NY
State University of New York at New Paltz, Samuel Dorsky Museum of Art, New Paltz NY
State University of New York at Plattsburgh, Art Museum, Plattsburgh NY
State University of New York College at Cortland, Dowd Fine Arts Gallery, Cortland NY
Staten Island Museum, Staten Island NY
Stauth Foundation & Museum, Stauth Memorial Museum, Montezuma KS
The Stewart Museum, Montreal PQ
Stone Quarry Hill Art Park, Winner Gallery, Cazenovia NY
Sturdivant Museum Association, Sturdivant Museum, Selma AL
The Summit County Historical Society of Akron, OH, Akron OH
Susquehanna University, Lore Degenstein Gallery, Selinsgrove PA
Swedish American Museum Association of Chicago, Chicago IL
Sweet Briar College, Art Collection & Galleries, Sweet Briar VA
Syracuse University, Art Collection, Syracuse NY
Syracuse University, SUArt Galleries, Syracuse NY
Szepmuveszeti Muzeum, Museum of Fine Arts Budapest, Budapest
Tacoma Art Museum, Tacoma WA
Tampa Museum of Art, Tampa FL
Temiskaming Art Gallery, Haileybury ON
The Temple-Tifereth Israel, The Temple Museum of Religious Art, Beachwood OH
Texas Tech University, Museum of Texas Tech University, Lubbock TX
Tohono Chul Park, Tucson AZ
Topeka & Shawnee County Public Library, Alice C Sabatini Gallery, Topeka KS
Turtle Bay Exploration Park, Redding CA
Tver Art Gallery, Tver
Tyne and Wear Archives & Museums, Sunderland Museum & Winter Gardens, Newcastle-upon-Tyne
Ukrainian Institute of Modern Art, Chicago IL
The Ukrainian Museum, New York NY
United States Capitol, Architect of the Capitol, Washington DC
United States Coast Guard Museum, New London CT
United States Figure Skating Association, World Figure Skating Museum & Hall of Fame, Colorado Springs CO
United States Military Academy, West Point Museum, West Point NY
United States Navy, Art Gallery, Washington DC
University of Alabama at Birmingham, Visual Arts Gallery, Birmingham AL
University of Arkansas at Little Rock, Art Galleries, Little Rock AR
University of California, Richard L Nelson Gallery & Fine Arts Collection, Davis CA
University of California, Berkeley, The Magnes Collection of Jewish Art & Life, Berkeley CA

University of California, Santa Barbara, University Art Museum, Santa Barbara CA
University of Chicago, Smart Museum of Art, Chicago IL
University of Cincinnati, DAAP Galleries-College of Design Architecture, Art & Planning, Cincinnati OH
University of Colorado, CU Art Museum, Boulder CO
University of Colorado at Colorado Springs, Gallery of Contemporary Art, Colorado Springs CO
University of Delaware, University Museums, Newark DE
University of Georgia, Georgia Museum of Art, Athens GA
University of Illinois at Urbana-Champaign, Krannert Art Museum and Kinkead Pavilion, Champaign IL
University of Indianapolis, Christel DeHaan Fine Arts Gallery, Indianapolis IN
University of Kansas, Spencer Museum of Art, Lawrence KS
University of Louisiana at Lafayette, Paul and Lulu Hilliard University Art Museum, Lafayette LA
University of Maine, Museum of Art, Bangor ME
University of Manchester, Whitworth Art Gallery, Manchester
University of Manitoba, Faculty of Architecture Exhibition Centre, Winnipeg MB
University of Mary Washington, University of Mary Washington Galleries, Fredericksburg VA
University of Massachusetts, Amherst, University Gallery, Amherst MA
University of Memphis, Art Museum, Memphis TN
University of Miami, Lowe Art Museum, Coral Gables FL
University of Michigan, Museum of Art, Ann Arbor MI
University of Minnesota, The Bell Museum of Natural History, Minneapolis MN
University of Minnesota Duluth, Tweed Museum of Art, Duluth MN
University of Missouri, Museum of Art & Archaeology, Columbia MO
University of Nevada, Reno, Sheppard Contemporary & University Galleries, Reno NV
University of New Brunswick, Art Centre, Fredericton NB
University of New Hampshire, Museum of Art, Durham NH
University of New Mexico, The Harwood Museum of Art, Taos NM
University of New Mexico, University of New Mexico Art Museum, Albuquerque NM
University of North Carolina at Chapel Hill, Ackland Art Museum, Chapel Hill NC
University of Pennsylvania, Arthur Ross Gallery, Philadelphia PA
University of Pittsburgh, University Art Gallery, Pittsburgh PA
University of Richmond, University Museums, Richmond VA
University of Saskatchewan, Diefenbaker Canada Centre, Saskatoon SK
University of Texas at Austin, Blanton Museum of Art, Austin TX
University of the South, University Art Gallery, Sewanee TN
University of Toronto, University of Toronto Art Centre, Toronto ON
University of Victoria, The Legacy Art Gallery, Victoria BC
University of Virginia, The Fralin Museum of Art at the University of Virginia, Charlottesville VA
University of Wisconsin-Eau Claire, Foster Gallery, Eau Claire WI
University of Wisconsin-Madison, Chazen Museum of Art, Madison WI
University of Wisconsin-Madison, Wisconsin Union Galleries, Madison WI
University of Wyoming, University of Wyoming Art Museum, Laramie WY
Ursinus College, Philip & Muriel Berman Museum of Art, Collegeville PA
Vassar College, The Frances Lehman Loeb Art Center, Poughkeepsie NY
Vero Beach Museum of Art, Vero Beach FL
Vesterheim Norwegian-American Museum, Decorah IA
Vietnam Fine Arts Museum, Hanoi
Virginia Museum of Fine Arts, Richmond VA
Walker Art Gallery, Liverpool
Washburn University, Mulvane Art Museum, Topeka KS
Washington University, Mildred Lane Kemper Art Museum, Saint Louis MO
Waterworks Visual Arts Center, Salisbury NC

Wellesley College, Davis Museum & Cultural Center, Wellesley MA
West Florida Historic Preservation, Inc/University of West Florida, T T Wentworth, Jr Florida State Museum; Historic Pensacola Village; Pensacola Historical Society & Resource Center, Pensacola FL
Wheaton College, Beard and Weil Galleries, Norton MA
Wichita State University, Ulrich Museum of Art, Wichita KS
Wildling Art Museum, Solvang CA
Wilfrid Laurier University, Robert Langen Art Gallery, Waterloo ON
Wiregrass Museum of Art, Dothan AL
Wisconsin Historical Society, Wisconsin Historical Museum, Madison WI
Woodlawn/The Pope-Leighey, Mount Vernon VA
Woodmere Art Museum Inc, Philadelphia PA
Worcester Art Museum, Worcester MA
World Erotic Art Museum, Miami Beach FL
Xavier University, Art Gallery, Cincinnati OH
Yale University, Yale Center for British Art, New Haven CT
Yarmouth County Historical Society, Yarmouth County Museum & Archives, Yarmouth NS
Yokohama Museum of Art, Yokohama
Yuma Fine Arts Association, Yuma Art Center, Yuma AZ
Zigler Art Museum, Jennings LA

ETHNOLOGY

African Art Museum of Maryland, Columbia MD
Al Ain National Museum, Al Ain
Alaska Department of Education, Division of Libraries, Archives & Museums, Sheldon Jackson Museum, Sitka AK
Alaska Heritage Museum at Wells Fargo, Anchorage AK
Anchorage Museum at Rasmuson Center, Anchorage AK
Arab American National Museum, Dearborn MI
Arizona Historical Society-Yuma, Sanguinetti House Museum & Garden, Yuma AZ
The Art Museum at the University of Kentucky, Lexington KY
Art Without Walls Inc, New York NY
ArtSpace/Lima, Lima OH
Aurora University, Schingoethe Center for Native American Cultures & The Schingoethe Art Gallery, Aurora IL
Autry National Center, Southwest Museum of the American Indian, Mt. Washington Campus, Los Angeles CA
Ball State University, Museum of Art, Muncie IN
Baroda Museum and Picture Gallery, Baroda
Berkshire Museum, Pittsfield MA
Brown University, Haffenreffer Museum of Anthropology, Providence RI
Bruce Museum, Inc, Greenwich CT
California State University, East Bay, C E Smith Museum of Anthropology, Hayward CA
Canadian Museum of Civilization, Gatineau PQ
Carson County Square House Museum, Panhandle TX
Carteret County Historical Society, The History Place, Morehead City NC
Centenary College of Louisiana, Meadows Museum of Art, Shreveport LA
Chhatrapati Shivaji Maharaj Vastu Sangrahalaya, Mumbai
Chief Plenty Coups Museum State Park, Pryor MT
City of Nome Alaska, Carrie M McLain Memorial Museum, Nome AK
City of Providence Parks Department, Roger Williams Park Museum of Natural History, Providence RI
City of Ukiah, Grace Hudson Museum & The Sun House, Ukiah CA
The College of Wooster, The College of Wooster Art Museum, Wooster OH
Colorado Historical Society, Colorado History Museum, Denver CO
Columbus Museum, Columbus GA
Cornell University, Herbert F Johnson Museum of Art, Ithaca NY
Craft and Folk Art Museum (CAFAM), Los Angeles CA
Davidson College, William H Van Every Jr & Edward M Smith Galleries, Davidson NC
Dawson City Museum & Historical Society, Dawson City YT
Denison University, Art Gallery, Granville OH

FLASKS & BOTTLES

The Israel Museum, Jerusalem, Jerusalem
Kenosha Public Museums, Kenosha WI
Kentucky Derby Museum, Louisville KY
Kereszteny Muzeum, Christian Museum, Esztergom
Kings County Historical Society & Museum, Hampton NB
The Long Island Museum of American Art, History & Carriages, Stony Brook NY
Louisiana State Exhibit Museum, Shreveport LA
Maysville, Kentucky Gateway Museum Center, Maysville KY
McLean County Historical Society, McLean County Museum of History, Bloomington IL
McMaster University, McMaster Museum of Art, Hamilton ON
Medina Railroad Museum, Medina NY
Ministry of the Arts & Multiculturalism, National Museum & Art Gallery, Port of Spain
Musees Royaux d'Art et d'Histoire, Royal Museums of Art and History, Brussels
The Museum, Greenwood SC
Museum of Decorative Arts in Prague, Prague
Museum of Fine Arts Houston, Bayou Bend Collection & Gardens, Houston TX
Museum of Fine Arts, Houston, Houston TX
Muzej za Umjetnost i Obrt, Museum of Arts & Crafts, Zagreb
Muzeul National Brukenthal, Brukenthal Palace & European Art Gallery, Sibiu
National Museum of Fine Arts of Moldova, Chisinau
National Society of Colonial Dames of America in the State of Maryland, Mount Clare Museum House, Baltimore MD
New Brunswick Museum, Saint John NB
New Jersey Historical Society, Newark NJ
New Jersey State Museum, Fine Art Bureau, Trenton NJ
Norwich Free Academy, Slater Memorial Museum, Norwich CT
Panhandle-Plains Historical Museum, Canyon TX
Philadelphia History Museum, Philadelphia PA
Pine Bluff/Jefferson County Historical Museum, Pine Bluff AR
Reading Public Museum, Reading PA
Rijksmuseum Twenthe, Rijksmuseum Twenthe, Enschede
Riley County Historical Society & Museum, Riley County Historical Museum, Manhattan KS
Saint Louis County Historical Society, St. Louis County Historical Society, Duluth MN
Saint Peter's College, Art Gallery, Jersey City NJ
The Sandwich Historical Society, Inc & Sandwich Glass Museum, Sandwich Glass Museum, Sandwich MA
The Speed Art Museum, Louisville KY
The State Museum of Fine Arts of Tatarstan Republic, Kazan
Staten Island Museum, Staten Island NY
Stauth Foundation & Museum, Stauth Memorial Museum, Montezuma KS
Sturdivant Museum Association, Sturdivant Museum, Selma AL
Suomen Kansallismuseo, National Museum of Finland, Helsinki
Switzerland County Historical Society Inc, Switzerland County Historical Museum, Vevay IN
Texas Tech University, Museum of Texas Tech University, Lubbock TX
Three Forks Area Historical Society, Headwaters Heritage Museum, Three Forks MT
Tohono Chul Park, Tucson AZ
Tver Art Gallery, Tver
United Society of Shakers, Shaker Museum, New Gloucester ME
University of California, Berkeley, Phoebe Apperson Hearst Museum of Anthropology, Berkeley CA
University of Pennsylvania, Museum of Archaeology & Anthropology, Philadelphia PA
University of Pittsburgh, University Art Gallery, Pittsburgh PA
University of Utah, Utah Museum of Fine Arts, Salt Lake City UT
Vesterheim Norwegian-American Museum, Decorah IA
Village of Potsdam, Potsdam Public Museum, Potsdam NY
Waterville Historical Society, Redington Museum, Waterville ME
West Florida Historic Preservation, Inc/University of West Florida, T T Wentworth, Jr Florida State Museum; Historic Pensacola Village; Pensacola Historical Society & Resource Center, Pensacola FL

Wheaton College, Beard and Weil Galleries, Norton MA
World Erotic Art Museum, Miami Beach FL
Yarmouth County Historical Society, Yarmouth County Museum & Archives, Yarmouth NS

FOLK ART

Adams County Historical Society, Gettysburg PA
Akron Art Museum, Akron OH
Albany Institute of History & Art, Albany NY
Albion College, Bobbitt Visual Arts Center, Albion MI
Albuquerque Museum of Art & History, Albuquerque NM
Allentown Art Museum, Allentown PA
Alton Museum of History & Art, Inc, Alton IL
American Art Museum, Smithsonian Institution, Washington DC
American Folk Art Museum, New York NY
American Museum of Ceramic Art, Pomona CA
American Swedish Historical Foundation & Museum, American Swedish Historical Museum, Philadelphia PA
American Swedish Institute, Minneapolis MN
Amherst Museum, Amherst NY
Amon Carter Museum of American Art, Fort Worth TX
Arizona Historical Society-Yuma, Sanguinetti House Museum & Garden, Yuma AZ
Arnold Mikelson Mind & Matter Art Gallery, White Rock BC
Art & Culture Center of Hollywood, Art Gallery/Multidisciplinary Cultural Center, Hollywood FL
Art Gallery of Calgary, Calgary AB
Art Gallery of Nova Scotia, Halifax NS
The Art Museum at the University of Kentucky, Lexington KY
Art Museum of Greater Lafayette, Lafayette IN
Art Museum of Southeast Texas, Beaumont TX
Art Without Walls Inc, New York NY
ArtSpace/Lima, Lima OH
Asheville Art Museum, Asheville NC
Aurora University, Schingoethe Center for Native American Cultures & The Schingoethe Art Gallery, Aurora IL
Autry National Center, Southwest Museum of the American Indian, Mt. Washington Campus, Los Angeles CA
Balzekas Museum of Lithuanian Culture, Chicago IL
Baroda Museum and Picture Gallery, Baroda
Bayerisches Nationalmuseum, Bavarian National Museum, Munich
Bellevue Arts Museum, Bellevue WA
Bennington Museum, Bennington VT
Berkshire Museum, Pittsfield MA
Besser Museum for Northeast Michigan, Alpena MI
Beverly Historical Society, Cabot, Hale & Balch House Museums, Beverly MA
Birmingham Museum of Art, Birmingham AL
Bone Creek Museum of Agrarian Art, David City NE
Brigham City Corporation, Brigham City Museum & Gallery, Brigham City UT
Bucks County Historical Society, Mercer Museum, Doylestown PA
Bush-Holley Historic Site & Storehouse Gallery, Greenwich Historical Society/ Bush-Holley House, Cos Cob CT
Cahoon Museum of American Art, Cotuit MA
California State University, Northridge, Art Galleries, Northridge CA
Cameron Art Museum, Wilmington NC
Canadian Clay and Glass Gallery, Waterloo ON
Canadian Museum of Civilization, Gatineau PQ
Carnegie Center for Art & History, New Albany IN
Carson County Square House Museum, Panhandle TX
Carteret County Historical Society, The History Place, Morehead City NC
Cartoon Art Museum, San Francisco CA
Center for Puppetry Arts, Atlanta GA
Central United Methodist Church, Swords Into Plowshares Peace Center & Gallery, Detroit MI
Chatham Historical Society, The Atwood House Museum, Chatham MA
Chesapeake Bay Maritime Museum, Saint Michaels MD
Chinese Culture Foundation, Center Gallery, San Francisco CA
Church of Jesus Christ of Latter-Day Saints, Museum of Church History & Art, Salt Lake City UT
City of Fayette, Alabama, Fayette Art Museum, Fayette AL

City of Gainesville, Thomas Center Galleries - Cultural Affairs, Gainesville FL
City of High Point, High Point Museum, High Point NC
City of Providence Parks Department, Roger Williams Park Museum of Natural History, Providence RI
City of San Antonio, San Antonio TX
City of Springdale, Shiloh Museum of Ozark History, Springdale AR
Columbus Museum, Columbus GA
Columbus Museum of Art, Columbus OH
Cornell Museum of Art and American Culture, Delray Beach FL
Cornwall Gallery Society, Cornwall Regional Art Gallery, Cornwall ON
Cortland County Historical Society, Suggett House Museum, Cortland NY
County of Henrico, Meadow Farm Museum, Glen Allen VA
Coutts Museum of Art, Inc, El Dorado KS
Craft and Folk Art Museum (CAFAM), Los Angeles CA
Craftsmen's Guild of Mississippi, Inc, Agriculture & Forestry Museum, Ridgeland MS
Craftsmen's Guild of Mississippi, Inc, Mississippi Crafts Center, Ridgeland MS
Cripple Creek District Museum, Cripple Creek CO
Crocker Art Museum, Sacramento CA
Crook County Museum & Art Gallery, Sundance WY
Culberson County Historical Museum, Van Horn TX
The Currier Museum of Art, Manchester NH
Danville Museum of Fine Arts & History, Danville VA
Davidson College, William H Van Every Jr & Edward M Smith Galleries, Davidson NC
Deines Cultural Center, Russell KS
Delta Blues Museum, Clarksdale MS
Deming-Luna Mimbres Museum, Deming NM
Denison University, Art Gallery, Granville OH
Denver Art Museum, Denver CO
Detroit Repertory Theatre Gallery, Detroit MI
East Carolina University, Wellington B Gray Gallery, Greenville NC
Eastern Illinois University, Tarble Arts Center, Charleston IL
Ellen Noel Art Museum of the Permian Basin, Odessa TX
Elmhurst Art Museum, Elmhurst IL
Erie Art Museum, Erie PA
Erie County Historical Society, Erie PA
The Ethel Wright Mohamed Stitchery Museum, Belzoni MS
Evansville Museum of Arts, History & Science, Evansville IN
Everhart Museum, Scranton PA
Fairbanks Museum & Planetarium, Saint Johnsbury VT
Farmington Village Green & Library Association, Stanley-Whitman House, Farmington CT
Ferenczy Muzeum, Szentendre
Fetherston Foundation, Packwood House Museum, Lewisburg PA
Fine Arts Center for the New River Valley, Pulaski VA
Fishkill Historical Society, Van Wyck Homestead Museum, Fishkill NY
Fisk University, Aaron Douglas Gallery, Nashville TN
Fisk University, Carl Van Vechten Gallery, Nashville TN
Flint Institute of Arts, Flint MI
Florida Southern College, Melvin Art Gallery, Lakeland FL
Folk Art Society of America, Richmond VA
Frankfort Community Public Library, Anna & Harlan Hubbard Gallery, Frankfort IN
Frontier Times Museum, Bandera TX
Frostburg State University, The Stephanie Ann Roper Gallery, Frostburg MD
Fruitlands Museum, Inc, Harvard MA
Fulton County Historical Society Inc, Fulton County Museum (Tetzlaff Reference Room), Rochester IN
Gadsden Museum of Fine Arts, Inc, Gadsden Museum of Art and History, Gadsden AL
Galeria de la Raza, Studio 24, San Francisco CA
Gem County Historical Society and Museum, Gem County Historical Village Museum, Emmett ID
General Board of Discipleship, The United Methodist Church, The Upper Room Chapel & Museum, Nashville TN
Genesee Country Village & Museum, John L Wehle Art Gallery, Mumford NY
Germanisches Nationalmuseum, Nuremberg
Wendell Gilley, Southwest Harbor ME
Gocseji Muzeum, Zalaegerszeg
Grand Rapids Art Museum, Grand Rapids MI

Pasadena Museum of History, Pasadena CA
Passaic County Historical Society, Lambert Castle
  Museum & Library, Paterson NJ
Pensacola Museum of Art, Pensacola FL
Philadelphia History Museum, Philadelphia PA
Philadelphia Museum of Art, Main Building,
  Philadelphia PA
The Phillips Collection, Washington DC
Pinacoteca Provinciale, Bari
Plains Art Museum, Fargo ND
Plainsman Museum, Aurora NE
Polish Museum of America, Chicago IL
Polk Museum of Art, Lakeland FL
Port Huron Museum, Port Huron MI
Prairie Art Gallery, Grande Prairie AB
Princeton University, Princeton University Art Museum,
  Princeton NJ
Queens College, City University of New York,
  Godwin-Ternbach Museum, Flushing NY
Rabindra Bhavan Art Gallery, Lalit Kala Akademi
  (National Academy of Art), New Delhi
Randolph College, Maier Museum of Art, Lynchburg
  VA
Rangeley Lakes Region Logging Museum, Rangeley
  ME
Reading Public Museum, Reading PA
Riley County Historical Society & Museum, Riley
  County Historical Museum, Manhattan KS
Riverside Metropolitan Museum, Riverside CA
Rock Ford Foundation, Inc, Rock Ford Plantation,
  Lancaster PA
Rollins College, George D & Harriet W Cornell Fine
  Arts Museum, Winter Park FL
The Rooms Corporation of Newfoundland & Labrador,
  Saint John's NF
Roswell Museum & Art Center, Roswell NM
C M Russell, Great Falls MT
Saco Museum, Saco ME
Saginaw Art Museum, Saginaw MI
Saint Augustine Historical Society, Oldest House
  Museum Complex, Saint Augustine FL
Saint Louis County Historical Society, St. Louis
  County Historical Museum, Duluth MN
Saint Mary's Romanian Orthodox Cathedral, Romanian
  Ethnic Museum, Cleveland OH
Saint Peter's College, Art Gallery, Jersey City NJ
Salisbury University, Ward Museum of Wildfowl Art,
  Salisbury MD
San Antonio Museum of Art, San Antonio TX
San Francisco Maritime National Historical Park,
  Maritime Museum, San Francisco CA
Shaker Village of Pleasant Hill, Harrodsburg KY
Shelburne Museum, Museum, Shelburne VT
Slovenska Narodna Galeria, Slovak National Gallery,
  Bratislava
South Carolina Artisans Center, Walterboro SC
South Carolina State Museum, Columbia SC
South Dakota State University, South Dakota Art
  Museum, Brookings SD
South Street Seaport Museum, New York NY
Southeastern Center for Contemporary Art, Winston
  Salem NC
Southern Ohio Museum Corporation, Southern Ohio
  Museum, Portsmouth OH
Spartanburg Art Museum, Spartanburg SC
The Speed Art Museum, Louisville KY
Spertus Institute of Jewish Studies, Chicago IL
Springfield Art Museum, Springfield MO
Springfield Museums, Connecticut Valley Historical
  Society, Springfield MA
The State Museum of Fine Arts of Tatarstan Republic,
  Kazan
State of North Carolina, Battleship North Carolina,
  Wilmington NC
Stauth Foundation & Museum, Stauth Memorial
  Museum, Montezuma KS
Stone Quarry Hill Art Park, Winner Gallery, Cazenovia
  NY
Stratford Historical Society, Catharine B Mitchell
  Museum, Stratford CT
The Summit County Historical Society of Akron, OH,
  Akron OH
Suomen Kansallismuseo, National Museum of Finland,
  Helsinki
Swedish American Museum Association of Chicago,
  Chicago IL
Switzerland County Historical Society Inc, Switzerland
  County Historical Museum, Vevay IN
Syracuse University, SUArt Galleries, Syracuse NY
Tallahassee Museum of History & Natural Science,
  Tallahassee FL
Tampa Museum of Art, Tampa FL

Texas Tech University, Museum of Texas Tech
  University, Lubbock TX
Tinkertown Museum, Sandia Park NM
Tohono Chul Park, Tucson AZ
Towson University, Asian Arts & Culture Center,
  Towson MD
Tver Art Gallery, Tver
Ukrainian Canadian Archives & Museum of Alberta,
  Edmonton AB
The Ukrainian Museum, New York NY
United Society of Shakers, Shaker Museum, New
  Gloucester ME
United States Military Academy, West Point Museum,
  West Point NY
Universalmuseum Joanneum GmbH, Graz
University of British Columbia, Museum of
  Anthropology, Vancouver BC
University of California, Berkeley, Berkeley Art
  Museum & Pacific Film Archive, Berkeley CA
University of California, Berkeley, Phoebe Apperson
  Hearst Museum of Anthropology, Berkeley CA
University of California, Berkeley, The Magnes
  Collection of Jewish Art & Life, Berkeley CA
University of California, Los Angeles, Fowler Museum
  at UCLA, Los Angeles CA
University of Colorado at Colorado Springs, Gallery of
  Contemporary Art, Colorado Springs CO
University of Georgia, Georgia Museum of Art, Athens
  GA
University of Illinois at Urbana-Champaign, Krannert
  Art Museum and Kinkead Pavilion, Champaign IL
University of Indianapolis, Christel DeHaan Fine Arts
  Gallery, Indianapolis IN
University of Louisiana at Lafayette, Paul and Lulu
  Hilliard University Art Museum, Lafayette LA
University of Memphis, Art Museum, Memphis TN
University of Missouri, Museum of Art & Archaeology,
  Columbia MO
University of Nebraska, Lincoln, Sheldon Memorial Art
  Gallery & Sculpture Garden, Lincoln NE
University of Nevada, Reno, Sheppard Contemporary
  & University Galleries, Reno NV
University of North Carolina at Chapel Hill, Ackland
  Art Museum, Chapel Hill NC
University of Pennsylvania, Museum of Archaeology &
  Anthropology, Philadelphia PA
University of Richmond, University Museums,
  Richmond VA
University of Rochester, Memorial Art Gallery,
  Rochester NY
The University of Texas at San Antonio, Institute of
  Texan Cultures, San Antonio TX
University of Victoria, The Legacy Art Gallery, Victoria
  BC
University of Wisconsin-Madison, Wisconsin Union
  Galleries, Madison WI
Ursinus College, Philip & Muriel Berman Museum of
  Art, Collegeville PA
Utah Arts Council, Chase Home Museum of Utah Folk
  Arts, Salt Lake City UT
Vesterheim Norwegian-American Museum, Decorah IA
Vietnam Fine Arts Museum, Hanoi
Vorres Museum of Contemporary Greek Art and Folk
  Art, Attica
VSA Arts of New Mexico, Very Special Arts Gallery,
  Albuquerque NM
Wake Forest University, Museum of Anthropology,
  Winston Salem NC
The Walker African American Museum & Research
  Center, Las Vegas NV
Waterworks Visual Arts Center, Salisbury NC
West Florida Historic Preservation, Inc/University of
  West Florida, T T Wentworth, Jr Florida State
  Museum; Historic Pensacola Village; Pensacola
  Historical Society & Resource Center, Pensacola FL
Western Kentucky University, Kentucky Library &
  Museum, Bowling Green KY
Wethersfield Historical Society Inc, Museum,
  Wethersfield CT
Whalers Village Museum, Lahaina HI
Whatcom Museum, Bellingham WA
Willard House & Clock Museum, Inc, North Grafton
  MA
Williams College, Museum of Art, Williamstown MA
Wiregrass Museum of Art, Dothan AL
Wisconsin Historical Society, Wisconsin Historical
  Museum, Madison WI
Witte Museum, San Antonio TX
Woodmere Art Museum Inc, Philadelphia PA
World Erotic Art Museum, Miami Beach FL
Yarmouth County Historical Society, Yarmouth County
  Museum & Archives, Yarmouth NS

FURNITURE

Academy of the New Church, Glencairn Museum, Bryn
  Athyn PA
Adams County Historical Society, Gettysburg PA
Adams National Historic Park, Quincy MA
African American Museum in Philadelphia,
  Philadelphia PA
African Art Museum of Maryland, Columbia MD
Alabama Department of Archives & History, Museum
  of Alabama, Montgomery AL
Albany Institute of History & Art, Albany NY
Albion College, Bobbitt Visual Arts Center, Albion MI
Albuquerque Museum of Art & History, Albuquerque
  NM
Allentown Art Museum, Allentown PA
Alton Museum of History & Art, Inc, Alton IL
American Art Museum, Smithsonian Institution,
  Washington DC
American Folk Art Museum, New York NY
American Swedish Historical Foundation & Museum,
  American Swedish Historical Museum, Philadelphia
  PA
Americas Society Art Gallery, New York NY
Amherst Museum, Amherst NY
Anna Maria College, Saint Luke's Gallery, Paxton MA
Anson County Historical Society, Inc, Wadesboro NC
Arab American National Museum, Dearborn MI
Arizona Historical Society-Yuma, Sanguinetti House
  Museum & Garden, Yuma AZ
Arnot Art Museum, Elmira NY
Art & Culture Center of Hollywood, Art
  Gallery/Multidisciplinary Cultural Center,
  Hollywood FL
Art Gallery of Calgary, Calgary AB
Art Gallery of South Australia, Adelaide
The Art Museum at the University of Kentucky,
  Lexington KY
Artesia Historical Museum & Art Center, Artesia NM
ArtSpace/Lima, Lima OH
Asheville Art Museum, Asheville NC
Athenaeum of Philadelphia, Philadelphia PA
Badisches Landesmuseum, Karlsruhe
Baldwin Historical Society Museum, Baldwin NY
Ball State University, Museum of Art, Muncie IN
The Baltimore Museum of Art, Baltimore MD
Barnes Foundation, Merion PA
Baroda Museum and Picture Gallery, Baroda
The Bartlett Museum, Amesbury MA
Bass Museum of Art, Miami Beach FL
Bayerisches Nationalmuseum, Bavarian National
  Museum, Munich
Beaverbrook Art Gallery, Fredericton NB
Belle Grove Inc., Belle Grove Plantation, Middletown
  VA
Bellevue Arts Museum, Bellevue WA
Bennington Museum, Bennington VT
Berkshire Museum, Pittsfield MA
Bertha V B Lederer Fine Arts Gallery-Suny Geneseo,
  Bertha V B Lederer Fine Arts Gallery, Geneseo NY
Besser Museum for Northeast Michigan, Alpena MI
Beverly Historical Society, Cabot, Hale & Balch House
  Museums, Beverly MA
Biggs Museum of American Art, Dover DE
Birmingham Museum of Art, Birmingham AL
Black River Academy Museum & Historical Society,
  Black River Academy Museum, Ludlow VT
Bodley-Bullock House Museum, Lexington KY
Brick Store Museum, Kennebunk ME
Brigham City Corporation, Brigham City Museum &
  Gallery, Brigham City UT
Bradford Brinton, Big Horn WY
Brooklyn Historical Society, Brooklyn OH
Bush-Holley Historic Site & Storehouse Gallery,
  Greenwich Historical Society/ Bush-Holley House,
  Cos Cob CT
Cabot's Old Indian Pueblo Museum, Desert Hot
  Springs CA
The California Historical Society, San Francisco CA
Cambria Historical Society, New Providence NJ
Cambridge Museum, Cambridge NE
Cameron Art Museum, Wilmington NC
Canadian Museum of Civilization, Gatineau PQ
Cape Ann Historical Association, Cape Ann Museum,
  Gloucester MA
Caramoor Center for Music & the Arts, Inc, Rosen
  House at Caramoor, Katonah NY
Carnegie Museums of Pittsburgh, Carnegie Museum of
  Art, Pittsburgh PA
Carson County Square House Museum, Panhandle TX
Carteret County Historical Society, The History Place,
  Morehead City NC

James Dick Foundation, Festival - Institute, Round Top TX

Jamestown-Yorktown Foundation, Jamestown Settlement, Williamsburg VA

Jefferson County Historical Society, Watertown NY

Jefferson County Open Space, Hiwan Homestead Museum, Evergreen CO

Thomas Jefferson, Monticello, Charlottesville VA

Jekyll Island Museum, Jekyll Island GA

Johns Hopkins University, Evergreen Museum & Library, Baltimore MD

Johns Hopkins University, Homewood Museum, Baltimore MD

Bob Jones University Museum & Gallery Inc, Greenville SC

Jordan National Gallery of Fine Arts, Amman

Joslyn Art Museum, Omaha NE

Judiciary History Center, Honolulu HI

Kelly-Griggs House Museum, Red Bluff CA

Kenosha Public Museums, Kenosha WI

Kentucky Museum of Art and Craft, Louisville KY

Kereszteny Muzeum, Christian Museum, Esztergom

Kings County Historical Society & Museum, Hampton NB

Kirchner Museum Davos, Davos

Kirkland Museum of Fine & Decorative Art, Denver CO

Knights of Columbus Supreme Council, Knights of Columbus Museum, New Haven CT

Koochiching Museums, International Falls MN

Kyiv Museum of Russian Art, Kyiv

LA County Museum of Art, Los Angeles CA

Lafayette Science Museum & Planetarium, Lafayette LA

Lahore Museum, Lahore

Landis Valley Village and Farm Museum, PA Historical & Museum Commission, Lancaster PA

Landmark Society of Western New York, Inc, The Campbell-Whittlesey House Museum, Rochester NY

Launceston City Council, Queen Victoria Museum and Art Gallery, Launceston

Le Grand Curtius, Musée d'Ansembourg, Liege

League of New Hampshire Craftsmen, Grodin Permanent Collection Museum, Concord NH

Leeds Museums & Galleries, Leeds

Lehigh Valley Heritage Center, Allentown PA

LeSueur County Historical Society, Chapter One, Elysian MN

Liberty Hall Historic Site, Liberty Hall Museum, Frankfort KY

Lightner Museum, Saint Augustine FL

Lincoln County Historical Association, Inc, 1811 Old Lincoln County Jail & Lincoln County Museum, Wiscasset ME

Lincolnshire County Council, Library & Heritage Services, Lincoln

Lincolnshire County Council, The Collection: Art & Archaeology in Lincolnshire, Lincoln

Livingston County Historical Society, Museum, Geneseo NY

Lockwood-Mathews Mansion Museum, Norwalk CT

The Long Island Museum of American Art, History & Carriages, Stony Brook NY

Longfellow's Wayside Inn Museum, Sudbury MA

Longfellow-Evangeline State Commemorative Area, Saint Martinville LA

Longue Vue House & Gardens, New Orleans LA

Los Angeles County Museum of Natural History, William S Hart Museum, Newhall CA

Louisiana Department of Culture, Recreation & Tourism, Louisiana State Museum, New Orleans LA

Louisiana State University, Museum of Art, Baton Rouge LA

Loveland Museum/Gallery, Loveland CO

Lyman Allyn Art Museum, New London CT

Magyar Nemzeti Muzeum - Hungarian National Museum, Budapest

Maine Historical Society, Wadsworth-Longfellow House, Portland ME

Maison Saint-Gabriel Museum, Montreal PQ

Manitoba Historical Society, Dalnavert Museum, Winnipeg MB

Marblehead Museum & Historical Society, Jeremiah Lee Mansion, Marblehead MA

Marblehead Museum & Historical Society, Marblehead MA

Jacques Marchais, Staten Island NY

Marquette University, Haggerty Museum of Art, Milwaukee WI

Maryhill Museum of Art, Goldendale WA

Marylhurst University, The Art Gym, Marylhurst OR

Massillon Museum, Massillon OH

Maude Kerns Art Center, Eugene OR

Maui Historical Society, Bailey House, Wailuku HI

Maysville, Kentucky Gateway Museum Center, Maysville KY

McCord Museum of Canadian History, Montreal PQ

McDowell House & Apothecary Shop, Danville KY

McLean County Historical Society, McLean County Museum of History, Bloomington IL

McPherson Museum and Arts Foundation, McPherson KS

Medina Railroad Museum, Medina NY

Meredith College, Frankie G Weems Gallery & Rotunda Gallery, Raleigh NC

Mesa Arts Center, Mesa Contemporary Arts Museum, Mesa AZ

Middle Border Museum & Oscar Howe Art Center, Mitchell SD

Milwaukee County War Memorial Inc., Villa Terrace Decorative Arts Museum, Milwaukee WI

Mingei International, Inc, Mingei International Museum - Balboa Park & Mingei International Museum - Escondido, San Diego CA

Ministry of Alberta Culture, Royal Alberta Museum, Edmonton AB

Ministry of Cultural Affairs, Bangladesh National Museum, Dhaka

Minnesota Historical Society, Minnesota State Capitol Historic Site, St Paul MN

The Mint Museum, Mint Museum of Craft & Design, Charlotte NC

Mission San Luis Rey de Francia, Mission San Luis Rey Museum, Oceanside CA

Mississippi River Museum at Mud-Island River Park, Memphis TN

Mississippi Valley Conservation Authority, R Tait McKenzie Memorial Museum, Almonte ON

Mobile Museum of Art, Mobile AL

Modern Art Museum, Fort Worth TX

Monroe County Historical Association, Elizabeth D Walters Library, Stroudsburg PA

James Monroe, Fredericksburg VA

Montana State University, Museum of the Rockies, Bozeman MT

Montreal Museum of Fine Arts, Montreal PQ

Moody County Historical Society, Moody County Museum, Pierre SD

Moravian Historical Society, Whitefield House Museum, Nazareth PA

Moravska Galerie v Brne, Moravian Gallery in Brno, Brno

Morris Museum of Art, Augusta GA

Morris-Jumel Mansion, Inc, New York NY

Mount Mary College, Marian Gallery, Milwaukee WI

Mount Vernon Hotel Museum & Garden, New York NY

Mount Vernon Ladies' Association of the Union, Mount Vernon VA

Munson-Williams-Proctor Arts Institute, Museum of Art, Utica NY

Murray State University, Art Galleries, Murray KY

Muscatine Art Center, Museum, Muscatine IA

Musea Brugge, Sint-Janshospitaal, Bruges

Musee Cognacq-Jay, Cognacq-Jay Museum, Paris

Musee des Beaux-Arts d'Orleans, Historical & Archaeological Museum of Orleans, Orleans

Musee des Beaux-Arts d'Orleans, Museum of Fine Arts, Orleans

Musee des Beaux-Arts/Palais des Archeveques, Museum of Fine Arts, Tours

Musee des Maitres et Artisans du Quebec, Montreal PQ

Musee Guimet, Paris

Musee National d'Histoire et d'Art Luxembourg, Luxembourg City

Musee Regional de lu Cote-Nord, Sept-Iles PQ

Musee Regional de Vaudreuil-Soulanges, Vaudreuil-Dorion PQ

Musee Royal Et Domaine De Mariemont, Morlanwelz

Museen der Stadt Koln, Museum Schnutgen, Cologne

Musees Royaux d'Art et d'Histoire, Royal Museums of Art and History, Brussels

Musei Capitolini, Rome

Musei Civici di Padova - Cappella Degli Scrovengni, Musei Civici Agli Eremitani (Civic Museum) - Scrovegni Chapel, Padua

Museo Cerralbo, Madrid

Museo De Las Americas, Denver CO

Museo Del Romanticismo, Museum of the Romantic Period, Madrid

Museu de Evora, Evora

Museu de Grao Vasco, Viseu

The Museum, Greenwood SC

Museum De Lakenhal, Leiden

Museum fur Angewandte Kunst Frankfurt, Museum of Applied Arts, Frankfurt

Museum fur Kunst und Gewerbe Hamburg, Hamburg

Museum of Art & History, Santa Cruz, Santa Cruz CA

Museum of Arts & Design, New York NY

The Museum of Arts & Sciences Inc, Daytona Beach FL

Museum of Contemporary Art, North Miami FL

Museum of Contemporary Craft, Portland OR

Museum of Decorative Arts in Prague, Prague

Museum of Fine Arts Houston, Bayou Bend Collection & Gardens, Houston TX

Museum of Fine Arts, Houston, Rienzi Center for European Decorative Arts, Houston TX

Museum of Fine Arts, Saint Petersburg, Florida, Inc, Saint Petersburg FL

Museum of Southern History, Houston TX

Museum of the City of New York, Museum, New York NY

Museum of Vancouver, Vancouver BC

Museum of West Louisiana, Leesville LA

Museum of Wisconsin Art, West Bend WI

Museum Plantin-Moretus/Prentenkabinet, Antwerp

Museum zu Allerheiligen, Schaffhausen

Muzej za Umjetnost i Obrt, Museum of Arts & Crafts, Zagreb

Muzeul de Istorie Nationala Si Arheologie Constanta, National History & Archaeology Museum, Constanta

Muzeul National Brukenthal, Blue House & Romanian Art Gallery, Sibiu

Muzeul National Brukenthal, Brukenthal Palace & European Art Gallery, Sibiu

Muzeum Narodowe, National Museum in Poznan, Poznan

Muzeum Narodowe W Kielcach, National Museum in Kielce, Kielce

National Galleries of Scotland, Scottish National Gallery, Edinburgh

National Gallery of Canada, Ottawa ON

National Museum of American Illustration, Newport RI

National Museums Scotland, National Museum of Scotland, Edinburgh

National Park Service, Weir Farm National Historic Site, Wilton CT

The National Park Service, United States Department of the Interior, Statue of Liberty National Monument & The Ellis Island Immigration Museum, Washington DC

National Society of Colonial Dames of America in the State of Maryland, Mount Clare Museum House, Baltimore MD

National Society of the Colonial Dames of America in The Commonwealth of Virginia, Wilton House Museum, Richmond VA

National Trust for Historic Preservation, Chesterwood, Stockbridge MA

National Trust for Historic Preservation, Decatur House, Washington DC

The National Trust for Historic Preservation, Lyndhurst, Tarrytown NY

National Trust for Historic Preservation, Shadows-on-the-Teche, New Iberia LA

National Trust for Historic Preservation, Washington DC

Nationalmuseum, Stockholm

Naval Historical Center, The Navy Museum, Washington DC

Nebraska Game and Parks Commission, Arbor Lodge State Historical Park & Morton Mansion, Nebraska City NE

Nebraska State Capitol, Lincoln NE

The Nelson-Atkins Museum of Art, Kansas City MO

The Nemours Foundatioin, Nemours Mansion & Gardens, Wilmington DE

Neustadt Collection of Tiffany Glass, Long Island City NY

Neville Public Museum of Brown County, Green Bay WI

New Brunswick Museum, Saint John NB

New Hampshire Antiquarian Society, Hopkinton Historical Society, Hopkinton NH

New Jersey Historical Society, Newark NJ

New Jersey State Museum, Fine Art Bureau, Trenton NJ

New Orleans Artworks at New Orleans Glassworks & Printmaking Studio, New Orleans LA

New Orleans Museum of Art, New Orleans LA

New World Art Center, T F Chen Cultural Center, New York NY

Museum; Historic Pensacola Village; Pensacola Historical Society & Resource Center, Pensacola FL
Wethersfield Historical Society Inc, Museum, Wethersfield CT
White House, Washington DC
Wichita State University, Ulrich Museum of Art, Wichita KS
Willard House & Clock Museum, Inc, North Grafton MA
William Morris Gallery, London
Woodrow Wilson, Washington DC
Wisconsin Historical Society, Wisconsin Historical Museum, Madison WI
Wistariahurst Museum, Holyoke MA
Witte Museum, San Antonio TX
Woodlawn/The Pope-Leighey, Mount Vernon VA
Woodmere Art Museum Inc, Philadelphia PA
Workman & Temple Family Homestead Museum, City of Industry CA
World Erotic Art Museum, Miami Beach FL
Yankton County Historical Society, Dakota Territorial Museum, Yankton SD
Yarmouth County Historical Society, Yarmouth County Museum & Archives, Yarmouth NS
Zurich University of the Arts (ZHdK), Museum Fuer Gestaltung Zurich (Museum of Design Zurich), Zurich

GLASS

A.E. Backus Museum of Art, Fort Pierce FL
Academy of the New Church, Glencairn Museum, Bryn Athyn PA
Adams County Historical Society, Gettysburg PA
Al Ain National Museum, Al Ain
Albany Institute of History & Art, Albany NY
Albion College, Bobbitt Visual Arts Center, Albion MI
Albuquerque Museum of Art & History, Albuquerque NM
Alton Museum of History & Art, Inc, Alton IL
American Art Museum, Smithsonian Institution, Washington DC
American Swedish Historical Foundation & Museum, American Swedish Historical Museum, Philadelphia PA
American Swedish Institute, Minneapolis MN
Amherst Museum, Amherst NY
Arab American National Museum, Dearborn MI
Archaeological Museum of the American University of Beirut, Beirut
Arizona Historical Society-Yuma, Sanguinetti House Museum & Garden, Yuma AZ
Arizona State University, ASU Art Museum, Tempe AZ
Arnot Art Museum, Elmira NY
Art & Culture Center of Hollywood, Art Gallery/Multidisciplinary Cultural Center, Hollywood FL
Art Community Center, Art Center of Corpus Christi, Corpus Christi TX
Art Gallery of Calgary, Calgary AB
Art Gallery of South Australia, Adelaide
The Art Museum at the University of Kentucky, Lexington KY
Arts Council of Fayetteville-Cumberland County, The Arts Center, Fayetteville NC
Arts Quest, Bethlehem PA
ArtSpace/Lima, Lima OH
Asbury College, Student Center Gallery, Wilmore KY
Asheville Art Museum, Asheville NC
Badisches Landesmuseum, Karlsruhe
Baldwin Historical Society Museum, Baldwin NY
Ball State University, Museum of Art, Muncie IN
Barker Character, Comic and Cartoon Museum, Cheshire CT
Baroda Museum and Picture Gallery, Baroda
Bayerisches Nationalmuseum, Bavarian National Museum, Munich
Baylor University, Martin Museum of Art, Waco TX
Bennington Museum, Bennington VT
Bergstrom-Mahler Museum, Neenah WI
Berkshire Museum, Pittsfield MA
Besser Museum for Northeast Michigan, Alpena MI
Beverly Historical Society, Cabot, Hale & Balch House Museums, Beverly MA
Birmingham Museum of Art, Birmingham AL
Black River Academy Museum & Historical Society, Black River Academy Museum, Ludlow VT
Brick Store Museum, Kennebunk ME
Brigham City Corporation, Brigham City Museum & Gallery, Brigham City UT
Brooklyn Historical Society, Brooklyn OH

The Buffalo Fine Arts Academy, Albright-Knox Art Gallery, Buffalo NY
Thornton W Burgess, Museum, Sandwich MA
Cambria Historical Society, New Providence NJ
Cameron Art Museum, Wilmington NC
Canadian Clay and Glass Gallery, Waterloo ON
Canadian Museum of Civilization, Gatineau PQ
Cape Cod Museum of Art Inc, Dennis MA
Carteret County Historical Society, The History Place, Morehead City NC
Center for Art & Education, Van Buren AR
Charleston Museum, Joseph Manigault House, Charleston SC
Charleston Museum, Charleston SC
Chatham Historical Society, The Atwood House Museum, Chatham MA
Chicago Athenaeum, Museum of Architecture & Design, Galena IL
Chrysler Museum of Art, Norfolk VA
City of Brea, Art Gallery, Brea CA
City of Gainesville, Thomas Center Galleries - Cultural Affairs, Gainesville FL
City of Mason City, Charles H MacNider Museum, Mason City IA
The City of Petersburg Museums, Petersburg VA
City of Pittsfield, Berkshire Artisans, Pittsfield MA
City of Port Angeles, Port Angeles Fine Arts Center & Webster Woods Art Park, Port Angeles WA
City of Springdale, Shiloh Museum of Ozark History, Springdale AR
Clark County Historical Society, Heritage Center of Clark County, Springfield OH
Clark County Historical Society, Pioneer - Krier Museum, Ashland KS
Sterling & Francine Clark, Williamstown MA
Clinton Art Association, River Arts Center, Clinton IA
Clinton County Historical Association, Clinton County Historical Museum, Plattsburgh NY
College of William & Mary, Muscarelle Museum of Art, Williamsburg VA
The College of Wooster, The College of Wooster Art Museum, Wooster OH
Columbus Chapel & Boal Mansion Museum, Boalsburg PA
Columbus Museum, Columbus GA
Columbus Museum of Art, Columbus OH
Cooper-Hewitt National Design Museum, Smithsonian Institution, New York NY
Coutts Museum of Art, Inc, El Dorado KS
Craft and Folk Art Museum (CAFAM), Los Angeles CA
Craftsmen's Guild of Mississippi, Inc, Agriculture & Forestry Museum, Ridgeland MS
Cripple Creek District Museum, Cripple Creek CO
Crocker Art Museum, Sacramento CA
Crook County Museum & Art Gallery, Sundance WY
Crow Wing County Historical Society, Brainerd MN
The Currier Museum of Art, Manchester NH
Danforth Museum of Art, Danforth Museum of Art, Framingham MA
DAR Museum, National Society Daughters of the American Revolution, Washington DC
Dartmouth College, Hood Museum of Art, Hanover NH
Dartmouth Heritage Museum, Dartmouth NS
Dawson City Museum & Historical Society, Dawson City YT
Delaware Archaeology Museum, Dover DE
Delaware Division of Historical & Cultural Affairs, Dover DE
Deming-Luna Mimbres Museum, Deming NM
Denver Art Museum, Denver CO
Department of Antiquities, Cyprus Museum, Nicosia
Designmuseum Danmark, Copenhagen
Detroit Institute of Arts, Detroit MI
Doncaster Museum and Art Gallery, Doncaster
Dundee City Council Leisure & Communities Department, The McManus: Dundee's Art Gallery & Museum, Dundee
Dundurn Castle, Hamilton ON
Emory University, Michael C Carlos Museum, Atlanta GA
Environment Canada - Parks Canada, Laurier House, National Historic Site, Ottawa ON
Evanston Historical Society, Charles Gates Dawes House, Evanston IL
Evansville Museum of Arts, History & Science, Evansville IN
Everhart Museum, Scranton PA
Farmington Village Green & Library Association, Stanley-Whitman House, Farmington CT
Fetherston Foundation, Packwood House Museum, Lewisburg PA

Fine Arts Center for the New River Valley, Pulaski VA
Fine Arts Museums of San Francisco, Legion of Honor, San Francisco CA
Flint Institute of Arts, Flint MI
Florence Museum, Florence SC
Florida Southern College, Melvin Art Gallery, Lakeland FL
Florida State University and Central Florida Community College, The Appleton Museum of Art, Ocala FL
Fondazione Musei Civici Di Venezia, Ca'Rezzonico, Museo del Settecento Veneziano, Venice
Fondazione Musei Civici Di Venezia, Galleria Internazionale d'Arte Moderna di Ca'Pesaro, Venice
Fondazione Musei Civici Di Venezia, Museo Correr, Venice
Edsel & Eleanor Ford, Grosse Pointe Shores MI
Forest Lawn Museum, Glendale CA
Fort Collins Museum of Art, Inc., Fort Collins CO
Freer Gallery of Art & Arthur M Sackler Gallery, Arthur M Sackler Gallery, Washington DC
The Frick Art & Historical Center, Inc, Frick Art Museum, Pittsburgh PA
Fuller Craft Museum, Brockton MA
Gadsden Museum, Mesilla NM
Gadsden Museum of Fine Arts, Inc, Gadsden Museum of Art and History, Gadsden AL
Gala-Salvador Dali Foundation Museums, Casa Museu Castell Gala Dali, Figueres
Gallery One Visual Arts Center, Ellensburg WA
Gem County Historical Society and Museum, Gem County Historical Village Museum, Emmett ID
Germanisches Nationalmuseum, Nuremberg
Girard College, Stephen Girard Collection, Philadelphia PA
Glanmore National Historic Site of Canada, Belleville ON
Glasmuseet Ebeltoft, Ebeltoft
Glessner House Museum, Chicago IL
Gonzaga University, Art Gallery, Spokane WA
Grand Rapids Art Museum, Grand Rapids MI
Grand Rapids Public Museum, Public Museum of Grand Rapids, Grand Rapids MI
Greek Ministry of Culture, Archaeological Museum of Thessaloniki, Thessaloniki
Greene County Historical Society, Bronck Museum, Coxsackie NY
Guilford College, Art Gallery, Greensboro NC
Halifax Historical Society, Inc, Halifax Historical Museum, Daytona Beach FL
Hammond-Harwood House Association, Inc, Hammond-Harwood House, Annapolis MD
Hancock County Trustees of Public Reservations, Woodlawn: Museum, Gardens & Park, Ellsworth ME
Hastings Museum of Natural & Cultural History, Hastings NE
Hawkes Bay Art Gallery and Museum, Napier
Haystack Mountain School of Crafts, Deer Isle ME
Headley-Whitney Museum, Lexington KY
Headquarters Fort Monroe, Dept of Army, Casemate Museum, Hampton VA
Heard Museum, Phoenix AZ
Heart of West Texas Museum, Colorado City TX
Hebrew Union College, Skirball Cultural Center, Los Angeles CA
Hecht Museum, Haifa
Henry County Museum & Cultural Arts Center, Clinton MO
Henry Morrison Flagler Museum, Palm Beach FL
Henry Sheldon Museum of Vermont History and Research Center, Middlebury VT
Heritage Glass Museum, Glassboro NJ
Heritage Museum Association, Inc, The Heritage Museum of Northwest Florida, Valparaiso FL
Hermitage Foundation Museum, Norfolk VA
Hershey Museum, Hershey PA
Edna Hibel, Hibel Museum of Art, Jupiter FL
Hickory Museum of Art, Inc, Hickory NC
Higgins Armory Museum, Worcester MA
Hill-Stead Museum, Farmington CT
Hillwood Museum & Gardens Foundation, Hillwood Estate Museum & Gardens, Washington DC
Historic Arkansas Museum, Little Rock AR
Historic Deerfield, Inc, Deerfield MA
The Historic New Orleans Collection, Royal Street Galleries, New Orleans LA
Historic Paris - Bourbon County, Inc, Hopewell Museum, Paris KY
Historical Society of Bloomfield, Bloomfield NJ
Historical Society of Cheshire County, Keene NH

Page-Walker Arts & History Center, Cary NC
Panhandle-Plains Historical Museum, Canyon TX
Pasadena Museum of History, Pasadena CA
The Pennsylvania State University, Palmer Museum of Art, University Park PA
Pensacola Museum of Art, Pensacola FL
Philadelphia History Museum, Philadelphia PA
Philadelphia Museum of Art, Main Building, Philadelphia PA
Philbrook Museum of Art, Tulsa OK
Phillips Academy, Addison Gallery of American Art, Andover MA
Phillips County Museum, Holyoke CO
Pilgrim Society, Pilgrim Hall Museum, Plymouth MA
Plains Art Museum, Fargo ND
Plainsman Museum, Aurora NE
Plumas County Museum, Quincy CA
Polk Museum of Art, Lakeland FL
Pope County Historical Society, Pope County Museum, Glenwood MN
Port Huron Museum, Port Huron MI
Porter-Phelps-Huntington Foundation, Inc, Historic House Museum, Hadley MA
Portland Museum of Art, Portland ME
Portsmouth Historical Society, John Paul Jones House & Discover Portsmouth, Portsmouth NH
Princeton University, Princeton University Art Museum, Princeton NJ
Principia College, School of Nations Museum, Elsah IL
Putnam Museum of History and Natural Science, Davenport IA
Queens College, City University of New York, Godwin-Ternbach Museum, Flushing NY
Rabindra Bhavan Art Gallery, Lalit Kala Akademi (National Academy of Art), New Delhi
Rahr-West Art Museum, Manitowoc WI
Rawls Museum Arts, Courtland VA
Reading Public Museum, Reading PA
Frederic Remington, Ogdensburg NY
Rijksmuseum Twenthe, Rijksmuseum Twenthe, Enschede
Riley County Historical Society & Museum, Riley County Historical Museum, Manhattan KS
The Rockwell Museum of Western Art, Corning NY
Rome Historical Society, Museum & Archives, Rome NY
The Rooms Corporation of Newfoundland & Labrador, Saint John's NF
Rose Lehrman Art Gallery, Harrisburg PA
Royal Pavilion & Museums, Brighton Museum & Art Gallery, Brighton
Ryerss Victorian Museum & Library, Philadelphia PA
Saco Museum, Saco ME
Saginaw Art Museum, Saginaw MI
Saint Augustine Historical Society, Oldest House Museum Complex, Saint Augustine FL
Saint Joseph Museum, Saint Joseph MO
Saint Louis County Historical Society, St. Louis County Historical Society, Duluth MN
Saint Peter's College, Art Gallery, Jersey City NJ
The Sandwich Historical Society, Inc & Sandwich Glass Museum, Sandwich Glass Museum, Sandwich MA
Scottsdale Cultural Council, Scottsdale Museum of Contemporary Art, Scottsdale AZ
Scripps College, Ruth Chandler Williamson Gallery, Claremont CA
Shaker Museum & Library, Old Chatham NY
Shirley Plantation Foundation, Charles City VA
Society for Contemporary Craft, Pittsburgh PA
The Society of the Cincinnati at Anderson House, Washington DC
Soprintendenza per I beni storici artistici ed etnoantropologici per le province di Mantova Brescia e Cremona, Museo di Palazzo Ducale, Mantua
South Carolina Artisans Center, Walterboro SC
South Dakota State University, South Dakota Art Museum, Brookings SD
Southeastern Center for Contemporary Art, Winston Salem NC
Southern Ohio Museum Corporation, Southern Ohio Museum, Portsmouth OH
The Speed Art Museum, Louisville KY
Spertus Institute of Jewish Studies, Chicago IL
Springfield Art Museum, Springfield MO
Stanford University, Cantor Arts Center at Stanford University, Stanford CA
Nelda C & H J Lutcher Stark, Stark Museum of Art, Orange TX
The State Museum of Fine Arts of Tatarstan Republic, Kazan

State University of New York at Binghamton, Binghamton University Art Museum, Binghamton NY
State University of New York at Geneseo, Bertha V B Lederer Gallery, Geneseo NY
State University of New York College at Buffalo, Buffalo NY
Staten Island Museum, Staten Island NY
Stauth Foundation & Museum, Stauth Memorial Museum, Montezuma KS
The Stewart Museum, Montreal PQ
Stone Quarry Hill Art Park, Winner Gallery, Cazenovia NY
Stratford Historical Society, Catharine B Mitchell Museum, Stratford CT
Suan Pakkad Palace Museum, Bangkok
The Summit County Historical Society of Akron, OH, Akron OH
Suomen Kansallismuseo, National Museum of Finland, Helsinki
Susquehanna University, Lore Degenstein Gallery, Selinsgrove PA
Swedish American Museum Association of Chicago, Chicago IL
Switzerland County Historical Society Inc, Switzerland County Historical Museum, Vevay IN
Syracuse University, Art Collection, Syracuse NY
Syracuse University, SUArt Galleries, Syracuse NY
Tacoma Art Museum, Tacoma WA
Tampa Museum of Art, Tampa FL
Lillian & Coleman Taube Museum of Art, Minot ND
The Temple-Tifereth Israel, The Temple Museum of Religious Art, Beachwood OH
Texas Tech University, Museum of Texas Tech University, Lubbock TX
Toledo Museum of Art, Toledo OH
Topeka & Shawnee County Public Library, Alice C Sabatini Gallery, Topeka KS
Triton Museum of Art, Santa Clara CA
Tryon Palace Historic Sites & Gardens, New Bern NC
Tulane University, Newcomb Art Gallery, New Orleans LA
Tver Art Gallery, Tver
Mark Twain, Hartford CT
Tyne and Wear Archives & Museums, Sunderland Museum & Winter Gardens, Newcastle-upon-Tyne
United Society of Shakers, Shaker Museum, New Gloucester ME
Universalmuseum Joanneum GmbH, Graz
University of California, Berkeley, Phoebe Apperson Hearst Museum of Anthropology, Berkeley CA
University of Chicago, Oriental Institute, Chicago IL
University of Chicago, Smart Museum of Art, Chicago IL
University of Colorado, CU Art Museum, Boulder CO
University of Colorado at Colorado Springs, Gallery of Contemporary Art, Colorado Springs CO
University of Georgia, Georgia Museum of Art, Athens GA
University of Illinois at Urbana-Champaign, Krannert Art Museum and Kinkead Pavilion, Champaign IL
University of Illinois at Urbana-Champaign, Spurlock Museum, Champaign IL
University of Kansas, Spencer Museum of Art, Lawrence KS
University of Louisiana at Lafayette, Paul and Lulu Hilliard University Art Museum, Lafayette LA
University of Miami, Lowe Art Museum, Coral Gables FL
University of Missouri, Museum of Art & Archaeology, Columbia MO
University of Nevada, Reno, Sheppard Contemporary & University Galleries, Reno NV
University of North Carolina at Chapel Hill, Ackland Art Museum, Chapel Hill NC
University of Pennsylvania, Museum of Archaeology & Anthropology, Philadelphia PA
University of Pittsburgh, University Art Gallery, Pittsburgh PA
University of Richmond, University Museums, Richmond VA
University of Saskatchewan, Diefenbaker Canada Centre, Saskatoon SK
University of Utah, Utah Museum of Fine Arts, Salt Lake City UT
University of Wisconsin-Madison, Chazen Museum of Art, Madison WI
University of Wisconsin-Madison, Wisconsin Union Galleries, Madison WI
Valentine Richmond History Center, Richmond VA
Vassar College, The Frances Lehman Loeb Art Center, Poughkeepsie NY

Vero Beach Museum of Art, Vero Beach FL
Vesterheim Norwegian-American Museum, Decorah IA
Victoria Mansion - Morse Libby House, Portland ME
Virginia Museum of Fine Arts, Richmond VA
Vorres Museum of Contemporary Greek Art and Folk Art, Attica
Walker Art Gallery, Liverpool
The Wallace Collection, London
Wallace State Community College, Evelyn Burrow Museum, Hanceville AL
Washburn University, Mulvane Art Museum, Topeka KS
Washington County Museum of Fine Arts, Hagerstown MD
Waterville Historical Society, Redington Museum, Waterville ME
Waterworks Visual Arts Center, Salisbury NC
Wayne County Historical Society, Museum, Honesdale PA
West Florida Historic Preservation, Inc/University of West Florida, T T Wentworth, Jr Florida State Museum; Historic Pensacola Village; Pensacola Historical Society & Resource Center, Pensacola FL
Westcott Bay Institute, Island Museum of Art & Westcott Bay Sculpture Park, Friday Harbor WA
Westfries Museum, Hoorn
Wheaton Arts & Cultural Center, Museum of American Glass, Millville NJ
Wheaton College, Beard and Weil Galleries, Norton MA
White House, Washington DC
Willard House & Clock Museum, Inc, North Grafton MA
Wiregrass Museum of Art, Dothan AL
Wistariahurst Museum, Holyoke MA
Woodlawn/The Pope-Leighey, Mount Vernon VA
World Erotic Art Museum, Miami Beach FL
Yarmouth County Historical Society, Yarmouth County Museum & Archives, Yarmouth NS
Yokohama Museum of Art, Yokohama
Yuma Fine Arts Association, Yuma Art Center, Yuma AZ
Zigler Art Museum, Jennings LA
Zurich University of the Arts (ZHdK), Museum Fuer Gestaltung Zurich (Museum of Design Zurich), Zurich

GOLD

Al Ain National Museum, Al Ain
Alaska Heritage Museum at Wells Fargo, Anchorage AK
American Art Museum, Smithsonian Institution, Washington DC
Archaeological Museum of the American University of Beirut, Beirut
Art & Culture Center of Hollywood, Art Gallery/Multidisciplinary Cultural Center, Hollywood FL
Art Gallery of Calgary, Calgary AB
The Baltimore Museum of Art, Baltimore MD
Banco de la Republica Museo del Oro, Museo del Oro, Bogota
Bayerisches Nationalmuseum, Bavarian National Museum, Munich
Bellevue Arts Museum, Bellevue WA
Beloit College, Wright Museum of Art, Beloit WI
Berman Museum, Anniston AL
Canadian Museum of Civilization, Gatineau PQ
City of Nome Alaska, Carrie M McLain Memorial Museum, Nome AK
City of Springdale, Shiloh Museum of Ozark History, Springdale AR
College of William & Mary, Muscarelle Museum of Art, Williamsburg VA
Cooper-Hewitt National Design Museum, Smithsonian Institution, New York NY
Cripple Creek District Museum, Cripple Creek CO
Crocker Art Museum, Sacramento CA
Denver Art Museum, Denver CO
Department of Antiquities, Cyprus Museum, Nicosia
Detroit Institute of Arts, Detroit MI
Forest Lawn Museum, Glendale CA
Galleria Nazionale dell'Umbria, Umbrian National Gallery, Perugia
Gem County Historical Society and Museum, Gem County Historical Village Museum, Emmett ID
Germanisches Nationalmuseum, Nuremberg
Glanmore National Historic Site of Canada, Belleville ON
Greek Ministry of Culture, Archaeological Museum of Thessaloniki, Thessaloniki

GRAPHICS

Gertrude Herbert, Augusta GA
Heritage Center, Inc, Pine Ridge SD
Edna Hibel, Hibel Museum of Art, Jupiter FL
Hickory Museum of Art, Inc, Hickory NC
Hidalgo County Historical Museum, Edinburg TX
Higgins Armory Museum, Worcester MA
Hillwood Museum & Gardens Foundation, Hillwood
  Estate Museum & Gardens, Washington DC
The Hispanic Society of America, Museum & Library,
  New York NY
Historisches und Volkerkundemuseum, Historical
  Museum, St Gallen
Hofstra University, Hofstra University Museum,
  Hempstead NY
Howard University, Gallery of Art, Washington DC
Hoyt Center for the Arts, New Castle PA
Huntington Museum of Art, Huntington WV
Illinois State Museum, ISM Lockport Gallery, Chicago
  Gallery & Southern Illinois Art Gallery, Springfield
  IL
Imperial Calcasieu Museum, Gibson-Barham Gallery,
  Lake Charles LA
Independence Seaport Museum, Philadelphia PA
Independent Administrative Institution National
  Institutes for Cultural Heritage, Tokyo National
  Museum, Tokyo
Institute of Puerto Rican Arts & Culture, Chicago IL
Institute of Puerto Rican Culture, Museo Fuerte Conde
  de Mirasol, Vieques PR
The Interchurch Center, Galleries at the Interchurch
  Center, New York NY
The Israel Museum, Jerusalem, Billy Rose Art Garden,
  Jerusalem
The Israel Museum, Jerusalem, Samuel & Saidye
  Bronfman Archaeology Wing, Jerusalem
The Israel Museum, Jerusalem, Jerusalem
J.M.W. Turner Museum, Sarasota FL
James Dick Foundation, Festival - Institute, Round Top
  TX
Japan Society, Inc, Japan Society Gallery, New York
  NY
The Jewish Museum, New York NY
Jordan National Gallery of Fine Arts, Amman
Joslyn Art Museum, Omaha NE
Juniata College Museum of Art, Huntingdon PA
Kenosha Public Museums, Kenosha WI
Kentucky Museum of Art and Craft, Louisville KY
Keystone Gallery, Scott City KS
Knights of Columbus Supreme Council, Knights of
  Columbus Museum, New Haven CT
Kunsthalle Bremen, Bremen Art Gallery, Bremen
Kunstmuseum Bern, Musee des Beaux-Arts de Berne,
  Bern
Kyiv Museum of Russian Art, Kyiv
L'Universite Laval, Ecole des Arts Visuels, Quebec PQ
La Salle University Art Museum, Philadelphia PA
Lafayette College, Lafayette College Art Galleries,
  Easton PA
Lafayette Science Museum & Planetarium, Lafayette
  LA
LaGrange Art Museum, LaGrange GA
Latino Art Museum, Pomona CA
Latvijas Nacionalais Makslas Muzejs, Arsenals
  Exhibition Hall, Riga
Lawrence University, Wriston Art Center Galleries,
  Appleton WI
Lehigh University Art Galleries, Museum Operation,
  Bethlehem PA
Lightner Museum, Saint Augustine FL
The Long Island Museum of American Art, History &
  Carriages, Stony Brook NY
Louisiana Arts & Science Museum, Baton Rouge LA
Louisiana Department of Culture, Recreation &
  Tourism, Louisiana State Museum, New Orleans
  LA
Louisiana State University, Museum of Art, Baton
  Rouge LA
Louisiana State University, School of Art - Glassell
  Gallery, Baton Rouge LA
Louisiana State University, Student Union Art Gallery,
  Baton Rouge LA
Magyar Nemzeti Muzeum - Hungarian National
  Museum, Budapest
Maitland Art Center, Maitland FL
The Mariners' Museum, Newport News VA
Maryland Art Place, Baltimore MD
Marylhurst University, The Art Gym, Marylhurst OR
Maude Kerns Art Center, Eugene OR
McCord Museum of Canadian History, Montreal PQ
McNay, San Antonio TX
Mennello Museum of American Art, Orlando FL
Midwest Museum of American Art, Elkhart IN

Ministry of Cultural Affairs, Bangladesh National
  Museum, Dhaka
Minot State University, Northwest Art Center, Minot
  ND
Mississippi River Museum at Mud-Island River Park,
  Memphis TN
Mobile Museum of Art, Mobile AL
Moderna Galerija, Gallery of Modern Art, Zagreb
Moravska Galerie v Brne, Moravian Gallery in Brno,
  Brno
Morris Museum of Art, Augusta GA
Mount Allison University, Owens Art Gallery, Sackville
  NB
Mount Saint Vincent University, MSVU Art Gallery,
  Halifax NS
Muscatine Art Center, Muscatine IA
Musee Carnavalet-Histoire de Paris, Paris
Musee des Beaux-Arts/Palais des Archeveques,
  Museum of Fine Arts, Tours
Musee et Chateau de Chantilly (MUSEE CONDE),
  Chantilly
Musee National d'Histoire et d'Art Luxembourg,
  Luxembourg City
Musee Royal Et Domaine De Mariemont, Morlanwelz
Museen der Stadt Koln, Museum Ludwig, Cologne
Museen der Stadt Koln, Wallraf-Richartz-Museum,
  Cologne
Musees Royaux d'Art et d'Histoire, Royal Museums of
  Art and History, Brussels
Musei Civici di Padova - Cappella Degli Scrovengni,
  Musei Civici Agli Eremitani (Civic Museum) -
  Scrovegni Chapel, Padua
Museo Cerralbo, Madrid
Museo Civico Giovanni Fattori, Livorno
Museo de Arte de Ponce, The Luis A Ferre Foundation
  Inc, Ponce PR
Museo De Las Americas, Denver CO
Museo Del Romanticismo, Museum of the Romantic
  Period, Madrid
Museum De Lakenhal, Leiden
Museum fur Kunst und Gewerbe Hamburg, Hamburg
Museum of Art, Fort Lauderdale, Fort Lauderdale FL
The Museum of Arts & Sciences Inc, Daytona Beach
  FL
Museum of Contemporary Art, North Miami FL
The Museum of Contemporary Art (MOCA), Moca
  Grand Avenue, Los Angeles CA
Museum of Decorative Arts in Prague, Prague
Museum of Discovery & Science, Fort Lauderdale FL
Museum of Florida Art, Deland FL
Museum of Latin American Art, Long Beach CA
Museum of Modern Art, New York NY
Museum of Northern British Columbia, Ruth Harvey
  Art Gallery, Prince Rupert BC
Museum of Northwest Art, La Conner WA
Museum of the City of New York, Museum, New York
  NY
Museum zu Allerheiligen, Schaffhausen
Muskegon Museum of Art, Muskegon MI
Muzej Moderne I Suvremene Umjetnosti, Museum of
  Modern and Contemporary Art, Rijeka
Muzej za Umjetnost i Obrt, Museum of Arts & Crafts,
  Zagreb
Muzeul de Istorie Nationala Si Arheologie Constanta,
  National History & Archaeology Museum,
  Constanta
Muzeul National Brukenthal, Blue House & Romanian
  Art Gallery, Sibiu
Muzeul National Brukenthal, Brukenthal Palace &
  European Art Gallery, Sibiu
Muzeum Narodowe, National Museum in Poznan,
  Poznan
Muzeum Narodowe W Kielcach, National Museum in
  Kielce, Kielce
Narodna Galerija, National Gallery of Slovenia,
  Ljubljana
Narodni Muzej Crne Gore, National Museum of
  Montenegro, Cetinje
National Art Museum of Sport, Indianapolis IN
National Baseball Hall of Fame & Museum, Inc, Art
  Collection, Cooperstown NY
National Gallery of Canada, Ottawa ON
National Museum of American Illustration, Newport RI
National Museum of Fine Arts of Moldova, Chisinau
The National Museum of Modern Art, Tokyo, Tokyo
National Museum, Monuments and Art Gallery,
  Gaborone
The National Park Service, United States Department
  of the Interior, Statue of Liberty National
  Monument & The Ellis Island Immigration
  Museum, Washington DC

National Society of Colonial Dames of America in the
  State of Maryland, Mount Clare Museum House,
  Baltimore MD
Naval Historical Center, The Navy Museum,
  Washington DC
Nelson Mandela Bay Municipality, Nelson Mandela
  Metropolitan Art Museum, Port Elizabeth
New Jersey State Museum, Fine Art Bureau, Trenton
  NJ
New Orleans Museum of Art, New Orleans LA
New Visions Gallery, Inc, Marshfield WI
New World Art Center, T F Chen Cultural Center, New
  York NY
New York State Military Museum and Veterans
  Research Center, Saratoga Springs NY
Niagara University, Castellani Art Museum, Niagara
  NY
The Noble Maritime Collection, Staten Island NY
North Dakota State University, Memorial Union
  Gallery, Fargo ND
Norwich Free Academy, Slater Memorial Museum,
  Norwich CT
Nova Scotia College of Art and Design, Anna
  Leonowens Gallery, Halifax NS
Noyes Art Gallery, Lincoln NE
The Ogden Museum of Southern Art, University of
  New Orleans, New Orleans LA
Ohio University, Kennedy Museum of Art, Athens OH
Owensboro Museum of Fine Art, Owensboro KY
Panhandle-Plains Historical Museum, Canyon TX
Pasadena Museum of California Art, Pasadena CA
The Pennsylvania State University, Palmer Museum of
  Art, University Park PA
Philadelphia History Museum, Philadelphia PA
Phillips Academy, Addison Gallery of American Art,
  Andover MA
The Phillips Collection, Washington DC
The Frank Phillips, Woolaroc Museum, Bartlesville OK
Plains Art Museum, Fargo ND
Plumas County Museum, Quincy CA
The Pomona College, Claremont CA
Portland Art Museum, Portland OR
Pretoria Art Museum, Municipal Art Gallery, Pretoria
Princeton University, Princeton University Art Museum,
  Princeton NJ
Putnam County Historical Society, Foundry School
  Museum, Cold Spring NY
Queen's University, Agnes Etherington Art Centre,
  Kingston ON
Queens College, City University of New York,
  Godwin-Ternbach Museum, Flushing NY
Queensborough Community College, Art Gallery,
  Bayside NY
Rahr-West Art Museum, Manitowoc WI
Rose Lehrman Art Gallery, Harrisburg PA
Roswell Museum & Art Center, Roswell NM
Saginaw Art Museum, Saginaw MI
Saint Joseph's Oratory, Museum, Montreal PQ
Saint Mary's College of California, Hearst Art Gallery,
  Moraga CA
Saint Peter's College, Art Gallery, Jersey City NJ
San Francisco Maritime National Historical Park,
  Maritime Museum, San Francisco CA
Santa Clara University, de Saisset Museum, Santa Clara
  CA
Savitsky Karakalpakstan State Art Museum, Nukus
School of Visual Arts, Visual Arts Museum, New York
  NY
Scripps College, Ruth Chandler Williamson Gallery,
  Claremont CA
Severoceska Galerie Vytvarneho Umeni v Litomericich,
  North Bohemian Gallery of Fine Arts in Litomerice,
  Litomerice
Simon Fraser University, Simon Fraser University
  Gallery, Burnaby BC
Norton Simon, Pasadena CA
Slovenska Narodna Galeria, Slovak National Gallery,
  Bratislava
The Society of the Cincinnati at Anderson House,
  Washington DC
South Dakota State University, South Dakota Art
  Museum, Brookings SD
Spertus Institute of Jewish Studies, Chicago IL
Springfield Museums, Michele & Donald D'Amour
  Museum of Fine Arts, Springfield MA
Staatliche Graphische Sammlung Munchen, Munich
Staatsgalerie Stuttgart, Stuttgart
Stanford University, Cantor Arts Center at Stanford
  University, Stanford CA
The State Museum of Fine Arts of Tatarstan Republic,
  Kazan

HISPANIC ART

Lillian & Coleman Taube Museum of Art, Minot ND
Texas Tech University, Museum of Texas Tech University, Lubbock TX
Tohono Chul Park, Tucson AZ
University of California, Los Angeles, Fowler Museum at UCLA, Los Angeles CA
University of Georgia, Georgia Museum of Art, Athens GA
University of Illinois at Urbana-Champaign, Krannert Art Museum and Kinkead Pavilion, Champaign IL
University of Miami, Lowe Art Museum, Coral Gables FL
University of New Mexico, The Harwood Museum of Art, Taos NM
University of Pennsylvania, Museum of Archaeology & Anthropology, Philadelphia PA
University of Puerto Rico, Museum of Anthropology, History & Art, Rio Piedras PR
University of Rochester, Memorial Art Gallery, Rochester NY
University of Texas at Austin, Blanton Museum of Art, Austin TX
University of Utah, Utah Museum of Fine Arts, Salt Lake City UT
University of Wisconsin-Madison, Chazen Museum of Art, Madison WI
Walker Art Gallery, Liverpool
Wellesley College, Davis Museum & Cultural Center, Wellesley MA
Wichita State University, Ulrich Museum of Art, Wichita KS
World Erotic Art Museum, Miami Beach FL
Yerba Buena Center for the Arts, San Francisco CA
Yuma Fine Arts Association, Yuma Art Center, Yuma AZ

HISTORICAL MATERIAL

Academy of the New Church, Glencairn Museum, Bryn Athyn PA
Adams County Historical Society, Gettysburg PA
Adams National Historic Park, Quincy MA
African American Museum of Iowa, Cedar Rapids IA
African American Museum in Philadelphia, Philadelphia PA
African Art Museum of Maryland, Columbia MD
Alabama Department of Archives & History, Museum of Alabama, Montgomery AL
Alaska Heritage Museum at Wells Fargo, Anchorage AK
Alaska Museum of Natural History, Anchorage AK
Albany Institute of History & Art, Albany NY
Albuquerque Museum of Art & History, Albuquerque NM
Allentown Art Museum, Allentown PA
Alton Museum of History & Art, Inc, Alton IL
American Textile History Museum, Lowell MA
Americas Society Art Gallery, New York NY
Amherst Museum, Amherst NY
Amon Carter Museum of American Art, Fort Worth TX
Anchorage Museum at Rasmuson Center, Anchorage AK
Ancient Spanish Monastery, North Miami Beach FL
Arab American National Museum, Dearborn MI
Archives & History Center of the United Methodist Church, Madison NJ
Arizona Historical Society-Yuma, Sanguinetti House Museum & Garden, Yuma AZ
Arnot Art Museum, Elmira NY
Art Gallery of Nova Scotia, Halifax NS
Art Without Walls Inc, New York NY
Artesia Historical Museum & Art Center, Artesia NM
Athenaeum of Philadelphia, Philadelphia PA
Atlanta Historical Society Inc, Atlanta History Center, Atlanta GA
Baker University, Old Castle Museum, Baldwin City KS
Baroda Museum and Picture Gallery, Baroda
The Bartlett Museum, Amesbury MA
Bay County Historical Society, Historical Museum of Bay County, Bay City MI
Baycrest Centre for Geriatric Care, The Morris & Sally Justein of Baycrest Heritage Museum, Toronto ON
Beverly Historical Society, Cabot, Hale & Balch House Museums, Beverly MA
Big Horn County Historical Museum, Hardin MT
Blanden Memorial Art Museum, Fort Dodge IA
Bodley-Bullock House Museum, Lexington KY
Booth Western Art Museum, Cartersville GA
Boston Public Library, Albert H Wiggin Gallery & Print Department, Boston MA

Brant Historical Society, Brant Museum & Archives, Brantford ON
Brick Store Museum, Kennebunk ME
Brigham City Corporation, Brigham City Museum & Gallery, Brigham City UT
Bronx Community College (CUNY), Hall of Fame for Great Americans, Bronx NY
Brookgreen Gardens, Murrells Inlet SC
Brooklyn Historical Society, Brooklyn OH
Bucknell University, Edward & Marthann Samek Art Gallery, Lewisburg PA
Buena Vista Museum of Natural History, Bakersfield CA
Bush-Holley Historic Site & Storehouse Gallery, Greenwich Historical Society/ Bush-Holley House, Cos Cob CT
Cabot's Old Indian Pueblo Museum, Desert Hot Springs CA
California State University Stanislaus, University Art Gallery, Turlock CA
Calvin College, Center Art Gallery, Grand Rapids MI
Cambridge Museum, Cambridge NE
Canadian Clay and Glass Gallery, Waterloo ON
Canadian Museum of Civilization, Gatineau PQ
Canadian War Museum, Ottawa ON
Canajoharie Library & Art Gallery, Arkell Museum of Canajoharie, Canajoharie NY
Cape Ann Historical Association, Cape Ann Museum, Gloucester MA
Carlsbad Museum & Art Center, Carlsbad NM
Carson County Square House Museum, Panhandle TX
Carteret County Historical Society, The History Place, Morehead City NC
Cartoon Art Museum, San Francisco CA
Casa Amesti, Monterey CA
Center for Puppetry Arts, Atlanta GA
Channel Islands Maritime Museum, Oxnard CA
Chatham Historical Society, The Atwood House Museum, Chatham MA
Chatillon-DeMenil House Foundation, Chatillon-DeMenil House, Saint Louis MO
Chelan County Public Utility District, Rocky Reach Dam, Wenatchee WA
Chesapeake Bay Maritime Museum, Saint Michaels MD
Chief Plenty Coups Museum State Park, Pryor MT
Church of Jesus Christ of Latter-Day Saints, Museum of Church History & Art, Salt Lake City UT
City of Atlanta, Atlanta Cyclorama & Civil War Museum, Atlanta GA
City of Austin Parks & Recreation, O. Henry Museum, Austin TX
City of Gainesville, Thomas Center Galleries - Cultural Affairs, Gainesville FL
City of High Point, High Point Museum, High Point NC
City of Ketchikan Museum Dept, Ketchikan AK
City of Nome Alaska, Carrie M McLain Memorial Museum, Nome AK
City of San Antonio, San Antonio TX
City of Springdale, Shiloh Museum of Ozark History, Springdale AR
City of Toronto Culture, The Market Gallery, Toronto ON
Clark County Historical Society, Heritage Center of Clark County, Springfield OH
Clark County Historical Society, Pioneer - Krier Museum, Ashland KS
Cliveden, Philadelphia PA
Cohasset Historical Society, Cohasset Maritime Museum, Cohasset MA
Cohasset Historical Society, Pratt Building (Society Headquarters), Cohasset MA
Cohasset Historical Society, Captain John Wilson Historical House, Cohasset MA
College of William & Mary, Muscarelle Museum of Art, Williamsburg VA
The College of Wooster, The College of Wooster Art Museum, Wooster OH
Colorado Historical Society, Colorado History Museum, Denver CO
Columbia County Historical Society, Columbia County Museum and Library, Kinderhook NY
Columbus Historic Foundation, Blewett-Harrison-Lee Museum, Columbus MS
Columbus Museum, Columbus GA
Communications and History Museum of Sutton, Sutton PQ
Concord Museum, Concord MA
Conrad-Caldwell House Museum, Louisville KY
Cooper-Hewitt National Design Museum, Smithsonian Institution, New York NY

Craigdarroch Castle Historical Museum Society, Victoria BC
Cranford Historical Society, Cranford NJ
Cripple Creek District Museum, Cripple Creek CO
Crook County Museum & Art Gallery, Sundance WY
The Currier Museum of Art, Manchester NH
Dacotah Prairie Museum, Lamont Art Gallery, Aberdeen SD
Danville Museum of Fine Arts & History, Danville VA
Davidson College, William H Van Every Jr & Edward M Smith Galleries, Davidson NC
Davistown Museum, Liberty Location, Liberty ME
Deines Cultural Center, Russell KS
Delaware Archaeology Museum, Dover DE
Delaware Division of Historical & Cultural Affairs, Dover DE
Deming-Luna Mimbres Museum, Deming NM
Department of Museums Malaysia, National Museum, Kuala Lumpur
Dickinson College, The Trout Gallery, Carlisle PA
The Dinosaur Museum, Blanding UT
Drew County Historical Society, Museum, Monticello AR
Dundee City Council Leisure & Communities Department, The McManus: Dundee's Art Gallery & Museum, Dundee
East Bay Asian Local Development Corp (EBALDC), Asian Resource Gallery, Oakland CA
East Tennessee State University, The Reece Museum, Johnson City TN
Eastern Washington State Historical Society, Northwest Museum of Arts & Culture, Spokane WA
Edgecombe County Cultural Arts Council, Inc, Blount-Bridgers House, Hobson Pittman Memorial Gallery, Tarboro NC
Egan Institute of Maritime Studies, Nantucket MA
Elmhurst Art Museum, Elmhurst IL
Erie County Historical Society, Erie PA
Essex Historical Society and Shipbuilding Museum, Essex MA
Evanston Historical Society, Charles Gates Dawes House, Evanston IL
Fairbanks Museum & Planetarium, Saint Johnsbury VT
Favell Museum of Western Art & Indian Artifacts, Klamath Falls OR
Fetherston Foundation, Packwood House Museum, Lewisburg PA
Fishkill Historical Society, Van Wyck Homestead Museum, Fishkill NY
Fitton Center for Creative Arts, Hamilton OH
Florence Museum, Florence SC
Folk Art Society of America, Richmond VA
Fort George G Meade Museum, Fort Meade MD
Fort Morgan Heritage Foundation, Fort Morgan CO
Fort Ticonderoga Association, Ticonderoga NY
Frontier Gateway Museum, Glendive MT
Frontier Times Museum, Bandera TX
Fulton County Historical Society Inc, Fulton County Museum (Tetzlaff Reference Room), Rochester IN
Gadsden Museum of Fine Arts, Inc, Gadsden Museum of Art and History, Gadsden AL
Gem County Historical Society and Museum, Gem County Historical Village Museum, Emmett ID
General Board of Discipleship, The United Methodist Church, The Upper Room Chapel & Museum, Nashville TN
Genesee Country Village & Museum, John L Wehle Art Gallery, Mumford NY
George Washington University, The Dimock Gallery, Washington DC
Georgetown University, Art Collection, Washington DC
Germanisches Nationalmuseum, Nuremberg
Germantown Historical Society, Philadelphia PA
Girard College, Stephen Girard Collection, Philadelphia PA
Glanmore National Historic Site of Canada, Belleville ON
Glasmuseet Ebeltoft, Ebeltoft
Glenbow Museum, Calgary AB
Glessner House Museum, Chicago IL
Gloridale Partnership, National Museum of Woodcarving, Custer SD
Gocseji Muzeum, Zalaegerszeg
Goshen Historical Society, Goshen CT
Grand Rapids Public Museum, Public Museum of Grand Rapids, Grand Rapids MI
Grand River Museum, Lemmon SD
Great Lakes Historical Society, Inland Seas Maritime Museum, Vermilion OH
Greene County Historical Society, Bronck Museum, Coxsackie NY
Gunston Hall Plantation, Mason Neck VA

Muzeul de Istorie Nationala Si Arheologie Constanta, National History & Archaeology Museum, Constanta

Muzeul National Brukenthal, Brukenthal Palace & European Art Gallery, Sibiu

Nanticoke Indian Museum, Millsboro DE

Napoleonic Society of America, Museum & Library, Saint Helena CA

Nara Kokuritsu Hakubutsu-Kan, Nara National Museum, Nara

Narodni Muzej Crne Gore, National Museum of Montenegro, Cetinje

Nathan Hale Homestead Museum, Coventry CT

National Archives & Records Administration, John F Kennedy Presidential Library & Museum, Boston MA

National Archives & Records Administration, Franklin D Roosevelt Museum, Hyde Park NY

National Baseball Hall of Fame & Museum, Inc, Art Collection, Cooperstown NY

National Gallery of Ireland, Dublin

National Heritage Museum, Lexington MA

National Museum of American Illustration, Newport RI

National Museum of the American Indian, George Gustav Heye Center, New York NY

National Museum of Wildlife Art of the Unites States, Jackson WY

National Park Service, Weir Farm National Historic Site, Wilton CT

The National Park Service, United States Department of the Interior, Statue of Liberty National Monument & The Ellis Island Immigration Museum, Washington DC

National Portrait Gallery, Smithsonian Institution, Washington DC

The National Shrine of the North American Martyrs, Fultonville NY

National Silk Art Museum, Weston MO

National Society of Colonial Dames of America in the State of Maryland, Mount Clare Museum House, Baltimore MD

Navajo Nation, Navajo Nation Museum, Window Rock AZ

Naval War College Museum, Newport RI

Nebraska Game and Parks Commission, Arbor Lodge State Historical Park & Morton Mansion, Nebraska City NE

Nebraska State Capitol, Lincoln NE

Neustadt Collection of Tiffany Glass, Long Island City NY

Nevada Northern Railway Museum, Ely NV

New Brunswick Museum, Saint John NB

New Canaan Historical Society, New Canaan CT

New England Maple Museum, Pittsford VT

The New England Museum of Telephony, Inc., The Telephone Museum, Ellsworth ME

New Hampshire Antiquarian Society, Hopkinton Historical Society, Hopkinton NH

New Jersey Historical Society, Newark NJ

New Jersey State Museum, Fine Art Bureau, Trenton NJ

New York State Office of Parks Recreation & Historic Preservation, John Jay Homestead State Historic Site, Katonah NY

Newburyport Maritime Society, Inc, Custom House Maritime Museum, Newburyport MA

Elisabet Ney, Austin TX

No Man's Land Historical Society, No Man's Land Museum, Goodwell OK

The Noble Maritime Collection, Staten Island NY

Norfolk Historical Society Inc, Museum, Norfolk CT

Norsk Sjøfartsmuseum, Norwegian Maritime Museum, Oslo

North Central Washington Museum, Wenatchee Valley Museum & Cultural Center, Wenatchee WA

Northeastern Nevada Museum, Elko NV

Norwich Free Academy, Slater Memorial Museum, Norwich CT

Ogden Union Station, Union Station Museums, Ogden UT

Ohio Historical Society, National Afro-American Museum & Cultural Center, Wilberforce OH

The Ohio Historical Society, Inc, Campus Martius Museum & Ohio River Museum, Marietta OH

Ohio University, Kennedy Museum of Art, Athens OH

Okefenokee Heritage Center, Inc, Waycross GA

Oklahoma Historical Society, State Museum of History, Oklahoma City OK

Old Barracks Museum, Trenton NJ

Old Dartmouth Historical Society, New Bedford Whaling Museum, New Bedford MA

The Old Jail Art Center, Albany TX

Old Salem Museums & Gardens, Museum of Early Southern Decorative Arts, Winston Salem NC

Opelousas Museum of Art, Inc (OMA), Opelousas LA

Osborne Homestead Museum, Derby CT

Oshkosh Public Museum, Oshkosh WI

Owen Sound Historical Society, Marine & Rail Heritage Museum, Owen Sound ON

Oysterponds Historical Society, Museum, Orient NY

Page-Walker Arts & History Center, Cary NC

Panhandle-Plains Historical Museum, Canyon TX

Pasadena Museum of History, Pasadena CA

Passaic County Historical Society, Lambert Castle Museum & Library, Paterson NJ

Pennsylvania Historical & Museum Commission, Railroad Museum of Pennsylvania, Harrisburg PA

Pennsylvania Historical & Museum Commission, The State Museum of Pennsylvania, Harrisburg PA

The Pennsylvania State University, Palmer Museum of Art, University Park PA

Penobscot Marine Museum, Searsport ME

Phelps County Historical Society, Nebraska Prairie Museum, Holdrege NE

Philadelphia History Museum, Philadelphia PA

Philbrook Museum of Art, Tulsa OK

Philipse Manor Hall State Historic Site, Yonkers NY

The Frank Phillips, Woolaroc Museum, Bartlesville OK

George Phippen, Phippen Museum - Art of the American West, Prescott AZ

Photographic Resource Center at Boston University, Boston MA

Pine Bluff/Jefferson County Historical Museum, Pine Bluff AR

Pioneer Historical Museum of South Dakota, Hot Springs SD

Plainsman Museum, Aurora NE

Plumas County Museum, Quincy CA

Polish Museum of America, Chicago IL

Pope County Historical Society, Pope County Museum, Glenwood MN

Porter-Phelps-Huntington Foundation, Inc, Historic House Museum, Hadley MA

Portsmouth Athenaeum, Joseph Copley Research Library, Portsmouth NH

Portsmouth Historical Society, John Paul Jones House & Discover Portsmouth, Portsmouth NH

Prairie Art Gallery, Grande Prairie AB

Putnam County Historical Society, Foundry School Museum, Cold Spring NY

Putnam Museum of History and Natural Science, Davenport IA

Queens College, City University of New York, Godwin-Ternbach Museum, Flushing NY

Rangeley Lakes Region Logging Museum, Rangeley ME

Red River Valley Museum, Vernon TX

RedMill Museum Village, Clinton NJ

Riley County Historical Society & Museum, Riley County Historical Museum, Manhattan KS

Ringwood Manor House Museum, Ringwood NJ

Roberson Museum & Science Center, Binghamton NY

Rosenborg Slot, The Danish Royal Collections, Copenhagen

Roswell Museum & Art Center, Roswell NM

Royal Arts Foundation, Belcourt Castle, Newport RI

Royal Ontario Museum, Toronto ON

C M Russell, Great Falls MT

Safety Harbor Museum of Regional History, Safety Harbor FL

Saginaw Art Museum, Saginaw MI

Saint Augustine Historical Society, Oldest House Museum Complex, Saint Augustine FL

Saint Louis County Historical Society, St. Louis County Historical Society, Duluth MN

St Mary Landmarks, Grevemberg House Museum, Franklin LA

Saint Mary's College of California, Hearst Art Gallery, Moraga CA

Salisbury House Foundation, Salisbury House and Garden, Des Moines IA

San Bernardino County Museum, Fine Arts Institute, Redlands CA

San Francisco Maritime National Historical Park, Maritime Museum, San Francisco CA

The Sandwich Historical Society, Inc & Sandwich Glass Museum, Sandwich Glass Museum, Sandwich MA

Schuyler Mansion State Historic Site, Albany NY

Sea Cliff Village Museum, Sea Cliff NY

Seattle Art Museum, Seattle Asian Art Museum, Seattle WA

Seneca Falls Historical Society Museum, Seneca Falls NY

Seneca-Iroquois National Museum, Salamanca NY

Shaker Museum & Library, Old Chatham NY

Shaker Village of Pleasant Hill, Harrodsburg KY

Shephela Museum, Post Kefar-Menahem

Ships of the Sea Maritime Museum, Savannah GA

Shirley Plantation Foundation, Charles City VA

Shoreline Historical Museum, Shoreline WA

Shores Memorial Museum, Lyndon Center VT

Shoshone Bannock Tribes, Shoshone Bannock Tribal Museum, Fort Hall ID

R L S Silverado Museum, Saint Helena CA

Sitka Historical Society, Sitka Historical Museum, Sitka AK

The Society of the Cincinnati at Anderson House, Washington DC

South Dakota State University, South Dakota Art Museum, Brookings SD

South Street Seaport Museum, New York NY

Southern Illinois University Carbondale, University Museum, Carbondale IL

Southern Lorain County Historical Society, Spirit of '76 Museum, Elyria OH

Southern Ohio Museum Corporation, Southern Ohio Museum, Portsmouth OH

Spertus Institute of Jewish Studies, Chicago IL

Springfield Museums, Connecticut Valley Historical Society, Springfield MA

St George Art Museum, Saint George UT

Stanford University, Cantor Arts Center at Stanford University, Stanford CA

State of North Carolina, Battleship North Carolina, Wilmington NC

State University of New York College at Buffalo, Buffalo NY

State University of New York College at Cortland, Dowd Fine Arts Gallery, Cortland NY

Staten Island Museum, Staten Island NY

Ste Genevieve Museum, Sainte Genevieve MO

Stedelijk Museum Alkmaar, Alkmaar Municipal Museum, Alkmaar

T C Steele, Nashville IN

The Stewart Museum, Montreal PQ

Stiftung Deutsches Historisches Museum, Berlin

Stone Quarry Hill Art Park, Winner Gallery, Cazenovia NY

Sturdivant Museum Association, Sturdivant Museum, Selma AL

The Summit County Historical Society of Akron, OH, Akron OH

Suomen Kansallismuseo, National Museum of Finland, Helsinki

Supreme Court of the United States, Office of the Curator, Washington DC

Susquehanna University, Lore Degenstein Gallery, Selinsgrove PA

Swedish American Museum Association of Chicago, Chicago IL

Switzerland County Historical Society Inc, Switzerland County Historical Museum, Vevay IN

Tallahassee Museum of History & Natural Science, Tallahassee FL

Taos, Ernest Blumenschein Home & Studio, Taos NM

Taos, La Hacienda de Los Martinez, Taos NM

The Temple-Tifereth Israel, The Temple Museum of Religious Art, Beachwood OH

Tennessee State Museum, Nashville TN

Texas Tech University, Museum of Texas Tech University, Lubbock TX

Three Forks Area Historical Society, Headwaters Heritage Museum, Three Forks MT

Towson University, Center for the Arts Gallery, Towson MD

Transylvania University, Morlan Gallery, Lexington KY

Trust Authority, Museum of the Great Plains, Lawton OK

Tryon Palace Historic Sites & Gardens, New Bern NC

Tubac Center of the Arts, Santa Cruz Valley Art Association, Tubac AZ

Tulane University, University Art Collection, New Orleans LA

Turtle Bay Exploration Park, Redding CA

Turtle Mountain Chippewa Historical Society, Turtle Mountain Heritage Center, Belcourt ND

Tver Art Gallery, Tver

Mark Twain, State Historic Site Museum, Florida MO

Tyne and Wear Archives & Museums, Sunderland Museum & Winter Gardens, Newcastle-upon-Tyne

Ukrainian Canadian Archives & Museum of Alberta, Edmonton AB

The Ukrainian Museum, New York NY

United Society of Shakers, Shaker Museum, New Gloucester ME

HISTORY OF ART & ARCHAEOLOGY

ILLUSTRATION

INTERIOR DESIGN

INTERMEDIA

ISLAMIC ART

Loyola University Chicago, Loyola University Museum of Art, Chicago IL

Mingei International, Inc, Mingei International Museum - Balboa Park & Mingei International Museum - Escondido, San Diego CA

Ministry of Cultural Affairs, Bangladesh National Museum, Dhaka

Mobile Museum of Art, Mobile AL

The Morgan Library & Museum, Museum, New York NY

Musee des Beaux-Arts/Palais des Archeveques, Museum of Fine Arts, Tours

Musee Royal Et Domaine De Mariemont, Morlanwelz

Musees Royaux d'Art et d'Histoire, Royal Museums of Art and History, Brussels

Museo Cerralbo, Madrid

Museo de Navarra, Pamplona

Museo di Capodimonte, Naples

Museu de Evora, Evora

Museum fur Angewandte Kunst Frankfurt, Museum of Applied Arts, Frankfurt

Museum fur Kunst und Gewerbe Hamburg, Hamburg

Museum of Fine Arts, Houston, Houston TX

Muzeul de Istorie Nationala Si Arheologie Constanta, National History & Archaeology Museum, Constanta

Muzeul National Brukenthal, Blue House & Romanian Art Gallery, Sibiu

Muzeul National Brukenthal, Brukenthal Palace & European Art Gallery, Sibiu

National Museum of the Philippines, Manila

National Museums Scotland, National Museum of Scotland, Edinburgh

Norwich Free Academy, Slater Memorial Museum, Norwich CT

Panhandle-Plains Historical Museum, Canyon TX

Princeton University, Princeton University Art Museum, Princeton NJ

Queens College, City University of New York, Godwin-Ternbach Museum, Flushing NY

Reading Public Museum, Reading PA

Stanford University, Cantor Arts Center at Stanford University, Stanford CA

The State Museum of Fine Arts of Tatarstan Republic, Kazan

The State Museum of Oriental Art, Moscow

State University of New York at New Paltz, Samuel Dorsky Museum of Art, New Paltz NY

Stone Quarry Hill Art Park, Winner Gallery, Cazenovia NY

Suomen Kansallismuseo, National Museum of Finland, Helsinki

Tver Art Gallery, Tver

University of California, Los Angeles, Fowler Museum at UCLA, Los Angeles CA

University of Chicago, Oriental Institute, Chicago IL

University of Illinois at Urbana-Champaign, Krannert Art Museum and Kinkead Pavilion, Champaign IL

University of Missouri, Museum of Art & Archaeology, Columbia MO

University of North Carolina at Chapel Hill, Ackland Art Museum, Chapel Hill NC

University of Pennsylvania, Museum of Archaeology & Anthropology, Philadelphia PA

University of Victoria, The Legacy Art Gallery, Victoria BC

University of Wisconsin-Madison, Chazen Museum of Art, Madison WI

Virginia Museum of Fine Arts, Richmond VA

Williams College, Museum of Art, Williamstown MA

IVORY

Academy of the New Church, Glencairn Museum, Bryn Athyn PA

African Art Museum of Maryland, Columbia MD

Alaska Department of Education, Division of Libraries, Archives & Museums, Sheldon Jackson Museum, Sitka AK

Alaska Heritage Museum at Wells Fargo, Anchorage AK

Albany Institute of History & Art, Albany NY

Anchorage Museum at Rasmuson Center, Anchorage AK

Archaeological Museum of the American University of Beirut, Beirut

Art & Culture Center of Hollywood, Art Gallery/Multidisciplinary Cultural Center, Hollywood FL

The Art Museum at the University of Kentucky, Lexington KY

Art Without Walls Inc, New York NY

Asian Art Museum of San Francisco, Chong-Moon Lee Ctr for Asian Art and Culture, San Francisco CA

Badisches Landesmuseum, Karlsruhe

Baroda Museum and Picture Gallery, Baroda

Bayerisches Nationalmuseum, Bavarian National Museum, Munich

Beloit College, Wright Museum of Art, Beloit WI

Blauvelt Demarest Foundation, Hiram Blauvelt Art Museum, Oradell NJ

Brown University, Haffenreffer Museum of Anthropology, Providence RI

Canadian Museum of Civilization, Gatineau PQ

Caramoor Center for Music & the Arts, Inc, Rosen House at Caramoor, Katonah NY

Billie Trimble Chandler, Texas State Museum of Asian Cultures, Corpus Christi TX

Chatham Historical Society, The Atwood House Museum, Chatham MA

Chhatrapati Shivaji Maharaj Vastu Sangrahalaya, Mumbai

City of Nome Alaska, Carrie M McLain Memorial Museum, Nome AK

Columbus Museum, Columbus GA

Cummer Museum of Art & Gardens, Museum & Library, Jacksonville FL

Department of Antiquities, Cyprus Museum, Nicosia

Detroit Institute of Arts, Detroit MI

Elmhurst Art Museum, Elmhurst IL

Fairbanks Museum & Planetarium, Saint Johnsbury VT

Fetherston Foundation, Packwood House Museum, Lewisburg PA

Fine Arts Museums of San Francisco, Legion of Honor, San Francisco CA

Flint Institute of Arts, Flint MI

Florence Museum, Florence SC

Florida State University and Central Florida Community College, The Appleton Museum of Art, Ocala FL

Forest Lawn Museum, Glendale CA

Galleria Nazionale dell'Umbria, Umbrian National Gallery, Perugia

Germanisches Nationalmuseum, Nuremberg

Glanmore National Historic Site of Canada, Belleville ON

Grand Rapids Public Museum, Public Museum of Grand Rapids, Grand Rapids MI

Greek Ministry of Culture, Archaeological Museum of Thessaloniki, Thessaloniki

Harvard University, Museum & Garden, Washington DC

Headley-Whitney Museum, Lexington KY

Hecht Museum, Haifa

Hillwood Museum & Gardens Foundation, Hillwood Estate Museum & Gardens, Washington DC

The Hispanic Society of America, Museum & Library, New York NY

Illinois State Museum, ISM Lockport Gallery, Chicago Gallery & Southern Illinois Art Gallery, Springfield IL

Independent Administrative Institution National Institutes for Cultural Heritage, Tokyo National Museum, Tokyo

The Israel Museum, Jerusalem, Billy Rose Art Garden, Jerusalem

The Israel Museum, Jerusalem, Samuel & Saidye Bronfman Archaeology Wing, Jerusalem

Jacksonville University, Alexander Brest Museum & Gallery, Jacksonville FL

Bob Jones University Museum & Gallery Inc, Greenville SC

Joslyn Art Museum, Omaha NE

Kenosha Public Museums, Kenosha WI

Kereszteny Muzeum, Christian Museum, Esztergom

Kings County Historical Society & Museum, Hampton NB

Knights of Columbus Supreme Council, Knights of Columbus Museum, New Haven CT

Koshare Indian Museum, Inc, La Junta CO

Kunsthistorisches Museum Vienna, Museum of Fine Arts, Vienna

Leeds Museums & Galleries, Leeds

Lightner Museum, Saint Augustine FL

Lizzadro Museum of Lapidary Art, Elmhurst IL

Loyola University Chicago, Loyola University Museum of Art, Chicago IL

Mabee-Gerrer Museum of Art, Shawnee OK

Manitoba Historical Society, Dalnavert Museum, Winnipeg MB

The Mariners' Museum, Newport News VA

Milwaukee County War Memorial Inc., Villa Terrace Decorative Arts Museum, Milwaukee WI

Mingei International, Inc, Mingei International Museum - Balboa Park & Mingei International Museum - Escondido, San Diego CA

Ministry of Cultural Affairs, Bangladesh National Museum, Dhaka

Ministry of Culture & Tourism, The Delphi Museum, 10th Ephorate of Prehistoric & Classical Antiquities, Delphi

Musee des Beaux-Arts d'Orleans, Museum of Fine Arts, Orleans

Musee des Beaux-Arts/Palais des Archeveques, Museum of Fine Arts, Tours

Musee Guimet, Paris

Musee Royal Et Domaine De Mariemont, Morlanwelz

Museen der Stadt Koln, Museum Schnutgen, Cologne

Musees Royaux d'Art et d'Histoire, Royal Museums of Art and History, Brussels

Musei Civici di Padova - Cappella Degli Scrovengni, Musei Civici Agli Eremitani (Civic Museum) - Scrovegni Chapel, Padua

Museo Cerralbo, Madrid

Museo de Navarra, Pamplona

Museo di Capodimonte, Naples

The Museum, Greenwood SC

Museum fur Kunst und Gewerbe Hamburg, Hamburg

The Museum of Arts & Sciences Inc, Daytona Beach FL

Museum of Vancouver, Vancouver BC

Museum zu Allerheiligen, Schaffhausen

Muzej za Umjetnost i Obrt, Museum of Arts & Crafts, Zagreb

The Namur Provincial Museum of Ancient Arts, Namur

National Archaeological Museum, Athens

National Museum of Fine Arts of Moldova, Chisinau

National Museum of the Philippines, Manila

National Museums Scotland, National Museum of Scotland, Edinburgh

National Palace Museum, Taiwan, R.O.C.

National Society of Colonial Dames of America in the State of Maryland, Mount Clare Museum House, Baltimore MD

Naval Historical Center, The Navy Museum, Washington DC

The Nelson-Atkins Museum of Art, Kansas City MO

New Jersey State Museum, Fine Art Bureau, Trenton NJ

Norwich Free Academy, Slater Memorial Museum, Norwich CT

Old Dartmouth Historical Society, New Bedford Whaling Museum, New Bedford MA

Omniplex Science Museum, Oklahoma City OK

Pacific - Asia Museum, Pasadena CA

Panhandle-Plains Historical Museum, Canyon TX

Princeton University, Princeton University Art Museum, Princeton NJ

Queens College, City University of New York, Godwin-Ternbach Museum, Flushing NY

Rabindra Bhavan Art Gallery, Lalit Kala Akademi (National Academy of Art), New Delhi

Rahr-West Art Museum, Manitowoc WI

Reading Public Museum, Reading PA

Rijksmuseum Twenthe, Rijksmuseum Twenthe, Enschede

Ryerss Victorian Museum & Library, Philadelphia PA

Saint Bonaventure University, Regina A Quick Center for the Arts, Saint Bonaventure NY

Saint John's University, Dr. M.T. Geoffrey Yeh Art Gallery, Queens NY

Saint Joseph's Oratory, Museum, Montreal PQ

San Francisco Maritime National Historical Park, Maritime Museum, San Francisco CA

Santa Clara University, de Saisset Museum, Santa Clara CA

Sheldon Museum & Cultural Center, Inc, Sheldon Museum & Cultural Center, Haines AK

The Society of the Cincinnati at Anderson House, Washington DC

Soprintendenza per I beni storici artistici ed etnoantropologici per le province di Mantova Brescia e Cremona, Museo di Palazzo Ducale, Mantua

The Speed Art Museum, Louisville KY

State University of New York at Binghamton, Binghamton University Art Museum, Binghamton NY

Staten Island Museum, Staten Island NY

Stauth Foundation & Museum, Stauth Memorial Museum, Montezuma KS

Suan Pakkad Palace Museum, Bangkok

Suomen Kansallismuseo, National Museum of Finland, Helsinki

Taft Museum of Art, Cincinnati OH

JADE

JEWELRY

Fetherston Foundation, Packwood House Museum, Lewisburg PA

Fine Arts Center for the New River Valley, Pulaski VA

Fishkill Historical Society, Van Wyck Homestead Museum, Fishkill NY

Fitton Center for Creative Arts, Hamilton OH

Florence Museum, Florence SC

Forest Lawn Museum, Glendale CA

Fuller Craft Museum, Brockton MA

Fulton County Historical Society Inc, Fulton County Museum (Tetzlaff Reference Room), Rochester IN

Gala-Salvador Dali Foundation Museums, Salvador Dali Foundation, Figueres

Galleria Nazionale dell'Umbria, Umbrian National Gallery, Perugia

Gallery One Visual Arts Center, Ellensburg WA

Glanmore National Historic Site of Canada, Belleville ON

Greek Ministry of Culture, Archaeological Museum of Thessaloniki, Thessaloniki

Hancock County Trustees of Public Reservations, Woodlawn: Museum, Gardens & Park, Ellsworth ME

Harvard University, Museum & Garden, Washington DC

Hawkes Bay Art Gallery and Museum, Napier

Haystack Mountain School of Crafts, Deer Isle ME

Headley-Whitney Museum, Lexington KY

Heard Museum, Phoenix AZ

Hebrew Union College, Skirball Cultural Center, Los Angeles CA

Hecht Museum, Haifa

Henry County Museum & Cultural Arts Center, Clinton MO

Heritage Center, Inc, Pine Ridge SD

Edna Hibel, Hibel Museum of Art, Jupiter FL

Hillwood Museum & Gardens Foundation, Hillwood Estate Museum & Gardens, Washington DC

The Hispanic Society of America, Museum & Library, New York NY

Holter Museum of Art, Helena MT

Hoyt Center for the Arts, New Castle PA

Hui No'eau Visual Arts Center, Gallery and Gift Shop, Makawao Maui HI

Imperial Calcasieu Museum, Gibson-Barham Gallery, Lake Charles LA

Independent Administrative Institution National Institutes for Cultural Heritage, Tokyo National Museum, Tokyo

Independent Administrative Institution National Museum of Art, The National Museum of Western Art, Tokyo

Institute of American Indian Arts, Museum of Contemporary Native Arts, Santa Fe NM

The Interchurch Center, Galleries at the Interchurch Center, New York NY

Iroquois Indian Museum, Howes Cave NY

The Israel Museum, Jerusalem, Billy Rose Art Garden, Jerusalem

The Israel Museum, Jerusalem, Samuel & Saidye Bronfman Archaeology Wing, Jerusalem

The Israel Museum, Jerusalem, Jerusalem

James Dick Foundation, Festival - Institute, Round Top TX

Kelly-Griggs House Museum, Red Bluff CA

Kenosha Public Museums, Kenosha WI

Kentucky Museum of Art and Craft, Louisville KY

Kereszteny Muzeum, Christian Museum, Esztergom

Keystone Gallery, Scott City KS

Kings County Historical Society & Museum, Hampton NB

Koochiching Museums, International Falls MN

Koshare Indian Museum, Inc, La Junta CO

Kunsthistorisches Museum Vienna, Museum of Fine Arts, Vienna

La Raza-Galeria Posada, Sacramento CA

Lac du Flambeau Band of Lake Superior Chippewa Indians, George W Brown Jr Ojibwe Museum & Cultural Center, Lac Du Flambeau WI

Latino Art Museum, Pomona CA

League of New Hampshire Craftsmen, Grodin Permanent Collection Museum, Concord NH

Leeds Museums & Galleries, Leeds

The Long Island Museum of American Art, History & Carriages, Stony Brook NY

Louisiana Department of Culture, Recreation & Tourism, Louisiana State Museum, New Orleans LA

Loveland Museum/Gallery, Loveland CO

Magyar Nemzeti Muzeum - Hungarian National Museum, Budapest

Manchester Bidwell Corporation, Manchester Craftsmen's Guild Youth & Arts Program, Pittsburgh PA

Manitoba Historical Society, Dalnavert Museum, Winnipeg MB

Marblehead Museum & Historical Society, Jeremiah Lee Mansion, Marblehead MA

Marblehead Museum & Historical Society, Marblehead MA

Maude Kerns Art Center, Eugene OR

Maysville, Kentucky Gateway Museum Center, Maysville KY

McCord Museum of Canadian History, Montreal PQ

McDowell House & Apothecary Shop, Danville KY

McLean County Historical Society, McLean County Museum of History, Bloomington IL

Meredith College, Frankie G Weems Gallery & Rotunda Gallery, Raleigh NC

Mesa Arts Center, Mesa Contemporary Arts Museum, Mesa AZ

Mexican Museum, San Francisco CA

Mezuraj Museum, Tirana

Mingei International, Inc, Mingei International Museum - Balboa Park & Mingei International Museum - Escondido, San Diego CA

Ministry of Alberta Culture, Royal Alberta Museum, Edmonton AB

Ministry of Cultural Affairs, Bangladesh National Museum, Dhaka

Ministry of Culture & Tourism, The Delphi Museum, 10th Ephorate of Prehistoric & Classical Antiquities, Delphi

The Mint Museum, Mint Museum of Craft & Design, Charlotte NC

Mississippi River Museum at Mud-Island River Park, Memphis TN

Missoula Art Museum, Missoula MT

Arthur Roy Mitchell, A.R. Mitchell Museum, Trinidad CO

Mobile Museum of Art, Mobile AL

James Monroe, Fredericksburg VA

Moravska Galerie v Brne, Moravian Gallery in Brno, Brno

Musee Cognacq-Jay, Cognacq-Jay Museum, Paris

Musee des Beaux-Arts/Palais des Archeveques, Museum of Fine Arts, Tours

Musee Guimet, Paris

Musee Royal Et Domaine De Mariemont, Morlanwelz

Museen der Stadt Koln, Romisch-Germanisches Museum, Cologne

Musees Royaux d'Art et d'Histoire, Royal Museums of Art and History, Brussels

Musei Civici di Padova - Cappella Degli Scrovegni, Musei Civici Agli Eremitani (Civic Museum) - Scrovegni Chapel, Padua

Museo Cerralbo, Madrid

Museo De Las Americas, Denver CO

Museo Del Romanticismo, Museum of the Romantic Period, Madrid

Museu de Evora, Evora

Museu Nacional D'Art De Catalunya, National Art Museum, Barcelona

Museum fur Angewandte Kunst Frankfurt, Museum of Applied Arts, Frankfurt

Museum fur Kunst und Gewerbe Hamburg, Hamburg

Museum of Arts & Design, New York NY

The Museum of Arts & Sciences Inc, Daytona Beach FL

Museum of Contemporary Art, North Miami FL

Museum of Contemporary Craft, Portland OR

Museum of Decorative Arts in Prague, Prague

Museum of Fine Arts Houston, Bayou Bend Collection & Gardens, Houston TX

Museum of Florida Art, Deland FL

Museum of Northern Arizona, Flagstaff AZ

Museum of Northern British Columbia, Ruth Harvey Art Gallery, Prince Rupert BC

Museum of Northwest Art, La Conner WA

Museum of Southern History, Houston TX

Museum of the City of New York, Museum, New York NY

Museum of Vancouver, Vancouver BC

Museum zu Allerheiligen, Schaffhausen

Muzej za Umjetnost i Obrt, Museum of Arts & Crafts, Zagreb

Muzeul de Istorie Nationala Si Arheologie Constanta, National History & Archaeology Museum, Constanta

Muzeul National Brukenthal, Brukenthal Palace & European Art Gallery, Sibiu

Muzeum Narodowe, National Museum in Poznan, Poznan

National Archaeological Museum, Athens

National Baseball Hall of Fame & Museum, Inc, Art Collection, Cooperstown NY

National Museum of the American Indian, Smithsonian Institution, Washington DC

National Museum of Women in the Arts, Washington DC

National Museums Scotland, National Museum of Scotland, Edinburgh

National Palace Museum, Taiwan, R.O.C.

National Society of Colonial Dames of America in the State of Maryland, Mount Clare Museum House, Baltimore MD

Navajo Nation, Navajo Nation Museum, Window Rock AZ

Nebraska Game and Parks Commission, Arbor Lodge State Historical Park & Morton Mansion, Nebraska City NE

Nelson Mandela Bay Municipality, Nelson Mandela Metropolitan Art Museum, Port Elizabeth

The Nelson-Atkins Museum of Art, Kansas City MO

New Brunswick Museum, Saint John NB

North Carolina State University, Gregg Museum of Art & Design, Raleigh NC

Norwich Free Academy, Slater Memorial Museum, Norwich CT

Nova Scotia College of Art and Design, Anna Leonowens Gallery, Halifax NS

The Ohio Historical Society, Inc, Campus Martius Museum & Ohio River Museum, Marietta OH

Ohio University, Kennedy Museum of Art, Athens OH

Okanagan Heritage Museum, Kelowna BC

Page-Walker Arts & History Center, Cary NC

Panhandle-Plains Historical Museum, Canyon TX

Plainsman Museum, Aurora NE

Port Huron Museum, Port Huron MI

Porter-Phelps-Huntington Foundation, Inc, Historic House Museum, Hadley MA

Princeton University, Princeton University Art Museum, Princeton NJ

Queens College, City University of New York, Godwin-Ternbach Museum, Flushing NY

Randall Junior Museum, San Francisco CA

Reading Public Museum, Reading PA

The Rooms Corporation of Newfoundland & Labrador, Saint John's NF

Royal Arts Foundation, Belcourt Castle, Newport RI

Ryerss Victorian Museum & Library, Philadelphia PA

Saint Peter's College, Art Gallery, Jersey City NJ

The Sandwich Historical Society, Inc & Sandwich Glass Museum, Sandwich Glass Museum, Sandwich MA

School for Advanced Research (SAR), Indian Arts Research Center, Santa Fe NM

Seneca-Iroquois National Museum, Salamanca NY

Shoshone Bannock Tribes, Shoshone Bannock Tribal Museum, Fort Hall ID

Slovenska Narodna Galeria, Slovak National Gallery, Bratislava

Society for Contemporary Craft, Pittsburgh PA

The Society of the Cincinnati at Anderson House, Washington DC

South Carolina Artisans Center, Walterboro SC

South Dakota State University, South Dakota Art Museum, Brookings SD

The Speed Art Museum, Louisville KY

Spertus Institute of Jewish Studies, Chicago IL

Stanford University, Cantor Arts Center at Stanford University, Stanford CA

State University of New York at Binghamton, Binghamton University Art Museum, Binghamton NY

State University of New York College at Buffalo, Buffalo NY

Staten Island Museum, Staten Island NY

Stauth Foundation & Museum, Stauth Memorial Museum, Montezuma KS

Ste Genevieve Museum, Sainte Genevieve MO

Suan Pakkad Palace Museum, Bangkok

Suomen Kansallismuseo, National Museum of Finland, Helsinki

Swedish American Museum Association of Chicago, Chicago IL

Tacoma Art Museum, Tacoma WA

Taft Museum of Art, Cincinnati OH

Lillian & Coleman Taube Museum of Art, Minot ND

Tohono Chul Park, Tucson AZ

Topeka & Shawnee County Public Library, Alice C Sabatini Gallery, Topeka KS

Tver Art Gallery, Tver

The Ukrainian Museum, New York NY

University of Chicago, Oriental Institute, Chicago IL

University of Georgia, Georgia Museum of Art, Athens GA
University of Illinois at Urbana-Champaign, Krannert Art Museum and Kinkead Pavilion, Champaign IL
University of Missouri, Museum of Art & Archaeology, Columbia MO
University of North Dakota, Hughes Fine Arts Center-Col Eugene Myers Art Gallery, Grand Forks ND
University of Pennsylvania, Museum of Archaeology & Anthropology, Philadelphia PA
University of Saskatchewan, Diefenbaker Canada Centre, Saskatoon SK
University of Utah, Utah Museum of Fine Arts, Salt Lake City UT
University of Victoria, The Legacy Art Gallery, Victoria BC
University of Wisconsin-Madison, Chazen Museum of Art, Madison WI
Valentine Richmond History Center, Richmond VA
Vancouver Public Library, Fine Arts & Music Department, Vancouver BC
Vassar College, The Frances Lehman Loeb Art Center, Poughkeepsie NY
Vesterheim Norwegian-American Museum, Decorah IA
Virginia Museum of Fine Arts, Richmond VA
Wadsworth Atheneum Museum of Art, Hartford CT
Wake Forest University, Museum of Anthropology, Winston Salem NC
The Walker African American Museum & Research Center, Las Vegas NV
Waterworks Visual Arts Center, Salisbury NC
Willard House & Clock Museum, Inc, North Grafton MA
Wiregrass Museum of Art, Dothan AL
Wisconsin Historical Society, Wisconsin Historical Museum, Madison WI
Woodlawn/The Pope-Leighey, Mount Vernon VA
World Erotic Art Museum, Miami Beach FL
Yuma Fine Arts Association, Yuma Art Center, Yuma AZ
Zacheta - National Gallery of Art, Kordegarda Gallery, Warsaw

JUDAICA

Arnot Art Museum, Elmira NY
Art & Culture Center of Hollywood, Art Gallery/Multidisciplinary Cultural Center, Hollywood FL
Art Without Walls Inc, New York NY
Arts Council of Fayetteville-Cumberland County, The Arts Center, Fayetteville NC
B'nai B'rith International, B'nai B'rith Klutznick National Jewish Museum, Washington DC
Barbara & Ray Alpert Jewish Community Center, Pauline & Zena Gatov Gallery, Long Beach CA
Baycrest Centre for Geriatric Care, The Morris & Sally Justein of Baycrest Heritage Museum, Toronto ON
Congregation Beth Israel's Plotkin Judaica Museum, Scottsdale AZ
Craft and Folk Art Museum (CAFAM), Los Angeles CA
Denver Art Museum, Denver CO
Detroit Institute of Arts, Detroit MI
Florence Museum, Florence SC
General Board of Discipleship, The United Methodist Church, The Upper Room Chapel & Museum, Nashville TN
Hebrew Union College, Skirball Cultural Center, Los Angeles CA
Hebrew Union College - Jewish Institute of Religion, Skirball Museum Cincinnati, Cincinnati OH
Hebrew Union College Museum, Jewish Institute of Religion Museum, New York NY
Hecht Museum, Haifa
Hillel Foundation, Hillel Jewish Student Center Gallery, Cincinnati OH
Hillwood Museum & Gardens Foundation, Hillwood Estate Museum & Gardens, Washington DC
The Hispanic Society of America, Museum & Library, New York NY
The Israel Museum, Jerusalem, Billy Rose Art Garden, Jerusalem
The Israel Museum, Jerusalem, Samuel & Saidye Bronfman Archaeology Wing, Jerusalem
The Israel Museum, Jerusalem, Jerusalem
The Jewish Museum, New York NY
Lightner Museum, Saint Augustine FL
Museo Cerralbo, Madrid
Museum fur Kunst und Gewerbe Hamburg, Hamburg

Muzej za Umjetnost i Obrt, Museum of Arts & Crafts, Zagreb
The National Park Service, United States Department of the Interior, Statue of Liberty National Monument & The Ellis Island Immigration Museum, Washington DC
New Brunswick Museum, Saint John NB
Norwich Free Academy, Slater Memorial Museum, Norwich CT
The Pennsylvania State University, Palmer Museum of Art, University Park PA
Reading Public Museum, Reading PA
The Rosenbach Museum & Library, Philadelphia PA
Sherwin Miller Museum of Jewish Art, Tulsa OK
Spertus Institute of Jewish Studies, Chicago IL
Stanford University, Cantor Arts Center at Stanford University, Stanford CA
Suomen Kansallismuseo, National Museum of Finland, Helsinki
The Temple-Tifereth Israel, The Temple Museum of Religious Art, Beachwood OH
Tver Art Gallery, Tver
University of California, Berkeley, The Magnes Collection of Jewish Art & Life, Berkeley CA
University of Illinois at Urbana-Champaign, Spurlock Museum, Champaign IL
Waterworks Visual Arts Center, Salisbury NC
World Erotic Art Museum, Miami Beach FL
Yeshiva University Museum, New York NY
Zidovske Muzeum, Jewish Museum, Prague

JUVENILE ART

Art Community Center, Art Center of Corpus Christi, Corpus Christi TX
Art Gallery of Calgary, Calgary AB
Art Without Walls Inc, New York NY
Arts Council of Fayetteville-Cumberland County, The Arts Center, Fayetteville NC
Canadian Museum of Civilization, Gatineau PQ
Cartoon Art Museum, San Francisco CA
Deines Cultural Center, Russell KS
Ellen Noel Art Museum of the Permian Basin, Odessa TX
Elmhurst Art Museum, Elmhurst IL
Erie Art Museum, Erie PA
Hebrew Union College, Skirball Cultural Center, Los Angeles CA
Hebrew Union College Museum, Jewish Institute of Religion Museum, New York NY
Higgins Armory Museum, Worcester MA
Iroquois Indian Museum, Howes Cave NY
Kenosha Public Museums, Kenosha WI
Kentucky Museum of Art and Craft, Louisville KY
LaGrange Art Museum, LaGrange GA
LeSueur County Historical Society, Chapter One, Elysian MN
The Long Island Museum of American Art, History & Carriages, Stony Brook NY
Manchester Bidwell Corporation, Manchester Craftsmen's Guild Youth & Arts Program, Pittsburgh PA
Meredith College, Frankie G Weems Gallery & Rotunda Gallery, Raleigh NC
Murray State University, Art Galleries, Murray KY
Musee Regional de lu Cote-Nord, Sept-Iles PQ
Museum of Florida Art, Deland FL
Museum of Northern Arizona, Flagstaff AZ
National Museum of Fine Arts of Moldova, Chisinau
New Visions Gallery, Inc, Marshfield WI
Opelousas Museum of Art, Inc (OMA), Opelousas LA
Owensboro Museum of Fine Art, Owensboro KY
Polk Museum of Art, Lakeland FL
School of Visual Arts, Visual Arts Museum, New York NY
South Carolina State Museum, Columbia SC
Southeastern Center for Contemporary Art, Winston Salem NC
Spartanburg Art Museum, Spartanburg SC
Lillian & Coleman Taube Museum of Art, Minot ND
Tohono Chul Park, Tucson AZ
University of Utah, Utah Museum of Fine Arts, Salt Lake City UT
The Walker African American Museum & Research Center, Las Vegas NV
Waterworks Visual Arts Center, Salisbury NC
Wiregrass Museum of Art, Dothan AL
Woodmere Art Museum Inc, Philadelphia PA
Yerba Buena Center for the Arts, San Francisco CA

LACES

Allentown Art Museum, Allentown PA
Art Gallery of South Australia, Adelaide
Art Without Walls Inc, New York NY
Artesia Historical Museum & Art Center, Artesia NM
Besser Museum for Northeast Michigan, Alpena MI
Brick Store Museum, Kennebunk ME
Brooklyn Historical Society, Brooklyn OH
Canadian Museum of Civilization, Gatineau PQ
Carson County Square House Museum, Panhandle TX
Clark County Historical Society, Pioneer - Krier Museum, Ashland KS
Cornwall Gallery Society, Cornwall Regional Art Gallery, Cornwall ON
Cripple Creek District Museum, Cripple Creek CO
Crook County Museum & Art Gallery, Sundance WY
Danville Museum of Fine Arts & History, Danville VA
Designmuseum Danmark, Copenhagen
Detroit Institute of Arts, Detroit MI
Doncaster Museum and Art Gallery, Doncaster
Evanston Historical Society, Charles Gates Dawes House, Evanston IL
Fine Arts Museums of San Francisco, Legion of Honor, San Francisco CA
Fishkill Historical Society, Van Wyck Homestead Museum, Fishkill NY
Flint Institute of Arts, Flint MI
Fuller Craft Museum, Brockton MA
Gem County Historical Society and Museum, Gem County Historical Village Museum, Emmett ID
Grand Rapids Public Museum, Public Museum of Grand Rapids, Grand Rapids MI
Halifax Historical Society, Inc, Halifax Historical Museum, Daytona Beach FL
Hebrew Union College, Skirball Cultural Center, Los Angeles CA
Henry Morrison Flagler Museum, Palm Beach FL
Heritage Museum Association, Inc, The Heritage Museum of Northwest Florida, Valparaiso FL
Hillwood Museum & Gardens Foundation, Hillwood Estate Museum & Gardens, Washington DC
The Hispanic Society of America, Museum & Library, New York NY
Historic Arkansas Museum, Little Rock AR
Illinois State Museum, ISM Lockport Gallery, Chicago Gallery & Southern Illinois Art Gallery, Springfield IL
Imperial Calcasieu Museum, Gibson-Barham Gallery, Lake Charles LA
Independent Administrative Institution National Institutes for Cultural Heritage, Tokyo National Museum, Tokyo
Indiana Landmarks, Morris-Butler House, Indianapolis IN
James Dick Foundation, Festival - Institute, Round Top TX
Kelly-Griggs House Museum, Red Bluff CA
Koochiching Museums, International Falls MN
Launceston City Council, Queen Victoria Museum and Art Gallery, Launceston
Leelanau Historical Museum, Leland MI
Lightner Museum, Saint Augustine FL
The Long Island Museum of American Art, History & Carriages, Stony Brook NY
Longfellow-Evangeline State Commemorative Area, Saint Martinville LA
Loveland Museum/Gallery, Loveland CO
Manitoba Historical Society, Dalnavert Museum, Winnipeg MB
Maysville, Kentucky Gateway Museum Center, Maysville KY
McCord Museum of Canadian History, Montreal PQ
McLean County Historical Society, McLean County Museum of History, Bloomington IL
Mississippi River Museum at Mud-Island River Park, Memphis TN
Moody County Historical Society, Moody County Museum, Pierre SD
Morris-Jumel Mansion, Inc, New York NY
Musea Brugge, Volkskunde Museum, Bruges
Musees Royaux d'Art et d'Histoire, Royal Museums of Art and History, Brussels
Museo Cerralbo, Madrid
The Museum, Greenwood SC
Museum of Arts & Design, New York NY
Muzej za Umjetnost i Obrt, Museum of Arts & Crafts, Zagreb
National Museum of Fine Arts of Moldova, Chisinau
National Society of Colonial Dames of America in the State of Maryland, Mount Clare Museum House, Baltimore MD
New Brunswick Museum, Saint John NB

North Carolina State University, Gregg Museum of Art & Design, Raleigh NC
Norwich Free Academy, Slater Memorial Museum, Norwich CT
Old Dartmouth Historical Society, New Bedford Whaling Museum, New Bedford MA
Plainsman Museum, Aurora NE
Portland Art Museum, Portland OR
Riley County Historical Society & Museum, Riley County Historical Museum, Manhattan KS
Saginaw Art Museum, Saginaw MI
Saint Louis County Historical Society, St. Louis County Historical Society, Duluth MN
Slater Mill, Old Slater Mill Association, Pawtucket RI
The Speed Art Museum, Louisville KY
The State Museum of Fine Arts of Tatarstan Republic, Kazan
Staten Island Museum, Staten Island NY
Ste Genevieve Museum, Sainte Genevieve MO
Suomen Kansallismuseo, National Museum of Finland, Helsinki
Syracuse University, Art Collection, Syracuse NY
Syracuse University, SUArt Galleries, Syracuse NY
Texas Tech University, Museum of Texas Tech University, Lubbock TX
Textile Museum of Canada, Toronto ON
Tohono Chul Park, Tucson AZ
Tver Art Gallery, Tver
University of California, Berkeley, The Magnes Collection of Jewish Art & Life, Berkeley CA
University of Georgia, Georgia Museum of Art, Athens GA
Valentine Richmond History Center, Richmond VA
Vesterheim Norwegian-American Museum, Decorah IA
Wadsworth Atheneum Museum of Art, Hartford CT
Washington County Museum of Fine Arts, Hagerstown MD
West Florida Historic Preservation, Inc/University of West Florida, T T Wentworth, Jr Florida State Museum; Historic Pensacola Village; Pensacola Historical Society & Resource Center, Pensacola FL
Wheaton College, Beard and Weil Galleries, Norton MA
Witte Museum, San Antonio TX
Woodmere Art Museum Inc, Philadelphia PA
Yarmouth County Historical Society, Yarmouth County Museum & Archives, Yarmouth NS

LANDSCAPE ARCHITECTURE

Crocker Art Museum, Sacramento CA
Establishment Public du Chateau du Rusee, Et du Dophine national de versailles, Versailles
Hancock County Trustees of Public Reservations, Woodlawn: Museum, Gardens & Park, Ellsworth ME
Patrick Henry, Red Hill National Memorial, Brookneal VA
J.M.W. Turner Museum, Sarasota FL
James Dick Foundation, Festival - Institute, Round Top TX
Johns Hopkins University, Evergreen Museum & Library, Baltimore MD
Jordan National Gallery of Fine Arts, Amman
Laumeier Sculpture Park, Saint Louis MO
Milwaukee County War Memorial Inc., Villa Terrace Decorative Arts Museum, Milwaukee WI
Morris Museum of Art, Augusta GA
Mount Saint Vincent University, MSVU Art Gallery, Halifax NS
Museu de Evora, Evora
Museum fur Kunst und Gewerbe Hamburg, Hamburg
Rabindra Bhavan Art Gallery, Lalit Kala Akademi (National Academy of Art), New Delhi
Rijksmuseum Twenthe, Rijksmuseum Twenthe, Enschede
St Mary's College of Maryland, The Dwight Frederick Boyden Gallery, St Mary's City MD
Saint Peter's College, Art Gallery, Jersey City NJ
Slovenska Narodna Galeria, Slovak National Gallery, Bratislava
Stone Quarry Hill Art Park, Winner Gallery, Cazenovia NY
Suomen rakennustaiteen museo, Museum of Finnish Architecture, Helsinki

LANDSCAPES

A.E. Backus Museum of Art, Fort Pierce FL
Academy Art Museum, Easton MD
Academy of the New Church, Glencairn Museum, Bryn Athyn PA

Albany Institute of History & Art, Albany NY
Albuquerque Museum of Art & History, Albuquerque NM
Allentown Art Museum, Allentown PA
Alton Museum of History & Art, Inc, Alton IL
American Art Museum, Smithsonian Institution, Washington DC
Amon Carter Museum of American Art, Fort Worth TX
Anchorage Museum at Rasmuson Center, Anchorage AK
Appaloosa Museum and Heritage Center, Moscow ID
Arnold Mikelson Mind & Matter Art Gallery, White Rock BC
Arnot Art Museum, Elmira NY
Art & Culture Center of Hollywood, Art Gallery/Multidisciplinary Cultural Center, Hollywood FL
Art Community Center, Art Center of Corpus Christi, Corpus Christi TX
Art Gallery of Calgary, Calgary AB
Art Gallery of Nova Scotia, Halifax NS
The Art Museum at the University of Kentucky, Lexington KY
Art Museum of Southeast Texas, Beaumont TX
Art Without Walls Inc, New York NY
Artesia Historical Museum & Art Center, Artesia NM
Arts Council of Fayetteville-Cumberland County, The Arts Center, Fayetteville NC
Asbury College, Student Center Gallery, Wilmore KY
Baroda Museum and Picture Gallery, Baroda
Baton Rouge Gallery, Center For Contemporary Art, Baton Rouge LA
Bay County Historical Society, Historical Museum of Bay County, Bay City MI
Bayerische Staatsgemaldesammlungen/Bavarian State Art Galleries, Alte Pinakothek, Munich
Bayerische Staatsgemaldesammlungen/Bavarian State Art Galleries, Neue Pinakothek, Munich
Belvedere Museum, Osterreichische Galerie Belvedere, Vienna
Berkshire Museum, Pittsfield MA
Besser Museum for Northeast Michigan, Alpena MI
Birmingham Museum of Art, Birmingham AL
Bone Creek Museum of Agrarian Art, David City NE
Booth Western Art Museum, Cartersville GA
Brandywine Conservancy, Brandywine River Museum, Chadds Ford PA
Brick Store Museum, Kennebunk ME
Brigham City Corporation, Brigham City Museum & Gallery, Brigham City UT
Brigham Young University, Museum of Art, Provo UT
Brooklyn Botanic Garden, Steinhardt Conservatory Gallery, Brooklyn NY
Bruce Museum, Inc, Greenwich CT
Bryan Memorial Gallery, Cambridge VT
Bucknell University, Edward & Marthann Samek Art Gallery, Lewisburg PA
Cahoon Museum of American Art, Cotuit MA
California Center for the Arts, Escondido Museum, Escondido CA
Calvin College, Center Art Gallery, Grand Rapids MI
Cambridge Museum, Cambridge NE
Cameron Art Museum, Wilmington NC
Canadian Museum of Civilization, Gatineau PQ
Canadian Museum of Contemporary Photography, Ottawa ON
Cape Ann Historical Association, Cape Ann Museum, Gloucester MA
Cedar Rapids Museum of Art, Cedar Rapids IA
Center for Art & Education, Van Buren AR
Central United Methodist Church, Swords Into Plowshares Peace Center & Gallery, Detroit MI
Centro de Arte Moderna, CAM - Calouste Gulbenkian Foundation, Lisbon
Chatham Historical Society, The Atwood House Museum, Chatham MA
Church of Jesus Christ of Latter-Day Saints, Museum of Church History & Art, Salt Lake City UT
Cincinnati Art Museum, Cincinnati Art Museum, Cincinnati OH
City of Brea, Art Gallery, Brea CA
City of Cedar Falls, Iowa, James & Meryl Hearst Center for the Arts & Sculpture Garden, Cedar Falls IA
City of Fayette, Alabama, Fayette Art Museum, Fayette AL
City of Gainesville, Thomas Center Galleries - Cultural Affairs, Gainesville FL
City of Mason City, Charles H MacNider Museum, Mason City IA
City of Nome Alaska, Carrie M McLain Memorial Museum, Nome AK

City of Pittsfield, Berkshire Artisans, Pittsfield MA
City of Port Angeles, Port Angeles Fine Arts Center & Webster Woods Art Park, Port Angeles WA
City of Toronto Culture, The Market Gallery, Toronto ON
Clark County Historical Society, Heritage Center of Clark County, Springfield OH
Sterling & Francine Clark, Williamstown MA
Colgate University, Picker Art Gallery, Hamilton NY
College of William & Mary, Muscarelle Museum of Art, Williamsburg VA
Columbus Museum, Columbus GA
Columbus Museum of Art, Columbus OH
Concordia University, Leonard & Bina Ellen Art Gallery, Montreal PQ
The Courtauld Institute of Art, The Courtauld Gallery, London
Coutts Museum of Art, Inc, El Dorado KS
Crocker Art Museum, Sacramento CA
Cummer Museum of Art & Gardens, Museum & Library, Jacksonville FL
The Currier Museum of Art, Manchester NH
Dahesh Museum of Art, Greenwich CT
Dartmouth College, Hood Museum of Art, Hanover NH
Daum Museum of Contemporary Art, Sedalia MO
Deines Cultural Center, Russell KS
Delaware Art Museum, Wilmington DE
Delaware Historical Society, Read House and Gardens, Wilmington DE
DeLeon White Gallery, Toronto ON
Denver Art Museum, Denver CO
Detroit Institute of Arts, Detroit MI
Dickinson College, The Trout Gallery, Carlisle PA
Dixie State College, Robert N & Peggy Sears Gallery, Saint George UT
Doncaster Museum and Art Gallery, Doncaster
Dundee City Council Leisure & Communities Department, The McManus: Dundee's Art Gallery & Museum, Dundee
Durham Art Guild, Durham NC
Eastern Illinois University, Tarble Arts Center, Charleston IL
George Eastman, Rochester NY
Egan Institute of Maritime Studies, Nantucket MA
Eiteljorg Museum of American Indians & Western Art, Indianapolis IN
Ellen Noel Art Museum of the Permian Basin, Odessa TX
Environment Canada - Parks Canada, Laurier House, National Historic Site, Ottawa ON
Erie Art Museum, Erie PA
Essex Historical Society and Shipbuilding Museum, Essex MA
Establishment Public du Chateau du Rusee, Et du Dophine national de versailles, Versailles
Evanston Historical Society, Charles Gates Dawes House, Evanston IL
Federal Reserve Board, Art Gallery, Washington DC
Fetherston Foundation, Packwood House Museum, Lewisburg PA
Fine Arts Center for the New River Valley, Pulaski VA
Fisher Art Gallery, Marshalltown IA
Fitton Center for Creative Arts, Hamilton OH
Flint Institute of Arts, Flint MI
Florence Museum, Florence SC
Florida Southern College, Melvin Art Gallery, Lakeland FL
Florida State University and Central Florida Community College, The Appleton Museum of Art, Ocala FL
Fondazione Musei Civici Di Venezia, Museo Correr, Venice
Forest Lawn Museum, Glendale CA
Fort Collins Museum of Art, Inc., Fort Collins CO
Fort Ticonderoga Association, Ticonderoga NY
Fruitlands Museum, Inc, Harvard MA
Gadsden Museum of Fine Arts, Inc, Gadsden Museum of Art and History, Gadsden AL
Galerie Montcalm, Gatineau PQ
Gallery One Visual Arts Center, Ellensburg WA
Germanisches Nationalmuseum, Nuremberg
The Ghent Museum of Fine Arts, Ghent
Glanmore National Historic Site of Canada, Belleville ON
Greene County Historical Society, Bronck Museum, Coxsackie NY
Guilford College, Art Gallery, Greensboro NC
Hammond-Harwood House Association, Inc, Hammond-Harwood House, Annapolis MD
Hancock County Trustees of Public Reservations, Woodlawn: Museum, Gardens & Park, Ellsworth ME

Roswell Artist-in-Residence Foundation, Anderson Museum of Contemporary Art, Roswell NM
Roswell Museum & Art Center, Roswell NM
Rutgers, The State University of New Jersey, Zimmerli Art Museum, Rutgers University, New Brunswick NJ
Ryerss Victorian Museum & Library, Philadelphia PA
Saco Museum, Saco ME
Saginaw Art Museum, Saginaw MI
Saint Augustine Historical Society, Oldest House Museum Complex, Saint Augustine FL
Saint Bonaventure University, Regina A Quick Center for the Arts, Saint Bonaventure NY
Saint Johnsbury Athenaeum, Saint Johnsbury VT
Saint Joseph College, Art Gallery, University of Saint Joseph, West Hartford CT
Saint Mary's College of California, Hearst Art Gallery, Moraga CA
Saint Olaf College, Flaten Art Museum, Northfield MN
Saint Peter's College, Art Gallery, Jersey City NJ
Schweinfurth Art Center, Auburn NY
Scripps College, Ruth Chandler Williamson Gallery, Claremont CA
Severoceska Galerie Vytvarneho Umeni v Litomericich, North Bohemian Gallery of Fine Arts in Litomerice, Litomerice
Shirley Plantation Foundation, Charles City VA
Norton Simon, Pasadena CA
Soprintendenza per I beni storici artistici ed etnoantropologici per le province di Mantova Brescia e Cremona, Museo di Palazzo Ducale, Mantua
South Dakota State University, South Dakota Art Museum, Brookings SD
Southeastern Center for Contemporary Art, Winston Salem NC
Southern Methodist University, Meadows Museum, Dallas TX
Southern Ohio Museum Corporation, Southern Ohio Museum, Portsmouth OH
Southern Oregon University, Schneider Museum of Art, Ashland OR
Spartanburg Art Museum, Spartanburg SC
The Speed Art Museum, Louisville KY
Springfield Art Museum, Springfield MO
Stanford University, Cantor Arts Center at Stanford University, Stanford CA
The State Museum of Fine Arts of Tatarstan Republic, Kazan
State University of New York at Binghamton, Binghamton University Art Museum, Binghamton NY
State University of New York at Geneseo, Bertha V B Lederer Gallery, Geneseo NY
State University of New York at Geneseo, Lockhart Gallery, Geneseo NY
State University of New York at New Paltz, Samuel Dorsky Museum of Art, New Paltz NY
State University of New York College at Cortland, Dowd Fine Arts Gallery, Cortland NY
Staten Island Museum, Staten Island NY
Stedelijk Museum Alkmaar, Alkmaar Municipal Museum, Alkmaar
T C Steele, Nashville IN
Stone Quarry Hill Art Park, Winner Gallery, Cazenovia NY
Suomen rakennustaiteen museo, Museum of Finnish Architecture, Helsinki
Susquehanna University, Lore Degenstein Gallery, Selinsgrove PA
Sweet Briar College, Art Collection & Galleries, Sweet Briar VA
Switzerland County Historical Society Inc, Life on the Ohio: River History Museum, Vevay IN
Syracuse University, Art Collection, Syracuse NY
Szepmuveszeti Muzeum, Museum of Fine Arts Budapest, Budapest
Tacoma Art Museum, Tacoma WA
Lillian & Coleman Taube Museum of Art, Minot ND
Temiskaming Art Gallery, Haileybury ON
The Temple-Tifereth Israel, The Temple Museum of Religious Art, Beachwood OH
Texas Tech University, Museum of Texas Tech University, Lubbock TX
Timken Museum of Art, San Diego CA
Tohono Chul Park, Tucson AZ
Topeka & Shawnee County Public Library, Alice C Sabatini Gallery, Topeka KS
Tubac Center of the Arts, Santa Cruz Valley Art Association, Tubac AZ
Tucson Museum of Art and Historic Block, Tucson AZ

Tulane University, Newcomb Art Gallery, New Orleans LA
Turtle Bay Exploration Park, Redding CA
Tver Art Gallery, Tver
Tyne and Wear Archives & Museums, Sunderland Museum & Winter Gardens, Newcastle-upon-Tyne
Ukrainian Canadian Archives & Museum of Alberta, Edmonton AB
The Ukrainian Museum, New York NY
United Society of Shakers, Shaker Museum, New Gloucester ME
United States Capitol, Architect of the Capitol, Washington DC
University of Alabama at Birmingham, Visual Arts Gallery, Birmingham AL
University of Cincinnati, DAAP Galleries-College of Design Architecture, Art & Planning, Cincinnati OH
University of Colorado at Colorado Springs, Gallery of Contemporary Art, Colorado Springs CO
University of Delaware, University Museums, Newark DE
University of Georgia, Georgia Museum of Art, Athens GA
University of Illinois at Urbana-Champaign, Krannert Art Museum and Kinkead Pavilion, Champaign IL
University of Indianapolis, Christel DeHaan Fine Arts Gallery, Indianapolis IN
University of Louisiana at Lafayette, Paul and Lulu Hilliard University Art Museum, Lafayette LA
University of Mary Washington, Gari Melchers Home and Studio, Fredericksburg VA
University of Mary Washington, University of Mary Washington Galleries, Fredericksburg VA
University of Miami, Lowe Art Museum, Coral Gables FL
University of Michigan, Museum of Art, Ann Arbor MI
University of Missouri, Museum of Art & Archaeology, Columbia MO
University of Nebraska-Lincoln, Great Plains Art Museum, Lincoln NE
University of Nevada, Reno, Sheppard Contemporary & University Galleries, Reno NV
University of New Hampshire, Museum of Art, Durham NH
University of New Mexico, The Harwood Museum of Art, Taos NM
University of North Carolina at Chapel Hill, Ackland Art Museum, Chapel Hill NC
University of Pittsburgh, University Art Gallery, Pittsburgh PA
University of Richmond, University Museums, Richmond VA
University of Rochester, Memorial Art Gallery, Rochester NY
University of Saskatchewan, Diefenbaker Canada Centre, Saskatoon SK
University of Toronto, University of Toronto Art Centre, Toronto ON
University of Utah, Utah Museum of Fine Arts, Salt Lake City UT
University of Virginia, The Fralin Museum of Art at the University of Virginia, Charlottesville VA
University of Wisconsin-Madison, Chazen Museum of Art, Madison WI
University of Wisconsin-Madison, Wisconsin Union Galleries, Madison WI
Ursinus College, Philip & Muriel Berman Museum of Art, Collegeville PA
Vancouver Art Gallery, Vancouver BC
Vesterheim Norwegian-American Museum, Decorah IA
Viridian Artists Inc, New York NY
Walker Art Gallery, Liverpool
Washington University, Mildred Lane Kemper Art Museum, Saint Louis MO
Waterworks Visual Arts Center, Salisbury NC
Wellesley College, Davis Museum & Cultural Center, Wellesley MA
West Florida Historic Preservation, Inc/University of West Florida, T T Wentworth, Jr Florida State Museum; Historic Pensacola Village; Pensacola Historical Society & Resource Center, Pensacola FL
Whatcom Museum, Bellingham WA
Wheaton College, Beard and Weil Galleries, Norton MA
Wichita State University, Ulrich Museum of Art, Wichita KS
Wildling Art Museum, Solvang CA
Wilfrid Laurier University, Robert Langen Art Gallery, Waterloo ON
Wiregrass Museum of Art, Dothan AL
Wistariahurst Museum, Holyoke MA
Woodmere Art Museum Inc, Philadelphia PA

Worcester Art Museum, Worcester MA
Yale University, Yale Center for British Art, New Haven CT
Yarmouth County Historical Society, Yarmouth County Museum & Archives, Yarmouth NS
Yokohama Museum of Art, Yokohama
Yuma Fine Arts Association, Yuma Art Center, Yuma AZ
Zigler Art Museum, Jennings LA

LATIN AMERICAN ART

Akron Art Museum, Akron OH
Albuquerque Museum of Art & History, Albuquerque NM
Americas Society Art Gallery, New York NY
Arizona State University, ASU Art Museum, Tempe AZ
Arnot Art Museum, Elmira NY
Art & Culture Center of Hollywood, Art Gallery/Multidisciplinary Cultural Center, Hollywood FL
Art Community Center, Art Center of Corpus Christi, Corpus Christi TX
The Art Museum at the University of Kentucky, Lexington KY
Art Museum of the University of Houston, Blaffer Gallery, Houston TX
Art Without Walls Inc, New York NY
Aurora University, Schingoethe Center for Native American Cultures & The Schingoethe Art Gallery, Aurora IL
Autry National Center, Southwest Museum of the American Indian, Mt. Washington Campus, Los Angeles CA
The Baltimore Museum of Art, Baltimore MD
Beloit College, Wright Museum of Art, Beloit WI
Bone Creek Museum of Agrarian Art, David City NE
Bucknell University, Edward & Marthann Samek Art Gallery, Lewisburg PA
California State University Stanislaus, University Art Gallery, Turlock CA
California State University, Northridge, Art Galleries, Northridge CA
Cartoon Art Museum, San Francisco CA
Center for Puppetry Arts, Atlanta GA
City of El Paso, El Paso TX
City of Gainesville, Thomas Center Galleries - Cultural Affairs, Gainesville FL
The Contemporary Austin, Austin TX
Cooper-Hewitt National Design Museum, Smithsonian Institution, New York NY
Coutts Museum of Art, Inc, El Dorado KS
Craft and Folk Art Museum (CAFAM), Los Angeles CA
Dartmouth College, Hood Museum of Art, Hanover NH
Davidson College, William H Van Every Jr & Edward M Smith Galleries, Davidson NC
Denver Art Museum, Denver CO
Detroit Institute of Arts, Detroit MI
East Carolina University, Wellington B Gray Gallery, Greenville NC
Emory University, Michael C Carlos Museum, Atlanta GA
En Foco, Inc, Bronx NY
Federal Reserve Board, Art Gallery, Washington DC
Fitton Center for Creative Arts, Hamilton OH
Florida International University, The Patricia & Phillip Frost Art Museum, Miami FL
Folk Art Society of America, Richmond VA
Forest Lawn Museum, Glendale CA
Galerie Montcalm, Gatineau PQ
Hidalgo County Historical Museum, Edinburg TX
The Hispanic Society of America, Museum & Library, New York NY
Institute of Puerto Rican Culture, Museo Fuerte Conde de Mirasol, Vieques PR
INTAR Gallery, New York NY
The Interchurch Center, Galleries at the Interchurch Center, New York NY
The Israel Museum, Jerusalem, Billy Rose Art Garden, Jerusalem
The Israel Museum, Jerusalem, Samuel & Saidye Bronfman Archaeology Wing, Jerusalem
The Israel Museum, Jerusalem, Jerusalem
Kalamazoo Institute of Arts, Kalamazoo MI
Kenosha Public Museums, Kenosha WI
Knights of Columbus Supreme Council, Knights of Columbus Museum, New Haven CT
Knoxville Museum of Art, Knoxville TN
LA County Museum of Art, Los Angeles CA
Latino Art Museum, Pomona CA

Lehigh University Art Galleries, Museum Operation, Bethlehem PA
Lehman College Art Gallery, Bronx NY
Loyola Marymount University, Laband Art Gallery, Los Angeles CA
Loyola University Chicago, Loyola University Museum of Art, Chicago IL
Marquette University, Haggerty Museum of Art, Milwaukee WI
Mesa Arts Center, Mesa Contemporary Arts Museum, Mesa AZ
Mexican Museum, San Francisco CA
Miami-Dade College, Kendal Campus, Art Gallery, Miami FL
Midwest Museum of American Art, Elkhart IN
Mission San Luis Rey de Francia, Mission San Luis Rey Museum, Oceanside CA
Modern Art Museum, Fort Worth TX
Museo de Arte de Puerto Rico, San Juan PR
Museo De Las Americas, Denver CO
Museo Nacional de Bellas Artes, National Museum of Fine Arts, Santiago
Museum of Art, Fort Lauderdale, Fort Lauderdale FL
The Museum of Arts & Sciences Inc, Daytona Beach FL
Museum of Contemporary Art, North Miami FL
The Museum of Contemporary Art (MOCA), Moca Grand Avenue, Los Angeles CA
Museum of Fine Arts, Houston, Houston TX
Museum of Fine Arts, Saint Petersburg, Florida, Inc, Saint Petersburg FL
Museum of Florida Art, Deland FL
Museum of Latin American Art, Long Beach CA
Museum of Northwest Art, La Conner WA
Museum zu Allerheiligen, Schaffhausen
Nassau County Museum of Art, Roslyn Harbor NY
National Museum of Mexican Art, Chicago IL
National Museum of the American Indian, George Gustav Heye Center, New York NY
National Museum of Women in the Arts, Washington DC
New Orleans Museum of Art, New Orleans LA
New World Art Center, T F Chen Cultural Center, New York NY
North Carolina State University, Gregg Museum of Art & Design, Raleigh NC
Okanagan Heritage Museum, Kelowna BC
Oklahoma City Museum of Art, Oklahoma City OK
Opelousas Museum of Art, Inc (OMA), Opelousas LA
Page-Walker Arts & History Center, Cary NC
Panhandle-Plains Historical Museum, Canyon TX
Phoenix Art Museum, Phoenix AZ
Polk Museum of Art, Lakeland FL
Princeton University, Princeton University Art Museum, Princeton NJ
Queens College, City University of New York, Godwin-Ternbach Museum, Flushing NY
Rabindra Bhavan Art Gallery, Lalit Kala Akademi (National Academy of Art), New Delhi
Reading Public Museum, Reading PA
Roswell Museum & Art Center, Roswell NM
C M Russell, Great Falls MT
Saint Joseph College, Art Gallery, University of Saint Joseph, West Hartford CT
Saint Mary's College of California, Hearst Art Gallery, Moraga CA
Saint Peter's College, Art Gallery, Jersey City NJ
San Antonio Museum of Art, San Antonio TX
Santa Barbara Museum of Art, Santa Barbara CA
Southeastern Center for Contemporary Art, Winston Salem NC
Southern Oregon University, Schneider Museum of Art, Ashland OR
Stanford University, Cantor Arts Center at Stanford University, Stanford CA
State University of New York at Geneseo, Bertha V B Lederer Gallery, Geneseo NY
State University of New York College at Cortland, Dowd Fine Arts Gallery, Cortland NY
Stauth Foundation & Museum, Stauth Memorial Museum, Montezuma KS
Stone Quarry Hill Art Park, Winner Gallery, Cazenovia NY
Tampa Museum of Art, Tampa FL
Lillian & Coleman Taube Museum of Art, Minot ND
Texas Tech University, Museum of Texas Tech University, Lubbock TX
Topeka & Shawnee County Public Library, Alice C Sabatini Gallery, Topeka KS
Tucson Museum of Art and Historic Block, Tucson AZ
Tulane University, Newcomb Art Gallery, New Orleans LA

University of California, Berkeley, Berkeley Art Museum & Pacific Film Archive, Berkeley CA
University of Colorado at Colorado Springs, Gallery of Contemporary Art, Colorado Springs CO
University of Georgia, Georgia Museum of Art, Athens GA
University of Miami, Lowe Art Museum, Coral Gables FL
University of Nevada, Reno, Sheppard Contemporary & University Galleries, Reno NV
University of North Carolina at Greensboro, Weatherspoon Art Museum, Greensboro NC
University of Pennsylvania, Museum of Archaeology & Anthropology, Philadelphia PA
University of Southern California, USC Fisher Museum of Art, Los Angeles CA
University of Texas at Austin, Blanton Museum of Art, Austin TX
University of Utah, Utah Museum of Fine Arts, Salt Lake City UT
University of Wisconsin-Madison, Chazen Museum of Art, Madison WI
Ursinus College, Philip & Muriel Berman Museum of Art, Collegeville PA
Wadsworth Atheneum Museum of Art, Hartford CT
Wake Forest University, Museum of Anthropology, Winston Salem NC
Wellesley College, Davis Museum & Cultural Center, Wellesley MA
Williams College, Museum of Art, Williamstown MA
Wiregrass Museum of Art, Dothan AL
Yerba Buena Center for the Arts, San Francisco CA
Yokohama Museum of Art, Yokohama
Yuma Fine Arts Association, Yuma Art Center, Yuma AZ

LEATHER

Albuquerque Museum of Art & History, Albuquerque NM
Appaloosa Museum and Heritage Center, Moscow ID
Art Without Walls Inc, New York NY
Artesia Historical Museum & Art Center, Artesia NM
Arts Council of Fayetteville-Cumberland County, The Arts Center, Fayetteville NC
Baroda Museum and Picture Gallery, Baroda
Canadian Museum of Civilization, Gatineau PQ
Carson County Square House Museum, Panhandle TX
City of Springdale, Shiloh Museum of Ozark History, Springdale AR
Cooper-Hewitt National Design Museum, Smithsonian Institution, New York NY
Craft and Folk Art Museum (CAFAM), Los Angeles CA
Craftsmen's Guild of Mississippi, Inc, Agriculture & Forestry Museum, Ridgeland MS
Craftsmen's Guild of Mississippi, Inc, Mississippi Crafts Center, Ridgeland MS
Cripple Creek District Museum, Cripple Creek CO
Crook County Museum & Art Gallery, Sundance WY
Culberson County Historical Museum, Van Horn TX
Deming-Luna Mimbres Museum, Deming NM
Detroit Institute of Arts, Detroit MI
Fitton Center for Creative Arts, Hamilton OH
Flint Institute of Arts, Flint MI
Fuller Craft Museum, Brockton MA
Glanmore National Historic Site of Canada, Belleville ON
Headquarters Fort Monroe, Dept of Army, Casemate Museum, Hampton VA
Henry County Museum & Cultural Arts Center, Clinton MO
Heritage Center, Inc, Pine Ridge SD
Hillwood Museum & Gardens Foundation, Hillwood Estate Museum & Gardens, Washington DC
Illinois State Museum, ISM Lockport Gallery, Chicago Gallery & Southern Illinois Art Gallery, Springfield IL
Independence Historical Museum & Art Center, Independence KS
Independent Administrative Institution National Institutes for Cultural Heritage, Tokyo National Museum, Tokyo
Iroquois Indian Museum, Howes Cave NY
Kelly-Griggs House Museum, Red Bluff CA
Kenosha Public Museums, Kenosha WI
Koshare Indian Museum, Inc, La Junta CO
Lac du Flambeau Band of Lake Superior Chippewa Indians, George W Brown Jr Ojibwe Museum & Cultural Center, Lac Du Flambeau WI
Lahore Museum, Lahore

League of New Hampshire Craftsmen, Grodin Permanent Collection Museum, Concord NH
Lehigh Valley Heritage Center, Allentown PA
LeSueur County Historical Society, Chapter One, Elysian MN
Lincolnshire County Council, Library & Heritage Services, Lincoln
The Long Island Museum of American Art, History & Carriages, Stony Brook NY
Magyar Nemzeti Muzeum - Hungarian National Museum, Budapest
Manchester Bidwell Corporation, Manchester Craftsmen's Guild Youth & Arts Program, Pittsburgh PA
Manitoba Historical Society, Dalnavert Museum, Winnipeg MB
Mexican Museum, San Francisco CA
Ministry of Cultural Affairs, Bangladesh National Museum, Dhaka
Moody County Historical Society, Moody County Museum, Pierre SD
Musee des Beaux-Arts/Palais des Archeveques, Museum of Fine Arts, Tours
Museo De Las Americas, Denver CO
Museum fur Kunst und Gewerbe Hamburg, Hamburg
Museum Plantin-Moretus/Prentenkabinet, Antwerp
Museum zu Allerheiligen, Schaffhausen
Muzej za Umjetnost i Obrt, Museum of Arts & Crafts, Zagreb
National Baseball Hall of Fame & Museum, Inc, Art Collection, Cooperstown NY
Naval Historical Center, The Navy Museum, Washington DC
Nebraska Game and Parks Commission, Arbor Lodge State Historical Park & Morton Mansion, Nebraska City NE
Nebraska State Capitol, Lincoln NE
New Brunswick Museum, Saint John NB
New Jersey State Museum, Fine Art Bureau, Trenton NJ
New York State Military Museum and Veterans Research Center, Saratoga Springs NY
Panhandle-Plains Historical Museum, Canyon TX
George Phippen, Phippen Museum - Art of the American West, Prescott AZ
Plainsman Museum, Aurora NE
Queens College, City University of New York, Godwin-Ternbach Museum, Flushing NY
The Rooms Corporation of Newfoundland & Labrador, Saint John's NF
Roswell Museum & Art Center, Roswell NM
Seneca-Iroquois National Museum, Salamanca NY
South Carolina Artisans Center, Walterboro SC
The Speed Art Museum, Louisville KY
The State Museum of Fine Arts of Tatarstan Republic, Kazan
Suomen Kansallismuseo, National Museum of Finland, Helsinki
The Temple-Tifereth Israel, The Temple Museum of Religious Art, Beachwood OH
Texas Tech University, Museum of Texas Tech University, Lubbock TX
Tver Art Gallery, Tver
United Society of Shakers, Shaker Museum, New Gloucester ME
University of Chicago, Oriental Institute, Chicago IL
University of Saskatchewan, Diefenbaker Canada Centre, Saskatoon SK
Vesterheim Norwegian-American Museum, Decorah IA
Wisconsin Historical Society, Wisconsin Historical Museum, Madison WI
Woodlawn/The Pope-Leighey, Mount Vernon VA
World Erotic Art Museum, Miami Beach FL

MANUSCRIPTS

Academy of the New Church, Glencairn Museum, Bryn Athyn PA
Adams County Historical Society, Gettysburg PA
African American Museum of Iowa, Cedar Rapids IA
Alabama Department of Archives & History, Museum of Alabama, Montgomery AL
Alaska Heritage Museum at Wells Fargo, Anchorage AK
Albany Institute of History & Art, Albany NY
Albin O Kuhn Library & Gallery, Baltimore MD
Albuquerque Museum of Art & History, Albuquerque NM
Alton Museum of History & Art, Inc, Alton IL
American Textile History Museum, Lowell MA
The Andy Warhol Museum, Museum, Pittsburgh PA
Appaloosa Museum and Heritage Center, Moscow ID

Arab American National Museum, Dearborn MI

Archives of American Art, Smithsonian Institution, Washington DC

Arizona Historical Society-Yuma, Sanguinetti House Museum & Garden, Yuma AZ

Arizona State University, ASU Art Museum, Tempe AZ

Art Without Walls Inc, New York NY

Artesia Historical Museum & Art Center, Artesia NM

Arts Council of Fayetteville-Cumberland County, The Arts Center, Fayetteville NC

Atlanta Historical Society Inc, Atlanta History Center, Atlanta GA

Autry National Center, Southwest Museum of the American Indian, Mt. Washington Campus, Los Angeles CA

Baldwin Historical Society Museum, Baldwin NY

Baroda Museum and Picture Gallery, Baroda

The Bartlett Museum, Amesbury MA

Besser Museum for Northeast Michigan, Alpena MI

Bone Creek Museum of Agrarian Art, David City NE

Brigham Young University, B F Larsen Gallery, Provo UT

Bucknell University, Edward & Marthann Samek Art Gallery, Lewisburg PA

Byzantine & Christian Museum, Athens, Athens

Canadian Museum of Civilization, Gatineau PQ

Cape Ann Historical Association, Cape Ann Museum, Gloucester MA

Caramoor Center for Music & the Arts, Inc, Rosen House at Caramoor, Katonah NY

Carson County Square House Museum, Panhandle TX

Cartoon Art Museum, San Francisco CA

Channel Islands Maritime Museum, Oxnard CA

Chatham Historical Society, The Atwood House Museum, Chatham MA

Chesapeake Bay Maritime Museum, Saint Michaels MD

Chhatrapati Shivaji Maharaj Vastu Sangrahalaya, Mumbai

City of Austin Parks & Recreation, O. Henry Museum, Austin TX

City of Cedar Falls, Iowa, James & Meryl Hearst Center for the Arts & Sculpture Garden, Cedar Falls IA

City of Nome Alaska, Carrie M McLain Memorial Museum, Nome AK

The City of Petersburg Museums, Petersburg VA

City of Springdale, Shiloh Museum of Ozark History, Springdale AR

City of Ukiah, Grace Hudson Museum & The Sun House, Ukiah CA

Clark County Historical Society, Heritage Center of Clark County, Springfield OH

Clark County Historical Society, Pioneer - Krier Museum, Ashland KS

Cohasset Historical Society, Pratt Building (Society Headquarters), Cohasset MA

Colgate University, Picker Art Gallery, Hamilton NY

College of William & Mary, Muscarelle Museum of Art, Williamsburg VA

Colorado Historical Society, Colorado History Museum, Denver CO

Columbia County Historical Society, Columbia County Museum and Library, Kinderhook NY

Concordia Historical Institute, Saint Louis MO

Cooper-Hewitt National Design Museum, Smithsonian Institution, New York NY

Craft and Folk Art Museum (CAFAM), Los Angeles CA

Cripple Creek District Museum, Cripple Creek CO

Crocker Art Museum, Sacramento CA

Crook County Museum & Art Gallery, Sundance WY

Crow Wing County Historical Society, Brainerd MN

Culberson County Historical Museum, Van Horn TX

The Currier Museum of Art, Manchester NH

Denison University, Art Gallery, Granville OH

Detroit Institute of Arts, Detroit MI

Eastern Washington State Historical Society, Northwest Museum of Arts & Culture, Spokane WA

Edgecombe County Cultural Arts Council, Inc, Blount-Bridgers House, Hobson Pittman Memorial Gallery, Tarboro NC

Egan Institute of Maritime Studies, Nantucket MA

Emory University, Michael C Carlos Museum, Atlanta GA

Erie County Historical Society, Erie PA

Evanston Historical Society, Charles Gates Dawes House, Evanston IL

Evansville Museum of Arts, History & Science, Evansville IN

Fetherston Foundation, Packwood House Museum, Lewisburg PA

Fitton Center for Creative Arts, Hamilton OH

Florence Museum, Florence SC

Fondazione Musei Civici Di Venezia, Museo Correr, Venice

Forest Lawn Museum, Glendale CA

Fort George G Meade Museum, Fort Meade MD

Fort Morgan Heritage Foundation, Fort Morgan CO

Fort Ticonderoga Association, Ticonderoga NY

Freer Gallery of Art & Arthur M Sackler Gallery, Freer Gallery of Art, Washington DC

Fruitlands Museum, Inc, Harvard MA

Fulton County Historical Society Inc, Fulton County Museum (Tetzlaff Reference Room), Rochester IN

Gem County Historical Society and Museum, Gem County Historical Village Museum, Emmett ID

General Board of Discipleship, The United Methodist Church, The Upper Room Chapel & Museum, Nashville TN

Germanisches Nationalmuseum, Nuremberg

Germantown Historical Society, Philadelphia PA

Glanmore National Historic Site of Canada, Belleville ON

Glessner House Museum, Chicago IL

Grand Rapids Public Museum, Public Museum of Grand Rapids, Grand Rapids MI

Hammond-Harwood House Association, Inc, Hammond-Harwood House, Annapolis MD

Hancock County Trustees of Public Reservations, Woodlawn: Museum, Gardens & Park, Ellsworth ME

Hancock Shaker Village, Inc, Pittsfield MA

Hawkes Bay Art Gallery and Museum, Napier

Headquarters Fort Monroe, Dept of Army, Casemate Museum, Hampton VA

Hebrew Union College, Skirball Cultural Center, Los Angeles CA

Hebrew Union College - Jewish Institute of Religion, Skirball Museum Cincinnati, Cincinnati OH

Hebrew Union College Museum, Jewish Institute of Religion Museum, New York NY

Hecht Museum, Haifa

Henry Sheldon Museum of Vermont History and Research Center, Middlebury VT

Heritage Glass Museum, Glassboro NJ

Hidalgo County Historical Museum, Edinburg TX

Higgins Armory Museum, Worcester MA

High Desert Museum, Bend OR

Hillwood Museum & Gardens Foundation, Hillwood Estate Museum & Gardens, Washington DC

The Hispanic Society of America, Museum & Library, New York NY

Historic Arkansas Museum, Little Rock AR

Historic Cherry Hill, Albany NY

The Historic New Orleans Collection, Royal Street Galleries, New Orleans LA

The Historic New Orleans Collection, Williams Research Center, New Orleans LA

Historic Newton, Newton MA

Historical Society of Cheshire County, Keene NH

Historical Society of Old Newbury, Cushing House Museum, Newburyport MA

Historical Society of Palm Beach County, The Richard and Pat Johnson Palm Beach County History Museum, West Palm Beach FL

History Museum of Mobile, Mobile AL

Huguenot Historical Society of New Paltz Galleries, New Paltz NY

The Huntington Library, Art Collections & Botanical Gardens, San Marino CA

Imperial Calcasieu Museum, Gibson-Barham Gallery, Lake Charles LA

Independence Seaport Museum, Philadelphia PA

Independent Administrative Institution National Institutes for Cultural Heritage, Tokyo National Museum, Tokyo

Indiana State Museum, Indianapolis IN

Institute of Puerto Rican Culture, Museo Fuerte Conde de Mirasol, Vieques PR

Iredell Museums, Statesville NC

Iroquois County Historical Society Museum, Old Courthouse Museum, Watseka IL

The Israel Museum, Jerusalem, Billy Rose Art Garden, Jerusalem

The Israel Museum, Jerusalem, Samuel & Saidye Bronfman Archaeology Wing, Jerusalem

The Israel Museum, Jerusalem, Jerusalem

J.M.W. Turner Museum, Sarasota FL

James Dick Foundation, Festival - Institute, Round Top TX

Jamestown-Yorktown Foundation, Jamestown Settlement, Williamsburg VA

Thomas Jefferson, Monticello, Charlottesville VA

Johns Hopkins University, Evergreen Museum & Library, Baltimore MD

Jordan National Gallery of Fine Arts, Amman

Judiciary History Center, Honolulu HI

Kenosha Public Museums, Kenosha WI

Kentucky Derby Museum, Louisville KY

Kings County Historical Society & Museum, Hampton NB

Knights of Columbus Supreme Council, Knights of Columbus Museum, New Haven CT

Koffler Centre of the Arts, Koffler Gallery, Toronto ON

Koochiching Museums, International Falls MN

Kunsthistorisches Museum Vienna, Museum of Fine Arts, Vienna

La Casa del Libro Museum, San Juan PR

Lac du Flambeau Band of Lake Superior Chippewa Indians, George W Brown Jr Ojibwe Museum & Cultural Center, Lac Du Flambeau WI

Lafayette Science Museum & Planetarium, Lafayette LA

Lahore Museum, Lahore

Leeds Museums & Galleries, Leeds

Leelanau Historical Museum, Leland MI

Lehigh Valley Heritage Center, Allentown PA

LeSueur County Historical Society, Chapter One, Elysian MN

Liberty Memorial Museum & Archives, The National Museum of World War I, Kansas City MO

Lincolnshire County Council, Library & Heritage Services, Lincoln

The Long Island Museum of American Art, History & Carriages, Stony Brook NY

Louisiana Department of Culture, Recreation & Tourism, Louisiana State Museum, New Orleans LA

Loveland Museum/Gallery, Loveland CO

Magyar Nemzeti Muzeum - Hungarian National Museum, Budapest

Maine Historical Society, Wadsworth-Longfellow House, Portland ME

The Mariners' Museum, Newport News VA

Maysville, Kentucky Gateway Museum Center, Maysville KY

McCord Museum of Canadian History, Montreal PQ

McLean County Historical Society, McLean County Museum of History, Bloomington IL

Mexican Museum, San Francisco CA

Ministry of Cultural Affairs, Bangladesh National Museum, Dhaka

Mission San Miguel Museum, San Miguel CA

Mississippi River Museum at Mud-Island River Park, Memphis TN

Mohave Museum of History & Arts, Kingman AZ

Moody County Historical Society, Moody County Museum, Pierre SD

Moravian Historical Society, Whitefield House Museum, Nazareth PA

Moravska Galerie v Brne, Moravian Gallery in Brno, Brno

The Morgan Library & Museum, Museum, New York NY

Mount Vernon Hotel Museum & Garden, New York NY

Musee des Beaux-Arts/Palais des Archeveques, Museum of Fine Arts, Tours

Musee et Chateau de Chantilly (MUSEE CONDE), Chantilly

Musee Guimet, Paris

Musee Royal Et Domaine De Mariemont, Morlanwelz

Museen der Stadt Koln, Museum Schnutgen, Cologne

Museo Cerralbo, Madrid

Museum fur Kunst und Gewerbe Hamburg, Hamburg

The Museum of Arts & Sciences Inc, Daytona Beach FL

Museum of Chinese in America, New York NY

Museum of the City of New York, Museum, New York NY

Museum Plantin-Moretus/Prentenkabinet, Antwerp

Museum zu Allerheiligen, Schaffhausen

Muzej za Umjetnost i Obrt, Museum of Arts & Crafts, Zagreb

Muzeul de Istorie Nationala Si Arheologie Constanta, National History & Archaeology Museum, Constanta

Muzeul National Brukenthal, Brukenthal Palace & European Art Gallery, Sibiu

The Namur Provincial Museum of Ancient Arts, Namur

Nara Kokuritsu Hakubutsu-Kan, Nara National Museum, Nara

Narodna Galerija, National Gallery of Slovenia, Ljubljana

MAPS

Colorado Historical Society, Colorado History Museum, Denver CO

Columbia County Historical Society, Columbia County Museum and Library, Kinderhook NY

Columbus Museum, Columbus GA

Cripple Creek District Museum, Cripple Creek CO

Crocker Art Museum, Sacramento CA

Crook County Museum & Art Gallery, Sundance WY

Crow Wing County Historical Society, Brainerd MN

Culberson County Historical Museum, Van Horn TX

Danville Museum of Fine Arts & History, Danville VA

Delta Blues Museum, Clarksdale MS

Detroit Institute of Arts, Detroit MI

Doncaster Museum and Art Gallery, Doncaster

Eastern Washington State Historical Society, Northwest Museum of Arts & Culture, Spokane WA

Edgecombe County Cultural Arts Council, Inc, Blount-Bridgers House, Hobson Pittman Memorial Gallery, Tarboro NC

Egan Institute of Maritime Studies, Nantucket MA

Erie County Historical Society, Erie PA

Essex Historical Society and Shipbuilding Museum, Essex MA

Evanston Historical Society, Charles Gates Dawes House, Evanston IL

Evansville Museum of Arts, History & Science, Evansville IN

Fairbanks Museum & Planetarium, Saint Johnsbury VT

Fetherston Foundation, Packwood House Museum, Lewisburg PA

Five Civilized Tribes Museum, Muskogee OK

Florida State University and Central Florida Community College, The Appleton Museum of Art, Ocala FL

Fondazione Musei Civici Di Venezia, Museo Correr, Venice

Fort George G Meade Museum, Fort Meade MD

Fort Ticonderoga Association, Ticonderoga NY

Fruitlands Museum, Inc, Harvard MA

Fulton County Historical Society Inc, Fulton County Museum (Tetzlaff Reference Room), Rochester IN

Gadsden Museum of Fine Arts, Inc, Gadsden Museum of Art and History, Gadsden AL

Germanisches Nationalmuseum, Nuremberg

Glanmore National Historic Site of Canada, Belleville ON

Grand Rapids Public Museum, Public Museum of Grand Rapids, Grand Rapids MI

Great Lakes Historical Society, Inland Seas Maritime Museum, Vermilion OH

Halifax Historical Society, Inc, Halifax Historical Museum, Daytona Beach FL

Hammond-Harwood House Association, Inc, Hammond-Harwood House, Annapolis MD

Hancock County Trustees of Public Reservations, Woodlawn: Museum, Gardens & Park, Ellsworth ME

Hancock Shaker Village, Inc, Pittsfield MA

Hawkes Bay Art Gallery and Museum, Napier

Headquarters Fort Monroe, Dept of Army, Casemate Museum, Hampton VA

Hebrew Union College Museum, Jewish Institute of Religion Museum, New York NY

Henry County Museum & Cultural Arts Center, Clinton MO

Henry Sheldon Museum of Vermont History and Research Center, Middlebury VT

Heritage Glass Museum, Glassboro NJ

Heritage Museum Association, Inc, The Heritage Museum of Northwest Florida, Valparaiso FL

Hermitage Foundation Museum, Norfolk VA

Hidalgo County Historical Museum, Edinburg TX

High Desert Museum, Bend OR

Hillwood Museum & Gardens Foundation, Hillwood Estate Museum & Gardens, Washington DC

The Hispanic Society of America, Museum & Library, New York NY

Historic Arkansas Museum, Little Rock AR

Historic Deerfield, Inc, Deerfield MA

Historic Hudson Valley, Pocantico Hills NY

The Historic New Orleans Collection, Royal Street Galleries, New Orleans LA

Historic Newton, Newton MA

Historical Society of Cheshire County, Keene NH

The History Center in Tompkins County, Ithaca NY

History Museum of Mobile, Mobile AL

Houston Baptist University, Museum of American Architecture and Decorative Arts, Houston TX

Hoyt Center for the Arts, New Castle PA

Huguenot Historical Society of New Paltz Galleries, New Paltz NY

Illinois State Museum, ISM Lockport Gallery, Chicago Gallery & Southern Illinois Art Gallery, Springfield IL

Imperial Calcasieu Museum, Gibson-Barham Gallery, Lake Charles LA

Independence Historical Museum & Art Center, Independence KS

Independence Seaport Museum, Philadelphia PA

Independent Administrative Institution National Institutes for Cultural Heritage, Tokyo National Museum, Tokyo

Institute of Puerto Rican Culture, Museo Fuerte Conde de Mirasol, Vieques PR

Iredell Museums, Statesville NC

Iroquois County Historical Society Museum, Old Courthouse Museum, Watseka IL

Iroquois Indian Museum, Howes Cave NY

The Israel Museum, Jerusalem, Billy Rose Art Garden, Jerusalem

The Israel Museum, Jerusalem, Samuel & Saidye Bronfman Archaeology Wing, Jerusalem

The Israel Museum, Jerusalem, Jerusalem

J.M.W. Turner Museum, Sarasota FL

Jackson County Historical Society, John Wornall House Museum, Independence MO

James Dick Foundation, Festival - Institute, Round Top TX

Jamestown-Yorktown Foundation, Jamestown Settlement, Williamsburg VA

Thomas Jefferson, Monticello, Charlottesville VA

Johns Hopkins University, Evergreen Museum & Library, Baltimore MD

Judiciary History Center, Honolulu HI

Kenosha Public Museums, Kenosha WI

Kings County Historical Society & Museum, Hampton NB

Knights of Columbus Supreme Council, Knights of Columbus Museum, New Haven CT

Koochiching Museums, International Falls MN

La Casa del Libro Museum, San Juan PR

Lac du Flambeau Band of Lake Superior Chippewa Indians, George W Brown Jr Ojibwe Museum & Cultural Center, Lac Du Flambeau WI

Lafayette Science Museum & Planetarium, Lafayette LA

Lehigh Valley Heritage Center, Allentown PA

LeSueur County Historical Society, Chapter One, Elysian MN

Liberty Memorial Museum & Archives, The National Museum of World War I, Kansas City MO

Lincoln County Historical Association, Inc, 1811 Old Lincoln County Jail & Lincoln County Museum, Wiscasset ME

Lincolnshire County Council, Library & Heritage Services, Lincoln

The Long Island Museum of American Art, History & Carriages, Stony Brook NY

Louisiana Department of Culture, Recreation & Tourism, Louisiana State Museum, New Orleans LA

Louisiana State Exhibit Museum, Shreveport LA

Magyar Nemzeti Muzeum - Hungarian National Museum, Budapest

Marblehead Museum & Historical Society, Jeremiah Lee Mansion, Marblehead MA

Marblehead Museum & Historical Society, Marblehead MA

Jacques Marchais, Staten Island NY

The Mariners' Museum, Newport News VA

Massachusetts Institute of Technology, MIT Museum, Cambridge MA

Maysville, Kentucky Gateway Museum Center, Maysville KY

McCord Museum of Canadian History, Montreal PQ

McDowell House & Apothecary Shop, Danville KY

McLean County Historical Society, McLean County Museum of History, Bloomington IL

McMaster University, McMaster Museum of Art, Hamilton ON

Medina Railroad Museum, Medina NY

Middle Border Museum & Oscar Howe Art Center, Mitchell SD

Milwaukee County War Memorial Inc., Villa Terrace Decorative Arts Museum, Milwaukee WI

Ministry of Cultural Affairs, Bangladesh National Museum, Dhaka

Ministry of the Arts & Multiculturalism, National Museum & Art Gallery, Port of Spain

Mississippi River Museum at Mud-Island River Park, Memphis TN

Moody County Historical Society, Moody County Museum, Pierre SD

Moravian Historical Society, Whitefield House Museum, Nazareth PA

Moto Moto Museum, Mbala

Mount Vernon Hotel Museum & Garden, New York NY

Muscatine Art Center, Museum, Muscatine IA

Musee des Beaux-Arts/Palais des Archeveques, Museum of Fine Arts, Tours

Musee National d'Histoire et d'Art Luxembourg, Luxembourg City

Musee Royal Et Domaine De Mariemont, Morlanwelz

Museo Cerralbo, Madrid

Museo De Las Americas, Denver CO

Museum De Lakenhal, Leiden

Museum fur Kunst und Gewerbe Hamburg, Hamburg

Museum Het Prinsenhof, Delft

Museum of Art & History, Santa Cruz, Santa Cruz CA

The Museum of Arts & Sciences Inc, Daytona Beach FL

Museum of Chinese in America, New York NY

Museum of Fine Arts Houston, Bayou Bend Collection & Gardens, Houston TX

Museum of New Mexico, Laboratory of Anthropology Library, Santa Fe NM

Museum of Northern British Columbia, Ruth Harvey Art Gallery, Prince Rupert BC

Museum of Southern History, Houston TX

Museum of the City of New York, Museum, New York NY

Museum Plantin-Moretus/Prentenkabinet, Antwerp

Museum zu Allerheiligen, Schaffhausen

Muzeul de Istorie Nationala Si Arheologie Constanta, National History & Archaeology Museum, Constanta

Muzeul National Brukenthal, Brukenthal Palace & European Art Gallery, Sibiu

The Namur Provincial Museum of Ancient Arts, Namur

National Museum of Wildlife Art of the Unites States, Jackson WY

The National Shrine of the North American Martyrs, Fultonville NY

National Society of the Colonial Dames of America in The Commonwealth of Virginia, Wilton House Museum, Richmond VA

Naval Historical Center, The Navy Museum, Washington DC

Naval War College Museum, Newport RI

New Brunswick Museum, Saint John NB

New Canaan Historical Society, New Canaan CT

New Hampshire Antiquarian Society, Hopkinton Historical Society, Hopkinton NH

New Jersey State Museum, Fine Art Bureau, Trenton NJ

New York State Office of Parks Recreation & Historic Preservation, John Jay Homestead State Historic Site, Katonah NY

Newburyport Maritime Society, Inc, Custom House Maritime Museum, Newburyport MA

The Noble Maritime Collection, Staten Island NY

Norfolk Historical Society Inc, Museum, Norfolk CT

Norwich Free Academy, Slater Memorial Museum, Norwich CT

Ogden Union Station, Union Station Museums, Ogden UT

Oklahoma City Museum of Art, Oklahoma City OK

Old Dartmouth Historical Society, New Bedford Whaling Museum, New Bedford MA

The Old Jail Art Center, Albany TX

Old Salem Museums & Gardens, Museum of Early Southern Decorative Arts, Winston Salem NC

Opelousas Museum of Art, Inc (OMA), Opelousas LA

Oshkosh Public Museum, Oshkosh WI

Oysterponds Historical Society, Museum, Orient NY

Page-Walker Arts & History Center, Cary NC

Panhandle-Plains Historical Museum, Canyon TX

Passaic County Historical Society, Lambert Castle Museum & Library, Paterson NJ

Pennsylvania Historical & Museum Commission, Railroad Museum of Pennsylvania, Harrisburg PA

Philadelphia History Museum, Philadelphia PA

Plainsman Museum, Aurora NE

Please Touch Museum, Philadelphia PA

Polish Museum of America, Chicago IL

Port Huron Museum, Port Huron MI

Porter-Phelps-Huntington Foundation, Inc, Historic House Museum, Hadley MA

Portsmouth Historical Society, John Paul Jones House & Discover Portsmouth, Portsmouth NH

Putnam County Historical Society, Foundry School Museum, Cold Spring NY

Putnam Museum of History and Natural Science, Davenport IA

Jack Richard Gallery, Almond Tea Museum & Jane Williams Galleries, Divisions of Studios of Jack Richard, Cuyahoga Falls OH

Riley County Historical Society & Museum, Riley County Historical Museum, Manhattan KS

Saco Museum, Saco ME

Safety Harbor Museum of Regional History, Safety Harbor FL

Saint Augustine Historical Society, Oldest House Museum Complex, Saint Augustine FL

Saint Johnsbury Athenaeum, Saint Johnsbury VT

San Francisco Maritime National Historical Park, Maritime Museum, San Francisco CA

The Sandwich Historical Society, Inc & Sandwich Glass Museum, Sandwich Glass Museum, Sandwich MA

Sea Cliff Village Museum, Sea Cliff NY

Seneca Falls Historical Society Museum, Seneca Falls NY

Seneca-Iroquois National Museum, Salamanca NY

Ella Sharp, Jackson MI

Shirley Plantation Foundation, Charles City VA

The Society of the Cincinnati at Anderson House, Washington DC

Soprintendenza per I beni storici artistici ed etnoantropologici per le province di Mantova Brescia e Cremona, Museo di Palazzo Ducale, Mantua

South Street Seaport Museum, New York NY

The Speed Art Museum, Louisville KY

Spertus Institute of Jewish Studies, Chicago IL

Stanford University, Cantor Arts Center at Stanford University, Stanford CA

The State Museum of Fine Arts of Tatarstan Republic, Kazan

State of North Carolina, Battleship North Carolina, Wilmington NC

State University of New York at Binghamton, Binghamton University Art Museum, Binghamton NY

Staten Island Museum, Staten Island NY

Stauth Foundation & Museum, Stauth Memorial Museum, Montezuma KS

Ste Genevieve Museum, Sainte Genevieve MO

Stone Quarry Hill Art Park, Winner Gallery, Cazenovia NY

Stratford Historical Society, Catharine B Mitchell Museum, Stratford CT

The Summit County Historical Society of Akron, OH, Akron OH

Switzerland County Historical Society Inc, Life on the Ohio: River History Museum, Vevay IN

Switzerland County Historical Society Inc, Switzerland County Historical Museum, Vevay IN

The Temple-Tifereth Israel, The Temple Museum of Religious Art, Beachwood OH

The Tokugawa Reimeikai Foundation, The Tokugawa Art Museum, Nagoya

Towson University, Center for the Arts Gallery, Towson MD

Trust Authority, Museum of the Great Plains, Lawton OK

Tryon Palace Historic Sites & Gardens, New Bern NC

Tulane University, University Art Collection, New Orleans LA

Turtle Bay Exploration Park, Redding CA

Turtle Mountain Chippewa Historical Society, Turtle Mountain Heritage Center, Belcourt ND

Tver Art Gallery, Tver

United Society of Shakers, Shaker Museum, New Gloucester ME

United States Department of the Interior, Interior Museum, Washington DC

University of Richmond, University Museums, Richmond VA

University of Saskatchewan, Diefenbaker Canada Centre, Saskatoon SK

Vermilion County Museum Society, Danville IL

Vesterheim Norwegian-American Museum, Decorah IA

Village of Potsdam, Potsdam Public Museum, Potsdam NY

Wadsworth Atheneum Museum of Art, Hartford CT

The Walker African American Museum & Research Center, Las Vegas NV

Waterville Historical Society, Redington Museum, Waterville ME

Wayne County Historical Society, Museum, Honesdale PA

West Baton Rouge Parish, West Baton Rouge Museum, Port Allen LA

West Florida Historic Preservation, Inc/University of West Florida, T T Wentworth, Jr Florida State

Museum; Historic Pensacola Village; Pensacola Historical Society & Resource Center, Pensacola FL

Westminster College, Winston Churchill Memorial & Library in the United States, Fulton MO

Wethersfield Historical Society Inc, Museum, Wethersfield CT

Peter & Catharine Whyte Foundation, Whyte Museum of the Canadian Rockies, Banff AB

Wistariahurst Museum, Holyoke MA

Woodlawn/The Pope-Leighey, Mount Vernon VA

Yale University, Yale Center for British Art, New Haven CT

MARINE PAINTING

American Art Museum, Smithsonian Institution, Washington DC

American Sport Art Museum and Archives, Daphne AL

Arnold Mikelson Mind & Matter Art Gallery, White Rock BC

Arnot Art Museum, Elmira NY

Art Community Center, Art Center of Corpus Christi, Corpus Christi TX

Art Gallery of Nova Scotia, Halifax NS

The Art Museum at the University of Kentucky, Lexington KY

Art Without Walls Inc, New York NY

Bayerische Staatsgemaldesammlungen/Bavarian State Art Galleries, Alte Pinakothek, Munich

Besser Museum for Northeast Michigan, Alpena MI

Beverly Historical Society, Cabot, Hale & Balch House Museums, Beverly MA

Brick Store Museum, Kennebunk ME

Brigham Young University, Museum of Art, Provo UT

Bruce Museum, Inc, Greenwich CT

The Butler Institute of American Art, Art Museum, Youngstown OH

Cahoon Museum of American Art, Cotuit MA

Canadian Museum of Civilization, Gatineau PQ

Cape Ann Historical Association, Cape Ann Museum, Gloucester MA

Carteret County Historical Society, The History Place, Morehead City NC

Channel Islands Maritime Museum, Oxnard CA

Chatham Historical Society, The Atwood House Museum, Chatham MA

Chesapeake Bay Maritime Museum, Saint Michaels MD

City of Mason City, Charles H MacNider Museum, Mason City IA

City of Toronto Culture, The Market Gallery, Toronto ON

Cohasset Historical Society, Cohasset Maritime Museum, Cohasset MA

Cohasset Historical Society, Pratt Building (Society Headquarters), Cohasset MA

College of William & Mary, Muscarelle Museum of Art, Williamsburg VA

Columbia River Maritime Museum, Astoria OR

Columbus Museum, Columbus GA

Crocker Art Museum, Sacramento CA

Detroit Institute of Arts, Detroit MI

Doncaster Museum and Art Gallery, Doncaster

Dundee City Council Leisure & Communities Department, The McManus: Dundee's Art Gallery & Museum, Dundee

Egan Institute of Maritime Studies, Nantucket MA

Erie County Historical Society, Erie PA

Essex Historical Society and Shipbuilding Museum, Essex MA

Federal Reserve Board, Art Gallery, Washington DC

Florida State University and Central Florida Community College, The Appleton Museum of Art, Ocala FL

Gallery One Visual Arts Center, Ellensburg WA

The Ghent Museum of Fine Arts, Ghent

Great Lakes Historical Society, Inland Seas Maritime Museum, Vermilion OH

Hammond-Harwood House Association, Inc, Hammond-Harwood House, Annapolis MD

The Heckscher Museum of Art, Huntington NY

Hickory Museum of Art, Inc, Hickory NC

Hillwood Museum & Gardens Foundation, Hillwood Estate Museum & Gardens, Washington DC

Historic Hudson Valley, Pocantico Hills NY

Hui No'eau Visual Arts Center, Gallery and Gift Shop, Makawao Maui HI

Independence Seaport Museum, Philadelphia PA

The Interchurch Center, Galleries at the Interchurch Center, New York NY

J.M.W. Turner Museum, Sarasota FL

Kyiv Museum of Russian Art, Kyiv

LaGrange Art Museum, LaGrange GA

The Long Island Museum of American Art, History & Carriages, Stony Brook NY

Louisiana Department of Culture, Recreation & Tourism, Louisiana State Museum, New Orleans LA

Maine Maritime Museum, Bath ME

Marblehead Museum & Historical Society, Jeremiah Lee Mansion, Marblehead MA

Marblehead Museum & Historical Society, Marblehead MA

The Mariners' Museum, Newport News VA

Maritime Museum of San Diego, San Diego CA

Massachusetts Institute of Technology, MIT Museum, Cambridge MA

Maysville, Kentucky Gateway Museum Center, Maysville KY

Mobile Museum of Art, Mobile AL

Moderna Galerija, Gallery of Modern Art, Zagreb

Monhegan Museum, Monhegan ME

Monterey History & Art Association, Maritime Museum of Monterey, Monterey CA

Morris Museum of Art, Augusta GA

Munson-Williams-Proctor Arts Institute, Museum of Art, Utica NY

Musee des Beaux-Arts/Palais des Archeveques, Museum of Fine Arts, Tours

Museo Nacional de Bellas Artes, National Museum of Fine Arts, Santiago

The Museum of Arts & Sciences Inc, Daytona Beach FL

Museum of Northwest Art, La Conner WA

Museum of the City of New York, Museum, New York NY

Muskegon Museum of Art, Muskegon MI

Muzeul National Brukenthal, Brukenthal Palace & European Art Gallery, Sibiu

National Art Museum of Sport, Indianapolis IN

National Museum of American Illustration, Newport RI

National Museum of Fine Arts of Moldova, Chisinau

Naval Historical Center, The Navy Museum, Washington DC

Naval War College Museum, Newport RI

Nelson Mandela Bay Municipality, Nelson Mandela Metropolitan Art Museum, Port Elizabeth

The Nemours Foundatioin, Nemours Mansion & Gardens, Wilmington DE

New Britain Museum of American Art, New Britain CT

New Brunswick Museum, Saint John NB

Newburyport Maritime Society, Inc, Custom House Maritime Museum, Newburyport MA

The Noble Maritime Collection, Staten Island NY

Norsk Sjøfartsmuseum, Norwegian Maritime Museum, Oslo

Norwich Free Academy, Slater Memorial Museum, Norwich CT

Nova Scotia Museum, Maritime Museum of the Atlantic, Halifax NS

The Ohio Historical Society, Inc, Campus Martius Museum & Ohio River Museum, Marietta OH

Old Dartmouth Historical Society, New Bedford Whaling Museum, New Bedford MA

Old Island Restoration Foundation Inc, Oldest House in Key West, Key West FL

Opelousas Museum of Art, Inc (OMA), Opelousas LA

Oysterponds Historical Society, Museum, Orient NY

Panhandle-Plains Historical Museum, Canyon TX

The Pennsylvania State University, Palmer Museum of Art, University Park PA

Penobscot Marine Museum, Searsport ME

Port Huron Museum, Port Huron MI

Portsmouth Athenaeum, Joseph Copley Research Library, Portsmouth NH

Portsmouth Historical Society, John Paul Jones House & Discover Portsmouth, Portsmouth NH

Princeton University, Princeton University Art Museum, Princeton NJ

Queens College, City University of New York, Godwin-Ternbach Museum, Flushing NY

Randolph College, Maier Museum of Art, Lynchburg VA

Reading Public Museum, Reading PA

Jack Richard Gallery, Almond Tea Museum & Jane Williams Galleries, Divisions of Studios of Jack Richard, Cuyahoga Falls OH

The Rooms Corporation of Newfoundland & Labrador, Saint John's NF

Saginaw Art Museum, Saginaw MI

Saint Joseph College, Art Gallery, University of Saint Joseph, West Hartford CT

St Mary's College of Maryland, The Dwight Frederick Boyden Gallery, St Mary's City MD
San Francisco Maritime National Historical Park, Maritime Museum, San Francisco CA
Scripps College, Ruth Chandler Williamson Gallery, Claremont CA
Ships of the Sea Maritime Museum, Savannah GA
Soprintendenza per I beni storici artistici ed etnoantropologici per le province di Mantova Brescia e Cremona, Museo di Palazzo Ducale, Mantua
South Street Seaport Museum, New York NY
The Speed Art Museum, Louisville KY
Stanford University, Cantor Arts Center at Stanford University, Stanford CA
State of North Carolina, Battleship North Carolina, Wilmington NC
Staten Island Museum, Staten Island NY
The Stewart Museum, Montreal PQ
Stratford Historical Society, Catharine B Mitchell Museum, Stratford CT
Switzerland County Historical Society Inc, Life on the Ohio: River History Museum, Vevay IN
Szepmuvezeti Muzeum, Museum of Fine Arts Budapest, Budapest
Timken Museum of Art, San Diego CA
Towson University, Center for the Arts Gallery, Towson MD
Tver Art Gallery, Tver
Tyne and Wear Archives & Museums, Sunderland Museum & Winter Gardens, Newcastle-upon-Tyne
United States Navy, Art Gallery, Washington DC
University of Georgia, Georgia Museum of Art, Athens GA
University of Illinois at Urbana-Champaign, Krannert Art Museum and Kinkead Pavilion, Champaign IL
University of Richmond, University Museums, Richmond VA
University of Rochester, Memorial Art Gallery, Rochester NY
University of Toronto, University of Toronto Art Centre, Toronto ON
University of Wisconsin-Madison, Chazen Museum of Art, Madison WI
Ursinus College, Philip & Muriel Berman Museum of Art, Collegeville PA
USS Constitution Museum, Boston MA
Vesterheim Norwegian-American Museum, Decorah IA
West Florida Historic Preservation, Inc/University of West Florida, T T Wentworth, Jr Florida State Museum; Historic Pensacola Village; Pensacola Historical Society & Resource Center, Pensacola FL
Wheaton College, Beard and Weil Galleries, Norton MA
Wichita State University, Ulrich Museum of Art, Wichita KS
Wilfrid Laurier University, Robert Langen Art Gallery, Waterloo ON
Yale University, Yale Center for British Art, New Haven CT
Yarmouth County Historical Society, Yarmouth County Museum & Archives, Yarmouth NS
Yuma Fine Arts Association, Yuma Art Center, Yuma AZ
Zigler Art Museum, Jennings LA

MEDIEVAL ART

Academy of the New Church, Glencairn Museum, Bryn Athyn PA
Arnot Art Museum, Elmira NY
Art Gallery of Nova Scotia, Halifax NS
The Art Museum at the University of Kentucky, Lexington KY
Art Without Walls Inc, New York NY
Badisches Landesmuseum, Karlsruhe
Baroda Museum and Picture Gallery, Baroda
Bayerische Staatsgemaldesammlungen/Bavarian State Art Galleries, Alte Pinakothek, Munich
Bayerisches Nationalmuseum, Bavarian National Museum, Munich
Beaverbrook Art Gallery, Fredericton NB
Beloit College, Wright Museum of Art, Beloit WI
Belvedere Museum, Osterreichische Galerie Belvedere, Vienna
Blanden Memorial Art Museum, Fort Dodge IA
Byzantine & Christian Museum, Athens, Athens
Caramoor Center for Music & the Arts, Inc, Rosen House at Caramoor, Katonah NY
Cincinnati Art Museum, Cincinnati Art Museum, Cincinnati OH
Colgate University, Picker Art Gallery, Hamilton NY

College of William & Mary, Muscarelle Museum of Art, Williamsburg VA
The Courtauld Institute of Art, The Courtauld Gallery, London
Cummer Museum of Art & Gardens, Museum & Library, Jacksonville FL
The Currier Museum of Art, Manchester NH
Denver Art Museum, Denver CO
Detroit Institute of Arts, Detroit MI
Duke University, Nasher Museum of Art at Duke University, Durham NC
Florida State University and Central Florida Community College, The Appleton Museum of Art, Ocala FL
Fondazione Musei Civici Di Venezia, Museo Correr, Venice
Forest Lawn Museum, Glendale CA
The Frick Art & Historical Center, Inc, Frick Art Museum, Pittsburgh PA
Galleria Nazionale dell'Umbria, Umbrian National Gallery, Perugia
Germanisches Nationalmuseum, Nuremberg
The Ghent Museum of Fine Arts, Ghent
Hebrew Union College, Skirball Cultural Center, Los Angeles CA
Hebrew Union College Museum, Jewish Institute of Religion Museum, New York NY
Heritage Malta, National Museum of Fine Arts, Valletta
The Hispanic Society of America, Museum & Library, New York NY
Independent Administrative Institution National Museum of Art, The National Museum of Western Art, Tokyo
The Israel Museum, Jerusalem, Billy Rose Art Garden, Jerusalem
The Israel Museum, Jerusalem, Samuel & Saidye Bronfman Archaeology Wing, Jerusalem
The Israel Museum, Jerusalem, Jerusalem
Bob Jones University Museum & Gallery Inc, Greenville SC
Joslyn Art Museum, Omaha NE
Kereszteny Muzeum, Christian Museum, Esztergom
Knoxville Museum of Art, Knoxville TN
Kunsthistorisches Museum Vienna, Museum of Fine Arts, Vienna
Kyiv Museum of Russian Art, Kyiv
Le Grand Curtius, Musée d'Ansembourg, Liege
Lincolnshire County Council, Library & Heritage Services, Lincoln
Mabee-Gerrer Museum of Art, Shawnee OK
Magyar Nemzeti Muzeum - Hungarian National Museum, Budapest
McNay, San Antonio TX
Menil Foundation, Inc, The Menil Collection, Houston TX
The Metropolitan Museum of Art, New York NY
Moravska Galerie v Brne, Moravian Gallery in Brno, Brno
The Morgan Library & Museum, Museum, New York NY
Mount Holyoke College, Art Museum, South Hadley MA
Musee des Augustins, Toulouse
Musee des Beaux-Arts d'Orleans, Historical & Archaeological Museum of Orleans, Orleans
Musee des Beaux-Arts d'Orleans, Museum of Fine Arts, Orleans
Musee des Beaux-Arts/Palais des Archeveques, Museum of Fine Arts, Tours
Musee National d'Histoire et d'Art Luxembourg, Luxembourg City
Museen der Stadt Koln, Museum Schnutgen, Cologne
Museen der Stadt Koln, Romisch-Germanisches Museum, Cologne
Museen der Stadt Koln, Wallraf-Richartz-Museum, Cologne
Musees Royaux d'Art et d'Histoire, Royal Museums of Art and History, Brussels
Musei Capitolini, Rome
Musei Civici di Padova - Cappella Degli Scrovengni, Musei Civici Agli Eremitani (Civic Museum) - Scrovegni Chapel, Padua
Museo Cerralbo, Madrid
Museo de Navarra, Pamplona
Museo di Capodimonte, Naples
Museu de Evora, Evora
Museu de Grao Vasco, Viseu
Museu Nacional D'Art De Catalunya, National Art Museum, Barcelona
Museum De Lakenhal, Leiden
Museum fur Kunst und Gewerbe Hamburg, Hamburg

The Museum of Arts & Sciences Inc, Daytona Beach FL
Museum zu Allerheiligen, Schaffhausen
Muzeul de Istorie Nationala Si Arheologie Constanta, National History & Archaeology Museum, Constanta
Muzeul National Brukenthal, Blue House & Romanian Art Gallery, Sibiu
Muzeul National Brukenthal, Brukenthal Palace & European Art Gallery, Sibiu
Muzeum Narodowe, National Museum in Poznan, Poznan
The Namur Provincial Museum of Ancient Arts, Namur
Narodna Galerija, National Gallery of Slovenia, Ljubljana
National Gallery of Canada, Ottawa ON
National Museum of Fine Arts of Moldova, Chisinau
National Museum of Serbia, Gallery of Frescoes, Beograd
National Museum of Wildlife Art of the Unites States, Jackson WY
The Nelson-Atkins Museum of Art, Kansas City MO
Opelousas Museum of Art, Inc (OMA), Opelousas LA
Panhandle-Plains Historical Museum, Canyon TX
The Pennsylvania State University, Palmer Museum of Art, University Park PA
Pinacoteca Provinciale, Bari
Princeton University, Princeton University Art Museum, Princeton NJ
Queens College, City University of New York, Godwin-Ternbach Museum, Flushing NY
Reading Public Museum, Reading PA
Rensselaer Newman Foundation Chapel + Cultural Center, The Gallery at the Chapel & Cultural Center, Troy NY
Royal Ontario Museum, Toronto ON
Saginaw Art Museum, Saginaw MI
Saint Mary's College of California, Hearst Art Gallery, Moraga CA
Severoceska Galerie Vytvarneho Umeni v Litomericich, North Bohemian Gallery of Fine Arts in Litomerice, Litomerice
Slovenska Narodna Galeria, Slovak National Gallery, Bratislava
Soprintendenza per I beni storici artistici ed etnoantropologici per le province di Mantova Brescia e Cremona, Museo di Palazzo Ducale, Mantua
Southern Methodist University, Meadows Museum, Dallas TX
The Speed Art Museum, Louisville KY
Staatsgalerie Stuttgart, Stuttgart
Stanford University, Cantor Arts Center at Stanford University, Stanford CA
The State Museum of Fine Arts of Tatarstan Republic, Kazan
State University of New York at Binghamton, Binghamton University Art Museum, Binghamton NY
Staten Island Museum, Staten Island NY
Stiftung Deutsches Historisches Museum, Berlin
Suomen Kansallismuseo, National Museum of Finland, Helsinki
Szepmuveszeti Muzeum, Museum of Fine Arts Budapest, Budapest
Taft Museum of Art, Cincinnati OH
Toledo Museum of Art, Toledo OH
Tver Art Gallery, Tver
University of Chicago, Oriental Institute, Chicago IL
University of Illinois at Urbana-Champaign, Krannert Art Museum and Kinkead Pavilion, Champaign IL
University of Kansas, Spencer Museum of Art, Lawrence KS
University of Miami, Lowe Art Museum, Coral Gables FL
University of Michigan, Museum of Art, Ann Arbor MI
University of Missouri, Museum of Art & Archaeology, Columbia MO
University of Rochester, Memorial Art Gallery, Rochester NY
University of Toronto, University of Toronto Art Centre, Toronto ON
University of Utah, Utah Museum of Fine Arts, Salt Lake City UT
University of Vermont, Robert Hull Fleming Museum, Burlington VT
University of Victoria, The Legacy Art Gallery, Victoria BC
University of Wisconsin-Madison, Chazen Museum of Art, Madison WI
Vassar College, The Frances Lehman Loeb Art Center, Poughkeepsie NY

Walker Art Gallery, Liverpool
Wellesley College, Davis Museum & Cultural Center, Wellesley MA
Williams College, Museum of Art, Williamstown MA
Worcester Art Museum, Worcester MA

METALWORK

Academy of the New Church, Glencairn Museum, Bryn Athyn PA
Albany Institute of History & Art, Albany NY
Albuquerque Museum of Art & History, Albuquerque NM
Arab American National Museum, Dearborn MI
Arnot Art Museum, Elmira NY
Art & Culture Center of Hollywood, Art Gallery/Multidisciplinary Cultural Center, Hollywood FL
Art Community Center, Art Center of Corpus Christi, Corpus Christi TX
Art Gallery of Calgary, Calgary AB
The Art Museum at the University of Kentucky, Lexington KY
Art Without Walls Inc, New York NY
Asheville Art Museum, Asheville NC
Asian Art Museum of San Francisco, Chong-Moon Lee Ctr for Asian Art and Culture, San Francisco CA
Atlanta International Museum of Art & Design, Museum of Design Atlanta, Atlanta GA
Banco de la Republica Museo del Oro, Museo del Oro, Bogota
Baroda Museum and Picture Gallery, Baroda
Bayerisches Nationalmuseum, Bavarian National Museum, Munich
Beloit College, Wright Museum of Art, Beloit WI
Belskie Museum, Closter NJ
Birmingham Museum of Art, Birmingham AL
Byzantine & Christian Museum, Athens, Athens
Canadian Museum of Civilization, Gatineau PQ
Center for Art & Education, Van Buren AR
City of Fayette, Alabama, Fayette Art Museum, Fayette AL
City of Mason City, Charles H MacNider Museum, Mason City IA
Clark County Historical Society, Pioneer - Krier Museum, Ashland KS
College of William & Mary, Muscarelle Museum of Art, Williamsburg VA
Columbus Museum, Columbus GA
Concord Museum, Concord MA
Cooper-Hewitt National Design Museum, Smithsonian Institution, New York NY
Craft and Folk Art Museum (CAFAM), Los Angeles CA
Craftsmen's Guild of Mississippi, Inc, Agriculture & Forestry Museum, Ridgeland MS
Craftsmen's Guild of Mississippi, Inc, Mississippi Crafts Center, Ridgeland MS
Cranbrook Art Museum, Bloomfield Hills MI
Crocker Art Museum, Sacramento CA
Davistown Museum, Liberty Location, Liberty ME
Denver Art Museum, Denver CO
Department of Antiquities, Cyprus Museum, Nicosia
Department of Museums Malaysia, National Museum, Kuala Lumpur
Detroit Institute of Arts, Detroit MI
Detroit Zoological Institute, Wildlife Interpretive Gallery, Royal Oak MI
Durham Art Guild, Durham NC
Evanston Historical Society, Charles Gates Dawes House, Evanston IL
Fetherston Foundation, Packwood House Museum, Lewisburg PA
Flint Institute of Arts, Flint MI
Florida State University and Central Florida Community College, The Appleton Museum of Art, Ocala FL
Edsel & Eleanor Ford, Grosse Pointe Shores MI
Forges du Saint-Maurice National Historic Site, Trois Rivieres PQ
Fort Collins Museum of Art, Inc., Fort Collins CO
Fuller Craft Museum, Brockton MA
Galerie Montcalm, Gatineau PQ
Gallery One Visual Arts Center, Ellensburg WA
Germanisches Nationalmuseum, Nuremberg
Glessner House Museum, Chicago IL
Grand Rapids Art Museum, Grand Rapids MI
Grassroots Art Center, Lucas KS
Greek Ministry of Culture, Archaeological Museum of Thessaloniki, Thessaloniki
Hammond-Harwood House Association, Inc, Hammond-Harwood House, Annapolis MD

Harvard University, Museum & Garden, Washington DC
Haystack Mountain School of Crafts, Deer Isle ME
Hebrew Union College, Skirball Cultural Center, Los Angeles CA
Hecht Museum, Haifa
Henry County Museum & Cultural Arts Center, Clinton MO
Heritage Center of Lancaster County Museum, Lancaster PA
Hillwood Museum & Gardens Foundation, Hillwood Estate Museum & Gardens, Washington DC
The Hispanic Society of America, Museum & Library, New York NY
Historic Arkansas Museum, Little Rock AR
Historic Hudson Valley, Pocantico Hills NY
Holter Museum of Art, Helena MT
Hoyt Center for the Arts, New Castle PA
Hui No'eau Visual Arts Center, Gallery and Gift Shop, Makawao Maui HI
Independence Historical Museum & Art Center, Independence KS
Independent Administrative Institution National Institutes for Cultural Heritage, Tokyo National Museum, Tokyo
Institute of American Indian Arts, Museum of Contemporary Native Arts, Santa Fe NM
Iredell Museums, Statesville NC
The Israel Museum, Jerusalem, Samuel & Saidye Bronfman Archaeology Wing, Jerusalem
Jamestown-Yorktown Foundation, Jamestown Settlement, Williamsburg VA
Johns Hopkins University, Evergreen Museum & Library, Baltimore MD
Kenosha Public Museums, Kenosha WI
Kereszteny Muzeum, Christian Museum, Esztergom
Kings County Historical Society & Museum, Hampton NB
Kirkland Museum of Fine & Decorative Art, Denver CO
Kyiv Museum of Russian Art, Kyiv
Launceston City Council, Queen Victoria Museum and Art Gallery, Launceston
Le Grand Curtius, Musée d'Ansembourg, Liege
League of New Hampshire Craftsmen, Grodin Permanent Collection Museum, Concord NH
LeSueur County Historical Society, Chapter One, Elysian MN
Lightner Museum, Saint Augustine FL
Lincolnshire County Council, Library & Heritage Services, Lincoln
Lincolnshire County Council, The Collection: Art & Archaeology in Lincolnshire, Lincoln
The Long Island Museum of American Art, History & Carriages, Stony Brook NY
Magyar Nemzeti Muzeum - Hungarian National Museum, Budapest
Manchester Bidwell Corporation, Manchester Craftsmen's Guild Youth & Arts Program, Pittsburgh PA
Manitoba Historical Society, Dalnavert Museum, Winnipeg MB
Jacques Marchais, Staten Island NY
Maryland Historical Society, Museum of Maryland History, Baltimore MD
McCord Museum of Canadian History, Montreal PQ
Mesa Arts Center, Mesa Contemporary Arts Museum, Mesa AZ
Milwaukee County War Memorial Inc., Villa Terrace Decorative Arts Museum, Milwaukee WI
Ministry of Cultural Affairs, Bangladesh National Museum, Dhaka
Ministry of Culture & Tourism, The Delphi Museum, 10th Ephorate of Prehistoric & Classical Antiquities, Delphi
The Mint Museum, Mint Museum of Craft & Design, Charlotte NC
Missoula Art Museum, Missoula MT
Mobile Museum of Art, Mobile AL
Modern Art Museum, Fort Worth TX
Moravska Galerie v Brne, Moravian Gallery in Brno, Brno
Musee des Beaux-Arts/Palais des Archeveques, Museum of Fine Arts, Tours
Musee des Maitres et Artisans du Quebec, Montreal PQ
Musee National d'Histoire et d'Art Luxembourg, Luxembourg City
Musee Regional de lu Cote-Nord, Sept-Iles PQ
Musee Royal Et Domaine De Mariemont, Morlanwelz
Museen der Stadt Koln, Romisch-Germanisches Museum, Cologne

Musees Royaux d'Art et d'Histoire, Royal Museums of Art and History, Brussels
Museo Cerralbo, Madrid
Museo De Las Americas, Denver CO
Museo di Capodimonte, Naples
Museu de Evora, Evora
Museum fur Kunst und Gewerbe Hamburg, Hamburg
Museum of Arts & Design, New York NY
Museum of Decorative Arts in Prague, Prague
Museum of Fine Arts Houston, Bayou Bend Collection & Gardens, Houston TX
Museum of Fine Arts, Houston, Rienzi Center for European Decorative Arts, Houston TX
Museum of Florida Art, Deland FL
Museum of Northwest Art, La Conner WA
Museum of the City of New York, Museum, New York NY
Museum zu Allerheiligen, Schaffhausen
Muzej za Umjetnost i Obrt, Museum of Arts & Crafts, Zagreb
Muzeul National Brukenthal, Brukenthal Palace & European Art Gallery, Sibiu
The Namur Provincial Museum of Ancient Arts, Namur
National Museums Scotland, National Museum of Scotland, Edinburgh
National Society of Colonial Dames of America in the State of Maryland, Mount Clare Museum House, Baltimore MD
Naval Historical Center, The Navy Museum, Washington DC
Neustadt Collection of Tiffany Glass, Long Island City NY
New Brunswick Museum, Saint John NB
New Jersey State Museum, Fine Art Bureau, Trenton NJ
New Orleans Artworks at New Orleans Glassworks & Printmaking Studio, New Orleans LA
New York State Office of Parks Recreation & Historic Preservation, John Jay Homestead State Historic Site, Katonah NY
North Carolina State University, Gregg Museum of Art & Design, Raleigh NC
Norwich Free Academy, Slater Memorial Museum, Norwich CT
Nova Scotia College of Art and Design, Anna Leonowens Gallery, Halifax NS
Noyes Art Gallery, Lincoln NE
Ohio University, Kennedy Museum of Art, Athens OH
Okanagan Heritage Museum, Kelowna BC
Olana State Historic Site, Hudson NY
Old Salem Museums & Gardens, Museum of Early Southern Decorative Arts, Winston Salem NC
Panhandle-Plains Historical Museum, Canyon TX
The Pennsylvania State University, Palmer Museum of Art, University Park PA
Philadelphia History Museum, Philadelphia PA
Pioneer Town, Pioneer Museum of Western Art, Wimberley TX
Plumas County Museum, Quincy CA
Pope County Historical Society, Pope County Museum, Glenwood MN
Princeton University, Princeton University Art Museum, Princeton NJ
Principia College, School of Nations Museum, Elsah IL
Queens College, City University of New York, Godwin-Ternbach Museum, Flushing NY
Rabindra Bhavan Art Gallery, Lalit Kala Akademi (National Academy of Art), New Delhi
Reading Public Museum, Reading PA
Rijksmuseum Twenthe, Rijksmuseum Twenthe, Enschede
Roswell Artist-in-Residence Foundation, Anderson Museum of Contemporary Art, Roswell NM
Rubin Museum of Art, New York NY
Saco Museum, Saco ME
Saint Clair County Community College, Jack R Hennesey Art Galleries, Port Huron MI
Saint Peter's College, Art Gallery, Jersey City NJ
Salisbury House Foundation, Salisbury House and Garden, Des Moines IA
San Francisco Maritime National Historical Park, Maritime Museum, San Francisco CA
Schweinfurth Art Center, Auburn NY
Seneca-Iroquois National Museum, Salamanca NY
Sheldon Museum & Cultural Center, Inc, Sheldon Museum & Cultural Center, Haines AK
Shirley Plantation Foundation, Charles City VA
Sloss Furnaces National Historic Landmark, Birmingham AL
Society for Contemporary Craft, Pittsburgh PA
The Society of the Cincinnati at Anderson House, Washington DC

South Carolina Artisans Center, Walterboro SC
Southeastern Center for Contemporary Art, Winston Salem NC
The Speed Art Museum, Louisville KY
Spertus Institute of Jewish Studies, Chicago IL
Staatliche Munzsammlung, State Coin Collection, Munich
Stanford University, Cantor Arts Center at Stanford University, Stanford CA
State University of New York at New Paltz, Samuel Dorsky Museum of Art, New Paltz NY
State University of New York College at Buffalo, Buffalo NY
Stauth Foundation & Museum, Stauth Memorial Museum, Montezuma KS
The Stewart Museum, Montreal PQ
Suan Pakkad Palace Museum, Bangkok
Suomen Kansallismuseo, National Museum of Finland, Helsinki
Syracuse University, SUArt Galleries, Syracuse NY
Taos, La Hacienda de Los Martinez, Taos NM
Lillian & Coleman Taube Museum of Art, Minot ND
The Temple-Tifereth Israel, The Temple Museum of Religious Art, Beachwood OH
Tokyo University of the Arts, The University Art Museum, Tokyo
Topeka & Shawnee County Public Library, Alice C Sabatini Gallery, Topeka KS
Towson University, Asian Arts & Culture Center, Towson MD
Tulane University, Newcomb Art Gallery, New Orleans LA
Tver Art Gallery, Tver
The Ukrainian Museum, New York NY
United States Naval Academy, USNA Museum, Annapolis MD
Universalmuseum Joanneum GmbH, Graz
University of California, Berkeley, The Magnes Collection of Jewish Art & Life, Berkeley CA
University of California, Los Angeles, Fowler Museum at UCLA, Los Angeles CA
University of Georgia, Georgia Museum of Art, Athens GA
University of Illinois at Urbana-Champaign, Krannert Art Museum and Kinkead Pavilion, Champaign IL
University of Indianapolis, Christel DeHaan Fine Arts Gallery, Indianapolis IN
University of Minnesota, Katherine E Nash Gallery, Minneapolis MN
University of Pennsylvania, Museum of Archaeology & Anthropology, Philadelphia PA
University of Toronto, University of Toronto Art Centre, Toronto ON
University of Wisconsin-Madison, Chazen Museum of Art, Madison WI
University of Wisconsin-Madison, Wisconsin Union Galleries, Madison WI
Vesterheim Norwegian-American Museum, Decorah IA
Walker Art Gallery, Liverpool
Westcott Bay Institute, Island Museum of Art & Westcott Bay Sculpture Park, Friday Harbor WA
White House, Washington DC
Wilfrid Laurier University, Robert Langen Art Gallery, Waterloo ON
Workman & Temple Family Homestead Museum, City of Industry CA
World Erotic Art Museum, Miami Beach FL
Yuma Fine Arts Association, Yuma Art Center, Yuma AZ

MEXICAN ART

Americas Society Art Gallery, New York NY
Arizona State University, ASU Art Museum, Tempe AZ
Art & Culture Center of Hollywood, Art Gallery/Multidisciplinary Cultural Center, Hollywood FL
Art Community Center, Art Center of Corpus Christi, Corpus Christi TX
The Art Museum at the University of Kentucky, Lexington KY
The Art Museum of Eastern Idaho, Idaho Falls ID
Art Museum of the University of Houston, Blaffer Gallery, Houston TX
Art Without Walls Inc, New York NY
Arts Council of Fayetteville-Cumberland County, The Arts Center, Fayetteville NC
Aurora University, Schingoethe Center for Native American Cultures & The Schingoethe Art Gallery, Aurora IL
The Baltimore Museum of Art, Baltimore MD

Brown University, Haffenreffer Museum of Anthropology, Providence RI
Bucknell University, Edward & Marthann Samek Art Gallery, Lewisburg PA
The Buffalo Fine Arts Academy, Albright-Knox Art Gallery, Buffalo NY
California State University, Northridge, Art Galleries, Northridge CA
City of El Paso, El Paso TX
The Contemporary Austin, Austin TX
Coutts Museum of Art, Inc, El Dorado KS
Craft and Folk Art Museum (CAFAM), Los Angeles CA
Crocker Art Museum, Sacramento CA
Dartmouth College, Hood Museum of Art, Hanover NH
Davidson College, William H Van Every Jr & Edward M Smith Galleries, Davidson NC
DeLeon White Gallery, Toronto ON
Denver Art Museum, Denver CO
Detroit Institute of Arts, Detroit MI
East Carolina University, Wellington B Gray Gallery, Greenville NC
Ellen Noel Art Museum of the Permian Basin, Odessa TX
Emory University, Michael C Carlos Museum, Atlanta GA
En Foco, Inc, Bronx NY
Figge Art Museum, Davenport IA
Flint Institute of Arts, Flint MI
Folk Art Society of America, Richmond VA
Edsel & Eleanor Ford, Grosse Pointe Shores MI
Fresno Arts Center & Museum, Fresno CA
General Board of Discipleship, The United Methodist Church, The Upper Room Chapel & Museum, Nashville TN
Gonzaga University, Art Gallery, Spokane WA
Guadalupe Historic Foundation, Santuario de Guadalupe, Santa Fe NM
Hartwick College, The Yager Museum, Oneonta NY
Heard Museum, Phoenix AZ
Hermitage Foundation Museum, Norfolk VA
Hidalgo County Historical Museum, Edinburg TX
High Desert Museum, Bend OR
The Hispanic Society of America, Museum & Library, New York NY
Independence Historical Museum & Art Center, Independence KS
INTAR Gallery, New York NY
The Interchurch Center, Galleries at the Interchurch Center, New York NY
The Israel Museum, Jerusalem, Billy Rose Art Garden, Jerusalem
Jefferson County Open Space, Hiwan Homestead Museum, Evergreen CO
Johns Hopkins University, Evergreen Museum & Library, Baltimore MD
Kenosha Public Museums, Kenosha WI
Knights of Columbus Supreme Council, Knights of Columbus Museum, New Haven CT
Knoxville Museum of Art, Knoxville TN
Koshare Indian Museum, Inc, La Junta CO
LA County Museum of Art, Los Angeles CA
La Raza-Galeria Posada, Sacramento CA
Latino Art Museum, Pomona CA
Mabee-Gerrer Museum of Art, Shawnee OK
Madison Museum of Contemporary Art, Madison WI
Mexican Museum, San Francisco CA
Mission San Luis Rey de Francia, Mission San Luis Rey Museum, Oceanside CA
Mission San Miguel Museum, San Miguel CA
Modern Art Museum, Fort Worth TX
Museo De Las Americas, Denver CO
Museo Frida Kahlo Casa Azul, Coyoacan
The Museum, Greenwood SC
The Museum of Contemporary Art (MOCA), Moca Grand Avenue, Los Angeles CA
Museum of Latin American Art, Long Beach CA
Museum of New Mexico, New Mexico Museum of Art, Unit of NM Dept of Cultural Affairs, Santa Fe NM
Muzeul National Brukenthal, Brukenthal Palace & European Art Gallery, Sibiu
National Museum of Mexican Art, Chicago IL
Opelousas Museum of Art, Inc (OMA), Opelousas LA
Palm Springs Art Museum, Palm Springs CA
Panhandle-Plains Historical Museum, Canyon TX
Phoenix Art Museum, Phoenix AZ
Purdue University Galleries, West Lafayette IN
Queens College, City University of New York, Godwin-Ternbach Museum, Flushing NY
Rabindra Bhavan Art Gallery, Lalit Kala Akademi (National Academy of Art), New Delhi
Reading Public Museum, Reading PA

Roswell Museum & Art Center, Roswell NM
C M Russell, Great Falls MT
Saint Joseph College, Art Gallery, University of Saint Joseph, West Hartford CT
Saint Mary's College of California, Hearst Art Gallery, Moraga CA
Saint Peter's College, Art Gallery, Jersey City NJ
San Angelo Museum of Fine Arts, San Angelo TX
San Antonio Museum of Art, San Antonio TX
Scripps College, Ruth Chandler Williamson Gallery, Claremont CA
The Speed Art Museum, Louisville KY
Stanford University, Cantor Arts Center at Stanford University, Stanford CA
Stone Quarry Hill Art Park, Winner Gallery, Cazenovia NY
Taos, La Hacienda de Los Martinez, Taos NM
Lillian & Coleman Taube Museum of Art, Minot ND
Tohono Chul Park, Tucson AZ
Topeka & Shawnee County Public Library, Alice C Sabatini Gallery, Topeka KS
Tucson Museum of Art and Historic Block, Tucson AZ
Tyler Museum of Art, Tyler TX
University of California, Los Angeles, Fowler Museum at UCLA, Los Angeles CA
University of Colorado at Colorado Springs, Gallery of Contemporary Art, Colorado Springs CO
University of Georgia, Georgia Museum of Art, Athens GA
University of Illinois at Urbana-Champaign, Krannert Art Museum and Kinkead Pavilion, Champaign IL
University of Miami, Lowe Art Museum, Coral Gables FL
University of Pennsylvania, Museum of Archaeology & Anthropology, Philadelphia PA
University of Southern California, USC Fisher Museum of Art, Los Angeles CA
University of Texas at Austin, Blanton Museum of Art, Austin TX
University of Utah, Utah Museum of Fine Arts, Salt Lake City UT
University of Wisconsin-Madison, Chazen Museum of Art, Madison WI
Wake Forest University, Museum of Anthropology, Winston Salem NC
Wichita Art Museum, Wichita KS
World Erotic Art Museum, Miami Beach FL
Yuma Fine Arts Association, Yuma Art Center, Yuma AZ

MILITARY ART

Adams County Historical Society, Gettysburg PA
African American Museum in Philadelphia, Philadelphia PA
Alabama Department of Archives & History, Museum of Alabama, Montgomery AL
Arizona Historical Society-Yuma, Sanguinetti House Museum & Garden, Yuma AZ
Arnot Art Museum, Elmira NY
Arts Council of Fayetteville-Cumberland County, The Arts Center, Fayetteville NC
Autry National Center, Southwest Museum of the American Indian, Mt. Washington Campus, Los Angeles CA
Bone Creek Museum of Agrarian Art, David City NE
Booth Western Art Museum, Cartersville GA
Canadian Museum of Civilization, Gatineau PQ
Carteret County Historical Society, The History Place, Morehead City NC
City of Brea, Art Gallery, Brea CA
Department of Antiquities, Cyprus Museum, Nicosia
Detroit Institute of Arts, Detroit MI
Evanston Historical Society, Charles Gates Dawes House, Evanston IL
Fairbanks Museum & Planetarium, Saint Johnsbury VT
Florence Museum, Florence SC
Fondazione Musei Civici Di Venezia, Museo Correr, Venice
Fort George G Meade Museum, Fort Meade MD
Fort Ticonderoga Association, Ticonderoga NY
Gadsden Museum, Mesilla NM
Germanisches Nationalmuseum, Nuremberg
Headquarters Fort Monroe, Dept of Army, Casemate Museum, Hampton VA
Henry County Museum & Cultural Arts Center, Clinton MO
Hillwood Museum & Gardens Foundation, Hillwood Estate Museum & Gardens, Washington DC
Huntington Museum of Art, Huntington WV
John Weaver Sculpture Collection, Hope BC
Kenosha Public Museums, Kenosha WI

MINIATURES

Portland Art Museum, Portland OR
Princeton University, Princeton University Art Museum, Princeton NJ
R W Norton Art Foundation, R W Norton Art Gallery, Shreveport LA
Rabindra Bhavan Art Gallery, Lalit Kala Akademi (National Academy of Art), New Delhi
Rijksmuseum Twenthe, Rijksmuseum Twenthe, Enschede
The Rosenbach Museum & Library, Philadelphia PA
Saco Museum, Saco ME
Saint Joseph's Oratory, Museum, Montreal PQ
Saint Louis County Historical Society, St. Louis County Historical Society, Duluth MN
Saint Olaf College, Flaten Art Museum, Northfield MN
Saint Peter's College, Art Gallery, Jersey City NJ
Slovenska Narodna Galeria, Slovak National Gallery, Bratislava
The Society of the Cincinnati at Anderson House, Washington DC
South Carolina State Museum, Columbia SC
The Speed Art Museum, Louisville KY
The State Museum of Oriental Art, Moscow
Staten Island Museum, Staten Island NY
The Stewart Museum, Montreal PQ
Suomen Kansallismuseo, National Museum of Finland, Helsinki
Supreme Court of the United States, Office of the Curator, Washington DC
Taft Museum of Art, Cincinnati OH
Tinkertown Museum, Sandia Park NM
Tohono Chul Park, Tucson AZ
Tver Art Gallery, Tver
United Society of Shakers, Shaker Museum, New Gloucester ME
University of Georgia, Georgia Museum of Art, Athens GA
University of Illinois at Urbana-Champaign, Krannert Art Museum and Kinkead Pavilion, Champaign IL
University of Louisiana at Lafayette, Paul and Lulu Hilliard University Art Museum, Lafayette LA
University of Wisconsin-Madison, Chazen Museum of Art, Madison WI
Vesterheim Norwegian-American Museum, Decorah IA
The Walker African American Museum & Research Center, Las Vegas NV
Walker Art Gallery, Liverpool
The Wallace Collection, London
Wistariahurst Museum, Holyoke MA
Woodlawn/The Pope-Leighey, Mount Vernon VA
World Erotic Art Museum, Miami Beach FL
Yale University, Yale Center for British Art, New Haven CT
Zigler Art Museum, Jennings LA

MIXED MEDIA

Art & Culture Center of Hollywood, Art Gallery/Multidisciplinary Cultural Center, Hollywood FL
Artspace, Richmond VA
Autry National Center, Southwest Museum of the American Indian, Mt. Washington Campus, Los Angeles CA
College of Saint Benedict, Gorecki Gallery & Gallery Lounge, Saint Joseph MN
Crocker Art Museum, Sacramento CA
Eula Mae Edwards Museum & Gallery, Clovis NM
Haystack Mountain School of Crafts, Deer Isle ME
J.M.W. Turner Museum, Sarasota FL
Jordan National Gallery of Fine Arts, Amman
LACE (Los Angeles Contemporary Exhibitions), Los Angeles CA
Latino Art Museum, Pomona CA
Palm Springs Art Museum, Palm Springs CA
Rabindra Bhavan Art Gallery, Lalit Kala Akademi (National Academy of Art), New Delhi
Jack Richard Gallery, Almond Tea Museum & Jane Williams Galleries, Divisions of Studios of Jack Richard, Cuyahoga Falls OH
Rijksmuseum Twenthe, Rijksmuseum Twenthe, Enschede
Slovenska Narodna Galeria, Slovak National Gallery, Bratislava
Society for Contemporary Craft, Pittsburgh PA
South Dakota State University, South Dakota Art Museum, Brookings SD
Spertus Institute of Jewish Studies, Chicago IL
Springfield Art Museum, Springfield MO
Stone Quarry Hill Art Park, Winner Gallery, Cazenovia NY

MOSAICS

Academy of the New Church, Glencairn Museum, Bryn Athyn PA
Arab American National Museum, Dearborn MI
Archaeological Museum of the American University of Beirut, Beirut
Art & Culture Center of Hollywood, Art Gallery/Multidisciplinary Cultural Center, Hollywood FL
Art Community Center, Art Center of Corpus Christi, Corpus Christi TX
Art Without Walls Inc, New York NY
The Baltimore Museum of Art, Baltimore MD
Baroda Museum and Picture Gallery, Baroda
Byzantine & Christian Museum, Athens, Athens
Cameron Art Museum, Wilmington NC
Canadian Museum of Civilization, Gatineau PQ
Craft and Folk Art Museum (CAFAM), Los Angeles CA
Craftsmen's Guild of Mississippi, Inc, Agriculture & Forestry Museum, Ridgeland MS
Dartmouth College, Hood Museum of Art, Hanover NH
Department of Antiquities, Cyprus Museum, Nicosia
Detroit Institute of Arts, Detroit MI
Flint Institute of Arts, Flint MI
Forest Lawn Museum, Glendale CA
Fuller Craft Museum, Brockton MA
Georgetown University, Art Collection, Washington DC
Grassroots Art Center, Lucas KS
Greek Ministry of Culture, Archaeological Museum of Thessaloniki, Thessaloniki
Harvard University, Museum & Garden, Washington DC
Hecht Museum, Haifa
Henry County Museum & Cultural Arts Center, Clinton MO
Higgins Armory Museum, Worcester MA
Illinois State Museum, ISM Lockport Gallery, Chicago Gallery & Southern Illinois Art Gallery, Springfield IL
The Interchurch Center, Galleries at the Interchurch Center, New York NY
The Israel Museum, Jerusalem, Billy Rose Art Garden, Jerusalem
The Israel Museum, Jerusalem, Samuel & Saidye Bronfman Archaeology Wing, Jerusalem
The Israel Museum, Jerusalem, Jerusalem
Johns Hopkins University, Evergreen Museum & Library, Baltimore MD
Bob Jones University Museum & Gallery Inc, Greenville SC
Kenosha Public Museums, Kenosha WI
Kentucky Museum of Art and Craft, Louisville KY
Knights of Columbus Supreme Council, Knights of Columbus Museum, New Haven CT
Latino Art Museum, Pomona CA
League of New Hampshire Craftsmen, Grodin Permanent Collection Museum, Concord NH
Lincolnshire County Council, The Collection: Art & Archaeology in Lincolnshire, Lincoln
Lizzadro Museum of Lapidary Art, Elmhurst IL
Manchester Bidwell Corporation, Manchester Craftsmen's Guild Youth & Arts Program, Pittsburgh PA
Mesa Arts Center, Mesa Contemporary Arts Museum, Mesa AZ
Ministry of Cultural Affairs, Bangladesh National Museum, Dhaka
Ministry of Culture & Tourism, The Delphi Museum, 10th Ephorate of Prehistoric & Classical Antiquities, Delphi
Musee National d'Histoire et d'Art Luxembourg, Luxembourg City
Musee Royal Et Domaine De Mariemont, Morlanwelz
Museen der Stadt Koln, Romisch-Germanisches Museum, Cologne
Musees Royaux d'Art et d'Histoire, Royal Museums of Art and History, Brussels
Musei Capitolini, Rome
Musei Civici di Padova - Cappella Degli Scrovegni, Musei Civici Agli Eremitani (Civic Museum) - Scrovegni Chapel, Padua
Museo de Navarra, Pamplona
Museum fur Kunst und Gewerbe Hamburg, Hamburg
Museum of Decorative Arts in Prague, Prague
Museum zu Allerheiligen, Schaffhausen
Muzeul de Istorie Nationala Si Arheologie Constanta, National History & Archaeology Museum, Constanta
National Museum of Ceramic Art & Glass, Baltimore MD

Nelson Mandela Bay Municipality, Nelson Mandela Metropolitan Art Museum, Port Elizabeth
New Jersey State Museum, Fine Art Bureau, Trenton NJ
Noyes Art Gallery, Lincoln NE
Panhandle-Plains Historical Museum, Canyon TX
The Frank Phillips, Woolaroc Museum, Bartlesville OK
Plainsman Museum, Aurora NE
Princeton University, Princeton University Art Museum, Princeton NJ
Queens College, City University of New York, Godwin-Ternbach Museum, Flushing NY
Rabindra Bhavan Art Gallery, Lalit Kala Akademi (National Academy of Art), New Delhi
Roswell Artist-in-Residence Foundation, Anderson Museum of Contemporary Art, Roswell NM
Saint Joseph's Oratory, Museum, Montreal PQ
Saint Peter's College, Art Gallery, Jersey City NJ
Slovenska Narodna Galeria, Slovak National Gallery, Bratislava
Society for Contemporary Craft, Pittsburgh PA
Soprintendenza per I beni storici artistici ed etnoantropologici per le province di Mantova Brescia e Cremona, Museo di Palazzo Ducale, Mantua
South Dakota State University, South Dakota Art Museum, Brookings SD
The Speed Art Museum, Louisville KY
Stanford University, Cantor Arts Center at Stanford University, Stanford CA
Tohono Chul Park, Tucson AZ
Tver Art Gallery, Tver
University of Manitoba, Faculty of Architecture Exhibition Centre, Winnipeg MB
University of Missouri, Museum of Art & Archaeology, Columbia MO
University of Pennsylvania, Museum of Archaeology & Anthropology, Philadelphia PA
University of Utah, Utah Museum of Fine Arts, Salt Lake City UT
University of Wisconsin-Madison, Chazen Museum of Art, Madison WI
Wadsworth Atheneum Museum of Art, Hartford CT
Waterworks Visual Arts Center, Salisbury NC
Wheaton College, Beard and Weil Galleries, Norton MA
Wiregrass Museum of Art, Dothan AL
Worcester Art Museum, Worcester MA

ORIENTAL ART

Academy of the New Church, Glencairn Museum, Bryn Athyn PA
Allentown Art Museum, Allentown PA
Arab American National Museum, Dearborn MI
Arnot Art Museum, Elmira NY
Art & Culture Center of Hollywood, Art Gallery/Multidisciplinary Cultural Center, Hollywood FL
Art Gallery of Greater Victoria, Victoria BC
Art Gallery of Nova Scotia, Halifax NS
The Art Museum at the University of Kentucky, Lexington KY
Art Without Walls Inc, New York NY
Arts Council of Fayetteville-Cumberland County, The Arts Center, Fayetteville NC
Asian Art Museum of San Francisco, Chong-Moon Lee Ctr for Asian Art and Culture, San Francisco CA
Badisches Landesmuseum, Karlsruhe
Baroda Museum and Picture Gallery, Baroda
Bates College, Museum of Art, Lewiston ME
Beloit College, Wright Museum of Art, Beloit WI
Birger Sandzen Memorial Gallery, Lindsborg KS
Birmingham Museum of Art, Birmingham AL
Blanden Memorial Art Museum, Fort Dodge IA
Bruce Museum, Inc, Greenwich CT
Bucknell University, Edward & Marthann Samek Art Gallery, Lewisburg PA
The Buffalo Fine Arts Academy, Albright-Knox Art Gallery, Buffalo NY
California State University Stanislaus, University Art Gallery, Turlock CA
California State University, Northridge, Art Galleries, Northridge CA
Carnegie Museums of Pittsburgh, Carnegie Museum of Art, Pittsburgh PA
Carolina Art Association, Gibbes Museum of Art, Charleston SC
Billie Trimble Chandler, Texas State Museum of Asian Cultures, Corpus Christi TX
Chhatrapati Shivaji Maharaj Vastu Sangrahalaya, Mumbai

PAINTING-AMERICAN

Abington Art Center, Jenkintown PA
Academy Art Museum, Easton MD
Academy of the New Church, Glencairn Museum, Bryn Athyn PA
African American Museum in Philadelphia, Philadelphia PA
Aidron Duckworth Art Preservation Trust, Aidron Duckworth Art Museum, Meriden NH
Akron Art Museum, Akron OH
Alabama Department of Archives & History, Museum of Alabama, Montgomery AL
Alaska Heritage Museum at Wells Fargo, Anchorage AK
Albany Institute of History & Art, Albany NY
Albany Museum of Art, Albany GA
Albin Polasek Museum & Sculpture Gardens, Winter Park FL
Albion College, Bobbitt Visual Arts Center, Albion MI
Albright College, Freedman Gallery, Reading PA
Albuquerque Museum of Art & History, Albuquerque NM
Allentown Art Museum, Allentown PA
Alton Museum of History & Art, Inc, Alton IL
American Art Museum, Smithsonian Institution, Washington DC
American Folk Art Museum, New York NY
American Sport Art Museum and Archives, Daphne AL
American University, Katzen Art Center Gallery, New York NY
Amon Carter Museum of American Art, Fort Worth TX
Anchorage Museum at Rasmuson Center, Anchorage AK
Walter Anderson, Ocean Springs MS
The Andy Warhol Museum, Museum, Pittsburgh PA
Anna Maria College, Saint Luke's Gallery, Paxton MA
Appaloosa Museum and Heritage Center, Moscow ID
ARC Gallery, Chicago IL
Arizona Museum For Youth, Mesa AZ
Arizona State University, ASU Art Museum, Tempe AZ
Arnot Art Museum, Elmira NY
Art & Culture Center of Hollywood, Art Gallery/Multidisciplinary Cultural Center, Hollywood FL
Art Community Center, Art Center of Corpus Christi, Corpus Christi TX
Art Complex Museum, Carl A. Weyerhaeuser Library, Duxbury MA
Art Gallery of Alberta, Edmonton AB
Art Gallery of Hamilton, Hamilton ON
Art Gallery of Nova Scotia, Halifax NS
Art Gallery of Ontario, Toronto ON
The Art Museum at the University of Kentucky, Lexington KY
The Art Museum of Eastern Idaho, Idaho Falls ID
Art Museum of Greater Lafayette, Lafayette IN
Art Museum of Southeast Texas, Beaumont TX
Art Museum of the University of Houston, Blaffer Gallery, Houston TX
Art Without Walls Inc, New York NY
Artesia Historical Museum & Art Center, Artesia NM
Artists' Cooperative Gallery, Omaha NE
Arts Council of Fayetteville-Cumberland County, The Arts Center, Fayetteville NC
Artspace, Richmond VA
Asbury College, Student Center Gallery, Wilmore KY
Asheville Art Museum, Asheville NC
Athenaeum of Philadelphia, Philadelphia PA
Attleboro Arts Museum, Attleboro MA
Auburn University, Julie Collins Smith Museum, Auburn AL
Augustana College, Augustana College Art Museum, Rock Island IL
Autry National Center, Southwest Museum of the American Indian, Mt. Washington Campus, Los Angeles CA
Avampato Discovery Museum, The Clay Center for Arts & Sciences, Charleston WV
Bakersfield Art Foundation, Bakersfield Museum of Art, Bakersfield CA
Baldwin Historical Society Museum, Baldwin NY
Baldwin-Wallace College, Fawick Art Gallery, Berea OH
Ball State University, Museum of Art, Muncie IN
Baltimore City Community College, Art Gallery, Baltimore MD
The Baltimore Museum of Art, Baltimore MD
Bard College, Center for Curatorial Studies and the Hessel Museum of Art, Annandale-on-Hudson NY
Barnes Foundation, Merion PA
John D Barrow, Skaneateles NY
The Bartlett Museum, Amesbury MA

Baruch College of the City University of New York, Sidney Mishkin Gallery, New York NY
Bass Museum of Art, Miami Beach FL
Bates College, Museum of Art, Lewiston ME
Baton Rouge Gallery, Center For Contemporary Art, Baton Rouge LA
Baylor University, Martin Museum of Art, Waco TX
Beaumont Art League, Beaumont TX
Belle Grove Inc., Belle Grove Plantation, Middletown VA
Beloit College, Wright Museum of Art, Beloit WI
Belskie Museum, Closter NJ
Bennington Museum, Bennington VT
Bergstrom-Mahler Museum, Neenah WI
Berkshire Museum, Pittsfield MA
Berman Museum, Anniston AL
Bertha V B Lederer Fine Arts Gallery-Suny Geneseo, Bertha V B Lederer Fine Arts Gallery, Geneseo NY
Besser Museum for Northeast Michigan, Alpena MI
Beverly Historical Society, Cabot, Hale & Balch House Museums, Beverly MA
Biggs Museum of American Art, Dover DE
Birger Sandzen Memorial Gallery, Lindsborg KS
Birmingham Museum of Art, Birmingham AL
Blanden Memorial Art Museum, Fort Dodge IA
Blauvelt Demarest Foundation, Hiram Blauvelt Art Museum, Oradell NJ
Board of Parks & Recreation, The Parthenon, Nashville TN
Boise Art Museum, Boise ID
Bone Creek Museum of Agrarian Art, David City NE
Booth Western Art Museum, Cartersville GA
Roy Boyd, Chicago IL
Brandywine Conservancy, Brandywine River Museum, Chadds Ford PA
Brick Store Museum, Kennebunk ME
Brigham City Corporation, Brigham City Museum & Gallery, Brigham City UT
Brigham Young University, B F Larsen Gallery, Provo UT
Brigham Young University, Museum of Art, Provo UT
L D Brinkman, Kerrville TX
Bradford Brinton, Big Horn WY
Brown University, David Winton Bell Gallery, Providence RI
Bruce Museum, Inc, Greenwich CT
Bryan Memorial Gallery, Cambridge VT
Bucknell University, Edward & Marthann Samek Art Gallery, Lewisburg PA
The Buffalo Fine Arts Academy, Albright-Knox Art Gallery, Buffalo NY
Burke Arts Council, Jailhouse Galleries, Morganton NC
Bush-Holley Historic Site & Storehouse Gallery, Greenwich Historical Society/ Bush-Holley House, Cos Cob CT
The Butler Institute of American Art, Art Museum, Youngstown OH
C W Post Campus of Long Island University, Hillwood Art Museum, Brookville NY
Cabot's Old Indian Pueblo Museum, Desert Hot Springs CA
California Center for the Arts, Escondido Museum, Escondido CA
California State University Stanislaus, University Art Gallery, Turlock CA
California State University, Northridge, Art Galleries, Northridge CA
Calvin College, Center Art Gallery, Grand Rapids MI
Cambridge Museum, Cambridge NE
Cameron Art Museum, Wilmington NC
Canadian Wildlife & Wilderness Art Museum, Ottawa ON
Canajoharie Library & Art Gallery, Arkell Museum of Canajoharie, Canajoharie NY
Canton Museum of Art, Canton OH
Cape Ann Historical Association, Cape Ann Museum, Gloucester MA
Cape Cod Museum of Art Inc, Dennis MA
Capital University, Schumacher Gallery, Columbus OH
Carleton College, Art Gallery, Northfield MN
Carlsbad Museum & Art Center, Carlsbad NM
Carnegie Center for Art & History, New Albany IN
Carnegie Museums of Pittsburgh, Carnegie Museum of Art, Pittsburgh PA
Carolina Art Association, Gibbes Museum of Art, Charleston SC
Carson County Square House Museum, Panhandle TX
Cartoon Art Museum, San Francisco CA
Cedar Rapids Museum of Art, Cedar Rapids IA
Center for Art & Education, Van Buren AR
Central Methodist University, Ashby-Hodge Gallery of American Art, Fayette MO

Central United Methodist Church, Swords Into Plowshares Peace Center & Gallery, Detroit MI
Channel Islands Maritime Museum, Oxnard CA
Charles Allis Art Museum, Milwaukee WI
Chatham Historical Society, The Atwood House Museum, Chatham MA
Chatillon-DeMenil House Foundation, Chatillon-DeMenil House, Saint Louis MO
Cheekwood-Tennessee Botanical Garden & Museum of Art, Nashville TN
Chrysler Museum of Art, Norfolk VA
Church of Jesus Christ of Latter-Day Saints, Museum of Church History & Art, Salt Lake City UT
City of Atlanta, Atlanta Cyclorama & Civil War Museum, Atlanta GA
City of Brea, Art Gallery, Brea CA
City of Cedar Falls, Iowa, James & Meryl Hearst Center for the Arts & Sculpture Garden, Cedar Falls IA
City of El Paso, El Paso TX
City of Fayette, Alabama, Fayette Art Museum, Fayette AL
City of Fremont, Olive Hyde Art Gallery, Fremont CA
City of Gainesville, Thomas Center Galleries - Cultural Affairs, Gainesville FL
City of Mason City, Charles H MacNider Museum, Mason City IA
The City of Petersburg Museums, Petersburg VA
City of Pittsfield, Berkshire Artisans, Pittsfield MA
City of Port Angeles, Port Angeles Fine Arts Center & Webster Woods Art Park, Port Angeles WA
City of Springdale, Shiloh Museum of Ozark History, Springdale AR
City of Ukiah, Grace Hudson Museum & The Sun House, Ukiah CA
Clark County Historical Society, Heritage Center of Clark County, Springfield OH
Clark County Historical Society, Pioneer - Krier Museum, Ashland KS
Sterling & Francine Clark, Williamstown MA
Clemson University, Rudolph E Lee Gallery, Clemson SC
The Cleveland Museum of Art, Cleveland OH
Clinton Art Association, River Arts Center, Clinton IA
Clinton County Historical Association, Clinton County Historical Museum, Plattsburgh NY
Coastal Arts League Museum, Half Moon Bay CA
Cohasset Historical Society, Pratt Building (Society Headquarters), Cohasset MA
Colgate University, Picker Art Gallery, Hamilton NY
College of Eastern Utah, Gallery East, Price UT
The College of Idaho, Rosenthal Art Gallery, Caldwell ID
College of Saint Rose, Art Gallery, Albany NY
College of William & Mary, Muscarelle Museum of Art, Williamsburg VA
The College of Wooster, The College of Wooster Art Museum, Wooster OH
Colorado Historical Society, Colorado History Museum, Denver CO
Columbia County Historical Society, Columbia County Museum and Library, Kinderhook NY
Columbia Museum of Art, Columbia SC
Columbus Chapel & Boal Mansion Museum, Boalsburg PA
Columbus Museum, Columbus GA
Columbus Museum of Art, Columbus OH
Concord Museum, Concord MA
Concordia Historical Institute, Saint Louis MO
Coos Art Museum, Coos Bay OR
Corcoran Gallery of Art, Washington DC
Cornell College, Peter Paul Luce Gallery, Mount Vernon IA
Cornell Museum of Art and American Culture, Delray Beach FL
Cornell University, Herbert F Johnson Museum of Art, Ithaca NY
Coutts Museum of Art, Inc, El Dorado KS
Craigdarroch Castle Historical Museum Society, Victoria BC
Cranbrook Art Museum, Bloomfield Hills MI
Crane Collection, Gallery of American Painting and Sculpture, Magnolia MA
Crary Art Gallery Inc, Grary Art Gallery, Warren PA
Crazy Horse Memorial, Indian Museum of North America, Native American Educational & Cultural Center & Crazy Horse Memorial Library (Reference), Crazy Horse SD
Creighton University, Lied Art Gallery, Omaha NE
Cripple Creek District Museum, Cripple Creek CO
Crocker Art Museum, Sacramento CA
Crook County Museum & Art Gallery, Sundance WY

Kirkland Museum of Fine & Decorative Art, Denver CO

Knights of Columbus Supreme Council, Knights of Columbus Museum, New Haven CT

Knoxville Museum of Art, Knoxville TN

Koochiching Museums, International Falls MN

Koshare Indian Museum, Inc, La Junta CO

La Salle University Art Museum, Philadelphia PA

Lafayette College, Lafayette College Art Galleries, Easton PA

Lafayette Science Museum & Planetarium, Lafayette LA

LaGrange Art Museum, LaGrange GA

Lamar University, Dishman Art Museum, Beaumont TX

Langston University, Melvin B Tolson Black Heritage Center, Langston OK

Laurentian University, Museum & Art Centre, Sudbury ON

Leanin' Tree Museum & Sculpture Garden of Western Art, Boulder CO

Leeds Museums & Galleries, Leeds

Lehigh University Art Galleries, Museum Operation, Bethlehem PA

Lehigh Valley Heritage Center, Allentown PA

LeMoyne Art Foundation, Center for the Visual Arts, Tallahassee FL

LeSueur County Historical Society, Chapter One, Elysian MN

Liberty Hall Historic Site, Liberty Hall Museum, Frankfort KY

Liberty Memorial Museum & Archives, The National Museum of World War I, Kansas City MO

Lightner Museum, Saint Augustine FL

Lincoln County Historical Association, Inc, 1811 Old Lincoln County Jail & Lincoln County Museum, Wiscasset ME

Livingston County Historical Society, Museum, Geneseo NY

Lockwood-Mathews Mansion Museum, Norwalk CT

Long Beach Museum of Art Foundation, Long Beach CA

The Long Island Museum of American Art, History & Carriages, Stony Brook NY

Longfellow's Wayside Inn Museum, Sudbury MA

Longfellow-Evangeline State Commemorative Area, Saint Martinville LA

Longue Vue House & Gardens, New Orleans LA

Longview Museum of Fine Art, Longview TX

Los Angeles County Museum of Art, Los Angeles CA

Los Angeles County Museum of Natural History, William S Hart Museum, Newhall CA

Louisiana Arts & Science Museum, Baton Rouge LA

Louisiana Department of Culture, Recreation & Tourism, Louisiana State Museum, New Orleans LA

Louisiana State University, Museum of Art, Baton Rouge LA

Louisiana State University, Student Union Art Gallery, Baton Rouge LA

Loveland Museum/Gallery, Loveland CO

Ludwig Museum - Museum of Contemporary Art, Budapest

Luther College, Fine Arts Collection, Decorah IA

Lycoming College Gallery, Williamsport PA

Lyman Allyn Art Museum, New London CT

Lyme Historical Society, Florence Griswold Museum, Old Lyme CT

Lynchburg College, Daura Gallery, Lynchburg VA

Mabee-Gerrer Museum of Art, Shawnee OK

Macalester College, Macalester College Art Gallery, Saint Paul MN

Madison Museum of Contemporary Art, Madison WI

Madison Museum of Fine Art, Madison GA

Maine College of Art, The Institute of Contemporary Art, Portland ME

Maine Historical Society, MHS Museum, Portland ME

Maitland Art Center, Maitland FL

Marblehead Museum & Historical Society, Jeremiah Lee Mansion, Marblehead MA

Marietta College, Grover M Hermann Fine Arts Center, Marietta OH

Marietta-Cobb Museum of Art, Marietta GA

Marine Corps University, National Museum of the Marine Corps, Triangle VA

The Mariners' Museum, Newport News VA

Marquette University, Haggerty Museum of Art, Milwaukee WI

Maryhill Museum of Art, Goldendale WA

Maryland Art Place, Baltimore MD

Maryland Historical Society, Museum of Maryland History, Baltimore MD

Marylhurst University, The Art Gym, Marylhurst OR

Maryville University Saint Louis, Morton J May Foundation Gallery, Saint Louis MO

Massachusetts Institute of Technology, List Visual Arts Center, Cambridge MA

Massillon Museum, Massillon OH

Mattatuck Historical Society, Mattatuck Museum, Waterbury CT

Maysville, Kentucky Gateway Museum Center, Maysville KY

McDowell House & Apothecary Shop, Danville KY

McLean County Historical Society, McLean County Museum of History, Bloomington IL

McMaster University, McMaster Museum of Art, Hamilton ON

McNay, San Antonio TX

McPherson College Gallery, McPherson KS

McPherson Museum and Arts Foundation, McPherson KS

Mendel Art Gallery & Civic Conservatory, Saskatoon SK

Menil Foundation, Inc, The Menil Collection, Houston TX

Mennello Museum of American Art, Orlando FL

Meredith College, Frankie G Weems Gallery & Rotunda Gallery, Raleigh NC

Meridian Museum of Art, Meridian MS

Merrick Art Gallery, New Brighton PA

Mesa Arts Center, Mesa Contemporary Arts Museum, Mesa AZ

The Metropolitan Museum of Art, New York NY

Miami University, Art Museum, Oxford OH

Miami-Dade College, Kendal Campus, Art Gallery, Miami FL

Michelson Museum of Art, Marshall TX

James A Michener, Doylestown PA

Middle Border Museum & Oscar Howe Art Center, Mitchell SD

Middlebury College, Museum of Art, Middlebury VT

Midwest Museum of American Art, Elkhart IN

Miller Art Center Foundation Inc, Miller Art Museum, Sturgeon Bay WI

Millikin University, Perkinson Gallery, Decatur IL

Mills College Art Museum, Oakland CA

Milwaukee Art Museum, Milwaukee WI

Ministry of Cultural Affairs, Bangladesh National Museum, Dhaka

Minneapolis Institute of Arts, Minneapolis MN

Minnesota Historical Society, Minnesota State Capitol Historic Site, St Paul MN

Minnesota Museum of American Art, Saint Paul MN

Minnesota State University, Mankato, Mankato MN

Minot State University, Northwest Art Center, Minot ND

The Mint Museum, Mint Museum of Craft & Design, Charlotte NC

Mission San Luis Rey de Francia, Mission San Luis Rey Museum, Oceanside CA

Mississippi University for Women, Fine Arts Gallery, Columbus MS

Missoula Art Museum, Missoula MT

Missouri Department of Natural Resources, Missouri State Museum, Jefferson City MO

Arthur Roy Mitchell, A.R. Mitchell Museum, Trinidad CO

Mobile Museum of Art, Mobile AL

Modern Art Museum, Fort Worth TX

Mohawk Valley Heritage Association, Inc, Walter Elwood Museum, Amsterdam NY

MonDak Heritage Center, History Library, Sidney MT

Monhegan Museum, Monhegan ME

Monroe County Historical Association, Elizabeth D Walters Library, Stroudsburg PA

Montclair Art Museum, Montclair NJ

Moravian College, Payne Gallery, Bethlehem PA

Moravian Historical Society, Whitefield House Museum, Nazareth PA

Morehead State University, Kentucky Folk Art Center, Morehead KY

Morris Museum, Morristown NJ

Morris Museum of Art, Augusta GA

Morris-Jumel Mansion, Inc, New York NY

Morven Museum & Garden, Princeton NJ

Mount Allison University, Owens Art Gallery, Sackville NB

Mount Holyoke College, Art Museum, South Hadley MA

Mount Vernon Hotel Museum & Garden, New York NY

Muchnic Foundation & Atchison Art Association, Muchnic Gallery, Atchison KS

Muhlenberg College, Martin Art Gallery, Allentown PA

Munson-Williams-Proctor Arts Institute, Museum of Art, Utica NY

Murray State University, Art Galleries, Murray KY

Muscatine Art Center, Museum, Muscatine IA

Muscatine Art Center, Muscatine IA

Musee des Beaux-Arts/Palais des Archeveques, Museum of Fine Arts, Tours

Musee National des Beaux Arts du Quebec, Quebec PQ

Musee Regional de Vaudreuil-Soulanges, Vaudreuil-Dorion PQ

Museo de Arte de Ponce, The Luis A Ferre Foundation Inc, Ponce PR

Museo De Las Americas, Denver CO

The Museum, Greenwood SC

Museum of Art & History, Santa Cruz, Santa Cruz CA

Museum of Art, Fort Lauderdale, Fort Lauderdale FL

The Museum of Arts & Sciences Inc, Daytona Beach FL

Museum of Arts & Sciences, Inc, Macon GA

Museum of Contemporary Art, Chicago IL

Museum of Contemporary Art, North Miami FL

The Museum of Contemporary Art (MOCA), Moca Grand Avenue, Los Angeles CA

Museum of Contemporary Art Jacksonville, Jacksonville FL

Museum of Contemporary Art San Diego, San Diego CA

Museum of Contemporary Art, San Diego, La Jolla CA

Museum of Decorative Arts in Prague, Prague

Museum of Fine Arts Houston, Bayou Bend Collection & Gardens, Houston TX

Museum of Fine Arts, Saint Petersburg, Florida, Inc, Saint Petersburg FL

Museum of Florida Art, Deland FL

Museum of Modern Art, New York NY

Museum of Northern Arizona, Flagstaff AZ

Museum of Northwest Art, La Conner WA

Museum of Southern History, Houston TX

Museum of the City of New York, Museum, New York NY

Museum of Ventura County, Ventura CA

Museum of Wisconsin Art, West Bend WI

Museum of York County, Rock Hill SC

Muskegon Museum of Art, Muskegon MI

Muzeul National Brukenthal, Blue House & Romanian Art Gallery, Sibiu

Nantucket Historical Association, Historic Nantucket, Nantucket MA

Napa Valley Museum, Yountville CA

Nassau County Museum of Art, Roslyn Harbor NY

Nathan Hale Homestead Museum, Coventry CT

National Air and Space Museum, Smithsonian Institution, Washington DC

National Art Museum of Sport, Indianapolis IN

National Audubon Society, John James Audubon Center at Mill Grove, Audubon PA

National Baseball Hall of Fame & Museum, Inc, Art Collection, Cooperstown NY

National Galleries of Scotland, Scottish National Gallery, Edinburgh

National Gallery of Canada, Ottawa ON

National Gallery of Ireland, Dublin

National Heritage Museum, Lexington MA

National Museum of American Illustration, Newport RI

National Museum of the American Indian, George Gustav Heye Center, New York NY

National Museum of Wildlife Art of the Unites States, Jackson WY

National Museum of Women in the Arts, Washington DC

National Park Service, Hubbell Trading Post National Historic Site, Ganado AZ

National Park Service, Weir Farm National Historic Site, Wilton CT

The National Park Service, United States Department of the Interior, Statue of Liberty National Monument & The Ellis Island Immigration Museum, Washington DC

National Portrait Gallery, Smithsonian Institution, Washington DC

The National Shrine of the North American Martyrs, Fultonville NY

National Society of Colonial Dames of America in the State of Maryland, Mount Clare Museum House, Baltimore MD

National Society of the Colonial Dames of America in The Commonwealth of Virginia, Wilton House Museum, Richmond VA

National Trust for Historic Preservation, Chesterwood, Stockbridge MA

Naval Historical Center, The Navy Museum, Washington DC

Springfield Museums, Connecticut Valley Historical Society, Springfield MA

Springfield Museums, Michele & Donald D'Amour Museum of Fine Arts, Springfield MA

Springville Museum of Art, Springville UT

St George Art Museum, Saint George UT

Stamford Museum & Nature Center, Stamford CT

Stanford University, Cantor Arts Center at Stanford University, Stanford CA

Stanley Museum, Inc, Kingfield ME

Nelda C & H J Lutcher Stark, Stark Museum of Art, Orange TX

State of North Carolina, Battleship North Carolina, Wilmington NC

State University of New York at Binghamton, Binghamton University Art Museum, Binghamton NY

State University of New York at Geneseo, Bertha V B Lederer Gallery, Geneseo NY

State University of New York at Geneseo, Lockhart Gallery, Geneseo NY

State University of New York at New Paltz, Samuel Dorsky Museum of Art, New Paltz NY

State University of New York at Oswego, Tyler Art Gallery, Oswego NY

State University of New York at Plattsburgh, Art Museum, Plattsburgh NY

The State University of New York at Potsdam, Roland Gibson Gallery, Potsdam NY

State University of New York at Ulster, Muroff-Kotler Visual Arts Gallery, Stone Ridge NY

State University of New York College at Buffalo, Buffalo NY

State University of New York College at Cortland, Dowd Fine Arts Gallery, Cortland NY

Staten Island Museum, Staten Island NY

T C Steele, Nashville IN

Stephens College, Lewis James & Nellie Stratton Davis Art Gallery, Columbia MO

Stratford Historical Society, Catharine B Mitchell Museum, Stratford CT

Sturdivant Museum Association, Sturdivant Museum, Selma AL

The Summit County Historical Society of Akron, OH, Akron OH

Susquehanna University, Lore Degenstein Gallery, Selinsgrove PA

SVACA - Sheyenne Valley Arts & Crafts Association, Bjarne Ness Gallery at Bear Creek Hall, Fort Ransom ND

Sweet Briar College, Art Collection & Galleries, Sweet Briar VA

Switzerland County Historical Society Inc, Life on the Ohio: River History Museum, Vevay IN

Switzerland County Historical Society Inc, Switzerland County Historical Museum, Vevay IN

Swope Art Museum, Terre Haute IN

Syracuse University, Art Collection, Syracuse NY

Syracuse University, SUArt Galleries, Syracuse NY

Tacoma Art Museum, Tacoma WA

Taft Museum of Art, Cincinnati OH

Tampa Museum of Art, Tampa FL

Taos, Ernest Blumenschein Home & Studio, Taos NM

Lillian & Coleman Taube Museum of Art, Minot ND

Texas A&M University, J Wayne Stark University Center Galleries, College Station TX

Texas Ranger Hall of Fame & Museum, Waco TX

Texas Tech University, Museum of Texas Tech University, Lubbock TX

Timken Museum of Art, San Diego CA

Tinkertown Museum, Sandia Park NM

Toledo Museum of Art, Toledo OH

Topeka & Shawnee County Public Library, Alice C Sabatini Gallery, Topeka KS

Triton Museum of Art, Santa Clara CA

Tubac Center of the Arts, Santa Cruz Valley Art Association, Tubac AZ

Tucson Museum of Art and Historic Block, Tucson AZ

Tufts University, Tufts University Art Gallery, Medford MA

Tulane University, Newcomb Art Gallery, New Orleans LA

Turtle Bay Exploration Park, Redding CA

Tver Art Gallery, Tver

Mark Twain, State Historic Site Museum, Florida MO

Mark Twain, Hartford CT

Twin City Art Foundation, Masur Museum of Art, Monroe LA

Tyler Museum of Art, Tyler TX

U Gallery, New York NY

Ucross Foundation, Big Red Barn Gallery, Clearmont WY

Ukrainian Institute of Modern Art, Chicago IL

UMLAUF Sculpture Garden & Museum, Austin TX

United States Capitol, Architect of the Capitol, Washington DC

United States Department of State, Diplomatic Reception Rooms, Washington DC

United States Department of the Interior, Interior Museum, Washington DC

United States Military Academy, West Point Museum, West Point NY

United States Naval Academy, USNA Museum, Annapolis MD

United States Navy, Art Gallery, Washington DC

University at Albany, State University of New York, University Art Museum, Albany NY

University of Alabama at Birmingham, Visual Arts Gallery, Birmingham AL

University of Alabama at Huntsville, Union Grove Gallery & University Center Gallery, Huntsville AL

University of Alaska, Museum of the North, Fairbanks AK

University of Arkansas at Little Rock, Art Galleries, Little Rock AR

University of California, Richard L Nelson Gallery & Fine Arts Collection, Davis CA

University of California, Berkeley, Berkeley Art Museum & Pacific Film Archive, Berkeley CA

University of California, Berkeley, The Magnes Collection of Jewish Art & Life, Berkeley CA

University of California, Los Angeles, UCLA at the Armand Hammer Museum of Art & Cultural Center, Los Angeles CA

University of California, Santa Barbara, University Art Museum, Santa Barbara CA

University of Chicago, Smart Museum of Art, Chicago IL

University of Cincinnati, DAAP Galleries-College of Design Architecture, Art & Planning, Cincinnati OH

University of Colorado, CU Art Museum, Boulder CO

University of Connecticut, William Benton Museum of Art, Storrs CT

University of Delaware, University Museums, Newark DE

University of Georgia, Georgia Museum of Art, Athens GA

University of Illinois at Urbana-Champaign, Krannert Art Museum and Kinkead Pavilion, Champaign IL

University of Indianapolis, Christel DeHaan Fine Arts Gallery, Indianapolis IN

University of Kansas, Spencer Museum of Art, Lawrence KS

University of Louisiana at Lafayette, Paul and Lulu Hilliard University Art Museum, Lafayette LA

University of Maine, Museum of Art, Bangor ME

University of Manitoba, Faculty of Architecture Exhibition Centre, Winnipeg MB

University of Mary Washington, Gari Melchers Home and Studio, Fredericksburg VA

University of Mary Washington, University of Mary Washington Galleries, Fredericksburg VA

University of Maryland, College Park, The Art Gallery, College Park MD

University of Massachusetts, Amherst, University Gallery, Amherst MA

University of Memphis, Art Museum, Memphis TN

University of Miami, Lowe Art Museum, Coral Gables FL

University of Michigan, Museum of Art, Ann Arbor MI

University of Minnesota, Katherine E Nash Gallery, Minneapolis MN

University of Minnesota, The Bell Museum of Natural History, Minneapolis MN

University of Minnesota, Frederick R Weisman Art Museum, Minneapolis MN

University of Minnesota Duluth, Tweed Museum of Art, Duluth MN

University of Missouri, Museum of Art & Archaeology, Columbia MO

University of Montana, Montana Museum of Art & Culture, Missoula MT

University of Nebraska, Lincoln, Sheldon Memorial Art Gallery & Sculpture Garden, Lincoln NE

University of Nebraska-Lincoln, Great Plains Art Museum, Lincoln NE

University of Nevada, Las Vegas, Donna Beam Fine Art Gallery, Las Vegas NV

University of Nevada, Reno, Sheppard Contemporary & University Galleries, Reno NV

University of New Hampshire, Museum of Art, Durham NH

University of New Mexico, The Harwood Museum of Art, Taos NM

University of New Mexico, University of New Mexico Art Museum, Albuquerque NM

University of North Carolina at Chapel Hill, Ackland Art Museum, Chapel Hill NC

University of North Carolina at Greensboro, Weatherspoon Art Museum, Greensboro NC

University of Northern Iowa, UNI Gallery of Art, Cedar Falls IA

University of Notre Dame, Snite Museum of Art, Notre Dame IN

University of Oregon, Jordan Schnitzer Museum of Art, Eugene OR

University of Pennsylvania, Arthur Ross Gallery, Philadelphia PA

University of Pittsburgh, University Art Gallery, Pittsburgh PA

University of Rhode Island, Fine Arts Center Galleries, Kingston RI

University of Richmond, University Museums, Richmond VA

University of South Florida, Contemporary Art Museum, Tampa FL

University of Southern California, USC Fisher Museum of Art, Los Angeles CA

University of Texas at Arlington, Gallery at UTA, Arlington TX

University of Texas at Austin, Blanton Museum of Art, Austin TX

University of Texas at El Paso, Stanlee & Gerald Rubin Center for the Visual Arts, El Paso TX

University of the South, University Art Gallery, Sewanee TN

University of Toronto, University of Toronto Art Centre, Toronto ON

University of Utah, Utah Museum of Fine Arts, Salt Lake City UT

University of Wisconsin-Eau Claire, Foster Gallery, Eau Claire WI

University of Wisconsin-Madison, Chazen Museum of Art, Madison WI

University of Wisconsin-Madison, Wisconsin Union Galleries, Madison WI

University of Wisconsin-Stout, J Furlong Gallery, Menomonie WI

University of Wyoming, University of Wyoming Art Museum, Laramie WY

Ursinus College, Philip & Muriel Berman Museum of Art, Collegeville PA

Utah Department of Natural Resources, Division of Parks & Recreation, Territorial Statehouse State Park Museum, Fillmore UT

Valentine Richmond History Center, Richmond VA

Valparaiso University, Brauer Museum of Art, Valparaiso IN

Vancouver Art Gallery, Vancouver BC

Vanderbilt University, Vanderbilt University Fine Arts Gallery, Nashville TN

Vassar College, The Frances Lehman Loeb Art Center, Poughkeepsie NY

Vero Beach Museum of Art, Vero Beach FL

Vesterheim Norwegian-American Museum, Decorah IA

Victoria Mansion - Morse Libby House, Portland ME

Village of Potsdam, Potsdam Public Museum, Potsdam NY

Viridian Artists Inc, New York NY

VSA Arts of New Mexico, Very Special Arts Gallery, Albuquerque NM

Wadsworth Atheneum Museum of Art, Hartford CT

Walker Art Center, Minneapolis MN

Warner House Association, MacPheadris-Warner House, Portsmouth NH

Washburn University, Mulvane Art Museum, Topeka KS

Washington & Lee University, Lee Chapel & Museum, Lexington VA

Washington County Museum of Fine Arts, Hagerstown MD

George Washington, Alexandria VA

Washington State University, Museum of Art, Pullman WA

Washington University, Mildred Lane Kemper Art Museum, Saint Louis MO

Waterloo Center of the Arts, Waterloo IA

Waterworks Visual Arts Center, Salisbury NC

Wayne Center for the Arts, Wooster OH

Wayne County Historical Society, Museum, Honesdale PA

Wellesley College, Davis Museum & Cultural Center, Wellesley MA

West Baton Rouge Parish, West Baton Rouge Museum, Port Allen LA

West Florida Historic Preservation, Inc/University of West Florida, T T Wentworth, Jr Florida State Museum; Historic Pensacola Village; Pensacola Historical Society & Resource Center, Pensacola FL
Western Illinois University, Western Illinois University Art Gallery, Macomb IL
Western State College of Colorado, Quigley Hall Art Gallery, Gunnison CO
Westminster College, Art Gallery, New Wilmington PA
Wethersfield Historical Society Inc, Museum, Wethersfield CT
Whatcom Museum, Bellingham WA
Wheaton College, Beard and Weil Galleries, Norton MA
White House, Washington DC
Whitney Museum of American Art, New York NY
Wichita Art Museum, Wichita KS
Wichita State University, Ulrich Museum of Art, Wichita KS
Widener University, Art Collection & Gallery, Chester PA
Wildling Art Museum, Solvang CA
Wilfrid Laurier University, Robert Langen Art Gallery, Waterloo ON
Wilkes Art Gallery, North Wilkesboro NC
Wilkes University, Sordoni Art Gallery, Wilkes-Barre PA
Willard House & Clock Museum, Inc, North Grafton MA
Woodrow Wilson, Staunton VA
Woodrow Wilson, Washington DC
The Winnipeg Art Gallery, Winnipeg MB
Winston-Salem State University, Diggs Gallery, Winston Salem NC
Wiregrass Museum of Art, Dothan AL
Wisconsin Historical Society, Wisconsin Historical Museum, Madison WI
Witte Museum, San Antonio TX
T W Wood, Montpelier VT
Woodlawn/The Pope-Leighey, Mount Vernon VA
Woodmere Art Museum Inc, Philadelphia PA
Worcester Art Museum, Worcester MA
World Erotic Art Museum, Miami Beach FL
Yale University, Yale University Art Gallery, New Haven CT
Yerba Buena Center for the Arts, San Francisco CA
Yokohama Museum of Art, Yokohama
York University, Art Gallery of York University, Toronto ON
Yuma Fine Arts Association, Yuma Art Center, Yuma AZ
Zigler Art Museum, Jennings LA

PAINTING-AUSTRALIAN

American Sport Art Museum and Archives, Daphne AL
Arizona State University, ASU Art Museum, Tempe AZ
Art & Culture Center of Hollywood, Art Gallery/Multidisciplinary Cultural Center, Hollywood FL
Art Gallery of South Australia, Adelaide
Art Museum of the University of Houston, Blaffer Gallery, Houston TX
Art Without Walls Inc, New York NY
Bakehouse Art Complex, Inc, Miami FL
California State University, Northridge, Art Galleries, Northridge CA
Central United Methodist Church, Swords Into Plowshares Peace Center & Gallery, Detroit MI
City of Fayette, Alabama, Fayette Art Museum, Fayette AL
College of William & Mary, Muscarelle Museum of Art, Williamsburg VA
Dartmouth College, Hood Museum of Art, Hanover NH
Detroit Institute of Arts, Detroit MI
Federal Reserve Board, Art Gallery, Washington DC
Fine Arts Center for the New River Valley, Pulaski VA
Iredell Museums, Statesville NC
Launceston City Council, Queen Victoria Museum and Art Gallery, Launceston
Longview Museum of Fine Art, Longview TX
Mobile Museum of Art, Mobile AL
Modern Art Museum, Fort Worth TX
The Museum of Arts & Sciences Inc, Daytona Beach FL
Museum of Decorative Arts in Prague, Prague
National Art Museum of Sport, Indianapolis IN
New Visions Gallery, Inc, Marshfield WI
New York Studio School of Drawing, Painting & Sculpture, Gallery, New York NY
Owensboro Museum of Fine Art, Owensboro KY
PS1 Contemporary Art Center, Long Island City NY

Queensborough Community College, Art Gallery, Bayside NY
Jack Richard Gallery, Almond Tea Museum & Jane Williams Galleries, Divisions of Studios of Jack Richard, Cuyahoga Falls OH
Saint Peter's College, Art Gallery, Jersey City NJ
Santa Monica Museum of Art, Santa Monica CA
The Speed Art Museum, Louisville KY
Stanford University, Cantor Arts Center at Stanford University, Stanford CA
University of Wisconsin-Madison, Chazen Museum of Art, Madison WI
Wadsworth Atheneum Museum of Art, Hartford CT

PAINTING-BRITISH

Anderson Park Art Gallery Inc, Art Gallery, Invercargill
Arnot Art Museum, Elmira NY
Art & Culture Center of Hollywood, Art Gallery/Multidisciplinary Cultural Center, Hollywood FL
Art Gallery of Greater Victoria, Victoria BC
Art Gallery of Hamilton, Hamilton ON
Art Gallery of Nova Scotia, Halifax NS
Art Gallery of South Australia, Adelaide
The Art Museum at the University of Kentucky, Lexington KY
Art Museum of the University of Houston, Blaffer Gallery, Houston TX
Art Without Walls Inc, New York NY
Bard College, Center for Curatorial Studies and the Hessel Museum of Art, Annandale-on-Hudson NY
Baroda Museum and Picture Gallery, Baroda
Bass Museum of Art, Miami Beach FL
Bates College, Museum of Art, Lewiston ME
Bayerische Staatsgemaldesammlungen/Bavarian State Art Galleries, Neue Pinakothek, Munich
Beaverbrook Art Gallery, Fredericton NB
Beloit College, Wright Museum of Art, Beloit WI
Berkshire Museum, Pittsfield MA
Birmingham Museum of Art, Birmingham AL
Blauvelt Demarest Foundation, Hiram Blauvelt Art Museum, Oradell NJ
Bradford Brinton, Big Horn WY
Bruce Museum, Inc, Greenwich CT
Bucknell University, Edward & Marthann Samek Art Gallery, Lewisburg PA
The Buffalo Fine Arts Academy, Albright-Knox Art Gallery, Buffalo NY
Capital University, Schumacher Gallery, Columbus OH
Channel Islands Maritime Museum, Oxnard CA
Chhatrapati Shivaji Maharaj Vastu Sangrahalaya, Mumbai
Sterling & Francine Clark, Williamstown MA
Colgate University, Picker Art Gallery, Hamilton NY
College of William & Mary, Muscarelle Museum of Art, Williamsburg VA
Columbus Museum, Columbus GA
Columbus Museum of Art, Columbus OH
Corcoran Gallery of Art, Washington DC
Cornell Museum of Art and American Culture, Delray Beach FL
The Courtauld Institute of Art, The Courtauld Gallery, London
Coutts Museum of Art, Inc, El Dorado KS
Crocker Art Museum, Sacramento CA
Cummer Museum of Art & Gardens, Museum & Library, Jacksonville FL
The Currier Museum of Art, Manchester NH
Dahesh Museum of Art, Greenwich CT
Dartmouth College, Hood Museum of Art, Hanover NH
Delaware Art Museum, Wilmington DE
Denver Art Museum, Denver CO
Detroit Institute of Arts, Detroit MI
The Dixon Gallery & Gardens, Memphis TN
Doncaster Museum and Art Gallery, Doncaster
Dundee City Council Leisure & Communities Department, The McManus: Dundee's Art Gallery & Museum, Dundee
Egan Institute of Maritime Studies, Nantucket MA
Evansville Museum of Arts, History & Science, Evansville IN
Figge Art Museum, Davenport IA
Fine Arts Center for the New River Valley, Pulaski VA
Flint Institute of Arts, Flint MI
Florence Museum, Florence SC
Fondazione Musei Civici Di Venezia, Museo Correr, Venice
The Frick Art & Historical Center, Inc, Frick Art Museum, Pittsburgh PA

General Board of Discipleship, The United Methodist Church, The Upper Room Chapel & Museum, Nashville TN
Glanmore National Historic Site of Canada, Belleville ON
Gunston Hall Plantation, Mason Neck VA
Hammond-Harwood House Association, Inc, Hammond-Harwood House, Annapolis MD
Hancock County Trustees of Public Reservations, Woodlawn: Museum, Gardens & Park, Ellsworth ME
The Heckscher Museum of Art, Huntington NY
Hillwood Museum & Gardens Foundation, Hillwood Estate Museum & Gardens, Washington DC
Huntington Museum of Art, Huntington WV
Independent Administrative Institution National Museum of Art, The National Museum of Western Art, Tokyo
Iredell Museums, Statesville NC
The Israel Museum, Jerusalem, Billy Rose Art Garden, Jerusalem
J.M.W. Turner Museum, Sarasota FL
Bob Jones University Museum & Gallery Inc, Greenville SC
Jordan National Gallery of Fine Arts, Amman
Joslyn Art Museum, Omaha NE
Juniata College Museum of Art, Huntingdon PA
La Salle University Art Museum, Philadelphia PA
Lafayette College, Lafayette College Art Galleries, Easton PA
Leeds Museums & Galleries, Leeds
Lehigh University Art Galleries, Museum Operation, Bethlehem PA
Lincolnshire County Council, Library & Heritage Services, Lincoln
Louisiana State University, Museum of Art, Baton Rouge LA
Manchester City Galleries, Manchester Art Gallery, Manchester
Marquette University, Haggerty Museum of Art, Milwaukee WI
Maryhill Museum of Art, Goldendale WA
McCord Museum of Canadian History, Montreal PQ
McMaster University, McMaster Museum of Art, Hamilton ON
Ministry of Cultural Affairs, Bangladesh National Museum, Dhaka
Mobile Museum of Art, Mobile AL
Modern Art Museum, Fort Worth TX
Mount Vernon Hotel Museum & Garden, New York NY
Musee Cognacq-Jay, Cognacq-Jay Museum, Paris
Museo Cerralbo, Madrid
Museo de Arte de Ponce, The Luis A Ferre Foundation Inc, Ponce PR
The Museum of Arts & Sciences Inc, Daytona Beach FL
Museum of Decorative Arts in Prague, Prague
Museum of Fine Arts, Houston, Rienzi Center for European Decorative Arts, Houston TX
Museum of Fine Arts, Saint Petersburg, Florida, Inc, Saint Petersburg FL
Muskegon Museum of Art, Muskegon MI
Muzej za Umjetnost i Obrt, Museum of Arts & Crafts, Zagreb
Muzeum Narodowe, National Museum in Poznan, Poznan
National Galleries of Scotland, Scottish National Gallery, Edinburgh
National Gallery of Canada, Ottawa ON
National Gallery of Ireland, Dublin
National Museum of Wildlife Art of the Unites States, Jackson WY
National Portrait Gallery, London
Nelson Mandela Bay Municipality, Nelson Mandela Metropolitan Art Museum, Port Elizabeth
The Nemours Foundatioin, Nemours Mansion & Gardens, Wilmington DE
New Brunswick Museum, Saint John NB
New York Studio School of Drawing, Painting & Sculpture, Gallery, New York NY
Niagara University, Castellani Art Museum, Niagara NY
Oklahoma City Museum of Art, Oklahoma City OK
Owensboro Museum of Fine Art, Owensboro KY
Panhandle-Plains Historical Museum, Canyon TX
Passaic County Community College, Broadway, LRC, and Hamilton Club Galleries, Paterson NJ
Philadelphia Museum of Art, John G Johnson Collection, Philadelphia PA
Phoenix Art Museum, Phoenix AZ
Piedmont Arts Association, Martinsville VA

Princeton University, Princeton University Art Museum, Princeton NJ

Queens College, City University of New York, Godwin-Ternbach Museum, Flushing NY

Queensborough Community College, Art Gallery, Bayside NY

Reading Public Museum, Reading PA

The Rosenbach Museum & Library, Philadelphia PA

Royal Arts Foundation, Belcourt Castle, Newport RI

Royal Museums of Fine Arts of Belgium, Brussels

Saginaw Art Museum, Saginaw MI

Saint Olaf College, Flaten Art Museum, Northfield MN

Saint Peter's College, Art Gallery, Jersey City NJ

Salisbury House Foundation, Salisbury House and Garden, Des Moines IA

San Diego Museum of Art, San Diego CA

Savitsky Karakalpakstan State Art Museum, Nukus

Shirley Plantation Foundation, Charles City VA

Slovenska Narodna Galeria, Slovak National Gallery, Bratislava

The Society of the Cincinnati at Anderson House, Washington DC

The Speed Art Museum, Louisville KY

Spertus Institute of Jewish Studies, Chicago IL

Springfield Art Museum, Springfield MO

Springfield Museums, Michele & Donald D'Amour Museum of Fine Arts, Springfield MA

Springville Museum of Art, Springville UT

Stanford University, Cantor Arts Center at Stanford University, Stanford CA

State University of New York at Binghamton, Binghamton University Art Museum, Binghamton NY

State University of New York at Oswego, Tyler Art Gallery, Oswego NY

Szepmuveszeti Muzeum, Museum of Fine Arts Budapest, Budapest

Tacoma Art Museum, Tacoma WA

Taft Museum of Art, Cincinnati OH

Tver Art Gallery, Tver

Tyne and Wear Archives & Museums, Sunderland Museum & Winter Gardens, Newcastle-upon-Tyne

University of California, Berkeley, Berkeley Art Museum & Pacific Film Archive, Berkeley CA

University of California, Los Angeles, UCLA at the Armand Hammer Museum of Art & Cultural Center, Los Angeles CA

University of Chicago, Smart Museum of Art, Chicago IL

University of Georgia, Georgia Museum of Art, Athens GA

University of Illinois at Urbana-Champaign, Krannert Art Museum and Kinkead Pavilion, Champaign IL

University of Kansas, Spencer Museum of Art, Lawrence KS

University of Manchester, Whitworth Art Gallery, Manchester

University of Miami, Lowe Art Museum, Coral Gables FL

University of Missouri, Museum of Art & Archaeology, Columbia MO

University of North Carolina at Chapel Hill, Ackland Art Museum, Chapel Hill NC

University of Notre Dame, Snite Museum of Art, Notre Dame IN

University of Pittsburgh, University Art Gallery, Pittsburgh PA

University of Southern California, USC Fisher Museum of Art, Los Angeles CA

University of Toronto, University of Toronto Art Centre, Toronto ON

University of Utah, Utah Museum of Fine Arts, Salt Lake City UT

University of Wisconsin-Madison, Chazen Museum of Art, Madison WI

University of Wyoming, University of Wyoming Art Museum, Laramie WY

Ursinus College, Philip & Muriel Berman Museum of Art, Collegeville PA

Vancouver Art Gallery, Vancouver BC

Wadsworth Atheneum Museum of Art, Hartford CT

Walker Art Gallery, Liverpool

The Wallace Collection, London

Washington University, Mildred Lane Kemper Art Museum, Saint Louis MO

Waterworks Visual Arts Center, Salisbury NC

Wellesley College, Davis Museum & Cultural Center, Wellesley MA

Wheaton College, Beard and Weil Galleries, Norton MA

Wilfrid Laurier University, Robert Langen Art Gallery, Waterloo ON

Wolverhampton Arts & Heritage, Wolverton Art Gallery, Wolverhampton

Woodlawn/The Pope-Leighey, Mount Vernon VA

Worcester Art Museum, Worcester MA

Yale University, Yale Center for British Art, New Haven CT

Yokohama Museum of Art, Yokohama

Zigler Art Museum, Jennings LA

PAINTING-CANADIAN

Americas Society Art Gallery, New York NY

Arizona State University, ASU Art Museum, Tempe AZ

Arnot Art Museum, Elmira NY

Art Gallery of Alberta, Edmonton AB

Art Gallery of Bancroft Inc, Bancroft ON

Art Gallery of Greater Victoria, Victoria BC

Art Gallery of Nova Scotia, Halifax NS

Art Gallery of Swift Current, Swift Current SK

Art Without Walls Inc, New York NY

Beaverbrook Art Gallery, Fredericton NB

Blauvelt Demarest Foundation, Hiram Blauvelt Art Museum, Oradell NJ

Bucknell University, Edward & Marthann Samek Art Gallery, Lewisburg PA

Canadian Museum of Civilization, Gatineau PQ

Canadian Museum of Nature, Musee Canadien de la Nature, Ottawa ON

Canadian War Museum, Ottawa ON

Cartoon Art Museum, San Francisco CA

Central United Methodist Church, Swords Into Plowshares Peace Center & Gallery, Detroit MI

City of Fayette, Alabama, Fayette Art Museum, Fayette AL

City of Port Angeles, Port Angeles Fine Arts Center & Webster Woods Art Park, Port Angeles WA

City of Toronto Culture, The Market Gallery, Toronto ON

Concordia University, Leonard & Bina Ellen Art Gallery, Montreal PQ

Confederation Centre Art Gallery and Museum, Charlottetown PE

Cornwall Gallery Society, Cornwall Regional Art Gallery, Cornwall ON

Craigdarroch Castle Historical Museum Society, Victoria BC

Dartmouth Heritage Museum, Dartmouth NS

DeLeon White Gallery, Toronto ON

Dundurn Castle, Hamilton ON

Environment Canada - Parks Canada, Laurier House, National Historic Site, Ottawa ON

Estevan National Exhibition Centre Inc, Estevan Art Gallery & Museum, Estevan SK

Frye Art Museum, Seattle WA

Galerie Montcalm, Gatineau PQ

Gallery Moos Ltd, Toronto ON

Glanmore National Historic Site of Canada, Belleville ON

Glenhyrst Art Gallery of Brant, Brantford ON

Henry Gallery Association, Henry Art Gallery, Seattle WA

Heritage Center, Inc, Pine Ridge SD

Huntington Museum of Art, Huntington WV

Huronia Museum, Gallery of Historic Huronia, Midland ON

The Israel Museum, Jerusalem, Billy Rose Art Garden, Jerusalem

Kamloops Art Gallery, Kamloops BC

Kings County Historical Society & Museum, Hampton NB

Kitchener-Waterloo Art Gallery, Kitchener ON

Knights of Columbus Supreme Council, Knights of Columbus Museum, New Haven CT

Laurentian University, Museum & Art Centre, Sudbury ON

The Lindsay Gallery Inc, Lindsay ON

Manitoba Historical Society, Dalnavert Museum, Winnipeg MB

McCord Museum of Canadian History, Montreal PQ

The Robert McLaughlin, Oshawa ON

McMaster University, McMaster Museum of Art, Hamilton ON

Mendel Art Gallery & Civic Conservatory, Saskatoon SK

Ministry of Cultural Affairs, Bangladesh National Museum, Dhaka

Mobile Museum of Art, Mobile AL

Modern Art Museum, Fort Worth TX

Moose Jaw Art Museum, Inc, Art & History Museum, Moose Jaw SK

Mount Saint Vincent University, MSVU Art Gallery, Halifax NS

Musee National des Beaux Arts du Quebec, Quebec PQ

Musee Regional de lu Cote-Nord, Sept-Iles PQ

Museum of Contemporary Canadian Art, Toronto ON

Museum of Decorative Arts in Prague, Prague

Museum of Fine Arts, Saint Petersburg, Florida, Inc, Saint Petersburg FL

Museum of Northern British Columbia, Ruth Harvey Art Gallery, Prince Rupert BC

National Art Museum of Sport, Indianapolis IN

National Gallery of Canada, Ottawa ON

National Museum of Wildlife Art of the Unites States, Jackson WY

New Brunswick Museum, Saint John NB

Niagara University, Castellani Art Museum, Niagara NY

Opelousas Museum of Art, Inc (OMA), Opelousas LA

Plains Art Museum, Fargo ND

Port Huron Museum, Port Huron MI

Prairie Art Gallery, Grande Prairie AB

Prince George Art Gallery, Prince George BC

PS1 Contemporary Art Center, Long Island City NY

Queensborough Community College, Art Gallery, Bayside NY

Radio-Canada SRC CBC, Georges Goguen CBC Art Gallery, Moncton NB

Red Deer & District Museum & Archives, Red Deer AB

Ross Memorial Museum, Saint Andrews NB

Saint Joseph's Oratory, Museum, Montreal PQ

Saint Peter's College, Art Gallery, Jersey City NJ

Santa Monica Museum of Art, Santa Monica CA

The Speed Art Museum, Louisville KY

Spertus Institute of Jewish Studies, Chicago IL

Stanford University, Cantor Arts Center at Stanford University, Stanford CA

State University of New York at Plattsburgh, Art Museum, Plattsburgh NY

Surrey Art Gallery, Surrey BC

Temiskaming Art Gallery, Haileybury ON

Ukrainian Institute of Modern Art, Chicago IL

University of Manitoba, Faculty of Architecture Exhibition Centre, Winnipeg MB

University of Minnesota Duluth, Tweed Museum of Art, Duluth MN

University of New Brunswick, Art Centre, Fredericton NB

University of Saskatchewan, Diefenbaker Canada Centre, Saskatoon SK

Vancouver Art Gallery, Vancouver BC

Vancouver Public Library, Fine Arts & Music Department, Vancouver BC

Wadsworth Atheneum Museum of Art, Hartford CT

Peter & Catharine Whyte Foundation, Whyte Museum of the Canadian Rockies, Banff AB

Wilfrid Laurier University, Robert Langen Art Gallery, Waterloo ON

The Winnipeg Art Gallery, Winnipeg MB

Yarmouth County Historical Society, Yarmouth County Museum & Archives, Yarmouth NS

York University, Art Gallery of York University, Toronto ON

Yuma Fine Arts Association, Yuma Art Center, Yuma AZ

PAINTING-DUTCH

Akademie der Bildenden Kunste Wien, Gemaldegalerie der Akademie der bildenden Kunste Wien, Vienna

Allentown Art Museum, Allentown PA

Arnot Art Museum, Elmira NY

Art & Culture Center of Hollywood, Art Gallery/Multidisciplinary Cultural Center, Hollywood FL

The Art Museum at the University of Kentucky, Lexington KY

Art Without Walls Inc, New York NY

Barnes Foundation, Merion PA

Baroda Museum and Picture Gallery, Baroda

Bass Museum of Art, Miami Beach FL

Bayerische Staatsgemaldesammlungen/Bavarian State Art Galleries, Neue Pinakothek, Munich

Berkshire Museum, Pittsfield MA

Birmingham Museum of Art, Birmingham AL

Brick Store Museum, Kennebunk ME

Bucknell University, Edward & Marthann Samek Art Gallery, Lewisburg PA

Calvin College, Center Art Gallery, Grand Rapids MI

Channel Islands Maritime Museum, Oxnard CA

Chrysler Museum of Art, Norfolk VA

Sterling & Francine Clark, Williamstown MA

College of William & Mary, Muscarelle Museum of Art, Williamsburg VA

PAINTING-EUROPEAN

Cornell Museum of Art and American Culture, Delray Beach FL

Cornell University, Herbert F Johnson Museum of Art, Ithaca NY

The Courtauld Institute of Art, The Courtauld Gallery, London

Coutts Museum of Art, Inc, El Dorado KS

Crocker Art Museum, Sacramento CA

Cummer Museum of Art & Gardens, Museum & Library, Jacksonville FL

Dahesh Museum of Art, Greenwich CT

Danville Museum of Fine Arts & History, Danville VA

Dartmouth College, Hood Museum of Art, Hanover NH

Dartmouth Heritage Museum, Dartmouth NS

Dayton Art Institute, Dayton OH

Denison University, Art Gallery, Granville OH

Denver Art Museum, Denver CO

Detroit Institute of Arts, Detroit MI

Duke University, Nasher Museum of Art at Duke University, Durham NC

Dundee City Council Leisure & Communities Department, The McManus: Dundee's Art Gallery & Museum, Dundee

Elverhoj Museum of History and Art, Solvang CA

Establishment Public du Chateau du Rusee, Et du Dophine national de versailles, Versailles

Evansville Museum of Arts, History & Science, Evansville IN

William A Farnsworth, Museum, Rockland ME

Felicien Rops Museum, Namur

Figge Art Museum, Davenport IA

Fine Arts Center for the New River Valley, Pulaski VA

Fisk University, Aaron Douglas Gallery, Nashville TN

Flint Institute of Arts, Flint MI

Florence Museum, Florence SC

Florida State University, John & Mable Ringling Museum of Art, Sarasota FL

Florida State University and Central Florida Community College, The Appleton Museum of Art, Ocala FL

Fondazione Musei Civici Di Venezia, Galleria Internazionale d'Arte Moderna di Ca'Pesaro, Venice

Fondazione Musei Civici Di Venezia, Museo Correr, Venice

Fondazione Scientifica Querini Stampalia, Venice

Frick Collection, New York NY

Friends of Historic Kingston, Fred J Johnston House Museum, Kingston NY

Galleria Doria Pamphilj, Rome

General Board of Discipleship, The United Methodist Church, The Upper Room Chapel & Museum, Nashville TN

Germanisches Nationalmuseum, Nuremberg

The Ghent Museum of Fine Arts, Ghent

Hancock County Trustees of Public Reservations, Woodlawn: Museum, Gardens & Park, Ellsworth ME

Hartwick College, The Yager Museum, Oneonta NY

Harvard University, Museum & Garden, Washington DC

Hecht Museum, Haifa

The Heckscher Museum of Art, Huntington NY

Henry Morrison Flagler Museum, Palm Beach FL

Heritage Malta, National Museum of Fine Arts, Valletta

Hermitage Foundation Museum, Norfolk VA

Higgins Armory Museum, Worcester MA

Hillwood Museum & Gardens Foundation, Hillwood Estate Museum & Gardens, Washington DC

The Hispanic Society of America, Museum & Library, New York NY

Hofstra University, Hofstra University Museum, Hempstead NY

Hyde Collection Trust, Glens Falls NY

Independent Administrative Institution National Museum of Art, The National Museum of Western Art, Tokyo

Indianapolis Museum of Art, Indianapolis IN

International Museum of Art & Science, McAllen TX

The Israel Museum, Jerusalem, Samuel & Saidye Bronfman Archaeology Wing, Jerusalem

The Israel Museum, Jerusalem, Jerusalem

J.M.W. Turner Museum, Sarasota FL

Bob Jones University Museum & Gallery Inc, Greenville SC

Joslyn Art Museum, Omaha NE

Kenosha Public Museums, Kenosha WI

Kereszteny Muzeum, Christian Museum, Esztergom

Kimbell Art Foundation, Kimbell Art Museum, Fort Worth TX

Kirchner Museum Davos, Davos

Kitchener-Waterloo Art Gallery, Kitchener ON

Knights of Columbus Supreme Council, Knights of Columbus Museum, New Haven CT

Knoxville Museum of Art, Knoxville TN

Koninklijk Museum voor Schone Kunsten Antwerpen, Royal Museum of Fine Arts, Antwerp

Kroller-Muller Museum, Otterlo

Kunsthalle Bremen, Bremen Art Gallery, Bremen

Kunsthistorisches Museum Vienna, Museum of Fine Arts, Vienna

Kunstmuseum Bern, Musee des Beaux-Arts de Berne, Bern

Kunstmuseum Solothurn, Solothurn Art Museum, Solothurn

La Salle University Art Museum, Philadelphia PA

Lafayette College, Lafayette College Art Galleries, Easton PA

Latino Art Museum, Pomona CA

Le Grand Curtius, Musée d'Ansembourg, Liege

Le Musee des Beaux-Arts, Brest

Leeds Museums & Galleries, Leeds

Lehigh University Art Galleries, Museum Operation, Bethlehem PA

Los Angeles County Museum of Art, Los Angeles CA

Louisiana Arts & Science Museum, Baton Rouge LA

Loyola University Chicago, Loyola University Museum of Art, Chicago IL

Lyman Allyn Art Museum, New London CT

Mabee-Gerrer Museum of Art, Shawnee OK

Macalester College, Macalester College Art Gallery, Saint Paul MN

Madison Museum of Fine Art, Madison GA

Magyar Nemzeti Muzeum - Hungarian National Museum, Budapest

Manchester City Galleries, Manchester Art Gallery, Manchester

Marquette University, Haggerty Museum of Art, Milwaukee WI

McMaster University, McMaster Museum of Art, Hamilton ON

McNay, San Antonio TX

Meredith College, Frankie G Weems Gallery & Rotunda Gallery, Raleigh NC

Merrick Art Gallery, New Brighton PA

The Metropolitan Museum of Art, New York NY

Middlebury College, Museum of Art, Middlebury VT

Milwaukee Art Museum, Milwaukee WI

Ministry of Cultural Affairs, Bangladesh National Museum, Dhaka

Minneapolis Institute of Arts, Minneapolis MN

Mission San Luis Rey de Francia, Mission San Luis Rey Museum, Oceanside CA

Mobile Museum of Art, Mobile AL

Modern Art Museum, Fort Worth TX

Moderna Galerija, Gallery of Modern Art, Zagreb

Moravska Galerie v Brne, Moravian Gallery in Brno, Brno

The Morgan Library & Museum, Museum, New York NY

Mount Holyoke College, Art Museum, South Hadley MA

Musea Brugge, Sint-Janshospitaal, Bruges

Musee d'art de Joliette, Joliette PQ

Musee des Augustins, Toulouse

Musee des Beaux-Arts d'Orleans, Museum of Fine Arts, Orleans

Musee des Beaux-Arts/Palais des Archeveques, Museum of Fine Arts, Tours

Musee et Chateau de Chantilly (MUSEE CONDE), Chantilly

Musee National d'Histoire et d'Art Luxembourg, Luxembourg City

Museen der Stadt Koln, Wallraf-Richartz-Museum, Cologne

Musei Capitolini, Rome

Musei Civici di Padova - Cappella Degli Scrovegni, Musei Civici Agli Eremitani (Civic Museum) - Scrovegni Chapel, Padua

Museo Cerralbo, Madrid

Museo de Navarra, Pamplona

Museu de Evora, Evora

Museu Nacional D'Art De Catalunya, National Art Museum, Barcelona

Museum De Lakenhal, Leiden

Museum Het Prinsenhof, Delft

The Museum of Arts & Sciences Inc, Daytona Beach FL

Museum of Arts & Sciences, Inc, Macon GA

Museum of Decorative Arts in Prague, Prague

Museum of Fine Arts, Houston, Rienzi Center for European Decorative Arts, Houston TX

Museum of Fine Arts, Saint Petersburg, Florida, Inc, Saint Petersburg FL

Museum zu Allerheiligen, Schaffhausen

Muskegon Museum of Art, Muskegon MI

Muzej za Umjetnost i Obrt, Museum of Arts & Crafts, Zagreb

Muzeul National Brukenthal, Brukenthal Palace & European Art Gallery, Sibiu

Muzeum Narodowe, National Museum in Poznan, Poznan

Muzeum Narodowe W Kielcach, National Museum in Kielce, Kielce

The Namur Provincial Museum of Ancient Arts, Namur

Narodna Galerija, National Gallery of Slovenia, Ljubljana

Nassau County Museum of Art, Roslyn Harbor NY

National Galleries of Scotland, Scottish National Gallery, Edinburgh

National Gallery of Canada, Ottawa ON

National Gallery of Ireland, Dublin

National Museum of Fine Arts of Moldova, Chisinau

National Museum of Wildlife Art of the Unites States, Jackson WY

National Trust for Historic Preservation, Chesterwood, Stockbridge MA

Nationalmuseum, Stockholm

Nelson Mandela Bay Municipality, Nelson Mandela Metropolitan Art Museum, Port Elizabeth

The Nemours Foundatioin, Nemours Mansion & Gardens, Wilmington DE

New Orleans Museum of Art, New Orleans LA

New World Art Center, T F Chen Cultural Center, New York NY

New York Studio School of Drawing, Painting & Sculpture, Gallery, New York NY

New York University, Grey Art Gallery, New York NY

North Country Museum of Arts, Park Rapids MN

North Dakota State University, Memorial Union Gallery, Fargo ND

Norwich Free Academy, Slater Memorial Museum, Norwich CT

Ohara Museum of Art, Kurashiki

Oklahoma City Museum of Art, Oklahoma City OK

Olana State Historic Site, Hudson NY

Panhandle-Plains Historical Museum, Canyon TX

Passaic County Community College, Broadway, LRC, and Hamilton Club Galleries, Paterson NJ

The Pennsylvania State University, Palmer Museum of Art, University Park PA

Philadelphia Museum of Art, John G Johnson Collection, Philadelphia PA

Philadelphia Museum of Art, Main Building, Philadelphia PA

Philbrook Museum of Art, Tulsa OK

The Phillips Collection, Washington DC

Phoenix Art Museum, Phoenix AZ

Piedmont Arts Association, Martinsville VA

Pinacoteca Provinciale, Bari

Port Huron Museum, Port Huron MI

Portland Art Museum, Portland OR

Portland Museum of Art, Portland ME

Prairie Art Gallery, Grande Prairie AB

Princeton University, Princeton University Art Museum, Princeton NJ

Purchase College, Neuberger Museum of Art, Purchase NY

Queens College, City University of New York, Godwin-Ternbach Museum, Flushing NY

Queensborough Community College, Art Gallery, Bayside NY

R W Norton Art Foundation, R W Norton Art Gallery, Shreveport LA

Radio-Canada SRC CBC, Georges Goguen CBC Art Gallery, Moncton NB

Reading Public Museum, Reading PA

Frederic Remington, Ogdensburg NY

Jack Richard Gallery, Almond Tea Museum & Jane Williams Galleries, Divisions of Studios of Jack Richard, Cuyahoga Falls OH

Rijksmuseum Twenthe, Rijksmuseum Twenthe, Enschede

Lauren Rogers, Laurel MS

Rollins College, George D & Harriet W Cornell Fine Arts Museum, Winter Park FL

Royal Arts Foundation, Belcourt Castle, Newport RI

Royal Museums of Fine Arts of Belgium, Brussels

Saginaw Art Museum, Saginaw MI

Saint Bonaventure University, Regina A Quick Center for the Arts, Saint Bonaventure NY

Saint Johnsbury Athenaeum, Saint Johnsbury VT

Saint Olaf College, Flaten Art Museum, Northfield MN

Saint Peter's College, Art Gallery, Jersey City NJ

San Antonio Museum of Art, San Antonio TX

San Diego Museum of Art, San Diego CA

PAINTING-FLEMISH

Pretoria Art Museum, Municipal Art Gallery, Pretoria
Princeton University, Princeton University Art Museum, Princeton NJ
Queens College, City University of New York, Godwin-Ternbach Museum, Flushing NY
Queensborough Community College, Art Gallery, Bayside NY
Reading Public Museum, Reading PA
Jack Richard Gallery, Almond Tea Museum & Jane Williams Galleries, Divisions of Studios of Jack Richard, Cuyahoga Falls OH
Royal Museums of Fine Arts of Belgium, Brussels
Saint Bonaventure University, Regina A Quick Center for the Arts, Saint Bonaventure NY
St Mary's College of Maryland, The Dwight Frederick Boyden Gallery, St Mary's City MD
Saint Peter's College, Art Gallery, Jersey City NJ
San Diego Museum of Art, San Diego CA
Santa Monica Museum of Art, Santa Monica CA
Shirley Plantation Foundation, Charles City VA
Norton Simon, Pasadena CA
Slovenska Narodna Galeria, Slovak National Gallery, Bratislava
Soprintendenza per I beni storici artistici ed etnoantropologici per le province di Mantova Brescia e Cremona, Museo di Palazzo Ducale, Mantua
The Speed Art Museum, Louisville KY
Stanford University, Cantor Arts Center at Stanford University, Stanford CA
State University of New York at Binghamton, Binghamton University Art Museum, Binghamton NY
Szepmuveszeti Muzeum, Museum of Fine Arts Budapest, Budapest
Taft Museum of Art, Cincinnati OH
Timken Museum of Art, San Diego CA
Tver Art Gallery, Tver
University of Chicago, Smart Museum of Art, Chicago IL
University of Illinois at Urbana-Champaign, Krannert Art Museum and Kinkead Pavilion, Champaign IL
University of Miami, Lowe Art Museum, Coral Gables FL
University of Michigan, Museum of Art, Ann Arbor MI
University of Missouri, Museum of Art & Archaeology, Columbia MO
University of North Carolina at Chapel Hill, Ackland Art Museum, Chapel Hill NC
University of Southern California, USC Fisher Museum of Art, Los Angeles CA
University of Utah, Utah Museum of Fine Arts, Salt Lake City UT
University of Virginia, The Fralin Museum of Art at the University of Virginia, Charlottesville VA
University of Wisconsin-Madison, Chazen Museum of Art, Madison WI
Ursinus College, Philip & Muriel Berman Museum of Art, Collegeville PA
Virginia Museum of Fine Arts, Richmond VA
Wadsworth Atheneum Museum of Art, Hartford CT
Walker Art Gallery, Liverpool
The Wallace Collection, London
Wellesley College, Davis Museum & Cultural Center, Wellesley MA
Worcester Art Museum, Worcester MA
Zigler Art Museum, Jennings LA

PAINTING-FRENCH

Akademie der Bildenden Kunste Wien, Gemaldegalerie der Akademie der bildenden Kunste Wien, Vienna
Arizona State University, ASU Art Museum, Tempe AZ
Arnot Art Museum, Elmira NY
Art & Culture Center of Hollywood, Art Gallery/Multidisciplinary Cultural Center, Hollywood FL
Art Museum of the University of Houston, Blaffer Gallery, Houston TX
Art Without Walls Inc, New York NY
Barnes Foundation, Merion PA
Baroda Museum and Picture Gallery, Baroda
Bates College, Museum of Art, Lewiston ME
Bayerische Staatsgemaldesammlungen/Bavarian State Art Galleries, Neue Pinakothek, Munich
Belvedere Museum, Osterreichische Galerie Belvedere, Vienna
Bertha V B Lederer Fine Arts Gallery-Suny Geneseo, Bertha V B Lederer Fine Arts Gallery, Geneseo NY
Birmingham Museum of Art, Birmingham AL
Brigham Young University, Museum of Art, Provo UT

Bucknell University, Edward & Marthann Samek Art Gallery, Lewisburg PA
The Buffalo Fine Arts Academy, Albright-Knox Art Gallery, Buffalo NY
Cartoon Art Museum, San Francisco CA
Centenary College of Louisiana, Meadows Museum of Art, Shreveport LA
Central United Methodist Church, Swords Into Plowshares Peace Center & Gallery, Detroit MI
Charles Allis Art Museum, Milwaukee WI
Chhatrapati Shivaji Maharaj Vastu Sangrahalaya, Mumbai
Chrysler Museum of Art, Norfolk VA
Cincinnati Art Museum, Cincinnati Art Museum, Cincinnati OH
City of El Paso, El Paso TX
Sterling & Francine Clark, Williamstown MA
Colgate University, Picker Art Gallery, Hamilton NY
College of William & Mary, Muscarelle Museum of Art, Williamsburg VA
The College of Wooster, The College of Wooster Art Museum, Wooster OH
Columbus Museum of Art, Columbus OH
Comune di Genova - Direzione Cultura Settore Musei, Museo di Strada Nuova Palazzo Rosso, Genoa
Corcoran Gallery of Art, Washington DC
The Courtauld Institute of Art, The Courtauld Gallery, London
Coutts Museum of Art, Inc, El Dorado KS
Crocker Art Museum, Sacramento CA
Cummer Museum of Art & Gardens, Museum & Library, Jacksonville FL
The Currier Museum of Art, Manchester NH
Dahesh Museum of Art, Greenwich CT
Dartmouth College, Hood Museum of Art, Hanover NH
DeLeon White Gallery, Toronto ON
Denison University, Art Gallery, Granville OH
Denver Art Museum, Denver CO
Dickinson College, The Trout Gallery, Carlisle PA
The Dixon Gallery & Gardens, Memphis TN
Doncaster Museum and Art Gallery, Doncaster
Drexel University, Drexel Collection, Philadelphia PA
Elmhurst Art Museum, Elmhurst IL
Establishment Public du Chateau du Rusee, Et du Dophine national de versailles, Versailles
Figge Art Museum, Davenport IA
Fine Arts Center for the New River Valley, Pulaski VA
Fisher Art Gallery, Marshalltown IA
Fisk University, Carl Van Vechten Gallery, Nashville TN
Flint Institute of Arts, Flint MI
Florence Museum, Florence SC
Florida State University and Central Florida Community College, The Appleton Museum of Art, Ocala FL
Edsel & Eleanor Ford, Grosse Pointe Shores MI
The Frick Art & Historical Center, Inc, Frick Art Museum, Pittsburgh PA
Frye Art Museum, Seattle WA
Galerie Montcalm, Gatineau PQ
Isabella Stewart Gardner, Boston MA
General Board of Discipleship, The United Methodist Church, The Upper Room Chapel & Museum, Nashville TN
The Ghent Museum of Fine Arts, Ghent
Glanmore National Historic Site of Canada, Belleville ON
Guggenheim Museum Soho, New York NY
Solomon R Guggenheim, New York NY
Hecht Museum, Haifa
The Heckscher Museum of Art, Huntington NY
Henry County Museum & Cultural Arts Center, Clinton MO
Henry Gallery Association, Henry Art Gallery, Seattle WA
Heritage Malta, National Museum of Fine Arts, Valletta
Hermitage Foundation Museum, Norfolk VA
Hill-Stead Museum, Farmington CT
Hillwood Museum & Gardens Foundation, Hillwood Estate Museum & Gardens, Washington DC
Hofstra University, Hofstra University Museum, Hempstead NY
Idemitsu Museum of Arts, Tokyo
Independent Administrative Institution National Museum of Art, The National Museum of Western Art, Tokyo
The Israel Museum, Jerusalem, Billy Rose Art Garden, Jerusalem
The Israel Museum, Jerusalem, Samuel & Saidye Bronfman Archaeology Wing, Jerusalem
The Israel Museum, Jerusalem, Jerusalem
J.M.W. Turner Museum, Sarasota FL

Johns Hopkins University, Evergreen Museum & Library, Baltimore MD
Bob Jones University Museum & Gallery Inc, Greenville SC
Jordan National Gallery of Fine Arts, Amman
Joslyn Art Museum, Omaha NE
Juniata College Museum of Art, Huntingdon PA
Kateri Tekakwitha Shrine/St. Francis Xavier Mission, Kahnawake PQ
Kunsthalle Bremen, Bremen Art Gallery, Bremen
Kunsthistorisches Museum Vienna, Museum of Fine Arts, Vienna
Kunstmuseum Bern, Musee des Beaux-Arts de Berne, Bern
Kunstmuseum Solothurn, Solothurn Art Museum, Solothurn
La Salle University Art Museum, Philadelphia PA
Lafayette College, Lafayette College Art Galleries, Easton PA
Le Musee des Beaux-Arts, Brest
Leeds Museums & Galleries, Leeds
Lehigh University Art Galleries, Museum Operation, Bethlehem PA
Liberty Memorial Museum & Archives, The National Museum of World War I, Kansas City MO
Lightner Museum, Saint Augustine FL
Lockwood-Mathews Mansion Museum, Norwalk CT
Longfellow-Evangeline State Commemorative Area, Saint Martinville LA
Loyola University Chicago, Loyola University Museum of Art, Chicago IL
Ludwig Museum - Museum of Contemporary Art, Budapest
Lyman Allyn Art Museum, New London CT
Madison Museum of Fine Art, Madison GA
The Mariners' Museum, Newport News VA
Marquette University, Haggerty Museum of Art, Milwaukee WI
McCord Museum of Canadian History, Montreal PQ
McMaster University, McMaster Museum of Art, Hamilton ON
Michelson Museum of Art, Marshall TX
Ministry of Cultural Affairs, Bangladesh National Museum, Dhaka
The Mint Museum, Charlotte NC
Mobile Museum of Art, Mobile AL
Modern Art Museum, Fort Worth TX
Moderna Galerija, Gallery of Modern Art, Zagreb
Muscatine Art Center, Museum, Muscatine IA
Muscatine Art Center, Muscatine IA
Musee Carnavalet-Histoire de Paris, Paris
Musee Cognacq-Jay, Cognacq-Jay Museum, Paris
Musee d'art moderne de Ceret, Ceret
Musee des Augustins, Toulouse
Musee des Beaux-Arts d'Orleans, Historical & Archaeological Museum of Orleans, Orleans
Musee des Beaux-Arts d'Orleans, Museum of Fine Arts, Orleans
Musee des Beaux-Arts/Palais des Archeveques, Museum of Fine Arts, Tours
Musee et Chateau de Chantilly (MUSEE CONDE), Chantilly
Musee National d'Histoire et d'Art Luxembourg, Luxembourg City
Museen der Stadt Koln, Wallraf-Richartz-Museum, Cologne
Museo Cerralbo, Madrid
Museo de Arte de Ponce, The Luis A Ferre Foundation Inc, Ponce PR
Museo di Capodimonte, Naples
Museo Nacional de Bellas Artes, National Museum of Fine Arts, Santiago
Museu de Evora, Evora
The Museum of Arts & Sciences Inc, Daytona Beach FL
Museum of Decorative Arts in Prague, Prague
Museum of Fine Arts, Saint Petersburg, Florida, Inc, Saint Petersburg FL
Museum of Modern Art, Ibaraki, Ibaraki
Muskegon Museum of Art, Muskegon MI
Muzej za Umjetnost i Obrt, Museum of Arts & Crafts, Zagreb
Muzeul National Brukenthal, Brukenthal Palace & European Art Gallery, Sibiu
Muzeum Narodowe, National Museum in Poznan, Poznan
Napoleonic Society of America, Museum & Library, Saint Helena CA
Narodna Galerija, National Gallery of Slovenia, Ljubljana
Nassau County Museum of Art, Roslyn Harbor NY

PAINTING-GERMAN

Museum of Fine Arts, Saint Petersburg, Florida, Inc, Saint Petersburg FL
Muskegon Museum of Art, Muskegon MI
Muzej za Umjetnost i Obrt, Museum of Arts & Crafts, Zagreb
Muzeul National Brukenthal, Brukenthal Palace & European Art Gallery, Sibiu
Muzeum Narodowe, National Museum in Poznan, Poznan
Narodna Galerija, National Gallery of Slovenia, Ljubljana
Nassau County Museum of Art, Roslyn Harbor NY
National Galleries of Scotland, Scottish National Gallery, Edinburgh
National Gallery of Canada, Ottawa ON
National Gallery of Ireland, Dublin
National Museum of Fine Arts of Moldova, Chisinau
Nationalmuseum, Stockholm
The Nemours Foundatioin, Nemours Mansion & Gardens, Wilmington DE
Niagara University, Castellani Art Museum, Niagara NY
Niigata Prefectural Museum of Modern Art, Niigata
Norwich Free Academy, Slater Memorial Museum, Norwich CT
Oklahoma City Museum of Art, Oklahoma City OK
The Old Jail Art Center, Albany TX
Opelousas Museum of Art, Inc (OMA), Opelousas LA
Panhandle-Plains Historical Museum, Canyon TX
Passaic County Community College, Broadway, LRC, and Hamilton Club Galleries, Paterson NJ
The Pennsylvania State University, Palmer Museum of Art, University Park PA
Philadelphia Museum of Art, John G Johnson Collection, Philadelphia PA
Piedmont Arts Association, Martinsville VA
Prairie Art Gallery, Grande Prairie AB
Princeton University, Princeton University Art Museum, Princeton NJ
PS1 Contemporary Art Center, Long Island City NY
Queens College, City University of New York, Godwin-Ternbach Museum, Flushing NY
Queensborough Community College, Art Gallery, Bayside NY
Reading Public Museum, Reading PA
Jack Richard Gallery, Almond Tea Museum & Jane Williams Galleries, Divisions of Studios of Jack Richard, Cuyahoga Falls OH
Saginaw Art Museum, Saginaw MI
Saint Joseph's Oratory, Museum, Montreal PQ
Saint Peter's College, Art Gallery, Jersey City NJ
Santa Monica Museum of Art, Santa Monica CA
Soprintendenza per I beni storici artistici ed etnoantropologici per le province di Mantova Brescia e Cremona, Museo di Palazzo Ducale, Mantua
The Speed Art Museum, Louisville KY
Spertus Institute of Jewish Studies, Chicago IL
Staatsgalerie Stuttgart, Stuttgart
Stanford University, Cantor Arts Center at Stanford University, Stanford CA
The State Museum of Fine Arts of Tatarstan Republic, Kazan
State University of New York at New Paltz, Samuel Dorsky Museum of Art, New Paltz NY
Stiftung Deutsches Historisches Museum, Berlin
Syracuse University, Art Collection, Syracuse NY
Telfair Museums' Jepson Center for the Arts Library, Savannah GA
Tver Art Gallery, Tver
United States Figure Skating Association, World Figure Skating Museum & Hall of Fame, Colorado Springs CO
Universalmuseum Joanneum GmbH, Graz
University of California, Berkeley, The Magnes Collection of Jewish Art & Life, Berkeley CA
University of Chicago, Smart Museum of Art, Chicago IL
University of Cincinnati, DAAP Galleries-College of Design Architecture, Art & Planning, Cincinnati OH
University of Illinois at Urbana-Champaign, Krannert Art Museum and Kinkead Pavilion, Champaign IL
University of Manitoba, Faculty of Architecture Exhibition Centre, Winnipeg MB
University of Mary Washington, Gari Melchers Home and Studio, Fredericksburg VA
University of Miami, Lowe Art Museum, Coral Gables FL
University of Utah, Utah Museum of Fine Arts, Salt Lake City UT
University of Virginia, The Fralin Museum of Art at the University of Virginia, Charlottesville VA

University of Wisconsin-Madison, Chazen Museum of Art, Madison WI
Ursinus College, Philip & Muriel Berman Museum of Art, Collegeville PA
Wadsworth Atheneum Museum of Art, Hartford CT
Walker Art Gallery, Liverpool
The Wallace Collection, London
Washington University, Mildred Lane Kemper Art Museum, Saint Louis MO
Wheaton College, Beard and Weil Galleries, Norton MA
World Erotic Art Museum, Miami Beach FL
Yokohama Museum of Art, Yokohama
Zentrum Paul Klee, Bern
Zigler Art Museum, Jennings LA

PAINTING-ISRAELI

Art Without Walls Inc, New York NY
The Baltimore Museum of Art, Baltimore MD
The Buffalo Fine Arts Academy, Albright-Knox Art Gallery, Buffalo NY
Central United Methodist Church, Swords Into Plowshares Peace Center & Gallery, Detroit MI
Cummer Museum of Art & Gardens, Museum & Library, Jacksonville FL
Detroit Institute of Arts, Detroit MI
Hebrew Union College - Jewish Institute of Religion, Skirball Museum Cincinnati, Cincinnati OH
Hebrew Union College Museum, Jewish Institute of Religion Museum, New York NY
Hecht Museum, Haifa
The Israel Museum, Jerusalem, Billy Rose Art Garden, Jerusalem
The Israel Museum, Jerusalem, Samuel & Saidye Bronfman Archaeology Wing, Jerusalem
The Israel Museum, Jerusalem, Jerusalem
Modern Art Museum, Fort Worth TX
Museum of Decorative Arts in Prague, Prague
Opelousas Museum of Art, Inc (OMA), Opelousas LA
Piedmont Arts Association, Martinsville VA
PS1 Contemporary Art Center, Long Island City NY
Queensborough Community College, Art Gallery, Bayside NY
Saint Peter's College, Art Gallery, Jersey City NJ
Santa Monica Museum of Art, Santa Monica CA
Shephela Museum, Post Kefar-Menahem
The Speed Art Museum, Louisville KY
Spertus Institute of Jewish Studies, Chicago IL
Stanford University, Cantor Arts Center at Stanford University, Stanford CA
The State Museum of Oriental Art, Moscow
The Temple-Tifereth Israel, The Temple Museum of Religious Art, Beachwood OH
University of California, Berkeley, The Magnes Collection of Jewish Art & Life, Berkeley CA
Ursinus College, Philip & Muriel Berman Museum of Art, Collegeville PA
Wadsworth Atheneum Museum of Art, Hartford CT
World Erotic Art Museum, Miami Beach FL

PAINTING-ITALIAN

Akademie der Bildenden Kunste Wien, Gemaldegalerie der Akademie der bildenden Kunste Wien, Vienna
Allentown Art Museum, Allentown PA
Arnot Art Museum, Elmira NY
Art & Culture Center of Hollywood, Art Gallery/Multidisciplinary Cultural Center, Hollywood FL
The Art Museum at the University of Kentucky, Lexington KY
Art Museum of the University of Houston, Blaffer Gallery, Houston TX
Art Without Walls Inc, New York NY
Baroda Museum and Picture Gallery, Baroda
Bates College, Museum of Art, Lewiston ME
Bayerische Staatsgemaldesammlungen/Bavarian State Art Galleries, Alte Pinakothek, Munich
Bayerische Staatsgemaldesammlungen/Bavarian State Art Galleries, Neue Pinakothek, Munich
Berkshire Museum, Pittsfield MA
Birmingham Museum of Art, Birmingham AL
Bucknell University, Edward & Marthann Samek Art Gallery, Lewisburg PA
The Buffalo Fine Arts Academy, Albright-Knox Art Gallery, Buffalo NY
Canton Museum of Art, Canton OH
Caramoor Center for Music & the Arts, Inc, Rosen House at Caramoor, Katonah NY
Chrysler Museum of Art, Norfolk VA

Cincinnati Art Museum, Cincinnati Art Museum, Cincinnati OH
City of El Paso, El Paso TX
Sterling & Francine Clark, Williamstown MA
Colgate University, Picker Art Gallery, Hamilton NY
College of William & Mary, Muscarelle Museum of Art, Williamsburg VA
Columbia Museum of Art, Columbia SC
Columbus Chapel & Boal Mansion Museum, Boalsburg PA
Columbus Museum of Art, Columbus OH
Comune di Genova - Direzione Cultura Settore Musei, Museo di Strada Nuova Palazzo Rosso, Genoa
The Courtauld Institute of Art, The Courtauld Gallery, London
Crocker Art Museum, Sacramento CA
Cuneo Foundation, Museum & Gardens, Vernon Hills IL
The Currier Museum of Art, Manchester NH
Dartmouth College, Hood Museum of Art, Hanover NH
Denison University, Art Gallery, Granville OH
Denver Art Museum, Denver CO
Detroit Institute of Arts, Detroit MI
Doncaster Museum and Art Gallery, Doncaster
Environment Canada - Parks Canada, Laurier House, National Historic Site, Ottawa ON
Fine Arts Center for the New River Valley, Pulaski VA
Flint Institute of Arts, Flint MI
Fondazione Musei Civici Di Venezia, Ca'Rezzonico, Museo del Settecento Veneziano, Venice
Fondazione Musei Civici Di Venezia, Galleria Internazionale d'Arte Moderna di Ca'Pesaro, Venice
Fondazione Scientifica Querini Stampalia, Venice
Edsel & Eleanor Ford, Grosse Pointe Shores MI
The Frick Art & Historical Center, Inc, Frick Art Museum, Pittsburgh PA
Frick Collection, New York NY
Frye Art Museum, Seattle WA
Galleria Doria Pamphilj, Rome
Galleria Nazionale dell'Umbria, Umbrian National Gallery, Perugia
Isabella Stewart Gardner, Boston MA
General Board of Discipleship, The United Methodist Church, The Upper Room Chapel & Museum, Nashville TN
The Ghent Museum of Fine Arts, Ghent
Guggenheim Museum Soho, New York NY
Solomon R Guggenheim, New York NY
Guilford College, Art Gallery, Greensboro NC
Hecht Museum, Haifa
Heritage Malta, National Museum of Fine Arts, Valletta
Hillwood Museum & Gardens Foundation, Hillwood Estate Museum & Gardens, Washington DC
Howard University, Gallery of Art, Washington DC
Hyde Collection Trust, Glens Falls NY
Independent Administrative Institution National Museum of Art, The National Museum of Western Art, Tokyo
Indiana Landmarks, Morris-Butler House, Indianapolis IN
The Israel Museum, Jerusalem, Billy Rose Art Garden, Jerusalem
The Israel Museum, Jerusalem, Samuel & Saidye Bronfman Archaeology Wing, Jerusalem
The Israel Museum, Jerusalem, Jerusalem
J.M.W. Turner Museum, Sarasota FL
Bob Jones University Museum & Gallery Inc, Greenville SC
Jordan National Gallery of Fine Arts, Amman
Joslyn Art Museum, Omaha NE
Juniata College Museum of Art, Huntingdon PA
Kereszteny Muzeum, Christian Museum, Esztergom
Knights of Columbus Supreme Council, Knights of Columbus Museum, New Haven CT
Kunsthistorisches Museum Vienna, Museum of Fine Arts, Vienna
Kunstmuseum Bern, Musee des Beaux-Arts de Berne, Bern
La Salle University Art Museum, Philadelphia PA
Latino Art Museum, Pomona CA
Le Musee des Beaux-Arts, Brest
Leeds Museums & Galleries, Leeds
Lightner Museum, Saint Augustine FL
Loyola University Chicago, Loyola University Museum of Art, Chicago IL
Lyman Allyn Art Museum, New London CT
Mabee-Gerrer Museum of Art, Shawnee OK
Madison Museum of Fine Art, Madison GA
Marquette University, Haggerty Museum of Art, Milwaukee WI
McMaster University, McMaster Museum of Art, Hamilton ON

PAINTING-JAPANESE

Seattle Art Museum, Downtown, Seattle WA
The Society of the Cincinnati at Anderson House,
    Washington DC
The Speed Art Museum, Louisville KY
Springfield Art Museum, Springfield MO
Stanford University, Cantor Arts Center at Stanford
    University, Stanford CA
The State Museum of Oriental Art, Moscow
State University of New York at New Paltz, Samuel
    Dorsky Museum of Art, New Paltz NY
The State University of New York at Potsdam, Roland
    Gibson Gallery, Potsdam NY
Tacoma Art Museum, Tacoma WA
Temiskaming Art Gallery, Haileybury ON
The Tokugawa Reimeikai Foundation, The Tokugawa
    Art Museum, Nagoya
Tokyo University of the Arts, The University Art
    Museum, Tokyo
Towson University, Asian Arts & Culture Center,
    Towson MD
Tver Art Gallery, Tver
Ukrainian Institute of Modern Art, Chicago IL
University of Chicago, Smart Museum of Art, Chicago
    IL
University of Illinois at Urbana-Champaign, Krannert
    Art Museum and Kinkead Pavilion, Champaign IL
University of Kansas, Spencer Museum of Art,
    Lawrence KS
University of Michigan, Museum of Art, Ann Arbor MI
University of Missouri, Museum of Art & Archaeology,
    Columbia MO
University of Pittsburgh, University Art Gallery,
    Pittsburgh PA
University of Utah, Utah Museum of Fine Arts, Salt
    Lake City UT
University of Virginia, The Fralin Museum of Art at
    the University of Virginia, Charlottesville VA
University of Wisconsin-Madison, Chazen Museum of
    Art, Madison WI
Ursinus College, Philip & Muriel Berman Museum of
    Art, Collegeville PA
Viridian Artists Inc, New York NY
Washington University, Mildred Lane Kemper Art
    Museum, Saint Louis MO
Yokohama Museum of Art, Yokohama
Zigler Art Museum, Jennings LA

PAINTING-NEW ZEALAND

Anderson Park Art Gallery Inc, Art Gallery, Invercargill
Art Without Walls Inc, New York NY
Detroit Institute of Arts, Detroit MI
Modern Art Museum, Fort Worth TX
Museum of Decorative Arts in Prague, Prague
Prairie Art Gallery, Grande Prairie AB
PS1 Contemporary Art Center, Long Island City NY
Queensborough Community College, Art Gallery,
    Bayside NY
Saint Peter's College, Art Gallery, Jersey City NJ
Santa Monica Museum of Art, Santa Monica CA
Stanford University, Cantor Arts Center at Stanford
    University, Stanford CA
University of Illinois at Urbana-Champaign, Krannert
    Art Museum and Kinkead Pavilion, Champaign IL

PAINTING-POLISH

Art & Culture Center of Hollywood, Art
    Gallery/Multidisciplinary Cultural Center,
    Hollywood FL
Art Without Walls Inc, New York NY
Bayerische Staatsgemaldesammlungen/Bavarian State
    Art Galleries, Neue Pinakothek, Munich
Bucknell University, Edward & Marthann Samek Art
    Gallery, Lewisburg PA
College of William & Mary, Muscarelle Museum of
    Art, Williamsburg VA
Detroit Institute of Arts, Detroit MI
Fine Arts Center for the New River Valley, Pulaski VA
Forest Lawn Museum, Glendale CA
Frye Art Museum, Seattle WA
Galerie Montcalm, Gatineau PQ
Grand Rapids Art Museum, Grand Rapids MI
Hecht Museum, Haifa
The Israel Museum, Jerusalem, Billy Rose Art Garden,
    Jerusalem
Knights of Columbus Supreme Council, Knights of
    Columbus Museum, New Haven CT
Laurentian University, Museum & Art Centre, Sudbury
    ON
Ludwig Museum - Museum of Contemporary Art,
    Budapest

Museum of Decorative Arts in Prague, Prague
Muzeum Narodowe, National Museum in Poznan,
    Poznan
Muzeum Narodowe W Kielcach, National Museum in
    Kielce, Kielce
Narodna Galerija, National Gallery of Slovenia,
    Ljubljana
National Museum of Fine Arts of Moldova, Chisinau
Panhandle-Plains Historical Museum, Canyon TX
Phoenix Art Museum, Phoenix AZ
Polish Museum of America, Chicago IL
PS1 Contemporary Art Center, Long Island City NY
Queensborough Community College, Art Gallery,
    Bayside NY
Reading Public Museum, Reading PA
Saginaw Art Museum, Saginaw MI
St Mary's Galeria, Orchard Lake MI
Saint Peter's College, Art Gallery, Jersey City NJ
Santa Monica Museum of Art, Santa Monica CA
The Speed Art Museum, Louisville KY
Spertus Institute of Jewish Studies, Chicago IL
Stanford University, Cantor Arts Center at Stanford
    University, Stanford CA
Tver Art Gallery, Tver
U Gallery, New York NY
University of California, Berkeley, The Magnes
    Collection of Jewish Art & Life, Berkeley CA
University of Georgia, Georgia Museum of Art, Athens
    GA
University of Wisconsin-Madison, Chazen Museum of
    Art, Madison WI
Walker Art Gallery, Liverpool
Zacheta - National Gallery of Art, Kordegarda Gallery,
    Warsaw
Zigler Art Museum, Jennings LA

PAINTING-RUSSIAN

Art & Culture Center of Hollywood, Art
    Gallery/Multidisciplinary Cultural Center,
    Hollywood FL
Art Without Walls Inc, New York NY
Baroda Museum and Picture Gallery, Baroda
Bayerische Staatsgemaldesammlungen/Bavarian State
    Art Galleries, Neue Pinakothek, Munich
Bucknell University, Edward & Marthann Samek Art
    Gallery, Lewisburg PA
Byzantine & Christian Museum, Athens, Athens
College of William & Mary, Muscarelle Museum of
    Art, Williamsburg VA
Concordia University Wisconsin, Fine Art Gallery,
    Mequon WI
Coutts Museum of Art, Inc, El Dorado KS
Crocker Art Museum, Sacramento CA
The Currier Museum of Art, Manchester NH
Detroit Institute of Arts, Detroit MI
Doncaster Museum and Art Gallery, Doncaster
Duke University, Nasher Museum of Art at Duke
    University, Durham NC
Fine Arts Center for the New River Valley, Pulaski VA
Frye Art Museum, Seattle WA
General Board of Discipleship, The United Methodist
    Church, The Upper Room Chapel & Museum,
    Nashville TN
Grand Rapids Art Museum, Grand Rapids MI
Guggenheim Museum Soho, New York NY
Solomon R Guggenheim, New York NY
Hebrew Union College Museum, Jewish Institute of
    Religion Museum, New York NY
Hillwood Museum & Gardens Foundation, Hillwood
    Estate Museum & Gardens, Washington DC
Hofstra University, Hofstra University Museum,
    Hempstead NY
Huntington Museum of Art, Huntington WV
The Israel Museum, Jerusalem, Billy Rose Art Garden,
    Jerusalem
The Israel Museum, Jerusalem, Samuel & Saidye
    Bronfman Archaeology Wing, Jerusalem
James Dick Foundation, Festival - Institute, Round Top
    TX
Johns Hopkins University, Evergreen Museum &
    Library, Baltimore MD
Bob Jones University Museum & Gallery Inc,
    Greenville SC
Jordan National Gallery of Fine Arts, Amman
Joslyn Art Museum, Omaha NE
Kereszteny Muzeum, Christian Museum, Esztergom
Knights of Columbus Supreme Council, Knights of
    Columbus Museum, New Haven CT
Kunstmuseum Bern, Musee des Beaux-Arts de Berne,
    Bern
Kyiv Museum of Russian Art, Kyiv

Latvijas Nacionalais Makslas Muzejs, Arsenals
    Exhibition Hall, Riga
Loyola University Chicago, Loyola University Museum
    of Art, Chicago IL
Ludwig Museum - Museum of Contemporary Art,
    Budapest
McMaster University, McMaster Museum of Art,
    Hamilton ON
Meredith College, Frankie G Weems Gallery &
    Rotunda Gallery, Raleigh NC
Michelson Museum of Art, Marshall TX
Ministry of Cultural Affairs, Bangladesh National
    Museum, Dhaka
The Mint Museum, Charlotte NC
Moravska Galerie v Brne, Moravian Gallery in Brno,
    Brno
The Museum of Arts & Sciences Inc, Daytona Beach
    FL
Museum of Decorative Arts in Prague, Prague
Muzeul National Brukenthal, Brukenthal Palace &
    European Art Gallery, Sibiu
Nassau County Museum of Art, Roslyn Harbor NY
National Gallery of Canada, Ottawa ON
National Museum of Fine Arts of Moldova, Chisinau
Noyes Art Gallery, Lincoln NE
Panhandle-Plains Historical Museum, Canyon TX
Pearson Lakes Art Center, Okoboji IA
The Phillips Collection, Washington DC
Princeton University, Princeton University Art Museum,
    Princeton NJ
PS1 Contemporary Art Center, Long Island City NY
Queens College, City University of New York,
    Godwin-Ternbach Museum, Flushing NY
Queensborough Community College, Art Gallery,
    Bayside NY
Reading Public Museum, Reading PA
Jack Richard Gallery, Almond Tea Museum & Jane
    Williams Galleries, Divisions of Studios of Jack
    Richard, Cuyahoga Falls OH
Rollins College, George D & Harriet W Cornell Fine
    Arts Museum, Winter Park FL
Rutgers, The State University of New Jersey, Zimmerli
    Art Museum, Rutgers University, New Brunswick
    NJ
Saginaw Art Museum, Saginaw MI
Saint Olaf College, Flaten Art Museum, Northfield MN
Saint Peter's College, Art Gallery, Jersey City NJ
Santa Monica Museum of Art, Santa Monica CA
The Speed Art Museum, Louisville KY
Spertus Institute of Jewish Studies, Chicago IL
Springville Museum of Art, Springville UT
Stanford University, Cantor Arts Center at Stanford
    University, Stanford CA
The State Museum of Fine Arts of Tatarstan Republic,
    Kazan
The State Museum of Oriental Art, Moscow
Timken Museum of Art, San Diego CA
Tver Art Gallery, Tver
University of California, Berkeley, The Magnes
    Collection of Jewish Art & Life, Berkeley CA
University of Cincinnati, DAAP Galleries-College of
    Design Architecture, Art & Planning, Cincinnati OH
University of Wisconsin-Madison, Chazen Museum of
    Art, Madison WI
Ursinus College, Philip & Muriel Berman Museum of
    Art, Collegeville PA
World Erotic Art Museum, Miami Beach FL
Yokohama Museum of Art, Yokohama

PAINTING-SCANDINAVIAN

American Swedish Historical Foundation & Museum,
    American Swedish Historical Museum, Philadelphia
    PA
American Swedish Institute, Minneapolis MN
Arnot Art Museum, Elmira NY
Art & Culture Center of Hollywood, Art
    Gallery/Multidisciplinary Cultural Center,
    Hollywood FL
Art Without Walls Inc, New York NY
Bayerische Staatsgemaldesammlungen/Bavarian State
    Art Galleries, Neue Pinakothek, Munich
Blauvelt Demarest Foundation, Hiram Blauvelt Art
    Museum, Oradell NJ
Bucknell University, Edward & Marthann Samek Art
    Gallery, Lewisburg PA
California State University, Northridge, Art Galleries,
    Northridge CA
Colgate University, Picker Art Gallery, Hamilton NY
Crocker Art Museum, Sacramento CA
Detroit Institute of Arts, Detroit MI
Fine Arts Center for the New River Valley, Pulaski VA

Atlanta Historical Society Inc, Atlanta History Center, Atlanta GA

The Bartlett Museum, Amesbury MA

Bartow-Pell Mansion Museum & Gardens, Bronx NY

Bay County Historical Society, Historical Museum of Bay County, Bay City MI

Belle Grove Inc., Belle Grove Plantation, Middletown VA

Belvedere Museum, Osterreichische Galerie Belvedere, Vienna

Blanden Memorial Art Museum, Fort Dodge IA

Bradford Brinton, Big Horn WY

Brooklyn Historical Society, Brooklyn OH

Bush-Holley Historic Site & Storehouse Gallery, Greenwich Historical Society/ Bush-Holley House, Cos Cob CT

Cabot's Old Indian Pueblo Museum, Desert Hot Springs CA

Cambridge Museum, Cambridge NE

Canadian Museum of Civilization, Gatineau PQ

Cape Ann Historical Association, Cape Ann Museum, Gloucester MA

Captain Forbes House Museum, Milton MA

Caramoor Center for Music & the Arts, Inc, Rosen House at Caramoor, Katonah NY

Carson County Square House Museum, Panhandle TX

Chateau Ramezay Museum, Montreal PQ

Chatham Historical Society, The Atwood House Museum, Chatham MA

Chatillon-DeMenil House Foundation, Chatillon-DeMenil House, Saint Louis MO

City of Austin Parks & Recreation, O. Henry Museum, Austin TX

City of Gainesville, Thomas Center Galleries - Cultural Affairs, Gainesville FL

City of Mason City, Charles H MacNider Museum, Mason City IA

The City of Petersburg Museums, Petersburg VA

City of San Antonio, San Antonio TX

City of Springdale, Shiloh Museum of Ozark History, Springdale AR

Clark County Historical Society, Pioneer - Krier Museum, Ashland KS

Clemson University, Fort Hill Plantation, Clemson SC

Cliveden, Philadelphia PA

Columbus Museum, Columbus GA

Comune di Genova - Direzione Cultura Settore Musei, Museo di Strada Nuova Palazzo Rosso, Genoa

Concord Museum, Concord MA

Congregation Beth Israel's Plotkin Judaica Museum, Scottsdale AZ

Conrad-Caldwell House Museum, Louisville KY

Craigdarroch Castle Historical Museum Society, Victoria BC

Crane Collection, Gallery of American Painting and Sculpture, Magnolia MA

Creek Council House Museum, Okmulgee OK

Cripple Creek District Museum, Cripple Creek CO

Crook County Museum & Art Gallery, Sundance WY

Culberson County Historical Museum, Van Horn TX

Cuneo Foundation, Museum & Gardens, Vernon Hills IL

Danville Museum of Fine Arts & History, Danville VA

DAR Museum, National Society Daughters of the American Revolution, Washington DC

Delaware Division of Historical & Cultural Affairs, Dover DE

Detroit Institute of Arts, Detroit MI

Dundurn Castle, Hamilton ON

East Tennessee State University, The Reece Museum, Johnson City TN

Edgecombe County Cultural Arts Council, Inc, Blount-Bridgers House, Hobson Pittman Memorial Gallery, Tarboro NC

Environment Canada - Parks Canada, Laurier House, National Historic Site, Ottawa ON

Erie County Historical Society, Erie PA

Evanston Historical Society, Charles Gates Dawes House, Evanston IL

Evansville Museum of Arts, History & Science, Evansville IN

Fondazione Musei Civici Di Venezia, Museo Correr, Venice

Edsel & Eleanor Ford, Grosse Pointe Shores MI

The Frick Art & Historical Center, Inc, Frick Art Museum, Pittsburgh PA

Friends of Historic Kingston, Fred J Johnston House Museum, Kingston NY

Frontier Gateway Museum, Glendive MT

Fruitlands Museum, Inc, Harvard MA

Fulton County Historical Society Inc, Fulton County Museum (Tetzlaff Reference Room), Rochester IN

Gem County Historical Society and Museum, Gem County Historical Village Museum, Emmett ID

Genesee Country Village & Museum, John L Wehle Art Gallery, Mumford NY

Gibson Society, Inc, Gibson House Museum, Boston MA

Girard College, Stephen Girard Collection, Philadelphia PA

Glanmore National Historic Site of Canada, Belleville ON

Glessner House Museum, Chicago IL

Grand Rapids Public Museum, Public Museum of Grand Rapids, Grand Rapids MI

Greene County Historical Society, Bronck Museum, Coxsackie NY

Hammond-Harwood House Association, Inc, Hammond-Harwood House, Annapolis MD

Hancock County Trustees of Public Reservations, Woodlawn: Museum, Gardens & Park, Ellsworth ME

Hancock Shaker Village, Inc, Pittsfield MA

Headquarters Fort Monroe, Dept of Army, Casemate Museum, Hampton VA

Heart of West Texas Museum, Colorado City TX

Henry County Museum & Cultural Arts Center, Clinton MO

Henry Morrison Flagler Museum, Palm Beach FL

Henry Sheldon Museum of Vermont History and Research Center, Middlebury VT

Hill-Stead Museum, Farmington CT

Historic Arkansas Museum, Little Rock AR

Historic Cherry Hill, Albany NY

Historic Deerfield, Inc, Deerfield MA

Historical Society of Cheshire County, Keene NH

Historical Society of Martin County, Elliott Museum, Stuart FL

Historical Society of Old Newbury, Cushing House Museum, Newburyport MA

Historisches und Volkerkundemuseum, Historical Museum, St Gallen

Hopewell Museum, Hopewell NJ

Houston Baptist University, Museum of American Architecture and Decorative Arts, Houston TX

Hoyt Center for the Arts, New Castle PA

Huguenot Historical Society of New Paltz Galleries, New Paltz NY

Huntington Museum of Art, Huntington WV

Stan Hywet, Akron OH

Idaho Historical Museum, Boise ID

Illinois State Museum, ISM Lockport Gallery, Chicago Gallery & Southern Illinois Art Gallery, Springfield IL

Imperial Calcasieu Museum, Gibson-Barham Gallery, Lake Charles LA

Imperial Calcasieu Museum, Lake Charles LA

Independence Historical Museum & Art Center, Independence KS

Independence National Historical Park, Philadelphia PA

Indiana Landmarks, Morris-Butler House, Indianapolis IN

Indianapolis Museum of Art, Indianapolis IN

Iroquois County Historical Society Museum, Old Courthouse Museum, Watseka IL

The Israel Museum, Jerusalem, Billy Rose Art Garden, Jerusalem

The Israel Museum, Jerusalem, Jerusalem

J.M.W. Turner Museum, Sarasota FL

Jackson County Historical Society, The 1859 Jail, Marshal's Home & Museum, Independence MO

James Dick Foundation, Festival - Institute, Round Top TX

Jamestown-Yorktown Foundation, Jamestown Settlement, Williamsburg VA

Johns Hopkins University, Homewood Museum, Baltimore MD

Bob Jones University Museum & Gallery Inc, Greenville SC

Jordan Historical Museum of The Twenty, Jordan ON

Kateri Tekakwitha Shrine/St. Francis Xavier Mission, Kahnawake PQ

Kelly-Griggs House Museum, Red Bluff CA

Kentucky Historical Society, Old State Capitol & Annex, Frankfort KY

Kings County Historical Society & Museum, Hampton NB

Knoxville Museum of Art, Knoxville TN

Koochiching Museums, International Falls MN

La Salle University Art Museum, Philadelphia PA

Landmark Society of Western New York, Inc, The Campbell-Whittlesey House Museum, Rochester NY

Leeds Museums & Galleries, Leeds

Lehigh Valley Heritage Center, Allentown PA

LeSueur County Historical Society, Chapter One, Elysian MN

Liberty Hall Historic Site, Liberty Hall Museum, Frankfort KY

Lincoln County Historical Association, Inc, 1811 Old Lincoln County Jail & Lincoln County Museum, Wiscasset ME

Lincolnshire County Council, Library & Heritage Services, Lincoln

Lockwood-Mathews Mansion Museum, Norwalk CT

Longfellow National Historic Site, Longfellow House - Washington's Headquarters, Cambridge MA

Longfellow's Wayside Inn Museum, Sudbury MA

Longfellow-Evangeline State Commemorative Area, Saint Martinville LA

Los Angeles County Museum of Natural History, William S Hart Museum, Newhall CA

Louisiana Department of Culture, Recreation & Tourism, Louisiana State Museum, New Orleans LA

Loveland Museum/Gallery, Loveland CO

Lyme Historical Society, Florence Griswold Museum, Old Lyme CT

Maine Historical Society, Wadsworth-Longfellow House, Portland ME

Marblehead Museum & Historical Society, Jeremiah Lee Mansion, Marblehead MA

Marblehead Museum & Historical Society, Marblehead MA

Jacques Marchais, Staten Island NY

McDowell House & Apothecary Shop, Danville KY

Middle Border Museum & Oscar Howe Art Center, Mitchell SD

Middlebury College, Museum of Art, Middlebury VT

Milwaukee County War Memorial Inc., Villa Terrace Decorative Arts Museum, Milwaukee WI

Minneapolis Institute of Arts, Minneapolis MN

The Mint Museum, Charlotte NC

Mission San Miguel Museum, San Miguel CA

Mississippi River Museum at Mud-Island River Park, Memphis TN

MonDak Heritage Center, History Library, Sidney MT

Monhegan Museum, Monhegan ME

Monroe County Historical Association, Elizabeth D Walters Library, Stroudsburg PA

Moody County Historical Society, Moody County Museum, Pierre SD

The Morgan Library & Museum, Museum, New York NY

Morris Museum, Morristown NJ

Morris-Jumel Mansion, Inc, New York NY

Morven Museum & Garden, Princeton NJ

Mount Vernon Hotel Museum & Garden, New York NY

Mount Vernon Ladies' Association of the Union, Mount Vernon VA

Muchnic Foundation & Atchison Art Association, Muchnic Gallery, Atchison KS

Munson-Williams-Proctor Arts Institute, Museum of Art, Utica NY

Muscatine Art Center, Museum, Muscatine IA

Musea Brugge, Stadhuis - Town Hall, Bruges

Musea Brugge, Volkskunde Museum, Bruges

Musee Carnavalet-Histoire de Paris, Paris

Musee des Beaux-Arts d'Orleans, Historical & Archaeological Museum of Orleans, Orleans

Museo Del Romanticismo, Museum of the Romantic Period, Madrid

Museu Nacional de Arte Contemporanea, National Museum of Contemporary Art, Museu Do Chiado, Lisbon

The Museum, Greenwood SC

Museum De Lakenhal, Leiden

Museum fur Kunst und Gewerbe Hamburg, Hamburg

Museum of Art, Fort Lauderdale, Fort Lauderdale FL

Museum of Chinese in America, New York NY

Museum of Fine Arts, Boston MA

Museum of Fine Arts Houston, Bayou Bend Collection & Gardens, Houston TX

Museum of Fine Arts, Saint Petersburg, Florida, Inc, Saint Petersburg FL

Museum of New Mexico, Palace of Governors, Santa Fe NM

Museum of Southern History, Houston TX

Museum Plantin-Moretus/Prentenkabinet, Antwerp

Museum zu Allerheiligen, Schaffhausen

Muzeul National Brukenthal, Brukenthal Palace & European Art Gallery, Sibiu

Nassau County Museum of Art, Roslyn Harbor NY

Nathan Hale Homestead Museum, Coventry CT

National Audubon Society, John James Audubon Center at Mill Grove, Audubon PA
National Museum of American Illustration, Newport RI
National Park Service, Hubbell Trading Post National Historic Site, Ganado AZ
National Society of Colonial Dames of America in the State of Maryland, Mount Clare Museum House, Baltimore MD
National Society of the Colonial Dames of America in The Commonwealth of Virginia, Wilton House Museum, Richmond VA
National Trust for Historic Preservation, Decatur House, Washington DC
National Trust for Historic Preservation, Shadows-on-the-Teche, New Iberia LA
Nebraska Game and Parks Commission, Arbor Lodge State Historical Park & Morton Mansion, Nebraska City NE
The Nelson-Atkins Museum of Art, Kansas City MO
Nevada Northern Railway Museum, Ely NV
New Brunswick Museum, Saint John NB
New Canaan Historical Society, New Canaan CT
New Orleans Museum of Art, New Orleans LA
New York State Office of Parks Recreation & Historic Preservation, John Jay Homestead State Historic Site, Katonah NY
New York State Office of Parks, Recreation & Historic Preservation, Staatsburgh State Historic Site, Staatsburg NY
Newport Art Museum and Association, Newport RI
Nichols House Museum, Inc, Boston MA
North Country Museum of Arts, Park Rapids MN
Norwich Free Academy, Slater Memorial Museum, Norwich CT
Oatlands Plantation, Leesburg VA
Oglebay Institute, Mansion Museum, Wheeling WV
The Ohio Historical Society, Inc, Campus Martius Museum & Ohio River Museum, Marietta OH
Okefenokee Heritage Center, Inc, Waycross GA
Oklahoma Historical Society, State Museum of History, Oklahoma City OK
Old Barracks Museum, Trenton NJ
Old Fort Harrod State Park Mansion Museum, Harrodsburg KY
Old Island Restoration Foundation Inc, Oldest House in Key West, Key West FL
Ordrupgaardsamlingen, Ordrupgaard, Charlottenlund
Owensboro Museum of Fine Art, Owensboro KY
Panhandle-Plains Historical Museum, Canyon TX
Pasadena Museum of History, Pasadena CA
Passaic County Community College, Broadway, LRC, and Hamilton Club Galleries, Paterson NJ
Passaic County Historical Society, Lambert Castle Museum & Library, Paterson NJ
Penobscot Marine Museum, Searsport ME
Peoria Historical Society, Peoria IL
Phelps County Historical Society, Nebraska Prairie Museum, Holdrege NE
Philadelphia Museum of Art, Main Building, Philadelphia PA
Piatt Castles, West Liberty OH
Pioneer Historical Museum of South Dakota, Hot Springs SD
Plainsman Museum, Aurora NE
Pope County Historical Society, Pope County Museum, Glenwood MN
Portsmouth Historical Society, John Paul Jones House & Discover Portsmouth, Portsmouth NH
Putnam County Historical Society, Foundry School Museum, Cold Spring NY
Rahr-West Art Museum, Manitowoc WI
Red Deer & District Museum & Archives, Red Deer AB
Riley County Historical Society & Museum, Riley County Historical Museum, Manhattan KS
Rock Ford Foundation, Inc, Rock Ford Plantation, Lancaster PA
Lauren Rogers, Laurel MS
Royal Arts Foundation, Belcourt Castle, Newport RI
Royal Museums of Fine Arts of Belgium, Brussels
C M Russell, Great Falls MT
Ryerss Victorian Museum & Library, Philadelphia PA
Saco Museum, Saco ME
Saint Augustine Historical Society, Oldest House Museum Complex, Saint Augustine FL
Saint Johnsbury Athenaeum, Saint Johnsbury VT
St Mary Landmarks, Grevemberg House Museum, Franklin LA
Saint-Gaudens National Historic Site, Cornish NH
Salisbury House Foundation, Salisbury House and Garden, Des Moines IA

The Sandwich Historical Society, Inc & Sandwich Glass Museum, Sandwich Glass Museum, Sandwich MA
Schuyler-Hamilton House, Morristown NJ
Seneca Falls Historical Society Museum, Seneca Falls NY
Shelburne Museum, Museum, Shelburne VT
Shirley Plantation Foundation, Charles City VA
Shoreline Historical Museum, Shoreline WA
Shores Memorial Museum, Lyndon Center VT
The Society of the Cincinnati at Anderson House, Washington DC
Sooke Region Museum & Art Gallery, Sooke BC
The Speed Art Museum, Louisville KY
Springville Museum of Art, Springville UT
Staatsgalerie Stuttgart, Stuttgart
State of North Carolina, Battleship North Carolina, Wilmington NC
State University of New York College at Buffalo, Buffalo NY
T C Steele, Nashville IN
Stratford Historical Society, Catharine B Mitchell Museum, Stratford CT
Sturdivant Museum Association, Sturdivant Museum, Selma AL
The Summit County Historical Society of Akron, OH, Akron OH
Suomen Kansallismuseo, National Museum of Finland, Helsinki
Tallahassee Museum of History & Natural Science, Tallahassee FL
Taos, Ernest Blumenschein Home & Studio, Taos NM
Taos, La Hacienda de Los Martinez, Taos NM
Taos, Taos NM
Telfair Museums' Jepson Center for the Arts Library, Savannah GA
Three Forks Area Historical Society, Headwaters Heritage Museum, Three Forks MT
Trust Authority, Museum of the Great Plains, Lawton OK
The Trustees of Reservations, The Mission House, Ipswich MA
Tryon Palace Historic Sites & Gardens, New Bern NC
Tucson Museum of Art and Historic Block, Tucson AZ
Mark Twain, Hartford CT
United Society of Shakers, Shaker Museum, New Gloucester ME
United States Capitol, Architect of the Capitol, Washington DC
Universalmuseum Joanneum GmbH, Graz
University of Mary Washington, Gari Melchers Home and Studio, Fredericksburg VA
University of Memphis, Art Museum, Memphis TN
University of Miami, Lowe Art Museum, Coral Gables FL
University of Saskatchewan, Diefenbaker Canada Centre, Saskatoon SK
Utah Department of Natural Resources, Division of Parks & Recreation, Territorial Statehouse State Park Museum, Fillmore UT
Vermilion County Museum Society, Danville IL
Vesterheim Norwegian-American Museum, Decorah IA
Victoria Mansion - Morse Libby House, Portland ME
Vizcaya Museum & Gardens, Miami FL
Wade House Historic Site-Wisconsin Historical Society, Wesley W. Jung Carriage Museum, Greenbush WI
Mamie McFaddin Ward, Beaumont TX
Warner House Association, MacPheadris-Warner House, Portsmouth NH
Washington & Lee University, Lee Chapel & Museum, Lexington VA
West Baton Rouge Parish, West Baton Rouge Museum, Port Allen LA
West Florida Historic Preservation, Inc/University of West Florida, T T Wentworth, Jr Florida State Museum; Historic Pensacola Village; Pensacola Historical Society & Resource Center, Pensacola FL
Westfries Museum, Hoorn
Wethersfield Historical Society Inc, Museum, Wethersfield CT
Whatcom Museum, Bellingham WA
White House, Washington DC
Willard House & Clock Museum, Inc, North Grafton MA
Woodrow Wilson, Staunton VA
Woodrow Wilson, Washington DC
Wistariahurst Museum, Holyoke MA
Woodlawn/The Pope-Leighey, Mount Vernon VA
Woodmere Art Museum Inc, Philadelphia PA
World Erotic Art Museum, Miami Beach FL
Yarmouth County Historical Society, Yarmouth County Museum & Archives, Yarmouth NS

PEWTER

Albany Institute of History & Art, Albany NY
Allentown Art Museum, Allentown PA
American Folk Art Museum, New York NY
Baker University, Old Castle Museum, Baldwin City KS
Beverly Historical Society, Cabot, Hale & Balch House Museums, Beverly MA
Cameron Art Museum, Wilmington NC
Canadian Museum of Civilization, Gatineau PQ
Cape Ann Historical Association, Cape Ann Museum, Gloucester MA
College of William & Mary, Muscarelle Museum of Art, Williamsburg VA
Concord Museum, Concord MA
Cooper-Hewitt National Design Museum, Smithsonian Institution, New York NY
Craftsmen's Guild of Mississippi, Inc, Mississippi Crafts Center, Ridgeland MS
The Currier Museum of Art, Manchester NH
DAR Museum, National Society Daughters of the American Revolution, Washington DC
Dartmouth College, Hood Museum of Art, Hanover NH
Detroit Institute of Arts, Detroit MI
The Dixon Gallery & Gardens, Memphis TN
Doncaster Museum and Art Gallery, Doncaster
Dundurn Castle, Hamilton ON
Gallery One Visual Arts Center, Ellensburg WA
Glanmore National Historic Site of Canada, Belleville ON
Grand Rapids Public Museum, Public Museum of Grand Rapids, Grand Rapids MI
Hammond-Harwood House Association, Inc, Hammond-Harwood House, Annapolis MD
Henry County Museum & Cultural Arts Center, Clinton MO
Henry Sheldon Museum of Vermont History and Research Center, Middlebury VT
Heritage Center of Lancaster County Museum, Lancaster PA
Hillwood Museum & Gardens Foundation, Hillwood Estate Museum & Gardens, Washington DC
Historic Deerfield, Inc, Deerfield MA
Historic Hudson Valley, Pocantico Hills NY
Historic Newton, Newton MA
Historical Society of Cheshire County, Keene NH
Hoyt Center for the Arts, New Castle PA
Huguenot Historical Society of New Paltz Galleries, New Paltz NY
Illinois State Museum, ISM Lockport Gallery, Chicago Gallery & Southern Illinois Art Gallery, Springfield IL
Imperial Calcasieu Museum, Gibson-Barham Gallery, Lake Charles LA
Independent Administrative Institution National Institutes for Cultural Heritage, Tokyo National Museum, Tokyo
James Dick Foundation, Festival - Institute, Round Top TX
Jamestown-Yorktown Foundation, Jamestown Settlement, Williamsburg VA
Johns Hopkins University, Homewood Museum, Baltimore MD
Kings County Historical Society & Museum, Hampton NB
Latino Art Museum, Pomona CA
Leeds Museums & Galleries, Leeds
Lehigh Valley Heritage Center, Allentown PA
Lincoln County Historical Association, Inc, 1811 Old Lincoln County Jail & Lincoln County Museum, Wiscasset ME
Livingston County Historical Society, Museum, Geneseo NY
Longfellow-Evangeline State Commemorative Area, Saint Martinville LA
Longue Vue House & Gardens, New Orleans LA
Loyola University Chicago, Loyola University Museum of Art, Chicago IL
McDowell House & Apothecary Shop, Danville KY
Mexican Museum, San Francisco CA
Mount Vernon Hotel Museum & Garden, New York NY
Musea Brugge, Sint-Janshospitaal, Bruges
Musee Royal Et Domaine De Mariemont, Morlanwelz
Musei Civici di Padova - Cappella Degli Scrovegni, Musei Civici Agli Eremitani (Civic Museum) - Scrovegni Chapel, Padua
Museo Cerralbo, Madrid
The Museum, Greenwood SC
Museum De Lakenhal, Leiden
The Museum of Arts & Sciences Inc, Daytona Beach FL

Museum of Fine Arts Houston, Bayou Bend Collection & Gardens, Houston TX
Museum of Fine Arts, Saint Petersburg, Florida, Inc, Saint Petersburg FL
Museum zu Allerheiligen, Schaffhausen
Muzej za Umjetnost i Obrt, Museum of Arts & Crafts, Zagreb
Muzeul National Brukenthal, Brukenthal Palace & European Art Gallery, Sibiu
National Society of Colonial Dames of America in the State of Maryland, Mount Clare Museum House, Baltimore MD
New Brunswick Museum, Saint John NB
New Canaan Historical Society, New Canaan CT
New Jersey State Museum, Fine Art Bureau, Trenton NJ
Norwich Free Academy, Slater Memorial Museum, Norwich CT
Oglebay Institute, Mansion Museum, Wheeling WV
The Ohio Historical Society, Inc, Campus Martius Museum & Ohio River Museum, Marietta OH
Panhandle-Plains Historical Museum, Canyon TX
George Phippen, Phippen Museum - Art of the American West, Prescott AZ
Pilgrim Society, Pilgrim Hall Museum, Plymouth MA
Porter-Phelps-Huntington Foundation, Inc, Historic House Museum, Hadley MA
Pump House Center for the Arts, Chillicothe OH
Rijksmuseum Twenthe, Rijksmuseum Twenthe, Enschede
Rollins College, George D & Harriet W Cornell Fine Arts Museum, Winter Park FL
The Rooms Corporation of Newfoundland & Labrador, Saint John's NF
Saco Museum, Saco ME
Shirley Plantation Foundation, Charles City VA
Society for Contemporary Craft, Pittsburgh PA
South Carolina Artisans Center, Walterboro SC
The Speed Art Museum, Louisville KY
Spertus Institute of Jewish Studies, Chicago IL
Springfield Museums, Connecticut Valley Historical Society, Springfield MA
The Stewart Museum, Montreal PQ
Stratford Historical Society, Catharine B Mitchell Museum, Stratford CT
Suomen Kansallismuseo, National Museum of Finland, Helsinki
Tryon Palace Historic Sites & Gardens, New Bern NC
Tver Art Gallery, Tver
United Society of Shakers, Shaker Museum, New Gloucester ME
United States Figure Skating Association, World Figure Skating Museum & Hall of Fame, Colorado Springs CO
University of Chicago, Smart Museum of Art, Chicago IL
University of Illinois at Urbana-Champaign, Krannert Art Museum and Kinkead Pavilion, Champaign IL
University of Saskatchewan, Diefenbaker Canada Centre, Saskatoon SK
Vesterheim Norwegian-American Museum, Decorah IA
Westfries Museum, Hoorn
Willard House & Clock Museum, Inc, North Grafton MA
Wisconsin Historical Society, Wisconsin Historical Museum, Madison WI
Woodlawn/The Pope-Leighey, Mount Vernon VA
World Erotic Art Museum, Miami Beach FL
Yarmouth County Historical Society, Yarmouth County Museum & Archives, Yarmouth NS

PHOTOGRAPHY

A.E. Backus Museum of Art, Fort Pierce FL
A.I.R. Gallery, Brooklyn NY
Abington Art Center, Jenkintown PA
Academy of the New Church, Glencairn Museum, Bryn Athyn PA
The Adirondack Historical Association, The Adirondack Museum, Blue Mountain Lake NY
African American Museum in Philadelphia, Philadelphia PA
African Art Museum of Maryland, Columbia MD
AKA Artist Run Centre, Saskatoon SK
Akron Art Museum, Akron OH
Alabama Department of Archives & History, Museum of Alabama, Montgomery AL
Alaska Heritage Museum at Wells Fargo, Anchorage AK
Alberta College of Art & Design, Illingworth Kerr Gallery, Calgary AB
Albin O Kuhn Library & Gallery, Baltimore MD

Albright College, Freedman Gallery, Reading PA
Albuquerque Museum of Art & History, Albuquerque NM
Allentown Art Museum, Allentown PA
American Art Museum, Smithsonian Institution, Washington DC
American Sport Art Museum and Archives, Daphne AL
American Textile History Museum, Lowell MA
Americas Society Art Gallery, New York NY
Amon Carter Museum of American Art, Fort Worth TX
Anchorage Museum at Rasmuson Center, Anchorage AK
Walter Anderson, Ocean Springs MS
The Andy Warhol Museum, Museum, Pittsburgh PA
Anthology Film Archives, New York NY
Appaloosa Museum and Heritage Center, Moscow ID
Arab American National Museum, Dearborn MI
Arizona Historical Society-Yuma, Sanguinetti House Museum & Garden, Yuma AZ
Arizona Museum For Youth, Mesa AZ
Arizona State University, ASU Art Museum, Tempe AZ
Arnot Art Museum, Elmira NY
Art & Culture Center of Hollywood, Art Gallery/Multidisciplinary Cultural Center, Hollywood FL
Art Center of Battle Creek, Battle Creek MI
Art Community Center, Art Center of Corpus Christi, Corpus Christi TX
Art Gallery of Alberta, Edmonton AB
Art Gallery of Bancroft Inc, Bancroft ON
Art Gallery of Hamilton, Hamilton ON
Art Gallery of Nova Scotia, Halifax NS
Art Gallery of South Australia, Adelaide
The Art Museum at the University of Kentucky, Lexington KY
Art Museum of Greater Lafayette, Lafayette IN
Art Museum of Southeast Texas, Beaumont TX
Art Museum of the University of Houston, Blaffer Gallery, Houston TX
Art Without Walls Inc, New York NY
Artesia Historical Museum & Art Center, Artesia NM
Arthur Griffin Center for Photographic Art, Griffin Museum of Photography, Winchester MA
Arts Council of Fayetteville-Cumberland County, The Arts Center, Fayetteville NC
Artspace, Richmond VA
Asbury College, Student Center Gallery, Wilmore KY
Asheville Art Museum, Asheville NC
Associates for Community Development, The Arts Center, Inc, Martinsburg WV
Atlanta Historical Society Inc, Atlanta History Center, Atlanta GA
Autry National Center, Southwest Museum of the American Indian, Mt. Washington Campus, Los Angeles CA
Baldwin Historical Society Museum, Baldwin NY
The Baltimore Museum of Art, Baltimore MD
Balzekas Museum of Lithuanian Culture, Chicago IL
Bard College, Center for Curatorial Studies and the Hessel Museum of Art, Annandale-on-Hudson NY
Baroda Museum and Picture Gallery, Baroda
Bates College, Museum of Art, Lewiston ME
Baton Rouge Gallery, Center For Contemporary Art, Baton Rouge LA
Bay County Historical Society, Historical Museum of Bay County, Bay City MI
Bellagio Resort & Casino, Bellagio Gallery of Fine Art, Las Vegas NV
Beloit College, Wright Museum of Art, Beloit WI
Belskie Museum, Closter NJ
Bemis Center for Contemporary Arts, Omaha NE
Berea College, Ulmann Doris Galleries, Berea KY
Besser Museum for Northeast Michigan, Alpena MI
Beverly Historical Society, Cabot, Hale & Balch House Museums, Beverly MA
Birger Sandzen Memorial Gallery, Lindsborg KS
Birmingham Museum of Art, Birmingham AL
Blanden Memorial Art Museum, Fort Dodge IA
Blauvelt Demarest Foundation, Hiram Blauvelt Art Museum, Oradell NJ
Blue Sky Gallery, Oregon Center for the Photographic Arts, Portland OR
Boise Art Museum, Boise ID
Bone Creek Museum of Agrarian Art, David City NE
Booth Western Art Museum, Cartersville GA
Boston Public Library, Albert H Wiggin Gallery & Print Department, Boston MA
Roy Boyd, Chicago IL
Brigham City Corporation, Brigham City Museum & Gallery, Brigham City UT
Brown University, David Winton Bell Gallery, Providence RI

Bruce Museum, Inc, Greenwich CT
Bucknell University, Edward & Marthann Samek Art Gallery, Lewisburg PA
The Buffalo Fine Arts Academy, Albright-Knox Art Gallery, Buffalo NY
Bush-Holley Historic Site & Storehouse Gallery, Greenwich Historical Society/ Bush-Holley House, Cos Cob CT
C W Post Campus of Long Island University, Hillwood Art Museum, Brookville NY
Cabot's Old Indian Pueblo Museum, Desert Hot Springs CA
California State University Stanislaus, University Art Gallery, Turlock CA
California State University, Long Beach, University Art Museum, Long Beach CA
California State University, Northridge, Art Galleries, Northridge CA
Calvin College, Center Art Gallery, Grand Rapids MI
Cameron Art Museum, Wilmington NC
Canadian Museum of Civilization, Gatineau PQ
Canadian Museum of Contemporary Photography, Ottawa ON
Canadian Museum of Nature, Musee Canadien de la Nature, Ottawa ON
Canajoharie Library & Art Gallery, Arkell Museum of Canajoharie, Canajoharie NY
Cape Ann Historical Association, Cape Ann Museum, Gloucester MA
Caramoor Center for Music & the Arts, Inc, Rosen House at Caramoor, Katonah NY
Carleton College, Art Gallery, Northfield MN
Carlsbad Museum & Art Center, Carlsbad NM
Carnegie Museums of Pittsburgh, Carnegie Museum of Art, Pittsburgh PA
Carson County Square House Museum, Panhandle TX
Cartoon Art Museum, San Francisco CA
Cedar Rapids Museum of Art, Cedar Rapids IA
Center for Puppetry Arts, Atlanta GA
Central Methodist University, Ashby-Hodge Gallery of American Art, Fayette MO
Centro Andaluz de Arte Contemporaneo, Sevilla
Centro de Arte Moderna, CAM - Calouste Gulbenkian Foundation, Lisbon
Channel Islands Maritime Museum, Oxnard CA
Chatham Historical Society, The Atwood House Museum, Chatham MA
Chesapeake Bay Maritime Museum, Saint Michaels MD
Chhatrapati Shivaji Maharaj Vastu Sangrahalaya, Mumbai
Chicago Athenaeum, Museum of Architecture & Design, Galena IL
Chinese Culture Foundation, Center Gallery, San Francisco CA
Chrysler Museum of Art, Norfolk VA
Church of Jesus Christ of Latter-Day Saints, Museum of Church History & Art, Salt Lake City UT
City of Brea, Art Gallery, Brea CA
City of Cedar Falls, Iowa, James & Meryl Hearst Center for the Arts & Sculpture Garden, Cedar Falls IA
City of El Paso, El Paso TX
City of Fremont, Olive Hyde Art Gallery, Fremont CA
City of Gainesville, Thomas Center Galleries - Cultural Affairs, Gainesville FL
City of High Point, High Point Museum, High Point NC
City of Mason City, Charles H MacNider Museum, Mason City IA
City of Nome Alaska, Carrie M McLain Memorial Museum, Nome AK
The City of Petersburg Museums, Petersburg VA
City of Pittsfield, Berkshire Artisans, Pittsfield MA
City of Port Angeles, Port Angeles Fine Arts Center & Webster Woods Art Park, Port Angeles WA
City of Springdale, Shiloh Museum of Ozark History, Springdale AR
Civic and Municipal Affairs Bureau of Macau, Macau Museum of Art, Nape
Clark County Historical Society, Pioneer - Krier Museum, Ashland KS
Sterling & Francine Clark, Williamstown MA
Clinton Art Association, River Arts Center, Clinton IA
Clinton County Historical Association, Clinton County Historical Museum, Plattsburgh NY
Coastal Arts League Museum, Half Moon Bay CA
Colgate University, Picker Art Gallery, Hamilton NY
College of Saint Benedict, Gorecki Gallery & Gallery Lounge, Saint Joseph MN
College of William & Mary, Muscarelle Museum of Art, Williamsburg VA

Lincoln County Historical Association, Inc, 1811 Old Lincoln County Jail & Lincoln County Museum, Wiscasset ME

Lincolnshire County Council, Library & Heritage Services, Lincoln

The Long Island Museum of American Art, History & Carriages, Stony Brook NY

Longfellow-Evangeline State Commemorative Area, Saint Martinville LA

Longview Museum of Fine Art, Longview TX

Louisiana Department of Culture, Recreation & Tourism, Louisiana State Museum, New Orleans LA

Louisiana State University, Museum of Art, Baton Rouge LA

Louisiana State University, Student Union Art Gallery, Baton Rouge LA

Loveland Museum/Gallery, Loveland CO

Loyola Marymount University, Laband Art Gallery, Los Angeles CA

Ludwig Museum - Museum of Contemporary Art, Budapest

Luther College, Fine Arts Collection, Decorah IA

Lyme Historical Society, Florence Griswold Museum, Old Lyme CT

Mabee-Gerrer Museum of Art, Shawnee OK

Macalester College, Macalester College Art Gallery, Saint Paul MN

Madison Museum of Contemporary Art, Madison WI

Magyar Nemzeti Muzeum - Hungarian National Museum, Budapest

Maine College of Art, The Institute of Contemporary Art, Portland ME

Maitland Art Center, Maitland FL

Manchester Bidwell Corporation, Manchester Craftsmen's Guild Youth & Arts Program, Pittsburgh PA

Marblehead Museum & Historical Society, Marblehead MA

Jacques Marchais, Staten Island NY

The Mariners' Museum, Newport News VA

Maryland Hall for the Creative Arts, Chaney Gallery, Annapolis MD

Marylhurst University, The Art Gym, Marylhurst OR

Massachusetts Institute of Technology, List Visual Arts Center, Cambridge MA

Massachusetts Institute of Technology, MIT Museum, Cambridge MA

Massillon Museum, Massillon OH

Mattatuck Historical Society, Mattatuck Museum, Waterbury CT

Maysville, Kentucky Gateway Museum Center, Maysville KY

The Robert McLaughlin, Oshawa ON

McLean County Historical Society, McLean County Museum of History, Bloomington IL

McMaster University, McMaster Museum of Art, Hamilton ON

Medina Railroad Museum, Medina NY

Mendel Art Gallery & Civic Conservatory, Saskatoon SK

Menil Foundation, Inc, The Menil Collection, Houston TX

Mennello Museum of American Art, Orlando FL

Meredith College, Frankie G Weems Gallery & Rotunda Gallery, Raleigh NC

Meridian Museum of Art, Meridian MS

Mesa Arts Center, Mesa Contemporary Arts Museum, Mesa AZ

The Metropolitan Museum of Art, New York NY

Mexican Museum, San Francisco CA

Miami University, Art Museum, Oxford OH

Miami-Dade College, Kendal Campus, Art Gallery, Miami FL

James A Michener, Doylestown PA

Middle Border Museum & Oscar Howe Art Center, Mitchell SD

Middle Tennessee State University, Baldwin Photographic Gallery, Murfreesboro TN

Middlebury College, Museum of Art, Middlebury VT

Midwest Museum of American Art, Elkhart IN

Miller Art Center Foundation Inc, Miller Art Museum, Sturgeon Bay WI

Mills College Art Museum, Oakland CA

Milwaukee Public Museum, Milwaukee WI

Ministry of Cultural Affairs, Bangladesh National Museum, Dhaka

Ministry of the Arts & Multiculturalism, National Museum & Art Gallery, Port of Spain

Minneapolis Institute of Arts, Minneapolis MN

Minnesota Museum of American Art, Saint Paul MN

Minot State University, Northwest Art Center, Minot ND

The Mint Museum, Charlotte NC

Mississippi Museum of Art, Jackson MS

Mississippi Valley Conservation Authority, R Tait McKenzie Memorial Museum, Almonte ON

Missoula Art Museum, Missoula MT

Arthur Roy Mitchell, A.R. Mitchell Museum, Trinidad CO

Mobile Museum of Art, Mobile AL

Moderna Galerija, Gallery of Modern Art, Zagreb

Monhegan Museum, Monhegan ME

Montclair Art Museum, Montclair NJ

Moody County Historical Society, Moody County Museum, Pierre SD

Moore College of Art & Design, The Galleries at Moore, Philadelphia PA

Moravian College, Payne Gallery, Bethlehem PA

Moravska Galerie v Brne, Moravian Gallery in Brno, Brno

The Morgan Library & Museum, Museum, New York NY

Morris Museum of Art, Augusta GA

Mount Saint Vincent University, MSVU Art Gallery, Halifax NS

Muhlenberg College, Martin Art Gallery, Allentown PA

Munson-Williams-Proctor Arts Institute, Museum of Art, Utica NY

Murray State University, Art Galleries, Murray KY

Muscatine Art Center, Museum, Muscatine IA

Musee Carnavalet-Histoire de Paris, Paris

Musee des Beaux-Arts/Palais des Archeveques, Museum of Fine Arts, Tours

Musee Guimet, Paris

Musee National d'Histoire et d'Art Luxembourg, Luxembourg City

Musee National des Beaux Arts du Quebec, Quebec PQ

Musee Regional de lu Cote-Nord, Sept-Iles PQ

Museen der Stadt Koln, Museum Ludwig, Cologne

Musees Royaux d'Art et d'Histoire, Royal Museums of Art and History, Brussels

Museo Cerralbo, Madrid

Museo de Arte de Ponce, The Luis A Ferre Foundation Inc, Ponce PR

Museo De Las Americas, Denver CO

Museo de Navarra, Pamplona

Museo Del Romanticismo, Museum of the Romantic Period, Madrid

Museo Frida Kahlo Casa Azul, Coyoacan

Museo Italo Americano, San Francisco CA

Museo Nacional de Bellas Artes, National Museum of Fine Arts, Santiago

Museu Nacional D'Art De Catalunya, National Art Museum, Barcelona

The Museum, Greenwood SC

Museum De Lakenhal, Leiden

Museum fur Kunst und Gewerbe Hamburg, Hamburg

Museum of Art & History, Santa Cruz, Santa Cruz CA

The Museum of Arts & Sciences Inc, Daytona Beach FL

Museum of Chinese in America, New York NY

Museum of Contemporary Art, Chicago IL

The Museum of Contemporary Art (MOCA), Moca Grand Avenue, Los Angeles CA

Museum of Contemporary Art Jacksonville, Jacksonville FL

Museum of Contemporary Art San Diego, San Diego CA

Museum of Contemporary Art, San Diego-Downtown, La Jolla CA

Museum of Decorative Arts in Prague, Prague

Museum of Fine Arts, Houston, Houston TX

Museum of Fine Arts, Saint Petersburg, Florida, Inc, Saint Petersburg FL

Museum of Florida Art, Deland FL

Museum of Modern Art, New York NY

Museum of New Mexico, New Mexico Museum of Art, Unit of NM Dept of Cultural Affairs, Santa Fe NM

Museum of New Mexico, Palace of Governors, Santa Fe NM

Museum of Northern Arizona, Flagstaff AZ

Museum of Northern British Columbia, Ruth Harvey Art Gallery, Prince Rupert BC

Museum of Northwest Art, La Conner WA

Museum of Photographic Arts, Edmund L. and Nancy K Dubois Library, San Diego CA

Museum of Southern History, Houston TX

Museum of the City of New York, Museum, New York NY

Museum of the Plains Indian & Crafts Center, Browning MT

Museum zu Allerheiligen, Schaffhausen

Muskegon Museum of Art, Muskegon MI

Muzej Moderne I Suvremene Umjetnosti, Museum of Modern and Contemporary Art, Rijeka

Muzej za Umjetnost i Obrt, Museum of Arts & Crafts, Zagreb

Muzeul de Istorie Nationala Si Arheologie Constanta, National History & Archaeology Museum, Constanta

Muzeul National Brukenthal, Brukenthal Palace & European Art Gallery, Sibiu

Muzeum Narodowe, National Museum in Poznan, Poznan

Muzeum Narodowe W Kielcach, National Museum in Kielce, Kielce

Nanticoke Indian Museum, Millsboro DE

Napa Valley Museum, Yountville CA

Narodna Galerija, National Gallery of Slovenia, Ljubljana

Narodni Muzej Crne Gore, National Museum of Montenegro, Cetinje

National Art Museum of Sport, Indianapolis IN

National Baseball Hall of Fame & Museum, Inc, Art Collection, Cooperstown NY

National Gallery of Canada, Ottawa ON

National Museum of Fine Arts of Moldova, Chisinau

National Museum of Mexican Art, Chicago IL

The National Museum of Modern Art, Tokyo, Tokyo

National Museum of the American Indian, George Gustav Heye Center, New York NY

National Museum of the American Indian, Smithsonian Institution, Washington DC

National Museum of Wildlife Art of the Unites States, Jackson WY

National Museum of Women in the Arts, Washington DC

National Museum, Monuments and Art Gallery, Gaborone

National Museums Scotland, National Museum of Scotland, Edinburgh

National Park Service, Hubbell Trading Post National Historic Site, Ganado AZ

The National Park Service, United States Department of the Interior, Statue of Liberty National Monument & The Ellis Island Immigration Museum, Washington DC

National Portrait Gallery, Smithsonian Institution, Washington DC

National Portrait Gallery, London

National Trust for Historic Preservation, Shadows-on-the-Teche, New Iberia LA

Naval Historical Center, The Navy Museum, Washington DC

Nebraska Game and Parks Commission, Arbor Lodge State Historical Park & Morton Mansion, Nebraska City NE

Nelson Mandela Bay Municipality, Nelson Mandela Metropolitan Art Museum, Port Elizabeth

The Nelson-Atkins Museum of Art, Kansas City MO

Neville Public Museum of Brown County, Green Bay WI

New Britain Museum of American Art, New Britain CT

New England Maple Museum, Pittsford VT

New Hampshire Antiquarian Society, Hopkinton Historical Society, Hopkinton NH

New Jersey Historical Society, Newark NJ

New Jersey State Museum, Fine Art Bureau, Trenton NJ

New Orleans Museum of Art, New Orleans LA

New Visions Gallery, Inc, Marshfield WI

New World Art Center, T F Chen Cultural Center, New York NY

New York State Military Museum and Veterans Research Center, Saratoga Springs NY

New York State Office of Parks Recreation & Historic Preservation, John Jay Homestead State Historic Site, Katonah NY

Newburyport Maritime Society, Inc, Custom House Maritime Museum, Newburyport MA

Newport Art Museum and Association, Newport RI

Niagara University, Castellani Art Museum, Niagara NY

Niigata Prefectural Museum of Modern Art, Niigata

Noordbrabants Museum, Hertogenbosch

Norfolk Historical Society Inc, Museum, Norfolk CT

Norman Rockwell Museum, Stockbridge MA

Norsk Sjøfartsmuseum, Norwegian Maritime Museum, Oslo

North Carolina State University, Gregg Museum of Art & Design, Raleigh NC

North Dakota State University, Memorial Union Gallery, Fargo ND

University of California, Berkeley, The Magnes Collection of Jewish Art & Life, Berkeley CA
University of California, Los Angeles, Fowler Museum at UCLA, Los Angeles CA
University of California, Santa Barbara, University Art Museum, Santa Barbara CA
University of Chicago, Oriental Institute, Chicago IL
University of Chicago, Smart Museum of Art, Chicago IL
University of Cincinnati, DAAP Galleries-College of Design Architecture, Art & Planning, Cincinnati OH
University of Colorado, CU Art Museum, Boulder CO
University of Colorado at Colorado Springs, Gallery of Contemporary Art, Colorado Springs CO
University of Georgia, Georgia Museum of Art, Athens GA
University of Illinois at Chicago, Gallery 400, Chicago IL
University of Illinois at Urbana-Champaign, Krannert Art Museum and Kinkead Pavilion, Champaign IL
University of Indianapolis, Christel DeHaan Fine Arts Gallery, Indianapolis IN
University of Kansas, Spencer Museum of Art, Lawrence KS
University of Louisiana at Lafayette, Paul and Lulu Hilliard University Art Museum, Lafayette LA
University of Maine, Museum of Art, Bangor ME
University of Manitoba, Faculty of Architecture Exhibition Centre, Winnipeg MB
University of Mary Washington, Gari Melchers Home and Studio, Fredericksburg VA
University of Mary Washington, University of Mary Washington Galleries, Fredericksburg VA
University of Maryland, College Park, Stamp Gallery, College Park MD
University of Massachusetts, Amherst, University Gallery, Amherst MA
University of Memphis, Art Museum, Memphis TN
University of Miami, Lowe Art Museum, Coral Gables FL
University of Michigan, Museum of Art, Ann Arbor MI
University of Minnesota, Katherine E Nash Gallery, Minneapolis MN
University of Minnesota Duluth, Tweed Museum of Art, Duluth MN
University of Missouri, Museum of Art & Archaeology, Columbia MO
University of Nebraska, Lincoln, Sheldon Memorial Art Gallery & Sculpture Garden, Lincoln NE
University of Nebraska-Lincoln, Great Plains Art Museum, Lincoln NE
University of Nevada, Las Vegas, Donna Beam Fine Art Gallery, Las Vegas NV
University of Nevada, Reno, Sheppard Contemporary & University Galleries, Reno NV
University of New Brunswick, Art Centre, Fredericton NB
University of New Hampshire, Museum of Art, Durham NH
University of New Mexico, The Harwood Museum of Art, Taos NM
University of North Carolina at Greensboro, Weatherspoon Art Museum, Greensboro NC
University of Notre Dame, Snite Museum of Art, Notre Dame IN
University of Oklahoma, Fred Jones Jr Museum of Art, Norman OK
University of Pennsylvania, Arthur Ross Gallery, Philadelphia PA
University of Pennsylvania, Museum of Archaeology & Anthropology, Philadelphia PA
University of Pittsburgh, University Art Gallery, Pittsburgh PA
University of Rhode Island, Fine Arts Center Galleries, Kingston RI
University of Richmond, University Museums, Richmond VA
University of Saskatchewan, Diefenbaker Canada Centre, Saskatoon SK
University of South Florida, Contemporary Art Museum, Tampa FL
University of the South, University Art Gallery, Sewanee TN
University of Utah, Utah Museum of Fine Arts, Salt Lake City UT
University of Victoria, The Legacy Art Gallery, Victoria BC
University of Virginia, The Fralin Museum of Art at the University of Virginia, Charlottesville VA
University of Washington, Henry Art Gallery, Seattle WA
University of West Florida, Art Gallery, Pensacola FL

University of Wisconsin-Eau Claire, Foster Gallery, Eau Claire WI
University of Wisconsin-Madison, Chazen Museum of Art, Madison WI
University of Wisconsin-Madison, Wisconsin Union Galleries, Madison WI
University of Wyoming, University of Wyoming Art Museum, Laramie WY
USS Constitution Museum, Boston MA
Utah Arts Council, Chase Home Museum of Utah Folk Arts, Salt Lake City UT
Utah Department of Natural Resources, Division of Parks & Recreation, Territorial Statehouse State Park Museum, Fillmore UT
Valentine Richmond History Center, Richmond VA
Vancouver Art Gallery, Vancouver BC
Vassar College, The Frances Lehman Loeb Art Center, Poughkeepsie NY
Vero Beach Museum of Art, Vero Beach FL
Vesterheim Norwegian-American Museum, Decorah IA
Victoria Mansion - Morse Libby House, Portland ME
Viridian Artists Inc, New York NY
VU Centre De Diffusion Et De Production De La Photographie, Quebec PQ
The Walker African American Museum & Research Center, Las Vegas NV
Walker Art Center, Minneapolis MN
Washington State University, Museum of Art, Pullman WA
Washington University, Mildred Lane Kemper Art Museum, Saint Louis MO
Waterworks Visual Arts Center, Salisbury NC
Wayne County Historical Society, Museum, Honesdale PA
Wellesley College, Davis Museum & Cultural Center, Wellesley MA
West Baton Rouge Parish, West Baton Rouge Museum, Port Allen LA
West Florida Historic Preservation, Inc/University of West Florida, T T Wentworth, Jr Florida State Museum; Historic Pensacola Village; Pensacola Historical Society & Resource Center, Pensacola FL
Wethersfield Historical Society Inc, Museum, Wethersfield CT
Whalers Village Museum, Lahaina HI
Whatcom Museum, Bellingham WA
Peter & Catharine Whyte Foundation, Whyte Museum of the Canadian Rockies, Banff AB
Wichita State University, Ulrich Museum of Art, Wichita KS
Wilfrid Laurier University, Robert Langen Art Gallery, Waterloo ON
The Winnipeg Art Gallery, Winnipeg MB
Winston-Salem State University, Diggs Gallery, Winston Salem NC
Wiregrass Museum of Art, Dothan AL
Woodmere Art Museum Inc, Philadelphia PA
World Erotic Art Museum, Miami Beach FL
Wounded Knee Museum, Wall SD
Yarmouth County Historical Society, Yarmouth County Museum & Archives, Yarmouth NS
Peter Yegen, Billings MT
Yeshiva University Museum, New York NY
Yokohama Museum of Art, Yokohama
Yosemite Museum, Yosemite National Park CA
Yuma Fine Arts Association, Yuma Art Center, Yuma AZ
Zigler Art Museum, Jennings LA
Zurich University of the Arts (ZHdK), Museum Fuer Gestaltung Zurich (Museum of Design Zurich), Zurich

PORCELAIN

Albany Institute of History & Art, Albany NY
Allentown Art Museum, Allentown PA
American Swedish Institute, Minneapolis MN
Arizona Historical Society-Yuma, Sanguinetti House Museum & Garden, Yuma AZ
Arnot Art Museum, Elmira NY
Art & Culture Center of Hollywood, Art Gallery/Multidisciplinary Cultural Center, Hollywood FL
Art Community Center, Art Center of Corpus Christi, Corpus Christi TX
Art Gallery of Nova Scotia, Halifax NS
Art Gallery of South Australia, Adelaide
The Art Museum at the University of Kentucky, Lexington KY
Art Museum of Greater Lafayette, Lafayette IN
Art Without Walls Inc, New York NY

Asian Art Museum of San Francisco, Chong-Moon Lee Ctr for Asian Art and Culture, San Francisco CA
Badisches Landesmuseum, Karlsruhe
Baroda Museum and Picture Gallery, Baroda
Beaverbrook Art Gallery, Fredericton NB
Bellevue Arts Museum, Bellevue WA
Bellingrath Gardens & Home, Theodore AL
Beloit College, Wright Museum of Art, Beloit WI
Besser Museum for Northeast Michigan, Alpena MI
Beverly Historical Society, Cabot, Hale & Balch House Museums, Beverly MA
Birmingham Museum of Art, Birmingham AL
Blanden Memorial Art Museum, Fort Dodge IA
Boise Art Museum, Boise ID
The Bradford Group, Niles IL
Brick Store Museum, Kennebunk ME
Bradford Brinton, Big Horn WY
Bush-Holley Historic Site & Storehouse Gallery, Greenwich Historical Society/ Bush-Holley House, Cos Cob CT
Calvin College, Center Art Gallery, Grand Rapids MI
Canadian Clay and Glass Gallery, Waterloo ON
Canadian Museum of Civilization, Gatineau PQ
Cape Ann Historical Association, Cape Ann Museum, Gloucester MA
Captain Forbes House Museum, Milton MA
Caramoor Center for Music & the Arts, Inc, Rosen House at Caramoor, Katonah NY
Chatham Historical Society, The Atwood House Museum, Chatham MA
Chatillon-DeMenil House Foundation, Chatillon-DeMenil House, Saint Louis MO
Cheekwood-Tennessee Botanical Garden & Museum of Art, Nashville TN
Chhatrapati Shivaji Maharaj Vastu Sangrahalaya, Mumbai
City of Austin Parks & Recreation, O. Henry Museum, Austin TX
Clark County Historical Society, Pioneer - Krier Museum, Ashland KS
Sterling & Francine Clark, Williamstown MA
Clinton County Historical Association, Clinton County Historical Museum, Plattsburgh NY
College of William & Mary, Muscarelle Museum of Art, Williamsburg VA
The College of Wooster, The College of Wooster Art Museum, Wooster OH
Columbus Museum, Columbus GA
Columbus Museum of Art, Columbus OH
Cooper-Hewitt National Design Museum, Smithsonian Institution, New York NY
Cornwall Gallery Society, Cornwall Regional Art Gallery, Cornwall ON
Craft and Folk Art Museum (CAFAM), Los Angeles CA
Cranbrook Art Museum, Bloomfield Hills MI
Cripple Creek District Museum, Cripple Creek CO
Crocker Art Museum, Sacramento CA
Cummer Museum of Art & Gardens, Museum & Library, Jacksonville FL
The Currier Museum of Art, Manchester NH
DAR Museum, National Society Daughters of the American Revolution, Washington DC
Dartmouth Heritage Museum, Dartmouth NS
Daum Museum of Contemporary Art, Sedalia MO
Denison University, Art Gallery, Granville OH
Designmuseum Danmark, Copenhagen
Detroit Institute of Arts, Detroit MI
The Dixon Gallery & Gardens, Memphis TN
Doncaster Museum and Art Gallery, Doncaster
Dundurn Castle, Hamilton ON
Ellen Noel Art Museum of the Permian Basin, Odessa TX
Elverhoj Museum of History and Art, Solvang CA
Erie Art Museum, Erie PA
Establishment Public du Chateau du Rusee, Et du Dophine national de versailles, Versailles
Evanston Historical Society, Charles Gates Dawes House, Evanston IL
Everhart Museum, Scranton PA
Everson Museum of Art, Syracuse NY
Fetherston Foundation, Packwood House Museum, Lewisburg PA
Fishkill Historical Society, Van Wyck Homestead Museum, Fishkill NY
Flint Institute of Arts, Flint MI
Florida State University and Central Florida Community College, The Appleton Museum of Art, Ocala FL
Fondazione Musei Civici Di Venezia, Ca'Rezzonico, Museo del Settecento Veneziano, Venice

Seattle Art Museum, Downtown, Seattle WA
Shirley Plantation Foundation, Charles City VA
Slovenska Narodna Galeria, Slovak National Gallery, Bratislava
The Society of the Cincinnati at Anderson House, Washington DC
Soprintendenza per I beni storici artistici ed etnoantropologici per le province di Mantova Brescia e Cremona, Museo di Palazzo Ducale, Mantua
South Carolina Artisans Center, Walterboro SC
South Dakota State University, South Dakota Art Museum, Brookings SD
Southern Ohio Museum Corporation, Southern Ohio Museum, Portsmouth OH
The Speed Art Museum, Louisville KY
Spertus Institute of Jewish Studies, Chicago IL
Nelda C & H J Lutcher Stark, Stark Museum of Art, Orange TX
The State Museum of Fine Arts of Tatarstan Republic, Kazan
State University of New York at Binghamton, Binghamton University Art Museum, Binghamton NY
State University of New York at Plattsburgh, Art Museum, Plattsburgh NY
Staten Island Museum, Staten Island NY
Stedelijk Museum Alkmaar, Alkmaar Municipal Museum, Alkmaar
Stone Quarry Hill Art Park, Winner Gallery, Cazenovia NY
Stratford Historical Society, Catharine B Mitchell Museum, Stratford CT
Sturdivant Museum Association, Sturdivant Museum, Selma AL
Suan Pakkad Palace Museum, Bangkok
Suomen Kansallismuseo, National Museum of Finland, Helsinki
Swedish American Museum Association of Chicago, Chicago IL
Switzerland County Historical Society Inc, Switzerland County Historical Museum, Vevay IN
Taft Museum of Art, Cincinnati OH
Lillian & Coleman Taube Museum of Art, Minot ND
Tohono Chul Park, Tucson AZ
Tokyo University of the Arts, The University Art Museum, Tokyo
Towson University, Asian Arts & Culture Center, Towson MD
Trenton City Museum, Trenton NJ
Tryon Palace Historic Sites & Gardens, New Bern NC
Tver Art Gallery, Tver
Tyne and Wear Archives & Museums, Sunderland Museum & Winter Gardens, Newcastle-upon-Tyne
United Society of Shakers, Shaker Museum, New Gloucester ME
United States Department of State, Diplomatic Reception Rooms, Washington DC
United States Figure Skating Association, World Figure Skating Museum & Hall of Fame, Colorado Springs CO
University of California, Berkeley, Phoebe Apperson Hearst Museum of Anthropology, Berkeley CA
University of Georgia, Georgia Museum of Art, Athens GA
University of Illinois at Urbana-Champaign, Krannert Art Museum and Kinkead Pavilion, Champaign IL
University of Mary Washington, Gari Melchers Home and Studio, Fredericksburg VA
University of Miami, Lowe Art Museum, Coral Gables FL
University of Michigan, Museum of Art, Ann Arbor MI
University of Notre Dame, Snite Museum of Art, Notre Dame IN
University of Richmond, University Museums, Richmond VA
University of Rochester, Memorial Art Gallery, Rochester NY
University of Tampa, Henry B Plant Museum, Tampa FL
University of Tennessee, McClung Museum of Natural History & Culture, Knoxville TN
University of Utah, Utah Museum of Fine Arts, Salt Lake City UT
University of Victoria, The Legacy Art Gallery, Victoria BC
University of Virginia, The Fralin Museum of Art at the University of Virginia, Charlottesville VA
University of Wisconsin-Madison, Chazen Museum of Art, Madison WI

Utah Department of Natural Resources, Division of Parks & Recreation, Territorial Statehouse State Park Museum, Fillmore UT
Vancouver Public Library, Fine Arts & Music Department, Vancouver BC
Vesterheim Norwegian-American Museum, Decorah IA
Victoria Mansion - Morse Libby House, Portland ME
Virginia Museum of Fine Arts, Richmond VA
Wadsworth Atheneum Museum of Art, Hartford CT
The Walker African American Museum & Research Center, Las Vegas NV
Walker Art Gallery, Liverpool
The Wallace Collection, London
Wallace State Community College, Evelyn Burrow Museum, Hanceville AL
Wayne Center for the Arts, Wooster OH
West Florida Historic Preservation, Inc/University of West Florida, T T Wentworth, Jr Florida State Museum; Historic Pensacola Village; Pensacola Historical Society & Resource Center, Pensacola FL
Westfries Museum, Hoorn
White House, Washington DC
Wichita Art Museum, Wichita KS
Wiregrass Museum of Art, Dothan AL
Woodlawn/The Pope-Leighey, Mount Vernon VA
Woodmere Art Museum Inc, Philadelphia PA
World Erotic Art Museum, Miami Beach FL
Yarmouth County Historical Society, Yarmouth County Museum & Archives, Yarmouth NS
Yokohama Museum of Art, Yokohama
Zigler Art Museum, Jennings LA

PORTRAITS

Academy of the New Church, Glencairn Museum, Bryn Athyn PA
Adams County Historical Society, Gettysburg PA
Adams National Historic Park, Quincy MA
African American Museum in Philadelphia, Philadelphia PA
Alabama Department of Archives & History, Museum of Alabama, Montgomery AL
Albany Institute of History & Art, Albany NY
Albuquerque Museum of Art & History, Albuquerque NM
American Art Museum, Smithsonian Institution, Washington DC
American Folk Art Museum, New York NY
The Andy Warhol Museum, Museum, Pittsburgh PA
Arizona Historical Society-Yuma, Sanguinetti House Museum & Garden, Yuma AZ
Arizona State University, ASU Art Museum, Tempe AZ
Arnot Art Museum, Elmira NY
Art & Culture Center of Hollywood, Art Gallery/Multidisciplinary Cultural Center, Hollywood FL
Art Community Center, Art Center of Corpus Christi, Corpus Christi TX
Art Gallery of Alberta, Edmonton AB
Art Gallery of Nova Scotia, Halifax NS
The Art Museum at the University of Kentucky, Lexington KY
The Art Museum of Eastern Idaho, Idaho Falls ID
Art Museum of Greater Lafayette, Lafayette IN
Art Without Walls Inc, New York NY
Arts Council of Fayetteville-Cumberland County, The Arts Center, Fayetteville NC
Asbury College, Student Center Gallery, Wilmore KY
Asheville Art Museum, Asheville NC
Asian Art Museum of San Francisco, Chong-Moon Lee Ctr for Asian Art and Culture, San Francisco CA
Augustana College, Augustana College Art Museum, Rock Island IL
Bakehouse Art Complex, Inc, Miami FL
The Baltimore Museum of Art, Baltimore MD
Baroda Museum and Picture Gallery, Baroda
The Bartlett Museum, Amesbury MA
Bayerische Staatsgemaldesammlungen/Bavarian State Art Galleries, Alte Pinakothek, Munich
Bayerische Staatsgemaldesammlungen/Bavarian State Art Galleries, Neue Pinakothek, Munich
Beaverbrook Art Gallery, Fredericton NB
Belle Grove Inc., Belle Grove Plantation, Middletown VA
Beloit College, Wright Museum of Art, Beloit WI
Belvedere Museum, Osterreichische Galerie Belvedere, Vienna
Bertha V B Lederer Fine Arts Gallery-Suny Geneseo, Bertha V B Lederer Fine Arts Gallery, Geneseo NY
Beverly Historical Society, Cabot, Hale & Balch House Museums, Beverly MA
Biggs Museum of American Art, Dover DE

Birmingham Museum of Art, Birmingham AL
Blanden Memorial Art Museum, Fort Dodge IA
Blauvelt Demarest Foundation, Hiram Blauvelt Art Museum, Oradell NJ
Boise Art Museum, Boise ID
Booth Western Art Museum, Cartersville GA
Boston Public Library, Albert H Wiggin Gallery & Print Department, Boston MA
Brick Store Museum, Kennebunk ME
Brigham City Corporation, Brigham City Museum & Gallery, Brigham City UT
Brigham Young University, Museum of Art, Provo UT
Bruce Museum, Inc, Greenwich CT
Bucknell University, Edward & Marthann Samek Art Gallery, Lewisburg PA
Cabot's Old Indian Pueblo Museum, Desert Hot Springs CA
Cahoon Museum of American Art, Cotuit MA
Calvin College, Center Art Gallery, Grand Rapids MI
Cameron Art Museum, Wilmington NC
Canadian Museum of Civilization, Gatineau PQ
Canadian Museum of Contemporary Photography, Ottawa ON
Canajoharie Library & Art Gallery, Arkell Museum of Canajoharie, Canajoharie NY
Canton Museum of Art, Canton OH
Cape Ann Historical Association, Cape Ann Museum, Gloucester MA
Caramoor Center for Music & the Arts, Inc, Rosen House at Caramoor, Katonah NY
Carnegie Center for Art & History, New Albany IN
Carolina Art Association, Gibbes Museum of Art, Charleston SC
Cartoon Art Museum, San Francisco CA
Cedar Rapids Museum of Art, Cedar Rapids IA
Chatham Historical Society, The Atwood House Museum, Chatham MA
Chatillon-DeMenil House Foundation, Chatillon-DeMenil House, Saint Louis MO
Chelan County Public Utility District, Rocky Reach Dam, Wenatchee WA
Chhatrapati Shivaji Maharaj Vastu Sangrahalaya, Mumbai
Church of Jesus Christ of Latter-Day Saints, Mormon Visitors' Center, Independence MO
Church of Jesus Christ of Latter-Day Saints, Museum of Church History & Art, Salt Lake City UT
City of Brea, Art Gallery, Brea CA
City of Cedar Falls, Iowa, James & Meryl Hearst Center for the Arts & Sculpture Garden, Cedar Falls IA
City of Fayette, Alabama, Fayette Art Museum, Fayette AL
City of Gainesville, Thomas Center Galleries - Cultural Affairs, Gainesville FL
City of Mason City, Charles H MacNider Museum, Mason City IA
The City of Petersburg Museums, Petersburg VA
City of Toronto Culture, The Market Gallery, Toronto ON
Clark County Historical Society, Pioneer - Krier Museum, Ashland KS
Sterling & Francine Clark, Williamstown MA
Clemson University, Fort Hill Plantation, Clemson SC
Clinton County Historical Association, Clinton County Historical Museum, Plattsburgh NY
Cohasset Historical Society, Cohasset Maritime Museum, Cohasset MA
Colgate University, Picker Art Gallery, Hamilton NY
College of William & Mary, Muscarelle Museum of Art, Williamsburg VA
The College of Wooster, The College of Wooster Art Museum, Wooster OH
Columbus Museum, Columbus GA
Columbus Museum of Art, Columbus OH
Comune di Genova - Direzione Cultura Settore Musei, Museo di Strada Nuova Palazzo Rosso, Genoa
Concord Museum, Concord MA
Cornwall Gallery Society, Cornwall Regional Art Gallery, Cornwall ON
The Courtauld Institute of Art, The Courtauld Gallery, London
Coutts Museum of Art, Inc, El Dorado KS
Cripple Creek District Museum, Cripple Creek CO
Crocker Art Museum, Sacramento CA
Crow Wing County Historical Society, Brainerd MN
Cummer Museum of Art & Gardens, Museum & Library, Jacksonville FL
The Currier Museum of Art, Manchester NH
Danville Museum of Fine Arts & History, Danville VA
DAR Museum, National Society Daughters of the American Revolution, Washington DC

Musee National des Beaux Arts du Quebec, Quebec PQ

Musee Regional de lu Cote-Nord, Sept-Iles PQ

Musee Regional de Vaudreuil-Soulanges, Vaudreuil-Dorion PQ

Museen der Stadt Koln, Wallraf-Richartz-Museum, Cologne

Musei Civici di Padova - Cappella Degli Scrovengni, Musei Civici Agli Eremitani (Civic Museum) - Scrovegni Chapel, Padua

Museo Cerralbo, Madrid

Museo De Las Americas, Denver CO

Museo de Navarra, Pamplona

Museo Del Romanticismo, Museum of the Romantic Period, Madrid

Museo di Capodimonte, Naples

Museo Frida Kahlo Casa Azul, Coyoacan

Museo Nacional de Bellas Artes, National Museum of Fine Arts, Santiago

Museu de Evora, Evora

Museu de Grao Vasco, Viseu

Museu Nacional de Arte Contemporanea, National Museum of Contemporary Art, Museu Do Chiado, Lisbon

Museum De Lakenhal, Leiden

Museum fur Kunst und Gewerbe Hamburg, Hamburg

Museum Het Prinsenhof, Delft

The Museum of Arts & Sciences Inc, Daytona Beach FL

Museum of Fine Arts Houston, Bayou Bend Collection & Gardens, Houston TX

Museum of Fine Arts, Houston, Rienzi Center for European Decorative Arts, Houston TX

Museum of Fine Arts, Saint Petersburg, Florida, Inc, Saint Petersburg FL

Museum of Florida Art, Deland FL

Museum of Latin American Art, Long Beach CA

Museum of Northern British Columbia, Ruth Harvey Art Gallery, Prince Rupert BC

Museum of Northwest Art, La Conner WA

Museum of Southern History, Houston TX

Museum Plantin-Moretus/Prentenkabinet, Antwerp

Museum zu Allerheiligen, Schaffhausen

Muskegon Museum of Art, Muskegon MI

Muzej za Umjetnost i Obrt, Museum of Arts & Crafts, Zagreb

Muzeul National Brukenthal, Brukenthal Palace & European Art Gallery, Sibiu

Muzeum Narodowe, National Museum in Poznan, Poznan

Muzeum Narodowe W Kielcach, National Museum in Kielce, Kielce

Narodna Galerija, National Gallery of Slovenia, Ljubljana

Narodni Muzej Crne Gore, National Museum of Montenegro, Cetinje

Nathan Hale Homestead Museum, Coventry CT

National Art Museum of Sport, Indianapolis IN

National Baseball Hall of Fame & Museum, Inc, Art Collection, Cooperstown NY

National Gallery of Canada, Ottawa ON

National Gallery of Ireland, Dublin

National Museum of American Illustration, Newport RI

National Museum of Fine Arts of Moldova, Chisinau

The National Museum of Modern Art, Tokyo, Tokyo

National Museum, Monuments and Art Gallery, Gaborone

National Palace Museum, Taiwan, R.O.C.

National Portrait Gallery, Smithsonian Institution, Washington DC

National Portrait Gallery, London

National Silk Art Museum, Weston MO

National Society of Colonial Dames of America in the State of Maryland, Mount Clare Museum House, Baltimore MD

National Society of the Colonial Dames of America in The Commonwealth of Virginia, Wilton House Museum, Richmond VA

National Trust for Historic Preservation, Chesterwood, Stockbridge MA

National Trust for Historic Preservation, Shadows-on-the-Teche, New Iberia LA

Nationalmuseum, Stockholm

Naval Historical Center, The Navy Museum, Washington DC

Nebraska Game and Parks Commission, Arbor Lodge State Historical Park & Morton Mansion, Nebraska City NE

Nelson Mandela Bay Municipality, Nelson Mandela Metropolitan Art Museum, Port Elizabeth

The Nemours Foundatioin, Nemours Mansion & Gardens, Wilmington DE

New Britain Museum of American Art, New Britain CT

New Canaan Historical Society, New Canaan CT

New Hampshire Antiquarian Society, Hopkinton Historical Society, Hopkinton NH

New Jersey Historical Society, Newark NJ

New Jersey State Museum, Fine Art Bureau, Trenton NJ

New Orleans Museum of Art, New Orleans LA

New World Art Center, T F Chen Cultural Center, New York NY

New York State Military Museum and Veterans Research Center, Saratoga Springs NY

New York State Office of Parks Recreation & Historic Preservation, John Jay Homestead State Historic Site, Katonah NY

Newburyport Maritime Society, Inc, Custom House Maritime Museum, Newburyport MA

Elisabet Ney, Austin TX

Norfolk Historical Society Inc, Museum, Norfolk CT

Norman Rockwell Museum, Stockbridge MA

North Carolina State University, Gregg Museum of Art & Design, Raleigh NC

North Dakota State University, Memorial Union Gallery, Fargo ND

Norwich Free Academy, Slater Memorial Museum, Norwich CT

Noyes Art Gallery, Lincoln NE

The Ogden Museum of Southern Art, University of New Orleans, New Orleans LA

The Ohio Historical Society, Inc, Campus Martius Museum & Ohio River Museum, Marietta OH

Oklahoma City Museum of Art, Oklahoma City OK

Old Dartmouth Historical Society, New Bedford Whaling Museum, New Bedford MA

Oshkosh Public Museum, Oshkosh WI

Owensboro Museum of Fine Art, Owensboro KY

Panhandle-Plains Historical Museum, Canyon TX

Paris Gibson Square, Museum of Art, Great Falls MT

Pasadena Museum of California Art, Pasadena CA

Pasadena Museum of History, Pasadena CA

Passaic County Historical Society, Lambert Castle Museum & Library, Paterson NJ

Pennsylvania Historical & Museum Commission, Railroad Museum of Pennsylvania, Harrisburg PA

The Pennsylvania State University, Palmer Museum of Art, University Park PA

Pensacola Museum of Art, Pensacola FL

Philadelphia History Museum, Philadelphia PA

Philadelphia Museum of Art, John G Johnson Collection, Philadelphia PA

Philipse Manor Hall State Historic Site, Yonkers NY

The Phillips Collection, Washington DC

George Phippen, Phippen Museum - Art of the American West, Prescott AZ

Phoenix Art Museum, Phoenix AZ

Piedmont Arts Association, Martinsville VA

Pilgrim Society, Pilgrim Hall Museum, Plymouth MA

Pinacoteca Provinciale, Bari

Plains Art Museum, Fargo ND

Plainsman Museum, Aurora NE

Pope County Historical Society, Pope County Museum, Glenwood MN

Port Huron Museum, Port Huron MI

Porter-Phelps-Huntington Foundation, Inc, Historic House Museum, Hadley MA

Presidential Museum & Leadership Library, Odessa TX

Princeton University, Princeton University Art Museum, Princeton NJ

Pump House Center for the Arts, Chillicothe OH

Putnam County Historical Society, Foundry School Museum, Cold Spring NY

Queens College, City University of New York, Godwin-Ternbach Museum, Flushing NY

R W Norton Art Foundation, R W Norton Art Gallery, Shreveport LA

Randolph College, Maier Museum of Art, Lynchburg VA

Rawls Museum Arts, Courtland VA

Reading Public Museum, Reading PA

Jack Richard Gallery, Almond Tea Museum & Jane Williams Galleries, Divisions of Studios of Jack Richard, Cuyahoga Falls OH

Rijksmuseum Twenthe, Rijksmuseum Twenthe, Enschede

Riley County Historical Society & Museum, Riley County Historical Museum, Manhattan KS

Rollins College, George D & Harriet W Cornell Fine Arts Museum, Winter Park FL

Ross Memorial Museum, Saint Andrews NB

Roswell Museum & Art Center, Roswell NM

Royal Ontario Museum, Dept of Western Art & Culture, Toronto ON

C M Russell, Great Falls MT

Rutgers, The State University of New Jersey, Zimmerli Art Museum, Rutgers University, New Brunswick NJ

Ryerss Victorian Museum & Library, Philadelphia PA

Saco Museum, Saco ME

Saginaw Art Museum, Saginaw MI

Saint Augustine Historical Society, Oldest House Museum Complex, Saint Augustine FL

Saint Johnsbury Athenaeum, Saint Johnsbury VT

Saint Joseph College, Art Gallery, University of Saint Joseph, West Hartford CT

St Mary Landmarks, Grevemberg House Museum, Franklin LA

St Mary's College of Maryland, The Dwight Frederick Boyden Gallery, St Mary's City MD

Saint Olaf College, Flaten Art Museum, Northfield MN

Saint Peter's College, Art Gallery, Jersey City NJ

Salisbury House Foundation, Salisbury House and Garden, Des Moines IA

The Sandwich Historical Society, Inc & Sandwich Glass Museum, Sandwich Glass Museum, Sandwich MA

Santa Monica Museum of Art, Santa Monica CA

Shirley Plantation Foundation, Charles City VA

R L S Silverado Museum, Saint Helena CA

Norton Simon, Pasadena CA

Slovenska Narodna Galeria, Slovak National Gallery, Bratislava

Smithsonian Institution, Washington DC

The Society of the Cincinnati at Anderson House, Washington DC

Sonoma State University, University Art Gallery, Rohnert Park CA

Soprintendenza per I beni storici artistici ed etnoantropologici per le province di Mantova Brescia e Cremona, Museo di Palazzo Ducale, Mantua

South Dakota State University, South Dakota Art Museum, Brookings SD

Southern Lorain County Historical Society, Spirit of '76 Museum, Elyria OH

Spartanburg Art Museum, Spartanburg SC

The Speed Art Museum, Louisville KY

Spertus Institute of Jewish Studies, Chicago IL

Springfield Art Museum, Springfield MO

Springfield Museums, Connecticut Valley Historical Society, Springfield MA

Springville Museum of Art, Springville UT

Stanford University, Cantor Arts Center at Stanford University, Stanford CA

The State Museum of Fine Arts of Tatarstan Republic, Kazan

State University of New York College at Cortland, Dowd Fine Arts Gallery, Cortland NY

Staten Island Museum, Staten Island NY

Stedelijk Museum Alkmaar, Alkmaar Municipal Museum, Alkmaar

T C Steele, Nashville IN

The Stewart Museum, Montreal PQ

Stone Quarry Hill Art Park, Winner Gallery, Cazenovia NY

Stratford Historical Society, Catharine B Mitchell Museum, Stratford CT

Gilbert Stuart, Gilbert Stuart Birthplace & Museum, Saunderstown RI

Sturdivant Museum Association, Sturdivant Museum, Selma AL

The Summit County Historical Society of Akron, OH, Akron OH

Suomen Kansallismuseo, National Museum of Finland, Helsinki

Supreme Court of the United States, Office of the Curator, Washington DC

Swedish American Museum Association of Chicago, Chicago IL

Switzerland County Historical Society Inc, Switzerland County Historical Museum, Vevay IN

Tacoma Art Museum, Tacoma WA

Taft Museum of Art, Cincinnati OH

Taos, Ernest Blumenschein Home & Studio, Taos NM

Lillian & Coleman Taube Museum of Art, Minot ND

Telfair Museums' Jepson Center for the Arts Library, Savannah GA

Temiskaming Art Gallery, Haileybury ON

The Temple-Tifereth Israel, The Temple Museum of Religious Art, Beachwood OH

Texas Tech University, Museum of Texas Tech University, Lubbock TX

POSTERS

The Israel Museum, Jerusalem, Jerusalem
J.M.W. Turner Museum, Sarasota FL
Joe Gish's Old West Museum, Fredericksburg TX
Juniata College Museum of Art, Huntingdon PA
Kenosha Public Museums, Kenosha WI
Kirkland Museum of Fine & Decorative Art, Denver CO
Knights of Columbus Supreme Council, Knights of Columbus Museum, New Haven CT
Kunstmuseum Thun, Thun
La Casa del Libro Museum, San Juan PR
Lac du Flambeau Band of Lake Superior Chippewa Indians, George W Brown Jr Ojibwe Museum & Cultural Center, Lac Du Flambeau WI
Lafayette Science Museum & Planetarium, Lafayette LA
Lakeview Museum of Arts & Sciences, Peoria IL
Latino Art Museum, Pomona CA
Latvijas Nacionalais Makslas Muzejs, Arsenals Exhibition Hall, Riga
Lehigh University Art Galleries, Museum Operation, Bethlehem PA
LeMoyne Art Foundation, Center for the Visual Arts, Tallahassee FL
LeSueur County Historical Society, Chapter One, Elysian MN
Liberty Memorial Museum & Archives, The National Museum of World War I, Kansas City MO
Livingston County Historical Society, Museum, Geneseo NY
The Long Island Museum of American Art, History & Carriages, Stony Brook NY
Longview Museum of Fine Art, Longview TX
Louisiana Department of Culture, Recreation & Tourism, Louisiana State Museum, New Orleans LA
Luther College, Fine Arts Collection, Decorah IA
Maitland Art Center, Maitland FL
The Mariners' Museum, Newport News VA
Marquette University, Haggerty Museum of Art, Milwaukee WI
Maysville, Kentucky Gateway Museum Center, Maysville KY
McLean County Historical Society, McLean County Museum of History, Bloomington IL
Medina Railroad Museum, Medina NY
Meredith College, Frankie G Weems Gallery & Rotunda Gallery, Raleigh NC
Ministry of Cultural Affairs, Bangladesh National Museum, Dhaka
Minnesota Museum of American Art, Saint Paul MN
Minot State University, Northwest Art Center, Minot ND
Mobile Museum of Art, Mobile AL
Moravska Galerie v Brne, Moravian Gallery in Brno, Brno
Musee Regional de lu Cote-Nord, Sept-Iles PQ
Museo De Las Americas, Denver CO
Museum fur Kunst und Gewerbe Hamburg, Hamburg
The Museum of Arts & Sciences Inc, Daytona Beach FL
Museum of Decorative Arts in Prague, Prague
Museum of Florida Art, Deland FL
Museum of Modern Art, New York NY
Museum of York County, Rock Hill SC
Museum zu Allerheiligen, Schaffhausen
Muskegon Museum of Art, Muskegon MI
Muzej Moderne I Suvremene Umjetnosti, Museum of Modern and Contemporary Art, Rijeka
Muzej za Umjetnost i Obrt, Museum of Arts & Crafts, Zagreb
Muzeul de Istorie Nationala Si Arheologie Constanta, National History & Archaeology Museum, Constanta
Muzeum Narodowe, National Museum in Poznan, Poznan
National Art Museum of Sport, Indianapolis IN
National Baseball Hall of Fame & Museum, Inc, Art Collection, Cooperstown NY
National Museum of American Illustration, Newport RI
The National Museum of Modern Art, Tokyo, Tokyo
National Museum, Monuments and Art Gallery, Gaborone
The National Park Service, United States Department of the Interior, Statue of Liberty National Monument & The Ellis Island Immigration Museum, Washington DC
National Portrait Gallery, Smithsonian Institution, Washington DC
The National Shrine of the North American Martyrs, Fultonville NY

Naval Historical Center, The Navy Museum, Washington DC
Nebraska State Capitol, Lincoln NE
Nelson Mandela Bay Municipality, Nelson Mandela Metropolitan Art Museum, Port Elizabeth
New Hampshire Antiquarian Society, Hopkinton Historical Society, Hopkinton NH
New Jersey Historical Society, Newark NJ
New Jersey State Museum, Fine Art Bureau, Trenton NJ
New Visions Gallery, Inc, Marshfield WI
New World Art Center, T F Chen Cultural Center, New York NY
Niigata Prefectural Museum of Modern Art, Niigata
Norman Rockwell Museum of Vermont, Rutland VT
North Dakota State University, Memorial Union Gallery, Fargo ND
The Ogden Museum of Southern Art, University of New Orleans, New Orleans LA
Oshkosh Public Museum, Oshkosh WI
Panhandle-Plains Historical Museum, Canyon TX
Pennsylvania Historical & Museum Commission, Railroad Museum of Pennsylvania, Harrisburg PA
The Pennsylvania State University, Palmer Museum of Art, University Park PA
Piedmont Arts Association, Martinsville VA
Plains Art Museum, Fargo ND
Princeton University, Princeton University Art Museum, Princeton NJ
Pump House Center for the Arts, Chillicothe OH
Queens College, City University of New York, Godwin-Ternbach Museum, Flushing NY
Radio-Canada SRC CBC, Georges Goguen CBC Art Gallery, Moncton NB
Rawls Museum Arts, Courtland VA
Jack Richard Gallery, Almond Tea Museum & Jane Williams Galleries, Divisions of Studios of Jack Richard, Cuyahoga Falls OH
Riley County Historical Society & Museum, Riley County Historical Museum, Manhattan KS
Saginaw Art Museum, Saginaw MI
Saint Joseph's Oratory, Museum, Montreal PQ
St Mary's College of Maryland, The Dwight Frederick Boyden Gallery, St Mary's City MD
Saint Peter's College, Art Gallery, Jersey City NJ
The Sandwich Historical Society, Inc & Sandwich Glass Museum, Sandwich Glass Museum, Sandwich MA
School of Visual Arts, Visual Arts Museum, New York NY
Slovenska Narodna Galeria, Slovak National Gallery, Bratislava
The Society of the Cincinnati at Anderson House, Washington DC
South Dakota State University, South Dakota Art Museum, Brookings SD
South Street Seaport Museum, New York NY
The Speed Art Museum, Louisville KY
Spertus Institute of Jewish Studies, Chicago IL
Staatsgalerie Stuttgart, Stuttgart
State University of New York at Binghamton, Binghamton University Art Museum, Binghamton NY
State University of New York at New Paltz, Samuel Dorsky Museum of Art, New Paltz NY
State University of New York at Oswego, Tyler Art Gallery, Oswego NY
Staten Island Museum, Staten Island NY
Stauth Foundation & Museum, Stauth Memorial Museum, Montezuma KS
Stiftung Deutsches Historisches Museum, Berlin
Stone Quarry Hill Art Park, Winner Gallery, Cazenovia NY
Stratford Historical Society, Catharine B Mitchell Museum, Stratford CT
Sweet Briar College, Art Collection & Galleries, Sweet Briar VA
Tver Art Gallery, Tver
Ukrainian Canadian Archives & Museum of Alberta, Edmonton AB
United Society of Shakers, Shaker Museum, New Gloucester ME
United States Figure Skating Association, World Figure Skating Museum & Hall of Fame, Colorado Springs CO
United States Military Academy, West Point Museum, West Point NY
United States Navy, Art Gallery, Washington DC
University of California, Richard L Nelson Gallery & Fine Arts Collection, Davis CA
University of California, Berkeley, Berkeley Art Museum & Pacific Film Archive, Berkeley CA

University of California, Berkeley, The Magnes Collection of Jewish Art & Life, Berkeley CA
University of California, Santa Barbara, University Art Museum, Santa Barbara CA
University of Cincinnati, DAAP Galleries-College of Design Architecture, Art & Planning, Cincinnati OH
University of Georgia, Georgia Museum of Art, Athens GA
University of Illinois at Chicago, Gallery 400, Chicago IL
University of Illinois at Urbana-Champaign, Krannert Art Museum and Kinkead Pavilion, Champaign IL
University of Maine, Museum of Art, Bangor ME
University of Nebraska-Lincoln, Great Plains Art Museum, Lincoln NE
University of Saskatchewan, Diefenbaker Canada Centre, Saskatoon SK
University of South Florida, Contemporary Art Museum, Tampa FL
University of Texas Pan American, Charles & Dorothy Clark Gallery; University Gallery, Edinburg TX
University of Texas Pan American, UTPA Art Galleries, Edinburg TX
University of Virginia, The Fralin Museum of Art at the University of Virginia, Charlottesville VA
University of Wisconsin-Madison, Chazen Museum of Art, Madison WI
Ursinus College, Philip & Muriel Berman Museum of Art, Collegeville PA
Utah Department of Natural Resources, Division of Parks & Recreation, Territorial Statehouse State Park Museum, Fillmore UT
The Walker African American Museum & Research Center, Las Vegas NV
Washington University, Mildred Lane Kemper Art Museum, Saint Louis MO
Waterworks Visual Arts Center, Salisbury NC
West Florida Historic Preservation, Inc/University of West Florida, T T Wentworth, Jr Florida State Museum; Historic Pensacola Village; Pensacola Historical Society & Resource Center, Pensacola FL
World Erotic Art Museum, Miami Beach FL
Zacheta - National Gallery of Art, Kordegarda Gallery, Warsaw
Zurich University of the Arts (ZHdK), Museum Fuer Gestaltung Zurich (Museum of Design Zurich), Zurich

POTTERY

Academy of the New Church, Glencairn Museum, Bryn Athyn PA
Albany Institute of History & Art, Albany NY
Albuquerque Museum of Art & History, Albuquerque NM
American Sport Art Museum and Archives, Daphne AL
Walter Anderson, Ocean Springs MS
Arab American National Museum, Dearborn MI
Arizona Historical Society-Yuma, Sanguinetti House Museum & Garden, Yuma AZ
Arnold Mikelson Mind & Matter Art Gallery, White Rock BC
Arnot Art Museum, Elmira NY
Art & Culture Center of Hollywood, Art Gallery/Multidisciplinary Cultural Center, Hollywood FL
The Art Association of Jacksonville, The David Strawn Art Gallery, Jacksonville IL
Art Community Center, Art Center of Corpus Christi, Corpus Christi TX
Art Gallery of Bancroft Inc, Bancroft ON
Art Gallery of Nova Scotia, Halifax NS
Art Gallery of South Australia, Adelaide
The Art Museum at the University of Kentucky, Lexington KY
Art Museum of Greater Lafayette, Lafayette IN
Art Without Walls Inc, New York NY
Artesia Historical Museum & Art Center, Artesia NM
Arts Council of Fayetteville-Cumberland County, The Arts Center, Fayetteville NC
Asbury College, Student Center Gallery, Wilmore KY
Asheville Art Museum, Asheville NC
Asian Art Museum of San Francisco, Chong-Moon Lee Ctr for Asian Art and Culture, San Francisco CA
Augustana College, Augustana College Art Museum, Rock Island IL
Autry National Center, Southwest Museum of the American Indian, Mt. Washington Campus, Los Angeles CA
Badisches Landesmuseum, Karlsruhe
Baker University, Old Castle Museum, Baldwin City KS

The Mint Museum, Mint Museum of Craft & Design, Charlotte NC
Mississippi River Museum at Mud-Island River Park, Memphis TN
Arthur Roy Mitchell, A.R. Mitchell Museum, Trinidad CO
Mobile Museum of Art, Mobile AL
Montclair Art Museum, Montclair NJ
Moody County Historical Society, Moody County Museum, Pierre SD
Moravian Historical Society, Whitefield House Museum, Nazareth PA
Moravska Galerie v Brne, Moravian Gallery in Brno, Brno
Morehead State University, Kentucky Folk Art Center, Morehead KY
Morris Museum, Morristown NJ
Morris Museum of Art, Augusta GA
Mount Saint Vincent University, MSVU Art Gallery, Halifax NS
Mount Vernon Hotel Museum & Garden, New York NY
Munson-Williams-Proctor Arts Institute, Museum of Art, Utica NY
Muscatine Art Center, Museum, Muscatine IA
Muscatine Art Center, Muscatine IA
Musea Brugge, Gruuthuse Museum, Bruges
Musee des Beaux-Arts/Palais des Archeveques, Museum of Fine Arts, Tours
Musee Guimet, Paris
Musee National d'Histoire et d'Art Luxembourg, Luxembourg City
Musee Regional de lu Cote-Nord, Sept-Iles PQ
Musee Regional de Vaudreuil-Soulanges, Vaudreuil-Dorion PQ
Musee Royal Et Domaine De Mariemont, Morlanwelz
Musees Royaux d'Art et d'Histoire, Royal Museums of Art and History, Brussels
Museo Cerralbo, Madrid
Museo De Las Americas, Denver CO
Museu de Evora, Evora
Museu de Grao Vasco, Viseu
The Museum, Greenwood SC
Museum De Lakenhal, Leiden
Museum fur Kunst und Gewerbe Hamburg, Hamburg
Museum Het Prinsenhof, Delft
Museum of Art & History, Santa Cruz, Santa Cruz CA
Museum of Arts & Design, New York NY
The Museum of Arts & Sciences Inc, Daytona Beach FL
Museum of Fine Arts Houston, Bayou Bend Collection & Gardens, Houston TX
Museum of Northern Arizona, Flagstaff AZ
Museum of Northwest Art, La Conner WA
Museum zu Allerheiligen, Schaffhausen
Muzej za Umjetnost i Obrt, Museum of Arts & Crafts, Zagreb
Muzeul de Istorie Nationala Si Arheologie Constanta, National History & Archaeology Museum, Constanta
Muzeul National Brukenthal, Brukenthal Palace & European Art Gallery, Sibiu
Muzeum Narodowe, National Museum in Poznan, Poznan
Nanticoke Indian Museum, Millsboro DE
National Baseball Hall of Fame & Museum, Inc, Art Collection, Cooperstown NY
National Museum of Ceramic Art & Glass, Baltimore MD
National Museum of Fine Arts of Moldova, Chisinau
National Museum of the American Indian, George Gustav Heye Center, New York NY
National Museum, Monuments and Art Gallery, Gaborone
National Museums Scotland, National Museum of Scotland, Edinburgh
National Palace Museum, Taiwan, R.O.C.
National Society of Colonial Dames of America in the State of Maryland, Mount Clare Museum House, Baltimore MD
Navajo Nation, Navajo Nation Museum, Window Rock AZ
Nelson Mandela Bay Municipality, Nelson Mandela Metropolitan Art Museum, Port Elizabeth
The Nelson-Atkins Museum of Art, Kansas City MO
The Nemours Foundatioin, Nemours Mansion & Gardens, Wilmington DE
New Hampshire Antiquarian Society, Hopkinton Historical Society, Hopkinton NH
New Jersey State Museum, Fine Art Bureau, Trenton NJ
New Visions Gallery, Inc, Marshfield WI

Niigata Prefectural Museum of Modern Art, Niigata
North Carolina State University, Gregg Museum of Art & Design, Raleigh NC
North Dakota State University, Memorial Union Gallery, Fargo ND
Norwich Free Academy, Slater Memorial Museum, Norwich CT
Noyes Art Gallery, Lincoln NE
The Ogden Museum of Southern Art, University of New Orleans, New Orleans LA
Ohara Museum of Art, Kurashiki
Ohio Historical Society, National Road-Zane Grey Museum, Columbus OH
The Ohio Historical Society, Inc, Campus Martius Museum & Ohio River Museum, Marietta OH
Olana State Historic Site, Hudson NY
Oshkosh Public Museum, Oshkosh WI
Owensboro Museum of Fine Art, Owensboro KY
Pacific - Asia Museum, Pasadena CA
Panhandle-Plains Historical Museum, Canyon TX
Paris Gibson Square, Museum of Art, Great Falls MT
Peoria Historical Society, Peoria IL
Phelps County Historical Society, Nebraska Prairie Museum, Holdrege NE
The Frank Phillips, Woolaroc Museum, Bartlesville OK
George Phippen, Phippen Museum - Art of the American West, Prescott AZ
Piedmont Arts Association, Martinsville VA
Pinacoteca Provinciale, Bari
Plains Art Museum, Fargo ND
Pretoria Art Museum, Municipal Art Gallery, Pretoria
Princeton University, Princeton University Art Museum, Princeton NJ
Pump House Center for the Arts, Chillicothe OH
Queens College, City University of New York, Godwin-Ternbach Museum, Flushing NY
R W Norton Art Foundation, R W Norton Art Gallery, Shreveport LA
Rabindra Bhavan Art Gallery, Lalit Kala Akademi (National Academy of Art), New Delhi
Rawls Museum Arts, Courtland VA
Reading Public Museum, Reading PA
Rijksmuseum Twenthe, Rijksmuseum Twenthe, Enschede
Riley County Historical Society & Museum, Riley County Historical Museum, Manhattan KS
The Rockwell Museum of Western Art, Corning NY
The Rooms Corporation of Newfoundland & Labrador, Saint John's NF
Roswell Museum & Art Center, Roswell NM
C M Russell, Great Falls MT
Saginaw Art Museum, Saginaw MI
Saint Augustine Historical Society, Oldest House Museum Complex, Saint Augustine FL
Saint Bonaventure University, Regina A Quick Center for the Arts, Saint Bonaventure NY
Saint Louis County Historical Society, St. Louis County Historical Society, Duluth MN
Saint Olaf College, Flaten Art Museum, Northfield MN
Santa Monica Museum of Art, Santa Monica CA
School for Advanced Research (SAR), Indian Arts Research Center, Santa Fe NM
Schweinfurth Art Center, Auburn NY
Seneca-Iroquois National Museum, Salamanca NY
Shirley Plantation Foundation, Charles City VA
Society for Contemporary Craft, Pittsburgh PA
South Carolina Artisans Center, Walterboro SC
South Dakota State University, South Dakota Art Museum, Brookings SD
Southern Baptist Theological Seminary, Joseph A Callaway Archaeological Museum, Louisville KY
Spartanburg Art Museum, Spartanburg SC
The Speed Art Museum, Louisville KY
Springfield Art Museum, Springfield MO
Springville Museum of Art, Springville UT
Stanford University, Cantor Arts Center at Stanford University, Stanford CA
State University of New York at Geneseo, Bertha V B Lederer Gallery, Geneseo NY
State University of New York at New Paltz, Samuel Dorsky Museum of Art, New Paltz NY
State University of New York at Oswego, Tyler Art Gallery, Oswego NY
Staten Island Museum, Staten Island NY
Stone Quarry Hill Art Park, Winner Gallery, Cazenovia NY
Suan Pakkad Palace Museum, Bangkok
The Summit County Historical Society of Akron, OH, Akron OH
Suomen Kansallismuseo, National Museum of Finland, Helsinki

Swedish American Museum Association of Chicago, Chicago IL
Switzerland County Historical Society Inc, Switzerland County Historical Museum, Vevay IN
Tallahassee Museum of History & Natural Science, Tallahassee FL
Taos, Ernest Blumenschein Home & Studio, Taos NM
Lillian & Coleman Taube Museum of Art, Minot ND
Temiskaming Art Gallery, Haileybury ON
The Temple-Tifereth Israel, The Temple Museum of Religious Art, Beachwood OH
Texas Tech University, Museum of Texas Tech University, Lubbock TX
Tokyo University of the Arts, The University Art Museum, Tokyo
Topeka & Shawnee County Public Library, Alice C Sabatini Gallery, Topeka KS
Towson University, Asian Arts & Culture Center, Towson MD
Tucson Museum of Art and Historic Block, Tucson AZ
Tulane University, Newcomb Art Gallery, New Orleans LA
Tulane University, University Art Collection, New Orleans LA
Tver Art Gallery, Tver
Tyne and Wear Archives & Museums, Sunderland Museum & Winter Gardens, Newcastle-upon-Tyne
Ukrainian Canadian Archives & Museum of Alberta, Edmonton AB
The Ukrainian Museum, New York NY
United Society of Shakers, Shaker Museum, New Gloucester ME
University of California, Berkeley, Phoebe Apperson Hearst Museum of Anthropology, Berkeley CA
University of Chicago, Oriental Institute, Chicago IL
University of Colorado, CU Art Museum, Boulder CO
University of Delaware, University Museums, Newark DE
University of Georgia, Georgia Museum of Art, Athens GA
University of Illinois at Urbana-Champaign, Krannert Art Museum and Kinkead Pavilion, Champaign IL
University of Louisiana at Lafayette, Paul and Lulu Hilliard University Art Museum, Lafayette LA
University of Manitoba, Faculty of Architecture Exhibition Centre, Winnipeg MB
University of Massachusetts, Amherst, University Gallery, Amherst MA
University of Miami, Lowe Art Museum, Coral Gables FL
University of Michigan, Kelsey Museum of Archaeology, Ann Arbor MI
University of Minnesota Duluth, Tweed Museum of Art, Duluth MN
University of Missouri, Museum of Art & Archaeology, Columbia MO
University of Nevada, Reno, Sheppard Contemporary & University Galleries, Reno NV
University of New Brunswick, Art Centre, Fredericton NB
University of New Mexico, The Harwood Museum of Art, Taos NM
University of Pennsylvania, Museum of Archaeology & Anthropology, Philadelphia PA
University of Pittsburgh, University Art Gallery, Pittsburgh PA
University of Richmond, University Museums, Richmond VA
University of Rochester, Memorial Art Gallery, Rochester NY
University of Tennessee, McClung Museum of Natural History & Culture, Knoxville TN
University of Virginia, The Fralin Museum of Art at the University of Virginia, Charlottesville VA
University of Washington, Henry Art Gallery, Seattle WA
University of Wisconsin-Madison, Chazen Museum of Art, Madison WI
University of Wisconsin-Madison, Wisconsin Union Galleries, Madison WI
Ursinus College, Philip & Muriel Berman Museum of Art, Collegeville PA
Utah Department of Natural Resources, Division of Parks & Recreation, Territorial Statehouse State Park Museum, Fillmore UT
Vesterheim Norwegian-American Museum, Decorah IA
Village of Potsdam, Potsdam Public Museum, Potsdam NY
Virginia Museum of Fine Arts, Richmond VA
Wake Forest University, Museum of Anthropology, Winston Salem NC

PRE-COLUMBIAN ART

PRIMITIVE ART

The Art Museum of Eastern Idaho, Idaho Falls ID
Artesia Historical Museum & Art Center, Artesia NM
Augustana College, Eide-Dalrymple Gallery, Sioux Falls SD
Birmingham Museum of Art, Birmingham AL
Bone Creek Museum of Agrarian Art, David City NE
Brown University, Haffenreffer Museum of Anthropology, Providence RI
Cabot's Old Indian Pueblo Museum, Desert Hot Springs CA
Canadian Museum of Civilization, Gatineau PQ
Capital University, Schumacher Gallery, Columbus OH
Carson County Square House Museum, Panhandle TX
Chhatrapati Shivaji Maharaj Vastu Sangrahalaya, Mumbai
Church of Jesus Christ of Latter-Day Saints, Museum of Church History & Art, Salt Lake City UT
City of Fayette, Alabama, Fayette Art Museum, Fayette AL
City of Springdale, Shiloh Museum of Ozark History, Springdale AR
Civic and Municipal Affairs Bureau of Macau, Macau Museum of Art, Nape
Colgate University, Picker Art Gallery, Hamilton NY
Columbus Museum, Columbus GA
Cornell University, Herbert F Johnson Museum of Art, Ithaca NY
Craft and Folk Art Museum (CAFAM), Los Angeles CA
Cripple Creek District Museum, Cripple Creek CO
Crocker Art Museum, Sacramento CA
Davidson College, William H Van Every Jr & Edward M Smith Galleries, Davidson NC
Delaware Archaeology Museum, Dover DE
Delta Blues Museum, Clarksdale MS
Dickinson College, The Trout Gallery, Carlisle PA
Discovery Place Inc, Nature Museum, Charlotte NC
Field Museum, Chicago IL
Fitton Center for Creative Arts, Hamilton OH
Florence Museum, Florence SC
Galerie Montcalm, Gatineau PQ
Gallery of Prehistoric Paintings, New York NY
Gem County Historical Society and Museum, Gem County Historical Village Museum, Emmett ID
Hawkes Bay Art Gallery and Museum, Napier
Heard Museum, Phoenix AZ
Heritage Museums & Gardens, Sandwich MA
Hermitage Foundation Museum, Norfolk VA
Edna Hibel, Hibel Museum of Art, Jupiter FL
Hickory Museum of Art, Inc, Hickory NC
Higgins Armory Museum, Worcester MA
High Desert Museum, Bend OR
The Hispanic Society of America, Museum & Library, New York NY
Illinois Historic Preservation Agency, Bishop Hill State Historic Site, Bishop Hill IL
Illinois State Museum, ISM Lockport Gallery, Chicago Gallery & Southern Illinois Art Gallery, Springfield IL
Independent Administrative Institution National Institutes for Cultural Heritage, Tokyo National Museum, Tokyo
Indiana Landmarks, Morris-Butler House, Indianapolis IN
Indiana University, Art Museum, Bloomington IN
Intuit: The Center for Intuitive & Outsider Art, Chicago IL
Iredell Museums, Statesville NC
The Israel Museum, Jerusalem, Billy Rose Art Garden, Jerusalem
Kenosha Public Museums, Kenosha WI
Kentucky Museum of Art and Craft, Louisville KY
Lafayette Science Museum & Planetarium, Lafayette LA
Lakeview Museum of Arts & Sciences, Peoria IL
Lamar University, Dishman Art Museum, Beaumont TX
Lehigh University Art Galleries, Museum Operation, Bethlehem PA
Louisiana Department of Culture, Recreation & Tourism, Louisiana State Museum, New Orleans LA
Luther College, Fine Arts Collection, Decorah IA
Mabee-Gerrer Museum of Art, Shawnee OK
The Mariners' Museum, Newport News VA
Menil Foundation, Inc, The Menil Collection, Houston TX
The Metropolitan Museum of Art, New York NY
Midwest Museum of American Art, Elkhart IN
Ministry of Cultural Affairs, Bangladesh National Museum, Dhaka
Moderna Galerija, Gallery of Modern Art, Zagreb

Morehead State University, Kentucky Folk Art Center, Morehead KY
Morris Museum, Morristown NJ
Morris Museum of Art, Augusta GA
Musees Royaux d'Art et d'Histoire, Royal Museums of Art and History, Brussels
The Museum, Greenwood SC
Museum fur Kunst und Gewerbe Hamburg, Hamburg
Museum of Art, Fort Lauderdale, Fort Lauderdale FL
The Museum of Arts & Sciences Inc, Daytona Beach FL
Museum of Northern British Columbia, Ruth Harvey Art Gallery, Prince Rupert BC
Muzeul de Istorie Nationala Si Arheologie Constanta, National History & Archaeology Museum, Constanta
Muzeul National Brukenthal, Brukenthal Palace & European Art Gallery, Sibiu
National Museum of the American Indian, Smithsonian Institution, Washington DC
National Museum, Monuments and Art Gallery, Gaborone
National Society of Colonial Dames of America in the State of Maryland, Mount Clare Museum House, Baltimore MD
The Ogden Museum of Southern Art, University of New Orleans, New Orleans LA
Olivet College, Armstrong Collection, Olivet MI
Panhandle-Plains Historical Museum, Canyon TX
Paris Gibson Square, Museum of Art, Great Falls MT
Princeton University, Princeton University Art Museum, Princeton NJ
Queens College, City University of New York, Godwin-Ternbach Museum, Flushing NY
Red Deer & District Museum & Archives, Red Deer AB
Riverside Metropolitan Museum, Riverside CA
Rollins College, George D & Harriet W Cornell Fine Arts Museum, Winter Park FL
Royal Ontario Museum, Toronto ON
Saint Peter's College, Art Gallery, Jersey City NJ
Scripps College, Ruth Chandler Williamson Gallery, Claremont CA
Seattle Art Museum, Downtown, Seattle WA
Springfield Museums, Michele & Donald D'Amour Museum of Fine Arts, Springfield MA
Stanford University, Cantor Arts Center at Stanford University, Stanford CA
The State Museum of Fine Arts of Tatarstan Republic, Kazan
Staten Island Museum, Staten Island NY
Stephens College, Lewis James & Nellie Stratton Davis Art Gallery, Columbia MO
Stone Quarry Hill Art Park, Winner Gallery, Cazenovia NY
Stratford Historical Society, Catharine B Mitchell Museum, Stratford CT
Suomen Kansallismuseo, National Museum of Finland, Helsinki
Tattoo Art Museum, San Francisco CA
Tohono Chul Park, Tucson AZ
Topeka & Shawnee County Public Library, Alice C Sabatini Gallery, Topeka KS
Tver Art Gallery, Tver
The Ukrainian Museum, New York NY
University of California, Richard L Nelson Gallery & Fine Arts Collection, Davis CA
University of California, Los Angeles, Fowler Museum at UCLA, Los Angeles CA
University of Illinois at Urbana-Champaign, Krannert Art Museum and Kinkead Pavilion, Champaign IL
University of Louisiana at Lafayette, Paul and Lulu Hilliard University Art Museum, Lafayette LA
University of Miami, Lowe Art Museum, Coral Gables FL
University of Missouri, Museum of Art & Archaeology, Columbia MO
University of Richmond, University Museums, Richmond VA
University of Rochester, Memorial Art Gallery, Rochester NY
University of Utah, Utah Museum of Fine Arts, Salt Lake City UT
University of Victoria, The Legacy Art Gallery, Victoria BC
University of Wisconsin-Madison, Chazen Museum of Art, Madison WI
University of Wyoming, University of Wyoming Art Museum, Laramie WY
Vietnam Fine Arts Museum, Hanoi
Wake Forest University, Museum of Anthropology, Winston Salem NC

Winston-Salem State University, Diggs Gallery, Winston Salem NC

PRINTS

A.E. Backus Museum of Art, Fort Pierce FL
Abington Art Center, Jenkintown PA
Academy Art Museum, Easton MD
The Adirondack Historical Association, The Adirondack Museum, Blue Mountain Lake NY
African American Museum in Philadelphia, Philadelphia PA
Alaska Heritage Museum at Wells Fargo, Anchorage AK
Albany Institute of History & Art, Albany NY
Albertina Museum, Vienna
Albion College, Bobbitt Visual Arts Center, Albion MI
Albright College, Freedman Gallery, Reading PA
Albuquerque Museum of Art & History, Albuquerque NM
Aldrich Museum of Contemporary Art, Ridgefield CT
Allentown Art Museum, Allentown PA
Alton Museum of History & Art, Inc, Alton IL
American Sport Art Museum and Archives, Daphne AL
American Textile History Museum, Lowell MA
American University, Katzen Art Center Gallery, New York NY
Americas Society Art Gallery, New York NY
Amon Carter Museum of American Art, Fort Worth TX
Anchorage Museum at Rasmuson Center, Anchorage AK
Appaloosa Museum and Heritage Center, Moscow ID
Arizona Museum For Youth, Mesa AZ
Arizona State University, ASU Art Museum, Tempe AZ
Arnot Art Museum, Elmira NY
Art Center of Battle Creek, Battle Creek MI
Art Complex Museum, Carl A. Weyerhaeuser Library, Duxbury MA
The Art Galleries of Ramapo College, Mahwah NJ
Art Gallery of Nova Scotia, Halifax NS
Art Gallery of South Australia, Adelaide
The Art Museum at the University of Kentucky, Lexington KY
Art Museum of Greater Lafayette, Lafayette IN
Art Museum of Southeast Texas, Beaumont TX
Art Without Walls Inc, New York NY
Artspace, Richmond VA
Asbury College, Student Center Gallery, Wilmore KY
Asheville Art Museum, Asheville NC
Attleboro Arts Museum, Attleboro MA
Auburn University, Julie Collins Smith Museum, Auburn AL
Augustana College, Augustana College Art Museum, Rock Island IL
Augustana College, Eide-Dalrymple Gallery, Sioux Falls SD
Austin College, Ida Green Gallery, Sherman TX
Baldwin-Wallace College, Fawick Art Gallery, Berea OH
Ball State University, Museum of Art, Muncie IN
The Baltimore Museum of Art, Baltimore MD
Balzekas Museum of Lithuanian Culture, Chicago IL
Baroda Museum and Picture Gallery, Baroda
Baruch College of the City University of New York, Sidney Mishkin Gallery, New York NY
Bates College, Museum of Art, Lewiston ME
Baylor University, Martin Museum of Art, Waco TX
Berea College, Ulmann Doris Galleries, Berea KY
Bertha V B Lederer Fine Arts Gallery-Suny Geneseo, Bertha V B Lederer Fine Arts Gallery, Geneseo NY
Besser Museum for Northeast Michigan, Alpena MI
Beverly Historical Society, Cabot, Hale & Balch House Museums, Beverly MA
Biggs Museum of American Art, Dover DE
Birger Sandzen Memorial Gallery, Lindsborg KS
Birmingham Museum of Art, Birmingham AL
Blanden Memorial Art Museum, Fort Dodge IA
Blauvelt Demarest Foundation, Hiram Blauvelt Art Museum, Oradell NJ
Boise Art Museum, Boise ID
Bone Creek Museum of Agrarian Art, David City NE
Booth Western Art Museum, Cartersville GA
Boston Public Library, Albert H Wiggin Gallery & Print Department, Boston MA
Roy Boyd, Chicago IL
Brandeis University, Rose Art Museum, Waltham MA
Brandywine Conservancy, Brandywine River Museum, Chadds Ford PA
Brevard College, Spiers Gallery, Brevard NC
Brigham City Corporation, Brigham City Museum & Gallery, Brigham City UT

Illinois State University, University Galleries, Normal IL

Illinois Wesleyan University, Merwin & Wakeley Galleries, Bloomington IL

Imperial Calcasieu Museum, Gibson-Barham Gallery, Lake Charles LA

Independence Seaport Museum, Philadelphia PA

Independent Administrative Institution National Institutes for Cultural Heritage, Tokyo National Museum, Tokyo

Independent Administrative Institution National Museum of Art, The National Museum of Western Art, Tokyo

Indiana Landmarks, Morris-Butler House, Indianapolis IN

Indiana University, Art Museum, Bloomington IN

Indianapolis Museum of Art, Indianapolis IN

Institute of American Indian Arts, Museum of Contemporary Native Arts, Santa Fe NM

Institute of Puerto Rican Culture, Museo Fuerte Conde de Mirasol, Vieques PR

International Clown Hall of Fame & Research Center, Inc, West Allis WI

International Museum of Art & Science, McAllen TX

Iowa State University, Brunnier Art Museum, Ames IA

Iredell Museums, Statesville NC

The Israel Museum, Jerusalem, Samuel & Saidye Bronfman Archaeology Wing, Jerusalem

The Israel Museum, Jerusalem, Jerusalem

J.M.W. Turner Museum, Sarasota FL

Jamestown-Yorktown Foundation, Jamestown Settlement, Williamsburg VA

Jersey City Museum, Jersey City NJ

Joe Gish's Old West Museum, Fredericksburg TX

The John L. Clarke Western Art Gallery & Memorial Museum, East Glacier Park MT

Johnson-Humrickhouse Museum, Coshocton OH

Jordan National Gallery of Fine Arts, Amman

Joslyn Art Museum, Omaha NE

Juniata College Museum of Art, Huntingdon PA

Kalamazoo Institute of Arts, Kalamazoo MI

Kamloops Art Gallery, Kamloops BC

Keene State College, Thorne-Sagendorph Art Gallery, Keene NH

Kenosha Public Museums, Kenosha WI

Kent State University, School of Art Galleries, Kent OH

Kentucky Museum of Art and Craft, Louisville KY

Kereszteny Muzeum, Christian Museum, Esztergom

Kings County Historical Society & Museum, Hampton NB

Kirchner Museum Davos, Davos

Kirkland Museum of Fine & Decorative Art, Denver CO

Kitchener-Waterloo Art Gallery, Kitchener ON

Knights of Columbus Supreme Council, Knights of Columbus Museum, New Haven CT

Knoxville Museum of Art, Knoxville TN

Koshare Indian Museum, Inc, La Junta CO

Kunstmuseum Thun, Thun

La Salle University Art Museum, Philadelphia PA

Lafayette College, Lafayette College Art Galleries, Easton PA

Lafayette Science Museum & Planetarium, Lafayette LA

LaGrange Art Museum, LaGrange GA

Lamar University, Dishman Art Museum, Beaumont TX

Latino Art Museum, Pomona CA

Latvijas Nacionalais Makslas Muzejs, Arsenals Exhibition Hall, Riga

Launceston City Council, Queen Victoria Museum and Art Gallery, Launceston

Lawrence University, Wriston Art Center Galleries, Appleton WI

Leeds Museums & Galleries, Leeds

Lehigh University Art Galleries, Museum Operation, Bethlehem PA

LeMoyne Art Foundation, Center for the Visual Arts, Tallahassee FL

Liberty Memorial Museum & Archives, The National Museum of World War I, Kansas City MO

Lincoln County Historical Association, Inc, 1811 Old Lincoln County Jail & Lincoln County Museum, Wiscasset ME

Lincolnshire County Council, The Collection: Art & Archaeology in Lincolnshire, Lincoln

Lindenwood University, Harry D Hendren Gallery, Saint Charles MO

Long Beach Museum of Art Foundation, Long Beach CA

The Long Island Museum of American Art, History & Carriages, Stony Brook NY

Longfellow's Wayside Inn Museum, Sudbury MA

Longfellow-Evangeline State Commemorative Area, Saint Martinville LA

Longue Vue House & Gardens, New Orleans LA

Longview Museum of Fine Art, Longview TX

Los Angeles County Museum of Art, Los Angeles CA

Louisiana Arts & Science Museum, Baton Rouge LA

Louisiana Department of Culture, Recreation & Tourism, Louisiana State Museum, New Orleans LA

Louisiana State University, School of Art - Glassell Gallery, Baton Rouge LA

Louisiana State University, Student Union Art Gallery, Baton Rouge LA

Loyola University Chicago, Loyola University Museum of Art, Chicago IL

Ludwig Museum - Museum of Contemporary Art, Budapest

Luther College, Fine Arts Collection, Decorah IA

Lycoming College Gallery, Williamsport PA

Lyman Allyn Art Museum, New London CT

Mabee-Gerrer Museum of Art, Shawnee OK

Macalester College, Macalester College Art Gallery, Saint Paul MN

Macdonald Stewart Art Centre, Guelph ON

Madison Museum of Contemporary Art, Madison WI

Madison Museum of Fine Art, Madison GA

Magyar Nemzeti Muzeum - Hungarian National Museum, Budapest

Maine College of Art, The Institute of Contemporary Art, Portland ME

Maitland Art Center, Maitland FL

Marietta-Cobb Museum of Art, Marietta GA

The Mariners' Museum, Newport News VA

Marquette University, Haggerty Museum of Art, Milwaukee WI

Maryhill Museum of Art, Goldendale WA

Marylhurst University, The Art Gym, Marylhurst OR

Massachusetts Institute of Technology, List Visual Arts Center, Cambridge MA

Maysville, Kentucky Gateway Museum Center, Maysville KY

The Robert McLaughlin, Oshawa ON

McLean County Historical Society, McLean County Museum of History, Bloomington IL

McMaster University, McMaster Museum of Art, Hamilton ON

McPherson College Gallery, McPherson KS

McPherson Museum and Arts Foundation, McPherson KS

Mendel Art Gallery & Civic Conservatory, Saskatoon SK

Menil Foundation, Inc, The Menil Collection, Houston TX

Mennello Museum of American Art, Orlando FL

Meridian Museum of Art, Meridian MS

Mesa Arts Center, Mesa Contemporary Arts Museum, Mesa AZ

Mexican Museum, San Francisco CA

Miami University, Art Museum, Oxford OH

Miami-Dade College, Kendal Campus, Art Gallery, Miami FL

Michelson Museum of Art, Marshall TX

James A Michener, Doylestown PA

Middle Border Museum & Oscar Howe Art Center, Mitchell SD

Middlebury College, Museum of Art, Middlebury VT

Midwest Museum of American Art, Elkhart IN

Miller Art Center Foundation Inc, Miller Art Museum, Sturgeon Bay WI

Millikin University, Perkinson Gallery, Decatur IL

Mills College Art Museum, Oakland CA

Ministry of Cultural Affairs, Bangladesh National Museum, Dhaka

Ministry of the Arts & Multiculturalism, National Museum & Art Gallery, Port of Spain

Minneapolis Institute of Arts, Minneapolis MN

Minnesota Museum of American Art, Saint Paul MN

Minnesota State University, Mankato, Mankato MN

Minot State University, Northwest Art Center, Minot ND

Mississippi Museum of Art, Jackson MS

Mississippi University for Women, Fine Arts Gallery, Columbus MS

Mobile Museum of Art, Mobile AL

Moderna Galerija, Gallery of Modern Art, Zagreb

Monhegan Museum, Monhegan ME

Montclair Art Museum, Montclair NJ

Moravian College, Payne Gallery, Bethlehem PA

Moravska Galerie v Brne, Moravian Gallery in Brno, Brno

Morehead State University, Claypool-Young Art Gallery, Morehead KY

The Morgan Library & Museum, Museum, New York NY

Morris Museum of Art, Augusta GA

Mount Holyoke College, Art Museum, South Hadley MA

Mount Mary College, Marian Gallery, Milwaukee WI

Mount Saint Vincent University, MSVU Art Gallery, Halifax NS

Mount Vernon Hotel Museum & Garden, New York NY

Muhlenberg College, Martin Art Gallery, Allentown PA

Munson-Williams-Proctor Arts Institute, Museum of Art, Utica NY

Murray State University, Art Galleries, Murray KY

Muscatine Art Center, Museum, Muscatine IA

Muscatine Art Center, Muscatine IA

Musee Carnavalet-Histoire de Paris, Paris

Musee d'art moderne de Ceret, Ceret

Musee des Beaux-Arts d'Orleans, Museum of Fine Arts, Orleans

Musee des Beaux-Arts/Palais des Archeveques, Museum of Fine Arts, Tours

Musee National d'Histoire et d'Art Luxembourg, Luxembourg City

Museen der Stadt Koln, Museum Ludwig, Cologne

Musees Royaux d'Art et d'Histoire, Royal Museums of Art and History, Brussels

Museo Civico Giovanni Fattori, Livorno

Museo de Arte de Ponce, The Luis A Ferre Foundation Inc, Ponce PR

Museo De Las Americas, Denver CO

Museum fur Kunst und Gewerbe Hamburg, Hamburg

Museum of American Glass in WV, Weston WV

Museum of Art & History, Santa Cruz, Santa Cruz CA

The Museum of Arts & Sciences Inc, Daytona Beach FL

Museum of Arts & Sciences, Inc, Macon GA

Museum of Contemporary Art, Chicago IL

The Museum of Contemporary Art (MOCA), Moca Grand Avenue, Los Angeles CA

Museum of Contemporary Art Jacksonville, Jacksonville FL

Museum of Contemporary Art San Diego, San Diego CA

Museum of Contemporary Art, San Diego-Downtown, La Jolla CA

Museum of Decorative Arts in Prague, Prague

Museum of Discovery & Science, Fort Lauderdale FL

Museum of Fine Arts, Boston MA

Museum of Fine Arts Houston, Bayou Bend Collection & Gardens, Houston TX

Museum of Fine Arts, Houston, Houston TX

Museum of Fine Arts, Saint Petersburg, Florida, Inc, Saint Petersburg FL

Museum of Florida Art, Deland FL

Museum of Latin American Art, Long Beach CA

Museum of Modern Art, New York NY

Museum of Modern Art, Ibaraki, Ibaraki

Museum of Northern British Columbia, Ruth Harvey Art Gallery, Prince Rupert BC

Museum of Northwest Art, La Conner WA

Museum of Southern History, Houston TX

Museum of the City of New York, Museum, New York NY

Museum of the Plains Indian & Crafts Center, Browning MT

Museum Plantin-Moretus/Prentenkabinet, Antwerp

Museum zu Allerheiligen, Schaffhausen

Muskegon Museum of Art, Muskegon MI

Muzej Moderne I Suvremene Umjetnosti, Museum of Modern and Contemporary Art, Rijeka

Muzeul National Brukenthal, Brukenthal Palace & European Art Gallery, Sibiu

Muzeum Narodowe, National Museum in Poznan, Poznan

Napoleonic Society of America, Museum & Library, Saint Helena CA

Narodna Galerija, National Gallery of Slovenia, Ljubljana

Nassau Community College, Firehouse Art Gallery, Garden City NY

Nassau County Museum of Art, Roslyn Harbor NY

National Air and Space Museum, Smithsonian Institution, Washington DC

National Art Museum of Sport, Indianapolis IN

National Audubon Society, John James Audubon Center at Mill Grove, Audubon PA

Supreme Court of the United States, Office of the Curator, Washington DC
Surrey Art Gallery, Surrey BC
Swedish American Museum Association of Chicago, Chicago IL
Sweet Briar College, Art Collection & Galleries, Sweet Briar VA
Swope Art Museum, Terre Haute IN
Syracuse University, SUArt Galleries, Syracuse NY
Tacoma Art Museum, Tacoma WA
Tampa Museum of Art, Tampa FL
Lillian & Coleman Taube Museum of Art, Minot ND
Texas Tech University, Museum of Texas Tech University, Lubbock TX
Tohono Chul Park, Tucson AZ
Toledo Museum of Art, Toledo OH
Topeka & Shawnee County Public Library, Alice C Sabatini Gallery, Topeka KS
Towson University, Asian Arts & Culture Center, Towson MD
Towson University, Center for the Arts Gallery, Towson MD
Triton Museum of Art, Santa Clara CA
Tryon Palace Historic Sites & Gardens, New Bern NC
Tucson Museum of Art and Historic Block, Tucson AZ
Tufts University, Tufts University Art Gallery, Medford MA
Tulane University, University Art Collection, New Orleans LA
Turtle Bay Exploration Park, Redding CA
Tver Art Gallery, Tver
Twin City Art Foundation, Masur Museum of Art, Monroe LA
Tyne and Wear Archives & Museums, Sunderland Museum & Winter Gardens, Newcastle-upon-Tyne
Ukrainian Canadian Archives & Museum of Alberta, Edmonton AB
United Society of Shakers, Shaker Museum, New Gloucester ME
United States Capitol, Architect of the Capitol, Washington DC
United States Figure Skating Association, World Figure Skating Museum & Hall of Fame, Colorado Springs CO
United States Military Academy, West Point Museum, West Point NY
United States Naval Academy, USNA Museum, Annapolis MD
United States Navy, Art Gallery, Washington DC
University of Albany, State University of New York, University Art Museum, Albany NY
University of Alabama at Birmingham, Visual Arts Gallery, Birmingham AL
University of Alabama at Huntsville, Union Grove Gallery & University Center Gallery, Huntsville AL
University of Arkansas at Little Rock, Art Galleries, Little Rock AR
University of California, Richard L Nelson Gallery & Fine Arts Collection, Davis CA
University of California, Berkeley, Berkeley Art Museum & Pacific Film Archive, Berkeley CA
University of California, Berkeley, The Magnes Collection of Jewish Art & Life, Berkeley CA
University of Chicago, Smart Museum of Art, Chicago IL
University of Cincinnati, DAAP Galleries-College of Design Architecture, Art & Planning, Cincinnati OH
University of Colorado, CU Art Museum, Boulder CO
University of Colorado at Colorado Springs, Gallery of Contemporary Art, Colorado Springs CO
University of Delaware, University Museums, Newark DE
University of Findlay, Dudley & Mary Marks Lea Gallery, Findlay OH
University of Georgia, Georgia Museum of Art, Athens GA
University of Illinois at Chicago, Gallery 400, Chicago IL
University of Illinois at Urbana-Champaign, Krannert Art Museum and Kinkead Pavilion, Champaign IL
University of Indianapolis, Christel DeHaan Fine Arts Gallery, Indianapolis IN
University of Kansas, Spencer Museum of Art, Lawrence KS
University of Louisiana at Lafayette, Paul and Lulu Hilliard University Art Museum, Lafayette LA
University of Louisville, Hite Art Institute, Louisville KY
University of Maine, Museum of Art, Bangor ME
University of Manchester, Whitworth Art Gallery, Manchester

University of Manitoba, Faculty of Architecture Exhibition Centre, Winnipeg MB
University of Mary Washington, University of Mary Washington Galleries, Fredericksburg VA
University of Maryland, College Park, The Art Gallery, College Park MD
University of Massachusetts, Amherst, University Gallery, Amherst MA
University of Memphis, Art Museum, Memphis TN
University of Miami, Lowe Art Museum, Coral Gables FL
University of Michigan, Museum of Art, Ann Arbor MI
University of Minnesota, Katherine E Nash Gallery, Minneapolis MN
University of Minnesota, The Bell Museum of Natural History, Minneapolis MN
University of Minnesota, Frederick R Weisman Art Museum, Minneapolis MN
University of Minnesota Duluth, Tweed Museum of Art, Duluth MN
University of Missouri, Museum of Art & Archaeology, Columbia MO
University of Nebraska at Omaha, UNO Art Gallery, Omaha NE
University of Nebraska, Lincoln, Sheldon Memorial Art Gallery & Sculpture Garden, Lincoln NE
University of Nebraska-Lincoln, Great Plains Art Museum, Lincoln NE
University of Nevada, Las Vegas, Donna Beam Fine Art Gallery, Las Vegas NV
University of Nevada, Reno, Sheppard Contemporary & University Galleries, Reno NV
University of New Brunswick, Art Centre, Fredericton NB
University of New Hampshire, Museum of Art, Durham NH
University of New Mexico, The Harwood Museum of Art, Taos NM
University of New Mexico, University of New Mexico Art Museum, Albuquerque NM
University of North Carolina at Greensboro, Weatherspoon Art Museum, Greensboro NC
University of Notre Dame, Snite Museum of Art, Notre Dame IN
University of Pennsylvania, Arthur Ross Gallery, Philadelphia PA
University of Pittsburgh, University Art Gallery, Pittsburgh PA
University of Rhode Island, Fine Arts Center Galleries, Kingston RI
University of Richmond, University Museums, Richmond VA
University of Rochester, Memorial Art Gallery, Rochester NY
University of Saskatchewan, Diefenbaker Canada Centre, Saskatoon SK
University of South Florida, Contemporary Art Museum, Tampa FL
University of Southern Colorado, College of Liberal & Fine Arts, Pueblo CO
University of Tennessee, McClung Museum of Natural History & Culture, Knoxville TN
University of Texas at Austin, Blanton Museum of Art, Austin TX
University of Texas at El Paso, Stanlee & Gerald Rubin Center for the Visual Arts, El Paso TX
University of Texas Pan American, Charles & Dorothy Clark Gallery; University Gallery, Edinburg TX
University of Texas Pan American, UTPA Art Galleries, Edinburg TX
University of the South, University Art Gallery, Sewanee TN
University of Vermont, Robert Hull Fleming Museum, Burlington VT
University of Washington, Henry Art Gallery, Seattle WA
University of West Florida, Art Gallery, Pensacola FL
University of Wisconsin Oshkosh, Allen R Priebe Gallery, Oshkosh WI
University of Wisconsin-Eau Claire, Foster Gallery, Eau Claire WI
University of Wisconsin-Madison, Chazen Museum of Art, Madison WI
University of Wisconsin-Madison, Wisconsin Union Galleries, Madison WI
University of Wisconsin-Stout, J Furlong Gallery, Menomonie WI
University of Wyoming, University of Wyoming Art Museum, Laramie WY
Ursinus College, Philip & Muriel Berman Museum of Art, Collegeville PA

Utah Department of Natural Resources, Division of Parks & Recreation, Territorial Statehouse State Park Museum, Fillmore UT
Valentine Richmond History Center, Richmond VA
Valparaiso University, Brauer Museum of Art, Valparaiso IN
Van Gogh Museum, Amsterdam
Vancouver Art Gallery, Vancouver BC
Vanderbilt University, Vanderbilt University Fine Arts Gallery, Nashville TN
Vero Beach Museum of Art, Vero Beach FL
Vesterheim Norwegian-American Museum, Decorah IA
Vietnam Fine Arts Museum, Hanoi
Viridian Artists Inc, New York NY
Wadsworth Atheneum Museum of Art, Hartford CT
The Walker African American Museum & Research Center, Las Vegas NV
Walker Art Center, Minneapolis MN
Walker Art Gallery, Liverpool
Washburn University, Mulvane Art Museum, Topeka KS
Washington County Museum of Fine Arts, Hagerstown MD
Washington State University, Museum of Art, Pullman WA
Washington University, Mildred Lane Kemper Art Museum, Saint Louis MO
Waterloo Center of the Arts, Waterloo IA
Waterworks Visual Arts Center, Salisbury NC
Wayne Center for the Arts, Wooster OH
Wayne State College, Nordstrand Visual Arts Gallery, Wayne NE
Wellesley College, Davis Museum & Cultural Center, Wellesley MA
West Baton Rouge Parish, West Baton Rouge Museum, Port Allen LA
West Florida Historic Preservation, Inc/University of West Florida, T T Wentworth, Jr Florida State Museum; Historic Pensacola Village; Pensacola Historical Society & Resource Center, Pensacola FL
Western Illinois University, Western Illinois University Art Gallery, Macomb IL
Western Michigan University, Gwen Frostic School of Art, Kalamazoo MI
Western State College of Colorado, Quigley Hall Art Gallery, Gunnison CO
Westminster College, Art Gallery, New Wilmington PA
Wheaton College, Beard and Weil Galleries, Norton MA
White House, Washington DC
Whitney Museum of American Art, New York NY
Peter & Catharine Whyte Foundation, Whyte Museum of the Canadian Rockies, Banff AB
Wichita Falls Museum & Art Center, Wichita Falls TX
Wichita State University, Ulrich Museum of Art, Wichita KS
Wildling Art Museum, Solvang CA
Wilfrid Laurier University, Robert Langen Art Gallery, Waterloo ON
The Winnipeg Art Gallery, Winnipeg MB
Winston-Salem State University, Diggs Gallery, Winston Salem NC
Wiregrass Museum of Art, Dothan AL
Wisconsin Historical Society, Wisconsin Historical Museum, Madison WI
Witter Gallery, Storm Lake IA
Woodmere Art Museum Inc, Philadelphia PA
Worcester Art Museum, Worcester MA
Yale University, Yale Center for British Art, New Haven CT
Yokohama Museum of Art, Yokohama
Yuma Fine Arts Association, Yuma Art Center, Yuma AZ
Zacheta - National Gallery of Art, Kordegarda Gallery, Warsaw
Zigler Art Museum, Jennings LA
Zurich University of the Arts (ZHdK), Museum Fuer Gestaltung Zurich (Museum of Design Zurich), Zurich

RELIGIOUS ART

Academy of the New Church, Glencairn Museum, Bryn Athyn PA
Adams County Historical Society, Gettysburg PA
African American Museum in Philadelphia, Philadelphia PA
Anchorage Museum at Rasmuson Center, Anchorage AK
Ancient Spanish Monastery, North Miami Beach FL
Arab American National Museum, Dearborn MI

Philadelphia Museum of Art, John G Johnson Collection, Philadelphia PA
Piedmont Arts Association, Martinsville VA
Pinacoteca Provinciale, Bari
Polish Museum of America, Chicago IL
Pope County Historical Society, Pope County Museum, Glenwood MN
Princeton University, Princeton University Art Museum, Princeton NJ
Queens College, City University of New York, Godwin-Ternbach Museum, Flushing NY
Rabindra Bhavan Art Gallery, Lalit Kala Akademi (National Academy of Art), New Delhi
Radio-Canada SRC CBC, Georges Goguen CBC Art Gallery, Moncton NB
Randolph College, Maier Museum of Art, Lynchburg VA
Reading Public Museum, Reading PA
Rensselaer Newman Foundation Chapel + Cultural Center, The Gallery at the Chapel & Cultural Center, Troy NY
Jack Richard Gallery, Almond Tea Museum & Jane Williams Galleries, Divisions of Studios of Jack Richard, Cuyahoga Falls OH
Rijksmuseum Twenthe, Rijksmuseum Twenthe, Enschede
Rubin Museum of Art, New York NY
Ryerss Victorian Museum & Library, Philadelphia PA
Saginaw Art Museum, Saginaw MI
Saint Bonaventure University, Regina A Quick Center for the Arts, Saint Bonaventure NY
Saint Johnsbury Athenaeum, Saint Johnsbury VT
Saint Joseph's Oratory, Museum, Montreal PQ
Saint Mary's College of California, Hearst Art Gallery, Moraga CA
Saint Olaf College, Flaten Art Museum, Northfield MN
Saint Peter's College, Art Gallery, Jersey City NJ
San Carlos Cathedral, Monterey CA
Seneca-Iroquois National Museum, Salamanca NY
Severoceska Galerie Vytvarneho Umeni v Litomericich, North Bohemian Gallery of Fine Arts in Litomerice, Litomerice
Shaker Village of Pleasant Hill, Harrodsburg KY
Norton Simon, Pasadena CA
Slovenska Narodna Galeria, Slovak National Gallery, Bratislava
The Society of the Cincinnati at Anderson House, Washington DC
Soprintendenza per I beni storici artistici ed etnoantropologici per le province di Mantova Brescia e Cremona, Museo di Palazzo Ducale, Mantua
Southern Baptist Theological Seminary, Joseph A Callaway Archaeological Museum, Louisville KY
Southern Methodist University, Meadows Museum, Dallas TX
The Speed Art Museum, Louisville KY
Spertus Institute of Jewish Studies, Chicago IL
Springville Museum of Art, Springville UT
Stanford University, Cantor Arts Center at Stanford University, Stanford CA
The State Museum of Fine Arts of Tatarstan Republic, Kazan
State University of New York at Binghamton, Binghamton University Art Museum, Binghamton NY
Staten Island Museum, Staten Island NY
Stone Quarry Hill Art Park, Winner Gallery, Cazenovia NY
Suomen Kansallismuseo, National Museum of Finland, Helsinki
Swedish American Museum Association of Chicago, Chicago IL
Switzerland County Historical Society Inc, Switzerland County Historical Museum, Vevay IN
Syracuse University, SUArt Galleries, Syracuse NY
Taft Museum of Art, Cincinnati OH
Taos, La Hacienda de Los Martinez, Taos NM
The Temple-Tifereth Israel, The Temple Museum of Religious Art, Beachwood OH
Texas Tech University, Museum of Texas Tech University, Lubbock TX
Timken Museum of Art, San Diego CA
Tohono Chul Park, Tucson AZ
Topeka & Shawnee County Public Library, Alice C Sabatini Gallery, Topeka KS
Tulane University, University Art Collection, New Orleans LA
Tver Art Gallery, Tver
Ukrainian Canadian Archives & Museum of Alberta, Edmonton AB
UMLAUF Sculpture Garden & Museum, Austin TX

United Society of Shakers, Shaker Museum, New Gloucester ME
Universalmuseum Joanneum GmbH, Graz
University of California, Berkeley, The Magnes Collection of Jewish Art & Life, Berkeley CA
University of California, Los Angeles, Fowler Museum at UCLA, Los Angeles CA
University of California, Santa Barbara, University Art Museum, Santa Barbara CA
University of Chicago, Oriental Institute, Chicago IL
University of Chicago, Smart Museum of Art, Chicago IL
University of Georgia, Georgia Museum of Art, Athens GA
University of Illinois at Urbana-Champaign, Krannert Art Museum and Kinkead Pavilion, Champaign IL
University of Miami, Lowe Art Museum, Coral Gables FL
University of Michigan, Museum of Art, Ann Arbor MI
University of Missouri, Museum of Art & Archaeology, Columbia MO
University of New Mexico, The Harwood Museum of Art, Taos NM
University of Texas at Austin, Blanton Museum of Art, Austin TX
University of Utah, Utah Museum of Fine Arts, Salt Lake City UT
University of Wisconsin-Madison, Chazen Museum of Art, Madison WI
Ursinus College, Philip & Muriel Berman Museum of Art, Collegeville PA
Valparaiso University, Brauer Museum of Art, Valparaiso IN
Vesterheim Norwegian-American Museum, Decorah IA
Vorarlberg Museum, Bregenz
Walker Art Gallery, Liverpool
Wallace State Community College, Evelyn Burrow Museum, Hanceville AL
Washington University, Mildred Lane Kemper Art Museum, Saint Louis MO
Waterworks Visual Arts Center, Salisbury NC
Wellesley College, Davis Museum & Cultural Center, Wellesley MA
Williams College, Museum of Art, Williamstown MA
Winston-Salem State University, Diggs Gallery, Winston Salem NC
Worcester Art Museum, Worcester MA
World Erotic Art Museum, Miami Beach FL
Yeshiva University Museum, New York NY
Zigler Art Museum, Jennings LA

RENAISSANCE ART

Arnot Art Museum, Elmira NY
Art Gallery of Nova Scotia, Halifax NS
The Art Museum at the University of Kentucky, Lexington KY
Art Without Walls Inc, New York NY
Badisches Landesmuseum, Karlsruhe
Ball State University, Museum of Art, Muncie IN
The Baltimore Museum of Art, Baltimore MD
Baroda Museum and Picture Gallery, Baroda
Bayerische Staatsgemaldesammlungen/Bavarian State Art Galleries, Alte Pinakothek, Munich
Beaverbrook Art Gallery, Fredericton NB
Birmingham Museum of Art, Birmingham AL
Blanden Memorial Art Museum, Fort Dodge IA
Brigham Young University, Museum of Art, Provo UT
Bucknell University, Edward & Marthann Samek Art Gallery, Lewisburg PA
Caramoor Center for Music & the Arts, Inc, Rosen House at Caramoor, Katonah NY
Charles Allis Art Museum, Milwaukee WI
Chhatrapati Shivaji Maharaj Vastu Sangrahalaya, Mumbai
Cincinnati Art Museum, Cincinnati Art Museum, Cincinnati OH
City of El Paso, El Paso TX
Colgate University, Picker Art Gallery, Hamilton NY
College of William & Mary, Muscarelle Museum of Art, Williamsburg VA
Columbia Museum of Art, Columbia SC
Columbus Museum of Art, Columbus OH
Comune di Genova - Direzione Cultura Settore Musei, Museo di Strada Nuova Palazzo Rosso, Genoa
The Courtauld Institute of Art, The Courtauld Gallery, London
Cummer Museum of Art & Gardens, Museum & Library, Jacksonville FL
The Currier Museum of Art, Manchester NH
Dartmouth College, Hood Museum of Art, Hanover NH
Denver Art Museum, Denver CO

Designmuseum Danmark, Copenhagen
Detroit Institute of Arts, Detroit MI
Dickinson College, The Trout Gallery, Carlisle PA
Duke University, Nasher Museum of Art at Duke University, Durham NC
Dundee City Council Leisure & Communities Department, The McManus: Dundee's Art Gallery & Museum, Dundee
East Los Angeles College, Vincent Price Art Museum, Monterey Park CA
Ellen Noel Art Museum of the Permian Basin, Odessa TX
Fairfield University, Thomas J Walsh Art Gallery, Fairfield CT
Flint Institute of Arts, Flint MI
Florence Museum, Florence SC
Fondazione Musei Civici Di Venezia, Museo Correr, Venice
Forest Lawn Museum, Glendale CA
The Frick Art & Historical Center, Inc, Frick Art Museum, Pittsburgh PA
Frick Collection, New York NY
Galleria Nazionale dell'Umbria, Umbrian National Gallery, Perugia
General Board of Discipleship, The United Methodist Church, The Upper Room Chapel & Museum, Nashville TN
Germanisches Nationalmuseum, Nuremberg
The Ghent Museum of Fine Arts, Ghent
Guadalupe Historic Foundation, Santuario de Guadalupe, Santa Fe NM
Guilford College, Art Gallery, Greensboro NC
Hartwick College, Foreman Gallery, Oneonta NY
Hartwick College, The Yager Museum, Oneonta NY
Edna Hibel, Hibel Museum of Art, Jupiter FL
Hillwood Museum & Gardens Foundation, Hillwood Estate Museum & Gardens, Washington DC
The Hispanic Society of America, Museum & Library, New York NY
Howard University, Gallery of Art, Washington DC
Independent Administrative Institution National Museum of Art, The National Museum of Western Art, Tokyo
The Israel Museum, Jerusalem, Samuel & Saidye Bronfman Archaeology Wing, Jerusalem
The Israel Museum, Jerusalem, Jerusalem
Bob Jones University Museum & Gallery Inc, Greenville SC
Joslyn Art Museum, Omaha NE
Kereszteny Muzeum, Christian Museum, Esztergom
Knights of Columbus Supreme Council, Knights of Columbus Museum, New Haven CT
Kunsthistorisches Museum Vienna, Museum of Fine Arts, Vienna
Kunstmuseum Solothurn, Solothurn Art Museum, Solothurn
La Salle University Art Museum, Philadelphia PA
Lahore Museum, Lahore
Le Grand Curtius, Musée d'Ansembourg, Liege
Leeds Museums & Galleries, Leeds
Mabee-Gerrer Museum of Art, Shawnee OK
Magyar Nemzeti Muzeum - Hungarian National Museum, Budapest
Marquette University, Haggerty Museum of Art, Milwaukee WI
Massillon Museum, Massillon OH
Menil Foundation, Inc, The Menil Collection, Houston TX
Milwaukee County War Memorial Inc., Villa Terrace Decorative Arts Museum, Milwaukee WI
Ministry of Cultural Affairs, Bangladesh National Museum, Dhaka
Moravska Galerie v Brne, Moravian Gallery in Brno, Brno
The Morgan Library & Museum, Museum, New York NY
Musea Brugge, Onze-Lieve-Vrouwekerk/Church of Our Lady, Bruges
Musee des Beaux-Arts d'Orleans, Historical & Archaeological Museum of Orleans, Orleans
Musee des Beaux-Arts d'Orleans, Museum of Fine Arts, Orleans
Musee des Beaux-Arts/Palais des Archeveques, Museum of Fine Arts, Tours
Musee et Chateau de Chantilly (MUSEE CONDE), Chantilly
Musee National d'Histoire et d'Art Luxembourg, Luxembourg City
Museen der Stadt Koln, Museum Schnutgen, Cologne
Museen der Stadt Koln, Wallraf-Richartz-Museum, Cologne

REPRODUCTIONS

Wiregrass Museum of Art, Dothan AL
World Erotic Art Museum, Miami Beach FL
Yokohama Museum of Art, Yokohama

RESTORATIONS

Amon Carter Museum of American Art, Fort Worth TX
Arnot Art Museum, Elmira NY
Art & Culture Center of Hollywood, Art Gallery/Multidisciplinary Cultural Center, Hollywood FL
Art Without Walls Inc, New York NY
Bakehouse Art Complex, Inc, Miami FL
Banco de la Republica Museo del Oro, Museo del Oro, Bogota
Bard College, Center for Curatorial Studies and the Hessel Museum of Art, Annandale-on-Hudson NY
Baroda Museum and Picture Gallery, Baroda
Belle Grove Inc., Belle Grove Plantation, Middletown VA
Belvedere Museum, Osterreichische Galerie Belvedere, Vienna
Canadian Museum of Civilization, Gatineau PQ
Center for Puppetry Arts, Atlanta GA
City of Austin Parks & Recreation, O. Henry Museum, Austin TX
City of Nome Alaska, Carrie M McLain Memorial Museum, Nome AK
City of San Antonio, San Antonio TX
City of San Rafael, Falkirk Cultural Center, San Rafael CA
Coastal Arts League Museum, Half Moon Bay CA
Craigdarroch Castle Historical Museum Society, Victoria BC
Cranford Historical Society, Cranford NJ
Cripple Creek District Museum, Cripple Creek CO
Crocker Art Museum, Sacramento CA
Culberson County Historical Museum, Van Horn TX
Denver Art Museum, Denver CO
Detroit Institute of Arts, Detroit MI
Dundurn Castle, Hamilton ON
Establishment Public du Chateau du Rusee, Et du Dophine national de versailles, Versailles
Florence Museum, Florence SC
Fondazione Musei Civici Di Venezia, Galleria Internazionale d'Arte Moderna di Ca'Pesaro, Venice
Galeria Mesta Bratislavy, Bratislava City Gallery, Bratislava
Genesee Country Village & Museum, John L Wehle Art Gallery, Mumford NY
Glanmore National Historic Site of Canada, Belleville ON
Glessner House Museum, Chicago IL
Gunston Hall Plantation, Mason Neck VA
Heard Museum, Phoenix AZ
Hecht Museum, Haifa
Heritage Museum & Cultural Center, Baker LA
Historic Hudson Valley, Pocantico Hills NY
Huguenot Historical Society of New Paltz Galleries, New Paltz NY
Illinois Historic Preservation Agency, Bishop Hill State Historic Site, Bishop Hill IL
Indiana Landmarks, Morris-Butler House, Indianapolis IN
The Israel Museum, Jerusalem, Billy Rose Art Garden, Jerusalem
J.M.W. Turner Museum, Sarasota FL
Thomas Jefferson, Monticello, Charlottesville VA
Joe Gish's Old West Museum, Fredericksburg TX
Johns Hopkins University, Homewood Museum, Baltimore MD
Kunstmuseum Thun, Thun
Lafayette Science Museum & Planetarium, Lafayette LA
Lahore Museum, Lahore
Landmark Society of Western New York, Inc, The Campbell-Whittlesey House Museum, Rochester NY
Latvijas Nacionalais Makslas Muzejs, Arsenals Exhibition Hall, Riga
Laumeier Sculpture Park, Saint Louis MO
Leeds Museums & Galleries, Leeds
Lincoln County Historical Association, Inc, 1811 Old Lincoln County Jail & Lincoln County Museum, Wiscasset ME
Lockwood-Mathews Mansion Museum, Norwalk CT
Magyar Nemzeti Muzeum - Hungarian National Museum, Budapest
Milwaukee County War Memorial Inc., Villa Terrace Decorative Arts Museum, Milwaukee WI
Ministry of Cultural Affairs, Bangladesh National Museum, Dhaka

Ministry of the Arts & Multiculturalism, National Museum & Art Gallery, Port of Spain
Minnesota Historical Society, Minnesota State Capitol Historic Site, St Paul MN
Mission San Luis Rey de Francia, Mission San Luis Rey Museum, Oceanside CA
Mission San Miguel Museum, San Miguel CA
Mohave Museum of History & Arts, Kingman AZ
Moravska Galerie v Brne, Moravian Gallery in Brno, Brno
Mount Vernon Hotel Museum & Garden, New York NY
Musee National d'Histoire et d'Art Luxembourg, Luxembourg City
Musei Civici di Padova - Cappella Degli Scrovegni, Musei Civici Agli Eremitani (Civic Museum) - Scrovegni Chapel, Padua
Museo Cerralbo, Madrid
Museum fur Kunst und Gewerbe Hamburg, Hamburg
Museum Het Prinsenhof, Delft
Museum of Chinese in America, New York NY
Museum Plantin-Moretus/Prentenkabinet, Antwerp
Museum zu Allerheiligen, Schaffhausen
Muzej za Umjetnost i Obrt, Museum of Arts & Crafts, Zagreb
Muzeul de Istorie Nationala Si Arheologie Constanta, National History & Archaeology Museum, Constanta
Muzeul National Brukenthal, Brukenthal Palace & European Art Gallery, Sibiu
Muzeum Narodowe, National Museum in Poznan, Poznan
Nara Kokuritsu Hakubutsu-Kan, Nara National Museum, Nara
Narodna Galerija, National Gallery of Slovenia, Ljubljana
National Museum of Fine Arts of Moldova, Chisinau
The National Park Service, United States Department of the Interior, Statue of Liberty National Monument & The Ellis Island Immigration Museum, Washington DC
National Society of Colonial Dames of America in the State of Maryland, Mount Clare Museum House, Baltimore MD
National Trust for Historic Preservation, Shadows-on-the-Teche, New Iberia LA
Nebraska State Capitol, Lincoln NE
Nelson Mandela Bay Municipality, Nelson Mandela Metropolitan Art Museum, Port Elizabeth
The Nelson-Atkins Museum of Art, Kansas City MO
Nevada Northern Railway Museum, Ely NV
New Hampshire Antiquarian Society, Hopkinton Historical Society, Hopkinton NH
New York State Office of Parks Recreation & Historic Preservation, John Jay Homestead State Historic Site, Katonah NY
Elisabet Ney, Austin TX
The Noble Maritime Collection, Staten Island NY
Norwich Free Academy, Slater Memorial Museum, Norwich CT
The Ohio Historical Society, Inc, Campus Martius Museum & Ohio River Museum, Marietta OH
Old Dartmouth Historical Society, New Bedford Whaling Museum, New Bedford MA
Page-Walker Arts & History Center, Cary NC
Panhandle-Plains Historical Museum, Canyon TX
Pennsylvania Historical & Museum Commission, Railroad Museum of Pennsylvania, Harrisburg PA
Piatt Castles, West Liberty OH
Please Touch Museum, Philadelphia PA
Queens College, City University of New York, Godwin-Ternbach Museum, Flushing NY
Rabindra Bhavan Art Gallery, Lalit Kala Akademi (National Academy of Art), New Delhi
Red Deer & District Museum & Archives, Red Deer AB
Jack Richard Gallery, Almond Tea Museum & Jane Williams Galleries, Divisions of Studios of Jack Richard, Cuyahoga Falls OH
Ringwood Manor House Museum, Ringwood NJ
Saint Peter's College, Art Gallery, Jersey City NJ
Savitsky Karakalpakstan State Art Museum, Nukus
Shirley Plantation Foundation, Charles City VA
Slovenska Narodna Galeria, Slovak National Gallery, Bratislava
Nelda C & H J Lutcher Stark, Stark Museum of Art, Orange TX
The State Museum of Fine Arts of Tatarstan Republic, Kazan
State University of New York at Binghamton, Binghamton University Art Museum, Binghamton NY

Switzerland County Historical Society Inc, Switzerland County Historical Museum, Vevay IN
Trust Authority, Museum of the Great Plains, Lawton OK
Tver Art Gallery, Tver
U Gallery, New York NY
United States Capitol, Architect of the Capitol, Washington DC
United States Figure Skating Association, World Figure Skating Museum & Hall of Fame, Colorado Springs CO
University of Michigan, Museum of Art, Ann Arbor MI
Vermilion County Museum Society, Danville IL
Victoria Mansion - Morse Libby House, Portland ME
Vietnam Fine Arts Museum, Hanoi
West Baton Rouge Parish, West Baton Rouge Museum, Port Allen LA
Wilfrid Laurier University, Robert Langen Art Gallery, Waterloo ON
Willard House & Clock Museum, Inc, North Grafton MA
Wistariahurst Museum, Holyoke MA
Woodlawn/The Pope-Leighey, Mount Vernon VA
Yarmouth County Historical Society, Yarmouth County Museum & Archives, Yarmouth NS

SCRIMSHAW

Academy of the New Church, Glencairn Museum, Bryn Athyn PA
Alaska Department of Education, Division of Libraries, Archives & Museums, Sheldon Jackson Museum, Sitka AK
Alaska Heritage Museum at Wells Fargo, Anchorage AK
American Folk Art Museum, New York NY
Autry National Center, Southwest Museum of the American Indian, Mt. Washington Campus, Los Angeles CA
Baroda Museum and Picture Gallery, Baroda
Blauvelt Demarest Foundation, Hiram Blauvelt Art Museum, Oradell NJ
Channel Islands Maritime Museum, Oxnard CA
Chatham Historical Society, The Atwood House Museum, Chatham MA
City of Nome Alaska, Carrie M McLain Memorial Museum, Nome AK
Craftsmen's Guild of Mississippi, Inc, Mississippi Crafts Center, Ridgeland MS
Dartmouth Heritage Museum, Dartmouth NS
Dawson City Museum & Historical Society, Dawson City YT
Denver Art Museum, Denver CO
Detroit Institute of Arts, Detroit MI
Dundee City Council Leisure & Communities Department, The McManus: Dundee's Art Gallery & Museum, Dundee
Eiteljorg Museum of American Indians & Western Art, Indianapolis IN
Gallery One Visual Arts Center, Ellensburg WA
Greenland National Museum & Archives, Nuuk
Heritage Museums & Gardens, Sandwich MA
Illinois State Museum, ISM Lockport Gallery, Chicago Gallery & Southern Illinois Art Gallery, Springfield IL
Independence Seaport Museum, Philadelphia PA
Iroquois Indian Museum, Howes Cave NY
The Israel Museum, Jerusalem, Billy Rose Art Garden, Jerusalem
Kings County Historical Society & Museum, Hampton NB
Koshare Indian Museum, Inc, La Junta CO
Launceston City Council, Queen Victoria Museum and Art Gallery, Launceston
Lincoln County Historical Association, Inc, 1811 Old Lincoln County Jail & Lincoln County Museum, Wiscasset ME
The Mariners' Museum, Newport News VA
Mennello Museum of American Art, Orlando FL
Ministry of Cultural Affairs, Bangladesh National Museum, Dhaka
The Museum, Greenwood SC
Muzeul de Istorie Nationala Si Arheologie Constanta, National History & Archaeology Museum, Constanta
National Museums Scotland, National Museum of Scotland, Edinburgh
Naval Historical Center, The Navy Museum, Washington DC
New Jersey State Museum, Fine Art Bureau, Trenton NJ

Norwich Free Academy, Slater Memorial Museum, Norwich CT
Old Dartmouth Historical Society, New Bedford Whaling Museum, New Bedford MA
Penobscot Marine Museum, Searsport ME
Porter-Phelps-Huntington Foundation, Inc, Historic House Museum, Hadley MA
Princeton University, Princeton University Art Museum, Princeton NJ
Pump House Center for the Arts, Chillicothe OH
Reading Public Museum, Reading PA
The Rooms Corporation of Newfoundland & Labrador, Saint John's NF
Saint Joseph Museum, Saint Joseph MO
San Francisco Maritime National Historical Park, Maritime Museum, San Francisco CA
Sheldon Museum & Cultural Center, Inc, Sheldon Museum & Cultural Center, Haines AK
Ships of the Sea Maritime Museum, Savannah GA
South Street Seaport Museum, New York NY
State University of New York at Binghamton, Binghamton University Art Museum, Binghamton NY
Staten Island Museum, Staten Island NY
Stauth Foundation & Museum, Stauth Memorial Museum, Montezuma KS
Suomen Kansallismuseo, National Museum of Finland, Helsinki
University of Alaska, Museum of the North, Fairbanks AK
University of Miami, Lowe Art Museum, Coral Gables FL
Whalers Village Museum, Lahaina HI
World Erotic Art Museum, Miami Beach FL

SCULPTURE

A.I.R. Gallery, Brooklyn NY
Abington Art Center, Jenkintown PA
Academy Art Museum, Easton MD
Academy of the New Church, Glencairn Museum, Bryn Athyn PA
African American Museum in Philadelphia, Philadelphia PA
Akron Art Museum, Akron OH
Alabama Department of Archives & History, Museum of Alabama, Montgomery AL
Alaska Heritage Museum at Wells Fargo, Anchorage AK
Albany Institute of History & Art, Albany NY
Alberta College of Art & Design, Illingworth Kerr Gallery, Calgary AB
Albin Polasek Museum & Sculpture Gardens, Winter Park FL
Albright College, Freedman Gallery, Reading PA
Albuquerque Museum of Art & History, Albuquerque NM
Allentown Art Museum, Allentown PA
American Sport Art Museum and Archives, Daphne AL
American Swedish Institute, Minneapolis MN
American University, Katzen Art Center Gallery, New York NY
Americas Society Art Gallery, New York NY
Amon Carter Museum of American Art, Fort Worth TX
Anchorage Museum at Rasmuson Center, Anchorage AK
Walter Anderson, Ocean Springs MS
Anna Maria College, Saint Luke's Gallery, Paxton MA
Arab American National Museum, Dearborn MI
ARC Gallery, Chicago IL
Arizona Museum For Youth, Mesa AZ
Arizona State University, ASU Art Museum, Tempe AZ
Arnold Mikelson Mind & Matter Art Gallery, White Rock BC
Arnot Art Museum, Elmira NY
Art & Culture Center of Hollywood, Art Gallery/Multidisciplinary Cultural Center, Hollywood FL
Art Center of Battle Creek, Battle Creek MI
Art Community Center, Art Center of Corpus Christi, Corpus Christi TX
Art Gallery of Alberta, Edmonton AB
Art Gallery of Bancroft Inc, Bancroft ON
Art Gallery of Nova Scotia, Halifax NS
Art Gallery of Ontario, Toronto ON
Art Gallery of South Australia, Adelaide
The Art Museum at the University of Kentucky, Lexington KY
Art Museum of Greater Lafayette, Lafayette IN
Art Museum of Southeast Texas, Beaumont TX
Art Without Walls Inc, New York NY

Arts Council of Fayetteville-Cumberland County, The Arts Center, Fayetteville NC
Asbury College, Student Center Gallery, Wilmore KY
Asian Art Museum of San Francisco, Chong-Moon Lee Ctr for Asian Art and Culture, San Francisco CA
Aspen Art Museum, Aspen CO
Associates for Community Development, The Arts Center, Inc, Martinsburg WV
Auburn University, Julie Collins Smith Museum, Auburn AL
Augustana College, Augustana College Art Museum, Rock Island IL
Avampato Discovery Museum, The Clay Center for Arts & Sciences, Charleston WV
Badisches Landesmuseum, Karlsruhe
Baldwin-Wallace College, Fawick Art Gallery, Berea OH
The Baltimore Museum of Art, Baltimore MD
Baroda Museum and Picture Gallery, Baroda
The Bartlett Museum, Amesbury MA
Baruch College of the City University of New York, Sidney Mishkin Gallery, New York NY
Bates College, Museum of Art, Lewiston ME
Baton Rouge Gallery, Center For Contemporary Art, Baton Rouge LA
Bayerische Staatsgemaldesammlungen/Bavarian State Art Galleries, Neue Pinakothek, Munich
Baylor University, Martin Museum of Art, Waco TX
Beaumont Art League, Beaumont TX
Bellagio Resort & Casino, Bellagio Gallery of Fine Art, Las Vegas NV
Bellevue Arts Museum, Bellevue WA
Beloit College, Wright Museum of Art, Beloit WI
Belskie Museum, Closter NJ
Belvedere Museum, Osterreichische Galerie Belvedere, Vienna
Bemis Center for Contemporary Arts, Omaha NE
The Benini Foundation & Sculpture Ranch, Johnson City TX
Bennington Museum, Bennington VT
Bergstrom-Mahler Museum, Neenah WI
Berman Museum, Anniston AL
Bethany College, Mingenback Art Center, Lindsborg KS
Biggs Museum of American Art, Dover DE
Birger Sandzen Memorial Gallery, Lindsborg KS
Birmingham Museum of Art, Birmingham AL
Blanden Memorial Art Museum, Fort Dodge IA
Blauvelt Demarest Foundation, Hiram Blauvelt Art Museum, Oradell NJ
Board of Parks & Recreation, The Parthenon, Nashville TN
Boise Art Museum, Boise ID
Bone Creek Museum of Agrarian Art, David City NE
Booth Western Art Museum, Cartersville GA
Roy Boyd, Chicago IL
Brandywine Conservancy, Brandywine River Museum, Chadds Ford PA
Bread & Puppet Theater, Bread & Puppet Museum, Barton VT
Brick Store Museum, Kennebunk ME
Brigham Young University, B F Larsen Gallery, Provo UT
Brigham Young University, Museum of Art, Provo UT
Bradford Brinton, Big Horn WY
Bronx Community College (CUNY), Hall of Fame for Great Americans, Bronx NY
Brookgreen Gardens, Murrells Inlet SC
Brown University, Haffenreffer Museum of Anthropology, Providence RI
Bruce Museum, Inc, Greenwich CT
Bucknell University, Edward & Marthann Samek Art Gallery, Lewisburg PA
Burke Arts Council, Jailhouse Galleries, Morganton NC
The Butler Institute of American Art, Art Museum, Youngstown OH
Cabot's Old Indian Pueblo Museum, Desert Hot Springs CA
California Center for the Arts, Escondido Museum, Escondido CA
California State University Stanislaus, University Art Gallery, Turlock CA
California State University, Long Beach, University Art Museum, Long Beach CA
California State University, Northridge, Art Galleries, Northridge CA
Calvin College, Center Art Gallery, Grand Rapids MI
Cameron Art Museum, Wilmington NC
Canadian Clay and Glass Gallery, Waterloo ON
Canadian Museum of Civilization, Gatineau PQ
Canadian Wildlife & Wilderness Art Museum, Ottawa ON

Canajoharie Library & Art Gallery, Arkell Museum of Canajoharie, Canajoharie NY
Canton Museum of Art, Canton OH
Cape Ann Historical Association, Cape Ann Museum, Gloucester MA
Cape Cod Museum of Art Inc, Dennis MA
Capital University, Schumacher Gallery, Columbus OH
Caramoor Center for Music & the Arts, Inc, Rosen House at Caramoor, Katonah NY
Carlsbad Museum & Art Center, Carlsbad NM
Carnegie Center for Art & History, New Albany IN
Carnegie Museums of Pittsburgh, Carnegie Museum of Art, Pittsburgh PA
Cedar Rapids Museum of Art, Cedar Rapids IA
Central Methodist University, Ashby-Hodge Gallery of American Art, Fayette MO
Centro de Arte Moderna, CAM - Calouste Gulbenkian Foundation, Lisbon
Chhatrapati Shivaji Maharaj Vastu Sangrahalaya, Mumbai
Chinati Foundation, Marfa TX
Chinese Culture Foundation, Center Gallery, San Francisco CA
Chrysler Museum of Art, Norfolk VA
Church of Jesus Christ of Latter-Day Saints, Museum of Church History & Art, Salt Lake City UT
Cincinnati Art Museum, Cincinnati Art Museum, Cincinnati OH
City of Antwerp, Middleheim Openluchtmuseum voor Beeldhouwkunst, Antwerp
City of Brea, Art Gallery, Brea CA
City of Cedar Falls, Iowa, James & Meryl Hearst Center for the Arts & Sculpture Garden, Cedar Falls IA
City of Fayette, Alabama, Fayette Art Museum, Fayette AL
City of Fremont, Olive Hyde Art Gallery, Fremont CA
City of Ketchikan Museum Dept, Ketchikan AK
City of Mason City, Charles H MacNider Museum, Mason City IA
The City of Petersburg Museums, Petersburg VA
City of Pittsfield, Berkshire Artisans, Pittsfield MA
City of Port Angeles, Port Angeles Fine Arts Center & Webster Woods Art Park, Port Angeles WA
Sterling & Francine Clark, Williamstown MA
The Cleveland Museum of Art, Cleveland OH
Clinton Art Association, River Arts Center, Clinton IA
Coastal Arts League Museum, Half Moon Bay CA
Colgate University, Picker Art Gallery, Hamilton NY
College of Saint Benedict, Gorecki Gallery & Gallery Lounge, Saint Joseph MN
College of Saint Rose, Art Gallery, Albany NY
College of William & Mary, Muscarelle Museum of Art, Williamsburg VA
Colorado Historical Society, Colorado History Museum, Denver CO
Columbia County Historical Society, Columbia County Museum and Library, Kinderhook NY
Columbus Museum, Columbus GA
Columbus Museum of Art, Columbus OH
Comune di Genova - Direzione Cultura Settore Musei, Museo di Strada Nuova Palazzo Rosso, Genoa
Concord Museum, Concord MA
Concordia University, Leonard & Bina Ellen Art Gallery, Montreal PQ
Congregation Beth Israel's Plotkin Judaica Museum, Scottsdale AZ
Coos Art Museum, Coos Bay OR
Cornell Museum of Art and American Culture, Delray Beach FL
Cornell University, Herbert F Johnson Museum of Art, Ithaca NY
Cornwall Gallery Society, Cornwall Regional Art Gallery, Cornwall ON
The Courtauld Institute of Art, The Courtauld Gallery, London
Coutts Museum of Art, Inc, El Dorado KS
Craft and Folk Art Museum (CAFAM), Los Angeles CA
Craftsmen's Guild of Mississippi, Inc, Mississippi Crafts Center, Ridgeland MS
Cranbrook Art Museum, Bloomfield Hills MI
Crazy Horse Memorial, Indian Museum of North America, Native American Educational & Cultural Center & Crazy Horse Memorial Library (Reference), Crazy Horse SD
Creighton University, Lied Art Gallery, Omaha NE
Cripple Creek District Museum, Cripple Creek CO
Crocker Art Museum, Sacramento CA
Cummer Museum of Art & Gardens, Museum & Library, Jacksonville FL
The Currier Museum of Art, Manchester NH

Dahesh Museum of Art, Greenwich CT
Danville Museum of Fine Arts & History, Danville VA
Dartmouth College, Hood Museum of Art, Hanover NH
Daum Museum of Contemporary Art, Sedalia MO
Davidson College, William H Van Every Jr & Edward
    M Smith Galleries, Davidson NC
Davistown Museum, Liberty Location, Liberty ME
Deines Cultural Center, Russell KS
Del Mar College, Joseph A Cain Memorial Art Gallery,
    Corpus Christi TX
Delaware Art Museum, Wilmington DE
DeLeon White Gallery, Toronto ON
Delta Blues Museum, Clarksdale MS
Denison University, Art Gallery, Granville OH
Denver Art Museum, Denver CO
Detroit Institute of Arts, Detroit MI
Detroit Zoological Institute, Wildlife Interpretive
    Gallery, Royal Oak MI
The Dinosaur Museum, Blanding UT
Dixie State College, Robert N & Peggy Sears Gallery,
    Saint George UT
Doncaster Museum and Art Gallery, Doncaster
Drexel University, Drexel Collection, Philadelphia PA
Dublin City Gallery The Hugh Lane, Dublin
Dundee City Council Leisure & Communities
    Department, The McManus: Dundee's Art Gallery
    & Museum, Dundee
Durham Art Guild, Durham NC
DuSable Museum of African American History,
    Chicago IL
Eastern Illinois University, Tarble Arts Center,
    Charleston IL
Edmundson Art Foundation, Inc, Des Moines Art
    Center, Des Moines IA
Eiteljorg Museum of American Indians & Western Art,
    Indianapolis IN
El Camino College Art Gallery, Torrance CA
Ellen Noel Art Museum of the Permian Basin, Odessa
    TX
Elmhurst Art Museum, Elmhurst IL
Emory University, Michael C Carlos Museum, Atlanta
    GA
Environment Canada - Parks Canada, Laurier House,
    National Historic Site, Ottawa ON
Erie Art Museum, Erie PA
Wharton Esherick, Paoli PA
Eskimo Museum, Churchill MB
Establishment Public du Chateau du Rusee, Et du
    Dophine national de versailles, Versailles
Eula Mae Edwards Museum & Gallery, Clovis NM
Evanston Historical Society, Charles Gates Dawes
    House, Evanston IL
Evansville Museum of Arts, History & Science,
    Evansville IN
Evergreen State College, Evergreen Gallery, Olympia
    WA
Everhart Museum, Scranton PA
Everson Museum of Art, Syracuse NY
Federal Reserve Board, Art Gallery, Washington DC
Ferenczy Muzeum, Szentendre
Fetherston Foundation, Packwood House Museum,
    Lewisburg PA
Fisk University, Aaron Douglas Gallery, Nashville TN
Fitton Center for Creative Arts, Hamilton OH
Five Civilized Tribes Museum, Muskogee OK
Flint Institute of Arts, Flint MI
Florida International University, The Patricia & Phillip
    Frost Art Museum, Miami FL
Florida State University, Museum of Fine Arts,
    Tallahassee FL
Florida State University, John & Mable Ringling
    Museum of Art, Sarasota FL
Florida State University and Central Florida
    Community College, The Appleton Museum of Art,
    Ocala FL
Fondazione Musei Civici Di Venezia, Galleria
    Internazionale d'Arte Moderna di Ca'Pesaro, Venice
Fondazione Musei Civici Di Venezia, Museo Correr,
    Venice
Fondo del Sol, Visual Art & Media Center, Washington
    DC
Edsel & Eleanor Ford, Grosse Pointe Shores MI
Forest Lawn Museum, Glendale CA
Fort Collins Museum of Art, Inc., Fort Collins CO
Fort Smith Regional Art Museum, Fort Smith AR
Fort Wayne Museum of Art, Inc, Fort Wayne IN
The Frick Art & Historical Center, Inc, Frick Art
    Museum, Pittsburgh PA
Frick Collection, New York NY
Fruitlands Museum, Inc, Harvard MA
Fuller Craft Museum, Brockton MA

Gadsden Museum of Fine Arts, Inc, Gadsden Museum
    of Art and History, Gadsden AL
Gala-Salvador Dali Foundation Museums, Casa Museu
    Castell Gala Dali, Figueres
Gala-Salvador Dali Foundation Museums, Salvador
    Dali Foundation, Figueres
Galerie Montcalm, Gatineau PQ
Galleria Nazionale dell'Umbria, Umbrian National
    Gallery, Perugia
Gallery Moos Ltd, Toronto ON
Gallery One Visual Arts Center, Ellensburg WA
Gaston County Museum of Art & History, Dallas NC
General Board of Discipleship, The United Methodist
    Church, The Upper Room Chapel & Museum,
    Nashville TN
Genesee Country Village & Museum, John L Wehle Art
    Gallery, Mumford NY
George Washington University, The Dimock Gallery,
    Washington DC
Georgetown College Gallery, Georgetown KY
Georgetown University, Art Collection, Washington DC
Georgian Court University, M Christina Geis Gallery,
    Lakewood NJ
Germanisches Nationalmuseum, Nuremberg
The Ghent Museum of Fine Arts, Ghent
Girard College, Stephen Girard Collection, Philadelphia
    PA
Glanmore National Historic Site of Canada, Belleville
    ON
Gloridale Partnership, National Museum of
    Woodcarving, Custer SD
Gocseji Muzeum, Zalaegerszeg
Gonzaga University, Art Gallery, Spokane WA
Greenville College, Richard W Bock Sculpture
    Collection, Almira College House, Greenville IL
Grounds for Sculpture, Hamilton NJ
Guggenheim Museum Soho, New York NY
Solomon R Guggenheim, New York NY
Guild Hall of East Hampton, Inc, Guild Hall Museum,
    East Hampton NY
Guilford College, Art Gallery, Greensboro NC
Hartwick College, Foreman Gallery, Oneonta NY
Hartwick College, The Yager Museum, Oneonta NY
Harvard University, Museum & Garden, Washington
    DC
Hawkes Bay Art Gallery and Museum, Napier
Headley-Whitney Museum, Lexington KY
Heard Museum, Phoenix AZ
Hebrew Union College, Skirball Cultural Center, Los
    Angeles CA
Hebrew Union College Museum, Jewish Institute of
    Religion Museum, New York NY
Hecht Museum, Haifa
Henry County Museum & Cultural Arts Center, Clinton
    MO
Henry Gallery Association, Henry Art Gallery, Seattle
    WA
Henry Morrison Flagler Museum, Palm Beach FL
Patrick Henry, Red Hill National Memorial, Brookneal
    VA
Gertrude Herbert, Augusta GA
Heritage Center of Lancaster County Museum,
    Lancaster PA
Heritage Center, Inc, Pine Ridge SD
Heritage Malta, National Museum of Fine Arts, Valletta
Hermitage Foundation Museum, Norfolk VA
Edna Hibel, Hibel Museum of Art, Jupiter FL
Hickory Museum of Art, Inc, Hickory NC
Higgins Armory Museum, Worcester MA
High Desert Museum, Bend OR
Hill-Stead Museum, Farmington CT
Hillwood Museum & Gardens Foundation, Hillwood
    Estate Museum & Gardens, Washington DC
The Hispanic Society of America, Museum & Library,
    New York NY
Historical Society of Cheshire County, Keene NH
Historisches und Volkerkundemuseum, Historical
    Museum, St Gallen
Hofstra University, Hofstra University Museum,
    Hempstead NY
Holter Museum of Art, Helena MT
Housatonic Community College, Housatonic Museum
    of Art, Bridgeport CT
Howard University, Gallery of Art, Washington DC
Hoyt Center for the Arts, New Castle PA
The Hudson River Museum, Yonkers NY
Hunter Museum of American Art, Chattanooga TN
Huntsville Museum of Art, Huntsville AL
Hyde Collection Trust, Glens Falls NY
Hyde Park Art Center, Chicago IL

Illinois State Museum, ISM Lockport Gallery, Chicago
    Gallery & Southern Illinois Art Gallery, Springfield
    IL
Illinois State University, University Galleries, Normal
    IL
Independence Historical Museum & Art Center,
    Independence KS
Independent Administrative Institution National
    Institutes for Cultural Heritage, Tokyo National
    Museum, Tokyo
Independent Administrative Institution National
    Museum of Art, The National Museum of Western
    Art, Tokyo
Indiana Landmarks, Morris-Butler House, Indianapolis
    IN
Indiana State Museum, Indianapolis IN
Institute of American Indian Arts, Museum of
    Contemporary Native Arts, Santa Fe NM
Institute of Puerto Rican Arts & Culture, Chicago IL
Institute of Puerto Rican Culture, Museo Fuerte Conde
    de Mirasol, Vieques PR
INTAR Gallery, New York NY
Iredell Museums, Statesville NC
Iroquois Indian Museum, Howes Cave NY
Irving Arts Center, Galleries & Sculpture Garden,
    Irving TX
The Israel Museum, Jerusalem, Billy Rose Art Garden,
    Jerusalem
The Israel Museum, Jerusalem, Samuel & Saidye
    Bronfman Archaeology Wing, Jerusalem
The Israel Museum, Jerusalem, Jerusalem
J.M.W. Turner Museum, Sarasota FL
Jacksonville University, Alexander Brest Museum &
    Gallery, Jacksonville FL
Japan Society, Inc, Japan Society Gallery, New York
    NY
Thomas Jefferson, Monticello, Charlottesville VA
Joe Gish's Old West Museum, Fredericksburg TX
John B Aird Gallery, Toronto ON
The John L. Clarke Western Art Gallery & Memorial
    Museum, East Glacier Park MT
John Weaver Sculpture Collection, Hope BC
Bob Jones University Museum & Gallery Inc,
    Greenville SC
Jordan National Gallery of Fine Arts, Amman
Joslyn Art Museum, Omaha NE
Kamloops Art Gallery, Kamloops BC
Kenosha Public Museums, Kenosha WI
Kent State University, School of Art Galleries, Kent
    OH
Kentucky Derby Museum, Louisville KY
Kentucky Museum of Art and Craft, Louisville KY
Keresztenny Muzeum, Christian Museum, Esztergom
Keystone Gallery, Scott City KS
Kimbell Art Foundation, Kimbell Art Museum, Fort
    Worth TX
Kings County Historical Society & Museum, Hampton
    NB
Kirchner Museum Davos, Davos
Kirkland Museum of Fine & Decorative Art, Denver
    CO
Kitchener-Waterloo Art Gallery, Kitchener ON
Knights of Columbus Supreme Council, Knights of
    Columbus Museum, New Haven CT
Knoxville Museum of Art, Knoxville TN
Koninklijk Museum voor Schone Kunsten Antwerpen,
    Royal Museum of Fine Arts, Antwerp
Krasl Art Center, Saint Joseph MI
Kroller-Muller Museum, Otterlo
Kunsthalle Bremen, Bremen Art Gallery, Bremen
Kunsthistorisches Museum Vienna, Museum of Fine
    Arts, Vienna
Kunstmuseum Bern, Musee des Beaux-Arts de Berne,
    Bern
Kunstmuseum Solothurn, Solothurn Art Museum,
    Solothurn
Kunstmuseum Thun, Thun
Kyiv Museum of Russian Art, Kyiv
L'Universite Laval, Ecole des Arts Visuels, Quebec PQ
La Salle University Art Museum, Philadelphia PA
Lafayette College, Lafayette College Art Galleries,
    Easton PA
Lafayette Science Museum & Planetarium, Lafayette
    LA
Langston University, Melvin B Tolson Black Heritage
    Center, Langston OK
Latino Art Museum, Pomona CA
Latvijas Nacionalais Makslas Muzejs, Arsenals
    Exhibition Hall, Riga
Latvijas Nacionalais Makslas Muzejs, Latvian National
    Museum of Art, Riga
Laumeier Sculpture Park, Saint Louis MO

National Museums Scotland, National Museum of
  Scotland, Edinburgh
The National Park Service, United States Department
  of the Interior, Statue of Liberty National
  Monument & The Ellis Island Immigration
  Museum, Washington DC
National Portrait Gallery, Smithsonian Institution,
  Washington DC
National Portrait Gallery, London
National Trust for Historic Preservation, Chesterwood,
  Stockbridge MA
Nationalmuseum, Stockholm
Navajo Nation, Navajo Nation Museum, Window Rock
  AZ
Naval Historical Center, The Navy Museum,
  Washington DC
Nebraska Game and Parks Commission, Arbor Lodge
  State Historical Park & Morton Mansion, Nebraska
  City NE
Nebraska State Capitol, Lincoln NE
Nebraska Wesleyan University, Elder Gallery, Lincoln
  NE
Nelson Mandela Bay Municipality, Nelson Mandela
  Metropolitan Art Museum, Port Elizabeth
The Nelson-Atkins Museum of Art, Kansas City MO
The Nemours Foundatioin, Nemours Mansion &
  Gardens, Wilmington DE
Neville Public Museum of Brown County, Green Bay
  WI
New Britain Museum of American Art, New Britain
  CT
New Brunswick Museum, Saint John NB
New Canaan Historical Society, New Canaan CT
New Jersey State Museum, Fine Art Bureau, Trenton
  NJ
New Orleans Artworks at New Orleans Glassworks &
  Printmaking Studio, New Orleans LA
New Orleans Museum of Art, New Orleans LA
New Visions Gallery, Inc, Marshfield WI
New York State Military Museum and Veterans
  Research Center, Saratoga Springs NY
New York State Office of Parks Recreation & Historic
  Preservation, John Jay Homestead State Historic
  Site, Katonah NY
New York Studio School of Drawing, Painting &
  Sculpture, Gallery, New York NY
Newport Art Museum and Association, Newport RI
Elisabet Ney, Austin TX
Niagara University, Castellani Art Museum, Niagara
  NY
Niigata Prefectural Museum of Modern Art, Niigata
No Man's Land Historical Society, No Man's Land
  Museum, Goodwell OK
Isamu Noguchi, Isamu Noguchi Garden Museum, Long
  Island City NY
Noordbrabants Museum, Hertogenbosch
Norsk Sjøfartsmuseum, Norwegian Maritime Museum,
  Oslo
North Carolina Central University, NCCU Art Museum,
  Durham NC
North Carolina State University, Gregg Museum of Art
  & Design, Raleigh NC
North Dakota State University, Memorial Union
  Gallery, Fargo ND
Northern Kentucky University, Galleries, Highland
  Heights KY
Northwestern College, Denler Art Gallery, Orange City
  IA
Norton Museum of Art, West Palm Beach FL
Norwich Free Academy, Slater Memorial Museum,
  Norwich CT
Nova Scotia College of Art and Design, Anna
  Leonowens Gallery, Halifax NS
Noyes Art Gallery, Lincoln NE
The Noyes Museum of Art, Oceanville NJ
Oakland Museum of California, Art Dept, Oakland CA
Oberlin College, Allen Memorial Art Museum, Oberlin
  OH
The Ogden Museum of Southern Art, University of
  New Orleans, New Orleans LA
Ogunquit Museum of American Art, Ogunquit ME
Ohio Historical Society, National Afro-American
  Museum & Cultural Center, Wilberforce OH
Ohio University, Kennedy Museum of Art, Athens OH
Oklahoma City Museum of Art, Oklahoma City OK
Olana State Historic Site, Hudson NY
Old Dartmouth Historical Society, New Bedford
  Whaling Museum, New Bedford MA
The Old Jail Art Center, Albany TX
Olivet College, Armstrong Collection, Olivet MI
Orlando Museum of Art, Orlando FL
Oshkosh Public Museum, Oshkosh WI

Otis College of Art & Design, Ben Maltz Gallery, Los
  Angeles CA
Owensboro Museum of Fine Art, Owensboro KY
Pacific - Asia Museum, Pasadena CA
Page-Walker Arts & History Center, Cary NC
Palm Springs Art Museum, Palm Springs CA
Panhandle-Plains Historical Museum, Canyon TX
Paris Gibson Square, Museum of Art, Great Falls MT
Parrish Art Museum, Water Mill NY
Patrimonio Nacional, Palacios de la Granja y Riofrio,
  Madrid
Pennsylvania Historical & Museum Commission,
  Railroad Museum of Pennsylvania, Harrisburg PA
The Pennsylvania State University, Palmer Museum of
  Art, University Park PA
Phelps County Historical Society, Nebraska Prairie
  Museum, Holdrege NE
Philadelphia History Museum, Philadelphia PA
Philadelphia Museum of Art, Rodin Museum of
  Philadelphia, Philadelphia PA
Philbrook Museum of Art, Tulsa OK
Phillips Academy, Addison Gallery of American Art,
  Andover MA
George Phippen, Phippen Museum - Art of the
  American West, Prescott AZ
Phoenix Art Museum, Phoenix AZ
Piedmont Arts Association, Martinsville VA
Pinacoteca Provinciale, Bari
Pioneer Town, Pioneer Museum of Western Art,
  Wimberley TX
Plains Art Museum, Fargo ND
Polish Museum of America, Chicago IL
Polk Museum of Art, Lakeland FL
The Pomona College, Claremont CA
Ponca City Cultural Center & Museum, Ponca City OK
Portland Art Museum, Portland OR
Portland Museum of Art, Portland ME
Pretoria Art Museum, Municipal Art Gallery, Pretoria
Prince George Art Gallery, Prince George BC
Princeton University, Princeton University Art Museum,
  Princeton NJ
PS1 Contemporary Art Center, Long Island City NY
Pump House Center for the Arts, Chillicothe OH
Purchase College, Neuberger Museum of Art, Purchase
  NY
Pyramid Hill Sculpture Park & Museum, Hamilton OH
Queen's University, Agnes Etherington Art Centre,
  Kingston ON
Queens College, City University of New York,
  Godwin-Ternbach Museum, Flushing NY
R W Norton Art Foundation, R W Norton Art Gallery,
  Shreveport LA
Rabindra Bhavan Art Gallery, Lalit Kala Akademi
  (National Academy of Art), New Delhi
Radio-Canada SRC CBC, Georges Goguen CBC Art
  Gallery, Moncton NB
Reading Public Museum, Reading PA
Real Art Ways (RAW), Hartford CT
Red River Valley Museum, Vernon TX
Frederic Remington, Ogdensburg NY
Rensselaer Newman Foundation Chapel + Cultural
  Center, The Gallery at the Chapel & Cultural
  Center, Troy NY
Reynolda House Museum of American Art,
  Winston-Salem NC
Jack Richard Gallery, Almond Tea Museum & Jane
  Williams Galleries, Divisions of Studios of Jack
  Richard, Cuyahoga Falls OH
Rider University, Art Gallery, Lawrenceville NJ
Rijksmuseum Twenthe, Rijksmuseum Twenthe,
  Enschede
Rogue Community College, Wiseman Gallery -
  FireHouse Gallery, Grants Pass OR
Rollins College, George D & Harriet W Cornell Fine
  Arts Museum, Winter Park FL
Roswell Artist-in-Residence Foundation, Anderson
  Museum of Contemporary Art, Roswell NM
Roswell Museum & Art Center, Roswell NM
Royal Arts Foundation, Belcourt Castle, Newport RI
Royal Museums of Fine Arts of Belgium, Brussels
Rubin Museum of Art, New York NY
C M Russell, Great Falls MT
Rutgers University, Stedman Art Gallery, Camden NJ
Rutgers, The State University of New Jersey, Zimmerli
  Art Museum, Rutgers University, New Brunswick
  NJ
Ryerss Victorian Museum & Library, Philadelphia PA
Saco Museum, Saco ME
Saginaw Art Museum, Saginaw MI
Saint Anselm College, Alva de Mars Megan Chapel Art
  Center, Manchester NH

Saint Augustine Historical Society, Oldest House
  Museum Complex, Saint Augustine FL
Saint Bonaventure University, Regina A Quick Center
  for the Arts, Saint Bonaventure NY
Saint Clair County Community College, Jack R
  Hennesey Art Galleries, Port Huron MI
Saint Johnsbury Athenaeum, Saint Johnsbury VT
Saint Joseph's Oratory, Museum, Montreal PQ
Saint Mary's College of California, Hearst Art Gallery,
  Moraga CA
St Mary's College of Maryland, The Dwight Frederick
  Boyden Gallery, St Mary's City MD
Saint Olaf College, Flaten Art Museum, Northfield MN
Saint Peter's College, Art Gallery, Jersey City NJ
Saint-Gaudens National Historic Site, Cornish NH
Salisbury House Foundation, Salisbury House and
  Garden, Des Moines IA
Salisbury University, Ward Museum of Wildfowl Art,
  Salisbury MD
San Carlos Cathedral, Monterey CA
San Diego Museum of Art, San Diego CA
San Diego State University, University Art Gallery, San
  Diego CA
San Francisco Museum of Modern Art, Artist Gallery,
  San Francisco CA
San Francisco Museum of Modern Art, San Francisco
  CA
San Jose Museum of Art, San Jose CA
Santa Barbara Museum of Art, Santa Barbara CA
Santa Clara University, de Saisset Museum, Santa Clara
  CA
Santa Monica Museum of Art, Santa Monica CA
Santarella Museum & Gardens, Tyringham MA
Savitsky Karakalpakstan State Art Museum, Nukus
Schweinfurth Art Center, Auburn NY
Scottsdale Cultural Council, Scottsdale Museum of
  Contemporary Art, Scottsdale AZ
Scripps College, Clark Humanities Museum, Claremont
  CA
Scripps College, Ruth Chandler Williamson Gallery,
  Claremont CA
Sculpture Space, Inc, Utica NY
Seattle Art Museum, Olympic Park, Seattle WA
Seneca-Iroquois National Museum, Salamanca NY
1708 Gallery, Richmond VA
Severoceska Galerie Vytvarneho Umeni v Litomericich,
  North Bohemian Gallery of Fine Arts in Litomerice,
  Litomerice
Ella Sharp, Jackson MI
Sheldon Art Galleries, Saint Louis MO
Norton Simon, Pasadena CA
Slovenska Narodna Galeria, Slovak National Gallery,
  Bratislava
The Society of the Cincinnati at Anderson House,
  Washington DC
Socrates Sculpture Park, Long Island City NY
Sonoma State University, University Art Gallery,
  Rohnert Park CA
Soprintendenza per I beni storici artistici ed
  etnoantropologici per le province di Mantova
  Brescia e Cremona, Museo di Palazzo Ducale,
  Mantua
South Carolina Artisans Center, Walterboro SC
South Carolina State Museum, Columbia SC
South Dakota State University, South Dakota Art
  Museum, Brookings SD
South Shore Arts, Munster IN
Southeastern Center for Contemporary Art, Winston
  Salem NC
Southern Baptist Theological Seminary, Joseph A
  Callaway Archaeological Museum, Louisville KY
Southern Illinois University Carbondale, University
  Museum, Carbondale IL
Southern Methodist University, Meadows Museum,
  Dallas TX
Southern Ohio Museum Corporation, Southern Ohio
  Museum, Portsmouth OH
Spartanburg Art Museum, Spartanburg SC
The Speed Art Museum, Louisville KY
Spertus Institute of Jewish Studies, Chicago IL
Springfield Art Museum, Springfield MO
Springfield Museums, Michele & Donald D'Amour
  Museum of Fine Arts, Springfield MA
Staatsgalerie Stuttgart, Stuttgart
Stamford Museum & Nature Center, Stamford CT
Stanford University, Cantor Arts Center at Stanford
  University, Stanford CA
The State Museum of Fine Arts of Tatarstan Republic,
  Kazan
State University of New York at Binghamton,
  Binghamton University Art Museum, Binghamton
  NY

Yale University, Yale Center for British Art, New Haven CT

Yale University, Yale University Art Gallery, New Haven CT

Yerba Buena Center for the Arts, San Francisco CA

Yeshiva University Museum, New York NY

Yokohama Museum of Art, Yokohama

York University, Art Gallery of York University, Toronto ON

Yuma Fine Arts Association, Yuma Art Center, Yuma AZ

Zacheta - National Gallery of Art, Kordegarda Gallery, Warsaw

Zigler Art Museum, Jennings LA

SILVER

Adams County Historical Society, Gettysburg PA

Alabama Department of Archives & History, Museum of Alabama, Montgomery AL

Albany Institute of History & Art, Albany NY

Albuquerque Museum of Art & History, Albuquerque NM

Allentown Art Museum, Allentown PA

Americas Society Art Gallery, New York NY

Arnot Art Museum, Elmira NY

Art & Culture Center of Hollywood, Art Gallery/Multidisciplinary Cultural Center, Hollywood FL

Art Gallery of South Australia, Adelaide

The Art Museum at the University of Kentucky, Lexington KY

Art Without Walls Inc, New York NY

The Baltimore Museum of Art, Baltimore MD

Baroda Museum and Picture Gallery, Baroda

The Bartlett Museum, Amesbury MA

Bayerisches Nationalmuseum, Bavarian National Museum, Munich

Biggs Museum of American Art, Dover DE

Birmingham Museum of Art, Birmingham AL

Bradford Brinton, Big Horn WY

Canadian Museum of Civilization, Gatineau PQ

Cape Ann Historical Association, Cape Ann Museum, Gloucester MA

Chatillon-DeMenil House Foundation, Chatillon-DeMenil House, Saint Louis MO

Cincinnati Art Museum, Cincinnati Art Museum, Cincinnati OH

The City of Petersburg Museums, Petersburg VA

Sterling & Francine Clark, Williamstown MA

College of William & Mary, Muscarelle Museum of Art, Williamsburg VA

Colorado Historical Society, Colorado History Museum, Denver CO

Columbus Museum, Columbus GA

Concord Museum, Concord MA

Congregation Beth Israel's Plotkin Judaica Museum, Scottsdale AZ

Cooper-Hewitt National Design Museum, Smithsonian Institution, New York NY

The Courtauld Institute of Art, The Courtauld Gallery, London

Craft and Folk Art Museum (CAFAM), Los Angeles CA

Cranbrook Art Museum, Bloomfield Hills MI

Crocker Art Museum, Sacramento CA

The Currier Museum of Art, Manchester NH

DAR Museum, National Society Daughters of the American Revolution, Washington DC

Dartmouth College, Hood Museum of Art, Hanover NH

Delaware Division of Historical & Cultural Affairs, Dover DE

Denison University, Art Gallery, Granville OH

Denver Art Museum, Denver CO

Designmuseum Danmark, Copenhagen

Detroit Institute of Arts, Detroit MI

Doncaster Museum and Art Gallery, Doncaster

Dundee City Council Leisure & Communities Department, The McManus: Dundee's Art Gallery & Museum, Dundee

Dundurn Castle, Hamilton ON

Ellen Noel Art Museum of the Permian Basin, Odessa TX

Elverhoj Museum of History and Art, Solvang CA

Environment Canada - Parks Canada, Laurier House, National Historic Site, Ottawa ON

Erie Art Museum, Erie PA

Erie County Historical Society, Erie PA

Evanston Historical Society, Charles Gates Dawes House, Evanston IL

Fetherston Foundation, Packwood House Museum, Lewisburg PA

Fishkill Historical Society, Van Wyck Homestead Museum, Fishkill NY

Fitton Center for Creative Arts, Hamilton OH

Flint Institute of Arts, Flint MI

Florence Museum, Florence SC

Fondazione Musei Civici Di Venezia, Museo Correr, Venice

Forest Lawn Museum, Glendale CA

The Frick Art & Historical Center, Inc, Frick Art Museum, Pittsburgh PA

Fuller Craft Museum, Brockton MA

Gadsden Museum of Fine Arts, Inc, Gadsden Museum of Art and History, Gadsden AL

Gallery One Visual Arts Center, Ellensburg WA

Georgetown University, Art Collection, Washington DC

Germanisches Nationalmuseum, Nuremberg

Girard College, Stephen Girard Collection, Philadelphia PA

Glanmore National Historic Site of Canada, Belleville ON

Glessner House Museum, Chicago IL

Hammond-Harwood House Association, Inc, Hammond-Harwood House, Annapolis MD

Hancock County Trustees of Public Reservations, Woodlawn: Museum, Gardens & Park, Ellsworth ME

Haystack Mountain School of Crafts, Deer Isle ME

Headley-Whitney Museum, Lexington KY

Headquarters Fort Monroe, Dept of Army, Casemate Museum, Hampton VA

Heard Museum, Phoenix AZ

Hecht Museum, Haifa

Henry Morrison Flagler Museum, Palm Beach FL

Patrick Henry, Red Hill National Memorial, Brookneal VA

Heritage Center of Lancaster County Museum, Lancaster PA

Heritage Center, Inc, Pine Ridge SD

Heritage Malta, National Museum of Fine Arts, Valletta

Heritage Museum Association, Inc, The Heritage Museum of Northwest Florida, Valparaiso FL

Hill-Stead Museum, Farmington CT

Hillwood Museum & Gardens Foundation, Hillwood Estate Museum & Gardens, Washington DC

The Hispanic Society of America, Museum & Library, New York NY

Historic Cherry Hill, Albany NY

Historic Deerfield, Inc, Deerfield MA

The Historic New Orleans Collection, Royal Street Galleries, New Orleans LA

Historic Newton, Newton MA

Historical Society of Cheshire County, Keene NH

History Museum of Mobile, Mobile AL

Hoyt Center for the Arts, New Castle PA

Hunter Museum of American Art, Chattanooga TN

Illinois State Museum, ISM Lockport Gallery, Chicago Gallery & Southern Illinois Art Gallery, Springfield IL

Independence Seaport Museum, Philadelphia PA

Independent Administrative Institution National Institutes for Cultural Heritage, Tokyo National Museum, Tokyo

Indiana Landmarks, Morris-Butler House, Indianapolis IN

Indiana State Museum, Indianapolis IN

Institute of American Indian Arts, Museum of Contemporary Native Arts, Santa Fe NM

Iroquois Indian Museum, Howes Cave NY

The Israel Museum, Jerusalem, Billy Rose Art Garden, Jerusalem

The Israel Museum, Jerusalem, Samuel & Saidye Bronfman Archaeology Wing, Jerusalem

Jamestown-Yorktown Foundation, Jamestown Settlement, Williamsburg VA

John B Aird Gallery, Toronto ON

Johns Hopkins University, Evergreen Museum & Library, Baltimore MD

Johns Hopkins University, Homewood Museum, Baltimore MD

Bob Jones University Museum & Gallery Inc, Greenville SC

Kenosha Public Museums, Kenosha WI

Kentucky Museum of Art and Craft, Louisville KY

Keresteny Muzeum, Christian Museum, Esztergom

Kings County Historical Society & Museum, Hampton NB

Kirkland Museum of Fine & Decorative Art, Denver CO

Knights of Columbus Supreme Council, Knights of Columbus Museum, New Haven CT

Kunsthistorisches Museum Vienna, Museum of Fine Arts, Vienna

Latino Art Museum, Pomona CA

Launceston City Council, Queen Victoria Museum and Art Gallery, Launceston

Le Grand Curtius, Musée d'Ansembourg, Liege

Leeds Museums & Galleries, Leeds

Liberty Hall Historic Site, Liberty Hall Museum, Frankfort KY

Lightner Museum, Saint Augustine FL

Lincoln County Historical Association, Inc, 1811 Old Lincoln County Jail & Lincoln County Museum, Wiscasset ME

Lincolnshire County Council, The Collection: Art & Archaeology in Lincolnshire, Lincoln

Livingston County Historical Society, Museum, Geneseo NY

The Long Island Museum of American Art, History & Carriages, Stony Brook NY

Longue Vue House & Gardens, New Orleans LA

Los Angeles County Museum of Natural History, William S Hart Museum, Newhall CA

Louisiana Department of Culture, Recreation & Tourism, Louisiana State Museum, New Orleans LA

Louisiana State University, Museum of Art, Baton Rouge LA

Loyola University Chicago, Loyola University Museum of Art, Chicago IL

Lyman Allyn Art Museum, New London CT

Magyar Nemzeti Muzeum - Hungarian National Museum, Budapest

Manchester City Galleries, Manchester Art Gallery, Manchester

Marblehead Museum & Historical Society, Jeremiah Lee Mansion, Marblehead MA

Marblehead Museum & Historical Society, Marblehead MA

Jacques Marchais, Staten Island NY

Maryland Historical Society, Museum of Maryland History, Baltimore MD

Maysville, Kentucky Gateway Museum Center, Maysville KY

McDowell House & Apothecary Shop, Danville KY

Mennello Museum of American Art, Orlando FL

Milwaukee County War Memorial Inc, Villa Terrace Decorative Arts Museum, Milwaukee WI

Ministry of Cultural Affairs, Bangladesh National Museum, Dhaka

Ministry of Culture & Tourism, The Delphi Museum, 10th Ephorate of Prehistoric & Classical Antiquities, Delphi

Mobile Museum of Art, Mobile AL

James Monroe, Fredericksburg VA

Montclair Art Museum, Montclair NJ

Mount Vernon Hotel Museum & Garden, New York NY

Munson-Williams-Proctor Arts Institute, Museum of Art, Utica NY

Musea Brugge, Gruuthuse Museum, Bruges

Musea Brugge, Sint-Janshospitaal, Bruges

Musee des Beaux-Arts d'Orleans, Museum of Fine Arts, Orleans

Musee des Beaux-Arts/Palais des Archeveques, Museum of Fine Arts, Tours

Musee des Maitres et Artisans du Quebec, Montreal PQ

Musee National d'Histoire et d'Art Luxembourg, Luxembourg City

Museen der Stadt Koln, Museum Schnutgen, Cologne

Musees Royaux d'Art et d'Histoire, Royal Museums of Art and History, Brussels

Museo Cerralbo, Madrid

Museo De Las Americas, Denver CO

Museo de Navarra, Pamplona

Museu de Evora, Evora

Museu de Grao Vasco, Viseu

Museum De Lakenhal, Leiden

Museum fur Kunst und Gewerbe Hamburg, Hamburg

Museum Het Prinsenhof, Delft

Museum of Arts & Design, New York NY

The Museum of Arts & Sciences Inc, Daytona Beach FL

Museum of Decorative Arts in Prague, Prague

Museum of Fine Arts, Boston MA

Museum of Fine Arts Houston, Bayou Bend Collection & Gardens, Houston TX

Museum of Fine Arts, Houston, Rienzi Center for European Decorative Arts, Houston TX

Museum of Fine Arts, Saint Petersburg, Florida, Inc, Saint Petersburg FL

Museum of Northern Arizona, Flagstaff AZ

Museum of Southern History, Houston TX

Museum zu Allerheiligen, Schaffhausen

SILVERSMITHING

SOUTHWESTERN ART

INTAR Gallery, New York NY
The Israel Museum, Jerusalem, Billy Rose Art Garden, Jerusalem
James Dick Foundation, Festival - Institute, Round Top TX
Jefferson County Open Space, Hiwan Homestead Museum, Evergreen CO
Kenosha Public Museums, Kenosha WI
Kentucky Museum of Art and Craft, Louisville KY
LA County Museum of Art, Los Angeles CA
Lakeview Museum of Arts & Sciences, Peoria IL
Leanin' Tree Museum & Sculpture Garden of Western Art, Boulder CO
Luther College, Fine Arts Collection, Decorah IA
Mabee-Gerrer Museum of Art, Shawnee OK
Mennello Museum of American Art, Orlando FL
Mesa Arts Center, Mesa Contemporary Arts Museum, Mesa AZ
Metropolitan State University of Denver, Center for Visual Art, Denver CO
Mexican Museum, San Francisco CA
Midwest Museum of American Art, Elkhart IN
Mills College Art Museum, Oakland CA
Ministry of Cultural Affairs, Bangladesh National Museum, Dhaka
Arthur Roy Mitchell, A.R. Mitchell Museum, Trinidad CO
Museo De Las Americas, Denver CO
Museum of New Mexico, Palace of Governors, Santa Fe NM
Museum of Northern Arizona, Flagstaff AZ
Narodni Muzej Crne Gore, National Museum of Montenegro, Cetinje
National Museum of Wildlife Art of the Unites States, Jackson WY
National Park Service, Hubbell Trading Post National Historic Site, Ganado AZ
New Mexico State University, Art Gallery, Las Cruces NM
New Visions Gallery, Inc, Marshfield WI
No Man's Land Historical Society, No Man's Land Museum, Goodwell OK
North Carolina State University, Gregg Museum of Art & Design, Raleigh NC
North Dakota State University, Memorial Union Gallery, Fargo ND
Northern Arizona University, Art Museum & Galleries, Flagstaff AZ
Ohio Historical Society, National Road-Zane Grey Museum, Columbus OH
Ohio University, Kennedy Museum of Art, Athens OH
Owensboro Museum of Fine Art, Owensboro KY
Panhandle-Plains Historical Museum, Canyon TX
The Frank Phillips, Woolaroc Museum, Bartlesville OK
George Phippen, Phippen Museum - Art of the American West, Prescott AZ
Piedmont Arts Association, Martinsville VA
Pope County Historical Society, Pope County Museum, Glenwood MN
Rabindra Bhavan Art Gallery, Lalit Kala Akademi (National Academy of Art), New Delhi
Riverside Metropolitan Museum, Riverside CA
Roswell Museum & Art Center, Roswell NM
Royal Ontario Museum, Toronto ON
C M Russell, Great Falls MT
Saginaw Art Museum, Saginaw MI
Salisbury House Foundation, Salisbury House and Garden, Des Moines IA
South Dakota State University, South Dakota Art Museum, Brookings SD
Springfield Art Museum, Springfield MO
Springville Museum of Art, Springville UT
Nelda C & H J Lutcher Stark, Stark Museum of Art, Orange TX
Stone Quarry Hill Art Park, Winner Gallery, Cazenovia NY
Taos, Ernest Blumenschein Home & Studio, Taos NM
Texas Ranger Hall of Fame & Museum, Waco TX
Texas Tech University, Museum of Texas Tech University, Lubbock TX
Tohono Chul Park, Tucson AZ
Towson University, Asian Arts & Culture Center, Towson MD
Trust Authority, Museum of the Great Plains, Lawton OK
Tucson Museum of Art and Historic Block, Tucson AZ
University of Colorado at Colorado Springs, Gallery of Contemporary Art, Colorado Springs CO
University of Georgia, Georgia Museum of Art, Athens GA
University of Illinois at Urbana-Champaign, Krannert Art Museum and Kinkead Pavilion, Champaign IL

University of Massachusetts, Amherst, University Gallery, Amherst MA
University of Miami, Lowe Art Museum, Coral Gables FL
University of Nevada, Reno, Sheppard Contemporary & University Galleries, Reno NV
University of New Mexico, The Harwood Museum of Art, Taos NM
University of New Mexico, University of New Mexico Art Museum, Albuquerque NM
University of Pennsylvania, Museum of Archaeology & Anthropology, Philadelphia PA
University of Texas at Austin, Blanton Museum of Art, Austin TX
University of Utah, Utah Museum of Fine Arts, Salt Lake City UT
University of Wisconsin-Madison, Chazen Museum of Art, Madison WI
Washburn University, Mulvane Art Museum, Topeka KS
Wichita Art Museum, Wichita KS
Yuma Fine Arts Association, Yuma Art Center, Yuma AZ

STAINED GLASS

Academy of the New Church, Glencairn Museum, Bryn Athyn PA
Adams County Historical Society, Gettysburg PA
Albuquerque Museum of Art & History, Albuquerque NM
American Art Museum, Smithsonian Institution, Washington DC
Art Community Center, Art Center of Corpus Christi, Corpus Christi TX
Art Gallery of Bancroft Inc, Bancroft ON
Art Without Walls Inc, New York NY
Asbury College, Student Center Gallery, Wilmore KY
Balzekas Museum of Lithuanian Culture, Chicago IL
Baroda Museum and Picture Gallery, Baroda
Bertha V B Lederer Fine Arts Gallery-Suny Geneseo, Bertha V B Lederer Fine Arts Gallery, Geneseo NY
Bronx Community College (CUNY), Hall of Fame for Great Americans, Bronx NY
Cameron Art Museum, Wilmington NC
Canadian Clay and Glass Gallery, Waterloo ON
Canadian Museum of Civilization, Gatineau PQ
Caramoor Center for Music & the Arts, Inc, Rosen House at Caramoor, Katonah NY
Chatham Historical Society, The Atwood House Museum, Chatham MA
Church of Jesus Christ of Latter-Day Saints, Museum of Church History & Art, Salt Lake City UT
City of Mason City, Charles H MacNider Museum, Mason City IA
The City of Petersburg Museums, Petersburg VA
Corcoran Gallery of Art, Washington DC
Craftsmen's Guild of Mississippi, Inc, Mississippi Crafts Center, Ridgeland MS
Craigdarroch Castle Historical Museum Society, Victoria BC
Cripple Creek District Museum, Cripple Creek CO
Detroit Institute of Arts, Detroit MI
Dundee City Council Leisure & Communities Department, The McManus: Dundee's Art Gallery & Museum, Dundee
Dundurn Castle, Hamilton ON
Erie County Historical Society, Erie PA
Evanston Historical Society, Charles Gates Dawes House, Evanston IL
Fetherston Foundation, Packwood House Museum, Lewisburg PA
Forest Lawn Museum, Glendale CA
Fuller Craft Museum, Brockton MA
Galleria Nazionale dell'Umbria, Umbrian National Gallery, Perugia
Gallery One Visual Arts Center, Ellensburg WA
General Board of Discipleship, The United Methodist Church, The Upper Room Chapel & Museum, Nashville TN
Germanisches Nationalmuseum, Nuremberg
Headquarters Fort Monroe, Dept of Army, Casemate Museum, Hampton VA
Hebrew Union College - Jewish Institute of Religion, Skirball Museum Cincinnati, Cincinnati OH
Henry County Museum & Cultural Arts Center, Clinton MO
Hermitage Foundation Museum, Norfolk VA
Higgins Armory Museum, Worcester MA
Historic Hudson Valley, Pocantico Hills NY
The History Center in Tompkins County, Ithaca NY
Hoyt Center for the Arts, New Castle PA

Hunter Museum of American Art, Chattanooga TN
Illinois State Museum, ISM Lockport Gallery, Chicago Gallery & Southern Illinois Art Gallery, Springfield IL
Iredell Museums, Statesville NC
Jekyll Island Museum, Jekyll Island GA
John B Aird Gallery, Toronto ON
Johns Hopkins University, Evergreen Museum & Library, Baltimore MD
Bob Jones University Museum & Gallery Inc, Greenville SC
Kenosha Public Museums, Kenosha WI
Kereszteny Muzeum, Christian Museum, Esztergom
Knights of Columbus Supreme Council, Knights of Columbus Museum, New Haven CT
LaGrange Art Museum, LaGrange GA
Latino Art Museum, Pomona CA
Le Grand Curtius, Musée d'Ansembourg, Liege
LeMoyne Art Foundation, Center for the Visual Arts, Tallahassee FL
Lightner Museum, Saint Augustine FL
Louisiana State University, Student Union Art Gallery, Baton Rouge LA
Loyola University Chicago, Loyola University Museum of Art, Chicago IL
Madison Museum of Fine Art, Madison GA
The Mariners' Museum, Newport News VA
Milwaukee County War Memorial Inc., Villa Terrace Decorative Arts Museum, Milwaukee WI
Musee National d'Histoire et d'Art Luxembourg, Luxembourg City
Museen der Stadt Koln, Museum Schnutgen, Cologne
Musees Royaux d'Art et d'Histoire, Royal Museums of Art and History, Brussels
Museo Cerralbo, Madrid
Museum De Lakenhal, Leiden
Museum of Arts & Design, New York NY
The Museum of Arts & Sciences Inc, Daytona Beach FL
Museum of the Plains Indian & Crafts Center, Browning MT
Museum zu Allerheiligen, Schaffhausen
Muzej za Umjetnost i Obrt, Museum of Arts & Crafts, Zagreb
Muzeul National Brukenthal, Blue House & Romanian Art Gallery, Sibiu
National Museum of Ceramic Art & Glass, Baltimore MD
Nebraska Game and Parks Commission, Arbor Lodge State Historical Park & Morton Mansion, Nebraska City NE
Nelson Mandela Bay Municipality, Nelson Mandela Metropolitan Art Museum, Port Elizabeth
Neustadt Collection of Tiffany Glass, Long Island City NY
New Jersey State Museum, Fine Art Bureau, Trenton NJ
Norwich Free Academy, Slater Memorial Museum, Norwich CT
Noyes Art Gallery, Lincoln NE
Owensboro Museum of Fine Art, Owensboro KY
Panhandle-Plains Historical Museum, Canyon TX
Piedmont Arts Association, Martinsville VA
Pilgrim Society, Pilgrim Hall Museum, Plymouth MA
Princeton University, Princeton University Art Museum, Princeton NJ
Pump House Center for the Arts, Chillicothe OH
Queens College, City University of New York, Godwin-Ternbach Museum, Flushing NY
Reading Public Museum, Reading PA
Frederic Remington, Ogdensburg NY
Rosemount Museum, Inc, Pueblo CO
Royal Arts Foundation, Belcourt Castle, Newport RI
Saint Louis County Historical Society, St. Louis County Historical Society, Duluth MN
Saint Peter's College, Art Gallery, Jersey City NJ
South Carolina Artisans Center, Walterboro SC
South Dakota State University, South Dakota Art Museum, Brookings SD
The Speed Art Museum, Louisville KY
Spertus Institute of Jewish Studies, Chicago IL
The State Museum of Fine Arts of Tatarstan Republic, Kazan
Suan Pakkad Palace Museum, Bangkok
Suomen Kansallismuseo, National Museum of Finland, Helsinki
Swedish American Museum Association of Chicago, Chicago IL
Switzerland County Historical Society Inc, Switzerland County Historical Museum, Vevay IN
Lillian & Coleman Taube Museum of Art, Minot ND

TAPESTRIES

University of Manitoba, Faculty of Architecture Exhibition Centre, Winnipeg MB
University of Michigan, Museum of Art, Ann Arbor MI
University of Pennsylvania, Museum of Archaeology & Anthropology, Philadelphia PA
University of Pittsburgh, University Art Gallery, Pittsburgh PA
University of San Diego, Founders' Gallery, San Diego CA
University of Utah, Utah Museum of Fine Arts, Salt Lake City UT
Ursinus College, Philip & Muriel Berman Museum of Art, Collegeville PA
Vesterheim Norwegian-American Museum, Decorah IA
Village of Potsdam, Potsdam Public Museum, Potsdam NY
Virginia Museum of Fine Arts, Richmond VA
Vizcaya Museum & Gardens, Miami FL
Walker Art Gallery, Liverpool
Wayne Center for the Arts, Wooster OH
Wilfrid Laurier University, Robert Langen Art Gallery, Waterloo ON
William Morris Gallery, London
World Erotic Art Museum, Miami Beach FL
Yokohama Museum of Art, Yokohama

TEXTILES

Abington Art Center, Jenkintown PA
Academy of the New Church, Glencairn Museum, Bryn Athyn PA
Adams County Historical Society, Gettysburg PA
African American Museum in Philadelphia, Philadelphia PA
African Art Museum of Maryland, Columbia MD
Alabama Department of Archives & History, Museum of Alabama, Montgomery AL
Albany Institute of History & Art, Albany NY
Albion College, Bobbitt Visual Arts Center, Albion MI
Albuquerque Museum of Art & History, Albuquerque NM
American Art Museum, Smithsonian Institution, Washington DC
American Folk Art Museum, New York NY
American Swedish Institute, Minneapolis MN
American Textile History Museum, Lowell MA
Americas Society Art Gallery, New York NY
Anchorage Museum at Rasmuson Center, Anchorage AK
Arab American National Museum, Dearborn MI
Arizona Historical Society-Yuma, Sanguinetti House Museum & Garden, Yuma AZ
Arizona Museum For Youth, Mesa AZ
Arnot Art Museum, Elmira NY
Art & Culture Center of Hollywood, Art Gallery/Multidisciplinary Cultural Center, Hollywood FL
Art Center of Battle Creek, Battle Creek MI
Art Gallery of Bancroft Inc, Bancroft ON
Art Gallery of Nova Scotia, Halifax NS
Art Gallery of South Australia, Adelaide
The Art Museum at the University of Kentucky, Lexington KY
Art Museum of Greater Lafayette, Lafayette IN
Art Without Walls Inc, New York NY
Artesia Historical Museum & Art Center, Artesia NM
Asian Art Museum of San Francisco, Chong-Moon Lee Ctr for Asian Art and Culture, San Francisco CA
Atlanta Historical Society Inc, Atlanta History Center, Atlanta GA
Augustana College, Augustana College Art Museum, Rock Island IL
Aurora University, Schingoethe Center for Native American Cultures & The Schingoethe Art Gallery, Aurora IL
The Baltimore Museum of Art, Baltimore MD
Balzekas Museum of Lithuanian Culture, Chicago IL
Banco de la Republica Museo del Oro, Museo del Oro, Bogota
Barnes Foundation, Merion PA
Baroda Museum and Picture Gallery, Baroda
Bay County Historical Society, Historical Museum of Bay County, Bay City MI
Bellevue Arts Museum, Bellevue WA
Berea College, Ulmann Doris Galleries, Berea KY
Besser Museum for Northeast Michigan, Alpena MI
Beverly Historical Society, Cabot, Hale & Balch House Museums, Beverly MA
Biggs Museum of American Art, Dover DE
Birmingham Museum of Art, Birmingham AL
Blanden Memorial Art Museum, Fort Dodge IA
Brick Store Museum, Kennebunk ME

Brooklyn Historical Society, Brooklyn OH
Brown University, Haffenreffer Museum of Anthropology, Providence RI
Bruce Museum, Inc, Greenwich CT
Burke Arts Council, Jailhouse Galleries, Morganton NC
Bush-Holley Historic Site & Storehouse Gallery, Greenwich Historical Society/ Bush-Holley House, Cos Cob CT
Byzantine & Christian Museum, Athens, Athens
C W Post Campus of Long Island University, Hillwood Art Museum, Brookville NY
Cabot's Old Indian Pueblo Museum, Desert Hot Springs CA
California State University, East Bay, C E Smith Museum of Anthropology, Hayward CA
California State University, Northridge, Art Galleries, Northridge CA
Calvin College, Center Art Gallery, Grand Rapids MI
Cameron Art Museum, Wilmington NC
Canadian Museum of Civilization, Gatineau PQ
Cape Ann Historical Association, Cape Ann Museum, Gloucester MA
Caramoor Center for Music & the Arts, Inc, Rosen House at Caramoor, Katonah NY
Carnegie Center for Art & History, New Albany IN
Charleston Museum, Charleston SC
Chatham Historical Society, The Atwood House Museum, Chatham MA
Chhatrapati Shivaji Maharaj Vastu Sangrahalaya, Mumbai
Chicago Athenaeum, Museum of Architecture & Design, Galena IL
Chinese Culture Foundation, Center Gallery, San Francisco CA
Church of Jesus Christ of Latter-Day Saints, Museum of Church History & Art, Salt Lake City UT
Cincinnati Art Museum, Cincinnati Art Museum, Cincinnati OH
City of Austin Parks & Recreation, O. Henry Museum, Austin TX
City of Brea, Art Gallery, Brea CA
City of Fayette, Alabama, Fayette Art Museum, Fayette AL
City of Fremont, Olive Hyde Art Gallery, Fremont CA
City of Gainesville, Thomas Center Galleries - Cultural Affairs, Gainesville FL
City of High Point, High Point Museum, High Point NC
City of Mason City, Charles H MacNider Museum, Mason City IA
City of Pittsfield, Berkshire Artisans, Pittsfield MA
City of San Antonio, San Antonio TX
City of Springdale, Shiloh Museum of Ozark History, Springdale AR
Clark County Historical Society, Pioneer - Krier Museum, Ashland KS
The Cleveland Museum of Art, Cleveland OH
Clinton County Historical Association, Clinton County Historical Museum, Plattsburgh NY
Cohasset Historical Society, Pratt Building (Society Headquarters), Cohasset MA
The College of Wooster, The College of Wooster Art Museum, Wooster OH
Colorado Historical Society, Colorado History Museum, Denver CO
Columbia Museum of Art, Columbia SC
Columbus Museum, Columbus GA
Columbus Museum of Art, Columbus OH
Concord Museum, Concord MA
Congregation Beth Israel's Plotkin Judaica Museum, Scottsdale AZ
Cooper-Hewitt National Design Museum, Smithsonian Institution, New York NY
Craft and Folk Art Museum (CAFAM), Los Angeles CA
Craftsmen's Guild of Mississippi, Inc, Mississippi Crafts Center, Ridgeland MS
Craigdarroch Castle Historical Museum Society, Victoria BC
Cranbrook Art Museum, Bloomfield Hills MI
Cranford Historical Society, Cranford NJ
Crocker Art Museum, Sacramento CA
Crook County Museum & Art Gallery, Sundance WY
The Currier Museum of Art, Manchester NH
Danbury Scott-Fanton Museum & Historical Society, Inc, Danbury CT
Danville Museum of Fine Arts & History, Danville VA
DAR Museum, National Society Daughters of the American Revolution, Washington DC
Dartmouth Heritage Museum, Dartmouth NS
Daum Museum of Contemporary Art, Sedalia MO

Davidson College, William H Van Every Jr & Edward M Smith Galleries, Davidson NC
Dawson County Historical Society, Museum, Lexington NE
Delaware Division of Historical & Cultural Affairs, Dover DE
Denison University, Art Gallery, Granville OH
Denver Art Museum, Denver CO
Designmuseum Danmark, Copenhagen
Detroit Institute of Arts, Detroit MI
Detroit Repertory Theatre Gallery, Detroit MI
Detroit Zoological Institute, Wildlife Interpretive Gallery, Royal Oak MI
Doncaster Museum and Art Gallery, Doncaster
Drexel University, Drexel Collection, Philadelphia PA
Dundee City Council Leisure & Communities Department, The McManus: Dundee's Art Gallery & Museum, Dundee
Dundurn Castle, Hamilton ON
Durham Art Guild, Durham NC
Edgecombe County Cultural Arts Council, Inc, Blount-Bridgers House, Hobson Pittman Memorial Gallery, Tarboro NC
Eiteljorg Museum of American Indians & Western Art, Indianapolis IN
Environment Canada - Parks Canada, Laurier House, National Historic Site, Ottawa ON
Erie Art Museum, Erie PA
Erie County Historical Society, Erie PA
Evanston Historical Society, Charles Gates Dawes House, Evanston IL
Evansville Museum of Arts, History & Science, Evansville IN
Evergreen State College, Evergreen Gallery, Olympia WA
Fairbanks Museum & Planetarium, Saint Johnsbury VT
Fashion Institute of Technology, The Museum at FIT, New York NY
Fetherston Foundation, Packwood House Museum, Lewisburg PA
Fine Arts Museums of San Francisco, Legion of Honor, San Francisco CA
Fishkill Historical Society, Van Wyck Homestead Museum, Fishkill NY
Fitton Center for Creative Arts, Hamilton OH
Flint Institute of Arts, Flint MI
Florence Museum, Florence SC
Florida State University and Central Florida Community College, The Appleton Museum of Art, Ocala FL
Fondazione Musei Civici Di Venezia, Ca'Rezzonico, Museo del Settecento Veneziano, Venice
Fondazione Musei Civici Di Venezia, Museo Correr, Venice
Fort George G Meade Museum, Fort Meade MD
Friends of Historic Kingston, Fred J Johnston House Museum, Kingston NY
Frontier Times Museum, Bandera TX
Fuller Craft Museum, Brockton MA
Fulton County Historical Society Inc, Fulton County Museum (Tetzlaff Reference Room), Rochester IN
Gadsden Museum, Mesilla NM
Galerie Montcalm, Gatineau PQ
Galleria Nazionale dell'Umbria, Umbrian National Gallery, Perugia
Gaston County Museum of Art & History, Dallas NC
General Board of Discipleship, The United Methodist Church, The Upper Room Chapel & Museum, Nashville TN
Genesee Country Village & Museum, John L Wehle Art Gallery, Mumford NY
Germanisches Nationalmuseum, Nuremberg
Glanmore National Historic Site of Canada, Belleville ON
Glessner House Museum, Chicago IL
Grand Rapids Public Museum, Public Museum of Grand Rapids, Grand Rapids MI
Grassroots Art Center, Lucas KS
Greene County Historical Society, Bronck Museum, Coxsackie NY
Hancock County Trustees of Public Reservations, Woodlawn: Museum, Gardens & Park, Ellsworth ME
Hancock Shaker Village, Inc, Pittsfield MA
Harvard University, Museum & Garden, Washington DC
Hawkes Bay Art Gallery and Museum, Napier
Haystack Mountain School of Crafts, Deer Isle ME
Headley-Whitney Museum, Lexington KY
Heard Museum, Phoenix AZ
Hebrew Union College - Jewish Institute of Religion, Skirball Museum Cincinnati, Cincinnati OH

Navajo Nation, Navajo Nation Museum, Window Rock AZ

Nelson Mandela Bay Municipality, Nelson Mandela Metropolitan Art Museum, Port Elizabeth

New Brunswick Museum, Saint John NB

New Canaan Historical Society, New Canaan CT

New Hampshire Antiquarian Society, Hopkinton Historical Society, Hopkinton NH

New Jersey State Museum, Fine Art Bureau, Trenton NJ

New York State Military Museum and Veterans Research Center, Saratoga Springs NY

New York State Office of Parks Recreation & Historic Preservation, John Jay Homestead State Historic Site, Katonah NY

Nichols House Museum, Inc, Boston MA

No Man's Land Historical Society, No Man's Land Museum, Goodwell OK

North Carolina State University, Gregg Museum of Art & Design, Raleigh NC

North Dakota State University, Memorial Union Gallery, Fargo ND

Norwich Free Academy, Slater Memorial Museum, Norwich CT

Nova Scotia College of Art and Design, Anna Leonowens Gallery, Halifax NS

Noyes Art Gallery, Lincoln NE

The Ogden Museum of Southern Art, University of New Orleans, New Orleans LA

Ohara Museum of Art, Kurashiki

The Ohio Historical Society, Inc, Campus Martius Museum & Ohio River Museum, Marietta OH

Ohio University, Kennedy Museum of Art, Athens OH

Okanagan Heritage Museum, Kelowna BC

Olana State Historic Site, Hudson NY

Old Colony Historical Society, Museum, Taunton MA

Old Island Restoration Foundation Inc, Oldest House in Key West, Key West FL

Owensboro Museum of Fine Art, Owensboro KY

Pacific - Asia Museum, Pasadena CA

Page-Walker Arts & History Center, Cary NC

Panhandle-Plains Historical Museum, Canyon TX

Pasadena Museum of History, Pasadena CA

Passaic County Historical Society, Lambert Castle Museum & Library, Paterson NJ

Pennsylvania Historical & Museum Commission, Railroad Museum of Pennsylvania, Harrisburg PA

Philadelphia History Museum, Philadelphia PA

Philadelphia University, Paley Design Center, Philadelphia PA

The Frank Phillips, Woolaroc Museum, Bartlesville OK

George Phippen, Phippen Museum - Art of the American West, Prescott AZ

Phoenix Art Museum, Phoenix AZ

Piedmont Arts Association, Martinsville VA

Plainsman Museum, Aurora NE

Polk Museum of Art, Lakeland FL

Pope County Historical Society, Pope County Museum, Glenwood MN

Port Huron Museum, Port Huron MI

Porter-Phelps-Huntington Foundation, Inc, Historic House Museum, Hadley MA

Pretoria Art Museum, Municipal Art Gallery, Pretoria

Principia College, School of Nations Museum, Elsah IL

Putnam Museum of History and Natural Science, Davenport IA

Quapaw Quarter Association, Inc, Villa Marre, Little Rock AR

Queens College, City University of New York, Godwin-Ternbach Museum, Flushing NY

Rabindra Bhavan Art Gallery, Lalit Kala Akademi (National Academy of Art), New Delhi

Randolph College, Maier Museum of Art, Lynchburg VA

Reading Public Museum, Reading PA

Red Deer & District Museum & Archives, Red Deer AB

Rhodes College, Clough-Hanson Gallery, Memphis TN

Rider University, Art Gallery, Lawrenceville NJ

Riley County Historical Society & Museum, Riley County Historical Museum, Manhattan KS

Riverside Metropolitan Museum, Riverside CA

Rollins College, George D & Harriet W Cornell Fine Arts Museum, Winter Park FL

The Rooms Corporation of Newfoundland & Labrador, Saint John's NF

Roswell Artist-in-Residence Foundation, Anderson Museum of Contemporary Art, Roswell NM

Roswell Museum & Art Center, Roswell NM

Royal Arts Foundation, Belcourt Castle, Newport RI

Saco Museum, Saco ME

Saginaw Art Museum, Saginaw MI

Saint Joseph's Oratory, Museum, Montreal PQ

Saint Louis County Historical Society, St. Louis County Historical Society, Duluth MN

St Mary's College of Maryland, The Dwight Frederick Boyden Gallery, St Mary's City MD

Saint Olaf College, Flaten Art Museum, Northfield MN

Saint Peter's College, Art Gallery, Jersey City NJ

Salisbury House Foundation, Salisbury House and Garden, Des Moines IA

Savitsky Karakalpakstan State Art Museum, Nukus

School for Advanced Research (SAR), Indian Arts Research Center, Santa Fe NM

Schweinfurth Art Center, Auburn NY

Scripps College, Clark Humanities Museum, Claremont CA

Scripps College, Ruth Chandler Williamson Gallery, Claremont CA

Shaker Museum & Library, Old Chatham NY

Shaker Village of Pleasant Hill, Harrodsburg KY

Shelburne Museum, Museum, Shelburne VT

Shirley Plantation Foundation, Charles City VA

Slater Mill, Old Slater Mill Association, Pawtucket RI

Slovenska Narodna Galeria, Slovak National Gallery, Bratislava

Society for Contemporary Craft, Pittsburgh PA

The Society of the Cincinnati at Anderson House, Washington DC

South Carolina Artisans Center, Walterboro SC

South Carolina State Museum, Columbia SC

South Dakota State University, South Dakota Art Museum, Brookings SD

Southern Baptist Theological Seminary, Joseph A Callaway Archaeological Museum, Louisville KY

Spartanburg Art Museum, Spartanburg SC

The Speed Art Museum, Louisville KY

Spertus Institute of Jewish Studies, Chicago IL

The State Museum of Fine Arts of Tatarstan Republic, Kazan

The State Museum of Oriental Art, Moscow

State of North Carolina, Battleship North Carolina, Wilmington NC

State University of New York at Binghamton, Binghamton University Art Museum, Binghamton NY

State University of New York College at Cortland, Dowd Fine Arts Gallery, Cortland NY

Staten Island Museum, Staten Island NY

Stauth Foundation & Museum, Stauth Memorial Museum, Montezuma KS

T C Steele, Nashville IN

Stiftung Deutsches Historisches Museum, Berlin

Stone Quarry Hill Art Park, Winner Gallery, Cazenovia NY

Stratford Historical Society, Catharine B Mitchell Museum, Stratford CT

The Summit County Historical Society of Akron, OH, Akron OH

Suomen Kansallismuseo, National Museum of Finland, Helsinki

Swedish American Museum Association of Chicago, Chicago IL

Syracuse University, SUArt Galleries, Syracuse NY

Tampa Museum of Art, Tampa FL

Taos, Ernest Blumenschein Home & Studio, Taos NM

Taos, La Hacienda de Los Martinez, Taos NM

Lillian & Coleman Taube Museum of Art, Minot ND

The Temple-Tifereth Israel, The Temple Museum of Religious Art, Beachwood OH

Texas Tech University, Museum of Texas Tech University, Lubbock TX

The Textile Museum, Washington DC

Textile Museum of Canada, Toronto ON

The Tokugawa Reimeikai Foundation, The Tokugawa Art Museum, Nagoya

Tokyo University of the Arts, The University Art Museum, Tokyo

Towson University, Asian Arts & Culture Center, Towson MD

Tubac Center of the Arts, Santa Cruz Valley Art Association, Tubac AZ

Tucson Museum of Art and Historic Block, Tucson AZ

Turtle Bay Exploration Park, Redding CA

Tver Art Gallery, Tver

Mark Twain, Hartford CT

Tyne and Wear Archives & Museums, Sunderland Museum & Winter Gardens, Newcastle-upon-Tyne

Ucross Foundation, Big Red Barn Gallery, Clearmont WY

Ukrainian Institute of Modern Art, Chicago IL

Ukrainian Canadian Archives & Museum of Alberta, Edmonton AB

The Ukrainian Museum, New York NY

United Society of Shakers, Shaker Museum, New Gloucester ME

Universalmuseum Joanneum GmbH, Graz

University of British Columbia, Museum of Anthropology, Vancouver BC

University of California, Berkeley, The Magnes Collection of Jewish Art & Life, Berkeley CA

University of Chicago, Oriental Institute, Chicago IL

University of Colorado at Colorado Springs, Gallery of Contemporary Art, Colorado Springs CO

University of Delaware, University Museums, Newark DE

University of Georgia, Georgia Museum of Art, Athens GA

University of Illinois at Urbana-Champaign, Krannert Art Museum and Kinkead Pavilion, Champaign IL

University of Kansas, Spencer Museum of Art, Lawrence KS

University of Manchester, Whitworth Art Gallery, Manchester

University of Manitoba, Faculty of Architecture Exhibition Centre, Winnipeg MB

University of Miami, Lowe Art Museum, Coral Gables FL

University of Michigan, Kelsey Museum of Archaeology, Ann Arbor MI

University of Minnesota Duluth, Tweed Museum of Art, Duluth MN

University of Missouri, Museum of Art & Archaeology, Columbia MO

University of Nevada, Reno, Sheppard Contemporary & University Galleries, Reno NV

University of New Brunswick, Art Centre, Fredericton NB

University of New Mexico, The Harwood Museum of Art, Taos NM

University of New Mexico, University of New Mexico Art Museum, Albuquerque NM

University of North Dakota, Hughes Fine Arts Center-Col Eugene Myers Art Gallery, Grand Forks ND

University of Oregon, Jordan Schnitzer Museum of Art, Eugene OR

University of Pennsylvania, Museum of Archaeology & Anthropology, Philadelphia PA

University of San Diego, Founders' Gallery, San Diego CA

University of Saskatchewan, Diefenbaker Canada Centre, Saskatoon SK

University of Texas at Austin, Blanton Museum of Art, Austin TX

University of Utah, Utah Museum of Fine Arts, Salt Lake City UT

University of Washington, Henry Art Gallery, Seattle WA

University of Wisconsin-Madison, Chazen Museum of Art, Madison WI

Ursinus College, Philip & Muriel Berman Museum of Art, Collegeville PA

Utah Department of Natural Resources, Division of Parks & Recreation, Territorial Statehouse State Park Museum, Fillmore UT

Vancouver Art Gallery, Vancouver BC

Vancouver Public Library, Fine Arts & Music Department, Vancouver BC

Vesterheim Norwegian-American Museum, Decorah IA

Victoria Mansion - Morse Libby House, Portland ME

Vietnam Fine Arts Museum, Hanoi

Village of Potsdam, Potsdam Public Museum, Potsdam NY

Vizcaya Museum & Gardens, Miami FL

Vorarlberg Museum, Bregenz

Wadsworth Atheneum Museum of Art, Hartford CT

Wake Forest University, Museum of Anthropology, Winston Salem NC

Waterworks Visual Arts Center, Salisbury NC

West Florida Historic Preservation, Inc/University of West Florida, T T Wentworth, Jr Florida State Museum; Historic Pensacola Village; Pensacola Historical Society & Resource Center, Pensacola FL

Wethersfield Historical Society Inc, Museum, Wethersfield CT

Whatcom Museum, Bellingham WA

Wheaton College, Beard and Weil Galleries, Norton MA

Peter & Catharine Whyte Foundation, Whyte Museum of the Canadian Rockies, Banff AB

Wichita Art Museum, Wichita KS

Wilfrid Laurier University, Robert Langen Art Gallery, Waterloo ON

Willard House & Clock Museum, Inc, North Grafton MA

WATERCOLORS

Illinois State Museum, ISM Lockport Gallery, Chicago Gallery & Southern Illinois Art Gallery, Springfield IL

Independence Historical Museum & Art Center, Independence KS

Independence Seaport Museum, Philadelphia PA

Independent Administrative Institution National Museum of Art, The National Museum of Western Art, Tokyo

Indiana Landmarks, Morris-Butler House, Indianapolis IN

Indianapolis Museum of Art, Indianapolis IN

Institute of American Indian Arts, Museum of Contemporary Native Arts, Santa Fe NM

Institute of Puerto Rican Culture, Museo Fuerte Conde de Mirasol, Vieques PR

International Museum of Art & Science, McAllen TX

Iredell Museums, Statesville NC

Irving Arts Center, Galleries & Sculpture Garden, Irving TX

The Israel Museum, Jerusalem, Billy Rose Art Garden, Jerusalem

The Israel Museum, Jerusalem, Samuel & Saidye Bronfman Archaeology Wing, Jerusalem

The Israel Museum, Jerusalem, Jerusalem

J.M.W. Turner Museum, Sarasota FL

Jacksonville University, Alexander Brest Museum & Gallery, Jacksonville FL

Janus Pannonius Muzeum, Pecs

Jersey City Museum, Jersey City NJ

John B Aird Gallery, Toronto ON

The John L. Clarke Western Art Gallery & Memorial Museum, East Glacier Park MT

John Weaver Sculpture Collection, Hope BC

Jordan National Gallery of Fine Arts, Amman

Joslyn Art Museum, Omaha NE

Juniata College Museum of Art, Huntingdon PA

Kalamazoo Institute of Arts, Kalamazoo MI

Kamloops Art Gallery, Kamloops BC

Kenosha Public Museums, Kenosha WI

Kentucky Museum of Art and Craft, Louisville KY

Kereszteny Muzeum, Christian Museum, Esztergom

Kings County Historical Society & Museum, Hampton NB

Kirchner Museum Davos, Davos

Kirkland Museum of Fine & Decorative Art, Denver CO

Kitchener-Waterloo Art Gallery, Kitchener ON

Knights of Columbus Supreme Council, Knights of Columbus Museum, New Haven CT

Knoxville Museum of Art, Knoxville TN

Koshare Indian Museum, Inc, La Junta CO

Kunstmuseum Solothurn, Solothurn Art Museum, Solothurn

Kunstmuseum Thun, Thun

Kyiv Museum of Russian Art, Kyiv

La Salle University Art Museum, Philadelphia PA

Lafayette College, Lafayette College Art Galleries, Easton PA

LaGrange Art Museum, LaGrange GA

Lahore Museum, Lahore

Lamar University, Dishman Art Museum, Beaumont TX

Latino Art Museum, Pomona CA

Latvijas Nacionalais Makslas Muzejs, Arsenals Exhibition Hall, Riga

Launceston City Council, Queen Victoria Museum and Art Gallery, Launceston

Leanin' Tree Museum & Sculpture Garden of Western Art, Boulder CO

Leeds Museums & Galleries, Leeds

Lehigh University Art Galleries, Museum Operation, Bethlehem PA

Lehigh Valley Heritage Center, Allentown PA

LeMoyne Art Foundation, Center for the Visual Arts, Tallahassee FL

Liberty Hall Historic Site, Liberty Hall Museum, Frankfort KY

Lightner Museum, Saint Augustine FL

Lincoln County Historical Association, Inc, 1811 Old Lincoln County Jail & Lincoln County Museum, Wiscasset ME

Lincolnshire County Council, Library & Heritage Services, Lincoln

Lincolnshire County Council, The Collection: Art & Archaeology in Lincolnshire, Lincoln

The Long Island Museum of American Art, History & Carriages, Stony Brook NY

Longview Museum of Fine Art, Longview TX

Los Angeles County Museum of Natural History, William S Hart Museum, Newhall CA

Louisiana Department of Culture, Recreation & Tourism, Louisiana State Museum, New Orleans LA

Louisiana State University, Museum of Art, Baton Rouge LA

Luther College, Fine Arts Collection, Decorah IA

Maitland Art Center, Maitland FL

Manchester Bidwell Corporation, Manchester Craftsmen's Guild Youth & Arts Program, Pittsburgh PA

Marblehead Museum & Historical Society, Jeremiah Lee Mansion, Marblehead MA

Marblehead Museum & Historical Society, Marblehead MA

The Mariners' Museum, Newport News VA

Maryland Hall for the Creative Arts, Chaney Gallery, Annapolis MD

Massachusetts Institute of Technology, MIT Museum, Cambridge MA

Massillon Museum, Massillon OH

Maysville, Kentucky Gateway Museum Center, Maysville KY

The Robert McLaughlin, Oshawa ON

McMaster University, McMaster Museum of Art, Hamilton ON

McPherson College Gallery, McPherson KS

Mennello Museum of American Art, Orlando FL

Meridian Museum of Art, Meridian MS

Mesa Arts Center, Mesa Contemporary Arts Museum, Mesa AZ

Michelson Museum of Art, Marshall TX

James A Michener, Doylestown PA

Middle Border Museum & Oscar Howe Art Center, Mitchell SD

Middlebury College, Museum of Art, Middlebury VT

Midwest Museum of American Art, Elkhart IN

Miller Art Center Foundation Inc, Miller Art Museum, Sturgeon Bay WI

Millikin University, Perkinson Gallery, Decatur IL

Ministry of Cultural Affairs, Bangladesh National Museum, Dhaka

Ministry of the Arts & Multiculturalism, National Museum & Art Gallery, Port of Spain

Minnesota Museum of American Art, Saint Paul MN

Minot State University, Northwest Art Center, Minot ND

Arthur Roy Mitchell, A.R. Mitchell Museum, Trinidad CO

Mobile Museum of Art, Mobile AL

Moderna Galerija, Gallery of Modern Art, Zagreb

Moore College of Art & Design, The Galleries at Moore, Philadelphia PA

Moravian College, Payne Gallery, Bethlehem PA

Moravian Historical Society, Whitefield House Museum, Nazareth PA

Moravska Galerie v Brne, Moravian Gallery in Brno, Brno

Morehead State University, Kentucky Folk Art Center, Morehead KY

Morris Museum, Morristown NJ

Morris Museum of Art, Augusta GA

Mount Saint Vincent University, MSVU Art Gallery, Halifax NS

Munson-Williams-Proctor Arts Institute, Museum of Art, Utica NY

Muscatine Art Center, Museum, Muscatine IA

Musee Cognacq-Jay, Cognacq-Jay Museum, Paris

Musee des Beaux-Arts d'Orleans, Museum of Fine Arts, Orleans

Musee des Beaux-Arts/Palais des Archeveques, Museum of Fine Arts, Tours

Musee National d'Histoire et d'Art Luxembourg, Luxembourg City

Musee Regional de lu Cote-Nord, Sept-Iles PQ

Museen der Stadt Koln, Wallraf-Richartz-Museum, Cologne

Museo Cerralbo, Madrid

Museo De Bellas Artes de Caracas, Museum of Fine Arts, Caracas

Museo De Las Americas, Denver CO

Museo Italo Americano, San Francisco CA

Museu de Evora, Evora

Museum of Art & History, Santa Cruz, Santa Cruz CA

The Museum of Arts & Sciences Inc, Daytona Beach FL

The Museum of Contemporary Art (MOCA), Moca Grand Avenue, Los Angeles CA

Museum of Contemporary Art, San Diego-Downtown, La Jolla CA

Museum of Contemporary Craft, Portland OR

Museum of Fine Arts Houston, Bayou Bend Collection & Gardens, Houston TX

Museum of Fine Arts, Saint Petersburg, Florida, Inc, Saint Petersburg FL

Museum of Florida Art, Deland FL

Museum of Latin American Art, Long Beach CA

Museum of Modern Art, Ibaraki, Ibaraki

Museum of Northwest Art, La Conner WA

Museum of Southern History, Houston TX

Museum of Wisconsin Art, West Bend WI

Museum Plantin-Moretus/Prentenkabinet, Antwerp

Museum zu Allerheiligen, Schaffhausen

Muskegon Museum of Art, Muskegon MI

Muzej za Umjetnost i Obrt, Museum of Arts & Crafts, Zagreb

Muzeul National Brukenthal, Blue House & Romanian Art Gallery, Sibiu

Muzeul National Brukenthal, Brukenthal Palace & European Art Gallery, Sibiu

Napa Valley Museum, Yountville CA

Narodna Galerija, National Gallery of Slovenia, Ljubljana

Nassau County Museum of Art, Roslyn Harbor NY

National Art Museum of Sport, Indianapolis IN

National Baseball Hall of Fame & Museum, Inc, Art Collection, Cooperstown NY

National Galleries of Scotland, Scottish National Gallery, Edinburgh

National Museum of Fine Arts of Moldova, Chisinau

The National Museum of Modern Art, Tokyo, Tokyo

National Museum of Wildlife Art of the Unites States, Jackson WY

National Museum, Monuments and Art Gallery, Gaborone

National Park Service, Weir Farm National Historic Site, Wilton CT

National Portrait Gallery, Smithsonian Institution, Washington DC

National Society of Colonial Dames of America in the State of Maryland, Mount Clare Museum House, Baltimore MD

Navajo Nation, Navajo Nation Museum, Window Rock AZ

Naval Historical Center, The Navy Museum, Washington DC

Nelson Mandela Bay Municipality, Nelson Mandela Metropolitan Art Museum, Port Elizabeth

The Nemours Foundatioin, Nemours Mansion & Gardens, Wilmington DE

Neville Public Museum of Brown County, Green Bay WI

New Britain Museum of American Art, New Britain CT

New Brunswick Museum, Saint John NB

New Hampshire Antiquarian Society, Hopkinton Historical Society, Hopkinton NH

New Jersey State Museum, Fine Art Bureau, Trenton NJ

New Visions Gallery, Inc, Marshfield WI

New York State Military Museum and Veterans Research Center, Saratoga Springs NY

New York Studio School of Drawing, Painting & Sculpture, Gallery, New York NY

New York University, Grey Art Gallery, New York NY

Newport Art Museum and Association, Newport RI

Niagara University, Castellani Art Museum, Niagara NY

Nihon Mingeikan, Japan Folk Crafts Museum, Tokyo

No Man's Land Historical Society, No Man's Land Museum, Goodwell OK

The Noble Maritime Collection, Staten Island NY

North Dakota State University, Memorial Union Gallery, Fargo ND

Northeastern Nevada Museum, Elko NV

Northern Illinois University, NIU Art Museum, DeKalb IL

Norwich Free Academy, Slater Memorial Museum, Norwich CT

Noyes Art Gallery, Lincoln NE

The Ogden Museum of Southern Art, University of New Orleans, New Orleans LA

Ohio University, Kennedy Museum of Art, Athens OH

Oklahoma City Museum of Art, Oklahoma City OK

The Old Jail Art Center, Albany TX

Owensboro Museum of Fine Art, Owensboro KY

Panhandle-Plains Historical Museum, Canyon TX

Paris Gibson Square, Museum of Art, Great Falls MT

Pasadena Museum of History, Pasadena CA

Passaic County Community College, Broadway, LRC, and Hamilton Club Galleries, Paterson NJ

Passaic County Historical Society, Lambert Castle Museum & Library, Paterson NJ

Pennsylvania Historical & Museum Commission, Railroad Museum of Pennsylvania, Harrisburg PA

WOODCARVINGS

A.E. Backus Museum of Art, Fort Pierce FL
A.I.R. Gallery, Brooklyn NY
Academy of the New Church, Glencairn Museum, Bryn Athyn PA
African American Museum in Philadelphia, Philadelphia PA
Alaska Department of Education, Division of Libraries, Archives & Museums, Sheldon Jackson Museum, Sitka AK
Albany Institute of History & Art, Albany NY
Albuquerque Museum of Art & History, Albuquerque NM
American Art Museum, Smithsonian Institution, Washington DC
American Swedish Institute, Minneapolis MN
Walter Anderson, Ocean Springs MS
Arab American National Museum, Dearborn MI
Arizona Museum For Youth, Mesa AZ
Arnold Mikelson Mind & Matter Art Gallery, White Rock BC
Arnot Art Museum, Elmira NY
Art & Culture Center of Hollywood, Art Gallery/Multidisciplinary Cultural Center, Hollywood FL
Art Gallery of Hamilton, Hamilton ON
Art Gallery of Nova Scotia, Halifax NS
The Art Museum at the University of Kentucky, Lexington KY
Art Museum of Greater Lafayette, Lafayette IN
Art Without Walls Inc, New York NY
Asian Art Museum of San Francisco, Chong-Moon Lee Ctr for Asian Art and Culture, San Francisco CA
Augustana College, Augustana College Art Museum, Rock Island IL
Balzekas Museum of Lithuanian Culture, Chicago IL
Baroda Museum and Picture Gallery, Baroda
Beaumont Art League, Beaumont TX
Bellevue Arts Museum, Bellevue WA
Blanden Memorial Art Museum, Fort Dodge IA
Blauvelt Demarest Foundation, Hiram Blauvelt Art Museum, Oradell NJ
Brigham Young University, Museum of Art, Provo UT
Bucknell University, Edward & Marthann Samek Art Gallery, Lewisburg PA
Cabot's Old Indian Pueblo Museum, Desert Hot Springs CA
Canadian Museum of Civilization, Gatineau PQ
Canadian Museum of Nature, Musee Canadien de la Nature, Ottawa ON
Cape Cod Museum of Art Inc, Dennis MA
Center for Puppetry Arts, Atlanta GA
Central United Methodist Church, Swords Into Plowshares Peace Center & Gallery, Detroit MI
Billie Trimble Chandler, Texas State Museum of Asian Cultures, Corpus Christi TX
Chatham Historical Society, The Atwood House Museum, Chatham MA
Chesapeake Bay Maritime Museum, Saint Michaels MD
Chinese Culture Foundation, Center Gallery, San Francisco CA
Church of Jesus Christ of Latter-Day Saints, Museum of Church History & Art, Salt Lake City UT
Cincinnati Art Museum, Cincinnati Art Museum, Cincinnati OH
City of Fayette, Alabama, Fayette Art Museum, Fayette AL
City of Gainesville, Thomas Center Galleries - Cultural Affairs, Gainesville FL
City of Nome Alaska, Carrie M McLain Memorial Museum, Nome AK
City of Springdale, Shiloh Museum of Ozark History, Springdale AR
Clark County Historical Society, Pioneer - Krier Museum, Ashland KS
Clinton Art Association, River Arts Center, Clinton IA
Columbus Museum, Columbus GA
Craft and Folk Art Museum (CAFAM), Los Angeles CA
Craftsmen's Guild of Mississippi, Inc, Mississippi Crafts Center, Ridgeland MS
Cripple Creek District Museum, Cripple Creek CO
Crook County Museum & Art Gallery, Sundance WY
The Currier Museum of Art, Manchester NH
Danville Museum of Fine Arts & History, Danville VA
Davidson College, William H Van Every Jr & Edward M Smith Galleries, Davidson NC
Delaware Archaeology Museum, Dover DE
Denison University, Art Gallery, Granville OH
Detroit Institute of Arts, Detroit MI
Detroit Repertory Theatre Gallery, Detroit MI

Doncaster Museum and Art Gallery, Doncaster
Dundee City Council Leisure & Communities Department, The McManus: Dundee's Art Gallery & Museum, Dundee
Dundurn Castle, Hamilton ON
Eastern Washington State Historical Society, Northwest Museum of Arts & Culture, Spokane WA
Ellen Noel Art Museum of the Permian Basin, Odessa TX
Elmhurst Art Museum, Elmhurst IL
Emory University, Michael C Carlos Museum, Atlanta GA
Wharton Esherick, Paoli PA
Essex Historical Society and Shipbuilding Museum, Essex MA
Establishment Public du Chateau du Rusee, Et du Dophine national de versailles, Versailles
Eula Mae Edwards Museum & Gallery, Clovis NM
Fetherston Foundation, Packwood House Museum, Lewisburg PA
Five Civilized Tribes Museum, Muskogee OK
Flint Institute of Arts, Flint MI
Florence Museum, Florence SC
Folk Art Society of America, Richmond VA
Fuller Craft Museum, Brockton MA
Fulton County Historical Society Inc, Fulton County Museum (Tetzlaff Reference Room), Rochester IN
Gadsden Museum, Mesilla NM
Gadsden Museum of Fine Arts, Inc, Gadsden Museum of Art and History, Gadsden AL
Galerie Montcalm, Gatineau PQ
General Board of Discipleship, The United Methodist Church, The Upper Room Chapel & Museum, Nashville TN
Germanisches Nationalmuseum, Nuremberg
Wendell Gilley, Southwest Harbor ME
Glessner House Museum, Chicago IL
Gloridale Partnership, National Museum of Woodcarving, Custer SD
Grassroots Art Center, Lucas KS
Hancock County Trustees of Public Reservations, Woodlawn: Museum, Gardens & Park, Ellsworth ME
Haystack Mountain School of Crafts, Deer Isle ME
Heard Museum, Phoenix AZ
Hecht Museum, Haifa
Henry County Museum & Cultural Arts Center, Clinton MO
Heritage Center, Inc, Pine Ridge SD
Hermitage Foundation Museum, Norfolk VA
Hershey Museum, Hershey PA
Higgins Armory Museum, Worcester MA
High Desert Museum, Bend OR
Hillwood Museum & Gardens Foundation, Hillwood Estate Museum & Gardens, Washington DC
Historic Royal Palaces, Hampton Court Palace, East Molesey
Hofstra University, Hofstra University Museum, Hempstead NY
Holter Museum of Art, Helena MT
Hong Kong University, University Museum and Art Gallery, Pokfulam
Hunter Museum of American Art, Chattanooga TN
Illinois State Museum, ISM Lockport Gallery, Chicago Gallery & Southern Illinois Art Gallery, Springfield IL
Independence Historical Museum & Art Center, Independence KS
Independence Seaport Museum, Philadelphia PA
Independent Administrative Institution National Institutes for Cultural Heritage, Tokyo National Museum, Tokyo
International Museum of Art & Science, McAllen TX
Iredell Museums, Statesville NC
Iroquois Indian Museum, Howes Cave NY
The Israel Museum, Jerusalem, Billy Rose Art Garden, Jerusalem
The Israel Museum, Jerusalem, Samuel & Saidye Bronfman Archaeology Wing, Jerusalem
The Israel Museum, Jerusalem, Jerusalem
Jacksonville University, Alexander Brest Museum & Gallery, Jacksonville FL
John B Aird Gallery, Toronto ON
The John L. Clarke Western Art Gallery & Memorial Museum, East Glacier Park MT
John Weaver Sculpture Collection, Hope BC
Bob Jones University Museum & Gallery Inc, Greenville SC
Jordan National Gallery of Fine Arts, Amman
Kalamazoo Institute of Arts, Kalamazoo MI
Kenosha Public Museums, Kenosha WI
Kentucky Museum of Art and Craft, Louisville KY

Kereszteny Muzeum, Christian Museum, Esztergom
Kirkland Museum of Fine & Decorative Art, Denver CO
Knights of Columbus Supreme Council, Knights of Columbus Museum, New Haven CT
Koshare Indian Museum, Inc, La Junta CO
Lac du Flambeau Band of Lake Superior Chippewa Indians, George W Brown Jr Ojibwe Museum & Cultural Center, Lac Du Flambeau WI
Lafayette Science Museum & Planetarium, Lafayette LA
LaGrange Art Museum, LaGrange GA
Lakeview Museum of Arts & Sciences, Peoria IL
Lamar University, Dishman Art Museum, Beaumont TX
Latino Art Museum, Pomona CA
Latvijas Nacionalais Makslas Muzejs, Arsenals Exhibition Hall, Riga
Lightner Museum, Saint Augustine FL
Lincoln County Historical Association, Inc, 1811 Old Lincoln County Jail & Lincoln County Museum, Wiscasset ME
The Long Island Museum of American Art, History & Carriages, Stony Brook NY
Los Angeles County Museum of Natural History, William S Hart Museum, Newhall CA
Louisiana Department of Culture, Recreation & Tourism, Louisiana State Museum, New Orleans LA
Louisiana State Exhibit Museum, Shreveport LA
Luther College, Fine Arts Collection, Decorah IA
Magyar Nemzeti Muzeum - Hungarian National Museum, Budapest
Maitland Art Center, Maitland FL
The Mariners' Museum, Newport News VA
Maryland Hall for the Creative Arts, Chaney Gallery, Annapolis MD
Maysville, Kentucky Gateway Museum Center, Maysville KY
McPherson Museum and Arts Foundation, McPherson KS
Mennello Museum of American Art, Orlando FL
Meredith College, Frankie G Weems Gallery & Rotunda Gallery, Raleigh NC
Middlebury College, Museum of Art, Middlebury VT
Miles B Carpenter Folk Art Museum, Waverly VA
Mills College Art Museum, Oakland CA
Ministry of Cultural Affairs, Bangladesh National Museum, Dhaka
Ministry of the Arts & Multiculturalism, National Museum & Art Gallery, Port of Spain
The Mint Museum, Mint Museum of Craft & Design, Charlotte NC
Mobile Museum of Art, Mobile AL
Moderna Galerija, Gallery of Modern Art, Zagreb
Moravska Galerie v Brne, Moravian Gallery in Brno, Brno
Morehead State University, Kentucky Folk Art Center, Morehead KY
Morris Museum of Art, Augusta GA
Moto Moto Museum, Mbala
Muscatine Art Center, Museum, Muscatine IA
Musea Brugge, Onze-Lieve-Vrouwekerk/Church of Our Lady, Bruges
Musee des Beaux-Arts d'Orleans, Historical & Archaeological Museum of Orleans, Orleans
Musee des Beaux-Arts/Palais des Archeveques, Museum of Fine Arts, Tours
Musee des Maitres et Artisans du Quebec, Montreal PQ
Musee et Chateau de Chantilly (MUSEE CONDE), Chantilly
Musee National des Beaux Arts du Quebec, Quebec PQ
Musee Regional de lu Cote-Nord, Sept-Iles PQ
Museen der Stadt Koln, Museum Schnutgen, Cologne
Museo Cerralbo, Madrid
Museo De Las Americas, Denver CO
Museu Nacional D'Art De Catalunya, National Art Museum, Barcelona
The Museum, Greenwood SC
Museum of Arts & Design, New York NY
Museum of Fine Arts Houston, Bayou Bend Collection & Gardens, Houston TX
Museum of Latin American Art, Long Beach CA
Museum of Northern Arizona, Flagstaff AZ
Museum of Northern British Columbia, Ruth Harvey Art Gallery, Prince Rupert BC
Museum of Northwest Art, La Conner WA
Museum of the Plains Indian & Crafts Center, Browning MT
Museum of York County, Rock Hill SC
Museum Plantin-Moretus/Prentenkabinet, Antwerp
Museum zu Allerheiligen, Schaffhausen

Muskegon Museum of Art, Muskegon MI
Muzeul National Brukenthal, Blue House & Romanian Art Gallery, Sibiu
Muzeul National Brukenthal, Brukenthal Palace & European Art Gallery, Sibiu
Nanticoke Indian Museum, Millsboro DE
Narodna Galerija, National Gallery of Slovenia, Ljubljana
National Art Museum of Sport, Indianapolis IN
National Museum of Fine Arts of Moldova, Chisinau
National Palace Museum, Taiwan, R.O.C.
National Portrait Gallery, Smithsonian Institution, Washington DC
The National Shrine of the North American Martyrs, Fultonville NY
Nebraska Game and Parks Commission, Arbor Lodge State Historical Park & Morton Mansion, Nebraska City NE
Nebraska State Capitol, Lincoln NE
Nelson Mandela Bay Municipality, Nelson Mandela Metropolitan Art Museum, Port Elizabeth
New Brunswick Museum, Saint John NB
New England Maple Museum, Pittsford VT
New Jersey State Museum, Fine Art Bureau, Trenton NJ
Noordbrabants Museum, Hertogenbosch
North Carolina State University, Gregg Museum of Art & Design, Raleigh NC
North Dakota State University, Memorial Union Gallery, Fargo ND
Norwich Free Academy, Slater Memorial Museum, Norwich CT
Noyes Art Gallery, Lincoln NE
The Ogden Museum of Southern Art, University of New Orleans, New Orleans LA
Ohrmann Museum and Gallery, Drummond MT
Olana State Historic Site, Hudson NY
Old Island Restoration Foundation Inc, Oldest House in Key West, Key West FL
Owensboro Museum of Fine Art, Owensboro KY
Pacific - Asia Museum, Pasadena CA
Panhandle-Plains Historical Museum, Canyon TX
Paris Gibson Square, Museum of Art, Great Falls MT
Phelps County Historical Society, Nebraska Prairie Museum, Holdrege NE
George Phippen, Phippen Museum - Art of the American West, Prescott AZ
Plains Art Museum, Fargo ND
Plainsman Museum, Aurora NE
Pope County Historical Society, Pope County Museum, Glenwood MN
Pretoria Art Museum, Municipal Art Gallery, Pretoria
Princeton University, Princeton University Art Museum, Princeton NJ
Pump House Center for the Arts, Chillicothe OH
Queens College, City University of New York, Godwin-Ternbach Museum, Flushing NY
Rabindra Bhavan Art Gallery, Lalit Kala Akademi (National Academy of Art), New Delhi
Radio-Canada SRC CBC, Georges Goguen CBC Art Gallery, Moncton NB
Randolph College, Maier Museum of Art, Lynchburg VA
Reading Public Museum, Reading PA
Rhodes College, Clough-Hanson Gallery, Memphis TN
Rijksmuseum Twenthe, Rijksmuseum Twenthe, Enschede
Roswell Artist-in-Residence Foundation, Anderson Museum of Contemporary Art, Roswell NM
Roswell Museum & Art Center, Roswell NM
Saginaw Art Museum, Saginaw MI
Saint Clair County Community College, Jack R Hennesey Art Galleries, Port Huron MI
Saint Louis County Historical Society, St. Louis County Historical Society, Duluth MN
St Mary's College of Maryland, The Dwight Frederick Boyden Gallery, St Mary's City MD
Salisbury University, Ward Museum of Wildfowl Art, Salisbury MD
Schweinfurth Art Center, Auburn NY
Seneca-Iroquois National Museum, Salamanca NY
Ella Sharp, Jackson MI
Sheldon Museum & Cultural Center, Inc, Sheldon Museum & Cultural Center, Haines AK
Shirley Plantation Foundation, Charles City VA
Soprintendenza per I beni storici artistici ed etnoantropologici per le province di Mantova Brescia e Cremona, Museo di Palazzo Ducale, Mantua
South Carolina Artisans Center, Walterboro SC
South Dakota State University, South Dakota Art Museum, Brookings SD

South Street Seaport Museum, New York NY
Southern Ohio Museum Corporation, Southern Ohio Museum, Portsmouth OH
Spartanburg Art Museum, Spartanburg SC
The Speed Art Museum, Louisville KY
Spertus Institute of Jewish Studies, Chicago IL
Springfield Art Museum, Springfield MO
The State Museum of Fine Arts of Tatarstan Republic, Kazan
Stauth Foundation & Museum, Stauth Memorial Museum, Montezuma KS
Stone Quarry Hill Art Park, Winner Gallery, Cazenovia NY
Suan Pakkad Palace Museum, Bangkok
SVACA - Sheyenne Valley Arts & Crafts Association, Bjarne Ness Gallery at Bear Creek Hall, Fort Ransom ND
Swedish American Museum Association of Chicago, Chicago IL
Tacoma Art Museum, Tacoma WA
Taos, La Hacienda de Los Martinez, Taos NM
Lillian & Coleman Taube Museum of Art, Minot ND
Texas Tech University, Museum of Texas Tech University, Lubbock TX
Tinkertown Museum, Sandia Park NM
Tohono Chul Park, Tucson AZ
Topeka & Shawnee County Public Library, Alice C Sabatini Gallery, Topeka KS
Tver Art Gallery, Tver
Mark Twain, Hartford CT
Ukrainian Institute of Modern Art, Chicago IL
The Ukrainian Museum, New York NY
UMLAUF Sculpture Garden & Museum, Austin TX
University of British Columbia, Museum of Anthropology, Vancouver BC
University of California, Richard L Nelson Gallery & Fine Arts Collection, Davis CA
University of Colorado, CU Art Museum, Boulder CO
University of Georgia, Georgia Museum of Art, Athens GA
University of Illinois at Urbana-Champaign, Krannert Art Museum and Kinkead Pavilion, Champaign IL
University of Indianapolis, Christel DeHaan Fine Arts Gallery, Indianapolis IN
University of Memphis, Art Museum, Memphis TN
University of Miami, Lowe Art Museum, Coral Gables FL
University of Nevada, Reno, Sheppard Contemporary & University Galleries, Reno NV
University of New Mexico, The Harwood Museum of Art, Taos NM
University of Pennsylvania, Museum of Archaeology & Anthropology, Philadelphia PA
University of Texas at Austin, Blanton Museum of Art, Austin TX
University of Utah, Utah Museum of Fine Arts, Salt Lake City UT
University of Wisconsin-Madison, Wisconsin Union Galleries, Madison WI
Vesterheim Norwegian-American Museum, Decorah IA
Vietnam Fine Arts Museum, Hanoi
Wadsworth Atheneum Museum of Art, Hartford CT
Warther Museum Inc, Dover OH
Washington University, Mildred Lane Kemper Art Museum, Saint Louis MO
Waterfront Museum, Brooklyn NY
Waterloo Center of the Arts, Waterloo IA
Waterworks Visual Arts Center, Salisbury NC
West Florida Historic Preservation, Inc/University of West Florida, T T Wentworth, Jr Florida State Museum; Historic Pensacola Village; Pensacola Historical Society & Resource Center, Pensacola FL
Westcott Bay Institute, Island Museum of Art & Westcott Bay Sculpture Park, Friday Harbor WA
Whatcom Museum, Bellingham WA
Wheaton College, Beard and Weil Galleries, Norton MA
Wichita Art Museum, Wichita KS
Wilfrid Laurier University, Robert Langen Art Gallery, Waterloo ON
Winston-Salem State University, Diggs Gallery, Winston Salem NC
Wiregrass Museum of Art, Dothan AL
Wisconsin Historical Society, Wisconsin Historical Museum, Madison WI
Yokohama Museum of Art, Yokohama
Yuma Fine Arts Association, Yuma Art Center, Yuma AZ
Zigler Art Museum, Jennings LA

WOODCUTS

A.E. Backus Museum of Art, Fort Pierce FL
A.I.R. Gallery, Brooklyn NY
Academy Art Museum, Easton MD
African American Museum in Philadelphia, Philadelphia PA
Alaska Heritage Museum at Wells Fargo, Anchorage AK
Albany Institute of History & Art, Albany NY
Albion College, Bobbitt Visual Arts Center, Albion MI
Albuquerque Museum of Art & History, Albuquerque NM
American Art Museum, Smithsonian Institution, Washington DC
American University, Katzen Art Center Gallery, New York NY
Amon Carter Museum of American Art, Fort Worth TX
Walter Anderson, Ocean Springs MS
Arizona Museum For Youth, Mesa AZ
Arnot Art Museum, Elmira NY
Art & Culture Center of Hollywood, Art Gallery/Multidisciplinary Cultural Center, Hollywood FL
Art Gallery of Alberta, Edmonton AB
Art Gallery of Nova Scotia, Halifax NS
Art Gallery of South Australia, Adelaide
The Art Museum at the University of Kentucky, Lexington KY
The Art Museum of Eastern Idaho, Idaho Falls ID
Art Museum of Greater Lafayette, Lafayette IN
Art Without Walls Inc, New York NY
ArtSpace/Lima, Lima OH
Asbury College, Student Center Gallery, Wilmore KY
Augustana College, Augustana College Art Museum, Rock Island IL
Balzekas Museum of Lithuanian Culture, Chicago IL
Bertha V B Lederer Fine Arts Gallery-Suny Geneseo, Bertha V B Lederer Fine Arts Gallery, Geneseo NY
Birger Sandzen Memorial Gallery, Lindsborg KS
Blanden Memorial Art Museum, Fort Dodge IA
Boise Art Museum, Boise ID
Bone Creek Museum of Agrarian Art, David City NE
Boston Public Library, Albert H Wiggin Gallery & Print Department, Boston MA
Brigham Young University, Museum of Art, Provo UT
Brown University, David Winton Bell Gallery, Providence RI
Bucknell University, Edward & Marthann Samek Art Gallery, Lewisburg PA
California State University, Northridge, Art Galleries, Northridge CA
Calvin College, Center Art Gallery, Grand Rapids MI
Canadian Museum of Civilization, Gatineau PQ
Cape Cod Museum of Art Inc, Dennis MA
Carleton College, Art Gallery, Northfield MN
Carnegie Mellon University, Hunt Institute for Botanical Documentation, Pittsburgh PA
Carnegie Museums of Pittsburgh, Carnegie Museum of Art, Pittsburgh PA
Carolina Art Association, Gibbes Museum of Art, Charleston SC
Centro de Arte Moderna, CAM - Calouste Gulbenkian Foundation, Lisbon
Billie Trimble Chandler, Texas State Museum of Asian Cultures, Corpus Christi TX
Chhatrapati Shivaji Maharaj Vastu Sangrahalaya, Mumbai
Church of Jesus Christ of Latter-Day Saints, Mormon Visitors' Center, Independence MO
Cincinnati Art Museum, Cincinnati Art Museum, Cincinnati OH
City of Cedar Falls, Iowa, James & Meryl Hearst Center for the Arts & Sculpture Garden, Cedar Falls IA
City of El Paso, El Paso TX
City of Fayette, Alabama, Fayette Art Museum, Fayette AL
City of Gainesville, Thomas Center Galleries - Cultural Affairs, Gainesville FL
City of Mason City, Charles H MacNider Museum, Mason City IA
City of Pittsfield, Berkshire Artisans, Pittsfield MA
City of Port Angeles, Port Angeles Fine Arts Center & Webster Woods Art Park, Port Angeles WA
Sterling & Francine Clark, Williamstown MA
Clinton Art Association, River Arts Center, Clinton IA
Colgate University, Picker Art Gallery, Hamilton NY
College of William & Mary, Muscarelle Museum of Art, Williamsburg VA
The College of Wooster, The College of Wooster Art Museum, Wooster OH
Columbus Museum, Columbus GA

Collections

Berman Collection
Lehigh University Art Galleries, Museum Operation, Bethlehem PA

Philip & Muriel Berman Collection
Ursinus College, Philip & Muriel Berman Museum of Art, Collegeville PA

Bernat Oriental Collection
Colby College, Museum of Art, Waterville ME

Joseph Beuys Collection
Walker Art Center, Minneapolis MN

Galen Biary Photograph Collection
Whatcom Museum, Bellingham WA

Melvin P Billups Glass Collection
New Orleans Museum of Art, New Orleans LA

Vyvyan Blackford Collection
Fort Hays State University, Moss-Thorns Gallery of Arts, Hays KS

Edwin M Blake Memorial Collection
Trinity College, Austin Arts Center, Widener Gallery, Hartford CT

Bloomsbury Collection of Kenneth Curry
Rollins College, George D & Harriet W Cornell Fine Arts Museum, Winter Park FL

Ernest L Blumenschein & Family Collection
Taos, Ernest Blumenschein Home & Studio, Taos NM

Boehm Collection
Bellingrath Gardens & Home, Theodore AL

Frederick T Bonham Collection
University of Tennessee, McClung Museum of Natural History & Culture, Knoxville TN

Sir Mackenzie Bowell Collection
Glanmore National Historic Site of Canada, Belleville ON

Bradley Collection
Milwaukee Art Museum, Milwaukee WI

Branch Collection of Renaissance Art
Virginia Museum of Fine Arts, Richmond VA

Broder Collection
University of Nebraska-Lincoln, Great Plains Art Museum, Lincoln NE

Saidye and Samuel Bronfman Collection of Contemporary Canadian Art
Montreal Museum of Fine Arts, Montreal PQ

Ailsa Mellon Bruce Collection of Decorative Arts
Virginia Museum of Fine Arts, Richmond VA

Pierre Brunet Collection
United States Figure Skating Association, World Figure Skating Museum & Hall of Fame, Colorado Springs CO

Ottilia Buerger Collection of Ancient Coins
Lawrence University, Wriston Art Center Galleries, Appleton WI

Charles E Burchfield Collection
State University of New York College at Buffalo, Buffalo NY

Charles Grove Burgoyne Collection
Halifax Historical Society, Inc, Halifax Historical Museum, Daytona Beach FL

Burnap Collection
The Nelson-Atkins Museum of Art, Kansas City MO

Burnap Collection of English Pottery
Village of Potsdam, Potsdam Public Museum, Potsdam NY

Burrison Folklife Collection
Atlanta Historical Society Inc, Atlanta History Center, Atlanta GA

Elizabeth Cole Butler Collection of Native American Art
Portland Art Museum, Portland OR

James F Byrnes Collection
University of South Carolina, McKissick Museum, Columbia SC

Earl Bailey Melorum Collection
Lunenburg Art Gallery Society, Lunenburg NS

Carol Barnes Collection
Sonoma County Museum, Santa Rosa CA

Basil & Elise Goulandris Collection
Museum of Contemporary Art, Basil and Elise Goulandris Foundation, Andros

Bayou Bend Collection
Museum of Fine Arts Houston, Bayou Bend Collection & Gardens, Houston TX

Sir Harold Beauchamp Collection
Museum of New Zealand Te Papa Tongarewa, Museum of New Zealand Te Papa Tongarewa, Wellington

Bertie Lord Collection
Ravalli County Museum, Hamilton MT

Biggs Collection
Biggs Museum of American Art, Dover DE

Bowen Collection of Antiquities
Bob Jones University Museum & Gallery Inc, Greenville SC

Bower Collection
Red Deer & District Museum & Archives, Red Deer AB

Luther W. Brady Collection
Colgate University, Picker Art Gallery, Hamilton NY

Bresler Collection
The Mint Museum, Mint Museum of Craft & Design, Charlotte NC

Broadfoot, Lennis L
Harlin Museum, West Plains MO

Donald Buchanan Art Collection
Southern Alberta Art Gallery, Lethbridge AB

Caplan Collection
The Children's Museum of Indianapolis, Indianapolis IN

Carnegie Collection of Prints
Dickinson College, The Trout Gallery, Carlisle PA

Miles B Carpenter Collection
Miles B Carpenter Folk Art Museum, Waverly VA

Carter & Eustis Collection of Furniture
Oatlands Plantation, Leesburg VA

Carter Collection of Pre-Columbian Art
Florida State University, Museum of Fine Arts, Tallahassee FL

Cesnola Collection
Stanford University, Cantor Arts Center at Stanford University, Stanford CA

George Chaplin Collection
Trinity College, Austin Arts Center, Widener Gallery, Hartford CT

Conrad Wise Chapman Oils Collection
Valentine Richmond History Center, Richmond VA

Alan Chasanoff Ceramic Collection
The Mint Museum, Mint Museum of Craft & Design, Charlotte NC

Chase Collection
Foosaner Art Museum, Melbourne FL

Winston Churchill Oil Painting Collection
Westminster College, Winston Churchill Memorial & Library in the United States, Fulton MO

Clark European Collection
Corcoran Gallery of Art, Washington DC

Clewell Pottery Collection
Besser Museum for Northeast Michigan, Alpena MI

Laura A Clubb Collection of Paintings
Philbrook Museum of Art, Tulsa OK

Cochran Collection of Windsor Chairs
Philipse Manor Hall State Historic Site, Yonkers NY

Cochrane Collection of American Art
Virginia Museum of Fine Arts, Richmond VA

Coe Collection
Coe College, Eaton-Buchan Gallery & Marvin Cone Gallery, Cedar Rapids IA

Colburn Collection of Indian Basketry
United States Department of the Interior, Interior Museum, Washington DC

Colburn Gemstone Collection
University of South Carolina, McKissick Museum, Columbia SC

Cole Collection of Oriental & Decorative Arts
Dickinson College, The Trout Gallery, Carlisle PA

George W Cole Smith & Wesson Gun Collection
Hastings Museum of Natural & Cultural History, Hastings NE

Joseph E Coleman Collection
African American Museum in Philadelphia, Philadelphia PA

Marvin Cone Alumni Collection
Coe College, Eaton-Buchan Gallery & Marvin Cone Gallery, Cedar Rapids IA

Cone Collection
The Baltimore Museum of Art, Baltimore MD

Coons Collection
City of Nome Alaska, Carrie M McLain Memorial Museum, Nome AK

Copeland Collection
Delaware Art Museum, Wilmington DE

Cosla Collection
Saint Mary's Romanian Orthodox Cathedral, Romanian Ethnic Museum, Cleveland OH

Cosla Collection of Renaissance Art
Montclair State University, Art Galleries, Upper Montclair NJ

F. Price Cossman Collection of Steuben Glass
Wichita Art Museum, Wichita KS

George Costakis Collection
State Museum of Contemporary Art, Thessaloniki

Costantini Collection
Museo de Arte Latinoamericano de Buenos Aires,
Buenos Aires

Cotter Collection
Saint Mary's College, Moreau Galleries, Notre Dame
IN

Couldery European Art Collection
Glanmore National Historic Site of Canada, Belleville
ON

Craig Collection of Edna Hibel's Work
Edna Hibel, Hibel Museum of Art, Jupiter FL

**Alexander M Craighead Collection of
European & American Military Art**
United States Military Academy, West Point Museum,
West Point NY

Crozier Collection of Chinese Art
Philadelphia Museum of Art, Main Building,
Philadelphia PA

**The Helen Warren & Willard Howe
Cummings Collection of American Art**
Colby College, Museum of Art, Waterville ME

Cybis Collection
Mercer County Community College, The Gallery, West
Windsor NJ

Czartoryski Collection
Muzeum Narodowe w Krakowie, National Museum in
Cracow, Krakow

**Cappadocia Collection of Southeast Asian
Textiles**
University of Montana, Montana Museum of Art &
Culture, Missoula MT

Cintas Foundation Collection
Florida International University, The Patricia & Phillip
Frost Art Museum, Miami FL
University of Miami, Lowe Art Museum, Coral Gables
FL

Clara Weaver Parish Collection
Sturdivant Museum Association, Sturdivant Museum,
Selma AL

The Clarendon Collection of Portraits
Plymouth City Museum and Art Gallery, Plymouth

Clifford M Clarke Collection
Agnes Scott College, Dalton Art Gallery, Decatur GA

Clowes Fund Collection
Indianapolis Museum of Art, Indianapolis IN

**Cohn Collection - 19th & 20th Century
Japanese Prints**
University of Louisiana at Lafayette, Paul and Lulu
Hilliard University Art Museum, Lafayette LA

Colorado Collection
University of Colorado, CU Art Museum, Boulder CO

Cone Collection
University of North Carolina at Greensboro,
Weatherspoon Art Museum, Greensboro NC

The Cottonian Collection
Plymouth City Museum and Art Gallery, Plymouth

**Samuel Courtauld Collection of Impressionist
& Post-Impressionist Art**
The Courtauld Institute of Art, The Courtauld Gallery,
London

Helen & Paul Covert Collection
Montana State University at Billings, Northcutt Steele
Gallery, Billings MT

Cowan Collection
Board of Parks & Recreation, The Parthenon, Nashville
TN

Chester Dale Collection
National Gallery of Art, Washington DC

Cyrus Dallin Bronze Collection
Springville Museum of Art, Springville UT

**Joseph E Davies Collection of Russian Icons
& Paintings**
University of Wisconsin-Madison, Chazen Museum of
Art, Madison WI

Norman Davis Collection of Classical Art
Seattle Art Museum, Downtown, Seattle WA

**Luis De Hoyos Collection of Pre-Columbian
Art**
Colgate University, Picker Art Gallery, Hamilton NY

Lockwood deForest Collection
Mark Twain, Hartford CT

**Agnes Delano Collection of Contemporary
American Watercolors & Prints**
Howard University, Gallery of Art, Washington DC

Percival DeLuce Memorial Collection
Northwest Missouri State University, DeLuce Art
Gallery, Maryville MO

Dicke Collection
University of Evansville, Krannert Gallery & Peterson
Gallery, Evansville IN

**Thomas S Dickey Civil War Ordnance
Collection**
Atlanta Historical Society Inc, Atlanta History Center,
Atlanta GA

Frank & Mary Alice Diener Collection
Fresno Metropolitan Museum, Fresno CA

Dillard Collection: Works on Paper
University of North Carolina at Greensboro,
Weatherspoon Art Museum, Greensboro NC

Maynard Dixon Collection
Brigham Young University, B F Larsen Gallery, Provo
UT

**F B Doane Collection of Western American
Art**
Frontier Times Museum, Bandera TX

Herman D Doochin Collection of Asian Art
Vanderbilt University, Vanderbilt University Fine Arts
Gallery, Nashville TN

Dorsky & Tannenbaum Collection
Fort Wayne Museum of Art, Inc, Fort Wayne IN

Dreyfus Collection of Paintings
Lehigh University Art Galleries, Museum Operation,
Bethlehem PA

DuBose Civil War Collection
Atlanta Historical Society Inc, Atlanta History Center,
Atlanta GA

Dunbarton Collection of Prints
Saint Mary's College, Moreau Galleries, Notre Dame
IN

**Dunnigan Collection of 19th Century
Etchings**
Parrish Art Museum, Water Mill NY

Duveneck Collection
Triton Museum of Art, Santa Clara CA

Harry L Dalton Collection
Agnes Scott College, Dalton Art Gallery, Decatur GA

Dana Collection of American Impressionists
University of Montana, Montana Museum of Art &
Culture, Missoula MT

De Beer Collection
Dunedin Public Art Gallery, Dunedin

Dorothy Adler Routh Collection of Cloisonne
Scripps College, Ruth Chandler Williamson Gallery,
Claremont CA

Anthony J Drexel Collection
Drexel University, Drexel Collection, Philadelphia PA

**Grace H Dreyfus Ancient Peruvian & Middle
Eastern Art Collection**
University of California, Santa Barbara, University Art
Museum, Santa Barbara CA

**Stella Duncan Collection of European
Paintings**
University of Montana, Montana Museum of Art &
Culture, Missoula MT

**Hogarth & Caroline Durieux Graphics
Collection**
Louisiana State University, Museum of Art, Baton
Rouge LA

George Eastman Legacy Collection
George Eastman, Rochester NY

The Edmond de Rothschild Collection
Musee du Jeu de Paume, Louvre Museum, Paris

Henry Eichheim Collection
Santa Barbara Museum of Art, Santa Barbara CA

Eisenstadt Collection
Lamar University, Dishman Art Museum, Beaumont
TX

Elkins Collection of Old Masters
Philadelphia Museum of Art, Main Building,
Philadelphia PA

The Bob & Mary Ernst Collection
Buena Vista Museum of Natural History, Bakersfield
CA

Erro Collection
Listasafan Reykjavikur - Reykjavik Art Museum,
Halfnarhus - Harbour House, Reykjavik

Esso Collection
University of Miami, Lowe Art Museum, Coral Gables
FL

Eteljorg Collection of African Art
Indianapolis Museum of Art, Indianapolis IN

William T Evans Collection
American Art Museum, Smithsonian Institution,
Washington DC

**Florence Naftzger Evans Collection of
Porcelain**
Wichita Art Museum, Wichita KS

**Mrs Arthur Kelly Evans Collection of Pottery
& Porcelain**
Virginia Museum of Fine Arts, Richmond VA

Ebnother Collection
Museum zu Allerheiligen, Schaffhausen

Eli Lilly Collection of Chinese Art
Indianapolis Museum of Art, Indianapolis IN

Elkins Collection
Casa Amesti, Monterey CA

Ellis Collection
Western Kentucky University, Kentucky Library & Museum, Bowling Green KY

Peter Carl Faberge Collection of Czarist Jewels
Virginia Museum of Fine Arts, Richmond VA

Fairbanks Collection
Fort Wayne Museum of Art, Inc, Fort Wayne IN

Dexter M Ferry Collection
Vassar College, The Frances Lehman Loeb Art Center, Poughkeepsie NY

Clark Field Collection of American Indian Crafts
Philbrook Museum of Art, Tulsa OK

Wally Findlay Collection
Northwood University, Jeannette Hare Art Gallery, West Palm Beach FL

Elizabeth Parke Firestone Collection of 18th Century Silver
Detroit Institute of Arts, Detroit MI

Fischer Collection of Expressionism
Virginia Museum of Fine Arts, Richmond VA

Elizabeth Holmes Fisher Collection
University of Southern California, USC Fisher Museum of Art, Los Angeles CA

Fisher Memorial Collection
Beloit College, Wright Museum of Art, Beloit WI

L L Fitzgerald Study Collection
University of Manitoba, School of Art Gallery, Winnipeg MB

Julius Fleischman Collection
University of Cincinnati, DAAP Galleries-College of Design Architecture, Art & Planning, Cincinnati OH

Robert Frank Photography Collection
Stanford University, Cantor Arts Center at Stanford University, Stanford CA

Simon Fraser Collection
Simon Fraser University, Simon Fraser University Gallery, Burnaby BC

Grace & Abigail French Collection
Rapid City Arts Council, Dahl Arts Center, Rapid City SD

Samuel Friedenberg Collection of Plaques & Medals
The Jewish Museum, New York NY

Patricia & Phillip Frost Collection
American Art Museum, Smithsonian Institution, Washington DC

Eugene Fuller Memorial Collection of Chinese Jades
Seattle Art Museum, Downtown, Seattle WA

Fearnside Collection of European Old Master Prints & Drawings
Lehigh University Art Galleries, Museum Operation, Bethlehem PA

Fedderson Collection of Rembrandt Collections
University of Notre Dame, Snite Museum of Art, Notre Dame IN

Edith H K Fetherston Collection
Fetherston Foundation, Packwood House Museum, Lewisburg PA

Flagg Collection of Haitian Art
Milwaukee Art Museum, Milwaukee WI

Forbes Family Collection
Captain Forbes House Museum, Milton MA

Dr C Ford Collection
Musee National, National Museum of Lebanon, Beirut

Fowler Collection
Gadsden Museum of Fine Arts, Inc, Gadsden Museum of Art and History, Gadsden AL

Harry J Stein-Samuel Friedenberg Collection
The Jewish Museum, New York NY

Gallatin Collection
Philadelphia Museum of Art, Main Building, Philadelphia PA

Garfield Collection
Sonoma State University, University Art Gallery, Rohnert Park CA

Garvan Collection of American Decorative Art
Yale University, Yale University Art Gallery, New Haven CT

Gebauer Collection of Cameroon Art
Portland Art Museum, Portland OR

The Matilda Geddings Gray Foundation Collection
New Orleans Museum of Art, New Orleans LA

Geesey Collection of Pennsylvania Dutch Folk Art
Philadelphia Museum of Art, Main Building, Philadelphia PA

John Gellatly Collection
American Art Museum, Smithsonian Institution, Washington DC

Harry L George Collection of Native American Art
Saint Joseph Museum, Saint Joseph MO

Gerard Collection of Bowling Green Photographs
Western Kentucky University, Kentucky Library & Museum, Bowling Green KY

Gerofsky Collection of African Art
Dickinson College, The Trout Gallery, Carlisle PA

Gibson Collection of Indian Materials
United States Department of the Interior, Interior Museum, Washington DC

Vivian & Gordon Gilkey Graphics Art Collection
Portland Art Museum, Portland OR

Gillert Collection of Ceramics
Philbrook Museum of Art, Tulsa OK

Arthur & Margaret Glasgow Collection of Renaissance Art
Virginia Museum of Fine Arts, Richmond VA

Harry C Goebel Collection
Saint John's University, Dr. M.T. Geoffrey Yeh Art Gallery, Queens NY

Barry M Goldwater Photograph Collection
Heard Museum, Phoenix AZ

The Lee Goodman Collection
Texas A&M University-Corpus Christi, Weil Art Gallery, Corpus Christi TX

Louisa Gordon Collection of Antiques
Frontier Times Museum, Bandera TX

Grace Collection of Paintings
Lehigh University Art Galleries, Museum Operation, Bethlehem PA

U S Grant Collection
George Washington University, The Dimock Gallery, Washington DC

Granville Collection
Musee des Beaux-Arts de Dijon, Museum of Fine Arts, Dijon

Charles A Greenfield Collection
The Metropolitan Museum of Art, New York NY

Ben & Abby Grey Foundation Collection of Contemporary Asian & Middle Eastern Art
New York University, Grey Art Gallery, New York NY

Grice Native American Ceramic Collection
The Mint Museum, Mint Museum of Craft & Design, Charlotte NC

Clara Champlain Griswold Toy Collection
Lyme Historical Society, Florence Griswold Museum, Old Lyme CT

Owen T Gromme Collection
University of Minnesota, The Bell Museum of Natural History, Minneapolis MN

Charles W Guildman Collection
University of Nebraska-Lincoln, Great Plains Art Museum, Lincoln NE

Irving R Gumbel Collection of Prints
Howard University, Gallery of Art, Washington DC

Robert Gumbiner Foundation Collection
Museum of Latin American Art, Long Beach CA

Gunther Collection
Saint Mary's Romanian Orthodox Cathedral, Romanian Ethnic Museum, Cleveland OH

Gurley Korean Pottery Collection
Beloit College, Wright Museum of Art, Beloit WI

Gussman Collection of African Sculpture
Philbrook Museum of Art, Tulsa OK

Gascoigne Collection
Leeds Museums & Galleries, Lotherton Hall, Leeds

Gillis Grafstrom Collection
United States Figure Skating Association, World Figure Skating Museum & Hall of Fame, Colorado Springs CO

Tom Golden's Christo Collection
Sonoma County Museum, Santa Rosa CA

The Gonor Collection
Allen Sapp, North Battleford SK

Gould Ivory Collection
University of the Ozarks, Stephens Gallery, Clarksville AR

Griffith Family Collection
Anacostia Community Museum, Smithsonian Institution, Washington DC

Gulbenkian Collection
Museu Calouste Gulbenkian, Lisbon

Gustav Holm Collection of Ammassalik in the 1880s
Greenland National Museum & Archives, Nuuk

Anka Gvozdanovic Coll
Muzej za Umjetnost i Obrt, Museum of Arts & Crafts, Zagreb

Paul M Hahn Collection of 18th Century English & American Silver
Berkshire Museum, Pittsfield MA

Mrs Virginia Bacher Haichol Artifact Collection
Hartnell College Gallery, Salinas CA

Frank M Hall Collection
University of Nebraska, Lincoln, Sheldon Memorial Art Gallery & Sculpture Garden, Lincoln NE

Vernon Hall Collection of European Medals
University of Wisconsin-Madison, Chazen Museum of Art, Madison WI

Hallmark Photographic Collection
The Nelson-Atkins Museum of Art, Kansas City MO

Hamilton Collection
Fort Wayne Museum of Art, Inc, Fort Wayne IN

Armand Hammer Collection
University of Southern California, USC Fisher Museum of Art, Los Angeles CA

Wilhelm Hansen Collection
Ordrupgaardsamlingen, Ordrupgaard, Charlottenlund

The Bill L Harbert Collection of European Art
Auburn University, Julie Collins Smith Museum, Auburn AL

Hartford Steam Boiler Collection of America
Lyme Historical Society, Florence Griswold Museum, Old Lyme CT

Marsden Hartley Memorial Collection
Bates College, Museum of Art, Lewiston ME

Fred Harvey Fine Arts Collection
Heard Museum, Phoenix AZ

Olga Hasbrouck Collection of Chinese Ceramics
Vassar College, The Frances Lehman Loeb Art Center, Poughkeepsie NY

Dr Ruth Wright Hayre Collection
African American Museum in Philadelphia, Philadelphia PA

William Randolph Hearst Collection of Arms & Armor & Flemish Tapestries
Detroit Institute of Arts, Detroit MI

Heeramaneck Collection of Asian Art
Virginia Museum of Fine Arts, Richmond VA

Heeramaneck Collection of Primitive Art
Seattle Art Museum, Downtown, Seattle WA

Herbert Waide Hemphill Jr Collection
American Art Museum, Smithsonian Institution, Washington DC

Herman Collection of Modern Chinese Woodcuts
Colgate University, Picker Art Gallery, Hamilton NY

Marieluise Hessel Collection
Bard College, Center for Curatorial Studies and the Hessel Museum of Art, Annandale-on-Hudson NY

Lida Hilton Print Collection
Montclair State University, Art Galleries, Upper Montclair NJ

Hinkhouse Collection of Contemporary Art
Coe College, Eaton-Buchan Gallery & Marvin Cone Gallery, Cedar Rapids IA

Hirschberg Collection of West African Arts
Topeka & Shawnee County Public Library, Alice C Sabatini Gallery, Topeka KS

Hirsh Collection of Oriental Rugs
Portland Art Museum, Portland OR

Gary M Hoffer '74 Memorial Photography Collection
Colgate University, Picker Art Gallery, Hamilton NY

Hogsett Collection
Fort Morgan Heritage Foundation, Fort Morgan CO

Alfred H & Eva Underhill Holbrook Collection of American Art
University of Georgia, Georgia Museum of Art, Athens GA

Willitts J Hole Collection
University of California, Los Angeles, UCLA at the Armand Hammer Museum of Art & Cultural Center, Los Angeles CA

Winslow Homer Collection
Colby College, Museum of Art, Waterville ME

Honda Collection of Southeast Asian Ceramics
Fukuoka Art Museum, Fukuoka

The Charlotte Stuart Hooker Collection
The Dixon Gallery & Gardens, Memphis TN

Hope Collection of Engraved Portraits
Oxford University, Ashmolean Museum, Oxford

Hosmer-Pillow-Vaughan Collection
Beaverbrook Art Gallery, Fredericton NB

F B Housser Memorial Collection
Museum London, London ON

J Harry Howard Gemstone Collection
University of South Carolina, McKissick Museum, Columbia SC

Joe & Lucy Howorth Collection
Delta State University, Fielding L Wright Art Center, Cleveland MS

Anna C Hoyt Collection of Old Masters
Vanderbilt University, Vanderbilt University Fine Arts Gallery, Nashville TN

William J Hubbard Drawings & Oils
Valentine Richmond History Center, Richmond VA

Winifred Kimball Hudnut Collection
University of Utah, Utah Museum of Fine Arts, Salt Lake City UT

Hudson & Carpenter Family Collection
City of Ukiah, Grace Hudson Museum & The Sun House, Ukiah CA

J Marvin Hunter Western Americana Collection
Frontier Times Museum, Bandera TX

Chapman H Hyams Collection
New Orleans Museum of Art, New Orleans LA

Hall Collection of American Folk Art
Milwaukee Art Museum, Milwaukee WI

Hammer Collections
University of California, Los Angeles, UCLA at the Armand Hammer Museum of Art & Cultural Center, Los Angeles CA

Haskell Collection of 19th-Century American & European Paintings
Frederic Remington, Ogdensburg NY

William Inge Memorabilia Collection
Independence Historical Museum & Art Center, Independence KS

Jene Isaacson Collection
California State University, Fullerton, Visual Arts Galleries, Fullerton CA

Henry & Martha Issacson Collection of 18th Century European Porcelain
Seattle Art Museum, Downtown, Seattle WA

William H Jackson Photo Collection
Colorado Historical Society, Colorado History Museum, Denver CO

Harry L Jackson Print Collection
Murray State University, Art Galleries, Murray KY

Jarves Collection of Italian Paintings
Yale University, Yale University Art Gallery, New Haven CT

Jeffersonian Collection
Thomas Jefferson, Monticello, Charlottesville VA

Jette Collection of American Painting in the Impressionist Period
Colby College, Museum of Art, Waterville ME

Jasper Johns Collection
Walker Art Center, Minneapolis MN

SC Johnson & Son Collection
American Art Museum, Smithsonian Institution, Washington DC

E Johnson Collection
Saint Louis County Historical Society, St. Louis County Historical Society, Duluth MN

Johnson Collection
Topeka & Shawnee County Public Library, Alice C Sabatini Gallery, Topeka KS

John G Johnson Collection of Old Masters
Philadelphia Museum of Art, Main Building, Philadelphia PA

Barbara Johnson Whaling Collection
San Francisco Maritime National Historical Park, Maritime Museum, San Francisco CA

Harriet Lane Johnston Collection
American Art Museum, Smithsonian Institution, Washington DC

Anna Russell Jones Collection
African American Museum in Philadelphia, Philadelphia PA

T Catesby Jones Collection of 20th Century European Art
Virginia Museum of Fine Arts, Richmond VA

Paul R Jones Collection of African American 20th Century Art
University of Delaware, University Museums, Newark DE

Raymond Jonson Reserved Retrospective Collection of Paintings
University of New Mexico, Raymond Jonson Collection & Archive, Albuquerque NM

Wilton Jaffee Roman Coin Collection
University of Colorado, CU Art Museum, Boulder CO

Jay Gould Collection
The National Trust for Historic Preservation, Lyndhurst, Tarrytown NY

Mrs James Johnson Collection of Contemporary American, British, Korean, Mexican & Japanese Ceramics
Scripps College, Ruth Chandler Williamson Gallery, Claremont CA

Era Katz Collection of Theatrical Marquis 1970's-1980's
Howard University, Gallery of Art, Washington DC

KATZEN COLLECTION
American University, Katzen Art Center Gallery, New York NY

The Edwin L & Ruth E Kennedy Southwest Native American Collection
Ohio University, Kennedy Museum of Art, Athens OH

Victor Kiam Painting Collection
New Orleans Museum of Art, New Orleans LA

Warren Kiefer Railroad Collection
Museum of Western Colorado, Museum of the West, Grand Junction CO

Kienbusch Collection of Arms & Armor
Philadelphia Museum of Art, Main Building, Philadelphia PA

Kloss Photo Collection
United States Figure Skating Association, World Figure Skating Museum & Hall of Fame, Colorado Springs CO

Koempel Spoon Collection
Passaic County Historical Society, Lambert Castle Museum & Library, Paterson NJ

Krannert Memorial Collection
University of Indianapolis, Christel DeHaan Fine Arts Gallery, Indianapolis IN

Samuel H Kress Collection
Allentown Art Museum, Allentown PA
City of El Paso, El Paso TX
National Gallery of Art, Washington DC
New Orleans Museum of Art, New Orleans LA
Philbrook Museum of Art, Tulsa OK
University of Miami, Lowe Art Museum, Coral Gables FL
Vanderbilt University, Vanderbilt University Fine Arts Gallery, Nashville TN

H Kress Collection of European Paintings
Seattle Art Museum, Downtown, Seattle WA

Kress Collection of Renaissance & Baroque Periods
City of El Paso, El Paso TX

Samuel H Kress Collection of Renaissance Painting & Sculpture
Portland Art Museum, Portland OR

Kress Study Collection
Howard University, Gallery of Art, Washington DC

Samuel H Kress Study Collection
Trinity College, Austin Arts Center, Widener Gallery, Hartford CT
University of Georgia, Georgia Museum of Art, Athens GA

Irma Kruse Collection
Hastings Museum of Natural & Cultural History, Hastings NE

Gordon Kuntz Collection
Will Rogers Memorial Museum & Birthplace Ranch, Claremore OK

Kurdian Collection of Pre-Columbian & Mexican Art
Wichita Art Museum, Wichita KS

Kusuma Collection of Textiles
Fukuoka Art Museum, Fukuoka

Kimura Teizo Collection
Aichi Prefectural Museum of Art, Nagoya

Kinne Water Turbine Collection
Jefferson County Historical Society, Watertown NY

Nan Kivell Collection of British Original Prints
Museum of New Zealand Te Papa Tongarewa, Museum of New Zealand Te Papa Tongarewa, Wellington

Kowalsky Collection
Ukrainian Institute of Modern Art, Chicago IL

Kraus II Collection of Modern & Contemporary Design
Philbrook Museum of Art, Tulsa OK

Kress Study Collection
University of Notre Dame, Snite Museum of Art, Notre Dame IN

Krone Collection
California State University, East Bay, C E Smith Museum of Anthropology, Hayward CA

Mary Andrews Ladd Collection of Japanese Prints
Portland Art Museum, Portland OR

Dr Paul Lamp Collection
Glanmore National Historic Site of Canada, Belleville ON

Larson Drawing Collection
Austin Peay State University, Mabel Larsen Fine Arts Gallery, Clarksville TN

Samuel K Lathrop Collection
University of Miami, Lowe Art Museum, Coral Gables FL

Latter-Schlesinger Miniature Collection
New Orleans Museum of Art, New Orleans LA

Roberta C Lawson Collection of Indian Costumes & Artifacts
Philbrook Museum of Art, Tulsa OK

Lawther Collection of Ethiopian Crosses
Portland Art Museum, Portland OR

Layman Glass Collection in Annie Pfeiffer Chapel
Florida Southern College, Melvin Art Gallery, Lakeland FL

Layton Collection
Milwaukee Art Museum, Milwaukee WI

Charles M Messer Leica Camera Collection
Miami University, Art Museum, Oxford OH

Roy C Leventritt Collection
Asian Art Museum of San Francisco, Chong-Moon Lee Ctr for Asian Art and Culture, San Francisco CA

Levin Collection
American Art Museum, Smithsonian Institution, Washington DC

Levy Collection
McMaster University, McMaster Museum of Art, Hamilton ON

Lewis Collection of Classical Antiquities
Portland Art Museum, Portland OR

Lewis-Kneberg Collection
University of Tennessee, McClung Museum of Natural History & Culture, Knoxville TN

Joans Lie Collection of Panama Canal Oils
United States Military Academy, West Point Museum, West Point NY

Jenny Lind Collection of Photos
The Barnum Museum, Bridgeport CT

Alain Locke Collection of African Art
Howard University, Gallery of Art, Washington DC

Locke Collection of Indian Artifacts
Roberts County Museum, Miami TX

Al Look Collection
Museum of Western Colorado, Museum of the West, Grand Junction CO

Loomis Wildlife Collection of Northeastern Birds and Mammals
Roberson Museum & Science Center, Binghamton NY

Lorimar Glass Collection
Philadelphia Museum of Art, Main Building, Philadelphia PA

Barry Lowen Collection
The Museum of Contemporary Art (MOCA), Moca Grand Avenue, Los Angeles CA

George A Lucas Collection
The Baltimore Museum of Art, Baltimore MD

Sir Hugh Lane Collection
Dublin City Gallery The Hugh Lane, Dublin

Langermann Collection of Pre-Columbian & Ethnographic Sculpture
Lehigh University Art Galleries, Museum Operation, Bethlehem PA

John D Lankenau Collection of 19th Century Paintings & Sculptures
Drexel University, Drexel Collection, Philadelphia PA

Lannan Foundation Collection
The Museum of Contemporary Art (MOCA), Moca Grand Avenue, Los Angeles CA

LeRoy M Backus Collection of Drawings & Paintings
Seattle Art Museum, Downtown, Seattle WA

Lee Archives
Washington & Lee University, Lee Chapel & Museum, Lexington VA

Lee Collection
California State University, East Bay, C E Smith Museum of Anthropology, Hayward CA

Lee Kong Chian Collection of Chinese Art
National University of Singapore Center for the Arts, Singapore

Lehman Collection, Medieval Art & The Cloisters
The Metropolitan Museum of Art, New York NY

Opal Leonard Collection of Chinese & Japanese Art
Montana State University at Billings, Northcutt Steele Gallery, Billings MT

Lucy Lewis Collection of Native American Pottery
Montclair State University, Art Galleries, Upper Montclair NJ

Linton-Surget Collection
Tulane University, University Art Collection, New Orleans LA

Lowe Collection - Outsider Art
University of Louisiana at Lafayette, Paul and Lulu Hilliard University Art Museum, Lafayette LA .

Lungren Collection
University of California, Santa Barbara, University Art Museum, Santa Barbara CA

Ernst Mahler Collection of Germanic Glass
Bergstrom-Mahler Museum, Neenah WI

Malcove Collection
University of Toronto, University of Toronto Art Centre, Toronto ON

Maltwood Collection of Decorative Art
University of Victoria, The Legacy Art Gallery, Victoria BC

Richard Mandell Collection
University of South Carolina, McKissick Museum, Columbia SC

Maness Collection of West and Central African Art
Guilford College, Art Gallery, Greensboro NC

Maningrida Collection of Aboriginal Art
Museum of Contemporary Art, Sydney

Edna Manley Memorial Collection
Institute of Jamaica, National Art Gallery of Jamaica, Kingston

Mildred Manty Memorial Collection
Mid-America All-Indian Center, Indian Center Museum, Wichita KS

Fred & Estelle Marer Contemporary Ceramics Collection
Scripps College, Ruth Chandler Williamson Gallery, Claremont CA

Marghab Linens Collection
South Dakota State University, South Dakota Art Museum, Brookings SD

John Marin Collection
Colby College, Museum of Art, Waterville ME

Markley Ancient Peruvian Ceramic Collection
The Pennsylvania State University, Palmer Museum of Art, University Park PA

Golda & Meyer B Marks Cobra Art Collection
Museum of Art, Fort Lauderdale, Fort Lauderdale FL

Matalon Collection
Institute of Jamaica, National Art Gallery of Jamaica, Kingston

Matsunaga Collection
Fukuoka Art Museum, Fukuoka

Andrew McClelland Collection of World Curiosities
Rosemount Museum, Inc, Pueblo CO

Bill McCoy Collection
Halifax Historical Society, Inc, Halifax Historical Museum, Daytona Beach FL

McFadden Collection of Old Masters
Philadelphia Museum of Art, Main Building, Philadelphia PA

Gladys McFerron Collection
United States Figure Skating Association, World Figure Skating Museum & Hall of Fame, Colorado Springs CO

McLain Collection
City of Nome Alaska, Carrie M McLain Memorial Museum, Nome AK

George F McMurray Collection
Trinity College, Austin Arts Center, Widener Gallery, Hartford CT

Paul McPharlin Collection of Theatre & Graphic Arts
Detroit Institute of Arts, Detroit MI

Mead Collection of Mammoth Bones & Fossils
Roberts County Museum, Miami TX

Ray Meadows Collection
Mid-America All-Indian Center, Indian Center Museum, Wichita KS

Algur H Meadows Collection of Spanish Paintings
Southern Methodist University, Meadows Museum, Dallas TX

Hamilton King Meek Memorial Collection
Museum London, London ON

Andrew W Mellon Collection
National Gallery of Art, Washington DC

Conger Metcalf Collection of Paintings
Coe College, Eaton-Buchan Gallery & Marvin Cone Gallery, Cedar Rapids IA

Michael Silver Collection
University of Utah, Utah Museum of Fine Arts, Salt Lake City UT

James & Mari Michener Collection of American Paintings
University of Texas at Austin, Blanton Museum of Art, Austin TX

Mielke Collection
City of Nome Alaska, Carrie M McLain Memorial Museum, Nome AK

The Louise Hauss & David Brent Miller Audubon Collection
Auburn University, Julie Collins Smith Museum, Auburn AL

Rose & Benjamin Mintz Collection of Eastern European Art
The Jewish Museum, New York NY

Moore Collection
Museum London, London ON

Marianne Moore Papers Collection
The Rosenbach Museum & Library, Philadelphia PA

Morse Collection
Beloit College, Wright Museum of Art, Beloit WI

Preston Morton Collection of American Art
Santa Barbara Museum of Art, Santa Barbara CA

Mourot Collection of Meissen Porcelain
Virginia Museum of Fine Arts, Richmond VA

The General Munthe Collection of Chinese Art
Vestlandske Kunstindustrimuseum, West Norway Museum of Decorative Art, Bergen

Roland P Murdock Collection of American Art
Wichita Art Museum, Wichita KS

Murphy Collection
University of California, Los Angeles, UCLA at the Armand Hammer Museum of Art & Cultural Center, Los Angeles CA

Eadweard Muybridge Photography Collection
Stanford University, Cantor Arts Center at Stanford University, Stanford CA

Madden Arnholz Collection
Irish Museum of Modern Art, Dublin

Marcia Simon Weisman Collection
The Museum of Contemporary Art (MOCA), Moca Grand Avenue, Los Angeles CA

Jane & Arthur Mason Collection
The Mint Museum, Mint Museum of Craft & Design, Charlotte NC

McGregor Collection of Rare Books
Western Kentucky University, Kentucky Library & Museum, Bowling Green KY

William McKendree Snyder Collection
Jefferson County Historical Society Museum, Madison IN

William Merritt Chase Collection
Parrish Art Museum, Water Mill NY

Meserve Collection
National Portrait Gallery, Smithsonian Institution, Washington DC

Mestrovich Collection
Fondazione Musei Civici Di Venezia, Ca'Rezzonico, Museo del Settecento Veneziano, Venice

Michener Collection of Prints & Paintings
Kent State University, School of Art Galleries, Kent OH

Milton Wichner Collection
Long Beach Museum of Art Foundation, Long Beach CA

Miriam Cowger Allen Doll Collection
The Art Association of Jacksonville, The David Strawn Art Gallery, Jacksonville IL

William C Mithoefer Collection of African Art
The College of Wooster, The College of Wooster Art Museum, Wooster OH

Mola's Collection - Donations & Acquisitions
Museum of Latin American Art, Long Beach CA

Monrad Collection of Early European Graphics
Museum of New Zealand Te Papa Tongarewa, Museum of New Zealand Te Papa Tongarewa, Wellington

Moore Collection
University of Illinois at Urbana-Champaign, Krannert Art Museum and Kinkead Pavilion, Champaign IL

C B Moore Collection
National Museum of the American Indian, Smithsonian Institution, Washington DC

Morgenroth Renaissance Medals & Plaquettes Collection
University of California, Santa Barbara, University Art Museum, Santa Barbara CA

Morrison Collection
University of Minnesota Duluth, Tweed Museum of Art, Duluth MN

Mrs Lynn Anna Louise Miller Collection of Contemporary United States Primitive
Viterbo University, Art Gallery, La Crosse WI

Musgrave Kinley Outsider Art Collection
Irish Museum of Modern Art, Dublin

M C Naftzger Collection of Charles M Russell Paintings
Wichita Art Museum, Wichita KS

Nagel Collection of Chinese & Tibetan Sculpture & Textiles
Scripps College, Clark Humanities Museum, Claremont CA

The Nagel Collection of Oriental Ceramics & Sculpture
University of California, Richard L Nelson Gallery & Fine Arts Collection, Davis CA

Elizabeth S Navas Papers
Wichita Art Museum, Wichita KS

Neese Fund Collection of Contemporary Art
Beloit College, Wright Museum of Art, Beloit WI

Harry Neigher Collection of Political Cartoons, 1928-1975
Colgate University, Picker Art Gallery, Hamilton NY

The Nelson and Joan Cousins Hartman Collection of Tibetan Bronzes
Auburn University, Julie Collins Smith Museum, Auburn AL

Nelson Maritime Arts Foundation Collection
Channel Islands Maritime Museum, Oxnard CA

Mrs Leslie Fenton Netsuke Collection
Hartnell College Gallery, Salinas CA

Newcomb Pottery Collection
West Baton Rouge Parish, West Baton Rouge Museum, Port Allen LA

Louise Norton Classic Design Collection
State University of New York at Plattsburgh, Art Museum, Plattsburgh NY

Harry T Norton Collection of Ancient Glass
Montreal Museum of Fine Arts, Montreal PQ

Alice B Nunn Silver Collection
Portland Art Museum, Portland OR

Neal Collection of Utopian Materials
Western Kentucky University, Kentucky Library & Museum, Bowling Green KY

Nelson International Ceramics
University of Minnesota Duluth, Tweed Museum of Art, Duluth MN

Nezu Kaichiro Sr Collection
Nezu Bijusukan, Nezu Museum, Tokyo

Bill & Polly Nordeen Collection of Western Art
University of Montana, Montana Museum of Art & Culture, Missoula MT

Oceanic Collection
Southern Illinois University Carbondale, University Museum, Carbondale IL

David T Owskley Collection of Ethnographic Art
Ball State University, Museum of Art, Muncie IN

Olsen Collection
University of Illinois at Urbana-Champaign, Krannert Art Museum and Kinkead Pavilion, Champaign IL

Oppenheimer Collection of Late Medieval & Early Renaissance Sculpture & Paintings
McNay, San Antonio TX

Oscar & Maria Salzer Collection of Still Life & Trompe l'oeil Paintings
Fresno Metropolitan Museum, Fresno CA

Overmyer Civil War Collection
Fulton County Historical Society Inc, Fulton County Museum (Tetzlaff Reference Room), Rochester IN

Kenan Ozbel Private Collections
Topkapi Palace Museum, Istanbul

A S Palmer Film Collection
San Francisco Maritime National Historical Park, Maritime Museum, San Francisco CA

Panza Collection
The Museum of Contemporary Art (MOCA), Moca Grand Avenue, Los Angeles CA

Parish Collection of Belter Furniture
Frederic Remington, Ogdensburg NY

Samuel Parrish Collection of Renaissance Art
Parrish Art Museum, Water Mill NY

Ralph M Parsons Foundation Photography Collection
The Museum of Contemporary Art (MOCA), Moca Grand Avenue, Los Angeles CA

The Paulson Collection of Ancient Near Eastern Coins
University of Georgia, Georgia Museum of Art, Athens GA

John Barton Payne Collection
Virginia Museum of Fine Arts, Richmond VA

Adelaide Pearson Collection
Colby College, Museum of Art, Waterville ME

Joseph Pennell Collection
George Washington University, The Dimock Gallery, Washington DC

Betty Laird Perry Emerging Artist Collection & Sculpture Park
Florida International University, The Patricia & Phillip Frost Art Museum, Miami FL

The Adler Pewter Collection
The Dixon Gallery & Gardens, Memphis TN

Phelps Collection of Andrew Wyeth Works
Delaware Art Museum, Wilmington DE

Lucile Pillow Porcelain Collection
Montreal Museum of Fine Arts, Montreal PQ

Bert Piso Collection
New Orleans Museum of Art, New Orleans LA

Pitkin Asian Art Collection
Beloit College, Wright Museum of Art, Beloit WI

Pohl Collection-German Expressionism
Lawrence University, Wriston Art Center Galleries, Appleton WI

Sigmar Polke Collection
Walker Art Center, Minneapolis MN

William J Pollock Collection of American Indian Art
Colby College, Museum of Art, Waterville ME

Porter-Phelps-Huntington Family Collection
Porter-Phelps-Huntington Foundation, Inc, Historic House Museum, Hadley MA

Potamkin Collection of 19th & 20th Century Work
Dickinson College, The Trout Gallery, Carlisle PA

Potlatch Collection of Royal Canadian Mounted Police Illustrations
University of Minnesota Duluth, Tweed Museum of Art, Duluth MN

J W Power Collection
Museum of Contemporary Art, Sydney

Powers Ceramics Collection
Cornell College, Peter Paul Luce Gallery, Mount Vernon IA

Charles Pratt Collection of Chinese Jades
Vassar College, The Frances Lehman Loeb Art Center, Poughkeepsie NY

Lillian Thomas Pratt Collection of Czarist Jewels
Virginia Museum of Fine Arts, Richmond VA

William Henry Price Memorial Collection of Oil Paintings
Oregon State University, Memorial Union Art Gallery, Corvallis OR

Putnam Collection
Timken Museum of Art, San Diego CA

Ike Parker Collection: Callie Hart
Henry County Museum & Cultural Arts Center, Clinton MO

Parker Lace Collection
Montreal Museum of Fine Arts, Montreal PQ

Pfeffer Moser Glass Collection
University of the Ozarks, Stephens Gallery, Clarksville AR

Pinto Collection
Birmingham Museums Trust, Birmingham Museums and Art Gallery, Birmingham

Pittman Collection of Oil, Watercolors, and Drawings
Edgecombe County Cultural Arts Council, Inc, Blount-Bridgers House, Hobson Pittman Memorial Gallery, Tarboro NC

Pope & Leighey Family Collections
Frank Lloyd Wright, Mount Vernon VA

Prasse Collection of Prints
Lehigh University Art Galleries, Museum Operation, Bethlehem PA

RA Young Collection
Oklahoma City Museum of Art, Oklahoma City OK

Natacha Rambova Egyptian Collection
University of Utah, Utah Museum of Fine Arts, Salt Lake City UT

Ramingining Collection of Aboriginal Art
Museum of Contemporary Art, Sydney

Rasmussen Collection of Eskimo Art
Portland Art Museum, Portland OR

Theo Redwood Blank Doll Collection
Houston Baptist University, Museum of American
Architecture and Decorative Arts, Houston TX

Remington Bronze Collection
Pioneer Town, Pioneer Museum of Western Art,
Wimberley TX

Frederic Remington Collection
R W Norton Art Foundation, R W Norton Art Gallery,
Shreveport LA

R J Reynolds Collection
Wake Forest University, Charlotte & Philip Hanes Art
Gallery, Winston Salem NC

Richards Coin Collection
Hastings Museum of Natural & Cultural History,
Hastings NE

David Roberts Collection
Riverside County Museum, Edward-Dean Museum &
Gardens, Cherry Valley CA

Evan H Roberts Sculpture Collection
Portland Art Museum, Portland OR

Marion Sharp Robinson Collection
University of Utah, Utah Museum of Fine Arts, Salt
Lake City UT

Sara Roby Foundation Collection
American Art Museum, Smithsonian Institution,
Washington DC

**Mr & Mrs John D Rockefeller 3D Collection
of Asian Art**
The Asia Society Museum, New York NY

Wilson Rockwell Collection
Museum of Western Colorado, Museum of the West,
Grand Junction CO

Robert F Rockwell Foundation Collection
The Rockwell Museum of Western Art, Corning NY

Rodman Collection of Popular Art
The Art Galleries of Ramapo College, Mahwah NJ

Guy Rowe Wax Drawings Collection
Angelo State University, Houston Harte University
Center, San Angelo TX

Roycroft Collection
State University of New York College at Buffalo,
Buffalo NY

Edmond R Ruben Film Study Collection
Walker Art Center, Minneapolis MN

Ruesch Collection of Whistler Lithographs
University of California, Richard L Nelson Gallery &
Fine Arts Collection, Davis CA

Charles M Russell Collection
R W Norton Art Foundation, R W Norton Art Gallery,
Shreveport LA

Rawlings Nelson Collection
University of Minnesota Duluth, Tweed Museum of
Art, Duluth MN

**J Henry Ray American Indian Artifacts
Collection**
Red River Valley Museum, Vernon TX

Reid Bill Collection
Bill Reid Gallery of Northwest Coast Art, Vancouver
BC

Reilly Collection of Old Master Drawings
University of Notre Dame, Snite Museum of Art, Notre
Dame IN

Frederic Remington Collection
Sid W Richardson, Sid Richardson Museum, Fort
Worth TX

Reuven Lipchitz Collection
The Israel Museum, Jerusalem, Billy Rose Art Garden,
Jerusalem

Rich Collection: Rare Books & Manuscripts
The Huntington Library, Art Collections & Botanical
Gardens, San Marino CA

Maurice & Esther Leah Ritz Collection
Milwaukee Art Museum, Milwaukee WI

Mr & Mrs Edward Rose Collection
Brandeis University, Rose Art Museum, Waltham MA

Charles M Russell Collection
Sid W Richardson, Sid Richardson Museum, Fort
Worth TX

Arthur M Sackler Collection
Freer Gallery of Art & Arthur M Sackler Gallery,
Arthur M Sackler Gallery, Washington DC

Sackler Collection
The Metropolitan Museum of Art, New York NY

**Evelyn McCurdy Salisbury Ceramic
Collection**
Lyme Historical Society, Florence Griswold Museum,
Old Lyme CT

**Oscar & Maria Salzer Collection of 16th &
17th Century Dutch & Flemish Paintings**
Fresno Metropolitan Museum, Fresno CA

Jonathan Sax Print Collection
University of Minnesota Duluth, Tweed Museum of
Art, Duluth MN

**Schiller Collection of Social Commentary Art
1930-1970**
Columbus Museum of Art, Columbus OH

**Schissler Antique Miniature Furniture
Collection**
Houston Baptist University, Museum of American
Architecture and Decorative Arts, Houston TX

Alice F Schott Doll Collection
Santa Barbara Museum of Art, Santa Barbara CA

Rita & Taft Schreiber Collection
The Museum of Contemporary Art (MOCA), Moca
Grand Avenue, Los Angeles CA

Schuette Woodland Indian Collection
Rahr-West Art Museum, Manitowoc WI

Hazel Schwentker Collection
Rapid City Arts Council, Dahl Arts Center, Rapid City
SD

Scotese Collection of Graphics
Columbia Museum of Art, Columbia SC

Isaac Scott Collection
Glessner House Museum, Chicago IL

A D Scott Collection
Institute of Jamaica, National Art Gallery of Jamaica,
Kingston

Seibels Collection of Renaissance Art
Columbia Museum of Art, Columbia SC

Maurice Sendak Archive
The Rosenbach Museum & Library, Philadelphia PA

**William Ludwell Sheppard Watercolor
Collection**
Valentine Richmond History Center, Richmond VA

**Philip Trammell Shutze Collection of
Decorative Arts**
Atlanta Historical Society Inc, Atlanta History Center,
Atlanta GA

Simmons Collection
Wake Forest University, Charlotte & Philip Hanes Art
Gallery, Winston Salem NC

Slathin Collection
State University of New York at Plattsburgh, Art
Museum, Plattsburgh NY

Sloan Collection
Valparaiso University, Brauer Museum of Art,
Valparaiso IN

Charles Small Puzzle Collection
Fresno Metropolitan Museum, Fresno CA

**Smith Collection of European & American
Paintings**
Woodmere Art Museum Inc, Philadelphia PA

**C R Smith Collection of Western American
Art**
University of Texas at Austin, Blanton Museum of Art,
Austin TX

Smith Watch Key Collection
Rollins College, George D & Harriet W Cornell Fine
Arts Museum, Winter Park FL

Hazel Smith Collection
Austin Peay State University, Mabel Larsen Fine Arts
Gallery, Clarksville TN

Smith-Patterson Memorial Collection
Delta State University, Fielding L Wright Art Center,
Cleveland MS

**Loti & Victor Smorgon Collection of
Contemporary Australian Art**
Museum of Contemporary Art, Sydney

Snelgrove Historical Collection
Gadsden Museum of Fine Arts, Inc, Gadsden Museum
of Art and History, Gadsden AL

Scott D F Spiegel Collection
The Museum of Contemporary Art (MOCA), Moca
Grand Avenue, Los Angeles CA

Anisoara Stan Collection
Saint Mary's Romanian Orthodox Cathedral, Romanian
Ethnic Museum, Cleveland OH

Stanford Family Collection
Stanford University, Cantor Arts Center at Stanford
University, Stanford CA

**Ann Louise Stanton Antique Dollhead
Collection**
Southern Ohio Museum Corporation, Southern Ohio
Museum, Portsmouth OH

**Stegeman Collection of Japanese Woodcut
Prints**
Northwestern College, Te Paske Gallery, Orange City
IA

Steinberg Collection
University of Texas at Austin, Blanton Museum of Art, Austin TX

Stern Collection
Philadelphia Museum of Art, Main Building, Philadelphia PA

Harold P Stern Collection of Oriental Art
Vanderbilt University, Vanderbilt University Fine Arts Gallery, Nashville TN

Carder Steuben Glass Collection
The Rockwell Museum of Western Art, Corning NY

Dorothy Stevens Collection
United States Figure Skating Association, World Figure Skating Museum & Hall of Fame, Colorado Springs CO

Alfred Stieglitz Center Collection of Photography
Philadelphia Museum of Art, Main Building, Philadelphia PA

Alfred Stieglitz Collection of Modern Art
Fisk University, Carl Van Vechten Gallery, Nashville TN

Thomas D Stimson Memorial Collection of Far Eastern Art
Seattle Art Museum, Downtown, Seattle WA

Stoddard Collection of Greek Vases
Yale University, Yale University Art Gallery, New Haven CT

Warda Stevens Stout Collection of 18th Century German Porcelain
The Dixon Gallery & Gardens, Memphis TN

Swallow Collection of Inuit and Indian Art
Red Deer & District Museum & Archives, Red Deer AB

Samuel H Kress Coll European Paintings & Sculpture
University of Wisconsin-Madison, Chazen Museum of Art, Madison WI

Samuel H Kress Collection of Renaissance Paintings
Columbia Museum of Art, Columbia SC
The Pomona College, Claremont CA

Sara Hilden Foundation Collection
Sara Hilden Art Museum, Tampere

Sawhill Artifact Collection
James Madison University, Sawhill Gallery, Harrisonburg VA

Sedgwick Collection
University of California, Santa Barbara, University Art Museum, Santa Barbara CA

Floyd & Josephine Segel Collection of Photography
Milwaukee Art Museum, Milwaukee WI

Sharp Collection of Period Glass, China, Silver & Cameos
Frederic Remington, Ogdensburg NY

Shuey Collection
Cranbrook Art Museum, Bloomfield Hills MI

Max Simon Comic Book Collection
The Children's Museum of Indianapolis, Indianapolis IN

Paul & Fanny Sinebrychoff Collection
Valtion Taidemuseo - Finnish National Art Gallery, Sinebrychoffin Taidemuseo - Sinebrychoff Art Museum, Helsinki

The Anna B & William H Singer Collection of Art & Antiquities
Vestlandske Kunstindustrimuseum, West Norway Museum of Decorative Art, Bergen

Sir John Ilott Collection of Prints
Museum of New Zealand Te Papa Tongarewa, Museum of New Zealand Te Papa Tongarewa, Wellington

Helen S Slosberg Collection
Brandeis University, Rose Art Museum, Waltham MA

Sonnenschein Collection of European Drawings
Cornell College, Peter Paul Luce Gallery, Mount Vernon IA

Marcia & Granvil Specks Collection
Milwaukee Art Museum, Milwaukee WI

Stuart M Speiser Collection of Photo Realist Art
National Air and Space Museum, Smithsonian Institution, Washington DC

Staples Collection of Indonesian Art
James Madison University, Sawhill Gallery, Harrisonburg VA

Stemmler Collection
Museum zu Allerheiligen, Schaffhausen

Stern-Davis Collection of Peruvian Painting
New Orleans Museum of Art, New Orleans LA

Sturzenegger Collection
Museum zu Allerheiligen, Schaffhausen

Suida-Manning Collection
University of Texas at Austin, Blanton Museum of Art, Austin TX

Tabor Collection of Oriental Art
Philbrook Museum of Art, Tulsa OK

Tamassy Collection of Old Masterworks on Paper
Northwood University, Jeannette Hare Art Gallery, West Palm Beach FL

Robert H Tannahill Collection of Impressionist & Post Impressionist Paintings
Detroit Institute of Arts, Detroit MI

Taos Society of Artists Collection
Taos, Ernest Blumenschein Home & Studio, Taos NM

Justin K Thannhauser Collection of Impressionist & Post-Impressionist Paintings
Solomon R Guggenheim, New York NY
Guggenheim Museum Soho, New York NY

Thatcher Family Collection
Rosemount Museum, Inc, Pueblo CO

Thieme Collection
Fort Wayne Museum of Art, Inc, Fort Wayne IN

Tobias Collection of African and Oceanic Art and Artifacts
William Paterson University, Ben Shahn Art Galleries, Wayne NJ

Tolliver Collection
Zigler Art Museum, Jennings LA

Tonkin Collection of Chinese Export Porcelain
The Pennsylvania State University, Palmer Museum of Art, University Park PA

James Townes Medal Collection
Delta State University, Fielding L Wright Art Center, Cleveland MS

Trovwer Silver Collection
University of Utah, Utah Museum of Fine Arts, Salt Lake City UT

Tucker Porcelain Collection
Philadelphia Museum of Art, Main Building, Philadelphia PA

J M W Turner Collection
Indianapolis Museum of Art, Indianapolis IN

Lyle Tuttle Collection
Tattoo Art Museum, San Francisco CA

George P Tweed Memorial Collection of American & European Paintings
University of Minnesota Duluth, Tweed Museum of Art, Duluth MN

Tyson Collection
Philadelphia Museum of Art, Main Building, Philadelphia PA

Joey and Toby Tanenbaum Collection
Art Gallery of Hamilton, Hamilton ON

Thanos Zintilis Cypriot art coll
Museum of Cycladic Art, Athens

The Olga Denison Collection - Anishinaabe art objects
Central Michigan University, University Art Gallery, Mount Pleasant MI

The Walt Disney-Tishman African Art Collection
National Museum of African Art, Smithsonian Institution, Washington DC

Thorvaldsen's Collection of Antiquities
Thorvaldsens Museum, Copenhagen

Tobin Theatre Arts Collection
McNay, San Antonio TX

Tokugawa Family Collection
The Tokugawa Reimeikai Foundation, The Tokugawa Art Museum, Nagoya

Tombaugh World War II Collection
Fulton County Historical Society Inc, Fulton County Museum (Tetzlaff Reference Room), Rochester IN

Trees Collection of European & American Painting
University of Illinois at Urbana-Champaign, Krannert Art Museum and Kinkead Pavilion, Champaign IL

Lorenzo Dow Turner Collection
Anacostia Community Museum, Smithsonian Institution, Washington DC

Turner Collection of Asian Art
Columbia Museum of Art, Columbia SC

Tyler Coverlet Collection
Jefferson County Historical Society, Watertown NY

Edward Virginius Valentine Sculpture Collection
Valentine Richmond History Center, Richmond VA

Catherine Van Rensselaer Bonney Collection of Oriental Decorative Art
Historic Cherry Hill, Albany NY

Carl Van Vechten Collection of Photographs
Fisk University, Carl Van Vechten Gallery, Nashville TN
Hammond Museum & Japanese Stroll Garden, Cross-Cultural Center, North Salem NY

Van Vleck Collection of Japenese Prints
University of Wisconsin-Madison, Chazen Museum of Art, Madison WI

Vanderpoel Collection of Asian Art
Norwich Free Academy, Slater Memorial Museum, Norwich CT

Matthew Vassar Collection
Vassar College, The Frances Lehman Loeb Art Center, Poughkeepsie NY

Vever Collection
Freer Gallery of Art & Arthur M Sackler Gallery, Arthur M Sackler Gallery, Washington DC

Voertman Collection
University of North Texas, Art Gallery, Denton TX

Rene von Schleintz Collection
Milwaukee Art Museum, Milwaukee WI

Vincent Van Gogh's Personal Collection: English & French Prints, Japanese Woodcuts
Van Gogh Museum, Amsterdam

Vogel Collection
University of Nevada, Las Vegas, Donna Beam Fine Art Gallery, Las Vegas NV

Wagner Collection of African Sculpture
Scripps College, Clark Humanities Museum, Claremont CA
Scripps College, Ruth Chandler Williamson Gallery, Claremont CA

Walker Collection of French Impressionists
Corcoran Gallery of Art, Washington DC

C G Wallace Collection
Heard Museum, Phoenix AZ

Cloud Wampler Collection of Oriental Art
Everson Museum of Art, Syracuse NY

Felix M Warburg Collection of Medieval Sculpture
Vassar College, The Frances Lehman Loeb Art Center, Poughkeepsie NY

Austen D Warburton Native American Art & Artifacts Collection
Triton Museum of Art, Santa Clara CA

Ernest C & Jane Werner Watson Collection of Indian Miniatures
University of Wisconsin-Madison, Chazen Museum of Art, Madison WI

Weatherhead Collection
Fort Wayne Museum of Art, Inc, Fort Wayne IN

Wedgwood Collection
R W Norton Art Foundation, R W Norton Art Gallery, Shreveport LA

Teresa Jackson Weill Collection
Brandeis University, Rose Art Museum, Waltham MA

J Alden Weir Collection
Brigham Young University, B F Larsen Gallery, Provo UT

Wellington Collection of Wood Engravings
Mobile Museum of Art, Mobile AL

Westheimer Family Collection
Oklahoma City Museum of Art, Oklahoma City OK

Candace Wheeler Collection
Mark Twain, Hartford CT

White Collection
Philadelphia Museum of Art, Main Building, Philadelphia PA

Katherine C White Collection of African Art
Seattle Art Museum, Downtown, Seattle WA

Whiting Collection of Phoenician Glass
Cornell College, Peter Paul Luce Gallery, Mount Vernon IA

Morgan-Whitney Collection of Chinese Jades
New Orleans Museum of Art, New Orleans LA

Grace Whitney-Hoff Collection of Fine Bindings
Detroit Institute of Arts, Detroit MI

Whittington Memorial Collection
Delta State University, Fielding L Wright Art Center, Cleveland MS

Wiant Collection of Chinese Art
Ohio State University, Wexner Center for the Arts, Columbus OH

Bartlett Wicks Collection
University of Utah, Utah Museum of Fine Arts, Salt Lake City UT

Widener Collection
National Gallery of Art, Washington DC

Albert H Wiggin Collection
Boston Public Library, Albert H Wiggin Gallery & Print Department, Boston MA

Wilder Collection of Art Nouveau Glass & Ceramics
Topeka & Shawnee County Public Library, Alice C Sabatini Gallery, Topeka KS

John Wiley Collection
Concordia University Wisconsin, Fine Art Gallery, Mequon WI

Will Collection of Paintings & Drawings
Jersey City Museum, Jersey City NJ

Adolph D & Wilkins C Williams Collection
Virginia Museum of Fine Arts, Richmond VA

Elizabeth Bayley Willis Collection of Textiles from India
University of Washington, Henry Art Gallery, Seattle WA

Ralph Wilson Collection of American Paintings and Graphics
Lehigh University Art Galleries, Museum Operation, Bethlehem PA

Robert E Wilson Collection of Paintings & Sculpture
Huntington University, Robert E Wilson Art Gallery, Huntington IN

Wilstach Collection of Old Masters
Philadelphia Museum of Art, Main Building, Philadelphia PA

Wingert Collection of African & Oceanic Art
Montclair State University, Art Galleries, Upper Montclair NJ

Larry Wirth Collection
Institute of Jamaica, National Art Gallery of Jamaica, Kingston

Grant Wood Collection
Coe College, Eaton-Buchan Gallery & Marvin Cone Gallery, Cedar Rapids IA

Howard E Wooden Papers
Wichita Art Museum, Wichita KS

Jack Woods Collection
Pioneer Town, Pioneer Museum of Western Art, Wimberley TX

Theodore Wores Collection
Triton Museum of Art, Santa Clara CA

W Lloyd Wright Collection
George Washington University, The Dimock Gallery, Washington DC

Lenoir C Wright Collection of Japanese Woodblock Prints
University of North Carolina at Greensboro, Weatherspoon Art Museum, Greensboro NC

Wyeth Family Collection
Brandywine Conservancy, Brandywine River Museum, Chadds Ford PA

Wachovia Permanent Collection
Burke Arts Council, Jailhouse Galleries, Morganton NC

Walter Jean & Paul Guillaume
Musee d'Orsay, Musee de Orangerie, Paris

Washington-Custis-Lee Art Collection
Washington & Lee University, Lee Chapel & Museum, Lexington VA

Wayne State Foundation Print Collection
Wayne State College, Nordstrand Visual Arts Gallery, Wayne NE

I Webb Surratt Jr Print Collection
University of Richmond, University Museums, Richmond VA

Weiss Collection
Northern Arizona University, Art Museum & Galleries, Flagstaff AZ

Weltkunst Foundation Collection
Irish Museum of Modern Art, Dublin

Wiiken Contemporary Glass Collection
University of Minnesota Duluth, Tweed Museum of Art, Duluth MN

William Keith Paintings Collection
Saint Mary's College of California, Hearst Art Gallery, Moraga CA

Mr & Mrs Franklin H Williams Collection of African Art
Lehigh University Art Galleries, Museum Operation, Bethlehem PA

Willis Print Collection
Lamar University, Dishman Art Museum, Beaumont TX

Wolfgang Gurlitt Collection
Lentos Art Museum, Linz

Wright Photography Collection
Grace Museum, Inc, Abilene TX

General Edward Young Collection of American Paintings
Scripps College, Ruth Chandler Williamson Gallery, Claremont CA

Mahonri Young Collection of Manuscripts
Brigham Young University, B F Larsen Gallery, Provo
UT

Zundel Collection of Oriental Materials
Southern Oregon University, Schneider Museum of Art,
Ashland OR

Hammer Honore's Daumier Collection
University of California, Los Angeles, Grunwald Center
for the Graphic Arts at Hammer Museum, Los
Angeles CA

W J Holliday Collection
Indianapolis Museum of Art, Indianapolis IN

Personal Index

Aaberg, Patricia, *Dir,* Liberty Village Arts Center & Gallery, Chester MT

Aakhus, Michael, *Prof,* University of Southern Indiana, Department of Art, Evansville IN (S)

Aaron, Billye, *Sr Chmn,* The APEX Museum, Atlanta GA

Aaronson, Lawrence R, *Dean Arts & Sciences,* Utica College of Syracuse University, Division of Art & Science, Utica NY (S)

Abbatiello, Darcie, *Registrar,* University at Albany, State University of New York, University Art Museum, Albany NY

Abbe, Ronald, *Prog Coordr,* Housatonic Community College, Art Dept, Bridgeport CT (S)

Abbot, James Archer, *Cur,* Johns Hopkins University, Evergreen Museum & Library, Baltimore MD

Abbott, Randy, *Head Reference Librn,* University of Evansville, University Library, Evansville IN

Abbott, Susannah, *Dir Devel,* Phillips Academy, Addison Gallery of American Art, Andover MA

Abbott, Terrence, *Adminr,* Brown University, David Winton Bell Gallery, Providence RI

Abdel-Malek, Laila, *Mgr Technical Svcs,* Museum of Fine Arts, William Morris Hunt Memorial Library, Boston MA

Abdo, George, *VPres Advancement,* The Huntington Library, Art Collections & Botanical Gardens, San Marino CA

Abdo, George, *VPres Advancement,* The Huntington Library, Art Collections & Botanical Gardens, Library, San Marino CA

Abdul-Musawwir, Najjar, *Assoc Prof & Head Undergrad Studies,* Southern Illinois University, School of Art & Design, Carbondale IL (S)

Abdur-Rahman, Uthman, *Head Dept Art,* Tuskegee University, Liberal Arts & Education, Tuskegee AL (S)

Abel, Charles, *Instr,* Springfield College, Dept of Visual & Performing Arts, Springfield MA (S)

Abel, Mickey, *Assoc Prof Art History,* University of North Texas, College of Visual Arts & Design, Denton TX (S)

Abell, E J, *Educ,* River Heritage Museum, Paducah KY

Abell, Mary, *Asst Prof Visual Arts,* Dowling College, Dept of Visual Arts, Oakdale NY (S)

Abellanosa, Ethelyn, *Human Resources,* University of Washington, Henry Art Gallery, Seattle WA

Aber, Lynn, *Librn,* Portsmouth Athenaeum, Joseph Copley Research Library, Portsmouth NH

Abercrombie, Bea, *Dir Admin Servs,* Witte Museum, San Antonio TX

Abercrombie, Karin Moen, *Exec Dir,* Swedish American Museum Association of Chicago, Chicago IL

Abersold, Lila, *Visual Arts Mgr,* Utah Arts Council, Chase Home Museum of Utah Folk Arts, Salt Lake City UT

Abia-Smith, Lisa, *Educ Dir,* University of Oregon, Jordan Schnitzer Museum of Art, Eugene OR

Abide, Joseph, *Assoc Prof,* Delta State University, Dept of Art, Cleveland MS (S)

Abiodun, Rowland O, *John C Newton Prof of Art & History of Art & Black Studies,* Amherst College, Dept of Art & the History of Art, Amherst MA (S)

Abler, Timothy, *Asst Prof,* Cardinal Stritch University, Art Dept, Milwaukee WI (S)

Abler, Timothy, *Chmn Art Dept,* Cardinal Stritch University, NM Gallery, Milwaukee WI

Abney, Brenda, *Dir,* North Central Washington Museum, Wenatchee Valley Museum & Cultural Center, Wenatchee WA

Abou-El-Haj, Barbara, *Chmn Dept,* State University of New York at Binghamton, Dept of Art History, Binghamton NY (S)

Abraham, Guenet, *Assoc Prof,* University of Maryland, Baltimore County, Imaging & Digital Arts (IMDA), Dept of Visual Arts, Baltimore MD (S)

Abraham, MJ, *Dir,* Riverside Art Museum, Library, Riverside CA

Abraham, Richard, *Instr,* Central Community College - Columbus Campus, Business & Arts Cluster, Columbus NE (S)

Abram, Antonia, *Dir Arts Prog,* The Children's Aid Society, Visual Arts Program of the Philip Coltoff Center at Green Arts and After School Program, New York NY (S)

Abram, Ronald, *Assoc Prof,* Denison University, Studio Art Program, Granville OH (S)

Abram, Trudi, *Instr Art History,* Glendale Community College, Visual & Performing Arts Div, Glendale CA (S)

Abrams, C, *Dir,* The Photon League of Holographers, Toronto ON

Abrams, Daniel, *Co-Dir,* Prince Street Gallery, New York NY

Abrams, Leslie, *Asst Prof,* Springfield College, Dept of Visual & Performing Arts, Springfield MA (S)

Abrams, Paul, *Instr,* Woodstock School of Art, Inc, Woodstock NY (S)

Abramson, Daniel, *Assoc Prof & Chmn,* Tufts University, Dept of Art & Art History, Medford MA (S)

Abreu, Vidal, *Librn,* Museum of Ossining Historical Society, Library, Ossining NY

Abshear, Debra, *Secy,* National Watercolor Society, San Pedro CA

Abstein, Teri, *Communs Coordr,* Florida State University, Museum of Fine Arts, Tallahassee FL

Accola, Kristin, *Dir Exhibitions,* Hunterdon Art Museum, Clinton NJ

Accurso, Li Ching, *Instr,* Columbia College, Fine Arts, Sonora CA (S)

Achey, Adam C, *Gallery Coordr,* Friends University, Riney Fine Arts Center Gallery, Wichita KS

Acita, Marcia, *Asst Dir,* Bard College, Center for Curatorial Studies and the Hessel Museum of Art, Annandale-on-Hudson NY

Ackerman, Andrew, *Exec Dir,* Children's Museum of Manhattan, New York NY

Ackermann, Paul, *Mus Specialist,* United States Military Academy, West Point Museum, West Point NY

Ackert, Stephen, *Head Music Dept,* National Gallery of Art, Washington DC

Ackiss, Holly, *Youth Prog Mgr,* Contemporary Art Center of Virginia, Virginia Beach VA

Acock, Anthony, *Asst Prof,* California State Polytechnic University, Pomona, Department of Art, Pomona CA (S)

Acosta, Ikuko, *Prog Dir Art Therapy,* New York University, Dept of Art & Art Professions, New York NY (S)

Acosta, Marie, *Dir,* La Raza-Galeria Posada, Sacramento CA

Acres, Al, *Asst Prof,* Georgetown University, Dept of Art & Art History, Washington DC (S)

Acs, Alajos, *Midwest Representative,* American Society of Artists, Inc, Palatine IL

Acton, David L, *Cur Prints, Drawings & Photography,* Worcester Art Museum, Worcester MA

Acuff, Michelle, *Asst Prof Art,* Whitman College, Art Dept, Walla Walla WA (S)

Acuna-Hansen, Chris, *Prof Photog,* Rio Hondo College, Visual Arts Dept, Whittier CA (S)

Acus-Smith, Jenn, *Educ Coordr,* Fitton Center for Creative Arts, Hamilton OH

Adains, Mac, *Chmn,* State University of New York College at Old Westbury, Visual Arts Dept, Old Westbury NY (S)

Adair, Cindy, *Office Mgr,* Pennsylvania Historical & Museum Commission, Railroad Museum of Pennsylvania, Harrisburg PA

Adair, Everl, *Dir Research & Rare Coll,* R W Norton Art Foundation, R W Norton Art Gallery, Shreveport LA

Adair, Macra, *Mus Shop Mgr,* Booth Western Art Museum, Cartersville GA

Adam, Mazih, *Asst Prof,* Community College of Rhode Island, Dept of Art, Warwick RI (S)

Adamcik-Huettel, Patricia, *Multimedia & Web Design,* Art Institute of Pittsburgh, Pittsburgh PA (S)

Adams, Andrew, *Educ & Events Dir,* Erie County Historical Society, Erie PA

Adams, Anne, *Registrar,* Menil Foundation, Inc, The Menil Collection, Houston TX

Adams, Annmarie, *Prof,* McGill University, School of Architecture, Montreal PQ (S)

Adams, Ashley, *Cur Educ,* Museum of Art & History, Santa Cruz, Santa Cruz CA

Adams, Bertha, *Project Archivist,* Philadelphia Museum of Art, Library & Archives, Philadelphia PA

Adams, Bev, *Cur,* Ravalli County Museum, Hamilton MT

Adams, Brad, *Asst Prof,* Berry College, Art Dept, Mount Berry GA (S)

Adams, Branden, *Asst Dir & Dir Exhib,* Piedmont Arts Association, Martinsville VA

Adams, Daniel, *Prof,* Harding University, Dept of Art & Design, Searcy AR (S)

Adams, Dean, *Asst Prof - Foundation,* Montana State University, School of Art, Bozeman MT (S)

Adams, Don, *Support Staff,* Knights of Columbus Supreme Council, Knights of Columbus Museum, New Haven CT

Adams, Donna, *Assoc Prof,* University of Indianapolis, Dept Art & Design, Indianapolis IN (S)

Adams, Dyane, *Asst Secy,* Artists' Cooperative Gallery, Omaha NE

Adams, Edward, *Instr,* Milwaukee Area Technical College, School of Media & Creative Arts, Milwaukee WI (S)

Adams, Gladys, *Bookings Mgr,* African American Museum in Philadelphia, Philadelphia PA

Adams, Gloria Rejune, *Dir,* Cornell Museum of Art and American Culture, Delray Beach FL

Adams, Helen, *Admin Asst,* State Capital Museum, Olympia WA

Adams, Helen, *Dir Visitor Services,* Clemson University, Fort Hill Plantation, Clemson SC

Adams, Henry, *Prof,* Case Western Reserve University, Dept of Art History & Art, Cleveland OH (S)

Adams, Holly, *Adjunct Instr,* Davis & Elkins College, Dept of Art, Elkins WV (S)

Adams, Idie, *Chmn & Ceramic Coordr,* Butte College, Dept of Fine Arts and Communication Tech, Oroville CA (S)

Adams, J Marshall, *Cur Educ,* Mississippi Museum of Art, Howorth Library, Jackson MS

Adams, J Marshall, *Dir Educ,* Vero Beach Museum of Art, Vero Beach FL

Adams, Jacqueline, *Supv Librn,* San Diego Public Library, Art, Music & Recreation, San Diego CA

Adams, James, *Asst Prof of Art,* Thomas University, Humanities Division, Thomasville GA (S)

Adams, Jamie, *Dept Head,* Judson College, Division of Fine and Performing Arts, Marion AL (S)

Adams, Jean, *Adjunct Prof,* Wilkes University, Dept of Art, Wilkes-Barre PA (S)

Adams, Jim, *Mng Dir Academy of the New Church,* Academy of the New Church, Glencairn Museum, Bryn Athyn PA

Adams, Kathryn, *Exec Dir,* Audrain County Historical Society, Graceland Museum & American Saddlehorse Museum, Mexico MO

Adams, Kathy, *Exec Dir,* Ponca City Cultural Center & Museum, Ponca City OK

Adams, Kathy, *Exec Dir,* Ponca City Cultural Center & Museum, Library, Ponca City OK

Adams, Keith, *Asst Chair,* Rowan University, Dept of Art, Glassboro NJ (S)

Adams, Kelly, *Dir,* East Carolina University, Media Center, Greenville NC

Adams, Laurie Schneider, *Prof,* City University of New York, PhD Program in Art History, New York NY (S)

Adams, Lee Ann, *Prog & Operations Mgr,* Association of Independent Colleges of Art & Design, Providence RI

Adams, Madge B, *Pres & CEO,* Shaker Village of Pleasant Hill, Harrodsburg KY

Adams, Marlin, *Instr,* Gordon College, Dept of Fine Arts, Barnesville GA (S)

Adams, Melanie, *Mng Dir Educ,* Missouri Historical Society, Missouri History Museum, Saint Louis MO

Adams, Nicholas, *Prof,* Vassar College, Art Dept, Poughkeepsie NY (S)

Adams, Nixon, *CEO & Dir,* Lake Pontchartrain Basin Maritime Museum, Madisonville LA

Adams, Pam, *Instr,* Bob Jones University, School of Fine Arts, Div of Art & Design, Greenville SC (S)

Adams, Patsy Baker, *Gallery Dir & Adminr,* New Orleans Academy of Fine Arts, Academy Gallery, New Orleans LA

Adams, Renee, *Arts Programmer,* Gallery One Visual Arts Center, Ellensburg WA

Adams, Rosemary, *Dir Publs,* Chicago History Museum, Chicago IL

Adams, Sharon, *Exec Dir,* Quickdraw Animation Society, Calgary AB

Adams, William R, *Chmn,* City of Saint Augustine, Saint Augustine FL

Adamson, John, *CEO, VChmn,* Strasburg Museum, Strasburg VA

Adamson, Rob, *Prof,* Salt Lake Community College, Graphic Design Dept, Salt Lake City UT (S)

Adams Ramsey, Susan, *Chmn,* Clinch Valley College of the University of Virginia, Visual & Performing Arts Dept, Wise VA (S)

Adamy, George E, *Dir,* Polyadam Concrete System Workshops, Ossining NY (S)

Adan, Elizabeth, *Asst Prof Art History,* California Polytechnic State University at San Luis Obispo, Dept of Art & Design, San Luis Obispo CA (S)

Adan, Joan, *Exhib Designer,* Forest Lawn Museum, Glendale CA

Adato, Linda, *Pres,* Society of American Graphic Artists, New York NY

Addison, Christopher, *Owner,* Addison/Ripley Fine Art, Washington DC

Addison, E W, *Dir,* Brewton-Parker College, Visual Arts, Mount Vernon GA (S)

Addison, Laura, *Cur Contemporary,* Museum of New Mexico, New Mexico Museum of Art, Unit of NM Dept of Cultural Affairs, Santa Fe NM

Addison, Lynne, *Registrar,* Yale University, Yale University Art Gallery, New Haven CT

Addiss, Stephen, *Prof,* University of Richmond, Dept of Art and Art History, Richmond VA (S)

Ade, Ken, *Coordr Opers,* Kenosha Public Museums, Kenosha WI

Adejumo, Christopher, *Asst Chair - Visual Art Studies,* University of Texas, Dept of Art & Art History, Austin TX (S)

Adelman, Charles, *Prof,* University of Northern Iowa, Dept of Art, Cedar Falls IA (S)

Adelman, Everett Mayo, *Instr,* North Carolina Wesleyan College, Dept of Visual & Performing Arts, Rocky Mount NC (S)

Adelson, Fred, *Chair,* Rowan University, Dept of Art, Glassboro NJ (S)

Adema, Polly, *Folklorist,* Dutchess County Arts Council, Poughkeepsie NY

Adgate, Brian, *Adj Instruc,* Quincy College, Art Dept, Quincy MA (S)

Adiletta, Dawn C, *Cur,* Harriet Beecher Stowe, Hartford CT

Adkins, Tim, *Dir Content Devel,* Industrial Designers Society of America, Herndon VA

Adler, Michelle, *Develop Asst,* Swope Art Museum, Research Library, Terre Haute IN

Adler, Michelle, *Develop Asst,* Swope Art Museum, Terre Haute IN

Adler, Pam, *Store Mgr,* South Dakota State University, South Dakota Art Museum, Brookings SD

Adlestein, Gary, *Assoc Prof,* Albright College, Dept of Art, Reading PA (S)

Adley, Allyson, *Coll & Educ Asst,* York University, Art Gallery of York University, Toronto ON

Adolph, Cheryl, *COO,* Staten Island Museum, Staten Island NY

Adolph, Cheryl, *Chief Operating Officer,* Staten Island Museum, Archives Library, Staten Island NY

Adrean, Louis, *Senior Librn,* The Cleveland Museum of Art, Ingalls Library, Cleveland OH

Adrian, Barbara, *Prof Theatre,* Marymount Manhattan College, Fine & Performing Arts Div, New York NY (S)

Adrian, Donna, *Instr,* La Sierra University, Art Dept, Riverside CA (S)

Aerbersold, Jane, *Cur of Ceramics,* University of Oklahoma, Fred Jones Jr Museum of Art, Norman OK

Aesoph, Jill, *Dir Develop,* Washington State University, Museum of Art, Pullman WA

Aframe, Debby, *Librn,* Worcester Art Museum, Library, Worcester MA

Aframe, Deborah, *Librn,* Worcester Art Museum, Worcester MA

Agamedia, Allan, *Technology,* Art Institute of Pittsburgh, Pittsburgh PA (S)

Agamy, Susan J, *Dir Develop,* The Barnum Museum, Bridgeport CT

Agar, Will, *Dir,* North Hennepin Community College, Joseph Gazzuolo Fine Arts Gallery, Brooklyn Park MN

Agar, Will, *Instr,* North Hennepin Community College, Art Dept, Brooklyn Park MN (S)

Agard, James, *Assoc Prof,* Gettysburg College, Dept of Visual Arts, Gettysburg PA (S)

Agarwal, Neha, *Asst Prof,* La Roche College, Division of Design, Pittsburgh PA (S)

Ageloff, Catherine, *Operations Mgr,* Essex Historical Society and Shipbuilding Museum, Essex MA

Ageloff, Scott, *Dean,* New York School of Interior Design, New York NY (S)

Aglio, Henry, *Asst Prof,* West Virginia University at Parkersburg, Art Dept, Parkersburg WV (S)

Agnew, Charlie, *Assoc Prof of Art,* Middle Georgia State College, Humanities Division, Dept of Art - School of Liberal Arts, Dept of Media, Culture & the Arts, Cochran GA (S)

Agnew, L Jack, *Prof,* Sullivan County Community College, Division of Commercial Art & Photography, Loch Sheldrake NY (S)

Agre-Kippenhan, Susan, *Assoc Prof,* Portland State University, Dept of Art, Portland OR (S)

Aguirre, David, *Dir,* Dinnerware Artist's Cooperative, Tucson AZ

Ahearn, Maureen, *Dir,* Keene State College, Thorne-Sagendorph Art Gallery, Keene NH

Ahern, Jack, *Dept Head,* University of Massachusetts, Amherst, Dept of Landscape Architecture & Regional Planning, Amherst MA (S)

Ahl, Diane Cole, *Dept Head,* Lafayette College, Dept of Art, Easton PA (S)

Ahlberg, Joanna, *Mng Ed,* The Drawing Center, New York NY

Ahnen, Phillip, *Facility Dir/Exhib Preparator,* Rochester Art Center, Rochester MN

Ahntholz, Richard, *Artist,* U Gallery, New York NY

Aho, Arnold, *Prof,* Norwich University, Dept of Architecture and Art, Northfield VT (S)

Aho, Paul, *Dean of School of Art,* Robert & Mary Montgomery Armory Art Center, Armory Art Center, West Palm Beach FL

Ahrens, Liz, *Dir,* Crooked Tree Arts Council, Virginia M McCune Community Arts Center, Petoskey MI

Ahrens, Todd, *Dir Develop,* University of Michigan, Museum of Art, Ann Arbor MI

Aide, Teri, *Controller,* Orlando Museum of Art, Orlando FL

Aiken, Jane, *Prof Emerita,* Virginia Polytechnic Institute & State University, Dept of Art & Art History, Blacksburg VA (S)

Aikens, Martha B, *Supt,* Independence National Historical Park, Library, Philadelphia PA

Aikey, Michael, *CEO & Dir,* New York State Military Museum and Veterans Research Center, Saratoga Springs NY

Aikin, Roger, *Instr Art History,* Creighton University, Fine & Performing Arts Dept, Omaha NE (S)

Aikman, John, *Instr,* Linn Benton Community College, Fine & Applied Art Dept, Albany OR (S)

Ainsworth, Sarah, *Prog & Develop Asst,* Belle Grove Inc., Belle Grove Plantation, Middletown VA

Airulla, Barbara, *Asst Prof,* University of Texas at Tyler, Department of Art, School of Visual & Performing Arts, Tyler TX (S)

Aistars, John, *Dir,* Cazenovia College, Chapman Art Center Gallery, Cazenovia NY

Aitali, Erin, *Exhib Mgr,* Pasadena Museum of California Art, Pasadena CA

Aitken, Molly, *Asst Prof,* City College of New York, Art Dept, New York NY (S)

Aitkens, Wendy, *Cur,* City of Lethbridge, Sir Alexander Galt Museum, Lethbridge AB

Aja, Adam, *Asst Cur,* Harvard University, Semitic Museum, Cambridge MA

Ajay, Abe, *Prof Emeritus,* Purchase College, State University of New York, School of Art+Design, Purchase NY (S)

Ajootian, Aileen, *Prof,* University of Mississippi, Department of Art, University MS (S)

Akbarnia, Ladan, *Hagop Kevorkian Assoc Cur Islamic Art,* Brooklyn Museum, Brooklyn NY

Akehurst, Leeanne, *Promotion,* Canada Science and Technology Museum, Ottawa ON

Akeley-Charron, Kim, *Mktg Coordr,* Loveland Museum/Gallery, Loveland CO

Akers, Norman, *Assoc Prof,* University of Kansas, The School of the Arts, Dept of Visual Art, Lawrence KS (S)

Akers, Rich, *Dept Head,* Contra Costa Community College, Dept of Art, San Pablo CA (S)

Akin-Kivanc, Esra, *Asst Prof,* University of South Florida, School The Arts, Tampa FL (S)

Akoor, Ravi, *Instr,* Kalamazoo Valley Community College, Center for New Media, Kalamazoo MI (S)

Alafat, Gary, *Security & Bldg Mgr,* Dartmouth College, Hood Museum of Art, Hanover NH

Alamiri, Laila, *Events & Mus Shop Coordr,* Asheville Art Museum, Asheville NC

Alanen, Marie, *Prof,* East Los Angeles College, Art Dept, Monterey Park CA (S)

Albacete, M J, *Exec Dir,* Canton Museum of Art, Art Library, Canton OH

Albacete, Manuel J, *Exec Dir,* Canton Museum of Art, Canton OH

Albacete, Manuel J, *Exec Dir,* Canton Museum of Art, Canton OH (S)

Albano, Albert, *Exec Dir,* Intermuseum Conservation Association, Cleveland OH

Albano, John, *Dean,* Merced College, Arts Division, Merced CA (S)

Albarran, Marco, *Preparator,* Mesa Arts Center, Mesa Contemporary Arts Museum, Mesa AZ

Albee, Becca, *Assoc Prof,* City College of New York, Art Dept, New York NY (S)

Albers, Jan, *Exec Dir,* Henry Sheldon Museum of Vermont History and Research Center, Middlebury VT

Albert, Karen, *Assoc Dir Exhibs & Coll,* Hofstra University, Hofstra University Museum, Hempstead NY

Alberti, Janet, *Deputy Dir,* Museum of Contemporary Art, Chicago IL

Albertson, Constant, *Assoc Prof,* University of Maine, Dept of Art, Orono ME (S)

Albertson, Rita, *Chief Conservator,* Worcester Art Museum, Worcester MA

Albin, Mark, *Deputy Dir Mktg,* Newark Museum Association, The Newark Museum, Newark NJ

Albinson, Cassandra, *Assoc Cur Paintings & Sculpture,* Yale University, Yale Center for British Art, New Haven CT

Albiston, Renee, *Commun Relations,* Kirkland Museum of Fine & Decorative Art, Denver CO

Albrecht, Carl, *Head Natural History,* Ohio Historical Society, Columbus OH

Albrecht, Ivan, *Asst Prof,* University of Miami, Dept of Art & Art History, Coral Gables FL (S)

Albrecht, Mary, *Sr Dir Devel,* Milwaukee Art Museum, Milwaukee WI

Albrecht, Matt, *Art Handler,* Columbus Museum, Columbus GA

Albrecht, Sterling, *Dir Libraries,* Brigham Young University, Harold B Lee Library, Provo UT

Albritton, Marty, *Develop Dir,* Eastern Shore Art Association, Inc, Eastern Shore Art Center, Fairhope AL

Albro, Colin, *Mus Aide,* 1890 House-Museum & Center for the Arts, Cortland NY

Alden, Donna, *Asst Prof,* University of Nebraska, Kearney, Dept of Art & Art History, Kearney NE (S)

Alderson, Julia, *Assoc Prof,* Humboldt State University, College of Arts & Humanities, Art Dept, Arcata CA (S)

Aldinger, Charlene, *Pub Rels Dir,* Honolulu Academy of Arts, The Art Center at Linekona, Honolulu HI (S)

Aldrich, Ginger, *Develop,* Haystack Mountain School of Crafts, Deer Isle ME

Aldrich, Ginger, *Develop Dir,* Haystack Mountain School of Crafts, Center for Community Programs Gallery, Deer Isle ME

Aldrich, Marvette, *Asst Prof,* Winston-Salem State University, Art Dept, Winston-Salem NC (S)

Aleci, Linda, *Assoc Prof,* Franklin & Marshall College, Art & Art History Dept, Lancaster PA (S)

Aleckson, Luke, *Dir,* Northwestern College, Denler Art Gallery, Orange City IA

Alegria, Christina, *Educ Asst,* California State University, Long Beach, University Art Museum, Long Beach CA

Alejandro, Brenda, *Prof,* University of Puerto Rico, Dept of Fine Arts, Rio Piedras PR (S)

Alejandro, Brenda, *Prof,* University of Puerto Rico, Dept of Fine Arts, Rio Piedras PR (S)

Alen, Casey, *Registrar,* Utah State University, Nora Eccles Harrison Museum of Art, Logan UT

Aleo, Nancy, *Pres Bd Trustees,* Attleboro Arts Museum, Attleboro MA

Alessi, Doreen, *Conservatory Coll Mgr,* The Adirondack Historical Association, The Adirondack Museum, Blue Mountain Lake NY

Alex, Kathleen, *Dir Fin,* Cultural Council of Palm Beach County, Lake Worth FL

Alexander, Carolyn, *Chmn Art,* Mount San Antonio College, Art Dept, Walnut CA (S)

Alexander, Catherine, *Gallery Dir,* Salem Art Association, Bush Barn Art Center, Salem OR

Alexander, Elizabeth, *Admin,* Dartmouth College, Dept of Art History, Hanover NH (S)

Alexander, Hope P, *Secy,* Newport Historical Society & Museum of Newport History, Newport RI

Alexander, Irene, *Cur,* Stephens College, Lewis James & Nellie Stratton Davis Art Gallery, Columbia MO

Alexander, James, *Prof,* University of Alabama at Birmingham, Dept of Art & Art History, Birmingham AL (S)

Alexander, Jane, *Dir Information Management & Tech Servs,* The Cleveland Museum of Art, Cleveland OH

Alexander, Janet, *Asst Dir,* Sarah Lawrence College Library, Esther Raushenbush Library, Bronxville NY

Alexander, Jean, *Head of Hunt Reference,* Carnegie Mellon University, Hunt Library, Pittsburgh PA

Alexander, Jenna, *Treas,* Dauphin & District Allied Arts Council, Watson Art Centre, Dauphin MB

Alexander, Julie, *Dir Finance,* Lighthouse ArtCenter Museum & School of Art, Tequesta FL

Alexander, Kathy, *In Charge Art Coll,* First Tennessee Bank, Memphis TN

Alexander, Melanie K, *Dir,* Muscatine Art Center, Museum, Muscatine IA

Alexander, Mellda, *Asst Registrar,* Columbus Museum, Columbus GA

Alexander, Pat, *Mus Educ,* Napa Valley Museum, Yountville CA

Alexander, Rebecca, *Media Asst,* San Francisco Art Institute, Anne Bremer Memorial Library, San Francisco CA

Alexander, Robbyn, *Faculty,* John F Kennedy, Department of Arts & Consciousness, Pleasant Hill CA (S)

Alexander, Ronald J, *Head Dept,* University of Louisiana at Monroe, Dept of Art, Monroe LA (S)

Alexander, Vikky, *Assoc Prof,* University of Victoria, Dept of Visual Arts, Victoria BC (S)

Alexenberg, Mel, *Dean Visual Arts,* New World School of the Arts, Gallery, Miami FL

Alexick, David, *Prof,* Christopher Newport University, Dept of Fine Performing Arts, Newport News VA (S)

Alferio, K, *Pres & Dir Programming,* The Cultural Arts Center at Glen Allen, Glen Allen VA

Alford, John, *Assoc Prof,* Carson-Newman College, Art Dept, Jefferson City TN (S)

Alford, John, *Asst Prof,* Mississippi University for Women, Division of Fine & Performing Arts, Columbus MS (S)

Alford, Keith, *VPres,* Mississippi Art Colony, Stoneville MS

Alfred, Darrin, *AIGA Asst Cur & Graphics,* Denver Art Museum, Denver CO

Alger, Erin, *Colls Mgr,* Museum of Northern British Columbia, Ruth Harvey Art Gallery, Prince Rupert BC

Alger, Erin, *Colls Mgr,* Museum of Northern British Columbia, Library, Prince Rupert BC

Alger, Jeff, *Librn,* Kansas State University, Paul Weigel Library of Architecture Planning & Design, Manhattan KS

Alhara, Chris, *Exec Dir,* Japanese American Cultural & Community Center, George J Doizaki Gallery, Los Angeles CA

Alice, Michele S, *Mus Security Officer,* Williams College, Museum of Art, Williamstown MA

Aliotti, Johnny, *Pres Bd,* Pacific Grove Art Center, Pacific Grove CA

Aliriza, Gulgan, *Treas,* Blue Mountain Gallery, New York NY

Alissandro, Laura D, *Head of Conservation,* University of Chicago, Oriental Institute, Chicago IL

Alix, Sylvie, *Librn,* Musee d'art Contemporain de Montreal, Mediatheque/ Media Centre, Centre for Research & Documentation on Contemporary Art, Montreal PQ

Allaben, Craig, *Gallery Mgr,* University of Massachusetts, Amherst, University Gallery, Amherst MA

Allaik, Khalil, *Asst Preparator,* Lehigh University Art Galleries, Museum Operation, Bethlehem PA

Allamby, Claire M, *Dir Institutional Advancement,* Independence Seaport Museum, Philadelphia PA

Allan, Elizabeth, *Cur Colls & Exhibits,* Morven Museum & Garden, Princeton NJ

Allan, Ken, *Asst Prof,* Seattle University, Dept of Fine Arts, Visual Art Division, Seattle WA (S)

Allan, Michele, *Prof,* California State University, Dominguez Hills, Art & Design Dept, Carson CA (S)

Allen, Angelo, *Instr,* Pierce College, Art Dept, Woodland Hills CA (S)

Allen, Anne, *Coordr of Fine Arts,* Indiana University-Southeast, Fine Arts Dept, New Albany IN (S)

Allen, Brian T, *Dir,* Phillips Academy, Addison Gallery of American Art, Andover MA

Allen, Brianna, *Admin Asst,* Bunnell Street AAS Center, Bunnell Street Arts Center, Homer AK

Allen, Brielly, *Asst to Dir,* The National Society of The Colonial Dames of America in the State of New Hampshire, Moffatt-Ladd House & Garden, Portsmouth NH

Allen, Bruce, *Chmn Dept & Prof,* Centenary College of Louisiana, Dept of Art, Shreveport LA (S)

Allen, Carl M, *Prof,* Ashland University, Art Dept, Ashland OH (S)

Allen, Catherine, *Studio Coordr,* Nova Scotia Centre for Craft & Design, Mary E Black Gallery, Halifax NS

Allen, Douglas, *Assoc Dean,* Georgia Institute of Technology, College of Architecture, Atlanta GA (S)

Allen, Elaine, *Accounting Mgr,* Contemporary Art Center of Virginia, Virginia Beach VA

Allen, Frank R, *Assoc Dir Admin,* University of Central Florida Libraries, Orlando FL

Allen, Greg, *Dir Finance & Admin,* American Craft Council, Minneapolis MN

Allen, Heidi, *Asst Prof,* Concordia College, Art Dept, Moorhead MN (S)

Allen, Jackie, *Head of Library,* Dallas Museum of Art, Mildred R & Frederick M Mayer Library, Dallas TX

Allen, James, *Media Arts & Animation,* Art Institute of Pittsburgh, Pittsburgh PA (S)

Allen, James, *Opers Supv,* Arizona State University, Architecture & Environmental Design Library, Tempe AZ

Allen, James, *Prof,* Daemen College, Art Dept, Amherst NY (S)

Allen, Jan, *Chief Cur & Cur Contemporary Art,* Queen's University, Agnes Etherington Art Centre, Kingston ON

Allen, Janice, *Office Adminr,* Auburn University, Julie Collins Smith Museum, Auburn AL

Allen, Jeff, *Preparator,* The Currier Museum of Art, Manchester NH

Allen, Jim, *Instr,* Springfield College in Illinois, Dept of Art, Springfield IL (S)

Allen, John, *Technical Dir,* University of Minnesota, Frederick R Weisman Art Museum, Minneapolis MN

Allen, Judith, *Pres,* Spirit Square Center for Arts & Education, Charlotte NC

Allen, Jules, *Asst Prof,* Queensborough Community College, Dept of Art & Photography, Bayside Hills NY (S)

Allen, Katy, *VP Human Resources & Organizational Devel,* The Children's Museum of Indianapolis, Indianapolis IN

Allen, Kay, *Assoc Dir,* University of Southern California, USC Fisher Museum of Art, Los Angeles CA

Allen, Kelly, *Dir Educ,* Academy of Fine Arts, Lynchburg VA

Allen, Kristie, *Museum Store Mgr,* Birmingham Museum of Art, Birmingham AL

Allen, Larry, *CFO,* Industrial Designers Society of America, Herndon VA

Allen, Lynne, *Dir School of Visual Arts,* Boston University, School for the Arts, Boston MA (S)

Allen, Mark, *Asst Prof,* Pomona College, Dept of Art & Art History, Claremont CA (S)

Allen, Mary B, *VP,* Gallery West Ltd, Alexandria VA

Allen, Michael, *Preparator,* Washburn University, Mulvane Art Museum, Topeka KS

Allen, Nash, *Chief Financial Officer,* BanCorp South, Art Collection, Tupelo MS

Allen, Pam, *Dir Finance & Facility,* Piedmont Arts Association, Martinsville VA

Allen, Pamela, *Asst Prof,* Troy State University, Dept of Art & Classics, Troy AL (S)

Allen, Rachel, *Deputy Dir,* American Art Museum, Smithsonian Institution, Washington DC

Allen, Regina, *Instr,* Wayne Art Center, Wayne PA (S)

Allen, Robert, *VPres,* South Arkansas Arts Center, El Dorado AR

Allen, Stan, *Chmn Div Urban Design,* Columbia University, Graduate School of Architecture, Planning & Preservation, New York NY (S)

Allen, Stan, *Dean,* Princeton University, School of Architecture, Princeton NJ (S)

Allen, Walter, *Div Chmn of Art,* James H Faulkner, Art Dept, Bay Minette AL (S)

Allen, William, *Prof,* Arkansas State University, Dept of Art, State University AR (S)

Alley, Ivy, *Cur Educ, Docents & Vols,* Mississippi Museum of Art, Jackson MS

Alley, Jon, *Instr,* Bucks County Community College, Fine Arts Dept, Newtown PA (S)

Alley-Bavaes, Royal, *Instr,* Seattle Central Community College, Humanities - Social Sciences Division, Seattle WA (S)

Allison, Andrea, *Librn,* Quetico Park, John B Ridley Research Library, Atikokan ON

Allison, Joseph, *Studio Mgr,* Austin College, Art Dept, Sherman TX (S)

Allison, Maya, *Cur,* Brown University, David Winton Bell Gallery, Providence RI

Allison, Wayne, *Instr & Chair,* North Iowa Area Community College, Dept of Art, Mason City IA (S)

Allman, Anne, *Prof,* College of the Ozarks, Dept of Art, Point Lookout MO (S)

Allman, Marion, *CEO,* The Art Institute of Cincinnati, AIC College of Design, Cincinnati OH (S)

Allman, William G, *Cur,* White House, Washington DC

Allmendinger, Carolyn, *Dir Acad Progs,* University of North Carolina at Chapel Hill, Ackland Art Museum, Chapel Hill NC

Ally, Art Perez, *Pres,* Xico Inc, Chandler AZ

Allyn, Anita, *Dept Chair,* The College of New Jersey, School of Arts & Sciences, Ewing NJ (S)

Alm, Rebecca, *Prof,* Minneapolis College of Art & Design, Minneapolis MN (S)

Almas, Bryan, *Asst,* Gallery Moos Ltd, Toronto ON

Almasi, Jesse, *Adjunct Prof,* Community College of Allegheny County, Boyce Campus, Art Dept, Monroeville PA (S)

Almon, Amanda, *Dept Head Biomedical Art,* Cleveland Institute of Art, Cleveland OH (S)

Alonso, Elisa, *Admin Asst to Exec Dir,* Bass Museum of Art, Miami Beach FL

Alonso, Idurre, *Cur,* Museum of Latin American Art, Long Beach CA

Alonzo, Juan, *Facilities Coordr,* Museum of Fine Arts, Houston, Rienzi Center for European Decorative Arts, Houston TX

Alpert, Gary J, *VPres Publs,* Old Salem Museums & Gardens, Museum of Early Southern Decorative Arts, Winston Salem NC

Alpert, L, *Assoc Prof,* University of Oregon, Dept of Fine & Applied Arts, Eugene OR (S)

Alphonso, Christina, *Mgr Admin,* The Metropolitan Museum of Art, The Cloisters Museum & Gardens, New York NY

Alpuche, Jose, *Master Printer,* Self Help Graphics, Los Angeles CA

Alsdorf, Marilynn B, *Pres,* The Arts Club of Chicago, Chicago IL

Alsobrook, David, *Dir,* History Museum of Mobile, Mobile AL

Alsobrook, Robert, *Asst Prof,* Taylor University, Visual Art Dept, Upland IN (S)

Alston, Leesha, *Registrar,* Phoenix Art Museum, Phoenix AZ

Alston, Littleton, *Instr Sculpture,* Creighton University, Fine & Performing Arts Dept, Omaha NE (S)

Alstrom, Eric, *Commun Chmn,* Guild of Book Workers, New York NY

Alswang, Hope, *Dir,* Norton Museum of Art, West Palm Beach FL

Alt, Marlene, *Prof,* Southern Oregon University, Art & Art History Dept, Ashland OR (S)

Altamura, Mauro, *Asst Prof,* New Jersey City University, Art Dept, Jersey City NJ (S)

Altemus, Anne R, *Asst Prof,* Johns Hopkins University, School of Medicine, Dept of Art as Applied to Medicine, Baltimore MD (S)

Altenau, Kristen Courtney, *Dept Head Interior Design,* Antonelli College, Cincinnati OH (S)

Alter-Muri, Simone, *Asst Prof,* Springfield College, Dept of Visual & Performing Arts, Springfield MA (S)

Althaver, Burt, *Chmn,* Artrain, Inc, Ann Arbor MI

Althouse, Shaun, *Asst Dir,* Carlsbad Museum & Art Center, Carlsbad NM

Altieri Haslinger, Myrian, *Pres (V),* Akron Art Museum, Akron OH

Altman, Phyllis, *Art Gallery Mgr,* Jewish Community Center of Greater Washington, Jane L & Robert H Weiner Judaic Museum, Rockville MD

Altmann, Helen, *Cur,* Chalet of the Golden Fleece, New Glarus WI

Altschul, Mark, *Secy,* National Association of Women Artists, Inc, N.A.W.A. Gallery, New York NY

Alvare, Gigi, *Dir Educ,* The Rockwell Museum of Western Art, Corning NY

Alvarez, Gina, *Gallery Dir,* St. Louis Artists' Guild, Saint Louis MO

Alvarez, Jose B, *Instr,* Inter American University of Puerto Rico, Dept of Art, San German PR (S)

Alvarez, Jose B, *Instr,* Inter American University of Puerto Rico, Dept of Art, San German PR (S)

Alvarez, Julio, *Security Mgr,* Florida International University, The Patricia & Phillip Frost Art Museum, Miami FL

Alvarez, Yetzenia, *Pub Rels Mgr,* Museo de Arte de Puerto Rico, San Juan PR

Alvarez, Yetzenia, *Pub Rels Mgr,* Museo de Arte de Puerto Rico, San Juan PR

Alves, C Douglass, *Dir,* Calvert Marine Museum, Solomons MD

Alvord, Ellen, *Coordr Acad Affairs,* Mount Holyoke College, Art Museum, South Hadley MA

Alvord, Ellen, *Educ Programs Dir,* Las Vegas Art Museum, Las Vegas NV

Alward, Sharon, *Prof,* University of Manitoba, School of Art, Winnipeg MB (S)

Amaro, Sophia, *Develop Dir,* Cooper-Hewitt National Design Museum, Smithsonian Institution, New York NY

Amassen, Laura, *Exhib Dir & Coll Coordr,* Goucher College, Rosenberg Gallery, Baltimore MD

Amato, Carol, *COO,* Virginia Museum of Fine Arts, Richmond VA

Amato, Micaela, *Prof Art & Women's Studies (Drawing/Painting),* Pennsylvania State University, University Park, Penn State School of Visual Arts, University Park PA (S)

Ambroge, Patti, *Assoc Prof,* Rochester Institute of Technology, School of Photographic Arts & Sciences, Rochester NY (S)

Ambrogio, Lucy Sant, *Cur,* Historical Society of Bloomfield, Bloomfield NJ

Ambrose, Andy, *Dir Research & Progs,* Atlanta Historical Society Inc, Atlanta History Center, Atlanta GA

Ambrose, Andy, *Exec Dir,* Tubman African American Museum, Macon GA

Ambrose, Pamela, *Dir Cultural Affairs,* Loyola University Chicago, Loyola University Museum of Art, Chicago IL

Ambrose, Richard, *Dir Exhibs/Cur Art,* Avampato Discovery Museum, The Clay Center for Arts & Sciences, Charleston WV

Ambrose, Vickie, *Archivist,* New Canaan Historical Society, New Canaan CT

Ambrosini, Lynne, *Chief Cur,* Taft Museum of Art, Cincinnati OH

Ambrosino, Thomas, *Prof,* Sullivan County Community College, Division of Commercial Art & Photography, Loch Sheldrake NY (S)

Amburgy, Patricia, *Assoc Prof Art Educ,* Pennsylvania State University, University Park, Penn State School of Visual Arts, University Park PA (S)

Amdursky, Saul, *Dir,* Public Library of Des Moines, Central Library Information Services, Des Moines IA

Ament, Elizabeth, *Asst Prof,* University of Wisconsin-Green Bay, Arts Dept, Green Bay WI (S)

Amentas, Peter, *Security Mgr,* Bard College, Center for Curatorial Studies and the Hessel Museum of Art, Annandale-on-Hudson NY

Ameri, Anan, *Dir,* Arab American National Museum, Dearborn MI

Ames, Charles C, *Chair,* Massachusetts Historical Society, Library, Boston MA

Ames-Bell, Linda, *Prof,* University of Toledo, Dept of Art, Toledo OH (S)

Amick, Alison, *Cur Colls,* Oklahoma City Museum of Art, Oklahoma City OK

Amidon, Catherine, *Dir,* Plymouth State University, Karl Drerup Art Gallery, Plymouth NH

Amies, Marian, *Assoc Prof,* University of Missouri, Saint Louis, Dept of Art & Art History, Saint Louis MO (S)

Amis, Anne, *Dir Finance & Operations,* Zeum, San Francisco CA

Amling, Diana, *Pres,* Coquille Valley Art Association, Library, Coquille OR

Ammons, Betty, *Asst Librn,* United Methodist Historical Society, Library, Baltimore MD

Ammons, John, *Adjunct Prof,* Louisiana College, Dept of Art, Pineville LA (S)

Ammons, Wendi, *Asst to Exec Dir & Mem Coord,* Carolina Art Association, Gibbes Museum of Art, Charleston SC

Ammons, Wendi, *Mem Mgr,* Gibbes Museum of Art, Charleston SC (S)

Amneus, Cynthia, *Cur Fashion & Textile,* Cincinnati Art Museum, Cincinnati Art Museum, Cincinnati OH

Amore, Shirley, *City Librn,* Denver Public Library, Reference, Denver CO

Amoroso, Kathy, *Dir Maine Memory Network,* Maine Historical Society, Portland ME

Amorous, Martin, *Dept Head,* Sam Houston State University, Art Dept, Huntsville TX (S)

Amos, Maria, *Admin Asst,* Oklahoma City University, Hulsey Gallery-Norick Art Center, Oklahoma City OK

Ams, Charles M, *Pres,* Southern Vermont Art Center, Manchester VT

Amsellem, Patrick, *Assoc Cur Photography,* Brooklyn Museum, Brooklyn NY

Amsler, Cory, *Cur Coll,* Bucks County Historical Society, Mercer Museum, Doylestown PA

Amsterdam, Susan, *Young People's Theatre Coordr,* Passaic County Community College, Broadway, LRC, and Hamilton Club Galleries, Paterson NJ

Amundsen, Christopher, *Exec Dir,* American Craft Council, Minneapolis MN

Amundson, Dale, *Dir,* University of Manitoba, School of Art, Winnipeg MB (S)

Amundson, David, *Instr,* Judson University, School of Art, Design & Architecture, Elgin IL (S)

Amundson, Jacob, *Asst Prof,* Greenville College, Art Dept, Greenville IL (S)

Amundson, Jhennifer A, *Prof,* Judson University, School of Art, Design & Architecture, Elgin IL (S)

Amyx, Guyla, *Instr,* Cuesta College, Art Dept, San Luis Obispo CA (S)

Anable, Susan, *Dir Educ Resources & Svcs,* Dayton Art Institute, Dayton OH

Anagnos, Christine, *Deputy Dir,* Association of Art Museum Directors, New York NY

Ananian, Michael, *Prof,* University of North Carolina at Greensboro, Art Dept, Greensboro NC (S)

Anasazi, Stacey, *Financial & Systems Coordr,* Smith College, Museum of Art, Northampton MA

Anawalt, Patricia, *Consulting Cur Costumes & Textiles,* University of California, Los Angeles, Fowler Museum at UCLA, Los Angeles CA

Andersen, David, *Designer/Preparator,* Willamette University, Hallie Ford Museum of Art, Salem OR

Andersen, Douglas, *Asst Prof,* University of Hartford, Hartford Art School, West Hartford CT (S)

Andersen, Jan-Henrik, *Asst Prof,* University of Michigan, Ann Arbor, School of Art & Design, Ann Arbor MI (S)

Andersen, Jeffrey, *Dir,* Lyme Historical Society, Library, Old Lyme CT

Andersen, Jeffrey W, *Dir,* Lyme Historical Society, Florence Griswold Museum, Old Lyme CT

Andersen, Jesse, *Digital Svcs Mgr,* Plains Art Museum, Fargo ND

Andersen, Patricia, *Asst Admin,* Washington Art Association, Washington Depot CT

Andersen, Rachel Klees, *Cur Exhibits,* Kenosha Public Museums, Kenosha WI

Anderson, Arthur, *Assoc Prof,* York College of the City University of New York, Fine & Performing Arts, Jamaica NY (S)

Anderson, Barbara, *Instr,* Concordia College, Art Dept, Moorhead MN (S)

Anderson, Barbara, *Assoc Dean,* Carnegie Mellon University, College of Fine Arts, Pittsburgh PA (S)

Anderson, Betsey, *Admin Asst,* Belle Grove Inc., Belle Grove Plantation, Middletown VA

Anderson, Betsy, *Pres,* The Art League Gallery & School, Alexandria VA

Anderson, Bjorn, *Asst Prof,* Minnesota State University-Moorhead, Dept of Art & Design, Moorhead MN (S)

Anderson, Blue, *Mus Shop Mgr,* San Bernardino County Museum, Fine Arts Institute, Redlands CA

Anderson, Blue, *Mus Shop Mgr,* Columbia River Maritime Museum, Astoria OR

Anderson, Bradley, *Children's Theatre,* Arkansas Arts Center, Museum, Little Rock AR (S)

Anderson, Brenda, *Gallery Cur,* North Seattle Community College, Art Dept, Seattle WA (S)

Anderson, Bruce, *Coll Mgr,* University of Regina, MacKenzie Art Gallery, Regina SK

Anderson, Catie, *Cur Educ,* Leigh Yawkey Woodson Art Museum, Wausau WI

Anderson, Chris, *Coll Information Mgr,* Museum of Wisconsin Art, West Bend WI

Anderson, Christopher, *Librn,* Archives & History Center of the United Methodist Church, Madison NJ

Anderson, Christopher J, *Head Librn,* Archives & History Center of the United Methodist Church, Library, Madison NJ

Anderson, Claire Jo, *Secy,* Frontier Times Museum, Bandera TX

Anderson, Craig, *Exec Dir,* Munoz Waxman Gallery - Center for Contemporary Arts, Santa Fe NM

Anderson, Craig A, *Bd Mem,* NAB Gallery, Chicago IL

Anderson, Cy, *Digital Media Production/Video Production,* Art Institute of Pittsburgh, Pittsburgh PA (S)

Anderson, Cynthia, *Mktg Dir,* South Texas Institute for the Arts, Art Museum of South Texas, Corpus Christi TX

Anderson, Daniel J, *Head Ceramic,* Southern Illinois University at Edwardsville, Dept of Art & Design, Edwardsville IL (S)

Anderson, David, *Dir,* Creek Council House Museum, Okmulgee OK

Anderson, David, *Dir,* Creek Council House Museum, Library, Okmulgee OK

Anderson, Deb, *Cur Educ,* Arts Midland Galleries & School, Alden B. Dow Museum of Science & Art, Midland MI

Anderson, Diana, *Exhibits Coordr,* Red Deer & District Museum & Archives, Red Deer AB

Anderson, Donald, *Prof Emeritus,* University of Louisville, Allen R Hite Art Institute, Louisville KY (S)

Anderson, Donald B, *CEO & Pres,* Roswell Artist-in-Residence Foundation, Anderson Museum of Contemporary Art, Roswell NM

Anderson, Donna, *Exec Dir,* The Exhibition Alliance, Hamilton NY

Anderson, Francine M, *Chief Arts Educ,* South Florida Cultural Consortium, Miami Dade County Dept of Cultural Affairs, Miami FL

Anderson, Gail Kana, *Asst Dir & Cur of Coll,* University of Oklahoma, Fred Jones Jr Museum of Art, Norman OK

Anderson, Glaire, *Asst Prof,* University of North Carolina at Chapel Hill, Art Dept, Chapel Hill NC (S)

Anderson, Hilary, *Dir Exhibits,* National Heritage Museum, Lexington MA

Anderson, Hugh B, *Dean of Arts,* Polk Community College, Art, Letters & Social Sciences, Winter Haven FL (S)

Anderson, Ingrid, *Dir Progs & Outreach,* Portland Children's Museum, Portland OR

Anderson, Jeffrey, *Exec Dir,* Alberta Foundation for the Arts, Edmonton AB

Anderson, Jennifer, *Admin Asst,* Scripps College, Ruth Chandler Williamson Gallery, Claremont CA

Anderson, Joanna, *Pres,* Daum Museum of Contemporary Art, Sedalia MO

Anderson, John, *Chairperson Div Creative Arts,* Monterey Peninsula College, Art Dept/Art Gallery, Monterey CA (S)

Anderson, John, *Prof,* Framingham State College, Art Dept, Framingham MA (S)

Anderson, Jon, *Prof,* Utah State University, Dept of Art, Logan UT (S)

Anderson, Joseph, *Librn,* Southern Alberta Art Gallery, Library, Lethbridge AB

Anderson, Ken, *Adjunct,* North Iowa Area Community College, Dept of Art, Mason City IA (S)

Anderson, Ken, *Chair Bd Trustees,* Santa Barbara Museum of Art, Library, Santa Barbara CA

Anderson, Ken, *Prof,* University of Missouri, Saint Louis, Dept of Art & Art History, Saint Louis MO (S)

Anderson, Kenneth, *Prof,* Peru State College, Art Dept, Peru NE (S)

Anderson, Kristin, *Chmn,* Augsburg College, Art Dept, Minneapolis MN (S)

Anderson, Larry, *Dir Performing Arts & Pub Progs,* Snug Harbor Cultural Center, Newhouse Center for Contemporary Arts, Staten Island NY

Anderson, Lawrence P, *Prof & Chmn,* Francis Marion University, Fine Arts Dept, Florence SC (S)

Anderson, Leslie, *Arts Librn,* California State University, Long Beach, University Library, Long Beach CA

Anderson, Linda, *Exec Dir,* Rapid City Arts Council, Dahl Arts Center, Rapid City SD

Anderson, Maggie, *Dir Educ,* Newport Art Museum, Coleman Center for Creative Studies, Newport RI (S)

Anderson, Margaret F, *VChmn,* Witte Museum, San Antonio TX

Anderson, Marge, *Sales Assoc,* Gene Roncka Willow Point Gallery/Museum, Ashland NE

Anderson, Mark, *Dir,* Texas A&M University-Corpus Christi, Weil Art Gallery, Corpus Christi TX

Anderson, Mark R, *Chmn,* Presbyterian College, Visual & Theater Arts, Clinton SC (S)

Anderson, Mark W, *Chmn,* Baylor University - College of Arts and Sciences, Dept of Art, Waco TX (S)

Anderson, Martin, *Dept Head,* Henry Ford Community College, McKenzie Fine Art Ctr, Dearborn MI (S)

Anderson, Mary Ann, *Admin Asst,* Purdue University Galleries, West Lafayette IN

Anderson, Maxwell, *Melvin and Bren Simon Dir & CEO,* Indianapolis Museum of Art, Indianapolis IN

Anderson, Nancy, *Asst Prof,* University at Buffalo, State University of New York, Dept of Visual Studies, Buffalo NY (S)

Anderson, Naura, *Pub Programs Dir,* Rochester Art Center, Rochester MN

Anderson, Neil, *Prof,* Bucknell University, Dept of Art, Lewisburg PA (S)

Anderson, Paul, *Asst Dir Library Admin Servs,* University of Delaware, Morris Library, Newark DE

Anderson, Peter, *Treas,* South County Art Association, Kingston RI

Anderson, Phelps, *Exec Dir,* Roswell Artist-in-Residence Foundation, Anderson Museum of Contemporary Art, Roswell NM

Anderson, Richita, *Librn,* Aesthetic Realism Foundation, Eli Siegel Collection, New York NY

Anderson, Richita, *Librn,* Aesthetic Realism Foundation, Aesthetic Realism Foundation Library, New York NY

Anderson, Robert, *Foundations Dir,* University of Texas, Dept of Art & Art History, Austin TX (S)

Anderson, Robert, *Prof,* West Virginia University, College of Creative Arts, School of Art & Design, Morgantown WV (S)

Anderson, Scott, *Dir Devel,* Museum of Contemporary Art Denver, Denver CO

Anderson, Stanford, *Head Dept,* Massachusetts Institute of Technology, School of Architecture and Planning, Cambridge MA (S)

Anderson, Steve, *Exec Dir,* Catfish Capital Visitors Center and Museum, Belzoni MS

Anderson, Steven R, *CEO & Dir,* Iowa Great Lakes Maritime Museum, Arnolds Park IA

Anderson, Susan, *Dir Finance & Admin,* South Shore Arts, Munster IN

Anderson, Susan B, *Treas,* Madison & Main Gallery, Greeley CO

Anderson, Susan K, *Archivist,* Philadelphia Museum of Art, Library & Archives, Philadelphia PA

Anderson, Sven, *Asst Prof,* State University of New York College at Oneonta, Dept of Art, Oneonta NY (S)

Anderson, Ted, *Design Dir,* The Exhibition Alliance, Hamilton NY

Anderson, Terri, *Dir Mus Coll,* National Trust for Historic Preservation, Washington DC

Anderson, Terry, *Instr,* Northeast Mississippi Junior College, Art Dept, Booneville MS (S)

Anderson, Tim, *Gallery Dir,* Cuesta College, Cuesta College Art Gallery, San Luis Obispo CA

Anderson, Tom, *Prof,* Florida State University, Art Education Dept, Tallahassee FL (S)

Anderson, Tom, *Team Leader Private Records,* Ministry of Alberta Culture, Provincial Archives of Alberta, Edmonton AB

Anderson, Tracey, *Exec Dir,* Yukon Historical & Museums Association, Whitehorse YT

Anderson, Wayne, *Dept Chair,* Wayne State College, Dept Art & Design, Wayne NE (S)

Anderson, Wayne, *Prof,* Wayne State College, Nordstrand Visual Arts Gallery, Wayne NE

Anderson, Whitney, *Computer Instr,* Ames Free-Easton's Public Library, North Easton MA

Anderson, Wyatt, *Dean,* University of Georgia, Franklin College of Arts & Sciences, Lamar Dodd School of Art, Athens GA (S)

Anderson-Fuller, Myrna, *Exec Dir,* Hammonds House Museum, Atlanta GA

Anderson-Himmelspach, Neil, *Asst Prof Music,* Harford Community College, Visual, Performing and Applied Arts Division, Bel Air MD (S)

Andersson, Christiane, *Prof,* Bucknell University, Dept of Art, Lewisburg PA (S)

Andison, Lois, *Asst Prof,* University of Waterloo, Fine Arts Dept, Waterloo ON (S)

Andreasen, Jason, *Exec Dir,* Baton Rouge Gallery, Center For Contemporary Art, Baton Rouge LA

Andres, Glenn, *Prof,* Middlebury College, History of Art & Architecture Dept, Middlebury VT (S)

Andress, Thomas, *Pres Print Selection Comt Chmn,* Print Club of Albany, Albany NY

Andrew, David, *Prof,* University of New Hampshire, Dept of Arts & Art History, Durham NH (S)

Andrews, Bill, *Instr,* Mississippi State University, Dept of Art, Starville MS (S)

Andrews, Debbie, *Educ Coordr,* Farmington Village Green & Library Association, Stanley-Whitman House, Farmington CT

Andrews, Edwin, *Assoc Prof,* Northeastern University, Dept of Art & Architecture, Boston MA (S)

Andrews, G Aseneth, *Instr Visual Arts Educ,* Madonna University, College of Arts & Humanities, Livonia MI (S)

Andrews, Gail, *Dir,* Birmingham Museum of Art, Birmingham AL

Andrews, Hazel, *Chmn,* Lynnwood Arts Centre, Simcoe ON

Andrews, Jim, *Instr,* Seton Hill University, Art Program, Greensburg PA (S)

Andrews, Jonathan, *Design Dept Head,* Bob Jones University, School of Fine Arts, Div of Art & Design, Greenville SC (S)

Andrews, Tim, *Dir Pub Rels,* Colonial Williamsburg Foundation, Williamsburg VA

Andrews, William, *Dir,* The Ogden Museum of Southern Art, University of New Orleans, New Orleans LA

Andrick, Annita, *Dir Library & Archives,* Erie County Historical Society, Erie PA

Andriulli, Robert, *Prof Drawing, Painting & Watercolor,* Millersville University, Dept of Art & Design, Millersville PA (S)

Andrus, Beryl, *Branch Adminr,* Las Vegas-Clark County Library District, Las Vegas NV

Andrus, Donna, *Finance Mgr,* Walter Anderson, Ocean Springs MS

Andrus, Lynda, *Prof,* Kansas State University, Art Dept, Manhattan KS (S)

Andrus, Maryanne, *Dir Educ,* Buffalo Bill Memorial Association, Buffalo Bill Historical Center, Cody WY

Andrzejewski, Anna V, *Asst Prof,* University of Wisconsin, Madison, Dept of Art History, Madison WI (S)

Angel, Catherine, *Prof,* University of Nevada, Las Vegas, Dept of Art, Las Vegas NV (S)

Angeloch, Eric, *Instr,* Woodstock School of Art, Inc, Woodstock NY (S)

Angert, Joe C, *Instr,* Saint Louis Community College at Forest Park, Art Dept, Saint Louis MO (S)

Anglin, B, *Asst Prof,* Christopher Newport University, Dept of Fine Performing Arts, Newport News VA (S)

Anglin, Barbara, *Technical Servs Librn,* Lee County Library, Tupelo MS

Anglin, John, *Dir,* East Central College, Art Dept, Union MO (S)

Anguilo, Marco, *Board VPres,* Centro Cultural De La Raza, San Diego CA

Angus, Scott, *Asst Prof Art,* Maryville University of Saint Louis, Art & Design Program, Saint Louis MO (S)

Anielski, Jennifer, *Librn, Tech Svcs,* The Mariners' Museum, Library, Newport News VA

Anke, Douglas, *Gen Educ,* Art Institute of Pittsburgh, Pittsburgh PA (S)

Annenberg, Wallis, *Dir,* Los Angeles County Museum of Art, Los Angeles CA

Anne Paul, Katherine, *Cur Asian Arts,* Newark Museum Association, The Newark Museum, Newark NJ

Anoushian, Suzanne E, *Chmn Commun Design,* Fashion Institute of Technology, Art & Design Division, New York NY (S)

Anreus, Alejandro, *Art Dept Chmn,* William Paterson University, Dept Arts, Wayne NJ (S)

Ansel, Erynne, *CEO & Dir,* Iroquois Indian Museum, Howes Cave NY

Ansell, Joseph P, *Interim Dean,* Auburn University, Dept of Art, Auburn AL (S)

Anstine, Michele, *Dir,* Delaware Historical Society, Read House and Gardens, Wilmington DE

Anstine, Michele, *Read House Site Admin,* Delaware Historical Society, Library, Wilmington DE

Antal, Bev, *Secy,* Regina Public Library, Dunlop Art Gallery, Regina SK

Antczak, Dorothy, *Summer Prog Dir,* Fine Arts Work Center, Provincetown MA

Anthony, Carolyn, *Dir,* Skokie Public Library, Skokie IL

Anthony, Clay, *Pub Relations,* Nicolaysen Art Museum & Discovery Center, Children's Discovery Center, Casper WY

Anthony, David, *Cur Anthropology,* Hartwick College, The Yager Museum, Oneonta NY

Anthony, David, *Dean,* Golden West College, Visual Art Dept, Huntington Beach CA (S)

Anthony, Kristina, *Exhibs Communs Mgr,* Hickory Museum of Art, Inc, Hickory NC

Anthony, Vincent, *Exec Dir,* Center for Puppetry Arts, Library, Atlanta GA

Antle, Sharon, *Chief Educ,* Ohio Historical Society, National Road-Zane Grey Museum, Columbus OH

Antle, Sharon, *Chief Educ Div,* Ohio Historical Society, Columbus OH

Anton, Don, *Prof,* Humboldt State University, College of Arts & Humanities, Art Dept, Arcata CA (S)

Anton, Janis K, *Dir Admis,* The Illinois Institute of Art - Chicago, Chicago IL (S)

Anton, Waldo, *Treas,* Guadalupe Historic Foundation, Santuario de Guadalupe, Santa Fe NM

Antonakis, Nick, *Dept Head Visual Arts,* Grand Rapids Community College, Visual Art Dept, Grand Rapids MI (S)

Antonelli, Karen, *Photog,* Art Institute of Pittsburgh, Pittsburgh PA (S)

Antonetti, Martin, *Lectr,* Smith College, Art Dept, Northampton MA (S)

Antonio, Carolyn, *Deputy Dir External Affairs,* Museum of Chinese in America, New York NY

Antonoff, Jeff, *Exec Dir,* Barbara & Ray Alpert Jewish Community Center, Pauline & Zena Gatov Gallery, Long Beach CA

Antonsen, Lasse, *Coordr Gallery,* University of Massachusetts Dartmouth, College of Visual & Performing Arts, North Dartmouth MA (S)

Antreasian, Tom, *Cur Exhib,* Albuquerque Museum of Art & History, Albuquerque NM

Anyah, Eric, *CFO,* Museum of Fine Arts, Houston, Houston TX

Anysas-Salkauskas, Ilse, *Mem Chmn,* Alberta Society of Artists, Calgary AB

Aoki, Katherine, *Assoc Prof,* Santa Clara University, Dept of Art & Art History, Santa Clara CA (S)

Aoki, Miho, *Assoc Prof,* University of Alaska-Fairbanks, Dept of Art, Fairbanks AK (S)

Aponte, Sandra, *Prof,* University of Puerto Rico, Mayaguez, Dept of Humanities, College of Fine Arts & Theory of Art Programs, Mayaguez PR (S)

Aponte, Sandra, *Prof,* University of Puerto Rico, Mayaguez, Dept of Humanities, College of Fine Arts & Theory of Art Programs, Mayaguez PR (S)

Apostolides, Nik, *Assoc Dir Opers,* National Portrait Gallery, Smithsonian Institution, Washington DC

Appel, Janet L, *Dir,* Shirley Plantation Foundation, Charles City VA

Appel, Kevin, *Prof Painting,* University of California, Irvine, Studio Art Dept, Irvine CA (S)

Appelhof, Ruth, *Exec Dir,* Guild Hall of East Hampton, Inc, Guild Hall Museum, East Hampton NY

Appiah, Krystal, *Cur African American History,* Library Company of Philadelphia, Philadelphia PA

Applebaun, Ronald, *Pres,* Kean University, James Howe Gallery, Union NJ

Applegate, Barbara, *Asst Dir,* C W Post Campus of Long Island University, Hillwood Art Museum, Brookville NY

Applegate, Barbara, *Treas,* Pemaquid Group of Artists, Pemaquid Art Gallery, Pemaquid Point ME

Applegate, Reed, *Resource Mgr,* California State University, Chico, Janet Turner Print Museum, CSU, Chicago, Chico CA

Appleton, Bill, *Asst Dir Pub Prog & Educ,* Saint Louis Art Museum, Saint Louis MO

Aquin, Stephane, *Cur Contemporary Art,* Montreal Museum of Fine Arts, Montreal PQ

Aquirre, Carlos, *Assoc Prof,* University of Miami, Dept of Art & Art History, Coral Gables FL (S)

Araki, Nancy, *Community Affairs,* Japanese American National Museum, Los Angeles CA

Aranda-Alvarado, Rocio, *Assoc Cur, Special Projects,* El Museo del Barrio, New York NY

Aravena, Lidia, *Conservator of Paintings,* Museo de Arte de Ponce, The Luis A Ferre Foundation Inc, Ponce PR

Aravena, Lidia, *Conservator of Paintings,* Museo de Arte de Ponce, The Luis A Ferre Foundation Inc, Ponce PR

Arbino, Larry, *Adjunct,* College of the Canyons, Art Dept, Santa Clarita CA (S)

Arbolino, Jamie, *Assoc Registrar,* United States Senate Commission on Art, Washington DC

Arbuckle, Linda, *Prof,* University of Florida, School of Art & Art History, Gainesville FL (S)

Arbury, Steve, *Chmn,* Radford University, Art Dept, Radford VA (S)

Arceneaux, Pamela D, *Senior Librn,* The Historic New Orleans Collection, Williams Research Center, New Orleans LA

Archabal, Nina M, *CEO & Dir,* Minnesota Historical Society, Saint Paul MN

Archer, Phil, *Dir Pub Prog,* Reynolda House Museum of American Art, Winston-Salem NC

Archer, Sarah, *Dir,* Greenwich House Pottery, Jane Hartsook Gallery, New York NY

Archer, Sarah, *Dir,* Greenwich House Pottery, Library, New York NY

Archias, Elise, *Asst Prof,* California State University, Chico, Department of Art & Art History, Chico CA (S)

Archibald, Courtney, *Accnt,* Willard Arts Center, Carr Gallery, Colonial Theater, Idaho Falls ID

Archibald, Robert, *Pres,* Missouri Historical Society, Missouri History Museum, Saint Louis MO

Arciniegas, Manuela, *Dir Educ,* Caribbean Cultural Center, Cultural Arts Organization & Resource Center, New York NY

Arday, Don, *Art Chair,* Rochester Institute of Technology, College of Imaging Arts & Sciences, Rochester NY (S)

Arena, Annie, *Instr,* Ocean City Arts Center, Ocean City NJ (S)

Arena Bell, Maria, *Co-Chair,* The Museum of Contemporary Art (MOCA), Moca Grand Avenue, Los Angeles CA

Arffmann, Kathleen, *Mgr Visitor Servs,* The Metropolitan Museum of Art, New York NY

Argabrite, Diana, *Dir Arts & Schools Prog,* De Anza College, Euphrat Museum of Art, Cupertino CA

Argall, Quinn, *Asst Cur,* City of Austin Parks & Recreation, O. Henry Museum, Austin TX

Argent, Lawrence, *Prof Sculpture,* University of Denver, School of Art & Art History, Denver CO (S)

Arice, Charles, *Instructional Asst,* Sullivan County Community College, Division of Commercial Art & Photography, Loch Sheldrake NY (S)

Arifin, Roni, *Mus Accnt,* Southern Methodist University, Meadows Museum, Dallas TX

Arike, Michael, *VPres,* Society of American Graphic Artists, New York NY

Aristarkhova, Irina, *Asst Prof Women's Studies & Art (Art Criticism),* Pennsylvania State University,

University Park, Penn State School of Visual Arts, University Park PA (S)

Arkin, Cynthia, *Pres,* Plastic Club, Art Club, Philadelphia PA

Arleth, Kim, *Office & Vol Coordr,* Intermedia Arts Minnesota, Minneapolis MN

Arleth, Kimberly, *Registrar,* Hamline University Studio Arts & Art History Depts, Gallery, Saint Paul MN

Armas-Garcia, Daisy, *Treas,* Miami Watercolor Society, Inc, Miami FL

Armborst, Tobias, *Asst Prof,* Vassar College, Art Dept, Poughkeepsie NY (S)

Armbrister, Clay, *Pres,* Girard College, Stephen Girard Collection, Philadelphia PA

Armendariz, Richard, *Assoc Prof,* University of Texas at San Antonio, Dept of Art & Art History, San Antonio TX (S)

Armento, Michael, *VPres Finance,* Please Touch Museum, Philadelphia PA

Arminio, Roberta Y, *Dir,* Museum of Ossining Historical Society, Ossining NY

Armistead, Julie, *Registrar,* Saint Mary's College of California, Hearst Art Gallery, Moraga CA

Armor, Joel, *Chief Preparator,* Contemporary Arts Center, Cincinnati OH

Armor, Kelly, *Dir Educ & Folk Art,* Erie Art Museum, Erie PA

Arms, Anneli, *Pres,* Federation of Modern Painters & Sculptors, New York NY

Armstrong, Barbara, *Mgr,* Seattle Public Library, Arts, Recreation & Literature Dept, Seattle WA

Armstrong, Christopher Drew, *Asst Prof,* University of Pittsburgh, Henry Clay Frick Dept History of Art & Architecture, Pittsburgh PA (S)

Armstrong, Chuck, *Contract Asst Prof Graphic Design,* University of Southern Indiana, Department of Art, Evansville IN (S)

Armstrong, Courtney, *Develop Officer,* Montgomery Museum of Fine Arts, Montgomery AL

Armstrong, David, *Pres & Founder,* American Museum of Ceramic Art, Pomona CA

Armstrong, Dirk, *Asst Cur,* Salvador Dali, Saint Petersburg FL

Armstrong, Elizabeth, *Dir Ctr for Alt Mus Practice & Cur Contemporary Art,* Minneapolis Institute of Arts, Minneapolis MN

Armstrong, Jean, *Mgr,* Portage and District Arts Council, Portage Arts Centre, Portage la Prairie MB

Armstrong, Joy, *Cur Asst,* Colorado Springs Fine Arts Center, Taylor Museum, Colorado Springs CO

Armstrong, June, *Corresp Secy,* Heritage Glass Museum, Glassboro NJ

Armstrong, Leatrice A, *Asst to Dir,* Wheelwright Museum of the American Indian, Santa Fe NM

Armstrong, Libbie, *Info & Pub Rels,* Higgins Armory Museum, Worcester MA

Armstrong, Lilian, *Prof,* Wellesley College, Art Dept, Wellesley MA (S)

Armstrong, Nadine, *2nd Vice Pres,* Cumberland Art Society Inc, Cookeville Art Gallery, Cookeville TN

Armstrong, Richard, *Dir Mus & Foundation,* Solomon R Guggenheim, New York NY

Armstrong-Gillis, Kathy, *Cur/Assoc,* Southwest School of Art, San Antonio TX

Armstutz, Bruce, *Prof,* Shoreline Community College, Humanities Division, Seattle WA (S)

Arnar, Anna, *Asst Prof,* Minnesota State University-Moorhead, Dept of Art & Design, Moorhead MN (S)

Arndt, Susan, *Art Instr,* Red Rocks Community College, Arts Dept, Lakewood CO (S)

Arneill, Porter, *Dir,* Kansas City Municipal Art Commission, Kansas City MO

Arnett, Jeff, *Mgr Develop Commun,* Columbia College Chicago, Museum of Contemporary Photography, Chicago IL

Arnholm, Ron, *Prof Graphic Design,* University of Georgia, Franklin College of Arts & Sciences, Lamar Dodd School of Art, Athens GA (S)

Arning, Bill, *Cur,* Massachusetts Institute of Technology, List Visual Arts Center, Cambridge MA

Arning, Bill, *Dir,* Contemporary Arts Museum Houston, Houston TX

Arnison, Steve, *Prof,* Munson-Williams-Proctor Arts Institute, Pratt MWP College of Art, Utica NY (S)

Arnold, Chester, *Chmn,* College of Marin, Dept of Art, Kentfield CA (S)

Arnold, Dorothea, *Lila Acheson Wallace,* The Metropolitan Museum of Art, New York NY

Arnold, Grant, *Sr Cur,* Vancouver Art Gallery, Vancouver BC

Arnold, Jan, *Library Dir,* Springfield Art Association of Edwards Place, Springfield IL

Arnold, Kristina, *Gallery Dir,* Western Kentucky University, University Gallery, Bowling Green KY

Arnold, Lee, *Chmn Art Dept,* Drew University, Elizabeth P Korn Gallery, Madison NJ

Arnold, Lee, *Dir Library,* Historical Society of Pennsylvania, Philadelphia PA

Arnold, Mark, *Exec Dir,* The Art Center of Waco, Waco TX

Arnold, Mark, *Exec Dir,* The Art Center of Waco, Library, Waco TX

Arnold, Pat, *Office Mgr,* Lehigh Valley Heritage Center, Allentown PA

Arnold, Patrick, *Instr,* Main Line Art Center, Haverford PA (S)

Arnold, Peter, *Pres & CEO,* Genesee Country Village & Museum, John L Wehle Art Gallery, Mumford NY

Arnold, Ralph, *Prof Emeritus,* Loyola University of Chicago, Fine Arts Dept, Chicago IL (S)

Arnold, Ramona, *Admin & Finance,* Institute of American Indian Arts, Museum of Contemporary Native Arts, Santa Fe NM (S)

Arnold, Robert, *Prof,* Ohio State University, Dept of Art Education, Columbus OH (S)

Arnold, Sara, *Cur Coll,* Gibbes Museum of Art, Charleston SC (S)

Arnold, Steven, *Asst Prof Graphic Design,* Middle Georgia State College, Humanities Division, Dept of Art - School of Liberal Arts, Dept of Media, Culture & the Arts, Cochran GA (S)

Aron, Kathy, *Exec Dir,* Society for Contemporary Photography, Kansas City MO

Aronoff, Mindy, *Dir Training & Resources,* Bay Area Video Coalition, Inc, San Francisco CA

Aronowitz, Richard, *Dean Grad & Continuing Educ,* Massachusetts College of Art, Boston MA (S)

Aronson, Julie, *Cur Am Painting & Sculpture,* Cincinnati Art Museum, Cincinnati Art Museum, Cincinnati OH

Arony, Joanne, *Exec Dir,* Landmark Society of Western New York, Inc, The Campbell-Whittlesey House Museum, Rochester NY

Arp, Kimberly, *Prof,* Louisiana State University, School of Art, Baton Rouge LA (S)

Arpad, Tori, *Assoc Prof,* Florida International University, School of Art & Art History, Miami FL (S)

Arpadi, Allen, *Instr,* Saint Louis Community College at Forest Park, Art Dept, Saint Louis MO (S)

Arquello, Lori, *Dir Mktg,* Putnam Museum of History and Natural Science, Davenport IA

Arquillos, Joel, *Exec Dir,* Social & Public Art Resource Center, (SPARC), Venice CA

Arquit, Kevin J, *Pres,* The Adirondack Historical Association, The Adirondack Museum, Blue Mountain Lake NY

Arrant, Christopher, *Exhibit Coordr,* Visual Arts Center of Northwest Florida, Visual Arts Center Library, Panama City FL

Arrasmith, Anne, *Co-Founder & Artist,* Space One Eleven, Inc, Birmingham AL

Arrasmith, Lynnda, *Cur & Registrar,* Canton Museum of Art, Art Library, Canton OH

Arrasmith, Lynnda, *Cur Coll & Registrar,* Canton Museum of Art, Canton OH

Arrasmith, Lynnda, *Cur Exhibits & Registrar,* Canton Museum of Art, Canton OH (S)

Arredondo, Richard, *Chmn,* San Antonio College, Visual Arts & Technology, San Antonio TX (S)

Arrington, Gerald C, *Prof,* Concord College, Fine Art Division, Athens WV (S)

Arroyo, Alexa, *Vis Lectr,* University of New Orleans-Lake Front, Dept of Fine Arts, New Orleans LA (S)

Arroyo, Rafael, *Office Mgr,* University of Oregon, Aperture Photo Gallery - EMU Art Gallery, Eugene OR

Arsenault, Roxanne, *Programming Coordr,* La Centrale Powerhouse Gallery, Montreal PQ

Arsenault, Todd, *Asst Prof,* Dickinson College, Dept of Art & Art History, Carlisle PA (S)

Arseneau, Laura, *Cur Educ,* Burlington Art Centre, Burlington ON

Arseneault, Celine, *Botanist & Librn,* Jardin Botanique de Montreal, Bibliotheque, Montreal PQ

Arseneault, Jacques, *Prof Printmaking,* Universite de Moncton, Dept of Visual Arts, Moncton NB (S)

Arteaga, Annabelle, *VPres Mem,* MEXIC-ARTE Museum, Austin TX

Arthur, Catherine, *Cur,* Johns Hopkins University, Homewood Museum, Baltimore MD

Arthur, Charmion, *Instr,* Fort Hays State University, Dept of Art & Design, Hays KS (S)

Arthur, Ellen, *Mus Mgr,* Biggs Museum of American Art, Dover DE

Arthur, Kathleen, *Prof,* James Madison University, School of Art & Art History, Harrisonburg VA (S)

Artimovich, Vicki, *Art History Instr,* Bellevue Community College, Art Dept, Bellevue WA (S)

Artzberger, John A, *Sr Cur,* Oglebay Institute, Mansion Museum, Wheeling WV

Artzberger, John A, *Sr Cur,* Oglebay Institute, Library, Wheeling WV

Arya, B N, *Dean,* University of Lucknow, College of Arts and Crafts, Faculty of Fine Arts, Lucknow UP (S)

Asbury, Jane, *Assoc Prof,* University of Kansas, The School of the Arts, Dept of Visual Art, Lawrence KS (S)

Ascenio, Mario, *Libr Dir,* Corcoran Gallery of Art, Corcoran Library, Washington DC

Aschkenes, Anna M, *Exec Dir,* Middlesex County Cultural & Heritage Commission, New Brunswick NJ

Asebedo, Anna, *Dept Chair,* City College of San Francisco, Art Dept, San Francisco CA (S)

Aselford, Catherine, *Develop Mgr,* Pyramid Atlantic, Silver Spring MD

Asel Ford, Catherine, *Exec Dir,* Northern Virginia Fine Arts Association, The Athenaeum, Alexandria VA

Ash, Carol, *Chair & NHT Commissioner,* New York Office of Parks, Recreation & Historic Preservation, Natural Heritage Trust, Albany NY

Ash, Scottie, *Store Mgr,* South Carolina State Museum, Columbia SC

Ashbaugh, Sue, *Educ Coordr,* Jefferson County Open Space, Hiwan Homestead Museum, Evergreen CO

Ashby, Andrea, *Librn Technician,* Independence National Historical Park, Library, Philadelphia PA

Ashby, Gil, *Chmn Illustration,* College for Creative Studies, Detroit MI (S)

Asher, Catherine, *Prof,* University of Minnesota, Minneapolis, Art History, Minneapolis MN (S)

Asher, Dorothy, *Dir,* Lizzadro Museum of Lapidary Art, Elmhurst IL

Asher, Frederick, *Prof,* University of Minnesota, Minneapolis, Art History, Minneapolis MN (S)

Ashkin, Michael, *Assoc Prof,* Cornell University, Dept of Art, Ithaca NY (S)

Ashley, Carrie, *Educ Coordr,* National Audubon Society, John James Audubon Center at Mill Grove, Audubon PA

Ashley, Janis, *Adminr,* Los Angeles County Museum of Natural History, William S Hart Museum, Newhall CA

Ashley, Paul, *Chmn Liberal Arts,* School of the Art Institute of Chicago, Chicago IL (S)

Ashley, Raymond, *Pres & CEO,* Maritime Museum of San Diego, San Diego CA

Ashline, Sue, *Matter & Frames,* University of Kansas, Spencer Museum of Art, Lawrence KS

Ashman, Stuart A, *Pres & CEO,* Museum of Latin American Art, Long Beach CA

Ashmore, Kathi, *Event Coordr,* Marian College, Allison Mansion, Indianapolis IN

Ashton, Jean, *Dir Libr Div,* New-York Historical Society, Library, New York NY

Ashton, Jean, *Sr Dir Resources & Progs,* New-York Historical Society, Museum, New York NY

Ashton, Lynn, *Exec Dir,* Kentucky Derby Museum, Louisville KY

Ashton Fisher, Helen, *Coll Cur,* William A Farnsworth, Library, Rockland ME

Asihene, Emmanuel, *Prof,* Clark-Atlanta University, School of Arts & Sciences, Atlanta GA (S)

Askew, Dan, *Lectr,* University of Texas of Permian Basin, Dept of Art, Odessa TX (S)

Askren, David L, *Treas,* Queen Sofia Spanish Institute, New York NY

Aslanova, Anya, *Dir Educ Develop,* Indianapolis Art Center, Marilyn K. Glick School of Art, Indianapolis IN

Asmoucha, Tobi, *Instr,* Toronto School of Art, Toronto ON (S)

Asmus, Collin, *Assoc Prof,* Bridgewater State College, Art Dept, Bridgewater MA (S)

Asmus, Collin, *Asst Prof,* Millsaps College, Dept of Art, Jackson MS (S)

Asmuth, Thomas, *Asst Prof,* University of West Florida, Dept of Art, Pensacola FL (S)

Aspness, Mary, *Instr,* Century College, Humanities Dept, White Bear Lake MN (S)

Asprodites, Gail, *Asst Dir for Admin & Fin,* New Orleans Museum of Art, New Orleans LA

Assad, Alan, *Industrial Design Technology,* Art Institute of Pittsburgh, Pittsburgh PA (S)

Assad, Cyril, *Industrial Design Technology,* Art Institute of Pittsburgh, Pittsburgh PA (S)

Assaf, Michele, *Dir Exhibitions & Collections,* Denver Art Museum, Denver CO

Asselin, Hedwidge, *Treas & Mem (Toronto),* International Association of Art Critics, AICA Canada, Inc, Toronto ON

Aste, Richard, *Cur European Art,* Brooklyn Museum, Brooklyn NY

Ataoguz, Kirsten, *Asst Prof,* Indiana-Purdue University, Dept of Fine Arts, Fort Wayne IN (S)

Atchison, Sandra, *Asst Dean,* University of North Texas, Libraries, Denton TX

Atencio, Thomas, *Chief Security,* Institute of American Indian Arts, Museum of Contemporary Native Arts, Santa Fe NM (S)

Atencio, Thomas, *Facilities & Security Mgr,* Institute of American Indian Arts, Museum of Contemporary Native Arts, Santa Fe NM

Atherholt, Wayne David, *Dir,* The Museum of Arts & Sciences Inc, Daytona Beach FL

Atheron, Cynthia, *Prof,* Middlebury College, History of Art & Architecture Dept, Middlebury VT (S)

Atherton, Jeff, *Photog Dept Chmn,* Art Center College of Design, Pasadena CA (S)

Atkins, Sharon Matt, *Mng Cur Exhibs,* Brooklyn Museum, Brooklyn NY

Atkinson, Conrad, *Prof Painting & Mixed Media,* University of California, Davis, Dept of Art & Art History, Davis CA (S)

Atkinson, Daniel, *Educ & Pub Progs Mgr,* Contemporary Arts Museum Houston, Houston TX

Atkinson, Dianne, *Instr,* Mount Mary College, Art & Design Division, Milwaukee WI (S)

Atkinson, Judith, *Dir Human Resources & Labor Relations,* Milwaukee Public Museum, Milwaukee WI

Atkinson, Lane, *Controller,* New Brunswick Museum, Saint John NB

Atkinson, Maggie, *Asst Prof,* Memorial University of Newfoundland, Division of Fine Arts, Visual Arts Program, Corner Brook NF (S)

Atkinson, Martha, *Educ Coordr,* The City of Petersburg Museums, Petersburg VA

Atkinson, Melanie, *Chmn,* Hinds Community College, Dept of Art, Raymond MS (S)

Atkinson, Melanie, *Dept Chmn, Painting & Drawing,* Hinds Community College District, Marie Hull Gallery, Raymond MS

Attenborough, Debra, *Librn,* Rodman Hall Arts Centre, Library, Saint Catharines ON

Attie, Diana, *Prof,* University of Toledo, Dept of Art, Toledo OH (S)

Attyah, David, *Instr,* Glendale Community College, Visual & Performing Arts Div, Glendale CA (S)

Atvur, Beste, *Gallery Mgr,* Ward-Nasse Gallery, New York NY

Atwater, H Brewster, *Chmn Bd,* Walker Art Center, Minneapolis MN

Atwell, Michael, *Asst Dir,* Purdue University Galleries, West Lafayette IN

Atwell, Michael, *Cur,* Art Museum of Greater Lafayette, Lafayette IN

Atwell, Patty, *Treas,* Frontier Gateway Museum, Glendive MT

Au, Jeri, *Asst Prof,* Webster University, Art Dept, Webster Groves MO (S)

Aubin, Rebeca, *Cur of Educ,* University of New Mexico, The Harwood Museum of Art, Taos NM

Aubourg, Vickie, *Asst Dir,* California Polytechnic State University, College of Architecture & Environmental Design-Architecture Collection, San Luis Obispo CA

Aucella, Frank J, *Exec Dir,* Woodrow Wilson, Washington DC

Audeh, Aida, *Dept Chair, Assoc Prof,* Hamline University, Dept of Studio Arts & Art History, Saint Paul MN (S)

Audette, Marc, *Cur,* York University, Glendon Gallery, Toronto ON

Audiss, Barb, *Develop Officer,* Oregon College of Art & Craft, Hoffman Gallery, Portland OR

Audley, Paul, *Pres,* Discovery Museum, Bridgeport CT

Audy, Heloise, *Treas,* Conseil des Arts du Quebec (CATQ), Diagonale, Centre des arts et des fibres du Quebec, Montreal PQ

Auerbach, Erik, *Dir Educ,* San Francisco Camerawork, San Francisco CA

Auerbach, Lisa Anne, *Asst Prof,* Pomona College, Dept of Art & Art History, Claremont CA (S)

Augaitis, Daina, *Chief Cur,* Vancouver Art Gallery, Vancouver BC

Augelli, John, *CEO, Exec Dir,* Rosenberg Library, Galveston TX

Augenbraum, Marjorie, *Liberal Arts Chair,* Montserrat College of Art, Beverly MA (S)

Augustine, Sylvia, *Mus Coordr,* Independence Historical Museum & Art Center, Independence KS

Auld, Michael, *Co-Chmn Exhibs,* Fondo del Sol, Visual Art & Media Center, Washington DC

Aulisi, Joe, *Dir,* National Museum of Racing, National Museum of Racing & Hall of Fame, Saratoga Springs NY

Aulisi, Joseph E, *Acting Dir,* National Museum of Racing, Reference Library, Saratoga Springs NY

Ault, Amanda, *Assoc Dir,* Southern Exposure, San Francisco CA

Ault, Amanda, *Prog & Mem Svcs Mgr,* National Alliance for Media Arts & Culture, San Francisco CA

Aumann, Karen, *Assoc Prof,* Philadelphia Community College, Dept of Art, Philadelphia PA (S)

Aune, Alison, *Asst Prof,* University of Minnesota, Duluth, Art Dept, Duluth MN (S)

Aunet, John, *Chmn Bd Dirs,* The American Film Institute, Center for Advanced Film & Television, Los Angeles CA (S)

Aunspaugh, Richard, *Chmn,* Young Harris College, Dept of Art, Young Harris GA (S)

Auping, Michael, *Chief Cur,* Modern Art Museum, Fort Worth TX

Aurandt, David, *Exec Dir,* The Robert McLaughlin, Oshawa ON

Aurbach, Michael, *Prof,* Vanderbilt University, Dept of Art, Nashville TN (S)

Aurles, Nereida, *Office Mgr,* Institute of Puerto Rican Arts & Culture, Chicago IL

Ausfeld, Margaret Lynne, *Cur Art,* Montgomery Museum of Fine Arts, Library, Montgomery AL

Ausfeld, Margaret Lynne, *Sr Cur Art,* Montgomery Museum of Fine Arts, Montgomery AL

Austen, Barbara, *Archivist,* Connecticut Historical Society, Library, Hartford CT

Austin, Beverly, *Asst Prof,* Harding University, Dept of Art & Design, Searcy AR (S)

Austin, David, *Dir,* Imago Galleries, Palm Desert CA

Austin, Howard, *Instr,* Milwaukee Area Technical College, School of Media & Creative Arts, Milwaukee WI (S)

Austin, Jerry, *Assoc Dean,* University of North Texas, College of Visual Arts & Design, Denton TX (S)

Austin, Lynn, *Archivist & Records Officer,* OCAD University, Dorothy H Hoover Library, Toronto ON

Austin, Marvin, *Div Chm,* Columbia State Community College, Dept of Art, Columbia TN (S)

Austin, Megan, *Office Asst,* Hamilton College, Emerson Gallery, Clinton NY

Austin, Sharyn, *Pres,* Art Center of Battle Creek, Battle Creek MI

Auston, Leisa, *Dir,* Imago Galleries, Palm Desert CA

Austrian, Sarah, *Deputy Dir & Gen Counsel,* Solomon R Guggenheim, New York NY

Auten, William, *Digital Colls Coordr,* University of Virginia, The Fralin Museum of Art at the University of Virginia, Charlottesville VA

Autenreith, Amy, *Mus Mgr,* Houston Museum of Decorative Arts, Chattanooga TN

Auther, Elissa, *Assoc Prof Visual Arts,* University of Colorado-Colorado Springs, Visual & Performing Arts Dept (VAPA), Colorado Springs CO (S)

Autry, Carolyn, *Assoc Prof,* University of Toledo, Dept of Art, Toledo OH (S)

Autry, Pamela, *Dir Human Resources,* Dallas Museum of Art, Dallas TX

Avery, Alyson, *Information Mgmt Specialist,* James A Michener, Doylestown PA

Avery, Elizabeth, *Vis Asst Prof,* Hamline University, Dept of Studio Arts & Art History, Saint Paul MN (S)

Avery, Laura, *Asst Dir,* Ringling College of Art & Design, Selby Gallery, Sarasota FL

Avery, Robert, *Dir,* Rome Historical Society, William E Scripture Memorial Library, Rome NY

Avery, Robert, *Exec Dir,* Rome Historical Society, Museum & Archives, Rome NY

Avila, Nicole, *Proj Mgr,* United States General Services Administration, Art in Architecture and Fine Arts, Washington DC

Aviles, Victoria, *Admin Asst,* University of Texas at El Paso, Stanlee & Gerald Rubin Center for the Visual Arts, El Paso TX

Avilla, Audre, *1st VPres,* Frontier Gateway Museum, Glendive MT

Avina, Maya, *Asst Prof,* University of Southern Colorado, Dept of Art, Pueblo CO (S)

Avril, Ellen, *Chief Cur & Cur Asian Art,* Cornell University, Herbert F Johnson Museum of Art, Ithaca NY

Awotona, Adenrele, *Dean,* Southern University A & M College, School of Architecture, Baton Rouge LA (S)

Axsom, Richard H, *Sr Cur Prints & Photographs,* Grand Rapids Art Museum, Grand Rapids MI

Axsom, Rick, *Exhib Cur,* Madison Museum of Contemporary Art, Madison WI

Axtman, Seb, *Cur,* South Dakota National Guard Museum, Pierre SD

Ayars, Lee, *Adjunct Asst Prof,* Spokane Falls Community College, Fine Arts Dept, Spokane WA (S)

Ayer, Elizabeth, *Asst Prof,* Hartwick College, Art Dept, Oneonta NY (S)

Ayers, Lucie, *Exhibit Coordr,* Tennessee Valley Art Association, Tuscumbia AL

Aylmer, Annabelle, *Instr,* Glendale Community College, Visual & Performing Arts Div, Glendale CA (S)

Aylward, Marci, *Gallery Dir,* Avila University, Thornhill Art Gallery, Kansas City MO

Aylward, Marci, *Instr,* Avila College, Art Division, Dept of Humanities, Kansas City MO (S)

Aynessazian, Tanya, *CEO,* Volcano Art Center Gallery, Hawaii Volcanoes National Park HI

Ayott, Diane, *Art Educ,* Montserrat College of Art, Beverly MA (S)

Ayotte, Tammy, *Clerk Typist,* Neville Public Museum of Brown County, Green Bay WI

Azar, John, *Philosophy,* Henry Ford Community College, McKenzie Fine Art Ctr, Dearborn MI (S)

Azbill, Penny, *Educ Coordr,* City of Cedar Falls, Iowa, James & Meryl Hearst Center for the Arts & Sculpture Garden, Cedar Falls IA

Azzolina, Elizabeth, *Secy,* Philadelphia Sketch Club, Philadelphia PA

Baab, Anthony, *Adjunct Assoc Prof Fine Art,* Johnson County Community College, Fine Arts Dept & Art History Dept, Overland Park KS (S)

Baba, Ronald, *Assoc Prof,* University of Wisconsin-Green Bay, Arts Dept, Green Bay WI (S)

Babb, Pamela, *Exec Dir,* Children's Art Carnival, New York NY

Babbitt, Steve, *Prof,* Black Hills State University, Art Dept, Spearfish SD (S)

Babcock, Catherine, *Dir,* Lansing Art Gallery, Lansing MI

Babcock, David, *Asst Prof,* Central Missouri State University, Dept Art & Design, Warrensburg MO (S)

Babcock, Elizabeth C, *VPres Educ & Library Coll,* Field Museum, Chicago IL

Babcock, Ryan, *Adjunct,* Idaho State University, Dept of Art & Pre-Architecture, Pocatello ID (S)

Babcock, Sidney, *Cur & Dept Head Seals & Tablets,* The Morgan Library & Museum, Museum, New York NY

Babcox, Wendy, *Assoc Prof,* University of South Florida, School The Arts, Tampa FL (S)

Baber, Desiree, *Asst to Dir,* Guggenheim Museum Soho, New York NY

Baber, Desiree, *Exec Asst to Dir,* Oklahoma City Museum of Art, Oklahoma City OK

Babila, Susan, *Prog Coordr,* Edna Hibel, Hibel Museum of Art, Jupiter FL

Baca, Judith F, *Artistic Dir,* Social & Public Art Resource Center, (SPARC), Venice CA

Bacci, Daniel, *Facility Coordr,* Kala Institute, Kala Art Institute, Berkeley CA

Bach, Beverly, *Museum Registrar,* Miami University, Art Museum, Oxford OH

Bach, Penny Balkin, *Exec Dir,* Fairmount Park Art Association, Philadelphia PA

Bacheller, Katch, *Exec Dir,* Alaska Museum of Natural History, Anchorage AK

Bachman, Dona, *Dir,* Southern Illinois University Carbondale, University Museum, Carbondale IL

Bachman, Donna N, *Chmn,* Park University, Dept of Art & Design, Parkville MO (S)

Bachmeier, Brad, *Asst Prof,* Minnesota State University-Moorhead, Dept of Art & Design, Moorhead MN (S)

Bachrach, Hanna, *Circ Mgr,* Parsons School of Design, Adam & Sophie Gimbel Design Library, New York NY

Bacigalupi, Don, *Dir,* Crystal Bridges Museum of American Art, Bentonville AR

Backus, Irene, *Asst Prof,* Oklahoma State University, Department of Art, Graphic Design and Art History, Stillwater OK (S)

Bacon, Larry, *Mem,* Newport Art Museum and Association, Newport RI

Bacon, Mardges, *Prof,* Northeastern University, Dept of Art & Architecture, Boston MA (S)

Bacon, Nancy M, *Pres,* San Antonio Art League, San Antonio Art League Museum, San Antonio TX

Bacot, Parrott, *Asst Prof,* Louisiana State University, School of Art, Baton Rouge LA (S)

Baczkowski, Steve, *Music Dir,* Hallwalls Contemporary Arts Center, Buffalo NY

Badalamenti, Kay, *Acting Chief,* Brooklyn Public Library, Art & Music Division, Brooklyn NY

Badder, Susan, *Cur Educ,* Corcoran Gallery of Art, Washington DC

Badeaux, Brynne, *Deputy Dir,* VSA Arts of New Mexico, Very Special Arts Gallery, Albuquerque NM

Badel, Julio, *Admin Asst,* San Francisco Museum of Modern Art, Artist Gallery, San Francisco CA

Baden, Laurence, *Deputy Chmn Mgmt & Budget,* National Endowment for the Arts, Washington DC

Baden, Linda, *Assoc Dir Editorial Servs,* Indiana University, Art Museum, Bloomington IN

Bader, Emily, *Dir,* Springfield City Library, Springfield MA

Bader, Jason, *Dept Chair,* Mt San Jacinto College, Art Dept, San Jacinto CA (S)

Badgett, Barry, *Interim Dir,* Wichita State University, School of Art & Design, Wichita KS (S)

Badoud, Jamie, *Exec Dir,* Hambidge Center for Creative Arts & Sciences, Rabun Gap GA

Badt, Pat, *Prof,* Cedar Crest College, Art Dept, Allentown PA (S)

Bae, Jaehan, *Asst Prof,* University of Wisconsin Oshkosh, Dept of Art, Oshkosh WI (S)

Baefsky, Laurie, *Arts Bridge Prog Dir,* Utah State University, Nora Eccles Harrison Museum of Art, Logan UT

Baer, Leslie, *VPres Mktg,* Natural History Museum of Los Angeles County, Los Angeles CA

Baer, Mark, *Exec Dir,* Monterey History & Art Association, Maritime Museum of Monterey, Monterey CA

Baer, Rhonda, *William & Ann Elfers Sr Cur Paintings,* Museum of Fine Arts, Boston MA

Baert, Renee, *Dir/Cur (gallery),* Saidye Bronfman, Liane & Danny Taran Gallery, Montreal PQ

Baetz, Catherine, *Mem Mgr,* Southern Methodist University, Meadows Museum, Dallas TX

Baez, Aida, *Librn,* Museo de Arte de Ponce, The Luis A Ferre Foundation Inc, Ponce PR

Baez, Aida, *Librn,* Museo de Arte de Ponce, The Luis A Ferre Foundation Inc, Ponce PR

Baez, Aida E, *Chief Librn,* Museo de Arte de Ponce, Library, Ponce PR

Baez, Aida E, *Chief Librn,* Museo de Arte de Ponce, Library, Ponce PR

Bafford, Rebecca, *Art Dir,* Howard Community College, The Rouse Company Foundation Gallery, Columbia MD

Baganz, Bruce, *Pres & Bd Trustees,* The Textile Museum, Washington DC

Baggett, Lynne, *Asst,* Louisiana State University, School of Art, Baton Rouge LA (S)

Baggs, Stephanie Robison, *Instr,* Marylhurst University, Art Dept, Marylhurst OR (S)

Baghy, Cathy, *Researcher,* Alton Museum of History & Art, Inc, Alton IL

Bagley, Robert, *Chmn,* Princeton University, Dept of Art & Archaeology, Princeton NJ (S)

Bagnal, Dianne R, *Asst Prof & Coordr Educ,* Converse College, School of the Arts, Dept of Art & Design, Spartanburg SC (S)

Bagnall, Mindi, *Registrar,* Western Michigan University, Gwen Frostic School of Art, Kalamazoo MI

Bagnatori, Paula, *Mng Dir,* Museo Italo Americano, San Francisco CA

Bagnoll, Martina, *Cur Medieval Art,* Walters Art Museum, Baltimore MD

Bahe, Norman, *Educ Cur,* Navajo Nation, Navajo Nation Museum, Window Rock AZ

Bahr, David, *Assoc Prof,* Baltimore City Community College, Dept of Fine Arts, Baltimore MD (S)

Bahrin, Adliana, *Prog & Web Mgr,* Asian American Arts Centre, New York NY

Baie, Sarah Kate, *Dir Programming & Chief of Fictions,* Museum of Contemporary Art Denver, Denver CO

Baigell, Matthew, *Prof,* Rutgers, The State University of New Jersey, Graduate Program in Art History, New Brunswick NJ (S)

Bailey, Alicia, *Treas,* Guild of Book Workers, New York NY

Bailey, Barry, *Prof,* Tulane University, Sophie H Newcomb Memorial College, New Orleans LA (S)

Bailey, Bradley, *Cur Teaching Fellow Japanese Prints,* Amherst College, Mead Art Museum, Amherst MA

Bailey, Carol, *Instr,* Midland College, Art Dept, Midland TX (S)

Bailey, Dan, *Prof & Dir Imaging Research Ctr,* University of Maryland, Baltimore County, Imaging & Digital Arts (IMDA), Dept of Visual Arts, Baltimore MD (S)

Bailey, David, *Cur History,* Museum of Western Colorado, Museum of the West, Grand Junction CO

Bailey, Debby, *Office Admin,* Yakima Valley Community College, Larson Gallery, Yakima WA

Bailey, Elizabeth, *Dept Head,* Virginia Western Community College, Communication Design, Fine Art & Photography, Roanoke VA (S)

Bailey, Erin, *Dir,* City of Atlanta, Gilbert House, Atlanta GA

Bailey, Erin, *Gallery Dir,* City of Atlanta, The Gallery @ Chastain Arts Center, Atlanta GA

Bailey, Hilton, *Archivist,* Caramoor Center for Music & the Arts, Inc, Rosen House at Caramoor, Katonah NY

Bailey, James, *Chmn, Assoc Prof,* University of Montana, Dept of Art, Missoula MT (S)

Bailey, Jann L M, *Exec Dir,* Kamloops Art Gallery, Kamloops BC

Bailey, Jeff, *Reference Librn,* Arkansas State University-Art Department, Jonesboro, Library, Jonesboro AR

Bailey, Laura W, *Exec Asst to Boards,* Jamestown-Yorktown Foundation, Jamestown Settlement, Williamsburg VA

Bailey, Lebe, *Asst Prof,* Wesleyan College, Art Dept, Macon GA (S)

Bailey, Lisa G, *Pres,* Rhode Island Watercolor Society, Pawtucket RI

Bailey, Lisbit, *Supervisory Archivist,* San Francisco Maritime National Historical Park, Maritime Museum, San Francisco CA

Bailey, Mike, *Past Pres,* National Watercolor Society, San Pedro CA

Bailey, Radcliffe, *Asst Prof Drawing & Painting,* University of Georgia, Franklin College of Arts & Sciences, Lamar Dodd School of Art, Athens GA (S)

Bailey, Rebecca, *Chmn,* Meredith College, Art Dept, Raleigh NC (S)

Bailey, Robert D, *Under Secy Designate for Finance & Admin,* Smithsonian Institution, Washington DC

Bailey, Ron, *Pub Rels & Treas,* St Mary Landmarks, Grevemberg House Museum, Franklin LA

Bailey, Scott, *Prof,* Wenatchee Valley College, Art Dept, Wenatchee WA (S)

Bailey, Shannon, *Dir,* Stephen F Austin State University, SFA Galleries, Nacogdoches TX

Bailey, Tina Garbo, *Dir,* Brownsville Art League, Brownsville Museum of Fine Art, Brownsville TX

Bailey, William, *Prof Emeritus,* Yale University, School of Art, New Haven CT (S)

Baillargeon, Claude, *Assoc Prof,* Oakland University, Dept of Art & Art History, Rochester MI (S)

Baillie, Charlyn, *Treas,* Association of Hawaii Artists, Honolulu HI

Baily, Mary Lou, *Conf Mgr,* Association of Collegiate Schools of Architecture, Washington DC

Bains, Sneh, *Library Dir,* Bayonne Free Public Library, Cultural Center, Bayonne NJ

Bair, Miles, *Dir,* Illinois Wesleyan University, School of Art, Bloomington IL (S)

Baird, George, *Dean,* University of Toronto, Faculty of Architecture, Landscape & Design, Toronto ON (S)

Baird, Jaime, *Asst Dir Admin & Develop,* Bard College, Center for Curatorial Studies and the Hessel Museum of Art, Annandale-on-Hudson NY

Baird, Jill, *Cur of Educ & Pub Prog,* University of British Columbia, Museum of Anthropology, Vancouver BC

Baird, M Duncan, *Asst Prof,* Delta State University, Dept of Art, Cleveland MS (S)

Baird, Nancy, *Ky Spec,* Western Kentucky University, Kentucky Library & Museum, Bowling Green KY

Baird, Roger, *Dir Coll Svcs,* Canadian Museum of Nature, Musee Canadien de la Nature, Ottawa ON

Baites, Bill, *Exec Dir,* Green Hill Center for North Carolina Art, Greensboro NC

Baize, Carissa, *Registrar,* Artesia Historical Museum & Art Center, Artesia NM

Bajko, Daria, *Admin Dir,* The Ukrainian Museum, New York NY

Bak, Susan K, *Sr Dir Mktg & Retail Opers,* Jamestown-Yorktown Foundation, Jamestown Settlement, Williamsburg VA

Baker, Aaron, *Cur & Bus Develop Dir,* Playboy Enterprises, Inc, Beverly Hills CA

Baker, Barry B, *Dir,* University of Central Florida Libraries, Orlando FL

Baker, Benjamin, *Chief Security,* Albany Museum of Art, Albany GA

Baker, Bernard, *Prof Emeritus,* California State University, Dominguez Hills, Art & Design Dept, Carson CA (S)

Baker, Bob, *Dir,* Art Community Center, Art Center of Corpus Christi, Corpus Christi TX

Baker, Cindy, *Prog Coordr,* AKA Artist Run Centre, Saskatoon SK

Baker, Cindy, *Program Coordr,* AKA Artist Run Centre, Library, Saskatoon SK

Baker, Darren, *Galleries & Coll Mgr,* Southern Ohio Museum Corporation, Southern Ohio Museum, Portsmouth OH

Baker, David, *Instr,* Kalamazoo Valley Community College, Center for New Media, Kalamazoo MI (S)

Baker, David, *Pres,* Canton Museum of Art, Canton OH

Baker, David R, *Instr,* Southwestern Michigan College, Fine & Performing Arts Dept, Dowagiac MI (S)

Baker, Doug, *Adjunct Prof Fine Art,* Johnson County Community College, Fine Arts Dept & Art History Dept, Overland Park KS (S)

Baker, Edward, *Exec Dir,* New London County Historical Society, Shaw Mansion, New London CT

Baker, Gary, *Prof,* Polk Community College, Art, Letters & Social Sciences, Winter Haven FL (S)

Baker, Griffith Aaron, *Dir & Cur,* Estevan National Exhibition Centre Inc, Estevan Art Gallery & Museum, Estevan SK

Baker, Helen, *Adminr,* University of Michigan, Kelsey Museum of Archaeology, Ann Arbor MI

Baker, James, *Prof,* Providence College, Art & Art History Dept, Providence RI (S)

Baker, James, *Exec Dir,* Pilchuck Glass School, Stanwood WA (S)

Baker, Janet, *Cur Asian Art,* Phoenix Art Museum, Phoenix AZ

Baker, Jim, *Pres,* Ste Genevieve Museum, Sainte Genevieve MO

Baker, Joe, *Dir,* Longue Vue House & Gardens, New Orleans LA

Baker, Judith, *Prof,* University of Wisconsin College - Marinette, Art Dept, Marinette WI (S)

Baker, Karen Z, *Registrar,* San Antonio Museum of Art, San Antonio TX

Baker, Kendall, *Dir,* Caldwell College, The Visceglia Art Gallery, Caldwell NJ

Baker, Kendall, *Prof,* Caldwell College, Dept of Fine Arts, Caldwell NJ (S)

Baker, Kim, *Project Mgr,* United States General Services Administration, Art in Architecture and Fine Arts, Washington DC

Baker, Linda, *1st VPres,* National Watercolor Society, San Pedro CA

Baker, Loren, *Chmn Dept & Asst Prof,* Biola University, Art Dept, La Mirada CA (S)

Baker, Loren, *Dir Art,* Roberts Wesleyan College, Art Dept, Rochester NY (S)

Baker, Malcolm, *Prof,* University of California, Riverside, Dept of the History of Art, Riverside CA (S)

Baker, Malissa Kay, *Admin Asst,* Art Community Center, Art Center of Corpus Christi, Corpus Christi TX

Baker, Marilyn, *Prof,* University of Manitoba, School of Art, Winnipeg MB (S)

Baker, Michelle, *Registrar,* South Carolina State Museum, Columbia SC

Baker, Nash, *Photographer,* Rice University, Rice Gallery, Houston TX

Baker, Nicole, *Admis/Gallery Store Coordr,* Kamloops Art Gallery, Kamloops BC

Baker, Opal, *Dir,* Fisk University, Library, Nashville TN

Baker, Robert, *Cur Natural Science Research Lab,* Texas Tech University, Museum of Texas Tech University, Lubbock TX

Baker, Sandra, *Asst Prof,* Brazosport College, Art Dept, Lake Jackson TX (S)

Baker, Sandra, *Dir Develop & Mktg,* Burlington Art Centre, Burlington ON

Baker, Sarah, *Cur Asst,* Denison University, Art Gallery, Granville OH

Baker, Scott, *Asst Dir,* Howard University, Gallery of Art, Washington DC

Baker, Steve, *Visual Arts & Humanities,* Grossmont Community College, Hyde Art Gallery, El Cajon CA

Baker, Wendy, *Exec Dir,* California State University, Los Angeles, Luckman Gallery, Los Angeles CA

Baker Horsey, Ann, *Cur Coll,* Delaware Division of Historical & Cultural Affairs, Dover DE

Bakke, Buck, *Information Technology,* Menil Foundation, Inc, The Menil Collection, Houston TX

Bakken, Mike, *Dir Comm Sch Arts,* Mayville State University, Northern Lights Art Gallery, Mayville ND

Bakker, Conrad, *Asst Dir Grad Studies, Assoc Prof,* University of Illinois, Urbana-Champaign, School of Art & Design, Champaign IL (S)

Bakos, Stephanie, *Dir,* Berkeley Heights Free Public Library, Berkeley Heights NJ

Bakst, Marilyn, *Recording Secy,* Miami Watercolor Society, Inc, Miami FL

Balabanoff, Doreen, *Dean Design,* OCAD University, Toronto ON (S)

Balakier, Ann, *Assoc Prof,* University of South Dakota, Department of Art, College of Fine Arts, Vermillion SD (S)

Balarezo-Badenjkl, Yina, *Dir Mem,* University of Miami, Lowe Art Museum, Coral Gables FL

Balasis, Michel, *Assoc Prof,* Loyola University of Chicago, Fine Arts Dept, Chicago IL (S)

Balboni, Kathleen, *Coordr Finance Servs,* College of Central Florida, Appleton Museum of Art, Ocala FL

Balcaen, Jo-Anne, *Exhib Coordr,* Concordia University, Leonard & Bina Ellen Art Gallery, Montreal PQ

Balch, Inge, *Prof Art,* Baker University, Dept of Mass Media & Visual Arts, Baldwin City KS (S)

Baldaia, Peter J, *Curatorial Affairs Dir,* Huntsville Museum of Art, Reference Library, Huntsville AL

Baldaia, Peter J, *Dir Cur Affairs,* Huntsville Museum of Art, Huntsville AL

Balderson, Patricia, *Mgr Mus Educ,* Colonial Williamsburg Foundation, Abby Aldrich Rockefeller Folk Art Museum, Williamsburg VA

Balderson, Patricia, *Mgr Mus Educ,* Colonial Williamsburg Foundation, DeWitt Wallace Decorative Arts Museum, Williamsburg VA

Baldissera, Lisa, *Chief Cur,* Mendel Art Gallery & Civic Conservatory, Saskatoon SK

Baldonieri, Amy, *Dir Develop & Finance,* Westmoreland Museum of American Art, Art Reference Library, Greensburg PA

Baldonieri, Amy B, *Dir Develop & Finance,* Westmoreland Museum of American Art, Greensburg PA

Baldridge, Mark, *Prof,* Longwood University, Dept of Art, Farmville VA (S)

Baldus, Jeff, *Lectr,* Briar Cliff University, Art Dept, Sioux City IA (S)

Baldwin, Dana, *Educ Dir,* Portland Museum of Art, Portland ME

Baldwin, David, *Dir,* University of New Mexico, Fine Arts Library, Albuquerque NM

Baldwin, Fred, *Chmn & Co-Founder,* Foto Fest International, Houston TX

Baldwin, Guy, *Assoc Prof,* University of Minnesota, Minneapolis, Dept of Art, Minneapolis MN (S)

Baldwin, K Read, *Assoc Prof,* Kenyon College, Art Dept, Gambier OH (S)

Baldwin, Leigh, *Commun Mgr,* San Antonio Museum of Art, San Antonio TX

Bale, Andrew, *Adjunct Faculty,* Dickinson College, Dept of Art & Art History, Carlisle PA (S)

Balestrieri Kohn, Beret, *Audio Visual Librn,* Milwaukee Art Museum, George Peckham Miller Art Research Library, Milwaukee WI

Balestrino, Richard, *Chmn Advertising & Mktg Communs,* Fashion Institute of Technology, Art & Design Division, New York NY (S)

Baley, Susan, *Cur Educ,* University of Oklahoma, Fred Jones Jr Museum of Art, Norman OK

Balfour, Alan, *Dean,* Rensselaer Polytechnic Institute, School of Architecture, Troy NY (S)

Balint, Valerie, *Assoc Cur,* Olana State Historic Site, Hudson NY

Balint, Valerie, *Cur,* Olana State Historic Site, Library, Hudson NY

Balise, Sett, *Technical Dir,* Davistown Museum, Liberty Location, Liberty ME

Balk, Moon-he, *Assoc Prof,* University of Louisville, Allen R Hite Art Institute, Louisville KY (S)

Balkema, Jenny, *Mem Assoc,* Tucson Museum of Art and Historic Block, Tucson AZ

Balkin, Ellen, *Educ,* The Ogden Museum of Southern Art, University of New Orleans, New Orleans LA

Ball, Allen, *Prof & Coordr Painting,* University of Alberta, Dept of Art & Design, Edmonton AB (S)

Ball, Amanda, *Dir Pub Rels,* The National Quilt Museum, Paducah KY

Ball, Deena, *Instr,* Wayne Art Center, Wayne PA (S)

Ball, Heather, *Librn,* Virginia Polytechnic Institute & State University, Art & Architecture Library, Blacksburg VA

Ball, Helena, *Mktg & PR Coordr,* Homer Watson, Kitchener ON

Ball, Isabel, *Dean,* Our Lady of the Lake University, Dept of Art, San Antonio TX (S)

Ball, Jeffrey, *Assoc Prof Art,* Harford Community College, Visual, Performing and Applied Arts Division, Bel Air MD (S)

Ball, Jennifer, *Prof,* City University of New York, PhD Program in Art History, New York NY (S)

Ball, Larry, *Prof,* University of Wisconsin-Stevens Point, Dept of Art & Design, Stevens Point WI (S)

Ball, Susan, *Deputy Dir,* Bruce Museum, Inc, Greenwich CT

Ball, Truly, *Ceramist Adjunct,* Iowa Wesleyan College, Art Dept, Mount Pleasant IA (S)

Ballangee-Morris, Christine, *Asst Prof,* Ohio State University, Dept of Art Education, Columbus OH (S)

Ballard, Jan, *Archivist,* Lehigh Valley Heritage Center, Allentown PA

Ballard, Jan, *Librn & Archivist,* Lehigh Valley Heritage Center, Scott Andrew Trexler II Library, Allentown PA

Ballate, Leo, *Dir ISS,* San Francisco Museum of Modern Art, San Francisco CA

Ballein, Chuck, *Dir Facilities,* Westmoreland Museum of American Art, Greensburg PA

Ballek, Susan, *Exec Dir,* Lyme Art Association, Inc, Old Lyme CT

Ballinger, James K, *Dir,* Phoenix Art Museum, Phoenix AZ

Ballinger, Kristi, *Pub Rels,* Museum of Science & History, Jacksonville FL

Ballinger, Patricia, *Gallery Dir,* University of Texas Pan American, Charles & Dorothy Clark Gallery; University Gallery, Edinburg TX

Ballinger, Patricia, *Gallery Dir,* University of Texas Pan American, UTPA Art Galleries, Edinburg TX

Ballou, Matthew, *Asst Tchg Prof,* University of Missouri - Columbia, Dept of Art, Columbia MO (S)

Balmer, Sarah, *Gallery Mgr,* Detroit Artists Market, Detroit MI

Baltmanis, George, *Dir Finance & Personnel,* Kalamazoo Institute of Arts, Kalamazoo MI

Baltmanis, George, *Dir Finance & Personnel,* Kalamazoo Institute of Arts, The Mary & Edwin Meader Fine Arts Library, Kalamazoo MI

Baltrushunas, John, *Assoc Prof Art & Prog Dir Studio Art,* Maryville University of Saint Louis, Art & Design Program, Saint Louis MO (S)

Baltrushunas, John, *Gallery Dir,* Maryville University Saint Louis, Morton J May Foundation Gallery, Saint Louis MO

Balzekas, Robert, *Dir Genealogy Dept,* Balzekas Museum of Lithuanian Culture, Chicago IL

Balzekas, Robert A, *Librn,* Balzekas Museum of Lithuanian Culture, Research Library, Chicago IL

Balzekas, Stanley, *Exec Dir & Pres,* Balzekas Museum of Lithuanian Culture, Chicago IL

Balzekas, Stanley, *Pres,* Balzekas Museum of Lithuanian Culture, Research Library, Chicago IL

Balzer, David, *Asst Ed,* Canadian Art Foundation, Toronto ON

Bambo-Kocze, Peter, *Bibliographer,* Corning Museum of Glass, Juliette K and Leonard S Rakow Research Library, Corning NY

Bambrough, Delmar, *Head Security,* Tucson Museum of Art and Historic Block, Tucson AZ

Bamburak, Michele, *Media Arts & Animation,* Art Institute of Pittsburgh, Pittsburgh PA (S)

Bambury, Jill, *Instr,* Southern University A & M College, School of Architecture, Baton Rouge LA (S)

Banasiak, John, *Prof,* University of South Dakota, Department of Art, College of Fine Arts, Vermillion SD (S)

Banay, Erin, *Asst Prof,* Case Western Reserve University, Dept of Art History & Art, Cleveland OH (S)

Bancroft, Katherine, *Dir Educ, Coll & Exhibs,* Port Huron Museum, Port Huron MI

Bancroft, Sarah, *Cur,* Orange County Museum of Art, Newport Beach CA

Bandar, Leila, *Dir,* Julian Scott Memorial Gallery, Johnson VT

Banduric, Pamela, *Instr Interior Design,* Henry Ford Community College, McKenzie Fine Art Ctr, Dearborn MI (S)

Banerjee, Deb, *Cur Exhibs, Progs & Webmaster,* Utah State University, Nora Eccles Harrison Museum of Art, Logan UT

Banerji, Naseem, *Asst Prof,* Weber State University, Dept of Visual Arts, Ogden UT (S)

Bang, Peggy, *Adjunct Emer,* North Iowa Area Community College, Dept of Art, Mason City IA (S)

Bangert, Shaun, *Asst Prof,* Saginaw Valley State University, Dept of Art & Design, University Center MI (S)

Baniassad, Essy, *Prof,* Dalhousie University, Faculty of Architecture, Halifax NS (S)

Banister, Kim, *Cur,* Rose Lehrman Art Gallery, Harrisburg PA

Bank, Larissa, *Instr,* Pierce College, Art Dept, Woodland Hills CA (S)

Banker, Amy, *Artist,* U Gallery, New York NY

Bankerd, Carol, *Assoc Prof,* Purchase College, State University of New York, School of Art+Design, Purchase NY (S)

Banko, Bernadette, *Dir Develop,* Edsel & Eleanor Ford, Grosse Pointe Shores MI

Banks, Carol, *Mgr,* Edgecombe County Cultural Arts Council, Inc, Blount-Bridgers House, Hobson Pittman Memorial Gallery, Tarboro NC

Bannard, Darby, *Prof,* University of Miami, Dept of Art & Art History, Coral Gables FL (S)

Bannon, Anthony, *Dir,* State University of New York College at Buffalo, Burchfield Penney Art Center, Buffalo NY

Bannon, Brian, *Commissioner,* Chicago Public Library, Harold Washington Library Center, Chicago IL

Bannos, Pamela, *Lectr,* Northwestern University, Evanston, Dept of Art Theory & Practice, Evanston IL (S)

Banocy-Payne, Marge, *Dean,* Tallahassee Community College, Art Dept, Tallahassee FL (S)

Banta, Beth, *Dir Develop,* Grand Rapids Public Museum, Public Museum of Grand Rapids, Grand Rapids MI

Bantens, Robert, *Art Historian,* University of South Alabama, Dept of Art & Art History, Mobile AL (S)

Bantle, Thomas, *Dir Exhibits & Facilities,* Grand Rapids Public Museum, Public Museum of Grand Rapids, Grand Rapids MI

Banz, Martha, *Dean Arts & Sciences,* Southern Nazarene University, Art & Design Department, Bethany OK (S)

Bao, Li-ying, *Prof Art & Design,* University of Wisconsin-Eau Claire, Dept of Art & Design, Eau Claire WI (S)

Baquir, Rose Christie, *Admis & Mem,* Craft and Folk Art Museum (CAFAM), Los Angeles CA

Baral, Jody, *Chmn & Prof,* Mount Saint Mary's College, Art Dept, Los Angeles CA (S)

Baral, Jody, *Gallery Dir,* Mount Saint Mary's College, Jose Drudis-Biada Art Gallery, Los Angeles CA

Baranski, Sarah, *Instr,* Judson University, School of Art, Design & Architecture, Elgin IL (S)

Barant, Jim, *Documentary Art & Photo Acquisition,* National Archives of Canada, Art & Photography Archives, Ottawa ON

Barattuci, Maurizio, *Gallery Chmn,* Santa Monica College, Pete & Susan Barrett Art Gallery, Santa Monica CA

Barbash, Yekaterina, *Asst Cur Egyptian Art,* Brooklyn Museum, Brooklyn NY

Barbee, Rebecca, *Operations Mgr,* Palo Alto Art Center, Palo Alto CA

Barber, Anne, *Asst Prof,* Albion College, Bobbitt Visual Arts Center, Albion MI

Barber, Carla, *Exec Dir,* McPherson Museum and Arts Foundation, McPherson KS

Barber, Diane, *Co-Dir,* Diverse Works, Houston TX

Barber, Lisa, *Asst Prof,* University of Wisconsin-Parkside, Art Dept, Kenosha WI (S)

Barber, Peter, *Board Pres,* Landis Valley Village and Farm Museum, PA Historical & Museum Commission, Lancaster PA

Barber, Rhonda, *Gallery Admin,* Calgary Contemporary Arts Society, Triangle Gallery of Visual Arts, Calgary AB

Barber, Robbie, *Assoc Prof,* Baylor University - College of Arts and Sciences, Dept of Art, Waco TX (S)

Barber, Vivian, *Preparator,* Moose Jaw Art Museum, Inc, Art & History Museum, Moose Jaw SK

Barbieri, Frances J, *Educ Dir,* Seneca Falls Historical Society Museum, Seneca Falls NY

Barcellona, Nina, *Advertising, Exhibs & Design,* Society for Photographic Education (SPE), SPE Gallery, Cleveland OH

Barch, Nancy, *Instr,* Wayne Art Center, Wayne PA (S)

Barch, Nancy, *VPres Exhib Submissions,* American Watercolor Society, Inc., New York NY

Barclay, Stacy, *Visual Resources Cur,* San Jose State University, Dr. Martin Luther King Jr. Library, San Jose CA

Bard, Sue, *Pres,* Beaumont Art League, Beaumont TX

Bardhan, Gail, *Reference Librn,* Corning Museum of Glass, Juliette K and Leonard S Rakow Research Library, Corning NY

Bardi, Gina, *Reference,* San Francisco Maritime National Historical Park, Maritime Library, San Francisco CA

Bardolph, Paige, *Asst Cur,* Autry National Center, Southwest Museum of the American Indian, Mt. Washington Campus, Los Angeles CA

Bareis, Arbe, *Instr & Fine & Performing Arts Spec,* Kirkwood Community College, Dept of Arts & Humanities, Cedar Rapids IA (S)

Barello, Julia, *Assoc Prof,* New Mexico State University, Art Dept, Las Cruces NM (S)

Barger, Peter, *Dean, Grad & Continuing Educ,* North Central College, Dept of Art, Naperville IL (S)

Barhaug, Shirley, *Pres,* Cody Country Art League, Cody WY

Barilleaux, Rene Paul, *Chief Cur & Cur Art after 1945,* McNay, San Antonio TX

Barilleaux, Rene Paul, *Deputy Dir Prog,* Mississippi Museum of Art, Howorth Library, Jackson MS

Barkai, Hagit, *Prof,* Davidson College, Art Dept, Davidson NC (S)

Barkee, Ken, *Co-Pres,* Klamath Art Association, Klamath Falls OR

Barker, Alex, *Dir,* University of Missouri, Museum of Art & Archaeology, Columbia MO

Barker, Angela, *Reg & Cur Permanent Coll,* California State University, Long Beach, University Art Museum, Long Beach CA

Barker, Anne, *Music,* University of Missouri, Art, Archaeology & Music Collection, Columbia MO

Barker, Bill, *Asst Archivist,* The Mariners' Museum, Library, Newport News VA

Barker, Elaine, *Pres Elect,* Arts Council of Greater Kingsport, Renaissance Center Main Gallery, Kingsport TN

Barker, Elizabeth E, *Dir,* Amherst College, Mead Art Museum, Amherst MA

Barker, Gloria, *Co-Founder,* Barker Character, Comic and Cartoon Museum, Cheshire CT

Barker, Herbert, *Co-Founder,* Barker Character, Comic and Cartoon Museum, Cheshire CT

Barker, James, *Pres,* Clemson University, College of Architecture, Arts & Humanities, Art Dept, Clemson SC (S)

Barker, Jimmy, *Prof,* Sam Houston State University, Art Dept, Huntsville TX (S)

Barker, Kandis, *Cur Educ,* Washburn University, Mulvane Art Museum, Topeka KS

Barker, Katherine, *Field Svcs Dir,* Textile Conservation Workshop Inc, South Salem NY

Barker, Keith, *Art Dept Chair, Instr,* Asbury University, Art Dept, Wilmore KY (S)

Barker, Keith, *Photography & Graphic Arts, Dept Chair,* Asbury College, Student Center Gallery, Wilmore KY

Barker, Lance, *Adjunct,* Feather River Community College, Art Dept, Quincy CA (S)

Barker, Marcia, *VPres,* Goshen Historical Society, Goshen CT

Barker, Norman, *Assoc Prof,* Johns Hopkins University, School of Medicine, Dept of Art as Applied to Medicine, Baltimore MD (S)

Barkley, Tim, *Registrar,* Contemporary Arts Museum Houston, Houston TX

Barletta, Barbara, *Prof,* University of Florida, School of Art & Art History, Gainesville FL (S)

Barletta, Bob, *Co-Treas,* Greenwich Art Society Inc, Greenwich CT

Barley, Gerlinde, *Coll Develop,* State University of New York at New Paltz, Sojourner Truth Library, New Paltz NY

Barlow, Anne, *Exec Dir,* Art in General, New York NY

Barlow Smedstad, Deborah, *Head Librn,* Museum of Fine Arts, William Morris Hunt Memorial Library, Boston MA

Barnaby, Martine, *Asst Prof,* State University of New York, College at Cortland, Dept Art & Art History, Cortland NY (S)

Barnard, Carissa, *Exhib Dir,* Contemporary Arts Center, Cincinnati OH

Barnard, Katie, *Cur Educ,* Westmoreland Museum of American Art, Art Reference Library, Greensburg PA

Barnard, Melissa, *Dir,* Grace A Dow, Fine Arts Dept, Midland MI

Barner, David L, *Chmn,* Westminster College, Art Dept, New Wilmington PA (S)

Barnes, Bernadine, *Prof,* Wake Forest University, Dept of Art, Winston-Salem NC (S)

Barnes, Bruce, *Dir,* George Eastman, Rochester NY

Barnes, Bruce, *Dir,* George Eastman, Museum, Rochester NY

Barnes, Gail, *Assoc Adminr,* Presidential Museum & Leadership Library, Odessa TX

Barnes, James, *Gallery Dir,* Rhode Island School of Design, Bayard Ewing Building Gallery, Providence RI

Barnes, Jonathan, *Dept Chmn,* Saint Petersburg College, Fine & Applied Arts at Clearwater Campus, Clearwater FL (S)

Barnes, Laurie, *Cur Chinese Art,* Norton Museum of Art, West Palm Beach FL

Barnes, Lucinda, *Chief Cur & Dir Progs & Colls,* University of California, Berkeley, Berkeley Art Museum & Pacific Film Archive, Berkeley CA

Barnes, Michael, *Grad Coordr,* Northern Illinois University, School of Art, DeKalb IL (S)

Barnes, Raymond S, *Asst Prof,* Muhlenberg College, Dept of Art, Allentown PA (S)

Barnes, Reinaldo, *Mgr,* Longfellow-Evangeline State Commemorative Area, Saint Martinville LA

Barnes, Sharron, *Assoc Prof,* Gulf Coast Community College, Division of Visual & Performing Arts, Panama City FL (S)

Barnes, Ted, *Dean,* University of Mary Hardin-Baylor, College of Visual & Performing Arts, Belton TX (S)

Barnes, Ted, *Prof,* Ouachita Baptist University, Dept of Visual Art, Arkadelphia AR (S)

Barnes, William, *Assoc Prof,* College of William & Mary, Dept of Fine Arts, Williamsburg VA (S)

Barnes, Wm, *Prof,* University of Saint Thomas, Dept of Art History, Saint Paul MN (S)

Barnet, Peter, *Chmn & Cur,* The Metropolitan Museum of Art, The Cloisters Museum & Gardens, New York NY

Barnett, Cheryl, *Prof 3-D Prog,* Merced College, Arts Division, Merced CA (S)

Barnett, John, *Prof,* California State University, Art Dept, Turlock CA (S)

Barnett, Loretta, *Prof,* Colby-Sawyer College, Dept of Fine & Performing Arts, New London NH (S)

Barnett, Mary, *Mus Store Mgr,* City of High Point, High Point Museum, High Point NC

Barnett, Nigel, *Preparator,* Queen's University, Agnes Etherington Art Centre, Kingston ON

Barnett, Redmond, *Cur Exhib,* State Capital Museum, Olympia WA

Barnett, Richard, *Prof,* College of Mount Saint Vincent, Fine Arts Dept, Riverdale NY (S)

Barnett, Robert, *Chmn Bd,* Chicago Children's Museum, Chicago IL

Barney, Cheryl, *Sr Dir Human Resources,* Genesee Country Village & Museum, John L Wehle Art Gallery, Mumford NY

Barney, Emily, *Asst Cur,* Elmhurst Art Museum, Elmhurst IL

Barney, Joan, *Spec Colls Family Historian,* New Bedford Free Public Library, Special Collections Dept: Art Collection, New Bedford MA

Barney, Win, *Cur,* Kanab Heritage Museum & Juniper Fine Arts Gallery, Kanab UT

Barnhard, Leah, *Exec Dir,* Wichita Public Library, Wichita KS

Barnhart, Jeff, *Chief Mus Officer,* Omaha Children's Museum, Omaha NE

Barnhart, Tom, *Mem Chmn,* Blacksburg Regional Art Association, Blacksburg VA

Barnhill, Georgia B, *Andrew W Mellon Cur Graphic Arts,* American Antiquarian Society, Worcester MA

Barnow, Penny, *Develop Co-Exec Dir,* Boulder Museum of Contemporary Art, Boulder CO

Baroff, Deborah, *Cur Spec Coll,* Trust Authority, Research Library, Lawton OK

Baroff, Deborah, *Head Cur,* Trust Authority, Museum of the Great Plains, Lawton OK

Barolsky, Paul, *Prof,* University of Virginia, McIntire Dept of Art, Charlottesville VA (S)

Baron, Alice, *Catalog & Reference Librn,* Becker College, William F Ruska Library, Worcester MA

Baron-Robbins, Ariel, *Vis Instr Painting,* Florida Atlantic University, D F Schmidt College of Arts & Letters Dept of Visual Arts & Art History, Boca Raton FL (S)

Barone, Matthew, *Pub Rels,* Harvard University, Harvard University Art Museums, Cambridge MA

Baronne, Geriod, *Pres,* New Orleans Artworks at New Orleans Glassworks & Printmaking Studio, New Orleans LA

Baroody, Julie, *Art Coordr,* Tallahassee Community College, Art Dept, Tallahassee FL (S)

Barquist, David, *Cur American Decorative Arts,* Philadelphia Museum of Art, Main Building, Philadelphia PA

Barr, Anne Q, *Coordr,* Greenville County Museum of Art Center for Museum Education, Greenville SC (S)

Barr, Brian, *Dir Horticulture,* Hillwood Museum & Gardens Foundation, Hillwood Estate Museum & Gardens, Washington DC

Barr, David, *Prof,* Macomb Community College, Art Dept, Warren MI (S)

Barr, Peter, *Assoc Prof Art History,* Siena Heights University, Studio Angelico-Art Dept, Adrian MI (S)

Barr, Peter, *Dir,* Siena Heights College, Klemm Gallery, Studio Angelico, Adrian MI

Barr, Zemie, *Exhibs Mgr,* Blue Sky Gallery, Oregon Center for the Photographic Arts, Portland OR

Barraclough, Bruce, *Bldg Mgr,* Fraunces Tavern Museum, New York NY

Barraclough, Dennis, *Assoc Prof,* Daemen College, Art Dept, Amherst NY (S)

Barraclough, Jeffrey, *Asst Exec Dir,* Manchester Historic Association, Millyard Museum, Manchester NH

Barraclough, Jeffrey, *Asst Exec Dir,* Manchester Historic Association, Library, Manchester NH

Barraza, Santa, *Chmn,* Texas A&M University-Kingsville, Art Dept, Kingsville TX (S)

Barraza, Santa, *Dir,* Texas A&M University, Art Gallery, Kingsville TX

Barre, Monica, *Security,* The Ogden Museum of Southern Art, University of New Orleans, New Orleans LA

Barrera, Lupita, *Dir Educ & Interpretation,* The University of Texas at San Antonio, Institute of Texan Cultures, San Antonio TX

Barrera, Roberto, *Auxiliary Prof,* University of Puerto Rico, Dept of Fine Arts, Rio Piedras PR (S)

Barrera, Roberto, *Auxiliary Prof,* University of Puerto Rico, Dept of Fine Arts, Rio Piedras PR (S)

Barreras, Petra, *Dir,* University of Puerto Rico, Museum of Anthropology, History & Art, Rio Piedras PR

Barreras, Petra, *Dir,* University of Puerto Rico, Museum of Anthropology, History & Art, Rio Piedras PR

Barret, Heidi, *Opers Mgr,* Ascension Lutheran Church Library, Milwaukee WI

Barreto, Brian, *Chief Preparator,* Capp Street Project, Wattis Institute, San Francisco CA

Barreto, Ricardo, *Exec Dir,* UrbanArts Institute at Massachusetts College of Art, Boston MA

Barrett, Dale, *Dir,* John B Aird Gallery, Toronto ON

Barrett, Michael, *CEO & Gen Dir,* Caramoor Center for Music & the Arts, Inc, Rosen House at Caramoor, Katonah NY

Barrett, Ned, *Humanities Chmn,* Idyllwild Arts Academy, Idyllwild CA (S)

Barrett, Terry, *Prof,* Ohio State University, Dept of Art Education, Columbus OH (S)

Barrett, Terry, *Prof Art Educ,* University of North Texas, College of Visual Arts & Design, Denton TX (S)

Barrick, William E, *Exec Dir,* Bellingrath Gardens & Home, Theodore AL

Barrie, Brooke, *Dir & Cur,* Grounds for Sculpture, Hamilton NJ

Barrie, Don, *Asst Prof,* Seattle Central Community College, Humanities - Social Sciences Division, Seattle WA (S)

Barrineau, Annette W, *VPres Student Servs,* Florida School of the Arts, Visual Arts, Palatka FL (S)

Barron, Jerry, *Dir Media Arts,* The Center for Contemporary Arts of Santa Fe, Santa Fe NM

Barron, Nancy, *Artistic Dir,* Kennebec Valley Art Association, Harlow Gallery, Hallowell ME

Barron, Robert, *Facilities Coordr,* Workman & Temple Family Homestead Museum, City of Industry CA

Barrot, Patricia, *Site Mgr Mabee Farm,* Schenectady County Historical Society, Museum of Schenectady History, Schenectady NY

Barrow, Dennis, *Librn,* Fairfield Historical Society, Library, Fairfield CT

Barrow, Jake, *Tech Dir Ritz Theater,* Tennessee Valley Art Association, Tuscumbia AL

Barrow, Jane, *Head Painting,* Southern Illinois University at Edwardsville, Dept of Art & Design, Edwardsville IL (S)

Barrow, Lee, *Dept Head,* North Georgia College & State University, Fine Arts Dept, Dahlonega GA (S)

Barrows, Jennifer, *Instr,* San Joaquin Delta College, Arts & Communication, Stockton CA (S)

Barrows, Scott, *Prog Coordr,* University of Illinois at Chicago, Biomedical Visualization, Chicago IL (S)

Barry, Bob, *Chmn,* Long Island University, Brooklyn Campus, Art Dept, Brooklyn NY (S)

Barry, Bruce, *Ceramic Studio Mgr,* DeCordova Museum School, Lincoln MA (S)

Barry, Claire M, *Chief Conservator,* Kimbell Art Foundation, Kimbell Art Museum, Fort Worth TX

Barry, Jill, *Deputy Dir Develop,* Montgomery Museum of Fine Arts, Library, Montgomery AL

Barry, Laura, *Asst Librn,* Historical Society of Washington DC, The City Museum of Washington DC, Washington DC

Barry, Laura, *Asst Librn,* Historical Society of Washington DC, Washington DC

Barry, Louise, *External Affairs Mgr,* Center for Book Arts, New York NY

Barry, Sandra, *VPres Operations,* New Hampshire Institute of Art, Manchester NH

Barry, Tim, *Contact,* Hot Shops Art Center, Omaha NE

Barry, William D, *Reference Asst,* Maine Historical Society, Library and Museum, Portland ME

Barryte, Bernard, *Cur European Art,* Stanford University, Cantor Arts Center at Stanford University, Stanford CA

Barsdate, Kelly J, *Chief Prog & Planning Officer,* National Assembly of State Arts Agencies, Washington DC

Barsness, Jim, *Asst Prof Drawing & Painting,* University of Georgia, Franklin College of Arts & Sciences, Lamar Dodd School of Art, Athens GA (S)

Barta, Andaleeb, *Cur American & European Art,* Oberlin College, Allen Memorial Art Museum, Oberlin OH

Barta, David, *Technician,* California State University, Chico, Department of Art & Art History, Chico CA (S)

Barta, Joy, *1st VPres,* Independence Historical Museum & Art Center, Independence KS

Bartel, Tom, *Asst Prof,* Viterbo College, Art Dept, La Crosse WI (S)

Bartels, Dennis, *Exec Dir,* Exploratorium, San Francisco CA

Bartels, Kathleen, *Dir,* Vancouver Art Gallery, Vancouver BC

Bartelt, Deborah, *Instr,* Marian University, Art Dept, Fond Du Lac WI (S)

Barten, Julie, *Conservator Colls & Exhibs,* Solomon R Guggenheim, New York NY

Bartenbach, Jennifer, *CFO,* Indianapolis Museum of Art, Indianapolis IN

Bartenhagen, Lynn, *Office Coordr,* Muscatine Art Center, Museum, Muscatine IA

Bartens, Helen, *Cur,* Norfolk Historical Society, Eva Brook Donly Museum & Archives, Simcoe ON

Barter, Judith, *Cur American Arts,* The Art Institute of Chicago, Chicago IL

Barth, Charles, *Prof,* Mount Mercy College, Art Dept, Cedar Rapids IA (S)

Barth, Uta, *Prof,* University of California, Riverside, Dept of Art, Riverside CA (S)

Barthelson, Karen, *Exec Dir,* Mystic Art Association, Inc, Mystic Art Center, Mystic CT

Bartlett, Alex, *Librn,* Germantown Historical Society, Philadelphia PA

Bartlett, Carly, *Pres,* National Society of Mural Painters, Inc, New York NY

Bartlett, Christopher, *Dir & Prof,* Towson University, Center for the Arts Gallery, Towson MD

Bartlett, David, *Prof,* Morehead State University, Art & Design Dept, Morehead KY (S)

Bartlett, Selina, *Asst Registrar,* Oberlin College, Allen Memorial Art Museum, Oberlin OH

Bartling, Mary, *Instr,* Mount Mary College, Art & Design Division, Milwaukee WI (S)

Bartman, Lori, *Develop Dir,* The Renaissance Society, Chicago IL

Bartmann, Christoph, *Dir,* Goethe-Institut New York, Mini/Goethe-Institut Curatorial Residencies Ludlow 38, New York NY

Bartner, Howard C, *Assoc Prof,* Johns Hopkins University, School of Medicine, Dept of Art as Applied to Medicine, Baltimore MD (S)

Barto, Betty, *Pres,* Long Beach Art League, Long Beach Library, Long Beach NY

Barton, Alan, *Dir Properties,* Wadsworth Atheneum Museum of Art, Hartford CT

Barton, David, *Multimedia & Web Design,* Art Institute of Pittsburgh, Pittsburgh PA (S)

Barton, Emerita Brigid, *Prof,* Santa Clara University, Dept of Art & Art History, Santa Clara CA (S)

Barton, Gary, *Assoc Chmn,* Brigham Young University, Dept of Visual Arts, Provo UT (S)

Barton, James, *Pres,* Johnson Atelier Technical Institute of Sculpture, Trenton NJ (S)

Barton, Matt, *Asst Prof Visual Arts,* University of Colorado-Colorado Springs, Visual & Performing Arts Dept (VAPA), Colorado Springs CO (S)

Barton, Max, *Mktg Dir,* Canton Museum of Art, Art Library, Canton OH

Barton-Navitsky, Elizabeth, *Dir,* Marcella Sembrich Memorial Association Inc, Marcella Sembrich Opera Museum, Bolton Landing NY

Barton Miller, Michael, *Prof Studio Art,* California Polytechnic State University at San Luis Obispo, Dept of Art & Design, San Luis Obispo CA (S)

Bartz, Marilyn K, *Interim Dir,* Safety Harbor Museum of Regional History, Safety Harbor FL

Barulich, Frances, *Cur Mary Hagler Cary Music Manuscripts & Dept Head,* The Morgan Library & Museum, Museum, New York NY

Barzman, Karen, *Assoc Prof,* State University of New York at Binghamton, Dept of Art History, Binghamton NY (S)

Basbas, Sarah, *Branch Mgr,* Manchester City Library, Manchester NH

Basgall, Janet, *Office Asst,* Fort Hays State University, Forsyth Library, Hays KS

Bashkoff, Tracy, *Cur Colls & Exhibs,* Solomon R Guggenheim, New York NY

Bashore Heeren, Elizabeth, *Instr,* South Dakota State University, Dept of Visual Arts, Brookings SD (S)

Basic, Julie W, *Senior Develop Officer,* Jamestown-Yorktown Foundation, Jamestown Settlement, Williamsburg VA

Basil, John, *Asst Prof Theatre,* Marymount Manhattan College, Fine & Performing Arts Div, New York NY (S)

Basile, Jennifer, *Instr,* Miami-Dade Community College, Arts & Philosophy Dept, Miami FL (S)

Basinger, Amy, *Events Coordr,* Bob Jones University Museum & Gallery Inc, Greenville SC

Baskin, Gene, *Co-Dir,* Detroit Focus, Royal Oak MI

Baskins, Cristelle, *Assoc Prof,* Tufts University, Dept of Art & Art History, Medford MA (S)

Basmadjian, Terry, *Instr,* Saginaw Valley State University, Dept of Art & Design, University Center MI (S)

Bass, Clayton, *Pres & CEO,* Huntsville Museum of Art, Huntsville AL

Bass, Judy, *Prof,* Marymount University, School of Arts & Sciences Div, Arlington VA (S)

Bass, Ruth, *Chmn,* Bronx Community College, Music & Art Dept, Bronx NY (S)

Bassanese, Lynn, *Deputy Dir,* National Archives & Records Administration, Franklin D Roosevelt Library, Hyde Park NY

Basseches, Josh, *Deputy Dir,* Peabody Essex Museum, Salem MA

Bassett, Joan, *Cur,* Nevada Northern Railway Museum, Ely NV

Bassett, Mark S, *CEO & Exec Dir,* Nevada Northern Railway Museum, Ely NV

Bassett, Ruth, *Librn,* Brandywine Conservancy, Library, Chadds Ford PA

Bassi, George, *Dir,* Lauren Rogers, Laurel MS

Basso, Judy, *Events Coordr,* Kamloops Art Gallery, Kamloops BC

Bassolos, Arturo, *Art Dept Chmn,* Delaware State College, Dept of Art & Art Education, Dover DE (S)

Bassuk, Jane, *Instr,* North Hennepin Community College, Art Dept, Brooklyn Park MN (S)

Bastidas, Hugo, *MFA,* New Jersey City University, Art Dept, Jersey City NJ (S)

Bastidas, Hugo Xavier, *Dir,* New Jersey City University, Courtney Art Gallery & Lemmerman Gallery, Jersey City NJ

Bastidas, Hugo Xavier, *Dir,* New Jersey City University, Lemmerman Art Gallery, Jersey City NJ

Bastos, Flavia, *Dir Art Educ Prog & Asst Prof Art Educ,* University of Cincinnati, School of Art, Cincinnati OH (S)

Basu, Chandreyi, *Assoc Prof,* St Lawrence University, Dept of Fine Arts, Canton NY (S)

Batchelder, Virginia, *Bd Pres,* Rome Historical Society, Museum & Archives, Rome NY

Batchelor, Anthony, *Prof,* Art Academy of Cincinnati, Cincinnati OH (S)

Batchelor, Betsey, *Assoc Prof,* Arcadia University, Dept of Fine Arts, Glenside PA (S)

Batdorff, Jon, *Head,* Goddard College, Dept of Art, Plainfield VT (S)

Bateman, Edward, *Asst Prof,* University of Utah, Dept of Art & Art History, Salt Lake City UT (S)

Bateman, Ellen, *Instr,* Toronto Art Therapy Institute, Toronto ON (S)

Bateman, Nell, *Supv,* Toronto Art Therapy Institute, Toronto ON (S)

Bater, John, *Area Head,* Kentucky State University, Jackson Hall Gallery, Frankfort KY

Bates, Bob, *Co-Founder & Artistic Dir,* Inner-City Arts, Los Angeles CA

Bates, Craig D, *Cur Ethnography,* Yosemite Museum, Yosemite National Park CA

Bates, Evelyne, *Visitor & Vol Relations,* Lighthouse ArtCenter Museum & School of Art, Tequesta FL

Bates, Julie, *Assoc Dir,* Intermedia Arts Minnesota, Minneapolis MN

Bates, Susan, *Bus Mgr,* Concord Museum, Concord MA

Bates, Thomas, *Assoc Prof,* La Roche College, Division of Design, Pittsburgh PA (S)

Bates, Ulko, *Head MA Prog,* Hunter College, Art Dept, New York NY (S)

Batey, Dorothy, *Asst Prof,* Clark-Atlanta University, School of Arts & Sciences, Atlanta GA (S)

Batista, Kenneth, *Assoc Prof,* University of Pittsburgh, Dept of Studio Arts, Pittsburgh PA (S)

Batkin, Jonathan, *Dir,* Wheelwright Museum of the American Indian, Santa Fe NM

Batkin, Jonathan, *Dir,* Wheelwright Museum of the American Indian, Mary Cabot Wheelwright Research Library, Santa Fe NM

Batkin, Norton, *Dean of Grad Studies,* Bard College, Center for Curatorial Studies Graduate Program, Annandale-on-Hudson NY (S)

Batt, Ted, *Exhib Cur,* Academy of Fine Arts, Lynchburg VA

Batten, Andrew, *Dir,* Fraunces Tavern Museum, New York NY

Batten, Chris, *Registrar,* Memorial University of Newfoundland, The Rooms Provincial Art Gallery, Saint John's NF

Battis, Nick, *Dir,* Pratt Institute, The Rubelle & Norman Schafler Gallery, Brooklyn NY

Battle, Kendra, *Visual Libr Tech,* Wake Forest University, A Lewis Aycock Visual Resource Library, Winston Salem NC

Batton, Susan, *Dir,* Dia Art Foundation, Beacon NY

Bauche, Dean, *Cur,* Allen Sapp, North Battleford SK

Bauer, Edward W, *Treas & Controller,* The Cleveland Museum of Art, Cleveland OH

Bauer, Marjorie, *Publications,* Historical Society of Rockland County, New City NY

Bauer, Marlene, *Instr,* Marylhurst University, Art Dept, Marylhurst OR (S)

Bauer, Sarah, *Assoc Prof,* University of Minnesota, Duluth, Art Dept, Duluth MN (S)

Baugh, Brian, *Asst Prof Art,* Monmouth College, Dept of Art, Monmouth IL (S)

Baugh, Chera, *Gallery Coordr,* Atlanta-Fulton Public Library, Central Library Art Gallery, Atlanta GA

Baulos, Doug, *Instr,* University of Alabama at Birmingham, Dept of Art & Art History, Birmingham AL (S)

Baum, Kelly, *Haskell Cur Modern & Contemporary Art,* Princeton University, Princeton University Art Museum, Princeton NJ

Bauman, Jan, *Dir Media & Pub,* Memphis Brooks Museum of Art, Memphis TN

Bauman, Janet, *2nd VPres,* Salmagundi Club, New York NY

Baumann, Caroline, *Assoc Dir,* Cooper-Hewitt National Design Museum, Smithsonian Institution, New York NY

Baumann, Richard, *Instr,* Columbia College, Art Dept, Columbia MO (S)

Baumann, Tanja, *Mktg & Pub Rels Dir,* Bellevue Arts Museum, Bellevue WA

Baumann, Timothy, *Cur Archaeology,* University of Tennessee, McClung Museum of Natural History & Culture, Knoxville TN

Baume, Nicholas, *Dir & Chief Cur,* Public Art Fund, Inc, New York NY

Baume, Nicholas, *Dir & Chief Cur,* Public Art Fund, Inc, Visual Archive, New York NY

Baumgartner, Nolan, *Instr,* University of Utah, Dept of Art & Art History, Salt Lake City UT (S)

Baumler, Christine Arle, *Asst Prof,* University of Minnesota, Minneapolis, Dept of Art, Minneapolis MN (S)

Baumler, Mark, *Preservation Officer,* Montana Historical Society, Helena MT

Bauske, Clay, *Mus Cur,* National Archives & Records Administration, Harry S Truman Museum and Library, Independence MO

Bavar, Ann, *Head Dept,* Manhattanville College, Art Dept, Purchase NY (S)

Bawel, Andy, *CFO,* The Children's Museum of Indianapolis, Indianapolis IN

Baxevanis, Susan, *Coll Mgr (Anthropology),* Texas Tech University, Museum of Texas Tech University, Lubbock TX

Baxter, Denise, *Chair, Dept Art Educ,* University of North Texas, College of Visual Arts & Design, Denton TX (S)

Baxter, Ellen, *Chief Conservator,* Carnegie Museums of Pittsburgh, Carnegie Museum of Art, Pittsburgh PA

Baxter, Gary, *Head Art Dept,* Houghton College, Art Dept, Houghton NY (S)

Baxter, Karen, *Visual Arts Librn,* California Institute of the Arts Library, Santa Clarita CA

Baxter, Kristin, *Prof,* Moravian College, Dept of Art, Bethlehem PA (S)

Baxter, William E, *Branch Librn,* National Air and Space Museum, Archives, Washington DC

Bay, Richard, *Asst Prof,* Radford University, Art Dept, Radford VA (S)

Bayersdorfer, Frederick, *Dir Gallery,* Old Dominion University, Art Dept, Norfolk VA (S)

Bayles, Jennifer, *Interim Head Develop,* The Buffalo Fine Arts Academy, Albright-Knox Art Gallery, Buffalo NY

Bayles, Justin, *Website,* Gallery XII, Wichita KS

Baylor, Trenton, *Asst Prof,* University of Wisconsin-Parkside, Art Dept, Kenosha WI (S)

Baymiller, Paula, *Art Library Asst,* Oberlin College, Clarence Ward Art Library, Oberlin OH

Baynes, Gloretta, *Asst to Dir,* Museum of the National Center of Afro-American Artists, Boston MA

Bayuzick, Dennis, *Assoc Prof,* University of Wisconsin-Parkside, Art Dept, Kenosha WI (S)

Beach, Gleny, *Dir Art,* Southeastern Oklahoma State University, Dept of Art, Communication & Theatre, Durant OK (S)

Beachley, Pati, *Instr,* Middle Tennessee State University, Art Dept, Murfreesboro TN (S)

Beachley, Patricia, *Assoc Prof,* Seton Hill University, Art Program, Greensburg PA (S)

Beachley, Patti, *Bd Pres,* Associated Artists of Pittsburgh, Pittsburgh PA

Beadle, Kristine, *Instr,* John C Calhoun, Department of Fine Arts, Tanner AL (S)

Beal, Graham WJ, *Dir,* Detroit Institute of Arts, Detroit MI

Beal, Melanie, *Mem & Educ Coordr,* Atlanta Contemporary Art Center, Atlanta GA

Beal, Stephen, *Pres,* California College of the Arts, San Francisco CA (S)

Beall-Fofana, Barbara, *Assoc Prof,* Assumption College, Dept of Art, Music & Theatre, Worcester MA (S)

Beals, Ruth, *Assoc Prof & Coordr Interior Design,* Converse College, School of the Arts, Dept of Art & Design, Spartanburg SC (S)

Beam, Michael J, *Cur Colls & Exhibs,* Niagara University, Castellani Art Museum, Niagara NY

Beamesdofer, Alice, *Assoc Dir Colls & Project Support,* Philadelphia Museum of Art, Main Building, Philadelphia PA

Beamish, Rollin, *Asst Prof - Painting & Drawing,* Montana State University, School of Art, Bozeman MT (S)

Bean, Robert, *Asst Prof,* Alabama A & M University, Art & Art Education Dept, Normal AL (S)

Bean, Roger, *Prof,* Illinois Central College, Arts & Communication Dept, East Peoria IL (S)

Bean, Steve, *Cur & Dir,* Okefenokee Heritage Center, Inc, Waycross GA

Beane, Frances A, *Deputy Dir,* Harvard University, William Hayes Fogg Art Museum, Cambridge MA

Beane, Frances A, *Deputy Dir,* Harvard University, Arthur M Sackler Museum, Cambridge MA

Beard, Deborah, *Chmn Technical Design,* Fashion Institute of Technology, Art & Design Division, New York NY (S)

Beard, Rick, *Exec Dir,* Atlanta Historical Society Inc, Atlanta History Center, Atlanta GA

Beardsley, Kelcey, *Dir,* Marylhurst University, Art Dept, Marylhurst OR (S)

Bearor, Karen, *Assoc Prof,* Florida State University, Art History Dept, Tallahassee FL (S)

Beasecker, Peter, *Asst Prof,* Southern Methodist University, Division of Art, Dallas TX (S)

Beasley, Todd, *Creative Dir,* Morris Museum of Art, Augusta GA

Beatly, Michael, *Assoc Prof,* College of the Holy Cross, Dept of Visual Arts, Worcester MA (S)

Beatty, Carol, *Dir,* Esplanade Arts & Heritage Centre, Medicine Hat AB

Beatty, Nicole, *Branch Coordr,* Indiana University, Fine Arts Library, Bloomington IN

Beatty, Tracy, *Exhibs Coordr,* Northeastern Nevada Museum, Elko NV

Beatty Adler, Frances, *Co Chmn,* The Drawing Center, New York NY

Beauchamp, Darrell, *Dean,* Navarro College, Gaston T Gooch Library & Learning Resource Center, Corsicana TX

Beauchamp, Darrell, *Dir,* C M Russell, Great Falls MT

Beauchamp, Darrell, *Exec Dir,* C M Russell, Frederic G Renner Memorial Library, Great Falls MT

Beaudry, Eve-Lyne, *Cur Contemporary Art,* Musee National des Beaux Arts du Quebec, Quebec PQ

Beaupre, Rachel, *Curatorial Asst,* Mount Holyoke College, Art Museum, South Hadley MA

Beausoleil, Deanne, *Adjunct,* Chemeketa Community College, Dept of Humanities & Communications, Art Program, Salem OR (S)

Beaver, Frank, *Assoc Chair,* University of Hawaii at Manoa, Dept of Art, Honolulu HI (S)

Beaver, Jeanne, *Asst Prof,* Murray State University, Dept of Art, Murray KY (S)

Beben, Sylvia, *Asst Dir,* Jordan Historical Museum of The Twenty, Jordan ON

Becenti, Pete, *Parks Supv,* Red Rock Park, Red Rock Museum, Church Rock NM

Becerra, Andrea, *Youth Prog Coordr,* City of Irvine, Irvine Fine Arts Center, Irvine CA

Bechand, Elizabeth, *Mus Shop Mgr,* Albany Institute of History & Art, Albany NY

Becher, Melissa, *Reference Team Leader,* American University, Jack I & Dorothy G Bender Library & Learning Resources Center, New York NY

Becherer, Joseph, *Prof,* Aquinas College, Art Dept, Grand Rapids MI (S)

Bechet, Ron, *Chmn,* Xavier University of Louisiana, Dept of Fine Arts, New Orleans LA (S)

Becht, Mary, *Dir,* Broward County Board of Commissioners, Cultural Div, Fort Lauderdale FL

Bechtell, MC, *Chmn,* Madison Museum of Fine Art, Madison GA

Bechtell, Michele, *CEO, Pres & Dir,* Madison Museum of Fine Art, Madison GA

Beck, Boyde, *Cur History,* Prince Edward Island Museum & Heritage Foundation, Charlottetown PE

Beck, David E, *Pres,* Middletown Arts Center, Middletown OH

Beck, Dylan, *Ceramics,* Oregon College of Art & Craft, Portland OR (S)

Beck, Jerry, *Dir Mktg,* Fitchburg Art Museum, Fitchburg MA

Beck, Kimberly, *Deputy Dir Opers,* Columbus Museum, Columbus GA

Beck, Tom, *Affiliate Assoc Prof, Chief Cur AOK Libr & Dir CBSA,* University of Maryland, Baltimore County, Imaging & Digital Arts (IMDA), Dept of Visual Arts, Baltimore MD (S)

Beck, Tom, *Chief Cur,* Albin O Kuhn Library & Gallery, Baltimore MD

Beck, Tracey, *Exec Dir,* American Swedish Historical Foundation & Museum, American Swedish Historical Museum, Philadelphia PA

Beck, Tracey, *Exec Dir,* American Swedish Historical Foundation & Museum, Nord Library, Philadelphia PA

Beckel, Margaret, *Interim Pres & CEO,* Canadian Museum of Nature, Musee Canadien de la Nature, Ottawa ON

Beckelman, John, *Chmn Art Dept,* Coe College, Eaton-Buchan Gallery & Marvin Cone Gallery, Cedar Rapids IA

Beckelman, John, *Prof,* Coe College, Dept of Art, Cedar Rapids IA (S)

Beckelman, Laurie, *Deputy Dir for Spec Projects,* Guggenheim Museum Soho, New York NY

Becker, Chuck, *1st Vice Pres,* Cumberland Art Society Inc, Cookeville Art Gallery, Cookeville TN

Becker, David, *Prof,* University of Wisconsin, Madison, Dept of Art, Madison WI (S)

Becker, Elizabeth, *Cur Educ,* Albuquerque Museum of Art & History, Albuquerque NM

Becker, Jack, *Dir,* Cheekwood-Tennessee Botanical Garden & Museum of Art, Museum of Art, Nashville TN

Becker, Jack, *Pres & CEO,* Cheekwood-Tennessee Botanical Garden & Museum of Art, Nashville TN

Becker, Jack F, *Exec Dir & CEO,* Joslyn Art Museum, Omaha NE

Becker, Janis, *Educ Coordr,* Mamie McFaddin Ward, Beaumont TX

Becker, Jim, *COO,* Taubman Museum of Art, Roanoke VA

Becker, Julia, *Prof Art,* University of Great Falls, Art Dept, Great Falls MT (S)

Becker, Lisa Tamiris, *Dir,* University of Colorado, CU Art Museum, Boulder CO

Becker, Thomas, *Pres,* Chautauqua Center for the Visual Arts, Chautauqua NY

Becket, Charlotte, *Prof,* Pace University, Dyson College of Arts & Sciences, Pleasantville NY (S)

Beckham, Donita, *Library & Archives Liaison,* Heard Museum, Billie Jane Baguley Library and Archives, Phoenix AZ

Beckham, Peggy, *Adjunct Prof,* Missouri Southern State University, Dept of Art, Joplin MO (S)

Beckham, Terry, *Designer,* Birmingham Museum of Art, Birmingham AL

Beckham, Terry A, *Exhibs Designer,* Birmingham Museum of Art, Clarence B Hanson Jr Library, Birmingham AL

Beckman, Jean, *Dean Arts & Sciences,* University of Evansville, Krannert Gallery & Peterson Gallery, Evansville IN

Beckman, Joy, *Dir,* Beloit College, Wright Museum of Art, Beloit WI

Beckstrom, Robert, *Chmn,* Lorain County Community College, Art Dept, Elyria OH (S)

Beckwith, Alice, *Assoc Prof,* Providence College, Art & Art History Dept, Providence RI (S)

Beckwith, Claudia, *Registrar Pub Rels,* Greenville County Museum of Art, Greenville SC

Beckwith, Patterson, *Lectr,* City College of New York, Art Dept, New York NY (S)

Bedard, Chantal, *Professional Develop & Exec Svcs Coordr/Privacy Officer,* Royal Architectural Institute of Canada, Ottawa ON

Bedard, Robert J, *Treas,* Art PAC, Washington DC

Beddow, Julie Ann, *Fine & Performing Arts,* University of Northern Iowa, Fine & Performing Arts Collection Rod Library, Cedar Falls IA

Beder, Louise, *Mem Coordr,* James A Michener, Doylestown PA

Beebe, Deryl, *Finance Mgr,* Coos Art Museum, Coos Bay OR

Beebe, Mary Livingstone, *Dir,* University of California, San Diego, Stuart Collection, La Jolla CA

Beecham, Bern, *VChmn,* Palo Alto Art Center, Palo Alto CA

Beeching, Lynne, *Develop Officer,* Hidalgo County Historical Museum, Edinburg TX

Beegan, Gerry, *Asst Prof,* Rutgers, The State University of New Jersey, Mason Gross School of the Arts, Visual Arts Dept, New Brunswick NJ (S)

Beegles, Anna, *Site Mgr,* County of Henrico, Library, Glen Allen VA

Beeler, Kristin, *Assoc Prof Jewelry & Metalwork, Program Coordr Applied Design,* Long Beach City College, Art & Photography Dept, Long Beach CA (S)

Beer, Chris, *Gallery Asst,* Pence Gallery, Davis CA

Beer, Gary, *Sr Bus Officer,* Smithsonian Institution, Washington DC

Beers, Debra, *Instr,* Lewis & Clark College, Dept of Art, Portland OR (S)

Beesch, Ruth, *Deputy Dir Prog Admin,* The Jewish Museum, New York NY

Beeson, Alison, *Assoc Cur,* Wiregrass Museum of Art, Dothan AL

Bega Foss, Joyce, *Chmn,* United States Department of the Interior, Indian Arts & Crafts Board, Washington DC

Begay, Clarenda, *Cur,* Navajo Nation, Navajo Nation Museum, Window Rock AZ

Begay, Lorenzo J, *Exec Dir,* Atlatl, Phoenix AZ

Begland, Mary Anne, *Chmn Graphic Design,* Rochester Institute of Technology, School of Design, Rochester NY (S)

Begley, John, *Gallery Dir,* University of Louisville, Hite Art Institute, Louisville KY

Begley, John, *Gallery Dir & Adjunct Assoc Prof,* University of Louisville, Allen R Hite Art Institute, Louisville KY (S)

Beglin, Patricia, *Instr,* Cazenovia College, Center for Art & Design Studies, Cazenovia NY (S)

Beglo, Jo, *Bibliographer,* National Gallery of Canada, Library, Ottawa ON

Begnaud, Joseph, *Assoc Prof,* University of North Carolina at Pembroke, Art Dept, Pembroke NC (S)

Behl, Diana, *Asst Prof,* South Dakota State University, Dept of Visual Arts, Brookings SD (S)

Behler, Mark, *Cur,* North Central Washington Museum, Wenatchee Valley Museum & Cultural Center, Wenatchee WA

Behnke, Betsy, *Secy,* Dillman's Creative Arts Foundation, Tom Lynch Resource Center, Lac Du Flambeau WI

Behnke, Henry, *Dir Mktg & External Affairs,* Staten Island Museum, Staten Island NY

Behrend, Rene, *Prof,* Saint Louis Community College at Meramec, Art Dept, Saint Louis MO (S)

Behrens, Fred, *Prof,* Columbia State Community College, Dept of Art, Columbia TN (S)

Behrens, Roy, *Prof,* University of Northern Iowa, Dept of Art, Cedar Falls IA (S)

Behrens, Todd, *Cur,* Sioux City Art Center, Sioux City IA (S)

Beibers, Sam, *Instr,* Belhaven College, Art Dept, Jackson MS (S)

Beidler, Anne, *Chmn,* Agnes Scott College, Dept of Art, Decatur GA (S)

Beidler, Anne, *Printmaker,* Agnes Scott College, Dalton Art Gallery, Decatur GA

Beim, David O, *VChmn,* Wave Hill, Bronx NY

Beiner, Susan, *Instr,* California State University, San Bernardino, Dept of Art, San Bernardino CA (S)

Beirdneau, Linda, *Office Mgr,* Las Vegas Natural History Museum, Las Vegas NV

Beirise, Elizabeth, *Mgr Publ & Pub Rels,* Art Services International, Alexandria VA

Beiter, Michael, *VPres,* Historic Cherry Hill, Albany NY

Beitz, Michael, *Asst Prof,* University of Wisconsin Oshkosh, Dept of Art, Oshkosh WI (S)

Belair, Phil, *Chmn 2D/4D Design,* Milwaukee Institute of Art & Design, Milwaukee WI (S)

Belan, Kyra, *Gallery Dir,* Broward Community College - South Campus, Art Gallery, Pembroke Pines FL

Beland, Mario, *Cur Early Quebec Art 1850-1900,* Musee National des Beaux Arts du Quebec, Quebec PQ

Belanger, Lyne, *Chief Librn,* Universite de Montreal, Bibliotheque d'Amenagement, Montreal PQ

Belanger, Pamela, *Cur 19th & 20th Century,* William A Farnsworth, Library, Rockland ME

Belanger, Sylvie, *Asst Prof,* University at Buffalo, State University of New York, Dept of Visual Studies, Buffalo NY (S)

Belanger, Tanya, *Fin Adminstr,* Beaverbrook Art Gallery, Fredericton NB

Belanger-Turner, Tammy, *Dir Finance,* Caramoor Center for Music & the Arts, Inc, Rosen House at Caramoor, Katonah NY

Belardo, John, *Pres,* Hudson Valley Art Association, Brooklyn NY

Belarger, Jessica, *Admin,* Conseil des Arts du Quebec (CATQ), Diagonale, Centre des arts et des fibres du Quebec, Montreal PQ

Belasco, Ruth, *Prof,* Spring Hill College, Department of Fine & Performing Arts, Mobile AL (S)

Belcher, Katie, *Prog Coordr,* Mount Saint Vincent University, MSVU Art Gallery, Halifax NS

Belcher, Laura, *Sr VP & CFO,* Arts & Science Council, Charlotte NC

Belcher, Patty, *Reference Librn,* Bernice Pauahi Bishop, Library, Honolulu HI

Belcher, Theta, *Asst to Dir,* San Jose State University, Natalie & James Thompson Art Gallery, San Jose CA

Belcher, Tracy, *Pub Rels,* Miami Art Museum, Miami FL

Belfort-Chalat, Jacqueline, *Chmn & Prof,* Le Moyne College, Fine Arts Dept, Syracuse NY (S)

Belisle, Patt, *Dir,* Middletown Arts Center, Middletown OH

Belknap, Beth, *Assoc,* College of Mount Saint Joseph, Art Dept, Cincinnati OH (S)

Bell, Adrienne, *Asst Prof Art History,* Marymount Manhattan College, Fine & Performing Arts Div, New York NY (S)

Bell, Caleb, *Pub Rel & Mktg,* Tyler Museum of Art, Tyler TX

Bell, Christine, *Lectr,* Northwestern University, Evanston, Dept of Art History, Evanston IL (S)

Bell, Daniel, *Pres,* Gilbert Stuart, Gilbert Stuart Birthplace & Museum, Saunderstown RI

Bell, Denise, *Dir Grants & Contracts,* California State University, Long Beach Foundation, Long Beach CA

Bell, Doug, *Preparator & Registrar,* Tufts University, Tufts University Art Gallery, Medford MA

Bell, Edwina, *Dir Devel,* Chrysler Museum of Art, Norfolk VA

Bell, Ford W, *Pres,* American Association of Museums, United States National Committee of the International Council of Museums (ICOM-US), Washington DC

Bell, Gloria, *Chief Historical Interpreter,* Old Barracks Museum, Trenton NJ

Bell, Joseph, *Dir Gen Serv,* Colorado Historical Society, Colorado History Museum, Denver CO

Bell, Jude, *Admin Asst,* University of California, Berkeley, College of Letters & Sciences-Art Practice Dept, Berkeley CA (S)

Bell, Judith, *Instr,* San Jose City College, School of Fine Arts, San Jose CA (S)

Bell, Kelley, *Asst Prof,* University of Maryland, Baltimore County, Imaging & Digital Arts (IMDA), Dept of Visual Arts, Baltimore MD (S)

Bell, Kurt, *Librn & Archivist,* Pennsylvania Historical & Museum Commission, Railroad Museum of Pennsylvania, Harrisburg PA

Bell, Leslie, *Prof Art,* Saint Ambrose University, Art Dept, Davenport IA (S)

Bell, Lynne, *Head,* University of Saskatchewan, Dept of Art & Art History, Saskatoon SK (S)

Bell, Maaji, *Prof,* Concordia University, Division of Performing & Visual Arts, Mequon WI (S)

Bell, Malcolm, *Prof,* University of Virginia, McIntire Dept of Art, Charlottesville VA (S)

Bell, Marybeth, *Dir,* State University of New York at Oswego, Penfield Library, Oswego NY

Bell, Maxine, *Commun Officer,* Ontario Crafts Council, OCC Gallery, Toronto ON

Bell, Michael, *Dir,* Carleton University, Dept of Art History, Ottawa ON (S)

Bell, Shauna, *Financial Asst,* Kamloops Art Gallery, Kamloops BC

Bell, Tom, *Dir Finance,* New Britain Museum of American Art, New Britain CT

Bell, Trevor, *Prof Emeritus,* Florida State University, Art Dept, Tallahassee FL (S)

Bellabia, Kim, *Dir,* Klamath County Museum, Klamath Falls OR

Bellabia, Kim, *Dir,* Klamath County Museum, Research Library, Klamath Falls OR

Bellabia, Kim, *Dir,* Klamath County Museum, Baldwin Hotel Museum Annex, Klamath Falls OR

Bellah, Suzzane, *Cultural Arts Supv,* Carnegie Art Museum, Oxnard CA

Bellais, Leslie, *Cur Costumes & Textiles,* Wisconsin Historical Society, Wisconsin Historical Museum, Madison WI

Bellard, Lauren, *Curatorial Asst,* Asheville Art Museum, Asheville NC

Bellas, Gerald, *Dir,* College of Mount Saint Joseph, Studio San Giuseppe, Cincinnati OH

Bellas, Gerry, *Asst Prof,* College of Mount Saint Joseph, Art Dept, Cincinnati OH (S)

Bellavance, Leslie, *Dean,* New York State College of Ceramics at Alfred University, School of Art & Design, Alfred NY (S)

Bellerby, Greg, *Cur,* Emily Carr Institute of Art & Design, The Charles H Scott Gallery, Vancouver BC

Bellerose, Richard, *CEO,* Musee d'art Contemporain de Montreal, Montreal PQ

Belletire, Steve, *Prof & Design Area Head,* Southern Illinois University, School of Art & Design, Carbondale IL (S)

Belleville, Patricia, *Prof,* Eastern Illinois University, Art Dept, Charleston IL (S)

Belli, Melia, *Asst Prof,* University of Texas at Arlington, Art & Art History Department, Arlington TX (S)

Bellingham, Susan, *Spec Coll Librn,* University of Waterloo, Dana Porter Library, Waterloo ON

Bellisio, Nina, *Asst Prof,* Saint Thomas Aquinas College, Art Dept, Sparkill NY (S)

Bellows, Joseph, *Dir,* Joseph Bellows Gallery, La Jolla CA

Bellum, Slade, *Dir Fin & Opers,* Armory Center for the Arts, Pasadena CA

Belluscio, Lynne, *Dir,* LeRoy Historical Society, The Jell-O Gallery, LeRoy NY

Belnap, Jeffrey, *Chmn,* Brigham Young University, Hawaii Campus, Division of Fine Arts, Laie HI (S)

Belson, Anne, *VPres,* New England Watercolor Society, Pembroke MA

Belson, Janer Danforth, *Pres,* Cleveland Institute of Art, Cleveland Art Association, Cleveland OH

Beltemacchi, Peter, *Assoc Prof,* Illinois Institute of Technology, College of Architecture, Chicago IL (S)

Beltke, Bridget, *Finance Mgr,* Pelham Art Center, Pelham NY

Belville, Scott, *Assoc Prof Drawing & Painting,* University of Georgia, Franklin College of Arts & Sciences, Lamar Dodd School of Art, Athens GA (S)

Belvo, Hazel, *Faculty,* Grand Marais Art Colony, Grand Marais MN (S)

Belzil-Normand, Carol-Ann, La Chambre Blanche, Quebec PQ

Belzile, Gervais, *Material Resources Tech,* Le Musee Regional de Rimouski, Centre National d'Exposition, Rimouski PQ

Beman, Lynn S, *Exec Dir,* Amherst Museum, Niederlander Research Library, Amherst NY

Ben-Haim, Sandra, *Cur Educ,* Plains Art Museum, Fargo ND

Ben-Horin, Barbara, *Dir Devel,* Santa Barbara Museum of Art, Santa Barbara CA

Ben-Horin, Barbara, *Dir Develop,* Santa Barbara Museum of Art, Library, Santa Barbara CA

Benally, Ailema, *Educ Dir,* National Park Service, Hubbell Trading Post National Historic Site, Ganado AZ

Benarde, Scott, *Dir Communs,* Norton Museum of Art, West Palm Beach FL

Benavides, James, *Pub Affairs,* The University of Texas at San Antonio, Institute of Texan Cultures, San Antonio TX

Benavides, Stacy, *Admin,* Ellen Noel Art Museum of the Permian Basin, Odessa TX

Benbassat, Karen, *Asst,* Community Arts Council of Vancouver, Vancouver BC

Benbow, Joyce, *Secy,* Switzerland County Historical Society Inc, Life on the Ohio: River History Museum, Vevay IN

Benbow, Joyce, *Secy,* Switzerland County Historical Society Inc, Switzerland County Historical Museum, Vevay IN

Bender, Christine, *Admin Asst,* Sun Gallery, Hayward CA

Bender, Heather, *Master Teacher,* University of Wyoming, University of Wyoming Art Museum, Laramie WY

Bender, Mark, *Graphic Design,* Art Institute of Pittsburgh, Pittsburgh PA (S)

Bender, Nathan, *House Cur,* Buffalo Bill Memorial Association, Harold McCracken Research Library, Cody WY

Bender, Neil, *Assoc Prof,* University of South Florida, School The Arts, Tampa FL (S)

Bender, Phil, *Dir,* Pirate-Contemporary Art, Denver CO

Benedetti, Joan M, *Librn,* LA County Museum of Art, Edith R Wyle Research Library of The Craft & Folk Art Museum, Los Angeles CA

Benedetto, Mark, *Pres,* University of Sioux Falls, Dept of Art, Sioux Falls SD (S)

Benedict, Dow, *Dean,* Shepherd University, Dept of Contemporary Art & Theater, Shepherdstown WV (S)

Benedict, Sean, *Media Arts & Animation,* Art Institute of Pittsburgh, Pittsburgh PA (S)

Beneditti, Joan, *Librn,* LA County Museum of Art, Los Angeles CA

Benefiel, Christian, *Coordr Sculpture,* Shepherd University, Dept of Contemporary Art & Theater, Shepherdstown WV (S)

Benefield, Richard, *Deputy Dir,* Harvard University, Harvard University Art Museums, Cambridge MA

Benehabane, Manel, *Gallery Asst,* Pointe Claire Cultural Centre, Stewart Hall Art Gallery, Pointe Claire PQ

Benero, Paul, *Adjunct Prof,* University of Texas at Arlington, Art & Art History Department, Arlington TX (S)

Benesh, Joseph, *Dir,* Phoenix Center for the Arts, Phoenix AZ

Benezra, Neal, *Dir SFMOMA,* San Francisco Museum of Modern Art, San Francisco CA

Benford, Benjamin, *Dean Liberal Arts,* Tuskegee University, Liberal Arts & Education, Tuskegee AL (S)

Bengston, Carl, *Dean Library Serv,* California State University Stanislaus, Vasche Library, Turlock CA

Bengston, Monee, *Registrar,* Contemporary Art Center of Virginia, Virginia Beach VA

Bengston, Rod, *Gallery Dir,* University of Akron, University Art Galleries, Akron OH

Benhisen, Louisa, *Prof 2-D Prog,* Merced College, Arts Division, Merced CA (S)

Benington-Kozlowski, Eliza, *Dir Communs & Visitor Engagement,* George Eastman, Rochester NY

Benini, Lorraine, *Pres,* The Benini Foundation & Sculpture Ranch, Johnson City TX

Benio, Pauleve, *Prof,* Adrian College, Art & Design Dept, Adrian MI (S)

Beniston, Susan, *Instr,* Toronto School of Art, Toronto ON (S)

Benitez-Booker, Alicia, *Admin Asst,* Nelda C & H J Lutcher Stark, Stark Museum of Art, Orange TX

Benjamin, Brent, *Dir,* Saint Louis Art Museum, Saint Louis MO

Benjamin, Jack, *Chmn,* University of South Carolina at Aiken, Dept of Visual & Performing Arts, Aiken SC (S)

Benjamin, Susan, *Chmn,* Pickens County Museum of Art & History, Pickens SC

Bennett, Dawn, *Exec Dir,* Urbanglass, Robert Lehman Gallery, Brooklyn NY

Bennett, Fernanda, *Registrar,* Nassau County Museum of Art, Roslyn Harbor NY

Bennett, Frank, *Exec Dir,* The National Quilt Museum, Paducah KY

Bennett, K Sharon, *Archivist,* Charleston Museum, Charleston SC

Bennett, Kate, *Dir Develop,* Wildling Art Museum, Solvang CA

Bennett, Michael, *Cur Greek & Roman Art,* The Cleveland Museum of Art, Cleveland OH

Bennett, Susan, *Exec Dir,* Port Huron Museum, Port Huron MI

Bennett, Susan, *Mus Opers Coordr,* Susquehanna Art Museum, Harrisburg PA

Bennett, Swannee, *Cur,* Historic Arkansas Museum, Library, Little Rock AR

Bennett, Swannee, *Cur Research,* Historic Arkansas Museum, Little Rock AR

Bennett, Tom D, *Cur,* Alaska Heritage Museum at Wells Fargo, Anchorage AK

Bennett, William, *Studio Faculty,* University of Virginia, McIntire Dept of Art, Charlottesville VA (S)

Bennett Easterson, Toni, *Visual Arts Specialist,* Northfield Arts Guild, Northfield MN

Benninghoff, Herman O, *VPres,* Burlington County Historical Society, Burlington NJ

Benoit, Jaye, *Outreach Coordr,* Latitude 53 Contemporary Visual Culture, Edmonton AB

Benso, Helen, *VPres Mktg,* Brookgreen Gardens, Murrells Inlet SC

Benson, Aaron Lee, *Chmn,* Union University, Dept of Art, Jackson TN (S)

Benson, Carla, *Treas,* The Art Museum of Eastern Idaho, Idaho Falls ID

Benson, Claire, *Dir,* Lyndon House Art, Athens GA

Benson, Dennis, *Assoc Dean,* Rutgers, The State University of New Jersey, Mason Gross School of the Arts, Visual Arts Dept, New Brunswick NJ (S)

Benson, Ilana, *Educator,* Yeshiva University Museum, New York NY

Benson, Mark, *Dept Head,* Auburn University Montgomery, Dept of Fine Arts, Montgomery AL (S)

Benson, Nicole, *Gallery Dir,* Portlock Galleries at SoNo, Chesapeake VA

Benson, Richard, *Dean,* Yale University, School of Art, New Haven CT (S)

Benson, Romona Riscoe, *Pres & CEO,* African American Museum in Philadelphia, Philadelphia PA

Benson, Timothy, *Cur,* Los Angeles County Museum of Art, Robert Gore Rifkind Center for German Expressionist Studies, Los Angeles CA

Bensur, Barbara J, *Assoc Prof Art Educ,* Millersville University, Dept of Art & Design, Millersville PA (S)

Bent, George, *Head,* Washington and Lee University, Div of Art, Lexington VA (S)

Bent, Nila, *Art Reference Librn,* The Society of the Four Arts, Gioconda & Joseph King Library, Palm Beach FL

Bentlage, Deb, *Colls Mgr,* George Phippen, Phippen Museum - Art of the American West, Prescott AZ

Bentley, Anne E, *Cur Art,* Massachusetts Historical Society, Boston MA

Bentley, Anne E, *Cur Art,* Massachusetts Historical Society, Library, Boston MA

Bentley, Bethany, *Pub Affairs Officer,* National Portrait Gallery, Smithsonian Institution, Washington DC

Bentley, Christine, *Exhib Coordr,* University of Indianapolis, Christel DeHaan Fine Arts Gallery, Indianapolis IN

Bentley, Eden R, *Librn,* Johnson Atelier Technical Institute of Sculpture, Johnson Atelier Library, Mercerville NJ

Bentley, Polly, *Mus Asst,* Vermont Historical Society, Museum, Montpelier VT

Bently, Christine, *Asst Prof,* University of Indianapolis, Dept Art & Design, Indianapolis IN (S)

Benton, Fran, *Cur,* Malaspina College, Nanaimo Art Gallery, Nanaimo BC

Benton, Janetta, *Prof,* Pace University, Dyson College of Arts & Sciences, Pleasantville NY (S)

Benton, Steve, *Dir,* Massachusetts Institute of Technology, Center for Advanced Visual Studies, Cambridge MA (S)

Bentor, Eli, *Asst Prof,* Appalachian State University, Dept of Art, Boone NC (S)

Bentz, Laura, *Asst Prof,* Chadron State College, Dept of Art, Chadron NE (S)

Benvenuto, Mary, *Dir Finance & Human Resources,* McMichael Canadian Art Collection, Kleinburg ON

Benzow, Jeff, *Assoc Prof,* University of Wisconsin-Green Bay, Arts Dept, Green Bay WI (S)

Beono, Tom, *Assoc Prof,* Texas State University - San Marcos, Dept of Art and Design, San Marcos TX (S)

Berben, Silvan, *Dir,* Owatonna Arts Center, Library, Owatonna MN

Berber, Sidney, *Dir Phillips Libr,* Peabody Essex Museum, Phillips Library, Salem MA

Berberich, Hugh, *Prof,* Manhattan College, School of Arts, Bronx NY (S)

Berbet, Theresa, *Asst Cur,* University of Louisville, Visual Resources Center, Louisville KY

Berelowitz, Jo-Anne, *Art History Grad Coordr,* San Diego State University, School of Art, Design & Art History, San Diego CA (S)

Berens, Stephen, *Prof,* Chapman University, Art Dept, Orange CA (S)

Berezansky, Tracey, *Asst Dir Government Records,* Alabama Department of Archives & History, Museum of Alabama, Montgomery AL

Berg, Irene, *Treas,* Malaspina College, Nanaimo Art Gallery, Nanaimo BC

Berg, John J, *Sr Vpres Finance & Opers,* National Academy Museum & School, New York NY

Berg, Kathy, *Admin Asst,* Sangre de Cristo Arts & Conference Center, Pueblo CO

Berg, Niels, *Sub Dir,* Ages of Man Foundation, Amenia NY

Berg-Gilbert, Tempy, *Instr,* Dallas Baptist University, Dept of Art, Dallas TX (S)

Bergboll, Barry, *Dir Grad Studies,* Columbia University, Dept of Art History & Archaeology, New York NY (S)

Bergeman, Rich, *Instr,* Linn Benton Community College, Fine & Applied Art Dept, Albany OR (S)

Bergen, Kim, *Head Registrar,* The Wolfsonian-Florida International University, Miami Beach FL

Berger, Carol, *Acting Chmn Div,* Saint Louis Community College at Florissant Valley, Liberal Arts Division, Ferguson MO (S)

Berger, Jerry, *Dir,* Southwest Missouri Museum Associates Inc, Springfield Art Museum, Springfield MO

Berger, Jerry A, *Dir,* Springfield Art Museum, Springfield MO

Berger, Kristin, *Dir Develop,* Sonoma County Museum, Santa Rosa CA

Berger, Lisa, *Develop & Commun,* Art Center Sarasota, Sarasota FL

Berger, Marilyn, *Head Librn,* McGill University, Blackader-Lauterman Library of Architecture and Art, Montreal PQ

Berger, Quindi, *Librn II, Prog Mgr,* San Francisco Public Library, Art & Music Center, San Francisco CA

Berger, Shelly, *Dir,* Mid-America All-Indian Center, Black Bear Bosin Resource Center, Wichita KS

Berger, Theodore, *Exec Dir,* New York Foundation for the Arts, Brooklyn NY

Bergeron, Suzanne K, *Asst Dir,* Bowdoin College, Museum of Art, Brunswick ME

Bergeron, Sylvie, *Treas,* Institut des Arts au Saguenay, Centre National D'Exposition a Jonquiere, Jonquiere PQ

Bergeron, Tom, *Chmn Creative Arts,* Western Oregon State College, Creative Arts Division, Visual Arts, Monmouth OR (S)

Bergess, Nancy, *Treas,* Clinton Art Association, River Arts Center, Clinton IA

Bergfeld, Mary Ann, *Assoc Prof,* Saint Xavier University, Dept of Art & Design, Chicago IL (S)

Berggren, Chris, *Develop Dir,* Maritime Museum of San Diego, San Diego CA

Bergman, Joseph, *Prof,* Siena Heights University, Studio Angelico-Art Dept, Adrian MI (S)

Bergman, Sky, *Dept Chmn, Prof Photog,* California Polytechnic State University at San Luis Obispo, Dept of Art & Design, San Luis Obispo CA (S)

Bergmann, Catherine, *Dir Adult Educ,* Dunedin Fine Art Center, Dunedin FL (S)

Bergmann, Malena, *Coordr Undergrad Educ,* University of North Carolina at Charlotte, Dept Art, Charlotte NC (S)

Bergquist, Dick, *Treas,* Snake River Heritage Center, Weiser ID

Bergsieker, David, *Instr,* Illinois Valley Community College, Division of Humanities & Fine Arts, Oglesby IL (S)

Bergstein, Scott, *Bd Mem,* The Mattress Factory, Pittsburgh PA

Bergstrom, Christopher (Kip), *Deputy Commissioner,* Department of Economic & Community Development, Eric Sloane Museum, Kent CT

Bergstrom, Doug, *Exhibs,* University of Kansas, Spencer Museum of Art, Lawrence KS

Berhard, Dianne B, *1st VPres,* Pastel Society of America, National Arts Club, Grand Gallery, New York NY

Beriault, Ginette, *Dir Exhibs,* Canada Science and Technology Museum, Ottawa ON

Berke, Joanne, *Prof,* Humboldt State University, College of Arts & Humanities, Art Dept, Arcata CA (S)

Berke, Lisa, *Fin Dir,* Yellowstone Art Museum, Billings MT

Berko, Linda, *Cur Colls,* Prince Edward Island Museum & Heritage Foundation, Charlottetown PE

Berley, Tanya, *Pres,* DuPage Art League School & Gallery, Wheaton IL

Berliant, Susan, *Acting Develop Dir,* Contemporary Arts Center, Cincinnati OH

Berlind, Robert, *Prof Emeritus,* Purchase College, State University of New York, School of Art+Design, Purchase NY (S)

Berlyn, Judith, *Librn,* Chateau Ramezay Museum, Library, Montreal PQ

Berman, Lawrence, *Calderwood Sr Cur Egyptian Nubian & Near Eastern Art,* Museum of Fine Arts, Boston MA

Berman, Nancy, *Dir Emerita,* Hebrew Union College, Skirball Cultural Center, Los Angeles CA

Berman, Patricia, *Chmn,* Wellesley College, Art Dept, Wellesley MA (S)

Bernal, Rudy, *Chief Preparator,* University of Chicago, Smart Museum of Art, Chicago IL

Bernard, Andre, *VPres & Sec,* John Simon Guggenheim, New York NY

Bernard, Geneive, *Cur Educ,* Mennello Museum of American Art, Orlando FL

Bernard, Lewis, *Chmn Bd Trustees,* American Museum of Natural History, New York NY

Bernardo, Celeste, *Dir Educ,* USS Constitution Museum, Boston MA

Bernatz, Michael, *Sr VPres Finance,* Milwaukee Public Museum, Milwaukee WI

Bernau, Bonnie, *Dir Educ,* University of Florida, Samuel P Harn Museum of Art, Gainesville FL

Bernberg, Bruce, *Pres,* Racine Art Museum, Racine WI

Berner, Andrew, *Dir & Cur Collections,* University Club Library, New York NY

Berner, Tracy, *Reg,* Illinois State University, University Galleries, Normal IL

Bernhard, Robin, *Coll Mgr & Registrar,* University of California, Richard L Nelson Gallery & Fine Arts Collection, Davis CA

Bernier, Elizabeth, *Asst to Dir,* Old Colony Historical Society, Museum, Taunton MA

Bernier, Monique, *Dir Human Resource,* Musee d'art Contemporain de Montreal, Montreal PQ

Bernis, Terry, *VPres,* Creek Council House Museum, Okmulgee OK

Berns, Marla C, *Dir,* University of California, Los Angeles, Fowler Museum at UCLA, Los Angeles CA

Bernstein, Alex, *Glass Dept Head,* Worcester Center for Crafts, Worcester MA (S)

Bernstein, Jill, *Dir Pub Rels,* Dallas Museum of Art, Dallas TX

Bernstein, Judith, *Assoc Prof Emeritus,* Purchase College, State University of New York, School of Art+Design, Purchase NY (S)

Bernstein, Roberta, *Prof,* State University of New York at Albany, Art Dept, Albany NY (S)

Bernstein, Sheri, *Dir Music & Educ,* Hebrew Union College, Skirball Cultural Center, Los Angeles CA

Bernstock, Judith E, *Assoc Prof,* Cornell University, Dept of the History of Art & Visual Studies, Ithaca NY (S)

Bernston, Ron, *Librn,* Nutana Collegiate Institute, Memorial Library and Art Gallery, Saskatoon SK

Bero, Jen, *Mktg & Dev Dir,* Bergstrom-Mahler Museum, Library, Neenah WI

Bero, Meg, *Dir,* Aurora University, Schingoethe Center for Native American Cultures & The Schingoethe Art Gallery, Aurora IL

Beroza, Barbara, *Coll Cur,* Yosemite Museum, Research Library, Yosemite National Park CA

Beroza, Barbara, *Coll Mgr,* Yosemite Museum, Yosemite National Park CA

Berreth, David, *Dir,* University of Mary Washington, Gari Melchers Home and Studio, Fredericksburg VA

Berrin, Kathleen, *Cur Africa, Oceania & American,* Fine Arts Museums of San Francisco, M H de Young Museum, San Francisco CA

Berrin, Kathleen, *Cur Africa, Oceania & American,* Fine Arts Museums of San Francisco, Legion of Honor, San Francisco CA

Berrones-Molina, Patricia, *Acting Dir,* Pimeria Alta Historical Society, Library, Nogales AZ

Berry, Ann, *Dir,* Pilgrim Society, Library, Plymouth MA

Berry, Ann, *Dir & Librn,* Pilgrim Society, Pilgrim Hall Museum, Plymouth MA

Berry, Ava, *Mgr Mktg,* Charles Allis Art Museum, Milwaukee WI

Berry, Christopher, *Assoc Prof,* Lakeland Community College, Fine Arts Department, Kirtland OH (S)

Berry, E Raymond, *Chmn,* Randolph-Macon College, Dept of the Arts, Ashland VA (S)

Berry, Ian, *Consulting Dir,* Hamilton College, Emerson Gallery, Clinton NY

Berry, Judith, *Lectr,* Wayne State College, Dept Art & Design, Wayne NE (S)

Berry, Linda, *Security Supvr,* Huntsville Museum of Art, Huntsville AL

Berry, Melanie, *Undergrad Prog Dir,* University of Maryland, Baltimore County, Imaging & Digital Arts (IMDA), Dept of Visual Arts, Baltimore MD (S)

Berry, Paul, *Librn,* Calvert Marine Museum, Library, Solomons MD

Berry, Rachel, *Exhib Coordr,* Visual Art Exchange, Raleigh NC

Berry, Sarah, *Pres,* Worcester Art Museum, Worcester MA

Berry, Shawn, *Mgr Arts & Cultural Educ,* Cultural Council of Palm Beach County, Lake Worth FL

Berryman, Jill, *Exec Dir,* Sierra Arts Foundation, Sierra Arts Gallery, Reno NV

Bershad, Deborah, *Exec Dir,* Design Commission of the City of New York, Associates of the Art Commission, Inc, New York NY

Berson, Ariel, *Dir Edu,* Palo Alto Art Center, Palo Alto CA

Berson, Ruth, *Deputy Dir Exhibs & Colls,* San Francisco Museum of Modern Art, San Francisco CA

Bert, James, *Dir,* Cuneo Foundation, Museum & Gardens, Vernon Hills IL

Bertalot, Daniel, *Exhibs Asst,* Lawndale Art Center, Houston TX

Bertini, Marieanne, *Pres,* 1890 House-Museum & Center for the Arts, Cortland NY

Bertis, Lori, *Mus Svcs Mgr,* Eastern Washington State Historical Society, Northwest Museum of Arts & Culture, Spokane WA

Berto, Kathleen, *Exec Asst,* University of Alberta, Dept of Art & Design, Edmonton AB (S)

Bertoia, Roberto, *Assoc Prof,* Cornell University, Dept of Art, Ithaca NY (S)

Besemer, Linda, *Prof,* Occidental College, Dept of Art History & Visual Arts, Los Angeles CA (S)

Bessa, Antonio Sergio, *Dir Progs,* Bronx Museum of the Arts, Bronx NY

Besselsen, Sandra, *Head Librn,* Interlochen Center for the Arts, Interlochen MI

Bessey, Richard B, *Dir,* The Rockwell Museum of Western Art, Library, Corning NY

Bessini, Matt, *Pres,* Art Guild of Burlington, Art Center, Burlington IA

Bessire, Mark, *Dir,* Portland Museum of Art, Portland ME

Besson, Ciara, *Finance & HR Mgr,* Public Art Fund, Inc, New York NY

Besson, Ciara, *Finance & Human Resource,* Public Art Fund, Inc, Visual Archive, New York NY

Best, Jonathan W, *Prof,* Wesleyan University, Dept of Art & Art History, Middletown CT (S)

Best, Kathryn, *Cur Educ,* Grace Museum, Inc, Abilene TX

Best, Linda Delone, *Coll Mgr,* Mount Holyoke College, Art Museum, South Hadley MA

Best, Mickey D, *Dean,* New Mexico Junior College, Arts & Sciences, Hobbs NM (S)

Best, Sherry L, *Gallery Dir,* Topeka & Shawnee County Public Library, Alice C Sabatini Gallery, Topeka KS

Betancourt, Michael, *Cur,* Sioux City Art Center, Sioux City IA

Betania, Daryl, *Mgr Colls,* Glenbow Museum, Calgary AB

Bethany, Adeline, *Chmn Dept,* Cabrini College, Dept of Fine Arts, Radnor PA (S)

Bethel, Molly, *Dir & Painting Teacher,* Locust Street Neighborhood Art Classes, Inc, Buffalo NY (S)

Bethel, Sky, *Instr,* Locust Street Neighborhood Art Classes, Inc, Buffalo NY (S)

Bethel, Suzanne, *Deputy Exec Dir,* The Art League Gallery & School, Alexandria VA

Bething, Dan, *Lectr,* University of Tennessee at Chattanooga, Dept of Art, Chattanooga TN (S)

Bethke, Jennifer, *Educ Cur,* Sonoma County Museum, Santa Rosa CA

Bethke, Karl, *Prof,* University of Minnesota, Minneapolis, Dept of Art, Minneapolis MN (S)

Betsch, William, *Asst Prof,* University of Miami, Dept of Art & Art History, Coral Gables FL (S)

Betsky, Aaron, *Dir,* Cincinnati Art Museum, Cincinnati Art Museum, Cincinnati OH

Bettis, Kathy, *Registrar,* Boise Art Museum, Boise ID

Betty, Claudia Michelle, *Reference & Pub Servs Librn,* Art Center College of Design, James Lemont Fogg Memorial Library, Pasadena CA

Betzen, R Eileen, *Co-Owner,* Gadsden Museum, Mesilla NM

Betzer, Sarah, *Assoc Prof Art History,* University of Virginia, McIntire Dept of Art, Charlottesville VA (S)

Beuhler, Sara, *Registrar,* James A Michener, Doylestown PA

Beura, Katherine, *Prof,* State College of Florida Manatee - Sarasota, Art, Design, Humanities, Bradenton FL (S)

Beutell, Jackie, *Visual Arts Comt Chair,* University of Minnesota, The Studio/Larson Gallery, Minneapolis MN

Beverly, Roberta, *Exec Dir,* Ogden Union Station, Union Station Museums, Ogden UT

Beverly, Roberta, *Exec Dir,* Ogden Union Station, Myra Powell Art Gallery & Gallery at the Station, Ogden UT

Beyer, Albin, *Prof,* University of South Carolina at Aiken, Dept of Visual & Performing Arts, Aiken SC (S)

Beyer, Linnea, *Dir Film/Video,* The Light Factory Contemporary Museum of Photography and Film, Charlotte NC

Bhasin, Roberta, *Pres (V),* Denver Art Museum, Denver CO

Bhatt, Vikram, *Prof,* McGill University, School of Architecture, Montreal PQ (S)

Biada, Charles, *Dir Operations,* National Academy Museum & School, New York NY

Biada, Charles, *Dir Operations,* National Academy Museum & School, Archives, New York NY

Bialy, Mark G, *Prof,* Passaic County Community College, Division of Humanities, Paterson NJ (S)

Bianco, Juliette, *Asst Dir,* Dartmouth College, Hood Museum of Art, Hanover NH

Bibas, David, *Technology Cur,* California Science Center, Los Angeles CA

Bibler, Carol, *Instr,* Chemeketa Community College, Dept of Humanities & Communications, Art Program, Salem OR (S)

Bickel, Barbara, *Asst Prof,* Southern Illinois University, School of Art & Design, Carbondale IL (S)

Bickford, Maggie, *Prof,* Brown University, Dept History of Art & Architecture, Providence RI (S)

Bickley, Steve, *Prof,* Virginia Polytechnic Institute & State University, Dept of Art & Art History, Blacksburg VA (S)

Bicknell, Sarah Lou, *Mus Gift Shop Mgr & Historian,* Cedarhurst Center for the Arts, Mitchell Museum, Mount Vernon IL

Biddiscombe, Jennae, *Registrar,* Louisiana Department of Culture, Recreation & Tourism, Louisiana State Museum, New Orleans LA

Biddle, Mark, *Prof,* Weber State University, Dept of Visual Arts, Ogden UT (S)

Bidstrup, Wendy, *Dir,* Marion Art Center, Cecil Clark Davis Gallery, Marion MA

Bidwell, John, *Astor Cur & Dept Head Printed Books & Bindings,* The Morgan Library & Museum, Museum, New York NY

Bieling, Cathleen, *Asst to the Chair,* The Sage Colleges, Dept Visual Arts, Albany NY (S)

Bieloh, David, *Instr,* Texas Woman's University, School of the Arts, Dept of Visual Arts, Denton TX (S)

Bielski, Sarah, *Contract Asst Prof Art,* University of Southern Indiana, Department of Art, Evansville IN (S)

Bierinckx, Cis, *Dir Film & Video,* Walker Art Center, Minneapolis MN

Biers, William R, *Prof Emeritus,* University of Missouri - Columbia, Art History & Archaeology Dept, Columbia MO (S)

Bieth, Ted, *Adjunct,* North Iowa Area Community College, Dept of Art, Mason City IA (S)

Biferie, Dan, *Prof,* Daytona Beach Community College, Dept of Fine Arts & Visual Arts, Daytona Beach FL (S)

Bigazzi, Anna, *Art Reference Librn,* University of Hartford, Mortensen Library, West Hartford CT

Bigazzi, Anna, *Art Reference Librn,* University of Hartford, Anne Bunce Cheney Art Collection, West Hartford CT

Bigelow, Brad, *Mus Store Mgr,* Seattle Art Museum, Downtown, Seattle WA

Bigelow, Brad, *Mus Store Mgr,* Seattle Art Museum, Dorothy Stimson Bullitt Library, Seattle WA

Biggs, George, *Instr,* New Mexico Junior College, Arts & Sciences, Hobbs NM (S)

Biggs, Tamara, *Dir Exhibs,* Chicago History Museum, Chicago IL

Biglane, Joanna, *Registrar,* Mississippi Museum of Art, Jackson MS

Bigley, Heather A, *Dir Gen Educ,* Art Institute of Pittsburgh, Pittsburgh PA (S)

Bilbo, Rebecca, *Chmn,* Thomas More College, Art Dept, Crestview Hills KY (S)

Bilello, Michelle, *Operations Asst,* Quapaw Quarter Association, Inc, Villa Marre, Little Rock AR

Bilello, Michelle, *Operations Asst,* Quapaw Quarter Association, Inc, Preservation Resource Center/ Historic Cannon Hall, Little Rock AR

Bilger, Wenzel, *Head Prog Dept,* Goethe-Institut New York, Mini/Goethe-Institut Curatorial Residencies Ludlow 38, New York NY

Billings, Cathy, *Librn,* Glendale Public Library, Brand Library & Art Center, Glendale CA

Billingslea, Renee, *Lectr,* Santa Clara University, Dept of Art & Art History, Santa Clara CA (S)

Billington, James H, *Librn,* Library of Congress, Prints & Photographs Division, Washington DC

Billington, Stephanie, *Mus Shop Mgr,* Frederic Remington, Ogdensburg NY

Billops, Camille, *Pres,* Hatch-Billops Collection, Inc, New York NY

Bills, Danny, *Cur Coll & Exhib,* Wichita Falls Museum & Art Center, Wichita Falls TX

Bilsky, Angela, *Registrar,* Cape Cod Museum of Art Inc, Dennis MA

Binder, Lisa, *Cur,* Museum for African Art, New York NY

Bindseil, Kenneth, *Chmn Humanities,* Quincy College, Art Dept, Quincy MA (S)

Bingham, Bob, *Assoc Head,* Carnegie Mellon University, School of Art, Pittsburgh PA (S)

Bingham, Pam, *Dept Head Bus Office Tech,* Antonelli College, Cincinnati OH (S)

Bingham, Susan, *Dir,* Thunderbird Foundation for the Arts, Mount Carmel UT

Bingman, Beth, *Mng Dir & Gallery Dir,* Appalshop Inc, Appalshop, Whitesburg KY

Binkard, Daniel, *Instr,* Chadron State College, Dept of Art, Chadron NE (S)

Binkowski, Kraig, *Head Librn,* Yale University, Yale Center for British Art, New Haven CT

Binks, Ronald, *Prof,* University of Texas at San Antonio, Dept of Art & Art History, San Antonio TX (S)

Binnington, Georgia, *Assoc Dean School,* Washington University, School of Art, Saint Louis MO (S)

Bintz, Carol, *COO,* Toledo Museum of Art, Toledo OH

Biondi, Priscilla, *Architectural Librn,* Wentworth Institute of Technology Library, Boston MA

Biondo-Gemmell, Susannah, *Prof,* Cornell College, Peter Paul Luce Gallery, Mount Vernon IA

Bippes, Bill, *Div Dir Music Arts,* Spring Arbor College, Art Dept, Spring Arbor MI (S)

Bippes, Will, *Instr,* Hillsdale College, Art Dept, Hillsdale MI (S)

Bird, Alan, *Pres,* Dubuque Museum of Art, Dubuque IA

Bird, Anne, *Dir Mem,* Society of Architectural Historians, Chicago IL

Bird, Donal, *Dean,* Howard Payne University, Dept of Art, Brownwood TX (S)

Bird, John, *Mgr Gen Servs,* Rothmans, Benson & Hedges, Art Collection, Don Mills ON

Bird, Joyce, *Catalogs,* Everson Museum of Art, Syracuse NY

Bird, Mary F, *Owner & Cur,* Gadsden Museum, Mesilla NM

Bird, Richard, *Chmn,* Chadron State College, Dept of Art, Chadron NE (S)

Bird, Richard, *Chair Performing & Visual Arts,* Chadron State College, Memorial Hall Main Gallery & Memorial Hall Gallery 239, Chadron NE

Birdsong, Daniel, *Instr,* Weatherford College, Dept of Speech Fine Arts, Weatherford TX (S)

Birdsong, Sherri, *Cur Coll,* Mamie McFaddin Ward, Beaumont TX

Birk, Sherry, *Cur Coll,* American Architectural Foundation, The Octagon Museum, Washington DC

Birkett, Barbara, *Prof,* Rochester Institute of Technology, School of Printing Management & Sciences, Rochester NY (S)

Birkett, Richard, *Cur,* Artists Space, New York NY

Birkett, William H, *Assoc Prof,* Rochester Institute of Technology, School of Printing Management & Sciences, Rochester NY (S)

Birkhofer, Denise, *Asst Cur Modern & Contemporary Art,* Oberlin College, Allen Memorial Art Museum, Oberlin OH

Birkner, Tom, *Adjunct Asst Prof,* Drew University, Art Dept, Madison NJ (S)

Birmingham, Mary, *Cur,* Visual Arts Center of New Jersey, Summit NJ

Birmingham, Pamela, *Cur Edn,* Woodmere Art Museum Inc, Philadelphia PA

Birmingham, Pamela, *Cur Educ,* Woodmere Art Museum Inc, Library, Philadelphia PA

Birmingham, Robbin, *Exec Asst,* Auburn University, Julie Collins Smith Museum, Auburn AL

Birnbaum, Nathan, *Exec Dir,* Angels Gate Cultural Center, Gallery A & Gallery G, San Pedro CA

Birnie, Jenny, *Exec Dir,* Center for the Arts Piper Gallery, Crested Butte CO

Birnie Danzker, Jo-Anne, *Dir,* Frye Art Museum, Seattle WA

Biro, Matthew, *Asst Prof,* University of Michigan, Ann Arbor, Dept of History of Art, Ann Arbor MI (S)

Bisbee, Fay, *Reg,* University of Wyoming, University of Wyoming Art Museum, Laramie WY

Bisbee, John, *Lectr,* Bowdoin College, Art Dept, Brunswick ME (S)

Bisbing, Roger, *Technician,* State University of New York at Albany, Art Dept, Albany NY (S)

Bisch, Jennifer, *Chief Prog Officer & Cur,* Manitoba Historical Society, Dalnavert Museum, Winnipeg MB

Bisenius, Jim, *Instr,* Morningside College, Art Dept, Sioux City IA (S)

Bishop, Allen, *Art Instr,* Crowder College, Longwell Museum/Art Department, Neosho MO (S)

Bishop, Barbara, *Mktg & Communs Dir,* Bush-Holley Historic Site & Storehouse Gallery, Greenwich Historical Society/ Bush-Holley House, Cos Cob CT

Bishop, Brian, *Asst Prof,* Framingham State College, Art Dept, Framingham MA (S)

Bishop, Brian, *Prof,* Lansing Community College, Visual Arts & Media Dept, Lansing MI (S)

Bishop, Bruce, *Dir,* Yarmouth County Historical Society, Yarmouth County Museum & Archives, Yarmouth NS

Bishop, Claire, *Prof,* City University of New York, PhD Program in Art History, New York NY (S)

Bishop, Henry, *Cur,* Society for the Protection & Preservation of Black Culture in Nova Scotia, Black Cultural Center for Nova Scotia, Dartmouth NS

Bishop, Janet, *Cur Painting & Sculpture,* San Francisco Museum of Modern Art, San Francisco CA

Bishop, Joe, *Dir Facility & Security,* National Museum of Wildlife Art of the Unites States, Jackson WY

Bishop, Michael, *Prof,* California State University, Chico, Department of Art & Art History, Chico CA (S)

Bishop, Rebecca, *Communs Mgr,* Eastern Washington State Historical Society, Northwest Museum of Arts & Culture, Spokane WA

Bishop, Ron, *Cur & Dir,* Edison State College, Bob Rauschenberg Gallery, Fort Myers FL

Bishop, Sam, *VPres,* Kappa Pi International Honorary Art Fraternity, Cleveland MS

Bishop, Steve, *Assoc Prof,* Murray State University, Dept of Art, Murray KY (S)

Bissell, R Ward, *Prof,* University of Michigan, Ann Arbor, Dept of History of Art, Ann Arbor MI (S)

Bissett, George Ann, *CFRE Exec Dir,* Dunedin Fine Art Center, Dunedin FL (S)

Bisson, Mariella, *Instr,* Woodstock School of Art, Inc, Woodstock NY (S)

Bissonnette, Daniel, *Dir,* Musee Regional de Vaudreuil-Soulanges, Vaudreuil-Dorion PQ

Bissonnette, Daniel, *Dir,* Musee Regional de Vaudreuil-Soulanges, Centre d'Histoire d'la Presqu'ile, Vaudreuil-Dorion PQ

Biswell, Lizz, *Educ & Outreach Coordr,* College of Charleston School of Arts, Halsey Institute of Contemporary Art, Charleston SC

Bithell, David, *Asst Prof Art,* Southern Oregon University, Art & Art History Dept, Ashland OR (S)

Bittel, Erica, *Instr,* Fort Hays State University, Dept of Art & Design, Hays KS (S)

Bitter, Ann, *Admin Dir,* Walker Art Center, Minneapolis MN

Bitters, Shawn (Daina), *Asst Prof,* University of Kansas, The School of the Arts, Dept of Visual Art, Lawrence KS (S)

Bittick, Ann, *Instr,* Southern Arkansas University at Magnolia, Dept of Art & Design, Magnolia AR (S)

Bittman, Dan, *Instr Computer Graphics,* The Art Institute of Cincinnati, AIC College of Design, Cincinnati OH (S)

Bittman, Lana, *Elec Resources & Serials,* Fashion Institute of Technology, Gladys Marcus Library - SUNY, New York NY

Bitz, Gwen, *Registrar,* Walker Art Center, Minneapolis MN

Bixler, Nancy, *Admin Asst,* Kennebec Valley Art Association, Harlow Gallery, Hallowell ME

Bizzarro, Tina Walduier, *Chmn Div,* Rosemont College, Art Program, Rosemont PA (S)

Bjarke, Amy, *Gallery Shop Mgr,* Fuller Lodge Art Center, Los Alamos NM

Bjarnesen, Lynne, *Exec Dir,* Danville Museum of Fine Arts & History, Danville VA

Bjelajac, David, *Prof,* George Washington University, Dept of Art of Fine Arts & Art History, Washington DC (S)

Bjorklund, Dana, *Technical Svcs Librn,* Cleveland Institute of Art, Jessica Gund Memorial Library, Cleveland OH

Bjornseth, Dick, *Cur,* Valdosta State University, Art Gallery, Valdosta GA

Bjurlin, Marvin, *Prof,* State University of New York at Fredonia, Dept of Art, Fredonia NY (S)

Blache, Gerard J, *Buildings & Grounds Supt,* National Trust for Historic Preservation, Chesterwood, Stockbridge MA

Block, Sarah, *Admin Support,* Mount Royal College, Dept of Interior Design, Calgary AB (S)

Blocker, Jane, *Assoc Prof,* University of Minnesota, Minneapolis, Art History, Minneapolis MN (S)

Blocksome, Rebecca, *Grant Writer,* University of Kansas, Spencer Museum of Art, Lawrence KS

Blocton, Lulu, *Chmn,* Eastern Connecticut State University, Fine Arts Dept, Willimantic CT (S)

Bloemink, Barbara, *Exec Dir,* Anderson Ranch Arts Center, Snowmass Village CO

Bloess, Elizabeth, *Mus Opers Supv,* Forest Lawn Museum, Glendale CA

Blomberg, Nancy, *Cur Native Arts,* Denver Art Museum, Denver CO

Blondin, Bruce, *Instr,* Solano Community College, Division of Fine & Applied Art & Behavioral Science, Fairfield CA (S)

Blondin, Jill, *Asst Prof,* University of Texas at Tyler, Department of Art, School of Visual & Performing Arts, Tyler TX (S)

Blood, Peggy, *Dir,* Savannah State University, Dept of Fine Arts, Savannah GA (S)

Bloodgood, Craig, *Contemporary Cur,* Art Complex Museum, Carl A. Weyerhaeuser Library, Duxbury MA

Bloodgood, Josephine, *Exec Dir & Cur Permanent Coll,* Woodstock Artists Association & Museum, Woodstock NY

Bloom, Beth, *Art Librn,* Seton Hall University, Walsh Gallery & Library, South Orange NJ

Bloom, Ken, *Dir,* University of Minnesota Duluth, Tweed Museum of Art, Duluth MN

Bloom, Sharon, *Chmn,* West Shore Community College, Division of Humanities & Fine Arts, Scottville MI (S)

Bloom, Sue, *Dept Head,* Western Maryland College, Dept of Art & Art History, Westminster MD (S)

Bloomenthal, Steven, *Asst to Dir,* The Guild of Boston Artists, Boston MA

Bloomer, Harlan, *Dir,* Minnesota State University, Mankato, Mankato MN

Bloomer, Jerry, *Secy-Treas,* R W Norton Art Foundation, Library, Shreveport LA

Bloomer, Jerry M, *Secy-Treas & Dir Pub Rels,* R W Norton Art Foundation, R W Norton Art Gallery, Shreveport LA

Bloomfield, Debra, *Instr,* Solano Community College, Division of Fine & Applied Art & Behavioral Science, Fairfield CA (S)

Bloomquist, Charly, *Instr,* Whitman College, Art Dept, Walla Walla WA (S)

Blosser, John, *Chmn,* Goshen College, Art Dept, Goshen IN (S)

Blount, Amy, *Instr,* Pierce College, Art Dept, Woodland Hills CA (S)

Blount, Wayne, *Bldg Supt,* Birmingham Museum of Art, Birmingham AL

Blount, Wayne, *Bldg Supt,* Birmingham Museum of Art, Clarence B Hanson Jr Library, Birmingham AL

Blue, Carol, *Cur Educ,* Branigan Cultural Center, Las Cruces NM

Bluemlein, Tom, *Pres,* Cincinnati Art Club, Cincinnati OH

Blue Spruce, George, *Secy,* Heard Museum, Billie Jane Baguley Library and Archives, Phoenix AZ

Bluewater, Marty, *Exec Dir,* United Indians of All Tribes Foundation, Daybreak Star Center Gallery, Seattle WA

Blum, Bernard, *Pres,* Leo Baeck, New York NY

Blum-Cumming, Nancy, *Lectr,* University of Wisconsin-Stout, Dept of Art & Design, Menomonie WI (S)

Blumberg, Adam, *Interim Preparator,* Temple University, Tyler School of Art-Galleries, Philadelphia PA

Blumberg, Linda, *Exec Dir,* Art Dealers Association of America, Inc, New York NY

Blume, Peter F, *Dir,* Ball State University, Museum of Art, Muncie IN

Boada, Maria, *Gen Educ,* Art Institute of Pittsburgh, Pittsburgh PA (S)

Board, Aaron, *Instr,* Mohawk Valley Community College, Utica NY (S)

Boatman, Linda, *Pres,* Palette & Chisel Academy of Fine Arts, Chicago IL

Bober, Jacqueline, *Cur,* City of Lubbock, Buddy Holly Center, Lubbock TX

Bober, Jonathan, *Sr Cur,* University of Texas at Austin, Blanton Museum of Art, Austin TX

Bobick, Bruce, *Chmn,* State University of West Georgia, Art Dept, Carrollton GA (S)

Bobo, Susan, *Architecture Librn,* Oklahoma State University, Architecture Library, Stillwater OK

Bocci, Roberto, *Prof,* Georgetown University, Dept of Art & Art History, Washington DC (S)

Bochicchio, Nicholas, *Dir Admin Servs,* Ferguson Library, Stamford CT

Bochnowski, Jean, *Dir,* National Audubon Society, John James Audubon Center at Mill Grove, Audubon PA

Bock, Sally, *Office Admin,* Eastern Illinois University, Tarble Arts Center, Charleston IL

Bockbrader, Nancy, *Prof, Chairperson,* Rhode Island College, Art Dept, Providence RI (S)

Bockelman, James, *Dir,* Concordia University, Marxhausen Art Gallery, Seward NE

Bockelman, Jim, *Prof,* Concordia University, Art Dept, Seward NE (S)

Bocz, George, *Assoc Prof,* Florida State University, Art Dept, Tallahassee FL (S)

Boden, Jim, *Prof Painting & Drawing,* Coker College, Art Dept, Hartsville SC (S)

Bodenheimer, Louise, *Asst Prof,* Southeast Missouri State University, Dept of Art, Cape Girardeau MO (S)

Bodily, Vince, *Instr,* Ricks College, Dept of Art, Rexburg ID (S)

Bodine, William, *Dir,* The Frick Art & Historical Center, Inc, Frick Art Museum, Pittsburgh PA

Bodish, Glenn, *Dir,* Butte Silver Bow Arts Chateau, Butte MT

Bodle, Kelli, *Asst Cur,* Boca Raton Museum of Art, Boca Raton FL

Bodorff, Richard, *Chmn,* Academy Art Museum, Easton MD

Boehler, Zack, *Educ Dir,* Ashford Hollow Foundation for Visual & Performing Arts, Griffis Sculpture Park, East Otto NY

Boehme, Doro, *Artists' Book Coll Specialist,* School of the Art Institute of Chicago, John M Flaxman Library, Chicago IL

Boehme, Sarah E, *Dir Stark Mus of Art,* Nelda C & H J Lutcher Stark, Stark Museum of Art, Orange TX

Boehr, Kay M, *Asst Prof,* Park University, Dept of Art & Design, Parkville MO (S)

Boerner, Anne, *Chief Enrol Officer,* Oregon College of Art & Craft, Portland OR (S)

Boerner, Steve, *Librn & Archivist,* East Hampton Library, Long Island Collection, East Hampton NY

Boettcher, Chris, *Exec Dir,* Randall Junior Museum, San Francisco CA

Boettcher, Graham, *Cur American Art,* Birmingham Museum of Art, Birmingham AL

Bogans, Alphonso, *Bldg & Grounds Mgr,* Albany Museum of Art, Albany GA

Bogart, Michele H, *Prof,* Stony Brook University, College of Arts & Sciences, Dept of Art, Stony Brook NY (S)

Bogdanov, Branka, *Dir Film & Video,* Institute of Contemporary Art, Boston MA

Bogdanov, Kristina, *Asst Prof,* Ohio Wesleyan University, Fine Arts Dept, Delaware OH (S)

Bogel, Ingrid E, *Exec Dir,* Conservation Center for Art & Historic Artifacts, Philadelphia PA

Bogen, David, *VPres Acad & Provost,* Emily Carr University of Art + Design, Vancouver BC (S)

Boger, Christyl, *Asst Prof,* Indiana University, Bloomington, Henry Radford Hope School of Fine Arts, Bloomington IN (S)

Boggess, Lynn, *Prof,* Fairmont State College, Div of Fine Arts, Fairmont WV (S)

Boggs, David, *Assoc Prof,* Concordia College, Art Dept, Moorhead MN (S)

Bogle, Bridgett, *Instr,* Sinclair Community College, Division of Fine & Performing Arts, Dayton OH (S)

Bognar, Pat, *Dir,* University of Portland, Buckley Center Gallery, Portland OR

Bogoniewski, Scott, *Chmn Entertainment Arts,* College for Creative Studies, Detroit MI (S)

Bogosian, David, *Chief Preparator,* Purchase College, Neuberger Museum of Art, Purchase NY

Bohan, Ruth, *Assoc Prof,* University of Missouri, Saint Louis, Dept of Art & Art History, Saint Louis MO (S)

Bohanon, Gloria, *Prof,* Los Angeles City College, Dept of Art, Los Angeles CA (S)

Bohlen, H David, *Asst Cur Zoology,* Illinois State Museum, Museum Store, Chicago IL

Bohlinger, Karen, *Exec Dir,* Holter Museum of Art, Helena MT

Bohls, Margaret, *Asst Prof,* University of Minnesota, Minneapolis, Dept of Art, Minneapolis MN (S)

Bohn, Babette, *Prof,* Texas Christian University, School of Art, Fort Worth TX (S)

Bohnert, Thomas, *Prof,* Mott Community College, Fine Arts & Social Sciences Division, Flint MI (S)

Bohr, Ted, *Gallery Dir,* Creighton University, Fine & Performing Arts Dept, Omaha NE (S)

Bohrer, Fred, *Assoc Prof,* Hood College, Dept of Art, Frederick MD (S)

Boisselle, Melissa, *Dir,* Wistariahurst Museum, Holyoke MA

Bokelman, Dorothy, *Dir,* Nazareth College of Rochester, Art Dept, Rochester NY (S)

Bol, Marsha, *Dir,* Museum of New Mexico, Museum of International Folk Art, Santa Fe NM

Boland, Lynn, *Cur European Art,* University of Georgia, Georgia Museum of Art, Athens GA

Bolcer, John, *Univ Archivist,* University of Washington, Univ of Washington Libraries, Special Collections, Seattle WA

Bolden, Joyce, *Chmn,* Alcorn State University, Dept of Fine Arts, Lorman MS (S)

Boldenow, John, *Theatre Develop,* Wichita Center for the Arts, Mary R Koch School of Visual Arts, Wichita KS (S)

Boldenow, John, *Theatre Dir,* Wichita Center for the Arts, Wichita KS

Bolding, Gary, *Prof,* Stetson University, Department of Creative Arts, Deland FL (S)

Bolduc, Leonard K, *Pres,* Springfield Art & Historical Society, The Miller Art Center, Springfield VT

Bolduc, Maureen, *Dir,* Springfield Art & Historical Society, The Miller Art Center, Springfield VT

Bolen, Jerry, *Dept Head,* Southwestern Illinois College, Art Dept, Belleville IL (S)

Bolen, Virginia, *Librn,* Schenectady County Historical Society, Museum of Schenectady History, Schenectady NY

Bolge, George, *CEO,* Museum of Florida Art, Deland FL

Bolger, Doreen, *Dir,* The Baltimore Museum of Art, Baltimore MD

Bolger, Laurie, *Conservation Librn,* University Club Library, New York NY

Bolker, Mare, *Vis Asst Prof Art,* Whitman College, Art Dept, Walla Walla WA (S)

Boll, Alicia, *Gallery Guard,* University of Wisconsin, Union Art Gallery, Milwaukee WI

Bollinger, Ben, *Dean of Faculty,* Citrus College, Art Dept, Glendora CA (S)

Bollmann, Marc, *Library Asst,* University of Rochester, Art/Music Library, Rochester NY

Bolon, Donald, *Treas,* Print Club of Albany, Albany NY

Bolourchi, Pati, *Librn,* Detroit Public Library, Art & Literature Dept, Detroit MI

Bolser, Barbara, *Asst Prof,* University of Illinois at Springfield, Visual Arts Program, Springfield IL (S)

Bolt, Ed, *Mill Site Mgr,* Pickens County Museum of Art & History, Pickens SC

Bolt, Macyn, *Preparator,* Fried, Frank, Harris, Shriver & Jacobson, Art Collection, New York NY

Boltan, Randy, *Head Dept Print Media,* Cranbrook Academy of Art, Bloomfield Hills MI (S)

Bolton, Bruce, *Dir Bus Opers,* Ministry of Alberta Culture, Royal Alberta Museum, Edmonton AB

Bolton, David, *Ceramics,* College of Lake County, Art Dept, Grayslake IL (S)

Bolton, Mary Rose, *Mem, Dir Fellows & Spec Prog,* Harvard University, Harvard University Art Museums, Cambridge MA

Bomberg, Nathalie, *Assoc Dir Laurel Opers,* Okanagan Heritage Museum, Kelowna BC

Bomberger, Bruce, *Cur,* Landis Valley Village and Farm Museum, PA Historical & Museum Commission, Lancaster PA

Bomberger, Bruce D, *Cur,* Landis Valley Village and Farm Museum, PA Historical & Museum Commission, Landis Collections Gallery, Lancaster PA

Bomford, David, *Acting Dir,* Getty Center, The J Paul Getty Museum, Los Angeles CA

Bomford, David, *Acting Dir,* Getty Center, The J Paul Getty Museum - Getty Villa, Los Angeles CA

Bomford, David, *Dir,* J Paul Getty Museum at the Getty Villa, Pacific Palisades CA

Bonanno, Michael, *Dir Educ,* USS Constitution Museum, Boston MA

Bonansinga, Kate, *Dir,* University of Texas at El Paso, Stanlee & Gerald Rubin Center for the Visual Arts, El Paso TX

Bonario, Bernard, *Chmn Art History,* University of Saint Thomas, Fine and Performing Arts Dept, Houston TX (S)

Bond, Anne Wainestein, *Dir Coll & Exhibits,* Colorado Historical Society, Colorado History Museum, Denver CO

Bond, Edith, *IT,* University of Kansas, Spencer Museum of Art, Lawrence KS

Bond, Hallie, *Cur,* The Adirondack Historical Association, The Adirondack Museum, Blue Mountain Lake NY

Bond, Janet, *Reference Librn,* Kutztown University, Rohrbach Library, Kutztown PA

Bond, Kener E, *Prof,* Rochester Institute of Technology, School of Design, Rochester NY (S)

Bond, Randall, *Fine Arts Librn,* Syracuse University, Syracuse University Library, Syracuse NY

Bondarchuk, Karen, *Foundation Area Coordr Sculpture,* Western Michigan University, Frostic School of Art, Kalamazoo MI (S)

Bonde, Sheila, *Prof,* Brown University, Dept History of Art & Architecture, Providence RI (S)

Bondil, Natalie, *Chief Conservator,* Montreal Museum of Fine Arts, Montreal PQ

Bone, Lloyd E, *Chmn,* Glenville State College, Dept of Fine Arts, Glenville WV (S)

Bongiovanni, Alessia, *Mem & Develop Coordr,* Canadian Conference of the Arts, Ottawa ON

Bonilla, Ileana, *Asst Cur,* Wells Fargo & Co, History Museum, Los Angeles CA

Bonin Pissarro, Frederic, *Instr Illustration & Design,* The Art Institute of Cincinnati, AIC College of Design, Cincinnati OH (S)

Bonjorni, Mary Ann, *Assoc Prof,* University of Montana, Dept of Art, Missoula MT (S)

Bonn, Claudia, *Dir Exec/Pres,* Wave Hill, Bronx NY

Bonnelly, Claude, *Dir Gen Library System,* L'Universite Laval, Library, Quebec PQ

Bonner, Charles, *Artist,* Keystone Gallery, Scott City KS

Bonner, Jean, *Dean Art Dept,* Schoolcraft College, Dept of Art & Design, Livonia MI (S)

Bonner, Judith H, *Sr Cur,* The Historic New Orleans Collection, Royal Street Galleries, New Orleans LA

Bonner, Logan, *Web Designer,* Keystone Gallery, Scott City KS

Bonner, Peter, *Adj Prof,* Saint Joseph's University, Art Dept, Philadelphia PA (S)

Bonning, Jack, *Exec Dir,* Dallas Historical Society, Hall of State, Dallas TX

Bonny, Francesca B, *Cur,* The Nemours Foundatioin, Nemours Mansion & Gardens, Wilmington DE

Bonsall, Mark B, *Vice Chair,* Heard Museum, Billie Jane Baguley Library and Archives, Phoenix AZ

Bontrager, Nick, *Prof,* Texas Christian University, School of Art, Fort Worth TX (S)

Bonzelaar, Helen, *Prof,* Calvin College, Art Dept, Grand Rapids MI (S)

Book, Michael, *Assoc Prof,* Louisiana State University, School of Art, Baton Rouge LA (S)

Booker, Mary Ames, *Cur Colls,* State of North Carolina, Battleship North Carolina, Wilmington NC

Booker, Robert, *Chief Security,* Brandywine Conservancy, Brandywine River Museum, Chadds Ford PA

Booker, Robert, *Exec Dir,* Arizona Commission on the Arts, Phoenix AZ

Booker, Robert C, *Exec Dir,* Arizona Commission on the Arts, Reference Library, Phoenix AZ

Bookout, Ann, *Regent,* Mount Vernon Ladies' Association of the Union, Mount Vernon VA

Bookwalter, Thomas, *Asst Prof,* Kansas State University, Art Dept, Manhattan KS (S)

Boone, Allyn, *Develop Dir,* Lauren Rogers, Laurel MS

Boone, Elizabeth, *Prof,* Tulane University, Sophie H Newcomb Memorial College, New Orleans LA (S)

Boord, Charlotte, *Mus Supv,* City of San Antonio, San Antonio TX

Boorsch, Suzanne, *Cur Prints, Drawings & Photographs,* Yale University, Yale University Art Gallery, New Haven CT

Boot, Lee, *Affiliate Assoc Prof & Assoc Dir Imaging Research Ctr,* University of Maryland, Baltimore County, Imaging & Digital Arts (IMDA), Dept of Visual Arts, Baltimore MD (S)

Booth, David W, *Instr,* Universite de Montreal, Dept of Art History, Montreal PQ (S)

Booth, Helen, *Cur & Dir,* Jordan Historical Museum of The Twenty, Jordan ON

Booth, Michael, *Chmn,* Blue Mountain Community College, Fine Arts Dept, Pendleton OR (S)

Booth, Paul, *Asst Prof,* Fort Lewis College, Art Dept, Durango CO (S)

Booth, Paula, *Dir Gallery,* Western Oregon University, Dan & Gail Cannon Gallery of Art, Monmouth OR

Booth, Peter, *Dir,* Museum of Western Colorado, Museum of the West, Grand Junction CO

Booth, Robert, *Prof,* State University of New York at Fredonia, Dept of Art, Fredonia NY (S)

Boothby, Ron, *Dir Facilities,* Kalamazoo Institute of Arts, Kalamazoo MI

Boothe, Berrisford, *Assoc Prof,* Lehigh University, Dept of Art, Architecture & Design, Bethlehem PA (S)

Boothe, Constance, *Instr,* Clark-Atlanta University, School of Arts & Sciences, Atlanta GA (S)

Boothe, Power, *Dir,* Ohio University, School of Art, Athens OH (S)

Bopp, Jay, *Chmn,* Bob Jones University, School of Fine Arts, Div of Art & Design, Greenville SC (S)

Boppel, Todd, *Prof,* University of Wisconsin-Stout, Dept of Art & Design, Menomonie WI (S)

Borato, Meghan, *Registrar,* Society for Photographic Education (SPE), SPE Gallery, Cleveland OH

Borchardt, Ali, *Dir Educ,* Columbia Museum of Art, Columbia SC

Borchardt, Susan, *Cur,* Gunston Hall Plantation, Library, Mason Neck VA

Borchardt, Susan A, *Asst Dir,* Gunston Hall Plantation, Mason Neck VA

Borcherbing, Kate, *Asst Prof,* Sam Houston State University, Art Dept, Huntsville TX (S)

Bordeaux, Mary, *Cur,* Heritage Center, Inc, Pine Ridge SD

Borden, Lee, *Events & Commun,* Western Colorado Center for the Arts, The Art Center, Grand Junction CO

Borden, Tamika, *Dir,* Cambria Historical Society, New Providence NJ

Bordowitz, Gregg, *Chmn Film, Video, New Media & Animation,* School of the Art Institute of Chicago, Chicago IL (S)

Boreen, Jean, *Assoc Dean,* Northern Arizona University, College of Arts & Letters, Flagstaff AZ (S)

Boresen, Gloria, *Gen Mgr,* Fort Collins Museum of Art, Inc., Fort Collins CO

Borge, John, *Instr,* Concordia College, Art Dept, Moorhead MN (S)

Borges, Seb, *Gen Mgr,* Providence Art Club, Providence RI

Borgeson, Jacquelyn, *Cur,* Martin and Osa Johnson, Imperato Collection of West African Artifacts, Chanute KS

Borgeson, Jacquelyn, *Cur,* Martin and Osa Johnson, Johnson Collection of Photographs, Movies & Memorabilia, Chanute KS

Borgeson, Jacquelyn, *Cur,* Martin and Osa Johnson, Selsor Art Gallery, Chanute KS

Borgeson, Jacquelyn, *Cur,* Martin and Osa Johnson, Scott Explorers Library, Chanute KS

Borgeson, Jacquelyn L, *Cur,* Martin and Osa Johnson, Chanute KS

Boring, Christine, *Exec Dir,* Arts on the Park, Lakeland Center for Creative Arts, Lakeland FL

Boris, Lexi, *Communs Dir,* Virginia Center for the Creative Arts, Amherst VA

Bork, Eric, *Exhibit Specialist/Preparator,* University of Memphis, Art Museum, Memphis TN

Borland, Jennifer, *Assoc Prof,* Oklahoma State University, Department of Art, Graphic Design and Art History, Stillwater OK (S)

Born, Nahamni, *Admin,* Huronia Museum, Gallery of Historic Huronia, Midland ON

Born, Richard A, *Sr Cur,* University of Chicago, Smart Museum of Art, Chicago IL

Bornarth, Philip W, *Prof,* Rochester Institute of Technology, School of Design, Rochester NY (S)

Borneman, Laura, *Assoc Prof,* Bakersfield College, Art Dept, Bakersfield CA (S)

Borntrager, Amy, *Develop Officer,* National Postal Museum, Smithsonian Institution, Washington DC

Borowy-Reeder, Elysia, *Exec Dir,* CAM Contemporary Art Museum, Raleigh NC

Borromeo, Gina, *Cur Ancient Art,* Rhode Island School of Design, Museum of Art, Providence RI

Borrowdale-Cox, Deborah, *Dir Educ,* The Art Museum at the University of Kentucky, Lexington KY

Borsanyi, Jackie, *Cur Exhibs,* Foosaner Art Museum, Melbourne FL

Borst, Kim, *Lectr,* University of Wisconsin-Superior, Programs in the Visual Arts, Superior WI (S)

Bortolussi, Jacquelyn, *Admin Asst,* Open Space, Victoria BC

Boruchov, Zoya, *Gallery Mgr,* Contemporary Art Gallery, Vancouver BC

Borys, Stephen D, *Dir,* The Winnipeg Art Gallery, Winnipeg MB

Bos, Rob, *Visual & Media Arts Coordr,* Organization of Saskatchewan Arts Councils (OSAC), Regina SK

Bos, Rosanne, *2nd VPres,* Frontier Gateway Museum, Glendive MT

Bos, Saskia, *Dean,* Cooper Union, School of Art, New York NY (S)

Bosch, Doug, *Assoc Prof, Found Coordr,* Rhode Island College, Art Dept, Providence RI (S)

Bosch, Jorge, *Pres,* New York Society of Architects, New York NY

Bosco, Bob, *Instr,* Creighton University, Fine & Performing Arts Dept, Omaha NE (S)

Bosco, Christine, *Dir Spec Events & Facility Rental,* Caramoor Center for Music & the Arts, Inc, Rosen House at Caramoor, Katonah NY

Bose, Arvn, *Assoc Prof,* Herbert H Lehman, Art Dept, Bronx NY (S)

Boshart, Jeff, *Prof,* Eastern Illinois University, Art Dept, Charleston IL (S)

Boshart, Jon D, *Chmn,* Saint Peter's College, Fine Arts Dept, Jersey City NJ (S)

Bosiak, Amanda, *Mem Svcs Coordr,* Saskatchewan Craft Council & Affinity Gallery, Saskatoon SK

Bosse, David C, *Librn,* Historic Deerfield, Inc, Henry N Flynt Library, Deerfield MA

Bosselmann, Peter, *Prof Urban Design in Architecture, Head Grad Adviser & Head Master Urban Design Prog,* University of California, Berkeley, College of Environmental Design, Berkeley CA (S)

Bosso, O Robert, *Thesis Adv,* Toronto Art Therapy Institute, Toronto ON (S)

Bosson, Jack, *Chmn Animation,* Woodbury University, Dept of Graphic Design, Burbank CA (S)

Bostick, Al, *Security Officer,* Morris Museum of Art, Augusta GA

Bostock, Bret, *Colls Mgr,* Academy of the New Church, Glencairn Museum, Bryn Athyn PA

Boston, Carmen, *Arts Educ Mgr,* National Assembly of State Arts Agencies, Washington DC

Bostrom, Antonia, *Sr Cur Sculpture & Decorative Arts,* Getty Center, The J Paul Getty Museum, Los Angeles CA

Bostrom, Jane, *Spec Events,* Eastern Shore Art Association, Inc, Eastern Shore Art Center, Fairhope AL

Bostrom, Leslie, *Assoc Prof,* Brown University, Dept of Visual Art, Providence RI (S)

Bostwick, Betsy, *Dir,* New Visions Gallery, Inc, Marshfield WI

Boswell, Tracy, *Adjunct Prof Art History,* Johnson County Community College, Fine Arts Dept & Art History Dept, Overland Park KS (S)

Bosworth, Barbara, *Chmn Media,* Massachusetts College of Art, Boston MA (S)

Botar, Oliver, *Assoc Prof,* University of Manitoba, School of Art, Winnipeg MB (S)

Bothwell, Anne, *Dir,* Texas Christian University, Moudy Gallery, Fort Worth TX

Botier, Saul, *Student Employee,* Manhattanville College, Brownson Gallery, Purchase NY

Botier, Saul, *Student Employee,* Manhattanville College, Arthur M Berger Gallery, Purchase NY

Botti-Salitsky, Rose, *Lectr,* Mount Ida College, Chamberlayne School of Design & Merchandising, Boston MA (S)

Bottinelli, Lora, *Exec Dir,* Salisbury University, Ward Museum of Wildfowl Art, Salisbury MD

Bottomley, Kristina, *Registrar,* Northwestern University, Mary & Leigh Block Museum of Art, Evanston IL

Bottomly-O'Looney, Jennifer, *Registrar,* Montana Historical Society, Helena MT

Botts, Carroll, *Head Reference Librn,* University of New Mexico, Fine Arts Library, Albuquerque NM

Botwinick, Michael, *Dir,* Newport Harbor Art Museum, Newport Beach CA

Botwinick, Michael, *Dir,* The Hudson River Museum, Yonkers NY

Bouc, Rod, *Deputy Dir Oper,* Columbus Museum of Art, Columbus OH

Bouchard, Karen, *Assoc Cur,* Brown University, Art Slide Library, Providence RI

Bouche, Anne-Marie, *Prof,* Princeton University, Dept of Art & Archaeology, Princeton NJ (S)

Bouche, Nicole, *Pacific Northwest Cur,* University of Washington, Univ of Washington Libraries, Special Collections, Seattle WA

Boucher, Barbara, *Dir,* Mohawk Valley Center for the Arts Inc, Little Falls NY

Boucher, Bruce, *Cur European Decorative Arts, Sculpture & Classical Art,* The Art Institute of Chicago, Chicago IL

Boucher, Bruce, *Dir,* University of Virginia, The Fralin Museum of Art at the University of Virginia, Charlottesville VA

Boucher, Kathryn, *Dir,* Converse College, Milliken Art Gallery, Spartanburg SC

Boudet, Daniel, *Web & eMktg Mgr,* Cultural Council of Palm Beach County, Lake Worth FL

Boughton, Douglas, *Dir School of Art,* Northern Illinois University, School of Art, DeKalb IL (S)

Bouknight, Alice, *Cur Educational Servs,* University of South Carolina, McKissick Museum, Columbia SC

Boulanger, Jennifer, *Dean,* Herkimer County Community College, Humanities Social Services, Herkimer NY (S)

Boulton, Anna, *Community Outreach Mgr,* Utah Arts Council, Chase Home Museum of Utah Folk Arts, Salt Lake City UT

Bourassa, Linda, *Prof,* Hiram College, Art Dept, Hiram OH (S)

Bourassa, Paul, *Dir Research & Coll,* Musee National des Beaux Arts du Quebec, Quebec PQ

Bourbeau, Melanie, *Cur,* Hill-Stead Museum, Farmington CT

Bourbon, Matthew, *Assoc Prof Drawing & Painting,* University of North Texas, College of Visual Arts & Design, Denton TX (S)

Bourcier, Paul, *Cur Political, Armaments,* Wisconsin Historical Society, Wisconsin Historical Museum, Madison WI

Bourdeau, Colleen, *Mktg & Special Events,* Auburn University, Julie Collins Smith Museum, Auburn AL

Bourdeau, James, *Mgr Fine Arts, Papers & Textiles,* Department of Canadian Heritage, Canadian Conservation Institute, Ottawa ON

Bourgault, Therese, *Librn Periodicals,* Montreal Museum of Fine Arts, Library, Montreal PQ

Bourgeau, Jef, *Contact,* Museum of New Art, Pontiac MI

Bourgeois, Amy, *Sales Mgr,* Vermont State Craft Center at Frog Hollow, Burlington VT

Bourgeois, Angi, *Asst Prof,* Mississippi State University, Dept of Art, Starville MS (S)

Bourque, Paul, *Technician,* Galerie d'art de l'Universite de Moncton, Moncton NB

Bouse, Heidi, *Dir Admin,* Arts Place, Inc., Hugh N Ronald Memorial Gallery, Portland IN

Bousquet, Laurence, *Pres Bd Trustees,* Everson Museum of Art, Syracuse NY

Bousson, Susie, *Admin,* Lannan Foundation, Santa Fe NM

Bouthillier, Rose, *Asst Cur,* Oakville Galleries, Centennial Square and Gairloch Gardens, Oakville ON

Bouw, Jonathan, *Assoc Prof,* Taylor University, Visual Art Dept, Upland IN (S)

Bouw, Jonathan, *Chmn,* Taylor University, Metcalf Art Gallery, Upland IN

Bowar, Sharon, *Assoc Prof,* Wilkes University, Dept of Art, Wilkes-Barre PA (S)

Bowcutt, Jason, *Performing Arts Coordr,* Utah Arts Council, Chase Home Museum of Utah Folk Arts, Salt Lake City UT

Bowden, Sue, *Mus Shop Mgr,* Sandwich Historical Society, Center Sandwich NH

Bowditch, Lucy, *Asst Prof,* College of Saint Rose, The Center For Art and Design, Albany NY (S)

Bowen, Betsy, *Mus Shop Mgr,* Grounds for Sculpture, Hamilton NJ

Bowen, Jeffrey, *Asst Dir External Affairs,* Art Museum of the University of Houston, Blaffer Gallery, Houston TX

Bowen, Jen, *Asst Mus Mgr,* Riverside County Museum, Edward-Dean Museum & Gardens, Cherry Valley CA

Bowen, Kasuya, *Assoc Prof,* Florida State University, Art Dept, Tallahassee FL (S)

Bowen, Katrina, *Reference,* Mason City Public Library, Mason City IA

Bowen, Ken, *Adjunct Instr,* Virginia Wesleyan College, Art Dept of the Humanities Div, Norfolk VA (S)

Bowen, Linnell R, *Exec Dir,* Maryland Hall for the Creative Arts, Chaney Gallery, Annapolis MD

Bowen, Nancy, *Assoc Prof,* Purchase College, State University of New York, School of Art+Design, Purchase NY (S)

Bowen, Tracey, *Coordr Art Placement,* Visual Arts Ontario, Toronto ON

Bower, Bob, *Div Dir,* Southwestern Oregon Community College, Visual Arts Dept, Coos Bay OR (S)

Bower, Brook, *Asst Cur,* Appalachian State University, Turchin Center for the Visual Arts, Boone NC

Bower, Gerald, *Prof,* Louisiana State University, School of Art, Baton Rouge LA (S)

Bower, Joe, *Dir Develop,* Kalamazoo Institute of Arts, Kalamazoo MI

Bower, Joe, *Dir Develop,* Kalamazoo Institute of Arts, The Mary & Edwin Meader Fine Arts Library, Kalamazoo MI

Bower, Mary, *Cur,* Evansville Museum of Arts, History & Science, Henry R Walker Jr Memorial Art Library, Evansville IN

Bower, Mary, *Cur Coll,* Evansville Museum of Arts, History & Science, Evansville IN

Bower-Peterson, Kathi, *Librn,* Library Association of La Jolla, Athenaeum Music & Arts Library, La Jolla CA

Bowerman, Douglas, *Bldg Operations Mgr,* Allentown Art Museum, Allentown PA

Bowers, Emma, *Dir,* Roberts County Museum, Miami TX

Bowers, John, *Asst Prof,* Oregon State University, Dept of Art, Corvallis OR (S)

Bowers, Paul, *Prof,* State University of New York at Fredonia, Dept of Art, Fredonia NY (S)

Bowers, Stacey, *Dir Bus Develop,* Special Libraries Association, Alexandria VA

Bowers, Tiffini, *Cur History,* California African-American Museum, Los Angeles CA

Bowhan, Elizabeth, *Pres,* The Art Museum of Eastern Idaho, Idaho Falls ID

Bowie, Barbara, *Dir Retail Svcs,* Witte Museum, San Antonio TX

Bowie, Elizabeth, *Cur Center for So Craft & Design,* The Ogden Museum of Southern Art, University of New Orleans, New Orleans LA

Bowie, Lucille, *Librn,* Southern University, Architecture Library, Baton Rouge LA

Bowie, Mary, *VPres Finance & Admin,* American Association of Museums, United States National Committee of the International Council of Museums (ICOM-US), Washington DC

Bowitz, John, *Chmn,* Morningside College, Art Dept, Sioux City IA (S)

Bowker, Jeanette, *Treas,* Blacksburg Regional Art Association, Blacksburg VA

Bowles, Johnson, *Asst Prof,* Longwood University, Dept of Art, Farmville VA (S)

Bowles, Kay Johnson, *Dir,* Longwood Center for the Visual Arts, Farmville VA

Bowles, Ron, *Dean Fine Arts,* Dallas Baptist University, Dept of Art, Dallas TX (S)

Bowles, Sandra, *Exec Dir & Ed,* Handweavers Guild of America, Suwanee GA

Bowman, Amy, *Adj Instr,* University of West Florida, Dept of Art, Pensacola FL (S)

Bowman, Amy, *Dir,* University of West Florida, Art Gallery, Pensacola FL

Bowman, Debbie, *Deputy Dir Opers,* Cincinnati Art Museum, Cincinnati Art Museum, Cincinnati OH

Bowman, Donna, *Vis Arts Librn,* University of Regina, Education/Fine Arts Library, Regina SK

Bowman, James, *Registrar & Exhib Preparator,* Dickinson College, The Trout Gallery, Carlisle PA

Bowman, Jaron, *House Mgr,* District of Columbia Arts Center (DCAC), Washington DC

Bowman, Jim, *Archivist,* Glenbow Museum, Library, Calgary AB

Bowman, John, *Assoc Prof Art (Drawing/Painting),* Pennsylvania State University, University Park, Penn State School of Visual Arts, University Park PA (S)

Bowman, Karmien, *Assoc Prof,* Tarrant County College, Art Dept, Hurst TX (S)

Bowman, Lee, *Instr,* Dallas Baptist University, Dept of Art, Dallas TX (S)

Bowman, Roger, *Prof,* University of Central Arkansas, Department of Art, Conway AR (S)

Bowman, Ruth, *Assoc Prof & Undergrad Coordr,* University of Kansas, The School of the Arts, Dept of Visual Art, Lawrence KS (S)

Bowman, Stephanie K, *Asst Prof,* Pittsburg State University, Art Dept, Pittsburg KS (S)

Bownan, JoAnn, *Cur,* Schuyler-Hamilton House, Morristown NJ

Bowser, Diane, *Gen Educ,* Art Institute of Pittsburgh, Pittsburgh PA (S)

Box, Beau, *Visitor Servs,* Tulane University, Newcomb Art Gallery, New Orleans LA

Boyadjian, Ani, *Dept Mgr,* Los Angeles Public Library, Art, Music, Recreation & Rare Books, Los Angeles CA

Boyce, David, *Mgr,* Oatlands Plantation, Leesburg VA

Boyd, Ann, *Co-Dir,* Roy Boyd, Chicago IL

Boyd, Chandra, *Senior Assoc Cur Educ & Mus School Admin,* Oklahoma City Museum of Art, Oklahoma City OK

Boyd, Jamie, *Adjunct Prof,* Community College of Allegheny County, Boyce Campus, Art Dept, Monroeville PA (S)

Boyd, Roy, *Dir,* Roy Boyd, Chicago IL

Boyd-Snee, Rancy, *Lectr,* Southeastern Louisiana University, Dept of Visual Arts, Hammond LA (S)

Boyer, Cindy, *Dir Mus,* Landmark Society of Western New York, Inc, The Campbell-Whittlesey House Museum, Rochester NY

Boyer, Irene, *Registrar Decorative Art,* Illinois State Museum, ISM Lockport Gallery, Chicago Gallery & Southern Illinois Art Gallery, Springfield IL

Boyer, John, *Exec Dir,* Mark Twain, Hartford CT

Boyer, John, *Exec Dir,* Mark Twain, Research Library, Hartford CT

Boyer, Nathan P, *Assoc Prof (Painting & Drawing),* University of Missouri - Columbia, Dept of Art, Columbia MO (S)

Boyer, Ron, *Deacon,* Kateri Tekakwitha Shrine/St. Francis Xavier Mission, Kahnawake PQ

Boyer, Sarah, *Oral Historian,* Cambridge Historical Commission, Research Library on Architectural Social History of Cambridge, Mass, Cambridge MA

Boyer-Reehlin, Nancy, *Cur,* Principia College, School of Nations Museum, Elsah IL

Boyes, Janet W, *Financial Adminr,* Newport Historical Society & Museum of Newport History, Newport RI

Boykin, Emily, *Educ Dir,* R W Norton Art Foundation, R W Norton Art Gallery, Shreveport LA

Boyle-Clapp, Dee, *Dir,* Arts Extension Service, Amherst MA

Boyles, Zoey, *Admin Prog Asst,* Southern Oregon University, Art & Art History Dept, Ashland OR (S)

Boylston, Kristen, *Dir Mktg & Pub Rels,* Telfair Museums' Jepson Center for the Arts Library, Telfair Academy of Arts & Sciences Library, Savannah GA

Boylston, Kristin, *Develop Dir,* Telfair Museums' Jepson Center for the Arts Library, Savannah GA

Bozicnik, Nina, *Asst Cur*, The Currier Museum of Art, Manchester NH

Brabham, Heather, *Mgr Operations & Mem*, University of Tampa, Henry B Plant Museum, Tampa FL

Bracalente, Anita, *Registrar*, Indiana University, Art Museum, Bloomington IN

Bracety, Steve, *Pres*, Prescott Fine Arts Association, Gallery, Prescott AZ

Brack, HG Skip, *Cur*, Davistown Museum, Liberty Location, Liberty ME

Brack, Lillie, *Dir Central Libr*, Kansas City Public Library, Kansas City MO

Brackbill, Eleanor, *Head Mus Educ*, Purchase College, Neuberger Museum of Art, Purchase NY

Brackett, David, *Asst Prof*, University of Kansas, The School of the Arts, Dept of Visual Art, Lawrence KS (S)

Brackman, Bob, *Dir Botanical Gardens*, Cheekwood Nashville's Home of Art & Gardens, Education Dept, Nashville TN (S)

Brackney, Kathryn S, *Head Librn*, Georgia Institute of Technology, College of Architecture Library, Atlanta GA

Bradburn, Douglas, *Libr Dir*, Mount Vernon Ladies' Association of the Union, The Fred W Smith National Library for the Study of George Washington, Mount Vernon VA

Bradbury, Leonie, *Gallery Dir*, Montserrat College of Art, Beverly MA (S)

Braddock, Alan, *Prof*, Syracuse University, Dept of Fine Arts (Art History), Syracuse NY (S)

Braden, Roger, *CEO & Gen Mgr*, Chelan County Public Utility District, Rocky Reach Dam, Wenatchee WA

Bradfield, Jan, *Asst Prof*, Southwestern Oklahoma State University, Art Dept, Weatherford OK (S)

Bradfield, Jan, *Asst Prof*, University of Wisconsin-Green Bay, Arts Dept, Green Bay WI (S)

Bradfield, Nancy, *Office Mgr*, First Tennessee Bank, Memphis TN

Bradford, Barry, *Head of Dept*, Chattanooga-Hamilton County Bicentennial Library, Fine Arts Dept, Chattanooga TN

Bradford, Blaine, *Recruiter*, Northern Illinois University, School of Art, DeKalb IL (S)

Bradham, Sharon, *Exec Dir*, Cedarhurst Center for the Arts, Mitchell Museum, Mount Vernon IL

Bradhead, Heather, *Librn*, Santa Barbara Museum of Art, Santa Barbara CA

Bradley, Alisa, *Museum Mgr*, Mississippi River Museum at Mud-Island River Park, Memphis TN

Bradley, Betsy, *Dir*, Mississippi Museum of Art, Howorth Library, Jackson MS

Bradley, Betsy, *Exec Dir*, Mississippi Museum of Art, Jackson MS

Bradley, Bob, *Cur Colls*, Alabama Department of Archives & History, Museum of Alabama, Montgomery AL

Bradley, David, *Pres*, Arizona Artists Guild, Phoenix AZ

Bradley, Diane, *Pres*, Saint Augustine Art Association and Art Gallery, Saint Augustine FL

Bradley, Douglas, *Cur*, University of Notre Dame, Snite Museum of Art, Notre Dame IN

Bradley, Jennifer, *Dean*, Kirkwood Community College, Dept of Arts & Humanities, Cedar Rapids IA (S)

Bradley, Katherine, *Mem*, Berks Art Alliance, Reading PA

Bradley, Laura E, *Exec Dir*, Germantown Historical Society, Philadelphia PA

Bradley, Laurel, *Dir & Cur*, Carleton College, Art Gallery, Northfield MN

Bradley, Maria, *Asst to Dir*, Academy Art Museum, Easton MD

Bradley, Michelle, *Dir*, Frankfort Community Public Library, Anna & Harlan Hubbard Gallery, Frankfort IN

Bradley, Ray, *Pres Bd*, Rock Ford Foundation, Inc, Rock Ford Plantation, Lancaster PA

Bradley, Richard, *Pres Bd Dirs*, Five Civilized Tribes Museum, Muskogee OK

Bradley, Ross, *Arts Prog Coordr*, Alberta Foundation for the Arts, Edmonton AB

Bradley, Steve, *Assoc Prof & Grad Prog Dir*, University of Maryland, Baltimore County, Imaging & Digital Arts (IMDA), Dept of Visual Arts, Baltimore MD (S)

Bradley, Thomas, *Assoc Dean*, University of Hartford, Hartford Art School, West Hartford CT (S)

Bradley, W Steven, *Assoc Prof*, Colorado Mesa University, Art Dept, Grand Junction CO (S)

Bradner, Anne, *Develop Dir*, Bush-Holley Historic Site & Storehouse Gallery, Greenwich Historical Society/ Bush-Holley House, Cos Cob CT

Bradshaw, Barbara, *Admin Asst*, Piedmont Arts Association, Martinsville VA

Bradshaw, Bruce, *Prin*, Nutana Collegiate Institute, Memorial Library and Art Gallery, Saskatoon SK

Bradshaw, Larry, *Prof*, University of Nebraska at Omaha, Dept of Art & Art History, Omaha NE (S)

Bradshaw, Mark, *Gallery Asst*, Art Association of Harrisburg, School & Galleries, Harrisburg PA

Bradt, Laurie, *Registrar*, Lyme Historical Society, Library, Old Lyme CT

Brady, Denise, *Coordr*, University of Nebraska at Omaha, UNO Art Gallery, Omaha NE

Brady, Edith, *Exec Dir*, City of High Point, High Point Museum, High Point NC

Brady, Elyse, *Exec Dir*, Saint Augustine Art Association and Art Gallery, Saint Augustine FL

Brady, Meghan, *Vis Asst Prof*, Bowdoin College, Art Dept, Brunswick ME (S)

Brady, Susan, *Librn*, Yale University, Yale Center for British Art Reference Library, New Haven CT

Brady-Rumble, Kelly, *Grants Specialist*, Florida International University, The Patricia & Phillip Frost Art Museum, Miami FL

Braff, Arnold, *Co-Treas*, Greenwich Art Society Inc, Greenwich CT

Bragg, Cheryl, *Dir*, Anniston Museum of Natural History, Anniston AL

Bragg, Terry A, *Exec Dir*, State of North Carolina, Battleship North Carolina, Wilmington NC

Braggins, Donna, *Assoc Dean Design Illustration & Photography*, Sheridan College, Faculty of Animation, Arts & Design, Oakville ON (S)

Braide, Carol, *Publs Mgr*, Museum for African Art, New York NY

Braille, A Charles, *Pres*, Art Gallery of Ontario, Toronto ON

Braisted, Todd, *VPres*, Bergen County Historical Society, Steuben House Museum, River Edge NJ

Brake, Karl, *Dir*, Rogue Community College, Wiseman Gallery - FireHouse Gallery, Grants Pass OR

Braman, Andrew, *Controller*, The Rockwell Museum of Western Art, Corning NY

Branaff, Cis, *Prog Mgr*, Pacific Northwest Art School, Gallery at the Wharf, Coupeville WA

Branagan, Carmine, *Dir*, National Academy Museum & School, New York NY

Branagan, Carmine, *Dir*, National Academy Museum & School, Archives, New York NY

Branch, Harrison, *Prof*, Oregon State University, Dept of Art, Corvallis OR (S)

Branchick, Thomas J, *Dir*, Williamstown Art Conservation Center, Williamstown MA

Branco, Susan, *Instr*, Wayne Art Center, Wayne PA (S)

Brandach, Joan, *Newsletter Ed*, North Country Museum of Arts, Park Rapids MN

Branden, Mack, *Chmn*, California Baptist University, Art Dept, Riverside CA (S)

Branden, Shirley, *Head Reference Dept*, University of Delaware, Morris Library, Newark DE

Brander, Susan, *Admin Dir*, Museum of the Hudson Highlands, Cornwall On Hudson NY

Brandman, Ann, *Cur Film*, Honolulu Academy of Arts, The Art Center at Linekona, Honolulu HI (S)

Brandon, Laura, *Acting Dir Research*, Canadian War Museum, Ottawa ON

Brandon, Reiko, *Cur Textiles*, Honolulu Academy of Arts, The Art Center at Linekona, Honolulu HI (S)

Brandrup, Jessica, *Mktg & Pub Rels*, Kimbell Art Foundation, Kimbell Art Museum, Fort Worth TX

Brandson, Lorraine, *Cur*, Eskimo Museum, Churchill MB

Brandson, Lorraine, *Cur*, Eskimo Museum, Library, Churchill MB

Brandt, Cathi, *Admin Dir*, Waterworks Visual Arts Center, Salisbury NC

Brandt, Elaine, *Instr*, California State University, Dominguez Hills, Art & Design Dept, Carson CA (S)

Brandt, Peter, *Area Coordr*, New York School of Interior Design, New York NY (S)

Brandt, Thomas, *Dir*, Highland Community College, Art Dept, Freeport IL (S)

Branham, Joan, *Prof*, Providence College, Art & Art History Dept, Providence RI (S)

Branning, Katherine, *Librn*, French Institute-Alliance Francaise, Library, New York NY

Brannon, Patrick, *Dept Head*, University of Saint Francis, Fine Arts Dept, Joliet IL (S)

Bransfield, Kevin, *Photog Instr*, Monterey Peninsula College, Art Dept/Art Gallery, Monterey CA (S)

Bransford, Jesse, *Prog Dir*, New York University, Dept of Art & Art Professions, New York NY (S)

Bransford, Pamela, *Registrar*, Montgomery Museum of Fine Arts, Montgomery AL

Branston, Stuart, *Chmn*, Oral Roberts University, Art Dept, Tulsa OK (S)

Brant, Nikki, *Exec Dir*, Burke Arts Council, Jailhouse Galleries, Morganton NC

Brant, Pip, *Assoc Prof*, Florida International University, School of Art & Art History, Miami FL (S)

Brantley, Royal, *Head Dept*, West Texas A&M University, Art, Theatre & Dance Dept, Canyon TX (S)

Braren, Lesley, *Admin Dir*, Essex Art Association, Inc, Essex CT

Brasch, Jean, *Bookkeeper*, Cultural Council of Palm Beach County, Lake Worth FL

Brase, Don, *Dir*, Chemeketa Community College, Dept of Humanities & Communications, Art Program, Salem OR (S)

Brashear, Jim, *Prof*, University of Alaska-Fairbanks, Dept of Art, Fairbanks AK (S)

Brashler, Cathy, *External Affairs Asst*, University of Kansas, Spencer Museum of Art, Lawrence KS

Brasier, Robert, *Deputy Dir Educ & Pub Progs*, Palm Springs Art Museum, Palm Springs CA

Brasile, Jeanne, *Gallery Dir*, Seton Hall University, Walsh Gallery & Library, South Orange NJ

Brassard, Lionel, *Pres*, Institut des Arts au Saguenay, Centre National D'Exposition a Jonquiere, Jonquiere PQ

Braswell, Tom, *Dir*, East Carolina University, Wellington B Gray Gallery, Greenville NC

Bratland, Don, *Instr*, Saint Olaf College, Art Dept, Northfield MN (S)

Brauer, Daniel R, *Publications Dir*, University of California, Los Angeles, Fowler Museum at UCLA, Los Angeles CA

Braun, Emily, *Prof*, City University of New York, PhD Program in Art History, New York NY (S)

Braun, Lon R, *Bus Mgr*, Fort Wayne Museum of Art, Inc, Fort Wayne IN

Braun, Mary E, *Dir*, St Mary's College of Maryland, The Dwight Frederick Boyden Gallery, St Mary's City MD

Braun, Matthew, *Exec Dir*, Philadelphia Museum of Art, Samuel S Fleisher Art Memorial, Philadelphia PA

Braunstein, Jack, *Dir of Develop*, State University of New York at Binghamton, Binghamton University Art Museum, Binghamton NY

Braunstein, Susan L, *Cur Archaeology*, The Jewish Museum, New York NY

Braverman, Marsha, *Dir Mktg & Communs*, Pennsylvania Academy of the Fine Arts, Philadelphia PA

Bravo, Joseph, *Exec Dir*, International Museum of Art & Science, McAllen TX

Bravo, Sheila, *Exec Dir*, Rehoboth Art League, Inc, Rehoboth Beach DE (S)

Brawner, Dan, *Asst Prof & Coordr Graphic Design*, Watkins College of Art, Design & Film, Nashville TN (S)

Bray, Kimberly, *Librn & Archivist*, The San Joaquin Pioneer & Historical Society, The Haggin Museum, Stockton CA

Bray, Kimberly D, *Librn, Archivist*, The San Joaquin Pioneer & Historical Society, Petzinger Memorial Library & Earl Rowland Art Library, Stockton CA

Brayman, Ruby, *Visual Arts Comt Chair*, University of Minnesota, The Studio/Larson Gallery, Minneapolis MN

Braysmith, Hilary, *Assoc Prof*, University of Southern Indiana, Department of Art, Evansville IN (S)

Brazil, Sally, *Chief Archives & Records Mgmt,* The Frick Collection, Frick Art Reference Library, New York NY

Brazile, Orella R, *Dir,* Southern University Library, Shreveport LA

Breault, Christina, *Mus Dir,* Lac du Flambeau Band of Lake Superior Chippewa Indians, George W Brown Jr Ojibwe Museum & Cultural Center, Lac Du Flambeau WI

Breaux, Robbie, *Pres,* Western Colorado Center for the Arts, Library, Grand Junction CO

Breazeale, Betty, *Secy,* University of Iowa, University of Iowa Museum of Art, Iowa City IA

Breaznell, Ann, *Assoc Prof,* College of Saint Rose, The Center For Art and Design, Albany NY (S)

Brechter, Bart, *Cur Gardens,* Museum of Fine Arts Houston, Bayou Bend Collection & Gardens, Houston TX

Brecken, Bradford A, *Pres Emeritus,* Newport Historical Society & Museum of Newport History, Newport RI

Breckenridge, Bruce, *Emer Prof,* University of Wisconsin, Madison, Dept of Art, Madison WI (S)

Breckenridge, Martha, *Asst Prof,* Northwest Missouri State University, Dept of Fine & Performing Arts, Maryville MO (S)

Bredbenner, Amanda, *Asst Develop Dir,* Contemporary Arts Museum Houston, Houston TX

Bredehoft, Wendy, *Cur Educ,* University of Wyoming, University of Wyoming Art Museum, Laramie WY

Bredendick, Joan, *Adjunct Prof,* North Central College, Dept of Art, Naperville IL (S)

Bredhoff, Stacey, *Cur,* National Archives & Records Administration, John F Kennedy Presidential Library & Museum, Boston MA

Breger, Christina, *Mktg & Promotions,* York University, Glendon Gallery, Toronto ON

Brehm, Georgia L, *Dir,* Black River Academy Museum & Historical Society, Black River Academy Museum, Ludlow VT

Breiling, Roy, *Instr,* Yavapai College, Visual & Performing Arts Div, Prescott AZ (S)

Breimayer, M Phyllis, *Dir,* Georgian Court University, M Christina Geis Gallery, Lakewood NJ

Breimayer, Mary Phyllis, *Assoc Prof,* Georgian Court University, Dept of Art, Lakewood NJ (S)

Breitenbach, Eric, *Prof,* Daytona Beach Community College, Dept of Fine Arts & Visual Arts, Daytona Beach FL (S)

Breitenberg, Mark, *Liberal Arts, Science, Grad & Acad Studies Chmn,* Art Center College of Design, Pasadena CA (S)

Breitner, Michael, *Dir,* University of Wisconsin - Platteville, Harry & Laura Nohr Gallery, Platteville WI

Brekke, Paul, *Asst Cur,* Gonzaga University, Art Gallery, Spokane WA

Breland, Evelyn, *Treas,* Mississippi Art Colony, Stoneville MS

Brener, Art, *Bd Mem,* American Color Print Society, Huntingdon Valley PA

Brengle, Anne, *Dir,* Old Dartmouth Historical Society, New Bedford Whaling Museum, New Bedford MA

Brennan, Anita, *CEO,* Schuyler-Hamilton House, Morristown NJ

Brennan, Anne, *Asst Dir,* Cameron Art Museum, Wilmington NC

Brennan, Joan, *Photo,* University of Colorado at Denver, College of Arts & Media Visual Arts Dept, Denver CO (S)

Brennan, Joe, *Dir Opers & Facilities,* San Francisco Museum of Modern Art, San Francisco CA

Brennan, Joe, *VPres & Gen Counsel,* Field Museum, Chicago IL

Brennan, Marnie, *Chmn Theatre,* Harrisburg Area Community College, Division of Communications, Humanities & the Arts, Harrisburg PA (S)

Brennan, Sandy, *Research Secy,* Livingston County Historical Society, Museum, Geneseo NY

Brennan, Shelia, *Pub Prog,* Naval Historical Center, The Navy Museum, Washington DC

Brenneman, David, *Chief Cur,* High Museum of Art, Atlanta GA

Brenneman, Jina, *Cur,* University of New Mexico, The Harwood Museum of Art, Taos NM

Brenner, Liza, *Assoc Prof,* Glenville State College, Dept of Fine Arts, Glenville WV (S)

Brenner, Susan, *Assoc Prof,* University of North Carolina at Charlotte, Dept Art, Charlotte NC (S)

Brenningmeyer, Todd, *Asst Prof Art History,* Maryville University of Saint Louis, Art & Design Program, Saint Louis MO (S)

Brenny, Barbara, *Visual Resources Librn,* North Carolina State University, Harrye Lyons Design Library, Raleigh NC

Bresler, Adrian, *Dir Finance & Admin,* USS Constitution Museum, Boston MA

Bresnahan, Edith, *Chmn,* Dominican College of San Rafael, Art Dept, San Rafael CA (S)

Bresowar, Jo-Ann, *Chmn,* Irving Arts Center, Galleries & Sculpture Garden, Irving TX

Breth, Renata, *Dir,* Santa Rosa Junior College, Art Gallery, Santa Rosa CA

Brett, Hillary, *Exec Dir,* LeMoyne Art Foundation, Center for the Visual Arts, Tallahassee FL

Brett-Smith, Sarah, *Assoc Prof,* Rutgers, The State University of New Jersey, Graduate Program in Art History, New Brunswick NJ (S)

Breuer, Karin, *Cur Prints & Drawings,* Achenbach Foundation for Graphic Arts, Fine Arts Museums of San Francisco, M H de Young Museum, San Francisco CA

Breuer, Karin, *Cur Prints & Drawings,* Achenbach Foundation for Graphic Arts, Fine Arts Museums of San Francisco, Legion of Honor, San Francisco CA

Breunig, Robert G, *Dir,* Museum of Northern Arizona, Flagstaff AZ

Breverman, Harvey, *Distinguished Prof Emeritus,* University at Buffalo, State University of New York, Dept of Visual Studies, Buffalo NY (S)

Brewer, Chris, *Gallery Mgr,* Washington County Arts Council, Gallery, Hagerstown MD

Brewer, Marty, *Facilities Mgr,* Springfield Museum of Art, Springfield OH

Brewer, Nan, *Cur Works on Paper,* Indiana University, Art Museum, Bloomington IN

Brewer, Piper, *Contact,* Shiawassee Arts Center, Owosso MI

Brewer, William, *Chmn,* Hutchinson Community College, Visual Arts Dept, Hutchinson KS (S)

Brewster, Carrie, *Dir,* Saint Mary's College of California, Hearst Art Gallery, Moraga CA

Breza, Michael, *Asst Dir,* Oshkosh Public Museum, Oshkosh WI

Brian, Cameron, *Instr,* Bakersfield College, Art Dept, Bakersfield CA (S)

Brian, Nancy K, *Chmn,* California State University, Fresno, Art & Design, Fresno CA (S)

Brickhouse, Ashley, *SIAMS Coordr/Brown Post-Bac Fel Mus Educ,* Smith College, Museum of Art, Northampton MA

Bridegam, Nathalie, *Cur Visual Coll,* University of Massachusetts, Amherst, Dorothy W Perkins Slide Library, Amherst MA

Bridenstine, James A, *Exec Dir,* Kalamazoo Institute of Arts, Kalamazoo MI

Bridenstine, James A, *Exec Dir,* Kalamazoo Institute of Arts, The Mary & Edwin Meader Fine Arts Library, Kalamazoo MI

Bridgeman, Amy, *Art Cur Asst,* Vanderbilt University, Vanderbilt University Fine Arts Gallery, Nashville TN

Bridgers, Ben, *Assoc Prof,* Barton College, Art & Design Dept, Wilson NC (S)

Bridges, Don, *Bookstore Mgr,* Irvine Museum, Irvine CA

Bridges, Edwin C, *Dir,* Alabama Department of Archives & History, Museum of Alabama, Montgomery AL

Bridges, Mary, *VPres Mktg & Communs,* Milwaukee Public Museum, Milwaukee WI

Bridges, Rebecca, *Registrar,* The Old Jail Art Center, Green Research Library, Albany TX

Brief, Martin, *Asst Prof,* Longwood University, Dept of Art, Farmville VA (S)

Brienen, Rebecca, *Dept Head Art & Art History,* Oklahoma State University, Department of Art, Graphic Design and Art History, Stillwater OK (S)

Brienen, Rebecca P, *Asst Prof,* University of Miami, Dept of Art & Art History, Coral Gables FL (S)

Brier, Ida, *Archivist & Librn,* Olana State Historic Site, Hudson NY

Brier, Ida, *Librn & Archivist,* Olana State Historic Site, Library, Hudson NY

Briggs, Jo, *Asst Cur 18th-19thc Art,* Walters Art Museum, Baltimore MD

Briggs, Karen, *Exec Dir,* LaGrange Art Museum, LaGrange GA

Briggs, Stephen R, *Pres,* Berry College, Moon Gallery, Mount Berry GA

Brigham, David, *Pres,* Pennsylvania Academy of the Fine Arts, Philadelphia PA

Brigham, David R, *CEO,* Pennsylvania Academy of the Fine Arts, Office of Admission, Philadelphia PA (S)

Brigham, Martha, *Deputy Dir Develop,* Fine Arts Museums of San Francisco, M H de Young Museum, San Francisco CA

Brigham, Martha, *Deputy Dir Develop,* Fine Arts Museums of San Francisco, Legion of Honor, San Francisco CA

Bright, Karen, *Assoc Prof,* Monmouth University, Dept of Art & Design, West Long Branch NJ (S)

Bright, Paul, *Asst Dir,* Wake Forest University, Charlotte & Philip Hanes Art Gallery, Winston Salem NC

Bright, Paul, *Gallery Dir,* Wake Forest University, Dept of Art, Winston-Salem NC (S)

Brightman, Katherine, *Cur Interpretation,* Tryon Palace Historic Sites & Gardens, New Bern NC

Briley, Jeff, *Asst Dir Coll,* Oklahoma Historical Society, State Museum of History, Oklahoma City OK

Brill, Margaret, *Prof,* Corning Community College, Division of Humanities, Corning NY (S)

Brilla, Maureen, *Assoc Prof,* Nazareth College of Rochester, Art Dept, Rochester NY (S)

Brin, Judith, *Mus Security,* The Art Museum at the University of Kentucky, Lexington KY

Brininger, Betsy, *Dir Institute of the Arts,* George Mason University, College of Humanities & Social Sciences, Dept of Art & Art History, Fairfax VA (S)

Brink, Annette, *Dir,* Tubac Center of the Arts, Library, Tubac AZ

Brinkerhoff, Dericksen M, *Prof Emeriti,* University of California, Riverside, Dept of the History of Art, Riverside CA (S)

Brinkman, L.D., *Trustee,* L D Brinkman, Kerrville TX

Brinkman, Lynn, *Instr,* Lourdes University, Art Dept, Sylvania OH (S)

Brinkman, Stacy, *Librn,* Miami University, Wertz Art & Architecture Library, Oxford OH

Brinson, Ericah, *Rental Coordr,* Historical Society of Martin County, Elliott Museum, Stuart FL

Brinson, Katherine, *Asst Cur,* Solomon R Guggenheim, New York NY

Brinton, Dean, *CEO,* Memorial University of Newfoundland, The Rooms Provincial Art Gallery, Saint John's NF

Briscoe, Eric, *Asst Cur,* Morgan State University, James E Lewis Museum of Art, Baltimore MD

Brisson, Christine, *Archivist & Exhib Coordr,* Chateau Ramezay Museum, Montreal PQ

Brittingham, John, *Interim Assoc Dir,* Montana State University, School of Architecture, Bozeman MT (S)

Britton, Benjamin, *Assoc Prof Fine Arts,* University of Cincinnati, School of Art, Cincinnati OH (S)

Britt Wang, May, *Asst to the Dir,* Marblehead Arts Association, Inc, Marblehead MA

Britz, Kevin, *VPres Progs & Exhibs Dir,* High Desert Museum, Bend OR

Brixey, Shawn, *Chair,* University of California, Berkeley, College of Letters & Sciences-Art Practice Dept, Berkeley CA (S)

Broad, David, *Dean,* Elgin Community College, Fine Arts Dept, Elgin IL (S)

Broadbeut, Alice, *Receptionist,* Rhode Island Watercolor Society, Pawtucket RI

Brock, Betsey, *Communs Mgr,* Henry Gallery Association, Henry Art Gallery, Seattle WA

Brock, Betsey, *Pub Information Mgr,* University of Washington, Henry Art Gallery, Seattle WA

Brockington, Lynn, *Librn,* Vancouver Art Gallery, Library, Vancouver BC

Brocklehurst, Eric, *Asst to Chmn/Arts Admin,* National Museum of American Illustration, Newport RI

Brockmann, J Nicholas, *Media Arts & Animation/Gen Educ,* Art Institute of Pittsburgh, Pittsburgh PA (S)

Brown, DeSoto, *Archivist*, Bernice Pauahi Bishop, Library, Honolulu HI

Brown, DeSoto, *Archivist*, Bernice Pauahi Bishop, Archives, Honolulu HI

Brown, Donald W, *Bibliographer*, Carnegie Mellon University, Hunt Institute for Botanical Documentation, Pittsburgh PA

Brown, Dorothy D, *Chmn*, Georgia College & State University, Art Dept, Milledgeville GA (S)

Brown, Dottie, *Instr*, Sierra Community College, Art Dept, Rocklin CA (S)

Brown, Elizabeth, *Chief Cur*, Henry Gallery Association, Henry Art Gallery, Seattle WA

Brown, Elizabeth A, *Sr Cur*, University of Washington, Henry Art Gallery, Seattle WA

Brown, Ellsworth, *Dir*, Wisconsin Historical Society, Wisconsin Historical Museum, Madison WI

Brown, Erika Jo, *Mgr Mktg & Commun*, University of Iowa, University of Iowa Museum of Art, Iowa City IA

Brown, Francine, *Office Specialist*, Vassar College, The Frances Lehman Loeb Art Center, Poughkeepsie NY

Brown, Geoffrey I, *Dir*, Navajo Nation, Navajo Nation Museum, Window Rock AZ

Brown, Geraldine, *Mus Prog Mgr*, Vermont Historical Society, Museum, Montpelier VT

Brown, Gerard, *Chmn Foundation Prog*, Temple University, Tyler School of Art, Philadelphia PA (S)

Brown, Glen R, *Prof*, Kansas State University, Art Dept, Manhattan KS (S)

Brown, Hilary, *VPres Inst Advancement*, Watkins College of Art, Design & Film, Brownlee O Currey Gallery, Nashville TN

Brown, Hillary, *Dir Communs*, University of Georgia, Georgia Museum of Art, Athens GA

Brown, Jack Perry, *Exec Dir Libraries*, The Art Institute of Chicago, Chicago IL

Brown, Jack Perry, *Exec Dir Libraries*, The Art Institute of Chicago, Ryerson & Burnham Libraries, Chicago IL

Brown, James, *Assoc Prof*, William Paterson University, Dept Arts, Wayne NJ (S)

Brown, James M, *Asst Dir Exhibits*, South Carolina State Museum, Columbia SC

Brown, Jana, *Educator Cur*, Trust Authority, Museum of the Great Plains, Lawton OK

Brown, Jasmine, *Exec Dir*, The Richmond Art Center, Richmond CA

Brown, Jason, *Assoc Prof*, Eastern Oregon University, School of Arts & Science, La Grande OR (S)

Brown, Jeff, *Chmn Fine Arts*, Jones County Junior College, Art Dept, Ellisville MS (S)

Brown, Jill, *Sales Mgr*, Stephen Huneck Gallery at Dog Mountain, Saint Johnsbury VT

Brown, Joe, *Dean, Theater Arts*, Texas Wesleyan University, Dept of Art, Fort Worth TX (S)

Brown, John, *Board VPres*, Cabot's Old Indian Pueblo Museum, Desert Hot Springs CA

Brown, Judith, *Dir Educ*, Davistown Museum, Liberty Location, Liberty ME

Brown, Judy, *Foundation Dept*, Montserrat College of Art, Beverly MA (S)

Brown, Julia, *Asst Prof*, George Washington University, Dept of Art of Fine Arts & Art History, Washington DC (S)

Brown, Karen, *Dir Mktg*, Chicago History Museum, Chicago IL

Brown, Karen F, *Libr Technician*, National Museum of African Art, Warren M Robbins Library, Washington DC

Brown, Kate, *Instr*, Toronto School of Art, Toronto ON (S)

Brown, Kenneth C, *Educ Dir*, Christina Cultural Arts Center, Inc, Wilmington DE

Brown, Larry, *Bd Mem*, Kennebec Valley Art Association, Harlow Gallery, Hallowell ME

Brown, Lenard, *Asst Prof Painting & Printmaking*, University of Texas Pan American, Art Dept, Edinburg TX (S)

Brown, Leslie E, *Instr Drawing*, Millersville University, Dept of Art & Design, Millersville PA (S)

Brown, Likassina, *Receptionist*, Lafayette Science Museum & Planetarium, Lafayette LA

Brown, Lindie K, *Dir Develop*, Anniston Museum of Natural History, Anniston AL

Brown, Lisa, *Instr Art Educ*, Eastern Oregon University, School of Arts & Science, La Grande OR (S)

Brown, Louise Freshman, *Prof*, University of North Florida, Dept of Communications & Visual Arts, Jacksonville FL (S)

Brown, Margaret, *Branch Librn*, Arlington County Department of Public Libraries, Fine Arts Section, Arlington VA

Brown, Marilyn R, *Prof*, Tulane University, Sophie H Newcomb Memorial College, New Orleans LA (S)

Brown, Michael K, *Cur*, Museum of Fine Arts Houston, Bayou Bend Collection & Gardens, Houston TX

Brown, Nancy, *Dir Human Resources*, Hillwood Museum & Gardens Foundation, Hillwood Estate Museum & Gardens, Washington DC

Brown, Nancy F, *Exec Dir & Cur*, Lillian & Coleman Taube Museum of Art, Minot ND

Brown, Pam, *Asst Prof Visual Arts*, Dowling College, Dept of Visual Arts, Oakdale NY (S)

Brown, Pam, *Cur of Ethnology & Media*, University of British Columbia, Museum of Anthropology, Vancouver BC

Brown, Patricia, *Exhib Chmn*, Delta State University, Fielding L Wright Art Center, Cleveland MS

Brown, Patricia, *Prof*, Delta State University, Dept of Art, Cleveland MS (S)

Brown, Patrick, *Chief Preparator & Exhib Designer*, Worcester Art Museum, Worcester MA

Brown, Rachel, *Educ*, Hidalgo County Historical Museum, Edinburg TX

Brown, Randy, *Admin Asst*, Wichita Center for the Arts, Wichita KS

Brown, Rebecca, *Asst Prof*, Saint Mary's College of Maryland, Art & Art History Dept, Saint Mary's City MD (S)

Brown, Robert, *Dir*, Historical Museum at Fort Missoula, Missoula MT

Brown, Robert B, *Secy & Treas*, National Museum of Ceramic Art & Glass, Baltimore MD

Brown, Sandra, *Office Mgr*, Women's Studio Workshop, Inc, Rosendale NY

Brown, Scott, *Color & Graphic Instr*, Hutchinson Community College, Visual Arts Dept, Hutchinson KS (S)

Brown, Sharon, *Co-Chair*, Santa Ana College, Art Dept, Santa Ana CA (S)

Brown, Sheena, *Cur*, Morris-Jumel Mansion, Inc, New York NY

Brown, Shirley B, *Adminr*, National Museum of Ceramic Art & Glass, Baltimore MD

Brown, Sonia, *Cur Educ*, California African-American Museum, Los Angeles CA

Brown, Stephen, *Assoc Prof*, University of Hartford, Hartford Art School, West Hartford CT (S)

Brown, Stephen, *VPres*, Shoreline Historical Museum, Shoreline WA

Brown, Steven, *Photog & Graphic Design*, Southern Illinois University at Edwardsville, Dept of Art & Design, Edwardsville IL (S)

Brown, Steven, *Prof*, University of Science & Arts of Oklahoma, Arts Dept, Chickasha OK (S)

Brown, Tim, *Cur Educ*, Columbus Museum, Columbus GA

Brown, Tim, *Cur Educ*, Montgomery Museum of Fine Arts, Library, Montgomery AL

Brown, Wendell, *Asst Prof*, Benedict College, School of Humanities, Arts & Social Sciences, Columbia SC (S)

Brown, William, *Chief Conservator*, North Carolina Museum of Art, Raleigh NC

Brown, William, *Dept Head, Prof*, University of Evansville, Art Dept, Evansville IN (S)

Brown, William, *Gallery Dir*, University of Evansville, Krannert Gallery & Peterson Gallery, Evansville IN

Brown-Urso, Rian, *Asst Prof*, Oberlin College, Dept of Art, Oberlin OH (S)

Browne, Charles C, *Dir*, Fairbanks Museum & Planetarium, Saint Johnsbury VT

Browne, Kelvin, *Exec Dir Mktg & Commercial Devel*, Royal Ontario Museum, Toronto ON

Browne, Mariane, *Co-2nd Vice Regent*, Schuyler-Hamilton House, Morristown NJ

Browne, Robert, *Pres*, Ontario Crafts Council, Artists in Stained Glass, Toronto ON

Brownell, Charles, *Assoc Prof*, Virginia Commonwealth University, Art History Dept, Richmond VA (S)

Brownell, Louise, *Registrar*, Maryland Historical Society, Library, Baltimore MD

Brownfield, Gail, *Pres*, Redlands Art Association, Redlands Art Association Gallery & Art Center, Redlands CA

Brownfield, John, *Chmn*, University of Redlands, Dept of Art, Redlands CA (S)

Browning, Alan, *Dir Develop*, Boulder History Museum, Museum of History, Boulder CO

Browning, Dawn C, *Dir*, Maysville, Kentucky Gateway Museum Center, Maysville KY

Browning, Kathleen, *Cur & Grants Mgr*, Star-Spangled Banner Flag House Association, Flag House & 1812 Museum, Baltimore MD

Browning, Kaye, *Cur Miniatures*, Maysville, Kentucky Gateway Museum Center, Maysville KY

Browning, Marion, *Receptionist*, Maysville, Kentucky Gateway Museum Center, Maysville KY

Browning, Terry, *Gallery Dir*, Ann Arbor Art Center, Art Center, Ann Arbor MI

Brozovich, Tom J, *Instr*, American River College, Dept of Art/Art New Media, Sacramento CA (S)

Brozynski, Dennis, *Coordr Fashion Design*, Columbia College, Art Dept, Chicago IL (S)

Bruce, Chris, *Dir*, Washington State University, Museum of Art, Pullman WA

Bruce, Donald, *Cur*, Cambria Historical Society, New Providence NJ

Bruce, Jeff, *Dir Exhib*, Tubman African American Museum, Macon GA

Brucker, Jane, *Prof*, Loyola Marymount University, Dept of Art & Art History, Los Angeles CA (S)

Bruegeman, Nancy, *Asst Coll Mgr*, University of British Columbia, Museum of Anthropology, Vancouver BC

Brueggeman, Mark, *Sr Lectr*, University of Wisconsin-Stevens Point, Dept of Art & Design, Stevens Point WI (S)

Brueggenhohann, Jean, *Prof (Graphic Design)*, University of Missouri - Columbia, Dept of Art, Columbia MO (S)

Bruhl, Win, *Chmn*, University of Arkansas at Little Rock, Art Slide Library and Galleries, Little Rock AR

Bruhl, Win, *Chmn*, University of Arkansas at Little Rock, Dept of Art, Little Rock AR (S)

Bruhn, Thomas P, *Cur*, University of Connecticut, William Benton Museum of Art, Storrs CT

Bruin, Joan, *Dir*, LA County Museum of Art, Los Angeles CA

Brumagen, Regan, *Reference & Emerging Tech Librn*, Corning Museum of Glass, Juliette K and Leonard S Rakow Research Library, Corning NY

Brumgardt, John R, *Dir*, Charleston Museum, Charleston SC

Brumley, Lizabeth, *Visitor Svcs Coordr*, Lauren Rogers, Laurel MS

Brumm, Tina, *Colls Asst*, Texas Ranger Hall of Fame & Museum, Waco TX

Brummett, Bill, *Pres*, Livingston County Historical Society, Museum, Geneseo NY

Brundage, Patricia L, *Dir Admin*, Art Dealers Association of America, Inc, New York NY

Brundage, Susan, *Dir Appraisals*, Art Dealers Association of America, Inc, New York NY

Brunelle, Jim, *Gallery Mgr*, Farmington Valley Arts Center, Avon CT

Bruner, Rich, *Coordr Photog*, Shepherd University, Dept of Contemporary Art & Theater, Shepherdstown WV (S)

Brunett, Keven, *Assoc Lect*, University of Wisconsin-Stevens Point, Dept of Art & Design, Stevens Point WI (S)

Brunetti, Sandra, *Admin Asst*, Custer County Art & Heritage Center, Miles City MT

Brungardt, Kevin, *Chmn Human & Fine Arts*, Garden City Community College, Art Dept, Garden City KS (S)

Bruni, Margaret, *Asst Dir Main Library*, Detroit Public Library, Art & Literature Dept, Detroit MI

Brunner, Christal, *Head Librn*, Mexico-Audrain County Library, Mexico MO

Brunner, Helen M, *Dir Spec Projects*, Art Resources International, Washington DC

Brunner, Ludwig, *Asst Dir*, Saint Bonaventure University, Regina A Quick Center for the Arts, Saint Bonaventure NY

Brunner, Wilfred, *Art Chair Tacoma Park,* Montgomery College, Dept of Art, Rockville MD (S)

Brunning, Dennis, *Art Specialist,* Arizona State University, ASU Library, Tempe AZ

Bruno, Lugene, *Cur Art,* Carnegie Mellon University, Hunt Institute for Botanical Documentation, Pittsburgh PA

Bruns, Craig, *Cur,* Independence Seaport Museum, Philadelphia PA

Brunscheen, Scott, *Dir,* Salisbury House Foundation, Salisbury House and Garden, Des Moines IA

Brunson, Ty, *Asst Prof,* Arkansas Tech University, Dept of Art, Russellville AR (S)

Brunt, Bonnie, *Dean,* Spokane Falls Community College, Fine Arts Dept, Spokane WA (S)

Bruntse, Line, *Asst Prof 2D & 3D Design, Drawing & Sculpture,* Millersville University, Dept of Art & Design, Millersville PA (S)

Brunvand, Sandy, *Instr,* University of Utah, Dept of Art & Art History, Salt Lake City UT (S)

Brusati, Celeste, *Prof,* University of Michigan, Ann Arbor, Dept of History of Art, Ann Arbor MI (S)

Brush, Gloria D, *Prof, Head Dept,* University of Minnesota, Duluth, Art Dept, Duluth MN (S)

Bruso, Arthur, *Cur,* Curious Matter, Jersey City NJ

Bruton, Julia, *Curatorial Asst,* Morris Museum of Art, Augusta GA

Brutschy, Sarah, *Dir Mem Svcs,* Henry Morrison Flagler Museum, Palm Beach FL

Bruttomesso, Patty, *Cur,* Louisa May Alcott Memorial Association, Orchard House, Concord MA

Brutvan, Cheryl, *Dir Curatorial Affairs, Cur Contemporary Art,* Norton Museum of Art, West Palm Beach FL

Bruya, Chris, *Assoc Dean,* Mount Hood Community College, Visual Arts Center, Gresham OR (S)

Bruya, Marilyn, *Prof,* University of Montana, Dept of Art, Missoula MT (S)

Bruzelius, Ellen, *Exec Dir,* Bartow-Pell Mansion Museum & Gardens, Bronx NY

Bryan, Betsy, *Dir Near Eastern & Egyptian Art,* Johns Hopkins University, Archaeological Collection, Baltimore MD

Bryan, Charles F, *CEO & Pres,* Virginia Historical Society, Richmond VA

Bryan, Jerry, *Chmn,* Western Oklahoma State College, Art Dept, Altus OK (S)

Bryan, John, *Chmn Art History,* University of South Carolina, Dept of Art, Columbia SC (S)

Bryan, John, *Pres,* CultureWorks, Richmond VA

Bryan, Paul, *Asst Security Supv,* University of Chicago, Smart Museum of Art, Chicago IL

Bryan, Tracy, *Va House Site Mgr,* Virginia Historical Society, Library, Richmond VA

Bryant, David, *Dir,* New Canaan Library, H. Pelham Curtis Gallery, New Canaan CT

Bryant, Jim, *Chmn,* Eastern New Mexico University, Dept of Art, Portales NM (S)

Bryant, Jo, *City Librn,* Toronto Public Library Board, Library, Toronto ON

Bryant, Keith, *Lectr,* University of North Carolina at Charlotte, Dept Art, Charlotte NC (S)

Bryant, Sampson, *Performance Coordr,* Museum of Northern British Columbia, Ruth Harvey Art Gallery, Prince Rupert BC

Bryant, Sampson, *Performance Coordr,* Museum of Northern British Columbia, Library, Prince Rupert BC

Bryck, Jack, *Pres,* Baldwin Historical Society Museum, Baldwin NY

Bryk, Jane, *Board Pres,* Mechanics' Institute, San Francisco CA

Bryner, Kyle, *Registrar & Colls Mgr,* Wake Forest University, Museum of Anthropology, Winston Salem NC

Brynjfson, Carol, *Conservator,* Museum of Vancouver, Vancouver BC

Brynolf, Anita, *Instr,* San Diego Mesa College, Fine Arts Dept, San Diego CA (S)

Brynteson, Susan, *Vice Provost & May Morris Dir Libraries,* University of Delaware, Morris Library, Newark DE

Bryon, Saskya, *Develop Dir,* Craft Alliance, Saint Louis MO

Bryson, Gregg, *Prof,* Virginia Polytechnic Institute & State University, Dept of Art & Art History, Blacksburg VA (S)

Brzozowski, Carole, *Dean,* Syracuse University, College of Visual & Performing Arts, Syracuse NY (S)

Bucci, Jonathan, *Coll Cur,* Willamette University, Hallie Ford Museum of Art, Salem OR

Buch, Wayna, *Dir Arts Based Pre-School,* Wichita Center for the Arts, Mary R Koch School of Visual Arts, Wichita KS (S)

Buchanan, Annette, *Admin Dir,* Anderson County Arts Council, Anderson SC

Buchanan, Donna, *Group Tour Sales Dir,* Edsel & Eleanor Ford, Grosse Pointe Shores MI

Buchanan, John, *Instr,* Alcorn State University, Dept of Fine Arts, Lorman MS (S)

Buchanan, John E, *Dir,* Fine Arts Museums of San Francisco, M H de Young Museum, San Francisco CA

Buchanan, John E, *Dir,* Fine Arts Museums of San Francisco, Legion of Honor, San Francisco CA

Buchanan, Mandy, *Cur Educ,* Lauren Rogers, Laurel MS

Buchanon, Mel, *Asst Cur 20th c Design,* Milwaukee Art Museum, Milwaukee WI

Bucher, Burt, *Prof,* Missouri Southern State University, Dept of Art, Joplin MO (S)

Buchloh, Benjamin, *Chmn,* Columbia University, Barnard College, New York NY (S)

Buchman, Bill, *Instr,* Art Center Sarasota, Sarasota FL (S)

Bucholz, Margaret, *VPres Activities,* DuPage Art League School & Gallery, Wheaton IL

Buchtel, John, *Spec Coll Librn,* Georgetown University, Lauinger Library-Special Collections Division, Washington DC

Bucino, Erika G, *Mus Shop Mgr,* Brandywine Conservancy, Brandywine River Museum, Chadds Ford PA

Buck, Audra, *Asst Prof,* University of Alabama at Birmingham, Dept of Art & Art History, Birmingham AL (S)

Buck, Rebecca, *Deputy Dir Coll,* Newark Museum Association, The Newark Museum, Newark NJ

Buck, Stephanie, *Librn & Archivist,* Cape Ann Historical Association, Cape Ann Museum, Gloucester MA

Buckingham, Daniel, *Prof,* Munson-Williams-Proctor Arts Institute, Pratt MWP College of Art, Utica NY (S)

Buckingham, Lark, *Registrar,* Historic Arkansas Museum, Little Rock AR

Buckland, Alex, *Instr,* Lincoln Memorial University, Division of Humanities, Harrogate TN (S)

Buckley, Donald G, *Asst Dir,* Westfield Athenaeum, Jasper Rand Art Museum, Westfield MA

Buckley, Kerry, *Exec Dir,* Historic Northampton Museum & Education Center, Northampton MA

Buckley, Laurene, *Asst Dir,* State University of New York at Oswego, Tyler Art Gallery, Oswego NY

Buckley, R F, *Prof,* Florida International University, School of Art & Art History, Miami FL (S)

Buckley, Robert, *Pres,* Inter-Society Color Council, Reston VA

Buckman, Barbara, *Dept Coordr MFA,* Niagara County Community College, Fine Arts Division, Sanborn NY (S)

Buckman, Pamela, *Sculpture Garden Mgr,* New Orleans Museum of Art, New Orleans LA

Buckner, Cindy, *Assoc Cur,* Grand Rapids Art Museum, Reference Library, Grand Rapids MI

Buckner, Marlene, *Deputy Dir,* Mobile Museum of Art, Mobile AL

Buckner, Marlene, *Deputy Dir,* Mobile Museum of Art, Library, Mobile AL

Buckner, Virginia, *Exec Advisor,* Halifax Historical Society, Inc, Halifax Historical Museum, Daytona Beach FL

Buckno, Joshua, *Asst Dir,* Florence & Chafetz Hillel House at Boston University, Boston University Art Gallery at the Stone Gallery, Boston MA

Bucuvalas, Tina, *Folk Arts Coordr,* Florida Folklife Programs, Tallahassee FL

Bucy, Carole S, *Secy,* Tennessee Historical Society, Nashville TN

Buczynski, Erin, *Gallery Dir,* Bradley University, Heuser Art Center, Peoria IL

Budahl, Lee P, *Assoc Prof,* Western Carolina University, Dept of Art/College of Arts & Science, Cullowhee NC (S)

Budde, Diana, *Prof,* University of Wisconsin College - Marinette, Art Dept, Marinette WI (S)

Budney, Jen, *Assoc Cur,* Mendel Art Gallery & Civic Conservatory, Saskatoon SK

Budoff, Nathan, *Instr,* University of Puerto Rico, Dept of Fine Arts, Rio Piedras PR (S)

Budoff, Nathan, *Instr,* University of Puerto Rico, Dept of Fine Arts, Rio Piedras PR (S)

Budrovich, Tony, *Deputy Dir Opers,* California Science Center, Los Angeles CA

Buechley, Mary, *Reference Technical Assoc,* Indiana University, Fine Arts Library, Bloomington IN

Buehner, Stacy, *Marketing & Develop,* South Dakota State University, South Dakota Art Museum, Brookings SD

Buenger, Barbara C, *Prof Art History,* University of Wisconsin, Madison, Dept of Art History, Madison WI (S)

Buentello, Mia Marisol, *Programming Officer,* Hidalgo County Historical Museum, Edinburg TX

Bueschel, Tiffanie, *Mus Dir,* American Numismatic Association, Edward C. Rochette Money Museum, Colorado Springs CO

Buescher, Jean, *Instr,* Siena Heights University, Studio Angelico-Art Dept, Adrian MI (S)

Buesgen, Linda, *Mem Coordr,* Lehigh Valley Heritage Center, Allentown PA

Buettner, Brigitte, *Prof,* Smith College, Art Dept, Northampton MA (S)

Bufano, Michelle, *Exec Dir,* Pratt Fine Arts Center, Gallery, Seattle WA

Bufano, Michelle, *Exec Dir,* City Art Works, Pratt Fine Arts Center, Seattle WA (S)

Buffalo, Jo, *Prof,* Cazenovia College, Center for Art & Design Studies, Cazenovia NY (S)

Bufferd, Lauren, *Dir Opers,* Board of Parks & Recreation, The Parthenon, Nashville TN

Buffington, Mel, *Instr Photog,* Eastern Oregon University, School of Arts & Science, La Grande OR (S)

Buffington, Ron, *Prof,* University of Tennessee at Chattanooga, Dept of Art, Chattanooga TN (S)

Buffington, Sean, *Pres,* The University of the Arts, Rosenwald-Wolf Gallery, Philadelphia PA

Buffington, Sean T, *Pres,* University of the Arts, Philadelphia Colleges of Art & Design, Performing Arts & Media & Communication, Philadelphia PA (S)

Bugler, Pam, *Dir Educ,* Wichita Center for the Arts, Mary R Koch School of Visual Arts, Wichita KS (S)

Bugslag, James, *Assoc Dir & Assoc Prof,* University of Manitoba, School of Art, Winnipeg MB (S)

Buhl, Gudrun, *Cur & Mus Dir,* Harvard University, Museum & Garden, Washington DC

Buhr, Margaret, *Dir Educ,* Dubuque Museum of Art, Dubuque IA

Buhr, Margaret, *Cur Exhibs,* Springfield Art Museum, Springfield MO

Buie, Sarah, *Dir,* Clark University, The Schiltkamp Gallery/Traina Center for the Arts, Worcester MA

Buie Niewyk, Ellen, *Cur,* Southern Methodist University, Hamon Arts Library, Dallas TX

Buis, Ed, *Lib Dir,* Southeast Missouri State University, Kent Library, Cape Girardeau MO

Buisch, Derrick, *Prof,* University of Wisconsin, Madison, Dept of Art, Madison WI (S)

Buisson, Rene, *Dir,* Le Musee Marc-Aurele Fortin, Montreal PQ

Buj, Otto, *Information Coordr,* Art Gallery of Windsor, Windsor ON

Bujacich, Marianne, *Office Admin,* Van Alen Institute, New York NY

Bukar, Nat, *VPres,* The National Art League, Douglaston NY

Bukowski, Lucy, *Deputy Dir Admin,* Heritage Museums & Gardens, Sandwich MA

Bukowski, William, *Head of Dept,* Bethany Lutheran College, Art Dept, Mankato MN (S)

Bul-Burton, Kim, *Dir,* Monterey Public Library, Art & Architecture Dept, Monterey CA

Bule, Sarah, *Prof,* Clark University, Dept of Visual & Performing Arts, Worcester MA (S)

Bulger, Stephen, *Dir,* Stephen Bulger Gallery, Toronto ON

Bullock, Jennifer, *Registrar,* Kitchener-Waterloo Art Gallery, Kitchener ON

Bullock, Katherine, *Educational Outreach Coordr,* Living Arts & Science Center, Inc, Lexington KY

Bulow, Harry, *Head of School (upa),* Purdue University, West Lafayette, Patti and Rusty Rueff School of Visual & Performing Arts, Art & Design Dept, West Lafayette IN (S)

Bumpass, Terry, *Cur,* Museum of New Mexico, Office of Cultural Affairs of New Mexico, The Governor's Gallery, Santa Fe NM

Bundock, Bruce, *Preparator,* Vassar College, The Frances Lehman Loeb Art Center, Poughkeepsie NY

Bundy, Annalee, *Exec Dir,* Ames Free-Easton's Public Library, North Easton MA

Bundy-Jost, Barbara, *Dir,* Rahr-West Art Museum, Manitowoc WI

Bunge, Jean, *Co-Dir,* Nobles County Art Center, Worthington MN

Bunge, Martin, *Co-Dir,* Nobles County Art Center, Worthington MN

Bunker, Gil, *Vol Archivist,* Girard College, Stephen Girard Collection, Philadelphia PA

Bunker, Sue, *Dir Museum Educ,* American Textile History Museum, Lowell MA

Bunn, Mike, *Assoc Cur History,* Columbus Museum, Columbus GA

Bunn, Steve, *Exhib Technician,* Bowdoin College, Peary-MacMillan Arctic Museum, Brunswick ME

Bunnell, Peter, *Prof,* Princeton University, Dept of Art & Archaeology, Princeton NJ (S)

Bunnenberg-Boehmer, Kay, *Instr,* Chemeketa Community College, Dept of Humanities & Communications, Art Program, Salem OR (S)

Bunner, Patty, *Instr,* Southwestern Michigan College, Fine & Performing Arts Dept, Dowagiac MI (S)

Buonaccorsi, Jim, *Assoc Prof Sculpture,* University of Georgia, Franklin College of Arts & Sciences, Lamar Dodd School of Art, Athens GA (S)

Buonagurio, Toby, *Prof,* Stony Brook University, College of Arts & Sciences, Dept of Art, Stony Brook NY (S)

Buonpastore, Andrew, *VPres Opers,* New-York Historical Society, Museum, New York NY

Buranakorn, Wanrudee, *Asst Prof,* University of Wisconsin-Eau Claire, Dept of Art & Design, Eau Claire WI (S)

Burbach, Sarah, *Chmn Bd,* Morgan County Foundation, Inc, Madison-Morgan Cultural Center, Madison GA

Burback, Bill, *VPres,* Garrison Art Center, Garrison NY

Burbul, Derrick, *Asst Prof,* University of Nebraska, Kearney, Dept of Art & Art History, Kearney NE (S)

Burchett, Jayme, *Prof,* College of the Ozarks, Dept of Art, Point Lookout MO (S)

Burchett, Kenneth, *Prof,* University of Central Arkansas, Department of Art, Conway AR (S)

Burchett, Theresa, *Dir,* East Tennessee State University, The Reece Museum, Johnson City TN

Burden, Jeff, *Chmn,* Columbus State University, Dept of Art, Fine Arts Hall, Columbus GA (S)

Burden, Jeffrey, *Prof,* University of Nevada, Las Vegas, Dept of Art, Las Vegas NV (S)

Burden, Rhonda, *ShopMgr,* Comox Valley Art Gallery, Courtenay BC

Burden Hart, Virginia, *Mus Specialist,* United States Department of State, Diplomatic Reception Rooms, Washington DC

Burdette, Phyllis, *Treas,* Women's Art Registry of Minnesota Gallery, Saint Paul MN

Burdick, Todd, *Interpretation & Educ,* Hancock Shaker Village, Inc, Pittsfield MA

Bureau, Pascale, *Dir,* VU Centre De Diffusion Et De Production De La Photographie, Quebec PQ

Burg, Pat, *Librn,* Illinois State Museum, Museum Store, Chicago IL

Burg, Patricia, *Librn,* Illinois State Museum, Library, Springfield IL

Burgard, Timothy Anglin, *Ednah Root Cur American Arts,* Fine Arts Museums of San Francisco, M H de Young Museum, San Francisco CA

Burgard, Timothy Anglin, *Ednah Root Cur American Arts,* Fine Arts Museums of San Francisco, Legion of Honor, San Francisco CA

Burge, Denise, *Foundations Coordr, Undergrad Adv & Assoc Prof Fine Arts,* University of Cincinnati, School of Art, Cincinnati OH (S)

Burge, Nolina, *Circ Supv,* Art Center College of Design, James Lemont Fogg Memorial Library, Pasadena CA

Burger, Thomas Julius, *Dir,* University of Bridgeport, Shintaro Akatsu School of Design, Bridgeport CT (S)

Burgess, Cynthia A, *Cur Books & Printed Material,* Baylor University, Armstrong Browning Library, Waco TX

Burgess, Margaret, *Cur Modern Art,* Portland Museum of Art, Portland ME

Burgett, Laurie, *Bd Pres,* Centro Cultural De La Raza, San Diego CA

Burggraf, Ray, *Prof & Assoc Chair,* Florida State University, Art Dept, Tallahassee FL (S)

Burgher, Elijah, *Asst,* The Art Institute of Chicago, Teacher Resource Center, Chicago IL

Burgner, Kelly, *Chmn,* Ricks College, Dept of Art, Rexburg ID (S)

Burk, George, *Assoc Prof Drawing & Painting,* University of Southern Maine, Dept of Art, Gorham ME (S)

Burk, Sue, *Regional Srvcs Dir,* Arts Place, Inc., Hugh N Ronald Memorial Gallery, Portland IN

Burk, Teresa, *Head Librn,* Savannah College of Art & Design - Atlanta, ACA Library of Atlanta, Atlanta GA

Burkard, Randall E, *Chmn, Buffalo Soc Natural Sci Bd Dirs,* Buffalo Museum of Science, Research Library, Buffalo NY

Burke, Bridget, *Cur Books & Manuscripts,* Colorado Historical Society, Colorado History Museum, Denver CO

Burke, Christina, *Cur Native American & Non-Western Art,* Philbrook Museum of Art, Tulsa OK

Burke, Daniel, *Chair, Prof,* Mercyhurst College, Dept of Art, Erie PA (S)

Burke, Gregory, *Exec Dir & CEO,* Mendel Art Gallery & Civic Conservatory, Saskatoon SK

Burke, J Martin, *Chmn (V),* Missoula Art Museum, Missoula MT

Burke, Jim, *VPres Finance & Admin,* Newberry Library, Chicago IL

Burke, Jo, *Dir,* Northern Illinois University, NIU Art Museum, DeKalb IL

Burke, John SJ, *Prof,* Longwood University, Dept of Art, Farmville VA (S)

Burke, Jonathan, *Dean Visual Commun,* Art Institute of Southern California, Laguna Beach CA (S)

Burke, Kathryn, *Exhib & Colls Mgr,* Muhlenberg College, Martin Art Gallery, Allentown PA

Burke, Ken, *Prof,* Mills College, Art Dept, Oakland CA (S)

Burke, Kristin, *Dir Mktg,* Museum of Florida Art, Deland FL

Burke, Marcus, *Sr Cur Paintings & Metalwork,* The Hispanic Society of America, Museum & Library, New York NY

Burke, Mary, *Dir,* Sid W Richardson, Sid Richardson Museum, Fort Worth TX

Burke, Mary, *Pres,* Fremont Center for the Arts, Canon City CO

Burke, Mary Ann, *Exec Dir,* Washington County Arts Council, Gallery, Hagerstown MD

Burke, Maryellen, *Exec Dir,* Portsmouth Historical Society, John Paul Jones House & Discover Portsmouth, Portsmouth NH

Burke, Matt, *Asst Prof,* University of Kansas, The School of the Arts, Dept of Visual Art, Lawrence KS (S)

Burke, Peggy, *Exec Dir,* Concord Museum, Concord MA

Burke, Shannon, *Dir Educ,* Harriet Beecher Stowe, Hartford CT

Burke, Shannon, *Educ & Visitor Svcs,* Harriet Beecher Stowe, Library, Hartford CT

Burke, Sheila, *Under Secy for American Museums and Nat'l Programs,* Smithsonian Institution, Washington DC

Burke, William J, *Exec Dir,* Philadelphia Art Commission, Philadelphia PA

Burke, William J, *Prof,* Florida International University, School of Art & Art History, Miami FL (S)

Burkhard, Catherine, *Sec,* Guild of Book Workers, New York NY

Burkhauser, Elizabeth, *Instr,* Keystone College, Fine Arts Dept, LaPlume PA (S)

Burkheimer, Karl, *Chair, MFA,* Oregon College of Art & Craft, Portland OR (S)

Burks, Amanda, *Instr,* Biola University, Art Dept, La Mirada CA (S)

Burks, James V, *Facilities Dir,* City of Los Angeles, Cultural Affairs Dept, Los Angeles CA

Burks, Jean, *Sr Cur,* Shelburne Museum, Library, Shelburne VT

Burks, Sarah L, *Preservation-Planner,* Cambridge Historical Commission, Research Library on Architectural Social History of Cambridge, Mass, Cambridge MA

Burleigh, Kimberly, *Dir MFA Prog, Chair & Prof Fine Arts,* University of Cincinnati, School of Art, Cincinnati OH (S)

Burlingham, Cynthia, *Dir,* University of California, Los Angeles, Grunwald Center for the Graphic Arts at Hammer Museum, Los Angeles CA

Burmeister, Alice, *Asst Prof,* Winthrop University, Dept of Art & Design, Rock Hill SC (S)

Burner, Janet, *Ceramics Instr,* Tucson Museum of Art and Historic Block, Tucson AZ

Burnes, Susan E, *Pres,* Grants Pass Museum of Art, Grants Pass OR

Burnet, Ralph W, *Pres,* Walker Art Center, Minneapolis MN

Burnett, Barbara, *VPres,* Grants Pass Museum of Art, Grants Pass OR

Burnett, Brian, *Instr & Dir,* Toronto School of Art, Toronto ON (S)

Burnett, Ingrid, *Registrar,* Nicolaysen Art Museum & Discovery Center, Children's Discovery Center, Casper WY

Burnett, Ron, *Pres,* Emily Carr Institute of Art & Design, The Charles H Scott Gallery, Vancouver BC

Burnett, Ronald, *Pres & Vice Chancellor,* Emily Carr University of Art + Design, Vancouver BC (S)

Burnett, Sandra, *Exec Dir,* Salem Art Association, Bush Barn Art Center, Salem OR

Burnett, Vernon, *Customer Svcs Mgr,* Light Work, Robert B Menschel Photography Gallery, Syracuse NY

Burnette, Karin, *Dir Fin & Opers,* Southeastern Center for Contemporary Art, Winston Salem NC

Burnette, Marshall, *Mus Aid,* Indian Arts & Crafts Board, US Dept of the Interior, Sioux Indian Museum, Rapid City SD

Burnette, Scott, *Instr,* Guilford Technical Community College, Commercial Art Dept, Jamestown NC (S)

Burnham, Helen, *Pamela & Peter Voss Cur Prints & Drawings,* Museum of Fine Arts, Boston MA

Burnham, Laura E, *Exec Dir,* Abington Art Center, Jenkintown PA

Burnham, Richard, *2nd VPres,* Newport Historical Society & Museum of Newport History, Newport RI

Burns, B Jane, *Dir,* Midwest Museum of American Art, Elkhart IN

Burns, Barry, *Asst Prof,* California Lutheran University, Art Dept, Thousand Oaks CA (S)

Burns, Billie, *Secy Grad Students,* New York State College of Ceramics at Alfred University, School of Art & Design, Alfred NY (S)

Burns, Courtney, *Chief Cur,* New York State Military Museum and Veterans Research Center, Saratoga Springs NY

Burns, Erin, *Digital Photog,* North Seattle Community College, Art Dept, Seattle WA (S)

Burns, Mark, *Prof & Chmn,* University of Nevada, Las Vegas, Dept of Art, Las Vegas NV (S)

Burns, Michelle, *VPres Develop,* Newberry Library, Chicago IL

Burns, Millie, *Asst Prof Art Dir Hewitt Gallery,* Marymount Manhattan College, Fine & Performing Arts Div, New York NY (S)

Burns, Millie, *Dir,* Marymount Manhattan College Hewitt Gallery, New York NY

Burns, Todd, *Asst Prof,* University of Louisville, Allen R Hite Art Institute, Louisville KY (S)

Burns, W James, *Exec Dir,* Maricopa County Historical Society, Desert Caballeros Western Museum, Wickenburg AZ

Burr, Josephine, *Studio Mgr,* Greenwich House Inc, Greenwich House Pottery, New York NY (S)

Burrell, Debra, *Arts Coordr,* City of Hampton, Hampton Arts Commission, Hampton VA

Burrell, Jane, *VP Educ & Pub Progs,* Los Angeles County Museum of Art, Los Angeles CA

Burrell, William, *Prof,* Amarillo College, Visual Art Dept, Amarillo TX (S)

Burritt-Peffer, Deanna, *Libr Specialist II,* Old Dominion University, Elise N Hofheimer Art Library, Norfolk VA

Burrough, Margaret T, *Founder,* DuSable Museum of African American History, Chicago IL

Burroughs, Sarah, *Interim Dir,* Fisk University, Carl Van Vechten Gallery, Nashville TN

Burrows, Geoff, *Pres,* Sandwich Historical Society, Center Sandwich NH

Burrows-Johnson, Susan, *Exec Dir & CEO,* City of Lethbridge, Sir Alexander Galt Museum, Lethbridge AB

Burrus, Bobby, *VPres,* Red River Valley Museum, Vernon TX

Burson, Max M, *Library Dir,* Friends University, Edmund Stanley Library, Wichita KS

Burson, Nancy, *Admin Asst,* Scripps College, Clark Humanities Museum, Claremont CA

Burt, Ann, *Dir,* Ormond Memorial Art Museum and Gardens, Ormond Beach FL

Burt, Helen, *Instr,* Toronto Art Therapy Institute, Toronto ON (S)

Burt, Sarah, *Cur,* C M Russell, Frederic G Renner Memorial Library, Great Falls MT

Burt, Sarah, *Dir Mktg,* Women's Studio Workshop, Inc, Rosendale NY

Burtleson, Stacie, *Interim Chmn Dept Architecture,* Judson University, School of Art, Design & Architecture, Elgin IL (S)

Burton, Douglas, *Asst Prof,* Lenoir Rhyne College, Dept of Art, Hickory NC (S)

Burton, Johanna, *Dir Grad Prog,* Bard College, Center for Curatorial Studies and the Hessel Museum of Art, Annandale-on-Hudson NY

Burton, Johanna, *Grad Comt,* Bard College, Center for Curatorial Studies Graduate Program, Annandale-on-Hudson NY (S)

Burton, Judith, *Dir,* Columbia University, Teachers Col Program in Art & Art Educ, New York NY (S)

Burton, Troy, *Exec Dir,* Eubie Blake, Baltimore MD

Burton, Troy, *Pres,* North Carolina Museums Council, Raleigh NC

Burtscher, Sarah, *Dir Sales,* Stephen Bulger Gallery, Toronto ON

Burwell, Joan, *Mem Chairperson,* Three Forks Area Historical Society, Headwaters Heritage Museum, Three Forks MT

Burwick, Georg, *Cur Digital Media,* University of California, California Museum of Photography, Riverside CA

Bury, Stephen, *Andrew W Mellon Chief Librn,* The Frick Collection, Frick Art Reference Library, New York NY

Burzcyk, Monika, *Instr,* Springfield College, Dept of Visual & Performing Arts, Springfield MA (S)

Busby, James, *Chmn,* Houston Baptist University, Dept of Art, Houston TX (S)

Busby, Leonard, *Board Chmn,* American Swedish Historical Foundation & Museum, American Swedish Historical Museum, Philadelphia PA

Busceme, Greg, *Dir,* The Art Studio Inc, Beaumont TX

Busceme, Greg, *Instr,* Lamar University, Art Dept, Beaumont TX (S)

Busch, Ellen Cone, *Dir,* Planting Fields Foundation, Coe Hall at Planting Fields Arboretum, Oyster Bay NY

Busch, Janet, *Dir,* Fisher Art Gallery, Marshalltown IA

Busch, Janet L, *Dir,* Central Iowa Art Association, Inc, Art Reference Library, Marshalltown IA

Busch, Jason, *Cur Decorative Arts,* Carnegie Museums of Pittsburgh, Carnegie Museum of Art, Pittsburgh PA

Busch, Liz, *Mktg Mgr,* Green Hill Center for North Carolina Art, Greensboro NC

Buschor, Elizabeth, *Sr Paper Conservator,* Midwest Art Conservation Center, Minneapolis MN

Buser, Tom, *Assoc Prof,* University of Louisville, Allen R Hite Art Institute, Louisville KY (S)

Bush, Dena, *Educ Supv,* West Florida Historic Preservation, Inc/University of West Florida, T T Wentworth, Jr Florida State Museum; Historic Pensacola Village; Pensacola Historical Society & Resource Center, Pensacola FL

Bush, Harold, *Head of Security,* University of Illinois at Urbana-Champaign, Spurlock Museum, Champaign IL

Bush, Robert, *Sr VP Cultural & Community Investment,* Arts & Science Council, Charlotte NC

Bushara, Leslie, *Deputy Dir Educ & Guest Svcs,* Children's Museum of Manhattan, New York NY

Bushelle, Renee, *Visitor Svcs Mgr,* Staten Island Museum, Staten Island NY

Bushman, Mark, *Educ Coordr,* Salisbury University, Ward Museum of Wildfowl Art, Salisbury MD

Bushuev, Marina, *Accnt,* Women's Art Association of Canada, Dignam Gallery, Toronto ON

Buss, Josh, *Educ Dir,* City Arts Center at Fair Park, Oklahoma City OK

Bussard, Kate, *Peter C. Bunell Cur Photog,* Princeton University, Princeton University Art Museum, Princeton NJ

Bussmann, Jeffrey, *Develop Admin Asst,* University of Pennsylvania, Institute of Contemporary Art, Philadelphia PA

Bussmann, Tom, *Owner,* Philip Slein Gallery, Saint Louis MO

Bustamante, Cody A, *Prof,* Southern Oregon University, Art & Art History Dept, Ashland OR (S)

Bustos, Betty, *Archivist & Librn,* Panhandle-Plains Historical Museum, Research Center, Canyon TX

Buszkiewicz, Kathy, *Dept Head Jewelry & Metals,* Cleveland Institute of Art, Cleveland OH (S)

Butckovitz, Dean, *Gallery Mgr,* University of North Carolina at Charlotte, Dept Art, Charlotte NC (S)

Butler, Ann, *Librn,* Bard College, Center for Curatorial Studies and the Hessel Museum of Art, Annandale-on-Hudson NY

Butler, Charles T, *Dir,* Columbus Museum, Columbus GA

Butler, Christine, *Supv,* Parsons School of Design, Adam & Sophie Gimbel Design Library, New York NY

Butler, David, *Exec Dir,* Knoxville Museum of Art, Knoxville TN

Butler, Erin, *Newsletter Ed & Bd Mem,* Women in the Arts Foundation, Inc, Staten Island NY

Butler, Erin, *Project Mgr,* Municipal Art Society of New York, Greenacre Reference Library, New York NY

Butler, Gordon, *Chief Financial Officer,* Canadian Museum of Civilization, Gatineau PQ

Butler, Janine, *Librn,* Art Gallery of Windsor, Reference Library, Windsor ON

Butler, Janine, *Registrar,* McMichael Canadian Art Collection, Kleinburg ON

Butler, Jerry E, *Chmn,* Madison Area Technical College, Art Dept, Madison WI (S)

Butler, Joshua, *Assoc Prof,* Colorado Mesa University, Art Dept, Grand Junction CO (S)

Butler, Karen K, *Asst Cur,* Washington University, Mildred Lane Kemper Art Museum, Saint Louis MO

Butler, Kent, *Assoc Prof,* Azusa Pacific University, College of Liberal Arts, Art Dept, Azusa CA (S)

Butler, Maria, *Exec Dir,* Pensacola Museum of Art, Harry Thornton Library, Pensacola FL

Butler, Owen, *Assoc Prof,* Rochester Institute of Technology, School of Photographic Arts & Sciences, Rochester NY (S)

Butler, Philip, *Cur Arms & Militaria,* The Stewart Museum, Montreal PQ

Butler, Ruth, *Emeritus Prof,* University of Massachusetts - Boston, Art Dept, Boston MA (S)

Butler, Stephen M, *Graphic Design,* Art Institute of Pittsburgh, Pittsburgh PA (S)

Butler, Susan, *Prog Coordr Photog Dept,* Pine Manor College, Visual Arts Dept, Chestnut Hill MA (S)

Butler-Ludwig, John L, *Cur,* University of Chicago, Visual Resources Collection, Chicago IL

Butt, Harlan, *Regents Prof Metals,* University of North Texas, College of Visual Arts & Design, Denton TX (S)

Buttacavoli, Eva, *Exec Dir,* Dayton Visual Arts Center, Dayton OH

Butterfield, Tom, *Art Dir,* Virginia Polytechnic Institute & State University, Perspective Gallery, Blacksburg VA

Butterill, Dale, *Pres,* Women's Art Association of Canada, Dignam Gallery, Toronto ON

Butts, H Daniel, *Art Dir,* Mansfield Fine Arts Guild, Library, Mansfield OH

Butts, H Daniel, *Dir,* Mansfield Fine Arts Guild, Mansfield Art Center, Mansfield OH

Butts, Patricia, *Asst to Dir,* Columbus Museum, Columbus GA

Buttwinick, Edward, *Dir,* Brentwood Art Center, Los Angeles CA (S)

Butz, Bob, *Pres,* Phelps County Historical Society, Nebraska Prairie Museum, Holdrege NE

Butz, Robert, *Pres,* Phelps County Historical Society, Donald O. Lindgren Library, Holdrege NE

Buxbaum, Melba, *Chmn,* Blackburn College, Dept of Art, Carlinville IL (S)

Buxkamper, Barry, *Instr,* Middle Tennessee State University, Art Dept, Murfreesboro TN (S)

Buxton, Eliza, *Admin,* Carolina Art Association, Gibbes Museum of Art, Charleston SC

Buxton, Sharon, *Registrar,* Johnson-Humrickhouse Museum, Coshocton OH

Buyers, Jane, *Prof,* University of Waterloo, Fine Arts Dept, Waterloo ON (S)

Buzzard, Colleen, *VPres,* Rochester Contemporary, Art Center, Rochester NY

Byars, Anna, *Office Mgr,* Fort Smith Regional Art Museum, Fort Smith AR

Byars, Jeffrey, *Dir Develop,* Ohio State University, Wexner Center for the Arts, Columbus OH

Byce, Joane, *Instr,* Pierce College, Art Dept, Woodland Hills CA (S)

Bychinski, Jan, *Mus Receptionist,* Washburn University, Mulvane Art Museum, Topeka KS

Bye, Elizabeth, *Head Dept,* University of Minnesota, Dept of Design, Housing & Apparel, Saint Paul MN (S)

Bye, Jenny, *Studio Prog Coordr,* Sioux City Art Center, Sioux City IA (S)

Byers, Bill, *Dir,* Brevard College, Spiers Gallery, Brevard NC

Byers, Bill, *Prof,* Brevard College, Department of Art, Brevard NC (S)

Byers, Jason, *Preparator,* Intermuseum Conservation Association, Cleveland OH

Byers, Larry, *Assoc Prof,* Saint Louis Community College at Florissant Valley, Liberal Arts Division, Ferguson MO (S)

Bykonen, Paula Lisa, *Mus Protection Visitor Svcs Supvr,* Alaska Department of Education, Division of Libraries, Archives & Museums, Sheldon Jackson Museum, Sitka AK

Byler, Cynthia, *Asst Prof,* Lincoln University, Dept Visual and Performing Arts, Jefferson City MO (S)

Byrd, Cathy, *Dir,* Georgia State University, Ernest G Welch Gallery, Atlanta GA

Byrd, Chris, *Mktg Coordr,* Southern Methodist University, Meadows Museum, Dallas TX

Byrd, Cindy, *Exhibits/Folklife,* Salisbury University, Ward Museum of Wildfowl Art, Salisbury MD

Byrd, Jeff, *Prof, Art Dept Head,* University of Northern Iowa, Dept of Art, Cedar Falls IA (S)

Byrd, Joan, *Prof,* Western Carolina University, Dept of Art/College of Arts & Science, Cullowhee NC (S)

Byrd, John, *Assoc Prof,* University of South Florida, School The Arts, Tampa FL (S)

Byrn, Brian D, *Cur Exhib & Educ,* Midwest Museum of American Art, Elkhart IN

Byrne, Alison, *Cur Educ,* Contemporary Art Center of Virginia, Virginia Beach VA

Byrne, Elizabeth, *Head,* University of California, Berkeley, Environmental Design Library, Berkeley CA

Byrne, Joseph, *Chmn, Prof Fine Arts,* Trinity College, Dept of Studio Arts, Hartford CT (S)

Byron, Michael, *Assoc Dean,* Washington University, School of Art, Saint Louis MO (S)

Bytof, Corey, *Pub Rels,* City of San Rafael, Falkirk Cultural Center, San Rafael CA

Bywaters, Diane, *Prof,* University of Wisconsin-Stevens Point, Dept of Art & Design, Stevens Point WI (S)

Cabral, Louis, *Exec Dir,* ASTED Inc, Montreal QC

Cabrera, Yvette, *Prof*, University of Puerto Rico, Mayaguez, Dept of Humanities, College of Fine Arts & Theory of Art Programs, Mayaguez PR (S)

Cabrera, Yvette, *Prof*, University of Puerto Rico, Mayaguez, Dept of Humanities, College of Fine Arts & Theory of Art Programs, Mayaguez PR (S)

Caceres, Pedro, *Preparator*, University of Colorado, CU Art Museum, Boulder CO

Cadaret, Marge, *VPres*, Spectrum Gallery, Toledo OH

Cadby-Sorensen, Robin, *Vol Dir, Cur & Mus Shop Mgr*, Three Forks Area Historical Society, Headwaters Heritage Museum, Three Forks MT

Caddell, Flo, *Arts Dir*, Frankfort Community Public Library, Anna & Harlan Hubbard Gallery, Frankfort IN

Cade, Leslie, *Archivist & Records Mgr*, The Cleveland Museum of Art, Ingalls Library, Cleveland OH

Cade, Michael, *Exec Dir*, Chilliwack Community Arts Council, Community Arts Centre, Chilliwack BC

Cadez, Robert, *Mgr Enrichment*, Henry Ford Community College, McKenzie Fine Art Ctr, Dearborn MI (S)

Cadger, Neil, *Dept Head & Assoc Prof (Performance - Theater)*, University of British Columbia Okanagan, Dept of Creative Studies, Kelowna BC (S)

Cadora, Francis, *Instr*, University of Evansville, Art Dept, Evansville IN (S)

Cadou, Carol, *Sr Cur & VPres*, Mount Vernon Ladies' Association of the Union, Mount Vernon VA

Cagenello, Cynthia, *Dir Communs*, Hill-Stead Museum, Farmington CT

Cagno, Michael, *Exec Dir*, The Noyes Museum of Art, Oceanville NJ

Cahalan, Joseph M, *VPres Xerox Foundation*, Xerox Corporation, Art Collection, Norwalk CT

Cahalan, Sarah Burke, *Spec Project & Reference Librn*, Harvard University, Dumbarton Oaks Research Library, Washington DC

Cahan, Susan, *Assoc Prof*, University of Missouri, Saint Louis, Dept of Art & Art History, Saint Louis MO (S)

Cahill, Kristen, *Mus Store & Cafe Mgr*, Henry Morrison Flagler Museum, Palm Beach FL

Cahill, Linda F, *Sr Adv*, American Museum of Natural History, New York NY

Cahill, Nicholas D, *Prof*, University of Wisconsin, Madison, Dept of Art History, Madison WI (S)

Cahill, Stephen, *Photog*, Pitzer College, Dept of Art, Claremont CA (S)

Cahill, Theresa, *Bus & Vocations Librn*, Long Beach Public Library, Long Beach NY

Cain, Asante, *Reference & Adult Svcs Coordr*, Grand Rapids Public Library, Grand Rapids MI

Cain, John, *Exec Dir*, South Shore Arts, Munster IN

Cain, Marcus, *Cur*, Kansas City Jewish Museum of Contemporary Art - Epsten Gallery, Overland Park KS

Cain, Meredith, *Registrar*, Art Services International, Alexandria VA

Cain, Paula, *Head Technical Svcs*, Ponca City Library, Art Dept, Ponca City OK

Cain, Peggy, Massachusetts Institute of Technology, School of Architecture and Planning, Cambridge MA (S)

Cain, Roger, *Maintenance*, Rosemount Museum, Inc, Pueblo CO

Caine, William, *Proj Mgr*, United States General Services Administration, Art in Architecture and Fine Arts, Washington DC

Cairns, Carol, *Performing Arts Coordr*, Organization of Saskatchewan Arts Councils (OSAC), Regina SK

Cairns, R Christopher, *Prof*, Haverford College, Fine Arts Dept, Haverford PA (S)

Cairns, Roger, *Assoc Prof*, Montgomery County Community College, Art Center, Blue Bell PA (S)

Caivano, Felice, *Cur*, Trinity College, Austin Arts Center, Widener Gallery, Hartford CT

Caivano, Nicholas, *Lectr*, Georgian Court University, Dept of Art, Lakewood NJ (S)

Cajigas, Idalia, *Acct*, Museum for African Art, New York NY

Calabrese, John A, *Prof*, Texas Woman's University, School of the Arts, Dept of Visual Arts, Denton TX (S)

Calabria, Debbie, *Mem & Special Events Mgr*, Cultural Council of Palm Beach County, Lake Worth FL

Calabria, Susan, *Educ Cur*, Brattleboro Museum & Art Center, Brattleboro VT

Calafiore, Robert, *Asst Dean*, University of Hartford, Hartford Art School, West Hartford CT (S)

Calamia, Libby, *Bd Mem*, American Color Print Society, Huntingdon Valley PA

Caldemeyer, Charles D, *Assoc Prof*, Ashland University, Art Dept, Ashland OH (S)

Calden, Lisa, *Coll & Exhib Admin*, University of California, Berkeley, Berkeley Art Museum & Pacific Film Archive, Berkeley CA

Calder, Jacqueline, *Cur*, Vermont Historical Society, Museum, Montpelier VT

Calderon, Christopher, *Gallery Mgr*, Eastern New Mexico University, Golden Library/Runnels Gallery, Portales NM

Calderon, Ismael, *Dir Science*, Newark Museum Association, The Newark Museum, Newark NJ

Calderon-Rosado, Vanessa, *CEO*, Inquilinos Boricuas en Accion, Boston MA

Calderwood, Jessica, *Asst Prof*, University of Wisconsin Oshkosh, Dept of Art, Oshkosh WI (S)

Calderwood, Kathy, *Assoc Prof*, Nazareth College of Rochester, Art Dept, Rochester NY (S)

Caldwell, Blaine, *Gallery Dir*, University of the Ozarks, Stephens Gallery, Clarksville AR

Caldwell, Blaine, *Prof*, University of the Ozarks, Dept of Art, Clarksville AR (S)

Caldwell, Brenda, *Acting Park Supt*, Tuskegee Institute National Historic Site, George Washington Carver & The Oaks, Montgomery AL

Caldwell, Joan G, *Cur*, Tulane University, University Art Collection, New Orleans LA

Caldwell, Melissa, *Dir Exhibs*, Philadelphia Art Alliance, Philadelphia PA

Caldwell, Michael, *Prof*, Seattle Pacific University, Art Dept, Seattle WA (S)

Caldwell, Peter, *VPres Admin*, OCAD University, Toronto ON (S)

Calhoun, Laura, *Prog Dir*, Portsmouth Historical Society, John Paul Jones House & Discover Portsmouth, Portsmouth NH

Calidonna, Richard, *First VPres*, Rome Historical Society, Museum & Archives, Rome NY

Califano, Cheryl, *Mem & Box Office Mgr*, Sangre de Cristo Arts & Conference Center, Pueblo CO

Calinescu, Adriana, *Cur Ancient Art*, Indiana University, Art Museum, Bloomington IN

Calisch, Doug, *Prof*, Wabash College, Art Dept, Crawfordsville IN (S)

Call, Elizabeth, *Special Coll Librn*, Brooklyn Historical Society, Othmer Library, Brooklyn NY

Callaghan, Karen, *Dean*, Barry University, Dept of Fine Arts, Miami Shores FL (S)

Callahan, Betty, *Vis Coordr*, Okefenokee Heritage Center, Inc, Waycross GA

Callahan, Colin J, *Dir Art Center*, Saint Paul's School, Art Center in Hargate, Concord NH

Callahan, David, *Chief Librn Circ Coll Mgr*, The New York Public Library, The New York Public Library for the Performing Arts, New York NY

Callahan, Debra, *Educ*, Birmingham Bloomfield Art Center, Art Center, Birmingham MI

Callahan, Diane, *Adjunct Prof*, Southwest Baptist University, Art Dept, Bolivar MO (S)

Callahan, Kelly, *Vol Mgr*, Brookgreen Gardens, Murrells Inlet SC

Callahan, Michele, *Dir Admin Affairs*, Minneapolis Institute of Arts, Minneapolis MN

Callahan, Nancy, *Instr*, State University of New York College at Oneonta, Dept of Art, Oneonta NY (S)

Callahan, Patrick, *Dir*, Purchase College, Library, Purchase NY

Callan, Borislava, *Dir*, Callan Contemporary, New Orleans LA

Callan, Scott, *Exec Dir*, The History Center in Tompkins County, Ithaca NY

Callan, Steven, *Owner*, Callan Contemporary, New Orleans LA

Callanan, Nina, *Develop Dir*, Georgia O'Keeffe Museum, Santa Fe NM

Callans, Jennifer, *Exec Dir*, Anton Art Center, Mount Clemens MI

Callas, Tom, *Registrar*, Museum of Photographic Arts, Edmund L. and Nancy K Dubois Library, San Diego CA

Callaway, Cathy, *Cur Educ*, University of Missouri, Museum of Art & Archaeology, Columbia MO

Callender, Alexis, *Asst Tchg Prof*, University of Missouri - Columbia, Dept of Art, Columbia MO (S)

Callewaert, Megan, *Colls Mgr*, Edsel & Eleanor Ford, Grosse Pointe Shores MI

Callina, Phyllis, *Colls Mgr*, Alaska Museum of Natural History, Anchorage AK

Callis, Daniel, *Assoc Prof*, Biola University, Art Dept, La Mirada CA (S)

Calloway, Edwin, *Chmn*, Truett-McConnell College, Fine Arts Dept & Arts Dept, Cleveland GA (S)

Calloway, William, *Exec Dir*, South Carolina State Museum, Columbia SC

Calluori Holcombe, Anna, *Prof*, University of Florida, School of Art & Art History, Gainesville FL (S)

Callupe, Eveline, *Mgr, Mem Develop*, Canadian Museums Association, Association des Musees Canadiens, Ottawa ON

Calo, Mary Ann, *Asst Prof*, Colgate University, Dept of Art & Art History, Hamilton NY (S)

Calvert, Ann, *Dean, Faculty Fine Arts*, University of Calgary, Dept of Art, Calgary AB (S)

Calvert, Emily, *Colls Management*, Museum of Latin American Art, Long Beach CA

Calvin, James, *Assoc Prof (Sculpture)*, University of Missouri - Columbia, Dept of Art, Columbia MO (S)

Calvin, Suzanne, *Admin Asst*, Ursinus College, Philip & Muriel Berman Museum of Art, Collegeville PA

Calza, Susan, *Prof Sculpture*, Johnson State College, Dept Fine & Performing Arts, Dibden Center for the Arts, Johnson VT (S)

Calzonetti, Jo Ann, *Head Librn*, West Virginia University, Evansdale Library, Morgantown WV

Camara, Esperanca, *Asst Prof*, University of Saint Francis, School of Creative Arts, Fort Wayne IN (S)

Cambareri, Marietta, *Cur Dec Arts & Sculpture*, Museum of Fine Arts, Boston MA

Cambre, Javier, *Asst Prof*, Queensborough Community College, Dept of Art & Photography, Bayside Hills NY (S)

Camden, Valerie, *Coordr Permanent Coll*, Galerie Montcalm, Gatineau PQ

Cameron, Ben, *Instr*, Columbia College, Art Dept, Columbia MO (S)

Cameron, Dan, *Guest Visual Arts Cur*, Contemporary Arts Center, New Orleans LA

Cameron, Linda, *Prog Mgr*, Minnesota Historical Society, Minnesota State Capitol Historic Site, St Paul MN

Cameron, Nick, *Chief Oper Officer*, Indianapolis Museum of Art, Indianapolis IN

Cameron, Sandy, *Acting Dir & Librn*, Regina Public Library, Art Dept, Regina SK

Cameron, Thomas, *Pres*, Long Branch Historical Museum, Long Branch NJ

Cammuso, Philomena M, *Exec Dir*, Seneca Falls Historical Society Museum, Seneca Falls NY

Camp, Ann, *Asst Cur Educ*, City of El Paso, El Paso TX

Camp, Carl, *Cur*, Utah Department of Natural Resources, Division of Parks & Recreation, Territorial Statehouse State Park Museum, Fillmore UT

Camp, Donna, *Mus Shop Dir*, C M Russell, Frederic G Renner Memorial Library, Great Falls MT

Camp, Kimberly, *Exec Dir*, Barnes Foundation, Merion PA

Camp, Roger, *Chmn & Instr*, Golden West College, Visual Art Dept, Huntington Beach CA (S)

Camp, Susan, *Adjunct Asst Prof*, University of Maine, Dept of Art, Orono ME (S)

Campagna, Barbara, *Architect*, National Trust for Historic Preservation, Washington DC

Campbell, Anna, *Asst Prof*, Grand Valley State University, Art & Design Dept, Allendale MI (S)

Campbell, Barbara, *Prof*, University of North Carolina at Greensboro, Art Dept, Greensboro NC (S)

Campbell, Bruce, *Ctr for Earth*, National Air and Space Museum, Smithsonian Institution, Washington DC

Campbell, C Jean, *Prof*, Emory University, Art History Dept, Atlanta GA (S)

Campbell, Carol, *Acting Mgr Exhib Svcs & Proj Mgr Temp Exhib*, Canadian Museum of Nature, Musee Canadien de la Nature, Ottawa ON

Campbell, Charles, *Instr*, Saint Mary's University of Minnesota, Art & Design Dept, Winona MN (S)

Campbell, Colin, *Pres*, Colonial Williamsburg Foundation, Williamsburg VA

Campbell, Critz, *Asst Prof*, Mississippi State University, Dept of Art, Starville MS (S)

Campbell, Cyndie, *Head Archives*, National Gallery of Canada, Library, Ottawa ON

Campbell, Deborah, *Instr*, Adrian College, Art & Design Dept, Adrian MI (S)

Campbell, Dennis, *Maintenance Tech*, Belle Grove Inc., Belle Grove Plantation, Middletown VA

Campbell, Elaine, *Educ Dir*, Gadsden Museum of Fine Arts, Inc, Gadsden Museum of Art and History, Gadsden AL

Campbell, Graham, *Chmn*, Brandeis University, Dept of Fine Arts, Waltham MA (S)

Campbell, Heather, *Cur Mus Progs*, University of Richmond, University Museums, Richmond VA

Campbell, Ina, *Pres*, Historical Society of Bloomfield, Bloomfield NJ

Campbell, James, *Librn*, New Haven Museum & Historical Society, Whitney Library, New Haven CT

Campbell, James W, *Librn*, New Haven Museum & Historical Society, New Haven CT

Campbell, Janet, *Bus Mgr*, Woodrow Wilson, Woodrow Wilson Presidential Library, Staunton VA

Campbell, Jayne, *Instr*, Glendale Community College, Visual & Performing Arts Div, Glendale CA (S)

Campbell, Jessica, *Educ Coordr*, Southern Alleghenies Museum of Art, Loretto Facility, Loretto PA

Campbell, Joel, *Educ Outreach Coordr*, The Robert McLaughlin, Oshawa ON

Campbell, Katharine H, *Dir*, The Sandwich Historical Society, Inc & Sandwich Glass Museum, Sandwich Glass Museum, Sandwich MA

Campbell, Kathleen, *Grant Writer*, University of Minnesota, Goldstein Museum of Design, Saint Paul MN

Campbell, Kay, *Assoc Prof*, Oregon State University, Dept of Art, Corvallis OR (S)

Campbell, L Kathleen, *Asst Prof*, Appalachian State University, Dept of Art, Boone NC (S)

Campbell, Laurel, *Asst Prof*, Indiana-Purdue University, Dept of Fine Arts, Fort Wayne IN (S)

Campbell, Mary, *Prof*, New Jersey City University, Art Dept, Jersey City NJ (S)

Campbell, Maryann, *Librr Dir*, Oregon Historical Society, Research Library, Portland OR

Campbell, Mei Wan, *Cur Ethnology & Textiles*, Texas Tech University, Museum of Texas Tech University, Lubbock TX

Campbell, Michael, *Asst Prof*, Shippensburg University, Art Dept, Shippensburg PA (S)

Campbell, Mona, *Admin Mgr*, The Arts Council of Winston-Salem & Forsyth County, Winston Salem NC

Campbell, Nancy, *Dir*, Wayne Art Center, Wayne PA

Campbell, Naomi, *VPres Painting*, Catharine Lorillard Wolfe, New York NY

Campbell, Sally, *Asst Prof*, University of Texas at Tyler, Department of Art, School of Visual & Performing Arts, Tyler TX (S)

Campbell, Stephen, *Chmn*, Spring Hill College, Department of Fine & Performing Arts, Mobile AL (S)

Campbell, Stephen, *Chmn*, Johns Hopkins University, Dept of the History of Art, Baltimore MD (S)

Campbell, Susan, *Adjunct Faculty*, University of Maryland, Baltimore County, Imaging & Digital Arts (IMDA), Dept of Visual Arts, Baltimore MD (S)

Campbell, Tom, *Instr*, Toronto School of Art, Toronto ON (S)

Campbell, Tony, *Vis Artist*, University of New Orleans-Lake Front, Dept of Fine Arts, New Orleans LA (S)

Campbell-Miller, Megan, *Production Coordr*, Cornish College of the Arts, Fisher Gallery, Seattle WA

Campognone, Andi, *Assoc Dir*, Riverside Art Museum, Riverside CA

Campos, Alexander, *Exec Dir*, Center for Book Arts, New York NY

Campos, Dee, *Progs Asst*, En Foco, Inc, Bronx NY

Canaves, Marie, *Prof*, Cape Cod Community College, Art Dept, West Barnstable MA (S)

Candee, Richard, *Pres*, Portsmouth Historical Society, John Paul Jones House & Discover Portsmouth, Portsmouth NH

Cane, Shannon Michael, *Distribution Asst*, Printed Matter, Inc, New York NY

Canfield, Linda, *Cur Arts*, University of Notre Dame, Snite Museum of Art, Notre Dame IN

Canfield, Megan, *Educ Coordr*, Liberty Hall Historic Site, Library, Frankfort KY

Cangelosi, Keith, *Chmn Memorial Hall Comt*, Confederate Memorial Hall, Confederate Museum, New Orleans LA

Caniff, Al, *Chmn*, Western State College of Colorado, Quigley Hall Art Gallery, Gunnison CO

Cann, Tyler, *Assoc Cur Contemp Art*, Columbus Museum of Art, Columbus OH

Cannady, Shelly, *CFO*, Telfair Museums' Jepson Center for the Arts Library, Telfair Academy of Arts & Sciences Library, Savannah GA

Cannady, Shelly, *Financial Officer*, Telfair Museums' Jepson Center for the Arts Library, Savannah GA

Cannell, Karen T., *FIT Spec Coll & Archives*, Fashion Institute of Technology, Gladys Marcus Library - SUNY, New York NY

Canniffe, Bernard, *Chair Design Dept*, Minneapolis College of Art & Design, Minneapolis MN (S)

Canning, Jonathan, *Cur Martin D'Arcy Col*, Loyola University Chicago, Loyola University Museum of Art, Chicago IL

Canning, Scott, *Dir Horticulture*, Wave Hill, Bronx NY

Canning, Stephanie, *Exhib & Educ Coordr*, Saskatchewan Craft Council & Affinity Gallery, Saskatoon SK

Canning, Susan, *Prof*, The College of New Rochelle, School of Arts & Sciences Art Dept, New Rochelle NY (S)

Cannizzo, Anna, *Cur Colls*, Denison University, Art Gallery, Granville OH

Cannon, Caley, *Ref Librn*, Savannah College of Art & Design - Atlanta, ACA Library of Atlanta, Atlanta GA

Cannon, Michael, *CFO*, Menil Foundation, Inc, The Menil Collection, Houston TX

Cannon, Robert, *Dir*, Public Library of Charlotte & Mecklenburg County, Charlotte NC

Cannon, Sara L, *Mus Educator*, Cultural Affairs Department, Los Angeles Municipal Art Gallery, Los Angeles CA

Cannuli, Richard, *Chmn*, Villanova University, Dept of Theater, Villanova PA (S)

Cannuli, Richard, *Dir*, Villanova University Art Gallery, The Art Gallery, Villanova PA

Cannup, John, *VPres Facilities Management*, The Mariners' Museum, Newport News VA

Cano, Rose Marie, *Exec Dir*, Plaza de la Raza Cultural Center, Los Angeles CA

Canright, Steve, *Cur Maritime History*, San Francisco Maritime National Historical Park, Maritime Museum, San Francisco CA

Cantella, Michael, *Multimedia & Web Design*, Art Institute of Pittsburgh, Pittsburgh PA (S)

Canter, Bruce, *Dir Opers*, Delaware Art Museum, Wilmington DE

Canter, Nancy, *Dean Creative Arts*, De Anza College, Creative Arts Division, Cupertino CA (S)

Canter, Stacy, *Bus Mgr*, The National Quilt Museum, Paducah KY

Cantieni, Graham, *Prof*, University of Quebec, Trois Rivieres, Fine Arts Section, Trois Rivieres PQ (S)

Cantley, John, *Dir*, County of Los Angeles, Century Gallery, Sylmar CA

Cantor, Mira, *Assoc Prof*, Northeastern University, Dept of Art & Architecture, Boston MA (S)

Cantrell, Jimmy, *Instr*, John C Calhoun, Department of Fine Arts, Tanner AL (S)

Cantu, Anthony, *Dean*, Fresno City College, Art Dept, Fresno CA (S)

Cantwell, Kevin, *Chmn*, Middle Georgia State College, Humanities Division, Dept of Art - School of Liberal Arts, Dept of Media, Culture & the Arts, Cochran GA (S)

Cantwell, Kyley, *Cur Coll*, Museum of East Texas, Lufkin TX

Cantwell, Louise, *Pres*, San Antonio Art League, Library, San Antonio TX

Canty, Scott, *Cur*, Cultural Affairs Department, Los Angeles Municipal Art Gallery, Los Angeles CA

Canty, Scott, *Exhib Dir*, Palos Verdes Art Center/Beverly G. Alpay Center for Arts Education, Rancho Palos Verdes CA

Canty-Jones, Eliza, *Ed*, Oregon Historical Society, Oregon History Museum, Portland OR

Cao, Nancy, *Develop Assoc*, Museum of African American History, Boston MA

Cao, Yvonne, *Asst Prof*, University of Mary Hardin-Baylor, College of Visual & Performing Arts, Belton TX (S)

Capasso, Nick, *Sr Cur*, DeCordova Museum & Sculpture Park, DeCordova Museum, Lincoln MA

Capawana, Sarah, *Chmn Art Dept*, Mesa Community College, Dept of Art, Mesa AZ (S)

Capehart, Lucy, *Reg*, University of Montana, Montana Museum of Art & Culture, Missoula MT

Capello, Stephanie, *VPres Develop*, Please Touch Museum, Philadelphia PA

Capener, Richard, *VP*, Art Gallery of Bancroft Inc, Bancroft ON

Caperton, John, *Cur*, The Print Center, Philadelphia PA

Caperton y Montoya, Will, *Dir Mktg & Devel*, City of Los Angeles, Cultural Affairs Dept, Los Angeles CA

Caplan, Alison, *Sr Educator*, Akron Art Museum, Akron OH

Caplan, Margi, *Mem & Mktg Dir*, Smith College, Museum of Art, Northampton MA

Capone, Truman, *Prof*, Virginia Polytechnic Institute & State University, Dept of Art & Art History, Blacksburg VA (S)

Capote, Melody, *Dir*, Caribbean Cultural Center, Cultural Arts Organization & Resource Center, New York NY

Capozzi, Gloria, *Prog Coordr*, Maitland Art Center, Library, Maitland FL

Cappellazzo, Amy, *Gallery Dir*, Miami-Dade Community College, Wolfson Galleries, Miami FL

Capper, Karen, *Trustee*, Merrick Art Gallery, New Brighton PA

Capps, John, *Interim Chmn Div Human*, Virginia Western Community College, Communication Design, Fine Art & Photography, Roanoke VA (S)

Cappuccio, Guy, *Brd Treas*, Mohawk Valley Heritage Association, Inc, Walter Elwood Museum, Amsterdam NY

Cappuccio, Thomas, *Prof*, Northern Michigan University, Dept of Art & Design, Marquette MI (S)

Capshaw, William, *Pres*, Oak Ridge Art Center, Oak Ridge TN

Capuano, James, *Supvr*, Newark Public Library, Reference, Newark NJ

Caputo, Victor, *Coordr Progs & Pub Rels*, Bryant Library, Roslyn NY

Carabell, Paula, *Asst Prof Art History*, Florida Atlantic University, D F Schmidt College of Arts & Letters Dept of Visual Arts & Art History, Boca Raton FL (S)

Caragol, Taina, *Cur Latino Art & History*, National Portrait Gallery, Smithsonian Institution, Washington DC

Caraska, Claire, *Communs Assoc*, Museum of Contemporary Art, San Diego, La Jolla CA

Caraska, Claire, *Communs Assoc*, Museum of Contemporary Art San Diego, San Diego CA

Carbone, David, *Assoc Prof*, State University of New York at Albany, Art Dept, Albany NY (S)

Carbone, Kathy, *Performing Arts Librn*, California Institute of the Arts Library, Santa Clarita CA

Carbone, Teresa A, *Andrew W Mellon Cur American Art; Mng Cur, Arts of the Americas & Europe*, Brooklyn Museum, Brooklyn NY

Carbonell, Marilyn, *Head Lib Svcs*, The Nelson-Atkins Museum of Art, Spencer Art Reference Library, Kansas City MO

Carboni, James, *Dir Curatorial Svcs*, Louisiana Department of Culture, Recreation & Tourism, Louisiana Historical Center Library, New Orleans LA

Cardell, Victor, *Music Librn*, San Diego Public Library, Art, Music & Recreation, San Diego CA

Cardenas, Cynthia, *Gift Shop Admin*, University of California, California Museum of Photography, Riverside CA

Cardenas, Virginia, *Secy*, Xico Inc, Chandler AZ

Cardinal, Jaré, *Dir,* Seneca-Iroquois National Museum, Salamanca NY

Cardoni, Edmund, *Dir,* Hallwalls Contemporary Arts Center, Buffalo NY

Cardoso, Orysia, *Pres,* Ukrainian Institute of Modern Art, Chicago IL

Cardot, Gary, *Asst Prof,* Mercyhurst College, Dept of Art, Erie PA (S)

Carey, Doreen, *Operations Mgr,* Academy of the New Church, Glencairn Museum, Bryn Athyn PA

Carey, Ellen, *Assoc Prof,* University of Hartford, Hartford Art School, West Hartford CT (S)

Carey, Frank, *Asst Head Librn,* Daemen College, Marian Library, Amherst NY

Carey, Linda, *Accounting Mgr,* Lannan Foundation, Santa Fe NM

Carfano, Georgiana, *Mem,* The Butler Institute of American Art, Art Museum, Youngstown OH

Cargill, Jennifer, *Dean LSU Libraries,* Louisiana State University, Library, Baton Rouge LA

Cargill, Jennifer, *Dean Libraries,* Louisiana State University, Middleton Library, Baton Rouge LA

Cargill, Jim, *Chmn,* Black Hills State University, Art Dept, Spearfish SD (S)

Cariglia, Andrew, *Head Bldgs & Grounds,* American Antiquarian Society, Worcester MA

Cariolano, Jody, *Assoc Prof,* Our Lady of the Lake University, Dept of Art, San Antonio TX (S)

Carl, Jeff, *Gallery Dir,* Judson University, School of Art, Design & Architecture, Elgin IL (S)

Carlano, Annie, *Dir,* The Mint Museum, Mint Museum of Craft & Design, Charlotte NC

Carlano, Annie, *Dir Craft & Design,* The Mint Museum, Charlotte NC

Carlano, Annie, *Dir Craft Design,* The Mint Museum, Art Organization & Library, Charlotte NC

Carlevaro, Giorgio, *Chief Preparator,* Santa Monica Museum of Art, Santa Monica CA

Carley, Brian, *Preparator,* Longwood Center for the Visual Arts, Farmville VA

Carley, Michal Ann, *Instr,* Cardinal Stritch University, Art Dept, Milwaukee WI (S)

Carlin, Brad, *Develop Dir,* Guadalupe Cultural Arts Center, San Antonio TX

Carlin Fogerty, Karen, *Instr,* Wayne Art Center, Wayne PA (S)

Carlisle, Roger, *Assoc Prof,* Arkansas State University, Dept of Art, State University AR (S)

Carlos, Gary, *Instr,* San Joaquin Delta College, Arts & Communication, Stockton CA (S)

Carlson, Arnold, *Prof Sculpture,* Northwestern College, Te Paske Gallery, Orange City IA

Carlson, Bettie, *Registrar,* Worcester Center for Crafts, Worcester MA (S)

Carlson, Brian, *Assoc Dean,* Milwaukee Area Technical College, School of Media & Creative Arts, Milwaukee WI (S)

Carlson, David, *Asst Prof,* Azusa Pacific University, College of Liberal Arts, Art Dept, Azusa CA (S)

Carlson, Eleanor, *Chmn Music Dept,* University of Massachusetts Dartmouth, College of Visual & Performing Arts, North Dartmouth MA (S)

Carlson, Elizabeth, *Assoc Prof,* Lawrence University, Dept of Art & Art History, Appleton WI (S)

Carlson, Helen, *Pres,* Legacy Ltd, Seattle WA

Carlson, Kristi, *Chair,* Waldorf College, Art Dept, Forest City IA (S)

Carlson, M Teresa, *Acting Dir,* University of Saskatchewan, Diefenbaker Canada Centre, Saskatoon SK

Carlson, Noel, *VChmn,* Plumas County Museum, Museum Archives, Quincy CA

Carlson, Warner, *Secy,* Phelps County Historical Society, Nebraska Prairie Museum, Holdrege NE

Carlson, Wayne E, *Chmn,* Ohio State University, Dept of Industrial Interior & Visual Communication Design, Columbus OH (S)

Carlson, William, *Secy,* Wellfleet Historical Society & Museum, Inc, Wellfleet MA

Carlson, William D., *Prof,* University of Miami, Dept of Art & Art History, Coral Gables FL (S)

Carman, Charles, *Assoc Prof,* University at Buffalo, State University of New York, Dept of Visual Studies, Buffalo NY (S)

Carmichael, Amber, *Office Mgr,* Willard Arts Center, Carr Gallery, Colonial Theater, Idaho Falls ID

Carmichael, Kris, *Supv,* Page-Walker Arts & History Center, Cary NC

Carmon, Elaine, *Fin Mgr,* Community Council for the Arts, Kinston NC

Carnage, Candice, *Dir Fin & Admin,* Children's Museum of Manhattan, New York NY

Carnahan, John, *VPres Develop & Mktg,* New York State Historical Association, Fenimore Art Museum, Cooperstown NY

Carnell, Brett, *Head Technical Svcs Section,* Library of Congress, Prints & Photographs Division, Washington DC

Carner, Bill, *Imaging Mgr,* University of Louisville, Ekstrom Library Photographic Archives, Louisville KY

Carney, Hoarce, *Chmn,* Alabama A & M University, Art & Art Education Dept, Normal AL (S)

Carney, Joseph T, *Dir Develop,* University of Rochester, Memorial Art Gallery, Rochester NY

Carney, Kathleen, *Dir,* College of the Holy Cross, Dinand Library, Worcester MA

Carney, Tiffany, *Mgr Special Events,* The American Federation of Arts, New York NY

Carns, Janet, *Asst to Dir,* Westmoreland Museum of American Art, Art Reference Library, Greensburg PA

Carnwath, Squeak, *Undergrad faculty adv,* University of California, Berkeley, College of Letters & Sciences-Art Practice Dept, Berkeley CA (S)

Carolan, Karen, *Exec Dir Appraisals,* Art Dealers Association of America, Inc, New York NY

Carothers, Mary, *Assoc Prof,* University of Louisville, Allen R Hite Art Institute, Louisville KY (S)

Carpenter, Edie, *Cur,* Green Hill Center for North Carolina Art, Greensboro NC

Carpenter, Karen, *Secy,* Portsmouth Historical Society, John Paul Jones House & Discover Portsmouth, Portsmouth NH

Carpenter, Ken, *Pres (Toronto),* International Association of Art Critics, AICA Canada, Inc, Toronto ON

Carpenter, Linda, *Dir Advancement,* American Textile History Museum, Lowell MA

Carpenter, Margot, *Exec Dir,* Aesthetic Realism Foundation, New York NY

Carpenter, Margot, *Exec Dir,* Aesthetic Realism Foundation, New York NY (S)

Carpenter, Richard, *Pres,* John C Calhoun, Art Gallery, Decatur AL

Carpenter, Syd, *Prof,* Swarthmore College, Dept of Art & Art History, Swarthmore PA (S)

Carpenter, William, *Asst Prof,* Indiana Wesleyan University, School of Arts & Humanities, Division of Art, Marion IN (S)

Carr, Annemarie Weyl, *VPres,* International Center of Medieval Art, New York NY

Carr, Dennis, *Lynch Cur Decorative Arts & Sculpture,* Museum of Fine Arts, Boston MA

Carr, Jeffrey, *Prof,* Saint Mary's College of Maryland, Art & Art History Dept, Saint Mary's City MD (S)

Carr, Jeffrey, *Registrar,* Ohio University, Kennedy Museum of Art, Athens OH

Carr, Mary Margaret, *Colls Mgr,* United States General Services Administration, Art in Architecture and Fine Arts, Washington DC

Carr, Mindi, *Pub Information Officer,* Phoenix Art Museum, Phoenix AZ

Carracio, Kathleen, *Lectr,* Coe College, Dept of Art, Cedar Rapids IA (S)

Carrageorge, Adrianne, *Asst Prof,* Rochester Institute of Technology, School of Photographic Arts & Sciences, Rochester NY (S)

Carranza, Nicolas, *Facilities Mgr,* Memphis Brooks Museum of Art, Memphis TN

Carraro, Francine, *Dir,* National Museum of Wildlife Art of the Unites States, Library, Jackson WY

Carrasco-Zanini, Adrian, *Instr,* Butte College, Dept of Fine Arts and Communication Tech, Oroville CA (S)

Carraway, Charles W, *Assoc Prof,* Jackson State University, Dept of Art, Jackson MS (S)

Carreiro, Joel, *Head MFA Prog,* Hunter College, Art Dept, New York NY (S)

Carrell, Dan, *Chmn,* Benedictine College, Art Dept, Atchison KS (S)

Carrico, Anita, *Head,* University of Maryland, College Park, Architecture Library, College Park MD

Carrillo, Alex, *Instr,* Pierce College, Art Dept, Woodland Hills CA (S)

Carrillo, Claudia, *Secy,* Modern Art Museum, Fort Worth TX

Carrillo, Laura, *Event Coordr & Gallery Asst,* Board of Parks & Recreation, The Parthenon, Nashville TN

Carrillo, Rhonda, *VPres,* Xico Inc, Chandler AZ

Carrion, Gwendolyn, *Mus Coord,* Glessner House Museum, Chicago IL

Carrizzi, Stacy, *Bus Mgr,* Urban Institute for Contemporary Arts, Grand Rapids MI

Carrlee, Ellen, *Conservator,* Alaska State Museum, Juneau AK

Carrlee, Scott, *Cur Mus Svcs,* Alaska State Museum, Juneau AK

Carroll, Charles, *Pres,* New Mexico Art League, Gallery & School, Albuquerque NM

Carroll, Christina, *Mgr Institutional Advancement,* College of William & Mary, Muscarelle Museum of Art, Williamsburg VA

Carroll, David, *Dir Coll & Exhibs,* University of Utah, Utah Museum of Fine Arts, Salt Lake City UT

Carroll, Holly, *Interim Dir,* Cleveland Public Library, Fine Arts & Special Collections Dept, Cleveland OH

Carroll, James F L, *Dir,* New Arts Program, Inc, NAP Museum, Gallery, Resource Library, Kutztown PA

Carroll, Joanne, *Admin Asst,* New Arts Program, Inc, NAP Museum, Gallery, Resource Library, Kutztown PA

Carroll, John, *Adjunct Prof Fine Art,* Johnson County Community College, Fine Arts Dept & Art History Dept, Overland Park KS (S)

Carroll, Julianne, *Dir Traditional Arts,* South Carolina Arts Commission, Columbia SC

Carroll, Karen, *Dir,* Maryland Institute, Art Education Graduate Studies, Baltimore MD (S)

Carroll, Margaret, *Prof,* Wellesley College, Art Dept, Wellesley MA (S)

Carroll, Mike, *Contact,* The Schoolhouse Gallery, Provincetown MA

Carroll, Theresa, *Educ Programmer, Sch,* Burnaby Art Gallery, Burnaby BC

Carron, Christian, *Dir Educ & Interpretation,* Grand Rapids Public Museum, Public Museum of Grand Rapids, Grand Rapids MI

Carroway, Rosemary, *Lectr,* Lambuth University, Dept of Human Ecology & Visual Arts, Jackson TN (S)

Carruthers, Meredith, *Asst to Dir/Cur,* Saidye Bronfman, Liane & Danny Taran Gallery, Montreal PQ

Carson, Cheryl, *Dir Develop,* Painted Bride Art Center Gallery, Philadelphia PA

Carson, David, *Pub Affairs Dir,* Henry Morrison Flagler Museum, Palm Beach FL

Carson, Denise, *Dir,* Bethany College, Wallerstedt Library, Lindsborg KS

Carson, JoAnne, *Dept Chair & Prof,* State University of New York at Albany, Art Dept, Albany NY (S)

Carson, John, *Head,* Carnegie Mellon University, School of Art, Pittsburgh PA (S)

Carson, Juli, *Assoc Prof Art History & Cur Studies,* University of California, Irvine, Studio Art Dept, Irvine CA (S)

Carson Pastan, Elizabeth, *Assoc Prof,* Emory University, Art History Dept, Atlanta GA (S)

Cart, Doran L, *Cur,* Liberty Memorial Museum & Archives, The National Museum of World War I, Kansas City MO

Cart, Ella, *VPres,* Glynn Art Association, Saint Simons Island GA

Cartagena, Jose, *Exhib Designer,* United States Military Academy, West Point Museum, West Point NY

Carte-Blanchenot, Suzanne, *Outreach Programmer,* University of Toronto at Mississauga, Blackwood Gallery, Mississauga ON

Carter, Alice, *Librn,* Montgomery Museum of Fine Arts, Montgomery AL

Carter, Alice T, *Librn,* Montgomery Museum of Fine Arts, Library, Montgomery AL

Carter, Blythe, *Store Mgr,* Sheldon Museum & Cultural Center, Inc, Sheldon Museum & Cultural Center, Haines AK

Carter, Bobbie, *Dir Human Resources,* Chicago History Museum, Chicago IL

Carter, Carol Ann, *Prof,* University of Kansas, The School of the Arts, Dept of Visual Art, Lawrence KS (S)

Carter, Charles Hill, *Owner,* Shirley Plantation Foundation, Charles City VA

Carter, Claire, *Asst Cur,* Scottsdale Cultural Council, Scottsdale Museum of Contemporary Art, Scottsdale AZ

Carter, Genevieve, *Photographer & Cur,* Huronia Museum, Gallery of Historic Huronia, Midland ON

Carter, Greg, *Temp Asst Prof,* Georgia Southern University, Dept of Art, Statesboro GA (S)

Carter, Joseph, *Dir,* Will Rogers Memorial Museum & Birthplace Ranch, Media Center Library, Claremore OK

Carter, Keith, *Prof,* Lamar University, Art Dept, Beaumont TX (S)

Carter, Lisa R, *Photographic Archivist,* The Art Museum at the University of Kentucky, Photographic Archives, Lexington KY

Carter, Lynn, *VPres,* The American-Scandinavian Foundation, Scandinavia House: The Nordic Center in America, New York NY

Carter, Mary, *Dir,* Museum of Neon Art, Los Angeles CA

Carter, Maureen, *Technical Svcs Librn,* OCAD University, Dorothy H Hoover Library, Toronto ON

Carter, Monica, *Office Mgr,* Glynn Art Association, Saint Simons Island GA

Carter, Nathan, *Fine Arts Dept Chmn,* Morgan State University, Dept of Art, Baltimore MD (S)

Carter, Patricia, *Temp Asst Prof,* Georgia Southern University, Dept of Art, Statesboro GA (S)

Carter, Randy, *Deputy Dir,* Shirley Plantation Foundation, Charles City VA

Carter, Susan, *Cur & Registrar,* University of Tampa, Henry B Plant Museum, Tampa FL

Carter, Tara Y, *Dean, Arts, Communs & Social Sciences,* Kishwaukee College, Art Dept, Malta IL (S)

Carter, Val, *Sr Instr,* University of Idaho/College of Art & Architecture, Dept of Art & Design, Moscow ID (S)

Carter Martine, Margaret, *Instr,* Appalachian State University, Dept of Art, Boone NC (S)

Carter Southard, Edna, *Cur Coll,* Miami University, Art Museum, Oxford OH

Cartier, Francois, *Cur History & Archives,* McCord Museum of Canadian History, Montreal PQ

Cartiere, Cameron, *Dean Faculty of Grad Studies,* Emily Carr University of Art + Design, Vancouver BC (S)

Cartland, Elizabeth, *Dir Develop,* Portland Museum of Art, Portland ME

Cartmell, Timothy, *Mus Store Mgr,* Board of Parks & Recreation, The Parthenon, Nashville TN

Carton, Deborah, *Librn,* Berkeley Public Library, Berkeley CA

Cartwright, Derrick R, *Dir,* Seattle Art Museum, McCaw Foundation Asian Art Library, Seattle WA

Cartwright, Derrick R, *Dir,* Seattle Art Museum, Ann P Wyckoff Teacher Resource Center, Seattle WA

Cartwright, Derrick R, *Dir,* Seattle Art Museum, Olympic Park, Seattle WA

Cartwright, Guenther, *Assoc Prof,* Rochester Institute of Technology, School of Photographic Arts & Sciences, Rochester NY (S)

Cartwright, Rick, *Dean,* University of Saint Francis, School of Creative Arts, John P Weatherhead Gallery & Lupke Gallery, Fort Wayne IN

Cartwright, Rick, *Dean,* University of Saint Francis, School of Creative Arts, Fort Wayne IN (S)

Cartwright, Roy, *Prof Fine Arts,* University of Cincinnati, School of Art, Cincinnati OH (S)

Caruso, Gina, *Cur Films & Dir Doris Duke Theatre,* Honolulu Museum of Art, Honolulu HI

Caruthers, Robert, *Prof,* West Texas A&M University, Art, Theatre & Dance Dept, Canyon TX (S)

Carvalho, Cheryl, *Admin Asst,* Newport Historical Society & Museum of Newport History, Newport RI

Carvalho, Joseph, *Exec Dir & Pres,* Springfield Museums, Springfield Science Museum, Springfield MA

Carvalho, Joseph, *Pres & Exec Dir,* Springfield Museums, Connecticut Valley Historical Society, Springfield MA

Carvalho, Mitjl, *Div Dean,* Rio Hondo College Art Gallery, Whittier CA

Carver, Cynthia, *Office Coordr,* Muscatine Art Center, Muscatine IA

Carver, Dan, *Mus Educ,* Springfield Art Museum, Springfield MO

Carver, Melvin, *Chmn,* North Carolina Central University, Art Dept, Durham NC (S)

Caryn, Laurel, *Asst Prof Lectr,* University of Utah, Dept of Art & Art History, Salt Lake City UT (S)

Casaletto, Kristin, *Assoc Prof,* Augusta State University, Dept of Art, Augusta GA (S)

Casarez, Carolyn, *Admin Asst,* International Museum of Art, El Paso TX

Casbarro, Shawn, *Instr,* Taylor University, Visual Art Dept, Upland IN (S)

Cascaito, James, *Chmn Foreign Languages,* Fashion Institute of Technology, Art & Design Division, New York NY (S)

Case, Niona, *Secy,* Pioneer Historical Museum of South Dakota, Hot Springs SD

Casebeer, Doug, *Chair Res Prog & Artistic Dir,* Anderson Ranch Arts Center, Snowmass Village CO

Casey, Candace, *Gallery Store,* Worcester Center for Crafts, Worcester MA (S)

Casey, John, *Chair Animation,* Lesley University, College of Art & Design, Boston MA (S)

Casey, Jonathan, *Archivist,* Liberty Memorial Museum & Archives, The National Museum of World War I, Kansas City MO

Casey, Sean, *Librn,* Boston Public Library, Rare Book & Manuscripts Dept, Boston MA

Cash, G Gerald, *Chmn Fine Arts Div,* Florida Keys Community College, Fine Arts Div, Key West FL (S)

Cash, Sarah, *Bechhoefer Cur American Art,* Corcoran Gallery of Art, Washington DC

Cashes, Sandra, *Asst Park Mgr,* Florida Department of Environmental Protection, Stephen Foster Folk Culture Center State Park, White Springs FL

Cashman, Carol, *Instr,* Bismarck State College, Fine Arts Dept, Bismarck ND (S)

Casid, Jill H, *Asst Prof,* University of Wisconsin, Madison, Dept of Art History, Madison WI (S)

Casillas, Emilia, *Gallery Adminr,* New Mexico State University, Art Gallery, Las Cruces NM

Casillas, Marlene Hernandez, *Exhib Designer,* Museo de las Americas, Viejo San Juan PR

Casillas, Marlene Hernandez, *Exhib Designer,* Museo de las Americas, Viejo San Juan PR

Casimiro, Charles, *Historic Site Asst,* Philipse Manor Hall State Historic Site, Yonkers NY

Casimiro, Olinda, *Admin,* The Robert McLaughlin, Oshawa ON

Caslin, Marci, *Registrar,* Amon Carter Museum of American Art, Fort Worth TX

Casolary, Terri, *Admin Asst,* Shasta College, Arts, Communications & Social Sciences Division, Redding CA (S)

Cason, Christine, *Visual Fine Arts Coordr,* Hill College, Fine Arts Dept, Hillsboro TX (S)

Casper, Joseph, *CEO,* Caspers, Inc, Art Collection, Tampa FL

Cass, Doug, *Dir Library & Archives,* Glenbow Museum, Calgary AB

Cass, William, *Lectr,* Northwestern University, Evanston, Dept of Art Theory & Practice, Evanston IL (S)

Cassaro, James P, *Head Librn,* University of Pittsburgh, Henry Clay Frick Fine Arts Library, Pittsburgh PA

Casselman, Carol Ann, *Portfolio of Makers Mgr,* Ontario Crafts Council, Craft Resource Centre, Toronto ON

Cassidy, Christopher, *Prof,* University of North Carolina at Greensboro, Art Dept, Greensboro NC (S)

Cassidy, Donna, *Prof Art Hist,* University of Southern Maine, Dept of Art, Gorham ME (S)

Cassidy, Laurie, *Admin Asst,* Lynchburg College, Daura Gallery, Lynchburg VA

Cassidy, Stephanie, *Archivist,* Art Students League of New York, New York NY

Cassone, John, *Assoc Prof,* Los Angeles Harbor College, Art Dept, Wilmington CA (S)

Casstevens, Margot, *Adjunct Asst Prof,* Spokane Falls Community College, Fine Arts Dept, Spokane WA (S)

Castagna, Peg, *Bookkeeper,* Ocean City Arts Center, Ocean City NJ (S)

Castagnacci, Vince, *Prof,* University of Michigan, Ann Arbor, School of Art & Design, Ann Arbor MI (S)

Castaldi, Margaret Louise, *Reference Librn,* The University of the Arts, University Libraries, Philadelphia PA

Castellani, Carla, *Asst Mus Shop Mgr,* Niagara University, Castellani Art Museum, Niagara NY

Castellani, Margaret, *Head Cataloger,* The Cleveland Museum of Art, Ingalls Library, Cleveland OH

Castellucci, Dale, *Adj Instr,* University of West Florida, Dept of Art, Pensacola FL (S)

Castelnuovo, Sheri, *Cur Educ & Pub Programming,* Madison Museum of Contemporary Art, Madison WI

Castilla, Carmen, *Co-Gallery Mgr,* Craftsmen's Guild of Mississippi, Inc, Mississippi Crafts Center, Ridgeland MS

Castillo, Christie, *Mem Svcs Mgr,* National Art Education Association, Reston VA

Castle, Charles, *Assoc Dir,* Museum of Contemporary Art, San Diego-Downtown, La Jolla CA

Castle, Charles, *Deputy Dir,* Museum of Contemporary Art, San Diego, Geisel Library, La Jolla CA

Castle, Charles, *Deputy Dir,* Museum of Contemporary Art San Diego, San Diego CA

Castle, Charles E, *Deputy Dir,* Museum of Contemporary Art, San Diego, La Jolla CA

Castle, Delphine, *Registrar & Technician,* Craigdarroch Castle Historical Museum Society, Victoria BC

Castle, Lynn, *Exec Dir,* Art Museum of Southeast Texas, Beaumont TX

Castle, Wendell, *Prof,* Rochester Institute of Technology, School of Design, Rochester NY (S)

Casto, S Michele, *Librn,* Public Library of the District of Columbia, Art Division, Washington DC

Castorano, Kerry, *Dir Develop,* Fruitlands Museum, Inc, Harvard MA

Castriota, David, *Faculty,* Sarah Lawrence College, Dept of Art History, Bronxville NY (S)

Castro, Milagros, *Dir,* Institute of Puerto Rican Culture, Parque Ceremonial Indigena de Caguana, San Juan PR

Castro, Milagros, *Dir,* Institute of Puerto Rican Culture, Parque Ceremonial Indigena de Caguana, San Juan PR

Castro, Ricardo, *Prof,* McGill University, School of Architecture, Montreal PQ (S)

Castro, Susannah, *Co-Dir,* Tubac Center of the Arts, Santa Cruz Valley Art Association, Tubac AZ

Casuso, Martin, *Assoc Preparator,* University of Miami, Lowe Art Museum, Coral Gables FL

Caswell, Ben, *Preparator & Bldg Mgr,* Woodstock Artists Association & Museum, Woodstock NY

Catalani, Stefano, *Dir Curatorial Affairs/Artistic Dir,* Bellevue Arts Museum, Bellevue WA

Catalano, Alan, *Vol Librn,* Higgins Armory Museum, Olive Higgins Prouty Library & Research Center, Worcester MA

Cataldo, Sabrina, *Communs Strategist,* Saskatchewan Arts Board, Regina SK

Catalfo, Jayne, *Bookkeeper,* Jacques Marchais, Staten Island NY

Catanach, Daniel, *Performing Arts Training Dir,* Henry Street Settlement, Abrons Art Center, New York NY

Catanese, Chris, *Dir Visitor Svcs,* New-York Historical Society, Museum, New York NY

Catchi, Benice, *Exec VPres,* New York Society of Women Artists, Inc, Westport CT

Cate, Barbara, *Prof,* Seton Hall University, College of Arts & Sciences, South Orange NJ (S)

Cateforts, David, *Assoc Prof,* University of Kansas, Kress Foundation Dept of Art History, Lawrence KS (S)

Cates, Jo, *Dean of Lib,* Columbia College Chicago, Library, Chicago IL

Cates, Lauren, *Mus Cafe Asst Mgr,* Oklahoma City Museum of Art, Oklahoma City OK

Cates, Marc, *VPres,* Chasen Galleries of Fine Art, Richmond VA

Cathcart, Anne, *Curatorial Asst,* National Trust for Historic Preservation, Chesterwood, Stockbridge MA

Catherall, Virginia, *Cur Educ,* University of Utah, Utah Museum of Fine Arts, Salt Lake City UT

Cathey, Jerry, *Dir,* Ponca City Art Association, Ponca City OK

Catizone, Richard, *Media Arts & Animation,* Art Institute of Pittsburgh, Pittsburgh PA (S)

Catlin, Jane, *Asst Prof,* Utah State University, Dept of Art, Logan UT (S)

Catling, William, *Chmn Dept,* Azusa Pacific University, College of Liberal Arts, Art Dept, Azusa CA (S)

Cato, Tom, *Chmn,* Armstrong Atlantic State University, Department of Art, Music & Theatre, Savannah GA (S)

Caton, Mary Anne, *Dir,* Mount Vernon Hotel Museum & Garden, New York NY

Catron, Joanna D, *Cur,* University of Mary Washington, Gari Melchers Home and Studio, Fredericksburg VA

Catterall, Kate, *Asst Chair - Design,* University of Texas, Dept of Art & Art History, Austin TX (S)

Catton, Deborah, *Calgary Branch Chmn,* Alberta Society of Artists, Calgary AB

Caulfield, Sean, *Coordr Printmaking & Drawing,* University of Alberta, Dept of Art & Design, Edmonton AB (S)

Caulkins, Beth, *Co-Owner & Creative Dir,* Frank Lloyd Wright Museum, AD German Warehouse, Richland Center WI

Cauna, Jacqueline, *VPres,* Rhode Island Watercolor Society, Pawtucket RI

Causey, Adera, *Cur Educ,* Hunter Museum of American Art, Chattanooga TN

Cauthen, Gene, *Chmn Dept Art,* Mount Wachusett Community College, East Wing Gallery, Gardner MA

Caux, Patrick, *Dir Communication & Develop,* Musee National des Beaux Arts du Quebec, Quebec PQ

Cavallaro, David, *Assoc Chair,* State University of New York at New Paltz, Art Education Program, New Paltz NY (S)

Cavallaro, Marie, *Assoc Prof,* Salisbury State University, Art Dept, Salisbury MD (S)

Cavallo, Steven, *Children's Librn,* Palisades Park Public Library, Palisades Park NJ

Cavanagh, T, *Assoc Prof,* Dalhousie University, Faculty of Architecture, Halifax NS (S)

Cavanaugh, Alden, *Chmn,* Indiana State University, Dept of Art, Terre Haute IN (S)

Cavanaugh, CJ, *Art Instr,* Tyler Junior College, Art Program, Tyler TX (S)

Cavanaugh, Marianne L, *Head Librn,* Saint Louis Art Museum, Richardson Memorial Library, Saint Louis MO

Cave, Mark, *Manuscripts,* The Historic New Orleans Collection, Williams Research Center, New Orleans LA

Cave, Nick, *Chmn Fashion Design,* School of the Art Institute of Chicago, Chicago IL (S)

Caveglia, Valerie, *Exec Dir,* Sun Gallery, Hayward CA

Cavendish, Kim L, *Pres,* Museum of Discovery & Science, Fort Lauderdale FL

Cavish, Jacquelyn, *Cur Arts,* Channel Islands Maritime Museum, Oxnard CA

Cawless, Heather, *Educ Dir,* Brookfield Craft Center, Inc, Gallery, Brookfield CT

Cawley, Sheila, *VPres Institutional Advancement,* Field Museum, Chicago IL

Cawthorne, Bonnie, *Library Technical Asst,* University of Maryland, College Park, Art Library, College Park MD

Cazabon, Lynn, *Assoc Chair & Assoc Prof,* University of Maryland, Baltimore County, Imaging & Digital Arts (IMDA), Dept of Visual Arts, Baltimore MD (S)

Cease, Bleu, *Exec Dir & Cur,* Rochester Contemporary, Art Center, Rochester NY

Cebulash, Glen, *Chair & Prof,* Wright State University, Dept of Art & Art History, Dayton OH (S)

Cecil, Andrew John, *Cur Coll,* Roswell Museum & Art Center, Roswell NM

Cecil, Rocky, *Preparator,* Owensboro Museum of Fine Art, Owensboro KY

Cecil-Satchwell, Breiana, *Educ Assoc,* Indianapolis Art Center, Marilyn K. Glick School of Art, Indianapolis IN

Cederna, Ann, *Asst Prof,* Catholic University of America, School of Architecture & Planning, Washington DC (S)

Cegelis, Linda, *Mktg Mgr,* Orlando Museum of Art, Orlando FL

Cegelis, Linda, *Mktg Mgr,* Orlando Museum of Art, Orlando Sentinel Library, Orlando FL

Celender, Donald, *Prof, Chair,* Macalester College, Art Dept, Saint Paul MN (S)

Celenko, Ted, *Cur Emeritus, Art of Africa, South Pacific, & the Americas,* Indianapolis Museum of Art, Indianapolis IN

Celentano, Denyce, *Asst Prof,* Louisiana State University, School of Art, Baton Rouge LA (S)

Celentano, Denyce, *Asst Dir School of Art,* Louisiana State University, School of Art - Glassell Gallery, Baton Rouge LA

Celestino, Vincent, *Vpres,* Saint Augustine Art Association and Art Gallery, Saint Augustine FL

Cembrola, Robert, *Cur,* Naval War College Museum, Newport RI

Cempellin, Leda, *Prof,* South Dakota State University, Dept of Visual Arts, Brookings SD (S)

Cendak, Sonja, *Exhib & PR Coordr,* Craft and Folk Art Museum (CAFAM), Los Angeles CA

Censky, Ellen, *Sr VPres Mus Progs,* Milwaukee Public Museum, Milwaukee WI

Centro, Mary, *Admin Asst,* Rome Historical Society, Museum & Archives, Rome NY

Cepluch, Henry, *Arts in Common Dir,* Fitton Center for Creative Arts, Hamilton OH

Cepluch, Henry, *Arts in Common Dir,* Fitton Center for Creative Arts, Hamilton OH (S)

Certo, Alberta Patella, *Gen Educ,* Art Institute of Pittsburgh, Pittsburgh PA (S)

Cervantes, James, *Cur Military History,* Heritage Museums & Gardens, Sandwich MA

Cervino, Anthony, *Asst Dir Exhib,* Maryland Institute, College of Art Exhibitions, Baltimore MD

Cervino, Anthony, *Asst Prof,* Dickinson College, Dept of Art & Art History, Carlisle PA (S)

Cestaro, Gina, *Adj Instr,* University of West Florida, Dept of Art, Pensacola FL (S)

Cetlin, Cynthia, *Prof,* Ohio Wesleyan University, Fine Arts Dept, Delaware OH (S)

Chabotar, Kent, *Pres,* Guilford College, Art Gallery, Greensboro NC

Chacon, Rafael, *Assoc Prof,* University of Montana, Dept of Art, Missoula MT (S)

Chadwick-Reid, Ann, *Chmn,* Skagit Valley College, Dept of Art, Mount Vernon WA (S)

Chafe, Perry, *Gen Prog Officer,* Memorial University of Newfoundland, The Rooms Provincial Art Gallery, Saint John's NF

Chaffee, Elissa, *Dir Develop,* American Craft Council, Minneapolis MN

Chaffee, Tom, *Prof,* Arkansas State University, Dept of Art, State University AR (S)

Chaffin, Cortney, *Prof,* University of Wisconsin-Stevens Point, Dept of Art & Design, Stevens Point WI (S)

Chait, Steven, *Treas,* National Antique & Art Dealers Association of America, Inc, New York NY

Chakola-Ramsey, Annah, *Develop Dir,* City Arts Center at Fair Park, Oklahoma City OK

Chalaron, Peggy, *Dept Head Educ Resources,* Louisiana State University, Middleton Library, Baton Rouge LA

Chalfie, David, *Dir Exhibs & Pub Programs,* Indianapolis Museum of Art, Indianapolis IN

Chalfont, Aubony, *Adjunct Prof,* Missouri Western State University, Art Dept, Saint Joseph MO (S)

Chalif, Lisa, *Cur,* The Heckscher Museum of Art, Huntington NY

Challoner, Pamela, *Mktg & Communs,* Peter & Catharine Whyte Foundation, Whyte Museum of the Canadian Rockies, Banff AB

Chalmers, Kim, *Dept Head,* Western Kentucky University, University Gallery, Bowling Green KY

Chalmers, Kim, *Dept Head,* Western Kentucky University, Art Dept, Bowling Green KY (S)

Chalmers, Lynn, *Head Dept Interior Design,* University of Manitoba, Faculty of Architecture, Winnipeg MB (S)

Chalmers, Pattie, *Asst Prof,* Southern Illinois University, School of Art & Design, Carbondale IL (S)

Chamberlain, Barbara, *VPres,* Madison County Historical Society, Cottage Lawn, Oneida NY

Chamberlin, Ed, *Cur,* National Park Service, Hubbell Trading Post National Historic Site, Ganado AZ

Chamberlin, Marsha, *CEO & Pres,* Ann Arbor Art Center, Art Center, Ann Arbor MI

Chamberlin, Patricia, *Exec Dir,* Long Beach Island Foundation of the Arts & Sciences, Loveladies NJ

Chambers, Barbara, *Treas,* Napoleonic Society of America, Museum & Library, Saint Helena CA

Chambers, Bryon, *Asst Educ Cur,* Oklahoma City Museum of Art, Oklahoma City OK

Chambers, Christine D, *Dir Fin & Admin,* The Frick Art & Historical Center, Inc, Frick Art Museum, Pittsburgh PA

Chambers, Jacqueline, *Develop Officer,* Laumeier Sculpture Park, Saint Louis MO

Chambers, Letitia, *Dir,* Heard Museum, Phoenix AZ

Chambers, Ruth, *Acting Head,* University of Regina, Visual Arts Dept, Regina SK (S)

Chambers, Sheila, *Prof,* Salt Lake Community College, Graphic Design Dept, Salt Lake City UT (S)

Chametzky, Peter, *Dir & Prof,* Southern Illinois University, School of Art & Design, Carbondale IL (S)

Chamness, Cay, *Libr Asst,* Maysville, Kentucky Gateway Museum Center, Maysville KY

Champagne, Aisha, *Dir Publications & Design,* New Orleans Museum of Art, New Orleans LA

Champagne, Anne, *Head Technical Svcs,* The Art Institute of Chicago, Ryerson & Burnham Libraries, Chicago IL

Champagne, Danielle, *Dir Communs,* Montreal Museum of Fine Arts, Montreal PQ

Champagne, Mickey, *Mus Aide,* Village of Potsdam, Potsdam Public Museum, Potsdam NY

Champion, Karin, *Develop Mgr,* Southern Alberta Art Gallery, Library, Lethbridge AB

Chan, Frances, *Admin Asst,* Queens College, City University of New York, Art Library, Flushing NY

Chan, Gaye, *Dept Chair,* University of Hawaii at Manoa, Dept of Art, Honolulu HI (S)

Chan, Irene, *Assoc Prof,* University of Maryland, Baltimore County, Imaging & Digital Arts (IMDA), Dept of Visual Arts, Baltimore MD (S)

Chan, Mitchell, *Mem Coordr,* Visual Arts Ontario, Toronto ON

Chan, Trish, *Exec Dir,* Craigdarroch Castle Historical Museum Society, Victoria BC

Chan, Ying Kit, *Prof,* University of Louisville, Allen R Hite Art Institute, Louisville KY (S)

Chan, Ying Kit, *Studio Program Head,* University of Louisville, Hite Art Institute, Louisville KY

Chance, Delores, *Gallery Dir,* Coe College, Eaton-Buchan Gallery & Marvin Cone Gallery, Cedar Rapids IA

Chancey, Jill, *Cur,* Lauren Rogers, Laurel MS

Chandler, Christine, *Cur Natural Science,* Putnam Museum of History and Natural Science, Davenport IA

Chandler, McKenzie, *Gallery Mgr,* Walker Fine Art, Denver CO

Chandler, Roger A, *Assoc Prof,* Northwestern State University of Louisiana, School of Creative & Performing Arts - Dept of Fine & Graphic Arts, Natchitoches LA (S)

Chandler, Susan T, *Asst Dir,* Arts Midwest, Minneapolis MN

Chandler-Mills, Leah, *Instr Theatre,* University of Colorado-Colorado Springs, Visual & Performing Arts Dept (VAPA), Colorado Springs CO (S)

Chaney, Robert, *Dir Cur Affairs,* University of Pennsylvania, Institute of Contemporary Art, Philadelphia PA

Chang, Albert, *Exec Dir,* Chinese Culture Foundation, Center Gallery, San Francisco CA

Chang, Anna, *Dir Finance & Opers,* American Numismatic Society, New York NY

Chang, Lauren, *Conservator,* The Art Institute of Chicago, Department of Textiles, Textile Society, Chicago IL

Chang, Li Fen, *Assoc Prof Fashion Design,* University of North Texas, College of Visual Arts & Design, Denton TX (S)

Chang, Willow Hai, *Dir Galleries,* China Institute in America, China Institute Gallery, New York NY

Chanin, Sherry, *Lethbridge Branch Chmn,* Alberta Society of Artists, Calgary AB

Chanlatte, Luis A, *Archaeologist,* University of Puerto Rico, Museum of Anthropology, History & Art, Rio Piedras PR

Chhangur, Emelie, *Asst Dir & Cur,* York University, Art Gallery of York University, Toronto ON

Chi, Ke-Hsin, *Assoc Prof,* Eastern Illinois University, Art Dept, Charleston IL (S)

Chiang, Jennifer, *Dir Finance & Admin,* Jamaica Center for Arts & Learning (JCAL), Jamaica NY

Chiasson, Hermenegilde, *Prof Art History,* Universite de Moncton, Dept of Visual Arts, Moncton NB (S)

Chiba Smith, Judith, *Colls Mgr,* Georgia O'Keeffe Museum, Santa Fe NM

Chibnik, Kitty, *Assoc Dir,* Columbia University, Avery Architectural & Fine Arts Library, New York NY

Chickering, F William, *Dean,* Pratt Institute, Art & Architecture Dept, Brooklyn NY

Chicoyne, Lisa, *Educ Coord,* Greenwich House Pottery, Jane Hartsook Gallery, New York NY

Chicquor, Isabell, *Prof,* North Carolina Central University, Art Dept, Durham NC (S)

Chidester, Paul, *Assoc Prof Art (Core Prog & Drawing/Painting),* Pennsylvania State University, University Park, Penn State School of Visual Arts, University Park PA (S)

Chieffo, Beverly, *Chmn & Assoc Prof Art,* Albertus Magnus College, Visual and Performing Arts, New Haven CT (S)

Chiego, William J, *Dir,* McNay, San Antonio TX

Chiesa, Wilfredo, *Prof,* University of Massachusetts - Boston, Art Dept, Boston MA (S)

Chi Hing Kwan, Billy, *Asst Library Dir,* Philadelphia Museum of Art, Library & Archives, Philadelphia PA

Child, Kent, *Gallery Adv & Humanities Div Dir,* Gavilan Community College, Art Gallery, Gilroy CA

Childers, Ann, *Southern Illinois Representative,* American Society of Artists, Inc, Palatine IL

Childress, Jennifer, *Asst Prof,* College of Saint Rose, The Center For Art and Design, Albany NY (S)

Childress, Mauree, *Dir Develop Mktg,* Neville Public Museum of Brown County, Green Bay WI

Childs, Peter, *Concert Coordr,* Academy of the New Church, Glencairn Museum, Bryn Athyn PA

Childs, Steve, *Vice Chmn,* American Society of Portrait Artists (ASOPA), Montgomery AL

Childs, William A P, *Chmn Prog in Classical Archaeology,* Princeton University, Dept of Art & Archaeology, Princeton NJ (S)

Chilla, Benigna, *Instr,* Berkshire Community College, Dept of Fine Arts, Pittsfield MA (S)

Chimirri-Russell, Geraldine, *Cur Numismatics,* University of Calgary, Nickle Galleries, Calgary AB

Chin, Caroline, *Assoc Dir Finance & Opers,* The American Federation of Arts, New York NY

Chin, Christina, *Art Edu,* Western Michigan University, Frostic School of Art, Kalamazoo MI (S)

Chin, Susan, *Assoct Registrar,* University of California, Los Angeles, Grunwald Center for the Graphic Arts at Hammer Museum, Los Angeles CA

Chin, Wanda W, *Coordr Exhib & Exhib Designer,* University of Alaska, Museum of the North, Fairbanks AK

Chinda, Dan-Horia, *Industrial Design Technology,* Art Institute of Pittsburgh, Pittsburgh PA (S)

Chinn, Jennie, *Exec Dir,* Kansas State Historical Society, Kansas Museum of History, Topeka KS

Chinn, Lori, *Curatorial Coordr,* Mills College Art Museum, Oakland CA

Chinov, Stefan, *Assoc Prof,* Wright State University, Dept of Art & Art History, Dayton OH (S)

Chioffi, David, *Div Chair Design Arts,* Memphis College of Art, Memphis TN (S)

Chipley, Sheila M, *Asst Prof,* Concord College, Fine Art Division, Athens WV (S)

Chisholm, Dorothy, *VPres Finance,* Society of Canadian Artists, Toronto ON

Chism, Sandy, *Assoc Prof,* Tulane University, Sophie H Newcomb Memorial College, New Orleans LA (S)

Chisolm, Sallie, *Museum Store Mgr,* Palm Beach County Parks & Recreation Department, Morikami Museum & Japanese Gardens, Delray Beach FL

Chiu, Melissa, *Museum Dir,* The Asia Society Museum, New York NY

Chmielewski, Wendy, *Cur Peace Coll,* Swarthmore College, Friends Historical Library of Swarthmore College, Swarthmore PA

Cho, Charlie, *Lectr,* Northwestern University, Evanston, Dept of Art Theory & Practice, Evanston IL (S)

Choate, Jerry, *Instr,* Northeastern State University, College of Arts & Letters, Tahlequah OK (S)

Choate, Steven B, *Assoc Prof Art,* Harding University, Dept of Art & Design, Searcy AR (S)

Choberka, Matthew, *Chair & Assoc Prof,* Weber State University, Dept of Visual Arts, Ogden UT (S)

Chodkowski, Henry, *Prof Emeritus,* University of Louisville, Allen R Hite Art Institute, Louisville KY (S)

Choen, Lewis, *Asst Prof,* College of William & Mary, Dept of Fine Arts, Williamsburg VA (S)

Choi, Sylvia, *Cataloger,* School of the Art Institute of Chicago, John M Flaxman Library, Chicago IL

Choi Beacon, Sandy, *Assoc Registrar,* University of California, Los Angeles, Fowler Museum at UCLA, Los Angeles CA

Choice, Thomas L, *Pres,* Kishwaukee College, Art Dept, Malta IL (S)

Chojecki, Randolph, *Ref Librn,* Daemen College, Marian Library, Amherst NY

Chom, Christina, *Vol Coordr,* Mobile Museum of Art, Mobile AL

Choma, Julie, *Coll Mgr,* Ursinus College, Philip & Muriel Berman Museum of Art, Collegeville PA

Chong, Alan, *Cur,* Isabella Stewart Gardner, Isabella Stewart Garden Museum Library & Archives, Boston MA

Chong, Elaine, *Adjunct Prof,* College of Saint Elizabeth, Art Dept, Morristown NJ (S)

Chong, Laurie Whitehill, *Spec Coll Librn,* Rhode Island School of Design, Fleet Library at RISD, Providence RI

Chong Kim, Hyun, *Assoc Prof,* Jackson State University, Dept of Art, Jackson MS (S)

Choo, Chunghi, *Prof Metalsmithing & Jewelry,* University of Iowa, School of Art & Art History, Iowa City IA (S)

Choo, Phil, *Assoc Prof,* Oklahoma State University, Department of Art, Graphic Design and Art History, Stillwater OK (S)

Choo, Philip, *Asst Prof,* University of Minnesota, Duluth, Art Dept, Duluth MN (S)

Chou, Wang-Ling, *Asst Prof,* Louisiana College, Dept of Art, Pineville LA (S)

Chouris, Vicki, *Develop & Mem,* Yesteryear Village, West Palm Beach FL

Chouteau, Suzanne, *Chair & Prof,* Xavier University, Dept of Art, Cincinnati OH (S)

Chovanec, Emily, *Assoc Dir External Affairs,* Museum of Chinese in America, New York NY

Chow, Alan, *Exec Dir,* Chinese-American Arts Council, New York NY

Choy, Lillian, *Asst Pub Prog Mgr,* Workman & Temple Family Homestead Museum, City of Industry CA

Chretien, Marc, *Dir Facilities Mgmt Svcs,* Canadian Museum of Nature, Musee Canadien de la Nature, Ottawa ON

Chrismas, Douglas, *Dir,* Ace Gallery, Los Angeles CA (S)

Christ, Ronald, *Grad Coordr,* Wichita State University, School of Art & Design, Wichita KS (S)

Christakos, Demetra, *Exec Dir,* Ontario Association of Art Galleries, Toronto ON

Christen, Derrick, *Asst Prof,* Northern Michigan University, Dept of Art & Design, Marquette MI (S)

Christensen, Audrey, *Archivist,* Exit Art, San Leandro CA

Christensen, Barbara C, *Dir,* Muscatine Art Center, Muscatine IA

Christensen, Candice, *Tour Registrar,* Minnesota Historical Society, Minnesota State Capitol Historic Site, St Paul MN

Christensen, Dan, *Treas & Exec Dir,* Phelps County Historical Society, Nebraska Prairie Museum, Holdrege NE

Christensen, Susan, *Pres,* Octagon Center for the Arts, Ames IA

Christensen, V A, *Prof,* Missouri Southern State University, Dept of Art, Joplin MO (S)

Christi, John, *Chmn,* Capitol Community Technical College, Humanities Division & Art Dept, Hartford CT (S)

Christian, Alix, *Instr,* Amarillo College, Visual Art Dept, Amarillo TX (S)

Christian, Ann, *Coordr Cultural Progs,* City of Scarborough, Cedar Ridge Creative Centre, Scarborough ON

Christian, Brantley B, *CEO & Dir,* Yesteryear Village, West Palm Beach FL

Christian, Kendall, *Mus Preparator,* Oberlin College, Allen Memorial Art Museum, Oberlin OH

Christian, Michele, *Univ Archivist,* South Dakota State University, Hilton M. Briggs Library, Brookings SD

Christian, Susan, *Chief Preparator & Installation Coordr,* Chrysler Museum of Art, Norfolk VA

Christiano, Melissa, *Instr,* Williams Baptist College, Dept of Art, Walnut Ridge AR (S)

Christiansen, Laura, *Dickson Librn,* Chrysler Museum of Art, Jean Outland Chrysler Library, Norfolk VA

Christianson, John, *Historic Houses Mgr,* Chrysler Museum of Art, Norfolk VA

Christie, Amanda Dawn, *Production Supvr, Faucet Media Arts,* Struts Gallery, Sackville NB

Christie, Jonathan, *Artist in Res,* Jacksonville University, Dept of Art, Theater, Dance, Jacksonville FL (S)

Christie, Leona, *Asst Prof,* State University of New York at Albany, Art Dept, Albany NY (S)

Christman, Linda, *Exec Dir,* Bismarck Art & Galleries Association, Bismarck ND

Christodoulou, Marilena, *Dir Finance & Admin,* Rubin Museum of Art, New York NY

Christopher, Nicholas J, *Registrar & Preparator,* Pensacola Museum of Art, Pensacola FL

Christopher, Theresa, *Registrar,* DuSable Museum of African American History, Chicago IL

Christovich, Mary Louise, *Chmn,* The Historic New Orleans Collection, Williams Research Center, New Orleans LA

Chu, Brian, *Asst Prof,* University of New Hampshire, Dept of Arts & Art History, Durham NH (S)

Chubb, Sara, *Security & Visitor Svcs Clerk,* Alaska State Museum, Juneau AK

Chubb, Tayrn, *Asst Prof,* East Central University, School of Fine Arts, Ada OK (S)

Chubrich, Michael, *Pres,* Portsmouth Athenaeum, Joseph Copley Research Library, Portsmouth NH

Chudzik, Theresa, *Instr,* Hibbing Community College, Art Dept, Hibbing MN (S)

Chuldenko, John, *Dept Head Illustration,* Cleveland Institute of Art, Cleveland OH (S)

Chumley, Jere, *Head,* Cleveland State Community College, Dept of Art, Cleveland TN (S)

Chundra, Fayiaz, *Head Communs & Mktg,* Museum of Contemporary Canadian Art, Toronto ON

Chung, Anita, *Cur Chinese Art,* The Cleveland Museum of Art, Cleveland OH

Chung, David, *Vis Assoc Prof,* University of Michigan, Ann Arbor, School of Art & Design, Ann Arbor MI (S)

Chung, Estella, *Cur Am Material Culture & Historian,* Hillwood Museum & Gardens Foundation, Hillwood Estate Museum & Gardens, Washington DC

Chung, Nogin, *Asst Prof,* Bloomsburg University, Dept of Art & Art History, Bloomsburg PA (S)

Chung, Robert Y, *Asst Prof,* Rochester Institute of Technology, School of Printing Management & Sciences, Rochester NY (S)

Chung, Sam, *Asst Prof,* Northern Michigan University, Dept of Art & Design, Marquette MI (S)

Chung, Wayne, *Dept Chmn,* Carnegie Mellon University, School of Design, Pittsburgh PA (S)

Chung, Youngmin, *Registrar,* Art Museum of the University of Houston, Blaffer Gallery, Houston TX

Chunko, Shelby, *Mus Shop Mgr,* Landis Valley Village and Farm Museum, PA Historical & Museum Commission, Lancaster PA

Chupa, Anna, *Assoc Prof,* Lehigh University, Dept of Art, Architecture & Design, Bethlehem PA (S)

Church, Angela, *Instr,* East Central University, School of Fine Arts, Ada OK (S)

Church, Fran, *Asst Prof,* Alabama A & M University, Art & Art Education Dept, Normal AL (S)

Church, Sharyn L, *Deputy Dir,* Inner-City Arts, Los Angeles CA

Churchwell, Marta, *Develop. Coordr,* George A Spiva, Joplin MO

Chute, Susan, *Supvr Libr Art & Picture Coll,* The New York Public Library, Mid-Manhattan Library, Art Collection, New York NY

Chyle, Lauren, *Cur,* Cayuga Museum of History & Art, Auburn NY

Chytilo, Lynne, *Chmn Dept Visual Arts,* Albion College, Dept of Visual Arts, Albion MI (S)

Chytilo, Lynne, *Prof,* Albion College, Bobbitt Visual Arts Center, Albion MI

Ciampa, John, *Chmn American Video Institute,* Rochester Institute of Technology, School of Photographic Arts & Sciences, Rochester NY (S)

Cichy, Barbara, *Instr,* Bismarck State College, Fine Arts Dept, Bismarck ND (S)

Cielo, Lauri, *Communs Coordr,* Historical Society of Pennsylvania, Philadelphia PA

Cigliano, Flavia, *Exec Dir,* Nichols House Museum, Inc, Boston MA

Ciesla, Maria, *Pres,* Polish Museum of America, Chicago IL

Ciesla, Maria, *Pres,* Polish Museum of America, Research Library, Chicago IL

Cieslewicz, Kathy C, *Cur & Collections Mgr,* Dixie State College, Robert N & Peggy Sears Gallery, Saint George UT

Ciganick, Jan, *Instr,* Moravian College, Dept of Art, Bethlehem PA (S)

Cioffoletti, Jessica, *Prog Mgr,* Pelham Art Center, Pelham NY

Ciotti, Angelo L, *Gen Educ, Graphic Design,* Art Institute of Pittsburgh, Pittsburgh PA (S)

Cipoletti, Christopher, *Exec Dir,* American Numismatic Association, Edward C. Rochette Money Museum, Colorado Springs CO

Cipolla, Vin, *Pres,* Municipal Art Society of New York, New York NY

Cipriano, M, *Chmn Dept,* Central Connecticut State University, Dept of Art, New Britain CT (S)

Cisco, Debra, *Pub Info Officer,* National Gallery of Art, Washington DC

Citron, Harvey, *Chmn,* New York Academy of Art, Graduate School of Figurative Art, New York NY (S)

Claassen, Garth, *Dir,* The College of Idaho, Rosenthal Art Gallery, Caldwell ID

Clair, Cynthia, *Exec Dir,* Silvermine Guild Arts Center, School of Art, New Canaan CT

Clair, Melina, *Exhibs Coordr,* LaGrange Art Museum, LaGrange GA

Claire, Michael, *Pres,* College of San Mateo, Creative Arts Dept, San Mateo CA (S)

Claire, William H, *Pres,* Coachella Valley History Museum, Indio CA

Clancey, Evin, *Assoc Cur,* Hebrew Union College, Skirball Cultural Center, Los Angeles CA

Clancy, Brian, *Chair & Asst Prof,* Colby-Sawyer College, Dept of Fine & Performing Arts, New London NH (S)

Clancy, Steven, *Chmn Art History,* Ithaca College, Handwerker Gallery of Art, Ithaca NY

Clapper, Michael, *Assoc Prof,* Franklin & Marshall College, Art & Art History Dept, Lancaster PA (S)

Clare, Mary, *Assoc Prof,* Sullivan County Community College, Division of Commercial Art & Photography, Loch Sheldrake NY (S)

Clareson, Tom, *Board Sec,* Heritage Preservation, The National Institute for Conservation, Washington DC

Clark, Abigail, *Admin Asst,* Public Art Fund, Inc, Visual Archive, New York NY

Clark, Benjamin L, *Exec Dir,* MonDak Heritage Center, History Library, Sidney MT

Clark, Benjamin L, *Exec Dir,* MonDak Heritage Center, Museum, Sidney MT

Clark, Bob, *Chief Archivist,* National Archives & Records Administration, Franklin D Roosevelt Museum, Hyde Park NY

Clark, Bob, *Instr,* Southwestern Community College, Advertising & Graphic Design, Sylva NC (S)

Clark, Brandi, *Dir Progs,* City Art Works, Pratt Fine Arts Center, Seattle WA (S)

Clark, Carol, *Chmn Wm McCall Vickery 1957 Prof History of Art & Amer Studies,* Amherst College, Dept of Art & the History of Art, Amherst MA (S)

Clark, Christa, *Cur Africa, Americas,* Newark Museum Association, The Newark Museum, Newark NJ

Clark, Christine, *Metals,* Oregon College of Art & Craft, Portland OR (S)

Clark, Donald, *Assoc Prof,* Minnesota State University-Moorhead, Dept of Art & Design, Moorhead MN (S)

Clark, Dwayne, *Exhibition Designer & Preparator,* Morris Museum of Art, Augusta GA

Clark, Eleanor, *Museum Cur,* Rosenberg Library, Galveston TX

Clark, Fred, *Prof,* Lansing Community College, Visual Arts & Media Dept, Lansing MI (S)

Clark, Ginenne, *Events & Publs Coordr,* Society for Photographic Education (SPE), SPE Gallery, Cleveland OH

Clark, Gregory, *Chmn Dept,* University of the South, Dept of Fine Arts, Sewanee TN (S)

Clark, James M, *Prof,* Blackburn College, Dept of Art, Carlinville IL (S)

Clark, Janet, *Instr,* Lakehead University, Dept of Visual Arts, Thunder Bay ON (S)

Clark, Joan, *Head Main Library,* Cleveland Public Library, Fine Arts & Special Collections Dept, Cleveland OH

Clark, John, *Head Adult Information Svcs,* Springfield City Library, Springfield MA

Clark, Joyce, *Cur Asst,* Regina Public Library, Dunlop Art Gallery, Regina SK

Clark, Judy, *Grad Coordr-Art Educ, Design, Studio Art,* University of Texas, Dept of Art & Art History, Austin TX (S)

Clark, Juleigh, *Pub Svcs Librn,* Colonial Williamsburg Foundation, John D Rockefeller, Jr Library, Williamsburg VA

Clark, Karen, *Sr Conservator,* Textile Conservation Workshop Inc, South Salem NY

Clark, Katreena, *Mus Opers Mgr,* University of Richmond, University Museums, Richmond VA

Clark, Laurie Beth, *Prof,* University of Wisconsin, Madison, Dept of Art, Madison WI (S)

Clark, Marcia, *Dir,* Blue Mountain Gallery, New York NY

Clark, Martha Fuller, *VPres,* Portsmouth Historical Society, John Paul Jones House & Discover Portsmouth, Portsmouth NH

Clark, Marylou, *Adj Prof,* Quincy College, Art Dept, Quincy MA (S)

Clark, Moira, *Instr,* Toronto School of Art, Toronto ON (S)

Clark, Monte, *Secy,* Art Dealers Association of Canada, Toronto ON

Clark, Nancy, *Registrar,* Yellowstone Art Museum, Billings MT

Clark, Nina, *Dir Colls & Exhibs,* American Swedish Institute, Minneapolis MN

Clark, Peter P, *Cur Coll,* National Baseball Hall of Fame & Museum, Inc, Art Collection, Cooperstown NY

Clark, Randy, *Assoc Prof,* South Dakota State University, Dept of Visual Arts, Brookings SD (S)

Clark, Raymond R, *Chmn Bd & Pres,* Cincinnati Institute of Fine Arts, Cincinnati OH

Clark, Robert, *Supervisory Archivist,* National Archives & Records Administration, Franklin D Roosevelt Library, Hyde Park NY

Clark, Ron, *Independent Study Prog Dir,* Whitney Museum of American Art, New York NY

Clark, Sara B, *Adjunct Instr,* Saginaw Valley State University, Dept of Art & Design, University Center MI (S)

Clark, Sharon, *Asst to Dir,* University of Rhode Island, Fine Arts Center Galleries, Kingston RI

Clark, Stephanie, *Adj Asst Prof,* University of Texas at Arlington, Art & Art History Department, Arlington TX (S)

Clark, Sussanne, *Secy,* Coppini Academy of Fine Arts, Library, San Antonio TX

Clark, William, *Asst Prof,* Cedar Crest College, Art Dept, Allentown PA (S)

Clark-Binder, Miranda, *Cur Educ,* La Salle University Art Museum, Philadelphia PA

Clark-Peck, Carrie, *Cur Educ,* Maryhill Museum of Art, Goldendale WA

Clarke, Adrienne, *Dept Admin,* Bryn Mawr College, Dept of the History of Art, Bryn Mawr PA (S)

Clarke, Alice, *Libr Tech,* National Portrait Gallery, Library, Washington DC

Clarke, Ann, *Prof,* Lakehead University, Dept of Visual Arts, Thunder Bay ON (S)

Clarke, Bede, *Prof (Ceramics),* University of Missouri - Columbia, Dept of Art, Columbia MO (S)

Clarke, Candace, *Deputy Dir,* James A Michener, Doylestown PA

Clarke, Jason, *Gen Mgr,* Arts and Letters Club of Toronto, Library, Toronto ON

Clarke, Jerrie, *Dir & Cur Sheldon Mus,* Sheldon Museum & Cultural Center, Inc, Sheldon Museum & Cultural Center, Haines AK

Clarke, Mollie, *Dir Educ,* Lyman Allyn Art Museum, New London CT

Clarke, Robert, *Assoc Prof,* Mohawk Valley Community College, Utica NY (S)

Clarkson, Larry, *Asst Prof,* Weber State University, Dept of Visual Arts, Ogden UT (S)

Clary, Marcia, *Interim Exec Dir,* Cascade County Historical Society, The History Museum, Great Falls MT

Clary, Owen, *CEO,* Aiken County Historical Museum, Aiken SC

Clause, Matthew, *Registrar,* Daum Museum of Contemporary Art, Sedalia MO

Clausen, Judy, *Dir Advancement,* Anderson Ranch Arts Center, Snowmass Village CO

Clausen, Nancy, *Archives Asst,* Northeastern Nevada Museum, Elko NV

Claussen, Louise Keith, *Fine Art Mgr,* Morris Communications Co. LLC, Corporate Collection, Augusta GA

Clavir, Miriam, *Sr Conservator,* University of British Columbia, Museum of Anthropology, Vancouver BC

Claxton, Dana, *Asst Prof,* University of British Columbia, Dept of Art History, Visual Art & Theory, Vancouver BC (S)

Claxton, Ronald, *Assoc Prof,* Central State University, Dept of Art, Wilberforce OH (S)

Clay, Joe, *Dir Progs,* Koshare Indian Museum, Inc, Library, La Junta CO

Claybourn, Bradford, *Mus Cur,* Mission San Luis Rey de Francia, Mission San Luis Rey Museum, Oceanside CA

Clayden, Stephen, *Cur Botany,* New Brunswick Museum, Saint John NB

Clayson, Hollis, *Prof,* Northwestern University, Evanston, Dept of Art History, Evanston IL (S)

Clayton, Beverley, *Mgr Admin Svcs,* Kamloops Art Gallery, Kamloops BC

Clayton, Christine, *Asst Librn,* Worcester Art Museum, Library, Worcester MA

Clayton, Debra, *Exec Dir,* Michigan Guild of Artists & Artisans, Michigan Guild Gallery, Ann Arbor MI

Clayton, Greg, *Assoc Prof Art,* Harding University, Dept of Art & Design, Searcy AR (S)

Clayton, Ron, *Prof & Interim Chmn,* Southeast Missouri State University, Dept of Art, Cape Girardeau MO (S)

Clearwater, Bonnie, *Dir,* Museum of Contemporary Art, North Miami FL

Clearwaters, Deb, *Dir Educ,* Asian Art Museum of San Francisco, Chong-Moon Lee Ctr for Asian Art and Culture, San Francisco CA

Cleary, Carole, *Dir,* Southampton Art Society, Southampton Art School, Southampton ON (S)

Cleary, John R, *Assoc Prof,* Salisbury State University, Art Dept, Salisbury MD (S)

Cleary, Manon, *Prof,* University of the District of Columbia, Dept of Mass Media, Visual & Performing Arts, Washington DC (S)

Cleary, Naomi, *Gallery Coordr,* Clay Studio, Philadelphia PA

Cleary, Tim, *Lectr,* University of Wisconsin-Superior, Programs in the Visual Arts, Superior WI (S)

Clelland, III, F Wesley, *Treas,* Heard Museum, Billie Jane Baguley Library and Archives, Phoenix AZ

Clem, Amanda, *Mem & Gallery Mgr,* Blue Sky Gallery, Oregon Center for the Photographic Arts, Portland OR

Clem, Debra, *Assoc Prof,* Indiana University-Southeast, Fine Arts Dept, New Albany IN (S)

Clem, Patricia, *Secy,* Strasburg Museum, Strasburg VA

Cleman, Rebecca, *Distribution Dir,* Electronic Arts Intermix (EAI), New York NY

Clemens, Lenore, *Arts Programmer,* Richmond Arts Centre, Richmond BC

Clemens Pedersen, Deanna, *Bus Mgr & CFO,* Cedar Rapids Museum of Art, Cedar Rapids IA

Clement, Constance, *Deputy Dir,* Yale University, Yale Center for British Art, New Haven CT

Clement, Louise, *Instr,* Samuel S Fleisher, Philadelphia PA (S)

Clement, Russell T, *Head Art Coll,* Northwestern University, Art Collection, University Library, Evanston IL

Clementi, Bobbie, *Prof,* Daytona Beach Community College, Dept of Fine Arts & Visual Arts, Daytona Beach FL (S)

Clements, Bob, *Digital Design,* Art Institute of Pittsburgh, Pittsburgh PA (S)

Clements, Elaine, *Exec Dir,* Andover Historical Society, Andover MA

Clements, Emmett, *Gallery Mgr,* Pasadena Museum of California Art, Pasadena CA

Clements, Martin, *Adjunct Instr,* New York Institute of Technology, Fine Arts Dept, Old Westbury NY (S)

Clements, Rodney, *Asst Dir,* Louisiana State Exhibit Museum, Shreveport LA

Cleminshaw, Doug, *Asst Prof,* Rochester Institute of Technology, School of Design, Rochester NY (S)

Clemmons, Leshari, *Youth Dir,* African American Atelier, Greensboro NC

Clemmons, Sarah, *VPres Instr,* Chipola College, Dept of Fine & Performing Arts, Marianna FL (S)

Clemons, Larry T, *Owner,* Purvis Young Museum, Fort Lauderdale FL

Clendenin, Juliana, *Asst Prof,* Adrian College, Art & Design Dept, Adrian MI (S)

Clendenin, Paula, *Asst Prof,* West Virginia State University, Art Dept, Institute WV (S)

Clercx, Byron, *Chmn,* Marshall University, Dept of Art & Design, Huntington WV (S)

Clervi, Paul, *Chmn,* William Woods-Westminster Colleges, Art Dept, Fulton MO (S)

Cleveland, Matt, *Dir Mem,* Arkansas Arts Center, Museum, Little Rock AR (S)

Clewell, Heather, *Archivist,* Winterthur Museum, Garden & Library, Library, Winterthur DE

Clews, Christina, *Chair Pub Rels Comt,* La Napoule Art Foundation, Chateau de la Napoule, Portsmouth NH

Clews, Christopher S, *Pres,* La Napoule Art Foundation, Chateau de la Napoule, Portsmouth NH

Clews, Noele M, *Exec Dir,* La Napoule Art Foundation, Chateau de la Napoule, Portsmouth NH

Cliff, Denis, *Instr,* Toronto School of Art, Toronto ON (S)

Clifford, Meena Khalili, *Asst Prof,* Virginia State University, Department of Art & Design, Petersburg VA (S)

Clifford, Michael, *VP Finance & Admin,* Emily Carr University of Art + Design, Vancouver BC (S)

Clifford, Mike, *1st VChmn,* Guild Hall of East Hampton, Inc, Guild Hall Museum, East Hampton NY

Clifford, Shaun Healy, *Bd Chmn,* National Art Museum of Sport, Indianapolis IN

Clift, Vicki, *Instr,* Appalachian State University, Dept of Art, Boone NC (S)

Clifton, Deborah, *Colls Cur,* Lafayette Science Museum & Planetarium, Lafayette LA

Cline, Holly, *Asst to Dir,* Wildling Art Museum, Solvang CA

Cline, Tricia, *Instr,* Woodstock School of Art, Inc, Woodstock NY (S)

Clinger, Melinda, *Dir Museum,* Fulton County Historical Society Inc, Fulton County Museum (Tetzlaff Reference Room), Rochester IN

Clinton, Lee, *Mem Records Coordr,* Columbia River Maritime Museum, Library, Astoria OR

Clive, Mark, *Sr Lectr,* University of Texas at Arlington, Art & Art History Department, Arlington TX (S)

Cloer, Garrett, *Park Ranger,* Longfellow National Historic Site, Longfellow House - Washington's Headquarters, Cambridge MA

Clonts, Jessy, *Pub Rels Mgr,* Wichita State University, Ulrich Museum of Art, Wichita KS

Close, John, *Instr,* Harriet FeBland, New York NY (S)

Clothier, Anne, *Dir Educ,* Saratoga County Historical Society, Brookside Museum, Ballston Spa NY

Clough, Jan, *Prof,* Western Illinois University, Department of Art, Macomb IL (S)

Clough, Sebastian, *Exhib Designer,* University of California, Los Angeles, Fowler Museum at UCLA, Los Angeles CA

Clouse, Danielle, *Dir Visual Arts,* Pearson Lakes Art Center, Okoboji IA

Clouten, Neville H, *Dean,* Lawrence Technological University, College of Architecture, Southfield MI (S)

Cloutier, Nadine, *Pres,* Hartland Art Council, Hartland MI

Clovis, John, *Prof,* Fairmont State College, Div of Fine Arts, Fairmont WV (S)

Clowe, Richard, *Treas,* Schenectady County Historical Society, Museum of Schenectady History, Schenectady NY

Clubb, Barbara, *Dir,* Ottawa Public Library, Fine Arts Dept, Ottawa ON

Cluett, Cora, *Asst Prof,* University of Waterloo, Fine Arts Dept, Waterloo ON (S)

Clum, Claire, *Cur Educ,* Boca Raton Museum of Art, Library, Boca Raton FL

Clum, Claire, *Dir Educ,* Boca Raton Museum of Art, Boca Raton FL

Clymer, Frances, *Librn,* Buffalo Bill Memorial Association, Harold McCracken Research Library, Cody WY

Coakley, Stephanie J, *Dir Educ,* Tucson Museum of Art and Historic Block, Tucson AZ

Coan, Michael, *Chmn Jewelry Design,* Fashion Institute of Technology, Art & Design Division, New York NY (S)

Coane, Amy, *Retail Cur,* Santa Monica Museum of Art, Santa Monica CA

Coaston, Shirley, *Head Librn,* Laney College Library, Art Section, Oakland CA

Coate, Pepper, *Exhib Initiatives Dir,* Chicago Artists' Coalition, Coalition Gallery, Chicago IL

Coates, James, *Chmn Dept,* University of Massachusetts Lowell, Dept of Art, Lowell MA (S)

Coates, Joseph, *Asst Prof,* California Polytechnic State University at San Luis Obispo, Dept of Art & Design, San Luis Obispo CA (S)

Coates, Ken, *Dean,* University of Waterloo, Fine Arts Dept, Waterloo ON (S)

Coates, Robert, *Asst Prof,* Sinclair Community College, Division of Fine & Performing Arts, Dayton OH (S)

Coates, Vivian, *Dir Mus Stores,* Colorado Historical Society, Colorado History Museum, Denver CO

Cobarruvias, Gerardo, *Asst Prof,* Del Mar College, Art Dept, Corpus Christi TX (S)

Cobb, Gary, *Chmn Fine Art,* Pepperdine University, Seaver College, Dept of Art, Malibu CA (S)

Cobb, Henry N, *VPres Art,* American Academy of Arts & Letters, New York NY

Cobb, June, *Dir Admin & Finance,* National Heritage Museum, Lexington MA

Cobb, Rebekah, *Guest Svcs,* Bob Jones University Museum & Gallery Inc, Greenville SC

Cobble, Kelly, *Cur,* Adams National Historic Park, Quincy MA

Cobb Wright, Carolina, *Exhib Prog,* Visual Arts Center of Richmond, Richmond VA

Coble, Cari, *Dance,* Jacksonville University, Dept of Art, Theater, Dance, Jacksonville FL (S)

Coblentz, Cassandra, *Assoc Cur,* Scottsdale Cultural Council, Scottsdale Museum of Contemporary Art, Scottsdale AZ

Coburn, Carol, *Chmn Humanities,* Avila College, Art Division, Dept of Humanities, Kansas City MO (S)

Coburn, Oakley H, *Dir,* Wofford College, Sandor Teszler Library Gallery, Spartanburg SC

Cocanougher, Robert L, *Assoc Prof,* University of North Florida, Dept of Communications & Visual Arts, Jacksonville FL (S)

Cochran, Dorothy, *Dir & Cur,* The Interchurch Center, Galleries at the Interchurch Center, New York NY

Cochran, Dorothy, *Dir & Cur Galleries,* The Interchurch Center, Library, New York NY

Cochran, Marie, *Asst Prof,* Georgia Southern University, Dept of Art, Statesboro GA (S)

Cochran, Michelle, *Instr,* Saint Mary's University of Minnesota, Art & Design Dept, Winona MN (S)

Cochran, Sara, *Cur Modern & Contemporary Art,* Phoenix Art Museum, Phoenix AZ

Cochrane, Charles, *Pres Bd Trustees,* Museum of Contemporary Art, San Diego-Downtown, La Jolla CA

Cochrane, George, *Faculty,* Fairleigh Dickinson University, Fine Arts Dept, Madison NJ (S)

Cochrane, Mike, *COO,* Confederation Centre Art Gallery and Museum, Charlottetown PE

Cocke, Dudley, *Theater Dir,* Appalshop Inc, Appalshop, Whitesburg KY

Cockerell, Priscilla, *2nd VChmn,* Maitland Art Center, Maitland FL

Cockerline, Neil, *Dir Preservation Svcs,* Midwest Art Conservation Center, Minneapolis MN

Coconaur, SC, *Chmn,* Barnard's Mill Art Museum, Glen Rose TX

Codding, Mitchell A, *Dir,* The Hispanic Society of America, Museum & Library, New York NY

Coddington Rast, Ann, *Assoc Prof,* Eastern Illinois University, Art Dept, Charleston IL (S)

Codell, Julie, *Dir,* Arizona State University, School of Art, Tempe AZ (S)

Codispot, Lawrence, *VPres,* Historical Society of Rockland County, New City NY

Codlin, Alex, *Exec Asst to Dir,* Las Vegas Art Museum, Las Vegas NV

Codney, Jean, *Pres (V),* Cottonlandia Museum, Greenwood MS

Cody, Chuck, *Div Mgr,* Columbus Metropolitan Library, Arts & Media Division Carnegie Gallery, Columbus OH

Cody, Dan, *Coll Mgr,* Rochester Historical Society, Rochester NY

Coerver, Chad, *Dir Graphic Design & Publs,* San Francisco Museum of Modern Art, San Francisco CA

Coes, Cara, *Dir,* Sunbury Shores Arts & Nature Centre, Inc, Gallery, Saint Andrews NB

Coester, Dan, *Exhibs,* University of Kansas, Spencer Museum of Art, Lawrence KS

Coffey, John, *Dep Dir Art Coll,* North Carolina Museum of Art, Raleigh NC

Coffey, Marylyn, *Staff Asst,* University of Alabama at Huntsville, Union Grove Gallery & University Center Gallery, Huntsville AL

Coffin, David, *Pres,* Old State House, Hartford CT

Coffin, Sarah, *Cur, Product Design & Dec Arts,* Cooper-Hewitt National Design Museum, Smithsonian Institution, New York NY

Coffman, Pam, *Educ Cur,* Museum of Florida Art, Deland FL

Coffman, Rebecca L, *Asst Prof,* Huntington College, Art Dept, Huntington IN (S)

Cofi, Dario, *Prof Emeritus,* University of Louisville, Allen R Hite Art Institute, Louisville KY (S)

Cofield, Carol, *Bookkeeper,* Creative Arts Guild, Dalton GA

Cogan, Kathryn, *Asst Dir,* Knights of Columbus Supreme Council, Knights of Columbus Museum, New Haven CT

Cogeval, Guy, *Dir,* Montreal Museum of Fine Arts, Montreal PQ

Coggeshall, Jan, *Pres,* Rosenberg Library, Galveston TX

Coggins, Paul, *Bd Pres,* Wilkes Art Gallery, North Wilkesboro NC

Cognato, Karen, *Librn,* New York Institute of Technology, Art & Architectural Library, Old Westbury NY

Cogswell, James, *Prof,* University of Michigan, Ann Arbor, School of Art & Design, Ann Arbor MI (S)

Cogswell, Peggy, *Lectr,* Southeastern Louisiana University, Dept of Visual Arts, Hammond LA (S)

Cohen, Ada, *Chair,* Dartmouth College, Dept of Art History, Hanover NH (S)

Cohen, Hallie, *Assoc Prof Art & Chair Art Dept,* Marymount Manhattan College, Fine & Performing Arts Div, New York NY (S)

Cohen, Janie, *Dir,* University of Vermont, Robert Hull Fleming Museum, Burlington VT

Cohen, Jody, *Mgr Exhib,* High Museum of Art, Atlanta GA

Cohen, John, *Prof Emeritus,* Purchase College, State University of New York, School of Art+Design, Purchase NY (S)

Cohen, Kara, *Admin Coordr,* National Architectural Accrediting Board, Inc, Washington DC

Cohen, Kathi, *Dir School,* The Art League Gallery & School, Alexandria VA

Cohen, Liz, *Head Photo Dept,* Cranbrook Academy of Art, Bloomfield Hills MI (S)

Cohen, Marianne, *Cir Corp Mems,* USS Constitution Museum, Boston MA

Cohen, Mildred Thaler, *Dir,* The Marbella Gallery Inc, New York NY

Cohen, Phyllis Samitz, *Dir Adopt-A-Monument/ Mural Progs,* Municipal Art Society of New York, New York NY

Cohen, Sarah, *Assoc Prof,* State University of New York at Albany, Art Dept, Albany NY (S)

Cohen, Stan, *Vice-Pres,* Rocky Mountain Museum of Military History, Missoula MT

Cohen-Stratyner, Barbara, *Cur Exhib,* The New York Public Library, The New York Public Library for the Performing Arts, New York NY

Cohlman, Jennifer, *Librn,* Cooper-Hewitt National Design Museum, Doris & Henry Dreyfuss Memorial Study Center Library & Archive, New York NY

Cohn, Diana, *Board Pres,* Yerba Buena Center for the Arts, San Francisco CA

Cohn, Marjorie B, *Acting Dir,* Harvard University, Harvard University Art Museums, Cambridge MA

Cohn, Marjorie B, *Cur Prints,* Harvard University, William Hayes Fogg Art Museum, Cambridge MA

Cohn, Michael, *CFO,* The Historic New Orleans Collection, Royal Street Galleries, New Orleans LA

Cohn, Peter, *Librn Urban Studies, Planning & Real Estate,* Massachusetts Institute of Technology, Rotch Library of Architecture & Planning, Cambridge MA

Cohn, Shelley, *Exec Dir,* Arizona Commission on the Arts, Phoenix AZ

Cohodas, Marvin, *Assoc Prof,* University of British Columbia, Dept of Art History, Visual Art & Theory, Vancouver BC (S)

Coin, Greg, *Dir Develop,* Delaware Historical Society, Library, Wilmington DE

Coker, Alyce, *Assoc Prof,* University of Minnesota, Duluth, Art Dept, Duluth MN (S)

Coker, Crystal, *Admin Asst & Rental Coordr,* Creative Arts Guild, Dalton GA

Coker, Rachel, *Dir Develop,* Storm King Art Center, Mountainville NY

Cokus, Patty, *Exec Asst,* Glass Art Society, Seattle WA

Colagross, John, *Dept Chair,* John C Calhoun, Art Gallery, Decatur AL

Colagross, John T, *Dept Chmn,* John C Calhoun, Department of Fine Arts, Tanner AL (S)

Colaguori, Louis A, *Pres,* Burlington County Historical Society, Burlington NJ

Colan, John, *Graphic Design,* Montserrat College of Art, Beverly MA (S)

Colangelo, Carmon, *Dir,* University of Georgia, Dept of Art Lamar Dodd School of Art, Athens GA

Colangelo, Carmon, *Dir,* University of Georgia, Franklin College of Arts & Sciences, Lamar Dodd School of Art, Athens GA (S)

Colarusso, Stefanie, *Dir Progs,* Everhart Museum, Scranton PA

Colbert, Charles, *Asst Prof,* Portland State University, Dept of Art, Portland OR (S)

Colbert, Cynthia, *Chmn Art Educ,* University of South Carolina, Dept of Art, Columbia SC (S)

Colbert, Tom, *Treas,* Wayne County Historical Society, Museum, Honesdale PA

Colborne, Allison, *Librn,* Museum of New Mexico, Laboratory of Anthropology Library, Santa Fe NM

Colburn, Cynthia, *Assoc Prof,* Pepperdine University, Seaver College, Dept of Art, Malibu CA (S)

Colburn, Richard, *Prof,* University of Northern Iowa, Dept of Art, Cedar Falls IA (S)

Colby, Chad, *Assoc Prof,* Fort Lewis College, Art Dept, Durango CO (S)

Colby, Gary, *Prof Photog,* University of La Verne, Dept of Art, La Verne CA (S)

Colby, James, *Dir,* Jamestown Community College, The Weeks, Jamestown NY

Colby-Stothart, Karen, *Deputy Dir Exhibs & Installations,* National Gallery of Canada, Ottawa ON

Coldiron, Lisa M, *Spec Projects Specialist,* National Gallery of Art, Department of Image Collections, Washington DC

Cole, Carol, *Instr,* Main Line Art Center, Haverford PA (S)

Cole, Caroline, *Curatorial Asst,* Museum of Fine Arts, Houston, Rienzi Center for European Decorative Arts, Houston TX

Cole, Charlene, *Dir Library Svcs,* Tougaloo College, Coleman Library, Tougaloo MS

Cole, Don, *Photographer,* University of California, Los Angeles, Fowler Museum at UCLA, Los Angeles CA

Cole, Harold D, *Prof Art History,* Baldwin-Wallace College, Dept of Art, Berea OH (S)

Cole, Jolyn S, *Pres,* Lafayette Museum Association, Lafayette Museum-Alexandre Mouton House, Lafayette LA

Cole, Marc, *Pres,* The Boston Printmakers, Boston MA

Cole, Mark, *Cur American Painting & Sculpture,* The Cleveland Museum of Art, Cleveland OH

Cole, Michael, *Instr,* De Anza College, Creative Arts Division, Cupertino CA (S)

Cole, Nancy, *Instr,* Dallas Baptist University, Dept of Art, Dallas TX (S)

Cole, Nita, *Cur,* Louisiana State Exhibit Museum, Shreveport LA

Cole, Robert A, *Prof,* Rochester Institute of Technology, School of Design, Rochester NY (S)

Cole, Steve, *Prof,* Birmingham Southern College, Doris Wainwright Kennedy Art Center, Birmingham AL

Cole, Steve, *Prof,* Birmingham-Southern College, Art & Art History, Birmingham AL (S)

Cole, Susan A, *Pres,* Montclair State University, Art Galleries, Upper Montclair NJ

Cole, Theresa, *Assoc,* Tulane University, Sophie H Newcomb Memorial College, New Orleans LA (S)

Cole-Cunningham, Ragan, *Dir Exhibs & Educ,* Contemporary Art Center of Virginia, Virginia Beach VA

Cole-Zielanski, Trudy, *Assoc Prof,* James Madison University, School of Art & Art History, Harrisonburg VA (S)

Colegrave, Jim, *Computer Systems Mgr,* Modern Art Museum, Fort Worth TX

Colegrove, Susan, *Admin Asst to Cur,* Modern Art Museum, Fort Worth TX

Colegrove, Ted, *Instr,* Moravian College, Dept of Art, Bethlehem PA (S)

Coleman, C Allen, *Exec Dir,* Pickens County Museum of Art & History, Pickens SC

Coleman, Christopher, *Gift Shop Mgr,* Delta Blues Museum, Clarksdale MS

Coleman, Clara Collins, *Cur Educ Interpretation,* Laumeier Sculpture Park, Saint Louis MO

Coleman, Dorothy, *Exec Dir,* Oil Pastel Association, Stockholm NJ

Coleman, Dorothy J, *Pres,* New Orleans Academy of Fine Arts, Academy Gallery, New Orleans LA

Coleman, Elizabeth, *Pres,* Bennington College, Visual Arts Division, Bennington VT (S)

Coleman, James S, *Pres & CEO,* American Textile History Museum, Lowell MA

Coleman, Johnny, *Assoc Prof,* Oberlin College, Dept of Art, Oberlin OH (S)

Coleman, Kathleen, *Cur,* Saratoga County Historical Society, Brookside Museum, Ballston Spa NY

Coleman, Laura, *Pub Rels & Mktg,* Kentucky Historical Society, Old State Capitol & Annex, Frankfort KY

Coleman, Michelle, *Dir Community Develop,* Idaho Commission on the Arts, Boise ID

Coleman, Myrlan, *Head Visual Arts & Instr,* Weatherford College, Dept of Speech Fine Arts, Weatherford TX (S)

Coleman, Rebekah, *Asst Educ,* San Angelo Museum of Fine Arts, San Angelo TX

Coleman, Richard, *Instr,* Glendale Community College, Visual & Performing Arts Div, Glendale CA (S)

Coleman, Romaula, *Mgr IL Artisans Shop,* Illinois State Museum, Illinois Artisans & Visitors Centers, Chicago IL

Coleman, Susan, *Dir Gallery,* Cornell College, Peter Paul Luce Gallery, Mount Vernon IA

Colenda, Marianne, *Dir Spec Events,* Thiel College, Weyers-Sampson Art Gallery, Greenville PA

Coletta, Natalie, *Prof,* Community College of Rhode Island, Dept of Art, Warwick RI (S)

Colgrove, Clare, *Staff Asst,* United States Senate Commission on Art, Washington DC

Colkitt, Brian, *Photog,* Art Institute of Pittsburgh, Pittsburgh PA (S)

Collard, Sara, *Develop Coordr,* Captain Forbes House Museum, Milton MA

Collens, David R, *Dir & Cur,* Storm King Art Center, Mountainville NY

Collette, Alfred T, *Dir,* Syracuse University, Art Collection, Syracuse NY

Colley, Brett, *Asst Prof,* Grand Valley State University, Art & Design Dept, Allendale MI (S)

Colley, Christine, *Prof,* Shorter College, Art Dept, Rome GA (S)

Collier, Denise, *Admin Mgr,* Cranbrook Art Museum, Bloomfield Hills MI

Collier, Jean, *Coll Mgr,* University of Virginia, The Fralin Museum of Art at the University of Virginia, Charlottesville VA

Collings, Ed, *Instr Photog & Ceramics,* Columbia College, Art Dept, Columbia MO (S)

Collins, Austin, *Chmn,* University of Notre Dame, Dept of Art, Art History & Design, Notre Dame IN (S)

Collins, D Cheryl, *Dir,* Riley County Historical Society & Museum, Seaton Library, Manhattan KS

Collins, D Cheryl, *Dir & Cur,* Riley County Historical Society & Museum, Riley County Historical Museum, Manhattan KS

Collins, Dana, *Instr,* Illinois Valley Community College, Division of Humanities & Fine Arts, Oglesby IL (S)

Collins, Doris, *Community Coordr,* Art Complex Museum, Carl A. Weyerhaeuser Library, Duxbury MA

Collins, Dylan, *Visiting Asst Prof,* West Virginia University, College of Creative Arts, School of Art & Design, Morgantown WV (S)

Collins, Garry, *Instr,* Locust Street Neighborhood Art Classes, Inc, Buffalo NY (S)

Collins, Gerry, *Prof Ceramics,* Universite de Moncton, Dept of Visual Arts, Moncton NB (S)

Collins, Jefferson, *Coll Mgr,* Agecroft Association, Museum, Richmond VA

Collins, Jennifer, *Office Mgr,* Indianapolis Art Center, Marilyn K. Glick School of Art, Indianapolis IN

Collins, Jill, *Admin Asst,* Sioux City Art Center, Library, Sioux City IA

Collins, Jill, *Admin Asst & Contact,* Sioux City Art Center, Sioux City IA

Collins, Joel, *Chmn,* Mount Union College, Dept of Art, Alliance OH (S)

Collins, John, *Dean,* Surry Community College, Art Dept, Dobson NC (S)

Collins, Kathleen, *Pres,* Kansas City Art Institute, Kansas City MO (S)

Collins, Kenlyn, *Librn,* The Winnipeg Art Gallery, Clara Lander Library, Winnipeg MB

Collins, Kristin, *Instr,* Marylhurst University, Art Dept, Marylhurst OR (S)

Collins, Kurt, *Instr,* California State University, San Bernardino, Dept of Art, San Bernardino CA (S)

Collins, Lisa, *Prof,* Vassar College, Art Dept, Poughkeepsie NY (S)

Collins, Lynda, *Mus Educ,* Springfield Museum of Art, Springfield OH

Collins, N Taylor, *National Pres,* National League of American Pen Women, Washington DC

Collins, Paul, *Artistic Dir,* Anderson Ranch Arts Center, Snowmass Village CO

Collins, Penny, *Chmn Fashion Design,* Woodbury University, Dept of Graphic Design, Burbank CA (S)

Collins, Phillip, *Chief Cur,* African American Museum, Dallas TX

Collins, Ruth, *Asst Deputy Dir Pub Svcs,* Buffalo & Erie County Public Library, Buffalo NY

Collins, Sarah, *Curatorial Asst,* Green Hill Center for North Carolina Art, Greensboro NC

Collins, Sherry, *Dir Finance,* The Currier Museum of Art, Manchester NH

Collins, Simon, *Dean School of Fashion,* Parsons The New School for Design, New York NY (S)

Collins, Susan, *State Archaeologist,* Colorado Historical Society, Colorado History Museum, Denver CO

Collins, Toni, *Adminr,* Pennsylvania Historical & Museum Commission, Brandywine Battlefield Park, Harrisburg PA

Collinsworth, Matt, *Dir,* Morehead State University, Kentucky Folk Art Center, Morehead KY

Collura, Bonnie, *Asst Prof Art (Sculpture),* Pennsylvania State University, University Park, Penn State School of Visual Arts, University Park PA (S)

Colo, Papo, *Co-Founder/Cultural Producer,* Exit Art, San Leandro CA

Colombik, Roger Bruce, *Prof,* Texas State University - San Marcos, Dept of Art and Design, San Marcos TX (S)

Colon, Doreen, *Educ,* Museo de Arte de Puerto Rico, San Juan PR

Colon, Doreen, *Educ,* Museo de Arte de Puerto Rico, San Juan PR

Coloto, Juan, *Cur,* Wells Fargo & Co, History Museum, Los Angeles CA

Colpitt, Frances, *Prof,* Texas Christian University, School of Art, Fort Worth TX (S)

Colpitts, GE, *Chmn Dept Art & Design,* Judson University, School of Art, Design & Architecture, Elgin IL (S)

Colquhoun, Peter, *VPres,* Federation of Modern Painters & Sculptors, New York NY

Colton, Stan, *Library Develop,* Las Vegas-Clark County Library District, Las Vegas NV

Coltrin, Chris, *Coordr Art History,* Shepherd University, Dept of Contemporary Art & Theater, Shepherdstown WV (S)

Coluntino, Diana, *Artistic Dir,* The Revolving Museum, Lowell MA

Colvard, Jane, *Asst Librn,* American Numismatic Association, Library, Colorado Springs CO

Colvin, Ann E, *Educ Coordr,* Maitland Art Center, Library, Maitland FL

Colvin, Kaersten, *Asst Prof,* Clarion University of Pennsylvania, Dept of Art, Clarion PA (S)

Colvin, Richard D, *Cur Coll,* Maitland Art Center, Maitland FL

Colvin, Richard D, *Cur Coll,* Maitland Art Center, Library, Maitland FL

Colvin, William E, *Acting Dept Chmn,* Alabama State University, Dept of Visual & Theatre Arts, Montgomery AL (S)

Comar, Catherine, *Dir Coll,* Shelburne Museum, Museum, Shelburne VT

Comba, Steve, *Asst Dir & Registrar,* The Pomona College, Claremont CA

Combs, Brian, *VPres,* Alton Museum of History & Art, Inc, Alton IL

Combs, Glenna, *Prog Admin Mgr,* Kentucky Guild of Artists & Craftsmen Inc, Berea KY

Combs, Thomas, *Operations & Finance,* George Eastman, Rochester NY

Comley, Ruth, *Computer Animation,* Art Institute of Pittsburgh, Pittsburgh PA (S)

Commoner, Lucy, *Textile Conservator,* Cooper-Hewitt National Design Museum, Smithsonian Institution, New York NY

Como, Thomas, *Prof, Chmn,* Slippery Rock University of Pennsylvania, Dept of Art, Slippery Rock PA (S)

Compton, Douglas, *Instr,* Joe Kubert, Dover NJ (S)

Comstock, Mary, *C&E Vermeule Cur & Keeper of Coins, Greek & Roman Art,* Museum of Fine Arts, Boston MA

Comstock, Richard, *Pres,* The Summit County Historical Society of Akron, OH, Akron OH

Conard, Susannah, *Facilities Coordr,* National Audubon Society, John James Audubon Center at Mill Grove, Audubon PA

Conaty, Gerald, *Dir Indigenous Studies,* Glenbow Museum, Calgary AB

Conaway, Stephanie, *Mgr Exhib,* Columbia College Chicago, Museum of Contemporary Photography, Chicago IL

Conaway, Susan, *Dir External Affairs,* Art Museum of the University of Houston, Blaffer Gallery, Houston TX

Concholar, Dan, *Pres & Dir,* Art Information Center, Inc, New York NY

Condict, Amanda, *Newsletter Ed,* Berks Art Alliance, Reading PA

Condon, Elisabeth, *Assoc Prof,* University of South Florida, School The Arts, Tampa FL (S)

Condon, Lorna, *Cur Library & Archives,* Historic New England, Library and Archives, Boston MA

Condon, Shawna, *CEO,* New Meriks Sketch Gallery, Richfield MN

Cone, Leslie, *Registrar & Collections Mgr,* Rollins College, George D & Harriet W Cornell Fine Arts Museum, Winter Park FL

Cone Busch, Ellen M, *Exec Dir,* Oysterponds Historical Society, Museum, Orient NY

Conelli, Maria, *Dir,* American Folk Art Museum, Shirley K. Schlafer Library, New York NY

Conelli, Maria Ann, *Dir,* American Folk Art Museum, New York NY

Confessore, Lisa-Marie, *Exec Dir,* Art Center Sarasota, Sarasota FL (S)

Conforti, Michael, *Dir,* Sterling & Francine Clark, Williamstown MA

Cong, Zhiyuan, *Assoc Prof,* William Paterson University, Dept Arts, Wayne NJ (S)

Congello, Joseph, *Mus Security Officer,* Williams College, Museum of Art, Williamstown MA

Conger, Bill, *Cur,* Illinois State University, University Galleries, Normal IL

Conger, Deniz H, *Sr Div Develop,* Museum of Contemporary Craft, Portland OR

Conger, Jeffrey, *Prof Graphic Design,* Montana State University, School of Art, Bozeman MT (S)

Conger, William, *Prof,* Northwestern University, Evanston, Dept of Art Theory & Practice, Evanston IL (S)

Conis, Pete, *Chmn,* Des Moines Area Community College, Art Dept, Boone IA (S)

Conklin, Donnelle, *Head Librn,* Lauren Rogers, Library, Laurel MS

Conklin, Jo-Ann, *Dir,* Brown University, David Winton Bell Gallery, Providence RI

Conklin-Wingfield, Cara, *Dir Educ,* Parrish Art Museum, Water Mill NY

Conlan, Teressa, *Asst Librn,* Toledo Museum of Art, Art Reference Library, Toledo OH

Conlee, Julie, *System Adminr & Sr Cataloger,* Colonial Williamsburg Foundation, John D Rockefeller, Jr Library, Williamsburg VA

Conley, B, *Instr,* Golden West College, Visual Art Dept, Huntington Beach CA (S)

Conley, Cort, *Dir Literature,* Idaho Commission on the Arts, Boise ID

Conley, Lisa, *Bus Mgr,* University of Georgia, Georgia Museum of Art, Athens GA

Conley, Mary, *Admin,* The Summit County Historical Society of Akron, OH, Akron OH

Conlin, Dan, *Cur Marine History,* Nova Scotia Museum, Maritime Museum of the Atlantic, Halifax NS

Conlon, Darby, *Mem Data Mgt,* Lighthouse ArtCenter Museum & School of Art, Tequesta FL

Conlon, William, *Div Chmn,* Fordham University, Art Dept, New York NY (S)

Connally, Abbie, *Accnt,* University of Wyoming, University of Wyoming Art Museum, Laramie WY

Connally, Betty, *Gift Shop Mgr,* San Angelo Museum of Fine Arts, San Angelo TX

Connally, Leslie, *Facility & Gallery Liaison,* The McKinney Avenue Contemporary (The MAC), Dallas TX

Connally, Leslie, *Prog Coordr,* The Dallas Contemporary, Dallas Visual Art Center, Dallas TX

Connell, Anne, *Dir School,* Silvermine Guild Arts Center, Silvermine Galleries, New Canaan CT

Connell, Anne, *Dir School,* Guild Arts Center, Silvermine, New Canaan CT (S)

Connell, Anne, *Dir Silvermine School,* Silvermine Guild Arts Center, School of Art, New Canaan CT

Connell, E Jane, *Sr Cur & Dir Colls & Exhib,* Muskegon Museum of Art, Muskegon MI

Connell, Emily, *Asst Librn,* The Baltimore Museum of Art, E Kirkbride Miller Art Library, Baltimore MD

Connell, Jim, *Assoc Prof,* Winthrop University, Dept of Art & Design, Rock Hill SC (S)

Connell, John, *Librn,* Yonkers Public Library, Fine Arts Dept, Yonkers NY

Connell, John, *Librn,* Yonkers Public Library, Will Library, Yonkers NY

Connell, Kevin, *Assoc Prof Theatre,* Marymount Manhattan College, Fine & Performing Arts Div, New York NY (S)

Connell, Steven, *Prof,* University of Montana, Dept of Art, Missoula MT (S)

Connelly, Adrienne, *Librn,* Alberta College of Art & Design, Luke Lindoe Library, Calgary AB

Connelly, David, *Dir Pub Rels,* Museum of Fine Arts, Saint Petersburg, Florida, Inc, Saint Petersburg FL

Connelly, Michael, *Asst Prof,* Montgomery County Community College, Art Center, Blue Bell PA (S)

Connelly, Trinity, *Curatorial Asst,* California State University, Chico, Janet Turner Print Museum, CSU, Chicago, Chico CA

Conner, Ann, *Prof,* University of North Carolina at Wilmington, Dept of Fine Arts - Division of Art, Wilmington NC (S)

Conner, Brittony, *Mem Coordr,* LaGrange Art Museum, LaGrange GA

Conner, Judy, *Dir Mktg & Commun,* Dallas Museum of Art, Dallas TX

Conner, Laura, *Pub Educ Prog,* University of Alaska, Museum of the North, Fairbanks AK

Conner, Margie, *Dir Mktg,* Anniston Museum of Natural History, Anniston AL

Conney, Lynne, *Acting Dir,* Florence & Chafetz Hillel House at Boston University, Boston University Art Gallery at the Stone Gallery, Boston MA

Conniff-O'Shea, Christine, *Conservation Tech,* The Art Institute of Chicago, Dept of Prints & Drawings, Chicago IL

Connolly, Felicia, *Office Admin,* Wenham Museum, Wenham MA

Connolly, Patrick, *Asst Prof,* La Roche College, Division of Design, Pittsburgh PA (S)

Connor, Colleen, *Develop Dir,* The Ogden Museum of Southern Art, University of New Orleans, New Orleans LA

Connor, Holly, *Cur American Art,* Newark Museum Association, The Newark Museum, Newark NJ

Connor, Kathy, *Cur Legacy Coll,* George Eastman, Museum, Rochester NY

Connor, Kathy, *House Cur,* George Eastman, Rochester NY

Connor, Scot, *Instr,* Mohawk Valley Community College, Utica NY (S)

Connor-Talasek, Catherine, *Assoc Prof,* Fontbonne University, Fine Art Dept, Saint Louis MO (S)

Connors, Andrew, *Cur Art,* Albuquerque Museum of Art & History, Albuquerque NM

Connors, Joseph, *Chmn,* Columbia University, Dept of Art History & Archaeology, New York NY (S)

Connors, Michael, *Prof,* University of Wisconsin, Madison, Dept of Art, Madison WI (S)

Connors McQuade, Margaret, *Asst Dir & Cur Decorative Arts,* The Hispanic Society of America, Museum & Library, New York NY

Connorton, Judy, *Architecture Librn,* City College of the City University of New York, Morris Raphael Cohen Library, New York NY

Connorton, Judy, *Librn,* City College of the City University of New York, Architecture Library, New York NY

Conour, Rachel, *Asst Dir,* Hoosier Salon Patrons Association, Inc, Art Gallery & Membership Organization, Indianapolis IN

Conrad, Eric, *Asst,* Emporia State University, Dept of Art, Emporia KS (S)

Conrad, Geoffrey W, *Dir,* Indiana University, The Mathers Museum of World Cultures, Bloomington IN

Conrad, Jennifer, *Mus Coordr,* University of Colorado, CU Art Museum, Boulder CO

Conrad, John, *Instr,* San Diego Mesa College, Fine Arts Dept, San Diego CA (S)

Conrad, Kristy, *Mem & Pub Progs Coordr,* Portland Art Museum, Northwest Film Center, Portland OR

Conradi, Jan, *Asst Prof,* State University of New York at Fredonia, Dept of Art, Fredonia NY (S)

Conrey, Joseph, *Coordr,* Ocean County College, Humanities Dept, Toms River NJ (S)

Conroy, Michel, *Prof,* Texas State University - San Marcos, Dept of Art and Design, San Marcos TX (S)

Conroy, Robyn, *Office Mgr,* St. Louis Artists' Guild, Saint Louis MO

Conroy, Shaun, *Exhibs Coordr,* George A Spiva, Joplin MO

Considine, Raymond, *Asst Dean Arts & Sciences,* Indian River Community College, Fine Arts Dept, Fort Pierce FL (S)

Consoli, Joseph, *Art Librn,* Rutgers, The State University of New Jersey, Art Library, New Brunswick NJ

Consolini, Marella, *Chief of Staff,* Whitney Museum of American Art, New York NY

Constantine, Gregory, *Chmn,* Andrews University, Dept of Art, Art History & Design, Berrien Springs MI (S)

Constantinou, Meghan R, *Librn,* Grolier Club Library, New York NY

Conte, Carolina, *Vis Asst Prof Film,* Jacksonville University, Dept of Art, Theater, Dance, Jacksonville FL (S)

Conte, Christine, *Exec Dir,* Tohono Chul Park, Tucson AZ

Conti, Fred, *Treas,* Mystic Art Association, Inc, Mystic Arts Center, Mystic CT

Conti, Nick, *Dir Information Technology,* American Antiquarian Society, Worcester MA

Contiguglia, Georgianna, *CEO,* Colorado Historical Society, Colorado History Museum, Denver CO

Contreras, Adriana, *Coordr,* Simon Fraser University, Simon Fraser University Gallery, Burnaby BC

Contreras, Adriana, *Mktg,* Brownsville Art League, Brownsville Museum of Fine Art, Brownsville TX

Contreras-Koterbay, Karlota, *Gallery Dir,* East Tennessee State University, College of Arts and Sciences, Dept of Art & Design, Johnson City TN (S)

Conway, Brenda, *Mem Asst,* Southern Oregon Historical Society, Library, Medford OR

Conway, Chris, *Sr Libr Asst,* Art Museum of the University of Houston, William R Jenkins Architecture & Art Library, Houston TX

Conway, Cindy, *VPres,* Wilmington Trust Company, Wilmington DE

Conway, Jan, *Adjunct Prof,* Wilkes University, Dept of Art, Wilkes-Barre PA (S)

Conway, Matthew, *Registrar,* Cornell University, Herbert F Johnson Museum of Art, Ithaca NY

Conyers, Wayne, *Chmn,* McPherson College, Art Dept, McPherson KS (S)

Conyers, Wayne, *Dir,* McPherson College Gallery, McPherson KS

Coogan, Michael, *Dir Publ,* Harvard University, Semitic Museum, Cambridge MA

Cook, Arthur, *Asst Prof,* Seton Hall University, College of Arts & Sciences, South Orange NJ (S)

Cook, Barbara, *Pub Rels,* Winterset Art Center, Winterset IA

Cook, Cathy, *Assoc Prof,* University of Maryland, Baltimore County, Imaging & Digital Arts (IMDA), Dept of Visual Arts, Baltimore MD (S)

Cook, David, *Chmn,* Sterling College, Art Dept, Sterling KS (S)

Cook, Gale, *Opers Mgr,* Northwestern Michigan College, Dennos Museum Center, Traverse City MI

Cook, Hope, *Gallery Coordr,* Mankato Area Arts Council, Carnegie Art Center, Mankato MN

Cook, James, *Prof,* Elmira College, Art Dept, Elmira NY (S)

Cook, Lakin, *Dir Performing Arts,* Avampato Discovery Museum, The Clay Center for Arts & Sciences, Charleston WV

Cook, Linda, *Supt,* National Park Service, Weir Farm National Historic Site, Wilton CT

Cook, Marlana L, *Registrar,* United States Military Academy, West Point Museum, West Point NY

Cook, Morris, *Park Svc Specialist,* Florida Department of Environmental Protection, Stephen Foster Folk Culture Center State Park, White Springs FL

Cook, Richard L, *Emeritus,* College of Santa Fe, Art Dept, Santa Fe NM (S)

Cook, Robert, *Sec,* Organization of Independent Artists, Inc, Brooklyn NY

Cook, Tom, *Pub Rels,* Montana Historical Society, Helena MT

Cooke, Edward, *Chmn,* Yale University, Dept of the History of Art, New Haven CT (S)

Cooke, Judy, *Instr,* Pacific Northwest College of Art, Portland OR (S)

Cooke, S Tucker, *Chmn,* University of North Carolina at Asheville, Dept of Art, Asheville NC (S)

Cooke, Samuel A, *VChmn,* Honolulu Academy of Arts, The Art Center at Linekona, Honolulu HI (S)

Cooksey, Susan, *Cur African Art,* University of Florida, Samuel P Harn Museum of Art, Gainesville FL

Cooley, Brian, *Facilities Mgr,* Oregon Historical Society, Oregon History Museum, Portland OR

Coolidge, Miles, *Chair & Assoc Prof Photog,* University of California, Irvine, Studio Art Dept, Irvine CA (S)

Coombe, JoAnne, *Exec Dir,* Saint Louis County Historical Society, St. Louis County Historical Society, Duluth MN

Coombs, Nancy, *Communs Coordr,* Fuller Lodge Art Center, Los Alamos NM

Coombs, Tamara, *Dir Progs & Tours,* Municipal Art Society of New York, New York NY

Coon, Alexandra Nicholis, *Exec,* Massillon Museum, Massillon OH

Coon, Cyndy, *Dir School-Work & Organization Develop,* Arizona Commission on the Arts, Phoenix AZ

Coones, R C, *Instr,* Northeastern State University, College of Arts & Letters, Tahlequah OK (S)

Cooney, Alice, *Anthony W & Lulu,* The Metropolitan Museum of Art, New York NY

Coonin, Victor, *Chmn, Asst Prof,* Rhodes College, Dept of Art, Memphis TN (S)

Cooper, Charisse, *Facility Coordr,* Philbrook Museum of Art, Tulsa OK

Cooper, Constance, *Chief Cur,* Delaware Historical Society, Delaware History Museum, Wilmington DE

Cooper, Cynthia, *Cur Costume,* McCord Museum of Canadian History, Montreal PQ

Cooper, David, *Instr,* Butte College, Dept of Fine Arts and Communication Tech, Oroville CA (S)

Cooper, Deb, *Registrar,* Brookfield Craft Center, Inc, Gallery, Brookfield CT

Cooper, Erika, *Librn Asst,* Johns Hopkins University, George Peabody Library, Baltimore MD

Cooper, Frederick A, *Prof,* University of Minnesota, Minneapolis, Art History, Minneapolis MN (S)

Cooper, Gina, *Mus Store Mgr,* Anniston Museum of Natural History, Anniston AL

Cooper, Ginny, *Exec Asst,* Gadsden Museum of Fine Arts, Inc, Gadsden Museum of Art and History, Gadsden AL

Cooper, Helen, *Cur American Painting,* Yale University, Yale University Art Gallery, New Haven CT

Cooper, Jacqueline, *Artistic Dir,* Sun Gallery, Hayward CA

Cooper, Janet, *Mktg Dir,* Bunte Gallery, Dublin OH

Cooper, Jeane, *Asst Prof Art, Graphic Design,* Florida Atlantic University, D F Schmidt College of Arts & Letters Dept of Visual Arts & Art History, Boca Raton FL (S)

Cooper, Kate, *Head Librn,* Montgomery College of Art & Design Library, Takoma Park MD

Cooper, Melody, *Instr,* Pierce College, Art Dept, Woodland Hills CA (S)

Cooper, Michael, *Instr,* De Anza College, Creative Arts Division, Cupertino CA (S)

Cooper, Neil B, *VPres,* Congregation Emanu-El, Bernard Judaica Museum, New York NY

Cooper, Nikki, *Publ Cur,* Fort Morgan Heritage Foundation, Fort Morgan CO

Cooper, Rebecca, *Educ Progs Coordr,* Biggs Museum of American Art, Dover DE

Cooper, Rhea, *Bookkeeper,* George A Spiva, Joplin MO

Cooper, Rhonda, *Dir,* State University of New York at Stony Brook, University Art Gallery, Stony Brook NY

Cooper, Valerie, *Pres & CEO,* Art Gallery of Calgary, Calgary AB

Cooper, Virginia, *Registrar,* Muscatine Art Center, Muscatine IA

Cooper, Virginia, *Registrar,* Muscatine Art Center, Museum, Muscatine IA

Cooperman, Lisa, *Cur Educ,* The San Joaquin Pioneer & Historical Society, The Haggin Museum, Stockton CA

Cooper Nadav, Jan, *Dir Educ,* Mizel Museum, Denver CO

Cooray, Dinali, *Cur,* University of Notre Dame, Snite Museum of Art, Notre Dame IN

Copas, Susan, *Dept Chair,* Seward County Community College, Art Dept, Liberal KS (S)

Cope, Abner, *Assoc Prof,* Central State University, Dept of Art, Wilberforce OH (S)

Cope, Steve, *Prof Painting,* Saint Joseph's University, Art Dept, Philadelphia PA (S)

Copeland, Huey, *Asst Prof,* Northwestern University, Evanston, Dept of Art History, Evanston IL (S)

Copeland, Jackie, *Dir Develop & Dir Educ,* Walters Art Museum, Baltimore MD

Copley, David C, *VPres Bd Trustees,* Museum of Contemporary Art, San Diego, La Jolla CA

Coppernoll, Lee, *Assoc Dir,* Marquette University, Haggerty Museum of Art, Milwaukee WI

Coppin, Kerry, *Assoc Prof,* Rochester Institute of Technology, School of Photographic Arts & Sciences, Rochester NY (S)

Copping, Lisette, *Chmn Fine Arts,* Delgado College, Dept of Fine Arts, New Orleans LA (S)

Coppinger, Ann, *Sr Conservator,* Fashion Institute of Technology, The Museum at FIT, New York NY

Copple, Carolyn, *Special Projects Coordr,* Wichita State University, Ulrich Museum of Art, Wichita KS

Corbett, Anne L, *Exec Dir,* Flashpoint, Washington DC

Corbett, M Timothy, *Vol Pres,* Hill-Stead Museum, Farmington CT

Corbin, George, *Prof Emertus,* City University of New York, PhD Program in Art History, New York NY (S)

Corbin, Tarrence, *Assoc Prof Fine Arts,* University of Cincinnati, School of Art, Cincinnati OH (S)

Corbus, Lili, *Prof Emeritus,* University of North Carolina at Charlotte, Dept Art, Charlotte NC (S)

Corcoran, Christine, *Mgr Individual Giving,* American Folk Art Museum, New York NY

Corcoran, Kathryn, *Librn,* Munson-Williams-Proctor Arts Institute, Museum of Art, Utica NY

Corcoran, Kathryn L, *Dir Library Svcs,* Munson-Williams-Proctor Arts Institute, Art Reference Library, Utica NY

Corcoran, Lambert, *Colls Mgmt,* Andy Warhol Foundation for the Visual Arts, New York NY

Cordell, Douglas, *Serials & Electronic Resources Librn,* Los Angeles County Museum of Art, Allan C Balch Art Research Library, Los Angeles CA

Cordero, Edwin, *Prof,* University of Puerto Rico, Mayaguez, Dept of Humanities, College of Fine Arts & Theory of Art Programs, Mayaguez PR (S)

Cordero, Edwin, *Prof,* University of Puerto Rico, Mayaguez, Dept of Humanities, College of Fine Arts & Theory of Art Programs, Mayaguez PR (S)

Cordova, Mary, *Office Mgr,* National YoungArts Foundation, Miami FL

Corea, Ellen, *Dir,* South Peace Art Society, Dawson Creek Art Gallery, Dawson Creek BC

Corell, Pam, *Asst Cur,* St Mary's University, Art Gallery, Halifax NS

Corey, Erika, *Finance & Mem Dir,* Visual Art Exchange, Raleigh NC

Corey, Karen M, *Interim Libr Dir,* Purdue University Calumet, Library Gallery, Hammond IN

Corey, Maureen, *Cur Art,* Loveland Museum/Gallery, Loveland CO

Corey, Sharon, *Prof,* Chapman University, Art Dept, Orange CA (S)

Cork, Sheila, *Librn,* New Orleans Museum of Art, New Orleans LA

Cork, Sheila, *Librn,* New Orleans Museum of Art, Felix J Dreyfous Library, New Orleans LA

Corle, Ed, *Dir,* University of Findlay, Dudley & Mary Marks Lea Gallery, Findlay OH

Corle, Jack (Ed), *Assoc Prof,* University of Findlay, Art Program, Findlay OH (S)

Corlett-Stahl, Claudia, *Assoc Dir,* University of Illinois at Urbana-Champaign, Krannert Art Museum and Kinkead Pavilion, Champaign IL

Cornejo, Cesar, *Asst Prof,* University of South Florida, School The Arts, Tampa FL (S)

Cornelius, Amy, *Develop Dir,* Huntsville Museum of Art, Reference Library, Huntsville AL

Cornelius, Camille, *Instr,* Pierce College, Art Dept, Woodland Hills CA (S)

Cornelius, Kim, *Treas,* Brown County Art Gallery Foundation, Nashville IN

Cornelius, Sally, *Prof,* Virginia Polytechnic Institute & State University, Dept of Art & Art History, Blacksburg VA (S)

Cornell, Daniell, *Deputy Dir Art, Sr Cur,* Palm Springs Art Museum, Palm Springs CA

Cornell, Thomas B, *Prof,* Bowdoin College, Art Dept, Brunswick ME (S)

Corner, Francie, *Pres,* The Art Institute of Chicago, The Woman's Board of the Art Institute of Chicago, Chicago IL

Cornish, Glenn, *Music Instr,* Edison Community College, Gallery of Fine Arts, Fort Myers FL (S)

Cornish, Jack, *Chmn,* Kean University, Fine Arts Dept, Union NJ (S)

Correa, Laura, *Dir,* Van Cortlandt House Museum, Bronx NY

Corrie, Rebecca, *Treas,* International Center of Medieval Art, New York NY

Corrie, Rebecca W, *Prof,* Bates College, Art & Visual Culture, Lewiston ME (S)

Corrigan, Caroline, *Educ & Exhibs Mgr,* The Arts Center of the Capital Region, Troy NY

Corrigan, David J, *Cur,* Connecticut State Library, Museum of Connecticut History, Hartford CT

Corrigan, Shannon K, *Dir,* Emmanuel Gallery, Denver CO

Corrigan, Sym, *Commun & Design,* Dalhousie University, Dalhousie Art Gallery, Halifax NS

Corrin, Lisa, *Deputy Dir Art,* Seattle Art Museum, Dorothy Stimson Bullitt Library, Seattle WA

Corrin, Lisa C, *Dir & Art Lect,* Williams College, Museum of Art, Williamstown MA

Corrock, Mary, *Special Events Coordr,* Boise Art Museum, Boise ID

Corry, Micquelle, *Mktg Dir,* Utah Lawyers for the Arts, Salt Lake City UT

Corsaro, James, *Librn,* Rensselaer County Historical Society, Hart-Cluett Mansion, 1827, Troy NY

Corso, Anne, *Dir Educ,* Reading Public Museum, Reading PA

Corso, John, *Asst Prof,* Oakland University, Dept of Art & Art History, Rochester MI (S)

Cortes, Monica, *Dir Internal Affairs,* Caribbean Cultural Center, Cultural Arts Organization & Resource Center, New York NY

Cortez, Diego, *Cur Photography,* New Orleans Museum of Art, New Orleans LA

Cortinas, Miguel, *Asst Prof,* University of the Incarnate Word, Art Dept, San Antonio TX (S)

Corwin, Sharon, *Cur,* Colby College, Museum of Art, Waterville ME

Cory, Joseph, *Asst Prof,* Judson University, School of Art, Design & Architecture, Elgin IL (S)

Cosentino, Cira, *Instr,* Indian River Community College, Fine Arts Dept, Fort Pierce FL (S)

Cosentino, Geraldine, *Dir,* Organization of Independent Artists, Inc, Brooklyn NY

Cosentino, Remo, *Design & Treas,* Organization of Independent Artists, Inc, Brooklyn NY

Cosner, Chris, *Assoc Prof,* Glenville State College, Dept of Fine Arts, Glenville WV (S)

Cost, Frank, *Assoc Dean,* Rochester Institute of Technology, College of Imaging Arts & Sciences, Rochester NY (S)

Cost, Steven, *Asst Prof,* Amarillo College, Visual Art Dept, Amarillo TX (S)

Costa, Denise, *Dir Communs,* High Desert Museum, Bend OR

Costa, Gina, *Mktg & Pub Rels,* University of Notre Dame, Snite Museum of Art, Notre Dame IN

Costa, Jennifer, *Prof, Dept Chair & Cur,* Illinois Central College, Arts & Communication Dept, East Peoria IL (S)

Costa, Jorge, *Instr,* Springfield College, Dept of Visual & Performing Arts, Springfield MA (S)

Costa, Lenora, *Cur,* Longue Vue House & Gardens, New Orleans LA

Costa, Mary Len, *Interim Dir & CEO,* Arts Council Of New Orleans, New Orleans LA

Costain, Charlie, *Assoc Dir Gen & Dir Conserv,* Department of Canadian Heritage, Canadian Conservation Institute, Ottawa ON

Costanza, Kristin, *Develop Assoc,* Whatcom Museum, Bellingham WA

Costanzo, Nancy, *Chmn Dept,* Our Lady of Elms College, Dept of Fine Arts, Chicopee MA (S)

Costello, Christy, *Dir Devel,* Museo De Las Americas, Denver CO

Costello, Joe, *VPres External Affairs,* Please Touch Museum, Philadelphia PA

Costello, Leslie, *Contact,* Essex Art Center, Lawrence MA

Costello, Lisa, *Gallery Dir,* Parkland College, Parkland Art Gallery, Champaign IL

Cote, Derek, *Asst Prof Fine Art,* Watkins College of Art, Design & Film, Nashville TN (S)

Cote, Jean-Francois, *Librn, Animation Instr (Quick Kids),* Quickdraw Animation Society, Calgary AB

Cote, Marc, *Chmn,* Framingham State College, Art Dept, Framingham MA (S)

Cothran, Brenna, *Registrar & Asst Cur,* Board of Parks & Recreation, The Parthenon, Nashville TN

Cothren, Michael, *Chmn & Prof,* Swarthmore College, Dept of Art & Art History, Swarthmore PA (S)

Cotner, Cynthia, *Reference Desk Coordr,* University of Missouri, Art, Archaeology & Music Collection, Columbia MO

Cotner, Teresa, *Chmn & Assoc Prof,* California State University, Chico, Department of Art & Art History, Chico CA (S)

Cott, Sharon H, *VPres & Secy,* The Metropolitan Museum of Art, New York NY

Cotten, Charles, *Admnr,* Presidential Museum & Leadership Library, Odessa TX

Cotter, Anita, *CSPWC Admnr,* Canadian Society of Painters In Watercolour, Toronto ON

Cotton, Laura, *Cur Art,* Paris Gibson Square, Museum of Art, Great Falls MT

Cotton, Laura, *Registrar/Cur,* The Adirondack Historical Association, The Adirondack Museum, Blue Mountain Lake NY

Cotton, Nancy, *VPres,* Allegany County Historical Society, Gordon-Roberts House, Cumberland MD

Cottong, Kathy, *Dir,* The Arts Club of Chicago, Reference Library, Chicago IL

Cottong, Kathy S, *Dir,* The Arts Club of Chicago, Chicago IL

Cottriall, Carrie, *Deputy Dir,* Timken Museum of Art, San Diego CA

Cottrill, Mary, *Mgr Hennage Auditorium,* Colonial Williamsburg Foundation, Abby Aldrich Rockefeller Folk Art Museum, Williamsburg VA

Cottrill, Mary, *Mgr Hennage Auditorium,* Colonial Williamsburg Foundation, DeWitt Wallace Decorative Arts Museum, Williamsburg VA

Cotts, Ross, *Mus Preparator,* University of Oklahoma, Fred Jones Jr Museum of Art, Norman OK

Couch, Dale, *Cur Decorative Art,* University of Georgia, Georgia Museum of Art, Athens GA

Couch, Jennie, *Asst Prof,* Alabama A & M University, Art & Art Education Dept, Normal AL (S)

Couch, Kirsten, *Instr,* Northeastern Oklahoma A & M College, Art Dept, Miami OK (S)

Couch, Rebecca, *Mgr Spec Projects & Bd Svcs,* McMichael Canadian Art Collection, Kleinburg ON

Couchon, Marie-Paule, *Archivist,* Musee des Augustines de l'Hotel Dieu de Quebec, Archive, Quebec PQ

Couer, Karen, *Archivist,* United States Figure Skating Association, World Figure Skating Museum & Hall of Fame, Colorado Springs CO

Coughlin, Joan Hopkins, *Cur,* Wellfleet Historical Society & Museum, Inc, Wellfleet MA

Coultas, Adah, *Pres,* The Art Association of Jacksonville, The David Strawn Art Gallery, Jacksonville IL

Coulter, Catherine, *Prog Coordr,* Rocky Mount Arts Center, Rocky Mount NC

Council, Dorothy, *VPres,* Rawls Museum Arts, Courtland VA

Countryman, Paul, *Exhibs Prep,* Illinois State Museum, Museum Store, Chicago IL

Coupolos-Selle, Stephanie, *Prof,* University of Wisconsin College - Marinette, Art Dept, Marinette WI (S)

Courchaine, Rocky, *Dir,* Crook County Museum & Art Gallery, Sundance WY

Cournoyel, Marie-France, *Secy,* Conseil des Arts du Quebec (CATQ), Diagonale, Centre des arts et des fibres du Quebec, Montreal PQ

Court, Elizabeth, *Chief Paintings Conservator,* Balboa Art Conservation Center, San Diego CA

Courtemanche, Marc, *Preparator,* University of Regina, MacKenzie Art Gallery, Regina SK

Courter, Anna, *Performing Arts Training Assoc,* Henry Street Settlement, Abrons Art Center, New York NY

Courtney, Janice, *Arts Advisor & Asst Dir,* Saint Cloud State University, Atwood Memorial Center Gallery, Saint Cloud MN

Courtney, Vernon S, *Dir,* Hampton University, University Museum, Hampton VA

Courtright, Nicola M, *Prof of Art & History of Art,* Amherst College, Dept of Art & the History of Art, Amherst MA (S)

Courts, Garland, *Mgr,* Branigan Cultural Center, Las Cruces NM

Couse, Jenny, *Admin Asst,* St Thomas-Elgin Public Art Centre, Saint Thomas ON

Cousino, Jennifer, *Cur History,* Loveland Museum/Gallery, Loveland CO

Coutu, Joan, *Assoc Prof,* University of Waterloo, Fine Arts Dept, Waterloo ON (S)

Coveney, Claire, *Communs Mgr,* ArtsConnection Inc, New York NY

Covert, Claudia, *Readers' Svcs Librn,* Rhode Island School of Design, Fleet Library at RISD, Providence RI

Covert, Nan, *Dept Head,* Bridgewater College, Art Dept, Bridgewater VA (S)

Coviello, Eliza, *Asst to Dir,* University of Pennsylvania, Institute of Contemporary Art, Philadelphia PA

Covitz, Bobby, *Outreach Coordr,* Hillel Foundation, Hillel Jewish Student Center Gallery, Cincinnati OH

Covo, David, *Prof,* McGill University, School of Architecture, Montreal PQ (S)

Cowan, Aaron J, *Dir,* University of Cincinnati, DAAP Galleries-College of Design Architecture, Art & Planning, Cincinnati OH

Cowan, Kathy, *Sr Reference Librn,* Maryland Institute, Decker Library, Baltimore MD

Cowan, Paula, *Lectr,* Mount Allison University, Dept of Fine Arts, Sackville NB (S)

Cowardin, Mark, *Asst Prof Fine Art & Sculpture Dept Coordr,* Johnson County Community College, Fine Arts Dept & Art History Dept, Overland Park KS (S)

Cowart, Jack, *Deputy Dir & Chief Cur,* Corcoran Gallery of Art, Washington DC

Cowden, Chris, *Exec Dir,* Women & Their Work, Austin TX

Cowden, Dorothy, *Dir Gallery,* University of Tampa, College of Arts & Letters, Tampa FL (S)

Cowden, Dorothy, *Dir of Galleries,* University of Tampa, Scarfone/Hartley Gallery, Tampa FL

Cowette, Thomas, *Assoc Prof,* University of Minnesota, Minneapolis, Dept of Art, Minneapolis MN (S)

Cowin, Kenneth A, *VPres,* Congregation Emanu-El, Bernard Judaica Museum, New York NY

Cox, Amanda, *Art Educ Dir,* Sumter Gallery of Art, Sumter SC

Cox, Amy, *Dir Interior Design & Assoc Prof,* Harding University, Dept of Art & Design, Searcy AR (S)

Cox, Andy, *Chmn,* Limestone College, Art Dept, Gaffney SC (S)

Cox, Anna, *Asst Prof,* Longwood University, Dept of Art, Farmville VA (S)

Cox, Bruce, *Asst Dir,* University of Missouri, Museum of Art & Archaeology, Columbia MO

Cox, Carolyn, *VPres,* Sturdivant Museum Association, Sturdivant Museum, Selma AL

Cox, Christopher, *Dean of Library Svcs,* University of Northern Iowa, Fine & Performing Arts Collection Rod Library, Cedar Falls IA

Cox, Cindy, *Develop Coordr,* Auburn University, Julie Collins Smith Museum, Auburn AL

Cox, Daniel, *Instr,* Kirkwood Community College, Dept of Arts & Humanities, Cedar Rapids IA (S)

Cox, Debra L, *Cur,* University of Washington, Art Slide Library, Seattle WA

Cox, Dennis, *Assoc Prof,* Pacific Lutheran University, Dept of Art, Tacoma WA (S)

Cox, Kim, *Performing Arts Training Assoc,* Henry Street Settlement, Abrons Art Center, New York NY

Cox, Michael, *Co-Dir,* University of Manitoba, Faculty of Architecture Exhibition Centre, Winnipeg MB

Cox, Michael, *Dean,* University of Manitoba, Faculty of Architecture, Winnipeg MB (S)

Cox, Patsy, *Pres,* National Council on Education for the Ceramic Arts (NCECA), Erie CO

Cox, Richard, *Prof,* Louisiana State University, School of Art, Baton Rouge LA (S)

Cox, Robert, *Lectr,* University of Tennessee at Chattanooga, Dept of Art, Chattanooga TN (S)

Cox, Sarah Beth, *Instr,* West Virginia University at Parkersburg, Art Dept, Parkersburg WV (S)

Cox, Sharon, *Chmn,* Jamestown College, Art Dept, Jamestown ND (S)

Cox, Sheri, *Event Coordr,* Craftsmen's Guild of Mississippi, Inc, Mississippi Crafts Center, Ridgeland MS

Coyle, Heather Campbell, *Cur American Art,* Delaware Art Museum, Wilmington DE

Coyle, Kathryn, *Technical Svcs,* The University of the Arts, University Libraries, Philadelphia PA

Coyne, Catherine, *Children's Librn,* Ames Free-Easton's Public Library, North Easton MA

Coyne, Janine, *Adj Assoc Prof*, College of Staten Island, Performing & Creative Arts Dept, Staten Island NY (S)

Coyne, Michael, *Prof*, Memorial University of Newfoundland, Division of Fine Arts, Visual Arts Program, Corner Brook NF (S)

Cozad Feehan, Jennifer, *Coordr Mem & Pub Rels*, The Pennsylvania State University, Palmer Museum of Art, University Park PA

Cozzi, Leslie, *Cur Assoc*, University of California, Los Angeles, Grunwald Center for the Graphic Arts at Hammer Museum, Los Angeles CA

Cozzolino, Robert, *Sr Cur*, Pennsylvania Academy of the Fine Arts, Philadelphia PA

Crabb, Patrick S, *Ceramics*, Santa Ana College, Art Dept, Santa Ana CA (S)

Crable, James, *Prof*, James Madison University, School of Art & Art History, Harrisonburg VA (S)

Cracco, Derek, *Asst Prof*, University of Alabama at Birmingham, Dept of Art & Art History, Birmingham AL (S)

Craft, Evelyn, *Dir*, Belger Arts Center, Kansas City MO

Craig, Briar, *Assoc Prof Visual Art*, University of British Columbia Okanagan, Dept of Creative Studies, Kelowna BC (S)

Craig, Debbie, *Pottery Dir*, Glynn Art Association, Saint Simons Island GA

Craig, Gerry, *Cur Educ*, Detroit Zoological Institute, Wildlife Interpretive Gallery, Royal Oak MI

Craig, James, *Art Dept Lead & Instr*, Columbia Basin College, Esvelt Gallery, Pasco WA (S)

Craig, Osubi, *Dir*, Lake Wales Arts Center, Lake Wales FL

Craig, Rob, *Mgr Family Events*, Newark Museum Association, Junior Museum, Newark NJ

Craig, Robert, *Chmn & Prof Art*, Drake University, Dept Art & Design, Des Moines IA (S)

Craig, Susan, *Dir*, Trinity College Library, Washington DC

Craig, Susan V, *Librn*, University of Kansas, Murphy Library of Art & Architecture, Lawrence KS

Craighill, Marcee F, *Cur*, United States Department of State, Diplomatic Reception Rooms, Washington DC

Crain, Brian, *Asst Prof Art*, Marian University, Visual Arts Dept, Indianapolis IN (S)

Crall, Steven, *Asst Prof*, South Carolina State University, Dept of Visual & Performing Arts, Orangeburg SC (S)

Cramer, George, *Emer Prof*, University of Wisconsin, Madison, Dept of Art, Madison WI (S)

Cramer, Lissa, *Exhib Coordr*, Tufts University, Tufts University Art Gallery, Medford MA

Cramer, Patricia T, *Dir*, Westfield Athenaeum, Jasper Rand Art Museum, Westfield MA

Cramer, Sam, *Instr & Coordr*, Luzerne County Community College, Commercial Art Dept, Nanticoke PA (S)

Crampton, Susanna, *PR Officer*, Historic New England, Boston MA

Crane, Anne, *Cataloging/Systems Admin*, Friends University, Edmund Stanley Library, Wichita KS

Crane, Bonnie L, *Owner, Dir & Pres*, Crane Collection, Gallery of American Painting and Sculpture, Magnolia MA

Crane, David, *Prof*, Virginia Polytechnic Institute & State University, Dept of Art & Art History, Blacksburg VA (S)

Crane, Diane, *Instr*, Viterbo College, Art Dept, La Crosse WI (S)

Crane, Kenneth, *Security Officer*, University of North Carolina at Greensboro, Weatherspoon Art Museum, Greensboro NC

Crane, Michael, *Dir*, Southern Oregon University, Schneider Museum of Art, Ashland OR

Crane, Michael, *Gallery Dir*, University of Central Missouri, Art Center Gallery, Warrensburg MO

Cranin, Tonya, *Mktg Dir*, Architects Design Group Inc, Winter Park FL

Cranston, Meg, *Chmn*, Otis College of Art & Design, Fine Arts, Los Angeles CA (S)

Craven, Allen, *Assoc Prof*, Fort Hays State University, Dept of Art & Design, Hays KS (S)

Craven, Katrina, *Pub Rels & Mktg Dir*, Hunter Museum of American Art, Chattanooga TN

Craven, Leigh, *Asst Prof*, Bridgewater State College, Art Dept, Bridgewater MA (S)

Craven Fernandez, Happy, *Pres*, Moore College of Art & Design, Philadelphia PA (S)

Cravens, Kate, *Cur Hall of Fame*, National Museum of Racing, National Museum of Racing & Hall of Fame, Saratoga Springs NY

Crawford, Barbara, *Head Dept*, Southern Virginia College, Division of Arts and Humanities, Buena Vista VA (S)

Crawford, Cameron, *Grad Adv & Prof*, California State University, Chico, Department of Art & Art History, Chico CA (S)

Crawford, Denton, *Lectr*, Humboldt State University, College of Arts & Humanities, Art Dept, Arcata CA (S)

Crawford, Gretchen, *Instr*, Capital University, Fine Arts Dept, Columbus OH (S)

Crawford, Henry B, *Cur History*, Texas Tech University, Museum of Texas Tech University, Lubbock TX

Crawford, James, *Cur*, Canajoharie Library & Art Gallery, Library, Canajoharie NY

Crawford, Margaret, *Educ*, The Walker African American Museum & Research Center, Las Vegas NV

Crawford, Nicole, *Cur Coll*, University of Wyoming, University of Wyoming Art Museum, Laramie WY

Crawford, Pam, *Gallery Mgr*, Brown County Art Gallery Foundation, Nashville IN

Crawford, Randal, *Prof*, Delta College, Art Dept, University Center MI (S)

Crawford, Romi, *Cur & Dir Educ & Pub Prog*, The Studio Museum in Harlem, New York NY

Creasman, Jody, *Dir Communs*, Oregon College of Art & Craft, Hoffman Gallery, Portland OR

Creasy, June, *Assoc Prof*, Lambuth University, Dept of Human Ecology & Visual Arts, Jackson TN (S)

Creedon, Denise, *Asst Dir*, Perkins Center for the Arts, Moorestown NJ

Cressman, Larry, *Assoc Prof*, University of Michigan, Ann Arbor, School of Art & Design, Ann Arbor MI (S)

Cresson, Pat, *Prof*, Monmouth University, Dept of Art & Design, West Long Branch NJ (S)

Creston, Bill, *Co-Dir*, eMediaLoft.org, New York NY

Crew, John, *Pres*, Wenatchee Valley College, Robert Graves Gallery, Wenatchee WA

Crews, Karen, *Asst Cur*, American Museum of Ceramic Art, Pomona CA

Cribelli, Susan, *Acad Dean Communs & Humanities*, Aims Community College, Visual & Performing Arts, Greeley CO (S)

Crickenberger, Jen, *Dir Educ*, The Light Factory Contemporary Museum of Photography and Film, Charlotte NC

Cridler, Kim, *Asst Prof*, University of Wisconsin, Madison, Dept of Art, Madison WI (S)

Crighton, Claire, *Assoc Ed*, Canadian Art Foundation, Toronto ON

Crilly, Trevor, *Pres*, Durham Art Gallery, Durham ON

Crimmins, Jaynie, *Pres*, Garrison Art Center, Garrison NY

Crimson, Linda, *Adjunct Asst Prof*, Indiana University South Bend, Fine Arts Dept, South Bend IN (S)

Crismon, David, *Asst Prof*, Oklahoma Christian University of Science & Arts, Dept of Art & Design, Oklahoma City OK (S)

Crissey, Jennifer, *Secy*, Polish Museum of America, Research Library, Chicago IL

Crittendon, Shelly, *Colls Mgr*, Texas Ranger Hall of Fame & Museum, Waco TX

Crivello, Peter, *Rector*, San Carlos Cathedral, Monterey CA

Croce, Judith, *Chmn*, Caldwell College, Dept of Fine Arts, Caldwell NJ (S)

Croce, Marianne Della, *Coll Mgr*, Planting Fields Foundation, Coe Hall at Planting Fields Arboretum, Oyster Bay NY

Crocker, Dusty, *Prof*, Texas Christian University, School of Art, Fort Worth TX (S)

Crocker, Elli, *Dir Studio Art Prog*, Clark University, Dept of Visual & Performing Arts, Worcester MA (S)

Crocker, Kyle, *Prof*, Bemidji State University, Visual Arts Dept, Bemidji MN (S)

Crockett, Candace, *Chmn*, San Francisco State University, Art Dept, San Francisco CA (S)

Croft, J W, *Exec VPres*, Field Museum, Chicago IL

Croft, Parker, *Vis Asst Prof*, Middlebury College, History of Art & Architecture Dept, Middlebury VT (S)

Croghan, Nicholas, *Gallery Dir*, University of West Florida, Dept of Art, Pensacola FL (S)

Croins, Sonya, *Office Mgr*, Mississippi Museum of Art, Howorth Library, Jackson MS

Cromley, Elizabeth, *Chmn*, Northeastern University, Dept of Art & Architecture, Boston MA (S)

Cromwell, Sara, *Pub Rels, Mem & Mktg Coordr*, Wake Forest University, Museum of Anthropology, Winston Salem NC

Cromwell, Sue, *Accnt*, Touchstone Center for Crafts, Hart Moore Museum, Farmington PA

Cronan, Todd, *Asst Prof*, Emory University, Art History Dept, Atlanta GA (S)

Cronin, Allison, *Mgr Loans & Proj*, University of British Columbia, Museum of Anthropology, Vancouver BC

Cronin, Betsy, *Prog Coordr for the Arts*, Wheaton College, Beard and Weil Galleries, Norton MA

Cronin, Jennifer, *Assoc Dir*, Museum of Fine Arts, Houston, Glassell School of Art, Houston TX (S)

Cronin, Mary W, *Supv Educ*, Brandywine Conservancy, Brandywine River Museum, Chadds Ford PA

Cronin, Ray, *Chief Exec Officer & Dir*, Art Gallery of Nova Scotia, Halifax NS

Croog, Elizabeth, *Secy & Gen Counsel*, National Gallery of Art, Washington DC

Crook, Lillian, *Librn Dir*, Dickinson State University, Stoxen Library, Dickinson ND

Cropper, Elizabeth, *Dean, Center for Advanced Study in Visual Arts*, National Gallery of Art, Washington DC

Crosby, Anna, *Bd Mem (Past Pres)*, Coquille Valley Art Association, Coquille OR

Crosby, Suzanne, *Dir*, Hillsborough Community College, Fine Arts Dept, Tampa FL (S)

Crosby-Hinds, Patricia, *Prof*, Antelope Valley College, Art Dept, Division of Fine Arts, Lancaster CA (S)

Crosman, Christopher B, *Dir*, William A Farnsworth, Museum, Rockland ME

Crosman, Christopher B, *Dir*, William A Farnsworth, Library, Rockland ME

Cross, Debbie, *Pres*, San Angelo Museum of Fine Arts, San Angelo TX

Cross, Louis, *Secy*, Contemporary Art Center of Virginia, Virginia Beach VA

Cross, Scott, *Archivist*, Oshkosh Public Museum, Oshkosh WI

Cross, Scott, *Archivist*, Oshkosh Public Museum, Library, Oshkosh WI

Cross, Tony, *Instr*, Cuyahoga Valley Art Center, Cuyahoga Falls OH (S)

Cross, Whitney, *Assoc Develop Officer*, Oklahoma City Museum of Art, Oklahoma City OK

Crossen, Kristine, *Pres & Cur*, Alaska Museum of Natural History, Anchorage AK

Crossman, Rodney, *Asst Prof*, Indiana Wesleyan University, School of Arts & Humanities, Division of Art, Marion IN (S)

Crosson, David, *Dir*, The California Historical Society, North Baker Research Library, San Francisco CA

Crosson, David, *Exec Dir*, The California Historical Society, San Francisco CA

Crotchett, Cut, *Art Appreciation*, Western Michigan University, Frostic School of Art, Kalamazoo MI (S)

Croteau, Jeffrey, *Mgr Lib*, National Heritage Museum, Lexington MA

Croton, Lynn, *Dean Visual & Performing Arts*, C W Post Campus of Long Island University, School of Visual & Performing Arts, Brookville NY (S)

Crotteau, Katie, *Contact*, Center for the Visual Arts, Gallery, Wausau WI

Crotty, John, *Dir Library*, Union for Reformed Judaism, Synagogue Art & Architectural Library, New York NY

Crouch, Dennis, *Instr*, Oklahoma State University, Graphic Arts Dept, Visual Communications, Okmulgee OK (S)

Crouch, Kaye, *Registrar*, Cheekwood-Tennessee Botanical Garden & Museum of Art, Nashville TN

Crouch, Kaye, *Registrar,* Cheekwood-Tennessee Botanical Garden & Museum of Art, Museum of Art, Nashville TN

Crouch, Robert, *Assoc Dir/Cur,* LACE (Los Angeles Contemporary Exhibitions), Los Angeles CA

Crouse, Michael, *Chmn Art & Art History Dept,* University of Alabama in Huntsville, Dept of Art and Art History, Huntsville AL (S)

Crouther, Betty, *Assoc Prof,* University of Mississippi, Department of Art, University MS (S)

Crow, James, *Asst Prof,* Lincoln University, Dept Visual and Performing Arts, Jefferson City MO (S)

Crow, James, *Instr,* East Central College, Art Dept, Union MO (S)

Crow, Lance, *Educ Dir,* Richmond Art Museum, Richmond IN

Crow, Linda, *Foundation Pres,* City of Port Angeles, Port Angeles Fine Arts Center & Webster Woods Art Park, Port Angeles WA

Crow, Paul, *Asst Prof,* Weber State University, Dept of Visual Arts, Ogden UT (S)

Crowe, Ann G, *Asst Prof,* Virginia Commonwealth University, Art History Dept, Richmond VA (S)

Crowe, Edith, *Art Reference Librn,* San Jose State University, Dr. Martin Luther King Jr. Library, San Jose CA

Crowe, John, *Chair Art Educ,* Massachusetts College of Art, Boston MA (S)

Crowe, Karen, *Dir Communs,* Municipal Art Society of New York, New York NY

Crowe, Shawn, *Educ Dir,* Butte Silver Bow Arts Chateau, Butte MT

Crowell, Megan, *Sales Mgr,* Society for Contemporary Craft, Pittsburgh PA

Crowell, Susan, *Assoc Prof,* University of Michigan, Ann Arbor, School of Art & Design, Ann Arbor MI (S)

Crowley, Evan, *Instr,* University of Evansville, Art Dept, Evansville IN (S)

Crowley, Gina, *Dir Spec Events & Rentals,* Museum of Contemporary Art, Chicago IL

Crowley, Jessica, *Librn,* Willet Hauser Architectural Glass Inc, Philadelphia PA

Crowley, John, *Gallery Dir,* Mayors Office of Arts, Tourism and Special Events, City Hall Galleries, Boston MA

Crowley, Tony, *Chmn,* Grinnell College, Dept of Art, Grinnell IA (S)

Crown, Cathleen, *Develop Coordr,* Old Barracks Museum, Trenton NJ

Crown, Patricia, *Prof Emeritus,* University of Missouri - Columbia, Art History & Archaeology Dept, Columbia MO (S)

Crowson, Belinda, *Visitor Svcs,* City of Lethbridge, Sir Alexander Galt Museum, Lethbridge AB

Crowston, Catherine, *Exec Dir & Chief Cur,* Art Gallery of Alberta, Edmonton AB

Croy, Mike, *Security Supv,* Historic Arkansas Museum, Little Rock AR

Croyle, Arthur, *Coordr Integrated Arts,* Iowa State University, Dept of Art & Design, Ames IA (S)

Crozier, Richard, *Studio Faculty,* University of Virginia, McIntire Dept of Art, Charlottesville VA (S)

Crum, Roger, *Assoc Prof,* University of Dayton, Visual Arts Dept, Dayton OH (S)

Crumby, F Todd, *Dir Archives & Libr,* Reynolda House Museum of American Art, Library, Winston-Salem NC

Crump, James, *Chief Cur & Cur Photography,* Cincinnati Art Museum, Cincinnati Art Museum, Cincinnati OH

Crutchfield, Margo, *Sr Adjunct Cur,* Museum of Contemporary Art Cleveland, Cleveland OH

Cruz, Alfredo, *Chmn,* Our Lady of the Lake University, Dept of Art, San Antonio TX (S)

Cruz, Dena, *Cur Educ,* Arizona Museum For Youth, Mesa AZ

Cruz, Michele A, *Instr,* North Carolina Wesleyan College, Dept of Visual & Performing Arts, Rocky Mount NC (S)

Cruz Souza, Luiz Antonio, *Vice Dir,* Universidade Federal de Minas Gerais (UFMG), Escola de Belas Artes, Belo Horizonte MG (S)

Crysler, Kevin, *Dir Develop,* Hirshhorn Museum & Sculpture Garden, Smithsonian Institution, Washington DC

Cubbage, John, *Prof Music,* University of Great Falls, Art Dept, Great Falls MT (S)

Cubina, Silvia Karmen, *Exec Dir & Chief Cur,* Bass Museum of Art, Miami Beach FL

Cudianat, Brian, *Spec Events Coordr & Vol Coordr,* University of Illinois at Urbana-Champaign, Spurlock Museum, Champaign IL

Cudnik, Carolyn, *Office Mgr,* Old Barracks Museum, Trenton NJ

Cuevas, Julianna, *Asst Dir,* Averill and Bernard Leviton A + D Gallery, Chicago IL

Cuffaro, Daniel, *Dept Head Industrial Design,* Cleveland Institute of Art, Cleveland OH (S)

Cui, Shanshan, *Asst Prof,* Bridgewater State College, Art Dept, Bridgewater MA (S)

Culbertson, Ben, *Coordr,* Hagerstown Junior College, Art Dept, Hagerstown MD (S)

Culbertson, Margaret, *Dir,* Museum of Fine Arts, Houston, Hirsch Library, Houston TX

Culbertson, Margaret, *Dir BB Library,* Museum of Fine Arts Houston, Bayou Bend Collection & Gardens, Houston TX

Culbreath, Gary, *VChmn,* South Carolina State Museum, Columbia SC

Culbreth, Kelvin, *Exhibits Coordr,* Arts Council of Fayetteville-Cumberland County, The Arts Center, Fayetteville NC

Culen, Lubos, *Curatorial Dir,* Vernon Art Gallery, Vernon BC

Cullen, Cecily, *Creative Dir,* Metropolitan State University of Denver, Center for Visual Art, Denver CO

Cullen, Deborah, *Dir Cur Progs,* El Museo del Barrio, New York NY

Culligan, Jenine, *Sr Cur,* Huntington Museum of Art, Huntington WV

Cullimore, Cheryl E, *Mus Properties Chmn,* The National Society of The Colonial Dames of America in the State of New Hampshire, Moffatt-Ladd House & Garden, Portsmouth NH

Cullinan, Deborah, *Dir,* Intersection for the Arts, San Francisco CA

Cullivan, Lynn, *Publ,* San Francisco Maritime National Historical Park, Maritime Museum, San Francisco CA

Cullum, Garrett, *IT & Network Admin,* Oklahoma City Museum of Art, Oklahoma City OK

Cullum, Marguerite, *Head Librn,* Crazy Horse Memorial, Indian Museum of North America, Native American Educational & Cultural Center & Crazy Horse Memorial Library (Reference), Crazy Horse SD

Culp, Ellie, *2nd VPres,* Independence Historical Museum & Art Center, Independence KS

Culp, Patti, *Hostess,* Alton Museum of History & Art, Inc, Alton IL

Culpepper, Diane, *Chmn,* Orlando Museum of Art, Orlando FL

Culpepper, Diane, *Pres,* Orlando Museum of Art, Orlando Sentinel Library, Orlando FL

Culver, Michael, *Dir & Cur,* Ogunquit Museum of American Art, Ogunquit ME

Culver, Michael, *Dir & Cur,* Ogunquit Museum of American Art, Reference Library, Ogunquit ME

Cumbo, Laurie, *Exec Dir,* MoCADA - The Museum of Contemporary African Diasporan Arts, Brooklyn NY

Cumming, Doug, *Prof,* University of Wisconsin-Stout, Dept of Art & Design, Menomonie WI (S)

Cummings, Alyson Amendola, *Exec Dir,* Erie County Historical Society, Erie PA

Cummings, DeAnna, *Contact,* Juxtaposition Arts, Minneapolis MN

Cummings, Heath, *Head Security & Facility,* Amherst College, Mead Art Museum, Amherst MA

Cummings, Mary Lou, *Cur & Registrar,* Knights of Columbus Supreme Council, Knights of Columbus Museum, New Haven CT

Cummings, Richard, *Assoc Prof,* College of the Ozarks, Dept of Art, Point Lookout MO (S)

Cummins, Heather, *Visual Resources Librn,* Academy of Art, University Library, San Francisco CA

Cummins, Joan, *Lisa & Bernard Selz Cur, Asian Art,* Brooklyn Museum, Brooklyn NY

Cummins, Joyce, *Supv Security & Registrar,* University of Oklahoma, Fred Jones Jr Museum of Art, Norman OK

Cunard, Gail, *Dir,* Harness Racing Museum & Hall of Fame, Goshen NY

Cunard, Jeffrey P, *Counsel,* College Art Association, New York NY

Cundall, Robert, *CFO,* Seattle Art Museum, Downtown, Seattle WA

Cundall, Robert, *CFO,* Seattle Art Museum, Dorothy Stimson Bullitt Library, Seattle WA

Cundiff, Linda, *Prof of Art,* Campbellsville University, Department of Art, Campbellsville KY (S)

Cunningham, Barb, *Pres,* Allied Arts Council of Lethbridge, Bowman Arts Center, Lethbridge AB

Cunningham, Barbara, *Gallery Mgr,* Vermont State Craft Center at Frog Hollow, Burlington VT

Cunningham, Ben J, *Asst Prof 2D Design & Drawing,* Millersville University, Dept of Art & Design, Millersville PA (S)

Cunningham, David, *Mgr Design & Exhibits,* University of British Columbia, Museum of Anthropology, Vancouver BC

Cunningham, Dennis, *Instr,* Marylhurst University, Art Dept, Marylhurst OR (S)

Cunningham, John, *Pres,* Cape Ann Historical Association, Cape Ann Museum, Gloucester MA

Cunningham, Richard, *Instr,* North Central Michigan College, Art Dept, Petoskey MI (S)

Cunningham, Stephanie, *Prof Art, Graphic Design,* Florida Atlantic University, D F Schmidt College of Arts & Letters Dept of Visual Arts & Art History, Boca Raton FL (S)

Cuno, James, *Adjunct Prof,* Northwestern University, Evanston, Dept of Art History, Evanston IL (S)

Cuno, James, *Dir,* Harvard University, William Hayes Fogg Art Museum, Cambridge MA

Cuno, James, *Dir,* Harvard University, Arthur M Sackler Museum, Cambridge MA

Cuno, James, *Pres & Dir,* The Art Institute of Chicago, Chicago IL

Curcic, Slobodan, *Prof,* Princeton University, Dept of Art & Archaeology, Princeton NJ (S)

Curfman, Robert, *Assoc Prof,* Indiana Wesleyan University, School of Arts & Humanities, Division of Art, Marion IN (S)

Curiel, Julia, *Program Coordr,* Lexington Art League, Inc, Lexington KY

Curley, John J, *Asst Prof,* Wake Forest University, Dept of Art, Winston-Salem NC (S)

Curnow, Kathy, *Assoc Prof,* Cleveland State University, Art Dept, Cleveland OH (S)

Curran, Annabelle, *Archivist,* Moore College of Art & Design, Library, Philadelphia PA

Curran, Brian, *Assoc Prof,* Pennsylvania State University, University Park, Dept of Art History, University Park PA (S)

Curran, Mary, *Asst to Dir,* Art Complex Museum, Carl A. Weyerhaeuser Library, Duxbury MA

Curran-Gawron, Marguerite, *Communs, Pub Rels & Vol Coordr,* Muskegon Museum of Art, Muskegon MI

Curren, Kerry, *Registrar,* Maine Photographic Workshops, The International T.V. & Film Workshops & Rockport College, Rockport ME (S)

Currie, Traci, *Secy,* Buckham Fine Arts Project, Gallery, Flint MI

Currie Jones, Amanda, *Mem & Develop Assoc,* Second Street Gallery, Charlottesville VA

Currier, Gail, *Develop Coordr,* Historical Society of Cheshire County, Keene NH

Currier, Richard, *Pres,* Willard House & Clock Museum, Inc, North Grafton MA

Currier, Tara, *Pub Rels,* Booth Western Art Museum, Cartersville GA

Curry, Alexis, *Head Librn,* Los Angeles County Museum of Art, Allan C Balch Art Research Library, Los Angeles CA

Curry, David Park, *Sr Cur Dec Arts & American Painting & Sculpture,* The Baltimore Museum of Art, Baltimore MD

Curry, Jeff, *VPres,* San Angelo Museum of Fine Arts, San Angelo TX

Curry, Michael P, *Dir,* City of Hampton, Hampton Arts Commission, Hampton VA

Curry-Evans, Kim, *Pub Art Coordr,* City of Raleigh Arts Commission, Miriam Preston Block Gallery, Raleigh NC

Curtin, Christopher, *Asst Prof,* Appalachian State University, Dept of Art, Boone NC (S)

Curtin, Donna, *Exec Dir,* Plymouth Antiquarian Society, Plymouth MA

Curtin, Nancy, *Dir,* Port Washington Public Library, Port Washington NY

Curtis, Amanda, *Prog Dir, Educ,* Intuit: The Center for Intuitive & Outsider Art, Chicago IL

Curtis, Brian, *Assoc Prof,* University of Miami, Dept of Art & Art History, Coral Gables FL (S)

Curtis, Gerard, *Assoc Prof,* Memorial University of Newfoundland, Division of Fine Arts, Visual Arts Program, Corner Brook NF (S)

Curtis, Julie, *Assoc Prof,* Northeastern University, Dept of Art & Architecture, Boston MA (S)

Curtis, Susan, *Coll Mgr,* University of Nebraska-Lincoln, Great Plains Art Museum, Lincoln NE

Curtis, Winifred, *Dir,* Harcum College, Fashion Design, Bryn Mawr PA (S)

Cusack, Mary, *Dean,* Mott Community College, Fine Arts & Social Sciences Division, Flint MI (S)

Cusack, Mary, *Pres,* Lansing Art Gallery, Lansing MI

Cushman, Brad, *Gallery Cur,* University of Arkansas at Little Rock, Art Slide Library and Galleries, Little Rock AR

Cushman, Brad, *Gallery Dir,* University of Arkansas at Little Rock, Art Galleries, Little Rock AR

Cushner, Steven, *Instr,* American University, Dept of Art, New York NY (S)

Cushnie, John Edward, *Dir,* Organization for the Development of Artists, Gallery Connexion, Fredericton NB

Cuthbertson, Christina, *Pub Rels Mgr,* Southern Alberta Art Gallery, Lethbridge AB

Cutler, Anthony, *Evan Pugh Prof,* Pennsylvania State University, University Park, Dept of Art History, University Park PA (S)

Cutler, Judy AG, *Dir,* National Museum of American Illustration, Newport RI

Cutler, Laurence S, *Chmn,* National Museum of American Illustration, Newport RI

Cutler-Lake, Karina, *Assoc Prof,* University of Wisconsin Oshkosh, Dept of Art, Oshkosh WI (S)

Cypriano, David, *Asst Educ Specialist,* Judiciary History Center, Honolulu HI

Cyr, Paul, *Head Spec Colls,* New Bedford Free Public Library, Special Collections Dept: Art Collection, New Bedford MA

Cyril, Jasmin, *Assoc Prof,* Benedict College, School of Humanities, Arts & Social Sciences, Columbia SC (S)

Cyrus, Jamal, *Educ Assoc,* Contemporary Arts Museum Houston, Houston TX

Czarnecki, James, *Assoc Prof,* University of Nebraska at Omaha, Dept of Art & Art History, Omaha NE (S)

Czechowski, Susan, *Asst Prof,* Western Illinois University, Department of Art, Macomb IL (S)

Czerkowicz, John, *Chmn,* Montclair State University, Fine Arts Dept, Montclair NJ (S)

Czichos, C L, *Dir Video,* Pioneer Town, Pioneer Museum of Western Art, Wimberley TX

Czichos, Raymond L, *Dir,* Pioneer Town, Pioneer Museum of Western Art, Wimberley TX

Dabakis, Melissa, *Prof,* Kenyon College, Art Dept, Gambier OH (S)

Dabash, Adrian G, *Assoc Prof,* Providence College, Art & Art History Dept, Providence RI (S)

D'Abate, Richard, *Exec Dir,* Maine Historical Society, MHS Museum, Portland ME

D'Abate, Richard, *Exec Dir,* Maine Historical Society, Wadsworth-Longfellow House, Portland ME

Dabb, Jean Ann, *Chair & Assoc Prof,* University of Mary Washington, Dept of Art & Art History, Fredericksburg VA (S)

Dablow, Dean, *Dir,* Louisiana Tech, School of Art, Ruston LA (S)

da Costa, Beatriz, *Assoc Prof Interactive Installation, & Programming,* University of California, Irvine, Studio Art Dept, Irvine CA (S)

da Costa-Meyer, Esther, *Prof,* Princeton University, Dept of Art & Archaeology, Princeton NJ (S)

Da Costa Nunes, Jadviga, *Chmn,* Muhlenberg College, Dept of Art, Allentown PA (S)

Daderko, Dean, *Cur,* Contemporary Arts Museum Houston, Houston TX

Dadi, Iftikhar, *Chair & Assoc Prof,* Cornell University, Dept of Art, Ithaca NY (S)

Dagdigian, Jamie, *Graphics Instr,* Monterey Peninsula College, Art Dept/Art Gallery, Monterey CA (S)

Dagon, Sonja, *Dir,* Contemporary Art Gallery, Vancouver BC

D'Agostino, Rachel, *Cur Printed Books,* Library Company of Philadelphia, Philadelphia PA

Dahl, Deb, *Chmn,* Arizona Museum For Youth, Mesa AZ

Dahm, Kristi, *Assoc Paper Conservator,* The Art Institute of Chicago, Dept of Prints & Drawings, Chicago IL

Dahms, David, *Technician,* Mount Saint Vincent University, MSVU Art Gallery, Halifax NS

Dahms, Rose, *Treas,* Cumberland Art Society Inc, Cookeville Art Gallery, Cookeville TN

Dai-Yu, Han, *Asst Prof,* Loyola Marymount University, Dept of Art & Art History, Los Angeles CA (S)

Dailey, John R, *NASM Dir,* National Air and Space Museum, Smithsonian Institution, Washington DC

Dailey, John R, *NASM Dir,* National Air And Space Museum, Steven F Udvar-Hazy Center, Chantilly VA

Daily, Julia, *Exec Dir,* Craftsmen's Guild of Mississippi, Inc, Agriculture & Forestry Museum, Ridgeland MS

Daily, Julia, *Exec Dir,* Craftsmen's Guild of Mississippi, Inc, Mississippi Crafts Center, Ridgeland MS

Dainard, Justine, *Librn,* University of British Columbia, Museum of Anthropology, Vancouver BC

Dainty, Linda, *Dir Art Dept,* Southwestern Community College, Art Dept, Creston IA (S)

Daix Westcoat, Bonna, *Assoc Prof,* Emory University, Art History Dept, Atlanta GA (S)

Dajani, Virginia, *Exec Dir,* American Academy of Arts & Letters, New York NY

Dake, Jason, *Educ Cur,* Northwestern Michigan College, Dennos Museum Center, Traverse City MI

Dakwar, Mohammad, *Dean,* Milwaukee Area Technical College, School of Media & Creative Arts, Milwaukee WI (S)

Dale, Alison, *Assoc Prof,* Seton Hall University, College of Arts & Sciences, South Orange NJ (S)

Dale, Gloria, *Accounting Mgr,* City Arts Center at Fair Park, Oklahoma City OK

Dale, Maria Saffiotti, *Cur Paintings, Sculpture, Decorative Arts,* University of Wisconsin-Madison, Chazen Museum of Art, Madison WI

Dale, Thomas E A, *Prof,* University of Wisconsin, Madison, Dept of Art History, Madison WI (S)

D'Alessandro, Mari, *Dir Progs & Communs,* Visual Arts Center of New Jersey, Summit NJ

Daley, Ginny, *Archivist,* Southern Highland Craft Guild, Folk Art Center, Asheville NC

Daley, Ken, *Prof,* Old Dominion University, Art Dept, Norfolk VA (S)

Daley, Sheila, *Asst Cur/Archivist,* Noah Webster House, Inc, Noah Webster House & West Hartford Historical Society, West Hartford CT

Dalkey, E, *Instr,* Sacramento City College, Art Dept, Sacramento CA (S)

D'Alleva, Anne, *Head Dept,* University of Connecticut, Dept of Art & Art History, Storrs CT (S)

Dallow, Jessica, *Asst Prof,* University of Alabama at Birmingham, Dept of Art & Art History, Birmingham AL (S)

Dally, Lynn, *Assoc Prof & Coordr Graphic Commun,* Tarrant County College, Art Dept, Hurst TX (S)

Dalton, Dennis, *Asst Prof,* University of Southern Colorado, Dept of Art, Pueblo CO (S)

Dalton, Laurie, *Dir,* Acadia University Art Gallery, Wolfville NS

Dalton, Sarah, *Asst,* Holland Tunnel Art Projects, Brooklyn NY

Daly, David, *Coll Mgr,* Longfellow National Historic Site, Longfellow House - Washington's Headquarters, Cambridge MA

Daly, Maureen, *Admin Cultural Arts,* Rocky Mount Arts Center, Rocky Mount NC

Daly, Terri, *Pub Rels,* Mount Vernon Hotel Museum & Garden, New York NY

Dalzell, Justin, *Tech Asst,* North Dakota Museum of Art, Grand Forks ND

D'Amato, Laura, *Dir Develop,* Racine Art Museum, Racine WI

Dambach, Cathy, *Ceramics,* Henry Ford Community College, McKenzie Fine Art Ctr, Dearborn MI (S)

D'Ambra, Eve, *Prof,* Vassar College, Art Dept, Poughkeepsie NY (S)

D'Ambrosio, Anna T, *Dir & Chief Cur,* Munson-Williams-Proctor Arts Institute, Museum of Art, Utica NY

D'Ambrosio, Paul, *Pres,* New York State Historical Association, Research Library, Cooperstown NY

Damer, Jack, *Prof,* University of Wisconsin, Madison, Dept of Art, Madison WI (S)

Damian, Carol, *Dir,* Florida International University, The Patricia & Phillip Frost Art Museum, Miami FL

Damian, Carol, *Prof,* Florida International University, School of Art & Art History, Miami FL (S)

Damkoehler, David, *Prof,* University of Wisconsin-Green Bay, Arts Dept, Green Bay WI (S)

Damm, Nancy, *Information Resources Supv,* University of Michigan, Fine Arts Library, Ann Arbor MI

Dampier, Elizabeth, *Dir,* Gaston County Museum of Art & History, Dallas NC

Damron, J, *Asst Prof,* Sierra Nevada College, Fine Arts Dept, Incline Village NV (S)

Damrosch, Eloise, *Exec Dir,* Regional Arts & Culture Council, Metropolitan Center for Public Arts, Portland OR

Dana, Robin, *Gallery Coordr,* University of Georgia, Franklin College of Arts & Sciences, Lamar Dodd School of Art, Athens GA (S)

Danahy, John, *Assoc Prof,* University of Toronto, Programme in Landscape Architecture, Toronto ON (S)

D'Anbrosio, Paul S, *Chief Cur,* New York State Historical Association, Fenimore Art Museum, Cooperstown NY

Dandridge, Peter, *Exec Asst Dir,* Memphis Brooks Museum of Art, Memphis TN

Dane, Kasarian, *Asst Prof,* St Lawrence University, Dept of Fine Arts, Canton NY (S)

Danford, Gerald, *VPres,* Fort Morgan Heritage Foundation, Fort Morgan CO

D'Angelo, John, *Exec Dir,* Mid-America All-Indian Center, Indian Center Museum, Wichita KS

D'Angelo, Starlyn, *Cur,* Shaker Museum & Library, Old Chatham NY

Daniel, Dwayne, *Asst Prof,* Central State University, Dept of Art, Wilberforce OH (S)

Daniel, Mike, *Instr,* Long Beach City College, Art & Photography Dept, Long Beach CA (S)

Daniel, Vesta, *Assoc Prof,* Ohio State University, Dept of Art Education, Columbus OH (S)

Daniels, Christopher, *Exhib Design,* Greenville Museum of Art, Inc, Greenville NC

Daniels, Diane, *Exec Dir,* Historical Society of Kent County, Chestertown MD

Daniels, Eve, *Cur & Registrar,* Roberson Museum & Science Center, Binghamton NY

Daniels, John P, *Dir,* Historic Pensacola Preservation Board, T.T. Wentworth Jr. Florida State Museum, Pensacola FL

Daniels, Maygene, *Gallery Archivist,* National Gallery of Art, Washington DC

Daniels, Ray, *Instr,* Lamar University, Art Dept, Beaumont TX (S)

Daniels, Stacie, *Asst Dir,* Mills College Art Museum, Oakland CA

Danielson, Deborah, *Prof,* Siena Heights University, Studio Angelico-Art Dept, Adrian MI (S)

Danielson, Sigrid, *Asst Prof,* Grand Valley State University, Art & Design Dept, Allendale MI (S)

Daniggelis, Chris, *Asst Prof,* University of Missouri - Columbia, Dept of Art, Columbia MO (S)

Danila, Joy, *Develop Assoc,* Bennington Museum, Bennington VT

Dankel, Jason, *Preparator,* The Robert McLaughlin, Oshawa ON

Danko, Linda A K, *Dir,* Biggs Museum of American Art, Dover DE

Danko-McGhee, Kathy, *Dir Educ,* Toledo Museum of Art, Toledo OH

Dannahower, Robin, *Mktg Dir,* A.E. Backus Museum of Art, Fort Pierce FL

Dannenberg, Penny, *Prog Dir,* New York Foundation for the Arts, Brooklyn NY

Danner, Anita, *Treas,* Switzerland County Historical Society Inc, Life on the Ohio: River History Museum, Vevay IN

Danner, Anita, *Treas,* Switzerland County Historical Society Inc, Switzerland County Historical Museum, Vevay IN

Dansberger, Dorothy, *Dir Finance & Opers,* Museum of Florida Art, Deland FL

Dantzic, Cynthia, *Prof,* Long Island University, Brooklyn Campus, Art Dept, Brooklyn NY (S)

Danziger, Maria, *Exec Dir,* The Art School at Old Church, Demarest NJ (S)

Darish, Patricia, *Asst Prof,* University of Kansas, Kress Foundation Dept of Art History, Lawrence KS (S)

Darlage, Jane, *Vol Dir & FSM Vols,* Indiana State Museum, Indianapolis IN

Darland, Carmen, *Exec Dir,* Quad City Arts Inc, Rock Island IL

Darley, Claire, *Chmn Foundation Dept,* Art Academy of Cincinnati, Cincinnati OH (S)

Darling, Barry, *Adjunct Asst Prof,* Le Moyne College, Fine Arts Dept, Syracuse NY (S)

Darling, Michael, *Chief Cur,* Museum of Contemporary Art, Chicago IL

Darling Pigat, Heather, *Coll Mgr,* University of Toronto, University of Toronto Art Centre, Toronto ON

Darnell, Polly, *Librn,* Shelburne Museum, Library, Shelburne VT

Da Rold, Joseph H, *Dir,* Plainfield Public Library, Plainfield NJ

Darr, Alan, *Cur European Sculpture & Decorative Arts,* Detroit Institute of Arts, Detroit MI

Darr, William, *Vol Coordr,* Bellingrath Gardens & Home, Theodore AL

Darraugh, Dave, *Asst Preparator,* Boise Art Museum, Boise ID

Darrow, Deb, *Exec Dir,* Rosemount Museum, Inc, Pueblo CO

Dart-Newton, Deana, *Cur Native Amer Ethnology,* University of Washington, Burke Museum of Natural History and Culture, Seattle WA

Darts, David, *Chmn,* New York University, Dept of Art & Art Professions, New York NY (S)

Dartt, Deana, *Cur Native American Art,* Portland Art Museum, Portland OR

Das, Urmilla, *Librn,* Surrey Art Gallery, Library, Surrey BC

Daschle, Thomas A, *VChmn,* United States Senate Commission on Art, Washington DC

Dasher, Glenn, *Prof,* University of Alabama in Huntsville, Dept of Art and Art History, Huntsville AL (S)

Dashnaw, Tom, *Mus Aide,* Village of Potsdam, Potsdam Public Museum, Potsdam NY

Dass, Carol, *Instr Visual Arts,* University of Colorado-Colorado Springs, Visual & Performing Arts Dept (VAPA), Colorado Springs CO (S)

Dass, Dean, *Studio Faculty,* University of Virginia, McIntire Dept of Art, Charlottesville VA (S)

Dates, Lynn, *Folk Arts,* Arts of the Southern Finger Lakes, Corning NY

Datlow, Dan, *Dir Operations & Security,* The Phillips Collection, Washington DC

Daubert, Debra, *Cur,* Oshkosh Public Museum, Oshkosh WI

Daubert, Debra, *Cur,* Oshkosh Public Museum, Library, Oshkosh WI

Daugherty, John, *Clinical Asst Prof,* University of Illinois at Chicago, Biomedical Visualization, Chicago IL (S)

Daugherty, Michael, *Dir,* Louisiana State University, School of Art, Baton Rouge LA (S)

Dauphin, Sylvie, *Cur Colls Mgmt,* The Stewart Museum, Montreal PQ

Dauphin, Sylvie, *Head of Colls,* The Stewart Museum, Library, Montreal PQ

Dave, Alfonzo, *VPres,* Museum of African American Art, Los Angeles CA

Davenny, Ward, *Assoc Prof,* Dickinson College, Dept of Art & Art History, Carlisle PA (S)

Davenport, A J, *Adminr,* Coos Art Museum, Coos Bay OR

Davenport, Kimberly, *Dir & Chief Cur,* Rice University, Rice Gallery, Houston TX

Davi, Susan A, *Subject Librn (Art & Art History),* University of Delaware, Morris Library, Newark DE

David, Lynn, *Dir Pub Rels,* Maysville, Kentucky Gateway Museum Center, Maysville KY

David, Michael, *Chair Fine Arts,* Lesley University, College of Art & Design, Boston MA (S)

David-West, Haig, *Head Div,* Chowan College, Division of Art, Murfreesboro NC (S)

Davidhazy, Andrew, *Chmn Imaging & Photographic Technology,* Rochester Institute of Technology, School of Photographic Arts & Sciences, Rochester NY (S)

Davidow, Joan, *Dir & Cur,* The Dallas Contemporary, Dallas Visual Art Center, Dallas TX

Davidson, Amanda, *Communs & Mktg Mgr,* Headlands Center for the Arts, Sausalito CA

Davidson, Andrea, *Dir & Librn,* The Temple-Tifereth Israel, Lee & Dolores Hartzmark Library, Beachwood OH

Davidson, Ben, *Dir,* Americans for the Arts, Library, New York NY

Davidson, Bobbie, *Dir Opers,* Safety Harbor Museum of Regional History, Safety Harbor FL

Davidson, Conrad, *Chmn Div Humanities,* Minot State University, Dept of Art, Division of Humanities, Minot ND (S)

Davidson, Gail, *Cur Drawings & Prints,* Cooper-Hewitt National Design Museum, Smithsonian Institution, New York NY

Davidson, Nancy, *Prof Emerita,* Purchase College, State University of New York, School of Art+Design, Purchase NY (S)

Davidson, Richard, *Chmn Trustees,* Longfellow's Wayside Inn Museum, Sudbury MA

Davidson, Susan, *Sr Cur Colls & Exhibs,* Solomon R Guggenheim, New York NY

Davidson, Thomas E, *Curatorial Servs Mgr,* Jamestown-Yorktown Foundation, Jamestown Settlement, Williamsburg VA

Davies, Bruce, *Cur,* Craigdarroch Castle Historical Museum Society, Victoria BC

Davies, Gail, *Office Mgr,* California College of the Arts, San Francisco CA (S)

Davies, Harry, *Chmn,* Adelphi University, Dept of Art & Art History, Garden City NY (S)

Davies, Hugh M, *David C Copley Dir,* Museum of Contemporary Art San Diego, San Diego CA

Davies, Hugh M, *Dir,* Museum of Contemporary Art, San Diego, La Jolla CA

Davies, Hugh M, *Dir,* Museum of Contemporary Art, San Diego, Geisel Library, La Jolla CA

Davies, Hugh M, *Dir,* Museum of Contemporary Art, San Diego-Downtown, La Jolla CA

Davies, Irene, *Asst to Dir,* Southern Methodist University, Meadows Museum, Dallas TX

Davies, Lauren, *Dir Exhib & Pub Progs,* Kala Institute, Kala Art Institute, Berkeley CA

Davies, Leigh, *Chmn & Dir Creative Arts,* Russell Sage College, Visual & Performing Arts Dept, Troy NY (S)

Davies, Melissa, *Educ,* Colgate University, Picker Art Gallery, Hamilton NY

Davies, Sandy, *Publicity,* Redlands Art Association, Redlands Art Association Gallery & Art Center, Redlands CA

Davies, Tricia, *Educ & Vis Servs,* American Swedish Historical Foundation & Museum, Nord Library, Philadelphia PA

Davila, Arturo, *Prof,* University of Puerto Rico, Dept of Fine Arts, Rio Piedras PR (S)

Davila, Arturo, *Prof,* University of Puerto Rico, Dept of Fine Arts, Rio Piedras PR (S)

Davila, Chris, *Exhibs Coordr,* Guadalupe Cultural Arts Center, San Antonio TX

Davis, Adria Crossen, *Coll Mgr,* California State University, Chico, Janet Turner Print Museum, CSU, Chicago, Chico CA

Davis, Arcenia, *Prof,* Winston-Salem State University, Art Dept, Winston-Salem NC (S)

Davis, Art, *Head Dept,* Grace College, Dept of Art, Winona Lake IN (S)

Davis, Bill, *Asst Prof,* Shippensburg University, Art Dept, Shippensburg PA (S)

Davis, Birgitta W, *Assoc Dir,* American Swedish Historical Foundation & Museum, American Swedish Historical Museum, Philadelphia PA

Davis, Birgitta W, *Assoc Dir,* American Swedish Historical Foundation & Museum, Nord Library, Philadelphia PA

Davis, Bruce, *Exec Dir,* Arts Council Silicon Valley, San Jose CA

Davis, Carla, *Mktg Dir,* Akron-Summit County Public Library, Fine Arts Division, Akron OH

Davis, Carol, *Dir Educ,* Edna Hibel, Hibel Museum of Art, Jupiter FL

Davis, Carol, *Dir Educ,* Edna Hibel, Hibel Museum Gallery, Jupiter FL

Davis, Charles, *Asst Prof Art,* Mississippi Valley State University, Fine Arts Dept, Itta Bena MS (S)

Davis, Christie, *Art Projects Mgr,* Lannan Foundation, Santa Fe NM

Davis, Christine, *Acting Exec Dir,* Philadelphia History Museum, Philadelphia PA

Davis, Danita, *Visual Resource Specialist,* Indiana University - Purdue University at Indianapolis, Herron School of Art Library, Indianapolis IN

Davis, Debbie, *Bus & Events Mgr,* Mount Holyoke College, Art Museum, South Hadley MA

Davis, Deborah, *Mus Mgr,* Aurora Regional Fire Museum, Aurora IL

Davis, Deborah A, *Secy,* Miles B Carpenter Folk Art Museum, Waverly VA

Davis, Don, *Assoc Prof,* East Tennessee State University, College of Arts and Sciences, Dept of Art & Design, Johnson City TN (S)

Davis, Dustin P, *Chair,* Frostburg State University, The Stephanie Ann Roper Gallery, Frostburg MD

Davis, Dustin P, *Head Dept,* Frostburg State University, Dept of Visual Arts, Frostburg MD (S)

Davis, E Holmes, *Treas,* Halifax Historical Society, Inc, Halifax Historical Museum, Daytona Beach FL

Davis, Eli, *Assoc Prof,* Illinois Central College, Arts & Communication Dept, East Peoria IL (S)

Davis, Gainor B, *Dir,* Vermont Historical Society, Library, Montpelier VT

Davis, Gainor B, *Pres & CEO,* Western Reserve Historical Society, Cleveland OH

Davis, Glenn Herbert, *Asst Prof, Photog,* University of Tulsa, School of Art, Tulsa OK (S)

Davis, Gloria, *Cur,* Muchnic Foundation & Atchison Art Association, Muchnic Gallery, Atchison KS

Davis, Gordon, *Dir,* Westminster College, Winston Churchill Memorial & Library in the United States, Fulton MO

Davis, Gordon, *Mem Bd Dir,* Hatch-Billops Collection, Inc, New York NY

Davis, Gordon, *Publicity,* Wiscasset, Waterville & Farmington Railway Museum (WW&F), Alna ME

Davis, Israel, *Clay Program Dir,* Urban Institute for Contemporary Arts, Grand Rapids MI

Davis, J Marshall, *Pres,* Indiana Landmarks, Information Center Library, Indianapolis IN

Davis, Jack R, *Chmn,* Oklahoma City University, Norick Art Center, Oklahoma City OK (S)

Davis, Jacqueline Z, *Dir,* The New York Public Library, The New York Public Library for the Performing Arts, New York NY

Davis, James, *Asst Prof,* Mississippi State University, Dept of Art, Starville MS (S)

Davis, Jeff, *Assoc Prof,* Texas State University - San Marcos, Dept of Art and Design, San Marcos TX (S)

Davis, Jeff, *Graphic Design,* Art Institute of Pittsburgh, Pittsburgh PA (S)

Davis, John, *Prof,* Smith College, Art Dept, Northampton MA (S)

Davis, Julie, *Asst Prof,* Oberlin College, Dept of Art, Oberlin OH (S)

Davis, Katherine M, *VPres,* Liberty Hall Historic Site, Library, Frankfort KY

Davis, Keahe, *Educ Specialist,* Judiciary History Center, Honolulu HI

Davis, Larry, *Faculty Coordr Fine Arts,* Florida Community College at Jacksonville, South Campus, Art Dept, Jacksonville FL (S)

Davis, Lauren, *Cur,* West Baton Rouge Parish, West Baton Rouge Museum, Port Allen LA

Davis, Lee Baxter, *Instr Printmaking,* Texas A&M University Commerce, Dept of Art, Commerce TX (S)

Davis, Lisa, *Mgr Educ Programs,* University of Chicago, Smart Museum of Art, Chicago IL

Davis, Lynn, *Admin Asst,* Patrick Henry, Red Hill National Memorial, Brookneal VA

Davis, Margo, *Assoc,* West Virginia Wesleyan College, Art Dept, Buckhannon WV (S)

Davis, Marsh, *Pres,* Indiana Landmarks, Morris-Butler House, Indianapolis IN

Davis, Meg, *Dir & Cur,* Gem County Historical Society and Museum, Gem County Historical Village Museum, Emmett ID

Davis, Meredith, *Assoc Prof Art History,* Ramapo College of New Jersey, School of Contemporary Arts, Mahwah NJ (S)

Davis, Meredith, *Sculpture Chair,* Montserrat College of Art, Beverly MA (S)

Davis, Michael P, *Interim Chmn,* Mount Holyoke College, Art Dept, South Hadley MA (S)

Davis, Nancy, *Cur Coll,* Maryland Historical Society, Library, Baltimore MD

Davis, Pam, Bechtler Museum of Modern Art, Charlotte NC

Davis, Pamela. *Exec Dir,* Silvermine Guild Arts Center, Silvermine Galleries, New Canaan CT

Davis, Paul, *Pres,* Billings Meriks Sculptors Society, Billings MT

Davis, Paula, *Events Coordr,* Longview Museum of Fine Art, Longview TX

Davis, Rebecca, *Asst Prof,* Mississippi State University, Dept of Art, Starville MS (S)

Davis, Rebecca, *Dir,* Bose Pacia, Brooklyn NY

Davis, Rebecca, *Registrar,* The Butler Institute of American Art, Art Museum, Youngstown OH

Davis, Richard, *Assoc Prof,* Monmouth University, Dept of Art & Design, West Long Branch NJ (S)

Davis, Richard, *Chmn,* Potomac State College, Dept of Art, Keyser WV (S)

Davis, Richard, *Prof Sculpture,* University of North Texas, College of Visual Arts & Design, Denton TX (S)

Davis, Robert, *Dir Develop,* Winterthur Museum, Winterthur Museum, Garden & Library, Winterthur DE

Davis, Rusty, *Facilities Mgr,* Springfield Museum of Art, Springfield OH

Davis, Scott, *Dir Exhibs and Design,* Museum of Photographic Arts, Edmund L. and Nancy K Dubois Library, San Diego CA

Davis, Sharon, *Librn,* Greenville College, The Richard W Bock Sculpture Collection & Art Library, Greenville IL

Davis, Sonya, *Exec Dir,* Pensacola Museum of Art, Pensacola FL

Davis, Stewart D, *Pres,* Rochester Contemporary, Art Center, Rochester NY

Davis, Susan S, *Dir,* Stanley Museum, Inc, Kingfield ME

Davis, Suzanne, *Conservator,* University of Michigan, Kelsey Museum of Archaeology, Ann Arbor MI

Davis, William, *Digital Media Photog Area Coordr,* Western Michigan University, Frostic School of Art, Kalamazoo MI (S)

Davis, William J, *Dir,* MacArthur Memorial, Norfolk VA

Davis, Zina, *Dir,* University of Hartford, Joseloff Gallery, West Hartford CT

Davis-Jones, Melanie, *Dir Mktg,* North Carolina Museum of Art, Raleigh NC

Davis-Rosenbaum, Kate, *Instr,* Midway College, Art Dept, Midway KY (S)

Davis-Rosenbaum, Steve, *Chmn,* Midway College, Art Dept, Midway KY (S)

Davish, Peggy, *Adminr,* Middletown Arts Center, Library, Middletown OH

Davison, Claudine, *Dir Baltimore Jewish Film Festival,* Norman and Sarah Brown Art Gallery, Baltimore MD

Davison, Darlene, *Asst Prof & Prog Dir, Interior Design,* Maryville University of Saint Louis, Art & Design Program, Saint Louis MO (S)

Davison, Liane, *Dir,* Surrey Art Gallery, Surrey BC

Davison, Liane, *Dir,* Surrey Art Gallery, Library, Surrey BC

Davison, Mark, *Chmn,* Clinton Community College, Art Dept, Plattsburgh NY (S)

Davison, Susan, *VPres Mktg & Develop,* Springfield Museums, Connecticut Valley Historical Society, Springfield MA

Davitt, Gail, *Dir Educ,* Dallas Museum of Art, Dallas TX

Davson, Victor, *Exec Dir,* Aljira Center for Contemporary Art, Newark NJ

Davy, Mark, *Preparator,* Pacific Grove Art Center, Pacific Grove CA

Dawes, John, *Asst Prof,* University of the Incarnate Word, Art Dept, San Antonio TX (S)

Dawn, Leslie, *Asst Prof,* University of Lethbridge, Div of Art, Lethbridge AB (S)

Daws, Russell S, *CEO & Exec Dir,* Tallahassee Museum of History & Natural Science, Museum, Tallahassee FL

Daws, Russell S, *Dir,* Tallahassee Museum of History & Natural Science, Tallahassee FL

Dawsari, Elizabeth, *Dir of Library,* Frank Lloyd Wright School, William Wesley Peters Library, Scottsdale AZ

Dawsey, Jill, *Cur,* University of Utah, Utah Museum of Fine Arts, Salt Lake City UT

Dawson, David, *Instr Animation,* Rio Hondo College, Visual Arts Dept, Whittier CA (S)

Dawson, Judy, *Dir Develop,* Honolulu Academy of Arts, The Art Center at Linekona, Honolulu HI (S)

Dawson, Kathleen, *Quilt Natl Dir,* The Dairy Barn Arts Center, Athens OH

Dawson, Will, *Pres,* Klamath Art Association, Klamath Falls OR

Day, Brenda, *Dir,* Baker University, Old Castle Museum, Baldwin City KS

Day, Gary, *Assoc Prof,* University of Nebraska at Omaha, Dept of Art & Art History, Omaha NE (S)

Day, Homer, *Pres,* Abraham Baldwin Agricultural College, Art & Humanities Dept, Tifton GA (S)

Day, Janet, *Pres,* Art Institute of Atlanta, Atlanta GA (S)

Day, Jennifer, *Registrar,* School for Advanced Research (SAR), Indian Arts Research Center, Santa Fe NM

Day, Jessica, *Guest Svcs Coordr,* Neville Public Museum of Brown County, Green Bay WI

Day, John, *Dir,* Fryeburg Academy, The Palmina F & Stephen S Pace Galleries of Art, Fryeburg ME

Day, John, *Chmn & Dean,* University of South Dakota, Department of Art, College of Fine Arts, Vermillion SD (S)

Day, Ross, *Acquisitions Coordr,* The Metropolitan Museum of Art, Museum Libraries, New York NY

Day, Russell, *Dept Chair,* Penn Foster College, School of Interior Design, Scranton PA (S)

Days, Russell, *Coordr Facilities,* College of Central Florida, Appleton Museum of Art, Ocala FL

Dayton, Arlene, *Pres,* Chinati Foundation, Marfa TX

Dayton, Gracia, *Pres,* New England Watercolor Society, Pembroke MA

de-Cossio, Renee, *Technical/Art Specialist,* San Francisco Museum of Modern Art, Artist Gallery, San Francisco CA

Deacy-Quinn, Christa, *Collections Mgr,* University of Illinois at Urbana-Champaign, Spurlock Museum, Champaign IL

Deadman, Pat, *Instr,* Art Center Sarasota, Sarasota FL (S)

Deadman, Patricia, *Acting Cur,* City of Woodstock, Woodstock Art Gallery, Woodstock ON

Deal, David, *Asst Prof Art & Graphic Design,* Eastern New Mexico University, Runnels Gallery, Golden Library, Portales NM

DeAlmeida, Claudia, *Circ Supv,* Roger Williams University, Architecture Library, Bristol RI

Dean, Amy, *Circ Asst,* Ames Free-Easton's Public Library, North Easton MA

Dean, Angel, *Admin Coordr & Archivist,* Providence Art Club, Providence RI

Dean, Catherine, *Cur,* Preservation Virginia, Richmond VA

Dean, Clay, *Dir Develop & Finance,* Museum of Biblical Art, New York NY

Dean, David K, *Assoc Dir Operations,* Texas Tech University, Museum of Texas Tech University, Lubbock TX

Dean, Emily, *Educ Cur,* University of Mississippi, University Museum & Historic Houses, Oxford MS

Dean, Jim, *Dean Admis,* Ringling School of Art & Design, Sarasota FL (S)

Dean, Kevin, *Dir,* Ringling College of Art & Design, Selby Gallery, Sarasota FL

Dean, Paul, *Asst Prof,* Louisiana State University, School of Art, Baton Rouge LA (S)

de Anda, Raquel, *Assoc Cur,* Galeria de la Raza, Studio 24, San Francisco CA

Deane, Dennis, *Assoc Prof,* Ohio University-Chillicothe Campus, Fine Arts & Humanities Division, Chillicothe OH (S)

DeAngelis, Anita, *Prof,* East Tennessee State University, College of Arts and Sciences, Dept of Art & Design, Johnson City TN (S)

DeAngelo, Darlene, *Dir Programming,* Huntington Beach Art Center, Huntington Beach CA

Deans, John, *Pres,* Jefferson Community College, Art Dept, Watertown NY (S)

Dearborn, Alan, *Asst Cur Physics,* Northern Maine Museum of Science, Presque Isle ME

Dearinger, David, *Susan Morse Hilles Cur Paintings & Sculpture & Head Art Dept,* Library of the Boston Athenaeum, Boston MA

Deaton, Judy, *Instr,* McMurry University, Art Dept, Abilene TX (S)

Deaton, Linda, *Chief Cur,* Tallahassee Museum of History & Natural Science, Museum, Tallahassee FL

Deaton, Linda, *Cur Coll & Exhib,* Tallahassee Museum of History & Natural Science, Tallahassee FL

De Backere, Jocelyn, *Program Coordr,* Visual Arts Ontario, Toronto ON

DeBaecke, Maggie, *Instr,* Wayne Art Center, Wayne PA (S)

Debardeleben, Patty, *Mus Shop Mgr,* Sturdivant Museum Association, Sturdivant Museum, Selma AL

Debarry, Christina, *Instr,* Woodstock School of Art, Inc, Woodstock NY (S)

Debarry, Christina, *VPres,* The Allied Artists of America, Inc, New York NY

DeBartolo, Rob, *Pres,* Essex Art Association, Inc, Essex CT

Debeer, Jan, *Mus Shop Mgr,* Nicolaysen Art Museum & Discovery Center, Children's Discovery Center, Casper WY

de Beer, Sue, *MFA Prog Dir,* New York University, Dept of Art & Art Professions, New York NY (S)

deBeixedon, Dianne, *Assoc Prof,* Old Dominion University, Art Dept, Norfolk VA (S)

Debela, Achameleh, *Prof,* North Carolina Central University, Art Dept, Durham NC (S)

DeBevoise, Frank, *VPres Historian,* Catharine Lorillard Wolfe, New York NY

de Bie, Melissa, *Registrar,* Las Vegas Art Museum, Las Vegas NV

Deblois, Annick, *Cur Educ,* Musee d'art de Joliette, Joliette PQ

DeBolt, Dean, *Dir Spec Coll,* University of West Florida, Library, Pensacola FL

DeBord, Betty, *Assoc Prof Art,* Lincoln Memorial University, Division of Humanities, Harrogate TN (S)

DeBow, Arthur, *Exhibs Dir,* Oregon College of Art & Craft, Hoffman Gallery, Portland OR

DeBow, Lynn, *VPres Develop,* American Museum of Natural History, New York NY

deBrer, Christian, *Asst Conservator,* University of California, Los Angeles, Fowler Museum at UCLA, Los Angeles CA

DeBruyne, Paul, *Co-Pres,* DeBruyne Fine Art, Naples FL

DeBruyne, Suzanne, *Co-Pres,* DeBruyne Fine Art, Naples FL

DeBus, Charles, *Asst Prof,* Southern Methodist University, Division of Art, Dallas TX (S)

deCamargo, Luiza, *Curatorial Asst,* Asheville Art Museum, Asheville NC

DeCarolis, Lisa, *Art Library Asst,* Smith College, Hillyer Art Library, Northampton MA

DeCat, Lisa, *Asst Prof Dance,* Lake Erie College, Fine Arts Dept, Painesville OH (S)

Decelestino, Blase, *Adjunct Instr,* New York Institute of Technology, Fine Arts Dept, Old Westbury NY (S)

Deci, Edward L, *Pres,* Monhegan Museum, Monhegan ME

DeCicco, Deb, *School Dir,* Sharon Arts Center, Sharon Arts Center Exhibition Gallery, Peterborough NH

Decicco, Stephanie, *Chmn,* Waubonsee Community College, Art Dept, Sugar Grove IL (S)

Decker, John, *Grad Dir,* Georgia State University, Ernest G Welch School of Art & Design, Atlanta GA (S)

Decker, Juilee, *Chmn,* Georgetown College Gallery, Georgetown KY

Decker, Julie, *Dir Exhibs,* Anchorage Museum at Rasmuson Center, Anchorage AK

Decker, Juliee, *Prof Art History & Dept Chair,* Georgetown College, Art Dept, Georgetown KY (S)

Decker, Thomas, *Treas,* Japanese American National Museum, Los Angeles CA

Decker, Timothy, *Coll Mgr,* New Jersey Historical Society, Newark NJ

Decklin, Tara, *Opers Mgr,* Society of North American Goldsmiths, Eugene OR

De Cocker, Dean, *Gallery Dir,* California State University Stanislaus, University Art Gallery, Turlock CA

DeCoker, Dean, *Prof,* California State University, Art Dept, Turlock CA (S)

Decoster, Patricia, *Registrar,* Kimbell Art Foundation, Kimbell Art Museum, Fort Worth TX

Decoteau, Pamela, *Head Art History,* Southern Illinois University at Edwardsville, Dept of Art & Design, Edwardsville IL (S)

DeCrescenzo, Robert, *Chmn,* Old State House, Hartford CT

DeDominicis, Jennifer, *VP Enrol & Student Servs Registrar,* Emily Carr University of Art + Design, Vancouver BC (S)

Deegan, Ann, *Cur History,* San Bernardino County Museum, Fine Arts Institute, Redlands CA

Deegan, Denis, *Prof,* Daytona Beach Community College, Dept of Fine Arts & Visual Arts, Daytona Beach FL (S)

Deegan, Denise, *Colls Mgr,* Avampato Discovery Museum, The Clay Center for Arts & Sciences, Charleston WV

Deek, Valentina, *VP,* Women's Art Association of Canada, Dignam Gallery, Toronto ON

Deer, Susan, *Assoc Dir Technical Serv,* New York State Historical Association, Research Library, Cooperstown NY

Deere, Bill, *Assoc Prof,* Purchase College, State University of New York, School of Art+Design, Purchase NY (S)

DeEsch, Vasti, *Coll Asst,* Lehigh University Art Galleries, Museum Operation, Bethlehem PA

de Fato, Elizabeth, *Librn,* Seattle Art Museum, Dorothy Stimson Bullitt Library, Seattle WA

DeFee, F Brooks, *Asst Prof,* Northwestern State University of Louisiana, School of Creative & Performing Arts - Dept of Fine & Graphic Arts, Natchitoches LA (S)

Defenbaugh, Deni, *Asst Prof,* Rochester Institute of Technology, School of Photographic Arts & Sciences, Rochester NY (S)

Defendi, Claudia, *Chief Cur,* Andy Warhol Foundation for the Visual Arts, New York NY

Defoor, T, *Music Instr,* Edison Community College, Gallery of Fine Arts, Fort Myers FL (S)

DeFord, Matt, *Asst Prof,* Northwestern State University of Louisiana, School of Creative & Performing Arts - Dept of Fine & Graphic Arts, Natchitoches LA (S)

De Fuchs, Mercedes Chacin, *Instr,* Toronto Art Therapy Institute, Toronto ON (S)

deFurio, Anne, *Reference Head,* Berkeley Heights Free Public Library, Berkeley Heights NJ

deGennaro, Cristina, *Assoc Prof,* The College of New Rochelle, School of Arts & Sciences Art Dept, New Rochelle NY (S)

DeGennaro, Frank J, *Graphic Design,* Art Institute of Pittsburgh, Pittsburgh PA (S)

DeGennaro, Mark, *Preparator,* Miami University, Art Museum, Oxford OH

DeGiacomo, Lynne, *Exec Admin,* Cohasset Historical Society, Captain John Wilson Historical House, Cohasset MA

DeGiacomo, Lynne, *Exec Dir,* Cohasset Historical Society, Pratt Building (Society Headquarters), Cohasset MA

DeGiacomo, Lynne, *Exec Dir,* Cohasset Historical Society, Cohasset Maritime Museum, Cohasset MA

Degler, Suzanne, *Dir,* Minneapolis College of Art & Design, Library, Minneapolis MN

DeGraaf, Lee, *Treas,* Canton Museum of Art, Canton OH

DeGraffenried, Judith, *Head Dept, Prof,* Middlesex Community College, Fine Arts Div, Middletown CT (S)

DeGroat, Mary, *Dir Mktg Communs,* Monterey Museum of Art, Monterey Museum of Art -Pacific Street, Monterey Museum of Art - La Mirada, Monterey CA

DeGroff, Jacqueline M, *Cur,* Drexel University, Drexel Collection, Philadelphia PA

De Groft, Aaron H, *Dir,* College of William & Mary, Muscarelle Museum of Art, Williamsburg VA

Degutis, Alan N, *Head Cataloging Svcs,* American Antiquarian Society, Worcester MA

de Habsburgo, Inmaculada, *Pres & CEO,* Queen Sofia Spanish Institute, New York NY

Dehan, Amy, *Assoc Cur Decorative Arts,* Cincinnati Art Museum, Cincinnati Art Museum, Cincinnati OH

DeHayes, Lisa, *Dir Mktg,* Indianapolis Art Center, Marilyn K. Glick School of Art, Indianapolis IN

Dehn, Brenda, *Dir,* Henry County Museum & Cultural Arts Center, Clinton MO

Dehne, Christine, *Faculty Cur,* Manhattanville College, Brownson Gallery, Purchase NY

Dehne, Christine, *Faculty Cur,* Manhattanville College, Arthur M Berger Gallery, Purchase NY

DeHoet, Robert, *Educ Prog Dir,* Southern Illinois University Carbondale, University Museum, Carbondale IL

De Hoff, William, *Asst Prof,* University of Wisconsin-Stout, Dept of Art & Design, Menomonie WI (S)

Deihl, Nancy, *Prog Dir Costume Studies,* New York University, Dept of Art & Art Professions, New York NY (S)

Deilke, Karen, *3rd VPres,* Miami Watercolor Society, Inc, Miami FL

Deily, Dave, *Dir MCG Youth & Arts,* Manchester Bidwell Corporation, Manchester Craftsmen's Guild Youth & Arts Program, Pittsburgh PA

Deines, Craig, *Chmn Art,* Mount San Antonio College, Art Dept, Walnut CA (S)

Deiss, Andrew, *Contact Person,* Utah Lawyers for the Arts, Salt Lake City UT

Deitch, Jeffrey, *Dir,* The Museum of Contemporary Art (MOCA), Moca Grand Avenue, Los Angeles CA

Deitrick, Pam, *Head Librn,* Public Library of Des Moines, Central Library Information Services, Des Moines IA

Deits, Katie, *Exec Dir,* Lighthouse ArtCenter Museum & School of Art, Not Profit Art Center, Tequesta FL

Deits, Katie, *Exec Dir & School of Art Interim Dir,* Lighthouse ArtCenter Museum & School of Art, Tequesta FL

Deitsch, Dina, *Assoc Cur Contemporary Art,* DeCordova Museum & Sculpture Park, DeCordova Museum, Lincoln MA

Deitsch, Elka, *Sr Cur,* Congregation Emanu-El, Bernard Judaica Museum, New York NY

Dejardin, Fiona, *Assoc Prof,* Hartwick College, Art Dept, Oneonta NY (S)

Dejardin, Fiona M, *Dir & Cur Fine Arts,* Hartwick College, The Yager Museum, Oneonta NY

de Jesus, Daniel, *Visual Arts Prog Mgr,* Taller Puertorriqueno Inc, Lorenzo Homar Gallery, Philadelphia PA

Delacretaz, Helen, *Chief Cur & Cur Decorative Art & Fine Art, Head Mus Servs,* The Winnipeg Art Gallery, Winnipeg MB

Delahanty, Patricia, *Exhibitions Dir,* National Sculpture Society, New York NY

de la Hidalga-Bartolomei, Ana M, *Mem/Art Travel,* Maitland Art Center, Library, Maitland FL

dela Houssaye, Isabella, *Pres,* Crowley Art Association, The Gallery, Crowley LA

del Alamo, Constancio, *Cur Archaeology & Sculpture,* The Hispanic Society of America, Museum & Library, New York NY

DeLamater, Peg, *Assoc Prof,* Winthrop University, Dept of Art & Design, Rock Hill SC (S)

del Amo, Yolanda, *Asst Prof Photo,* Ramapo College of New Jersey, School of Contemporary Arts, Mahwah NJ (S)

DeLaney, Chuck, *Dir,* New York Institute of Photography, New York NY (S)

Delaney, Esmeralda, *Asst Prof Art,* Grand Canyon University, Art Dept, Phoenix AZ (S)

DeLaney, Phyllis, *Dir Develop,* University of Florida, Samuel P Harn Museum of Art, Gainesville FL

Delaney, Susan, *Art History Instr,* Miracosta College, Art Dept, Oceanside CA (S)

Delaney, Trish, *Instr,* Toronto School of Art, Toronto ON (S)

DeLang, Val, *Dir Educ,* San Jose Museum of Art, Library, San Jose CA

Delano, Pablo, *Asst Prof,* Trinity College, Dept of Studio Arts, Hartford CT (S)

Delanoy, Geoff, *Assoc Prof,* College of Notre Dame of Maryland, Art Dept, Baltimore MD (S)

DeLap, Amy, *Prof,* Vincennes University Junior College, Humanities Art Dept, Vincennes IN (S)

de la Renta, Oscar, *Chmn,* Queen Sofia Spanish Institute, New York NY

DeLaria, Nicole, *Librn,* The Bostonian Society, Library, Boston MA

deLarosa, Francise, *Asst Prof,* Wesleyan College, Art Dept, Macon GA (S)

de la Serna, Arlette, *Assoc Cur,* Museo de Arte de Ponce, The Luis A Ferre Foundation Inc, Ponce PR

de la Serna, Arlette, *Assoc Cur,* Museo de Arte de Ponce, The Luis A Ferre Foundation Inc, Ponce PR

de la Torre, David J, *Assoc Dir,* Honolulu Academy of Arts, The Art Center at Linekona, Honolulu HI (S)

de la Torre, Marta, *Dir Museum Studies,* Florida International University, School of Art & Art History, Miami FL (S)

DeLaura, Angela, *Asst Prof,* William Paterson University, Dept Arts, Wayne NJ (S)

Delavaux, Denise, *Adjunct,* College of the Canyons, Art Dept, Santa Clarita CA (S)

Delavega, Jan, *Shop Mgr,* Kauai Museum Association, Ltd., Lihue HI

DeLay, Matthew, *Educ Coordr,* Iowa State University, Brunnier Art Museum, Ames IA

Delbo, Jose, *Instr,* Joe Kubert, Dover NJ (S)

Del Deo, Frank, *Sr VPres & Assoc Dir,* M Knoedler, Library, New York NY

Deleary, Mary, *Primitive Edge Gallery Coordr,* Institute of American Indian Arts, Museum of Contemporary Native Arts, Santa Fe NM (S)

Delehanty, Suzanne, *Dir,* Rutgers, The State University of New Jersey, Zimmerli Art Museum, Rutgers University, New Brunswick NJ

DeLelys, Mark, *Dir Retail Sales,* Pennsylvania Academy of the Fine Arts, Philadelphia PA

De Leon, Denisse, *Coordr Mus Visitor & Tour Srvcs,* University of Richmond, University Museums, Richmond VA

Delfino, Christine, *Admin Asst,* Bard College, Center for Curatorial Studies and the Hessel Museum of Art, Annandale-on-Hudson NY

Delgado, Iris, *Chmn,* St Francis Xavier University, Fine Arts Dept, Antigonish NS (S)

Delgado, Jessica, *Comm & Mktg Mgr,* Florida International University, The Patricia & Phillip Frost Art Museum, Miami FL

Delgado, John, *Instr,* Southern University A & M College, School of Architecture, Baton Rouge LA (S)

Delgado, Sally, *Cur Educ,* Ohio University, Kennedy Museum of Art, Athens OH

Delgado, Steve, *VPres,* Second Street Gallery, Charlottesville VA

Delimont, William, *Bd Pres,* Coos Art Museum, Coos Bay OR

Delisle, Andre, *Exec Dir & Cur,* Chateau Ramezay Museum, Montreal PQ

Delker, Kathy, *Asst Library Dir Reference,* Friends University, Edmund Stanley Library, Wichita KS

Dell, Jeff, *Assoc Prof,* Texas State University - San Marcos, Dept of Art and Design, San Marcos TX (S)

Dell, Jery, *Prof,* University of Wisconsin-Green Bay, Arts Dept, Green Bay WI (S)

Dell, Urve, *Chmn,* Saint Olaf College, Art Dept, Northfield MN (S)

Dellapina, Ardath, *Dir Educ & Progs,* Clark County Historical Society, Heritage Center of Clark County, Springfield OH

Dellatte, Cara, *Archivist,* Staten Island Museum, Archives Library, Staten Island NY

Dellavalle, Jacques A, *Prof,* Daytona Beach Community College, Dept of Fine Arts & Visual Arts, Daytona Beach FL (S)

Deller, Harris, *Prof,* Southern Illinois University, School of Art & Design, Carbondale IL (S)

Delli, Lyn Quadri, *Exec Dir Graphics & Communs Svcs,* The Art Institute of Chicago, Chicago IL

Dellinger, Adrienne, *Exec Dir,* Clayworks Gallery, Charlotte NC

Dell'Olio, L, *Prof,* Camden County College, Visual & Performing Arts Dept, Blackwood NJ (S)

Delman, Kirk, *Coll Mgr, Registrar,* Scripps College, Ruth Chandler Williamson Gallery, Claremont CA

Delois, Patti, *AV Mgr,* Portland Public Library, Art - Audiovisual Dept, Portland ME

De Long, Paul, *Prof,* University of Wisconsin-Stout, Dept of Art & Design, Menomonie WI (S)

DeLorme, Harry, *Cur Educ,* Telfair Museums' Jepson Center for the Arts Library, Telfair Academy of Arts & Sciences Library, Savannah GA

DeLorme, Harry H, *Chief Cur Educ,* Telfair Museums' Jepson Center for the Arts Library, Savannah GA

Delos, Kate, *Instr,* Solano Community College, Division of Fine & Applied Art & Behavioral Science, Fairfield CA (S)

De Los Santos, Ofelia, *Chief Financial Officer,* Inner-City Arts, Los Angeles CA (S)

Delto, Byron, *Instr,* Glendale Community College, Visual & Performing Arts Div, Glendale CA (S)

Delucca, Sharon, *Assoc Prof,* Roger Williams University, Visual Art Dept, Bristol RI (S)

DeLucia, Angela, *Interim Dir,* Youngstown State University, The John J McDonough Museum of Art, Youngstown OH

de Luise, Alexandra, *Cur,* Queens College, City University of New York, Queens College Art Center, Flushing NY

DeLura, Mark, *Prep,* Bard College, Center for Curatorial Studies and the Hessel Museum of Art, Annandale-on-Hudson NY

Del Valle, Andrea, *Dir Educ,* Brooklyn Historical Society, Brooklyn NY

del Valle, Ed, *Prof,* Florida International University, School of Art & Art History, Miami FL (S)

DelValle, Helen, *VPres,* American Society of Artists, Inc, Palatine IL

Delvin, Robert C, *Fine Arts Librn,* Illinois Wesleyan University, Sheean Library, Bloomington IL

DeManuelle, Stephanie, *Chmn Fine Arts,* Fashion Institute of Technology, Art & Design Division, New York NY (S)

De Marcos, Sally, *Asst Prof,* Baltimore City Community College, Dept of Fine Arts, Baltimore MD (S)

de Maria, Blake, *Chmn, Assoc Prof,* Santa Clara University, Dept of Art & Art History, Santa Clara CA (S)

Demarjian, Haig, *Assoc Prof,* Salem State University, Art & Design Department, Salem MA (S)

DeMarsche, Kay, *Head,* Mississippi State University, Dept of Art, Starville MS (S)

DeMarte, Jason, *Asst Prof,* Mississippi State University, Dept of Art, Starville MS (S)

deMartin, Jon, *Instr,* Woodstock School of Art, Inc, Woodstock NY (S)

Demas, Sara, *Instr,* Mohawk Valley Community College, Utica NY (S)

DeMay, Susan, *Sr Lectr,* Vanderbilt University, Dept of Art, Nashville TN (S)

Demel, August, *Instr,* Judson University, School of Art, Design & Architecture, Elgin IL (S)

Demerling, Rod, *Dir,* Lynnwood Arts Centre, Simcoe ON

Demeroukas, Marie, *Librn,* City of Springdale, Shiloh Museum of Ozark History, Springdale AR

Demers, Sheryl, *Bus Mgr,* Fitchburg Art Museum, Fitchburg MA

Demerson, Bamidele, *Museum Liaison,* National Conference of Artists, Michigan Chapter Gallery, Detroit MI

Demeter, Frank, *Sales,* Gene Roncka Willow Point Gallery/Museum, Ashland NE

DeMichiel, Helen, *Co-Dir,* National Alliance for Media Arts & Culture, San Francisco CA

DeMong, Temesa Ann, *Office & Progs Mgr,* University of Saskatchewan, Diefenbaker Canada Centre, Saskatoon SK

de Montebello, Philippe, *Dir & CEO,* The Metropolitan Museum of Art, New York NY

DeMots, Lois, *Instr,* Siena Heights University, Studio Angelico-Art Dept, Adrian MI (S)

Dempsey, Connie, *Chief Certification Officer,* Penn Foster College, School of Interior Design, Scranton PA (S)

Dempsey, David, *Assoc Dir Museum Svcs,* Smith College, Museum of Art, Northampton MA

Dempsey, John, *Prof,* Mott Community College, Fine Arts & Social Sciences Division, Flint MI (S)

Dempster, Donna, *Dir Develop,* Knoxville Museum of Art, Knoxville TN

Demulder, Kim, *Instr,* Joe Kubert, Dover NJ (S)

Denaci, Mark, *Asst Prof,* St Lawrence University, Dept of Fine Arts, Canton NY (S)

Denby, Greg, *Chief Preparator,* University of Notre Dame, Snite Museum of Art, Notre Dame IN

Dene English, Donna, *Area Coordr,* Saint Mary-of-the-Woods College, Art Dept, Saint Mary of the Woods IN (S)

Dengler, Jana, *Dir Facilities & Security,* Institute of Contemporary Art, Boston MA

den Hartog, Jacci, *Prog Dir Sculpture/New Genres,* Otis College of Art & Design, Fine Arts, Los Angeles CA (S)

Denis, Paul, *Dept Head,* Royal Ontario Museum, Dept of Western Art & Culture, Toronto ON

Denison, Dirk, *Studio Prof,* Illinois Institute of Technology, College of Architecture, Chicago IL (S)

Denk, Leslie, *Dir Pub Affairs,* Norton Simon, Pasadena CA

Denk-Leigh, Margaret, *Dept Head Printmaking,* Cleveland Institute of Art, Cleveland OH (S)

Denlsnap, Susan, *Lectr,* Bates College, Art & Visual Culture, Lewiston ME (S)

Denney, Gaylon, *Sr Admin,* Rice University, Visual & Dramatic Arts, Houston TX (S)

Denning, Elizabeth, *Pres,* Fall River Historical Society, Fall River MA

Denning, Kylee, *Cur Coll,* The San Joaquin Pioneer & Historical Society, The Haggin Museum, Stockton CA

Denninger, Nina, *Assoc Prof,* Seton Hill University, Art Program, Greensburg PA (S)

Dennis, Donna, *Prof,* Purchase College, State University of New York, School of Art+Design, Purchase NY (S)

Dennis, Fred, *Senior Cur,* Fashion Institute of Technology, The Museum at FIT, New York NY

Dennis, Linda, *Exec Dir,* Rockford Art Museum, Rockford IL

Dennis, Mac, *Asst Prof,* Elmira College, Art Dept, Elmira NY (S)

Dennis, Ryan, *Traveling Exhibit Coordr,* Museum for African Art, New York NY

Dennis, Terry, *Instr,* Rochester Community & Technical College, Art Dept, Rochester MN (S)

Dennis, Tom, *Assoc Prof,* University of Nebraska, Kearney, Dept of Art & Art History, Kearney NE (S)

Dennison, Lisa, *Deputy Dir & Sr Cur,* Guggenheim Museum Soho, New York NY

Denniston, Donna, *VPres,* Boothbay Region Art Foundation, Boothbay Harbor ME

Denny, Katie, *Dir Develop & Communs,* Socrates Sculpture Park, Long Island City NY

Denny, Walter B, *Prof,* University of Massachusetts, Amherst, Art History Program, Amherst MA (S)

DeNooyer, Caroline, *Events Coordr,* Kalamazoo Institute of Arts, Kalamazoo MI

Densmore, Christopher, *Cur,* Swarthmore College, Friends Historical Library of Swarthmore College, Swarthmore PA

Denton, Elaine, *First VPres,* Art Centre of New Jersey, Livingston NJ (S)

Denton, Margaret, *Assoc Prof,* University of Richmond, Dept of Art and Art History, Richmond VA (S)

Denton, William, *Librn,* Arts and Letters Club of Toronto, Toronto ON

D'entremont, Nil, *Corp Controller,* Art Gallery of Nova Scotia, Halifax NS

De Nunzio, John, *Chmn,* Lackawanna College, Fine Arts Dept, Scranton PA (S)

Denyer, Alison, *Asst Prof,* University of Utah, Dept of Art & Art History, Salt Lake City UT (S)

Denyes, Kaaren, *Dept Head,* Ferris State University, Visual Communication Dept, Big Rapids MI (S)

DeNyse, Deanne, *Asst Dir,* Queensborough Community College, Art Gallery, Bayside NY

dePeaux, Dick, *Painting Area Coordr,* Western Michigan University, Frostic School of Art, Kalamazoo MI

DePrisco, Michael, *Pres,* Art Institute of Philadelphia, Philadelphia PA (S)

Deragon, Rick, *Exec Dir,* Napa Valley Museum, Yountville CA

Derbentli, Betty Ann, *Asst Prof Visual Arts,* Dowling College, Dept of Visual Arts, Oakdale NY (S)

Derbes, Anne, *Chmn,* Hood College, Dept of Art, Frederick MD (S)

Derby, John, *Asst Prof,* University of Kansas, The School of the Arts, Dept of Visual Art, Lawrence KS (S)

Derezinski, Matthew, *Asst Prof,* Emporia State University, Dept of Art, Emporia KS (S)

Derksen, Karen, *Asst Gallery Dir,* Winthrop University Galleries, Rock Hill SC

Dernehl, Maggie, *Exhib Technician,* Neville Public Museum of Brown County, Green Bay WI

DeRosa, Donald, *Pres,* University of the Pacific, Jeannette Powell Art Center, Stockton CA

De Rosa, Elizabeth, *Sec,* Neustadt Collection of Tiffany Glass, Long Island City NY

DeRosa, Michael, *Head Dept,* Coffeyville Community College, Art Dept, Coffeyville KS (S)

Derr, Mary, *Press Liaison,* Independent Curators International, New York NY

Derrevere, William, *Instr,* Tulsa Community College, Art Dept, Tulsa OK (S)

Derring, Tonia M, *Asst Mgr,* Columbus Metropolitan Library, Arts & Media Division Carnegie Gallery, Columbus OH

Derry, Rebecca, *Traveling Exhibs,* Glenbow Museum, Calgary AB

Derstine, Andria, *Dir,* Oberlin College, Allen Memorial Art Museum, Oberlin OH

DeRuiter, Melissa, *Exec VPres,* Pennsylvania Academy of the Fine Arts, Philadelphia PA

Deruosi, Jessica, *Mus Shop Mgr,* Virginia Historical Society, Library, Richmond VA

DeRuvo, Janet, *Mktg,* Colorado Historical Society, Colorado History Museum, Denver CO

Dery, Joanne, *Head Librn,* Montreal Museum of Fine Arts, Library, Montreal PQ

Dery, Louise, *Pres,* Artexte Information Centre, Documentation Centre, Montreal PQ

Desabritas, Elizabeth, *Instr,* Centenary College, Humanities Dept, Hackettstown NJ (S)

Desai, Dipti, *Prog Dir Art Educ & PhD,* New York University, Dept of Art & Art Professions, New York NY (S)

Desai, Madhuri, *Asst Prof,* Pennsylvania State University, University Park, Dept of Art History, University Park PA (S)

Desai, Smita, *Sec,* Passaic County Community College, Broadway, LRC, and Hamilton Club Galleries, Paterson NJ

de Sales Dinneen, Marie, *Chmn,* Regis College, Dept of Art, Weston MA (S)

DeSalvo, Donna, *Chief Cur,* Whitney Museum of American Art, New York NY

Deschamps, Yves, *Instr,* Universite de Montreal, Dept of Art History, Montreal PQ (S)

de Sciora, Susan, *Dir,* Hewlett-Woodmere Public Library, Hewlett NY

Descoteaux, Ann, *Dir Docents,* Fitchburg Art Museum, Fitchburg MA

Desgagnes, Alexis, *Artist & Dir,* VU Centre De Diffusion Et De Production De La Photographie, Quebec PQ

Deshauteurs, Aurora, *Librn,* Pennsylvania Academy of the Fine Arts, Library, Philadelphia PA

DeSiano, Michael, *Coordr Art Educ,* Kean University, Fine Arts Dept, Union NJ (S)

Desiderio, Vincent, *Instr,* New York Academy of Art, Graduate School of Figurative Art, New York NY (S)

de Silva, Kauka, *Chmn,* University of Hawaii, Kapiolani Community College, Honolulu HI (S)

De Silvo, Verneal, *Prof,* Compton Community College, Art Dept, Compton CA (S)

Desjatlais, Sandi, *Exec Asst,* Saskatchewan Arts Board, Regina SK

Deslis, Konstantine, *Develop Dir,* Kimball Art Center, Park City UT

DeSloover, Rose, *Dean,* Marygrove College, Department of Art, Detroit MI (S)

de Smet, Louis, *Treas,* Art Centre of New Jersey, Livingston NJ (S)

Desmett, Don, *Exhib Dir,* Western Michigan University, Gwen Frostic School of Art, Kalamazoo MI

Desmond, Kathleen, *Prof,* Central Missouri State University, Dept Art & Design, Warrensburg MO (S)

Desormeau, Monique, *Cur Educ,* Flint Institute of Arts, Flint MI

Desormeau, Monique, *Cur Educ,* Flint Institute of Arts, Library, Flint MI

Desrochers, Donna, *Dir Mktg,* Rhode Island School of Design, Museum of Art, Providence RI

Des Rochers, Jacques, *Cur Canadian Art,* Montreal Museum of Fine Arts, Montreal PQ

Des Roches, Anne-Marie, *Assoc Dir & Sr Policy Advisor,* Canadian Conference of the Arts, Ottawa ON

Dessornes, Maria, *CEO & VPres,* Conejo Valley Art Museum, Thousand Oaks CA

Dessureault, Pierre, *Assoc Cur,* Canadian Museum of Contemporary Photography, Ottawa ON

Desy, Margherita, *Cur,* USS Constitution Museum, Boston MA

DeTample, Kelly, *Shop Assoc,* Belle Grove Inc., Belle Grove Plantation, Middletown VA

Detkin, Margie, *Secy,* Marblehead Arts Association, Inc, Marblehead MA

Detrich, David, *Grad Coordr,* Clemson University, College of Architecture, Arts & Humanities, Art Dept, Clemson SC (S)

DeTurk, Sabrina, *Adj Prof,* Saint Joseph's University, Art Dept, Philadelphia PA (S)

Detweiler, Kelly, *Chmn, Prof,* Santa Clara University, Dept of Art & Art History, Santa Clara CA (S)

Deupi, Jill, *Dir,* Fairfield University, Thomas J Walsh Art Gallery, Fairfield CT

Deutsch, Sanna Saks, *Registrar,* Honolulu Academy of Arts, The Art Center at Linekona, Honolulu HI (S)

Deutsch, Todd, *Chmn & Assoc Prof,* St. Catherine University, Art & Art History Dept, Saint Paul MN (S)

Devening, Dan, *Lectr,* Northwestern University, Evanston, Dept of Art Theory & Practice, Evanston IL (S)

Devereaux, Kent, *Dept Chair,* Cornish College of the Arts, Fisher Gallery, Seattle WA

Devereaux Lewis, Caitlain, *Visual Resources Cur,* University of Albany, State University of New York, Visual Resources Library, Albany NY

De Verges, Jolene, *Librn Architecture & Visual Arts,* Massachusetts Institute of Technology, Rotch Library of Architecture & Planning, Cambridge MA

de Ville, Roy V, *Dir University Gallery,* Louisiana State University at Alexandria, University Gallery, Alexandria LA

deVille, Roy V, *Prof Art,* Louisiana State University at Alexandria, Dept of Fine Arts & Design, Alexandria LA (S)

Devine, Jack, *Bd Pres,* Ocean City Art Center, Ocean City NJ

DeVine, Meta, *Mus Shop Mgr,* Minnesota Historical Society, Saint Paul MN

Devine, Michael, *Acting Dir,* National Archives & Records Administration, Harry S Truman Museum and Library, Independence MO

Devine, Michelle, *Develop Officer Grant Funding,* Contemporary Arts Center, Cincinnati OH

Devinney, Rosemary A, *Mgr & Coordr,* Shoshone Bannock Tribes, Shoshone Bannock Tribal Museum, Fort Hall ID

DeVinny, Douglas, *Prof,* University of Wisconsin-Parkside, Art Dept, Kenosha WI (S)

de Vletter, Martien, *Assoc Dir Coll,* Canadian Centre for Architecture, Library, Montreal PQ

Devlin, Eric, *Pres,* Musee des Maitres et Artisans du Quebec, Montreal PQ

Devlin, Peter, *Tour Interpreter,* Farmington Village Green & Library Association, Stanley-Whitman House, Farmington CT

Devlin, Teresa, *Pub Rel Dir,* The Historic New Orleans Collection, Williams Research Center, New Orleans LA

Devon, Marjorie, *Dir,* University of New Mexico, Tamarind Institute, Albuquerque NM (S)

Devono, Lanny, *Chmn,* Eastern Washington University, Dept of Art, Cheney WA (S)

DeVries, Karl, *Asst Dir,* Ships of the Sea Maritime Museum, Savannah GA

Dewaele, Robert, *Pres,* Artists' Cooperative Gallery, Omaha NE

Dewald, Ann, *Dir,* Archaeological Society of Ohio, Indian Museum of Lake County, Ohio, Willoughby OH

Dewald, Ann, *Dir,* Archaeological Society of Ohio, Indian Museum of Lake County Library, Willoughby OH

DeWalt, James D, *Head,* Free Library of Philadelphia, Rare Book Dept, Philadelphia PA

DeWeese, Josh, *Asst Prof Ceramics,* Montana State University, School of Art, Bozeman MT (S)

Dewell, Judith, *Assoc Prof,* Loyola University of Chicago, Fine Arts Dept, Chicago IL (S)

Dewey, Dennis, *COO & CFO,* National Assembly of State Arts Agencies, Washington DC

Dewey, Kevin, *Music,* Henry Ford Community College, McKenzie Fine Art Ctr, Dearborn MI (S)

Dewey, Toby, *Dir,* Charles River School, Creative Arts Program, Dover MA (S)

Dewey II, Tom, *Assoc Prof,* University of Mississippi, Department of Art, University MS (S)

Dewhurst, Marit, *Prog Dir Art Ed Asst Prof,* City College of New York, Art Dept, New York NY (S)

de Witt, David, *Bader Cur European Art,* Queen's University, Agnes Etherington Art Centre, Kingston ON

DeWitt, Karen, *Head Design Library,* North Carolina State University, Harrye Lyons Design Library, Raleigh NC

DeWitt, Lloyd, *Assoc Cur,* Philadelphia Museum of Art, John G Johnson Collection, Philadelphia PA

DeWitt, Marcia, *Pres Board,* Rehoboth Art League, Inc, Rehoboth Beach DE

Dewitte, Debra, *Adj Asst Prof,* University of Texas at Arlington, Art & Art History Department, Arlington TX (S)

DeWitte, Elizabeth, *Instr,* University of Utah, Dept of Art & Art History, Salt Lake City UT (S)

Dey, Barbara, *Ref Librn,* Colorado Historical Society, Stephen H Hart Library, Denver CO

Deyasi, Marco, *Asst Prof,* University of Idaho/College of Art & Architecture, Dept of Art & Design, Moscow ID (S)

De Young, Jim, *Sr Conservator,* Milwaukee Art Museum, Milwaukee WI

DeYoung Kohler, Ruth, *Dir,* Sheboygan Arts Foundation, Inc, John Michael Kohler Arts Center, Sheboygan WI

d'Harnoncourt, Anne, *The George D Widener Dir & CEO,* Philadelphia Museum of Art, Main Building, Philadelphia PA

d'Humieres, Chislain, *Dir,* The Speed Art Museum, Louisville KY

Diamantopoulos, Aella, *Chief Conservator,* Pennsylvania Academy of the Fine Arts, Philadelphia PA

Diamato, Paul, *Instr,* Maine College of Art, Portland ME (S)

Diamond, Julie, *Dir Pub Rels,* The Long Island Museum of American Art, History & Carriages, Stony Brook NY

Diamond, Pamela, *Dir Mktg,* American Craft Council, Minneapolis MN

Diamond, Sara, *Pres,* OCAD University, Toronto ON (S)

Diamond, Tom, *Head Ref & Coll Develop Svcs,* Louisiana State University, Middleton Library, Baton Rouge LA

Diamond-Nigh, John, *Asst,* Elmira College, Art Dept, Elmira NY (S)

Diaz, Alfred, *Student Aid Coordr,* Escuela de Artes Plasticas de Puerto Rico, San Juan PR (S)

Diaz, Alfred, *Student Aid Coordr,* Escuela de Artes Plasticas de Puerto Rico, San Juan PR (S)

Diaz, Eduardo, *CEO & Dir,* National Hispanic Cultural Center, Art Museum, Albuquerque NM

Diaz, Josef, *Cur,* Museum of New Mexico, Palace of Governors, Santa Fe NM

Diaz, Julius, *Dir Educ,* Social & Public Art Resource Center, (SPARC), Venice CA

Diaz, Lynette, *Jr Mus Supv,* Newark Museum Association, Junior Museum, Newark NJ

Dibble, Valerie, *Community Coordr,* American Print Alliance, Peachtree City GA

Dibley, Jason, *Exhibs Coordr,* Houston Center For Photography, Houston TX

DiCapua, Ray, *Assoc Head,* University of Connecticut, Dept of Art & Art History, Storrs CT (S)

DiCicco, John, *Slide Librn,* Providence College, Art & Art History Dept, Providence RI (S)

DiCindio, Carissa, *Cur Educ,* University of Georgia, Georgia Museum of Art, Athens GA

Dick, James, *Founder & Dir,* James Dick Foundation, Festival - Institute, Round Top TX

Dickenson, Victoria, *Exec Dir,* McCord Museum of Canadian History, Montreal PQ

Dickerson, Roger, *Music,* Southern University in New Orleans, Fine Arts & Philosophy Dept, New Orleans LA (S)

Dickerson, Vermell, *Accounting Officer,* Salisbury University, Ward Museum of Wildfowl Art, Salisbury MD

Dickes, Rodger, *MFA,* Glendale Community College, Visual & Performing Arts Div, Glendale CA (S)

Dickey, Mike, *Adminr,* Arrow Rock State Historic Site, Arrow Rock MO

Dickey, Shawn, *Recorder,* Mississippi University for Women, Fine Arts Gallery, Columbus MS

Dickinson, Carolyn, *Head Fine Arts & Av Dept,* Salt Lake City Public Library, Fine Arts & Audiovisual Dept and Atrium Gallery, Salt Lake City UT

Dickinson, James L, *Vol Pres,* Medina Railroad Museum, Medina NY

Dickinson, John, *Asst Prof,* Wright State University, Dept of Art & Art History, Dayton OH (S)

Dickinson, Nancy, *Dir's Admin Asst,* Cornell University, Herbert F Johnson Museum of Art, Ithaca NY

Dickinson, Pat, *Coordr,* Baycrest Centre for Geriatric Care, The Morris & Sally Justein of Baycrest Heritage Museum, Toronto ON

Dickinson, Susan, *Admin Asst,* Rodman Hall Arts Centre, Saint Catharines ON

Dickson, Lu, *Sales Gallery Coordr,* Green Hill Center for North Carolina Art, Greensboro NC

Dickson, Mary, *Instr,* Oklahoma State University, Graphic Arts Dept, Visual Communications, Okmulgee OK (S)

Dickson, Rachael, *Events Coordr,* University of California, Berkeley, The Magnes Collection of Jewish Art & Life, Berkeley CA

DiCola Matos, Jennifer, *Dir Educ,* Noah Webster House, Inc, Noah Webster House & West Hartford Historical Society, West Hartford CT

DiCosola, Angela, *Prof Art, Ceramics,* Florida Atlantic University, D F Schmidt College of Arts & Letters Dept of Visual Arts & Art History, Boca Raton FL (S)

DiDiego, Charles, *Adjunct Asst Prof,* New York Institute of Technology, Fine Arts Dept, Old Westbury NY (S)

Diduk, Barbara, *Prof,* Dickinson College, Dept of Art & Art History, Carlisle PA (S)

Diebold, William J, *Chmn Art History & Humanities,* Reed College, Dept of Art, Portland OR (S)

Diedrich, Norah, *Exec Dir,* Evanston Art Center, Evanston IL

Diehl, Kathy, *Mgr,* Indianapolis Marion County Public Library, Central Library, Indianapolis IN

Diehl, Lindsay, *Exec Dir,* Wenham Museum, Timothy Pickering Library, Wenham MA

Diehl, Steve, *Assoc Prof,* Rochester Institute of Technology, School of Photographic Arts & Sciences, Rochester NY (S)

Diel, Lori, *Prof,* Texas Christian University, School of Art, Fort Worth TX (S)

DiEleuterio, Rachael, *Head Librn,* Delaware Art Museum, Helen Farr Sloan Library, Wilmington DE

Diemente, Deborah, *Registrar,* Worcester Art Museum, Worcester MA

Dienes, Claire, *Assoc Mus Librn,* The Metropolitan Museum of Art, Image Library, New York NY

Diercks, Robert, *Co-Chmn,* Franklin Pierce College, Dept of Fine Arts & Graphic Communications, Rindge NH (S)

Dierdorf, Jenn, *Gallery Dir,* Soho 20 Gallery, New York NY

Dierdorff, Jo, *Dance Chmn,* Riverside Community College, Dept of Art & Mass Media, Riverside CA (S)

Dieringer, Holland, *Dir,* Florence & Chafetz Hillel House at Boston University, Rubin-Frankel Gallery , Boston MA

Dierks, Chris, *Archive Mgr,* Van Alen Institute, New York NY

Diersen, Jenny, *Art Educ Coordr,* Kimball Art Center, Park City UT

Dieter, Joseph, *Lectr,* Johns Hopkins University, School of Medicine, Dept of Art as Applied to Medicine, Baltimore MD (S)

Diethorn, Karie, *Chief Cur,* Independence National Historical Park, Library, Philadelphia PA

Diethorn, Karie, *Chief Mus Branch,* Independence National Historical Park, Philadelphia PA

Dietrich, Gretchen, *Exec Dir,* University of Utah, Utah Museum of Fine Arts, Salt Lake City UT

Dietrich, Julia, *Dir Mktg,* Robert & Mary Montgomery Armory Art Center, Armory Art Center, West Palm Beach FL

Dietz, Kirk, *Mus Specialist,* United States Department of the Interior, Interior Museum, Washington DC

Dietz, Ulysses G, *Cur Decorative Arts,* Newark Museum Association, The Newark Museum, Newark NJ

Dietze, Christine, *Deputy Dir Finance & Admin,* The Baltimore Museum of Art, Baltimore MD

Dietzel, Tracy, *Instr,* Edgewood College, Art Dept, Madison WI (S)

Dietzel, Tracy Doreen, *Dir Exhibs,* St. Johns University, Alice R Rogers/Target Galleries, Collegeville MN

DiFabatino, Peter, *Co-Chmn,* Art Center College of Design, Pasadena CA (S)

Difee, Nancy, *Chmn,* GumTree Museum of Art, Tupelo MS

DiGennaro, Amy, *Instr,* Macalester College, Art Dept, Saint Paul MN (S)

Diggle, Justin, *Assoc Prof,* University of Utah, Dept of Art & Art History, Salt Lake City UT (S)

DiGirolamo, Michele, *Dir Communs,* Independence Seaport Museum, Philadelphia PA

Dignan, Paul, *Instr,* University of Waterloo, Fine Arts Dept, Waterloo ON (S)

Dillard Rech, Lori, *CEO & Pres,* Independence Seaport Museum, Philadelphia PA

Dillaway, Brandelyn, *Dir,* Mt San Jacinto College, Fine Art Gallery, San Jacinto CA

Dillaway, Brandelyn, *Gallery Dir,* Mt San Jacinto College, Art Dept, San Jacinto CA (S)

Dillon, David, *Exhib Coordr,* Contemporary Arts Center, Cincinnati OH

Dillon, Heather, *Cur Educ,* Florence Museum, Florence SC

Dillon, Sheila, *Assoc Prof & Dir Undergrad Studies,* Duke University, Dept of Art, Art History & Visual Studies, Durham NC (S)

Dillon, Tambra, *Dir,* Bard College, Fisher Art Center, Annandale-on-Hudson NY

Dillon, Tremenda, *Sandzen Foundation Pres & CEO,* Birger Sandzen Memorial Gallery, Lindsborg KS

Dills, Keith, *Prof,* California Polytechnic State University at San Luis Obispo, Dept of Art & Design, San Luis Obispo CA (S)

DiLoreto, Lauren, *Exhib Mgr,* Whitney Museum of American Art, New York NY

Dilworth, Robert, *Interim Chair Art & Art History,* University of Rhode Island, Fine Arts Center Galleries, Kingston RI

DiManno, Marie, *Mus Shop Mgr,* American Folk Art Museum, New York NY

DiMaria, Tom, *Exec Dir,* Creative Growth Art Center, Oakland CA

DiMattia, Ernest A, *Pres,* Ferguson Library, Stamford CT

Dimattio, Vincent, *Chmn,* Monmouth University, Dept of Art & Design, West Long Branch NJ (S)

DiMeo Carlozzi, Annette, *Dep Dir Arts & Progs,* University of Texas at Austin, Blanton Museum of Art, Austin TX

Dimock, George, *Prof,* University of North Carolina at Greensboro, Art Dept, Greensboro NC (S)

Dimond, Thomas, *Prof Art,* Eastern Oregon University, School of Arts & Science, La Grande OR (S)

Dimond, V Scott, *Cur Visual Arts,* Southern Alleghenies Museum of Art, Loretto Facility, Loretto PA

DiNardo, Matt, *Campus Mgr,* Touchstone Center for Crafts, Hart Moore Museum, Farmington PA

Dinces, Anna, *Mktg Dir,* Creative Time, New York NY

Dineen, Benjamin, *Chmn of Brd,* Jersey City Museum, Jersey City NJ

Dines, Diana, *Treas,* Lunenburg Art Gallery Society, Lunenburg NS

Dingilian, Sonia, *Registrar,* Fashion Institute of Technology, The Museum at FIT, New York NY

Dingwerth, Shaun T, *Exec Dir,* Richmond Art Museum, Richmond IN

Dingwerth, Shaun T, *Exec Dir,* Richmond Art Museum, Library, Richmond IN

Dininno, Steve, *Instr,* Woodstock School of Art, Inc, Woodstock NY (S)

Dinkins, Stephanie, *Assoc Prof,* Stony Brook University, College of Arts & Sciences, Dept of Art, Stony Brook NY (S)

DiNoble, Lisa, *Head Colls & Database Mgr,* National Gallery of Canada, Library, Ottawa ON

Dinschel, Elizabeth, *Educ Specialist,* National Archives & Records Administration, Herbert Hoover Presidential Library - Museum, West Branch IA

Dion, Francois, *Dir,* Artexte Information Centre, Documentation Centre, Montreal PQ

Dion, Phil, *Preparator,* Contemporary Art Gallery Society of British Columbia, Vancouver BC

Diope, Corinne, *Asst Prof,* James Madison University, School of Art & Art History, Harrisonburg VA (S)

DiOrio, Barbara, *Adj,* University of Saint Joseph, Connecticut, Dept of Fine Arts, West Hartford CT (S)

DiPietro, David, *Assoc Prof Art (Fayette Campus),* Pennsylvania State University, University Park, Penn State School of Visual Arts, University Park PA (S)

Dirado, Stephen, *Instr,* Clark University, Dept of Visual & Performing Arts, Worcester MA (S)

Diresta, Kathleen, *Mus Shop Mgr,* Sea Cliff Village Museum, Sea Cliff NY

Dirican, Alan, *Deputy Dir Operations & Capital Planning,* The Baltimore Museum of Art, Baltimore MD

DiRisio, Tony, *Dir,* Nova Scotia College of Art and Design, Anna Leonowens Gallery, Halifax NS

DiRito, Ron, *Photog,* Montserrat College of Art, Beverly MA (S)

Dirocco, Rose, *Dir,* Lycoming College Gallery, Williamsport PA

Disbro, Bill, *Art Coordr,* Jamestown Community College, Arts, Humanities & Health Sciences Division, Jamestown NY (S)

Disney, Betty, *Dir,* Cypress College, Fine Arts Gallery, Cypress CA

DiSpigna, Antonio, *Adjunct Assoc Prof,* New York Institute of Technology, Fine Arts Dept, Old Westbury NY (S)

Disviscour, Jeannine, *Deputy Dir & Chief Cur,* Maryland Historical Society, Museum of Maryland History, Baltimore MD

Ditmore, Patricia, *Office Mgr,* Grace Museum, Inc, Abilene TX

Dito, Norman E, *Retail PM & Dir Mktg,* Boston Properties LLC, San Francisco CA

DiTommaso, Francis, *Dir,* School of Visual Arts, Visual Arts Museum, New York NY

Dittman, Emily, *Coll & Exhib Coordr,* Syracuse University, SUArt Galleries, Syracuse NY

Dittman, Marilyn, *Dir Develop,* New Orleans Museum of Art, New Orleans LA

Dittmer, Ryan, *Film Program Mgr,* Urban Institute for Contemporary Arts, Grand Rapids MI

Dittrich, Dennis, *MFA,* New Jersey City University, Art Dept, Jersey City NJ (S)

Dittrich, Dennis, *Pres,* Society of Illustrators, New York NY

Dittrich, Dennis, *Pres,* Society of Illustrators, Museum of American Illustration, New York NY

Diviney, David, *Asst Cur,* Southern Alberta Art Gallery, Library, Lethbridge AB

Divola, John, *Prof,* University of California, Riverside, Dept of Art, Riverside CA (S)

Dixie, Gwen, *Art Librn,* J Eric Johnson, Fine Arts Division, Dallas TX

Dixon, Bob, *Assoc Prof,* University of Illinois at Springfield, Visual Arts Program, Springfield IL (S)

Dixon, David, *Assoc Prof,* East Tennessee State University, College of Arts and Sciences, Dept of Art & Design, Johnson City TN (S)

Dixon, David, *Communs Coordr,* Rockford Art Museum, Rockford IL

Dixon, Jenny, *Exec Dir,* Isamu Noguchi, Isamu Noguchi Garden Museum, Long Island City NY

Dixon, Laurinda, *Prof,* Syracuse University, Dept of Fine Arts (Art History), Syracuse NY (S)

Dixon, Lorrainne, *Pres,* Art Gallery of Greater Victoria, Victoria BC

Dixon, Melanie, *COO,* National Art Education Association, Reston VA

Dixon, Michael, *Asst Prof,* Albion College, Bobbitt Visual Arts Center, Albion MI

Dixon, Susan M, *Asst Prof, Art Hist,* University of Tulsa, School of Art, Tulsa OK (S)

Dixon, Terry, *Computer Art,* College of Lake County, Art Dept, Grayslake IL (S)

Dixon, Yvonne, *Prof,* Trinity College, Fine Arts Program, Washington DC (S)

Dixson, Ronna, *Coll Mgr,* New York State Office of Parks, Recreation and Historic Preservation, Bureau of Historic Sites, Waterford NY

Dizik, Elizabeth, *Library Asst,* Cranbrook Art Museum, Library, Bloomfield Hills MI

Djoka, Mimi, *Lectr,* Humboldt State University, College of Arts & Humanities, Art Dept, Arcata CA (S)

Dluhy, Deborah H, *Dean,* School of the Museum of Fine Arts, Boston MA (S)

Dmytriw, Charles, *Prof,* Northwestern Connecticut Community College, Fine Arts Dept, Winsted CT (S)

Doane, Maureen, *Operations Coordr,* The Dallas Contemporary, Dallas Visual Art Center, Dallas TX

Dobbin, Glenn, *Deputy Dir Opers,* Royal Ontario Museum, Toronto ON

Dobbins, John, *Prof,* University of Virginia, McIntire Dept of Art, Charlottesville VA (S)

Dobbs, Christopher, *Dir,* Noah Webster House, Inc, Noah Webster House & West Hartford Historical Society, West Hartford CT

Dobbs, Jennifer, *Dir Develop,* Erie Art Museum, Erie PA

Dobbs, Paul, *Library Dir,* Massachusetts College of Art, Morton R Godine Library, Boston MA

Dobrea, George, *Dir,* Saint Mary's Romanian Orthodox Cathedral, Romanian Ethnic Museum, Cleveland OH

Dobson, Jenni, *Coordr Educ,* Loveland Museum/Gallery, Loveland CO

Docherty, Linda, *Prof,* Bowdoin College, Art Dept, Brunswick ME (S)

Docktor, Mali, *Provincial Exhibs Chmn,* Alberta Society of Artists, Calgary AB

Dodd, Beth, *Cur & Librn,* Society for Commercial Archeology, Little AR

Dodd, Beth, *Head Librn & Cur Alexander Architectural Archive,* University of Texas at Austin, Architecture & Planning Library, Austin TX

Dodd, Jerry, *Instr Sculpture,* Texas A&M University Commerce, Dept of Art, Commerce TX (S)

Dodds, Jerrilynn, *Dean,* Sarah Lawrence College, Dept of Art History, Bronxville NY (S)

Dodds, Richard J, *Cur Maritime History,* Calvert Marine Museum, Solomons MD

Dodge, John W, *Registrar,* The First National Bank of Chicago, Art Collection, Chicago IL

Dodge, Robert, *Instr,* Bucks County Community College, Fine Arts Dept, Newtown PA (S)

Dodge-Peters Daiss, Susan, *Dir Educ,* University of Rochester, Memorial Art Gallery, Rochester NY

Dodson, Angie, *COO, Assoc & Dir Interpretation & Vis Svcs,* Hillwood Museum & Gardens Foundation, Hillwood Estate Museum & Gardens, Washington DC

Dodson, Drew, *Asst Prof,* Radford University, Art Dept, Radford VA (S)

Dodson, Howard, *Dir,* The New York Public Library, Schomburg Center for Research in Black Culture, New York NY

Dodson, Karen, *Vol Coordr,* Erie Art Museum, Erie PA

Dodson, Linda, *Registrar,* Washington County Museum of Fine Arts, Hagerstown MD

Doell, Margaret, *Head Chair & Prof Art,* Adams State College, Dept of Visual Arts, Alamosa CO (S)

Doering, James, *Instr Music,* Randolph-Macon College, Dept of the Arts, Ashland VA (S)

Doern-Danko, Maura, *Gen Educ,* Art Institute of Pittsburgh, Pittsburgh PA (S)

Doerner, Richard L, *Museum Specialist,* United States Senate Commission on Art, Washington DC

Doherty, Deirdre, *Dir Develop*, The Long Island Museum of American Art, History & Carriages, Stony Brook NY

Doherty, Dornith, *Prof Photog*, University of North Texas, College of Visual Arts & Design, Denton TX (S)

Doherty, Laura, *Communs Coordr*, Art Complex Museum, Carl A. Weyerhaeuser Library, Duxbury MA

Doherty, Meghan C, *Dir & Asst Prof*, Berea College, Art & Art History Program, Berea KY (S)

Doherty, Meghan C, *Dir & Cur*, Berea College, Ulmann Doris Galleries, Berea KY

Doherty, Richard, *Assoc Prof Photog*, Tarrant County College, Art Dept, Hurst TX (S)

Doherty, Ryan, *Cur*, Southern Alberta Art Gallery, Lethbridge AB

Doiron, Julie Cormier, *Mgr Communs*, Canadian Museums Association, Association des Musees Canadiens, Ottawa ON

Doktorski, Eileen, *Dept Chair*, Mt San Jacinto College, Art Dept, San Jacinto CA (S)

Dolan, Anne R, *Dir*, Lincoln County Historical Association, Inc, Library, Wiscasset ME

Dolan, Douglas, *Exec Dir*, Bucks County Historical Society, Mercer Museum, Doylestown PA

Dolan, Julia, *Minor White Cur Photog*, Portland Art Museum, Portland OR

Dolan, Susan, *Coll Mgr & Registrar*, Tucson Museum of Art and Historic Block, Tucson AZ

Doland, Deborah, *Mus Protection Visitor Svcs Asst*, Alaska Department of Education, Division of Libraries, Archives & Museums, Sheldon Jackson Museum, Sitka AK

Dolbin, Steve, *Dir*, Shippensburg University, Kauffman Gallery, Shippensburg PA

Dolbin, Steven, *Asst Prof*, Shippensburg University, Art Dept, Shippensburg PA (S)

Dolby, Billann, *Bd Mem*, Kennebec Valley Art Association, Harlow Gallery, Hallowell ME

Dole, Donnae, *Exec Dir*, Hoosier Salon Patrons Association, Inc, Art Gallery & Membership Organization, Indianapolis IN

Dolembo, Marie, *Adjunct Asst Prof Art History*, Johnson County Community College, Fine Arts Dept & Art History Dept, Overland Park KS (S)

Dolgos, Charles, *Prof*, Miami-Dade Community College, Arts & Philosophy Dept, Miami FL (S)

Doll, Don, *Instr*, Creighton University, Fine & Performing Arts Dept, Omaha NE (S)

Doll, Linda, *Asst Dir*, Wichita State University, Ulrich Museum of Art, Wichita KS

Doll, Linda A, *Pres*, National Watercolor Society, San Pedro CA

Doll, Nancy, *Dir*, University of North Carolina at Greensboro, Weatherspoon Art Museum, Greensboro NC

Dollar, Betsy, *Exec Dir*, Springfield Art Association of Edwards Place, Springfield IL

Dollard, Mehri Rae, *Dir*, The Society of Layerists in Multi-Media (SLMM), Albuquerque NM

Dolman, Marjorie, *Admin Asst*, Charles B Goddard, Ardmore OK

Dolton, Dennis, *Dir Gallery*, University of Southern Colorado, College of Liberal & Fine Arts, Pueblo CO

Dombrowski, Mark, *Cataloging*, Siena Heights College, Art Library, Adrian MI

Domen, Dennis, *Exhib Coordr*, Okanagan Heritage Museum, Kelowna BC

Domencil, Laura, *Dir*, Pittsburgh Center for the Arts, Pittsburgh PA

Domine, Doug, *Chmn Dept*, Northwestern Michigan College, Art Dept, Traverse City MI (S)

Domingo, Beatrice Santo, *VChmn*, Queen Sofia Spanish Institute, New York NY

Dominguez, Frank, *Chmn*, Bucks County Community College, Hicks Art Center, Newtown PA

Dominguez, Frank, *Chmn Dept*, Bucks County Community College, Fine Arts Dept, Newtown PA (S)

Dominguez, Jose, *Dir*, Pyramid Atlantic, Silver Spring MD

Dominguez, Sonia, *Treas*, Museo de Arte de Puerto Rico, San Juan PR

Dominguez, Sonia, *Treas*, Museo de Arte de Puerto Rico, San Juan PR

Dominique, Gina, *Assoc Prof & Dept Chmn*, Delta College, Art Dept, University Center MI (S)

Domino, Dusty, *Dir Art Dept*, North Arkansas Community-Technical College, Art Dept, Harrison AR (S)

Domkoski, David, *Mgr Community Rels*, Tacoma Public Library, Handforth Gallery, Tacoma WA

Domkowski, Dorothy, *Graphics Design & Editor*, The National Shrine of the North American Martyrs, Fultonville NY

Dompierre, Louise, *Pres & CEO*, Art Gallery of Hamilton, Hamilton ON

Donadio, Emmie, *Chief Cur*, Middlebury College, Museum of Art, Middlebury VT

Donaher, Sean, *interim Exec & Artistic Dir*, Center for Exploratory & Perceptual Art, CEPA Gallery, Buffalo NY

Donaher, Sean, *Artistic Dir*, Center for Exploratory & Perceptual Art, CEPA Library, Buffalo NY

Donahue, Deirdre, *Librn*, International Center of Photography, Research Center, New York NY

Donahue, Gail, *Asst Dir*, Frank Lloyd Wright, Mount Vernon VA

Donahue, Gail, *Asst Dir*, Woodlawn/The Pope-Leighey, Mount Vernon VA

Donahue, Kevin, *Drawing*, Henry Ford Community College, McKenzie Fine Art Ctr, Dearborn MI (S)

Donahue, Marsha, *Founder*, North Light Gallery, Millinocket ME

Donahue, Mary, *Asst Prof*, Chadron State College, Dept of Art, Chadron NE (S)

Donahue, Michael, *Chmn*, Temple College, Art Dept, Temple TX (S)

Donahue-Semenza, Stacey, *Art Dept Coordr*, Keystone College, Fine Arts Dept, LaPlume PA (S)

Donahue-Wallace, Kelly, *Assoc Prof Art History*, University of North Texas, College of Visual Arts & Design, Denton TX (S)

Donaldson, Jeff, *Cur*, Booth Western Art Museum, Cartersville GA

Donaldson, Margo, *Sr Develop Mgr*, Museum for African Art, New York NY

Donaldson, P, *Instr*, Golden West College, Visual Art Dept, Huntington Beach CA (S)

Donaldson, Thomas E, *Prof*, Cleveland State University, Art Dept, Cleveland OH (S)

Donatelli, Kara, *Asst Prof*, South Plains College, Fine Arts Dept, Levelland TX (S)

Donati, Grace, *Mem Svcs Coordr*, Ontario Crafts Council, OCC Gallery, Toronto ON

Dondero, Mary, *Asst Prof*, Bridgewater State College, Art Dept, Bridgewater MA (S)

Donegan, Pamela, *Librn/Cataloger*, Institute of American Indian Arts, College of Contemporary Native Arts Library and Archives, Santa Fe NM

Donelson, Gretchen, *Asst*, Ohio State University, Fine Arts Library, Columbus OH

Donesky, Grant, *Design Dept Chair*, Cornish College of the Arts, Art Dept, Seattle WA (S)

Doney, Todd, *Adjunct Prof*, College of Saint Elizabeth, Art Dept, Morristown NJ (S)

Donick, Carol, *Library Dir*, Alice Curtis Desmond, Hudson River Reference Collection, Garrison NY

Donjuan, Carlos, *Adj Asst Prof*, University of Texas at Arlington, Art & Art History Department, Arlington TX (S)

Donkersley, Vicki, *Cur Exhibits*, Tohono Chul Park, Tucson AZ

Donley, Robert, *Prof*, DePaul University, Dept of Art, Chicago IL (S)

Donley, Thomas, *Photog*, Art Institute of Pittsburgh, Pittsburgh PA (S)

Donnelly, Daniel, *Co-Chair ADAD Dept*, Butte College, Art Gallery, Oroville CA

Donnelly, John, *Instr*, Mount Vernon Nazarene University, Art Dept, Mount Vernon OH (S)

Donnelly, Peter, *Pres*, Corporate Council for the Arts/Arts Fund, Seattle WA

Donner, Heidi, *Community Relations & Educ Programs*, Saint Mary's College of California, Hearst Art Gallery, Moraga CA

Donohoe, Kevin, *Chmn Bd*, Pennsylvania Academy of the Fine Arts, Philadelphia PA

Donohue, Adrienne, *Designer*, Concord Museum, Concord MA

Donohue, Bill, *Exec Dir Jekyll Island*, Jekyll Island Museum, Jekyll Island GA

Donovan, Jeremiah, *Prof*, State University of New York, College at Cortland, Dept Art & Art History, Cortland NY (S)

Donovan, Margaret, *Dir Pub Rels*, Southern Vermont Art Center, Manchester VT

Donovan, Margie, *Develop Assoc*, Contemporary Art Center of Virginia, Virginia Beach VA

Donovan, Maureen, *Registrar*, Harvard University, Harvard University Art Museums, Cambridge MA

Donovan, Michael, *Asst Dir*, Missouri Arts Council, Saint Louis MO

Donovan Fisher, Jeanne, *Chair*, Bard College, Fisher Art Center, Annandale-on-Hudson NY

Dooley, Beth, *Treas*, Kent Art Association, Gallery, Kent CT

Dooley, Michael, *Instr*, University of Utah, Dept of Art & Art History, Salt Lake City UT (S)

Dooley, Tim, *Assoc Prof*, University of Northern Iowa, Dept of Art, Cedar Falls IA (S)

Dooley, William, *Dir*, University of Alabama, Sarah Moody Gallery of Art, Tuscaloosa AL

Dooling, Daniella, *Asst Prof*, Colgate University, Dept of Art & Art History, Hamilton NY (S)

Dooner, Steve, *Asst Prof*, Quincy College, Art Dept, Quincy MA (S)

Doran, Camille, *Registrar*, University of Minnesota Duluth, Tweed Museum of Art, Duluth MN

Doran, Faye, *Prof*, Harding University, Dept of Art & Design, Searcy AR (S)

Doran, Marie Andree, *Dir Visual Arts*, Universite Quebec Cite Universitaire, School of Visual Arts, Quebec PQ (S)

Dorant, Liz, *Graphic Designer*, Kitchener-Waterloo Art Gallery, Kitchener ON

Dorazewski-Smouse, Kimberly, *Colls Mgr & Registrar*, University of Colorado, CU Art Museum, Boulder CO

Dorcey-Naber, Penny, *Secy*, Monroe County Community College, Humanities Division, Monroe MI (S)

Dorethy, Rex, *Prof*, University of Wisconsin-Stevens Point, Dept of Art & Design, Stevens Point WI (S)

Dorey, Audrey, *Admin Secy*, Acadia University, Art Dept, Wolfville NS (S)

Dorfman, Geoffrey, *Adj Assoc Prof*, College of Staten Island, Performing & Creative Arts Dept, Staten Island NY (S)

Dorfmann, Tracey, *Prog Dir*, Jewish Community Center of Greater Washington, Jane L & Robert H Weiner Judaic Museum, Rockville MD

Dorman, Dana, *Dir*, Beaumont Art League, Beaumont TX

Dorman, Nicholas, *Conservator*, Seattle Art Museum, Downtown, Seattle WA

Dorman, Nicholas, *Conservator*, Seattle Art Museum, Dorothy Stimson Bullitt Library, Seattle WA

Dormon, Jessica, *Dir Publications*, The Historic New Orleans Collection, Williams Research Center, New Orleans LA

Dorn, Rachel, *Faculty*, Yakima Valley Community College, Dept of Visual Arts, Yakima WA (S)

Dornbush, Talya, *Edu Dir*, Metropolitan State University of Denver, Center for Visual Art, Denver CO

Dornfeld, Mary, *Communs Asst*, Marquette University, Haggerty Museum of Art, Milwaukee WI

Doroshenko, Peter, *Dir*, University of Wisconsin, Institute of Visual Arts, (INOVA), Milwaukee WI

Dorough, Bonny, *Finance & Operation*, Albany Museum of Art, Albany GA

Dorrien, Carlos, *Prof*, Wellesley College, Art Dept, Wellesley MA (S)

Dorrill, Lisa, *Adjunct Faculty*, Dickinson College, Dept of Art & Art History, Carlisle PA (S)

Dorrill, Lisa, *Instr*, Gettysburg College, Dept of Visual Arts, Gettysburg PA (S)

D'Orsaneo, Terri, *Adminr*, Polk Museum of Art, Lakeland FL

Dorsett, Wendy, *Publs & Mem*, Anthology Film Archives, New York NY

Dorsey, Henry, *Chmn*, Coahoma Community College, Art Education & Fine Arts Dept, Clarksdale MS (S)

Dorsey, Rachael, *Assoc Dir Press & Mktg*, PS1 Contemporary Art Center, Long Island City NY

Dorsky, David, *Dir*, Dorsky Gallery, Dorsky Gallery Curatorial Programs, Long Island City NY

Dosik, Jeff, *Library Technician,* The National Park Service, United States Department of the Interior, Statue of Liberty National Monument & The Ellis Island Immigration Museum, Washington DC

Dougan, Jay, *Asst Prof,* Fort Lewis College, Art Dept, Durango CO (S)

Dougherty, Linda, *Chief Cur,* North Carolina Museum of Art, Raleigh NC

Dougherty, Molly, *Exec Dir,* Philadelphia Art Alliance, Philadelphia PA

Dougherty, Peggy, *Deputy Dir Develop,* Newark Museum Association, The Newark Museum, Newark NJ

Dougherty, Richard, *Chmn,* Murray State University, Dept of Art, Murray KY (S)

Douglas, Alison, *Conservator,* McMichael Canadian Art Collection, Kleinburg ON

Douglas, Deanna, *Prof,* University of Southern Mississippi, Dept of Art & Design, Hattiesburg MS (S)

Douglas, Deborah, *Cur Science & Technology,* Massachusetts Institute of Technology, MIT Museum, Cambridge MA

Douglas, Kris, *Chief Cur,* Rochester Art Center, Rochester MN

Douglas, Lourdes, *Mem Mgr,* University of Rochester, Memorial Art Gallery, Rochester NY

Douglas, Mark, *Asst Prof & Chair,* Fontbonne University, Fine Art Dept, Saint Louis MO (S)

Douglas, Peggy Lea, *Office Supv,* University of Delaware, University Museums, Newark DE

Douglas, Robert, *Prof,* University of Louisville, Allen R Hite Art Institute, Louisville KY (S)

Douley, Scott, *Asst Prof,* Wittenberg University, Art Dept, Springfield OH (S)

Doumato, Lamia, *Head Reader Svcs,* National Gallery of Art, Library, Washington DC

Doutrick, Reba, *Vol Chmn,* Riverside, the Farnsley-Moremen Landing, Louisville KY

Dove, Daniel, *Asst Prof Studio Art,* California Polytechnic State University at San Luis Obispo, Dept of Art & Design, San Luis Obispo CA (S)

Dove, Elizabeth, *Asst Prof,* University of Montana, Dept of Art, Missoula MT (S)

Dover, Conilia, *Guest Svcs,* Tellus Northwest Georgia Science Museum, Cartersville GA

Dowbenka, Michael, *Exhib & Outreach Technician,* City of Toronto Culture, The Market Gallery, Toronto ON

Dowbiggin, Valerie, *Develop Officer,* Art Gallery of Peel, Peel Heritage Complex, Brampton ON

Dowdle, Paul, *VPres Information Technology,* Bowers Museum, Santa Ana CA

Dowdy, Dru, *Publications Officer,* National Portrait Gallery, Smithsonian Institution, Washington DC

Dowdy, William, *Chmn Dept,* Blue Mountain College, Art Dept, Blue Mountain MS (S)

Dowell-Dennis, Terri, *Assoc Cur of Educ,* University of North Carolina at Greensboro, Weatherspoon Art Museum, Greensboro NC

Dowhaniuk, Valerie, *Technician,* Alberta College of Art & Design, Illingworth Kerr Gallery, Calgary AB

Dowhie, Leonard, *Prof Emeritus,* University of Southern Indiana, Department of Art, Evansville IN (S)

Dowling, Russell, *Chmn Bd,* High Plains Museum, McCook NE

Dowling, Teri, *Librn,* California College of the Arts, Libraries, Oakland CA

Dowling, Tom, *Prof Drawing & Painting,* Orange Coast College, Visual & Performing Arts Division, Costa Mesa CA (S)

Down, Chris, *Asst Prof,* Mount Allison University, Dept of Fine Arts, Sackville NB (S)

Downey, Martha J, *Site Mgr,* Illinois Historic Preservation Agency, Bishop Hill State Historic Site, Bishop Hill IL

Downey-Schilling, Joanna, *Dean,* Rio Hondo College, Visual Arts Dept, Whittier CA (S)

Downing, Milton, *Visual Arts,* Christina Cultural Arts Center, Inc, Wilmington DE

Downs, Clyde, *Prof,* Northwestern State University of Louisiana, School of Creative & Performing Arts - Dept of Fine & Graphic Arts, Natchitoches LA (S)

Downs, Linda, *Exec Dir,* College Art Association, New York NY

Downs, Stuart, *Instr,* James Madison University, School of Art & Art History, Harrisonburg VA (S)

Downward, Pat, *Museum Store Mgr,* San Jose Museum of Art, San Jose CA

Dowsett, Robert C, *Secy,* McMichael Canadian Art Collection, Kleinburg ON

Doxey, Mary Denise, *Cur Ancient Egyptian, Nubian, & Near Eastern Art,* Museum of Fine Arts, Boston MA

Doyle, Christopher, *Facilities Mgr,* Headlands Center for the Arts, Sausalito CA

Doyle, J Casey, *Asst Prof,* University of Idaho/College of Art & Architecture, Dept of Art & Design, Moscow ID (S)

Doyle, Kay, *Educ Coordr,* Art Center of Battle Creek, Battle Creek MI

Doyle, Kay, *Educ Coordr,* Art Center of Battle Creek, Michigan Art & Artist Archives, Battle Creek MI

Doyle, Kerry, *Asst Dir,* University of Texas at El Paso, Stanlee & Gerald Rubin Center for the Visual Arts, El Paso TX

Doyle, Leo, *Instr,* California State University, San Bernardino, Dept of Art, San Bernardino CA (S)

Doyle, Michele, *Librn,* Old Salem Museums & Gardens, Library and Research Center, Winston Salem NC

Doyle, Richard, *VPres & Cur,* San Fernando Valley Historical Society, Mission Hills CA

Doyle, Richard, *Pres & Cur,* San Fernando Valley Historical Society, Mark Harrington Library, Mission Hills CA

Doyle, Wanda, *Interim Dept Sec,* Millersville University, Dept of Art & Design, Millersville PA (S)

Doyon, Lina, *Documentation Tech,* Musee National des Beaux Arts du Quebec, Bibliotheque, Quebec PQ

Doyon, Pierre-Simon, *Dir Dept Arts,* University of Quebec, Trois Rivieres, Fine Arts Section, Trois Rivieres PQ (S)

Doyon, Suzette J, *Assoc Prof,* University of West Florida, Dept of Art, Pensacola FL (S)

Dozier, Kelly, *Pres,* LeMoyne Art Foundation, Center for the Visual Arts, Tallahassee FL

Drachler, Carole, *Instr,* Mesa Community College, Dept of Art, Mesa AZ (S)

Draffen, Jennifer, *Chief Registrar & Exhib Mgr,* Museum of Contemporary Art, Chicago IL

Dragonfly, David, *Cur,* Museum of the Plains Indian & Crafts Center, Browning MT

Drake, Amy, *Cur Special Projects,* Southern Oregon Historical Society, Library, Medford OR

Drake, Susan R, *Dir Finance & Admin,* Kimbell Art Foundation, Kimbell Art Museum, Fort Worth TX

Drapeau, Judy, *Asst Librn,* Saint Augustine Historical Society, Library, Saint Augustine FL

Draper, James David, *Cur Henry R Kravis,* The Metropolitan Museum of Art, New York NY

Draper, Jerry L, *Dean School Visual Arts,* Florida State University, Art History Dept, Tallahassee FL (S)

Draper, Stacy F Pomeroy, *Cur,* Rensselaer County Historical Society, Hart-Cluett Mansion, 1827, Troy NY

Drayman-Weisser, Terry, *Dir Conservation,* Walters Art Museum, Library, Baltimore MD

Dreher, Derick, *Dir,* The Rosenbach Museum & Library, Philadelphia PA

Dreiling, Janet, *Registrar,* University of Kansas, Spencer Museum of Art, Lawrence KS

Dreishpon, Douglas, *Chief Cur,* The Buffalo Fine Arts Academy, Albright-Knox Art Gallery, Buffalo NY

Dreiss, Joseph, *Prof,* University of Mary Washington, Dept of Art & Art History, Fredericksburg VA (S)

Dreith, Corey, *Asst Prof Visual Arts,* University of Colorado-Colorado Springs, Visual & Performing Arts Dept (VAPA), Colorado Springs CO (S)

Drennan, Cohn, *Dir,* Wichita Falls Museum & Art Center, Wichita Falls TX

Drennan, Emily, *Cur, Registrar,* City of Cedar Falls, Iowa, James & Meryl Hearst Center for the Arts & Sculpture Garden, Cedar Falls IA

Drennen, Barbara, *Prof,* Malone University, Dept of Art, Canton OH (S)

Dresbach, Chad, *Asst Prof,* Winthrop University, Dept of Art & Design, Rock Hill SC (S)

Drescher, Judith, *Dir,* Memphis-Shelby County Public Library & Information Center, Dept of Art, Music & Films, Memphis TN

Drescher, William, *Assoc Prof,* Elizabeth City State University, School of Arts & Humanities, Dept of Art, Elizabeth City NC (S)

Dressel, Barry, *CEO & Pres,* Indiana State Museum, Indianapolis IN

Dressler, Rachel, *Asst Prof,* State University of New York at Albany, Art Dept, Albany NY (S)

Drewal, Henry J, *Prof,* University of Wisconsin, Madison, Dept of Art History, Madison WI (S)

Drewett, Heidi, *Mktg & Commun,* Art Gallery of Calgary, Calgary AB

Dreyer, Carl, *VPres Fin & Admin & CFO,* Museum of the City of New York, Research Room, New York NY

Dreyer, Chris, *Pres,* Martha's Vineyard Center for the Visual Arts, Firehouse Gallery, Oak Bluffs MA

Dreyer, Tina L, *Exec Dir,* Visual Arts Center of Northwest Florida, Visual Arts Center Library, Panama City FL

Dreyfus, Renee, *Cur Ancient Art & Interpretation,* Fine Arts Museums of San Francisco, M H de Young Museum, San Francisco CA

Dreyfus, Renee, *Cur Ancient Art & Interpretation,* Fine Arts Museums of San Francisco, Legion of Honor, San Francisco CA

Dreyfuss, Elizabeth K, *Treas,* John D Barrow, Skaneateles NY

Drieband, Laurence, *Fine Arts Dept Chmn,* Art Center College of Design, Pasadena CA (S)

Driesbach, Janice, *Dir,* Dayton Art Institute, Dayton OH

Drinan, Patricia, *Chmn,* University of San Diego, Art Dept, San Diego CA (S)

Drinkard, Nisha, *Asst Prof,* William Paterson University, Dept Arts, Wayne NJ (S)

Driscoll, Amy, *Asst Cur Educ,* Dartmouth College, Hood Museum of Art, Hanover NH

Driscoll, David, *Cur Bus & Technology,* Wisconsin Historical Society, Wisconsin Historical Museum, Madison WI

Driscoll, Heather Dawn, *Circ Mgr,* Maine College of Art, Joanne Waxman Library, Portland ME

Driver, David, *Coll Mgr,* State University of New York at Plattsburgh, Art Museum, Plattsburgh NY

Driver, Katrina, *Visual Arts Coordr,* Place des Arts at Heritage Square, Coquitlam BC

Droega, Anthony, *Adjunct Asst Prof,* Indiana University South Bend, Fine Arts Dept, South Bend IN (S)

Drogoul, Laure, *Adjunct,* York College of Pennsylvania, Dept of Music, Art & Speech Communications, York PA (S)

Drolsum, Chris, *Reference Librn,* Maryland Institute, Decker Library, Baltimore MD

Drost, Lise, *Chair, Assoc Prof,* University of Miami, Dept of Art & Art History, Coral Gables FL (S)

Droth, Martina, *Head Research & Cur Sculpture,* Yale University, Yale Center for British Art, New Haven CT

Drought, Michael H, *Dir,* East Carolina University, School of Art & Design, Greenville NC (S)

Drouin, Daniel, *Cur Early Quebec Art before 1850,* Musee National des Beaux Arts du Quebec, Quebec PQ

Drouin-Brisebois, Josee, *Cur, Contemp Art,* National Gallery of Canada, Ottawa ON

Drucker, Barbara, *Chmn,* University of California, Los Angeles, Dept of Art, Los Angeles CA (S)

Druckman, Nicole, *Grants Mgr,* Northwestern University, Mary & Leigh Block Museum of Art, Evanston IL

Druick, Douglas W, *Cur European Painting & Prints & Drawings,* The Art Institute of Chicago, Chicago IL

Drumheller, Grant, *Assoc Prof,* University of New Hampshire, Dept of Arts & Art History, Durham NH (S)

Drumm, Charlotte, *Asst Prof,* Sam Houston State University, Art Dept, Huntsville TX (S)

Drummey, Peter, *Librn,* Massachusetts Historical Society, Library, Boston MA

Drummond, Derek, *Prof (Emeritus),* McGill University, School of Architecture, Montreal PQ (S)

Drummond, Merlyn, *Pub Svcs,* Trinity College Library, Washington DC

Drummond, Sheila, *Head Reference Svcs,* Medicine Hat Public Library, Medicine Hat AB

Drury, Ann, *Office Coordr,* Kentucky Museum of Art and Craft, Louisville KY

Dryburgh, Mary, *Dir Gallery & Instr,* Columbia Basin College, Esvelt Gallery, Pasco WA (S)

Dryfhout, John H, *Supt & Cur,* Saint-Gaudens National Historic Site, Cornish NH

D'Souza, Aruna, *Assoc Prof,* State University of New York at Binghamton, Dept of Art History, Binghamton NY (S)

Duarte, Dora, *Rentals,* Brownsville Art League, Brownsville Museum of Fine Art, Brownsville TX

Duarte, Joseph, *Asst Prep,* Blue Star Contemporary Art Center, San Antonio TX

Duarte, Yvette, *Custodian,* Artesia Historical Museum & Art Center, Artesia NM

Dubansky, Mindell, *Conservation Librn,* The Metropolitan Museum of Art, Museum Libraries, New York NY

Dube, Ilene, *Dir Mktg,* James A Michener, Doylestown PA

Dubler, Linda, *Cur Media Arts,* High Museum of Art, Atlanta GA

Dubnicka, Eric, *Preparator,* University of Minnesota Duluth, Tweed Museum of Art, Duluth MN

DuBois, William, *Dir,* Rochester Institute of Technology, School of Photographic Arts & Sciences, Rochester NY (S)

Dubose, Susan, *Cur Educ,* Alabama Department of Archives & History, Museum of Alabama, Montgomery AL

Dubreuil, Nicole, *Instr,* Universite de Montreal, Dept of Art History, Montreal PQ (S)

Dubreuil, Steve, *Conservateur,* Musee Regional de lu Cote-Nord, Sept-Iles PQ

Dubrevil, Patrick, *Instr,* Lourdes University, Art Dept, Sylvania OH (S)

Dubrowski, Bevin Bering, *Exec Dir,* Houston Center For Photography, Houston TX

Dubsky, Shelagh, *Dance Dept Coordr,* Ashtabula Arts Center, Ashtabula OH

Duckett, Dejay B, *Assoc Dir,* University of Pennsylvania, Arthur Ross Gallery, Philadelphia PA

Duckworth, Chris, *Dir Publs,* Columbus Museum of Art, Columbus OH

Duckworth, Harry W, *Pres,* Manitoba Historical Society, Dalnavert Museum, Winnipeg MB

Duda, Jana, *Library Tech Servs,* Fashion Institute of Technology, Gladys Marcus Library - SUNY, New York NY

Duddy, David A, *Dir Retail Opers,* DeCordova Museum & Sculpture Park, DeCordova Museum, Lincoln MA

Dudek, Steve, *Dir,* Barton County Community College, Fine Arts Dept, Great Bend KS (S)

Dudics, Kitty, *Prof,* Del Mar College, Art Dept, Corpus Christi TX (S)

Dudley, Ian, *Touring Exhib Coordr,* University of Minnesota, The Bell Museum of Natural History, Minneapolis MN

Dudley, Janice Stafford, *Admin Asst,* MacArthur Memorial, Norfolk VA

Dudley, Mary, *Prof,* Howard College, Art Dept, Big Spring TX (S)

Dudley, Russell, *Dir Gallery,* Sierra Nevada College, Fine Arts Dept, Incline Village NV (S)

Duerr, Mark, *Dir,* Steep & Brew Gallery, Madison WI

Duff, Ana, *Pres,* Van Cortlandt House Museum, Bronx NY

Duff, Barb, *Coordr Library Svcs,* The Robert McLaughlin, Library, Oshawa ON

Duff, Charles, *Act Dept Head,* Ancilla College, Art Dept, Donaldson IN (S)

Duff, James, *Treas,* National Gallery of Art, Washington DC

Duffy, Brian R, *Chmn,* Villa Maria College of Buffalo, Art Dept, Buffalo NY (S)

Duffy, Henry, *Cur,* Saint-Gaudens National Historic Site, Cornish NH

Duffy, Henry J, *Cur & Div Chief,* Saint-Gaudens National Historic Site, Library, Cornish NH

Duffy, Jim, *Cur & Caretaker,* South County Art Association, Kingston RI

Duffy-Zeballos, Lisa, *Art Research Dir,* International Foundation for Art Research, Inc (IFAR), New York NY

Dufilho, Diane, *Dir,* Centenary College of Louisiana, Meadows Museum of Art, Shreveport LA

Dufilho, Diane, *Instr,* Centenary College of Louisiana, Dept of Art, Shreveport LA (S)

Dufresne, Daphne, *Dir,* Universite du Quebec, Bibliotheque des Arts, Montreal PQ

Dufresne, Nancy, *Assoc Prof,* Winthrop University, Dept of Art & Design, Rock Hill SC (S)

Dugal, Rod, *Prog Chair,* Sheridan College, Art Dept, Sheridan WY (S)

Dugan, Joel, *Prof,* Fort Hays State University, Dept of Art & Design, Hays KS (S)

Dugan, Steve, *Vol Coordr,* Workman & Temple Family Homestead Museum, City of Industry CA

Dugaune, Erica, *Asst Prof,* Texas State University - San Marcos, Dept of Art and Design, San Marcos TX (S)

Dugdale, James, *Instr,* Joliet Junior College, Fine Arts Dept, Joliet IL (S)

Duggan, Ervin S, *Pres,* The Society of the Four Arts, Palm Beach FL

Duggan, Jenny, *Vis Svcs,* The Dixon Gallery & Gardens, Memphis TN

Duggan, Lynn, *Prof,* Nazareth College of Rochester, Art Dept, Rochester NY (S)

Duggins, Stephen, *Mus Preparator,* University of Richmond, University Museums, Richmond VA

Duguense, Chuck, *AV Specialist,* Moore College of Art & Design, Library, Philadelphia PA

Duhan, Peter, *Programming Dir,* Artists Talk on Art, New York NY

Duillo, John, *Pres,* Society of American Historical Artists, Oyster Bay NY

Dujin, Veljko, *Coll Cur,* Palm Beach County Parks & Recreation Department, Morikami Museum & Japanese Gardens, Delray Beach FL

Duke, Linda, *Dir Educ & Community Develop,* University of California, Los Angeles, UCLA at the Armand Hammer Museum of Art & Cultural Center, Los Angeles CA

Duke, Linda, *Dir Education,* Indianapolis Museum of Art, Indianapolis IN

Duley, Kathy, *Dir,* Duley-Jones Gallery, Paradise Valley AZ

Dulic, Aleksandra, *Asst Prof (Visual Art),* University of British Columbia Okanagan, Dept of Creative Studies, Kelowna BC (S)

Dull, Keith A, *Asst Prof,* Ashland University, Art Dept, Ashland OH (S)

Dumas, Tanya, *Vis Svcs,* The Dixon Gallery & Gardens, Memphis TN

Dumbadze, Alexander, *Asst Prof,* George Washington University, Dept of Art of Fine Arts & Art History, Washington DC (S)

Dumohoo, Andrew, *Educ,* Fort Morgan Heritage Foundation, Fort Morgan CO

Dumouchelle, Kevin D, *Asst Cur, Arts of Africa & the Pacific Islands,* Brooklyn Museum, Brooklyn NY

Dunagan, Casey, *Vis Serv & Retail Mgr,* Cedar Rapids Museum of Art, Cedar Rapids IA

Dunbar, Lisa, *Museum Cur,* Historic Pensacola Preservation Board, T.T. Wentworth Jr. Florida State Museum, Pensacola FL

Dunbar, Richard, *Vice Pres Finance,* Springfield Museums, Connecticut Valley Historical Society, Springfield MA

Dunbeck, Helen, *Dir of Admin,* Museum of Contemporary Art, Chicago IL

Duncan, Chris, *Chmn Visual Arts,* Union College, Dept of Visual Arts, Schenectady NY (S)

Duncan, Diana Duke, *Dir Develop,* Dallas Museum of Art, Dallas TX

Duncan, Donald, *Asst Prof,* Capital University, Fine Arts Dept, Columbus OH (S)

Duncan, Joyce, *Treas,* Hendricks Hill Museum, Southport ME

Duncan, Karen, *Registrar,* University of Minnesota, Frederick R Weisman Art Museum, Minneapolis MN

Duncan, Martina, *Assoc Dir,* Bowdoin College, Museum of Art, Brunswick ME

Duncan, Norine, *Cur,* Brown University, Art Slide Library, Providence RI

Duncan, Richard, *Pres Bd Trustees,* Zanesville Museum of Art, Zanesville OH

Duncan, Samuel, *Library Dir,* Amon Carter Museum of American Art, Fort Worth TX

Duncan, Samuel, *Library Dir,* Amon Carter Museum of American Art, Research Library, Fort Worth TX

Duncan, Warren, *Chmn Fine & Performing Arts,* Tuskegee University, Liberal Arts & Education, Tuskegee AL (S)

Dunfey, Patrick, *Exhibitions Designer,* Dartmouth College, Hood Museum of Art, Hanover NH

Dungey, Jan, *Library Dir,* Springfield Art Association of Edwards Place, Michael Victor II Art Library, Springfield IL

Dunkelman, Arthur, *Dir,* Jay I Kislak Foundation, Miami Lakes FL

Dunkley, Diane, *Dir & Chief Cur,* DAR Museum, National Society Daughters of the American Revolution, Washington DC

Dunkley, Diane, *Dir & Chief Cur,* DAR Museum, Library, Washington DC

Dunlap, Ellen S, *Pres,* American Antiquarian Society, Worcester MA

Dunlap, Margo, *Exec Dir,* Pro Arts, Oakland CA

Dunn, B J, *Supt,* Saint-Gaudens National Historic Site, Library, Cornish NH

Dunn, Chuck, *VChmn,* Mississippi Museum of Art, Howorth Library, Jackson MS

Dunn, David, *Mus Dir,* Pennsylvania Historical & Museum Commission, The State Museum of Pennsylvania, Harrisburg PA

Dunn, David W, *Dir,* Pennsylvania Historical & Museum Commission, Railroad Museum of Pennsylvania, Harrisburg PA

Dunn, David W, *Mus Dir,* Pennsylvania Historical & Museum Commission, The State Museum of Pennsylvania, Harrisburg PA

Dunn, Elizabeth C, *Gen Educ,* Art Institute of Pittsburgh, Pittsburgh PA (S)

Dunn, Jamila, *Artists In Schools Prog Coordr,* Kala Institute, Kala Art Institute, Berkeley CA

Dunn, Jodi, *Instr,* Keystone College, Fine Arts Dept, LaPlume PA (S)

Dunn, Madeline, *Cur Educ,* Delaware Division of Historical & Cultural Affairs, Dover DE

Dunn, Marilyn, *Assoc Prof,* Loyola University of Chicago, Fine Arts Dept, Chicago IL (S)

Dunn, Michael, *Photo Branch,* United States Capitol, Architect of the Capitol, Washington DC

Dunn, Nancy, *Mus Mgr,* Artesia Historical Museum & Art Center, Artesia NM

Dunn, Robert, *VPres,* National Society of Painters in Casein & Acrylic, Inc, Whitehall PA

Dunn, Roger, *Prof,* Bridgewater State College, Art Dept, Bridgewater MA (S)

Dunn, Sharon, *VPres Educ,* New-York Historical Society, Museum, New York NY

Dunn-Froebig, Eva, *Admin Officer,* Missoula Art Museum, Missoula MT

Dunnahoe, Donna, *Exec Dir,* The Fine Arts Center of Hot Springs, Hot Springs AR

Dunne, Charles S, *Pres & Dir,* The New England Museum of Telephony, Inc., The Telephone Museum, Ellsworth ME

Dunne, Laura, *Treas,* Chicago Children's Museum, Chicago IL

Dunne, Linda, *Chief Admin Officer,* American Folk Art Museum, New York NY

Dunnell, Molly, *Mktg Assoc,* University of Wyoming, University of Wyoming Art Museum, Laramie WY

Dunnewold, Jane, *Pres,* Surface Design Association, Inc, Sebastopol CA

Dunnill, Andrew, *Prof,* University of North Carolina at Greensboro, Art Dept, Greensboro NC (S)

Dunning, Alan, *Acad Head Media Arts,* Alberta College of Art & Design, Calgary AB (S)

Dunning, Jeanne, *Assoc Prof,* Northwestern University, Evanston, Dept of Art Theory & Practice, Evanston IL (S)

Dunsuir, Linda, *Financial Adminr,* Hunterdon Art Museum, Clinton NJ

Dunwoody, Lorri, *Registrar,* Indiana State Museum, Indianapolis IN

Duperry, Robin, *Library Coordr,* Colby College, Bixler Art & Music Library, Waterville ME

Dupont, Daniel, *Dir Develop,* Barnes Foundation, Merion PA

Dupont, Inge, *Head Reader Svcs,* The Morgan Library & Museum, Library, New York NY

Dupper, Ervin, *VChmn & VPres,* Klein Museum, Mobridge SD

Dupra, Rheba, *Information Services,* University of Alaska, Elmer E Rasmuson Library, Fairbanks AK

Dupre, Kelly, *Faculty,* Grand Marais Art Colony, Grand Marais MN (S)

DuPrey, Michelle, *Admin Asst,* Ames Free-Easton's Public Library, North Easton MA

Duquette, Anita, *Secy,* Belskie Museum, Closter NJ

Durand, Lydia, *Communs Mgr,* Utah Arts Council, Chase Home Museum of Utah Folk Arts, Salt Lake City UT

Durand, Mark, *Librn,* Playboy Enterprises, Inc, Library, Beverly Hills CA

Durant, John, *Dir,* Massachusetts Institute of Technology, MIT Museum, Cambridge MA

Durant, Mark Alice, *Prof,* University of Maryland, Baltimore County, Imaging & Digital Arts (IMDA), Dept of Visual Arts, Baltimore MD (S)

Durben, Silvan A, *Dir & Cur,* Owatonna Arts Center, Owatonna MN

Durden, Bob, *Senior Cur,* Yellowstone Art Museum, Billings MT

Durden, Joan, *Asst Prof,* Appalachian State University, Dept of Art, Boone NC (S)

Duren, Paula, *Instr,* Hinds Community College, Dept of Art, Raymond MS (S)

Duren, Paula L, *Gallery Dir,* Hinds Community College District, Marie Hull Gallery, Raymond MS

Durham, Bill, *Security,* University of California, Santa Barbara, University Art Museum, Santa Barbara CA

Durham, Jonathan, *Visual Arts Dir,* Henry Street Settlement, Abrons Art Center, New York NY

Durham, Robert, *Lectr,* Vanderbilt University, Dept of Art, Nashville TN (S)

During, Helen Klisser, *Dir Visual Arts,* Westport Arts Center, Westport CT

During, Helen Klisser, *Gallery Dir,* Silvermine Guild Arts Center, School of Art, New Canaan CT

Durkin, Brigid, *Cur Specialist,* Danbury Scott-Fanton Museum & Historical Society, Inc, Danbury CT

Durkin, Brigid, *Cur Specialist,* Danbury Scott-Fanton Museum & Historical Society, Inc, Library, Danbury CT

Durlac, Bob, *Asst Prof,* Southwestern Oklahoma State University, Art Dept, Weatherford OK (S)

Durocher, Kristina, *Dir,* University of New Hampshire, Museum of Art, Durham NH

Durrant, Doug, *Chmn,* Palomar Community College, Art Dept, San Marcos CA (S)

Dursum, Brian A, *Dir,* University of Miami, Lowe Art Museum, Coral Gables FL

Dusang, LeAnn, *Shop Mgr,* Louisiana State University, Museum of Art, Baton Rouge LA

Duse, Kathy, *Convention & Progs Coordr,* National Art Education Association, Reston VA

Dusenbury, Carolyn, *Dir,* California State University, Chico, Meriam Library, Chico CA

DuSold, Paul, *Instr,* Wayne Art Center, Wayne PA (S)

Duson, Virginia, *VPres,* Crowley Art Association, The Gallery, Crowley LA

Dussart, Christel, *Cur Visual Arts,* Sangre de Cristo Arts & Conference Center, Pueblo CO

Dussault, Carole, *Coordr-Communs,* Guilde canadienne des metiers d'art, Canadian Guild of Crafts, Montreal PQ

Dussault, Chantal, *Head Archives, Records & Libr,* Canadian Museum of Nature, Musee Canadien de la Nature, Ottawa ON

Dutiel, Robert, *Assoc Prof Theatre,* Marymount Manhattan College, Fine & Performing Arts Div, New York NY (S)

Dutlinger, Anne, *Chmn Art Dept,* Moravian College, Payne Gallery, Bethlehem PA

Dutremaine, James, *Art Educ,* University of Texas Pan American, Art Dept, Edinburg TX (S)

Dutschke, Alithia, *Mgr Annual Giving,* Caramoor Center for Music & the Arts, Inc, Rosen House at Caramoor, Katonah NY

Dutton, Jeff, *Preparator & Designer,* Montgomery Museum of Fine Arts, Montgomery AL

Duval, Cynthia, *Chief Cur,* The Museum of Arts & Sciences Inc, Daytona Beach FL

Duval, Douglas P, *Facilities Mgr,* Jamestown-Yorktown Foundation, Jamestown Settlement, Williamsburg VA

DuVerneay, Jessica, *Information Resources Specialist,* University of Michigan, Fine Arts Library, Ann Arbor MI

Duychak, Linda, *Reference Librn,* University of Wisconsin-Madison, Kohler Art Library, Madison WI

Dwiggins, David, *Systems Librn & Archivist,* Historic New England, Library and Archives, Boston MA

Dwight, Dorothy, *Assoc Prof,* Loyola University of Chicago, Fine Arts Dept, Chicago IL (S)

Dworin, Arthur, *VPres,* Viridian Artists Inc, New York NY

Dwyer, Eugene J, *Prof,* Kenyon College, Art Dept, Gambier OH (S)

Dwyer, Rob, *Dir,* Quincy Society of Fine Arts, Quincy IL

Dyas, Sandy, *Instr,* Cornell College, Peter Paul Luce Gallery, Mount Vernon IA

Dybdahl, Tammy, *Financial Aid,* Rocky Mountain College of Art & Design, Lakewood CO (S)

Dyckes, Martha, *Dir Interpretive Servs,* Colorado Historical Society, Colorado History Museum, Denver CO

Dye, Joseph, *Lectr,* College of William & Mary, Dept of Fine Arts, Williamsburg VA (S)

Dye, Joseph M, *Cur Chair & Cur S Asian & Islamic Art,* Virginia Museum of Fine Arts, Richmond VA

Dyer, Deb, *Exec Dir,* National Institute of Art & Disabilities (NIAD), Florence Ludins-Katz Gallery, Richmond CA

Dyer, Eric, *Asst Prof,* University of Maryland, Baltimore County, Imaging & Digital Arts (IMDA), Dept of Visual Arts, Baltimore MD (S)

Dyer, M Wayne, *Prof,* East Tennessee State University, College of Arts and Sciences, Dept of Art & Design, Johnson City TN (S)

Dyer, Suzy, *Develop Asst,* Museum of Ventura County, Ventura CA

Dykhuis, Peter, *Dir & Cur,* Dalhousie University, Dalhousie Art Gallery, Halifax NS

Dyki, Judy, *Dir Library,* Cranbrook Art Museum, Library, Bloomfield Hills MI

Dyment, James, *Exhibits Mgr,* Lowell Art Association, Inc, Whistler House Museum of Art, Lowell MA

Dynak, Sharon, *Exec Dir,* Ucross Foundation, Big Red Barn Gallery, Clearmont WY

Dyrhaug, Kurt, *Assoc Prof,* Lamar University, Art Dept, Beaumont TX (S)

Dzenko, Corey, *Lectr,* University of North Carolina at Greensboro, Art Dept, Greensboro NC (S)

Eacret-Simmons, Carol, *Dir,* Dickinson State University, Art Gallery, Dickinson ND

Eacret-Simmons, Carol, *Gallery Dir & Assoc Prof Art,* Dickinson State University, Dept of Art, Dickinson ND (S)

Eagle, Scott, *Asst Dir,* East Carolina University, School of Art & Design, Greenville NC (S)

Eagleton, Tod, *Registrar,* McLean County Historical Society, McLean County Museum of History, Bloomington IL

Earenfight, Phillip, *Dir,* Dickinson College, The Trout Gallery, Carlisle PA

Earle, Edward, *Cur Coll,* International Center of Photography, Museum, New York NY

Earle, Joe, *Vice Pres & Gallery Dir,* Japan Society, Inc, Japan Society Gallery, New York NY

Earle, Susan, *Cur European & American Art,* University of Kansas, Spencer Museum of Art, Lawrence KS

Earls, Elliott, *Head 2-D Design Dept,* Cranbrook Academy of Art, Bloomfield Hills MI (S)

Early, Susan, *Fundraising,* Visual Arts Center of Richmond, Richmond VA

Earnest, Greta K, *Assoc Dir,* Fashion Institute of Technology, Gladys Marcus Library - SUNY, New York NY

Earnest, Royce, *Grad Coordr,* Judson University, School of Art, Design & Architecture, Elgin IL (S)

Earnhart, Kathy, *Pub Rels,* The Butler Institute of American Art, Art Museum, Youngstown OH

Easby, Rebecca, *Chmn & Assoc Prof,* Trinity College, Fine Arts Program, Washington DC (S)

Easley, Debbie, *Outreach Mgr,* Union County Public Library Union Room, Monroe NC

East, Ramona, *Registrar,* University of Louisiana at Lafayette, Paul and Lulu Hilliard University Art Museum, Lafayette LA

Eastep, Jim, *Sr Develop Officer,* Oklahoma City Museum of Art, Oklahoma City OK

Easter, Earl, *Graphic Design,* Art Institute of Pittsburgh, Pittsburgh PA (S)

Easto, Elizabeth, *Cur Coll,* Aurora University, Schingoethe Center for Native American Cultures & The Schingoethe Art Gallery, Aurora IL

Easton-Moore, Barbara, *Exec Dir,* Rawls Museum Arts, Courtland VA

Eatmon, Cheryl, *Dept Secy, Grad Prog Asst,* North Carolina State University at Raleigh, School of Design, Raleigh NC (S)

Eaton, Aurore, *Exec Dir,* Manchester Historic Association, Millyard Museum, Manchester NH

Eaton, Aurore, *Exec Dir,* Manchester Historic Association, Library, Manchester NH

Eaton, Jeff, *Curatorial Assoc,* White Columns, White Columns Curated Artist Registry, New York NY

Eaton, Jennifer, *Mktg Coordr,* Fraunces Tavern Museum, New York NY

Eaton, Linda, *Dir Colls,* Winterthur Museum, Winterthur Museum, Garden & Library, Winterthur DE

Eaton, Lynn, *Reference Archivist,* Duke University Library, Hartman Center for Sales, Advertising & Marketing History, Durham NC

Eber, Frank, *2nd VPres,* National Watercolor Society, San Pedro CA

Eberhardt, Brett, *Assoc Prof Art,* Western Illinois University, Department of Art, Macomb IL (S)

Eberhardt, Herman, *Cur,* National Archives & Records Administration, Franklin D Roosevelt Museum, Hyde Park NY

Eberhardt, Herman, *Cur,* National Archives & Records Administration, Franklin D Roosevelt Library, Hyde Park NY

Eberhart, Karen, *Spec Coll Cur,* Rhode Island Historical Society, Library, Providence RI

Eberle-Nielander, Lilith, *Instr,* Appalachian State University, Dept of Art, Boone NC (S)

Ebersole, Noriko, *Visual Resource Librn,* The Nelson-Atkins Museum of Art, Spencer Art Reference Library, Kansas City MO

Ebert, D, *Instr,* Golden West College, Visual Art Dept, Huntington Beach CA (S)

Ebert, Howard, *Dir,* Saint Norbert College, Div of Humanities & Fine Arts, De Pere WI (S)

Ebert, Loretta, *Research Lib Dir,* New York State Library, Manuscripts & Special Collections, Albany NY

Ebitz, David, *Assoc Prof Art & Art Educ,* Pennsylvania State University, University Park, Penn State School of Visual Arts, University Park PA (S)

Ebner, Martha, *Web & Mktg Coordr,* Smith College, Museum of Art, Northampton MA

Ebner, Stella, *Asst Prof,* Purchase College, State University of New York, School of Art+Design, Purchase NY (S)

Eccles, Tom, *Exec Dir,* Bard College, Center for Curatorial Studies and the Hessel Museum of Art, Annandale-on-Hudson NY

Echevery, Santiago, *Prof,* University of Tampa, College of Arts & Letters, Tampa FL (S)

Echols, Joralyn, *Outreach & Pub Rels Coordr,* Academy of the New Church, Glencairn Museum, Bryn Athyn PA

Echtner, Mark, *Prof,* Sinclair Community College, Division of Fine & Performing Arts, Dayton OH (S)

Ecker, Heather, *Cur Islamic Art,* Detroit Institute of Arts, Detroit MI

Eckersley, Robyn D, *Educ Coordr,* Lighthouse ArtCenter Museum & School of Art, Tequesta FL

Eckert, Cathy Lee, *Treas,* Booth Western Art Museum, Cartersville GA

Eckert, Mitch, *Assoc Prof,* University of Louisville, Allen R Hite Art Institute, Louisville KY (S)

Eckhardt, Marcus, *Cur Mus,* National Archives & Records Administration, Herbert Hoover Presidential Library - Museum, West Branch IA

Eckhardt, Susan, *Dir Mus Educ,* Kalamazoo Institute of Arts, Kalamazoo MI

Eckhardt, Susan, *Dir Museum Educ,* Kalamazoo Institute of Arts, The Mary & Edwin Meader Fine Arts Library, Kalamazoo MI

Eckley, Laura, *Dir Library,* Bronxville Public Library, Bronxville NY

Eckman, Chuck, *Univ Librn,* Simon Fraser University, W A C Bennett Library, Burnaby BC

Eckmann, Sabine, *Dir & Chief Cur,* Washington University, Mildred Lane Kemper Art Museum, Saint Louis MO

Eckmann, Teresa, *Asst Prof,* University of Texas at San Antonio, Dept of Art & Art History, San Antonio TX (S)

Eckstein, Eileen, *Corresp Secy,* Plastic Club, Art Club, Philadelphia PA

Economon, Barbara, *Visual Resources Librn,* Walker Art Center, Staff Reference Library, Minneapolis MN

Edberg, Jane, *Chmn & Prof,* Gavilan Community College, Art Dept, Gilroy CA (S)

Edberg, Jane, *Prof Art & New Technology,* Gavilan Community College, Art Gallery, Gilroy CA

Edborg, Judy A, *American Artisans Dir,* American Society of Artists, Inc, Palatine IL

Eddey, Roy, *Deputy Dir Finance & Adminr,* Guggenheim Museum Soho, New York NY

Eddings, Melissa, *Assoc Prof Art,* Ohio Northern University, Dept of Art & Design, Ada OH (S)

Eddins, Rebecca, *Dir Colls Management,* Reynolda House Museum of American Art, Winston-Salem NC

Eddy, Cheri, *Facilities Mgr,* Bank One Wisconsin, Milwaukee WI

Eddy, Dave, *Asst Prof Lectr,* University of Utah, Dept of Art & Art History, Salt Lake City UT (S)

Edelen, Dawn, *Cur Educ,* Lafayette Science Museum & Planetarium, Lafayette LA

Edelson, Gilbert S, *Admin VPres & Counsel,* Art Dealers Association of America, Inc, New York NY

Eden, John, *Adjunct Prof,* University of Maine, Dept of Art, Orono ME (S)

Eden, Xandra, *Cur of Exhib,* University of North Carolina at Greensboro, Weatherspoon Art Museum, Greensboro NC

Edgar, David, *Chmn,* Ashland University, Art Dept, Ashland OH (S)

Edgar, David, *Prof,* University of North Carolina at Charlotte, Dept Art, Charlotte NC (S)

Edgar, William R, *Dir Interior Design, Industrial Design Tech,* The Art Institutes, The Art Institute of Seattle, Seattle WA (S)

Edgecombe, Wallace I, *Dir,* Hostos Center for the Arts & Culture, Bronx NY

Edidin, Stephen, *Chief Cur Mus Div,* New-York Historical Society, Museum, New York NY

Edinberg, Lucinda, *Outreach Coordr,* St John's College, Elizabeth Myers Mitchell Art Gallery, Annapolis MD

Edison, Carol, *Folk Arts Mgr,* Utah Arts Council, Chase Home Museum of Utah Folk Arts, Salt Lake City UT

Edison, Diane, *Assoc Prof Drawing & Painting,* University of Georgia, Franklin College of Arts & Sciences, Lamar Dodd School of Art, Athens GA (S)

Edkins, Diana, *Dir Exhibitions,* Aperture Foundation, New York NY

Edmondson, Jo, *Educ Coordr,* Tubac Center of the Arts, Santa Cruz Valley Art Association, Tubac AZ

Edmonson, Chris, *Reference Librn,* The Cleveland Museum of Art, Ingalls Library, Cleveland OH

Edmonson, Randall W, *Prof,* Longwood University, Dept of Art, Farmville VA (S)

Edmunds, Allan L, *Pres & Exec Dir,* Brandywine Workshop, Center for the Visual Arts, Philadelphia PA

Edmundson, Jane, *Chief Preparator,* University of Lethbridge, Art Gallery, Lethbridge AB

Edmundson, Jane, *Curatorial Researcher & Preparator,* University of Lethbridge, Art Gallery, Lethbridge AB

Edmundson, John, *Exhibits Mgr,* Witte Museum, San Antonio TX

Edson, Erik, *Assoc Prof,* Mount Allison University, Dept of Fine Arts, Sackville NB (S)

Edson, Gary, *Exec Dir,* Texas Tech University, Museum of Texas Tech University, Lubbock TX

Edward, Whit, *Dir Educ,* Oklahoma Historical Society, Library Resources Division, Oklahoma City OK

Edwards, Adam, *Security Chief,* Oklahoma City Museum of Art, Oklahoma City OK

Edwards, Byron, *VPres Acad Affairs,* Nossi College of Art, Nashville TN (S)

Edwards, Glen, *Prof,* Utah State University, Dept of Art, Logan UT (S)

Edwards, June, *Prof,* Slippery Rock University of Pennsylvania, Dept of Art, Slippery Rock PA (S)

Edwards, Kathleen, *Chief Cur,* University of Iowa, University of Iowa Museum of Art, Iowa City IA

Edwards, Kathy, *Circulation Mgr,* Friends University, Edmund Stanley Library, Wichita KS

Edwards, Kathy, *Ref Librn,* Clemson University, Emery A Gunnin Architectural Library, Clemson SC

Edwards, Kirsti Scutt, *Exhib Mgr,* Berkshire Museum, Pittsfield MA

Edwards, Maggie, *Curatorial Asst,* Norton Museum of Art, West Palm Beach FL

Edwards, Nancy, *Cur European Art & Head Acad Svcs,* Kimbell Art Foundation, Kimbell Art Museum, Fort Worth TX

Edwards, Norman, *Opers Mgr,* Museum of New Mexico, Palace of Governors, Santa Fe NM

Edwards, Pam, *Dir Vis Svcs & Vols,* Columbus Museum of Art, Columbus OH

Edwards, Patricia, *Asst Prof,* University of Saint Francis, School of Creative Arts, Fort Wayne IN (S)

Edwards, Patricia, *Lect,* Old Dominion University, Art Dept, Norfolk VA (S)

Edwards, Philip, *Reference Lib,* National Air and Space Museum, Archives, Washington DC

Edwards, Rebecca, *Adjunct,* College of the Canyons, Art Dept, Santa Clarita CA (S)

Edwards, Rebecca, *Educ Mgr,* Pacific - Asia Museum, Pasadena CA

Edwards, Richard, *Dir,* Baldwin Gallery, Aspen CO

Edwards, Sara Foley, *Pub Progs Mgr,* Museum of Fine Arts, Houston, Rienzi Center for European Decorative Arts, Houston TX

Edwards, Skip, *Master Woodcarver,* Calvert Marine Museum, Solomons MD

Edwards, Susan C S, *Dir Historic Resources,* The Trustees of Reservations, The Mission House, Ipswich MA

Edwards, Taryn, *Reference Librn,* Mechanics' Institute, San Francisco CA

Edwards, Wanda, *Registrar,* Museum of New Mexico, Palace of Governors, Santa Fe NM

Edwards, Wendy, *Chmn,* Brown University, Dept of Visual Art, Providence RI (S)

Edwins, Steve, *Asst Prof,* Saint Olaf College, Art Dept, Northfield MN (S)

Efimova, Alla, *Dir,* University of California, Berkeley, The Magnes Collection of Jewish Art & Life, Berkeley CA

Efland, Arthur, *Prof Emeritus,* Ohio State University, Dept of Art Education, Columbus OH (S)

Egami, Renay, *Asst Prof (Visual Art),* University of British Columbia Okanagan, Dept of Creative Studies, Kelowna BC (S)

Egami, Yash, *Ed-in-Chief,* The One Club, New York NY

Egan, Cara, *Dir Pub Rels,* Seattle Art Museum, Downtown, Seattle WA

Egan, Gary, *Deputy Dir Admin,* Phoenix Art Museum, Phoenix AZ

Egan, Gary, *VPres Finance & Admin,* The Mariners' Museum, Newport News VA

Egan, Natasha, *Assoc Dir,* Columbia College Chicago, Museum of Contemporary Photography, Chicago IL

Egan Stalfort, Heather, *Communs Dir,* Johns Hopkins University, Homewood Museum, Baltimore MD

Egbert, Elizabeth, *CEO & Pres,* Staten Island Museum, Archives Library, Staten Island NY

Egelston, Rachel, *Children's Progs Mgr,* Western Colorado Center for the Arts, The Art Center, Grand Junction CO

Eggebrecht, David, *Acad Dean,* Concordia University Wisconsin, Fine Art Gallery, Mequon WI

Eggener, Keith, *Assoc Prof,* University of Missouri - Columbia, Art History & Archaeology Dept, Columbia MO (S)

Eggers, Jill, *Assoc Prof,* Grand Valley State University, Art & Design Dept, Allendale MI (S)

Eglinski, Edmund, *Assoc Prof,* University of Kansas, Kress Foundation Dept of Art History, Lawrence KS (S)

Egloff, Fred R, *Librn,* The Museum of Western Art, Museum of Western Art & Research Library, Kerrville TX

Ehlers, Marla, *Asst Library Dir,* Grand Rapids Public Library, Grand Rapids MI

Ehnbom, Daniel, *Art History Instr,* University of Virginia, McIntire Dept of Art, Charlottesville VA (S)

Ehrhardt, Ursula M, *Asst Prof,* Salisbury State University, Art Dept, Salisbury MD (S)

Ehrhart, Megan, *Dept Head TIME Digital Arts,* Cleveland Institute of Art, Cleveland OH (S)

Ehrin, Leslie, *Pres,* Wayne Art Center, Wayne PA (S)

Ehrlund, Jake, *Mus Registrar & Preparator,* Asheville Art Museum, Asheville NC

Ehrnst, Elizabeth, *Archives & Digital Colls Librn,* Georgia O'Keeffe Museum, Research Center, Santa Fe NM

Eichelberg, Ann, *Registrar,* Portland Art Museum, Portland OR

Eichenberg, Iris, *Head Metalsmithing Dept,* Cranbrook Academy of Art, Bloomfield Hills MI (S)

Eichenberg, Roberta, *Assoc Prof of Art & Galleries Dir,* Emporia State University, Norman R Eppink Art Gallery, Emporia KS

Eichenberg, Roberta, *Asst,* Emporia State University, Dept of Art, Emporia KS (S)

Eichensehr, Kasey, *Cur,* Clark County Historical Society, Heritage Center of Clark County, Springfield OH

Eichman, Shawn, *Cur Asian Art,* Honolulu Museum of Art, Honolulu HI

Eichner, Timothy, *Graphic Design Chmn,* Palm Beach Community College, Dept of Art, Lake Worth FL (S)

Eickhorst, William S, *Exec Dir,* Print Consortium, Kansas City MO

Eickmeier, Valerie, *Dean,* Indiana University-Purdue University, Indianapolis, Herron School of Art & Design, Indianapolis IN (S)

Eide, John, *Instr,* Maine College of Art, Portland ME (S)

Eifert, Marie, *Dir Develop,* Fort Wayne Museum of Art, Inc, Fort Wayne IN

Eifler, David, *Planning & Instruction Librn,* University of California, Berkeley, Environmental Design Library, Berkeley CA

Eike, Claire, *Dir,* School of the Art Institute of Chicago, John M Flaxman Library, Chicago IL

Eikmeier, Linda, *Asst Site Mgr,* County of Henrico, Meadow Farm Museum, Glen Allen VA

Eiland, William, *Museum Dir,* University of Georgia, Georgia Museum of Art, Athens GA

Eilertsen, Kate, *Exec Dir,* Sonoma Valley Museum of Art, Sonoma CA ·

Einfalt, Linda, *Assoc Prof Fine Arts,* University of Cincinnati, School of Art, Cincinnati OH (S)

Eis, Andrea, *Chmn Dept & Spec Instr,* Oakland University, Dept of Art & Art History, Rochester MI (S)

Eisenbach, Diane, *Ceramics Instr,* Monterey Peninsula College, Art Dept/Art Gallery, Monterey CA (S)

Eisenbach-Bush, Laurie, *Instr Graphic Design,* Maryville University of Saint Louis, Art & Design Program, Saint Louis MO (S)

Eisenhauer, Paul, *Cur,* Wharton Esherick, Paoli PA

Eisenman, Stephen, *Prof,* Northwestern University, Evanston, Dept of Art History, Evanston IL (S)

Eisinger, Marguerite, *Docent Coordr,* State University of New York at Plattsburgh, Art Museum, Plattsburgh NY

Eisman, Hy, *Instr,* Joe Kubert, Dover NJ (S)

Eitel, Sydney, *Pres,* Colorado Watercolor Society, Denver CO

Ekechi, Lawrence, *Community Outreach Liaison,* Museum for African Art, New York NY

Eklund, Brian, *Commun & Mktg Dir,* Hockaday Museum of Art, Kalispell MT

Eklund, Lori, *COO,* Amon Carter Museum of American Art, Fort Worth TX

Eklund, Lori, *Cur Educ,* City of El Paso, El Paso TX

Elam, Chris, *Mem Coordr,* The Dallas Contemporary, Dallas Visual Art Center, Dallas TX

Elarfi, Meredith, *Mktg,* Tampa Museum of Art, Tampa FL

Elder, Beth, *Dir,* Salt Lake City Public Library, Fine Arts & Audiovisual Dept and Atrium Gallery, Salt Lake City UT

Elder, Carol, *Mem Assoc,* Historical Society of Palm Beach County, The Richard and Pat Johnson Palm Beach County History Museum, West Palm Beach FL

Elder, Donald, *Instr,* Woodstock School of Art, Inc, Woodstock NY (S)

Elder, Douglas Shaw, *Exec Dir,* Firehouse Art Center, Norman OK

Elder, Marianne, *Sr Cur,* Art Gallery of Calgary, Calgary AB

Elder, Sarah, *Cur Educ,* Saint Joseph Museum, Library, Saint Joseph MO

Elder, Sarah M, *Cur Collections,* Saint Joseph Museum, Saint Joseph MO

Elder, Tanya, *Sr Archivist,* American Jewish Historical Society, The Center for Jewish History, New York NY

Eldin, Marie, *Adj Prof,* Saint Joseph's University, Art Dept, Philadelphia PA (S)

Eldredge, Charles, *Prof,* University of Kansas, Kress Foundation Dept of Art History, Lawrence KS (S)

Eldridge, Jan, *Instr,* Solano Community College, Division of Fine & Applied Art & Behavioral Science, Fairfield CA (S)

Eldridge, Laura, *Dir Intern Progs,* Fondo del Sol, Visual Art & Media Center, Washington DC

Eldridge, Todd, *Art Instr,* East Central Community College, Art Dept, Decatur MS (S)

Elesh, James, *Bd Chmn,* Northwestern University, Mary & Leigh Block Museum of Art, Evanston IL

Elet, Yvonne, *Asst Prof,* Vassar College, Art Dept, Poughkeepsie NY (S)

Elhenny, James, *Painting & Drawing,* University of Colorado at Denver, College of Arts & Media Visual Arts Dept, Denver CO (S)

Elias, Arthur, *Treas,* Prince Street Gallery, New York NY

Elias, Bridget, *Chief Financial Officer,* Whitney Museum of American Art, New York NY

Elkeslassi, Rosette, *Admin Asst,* Concordia University, Leonard & Bina Ellen Art Gallery, Montreal PQ

Elkington, Richard, *Asst Prof,* Providence College, Art & Art History Dept, Providence RI (S)

Elkins, Nathan, *Asst Prof,* Baylor University - College of Arts and Sciences, Dept of Art, Waco TX (S)

Ellason, Craig, *Prof,* University of Saint Thomas, Dept of Art History, Saint Paul MN (S)

Ellenbogen, Josh, *Asst Prof,* University of Pittsburgh, Henry Clay Frick Dept History of Art & Architecture, Pittsburgh PA (S)

Eller, Carolyn, *Dir Mktg & Pub Rels,* Erie Art Museum, Erie PA

Eller, John W, *COO,* Maryland Historical Society, Library, Baltimore MD

Ellerbroek, Betsey, *Educ Dir,* Columbia River Maritime Museum, Astoria OR

Ellerby, Laura, *Mus Shop Mgr,* Institute of American Indian Arts, Museum of Contemporary Native Arts, Santa Fe NM (S)

Ellerby, Laura, *Mus Store Mgr,* Institute of American Indian Arts, Museum of Contemporary Native Arts, Santa Fe NM

Ellett, Tommy, *Pres,* Cottonlandia Museum, Greenwood MS

Elligott, Michelle, *Archivist,* Museum of Modern Art, Library and Museum Archives, New York NY

Ellinghausen, Judy, *Archivist,* Cascade County Historical Society, The History Museum, Great Falls MT

Ellingson, Bruce, *VPres,* Witter Gallery, Storm Lake IA

Ellington, Howard W, *Exec Dir,* Wichita Center for the Arts, Wichita KS

Ellington, Howard W, *Exec Dir,* Wichita Center for the Arts, Maude Schollenberger Memorial Library, Wichita KS

Ellington, Howard W, *Exec Dir,* Wichita Center for the Arts, Mary R Koch School of Visual Arts, Wichita KS (S)

Ellington, Sam, *Pres,* Carnegie Center for Art & History, New Albany IN

Elliot, Gregory, *Asst Prof,* Louisiana State University, School of Art, Baton Rouge LA (S)

Elliot, John, *Asst Prof,* University of South Carolina at Aiken, Dept of Visual & Performing Arts, Aiken SC (S)

Elliot, Sandy, *Secy,* Western Art Association, Ellensburg WA

Elliot, Sheila, *VPres Mktg,* Edward Hopper, Nyack NY

Elliot, Steve, *Prof,* Wayne State College, Dept Art & Design, Wayne NE (S)

Elliott, Bill, *Mgr Bus Opers & Servs,* The Winnipeg Art Gallery, Winnipeg MB

Elliott, Bob, *Instr,* William Woods-Westminster Colleges, Art Dept, Fulton MO (S)

Elliott, Bonnie, *Ed,* Dartmouth Heritage Museum, Dartmouth NS

Elliott, D Stephen, *Pres & CEO,* New York State Historical Association, Fenimore Art Museum, Cooperstown NY

Elliott, Danial, *Arcadia Dir Libr & Archives,* Philadelphia Museum of Art, Library & Archives, Philadelphia PA

Elliott, Diann, *Asst Cur,* Eskimo Museum, Library, Churchill MB

Elliott, Gregory, *Dept Chair,* University of Texas at San Antonio, Dept of Art & Art History, San Antonio TX (S)

Elliott, John, *Pres,* Oil Pastel Association, Stockholm NJ

Elliott, John R, *Genealogist,* Kings County Historical Society & Museum, Hampton NB

Elliott, Joseph, *Asst Prof,* Muhlenberg College, Dept of Art, Allentown PA (S)

Elliott, Kate, *Cur,* Luther College, Fine Arts Collection, Decorah IA

Elliott, Scott, *Dir Develop,* Vancouver Art Gallery, Vancouver BC

Elliott, Vanessa, *Admin Asst,* Ormond Memorial Art Museum and Gardens, Ormond Beach FL

Ellis, Anita, *Deputy Dir Cur Affairs,* Cincinnati Art Museum, Cincinnati Art Museum, Cincinnati OH

Ellis, Bryan, *Lectr,* University of North Carolina at Greensboro, Art Dept, Greensboro NC (S)

Ellis, Eric, *Proj Mgr,* Association of Collegiate Schools of Architecture, Washington DC

Ellis, George R, *Dir, CEO & Pres,* Honolulu Academy of Arts, The Art Center at Linekona, Honolulu HI (S)

Ellis, Greg, *Archivist,* City of Lethbridge, Sir Alexander Galt Museum, Lethbridge AB

Ellis, Jack, *Co-Chmn Theater,* Western New Mexico University, Dept of Expressive Arts, Silver City NM (S)

Ellis, Jesika, *Instr,* University of Evansville, Art Dept, Evansville IN (S)

Ellis, Jim, *Instr,* Kirkwood Community College, Dept of Arts & Humanities, Cedar Rapids IA (S)

Ellis, Joe, *Dir,* Nicolaysen Art Museum & Discovery Center, Museum, Casper WY

Ellis, Lori, *Chmn & Prof,* State University of New York, College at Cortland, Dept Art & Art History, Cortland NY (S)

Ellis, Lori, *Cur,* Art Gallery of Calgary, Calgary AB

Ellis, Mac, *Custodian,* Glanmore National Historic Site of Canada, Belleville ON

Ellis, Rhianna, *Asst Cur,* Nassau County Museum of Art, Roslyn Harbor NY

Ellis, Rudy, *Cur,* Charles B Goddard, Ardmore OK

Ellis, Timothy, *Bd Pres,* Ogunquit Museum of American Art, Reference Library, Ogunquit ME

Ellison, Julie, *Prof,* University of Michigan, Ann Arbor, School of Art & Design, Ann Arbor MI (S)

Ellison, Rosemary, *Chief Cur,* Southern Plains Indian Museum, Anadarko OK

Ellison, Scott, *VPres Exec Comt,* Bank of Oklahoma NA, Art Collection, Tulsa OK

Ellisor, Megan, *Dir Opers,* Long Beach Museum of Art Foundation, Long Beach CA

Elloian, Peter, *Prof,* University of Toledo, Dept of Art, Toledo OH (S)

Ellsworth, Lisa, *Cur,* Palo Alto Art Center, Palo Alto CA

Elmendorf, Dana, *Asst,* Seton Hill University, Art Program, Greensburg PA (S)

Elmquist, Dana, *Assoc Producer Theater Progs,* Museum for African Art, New York NY

Elnimeiri, Mahjoub, *Prof,* Illinois Institute of Technology, College of Architecture, Chicago IL (S)

Elsishans, Nicholas, *CFO,* Fine Arts Museums of San Francisco, M H de Young Museum, San Francisco CA

Elsishans, Nicholas, *CFO,* Fine Arts Museums of San Francisco, Legion of Honor, San Francisco CA

Elsmo, Nancy, *Librn,* Wustum Museum Art Association, Wustum Art Library, Racine WI

Elsner, Linda, *Pres,* Kelly-Griggs House Museum, Red Bluff CA

Elvert, Jon, *Planetarium Dir,* Louisiana Arts & Science Museum, Baton Rouge LA

Emack-Cambra, Jane, *Cur,* Old Colony Historical Society, Museum, Taunton MA

Emack-Cambra, Jane, *Cur,* Old Colony Historical Society, Library, Taunton MA

Embree, Anna, *Guild Librn,* Guild of Book Workers, Library, New York NY

Emerick, Judson, *Prof,* Pomona College, Dept of Art & Art History, Claremont CA (S)

Emerson, Alice, *Mgr External Relations,* The Rosenbach Museum & Library, Philadelphia PA

Emerson, Bert, *Asst Prof,* Salve Regina University, Art Dept, Newport RI (S)

Emerson, Julie, *Cur Drawings,* Seattle Art Museum, Downtown, Seattle WA

Emerson, Julie, *Ruth J Nutt Cur Drawings,* Seattle Art Museum, Dorothy Stimson Bullitt Library, Seattle WA

Emerson, Melanie, *Head Reader Servs,* The Art Institute of Chicago, Ryerson & Burnham Libraries, Chicago IL

Emerson, Philip G, *Exec Dir,* Jamestown-Yorktown Foundation, Jamestown Settlement, Williamsburg VA

Emert, Carol, *Cur,* Washburn University, Mulvane Art Museum, Topeka KS

Emery, Brian E, *Chmn Photog,* Fashion Institute of Technology, Art & Design Division, New York NY (S)

Emery, Lea, *Acting Dir,* Purchase College, Neuberger Museum of Art, Purchase NY

Emery, Marty, *Pub Rels Mgr,* National Postal Museum, Smithsonian Institution, Washington DC

Emison, John, *Contact,* Sculpture Center School, Studios & Gallery, Long Island City NY (S)

Emison, Patricia, *Assoc Prof,* University of New Hampshire, Dept of Arts & Art History, Durham NH (S)

Emme, Mary-Jane, *Secy Gen,* Canadian Society for Education Through Art, Victoria BC

Emmons, Carol, *Prof,* University of Wisconsin-Green Bay, Arts Dept, Green Bay WI (S)

Emmons, Deborah, *Cur,* Historic Cherry Hill, Albany NY

Emmons, Nicole, *Ed & Publications Coordr,* Oklahoma City Museum of Art, Oklahoma City OK

Emmons-Andarawl, Deborah, *Interpreter,* Schuyler Mansion State Historic Site, Albany NY

Emodi, T, *Dean,* Dalhousie University, Faculty of Architecture, Halifax NS (S)

Emrich, Liz, *Cur Asst Rights & Repros,* Cornell University, Herbert F Johnson Museum of Art, Ithaca NY

Emsley, Tara, *Registrar,* Rhode Island School of Design, Museum of Art, Providence RI

Enabnit, Kenneth, *Art Librn,* Mason City Public Library, Mason City IA

Encina, Sebastian, *Mus Coll Mgr,* University of Michigan, Kelsey Museum of Archaeology, Ann Arbor MI

Endersby, Linda, *Asst Dir,* Missouri Department of Natural Resources, Missouri State Museum, Jefferson City MO

Endersby, Linda, *Asst Dir,* Missouri Department of Natural Resources, Elizabeth Rozier Gallery, Jefferson City MO

Endslow, Ellen, *Dir Coll & Cur,* Chester County Historical Society, West Chester PA

Engel, Dianne, *Coordr Coll,* Shell Canada Ltd, Calgary AB

Engel, Scott, *Chmn,* Arapahoe Community College, Colorado Gallery of the Arts, Littleton CO

Engelbert, John P, *Pres,* First State Bank, They Also Ran Gallery, Norton KS

Engelmann, Lothar K, *Prof,* Rochester Institute of Technology, School of Photographic Arts & Sciences, Rochester NY (S)

Engglezos, Yvonne, *Dir,* Bowne House Historical Society, Flushing NY

Engh, Michael, *Acad Pres,* Santa Clara University, de Saisset Museum, Santa Clara CA

England, Ann, *Cur,* Georgia State University, School of Art & Design, Visual Resource Center, Atlanta GA

England, Susan, *Prog Asst,* Kentucky Guild of Artists & Craftsmen Inc, Berea KY

Englebach, Fred, *Treas,* Portsmouth Historical Society, John Paul Jones House & Discover Portsmouth, Portsmouth NH

Engler, Dara, *Asst Gallery Dir,* University of Louisiana at Monroe, Bry Gallery, Monroe LA

English, Anderson B, *Photog,* Art Institute of Pittsburgh, Pittsburgh PA (S)

English, Darby, *Dir Research & Acad Progs,* Sterling & Francine Clark, Williamstown MA

English, Steve, *1st VPres,* Columbus Museum of Art, Columbus OH

Engman, Berin, *Assoc Prof,* Colby College, Art Dept, Waterville ME (S)

Engman, Kerstin, *Adjunct Asst Prof,* University of Maine, Dept of Art, Orono ME (S)

Engstrom, Mark, *Deputy Dir Coll & Res,* Royal Ontario Museum, Toronto ON

Ennen, Rita, *Dir Acquisition & Cataloging,* Dickinson State University, Stoxen Library, Dickinson ND

Ennis, Betsy, *Dir Pub Affairs,* Guggenheim Museum Soho, New York NY

Ennis, Ciara, *Cur Exhibs,* University of California, California Museum of Photography, Riverside CA

Ennis, Ciara, *Dir,* Pitzer College, Pitzer Art Galleries, Claremont CA (S)

Ennis, Elissa, *Dir Educ & Visitor Svcs,* Long Beach Museum of Art Foundation, Long Beach CA

Enniss, Stephen, *Librn,* Folger Shakespeare, Washington DC

Enos, Chris, *Assoc Prof,* University of New Hampshire, Dept of Arts & Art History, Durham NH (S)

Enright, Robyn, *Dir Pub Events,* The Albrecht-Kemper Museum of Art, Saint Joseph MO

Enriquez, Carola Rupert, *Dir,* Kern County Museum, Bakersfield CA

Enriquez, Carola Rupert, *Dir,* Kern County Museum, Library, Bakersfield CA

Enstice, Wayne, *Prof Fine Arts,* University of Cincinnati, School of Art, Cincinnati OH (S)

Entin, Daniel, *Exec Dir,* Nicholas Roerich, New York NY

Enyeart, James, *Asst Prof,* College of Santa Fe, Art Dept, Santa Fe NM (S)

Enzenaurer, Julie, *Admin Asst,* Owatonna Arts Center, Library, Owatonna MN

Epley, Brad, *Chief Conservator,* Menil Foundation, Inc, The Menil Collection, Houston TX

Eppley, Brenda, *Instr,* Harrisburg Area Community College, Division of Communications, Humanities & the Arts, Harrisburg PA (S)

Epps, Linda, *Pres,* New Jersey Historical Society, Newark NJ

Epps, Michelle, *Office Admin,* SPACES, Cleveland OH

Epstein, Ruth, *Thesis Adv,* Toronto Art Therapy Institute, Toronto ON (S)

Epstein, Sharon, *Instr,* Toronto School of Art, Toronto ON (S)

Erard, Mary Jane, *1st VPres,* Spectrum Gallery, Toledo OH

Erazmus, Alison, *Dir,* University of South Dakota, University Art Galleries, Vermillion SD

Erbes, Scott, *Dir Coll & Exhibs,* The Speed Art Museum, Louisville KY

Erbolato-Ramsey, Christiane, *Fine Arts Librn,* Brigham Young University, Harold B Lee Library, Provo UT

Ercums, Kris, *Cur Global Cont & Asian Art,* University of Kansas, Spencer Museum of Art, Lawrence KS

Erda, Andrea F, *Mgr,* Westover Plantation, Charles City VA

Erdelsky, Pat, *Asst Pub & Finance,* Westmoreland Museum of American Art, Art Reference Library, Greensburg PA

Erdman, Lindsay, *Chair,* Vesterheim Norwegian-American Museum, Decorah IA

Erdmann, Mariella, *Prof, Chmn,* Silver Lake College, Art Dept, Manitowoc WI (S)

Erdmann, Steven F, *Cur Colls,* Historical Society of Palm Beach County, The Richard and Pat Johnson Palm Beach County History Museum, West Palm Beach FL

Erf, Greg, *Asst Prof,* Eastern New Mexico University, Dept of Art, Portales NM (S)

Erf, Greg, *Prof Art & Animation,* Eastern New Mexico University, Runnels Gallery, Golden Library, Portales NM

Erf, Lisa K, *Dir Art Prog & Cur,* The First National Bank of Chicago, Art Collection, Chicago IL

Erf, Lisa K, *Dir Art Prog,* The JPMorgan Chase, Art Collection, New York NY

Erhard, Peter, *Prof,* La Sierra University, Art Dept, Riverside CA (S)

Erickson, Alyssa, *Coordr Project Look!,* Palo Alto Art Center, Palo Alto CA

Erickson, Ann Marie, *VChair,* Pewabic Society Inc, Pewabic Pottery, Detroit MI

Erickson, Christa, *Assoc Prof,* Stony Brook University, College of Arts & Sciences, Dept of Art, Stony Brook NY (S)

Erickson, David, *Pres,* Lincoln Arts Council, Lincoln NE

Erickson, Edmund, *Dir Library,* Black Hills State University, Library, Spearfish SD

Erickson, Elizabeth, *Prof,* Minneapolis College of Art & Design, Minneapolis MN (S)

Erickson, Gary, *Instr,* Macalester College, Art Dept, Saint Paul MN (S)

Erickson, Ingrid, *Educ Coordr,* Waterworks Visual Arts Center, Salisbury NC

Erickson, Jeffrey, *Visual Resources Cur,* Davidson College, Katherine & Tom Belk Visual Arts Center, Davidson NC

Erickson, John, *Asst Prof Lectr,* University of Utah, Dept of Art & Art History, Salt Lake City UT (S)

Erickson, Joyce, *Dean Col Arts & Sciences,* Seattle Pacific University, Art Dept, Seattle WA (S)

Erickson, Kathy, *Colls Mgr,* United States General Services Administration, Art in Architecture and Fine Arts, Washington DC

Erickson, Pam, *Bookkeeper,* Fuller Lodge Art Center, Los Alamos NM

Erickson, Paul J, *Dir Acad Programs,* American Antiquarian Society, Worcester MA

Erickson, Robert, *Prof,* University of Wisconsin-Stevens Point, Dept of Art & Design, Stevens Point WI (S)

Erickson, Russanne, *Educ,* Hastings Museum of Natural & Cultural History, Hastings NE

Ericksson, Lynn, *Mem Coordr,* University of Connecticut, William Benton Museum of Art, Storrs CT

Ericson, Margaret, *Librn,* Colby College, Bixler Art & Music Library, Waterville ME

Ericta, Cecille, *Fin & Office Mgr,* Alternate ROOTS, Inc, Atlanta GA

Eriksen, Lisa, *Dir Educ & Pub Progs,* The California Historical Society, San Francisco CA

Eriksen, Roger, *Assoc Prof Art,* Adams State College, Dept of Visual Arts, Alamosa CO (S)

Erikson, Bruce, *Assoc Prof,* Xavier University, Dept of Art, Cincinnati OH (S)

Erlandson, Molly, *Asst Prof,* West Virginia State University, Art Dept, Institute WV (S)

Erlebacher, Martha Mayer, *Instr,* New York Academy of Art, Graduate School of Figurative Art, New York NY (S)

Erlendson, Chandra, *Dir Educ & Pub Progs,* Homer Watson, Kitchener ON

Erlinger, Lauren, *Develop Dir,* Kirkland Arts Center, Kirkland WA

Ermansons, Taiga, *Educ Prog Planner,* Smith College, Museum of Art, Northampton MA

Ernst-Croskrey, Wendy, *Assoc Prof,* University of Alaska-Fairbanks, Dept of Art, Fairbanks AK (S)

Ershig, Janet, *Store Mgr,* Whatcom Museum, Bellingham WA

Erskine, Pamela, *Lib Specialist,* Cornish College of the Arts, Cornish Library, Seattle WA

Erskins, Eleanor, *Assoc Prof,* Portland State University, Dept of Art, Portland OR (S)

Erway, Janet, *Dir,* Cooperstown Art Association, Cooperstown NY

Erwin, Sarah, *Cur Archival Coll,* University of Tulsa, Library, Tulsa OK

Escalada, Kathleen, *Pres,* Pimeria Alta Historical Society, Nogales AZ

Escalante, Jim, *Prof,* University of Wisconsin, Madison, Dept of Art, Madison WI (S)

Escallon, Ana Maria, *Dir,* Art Museum of the Americas, Washington DC

Escarsega, Edward, *Admin & Mem Mgr,* American Museum of Ceramic Art, Pomona CA

Eschapasse, Anne, *Dir Exhibs & Publs,* Musee National des Beaux Arts du Quebec, Quebec PQ

Escobar, Gloria, *Chmn,* Hartwick College, Art Dept, Oneonta NY (S)

Escobar, Gloria, *Cur of Foreman Gallery,* Hartwick College, The Yager Museum, Oneonta NY

Escobar, Jesus, *Assoc Prof,* Northwestern University, Evanston, Dept of Art History, Evanston IL (S)

Escoveda, Lisa, *Registrar,* Norton Simon, Pasadena CA

Esdrin, Debbie, *Dir Develop,* Koffler Centre of the Arts, Koffler Gallery, Toronto ON

Eshleman, Janet, *Pres,* Carteret County Historical Society, The History Place, Morehead City NC

Eshraghi-Yazdi, Ramin, *Career & Life Counselor (YA! Project),* Quickdraw Animation Society, Calgary AB

Eskildsen, Noreen, *Lectr,* Briar Cliff University, Art Dept, Sioux City IA (S)

Eskilson, Stephen, *Prof,* Eastern Illinois University, Art Dept, Charleston IL (S)

Eskridge, Robert, *Dir Museum Educ,* The Art Institute of Chicago, Kraft Education Center/Museum Education, Chicago IL

Eskridge, Robert, *Exec Dir Mus Educ,* The Art Institute of Chicago, Chicago IL

Esler, Jennifer, *Pres & CEO,* Historical Society of Martin County, Elliott Museum, Stuart FL

Esmaye, Rodayne, *Prof,* Salt Lake Community College, Graphic Design Dept, Salt Lake City UT (S)

Esmond, Judi, *Educ Coordr,* State University of New York at New Paltz, Samuel Dorsky Museum of Art, New Paltz NY

Esmonde, Gary, *Librn,* Cleveland Botanical Garden, Eleanor Squire Library, Cleveland OH

Espey, Jule Adele, *Assoc Prof,* Our Lady of the Lake University, Dept of Art, San Antonio TX (S)

Espinosa, Christopher, *Gen Mgr,* El Pueblo de Los Angeles Historical Monument, Los Angeles CA

Espinosa, Fred, *Maintenance,* Museum of Western Colorado, Museum of the West, Grand Junction CO

Espinoza, Dyanna, *Instr,* Biola University, Art Dept, La Mirada CA (S)

Esposito, Cecilia, *Dir,* State University of New York at Plattsburgh, Art Museum, Plattsburgh NY

Esposito, Dan, *Asst Security & Facility Mgr,* The Pennsylvania State University, Palmer Museum of Art, University Park PA

Esprit, Raymond Vincent, *Pastor,* Kateri Tekakwitha Shrine/St. Francis Xavier Mission, Kahnawake PQ

Esquibel, George A, *Instr,* Sacramento City College, Art Dept, Sacramento CA (S)

Esser, Joe, *Designer & Preparator,* The Long Island Museum of American Art, History & Carriages, Stony Brook NY

Esser, Joseph, *Exhib Designer,* The Long Island Museum of American Art, History & Carriages, Library, Stony Brook NY

Essig, Joseph, *Treas,* Society of American Graphic Artists, New York NY

Essinger, Catherine, *Libr Coordr,* Art Museum of the University of Houston, William R Jenkins Architecture & Art Library, Houston TX

Esslinger, Claudia, *Prof,* Kenyon College, Art Dept, Gambier OH (S)

Estomin, B Lynn, *Chmn,* Lycoming College, Art Dept, Williamsport PA (S)

Etchieson, David, *Historic Site Specialist,* Historic Arkansas Museum, Little Rock AR

Etheridge, Frank, *Pub Rels Coordr,* Columbus Museum, Columbus GA

Ethington, Bob, *Mgr History & Humanities Div,* Akron-Summit County Public Library, Fine Arts Division, Akron OH

Etling, Russell, *Cultural Affairs Progs Coordr,* City of Gainesville, Thomas Center Galleries - Cultural Affairs, Gainesville FL

Ettema, Michael, *Dir,* Maricopa County Historical Society, Eleanor Blossom Memorial Library, Wickenburg AZ

Etter, Ann, *Theater Specialist,* Northfield Arts Guild, Northfield MN

Eubank, Larry, *Opers Mgr,* Kimbell Art Foundation, Kimbell Art Museum, Fort Worth TX

Eubanks, Jenifer, *Dir,* Pomerene Center for the Arts, Coshocton OH

Eubanks, W Ralph, *Dir Publ Office*, Library of Congress, Prints & Photographs Division, Washington DC

Eudenbach, Peter, *Assoc Prof*, Old Dominion University, Art Dept, Norfolk VA (S)

Eure, Dana, *Asst Dir*, Union County Public Library Union Room, Monroe NC

Evaleuko, Suz, *Pres*, First Street Gallery, New York NY

Evangelista, Kristen, *Dir*, William Paterson University, Ben Shahn Art Galleries, Wayne NJ

Evanisko, Sonya, *Coordr Painting*, Shepherd University, Dept of Contemporary Art & Theater, Shepherdstown WV (S)

Evans, Ali, *Pub Rels Mgr*, The Studio Museum in Harlem, New York NY

Evans, Allison, *Registrar*, Nelda C & H J Lutcher Stark, Stark Museum of Art, Orange TX

Evans, Barbara, *Dir Develop*, Telfair Museums' Jepson Center for the Arts Library, Telfair Academy of Arts & Sciences Library, Savannah GA

Evans, Brett, *Dir Develop*, Auburn University, Julie Collins Smith Museum, Auburn AL

Evans, Catherine, *Cur Photography*, Columbus Museum of Art, Columbus OH

Evans, Colleen, *VPres External Affairs & Develop*, Alberta College of Art & Design, Calgary AB (S)

Evans, Craig, *CEO*, Sandwich Historical Society, Center Sandwich NH

Evans, Diane, *Exec Dir*, Sonoma County Museum, Santa Rosa CA

Evans, Donald H, *Prof Emeritus*, Vanderbilt University, Dept of Art, Nashville TN (S)

Evans, Douglas R, *Registrar*, Westmoreland Museum of American Art, Art Reference Library, Greensburg PA

Evans, Douglas W, *Colls Mgr*, Westmoreland Museum of American Art, Greensburg PA

Evans, Jon, *Ref Librn*, Museum of Fine Arts, Houston, Hirsch Library, Houston TX

Evans, Julie, *Instr*, Guilford Technical Community College, Commercial Art Dept, Jamestown NC (S)

Evans, Kenya, *Gallery Supervisor*, Contemporary Arts Museum Houston, Houston TX

Evans, Lee, *Chmn*, Pace University, Theatre & Fine Arts Dept, New York NY (S)

Evans, Lois, *Librn*, J T & E J Crumbaugh, Le Roy IL

Evans, Oliver H, *Pres*, Kendall College of Art & Design, Grand Rapids MI (S)

Evans, Pat, *Registrar*, Scottsdale Cultural Council, Scottsdale Museum of Contemporary Art, Scottsdale AZ

Evans, Peggy, *Bd Mem*, French Art Colony, Gallipolis OH

Evans, Scott, *Faculty*, Idaho State University, Dept of Art & Pre-Architecture, Pocatello ID (S)

Evans, Scott, *VPres*, Long Beach Art League, Long Beach Island NY

Evans, Sharon, *Interim Dean Fine Arts & Commun*, Western Illinois University, Department of Art, Macomb IL (S)

Evans, Susan, *Asst Prof*, Oakland University, Dept of Art & Art History, Rochester MI (S)

Evans-Cantrell, Deborah, *Catalog/Reference Librn*, Indianapolis Museum of Art, Stout Reference Library, Indianapolis IN

Evans-Cross, Lorraine, *Office Mgr*, Red Deer & District Museum & Archives, Red Deer AB

Evanson, Barbara, *Community Serv Dir*, Rapid City Arts Council, Dahl Arts Center, Rapid City SD

Evarts, Wilbur, *Cur*, Paint 'N Palette Club, Grant Wood Memorial Park & Gallery, Anamosa IA

Even, Yael, *Prof*, University of Missouri, Saint Louis, Dept of Art & Art History, Saint Louis MO (S)

Evenden, Kirstin, *Pres & CEO*, Glenbow Museum, Calgary AB

Evenhouse, Anna Hayes, *Assoc Dir Exhibs*, The American Federation of Arts, New York NY

Evenhouse, Raymond, *Clinical Asst Prof*, University of Illinois at Chicago, Biomedical Visualization, Chicago IL (S)

Everett, Eileen, *Dir Liberal Arts & Grad Studies*, Academy of Art University, Fine Arts Dept, San Francisco CA (S)

Everett, Terry, *Educ*, Tellus Northwest Georgia Science Museum, Cartersville GA

Everett, William, *Gallery Dir*, The Guild of Boston Artists, Boston MA

Everett Zamora, Kristie, *Exhib Coordr*, Flint Institute of Arts, Library, Flint MI

Everhart, Sarah, *Photo Librn*, Colorado Historical Society, Stephen H Hart Library, Denver CO

Everly, Lynne, *Ranger Coordr*, Bluemont Historical Railroad Junction, Arlington VA

Evers, Renate, *Librn*, Leo Baeck, Library, New York NY

Everson, Dave, *Instr*, Cuyahoga Valley Art Center, Cuyahoga Falls OH (S)

Everson, David, *Interim Dept Head*, Southeastern Louisiana University, Dept of Visual Arts, Hammond LA (S)

Everson, Kevin, *Studio Faculty*, University of Virginia, McIntire Dept of Art, Charlottesville VA (S)

Evins, Jennifer, *Pres & COO*, Arts Partnership of Greater Spartanburg, Inc, Chapman Cultural Center, Spartanburg SC

Evnin, Judy, *Chmn Bd Trustees*, Caramoor Center for Music & the Arts, Inc, Rosen House at Caramoor, Katonah NY

Ewald, Jill, *Dir*, Saint Olaf College, Flaten Art Museum, Northfield MN

Ewald, Jill, *Museum Dir*, Saint Olaf College, Art Dept, Northfield MN (S)

Ewan, Jeanette Cousins, *Registrar*, Museum London, London ON

Ewers, Don, *Lectr*, University of the Incarnate Word, Art Dept, San Antonio TX (S)

Ewers, William, *Exec Dir*, Palette & Chisel Academy of Fine Arts, Chicago IL

Ewert, George, *Dir*, History Museum of Mobile, Reference Library, Mobile AL

Ewert, George, *Dir*, History Museum of Mobile, Carlen House, Mobile AL

Ewert, Linda, *Educ Dir*, Yellowstone Art Museum, Billings MT

Ewing, Calum, *Dir Mus Opers*, Nova Scotia Museum, Maritime Museum of the Atlantic, Halifax NS

Ewing, Lauren, *Prof*, Rutgers, The State University of New Jersey, Mason Gross School of the Arts, Visual Arts Dept, New Brunswick NJ (S)

Ewing, Rick, *Main Library Gen Mgr*, Akron-Summit County Public Library, Fine Arts Division, Akron OH

Ewing, Rosemary, *Chmn*, Louisiana Department of Culture, Recreation & Tourism, Louisiana State Museum, New Orleans LA

Ex, Jim, *Assoc Exec Dir*, United States Figure Skating Association, World Figure Skating Museum & Hall of Fame, Colorado Springs CO

Exline, J, *Adjunct Prof*, Le Moyne College, Fine Arts Dept, Syracuse NY (S)

Exxon, Randall L, *Prof*, Swarthmore College, Dept of Art & Art History, Swarthmore PA (S)

Eyerdam, Pamela J, *Mgr*, Cleveland Public Library, Fine Arts & Special Collections Dept, Cleveland OH

Eyermann, Linda, *Dir Educ*, South Shore Arts, Munster IN

Eyjolfsson, Kristjana, *Dir Educ*, Historical Museum at Fort Missoula, Missoula MT

Eyland, Cliff, *Faculty*, University of Manitoba, School of Art, Winnipeg MB (S)

Eyler, Carolyn, *Dir Exhibs*, University of Southern Maine, Dept of Art, Gorham ME (S)

Ezell, Liz, *Mus Dir*, Marine Corps University, National Museum of the Marine Corps, Triangle VA

Ezell, Lynn, *Publications Mgr*, National Art Education Association, Reston VA

Ezell-Gilson, Carol, *Cur*, City of Charleston, City Hall Council Chamber Gallery, Charleston SC

Fabbri Butera, Virginia, *Chmn Dept*, College of Saint Elizabeth, Art Dept, Morristown NJ (S)

Fabbro, Robert, *Reference & Access Svcs Librn*, OCAD University, Dorothy H Hoover Library, Toronto ON

Faber, David, *Assoc Prof*, Wake Forest University, Dept of Art, Winston-Salem NC (S)

Faberman, Hilarie, *Cur Modern & Contemporary*, Stanford University, Cantor Arts Center at Stanford University, Stanford CA

Fabian, Carole Ann, *Dir*, Columbia University, Avery Architectural & Fine Arts Library, New York NY

Fabiano, Steve, *Dir Fin & Admin*, DeCordova Museum & Sculpture Park, DeCordova Museum, Lincoln MA

Fabiszak, Dennis, *Dir*, East Hampton Library, Long Island Collection, East Hampton NY

Fabo, Andy, *Instr*, Toronto School of Art, Toronto ON (S)

Fabozzi, Paul, *Chmn*, Saint John's University, Dept of Fine Arts, Jamaica NY (S)

Fabricand-Person, Nicole, *Japanese Art Specialist*, Princeton University, Marquand Library of Art & Archaeology, Princeton NJ

Fabrick, Lane, *Assoc Prof*, Southeast Missouri State University, Dept of Art, Cape Girardeau MO (S)

Facchini, Gina, *Asst Dir*, Wynick Tuck Gallery, Toronto ON

Faccinto, Victor, *Dir*, Wake Forest University, Charlotte & Philip Hanes Art Gallery, Winston Salem NC

Facio, Isaac, *Dept Specialist*, The Art Institute of Chicago, Department of Textiles, Textile Society, Chicago IL

Fagaly, William A, *Cur African Art*, New Orleans Museum of Art, New Orleans LA

Fagan, Barry, *Financial Coordr*, Queen's University, Agnes Etherington Art Centre, Kingston ON

Fagan, Sha, *Dir Lib & Acad Computing*, Sarah Lawrence College Library, Esther Raushenbush Library, Bronxville NY

Fagan, Tricia, *Cur*, Mercer County Community College, Arts, Communication & Engineering Technology, West Windsor NJ (S)

Fagan, Tricia, *Dir*, Artworks, The Visual Art School of Trenton, Trenton NJ

Fagan, Tricia, *Dir*, Artworks, The Visual Art School of Trenton, Library, Trenton NJ

Fagan, Tricia, *Gallery Dir*, Mercer County Community College, The Gallery, West Windsor NJ

Fagan Affleck, Diane, *Dir Exhib*, American Textile History Museum, Lowell MA

Faggioli, Renzo, *Instr*, Moravian College, Dept of Art, Bethlehem PA (S)

Fahlund, Michael, *Deputy Dir*, College Art Association, New York NY

Fahnestock, Jon, *Assoc Prof Interactive Design*, Maryville University of Saint Louis, Art & Design Program, Saint Louis MO (S)

Fahy, Deborah, *Exec Dir*, Kennebec Valley Art Association, Harlow Gallery, Hallowell ME

Fahy, Everett, *John Pope Henness Chmn*, The Metropolitan Museum of Art, New York NY

Faillace, Rachael, *Dir Gallery*, The Art School at Old Church, Demarest NJ (S)

Fair, Sherry, *Admin Dir*, City Arts Center at Fair Park, Oklahoma City OK

Fairall, Tiffany, *Assoc Cur*, Mesa Arts Center, Mesa Contemporary Arts Museum, Mesa AZ

Fairchild, Pat, *Head Cataloging*, University of New Mexico, Fine Arts Library, Albuquerque NM

Fairlie, Carol, *Asst Prof*, Sul Ross State University, Dept of Fine Arts & Communications, Alpine TX (S)

Fairman, Elisabeth, *Sr Cur Rare Books & Manuscripts*, Yale University, Yale Center for British Art, New Haven CT

Fairman, Hugh, *Treas*, Inter-Society Color Council, Reston VA

Fairweather, Paula, *Dir Mktg*, Bill Reid Gallery of Northwest Coast Art, Vancouver BC

Faison, Michael, *Exec Dir*, Idaho Commission on the Arts, Boise ID

Faist, Jennifer, *Photo Research Cur*, Art Center College of Design, James Lemont Fogg Memorial Library, Pasadena CA

Fajardo, Carlos, *Prof*, University of Puerto Rico, Mayaguez, Dept of Humanities, College of Fine Arts & Theory of Art Programs, Mayaguez PR (S)

Fajardo, Carlos, *Prof*, University of Puerto Rico, Mayaguez, Dept of Humanities, College of Fine Arts & Theory of Art Programs, Mayaguez PR (S)

Fajardo, Rafael, *Assoc Prof Electronic Media Arts & Design*, University of Denver, School of Art & Art History, Denver CO (S)

Fajardo-Hill, Cecilia, *VPres Curatorial Affairs & Chief Cur*, Museum of Latin American Art, Long Beach CA

Fakundiny, Robert, *Chief Geological Survey*, New York State Museum, Albany NY

Falcaro, Millie, *Assoc Prof Art,* Marymount Manhattan College, Fine & Performing Arts Div, New York NY (S)

Falcone-Hall, Kelly, *Vice Pres,* Western Reserve Historical Society, Cleveland OH

Falconer, Jim, *Registrar,* Lyme Academy College of Fine Arts, Old Lyme CT (S)

Fales, Christine, *Acad Affairs Asst,* New Hampshire Institute of Art, Manchester NH

Fales, Melanie, *Exec Dir,* Boise Art Museum, Boise ID

Falgner, Susan M, *Head Pub Svcs,* College of Mount Saint Joseph, Archbishop Alter Library, Cincinnati OH

Falk, Karen, *Gallery Dir,* Jewish Community Center of Greater Washington, Jane L & Robert H Weiner Judaic Museum, Rockville MD

Falk, Lorne, *Dean Faculty,* School of the Museum of Fine Arts, Boston MA (S)

Falk, Louie, *Chmn Bd,* North Country Museum of Arts, Park Rapids MN

Falke, Emily, *Cur,* Bakersfield Art Foundation, Bakersfield Museum of Art, Bakersfield CA

Falkenstein, Jaclyn, *Pub Rels Coordr,* The Children's Museum of Indianapolis, Indianapolis IN

Falkenstien-Doyle, Cheri, *Cur,* Wheelwright Museum of the American Indian, Santa Fe NM

Falkenstien-Doyle, Cheri, *Cur,* Wheelwright Museum of the American Indian, Mary Cabot Wheelwright Research Library, Santa Fe NM

Falkner, Avery, *Prof,* Pepperdine University, Seaver College, Dept of Art, Malibu CA (S)

Falkner, Lorett, *Asst Prof,* Rochester Institute of Technology, School of Photographic Arts & Sciences, Rochester NY (S)

Falkner Mercurio, Melissa, *Registrar,* Birmingham Museum of Art, Birmingham AL

Falkner Mercurio, Melissa, *Registrar,* Birmingham Museum of Art, Clarence B Hanson Jr Library, Birmingham AL

Fallacaro, Bill, *Facilities Mgr,* Henry Morrison Flagler Museum, Palm Beach FL

Fallon, Roberta, *Adj Prof,* Saint Joseph's University, Art Dept, Philadelphia PA (S)

Falls, David, *Installations Officer & Registrar,* University of Western Ontario, McIntosh Gallery, London ON

Falls, Jo, *Dir Pub Progs,* Tohono Chul Park, Tucson AZ

Faloon, Ronda, *Dir,* Cape Ann Historical Association, Cape Ann Museum, Gloucester MA

Falsetta, Vincent, *Prof Drawing & Painting,* University of North Texas, College of Visual Arts & Design, Denton TX (S)

Falvey, Tom, *Dir Science & Outreach,* South Carolina State Museum, Columbia SC

Falzon, Patrizia, *Dir Develop,* Orange County Museum of Art, Newport Beach CA

Familian, David, *Asst Dir,* University of California, Irvine, Beall Center for Art + Technology, and University Art Gallery, Irvine CA

Famula, Linda, *Mktg & Pub Rels Mgr,* United States Figure Skating Association, World Figure Skating Museum & Hall of Fame, Colorado Springs CO

Fancher, Ollie, *Instr,* Middle Tennessee State University, Art Dept, Murfreesboro TN (S)

Fanelli, Doris, *Chief Cultural Resources,* Independence National Historical Park, Library, Philadelphia PA

Fang, Miho, *Gallery Asst,* Japan Society, Inc, Japan Society Gallery, New York NY

Fankhauser, Teresa, *Exec Dir,* Allied Arts Council of St Joseph, Saint Joseph MO

Fannon, Megan, *VPres,* Rensselaer Newman Foundation Chapel + Cultural Center, The Gallery at the Chapel & Cultural Center, Troy NY

Faraci, Carolyn, *Deputy Dir,* Huntsville Museum of Art, Huntsville AL

Farago, Andrew, *Gallery Mgr,* Cartoon Art Museum, San Francisco CA

Farber, Ellen, *Instr,* State University of New York College at Oneonta, Dept of Art, Oneonta NY (S)

Farber, Leslie, *Assoc Prof,* William Paterson University, Dept Arts, Wayne NJ (S)

Farbstein, Tracy, *Library Asst,* University of California, Berkeley, Architecture Visual Resources Library, Berkeley CA

Farina, John, *Dir Develop,* Beck Center for the Arts, Lakewood OH

Farley, Danica, *Communs Dir,* Salt Lake Art Center, Utah Museum of Contemporary Art, Salt Lake City UT

Farley, Gale, *Asst Prof,* Herkimer County Community College, Humanities Social Services, Herkimer NY (S)

Farley, Joy, *Registrar,* Institute of American Indian Arts, Museum of Contemporary Native Arts, Santa Fe NM (S)

Farley Harger, Sara, *Exec Dir,* Liberty Hall Historic Site, Library, Frankfort KY

Farlow, Shannon, *Dir Mktg,* Waterloo Center of the Arts, Waterloo IA

Farlowe, Allie, *Asst Cur,* The Mint Museum, Mint Museum of Craft & Design, Charlotte NC

Farmar, Angela, *Head Info & Reference,* Public Library of Cincinnati & Hamilton County, Info & Reference Dept, Cincinnati OH

Farmer, Dustin, *Art Instr,* Seward County Community College, Art Dept, Liberal KS (S)

Farmer, James, *Asst Prof,* Virginia Commonwealth University, Art History Dept, Richmond VA (S)

Farmer, Laura, *Facilities Use Coordr,* California African-American Museum, Los Angeles CA

Farmer, Marni, *Dir Communs,* Laguna Art Museum, Laguna Beach CA

Farmer, Rosella, *Mem Chair,* Manitoba Society of Artists, Winnipeg MB

Farn, George, *Treas,* Bowne House Historical Society, Flushing NY

Farndon, Gail, *Opers Mgr,* Art Gallery of Mississauga, Mississauga ON

Farnia, Ahmad, *Mus Cafe Mgr,* Oklahoma City Museum of Art, Oklahoma City OK

Farnsworth, Craig, *Instr,* Judson University, School of Art, Design & Architecture, Elgin IL (S)

Farr, Christopher J, *Exec Dir,* Brick Store Museum, Kennebunk ME

Farr, Jeanette, *Instr,* Glendale Community College, Visual & Performing Arts Div, Glendale CA (S)

Farr, Libby, *Instr,* Marylhurst University, Art Dept, Marylhurst OR (S)

Farral, Tammy, *Secy,* Bertha V B Lederer Fine Arts Gallery-Suny Geneseo, Bertha V B Lederer Fine Arts Gallery, Geneseo NY

Farral, Tommy, *Sec,* State University of New York at Geneseo, Lockhart Gallery, Geneseo NY

Farrar, Paula, *Reference Librn,* University of British Columbia, Art & Architecture Planning, UBC Library, Vancouver BC

Farrar-Wegener, Louise, *Instr,* Marylhurst University, Art Dept, Marylhurst OR (S)

Farrell, Anne, *Dir Develop,* Museum of Contemporary Art, San Diego-Downtown, La Jolla CA

Farrell, Anne, *Dir External Affairs,* Museum of Contemporary Art, San Diego, Geisel Library, La Jolla CA

Farrell, Cynthia, *Admin Asst,* University of New Hampshire, Museum of Art, Durham NH

Farrell, Donald M, *Treas,* Belskie Museum, Closter NJ

Farrell, Jennifer, *Cur Exhibs,* University of Virginia, The Fralin Museum of Art at the University of Virginia, Charlottesville VA

Farrell, Mary, *Prof,* Gonzaga University, Dept of Art, Spokane WA (S)

Farrell, Michael J, *Prof,* University of Windsor, Visual Arts, Windsor ON (S)

Farrell, Peggy, *Secy,* Pemaquid Group of Artists, Pemaquid Art Gallery, Pemaquid Point ME

Farrell, Peter C, *Pres Board Trustees,* Museum of Contemporary Art, San Diego, La Jolla CA

Farrell, William, *Industrial Design Technology,* Art Institute of Pittsburgh, Pittsburgh PA (S)

Farrier, Sanford, *Chmn, Visual Communs,* Endicott College, School of Visual & Performing Arts, Beverly MA (S)

Farrington, Jennifer, *Pres & CEO,* Chicago Children's Museum, Chicago IL

Farrington, Rusty, *Chmn,* Iowa Central Community College, Dept of Art, Fort Dodge IA (S)

Farriss, Adra, *Prog Coordr,* Edna Hibel, Hibel Museum Gallery, Jupiter FL

Farrokhi, Abdollah, *Instr,* Black Hills State University, Art Dept, Spearfish SD (S)

Farthing, Stephen, *Exec Dir,* New York Academy of Art, Graduate School of Figurative Art, New York NY (S)

Farver, Jane, *Dir,* Massachusetts Institute of Technology, List Visual Arts Center, Cambridge MA

Farynyk, Diane, *Registrar,* Frick Collection, New York NY

Fasoldt, Staats, *Instr,* Woodstock School of Art, Inc, Woodstock NY (S)

Fass, Philip, *Prof,* University of Northern Iowa, Dept of Art, Cedar Falls IA (S)

Fasse, Jane, *Instr,* Edgewood College, Art Dept, Madison WI (S)

Fassett, Brian, *Instr,* University of Louisiana at Monroe, Dept of Art, Monroe LA (S)

Faubert, Alison, *Cur,* Passaic County Historical Society, Lambert Castle Museum & Library, Paterson NJ

Faubert, Claude, *Dir Gen,* Canada Science and Technology Museum, Ottawa ON

Faude, Wilson H, *Exec Dir,* Old State House, Hartford CT

Faudie, Fred, *Prof,* University of Massachusetts Lowell, Dept of Art, Lowell MA (S)

Faught, Jana, *MoFAB Mgr,* Butte Silver Bow Arts Chateau, Butte MT

Faulds, W Rod, *Dir University Galleries,* Florida Atlantic University, University Galleries/Ritter Art Gallery/Schmidt Center Gallery, Boca Raton FL

Faulkes, Eve, *Prof,* West Virginia University, College of Creative Arts, School of Art & Design, Morgantown WV (S)

Faulkner, Phillip, *Vis Artist,* Finlandia Univ, International School of Art and Design, Hancock MI (S)

Faure, Ben, *Park Mgr,* Florida Department of Environmental Protection, Stephen Foster Folk Culture Center State Park, White Springs FL

Faurot, Carlis, *Facilities Mgr,* Cedar Rapids Museum of Art, Cedar Rapids IA

Fausone, Lynn G, *Adjunct Asst Prof,* Oakland University, Dept of Art & Art History, Rochester MI (S)

Favata, Alexa A, *Deputy Dir,* University of South Florida, Contemporary Art Museum, Tampa FL

Favela, Maria, *Deputy Security Supv,* Institute of American Indian Arts, Museum of Contemporary Native Arts, Santa Fe NM

Favella, Maria, *Dep Security Office,* Institute of American Indian Arts, Museum of Contemporary Native Arts, Santa Fe NM (S)

Favier, Pieter, *Sculptor,* University of South Alabama, Dept of Art & Art History, Mobile AL (S)

Favret, John, *Faculty,* Housatonic Community College, Art Dept, Bridgeport CT (S)

Favrholdt, Linda, *Prog Coordr,* Kamloops Art Gallery, Kamloops BC

Fawcett, Mim Brooks, *Exec Dir,* Attleboro Arts Museum, Attleboro MA

Fawkes, Tom, *Instr,* Pacific Northwest College of Art, Portland OR (S)

Faxon, Susan, *Cur (art before 1950),* Phillips Academy, Addison Gallery of American Art, Andover MA

Fay, Bob, *VPres,* The San Joaquin Pioneer & Historical Society, The Haggin Museum, Stockton CA

Fay, Ming, *Prof,* William Paterson University, Dept Arts, Wayne NJ (S)

Faye, Chris, *Cur,* Kauai Museum Association, Ltd., Lihue HI

Fayerman, Faye, *Prof,* New York Institute of Technology, Fine Arts Dept, Old Westbury NY (S)

Fazio, Ellissa, *Exec Dir,* Queens Historical Society, Kingsland Homestead, Flushing NY

Fazzino, Joseph, *Dir Pub Rels & Mktg,* Mark Twain, Hartford CT

Feagins, J R, *Chief Security,* Birmingham Museum of Art, Birmingham AL

Fear, Janet, *Reference,* Sheridan College of Applied Arts and Technology, Trafalgar Campus Library, Oakville ON

Feast, Terra, *Cur Educ,* Boise Art Museum, Boise ID

Feather, Meghan, *Admin Asst,* Touchstone Center for Crafts, Hart Moore Museum, Farmington PA

Feavyour, Dawn, *Prog Coordr,* Maitland Art Center, Maitland FL

FeBland, Harriet, *Dir & Instruc,* Harriet FeBland, New York NY (S)

FeBland, Harriet, *Pres Emerita,* American Society of Contemporary Artists (ASCA), Yorktown Heights NY

Febo, Samuel, *Dir,* Institute of Puerto Rican Culture, Dr Jose C Barbosa Museum, San Juan PR

Febo, Samuel, *Dir,* Institute of Puerto Rican Culture, Dr Jose C Barbosa Museum, San Juan PR

Febo-Cotto, Samuel D, *Dir,* Institute of Puerto Rican Culture, Museo y Parque Historico Ruinas de Caparra, San Juan PR

Febo-Cotto, Samuel D, *Dir,* Institute of Puerto Rican Culture, Museo y Parque Historico Ruinas de Caparra, San Juan PR

Febraro, Sarah, *Community Arts Programmer,* Oakville Galleries, Centennial Square and Gairloch Gardens, Oakville ON

Febre, Ricardo, *Asst Prof,* Humboldt State University, College of Arts & Humanities, Art Dept, Arcata CA (S)

Fecho, Susan C, *Chmn,* Barton College, Art & Design Dept, Wilson NC (S)

Fechter, Earl, *Prof,* Norwich University, Dept of Architecture and Art, Northfield VT (S)

Fecter, Eric, *VPres Finance,* Alberta College of Art & Design, Calgary AB (S)

Fedders, Kristin, *Asst Prof,* University of Saint Francis, School of Creative Arts, Fort Wayne IN (S)

Fedders, Kristin, *Convener,* Earlham College, Art Dept, Richmond IN (S)

Fedeler, Barbara, *Asst Prof,* Wartburg College, Dept of Art, Waverly IA (S)

Federici, Mario, *Chmn Production Mgmt,* Fashion Institute of Technology, Art & Design Division, New York NY (S)

Fedor, Stefanie, *Exec Dir,* Arlington Arts Center (AAC), Arlington VA

Fedor, Stephanie, *Asst Dir,* American University, Katzen Art Center Gallery, New York NY

Fedorak, Lisa, *Prog Coordr,* Contemporary Art Gallery Society of British Columbia, Vancouver BC

Fedorchenko, Xenia, *Asst Prof,* Lamar University, Art Dept, Beaumont TX (S)

Fee, Walker, *Artist,* U Gallery, New York NY

Feeler, William, *Dean,* Midland College, Art Dept, Midland TX (S)

Fefee, Claudette, *Secy,* The State University of New York at Potsdam, Roland Gibson Gallery, Potsdam NY

Feher-Simonelli, Brenda, *Gallery Coordr,* Texas A&M University Commerce, Dept of Art, Commerce TX (S)

Fehlau, Fred, *Computer Graphics Chmn,* Art Center College of Design, Pasadena CA (S)

Fehlner, Jacqueline, *Instr & Supv,* Toronto Art Therapy Institute, Toronto ON (S)

Fehon, Diane, *Educ Coordr,* Academy of the New Church, Glencairn Museum, Bryn Athyn PA

Feig, Randy, *Asst Prof,* Edgewood College, Art Dept, Madison WI (S)

Feige, Juliet, *Adjunct,* Idaho State University, Dept of Art & Pre-Architecture, Pocatello ID (S)

Fein, Ruth, *Asst Cur,* National Gallery of Art, Index of American Design, Washington DC

Feinberg, David, *Assoc Prof,* University of Minnesota, Minneapolis, Dept of Art, Minneapolis MN (S)

Feinberg, Jonathan, *Dir Events,* American Institute of Graphic Arts, New York NY

Feinberg, Larry, *Cur European Painting,* The Art Institute of Chicago, Chicago IL

Feinberg, Larry J, *Dir,* Santa Barbara Museum of Art, Santa Barbara CA

Feinberg, Larry J, *Dir,* Santa Barbara Museum of Art, Library, Santa Barbara CA

Feinstein, Michael, *Chief Operating Officer,* Jewish Community Center of Greater Washington, Jane L & Robert H Weiner Judaic Museum, Rockville MD

Feinstein, Rochelle, *Prof,* Yale University, School of Art, New Haven CT (S)

Feintuch, Robert, *Senior Lectr,* Bates College, Art & Visual Culture, Lewiston ME (S)

Feiro, Christopher, *Asst Prof & Head Art Dept,* Philadelphia Community College, Dept of Art, Philadelphia PA (S)

Feisal, Marcia M, *Dept Chair,* Southern Nazarene University, Art & Design Department, Bethany OK (S)

Fejes, Yolande, *Owner,* Alaska House Art Gallery, Fairbanks AK

Fekete, Ron, *Asst Office Mgr & Exhib Dir,* Safety Harbor Museum of Regional History, Safety Harbor FL

Feklman, Bruce, *Chmn Photog,* College for Creative Studies, Detroit MI (S)

Fekner, John, *Asst Prof,* C W Post Campus of Long Island University, School of Visual & Performing Arts, Brookville NY (S)

Felder, Wendy, *Coordr Traveling Exhibs & Registrar,* Ohio Historical Society, National Afro-American Museum & Cultural Center, Wilberforce OH

Feldman, Arthur M, *Exec Dir,* Sherwin Miller Museum of Jewish Art, Tulsa OK

Feldman, Bob, *Pres,* Key West Art & Historical Society, East Martello Museum & Gallery, Key West FL

Feldman, Devin, *Coordr Technical Svcs,* Queensborough Community College Library, Kurt R Schmeller Library, Flushing NY

Feldman, Hannah, *Asst Prof,* Northwestern University, Evanston, Dept of Art History, Evanston IL (S)

Feldman, Jaclyn, *VPres,* Long Beach Art League, Long Beach Library, Long Beach NY

Feldman, Joan, *Adjunct Faculty,* University of Maryland, Baltimore County, Imaging & Digital Arts (IMDA), Dept of Visual Arts, Baltimore MD (S)

Feldman, Kaywin, *Dir & Pres,* Minneapolis Institute of Arts, Minneapolis MN

Feldman, Sally, *Branch Admnr,* Las Vegas-Clark County Library District, Las Vegas NV

Feliciano, Awilda, *Instr,* Guilford Technical Community College, Commercial Art Dept, Jamestown NC (S)

Felix, Amanda, *Mus Mgr,* Ogden Union Station, Union Station Museums, Ogden UT

Fell, Carolyn, *Asst,* Gallery North, Setauket NY

Fellows, Cameron, *Deputy Dir & Dir Admin & Fin,* Tacoma Art Museum, Tacoma WA

Fellows, Leslie, *Gallery Mgr,* University of California at Santa Cruz, Eloise Pickard Smith Gallery, Santa Cruz CA

Felos, Charlene, *Chairperson,* Cypress College, Cypress CA (S)

Felshin, Nina, *Cur Exhib,* Wesleyan University, Ezra & Cecile Zilkha Gallery, Middletown CT

Felt, Tom, *Archivist,* Museum of American Glass in WV, Weston WV

Felton, Craig, *Prof,* Smith College, Art Dept, Northampton MA (S)

Fencl, Brian, *Asst Prof,* West Liberty State College, Div Art, West Liberty WV (S)

Fender, Kimber L, *Dir,* Public Library of Cincinnati & Hamilton County, Info & Reference Dept, Cincinnati OH

Fenety, Lois, *Dir,* Sunbury Shores Arts & Nature Centre, Inc, Library, Saint Andrews NB

Feng, ZL, *MFA,* Radford University, Art Dept, Radford VA (S)

Fengin, Christle, *Events Coordr,* Art Museum of Southeast Texas, Beaumont TX

Fennell, Nancy, *Pres,* Nevada Museum of Art, Reno NV

Fennell, Patricia, *Emer Prof,* University of Wisconsin, Madison, Dept of Art, Madison WI (S)

Fenney, Stephen, *Registrar,* Fraunces Tavern Museum, New York NY

Fenske, Gail, *Second VPres,* Society of Architectural Historians, Chicago IL

Fenske, Hannah, *Dir,* Western Washington University, Viking Union Gallery, Bellingham WA

Fenster, Fred, *Emer Prof,* University of Wisconsin, Madison, Dept of Art, Madison WI (S)

Fenton, Susan, *Photog,* Saint Joseph's University, Art Dept, Philadelphia PA (S)

Fenton, Wendell, *VPres,* Brandywine Conservancy, Brandywine River Museum, Chadds Ford PA

Ferber, Linda S, *VPres & Sr Art Historian,* New-York Historical Society, Museum, New York NY

Feren, Steve, *Prof,* University of Wisconsin, Madison, Dept of Art, Madison WI (S)

Ferentz, Nicole, *Assoc Prof,* Loyola University of Chicago, Fine Arts Dept, Chicago IL (S)

Fergus, Victoria, *Prof,* West Virginia University, College of Creative Arts, School of Art & Design, Morgantown WV (S)

Ferguson, Alan, *Digital Production Coordr, Instr,* Quickdraw Animation Society, Calgary AB

Ferguson, Barbara, *Admin Asst,* Dunedin Fine Art Center, Dunedin FL (S)

Ferguson, Janene, *Mus Supv,* Torrance Art Museum, Torrance CA

Ferguson, Judy, *Pres,* Witter Gallery, Storm Lake IA

Ferguson, Kathleen, *Asst to Dir,* International Foundation for Art Research, Inc (IFAR), New York NY

Ferguson, Melissa, *Dir Mktg & Communs,* Columbus Museum of Art, Columbus OH

Ferguson, Scott, *Colls Mgmt,* Andy Warhol Foundation for the Visual Arts, New York NY

Fergusson, Mary E D'Aquin, *Asst Dir,* Longue Vue House & Gardens, New Orleans LA

Fergusson, Peter J, *Prof,* Wellesley College, Art Dept, Wellesley MA (S)

Fermoile, Kate, *VP Exhibs & Educ,* Brooklyn Historical Society, Brooklyn NY

Fernandes, Irene, *Gift Shop Mgr,* Museum of Northern British Columbia, Ruth Harvey Art Gallery, Prince Rupert BC

Fernandez, Alexandra, *Cur Asst,* University of Tampa, Henry B Plant Museum, Tampa FL

Fernandez, Dolores, *Pres,* Hostos Center for the Arts & Culture, Bronx NY

Fernandez, George, *Asst Prof,* State University of New York at Farmingdale, Visual Communications, Farmingdale NY (S)

Fernandez, Gracie, *Exec,* San Angelo Museum of Fine Arts, San Angelo TX

Fernandez, Jacqueline, *Cur of Coll,* Alaska Department of Education, Division of Libraries, Archives & Museums, Sheldon Jackson Museum, Sitka AK

Fernandez, Maria Ester, *Cur Educ,* Triton Museum of Art, Santa Clara CA

Fernandez-Keys, Alba, *Head Librn,* Indianapolis Museum of Art, Indianapolis IN

Fernandez-Keys, Alba, *Head of Lib & Archives,* Indianapolis Museum of Art, Stout Reference Library, Indianapolis IN

Ferrante, Krista S, *First Democratization Project Coordr,* American Antiquarian Society, Worcester MA

Ferrante, Virginia, *Instr,* Johns Hopkins University, School of Medicine, Dept of Art as Applied to Medicine, Baltimore MD (S)

Ferrara, Linda, *Dir Human Resources,* Honolulu Museum of Art, Honolulu HI

Ferrari, Gerard, *Asst Prof,* North Central College, Dept of Art, Naperville IL (S)

Ferrari, Roberto, *Assoc Mus Librn,* The Metropolitan Museum of Art, Image Library, New York NY

Ferrell, Brian, *Instr,* Seton Hill University, Art Program, Greensburg PA (S)

Ferrell, Walt, *Pub Rels,* National Air and Space Museum, Smithsonian Institution, Washington DC

Ferrer, Elizabeth, *Dir,* BRIC - Brooklyn Information & Culture, Rotunda Gallery, Brooklyn NY

Ferres, Kathleen, *Registrar,* Grand Rapids Art Museum, Grand Rapids MI

Ferri, Rita, *Asst Dir,* Santa Barbara Contemporary Arts Forum, Santa Barbara CA

Ferriso, Brian J, *Dir,* Portland Art Museum, Portland OR

Ferro, Anthony, *Assoc Prof Dance,* Marymount Manhattan College, Fine & Performing Arts Div, New York NY (S)

Ferry, Jane, *Cur of Educ,* Orlando Museum of Art, Orlando FL

Ferry, Jane, *Cur of Educ,* Orlando Museum of Art, Orlando Sentinel Library, Orlando FL

Fertitta, Becky, *Mgr Visitor Center,* Mamie McFaddin Ward, Beaumont TX

Festa, Lisa, *Asst Prof,* Georgian Court University, Dept of Art, Lakewood NJ (S)

Fetig, Kathy, *Admin Asst,* Bismarck Art & Galleries Association, Bismarck ND

Fetterman-Mulvey, Mia, *Assoc Prof,* University of Denver, School of Art & Art History, Denver CO (S)

Fettes, John, *Head Dept,* Magnum Opus, Sterling VA (S)

Feught, Johann, *Assoc Prof (Visual Art),* University of British Columbia Okanagan, Dept of Creative Studies, Kelowna BC (S)

Fey, Michael, *Dir Exhibits,* South Carolina State Museum, Columbia SC

Feye, Cornelia, *School Dir,* Library Association of La Jolla, Athenaeum Music & Arts Library, La Jolla CA

Ffrench, Courtney, *Gen Mgr, JPAC,* Jamaica Center for Arts & Learning (JCAL), Jamaica NY

Fiak, Jose, *Interim Dir,* Wethersfield Historical Society Inc, Old Academy Library, Wethersfield CT

Fich, Dean K, *IMAX Theater Mgr,* Putnam Museum of History and Natural Science, Davenport IA

Fichner-Rathus, Lois, *Chmn & Prof,* College of New Jersey, Art Gallery, Ewing NJ

Fichner-Rathus, Lois, *Chmn Dept,* The College of New Jersey, School of Arts & Sciences, Ewing NJ (S)

Fichter, Mary, *Dir Communs,* National Academy Museum & School, Archives, New York NY

Fichter, Robert, *Prof,* Florida State University, Art Dept, Tallahassee FL (S)

Ficke, Bob, *Treas,* Iroquois County Historical Society Museum, Old Courthouse Museum, Watseka IL

Ficke, Judy, *Office Mgr,* Iroquois County Historical Society Museum, Old Courthouse Museum, Watseka IL

Fidler, Spencer, *Dept Head,* New Mexico State University, Art Dept, Las Cruces NM (S)

Fiegel, Kay, *Asst Dir Opers & Pub Rels, Cur Cross Orchard, Gift Shop Mgr,* Museum of Western Colorado, Museum of the West, Grand Junction CO

Field, Charles, *Prof Emeritus,* University of Texas at San Antonio, Dept of Art & Art History, San Antonio TX (S)

Field, John, *Dean of Humanities & Fine Arts,* Holyoke Community College, Dept of Art, Holyoke MA (S)

Field, Philip S, *Prof Painting,* University of Texas Pan American, Art Dept, Edinburg TX (S)

Field, Richard, *Dir Gallery,* Indiana University of Pennsylvania, Kipp Gallery, Indiana PA

Fielder, Daniel, *Head Dept,* Eastern Wyoming College, Art Dept, Torrington WY (S)

Fields, Carl, *Interim Exec Dir,* Jamaica Center for Arts & Learning (JCAL), Jamaica NY

Fields, Catherine Keene, *Dir,* Litchfield History Museum, Litchfield CT

Fields, Catherine Keene, *Dir,* Litchfield History Museum, Ingraham Memorial Research Library, Litchfield CT

Fields, Laura Kemper, *Dir Art Coll,* Commerce Bancshares, Inc, Fine Art Collection, Kansas City MO

Fields, Robert, *Prof,* Virginia Polytechnic Institute & State University, Dept of Art & Art History, Blacksburg VA (S)

Fieramosea, Kathy Krantz, *Treas,* Catharine Lorillard Wolfe, New York NY

Fierst, Eva, *Educ Cur,* University of Massachusetts, Amherst, University Gallery, Amherst MA

Fife Harbert, Laurie G, *Cur,* North Canton Public Library, The Little Art Gallery, North Canton OH

Figenshow Koss, Pamela, *Exec Dir,* Glass Art Society, Seattle WA

Figueroa, Mencia, *Coordr Develop & Pub Relations,* The Hispanic Society of America, Museum & Library, New York NY

Fihs, Catherine E, *Cur,* Supreme Court of the United States, Office of the Curator, Washington DC

Filer, Felicia, *Pub Art Dir,* City of Los Angeles, Cultural Affairs Dept, Los Angeles CA

Filip, Mona, *Cur,* Koffler Centre of the Arts, Koffler Gallery, Toronto ON

Filippi, Jo Ann, *Registrar,* Plumas County Museum, Museum Archives, Quincy CA

Filippone, Christine, *Asst Prof Art History,* Millersville University, Dept of Art & Design, Millersville PA (S)

Fillebrown, Tom, *Instr,* Sierra Community College, Art Dept, Rocklin CA (S)

Filo, Barbara, *Fine Arts Dept Chmn & Asst Prof,* Whitworth College, Art Dept, Spokane WA (S)

Finamore, Michelle, *Cur Fashion Arts,* Museum of Fine Arts, Boston MA

Finch, Richard D, *Dir,* Illinois State University, Normal Editions Workshop, Normal IL

Finch, Robert, *Instr,* Main Line Art Center, Haverford PA (S)

Findikoglu, Ziki, *Art Chair Germantown,* Montgomery College, Dept of Art, Rockville MD (S)

Findlay, Kimberly, *Pres & CEO,* Putnam Museum of History and Natural Science, Davenport IA

Findlay, Michael, *VPres,* Art Dealers Association of America, Inc, New York NY

Fine, Christy, *Dir Pub Progs,* Alaska Museum of Natural History, Anchorage AK

Fine, Peter, *Asst Prof,* New Mexico State University, Art Dept, Las Cruces NM (S)

Fineman, Richard, *Prof,* Northwestern Connecticut Community College, Fine Arts Dept, Winsted CT (S)

Fink, Charles, *Prof,* Miami-Dade Community College, Arts & Philosophy Dept, Miami FL (S)

Fink, Courtney, *Dir,* Southern Exposure, San Francisco CA

Fink, Sue, *Dir Educ,* North Dakota Museum of Art, Grand Forks ND

Finkelpearl, Tom, *Exec Dir,* The Queens Museum of Art, Flushing NY

Finkelstein, Christine E, *Cur Educ,* Grounds for Sculpture, Hamilton NJ

Finlan, Cathey, *Pres,* Denver Art Museum, Denver CO

Finlay, Nancy, *Cur Graphics,* Connecticut Historical Society, Hartford CT

Finlay, Nancy, *Cur Graphics,* Connecticut Historical Society, Library, Hartford CT

Finley, Greg, *Asst,* Plymouth State University, Karl Drerup Art Gallery, Plymouth NH

Finley, Kristi, *Commun Mgr,* Swope Art Museum, Terre Haute IN

Finley, Kristi, *Commun Mgr,* Swope Art Museum, Research Library, Terre Haute IN

Finley, Lisa, *Instr,* Tidewater Community College, Visual Arts Center, Portsmouth VA (S)

Finley, Patrick, *Asst Prof,* Oklahoma State University, Department of Art, Graphic Design and Art History, Stillwater OK (S)

Finley-Stansbury, Kim, *Asst Prof,* Southeastern Louisiana University, Dept of Visual Arts, Hammond LA (S)

Finn, Candice, *Website/Communs,* National Council on Education for the Ceramic Arts (NCECA), Erie CO

Finn, David, *Prof,* Wake Forest University, Dept of Art, Winston-Salem NC (S)

Finn, Matthew, *Asst Prof,* Saint Thomas Aquinas College, Art Dept, Sparkill NY (S)

Finnamore, Albert, *Dir Colls,* Ministry of Alberta Culture, Royal Alberta Museum, Edmonton AB

Finnegan, Jacqueline, *Exhibs & Colls Mgr,* University of New Hampshire, Museum of Art, Durham NH

Finnegan, Kate, *Dir & Adminr,* Kaji Aso Studio, Gallery Nature & Temptation, Boston MA

Finnegan, Patrick, *Vol Treas,* Three Forks Area Historical Society, Headwaters Heritage Museum, Three Forks MT

Finnemore, Bonny, *Resident Custodian,* Waterville Historical Society, Redington Museum, Waterville ME

Finnemore, Bryan, *Resident Custodian,* Waterville Historical Society, Redington Museum, Waterville ME

Finner, Leigh, *Admin Asst,* Halifax Historical Society, Inc, Halifax Historical Museum, Daytona Beach FL

Finneran, Mary, *Asst Prof,* Eastern New Mexico University, Dept of Art, Portales NM (S)

Finnerty, Sinead, *Artistic Dir, Contact,* Gallery 825/Los Angeles Art Association, Gallery 825, Los Angeles CA

Finnerty-Pyne, Sinead, *Gallery Progs Mgr,* Armory Center for the Arts, Pasadena CA

Finney, Eugene, *Assoc Preparator,* DeCordova Museum & Sculpture Park, DeCordova Museum, Lincoln MA

Fiorani, Francesca, *Assoc Prof & Chair,* University of Virginia, McIntire Dept of Art, Charlottesville VA (S)

Fiorentino, Brian, *Assoc Prof,* Loyola University of Chicago, Fine Arts Dept, Chicago IL (S)

Fiorenza, Giancarlo, *Asst Prof Art History,* California Polytechnic State University at San Luis Obispo, Dept of Art & Design, San Luis Obispo CA (S)

Fiorenza, Lily, *Kateria Media Center Mgr,* The National Shrine of the North American Martyrs, Fultonville NY

Fiorese, Lisa, *Bus Mgr,* Dutchess County Arts Council, Poughkeepsie NY

Fiori, Dennis, *CEO,* Maryland Historical Society, Library, Baltimore MD

Fiori, Dennis, *Pres,* Massachusetts Historical Society, Boston MA

Fiori, Dennis A, *Pres,* Massachusetts Historical Society, Library, Boston MA

Fiori, Kelly, *Library Dir,* Carteret County Historical Society, The History Place, Morehead City NC

Fiormo, Julia, *Pub Rels Coordr,* Monmouth Museum & Cultural Center, Lincroft NJ

Firestone, Evan, *Prof Art History,* University of Georgia, Franklin College of Arts & Sciences, Lamar Dodd School of Art, Athens GA (S)

Firestone, Laura, *Mus Shop Mgr,* Akron Art Museum, Akron OH

Firestone, Pattie, *Pres,* Washington Sculptors Group, Washington DC

Firmani, Domenico, *Chmn Prof,* College of Notre Dame of Maryland, Art Dept, Baltimore MD (S)

First, Alison, *Educ Coordr,* The Summit County Historical Society of Akron, OH, Akron OH

Firstenberg, Jean, *Dir & CEO,* The American Film Institute, Center for Advanced Film & Television, Los Angeles CA (S)

Fischel, Sharo, *Instr,* American University, Dept of Art, New York NY (S)

Fischer, Andrea, *Dir,* Transylvania University, Morlan Gallery, Lexington KY

Fischer, Barbara, *Dir & Cur,* University of Toronto, Justina M Barnicke Gallery, Toronto ON

Fischer, Brian, *Facility Coordr,* Lockwood-Mathews Mansion Museum, Norwalk CT

Fischer, Diane P, *Chief Cur,* Allentown Art Museum, Allentown PA

Fischer, Joshua, *Asst Cur,* Rice University, Rice Gallery, Houston TX

Fischer-Carlson, Lynn, *Prof,* Rock Valley College, Humanities and Fine Arts Division, Rockford IL (S)

Fischli, Ron, *Dean College of Fine Arts,* Midwestern State University, Lamar D. Fain College of Fine Arts, Wichita Falls TX (S)

Fish, Alida, *Interim Dean, College of Art & Design,* University of the Arts, Philadelphia Colleges of Art & Design, Performing Arts & Media & Communication, Philadelphia PA (S)

Fish, Lillian, *Vis Instr Art History,* Watkins College of Art, Design & Film, Nashville TN (S)

Fishbein, Ellen, *Treas,* The Art League Gallery & School, Alexandria VA

Fishel, Teresa, *Dir Library,* Macalester College, DeWitt Wallace Library, Saint Paul MN

Fisher, Alan, *Assoc Prof,* Dakota State University, College of Liberal Arts, Madison SD (S)

Fisher, Andrea, *Gallery Dir,* Transylvania University, Art Program, Lexington KY (S)

Fisher, Anne, *VPres,* Lancaster County Art Association, Inc, Strasburg PA

Fisher, Beverly, *Adj Prof,* Saint Joseph's University, Art Dept, Philadelphia PA (S)

Fisher, Bob, *Cur Coll,* Wing Luke Asian Museum, Governor Gary Locke Library and Community Heritage Center, Seattle WA

Fisher, Carolyn, *Pres,* Kent Art Association, Gallery, Kent CT

Fisher, Dale William, *Dir Educ,* University of Iowa, University of Iowa Museum of Art, Iowa City IA

Fisher, Debra, *Chmn,* State University of New York College at Brockport, Dept of Art, Brockport NY (S)

Fisher, Ellen, *Assoc Dean,* New York School of Interior Design, New York NY (S)

Fisher, Gabrielle, *Communs,* Public Art Fund, Inc, Visual Archive, New York NY

Fisher, Gabrielle, *Communs Dir,* Public Art Fund, Inc, New York NY

Fisher, Helen Ashton, *Coll Cur,* William A Farnsworth, Museum, Rockland ME

Fisher, Jane, *Finance Dir,* Contemporary Arts Center, Cincinnati OH

Fisher, Jay, *Deputy Dir Curatorial Affairs,* The Baltimore Museum of Art, Baltimore MD

Fisher, June, *Dir Fashion Design,* Art Institute of Fort Lauderdale, Fort Lauderdale FL (S)

Fisher, Kate, *Vis Asst Prof,* Hamline University, Dept of Studio Arts & Art History, Saint Paul MN (S)

Fisher, Katie, *Admin,* Art Gallery of Calgary, Calgary AB

Fisher, Lawrence A, *Exec Dir,* The Barnum Museum, Bridgeport CT

Fisher, Linda, *Coordr Interior Design,* Kean University, Fine Arts Dept, Union NJ (S)

Fisher, Mike, *Chmn Art Dept,* Sullivan County Community College, Division of Commercial Art & Photography, Loch Sheldrake NY (S)

Fisher, Richard, *Asst Prof,* College of Santa Fe, Art Dept, Santa Fe NM (S)

Fisher, Robert A, *Dir,* Yakima Valley Community College, Dept of Visual Arts, Yakima WA (S)

Fisher, Stephen, *Colls Mgr,* Amherst College, Mead Art Museum, Amherst MA

Fisher, Stephen, *Prof,* Rhode Island College, Art Dept, Providence RI (S)

Fisher, Steven M, *Prof Art,* The College of Idaho, Rosenthal Art Gallery, Caldwell ID

Fisher, Susan, *Dir,* The Renee & Chaim Gross Foundation, Chaim Gross Studio, New York NY

Fisher, Tim, *Assoc Prof,* Grand Valley State University, Art & Design Dept, Allendale MI (S)

Fisher, Will, *Instr,* Yavapai College, Visual & Performing Arts Div, Prescott AZ (S)

Fisherkeller, Margaret, *Cur Geology,* Indiana State Museum, Indianapolis IN

Fishman, Bernard P, *Exec Dir,* Rhode Island Historical Society, Providence RI

Fishman, Bernard P, *Exec Dir,* Rhode Island Historical Society, John Brown House, Providence RI

Fishman, Bernard P, *Exec Dir,* Rhode Island Historical Society, Aldrich House, Providence RI

Fishman, Beverly, *Head Painting Dept,* Cranbrook Academy of Art, Bloomfield Hills MI (S)

Fishman, Richard, *Prof,* Brown University, Dept of Visual Art, Providence RI (S)

Fisk, Lars, *Studio Mgr,* Socrates Sculpture Park, Long Island City NY

Fiske, Marin, *Events Mgr,* Southern Methodist University, Meadows Museum, Dallas TX

Fisler, Ben, *Assoc Prof Theatre,* Harford Community College, Visual, Performing and Applied Arts Division, Bel Air MD (S)

Fister, Cherie, *Prof Art & Prog Dir Graphic Design,* Maryville University of Saint Louis, Art & Design Program, Saint Louis MO (S)

Fitch, Carlana, *Dir,* Kemp Center for the Arts, Wichita Falls TX

Fitch, Kenneth W, *Librn,* Salmagundi Club, Library, New York NY

Fitch, Steve, *Adjunct Assoc,* College of Santa Fe, Art Dept, Santa Fe NM (S)

Fitch, Wendy, *Exec Dir,* Museums Association of Saskatchewan, Regina SK

Fithian, Charles, *Cur Archaeology,* Delaware Division of Historical & Cultural Affairs, Dover DE

Fithian, David, *Exhibitions,* Museum of Florida Art, Deland FL

Fitz, Charlotte, *Educ Dir,* Greenville Museum of Art, Inc, Greenville NC

Fitz, Gregory, *Gallery Cur,* Macalester College, Macalester College Art Gallery, Saint Paul MN

Fitzgerald, Angela, *Asst Gallery Mgr,* African American Atelier, Greensboro NC

Fitzgerald, Barnaby, *Prof,* Southern Methodist University, Division of Art, Dallas TX (S)

Fitzgerald, Betty, *Exhibit Chmn,* National Oil & Acrylic Painters Society, Osage Beach MO

Fitzgerald, Ginny, *Dir Visitor Servs,* Chicago History Museum, Chicago IL

Fitzgerald, Kenneth, *Grad Prog Dir & Assoc Prof,* Old Dominion University, Art Dept, Norfolk VA (S)

Fitzgerald, Mary Ann, *Exhib Coordr,* University of Wisconsin-Madison, Chazen Museum of Art, Madison WI

Fitzgerald, Sally, *Chmn,* Chabot College, Humanities Division, San Leandro CA (S)

Fitzgerald, Shannon, *Exec Dir,* Rochester Art Center, Rochester MN

Fitzgerald, Sharon, *Cur Mineralogical Mus,* University of Delaware, University Museums, Newark DE

FitzGibbons, Bill, *Pres/Exec Dir,* Blue Star Contemporary Art Center, San Antonio TX

Fitzpatrick, Ann, *VPres Communs,* Edsel & Eleanor Ford, Grosse Pointe Shores MI

Fitzpatrick, Susan, *Admin Asst,* University of Notre Dame, Snite Museum of Art, Notre Dame IN

Fitzpatrick, Tracy, *Cur & Asst Prof Art History,* Purchase College, Neuberger Museum of Art, Purchase NY

Fitzsimmons, Claire, *Deputy Dir,* Capp Street Project, Wattis Institute, San Francisco CA

Fitzsimmons, Julie, *College Asst Prof,* New Mexico State University, Art Dept, Las Cruces NM (S)

Fitzsimons, Constance, *Dean Div,* El Camino College, Division of Fine Arts, Torrance CA (S)

Flack, James, *Exec Dir,* Mechanics' Institute, San Francisco CA

Flageolle, Andree, *Asst Prof,* Pittsburg State University, Art Dept, Pittsburg KS (S)

Flaherty, Barbara, *Chair,* University of the Pacific, Jeannette Powell Art Center, Stockton CA

Flaherty, Barbara, *Chmn,* University of the Pacific, College of the Pacific, Dept of Art & Art History, Stockton CA (S)

Flaherty, Linda, *Educ,* Blanden Memorial Art Museum, Fort Dodge IA

Flaherty, Patrick, *Dir Exhibs & Artist Srvcs,* Indianapolis Art Center, Marilyn K. Glick School of Art, Indianapolis IN

Flahive, Ryan, *Archivist,* Institute of American Indian Arts, College of Contemporary Native Arts Library and Archives, Santa Fe NM

Flam, Jack, *Prof Emeritus,* City University of New York, PhD Program in Art History, New York NY (S)

Flamm, Eugene S, *Pres,* Grolier Club Library, New York NY

Flamm, Susan, *Dir Pub Rels,* American Folk Art Museum, New York NY

Flanagan, Daly, *Dir School,* Rockland Center for the Arts, West Nyack NY (S)

Flanagan, Daly, *School Dir,* Rockland Center for the Arts, West Nyack NY (S)

Flanagan, Jeanne, *Dir,* College of Saint Rose, Art Gallery, Albany NY

Flanagan, Maureen, *Adminr,* Hussian School of Art, Commercial Art Dept, Philadelphia PA (S)

Flanagan, Michael, *Asst Dir,* State University of New York at Oswego, Tyler Art Gallery, Oswego NY

Flanagan, Michael, *Dir,* University of Wisconsin-Whitewater, Crossman Gallery, Whitewater WI

Flanagan, Patrick, *Facilities & Security Supv,* University of Chicago, Smart Museum of Art, Chicago IL

Flanagan, Sheila, *Asst Dir,* History Museum of Mobile, Mobile AL

Flanigan, James F, *Cur,* University of Notre Dame, Snite Museum of Art, Notre Dame IN

Flanigan, Theresa, *Asst Prof,* College of Saint Rose, The Center For Art and Design, Albany NY (S)

Flannery, Richard, *Pres,* Hoyt Center for the Arts, New Castle PA

Flannigan, Sean, *Registrar/Preparator,* University of Maine, Museum of Art, Bangor ME

Flashner, Dale, *Asst Prof,* Adelphi University, Dept of Art & Art History, Garden City NY (S)

Flathu, Ryan, *Art Instr,* Kellogg Community College, Arts & Communication Dept, Battle Creek MI (S)

Fleck, Rudolf, *Prof,* Loyola Marymount University, Dept of Art & Art History, Los Angeles CA (S)

Flecky, Michael, *Assoc Chair,* Creighton University, Fine & Performing Arts Dept, Omaha NE (S)

Fleeher, Kathy, *Asst Cur & Mus Guild Coordr,* Canton Museum of Art, Canton OH

Fleischer, Arthur, *Chmn,* Fried, Frank, Harris, Shriver & Jacobson, Art Collection, New York NY

Fleischer, Mary, *Prof & Chair Theatre,* Marymount Manhattan College, Fine & Performing Arts Div, New York NY (S)

Fleischer, Roland E, *Prof Emeritus,* Pennsylvania State University, University Park, Dept of Art History, University Park PA (S)

Fleischman, Martha, *Pres,* Kennedy Galleries, Kennedy Galleries, Inc, New York NY

Fleischman, Stephen, *Dir,* Madison Museum of Contemporary Art, Madison WI

Fleischmann, Jo, *Admin Asst,* The Arts Council of Wayne County, Goldsboro NC (S)

Fleischmann, Laura, *Sr Registrar,* The Buffalo Fine Arts Academy, Albright-Knox Art Gallery, Buffalo NY

Fleming, Alison, *Asst Prof,* College of the Holy Cross, Dept of Visual Arts, Worcester MA (S)

Fleming, Anne, *Assoc Prof (Creative Writing),* University of British Columbia Okanagan, Dept of Creative Studies, Kelowna BC (S)

Fleming, Elizabeth, *Cur of Coll,* C W Post Campus of Long Island University, Hillwood Art Museum, Brookville NY

Fleming, Elma, *Prin HS,* Forest Hills Adult and Youth Center, Forest Hills NY (S)

Fleming, Erika, *Pres College,* International Fine Arts College, Miami FL (S)

Fleming, Jeff, *Dir,* Edmundson Art Foundation, Inc, Des Moines Art Center, Des Moines IA

Fleming, Joe, *Instr,* Toronto School of Art, Toronto ON (S)

Fleming, Marnie, *Cur Contemporary Art,* Oakville Galleries, Centennial Square and Gairloch Gardens, Oakville ON

Fleming, Nan, *Mus Store Mgr,* Smith College, Museum of Art, Northampton MA

Fleming, Nancy, *Graphic Design,* Roswell Artist-in-Residence Foundation, Anderson Museum of Contemporary Art, Roswell NM

Fleming, Robyn, *Interlibrary Servs Librn,* The Metropolitan Museum of Art, Museum Libraries, New York NY

Fleming, Tom, *Prof,* University of Wisconsin College - Marinette, Art Dept, Marinette WI (S)

Fleming, Tricia, *Dir Educ,* Antonelli Institute, Professional Photography & Commercial Art, Erdenheim PA (S)

Flentje, Rachel D, *Visual Arts Dir,* Bloomington Theatre & Art Center, Inez Greenberg Gallery, Bloomington MN

Flescher, Sharon, *Dir,* International Foundation for Art Research, Inc (IFAR), Authentication Service, New York NY

Flescher, Sharon, *Exec Dir, Ed in Chief,* International Foundation for Art Research, Inc (IFAR), New York NY

Flesher, Karen, *Prog Coordr,* University of Illinois at Urbana-Champaign, Spurlock Museum, Champaign IL

Flester, Inge, *Office Mgr,* Colonial Williamsburg Foundation, John D Rockefeller, Jr Library, Williamsburg VA

Fletcher, Carrol, *CEO,* Harrison County Historical Museum, Marshall TX

Fletcher, Dorothy, *Dir Undergrad Studies & Sr Lectr,* Emory University, Art History Dept, Atlanta GA (S)

Fletcher, Jacqueline, *Coll Mgr,* Morris Museum, Morristown NJ

Fletcher, Marylynn, *Head Dept,* Victoria College, Fine Arts Dept, Victoria TX (S)

Fletcher, Pamela, *Asst Prof,* Bowdoin College, Art Dept, Brunswick ME (S)

Fletcher, Peter, *Prof,* Viterbo College, Art Dept, La Crosse WI (S)

Fleurov, Ellen, *Exec Dir,* Silver Eye Center for Photography, Pittsburgh PA

Flexner, Paul, *Chmn,* Salisbury State University, Art Dept, Salisbury MD (S)

Flicker, Melissa, *Asst,* California State Polytechnic University, Pomona, Department of Art, Pomona CA (S)

Fliegel, Stephen, *Cur Medieval Art,* The Cleveland Museum of Art, Cleveland OH

Flint, Jean, *Instr,* Arkansas State University, Dept of Art, State University AR (S)

Flint, Matt, *Prof 2-D,* Central Wyoming College, Art Center, Riverton WY (S)

Flint, Russ, *Adjunct,* Feather River Community College, Art Dept, Quincy CA (S)

Flint, Suzanne, *Cur,* Pocumtuck Valley Memorial Association, Memorial Hall Museum, Deerfield MA

Fliss, Eric B, *South Miami-Dade Cultural Arts Ctr,* South Florida Cultural Consortium, Miami Dade County Dept of Cultural Affairs, Miami FL

Fliss, Roberta Behrendt, *Dir Productions,* National YoungArts Foundation, Miami FL

Flitcroft, Holly, *Office Mgr,* Sculpture Space, Inc, Utica NY

Flitner, Jane V, *Asst Educ,* Brandywine Conservancy, Brandywine River Museum, Chadds Ford PA

Flood, James, *Dept Chmn,* Towson State University, Dept of Art, Towson MD (S)

Flood, Richard, *Chief Cur,* Walker Art Center, Minneapolis MN

Flook, Kimberly, *Historic Site Mgr,* Olana State Historic Site, Library, Hudson NY

Flora, Judith, *Dir Finance,* Mystic Art Association, Inc, Mystic Arts Center, Mystic CT

Flora, Karen, *Instr,* Bob Jones University, School of Fine Arts, Div of Art & Design, Greenville SC (S)

Florentin, Bryan, *Sr Lectr,* University of Texas at Arlington, Art & Art History Department, Arlington TX (S)

Flores, Jessica, *Assoc Cur Contemporary,* Cincinnati Art Museum, Cincinnati Art Museum, Cincinnati OH

Flores, Richard, *Instr,* College of the Sequoias, Art Dept, Visalia CA (S)

Flores, Tobias, *Asst Prof,* Fort Hays State University, Dept of Art & Design, Hays KS (S)

Florez, Betty L, *Admin Support Asst,* Mesa Arts Center, Mesa Contemporary Arts Museum, Mesa AZ

Flowers, Randolph, *Prof,* Del Mar College, Art Dept, Corpus Christi TX (S)

Flowers, Randy, *Gallery Dir,* Del Mar College, Joseph A Cain Memorial Art Gallery, Corpus Christi TX

Floyd, Rick, *Registrar,* Modern Art Museum, Fort Worth TX

Floyd, Tiffany, *Secy,* Artspace, Richmond VA

Flug, Janice, *Acting Asst University Librn,* American University, Jack I & Dorothy G Bender Library & Learning Resources Center, New York NY

Flury, Jane, *VPres,* Pacific Grove Art Center, Pacific Grove CA

Flyhn, Marissa, *Asst Dir,* Kansas City Artists Coalition, Kansas City MO

Flynn, Christopher, *Instr Graphic Commun,* Tarrant County College, Art Dept, Hurst TX (S)

Flynn, Kathleen, *Exec Dir,* Dieu Donne Papermill, Inc, Gallery, New York NY

Focht, Brenda, *Cur Coll & Exhib,* Riverside Metropolitan Museum, Riverside CA

Fogarty, Lori, *Exec Dir,* Oakland Museum of California, Art Dept, Oakland CA

Fogel, Jerise, *Registrar,* Society of Scribes, Ltd, New York NY

Fogerty, Lee, *Asst Dir,* Springfield City Library, Springfield MA

Fogher, Valentina, *Cur,* Museo Italo Americano, Library, San Francisco CA

Fogt, Rex, *Assoc Prof,* University of Toledo, Dept of Art, Toledo OH (S)

Foisy, Marie-Helene, *Registrar,* Musee d'art de Joliette, Joliette PQ

Folda, Jaroslav, *Prof,* University of North Carolina at Chapel Hill, Art Dept, Chapel Hill NC (S)

Foldes, Lance, *Dir,* Berry College, Memorial Library, Mount Berry GA

Foley, Bridget, *Mgr Opers & Admin,* Museum for African Art, New York NY

Foley, Cynthia Meyers, *Dir Educ,* Columbus Museum of Art, Columbus OH

Foley, Jodie, *Archivist,* Montana Historical Society, Helena MT

Foley, Kathy Kelsey, *Dir,* Leigh Yawkey Woodson Art Museum, Wausau WI

Foley, Lori, *VPres Emergency Progs,* Heritage Preservation, The National Institute for Conservation, Washington DC

Foley, Mike, *Design Ctr Adjunct,* Iowa Wesleyan College, Art Dept, Mount Pleasant IA (S)

Foley, Tara, *Artists in Educ Mgr,* Southern Exposure, San Francisco CA

Foley, William, *Asst Prof Art,* Marian University, Visual Arts Dept, Indianapolis IN (S)

Folger, Kelly, *Secy,* Naval War College Museum, Newport RI

Folk, Amy, *Colls Mgr,* Oysterponds Historical Society, Museum, Orient NY

Folkestad, William, *Chmn,* Central Washington University, Dept of Art, Ellensburg WA (S)

Folsom, James, *Dir Botanical Gardens,* The Huntington Library, Art Collections & Botanical Gardens, San Marino CA

Folsom, James, *Dir Botanical Gardens,* The Huntington Library, Art Collections & Botanical Gardens, Library, San Marino CA

Folts, James, *Chmn,* Oregon State University, Dept of Art, Corvallis OR (S)

Foltz, Amy, *Instr,* Morningside College, Art Dept, Sioux City IA (S)

Folwell, Sue, *Mus Shop Mgr,* Putnam Museum of History and Natural Science, Davenport IA

Folz, Christine, *Weaving,* Worcester Center for Crafts, Worcester MA (S)

Fombella, Trinidad, *Exhib Mgr & Asst Cur,* El Museo del Barrio, New York NY

Fomin, Elizabeth, *Asst Prof,* Rochester Institute of Technology, School of Design, Rochester NY (S)

Fondren, Jennifer, *Cur Educ,* History Museum of Mobile, Mobile AL

Fonfara, Chad, *Asst Prof,* University of Nebraska, Kearney, Dept of Art & Art History, Kearney NE (S)

Fong, Mimi, *Instr,* Sacramento City College, Art Dept, Sacramento CA (S)

Fong, Yem, *Art & Architecture Librn,* University of Colorado, Art & Architecture Library, Boulder CO

Fontaine-White, Barbar, *Prof,* University of Mary Hardin-Baylor, College of Visual & Performing Arts, Belton TX (S)

Fontana, Jeffrey, *Prof,* Austin College, Art Dept, Sherman TX (S)

Fontana, Leslie, *Adjunct Prof Art,* University of Great Falls, Art Dept, Great Falls MT (S)

Fontanella, Megan, *Asst Cur,* Solomon R Guggenheim, New York NY

Fontant, Lilia, *Acting Dir,* Miami-Dade College, Kendal Campus, Art Gallery, Miami FL

Fontenot-Jamerson, Berlinda, *Pres,* Museum of African American Art, Los Angeles CA

Foote, Vincent M, *Prof,* North Carolina State University at Raleigh, School of Design, Raleigh NC (S)

Forbes, Dawn, *Instr,* Whitman College, Art Dept, Walla Walla WA (S)

Forbes, Susan, *Div Chmn,* Wells College, Dept of Art, Aurora NY (S)

Force, Leah, *Lectr,* Baylor University - College of Arts and Sciences, Dept of Art, Waco TX (S)

Ford, Ann, *Asst Prof,* Virginia State University, Department of Art & Design, Petersburg VA (S)

Ford, Beth, *Prof Emerita,* Florida Southern College, Melvin Art Gallery, Lakeland FL

Ford, Beth, *Prof Emerita,* Florida Southern College, Department of Art & Art History, Lakeland FL (S)

Ford, Cindi, *Contact,* Van Ingel Fine Arts Center, Gainey Gallery, Byron Center MI

Ford, Inga, *Communs Coordr,* Boca Raton Museum of Art, Boca Raton FL

Ford, Janice, *Gallery Dir,* Pikeville College, Humanities Division, Pikeville KY (S)

Ford, John, *Asst Prof,* University of North Carolina at Charlotte, Dept Art, Charlotte NC (S)

Ford, Kelly, *Dir Develop,* Arkansas Arts Center, Little Rock AR

Ford, Margaret, *Tech Svcs Librn,* Museum of Fine Arts, Houston, Hirsch Library, Houston TX

Ford, Ryan, *Treas,* Second Street Gallery, Charlottesville VA

Ford, Sarah, *COO,* Art Center Sarasota, Sarasota FL

Ford, Tim, *Instr,* Appalachian State University, Dept of Art, Boone NC (S)

Forde, Ed, *Chmn,* California State University, Los Angeles, Art Dept, Los Angeles CA (S)

Forde, Ed, *Chmn Dept,* University of Nebraska-Lincoln, Dept of Art & Art History, Lincoln NE (S)

Fordham, Douglas, *Assoc Prof Art History,* University of Virginia, McIntire Dept of Art, Charlottesville VA (S)

Foreman, Brian, *Asst Cur,* Surrey Art Gallery, Library, Surrey BC

Foreman, Hank T, *Dir & Chief Cur,* Appalachian State University, Turchin Center for the Visual Arts, Boone NC

Foreman, Henry T, *Instr,* Appalachian State University, Dept of Art, Boone NC (S)

Forer, Taj, *Dir,* Durham Art Guild, Durham NC

Forero, Juliana, *Asst Dir Educ,* Houston Center For Photography, Houston TX

Forest Wilson, Ernest, *Prof,* Catholic University of America, School of Architecture & Planning, Washington DC (S)

Forgang, David M, *Chief Cur,* Yosemite Museum, Yosemite National Park CA

Forgeng, Jeffrey, *Cur,* Higgins Armory Museum, Olive Higgins Prouty Library & Research Center, Worcester MA

Forgeng, Jeffrey, *Paul S Morgan Cur,* Higgins Armory Museum, Worcester MA

Forgit, Susan, *Finance Dir,* American Antiquarian Society, Worcester MA

Forino, Belle, *Spec Events & Vols,* Boca Raton Museum of Art, Boca Raton FL

Forman, Lois, *Tour Coordr,* Frederick R Weisman, Los Angeles CA

Forman, Melanie, *Dir Develop,* Guggenheim Museum Soho, New York NY

Fornandez, Fabio J, *Exhib Mgr,* The Society of Arts & Crafts, Boston MA

Fornaro, Michael, *Asst Prof Interior Design,* Converse College, School of the Arts, Dept of Art & Design, Spartanburg SC (S)

Fornell, Julie, *Asst Mgr,* Detroit Public Library, Art & Literature Dept, Detroit MI

Forney, Darrell, *Instr,* Sacramento City College, Art Dept, Sacramento CA (S)

Forney, Shawna, *Pub Relations & Mktg Mgr,* Diverse Works, Houston TX

Forrest, Anne, *Head Children's Prog,* Kalamazoo Institute of Arts, KIA School, Kalamazoo MI (S)

Forrester, Gillian, *Cur Prints & Drawings,* Yale University, Yale Center for British Art, New Haven CT

Forrester, James, *Head Library Systems & Technical Svcs,* OCAD University, Dorothy H Hoover Library, Toronto ON

Forsberg, Diane, *Chief Cur,* Canajoharie Library & Art Gallery, Arkell Museum of Canajoharie, Canajoharie NY

Forsberg, Diane, *Cur,* Mark Twain, Research Library, Hartford CT

Forschler, Anne, *Cur Decorative Arts,* Birmingham Museum of Art, Birmingham AL

Forschler, Anne M, *Cur Decorative Arts,* Birmingham Museum of Art, Clarence B Hanson Jr Library, Birmingham AL

Forsgren, Emily, *Asst to Dir,* Northwestern University, Mary & Leigh Block Museum of Art, Evanston IL

Forshaw, Natalie, *Head Bibliographic Access Management,* University of Alaska, Elmer E Rasmuson Library, Fairbanks AK

Forshay, Patrick, *Instr,* Hillsdale College, Art Dept, Hillsdale MI (S)

Forster-Hahn, Francoise, *Prof Emeriti,* University of California, Riverside, Dept of the History of Art, Riverside CA (S)

Forsyth, Alex, *Instr,* Guilford Technical Community College, Commercial Art Dept, Jamestown NC (S)

Forsyth, Amy, *Assoc Prof,* Lehigh University, Dept of Art, Architecture & Design, Bethlehem PA (S)

Fort, Bernadette, *Adjunct Prof,* Northwestern University, Evanston, Dept of Art History, Evanston IL (S)

Fort, Lifran, *Chmn & Instr,* Fisk University, Art Dept, Nashville TN (S)

Fort, Thomas A, *Asst Dir & Cur Exhibits,* Hidalgo County Historical Museum, Edinburg TX

Forte, Joseph C, *Faculty,* Sarah Lawrence College, Dept of Art History, Bronxville NY (S)

Fortenberry, Tobin, *Registrar,* Mississippi Museum of Art, Howorth Library, Jackson MS

Fortenot, Michelle, *Mus Coll Mgr,* University of Michigan, Kelsey Museum of Archaeology, Ann Arbor MI

Fortescue, Ann, *Dir,* Springfield Museum of Art, Springfield OH (S)

Fortier, Jerome, *Asst Cur,* Marquette University, Haggerty Museum of Art, Milwaukee WI

Fortier, Rollin, *Designer,* University of California, Santa Barbara, University Art Museum, Santa Barbara CA

Fortier, Suzanne, *Dir Devel,* Rhode Island School of Design, Museum of Art, Providence RI

Fortini-Brown, Patricia, *Chmn,* Princeton University, Dept of Art & Archaeology, Princeton NJ (S)

Fortney, Kim, *Cur Educ,* Heritage Center of Lancaster County Museum, Lancaster PA

Fortriede, Steven, *Assoc Dir,* Allen County Public Library, Art, Music & Audiovisual Services, Fort Wayne IN

Fortune, Brandon B, *Chief Cur,* National Portrait Gallery, Smithsonian Institution, Washington DC

Fortune, Janice, *Gallery Opers Asst,* Art Gallery of Peterborough, Peterborough ON

Fortushniak, Ivan, *Asst Prof,* Indiana University of Pennsylvania, College of Fine Arts, Indiana PA (S)

Fortwengler, Nancy, *VPres,* The Art League Gallery & School, Alexandria VA

Fosdick, Rose, *Commissioner,* United States Department of the Interior, Indian Arts & Crafts Board, Washington DC

Foshay, Susan MacAlpine, *Dir,* Nova Scotia Centre for Craft & Design, Mary E Black Gallery, Halifax NS

Fosmire, Ed, *Deputy Dir,* Laguna Art Museum, Laguna Beach CA

Fosque, William, *Prof,* Portland State University, Dept of Art, Portland OR (S)

Foss, Pauline, *Instr Visual Arts,* University of Colorado-Colorado Springs, Visual & Performing Arts Dept (VAPA), Colorado Springs CO (S)

Foster, April, *Instr,* Art Academy of Cincinnati, Cincinnati OH (S)

Foster, Bill, *Dir,* Portland Art Museum, Northwest Film Center, Portland OR

Foster, Carter, *Cur Drawings,* Whitney Museum of American Art, New York NY

Foster, Daniel, *Exec Dir,* Riverside Art Museum, Riverside CA

Foster, David, *Chmn Art Dept,* Lake Tahoe Community College, Art Dept, South Lake Tahoe CA (S)

Foster, Eryn, *Dir,* Eye Level Gallery, Halifax NS

Foster, Frank, *Chmn,* Victor Valley Community College, Art Dept, Victorville CA (S)

Foster, Frank, *Treas,* Philadelphia Sketch Club, Philadelphia PA

Foster, H Eugene, *Facilities Supv,* International Center of Photography, School, New York NY (S)

Foster, Hal, *Prof,* Princeton University, Dept of Art & Archaeology, Princeton NJ (S)

Foster, James, *Mgr Security Svcs,* Northwestern University, Mary & Leigh Block Museum of Art, Evanston IL

Foster, Jill, *Admin Staff,* Greenwich Art Society Inc, Greenwich CT

Foster, John R, *Cur Paleontology,* Museum of Western Colorado, Museum of the West, Grand Junction CO

Foster, Kenneth, *Exec Dir,* Yerba Buena Center for the Arts, San Francisco CA

Foster, Laura, *Dir & Cur,* Frederic Remington, Ogdensburg NY

Foster, Laura, *Pres & CEO,* Please Touch Museum, Philadelphia PA

Foster, Marlon, *Vis Servs Coordr,* Cultural Council of Palm Beach County, Lake Worth FL

Foster, Mary, *Office Coordr,* University of Notre Dame, Dept of Art, Art History & Design, Notre Dame IN (S)

Foster, Megan, *Dir, Lectr,* City College of New York, Art Dept, New York NY (S)

Foster, Robert, *Gallery Dir,* Artists Association of Nantucket, Nantucket MA

Foster, Scott, *Asst Prof Painting & Drawing,* Siena College, Dept of Creative Arts, Loudonville NY (S)

Foster, Stephen, *Assoc Prof (Visual Art),* University of British Columbia Okanagan, Dept of Creative Studies, Kelowna BC (S)

Foster-Campbell, Megan, *Asst Prof,* Illinois Central College, Arts & Communication Dept, East Peoria IL (S)

Fostor, Kathy, *McNeil Cur American Art,* Philadelphia Museum of Art, Main Building, Philadelphia PA

Foti, Silvana, *Chmn,* Methodist College, Art Dept, Fayetteville NC (S)

Fought, Rick, *Librn,* Art Institute of Fort Lauderdale, Technical Library, Fort Lauderdale FL

Foughty, John, *Admin,* Washington University, Mildred Lane Kemper Art Museum, Saint Louis MO

Foulds, Don, *Assoc Prof,* Memorial University of Newfoundland, Division of Fine Arts, Visual Arts Program, Corner Brook NF (S)

Foumberg, Jason, *Dept Sec,* The Art Institute of Chicago, Dept of Prints & Drawings, Chicago IL

Fountain, Benny, *Asst Prof,* Baylor University - College of Arts and Sciences, Dept of Art, Waco TX (S)

Fourhman-Shaull, Lila, *Dir Libr & Archives,* The York County Heritage Trust, York PA

Fourhman-Shaull, Lila, *Librn,* The York County Heritage Trust, Library, York PA

Fournier, Celia, *Bus Mgr,* Museum of Western Colorado, Museum of the West, Grand Junction CO

Foushee, Sean, *Instr Graphic Commun,* Tarrant County College, Art Dept, Hurst TX (S)

Foust, Andrea, *Mem/Pub Rels Mgr,* Willamette University, Hallie Ford Museum of Art, Salem OR

Fowle, Bruce, *Pres,* National Academy Museum & School, New York NY

Fowle, Kate, *Exec Dir,* Independent Curators International, New York NY

Fowler, Patricia, *Asst Ed,* Handweavers Guild of America, Suwanee GA

Fowler, Sherry, *Asst Prof,* Lewis & Clark College, Dept of Art, Portland OR (S)

Fox, Allison, *Office Mgr,* R L S Silverado Museum, Reference Library, Saint Helena CA

Fox, Andrew, *Webmaster,* Fine Arts Museums of San Francisco, Legion of Honor, San Francisco CA

Fox, Andrew, *Webmaster,* Fine Arts Museums of San Francisco, M H de Young Museum, San Francisco CA

Fox, Broderick, *Prof,* Occidental College, Dept of Art History & Visual Arts, Los Angeles CA (S)

Fox, Carson, *Instr,* Main Line Art Center, Haverford PA (S)

Fox, Christopher D, *Cur,* Fort Ticonderoga Association, Ticonderoga NY

Fox, Edward, *Prof,* Nassau Community College, Art Dept, Garden City NY (S)

Fox, Elizabeth, *Educational Outreach Coordr,* Rawls Museum Arts, Courtland VA

Fox, Hugh R, *Asst Prof,* Rochester Institute of Technology, School of Printing Management & Sciences, Rochester NY (S)

Fox, Jennifer, *Dir Fin & Opers,* Marietta-Cobb Museum of Art, Marietta GA

Fox, Jennifer, *Mktg Coordr,* Las Vegas Natural History Museum, Las Vegas NV

Fox, John, *Asst Prof,* Finger Lakes Community College, Visual & Performing Arts Dept, Canandaigua NY (S)

Fox, Josh, *Colls Mgr,* Independence Seaport Museum, Library, Philadelphia PA

Fox, Kate, *Mus Shop Mgr,* Cleveland Botanical Garden, Eleanor Squire Library, Cleveland OH

Fox, Michael, *Asst Dir Library,* Minnesota Historical Society, Library, Saint Paul MN

Fox, Michael, *Cur History,* Montana State University, Museum of the Rockies, Bozeman MT

Fox, Michael, *Deputy Dir,* Minnesota Historical Society, Saint Paul MN

Fox, Pamela, *Dean School Fine Arts,* Miami University, Art Dept, Oxford OH (S)

Fox, Paulette, *Dir Pub Rels,* Tennessee State Museum, Nashville TN

Fox, Randall, *Supt,* Nebraska Game and Parks Commission, Arbor Lodge State Historical Park & Morton Mansion, Nebraska City NE

Fox, Richard, *Art Librn,* Hewlett-Woodmere Public Library, Hewlett NY

Fox, Sharon, *Publications,* Palo Alto Art Center, Palo Alto CA

Fox, Sheila, *Dir Educ,* UMLAUF Sculpture Garden & Museum, Austin TX

Fox, Stacey, *Lectr,* University of Kansas, The School of the Arts, Dept of Visual Art, Lawrence KS (S)

Fox, Terri, *Coll Mgr,* Nelda C & H J Lutcher Stark, Stark Museum of Art, Orange TX

Fox, William L, *Dir Center for Art & Environ,* Nevada Museum of Art, Reno NV

Fox-Pfeiffer, Lisa, *Exec Dir,* Burlington County Historical Society, Burlington NJ

Foxworth, Judith, *Assoc Librn,* Saint Augustine Historical Society, Library, Saint Augustine FL

Foye, Noelle, *Dir Educ,* Fuller Craft Museum, Brockton MA

Fraas, Kathleen, *Registrar,* Niagara University, Castellani Art Museum, Niagara NY

Fraenkel, Jeffrey, *Secy,* Art Dealers Association of America, Inc, New York NY

Fraher, David J, *Exec Dir,* Arts Midwest, Minneapolis MN

Fraizer, Stephen, *Preparator & Registrar,* Southern Oregon University, Schneider Museum of Art, Ashland OR

Fraker, Pat, *Cataloger,* Colorado Historical Society, Stephen H Hart Library, Denver CO

Frakes, Jim, *Asst Prof,* University of North Carolina at Charlotte, Dept Art, Charlotte NC (S)

Fraleigh, Angela, *Chmn,* Moravian College, Dept of Art, Bethlehem PA (S)

Frame, Susan, *Faculty,* Grand Marais Art Colony, Grand Marais MN (S)

Franc, Julie, *Opers Mgr,* Walter Anderson, Ocean Springs MS

Franchino, Mark, *Asst Prof,* Clarion University of Pennsylvania, Dept of Art, Clarion PA (S)

Francik, Jeff, *Visitor Svcs Coordr,* Elmhurst Art Museum, Elmhurst IL

Francis, Ed, *Asst Prof,* Tidewater Community College, Visual Arts Center, Portsmouth VA (S)

Francis, Frances, *Registrar,* High Museum of Art, Atlanta GA

Francis, Jacqueline, *Asst Prof,* University of Michigan, Ann Arbor, Dept of History of Art, Ann Arbor MI (S)

Francisco, Jason, *Asst Prof,* Rutgers, The State University of New Jersey, Mason Gross School of the Arts, Visual Arts Dept, New Brunswick NJ (S)

Francisco-Abitz, Lisa, *Asst Dir,* University of Memphis, Art Museum, Memphis TN

Franco, Andi, *Pres,* Art Center Manatee, Bradenton FL

Franco, Pamela, *Asst Prof,* Tulane University, Sophie H Newcomb Memorial College, New Orleans LA (S)

Francuz, Liliane, *Visual Arts Prog Mgr,* Department of Commerce, Wyoming Arts Council Gallery, Cheyenne WY

Franczak, John, *Lectr,* University of Nebraska, Kearney, Dept of Art & Art History, Kearney NE (S)

Franczyk, Jean, *Dir Educ,* Museum of Science & Industry, Chicago IL

Frandrup, Dennis, *Chmn,* College of Saint Benedict, Art Dept, Saint Joseph MN (S)

Frandrup, Dennis, *Prof,* Saint John's University, Art Dept, Collegeville MN (S)

Frank, Barbara, *Prof,* Stony Brook University, College of Arts & Sciences, Dept of Art, Stony Brook NY (S)

Frank, David, *Prof,* Mississippi University for Women, Division of Fine & Performing Arts, Columbus MS (S)

Frank, Denise, *Dir Fine Arts,* Chattanooga State Technical Community College, Advertising Arts Dept, Chattanooga TN (S)

Frank, Eric, *Prof,* Occidental College, Dept of Art History & Visual Arts, Los Angeles CA (S)

Frank, Ilene, *Art Reference Librn,* University of South Florida, Library, Tampa FL

Frank, Ilene, *Pub Program Mgr,* Rensselaer County Historical Society, Hart-Cluett Mansion, 1827, Troy NY

Frank, Jacqueline, *Assoc Prof,* C W Post Campus of Long Island University, School of Visual & Performing Arts, Brookville NY (S)

Frank, Jean, *Gift Gallery Mgr,* Delaplaine Visual Arts Education Center, Frederick MD

Frank, Patrick, *Asst Prof,* University of Kansas, Kress Foundation Dept of Art History, Lawrence KS (S)

Frank, Peter, *Sr Cur,* Riverside Art Museum, Riverside CA

Franke, John C, *Gen Educ,* Art Institute of Pittsburgh, Pittsburgh PA (S)

Frankel, Nancy, *Treas,* Washington Sculptors Group, Washington DC

Franki, Jamie, *Assoc Prof,* University of North Carolina at Charlotte, Dept Art, Charlotte NC (S)

Franklin, David, *Deputy Dir, Chief Cur Colls & Research, Cur Prints & Drawings,* National Gallery of Canada, Ottawa ON

Franklin, David, *Dir, Pres & CEO,* The Cleveland Museum of Art, Cleveland OH

Franklin, Dick, *VPres,* State Historical Society of Missouri, Gallery and Library, Columbia MO

Franklin, Jamie, *Cur Coll,* Bennington Museum, Bennington VT

Franklin, Jonathan, *Chief Librn,* National Gallery of Canada, Library, Ottawa ON

Franklin, Julia, *Dept Coordr & Assoc Prof,* Graceland University, Fine Arts Div, Lamoni IA (S)

Franklin, Julie, *Exhib Coordr,* University of California, Berkeley, The Magnes Collection of Jewish Art & Life, Berkeley CA

Franklin, Laura L, *Chair Div Fine Arts,* Brevard College, Department of Art, Brevard NC (S)

Franklin, Marjorie, *Assoc Prof,* University of Minnesota, Minneapolis, Dept of Art, Minneapolis MN (S)

Franklin, Yoriko, *Admin Asst,* Grounds for Sculpture, Hamilton NJ

Franklin-David, Amy, *Cur Educ,* University of Tampa, Henry B Plant Museum, Tampa FL

Franko, Joseph, *Assoc Dean Arts & Science,* Pace University, Dyson College of Arts & Sciences, Pleasantville NY (S)

Franks, Pamela, *Cur Acad Initiatives,* Yale University, Yale University Art Gallery, New Haven CT

Franson, Scott, *Instr,* Ricks College, Dept of Art, Rexburg ID (S)

Frantz, April, *Interpretation Supvr,* Landis Valley Village and Farm Museum, PA Historical & Museum Commission, Lancaster PA

Frantz, Barry, *Instr,* Cuesta College, Art Dept, San Luis Obispo CA (S)

Frantz, James H, *Conservator In Charge,* The Metropolitan Museum of Art, New York NY

Frantz, Paul, *Pres Bd Trustees,* Taubman Museum of Art, Roanoke VA

Franzini, Robert, *Chmn,* Morehead State University, Claypool-Young Art Gallery, Morehead KY

Franzini, Robert, *Chmn,* Morehead State University, Art & Design Dept, Morehead KY (S)

Frasco, Michael, *Dir Finance,* Montclair Art Museum, Montclair NJ

Frasconi, Antonio, *Prof Emeritus,* Purchase College, State University of New York, School of Art+Design, Purchase NY (S)

Fraser, Bob, *CEO,* The Frank Phillips, Woolaroc Museum, Bartlesville OK

Fraser, Elisabeth, *Prof,* University of South Florida, School The Arts, Tampa FL (S)

Fraser, Karen, *Asst Prof,* Santa Clara University, Dept of Art & Art History, Santa Clara CA (S)

Fraser, Lydia, *Librn,* The Textile Museum, Arthur D Jenkins Library of Textile Arts, Washington DC

Fraser, Sandra, *Assoc Cur,* Mendel Art Gallery & Civic Conservatory, Saskatoon SK

Fraser, Sarah E, *Chmn & Assoc Prof,* Northwestern University, Evanston, Dept of Art History, Evanston IL (S)

Frasier, Stephanie, *Assoc Prof,* University of Evansville, Art Dept, Evansville IN (S)

Fratello, Bradley, *Prof,* Saint Louis Community College at Meramec, Art Dept, Saint Louis MO (S)

Frauenberger, Michelle, *Coll Mgr,* National Archives & Records Administration, Franklin D Roosevelt Library, Hyde Park NY

Frauenberger, Michelle, *Registrar,* National Archives & Records Administration, Franklin D Roosevelt Museum, Hyde Park NY

Fraver, Kellie, *Pub Rel Mgr,* George Eastman, Rochester NY

Frazer, Nicole, *Coll & Admin Clerk,* American Museum of Ceramic Art, Pomona CA

Frazier, Clifton T, *Assoc Prof,* Rochester Institute of Technology, School of Printing Management & Sciences, Rochester NY (S)

Frazier, L'Merchie, *Dir Educ,* Museum of African American History, Boston MA

Frazier, Nancy, *Lectr,* Humboldt State University, College of Arts & Humanities, Art Dept, Arcata CA (S)

Frechette, Alain, *Head Educ & Cultural Progs,* The Stewart Museum, Montreal PQ

Frechette, Suzy Enns, *Mgr Fine Arts Dept,* Saint Louis Public Library, Saint Louis MO

Fredendall, Phyllis, *Prof,* Finlandia Univ, International School of Art and Design, Hancock MI (S)

Frederick, Frances A, *Exec Dir,* Associated Artists of Pittsburgh, Pittsburgh PA

Frederick, Jennie, *Head Dept,* Maple Woods Community College, Dept of Art & Art History, Kansas City MO (S)

Frederick, Karen, *Cur & Exhib Coordr,* Bush-Holley Historic Site & Storehouse Gallery, Greenwich Historical Society/ Bush-Holley House, Cos Cob CT

Frederick, Margaretta S, *Cur Bancroft Coll Pre-Raphaelite Art,* Delaware Art Museum, Wilmington DE

Fredericksen, Eric, *Contact,* Western Bridge, Seattle WA

Fredericksen, Renee, *Vol Dir,* Salisbury University, Ward Museum of Wildfowl Art, Salisbury MD

Fredette, Chantal, *Mem Coordr,* Royal Architectural Institute of Canada, Ottawa ON

Fredrick, Charles, *Prof Emer,* California State Polytechnic University, Pomona, Department of Art, Pomona CA (S)

Fredrick, Kathleen P, *Dir,* A.E. Backus Museum of Art, Fort Pierce FL

Freeburg, Gary, *Gallery Dir,* James Madison University, Sawhill Gallery, Harrisonburg VA

Freed, Wayne, *Assoc Prof,* Mohawk Valley Community College, Utica NY (S)

Freedman, Ann, *Pres & Dir,* M Knoedler, Library, New York NY

Freedman, Jacqueline, *Assoc Prof,* Cuyahoga Community College, Dept of Art, Cleveland OH (S)

Freedman, Joan A, *Lectr,* Johns Hopkins University, School of Medicine, Dept of Art as Applied to Medicine, Baltimore MD (S)

Freedman, Kerry, *Div Head Art Educ,* Northern Illinois University, School of Art, DeKalb IL (S)

Freedman, Phyllis, *Curatorial Asst,* Hebrew Union College Museum, Jewish Institute of Religion Museum, New York NY

Freedman, Susan K, *Pres,* Public Art Fund, Inc, New York NY

Freedman, Susan K, *Pres,* Public Art Fund, Inc, Visual Archive, New York NY

Freeman, Aimee, *Dir Devel,* Arts Council Of New Orleans, New Orleans LA

Freeman, Amy, *Vis Asst Prof,* University of Florida, School of Art & Art History, Gainesville FL (S)

Freeman, Dana, *Assoc Prof & Dir Exhibs,* Aquinas College, Art Dept, Grand Rapids MI (S)

Freeman, Dave, *Interim Dir,* Cottonlandia Museum, Greenwood MS

Freeman, David, *Prof,* Winthrop University, Dept of Art & Design, Rock Hill SC (S)

Freeman, Deborah, *Finance,* Fusion: The Ontario Clay & Glass Association, Fusion Clay & Glass Association, Toronto ON

Freeman, Dorothy, *Pub Rels & Publ Coordr,* The Art Museum at the University of Kentucky, Lexington KY

Freeman, Gary, *Dept Chmn,* Gaston College, Art Dept, Dallas NC (S)

Freeman, Heather, *Asst Prof,* University of North Carolina at Charlotte, Dept Art, Charlotte NC (S)

Freeman, Jeff, *Prof,* University of South Dakota, Department of Art, College of Fine Arts, Vermillion SD (S)

Freeman, Joanne, *Information Systems,* The National Shrine of the North American Martyrs, Fultonville NY

Freeman, John C, *Assoc Prof,* University of Massachusetts Lowell, Dept of Art, Lowell MA (S)

Freeman, K Genevieve, *Asst Prof,* Pepperdine University, Seaver College, Dept of Art, Malibu CA (S)

Freeman, Kirk, *Prof,* Bethel College, Dept of Art, Saint Paul MN (S)

Freeman, Kristin, *Mgr Col,* Columbia College Chicago, Museum of Contemporary Photography, Chicago IL

Freeman, Lynda, *Secy,* Arlington Museum of Art, Arlington TX

Freeman, McArthur, *Asst Prof,* University of South Florida, School The Arts, Tampa FL (S)

Freeman, Robert, *Exec Dir & Cur,* Art Gallery of Mississauga, Mississauga ON

Freeman, Rusty, *Dir Visual Arts,* Cedarhurst Center for the Arts, Mitchell Museum, Mount Vernon IL

Freeman, Rusty, *VP Cur,* Plains Art Museum, Fargo ND

Freeman, Sandi, *Exec Asst,* University of Tulsa, Gilcrease Museum, Tulsa OK

Freeman, Suzanne H, *Head Fine Arts Librn,* Virginia Museum of Fine Arts, Margaret R & Robert M Freeman Library, Richmond VA

Freeman, Turner, *Film & Video Librn,* Public Library of the District of Columbia, Audiovisual Division, Washington DC

Freer, Elene J, *Cur,* Muskoka Arts & Crafts Inc, Chapel Gallery, Bracebridge ON

Freese, David, *Adj Prof,* Saint Joseph's University, Art Dept, Philadelphia PA (S)

Fregin, Nancy J, *Pres,* American Society of Artists, Inc, Palatine IL

Freiberg, Jack, *Asst Prof,* Florida State University, Art History Dept, Tallahassee FL (S)

Freilach, David, *Admin Officer,* Massachusetts Institute of Technology, List Visual Arts Center, Cambridge MA

Freiman, Lisa, *Chair Dept of Contemporary Art,* Indianapolis Museum of Art, Indianapolis IN

Freitag, April, *Vol & Event Coordr,* Fort Collins Museum of Art, Inc., Fort Collins CO

Freitag, Sally, *Registrar,* National Gallery of Art, Washington DC

Frembling, Jonathan, *Archivist & Reference Serv Mgr,* Amon Carter Museum of American Art, Fort Worth TX

Frembling, Jonathan, *Archivist & Reference Serv Mgr,* Amon Carter Museum of American Art, Research Library, Fort Worth TX

French, Annette, *Visitor Info Center,* Mississippi Museum of Art, Howorth Library, Jackson MS

French, Elizabeth, *Admin Asst,* The Art Studio Inc, Beaumont TX

French, Eva, *Dir,* Storefront for Art & Architecture, New York NY

French, Heather, *Mus Shop Mgr,* Riverside, the Farnsley-Moremen Landing, Louisville KY

French, Hugh, *Dir,* Tides Institute & Museum of Art, Eastport ME

French, Jeannie, *Prof,* South Dakota State University, Dept of Visual Arts, Brookings SD (S)

French, Kate Pearson, *Pres,* Wave Hill, Bronx NY

French, Katherine, *Dir,* Danforth Museum of Art, Danforth Museum of Art, Framingham MA

French, Katherine, *Dir,* Danforth Museum of Art, Library, Framingham MA

French, Susanne, *Gallery Dir,* Merced College, Arts Division, Merced CA (S)

Frenette, Guy, *Library Tech,* Jardin Botanique de Montreal, Bibliotheque, Montreal PQ

Fretz, Phelan, *VPres Prog,* Museum of Science & Industry, Chicago IL

Freund, Louise, *Publicity,* Gallery 9, Los Altos CA

Frew, Craig, *Chmn (V),* The Barnum Museum, Bridgeport CT

Frewaldt, Shannon, *Instr,* South Dakota State University, Dept of Visual Arts, Brookings SD (S)

Frey, Barbara, *Dir,* Texas A&M University - Commerce, University Gallery, Commerce TX

Frey, Barbara, *Instr Ceramics,* Texas A&M University Commerce, Dept of Art, Commerce TX (S)

Frey, Erick, *Treas,* Kelly-Griggs House Museum, Red Bluff CA

Frey, Mary, *Assoc Prof,* University of Hartford, Hartford Art School, West Hartford CT (S)

Frey, Michael, *Contact,* Edina Art Center, Margaret Foss Gallery, Edina MN

Frey, Victoria, *Dir,* Quartersaw Gallery, Portland OR

Freyberger, Erica, *Opers Mgr,* Storefront for Art & Architecture, New York NY

Frias, Jennifer, *Gallery Mgr,* University of California, Sweeney Art Gallery, Riverside CA

Fricke, Verna, *Group Coordr,* Green Hill Center for North Carolina Art, Greensboro NC

Fricker, Geoff, *Instr,* Butte College, Dept of Fine Arts and Communication Tech, Oroville CA (S)

Fridlington, Bob, *Dir,* Cranford Historical Society, Cranford NJ

Fried, June A, *Trustee,* Miami Watercolor Society, Inc, Miami FL

Frieder, Braden, *Asst Prof,* Morehead State University, Art & Design Dept, Morehead KY (S)

Friedle, Kathy, *Educator,* Sheldon Museum & Cultural Center, Inc, Sheldon Museum & Cultural Center, Haines AK

Friedman, Alice T, *Prof,* Wellesley College, Art Dept, Wellesley MA (S)

Friedman, Ann, *Dir,* Evergreen State College, Evergreen Gallery, Olympia WA

Friedman, Avi, *Prof,* McGill University, School of Architecture, Montreal PQ (S)

Friedman, Barbara, *Prof,* Pace University, Dyson College of Arts & Sciences, Pleasantville NY (S)

Friedman, Betty, *Art Dept Chair*, Notre Dame de Namur University, Wiegand Gallery, Belmont CA (S)

Friedman, Cheri, *Exec Dir*, Prescott Fine Arts Association, Gallery, Prescott AZ

Friedman, Jennifer, *Instruction Librn*, Ringling College of Art & Design, Verman Kimbrough Memorial Library, Sarasota FL

Friedman, Jennifer, *Librn Architecture & Visual Arts*, Massachusetts Institute of Technology, Rotch Library of Architecture & Planning, Cambridge MA

Friedman, Joel, *Asst Prof*, Seton Hall University, College of Arts & Sciences, South Orange NJ (S)

Friedman, Nancy, *Mus Shop Mgr*, Hunterdon Art Museum, Clinton NJ

Friedman, Rebecca K, *Asst Librn*, Princeton University, Marquand Library of Art & Archaeology, Princeton NJ

Friedman, Robert, *Dir*, Stephens College, Lewis James & Nellie Stratton Davis Art Gallery, Columbia MO

Friedman, Robert, *Instr*, Stephens College, Art Dept, Columbia MO (S)

Frieling, Rudolf, *Cur Media Arts*, San Francisco Museum of Modern Art, San Francisco CA

Friesen, Leslie, *Power Creative Designer-in-Residence*, University of Louisville, Allen R Hite Art Institute, Louisville KY (S)

Friesen, Paul, *Faculty Emeritus*, Hesston College, Art Dept, Hesston KS (S)

Frieser, Hannah, *Dir*, Light Work, Robert B Menschel Photography Gallery, Syracuse NY

Frieseu, Jacqueline, *Chief Admin Officer*, Manitoba Historical Society, Dalnavert Museum, Winnipeg MB

Frigard, Kelly, *Asst Prof*, McPherson College, Art Dept, McPherson KS (S)

Frisbee Johnson, Mary, *Prof*, University of Northern Iowa, Dept of Art, Cedar Falls IA (S)

Frisby, Rachel, *Cur*, Albin Polasek Museum & Sculpture Gardens, Winter Park FL

Frisch, Marianne Brunson, *Cur*, The Reader's Digest Association Inc, New York NY

Frischkorn, Shauna L, *Assoc Prof Photog*, Millersville University, Dept of Art & Design, Millersville PA (S)

Frish, Scott, *Asst Prof*, West Texas A&M University, Art, Theatre & Dance Dept, Canyon TX (S)

Frith, Deidre, *Dir Community Rels*, Wiregrass Museum of Art, Dothan AL

Fritsch, Jodi, *Dir Pub Rel and Mktg*, Fitton Center for Creative Arts, Hamilton OH

Fritz, Don, *Asst Prof*, Santa Clara University, Dept of Art & Art History, Santa Clara CA (S)

Fritz, James, *Prof*, Southwestern Oregon Community College, Visual Arts Dept, Coos Bay OR (S)

Fritz, Lisa, *Instr*, Indian Hills Community College, Ottumwa Campus, Dept of Art, Ottumwa IA (S)

Fritz, Natalie, *Asst Cur*, Clark County Historical Society, Heritage Center of Clark County, Springfield OH

Fritzsch, Laurel, *Cur Fine Art*, Kansas State Historical Society, Kansas Museum of History, Topeka KS

Frizzell, Deborah, *Asst Prof*, William Paterson University, Dept Arts, Wayne NJ (S)

Frocheur, Nicole, *Adj Asst Prof*, College of Staten Island, Performing & Creative Arts Dept, Staten Island NY (S)

Froehlich, Conrad G, *Dir*, Martin and Osa Johnson, Chanute KS

Froehlich, Conrad G, *Dir*, Martin and Osa Johnson, Imperato Collection of West African Artifacts, Chanute KS

Froehlich, Conrad G, *Dir*, Martin and Osa Johnson, Johnson Collection of Photographs, Movies & Memorabilia, Chanute KS

Froehlich, Conrad G, *Dir*, Martin and Osa Johnson, Selsor Art Gallery, Chanute KS

Froehlich, Conrad G, *Dir*, Martin and Osa Johnson, Scott Explorers Library, Chanute KS

Froehlich, Kristen, *Dir of Coll*, Philadelphia History Museum, Philadelphia PA

From, Kristy, *Gallery Adminr*, University of Alabama at Huntsville, Union Grove Gallery & University Center Gallery, Huntsville AL

Froman, David, *Chmn*, Northeastern Oklahoma A & M College, Art Dept, Miami OK (S)

Fromm, Martin, *Assoc Prof*, University of Montana, Dept of Art, Missoula MT (S)

Frontz, Stephanie J, *Librn*, University of Rochester, Art/Music Library, Rochester NY

Frorup, Kendra, *Prof*, University of Tampa, College of Arts & Letters, Tampa FL (S)

Frost, Darrel R, *Assoc Dean Science*, American Museum of Natural History, New York NY

Frost, Donna, *Dir Admin & Finance*, Museum of Contemporary Art Denver, Denver CO

Frost, Judy, *Accnt*, Whatcom Museum, Library, Bellingham WA

Frost, Krisanne, *Gal Liaison*, Blue Star Contemporary Art Center, San Antonio TX

Frudakis, Tony, *Asst Prof*, Hillsdale College, Art Dept, Hillsdale MI (S)

Frus, Brian, *Vis Asst Prof of Glass*, Jacksonville University, Dept of Art, Theater, Dance, Jacksonville FL (S)

Frusier, Stephanie, *Chmn Art Dept*, University of Evansville, Krannert Gallery & Peterson Gallery, Evansville IN

Fry, Amy, *Exec Dir*, Lahaina Arts Society, Art Organization, Lahaina HI

Fry, Ashley, *Prog Specialist*, United States Department of the Interior, Indian Arts & Crafts Board, Washington DC

Fry, Betzy, *Dir Develop & External Affairs*, Portland Children's Museum, Portland OR

Fry, Matt, *Dir Mktg & Commun*, Walters Art Museum, Library, Baltimore MD

Fry, Matthew, *Dir Mktg*, Walters Art Museum, Baltimore MD

Frye, Todd, *Gallery Dir*, Brigham Young University, B F Larsen Gallery, Provo UT

Frykman, Sharon, *Faculty*, Grand Marais Art Colony, Grand Marais MN (S)

Frykman, Steve, *Faculty*, Grand Marais Art Colony, Grand Marais MN (S)

Fuchs, Angelee, *Prof*, Mount Mary College, Art & Design Division, Milwaukee WI (S)

Fuentes, Elvis, *Cur*, El Museo del Barrio, New York NY

Fuentes, Leo, *Asst Prof*, City College of New York, Art Dept, New York NY (S)

Fuentes, Monique, *Retail Opers Mgr*, Museum of Contemporary Art, San Diego, La Jolla CA

Fuentes, Tina, *Dir & Prof*, Texas Tech University, Dept of Art, Lubbock TX (S)

Fuerst, Judy, *Cur*, Barker Character, Comic and Cartoon Museum, Cheshire CT

Fuhrman, Robert, *Dir*, Clark County Historical Society, Library, Springfield OH

Fuhrman Bragg, Elizabeth, *Registrar*, Evansville Museum of Arts, History & Science, Evansville IN

Fuhro, Laura, *Asst Dir*, Berkeley Heights Free Public Library, Berkeley Heights NJ

Fujita, Rachel, *Asst Prof*, University of Idaho/College of Art & Architecture, Dept of Art & Design, Moscow ID (S)

Fukawa, Hirokazu, *Asst Prof*, University of Hartford, Hartford Art School, West Hartford CT (S)

Fulda, Caryn, *Exec Asst*, Museum of Fine Arts Houston, Bayou Bend Collection & Gardens, Houston TX

Fuller, Cara, *Asst Prof*, Alabama A & M University, Art & Art Education Dept, Normal AL (S)

Fuller, Charles, *Dean School Fine Arts*, Ouachita Baptist University, Dept of Visual Art, Arkadelphia AR (S)

Fuller, Cindy, *Bd Pres*, North Shore Art League, Winnetka IL (S)

Fuller, Corey, *Asst Prof*, Oklahoma Baptist University, Art Dept, Shawnee OK (S)

Fuller, Dan, *Instr*, University of Wisconsin, Madison, Dept of Art History, Madison WI (S)

Fuller, Daniel, *Dir*, Maine College of Art, The Institute of Contemporary Art, Portland ME

Fuller, Elizabeth E, *Librn*, The Rosenbach Museum & Library, Philadelphia PA

Fuller, Lori, *Assoc Librn Coll Mgmt*, Corning Museum of Glass, Juliette K and Leonard S Rakow Research Library, Corning NY

Fuller, Stacy, *Head Educ*, Amon Carter Museum of American Art, Fort Worth TX

Fuller-Sutherland, Susan, *Bd Mem*, Arlington Museum of Art, Arlington TX

Fullerton, Deborah, *Cur*, South Texas Institute for the Arts, Art Museum of South Texas, Corpus Christi TX

Fullerton, Deborah, *Cur Exhibs*, South Texas Institute for the Arts, Art Museum of South Texas, Corpus Christi TX

Fullerton, Jane, *CEO*, New Brunswick Museum, Saint John NB

Fullerton, Monica, *Instr*, Kenyon College, Art Dept, Gambier OH (S)

Fullmer, Mark, *VPres*, Contemporary Arts Center, New Orleans LA

Fulmer, Mara, *Prof*, Mott Community College, Fine Arts & Social Sciences Division, Flint MI (S)

Fulton, Andrea, *Dir Communs*, Denver Art Museum, Denver CO

Fulton, Brianne, *Art Faculty*, Cottey College, Art Dept, Nevada MO (S)

Fulton, Carol, *Exhibition Designer*, LA County Museum of Art, Los Angeles CA

Fulton, Christopher, *Assoc Prof*, University of Louisville, Allen R Hite Art Institute, Louisville KY (S)

Funderburk, Brent, *Prof*, Mississippi State University, Dept of Art, Starville MS (S)

Funderburk, Danielle, *Registrar*, Auburn University, Julie Collins Smith Museum, Auburn AL

Fung, Adam, *Prof*, Texas Christian University, School of Art, Fort Worth TX (S)

Fung, Ming, *Grad Dir*, Southern California Institute of Architecture, Los Angeles CA (S)

Funk, Carla, *Dir Univ Mus*, Foosaner Art Museum, Melbourne FL

Funk, Patricia, *Progs & Mem*, Springfield Museum of Art, Springfield OH

Funke, Marti, *Coll Mgr/Registrar*, University of Mississippi, University Museum & Historic Houses, Oxford MS

Funkenstein, Susan, *Asst Prof*, University of Wisconsin-Parkside, Art Dept, Kenosha WI (S)

Funkhouser, Kate, *Fine Arts Dept Chmn*, Brazosport College, Art Dept, Lake Jackson TX (S)

Funnell, Jeff, *Prof*, University of Manitoba, School of Art, Winnipeg MB (S)

Fuqua, Dana, *Dir Fin & CFO*, Chrysler Museum of Art, Norfolk VA

Furber, Rich, *Dir*, Chief Plenty Coups Museum State Park, Pryor MT

Furgol, Edward, *Cur*, Naval Historical Center, The Navy Museum, Washington DC

Furlong, Jim, *Gallery Dir*, Hudson Guild, Hudson Guild Gallery, New York NY

Furlong, Patrick, *Dir Finance & Admis*, Chicago Architecture Foundation, Chicago IL

Furman, David, *Prof Ceramics*, Pitzer College, Dept of Art, Claremont CA (S)

Furqueron, Reagan, *Asst Prof, Dir Foundation*, Indiana University-Purdue University, Indianapolis, Herron School of Art & Design, Indianapolis IN (S)

Furry, Stephanie, *Instr*, John C Calhoun, Department of Fine Arts, Tanner AL (S)

Furst, Donald, *Prof*, University of North Carolina at Wilmington, Dept of Fine Arts - Division of Art, Wilmington NC (S)

Furtak, Rosemary, *Librn*, Walker Art Center, Staff Reference Library, Minneapolis MN

Furtkamp, Darryl, *Asst Prof*, New England College, Art & Art History, Henniker NH (S)

Fuscarino, Elise, *Dir*, Printmaking Council of New Jersey, Branchburg NJ

Fusco, Peter, *Cur of European Sculpture & Works of Art*, Getty Center, Trust Museum, Los Angeles CA

Fusey, Jean-Francois, *Dir Admin*, Musee National des Beaux Arts du Quebec, Quebec PQ

Fuson, Eric, *Instr*, Missouri Western State University, Art Dept, Saint Joseph MO (S)

Fuson, Paul, *Dir*, Valley Art Center Inc, Clarkston WA

Fussa, Nilsevady, *Auxiliary Prof*, University of Puerto Rico, Dept of Fine Arts, Rio Piedras PR (S)

Fussa, Nilsevady, *Auxiliary Prof*, University of Puerto Rico, Dept of Fine Arts, Rio Piedras PR (S)

Futernick, Robert, *Assoc Dir*, Fine Arts Museums of San Francisco, M H de Young Museum, San Francisco CA

Futernick, Robert, *Assoc Dir*, Fine Arts Museums of San Francisco, Legion of Honor, San Francisco CA

Futter, Ellen V, *Pres,* American Museum of Natural History, New York NY

Futtner, Joseph, *Acting Area Head History,* Pasadena City College, Visual Arts and Media Studies Division, Pasadena CA (S)

Fye, Rebecca, *Dir,* Jackson County Historical Society, John Wornall House Museum, Independence MO

Fyffe, Ben, *Asst Cur Coll,* City of El Paso, El Paso Museum of Art, El Paso TX

Fyffe, Louise, *Pres,* Kings County Historical Society & Museum, Hampton NB

Gaa, David, *Exec Dir,* Mission San Luis Rey de Francia, Mission San Luis Rey Museum, Oceanside CA

Gaasch, Cynnie, *Exec & Artistic Dir,* Chautauqua Center for the Visual Arts, Chautauqua NY

Gabany, Donald, *Video Production,* Art Institute of Pittsburgh, Pittsburgh PA (S)

Gabarra, Ed, *Admin,* Mission San Luis Rey de Francia, Mission San Luis Rey Museum, Oceanside CA

Gabbard, Paula, *Sr Bibliographer,* Columbia University, Avery Architectural & Fine Arts Library, New York NY

Gabbert, Tammy, *Art at Work,* Eastern Washington State Historical Society, Northwest Museum of Arts & Culture, Spokane WA

Gach Peelle, Susie, *Recording Secy,* American Artists Professional League, Inc, New York NY

Gacummo, Beth, *Mus Exhibs Dir,* Islip Art Museum, East Islip NY

Gaddy, Janet, *Instr Art,* Greensboro College, Irene Cullis Gallery, Greensboro NC

Gadsden, Eleanore, *Weems Sr Cur Decorative Arts & Sculpture AOA,* Museum of Fine Arts, Boston MA

Gadzia, Jimi, *VPres,* Roswell Museum & Art Center, Roswell NM

Gaffin, Harold, *Dir,* Rochester Institute of Technology, School of Printing Management & Sciences, Rochester NY (S)

Gaffney, Gary, *Instr,* Art Academy of Cincinnati, Cincinnati OH (S)

Gaffney, Nicholas, *Asst Prof,* Colby-Sawyer College, Dept of Fine & Performing Arts, New London NH (S)

Gage, Russ, *Opers & Event Develop Mgr,* Portland Art Museum, Northwest Film Center, Portland OR

Gage, Stacy, *Mgr Coll & Exhibs,* Dubuque Museum of Art, Dubuque IA

Gagne, Prudence, *Finance Dir,* League of New Hampshire Craftsmen, Grodin Permanent Collection Museum, Concord NH

Gagne, Tami, *Financial Dir,* Riverside Arts Center, Riverside IL (S)

Gagnon, Francois Marc, *Instr,* Universite de Montreal, Dept of Art History, Montreal PQ (S)

Gagnon, Vicky Chainey, *Dir & Cur,* Bishop's University, Foreman Art Gallery, Sherbrooke PQ

Gahagan, Sean, *VPres,* National Baseball Hall of Fame & Museum, Inc, Art Collection, Cooperstown NY

Gaiber, Maxine, *Exec Dir,* Delaware Center for the Contemporary Arts, Wilmington DE

Gaines, Anne, *Adjunct Asst Prof,* Drew University, Art Dept, Madison NJ (S)

Gaither, Edmund, *Dir/Cur NCAAA Art of the Americas,* Museum of Fine Arts, Boston MA

Gaither, Edmund B, *Dir & Cur,* Museum of the National Center of Afro-American Artists, Boston MA

Gaito, Elaine, *Mktg & Communs,* Canadian Art Foundation, Toronto ON

Gajewski, Czary, *Chair,* University of Alberta, Dept of Art & Design, Edmonton AB (S)

Galante, Frances, *Instr,* Wayne Art Center, Wayne PA (S)

Galante, Peter, *Asst Prof,* Cardinal Stritch University, Art Dept, Milwaukee WI (S)

Galante, Thomas, *Lib Dir,* Queens Borough Public Library, Fine Arts & Recreation Division, Jamaica NY

Galanti, Tera, *Asst Prof Studio Art,* California Polytechnic State University at San Luis Obispo, Dept of Art & Design, San Luis Obispo CA (S)

Galassi, Susan Grace, *Cur,* Frick Collection, New York NY

Galazka, Suzanne, *Gallery Asst,* Artlink, Inc, Auer Center for Arts & Culture, Fort Wayne IN

Galbraith, James, *Chief Librn,* Corning Museum of Glass, Juliette K and Leonard S Rakow Research Library, Corning NY

Galbraith, Jeanne, *Research Sec,* Livingston County Historical Society, Museum, Geneseo NY

Galbreath, Joseph, *Asst Prof,* West Virginia University, College of Creative Arts, School of Art & Design, Morgantown WV (S)

Galczenski, Marian, *Instr,* Cuesta College, Art Dept, San Luis Obispo CA (S)

Galehouse, Ida, *Librn,* Cheekwood-Tennessee Botanical Garden & Museum of Art, Botanic Hall Library, Nashville TN

Galembo, Phyllis, *Prof,* State University of New York at Albany, Art Dept, Albany NY (S)

Galeno, Ciro, *Asst Dir,* The Noble Maritime Collection, Staten Island NY

Gales, Melinda, *Registrar,* Morris Museum of Art, Augusta GA

Galey, Chuck, *Lectr,* Mississippi State University, Dept of Art, Starville MS (S)

Galioto, Kristin, *Communs Mgr,* Glass Art Society, Seattle WA

Galizia, Ed, *Dir Music & Video Bus,* Art Institute of Fort Lauderdale, Fort Lauderdale FL (S)

Gall, Dolores, *Pres,* New Haven Paint & Clay Club, Inc, New Haven CT

Gallagher, Brian, *Cur Decorative Arts,* The Mint Museum, Charlotte NC

Gallagher, Edward, *Dir Educ,* Beck Center for the Arts, Lakewood OH

Gallagher, Edward, *Pres,* The American-Scandinavian Foundation, Scandinavia House: The Nordic Center in America, New York NY

Gallagher, Jean, *Prof,* California State University, Chico, Department of Art & Art History, Chico CA (S)

Gallagher, Laraine, *Fiscal Officer,* Visual Studies Workshop, Rochester NY (S)

Gallagher, Sean, *Instr,* Judson University, School of Art, Design & Architecture, Elgin IL (S)

Gallagher, Sean, *Secy,* Madison Museum of Fine Art, Madison GA

Gallagher, Tim, *VPres,* Arts on the Park, Lakeland Center for Creative Arts, Lakeland FL

Gallagher Landis, Gary, *Deputy Dir of Extended Affairs,* San Jose Museum of Art, Library, San Jose CA

Gallant, Aprile, *Cur Prints, Drawings & Photographs,* Smith College, Museum of Art, Northampton MA

Gallant, Michele, *Registrar & Preparator,* Dalhousie University, Dalhousie Art Gallery, Halifax NS

Gallardo, Evonne, *Exec Dir,* Self Help Graphics, Los Angeles CA

Gallas, Ron, *Assoc Prof,* Saint Olaf College, Art Dept, Northfield MN (S)

Gallavan, Teresa, *Mus Mgr,* Riverside County Museum, Edward-Dean Museum & Gardens, Cherry Valley CA

Gallaway, Natasha, *Chair Residency Comt,* La Napoule Art Foundation, Chateau de la Napoule, Portsmouth NH

Gallegos, Ximena, *Mem Coordr,* Florida International University, The Patricia & Phillip Frost Art Museum, Miami FL

Gallerani, Elizabeth, *Coordr Mellon Acad Programs,* Williams College, Museum of Art, Williamstown MA

Gallery, Julie, *Accounting Asst,* Sangre de Cristo Arts & Conference Center, Pueblo CO

Galley, Sandra, *VPres & Dir,* The New England Museum of Telephony, Inc., The Telephone Museum, Ellsworth ME

Galliardt, Jan, *Chief Preparator/ Exhib Technician,* Bass Museum of Art, Miami Beach FL

Galligan, David M, *Exec VPres & COO,* The Museum of Contemporary Art (MOCA), Moca Grand Avenue, Los Angeles CA

Gallina, Brenda, *Exec Dir,* Atlanta International Museum of Art & Design, Museum of Design Atlanta, Atlanta GA

Gallini, Karen, *Head Circulation Dept,* Springfield Free Public Library, Donald B Palmer Museum, Springfield NJ

Galloway, Elizabeth, *VPres & Dir,* Art Center College of Design, James Lemont Fogg Memorial Library, Pasadena CA

Galloway, Julia, *School for American Crafts Chair,* Rochester Institute of Technology, College of Imaging Arts & Sciences, Rochester NY (S)

Galloway, Kat, *Prof Art,* Eastern Oregon University, School of Arts & Science, La Grande OR (S)

Galloway, Mary Lou, *Dir SIACM,* Illinois State Museum, Illinois Artisans & Visitors Centers, Chicago IL

Galloway, Robert, *Instr,* Mesa Community College, Dept of Art, Mesa AZ (S)

Galloway, Thomas D, *Dean,* Georgia Institute of Technology, College of Architecture, Atlanta GA (S)

Gallucci, Mario, *ArtQuest Educ Cur,* Green Hill Center for North Carolina Art, Greensboro NC

Galpin, Amy, *Proj Cur,* San Diego Museum of Art, San Diego CA

Galtere, Roberto, *Head Opers & Finance,* The Stewart Museum, Montreal PQ

Gamble, Jeanne, *Library & Archives Specialist,* Historic New England, Library and Archives, Boston MA

Gamble, Shweta, *Exec Dir,* Kentuck Museum Association, Inc., Kentuck Art Center & Festival of the Arts, Northport AL

Gamble, Steven G, *Pres,* Southern Arkansas University, Art Dept Gallery & Magale Art Gallery, Magnolia AR

Gamler, Steve, *Registrar,* Lafayette College, Lafayette College Art Galleries, Easton PA

Gammell, Brad, *Prog Coordr,* The Names Project Foundation AIDS Memorial Quilt, Atlanta GA

Gammon, Lynda, *Chmn & Assoc Prof,* University of Victoria, Dept of Visual Arts, Victoria BC (S)

Gamon, Patricia, *Instr,* California State University, Dominguez Hills, Art & Design Dept, Carson CA (S)

Gamse, Barbara, *Mus Shop Mgr,* Maryland Historical Society, Library, Baltimore MD

Gamwell, Lynn, *Dir,* State University of New York at Binghamton, Binghamton University Art Museum, Binghamton NY

Gancz, Sheri, *Visitor Relations,* Lighthouse ArtCenter Museum & School of Art, Tequesta FL

Gandara, Nancy, *Asst Dir,* Central Library, Dept of Fine Arts, San Antonio TX

Gandee, Cynthia, *Dir,* University of Tampa, Henry B Plant Museum, Tampa FL

Gander, Chris, *Instr,* Pacific Northwest College of Art, Portland OR (S)

Gandee, Cynthia, *Art Historian,* University of South Alabama, Dept of Art & Art History, Mobile AL (S)

Gandy, Janice, *Art Historian,* University of South Alabama, Dept of Art & Art History, Mobile AL (S)

Gandy, Jim, *Archivist,* New York State Military Museum and Veterans Research Center, Saratoga Springs NY

Gangarosa, Louis P, *Finance Officer,* Morris Museum of Art, Augusta GA

Gannon, Stacey, *Exec Dir,* Saginaw Art Museum, Saginaw MI

Ganong, Overton G, *Exec Dir,* South Carolina State Museum, Columbia SC

Gans, Lucy, *Prof,* Lehigh University, Dept of Art, Architecture & Design, Bethlehem PA (S)

Ganstrom, Linda, *Asst Prof,* Fort Hays State University, Dept of Art & Design, Hays KS (S)

Gant, Ella, *Assoc Prof Art,* Hamilton College, Art Dept, Clinton NY (S)

Gant, Sally, *Dir Educ & Spec Progs,* Old Salem Museums & Gardens, Museum of Early Southern Decorative Arts, Winston Salem NC

Ganther, Becky, *Mktg & Pub Rels Mgr,* Golden State Mutual Life Insurance Company, Afro-American Art Collection, Los Angeles CA

Gantner, Ellen, *Dir,* Illinois State Museum, Illinois Artisans & Visitors Centers, Chicago IL

Gantner, Robert, *Treas,* Essex Art Association, Inc, Essex CT

Gantt, Nancy, *Cur,* Sturdivant Museum Association, Sturdivant Museum, Selma AL

Gantt, Richard, *Lectr,* University of North Carolina at Greensboro, Art Dept, Greensboro NC (S)

Ganz, Cheryl, *Cur,* National Postal Museum, Smithsonian Institution, Washington DC

Ganz, Christopher, *Assoc Prof,* Indiana-Purdue University, Dept of Fine Arts, Fort Wayne IN (S)

Ganz, Sarah, *Dir Educ,* Rhode Island School of Design, Museum of Art, Providence RI

Gappmayer, Sam, *Exec Dir,* Sun Valley Center for the Arts, Dept of Fine Art, Sun Valley ID (S)

Gappmayer, Sam, *Pres & CEO,* Colorado Springs Fine Arts Center, Taylor Museum, Colorado Springs CO

Gappmayer, Sam, *Pres & CEO,* Colorado Springs Fine Arts Center, Bemis School of Art, Colorado Springs CO

Gara, James, *Asst Treas,* Museum of Modern Art, New York NY

Garand, Betsey, *Prof, Resident Artist,* Amherst College, Dept of Art & the History of Art, Amherst MA (S)

Garay, Olga, *Dir Cultural Affairs,* Miami-Dade Community College, Wolfson Galleries, Miami FL

Garay-English, Olga, *Exec Dir,* City of Los Angeles, Cultural Affairs Dept, Los Angeles CA

Garber, Kari, *External Relations & Events Coordr,* Touchstone Center for Crafts, Hart Moore Museum, Farmington PA

Garcia, Christopher, *Prof,* Antioch College, Visual Arts Dept, Yellow Springs OH (S)

Garcia, Cynthia, *Asst Dir,* Albuquerque Museum of Art & History, Albuquerque NM

Garcia, Edward, *Exhib Supv,* California African-American Museum, Los Angeles CA

Garcia, Emeren, *Traveling Exhib Officer,* Musee d'art Contemporain de Montreal, Montreal PQ

Garcia, Joel, *Prog Mgr,* Self Help Graphics, Los Angeles CA

Garcia, Juan R, *Asst Prof,* Johns Hopkins University, School of Medicine, Dept of Art as Applied to Medicine, Baltimore MD (S)

Garcia, Magdalena, *Exec Dir,* El Museo Latino, Omaha NE

Garcia, Martin, *Assoc Prof,* University of Puerto Rico, Dept of Fine Arts, Rio Piedras PR (S)

Garcia, Martin, *Assoc Prof,* University of Puerto Rico, Dept of Fine Arts, Rio Piedras PR (S)

Garcia, Miki, *Exec Dir,* Santa Barbara Contemporary Arts Forum, Santa Barbara CA

Garcia, Monica, *Dir Educ & Pub Progs,* Anchorage Museum at Rasmuson Center, Anchorage AK

Garcia, Ofelia, *Prof,* William Paterson University, Dept Arts, Wayne NJ (S)

Garcia, Pam, *Dir Fin,* The California Historical Society, San Francisco CA

Garcia, Robert, *Coll & Exhib,* Hidalgo County Historical Museum, Edinburg TX

Garcia, Serena, *Adm & Communs Mgr,* Hammonds House Museum, Atlanta GA

Garcia-Nuthmann, Andre, *Chmn,* New Mexico Highlands University, Dept of Communications & Fine Arts, Las Vegas NM (S)

Garcia-Roil, Lilian, *Assoc Prof,* Florida State University, Art Dept, Tallahassee FL (S)

Garcia-Sola, Arturo, *Vol Pres Bd Trustees,* Museo de Arte de Puerto Rico, San Juan PR

Garcia-Sola, Arturo, *Vol Pres Bd Trustees,* Museo de Arte de Puerto Rico, San Juan PR

Gardiner, Diana, *Instr,* University of Utah, Dept of Art & Art History, Salt Lake City UT (S)

Gardiner, Jennifer, *Develop & Outreach Assoc,* Laguna Art Museum, Laguna Beach CA

Gardinier, Paul, *Cur Exhib,* Alaska State Museum, Juneau AK

Gardner, Anthony, *Exec Dir,* New Jersey State Museum, Fine Art Bureau, Trenton NJ

Gardner, Ben, *Preparator,* McLean County Art Association, McLean County Arts Center, Bloomington IL

Gardner, Carla, *Accounting Specialist,* University of Kansas, Spencer Museum of Art, Lawrence KS

Gardner, Courtney, *Exec Dir,* Peninsula Fine Arts Center, Newport News VA

Gardner, Jacquie, *Gallery Clerk,* City of Toronto Culture, The Market Gallery, Toronto ON

Gardner, Kevin N, *Asst Prof,* Berea College, Art & Art History Program, Berea KY (S)

Gardner, Margaret, *Instr,* Wayne Art Center, Wayne PA (S)

Gardner, Symmes, *Affiliate Assoc Prof & Dir Ctr for Art Design & Visual Culture,* University of Maryland, Baltimore County, Imaging & Digital Arts (IMDA), Dept of Visual Arts, Baltimore MD (S)

Gardner, Symmes, Center for Art Design and Visual Culture, Baltimore MD

Gardner, William F, *Instr,* North Florida Community College, Dept Humanities & Art, Madison FL (S)

Garfield, Ellen, *Assoc Prof,* Monmouth University, Dept of Art & Design, West Long Branch NJ (S)

Garfinkel, Barry H, *Secy,* Aperture Foundation, New York NY

Gargasz, Joseph, *Dir Exhib & Collections,* Emory University, Michael C Carlos Museum, Atlanta GA

Garhart, Karen M, *Vis Assoc Prof Art,* Kenyon College, Art Dept, Gambier OH (S)

Gariff, David, *Asst Prof,* University of Wisconsin-Stout, Dept of Art & Design, Menomonie WI (S)

Garis, Jane, *Archival Records Coordr & Cur,* North Tonawanda History Museum, North Tonawanda NY

Garland, James, *Assoc VPres of Univ Rels,* University of Bridgeport Gallery, Bridgeport CT

Garland, Jeff, *Head Dept,* Springfield College in Illinois, Dept of Art, Springfield IL (S)

Garmendia, Tatiana, *Prof,* Seattle Central Community College, Humanities - Social Sciences Division, Seattle WA (S)

Garmon, Carole, *Sr Lectr,* University of Mary Washington, Dept of Art & Art History, Fredericksburg VA (S)

Garmon, Christina, *Educ Assoc,* Indianapolis Art Center, Marilyn K. Glick School of Art, Indianapolis IN

Garneau, Neil, *Cur,* Owen Sound Historical Society, Marine & Rail Heritage Museum, Owen Sound ON

Garner, Emily, *School Dir,* DeCordova Museum School, Lincoln MA (S)

Garner, Judy, *Dir,* American Jewish Historical Society, Lee M Friedman Memorial Library, New York NY

Garner, Rebecca, *Program & Publ Coordr,* University of Montana, Montana Museum of Art & Culture, Missoula MT

Garner, Sharon, *Mus Aide,* Historical Museum at Fort Missoula, Missoula MT

Garner, Teresa S, *Dept Head,* Colorado Mesa University, Art Dept, Grand Junction CO (S)

Garnet, Carla, *Cur,* Art Gallery of Peterborough, Peterborough ON

Garnett, Diana, *Accounting Specialist,* University of Virginia, The Fralin Museum of Art at the University of Virginia, Charlottesville VA

Garnett, Leah, *Asst Prof,* Mount Allison University, Dept of Fine Arts, Sackville NB (S)

Garniewicz, Rex, *Dir Collections & Interpretation,* Indiana State Museum, Indianapolis IN

Garoian, Charles, *Dir & Prof Art Educ,* Pennsylvania State University, University Park, Penn State School of Visual Arts, University Park PA (S)

Garoutte, Claire, *Asst Prof,* Seattle University, Dept of Fine Arts, Visual Art Division, Seattle WA (S)

Garoza, Valdis, *Chmn,* Marietta College, Grover M Hermann Fine Arts Center, Marietta OH

Garoza, Valdis, *Chmn,* Marietta College, Art Dept, Marietta OH (S)

Garr, Robin, *Dir Educ,* Bruce Museum, Inc, Greenwich CT

Garrard, Mary, *Prof,* American University, Dept of Art, New York NY (S)

Garrels, Gary, *Sr Cur Painting & Sculpture,* San Francisco Museum of Modern Art, San Francisco CA

Garrepy, Ken, *Bus Mgr,* Providence Athenaeum, Providence RI

Garrera, Joseph, *Exec Dir,* Lehigh Valley Heritage Center, Allentown PA

Garretson, Susan, *Chair Bd Trustees,* Museum of Northern Arizona, Flagstaff AZ

Garrett, Jeff, *Art School Dir,* Flint Institute of Arts, Flint MI

Garrett, Jural J, *Chief Deputy Dir,* Natural History Museum of Los Angeles County, Los Angeles CA

Garrett, Michael, *Head Dept,* Mississippi University for Women, Division of Fine & Performing Arts, Columbus MS (S)

Garrett, Tom, *Prof Design Dept,* Minneapolis College of Art & Design, Minneapolis MN (S)

Garrison, Denzil, *VChmn,* Oklahoma Historical Society, Library Resources Division, Oklahoma City OK

Garrison, Elizabeth, *Educ Cur,* Willamette University, Hallie Ford Museum of Art, Salem OR

Garrison, Helen, *Dean Liberal Arts,* Art Institute of Southern California, Laguna Beach CA (S)

Garrison, Jim, *Instr,* Mesa Community College, Dept of Art, Mesa AZ (S)

Garrison, Jodie, *Head Art Dept,* Western Oregon University, Dan & Gail Cannon Gallery of Art, Monmouth OR

Garrison, Jodie, *Instr Painting,* Columbia College, Art Dept, Columbia MO (S)

Garrison, Laura, *Asst Dir,* Rensselaer Polytechnic Institute, Eye Ear Studio Dept of Art, Troy NY (S)

Garrison, Lee Ann, *Chair,* University of Wisconsin-Milwaukee, Peck School of the Arts, Dept of Art & Design, Milwaukee WI (S)

Garrison, Natalie, *Asst Cur,* Charles B Goddard, Ardmore OK

Garrity, Noreen Scott, *Cur Educ,* Rutgers University, Stedman Art Gallery, Camden NJ

Garrow, Kelly Fritz, *Communs Dir,* Toledo Museum of Art, Toledo OH

Garry, Eileen, *Exec Dir,* Kansas City Jewish Museum of Contemporary Art - Epsten Gallery, Overland Park KS

Garside, Anne, *Dir Communs,* Maryland Historical Society, Museum of Maryland History, Baltimore MD

Gartenmann, Donna, *City of Boulder Arts Commission & Dir Cultural Programs,* Boulder Public Library & Gallery, Arts Gallery, Boulder CO

Garthwaite, Ernest, *Assoc Prof,* York College of the City University of New York, Fine & Performing Arts, Jamaica NY (S)

Gartner, Jackie, *Archivist,* Pope County Historical Society, Pope County Museum, Glenwood MN

Garver, Grace, *Deputy Dir Finance,* Museum of Contemporary Art Cleveland, Cleveland OH

Garvey, Regis, *Develop Coordr,* Sioux City Art Center, Sioux City IA (S)

Garvey, Timothy, *Instr,* Illinois Wesleyan University, School of Art, Bloomington IL (S)

Garwood, Jo, *Bus Mgr,* Modern Art Museum, Fort Worth TX

Garwood, Virginia, *Instr,* Wayne Art Center, Wayne PA (S)

Gary, Anne-Bridget, *Prof,* University of Wisconsin-Stevens Point, Dept of Art & Design, Stevens Point WI (S)

Gary, Grace, *Exec Dir,* The Nemours Foundatioin, Nemours Mansion & Gardens, Wilmington DE

Garza, Amorette, *Assoc Prof,* Del Mar College, Art Dept, Corpus Christi TX (S)

Garza, Bertha, *Pres,* Brownsville Art League, Brownsville Museum of Fine Art, Brownsville TX

Garza, Monica, *Dir Educ,* Institute of Contemporary Art, Boston MA

Garzillo, Robert, *Technical Svcs Librn,* Rhode Island School of Design, Fleet Library at RISD, Providence RI

Garzon, Gerry, *Assoc Dir,* Oakland Public Library, Art, Music, History & Literature Section, Oakland CA

Gascogne, Laura-Harris, *Assoc Prof Fine Art & Ceramic Dept Coordr,* Johnson County Community College, Fine Arts Dept & Art History Dept, Overland Park KS (S)

Gaske, Fred, *Bureau Chief,* Florida Folklife Programs, Tallahassee FL

Gaskell, Ivan, *Cur Painting,* Harvard University, William Hayes Fogg Art Museum, Cambridge MA

Gaskil, Darlene, *Adj Prof,* Oral Roberts University, Art Dept, Tulsa OK (S)

Gasparri, Vince, *Exec Dir,* Where Edmonton Community Artists Network Society, Harcourt House Arts Centre, Edmonton AB

Gasparro, Frank, *Instr,* Samuel S Fleisher, Philadelphia PA (S)

Gassinger, Ilse, *Dir,* Durham Art Gallery, Durham ON

Gast, Claudia, *Office Mgr,* Toledo Artists' Club, Toledo Artists' Club & Gallery, Toledo OH

Gaston, Elizabeth, *Asst Prof,* Mount Mary College, Art & Design Division, Milwaukee WI (S)

Gaston, Elizabeth, *Cur,* Mount Mary College, Marian Gallery, Milwaukee WI

Gastonguay, Nicole, *Documentation Tech,* Musee National des Beaux Arts du Quebec, Bibliotheque, Quebec PQ

Gatchalian, Raphael, *Admin Asst,* University of Southern California, USC Fisher Museum of Art, Los Angeles CA

Gates, James L, *Librn,* National Baseball Hall of Fame & Museum, Inc, Art Collection, Cooperstown NY

Gates, Jordene, *Interior Design,* Art Institute of Pittsburgh, Pittsburgh PA (S)

Gates, Nadine, *Cur,* Yarmouth County Historical Society, Yarmouth County Museum & Archives, Yarmouth NS

Gates, Rebecca, *Colls Asst,* Kirkland Museum of Fine & Decorative Art, Denver CO

Gates, Sue, *Dir,* Dacotah Prairie Museum, Lamont Art Gallery, Aberdeen SD

Gates, Sue, *Dir,* Dacotah Prairie Museum, Ruth Bunker Memorial Library, Aberdeen SD

Gates, William, *Cur History,* Ohio Historical Society, National Road-Zane Grey Museum, Columbus OH

Gatewood, Caterine, *Events Coordr,* The Buffalo Fine Arts Academy, Albright-Knox Art Gallery, Buffalo NY

Gatewood, Nicolet, *Assoc Dir Institutional Giving,* Museum for African Art, New York NY

Gatlin, Janice, *Dir Progs,* The Multicultural Center of the South, Shreveport LA

Gatten, Jeff, *Dean,* California Institute of the Arts Library, Santa Clarita CA

Gatti, Stanlee, *Pres,* San Francisco City & County Art Commission, San Francisco CA

Gatto, Holly, *Systems & Online Resources Librn,* Academy of Art, University Library, San Francisco CA

Gatzke, Donald, *Dean,* Tulane University, School of Architecture, New Orleans LA (S)

Gaucher, Jeremy, *Pub Arts Admin,* Cambridge Arts Council, CAC Gallery, Cambridge MA

Gaudelius, Yvonne, *Prof Art Educ,* Pennsylvania State University, University Park, Penn State School of Visual Arts, University Park PA (S)

Gaudette, Mary, *Gallery Asst,* Saint Paul's School, Art Center in Hargate, Concord NH

Gaudieri, Millicent Hall, *Exec Dir,* Association of Art Museum Directors, New York NY

Gaudin, Susanne, *Grants & Fund-raising Adv to Bd,* Brown County Art Gallery Foundation, Nashville IN

Gaudio, Michael, *Asst Prof,* University of Minnesota, Minneapolis, Art History, Minneapolis MN (S)

Gaudreault, Andre, *Instr,* Universite de Montreal, Dept of Art History, Montreal PQ (S)

Gaugler, Jonathan, *Asst Dir Mktg & Communs,* Carnegie Museums of Pittsburgh, Carnegie Museum of Art, Pittsburgh PA

Gaul, Elaine, *Co-Cur Exhibs,* Indiana University, The Mathers Museum of World Cultures, Bloomington IN

Gaumond, Lisa, *Gallery Mgr,* University of Hartford, Joseloff Gallery, West Hartford CT

Gaunce, Nancy, *Secy,* Waterville Historical Society, Redington Museum, Waterville ME

Gause, Conni, *Admin Asst,* Grinnell College, Faulconer Gallery, Grinnell IA

Gauthier, Caroline, *Documentation Tech,* Musee National des Beaux Arts du Quebec, Bibliotheque, Quebec PQ

Gauthier, Shelley, *Mem Svcs Coordr,* British Columbia Museums Association, Victoria BC

Gauthier, Sue, *Museum Store Mgr,* University of Tampa, Henry B Plant Museum, Tampa FL

Gautreaux, Hurley, *Secy,* Crowley Art Association, The Gallery, Crowley LA

Gawronski, Bryan, *Interim Head Opers,* The Buffalo Fine Arts Academy, Albright-Knox Art Gallery, Buffalo NY

Gawronski, Jenny, *Asst Prof,* Adams State College, Dept of Visual Arts, Alamosa CO (S)

Gay, Richard, *Chair,* University of North Carolina at Pembroke, Art Dept, Pembroke NC (S)

Gaya, Kieran, *Asst Prof,* Azusa Pacific University, College of Liberal Arts, Art Dept, Azusa CA (S)

Gaynor, Emily, *Pub Rels & Mktg Officer,* The Drawing Center, New York NY

Gayson, Saisha M, *Asst Cur, Elizabeth A Sackler Center for Feminist Art,* Brooklyn Museum, Brooklyn NY

Gazda, Elaine K, *Cur,* University of Michigan, Kelsey Museum of Archaeology, Ann Arbor MI

Gazda, Elaine K, *Dir Kelsey Museum & Prof,* University of Michigan, Ann Arbor, Dept of History of Art, Ann Arbor MI (S)

Gazzo, Bridget, *Pre-Columbian Studies Librn,* Harvard University, Dumbarton Oaks Research Library, Washington DC

Gealt, Adelheid, *Dir,* Indiana University, Art Museum, Bloomington IN

Gearding, Dave, *Facility Dir,* Contemporary Arts Center, Cincinnati OH

Geary, Christraud, *Teal Sr Cur African & Oceanic Art,* Museum of Fine Arts, Boston MA

Geary, Donnita, *Treas,* Cincinnati Art Club, Cincinnati OH

Gebb, Wayne, *Instr Music & Choir,* Midway College, Art Dept, Midway KY (S)

Gebhardt, Denise, *Cur,* Central Methodist University, Ashby-Hodge Gallery of American Art, Fayette MO

Gebhardt, Matt, *Cur,* Bergen County Historical Society, Steuben House Museum, River Edge NJ

Gebhart, Tina M, *Asst Prof,* Berea College, Art & Art History Program, Berea KY (S)

Geddes, Mathew, *Instr,* Ricks College, Dept of Art, Rexburg ID (S)

Gedeon, Lucinda H, *Exec Dir,* Vero Beach Museum of Art, Vero Beach FL

Gee, Dwight, *VPres Community Affairs,* Corporate Council for the Arts/Arts Fund, Seattle WA

Gee, Erika, *Dir Educ & Pub Progs,* Museum for African Art, New York NY

Gee, Norman, *Prof Emer,* University of Kansas, The School of the Arts, Dept of Visual Art, Lawrence KS (S)

Gee, Regina, *Asst Prof - Art History,* Montana State University, School of Art, Bozeman MT (S)

Geehr, Ethan, *Chair,* Association of Medical Illustrators, Lexington KY

Geelhood, Lisa, *Dir Educ,* Huntington Museum of Art, Huntington WV

Geffen, Amara, *Chair Art Dept,* Allegheny College, Art Dept, Meadville PA (S)

Gehnrich, Babette, *Chief Conservator,* American Antiquarian Society, Worcester MA

Gehrm, Barbara, *Registrar,* Salisbury University, Ward Museum of Wildfowl Art, Salisbury MD

Geib,. Scott, *Instr,* Langara College, Department of Design: Design Formation, Vancouver BC (S)

Geiger, Gail L, *Prof, Dept Chmn,* University of Wisconsin, Madison, Dept of Art History, Madison WI (S)

Geiger, Justin, *Vis Svcs Coordr,* University of Mary Washington, University of Mary Washington Galleries, Fredericksburg VA

Geiger, Karin, *Exec Dir,* Studio Channel Islands Art Center, Camarillo CA

Geiger, Mark, *Pres,* Frontier Gateway Museum, Glendive MT

Geiger, Philip, *Studio Faculty,* University of Virginia, McIntire Dept of Art, Charlottesville VA (S)

Geils, Laurelle, *Dir,* McGroarty Cultural Art Center, Tujunga CA (S)

Geimzer, Eugene, *Chmn Fine Arts Dept,* Loyola University of Chicago, Fine Arts Dept, Chicago IL (S)

Geisbrecht, Miles, *Technician,* Open Space, Victoria BC

Geisinger, William, *Instr,* De Anza College, Creative Arts Division, Cupertino CA (S)

Geisler, Carol, *Fiscal Officer & Admin Assoc,* University of Missouri, Museum of Art & Archaeology, Columbia MO

Geisler, Joelle, *Dir Opers,* UMLAUF Sculpture Garden & Museum, Austin TX

Geisser, Gail, *Interlibrary Loan,* Rhode Island School of Design, Fleet Library at RISD, Providence RI

Geist, Aimee, *Cur of Educ,* Wichita State University, Ulrich Museum of Art, Wichita KS

Geist, Doe, *Supv Coll,* Central Methodist University, Ashby-Hodge Gallery of American Art, Fayette MO

Geist, Ronnie, *Dir Programming,* Women's Interart Center, Inc, Interart Gallery, New York NY

Geldin, Sherri, *Dir,* Ohio State University, Wexner Center for the Arts, Columbus OH

Geller, Beatrice, *Assoc Prof,* Pacific Lutheran University, Dept of Art, Tacoma WA (S)

Gelotte, Susan, *Asst Mus Shop Mgr,* Smith College, Museum of Art, Northampton MA

Gelover, Cheryl, *Asst Prof,* Montgomery County Community College, Art Center, Blue Bell PA (S)

Gemmell, Sarah McKee, *Dir Mktg & Develop,* Delaplaine Visual Arts Education Center, Frederick MD

Gendreau, Andree, *Coll & Research,* Musee de l'Amerique Francaise, Quebec PQ

Gendron, Heather, *Art Librn,* University of North Carolina at Chapel Hill, Joseph Curtis Sloane Art Library, Chapel Hill NC

Genevro, Rosalie, *Exec Dir,* Architectural League of New York, New York NY

Geng, Barbara Merry, *Dir & Cur,* Lamama La Galleria, New York NY

Gengler, Matthew, *Access Servs Librn,* The Cleveland Museum of Art, Ingalls Library, Cleveland OH

Gengler, Tom, *Coll Asst,* Spertus Institute of Jewish Studies, Chicago IL

Genik, Chris, *Undergrad Dir,* Southern California Institute of Architecture, Los Angeles CA (S)

Genshaft, Carole, *Adjunct Cur,* Columbus Museum of Art, Columbus OH

Genszler, Leslie, *Gallery Shop Mgr,* Madison Museum of Contemporary Art, Madison WI

Gentele, Glen, *Pres & CEO,* Oklahoma City Museum of Art, Oklahoma City OK

Genteman, Sheila, *Gallery Dir,* Saint Mary-of-the-Woods College, Art Dept, Saint Mary of the Woods IN (S)

Gentile, Karen A, *Chmn Textile/Surface Design,* Fashion Institute of Technology, Art & Design Division, New York NY (S)

Gentilini, David, *Asst Dir,* Capital University, Schumacher Gallery, Columbus OH

Gentis, Thierry, *Assoc Cur & Coll Mgr,* Brown University, Haffenreffer Museum of Anthropology, Providence RI

Gentry, David, *Instr & Gallery Dir,* Shasta College, Arts, Communications & Social Sciences Division, Redding CA (S)

Gentry, James, *Instr,* Eastern Arizona College, Art Dept, Thatcher AZ (S)

Gentry, Liz, *Librn & Archivist,* Booth Western Art Museum, Cartersville GA

Gentry, Sandra J, *Exec Asst,* Pensacola Museum of Art, Harry Thornton Library, Pensacola FL

Geo, Lisa, *Visual Arts Comt Chair,* Duke University Union, Louise Jones Brown Gallery, Durham NC

Geoffino, Tom, *Dir,* New Rochelle Public Library, Art Section, New Rochelle NY

George, David N, *Prof,* Truett-McConnell College, Fine Arts Dept & Arts Dept, Cleveland GA (S)

George, Hardy, *Consulting Cur,* Oklahoma City Museum of Art, Oklahoma City OK

George, Ivana, *Asst Prof,* Bridgewater State College, Art Dept, Bridgewater MA (S)

George, Valerie, *Asst Prof,* University of West Florida, Dept of Art, Pensacola FL (S)

Georgeadis, Socrates J, *Treas,* Reading Public Museum, Reading PA

Georger, Lauren, *Archivist, Spec Colls Librn,* Manhattanville College, Library, Purchase NY

Georgiades, Aristotle, *Prof,* University of Wisconsin, Madison, Dept of Art, Madison WI (S)

Georgiou, Tyrone, *Prof,* University at Buffalo, State University of New York, Dept of Visual Studies, Buffalo NY (S)

Geppert, Melissa, *Asst Prof,* Southern Oregon University, Art & Art History Dept, Ashland OR (S)

Geraci, Phil, *Asst Prof,* Eastern New Mexico University, Dept of Art, Portales NM (S)

Geralds, John, *Trustee,* Brooklyn Historical Society, Brooklyn OH

Gerard, Mira, *Assoc Prof,* East Tennessee State University, College of Arts and Sciences, Dept of Art & Design, Johnson City TN (S)

Gerber, Corinn, *Dir,* Art Metropole, Toronto ON

Gerber, Emilie, *Gallery Dir, Coordr,* Portland State University, White Gallery, Portland OR

Gerbracht, Grady, *Asst Prof,* Stony Brook University, College of Arts & Sciences, Dept of Art, Stony Brook NY (S)

Gerdes, Kirsten, *Assoc Cur,* Boulder Museum of Contemporary Art, Boulder CO

Gerety, Lorraine, *Visual Resources Cur,* Visual Arts Library, New York NY

Gerhardt, Stephanie, *Cur Educ,* Evansville Museum of Arts, History & Science, Evansville IN

Geritz, Kathy, *Assoc Film Cur,* University of California, Berkeley, Pacific Film Archive, Berkeley CA

Geritz, Kathy, *Cur Film,* University of California, Berkeley, Berkeley Art Museum & Pacific Film Archive, Berkeley CA

Gerlach, Monte, *Assoc Prof,* Saint Xavier University, Dept of Art & Design, Chicago IL (S)

Gerling, Don, *Opers Mgr,* Laumeier Sculpture Park, Saint Louis MO

Gerlough, Kate, *Mgr Sales & Info,* Frick Collection, New York NY

Germano, Thomas, *Assoc Prof,* State University of New York at Farmingdale, Visual Communications, Farmingdale NY (S)

Germer, Mark, *Music Librn,* The University of the Arts, University Libraries, Philadelphia PA

Germi, Heather, *Gallery Coordr,* The ArtsCenter, The Nicholson Gallery at the Arts Center, Carrboro NC

Gerrard, Susan, *Dir Mktg,* Museum of Ventura County, Ventura CA

Gerring, Andrea, *Instr,* North Central Michigan College, Art Dept, Petoskey MI (S)

Gerring, Todd, *Coordr of Mus Visitor Programs,* University of Michigan, Kelsey Museum of Archaeology, Ann Arbor MI

Gerry, Rip, *Exhib Designer & Photo Archivist,* Brown University, Haffenreffer Museum of Anthropology, Providence RI

Gershfeld, Yelena, *Asst Dean Visual Arts,* New World School of the Arts, Miami FL (S)

Gerson, Denise M, *Assoc Dir,* University of Miami, Lowe Art Museum, Coral Gables FL

Gerson, Paula, *Chmn,* Florida State University, Art History Dept, Tallahassee FL (S)

Gerstein, Beth Ann, *Exec Dir,* The Society of Arts & Crafts, Boston MA

Gerstein, Marc, *Assoc Prof,* University of Toledo, Dept of Art, Toledo OH (S)

Gerstheimer, Christian, *Cur Coll,* City of El Paso, El Paso Museum of Art, El Paso TX

Gerth, Troy, *Asst Prof,* Mount Mary College, Art & Design Division, Milwaukee WI (S)

Gertjejansen, Doyle, *Gallery Dir,* University of New Orleans, Fine Arts Gallery, New Orleans LA

Gertjejansen, Doyle J, *Prof Emeritus,* University of New Orleans-Lake Front, Dept of Fine Arts, New Orleans LA (S)

Gertsman, Elina, *Asst Prof,* Case Western Reserve University, Dept of Art History & Art, Cleveland OH (S)

Gervais, Christine, *Assoc Cur Decorative Arts,* Museum of Fine Arts, Houston, Rienzi Center for European Decorative Arts, Houston TX

Gervais, Rachel, *Coordr Traveling Exhibs,* Canadian Museum of Nature, Musee Canadien de la Nature, Ottawa ON

Gervits, Maya, *Dir,* New Jersey Institute of Technology, Littman Architecture & Design Library, Newark NJ

Gessner, Andrew P, *Chief Librn,* The Metropolitan Museum of Art, Image Library, New York NY

Gessner, Mark, *Maintenance,* Historical Museum at Fort Missoula, Missoula MT

Getek, Lauren Marie, *Dir,* Rome Art & Community Center, Rome NY

Geter, Tyrone, *Prof Art & Dir Ponder Gallery,* Benedict College, School of Humanities, Arts & Social Sciences, Columbia SC

Gette, Timothy J, *Exec Dir,* The University of Texas at San Antonio, Institute of Texan Cultures, San Antonio TX

Gevas, Sophia, *Dir,* Sacred Heart University, Gallery of Contemporary Art, Fairfield CT

Gever, Martha, *Assoc Prof Media Histories,* University of California, Irvine, Studio Art Dept, Irvine CA (S)

Gevins, Jack, *Instr,* Bucks County Community College, Fine Arts Dept, Newtown PA (S)

Gevurtz, Sara, *Adj Instr,* University of West Florida, Dept of Art, Pensacola FL (S)

Geyer, Nancy, *Exec Dir,* Boulder History Museum, Museum of History, Boulder CO

Ghelerter, Donna, *Assoc Dir Curatorial Affairs,* Museum for African Art, New York NY

Ghirardo, Raymond, *Prof,* Ithaca College, Fine Art Dept, Ithaca NY (S)

Ghize, Shannon, *Admin Aid,* Frederic Remington, Ogdensburg NY

Ghose, Madhuvanti, *Assoc Cur Indian, SE Asian, Himalayan & Islamic Art,* The Art Institute of Chicago, Department of Asian Art, Chicago IL

Ghosh, Pika, *Assoc Prof,* University of North Carolina at Chapel Hill, Art Dept, Chapel Hill NC (S)

Giacopuzzi, Michelle, *Exhib Coordr,* California State University, Northridge, Art Galleries, Northridge CA

Giambi, M Dina, *Asst Dir Library Technical Servs,* University of Delaware, Morris Library, Newark DE

Giancola, Deborah, *Graphic Design,* Art Institute of Pittsburgh, Pittsburgh PA (S)

Giandomenico, Jolene, *Asst. Dir.,* 1708 Gallery, Richmond VA

Giangaspero, Maric, *Chief of Staff,* Jack Richard Gallery, Almond Tea Museum & Jane Williams Galleries, Divisions of Studios of Jack Richard, Cuyahoga Falls OH

Giangaspero, Mark, *Chief of Staff,* Jack Richard Gallery, Almond Tea Museum & Jane Williams Galleries, Library, Cuyahoga Falls OH

Giannelli, Gary, *Dir Computer Svcs,* Ferguson Library, Stamford CT

Giannotti, John, *Chmn,* Rutgers University, Camden, Art Dept, Camden NJ (S)

Giaquinto, Michael, *Mgr Exhib,* Cape Cod Museum of Art Inc, Dennis MA

Giard, Elizabeth, *Collections Mgr,* Harriet Beecher Stowe, Hartford CT

Giarda, Robert, *Park Svc Specialist,* Florida Department of Environmental Protection, Stephen Foster Folk Culture Center State Park, White Springs FL

Giardina, Lynn, *Dir Develop,* Washington University, Mildred Lane Kemper Art Museum, Saint Louis MO

Giarrizzo, John, *Assoc Prof,* Northwest Community College, Dept of Art, Powell WY (S)

Giasson, Patrice, *Cur Art of the Americas,* Purchase College, Neuberger Museum of Art, Purchase NY

Gibb, Melanie, *Asst Prof,* Judson University, School of Art, Design & Architecture, Elgin IL (S)

Gibb-Roff, Samantha, *Adminr,* William Bonifas, Alice Powers Art Gallery, Escanaba MI

Gibbons, Arthur, *Dir,* Bard College, Milton Avery Graduate School of the Arts, Annandale-on-Hudson NY (S)

Gibbons, Bud, *Assoc Prof Art,* Pennsylvania State University at New Kensington, Depts of Art & Architecture, Upper Burrell PA (S)

Gibbons, Connie, *Dir,* Washburn University, Mulvane Art Museum, Topeka KS

Gibbons, Lari, *Asst Prof,* University of Dayton, Visual Arts Dept, Dayton OH (S)

Gibbons, Larry, *Assoc Prof Printmaking,* University of North Texas, College of Visual Arts & Design, Denton TX (S)

Gibbons, Michael, *Cur,* Yaquina River Museum of Art, Toledo OR

Gibbs, Andrea, *Dep Chief & Architecture Specialist,* National Gallery of Art, Department of Image Collections, Washington DC

Gibbs, Carrie, *Dir Shrode Art Center,* Cedarhurst Center for the Arts, Mitchell Museum, Mount Vernon IL

Gibbs, Ed, *Dir,* Tidewater Community College, Visual Arts Center, Portsmouth VA (S)

Gibbs, Gaile Snow, *VPres Catalog,* Catharine Lorillard Wolfe, New York NY

Gibbs, Jason, *Librn II, Prog Mgr,* San Francisco Public Library, Art & Music Center, San Francisco CA

Gibbs, Judith, *Deputy Dir Develop,* The Baltimore Museum of Art, Baltimore MD

Gibbs, Steve, *Owner,* The Art Spirit Gallery, Coeur D Alene ID

Gibbs, Tom, *Instr,* Loras College, Dept of Art, Dubuque IA (S)

Gibbs-Riley, Brandy, *Asst Prof,* Colby-Sawyer College, Dept of Fine & Performing Arts, New London NH (S)

Giberga, Ovidio, *Assoc Prof,* University of Texas at San Antonio, Dept of Art & Art History, San Antonio TX (S)

Gibney, Katherine, *VPres Develop,* Americans for the Arts, New York NY

Gibson, Barbara, *Pres Bd & Dir,* Associates for Community Development, The Arts Center, Inc, Martinsburg WV

Gibson, Ben, *Fine Arts Representative,* Edinboro University of Pennsylvania, Art Dept, Edinboro PA (S)

Gibson, Edward, *Dir,* Jones Memorial Library, Lynchburg VA

Gibson, Ingrid, *Interlibrary Loan Librn,* Harvard University, Dumbarton Oaks Research Library, Washington DC

Gibson, Jen, *Database Coordr,* Glanmore National Historic Site of Canada, Belleville ON

Gibson, Jennifer, *Dir,* United States General Services Administration, Art in Architecture and Fine Arts, Washington DC

Gibson, Jonathan, *Assoc Prof,* Xavier University, Dept of Art, Cincinnati OH (S)

Gibson, Julia, *Faculty,* Florida College, Division of Art, Temple Terrace FL (S)

Gibson, Michael, *Assoc Prof Comm Design,* University of North Texas, College of Visual Arts & Design, Denton TX (S)

Gibson, Michael, *Pres,* Art Dealers Association of Canada, Toronto ON

Gibson, Nancy, *Cur Textiles,* DAR Museum, Library, Washington DC

Gibson, Robert, *Asst Prof,* Mississippi University for Women, Division of Fine & Performing Arts, Columbus MS (S)

Gibson, Robin, *Assoc Prof Art (Printmaking),* Pennsylvania State University, University Park, Penn State School of Visual Arts, University Park PA (S)

Gibson, Steve, *Asst Prof,* University of Victoria, Dept of Visual Arts, Victoria BC (S)

Gibson-Wood, Carol, *Chair,* University of Victoria, Dept of History in Art, Victoria BC (S)

Gick, Jen, *Dir Programs,* Longue Vue House & Gardens, New Orleans LA

Giddens, Phyllis, *Dir External Affairs,* Morris Museum of Art, Augusta GA

Giebel, Douglas, *Assoc Prof,* Roberts Wesleyan College, Art Dept, Rochester NY (S)

Gieber, Terry, *Chmn,* Gonzaga University, Dept of Art, Spokane WA (S)

Giersdorf, Jens, *Assoc Prof Dance,* Marymount Manhattan College, Fine & Performing Arts Div, New York NY (S)

Gierster, Patrick, *Dean Humanities & Social Science,* San Jose City College, School of Fine Arts, San Jose CA (S)

Giese, Billie, *Div Head FA Studio,* Northern Illinois University, School of Art, DeKalb IL (S)

Gifford, Caroline, *Librn,* The New York Public Library, Art & Architecture Collection, New York NY

Giffuni, Flora B, *Founder & Hon Chair,* Pastel Society of America, National Arts Club, Grand Gallery, New York NY

Gigante, Linda, *Art History Program Head,* University of Louisville, Hite Art Institute, Louisville KY

Gigante, Linda, *Assoc Prof,* University of Louisville, Allen R Hite Art Institute, Louisville KY (S)

Giguere, Marie, *Bd Mem,* Kennebec Valley Art Association, Harlow Gallery, Hallowell ME

Gikas, Carol S, *Exec Dir,* Louisiana Arts & Science Museum, Baton Rouge LA

Gikas, Carol S, *Exec Dir,* Louisiana Arts & Science Museum, Library, Baton Rouge LA

Gilats, Andrea, *Dir,* University of Minnesota, Minneapolis, Split Rock Arts Program, Minneapolis MN (S)

Gilbert, Barbara, *Project Coordr,* Ontario Association of Art Galleries, Toronto ON

Gilbert, Courtney, *Cur Visual Arts,* Sun Valley Center for the Arts, Dept of Fine Art, Sun Valley ID (S)

Gilbert, Edi, *Tour Scheduling,* Lafayette Science Museum & Planetarium, Lafayette LA

Gilbert, Gail, *Art Librn,* University of Louisville, Hite Art Institute, Louisville KY

Gilbert, Gail R, *Dir Art Library,* University of Louisville, Margaret M Bridwell Art Library, Louisville KY

Gilbert, Johnnie Mae, *Chair,* Tougaloo College, Art Collection, Tougaloo MS

Gilbert, Kathy, *Adjunct Prof,* Community College of Allegheny County, Boyce Campus, Art Dept, Monroeville PA (S)

Gilbert, Nancy, *Secy,* Shawinigan Art Center, Shawinigan PQ

Gilbert, Paula, *Dir Operations,* Martin Memorial Library, York PA

Gilbert, Peg, *Staff Asst,* Grassroots Art Center, Lucas KS

Gilbert, Suzanne, *Gallery Dir,* North Shore Arts Association, Inc, Gloucester MA

Gilbert, Sylvie, *Cur,* Saidye Bronfman, Liane & Danny Taran Gallery, Montreal PQ

Gilbertson, Claire, *Library Asst,* Vermont Historical Society, Library, Montpelier VT

Gilbertson, Greg, *Instr,* Pierce College, Art Dept, Woodland Hills CA (S)

Gilbertson, Lauran, *Chief Cur,* Vesterheim Norwegian-American Museum, Decorah IA

Gilbertson, Leanne, *Gallery Dir,* Montana State University at Billings, Northcutt Steele Gallery, Billings MT

Gilbo, Lacey, *Cur Prog,* City of Ketchikan Museum, Tongass Historical Museum, Ketchikan AK

Gilbo, Lacey, *Sr Cur Prog,* City of Ketchikan Museum Dept, Ketchikan AK

Gilboe, Roberta Frey, *Registrar,* Cranbrook Art Museum, Bloomfield Hills MI

Gilchrist, Preston, *Adjunct Prof,* Louisiana College, Dept of Art, Pineville LA (S)

Gilchrist, Rod, *Exec Dir,* Cartoon Art Museum, San Francisco CA

Giles, Kirsti, *Coll Mgr,* East Tennessee State University, The Reece Museum, Johnson City TN

Giles, Laura, *Cur Prints & Drawings,* Princeton University, Princeton University Art Museum, Princeton NJ

Gilfillan, Tim, *Preparator,* Amherst College, Mead Art Museum, Amherst MA

Gilg, Karen, *Prof,* University of Maine at Augusta, College of Arts & Humanities, Augusta ME (S)

Gilgan, Elizabeth, *Prog & Svcs Dir,* Archaeological Institute of America, Boston MA

Gilgore, Susan, *Exec Dir,* Lockwood-Mathews Mansion Museum, Norwalk CT

Gill, Cecil, *Exec Dir,* Roberts County Museum, Miami TX

Gill, Charlene, *Pres Emeritus,* Alton Museum of History & Art, Inc, Alton IL

Gill, Edward A, *VPres, Dean Educ,* Art Institute of Pittsburgh, Pittsburgh PA (S)

Gill, Valerie, *Art Cur,* Musee Regional de lu Cote-Nord, Sept-Iles PQ

Gill, Vanessa, *Develop Dir,* Calvert Marine Museum, Solomons MD

Gillan, Maria Mazziotti, *Exec Dir Cultural Affairs,* Passaic County Community College, Broadway, LRC, and Hamilton Club Galleries, Paterson NJ

Gillcrist, Christopher, *Exec Dir,* Great Lakes Historical Society, Inland Seas Maritime Museum, Vermilion OH

Gillenwater, Karen, *Cur,* Carnegie Center for Art & History, New Albany IN

Gillepsie, Marilyn, *Exec Dir,* Las Vegas Natural History Museum, Las Vegas NV

Gillespie, Clark, *Asst Cur,* Knoxville Museum of Art, Knoxville TN

Gillespie, Dan, *Coordr Opers,* The Drawing Center, New York NY

Gillespie, David M, *Dir,* Frostburg State University, Lewis J Ort Library, Frostburg MD

Gillespie, Michael, *Dir Mktg & Commun,* Montclair Art Museum, Montclair NJ

Gillespie, Pamela, *Chief Librn,* City College of the City University of New York, Morris Raphael Cohen Library, New York NY

Gillette, Allison, *Librn,* The Speed Art Museum, Art Reference Library, Louisville KY

Gillette, Annie, *2nd VPres Shows,* Scottsdale Artists' League, Scottsdale AZ

Gillette, David D, *Colbert Cur Paleontology,* Museum of Northern Arizona, Flagstaff AZ

Gillette, Jonathan, *Instr,* Union University, Dept of Art, Jackson TN (S)

Gillette-Woodard, Helene, *Objects Conservator & Dept Head,* Williamstown Art Conservation Center, Williamstown MA

Gillham, Andrew, *Assoc Prof,* Indiana University of Pennsylvania, College of Fine Arts, Indiana PA (S)

Gillham, Will, *Dir Publ,* Amon Carter Museum of American Art, Fort Worth TX

Gilliam, Georgen, *Cur Library & Archives,* Nantucket Historical Association, Historic Nantucket, Nantucket MA

Gilliam, Jan, *Mgr Exhibits Planning,* Colonial Williamsburg Foundation, Abby Aldrich Rockefeller Folk Art Museum, Williamsburg VA

Gilliam, Jan, *Mgr Exhibs Planning,* Colonial Williamsburg Foundation, DeWitt Wallace Decorative Arts Museum, Williamsburg VA

Gilliam, Kevin, *Exhib Mgr,* College of William & Mary, Muscarelle Museum of Art, Williamsburg VA

Gilliam, Wren, *Spec Events,* Columbus Museum, Columbus GA

Gillick, Liam, *Grad Comt,* Bard College, Center for Curatorial Studies Graduate Program, Annandale-on-Hudson NY (S)

Gilliland, Cynthia, *Asst Registrar,* Dartmouth College, Hood Museum of Art, Hanover NH

Gillis, Jeanie, *Cur Botanical Science,* Heritage Museums & Gardens, Sandwich MA

Gillison, David, *Asst Prof,* Herbert H Lehman, Art Dept, Bronx NY (S)

Gillispie, John, *Pub Rels,* Huntington Museum of Art, Huntington WV

Gilly, Elizabeth, *Outreach & Pub Progs Coordr,* Moore College of Art & Design, The Galleries at Moore, Philadelphia PA

Gilman, Amy, *Assoc Cur Modern & Contemporary Art, Asst Dir Coll Exhib,* Toledo Museum of Art, Toledo OH

Gilman, Claire, *Cur,* The Drawing Center, New York NY

Gilmarten, Danee, *Prog Coord,* Edward Hopper, Nyack NY

Gilmor, Jane, *Prof,* Mount Mercy College, Art Dept, Cedar Rapids IA (S)

Gilmore, Barton, *Asst Prof,* Saint Petersburg College, Fine & Applied Arts at Clearwater Campus, Clearwater FL (S)

Gilmore, Jean A, *Registrar,* Brandywine Conservancy, Brandywine River Museum, Chadds Ford PA

Gilmore, Kate, *Asst Prof,* Purchase College, State University of New York, School of Art+Design, Purchase NY (S)

Gilmore, R, *Prof,* Gonzaga University, Dept of Art, Spokane WA (S)

Gilo, Anthony, *Dept Tech Dir,* Sierra Community College, Art Dept, Rocklin CA (S)

Gilomen, Jennifer, *Dir Pub Media Initiatives,* Bay Area Video Coalition, Inc, San Francisco CA

Gilwood, Deborah, *Asst Prof,* Seton Hall University, College of Arts & Sciences, South Orange NJ (S)

Gimeson, Dewayne, *Instr,* Chadron State College, Dept of Art, Chadron NE (S)

Gimse, Malcolm, *Prof,* Saint Olaf College, Art Dept, Northfield MN (S)

Gindhart, Maria, *Assoc Dir,* Georgia State University, Ernest G Welch School of Art & Design, Atlanta GA (S)

Gingerich, Ron, *Chmn,* Dickinson State University, Dept of Art, Dickinson ND (S)

Gingles, Mack, *Asst Prof,* Baylor University - College of Arts and Sciences, Dept of Art, Waco TX (S)

Ginsburg, Sigmund G, *Sr VPres Fin,* American Museum of Natural History, New York NY

Ginther, Gary, *Art Librn,* Ohio University, Fine Arts Library, Athens OH

Gioffre, Dolores, *Chmn,* Woodbridge Township Cultural Arts Commission, Barron Arts Center, Woodbridge NJ

Gionet, Bruce, *Asst Prof,* William Paterson University, Dept Arts, Wayne NJ (S)

Giordana, Enrico, *Chmn & Prof,* College of Mount Saint Vincent, Fine Arts Dept, Riverdale NY (S)

Giordano, Patti, *Pub Rels Mgr,* University of Rochester, Memorial Art Gallery, Rochester NY

Giordano, Susan, *Mus Shop Mgr,* Worcester Art Museum, Worcester MA

Giorgio, Michael, *Pub Rels,* Vermont State Craft Center at Frog Hollow, Burlington VT

Gipe, Thomas D, *Head Sculpture,* Southern Illinois University at Edwardsville, Dept of Art & Design, Edwardsville IL (S)

Girard, Jack, *Prof, Div Chair,* Transylvania University, Art Program, Lexington KY (S)

Girard, Kathryn, *Chief of Staff,* Hebrew Union College, Skirball Cultural Center, Los Angeles CA

Girard, Louise, *Colls Asst,* The Stewart Museum, Library, Montreal PQ

Girard, Louise, *Head Visitor Svcs,* The Stewart Museum, Montreal PQ

Girard, Lyne, *Pres,* Conseil des Arts du Quebec (CATQ), Diagonale, Centre des arts et des fibres du Quebec, Montreal PQ

Girmschied, Mary Kay, *Mus Shop Mgr,* Trenton City Museum, Trenton NJ

Giroir Luckett, Jeannie, *Educ Cur,* West Baton Rouge Parish, West Baton Rouge Museum, Port Allen LA

Girshman, Beth, *Adult Svc Librn,* Jones Library, Inc, Amherst MA

Gish, Joe, *Owner,* Joe Gish's Old West Museum, Fredericksburg TX

Gittenstein, R Barbara, *Pres,* College of New Jersey, Art Gallery, Ewing NJ

Giuel, Rosanne, *Dir Visual Communs,* Art Institute of Fort Lauderdale, Fort Lauderdale FL (S)

Giuffrida, Noelle, *Asst Prof,* Case Western Reserve University, Dept of Art History & Art, Cleveland OH (S)

Giuliani, David S, *Graphic Design,* Art Institute of Pittsburgh, Pittsburgh PA (S)

Giuliano, Marie, *Bus Office Supv,* Ferguson Library, Stamford CT

Giuntini, Gilles, *Assoc Prof,* University of Hartford, Hartford Art School, West Hartford CT (S)

Giuntini, Trey, *Gen Mgr,* Mississippi River Museum at Mud-Island River Park, Memphis TN

Giuriceo, Judy, *Cur Exhibs & Media,* The National Park Service, United States Department of the Interior, Statue of Liberty National Monument & The Ellis Island Immigration Museum, Washington DC

Giurini, John, *Asst Dir Pub Affairs,* Getty Center, The J Paul Getty Museum, Los Angeles CA

Givens, Jean, *Assoc Head,* University of Connecticut, Dept of Art & Art History, Storrs CT (S)

Giviskos, Christine, *Assoc Cur European Art,* Rutgers, The State University of New Jersey, Zimmerli Art Museum, Rutgers University, New Brunswick NJ

Gjertson, Sarah, *Dir, Assoc Prof Foundations,* University of Denver, School of Art & Art History, Denver CO (S)

Gjovick, Peder, *Asst Prof,* Northwest Community College, Dept of Art, Powell WY (S)

Glab, Tracee, *Assoc Cur Exhibs,* Flint Institute of Arts, Flint MI

Glabicki, Paul, *Prof,* University of Pittsburgh, Dept of Studio Arts, Pittsburgh PA (S)

Gladdys, Katerie, *Assoc Prof,* University of Florida, School of Art & Art History, Gainesville FL (S)

Gladstone, Caroline T, *Mgr Vol Servs,* Philadelphia Museum of Art, Mount Pleasant, Philadelphia PA

Glanzer, Harvey W, *Co-Owner, Mgr & Dir,* Frank Lloyd Wright Museum, AD German Warehouse, Richland Center WI

Glasby, Becky, *Cur Educ,* The National Quilt Museum, Paducah KY

Glascock, Zoe, *Publicist,* Longview Museum of Fine Art, Longview TX

Glaser, Heather M, *Asst Librn,* University of Pennsylvania, Fisher Fine Arts Library, Philadelphia PA

Glaser, Lewis, *Prof,* Texas Christian University, School of Art, Fort Worth TX (S)

Glaser, Samantha, *Dir,* Michael Kohn Gallery, Los Angeles CA

Glasgow, Isti Haroh, *Dir,* Cultural Affairs Department City of Los Angeles/Barnsdall Art Centers/Junior Arts Center, Los Angeles CA

Glasgow, Linda, *Cur Archives & Libr,* Riley County Historical Society & Museum, Riley County Historical Museum, Manhattan KS

Glasgow, Linda, *Library Archivist,* Riley County Historical Society & Museum, Seaton Library, Manhattan KS

Glasgow, Paul, *Chmn Dept,* Community College of Baltimore County, Art Dept, Catonsville MD (S)

Glaske, Sheila, *Cur Horticulture,* Paine Art Center & Gardens, Oshkosh WI

Glass, Dorothy F, *Pres,* International Center of Medieval Art, New York NY

Glass, Kathleen, *Communications Mgr,* Asheville Art Museum, Asheville NC

Glass, Michelle, *Prog Dir,* Side Street Projects, Pasadena CA

Glass, Richard, *Bookeeper,* Virginia Center for the Creative Arts, Amherst VA

Glass, Simon, *Instr,* Toronto School of Art, Toronto ON (S)

Glasser, Dale, *Dir, Synagogue Mgr,* Union for Reformed Judaism, Synagogue Art & Architectural Library, New York NY

Glasser, Susan, *Dir Educ,* North Carolina Museum of Art, Raleigh NC

Glassford, C, *Instr,* Golden West College, Visual Art Dept, Huntington Beach CA (S)

Glasson, Lloyd, *Prof,* University of Hartford, Hartford Art School, West Hartford CT (S)

Glatz, Lindsay, *Dir Mktg & Communs,* Arts Council Of New Orleans, New Orleans LA

Glaubinger, Jane, *Cur Prints,* The Cleveland Museum of Art, Cleveland OH

Glaubinger, Jane, *Cur Prints & Mem,* The Cleveland Museum of Art, Print Club of Cleveland, Cleveland OH

Glavin, Ellen, *Prof,* Emmanuel College, Art Dept, Boston MA (S)

Glavin, Eric, *Instr,* Toronto School of Art, Toronto ON (S)

Glazer, Steve, *Asst Prof,* Concord College, Fine Art Division, Athens WV (S)

Gleaves, Spray, *Instr,* Dallas Baptist University, Dept of Art, Dallas TX (S)

Glen, Marilyn, *Admin Coordr,* Where Edmonton Community Artists Network Society, Harcourt House Arts Centre, Edmonton AB

Glen, Tony, *Dir Colls,* Canadian War Museum, Ottawa ON

Glendinning, Chanda, *Vis Instr Ceramics,* Florida Atlantic University, D F Schmidt College of Arts & Letters Dept of Visual Arts & Art History, Boca Raton FL (S)

Glenn, Barbara, *Head Art Prog,* J Sargeant Reynolds Community College, Humanities & Social Science Division, Richmond VA (S)

Glenn, Bridgett, *Chmn,* Lock Haven University, Dept of Fine Arts, Lock Haven PA (S)

Glenn, Diane, *Finance Asst,* Oklahoma City Museum of Art, Oklahoma City OK

Glenn, Jim, *Pub Arts & Design Arts Mgr,* Utah Arts Council, Chase Home Museum of Utah Folk Arts, Salt Lake City UT

Glenn, Ralph F, *Instr Art History,* Madonna University, College of Arts & Humanities, Livonia MI (S)

Glenn, Rebecca, *Asst Prof,* Southern Arkansas University at Magnolia, Dept of Art & Design, Magnolia AR (S)

Glenn, T, *Assoc Prof,* McGill University, Dept of Art History, Montreal PQ (S)

Glenn Norris, Laurie, *Mgr Communs & Outreach,* Beaverbrook Art Gallery, Fredericton NB

Glennon, Michael L, *Chairperson,* Northport-East Northport Public Library, Northport NY

Glennon, Rose M, *Cur Educ,* McNay, San Antonio TX

Glick, Michael, *VPres Opers,* Go Antiques, Inc, Atlanta GA

Glidden, Craig, *Chmn Fine Arts Prog,* Westminster College of Salt Lake City, Dept of Arts, Salt Lake City UT (S)

Gliniecki, Anita, *VPres Acad Svcs,* Saint Clair County Community College, Jack R Hennesey Art Dept, Port Huron MI (S)

Gloeckler, Terry, *Assoc Prof,* Eastern Oregon University, School of Arts & Science, La Grande OR (S)

Gloeckner, Phoebe, *Asst Prof,* University of Michigan, Ann Arbor, School of Art & Design, Ann Arbor MI (S)

Gloman, David I, *Prof, Resident Artist,* Amherst College, Dept of Art & the History of Art, Amherst MA (S)

Glotzhober, Robert, *Cur Natural History,* Ohio Historical Society, National Road-Zane Grey Museum, Columbus OH

Glover, Cherie, *Co-Owner,* Joe Gish's Old West Museum, Fredericksburg TX

Glover, David, *Instr,* Pierce College, Art Dept, Woodland Hills CA (S)

Glover, Hugh, *Furniture Conservator & Dept Head,* Williamstown Art Conservation Center, Williamstown MA

Glover, Jack, *Owner & Cur,* Joe Gish's Old West Museum, Fredericksburg TX

Glover, Jamie, *Museum Shop Mgr,* The Studio Museum in Harlem, New York NY

Glover, Stephanie, *Opers Dir,* Touchstone Center for Crafts, Hart Moore Museum, Farmington PA

Glover, Susan, *Keeper of Special Colls,* Boston Public Library, Central Library, Boston MA

Glowacki, Martha, *Dir,* Wisconsin Academy of Sciences, Arts & Letters, James Watrous Gallery, Madison WI

Glowacki, Michael, *Instr,* Delta College, Art Dept, University Center MI (S)

Gluck, Nahan, *VPres,* Japanese American National Museum, Los Angeles CA

Glueckert, Stephen, *Cur Exhibit,* Missoula Art Museum, Missoula MT

Glushien, Scott, *Asst Prof,* Assumption College, Dept of Art, Music & Theatre, Worcester MA (S)

Gochenour, Anne, *Gallery Dir,* Central Michigan University, University Art Gallery, Mount Pleasant MI

Gochman, Julie, *International Planning Dir,* International Council for Cultural Exchange (ICCE), Brookhaven NY (S)

Gochman, Stanley I, *Prog Coordr,* International Council for Cultural Exchange (ICCE), Brookhaven NY (S)

Godbout, Helene, *Reference Agent,* Musee National des Beaux Arts du Quebec, Bibliotheque, Quebec PQ

Goddard, Elizabeth, *Exec Dir,* Newport Art Museum and Association, Newport RI

Goddard, Elizabeth, *Exec Dir,* Newport Art Museum, Coleman Center for Creative Studies, Newport RI (S)

Goddard, Elizabeth, *Mgr Educ,* Urban Institute for Contemporary Arts, Grand Rapids MI

Goddard, Janet D, *Museum Store Mgr,* McNay, San Antonio TX

Goddard, Leslie, *Educ Officer,* Evanston Historical Society, Charles Gates Dawes House, Evanston IL

Goddard, Stephen, *Assoc Dir,* University of Kansas, Spencer Museum of Art, Lawrence KS

Goddard, Stephen, *IPCR Proj Coordr,* Print Council of America, Chicago IL

Goddard, Stephen, *Prof,* University of Kansas, Kress Foundation Dept of Art History, Lawrence KS (S)

Godeke, Jason, *Assoc Prof,* Bloomsburg University, Dept of Art & Art History, Bloomsburg PA (S)

Goders, John, *Prof Emeritus,* California State University, Dominguez Hills, Art & Design Dept, Carson CA (S)

Godfrey, Judith, *Pres & CEO,* Grace Museum, Inc, Abilene TX

Godfrey, Robert, *Head Dept,* Western Carolina University, Dept of Art/College of Arts & Science, Cullowhee NC (S)

Godfrey, Stephen, *Cur Paleontology,* Calvert Marine Museum, Solomons MD

Godfrey, William R, *Pres,* Environic Foundation International Library, South Bend IN

Godlewska, Maja, *Asst Prof,* University of North Carolina at Charlotte, Dept Art, Charlotte NC (S)

Godlewski, Henry, *Assoc Prof,* Mohawk Valley Community College, Utica NY (S)

Godollei, Ruthann, *Prof,* Macalester College, Art Dept, Saint Paul MN (S)

Godsey, William, *Instr,* John C Calhoun, Department of Fine Arts, Tanner AL (S)

Godwin, Stan, *Asst Prof,* Texas A&M University Commerce, Dept of Art, Commerce TX (S)

Goebel Bain, Angela, *Asst Cur Decorative Arts,* Illinois State Museum, ISM Lockport Gallery, Chicago Gallery & Southern Illinois Art Gallery, Springfield IL

Goedde, Gayle, *Librn, Asst Cur Colls,* Alaska State Library, Alaska Historical Collections, Juneau AK

Goedde, Lawrence, *Art History Instr,* University of Virginia, McIntire Dept of Art, Charlottesville VA (S)

Goering, Douglas, *Prof,* Albion College, Dept of Visual Arts, Albion MI (S)

Goering, Douglas, *Prof Emeritus,* Albion College, Bobbitt Visual Arts Center, Albion MI

Goering, Karen M, *Mng Dir Opers,* Missouri Historical Society, Missouri History Museum, Saint Louis MO

Goeser, Caroline, *Dir Educ & Interpretation,* The Cleveland Museum of Art, Cleveland OH

Goetz, Becky, *Pres,* Grand Prairie Arts Council, Inc, Arts Center of the Grand Prairie, Stuttgart AR

Goetz, Mary Anna, *Instr,* Woodstock School of Art, Inc, Woodstock NY (S)

Goff, Allison, *Educ Dir,* Henry Morrison Flagler Museum, Palm Beach FL

Goff, Terri, *Communs Dir,* Associated Artists of Winston-Salem, Winston Salem NC

Goffen, Rona, *Prof,* Rutgers, The State University of New Jersey, Graduate Program in Art History, New Brunswick NJ (S)

Goffin, Jordan, *Asst Reference Librn,* Rhode Island Historical Society, Library, Providence RI

Gogan, Susan, *Exec Dir,* Wheaton Arts & Cultural Center, Museum of American Glass, Millville NJ

Goganian, Susan, *Dir,* Beverly Historical Society, Library, Beverly MA

Goganian, Susan J, *Dir & Cur,* Beverly Historical Society, Cabot, Hale & Balch House Museums, Beverly MA

Goger, Elizabeth, *VPres Human Resources,* Canadian Museum of Civilization, Gatineau PQ

Goggin, James, *Dir Design,* Museum of Contemporary Art, Chicago IL

Goggin, Nan, *Dir, Prof,* University of Illinois, Urbana-Champaign, School of Art & Design, Champaign IL (S)

Goguen, George, *Dir,* Radio-Canada SRC CBC, Georges Goguen CBC Art Gallery, Moncton NB

Gohde, Kurt, *Assoc Prof, Prog Dir,* Transylvania University, Art Program, Lexington KY (S)

Goheen, Marion, *Pres,* Allied Arts Association, Allied Arts Center & Gallery, Richland WA

Goin, Peter, *Art Dept Chmn,* University of Nevada, Reno, Sheppard Contemporary & University Galleries, Reno NV

Goire, Eric, *Dep Dir Facilities,* The Museum of Arts & Sciences Inc, Daytona Beach FL

Goitia, Michael, *Exhib Mgr,* Fashion Institute of Technology, The Museum at FIT, New York NY

Golahny, Amy, *Prof,* Lycoming College, Art Dept, Williamsport PA (S)

Golan, Romy, *Prof,* City University of New York, PhD Program in Art History, New York NY (S)

Golas, Theresa, *Exec Dir,* Iredell Museums, Statesville NC

Gold, Allyssa, *Asst Prof Fine Arts Metals,* Millersville University, Dept of Art & Design, Millersville PA (S)

Gold, Dawn, *Instr,* Dallas Baptist University, Dept of Art, Dallas TX (S)

Gold, Elaine Kiernan, *Librn,* Newark Public Library, Reference, Newark NJ

Gold, Lawrence, *Assoc Prof,* Pacific Lutheran University, Dept of Art, Tacoma WA (S)

Gold, Umber, *Interpreter,* Schuyler Mansion State Historic Site, Albany NY

Gold-Smith, Susan, *Prof,* University of Windsor, Visual Arts, Windsor ON (S)

Goldberg, Beth, *Cur,* City of San Rafael, Falkirk Cultural Center, San Rafael CA

Goldberg, Carol, *Instr,* American University, Dept of Art, New York NY (S)

Goldberg, Glenn, *Instr,* American University, Dept of Art, New York NY (S)

Goldberg, Ira, *Exec Dir,* Art Students League of New York, New York NY

Goldberg, Joan, *Instr,* Daemen College, Art Dept, Amherst NY (S)

Goldberg, Kenneth P, *Librn,* Northeast Ohio Areawide Coordinating Agency (NOACA), Information Resource Center, Cleveland OH

Goldberg, Linda, *Develop Officer,* Fraunces Tavern Museum, New York NY

Goldberg, Liz, *Instr,* Main Line Art Center, Haverford PA (S)

Goldberg, Margery, *Dir,* Zenith Gallery, Washington DC

Goldberg, Marsea, *Dir,* New Image Art, West Hollywood CA

Goldberg, Mitchell J, *Treas,* New York Society of Architects, New York NY

Goldberg, Sara, *Cur Manuscripts,* Historic Newton, Newton MA

Golden, Jacqueline, *Assoc Prof,* University of Arkansas, Art Dept, Fayetteville AR (S)

Golden, Jennifer, *Dir Educ,* Tallahassee Museum of History & Natural Science, Tallahassee FL

Golden, Kenneth, *Assoc Prof,* Queensborough Community College, Dept of Art & Photography, Bayside Hills NY (S)

Golden, Nancy, *Cur,* Hartwick College, Foreman Gallery, Oneonta NY

Golden, Susan, *VPres Communs,* Museum of Latin American Art, Long Beach CA

Golden, Thelma, *Dir & Chief Cur,* The Studio Museum in Harlem, New York NY

Golden, Vincent L, *Cur Newspapers & Periodicals,* American Antiquarian Society, Worcester MA

Goldfarb, Alvin, *Pres,* Western Illinois University, Western Illinois University Art Gallery, Macomb IL

Goldfarb, Barbara, *Second VPres,* Monmouth Museum & Cultural Center, Lincroft NJ

Goldfarb, Hilliard T, *Cur Old Master, Prints & Drawings,* Montreal Museum of Fine Arts, Montreal PQ

Goldhar, Eleanor, *Deputy Dir & Chief Global Commun,* Solomon R Guggenheim, New York NY

Golding, Deeno, *Assoc Prof,* Morehead State University, Art & Design Dept, Morehead KY (S)

Goldman, Nancy, *Library Head,* University of California, Berkeley, Pacific Film Archive, Berkeley CA

Goldman, Steven, *Pres,* Art Institutes International at Portland, Portland OR

Goldner, George R, *Chmn,* The Metropolitan Museum of Art, Dept of Drawings & Prints, New York NY

Goldner, George R, *Drue Heinz Chmn Dr,* The Metropolitan Museum of Art, New York NY

Goldsleger, Cheryl, *Dept Head,* Piedmont College, Art Dept, Demorest GA (S)

Goldsmith, Alan, *Assoc Prof,* University of Wisconsin-Parkside, Art Dept, Kenosha WI (S)

Goldsmith, Robert B, *Deputy Dir,* Frick Collection, New York NY

Goldstein, Alan, *Instr,* Bucks County Community College, Fine Arts Dept, Newtown PA (S)

Goldstein, Andrea, *Librn,* Temple University, Tyler School of Art Library, Philadelphia PA

Goldstein, Carl, *Prof,* University of North Carolina at Greensboro, Art Dept, Greensboro NC (S)

Goldstein, Fred, *VP & Gen Counsel,* Los Angeles County Museum of Art, Los Angeles CA

Goldstein, Homeira, *Chair,* Fellows of Contemporary Art, Los Angeles CA

Goldstein, Iris, *Pres,* ARC Gallery, Chicago IL

Goldstein, Marilyn, *Prof,* C W Post Campus of Long Island University, School of Visual & Performing Arts, Brookville NY (S)

Goldstein, Mark, *Library Technician,* San Francisco Maritime National Historical Park, Maritime Library, San Francisco CA

Goldstein, Norma, *Dean,* Shoreline Community College, Humanities Division, Seattle WA (S)

Goldstein, Sara June, *Dir Literary Arts,* South Carolina Arts Commission, Columbia SC

Goldstone, Elissa, *Exhibs Prog Mgr,* Socrates Sculpture Park, Long Island City NY

Golik, Jay, *Prof,* Napa Valley College, Art Dept, Napa CA (S)

Golisek, Lisa, *Security & Visitor Svcs Coordr,* Alaska State Museum, Juneau AK

Goliti, Susie, *Dir Opers,* Inner-City Arts, Los Angeles CA (S)

Gollini, Michael, *Interim Environment Chmn, Dept Head Interior Design,* Cleveland Institute of Art, Cleveland OH (S)

Golubov, Nicholas, *Research Curatorial Asst,* Historical Society of Palm Beach County, The Richard and Pat Johnson Palm Beach County History Museum, West Palm Beach FL

Gombert, Carl, *Asst Prof,* Maryville College, Dept of Fine Arts, Maryville TN (S)

Gomes, Agnes, *Mktg & Pub Rels,* Pacific - Asia Museum, Pasadena CA

Gomes, Lyle, *Prof Photog,* College of San Mateo, Creative Arts Dept, San Mateo CA (S)

Gomez, Andrea, *Educ & Programs,* Delaware Historical Society, Library, Wilmington DE

Gomez, Aurelia, *Dir Educ,* Museum of New Mexico, Museum of International Folk Art, Santa Fe NM

Gomez, Drake, *Assoc Prof,* Keystone College, Fine Arts Dept, LaPlume PA (S)

Gomez, Jewelle, *Dir Cultural Equity Grants,* San Francisco City & County Art Commission, San Francisco CA

Gomez, Julian, *Deputy Dir Finance, Opers & Admin,* The Wolfsonian-Florida International University, Miami Beach FL

Gomez, Mercedes, *Dir,* Institute of Puerto Rican Culture, Instituto de Cultura Puertorriquena, San Juan PR

Gomez, Mercedes, *Dir,* Institute of Puerto Rican Culture, Instituto de Cultura Puertorriquena, San Juan PR

Gomez, Mirta, *Prof,* Florida International University, School of Art & Art History, Miami FL (S)

Gomez, Sergio, *Exhib Designer,* Pasadena Museum of California Art, Pasadena CA

Gomez-Ibanez, Miguel, *Treas,* Haystack Mountain School of Crafts, Deer Isle ME

Gomez Marrero, Mercedes, *Exec Dir Institute of Culture,* Institute of Puerto Rican Culture, National Gallery, San Juan PR

Gomez Marrero, Mercedes, *Exec Dir Institute of Culture,* Institute of Puerto Rican Culture, National Gallery, San Juan PR

Gomula, Jessica, *Prof,* California State University, Art Dept, Turlock CA (S)

Gonchar, Nancy, *Asst Dir,* San Francisco City & County Art Commission, San Francisco CA

Goncharov, Kathleen, *Cur,* Boca Raton Museum of Art, Boca Raton FL

Goncharov, Kathleen, *Pub Art Cur,* Massachusetts Institute of Technology, List Visual Arts Center, Cambridge MA

Goncharov, Kathy, *Cur Exhibs & Audience Engagement,* Boca Raton Museum of Art, Library, Boca Raton FL

Gondek, Tom, *Chmn Foundation Fine Arts,* Kendall College of Art & Design, Grand Rapids MI (S)

Gonsalves, Priscilla, *Exec Dir Lahaina Arts Assoc,* Lahaina Arts Society, Art Organization, Lahaina HI

Gonsiorowski, Joy, *2nd VPres,* Columbus Museum of Art, Columbus OH

Gonzales, Edward, *VPres,* Guadalupe Historic Foundation, Santuario de Guadalupe, Santa Fe NM

Gonzales, Quinton, *Painting & Drawing,* University of Colorado at Denver, College of Arts & Media Visual Arts Dept, Denver CO (S)

Gonzales, Sara, *Coordr Conservation Assessment Prog,* Heritage Preservation, The National Institute for Conservation, Washington DC

Gonzalez, Alfred James, *Acting Area Head Ceramics,* Pasadena City College, Visual Arts and Media Studies Division, Pasadena CA (S)

Gonzalez, Cristina, *Assoc Prof,* Oklahoma State University, Department of Art, Graphic Design and Art History, Stillwater OK (S)

Gonzalez, Denise, *Instr,* Wayne Art Center, Wayne PA (S)

Gonzalez, Jorge, *Adjunct Asst Prof,* University of Maine, Dept of Art, Orono ME (S)

Gonzalez, Maria Del Pilar, *Prof,* University of Puerto Rico, Dept of Fine Arts, Rio Piedras PR (S)

Gonzalez, Maria Del Pilar, *Prof,* University of Puerto Rico, Dept of Fine Arts, Rio Piedras PR (S)

Gonzalez, Nathan, *Assoc Archivist,* Lincoln Memorial Shrine, Redlands CA

Gonzalez, Pedro, *Instr,* Amarillo College, Visual Art Dept, Amarillo TX (S)

Gonzalez, Vanessa, *Gallery Asst,* Bronx Council on the Arts, Longwood Arts Gallery @ Hostos, Bronx NY

Gonzalez-Cid, Malena, *Exec Dir,* Centro Cultural Aztlan, San Antonio TX

Gonzalez-Falla, Cleso, *Chmn,* Aperture Foundation, New York NY

Gonzalez-Lazo, Alvaro, *Cur Prints,* The New York Public Library, Print Room, New York NY

Gonzalez Palacios, Martha, *Archit & Planning Librn,* University of Texas at Austin, Architecture & Planning Library, Austin TX

Gonzolas, Diane, *VP Prog,* Lincoln Arts Council, Lincoln NE

Gooch, Peter, *Assoc Prof,* University of Dayton, Visual Arts Dept, Dayton OH (S)

Good, Aimee, *Educ Dir,* The Drawing Center, New York NY

Good, Cipperly, *Colls Mgr,* Penobscot Marine Museum, Stephen Phillips Memorial Library, Searsport ME

Good, Diane L, *Dir Develop,* Martin and Osa Johnson, Chanute KS

Good, Megan, *Library Dir,* Independence Seaport Museum, Library, Philadelphia PA

Good, Olivia, *Asst Dir,* Pratt Institute, The Rubelle & Norman Schafler Gallery, Brooklyn NY

Good, Sara C, *Colls Mgr,* Bucks County Historical Society, Mercer Museum Library, Doylestown PA

Goodarzi, Shoki, *Lectr,* Stony Brook University, College of Arts & Sciences, Dept of Art, Stony Brook NY (S)

Goodbar, Paula, *Gallery Dir,* Emerald Empire Art Association, Emerald Art Center, Springfield OR

Goode, Jamie, *Instr,* Siena Heights University, Studio Angelico-Art Dept, Adrian MI (S)

Goode-Walker, Vaughnette, *Dir Diversity & Access,* Telfair Museums' Jepson Center for the Arts Library, Savannah GA

Goodell, Tom, *Ceramic Studio Asst,* North Central College, Dept of Art, Naperville IL (S)

Goodhue, Timothy, *Registrar,* Yale University, Yale Center for British Art, New Haven CT

Goodkind, Joan, *Librn,* Bard College at Simon's Rock, Library, Great Barrington MA

Goodman, Bill, *Instr,* Hibbing Community College, Art Dept, Hibbing MN (S)

Goodman, Dan, *Registrar,* Museum of New Mexico, New Mexico Museum of Art, Unit of NM Dept of Cultural Affairs, Santa Fe NM

Goodman, Dana, *Chmn,* Indiana-Purdue University, Dept of Fine Arts, Fort Wayne IN (S)

Goodman, Frances, *Chmn Bd,* Cameron Art Museum, Wilmington NC

Goodman, Herb, *Asst Prof,* Louisiana State University, School of Art, Baton Rouge LA (S)

Goodman, Michael, *Dir Information Technology,* College Art Association, New York NY

Goodman, Rhonna, *Dir,* Manhattanville College, Library, Purchase NY

Goodman, Robin, *Registrar,* Kalamazoo Institute of Arts, Kalamazoo MI

Goodman, Robin, *Registrar,* Kalamazoo Institute of Arts, The Mary & Edwin Meader Fine Arts Library, Kalamazoo MI

Goodman, Sarah, *Mktg Coordr,* Palo Alto Art Center, Palo Alto CA

Goodman, Seth, *Prof,* Lycoming College, Art Dept, Williamsport PA (S)

Goodman, Sherry, *Cur Educ,* University of California, Berkeley, Berkeley Art Museum & Pacific Film Archive, Berkeley CA

Goodman, Ted, *Ed, Avery Index,* Columbia University, Avery Architectural & Fine Arts Library, New York NY

Goodman, Toni, *CEO,* Jewish Community Center of Greater Washington, Jane L & Robert H Weiner Judaic Museum, Rockville MD

Goodman, William, *Prof,* Indiana Wesleyan University, School of Arts & Humanities, Division of Art, Marion IN (S)

Goodrich, Jonathan, *Registrar,* Northeast Document Conservation Center, Inc, Andover MA

Goodrich, Laura, *Asst Mgr,* New England Maple Museum, Pittsford VT

Goodrow, Janice, *Dir Mem,* Fitchburg Art Museum, Fitchburg MA

Goodson, Lucy, *Asst Prof,* Coe College, Dept of Art, Cedar Rapids IA (S)

Goodstein, Richard E (Rick), *Dean, CAAH,* Clemson University, College of Architecture, Arts & Humanities, Art Dept, Clemson SC (S)

Goodwik, Sorrel, *Registrar,* Alaska State Museum, Juneau AK

Goodwillie, Christian, *Cur Coll,* Hancock Shaker Village, Inc, Pittsfield MA

Goodwin, Daniel, *Asst Prof,* State University of New York at Albany, Art Dept, Albany NY (S)

Goodwin, Mary, *Assoc Prof,* University of Alaska-Fairbanks, Dept of Art, Fairbanks AK (S)

Goodwin, Stewart, *Dir,* Heritage Museums & Gardens, Sandwich MA

Goody, Dick, *Dir,* Oakland University, Oakland University Art Gallery, Rochester MI

Goody, Stephen, *Gallery Dir & Spec Instr,* Oakland University, Dept of Art & Art History, Rochester MI (S)

Goodyear, Anne Collins, *Co-Dir,* Bowdoin College, Museum of Art, Brunswick ME

Goodyear, Anne Collins, *Pres,* College Art Association, New York NY

Goodyear, Frank, *Co-Dir,* Bowdoin College, Museum of Art, Brunswick ME

Gootee, Marita, *Prof,* Mississippi State University, Dept of Art, Starville MS (S)

Gopaul, Merika Adams, *Exec Dir,* Irvine Museum, Irvine CA

Gorbelt, Mandi, *Gallery Coordr,* Spectrum Gallery, Toledo OH

Gorcica, Bill, *Gallery Dir,* Saint Cloud State University, Kiehle Gallery, Saint Cloud MN

Gordilio, Nicole, *Develop Assoc,* 18th Street Arts Complex, Santa Monica CA

Gordon, Charlotte, *Cur,* Springfield Museum of Art, Springfield OH (S)

Gordon, Charlotte, *Cur,* Springfield Museum of Art, Springfield OH

Gordon, Cheryl, *Prog Coordr,* Arts Midland Galleries & School, Midland MI

Gordon, David, *Asst Dir,* Bakersfield Art Foundation, Bakersfield Museum of Art, Bakersfield CA

Gordon, Edmund, *Interim Dean,* Columbia University, Teachers Col Program in Art & Art Educ, New York NY (S)

Gordon, Edward, *Dir Educ,* Gibson Society, Inc, Gibson House Museum, Boston MA

Gordon, Heather M, *City Archivist,* Vancouver City Archives, Vancouver BC

Gordon, J, *Cur Coordr,* Delaware Center for the Contemporary Arts, Wilmington DE

Gordon, James, *Mktg Coordr,* Kamloops Art Gallery, Kamloops BC

Gordon, Jennifer, *Asst Dean,* University of Lethbridge, Div of Art, Lethbridge AB (S)

Gordon, Kathy, *Dir,* Colby Community College, Visual Arts Dept, Colby KS (S)

Gordon, Lida, *Prof,* University of Louisville, Allen R Hite Art Institute, Louisville KY (S)

Gordon, Lola, *Cur,* Pine Bluff/Jefferson County Historical Museum, Pine Bluff AR

Gordon, Mark, *Assoc Prof,* Barton College, Art & Design Dept, Wilson NC (S)

Gordon, Martha, *Chair & Assoc Prof,* Tarrant County College, Art Dept, Hurst TX (S)

Gordon, Myles, *VPres Educ,* American Museum of Natural History, New York NY

Gordon, Nadeane, *Pres,* Allegany County Historical Society, Gordon-Roberts House, Cumberland MD

Gordon, Richard, *Asst Cur,* Alberta College of Art & Design, Illingworth Kerr Gallery, Calgary AB

Gordon, Robert, *Assoc Prof Film & Instr Community Educ,* Watkins College of Art, Design & Film, Nashville TN (S)

Gordon, Steve, *Pres,* Barbara & Ray Alpert Jewish Community Center, Pauline & Zena Gatov Gallery, Long Beach CA

Gordon, Susan, *Develop Dir,* University of California, Los Angeles, Fowler Museum at UCLA, Los Angeles CA

Gordon, Wendy, *Assoc Dir,* Boulder History Museum, Museum of History, Boulder CO

Gore, Allison, *Mus Shop Mgr,* Alabama Department of Archives & History, Museum of Alabama, Montgomery AL

Gore, Caroline, *Jewelry/Metals Area Coordr,* Western Michigan University, Frostic School of Art, Kalamazoo MI (S)

Gore, Joyce, *Admin Asst,* University of Wyoming, University of Wyoming Art Museum, Laramie WY

Gore, Robert, *Librn for Art,* University of California, Los Angeles, Arts Library, Los Angeles CA

Gorewitz, Shalom, *Dir,* The Art Galleries of Ramapo College, Mahwah NJ

Gorham-Smith, Karen, *Assoc Cur,* Patrick Henry, Red Hill National Memorial, Brookneal VA

Goring, Rich, *Historic Site Mgr,* New York State Office of Parks: Recreation and Historic Preservation, Senate House State Historic Site, Kingston NY

Goring, Rich, *Historic Site Mgr,* New York State Office of Parks: Recreation and Historic Preservation, Reference Library, Kingston NY

Gorman, Amy, *Cur Educ & New Media,* College of William & Mary, Muscarelle Museum of Art, Williamsburg VA

Gorman, Carma, *Assoc Prof & Acad Area Head,* Southern Illinois University, School of Art & Design, Carbondale IL (S)

Gorman, Joan, *Sr Paintings Conservator,* Midwest Art Conservation Center, Minneapolis MN

Gormel, Donna M, *Vol Coordr,* Brandywine Conservancy, Brandywine River Museum, Chadds Ford PA

Gormley, Jim, *Assoc Prof,* Saint Louis Community College at Florissant Valley, Liberal Arts Division, Ferguson MO (S)

Gormley, Nina Z, *Exec Dir,* Wendell Gilley, Southwest Harbor ME

Goro-Rapoport, Victoria, *Asst Prof,* University of Nebraska, Kearney, Dept of Art & Art History, Kearney NE (S)

Gorse, George, *Prof,* Pomona College, Dept of Art & Art History, Claremont CA (S)

Gort, Gene, *Asst Prof,* University of Hartford, Hartford Art School, West Hartford CT (S)

Gorzegno, Janet, *Prof,* University of Southern Mississippi, Dept of Art & Design, Hattiesburg MS (S)

Gosar, Kris, *PT Instr,* Adams State College, Dept of Visual Arts, Alamosa CO (S)

Goss, Charles, *Prof & Chmn,* Cazenovia College, Center for Art & Design Studies, Cazenovia NY (S)

Gossel, Deborah, *Develop Dir,* Flint Institute of Arts, Library, Flint MI

Gothard, Paul, *Prof,* Lake Erie College, Fine Arts Dept, Painesville OH (S)

Gotlieb, Albert, *Graphic Design,* Art Institute of Pittsburgh, Pittsburgh PA (S)

Gotlieb, Marc, *Chmn,* University of Toronto, Dept of Fine Art, Toronto ON (S)

Gotlieb, Rachel, *Assoc Cur,* George R Gardiner, Toronto ON

Gott, Wesley A, *Chmn,* Southwest Baptist University, Art Dept, Bolivar MO (S)

Gottesfeld, Linda, *Prof,* Pace University, Dyson College of Arts & Sciences, Pleasantville NY (S)

Gottlieb, Dan, *Dir Planning & Design,* North Carolina Museum of Art, Raleigh NC

Gottlieb, Peter, *Dir & Archivist,* Wisconsin Historical Society, Wisconsin Historical Museum, Archives, Madison WI

Gottlieb, Wendy P, *Mgr Publications,* Kimbell Art Foundation, Kimbell Art Museum, Fort Worth TX

Gottsegen, Mark D, *Materials Res Dir,* Intermuseum Conservation Association, Cleveland OH

Goudey, Stephen, *Dir Admin,* New Brunswick College of Craft & Design, Library, Fredericton NB

Goudswaard, Ann, *Mktg Mgr,* Chilliwack Community Arts Council, Community Arts Centre, Chilliwack BC

Gough, Maria, *Asst Prof,* University of Michigan, Ann Arbor, Dept of History of Art, Ann Arbor MI (S)

Gould, Claudia, *Dir,* The Jewish Museum, New York NY

Gould, Claudia, *Dir,* University of Pennsylvania, Institute of Contemporary Art, Philadelphia PA

Gould, Gina, *Cur Sci,* Bruce Museum, Inc, Greenwich CT

Gould, Meggan, *Vis Asst Prof,* Bowdoin College, Art Dept, Brunswick ME (S)

Gould, Peter, *Deputy Dir Fin & Admin,* Cornell University, Herbert F Johnson Museum of Art, Ithaca NY

Gould, Rosemary, *Instr,* North Central Michigan College, Art Dept, Petoskey MI (S)

Goulding, Daniel, *Chmn,* Oberlin College, Dept of Art, Oberlin OH (S)

Goulding, Megan, *Assoc Dir Devel,* Long Beach Museum of Art Foundation, Long Beach CA

Goulin, Denise, *Asst to Dir,* Delaplaine Visual Arts Education Center, Frederick MD

Gourley, Julia, *Exec Dir,* Krasl Art Center, Saint Joseph MI

Gouveia, David F, *VPres,* Old Colony Historical Society, Museum, Taunton MA

Govan, Michael, *CEO,* Los Angeles County Museum of Art, Los Angeles CA

Gove, Emily, *Bilingual Educ Officer,* Oakville Galleries, Centennial Square and Gairloch Gardens, Oakville ON

Gove, Wayne, *Treas (V),* The Bartlett Museum, Amesbury MA

Gow, David, *Conservator,* Willard House & Clock Museum, Inc, North Grafton MA

Goward, Rick, *Div Dir,* Henry Ford Community College, McKenzie Fine Art Ctr, Dearborn MI (S)

Gowen, John R, *Prof,* Ocean County College, Humanities Dept, Toms River NJ (S)

Goyette, Caroline, *Ed Arts Quarterly,* New Orleans Museum of Art, New Orleans LA

Gozani, Tal, *Assoc Cur,* Hebrew Union College, Skirball Cultural Center, Los Angeles CA

Grabbe, Kaye, *Admin Librn,* Lake Forest Library, Fine Arts Dept, Lake Forest IL

Grabiec, Alex, *Exhib Mgr,* Longwood Center for the Visual Arts, Farmville VA

Grabill, Vin, *Assoc Prof & Chair,* University of Maryland, Baltimore County, Imaging & Digital Arts (IMDA), Dept of Visual Arts, Baltimore MD (S)

Grabner, Michelle, *Chmn Painting & Drawing,* School of the Art Institute of Chicago, Chicago IL (S)

Grabowski, Beth, *Asst Chm & Prof,* University of North Carolina at Chapel Hill, Art Dept, Chapel Hill NC (S)

Grabowski, John, *Dir Research,* Western Reserve Historical Society, Library, Cleveland OH

Grace, Alfred, *Pres & CEO,* Polynesian Cultural Center, Laie HI

Grace, Debbie, *Library Technician,* San Francisco Maritime National Historical Park, Maritime Library, San Francisco CA

Grace, James F, *Exec Dir,* Volunteer Lawyers for the Arts of Massachusetts Inc, Boston MA

Grace, Kathy, *Admin Officer,* National Archives & Records Administration, Herbert Hoover Presidential Library - Museum, West Branch IA

Grace, Kyla, *Vis Servs,* Walter Anderson, Ocean Springs MS

Grace, Laura, *Slide Cur,* University of Arkansas at Little Rock, Art Slide Library and Galleries, Little Rock AR

Gracey, Patty, *Operations Mgr,* Rose Center & Council for the Arts, Morristown TN

Grachos, Louis, *Dir,* The Buffalo Fine Arts Academy, Albright-Knox Art Gallery, Buffalo NY

Grachos, Louis, *Exec Dir,* The Contemporary Austin, Austin TX

Graciano, Matilde, *Dir Educ,* Inquilinos Boricuas en Accion, Boston MA

Gracie, David, *Asst Prof,* Nebraska Wesleyan University, Art Dept, Lincoln NE (S)

Gradle, Sally, *Assoc Prof,* Southern Illinois University, School of Art & Design, Carbondale IL (S)

Grady, Ann, *Collections Mgr,* Pope County Historical Society, Pope County Museum, Glenwood MN

Grady, Christine, *Pres,* Mystic Art Association, Inc, Mystic Arts Center, Mystic CT

Grady, Edward, *Asst Cur Tolson Ctr,* Langston University, Melvin B Tolson Black Heritage Center, Langston OK

Grady, John, *Instr,* Elgin Community College, Fine Arts Dept, Elgin IL (S)

Grady, Thomas, *Vis Asst Prof,* Assumption College, Dept of Art, Music & Theatre, Worcester MA (S)

Graesser, Bill, *CFO,* Royal Ontario Museum, Toronto ON

Graf, Dean, *Prof,* Concordia University, Division of Performing & Visual Arts, Mequon WI (S)

Graf, Jaz, *VPres,* Manhattan Graphics Center, New York NY (S)

Grafe, Steven L., *Cur Art,* Maryhill Museum of Art, Goldendale WA

Graff, Terry, *Cur & Deputy Dir,* Beaverbrook Art Gallery, Fredericton NB

Graffam, Olive, *Cur Coll,* DAR Museum, Library, Washington DC

Gragert, Steven, *Library & Colls,* Will Rogers Memorial Museum & Birthplace Ranch, Claremore OK

Graham, Alice, *VPres,* Zanesville Museum of Art, Zanesville OH

Graham, Amy, *Head Gardener*, Longue Vue House & Gardens, New Orleans LA

Graham, Ann, *Visual Resources Cur*, University of North Texas, Visual Resources Collection, Denton TX

Graham, Brenda, *Asst Prof*, Oakland City University, Division of Fine Arts, Oakland City IN (S)

Graham, Cathy, *Secy*, Shippensburg University, Kauffman Gallery, Shippensburg PA

Graham, Conrad, *Cur Decorative Arts*, McCord Museum of Canadian History, Montreal PQ

Graham, Isis Marina, *Chief Cur & Trustee*, J.M.W. Turner Museum, Sarasota FL

Graham, Jan, *Reg & Prog Dir*, Pacific Northwest Art School, Gallery at the Wharf, Coupeville WA

Graham, John R, *Cur Exhib*, Western Illinois University, Western Illinois University Art Gallery, Macomb IL

Graham, Juliet, *Registrar*, University of Lethbridge, Art Gallery, Lethbridge AB

Graham, Kim, *Family Svc Dir*, Christina Cultural Arts Center, Inc, Wilmington DE

Graham, Kurt, *Cur McCracken Research Library*, Buffalo Bill Memorial Association, Buffalo Bill Historical Center, Cody WY

Graham, Lisa, *Assoc Prof*, University of Texas at Arlington, Art & Art History Department, Arlington TX (S)

Graham, Lonnie, *Asst Prof Art (Photog)*, Pennsylvania State University, University Park, Penn State School of Visual Arts, University Park PA (S)

Graham, Mark, *Dir Research Svcs*, Canadian Museum of Nature, Musee Canadien de la Nature, Ottawa ON

Graham, Mark M, *Interim Head*, Auburn University, Dept of Art, Auburn AL (S)

Graham, Michael, *Assoc Prof*, American University, Dept of Art, New York NY (S)

Graham, Michael, *Dir & Cur*, United Society of Shakers, The Shaker Library, New Gloucester ME

Graham, Michael S, *Dir & Cur*, United Society of Shakers, Shaker Museum, New Gloucester ME

Graham, Patricia, *Archivist*, Midwest Art History Society, Waco TX

Graham, Richard, *Instr*, Salt Lake Community College, Graphic Design Dept, Salt Lake City UT (S)

Graham, Robert, *Prof*, Virginia Polytechnic Institute & State University, Dept of Art & Art History, Blacksburg VA (S)

Graham, Sandra, *Dean Acad Affairs*, The Illinois Institute of Art - Chicago, Chicago IL (S)

Graham, Shelby, *Dir*, University of California at Santa Cruz, Mary Porter Sesnon Art Gallery, Santa Cruz CA

Graham, Susan, *Spec Coll Librn*, Albin O Kuhn Library & Gallery, Baltimore MD

Graham, Tracy, *Asst Registrar*, Bucknell University, Edward & Marthann Samek Art Gallery, Lewisburg PA

Grajek-Specter, Bambi, *Dir Visitor Experience*, Milwaukee Art Museum, Milwaukee WI

Gralnick, Lisa, *Prof*, University of Wisconsin, Madison, Dept of Art, Madison WI (S)

Grame, Robert, *Assoc Prof*, Finlandia Univ, International School of Art and Design, Hancock MI (S)

Granby, Karen, *Dir Human Resources*, The Jewish Museum, New York NY

Grand, Stanley I, *Dir*, Lancaster Museum of Art, Lancaster PA

Granda, Margaret, *Grants Coordr*, Cultural Council of Palm Beach County, Lake Worth FL

Grandbois, Michele, *Cur Modern Art*, Musee National des Beaux Arts du Quebec, Quebec PQ

Grande, Lance, *Sr VPres Colls & Research*, Field Museum, Chicago IL

Granderson, Eddie, *Prog Adminr*, City of Atlanta, Office of Cultural Affairs, Atlanta GA

Grandmaitre, Robert, *Chief Coll Consultation*, National Archives of Canada, Art & Photography Archives, Ottawa ON

Grando, Connie, *VPres*, Baldwin Historical Society Museum, Baldwin NY

Grando, Robert, *Treas*, Baldwin Historical Society Museum, Baldwin NY

Graney, Carol H, *Library Dir*, The University of the Arts, University Libraries, Philadelphia PA

Granger, Steven T, *Archivist*, Archives of the Archdiocese of St Paul & Minneapolis, Saint Paul MN

Grannis, Pete, *Commissioner Dept Environmental Conservation*, New York Office of Parks, Recreation & Historic Preservation, Natural Heritage Trust, Albany NY

Grannis, Sue Ellen, *Cur Books & Art*, Maysville, Kentucky Gateway Museum Center, Maysville KY

Grano, Dee, *Mktg Dir*, The Light Factory Contemporary Museum of Photography and Film, Charlotte NC

Granof, Corinne, *Cur*, Northwestern University, Mary & Leigh Block Museum of Art, Evanston IL

Granquist, Paula, *Literary Arts Specialist*, Northfield Arts Guild, Northfield MN

Granson, Robert, *Dir Finance*, Museum of Art, Fort Lauderdale, Library, Fort Lauderdale FL

Grant, Hugh, *Dir*, Kirkland Museum of Fine & Decorative Art, Denver CO

Grant, Jacqueline, *Dir*, Museum of the Hudson Highlands, Cornwall On Hudson NY

Grant, Jerry, *Librn*, Shaker Museum & Library, Emma B King Library, Old Chatham NY

Grant, Jim, *Pres*, Okanagan Heritage Museum, Kelowna BC

Grant, Scott, *Bldg Engineer*, Modern Art Museum, Fort Worth TX

Grant, Susan Kae, *Prof*, Texas Woman's University, School of the Arts, Dept of Visual Arts, Denton TX (S)

Grantham, Shirlyn, *Bus Mgr*, Carson County Square House Museum, Panhandle TX

Granzow, Carl, *Assoc Prof*, University of Lethbridge, Div of Art, Lethbridge AB (S)

Grash, Valerie, *Dept Head*, University of Pittsburgh at Johnstown, Dept of Fine Arts, Johnstown PA (S)

Grass, Kevin, *Assoc Prof*, Saint Petersburg College, Fine & Applied Arts at Clearwater Campus, Clearwater FL (S)

Grattan, David, *Mgr Conserv Research Svcs*, Department of Canadian Heritage, Canadian Conservation Institute, Ottawa ON

Graubman, Daniel, *Research Assoc*, Belz Museum of Asian & Judaic Art, Memphis TN

Grauer, Michael R, *Art Cur*, Panhandle-Plains Historical Museum, Canyon TX

Graves, Beverly, *Operations Mgr*, Portraits South, Raleigh NC

Graves, Chris, *Asst Prof*, Northwest Missouri State University, Dept of Fine & Performing Arts, Maryville MO (S)

Graves, Jerrold, *Acting Area Head Design*, Pasadena City College, Visual Arts and Media Studies Division, Pasadena CA (S)

Graves, Judy, *Dir Educ & Research*, Portland Children's Museum, Portland OR

Graves, Maurice, *Foundations*, Art Institute of Pittsburgh, Pittsburgh PA (S)

Graves, Robert, *Dean*, University of Illinois, Urbana-Champaign, College of Fine & Applied Arts, Champaign IL (S)

Graves, Travis, *Asst Prof*, East Tennessee State University, College of Arts and Sciences, Dept of Art & Design, Johnson City TN (S)

Gray, Amy, *Program Admin*, Wesley Theological Seminary, Henry Luce III Center for the Arts & Religion, Dadian Gallery, Washington DC

Gray, Chris, *Assoc Dean*, Illinois Central College, Arts & Communication Dept, East Peoria IL (S)

Gray, Debi, *Exec Dir*, Contemporary Art Center of Virginia, Virginia Beach VA

Gray, Elmer, *Commissioner*, United States Department of the Interior, Indian Arts & Crafts Board, Washington DC

Gray, Frances B, *VPres*, Miles B Carpenter Folk Art Museum, Waverly VA

Gray, Jamie, *Asst Prof*, Kansas City Art Institute, Kansas City MO (S)

Gray, Jane, *Exec Dir*, Kauai Museum Association, Ltd., Lihue HI

Gray, Jim, *Adminr*, University of South Florida, Library, Tampa FL

Gray, John L, *Pres & CEO*, Autry National Center, Museum of the American West, Griffith Park, Los Angeles CA

Gray, Johnnie, *Chmn Fine Arts Dept*, Mississippi Gulf Coast Community College-Jackson County Campus, Art Dept, Gautier MS (S)

Gray, Lee, *Cur*, University of Louisiana at Lafayette, Paul and Lulu Hilliard University Art Museum, Lafayette LA

Gray, Lynn, *Assoc Prof*, University of Minnesota, Minneapolis, Dept of Art, Minneapolis MN (S)

Gray, Mary Ann, *Head Archivist*, Chatham Historical Society, The Atwood House Museum, Chatham MA

Gray, Mary Kathryn, *Treas*, North Shore Arts Association, Inc, Gloucester MA

Gray, Nancy, *Exhibits Coordr*, Tryon Palace Historic Sites & Gardens, New Bern NC

Gray, Richard, *Grad Dir*, University of Notre Dame, Dept of Art, Art History & Design, Notre Dame IN (S)

Gray, Sara, *Mgr*, Stremmel Gallery, Reno NV

Gray, Sharon, *Admin Asst*, Frostburg State University, The Stephanie Ann Roper Gallery, Frostburg MD

Gray-Young, Rhonda, *Fine Arts Prog Asst*, Federal Reserve Board, Art Gallery, Washington DC

Graybill, Lela, *Asst Prof*, University of Utah, Dept of Art & Art History, Salt Lake City UT (S)

Graybill, Maribeth, *Arlene & Harold Schnitzer Cur Asian Art*, Portland Art Museum, Portland OR

Graydon, Elisa, *Cataloging Librn*, Moore College of Art & Design, Library, Philadelphia PA

Graydon Smith, John, *Dir & CEO*, Reading Public Museum, Reading PA

Grayson, Jan, *Vice Chmn*, Chicago Architecture Foundation, Chicago IL

Graziano, Laura, *Registrar & Coll Mgr*, Museum of Contemporary Art, San Diego, La Jolla CA

Grazzini, Patricia J, *Deputy Dir*, Minneapolis Institute of Arts, Minneapolis MN

Greaser, KP, *Pub Rels Dir*, The Barnum Museum, Bridgeport CT

Grebl, James, *Library Mgr*, San Diego Museum of Art, Art Reference Library & Archives, San Diego CA

Greco, Anna, *Educ Cur*, Bush-Holley Historic Site & Storehouse Gallery, Greenwich Historical Society/Bush-Holley House, Cos Cob CT

Greco, Lucas, *Instr*, Tulsa Community College, Art Dept, Tulsa OK (S)

Gredinger, Martin, *CFO*, Fuller Craft Museum, Brockton MA

Greel, Deborah, *Exec Dir*, Marblehead Arts Association, Inc, Marblehead MA

Greeley, Andrew M, *Gallery Opers & Outreach*, Second Street Gallery, Charlottesville VA

Green, Amanda, *Asst Prof Photog & Video*, Siena College, Dept of Creative Arts, Loudonville NY (S)

Green, Amy, *Adjunct*, College of the Canyons, Art Dept, Santa Clarita CA (S)

Green, Amy, *Dir Opers*, Georgia O'Keeffe Museum, Santa Fe NM

Green, Art, *Prof*, University of Waterloo, Fine Arts Dept, Waterloo ON (S)

Green, Aylin, *Coordr (V)*, Grounds for Sculpture, Hamilton NJ

Green, Bill, *Interim Dir*, Carson County Square House Museum, Panhandle TX

Green, Christina, *Coll Mgr*, George R Gardiner, Toronto ON

Green, Gregory, *Assoc Prof*, University of South Florida, School The Arts, Tampa FL (S)

Green, Harriett, *Dir Visual Arts*, South Carolina Arts Commission, Columbia SC

Green, Heather, *Gallery Coordr*, Rogue Community College, Wiseman Gallery - FireHouse Gallery, Grants Pass OR

Green, Holly, *Mktg Dir*, Lauren Rogers, Laurel MS

Green, Jack, *Museum Chief Cur*, University of Chicago, Oriental Institute, Chicago IL

Green, James N, *Librn*, Library Company of Philadelphia, Philadelphia PA

Green, Jeffrey, *Chmn*, Georgia Southwestern State University, Art Gallery, Americus GA

Green, John, *Instr*, East Central University, School of Fine Arts, Ada OK (S)

Green, Jonathan W, *Prof*, University of California, Riverside, Dept of the History of Art, Riverside CA (S)

Green, Joshua, *Exec Dir*, National Council on Education for the Ceramic Arts (NCECA), Erie CO

Green, Julie, *Asst Prof,* Oregon State University, Dept of Art, Corvallis OR (S)

Green, Karen, *Gallery Coordr,* College of Eastern Utah, Gallery East, Price UT

Green, Krista, *Asst Dir Cultural Affairs,* School 33 Art Center, Baltimore MD

Green, Leamon, *Assoc Prof,* Texas Southern University, College of Liberal Arts & Behavioral Sciences, Houston TX (S)

Green, Louise, *Reference Librn,* University of Maryland, College Park, Art Library, College Park MD

Green, Maggie, *Dir Educ,* Fruitlands Museum, Inc, Harvard MA

Green, Mary-Ellen, *Pres,* Organization for the Development of Artists, Gallery Connexion, Fredericton NB

Green, Mike, *Chmn,* College of Southern Idaho, Art Dept, Twin Falls ID (S)

Green, Mimi, *Instr,* Wayne Art Center, Wayne PA (S)

Green, Nancy E, *Sr Cur Prints, Drawings & Photographs,* Cornell University, Herbert F Johnson Museum of Art, Ithaca NY

Green, Nancy W, *Interim Librn,* American Numismatic Association, Library, Colorado Springs CO

Green, Peter, *Instr Music,* Glendale Community College, Visual & Performing Arts Div, Glendale CA (S)

Green, Rebecca, *Communs Mgr,* Quad City Arts Inc, Rock Island IL

Green, Richard, *Instr,* Eastern Arizona College, Art Dept, Thatcher AZ (S)

Green, Robert, *Prof,* Abilene Christian University, Dept of Art & Design, Abilene TX (S)

Green, Seth, *Art Instr,* Morehead State University, Art & Design Dept, Morehead KY (S)

Green, Tom, *Pres,* Polk County Heritage Gallery, Heritage Art Gallery, Des Moines IA

Green, Virginia, *Asst Prof,* Baylor University - College of Arts and Sciences, Dept of Art, Waco TX (S)

Green, William, *Assoc Prof,* New Mexico State University, Art Dept, Las Cruces NM (S)

Green-Price, Tina, *Gallery Cur,* Oregon State University, Giustina Gallery, Corvallis OR

Greenbaum, Susan, *Conservator,* Neustadt Collection of Tiffany Glass, Long Island City NY

Greenberg, Gary, *Asst Prof & Chmn,* Clarion University of Pennsylvania, Dept of Art, Clarion PA (S)

Greenberg, Ira, *Asst Prof,* Seton Hall University, College of Arts & Sciences, South Orange NJ (S)

Greenberg, Karen, *VPres,* Congregation Emanu-El, Bernard Judaica Museum, New York NY

Greenberg, Suzy, *Contact,* Soo Visual Arts Center, Minneapolis MN

Greenblatt, Arthur, *Dir,* Dundas Valley School of Art, DVSA Gallery, Dundas ON (S)

Greene, Amy Gundrum, *Dir & Cur,* Headley-Whitney Museum, Lexington KY

Greene, Casey, *Head Spec Coll,* Rosenberg Library, Galveston TX

Greene, Fred, *Admin Mgr,* University of Lethbridge, Art Gallery, Lethbridge AB

Greene, Joseph A, *Asst Dir,* Harvard University, Semitic Museum, Cambridge MA

Greene, Kathleen Ogilvie, *Mgr Adult Progs,* Philadelphia Museum of Art, Samuel S Fleisher Art Memorial, Philadelphia PA

Greene, Ken, *Instr,* William Woods-Westminster Colleges, Art Dept, Fulton MO (S)

Greene, Lois, *Chmn,* University of Kansas, Dept of Design, Lawrence KS (S)

Greene, Lois, *Chmn Dept,* University of Kansas, Dept of Art & Music Education & Music Therapy, Lawrence KS (S)

Greene, Marjorie, *Instr,* Saint Petersburg College, Fine & Applied Arts at Clearwater Campus, Clearwater FL (S)

Greene, Rhonda, *Co-Site Supv,* Fort Totten State Historic Site, Pioneer Daughters Museum, Fort Totten ND

Greene, Tracy, *Pub Information,* Amon Carter Museum of American Art, Fort Worth TX

Greene, Vivian, *Cur 19th & Early 20th c Art,* Solomon R Guggenheim, New York NY

Greene, Warren, *Gallery Dir,* Austin Peay State University, Art Dept Library, Clarksville TN

Greene Bowman, Leslie, *Pres,* Thomas Jefferson, Monticello, Charlottesville VA

Greenfield, Dorothy, *Treas,* Historical Society of Bloomfield, Bloomfield NJ

Greenfield, Mark Steven, *Dir,* Cultural Affairs Department, Los Angeles Municipal Art Gallery, Los Angeles CA

Greening, Cynthia, *Instr,* Mesa Community College, Dept of Art, Mesa AZ (S)

Greening, Suzanne E, *Arts Coordr,* Richmond Arts Centre, Richmond BC

Greenlaw, William (Bill), *Pres,* Canadian Museums Association, Association des Musees Canadiens, Ottawa ON

Greennagle, Dave, *Dir Coral Act,* Randolph-Macon College, Dept of the Arts, Ashland VA (S)

Greenough, Sara, *Chief Photographic Svcs,* National Gallery of Art, Washington DC

Greenwall, Steven R, *Dept Head,* Allen County Community College, Art Dept, Iola KS (S)

Greenwalt, Rose, *Receptionist,* Frontier Times Museum, Bandera TX

Greenwell, Matt, *Head & Prof,* University of Tennessee at Chattanooga, Dept of Art, Chattanooga TN (S)

Greenwold, Mark, *Assoc Prof,* State University of New York at Albany, Art Dept, Albany NY (S)

Greer, Ann, *Dir Mktg & Communs,* The Phillips Collection, Washington DC

Greer, Ippy, *Assoc Prof,* South Plains College, Fine Arts Dept, Levelland TX (S)

Greer, Rina, *Dir,* Toronto Sculpture Garden, Toronto ON

Grefe, C Morgan, *Dir Educ,* Rhode Island Historical Society, Aldrich House, Providence RI

Grefe, C Morgan, *Dir Educ & Pub Programming,* Newport Historical Society & Museum of Newport History, Newport RI

Grefe, C Morgan, *Educ Dir,* Rhode Island Historical Society, Providence RI

Grefe, Dick, *Sr Reference Librn,* Washington & Lee University, Leyburn Library, Lexington VA

Grefe, Morgan, *Dir Goff Institute,* Rhode Island Historical Society, John Brown House, Providence RI

Grefe, Richard, *Exec Dir,* American Institute of Graphic Arts, New York NY

Grefe, Richard, *Exec Dir,* American Institute of Graphic Arts, Library, New York NY

Gregersen, Thomas, *Cultural Dir,* Palm Beach County Parks & Recreation Department, Morikami Museum & Japanese Gardens, Delray Beach FL

Gregg, Rebecca, *Instr,* Sierra Community College, Art Dept, Rocklin CA (S)

Gregoire, Mathieu, *Project Mgr,* University of California, San Diego, Stuart Collection, La Jolla CA

Gregorio, Teresa, *Information Officer,* McMaster University, McMaster Museum of Art, Hamilton ON

Gregorski, Peggy, *Deputy Dir,* Kenosha Public Museums, Kenosha WI

Gregory, Dale, *VPres Pub Prog,* New-York Historical Society, Museum, New York NY

Gregory, Maggie, *Registrar,* North Carolina Museum of Art, Raleigh NC

Gregory, Shirley, *Dir,* Barton College, Library, Wilson NC

Gregson, Chris, *Historic Preservation Supv,* County of Henrico, Meadow Farm Museum, Glen Allen VA

Gregson, Sandra, *Instr,* Toronto School of Art, Toronto ON (S)

Grehan, John, *Dir Science,* Buffalo Museum of Science, Research Library, Buffalo NY

Greig, Charmayne, *Bookkeeper,* Canadian Clay and Glass Gallery, Waterloo ON

Greig, Rick E, *Dir Prog,* Angelo State University, Houston Harte University Center, San Angelo TX

Greiner, William, *Prof & Chair,* Olivet Nazarene University, Dept of Art, Bourbonnais IL (S)

Grell, Krystyna, *Librn,* Polish Museum of America, Research Library, Chicago IL

Greminger, Gretchen, *Cur Educ,* Jekyll Island Museum, Jekyll Island GA

Grenda, C, *Prof,* City Colleges of Chicago, Daley College, Chicago IL (S)

Grenda, Rick, *Pres Bd Trustees,* Heritage Glass Museum, Glassboro NJ

Grenville, Bruce, *Sr Cur,* Vancouver Art Gallery, Vancouver BC

Gresh, Laura, *Mus Admin,* Gibson Society, Inc, Gibson House Museum, Boston MA

Gresham, Jodi Hays, *Asst to Dir,* Cambridge Art Association, Cambridge MA

Greshem, Emily, *Cur Educ,* Longwood Center for the Visual Arts, Farmville VA

Gretizer, Michael, *Chmn,* Dayton Art Institute, Dayton OH

Grey, Emily, *Cur Annual Exhibs,* Monhegan Museum, Monhegan ME

Grey, Stephanie, *Develop Dir,* Anthology Film Archives, New York NY

Grey, Wilma, *Dir,* Newark Public Library, Reference, Newark NJ

Greyson, Peter, *Dir & Cur,* Temiskaming Art Gallery, Haileybury ON

Grezdo, Stanislav, *Cur,* Ukrainian Institute of Modern Art, Chicago IL

Gribbon, Deborah, *Assoc Dir,* Getty Center, Trust Museum, Los Angeles CA

Grief, Kathy, *Mktg,* Salvador Dali, Library, Saint Petersburg FL

Grief, Steve, *VPres,* Coos County Historical Society Museum, North Bend OR

Grieger, Scott, *Prog Dir Painting,* Otis College of Art & Design, Fine Arts, Los Angeles CA (S)

Griep, Mary, *Assoc Prof,* Saint Olaf College, Art Dept, Northfield MN (S)

Griesheimer, Martha, *Vol Coordr,* Vesterheim Norwegian-American Museum, Decorah IA

Griesinger, Pamela, *Prof,* Daytona Beach Community College, Dept of Fine Arts & Visual Arts, Daytona Beach FL (S)

Griffen, Sara, *Pres Olana Partnership,* Olana State Historic Site, Library, Hudson NY

Griffen, Sara, *Pres The Olana,* Olana State Historic Site, Hudson NY

Griffin, Cathryn, *Assoc Prof,* Western Carolina University, Dept of Art/College of Arts & Science, Cullowhee NC (S)

Griffin, David, *Prof,* Eastern Illinois University, Art Dept, Charleston IL (S)

Griffin, Eve, *Cur Fine Arts,* Boston Public Library, Central Library, Boston MA

Griffin, Eve, *Cur Fine Arts,* Boston Public Library, Arts Reference Department, Boston MA

Griffin, Gail, *Dir Gardens & Grounds,* Harvard University, Museum & Garden, Washington DC

Griffin, Gerald, *Instr,* Ricks College, Dept of Art, Rexburg ID (S)

Griffin, Gerry, *Cur,* Baldwin Historical Society Museum, Baldwin NY

Griffin, Jennifer, *Instr,* Sacramento City College, Art Dept, Sacramento CA (S)

Griffin, Jerri, *Ceramics & Sculpture Instr,* Hutchinson Community College, Visual Arts Dept, Hutchinson KS (S)

Griffin, Julie, *Bookkeeper,* Springfield Museum of Art, Springfield OH (S)

Griffin, Kathy, *Gen Educ,* Art Institute of Pittsburgh, Pittsburgh PA (S)

Griffin, Leah, *Assoc Cur,* Pensacola Museum of Art, Pensacola FL

Griffin, Linda Smith, *Dept Head Cataloging,* Louisiana State University, Middleton Library, Baton Rouge LA

Griffin, Penny, *Asst Prof,* Salem Academy & College, Art Dept, Winston Salem NC (S)

Griffin, Shirley, *Treas,* Crowley Art Association, The Gallery, Crowley LA

Griffin, Steve, *Assoc Prof,* University of Mary Washington, Dept of Art & Art History, Fredericksburg VA (S)

Griffin, Tim, *Exec Dir,* The Kitchen, New York NY

Griffis, Damian, *Sculpture Park Dir,* Ashford Hollow Foundation for Visual & Performing Arts, Griffis Sculpture Park, East Otto NY

Griffis, Larry L, *Dir,* Birger Sandzen Memorial Gallery, Lindsborg KS

Griffis, Mark, *Essex Arts Center Dir,* Ashford Hollow Foundation for Visual & Performing Arts, Griffis Sculpture Park, East Otto NY

Griffis Lampman, Nila, *Exec Dir,* Ashford Hollow Foundation for Visual & Performing Arts, Griffis Sculpture Park, East Otto NY

Griffith, Bill, *Prog Dir,* Arrowmont School of Arts & Crafts, Arrowmont School of Arts & Crafts, Gatlinburg TN (S)

Griffith, Cable, *Exhibs Dir,* Kirkland Arts Center, Kirkland WA

Griffith, John, *Asst Prof,* College of Mount Saint Joseph, Art Dept, Cincinnati OH (S)

Griffith, Laura S, *Asst Dir,* Fairmount Park Art Association, Philadelphia PA

Griffith, Lesa, *Dir Communs,* Honolulu Museum of Art, Honolulu HI

Griffith, Margaret, *Asst Prof Painting & Drawing,* Rio Hondo College, Visual Arts Dept, Whittier CA (S)

Griffith, Roberta, *Prof,* Hartwick College, Art Dept, Oneonta NY (S)

Griffith, William, *Cur,* University of Mississippi, Rowan Oak, Home of William Faulkner, Oxford MS

Griffith, William, *Rowan Oak Cur & Colls Mgr,* University of Mississippi, University Museum & Historic Houses, Oxford MS

Grigg, Susan, *Head Alaska & Polar Regions Colls,* University of Alaska, Elmer E Rasmuson Library, Fairbanks AK

Griggs, Miyai Abe, *Dir,* The Art Museum of Eastern Idaho, Idaho Falls ID

Grigsby, Eddy, *Asst Dir,* City of Lubbock, Buddy Holly Center, Lubbock TX

Grill, J Brett, *Assoc Prof, Dir Grad Studies (Painting & Drawing),* University of Missouri - Columbia, Dept of Art, Columbia MO (S)

Grillo, Janet, *Educ Dir,* Order Sons of Italy in America, Garibaldi & Meucci Museum, Staten Island NY

Grillo, Michael, *Assoc Prof & Chair,* University of Maine, Dept of Art, Orono ME (S)

Grim, Ruth, *Cur,* College of Central Florida, Appleton Museum of Art, Ocala FL

Grim, Ruth, *Cur of Exhibs,* College of Central Florida, Appleton Museum of Art, Ocala FL

Grimaldi, Ann, *Cur Educ,* University of North Carolina at Greensboro, Weatherspoon Art Museum, Greensboro NC

Grimaldi, Scott, *Prof,* Manhattan College, School of Arts, Bronx NY (S)

Grimes, Ann, *Bookmobile Librn,* Lee County Library, Tupelo MS

Grimes, Margaret, *MFA Coordr,* Western Connecticut State University, School of Visual & Performing Arts, Danbury CT (S)

Grimes, Sharon, *Dir,* Greenville College, Art Dept, Greenville IL (S)

Grimes, Sharon, *Dir & Cur,* Greenville College, Richard W Bock Sculpture Collection, Almira College House, Greenville IL

Grimm, Amy, *Cur Coll,* City of El Paso, El Paso Museum of Art, El Paso TX

Grimm, Kristin, *Gallery Coordr,* Providence Art Club, Providence RI

Grimmer, Jean, *Dir Develop,* Nantucket Historical Association, Historic Nantucket, Nantucket MA

Grimsley, Meredith, *Asst Prof,* Bloomsburg University, Dept of Art & Art History, Bloomsburg PA (S)

Grimsley, Molly, *Registrar Exhibs & Loans,* National Portrait Gallery, Smithsonian Institution, Washington DC

Grinage, Jeanine, *Head Educ,* New York State Museum, Albany NY

Gringras-Taylor, Lynn, *Youth & Family Progs Coordr,* Figge Art Museum, Davenport IA

Grinna, Steve, *Develop Dir,* Vesterheim Norwegian-American Museum, Decorah IA

Grinnan, Karen P, *VPres Mktg,* The Mariners' Museum, Newport News VA

Grinnell, Nancy, *Cur,* Newport Art Museum and Association, Newport RI

Grisaitis, Olga, *Dir,* Art Directors Club, New York NY

Grissano, Joan, *Reference Coordr,* New York City Technical College, Ursula C Schwerin Library, Brooklyn NY

Grissim, Mary, *Dir Educ,* Cheekwood Nashville's Home of Art & Gardens, Education Dept, Nashville TN (S)

Grissom, Mary, *Dir Educ,* Cheekwood-Tennessee Botanical Garden & Museum of Art, Nashville TN

Griswold, Joan, *Treas,* New England Watercolor Society, Pembroke MA

Griswold, Justin, *Coll Registrar,* University of Massachusetts, Amherst, University Gallery, Amherst MA

Grittner, James, *Chmn,* University of Wisconsin-Superior, Programs in the Visual Arts, Superior WI (S)

Gritton, Joy, *Assoc Prof,* Morehead State University, Art & Design Dept, Morehead KY (S)

Grivetti, Al, *Assoc Prof,* Clarke College, Dept of Art, Dubuque IA (S)

Grobes, Thelma, *Bd Mem,* American Color Print Society, Huntingdon Valley PA

Groce, Susan, *Prof,* University of Maine, Dept of Art, Orono ME (S)

Grodenchik, Barly, *VPres,* Bowne House Historical Society, Flushing NY

Groenert, Diane, *Gallery Receptionist,* Artlink, Inc, Auer Center for Arts & Culture, Fort Wayne IN

Groeninger, Scott, *Asst Prof,* Florida State University, Art Dept, Tallahassee FL (S)

Groff, Jeff, *Dir Pub Progs,* Winterthur Museum, Winterthur Museum, Garden & Library, Winterthur DE

Groft, Tammis K, *Deputy Dir Coll & Exhibs,* Albany Institute of History & Art, Albany NY

Grogan, Cynthia, *Pub Info Officer,* Louisiana State Exhibit Museum, Shreveport LA

Grogan, Geoffrey, *Asst Prof,* Adelphi University, Dept of Art & Art History, Garden City NY (S)

Grogan, Kevin, *Exec Dir,* Morris Museum of Art, Augusta GA

Groh, Barton, *COO,* Mount Vernon Ladies' Association of the Union, Mount Vernon VA

Gron, Jack, *Chmn,* University of Kentucky, Dept of Art, Lexington KY (S)

Gronau, Jane, *Educ & Pub Rels Coordr,* Mount Holyoke College, Art Museum, South Hadley MA

Groning, Adele, *Asst Dir,* Bunnell Street AAS Center, Bunnell Street Arts Center, Homer AK

Gronsdahl, Troy, *Admin Coordr,* AKA Artist Run Centre, Saskatoon SK

Gronsdahl, Troy, *Admin Coordr,* AKA Artist Run Centre, Library, Saskatoon SK

Groom, Gloria, *Cur European Painting,* The Art Institute of Chicago, Chicago IL

Groover, Charles, *Head,* Jacksonville State University, Art Dept, Jacksonville AL (S)

Grose, Donald, *Dean,* University of North Texas, Libraries, Denton TX

Groshong, Mae, *Sec,* Cambridge Museum, Cambridge NE

Grosland, Roberta, *Registrar,* City of Woodstock, Woodstock Art Gallery, Woodstock ON

Grosowsky, Vera, *Instr,* Solano Community College, Division of Fine & Applied Art & Behavioral Science, Fairfield CA (S)

Gross, Benjamin, *Chmn Dept,* Salem State University, Art & Design Department, Salem MA (S)

Gross, Betsy, *Coordr Bd Mem,* Women in the Arts Foundation, Inc, Staten Island NY

Gross, Erik, *VPres Finance,* New Hampshire Institute of Art, Manchester NH

Gross, Jennifer, *Cur Modern & Contemporary Art,* Yale University, Yale University Art Gallery, New Haven CT

Gross, Julie, *Communs Dir,* Kentucky Museum of Art and Craft, Louisville KY

Gross, Katie, *Exec Admin,* The Stained Glass Association of America, Raytown MO

Gross, Kelly M, *Dir,* The Art Association of Jacksonville, The David Strawn Art Gallery, Jacksonville IL

Gross, Mimi, *Pres,* The Renee & Chaim Gross Foundation, Chaim Gross Studio, New York NY

Gross, Sarah, *Asst Prof,* Berea College, Art & Art History Program, Berea KY (S)

Grosser, Jean, *Prof Art, Chair,* Coker College, Art Dept, Hartsville SC (S)

Grossman, Arlene, *Chair Foundation,* Lesley University, College of Art & Design, Boston MA (S)

Grossman, Gilda S, *Dir Acad Prog & Internships,* Toronto Art Therapy Institute, Toronto ON (S)

Grossman, Grace Cohen, *Sr Cur,* Hebrew Union College, Skirball Cultural Center, Los Angeles CA

Grossman, Jim, *VPres Research & Educ,* Newberry Library, Chicago IL

Grossman, JoAnn, *Tour Coordr,* Frederick R Weisman, Los Angeles CA

Grosswiler, Shannon, *Dir Communs & Mktg,* Portland Children's Museum, Portland OR

Groth, Chuck, *Prof,* Saint Louis Community College at Meramec, Art Dept, Saint Louis MO (S)

Grou, Claude, *Oratory Rector,* Saint Joseph's Oratory, Museum, Montreal PQ

Grove, Lisa, *Deputy Dir,* Contemporary Art Museum St Louis, Saint Louis MO

Grove, Nancy, *Prof,* Long Island University, Brooklyn Campus, Art Dept, Brooklyn NY (S)

Grover, Kevin, *Dir,* National Museum of the American Indian, George Gustav Heye Center, New York NY

Grover, Ruth, *Dir & Cur,* University of Tennessee at Chattanooga, Cress Gallery of Art, Chattanooga TN

Grover, Ryan, *Cur,* Biggs Museum of American Art, Dover DE

Groves, Anne K, *Chair,* Historic Deerfield, Inc, Deerfield MA

Grow, Charlie, *Dep Dir,* Marine Corps University, National Museum of the Marine Corps, Triangle VA

Grow, Lana L, *Dir,* The Society of Layerists in Multi-Media (SLMM), Albuquerque NM

Grow, Stephanie, *Asst Exec Dir,* Elmhurst Art Museum, Elmhurst IL

Growborg, Erik, *Instr,* Miracosta College, Art Dept, Oceanside CA (S)

Groyl, Frank, *Instr,* Keystone College, Fine Arts Dept, LaPlume PA (S)

Grubb, Troy, *Asst Educ,* Pennsylvania Historical & Museum Commission, Railroad Museum of Pennsylvania, Harrisburg PA

Grubbs, Emily, *Cur Asst,* Southern Methodist University, Hamon Arts Library, Dallas TX

Grubbs, Kristen, *Educ Coordr,* Delaplaine Visual Arts Education Center, Frederick MD

Grubbs, Rhonda, *Instr,* Ohio Northern University, Dept of Art & Design, Ada OH (S)

Gruber, Doris, *Periodicals,* Trinity College Library, Washington DC

Gruber, John, *Asst Prof,* Southwest Baptist University, Art Dept, Bolivar MO (S)

Gruber, Linda, *Dir Information Servs & Electronic Systems,* Milwaukee Public Museum, Milwaukee WI

Grubola, James, *Chmn,* University of Louisville, Hite Art Institute, Louisville KY

Grubola, James T, *Chmn Dept Fine Arts, Dir Hite Art Institute,* University of Louisville, Allen R Hite Art Institute, Louisville KY (S)

Grubola, Kay, *Artistic Dir,* Louisville Visual Art Association, Louisville KY

Gruen, Vanessa, *Dir Special Projs,* Municipal Art Society of New York, New York NY

Gruendell, Lana, *Instr,* Salt Lake Community College, Graphic Design Dept, Salt Lake City UT (S)

Gruener, Mark, *Instr,* Wayne Art Center, Wayne PA (S)

Gruenwald, Helen, *Prof,* Kirkwood Community College, Dept of Arts & Humanities, Cedar Rapids IA (S)

Grumbine-Hornock, Penelope, *Adjunct,* York College of Pennsylvania, Dept of Music, Art & Speech Communications, York PA (S)

Grundy, Jane, *Asst Prof,* New York Institute of Technology, Fine Arts Dept, Old Westbury NY (S)

Gruner, Charles J, *Dir Lect & Demonstration Serv,* American Society of Artists, Inc, Palatine IL

Gruninger, Sandi, *Pres,* Wood Tobe-Coburn School, New York NY (S)

Gruol, David, *Pres,* Blackwell Street Center for the Arts, Denville NJ

Grupp, Carl A, *Chmn,* Augustana College, Art Dept, Sioux Falls SD (S)

Grutzeck, Laura, *Visual Resources & Special Colls Librn,* The University of the Arts, University Libraries, Philadelphia PA

Grynsztejn, Madeleine, *Dir,* Museum of Contemporary Art, Chicago IL

Grzesiak, Marion, *Cur & Dir,* Fraunces Tavern Museum, New York NY

Grzesiak, Marion, *Exec Dir,* Visual Arts Center of New Jersey, Summit NJ

Grzybek, Heather, *Horticulture Supv,* Palm Beach County Parks & Recreation Department, Morikami Museum & Japanese Gardens, Delray Beach FL

Grzywaca, Linda, *Annual Fund Coordr,* Honolulu Academy of Arts, The Art Center at Linekona, Honolulu HI (S)

Gu, Xiong, *Prof,* University of British Columbia, Dept of Art History, Visual Art & Theory, Vancouver BC (S)

Gu, Zhe, *Exec Dir,* Gallery Stratford, Stratford ON

Guadamuz, Susan, *Registrar Colls,* California African-American Museum, Los Angeles CA

Guajardo, Ruth M., *Arts Prog Dir,* Centro Cultural Aztlan, San Antonio TX

Guan, Zhimin, *Assoc Prof,* Minnesota State University-Moorhead, Dept of Art & Design, Moorhead MN (S)

Guarneiri, Sarisha, *Registrar,* Colgate University, Picker Art Gallery, Hamilton NY

Guava, Sig, *Prof,* Columbia University, Graduate School of Architecture, Planning & Preservation, New York NY (S)

Gubala, Darius, *Dir,* U Gallery, New York NY

Gubser, Rose Mary, *Exec Asst,* Manchester Bidwell Corporation, Manchester Craftsmen's Guild Youth & Arts Program, Pittsburgh PA

Guckes, Patty, *Instr,* Ocean City Arts Center, Ocean City NJ (S)

Gudenrath, William, *RA,* Corning Museum of Glass, The Studio, Corning NY

Gudmundsen, F Tor, *Instr,* Woodstock School of Art, Inc, Woodstock NY (S)

Guelce, Yvel, *Dir IT,* Indianapolis Museum of Art, Indianapolis IN

Guenther, Bruce, *Chief Cur & The Robert & Mercedes Eichholz Cur of Modern & Contemporary Art,* Portland Art Museum, Portland OR

Guenthler, John R, *Assoc Prof,* Indiana University-Southeast, Fine Arts Dept, New Albany IN (S)

Guerdat, Chelsea, *Registrar & Exhib Mgr,* Bass Museum of Art, Miami Beach FL

Guerin, Charles A, *Exec Dir,* University of Arizona, Museum of Art & Archive of Visual Arts, Tucson AZ

Guerin, Francesca Schuler, *Dir,* Schuler School of Fine Arts, Baltimore MD (S)

Guerin, Hans Schuler, *Asst Dir,* Schuler School of Fine Arts, Baltimore MD (S)

Guerin, Manon, *Dir,* Institut des Arts au Saguenay, Centre National D'Exposition a Jonquiere, Jonquiere PQ

Guernsey, Dan, *Assoc Prof,* Florida International University, School of Art & Art History, Miami FL (S)

Guernsey, Dawn, *Prof,* University of Kansas, The School of the Arts, Dept of Visual Art, Lawrence KS (S)

Guerrero, Francheska, *Interim Chair, Undergrad Design,* Corcoran School of Art, Washington DC (S)

Guerrero, Francisco, *Assoc Prof,* Seattle University, Dept of Fine Arts, Visual Art Division, Seattle WA (S)

Guerrero, Irma, *Dir Pub Rels,* Witte Museum, San Antonio TX

Guerrero, Tony, *Dir Operations,* PS1 Contemporary Art Center, Long Island City NY

Guess, Erika, *Pub Rels Assoc,* Contemporary Art Center of Virginia, Virginia Beach VA

Guest, Gerald, *Chmn,* John Carroll University, Dept of Art History & Humanities, University Heights OH (S)

Guest, Raechel, *Cur,* Lockwood-Mathews Mansion Museum, Norwalk CT

Guffin, R L, *Prof,* Stillman College, Stillman Art Gallery & Art Dept, Tuscaloosa AL (S)

Gugenheim, Lisa J, *VPres Government,* American Museum of Natural History, New York NY

Gugino, Jeanne, *Ceramic Dir,* Kaji Aso Studio, Gallery Nature & Temptation, Boston MA

Guglielmo, Rudy, *Expansion Arts Dir,* Arizona Commission on the Arts, Phoenix AZ

Guheen, Elizabeth, *Pres,* Ucross Foundation, Big Red Barn Gallery, Clearmont WY

Guichet, Melody, *Prof,* Louisiana State University, School of Art, Baton Rouge LA (S)

Guido, Jeff, *Artistic Dir,* Clay Studio, Philadelphia PA

Guidry, Keith J, *Cur,* Opelousas Museum of Art, Inc (OMA), Opelousas LA

Guigmon, Norah, *Marketing Mgr,* Society for Contemporary Craft, Pittsburgh PA

Guijarro, Charlie, *Opers Mgr,* Southern Methodist University, Meadows Museum, Dallas TX

Guilarte, Margarida, *Office Mgr,* Artists Talk on Art, New York NY

Guild, Henley, *Mus Preparator,* University of Richmond, University Museums, Richmond VA

Guild, Jennifer, *Media Rel Spec,* Virginia Historical Society, Library, Richmond VA

Guillot, Charlotte, *Asst Cur,* Lafayette Science Museum & Planetarium, Lafayette LA

Guilmette, Joanne, *Dir Commun,* New York State Museum, Albany NY

Guin, David S, *Exec Dir,* Bunte Gallery, Dublin OH

Guinn, Michael, *3rd VPres,* Plastic Club, Art Club, Philadelphia PA

Guinnee, Eli, *Dir,* Patterson Library & Art Gallery, Westfield NY

Guip, David, *Chmn,* University of Toledo, Dept of Art, Toledo OH (S)

Guleranson, Jim, *VPres,* San Fernando Valley Historical Society, Mark Harrington Library, Mission Hills CA

Gulezian, Mark, *Chief Photographer,* National Portrait Gallery, Smithsonian Institution, Washington DC

Gulley, Cheryl, *Assoc Prof Interior Design,* Watkins College of Art, Design & Film, Nashville TN (S)

Gulley, Christie, *Educ Asst,* The Center for Visual Artists - Greensboro, Greensboro NC

Gumerman, George J, *VPres,* Amerind Foundation, Inc, Amerind Museum, Fulton-Hayden Memorial Art Gallery, Dragoon AZ

Gummel, Rob, *Instr Guitar,* Ocean City Arts Center, Ocean City NJ (S)

Gumpert, Julie, *Gallery Mgr,* Academy of Motion Picture Arts & Sciences, The Academy Gallery, Beverly Hills CA

Gumpert, Lynn, *Dir,* New York University, Grey Art Gallery, New York NY

Gunderson, Barry, *Prof,* Kenyon College, Art Dept, Gambier OH (S)

Gunderson, Dan, *Prof,* Stetson University, Department of Creative Arts, Deland FL (S)

Gunderson, Jeff, *Librn,* San Francisco Art Institute, Anne Bremer Memorial Library, San Francisco CA

Gunderson, Keith, *Instr,* Woodstock School of Art, Inc, Woodstock NY (S)

Gunn, Barbara D, *Sr VPres Oper,* American Museum of Natural History, New York NY

Gunn, Don, *Dir Admin,* Allentown Art Museum, Allentown PA

Gunn, Kevin, *Head Humanities Div,* Catholic University of America, Humanities Library, Mullen Library, Washington DC

Gunn, Nancy, *Dir Museum Develop & Mem,* Wellesley College, Davis Museum & Cultural Center, Wellesley MA

Gunsch, Kathryn, *Assoc Cur & Dept Head Art of Africa, Asia, The Americas & Pacific Islands,* The Baltimore Museum of Art, Baltimore MD

Gunter, Michelle, *Dir Outreach,* Indianapolis Art Center, Marilyn K. Glick School of Art, Indianapolis IN

Guo, Feng, *Monitor/Technical Asst,* McMaster University, McMaster Museum of Art, Hamilton ON

Guppy, Susan, *Asst Prof,* Dalhousie University, Faculty of Architecture, Halifax NS (S)

Gura, Judith, *Area Coordr,* New York School of Interior Design, New York NY (S)

Guraedy, J Bruce, *Head Dept,* East Central Community College, Art Dept, Decatur MS (S)

Gureckas, Vytenis A, *Assoc Prof,* Catholic University of America, School of Architecture & Planning, Washington DC (S)

Gurley, Diana, *Pres,* Art Gallery of Bancroft Inc, Bancroft ON

Gurman, Deb, *Rec Secy,* Berks Art Alliance, Reading PA

Gurman, Fred, *Pres,* Berks Art Alliance, Reading PA

Gurney, A R, *VPres Literature,* American Academy of Arts & Letters, New York NY

Gurney, Janice, *Instr,* Toronto School of Art, Toronto ON (S)

Gurvets, Joseph, *Dir Technology,* John Simon Guggenheim, New York NY

Gurwitz, Danny, *Chmn Board Trustees,* Hidalgo County Historical Museum, Edinburg TX

Gury, Al, *Painting Dept Chair,* Pennsylvania Academy of the Fine Arts, Office of Admission, Philadelphia PA (S)

Gusler, Cyndi, *Chair,* Eastern Mennonite University, Art Dept, Harrisonburg VA (S)

Gussak, David, *Chmn Art Educ Dept,* Florida State University, Art Education Dept, Tallahassee FL (S)

Gustafson, Brian, *MFA,* New Jersey City University, Art Dept, Jersey City NJ (S)

Gustafson, Crandon, *Dept Chair,* Harrington Institute of Interior Design, Chicago IL (S)

Gustafson, Donna, *Dir Exhib,* Hunterdon Art Museum, Clinton NJ

Gustafson, Donna, *Liaison Acad Progs & Cur,* Rutgers, The State University of New Jersey, Zimmerli Art Museum, Rutgers University, New Brunswick NJ

Gustafson, Elaine, *Chief Cur,* Tampa Museum of Art, Tampa FL

Gustafson, Elaine D, *Cur Coll,* University of North Carolina at Greensboro, Weatherspoon Art Museum, Greensboro NC

Gustafson, Gary, *Asst Dir,* Plainsman Museum, Aurora NE

Gustafson, Julie, *Dir,* College of Marin, Art Gallery, Kentfield CA

Gustafson, Lisa, *IT,* Noyes Art Gallery, Lincoln NE

Gustafson, Maureen, *Dir,* Rockford College Art Gallery, Rockford IL

Gustafson, Paul, *Assoc Prof,* State University of New York at Farmingdale, Visual Communications, Farmingdale NY (S)

Gustafson, Peter, *Develop Coord,* See Science Center, Manchester NH

Gustafson, Roger, *Instr,* Elgin Community College, Fine Arts Dept, Elgin IL (S)

Gustavson, Carrie, *Cur Archival Coll,* Bisbee Arts & Humanities Council, Lemuel Shattuck Memorial Library, Bisbee AZ

Gustavson, Todd, *Cur Technology,* George Eastman, Museum, Rochester NY

Gustavson, Todd, *Cur Technology Coll,* George Eastman, Rochester NY

Guthier, Amy, *Develop Specialist,* University of Wisconsin-Madison, Chazen Museum of Art, Madison WI

Guthier, Mark, *Union Dir,* University of Wisconsin-Madison, Wisconsin Union Galleries, Madison WI

Guthrie, Emily, *Librn Printed Books & Periodical Coll,* Winterthur Museum, Garden & Library, Library, Winterthur DE

Guthrie, JoAnn, *Exec Adminr,* George Washington, Alexandria VA

Guthrie, Mareca, *Coordr Fine Arts,* University of Alaska, Museum of the North, Fairbanks AK

Guthworth, Sarah, *Asst Prof,* Murray State University, Dept of Art, Murray KY (S)

Gutierrez, Joe, *VPres Finance & CFO,* National YoungArts Foundation, Miami FL

Gutman, Bertha, *Prof,* Delaware County Community College, Communications, Art & Humanities, Media PA (S)

Guy, Heather, *Prog Dir,* Sloss Furnaces National Historic Landmark, Birmingham AL

Guy, Jody, *Instr Art Educ,* Pennsylvania State University, University Park, Penn State School of Visual Arts, University Park PA (S)

Guy, Leslie, *Cur Colls,* African American Museum in Philadelphia, Philadelphia PA

Guyer, Cynthia, *Dir External Affairs,* Rubin Museum of Art, New York NY

Guyer, Paul, *Pres,* American Society for Aesthetics, Pooler GA

Guyer, Rod, *Instr,* Solano Community College, Division of Fine & Applied Art & Behavioral Science, Fairfield CA (S)

Guynes, Jason, *Chmn,* University of West Alabama, Division of Fine Arts, Livingston AL (S)

Guynn, Janet, *Graphic Designer,* Auburn University, Julie Collins Smith Museum, Auburn AL

Guynn, Tod, *Asst Prof,* Cazenovia College, Center for Art & Design Studies, Cazenovia NY (S)

Guzman, Andy, *Commun Dir,* Sierra Arts Foundation, Sierra Arts Gallery, Reno NV

Guzman, Juana, *Assoc Dir*, National Museum of Mexican Art, Chicago IL

Gwynne, James, *Chmn & Prof*, County College of Morris, Art Dept, Randolph NJ (S)

Gylfe, Per, *Digital Media Labs*, International Center of Photography, School, New York NY (S)

Gylfe, Per, *Facilities Supv*, International Center of Photography, Rita K Hillman Education Gallery, New York NY

Gyllenhaal, C Edward, *Cur*, Academy of the New Church, Glencairn Museum, Bryn Athyn PA

Gyllensvard, Katherine, *Archival*, Cambridge Historical Commission, Research Library on Architectural Social History of Cambridge, Mass, Cambridge MA

Gyorody, Ninette, *Exec Dir*, Orillia Museum of Art & History, Orillia ON

Ha, Paul, *Exec Dir*, Contemporary Art Museum St Louis, Saint Louis MO

Haag, Pat, *Asst Dean*, Herkimer County Community College, Humanities Social Services, Herkimer NY (S)

Haag, Patty, *Asst Prof*, Spokane Falls Community College, Fine Arts Dept, Spokane WA (S)

Haagenson, Lynne, *Prof*, University of Idaho/College of Art & Architecture, Dept of Art & Design, Moscow ID (S)

Haapanen, Lawrence, *Prof*, Lewis-Clark State College, Art Dept, Lewiston ID (S)

Haar, Annemarie, *Digital Archivist*, California College of the Arts, Libraries, Oakland CA

Haarer, Anne, *Assoc Prof*, College of Saint Elizabeth, Art Dept, Morristown NJ (S)

Haas, David, *Instr*, Muhlenberg College, Dept of Art, Allentown PA (S)

Haas, Emma, *Asst to Dir Emer*, New Orleans Museum of Art, New Orleans LA

Haas, Karen, *Lane Coll Curator Photographs*, Museum of Fine Arts, Boston MA

Haas, Tara, *Visual Resources Librn*, Columbus College of Art & Design, Packard Library, Columbus OH

Haas, V Heidi, *Head Reference Coll*, The Morgan Library & Museum, Library, New York NY

Haase, William, *VPres*, National Baseball Hall of Fame & Museum, Inc, Art Collection, Cooperstown NY

Habarth, Gerald, *Assoc Prof*, West Virginia University, College of Creative Arts, School of Art & Design, Morgantown WV (S)

Habeger, Hans, *Drawing & Design*, College of Lake County, Art Dept, Grayslake IL (S)

Haberle, Mary, *Proj Cataloguer*, Franklin Furnace Archive, Inc, Brooklyn NY

Haberman, Donna, *Sr Objects Conservator*, Midwest Art Conservation Center, Minneapolis MN

Haberman, Lise, *Office Mgr*, The Renaissance Society, Chicago IL

Haberman, Patty, *Cur*, Mesa Arts Center, Mesa Contemporary Arts Museum, Mesa AZ

Hachey, Michael C, *Assoc Prof*, Worcester State College, Visual & Performing Arts Dept, Worcester MA (S)

Hachmeister, John, *Assoc Prof*, University of Kansas, The School of the Arts, Dept of Visual Art, Lawrence KS (S)

Hackbardt, Marcella M, *Assoc Prof*, Kenyon College, Art Dept, Gambier OH (S)

Hacker, Katherine, *Asst Prof*, University of British Columbia, Dept of Art History, Visual Art & Theory, Vancouver BC (S)

Hacker, Kathy, *Exec Asst to Pres*, The Huntington Library, Art Collections & Botanical Gardens, Library, San Marino CA

Hacker, Robert G, *Paul & Louise Miller Prof*, Rochester Institute of Technology, School of Printing Management & Sciences, Rochester NY (S)

Hackwelder, Michell, *Information Serv Supv*, Ferguson Library, Stamford CT

Hacleer, Kathy, *Exec Asst to Pres*, The Huntington Library, Art Collections & Botanical Gardens, San Marino CA

Hadacek, Lori, *Adjunct*, Waldorf College, Art Dept, Forest City IA (S)

Hadaway, Sandra S, *Admin*, Telfair Museums' Jepson Center for the Arts Library, Savannah GA

Hadaway, Sandra S, *Admin*, Telfair Museums' Jepson Center for the Arts Library, Telfair Academy of Arts & Sciences Library, Savannah GA

Haddad, Farid A, *Prof*, New England College, Art & Art History, Henniker NH (S)

Hadden, Helen, *Librn*, Art Gallery of Hamilton, Muriel Isabel Bostwick Library, Hamilton ON

Hadler, Mona, *Prof*, City University of New York, PhD Program in Art History, New York NY (S)

Hadley, Richard, *Dir Mus Exhibs & Opers*, Colonial Williamsburg Foundation, Abby Aldrich Rockefeller Folk Art Museum, Williamsburg VA

Hadley, Richard, *Dir Mus Exhibs & Opers*, Colonial Williamsburg Foundation, DeWitt Wallace Decorative Arts Museum, Williamsburg VA

Hadsel, Alice, *Mus Store Mgr*, Alaska State Museum, Juneau AK

Hafemann, Amy, *Graphic Designer*, Museum of Wisconsin Art, West Bend WI

Hafer, Linda, *Exec Dir*, The Art League Gallery & School, Alexandria VA

Hafer, Mark K, *Pres*, Victor Heritage Museum, Victor MT

Haffar, Nadra E, *Educ Cur*, Utah State University, Nora Eccles Harrison Museum of Art, Logan UT

Hagan, Angela, *Develop Dir*, Kentucky Museum of Art and Craft, Louisville KY

Hagan, Kathy, *Chmn 3-D Studies*, Bowling Green State University, School of Art, Bowling Green OH (S)

Hage, Emily, *Prof Art History*, Saint Joseph's University, Art Dept, Philadelphia PA (S)

Hagedorn, Bernard, *Assoc Prof*, Vincennes University Junior College, Humanities Art Dept, Vincennes IN (S)

Hagedorn, Christine, *Instr*, Marygrove College, Department of Art, Detroit MI (S)

Hagedorn, Deborah, *Assoc Prof*, Vincennes University Junior College, Humanities Art Dept, Vincennes IN (S)

Hageman, George, *Prof*, Sinclair Community College, Division of Fine & Performing Arts, Dayton OH (S)

Hageman, George, *Vice Pres*, Cincinnati Art Club, Cincinnati OH

Hagemeyer, Jim, *Chmn*, Heidelberg College, Dept of Art, Tiffin OH (S)

Hager, Greg, *Dir*, Willard Library, Dept of Fine Arts, Evansville IN

Hager, Hellmut, *Evan Pugh Prof Emeritus*, Pennsylvania State University, University Park, Dept of Art History, University Park PA (S)

Hager, Michael, *Asst Prof*, Washburn University of Topeka, Dept of Art, Topeka KS (S)

Hagerman, Sharon, *Admin Asst*, Owensboro Museum of Fine Art, Owensboro KY

Haggerty, Barbara, *Pres*, Erie Art Museum, Erie PA

Haggerty, Christine, *Prof*, Marymount University, School of Arts & Sciences Div, Arlington VA (S)

Hagood, John, *Reference Librn*, National Gallery of Art, Library, Washington DC

Hahn, Alex, *Secy & Office Coordr*, Syracuse University, SUArt Galleries, Syracuse NY

Hahn, Bryan, *Gallery Mgr*, Eastern New Mexico University, Runnels Gallery, Golden Library, Portales NM

Hahn, Cynthia J, *Prof*, Florida State University, Art History Dept, Tallahassee FL (S)

Hahn, Dorothy, *Instr*, Hannibal La Grange College, Art Dept, Hannibal MO (S)

Hahn, Elizabeth, *Librn*, American Numismatic Society, Library, New York NY

Hahn, Eric, *Industrial Design Technology*, Art Institute of Pittsburgh, Pittsburgh PA (S)

Hahn, Mary, *Pres & Dance Specialist*, Northfield Arts Guild, Northfield MN

Hahne, Freddie, *Pres*, Eyes & Ears Foundation, San Francisco CA

Haidet, Mark, *Develop Officer*, Minnesota Historical Society, Saint Paul MN

Haien, Gretchen, *Instr*, Belhaven College, Art Dept, Jackson MS (S)

Haigh, Kathryn, *Chief Registrar*, Indianapolis Museum of Art, Indianapolis IN

Haight, Bonnie, *Gallery Mgr*, Creative Growth Art Center, Oakland CA

Hailey, Dabney, *Cur*, Wellesley College, Davis Museum & Cultural Center, Wellesley MA

Haiman, Kurt, *Pres*, Belskie Museum, Closter NJ

Haimes, Ann, *Acting Dir*, Atlanta-Fulton Public Library, Central Library Art Gallery, Atlanta GA

Hainanaka, Mayumi, *Commus Mgr & Registrar*, Kala Institute, Kala Art Institute, Berkeley CA

Haines, Annette, *Art & Design Field Librn*, University of Michigan, Media Union Library, Ann Arbor MI

Haines, Lee, *Dir Pub Rels*, Buffalo Bill Memorial Association, Buffalo Bill Historical Center, Cody WY

Hairston, Michael, *Dir Finance*, Historical Society of Pennsylvania, Philadelphia PA

Haizlett, Jim, *Assoc Prof*, West Liberty State College, Div Art, West Liberty WV (S)

Hajian, Paul, *Chair Environmental Design*, Massachusetts College of Art, Boston MA (S)

Hake, Carol, *Exhibits Chmn*, Gallery 9, Los Altos CA

Hakim, Sy, *Pub Chmn*, American Color Print Society, Huntingdon Valley PA

Hakimzadeh, Heather, *Assoc Cur*, Contemporary Art Center of Virginia, Virginia Beach VA

Hala, Natalie A, *Exec Dir*, San Francisco Arts Education Project, San Francisco CA

Halaby, Raouf, *Prof*, Ouachita Baptist University, Dept of Visual Art, Arkadelphia AR (S)

Halbert, Nancy, *Dir*, Muse Art Gallery, Philadelphia PA

Halbreich, Kathy, *Dir*, Walker Art Center, Minneapolis MN

Hale, Alma, *Asst Prof*, Murray State University, Dept of Art, Murray KY (S)

Hale, Ann, *Advancement Dir*, Anchorage Museum at Rasmuson Center, Anchorage AK

Hale, Christine, *Dir Mktg*, University of Florida, Samuel P Harn Museum of Art, Gainesville FL

Hale, David, *Instr*, Goddard College, Dept of Art, Plainfield VT (S)

Hale, Jack, *1st VPres*, Fishkill Historical Society, Van Wyck Homestead Museum, Fishkill NY

Hale, Linda, *Adjunct*, Feather River Community College, Art Dept, Quincy CA (S)

Hale, Marlene, *Admin Asst*, McDowell House & Apothecary Shop, Danville KY

Hale, Nathan Cabot, *Pres*, Ages of Man Foundation, Amenia NY

Hales, Andrea, *Librn*, Museum of Contemporary Art, San Diego, Geisel Library, La Jolla CA

Halevy, Richard, *Dir Community Devel*, The Hudson River Museum, Yonkers NY

Haley, Laura, *Vol Treas*, Rangeley Lakes Region Logging Museum, Rangeley ME

Haley, Pat, *VPres*, Coquille Valley Art Association, Coquille OR

Halford-MacLeod, Johanna, *Ed-in-Chief*, The Phillips Collection, Washington DC

Hall, Alana, *Gift Shop Mgr & Admin Asst*, South Peace Art Society, Dawson Creek Art Gallery, Dawson Creek BC

Hall, Andy, *Chmn Architecture - Interior Architecture & Designed Objects*, School of the Art Institute of Chicago, Chicago IL (S)

Hall, Brenda, *Office Mgr*, Morris Museum of Art, Augusta GA

Hall, Christopher, *Cur*, Maine Maritime Museum, Bath ME

Hall, Dale, *Dir*, Oklahoma City University, Scheme Shop, Oklahoma City OK

Hall, Daniel, *Asst Prof*, Indiana Wesleyan University, School of Arts & Humanities, Division of Art, Marion IN (S)

Hall, Doug, *Prof*, Kirkwood Community College, Dept of Arts & Humanities, Cedar Rapids IA (S)

Hall, Eli M, *Asst Prof*, Colorado Mesa University, Art Dept, Grand Junction CO (S)

Hall, Frances, *Librn*, Vizcaya Museum & Gardens, Vizcaya Volunteer Guides Library, Miami FL

Hall, Gail, *Pres*, Dawson County Historical Society, Museum, Lexington NE

Hall, Gaines, *Assoc Dean*, University of Illinois, Urbana-Champaign, College of Fine & Applied Arts, Champaign IL (S)

Hall, Harry, *Pres*, Wiregrass Museum of Art, Dothan AL

Hall, Katherine, *Admin*, Utah Valley University, Woodbury Art Museum, Orem UT

Hall, Kit, *Dean Art Dept*, Texas Wesleyan University, Dept of Art, Fort Worth TX (S)

Hall, Lauren, *Visual Arts Mgr*, The Cultural Arts Center at Glen Allen, Glen Allen VA

Hall, Laurilyn, *Instr*, Bob Jones University, School of Fine Arts, Div of Art & Design, Greenville SC (S)

Hall, Lisa H, *VPres,* Marcella Sembrich Memorial Association Inc, Marcella Sembrich Opera Museum, Bolton Landing NY

Hall, Mark, *Chmn,* Maryville College, Fine Arts Center Gallery, Maryville TN

Hall, Mark, *Instr,* Butte College, Dept of Fine Arts and Communication Tech, Oroville CA (S)

Hall, Mark, *Mgr Art, Music, Bus & Technical Science,* San Francisco Public Library, Art & Music Center, San Francisco CA

Hall, Mary-Anne, *Cur Educ,* Norwich Free Academy, Slater Memorial Museum, Norwich CT

Hall, Michael, *Adjunct Cur Folk Art,* Columbus Museum of Art, Columbus OH

Hall, Ray, *Dir,* Mexico-Audrain County Library, Mexico MO

Hall, Richard, *Sr Preparator,* The Pennsylvania State University, Palmer Museum of Art, University Park PA

Hall, Robert, *Acting Dir Educ & Outreach,* Anacostia Community Museum, Smithsonian Institution, Washington DC

Hall, Sarah, *Dir Cur Affairs,* The Frick Art & Historical Center, Inc, Frick Art Museum, Pittsburgh PA

Hall, Steven B, *Dir,* Regis College, Carney Gallery, Weston MA

Hall, Suzanne, *Assoc Dir Communs & Mktg,* Virginia Museum of Fine Arts, Richmond VA

Hall, Thom, *Registrar,* Arkansas Arts Center, Little Rock AR

Hall, Thom, *Registrar,* Arkansas Arts Center, Museum, Little Rock AR (S)

Hall, Verna, *Pres,* Tyler Museum of Art, Tyler TX

Hall, Walter, *Assoc Prof,* University of Hartford, Hartford Art School, West Hartford CT (S)

Hall, Wanda, *Asst Librn,* United Methodist Historical Society, Lovely Lane Museum, Baltimore MD

Hall, Wayne, *Adjunct Asst Prof,* University of Maine, Dept of Art, Orono ME (S)

Hall-Cheathan, Tomella, *Bus Mgr,* Craftsmen's Guild of Mississippi, Inc, Mississippi Crafts Center, Ridgeland MS

Hallahan, Ed, *Preparator,* The Butler Institute of American Art, Art Museum, Youngstown OH

Hallam, John, *Chmn,* Pacific Lutheran University, Dept of Art, Tacoma WA (S)

Hallatt, Kim, *Dir Admin,* University of Rochester, Memorial Art Gallery, Rochester NY

Halleck, Charles W, *Treas,* Gallery 9, Los Altos CA

Haller, Robert A, *Dir Colls & Spec Projs,* Anthology Film Archives, New York NY

Hallet, Stanley I, *Prof,* Catholic University of America, School of Architecture & Planning, Washington DC (S)

Hallett, Megan, *Cur Educ,* University of Utah, Utah Museum of Fine Arts, Salt Lake City UT

Hallett, Phyllis, *Secy,* Moncur Gallery, Boissevain MB

Halliday, Betsy, *Mktg Dir,* Brookfield Craft Center, Inc, Gallery, Brookfield CT

Hallman, Gary, *Assoc Prof,* University of Minnesota, Minneapolis, Dept of Art, Minneapolis MN (S)

Hallman, Kirk, *Develop Officer,* Muskegon Museum of Art, Muskegon MI

Hallman, Linda D, *Exec Dir,* American Association of University Women, Washington DC

Hallman, Tim, *Pub Rels Mgr,* Asian Art Museum of San Francisco, Chong-Moon Lee Ctr for Asian Art and Culture, San Francisco CA

Hallock, Robert, *Pres,* Greene County Historical Society, Bronck Museum, Coxsackie NY

Hall Smith, Beverly, *Asst Prof,* Marygrove College, Department of Art, Detroit MI (S)

Halman, Doug, *Dir Finance,* Indianapolis Art Center, Marilyn K. Glick School of Art, Indianapolis IN

Halpern, Emily, *Dir Communs,* The Dixon Gallery & Gardens, Memphis TN

Halpern, Robert, *Theater Mgr,* Art & Culture Center of Hollywood, Art Gallery/Multidisciplinary Cultural Center, Hollywood FL

Halter, Susan, *Contact,* Lynn Arts, Lynn MA

Haltman, Kenneth, *Prog Head,* Michigan State University, Dept of Art & Art History, East Lansing MI (S)

Halushak, Richard, *Pres,* Art Center College of Design, Pasadena CA (S)

Halverson, Jackie, *Instr,* Mount Mary College, Art & Design Division, Milwaukee WI (S)

Halvorson, Liza, *Ceramics,* North Seattle Community College, Art Dept, Seattle WA (S)

Halvorson, Richard, *Museum Coordr,* Brown County Art Gallery Foundation, Nashville IN

Ham, Ethan, *Assoc Prof,* City College of New York, Art Dept, New York NY (S)

Hamanaka, Takuji, *Instr,* Manhattan Graphics Center, New York NY (S)

Hamann, Brad, *Chair Art, Asst Prof Art & Graphic Design,* Eastern New Mexico University, Runnels Gallery, Golden Library, Portales NM

Hambleton, Judy, *Dir Educ,* Newport Art Museum and Association, Newport RI

Hamblin, Diane, *Doll Cur,* Wenham Museum, Wenham MA

Hambourg, Maria Morris, *Cur In Charge Photog,* The Metropolitan Museum of Art, New York NY

Hamburb, Paul, *Librn,* University of California, Berkeley, Blumenthal Rare Book & Manuscript Library, Berkeley CA

Hamby, Thomas L, *Chmn,* Birmingham Museum of Art, Birmingham AL

Hamel, Joanne, *Mem Svcs,* Alberta Craft Council, Edmonton AB

Hamel, Teresa, *Treas,* Warwick Museum of Art, Warwick RI

Hamer, Fritz, *Cultural History Chief Cur,* South Carolina State Museum, Columbia SC

Hamer, Linnea, *Cur Exhibits,* American Architectural Foundation, The Octagon Museum, Washington DC

Hamerman, Jesse, *Project Mgr,* Public Art Fund, Inc, New York NY

Hamerman, Jesse, *Project Mgr,* Public Art Fund, Inc, Visual Archive, New York NY

Hamilton, Cindi, *Exec Dir,* Carteret County Historical Society, The History Place, Morehead City NC

Hamilton, Cindy, *Visitor Svcs,* University of Louisiana at Lafayette, Paul and Lulu Hilliard University Art Museum, Lafayette LA

Hamilton, Dotty, *Visual Commun Chair,* Avila University, Thornhill Art Gallery, Kansas City MO

Hamilton, Douglas, *Pres,* Walters Art Museum, Library, Baltimore MD

Hamilton, Douglas W, *Pres Bd Trustees,* Walters Art Museum, Baltimore MD

Hamilton, Frederic C, *Chmn,* Denver Art Museum, Denver CO

Hamilton, J Hank, *Fine Arts Dept Chmn,* Cheyney University of Pennsylvania, Dept of Art, Cheyney PA (S)

Hamilton, Jennifer, *Dir,* Appaloosa Museum and Heritage Center, Moscow ID

Hamilton, Kathy, *COO,* Bowers Museum, Santa Ana CA

Hamilton, Ken, *Pres,* New Jersey Watercolor Society, Parsippany NJ

Hamilton, Laurie, *Fine Arts Conservator,* Art Gallery of Nova Scotia, Halifax NS

Hamilton, Lynn, *Dir Admin,* Discovery Museum, Bridgeport CT

Hamilton, Paula, *Head Librn,* Mount Angel Abbey Library, Saint Benedict OR

Hamilton, Roy, *Cur Asian & Pacific Art,* University of California, Los Angeles, Fowler Museum at UCLA, Los Angeles CA

Hamilton, Wendy, *Dir,* Central United Methodist Church, Swords Into Plowshares Peace Center & Gallery, Detroit MI

Hamlin, Amy, *Asst Prof,* St. Catherine University, Art & Art History Dept, Saint Paul MN (S)

Hamm, Beccy, *Educ & Special Events,* Rose Center & Council for the Arts, Morristown TN

Hamm, Harry, *Colls Coordr,* St Mary's University, Art Gallery, Halifax NS

Hamm, Monte, *Acting Chmn,* Kentucky Wesleyan College, Dept Art, Owensboro KY (S)

Hamm, Rachel, *Bus Mgr,* Utah State University, Nora Eccles Harrison Museum of Art, Logan UT

Hammer, Karen, *Dir Art Educ,* Coos Art Museum, Coos Bay OR

Hammer, Karen, *Dir Art Educ,* Coos Art Museum, Coos Bay OR (S)

Hammerstrom, Kirsten, *Coll Cur,* Rhode Island Historical Society, Providence RI

Hammerstrom, Kirsten, *Cur,* Rhode Island Historical Society, John Brown House, Providence RI

Hammerstrom, Kirsten, *Deputy Dir Colls,* Rhode Island Historical Society, Library, Providence RI

Hammett, Beverly, *Dir,* Webster Parish Library, Minden LA

Hammett, Kevin, *Prog Management Specialist,* University of Maryland, College Park, National Trust for Historic Preservation Library Collection, College Park MD

Hammock, April, *Lectr,* Southeastern Louisiana University, Dept of Visual Arts, Hammond LA (S)

Hammock, Hill, *Vice Chmn,* Chicago History Museum, Chicago IL

Hammond, Amy, *Exhibs Mgr,* Susquehanna Art Museum, Harrisburg PA

Hammond, Jennifer, *Dir Educ,* Museum of Fine Arts Houston, Bayou Bend Collection & Gardens, Houston TX

Hammond, Susan G, *Exec Dir,* National Association of Women Artists, Inc, N.A.W.A. Gallery, New York NY

Hammond, Theresa, *Dir & Cur,* Guilford College, Art Gallery, Greensboro NC

Hammond, Wayne G, *Asst Librn,* Williams College, Chapin Library, Williamstown MA

Hammond-Hagman, Hannah, *Dir Educ,* Munroe Center for the Arts, Lexington MA (S)

Hammonds, Hollis, *Dir,* Saint Edward's University, Fine Arts Gallery, Austin TX

Hammontree, Eddie, *Librn,* Webster Parish Library, Minden LA

Hamm Walsh, Dawna, *Head Art Dept,* Dallas Baptist University, Dept of Art, Dallas TX (S)

Hamon, Amanda Martin, *Docent Coordr,* University of Kansas, Spencer Museum of Art, Lawrence KS

Hamon, Rodney, *Educ Dir,* University of New Mexico, Tamarind Institute, Albuquerque NM (S)

Hampton, Dan, *Graphics Dir,* Gadsden Museum of Fine Arts, Inc, Gadsden Museum of Art and History, Gadsden AL

Hampton, Sandra, *Bookkeeper,* Southern Alleghenies Museum of Art, Loretto Facility, Loretto PA

Hamrick Ferrara, Dana, *Instr,* Dallas Baptist University, Dept of Art, Dallas TX (S)

Hamwi, Richard, *Asst Prof,* Albright College, Dept of Art, Reading PA (S)

Han, Angela, *Dir Res,* National Assembly of State Arts Agencies, Washington DC

Han, Helen, *Mktg Coordr,* Boston Properties LLC, San Francisco CA

Hanahan, Martin, *Registrar,* Boca Raton Museum of Art, Boca Raton FL

Hanami, Clement, *Dir Support Svcs,* Japanese American National Museum, Los Angeles CA

Hanbury-Tenison, William, *Asst Dir,* Pacific - Asia Museum, Pasadena CA

Hancock, Blair, *Dir,* Wilkes Community College, Arts & Science Division, Wilkesboro NC (S)

Hancock, John, *Prof,* University of Mary Hardin-Baylor, College of Visual & Performing Arts, Belton TX (S)

Hancock, Kathleen, *Asst Prof,* Roger Williams University, Visual Art Dept, Bristol RI (S)

Hancock, Mariko, *Coordr,* Castleton State College, Art Dept, Castleton VT (S)

Hancock, Sherry, *Dept Chmn,* Langara College, Department of Design: Design Formation, Vancouver BC (S)

Hand, Jamie, *Dir Progs & Devel,* Van Alen Institute, New York NY

Hand-Evans, Dana, *Cur,* National Society of the Colonial Dames of America in The Commonwealth of Virginia, Wilton House Museum, Richmond VA

Handel, Cynthia, *Asst Prof,* Louisiana State University, School of Art, Baton Rouge LA (S)

Handelsman, Rebecca, *Sr Mktg & Commun Mgr,* Museum of Contemporary Art San Diego, San Diego CA

Handelsman, Rebecca, *Sr Communs & Mktg Mgr,* Museum of Contemporary Art, San Diego, La Jolla CA

Handler, Linda, *Dir,* Phoenix Gallery, New York NY

Handman, Gary, *Pub Servs Coordr,* University of California, Berkeley, The Magnes Collection of Jewish Art & Life, Berkeley CA

Handsloser, Diane, *Chmn,* Santa Barbara City College, Fine Arts Dept, Santa Barbara CA (S)

Handy, Christopher, *Technical Servs Librn,* Saint Louis Art Museum, Richardson Memorial Library, Saint Louis MO

Handy, Ellen, *Assoc Prof,* City College of New York, Art Dept, New York NY (S)

Handysides, Barb, *Pres,* South Peace Art Society, Dawson Creek Art Gallery, Dawson Creek BC

Hane, Maria, *Exec Dir,* Museum of Science & History, Jacksonville FL

Hanel, Jodi, *Dir Devel,* The Queens Museum of Art, Flushing NY

Hanen, Jenifer, *Instr,* Biola University, Art Dept, La Mirada CA (S)

Haney, Judith, *Mem & Develop Coordr,* Canadian Conference of the Arts, Ottawa ON

Haney, Kristine, *Assoc Prof,* University of Massachusetts, Amherst, Art History Program, Amherst MA (S)

Haney, Lou, *Asst Prof,* University of Mississippi, Department of Art, University MS (S)

Haney, Nick, *Adjunct Assoc Prof Fine Art,* Johnson County Community College, Fine Arts Dept & Art History Dept, Overland Park KS (S)

Haney, Rich, *VPres Educ Affairs,* College of Lake County, Art Dept, Grayslake IL (S)

Hanger, Anne, *Vis Artist,* Mary Baldwin College, Dept of Art & Art History, Staunton VA (S)

Hanger, Barbara, *Assoc Prof,* University of Louisville, Allen R Hite Art Institute, Louisville KY (S)

Hankewych, Jaroslaw J, *Dir & Pres,* Ukrainian National Museum & Library, Chicago IL

Hankins, Roger, *Dir,* University of California, Memorial Union Art Gallery, Davis CA

Hanks, Richard, *Assoc Archivist,* Lincoln Memorial Shrine, Redlands CA

Hanlon, David, *Prof,* Saint Louis Community College at Meramec, Art Dept, Saint Louis MO (S)

Hann, Richard, *Chmn Dept Humanities,* Imperial Valley College, Art Dept, Imperial CA (S)

Hanna, Annette Adrian, *VPres,* Blackwell Street Center for the Arts, Denville NJ

Hanna, Emily, *Cur Americas & Africa,* Birmingham Museum of Art, Clarence B Hanson Jr Library, Birmingham AL

Hanna, Emily, *Cur Arts of Africa & Americas,* Birmingham Museum of Art, Birmingham AL

Hanna, Fred, *Chmn Fine & Performing Arts Dept,* Creighton University, Lied Art Gallery, Omaha NE

Hanna, Martha, *Dir,* Canadian Museum of Contemporary Photography, Ottawa ON

Hanna, Matthew, *Gallery Asst,* Detroit Artists Market, Detroit MI

Hanna, William, *Dean,* Humber College of Applied Arts & Technology, The School of Media Studies, Toronto ON (S)

Hannaford, Joey, *Acad Professional Graphic Design,* University of Georgia, Franklin College of Arts & Sciences, Lamar Dodd School of Art, Athens GA (S)

Hannah, Cassie, *Instr,* Weatherford College, Dept of Speech Fine Arts, Weatherford TX (S)

Hannah, Kimberly, *Libr Asst,* New York University, Stephen Chan Library of Fine Arts, New York NY

Hannah, Will, *Systems Librn,* The Cleveland Museum of Art, Ingalls Library, Cleveland OH

Hannan, Catalina, *Librn,* Historic Hudson Valley, Pocantico Hills NY

Hannan, Catalina, *Librn,* Historic Hudson Valley, Library, Pocantico Hills NY

Hannan, Sarah, *Dir,* South Shore Art Center, Cohasset MA

Hanner, Erika, *Educ Dir,* Museum of Contemporary Art, Chicago IL

Hanni, Jane, *Asst Cur Educ,* Washburn University, Mulvane Art Museum, Topeka KS

Hannibal, Joe, *Prof,* California State Polytechnic University, Pomona, Department of Art, Pomona CA (S)

Hanninen, Kim, *Registrar,* Northwestern Michigan College, Dennos Museum Center, Traverse City MI

Hanor, Stephanie, *Cur,* Museum of Contemporary Art, San Diego, Geisel Library, La Jolla CA

Hanor, Stephanie, *Dir,* Mills College Art Museum, Oakland CA

Hanover, Lisa Tremper, *Dir,* James A Michener, Doylestown PA

Han Palermo, Toni, *Programs Specialist,* Judiciary History Center, Honolulu HI

Hanrahan, Thomas, *Dean,* Pratt Institute, School of Architecture, Brooklyn NY (S)

Hanru, Hou, *Dir Exhibs & Pub Progs,* San Francisco Art Institute, Galleries, San Francisco CA

Hansalik, Konrad, *Pres,* American Artists Professional League, Inc, New York NY

Hansberry, Jane, *Managing Dir,* Think 360 Art Complete Education, Colo Chapter, Denver CO

Hansel, Debbie, *Asst,* North Canton Public Library, The Little Art Gallery, North Canton OH

Hansen, Al, *Instr Pottery,* Bay De Noc Community College, Art Dept, Escanaba MI (S)

Hansen, Cindy, *Admin Asst,* University of Chicago, Smart Museum of Art, Chicago IL

Hansen, Elaine, *Pres,* Bates College, Art & Visual Culture, Lewiston ME (S)

Hansen, Gregory, *Folklife Adminr,* Florida Folklife Programs, Tallahassee FL

Hansen, Harry, *Asst Chmn,* University of South Carolina, Dept of Art, Columbia SC (S)

Hansen, Hugh, *Accounting Mgr,* The Winnipeg Art Gallery, Winnipeg MB

Hansen, Linda, *Metals Dept Head,* Worcester Center for Crafts, Worcester MA (S)

Hansen, Lorraine, *Exec Dir,* Ocean City Art Center, Ocean City NJ

Hansen, Lorraine, *Exec Dir,* Ocean City Arts Center, Ocean City NJ (S)

Hansen, Matt, *Preservation Architect,* Nebraska State Capitol, Lincoln NE

Hansen, Moya, *Cur Decorative & Fine Arts,* Colorado Historical Society, Colorado History Museum, Denver CO

Hansen, Pearl, *Chmn Art,* Wayne State College, Nordstrand Visual Arts Gallery, Wayne NE

Hansen, Pearl, *Prof,* Wayne State College, Dept Art & Design, Wayne NE (S)

Hansen, Richard, *Assoc Prof,* University of Southern Colorado, Dept of Art, Pueblo CO (S)

Hansen, Roland C, *Head Access Serv,* Columbia College Chicago, Library, Chicago IL

Hansen, Sandi, *Dir,* Sonoma Valley Historical Society, Depot Park Museum, Sonoma CA

Hansen, Steve, *Prof,* Andrews University, Dept of Art, Art History & Design, Berrien Springs MI (S)

Hansen, Victoria, *Assoc Prof,* University of Southern Colorado, Dept of Art, Pueblo CO (S)

Hanson, Brent, *Chmn,* Dixie College, Art Dept, Saint George UT (S)

Hanson, Colleen W, *Dir & Cur,* Gallery North, Setauket NY

Hanson, Doug, *Prof,* Cornell College, Peter Paul Luce Gallery, Mount Vernon IA

Hanson, Elizabeth, *Asst Cur,* California State University, Long Beach, University Art Museum, Long Beach CA

Hanson, Emma, *Cur Plains Indian Museum,* Buffalo Bill Memorial Association, Buffalo Bill Historical Center, Cody WY

Hanson, Jacquelyn, *Adjunct Asst Prof Art Educ,* Florida Southern College, Melvin Art Gallery, Lakeland FL

Hanson, Jacquelyn, *Adjunct Asst Prof Art Educ,* Florida Southern College, Department of Art & Art History, Lakeland FL (S)

Hanson, Jennifer, *Office Mgr,* Schenectady County Historical Society, Museum of Schenectady History, Schenectady NY

Hanson, Jody, *Sr Art Preparator,* The Buffalo Fine Arts Academy, Albright-Knox Art Gallery, Buffalo NY

Hanson, Lars, *VPres,* Wayne County Historical Society, Museum, Honesdale PA

Hanson, Lowell, *Instr Art,* Everett Community College, Art Dept, Everett WA (S)

Hanson, Robert, *Instr,* Pacific Northwest College of Art, Portland OR (S)

Hanson, Shannon, *Mktg Mgr,* Georgia O'Keeffe Museum, Santa Fe NM

Hantman, Alan M, *Architect of the Capitol,* United States Capitol, Architect of the Capitol, Washington DC

Hanworth, John, *Dir Heye Ctr,* National Museum of the American Indian, George Gustav Heye Center, New York NY

Hanzel, Yvette A, *Dir Mktg,* Beck Center for the Arts, Lakewood OH

Hanzich, Kim, *Info Mgr,* Art Directors Club, New York NY

Hapgood, Susan, *Exhib Dir,* Independent Curators International, New York NY

Hapgood, Thomas, *Asst Prof,* University of Arkansas, Art Dept, Fayetteville AR (S)

Harada, Gwen, *Keeper Lending,* Honolulu Academy of Arts, The Art Center at Linekona, Honolulu HI (S)

Harbage-Page, Susan, *Instr,* University of North Carolina at Chapel Hill, Art Dept, Chapel Hill NC (S)

Harber, Laine, *Bus Mgr,* Arkansas Arts Center, Museum, Little Rock AR (S)

Harber, Laine, *CFO,* Arkansas Arts Center, Little Rock AR

Harbison, Burt, *Gallery Dir,* Oklahoma City University, Hulsey Gallery-Norick Art Center, Oklahoma City OK

Harbison, Craig, *Prof,* University of Massachusetts, Amherst, Art History Program, Amherst MA (S)

Harbison, Mary Jane, *Library Technical Servs Coordr,* Amon Carter Museum of American Art, Research Library, Fort Worth TX

Harbour, Robert, *Mktg,* World Erotic Art Museum, Miami Beach FL

Harcourt, Carolyn, *Asst to Dir,* Willamette University, Hallie Ford Museum of Art, Salem OR

Hard, Michael W, *Pres,* Amerind Foundation, Inc, Amerind Museum, Fulton-Hayden Memorial Art Gallery, Dragoon AZ

Hard, Nicole, *Asst Prof,* Murray State University, Dept of Art, Murray KY (S)

Harde, Grace, *Trustee & Dir,* Aidron Duckworth Art Preservation Trust, Aidron Duckworth Art Museum, Meriden NH

Harden, Andrea Griffa, *HR Mgr,* The Buffalo Fine Arts Academy, Albright-Knox Art Gallery, Buffalo NY

Harders, Faith, *Librn,* University of Kentucky, Hunter M Adams Architecture Library, Lexington KY

Hardesty, Tony, *Registrar,* Owensboro Museum of Fine Art, Owensboro KY

Hardiman, Tom, *Keeper,* Portsmouth Athenaeum, Joseph Copley Research Library, Portsmouth NH

Hardin, Cable, *Asst Prof,* South Dakota State University, Dept of Visual Arts, Brookings SD (S)

Hardin, Jennifer, *Asst Librn,* Cincinnati Art Museum, Mary R Schiff Library & Archives, Cincinnati OH

Hardin, Jennifer, *Chief Cur,* Museum of Fine Arts, Saint Petersburg, Florida, Inc, Saint Petersburg FL

Harding, Beverly, *Mus Educator,* Seattle Art Museum, Dorothy Stimson Bullitt Library, Seattle WA

Harding, Catherine, *Asst Prof,* University of Victoria, Dept of History in Art, Victoria BC (S)

Harding, Jim, *Exec Dir,* British Columbia Museums Association, Victoria BC

Harding, Liz, *Assoc Cur,* Yellowstone Art Museum, Billings MT

Harding, Megan, *Publications & Media,* Oberlin College, Allen Memorial Art Museum, Oberlin OH

Hardison, Kathleen, *Finance Mgr,* Delaplaine Visual Arts Education Center, Frederick MD

Hardmon, Frank, *Assoc Prof Art,* Mississippi Valley State University, Fine Arts Dept, Itta Bena MS (S)

Hardwick, M Susan, *Pres Bd Dir,* Evansville Museum of Arts, History & Science, Evansville IN

Hardwig, Scott, *Prof,* Roanoke College, Fine Arts Dept-Art, Salem VA (S)

Hardwood, Edward S, *Assoc Prof,* Bates College, Art & Visual Culture, Lewiston ME (S)

Hardy, Bea, *Head Librn,* Maryland Historical Society, Library, Baltimore MD

Hardy, Beatriz, *Dean of Libraries & Instructional Resources,* Salisbury University, Blackwell Library, Salisbury MD

Hardy, Chantal, *Instr,* Universite de Montreal, Dept of Art History, Montreal PQ (S)

Hardy, Jacqueline, *Mem Svcs,* National Council on Education for the Ceramic Arts (NCECA), Erie CO

Hardy, Linda, *Museum Store Mgr,* Key West Art & Historical Society, East Martello Museum & Gallery, Key West FL

Hardy, Mariela, *Coordr Exhibs & Pub Progs,* Americas Society Art Gallery, New York NY

Hardy, Mary, *Instr (2-D),* Mississippi Gulf Coast Community College-Jackson County Campus, Art Dept, Gautier MS (S)

Hardy, Michele, *Cur Decorative Arts,* University of Calgary, Nickle Galleries, Calgary AB

Hardy, Myra, *Librn,* Maysville, Kentucky Gateway Museum Center, Maysville KY

Hardy, Saralyn Reece, *Dir,* University of Kansas, Spencer Museum of Art, Lawrence KS

Harger, Sara, *Dir,* Liberty Hall Historic Site, Orlando Brown House, Frankfort KY

Hargett, Brian, *Reference Librn,* Lee County Library, Tupelo MS

Hargrave, Mary, *Corresp Secy,* Pastel Society of America, National Arts Club, Grand Gallery, New York NY

Hargrave, Michelle, *Cur,* The American Federation of Arts, New York NY

Hargraves, Matthew, *Assoc Cur Colls Research,* Yale University, Yale Center for British Art, New Haven CT

Hargreaves, Eddie, *Webmaster, Publicity,* The San Joaquin Pioneer & Historical Society, The Haggin Museum, Stockton CA

Hargrove, James, *Asst Prof,* Roanoke College, Fine Arts Dept-Art, Salem VA (S)

Hargrove, June, *Chmn,* University of Maryland, Dept of Art History & Archaeology, College Park MD (S)

Hargrove, Kristi, *Asst Prof & Chair of Fine Art,* Watkins College of Art, Design & Film, Nashville TN (S)

Haring, Valerie, *Instr,* Butler County Community College, Art Dept, El Dorado KS (S)

Hark, Mary, *Instr,* Macalester College, Art Dept, Saint Paul MN (S)

Harker, Barbara, *Admin Asst,* Children's Art Foundation, Museum of International Children's Art, Santa Cruz CA

Harkness, Ed, *Ceramics Area Coordr,* Western Michigan University, Frostic School of Art, Kalamazoo MI (S)

Harks, Frank, *Chmn,* Mount Royal College, Dept of Interior Design, Calgary AB (S)

Harlacher, Sherry, *Dir,* Denison University, Art Gallery, Granville OH

Harlan, Susan, *Assoc Prof,* Portland State University, Dept of Art, Portland OR (S)

Harle, Matt, *Vis Asst Prof,* Connecticut College, Dept of Art, New London CT (S)

Harleman, Kathleen, *Dir,* University of Illinois at Urbana-Champaign, Krannert Art Museum and Kinkead Pavilion, Champaign IL

Harley, Alice, *Educ Liaison,* Sioux City Art Center, Sioux City IA (S)

Harley, Matt, *Preparator,* Rodman Hall Arts Centre, Saint Catharines ON

Harley-Wilson, Theresa, *Registrar,* Indiana University, The Mathers Museum of World Cultures, Bloomington IN

Harman, Pam, *Coordr Educ Prog,* Grace Museum, Inc, Abilene TX

Harmon, Darla, *Exec Dir,* Center for Contemporary Arts, Abilene TX

Harmon, J Scott, *Dir,* United States Naval Academy, USNA Museum, Annapolis MD

Harmon, J Scott, *Dir,* United States Naval Academy, Naval Academy Museum, Annapolis MD

Harmon, Megan Ann, *Alumni Rels Mgr,* National YoungArts Foundation, Miami FL

Harnden, Joann, *Coordr Educ Programs,* Williams College, Museum of Art, Williamstown MA

Harold, Dorothy, *Clay Instr,* Locust Street Neighborhood Art Classes, Inc, Buffalo NY (S)

Harold, Lizzy, *Interim Exec Dir,* Hillel Foundation, Hillel Jewish Student Center Gallery, Cincinnati OH

Harpaz, Nathan, *Cur Gallery,* Oakton Community College, Language Humanities & Art Divisions, Des Plaines IL (S)

Harpe, Annie, *Dir,* Tanner Hill Gallery, Chattanooga TN

Harper, Colleen, *Mgr Mem, Events & Fundraisers,* College of Central Florida, Appleton Museum of Art, Ocala FL

Harper, Dennis, *Cur,* Auburn University, Julie Collins Smith Museum, Auburn AL

Harper, Donna, *Adj Instr,* University of West Florida, Dept of Art, Pensacola FL (S)

Harper, Katherine, *Assoc Prof,* Loyola Marymount University, Dept of Art & Art History, Los Angeles CA (S)

Harper, Kinsey, *Dir Develop,* Atlanta Historical Society Inc, Atlanta History Center, Atlanta GA

Harper, Lucy Bjorklund, *Librn,* University of Rochester, Charlotte W Allen Library-Memorial Art Gallery, Rochester NY

Harper, Pat, *Library Mgr,* Southern Oregon Historical Society, Library, Medford OR

Harper, Paula, *Assoc Prof,* University of Miami, Dept of Art & Art History, Coral Gables FL (S)

Harper, Wallace G, *1st VChmn,* Maitland Art Center, Maitland FL

Harpin, Robert, *Prog Officer,* Latitude 53 Contemporary Visual Culture, Edmonton AB

Harr, Jemima, *Exec Dir & Cur,* Humboldt Arts Council, Morris Graves Museum of Art, Eureka CA

Harrington, Bernadette, *Library Asst,* Vermont Historical Society, Library, Montpelier VT

Harrington, Christi, *Instr,* Mohawk Valley Community College, Utica NY (S)

Harrington, Ellen, *Gallery Dir,* Academy of Motion Picture Arts & Sciences, The Academy Gallery, Beverly Hills CA

Harrington, Heather, *Asst Librn,* Historic Deerfield, Inc, Henry N Flynt Library, Deerfield MA

Harrington, Karen, *Vis Scvs,* Bennington Museum, Bennington VT

Harrington, Leslie, *Exec Dir,* Color Association of the US, New York NY

Harrington, Meredith, *Exec Dir,* Greenville Museum of Art, Inc, Greenville NC

Harrington, Richard A, *VPres,* Philadelphia Sketch Club, Philadelphia PA

Harrington, Sara, *Asst Librn,* Rutgers, The State University of New Jersey, Art Library, New Brunswick NJ

Harrington, Susan, *Prof,* Texas Christian University, School of Art, Fort Worth TX (S)

Harris, Adam D, *Cur Art,* National Museum of Wildlife Art of the Unites States, Jackson WY

Harris, Alison, *Asst Prof,* Colorado Mesa University, Art Dept, Grand Junction CO (S)

Harris, Beth R, *Dir Library,* Paier College of Art, Inc, Library, Hamden CT

Harris, Caroline, *Assoc Dir Educ,* Princeton University, Princeton University Art Museum, Princeton NJ

Harris, Damon, *Adjunct Faculty,* Southern Oregon University, Art & Art History Dept, Ashland OR (S)

Harris, David, *Asst Prof,* Missouri Western State University, Art Dept, Saint Joseph MO (S)

Harris, Debra, *Fiscal Officer,* California African-American Museum, Los Angeles CA

Harris, Dianne, *Pres,* Society of Architectural Historians, Chicago IL

Harris, Edward J, *VPres Admin,* American Antiquarian Society, Worcester MA

Harris, Elizabeth, *Instr,* Walla Walla Community College, Fine Arts Dept, Walla Walla WA (S)

Harris, George, *Cur,* Prince George Art Gallery, Prince George BC

Harris, J C, *Gen Mgr,* World Erotic Art Museum, Miami Beach FL

Harris, Jada, *Dir Progs,* The Names Project Foundation AIDS Memorial Quilt, Atlanta GA

Harris, Jeff, *Instr,* Whitworth College, Art Dept, Spokane WA (S)

Harris, Julie, *Exec Dir & Mus Shop Mgr,* River Heritage Museum, Paducah KY

Harris, Kevin, *Assoc Prof,* Sinclair Community College, Division of Fine & Performing Arts, Dayton OH (S)

Harris, Kyle, *Coordr Educ,* Los Angeles County Museum of Natural History, William S Hart Museum, Newhall CA

Harris, Lance, *Dir,* University of Louisiana at Lafayette, Paul and Lulu Hilliard University Art Museum, Lafayette LA

Harris, Lew, *Prof,* University of Tampa, College of Arts & Letters, Tampa FL (S)

Harris, Lois, *Provost,* Cornish College of the Arts, Art Dept, Seattle WA (S)

Harris, Marie Joan, *Acad Dean,* Avila University, Thornhill Art Gallery, Kansas City MO

Harris, Mark, *Dir, School of Art & Prof Fine Arts,* University of Cincinnati, School of Art, Cincinnati OH (S)

Harris, Melissa, *Magazine Ed,* Aperture Foundation, New York NY

Harris, Pamela, *Communs Coordr,* Salina Art Center, Salina KS

Harris, Rene, *Colls & Educ Progs Mgr,* Museum of New Mexico, Palace of Governors, Santa Fe NM

Harris, Rich, *Contact,* The Dairy Center for the Arts, Boulder CO

Harris, Robert A, *Dir,* Helen M Plum, Lombard IL

Harris, Ronna, *Assoc Prof,* Tulane University, Sophie H Newcomb Memorial College, New Orleans LA (S)

Harris, Steven, *Prof, Grad Programs,* University of Alberta, Dept of Art & Design, Edmonton AB (S)

Harris, Sue, *Pres,* Quincy College, Art Dept, Quincy MA (S)

Harris, Tamara Winfrey, *VPres Communs & Mktg,* Eiteljorg Museum of American Indians & Western Art, Indianapolis IN

Harris, Teresa, *Assoc Prof,* Missouri Western State University, Art Dept, Saint Joseph MO (S)

Harris, Thomas N, *Pres,* Porter-Phelps-Huntington Foundation, Inc, Historic House Museum, Hadley MA

Harris, William, *Sr VPres Develop & Mktg,* California Science Center, Los Angeles CA

Harris-Fernandez, Al, *Dir,* Sioux City Art Center, Sioux City IA

Harris-Fernandez, Al, *Dir,* Sioux City Art Center, Sioux City IA (S)

Harrison, Anne, *Mgr Children & Youth Progs,* Philadelphia Museum of Art, Samuel S Fleisher Art Memorial, Philadelphia PA

Harrison, Barbara, *Mus Shop Mgr,* Brookgreen Gardens, Murrells Inlet SC

Harrison, Eugene, *Prof,* Eastern Illinois University, Art Dept, Charleston IL (S)

Harrison, Helen, *Lectr,* Stony Brook University, College of Arts & Sciences, Dept of Art, Stony Brook NY (S)

Harrison, Jeff, *Dir,* Chrysler Museum of Art, Norfolk VA

Harrison, Myra, *Supt,* Longfellow National Historic Site, Longfellow House - Washington's Headquarters, Cambridge MA

Harrison, Stephen, *Cur Decorative Art & Design,* The Cleveland Museum of Art, Cleveland OH

Harrison, Stephen, *Cur Decorative Arts,* High Museum of Art, Atlanta GA

Harrison, Tanja, *Contact,* Nova Scotia College of Art and Design, Library, Halifax NS

Harrison, Verne, *Gallery Coordr,* Macdonald Stewart Art Centre, Guelph ON

Harrity, Gail, *COO,* Philadelphia Museum of Art, Main Building, Philadelphia PA

Harrop, Patrick, *Co-Dir & Prof,* University of Manitoba, Faculty of Architecture Exhibition Centre, Winnipeg MB

Harrow, Del, *Asst Prof Art (Ceramics),* Pennsylvania State University, University Park, Penn State School of Visual Arts, University Park PA (S)

Harry, Christine, *Marketing & Pub Rels,* Ocean City Arts Center, Ocean City NJ (S)

Harsch, Janna, *Cur,* Noyes Art Gallery, Lincoln NE

Harsh, Michael, *Actg Chief Coll,* Ohio Historical Society, National Road-Zane Grey Museum, Columbus OH

Harsh, Michael, *Head Collections,* Ohio Historical Society, Archives-Library Division, Columbus OH

Harshman, Melissa, *Assoc Prof Printmaking,* University of Georgia, Franklin College of Arts & Sciences, Lamar Dodd School of Art, Athens GA (S)

Hart, Alice, *Cur,* Grand Teton National Park Service, Colter Bay Indian Arts Museum, Moose WY

Hart, Ashley, *Mgr Tour Svcs,* Agecroft Association, Museum, Richmond VA

Hart, Barbie, *Pres,* Maryland Art Place, Baltimore MD

Hart, Diane M, *Dir Mus Reg,* Williams College, Museum of Art, Williamstown MA

Hart, Erdell, *Mus Shop Mgr,* Mississippi Museum of Art, Howorth Library, Jackson MS

Hart, Imogen, *Assoc Cur Exhibs & Publs,* Yale University, Yale Center for British Art, New Haven CT

Hart, Jane, *Cur,* Art & Culture Center of Hollywood, Art Gallery/Multidisciplinary Cultural Center, Hollywood FL

Hart, John, *Dir Research & Coll,* New York State Museum, Albany NY

Hart, Katherine, *Assoc Dir & Cur Acad Programming & Registrar & Colls Mgr,* Dartmouth College, Hood Museum of Art, Hanover NH

Hart, Kelly, *Admin Assoc,* University of Montana, Montana Museum of Art & Culture, Missoula MT

Hart, Kerry, *Dean,* Laramie County Community College, Division of Arts & Humanities, Cheyenne WY (S)

Hart, Naomi, *Faculty,* Grand Marais Art Colony, Grand Marais MN (S)

Hart, Nicki, *Mktg Specialist,* Sangre de Cristo Arts & Conference Center, Pueblo CO

Hart, Peggy, *Librn,* Detroit Public Library, Art & Literature Dept, Detroit MI

Hart, Sharon, *Asst Prof Art & Photography,* Florida Atlantic University, D F Schmidt College of Arts & Letters Dept of Visual Arts & Art History, Boca Raton FL (S)

Hart, Sidney, *Senior Historian,* National Portrait Gallery, Smithsonian Institution, Washington DC

Hart, Tara, *Archivist,* Public Art Fund, Inc, New York NY

Hart, Tara, *Archivist,* Public Art Fund, Inc, Visual Archive, New York NY

Harter, Gene, *Exec Dir,* Channel Islands Maritime Museum, Oxnard CA

Harth, Freddy, *Chief Preparator,* Oklahoma City Museum of Art, Oklahoma City OK

Harthorn, Sandy, *Cur Art,* Boise Art Museum, Boise ID

Hartigan, Grace, *Dir,* Maryland Institute, Hoffberger School of Painting, Baltimore MD (S)

Hartigan, Lynda, *Chief Cur,* Peabody Essex Museum, Salem MA

Hartke, Becki, *Dir Exhib,* Missouri Historical Society, Missouri History Museum, Saint Louis MO

Hartley, Blair, *Dir Develop,* American Folk Art Museum, New York NY

Hartling, Sandi, *Registrar,* Confederation Centre Art Gallery and Museum, Charlottetown PE

Hartman, Diane A, *Dir Resource Initiative,* University of Arizona, Museum of Art & Archive of Visual Arts, Tucson AZ

Hartman, Jeanne, *Secy,* Brooklyn Historical Society, Brooklyn OH

Hartman, Joanne, *Adjunct Asst Prof,* New York Institute of Technology, Fine Arts Dept, Old Westbury NY (S)

Hartman, Mark, *Prof,* University of Nebraska, Kearney, Dept of Art & Art History, Kearney NE (S)

Hartman, Tanya, *Assoc Prof & Grad Dir,* University of Kansas, The School of the Arts, Dept of Visual Art, Lawrence KS (S)

Hartman, Terry L, *Instr,* Modesto Junior College, Arts Humanities & Communications Division, Modesto CA (S)

Hartman, Vladmir, *Photog,* Antonelli Institute, Professional Photography & Commercial Art, Erdenheim PA (S)

Hartmann, Bonnie, *Dir,* Miller Art Center Foundation Inc, Miller Art Museum, Sturgeon Bay WI

Hartranft, Janet, *Asst Prof Art,* Pennsylvania State University, University Park, Penn State School of Visual Arts, University Park PA (S)

Hartshorn, Mark, *Asst Prof,* Community College of Rhode Island, Dept of Art, Warwick RI (S)

Hartshorn, Willis, *Dir,* International Center of Photography, Museum, New York NY

Hartt, Jodan, *Dir Progs,* Centrum Arts & Creative Education, Port Townsend WA

Hartwell, Janice E, *Assoc Prof,* Florida State University, Art Dept, Tallahassee FL (S)

Hartz, Jill, *Exec Dir,* University of Oregon, Jordan Schnitzer Museum of Art, Eugene OR

Hartzold, Susan, *Cur,* McLean County Historical Society, McLean County Museum of History, Bloomington IL

Harvath, John, *Mgr Fine Arts & Recreation,* Houston Public Library, Houston TX

Harvey, Alan, *Dean,* Foothill College, Fine Arts & Communications Div, Los Altos Hills CA (S)

Harvey, Archer, *Assoc Prof,* Rutgers, The State University of New Jersey, Graduate Program in Art History, New Brunswick NJ (S)

Harvey, Ben, *Asst Prof,* Mississippi State University, Dept of Art, Starville MS (S)

Harvey, Beth, *Mktg Specialist,* The Rockwell Museum of Western Art, Corning NY

Harvey, Bruce, *Dir,* Housatonic Community College, Library, Bridgeport CT

Harvey, Bunny, *Prof,* Wellesley College, Art Dept, Wellesley MA (S)

Harvey, Dale, *Prof Art,* Rio Hondo College, Visual Arts Dept, Whittier CA (S)

Harvey, David, *VPres Exhibition,* American Museum of Natural History, New York NY

Harvey, Eleanor, *Chief Cur,* American Art Museum, Smithsonian Institution, Washington DC

Harvey, Emily, *Discipline Coordr,* Rockland Community College, Graphic Arts & Advertising Tech Dept, Suffern NY (S)

Harvey, Gregory M, *VPres,* Fairmount Park Art Association, Philadelphia PA

Harvey, Marjorie, *Dir Architectural Planning & Design,* High Museum of Art, Atlanta GA

Harvey, Tobe, *Adjunct Asst Prof,* Spokane Falls Community College, Fine Arts Dept, Spokane WA (S)

Harwood, Barry R, *Cur, Decorative Arts,* Brooklyn Museum, Brooklyn NY

Harwood, Charles, *Commissioner,* United States Department of the Interior, Indian Arts & Crafts Board, Washington DC

Harwood, Roger, *Pres,* Clinton County Historical Association, Clinton County Historical Museum, Plattsburgh NY

Harwood, Ruth Schilling, *Asst Dir,* Maryland-National Capital Park & Planning Commission, Montpelier Arts Center, Laurel MD

Hasbun, Muriel, *Chair Fine Art Photog,* Corcoran School of Art, Washington DC (S)

Hasegawa, John, *Lectr,* Emporia State University, Dept of Art, Emporia KS (S)

Hasen, Irwin, *Instr,* Joe Kubert, Dover NJ (S)

Hasenberg, Tina, *Educ Dir,* City of Brea, Art Gallery, Brea CA

Hashimoto, Alan, *Asst Prof,* Utah State University, Dept of Art, Logan UT (S)

Haskel, Diane, *Mus Shop Mgr,* Dayton Art Institute, Dayton OH

Haskell, Barbara, *Cur Prewar Art,* Whitney Museum of American Art, New York NY

Haskell, Eric, *Dir,* Scripps College, Clark Humanities Museum, Claremont CA

Haskell, Heather, *Dir,* Springfield Museums, Michele & Donald D'Amour Museum of Fine Arts, Springfield MA

Hassan, Thomas E, *Prin,* Phillips Exeter Academy, Frederick R. Mayer Art Center, Lamont Gallery, Exeter NH

Hassel, Patricia, *Finance Dir,* Taft Museum of Art, Cincinnati OH

Hasselbalch, Kurt, *Cur,* Massachusetts Institute of Technology, Hart Nautical Galleries & Collections, Cambridge MA

Hasselbalch, Kurt, *Cur Hart Nautical Coll,* Massachusetts Institute of Technology, MIT Museum, Cambridge MA

Hassen, Carol, *Exec Dir,* Gallery One Visual Arts Center, Ellensburg WA

Hassett, Barbara, *Admin Asst,* Folk Art Society of America, Richmond VA

Hassinger, John L, *Graphic Design,* Art Institute of Pittsburgh, Pittsburgh PA (S)

Hassinger, Maren, *Dir,* Maryland Institute, Rinehart School of Sculpture, Baltimore MD (S)

Hassler, Donna, *Dir,* National Trust for Historic Preservation, Chesterwood, Stockbridge MA

Hassler, Donna, *Dir,* Rensselaer County Historical Society, Hart-Cluett Mansion, 1827, Troy NY

Hassler, Hilda, *Treas,* Phillips County Museum, Holyoke CO

Hastedt, Catherine A, *Dir,* Texas A&M University, J Wayne Stark University Center Galleries, College Station TX

Hastedt, Monica, *Admin Coord,* Schweinfurth Art Center, Auburn NY

Hastings, Bill, *Lectr,* Ithaca College, Fine Art Dept, Ithaca NY (S)

Hastings, Tina, *Dir,* State University of New York College at Fredonia, Cathy and Jesse Marion Art Gallery, Fredonia NY

Haston, Brady, *Asst Prof Fine Art & Studio Facilities Mgr,* Watkins College of Art, Design & Film, Nashville TN (S)

Hata, Stuart, *Mus Shop Mgr,* Fine Arts Museums of San Francisco, M H de Young Museum, San Francisco CA

Hata, Stuart, *Mus Shop Mgr,* Fine Arts Museums of San Francisco, Legion of Honor, San Francisco CA

Hatalski, Jon-Chris, *Grants Coordr,* Historical Society of Pennsylvania, Philadelphia PA

Hatch, Bill, *Dept Chmn,* San Juan College, Art Dept, Farmington NM (S)

Hatch, Carla, *Asst Bus Mgr,* Museum of Western Colorado, Museum of the West, Grand Junction CO

Hatch, Greg, *Head Fine Arts,* University of Utah, Katherine W Dumke Architecture Library, Marriott Library, Salt Lake City UT

Hatch, James V, *Mem Bd Dir,* Hatch-Billops Collection, Inc, New York NY

Hatch, Jeremy, *Assoc Dir Develop,* Indiana University, Art Museum, Bloomington IN

Hatch, Jeremy, *Assoc Prof Ceramics,* Montana State University, School of Art, Bozeman MT (S)

Hatchadoorian, Lisa, *Cur,* Nicolaysen Art Museum & Discovery Center, Children's Discovery Center, Casper WY

Hatcher, Adriane, *Dir,* Baker Arts Center, Liberal KS

Hatcher, Alison, *Cur,* McLean County Art Association, McLean County Arts Center, Bloomington IL

Hatcher, Gary C, *Assoc Prof & Chmn,* University of Texas at Tyler, Department of Art, School of Visual & Performing Arts, Tyler TX (S)

Hatcher, Steven, *Dir Folk & Trade Arts,* Idaho Commission on the Arts, Boise ID

Hatchett, Dana, *Instr,* Daemen College, Art Dept, Amherst NY (S)

Hatfield, John, *Exec Dir,* Socrates Sculpture Park, Long Island City NY

Hatley, Pam, *Head Publs,* The Buffalo Fine Arts Academy, Albright-Knox Art Gallery, Buffalo NY

Hattendorf, John B., *Dir,* Naval War College Museum, Newport RI

Hatter, Richard, *Dir Develop & Pub Rels,* John Simon Guggenheim, New York NY

Hattersley, Pat, *Secy,* Searchlight Historic Museum & Mining Park, Searchlight NV

Hau, Amy, *Admin Dir,* Isamu Noguchi, Isamu Noguchi Garden Museum, Long Island City NY

Haubach, Janna L, *Gen Educ,* Art Institute of Pittsburgh, Pittsburgh PA (S)

Hauber, Amy, *Asst Prof,* St Lawrence University, Dept of Fine Arts, Canton NY (S)

Haubold, Susan, *Lectr,* Lambuth University, Dept of Human Ecology & Visual Arts, Jackson TN (S)

Hauck, Allison, *Dir Develop,* Washington Pavilion of Arts & Science, Visual Arts Center, Sioux Falls SD

Hauerstein, Suzanne, *Vol Coordr,* Newport Art Museum and Association, Newport RI

Haugaard, David, *Dir Research,* Historical Society of Pennsylvania, Philadelphia PA

Haugen, Eunice, *Registrar,* University of Minnesota, Goldstein Museum of Design, Saint Paul MN

Haught, Roy, *Chmn & Prof,* Loras College, Dept of Art, Dubuque IA (S)

Haughton, Quincy, *Assoc Dir Exhibs & Pub Progs,* Getty Center, The J Paul Getty Museum, Los Angeles CA

Haupt, Jeffrey, *Assoc Prof,* Mississippi State University, Dept of Art, Starville MS (S)

Hause, Melissa, *Asst Prof Art History,* Belhaven College, Art Dept, Jackson MS (S)

Hauser, Mary, *Registrar,* North Carolina State University, Gregg Museum of Art & Design, Raleigh NC

Hausey, Robert, *Prof,* Louisiana State University, School of Art, Baton Rouge LA (S)

Hausman, Mariah, *Instr,* University of Miami, Dept of Art & Art History, Coral Gables FL (S)

Haust, Bill, *Head Dept,* Plymouth State College, Art Dept, Plymouth NH (S)

Hauth, Paul, *Pres,* Buckham Fine Arts Project, Gallery, Flint MI

Hauus, Paula, *Adjunct,* North Iowa Area Community College, Dept of Art, Mason City IA (S)

Havekost, Niki, *Instr,* Siena Heights University, Studio Angelico-Art Dept, Adrian MI (S)

Havel, Joseph, *Dir,* Museum of Fine Arts, Houston, Glassell School of Art, Houston TX (S)

Havelak, Sharon, *Instr,* Lourdes University, Art Dept, Sylvania OH (S)

Havemeyer, Ann, *Cur,* Norfolk Historical Society Inc, Museum, Norfolk CT

Haven, Mark, *Assoc Prof,* Rochester Institute of Technology, School of Photographic Arts & Sciences, Rochester NY (S)

Haven, Sarah, *Retail Mgr,* Gallery One Visual Arts Center, Ellensburg WA

Havener, Jon, *Prof,* University of Kansas, The School of the Arts, Dept of Visual Art, Lawrence KS (S)

Havers, Robert, *Exec Dir,* Westminster College, Winston Churchill Memorial & Library in the United States, Fulton MO

Havice, Christine, *Dir,* Kent State University, School of Art, Kent OH (S)

Havice, Christine, *School of Art Dir,* Kent State University, School of Art Galleries, Kent OH

Havinga, Anne, *Estrellita & Yousuf Karsh Sr Cur Photographs,* Museum of Fine Arts, Boston MA

Havlena, Janice M, *Asst Prof,* Edgewood College, Art Dept, Madison WI (S)

Havv, Jane, *Cur Gallery,* Passaic County Community College, Division of Humanities, Paterson NJ (S)

Haw, Jane, *Gallery Cur,* Passaic County Community College, Broadway, LRC, and Hamilton Club Galleries, Paterson NJ

Haw, Kate, *Exec Dir Develop & Admin,* Skowhegan School of Painting & Sculpture, New York NY (S)

Hawk, William, *Assoc Prof (Painting & Drawing),* University of Missouri - Columbia, Dept of Art, Columbia MO (S)

Hawke, Nadine, *Instr,* Arkansas State University, Dept of Art, State University AR (S)

Hawken, Edwin F, *Treas,* McMichael Canadian Art Collection, Kleinburg ON

Hawken, George, *Undergrad Coordr Visual Studies,* University of Toronto, Dept of Fine Art, Toronto ON (S)

Hawkes, Amy, *Mus Outreach Coordr,* Bowdoin College, Peary-MacMillan Arctic Museum, Brunswick ME

Hawkes, Carol, *Dean,* Western Connecticut State University, School of Visual & Performing Arts, Danbury CT (S)

Hawkes, Rob, *Prof,* Tidewater Community College, Visual Arts Center, Portsmouth VA (S)

Hawkins, Amy Harris, *Asst Cur,* The Ethel Wright Mohamed Stitchery Museum, Belzoni MS

Hawkins, Cynthia, *Dir Galleries,* Bertha V B Lederer Fine Arts Gallery-Suny Geneseo, Bertha V B Lederer Fine Arts Gallery, Geneseo NY

Hawkins, Cynthia, *Dir Galleries,* State University of New York at Geneseo, Lockhart Gallery, Geneseo NY

Hawkins, Cynthia, *Dir of Galleries,* State University of New York at Geneseo, Bertha V B Lederer Gallery, Geneseo NY

Hawkins, Laurie, *Deputy Dir Develop & Endowments,* Timken Museum of Art, San Diego CA

Hawkins, Pamela, *Coordr Bd Mem,* Women in the Arts Foundation, Inc, Staten Island NY

Hawkins, Renee, *Dir,* Longview Museum of Fine Art, Longview TX

Hawkins, Susan, *Art Instr,* Morehead State University, Art & Design Dept, Morehead KY (S)

Hawley, Anne, *Dir,* Isabella Stewart Gardner, Boston MA

Hawley, Hilarie V, *Pres,* Pennsylvania Academy of the Fine Arts, Fellowship of the Pennsylvania Academy of the Fine Arts, Philadelphia PA

Hawley, Nancy, *Communs Specialist,* Tryon Palace Historic Sites & Gardens, New Bern NC

Hawthorne, Frances, *Lectr,* University of North Carolina at Charlotte, Dept Art, Charlotte NC (S)

Hawthorne, Jeff, *Dir Commun Affairs,* Regional Arts & Culture Council, Metropolitan Center for Public Arts, Portland OR

Hayashi, Masumi, *Prof,* Cleveland State University, Art Dept, Cleveland OH (S)

Hayashi-Smith, Donna, *Coll Mgr,* White House, Washington DC

Hayden, Carla, *Dir,* Enoch Pratt, Baltimore MD

Hayden, Casey, *Adv,* Western Washington University, Viking Union Gallery, Bellingham WA

Hayden, Diane, *Financial Admin,* Sharon Arts Center, Sharon Arts Center Exhibition Gallery, Peterborough NH

Hayden, Jason, *Dir Operations,* Owensboro Museum of Fine Art, Owensboro KY

Hayden, John, *Pres,* Antonelli Institute, Professional Photography & Commercial Art, Erdenheim PA (S)

Hayden, Leanne, *Colls Mgr,* Berkshire Museum, Pittsfield MA

Hayden, William, *Dir & Pres,* Hayden Museum of American Art, Paris TX

Haydu, John, *Prof,* Central Missouri State University, Dept Art & Design, Warrensburg MO (S)

Hayes, Ann Marie, *Dir Educ,* Figge Art Museum, Art Reference Library, Davenport IA

Hayes, Bonnie, *Asst Prof,* Arcadia University, Dept of Fine Arts, Glenside PA (S)

Hayes, Cheryl A, *Chair & Assoc Prof,* University of New Orleans-Lake Front, Dept of Fine Arts, New Orleans LA (S)

Hayes, Daniel T, *Pres,* Finger Lakes Community College, Visual & Performing Arts Dept, Canandaigua NY (S)

Hayes, Greg, *Supv Ranger,* Jack London, House of Happy Walls, Glen Ellen CA

Hayes, Julia, *Asst Cur Visual Resources Coll,* Toledo Museum of Art, Toledo OH

Hayes, Julia Chytil, *Instr,* Lourdes University, Art Dept, Sylvania OH (S)

Hayes, Martha, *VPres & Publicity,* Clinton Art Association, River Arts Center, Clinton IA

Hayes, Meredith, *Dir Pub Rels & Mktg,* Tucson Museum of Art and Historic Block, Tucson AZ

Hayes, Richard, *Instr,* University of Louisiana at Monroe, Dept of Art, Monroe LA (S)

Hayes-Benjamin, Tritobia, *Dir,* Howard University, Gallery of Art, Washington DC

Hayes-Hawkinson, Ann Marie, *Cur Educ,* Figge Art Museum, Davenport IA

Hayes-Thumann, Karen, *Asst Dir Undergrad,* University of Oklahoma, School of Art, Norman OK (S)

Haymaker, James, *Dir,* Pfeiffer University, Art Program, Misenheimer NC (S)

Hayman, Marc, *Chief Interpretation,* San Francisco Maritime National Historical Park, Maritime Museum, San Francisco CA

Haymon, Elizabeth G, *Dir Develp & Mktg,* Allentown Art Museum, Allentown PA

Haymond, Lizzy, *Tours,* First Horizon National Corp, First Tennessee Heritage Collection, Memphis TN

Hayner, Judith, *Exec Dir,* Muskegon Museum of Art, Muskegon MI

Haynes, Carol, *Pres,* Phillips County Museum, Holyoke CO

Haynes, Chris, *Asst Prof,* Springfield College, Dept of Visual & Performing Arts, Springfield MA (S)

Haynes, Deborah, *Data Mgr,* Dartmouth College, Hood Museum of Art, Hanover NH

Haynes, Jennifer, *Art Dir,* Hill Country Arts Foundation, Duncan-McAshan Visual Arts Center, Ingram TX

Haynes, Michaele, *Cur History & Textiles,* Witte Museum, San Antonio TX

Haynes, Peggy, *Mktg,* Art Center Manatee, Bradenton FL

Haynes, Sandra, *Acting Area Head History,* Pasadena City College, Visual Arts and Media Studies Division, Pasadena CA (S)

Haynes, Thomas, *Educ Dir,* Historical Society of Cheshire County, Keene NH

Hays, Michelle, *Asst Prof,* Texas State University - San Marcos, Dept of Art and Design, San Marcos TX (S)

Hays, Philip, *Illustration Chmn,* Art Center College of Design, Pasadena CA (S)

Hays, Sarah, *Library Dir,* New Hampshire Historical Society, Library of History & Genealogy, Concord NH

Hays-Gilpin, Kelley, *Danson Cur Anthropology,* Museum of Northern Arizona, Flagstaff AZ

Hayton, Greg, *Chief Librn,* Cambridge Public Library and Gallery, Cambridge ON

Hayward, Justin, *Instr,* Casper College, Dept of Visual Arts, Casper WY (S)

Haywood, Heather, *Dir Mktg,* Arkansas Arts Center, Museum, Little Rock AR (S)

Hayworth, Kathleen, *Head Mktg & Pub Rels,* State University of New York College at Buffalo, Buffalo NY

Hazelwood, Donna, *Prof,* Oakland City University, Division of Fine Arts, Oakland City IN (S)

Hazen, Vince, *Cur Art Center,* Honolulu Museum of Art, Honolulu HI

Hazen, Wayne, *Chmn,* Southern Adventist University, Art Dept, Collegedale TN (S)

Heaberlin, Tim, *Corporate Art Admin,* Ashland Inc, Ashland KY

Headrick, Annabeth, *Assoc Prof Art History,* University of Denver, School of Art & Art History, Denver CO (S)

Heald, David, *Photographer,* Guggenheim Museum Soho, New York NY

Healey, Marilyn, *Art Librn,* University of Georgia, University of Georgia Libraries, Athens GA

Healy, Anne, *Undergrad faculty adv,* University of California, Berkeley, College of Letters & Sciences-Art Practice Dept, Berkeley CA (S)

Healy, Patricia, *Asst Cur,* University of Texas at Arlington, Gallery at UTA, Arlington TX

Heaps, Douglas N, *Prog Chmn Digital Media Production,* Art Institute of Pittsburgh, Pittsburgh PA (S)

Heard, Catherine, *Instr,* Toronto School of Art, Toronto ON (S)

Heard, Chris, *Asst Prof Photog,* Harford Community College, Visual, Performing and Applied Arts Division, Bel Air MD (S)

Heard, Ruthie, *Secy,* St Mary Landmarks, Grevemberg House Museum, Franklin LA

Hearn, Brian, *Film Cur,* Oklahoma City Museum of Art, Oklahoma City OK

Hearne, Pardee, *Prof Painting,* University of California, Davis, Dept of Art & Art History, Davis CA (S)

Hearon, Kim, *Office Coordr,* Southern Oregon University, Schneider Museum of Art, Ashland OR

Hearst, George R, *Chair Bd Trustees,* Albany Institute of History & Art, Albany NY

Hearst, William Randolph, *Cur Educ,* Norton Museum of Art, West Palm Beach FL

Heasley, Charles, *Prof,* State University of New York, College at Cortland, Dept Art & Art History, Cortland NY (S)

Heath, Angela, *Assoc Prof,* South Plains College, Fine Arts Dept, Levelland TX (S)

Heath, Heather, *Exec Dir,* Golden Isles Arts & Humanities Association, Brunswick GA

Heath, Margo, *Auxiliary VPres,* Mississippi Museum of Art, Howorth Library, Jackson MS

Heath-Wiersma, Anne, *Asst Prof,* Hope College, Dept of Art & Art History, Holland MI (S)

Heathington, Mary Dell, *Chmn,* North Central Texas College, Division of Communications & Fine Arts, Gainesville TX (S)

Heatly, Stanley, *Pres Bd Dirs,* Red River Valley Museum, Vernon TX

Heaton, Debbie, *Dir Devel,* Delaware Center for the Contemporary Arts, Wilmington DE

Heaton, Nancy, *Dir,* Bay Arts, Inc., Bay Village OH

Hebb, David, *Instr,* North Hennepin Community College, Art Dept, Brooklyn Park MN (S)

Hebermehl, Tom, *Chmn & Pres (V),* Bicentennial Art Center & Museum, Paris IL

Hebert, Melissa, *Instr,* Black Hawk College, Art Dept, Moline IL (S)

Heck, Joey, *Exhibits Mgr,* Herrett Center for Arts & Sciences, Jean B King Art Gallery, Twin Falls ID

Heckel, Inge, *Pres,* New York School of Interior Design, New York NY (S)

Heckerman, Maureen, *Exec Dir,* Institute for Arts & Humanities Education, New Jersey Summer Arts Institute, Staten Island NY (S)

Heckle, Shay, *Treas,* Glynn Art Association, Saint Simons Island GA

Heckscher, Morrison H, *Lawrence A Fleisch,* The Metropolitan Museum of Art, New York NY

Hedges, Kimberly, *VPres Mktg, Communs & Technology,* Americans for the Arts, New York NY

Hedin, Thomas F, *Prof,* University of Minnesota, Duluth, Art Dept, Duluth MN (S)

Heermans, Debra, *Asst Prof,* Mount Mary College, Art & Design Division, Milwaukee WI (S)

Heermans, Debra, *Prog Dir Fine Art,* Mount Mary College, Marian Gallery, Milwaukee WI

Hees, Lisa, *Dir,* The McKinney Avenue Contemporary (The MAC), Dallas TX

Heffernan, Mary Beth, *Prof,* Occidental College, Dept of Art History & Visual Arts, Los Angeles CA (S)

Heffner, Jennifer, *Senior Registrar,* The American Federation of Arts, New York NY

Heffner, Jinger, *Exhib Coordr & Gallery Registrar,* Otis College of Art & Design, Ben Maltz Gallery, Los Angeles CA

Heffner, Terry, *Assoc Dir,* Meredith Gallery, Baltimore MD

Hefley, Kara, *Dir Devel,* Tacoma Art Museum, Tacoma WA

Heft, Caren, *Dir,* University of Wisconsin-Stevens Point, Carlsten Art Gallery, Stevens Point WI

Heft, Caren, *Dir Gallery,* University of Wisconsin-Stevens Point, Dept of Art & Design, Stevens Point WI (S)

Heft, Carol, *Instr,* Muhlenberg College, Dept of Art, Allentown PA (S)

Heggemeyer, Amy, *Asst Registrar,* University of Illinois at Urbana-Champaign, Spurlock Museum, Champaign IL

Heher, Jody, *Assoc Dir Museum Admin,* Yeshiva University Museum, New York NY

Heidel, Gail, *Programs Coordr,* Greenwich House Inc, Greenwich House Pottery, New York NY (S)

Heideman, Sally, *Vol Pres,* Kenosha Public Museums, Kenosha WI

Heiden, Stacie, *Bd Dir Treas,* Plains Art Museum, Fargo ND

Heider, Nate, *Develop Mem & Pub Rels,* River Heritage Museum, Paducah KY

Heighton, Jennifer, *Exec Dir,* Santa Paula Art Museum, Santa Paula CA

Heikens, Joan A, *Sr Sales & Promotions Mgr,* Jamestown-Yorktown Foundation, Jamestown Settlement, Williamsburg VA

Heil, Elizabeth, *Assoc Prof,* Roanoke College, Fine Arts Dept-Art, Salem VA (S)

Heil, Harry, *Dir Gallery,* Western State College of Colorado, Quigley Hall Art Gallery, Gunnison CO

Heil, Mary Colleen, *Pres,* Pennsylvania School of Art & Design, Lancaster PA (S)

Heilmer, Steve, *Dept Head,* Greenville College, Art Dept, Greenville IL (S)

Heiman, Richard SV, *CFO,* Virginia Historical Society, Library, Richmond VA

Heimann, Nora, *Asst Prof,* Catholic University of America, Dept of Art, Washington DC (S)

Heimerdinger, Barbara, *Exec Dir,* Illinois Alliance for Arts Education (IAAE), DeKalb IL

Heimerman, Ebon, *Facilities Mgr,* Museum of Wisconsin Art, West Bend WI

Heimsch, Barbara, *Dir Gallery,* Mount Mary College, Marian Gallery, Milwaukee WI

Heine, Yvonne, *Office Mgr,* Santa Barbara Contemporary Arts Forum, Santa Barbara CA

Heineman, Stephanie, *Dir,* Northport-East Northport Public Library, Northport NY

Heinlein, Douglas, *Dir Graphic Design, Web Design & Interactive Media, Digital Design,* The Art Institutes, The Art Institute of Seattle, Seattle WA (S)

Heinrich, Christoph, *Frederick & Jan Mayer Dir & Cur Modern & Contemporary Art,* Denver Art Museum, Denver CO

Heinrich, Milton, *Chmn,* Dana College, Art Dept, Blair NE (S)

Heinrich, Tanya, *Dir Publications,* American Folk Art Museum, New York NY

Heinritz, Ryan, *Exec Dir,* Paradise Center for the Arts, Faribault MN

Heinson, Lillian, *Slide Librn,* York University, Fine Arts Phase II Slide Library, Toronto ON

Heipp, Richard, *Prof & Dir,* University of Florida, School of Art & Art History, Gainesville FL (S)

Heischman, Robert, *Prof,* Rochester Institute of Technology, School of Design, Rochester NY (S)

Heise, Donalyn, *Prof,* University of Nebraska at Omaha, Dept of Art & Art History, Omaha NE (S)

Heisler, Virginia, *Prof,* Saint Louis Community College at Meramec, Art Dept, Saint Louis MO (S)

Heiss, Alanna, *Exec Dir,* PS1 Contemporary Art Center, Long Island City NY

Heiss, Wesley, *Asst Prof,* Lehigh University, Dept of Art, Architecture & Design, Bethlehem PA (S)

Heist, Eric, *Dir,* Momenta Art, Brooklyn NY

Heitzenroder, Sharon, *Print Studio & Custom Printing Mgr,* Kala Institute, Kala Art Institute, Berkeley CA

Helay, Ryan M, *Librn,* The New York Public Library, Art & Architecture Collection, New York NY

Helbert, Theresa, *Treas,* Frontier Times Museum, Bandera TX

Held, Peter, *Ceramics Cur,* Arizona State University, ASU Art Museum, Tempe AZ

Helfand, Fern, *Assoc Prof (Visual Art),* University of British Columbia Okanagan, Dept of Creative Studies, Kelowna BC (S)

Helfenstein, Josef, *Dir,* Menil Foundation, Inc, The Menil Collection, Houston TX

Helfrich, Kurt, *Cur Architectural Drawings,* University of California, Santa Barbara, University Art Museum, Santa Barbara CA

Helfrich, Richard, *Asst Prof,* La Roche College, Division of Design, Pittsburgh PA (S)

Helgesen, Brita, *Research Asst,* Queens College, City University of New York, Godwin-Ternbach Museum, Flushing NY

Heller, Barbara, *Head Conservator,* Detroit Institute of Arts, Detroit MI

Heller, Dulcey, *Libr Asst,* American Craft Council, Library, Minneapolis MN

Heller, Ena, *Dir,* Rollins College, George D & Harriet W Cornell Fine Arts Museum, Winter Park FL

Heller, Ena, *Exec Dir,* Museum of Biblical Art, New York NY

Hellier, Bob, *Preparator,* Tampa Museum of Art, Tampa FL

Hellige, Kristan, *Commun Coordr,* Cedar Rapids Museum of Art, Cedar Rapids IA

Hellyer-Heinz, Cynthia, *Foundations Coordr,* Northern Illinois University, School of Art, DeKalb IL (S)

Helm, Alison, *Assoc Prof, Dir,* West Virginia University, College of Creative Arts, School of Art & Design, Morgantown WV (S)

Helm, Alison, *Prof & Dir of Art,* West Virginia University, College of Creative Arts, School of Art & Design, Morgantown WV (S)

Helm, Amanda, *Develop Dir,* Nicolaysen Art Museum & Discovery Center, Children's Discovery Center, Casper WY

Helm, Charles R, *Dir Performing Arts,* Ohio State University, Wexner Center for the Arts, Columbus OH

Helm, Dannie, *Dir,* Saint Augustine Historical Society, Oldest House Museum Complex, Saint Augustine FL

Helm, David, *Prof,* University of Nebraska at Omaha, Dept of Art & Art History, Omaha NE (S)

Helm, Elizabeth, *Admin Asst,* National Sculpture Society, New York NY

Helmer, Matthew S, *Dir,* Colorado State University, Curfman Gallery, Fort Collins CO

Helmke, George E, *Cur Emeritus,* Fleetwood Museum, North Plainfield NJ

Helmreich, Anne, *Assoc Prof,* Case Western Reserve University, Dept of Art History & Art, Cleveland OH (S)

Helton, Jo-Lyn, *Bus Mgr,* Lauren Rogers, Laurel MS

Hemeon, Debra, *Deputy Dir,* Cape Cod Museum of Art Inc, Dennis MA

Hemmelgarn, Elaine, *Dir Develop,* Fitton Center for Creative Arts, Hamilton OH

Hempel, Melissa, *Interim Dir,* Utah Valley University, Woodbury Art Museum, Orem UT

Hemsworth, Sandra, *Gallery Cur,* City of Fremont, Olive Hyde Art Gallery, Fremont CA

Hemzik, Pamela, *Coordr Div Arts,* York College of Pennsylvania, Dept of Music, Art & Speech Communications, York PA (S)

Hendee, Stephen, *Asst Prof,* University of Nevada, Las Vegas, Dept of Art, Las Vegas NV (S)

Hendershot, James, *Assoc Prof,* Saint John's University, Art Dept, Collegeville MN (S)

Hendershot, James, *Assoc Prof,* College of Saint Benedict, Art Dept, Saint Joseph MN (S)

Hendershot, Leann, *Secy,* The Ohio Historical Society, Inc, Campus Martius Museum & Ohio River Museum, Marietta OH

Hendershot, Susan, *Lectr,* Saint John's University, Art Dept, Collegeville MN (S)

Henderson, Adele, *Prof,* University at Buffalo, State University of New York, Dept of Visual Studies, Buffalo NY (S)

Henderson, Avis, *Exec Dir,* Monmouth Museum & Cultural Center, Lincroft NJ

Henderson, Barry, *Librn,* Beaverbrook Art Gallery, Library, Fredericton NB

Henderson, Brian, *Dir,* Academy of the New Church, Glencairn Museum, Bryn Athyn PA

Henderson, Brooke, *Art Librn,* Wellesley College, Art Library, Wellesley MA

Henderson, Bruce, *Photog,* Art Institute of Pittsburgh, Pittsburgh PA (S)

Henderson, Cathy, *Assoc Dir,* University of Texas at Austin, Harry Ransom Humanities Research Center, Austin TX

Henderson, Douglas, *Dir Entertainment Technology Center,* Art Institute of Pittsburgh, Pittsburgh PA (S)

Henderson, Garry, *Gallery Cur,* Riverside Arts Center, Riverside IL (S)

Henderson, Ivan, *Educ Dir,* African American Museum in Philadelphia, Philadelphia PA

Henderson, Jackie, *Cur Educ,* Sangre de Cristo Arts & Conference Center, Pueblo CO

Henderson, Jesse, *Technology Coordr,* Colgate University, Picker Art Gallery, Hamilton NY

Henderson, Jessica, *Asst Prof,* Bethel College, Dept of Art, Saint Paul MN (S)

Henderson, Jill, *Gallery Coordr,* Contemporary Art Gallery Society of British Columbia, Vancouver BC

Henderson, Jim, *Pres,* Owen Sound Historical Society, Marine & Rail Heritage Museum, Owen Sound ON

Henderson, Maren, *Prof Emer,* California State Polytechnic University, Pomona, Department of Art, Pomona CA (S)

Henderson, Mike, *Prof Painting,* University of California, Davis, Dept of Art & Art History, Davis CA (S)

Henderson, Paul, *Mgr Faucet Media Arts,* Struts Gallery, Sackville NB

Henderson, Sophie, *VPres External Affairs,* Museum of Arts & Design, New York NY

Hendigg, Arthur, *Secy,* Bromfield Art Gallery, Boston MA

Hendon, Karen Crews, *Cur,* Monterey Museum of Art, Monterey Museum of Art -Pacific Street, Monterey Museum of Art - La Mirada, Monterey CA

Hendren, Eileen, *Asst Dir,* Pence Gallery, Davis CA

Hendren, Greg, *Asst Dir,* Artists Space, Artists Space Gallery, New York NY

Hendrick, Joe, *Assoc Prof,* Monroe Community College, Art Dept, Rochester NY (S)

Hendricks, Barkley L, *Prof,* Connecticut College, Dept of Art, New London CT (S)

Hendricks, Becky, *Finance Dir,* Hill-Stead Museum, Farmington CT

Hendricks, Janet, *Dir Progs & Design,* Academy Art Museum, Easton MD

Hendricks, Leta, *Librn,* Ohio State University, The Education, Human Ecology, Psychology and Social Work Library, Columbus OH

Hendricks, Susan, *Dir Communs,* Lyman Allyn Art Museum, New London CT

Hendrickson, Ted, *Assoc Prof,* Connecticut College, Dept of Art, New London CT (S)

Hendrickx, Jim, *Chmn,* Mount Vernon Nazarene University, Art Dept, Mount Vernon OH (S)

Hendrix, Janel, *Cur,* Historical Society of Martin County, Elliott Museum, Stuart FL

Hendrix, Lee, *Sr Cur Drawings,* Getty Center, The J Paul Getty Museum, Los Angeles CA

Hendry, Leigh, *External Affairs,* Tennessee State Museum, Nashville TN

Hendry, Thomas, *Instr,* Toronto School of Art, Toronto ON (S)

Heneghan, Marguerite, *Maintainer,* Osborne Homestead Museum, Derby CT

Henessey, Colleen, *Archives Asst,* The Phillips Collection, Library, Washington DC

Hengal, Brenda, *Dir Prog,* Arts & Science Center for Southeast Arkansas, Pine Bluff AR

Hershey, David, *Asst Coll Mgr,* University of Richmond, University Museums, Richmond VA

Hershman, Lynn, *Prof Electronic & Digital Arts,* University of California, Davis, Dept of Art & Art History, Davis CA (S)

Hershour, Jenny, *Mng Dir,* Citizens for the Arts in Pennsylvania, Harrisburg PA

Hertel, Heather, *Prof,* Slippery Rock University of Pennsylvania, Dept of Art, Slippery Rock PA (S)

Hertzberg, Lesley, *Collections Mgr,* Hancock Shaker Village, Inc, Pittsfield MA

Hertzel, David, *Mgr Library Operations,* University of New Mexico, Fine Arts Library, Albuquerque NM

Hertzlieb, Gregg, *Dir & Cur,* Valparaiso University, Brauer Museum of Art, Valparaiso IN

Hertzson, Joyce, *Chmn Foundation Studies,* Rochester Institute of Technology, School of Design, Rochester NY (S)

Hertzson, Joyce, *Foundations Chair,* Rochester Institute of Technology, College of Imaging Arts & Sciences, Rochester NY (S)

Herwitz, Daniel, *Prof,* University of Michigan, Ann Arbor, School of Art & Design, Ann Arbor MI (S)

Herz, Rebecca, *Head Educ,* Isamu Noguchi, Isamu Noguchi Garden Museum, Long Island City NY

Herzog, Elaine, *Pres,* Wayne County Historical Society, Museum, Honesdale PA

Herzog, Erin, *Vis Resource Specialist,* California State University, Chico, Department of Art & Art History, Chico CA (S)

Herzog, Melanie, *Assoc Prof,* Edgewood College, Art Dept, Madison WI (S)

Heslin, Linda, *Branch Dir,* New York Institute of Technology, Art & Architectural Library, Old Westbury NY

Hess, Catherine, *Cur British & Continental Art,* The Huntington Library, Art Collections & Botanical Gardens, San Marino CA

Hess, Donnalynn, *Dir Educ,* Bob Jones University Museum & Gallery Inc, Greenville SC

Hess, Honee A, *Dir Educ,* Worcester Art Museum, Worcester MA

Hess, Lali, *Gallery Dir,* Wabash College, Art Dept, Crawfordsville IN (S)

Hess, Mary, *Prog Mgmt Specialist,* University of Maryland, Baltimore County, Imaging & Digital Arts (IMDA), Dept of Visual Arts, Baltimore MD (S)

Hess, Paul, *School of Art Dir,* University of Manitoba, School of Art Gallery, Winnipeg MB

Hess, Richard, *Secy,* Brown County Art Gallery Foundation, Nashville IN

Hess, Sara, *VPres,* Brown County Art Gallery Foundation, Nashville IN

Hess, Teresa, *Prof,* Lakeland Community College, Fine Arts Department, Kirtland OH (S)

Hessburg, Aloyse, *Assoc Prof,* Mount Mary College, Art & Design Division, Milwaukee WI (S)

Hessel, Jan, *Facilities Mgr & Art Preparator,* Washington University, Mildred Lane Kemper Art Museum, Saint Louis MO

Hesseldenz, Kate, *Cur,* Liberty Hall Historic Site, Liberty Hall Museum, Frankfort KY

Hesselgrave, Joyce, *Lectr,* California State Polytechnic University, Pomona, Department of Art, Pomona CA (S)

Hesseltine, Doug, *FT Lectr,* University of Michigan, Ann Arbor, School of Art & Design, Ann Arbor MI (S)

Hessemer, Peter, *Assoc Prof,* Oakton Community College, Language Humanities & Art Divisions, Des Plaines IL (S)

Hessling, Joanie, *Co-Dir,* Arthur Roy Mitchell, A.R. Mitchell Museum, Trinidad CO

Hester, Cash, *Bright Starts Coordr,* School 33 Art Center, Baltimore MD

Heston, Sally, *Instr,* Cuyahoga Valley Art Center, Cuyahoga Falls OH (S)

Hethcox, Rhonda, *Vol Coordr,* Birmingham Museum of Art, Birmingham AL

Hethorn, Janet, *Chair,* University of Delaware, Dept of Art, Newark DE (S)

Heubach, Merrill, *Secy,* Lunenburg Art Gallery Society, Lunenburg NS

Heuck, Roger, *Cur,* Cincinnati Art Club, Cincinnati OH

Heuer, Curt, *Chmn,* University of Wisconsin-Green Bay, Arts Dept, Green Bay WI (S)

Heuker, Jennifer, *Prof,* State University of New York College at Brockport, Dept of Art, Brockport NY (S)

Heuser, Douglas, *Dir,* See Science Center, Manchester NH

Hever, Amy, *Dir Advancement,* Palm Beach County Parks & Recreation Department, Morikami Museum & Japanese Gardens, Delray Beach FL

Hewen, Tony, *Head Communs,* Koffler Centre of the Arts, Koffler Gallery, Toronto ON

Hewett, Daphne, *Mus Shop Mgr,* Memphis Brooks Museum of Art, Memphis TN

Hewitt, David, *Studio Grad Coordr,* San Diego State University, School of Art, Design & Art History, San Diego CA (S)

Hewitt, Duncan, *Prof Sculpture,* University of Southern Maine, Dept of Art, Gorham ME (S)

Hext, Charles R, *Prof,* Sul Ross State University, Dept of Fine Arts & Communications, Alpine TX (S)

Heying, Philip, *Adjunct Asst Prof Photog,* Johnson County Community College, Fine Arts Dept & Art History Dept, Overland Park KS (S)

Heyl de Ortiz, Richard, *Communs Specialist,* Huguenot Historical Society of New Paltz Galleries, New Paltz NY

Heyler, Joanne, *Acting Cur,* SunAmerica, Inc, The SunAmerica Collection, Los Angeles CA

Heyman, Joy, *Dir Develop,* Walters Art Museum, Baltimore MD

Heyning, John, *Deputy Dir Research,* Natural History Museum of Los Angeles County, Los Angeles CA

Heyrman, Joy, *Dir Develop,* Walters Art Museum, Library, Baltimore MD

Heywood, Ben, *Contact,* Soap Factory, Minneapolis MN

Heywood, Stephen, *Prof,* Florida Community College at Jacksonville, South Campus, Art Dept, Jacksonville FL (S)

Hiatt, Akemi, *Prog Assoc,* Center for Photography at Woodstock Inc, Woodstock NY

Hickerson, Robert, *Info Coordr,* University of Kansas, Spencer Museum of Art, Lawrence KS

Hickey, Andria, *Cur,* Art in General, New York NY

Hickey, Christopher, *Assoc Prof,* Clark-Atlanta University, School of Arts & Sciences, Atlanta GA (S)

Hickey, Nichole, *Mgr Artist Servs,* Cultural Council of Palm Beach County, Lake Worth FL

Hickman, Paul, *Asst Prof,* Arkansas State University, Dept of Art, State University AR (S)

Hickman, Wanda, *Rec Secy,* Northwest Watercolor Society, Woodinville WA

Hickok, Paul, *Pres,* Pioneer Historical Museum of South Dakota, Hot Springs SD

Hicks, Audrey, *Treas,* Moncur Gallery, Boissevain MB

Hicks, David, *Asst Prof,* University of North Carolina at Pembroke, Art Dept, Pembroke NC (S)

Hicks, Laurie E, *Prof,* University of Maine, Dept of Art, Orono ME (S)

Hicks, Patsy, *Cur Educ,* Santa Barbara Museum of Art, Santa Barbara CA

Hicks, Patsy, *Dir Educ,* Santa Barbara Museum of Art, Library, Santa Barbara CA

Hicks, Steve, *Chmn,* Oklahoma Baptist University, Art Dept, Shawnee OK (S)

Hickson, Patricia, *Cur Contemporary Art,* Wadsworth Atheneum Museum of Art, Hartford CT

Hickson-Stevenson, Pam, *Asst Dir,* Akron-Summit County Public Library, Fine Arts Division, Akron OH

Hidalgo, William, *Visitor Svcs & Educ Asst,* University of Pennsylvania, Institute of Contemporary Art, Philadelphia PA

Hieblinger, Faith, *Exec Dir,* Homer Watson, Kitchener ON

Hiedeman, Katie, *Dir Fin & Admin,* Tucson Museum of Art and Historic Block, Tucson AZ

Hiemstra, Janna, *Cur,* Ontario Crafts Council, OCC Gallery, Toronto ON

Hiester, Jan, *Registrar,* Charleston Museum, Charleston SC

Higa, Karin, *Dir Cur & Exhib,* Japanese American National Museum, Los Angeles CA

Higbee, Brad, *Technical Dir,* Willard Arts Center, Carr Gallery, Colonial Theater, Idaho Falls ID

Higby, Sue, *Exec Dir,* Studio Place Arts, Barre VT

Higdon, Debbie, *CFO,* Huntsville Museum of Art, Huntsville AL

Higginbotham, Carmenita, *Assoc Prof,* University of Virginia, McIntire Dept of Art, Charlottesville VA (S)

Higginbotham, Colleen, *Dir Visitor Svcs,* Chrysler Museum of Art, Norfolk VA

Higgins, David, *Prof,* Corning Community College, Division of Humanities, Corning NY (S)

Higgins, Janet, *Instr,* Middle Tennessee State University, Art Dept, Murfreesboro TN (S)

Higgins, Larkin, *Prof,* California Lutheran University, Art Dept, Thousand Oaks CA (S)

Higgins, Marcia, *Pres,* Marin Society of Artists Inc, Ross CA

Higgins, Melissa, *Dir Educ,* Akron Art Museum, Akron OH

Higgins, Padraig, *Staff Asst,* Delaplaine Visual Arts Education Center, Frederick MD

Higgins, Wesley, *VPres,* Snake River Heritage Center, Weiser ID

Higgins-Jacob, Coleen, *VPres, Chief Finance, & Treas,* John Simon Guggenheim, New York NY

Higgs, Jamie, *Chmn,* Marian University, Visual Arts Dept, Indianapolis IN (S)

Higgs, Matthew, *Dir & Chief Cur,* White Columns, White Columns Curated Artist Registry, New York NY

High, Steven, *Dir & CEO,* Telfair Museums' Jepson Center for the Arts Library, Telfair Academy of Arts & Sciences Library, Savannah GA

Highet, Alan, *Dir Fin,* Bronx Museum of the Arts, Bronx NY

Highland, Margaret, *Educ Dir & Cur,* Bartow-Pell Mansion Museum & Gardens, Bronx NY

Hight, Eleanor, *Assoc Prof,* University of New Hampshire, Dept of Arts & Art History, Durham NH (S)

Hightower, John B, *Pres,* The Mariners' Museum, Newport News VA

Higonnet, Anne, *Assoc Prof,* Wellesley College, Art Dept, Wellesley MA (S)

Hild, Glenn, *Dept Chmn,* Eastern Illinois University, Art Dept, Charleston IL (S)

Hildebrandt, A Thomas, *Chair, Bd Trustees,* Genesee Country Village & Museum, John L Wehle Art Gallery, Mumford NY

Hile, Jeanette, *Prof,* Seton Hall University, College of Arts & Sciences, South Orange NJ (S)

Hileman, Jayne, *Chmn,* Saint Xavier University, Dept of Art & Design, Chicago IL (S)

Hileman, Kristen, *Cur Contemporary,* The Baltimore Museum of Art, Baltimore MD

Hiles, Jean, *VPres,* Iroquois County Historical Society Museum, Old Courthouse Museum, Watseka IL

Hiles, Tim, *Assoc Dir,* University of Tennessee, Knoxville, School of Art, Knoxville TN (S)

Hilgers, Ross, *Asst Prof,* Concordia College, Art Dept, Moorhead MN (S)

Hilken, Helen, *Dir Develop,* Northwestern University, Mary & Leigh Block Museum of Art, Evanston IL

Hilkin, Danielle, *Outreach Coordr,* Queens Historical Society, Kingsland Homestead, Flushing NY

Hill, Amelia, *Develop Asst,* McLean County Historical Society, McLean County Museum of History, Bloomington IL

Hill, Annegreth, *Chief Cur,* Museum of Art, Fort Lauderdale, Fort Lauderdale FL

Hill, Beth, *Exec Dir,* Fort Ticonderoga Association, Ticonderoga NY

Hill, Bill, *Dean,* Jacksonville University, Dept of Art, Theater, Dance, Jacksonville FL (S)

Hill, Bonnie, *Instr,* North Central Michigan College, Art Dept, Petoskey MI (S)

Hill, Brian O, *Dir & Cur,* Trenton City Museum, Trenton NJ

Hill, C T, *Pres,* Crestar Bank, Art Collection, Richmond VA

Hill, Charlie, *Cur, Canadian Art,* National Gallery of Canada, Ottawa ON

Hill, Craig, *Vis Asst Prof,* Kenyon College, Art Dept, Gambier OH (S)

Hill, Daniel G, *Pres,* American Abstract Artists, Brooklyn NY

Hill, David, *Asst Pro,* University of Mary Hardin-Baylor, College of Visual & Performing Arts, Belton TX (S)

Hill, Dennis, *Music Instr*, Edison Community College, Gallery of Fine Arts, Fort Myers FL (S)

Hill, Greg A, *Audain Cur Indigenous Art*, National Gallery of Canada, Ottawa ON

Hill, Jake, *Instr*, Langara College, Department of Design: Design Formation, Vancouver BC (S)

Hill, Lisa, *Spec Progs Coordr*, Santa Barbara Museum of Art, Library, Santa Barbara CA

Hill, Lynn, *Asst Prof*, Elmhurst College, Art Dept, Elmhurst IL (S)

Hill, Martha L, *VPres Pub Progs & Vis Experience*, Eiteljorg Museum of American Indians & Western Art, Indianapolis IN

Hill, Michael, *Instr*, University of South Dakota, Department of Art, College of Fine Arts, Vermillion SD (S)

Hill, Michele, *Admin Officer*, United States Department of the Interior, Indian Arts & Crafts Board, Washington DC

Hill, Nicholas, *Chmn*, Otterbein College, Art Dept, Westerville OH (S)

Hill, Nicole Jean, *Assoc Prof*, Humboldt State University, College of Arts & Humanities, Art Dept, Arcata CA (S)

Hill, Penny, *Dir Annual Exhib, Opening Reception Facilitator, Dir Demonstration Series*, National Watercolor Society, San Pedro CA

Hill, Phyllis, *Asst Prof Art Educ*, Elizabeth City State University, School of Arts & Humanities, Dept of Art, Elizabeth City NC (S)

Hill, Rosemary, *Assoc Prof*, Tidewater Community College, Visual Arts Center, Portsmouth VA (S)

Hill, Sherri, *Prof*, State College of Florida Manatee - Sarasota, Art, Design, Humanities, Bradenton FL (S)

Hill, Steve, *Pub Rels*, Shakespeare Ghost Town, Lordsburg NM

Hill, Thomas, *Librn*, Vassar College, Art Library, Poughkeepsie NY

Hillard, Caroline, *Asst Prof*, Wright State University, Dept of Art & Art History, Dayton OH (S)

Hillbruner, Fred, *Head Technical Svcs*, School of the Art Institute of Chicago, John M Flaxman Library, Chicago IL

Hillhouse, Susan, *Cur Exhib*, Museum of Art & History, Santa Cruz, Santa Cruz CA

Hilliard, Greg, *Dir Operations*, Cedarhurst Center for the Arts, Mitchell Museum, Mount Vernon IL

Hilliard, Mark, *Asst Prof*, Wayland Baptist University, Dept of Art, School of Fine Art, Plainview TX (S)

Hilliard, Scott, *Exec Dir*, Touchstone Center for Crafts, Hart Moore Museum, Farmington PA

Hillier, John, *Chmn*, Kilgore College, Visual Arts Dept, Kilgore TX (S)

Hillings, Valerie, *Assoc Cur Colls & Exhibs, Abu Dhabi Proj*, Solomon R Guggenheim, New York NY

Hillman, Arthur, *Prof*, Simon's Rock College of Bard, Visual Arts Dept, Great Barrington MA (S)

Hillman, Eric, *VPres*, Southern Alberta Art Gallery, Lethbridge AB

Hillmann, Elizabeth, *Educ Coordr*, Art Center Sarasota, Sarasota FL

Hillquist, Rebecca, *Instr*, Glendale Community College, Visual & Performing Arts Div, Glendale CA (S)

Hills, Matthew, *Admin Coordr*, Queen's University, Agnes Etherington Art Centre, Kingston ON

Hillstrom, Richard L, *Consultant & Cur*, Thrivent Financial for Lutherans, Gallery of Religious Art, Minneapolis MN

Hilsdale, Cecily J, *Asst Prof*, Northwestern University, Evanston, Dept of Art History, Evanston IL (S)

Hilsdon, Teta, *Opers Mgr*, Brattleboro Museum & Art Center, Brattleboro VT

Hilsinger, Laurie, *Asst to Dir*, University of Virginia, The Fralin Museum of Art at the University of Virginia, Charlottesville VA

Hilson, Douglas, *Chmn*, Hofstra University, Department of Fine Arts, Hempstead NY (S)

Hiltl-Cohen, Gabriele, *Gallery Coordr*, Drew University, Elizabeth P Korn Gallery, Madison NJ

Hilton, Alison, *Chmn & Prof*, Georgetown University, Dept of Art & Art History, Washington DC (S)

Hilty, Thomas, *Instr*, Lourdes University, Art Dept, Sylvania OH (S)

Hilty, Tomas, *Dir*, Bowling Green State University, School of Art, Bowling Green OH (S)

Hilyard, Stephen, *Assoc Prof*, University of Wisconsin, Madison, Dept of Art, Madison WI (S)

Himes, Gary, *Develop Dir*, Caramoor Center for Music & the Arts, Inc, Rosen House at Caramoor, Katonah NY

Himmelman, Ken, *Dean Admissions & Fin Aid*, Bennington College, Visual Arts Division, Bennington VT (S)

Hinckley, Bunny, *Head Docent*, The Historic New Orleans Collection, Royal Street Galleries, New Orleans LA

Hinckley, Robert L, *Exec VPres*, Wendell Gilley, Southwest Harbor ME

Hindman, James, *Dir & COO*, The American Film Institute, Center for Advanced Film & Television, Los Angeles CA (S)

Hindmarch, Sara, *Assoc Registrar*, University of Chicago, Smart Museum of Art, Chicago IL

Hinds, Jill, *Instr*, Northwestern Michigan College, Art Dept, Traverse City MI (S)

Hindson, Bradley T, *Assoc Prof*, Rochester Institute of Technology, School of Photographic Arts & Sciences, Rochester NY (S)

Hine, Charles, *Dir*, Salvador Dali, Library, Saint Petersburg FL

Hine, Hank, *Exec Dir*, Salvador Dali, Saint Petersburg FL

Hines, Jessica, *Assoc Prof*, Georgia Southern University, Dept of Art, Statesboro GA (S)

Hines, Karen, *Asst Registrar*, Vassar College, The Frances Lehman Loeb Art Center, Poughkeepsie NY

Hines, Rich, *Dir*, University of Portland, Wilson W Clark Memorial Library, Portland OR

Hines, Sondra, *Cur Educ*, Holter Museum of Art, Helena MT

Hines Cowan, Marie, *1st VPres*, National Association of Women Artists, Inc, N.A.W.A. Gallery, New York NY

Hingle, Peter, *Gift Shop Coordr*, Lewistown Art Center, Lewistown MT

Hinken, Susan, *Technical Svcs Librn*, University of Portland, Wilson W Clark Memorial Library, Portland OR

Hinkle, Brian, *Dir Gallery*, Wichita Center for the Arts, Mary R Koch School of Visual Arts, Wichita KS (S)

Hinkson, Lauren, *Asst Cur Colls*, Solomon R Guggenheim, New York NY

Hinojos, Erica, *Mus Shop Mgr*, Kern County Museum, Library, Bakersfield CA

Hinson, Mary Joan, *Prof*, Florida Community College at Jacksonville, South Campus, Art Dept, Jacksonville FL (S)

Hinson, Peggy S, *Prof*, Methodist College, Art Dept, Fayetteville NC (S)

Hinton, Al, *Prof*, University of Michigan, Ann Arbor, School of Art & Design, Ann Arbor MI (S)

Hinton, Darla, *Receptionist*, Frontier Times Museum, Bandera TX

Hinton, William, *Dir & Cur*, Louisburg College, Art Gallery, Louisburg NC

Hintz, Glen, *Asst Prof*, Rochester Institute of Technology, School of Design, Rochester NY (S)

Hintz, Jayna, *Cur Educ*, Leigh Yawkey Woodson Art Museum, Wausau WI

Hintz, Josh, *Artist*, Walker's Point Artists Assoc Inc, Gallery 218, Milwaukee WI

Hinze, Roxanne, *Adjunct Instr*, Northern State University, Art Dept, Aberdeen SD (S)

Hiott, Will, *Dir Historic Houses & Cur*, Clemson University, Fort Hill Plantation, Clemson SC

Hipp, Francis M, *Pres*, Liberty Life Insurance Company, Greenville SC

Hipps, Will, *Gallery Dir*, Maryland Institute, College of Art Exhibitions, Baltimore MD

Hirabayashi, James, *Prog Adv*, Japanese American National Museum, Los Angeles CA

Hiramoto, Judy, *Instr*, American River College, Dept of Art/Art New Media, Sacramento CA (S)

Hiratsuka, Yuji, *Asst Prof*, Oregon State University, Dept of Art, Corvallis OR (S)

Hirayama, Mikiko, *Asst Prof Art History*, University of Cincinnati, School of Art, Cincinnati OH (S)

Hirsch, Barron, *Prof*, Saginaw Valley State University, Dept of Art & Design, University Center MI (S)

Hirsch, Edward, *Pres*, John Simon Guggenheim, New York NY

Hirsch, Elizabeth, *Mgr Communs*, Artists Space, New York NY

Hirsch, Erin, *Dir HR*, San Francisco Museum of Modern Art, San Francisco CA

Hirsch, Marjorie, *Dir*, Clark College, Archer Gallery/Gaiser Hall, Vancouver WA

Hirsch, Richard, *Prof*, Rochester Institute of Technology, School of Design, Rochester NY (S)

Hirsch, Robin, *Assoc Dir*, Art Saint Louis, Saint Louis MO

Hirschel, Anthony, *Dir*, University of Chicago, Smart Museum of Art, Chicago IL

Hirschfeld, Barbara, *Exec Dir*, Paine Art Center & Gardens, Oshkosh WI

Hirschfield, Jim, *Prof*, University of North Carolina at Chapel Hill, Art Dept, Chapel Hill NC (S)

Hirshler, Erica, *Croll Sr Cur Paintings Art of the Americas*, Museum of Fine Arts, Boston MA

Hirshon, Stephen, *Asst Prof*, Shippensburg University, Art Dept, Shippensburg PA (S)

Hirt, Brian, *Chair Ceramics*, Kalamazoo Institute of Arts, KIA School, Kalamazoo MI (S)

Hirz, Aimee C, *Pub Rels Asst*, Williams College, Museum of Art, Williamstown MA

Hisa, Asuka, *Dir Educ*, Santa Monica Museum of Art, Santa Monica CA

Hisey, Scott, *Dir Mktg*, Cincinnati Art Museum, Cincinnati Art Museum, Cincinnati OH

Hiskey, Lynnette, *Asst Dir*, Utah Arts Council, Chase Home Museum of Utah Folk Arts, Salt Lake City UT

Hiss, Nancy, *Instr*, Marylhurst University, Art Dept, Marylhurst OR (S)

Hissey, Carey, *Assoc Prof*, Oklahoma State University, Department of Art, Graphic Design and Art History, Stillwater OK (S)

Hitchcock, Alix, *Instr*, Wake Forest University, Dept of Art, Winston-Salem NC (S)

Hitchcock, John, *Assoc Prof*, University of Wisconsin, Madison, Dept of Art, Madison WI (S)

Hitchcock, Julia, *Assoc Prof*, Baylor University - College of Arts and Sciences, Dept of Art, Waco TX (S)

Hites, Thomas, *Treas*, Brooklyn Historical Society, Brooklyn OH

Hittinger, Lauren, *Mktg & Develop Mgr*, The Arts Center of the Capital Region, Troy NY

Hixon, Karen, *Chmn Bd Trustees*, San Antonio Museum of Art, San Antonio TX

Hixson, Maiza, *Cur Contemporary Art*, Delaware Center for the Contemporary Arts, Wilmington DE

Hixson, Steven Driscoll, *Asst Prof*, University of Wisconsin, Madison, Dept of Art, Madison WI (S)

Hlady, Maria, *Instr*, Toronto School of Art, Toronto ON (S)

Hlowatzki, William, *Pub Rels*, Canadian Clay and Glass Gallery, Waterloo ON

Hnateyko, Olha, *Pres (V)*, The Ukrainian Museum, New York NY

Hnatysh, Walter, *Prof Art, Painting/Drawing*, Florida Atlantic University, D F Schmidt College of Arts & Letters Dept of Visual Arts & Art History, Boca Raton FL (S)

Hoagland, Eleanor T M, *Pres*, Wendell Gilley, Southwest Harbor ME

Hoar, Bill, *Prof*, Northern State University, Art Dept, Aberdeen SD (S)

Hoard, Curtis, *Prof*, University of Minnesota, Minneapolis, Dept of Art, Minneapolis MN (S)

Hobbs, Frank, *Asst Prof*, Ohio Wesleyan University, Fine Arts Dept, Delaware OH (S)

Hobbs, Jon F, *Exec Dir*, Royal Architectural Institute of Canada, Ottawa ON

Hobbs, Katelyn, *Cur Asst*, University of Virginia, The Fralin Museum of Art at the University of Virginia, Charlottesville VA

Hobbs, Mary Alice, *Publicity & Heritage Writer*, Brigham City Corporation, Brigham City Museum & Gallery, Brigham City UT

Hobbs, Patricia, *Dir*, Washington & Lee University, Lee Chapel & Museum, Lexington VA

Hobbs, Robert, *Prof*, Virginia Commonwealth University, Art History Dept, Richmond VA (S)

Hobby, Janet, *Pres*, Menil Foundation, Inc, The Menil Collection, Houston TX

Hobday, John, *Exec Dir (SBC)*, Saidye Bronfman, Liane & Danny Taran Gallery, Montreal PQ

Hobgood, Wade, *Dean*, California State University, Long Beach, Design Dept, Long Beach CA (S)

Hobin, Timothy J, *Admin Asst*, Center for Exploratory & Perceptual Art, CEPA Library, Buffalo NY

Hobruecker, Uli, *Book-Keeper*, Contemporary Art Gallery Society of British Columbia, Vancouver BC

Hochhalter, Lindsay, *Develop Coordr*, Arizona Museum For Youth, Mesa AZ

Hochradel, Rebecca, *Fiscal Mgr*, Historic Arkansas Museum, Little Rock AR

Hock, John, *Dir*, Saint Paul Western Sculpture Park, Saint Paul MN

Hock, Rick, *Exhibs Coordr*, Visual Studies Workshop, Rochester NY (S)

Hockensmith, Josh, *Libr Technical Asst*, University of North Carolina at Chapel Hill, Joseph Curtis Sloane Art Library, Chapel Hill NC

Hocket, Esther, *Dir*, North Dakota State University, Memorial Union Gallery, Fargo ND

Hockett, Roland L, *Assoc Prof*, Gulf Coast Community College, Division of Visual & Performing Arts, Panama City FL (S)

Hockhousen, Jim, *Dir Finance & Admin*, Newport Art Museum and Association, Newport RI

Hocking, Christopher, *Assoc Prof Foundations*, University of Georgia, Franklin College of Arts & Sciences, Lamar Dodd School of Art, Athens GA (S)

Hockwelt, Helen, *Cur*, Pickens County Museum of Art & History, Pickens SC

Hodge, Beth, *Exec Dir*, Stauton Augusta Art Center, Staunton VA

Hodge, Patricia, *Vol Svcs Coordr*, Rodman Hall Arts Centre, Saint Catharines ON

Hodgens, Mary Lee, *Prog Mgr*, Light Work, Robert B Menschel Photography Gallery, Syracuse NY

Hodges, Jeanne, *Admin Asst*, Prince George Art Gallery, Prince George BC

Hodges, Pat, *Manuscript Librn*, Western Kentucky University, Kentucky Library & Museum, Bowling Green KY

Hodges, Richard, *Dir*, University of Pennsylvania, Museum of Archaeology & Anthropology, Philadelphia PA

Hodges, V. Pauline, *VPres*, No Man's Land Historical Society, No Man's Land Museum, Goodwell OK

Hodgson, Terri, *Admin Asst*, University of Redlands, Peppers Art Gallery, Redlands CA

Hodik, Barbara, *Prof*, Rochester Institute of Technology, School of Design, Rochester NY (S)

Hodson, Carol, *Asst Prof*, Webster University, Art Dept, Webster Groves MO (S)

Hodson, Janice, *Cur Art*, New Bedford Free Public Library, Special Collections Dept: Art Collection, New Bedford MA

Hoechstetter, Marissa, *Events & Pub Rels*, Archives of American Art, New York Regional Center, Washington DC

Hoefferie, Mary, *Asst Prof*, University of Wisconsin Oshkosh, Dept of Art, Oshkosh WI (S)

Hoefle, Krista, *Gallery Dir*, Saint Mary's College, Moreau Galleries, Notre Dame IN

Hoeltzel, Susan, *Dir*, Lehman College Art Gallery, Bronx NY

Hofacket, Katy, *Coordr*, Deming-Luna Mimbres Museum, Deming NM

Hoffeld, Jeffrey, *Assoc Dean*, New York Studio School of Drawing, Painting & Sculpture, Gallery, New York NY

Hoffer, Larry, *Deputy Exec Dir & COO*, Industrial Designers Society of America, Herndon VA

Hoffman, Angela, *Dir School of Art*, Palos Verdes Art Center/Beverly G. Alpay Center for Arts Education, Rancho Palos Verdes CA

Hoffman, Clair, *Individual Giving Assoc*, Museum for African Art, New York NY

Hoffman, Diane, *Assoc Prof*, Rhodes College, Dept of Art, Memphis TN (S)

Hoffman, Erin, *Prog Coordr*, Muskegon Community College, Dept of Creative & Performing Arts, Muskegon MI (S)

Hoffman, Eva, *Asst Prof*, Tufts University, Dept of Art & Art History, Medford MA (S)

Hoffman, Geralyn, *Cur Progs & Educ*, Brown University, Haffenreffer Museum of Anthropology, Providence RI

Hoffman, Jens, *Deputy Dir Exhibs & Pub progs*, The Jewish Museum, New York NY

Hoffman, Jens, *Dir*, Capp Street Project, Wattis Institute, San Francisco CA

Hoffman, Joel M, *Exec Dir*, Vizcaya Museum & Gardens, Miami FL

Hoffman, Kate, *Dir*, Huntington Beach Art Center, Huntington Beach CA

Hoffman, Katherine, *Chmn*, Saint Anselm College, Dept of Fine Arts, Manchester NH (S)

Hoffman, Kim, *Prof*, Western Oregon State College, Creative Arts Division, Visual Arts, Monmouth OR (S)

Hoffman, Mark, *COO*, The Buffalo Fine Arts Academy, Albright-Knox Art Gallery, Buffalo NY

Hoffman, Michael, *Div Head & Assoc Prof*, Norwich University, Dept of Architecture and Art, Northfield VT (S)

Hoffman, Neil, *Pres*, Milwaukee Institute of Art & Design, Milwaukee WI (S)

Hoffman, Randy, *Treas*, Independence Historical Museum & Art Center, Independence KS

Hoffman, Sheila, *Cur*, The Rockwell Museum of Western Art, Corning NY

Hoffman, Tom, *Instr*, University of Utah, Dept of Art & Art History, Salt Lake City UT (S)

Hoffman, Tom, *Prof*, University of Maine at Augusta, College of Arts & Humanities, Augusta ME (S)

Hofmann, Sally, *Visual Arts Coordr*, Beaufort County Arts Council, Washington NC

Hofstedt, Matthew, *Assoc Cur*, Supreme Court of the United States, Office of the Curator, Washington DC

Hofstetter, Philip, *Dir*, California State University, East Bay, University Art Gallery, Hayward CA

Hoftstetter, Mary, *Pres & CEO*, Banff Centre, Walter Phillips Gallery, Banff AB

Hogan, Carrie, *Cur*, American Swedish Historical Foundation & Museum, American Swedish Historical Museum, Philadelphia PA

Hogan, Carrie, *Cur Exhib*, American Swedish Historical Foundation & Museum, Nord Library, Philadelphia PA

Hogan, Erin, *Dir Pub Affairs*, The Art Institute of Chicago, Chicago IL

Hogan, Gilbert F, *Pres*, New Haven Museum & Historical Society, Whitney Library, New Haven CT

Hogan, Jacqueline, *Asst Dir*, State University of New York at Binghamton, Binghamton University Art Museum, Binghamton NY

Hogan, John, *Dir Opers*, Museum of Photographic Arts, Edmund L. and Nancy K Dubois Library, San Diego CA

Hogan-Finlay, Onya, *Programming Asst*, La Centrale Powerhouse Gallery, Montreal PQ

Hogan-Schofield, Dorothy, *Cur Colls*, The Sandwich Historical Society, Inc & Sandwich Glass Museum, Sandwich Glass Museum, Sandwich MA

Hogarth, Brian, *Adjunct Asst Prof Art History*, Johnson County Community College, Fine Arts Dept & Art History Dept, Overland Park KS (S)

Hoge, Joan, *Exec Dir*, Delaware Historical Society, Library, Wilmington DE

Hogg, John, *Pres*, MEXIC-ARTE Museum, Austin TX

Hogg, Lois, *Secy*, Manitoba Society of Artists, Winnipeg MB

Hogu, Barbara J, *Asst Prof*, City Colleges of Chicago, Malcolm X College, Chicago IL (S)

Hogya, G, *Dean*, University of Victoria, Dept of History in Art, Victoria BC (S)

Hohenberg, Alane, *Dir Develop*, Rensselaer County Historical Society, Hart-Cluett Mansion, 1827, Troy NY

Hohmann, Glynys, *Team Leader Government Records*, Ministry of Alberta Culture, Provincial Archives of Alberta, Edmonton AB

Hoinski, Michael, *Educ Coordr*, City of Austin Parks & Recreation, O. Henry Museum, Austin TX

Hoisington, Rena, *Assoc Cur Drawings & Photographs*, The Baltimore Museum of Art, Baltimore MD

Hojonsky, Patrick, *Prof*, Southwestern University, Sarofim School of Fine Art, Dept of Art & Art History, Georgetown TX (S)

Hokanson, Taylor, *Asst Prof*, Oakland University, Dept of Art & Art History, Rochester MI (S)

Holahan, Mary F, *Cur Colls*, Delaware Art Museum, Wilmington DE

Holbach, Joseph, *Chief Registrar*, The Phillips Collection, Washington DC

Holbert, Kelly, *Exhib Coordr*, Smith College, Museum of Art, Northampton MA

Holbrook-Shaw, Chanelle, *Contact*, Monarch Contemporary Art Center & Sculpture Park, Olympia WA

Holbrow, Dan, *Professional Develop Coordr*, Museums Association of Saskatchewan, Regina SK

Holbrow, Katherine, *Conservator*, Asian Art Museum of San Francisco, Chong-Moon Lee Ctr for Asian Art and Culture, San Francisco CA

Holbus, Heather, *Prog Coordr*, Intuit: The Center for Intuitive & Outsider Art, Chicago IL

Holcomb, Grant, *Dir*, University of Rochester, Memorial Art Gallery, Rochester NY

Holcombe, Anna Calluori, *Prof*, Kansas State University, Art Dept, Manhattan KS (S)

Holden, Daniel, *Gallery Asst*, St Mary's College of Maryland, The Dwight Frederick Boyden Gallery, St Mary's City MD

Holden, John, *Asst Prof*, Bemidji State University, Visual Arts Dept, Bemidji MN (S)

Holden, Wendy, *Sr Assoc Cur*, University of Michigan, Asian Art Archives, Ann Arbor MI

Holder, Teresa, *Lectr*, Oklahoma State University, Department of Art, Graphic Design and Art History, Stillwater OK (S)

Holder, Thomas J, *Prof*, University of Nevada, Las Vegas, Dept of Art, Las Vegas NV (S)

Holderbaum, Linda, *Exec Dir*, Art Center of Battle Creek, Battle Creek MI

Holderbaum, Linda, *Exec Dir*, Art Center of Battle Creek, Michigan Art & Artist Archives, Battle Creek MI

Holdorf, Ellen, *Registrar*, Museum of Arts & Design, New York NY

Holeu, Alisa, *Asst Prof Art*, University of Southern Indiana, Department of Art, Evansville IN (S)

Holian, Heather, *Prof*, University of North Carolina at Greensboro, Art Dept, Greensboro NC (S)

Holker, Lynda, *Spec Events Mgr*, Museum of Russian Art, Minneapolis MN

Holl, James, *Assoc Prof Art*, Marymount Manhattan College, Fine & Performing Arts Div, New York NY (S)

Holland, Barbara, *Art Instr*, Tyler Junior College, Art Program, Tyler TX (S)

Holland, Hillary, *Dir Pub Rels*, Brandywine Conservancy, Brandywine River Museum, Chadds Ford PA

Holland, Joy, *Adj Instr*, University of West Florida, Dept of Art, Pensacola FL (S)

Holland, Raymond, *VPres*, Lehigh Valley Heritage Center, Allentown PA

Hollander, Barbara J, *Altoona Coordr*, Southern Alleghenies Museum of Art, Altoona Facility, Loretto PA

Hollander, Joel, *Instr*, University of Miami, Dept of Art & Art History, Coral Gables FL (S)

Hollander, Katie, *Deputy Dir*, Creative Time, New York NY

Hollander, Stacy, *Dir Exhibs & Sr Cur*, American Folk Art Museum, New York NY

Holliday, Paul, *Acad Prog Asst*, Southern California Institute of Architecture, Los Angeles CA (S)

Holliday, Stuart, *Pres*, Meridian International Center, Cafritz Galleries, Washington DC

Hollingsworth, Mar, *Prog Mgr Visual Arts*, California African-American Museum, Los Angeles CA

Hollingsworth, Priscilla, *Prof*, Augusta State University, Dept of Art, Augusta GA (S)

Hollingwood, Keith, *Adjunct Faculty*, Mount Wachusett Community College, East Wing Gallery, Gardner MA

Hollins, Hunter, *Coordr*, United States Department of the Interior, Interior Museum, Washington DC

Hollis, Sara, *Chmn*, Southern University in New Orleans, Fine Arts & Philosophy Dept, New Orleans LA (S)

Hollister, Philip, *Mus Technician*, University of Connecticut, William Benton Museum of Art, Storrs CT

Horne, Prudence, *Cur,* Grossmont Community College, Hyde Art Gallery, El Cajon CA

Horne-Leshinsky, Jody, *Community Develop Dir,* Broward County Board of Commissioners, Cultural Div, Fort Lauderdale FL

Horne Garland, Traci, *Gallery Coordr,* Virginia Commonwealth University, Anderson Gallery, Richmond VA

Horner, Edward W, *Exec VPres Develop & Pub Affairs,* The Art Institute of Chicago, Chicago IL

Horner, Garin, *Asst Prof,* Adrian College, Art & Design Dept, Adrian MI (S)

Horner, Gerald, *Deputy Dir,* Kirkland Museum of Fine & Decorative Art, Denver CO

Horner, Marge, *Educ Dir,* Abington Art Center, Jenkintown PA

Hornik, Heidi, *Dir,* Baylor University, Martin Museum of Art, Waco TX

Hornik, Heidi, *Treas,* Midwest Art History Society, Waco TX

Hornik, Heidi J, *Prof,* Baylor University - College of Arts and Sciences, Dept of Art, Waco TX (S)

Horning, Jerry, *Instr,* Creighton University, Fine & Performing Arts Dept, Omaha NE (S)

Horning, Lisa, *Prof,* Ocean County College, Humanities Dept, Toms River NJ (S)

Hornor, Elizabeth S, *Dir Educ,* Emory University, Michael C Carlos Museum, Atlanta GA

Horodner, Stuart, *Artistic Dir,* Atlanta Contemporary Art Center, Atlanta GA

Horoschak, Lynne, *Chmn Art Educ,* Moore College of Art & Design, Philadelphia PA (S)

Horovitz, Ellen, *Assoc Prof,* Nazareth College of Rochester, Art Dept, Rochester NY (S)

Horowitz, Amy, *Clerk Specialist,* Rensselaer Polytechnic Institute, Eye Ear Studio Dept of Art, Troy NY (S)

Horrigan, William, *Cur Media Arts,* Ohio State University, Wexner Center for the Arts, Columbus OH

Horsbrugh, Patrick, *Founder,* Environic Foundation International Library, South Bend IN

Horst, Randy, *Chmn Dept,* The University of Montana Western, Art Program, Dillon MT (S)

Horst, Randy, *Dir,* The University of Montana - Western, Art Gallery Museum, Dillon MT

Horsting, Archana, *Exec Dir,* Kala Institute, Kala Art Institute, Berkeley CA

Horstmann, Joy, *VPres,* Marion Art Center, Cecil Clark Davis Gallery, Marion MA

Horton, Amanda, *Mem & Commun Assoc,* Kentucky Museum of Art and Craft, Louisville KY

Horton, Angie, *Instr,* Bakersfield College, Art Dept, Bakersfield CA (S)

Horton, Christopher, *Assoc Prof,* University of Hartford, Hartford Art School, West Hartford CT (S)

Horton, David, *Assoc Prof,* William Paterson University, Dept Arts, Wayne NJ (S)

Horton, Lindsay, *Receptionist,* Contemporary Art Center of Virginia, Virginia Beach VA

Horton-Lopez, Ann, *Assoc Prof & Dir Grad Art Educ,* University of North Carolina at Pembroke, Art Dept, Pembroke NC (S)

Horvat, Krisjohn O, *Prof,* Rhode Island College, Art Dept, Providence RI (S)

Horvath, Sharon, *Assoc Prof,* Purchase College, State University of New York, School of Art+Design, Purchase NY (S)

Horvay, Henrietta C, *Pres & Cur,* Goshen Historical Society, Goshen CT

Hose, Don, *Photographer,* City of Springdale, Shiloh Museum of Ozark History, Springdale AR

Hosey, Terrie, *Cur,* Art Association of Harrisburg, School & Galleries, Harrisburg PA

Hosford, John, *Visual Resources Cur,* New York State College of Ceramics at Alfred University, Scholes Library of Ceramics, Alfred NY

Hoskins, W E, *Exec Dir,* San Francisco African-American Historical & Cultural Society, San Francisco CA

Hosterman, Bill, *Assoc Prof,* Grand Valley State University, Art & Design Dept, Allendale MI (S)

Hostetler, Lisa, *Cur Photographs,* Milwaukee Art Museum, Milwaukee WI

Hostetler, Soo, *Asst Prof,* University of Northern Iowa, Dept of Art, Cedar Falls IA (S)

Hostetter, David, *Cur Planetarium,* Lafayette Science Museum & Planetarium, Lafayette LA

Hotchkiss, Margit, *Dir Mktg & Communs,* Norman Rockwell Museum, Stockbridge MA

Hotchkiss, Patricia, *Libr Dir,* Cochise College, Charles Di Peso Library, Douglas AZ

Hottle, Max, *Guardian,* Mission San Miguel Museum, San Miguel CA

Hou, Lucia, *Pres,* New World Art Center, T F Chen Cultural Center, New York NY

Houben, Anden, *Opers Mgr,* Kentuck Museum Association, Inc., Kentuck Art Center & Festival of the Arts, Northport AL

Houck, Gayla, *Mgr,* Omaha Children's Museum, Omaha NE

Houdek, Alesh, *Mktg & Design Mgr,* Art & Culture Center of Hollywood, Art Gallery/Multidisciplinary Cultural Center, Hollywood FL

Hough, Emanuel D, *Dir & Pres,* Shakespeare Ghost Town, Lordsburg NM

Hough, Katherine, *Chief Cur,* Palm Springs Art Museum, Palm Springs CA

Houghtaling, Kim, *Dir & Cur,* Art Gallery of Swift Current, Swift Current SK

Houghton, Charlotte, *Assoc Prof,* Pennsylvania State University, University Park, Dept of Art History, University Park PA (S)

Houghton, Melissa, *VPres,* American Architectural Foundation, Museum, Washington DC

Houle, Joy, *Exec Dir,* Saratoga County Historical Society, Brookside Museum, Ballston Spa NY

Houle, Matthew, *Cur Mus Coll,* University of Richmond, University Museums, Richmond VA

Houle, Michel, *Dir Fin Mgmt Svcs & Interim VP,* Canadian Museum of Nature, Musee Canadien de la Nature, Ottawa ON

Hourahan, Richard, *Coll Mgr,* Queens Historical Society, Kingsland Homestead, Flushing NY

Hourihane, Colum, *Dir,* Princeton University, Index of Christian Art, Princeton NJ

House, John, *Chair Prof,* University of Southern Mississippi, Dept of Art & Design, Hattiesburg MS (S)

Housefield, James, *Assoc Prof,* Texas State University - San Marcos, Dept of Art and Design, San Marcos TX (S)

Houser, Craig, *Lectr,* City College of New York, Art Dept, New York NY (S)

Houser, Thom, *Assoc Prof Interior Design,* University of Georgia, Franklin College of Arts & Sciences, Lamar Dodd School of Art, Athens GA (S)

Houston, Gay, *Pres,* Heart of West Texas Museum, Colorado City TX

Houston, Joe, *Cur,* Hallmark Cards, Inc, Hallmark Art Collection, Kansas City MO

Houston, William, *Artist-in-Residence,* Carson-Newman College, Art Dept, Jefferson City TN (S)

Houze, Rebecca, *Div Head Art History,* Northern Illinois University, School of Art, DeKalb IL (S)

Hovde, Amy, *Bus Mgr,* North Dakota Museum of Art, Grand Forks ND

Hovey, David, *Assoc Prof,* Illinois Institute of Technology, College of Architecture, Chicago IL (S)

Hovins, Kristen, *Prof,* Middlebury College, History of Art & Architecture Dept, Middlebury VT (S)

Howard, Andrew, *Chmn Dept,* Wheaton College, Art Dept, Norton MA (S)

Howard, Angela, *Assoc Prof,* Rutgers, The State University of New Jersey, Graduate Program in Art History, New Brunswick NJ (S)

Howard, Bryan, *Dir Exhib & Coll,* The University of Texas at San Antonio, Institute of Texan Cultures, San Antonio TX

Howard, Carolyn, *Instr,* Wayne Art Center, Wayne PA (S)

Howard, Debbie, *Bus Mgr,* LaGrange Art Museum, LaGrange GA

Howard, Deborah, *Assoc Prof Drawing & Painting,* University of Denver, School of Art & Art History, Denver CO (S)

Howard, Jack, *Far Eastern Librn,* Royal Ontario Museum, Library & Archives, Toronto ON

Howard, Jan, *Cur Prints, Drawings & Photos,* Rhode Island School of Design, Museum of Art, Providence RI

Howard, Richard, *Bus Mgr,* 18th Street Arts Complex, Santa Monica CA

Howard, William, *Asst Prof,* Western Illinois University, Department of Art, Macomb IL (S)

Howard-Rogers, Kathryn, *Asst Prof,* Oakton Community College, Language Humanities & Art Divisions, Des Plaines IL (S)

Howe, Farrell, *Coordr Mktg,* Kalamazoo Institute of Arts, Kalamazoo MI

Howe, Katherine S, *Dir,* Museum of Fine Arts, Houston, Rienzi Center for European Decorative Arts, Houston TX

Howe, Kathleen, *Dir,* The Pomona College, Claremont CA

Howe, Lisa, *Educ Coordr,* City of Lubbock, Buddy Holly Center, Lubbock TX

Howe, Scott, *Dir Educ & Pub Progs,* Chrysler Museum of Art, Norfolk VA

Howe, Thomas, *Co-Chmn Prof,* Southwestern University, Sarofim School of Fine Art, Dept of Art & Art History, Georgetown TX (S)

Howe, Wayne, *Archives Chmn,* Jericho Historical Society, Jericho VT

Howell, Jason, *Asst Prof,* Oral Roberts University, Art Dept, Tulsa OK (S)

Howell, Joyce B, *Assoc Prof,* Virginia Wesleyan College, Art Dept of the Humanities Div, Norfolk VA (S)

Howell, Marta, *Exec Dir,* Hershey Museum, Hershey PA

Howell, Maureen, *Grad Coordr-Art History,* University of Texas, Dept of Art & Art History, Austin TX (S)

Howell, Michael, *Collections Mgr & Registrar,* Colorado Springs Fine Arts Center, Taylor Museum, Colorado Springs CO

Howell, Michael, *Dir,* Albright College, Freedman Gallery, Reading PA

Howell, Robert, *Prof Photog,* California Polytechnic State University at San Luis Obispo, Dept of Art & Design, San Luis Obispo CA (S)

Howell, Tom, *Chmn,* Porterville College, Dept of Fine Arts, Porterville CA (S)

Howenstein, Drea, *Chmn Art Education,* School of the Art Institute of Chicago, Chicago IL (S)

Hower, Robert, *Chmn,* University of Texas at Arlington, Art & Art History Department, Arlington TX (S)

Hower, Rolland, *Pres,* Mattawoman Creek Art Center, Marbury MD

Howes, Ann, *Instr,* Wayne Art Center, Wayne PA (S)

Howes, Stephen, *Chmn,* Town of Cummington Historical Commission, Kingman Tavern Historical Museum, Cummington MA

Howick, Laura, *Dir Educ,* Fitchburg Art Museum, Fitchburg MA

Howk, Cynthia, *Res Coordr,* Landmark Society of Western New York, Inc, Wenrich Memorial Library, Rochester NY

Howkins, Mary Ball, *Prof,* Rhode Island College, Art Dept, Providence RI (S)

Howland, Margaret, *Visitor Servs,* Harvard University, Harvard University Art Museums, Cambridge MA

Hownion, Morris, *Chief Cataloguer,* New York City Technical College, Ursula C Schwerin Library, Brooklyn NY

Howorth, Ted, *Lectr,* University of Manitoba, School of Art, Winnipeg MB (S)

Howorth-Bouman, Katherine, *Dir Educ,* Roberson Museum & Science Center, Binghamton NY

Howse, Beth, *Ref Librn Special Collections,* Fisk University, Library, Nashville TN

Hoydysh, Walter, *Dir Prog,* Ukrainian Institute of America, Inc, New York NY

Hoyer, Lindy, *Exec Dir,* Omaha Children's Museum, Omaha NE

Hoyle, Haruko, *Gallery Officer,* Japan Society, Inc, Japan Society Gallery, New York NY

Hoyt, Edward, *Pres,* Museum of the Hudson Highlands, Cornwall On Hudson NY

Hrehov, John, *Prof,* Indiana-Purdue University, Dept of Fine Arts, Fort Wayne IN (S)

Hrenko, Kelly, *Asst Prof Art Educ,* University of Southern Maine, Dept of Art, Gorham ME (S)

Hriso, Peter, *Assoc Prof,* Missouri Western State University, Art Dept, Saint Joseph MO (S)

Hriunak, John, *Instr,* Judson University, School of Art, Design & Architecture, Elgin IL (S)

Hrivnak, Tom, *Dir Horticulture,* Stan Hywet, Akron OH

Hron, Vincent, *Assoc Prof*, Bloomsburg University, Dept of Art & Art History, Bloomsburg PA (S)

Hruby, Julie A, *Asst Prof*, Berea College, Art & Art History Program, Berea KY (S)

Hrushetska, Maryna, *Exec Dir*, Craft and Folk Art Museum (CAFAM), Los Angeles CA

Hrycelak, George, *Dir*, Ukrainian National Museum & Library, Chicago IL

Hsin-Mei, Agnes, *Dir Arts & Culture Progs*, China Institute in America, China Institute Gallery, New York NY

Hsiung, Robert, *VPres*, New England Watercolor Society, Pembroke MA

Hsu, Lillian, *Dir Pub Art*, Cambridge Arts Council, CAC Gallery, Cambridge MA

Hu, Li, *Prof*, University of Wisconsin Oshkosh, Dept of Art, Oshkosh WI (S)

Hu, Xinran, *Asst Prof*, University of Southern Indiana, Department of Art, Evansville IN (S)

Hu, Zheng, *Exhib Designer*, University at Albany, State University of New York, University Art Museum, Albany NY

Huacuja-Person, Judith, *Asst Prof*, University of Dayton, Visual Arts Dept, Dayton OH (S)

Huang, Binggi, *Asst Prof*, University at Buffalo, State University of New York, Dept of Visual Studies, Buffalo NY (S)

Huang, Tien, *Dir*, Bau-Xi Gallery, Toronto ON

Huang, Vivian, *Gallery Cur*, Chinese-American Arts Council, New York NY

Hubbard, John D, *Prof*, Northern Michigan University, Dept of Art & Design, Marquette MI (S)

Hubbard, Michael, *Instr*, Midland College, Art Dept, Midland TX (S)

Hubbard, Paul, *Chmn Fine Arts*, Moore College of Art & Design, Philadelphia PA (S)

Hubbard, Quatro, *Archivist*, Virginia Dept Historic Resources, Research Library, Richmond VA

Hubbard, Walter, *VPres*, Belskie Museum, Closter NJ

Hubbartt, Beth, *Dir Merchandising*, Chicago History Museum, Chicago IL

Huber, Fran, *Asst Dir Coll*, Louisiana State University, Museum of Art, Baton Rouge LA

Huber, Mary, *Dir*, City of Cedar Falls, Iowa, James & Meryl Hearst Center for the Arts & Sculpture Garden, Cedar Falls IA

Huberman, Anthony, *Dir*, California College of the Arts, CCAC Wattis Institute for Contemporary Arts, San Francisco CA

Huberman, Brian, *Assoc Prof*, Rice University, Visual & Dramatic Arts, Houston TX (S)

Hubert, Thomas, *Assoc Prof*, Mercyhurst College, Dept of Art, Erie PA (S)

Hubert, William Post, *Assoc Pres*, Marcella Sembrich Memorial Association Inc, Marcella Sembrich Opera Museum, Bolton Landing NY

Huchko, Michael, *Library Asst*, Rome Historical Society, Museum & Archives, Rome NY

Huchko, Michael, *Library Asst*, Rome Historical Society, William E Scripture Memorial Library, Rome NY

Huckaby, Sedrick, *Vis Asst Prof*, University of Texas at Arlington, Art & Art History Department, Arlington TX (S)

Hudak, Jane R, *Assoc Prof*, Georgia Southern University, Dept of Art, Statesboro GA (S)

Hudec, Susan, *Mus Educ*, University of Minnesota Duluth, Tweed Museum of Art, Duluth MN

Hudgins, Don, *Exec Dir*, Center on Contemporary Art, Seattle WA

Hudson, Eldred, *Assoc Prof*, University of North Carolina at Charlotte, Dept Art, Charlotte NC (S)

Hudson, Ernest, *Accnt*, Birmingham Museum of Art, Birmingham AL

Hudson, James, *Video Production*, Art Institute of Pittsburgh, Pittsburgh PA (S)

Hudson, Kelly, *Deputy Dir*, Montalvo Center for the Arts, Saratoga CA

Hudson, Myrtle, *Information Resources Asst*, University of Michigan, Fine Arts Library, Ann Arbor MI

Hudson, Rebecca, *Budget Officer & Gallery Mgr*, The Art Museum at the University of Kentucky, Lexington KY

Hudson-Connors, Jenniffer, *Librn*, Nelda C & H J Lutcher Stark, Stark Museum of Art, Orange TX

Hudzan, Andriy, *Adminr*, Ukrainian Institute of Modern Art, Chicago IL

Huebner, Carla, *Assoc Prof*, Mount Mary College, Art & Design Division, Milwaukee WI (S)

Huebner, Gregory, *Chmn*, Wabash College, Art Dept, Crawfordsville IN (S)

Huebner, Karla, *Asst Prof*, Wright State University, Dept of Art & Art History, Dayton OH (S)

Huebner, Rosemarita, *Prof*, Mount Mary College, Art & Design Division, Milwaukee WI (S)

Huebner-Venezia, Carol, *Asst Prof*, C W Post Campus of Long Island University, School of Visual & Performing Arts, Brookville NY (S)

Huelsbergen, Deborah, *Prof, Dir Undergrad Studies (Graphic Design)*, University of Missouri - Columbia, Dept of Art, Columbia MO (S)

Huelsmann, Mary, *Prof*, Saint Louis Community College at Meramec, Art Dept, Saint Louis MO (S)

Huerta, Benito, *Assoc Prof*, University of Texas at Arlington, Art & Art History Department, Arlington TX (S)

Huerta, Benito, *Dir & Cur*, University of Texas at Arlington, Gallery at UTA, Arlington TX

Hueting, Melissa, *Outreach Progs Coordr*, Figge Art Museum, Davenport IA

Hufbauer, Ben, *Assoc Prof*, University of Louisville, Allen R Hite Art Institute, Louisville KY (S)

Huff, David, *Educ*, Tom Thomson, Library/Archives, Owen Sound ON

Huff, David, *Mgr Pub Progs*, Tom Thomson, Owen Sound ON

Huff, Mark, *Chmn*, State University of New York College at Potsdam, Dept of Fine Arts, Potsdam NY (S)

Huff, Richard E, *Exec Dir*, Irving Arts Center, Galleries & Sculpture Garden, Irving TX

Huff, Robert, *Chmn*, Miami-Dade Community College, Arts & Philosophy Dept, Miami FL (S)

Huff, Sam, *Exec Dir*, Buckham Fine Arts Project, Gallery, Flint MI

Huffman, Bill, *Admin Dir*, A Space, Toronto ON

Huffman, Bill, *Dir*, Laurentian University, Museum & Art Centre, Sudbury ON

Huffman, Bill, *Dir & Cur*, Laurentian University, Art Centre Library, Sudbury ON

Huffman, Joan, *Park Supt*, Old Fort Harrod State Park Mansion Museum, Harrodsburg KY

Huffman, John, *Site Adminr*, Mark Twain, State Historic Site Museum, Florida MO

Huffman, Leslie, *Admin Mgr*, CultureWorks, Richmond VA

Huffman, Lorilee, *Cur Colls*, Southern Illinois University Carbondale, University Museum, Carbondale IL

Huffstutler, Rebecca, *Cur Archives & Registrar*, Witte Museum, San Antonio TX

Huffstutler Norton, Rebecca, *Exec Dir*, Frontier Times Museum, Bandera TX

Huftalen, Alison L, *Head Librn*, Toledo Museum of Art, Art Reference Library, Toledo OH

Huggett, Gretchen, *Head Weaving Dept*, Kalamazoo Institute of Arts, KIA School, Kalamazoo MI (S)

Huggins, Anita, *Admin Secy*, University of Memphis, Art Museum, Memphis TN

Huggins, Marvin A, *Assoc Dir Archives*, Concordia Historical Institute, Saint Louis MO

Huggins, Melanie, *Library Dir*, Saint Paul Public Library, Central Adult Public Services, Saint Paul MN

Huggins, Tavia, *Deputy Dir Fin*, ArtsConnection Inc, New York NY

Huggins, William, *Access Svcs Supvr*, University of California, Los Angeles, Arts Library, Los Angeles CA

Hughes, Amanda, *Dir External Affairs*, University of North Carolina at Chapel Hill, Ackland Art Museum, Chapel Hill NC

Hughes, Ava, *Dir Arts Educ*, Arts Partnership of Greater Spartanburg, Inc, Chapman Cultural Center, Spartanburg SC

Hughes, Dewane, *Asst Prof*, University of Texas at Tyler, Department of Art, School of Visual & Performing Arts, Tyler TX (S)

Hughes, Elaine R, *Coll Mgr*, Museum of Northern Arizona, Flagstaff AZ

Hughes, Eleanor, *Assoc Cur & Head Exhibs & Publs*, Yale University, Yale Center for British Art, New Haven CT

Hughes, Gary, *History & Technology Cur*, New Brunswick Museum, Saint John NB

Hughes, George, *Asst Prof*, University at Buffalo, State University of New York, Dept of Visual Studies, Buffalo NY (S)

Hughes, Hillary, *Asst to Dir*, Pensacola Museum of Art, Pensacola FL

Hughes, Holly, *Assoc Prof*, University of Michigan, Ann Arbor, School of Art & Design, Ann Arbor MI (S)

Hughes, Holly E, *Coll Cur*, The Buffalo Fine Arts Academy, Albright-Knox Art Gallery, Buffalo NY

Hughes, Jayne, *Educ Coordr*, Buffalo Arts Studio, Art Gallery, Buffalo NY

Hughes, Jeffrey, *Asst Prof*, Webster University, Art Dept, Webster Groves MO (S)

Hughes, Julie, *Lectr*, Santa Clara University, Dept of Art & Art History, Santa Clara CA (S)

Hughes, Kevin, *Dir Admin*, Connecticut Historical Society, Hartford CT

Hughes, Margaret, *Head Dept*, Butte College, Dept of Performing Arts, Oroville CA (S)

Hughes, Mary Jo, *Chief Cur*, Art Gallery of Greater Victoria, Victoria BC

Hughes, Mary Jo, *Dir*, University of Victoria, The Legacy Art Gallery, Victoria BC

Hughes, Michael, *Develop Dir*, Florida International University, The Patricia & Phillip Frost Art Museum, Miami FL

Hughes, Michael, *Libr Serv Supv*, New York University, Stephen Chan Library of Fine Arts, New York NY

Hughes, Sharon, *Educ Coordr*, Danville Museum of Fine Arts & History, Danville VA

Hughley, John, *Prof*, North Carolina Central University, Art Dept, Durham NC (S)

Hughson, John, *Prof*, State University of New York at Fredonia, Dept of Art, Fredonia NY (S)

Hughston, Milan, *Chief Library & Mus Archives*, Museum of Modern Art, Library and Museum Archives, New York NY

Hugo, Corina, *Cur Coll & Registrar*, Riley County Historical Society & Museum, Riley County Historical Museum, Manhattan KS

Hugo, Corina, *Registrar*, Riley County Historical Society & Museum, Seaton Library, Manhattan KS

Huie, Patricia, *Treas*, National Association of Women Artists, Inc, N.A.W.A. Gallery, New York NY

Huisman, Carl, *Chmn Dept*, Calvin College, Art Dept, Grand Rapids MI (S)

Hukman, Ian, *Instr*, Judson University, School of Art, Design & Architecture, Elgin IL (S)

Hulen, Jeannie, *Dept Chair & Assoc Prof*, University of Arkansas, Art Dept, Fayetteville AR (S)

Hull, David, *Prin Librn*, San Francisco Maritime National Historical Park, Maritime Museum, San Francisco CA

Hull, John, *Chmn*, University of Colorado at Denver, College of Arts & Media Visual Arts Dept, Denver CO (S)

Hull, Lynne, *Jewelry & Metal Design*, North Seattle Community College, Art Dept, Seattle WA (S)

Hull, Vida, *Prof*, East Tennessee State University, College of Arts and Sciences, Dept of Art & Design, Johnson City TN (S)

Hull, William, *Pres Bd*, Hermitage Foundation Museum, Norfolk VA

Hulse, Toni, *Registrar*, University of Connecticut, William Benton Museum of Art, Storrs CT

Hulsey, Shelley, *Shop Sales Mgr*, Kentucky Museum of Art and Craft, Louisville KY

Hulst, Connie, *Office Mgr*, North Dakota Museum of Art, Grand Forks ND

Humber, Sarah, *Cur*, Howard University, Architecture & Planning Library, Washington DC

Humbertson, Margaret, *Head Library & Archive Coll*, Springfield Museums, Connecticut Valley Historical Society, Springfield MA

Hume, Karen, *Exec Dir*, Capitol Arts Alliance, Houchens Gallery, Bowling Green KY

Hume, Naomi, *Asst Prof*, Seattle University, Dept of Fine Arts, Visual Art Division, Seattle WA (S)

Humphery, Meeghan, *Art Coordr*, Ashtabula Arts Center, Ashtabula OH

Humphrey, Beth, *Educ Cur*, Woodstock Artists Association & Museum, Woodstock NY

Humphrey, Charlie, *Exec Dir*, Pittsburgh Center for the Arts, Pittsburgh PA

Humphrey, Corinne, *Pub Rels,* Kimball Art Center, Park City UT

Humphrey, G Watts, *VChmn Bd,* Shaker Village of Pleasant Hill, Harrodsburg KY

Humphrey, Judy, *Prof,* Appalachian State University, Dept of Art, Boone NC (S)

Humphrey, Sally, *Visitor Svcs Clerk,* Belle Grove Inc., Belle Grove Plantation, Middletown VA

Huneck, Gwendolyn, *Art Dir,* Stephen Huneck Gallery at Dog Mountain, Saint Johnsbury VT

Hung, Wu, *Consulting Cur,* University of Chicago, Smart Museum of Art, Chicago IL

Hungerford, Constance Cain, *Prof,* Swarthmore College, Dept of Art & Art History, Swarthmore PA (S)

Hunisak, John, *Prof,* Middlebury College, History of Art & Architecture Dept, Middlebury VT (S)

Hunley, Pam, *Pres,* The Museum, Greenwood SC

Hunsberger, Alice, *Assoc Dir Develop,* The American Federation of Arts, New York NY

Hunsinger, Pat, *Lectr,* Ithaca College, Fine Art Dept, Ithaca NY (S)

Hunt, Aimee, *Assoc Acad Cur,* University of Virginia, The Fralin Museum of Art at the University of Virginia, Charlottesville VA

Hunt, Amy, *Educator,* Washington County Museum of Fine Arts, Hagerstown MD

Hunt, Barb, *Prof,* Memorial University of Newfoundland, Division of Fine Arts, Visual Arts Program, Corner Brook NF (S)

Hunt, Barbara, *Dir,* Artists Space, Artists Space Gallery, New York NY

Hunt, Barbara, *Dir,* Artists Space, Irving Sandler Artists File, New York NY

Hunt, Benjamin, *Vis Asst Lectr,* Idaho State University, Dept of Art & Pre-Architecture, Pocatello ID (S)

Hunt, Daniel, *Assoc Prof,* Kansas State University, Art Dept, Manhattan KS (S)

Hunt, Gregory K, *Dean,* Catholic University of America, School of Architecture & Planning, Washington DC (S)

Hunt, Janice, *Bd Pres (V),* The Trustees of Reservations, The Mission House, Ipswich MA

Hunt, John Dixon, *Chmn,* University of Pennsylvania, Dept of Landscape Architecture & Regional Planning, Philadelphia PA (S)

Hunt, Kat, *Coordr,* Society of Photographers & Artists Representatives, New York NY

Hunt, Kathy, *Bus Mgr,* Peoria Art Guild, Peoria IL

Hunt, Margaret, *Exec Dir,* Utah Arts Council, Chase Home Museum of Utah Folk Arts, Salt Lake City UT

Hunt, Rebecca, *Educ Progs Coordr,* Krasl Art Center, Saint Joseph MI

Hunt, Susan, *Prof,* University of Wisconsin-Stout, Dept of Art & Design, Menomonie WI (S)

Hunt Blanc, Elizabeth, *Deputy Dir,* Southern Methodist University, Meadows Museum, Dallas TX

Hunter, David, *Music Librn,* University of Texas at Austin, Fine Arts Library, Austin TX

Hunter, Debora, *Asst Prof,* Southern Methodist University, Division of Art, Dallas TX (S)

Hunter, James, *Dir,* Huronia Museum, Gallery of Historic Huronia, Midland ON

Hunter, John, *Chief Cur,* Jekyll Island Museum, Jekyll Island GA

Hunter, John, *Chmn,* Cleveland State University, Art Dept, Cleveland OH (S)

Hunter, Kathleen, *Educ Coordr,* Old State House, Hartford CT

Hunter, Lissa Ann, *Chmn Bd,* Haystack Mountain School of Crafts, Deer Isle ME

Hunter-Smith, Lauren, *Cur Educ,* Headley-Whitney Museum, Lexington KY

Huntington Fenn, Dan, *VPres,* Porter-Phelps-Huntington Foundation, Inc, Historic House Museum, Hadley MA

Huntley, Patty, *Mus Store Mgr,* The San Joaquin Pioneer & Historical Society, The Haggin Museum, Stockton CA

Huntley, Sondra, *Archivist,* Town of Cummington Historical Commission, Kingman Tavern Historical Museum, Cummington MA

Huntoon, Katherine, *Dir Gallery,* Old Dominion University, Art Dept, Norfolk VA

Huntoon, Perry, *Admin Asst,* Arts Extension Service, Amherst MA

Huot, Andrew, *Pres,* Guild of Book Workers, New York NY

Hupfel, Gretchen, *Asst Prof Foundations,* University of Georgia, Franklin College of Arts & Sciences, Lamar Dodd School of Art, Athens GA (S)

Hurd, J R, *Pres,* McNay, San Antonio TX

Hurlburt, Roger, *Vis Instr Art History,* Florida Atlantic University, D F Schmidt College of Arts & Letters Dept of Visual Arts & Art History, Boca Raton FL (S)

Hurley, Brennan, *Gen Mgr,* Arts Club of Washington, James Monroe House, Washington DC

Hurley, Carole, *Pres,* Moody County Historical Society, Moody County Museum, Pierre SD

Hurley, Steven, *Preparator,* University of New Mexico, University of New Mexico Art Museum, Albuquerque NM

Hurliman, Ted, *Exhib Asst,* Portland Art Museum, Northwest Film Center, Portland OR

Hurry, Robert J, *Registrar,* Calvert Marine Museum, Solomons MD

Hurry, Robert J, *Registrar,* Calvert Marine Museum, Library, Solomons MD

Hurst, Larry, *Adjunct,* College of the Canyons, Art Dept, Santa Clarita CA (S)

Hurst, Ronald, *VPres Coll & Museums,* Colonial Williamsburg Foundation, Williamsburg VA

Hurst, Ronald, *VPres Conservation, Colls & Mus,* Colonial Williamsburg Foundation, Abby Aldrich Rockefeller Folk Art Museum, Williamsburg VA

Hurst, Ronald, *VPres Conservation, Colls & Mus,* Colonial Williamsburg Foundation, DeWitt Wallace Decorative Arts Museum, Williamsburg VA

Hurst, William, *Dir Dept Arts & Science,* Dominican College of Blauvelt, Art Dept, Orangeburg NY (S)

Hurst-Wender, Jennifer, *Assoc Dir Mus Operations & Educ,* Preservation Virginia, John Marshall House, Richmond VA

Hurston, Robin, *Bd Mem,* Coquille Valley Art Association, Coquille OR

Hurt, Cynthia, *Assoc Prof,* Tarrant County College, Art Dept, Hurst TX (S)

Hurt, Lee Anne, *Asst Cur Pre Columbian & Native American Art,* Virginia Museum of Fine Arts, Richmond VA

Hurt, Shannon L, *Activities & Communs Dir,* Arts Council of Southwestern Indiana, The Bower-Suhrheinrich Foundation Gallery, Evansville IN

Hurt, Susanne, *Corresp Secy,* American Artists Professional League, Inc, New York NY

Hurwitz, Jeffrey, *Instr,* Moravian College, Dept of Art, Bethlehem PA (S)

Husar, Janet, *Gift Shop Coordr,* Mankato Area Arts Council, Carnegie Art Center, Mankato MN

Husarek, Kandi, *Treas,* DuPage Art League School & Gallery, Wheaton IL

Husband, Timothy, *Cur,* The Metropolitan Museum of Art, The Cloisters Museum & Gardens, New York NY

Husch, Gail, *Prof,* Goucher College, Art & Art History Dept, Baltimore MD (S)

Hushion, Anthony, *VPres Exhibits, Educ & New Media,* Royal Ontario Museum, Toronto ON

Hushka, Rock, *Dir Cur Admin & Cur Contemporary & Northwest Art,* Tacoma Art Museum, Tacoma WA

Huss, Kathryn, *Chief Admin Officer,* University of Michigan, Museum of Art, Ann Arbor MI

Hussain, Tasmia, *Coordr Family Progs & Outreach,* Palo Alto Art Center, Palo Alto CA

Hussey, Kathryn, *Registrar,* Brick Store Museum, Kennebunk ME

Hussman, Dale, *Chmn Dept of Art,* Carlow College, Art Dept, Pittsburgh PA (S)

Hussy, Hawley, *Dir Educ,* BRIC - Brooklyn Information & Culture, Rotunda Gallery, Brooklyn NY

Huston, Alan, *Assoc Prof,* Winthrop University, Dept of Art & Design, Rock Hill SC (S)

Huston, John, *Assoc Prof Theater,* Lake Erie College, Fine Arts Dept, Painesville OH (S)

Hutchens, James, *Chmn Dept,* Ohio State University, Dept of Art Education, Columbus OH (S)

Hutchins, Addie, *Art School Dir,* Spartanburg Art Museum, Spartanburg SC

Hutchins, Grover M, *Prof Pathology,* Johns Hopkins University, School of Medicine, Dept of Art as Applied to Medicine, Baltimore MD (S)

Hutchins, Monalea, *Instr,* Cuyahoga Valley Art Center, Cuyahoga Falls OH (S)

Hutchinson, Becka, *Mus Shop Mgr,* Creek Council House Museum, Okmulgee OK

Hutchinson, James, *CFO,* Santa Barbara Museum of Art, Library, Santa Barbara CA

Hutchinson, Jim, *Asst Prof,* Dallas Baptist University, Dept of Art, Dallas TX (S)

Hutchinson, Linda, *Instr,* Cuyahoga Valley Art Center, Cuyahoga Falls OH (S)

Hutchison, Jane C, *Prof,* University of Wisconsin, Madison, Dept of Art History, Madison WI (S)

Hutchison, Johannah, *Exec Dir,* International Sculpture Center, Hamilton NJ

Huth, Nancy, *Cur Educ,* Taft Museum of Art, Cincinnati OH

Hutlova-Foy, Zora, *Mgr Exhibitions,* Seattle Art Museum, Downtown, Seattle WA

Hutlova-Foy, Zora, *Mgr Exhibitions,* Seattle Art Museum, Dorothy Stimson Bullitt Library, Seattle WA

Hutson, Bill, *Instr,* Creighton University, Fine & Performing Arts Dept, Omaha NE (S)

Hutter, Cherie, *Chair,* Grace A Dow, Fine Arts Dept, Midland MI

Hutterer, Maile, *Asst Prof Art,* Western Illinois University, Department of Art, Macomb IL (S)

Hutton, Brett, *Secy,* Rensselaer Newman Foundation Chapel + Cultural Center, The Gallery at the Chapel & Cultural Center, Troy NY

Hutton, John, *Prof,* Salem Academy & College, Art Dept, Winston Salem NC (S)

Hutton, Kathleen, *Dir Educ,* Reynolda House Museum of American Art, Winston-Salem NC

Hutzel, Renaie, *Bd Pres,* Central Iowa Art Association, Inc, Art Reference Library, Marshalltown IA

Huun, Kathleen, *Instr,* Marylhurst University, Art Dept, Marylhurst OR (S)

Huxhold, Stacey, *Art, Music & Av Mgr,* Allen County Public Library, Art, Music & Audiovisual Services, Fort Wayne IN

Huxley, Geralyn, *Cur Film & Video,* The Andy Warhol Museum, Museum, Pittsburgh PA

Huynh, Phung, *Gallery Mgr,* Los Angeles Valley College, Art Gallery, Valley Glen CA

Hwang, Karen, *Asst Prof,* Vassar College, Art Dept, Poughkeepsie NY (S)

Hwang, Lydia, *Vis Lectr Art,* North Central College, Dept of Art, Naperville IL (S)

Hwangho, Imi, *Assoc Prof Sculpture,* University of Georgia, Franklin College of Arts & Sciences, Lamar Dodd School of Art, Athens GA (S)

Hyams, L Collier, *Asst Prof,* Georgetown University, Dept of Art & Art History, Washington DC (S)

Hyche, Jessica, *Dir Finance,* Pensacola Museum of Art, Pensacola FL

Hyde, Budge, *Prof,* Greenfield Community College, Art Dept, Greenfield MA (S)

Hyde, Marion, *Assoc Prof,* Utah State University, Dept of Art, Logan UT (S)

Hyde, Melissa, *Prof,* University of Florida, School of Art & Art History, Gainesville FL (S)

Hyde, Robb, *Exec Dir,* Wayne Center for the Arts, Wooster OH

Hyland, Alice R M, *Consulting Cur,* Art Complex Museum, Carl A. Weyerhaeuser Library, Duxbury MA

Hyland, Douglas, *Dir,* New Britain Museum of American Art, New Britain CT

Hyland, Matthew, *Dir,* Oakville Galleries, Centennial Square and Gairloch Gardens, Oakville ON

Hylen, Beth, *Reference & Educ Librn,* Corning Museum of Glass, Juliette K and Leonard S Rakow Research Library, Corning NY

Hylton, David, *Prof,* California State Polytechnic University, Pomona, Department of Art, Pomona CA (S)

Hynes, William, *Chmn Art Dept,* Shippensburg University, Art Dept, Shippensburg PA (S)

Hyslin, Richard P, *Prof Sculpture,* University of Texas Pan American, Art Dept, Edinburg TX (S)

Iacono, Domenic J, *Assoc Dir,* Syracuse University, Art Collection, Syracuse NY

Iacono, Domenic J, *Dir,* Syracuse University, SUArt Galleries, Syracuse NY

Iannacchione, Anita, *Pres & Mktg Mgr,* Public Art Fund, Inc, Visual Archive, New York NY

Iannucci, Heather, *Historic Site Mgr,* New York State Office of Parks Recreation & Historic Preservation, John Jay Homestead State Historic Site, Katonah NY

Iannucci, Heather, *Historic Site Mgr,* Philipse Manor Hall State Historic Site, Yonkers NY

Ianuzzelli, Nicole, *Proj Mgr,* Rutgers, The State University of New Jersey, Mary H Dana Women Artists Series, a Partnership of the Institute for Women & Art and the Rutgers University Libraries, New Brunswick NJ

Iavicoli, Vincenzo, *Chair Product Design,* College for Creative Studies, Detroit MI (S)

Ibbitson, Roxie, *Registrar/Preparator,* Mount Allison University, Owens Art Gallery, Sackville NB

Iberti, Elissa, *Dept Chair, Coordr Visual Communs Prog & Asst Prof Visual Arts,* Dowling College, Dept of Visual Arts, Oakdale NY (S)

Ibur, James, *Prof,* Saint Louis Community College at Meramec, Art Dept, Saint Louis MO (S)

Ickes, Jennifer, *Asst Registrar,* New Orleans Museum of Art, New Orleans LA

Ida, Richard, *Div Dean,* Solano Community College, Division of Fine & Applied Art & Behavioral Science, Fairfield CA (S)

Idelson, Jeffrey L, *Pres,* National Baseball Hall of Fame & Museum, Inc, Art Collection, Cooperstown NY

Idrogo, Curt, *Prin Librn,* Newark Public Library, Reference, Newark NJ

Igna, Mary Ann, *Cur,* Maricopa County Historical Society, Desert Caballeros Western Museum, Wickenburg AZ

Ignat, Lavinia, *Visitor Servs Mgr,* Museum of Fine Arts Houston, Bayou Bend Collection & Gardens, Houston TX

Ignatowich, William, *CFO,* Dahesh Museum of Art, Greenwich CT

Igoe, Kim, *Exec VPres,* American Association of Museums, United States National Committee of the International Council of Museums (ICOM-US), Washington DC

Igwe, Kod, *Assoc Prof,* Claflin College, Dept of Art, Orangeburg SC (S)

Ihrke, Josephine, *Field Serv Project Mgr,* Balboa Art Conservation Center, San Diego CA

Ikeda, Ken, *Exec Dir,* Bay Area Video Coalition, Inc, San Francisco CA

Ikeda, Ken, *Exec Dir,* Boston Properties LLC, San Francisco CA

Ikeda, Seiji, *Asst Prof,* University of Texas at Arlington, Art & Art History Department, Arlington TX (S)

Ikeda, Yoshiro, *Prof,* Kansas State University, Art Dept, Manhattan KS (S)

Ikemiya, Cheryl, *Dir Develop,* Japanese American National Museum, Los Angeles CA

Ilchman, Frederick, *Mrs Russel W Baker Cur Paintings,* Museum of Fine Arts, Boston MA

Iler, Henry, *Assoc Prof,* Georgia Southern University, Dept of Art, Statesboro GA (S)

Iles, Chrissie, *Cur Film & Video,* Whitney Museum of American Art, New York NY

Iliescu, Sanda, *Studio Faculty,* University of Virginia, McIntire Dept of Art, Charlottesville VA (S)

Iliff, Lori, *Registrar,* Denver Art Museum, Denver CO

Illig, Laura, *Office Asst,* Arts of the Southern Finger Lakes, Corning NY

Im, Sooyun, *Asst Prof,* University of Wisconsin-Eau Claire, Dept of Art & Design, Eau Claire WI (S)

Imami-Paydar, Niloo, *Cur of Textile & Fashion Arts,* Indianapolis Museum of Art, Indianapolis IN

Imboden, Elis, *Sr Admin,* Stanford University, Dept of Art & Art History, Stanford CA (S)

Imeson, Katie, *Sec,* Florida Southern College, Department of Art & Art History, Lakeland FL (S)

Imm-Stroukoff, Eumie, *Emily Fisher Landau Dir, Librn & Asst Dir Research Ctr,* Georgia O'Keeffe Museum, Research Center, Santa Fe NM

Inabinett, Marian, *Cur Colls,* City of High Point, High Point Museum, High Point NC

Inada, Miles, *Prof,* Southern Oregon University, Art & Art History Dept, Ashland OR (S)

Incandela, Daniel, *Dir New Media,* Indianapolis Museum of Art, Indianapolis IN

Inch, Jeanne, *Dir Gen & COO,* Department of Canadian Heritage, Canadian Conservation Institute, Ottawa ON

Indeck, Karen, *Cur Asst,* The First National Bank of Chicago, Art Collection, Chicago IL

Indych-Lopez, Anna, *Assoc Prof & Chair,* City College of New York, Art Dept, New York NY (S)

Infinger, Jennifer, *Educ Dir,* LeMoyne Art Foundation, Center for the Visual Arts, Tallahassee FL

Ingalls, Sherrill, *Dir Communs,* San Jose Museum of Art, San Jose CA

Ingber, Rabbi Abie, *Rabbi Emeritus,* Hillel Foundation, Hillel Jewish Student Center Gallery, Cincinnati OH

Ingberman, Jeannette, *Co-founder/Dir,* Exit Art, San Leandro CA

Ingbretson, Paul, *Pres,* The Guild of Boston Artists, Boston MA

Ingelright, Kelly, *Vis Asst Prof,* University of Texas at Arlington, Art & Art History Department, Arlington TX (S)

Inglis, Erik, *Asst Prof,* Oberlin College, Dept of Art, Oberlin OH (S)

Ingram, Millard, *Chmn,* Charles B Goddard, Ardmore OK

Inlow, Terry, *Prof,* Wilmington College, Art Dept, Wilmington OH (S)

Inman, Jan, *Instr,* La Sierra University, Art Dept, Riverside CA (S)

Inman, Jessie, *CEO,* Confederation Centre Art Gallery and Museum, Charlottetown PE

Inman, Marcie J, *Dir Exhibs & Educ Progs,* Irving Arts Center, Galleries & Sculpture Garden, Irving TX

Innella, Valerie, *Instr,* Casper College, Dept of Visual Arts, Casper WY (S)

Inselmann, Andrea, *Cur Modern & Contemporary Art,* Cornell University, Herbert F Johnson Museum of Art, Ithaca NY

Intersoll, Joanne Dolan, *Cur Costumes & Textiles,* Rhode Island School of Design, Museum of Art, Providence RI

Inuzuka, Sadashi, *Assoc Prof,* University of Michigan, Ann Arbor, School of Art & Design, Ann Arbor MI (S)

Inwood, Judy, *Art & Music Dept,* Public Library of Cincinnati & Hamilton County, Info & Reference Dept, Cincinnati OH

Iolascon, Filomena, *Educ & Outreach Mgr,* Pelham Art Center, Pelham NY

Ipson, Daniel A, *Dean Fine Arts,* Hartnell College, Art & Photography Dept, Salinas CA (S)

Irby, Frank, *Instr,* Pacific Northwest College of Art, Portland OR (S)

Ireland, Lynda, *Cur,* Autozone, Autozone Corporation Collection, Memphis TN

Irick, Andy, *Pres,* Springfield Museum of Art, Springfield OH

Irick, Chris, *Prof,* Munson-Williams-Proctor Arts Institute, Pratt MWP College of Art, Utica NY (S)

Irish, Jane, *Grad Prog Coordr,* University of Pennsylvania, Graduate School of Fine Arts, Philadelphia PA (S)

Irizarry, Rafael, *Develop Dir,* Museo de Arte de Ponce, The Luis A Ferre Foundation Inc, Ponce PR

Irizarry, Rafael, *Develop Dir,* Museo de Arte de Ponce, The Luis A Ferre Foundation Inc, Ponce PR

Irrgang, William, *Dir Finance,* Minnesota Historical Society, Saint Paul MN

Irvin, Kate, *Dept Head & Cur Costumes & Textiles,* Rhode Island School of Design, Museum of Art, Providence RI

Irvine, Karen, *Cur,* Columbia College Chicago, Museum of Contemporary Photography, Chicago IL

Irvine, Mary, *Asst to Visitor Svcs,* Alaska State Museum, Juneau AK

Irvine-Stiver, Debra, *Instr,* Adrian College, Art & Design Dept, Adrian MI (S)

Irwin, Terry, *Head,* Carnegie Mellon University, School of Design, Pittsburgh PA (S)

Isaac, Joanne, *Mus Admin,* American Numismatic Society, New York NY

Isaacs, J Susan, *Cur Special Projs,* Delaware Center for the Contemporary Arts, Wilmington DE

Isaacs, Judy, *Office Mgr & Bookkeeper,* Liberty Hall Historic Site, Liberty Hall Museum, Frankfort KY

Isaacson, Lynn, *Pres,* Snake River Heritage Center, Weiser ID

Isaacson, Stan, *Dir Develop,* Brandywine Workshop, Center for the Visual Arts, Philadelphia PA

Isenbarger, Stacy, *Asst Prof,* University of Idaho/College of Art & Architecture, Dept of Art & Design, Moscow ID (S)

Isenberg, E Duane, *Assoc Prof,* Mohawk Valley Community College, Utica NY (S)

Isenstein, Laura, *Dir,* Central Library, Dept of Fine Arts, San Antonio TX

Isgett, Kevin, *Instr,* Bob Jones University, School of Fine Arts, Div of Art & Design, Greenville SC (S)

Isham, Nina, *Colls Technician,* Lac du Flambeau Band of Lake Superior Chippewa Indians, George W Brown Jr Ojibwe Museum & Cultural Center, Lac Du Flambeau WI

Ishikawa, Chiyo, *Cur European Painting,* Seattle Art Museum, Dorothy Stimson Bullitt Library, Seattle WA

Ishikawa, Chiyo, *Deputy Dir Art,* Seattle Art Museum, Downtown, Seattle WA

Ishino, Catherine, *Asst Prof,* University of Minnesota, Duluth, Art Dept, Duluth MN (S)

Isman, Bonnie, *Dir,* Jones Library, Inc, Amherst MA

Isom, Carol, *Mgr (V),* Arkansas Arts Center, Museum, Little Rock AR (S)

Ison, Judy, *Exec Dir,* Fine Arts Center for the New River Valley, Pulaski VA

Ison, Susan, *Dir Cultural Svcs,* Loveland Museum/Gallery, Loveland CO

Isovitsch, Emily, *Mng Dir,* The One Club, New York NY

Israel, Hannah, *Gallery Dir,* Columbus State University, Norman Shannon and Emmy Lou P Illges Gallery, Columbus GA

Ito, Lauren, *Admin Asst to Dir,* Fine Arts Museums of San Francisco, M H de Young Museum, San Francisco CA

Ito, Lauren, *Admin Asst to Dir,* Fine Arts Museums of San Francisco, Legion of Honor, San Francisco CA

Ittelson, Lane, *Dir Colo Hist Found,* Colorado Historical Society, Colorado History Museum, Denver CO

Ivan, Sorina, *Instr Visual Arts,* Dowling College, Dept of Visual Arts, Oakdale NY (S)

Ivanova, Elena, *Chief Educ,* Nelda C & H J Lutcher Stark, Stark Museum of Art, Orange TX

Ivanova, Silvia, *Cur Educ,* State University of New York at Binghamton, Binghamton University Art Museum, Binghamton NY

Ivers, Louise, *Prof Emeritus,* California State University, Dominguez Hills, Art & Design Dept, Carson CA (S)

Iverson, Marsha, *Educ Dir,* Meridian Museum of Art, Meridian MS

Ives, Laura, *Chmn,* Appalachian State University, Dept of Art, Boone NC (S)

Ives Hunter, Elizabeth, *Exec Dir,* Cape Cod Museum of Art Inc, Dennis MA

Ivins, Jerry, *Acting Div Chmn & Dean Fine Arts,* San Jacinto Junior College, Division of Fine Arts, Pasadena TX (S)

Ivy, Carol Mohamed, *Cur,* The Ethel Wright Mohamed Stitchery Museum, Belzoni MS

Ivy, Krista, *Art Selector,* University of California, Tomas Rivera Library, Riverside CA

Ivy, Meredith, *Events Coordr,* Mobile Museum of Art, Mobile AL

Iwamura, Alan, *Interim Dir Educ,* Urbanglass, Robert Lehman Gallery, Brooklyn NY

Iwata, Chris, *Dir Humanities & Fine Arts,* Sacramento City College, Art Dept, Sacramento CA (S)

Iwerson, Kathleen, *Dir Develop,* Whatcom Museum, Library, Bellingham WA

Izes, Doris, *Exec Asst to Dean,* Temple University, Tyler School of Art, Philadelphia PA (S)

Izzo, Michele, *VPres & Treas,* American Watercolor Society, Inc., New York NY

Jaber, George, *Chmn,* Community College of Allegheny County, Fine Arts Dept, West Mifflin PA (S)

Jablonski, Joyce, *Prof,* Central Missouri State University, Dept Art & Design, Warrensburg MO (S)

Jablonski, Keith, *Cur,* Federal Reserve Bank of Minneapolis, Minneapolis MN

Jablonski, Mary Kathryn, *Asst Dir,* Skidmore College, Schick Art Gallery, Saratoga Springs NY

Jablow, Lisa, *Assoc Prof,* Johnson State College, Dept Fine & Performing Arts, Dibden Center for the Arts, Johnson VT (S)

Jabra, Linda, *Gallery Dir,* VSA Arts of New Mexico, Very Special Arts Gallery, Albuquerque NM

Jack, Deborah, *MFA,* New Jersey City University, Art Dept, Jersey City NJ (S)

Jack, Jill, *Dir Library Svcs,* Coe College, Stewart Memorial Library & Gallery, Cedar Rapids IA

Jack, Marlene, *Assoc Prof,* College of William & Mary, Dept of Fine Arts, Williamsburg VA (S)

Jack, Meredith M, *Prof,* Lamar University, Art Dept, Beaumont TX (S)

Jacklitch, Paul, *Dir,* Baldwin-Wallace College, Fawick Art Gallery, Berea OH

Jacks, Philip, *Assoc Prof,* George Washington University, Dept of Art of Fine Arts & Art History, Washington DC (S)

Jackson, Anke, *Asst Dir,* Parrish Art Museum, Water Mill NY

Jackson, Arnold, *Dir Promotional Svcs,* American Society of Artists, Inc, Palatine IL

Jackson, Barbara, *Asst Librn & Pub Services,* University of Virginia, Fiske Kimball Fine Arts Library, Charlottesville VA

Jackson, Bob, *1st VPres,* Plastic Club, Art Club, Philadelphia PA

Jackson, Charles Terry, *Chm (V),* Biggs Museum of American Art, Dover DE

Jackson, Christopher, *Dean,* Concordia University, Faculty of Fine Arts, Montreal PQ (S)

Jackson, David, *Dir Archives,* Jackson County Historical Society, Research Library & Archives, Independence MO

Jackson, Duke, *Chmn,* Georgia Southwestern State University, Dept of Fine Arts, Americus GA (S)

Jackson, Fairleigh, *Assoc Dir Develop,* Louisiana State University, Museum of Art, Baton Rouge LA

Jackson, James, *Dir Security & Plant Operations,* Bob Jones University Museum & Gallery Inc, Greenville SC

Jackson, Jo Anne, *Dir Fin,* Christina Cultural Arts Center, Inc, Wilmington DE

Jackson, Joe, *Dir,* New Image Art, West Hollywood CA

Jackson, Julian, *Secy,* American Abstract Artists, Brooklyn NY

Jackson, Julie, *MOWA Shop Mgr,* Museum of Wisconsin Art, West Bend WI

Jackson, Kelli, *Head Jewelry Dept,* Kalamazoo Institute of Arts, KIA School, Kalamazoo MI (S)

Jackson, Lora, *Educ Cur,* City of El Paso, El Paso Museum of Archaeology, El Paso TX

Jackson, Marcie, *Dir Educ & Curatorial Svcs,* Hill-Stead Museum, Farmington CT

Jackson, Marian, *Chmn,* Wayne State University, Dept of Art & Art History, Detroit MI (S)

Jackson, Pamela, *Catalog Librn,* San Francisco Art Institute, Anne Bremer Memorial Library, San Francisco CA

Jackson, Philip, *Asst Prof,* University of Mississippi, Department of Art, University MS (S)

Jackson, Phyllis, *Assoc Prof,* Pomona College, Dept of Art & Art History, Claremont CA (S)

Jackson, Rafael, *Dir,* University of Puerto Rico, Mayaguez, Dept of Humanities, College of Fine Arts & Theory of Art Programs, Mayaguez PR (S)

Jackson, Rafael, *Dir,* University of Puerto Rico, Mayaguez, Dept of Humanities, College of Fine Arts & Theory of Art Programs, Mayaguez PR (S)

Jackson, Richard, *Preparator,* University of Nevada, Reno, Sheppard Contemporary & University Galleries, Reno NV

Jackson, Robbyn, *Chief of Cultural Resources,* San Francisco Maritime National Historical Park, Maritime Library, San Francisco CA

Jackson, Robert, *Asst Prof Jewelry & Metalwork,* University of Georgia, Franklin College of Arts & Sciences, Lamar Dodd School of Art, Athens GA (S)

Jackson, Robin, *Chmn,* Treasure Valley Community College, Art Dept, Ontario OR (S)

Jackson, Shaun, *Assoc Prof,* University of Michigan, Ann Arbor, School of Art & Design, Ann Arbor MI (S)

Jackson, Stefanie, *Assoc Prof Drawing & Painting,* University of Georgia, Franklin College of Arts & Sciences, Lamar Dodd School of Art, Athens GA (S)

Jackson, Steve, *Assoc Cur Art & Photog,* Montana State University, Museum of the Rockies, Bozeman MT

Jackson, Steven, *Dir Finance & Admin,* American Textile History Museum, Lowell MA

Jackson, Thomas, *Chmn,* George Eastman, Rochester NY

Jackson, W Herbert, *Emeritus Prof,* Davidson College, Art Dept, Davidson NC (S)

Jackson, William D, *Prof,* Simon's Rock College of Bard, Visual Arts Dept, Great Barrington MA (S)

Jackson-Dumont, Sandra, *Dir Educ,* Seattle Art Museum, Downtown, Seattle WA

Jackson-Reese, Carla, *Instr,* Tuskegee University, Liberal Arts & Education, Tuskegee AL (S)

Jacob, George, *Dir,* Ellen Noel Art Museum of the Permian Basin, Odessa TX

Jacob, Preminda, *Assoc Prof & Assoc Chair,* University of Maryland, Baltimore County, Imaging & Digital Arts (IMDA), Dept of Visual Arts, Baltimore MD (S)

Jacobs, Amy, *Studio Mgr & Collaborator,* Dieu Donne Papermill, Inc, Gallery, New York NY

Jacobs, Anita, *Dir Pub Progs,* Brooklyn Botanic Garden, Steinhardt Conservatory Gallery, Brooklyn NY

Jacobs, Bud, *Prof,* Niagara County Community College, Fine Arts Division, Sanborn NY (S)

Jacobs, Dan, *Dir Gallery,* University of Denver, School of Art & Art History, Denver CO (S)

Jacobs, Del, *Prof, Film,* State College of Florida Manatee - Sarasota, Art, Design, Humanities, Bradenton FL (S)

Jacobs, Fredrika H, *Assoc Prof,* Virginia Commonwealth University, Art History Dept, Richmond VA (S)

Jacobs, Jack, *Production Mgr,* Hostos Center for the Arts & Culture, Bronx NY

Jacobs, John, *Cur Science,* Neville Public Museum of Brown County, Green Bay WI

Jacobs, Joyce, *Asst Prof,* Georgian Court University, Dept of Art, Lakewood NJ (S)

Jacobs, Lynn, *Prof,* University of Arkansas, Art Dept, Fayetteville AR (S)

Jacobs, Rich, *Dir,* New Image Art, West Hollywood CA

Jacobs, William, *Chief Interpretive,* Library of Congress, Prints & Photographs Division, Washington DC

Jacobsen, Carol, *Assoc Prof,* University of Michigan, Ann Arbor, School of Art & Design, Ann Arbor MI (S)

Jacobsen, Don, *Dir Library,* Englewood Library, Fine Arts Dept, Englewood NJ

Jacobsen, Terry D, *Asst Dir,* Carnegie Mellon University, Hunt Institute for Botanical Documentation, Pittsburgh PA

Jacobsen, Virgil E, *Asst Dir & Cur Educ,* Springville Museum of Art, Springville UT

Jacobsen Bates, Esther, *CEO,* Elverhoj Museum of History and Art, Solvang CA

Jacobson, Cody, *Graphic Designer,* Plains Art Museum, Fargo ND

Jacobson, Jake, *Assoc Prof,* University of Nebraska, Kearney, Dept of Art & Art History, Kearney NE (S)

Jacobson, Kathy, *Develop Assoc,* The California Historical Society, San Francisco CA

Jacobson, Lee, *Instr,* Chemeketa Community College, Dept of Humanities & Communications, Art Program, Salem OR (S)

Jacobson, Pam, *Cur Outreach,* Plains Art Museum, Fargo ND

Jacobson, Paul, *Chmn Div Language,* Western Nebraska Community College, Division of Language & Arts, Scottsbluff NE (S)

Jacobson, Thora E, *Dir,* Samuel S Fleisher, Philadelphia PA (S)

Jacobson-Sive, Emma, *Pub Rels,* Pasadena Museum of California Art, Pasadena CA

Jacoby, Mark, *1st VPres,* National Antique & Art Dealers Association of America, Inc, New York NY

Jacoby, Thomas J, *Art & Design Librn,* University of Connecticut, Art & Design Library, Storrs CT

Jacquemain, Patti, *Pres,* Wildling Art Museum, Solvang CA

Jacques, Kathy, *Dir Finance,* Lyman Allyn Art Museum, New London CT

Jacques, M, *Chief Cur,* Art Gallery of Greater Victoria, Library, Victoria BC

Jacuson, Georgina, *Dir Exhibs,* Mercer Union, A Centre for Contemporary Art, Toronto ON

Jaeger, Philip, *VPres,* Passaic County Historical Society, Lambert Castle Museum & Library, Paterson NJ

Jaeger, Steven D, *Gallery Mgr,* University of Wisconsin, Union Art Gallery, Milwaukee WI

Jaeger, Tim, *Gallery Asst,* Ringling College of Art & Design, Selby Gallery, Sarasota FL

Jaehn, Tomas, *Head Librn,* Museum of New Mexico, Fray Angelico Chavez History Library, Santa Fe NM

Jaehn, Tomas, *Library,* Museum of New Mexico, Palace of Governors, Santa Fe NM

Jaffe, Amanda, *Dir Ceramics,* New Mexico State University, Art Dept, Las Cruces NM (S)

Jaffe, John G, *Dir,* Sweet Briar College, Mary Helen Cochran Library, Sweet Briar VA

Jaffe, Scot, *Assoc Dir Exhibs & Colls,* San Diego Museum of Art, San Diego CA

Jaffe, Vicky, *Mktg & Pub Rels,* The Currier Museum of Art, Manchester NH

Jager, Edwin, *Chmn,* University of Wisconsin Oshkosh, Dept of Art, Oshkosh WI (S)

Jagoda, Peter, *Adjunct Asst Prof,* Spokane Falls Community College, Fine Arts Dept, Spokane WA (S)

Jahns, Tim, *Educ Coordr,* City of Irvine, Irvine Fine Arts Center, Irvine CA (S)

Jahos, Catherine, *Asst to Dir,* Monmouth Museum & Cultural Center, Lincroft NJ

Jaimes, Manuel, *Dir Archives/Media Resource Center,* Caribbean Cultural Center, Cultural Arts Organization & Resource Center, New York NY

Jakes, Carolee, *Treas,* Studio Gallery, Washington DC

Jakubek, Frances, *Assoc Dir,* Arthur Griffin Center for Photographic Art, Griffin Museum of Photography, Winchester MA

James, Beth, *Exec Dir,* South Arkansas Arts Center, El Dorado AR

James, Dan, *Dean Fine & Liberal Arts,* Rocky Mountain College of Art & Design, Lakewood CO (S)

James, David, *Prof,* University of Montana, Dept of Art, Missoula MT (S)

James, Dora, *Cur Educ,* Irvine Museum, Irvine CA

James, Gareth, *Assoc Prof,* University of British Columbia, Dept of Art History, Visual Art & Theory, Vancouver BC (S)

James, Hugh F, *VPres, Dir & Pub Rels & Mus Shop Mgr,* Medina Railroad Museum, Medina NY

James, Juanita, *Pres,* Stamford Museum & Nature Center, Stamford CT

James, Louise, *Dir & Cur,* Plains Indians & Pioneers Historical Foundation, Museum & Art Center, Woodward OK

James, Paige, *Mus Shop Mgr,* Historic Arkansas Museum, Little Rock AR

James, Portia P, *Historian,* Anacostia Community Museum, Smithsonian Institution, Washington DC

James, Ray, *Facilities Mgr,* Rose Center & Council for the Arts, Morristown TN

James, Sara N, *Assoc Prof,* Mary Baldwin College, Dept of Art & Art History, Staunton VA (S)

James, Scott, *Archivist,* Arts and Letters Club of Toronto, Toronto ON

Jameson, Kathleen V, *Exec Dir,* The Mint Museum, Art Organization & Library, Charlotte NC

Jamison, Margaret, *Instr,* Walla Walla Community College, Fine Arts Dept, Walla Walla WA (S)

Jammes, Michelle, *Mgr,* College of New Rochelle, Castle Gallery, New Rochelle NY

Jamra, Mark, *Instr,* Maine College of Art, Portland ME (S)

Jancosek, Pat, *Asst Prof,* Saint Mary-of-the-Woods College, Art Dept, Saint Mary of the Woods IN (S)

Jancourt, Jan, *Prof,* Minneapolis College of Art & Design, Minneapolis MN (S)

Janecek, James, *Asst Prof,* Providence College, Art & Art History Dept, Providence RI (S)

Janes, Todd, *Exec Dir,* Latitude 53 Contemporary Visual Culture, Edmonton AB

Janick, Richard, *Art Hist Instr,* Monterey Peninsula College, Art Dept/Art Gallery, Monterey CA (S)

Jankauskas, Jennifer, *Cur Art,* Montgomery Museum of Fine Arts, Library, Montgomery AL

Janke, James, *Assoc Prof,* Dakota State University, College of Liberal Arts, Madison SD (S)

Janken, Amy, *Educ Coordr,* Elmhurst Art Museum, Elmhurst IL

Jankowski, Edward, *Asst Prof,* Monmouth University, Dept of Art & Design, West Long Branch NJ (S)

Jankowski, Leslie, *Tech Svcs Librn,* Columbus College of Art & Design, Packard Library, Columbus OH

Janoskey, Pam, *Treas,* Carteret County Historical Society, The History Place, Morehead City NC

Janosy, Mimi, *Photog,* Antonelli Institute, Professional Photography & Commercial Art, Erdenheim PA (S)

Janov, Danie, *VPres,* Blacksburg Regional Art Association, Blacksburg VA

Janovy, Karen, *Dir Educ,* University of Nebraska, Lincoln, Sheldon Memorial Art Gallery & Sculpture Garden, Lincoln NE

Janowich, Ron, *Assoc Prof,* University of Florida, School of Art & Art History, Gainesville FL (S)

Janquith, Stephanie, *Cur,* Ohio State University, Visual Resources Library, Columbus OH

Jans-Duffy, Kathleen, *Colls Mgr,* Seneca Falls Historical Society Museum, Seneca Falls NY

Jansen, Catherine, *Instr,* Bucks County Community College, Fine Arts Dept, Newtown PA (S)

Jansen, Charles, *Instr,* Middle Tennessee State University, Art Dept, Murfreesboro TN (S)

Jansen, Holley, *Cur Colls,* History Museum of Mobile, Mobile AL

Jansma, Linda, *Cur,* The Robert McLaughlin, Oshawa ON

Janssen, Suzanne, *Bus Svcs,* Loveland Museum/Gallery, Loveland CO

Janz, Joni, *VPres Develop & Mktg,* Plains Art Museum, Fargo ND

Janz, Rita, *Art Dir,* Balzekas Museum of Lithuanian Culture, Chicago IL

Janzen, Gesine, *Asst Prof Printmaking,* Montana State University, School of Art, Bozeman MT (S)

J'Arbeloff, PA, *Dir Cambridge Science Festival,* Massachusetts Institute of Technology, MIT Museum, Cambridge MA

Jarboe, Kate, *Reference Librn,* School of the Art Institute of Chicago, John M Flaxman Library, Chicago IL

Jarnot, Jenn, *Instr Art,* Baker University, Dept of Mass Media & Visual Arts, Baldwin City KS (S)

Jarosi, Susan, *Asst Prof,* University of Louisville, Allen R Hite Art Institute, Louisville KY (S)

Jarvis, Doug, *Prog Coordr,* Open Space, Victoria BC

Jarvis, Dwayne, *Dir Finance,* Storm King Art Center, Mountainville NY

Jarvis, John, *Dir,* Bay Path College, Dept of Art, Longmeadow MA (S)

Jarvis, Muriel, *Pres,* Sunbury Shores Arts & Nature Centre, Inc, Gallery, Saint Andrews NB

Jarvis, Tripp, *Preparator,* Rocky Mount Arts Center, Rocky Mount NC

Jaskot, Paul, *Asst Prof,* DePaul University, Dept of Art, Chicago IL (S)

Jaskowiak, Jennifer, *Asst Cur ISM Lockport,* Illinois State Museum, ISM Lockport Gallery, Chicago Gallery & Southern Illinois Art Gallery, Springfield IL

Jaskulski, Faith, *Research Coordr,* North Tonawanda History Museum, North Tonawanda NY

Jaspers, Annika, *Pres,* Swedish American Museum Association of Chicago, Chicago IL

Jauch, Stephanie, *Dir Finance,* Artists Space, New York NY

Jaus, Bonme, *Gift Shop Mgr,* Tubac Center of the Arts, Santa Cruz Valley Art Association, Tubac AZ

Javorski, Susanne, *Art Librn,* Wesleyan University, Art Library, Middletown CT

Jay, Tonya, *Sales Assoc,* Providence Gallery, Charlotte NC

Jayaram, Carolina O, *Exec Dir,* Chicago Artists' Coalition, Coalition Gallery, Chicago IL

Jebsen, Mary, *Asst Dir,* Museum of New Mexico, New Mexico Museum of Art, Unit of NM Dept of Cultural Affairs, Santa Fe NM

Jedda McNab, Barbara, *Cur & Mgr,* American Kennel Club, Museum of the Dog, Saint Louis MO

Jeff-Bouska, Marcia, *Bd Mem,* Artists' Cooperative Gallery, Omaha NE

Jefferies, Eric, *Head Dept,* Atlanta Technical Institute, Visual Communications Class, Atlanta GA (S)

Jeffers, Jim, *Adjunct Asst Prof,* Drew University, Art Dept, Madison NJ (S)

Jeffers, Susan, *Gallery Coordr,* State University of New York at Ulster, Muroff-Kotler Visual Arts Gallery, Stone Ridge NY

Jefferson, Calandra S, *Mus Svcs Coordr,* Albany Museum of Art, Albany GA

Jefferson, Charmaine, *Exec Dir,* California African-American Museum, Los Angeles CA

Jefferson, Charmaine, *Exec Dir,* California African-American Museum, Research Library, Los Angeles CA

Jeffery, Jonathan, *Librn,* Western Kentucky University, Kentucky Library & Museum, Bowling Green KY

Jeffery, Mary, *Board Chmn,* The Lindsay Gallery Inc, Lindsay ON

Jeffett, William, *Cur Exhibs,* Salvador Dali, Library, Saint Petersburg FL

Jeffries, Bill, *Dir & Cur,* Simon Fraser University, Simon Fraser University Gallery, Burnaby BC

Jehle, Michael, *CEO,* Fairfield Historical Society, Fairfield Museum & History Center, Fairfield CT

Jehle, Michael, *Cur,* Old Dartmouth Historical Society, New Bedford Whaling Museum, New Bedford MA

Jemison, Kyla, *Music Librn,* Banff Centre, Paul D Fleck Library & Archives, Banff AB

Jemmson-Pollard, Dianne, *Chmn,* Texas Southern University, College of Liberal Arts & Behavioral Sciences, Houston TX (S)

Jendrzejewski, Andrew, *Chmn,* Vincennes University Junior College, Humanities Art Dept, Vincennes IN (S)

Jenkens, Lawrence, *Head,* University of North Carolina at Greensboro, Art Dept, Greensboro NC (S)

Jenkins, Andre, *Prog Asst,* Rocky Mount Arts Center, Rocky Mount NC

Jenkins, Delanie, *Assoc Prof,* University of Pittsburgh, Dept of Studio Arts, Pittsburgh PA (S)

Jenkins, Erik, *Asst Dean/Asst Prof,* Catholic University of America, School of Architecture & Planning, Washington DC (S)

Jenkins, Greg, *Dir Opers,* Gibbes Museum of Art, Charleston SC (S)

Jenkins, John, *Pres,* The Illinois Institute of Art - Chicago, Chicago IL (S)

Jenkins, Paul, *Dir,* College of Mount Saint Joseph, Archbishop Alter Library, Cincinnati OH

Jenkins, Rick, *Park Ranger,* Longfellow National Historic Site, Longfellow House - Washington's Headquarters, Cambridge MA

Jenkins, Rupert, *Exec Dir,* Colorado Photographic Arts Center, Denver CO

Jenkins, Ulysses, *Assoc Prof Video,* African American Studies, University of California, Irvine, Studio Art Dept, Irvine CA (S)

Jenkins, Virginia, *Chmn,* Grand Valley State University, Art & Design Dept, Allendale MI (S)

Jenkins, Virginia, *Dir of Mktg & Develop,* Morgan State University, James E Lewis Museum of Art, Baltimore MD

Jenkner, Ingrid, *Dir Art Gallery,* Mount Saint Vincent University, MSVU Art Gallery, Halifax NS

Jenneman, Eugene A, *Dir Mus,* Northwestern Michigan College, Dennos Museum Center, Traverse City MI

Jennings, Corrine, *Dir,* Kenkeleba House, Inc, Kenkeleba Gallery, New York NY

Jennings, David, *Dir,* Akron-Summit County Public Library, Fine Arts Division, Akron OH

Jennings, DeAnn, *Instr,* Los Angeles Harbor College, Art Dept, Wilmington CA (S)

Jennings, Patrick, *Educ Coordr,* Pensacola Museum of Art, Pensacola FL

Jensen, Carl, *Asst Prof,* University of Southern Colorado, Dept of Art, Pueblo CO (S)

Jensen, David, *Pres,* The Currier Museum of Art, Manchester NH

Jensen, Elisa, *Dir Prog,* New York Studio School of Drawing, Painting & Sculpture, New York NY (S)

Jensen, Heidi, *Prof,* University of Wisconsin College - Marinette, Art Dept, Marinette WI (S)

Jensen, Hilbert J, *Mus Asst,* The Agricultural Memories Museum, Penn Yan NY

Jensen, James, *Assoc Prof,* Loyola University of Chicago, Fine Arts Dept, Chicago IL (S)

Jensen, James F, *Deputy Dir Exhibs & Colls,* The Contemporary Museum, Honolulu HI

Jensen, Jennifer R, *Owner & Operator,* The Agricultural Memories Museum, Penn Yan NY

Jensen, Leslie D, *Cur Weapons,* United States Military Academy, West Point Museum, West Point NY

Jensen, Pam, *Site Supervisor,* Jeffers Petroglyphs Historic Site, Comfrey MN

Jensen, Per Haubro, *VPres,* M Knoedler, Library, New York NY

Jensen-Inman, Leslie, *Lectr,* University of Tennessee at Chattanooga, Dept of Art, Chattanooga TN (S)

Jent, Deanna, *Assoc Prof,* Fontbonne University, Fine Art Dept, Saint Louis MO (S)

Jercich, George, *Prof Studio Art,* California Polytechnic State University at San Luis Obispo, Dept of Art & Design, San Luis Obispo CA (S)

Jerez, Cesar, *Chair Oils,* Hudson Valley Art Association, Brooklyn NY

Jerger, Holly, *Educ Dir,* Craft and Folk Art Museum (CAFAM), Los Angeles CA

Jernegan, Jeremy, *Assoc Prof,* Tulane University, Sophie H Newcomb Memorial College, New Orleans LA (S)

Jernegan, Jeremy, *Interim Dir,* Tulane University, Newcomb Art Gallery, New Orleans LA

Jerolmon, Linda, *Mem,* Yale University, Yale University Art Gallery, New Haven CT

Jerry, Jane, *Pres,* Cheekwood Nashville's Home of Art & Gardens, Education Dept, Nashville TN (S)

Jery, Jane, *Dir,* The Bascomb, Highlands NC

Jesse, Sarah, *Dir Educ & Pub Prog,* Philbrook Museum of Art, Tulsa OK

Jessen, Mark, *Security & Maintenance,* Blanden Memorial Art Museum, Fort Dodge IA

Jesso, Stacy Sumner, *Dir Develop,* The Mint Museum, Charlotte NC

Jessop, F Bradley, *Chair,* East Central University, School of Fine Arts, Ada OK (S)

Jessup, Robert, *Prof Drawing & Painting,* University of North Texas, College of Visual Arts & Design, Denton TX (S)

Jette, Carol, *Dir,* Copper Village Museum & Arts Center, Library, Anaconda MT

Jetzer, Gianni, *Dir,* Swiss Institute, New York NY

Jewell, Christine, *Dir Educ,* Fairfield Historical Society, Fairfield Museum & History Center, Fairfield CT

Jewell, Elizabeth A, *Exec Dir,* Worthington Arts Council, Columbus OH

Jewell, Jeff, *Photo Archives Historian,* Whatcom Museum, Bellingham WA

Jewell, Linda, *Chair, Dept Landscape Architecture & Environmental Planning & Prof Landscape Architecture & Urban Design,* University of California, Berkeley, College of Environmental Design, Berkeley CA (S)

Jewell, Robert, *CEO & Pres,* Brookgreen Gardens, Murrells Inlet SC

Jhashi, Tamara, *Assoc Prof,* Oakland University, Dept of Art & Art History, Rochester MI (S)

Jian, Li, *Cur E Asian Art,* Virginia Museum of Fine Arts, Richmond VA

JianXin, Xue, *Cur Chinese Art,* New England Center for Contemporary Art, Brooklyn CT

Jicha, Jon, *Prof,* Western Carolina University, Dept of Art/College of Arts & Science, Cullowhee NC (S)

Jilg, Joyce, *Instr,* Fort Hays State University, Dept of Art & Design, Hays KS (S)

Jimenez, Dan'etta, *Youth Progs Coordr,* Museum for African Art, New York NY

Jimenez, Ingrid, *Assoc Prof,* University of Puerto Rico, Dept of Fine Arts, Rio Piedras PR (S)

Jimenez, Ingrid, *Assoc Prof,* University of Puerto Rico, Dept of Fine Arts, Rio Piedras PR (S)

Jimenez, Pancho, *Lectr,* Santa Clara University, Dept of Art & Art History, Santa Clara CA (S)

Jimerson, Nadine, *Shop Mgr,* Seneca-Iroquois National Museum, Salamanca NY

Jiminez, Gabriel, *Admin Office Asst,* Plaza de la Raza Cultural Center, Los Angeles CA

Jiminez, Jill Berk, *CEO & Dir,* Berkeley Art Center, Berkeley CA

Jiminez-Torres, Maria, *Educ Dir,* Plaza de la Raza Cultural Center, Los Angeles CA

Jimison, Tom, *Cur,* Middle Tennessee State University, Baldwin Photographic Gallery, Murfreesboro TN

Jipson, Jim, *Assoc Prof,* University of West Florida, Dept of Art, Pensacola FL (S)

Jirges, Barbara, *Dir,* Bismarck State College, The Else Forde Gallery, Bismarck ND (S)

Jo, Kate, *Gallery Dir,* Montana State University, Helen E Copeland Gallery, Bozeman MT

Jo-Smith, Tyler, *Assoc Prof Art History,* University of Virginia, McIntire Dept of Art, Charlottesville VA (S)

Joassin, Odile, *Asst Cur,* The Art Institute of Chicago, Department of Textiles, Textile Society, Chicago IL

Jobe, Barbara, *Educator Group Tours,* Chester County Historical Society, West Chester PA

Jobe, Gary, *Instr,* Oklahoma State University, Graphic Arts Dept, Visual Communications, Okmulgee OK (S)

Joeger, Tom, *Instr,* Judson University, School of Art, Design & Architecture, Elgin IL (S)

Johaneman, Elaine, *Bookkeeper,* Lehigh Valley Heritage Center, Allentown PA

Johanowicz, Steve, *Preparator,* University of Wisconsin-Madison, Chazen Museum of Art, Madison WI

Johansen, Chris, *Dir,* New Image Art, West Hollywood CA

Johanson, David, *Asst Prof,* North Park University, Art Dept, Chicago IL (S)

Johanson, Melanie, *Mus Asst,* Cornell Museum of Art and American Culture, Delray Beach FL

Johanssen, Betty, *Art Instr,* Big Bend Community College, Art Dept, Moses Lake WA (S)

John, Jessy, *Chmn,* Troy State University, Dept of Art & Classics, Troy AL (S)

John, Madison, *Admin Asst,* Tucson Museum of Art and Historic Block, Tucson AZ

Johns, Jennifer, *Cur,* Ruthmere Museum, Robert B. Beardsley Arts Reference Library, Elkhart IN

Johns, Karl, *Librn,* Los Angeles County Museum of Art, Robert Gore Rifkind Center for German Expressionist Studies, Los Angeles CA

Johns, Shellie, *Coordr Conf,* Chadron State College, Memorial Hall Main Gallery & Memorial Hall Gallery 239, Chadron NE

Johns, Tim, *Pres & CEO,* Bernice Pauahi Bishop, Honolulu HI

Johnsen, Emily, *Prog Asst,* William Paterson University, Ben Shahn Art Galleries, Wayne NJ

Johnson, Alford, *Pres,* Taos Center for the Arts, Stables Gallery, Taos NM

Johnson, Amber, *Graphic Design & Mktg Coordr,* Pensacola Museum of Art, Pensacola FL

Johnson, Amy Jo, *Dir Gallery,* Idaho State University, John B Davis Gallery of Fine Art, Pocatello ID

Johnson, Anne, *Instr,* Pacific Northwest College of Art, Portland OR (S)

Johnson, Anne-Marie, *Visitor Experience Mgr,* Environment Canada - Parks Canada, Laurier House, National Historic Site, Ottawa ON

Johnson, Ben, *Asst Exhibits Cur,* Tohono Chul Park, Tucson AZ

Johnson, Ben, *Instr,* Kirkwood Community College, Dept of Arts & Humanities, Cedar Rapids IA (S)

Johnson, Bob, *Trustee,* J.M.W. Turner Museum, Sarasota FL

Johnson, Brad, *Exhibs Dir,* Oglebay Institute, Stifel Fine Arts Center, Wheeling WV

Johnson, Brad, *Instr,* West Liberty State College, Div Art, West Liberty WV (S)

Johnson, Brett John, *Dir Visual Arts,* Lorton Arts Foundation, Workhouse Arts Center, Lorton VA

Johnson, Bruce, *Cur,* Memorial University of Newfoundland, The Rooms Provincial Art Gallery, Saint John's NF

Johnson, Byron, *Exec Dir,* Texas Ranger Hall of Fame & Museum, Waco TX

Johnson, Carl, *Dir Museum,* Le Musee Regional de Rimouski, Centre National d'Exposition, Rimouski PQ

Johnson, Carl, *Dir Museum,* Le Musee Regional de Rimouski, Library, Rimouski PQ

Johnson, Carla C, *Dir,* New York State College of Ceramics at Alfred University, Scholes Library of Ceramics, Alfred NY

Johnson, Carlyle, *Instr,* Middle Tennessee State University, Art Dept, Murfreesboro TN (S)

Johnson, Charles, *Res Librn,* Museum of Ventura County, Ventura CA

Johnson, Charlie, *Instr,* Southern University in New Orleans, Fine Arts & Philosophy Dept, New Orleans LA (S)

Johnson, Cherry, *Registrar & Archivist,* Tellus Northwest Georgia Science Museum, Cartersville GA

Johnson, Christy, *Dir, Cur,* American Museum of Ceramic Art, Pomona CA

Johnson, Colleen, *Admin Asst,* Keene State College, Thorne-Sagendorph Art Gallery, Keene NH

Johnson, Craig, *Acting Head,* Utah State University, Dept of Landscape Architecture Environmental Planning, Logan UT (S)

Johnson, Cynthia A, *Dir Reader Svcs,* Pratt Institute, Art & Architecture Dept, Brooklyn NY

Johnson, Dale, *Dir,* Moody County Historical Society, Moody County Museum, Pierre SD

Johnson, David, *Instr,* Indian Hills Community College, Dept of Art, Centerville IA (S)

Johnson, David G, *Co-Chair,* The Museum of Contemporary Art (MOCA), Moca Grand Avenue, Los Angeles CA

Johnson, David J, *Mus Specialist,* Headquarters Fort Monroe, Dept of Army, Casemate Museum, Hampton VA

Johnson, Dawn, *Cur Educ,* Tampa Museum of Art, Tampa FL

Johnson, Dawn, *Cur Educ,* Tampa Museum of Art, Judith Rozier Blanchard Library, Tampa FL

Johnson, Deborah, *Asst Prof,* Providence College, Art & Art History Dept, Providence RI (S)

Johnson, Denise, *Registrar,* Phillips Academy, Addison Gallery of American Art, Andover MA

Johnson, Diane, *Librn,* Waterville Historical Society, Redington Museum, Waterville ME

Johnson, Donna, *Archivist,* Okanagan Heritage Museum, Kelowna BC

Johnson, Donna, *Archivist,* Okanagan Heritage Museum, Kelowna Public Archives, Kelowna BC

Johnson, Doro, *Recording Secy,* San Bernardino Art Association, Inc, Sturges Fine Arts Center, San Bernardino CA

Johnson, Dorothy, *Dir,* University of Iowa, School of Art & Art History, Iowa City IA (S)

Johnson, Douglas C, *Exec Dir,* McLean County Art Association, McLean County Arts Center, Bloomington IL

Johnson, Edward, *Dir Science,* Staten Island Museum, Staten Island NY

Johnson, Eileen, *Cur Anthropology,* Texas Tech University, Museum of Texas Tech University, Lubbock TX

Johnson, Elizabeth, *Cur Ethnology & Document,* University of British Columbia, Museum of Anthropology, Vancouver BC

Johnson, Eric, *Dean,* Dakota State University, College of Liberal Arts, Madison SD (S)

Johnson, Eric, *Prof Photog,* California Polytechnic State University at San Luis Obispo, Dept of Art & Design, San Luis Obispo CA (S)

Johnson, Ezra, *Asst Prof,* University of South Florida, School The Arts, Tampa FL (S)

Johnson, Frederic P, *Pres Historical Society,* Waterville Historical Society, Redington Museum, Waterville ME

Johnson, Gloria J, *Security Chief,* United States Military Academy, West Point Museum, West Point NY

Johnson, Harvey, *Art Coordr & Assoc Prof,* Texas Southern University, College of Liberal Arts & Behavioral Sciences, Houston TX (S)

Johnson, Heather, *Residency Program Mgr,* Bemis Center for Contemporary Arts, Omaha NE

Johnson, Herbert H, *Assoc Prof,* Rochester Institute of Technology, School of Printing Management & Sciences, Rochester NY (S)

Johnson, Hope, *Asst Dir,* Academy of Art, University Library, San Francisco CA

Johnson, Isabelle, *Librn,* Women's Art Association of Canada, Library, Toronto ON

Johnson, James, *Chmn,* University of Colorado, Boulder, Dept of Art & Art History, Boulder CO (S)

Johnson, James, *Chmn Photog & Digital Arts,* Moore College of Art & Design, Philadelphia PA (S)

Johnson, Jane, *Admin Asst,* Friends University, Edmund Stanley Library, Wichita KS

Johnson, Jane, *Community Svcs,* Westerly Public Library, Hoxie Gallery, Westerly RI

Johnson, Jeanne, *Exec Dir,* Thornton W Burgess, Museum, Sandwich MA

Johnson, Jennifer, *Arts Adminr,* Columbus Cultural Arts Center, Columbus OH

Johnson, Jeremy W, *Pres & CEO,* Historical Society of Palm Beach County, The Richard and Pat Johnson Palm Beach County History Museum, West Palm Beach FL

Johnson, Jerry, *Exec Dir,* Art Guild of Burlington, Art Center, Burlington IA

Johnson, Jim, *Dean Div,* Modesto Junior College, Arts Humanities & Communications Division, Modesto CA (S)

Johnson, Joan, *Dir Central Library Svcs,* Milwaukee Public Library, Art, Music & Recreation Dept, Milwaukee WI

Johnson, Joe, *Asst Prof (Photog),* University of Missouri - Columbia, Dept of Art, Columbia MO (S)

Johnson, Joyce, *Archaeology Asst Cur,* University of British Columbia, Museum of Anthropology, Vancouver BC

Johnson, Judith E, *Genealogist,* Connecticut Historical Society, Library, Hartford CT

Johnson, Judith Ellen, *Genealogist,* Connecticut Historical Society, Hartford CT

Johnson, Julie, *Asst Prof,* University of Texas at San Antonio, Dept of Art & Art History, San Antonio TX (S)

Johnson, Julie, *Asst Prof,* Utah State University, Dept of Art, Logan UT (S)

Johnson, Justin, *Gallery Dir,* University of Saint Francis, School of Creative Arts, John P Weatherhead Gallery & Lupke Gallery, Fort Wayne IN

Johnson, Karen, *Treas,* Kennebec Valley Art Association, Harlow Gallery, Hallowell ME

Johnson, Kate, *Dir,* Fullerton College, Division of Fine Arts, Fullerton CA (S)

Johnson, Kaytie, *Dir & Chief Cur,* Moore College of Art & Design, The Galleries at Moore, Philadelphia PA

Johnson, Kendra, *Project Coordr,* McLean County Art Association, McLean County Arts Center, Bloomington IL

Johnson, Kristi, *Artist in Res,* Jacksonville University, Dept of Art, Theater, Dance, Jacksonville FL (S)

Johnson, Larry, *Chmn Dept,* California State University, Fullerton, Art Dept, Fullerton CA (S)

Johnson, Lee, *Art Area Coordr,* Western State College of Colorado, Quigley Hall Art Gallery, Gunnison CO

Johnson, Lia, *Assoc Prof,* University of Wisconsin-Eau Claire, Dept of Art & Design, Eau Claire WI (S)

Johnson, Linda, *Chair, Prof Art, Graphic Design,* Florida Atlantic University, D F Schmidt College of Arts & Letters Dept of Visual Arts & Art History, Boca Raton FL (S)

Johnson, Lisa, *Dir,* Farmington Village Green & Library Association, Stanley-Whitman House, Farmington CT

Johnson, Lori, *Asst Prof,* University at Buffalo, State University of New York, Dept of Visual Studies, Buffalo NY (S)

Johnson, Lorna, *Mgr,* Red Deer & District Museum & Archives, Red Deer AB

Johnson, Lydia, *Dir,* Southern Utah University, Braithwaite Fine Arts Gallery, Cedar City UT

Johnson, Lynne, *Chmn,* Honolulu Museum of Art, Honolulu HI

Johnson, Margaret, *Assoc Prof,* Winthrop University, Dept of Art & Design, Rock Hill SC (S)

Johnson, Margaret, *Prog Dir Art Educ,* State University of New York at New Paltz, Art Education Program, New Paltz NY (S)

Johnson, Mark, *Board Pres,* Peoria Historical Society, Peoria IL

Johnson, Mark, *Instr,* Maine College of Art, Portland ME (S)

Johnson, Mark M, *Dir,* Montgomery Museum of Fine Arts, Montgomery AL

Johnson, Mark M, *Dir,* Montgomery Museum of Fine Arts, Library, Montgomery AL

Johnson, Martha K, *Dir,* Randolph College, Maier Museum of Art, Lynchburg VA

Johnson, Mary, *Bookkeeper,* Hickory Museum of Art, Inc, Hickory NC

Johnson, Mary, *Registrar,* California Center for the Arts, Escondido Museum, Escondido CA

Johnson, Mary Ellyn, *Asst Cur,* San Francisco Art Institute, Galleries, San Francisco CA

Johnson, Megan, *Facility Rental Mgr,* Museum of Wisconsin Art, West Bend WI

Johnson, Melissa, *Educ Dir,* Walter Anderson, Ocean Springs MS

Johnson, Melvin, *Asst Preparator,* Mississippi Museum of Art, Howorth Library, Jackson MS

Johnson, Michael, *Assoc Prof,* Murray State University, Dept of Art, Murray KY

Johnson, Mimi, *Acad Dept Assoc,* University of Wisconsin-Stevens Point, Dept of Art & Design, Stevens Point WI (S)

Johnson, Nancy, *Mus Shop Mgr,* Aiken County Historical Museum, Aiken SC

Johnson, Neil, *Lectr,* Centenary College of Louisiana, Dept of Art, Shreveport LA (S)

Johnson, Pam, *Instr,* Sierra Community College, Art Dept, Rocklin CA (S)

Johnson, Pamela, *Assoc Prof,* Bates College, Art & Visual Culture, Lewiston ME (S)

Johnson, Patricia, *Assoc Div Chmn,* J Sargeant Reynolds Community College, Humanities & Social Science Division, Richmond VA (S)

Johnson, Paul, *VPres Exhibit Design & & Fabrication,* Bowers Museum, Santa Ana CA

Johnson, Quinn, *Exhibs Preparator,* Loveland Museum/Gallery, Loveland CO

Johnson, Ray, *Preparator,* The Butler Institute of American Art, Art Museum, Youngstown OH

Johnson, Raymond, *Chmn,* Museum of Russian Art, Minneapolis MN

Johnson, Richard, *Assoc Dir,* University of Georgia, Franklin College of Arts & Sciences, Lamar Dodd School of Art, Athens GA (S)

Johnson, Richard A, *Prof,* University of New Orleans-Lake Front, Dept of Fine Arts, New Orleans LA (S)

Johnson, Rick, *Chmn,* Iowa Great Lakes Maritime Museum, Arnolds Park IA

Johnson, Robert, *Instr,* Judson University, School of Art, Design & Architecture, Elgin IL (S)

Johnson, Robert S, *Cur,* Fort George G Meade Museum, Fort Meade MD

Johnson, Rolf, *Dir,* Neville Public Museum of Brown County, Green Bay WI

Johnson, Sallie, *Deputy Dir,* Memphis-Shelby County Public Library & Information Center, Dept of Art, Music & Films, Memphis TN

Johnson, Sam, *CEO & Dir,* Columbia River Maritime Museum, Astoria OR

Johnson, Sara, *Chief Cur,* Southern Ohio Museum Corporation, Southern Ohio Museum, Portsmouth OH

Johnson, Stephen, *Installationist,* Arizona State University, ASU Art Museum, Tempe AZ

Johnson, Steven, *Exec Dir,* Vesterheim Norwegian-American Museum, Decorah IA

Johnson, Sue, *Dept Chmn,* Saint Mary's College of Maryland, Art & Art History Dept, Saint Mary's City MD (S)

Johnson, Suni, *Librn,* United Methodist Historical Society, Library, Baltimore MD

Johnson, Susan, *Dir Develop,* The Dixon Gallery & Gardens, Memphis TN

Johnson, Susan, *Dir Opers,* C M Russell, Frederic G Renner Memorial Library, Great Falls MT

Johnson, Tama, *Admin Asst to Dir Univ Mus,* Foosaner Art Museum, Melbourne FL

Johnson, Tammy, *Cur Art Educ,* Louisiana Arts & Science Museum, Baton Rouge LA

Johnson, Teresa, *Treas,* Almond Historical Society, Inc, Hagadorn House, The 1800-37 Museum, Almond NY

Johnson, Tora, *Pres,* Watercolor Society of Alabama, Town Creek AL

Johnson, Trudi Ludwig, *Cur,* Wesley Theological Seminary, Henry Luce III Center for the Arts & Religion, Dadian Gallery, Washington DC

Johnson, Tullis, *Archives & Info Resource Mgr,* State University of New York College at Buffalo, Buffalo NY

Johnson, Valerie, *Asst Exec Dir,* Boca Raton Museum of Art, Boca Raton FL

Johnson, Wanda, *Dir,* Beaufort County Arts Council, Washington NC

Johnson-Dibb, Rebecca, *Conservator,* Textile Conservation Workshop Inc, South Salem NY

Johnson Jr, Charles W, *Chmn,* University of Richmond, Dept of Art and Art History, Richmond VA (S)

Johnston, Amanda, *Gallery Asst,* Pointe Claire Cultural Centre, Stewart Hall Art Gallery, Pointe Claire PQ

Johnston, Aron, *Instr,* Moravian College, Dept of Art, Bethlehem PA (S)

Johnston, Ben, *Art Installer/Driver,* San Francisco Museum of Modern Art, Artist Gallery, San Francisco CA

Johnston, Benjamin, *Asst Prof,* Delta State University, Dept of Art, Cleveland MS (S)

Johnston, Byron, *Assoc Prof (Visual Art),* University of British Columbia Okanagan, Dept of Creative Studies, Kelowna BC (S)

Johnston, Eileen, *Registrar,* Howard University, Gallery of Art, Washington DC

Johnston, Jeff, *Prof,* College of the Ozarks, Dept of Art, Point Lookout MO (S)

Johnston, Lisa N, *Pub Svcs,* Sweet Briar College, Mary Helen Cochran Library, Sweet Briar VA

Johnston, Marc, *Pres,* Yukon Historical & Museums Association, Whitehorse YT

Johnston, Maryalice, *Visual Coordr,* Fine Arts Work Center, Provincetown MA

Johnston, Matthew, *Asst Prof,* Radford University, Art Dept, Radford VA (S)

Johnston, Michael W, *Chmn,* McMichael Canadian Art Collection, Kleinburg ON

Johnston, Patricia, *Prof,* Salem State University, Art & Design Department, Salem MA (S)

Johnston, Rebecca, *Paper Conservator,* Williamstown Art Conservation Center, Williamstown MA

Johnston, Robert C, *Library Dir,* Le Moyne College, Wilson Art Gallery, Syracuse NY

Johnston, Sally, *Dir,* Star-Spangled Banner Flag House Association, Flag House & 1812 Museum, Baltimore MD

Johnston, Sally S, *Dir,* Star-Spangled Banner Flag House Association, Museum, Baltimore MD

Johnston, Sona, *Sr Cur Painting & Sculpture Emeritus,* The Baltimore Museum of Art, Baltimore MD

Johnston, Sue, *Dir Mem,* California Watercolor Association, Gallery Concord, Concord CA

Johnston, Thomas, *Chmn Dept Art,* Western Washington University, Art Dept, Bellingham WA (S)

Joice, Gail, *Sr Deputy Dir,* Seattle Art Museum, Dorothy Stimson Bullitt Library, Seattle WA

Jolicoeur, Anne, *Nat & International Prog Mgr,* Canadian Museum of Contemporary Photography, Ottawa ON

Jolly, Marilyn, *Assoc Prof,* University of Texas at Arlington, Art & Art History Department, Arlington TX (S)

Jolly, Mike, *Mus Technician,* Tuskegee Institute National Historic Site, George Washington Carver & The Oaks, Montgomery AL

Jonason, Maureen Kelly, *Exec Dir,* Historical and Cultural Society of Clay County, Hjemkomst Center, Moorhead MN

Jonckheere, Sherry, *Mus Shop Mgr,* Montana Historical Society, Helena MT

Jones, Amber, *Mktg & Vol Coordr,* 18th Street Arts Complex, Santa Monica CA

Jones, Andy, *Dir,* Society of Decorative Painters, Inc, Decorative Arts Collection Museum, Atlanta GA

Jones, Anita, *Cur Textiles,* The Baltimore Museum of Art, Baltimore MD

Jones, Ann, *Librn,* McNay, San Antonio TX

Jones, Ann, *Librn,* McNay, McNay Art Museum Library & Archives, San Antonio TX

Jones, Anna Bell, *Operations & Sales,* Longue Vue House & Gardens, New Orleans LA

Jones, Antwan, *Asst Cur Educ,* Contemporary Arts Center, Cincinnati OH

Jones, Barbara L, *Cur,* Westmoreland Museum of American Art, Greensburg PA

Jones, Barbara L, *Cur,* Westmoreland Museum of American Art, Art Reference Library, Greensburg PA

Jones, Barry, *Opers Mgr,* African American Museum, Dallas TX

Jones, Ben, *Prof,* New Jersey City University, Art Dept, Jersey City NJ (S)

Jones, Beth, *Develop Dir,* Academy Art Museum, Easton MD

Jones, Bob, *Chmn Bd,* Bob Jones University Museum & Gallery Inc, Greenville SC

Jones, Bob, *Prof,* Delaware County Community College, Communications, Art & Humanities, Media PA (S)

Jones, Catherine, *Educ Fellow,* Bates College, Museum of Art, Lewiston ME

Jones, Chad, *Develop & Communs Mgr,* San Francisco Arts Education Project, San Francisco CA

Jones, Charles E, *Librn,* University of Chicago, Oriental Institute Research Archives, Chicago IL

Jones, Dana, *Assoc Dir Admis,* Virginia Center for the Creative Arts, Amherst VA

Jones, Dennis, *Dir,* University of Arizona, Dept of Art, Tucson AZ (S)

Jones, Diem, *Deputy Dir,* Arts Council Silicon Valley, San Jose CA

Jones, Don R, *Chmn,* Iowa Wesleyan College, Art Dept, Mount Pleasant IA (S)

Jones, Elliott, *Assoc Prof,* Old Dominion University, Art Dept, Norfolk VA (S)

Jones, Emily, *Deputy Dir,* San Antonio Museum of Art, San Antonio TX

Jones, Emily, *Archivist,* Woodstock Artists Association & Museum, Woodstock NY

Jones, Eric S, *Registrar,* Southern Illinois University Carbondale, University Museum, Carbondale IL

Jones, Erin, *Dir,* Bob Jones University Museum & Gallery Inc, Greenville SC

Jones, Frederick N, *Instr,* Guilford Technical Community College, Commercial Art Dept, Jamestown NC (S)

Jones, Greg, *Exhib Designer,* Columbus Museum of Art, Columbus OH

Jones, Gregory, *Instr,* Adrian College, Art & Design Dept, Adrian MI (S)

Jones, Jim, *Head Board of Dirs,* Meridian International Center, Cafritz Galleries, Washington DC

Jones, Jo Ann, *Gift Shop Mgr,* Koshare Indian Museum, Inc, La Junta CO

Jones, Joanne, *Instr,* University of Arkansas, Art Dept, Fayetteville AR (S)

Jones, Joyce, *Dir Finance,* Knoxville Museum of Art, Knoxville TN

Jones, Julie, *Cur in Charge Arts,* The Metropolitan Museum of Art, New York NY

Jones, Keith, *Asst Prof,* University of Alabama in Huntsville, Dept of Art and Art History, Huntsville AL (S)

Jones, Kelly, *Dir Undergrad Studies,* Yale University, Dept of the History of Art, New Haven CT (S)

Jones, Kenneth, *Assoc Prof Art,* Harford Community College, Visual, Performing and Applied Arts Division, Bel Air MD (S)

Jones, Kent, *Prof & Chair Visual Arts,* Memorial University of Newfoundland, Division of Fine Arts, Visual Arts Program, Corner Brook NF (S)

Jones, Kent, *VPres Retail Opers,* California Science Center, Los Angeles CA

Jones, Kimberly Koller, *Exec Dir,* Hoyt Center for the Arts, New Castle PA

Jones, Lewis L, *VPres Acad Affairs,* Tougaloo College, Art Collection, Tougaloo MS

Jones, Lial A, *Mus Dir,* Crocker Art Museum, Sacramento CA

Jones, Lindsey, *Visitor Svcs Team Leader,* Contemporary Arts Center, Cincinnati OH

Jones, Lisa, *Visual Resource Cur,* East Tennessee State University, College of Arts and Sciences, Dept of Art & Design, Johnson City TN (S)

Jones, Lynda, *Dir Human Resources,* Historic Hudson Valley, Pocantico Hills NY

Jones, Lynn M, *Art & Design Chair,* Brenau University, Art & Design Dept, Gainesville GA (S)

Jones, Marilyn, *Asst Prof,* Lehigh University, Dept of Art, Architecture & Design, Bethlehem PA (S)

Jones, Marvin H, *Prof,* Cleveland State University, Art Dept, Cleveland OH (S)

Jones, Megan, *Visitor Prog Mgr,* Supreme Court of the United States, Office of the Curator, Washington DC

Jones, Michael, *Animal Cur,* Tallahassee Museum of History & Natural Science, Tallahassee FL

Jones, Mike, *Prof & Chmn,* Hardin-Simmons University, Art Dept, Abilene TX (S)

Jones, Nancy, *Dir Educ,* Detroit Institute of Arts, Detroit MI

Jones, Pamela, *Assoc Prof,* University of Massachusetts - Boston, Art Dept, Boston MA (S)

Jones, Patty Sue, *International Child Art Coordr,* Cultural Affairs Department City of Los Angeles/Barnsdall Art Centers/Junior Arts Center, Los Angeles CA

Jones, Peggy, *Instr Digital Art,* Miracosta College, Art Dept, Oceanside CA (S)

Jones, Phillip J, *Librn,* University of Arkansas, Fine Arts Library, Fayetteville AR

Jones, Rachel, *Library Mgr,* Maine Photographic Workshops/Rockport College, Carter-Haas Library, Rockport ME

Jones, Randal, *Pub Rels Coordr,* Tennessee State Museum, Nashville TN

Jones, Randy, *Dir,* Duley-Jones Gallery, Paradise Valley AZ

Jones, Reba, *Coll Mgr,* Amarillo Art Association, Amarillo Museum of Art, Amarillo TX

Jones, Rick H, *Exec Dir,* Fitton Center for Creative Arts, Hamilton OH

Jones, Rick H, *Exec Dir,* Fitton Center for Creative Arts, Hamilton OH (S)

Jones, Robert L, *Head Div Fine Arts,* Truman State University, Art Dept, Kirksville MO (S)

Jones, Ron, *Pres,* Memphis College of Art, Memphis TN (S)

Jones, Ronald, *Chmn,* Columbia University, School of the Arts, Division of Visual Arts, New York NY (S)

Jones, Shalonda, *Financial Secy,* The Walker African American Museum & Research Center, Las Vegas NV

Jones, Shawn, *Arts Prog Coordr,* Danville Museum of Fine Arts & History, Danville VA

Jones, Sonja, *Asst Curator,* The Robert McLaughlin, Library, Oshawa ON

Jones, Steve, *Asst Prof,* Florida State University, Art Dept, Tallahassee FL (S)

Jones, Steven, *Instr,* Millsaps College, Dept of Art, Jackson MS (S)

Jones, Susan Henshaw, *Pres & Dir,* Museum of the City of New York, Research Room, New York NY

Jones, Suzi, *Deputy Dir,* Anchorage Museum at Rasmuson Center, Anchorage AK

Jones, Tate, *Exec Dir,* Rocky Mountain Museum of Military History, Missoula MT

Jones, Thomas, *Exec Dir,* The Old Jail Art Center, Green Research Library, Albany TX

Jones, Tom, *Asst Prof,* University of Wisconsin, Madison, Dept of Art, Madison WI (S)

Jones, Tom, *Instr,* Cuyahoga Valley Art Center, Cuyahoga Falls OH (S)

Jones, Tracey, *Asst Prof,* College of Staten Island, Performing & Creative Arts Dept, Staten Island NY (S)

Jones, Viki, *Bus Mgr,* Anderson Fine Arts Center, The Anderson Center for the Arts, Anderson IN

Jones, Win, *Instr,* Art Center Sarasota, Sarasota FL (S)

Jones-Avery, H Raye, *Dir,* Christina Cultural Arts Center, Inc, Wilmington DE

Jonte-Pace, Diane, *Vice Provost for Acad Affairs,* Santa Clara University, de Saisset Museum, Santa Clara CA

Jonus, Chris, *Cur & Dir Installation & Performance Arts,* The Center for Contemporary Arts of Santa Fe, Santa Fe NM

Jordahl, Irene, *Recreation Supvr II,* City of Fremont, Olive Hyde Art Gallery, Fremont CA

Jordan, Brenda, *Asst Prof,* Florida State University, Art History Dept, Tallahassee FL (S)

Jordan, Bryan, *CEO,* First Horizon National Corp, First Tennessee Heritage Collection, Memphis TN

Jordan, Candace, *Librn & Mus Library Cataloger,* Roswell Museum & Art Center, Library, Roswell NM

Jordan, Debbie, *Asst Prof,* Jacksonville University, Dept of Art, Theater, Dance, Jacksonville FL (S)

Jordan, Edward, *Instr,* Southern University in New Orleans, Fine Arts & Philosophy Dept, New Orleans LA (S)

Jordan, Jennifer, *Develop & Communs Mgr,* San Francisco Camerawork, San Francisco CA

Jordan, Mary Anne, *Prof & Chair,* University of Kansas, The School of the Arts, Dept of Visual Art, Lawrence KS (S)

Jordan, Maryann, *Vice Dir,* Seattle Art Museum, Downtown, Seattle WA

Jordan, Patricia, *Instr,* Wayne Art Center, Wayne PA (S)

Jordan, Shirley, *VPres,* Northwest Watercolor Society, Woodinville WA

Jordan, Tiffany, *Develop & Mem Coordr,* Hofstra University, Hofstra University Museum, Hempstead NY

Jordan-Smith, Latonya, *Community Arts Coordr,* Arizona Museum For Youth, Mesa AZ

Jordon, Shelley, *Assoc Prof,* Oregon State University, Dept of Art, Corvallis OR (S)

Jorgensen, Joseph, *Assoc Prof,* Culver-Stockton College, Art Dept, Canton MO (S)

Jorgensen, Roy, *Librn,* Fishkill Historical Society, Van Wyck Homestead Museum, Fishkill NY

Jorgenson, Tim, *Events Coordr,* Historical and Cultural Society of Clay County, Hjemkomst Center, Moorhead MN

Joselit, David, *Prof,* City University of New York, PhD Program in Art History, New York NY (S)

Joseph, Ellis, *Treas,* San Francisco African-American Historical & Cultural Society, Library, San Francisco CA

Joseph, Ellis, *Treasurer,* San Francisco African-American Historical & Cultural Society, San Francisco CA

Joseph, Phil, *Art Coordr,* Miami University, Dept Fine Arts, Hamilton OH (S)

Joseph, Sarah, *Dir Exhibitions,* Kendall College of Art & Design, Kendall Gallery, Grand Rapids MI

Josephson, Jack A, *Chmn,* International Foundation for Art Research, Inc (IFAR), New York NY

Joslin, Kelly, *Chair Arts & Asst Prof,* Sinclair Community College, Division of Fine & Performing Arts, Dayton OH (S)

Joslyn, Catherine, *Prof,* Clarion University of Pennsylvania, Dept of Art, Clarion PA (S)

Jost, Stephan, *Dir,* Honolulu Museum of Art, Honolulu HI

Jovanelli, Kathryn, *Asst Mus Coordr & Mem Mgr,* University of Maine, Museum of Art, Bangor ME

Joy, Carol, *Chmn,* Laney College, Art Dept, Oakland CA (S)

Joy, Diane Chisnall, *Dir,* Osborne Homestead Museum, Derby CT

Joy, Jason, *Gen Educ,* Art Institute of Pittsburgh, Pittsburgh PA (S)

Joyaux, Aimee, *Prog Dir,* Visual Arts Center of Richmond, Richmond VA

Joyce, Daniel, *Dir,* Kenosha Public Museums, Kenosha WI

Joyce, Julie, *Cur Contemporary Art,* Santa Barbara Museum of Art, Santa Barbara CA

Joyce, Julie, *Cur Contemporary Art,* Santa Barbara Museum of Art, Library, Santa Barbara CA

Joyce, Larry, *Chmn & Pres,* Iroquois Indian Museum, Howes Cave NY

Joyce, Lillian, *Asst Prof,* University of Alabama in Huntsville, Dept of Art and Art History, Huntsville AL (S)

Joyce, Lisa, *Visual Resources Cur,* State University of New York College at Cortland, Visual Resources Collection, Cortland NY

Joyce, Rosemary, *Dir,* University of California, Berkeley, Phoebe Apperson Hearst Museum of Anthropology, Berkeley CA

Joyner, Alexis, *Chair,* Elizabeth City State University, School of Arts & Humanities, Dept of Art, Elizabeth City NC (S)

Joyner, Gary T, *Sr Retail Opers Mgr,* Jamestown-Yorktown Foundation, Jamestown Settlement, Williamsburg VA

Joyner, J Brooks, *Pres & CEO,* Allentown Art Museum, Allentown PA

Jozoff, Jane, *Chmn,* Arizona Commission on the Arts, Phoenix AZ

Juarez, Jaime, *Dir Protection Servs,* The Cleveland Museum of Art, Cleveland OH

Juarez, Miguel, *Librn,* University of Arizona, Library, Tucson AZ

Juchniewich, Daniel, *Asst Dir,* Rahr-West Art Museum, Manitowoc WI

Judge, Vaughan, *Dir School of Art,* Montana State University, Helen E Copeland Gallery, Bozeman MT

Judge, Vaughan, *Dir School of Art,* Montana State University, School of Art, Bozeman MT (S)

Judge McCalpin, Sara, *Pres,* China Institute in America, China Institute Gallery, New York NY

Jue, Sharon, *Event Rental & Admin Mgr,* Kala Institute, Kala Art Institute, Berkeley CA

Juergens, Karyn, *Gallery Shop Mgr,* Kalamazoo Institute of Arts, Kalamazoo MI

Jueschke, Rainie, *Dir Devel,* Center for Puppetry Arts, Atlanta GA

Juhasz, Victor, *VPres,* Society of Illustrators, New York NY

Juliusburger, Thomas, *Art Dept Chmn,* University of Bridgeport Gallery, Bridgeport CT

Jull, Emily, *Retail Mgr,* Canadian Clay and Glass Gallery, Waterloo ON

Juneau, Madeleine, *Gen Mgr,* Maison Saint-Gabriel Museum, Montreal PQ

Jung, Hyun Tae, *Asst Prof,* Lehigh University, Dept of Art, Architecture & Design, Bethlehem PA (S)

Jung, Nancy, *Office Mgr,* Cultural Affairs Department City of Los Angeles/Barnsdall Art Centers/Junior Arts Center, Library, Los Angeles CA

Jungen, Bettina, *Senior Cur & Cur Russian Art,* Amherst College, Mead Art Museum, Amherst MA

Junor, Maggi, *Asst to Dir,* Mizel Museum, Denver CO

Juorio, Alex, *Dir,* John M Cuelenaere, Grace Campbell Gallery, Prince Albert SK

Jurakic, Ivan, *Dir & Cur,* University of Waterloo, University of Waterloo Art Gallery, Waterloo ON

Jurgemeyer, Marne, *Dir,* Fort Morgan Heritage Foundation, Fort Morgan CO

Jurgena, Jason, *Cur,* City of El Paso, El Paso Museum of Archaeology, El Paso TX

Jurgensmeier, Charles, *Instr Music,* Creighton University, Fine & Performing Arts Dept, Omaha NE (S)

Juroszek, Steven, *Interim Dir,* Montana State University, School of Architecture, Bozeman MT (S)

Jurovics, Toby, *Chief Cur,* Joslyn Art Museum, Omaha NE

Jurus, Richard, *Prof,* Sinclair Community College, Division of Fine & Performing Arts, Dayton OH (S)

Jurvais, Roger, *Chief,* Universite de Moncton, Campus d'Edmundston, Dept of Visual Arts Arts & Lettres, Edmundston NB (S)

Jussila, Neil, *Prof of Art,* Montana State University at Billings, Northcutt Steele Gallery, Billings MT

Just, Bryan, *Cur & Lectr Art of Ancient Americas,* Princeton University, Princeton University Art Museum, Princeton NJ

Justice, Adam, *Cur Art,* Polk Museum of Art, Lakeland FL

Juszczyk, James, *Treas,* American Abstract Artists, Brooklyn NY

Kabala, Irene, *Assoc Prof,* Indiana University of Pennsylvania, College of Fine Arts, Indiana PA (S)

Kabot, Sarah, *Head Drawing,* Cleveland Institute of Art, Cleveland OH (S)

Kabriel, J Ronald, *Asst Prof,* Catholic University of America, School of Architecture & Planning, Washington DC (S)

Kacerguis, Ed, *Treas,* Rensselaer Newman Foundation Chapel + Cultural Center, The Gallery at the Chapel & Cultural Center, Troy NY

Kachur, Louis, *Coordr Art History,* Kean University, Fine Arts Dept, Union NJ (S)

Kaczmarczyk, Madeline, *Adjunct Instr Ceramics,* Aquinas College, Art Dept, Grand Rapids MI (S)

Kaczmarek, Sheila, *VPres,* New Haven Paint & Clay Club, Inc, New Haven CT

Kadish, Skip, *Adjunct,* Monterey Peninsula College, Art Dept/Art Gallery, Monterey CA (S)

Kadoche, Salomon, *Second VPres,* Art Centre of New Jersey, Livingston NJ (S)

Kadow, Joan, *Instr,* Mount Mary College, Art & Design Division, Milwaukee WI (S)

Kaellgren, Peter, *Interim Chief Cur,* George R Gardiner, Toronto ON

Kaffenberger, Vicki, *Mng Dir Institutional Advancement,* Missouri Historical Society, Missouri History Museum, Saint Louis MO

Kagan, Judy, *Asst Dir,* Wooster Community Art Center, Danbury CT

Kagerer, Sally, *VPres,* Buckham Fine Arts Project, Gallery, Flint MI

Kaha, Myra, *Educ Dir,* Kirkland Arts Center, Kirkland WA

Kahan, Mitchell, *Dir & CEO,* Akron Art Museum, Akron OH

Kahle, David, *Dept Head,* Mount Marty College, Art Dept, Yankton SD (S)

Kahle, David, *Dir,* Bede Art Gallery, Yankton SD

Kahle, Patricia, *Dir,* National Trust for Historic Preservation, Shadows-on-the-Teche, New Iberia LA

Kahler, Bruce, *Dr,* Bethany College, Art Dept, Lindsborg KS (S)

Kahler, Bruce, *Prof,* Bethany College, Mingenback Art Center, Lindsborg KS

Kahler, Caroline, *Head Art Dept,* Bethany College, Art Dept, Lindsborg KS (S)

Kahler, Caroline, *Prof,* Bethany College, Mingenback Art Center, Lindsborg KS

Kahler, Chris, *Prof,* Eastern Illinois University, Art Dept, Charleston IL (S)

Kahn, Bibi, *Asst Cur,* Andy Warhol Foundation for the Visual Arts, New York NY

Kahn, David, *Dir,* The Adirondack Historical Association, The Adirondack Museum, Blue Mountain Lake NY

Kahn, David, *Exec Dir,* Connecticut Historical Society, Hartford CT

Kahn, Deborah, *Assoc Prof,* American University, Dept of Art, New York NY (S)

Kahn, Eunice, *Archivist,* Navajo Nation, Navajo Nation Museum, Window Rock AZ

Kahn, Leo, *Pres,* Guadalupe Historic Foundation, Santuario de Guadalupe, Santa Fe NM

Kahn, Leslie, *Supvr,* Newark Public Library, Reference, Newark NJ

Kahng, Eik, *Chief Cur,* Santa Barbara Museum of Art, Santa Barbara CA

Kahute, Robert M, *Assoc Prof,* Rochester Institute of Technology, School of Design, Rochester NY (S)

Kaier, Dale A, *Office Mgr,* Rome Art & Community Center, Rome NY

Kaigler, Doug, *Prof Art,* Eastern Oregon University, School of Arts & Science, La Grande OR (S)

Kaimal, Padma, *Asst Prof,* Colgate University, Dept of Art & Art History, Hamilton NY (S)

Kain, Evelyn, *Prof,* Ripon College, Art Dept, Ripon WI (S)

Kain, Karen, *Chmn,* Canada Council for the Arts, Conseil des Arts du Canada, Ottawa ON

Kaineg, Kristin, *Coordr Design,* Shepherd University, Dept of Contemporary Art & Theater, Shepherdstown WV (S)

Kaino, Glen, *Co-Pres,* Los Angeles Center for Photographic Studies, Los Angeles CA

Kaiser, Allison, *Exec Dir,* Lexington Art League, Inc, Lexington KY

Kaiser, Karen, *Asst Cur Educ,* Jundt Art Museum, Spokane WA

Kaiser, Kurt, *Assoc Prof,* Aquinas College, Art Dept, Grand Rapids MI (S)

Kaiser, Michael M, *Pres,* The John F Kennedy, Washington DC

Kaiser, Michel, *Instr Commercial Art,* Honolulu Community College, Commercial Art Dept, Honolulu HI (S)

Kajer, Andrea, *Deputy Dir External Relations,* Minnesota Historical Society, Saint Paul MN

Kajitani, Nobuko, *Conservator In charge,* The Metropolitan Museum of Art, New York NY

Kakas, Karen, *Chmn Art Educ,* Bowling Green State University, School of Art, Bowling Green OH (S)

Kalaman, Megan, *Event Mgr,* Canadian Art Foundation, Toronto ON

Kalavrezou, Ioli, *Chmn Dept,* Harvard University, Dept of History of Art & Architecture, Cambridge MA (S)

Kalb, Kent, *VPres,* Maysville, Kentucky Gateway Museum Center, Maysville KY

Kalba, Laura, *Asst Prof,* Smith College, Art Dept, Northampton MA (S)

Kaldahl, Eric, *Chief Cur,* Amerind Foundation, Inc, Amerind Museum, Fulton-Hayden Memorial Art Gallery, Dragoon AZ

Kaldahl, Eric, *Cur,* Amerind Foundation, Inc, Fulton-Hayden Memorial Library & Art Gallery, Dragoon AZ

Kaldany, Mary, *Sr Conservator,* Textile Conservation Workshop Inc, South Salem NY

Kaldor, Cynthia, *Dir,* Mayville State University, Northern Lights Art Gallery, Mayville ND

Kalin, Amelia, *Library Dir,* Valley Cottage Library, Gallery, Valley Cottage NY

Kalinovska, Milena, *Dir Pub Programs,* Hirshhorn Museum & Sculpture Garden, Smithsonian Institution, Washington DC

Kalk, Bethany, *Art Instr,* Morehead State University, Art & Design Dept, Morehead KY (S)

Kalke, Ed, *Chmn,* Carthage College, Art Dept, Kenosha WI (S)

Kallan, Linda, *Dept Chmn,* East Los Angeles College, Art Dept, Monterey Park CA (S)

Kallenberger, Christine, *Dir Exhib & Coll,* Philbrook Museum of Art, Tulsa OK

Kallenberger, Klaus, *Instr,* Middle Tennessee State University, Art Dept, Murfreesboro TN (S)

Kallsen, Mark, *Asst Prof,* University of Wisconsin-Stout, Dept of Art & Design, Menomonie WI (S)

Kalmar, Stefan, *Dir,* Artists Space, New York NY

Kalmbach, Ann, *Exec Dir,* Women's Studio Workshop, Inc, Rosendale NY

Kalogeros-Chattan, Charles, *Dir,* Mesa Public Library Art Gallery, Los Alamos NM

Kaloyanides, Michael G, *Chmn,* University of New Haven, Dept of Visual & Performing Arts & Philosophy, West Haven CT (S)

Kalra, Raji, *CFO,* Museum for African Art, New York NY

Kaltenbach, Jim, *Pres Mem Guild,* High Museum of Art, Atlanta GA

Kam, D Vanessa, *Head Librn,* University of British Columbia, Art & Architecture Planning, UBC Library, Vancouver BC

Kama-Drake, Lyah, *Mem Mgr/Admin,* Kauai Museum Association, Ltd., Lihue HI

Kamalipour, Yahya R, *Head,* Purdue University Calumet, Dept of Communication & Creative Arts, Hammond IN (S)

Kamansky, David, *Exec Dir,* Pacific - Asia Museum, Pasadena CA

Kamas, Louise, *Prof Art,* Clarke College, Dept of Art, Dubuque IA (S)

Kamen, Brian, *Preparator,* University of Delaware, University Museums, Newark DE

Kamerer, Tracy, *Chief Cur,* Henry Morrison Flagler Museum, Palm Beach FL

Kamerling, Leonard J, *Cur Alaska Ctr for Documentary Film,* University of Alaska, Museum of the North, Fairbanks AK

Kaminishi, Ikumi, *Assoc Prof,* Tufts University, Dept of Art & Art History, Medford MA (S)

Kamiya, Takashi, *Chmn Interior Design,* Fashion Institute of Technology, Art & Design Division, New York NY (S)

Kamm, David, *Gallery Coordr,* Luther College, Fine Arts Collection, Decorah IA

Kammer, Greg, *Dir,* Everett Community College, Art Dept, Everett WA (S)

Kammerer, Steve, *Bd Trustees,* Sioux City Art Center, Sioux City IA

Kammerzell, Kay, *Dir,* Westcott Bay Institute, Island Museum of Art & Westcott Bay Sculpture Park, Friday Harbor WA

Kamniker, Jim, *Pres,* Go Antiques, Inc, Atlanta GA

Kamniker, Kathy, *Sr VPres Bus Develop,* Go Antiques, Inc, Atlanta GA

Kampf, Ray, *Assoc Prof,* California State Polytechnic University, Pomona, Department of Art, Pomona CA (S)

Kamphaus, Lisa, *Asst Prof,* La Roche College, Division of Design, Pittsburgh PA (S)

Kamphuis, Mark, *IT Mgr,* Contemporary Arts Center, Cincinnati OH

Kamps, Toby, *Cur,* Menil Foundation, Inc, The Menil Collection, Houston TX

Kanbara, Bryce, *Cur,* Glenhyrst Art Gallery of Brant, Brantford ON

Kandianis, Patricia, *Ed,* Lehigh University Art Galleries, Museum Operation, Bethlehem PA

Kandiuk, Patricia, *Subject Librn,* York University, Fine Arts Phase II Slide Library, Toronto ON

Kane, Allen, *Dir,* National Postal Museum, Smithsonian Institution, Washington DC

Kane, Julie, *Technical Svcs,* Sweet Briar College, Mary Helen Cochran Library, Sweet Briar VA

Kane, Katherine, *Exec Dir,* Harriet Beecher Stowe, Library, Hartford CT

Kane, Katherine, *Dir,* Harriet Beecher Stowe, Hartford CT

Kane, Marie Louise, *Assoc Dir,* Salisbury House Foundation, Salisbury House and Garden, Des Moines IA

Kane, Patricia, *Cur American Decorative Arts,* Yale University, Yale University Art Gallery, New Haven CT

Kane, Susan, *Assoc Prof,* Oberlin College, Dept of Art, Oberlin OH (S)

Kane, Virginia Rose, *Outreach Mgr & Dir Educ,* Delaplaine Visual Arts Education Center, Frederick MD

Kaneshiro, Alexis, *Mktg & Outreach Coordr,* Pasadena Museum of California Art, Pasadena CA

Kang, Sung Yung, *Coordr Graphic Design,* Iowa State University, Dept of Art & Design, Ames IA (S)

Kanganis, Charles, *Assoc Prof Film,* Watkins College of Art, Design & Film, Nashville TN (S)

Kanigan-Fairen, Joan, *Exec Dir,* Brant Historical Society, Library, Brantford ON

Kanjo, Kathryn, *Chief Cur,* Museum of Contemporary Art, San Diego, La Jolla CA

Kanjo, Kathryn, *Chief Cur,* Museum of Contemporary Art San Diego, San Diego CA

Kann, Andrea, *Assoc Prof,* Coe College, Dept of Art, Cedar Rapids IA (S)

Kanschat, Melody, *Pres,* Los Angeles County Museum of Art, Los Angeles CA

Kanter, Janis, *Chmn,* Hyde Park Art Center, Chicago IL

Kanter, Joshua S, *Chmn Bd,* International Sculpture Center, Hamilton NJ

Kanter, Laurence B, *Cur In Charge Robert Lehman Coll,* The Metropolitan Museum of Art, New York NY

Kanter, Lawrence, *Cur European Art,* Yale University, Yale University Art Gallery, New Haven CT

Kantgias, Amy, *Exhib,* Birmingham Bloomfield Art Center, Art Center, Birmingham MI

Kanwischer, Charlie, *Dir Grad Studies,* Bowling Green State University, School of Art, Bowling Green OH (S)

Kapalka, Kim, *Educ & Tours,* C M Russell, Frederic G Renner Memorial Library, Great Falls MT

Kapitan, Lynn, *Chmn,* Mount Mary College, Art & Design Division, Milwaukee WI (S)

Kaplan, Flora, *Dir,* Dahesh Museum of Art, Greenwich CT

Kaplan, Ilee, *Assoc Dir,* California State University, Long Beach, University Art Museum, Long Beach CA

Kaplan, Julius, *Instr,* California State University, San Bernardino, Dept of Art, San Bernardino CA (S)

Kaplan, Susan A, *Dir,* Bowdoin College, Peary-MacMillan Arctic Museum, Brunswick ME

Kapler, Joseph, *Cur Art Coll,* Wisconsin Historical Society, Wisconsin Historical Museum, Madison WI

Kaplin, Judith, *Recording Secy,* South County Art Association, Kingston RI

Kaplowitz, Kenneth, *Assoc Prof,* The College of New Jersey, School of Arts & Sciences, Ewing NJ (S)

Kapnik, Deanne, *Spec Events,* Mizel Museum, Denver CO

Kapp, David, *Bd Chmn,* National Academy Museum & School, New York NY

Kapplinger, Kent, *Lectr,* North Dakota State University, Division of Fine Arts, Fargo ND (S)

Karabin, Alexa, *Head Printmaking,* Kalamazoo Institute of Arts, KIA School, Kalamazoo MI (S)

Karagheusian-Murphy, Marsha, *Prof,* Xavier University, Dept of Art, Cincinnati OH (S)

Karakalos, Ariane, *Asst Cur,* Museum of Ventura County, Ventura CA

Karalias, Ioannis, *VPres,* Chicago Athenaeum, Museum of Architecture & Design, Galena IL

Karberg, Richard, *Assoc Prof,* Cuyahoga Community College, Dept of Art, Cleveland OH (S)

Kardon, Carol, *Instr,* Main Line Art Center, Haverford PA (S)

Kardos, Ann, *Librn/Archivist,* Historic New England, Library and Archives, Boston MA

Karges, Sylvia, *Cur Asst,* American Numismatic Society, New York NY

Karibo, Lou, *Cur,* Kentucky New State Capitol, Division of Historic Properties, Frankfort KY

Karimi-Hakak, Mahmood, *Prof Theatre,* Siena College, Dept of Creative Arts, Loudonville NY (S)

Karlotski, William, *Instr,* Luzerne County Community College, Commercial Art Dept, Nanticoke PA (S)

Karlstrom, Ann Heath, *Publications,* Fine Arts Museums of San Francisco, M H de Young Museum, San Francisco CA

Karlstrom, Ann Heath, *Publications,* Fine Arts Museums of San Francisco, Legion of Honor, San Francisco CA

Karnes, Andrea, *Cur,* Modern Art Museum, Fort Worth TX

Karns, Lynn, *Art Instr,* Grand Canyon University, Art Dept, Phoenix AZ (S)

Karp, Diane R, *Dir,* Santa Fe Arts Institute, Santa Fe NM (S)

Karp, Jonathan, *Exec Dir,* American Jewish Historical Society, The Center for Jewish History, New York NY

Karp, Marilynn, *Faculty Dir,* New York University, Washington Square East Galleries, New York NY

Karp, Susan C Katz, *Adminr,* International Center of Medieval Art, New York NY

Karpen, John E, *Prof,* Rochester Institute of Technology, School of Photographic Arts & Sciences, Rochester NY (S)

Karras, Deana, *Dir Retail Operations,* The Baltimore Museum of Art, Baltimore MD

Karson, Richard, *Chief Design & Installations,* San Jose Museum of Art, Library, San Jose CA

Karstadt, Bruce, *Dir,* American Swedish Institute, Minneapolis MN

Karsten, Sharon, *Exec Dir,* Comox Valley Art Gallery, Courtenay BC

Karszewski, Jim, *VPres Buildings & Grounds,* DuPage Art League School & Gallery, Wheaton IL

Kart, Susan, *Asst Prof,* Lehigh University, Dept of Art, Architecture & Design, Bethlehem PA (S)

Kart, Susan, *Faculty,* Sarah Lawrence College, Dept of Art History, Bronxville NY (S)

Kasfir, Sidney L, *Prof,* Emory University, Art History Dept, Atlanta GA (S)

Kashatus, William C, *Dir Pub Prog,* Chester County Historical Society, West Chester PA

Kasl, Ronda, *Senior Cur Painting & Sculpture Before 1800,* Indianapolis Museum of Art, Indianapolis IN

Kaspar, Thomas L, *Preservation Architect,* Nebraska State Capitol, Lincoln NE

Kasper, Jamie, *State Advisor,* Pennsylvania Department of Education, Arts in Education Program, Harrisburg PA

Kasper, Michael, *Reference & Fine Arts Librn,* Amherst College, Robert Frost Library, Amherst MA

Kass, Emily, *Dir,* University of North Carolina at Chapel Hill, Ackland Art Museum, Chapel Hill NC

Kass, Ray, *Prof,* Virginia Polytechnic Institute & State University, Dept of Art & Art History, Blacksburg VA (S)

Kastell, Christina, *Cur Hist & Anthropology,* Putnam Museum of History and Natural Science, Davenport IA

Kastner, Carolyn, *Assoc Cur,* Georgia O'Keeffe Museum, Santa Fe NM

Kasumi, Naomi, *Assoc Prof,* Seattle University, Dept of Fine Arts, Visual Art Division, Seattle WA (S)

Kaszubski, Lynda, *Exec Asst,* Center for Exploratory & Perceptual Art, CEPA Gallery, Buffalo NY

Katagi, John, *Dir Admin,* Japanese American National Museum, Los Angeles CA

Katani, Kim, *Deputy Dir & Dir Educ,* Solomon R Guggenheim, New York NY

Katchadourian, Nina, *Cur Viewing Prog,* The Drawing Center, New York NY

Katchen, Cornelia, *Vis Servs & Mus Shop Mgr,* Asheville Art Museum, Asheville NC

Katchen, Michael, *Sr Archivist,* Franklin Furnace Archive, Inc, Brooklyn NY

Kates, Michael, *Dir,* African American Museum of Iowa, Cedar Rapids IA

Kather, Jan, *Asst,* Elmira College, Art Dept, Elmira NY (S)

Kato, Bruce, *Chief Cur,* Alaska State Museum, Juneau AK

Katsiaficas, Mary Diane, *Prof,* University of Minnesota, Minneapolis, Dept of Art, Minneapolis MN (S)

Katsolis, Christina, *Educ Dept,* Daytona State College, Southeast Museum of Photography, Daytona Beach FL

Katsourides, Andrew, *Prof,* Central Missouri State University, Dept Art & Design, Warrensburg MO (S)

Kattenbach, Ryan, *Deputy Dir & Asst Cur,* Saginaw Art Museum, Saginaw MI

Katz, Barbara P, *VPres,* Maryland Historical Society, Library, Baltimore MD

Katz, Cima, *Prof,* University of Kansas, The School of the Arts, Dept of Visual Art, Lawrence KS (S)

Katz, Janice, *Asst Cur Japanese Art,* The Art Institute of Chicago, Department of Asian Art, Chicago IL

Katz, Jill, *Dir Mktg & Communs,* University of Pennsylvania, Institute of Contemporary Art, Philadelphia PA

Katz, Jonathan, *CEO,* National Assembly of State Arts Agencies, Washington DC

Katz, Lynda, *Instr,* Southeastern Louisiana University, Dept of Visual Arts, Hammond LA (S)

Katz, Paula, *Gallery Dir,* Indiana University-Purdue University, Indianapolis, Herron School of Art & Design, Indianapolis IN (S)

Katz, Paula, *Gallery Dir & Cur,* Indiana University - Purdue University at Indianapolis, Herron Galleries, Indianapolis IN

Katz, Robert, *Prof,* University of Maine at Augusta, College of Arts & Humanities, Augusta ME (S)

Katz-Harris, Felicia, *Cur Asian & Mid East,* Museum of New Mexico, Museum of International Folk Art, Santa Fe NM

Kauffman, Elizabeth, *Dir of Galleries,* Salisbury University, Salisbury University Art Galleries, Salisbury MD

Kauffman, Ingrid, *Head Art Prog,* Arlington County Department of Public Libraries, Fine Arts Section, Arlington VA

Kaufman, Claudia, *VPres,* Marblehead Arts Association, Inc, Marblehead MA

Kaufman, Glen, *Prof Fabric Design,* University of Georgia, Franklin College of Arts & Sciences, Lamar Dodd School of Art, Athens GA (S)

Kaufman, Jolene, *Bus Mgr,* Oregon Trail Museum Association, Scotts Bluff National Monument, Gering NE

Kaufman, Linda, *Pres,* Evanston Art Center, Evanston IL

Kaufmann, Cynthia, *Chief Horticulture,* National Gallery of Art, Washington DC

Kaufmann, Faith, *Arts & Music Librn,* Forbes Library, Northampton MA

Kaufmann, Gina, *Pub Info Liaison,* University of Kansas, Spencer Museum of Art, Lawrence KS

Kaufmann, Thomas, *Prof,* Princeton University, Dept of Art & Archaeology, Princeton NJ (S)

Kaur, Amrita, *Library Asst,* University of Maryland, College Park, Art Library, College Park MD

Kaur, Ina, *Prof,* University of Tampa, College of Arts & Letters, Tampa FL (S)

Kauten, Heather, *Adjunct Asst Prof Art History,* Johnson County Community College, Fine Arts Dept & Art History Dept, Overland Park KS (S)

Kavanagh, Robert, *Prin,* New Brunswick College of Craft & Design, Library, Fredericton NB

Kaven, Dennis, *Dept Head,* Grand View College, Art Dept, Des Moines IA (S)

Kawaiaea, Sachiyo, *Librn,* Honolulu Museum of Art, Honolulu HI

Kawaiaea, Sachiyo, *Librn,* Honolulu Museum of Art, Robert Allerton Art Library, Honolulu HI

Kawamoto, Wayne, *Design Asst,* University of Hawaii at Manoa, Art Gallery, Honolulu HI

Kay, Ceyrona, *Dir,* Maharishi University of Management, Department of Art, Fairfield IA

Kay, David, *Dir Devel,* Inquilinos Boricuas en Accion, Boston MA

Kay, Donald, *Prof Art/Applied Multimedia,* Southern Oregon University, Art & Art History Dept, Ashland OR (S)

Kay, Jaeson, *Assoc Dir,* American Museum of Cartoon Art, Inc, Sunland CA

Kay, Jeremy, *Dir & Cur,* American Museum of Cartoon Art, Inc, Sunland CA

Kay, Liz, *Treas,* American Museum of Cartoon Art, Inc, Sunland CA

Kay, Mary, *Assoc Prof,* Bethany College, Mingenback Art Center, Lindsborg KS

Kay, Mary, *Prof,* Bethany College, Art Dept, Lindsborg KS (S)

Kay, Pamela, *Bus Office,* Blanden Memorial Art Museum, Fort Dodge IA

Kays, Elena, *Asst Prof Interior Design,* Centenary College, Humanities Dept, Hackettstown NJ (S)

Kayser, Robert, *Assoc Prof,* Rochester Institute of Technology, School of Photographic Arts & Sciences, Rochester NY (S)

Kazan, Katie, *Dir Pub Information,* Madison Museum of Contemporary Art, Madison WI

Keane, MaryAnn, *Mus Shop Mgr,* Orlando Museum of Art, Orlando FL

Keane, MaryAnn, *Mus Shop Mgr,* Orlando Museum of Art, Orlando Sentinel Library, Orlando FL

Keane, Patricia, *Dir Fin,* Katonah Museum of Art, Katonah NY

Kear, Andrew, *Cur Historical Art,* The Winnipeg Art Gallery, Winnipeg MB

Kearnan, Kathleen, *Assoc Dir,* Center for Exploratory & Perceptual Art, CEPA Library, Buffalo NY

Kearney, Judy, *Reference Archivist,* Bernice Pauahi Bishop, Library, Honolulu HI

Kearney, Kathleen, *Bus Mgr,* University of Arizona, Museum of Art & Archive of Visual Arts, Tucson AZ

Kearns, Heather, *Gallery Assoc,* Topeka & Shawnee County Public Library, Alice C Sabatini Gallery, Topeka KS

Kearns, Kate, *Colls Management Imaging Proj Coordr,* Smith College, Museum of Art, Northampton MA

Kearns, Martha, *Instr,* Moravian College, Dept of Art, Bethlehem PA (S)

Kearse, Mary Boyd, *VPres Bd Dir,* Associates for Community Development, The Arts Center, Inc, Martinsburg WV

Keating, Jeffrey, *VPres,* El Museo Latino, Omaha NE

Keckeisen, Robert, *Dir Mus,* Kansas State Historical Society, Kansas Museum of History, Topeka KS

Kee, Cynthia, *Instr,* University of Louisiana at Monroe, Dept of Art, Monroe LA (S)

Keebler, Catherine, *VPres,* The Society of Layerists in Multi-Media (SLMM), Albuquerque NM

Keech, John, *Prof,* Arkansas State University, Dept of Art, State University AR (S)

Keefe, John W, *Cur Decorative Arts,* New Orleans Museum of Art, New Orleans LA

Keegan, Daniel T, *Exec Dir,* San Jose Museum of Art, Library, San Jose CA

Keegan, Daniel T, *Exec Dir,* Milwaukee Art Museum, Milwaukee WI

Keegan, Larry, *Prof,* Rensselaer Polytechnic Institute, Eye Ear Studio Dept of Art, Troy NY (S)

Keegan, Trish, *Registrar & Coll Coordr,* Kamloops Art Gallery, Kamloops BC

Keeler, Emily, *Artistic Dir,* San Francisco Arts Education Project, San Francisco CA

Keeler, William, *Librn,* Rochester Historical Society, Rochester NY

Keeling, Bob, *Instr,* Southwestern Community College, Advertising & Graphic Design, Sylva NC (S)

Keeling, Bruce, *Chmn,* South Plains College, Fine Arts Dept, Levelland TX (S)

Keenan, James P, *Dir,* American Society of Bookplate Collectors & Designers, Tucson AZ

Keenan, Jon, *Prof,* Colby-Sawyer College, Dept of Fine & Performing Arts, New London NH (S)

Keenan, Joseph, *Dir,* Free Public Library of Elizabeth, Fine Arts Dept, Elizabeth NJ

Keenan, Patrick, *Dir,* Willard House & Clock Museum, Inc, North Grafton MA

Keeney, Bill, *Chmn Graphic Design,* Woodbury University, Dept of Graphic Design, Burbank CA (S)

Keenlyside, David, *Exec Dir,* Prince Edward Island Museum & Heritage Foundation, Charlottetown PE

Kennedy, Kari, *Mus Educator,* Seneca-Iroquois National Museum, Salamanca NY

Kennedy, Kimberly, *Cur,* Historical Society of Rockland County, New City NY

Kennedy, Mary, *Cur,* Iowa Great Lakes Maritime Museum, Arnolds Park IA

Kennedy, Patricia, *Prof,* Ocean County College, Humanities Dept, Toms River NJ (S)

Kennedy, Philip, *Exhibs Designer,* Illinois State Museum, ISM Lockport Gallery, Chicago Gallery & Southern Illinois Art Gallery, Springfield IL

Kennedy, Robyn, *Chief,* American Art Museum, Renwick Gallery, Washington DC

Kennedy, Robyn, *Chief Renwick Gallery,* American Art Museum, Smithsonian Institution, Washington DC

Kennedy, Ronald, *Prof,* Southeastern Louisiana University, Dept of Visual Arts, Hammond LA (S)

Kennedy, Sharon, *Coll Cur,* University of Nebraska, Lincoln, Sheldon Memorial Art Gallery & Sculpture Garden, Lincoln NE

Kennedy III, John, *VPres & Bd of Trustees,* Telfair Museums' Jepson Center for the Arts Library, Telfair Academy of Arts & Sciences Library, Savannah GA

Kennedy Zeller, Susan, *Assoc Cur, Native American Art,* Brooklyn Museum, Brooklyn NY

Kennerk, Emily, *Asst Prof,* University of Nevada, Las Vegas, Dept of Art, Las Vegas NV (S)

Kenney, Christopher, *Cur Educ,* Historical Society of Rockland County, New City NY

Kenney, Denise, *Asst Prof (Performance Theatre),* University of British Columbia Okanagan, Dept of Creative Studies, Kelowna BC (S)

Kenney, Eliza, *Assoc Prof,* Loyola University of Chicago, Fine Arts Dept, Chicago IL (S)

Kenny, Mary, *Asst Prof,* Sierra Nevada College, Fine Arts Dept, Incline Village NV (S)

Kent, Dale, *Pres,* Museum of Wisconsin Art, West Bend WI

Kent, Jo Anne, *Coll Mgr,* Koshare Indian Museum, Inc, La Junta CO

Kent, Liz, *Exec Asst,* African American Museum in Philadelphia, Philadelphia PA

Kent, Liz, *Serials Librn,* Sweet Briar College, Mary Helen Cochran Library, Sweet Briar VA

Kent, Richard K, *Prof,* Franklin & Marshall College, Art & Art History Dept, Lancaster PA (S)

Kenworthy, Steve, *Dir,* Rhinelander District Library, Rhinelander WI

Kenyon, Matthew, *Asst Prof Art (New Media),* Pennsylvania State University, University Park, Penn State School of Visual Arts, University Park PA (S)

Kenyon, Paula, *Interim Exec Dir,* Museum of Art & History, Santa Cruz, Santa Cruz CA

Keogh, Michael, *Instr,* Casper College, Dept of Visual Arts, Casper WY (S)

Keough, Jane, *Dir Corporate Mem Svcs,* Fitchburg Art Museum, Fitchburg MA

Keough, Tracey, *Dir,* City of Providence Parks Department, Roger Williams Park Museum of Natural History, Providence RI

Keown, Gary, *Asst Prof,* Southeastern Louisiana University, Dept of Visual Arts, Hammond LA (S)

Kephart, Any, *Adjunct Assoc Prof Fine Art,* Johnson County Community College, Fine Arts Dept & Art History Dept, Overland Park KS (S)

Kephart, Betsy, *Exec Dir,* Historic Paris - Bourbon County, Inc, Hopewell Museum, Paris KY

Kerber, Gwen, *Instr,* Bucks County Community College, Fine Arts Dept, Newtown PA (S)

Keris, Holly, *Cur,* Cummer Museum of Art & Gardens, Museum & Library, Jacksonville FL

Kermond, Adrienne, *Tour Coordr,* Dartmouth College, Hood Museum of Art, Hanover NH

Kern, Amy, *Graphic Design,* Art Institute of Pittsburgh, Pittsburgh PA (S)

Kern, Karen, *Grants Mgr,* Arts Council Of New Orleans, New Orleans LA

Kern, Steve, *Exec Dir,* Everson Museum of Art, Syracuse NY

Kern Paster, Gail, *Dir,* Folger Shakespeare, Washington DC

Kerns, Ed, *Prof Art,* Lafayette College, Dept of Art, Easton PA (S)

Keropian, Michael, *Chair Sculpture,* Hudson Valley Art Association, Brooklyn NY

Kerr, Beth, *Theatre & Dance Librn,* University of Texas at Austin, Fine Arts Library, Austin TX

Kerr, Don, *Adjunct Prof,* Aquinas College, Art Dept, Grand Rapids MI (S)

Kerr, James, *Pres,* Morris-Jumel Mansion, Inc, New York NY

Kerr, Joellen, *Dir,* University of Charleston, Carleton Varney Dept of Art & Design, Charleston WV (S)

Kerr, Larry, *Pres,* Cuyahoga Valley Art Center, Cuyahoga Falls OH (S)

Kerr, Norwood, *Archival Librn,* Alabama Department of Archives & History, Library, Montgomery AL

Kerr, Pat, *Instr,* Wayne Art Center, Wayne PA (S)

Kerr, Sunny, *Student & Educ Coordr,* University of Toronto, University of Toronto Art Centre, Toronto ON

Kersavage, Lisa, *Sr Dir Preservation & Sustainability,* Municipal Art Society of New York, New York NY

Kersey, Barbara, *Pres,* Crary Art Gallery Inc, Grary Art Gallery, Warren PA

Kersey, Lynda, *Park Ranger II,* Bluemont Historical Railroad Junction, Arlington VA

Kersh, Joanne, *Asst Dir Research Servs,* Association of Independent Colleges of Art & Design, Providence RI

Kershaw, Mary, *Dir,* Museum of New Mexico, New Mexico Museum of Art, Unit of NM Dept of Cultural Affairs, Santa Fe NM

Kershaw, Mary, *Dir,* Museum of New Mexico, New Mexico Museum of Art, Santa Fe NM

Kerven, Don, *Facilities Mgr,* Museum of Western Colorado, Museum of the West, Grand Junction CO

Kesling, Ashley, *Outreach Coordr,* Passaic County Community College, Broadway, LRC, and Hamilton Club Galleries, Paterson NJ

Kessel, Suzan, *Dir,* Fairfield Art Association, Fairfield IA

Kessler, Jamie Paul, *Instr,* Lamar University, Art Dept, Beaumont TX (S)

Kessmann, Dean, *Assoc Prof,* George Washington University, Dept of Art of Fine Arts & Art History, Washington DC (S)

Kestenbaum, Joy, *Art & Architecture Librn,* Pratt Institute, Art & Architecture Dept, Brooklyn NY

Kestenbaum, Joy, *Dir,* Parsons School of Design, Adam & Sophie Gimbel Design Library, New York NY

Kestenbaum, Stuart J, *Dir,* Haystack Mountain School of Crafts, Deer Isle ME

Kestenbaum, Stuart J, *Dir,* Haystack Mountain School of Crafts, Center for Community Programs Gallery, Deer Isle ME

Kestenbaum, Stuart J, *Dir,* Haystack Mountain School of Crafts, Deer Isle ME (S)

Kester, Marilyn, *Pres,* Cambridge Museum, Cambridge NE

Kester, Susanne, *Media Resources Coordr,* Hebrew Union College, Skirball Cultural Center, Los Angeles CA

Kesterson-Bullen, Sharon, *Prof,* College of Mount Saint Joseph, Art Dept, Cincinnati OH (S)

Kestner, R Steven, *Chmn of Brd,* The Cleveland Museum of Art, Cleveland OH

Ketcham, Maria, *Dept Head,* Detroit Institute of Arts, Research Library & Archives, Detroit MI

Ketchum, Cavaliere, *Emer Prof,* University of Wisconsin, Madison, Dept of Art, Madison WI (S)

Kets de Vries, Henriette, *Cunningham Center Mgr,* Smith College, Museum of Art, Northampton MA

Ketter, Cathy, *Opers Mgr,* Allied Arts Council of St Joseph, Saint Joseph MO

Kettering, Alison, *Chmn,* Carleton College, Dept of Art & Art History, Northfield MN (S)

Kettler, Kim, *Pres,* Truro Center for the Arts at Castle Hill, Inc, Truro MA (S)

Keville, Jim, *Chmn & Assoc Prof,* California State University, Dominguez Hills, Art & Design Dept, Carson CA (S)

Kewl-Durfey, Grace, *Community Develop Arts Educ,* Broward County Board of Commissioners, Cultural Div, Fort Lauderdale FL

Key, Bonnie, *Office Mgr,* Embroiderers Guild of America, Dorothy Babcock Memorial Library, Louisville KY

Key, Lisa, *Dir Foundation & Corporate Rels,* The Art Institute of Chicago, Chicago IL

Keyes, David, *Prof,* Pacific Lutheran University, Dept of Art, Tacoma WA (S)

Keyes, George, *Cur European Painting,* Detroit Institute of Arts, Detroit MI

Keyes, Ute, *Gen Mgr,* Museum of Biblical Art, New York NY

Keyes, William, *Dir Historic Sites,* Minnesota Historical Society, Saint Paul MN

Keys, Den, *Mus Shop Mgr,* Pickens County Museum of Art & History, Pickens SC

Keyser, William, *Prof,* Rochester Institute of Technology, School of Design, Rochester NY (S)

Khachatoorian, Haig, *Head Design & Technology Dept,* North Carolina State University at Raleigh, School of Design, Raleigh NC (S)

Khaki, Shlrin, *Libr Asst,* New York University, Stephen Chan Library of Fine Arts, New York NY

Khalidi, Omar, *Librn Aga Khan Prog,* Massachusetts Institute of Technology, Rotch Library of Architecture & Planning, Cambridge MA

Khalsa, Sant, *Instr,* California State University, San Bernardino, Dept of Art, San Bernardino CA (S)

Khan, Baseera, *Gallery Mgr,* BRIC - Brooklyn Information & Culture, Rotunda Gallery, Brooklyn NY

Khan, Beverly, *Acting Dean,* Fairfield University, Visual & Performing Arts, Fairfield CT (S)

Khan, Sabir, *Assoc Dean,* Georgia Institute of Technology, College of Architecture, Atlanta GA (S)

Khanam, Ferdousi, *Sec,* United States Department of the Interior, Indian Arts & Crafts Board, Washington DC

Khang, Eik, *Chief Cur,* Santa Barbara Museum of Art, Library, Santa Barbara CA

Khewhok, Carol, *Cur Art Ctr,* Honolulu Academy of Arts, The Art Center at Linekona, Honolulu HI (S)

Khewhok, Sanit, *Cur,* Hawaii Pacific University, Gallery, Kaneohe HI

Kiaer, Christina, *Assoc Prof,* Northwestern University, Evanston, Dept of Art History, Evanston IL (S)

Kibler, Brian, *Dir Operations,* Urbanglass, Robert Lehman Gallery, Brooklyn NY

Kibler, Robert, *Prof of Art,* Glendale Community College, Visual & Performing Arts Div, Glendale CA (S)

Kidd, J Benton, *Cur Ancient Art,* University of Missouri, Museum of Art & Archaeology, Columbia MO

Kidd, Mark, *Communs Dir,* Appalshop Inc, Appalshop, Whitesburg KY

Kidd, Sandra K, *Dir Mus Advan,* High Museum of Art, Atlanta GA

Kiddie, David, *Chmn,* Chapman University, Art Dept, Orange CA (S)

Kidwell, Michael, *Asst Prof,* Kansas City Art Institute, Kansas City MO (S)

Kiefer, Brenda, *Cur Exhib,* Kentucky Derby Museum, Louisville KY

Kiehl, David, *Cur Prints,* Whitney Museum of American Art, New York NY

Kiel, Dennis, *Chief Cur,* The Light Factory Contemporary Museum of Photography and Film, Charlotte NC

Kiel, Martha, *Prof,* Hardin-Simmons University, Art Dept, Abilene TX (S)

Kiely, Declan, *Robert H Taylor Cur & Dept Head,* The Morgan Library & Museum, Museum, New York NY

Kiely, Mary, *Dir Fin & Opers,* Danforth Museum of Art, Danforth Museum of Art, Framingham MA

Kiely, Paula, *Library Dir,* Milwaukee Public Library, Art, Music & Recreation Dept, Milwaukee WI

Kiendl, Anthony, *Dir,* Plug In, Institute of Contemporary Art, Winnipeg MB

Kienzle, Karen, *Dir,* Palo Alto Art Center, Palo Alto CA

Kiernan, Brian, *Mus Technician,* Mount Holyoke College, Art Museum, South Hadley MA

Kiesel, Izumi, *Bookkeeper,* Museum of Ventura County, Ventura CA

Kiger, Robert W, *Dir,* Carnegie Mellon University, Hunt Institute for Botanical Documentation, Pittsburgh PA

Kihata, Hideki, *Chmn Dept, Prof,* Saginaw Valley State University, Dept of Art & Design, University Center MI (S)

Kikuchi, Hiroko, *Educ/Outreach Coordr,* Massachusetts Institute of Technology, List Visual Arts Center, Cambridge MA

Kiland, Lance, *Instr,* North Hennepin Community College, Art Dept, Brooklyn Park MN (S)

Kilbane, Nora, *Asst,* Ohio State University, Visual Resources Library, Columbus OH

Kilburn, Jan, *Vice Pres,* Pemaquid Group of Artists, Pemaquid Art Gallery, Pemaquid Point ME

Kilcup, Anne, *Bd Pres,* Bellevue Arts Museum, Bellevue WA

Kile, Karen M, *Exec Dir,* San Luis Obispo Museum of Art, San Luis Obispo CA

Kilgallen, Caitlin, *Assoc Dir Library,* Visual Arts Library, New York NY

Kilgore, Ron, *Studio Mgr,* Creative Growth Art Center, Oakland CA

Kilgore, Sydney, *Media Coord, Images,* University of Texas at Austin, Fine Arts Library, Austin TX

Kilgour-Walsh, Laurie, *Educator,* Art Gallery of Hamilton, Hamilton ON

Kilian, Peter, *Prof & Coordr,* Northern State University, Art Dept, Aberdeen SD (S)

Killhour, Caroline, *Exec Dir,* Hui No'eau Visual Arts Center, Gallery and Gift Shop, Makawao Maui HI

Killion, Robert, *Coll Mgr,* Peoria Historical Society, Peoria IL

Killough, Ellen, *Exec Dir,* Visual Arts Center of Northwest Florida, Panama City FL

Kim, Christine Y, *Assoc Cur,* The Studio Museum in Harlem, New York NY

Kim, Heemong, *Prof,* Rhode Island College, Art Dept, Providence RI (S)

Kim, Kyu Hugh, *Chief Librn,* Queensborough Community College Library, Kurt R Schmeller Library, Flushing NY

Kim, Nanhee, *Asst Prof,* University of North Alabama, Dept of Art, Florence AL (S)

Kim, Sei Young, *Progs Dir,* Lower East Side Printshop Inc, New York NY (S)

Kim, Soo, *Prog Dir Photog,* Otis College of Art & Design, Fine Arts, Los Angeles CA (S)

Kimball, Cathy, *Dir,* San Jose Institute of Contemporary Art, San Jose CA

Kimball, Justin, *Vis Asst Prof,* Amherst College, Dept of Art & the History of Art, Amherst MA (S)

Kimball, Kathryn, *Upper Room Cur,* General Board of Discipleship, The United Methodist Church, The Upper Room Chapel & Museum, Nashville TN

Kimball, Richard, *Cur Mathematics,* Northern Maine Museum of Science, Presque Isle ME

Kimball, Tevis, *Cur,* Jones Library, Inc, Amherst MA

Kimes, Diane, *Dir Develop,* Historical Society of Martin County, Elliott Museum, Stuart FL

Kimes, Don, *Chmn Dept & Prof,* American University, Dept of Art, New York NY (S)

Kimes, Don, *Dir Art School,* Chautauqua Institution, School of Art, Chautauqua NY (S)

Kim Han, Hyonjeong, *Cur Korean Art,* Asian Art Museum of San Francisco, Chong-Moon Lee Ctr for Asian Art and Culture, San Francisco CA

Kincaid, Amy, *Pres Bd Dir,* Pyramid Atlantic, Silver Spring MD

Kincaid, Carol, *VPres Finance,* DuPage Art League School & Gallery, Wheaton IL

Kincaid, Merna, *Treas,* Big Horn County Historical Museum, Hardin MT

Kincannon, Romald, *Pres,* No Man's Land Historical Society, No Man's Land Museum, Goodwell OK

Kindall, Elizabeth, *Prof,* University of Saint Thomas, Dept of Art History, Saint Paul MN (S)

Kinder, Ben, *Preparator,* Confederation Centre Art Gallery and Museum, Charlottetown PE

Kindred, Ann, *Assoc Dir,* R L S Silverado Museum, Saint Helena CA

Kindstedt, Susan S, *Archival Project,* Portsmouth Athenaeum, Joseph Copley Research Library, Portsmouth NH

Kindt, Diane, *Mus Shop Mgr,* Klein Museum, Mobridge SD

King, Alan, *Mgr,* Ohio Historical Society, National Road-Zane Grey Museum, Columbus OH

King, Angie, *Outreach Educ Coordr,* Lauren Rogers, Laurel MS

King, Anthony, *Deputy Dir,* Sterling & Francine Clark, Williamstown MA

King, Bob, *Pres,* Thornton W Burgess, Museum, Sandwich MA

King, Codie, *CEO & Dir,* Wailoa Arts & Cultural Center, Hilo HI

King, Cornelia S, *Chief of Ref,* Library Company of Philadelphia, Philadelphia PA

King, Diana, *Librn for Film, TV & Theater,* University of California, Los Angeles, Arts Library, Los Angeles CA

King, Duane, *Exec Dir,* University of Tulsa, Gilcrease Museum, Tulsa OK

King, Gwen G, *Dir Emeritus,* Archaeological Society of Ohio, Indian Museum of Lake County, Ohio, Willoughby OH

King, Heather, *Mus Store Assoc,* Oklahoma City Museum of Art, Oklahoma City OK

King, Jack, *Prof,* University of Tampa, College of Arts & Letters, Tampa FL (S)

King, Jacqueline P. *Community Rels Mgr,* High Museum of Art, Atlanta GA

King, Jeanne, *Prof,* Cazenovia College, Center for Art & Design Studies, Cazenovia NY (S)

King, John J, *Chmn,* Chatham Historical Society, The Atwood House Museum, Chatham MA

King, Johnny, *Exhib Mgr,* Contemporary Arts Center, New Orleans LA

King, Juliet, *Asst Prof, Dir Art Therapy,* Indiana University-Purdue University, Indianapolis, Herron School of Art & Design, Indianapolis IN (S)

King, Karen, *Cur Historic Houses,* Charleston Museum, Charleston SC

King, Kathleen, *Assoc Prof,* Kansas State University, Art Dept, Manhattan KS (S)

King, Landa, *Asst Prof,* Texas Lutheran University, Dept of Visual Arts, Seguin TX (S)

King, Linda, *Instr,* Long Beach City College, Art & Photography Dept, Long Beach CA (S)

King, Lindsay, *Pub Svcs Librn,* Northwestern University, Art Collection, University Library, Evanston IL

King, Lyndel, *Dir,* University of Minnesota, Frederick R Weisman Art Museum, Minneapolis MN

King, Margery, *Cur,* The American Federation of Arts, New York NY

King, Maureen, *Secy,* Cypress College, Fine Arts Gallery, Cypress CA

King, Morgana, *Pub Art Mgr,* Arts Council Of New Orleans, New Orleans LA

King, Pam, *Bd Dir,* Artists' Cooperative Gallery, Omaha NE

King, Sam, *Gallery Dir,* University of Arkansas, Fine Arts Center Gallery, Fayetteville AR

King, Sharon, *Prof,* Sam Houston State University, Art Dept, Huntsville TX (S)

King, Valeria, *Music,* Southern University in New Orleans, Fine Arts & Philosophy Dept, New Orleans LA (S)

King, Wade, *Dept Head,* North Dakota State College of Science, Dept of Graphic Arts, Wahpeton ND (S)

King-Nero, Sally, *Cur Drawings & Photography,* Andy Warhol Foundation for the Visual Arts, New York NY

Kinghorn, George, *Dir,* University of Maine, Museum of Art, Bangor ME

Kingsley, Evan, *Deputy Dir External Affairs,* International Center of Photography, Museum, New York NY

Kingsley, Orson, *Librn,* Henry Sheldon Museum of Vermont History and Research Center, Middlebury VT

Kingston, Donna, *Office Mgr,* Osborne Homestead Museum, Derby CT

Kingston, John, *Prof Ceramics,* Simon's Rock College of Bard, Visual Arts Dept, Great Barrington MA (S)

Kingston, Kitty, *Prof & Chmn,* University of Wisconsin College - Marinette, Art Dept, Marinette WI (S)

Kingston, Robert, *Instr,* Pierce College, Art Dept, Woodland Hills CA (S)

Kinkead, John, *Dir,* Kinkead Contemporary, Los Angeles CA

Kinkley, Melissa, *Mgr Family & New Media Interpretation,* University of Chicago, Smart Museum of Art, Chicago IL

Kinne, Carol, *Asst Prof,* Colgate University, Dept of Art & Art History, Hamilton NY (S)

Kinnear, Guy, *Assoc Prof,* Azusa Pacific University, College of Liberal Arts, Art Dept, Azusa CA (S)

Kinney, Karen, *Mus Store Mgr,* Craigdarroch Castle Historical Museum Society, Victoria BC

Kinney, Susan, *Museum Mgr,* Center for Puppetry Arts, Library, Atlanta GA

Kinsey, Amy, *Cur Landscape,* George Eastman, Rochester NY

Kinsey, Amy, *Cur Landscape,* George Eastman, Museum, Rochester NY

Kinsky, Katie, *Library Asst,* University of Rochester, Art/Music Library, Rochester NY

Kinslea, Michael, *Treas,* Portsmouth Athenaeum, Joseph Copley Research Library, Portsmouth NH

Kinsolving, Lucie, *Chief Conservator,* National Academy Museum & School, New York NY

Kinsolving, Lucie, *Chief Conservator,* National Academy Museum & School, Archives, New York NY

Kintzer, Jane, *Interim Dir Educ,* Allentown Art Museum, Allentown PA

Kinzel, Laura, *Pub Progs Coordr,* Mendel Art Gallery & Civic Conservatory, Saskatoon SK

Kira, Keiko, *Adjunct Prof Fine Art,* Johnson County Community College, Fine Arts Dept & Art History Dept, Overland Park KS (S)

Kirby, Catherine, *Asst Prof,* Nazareth College of Rochester, Art Dept, Rochester NY (S)

Kirby, Jenni, *Contact,* Crossroads Art Center Gallery, Richmond VA

Kirby, Julia, *Asst Dir,* Victoria Mansion - Morse Libby House, Portland ME

Kirby, Michael, *Pres,* This Century Art Gallery, Williamsburg VA

Kirch, Lisa, *Asst Prof,* University of North Alabama, Dept of Art, Florence AL (S)

Kircher, Ashley, *Cur Coll & Exhibs,* Sitka Historical Society, Sitka Historical Museum, Sitka AK

Kirchhefer, Dan R, *Prof,* Emporia State University, Dept of Art, Emporia KS (S)

Kirchman, Kim, *Asst Prof,* Saint Petersburg College, Fine & Applied Arts at Clearwater Campus, Clearwater FL (S)

Kirin, Asen, *Asst Prof Art History,* University of Georgia, Franklin College of Arts & Sciences, Lamar Dodd School of Art, Athens GA (S)

Kirjakovic, Dusica, *Exec Dir,* Lower East Side Printshop Inc, New York NY (S)

Kirk, Judith, *Asst Dir,* Indiana University, The Mathers Museum of World Cultures, Bloomington IN

Kirk, Paula, *Accnt,* Embroiderers Guild of America, Margaret Parshall Gallery, Louisville KY

Kirkeby, Gary, *Chmn,* Prince George's Community College, Art Dept, Largo MD (S)

Kirking, Clayton, *Chief, Art Info Resources,* The New York Public Library, Humanities Department, New York NY

Kirking, Clayton C, *Chief Art Information Resources,* The New York Public Library, Art & Architecture Collection, New York NY

Kirkland, Jacqlyn, *Mus Relations Officer,* History Museum of Mobile, Mobile AL

Kirkland, Jane, *Serials Librn,* The Cleveland Museum of Art, Ingalls Library, Cleveland OH

Kirkland, Scotty, *Cur History,* History Museum of Mobile, Mobile AL

Kirkland, Stefanie, *Dir Exhibs,* Craft Alliance, Saint Louis MO

Kirklin, Deborah, *Chmn,* Santa Rosa Junior College, Art Dept, Santa Rosa CA (S)

Kirkpatrick, Diane, *Interim Chmn,* University of Michigan, Ann Arbor, Dept of History of Art, Ann Arbor MI (S)

Kirkpatrick, Garland, *Asst Prof,* Loyola Marymount University, Dept of Art & Art History, Los Angeles CA (S)

Kirkwood, Heather, *Art Librn,* Purchase College, Library, Purchase NY

Kirkwood, Jane, *Gallery Dir,* East End Arts & Humanities Council, Riverhead NY

Kirsch, Edith, *Assoc Prof,* Colorado College, Dept of Art, Colorado Springs CO (S)

Kirsch, Eva, *Dir Mus,* California State University, San Bernardino, Dept of Art, San Bernardino CA (S)

Kirsch, Eva, *Dir Gallery,* California State University, San Bernardino, San Bernardino CA

Kirschbaum, Robert, *Prof Fine Arts,* Trinity College, Dept of Studio Arts, Hartford CT (S)

Kirschtel-Taylor, Debbye, *Coll Cur, Registrar,* Florida International University, The Patricia & Phillip Frost Art Museum, Miami FL

Kirshenbaum, Esther, *Gallery Coordr,* Michigan Guild of Artists & Artisans, Michigan Guild Gallery, Ann Arbor MI

Kirshner, Andy, *Asst Prof,* University of Michigan, Ann Arbor, School of Art & Design, Ann Arbor MI (S)

Kirstel, Harvey, *Affiliate Assoc Prof,* University of Maryland, Baltimore County, Imaging & Digital Arts (IMDA), Dept of Visual Arts, Baltimore MD (S)

Kirton, Doug, *Asst Prof,* University of Waterloo, Fine Arts Dept, Waterloo ON (S)

Kirwin, Liza, *Cur Manuscripts,* Archives of American Art, Smithsonian Institution, Washington DC

Kiser, Joy M, *Librn,* National Endowment for the Arts, Library, Washington DC

Kisielewska, Lara, *Sec,* Graphic Artists Guild, New York NY

Kisiow, Karen, *Registrar,* The Winnipeg Art Gallery, Winnipeg MB

Kisor, Doug, *Chmn Graphic Design,* College for Creative Studies, Detroit MI (S)

Kissick, John D, *Dir,* University of Guelph, School of Fine Art & Music (SOFAM), Guelph ON (S)

Kistler, Ashley, *Dir,* Virginia Commonwealth University, Anderson Gallery, Richmond VA

Kitagawa, Anne Rose, *Chief Cur,* University of Oregon, Jordan Schnitzer Museum of Art, Eugene OR

Kitchen, Larry, *Instr,* Kilgore College, Visual Arts Dept, Kilgore TX (S)

Kitchin, Cameron, *Dir,* Memphis Brooks Museum of Art, Memphis TN

Kite, Cheryl, *Dir Develop,* Tryon Palace Historic Sites & Gardens, New Bern NC

Kittelson, Karen, *Asst Prof,* Southern Methodist University, Division of Art, Dallas TX (S)

Kitteredge, Frank, *Asst Cur Mathematics,* Northern Maine Museum of Science, Presque Isle ME

Kittinger, Susan, *Colls Mgr,* Rosemount Museum, Inc, Pueblo CO

Kittlaus, Jennifer, *Library Asst,* Mount Vernon Ladies' Association of the Union, Library, Mount Vernon VA

Kittleson, Michelle, *Commun Coordr,* Historical and Cultural Society of Clay County, Hjemkomst Center, Moorhead MN

Kjaer, Lise, *Lectr,* City College of New York, Art Dept, New York NY (S)

Kjaer, Merete, *Asst Dir,* University of California-San Diego, University Art Gallery, La Jolla CA

Kjellman-Chapin, Monica, *Asst,* Emporia State University, Dept of Art, Emporia KS (S)

Kjorlien, Melanie, *VPres Access Colls & Exhibs,* Glenbow Museum, Calgary AB

Klabe, Kim, *Educ Dir,* Rehoboth Art League, Inc, Rehoboth Beach DE (S)

Klaff, Len, *Pres,* Ojai Art Center, Ojai CA

Klages, Ricki, *Head Dept,* University of Wyoming, Dept of Art, Laramie WY (S)

Klahn, Jennifer, *Dir Devel,* Archaeological Institute of America, Boston MA

Klapperich, Leah, *Instr,* Marian University, Art Dept, Fond Du Lac WI (S)

Klapthor, Frances, *Assoc Cur Art of Africa, Asia, the Americas & Pacific Islands,* The Baltimore Museum of Art, Baltimore MD

Klaptocz, Veronika, *Coordr,* Simon Fraser University, Simon Fraser University Gallery, Burnaby BC

Klaric, Arlette, *Cur Exhibs,* Mid America Arts Alliance & Exhibits USA, Kansas City MO

Klatt, Lori, *Admin Coordr,* Nicolaysen Art Museum & Discovery Center, Children's Discovery Center, Casper WY

Klaus, Marianne, *Archives,* Maui Historical Society, Bailey House, Wailuku HI

Klawans, Alan J, *2nd VPres,* Plastic Club, Art Club, Philadelphia PA

Klawans, Alan J, *Bd Mem,* American Color Print Society, Huntingdon Valley PA

Klee, Susan, *Pres (V),* Berkeley Art Center, Berkeley CA

Kleeblatt, Norman, *Chief Cur,* The Jewish Museum, New York NY

Klein, Aimee, *Admin Asst,* Longview Museum of Fine Art, Longview TX

Klein, Carol, *Assoc Cur,* University of Tulsa, Gilcrease Museum, Tulsa OK

Klein, Emanuel, *Pres,* Brown County Art Gallery Foundation, Nashville IN

Klein, Holger A, *Dept Chair,* Columbia University, Dept of Art History & Archaeology, New York NY

Klein, Joy, *Prog Coordr,* Arizona State University, Memorial Union Gallery, Tempe AZ

Klein, Mary Anne, *Correspondence Secy,* The National Art League, Douglaston NY

Klein, Michelle, *Asst Cur & Registrar,* Guild Hall of East Hampton, Inc, Guild Hall Museum, East Hampton NY

Klein, Nancy, *Cur Villa Philmont,* Philmont Scout Ranch, Philmont Museum - Seton Memorial Library, Cimarron NM

Klein, Richard, *Exhib Dir,* Aldrich Museum of Contemporary Art, Ridgefield CT

Klein, Richard, *Gallery Guard,* University of Wisconsin, Union Art Gallery, Milwaukee WI

Klein, Robert, *Owner,* Robert Klein Gallery, Boston MA

Klein, Ron, *Prof Sculpture/ 3D,* Saint Joseph's University, Art Dept, Philadelphia PA (S)

Klein, Terry M, *Pres,* Fairfield Art Association, Fairfield IA

Kleinberg, Joanna, *Asst Cur,* The Drawing Center, New York NY

Kleinfelder, Arthur, *Dept Head,* Suffolk County Community College, Art Dept, Selden NY (S)

Klem, Alan, *Assoc Chair Performing Arts,* Creighton University, Fine & Performing Arts Dept, Omaha NE (S)

Klema, Stephen A, *Graphic Design Coordr,* Tunxis Community Technical College, Graphic Design Dept, Farmington CT (S)

Klemchuk, Ray, *Preparator,* University of Chicago, Smart Museum of Art, Chicago IL

Klepacz, Kristina, *Archivist,* Dayton Art Institute, Library, Dayton OH

Kleppin, Jeri, *Secy,* Snake River Heritage Center, Weiser ID

Kleppinger, Kathleen, *Chmn,* Reading Public Museum, Reading PA

Kletchka, Dana Carlisle, *Cur Educ,* The Pennsylvania State University, Palmer Museum of Art, University Park PA

Kleviter, Lora, *Vis Lectr Art,* North Central College, Dept of Art, Naperville IL (S)

Klick, Samantha, *Asst to Dir,* Phoenix Art Museum, Phoenix AZ

Kligensmith, Ann, *Chmn Fine Arts Div,* Iowa Wesleyan College, Art Dept, Mount Pleasant IA (S)

Kligman, Mikhail, *Adjunct Prof,* Missouri Western State University, Art Dept, Saint Joseph MO (S)

Kligman, Misha, *Adjunct Asst Prof Fine Art,* Johnson County Community College, Fine Arts Dept & Art History Dept, Overland Park KS (S)

Klihdt, Steve, *Dev,* Tampa Museum of Art, Tampa FL

Klimaszewski, Cathy, *Assoc Dir Progs & Cur Educ,* Cornell University, Herbert F Johnson Museum of Art, Ithaca NY

Klimiades, Mario Nick, *Library Archives Dir,* Heard Museum, Billie Jane Baguley Library and Archives, Phoenix AZ

Klimiades, Mario Nick, *Librn & Archivist,* Heard Museum, Phoenix AZ

Kline, Carole, *Bd Dir Secy,* Plains Art Museum, Fargo ND

Kline, Phil, *Exec Dir,* The Mint Museum, Charlotte NC

Klingman, Berry J, *Prof,* Baylor University - College of Arts and Sciences, Dept of Art, Waco TX (S)

Klink, Peter J, *Pres,* Heritage Center, Inc, Pine Ridge SD

Klinker, Scott, *Head 3-D Design Dept,* Cranbrook Academy of Art, Bloomfield Hills MI (S)

Klinkon, Heinz, *Asst Prof,* Rochester Institute of Technology, School of Design, Rochester NY (S)

Klinkow, Meg, *Cur,* University of Chicago, Max Epstein Archive, Chicago IL

Klobe, Tom, *Dir Gallery,* University of Hawaii at Manoa, Dept of Art, Honolulu HI (S)

Klochko, Deborah, *Exec Dir,* Museum of Photographic Arts, Edmund L. and Nancy K Dubois Library, San Diego CA

Klocke, Dave, *Historian,* Cincinnati Art Club, Cincinnati OH

Klocke, Richard, *Exhib Designer,* University of Kansas, Spencer Museum of Art, Lawrence KS

Kloner, Jay, *Assoc Prof,* University of Louisville, Allen R Hite Art Institute, Louisville KY (S)

Klontz, Lauren, *Educ Dir,* McDowell House & Apothecary Shop, Danville KY

Klooz, Donan, *Cur Exhibs,* Mobile Museum of Art, Library, Mobile AL

Klooz, Donan, *Cur Exhibs,* Mobile Museum of Art, Mobile AL

Klopfer, Dennis, *Assoc Prof,* Mount Mary College, Art & Design Division, Milwaukee WI (S)

Klopfer, Mary, *Assoc Prof,* University of Saint Francis, School of Creative Arts, Fort Wayne IN (S)

Klos, Jennifer, *Assoc Cur & Dept Coordr,* Oklahoma City Museum of Art, Oklahoma City OK

Klos, Sheila, *Dir Libr,* Harvard University, Dumbarton Oaks Research Library, Washington DC

Klosky, Peter, *Dir Exhibits,* Roberson Museum & Science Center, Binghamton NY

Kluba, William, *Assoc Prof,* Tunxis Community Technical College, Graphic Design Dept, Farmington CT (S)

Klueg, James, *Prof,* University of Minnesota, Duluth, Art Dept, Duluth MN (S)

Klundt, Michelle, *Interim Exec Dir,* Paris Gibson Square, Museum of Art, Great Falls MT

Kluttz, Ann, *Lectr,* University of North Carolina at Charlotte, Dept Art, Charlotte NC (S)

Kmelnitsky, Dmitry, *Asst Prof,* Loyola Marymount University, Dept of Art & Art History, Los Angeles CA (S)

Kmet, Kathryn, *Artist,* Walker's Point Artists Assoc Inc, Gallery 218, Milwaukee WI

Kmetz, Janice, *Assoc Prof,* University of Minnesota, Duluth, Art Dept, Duluth MN (S)

Knaack, Beth, *Dir Visitor Svcs,* Putnam Museum of History and Natural Science, Davenport IA

Knapp, Cindy, *Dir Opers,* Regional Arts & Culture Council, Metropolitan Center for Public Arts, Portland OR

Knapp, Dana M, *Dir Progs,* Mid America Arts Alliance & Exhibits USA, Kansas City MO

Knapp, Jacquelyn, *Chmn, Assoc Prof Art,* University of Science & Arts of Oklahoma, Arts Dept, Chickasha OK (S)

Knapp, M Jason, *Chmn,* Anderson University, Art Dept, Anderson IN (S)

Knapp, Martha, *Mus Spec,* Saint-Gaudens National Historic Site, Library, Cornish NH

Knapp, Melinda, *Chief Registrar & Exhib Mgr,* Columbus Museum of Art, Columbus OH

Knapp, Tim, *Asst Dir,* Cleveland State University, Art Gallery, Cleveland OH

Knappe, Brett, *Chair & Asst Prof Art History,* Baker University, Dept of Mass Media & Visual Arts, Baldwin City KS (S)

Knapple, Barb, *Sec,* Dawson County Historical Society, Museum, Lexington NE

Knavel, Jenny, *Prof,* Western Illinois University, Department of Art, Macomb IL (S)

Knebelsberger, Caroline, *Asst Dir,* Roswell Museum & Art Center, Library, Roswell NM

Knecht, John, *Chmn,* Colgate University, Dept of Art & Art History, Hamilton NY (S)

Knecht, Michael S, *Dir,* Laurel Arts, Somerset PA

Knecht, Samuel, *Dir,* Hillsdale College, Art Dept, Hillsdale MI (S)

Knechtel, Nancy, *Prof,* Niagara County Community College, Fine Arts Division, Sanborn NY (S)

Knepper, Alice, *Adjunct Prof,* Missouri Southern State University, Dept of Art, Joplin MO (S)

Knibb, Nicole, *Information Officer,* McMaster University, McMaster Museum of Art, Hamilton ON

Knicely, Carol, *Asst Prof,* University of British Columbia, Dept of Art History, Visual Art & Theory, Vancouver BC (S)

Knickmeyer, Hank, *Prof,* Fontbonne University, Fine Art Dept, Saint Louis MO (S)

Knight, Anne, *Pres,* Sturdivant Museum Association, Sturdivant Museum, Selma AL

Knight, Charles R, *Cur,* MacArthur Memorial, Norfolk VA

Knight, Clarence, *Chmn,* Bowie State University, Fine & Performing Arts Dept, Bowie MD (S)

Knight, Cynthia, *Dir,* Woodbridge Township Cultural Arts Commission, Barron Arts Center, Woodbridge NJ

Knight, David, *Dir Exhib & Colls,* Northern Kentucky University, Galleries, Highland Heights KY

Knight, Dean, *Librn,* Tryon Palace Historic Sites & Gardens, Library, New Bern NC

Knight, Dean, *Registrar,* Tryon Palace Historic Sites & Gardens, New Bern NC

Knight, James, *Chief Cur Natural History,* South Carolina State Museum, Columbia SC

Knight, Lynn, *Dir of Events Coordr,* Earlham College, Leeds Gallery, Richmond IN

Knight, Mary Ann, *Music & Arts Specialist,* Berkshire Athenaeum, Reference Dept, Pittsfield MA

Knight, Michael, *Cur Chinese Art,* Asian Art Museum of San Francisco, Chong-Moon Lee Ctr for Asian Art and Culture, San Francisco CA

Knight, Nancy, *Dir,* Belz Museum of Asian & Judaic Art, Memphis TN

Knight, Robert E, *Exec Dir,* Tucson Museum of Art and Historic Block, Tucson AZ

Knight, Wanda, *Assoc Prof Art Educ,* Pennsylvania State University, University Park, Penn State School of Visual Arts, University Park PA (S)

Knight-Gillum, Shari, *Sales & Rental Coordr,* Gibbes Museum of Art, Charleston SC (S)

Knipp, Tammy, *Assoc Prof Art, Graphic Design,* Florida Atlantic University, D F Schmidt College of Arts & Letters Dept of Visual Arts & Art History, Boca Raton FL (S)

Knittel, K D, *Asst Prof,* Seton Hall University, College of Arts & Sciences, South Orange NJ (S)

Knoblauch, Ann-Marie, *Prof,* Virginia Polytechnic Institute & State University, Dept of Art & Art History, Blacksburg VA (S)

Knobloch-Nelson, Leona, *Prog Dir Interior Design,* Mount Mary College, Marian Gallery, Milwaukee WI

Knode, Marilu, *Dir,* Laumeier Sculpture Park, Saint Louis MO

Knode, Marilu, *Sr Cur,* University of Wisconsin, Institute of Visual Arts, (INOVA), Milwaukee WI

Knoedler, J, *Educ Dir,* The Barnum Museum, Bridgeport CT

Knoles, Thomas G, *Marcus A McCorison Librn,* American Antiquarian Society, Worcester MA

Knoll, Ann, *Assoc Dir,* University of Notre Dame, Snite Museum of Art, Notre Dame IN

Knopf, David, *CFO,* The Speed Art Museum, Louisville KY

Knopke, Liz, *Mem Coordr,* Museum of Wisconsin Art, West Bend WI

Knopp, Michael, *Cur Chemistry,* Northern Maine Museum of Science, Presque Isle ME

Knopp, Stephanie, *Chmn Graphic Arts & Design,* Temple University, Tyler School of Art, Philadelphia PA (S)

Knothe, Florian, *Cur European Glass,* Corning Museum of Glass, Museum, Corning NY

Knowles, Amanda, *Printmaking & Drawing,* North Seattle Community College, Art Dept, Seattle WA (S)

Knowles, Brigitte, *Sr Assoc Dean,* Temple University, Tyler School of Art, Philadelphia PA (S)

Knowles, Craig, *Caretaker Bldgs & Grounds,* National Museum of American Illustration, Newport RI

Knowles, Elizabeth, *Exec Dir,* Wildling Art Museum, Solvang CA

Knowles, Elizabeth, *Secy,* Sculptors Guild, Inc, Brooklyn NY

Knowles, Thomas G, *Cur Manuscripts,* American Antiquarian Society, Worcester MA

Knowlton, Kenn, *Instr,* Art Academy of Cincinnati, Cincinnati OH (S)

Knowlton, Paul, *Tech,* Keene State College, Thorne-Sagendorph Art Gallery, Keene NH

Knox, Alexandra, *Asst Prof,* East Central University, School of Fine Arts, Ada OK (S)

Knox, Gordon, *Dir,* Arizona State University, ASU Art Museum, Tempe AZ

Knox, John, *Dir Opers,* North Carolina Museum of Art, Raleigh NC

Knox, Tyra, *Exec Secy,* Springfield Art Museum, Springfield MO

Knudsen, Dean, *Historian,* Oregon Trail Museum Association, Scotts Bluff National Monument, Gering NE

Knudson, Brittany, *Communications Coordr,* Museums Association of Saskatchewan, Regina SK

Knudson, Ellen, *Assoc Prof,* University of Florida, School of Art & Art History, Gainesville FL (S)

Knutas, Per, *Chief Conservator,* The Cleveland Museum of Art, Cleveland OH

Knutsen, Jim, *Dir,* Black Hills State University, Ruddell Gallery, Spearfish SD

Knutson, Audrey, *Pres,* LeSueur County Historical Society, Chapter One, Elysian MN

Knutson, James, *Prof,* Black Hills State University, Art Dept, Spearfish SD (S)

Knutson, Karen, *Faculty,* Grand Marais Art Colony, Grand Marais MN (S)

Knutson, Michael, *Prof Art,* Reed College, Dept of Art, Portland OR (S)

Koach, Jennifer, *Educ,* Liberty Hall Historic Site, Liberty Hall Museum, Frankfort KY

Kobik, Steven, *Pres,* The Huntington Library, Art Collections & Botanical Gardens, Library, San Marino CA

Koblas, Alyson, *Mem & Mktg Dir,* Chicago Artists' Coalition, Coalition Gallery, Chicago IL

Koblik, Steven S, *Pres,* The Huntington Library, Art Collections & Botanical Gardens, San Marino CA

Kobrynich, Bill, *Dir Interior Design,* Art Institute of Fort Lauderdale, Fort Lauderdale FL (S)

Koch, Arthur, *Assoc Prof,* Southern Methodist University, Division of Art, Dallas TX (S)

Koch, Brittany, *Mem Coordr,* Athenaeum of Philadelphia, Philadelphia PA

Koch, Cynthia, *Dir,* National Archives & Records Administration, Franklin D Roosevelt Museum, Hyde Park NY

Koch, Cynthia M, *Dir,* National Archives & Records Administration, Franklin D Roosevelt Library, Hyde Park NY

Koch, Doug, *Adjunct Asst Prof Photog,* Johnson County Community College, Fine Arts Dept & Art History Dept, Overland Park KS (S)

Koch, Richard, *Performing Arts Mgr & Technical Dir,* The Cultural Arts Center at Glen Allen, Glen Allen VA

Kochan, Roman V, *Dean Lib & Acad Tech,* California State University, Long Beach, University Library, Long Beach CA

Kocs, Constance, *Instr,* Pierce College, Art Dept, Woodland Hills CA (S)

Koda, Harold, *Cur In Charge Cost,* The Metropolitan Museum of Art, New York NY

Koefoed, Lori, *Instr,* Pierce College, Art Dept, Woodland Hills CA (S)

Koehler, Catherin, *Secy,* Kappa Pi International Honorary Art Fraternity, Cleveland MS

Koehler, Keri, *Colls Mgr,* San Francisco Maritime National Historical Park, Maritime Library, San Francisco CA

Koehler, Ron, *Chmn,* Delta State University, Dept of Art, Cleveland MS (S)

Koehler, Ron, *Pres,* Kappa Pi International Honorary Art Fraternity, Cleveland MS

Koehler, Ronald G, *Chmn Dept,* Delta State University, Fielding L Wright Art Center, Cleveland MS

Koen, Michael, *Pres,* Kemp Center for the Arts, Wichita Falls TX

Koenig, Richard, *Prof,* Kalamazoo College, Art Dept, Kalamazoo MI (S)

Koenig, Wendy, *Assoc Prof Art,* North Central College, Dept of Art, Naperville IL (S)

Koeninger, Kay, *Asst Prof,* Sinclair Community College, Division of Fine & Performing Arts, Dayton OH (S)

Koerbler, Sasha, *VPres,* Malaspina College, Nanaimo Art Gallery, Nanaimo BC

Koester, Chris, *Dir Human Resources,* Royal Ontario Museum, Toronto ON

Koeth, David M, *Chair, Prof Art,* Bakersfield College, Art Dept, Bakersfield CA (S)

Koetting, Delores, *Treas,* Ste Genevieve Museum, Sainte Genevieve MO

Koga, Kim, *Exec Dir,* Museum of Neon Art, Los Angeles CA

Kogn, Lee, *Cur Spec Projects,* American Folk Art Museum, Shirley K. Schlafer Library, New York NY

Koh, Cindy, *Preparator,* George R Gardiner, Toronto ON

Koh, Helen, *Exec Dir,* Museum of Chinese in America, New York NY

Kohl, Allan, *Slide Librn,* Minneapolis College of Art & Design, Library, Minneapolis MN

Kohl, Jeanette, *Assoc Prof,* University of California, Riverside, Dept of the History of Art, Riverside CA (S)

Kohl, Kurt C, *Treas,* The Art Cafe, Davison MI

Kohl, Laura, *Admin,* Museum of New Mexico, New Mexico Museum of Art, Unit of NM Dept of Cultural Affairs, Santa Fe NM

Kohler, Ruth, *Dir,* Kohler Co, John Michael Kohler Arts Center - Arts/Industry Program, Sheboygan WI

Kohrman, Louise, *Mem & Gifts Asst,* Smith College, Museum of Art, Northampton MA

Kohut, Khrystia, *2nd VP,* Ukrainian Canadian Archives & Museum of Alberta, Edmonton AB

Kois, Dennis, *Mus Dir,* DeCordova Museum & Sculpture Park, DeCordova Museum, Lincoln MA

Kois, Dennis, *Mus Dir,* DeCordova Museum & Sculpture Park, Sculpture Park, Lincoln MA

Koivisto, Chris, *Instr,* Vermilion Community College, Art Dept, Ely MN (S)

Koizumi, Anne, *Production Technician (YA! Project),* Quickdraw Animation Society, Calgary AB

Kokoris, Eva J, *Pres,* Society of Scribes, Ltd, New York NY

Kolar, Mary, *Gallery Operations Mgr,* Madison Museum of Contemporary Art, Madison WI

Kolasinski, Jacek, *Asst Prof,* Florida International University, School of Art & Art History, Miami FL (S)

Kolasinski, Sheryl, *Deputy Dir & COO,* Menil Foundation, Inc, The Menil Collection, Houston TX

Kolb, Britta, *Mktg Commus Coordr,* University of California, Berkeley, The Magnes Collection of Jewish Art & Life, Berkeley CA

Kolb, Jennifer, *Cur Native American,* Wisconsin Historical Society, Wisconsin Historical Museum, Madison WI

Kolber, Georgina, *Cur,* Mizel Museum, Denver CO

Kolbo, John, *Instr,* Morningside College, Art Dept, Sioux City IA (S)

Kolbo, Scott, *Assoc Prof,* Whitworth College, Art Dept, Spokane WA (S)

Kolczynski, Charlotte, *Sr Music Reference Librn,* Boston Public Library, Arts Reference Department, Boston MA

Koles, Jeanne, *Publs Coordr,* Tufts University, Tufts University Art Gallery, Medford MA

Koletsky, Susan, *Dir Mus,* The Temple-Tifereth Israel, The Temple Museum of Religious Art, Beachwood OH

Kolla, Stephanie, *Cur Asst,* Banff Centre, Walter Phillips Gallery, Banff AB

Kollmeyer, Mary, *1st VPres,* San Angelo Art Club, Helen King Kendall Memorial Art Gallery, San Angelo TX

Kolmer, Brandy, *Dir Develop,* Mystic Art Association, Inc, Mystic Arts Center, Mystic CT

Kolowski, Janet, *Security & Visitor Svcs Clerk,* Alaska State Museum, Juneau AK

Kolster, Michael, *Asst Prof,* Bowdoin College, Art Dept, Brunswick ME (S)

Kolsters, Stephanie, *Cur,* Mississippi Valley Conservation Authority, R Tait McKenzie Memorial Museum, Almonte ON

Kolt, Ingrid, *Cur Prog,* Surrey Art Gallery, Library, Surrey BC

Kolt, Ingrid, *Cur Progs,* Surrey Art Gallery, Surrey BC

Komanski, Debbie, *Exec Dir,* Albin Polasek Museum & Sculpture Gardens, Winter Park FL

Komatsuka, Carol, *VPres External,* Japanese American National Museum, Los Angeles CA

Kominos, Nicolette, *Sunday Coordr,* Cultural Affairs Department City of Los Angeles/Barnsdall Art Centers/Junior Arts Center, Los Angeles CA

Komodore, Bill, *Prof,* Southern Methodist University, Division of Art, Dallas TX (S)

Kondoleon, Christine, *George D & Margo Behrakis Sr Cur Greek & Roman Art,* Museum of Fine Arts, Boston MA

Kong, Praseth, *Circ Mgr,* Indiana University - Purdue University at Indianapolis, Herron School of Art Library, Indianapolis IN

Konrad, Michael, *Information Svc Asst,* New York University, Institute of Fine Arts Visual Resources Collection, New York NY

Kontar, Diane, *Asst Prof,* University of Findlay, Art Program, Findlay OH (S)

Konya, Seiko, *Corresp Secy,* Northwest Watercolor Society, Woodinville WA

Koob, Pam, *Cur,* Art Students League of New York, New York NY

Kook-Anderson, Grace, *Cur Contemporary Art,* Laguna Art Museum, Laguna Beach CA

Koonce, Lou Mecia, *Asst Gallery Mgr,* African American Atelier, Greensboro NC

Koons McCullough, Hollis, *Cur Fine Arts & Exhibits,* Telfair Museums' Jepson Center for the Arts Library, Telfair Academy of Arts & Sciences Library, Savannah GA

Koop, Kathy, *Dir,* Westminster College, Art Gallery, New Wilmington PA

Koop, Ken, *Dir Retail Svcs,* Vesterheim Norwegian-American Museum, Decorah IA

Koop, Rebecca, *Instr,* William Jewell College, Art Dept, Liberty MO (S)

Koos, Greg, *Exec Dir,* McLean County Historical Society, McLean County Museum of History, Bloomington IL

Koostra, Barbara, *Dir,* University of Montana, Montana Museum of Art & Culture, Missoula MT

Kopatz, Kim, *Visual Resources Cur,* University of Rochester, Art/Music Library, Rochester NY

Kopczak, Chuck, *Cur World Ecology,* California Science Center, Los Angeles CA

Kopczynski, Carol, *Admin & Colls Asst,* North Tonawanda History Museum, North Tonawanda NY

Kopelman, Arie, *VPres,* Nantucket Historical Association, Historic Nantucket, Nantucket MA

Koper, Rachel, *Prog Dir,* Women & Their Work, Austin TX

Koperski, Kate, *Dir,* Niagara University, Castellani Art Museum, Niagara NY

Kopet, Donna, *Tour Coordr,* Anniston Museum of Natural History, Anniston AL

Kopielski, Camille, *Treas,* Polish Museum of America, Research Library, Chicago IL

Koplin, Bruce M, *Chmn,* Virginia Commonwealth University, Art History Dept, Richmond VA (S)

Koppy, Ann, *Dir,* Coos County Historical Society Museum, North Bend OR

Kopren, Eileen, *Dir Pub Svcs,* Dickinson State University, Stoxen Library, Dickinson ND

Korchinski, Kevin, *Exec Dir,* Organization of Saskatchewan Arts Councils (OSAC), Regina SK

Kordich, Diane D, *Prof,* Northern Michigan University, Dept of Art & Design, Marquette MI (S)

Kordiuk, Ania, *Exec Dir Vis Rels,* Royal Ontario Museum, Toronto ON

Kordos, Richard S, *Exec Dir,* Academy of Fine Arts, Lynchburg VA

Koren, Cynthia, *Assoc Prof,* Munson-Williams-Proctor Arts Institute, Pratt MWP College of Art, Utica NY (S)

Korenblat, Ellen, *Communs Dir,* Historic Arkansas Museum, Library, Little Rock AR

Korenblat, Ellen, *Dir Communs,* Historic Arkansas Museum, Little Rock AR

Korenic, Lyn, *Dir,* University of Wisconsin-Madison, Kohler Art Library, Madison WI

Korff, David, *Coordr Galleries & Exhibits,* Saint Clair County Community College, Jack R Hennesey Art Galleries, Port Huron MI

Korff, David, *Dept Chmn,* Saint Clair County Community College, Jack R Hennesey Art Dept, Port Huron MI (S)

Korherr, Johannes, *Admin Mgr,* Austrian Cultural Forum Gallery, New York NY

Korman, Jaymie, *Site Supv,* Minnesota Historical Society, Minnesota State Capitol Historic Site, St Paul MN

Kornek, Jay, *Radio,* Henry Ford Community College, McKenzie Fine Art Ctr, Dearborn MI (S)

Kornfeld, Abby, *Asst Prof,* City College of New York, Art Dept, New York NY (S)

Kornfeld, Fran, *Pub Rels,* Holland Tunnel Art Projects, Brooklyn NY

Kornhauser, Stephen, *Conservator,* Wadsworth Atheneum Museum of Art, Hartford CT

Kornick, Brenda, *Registrar,* C M Russell, Frederic G Renner Memorial Library, Great Falls MT

Kornstein, Jeffrey, *Controller,* American Jewish Historical Society, The Center for Jewish History, New York NY

Koroscik, Judith, *Dean Col,* Ohio State University, College of the Arts, Columbus OH (S)

Koroscik, Judith, *Prof,* Ohio State University, Dept of Art Education, Columbus OH (S)

Korow, Elinore, *Instr,* Cuyahoga Valley Art Center, Cuyahoga Falls OH (S)

Korzon, John, *Chmn & Instr,* Southwestern Michigan College, Fine & Performing Arts Dept, Dowagiac MI (S)

Kosak, Jackie, *Coll Mgr,* Liberty Mutual, Safeco Insurance Co Art Collection, Boston MA

Koshar, Summerlea, *Admin Coordr,* Cartoon Art Museum, San Francisco CA

Kosharek, Daniel, *Photo Archives,* Museum of New Mexico, Palace of Governors, Santa Fe NM

Koshinsky, Deborah, *Adminr & Asc Librn,* Arizona State University, Architecture & Environmental Design Library, Tempe AZ

Koshinsky, Deborah, *Architecture Librn,* Arizona State University, ASU Library, Tempe AZ

Kosinski, Dorothy, *Sr Cur European Art,* Dallas Museum of Art, Dallas TX

Kosinski, Dorothy M, *Dir,* The Phillips Collection, Washington DC

Kositany-Buckner, Cheptoo, *Dep Exec Dir,* Kansas City Public Library, Kansas City MO

Koski, Elizabeth, *Exec Dir,* Ashtabula Arts Center, Ashtabula OH

Kosmere, Ellen, *Prof,* Worcester State College, Visual & Performing Arts Dept, Worcester MA (S)

Koss, Gene H, *Prof,* Tulane University, Sophie H Newcomb Memorial College, New Orleans LA (S)

Kossar, Carolyn, *Gallery Dir,* Hillsborough Community College, Fine Arts Dept, Tampa FL (S)

Kostelny, Elizabeth, *Exec Dir,* Preservation Virginia, Richmond VA

Kostelny, Elizabeth, *Exec Dir,* Preservation Virginia, John Marshall House, Richmond VA

Kosten, Andrew, *Contract Asst Prof Art,* University of Southern Indiana, Department of Art, Evansville IN (S)

Koster, Julia, *Mus Shop Mgr,* Naval War College Museum, Newport RI

Kostman, Lynne, *Managing Ed,* University of California, Los Angeles, Fowler Museum at UCLA, Los Angeles CA

Kosuge, Michihiro, *Dept Chmn, Prof,* Portland State University, Dept of Art, Portland OR (S)

Kot, Malgorzata, *Head Librn,* Polish Museum of America, Research Library, Chicago IL

Kot, Matgorzata, *Head Librn,* Polish Museum of America, Chicago IL

Koterbay, Scott, *Assoc Prof,* East Tennessee State University, College of Arts and Sciences, Dept of Art & Design, Johnson City TN (S)

Kotsch, Kristine, *Instr,* Moravian College, Dept of Art, Bethlehem PA (S)

Kotting, Joey, *Dir,* California State University, Bakersfield, Todd Madigan Gallery, Bakersfield CA

Kotz, Liz, *Assoc Prof,* University of California, Riverside, Dept of the History of Art, Riverside CA (S)

Kouba, Don, *Dept Chmn,* Prairie State College, Art Dept, Chicago Heights IL (S)

Koucky, Charles J, *Dir,* Koucky Gallery, Charlevoix MI

Koumijian, Jeanette, *Sec,* Catharine Lorillard Wolfe, New York NY

Kourasis, Betty, *Dean Student Affairs,* The Illinois Institute of Art - Chicago, Chicago IL (S)

Kourelis, Kostis, *Asst Prof,* Franklin & Marshall College, Art & Art History Dept, Lancaster PA (S)

Koutecky, Judy, *Admin Asst & Mgr Vol Resources,* Mendel Art Gallery & Civic Conservatory, Saskatoon SK

Kouvaris, Lindsey, *Cur Exhibits & Coll,* Santa Clara University, de Saisset Museum, Santa Clara CA

Kovacs, Rudy, *Chair,* Idaho State University, John B Davis Gallery of Fine Art, Pocatello ID

Kovacs, Rudy, *Chmn,* Idaho State University, Dept of Art & Pre-Architecture, Pocatello ID (S)

Koval, Anne, *Assoc Prof,* Mount Allison University, Dept of Fine Arts, Sackville NB (S)

Kovarik, Jennifer, *Registrar & Librn,* Vesterheim Norwegian-American Museum, Decorah IA

Koverman, Jill, *Cur Colls,* University of South Carolina, McKissick Museum, Columbia SC

Kowal, Calvin, *Instr,* Art Academy of Cincinnati, Cincinnati OH (S)

Kowal, Jill, *Educ Coordr,* Art Center Sarasota, Sarasota FL (S)

Kowalchek, Elizabeth, *Asst Prof,* University of Kansas, Dept of Art & Music Education & Music Therapy, Lawrence KS (S)

Kowalchuk, Anna, *Mus Admin,* Livingston County Historical Society, Museum, Geneseo NY

Kowalchuk, Elizabeth, *Assoc Prof & Assoc Dean,* University of Kansas, The School of the Arts, Dept of Visual Art, Lawrence KS (S)

Kowalczyk, Tracie, *Dir Event and Culinary Service,* Indianapolis Museum of Art, Indianapolis IN

Kowalick, Stephanie, *Coll Mgr, Registrar,* University of Southern California, USC Fisher Museum of Art, Los Angeles CA

Kowalski, Jesse, *Dir Exhibs,* The Andy Warhol Museum, Museum, Pittsburgh PA

Kowski, Robert, *Prof,* Greensboro College, Dept of Art, Division of Fine Arts, Greensboro NC (S)

Koyne, Paul, *Assoc Prof Music,* Siena College, Dept of Creative Arts, Loudonville NY (S)

Kozbial, Ardys, *Librn,* Payette Associates, Library, Boston MA

Kozel, Melinda Wriedt, *Prog Coordr,* Norfolk Arts Center, Norfolk NE

Kozionnyi, Alexander, *Dir Exhib Installation & Architect,* Chicago Athenaeum, Museum of Architecture & Design, Galena IL

Kozman, Kathryn Hubner, *Instr & Supvr,* Toronto Art Therapy Institute, Toronto ON (S)

Kozokoff, Neil, *Chmn,* Chicago Athenaeum, Museum of Architecture & Design, Galena IL

Kraball, Merrill, *Chmn,* Bethel College, Dept of Art, North Newton KS (S)

Kraczon, Kate, *Asst Cur,* University of Pennsylvania, Institute of Contemporary Art, Philadelphia PA

Kraeger, Markus, *Dir Visitor Svcs,* Historical and Cultural Society of Clay County, Hjemkomst Center, Moorhead MN

Kraemer, Amanda, *Educ Asst,* Bartow-Pell Mansion Museum & Gardens, Bronx NY

Kraemer, Pat, *Instr,* Rochester Community & Technical College, Art Dept, Rochester MN (S)

Kraft, Brian, *Head Reg,* Minneapolis Institute of Arts, Minneapolis MN

Kraft, Heather, *Mem Servs/Registrar,* Glass Art Society, Seattle WA

Kraft, Michelle, *Chmn & Instr,* Lubbock Christian University, Dept of Communication & Fine Art, Lubbock TX (S)

Kraft, Toni Lee, *Registrar,* Tyler Museum of Art, Reference Library, Tyler TX

Krainak, Paul, *Chair,* Bradley University, Dept of Art, Peoria IL (S)

Krainak, Paul, *Chmn Art Dept,* Bradley University, Heuser Art Center, Peoria IL

Kralickova, Petra, *Cur,* Ohio University, Kennedy Museum of Art, Athens OH

Kralisz, Victor, *Mgr Fine Art Div,* J Eric Johnson, Fine Arts Division, Dallas TX

Kramer, Cheryl, *Gallery Dir,* Ithaca College, Handwerker Gallery of Art, Ithaca NY

Kramer, Don, *Art Educ Adjunct,* Iowa Wesleyan College, Art Dept, Mount Pleasant IA (S)

Kramer, Edith, *Cur Film,* University of California, Berkeley, Pacific Film Archive, Berkeley CA

Kramer, Gerald, *Coordr Fine Art Prog,* Cuyahoga Community College, Dept of Art, Cleveland OH (S)

Kramer, Jane, *Prog Mgr,* Lansing Art Gallery, Lansing MI

Kramer, Kathryn, *Assoc Prof,* State University of New York, College at Cortland, Dept Art & Art History, Cortland NY (S)

Kramer, Leslie, *Asst Prof,* Elmira College, Art Dept, Elmira NY (S)

Kramer, Leslie, *Dir,* Elmira College, George Waters Gallery, Elmira NY

Kramer, Steve, *Head Dept South Campus,* Austin Community College, Dept of Commercial Art, North Ridge Campus, Austin TX (S)

Kramer, William, *Preparator,* Syracuse University, Art Collection, Syracuse NY

Kramer DeBalko, Brittany, *Interim Dir,* Wilkes University, Sordoni Art Gallery, Wilkes-Barre PA

Krammes, Barry, *Prof,* Biola University, Art Dept, La Mirada CA (S)

Kramp, Rachael, *Educ Prog Coordr,* McLean County Historical Society, McLean County Museum of History, Bloomington IL

Krane, Susan, *Exec Dir,* San Jose Museum of Art, San Jose CA

Krannig, Dora, *Instr Dance,* Glendale Community College, Visual & Performing Arts Div, Glendale CA (S)

Krantz, Kevin, *Dir,* Lafayette Science Museum & Planetarium, Lafayette LA

Krantzler, Robert, *Prof,* Miami-Dade Community College, Arts & Philosophy Dept, Miami FL (S)

Kraskin, Sandra, *Dir,* Baruch College of the City University of New York, Sidney Mishkin Gallery, New York NY

Kraus, Corrine, *Instr,* Milwaukee Area Technical College, School of Media & Creative Arts, Milwaukee WI (S)

Kraus, Heidi, *Dir,* Hope College, DePree Art Center & Gallery, Holland MI

Kraus, Heidi, *Gallery Dir,* Hope College, Dept of Art & Art History, Holland MI (S)

Kraus, Russell C, *Prof,* Rochester Institute of Technology, School of Photographic Arts & Sciences, Rochester NY (S)

Krause, Joann, *Instr,* Grand Marais Art Colony, Grand Marais MN (S)

Krause, Kim, *Instr,* Art Academy of Cincinnati, Cincinnati OH (S)

Krause, Marty, *Cur Prints, Drawings, & Photographs,* Indianapolis Museum of Art, Indianapolis IN

Krause, Rose, *Cur of Special,* Eastern Washington State Historical Society, Northwest Museum of Arts & Culture, Spokane WA

Kraushaar, Andy, *Cur Visual Materials,* Wisconsin Historical Society, Wisconsin Historical Museum, Madison WI

Krauss, James A, *Chmn & Prof,* Oakton Community College, Language Humanities & Art Divisions, Des Plaines IL (S)

Krauss, Jeff, *Dir Finance & Admin,* Montana State University, Museum of the Rockies, Bozeman MT

Krauss, Sharon, *Asst Dir,* Becker College, William F Ruska Library, Worcester MA

Krausz, Peter, *Instr,* Universite de Montreal, Dept of Art History, Montreal PQ (S)

Kravitz, M, *Prof,* George Mason University, College of Humanities & Social Sciences, Dept of Art & Art History, Fairfax VA (S)

Kravitz, Walter, *Dir,* George Mason University, College of Visual & Performing Arts, Fine Arts Gallery, Fairfax VA (S)

Kray, Hazele, *Cur,* The Bartlett Museum, Amesbury MA

Krazer, Kim A, *Registrar,* Newport Historical Society & Museum of Newport History, Newport RI

Krazmien, Mindy, *Exec Dir,* Putnam County Historical Society, Foundry School Museum, Cold Spring NY

Kreager, Tom, *Prof,* Hastings College, Art Dept, Hastings NE (S)

Kreger, Philip, *Dir Exhib,* Tennessee State Museum, Nashville TN

Krehbiel, Bryce, *Pres,* Maude Kerns Art Center, Eugene OR

Krehbiel, James, *Chmn,* Ohio Wesleyan University, Fine Arts Dept, Delaware OH (S)

Krehmeier, Bill, *Instr,* Hannibal La Grange College, Art Dept, Hannibal MO (S)

Kreidler, Nicole Bieak, *Asst Prof & Dept Chair Interior Design,* La Roche College, Division of Design, Pittsburgh PA (S)

Kreimer, Julian, *Asst Prof,* Purchase College, State University of New York, School of Art+Design, Purchase NY (S)

Kreiner, Mary Beth, *Librn,* Cranbrook Art Museum, Library, Bloomfield Hills MI

Kreischer, Patricia, *Graphic Artist,* Lake Forest Library, Fine Arts Dept, Lake Forest IL

Krejcarek, Philip, *Assoc Prof,* Carroll College, Art Dept, Waukesha WI (S)

Krejci, Mark, *Instr Set Design,* Creighton University, Fine & Performing Arts Dept, Omaha NE (S)

Kremer, Gary R, *Exec Dir,* State Historical Society of Missouri, Columbia MO

Kremer, Gary R, *Exec Dir,* State Historical Society of Missouri, Gallery and Library, Columbia MO

Kremers, Michele, *Instr,* Marylhurst University, Art Dept, Marylhurst OR (S)

Krempel, Sara, *Prof,* Central Oregon Community College, Dept of Art, Bend OR (S)

Kren, Thom, *Cur Manuscripts,* Getty Center, Trust Museum, Los Angeles CA

Kren, Thomas, *Interim Assoc Dir Colls,* Getty Center, The J Paul Getty Museum, Los Angeles CA

Krenisky, Paul, *Dir Facilities,* The Cleveland Museum of Art, Cleveland OH

Krenos, Elizabeth, *Instr,* Moravian College, Dept of Art, Bethlehem PA (S)

Krens, Thomas, *Dir,* Guggenheim Museum Soho, New York NY

Krensky, Beth, *Asst Prof,* University of Utah, Dept of Art & Art History, Salt Lake City UT (S)

Krepps, Jerald, *Assoc Prof,* University of Minnesota, Minneapolis, Dept of Art, Minneapolis MN (S)

Kreps, Dennis, *Librn,* Kalamazoo Institute of Arts, Kalamazoo MI

Kress, Katherine, *Mus Shop Mgr,* Northwood University, Jeannette Hare Art Gallery, West Palm Beach FL

Kret, Robert A, *Dir,* Georgia O'Keeffe Museum, Santa Fe NM

Kret, Robert A, *Dir,* Hunter Museum of American Art, Reference Library, Chattanooga TN

Kreutzer-Hodson, Teresa, *Cur & Coll,* Hastings Museum of Natural & Cultural History, Hastings NE

Krevens, Frank, *Asst Prof Art,* Brescia University, Art Dept, Owensboro KY (S)

Krevens, Frank, *Asst Prof of Art,* Brescia University, Anna Eaton Stout Memorial Art Gallery, Owensboro KY

Krevolin, Benjamin, *Pres,* Dutchess County Arts Council, Poughkeepsie NY

Kreymer, Oleg, *Systems Librn,* The Metropolitan Museum of Art, Museum Libraries, New York NY

Krezel, Cindy, *Dir Develop,* Planting Fields Foundation, Coe Hall at Planting Fields Arboretum, Oyster Bay NY

Krichman, Michael, *Exec Dir,* Installation Gallery, San Diego CA

Krick, Jessa J, *Colls Mgr,* Historic Hudson Valley, Pocantico Hills NY

Krieger, Louise, *Admin Asst,* Smith College, Museum of Art, Northampton MA

Krieger, Stella, *Mus Store Mgr,* University of California, Los Angeles, Fowler Museum at UCLA, Los Angeles CA

Kriff, Leslie, *Registrar,* Rutgers, The State University of New Jersey, Zimmerli Art Museum, Rutgers University, New Brunswick NJ

Kriley, Jessica, *Dir Visitor Svcs & Events,* DeCordova Museum & Sculpture Park, DeCordova Museum, Lincoln MA

Kriner, Lisa L, *Chmn,* Berea College, Art & Art History Program, Berea KY (S)

Kripal, Nick, *Chmn Crafts,* Temple University, Tyler School of Art, Philadelphia PA (S)

Krische, Christine Tripoli, *Sr Dir Pub Progs,* Municipal Art Society of New York, New York NY

Kristof, Jane, *Assoc Prof,* Portland State University, Dept of Art, Portland OR (S)

Kritselis, Alexander, *Div Dean,* Pasadena City College, Visual Arts and Media Studies Division, Pasadena CA (S)

Krivak, Andrea, *Publ Coordr,* Erie Art Museum, Erie PA

Kriz, K Dian, *Chmn, Prof,* Brown University, Dept History of Art & Architecture, Providence RI (S)

Krody, Sumru Belger, *Senior Cur Eastern Hemisphere,* The Textile Museum, Washington DC

Kroeker, Richard, *Assoc Prof,* Dalhousie University, Faculty of Architecture, Halifax NS (S)

Kroemer, Angela, *Secy,* University of Northern Iowa, Dept of Art, Cedar Falls IA (S)

Kroft, David, *Chmn,* Concordia University, Dept of Fine Arts, Austin TX (S)

Krohn-Andros, Laurie, *Cafe Mgr,* Worcester Art Museum, Worcester MA

Krol, Debra Utacia, *Ed,* Heard Museum, Billie Jane Baguley Library and Archives, Phoenix AZ

Krol, Penne, *Prof,* Greenfield Community College, Art Dept, Greenfield MA (S)

Krolak, K Malia, *Dir,* Louisiana State University School of Art, Alfred C Glassell Jr Exhibition Gallery, Baton Rouge LA

Krolak, Kristin Malia, *Gallery Coordr,* Louisiana State University, School of Art - Glassell Gallery, Baton Rouge LA

Kroll, Jim, *Mgr - Western History & Genealogy,* Denver Public Library, Reference, Denver CO

Kroloff, Reed, *Dir,* Cranbrook Academy of Art, Bloomfield Hills MI (S)

Krom, Nicole, *Mgr Vis Svcs & Rentals Coordr,* Philadelphia Museum of Art, Samuel S Fleisher Art Memorial, Philadelphia PA

Kromer, Lindsay, *Media Productions Coordr,* University of Tennessee, McClung Museum of Natural History & Culture, Knoxville TN

Krone, Ted, *Chmn,* Friends University, Art Dept, Wichita KS (S)

Kronewetter, Justin, *Dir,* Richard M Ross Art Museum at Wesleyan University, Delaware OH

Kroning, Melissa, *Registrar,* American Art Museum, Smithsonian Institution, Washington DC

Kronkite, Dale, *Head Conservation,* Georgia O'Keeffe Museum, Santa Fe NM

Kropf, Joan R, *Deputy Dir & Cur,* Salvador Dali, Library, Saint Petersburg FL

Kropf, Joan R, *Deputy Dir & Cur Coll,* Salvador Dali, Saint Petersburg FL

Kroupa, Sandra, *Book Arts & Rare Books Cur,* University of Washington, Univ of Washington Libraries, Special Collections, Seattle WA

Kruck, Martin, *Printmaking Prof,* New Jersey City University, Art Dept, Jersey City NJ (S)

Krucoff, Carole, *Head of Museum Educ,* University of Chicago, Oriental Institute, Chicago IL

Krudy, Catherine, *Dir,* Printed Matter, Inc, New York NY

Krueger, Dana, *Registrar,* Hamilton College, Emerson Gallery, Clinton NY

Krueger, David, *Preparator,* Rice University, Rice Gallery, Houston TX

Krueger, Karl, *Dir Library,* Lutheran Theological Seminary, Krauth Memorial Library, Philadelphia PA

Krueger, Michael, *Assoc Prof,* University of Kansas, The School of the Arts, Dept of Visual Art, Lawrence KS (S)

Krueger, Raymond R, *Pres Bd Trustees,* Milwaukee Art Museum, Milwaukee WI

Krueger, September, *Instr, Chair,* Southeastern Community College, Dept of Art, Whiteville NC (S)

Krueger-Corrado, Kristen, *Mktg & Communs Mgr,* Grand Rapids Public Library, Grand Rapids MI

Krug, Don, *Assoc Prof,* Ohio State University, Dept of Art Education, Columbus OH (S)

Krug, Kersti, *Mgr Directed Studies & the Critical Curatorial Studies Prog,* University of British Columbia, Museum of Anthropology, Vancouver BC

Kruger, Betty, *Cur,* Cambridge Museum, Cambridge NE

Kruger, Diane, *Pres,* Arts and Letters Club of Toronto, Toronto ON

Kruger, Laura, *Cur,* Hebrew Union College Museum, Jewish Institute of Religion Museum, New York NY

Kruizenga, Leonie, *Head Develop,* Swiss Institute, New York NY

Krule, Bernard K, *Assoc Prof,* Oakton Community College, Language Humanities & Art Divisions, Des Plaines IL (S)

Krull, Jeffrey R, *Dir,* Allen County Public Library, Art, Music & Audiovisual Services, Fort Wayne IN

Krush, Wayne, *Dept Chmn,* State University of New York at Farmingdale, Visual Communications, Farmingdale NY (S)

Kuan, Baulu, *Assoc Prof,* Saint John's University, Art Dept, Collegeville MN (S)

Kuan, Baulu, *Assoc Prof,* College of Saint Benedict, Art Dept, Saint Joseph MN (S)

Kubert, Joe, *Pres,* Joe Kubert, Dover NJ (S)

Kubiski, Joyce, *Art History Area Coordr,* Western Michigan University, Frostic School of Art, Kalamazoo MI (S)

Kucharski, Malcolm E, *Assoc Prof,* Pittsburg State University, Art Dept, Pittsburg KS (S)

Kuchler, Lee, *Instr,* Ocean City Arts Center, Ocean City NJ (S)

Kuderle, Chris, *Admin Dir,* Malaspina College, Nanaimo Art Gallery, Nanaimo BC

Kudryavtseva, Ekaterina, *Asst Prof,* Stetson University, Department of Creative Arts, Deland FL (S)

Kuebel-Stanky, Melanie, *Dir Visitor & Mem Svcs,* Erie County Historical Society, Erie PA

Kueber, Rita, *Dir Mktg & Communs,* Western Reserve Historical Society, Library, Cleveland OH

Kuehn, David, *Dir,* Cotuit Center for the Arts, Cotuit MA

Kuehn, Gary, *Prof,* Rutgers, The State University of New Jersey, Mason Gross School of the Arts, Visual Arts Dept, New Brunswick NJ (S)

Kuehn, Trena, *Asst Cur,* Frontier Gateway Museum, Glendive MT

Kuehner, Jennifer, *Asst Cur Educ,* Illinois State Museum, Museum Store, Chicago IL

Kuenstner, Molli E, *Northern & Central Europe Specialist,* National Gallery of Art, Department of Image Collections, Washington DC

Kuentzel, Peter, *Prof,* Miami-Dade Community College, Arts & Philosophy Dept, Miami FL (S)

Kufahl, Kim, *Pub Rels,* Wichita Center for the Arts, Mary R Koch School of Visual Arts, Wichita KS (S)

Kuharic, Katharine, *Kevin Kennedy Assoc Prof Art,* Hamilton College, Art Dept, Clinton NY (S)

Kuhman, Darla, *Gallery Asst,* The Art Spirit Gallery, Coeur D Alene ID

Kuhr, Alexis, *Assoc Prof,* University of Minnesota, Minneapolis, Dept of Art, Minneapolis MN (S)

Kuhre, Margo, *Publications Mgr,* Santa Cruz Art League, Inc, Center for the Arts, Santa Cruz CA

Kuhu, Heather, *Dir Mktg & Pub Rels,* Grace Museum, Inc, Abilene TX

Kuiper, Adriana, *Asst Prof,* Mount Allison University, Dept of Fine Arts, Sackville NB (S)

Kuiper, James, *Prof,* California State University, Chico, Department of Art & Art History, Chico CA (S)

Kujawa, Richard, *Opers Mgr,* Polish Museum of America, Research Library, Chicago IL

Kujiper, Trix, *Co-Chmn,* Studio Gallery, Washington DC

Kukee, Laura, *Olive DeLuce Art Gallery Coll Cur,* Northwest Missouri State University, DeLuce Art Gallery, Maryville MO

Kukella, Joseph, *Asst Prof & Chmn,* Daemen College, Art Dept, Amherst NY (S)

Kukharenko, Julie, *Mem, Finance & Opers Mgr,* Photographic Resource Center at Boston University, Boston MA

Kukla, Jon, *Exec Dir,* Patrick Henry, Red Hill National Memorial, Brookneal VA

Kulhavy, Valerie, *Acting Dir,* Nicolaysen Art Museum & Discovery Center, Children's Discovery Center, Casper WY

Kuluk, Tony, *VPres,* Manitoba Society of Artists, Winnipeg MB

Kumagai, Mitsu, *Youth & Arts Prog Mgr,* Arts Council Silicon Valley, San Jose CA

Kumao, Heidi, *Asst Prof,* University of Michigan, Ann Arbor, School of Art & Design, Ann Arbor MI (S)

Kumar, Vijay, *Instr,* Manhattan Graphics Center, New York NY (S)

Kumle, Aden, *Dir Grad Studies,* University of Chicago, Dept of Art History, Chicago IL (S)

Kummerow, Bill, *Web Designer,* University of Kansas, Spencer Museum of Art, Lawrence KS

Kumnick, Charles, *Assoc Prof,* The College of New Jersey, School of Arts & Sciences, Ewing NJ (S)

Kundar, Cynthia A, *Dir & Educ Dir,* Merrick Art Gallery, New Brighton PA

Kuniholm, Peter I, *Assoc Prof,* Cornell University, Dept of the History of Art & Visual Studies, Ithaca NY (S)

Kuntz, Margaret, *Asst Prof,* Drew University, Art Dept, Madison NJ (S)

Kuntz, Melissa, *Asst Prof,* Clarion University of Pennsylvania, Dept of Art, Clarion PA (S)

Kuntzman, Lauren, *Coordr Educ,* Canton Museum of Art, Canton OH

Kuntzman, Lauren, *Cur Educ,* Canton Museum of Art, Canton OH (S)

Kunzendorf, Eric, *Asst Prof of Animation,* Jacksonville University, Dept of Art, Theater, Dance, Jacksonville FL (S)

Kupper, Ketti, *Asst Prof,* University of Bridgeport, Shintaro Akatsu School of Design, Bridgeport CT (S)

Kurahashi, Eileen, *VPres National Ctr,* Japanese American National Museum, Los Angeles CA

Kuratnick, Jeff, *Cur Educ,* Paris Gibson Square, Museum of Art, Great Falls MT

Kuretsky, Susan D, *Prof,* Vassar College, Art Dept, Poughkeepsie NY (S)

Kurnit, Daniel, *Admin Asst,* School for Advanced Research (SAR), Indian Arts Research Center, Santa Fe NM

Kuronen, Darcy, *Pappalardo Cur Musical Instruments,* Museum of Fine Arts, Boston MA

Kurtz, Carla, *Office & Accts Mgr,* Society for Photographic Education (SPE), SPE Gallery, Cleveland OH

Kurtz, Howard, *Asst Cur Costumes & Textiles,* Hillwood Museum & Gardens Foundation, Hillwood Estate Museum & Gardens, Washington DC

Kurtz, Katie J, *Prog Dir,* Center on Contemporary Art, Seattle WA

Kurtz, Steven, *Assoc Prof,* University at Buffalo, State University of New York, Dept of Visual Studies, Buffalo NY (S)

Kusaba, Yoshio, *Prof Emeritus,* California State University, Chico, Department of Art & Art History, Chico CA (S)

Kusaba, Yoshio, *Prof Emeritus Art History Research,* California State University, Chico, Janet Turner Print Museum, CSU, Chico, Chico CA

Kuspit, Donald B, *Prof,* Stony Brook University, College of Arts & Sciences, Dept of Art, Stony Brook NY (S)

Kussack, John, *Admin Mgr,* Oregon Trail Museum Association, Scotts Bluff National Monument, Gering NE

Kusser, Robert L, *Dir,* South Dakota National Guard Museum, Pierre SD

Kusserow, Karl, *Cur American Art,* Princeton University, Princeton University Art Museum, Princeton NJ

Kuster, Deborah, *Assoc Prof,* University of Central Arkansas, Department of Art, Conway AR (S)

Kuster, Diane, *Archivist,* Art Gallery of Peel, Archives, Brampton ON

Kutbay, Bonnie, *Asst Prof & Chmn Dept,* Mansfield University, Art Dept, Mansfield PA (S)

Kutka, Catherine, *Asst Dir,* University of Wisconsin - Platteville, Harry & Laura Nohr Gallery, Platteville WI

Kuzler, Jen Larkin, *Dir Awards Progs,* Art Directors Club, New York NY

Kvapi, Jay, *Chmn,* California State University, Long Beach, Art Dept, Long Beach CA (S)

Kvarnstrom, Arthur, *Co-Dir,* Prince Street Gallery, New York NY

Kveton, Alex, *Instr,* Woodstock School of Art, Inc, Woodstock NY (S)

Kwan, Billy, *Assoc Mus Librn,* The Metropolitan Museum of Art, Image Library, New York NY

Kwiatkowski, Helen, *Prof,* University of Mary Hardin-Baylor, College of Visual & Performing Arts, Belton TX (S)

Kwler, Nicholas, *Graphic Design,* Western Michigan University, Frostic School of Art, Kalamazoo MI (S)

Kwok, Zoe, *Asst Cur Asian Art,* Princeton University, Princeton University Art Museum, Princeton NJ

Kwong, Maria, *Dir Retail & Visitors,* Japanese American National Museum, Los Angeles CA

Kyger, Linda, *Office Mgr,* George A Spiva, Joplin MO

Kyle, Nick, *Dept Head,* Missouri Southern State University, Dept of Art, Joplin MO (S)

Kyoung Kim, Sun, *Asst Prof,* Southern Illinois University, School of Art & Design, Carbondale IL (S)

Kyu Kim, Jong, *Exhib Coordr,* Philadelphia Museum of Art, Samuel S Fleisher Art Memorial, Philadelphia PA

Labadie, John Antoine, *Prof,* University of North Carolina at Pembroke, Art Dept, Pembroke NC (S)

LaBarbera, Anne, *Museum Shop Mgr,* Niagara University, Castellani Art Museum, Niagara NY

LaBarre, Rebecca Young, *Asst Cur,* Glessner House Museum, Chicago IL

LaBarrett, Joye, *Mng Dir,* Billie Trimble Chandler, Texas State Museum of Asian Cultures, Corpus Christi TX

Labe, Paul, *Dean,* Harford Community College, Visual, Performing and Applied Arts Division, Bel Air MD (S)

Labelle, Diane, *Mng Dir,* Guilde canadienne des metiers d'art, Canadian Guild of Crafts, Montreal PQ

Laber, Phil, *Prof,* Northwest Missouri State University, Dept of Fine & Performing Arts, Maryville MO (S)

Laber, Philip, *Chmn Dept Art,* Northwest Missouri State University, DeLuce Art Gallery, Maryville MO

LaBlanc, Necol, *Secy,* Galerie d'art de l'Universite de Moncton, Moncton NB

Labode, Modupe, *Historian,* Colorado Historical Society, Colorado History Museum, Denver CO

Labonuit, Melanie, *Acting Mus Dir,* Indian Pueblo Cultural Center, Albuquerque NM

LaBossiere, Holly, *Dir,* Ponca City Library, Art Dept, Ponca City OK

Labranche, Robert, *Lectr,* Southeastern Louisiana University, Dept of Visual Arts, Hammond LA (S)

Labuz, Ronald, *Prof,* Mohawk Valley Community College, Utica NY (S)

Lachance, Janice R, *CEO,* Special Libraries Association, Alexandria VA

LaChance, Patti, *Design Chair,* Rochester Institute of Technology, College of Imaging Arts & Sciences, Rochester NY (S)

Lacina, Ray, *Pres,* Owatonna Arts Center, Owatonna MN

Lacroix, Emily, *Vol Coordr,* Palo Alto Art Center, Palo Alto CA

Lacy, Tandy, *Dir Educ,* University of Illinois at Urbana-Champaign, Spurlock Museum, Champaign IL

Laczko, Gina, *Educ Servs Mgr,* Heard Museum, Phoenix AZ

Ladd, Spencer, *Chmn Design,* University of Massachusetts Dartmouth, College of Visual & Performing Arts, North Dartmouth MA (S)

Ladd-Simmons, Marilyn, *Gallery Mgr,* SPACES, Cleveland OH

Ladis, Andrew, *Franklin Prof Art History,* University of Georgia, Franklin College of Arts & Sciences, Lamar Dodd School of Art, Athens GA (S)

Ladkin, Nicola, *Registrar,* Texas Tech University, Museum of Texas Tech University, Lubbock TX

Ladnier, Paul, *Assoc Prof,* University of North Florida, Dept of Communications & Visual Arts, Jacksonville FL (S)

Ladson, Jack, *Secy,* Inter-Society Color Council, Reston VA

Ladu, Jen, *Coordr Outreach Educ,* Hebrew Union College - Jewish Institute of Religion, Skirball Museum Cincinnati, Cincinnati OH

Laducer, Jeremy, *Chm Bd,* Turtle Mountain Chippewa Historical Society, Turtle Mountain Heritage Center, Belcourt ND

Laehowski, Michael, *Pub Rels Coordr,* University of Georgia, Georgia Museum of Art, Athens GA

LaFarge, Antoinette, *Assoc Prof Digital Media,* University of California, Irvine, Studio Art Dept, Irvine CA (S)

Lafargue, Philippe, *Deputy Dir,* Tryon Palace Historic Sites & Gardens, New Bern NC

LaFavre, Ruth Ann, *First VPres,* Arizona Artists Guild, Phoenix AZ

Lafferty, Susan, *Dir Educ,* The Huntington Library, Art Collections & Botanical Gardens, San Marino CA

Lafferty, Susan, *Dir Educ,* The Huntington Library, Art Collections & Botanical Gardens, Library, San Marino CA

Laffitte, Polly, *Chief Cur Art,* South Carolina State Museum, Columbia SC

Lane, Barbara, *Prof*, City University of New York, PhD Program in Art History, New York NY (S)

Lane, Bruce, *Asst Prof*, Rochester Institute of Technology, School of Photographic Arts & Sciences, Rochester NY (S)

Lane, Christina, *Mktg Dir*, The Museum of Arts & Sciences Inc, Daytona Beach FL

Lane, Helen T., *Head Research Instr Servs*, Fashion Institute of Technology, Gladys Marcus Library - SUNY, New York NY

Lane, Hugh C, *Pres*, Charleston Museum, Charleston SC

Lane, Jenny, *Communs Mgr*, Huntsville Museum of Art, Huntsville AL

Lane, Joshua, *Cur Furniture*, Historic Deerfield, Inc, Deerfield MA

Lane, Lisa, *Develop Dir/Mem*, Beyond Baroque Foundation, Beyond Baroque Literary Arts Center, Venice CA

Lane, Mikki, *Events Outreach Coordr*, Middlebury College, Museum of Art, Middlebury VT

Lane, Thomas, *Assoc Prof*, University of Minnesota, Minneapolis, Dept of Art, Minneapolis MN (S)

Lane, William, *Gallery Dir*, Rio Hondo College Art Gallery, Whittier CA

Lanes, Susan, *Grant Writer*, Copper Village Museum & Arts Center, Anaconda MT

Laneve, Art, *Treas*, Erie Art Museum, Erie PA

Lang, Alyssa, *Assoc Prof*, California State Polytechnic University, Pomona, Department of Art, Pomona CA (S)

Lang, Brian, *Chief Cur*, Arkansas Arts Center, Little Rock AR

Lang, Brian J, *Art Dir*, Bank of NY Mellon Corporation, Pittsburgh PA

Lang, Michale, *Exec Dir & Chief Cur*, Peter & Catharine Whyte Foundation, Whyte Museum of the Canadian Rockies, Banff AB

Lang, Nick, *Chief Preparator*, Laumeier Sculpture Park, Saint Louis MO

Lang, Nico, *Dir Progs & Arts Svcs*, Dutchess County Arts Council, Poughkeepsie NY

Lang, Paul, *Deputy Dir & Chief Cur*, National Gallery of Canada, Ottawa ON

Lang, Sandra, *Prog Dir Visual Arts Admin*, New York University, Dept of Art & Art Professions, New York NY (S)

Lang, Tom, *Chmn*, Webster University, Art Dept, Webster Groves MO (S)

Lang, Tom, *Dept Chair*, Webster University, Cecille R Hunt Gallery, Webster Groves MO

Langa, Helen, *Asst Prof*, American University, Dept of Art, New York NY (S)

Langan, Katie, *Assoc Prof & Chair Dance*, Marymount Manhattan College, Fine & Performing Arts Div, New York NY (S)

Langdon, Rita, *Pub Rels*, C W Post Campus of Long Island University, Hillwood Art Museum, Brookville NY

Langdon, Susan, *Assoc Prof*, University of Missouri - Columbia, Art History & Archaeology Dept, Columbia MO (S)

Lange, Amanda E, *Cur Chair*, Historic Deerfield, Inc, Deerfield MA

Lange, Gerard, *Asst Prof*, Barton College, Art & Design Dept, Wilson NC (S)

Lange, Jane, *Dir*, City of San Rafael, Falkirk Cultural Center, San Rafael CA

Lange, Stephanie, *Prog Coord*, Schweinfurth Art Center, Auburn NY

Langehough, Steve, *Registrar*, Cooper-Hewitt National Design Museum, Smithsonian Institution, New York NY

Langelier, Nathalie, *Coll Archivist*, Le Musee Regional de Rimouski, Centre National d'Exposition, Rimouski PQ

Langeneckert, Mark, *Asst Tchs Prof & Dir Florence Prog*, University of Missouri - Columbia, Dept of Art, Columbia MO (S)

Langer, James V, *Asst Prof Art*, Greensboro College, Irene Cullis Gallery, Greensboro NC

Langer, James V, *Instr*, Greensboro College, Dept of Art, Division of Fine Arts, Greensboro NC (S)

Langer-Holt, Una Charlene, *Prof Foundations Studies*, Art Institute of Pittsburgh, Pittsburgh PA (S)

Langevin, Ann, *Exten Svcs*, Las Vegas-Clark County Library District, Las Vegas NV

Langley, James L, *Exhib Designer*, Calvert Marine Museum, Solomons MD

Langley, John, *Secy*, Alton Museum of History & Art, Inc, Alton IL

Langley, Judy, *Secy*, Birger Sandzen Memorial Gallery, Lindsborg KS

Langmann, Jeanette, *VPres & Treas*, Art Dealers Association of Canada, Toronto ON

Langnas, Bob, *Assoc Prof*, Saint Louis Community College at Florissant Valley, Liberal Arts Division, Ferguson MO (S)

Langston, Judy, *Asst Prof*, Oakton Community College, Language Humanities & Art Divisions, Des Plaines IL (S)

Langton, Charlie, *Ed*, Vesterheim Norwegian-American Museum, Decorah IA

Lanier, Chris, *Asst Prof*, Sierra Nevada College, Fine Arts Dept, Incline Village NV (S)

Lank, Katie, *Educ Dir*, The Center for Visual Artists - Greensboro, Greensboro NC

Lanka, Jason, *Asst Prof*, University of Wisconsin-Eau Claire, Dept of Art & Design, Eau Claire WI (S)

Lankford, E Louis, *Des Lee Foundation Prof Art Educ*, University of Missouri, Saint Louis, Dept of Art & Art History, Saint Louis MO (S)

Lankford, Nelson D, *VPres Prog*, Virginia Historical Society, Library, Richmond VA

Lankin-Hayes, Mollie, *Prog Adminr*, Arizona Commission on the Arts, Phoenix AZ

Lanman, Jennifer, *Coll Mgr*, Swope Art Museum, Research Library, Terre Haute IN

Lanman, Jennifer, *Collections Mgr*, Swope Art Museum, Terre Haute IN

Lannan, J Patrick, *Pres*, Lannan Foundation, Santa Fe NM

Lanni, Nanci, *Dir*, Pyramid Hill Sculpture Park & Museum, Hamilton OH

Lanning, Anne, *VPres Mus Affairs*, Historic Deerfield, Inc, Deerfield MA

Lannon, Evelyn W, *Sr Fine Arts Reference Librn*, Boston Public Library, Arts Reference Department, Boston MA

Lannon, John H, *Assoc Dir & Cur Maps*, Library of the Boston Athenaeum, Boston MA

Lansbury, Edgar, *Pres*, Nicholas Roerich, New York NY

Lansdown, Robert R, *Dir*, The Frank Phillips, Library, Bartlesville OK

Lansing, Amy Kurtz, *Cur*, Lyme Historical Society, Florence Griswold Museum, Old Lyme CT

Lanteigne, Charlene, *Dir*, Galerie Restigouche Gallery, Campbellton NB

Lantz, Dona, *Acad Dean*, Moore College of Art & Design, Philadelphia PA (S)

Lantz, Elizabeth, *Dir Library & Archives*, The Cleveland Museum of Art, Cleveland OH

Lantz, Elizabeth A, *Dir Libr & Archives*, The Cleveland Museum of Art, Ingalls Library, Cleveland OH

Lantzas, Jennifer, *Cur*, City of New York Parks & Recreation, Arsenal Gallery, New York NY

Lanyon, Scott M, *Dir*, University of Minnesota, The Bell Museum of Natural History, Minneapolis MN

Lanzl, Christina, *Project Mgr*, UrbanArts Institute at Massachusetts College of Art, Boston MA

Lanzo, Juanita, *Dir & Cur*, Bronx Council on the Arts, Longwood Arts Gallery @ Hostos, Bronx NY

Lapaeva, Olga, *Gift Shop Mgr*, Knights of Columbus Supreme Council, Knights of Columbus Museum, New Haven CT

Lapaite, Livija, *Dir BAC Educ*, Cultural Affairs Department City of Los Angeles/Barnsdall Art Centers/Junior Arts Center, Library, Los Angeles CA

Lapalombara, David, *Prof*, Antioch College, Visual Arts Dept, Yellow Springs OH (S)

Lape, Peter, *Cur Archaeology*, University of Washington, Burke Museum of Natural History and Culture, Seattle WA

Lapierre, Renee, *Exec Dir*, Vernon Art Gallery, Vernon BC

LaPlante, Dave, *Supvr Exhibit Production*, New York State Museum, Albany NY

Laplante, Louise, *Registrar, Coll Mgr*, Smith College, Museum of Art, Northampton MA

LaPointe, Andre, *Chmn Sculpture Dept*, Universite de Moncton, Dept of Visual Arts, Moncton NB (S)

Lapointe, Andre, *Pres*, Association professionnelle des designers d'interieur du Quebec, Montreal PQ

Lapointe, Jon, *Dir Communs*, Armory Center for the Arts, Pasadena CA

Lapointe, Jon, *Pres Bd Dir*, Side Street Projects, Pasadena CA

Laporte, Andrea, *Chair Bd Trustees*, Walters Art Museum, Baltimore MD

Laporte, Andrea B, *Chmn*, Walters Art Museum, Library, Baltimore MD

LaPorte, Angela M, *Assoc Prof*, University of Arkansas, Art Dept, Fayetteville AR (S)

LaPorte, Chris, *Adjunct Assoc Prof*, Aquinas College, Art Dept, Grand Rapids MI (S)

Laporte, Claire, *Mgr Pub Affairs*, Museum of Arts & Design, New York NY

LaPorte, Mary, *Prof Graphic Design*, California Polytechnic State University at San Luis Obispo, Dept of Art & Design, San Luis Obispo CA (S)

Lappie, Joseph, *Asst Prof Art*, Saint Ambrose University, Art Dept, Davenport IA (S)

Lapthisophon, Stephen, *Vis Asst Prof*, University of Texas at Arlington, Art & Art History Department, Arlington TX (S)

Laputka, Dolores A, *Chmn*, Allentown Art Museum, Allentown PA

Lara, Rosa, *Dir Educ*, Blauvelt Demarest Foundation, Hiram Blauvelt Art Museum, Oradell NJ

Lard, Jim, *Instr*, Harrisburg Area Community College, Division of Communications, Humanities & the Arts, Harrisburg PA (S)

Large, Anne Marie, *Cataloger*, Ames Free-Easton's Public Library, North Easton MA

Large, David, *Pres*, International Society of Marine Painters, Puryear TN

Laris, Elisa, *Dir Devel*, Armory Center for the Arts, Pasadena CA

Laris, Jeorgia, *Instr*, San Diego Mesa College, Fine Arts Dept, San Diego CA (S)

Larken, Dan, *Lectr*, Rochester Institute of Technology, School of Photographic Arts & Sciences, Rochester NY (S)

Larkin, Alan, *Prof*, Indiana University South Bend, Fine Arts Dept, South Bend IN (S)

Larkin, Annie, *Cur*, Bisbee Arts & Humanities Council, Lemuel Shattuck Memorial Library, Bisbee AZ

Larkin, Claire, *Acting Chief of Exhibs*, American Art Museum, Smithsonian Institution, Washington DC

Larkin, Ric, *Horticulturist*, The Nemours Foundatioin, Nemours Mansion & Gardens, Wilmington DE

Larkin, Todd, *Prof Art History*, Montana State University, School of Art, Bozeman MT (S)

Larmann, Ralph, *Assoc Prof*, University of Evansville, Art Dept, Evansville IN (S)

Larned, Ron, *Chmn*, Rollins College, Dept of Art, Main Campus, Winter Park FL (S)

LaRoche, Lynda, *Asst Prof*, Indiana University of Pennsylvania, College of Fine Arts, Indiana PA (S)

Larochelle, Steven, *Librn*, Thomas College, Mariner Library, Waterville ME

Larocque, Paul, *Assoc Dir*, Vancouver Art Gallery, Vancouver BC

Larocque, Peter, *Cur New Brunswick Cultural History & Art*, New Brunswick Museum, Saint John NB

LaRose, Matthew, *Head, Assoc Prof*, Davis & Elkins College, Dept of Art, Elkins WV (S)

LaRose, Steven, *Adjunct Faculty*, Southern Oregon University, Art & Art History Dept, Ashland OR (S)

Larose, Thomas, *Chmn & Dir*, Virginia State University, Department of Art & Design, Petersburg VA (S)

LaRou, George, *Instr*, Maine College of Art, Portland ME (S)

Larouche, Michel, *Dir*, Universite de Montreal, Dept of Art History, Montreal PQ (S)

Larrow, James, *Treas*, Toledo Artists' Club, Toledo Artists' Club & Gallery, Toledo OH

Larrow, Sharon, *Secy*, Toledo Artists' Club, Toledo Artists' Club & Gallery, Toledo OH

Larry, Charles, *Arts Librn*, Northern Illinois University, The University Libraries, DeKalb IL

Larsen, Adam, *Dir*, Snow College Art Gallery, Ephraim UT

Larsen, Devon, *Registrar*, Tampa Museum of Art, Tampa FL

Lawrence, Priscilla, *Dir The Historic New Orleans Collection,* The Historic New Orleans Collection, Williams Research Center, New Orleans LA

Lawrence, Priscilla, *Exec Dir,* The Historic New Orleans Collection, Royal Street Galleries, New Orleans LA

Lawrence, Randy, *Dir,* Olympic College, Social Sciences & Humanities Div, Bremerton WA (S)

Lawrence, Robert, *Assoc Prof,* University of South Florida, School The Arts, Tampa FL (S)

Lawrence, Sally, *Pres,* Pacific Northwest College of Art, Portland OR (S)

Lawrence, Sarah, *Dean School of Art & Design,* Parsons The New School for Design, New York NY (S)

Laws, Holly, *Asst Prof,* University of Central Arkansas, Department of Art, Conway AR (S)

Lawson, Darren, *Dean,* Bob Jones University, School of Fine Arts, Div of Art & Design, Greenville SC (S)

Lawson, Karol, *Dir,* Sweet Briar College, Art Collection & Galleries, Sweet Briar VA

Lawson, Mary, *Develop,* Greenville County Museum of Art, Greenville SC

Lawson, Roger, *Admin Librn,* National Gallery of Art, Library, Washington DC

Lawson, Scott, *CEO,* Plumas County Museum, Museum Archives, Quincy CA

Lawson, Scott, *Dir,* Plumas County Museum, Quincy CA

Lawson, Thomas, *Dean,* California Institute of the Arts, School of Art, Valencia CA (S)

Lawton, Carol, *Chmn,* Lawrence University, Dept of Art & Art History, Appleton WI (S)

Lawton, Cheryl, *Ranger,* Jack London, House of Happy Walls, Glen Ellen CA

Lawton, Mary, *Lectr,* Lake Forest College, Dept of Art, Lake Forest IL (S)

Lawton, Pamela, *Asst Prof,* University of North Carolina at Charlotte, Dept Art, Charlotte NC (S)

Lawton, Rebecca, *Cur Paintings & Sculpture,* Amon Carter Museum of American Art, Fort Worth TX

Laxton, Susan, *Asst Prof,* University of California, Riverside, Dept of the History of Art, Riverside CA (S)

Lay, Bill, *Security Officer,* Morris Museum of Art, Augusta GA

Lay, Daniel, *Preparator,* Mabee-Gerrer Museum of Art, Shawnee OK

Lay, Gary, *Media Coordr, Audio Visual,* University of Texas at Austin, Fine Arts Library, Austin TX

Lay, Howard, *Asst Prof,* University of Michigan, Ann Arbor, Dept of History of Art, Ann Arbor MI (S)

Laycock, Natal, *Mem Services Coordr,* Saskatchewan Association of Architects, Saskatoon SK

Layne, Margaret Mary, *Dir Develop,* Huntington Museum of Art, Huntington WV

Layton, Jo Ellen, *Western Representative,* Arizona Watercolor Association, Phoenix AZ

Layton, Kevin D, *Exec Dir,* Custer County Art & Heritage Center, Miles City MT

Lazar, Howard, *Dir Street Artist Prog,* San Francisco City & County Art Commission, San Francisco CA

Lazarus, Fred, *Pres,* Maryland Institute, College of Art Exhibitions, Baltimore MD

Lazarus, Fred, *Pres,* Maryland Institute, College of Art, Baltimore MD

Laziza, William, *Technical Dir,* Promote Art Works Inc (PAWI), Job Readiness in the Arts-Media-Communication, Brooklyn NY (S)

Lazzaro, Claudia, *Assoc Prof,* Cornell University, Dept of the History of Art & Visual Studies, Ithaca NY (S)

Le, Anh, *Cur,* Comox Valley Art Gallery, Courtenay BC

Lea, Ike, *Prof,* Lansing Community College, Visual Arts & Media Dept, Lansing MI (S)

Leach, Ann, *Bd Pres,* George A Spiva, Joplin MO

Leach, Brendan, *Asst Dir,* The Children's Aid Society, Visual Arts Program of the Philip Coltoff Center at Green Arts and After School Program, New York NY (S)

Leach, David, *Develop,* Worcester Center for Crafts, Krikorian Gallery, Worcester MA

Leach, Davie R, *Exec Dir,* Worcester Center for Crafts, Worcester MA (S)

Leach, Jessica, *Educ Dir,* Oglebay Institute, Stifel Fine Arts Center, Wheeling WV

Leach, Mark R, *Exec Dir,* Southeastern Center for Contemporary Art, Winston Salem NC

Leach, Patricia, *Dir,* Whatcom Museum, Bellingham WA

Leach, Robert, *Instr,* Sacramento City College, Art Dept, Sacramento CA (S)

Leache, Adam, *Cur Genetic Resources,* University of Washington, Burke Museum of Natural History and Culture, Seattle WA

Leacock, Kathryn, *Cur Coll,* Buffalo Museum of Science, Research Library, Buffalo NY

Leader, Karen, *Asst Prof Art History,* Florida Atlantic University, D F Schmidt College of Arts & Letters Dept of Visual Arts & Art History, Boca Raton FL (S)

Leahy, Debby, *Exec Dir,* Salem Art Association, Salem OR

Leahy, Margaret, *Chmn Interior Design,* Moore College of Art & Design, Philadelphia PA (S)

Leak, Carol, *Chmn,* Loyola University of New Orleans, Dept of Visual Arts, New Orleans LA (S)

Leal, Teresa, *Acting Dir,* Pimeria Alta Historical Society, Nogales AZ

Lean, Larry, *Chmn,* Mount Olive College, Dept of Art, Mount Olive NC (S)

Learmonth, Stephanie, *Registrar,* Triton Museum of Art, Santa Clara CA

Leary, Desiree, *Media Art Coll Mgr,* Electronic Arts Intermix (EAI), New York NY

Leary, Nadine, *Admin,* Captain Forbes House Museum, Milton MA

Lease, Michael, *Exhib Mgr,* Virginia Commonwealth University, Anderson Gallery, Richmond VA

Leatherbarrow, David, *Chmn Grad Group,* University of Pennsylvania, Dept of Architecture, Philadelphia PA (S)

Leavens, Ileana, *Prof,* Seattle Central Community College, Humanities - Social Sciences Division, Seattle WA (S)

Lebel, Christine, *Educ,* Musee Regional de lu Cote-Nord, Sept-Iles PQ

LeBlanc, Alice, *Admin Asst,* West Baton Rouge Parish, West Baton Rouge Museum, Port Allen LA

LeBlanc, France, *Educ & Culture,* Le Musee Regional de Rimouski, Centre National d'Exposition, Rimouski PQ

LeBlanc, Lajla, *Dir Commuins,* Sharon Arts Center, Sharon Arts Center Exhibition Gallery, Peterborough NH

LeBlanc, Pierre, *Assoc Prof,* Memorial University of Newfoundland, Division of Fine Arts, Visual Arts Program, Corner Brook NF (S)

Leblanc, Therese, *Pres,* Nova Scotia Association of Architects, Halifax NS

Leblond, Helene, *Archiviste,* Saint Joseph's Oratory, Centre d'archives et de Documentation Roland-Guthier, Montreal PQ

LeBras, Carol, *Fine Arts Librn,* Chicago Public Library, Harold Washington Library Center, Chicago IL

Leca, Benedict, *Cur European Painting & Sculpture,* Cincinnati Art Museum, Cincinnati Art Museum, Cincinnati OH

Leca, Benedict, *Dir Curatorial Affairs,* Art Gallery of Hamilton, Hamilton ON

Leck-Grela, Janie, *Dir After School & Educ Projects,* Arizona Commission on the Arts, Phoenix AZ

Leckey, Colun, *Chmn Humanities,* Lincoln Memorial University, Division of Humanities, Harrogate TN (S)

LeClair, Laura, *Pres,* Arts & Crafts Association of Meriden Inc, Gallery 53, Meriden CT

LeClair, Paul, *Chmn,* St Michael's College, Fine Arts Dept, Colchester VT (S)

Leclerc, Erin, *Prof,* Saint Louis Community College at Meramec, Art Dept, Saint Louis MO (S)

Leclere, Mary, *Assoc Dir Core Residency Prog,* Museum of Fine Arts, Houston, Glassell School of Art, Houston TX (S)

LeCount, Chuck, *Sr Dir Progs & Colls,* Genesee Country Village & Museum, John L Wehle Art Gallery, Mumford NY

L'Ecuyer, Kelly, *Ellyn McColgan Cur Decorative Arts,* Museum of Fine Arts, Boston MA

Ledee, Kimberly, *Asst Prof,* South Carolina State University, Dept of Visual & Performing Arts, Orangeburg SC (S)

Lederer, Carrie, *Cur,* Dean Lesher, Bedford Gallery, Walnut Creek CA

Lederer, Robert, *Coordr Industrial Design,* University of Alberta, Dept of Art & Design, Edmonton AB (S)

Ledford, Victoria, *Visual Art Educ,* Rapid City Arts Council, Dahl Arts Center, Rapid City SD

Ledgerwood, Judy, *Assoc Prof,* Northwestern University, Evanston, Dept of Art Theory & Practice, Evanston IL (S)

Ledot, Laura, *Educ Coordr,* Tulane University, Newcomb Art Gallery, New Orleans LA

LeDuc, Aimee, *Gallery Mgr,* San Francisco Arts Commission, Gallery, San Francisco CA

Leduc, Philip, *Dir Opers,* McCord Museum of Canadian History, Montreal PQ

Leduc, Rebecca, *Asst Dir,* San Luis Obispo Museum of Art, San Luis Obispo CA

Ledward, Lynne, *Admin,* Hawaii Pacific University, Gallery, Kaneohe HI

Lee, Barbara Brown, *Chief Educ,* Milwaukee Art Museum, Milwaukee WI

Lee, Beverly, *Prog Asst,* Piatt Castles, West Liberty OH

Lee, Billy, *Prof,* University of North Carolina at Greensboro, Art Dept, Greensboro NC (S)

Lee, Bovey, *Asst Prof,* University of Pittsburgh, Dept of Studio Arts, Pittsburgh PA (S)

Lee, Christine, *Office Mgr,* Gallery Stratford, Stratford ON

Lee, Christopher, *CEO,* Columbus Chapel & Boal Mansion Museum, Boalsburg PA

Lee, Chui-Chun, *Dir,* State University of New York at New Paltz, Sojourner Truth Library, New Paltz NY

Lee, De-Nin, *Asst Prof,* Bowdoin College, Art Dept, Brunswick ME (S)

Lee, Diane, *Coll Mgr,* Connecticut Historical Society, Library, Hartford CT

Lee, Elizabeth, *Asst Prof,* Dickinson College, Dept of Art & Art History, Carlisle PA (S)

Lee, Ellen, *Wood-Pulliam Dist Senior Cur,* Indianapolis Museum of Art, Indianapolis IN

Lee, Eric M, *Dir,* Kimbell Art Foundation, Kimbell Art Museum, Fort Worth TX

Lee, Eric M, *Dir & Chief Cur,* University of Oklahoma, Fred Jones Jr Museum of Art, Norman OK

Lee, Esther, *Div Mgr,* Queens Borough Public Library, Fine Arts & Recreation Division, Jamaica NY

Lee, Hoon, *Asst Prof,* Grand Valley State University, Art & Design Dept, Allendale MI (S)

Lee, Jack, *Dir,* Taipei Economic & Cultural Office, Chinese Information & Culture Center Library, New York NY

Lee, Jason, *Assoc Prof,* West Virginia University, College of Creative Arts, School of Art & Design, Morgantown WV (S)

Lee, Jennifer, *Dir,* Peoria Art Guild, Peoria IL

Lee, Jill L, *Circ Librn,* Athenaeum of Philadelphia, Philadelphia PA

Lee, Jim, *Assoc Prof,* University of Hartford, Hartford Art School, West Hartford CT (S)

Lee, Jiwon, *Asst Prof,* Old Dominion University, Art Dept, Norfolk VA (S)

Lee, Jiyong, *Assoc Prof,* Southern Illinois University, School of Art & Design, Carbondale IL (S)

Lee, Joe A, *Pres,* Tougaloo College, Art Collection, Tougaloo MS

Lee, Junghee, *Assoc Prof,* Portland State University, Dept of Art, Portland OR (S)

Lee, Kristie, *Graphic Designer,* University of Missouri, Museum of Art & Archaeology, Columbia MO

Lee, Lexi, *Koch Cur Fellow,* DeCordova Museum & Sculpture Park, DeCordova Museum, Lincoln MA

Lee, Liz, *Prof,* State University of New York at Fredonia, Dept of Art, Fredonia NY (S)

Lee, Lydia, *VPres & Mgr,* Bank One Arizona, Phoenix AZ

Lee, Margaret, *Educ Coordr,* Lillian & Coleman Taube Museum of Art, Minot ND

Lee, Marilyn, *Assoc Prof,* Dickinson State University, Dept of Art, Dickinson ND (S)

Lee, Michelle, *Develop & Communs,* Craft and Folk Art Museum (CAFAM), Los Angeles CA

Lee, Paul, *Chmn,* Washington State University, Fine Arts Dept, Pullman WA (S)

Lee, Paul, *Dir School of Art,* University of Tennessee, Knoxville, School of Art, Knoxville TN (S)

Lee, Robert, *Exec Dir,* Asian American Arts Centre, New York NY

Lee, Rodney, *Dir,* Mount Vernon Public Library, Fine Art Dept, Mount Vernon NY

Lee, Rodney, *Finance Dir,* Oklahoma City Museum of Art, Oklahoma City OK

Lee, Shirley, *Bd Mem,* Coquille Valley Art Association, Coquille OR

Lee, Steph D, *CAS Gen,* Columbus Historic Foundation, Blewett-Harrison-Lee Museum, Columbus MS

Lee, Stephen, *Head,* Carnegie Mellon University, School Architecture, Pittsburgh PA (S)

Lee, Su-Ying, *Asst Cur,* Museum of Contemporary Canadian Art, Toronto ON

Lee, Susan, *Technical Svcs Adminr,* Miami-Dade Public Library, Miami FL

Lee, Talice, *Archivist & Develop Assoc,* Asian American Arts Centre, New York NY

Lee, Tetia, *Asst Dir,* Arts Place, Inc., Hugh N Ronald Memorial Gallery, Portland IN

Lee, Thom, *Instr Art,* Everett Community College, Art Dept, Everett WA (S)

Lee, Yachin Crystal, *Assoc Prof,* California State Polytechnic University, Pomona, Department of Art, Pomona CA (S)

Lee-Warren, S, *Instr,* Golden West College, Visual Art Dept, Huntington Beach CA (S)

Lee Brosseau, Carol, *Dir,* Joseph Bellows Gallery, La Jolla CA

Leech, Tom, *Palace Press,* Museum of New Mexico, Palace of Governors, Santa Fe NM

Leedy, James, *Exec Dir,* Leedy-Voulkos Art Center, Kansas City MO

Leedy Jr, Walter, *Prof,* Cleveland State University, Art Dept, Cleveland OH (S)

Leen, Mary, *Assoc Dir,* Massachusetts Institute of Technology, MIT Museum, Cambridge MA

Lees, Gary P, *Dir Dept,* Johns Hopkins University, School of Medicine, Dept of Art as Applied to Medicine, Baltimore MD (S)

Leete, William C, *Prof,* Northern Michigan University, Dept of Art & Design, Marquette MI (S)

Leete Smith, Avery, *Pres Bd,* Friends of Historic Kingston, Fred J Johnston House Museum, Kingston NY

Leeuwrik, Linda, *Instr,* Idaho State University, Dept of Art & Pre-Architecture, Pocatello ID (S)

Lefebvrre-Carter, Michelle, *Dir,* Will Rogers Memorial Museum & Birthplace Ranch, Claremore OK

Leff, Cathy, *Dir,* The Wolfsonian-Florida International University, Miami Beach FL

Leffel, Joann, *Instr Art History,* Bay De Noc Community College, Art Dept, Escanaba MI (S)

LeFlore, Gail, *Sr Svcs Coordr,* City of Cedar Falls, Iowa, James & Meryl Hearst Center for the Arts & Sculpture Garden, Cedar Falls IA

Legere, Phoebe, *Artist,* U Gallery, New York NY

Legette, Lee David, *Interim Chmn,* Winston-Salem State University, Art Dept, Winston-Salem NC (S)

Legg, Kate, *Educ Asst,* DeCordova Museum School, Lincoln MA (S)

Legge, Katie Frinkle, *Pres (V),* Artists Association of Nantucket, Nantucket MA

Legleiter, Kim, *Dir & Financial Dir,* Stauth Foundation & Museum, Stauth Memorial Museum, Montezuma KS

Lehane, Debra, *Mgr Civic Art Coll,* San Francisco City & County Art Commission, San Francisco CA

Lehman, Arnold L, *Dir,* Brooklyn Museum, Brooklyn NY

Lehman, Linda, *Instr,* Ohio Northern University, Dept of Art & Design, Ada OH (S)

Lehman, Marie, *Instr,* Toronto School of Art, Toronto ON (S)

Lehman, Tina, *Johnstown Coordr,* Southern Alleghenies Museum of Art, Johnstown Gallery, Loretto PA

Lehmbeck, Leah, *Cur,* Norton Simon, Pasadena CA

Lehner, Warren, *Prof,* Purchase College, State University of New York, School of Art+Design, Purchase NY (S)

Lehr, John, *Asst Prof,* Purchase College, State University of New York, School of Art+Design, Purchase NY (S)

Lehr, Lydia, *Instr,* Main Line Art Center, Haverford PA (S)

Lehr, Paul T, *Pres & CEO,* National YoungArts Foundation, Miami FL

Lehrecke, Barbara, *Conservator,* Textile Conservation Workshop Inc, South Salem NY

Leibert, Peter, *Prof,* Connecticut College, Dept of Art, New London CT (S)

Leibold, Cheryl, *Archivist,* Pennsylvania Academy of the Fine Arts, Archives, Philadelphia PA

Leibsohn, Dana, *Prof,* Smith College, Art Dept, Northampton MA (S)

Leidich, David, *Asst to Dir,* Moravian College, Payne Gallery, Bethlehem PA

Leigh, Emily, *Asst Dir,* Kentuck Museum Association, Inc., Kentuck Art Center & Festival of the Arts, Northport AL

Leigh, Karon, *Weekend Supv,* Tubac Center of the Arts, Santa Cruz Valley Art Association, Tubac AZ

Leigh, Sheri, *Dir Summer Arts,* Sierra Nevada College, Fine Arts Dept, Incline Village NV (S)

Lein, Sharon, *Dir,* Deming-Luna Mimbres Museum, Deming NM

Leinaweaver, Chad, *Dir Library,* New Jersey Historical Society, Library, Newark NJ

Leinaweaver, Chad, *Library Dir,* New Jersey Historical Society, Newark NJ

Leinbach, Charles, *Chmn,* California State University, Long Beach, Design Dept, Long Beach CA (S)

Leiner, Virginia, *Mus Shop Mgr,* Westmoreland Museum of American Art, Greensburg PA

Leiner, Virginia, *Mus Shop Mgr,* Westmoreland Museum of American Art, Art Reference Library, Greensburg PA

Leininger, Matthew, *Head Exhibits & Reg,* Cincinnati Art Museum, Cincinnati Art Museum, Cincinnati OH

Leininger-Miller, Theresa, *Dir Art Hist Prog & Asst Prof Art Educ,* University of Cincinnati, School of Art, Cincinnati OH (S)

Leinroth, Martha, *Asst Prof,* Rochester Institute of Technology, School of Photographic Arts & Sciences, Rochester NY (S)

Leipert, Kristen, *Asst Archivist,* Whitney Museum of American Art, Frances Mulhall Achilles Library, New York NY

Leipzig, Mel, *Prof,* Mercer County Community College, Arts, Communication & Engineering Technology, West Windsor NJ (S)

Leiser, Amy, *Exec Dir,* Monroe County Historical Association, Elizabeth D Walters Library, Stroudsburg PA

Leisten, Thomas, *Prof,* Princeton University, Dept of Art & Archaeology, Princeton NJ (S)

Leister, Claudia, *Coll Mgr,* Delaware Division of Historical & Cultural Affairs, Dover DE

Leithauser, Mark, *Chief Design & Installation,* National Gallery of Art, Washington DC

Leither, Luke, *Fine Arts Librn,* University of Utah, Katherine W Dumke Architecture Library, Marriott Library, Salt Lake City UT

Lemay, Bonnie White, *Adminr,* Palm Beach County Parks & Recreation Department, Morikami Museum & Japanese Gardens, Delray Beach FL

Lemay, Brian, *Exec Dir,* The Bostonian Society, Old State House Museum, Boston MA

Lemay, Guislaine, *Cur Material Culture,* McCord Museum of Canadian History, Montreal PQ

Lemberg, Jessica, *Educ Asst,* Museum of Wisconsin Art, West Bend WI

Le Mense, Montserrat, *Paintings Conservator,* Williamstown Art Conservation Center, Williamstown MA

Lemieox, Jeff, *Secy,* Glynn Art Association, Saint Simons Island GA

Lemke, Melissa Beck, *Italian Specialist,* National Gallery of Art, Department of Image Collections, Washington DC

Lemmon, Alfred, *Dir Williams Research Ctr,* The Historic New Orleans Collection, Williams Research Center, New Orleans LA

LeMoine, Genevieve, *Cur,* Bowdoin College, Peary-MacMillan Arctic Museum, Brunswick ME

Lemonedes, Heather, *Cur Drawings,* The Cleveland Museum of Art, Cleveland OH

Lemons, Charles R, *Cur,* Cavalry-Armor Foundation, Patton Museum of Cavalry & Armor, Fort Knox KY

Lemos da Cunha, Evandro Jose, *Dir,* Universidade Federal de Minas Gerais (UFMG), Escola de Belas Artes, Belo Horizonte MG (S)

Lemp, Frank J, *Chmn,* Ottawa University, Dept of Art, Ottawa KS (S)

Lempka, Wayne, *Coll Mgr,* State University of New York at New Paltz, Samuel Dorsky Museum of Art, New Paltz NY

Lenaghan, Patrick, *Cur Prints & Photographs,* The Hispanic Society of America, Museum & Library, New York NY

Lenderman, Max, *Prof,* Rochester Institute of Technology, School of Design, Rochester NY (S)

Lenfestey, Harold, *Asst Prof,* West Texas A&M University, Art, Theatre & Dance Dept, Canyon TX (S)

L'Engle, Madeleine, *Vol Librn,* Cathedral of Saint John the Divine, Library, New York NY

Lenhardt, Barbara, *Mus Shop Mgr,* Virginia Museum of Fine Arts, Richmond VA

Lenharth, Amy, *Adjunct Prof,* Missouri Western State University, Art Dept, Saint Joseph MO (S)

Lenihan, Teresa, *Asst Prof,* Loyola Marymount University, Dept of Art & Art History, Los Angeles CA (S)

Lennon, Madeline, *Chmn,* University of Western Ontario, John Labatt Visual Arts Centre, London ON (S)

Lenoir, Susan, *Dir Workshops,* California Watercolor Association, Gallery Concord, Concord CA

Lenore, Leila, *Exec Dir,* Charles B Goddard, Ardmore OK

Lent, Amy, *Exec Dir,* Maine Maritime Museum, Bath ME

Lentz, Craig, *VPres,* Hammond Castle Museum, Gloucester MA

Lentz, Lamar, *Dir Library & Mus,* James Dick Foundation, Festival - Institute, Round Top TX

Lentz, Thomas, *Dir Int'l Art Museums,* Smithsonian Institution, Washington DC

Lenz, William, *Dir Fine & Performing Arts,* Chatham College, Art Gallery, Pittsburgh PA

Lenzi, Kristina, *Instr,* University of Utah, Dept of Art & Art History, Salt Lake City UT (S)

Lenz Kothe, Elsa, *Educ,* Whatcom Museum, Bellingham WA

Leonard, Anne, *Cur & Mellon Prog Coordr,* University of Chicago, Smart Museum of Art, Chicago IL

Leonard, Brandie, *Develop Dir,* Willard Arts Center, Carr Gallery, Colonial Theater, Idaho Falls ID

Leonard, Donald, *Registrar,* United States Naval Academy, USNA Museum, Annapolis MD

Leonard, Glen, *Dir,* Church of Jesus Christ of Latter-Day Saints, Museum of Church History & Art, Salt Lake City UT

Leonard, Joanne, *Prof,* University of Michigan, Ann Arbor, School of Art & Design, Ann Arbor MI (S)

Leonard, John, *Instr,* Toronto School of Art, Toronto ON (S)

Leonard, Mary, *Reference Librn,* Dallas Museum of Art, Mildred R & Frederick M Mayer Library, Dallas TX

Leonard, Nancy, *Mgr,* Rosicrucian Egyptian Museum & Planetarium, Rosicrucian Order, A.M.O.R.C., San Jose CA

Leonard, Rebecca, *Asst Librn,* Japan Society, Inc, C.V. Starr Library, New York NY

Leonard, Sandra Blake, *Pres,* Hancock County Trustees of Public Reservations, Woodlawn: Museum, Gardens & Park, Ellsworth ME

Leonard, Susan, *Dir,* South Carolina Arts Commission, Media Center, Columbia SC

Leonard, Susan, *Librn,* Bard College, Center For Curatorial Studies Library, Annandale-on-Hudson NY

Leonard, Yvonne, *Asst Prof,* Community College of Rhode Island, Dept of Art, Warwick RI (S)

Leonard-Cravens, Mary, *Prof,* Eastern Illinois University, Art Dept, Charleston IL (S)

Leonardo, Shaun, *Dir of Pub Progs & Community Rels,* Socrates Sculpture Park, Long Island City NY

Leong, Lampo, *Prof (Painting & Drawing)*, University of Missouri - Columbia, Dept of Art, Columbia MO (S)

Leong, Russell, *Pres*, Chinese Culture Foundation, Center Gallery, San Francisco CA

Leousis, Kasia, *Art Librn*, Washington University, Art & Architecture Library, Saint Louis MO

Le Page, Carmen D, *Supt*, Forges du Saint-Maurice National Historic Site, Trois Rivieres PQ

L'Eplattenier, Elizabeth, *Exec Asst*, University of North Carolina at Greensboro, Weatherspoon Art Museum, Greensboro NC

LePore, Ann, *Assoc Prof 3D Design & Animation*, Ramapo College of New Jersey, School of Contemporary Arts, Mahwah NJ (S)

LePore, William, *Asst Prof*, Portland State University, Dept of Art, Portland OR (S)

Lepper, Sandra, *Dir*, Russell Day Gallery, Everett WA

Lepper, Sandra, *Instr Art*, Everett Community College, Art Dept, Everett WA (S)

Leppky, Raenel, *Office Admin*, Royal Canadian Academy of Arts, Toronto ON

Leppmann, Erika, *Assoc Prof*, Southern Oregon University, Art & Art History Dept, Ashland OR (S)

Lere, Dan, *Exec Dir*, Sangre de Cristo Arts & Conference Center, Pueblo CO

Lerer, Seth, *Dean*, University of California, San Diego, Visual Arts Dept, La Jolla CA (S)

LeRiche, Sharon, *Gallery Coordr*, Craft Council of Newfoundland & Labrador, Saint John's NF

Lerma, Liz, *Dir Community Arts & Educ*, San Francisco City & County Art Commission, San Francisco CA

Lerner, A, *Prof*, City Colleges of Chicago, Daley College, Chicago IL (S)

Lerner, Adam, *Dir & Chief Animator*, Museum of Contemporary Art Denver, Denver CO

Lerner, Lynne, *Asst Dir*, Greenwich House Pottery, First Floor Gallery, New York NY

Lerner, Lynne, *Asst Dir*, Greenwich House Inc, Greenwich House Pottery, New York NY (S)

Lesher, Pete, *Cur*, Chesapeake Bay Maritime Museum, Saint Michaels MD

Lesher, Pete, *Cur*, Chesapeake Bay Maritime Museum, Howard I Chapelle Memorial Library, Saint Michaels MD

Leshnoff, Susan, *Asst Prof*, Seton Hall University, College of Arts & Sciences, South Orange NJ (S)

LeShock, Ed, *Asst Prof*, Radford University, Art Dept, Radford VA (S)

Lesinski, Peg, *Head Acquisitions*, American Antiquarian Society, Worcester MA

Leskard, Marta, *Conservator*, Okanagan Heritage Museum, Kelowna BC

Lesko, Jim, *Assoc Prof*, University of Bridgeport, Shintaro Akatsu School of Design, Bridgeport CT (S)

Lesley, Kimberly, *Access Servs Librn*, The University of the Arts, University Libraries, Philadelphia PA

Lesley, Nick, *Distribution Mgr*, Electronic Arts Intermix (EAI), New York NY

Leslie, Ken, *Dept Painting*, Johnson State College, Dept Fine & Performing Arts, Dibden Center for the Arts, Johnson VT (S)

Leslie, Matt, *Exhib & Educ Adminr*, Muckenthaler Cultural Center, Fullerton CA

Leslie, Richard, *Vis Assoc Prof*, Stony Brook University, College of Arts & Sciences, Dept of Art, Stony Brook NY (S)

Lester, Audra, *Treas*, Saint Augustine Art Association and Art Gallery, Saint Augustine FL

Lester, Barri, *Asst Prof*, Kansas State University, Art Dept, Manhattan KS (S)

Lester, DeeGee, *Dir Educ*, Board of Parks & Recreation, The Parthenon, Nashville TN

Lester, Howard, *Chmn Film/Video*, Rochester Institute of Technology, School of Photographic Arts & Sciences, Rochester NY (S)

Lester, Laurie, *Gift Shop & Mem Mgr*, Western Colorado Center for the Arts, The Art Center, Grand Junction CO

Lester, William Carey, *Prof*, Delta State University, Dept of Art, Cleveland MS (S)

LeSuer, Sharon, *Acad Dean*, Tunxis Community Technical College, Graphic Design Dept, Farmington CT (S)

Lesztak, Elizabeth, *Sculptor*, John Weaver Sculpture Collection, Hope BC

Lesztak, Sara, *Cur*, John Weaver Sculpture Collection, Hope BC

Lethbridge, York, *Dir Opers*, Mercer Union, A Centre for Contemporary Art, Toronto ON

Lethen, Paulien, *Dir*, Holland Tunnel Art Projects, Brooklyn NY

Lethen, Roy, *Graphic Designer*, Holland Tunnel Art Projects, Brooklyn NY

Letizia, Christopher, *Conservator*, Boston Public Library, Rare Book & Manuscripts Dept, Boston MA

Letocha, Louise Dusseault, *Dept Head*, Universite du Quebec a Montreal, Famille des Arts, Montreal PQ (S)

Letson, Carol, *Pres*, Pocumtuck Valley Memorial Association, Memorial Hall Museum, Deerfield MA

Lettenstrom, Dean R, *Prof*, University of Minnesota, Duluth, Art Dept, Duluth MN (S)

Lettieri, Robert, *Chair*, Citizens for the Arts in Pennsylvania, Harrisburg PA

Lettieri, Robin, *Dir*, Port Chester-Rye Brook Public Library, Port Chester NY

Letton, Laura, *Dir Planned Gifts & Mem Coordr*, Dayton Art Institute, Dayton OH

Leubke, Thomas, *Secy*, United States Commission of Fine Arts, Washington DC

Leuchak, Rebecca, *Asst Prof*, Roger Williams University, Visual Art Dept, Bristol RI (S)

Leung, Simon, *Assoc Prof Contemporary Art History*, University of California, Irvine, Studio Art Dept, Irvine CA (S)

Leusch, Kelly, *Develop Dir*, Cedar Rapids Museum of Art, Cedar Rapids IA

Leuthold, Marc, *Asst Prof*, State University of New York College at Potsdam, Dept of Fine Arts, Potsdam NY (S)

Leuthold, Steve, *Asst Prof*, Northern Michigan University, Dept of Art & Design, Marquette MI (S)

LeVan, Susan, *Chair Illustration*, Lesley University, College of Art & Design, Boston MA (S)

LeVant, Howard, *Assoc Prof*, Rochester Institute of Technology, School of Photographic Arts & Sciences, Rochester NY (S)

Levasseur, Marie-Andree, *Dir*, Maison de la Culture, Centre d'exposition Raymond-Lasnier, Trois Rivieres PQ

LeVeille, Fayn (no e), *Mus Dir*, Halifax Historical Society, Inc, Halifax Historical Museum, Daytona Beach FL

Levengood, Paul A, *Pres*, Virginia Historical Society, Library, Richmond VA

Lever, Briles, *Instr Graphics*, Lander University, College of Arts & Humanities, Greenwood SC (S)

Leverette, Carlton, *Coordr Arts*, Baltimore City Community College, Art Gallery, Baltimore MD

Levesque, Josyka, *Commun*, Le Musee Regional de Rimouski, Centre National d'Exposition, Rimouski PQ

Levesque, Kristen, *Dir Pub Rels*, Portland Museum of Art, Portland ME

Levesque, Richard, *VPres*, International Society of Marine Painters, Puryear TN

Levesque, Sophie, *Boutique Mgr*, Musee Regional de lu Cote-Nord, Sept-Iles PQ

Levett, Jude, *Admin Asst*, McMaster University, McMaster Museum of Art, Hamilton ON

Levin, Brett M, *Cur & Dir*, University of Alabama at Birmingham, Visual Arts Gallery, Birmingham AL

Levin, Gail, *Prof*, City University of New York, PhD Program in Art History, New York NY (S)

Levin, John, *Treas*, Birger Sandzen Memorial Gallery, Lindsborg KS

Levine, Adam, *Interim Head Visitor Engagement*, Toledo Museum of Art, Toledo OH

Levine, Cary, *Asst Prof*, University of North Carolina at Chapel Hill, Art Dept, Chapel Hill NC (S)

Levine, Francis, *Dir*, Museum of New Mexico, Palace of Governors, Santa Fe NM

Levine, Jeffrey, *Dir Communs*, Whitney Museum of American Art, New York NY

Levine, Julius S, *Assoc Prof*, Catholic University of America, School of Architecture & Planning, Washington DC (S)

Levine, Kathy, *Assoc Prof Visual Arts*, Dowling College, Dept of Visual Arts, Oakdale NY (S)

Levine, Martin, *Asst Prof*, Stony Brook University, College of Arts & Sciences, Dept of Art, Stony Brook NY (S)

Levine, Phyllis, *Dir Communs*, International Center of Photography, Museum, New York NY

Levine, Yasemin Celik, *Chmn Social Science*, Fashion Institute of Technology, Art & Design Division, New York NY (S)

Levine, Zachary, *Asst Cur*, Yeshiva University Museum, New York NY

Leviness, Bobbie, *Site Coordr*, Preservation Virginia, John Marshall House, Richmond VA

Levinthal, Beth E, *Exec Dir*, Hofstra University, Hofstra University Museum, Hempstead NY

Levinthal, Beth E, *Exec Dir*, The Heckscher Museum of Art, Library, Huntington NY

Levister, Delores, *Grad & undergrad advising asst*, University of California, Berkeley, College of Letters & Sciences-Art Practice Dept, Berkeley CA (S)

Levit, Robert, *Master Urban Design*, University of Toronto, Faculty of Architecture, Landscape & Design, Toronto ON (S)

Levitov, Karen, *Curatorial Mgr*, The Jewish Museum, New York NY

Levitt, Viera, *Dir*, Community College of Rhode Island, Knight Campus Art Gallery, Warwick RI

Levitz, Dale R, *Asst Prof*, Johns Hopkins University, School of Medicine, Dept of Art as Applied to Medicine, Baltimore MD (S)

Levkoff, Mary, *Cur Sculpture & Decorative Arts*, National Gallery of Art, Washington DC

Levrant-Bretteville, Sheila, *Prof*, Yale University, School of Art, New Haven CT (S)

Levy, David C, *Pres & Dir*, Corcoran Gallery of Art, Washington DC

Levy, Gady, *Dir*, University of Judaism, Dept of Continuing Education, Los Angeles CA (S)

Levy, Sue, *Colls Mgr*, Independence Seaport Museum, Philadelphia PA

Levy, Tracey, *Opers Mgr Gallery Shop*, The Buffalo Fine Arts Academy, Albright-Knox Art Gallery, Buffalo NY

Lew, Karen, *Dir Educ*, Museum of Chinese in America, New York NY

Lewandowicz, Galina, *Head Library & Archives*, Cincinnati Art Museum, Cincinnati Art Museum, Cincinnati OH

Lewandowicz, Galina, *Head Librn*, Cincinnati Art Museum, Mary R Schiff Library & Archives, Cincinnati OH

Lewang, Debbi, *Controller*, Seattle Art Museum, Dorothy Stimson Bullitt Library, Seattle WA

Lewars, James, *Dir*, Landis Valley Village and Farm Museum, PA Historical & Museum Commission, Landis Collections Gallery, Lancaster PA

Lewellyn, Michaela, *Prog Mgr*, Kentuck Museum Association, Inc., Kentuck Art Center & Festival of the Arts, Northport AL

Lewin, Jackie, *Cur History*, Saint Joseph Museum, Saint Joseph MO

Lewin, Rod, *Pres*, Fitchburg Art Museum, Fitchburg MA

Lewin, Sarah, *Dir Develop*, The Adirondack Historical Association, The Adirondack Museum, Blue Mountain Lake NY

Lewis, Andrea, *Exec Dir*, The Dairy Barn Arts Center, Athens OH

Lewis, Anissa, *Dir Educ*, Perkins Center for the Arts, Moorestown NJ

Lewis, Ann-Eliza, *Exec Dir*, Columbia County Historical Society, Columbia County Museum and Library, Kinderhook NY

Lewis, Ann-Eliza, *Exec Dir*, Columbia County Historical Society, Luykas Van Alen House, Kinderhook NY

Lewis, Audrey, *Assoc Cur*, Brandywine Conservancy, Brandywine River Museum, Chadds Ford PA

Lewis, Barbara, *Prof*, James Madison University, School of Art & Art History, Harrisonburg VA (S)

Lewis, C Stanley, *Prof*, American University, Dept of Art, New York NY (S)

Lewis, Carolyn, *Instr*, Cuyahoga Valley Art Center, Cuyahoga Falls OH (S)

Lewis, Cathleen, *VPres Educ*, Museum of Arts & Design, New York NY

Lewis, Chris, *Media Librn,* American University, Jack I & Dorothy G Bender Library & Learning Resources Center, New York NY

Lewis, Cindi, *Treas,* Gallery West Ltd, Alexandria VA

Lewis, Cynthia, *Asst Prof Art History,* Rio Hondo College, Visual Arts Dept, Whittier CA (S)

Lewis, David, *Cur,* Aurora Regional Fire Museum, Aurora IL

Lewis, David, *Chair,* Hampden-Sydney College, Fine Arts Dept, Hampden Sydney VA (S)

Lewis, Diane, *Pub Rels,* University of Connecticut, William Benton Museum of Art, Storrs CT

Lewis, Dorothy H (Dee Dee), *Budget Admin & Asst to Deputy Dir,* Williams College, Museum of Art, Williamstown MA

Lewis, Eileen, *Gift Shop Mgr,* Ships of the Sea Maritime Museum, Savannah GA

Lewis, Elma, *Artistic Dir,* Museum of the National Center of Afro-American Artists, Boston MA

Lewis, Frank, *Cur & Dir,* Lawrence University, Wriston Art Center Galleries, Appleton WI

Lewis, Glen, *Prof,* North Carolina State University at Raleigh, School of Design, Raleigh NC (S)

Lewis, Hal M, *Pres & CEO,* Spertus Institute of Jewish Studies, Chicago IL

Lewis, Jack R, *Art Coordr,* Georgia Southwestern State University, Art Gallery, Americus GA

Lewis, Janice, *Chmn Fashion Design,* Moore College of Art & Design, Philadelphia PA (S)

Lewis, Jerry, *Chmn Dept,* Joliet Junior College, Fine Arts Dept, Joliet IL (S)

Lewis, Joe, *Dept Chmn,* California State University, Northridge, Dept of Art, Northridge CA (S)

Lewis, Joseph S, *Dir,* University of California, Irvine, Beall Center for Art + Technology, and University Art Gallery, Irvine CA

Lewis, Lara, *Dirk Mktg & Pub Relations,* Montgomery Museum of Fine Arts, Library, Montgomery AL

Lewis, Lara, *Dir Mktg & Pub Rels,* Montgomery Museum of Fine Arts, Montgomery AL

Lewis, Lawrence R, *Opers Mgr,* Center for Photography at Woodstock Inc, Woodstock NY

Lewis, Leslie, *Asst Prof,* South Plains College, Fine Arts Dept, Levelland TX (S)

Lewis, Lynn, *Gallery Coordr,* Florida State College at Jacksonville, South Gallery, Jacksonville FL

Lewis, Mary, *Dir Develop,* Cultural Council of Palm Beach County, Lake Worth FL

Lewis, Michael H, *Prof,* University of Maine, Dept of Art, Orono ME (S)

Lewis, Morgan, *Arts Adminr,* Florida Department of State, Division of Cultural Affairs, Florida Council on Arts & Culture, Tallahassee FL

Lewis, Naomi, *Outreach Coordr,* University at Albany, State University of New York, University Art Museum, Albany NY

Lewis, Richard, *Prof,* Salem State University, Art & Design Department, Salem MA (S)

Lewis, Russell, *Deputy Dir Research,* Chicago History Museum, Chicago IL

Lewis, Ryan, *Graphic Design,* Western Michigan University, Frostic School of Art, Kalamazoo MI (S)

Lewis, Samella, *Founder,* Museum of African American Art, Los Angeles CA

Lewis, Steve, *Head,* Allan Hancock College, Fine Arts Dept, Santa Maria CA (S)

Lewis, Steve, *VPres,* Michelson Museum of Art, Marshall TX

Lewis, Susan, *Chief Librn,* Boston Architectural College, Library, Boston MA

Lewiston, Cal, *Head Speech & Fine Arts,* Weatherford College, Dept of Speech Fine Arts, Weatherford TX (S)

Lewitin, Margot, *Artistic Dir,* Women's Interart Center, Inc, Interart Gallery, New York NY

Lewthwaite, Barbara-Jayne, *Pres,* Centenary College, Humanities Dept, Hackettstown NJ (S)

Leys, Dale, *Prof,* Murray State University, Dept of Art, Murray KY (S)

Leyva, Karla, *Gallery Educator II,* California African-American Museum, Los Angeles CA

Leyva, Maria, *Cur,* Art Museum of the Americas, Archive of Contemporary Latin American Art, Washington DC

Leyva, Maria, *Cur Reference Center,* Art Museum of the Americas, Washington DC

L'Heureux, Stephanie, *Dir,* Conseil des Arts du Quebec (CATQ), Diagonale, Centre des arts et des fibres du Quebec, Montreal PQ

Li, Chu-tsing, *Prof Emeritus,* University of Kansas, Kress Foundation Dept of Art History, Lawrence KS (S)

Li, Dougfeng, *Asst Prof,* Morehead State University, Art & Design Dept, Morehead KY (S)

Li, Yu, *Librn,* The University of Texas at San Antonio, Institute of Texan Cultures, San Antonio TX

Liao, James S J, *VP Fin & Admin,* Municipal Art Society of New York, New York NY

Liao, Jing, *Asst Librn,* University of Illinois at Urbana-Champaign, Ricker Library of Architecture & Art, Champaign IL

Libbey, Lizabeth, *Prof,* University of Maine at Augusta, College of Arts & Humanities, Augusta ME (S)

Libby, Eileen, *VPres,* California Watercolor Association, Gallery Concord, Concord CA

Liberman, Jack, *Instr,* Cuyahoga Valley Art Center, Cuyahoga Falls OH (S)

Libke, Audrey, *Receptionist,* Michigan Guild of Artists & Artisans, Michigan Guild Gallery, Ann Arbor MI

Licata, Chris, *Assoc Prof,* Saint Louis Community College at Florissant Valley, Liberal Arts Division, Ferguson MO (S)

Lichtendorf, Victoria, *Dir Edu & Pub Progs,* Storm King Art Center, Mountainville NY

Lichtenfeld, Danny, *Dir,* Brattleboro Museum & Art Center, Brattleboro VT

Licka, Sean, *Chmn,* University of Alaska Anchorage, Dept of Art, Anchorage AK (S)

Liddell, Ana Marie, *Exhibs Coordr,* University of Virginia, The Fralin Museum of Art at the University of Virginia, Charlottesville VA

Liddle, Donna Eastman, *Second VPres,* Arizona Watercolor Association, Phoenix AZ

Liddle, Matt, *Asst Prof,* Western Carolina University, Dept of Art/College of Arts & Science, Cullowhee NC (S)

Liddy, Tim, *Assoc Prof,* Fontbonne University, Fine Art Dept, Saint Louis MO (S)

Lie, Henry, *Dir Straus Center Conservation,* Harvard University, Harvard University Art Museums, Cambridge MA

Lieberman, Andi, *Instr,* Wayne Art Center, Wayne PA (S)

Lieberman, Arlene, *Chmn Board of Trustees,* Newark Museum Association, The Newark Museum, Newark NJ

Lieberman, William S, *Jacques & Natasha,* The Metropolitan Museum of Art, New York NY

Lieber Mays, Jane, *Adjunct,* Chemeketa Community College, Dept of Humanities & Communications, Art Program, Salem OR (S)

Liebler, Michele, *Mem Dir,* First Street Gallery, New York NY

Liebling, Alex, *Pres,* Harrison County Historical Museum, Marshall TX

Liebman, Stuart, *Prof Emeritus,* City University of New York, PhD Program in Art History, New York NY (S)

Liebowitz, Rachel, *Asst Cur,* The Drawing Center, New York NY

Lien, Fu-Chia-Wen, *Asst Prof,* Lamar University, Art Dept, Beaumont TX (S)

Lien, Kim, *VPres,* Dacotah Prairie Museum, Lamont Art Gallery, Aberdeen SD

Lien, Krist, *Head Dept,* Pensacola State College, Visual Arts Dept, Pensacola FL (S)

Lietch, Jennifer, *Develop Coordr,* University of California, Los Angeles, Fowler Museum at UCLA, Los Angeles CA

Liford, Melissa, *Instr Visual Arts Educ,* Madonna University, College of Arts & Humanities, Livonia MI (S)

Ligan, Eric, *Assoc Dean & Distinguished Teaching Prof,* University of North Texas, College of Visual Arts & Design, Denton TX (S)

Light, Flash, *IT Dir,* Artists Talk on Art, New York NY

Light, Rolland, *Pres & Chmn Mgmt Comt,* Iroquois County Historical Society Museum, Old Courthouse Museum, Watseka IL

Lightfoot, Thomas, *Asst Prof,* Rochester Institute of Technology, School of Design, Rochester NY (S)

Lightfoot, Tulla, *Prof & Coordr Undergrad Art Educ,* University of North Carolina at Pembroke, Art Dept, Pembroke NC (S)

Lightner, Karen, *Head,* Free Library of Philadelphia, Print & Picture Collection, Philadelphia PA

Lightner, Karen, *Head Librn Art, Dept,* Free Library of Philadelphia, Art Dept, Philadelphia PA

Ligo, Larry L, *Prof,* Davidson College, Art Dept, Davidson NC (S)

Ligon, Eric, *Assoc Dean,* University of North Texas, College of Visual Arts & Design, Denton TX (S)

Lillehoj, Elizabeth, *Assoc Prof,* DePaul University, Dept of Art, Chicago IL (S)

Lillich, Meredith, *Prof,* Syracuse University, Dept of Fine Arts (Art History), Syracuse NY (S)

Lilly, Tina, *Interim Dir,* Morgan County Foundation, Inc, Madison-Morgan Cultural Center, Madison GA

Lily, Jane, *Asst Prof Interior Design,* University of Georgia, Franklin College of Arts & Sciences, Lamar Dodd School of Art, Athens GA (S)

Lilyard-Mitchell, Corinne, *Asst Prof,* Tidewater Community College, Visual Arts Center, Portsmouth VA (S)

Lim, Eun-Hee, *Prof,* University of North Carolina at Greensboro, Art Dept, Greensboro NC (S)

Lima, Benjamin, *Asst Prof,* University of Texas at Arlington, Art & Art History Department, Arlington TX (S)

Lima, Jennifer, *Gallery Registrar & Mgr,* China Institute in America, China Institute Gallery, New York NY

Lima-Coelho, Ken, *VPres Develop,* Glenbow Museum, Calgary AB

Limbaugh, Stephen N, *Vol Pres,* State Historical Society of Missouri, Columbia MO

Limoges, Justin, *Chief Preparator,* California College of the Arts, CCAC Wattis Institute for Contemporary Arts, San Francisco CA

Limouze, Dorothy, *Assoc Prof,* St Lawrence University, Dept of Fine Arts, Canton NY (S)

Lin, Cynthia, *Asst Prof,* Southern Methodist University, Division of Art, Dallas TX (S)

Lin, Cynthia, *Vis Assoc Prof,* Purchase College, State University of New York, School of Art+Design, Purchase NY (S)

Lin, Jasper, *Graphics Lab,* Fashion Institute of Technology, Gladys Marcus Library - SUNY, New York NY

Linabury, Sandy, *Vol Coordr,* Kalamazoo Institute of Arts, Kalamazoo MI

Lincoln, Justin, *Asst Prof Art,* Whitman College, Art Dept, Walla Walla WA (S)

Lind, C J, *Pub Rel & Mktg Mgr,* University of Chicago, Smart Museum of Art, Chicago IL

Lind, Ed, *Interim Dir & Assoc,* Brigham Young University, Museum of Art, Provo UT

Lind, Frank, *Dean,* Pratt Institute, School of Art & Design, Brooklyn NY (S)

Lind, Maggie, *Assoc Educator Acad Progs,* Smith College, Museum of Art, Northampton MA

Lind, Maria, *Dir,* Bard College, Center for Curatorial Studies Graduate Program, Annandale-on-Hudson NY (S)

Lindale, Paul, *Dept Chair,* Greenfield Community College, Art Dept, Greenfield MA (S)

Lindall, Terrance, *Pres & Exec Dir,* Williamsburg Art & Historical Center, Brooklyn NY

Lindblad, Karen, *First VPres,* Swedish American Museum Association of Chicago, Chicago IL

Lindblade, Michael, *Registrar,* McPherson Museum and Arts Foundation, McPherson KS

Lindblom, Michelle, *Instr,* Bismarck State College, Fine Arts Dept, Bismarck ND (S)

Lindblom, Ronald Allan, *Chmn,* Point Park College, Performing Arts Dept, Pittsburgh PA (S)

Lindbloom, Terri, *Assoc Prof,* Florida State University, Art Dept, Tallahassee FL (S)

Lindell, Ann, *Architecture Fine Arts Bibliographer & Head Librn,* University of Florida, Architecture & Fine Arts Library, Gainesville FL

Lindeman, Leslie, *Dir Mktg,* Newport Historical Society & Museum of Newport History, Newport RI

Lindemann, J, *Assoc Prof,* Lawrence University, Dept of Art & Art History, Appleton WI (S)

Linden, Elizabeth, *Proj Mgr,* Public Art Fund, Inc, New York NY

Linden, Elizabeth, *Project Mgr,* Public Art Fund, Inc, Visual Archive, New York NY

Lindenberger, Beth, *Instr,* Cuyahoga Valley Art Center, Cuyahoga Falls OH (S)

Lindenheim, Diane, *Instr,* Bucks County Community College, Fine Arts Dept, Newtown PA (S)

Linder, Erin, *Exhib Coordr,* Kimball Art Center, Park City UT

Linder, Joan, *Asst Prof,* University at Buffalo, State University of New York, Dept of Visual Studies, Buffalo NY (S)

Linder, Timothy, *Prof,* Saint Louis Community College at Meramec, Art Dept, Saint Louis MO (S)

Lindland, Pauline, *Art Cur,* Petro-Canada, Corporate Art Programme, Calgary AB

Lindner, Harry, *Instr,* Northeast Community College, Dept of Liberal Arts, Norfolk NE (S)

Lindner, Stacie, *Mng Dir,* Atlanta Contemporary Art Center, Atlanta GA

Lindo, Angela, *Foundations Government Relations Mgr,* University of Washington, Henry Art Gallery, Seattle WA

Lindou, Angela, *Foundation & Corp Giving Mgr,* Henry Gallery Association, Henry Art Gallery, Seattle WA

Lindquist, Evan, *Prof,* Arkansas State University, Dept of Art, State University AR (S)

Lindsay, Betsy, *Instr,* Pacific Northwest College of Art, Portland OR (S)

Lindsay, Mark, *Pres,* Essex Historical Society and Shipbuilding Museum, Essex MA

Lindsay, Opal, *Acting Dir,* Mount Vernon Public Library, Fine Art Dept, Mount Vernon NY

Lindsey, Anne, *Prof,* University of Tennessee at Chattanooga, Dept of Art, Chattanooga TN (S)

Lindsey, George, *Dir Finance & Opers,* University of Utah, Utah Museum of Fine Arts, Salt Lake City UT

Lindsey, Jack, *Cur American Decorative Arts,* Philadelphia Museum of Art, Mount Pleasant, Philadelphia PA

Lindsey, Jeremy, *Instr,* Judson University, School of Art, Design & Architecture, Elgin IL (S)

Lindsey, Sheila, *Dir Bus Oper,* Port Huron Museum, Port Huron MI

Lindstrom, Eric, *Dean Educ,* Art Institutes International at Portland, Portland OR

Lindstrom, Janet, *Exec Dir,* New Canaan Historical Society, New Canaan CT

Lineberry, Heather, *Sr Cur,* Arizona State University, ASU Art Museum, Tempe AZ

Linehan, Chaitra, *Adj Asst Prof,* University of Texas at Arlington, Art & Art History Department, Arlington TX (S)

Linehan, James, *Prof,* University of Maine, Dept of Art, Orono ME (S)

Linehan, Karen, *Adjunct Asst Prof,* University of Maine, Dept of Art, Orono ME (S)

Linehan, Monika, *Asst Prof,* Cameron University, Art Dept, Lawton OK (S)

Linehan, Thomas E, *Pres,* Ringling School of Art & Design, Sarasota FL (S)

Lines, Barbara, *Instr,* West Texas A&M University, Art, Theatre & Dance Dept, Canyon TX (S)

Linforth, Jennifer, *Educator,* Wendell Gilley, Southwest Harbor ME

Lingen, Joan, *Chmn & Prof Art,* Clarke College, Dept of Art, Dubuque IA (S)

Lingenfelter, Jessica, *Gallery Coordr,* Crowder College, Longwell Museum/Art Department, Neosho MO (S)

Lingner, Richard, *Librn & Asst Cur,* Isabella Stewart Gardner, Isabella Stewart Garden Museum Library & Archives, Boston MA

Link, Emily, *Community Relations Coordr,* Lawndale Art Center, Houston TX

Link, Michael, *VPres,* Halifax Historical Society, Inc, Halifax Historical Museum, Daytona Beach FL

Link, Sarah, *Instr,* Lakehead University, Dept of Visual Arts, Thunder Bay ON (S)

Linker, Wayne, *Exec VPres,* American Academy in Rome, New York NY (S)

Linn, Patti, *CEO & Dir,* Riverside, the Farnsley-Moremen Landing, Louisville KY

Linnehan, Genevieve, *Institutional Advancement Assoc,* Guild Hall of East Hampton, Inc, Guild Hall Museum, East Hampton NY

Linnell, Eric, *Pres,* Parson Fisher House, Jonathan Fisher Memorial, Inc, Blue Hill ME

Linnell, Sandra, *Adminr,* Parson Fisher House, Jonathan Fisher Memorial, Inc, Blue Hill ME

Linnenberg, David, *Dir Develop,* Cincinnati Art Museum, Cincinnati Art Museum, Cincinnati OH

Linskey-Deegan, Mara, *Assoc Cur & Registrar,* City of Mason City, Charles H MacNider Museum, Mason City IA

Linsky, Carol, *Exec Dir,* Rockport Art Association, Rockport MA

Linster, Debbie, *CFO,* Colorado Springs Fine Arts Center, Taylor Museum, Colorado Springs CO

Linsz Ross, Judith, *Dir Mktg & Vis Svcs,* Westmoreland Museum of American Art, Greensburg PA

Lint, Suzanne, *Exec Dir,* Allied Arts Council of Lethbridge, Bowman Arts Center, Lethbridge AB

Linton, Henri, *Dept Chmn,* University of Arkansas at Pine Bluff, Art Dept, Pine Bluff AR (S)

Linton, Meg, *Dir Galleries & Exhibs,* Otis College of Art & Design, Ben Maltz Gallery, Los Angeles CA

Linz Ross, Judy, *Dir Mktg & Pub Rels,* Westmoreland Museum of American Art, Art Reference Library, Greensburg PA

Liokatis, Ariadni A, *Cur,* University of Southern California, USC Fisher Museum of Art, Los Angeles CA

Liontas-Warren, Kathy, *Assoc Prof,* Cameron University, Art Dept, Lawton OK (S)

Lipfert, Nathan, *Dir Library,* Maine Maritime Museum, Bath ME

Lipfert, Nathan, *Senior Cur,* Maine Maritime Museum, Archives Library, Bath ME

Lipinski, Lisa, *Interim Chair, Arts & Humanities,* Corcoran School of Art, Washington DC (S)

Lipinski, Marlene, *Coordr Graphics,* Columbia College, Art Dept, Chicago IL (S)

Lipp, Frederick, *Prof,* Rochester Institute of Technology, School of Design, Rochester NY (S)

Lippincott, Bertram, *Librn,* Newport Historical Society & Museum of Newport History, Library, Newport RI

Lippincott, Louise W, *Cur Fine Art,* Carnegie Museums of Pittsburgh, Carnegie Museum of Art, Pittsburgh PA

Lippincott III, Bert, *Reference Librn & Genealogist,* Newport Historical Society & Museum of Newport History, Newport RI

Lippman, Irvin, *Exec Dir & Pres,* Museum of Art, Fort Lauderdale, Fort Lauderdale FL

Lippman, Judith, *Dir,* Meredith Gallery, Baltimore MD

Lippman, Paula, *Representative,* Art Without Walls Inc, New York NY

Lippman, Sharon, *Exec Dir,* Art Without Walls Inc, New York NY

Lipschutz, Jeff, *Prof,* University of Wisconsin Oshkosh, Dept of Art, Oshkosh WI (S)

Lipscomb, Diane, *Chmn,* Feather River Community College, Art Dept, Quincy CA (S)

Lipsey, Ellen, *Secy,* Culberson County Historical Museum, Van Horn TX

Lipsky, Patricia, *Assoc Prof,* University of Hartford, Hartford Art School, West Hartford CT (S)

Liput, Peg, *Dir Finance & Admin,* University of Chicago, Smart Museum of Art, Chicago IL

Lipzin, Janice, *Dir Visual Art & Educ,* Arts Quest, Bethlehem PA

Lisak, Pamela A, *Interior Design,* Art Institute of Pittsburgh, Pittsburgh PA (S)

Liscomb, Kathlyn, *Assoc Prof,* University of Victoria, Dept of History in Art, Victoria BC (S)

Liscomb, Trish, *Admin Asst,* Oklahoma Historical Society, State Museum of History, Oklahoma City OK

Lisi, Peter, *Dir External Affairs,* Connecticut Historical Society, Hartford CT

Lisiecki, Denise, *Dir KIA School,* Kalamazoo Institute of Arts, KIA School, Kalamazoo MI (S)

Lisiecki, Denise, *School Dir,* Kalamazoo Institute of Arts, Kalamazoo MI

Lisiecki, Denise, *Dir of School,* Kalamazoo Institute of Arts, The Mary & Edwin Meader Fine Arts Library, Kalamazoo MI

Lisk, Susan J, *Exec Dir,* Porter-Phelps-Huntington Foundation, Inc, Historic House Museum, Hadley MA

Liss, David, *Artistic Dir & Cur,* Museum of Contemporary Canadian Art, Toronto ON

Liss, Kay, *Gallery Mgr,* Lincoln County Historical Association, Inc, Maine Art Gallery, Wiscasset ME

Liss, Laurence A, *Pres,* Wharton Esherick, Paoli PA

Lissoway, Brenna, *Archivist,* Yosemite Museum, Research Library, Yosemite National Park CA

List, Kara, *Reference Librn,* University of Oregon, Architecture & Allied Arts Library, Eugene OR

List, Kathleen, *Dir Library,* Ringling College of Art & Design, Verman Kimbrough Memorial Library, Sarasota FL

Lister, Ardele, *Assoc Prof,* Rutgers, The State University of New Jersey, Mason Gross School of the Arts, Visual Arts Dept, New Brunswick NJ (S)

Listor, Jane, *VPres,* Marin Society of Artists Inc, Ross CA

Litch, Debbie, *Dir Develop,* Memphis Brooks Museum of Art, Memphis TN

Litchfield, Jennifer, *Pres,* Boothbay Region Art Foundation, Boothbay Harbor ME

Litow, Joseph, *Asst Prof Arts & Communs,* Orange County Community College, Arts & Communication, Middletown NY (S)

Littell, David, *Instr,* Saginaw Valley State University, Dept of Art & Design, University Center MI (S)

Little, Adriane, *Photo/Intermedia,* Western Michigan University, Frostic School of Art, Kalamazoo MI (S)

Little, Bruce, *Assoc Prof,* Georgia Southern University, Dept of Art, Statesboro GA (S)

Little, Christine, *Library & Archives Asst,* New Brunswick Museum, Archives & Research Library, Saint John NB

Little, Cynthia, *Historian, Dir Interpretive Programming,* Philadelphia History Museum, Philadelphia PA

Little, David, *Cur Photography & New Media,* Minneapolis Institute of Arts, Minneapolis MN

Little, David, *Dir Educ,* Whitney Museum of American Art, New York NY

Little, Ken, *Prof,* University of Texas at San Antonio, Dept of Art & Art History, San Antonio TX (S)

Little, Mark A, *Proj Dir,* Atlatl, Phoenix AZ

Little, Melanie, *Show Dir,* American Craft Council, Minneapolis MN

Little, Nancy, *School Dir,* National Academy Museum & School, Archives, New York NY

Little, Paula, *Co-Dir,* Arthur Roy Mitchell, A.R. Mitchell Museum, Trinidad CO

Little, Polly, *Dir Develop,* Hallwalls Contemporary Arts Center, Buffalo NY

Little, Tess, *Prof Reach Coordr,* Sinclair Community College, Division of Fine & Performing Arts, Dayton OH (S)

Littlefield, Robert, *Adj Instr,* Quincy College, Art Dept, Quincy MA (S)

Littleton, Harvey K, *Dir,* Maurine Littleton Gallery, Washington DC

Littman, Brett, *Exec Dir,* The Drawing Center, New York NY

Littman, Mara, *Dir Mktg & Pub Rels,* Cambridge Arts Council, CAC Gallery, Cambridge MA

Litts, Doug, *Acting Head Librn,* National Portrait Gallery, Library, Washington DC

Litts, Doug, *Librn,* American Art Museum, Library of the Smithsonian American Art Museum & National Portrait Gallery, Washington DC

Litts, Niki, *Dir Educ & Exhibs,* Community Council for the Arts, Kinston NC

Litwinsky, Robin, *Chmn Fashion Merchandising Mgmt,* Fashion Institute of Technology, Art & Design Division, New York NY (S)

Litzer, Doris, *Chmn,* Linn Benton Community College, Fine & Applied Art Dept, Albany OR (S)

Liu, An Te, *Dir Master of Archit,* University of Toronto, Faculty of Architecture, Landscape & Design, Toronto ON (S)

Liu, Cary, *Cur Asian Art,* Princeton University, Princeton University Art Museum, Princeton NJ

Liu, Frank, *Dir Tech,* Museum of Chinese in America, New York NY

Liu, Heping, *Asst Prof,* Wellesley College, Art Dept, Wellesley MA (S)

Liu, Hung, *Prof,* Mills College, Art Dept, Oakland CA (S)

Longman, Jenanne, *Office Adminr,* Fusion: The Ontario Clay & Glass Association, Fusion Clay & Glass Association, Toronto ON

Longo, Julie, *Chmn Liberal Arts,* College for Creative Studies, Detroit MI (S)

Longon, Jennifer, *Library & Archives Asst,* New Brunswick Museum, Archives & Research Library, Saint John NB

Longshore, Jennifer, *Instr,* Southern Oregon University, Art & Art History Dept, Ashland OR (S)

Longwell, Alicia, *Lewis B & Dorothy Cullman Chief Cur Art & Educ,* Parrish Art Museum, Water Mill NY

Longwell, David, *Preparator,* Tucson Museum of Art and Historic Block, Tucson AZ

Lonnberg, Tom, *Cur History,* Evansville Museum of Arts, History & Science, Evansville IN

Loomer, Dennis, *Dir Finance,* Kentucky Derby Museum, Louisville KY

Loomis, Judith, *Pres,* Allied Arts Association, Allied Arts Center & Gallery, Richland WA

Loomis, Rosemary, *Reference Librn,* Jones Library, Inc, Amherst MA

Loomis, Ryan, *Cur & CEO,* North Country Museum of Arts, Park Rapids MN

Loomis, Tom, *Assoc Prof,* Mansfield University, Art Dept, Mansfield PA (S)

Looney, Mary Beth, *Studio Arts Prog Dir,* Brenau University, Art & Design Dept, Gainesville GA (S)

Loonsk, Susan, *Assoc Prof,* University of Wisconsin-Superior, Programs in the Visual Arts, Superior WI (S)

Looper, Matt, *Prof,* California State University, Chico, Department of Art & Art History, Chico CA (S)

Loos, Jen, *Dir Opers,* Washington Pavilion of Arts & Science, Visual Arts Center, Sioux Falls SD

Lopes, Dominic Melver, *VPres,* American Society for Aesthetics, Pooler GA

Lopez, Alex, *Asst Prof,* Southern Illinois University, School of Art & Design, Carbondale IL (S)

Lopez, Ana, *Assoc Prof Metals,* University of North Texas, College of Visual Arts & Design, Denton TX (S)

Lopez, Donald, *Deputy Dir,* National Air and Space Museum, Smithsonian Institution, Washington DC

Lopez, Frank, *Librn,* Palm Springs Art Museum, Palm Springs CA

Lopez, J Tomas, *Prof,* University of Miami, Dept of Art & Art History, Coral Gables FL (S)

Lopez, John, *Bd Dir,* Grand River Museum, Lemmon SD

Lopez, Juan C, *Cur,* Museo de Arte de Puerto Rico, San Juan PR

Lopez, Juan C, *Cur,* Museo de Arte de Puerto Rico, San Juan PR

Lopez, Mario Gee, *Treas,* Latino Art Museum, Pomona CA

Lopez, Ramon, *Prof,* University of Puerto Rico, Mayaguez, Dept of Humanities, College of Fine Arts & Theory of Art Programs, Mayaguez PR (S)

Lopez, Ramon, *Prof,* University of Puerto Rico, Mayaguez, Dept of Humanities, College of Fine Arts & Theory of Art Programs, Mayaguez PR (S)

Lopez, Robert A, *Asst Prof,* Southern Illinois University, School of Art & Design, Carbondale IL (S)

Lopez, Teresa, *Acting Dean Acad/Study Affairs,* Escuela de Artes Plasticas de Puerto Rico, San Juan PR (S)

Lopez, Teresa, *Acting Dean Acad/Study Affairs,* Escuela de Artes Plasticas de Puerto Rico, San Juan PR (S)

Lopez, Teresa, *CFO,* College Art Association, New York NY

Lopez, Tom, *Asst Prof,* Rochester Institute of Technology, School of Photographic Arts & Sciences, Rochester NY (S)

Lopez, Jr., Albert, *Opers Dir,* Orange County Museum of Art, Newport Beach CA

Lopez-Isnardi, C Sandy, *Asst Prof,* Alma College, Clack Art Center, Dept of Art & Design, Alma MI (S)

Lorance, Jane, *Branch Adminr,* Las Vegas-Clark County Library District, Las Vegas NV

Lorance, Leslie, *New Media Mgr,* Indiana State Museum, Indianapolis IN

Lord, Allyn, *Dir,* City of Springdale, Shiloh Museum of Ozark History, Springdale AR

Lord, Catherine, *Prof Critical Theory, Feminism, Photog,* University of California, Irvine, Studio Art Dept, Irvine CA (S)

Lord, Evelyn, *Catalog & Systems Librn,* Laney College Library, Art Section, Oakland CA

Lord, Keith, *Asst Prof Art,* University of La Verne, Dept of Art, La Verne CA (S)

Lord, Richard, *Vol Treas,* Macartney House Museum, Oakland ME

Lord, Shelley, *Dir,* Cando Arts Center, Cando ND

Lord, Sue, *Office Mgr,* Prescott Fine Arts Association, Gallery, Prescott AZ

Lordi, Michael, *Assoc Dir Librn,* California College of the Arts, Libraries, Oakland CA

Lorence, Marian, *Adjunct,* York College of Pennsylvania, Dept of Music, Art & Speech Communications, York PA (S)

Lorenson, Rob, *Assoc Prof,* Bridgewater State College, Art Dept, Bridgewater MA (S)

Lorenz, Elaine, *Asst Prof,* William Paterson University, Dept Art, Wayne NJ (S)

Lorenz, Hilary, *Prof,* Long Island University, Brooklyn Campus, Art Dept, Brooklyn NY (S)

Lorenz, Kate, *Exec Dir,* Hyde Park Art Center, Chicago IL

Lorenz, Marianne, *Exec Dir,* Fort Collins Museum of Art, Inc., Fort Collins CO

Lorenz, Michael, *Prof,* Saint Louis Community College at Meramec, Art Dept, Saint Louis MO (S)

Loret, Avril, *Sr Project Officer,* Visual Arts Ontario, Toronto ON

Loria, Mark, *Mgr Pub Affairs & Dir Develop,* Art Gallery of Greater Victoria, Victoria BC

Lorigan, Jim, *Chair,* College of the Canyons, Art Dept, Santa Clarita CA (S)

Lorimer, Cal, *Office Admin,* Women's Art Association of Canada, Dignam Gallery, Toronto ON

Loring, Karla, *Dir Pub Rels,* Museum of Contemporary Art, Chicago IL

Lorini, Frederick, *Gen Educ,* Art Institute of Pittsburgh, Pittsburgh PA (S)

Lorren, Margaret N, *VPres,* Pensacola Museum of Art, Harry Thornton Library, Pensacola FL

Lorys, Jan M, *Dir,* Polish Museum of America, Chicago IL

Lorys, Jan M, *Dir,* Polish Museum of America, Research Library, Chicago IL

Losavio, Sam, *Asst Dir,* Louisiana Arts & Science Museum, Baton Rouge LA

Losavio, Sam, *Asst Dir,* Louisiana Arts & Science Museum, Library, Baton Rouge LA

Losch, Michael, *Assoc Prof,* Western Maryland College, Dept of Art & Art History, Westminster MD (S)

Losch, Michael, *Dir,* McDaniel College, Esther Prangley Rice Gallery, Westminster MD

LoSchiavo, Joseph A, *Exec Dir,* Saint Bonaventure University, Regina A Quick Center for the Arts, Saint Bonaventure NY

Loscuito, John, *Registrar,* Marquette University, Haggerty Museum of Art, Milwaukee WI

Losinski, Patrick, *CEO,* Columbus Metropolitan Library, Arts & Media Division Carnegie Gallery, Columbus OH

Lossmann, Robert, *Painting & Watercolor,* College of Lake County, Art Dept, Grayslake IL (S)

Lothamer, Mary Ellen, *VPres Fin,* Watkins College of Art, Design & Film, Brownlee O Currey Gallery, Nashville TN

Loto, Judith, *Cur,* Litchfield History Museum, Litchfield CT

Lott, Linda, *Rare Book Librn,* Harvard University, Dumbarton Oaks Research Library, Washington DC

Lott, Robin, *Dir Retail & Vis Servs,* Genesee Country Village & Museum, John L Wehle Art Gallery, Mumford NY

Lotz, Stacy, *Dept Chair & Assoc Prof Art,* Monmouth College, Dept of Art, Monmouth IL (S)

Lou, Julie, *Dir Fin,* The Queens Museum of Art, Flushing NY

Lou, Nils, *Prof,* Linfield College, Department of Art & Visual Culture, McMinnville OR (S)

Lou, Richard, *Chmn,* San Diego Mesa College, Fine Arts Dept, San Diego CA (S)

Louckes, Theresa, *Mktg Coordr,* Cultural Council of Palm Beach County, Lake Worth FL

Loud, Patricia Cummings, *Cur Emer Architecture/Archivist,* Kimbell Art Foundation, Kimbell Art Museum, Fort Worth TX

Louden, William F, *Librn,* University of Evansville, University Library, Evansville IN

Loudenback, Brad, *Asst Prof,* Webster University, Art Dept, Webster Groves MO (S)

Louder, John, *Prof,* Central Missouri State University, Dept Art & Design, Warrensburg MO (S)

Loudermilk, Wanda, *Ex Dir,* Grand Prairie Arts Council, Inc, Arts Center of the Grand Prairie, Stuttgart AR

Loudon, Sarah, *Sr Mus Educator,* Seattle Art Museum, Dorothy Stimson Bullitt Library, Seattle WA

Loughlin, Deborah, *AAI/Outreach,* University of Southern Maine, Dept of Art, Gorham ME (S)

Loughridge, Martha, *Develop Dir,* SPACES, Cleveland OH

Loughridge, Sally, *Pres,* Pemaquid Group of Artists, Pemaquid Art Gallery, Pemaquid Point ME

Loughridge Bush, Sally, *Bd Pres,* Lincoln County Historical Association, Inc, Maine Art Gallery, Wiscasset ME

Louis, Alan, *Educ & Mus Progs Dir,* Center for Puppetry Arts, Atlanta GA

Louis, Elizabeth, *Gallery Coordr,* Florida Community College at Jacksonville, South Campus, Art Dept, Jacksonville FL (S)

Louisdhon-Lovinis, Lucrece, *Youth Svcs Adminr,* Miami-Dade Public Library, Miami FL

Lourdes Solomon, Maria, *Dir,* Montgomery County Guild of Professional Artists, Conshohocken PA

Lourse, Margaret, *Communs Ed,* University of Michigan, Kelsey Museum of Archaeology, Ann Arbor MI

Lousplain, Mary, *Coordr,* Middlebury College, History of Art & Architecture Dept, Middlebury VT (S)

Lovaglio Costello, Enrica, *Asst Prof Digital Media,* California Polytechnic State University at San Luis Obispo, Dept of Art & Design, San Luis Obispo CA (S)

Love, Angela, *Media Arts & Animation,* Art Institute of Pittsburgh, Pittsburgh PA (S)

Love, Camille, *Dir,* City of Atlanta, City Gallery East, Atlanta GA

Love, Ed, *Prof Emeritus,* Florida State University, Art Dept, Tallahassee FL (S)

Love, Georgina, *Exhib Coordr,* A.E. Backus Museum of Art, Fort Pierce FL

Love, Jeff, *Board Pres,* Art Museum of Greater Lafayette, Lafayette IN

Love, M Jordan, *Acad Cur,* University of Virginia, The Fralin Museum of Art at the University of Virginia, Charlottesville VA

Loveday, Amos, *Head Historic Preservation,* Ohio Historical Society, Columbus OH

Lovejoy, Barbara, *Registrar,* The Art Museum at the University of Kentucky, Lexington KY

Lovejoy, Claudine, *Admin Asst,* Museum of East Texas, Lufkin TX

Lovejoy, Margot, *Prof Emerita,* Purchase College, State University of New York, School of Art+Design, Purchase NY (S)

Lovelace, Joan, *Admin Opers Dir,* Rochester Art Center, Rochester MN

Loveless, Jim, *Prof,* Colgate University, Dept of Art & Art History, Hamilton NY (S)

Lovell, Carol, *Cur,* Stratford Historical Society, Catharine B Mitchell Museum, Stratford CT

Lovell, Carol W, *Cur,* Stratford Historical Society, Genealogical Library, Stratford CT

Lovell, Lorry, *Dir Mktg & Pub Rels,* Louisiana Department of Culture, Recreation & Tourism, Louisiana Historical Center Library, New Orleans LA

Loven, Del Rey, *Dept Head,* University of Akron, Myers School of Art, Akron OH (S)

Lovering-Brown, Theresa, *Jewelry & Metals Instr,* Monterey Peninsula College, Art Dept/Art Gallery, Monterey CA (S)

Lovett, Beverly, *Parks Specialist,* Red Rock Park, Red Rock Museum, Church Rock NM

Lovett, O Rufus, *Instr,* Kilgore College, Visual Arts Dept, Kilgore TX (S)

Loving, Charles R, *Dir & Cur,* University of Notre Dame, Snite Museum of Art, Notre Dame IN

Loving, Glenna, *Mus Shop Mgr*, Strasburg Museum, Strasburg VA

Lovingood, Melissa, *Instr*, North Iowa Area Community College, Dept of Art, Mason City IA (S)

Lovington, Nan, *Dir of Outreach*, California Watercolor Association, Gallery Concord, Concord CA

Low, Bill, *Cur Coll*, Bates College, Museum of Art, Lewiston ME

Low, Peter, *Assoc Prof, Chair*, Williams College, Dept of Art, Williamstown MA (S)

Lowe, Arline, *Asst Prof*, Seton Hall University, College of Arts & Sciences, South Orange NJ (S)

Lowe, Constance, *Prof*, University of Texas at San Antonio, Dept of Art & Art History, San Antonio TX (S)

Lowe, Damon, *Cur Biology*, Indiana State Museum, Indianapolis IN

Lowe, Karen, *Dir*, City of Atlanta, Chastain Arts Center & Gallery, Atlanta GA

Lowe, Matt, *Technical Svcs Mgr*, Bemis Center for Contemporary Arts, Omaha NE

Lowe, Nicholas, *Chmn Arts Admin*, School of the Art Institute of Chicago, Chicago IL (S)

Lowe, Patricia, *Librn*, Will Rogers Memorial Museum & Birthplace Ranch, Media Center Library, Claremore OK

Lowe, Phillip, *Coordr Fine Arts*, Hill College, Fine Arts Dept, Hillsboro TX (S)

Lowe, Ruth E, *Adminr*, Dauphin & District Allied Arts Council, Watson Art Centre, Dauphin MB

Lowe, Truman, *Emer Prof*, University of Wisconsin, Madison, Dept of Art, Madison WI (S)

Lowe-Stockwell, Susie, *Dir*, League of New Hampshire Craftsmen, Grodin Permanent Collection Museum, Concord NH

Lowe-Stockwell, Susie, *Dir*, League of New Hampshire Craftsmen, Kira Fournier Resource Library Center, Concord NH

Lowenberg, Susan, *Info Resources Librn*, California Institute of the Arts Library, Santa Clarita CA

Lowery, Liz, *Dept Chair*, Howard College, Art Dept, Big Spring TX (S)

Lowery, Stephen, *Prof*, Aurora University, Art Dept, Aurora IL (S)

Lowley, Scott, *Chmn*, Mars Hill College, Art Dept, Mars Hill NC (S)

Lowly, Tim, *Dir Gallery*, North Park University, Carlson Tower Gallery, Chicago IL

Lowrance, Melanie, *Instr*, Central Missouri State University, Dept Art & Design, Warrensburg MO (S)

Lowrance, Sandy, *Acting Chmn*, University of Memphis, Art Dept, Memphis TN (S)

Lowry, William, *Secy*, Chicago Children's Museum, Chicago IL

Lowy, Melinda, *Treas*, Surface Design Association, Inc, Sebastopol CA

Loy, Jessica, *Asst Prof*, College of Saint Rose, The Center For Art and Design, Albany NY (S)

Loye, David, *Chief Operating Officer*, Canadian Museum of Civilization, Gatineau PQ

Loyola, Walter, *Assoc Prof*, College of Mount Saint Joseph, Art Dept, Cincinnati OH (S)

Lozar, Carmen, *Dir*, Illinois Wesleyan University, Merwin & Wakeley Galleries, Bloomington IL

Lozito, Frank, *Security Officer*, Morris Museum of Art, Augusta GA

Luark, Carolyn, *Dept Chmn*, Bellevue Community College, Art Dept, Bellevue WA (S)

Lubar, Robert, *Dir Masters Studies*, New York University, Institute of Fine Arts, New York NY (S)

Lubensky, Gerald, *Prof*, University of Kansas, The School of the Arts, Dept of Visual Art, Lawrence KS (S)

Luber, Patrick, *Chmn*, University of North Dakota, Art Department, Grand Forks ND (S)

Lubin, David M, *Charlotte C Weber Prof Art*, Wake Forest University, Dept of Art, Winston-Salem NC (S)

Luca, Frank, *Head Librn*, The Wolfsonian-Florida International University, Miami Beach FL

Lucarelli, Vincent, *Instr*, Illinois Benedictine University, Department of Fine Arts, Lisle IL (S)

Lucas, Barb, *Dir Finance & Admin*, Art Gallery of Greater Victoria, Victoria BC

Lucas, Cindy, *Asst to Dir*, College of William & Mary, Muscarelle Museum of Art, Williamsburg VA

Lucas, June, *Dir Research*, Old Salem Museums & Gardens, Library and Research Center, Winston Salem NC

Lucas, June, *Librn & Cur Research Coll*, Old Salem Museums & Gardens, Museum of Early Southern Decorative Arts, Winston Salem NC

Lucas, Laura, *Patron Svcs Coordr*, Huguenot Historical Society of New Paltz Galleries, New Paltz NY

Lucas, Paula, *Instr*, West Liberty State College, Div Art, West Liberty WV (S)

Lucas, Thomas, *Dir & Cur*, The University of San Francisco Thacher Gallery, San Francisco CA

Lucchesi, Joe, *Asst Prof*, Saint Mary's College of Maryland, Art & Art History Dept, Saint Mary's City MD (S)

Luce, Donald T, *Cur Exhib*, University of Minnesota, The Bell Museum of Natural History, Minneapolis MN

Luce, Ken, *Instr*, San Jacinto College-North, Art Dept, Houston TX (S)

Luce, Lara, *Dir Develop*, Blue Star Contemporary Art Center, San Antonio TX

Lucenti, Lisa, *Bd Pres*, North Shore Art League, Winnetka IL

Lucere, Lisa, *Park Supt*, Red Rock Park, Library, Church Rock NM

Lucey, Susan, *Assoc Prof*, University of Minnesota, Minneapolis, Dept of Art, Minneapolis MN (S)

Luchans, Miriam, *Registrar*, Yosemite Museum, Research Library, Yosemite National Park CA

Lucic, Karen, *Prof*, Vassar College, Art Dept, Poughkeepsie NY (S)

Lucke, Susan, *Registrar*, University of California, Santa Barbara, University Art Museum, Santa Barbara CA

Lucker, Amy, *Head Librn*, New York University, Stephen Chan Library of Fine Arts, New York NY

Luckett, Sandra, *Asst Prof*, University of Central Arkansas, Department of Art, Conway AR (S)

Luderowski, Barbara, *Bd Mem, Co-Dir*, The Mattress Factory, Pittsburgh PA

Ludke, Amy, *Fin Assoc*, Tucson Museum of Art and Historic Block, Tucson AZ

Ludwig, Daniel, *Assoc Prof*, Salve Regina University, Art Dept, Newport RI (S)

Ludwig, Jeffrey, *Preparator*, Lehigh University Art Galleries, Museum Operation, Bethlehem PA

Ludwig, Justin, *Asst Cur*, Contemporary Arts Center, Cincinnati OH

Ludwig, Robert, *Adj Asst Prof*, College of Staten Island, Performing & Creative Arts Dept, Staten Island NY (S)

Lue, Joanne, *Admin Asst*, University at Albany, State University of New York, University Art Museum, Albany NY

Luebbers, Leslie L, *Dir*, University of Memphis, Art Museum, Memphis TN

Luecking, Stephen, *Chmn Dept*, DePaul University, Dept of Art, Chicago IL (S)

Luedtke, Julie, *VPres Exhibits*, DuPage Art League School & Gallery, Wheaton IL

Luehrman, Mick, *Chair Dept*, Central Missouri State University, Dept Art & Design, Warrensburg MO (S)

Luft, Alan, *Asst Prof*, Edgewood College, Art Dept, Madison WI (S)

Luginbuhl, Gregg, *Chair*, Bluffton University, Art Dept, Bluffton OH (S)

Lugo, Mark-Elliott, *Visual Arts Librn*, San Diego Public Library, Art, Music & Recreation, San Diego CA

Luhikhuizen, Henry, *Prof*, Calvin College, Art Dept, Grand Rapids MI (S)

Luhring, Lawrence, *Treas*, Art Dealers Association of America, Inc, New York NY

Lujan, Melisa, *Registrar*, El Museo del Barrio, New York NY

Lujan, Vernon, *Dir*, Pueblo of Pojoaque, Poeh Museum, Santa Fe NM

Luk, Cynthia, *Paintings Conservator & Internatl Projs Specialist*, Williamstown Art Conservation Center, Williamstown MA

Luka, Nik, *Prof*, McGill University, School of Architecture, Montreal PQ (S)

Lukacher, Brian, *Assoc Prof*, Vassar College, Art Dept, Poughkeepsie NY (S)

Lukasek, Edward, *Catalog Librn*, Museum of Fine Arts, Houston, Hirsch Library, Houston TX

Lukasiewicz, Nancy, *Cur*, Lyndon House Art, Athens GA

Lukaszewski, Laurel, *Sec*, Washington Sculptors Group, Washington DC

Luke, Margie L, *Archivist*, St Mary Landmarks, Grevemberg House Museum, Franklin LA

Luke, Suzanne, *Cur & Mgr*, Wilfrid Laurier University, Robert Langen Art Gallery, Waterloo ON

Luker, Amanda, *Graphic Designer*, Utah Valley University, Woodbury Art Museum, Orem UT

Lukkas, Lynn, *Asst Prof*, University of Minnesota, Minneapolis, Dept of Art, Minneapolis MN (S)

Lukoff, Ashlee, *Dir Special Events & Mem Svcs*, Delaware Center for the Contemporary Arts, Wilmington DE

Luman, Mitch, *Dir Science Planetarium*, Evansville Museum of Arts, History & Science, Evansville IN

Lumbria-McDonald, Julie, *Library Coordr*, New Brunswick College of Craft & Design, Library, Fredericton NB

Lumpe, Laurence L, *Exec Dir*, Concordia Historical Institute, Saint Louis MO

Lumpkin, Libby, *Dir*, Las Vegas Art Museum, Las Vegas NV

Luna, Sandra, *Receptionist*, Hidalgo County Historical Museum, Edinburg TX

Lundberg, Nozomi, *Admin Asst*, Billie Trimble Chandler, Texas State Museum of Asian Cultures, Corpus Christi TX

Lunde, Mary Lee, *Chmn*, State University of New York at Fredonia, Dept of Art, Fredonia NY (S)

Lundegard, Stephanie, *Admin Asst*, Order Sons of Italy in America, Garibaldi & Meucci Museum, Staten Island NY

Lunderman, Ron, *Pres*, Plymouth Antiquarian Society, Plymouth MA

Lundgren, Jodi, *Cur Exhibs*, South Dakota State University, South Dakota Art Museum, Brookings SD

Lundskow, Pete, *Cur Coll*, Boulder History Museum, Museum of History, Boulder CO

Luner, Karin, *Dir Opers*, Women's Caucus For Art, New York NY

Lunsford, John J, *Deputy Dir Admin*, Jamestown-Yorktown Foundation, Jamestown Settlement, Williamsburg VA

Lunt, Eve, *Gallery Dir*, Barbara & Ray Alpert Jewish Community Center, Pauline & Zena Gatov Gallery, Long Beach CA

Luo, Jian, *Assoc Prof*, University of Wisconsin-Eau Claire, Dept of Art & Design, Eau Claire WI (S)

Luong, Renata, *Contact*, Rhode Island Historical Society, Aldrich House, Providence RI

Lupher, Vance, *Registrar*, Erie Art Museum, Erie PA

Lupi, Ginnie, *Exec Dir*, Arts of the Southern Finger Lakes, Corning NY

Lupo, Joseph, *Prof*, West Virginia University, College of Creative Arts, School of Art & Design, Morgantown WV (S)

Lupton, Ellen, *Cur Contemporary Design*, Cooper-Hewitt National Design Museum, Smithsonian Institution, New York NY

Lurie, Evan, *Dir*, Evan Lurie Fine Art Gallery, Carmel IN

Lurie, Janice Lea, *Head Librn*, Minneapolis Institute of Arts, Art Research & Reference Library, Minneapolis MN

Lurowist, Peter, *Librn*, Ryerss Victorian Museum & Library, Philadelphia PA

Lush, Brian, *Mem Coordr*, Indian Arts & Crafts Association, Albuquerque NM

Lush, Colleen, *Bookkeeper*, The Robert McLaughlin, Oshawa ON

Lushington, Nancy, *Artist in Res, Dance*, Marymount Manhattan College, Fine & Performing Arts Div, New York NY (S)

Lusk, Kyle, *Assoc Prof*, Brevard College, Department of Art, Brevard NC (S)

Lustig, Steven, *Pres*, Jewish Community Center of Greater Washington, Jane L & Robert H Weiner Judaic Museum, Rockville MD

Luth, Nicki Byram, *Bd Secy*, Artists' Cooperative Gallery, Omaha NE

Luther, Olivia, *Mus Dir*, California Center for the Arts, Escondido Museum, Escondido CA

Luther, Sherry, *Exec Dir,* Saskatchewan Craft Council & Affinity Gallery, Saskatoon SK

Lutomski, James, *Asst Prof,* Marygrove College, Department of Art, Detroit MI (S)

Lutsch, Gail, *Assoc Prof,* Bethel College, Dept of Art, North Newton KS (S)

Luttikhuizen, Henry, *Secy,* Midwest Art History Society, Waco TX

Lutz, Barbara, *Admin Asst,* University of Minnesota, Goldstein Museum of Design, Saint Paul MN

Lutz, Jim, *Prof,* Rhodes College, Dept of Art, Memphis TN (S)

Lutz, Penny, *Gallery Asst,* Pennsylvania College of Technology, The Gallery at Penn College, Williamsport PA (S)

Lutz, Tina, *Exec Dir & Pub Rels,* GumTree Museum of Art, Tupelo MS

Lutze, Margaret, *Treas,* Women's Caucus For Art, New York NY

Luukkonen, John, *School of Design,* Art Institute of Houston, Houston TX (S)

Lux, Sam, *Artist,* Walker's Point Artists Assoc Inc, Gallery 218, Milwaukee WI

Luxenberg, Alisa, *Asst Prof Art History,* University of Georgia, Franklin College of Arts & Sciences, Lamar Dodd School of Art, Athens GA (S)

Lybarger, Mary, *Instr,* Edgewood College, Art Dept, Madison WI (S)

Lydecker, Kent, *Assoc Dir Educ,* The Metropolitan Museum of Art, New York NY

Lyders, Laurie S, *Treas,* Liberty Village Arts Center & Gallery, Chester MT

Lydon, Catherine, *Instr,* Springfield College, Dept of Visual & Performing Arts, Springfield MA (S)

Lydon, Kate, *Dir Exhibs,* Society for Contemporary Craft, Pittsburgh PA

Lyford, Amy, *Prof,* Occidental College, Dept of Art History & Visual Arts, Los Angeles CA (S)

Lyke, Linda, *Pres,* Occidental College, Weingart Galleries, Los Angeles CA

Lyke, Linda, *Prof,* Occidental College, Dept of Art History & Visual Arts, Los Angeles CA (S)

Lykins, Jere, *Asst Prof,* Berry College, Art Dept, Mount Berry GA (S)

Lykins, Jere, *Dir,* Berry College, Moon Gallery, Mount Berry GA

Lyles, Cornelia, *Dr,* Compton Community College, Art Dept, Compton CA (S)

Lyman, Christy, *Mktg & Develop Coordr,* Museum of Northwest Art, La Conner WA

Lyman, Daniel, *Interim Pres,* New Hampshire Institute of Art, Manchester NH

Lyman, Daniel, *Interim Pres,* New Hampshire Institute of Art, Manchester NH (S)

Lyman, David H, *Founder & Dir,* Maine Photographic Workshops/Rockport College, Rockport ME

Lyman, David H, *Founder & Dir,* Maine Photographic Workshops, The International T.V. & Film Workshops & Rockport College, Rockport ME (S)

Lynch, Beth, *Martyrs Mus Mgr,* The National Shrine of the North American Martyrs, Fultonville NY

Lynch, Fred, *Illustration,* Montserrat College of Art, Beverly MA (S)

Lynch, Harry P, *Pres & CEO,* Stan Hywet, Akron OH

Lynch, James, *Asst Archivist,* Bethel College, Mennonite Library & Archives, North Newton KS

Lynch, Jill, *Media Rels,* Fine Arts Museums of San Francisco, M H de Young Museum, San Francisco CA

Lynch, Jill, *Media Rels,* Fine Arts Museums of San Francisco, Legion of Honor, San Francisco CA

Lynch, Jo, *Lectr,* Oklahoma State University, Department of Art, Graphic Design and Art History, Stillwater OK (S)

Lynch, John, *Assoc Prof,* Central Missouri State University, Dept Art & Design, Warrensburg MO (S)

Lynch, Laura, *Dir Educ,* Nassau County Museum of Art, Roslyn Harbor NY

Lynch, Mary, *Library Assoc,* New York School of Interior Design, New York School of Interior Design Library, New York NY

Lynch, Matthew, *Asst Prof Fine Arts,* University of Cincinnati, School of Art, Cincinnati OH (S)

Lynch, Robert, *Chmn 3D Design,* Milwaukee Institute of Art & Design, Milwaukee WI (S)

Lynch, Robert, *Pres & CEO,* Americans for the Arts, New York NY

Lynch, Robert L, *Pres & CEO,* Americans for the Arts, Washington DC

Lynch, Robin, *Assoc Prof,* Purchase College, State University of New York, School of Art+Design, Purchase NY (S)

Lynch, Shelia, *Prof Art & Art History,* Rio Hondo College, Visual Arts Dept, Whittier CA (S)

Lynch, Steve, *Pres,* Fishkill Historical Society, Van Wyck Homestead Museum, Fishkill NY

Lynch-Maas, Rebecca, *Capital Campaign Coordr,* Asheville Art Museum, Asheville NC

Lynch-McWhite, Wyona, *Dir,* Fuller Craft Museum, Brockton MA

Lynch-McWhite, Wyona, *Exec Dir,* Fuller Craft Museum, Library, Brockton MA

Lynch-McWhite, Wyona, *Exec Dir,* Fruitlands Museum, Inc, Harvard MA

Lynde, Richard, *VPres,* Montclair State University, Art Galleries, Upper Montclair NJ

Lynes, Lisa, *Instr,* North Idaho College, Art Dept, Coeur D'Alene ID (S)

Lyness, Jessica, *Pub Rels & Mktg Mgr,* Portland Art Museum, Northwest Film Center, Portland OR

Lynn, Billie G, *Asst Prof,* University of Miami, Dept of Art & Art History, Coral Gables FL (S)

Lynn, Judy G, *Exec Dir,* Pacific Northwest Art School, Gallery at the Wharf, Coupeville WA

Lynne, Michael, *2nd VChmn,* Guild Hall of East Hampton, Inc, Guild Hall Museum, East Hampton NY

Lynx, David, *Dir,* Yakima Valley Community College, Larson Gallery, Yakima WA

Lyon, Joyce, *Assoc Prof,* University of Minnesota, Minneapolis, Dept of Art, Minneapolis MN (S)

Lyon, Robert F, *Chmn,* University of South Carolina, Dept of Art, Columbia SC (S)

Lyons, Heather, *Exec Dir,* Living Arts & Science Center, Inc, Lexington KY

Lyons, Keith, *Mem Coordr,* Historical Society of Pennsylvania, Philadelphia PA

Lyons, Kenneth H, *Pres Emeritus,* Newport Historical Society & Museum of Newport History, Newport RI

Lyons, Matthew, *Dir Archives,* Historical Society of Pennsylvania, Philadelphia PA

Lysak, Wendy, *Mgr, Financial & Facility Svcs,* Kamloops Art Gallery, Kamloops BC

Lytle, Richard, *Prof,* Yale University, School of Art, New Haven CT (S)

M, Jackie, *Dir Educ,* Georgia O'Keeffe Museum, Santa Fe NM

M.C. Randolph, Angus, *Dir,* Springfield Museum of Art, Springfield OH

Ma, Yue, *Assoc Dir Coll,* Museum of Chinese in America, New York NY

Ma, Yue, *Mgr AA Educ Prog (DCTA),* China Institute in America, China Institute Gallery, New York NY

Maag, Albert, *Dir,* Capital University, Art Library, Columbus OH

Maas, Bernard, *Chmn Crafts,* Edinboro University of Pennsylvania, Art Dept, Edinboro PA (S)

Maas, Suzanne, *Exec Dir,* Higgins Armory Museum, Worcester MA

Mabee, Kim A, *VPres,* Schenectady County Historical Society, Museum of Schenectady History, Schenectady NY

Mabee, Laura, *Research & Archive Coordr,* Homer Watson, Kitchener ON

Maberry, Sue, *Dir,* Otis College of Art & Design, Millard Sheets Library, Los Angeles CA

MacAdam, Barbara J, *Cur American Art,* Dartmouth College, Hood Museum of Art, Hanover NH

Macapia, Paul, *Mus Photography,* Seattle Art Museum, Dorothy Stimson Bullitt Library, Seattle WA

Macara, Peter, *Registrar,* Provincetown Art Association & Museum, Provincetown MA

Macaulay, Lorinda, *Educ Asst,* Lehigh Valley Heritage Center, Allentown PA

Macaulay, Sally, *Exec Dir,* Marietta-Cobb Museum of Art, Marietta GA

MacAulay, Suzanne, *Chair, Visual & Performing Arts,* University of Colorado-Colorado Springs, Visual & Performing Arts Dept (VAPA), Colorado Springs CO (S)

MacBain, Ken, *Jewelry & Metals Prof,* New Jersey City University, Art Dept, Jersey City NJ (S)

MacBoggs, Mayo, *Prof Studio Art,* Converse College, School of the Arts, Dept of Art & Design, Spartanburg SC (S)

MacCallum, Marlene, *Prof,* Memorial University of Newfoundland, Division of Fine Arts, Visual Arts Program, Corner Brook NF (S)

MacCann, Brynne, *Facilities Mktg Coordr,* Birmingham Museum of Art, Birmingham AL

Macdonald, Christine, *Bus Asst,* Dartmouth College, Hood Museum of Art, Hanover NH

Macdonald, Christopher, *Dir,* University of British Columbia, School of Architecture, Vancouver BC (S)

MacDonald, Denise, *Commun & Outreach,* Royal Architectural Institute of Canada, Ottawa ON

Macdonald, Eileen, *Assoc Prof,* California State University, Chico, Department of Art & Art History, Chico CA (S)

MacDonald, Elizabeth H, *VPres, Color Proof Ed & Treas,* American Color Print Society, Huntingdon Valley PA

MacDonald, Ian, *Head Dept Architecture,* University of Manitoba, Faculty of Architecture, Winnipeg MB (S)

MacDonald, Lucy, *Cur Educ,* Mount Allison University, Owens Art Gallery, Sackville NB

MacDonald, Neal, *Asst Prof,* University of Maryland, Baltimore County, Imaging & Digital Arts (IMDA), Dept of Visual Arts, Baltimore MD (S)

MacDonald, Sara, *Pub Services Librn,* The University of the Arts, University Libraries, Philadelphia PA

MacDonald, Scott, *Dir Educ & Prog,* McMichael Canadian Art Collection, Kleinburg ON

MacDonald, Susan, *Instr,* North Hennepin Community College, Art Dept, Brooklyn Park MN (S)

MacDonnell, Robert A, *Deputy Dir Develop,* Cliveden, Philadelphia PA

MacDonnell, Virginia, *Cur,* DeLeon White Gallery, Toronto ON

MacDougall, Jean, *Coll Mgr,* Santa Clara University, de Saisset Museum, Santa Clara CA

MacDowall, Cyndra, *Prof,* University of Windsor, Visual Arts, Windsor ON (S)

Macechak, Jeffrey, *Educ Dir,* Burlington County Historical Society, Burlington NJ

Macella, Bruce, *Prof,* Oklahoma City University, Norick Art Center, Oklahoma City OK (S)

MacElwee, John A, *Exec Dir,* Centrum Arts & Creative Education, Port Townsend WA

Macgil, Hugh, *VPres,* Connecticut Historical Society, Hartford CT

MacGuffie, Larry, *VPres,* Western Art Association, Ellensburg WA

Machek, Frank, *Prof Emer,* Albion College, Bobbitt Visual Arts Center, Albion MI

Machell, Iain, *Chmn,* Ulster County Community College/Suny Ulster, Dept of Art, Design, Music, Theatre & Communication, Stone Ridge NY (S)

Machin, Jana, *Dir Mus Store,* San Francisco Museum of Modern Art, San Francisco CA

Machlin, Daniel, *Exec Dir,* Segue Foundation, Reading Room-Archive, New York NY

Machlis, Sally, *Dept Chair,* University of Idaho/College of Art & Architecture, Dept of Art & Design, Moscow ID (S)

Machtan, James, *Asst Dir,* New Visions Gallery, Inc, Marshfield WI

Maciarello, Sarah, *Exec Admin Asst,* Salisbury University, Ward Museum of Wildfowl Art, Salisbury MD

Macias, Irene, *Lib Dir,* Santa Barbara Public Central Library, Faulkner Memorial Art Wing, Santa Barbara CA

Macias, Maria Elena, *Cur,* International Museum of Art & Science, McAllen TX

Macias, Nanette Yannuzzi, *Assoc Prof,* Oberlin College, Dept of Art, Oberlin OH (S)

Macias, Pat Kemeny, *Exec Dir,* 1078 Gallery, Chico CA

Maciejunes, Nannette V, *Exec Dir,* Columbus Museum of Art, Columbus OH

MacInnes, Roddy, *Assoc Prof Photog,* University of Denver, School of Art & Art History, Denver CO (S)

MacInnis, Karen, *Cur,* Marblehead Museum & Historical Society, Marblehead MA

MacInnis, Karen, *Cur,* Marblehead Museum & Historical Society, John Orne Johnson Frost Gallery, Marblehead MA

MacInnis, Karen, *Cur,* Marblehead Museum & Historical Society, Jeremiah Lee Mansion, Marblehead MA

MacInnis, Karen, *Cur,* Marblehead Museum & Historical Society, Archives, Marblehead MA

Macintosh, Matt, *Exhibs Mgr,* Orillia Museum of Art & History, Orillia ON

MacIntyre, Robert, *Exhib Coordr & Preparator,* Burnaby Art Gallery, Burnaby BC

Mack, Angela, *Dir,* Carolina Art Association, Library, Charleston SC

Mack, Angela D, *Exec Dir,* Gibbes Museum of Art, Charleston SC (S)

Mack, Angela D, *Exec Dir & Chief Cur,* Carolina Art Association, Gibbes Museum of Art, Charleston SC

Mack, Anissa, *Asst Prof,* Queensborough Community College, Dept of Art & Photography, Bayside Hills NY (S)

Mack, Honour, *Instr,* Maine College of Art, Portland ME (S)

Mack, James, *Chmn,* City Colleges of Chicago, Wright College, Chicago IL (S)

Mack, Joanne, *Cur,* University of Notre Dame, Snite Museum of Art, Notre Dame IN

Mack, Laurce, *Instr,* Chemeketa Community College, Dept of Humanities & Communications, Art Program, Salem OR (S)

Mack, Mary Lynn, *Pub Rels Mgr,* Delaware Historical Society, Delaware History Museum, Wilmington DE

Mack, MaryLynn, *Dir Pub Rels,* Delaware Historical Society, Library, Wilmington DE

Mack, Rita, *Office Mgr,* Nassau County Museum of Art, Roslyn Harbor NY

Mack-Harvin, Dionne, *Exec Dir,* Brooklyn Public Library, Art & Music Division, Brooklyn NY

MacKay, Anne, *Chief Conservator,* McCord Museum of Canadian History, Montreal PQ

MacKay, Camilla, *Head Librn,* Bryn Mawr College, Rhys Carpenter Library for Art, Archaeology, Classics & Cities, Bryn Mawr PA

Mackay, Chris, *Pres (2013),* Emerald Empire Art Association, Emerald Art Center, Springfield OR

Mackay, John L, *CEO,* Discovery Place Inc, Nature Museum, Charlotte NC

Mackay-Collins, Dorothy, *Cur,* R L S Silverado Museum, Saint Helena CA

Mackay-Collins, Dorothy, *Dir/Archivist,* R L S Silverado Museum, Reference Library, Saint Helena CA

MacKay-Lyons, B, *Prof,* Dalhousie University, Faculty of Architecture, Halifax NS (S)

MacKay-Smith, Kyla, *Museum Asst,* Gibson Society, Inc, Gibson House Museum, Boston MA

Mackenzie, Colin, *Robert P Youngman Cur Asian Art,* Middlebury College, History of Art & Architecture Dept, Middlebury VT (S)

Mackenzie, Linda, *Dir Research & Reference,* Toronto Public Library Board, Library, Toronto ON

Mackey, Cindy, *Asst Registrar,* The Currier Museum of Art, Manchester NH

Mackey, David, *Pres,* Hopewell Museum, Hopewell NJ

Mackie, Elizabeth, *Assoc Prof,* The College of New Jersey, School of Arts & Sciences, Ewing NJ (S)

Mackie, Karen, *Dir Visitor Experience,* Ministry of Alberta Culture, Royal Alberta Museum, Edmonton AB

Mackie, Louise, *Cur Textiles & Islamic Art,* The Cleveland Museum of Art, Cleveland OH

Mackie, Peter F, *Chmn,* Arts & Education Council of Greater Saint Louis, Saint Louis MO

Macko, Nancy, *Chmn Dept,* Scripps College, Millard Sheets Art Center-Williamson Gallery, Claremont CA (S)

Mack Weber, Carey, *Registrar,* Fairfield University, Thomas J Walsh Art Gallery, Fairfield CT

MacLaird, Pam, *Gallery Mgr,* Rancho Santa Fe Art Guild, Rancho Santa Fe CA

MacLaren, Shelly, *Gallery Dir,* University of the South, University Art Gallery, Sewanee TN

MacLellan, Iain, *Dir,* Saint Anselm College, Alva de Mars Megan Chapel Art Center, Manchester NH

MacLennan, Toby, *Assoc Prof,* Rutgers, The State University of New Jersey, Mason Gross School of the Arts, Visual Arts Dept, New Brunswick NJ (S)

Macleod Farley, Pauline, *Mgr Devel,* Tom Thomson, Owen Sound ON

Mac Low, Mordecai-Mark, *Chair Dept Physical Sciences,* American Museum of Natural History, Rose Center for Earth & Space, New York NY

MacMillan, Sean, *Prof,* Slippery Rock University of Pennsylvania, Dept of Art, Slippery Rock PA (S)

MacMillan, William, *Conservator,* Higgins Armory Museum, Worcester MA

MacNamara, Aoife, *Dean Faculty of Visual Art & Material Practice,* Emily Carr University of Art + Design, Vancouver BC (S)

MacNulty, Thomas, *Assoc Prof,* Adelphi University, Dept of Art & Art History, Garden City NY (S)

Macpherson, Kate, *Develop Officer,* Homer Watson, Kitchener ON

MacPherson, Kathy, *Gallery Mgr & Outreach Coordr,* Otis College of Art & Design, Ben Maltz Gallery, Los Angeles CA

Macrae, Laurie, *Librn,* Taos Public Library, Fine Art Collection, Taos NM

MacTaggart, Alan, *Chair,* Augusta State University, Dept of Art, Augusta GA (S)

MacTaggart, Alan C, *Prof Art,* Lander University, College of Arts & Humanities, Greenwood SC (S)

Macy, Christine, *Assoc Prof,* Dalhousie University, Faculty of Architecture, Halifax NS (S)

Madar, Heather, *Assoc Prof,* Humboldt State University, College of Arts & Humanities, Art Dept, Arcata CA (S)

Madden, Jack, *Facility Opers Dir,* Oklahoma City Museum of Art, Oklahoma City OK

Madden, Julie, *Dir Community Arts,* Cambridge Arts Council, CAC Gallery, Cambridge MA

Madden, Mimi, *Dir Poetry Festival,* Hill-Stead Museum, Farmington CT

Madden, Susan, *VPres Develop,* Museum of the City of New York, Research Room, New York NY

Madden, Tom, *Chmn Crafts,* College for Creative Studies, Detroit MI (S)

Maddock, Pam, *Spokesperson,* American River College, Dept of Art/Art New Media, Sacramento CA (S)

Maddox, Caroline, *Dir Develop,* University of Georgia, Georgia Museum of Art, Athens GA

Maddox, Gene, *Instr,* College of the Sequoias, Art Dept, Visalia CA (S)

Maddox, Jerrold, *Prof Art (Gen Educ),* Pennsylvania State University, University Park, Penn State School of Visual Arts, University Park PA (S)

Mader, Daniel, *Chmn,* College of Mount Saint Joseph, Art Dept, Cincinnati OH (S)

Madigan, Emily, *Assoc Prof,* Bakersfield College, Art Dept, Bakersfield CA (S)

Madill, Shirley, *Exec Dir,* Kitchener-Waterloo Art Gallery, Kitchener ON

Madill, Shirley, *Sr Cur,* Art Gallery of Hamilton, Muriel Isabel Bostwick Library, Hamilton ON

Madison, Kurt, *Adjunct Asst Prof,* Spokane Falls Community College, Fine Arts Dept, Spokane WA (S)

Madison, Nina, *Dir Special Events,* Parrish Art Museum, Water Mill NY

Madkour, Christopher, *Dir,* Huntsville Museum of Art, Reference Library, Huntsville AL

Madkour, Christopher, *Dir,* Southern Vermont Art Center, Manchester VT

Madkour, Christopher, *Dir,* Southern Vermont Art Center, Library, Manchester VT

Madsen, Barbara, *Assoc Prof,* Rutgers, The State University of New Jersey, Mason Gross School of the Arts, Visual Arts Dept, New Brunswick NJ (S)

Madson, Barbara, *Reference,* Mason City Public Library, Mason City IA

Madura, Nancy, *Instr,* Casper College, Dept of Visual Arts, Casper WY (S)

Maeckelbergh, Kenneth, *Chmn,* Century College, Humanities Dept, White Bear Lake MN (S)

Maeda, John, *Pres,* Rhode Island School of Design, Providence RI (S)

Maeglin, William, *Chmn,* Bucks County Historical Society, Mercer Museum, Doylestown PA

Maegowan, Ciaran, *Instr,* San Jose City College, School of Fine Arts, San Jose CA (S)

Maeson Yang, Jessica, *Educ Dir,* Angels Gate Cultural Center, Gallery A & Gallery G, San Pedro CA

Maestas, Ileana, *Museum Cur,* California State Parks, State Indian Museum, Sacramento CA

Magee, Carol, *Asst Prof,* University of North Carolina at Chapel Hill, Art Dept, Chapel Hill NC (S)

Magee, Eileen, *Asst Dir Progs,* Athenaeum of Philadelphia, Philadelphia PA

Magee, Noel, *Chmn Fine Arts & Music,* Roberts Wesleyan College, Art Dept, Rochester NY (S)

Maggio, John, *Prof,* University of North Carolina at Greensboro, Art Dept, Greensboro NC (S)

Maggio, Ronald, *Chmn,* Springfield College, William Blizard Gallery, Springfield MA

Maggio, Ronald, *Chmn,* Springfield College, Dept of Visual & Performing Arts, Springfield MA (S)

Magill, John, *Historian & Cur,* The Historic New Orleans Collection, Williams Research Center, New Orleans LA

Maginnis, Ken, *Assoc Prof Design,* Coker College, Art Dept, Hartsville SC (S)

Magistro, Charles, *Prof,* William Paterson University, Dept Arts, Wayne NJ (S)

Magley, Betsy, *Dir Devel,* The Andy Warhol Museum, Museum, Pittsburgh PA

Magnan, Oscar, *Dir,* Saint Peter's College, Art Gallery, Jersey City NJ

Magnani, Patricia, *Registrar,* Purchase College, Neuberger Museum of Art, Purchase NY

Magnat, Virginie, *Asst Prof (Performance - Theater),* University of British Columbia Okanagan, Dept of Creative Studies, Kelowna BC (S)

Magner, Nancy, *Prof Art,* Bakersfield College, Art Dept, Bakersfield CA (S)

Magnuson, Roz, *Archivist,* Brick Store Museum, Kennebunk ME

Magnusson, Mishell, *Pres,* Madison County Historical Society, Cottage Lawn, Oneida NY

Magrath, Lauren, *Dir Admissions,* Bennington College, Visual Arts Division, Bennington VT (S)

Magri, Ken, *Instr,* American River College, Dept of Art/Art New Media, Sacramento CA (S)

Magrin, Roger, *Sr Dir Facilities & Grounds,* Genesee Country Village & Museum, John L Wehle Art Gallery, Mumford NY

Maguire, Catherine, *Asst Dir,* National Museum of Racing, Reference Library, Saratoga Springs NY

Maguire, Eunice, *Cur,* Johns Hopkins University, Archaeological Collection, Baltimore MD

Maguire, George, *Pres,* South Arkansas Arts Center, El Dorado AR

Maguire, Marsha, *Manuscripts & Spec Collections Cataloging Librn,* University of Washington, Univ of Washington Libraries, Special Collections, Seattle WA

Maguire, William, *Prof,* Florida International University, School of Art & Art History, Miami FL (S)

Mahaffey, Richard, *Art Dept Chmn,* Tacoma Community College, Art Dept, Tacoma WA (S)

Maher, Christine F, *Mus Shop Asst,* Williams College, Museum of Art, Williamstown MA

Maher, Kathleen, *Cur,* The Barnum Museum, Bridgeport CT

Maher, Tim, *Pres,* Art Centre of New Jersey, Livingston NJ (S)

Mahitas, Frank, *Dept Head,* Fort Valley State College, H A Hunt Memorial Library, Fort Valley GA

Mahle, Curtis, *Preparator,* Whatcom Museum, Bellingham WA

Mahnke, Helen, *Mus Educ,* Pennsylvania Historical & Museum Commission, Brandywine Battlefield Park, Harrisburg PA

Mahnken, Cecelia, *Accounting,* Fraunces Tavern Museum, New York NY

Mahoney, James, *Affiliate Assoc Prof,* University of Maryland, Baltimore County, Imaging & Digital Arts (IMDA), Dept of Visual Arts, Baltimore MD (S)

Mahoney, Julie, *Prof,* Western Illinois University, Department of Art, Macomb IL (S)

Mahoney, Meredith, *Asst Cur Zoology,* Illinois State Museum, Museum Store, Chicago IL

Mahoney, Olivia, *Dir Historical Documentation,* Chicago History Museum, Chicago IL

Mahoney, Ryan, *Cur,* Schenectady County Historical Society, Library, Schenectady NY

Mai, Josie, *Prof,* Missouri Southern State University, Dept of Art, Joplin MO (S)

Maidenberg, Sharon, *Exec Dir,* Headlands Center for the Arts, Sausalito CA

Maier, Joan, *Bus Mgr,* Moose Jaw Art Museum, Inc, Art & History Museum, Moose Jaw SK

Maietta, Andrew, *Video Production,* Art Institute of Pittsburgh, Pittsburgh PA (S)

Main, Sally, *Cur,* Tulane University, Newcomb Art Gallery, New Orleans LA

Mainardi, Patricia, *Prof Emerita,* City University of New York, PhD Program in Art History, New York NY (S)

Maines, Clark, *Prof,* Wesleyan University, Dept of Art & Art History, Middletown CT (S)

Maines, Renee, *Bookkeeper,* Belle Grove Inc, Belle Grove Plantation, Middletown VA

Maiolo, Mimmo, *Preparator,* Banff Centre, Walter Phillips Gallery, Banff AB

Maitzen, Dolly, *Recording Sec,* Arizona Watercolor Association, Phoenix AZ

Majewski, Andrea, *Educ Coordr,* Delaware Historical Society, Read House and Gardens, Wilmington DE

Majewski, David, *Chmn,* Richard Bland College, Art Dept, Petersburg VA (S)

Majewski, Sally, *Dir Mktg,* Hancock Shaker Village, Inc, Pittsfield MA

Majoli, Monica, *Assoc Prof Painting,* University of California, Irvine, Studio Art Dept, Irvine CA (S)

Major, James, *Dean,* Illinois State University, College of Fine Arts, Normal IL (S)

Mak, Jennifer, *Daytime Access Servs Mgr,* Fashion Institute of Technology, Gladys Marcus Library - SUNY, New York NY

Makholm, Kristin, *Contact,* Highpoint Center for Printmaking, Minneapolis MN

Makholm, Kristin, *Exec Dir,* Minnesota Museum of American Art, Saint Paul MN

Maklansky, Steven, *Dir,* Boca Raton Museum of Art, Library, Boca Raton FL

Maklansky, Steven, *Exec Dir,* Boca Raton Museum of Art, Boca Raton FL

Makov, Susan, *Prof,* Weber State University, Dept of Visual Arts, Ogden UT (S)

Makrandi, Nandini, *Clinical Prof,* University of Tennessee at Chattanooga, Dept of Art, Chattanooga TN (S)

Maksymiuk, Catherine, *Mgr Communs & Mktg,* The Winnipeg Art Gallery, Winnipeg MB

Maksymowicz, Virginia A, *Dept Chair,* Franklin & Marshall College, Art & Art History Dept, Lancaster PA (S)

Makuch, Nestor, *1st VP,* Ukrainian Canadian Archives & Museum of Alberta, Edmonton AB

Makuuchi, Yuko, *Mus Shop Dir,* Craft and Folk Art Museum (CAFAM), Los Angeles CA

Malak, Gregory, *Cur,* Will Rogers Memorial Museum & Birthplace Ranch, Claremore OK

Malak, Gregory, *Cur,* Will Rogers Memorial Museum & Birthplace Ranch, Media Center Library, Claremore OK

Malbin, Susan, *Dir Library & Archives,* American Jewish Historical Society, The Center for Jewish History, New York NY

Malcolm, Pamela, *Historic Site Mgr,* New York State Office of Parks, Recreation & Historic Preservation, Staatsburgh State Historic Site, Staatsburg NY

Malec, Jacek, *Dir & Cur,* Calgary Contemporary Arts Society, Triangle Gallery of Visual Arts, Calgary AB

Malec, Mariah, *Vis Asst Prof,* Jacksonville University, Dept of Art, Theater, Dance, Jacksonville FL (S)

Malenke, Patti, *Dir,* Johnson-Humrickhouse Museum, Coshocton OH

Malgeri, Dina G, *Dir & Librn,* Malden Public Library, Art Dept & Gallery, Malden MA

Malinee, Christine, *Dir Mktg & Develop,* Art Saint Louis, Saint Louis MO

Maling, Kathy, *1st VPres & Co-Chmn,* Miami Watercolor Society, Inc, Miami FL

Malinowski, Monica, *Sr Librn,* Newark Public Library, Reference, Newark NJ

Malkin, Hamish, *Pres,* Community Arts Council of Vancouver, Vancouver BC

Malkovich, Mark P, *Pres,* Royal Arts Foundation, Belcourt Castle, Newport RI

Mall, Andrea, *Reg,* Toledo Museum of Art, Toledo OH

Mall, Bonita, *Dir Pub Program,* Chicago Architecture Foundation, Chicago IL

Malle, Michael, *Graphic Design,* Art Institute of Pittsburgh, Pittsburgh PA (S)

Mallette, Carol S, *Admin Asst,* City of Raleigh Arts Commission, Miriam Preston Block Gallery, Raleigh NC

Mallette, Wallace, *Coordr,* Mississippi Delta Community College, Dept of Fine Arts, Moorhead MS (S)

Malley, Diane, *Dir,* Clarion University, Hazel Sandford Gallery, Clarion PA

Malley, Richard, *Head of Collections,* Connecticut Historical Society, Library, Hartford CT

Mallory, Cathryn, *Co-Chair,* University of Montana, Dept of Art, Missoula MT (S)

Mallory, Deana, *Pub Programs Dir,* Bennington Museum, Bennington VT

Mallory, Jess, *Support Staff,* Knights of Columbus Supreme Council, Knights of Columbus Museum, New Haven CT

Mallory, Michael, *Chmn,* Brooklyn College, Art Dept, Brooklyn NY (S)

Mallory Kotz, Vanessa, *Grants Mgr,* Tucson Museum of Art and Historic Block, Tucson AZ

Malloy, Jeanne, *Educ Specialist,* Ormond Memorial Art Museum and Gardens, Ormond Beach FL

Malloy, Joe, *Bibliographic Instruction & Branch Librn,* Sweet Briar College, Mary Helen Cochran Library, Sweet Briar VA

Malloy, Kip, *Exec Asst,* James A Michener, Doylestown PA

Malloy, Mark, *Prof,* Salem State University, Art & Design Department, Salem MA (S)

Malloy, Nancy, *Dir Artist Mem,* National Academy Museum & School, Archives, New York NY

Mally, Christine, *Dir Develop,* Boca Raton Museum of Art, Library, Boca Raton FL

Malon, Louis J, *Dir Properties,* Preservation Virginia, Richmond VA

Malon, Louis J, *Dir Properties,* Preservation Virginia, Library, Richmond VA

Malone, Carolyn, *Chair,* University of Southern California, College of Letters, Arts & Sciences, Los Angeles CA (S)

Malone, Meredith, *Assoc Cur,* Washington University, Mildred Lane Kemper Art Museum, Saint Louis MO

Malone, Peter, *Dir,* Kingsborough Community College, CUNY, Art Gallery, Brooklyn NY

Malone, Robert R, *Head Printmaking,* Southern Illinois University at Edwardsville, Dept of Art & Design, Edwardsville IL (S)

Malone, Ronald, *Program Dir,* Eubie Blake, Baltimore MD

Malone, Roxanne, *Asst Prof,* College of Santa Fe, Art Dept, Santa Fe NM (S)

Malone, Terry, *Exec Dir,* Sooke Region Museum & Art Gallery, Sooke BC

Maloney, Agnes, *Bus Mgr,* Cahoon Museum of American Art, Cotuit MA

Maloney, Courtney, *Chmn Writing & Humanities,* Milwaukee Institute of Art & Design, Milwaukee WI (S)

Maloney, Judy, *Dir,* Juniata College Museum of Art, Huntingdon PA

Maloney, Richard, *Prof,* Boston University, Graduate Program - Arts Administration, Boston MA (S)

Maloney, Stephanie, *Prof,* University of Louisville, Allen R Hite Art Institute, Louisville KY (S)

Malovany, Bernie, *VPres Organization,* DuPage Art League School & Gallery, Wheaton IL

Malshibini, Deborah, *Dir,* VSA Arts of New Mexico, Enabled Arts Center, Albuquerque NM (S)

Maltais, Marie, *Dir,* University of New Brunswick, Art Centre, Fredericton NB

Maltese, Vinnie, *Dean,* Monroe County Community College, Fine Arts Council, Monroe MI

Malus, Mary June, *Coordr,* Imperial Calcasieu Museum, Gibson-Barham Gallery, Lake Charles LA

Malus, Mary June, *Coordr,* Imperial Calcasieu Museum, Gibson Library, Lake Charles LA

Malvern, Fred, *Coordr Interior Design,* Iowa State University, Dept of Art & Design, Ames IA (S)

Malyk, Mike, *Human Resources Mgr,* The Winnipeg Art Gallery, Winnipeg MB

Mamangakis, Georgia, *Mus Shop Mgr,* The Mariners' Museum, Newport News VA

Mambo, Marjorie, *Assoc Prof,* Indiana University of Pennsylvania, College of Fine Arts, Indiana PA (S)

Mammel, Jim, *Pres,* El Museo Latino, Omaha NE

Manaffey, Ellen, *Instr,* Lake Tahoe Community College, Art Dept, South Lake Tahoe CA (S)

Manbeck, Brooks, *Exhibs Preparator,* Long Beach Museum of Art Foundation, Long Beach CA

Manchester, Carri, *Head Educ,* Olana State Historic Site, Hudson NY

Mancinelli, Diane, *Dance,* Henry Ford Community College, McKenzie Fine Art Ctr, Dearborn MI (S)

Mancini, Ellen, *Receptionist,* Hammond Museum & Japanese Stroll Garden, Cross-Cultural Center, North Salem NY

Mancuso, William, *Asst Prof Art,* Ohio Northern University, Dept of Art & Design, Ada OH (S)

Mandel, Gerry, *VPres,* Children's Art Foundation, Museum of International Children's Art, Santa Cruz CA

Manderen, Elizabeth, *Exec Dir,* Firelands Association for the Visual Arts, Oberlin OH

Mandeville, Lynn, *Dir of Develop,* Museum of Art, Fort Lauderdale, Library, Fort Lauderdale FL

Mandeville-Gamble, Steven, *Univ Librn,* University of California, Tomas Rivera Library, Riverside CA

Maneen, Thomas, *Instr,* Mohawk Valley Community College, Utica NY (S)

Manega, Antonio, *Designer,* Rice University, Rice Gallery, Houston TX

Manella, Mary Alice, *Budget & Finance Mgr,* Florida International University, The Patricia & Phillip Frost Art Museum, Miami FL

Manfredi, John, *Chmn (V),* Creative Arts Center, Pontiac MI

Mangan, Kelly, *Fin Asst / DBA,* Historical Society of Martin County, Elliott Museum, Stuart FL

Mangubi, Marina, *Assoc Prof,* The College of Wooster, Dept of Art and Art History, Wooster OH (S)

Manion, Shelia, *Acting Asst Dir Develop,* Saint Louis Art Museum, Saint Louis MO

Maniscalco, Nelson, *Prof,* Cedar Crest College, Art Dept, Allentown PA (S)

Manister, Craig, *Adj Asst Prof,* College of Staten Island, Performing & Creative Arts Dept, Staten Island NY (S)

Mankin, Diane, *Assoc Prof Fine Arts,* University of Cincinnati, School of Art, Cincinnati OH (S)

Manley, Jason, *Asst Prof,* Weber State University, Dept of Visual Arts, Ogden UT (S)

Manley, Juniper, *Develop Officer,* University of New Mexico, The Harwood Museum of Art, Taos NM

Manley, Mary, *Assoc Dir,* Henry Sheldon Museum of Vermont History and Research Center, Middlebury VT

Manley, Roger, *Dir,* North Carolina State University, Gregg Museum of Art & Design, Raleigh NC

Mann, Jack, *Prof,* Wittenberg University, Art Dept, Springfield OH (S)

Mann, Janice, *Prof,* Bucknell University, Dept of Art, Lewisburg PA (S)

Mann, Laura, *Exec Dir,* Dawson City Museum & Historical Society, Klondike History Library, Dawson City YT

Mann, Tina, *Instr,* William Woods-Westminster Colleges, Art Dept, Fulton MO (S)

Mannarino, Amy, *Mgr Communs & Mktg,* National Museum of Women in the Arts, Washington DC

Mannell, Steven, *Asst Prof,* Dalhousie University, Faculty of Architecture, Halifax NS (S)

Manning, Albina, *Dir,* School of Art Institute of Chicago, Video Data Bank, Chicago IL

Manning, Cynthia, *Develop,* Discovery Museum, Bridgeport CT

Manning, Jackie, *Exhibits Designer,* Alaska State Museum, Juneau AK

Manning, Maureen, *Librn,* University Club Library, New York NY

Mannion, John, *Digital Lab Mgr,* Light Work, Robert B Menschel Photography Gallery, Syracuse NY

Mannix, Anne, *Dir Communs,* The Baltimore Museum of Art, Baltimore MD

Mannix, Christine, *Pub Svcs Librn,* Columbus College of Art & Design, Packard Library, Columbus OH

Manns, Suzanne, *Chmn Studio Arts,* University of Saint Thomas, Fine and Performing Arts Dept, Houston TX (S)

Manoguerra, Paul, *Dir & Cur,* Jundt Art Museum, Spokane WA

Mansfield, Gregory, *Cur,* Ancient Spanish Monastery, North Miami Beach FL

Mansfield, Marcia, *Treas,* Lincoln County Historical Association, Inc, Maine Art Gallery, Wiscasset ME

Mansfield, Phil, *Digital Lab Mgr,* Center for Photography at Woodstock Inc, Woodstock NY

Mansfield, Steve, *Div & Dept Chair,* Salt Lake Community College, Graphic Design Dept, Salt Lake City UT (S)

Mansolino, Ann, *Instr Photog,* Rio Hondo College, Visual Arts Dept, Whittier CA (S)

Mansoor, Jaleh, *Asst Prof,* University of British Columbia, Dept of Art History, Visual Art & Theory, Vancouver BC (S)

Mantell, Nancy, *Curatorial Asst,* Hebrew Union College Museum, Jewish Institute of Religion Museum, New York NY

Manthorne, Katherine, *Prof,* City University of New York, PhD Program in Art History, New York NY (S)

Mantin, Regina, *Mgr Temporary Exhibits,* New Brunswick Museum, Saint John NB

Manton, Jill, *Dir Pub Art Prog,* San Francisco City & County Art Commission, San Francisco CA

Manuel, Anne, *Exec Dir,* Craft Council of Newfoundland & Labrador, Saint John's NF

Manuel, Chuck, *Instr,* Graceland University, Fine Arts Div, Lamoni IA (S)

Manuele, Lisa, *Instr,* Springfield College in Illinois, Dept of Art, Springfield IL (S)

Maphet, Tony, *CEO,* Clark County Historical Society, Pioneer - Krier Museum, Ashland KS

Mar, Louis, *Art Dir,* Coppini Academy of Fine Arts, Library, San Antonio TX

Maranci, Christina, *Assoc Prof,* Tufts University, Dept of Art & Art History, Medford MA (S)

Maranda, Lynn, *Cur Anthropology,* Museum of Vancouver, Vancouver BC

Maranda, Michael, *Asst Cur,* York University, Art Gallery of York University, Toronto ON

Marantz, Kenneth, *Prof Emeritus,* Ohio State University, Dept of Art Education, Columbus OH (S)

Marasco, Rose, *Prof Photog,* University of Southern Maine, Dept of Art, Gorham ME (S)

Marble, Lori, *PR Coordr,* George A Spiva, Joplin MO

Marblo, Christopher, *Pres,* The Arts Center of the Capital Region, Troy NY

Marcantel, Gregory, *Pres Bd Trustees,* Zigler Art Museum, Jennings LA

Marcereau DeGalan, Aimee, *Cur,* University of Vermont, Robert Hull Fleming Museum, Burlington VT

Marcet, David, *Instr,* Illinois Benedictine University, Department of Fine Arts, Lisle IL (S)

Marcey, Sheyna, *Educ,* West Florida Historic Preservation, Inc/University of West Florida, T T Wentworth, Jr Florida State Museum; Historic Pensacola Village; Pensacola Historical Society & Resource Center, Pensacola FL

Marche, Theresa, *Assoc Prof,* University of Wisconsin, Madison, Dept of Art, Madison WI (S)

Marchessault, Lesley, *Cur,* LeMoyne Art Foundation, Center for the Visual Arts, Tallahassee FL

Marchi, Riccardo, *Assoc Prof,* University of South Florida, School The Arts, Tampa FL (S)

Marchione, Ken, *Prof,* Munson-Williams-Proctor Arts Institute, Pratt MWP College of Art, Utica NY (S)

Marchione, Kenneth, *Dir Art,* Stamford Museum & Nature Center, Stamford CT

Marciari, John, *Cur European Art & Head Provenance Research,* San Diego Museum of Art, San Diego CA

Marciari Alexander, Julia, *Deputy Dir, Cur Affairs & Educ,* San Diego Museum of Art, San Diego CA

Marcincowski, David, *Dir,* Pratt Institute, Pratt Manhattan, New York NY (S)

Marcinowski, Gary, *Assoc Prof,* University of Dayton, Visual Arts Dept, Dayton OH (S)

Marconi, Richard A, *Cur Educ,* Historical Society of Palm Beach County, The Richard and Pat Johnson Palm Beach County History Museum, West Palm Beach FL

Marcotte, Christian, *Dir,* Musee Regional de lu Cote-Nord, Sept-Iles PQ

Marcou, George T, *Prof,* Catholic University of America, School of Architecture & Planning, Washington DC (S)

Marcum-Estes, Leah, *Dir,* Oak Ridge Art Center, Oak Ridge TN

Marcum-Estes, Leah, *Dir,* Oak Ridge Art Center, Library, Oak Ridge TN

Marcus, Louis, *Prof,* University of South Florida, School The Arts, Tampa FL (S)

Marcy, Jane, *Adj Prof,* Saint Thomas Aquinas College, Art Dept, Sparkill NY (S)

Marder, Tod, *Prof,* Rutgers, The State University of New Jersey, Graduate Program in Art History, New Brunswick NJ (S)

Mardikos, JoAnn, *Acting Pres & CEO,* Snug Harbor Cultural Center, Newhouse Center for Contemporary Art, Staten Island NY

Mare, Linda, *Cur Educ,* New Britain Museum of American Art, New Britain CT

Marentette, Kara, *Develop Coordr,* The Light Factory Contemporary Museum of Photography and Film, Charlotte NC

Maresca, Mary, *Asst Dir,* Nichols House Museum, Inc, Boston MA

Margalit, Nathan, *Vis Assoc Prof,* Trinity College, Dept of Studio Arts, Hartford CT (S)

Margeson, Hank, *Asst Prof,* North Georgia College & State University, Fine Arts Dept, Dahlonega GA (S)

Margol, Deborah J, *Deputy Dir,* South Florida Cultural Consortium, Miami Dade County Dept of Cultural Affairs, Miami FL

Margolis, Gerald, *Deputy Dir,* University of Pennsylvania, Museum of Archaeology & Anthropology, Philadelphia PA

Margolis, Margo, *Chmn Painting, Drawing, & Sculpture,* Temple University, Tyler School of Art, Philadelphia PA (S)

Marianne, Jo Ann, *Exec Dir,* Gulf Beach Art Center, Indian Rocks Beach FL

Marichal, Flavia, *Cur Art,* University of Puerto Rico, Museum of Anthropology, History & Art, Rio Piedras PR

Marichal, Flavia, *Cur Art,* University of Puerto Rico, Museum of Anthropology, History & Art, Rio Piedras PR

Marien, Mary, *Prof,* Syracuse University, Dept of Fine Arts (Art History), Syracuse NY (S)

Marinaro, Lou, *Prof,* University of Michigan, Ann Arbor, School of Art & Design, Ann Arbor MI (S)

Marinas, Silvia, *Conservator,* New Mexico State University, Art Gallery, Las Cruces NM

Marincol, Michele, *Sherman Fairchild Chmn,* New York University, Institute of Fine Arts, New York NY (S)

Marine, Rose, *Controller,* Independence Seaport Museum, Philadelphia PA

Marinello, Marcia, *Dir,* Glynn Art Association, Saint Simons Island GA

Marini, Gina, *Adminr Mgr,* Heritage Museum Association, Inc, The Heritage Museum of Northwest Florida, Valparaiso FL

Marinsky, Jane, *Instr,* Daemen College, Art Dept, Amherst NY (S)

Marion, Joanne, *Cur Art,* Esplanade Arts & Heritage Centre, Medicine Hat AB

Marion, Nancy, *Treas,* Octagon Center for the Arts, Ames IA

Mariona, Myrna, *Mgr Human Resources,* Japanese American National Museum, Los Angeles CA

Marioni, Tom, *Dir,* Archives of MOCA (Museum of Conceptual Art), Society of Independent Artists, San Francisco CA

Marioni, Tom, *Dir,* Archives of MOCA (Museum of Conceptual Art), Library, San Francisco CA

Mariscal, Joe, *Instr,* San Joaquin Delta College, Arts & Communication, Stockton CA (S)

Mark, Peter, *Prof,* Wesleyan University, Dept of Art & Art History, Middletown CT (S)

Markert, Kate, *Exec Dir & CEO,* Hillwood Museum & Gardens Foundation, Hillwood Estate Museum & Gardens, Washington DC

Markey, Mike, *Instr Arts Mgmt,* Creighton University, Fine & Performing Arts Dept, Omaha NE (S)

Markey, Teresa L, *Gallery Asst,* Grossmont Community College, Hyde Art Gallery, El Cajon CA

Markin, Linda, *Sr VPres,* Discovery Museum, Bridgeport CT

Markoe, Glenn E, *Cur Classical, Near Eastern Art,* Cincinnati Art Museum, Cincinnati Art Museum, Cincinnati OH

Markow, Julianne, *Deputy Dir Fin & Opers,* San Diego Museum of Art, San Diego CA

Markowitz, Joan, *Sr Cur,* Boulder Museum of Contemporary Art, Boulder CO

Markowitz, John, *Program Dir,* University of West Florida, Dept of Art, Pensacola FL (S)

Markowitz, Yvonne, *Rita J Kaplan Cur Jewelry,* Museum of Fine Arts, Boston MA

Markowski, Eugene D, *Lectr,* Trinity College, Fine Arts Program, Washington DC (S)

Markowsky, Chris, *Animation Instr (YA! Project),* Quickdraw Animation Society, Calgary AB

Marks, Andrea, *Asst Prof,* Oregon State University, Dept of Art, Corvallis OR (S)

Marks, Laura, *Dir Visitor Svcs,* Hancock Shaker Village, Inc, Pittsfield MA

Marks, Pamela, *Assoc Prof,* Connecticut College, Dept of Art, New London CT (S)

Markwalter, Mary, *Dir,* Mason City Public Library, Mason City IA

Markwith, Jillian, *Mktg & Special Events,* Historical Society of Palm Beach County, The Richard and Pat Johnson Palm Beach County History Museum, West Palm Beach FL

Marlais, Michael, *Prof,* Colby College, Art Dept, Waterville ME (S)

Marlatt, Megan, *Studio Faculty,* University of Virginia, McIntire Dept of Art, Charlottesville VA (S)

Marling, Karal Ann, *Prof,* University of Minnesota, Minneapolis, Art History, Minneapolis MN (S)

Marling, Michael, *Instr,* Brenau University, Art & Design Dept, Gainesville GA (S)

Marling de Cuellar, Michael, *Asst Prof,* North Georgia College & State University, Fine Arts Dept, Dahlonega GA (S)

Marlowe, Claudia, *Catalog Asst,* San Francisco Art Institute, Anne Bremer Memorial Library, San Francisco CA

Marmon, Betty, *Dir Develop,* Philadelphia Museum of Art, Main Building, Philadelphia PA

Maron, Deborah, *Digitization Specialist,* Harvard University, Image Collection & Fieldwork Archives, Washington DC

Marotta, Joseph, *Prof,* University of Utah, Dept of Art & Art History, Salt Lake City UT (S)

Marquardt-Cherry, Janet, *Prof,* Eastern Illinois University, Art Dept, Charleston IL (S)

Marquet, Cynthia, *Librn,* Historical Society of the Cocalico Valley, Ephrata PA

Marquez, Jose, *Coll Mgr,* Foosaner Art Museum, Melbourne FL

Marquez, Lorrie, *Facilities & Beverage Mgr,* Sangre de Cristo Arts & Conference Center, Pueblo CO

Marquez, Marco, *Lectr,* Santa Clara University, Dept of Art & Art History, Santa Clara CA (S)

Marquez, Phillip, *Interim Gallery Dir,* Santa Ana College, Art Gallery, Santa Ana CA

Marquis, David, *Sr Paintings Conservator,* Midwest Art Conservation Center, Minneapolis MN

Marrin, Elizabeth, *Asst Prof,* University of Massachusetts - Boston, Art Dept, Boston MA (S)

Marriott, Bill, *Assoc Prof Drawing & Painting,* University of Georgia, Franklin College of Arts & Sciences, Lamar Dodd School of Art, Athens GA (S)

Marsalis, Nelson, *Asst Prof,* Xavier University of Louisiana, Dept of Fine Arts, New Orleans LA (S)

Marschalek, Doug, *Prof,* University of Wisconsin, Madison, Dept of Art, Madison WI (S)

Marsden, Susan, *Cur,* Museum of Northern British Columbia, Ruth Harvey Art Gallery, Prince Rupert BC

Marsden-Atlass, Lynn, *Dir & Univ Cur,* University of Pennsylvania, Arthur Ross Gallery, Philadelphia PA

Marsder, Susan, *Cur,* Museum of Northern British Columbia, Library, Prince Rupert BC

Marsee, Todd, *Instr,* Siena Heights University, Studio Angelico-Art Dept, Adrian MI (S)

Marsh, Cindy, *Chair,* Austin Peay State University, Dept of Art, Clarksville TN (S)

Marsh, Jeanne, *Comptroller,* Greenville County Museum of Art, Greenville SC

Marsh, Jennifer, *Catron Prof of Art,* Washburn University of Topeka, Dept of Art, Topeka KS (S)

Marsh, Jennifer, *Coordr Child Art,* Palo Alto Art Center, Palo Alto CA

Marsh, Robert, *Prof,* Averett College, Art Dept, Danville VA (S)

Marshall, Alison, *Dir Educ,* Arizona Commission on the Arts, Phoenix AZ

Marshall, Amy, *Archivist Spec Coll,* Art Gallery of Ontario, Edward P Taylor Research Library & Archives, Toronto ON

Marshall, Ann, *Dir Research,* Heard Museum, Phoenix AZ

Marshall, Heidi, *Head Col Archives & Digital Colls,* Columbia College Chicago, Library, Chicago IL

Marshall, Howard, *Prof Emeritus,* University of Missouri - Columbia, Art History & Archaeology Dept, Columbia MO (S)

Marshall, Janet, *Admin Asst, BB,* Museum of Fine Arts Houston, Bayou Bend Collection & Gardens, Houston TX

Marshall, John Dudley, *Projectionist & Film Asst,* Oklahoma City Museum of Art, Oklahoma City OK

Marshall, Linda, *Prog Dir,* Cape Ann Historical Association, Cape Ann Museum, Gloucester MA

Marshall, Michael, *Asst Prof Photog,* University of Georgia, Franklin College of Arts & Sciences, Lamar Dodd School of Art, Athens GA (S)

Marshall, Nancy R, *Assoc Prof,* University of Wisconsin, Madison, Dept of Art History, Madison WI (S)

Marshall, Piper, *Asst Cur,* Swiss Institute, New York NY

Marshall, Sally, *Dir Devel,* Brooklyn Historical Society, Brooklyn NY

Marshall, Tom, *Asst,* Noyes Art Gallery, Lincoln NE

Marshall, William J, *Dir Spec Coll & Archives,* The Art Museum at the University of Kentucky, Photographic Archives, Lexington KY

Marsolais, Gilles, *Instr,* Universite de Montreal, Dept of Art History, Montreal PQ (S)

Marsten, Heidi M, *Media & Exhibitions Coordr,* Bromfield Art Gallery, Boston MA

Marston, Pamela, *Secy,* East Tennessee State University, The Reece Museum, Johnson City TN

Martel, Bastien, *Secy,* Sculptor's Society of Canada, Canadian Sculpture Centre, Toronto ON

Martel, Jean, *Admin Dir,* Ottawa Public Library, Fine Arts Dept, Ottawa ON

Martel, Ralph, *Prof,* College of Staten Island, Performing & Creative Arts Dept, Staten Island NY (S)

Martel, Richard, *Coordr,* Les Editions Intervention, Inter-Le Lieu, Documentation Center, Quebec PQ

Martell, Danielle, *Mem Asst,* Museum of Ventura County, Ventura CA

Martello, Anita, *Prog Coordr,* Gonzaga University, Art Gallery, Spokane WA

Martello, Anita, *Prog Coordr,* Jundt Art Museum, Spokane WA

Marten, Robert, *Interim Chmn,* Wayne State University, Dept of Art & Art History, Detroit MI (S)

Martens, Darrin, *Dir & Cur,* Burnaby Art Gallery, Burnaby BC

Martens-Haworth, Megan, *Asst Prof,* Spokane Falls Community College, Fine Arts Dept, Spokane WA (S)

Martin, Allan, *Restoration Mgr,* Pennsylvania Historical & Museum Commission, Railroad Museum of Pennsylvania, Harrisburg PA

Martin, Amy, *Dir Fin,* Historical Society of Martin County, Elliott Museum, Stuart FL

Martin, Andrew, *Assoc Dir & Assoc Prof,* Texas Tech University, Dept of Art, Lubbock TX (S)

Martin, Anna, *Reg,* The Drawing Center, New York NY

Martin, Anya, *Vis Artist,* University of New Orleans-Lake Front, Dept of Fine Arts, New Orleans LA (S)

Martin, Art, *Assoc Cur & Mgr Coll,* Muskegon Museum of Art, Muskegon MI

Martin, Barbara, *Alfond Cur Educ,* Museum of Fine Arts, Boston MA

Martin, Bobby, *Instr,* Northeastern State University, College of Arts & Letters, Tahlequah OK (S)

Martin, Charlotte, *Instr,* Wayne Art Center, Wayne PA (S)

Martin, Chas E, *Dept Head Photog,* Antonelli College, Cincinnati OH (S)

Martin, Craig, *Dir Gallery,* Purdue University Galleries, West Lafayette IN

Martin, Crystal, *Cur,* Dartmouth Heritage Museum, Dartmouth NS

Martin, Dan, *Interim Dean,* Carnegie Mellon University, College of Fine Arts, Pittsburgh PA (S)

Martin, Darlene Fossum, *Educ Specialist-Folk Art,* Vesterheim Norwegian-American Museum, Decorah IA

Martin, David, *Provost,* Milwaukee Institute of Art & Design, Milwaukee WI (S)

Martin, Don, *Chmn,* Flagler College, Visual Arts Dept, Saint Augustine FL (S)

Martin, Erin L, *CEO,* Historical Society of Rockland County, New City NY

Martin, Frank, *Instr,* South Carolina State University, Dept of Visual & Performing Arts, Orangeburg SC (S)

Martin, George, *Pres,* North Shore Arts Association, Inc, Gloucester MA

Martin, George-McKinley, *Chief Art Div,* Public Library of the District of Columbia, Art Division, Washington DC

Martin, Gordon, *Bd Pres,* Montgomery Museum of Fine Arts, Montgomery AL

Martin, Hal, *Pres,* Coppini Academy of Fine Arts, Library, San Antonio TX

Martin, Jane, *Assoc Prof,* University of Saint Francis, School of Creative Arts, Fort Wayne IN (S)

Martin, Jane, *Librn,* Martin and Osa Johnson, Scott Explorers Library, Chanute KS

Martin, Jeff, *Mgr Exhib & Colls,* University of Iowa, University of Iowa Museum of Art, Iowa City IA

Martin, Jennifer, *Dir Educ & Opers,* Clay Studio, Philadelphia PA

Martin, Julie, *Develop & Pub Rels Coordr,* Northeast Document Conservation Center, Inc, Andover MA

Martin, Kate, *Dir Gallery,* Ventura College, Art Galleries, Ventura CA

Martin, Kate, *Head Colls & Mus,* University of Northern Iowa, Fine & Performing Arts Collection Rod Library, Cedar Falls IA

Martin, Kathy, *Dir Educ,* Hockaday Museum of Art, Kalispell MT

Martin, Leslie, *Book Publisher,* Aperture Foundation, New York NY

Martin, Lisa, *Exec Asst,* Blue Lake Fine Arts Camp, Art Dept, Twin Lake MI (S)

Martin, Louise, *Gen Dir,* Shawinigan Art Center, Shawinigan PQ

Martin, Lyn, *Spec Coll,* Willard Library, Dept of Fine Arts, Evansville IN

Martin, Margaret, *Admin,* Chatham Historical Society, The Atwood House Museum, Chatham MA

Martin, Marianne, *Visual Resources Editorial Librn,* Colonial Williamsburg Foundation, John D Rockefeller, Jr Library, Williamsburg VA

Martin, Martha Kent, *Instr,* Main Line Art Center, Haverford PA (S)

Martin, Mary, *Asst Prof Art History,* Johnson State College, Dept Fine & Performing Arts, Dibden Center for the Arts, Johnson VT (S)

Martin, Michael, *Coordr Colls & Exhibs,* Flint Institute of Arts, Flint MI

Martin, Nicholas A, *French Specialist,* National Gallery of Art, Department of Image Collections, Washington DC

Martin, Nicole, *Creative Resources Dir,* Sierra Arts Foundation, Sierra Arts Gallery, Reno NV

Martin, Patrick, *Asst Prof,* Emporia State University, Dept of Art, Emporia KS (S)

Martin, Ray, *Assoc Prof,* Greensboro College, Dept of Art, Division of Fine Arts, Greensboro NC (S)

Martin, Ray, *Prof Art,* Greensboro College, Irene Cullis Gallery, Greensboro NC

Martin, Rebecca, *Coll Mgr,* Kansas State Historical Society, Kansas Museum of History, Topeka KS

Martin, Rebecca, *Educ Coordr,* Litchfield History Museum, Litchfield CT

Martin, Roly, *Instr,* Lakehead University, Dept of Visual Arts, Thunder Bay ON (S)

Martin, Sarah, *Prof,* University of North Carolina at Greensboro, Art Dept, Greensboro NC (S)

Martin, Sarah, *VPres Opers,* Avampato Discovery Museum, The Clay Center for Arts & Sciences, Charleston WV

Martin, Terry, *Anthropology Chmn,* Illinois State Museum, Museum Store, Chicago IL

Martin, Terry, *Instr,* William Woods-Westminster Colleges, Art Dept, Fulton MO (S)

Martin, Terry, *Instr,* Salt Lake Community College, Graphic Design Dept, Salt Lake City UT (S)

Martin, Tony, *Faculty,* Idaho State University, Dept of Art & Pre-Architecture, Pocatello ID (S)

Martin, Victoria, *Acting Area Head Photog,* Pasadena City College, Visual Arts and Media Studies Division, Pasadena CA (S)

Martin, Wilbert R, *Prof Printmaking & Drawing,* University of Texas Pan American, Art Dept, Edinburg TX (S)

Martin, William, *Dir,* Valentine Richmond History Center, Richmond VA

Martin, William, *Prof,* Rhode Island College, Art Dept, Providence RI (S)

Martin-Mathewson, Nancy, *Bus Mgr,* Hartwick College, The Yager Museum, Oneonta NY

Martin-Wicoff, Jenny, *Fine Art & Cultural History Registrar,* New Jersey State Museum, Fine Art Bureau, Trenton NJ

Martindale, Robin, *Prof,* Appalachian State University, Dept of Art, Boone NC (S)

Martinez, Andy, *Archivist,* Rhode Island School of Design, Fleet Library at RISD, Providence RI

Martinez, Carmen, *Dir Library Svcs,* Oakland Public Library, Art, Music, History & Literature Section, Oakland CA

Martinez, Charmaine, *Asst Prof Graphic Design,* California Polytechnic State University at San Luis Obispo, Dept of Art & Design, San Luis Obispo CA (S)

Martinez, Dan, *Chmn,* Cabrillo College, Visual & Performing Arts Division, Aptos CA (S)

Martinez, Daniel, *Prof Pub Art, Sculpture,* University of California, Irvine, Studio Art Dept, Irvine CA (S)

Martinez, Dennis, *Asst Prof,* Dixie College, Art Dept, Saint George UT (S)

Martinez, Ed W, *Chmn Dept,* University of Nevada, Reno, Art Dept, Reno NV (S)

Martinez, Joyce, *Mus Tech,* Fort Morgan Heritage Foundation, Fort Morgan CO

Martinez, Juan, *Prof,* Florida International University, School of Art & Art History, Miami FL (S)

Martinez, Katharine, *Dir,* University of Arizona, Center for Creative Photography, Tucson AZ

Martinez, Kim, *Assoc Prof,* University of Utah, Dept of Art & Art History, Salt Lake City UT (S)

Martinez, Magda, *Dir Educ & Community Engagement,* Philadelphia Museum of Art, Samuel S Fleisher Art Memorial, Philadelphia PA

Martinez, Manual, *Instr,* Cochise College, Art Dept, Douglas AZ (S)

Martinez, Matt, *Chmn,* National Hispanic Cultural Center, Art Museum, Albuquerque NM

Martinez, Peggy Halbig, *Instr,* Lourdes University, Art Dept, Sylvania OH (S)

Martinez, Reuben, *Colls Mgr,* Pueblo of Pojoaque, Poeh Museum, Santa Fe NM

Martinez, Teresa, *Prog Asst,* Heritage Preservation, The National Institute for Conservation, Washington DC

Martinez, Val, *Discovery Center Coordr,* Nicolaysen Art Museum & Discovery Center, Museum, Casper WY

Martinez-Lemke, Tania, *Dir,* Los Angeles Center for Photographic Studies, Los Angeles CA

Martinez Wormser, Jennifer, *Head Librn,* Laguna College of Art & Design, Dennis & Leslie Power Library, Laguna Beach CA

Martini, Dino, *Pres,* Center on Contemporary Art, Seattle WA

Martini, Kathryn, *Registrar,* Independent Curators International, New York NY

Martins, Michael, *Cur,* Fall River Historical Society, Fall River MA

Martinson, Kate, *Head Dept,* Luther College, Art Dept, Decorah IA (S)

Martiny, Sandy, *Cur Educ,* National Academy Museum & School, Archives, New York NY

Martonis, Stephen, *Exhibs, Facilities & Securities Mgr,* University of Colorado, CU Art Museum, Boulder CO

Martorell, Penni, *Cur & City Hist,* Wistariahurst Museum, Holyoke MA

Martyka, Paul, *Assoc Prof,* Winthrop University, Dept of Art & Design, Rock Hill SC (S)

Martz, Genie, *Week-End Mgr,* Walter Anderson, Ocean Springs MS

Martz, Jean-Marie, *Chmn Dance,* Idyllwild Arts Academy, Idyllwild CA (S)

Martz, Mary J, *Coordr Handicapped Svcs,* Cultural Affairs Department City of Los Angeles/Barnsdall Art Centers/Junior Arts Center, Los Angeles CA

Marvel, Kate, *Secy,* Marion Art Center, Cecil Clark Davis Gallery, Marion MA

Marvin, Judy, *Registrar,* Susquehanna University, Lore Degenstein Gallery, Selinsgrove PA

Marvin, Miranda, *Prof,* Wellesley College, Art Dept, Wellesley MA (S)

Marx, Bridget, *Colls Mgr & Cur Exhibs,* Southern Methodist University, Meadows Museum, Dallas TX

Marzan, Mario, *Asst Prof,* University of North Carolina at Chapel Hill, Art Dept, Chapel Hill NC (S)

Marzan, Nathan, *Colls Mgr,* Allentown Art Museum, Allentown PA

Marzolf, Helen, *Exec Dir,* Open Space, Victoria BC

Mas, Deborah, *Dean Acad Affairs,* International Fine Arts College, Miami FL (S)

Maschino, David, *Exhib Coordr,* Bowdoin College, Peary-MacMillan Arctic Museum, Brunswick ME

Masich, Andrew, *PHMC Chmn,* Pennsylvania Historical & Museum Commission, The State Museum of Pennsylvania, Harrisburg PA

Masino, Al, *Dir Exhibs, Design, & Spec Projects,* Hirshhorn Museum & Sculpture Garden, Smithsonian Institution, Washington DC

Masler, Marilyn, *Assoc Registrar,* Memphis Brooks Museum of Art, Memphis TN

Mason, Bonnie C, *Cur Educ,* Miami University, Art Museum, Oxford OH

Mason, Dan, *Instr,* North Hennepin Community College, Art Dept, Brooklyn Park MN (S)

Mason, Henri, *Dir,* Drew County Historical Society, Museum, Monticello AR

Mason, Joel, *Chmn,* New York City College of Technology of the City University of New York, Dept of Advertising Design & Graphic Arts, Brooklyn NY (S)

Mason, John, *Pres & CEO,* Lorton Arts Foundation, Workhouse Arts Center, Lorton VA

Mason, Kelvin, *Assoc Prof,* Augustana College, Art Dept, Rock Island IL (S)

Mason, Kelvin, *Assoc Prof Art,* North Central College, Dept of Art, Naperville IL (S)

Mason, Kelvin, *Chmn & Assoc Prof,* West Virginia Wesleyan College, Art Dept, Buckhannon WV (S)

Mason, Laura, *Admin Asst,* Morris Museum of Art, Augusta GA

Mason, Noelle, *Asst Prof,* University of South Florida, School The Arts, Tampa FL (S)

Mason, Robert, *Instr,* Andrews University, Dept of Art, Art History & Design, Berrien Springs MI (S)

Mason, Sara, *Library Asst,* Chrysler Museum of Art, Jean Outland Chrysler Library, Norfolk VA

Mason, Sarah, *Mem, Grants & Vis Svcs Coordr,* CAM Contemporary Art Museum, Raleigh NC

Mason, Terry J, *Dir,* Douglas Art Association, The Gallery and Gift Shop, Douglas AZ

Mason, Trapeta, *VPres Educ & Family Learning,* Please Touch Museum, Philadelphia PA

Mason, Wally, *Dir,* Marquette University, Haggerty Museum of Art, Milwaukee WI

Massaro, Marilyn R, *Cur,* City of Providence Parks Department, Roger Williams Park Museum of Natural History, Providence RI

Massaroni, Dino, *Instr,* Cuyahoga Valley Art Center, Cuyahoga Falls OH (S)

Masse, Joanne, *Mgr Financial Servs,* Northeast Document Conservation Center, Inc, Andover MA

Massen, Suzannah, *Chief Pub Servs,* The Frick Collection, Frick Art Reference Library, New York NY

Massett, Sarah, *Dir Pub Rels,* Everson Museum of Art, Syracuse NY

Massey, Allyn, *Prof, Chair,* Goucher College, Art & Art History Dept, Baltimore MD (S)

Massey, Bryan, *Prof,* University of Central Arkansas, Department of Art, Conway AR (S)

Massey, Debra, *Staff Asst,* National Gallery of Art, Department of Image Collections, Washington DC

Massey, Lew, *Property Mgr,* Bank One Fort Worth, Fort Worth TX

Massey, Scott, *Asst Prof,* University of Louisville, Allen R Hite Art Institute, Louisville KY (S)

Massey, Scott, *Sculpture,* University of Colorado at Denver, College of Arts & Media Visual Arts Dept, Denver CO (S)

Massey, Shari, *Dir Accounting,* Chicago History Museum, Chicago IL

Massey, Tim, *Asst Prof,* State University of New York College at Brockport, Dept of Art, Brockport NY (S)

Massey, Walter, *Pres,* School of the Art Institute of Chicago, Chicago IL (S)

Massie, Amanda, *Asst Cur,* New York State Office of Parks, Recreation and Historic Preservation, Bureau of Historic Sites, Waterford NY

Massie, Donna Jo, *Treas,* Alberta Society of Artists, Calgary AB

Massie, William, *Head Archit Dept,* Cranbrook Academy of Art, Bloomfield Hills MI (S)

Massie Lane, Rebecca, *Dir,* Washington County Museum of Fine Arts, Hagerstown MD

Massier, John, *Visual Arts Cur,* Hallwalls Contemporary Arts Center, Buffalo NY

Massman, Denise, *Asst Prof Theatre Design,* Siena College, Dept of Creative Arts, Loudonville NY (S)

Mast, Sarah, *Asst Prof Painting,* Montana State University, School of Art, Bozeman MT (S)

Mastandrea, Eva, *Prof,* The University of Montana Western, Art Program, Dillon MT (S)

Master, Diane, *Mus Shop Mgr,* Palo Alto Art Center, Palo Alto CA

Masters, Bonnie, *Sec,* Cumberland Art Society Inc, Cookeville Art Gallery, Cookeville TN

Masters, Jonelle, *Chmn,* Bismarck State College, Fine Arts Dept, Bismarck ND (S)

Masters, Richard, *Prof,* University of Wisconsin Oshkosh, Dept of Art, Oshkosh WI (S)

Masterson, Dan, *Asst Mem & Box Office Mgr,* Sangre de Cristo Arts & Conference Center, Pueblo CO

Masterson, Judith P, *Gallery Coordr,* College of New Jersey, Art Gallery, Ewing NJ

Masterson, Kate, *Coordr Mem,* Boise Art Museum, Boise ID

Masterson, Mike, *Chmn,* Northwest Community College, Dept of Art, Powell WY (S)

Mastin, Catherine, *Dir,* Art Gallery of Windsor, Windsor ON

Mastin, Lauren, *Mus Shop Mgr,* Historic Cherry Hill, Albany NY

Mastroeini, Georgia, *Cur Educ,* Cameron Art Museum, Wilmington NC

Masuoka, Mark, *Exec Dir & Chief Cur,* Bemis Center for Contemporary Arts, Omaha NE

Mata, Nancy R, *Assoc Prof Graphic Design,* Millersville University, Dept of Art & Design, Millersville PA (S)

Mates, Judy, *Instr,* Joe Kubert, Dover NJ (S)

Matheison, Rhonda, *Dir Finance & Opers,* High Museum of Art, Atlanta GA

Matheny, Paul, *Chief Cur Art,* South Carolina State Museum, Columbia SC

Mather, Charles E, *Pres,* Fairmount Park Art Association, Philadelphia PA

Mather, Tim, *Dir, Assoc Prof,* Indiana University, Bloomington, Henry Radford Hope School of Fine Arts, Bloomington IN (S)

Mathers, W Nicholas V, *Vice Chmn,* Colorado Historical Society, Colorado History Museum, Denver CO

Matheson, Pat, *Cur,* University of Regina, Visual Resource Center, Regina SK

Matheson, Susan, *Cur Ancient Art,* Yale University, Yale University Art Gallery, New Haven CT

Mathews, John, *Instr,* Bucks County Community College, Fine Arts Dept, Newtown PA (S)

Mathews, Karen, *Asst Prof,* University of Colorado at Denver, College of Arts & Media Visual Arts Dept, Denver CO (S)

Mathews, Patricia, *Assoc Prof,* Oberlin College, Dept of Art, Oberlin OH (S)

Mathews, Susan, *Treas,* Graphic Artists Guild, New York NY

Mathews, Susie, *Dir Educ,* Peoria Art Guild, Peoria IL

Mathez, Rene, *Chmn Science & Math,* Fashion Institute of Technology, Art & Design Division, New York NY (S)

Mathias, Eve Page, *Coordr Fine Arts,* San Jose City College, School of Fine Arts, San Jose CA (S)

Mathiason, Jerry, *Instr,* North Hennepin Community College, Art Dept, Brooklyn Park MN (S)

Mathie, William, *Dir Gallery,* Edinboro University of Pennsylvania, Art Dept, Edinboro PA (S)

Mathies, Linda, *Tour Coordr,* Old Barracks Museum, Trenton NJ

Mathis, Jaci, *Instr,* Northeastern Junior College, Art Department, Sterling CO (S)

Mathis, Natalie, *Dir Institutional Advancement,* Taft Museum of Art, Cincinnati OH

Mathison, Tara, *Asst Cur,* Queens College, City University of New York, Queens College Art Center, Flushing NY

Matijcio, Steven, *Cur Contemporary Art,* Southeastern Center for Contemporary Art, Winston Salem NC

Matilsky, Barbara, *Cur Art,* Whatcom Museum, Bellingham WA

Matis, Walter, *Prog & Vol Coordr,* Fairfield Historical Society, Fairfield Museum & History Center, Fairfield CT

Matlock, Ann, *Assoc Prof,* Lamar University, Art Dept, Beaumont TX (S)

Mato, Nancy, *Exec VPres,* The Society of the Four Arts, Palm Beach FL

Matson, Karen, *Coordr Technical Communs,* Kalamazoo Valley Community College, Center for New Media, Kalamazoo MI (S)

Matsubara, Fuyuko, *Assoc Prof,* Indiana University of Pennsylvania, College of Fine Arts, Indiana PA (S)

Mattason, Michael, *Gallery Mgr,* District of Columbia Arts Center (DCAC), Washington DC

Mattei, Edwin J, *Head Dept,* Pontifical Catholic University of Puerto Rico, Dept of Fine Arts, Ponce PR (S)

Mattei, Edwin J, *Head Dept,* Pontifical Catholic University of Puerto Rico, Dept of Fine Arts, Ponce PR (S)

Mattern, Tom, *C+CC Dir,* Rensselaer Newman Foundation Chapel + Cultural Center, The Gallery at the Chapel & Cultural Center, Troy NY

Mattern, Yvette, *Asst Prof,* State University of New York at Albany, Art Dept, Albany NY (S)

Matteson, Todd A, *Chmn Fine Arts,* Lourdes University, Art Dept, Sylvania OH (S)

Matthews, Harriett, *Prof,* Colby College, Art Dept, Waterville ME (S)

Matthews, Marsha, *Dir Pub Servs,* Oregon Historical Society, Oregon History Museum, Portland OR

Matthews, Nancy, *Sr Cur Educ,* Kenosha Public Museums, Kenosha WI

Matthews, Paula, *Dir & Librn,* Library of the Boston Athenaeum, Boston MA

Matthias, Diana, *Cur Educ,* University of Notre Dame, Snite Museum of Art, Notre Dame IN

Matthis, Rose, *Instr,* Lamar University, Art Dept, Beaumont TX (S)

Mattice, Matt, *Exec Dir,* Judiciary History Center, Honolulu HI

Mattice, Shelby, *Mus Mgr,* Greene County Historical Society, Bronck Museum, Coxsackie NY

Mattke, Brittani, *Dir Mktg & Pub Rels,* Museum of Wisconsin Art, West Bend WI

Mattox, Diane, *Instr,* Bob Jones University, School of Fine Arts, Div of Art & Design, Greenville SC (S)

Mattson, John, *Co-Site Supvr,* Fort Totten State Historic Site, Pioneer Daughters Museum, Fort Totten ND

Mattson, John, *Preparator,* San Angelo Museum of Fine Arts, San Angelo TX

Mattson, Robert, *Chmn Art Dept & Coordr Art Gallery,* Ridgewater College, Art Dept, Willmar MN (S)

Mattys, Joe, *Assoc Prof,* Randolph-Macon College, Dept of the Arts, Ashland VA (S)

Matulewich, Vincent, *Co-Pres,* Guild of Creative Art, Shrewsbury NJ (S)

Matus, Edward M, *Gen Educ,* Art Institute of Pittsburgh, Pittsburgh PA (S)

Matuscak, Melissa, *Mus Dir & Cur,* Northern Michigan University, De Vos Art Museum, Marquette MI

Matvey, Richard, *Gen Educ,* Art Institute of Pittsburgh, Pittsburgh PA (S)

Matyas, Diane, *Dir Exhib & Programs,* Staten Island Museum, Staten Island NY

Matyas, Diane, *Dir Exhibs & Programs,* Staten Island Museum, Archives Library, Staten Island NY

Maude, Marshall, *Asst Prof,* University of Kansas, The School of the Arts, Dept of Visual Art, Lawrence KS (S)

Mauersberger, George, *Chmn & Assoc Prof,* Cleveland State University, Art Dept, Cleveland OH (S)

Mauk, Patrick, *Gallery Mgr,* Dayton Visual Arts Center, Dayton OH

Maul, John, *Asst Prof,* Oregon State University, Dept of Art, Corvallis OR (S)

Mauldin, Barbara, *Cur Latin American Folk Art,* Museum of New Mexico, Museum of International Folk Art, Santa Fe NM

Mauldin, Stephen L, *Instr,* Saint Gregory's University, Dept of Art, Shawnee OK (S)

Mault, Natalie, *Cur,* Louisiana State University, Museum of Art, Baton Rouge LA

Maupin, Sandra, *Adjunct Prof,* Southwest Baptist University, Art Dept, Bolivar MO (S)

Mauren, Paul, *Chmn,* College of Saint Rose, The Center For Art and Design, Albany NY (S)

Maurer, KC, *CFO & Treas,* Andy Warhol Foundation for the Visual Arts, New York NY

Maurer, Steven P, *Mktg,* The Nemours Foundatioin, Nemours Mansion & Gardens, Wilmington DE

Maurer, Tracy, *Instr,* University of Evansville, Art Dept, Evansville IN (S)

Maurier, Adele, *Opers & Design,* See Science Center, Manchester NH

Mauro, Robert, *Chmn,* Arcadia University, Dept of Fine Arts, Glenside PA (S)

Maury, Kate, *Asst Prof,* University of Wisconsin-Stout, Dept of Art & Design, Menomonie WI (S)

Maury, Nichole, *Printing Area Coordr,* Western Michigan University, Frostic School of Art, Kalamazoo MI (S)

Maus, Andy, *Cur Pub Programming,* Plains Art Museum, Fargo ND

Maute, Mary Jo, *Educ,* Whatcom Museum, Bellingham WA

Mavers, Steve, *Cur Educ,* Museum London, London ON

Mavery, Andy, *Assoc Prof,* University of Maine, Dept of Art, Orono ME (S)

Mawani, Salma, *Shop Mgr Wholesale & Supvr Admin,* University of British Columbia, Museum of Anthropology, Vancouver BC

Maxedon, Ed, *Cur Educ,* Indiana University, Art Museum, Bloomington IN

Maxion, Cornelia, *Instr,* Wayne Art Center, Wayne PA (S)

Maxon, Jennifer, *Assoc Librn & Archivist,* Museum of Ventura County, Ventura CA

Maxon, Mary, *Cur,* Rapid City Arts Council, Dahl Arts Center, Rapid City SD

Maxwell, Alison, *Exec Dir,* Providence Athenaeum, Providence RI

Maxwell, Betty, *Asst Dir,* Henry County Museum & Cultural Arts Center, Clinton MO

Maxwell, Deborah, *Lectr,* Emporia State University, Dept of Art, Emporia KS (S)

Maxwell, Jack, *Head Dept & Chmn,* Abilene Christian University, Dept of Art & Design, Abilene TX (S)

Maxwell, Kathleen, *Assoc Prof,* Santa Clara University, Dept of Art & Art History, Santa Clara CA (S)

Maxwell, Robert, *Asst Prof,* University of Michigan, Ann Arbor, Dept of History of Art, Ann Arbor MI (S)

Maxwell, Stephanie, *Asst Prof,* Rochester Institute of Technology, School of Photographic Arts & Sciences, Rochester NY (S)

Maxwell, Susan, *Assoc Prof,* University of Wisconsin Oshkosh, Dept of Art, Oshkosh WI (S)

Maxwell, Susie, *VPres Develop,* Eiteljorg Museum of American Indians & Western Art, Indianapolis IN

Maxwell, William C, *Prof,* The College of New Rochelle, School of Arts & Sciences Art Dept, New Rochelle NY (S)

Maxwell Lane, Marty, *Asst Prof,* Kansas City Art Institute, Kansas City MO (S)

May, Bill, *Dir,* Arrowmont School of Arts & Crafts, Arrowmont School of Arts & Crafts, Gatlinburg TN (S)

May, Cheryl, *Head Cur,* Brigham Young University, Museum of Art, Provo UT

May, Dan, *Chair,* Southern Arkansas University at Magnolia, Dept of Art & Design, Magnolia AR (S)

May, Daniel, *Chmn,* Newburyport Maritime Society, Inc, Custom House Maritime Museum, Newburyport MA

May, Jessica, *Asst Cur Photographs,* Amon Carter Museum of American Art, Fort Worth TX

May, Jessica, *Cur Contemporary & Modern Art,* Portland Museum of Art, Portland ME

May, Jill, *Dir Develop,* Urban Institute for Contemporary Arts, Grand Rapids MI

May, Jim, *VPres Programs,* Indiana State Museum, Indianapolis IN

May, Joyce, *Instr,* Northeastern Junior College, Art Department, Sterling CO (S)

May, Julia, *Cur,* Earlham College, Ronald Gallery, Richmond IN

May, Ken, *Exec Dir,* South Carolina Arts Commission, Columbia SC

May, Larry, *Instr,* Art Academy of Cincinnati, Cincinnati OH (S)

Maya, Gloria, *Prof,* Western New Mexico University, Dept of Expressive Arts, Silver City NM (S)

Mayar, Patricia, *Dir Visual Arts,* Rutgers, The State University of New Jersey, Mason Gross School of the Arts, Visual Arts Dept, New Brunswick NJ (S)

Mayberry, Martha T, *Registrar,* The Mint Museum, Charlotte NC

Maycock, Susan E, *Dir Survey,* Cambridge Historical Commission, Research Library on Architectural Social History of Cambridge, Mass, Cambridge MA

Mayer, Bob, *Instr,* University of Saint Francis, School of Creative Arts, Fort Wayne IN (S)

Mayer, Carol, *Cur Ethnology & Ceramics,* University of British Columbia, Museum of Anthropology, Vancouver BC

Mayer, Edward, *Prof,* State University of New York at Albany, Art Dept, Albany NY (S)

Mayer, John, *Cur,* Maine Historical Society, Portland ME

Mayer, John, *Mus Cur,* Maine Historical Society, Library and Museum, Portland ME

Mayer, Marc, *Dir,* National Gallery of Canada, Ottawa ON

Mayer, William, *Prof,* Hope College, Dept of Art & Art History, Holland MI (S)

Mayer, William A, *University Librn,* American University, Jack I & Dorothy G Bender Library & Learning Resources Center, New York NY

Mayes, Dewey, *Instr,* Wilkes Community College, Arts & Science Division, Wilkesboro NC (S)

Mayes, Steven, *Dir,* Arkansas State University-Art Department, Jonesboro, Fine Arts Center Gallery, Jonesboro AR

Mayes, Steven L, *Prof,* Arkansas State University, Dept of Art, State University AR (S)

Mayfield, Kimberly, *Pub Affairs,* National Museum of African Art, Smithsonian Institution, Washington DC

Mayhew, Rebecca, *Educ & Mem,* See Science Center, Manchester NH

Mayhugh, Cathy, *Exhib,* Fitton Center for Creative Arts, Hamilton OH

Mayhugh, Cathy, *Exhib,* Fitton Center for Creative Arts, Hamilton OH (S)

Maynard, George, *Asst,* GumTree Museum of Art, Tupelo MS

Maynard, Margaret, *Dir Visitor Experience & Interpreter,* San Jose Museum of Art, Library, San Jose CA

Maynard, Margie, *Educ & Pub Progs Dir,* Sonoma Valley Museum of Art, Sonoma CA

Maynard, Michael, *Chmn,* George Brown College of Applied Arts & Technology, Dept of Graphics, Toronto ON (S)

Mayne, Debby, *Asst Dir,* University of Louisiana at Lafayette, Paul and Lulu Hilliard University Art Museum, Lafayette LA

Maynes, Bill, *Dir,* The Fields Sculpture Park at Omi International Arts Center, Ghent NY

Mayo, Ann, *Mgr Security & Guest Servs,* Smith College, Museum of Art, Northampton MA

Mayo, Doug, *Assoc Librn,* Colonial Williamsburg Foundation, John D Rockefeller, Jr Library, Williamsburg VA

Mayocole, Lynne, *Pres,* Artists Talk on Art, New York NY

Mayor, Babette, *Prof,* California State Polytechnic University, Pomona, Department of Art, Pomona CA (S)

Mayrhofer, Ingrid, *Dir Prog,* A Space, Toronto ON

Mays, Brian, *Adjunct Prof,* Southern Nazarene University, Art & Design Department, Bethany OK (S)

Mays, Gayle, *Librr Asst,* Fort Worth Public Library Arts & Humanities, Fine Arts Section, Fort Worth TX

Mays, Peter, *Exec Dir,* Gallery 825/Los Angeles Art Association, Gallery 825, Los Angeles CA

Mayse, Kevin, *Chmn Performing Arts & Media,* Riverside Community College, Dept of Art & Mass Media, Riverside CA (S)

Maywood, John, *Cur,* Multicultural Heritage Centre, Public Art Gallery, Stony Plain AB

Maza, James, *Chief Technology Officer,* Walters Art Museum, Baltimore MD

Mazellen, Ron, *Prof,* Indiana Wesleyan University, School of Arts & Humanities, Division of Art, Marion IN (S)

Mazonowicz, Douglas, *Dir,* Gallery of Prehistoric Paintings, New York NY

Mazonowicz, Douglas, *Dir,* Gallery of Prehistoric Paintings, Library, New York NY

Mazow, Alissa, *Asst Prof,* University of Arkansas, Art Dept, Fayetteville AR (S)

Mazow, Leo, *Assoc Prof,* University of Arkansas, Art Dept, Fayetteville AR (S)

Mazur, Catherine, *Educ & Publicity Coordr,* University of New Hampshire, Museum of Art, Durham NH

Mazur, Michael, *Exec Dir,* Fresno Arts Center & Museum, Fresno CA

Mazur, Zachary, *Asst Cur,* Washington State University, Museum of Art, Pullman WA

Mazzaccaro, Paul R, *Asst Dir & COO,* Westport Public Library, Westport CT

Mazzei, Justin, *Teaching Artist Coordr,* Manchester Bidwell Corporation, Manchester Craftsmen's Guild Youth & Arts Program, Pittsburgh PA

Mazziotti Gillan, Maria, *Exec Dir Cultural Arts,* Passaic County Community College, Division of Humanities, Paterson NJ (S)

Mazzo, Kathryn, *Mus Shop Mgr,* Connecticut Historical Society, Hartford CT

McAdams, Holly, *Community Arts Prog Mgr,* Bemis Center for Contemporary Arts, Omaha NE

McAdams, Margaret, *Assoc Prof,* Ohio University-Chillicothe Campus, Fine Arts & Humanities Division, Chillicothe OH (S)

McAdams, Shane, *Instr,* Marian University, Art Dept, Fond Du Lac WI (S)

McAfee, Melissa, *Library Dir,* New York State Historical Association, Fenimore Art Museum, Cooperstown NY

Mcafee, Michael, *Cur History,* United States Military Academy, West Point Museum, West Point NY

McAffee, Dionne, *Co-Dir,* YYZ Artists' Outlet, Toronto ON

McAleer-Keeler, Kerry, *Dir Art & The Book,* Corcoran School of Art, Washington DC (S)

McAlister, Richard A, *Assoc Prof,* Providence College, Art & Art History Dept, Providence RI (S)

McAllister, Connie, *Dir Community Engagement,* Contemporary Arts Museum Houston, Houston TX

McAllister, Kay, *Bus Mgr,* Canton Museum of Art, Canton OH (S)

McAllister, Kay, *Bus, Admin & Mus Shop Mgr,* Canton Museum of Art, Canton OH

McAllister, Michael F, *Legal Advisor,* Art Services International, Alexandria VA

McAlpine, Donald, *Cur Zoology,* New Brunswick Museum, Saint John NB

McAlpine, Eleanor, *Educ & Events Coordr,* St Thomas-Elgin Public Art Centre, Saint Thomas ON

McAn, Robert, *Spec Events & Mem Mgr,* Kimbell Art Foundation, Kimbell Art Museum, Fort Worth TX

McAndrew, Nancy, *International Prog Coordr,* Virginia Center for the Creative Arts, Amherst VA

McArdle, Karen, *Assoc Prof,* University of Saint Francis, School of Creative Arts, Fort Wayne IN (S)

McArt, Craig, *Prof,* Rochester Institute of Technology, School of Design, Rochester NY (S)

McArthur, Andrew, *Pres Bd Dir,* Boulder Museum of Contemporary Art, Boulder CO

McArthur, Damon, *Asst Prof,* Western Illinois University, Department of Art, Macomb IL (S)

McArthur, Meher, *Cur East Asian Art,* Pacific - Asia Museum, Pasadena CA

McAsey, Veronica, *Lib Dir,* Southwestern College, Deets Library - Art Dept, Winfield KS

McAuliffe, Alice, *Mus Shop Mgr,* Walters Art Museum, Library, Baltimore MD

McAvey, Suzette, *Chief Cur,* William A Farnsworth, Museum, Rockland ME

McAvity, John G, *Exec Dir,* Canadian Museums Association, Association des Musees Canadiens, Ottawa ON

McAvoy, Kenneth J, *Chmn,* American Textile History Museum, Lowell MA

McAvoy, Suzette, *Dir,* CMCA-Center for Maine Contemporary Art, Art Gallery, Rockport ME

McAvoy, Suzette L, *Chief Cur,* William A Farnsworth, Library, Rockland ME

McBratney-Stapleton, Deborah, *Exec Dir,* Anderson Fine Arts Center, The Anderson Center for the Arts, Anderson IN

McBride, Carolyn N, *Secy,* National Hall of Fame for Famous American Indians, Anadarko OK

McBride, Debbie, *Admin Asst,* Alaska State Museum, Juneau AK

McBride, Joe, *Dir & Exec VPres,* National Hall of Fame for Famous American Indians, Anadarko OK

McBryde, Malcolm, *Head Librn,* Kalamazoo Institute of Arts, The Mary & Edwin Meader Fine Arts Library, Kalamazoo MI

McCabe, Caroline, *Gallery Coordr,* Santa Ana College, Art Gallery, Santa Ana CA

McCabe, Mary Kennedy, *Exec Dir,* Mid America Arts Alliance & Exhibits USA, Kansas City MO

McCabe, Maureen, *Prof,* Connecticut College, Dept of Art, New London CT (S)

McCabe, Michael M, *Library Dir,* Brevard College, Spiers Gallery, Brevard NC

McCabe, Michael M, *Library Dir,* Brevard College, James A Jones Library, Brevard NC

McCabe, Shauna, *Exec Dir,* Textile Museum of Canada, Toronto ON

McCafferty, Jay, *Instr,* Los Angeles Harbor College, Art Dept, Wilmington CA (S)

McCafferty, Michael, *Exhibitions Designer,* Seattle Art Museum, Downtown, Seattle WA

McCafferty, Michael, *Exhibitions Designer,* Seattle Art Museum, Dorothy Stimson Bullitt Library, Seattle WA

McCaffrey, Moira, *VPres Research & Coll,* Canadian Museum of Civilization, Gatineau PQ

McCain, Diane, *Head of Research Center,* Connecticut Historical Society, Library, Hartford CT

McCall, Ann, *Pres,* Royal Canadian Academy of Arts, Toronto ON

McCall, Janet, *Exec Dir,* Society for Contemporary Craft, Pittsburgh PA

McCall, Robert, *Prof,* Saint Mary's University of Minnesota, Art & Design Dept, Winona MN (S)

McCall, William, *Treas,* Fairmount Park Art Association, Philadelphia PA

McCalla, Mary Bea, *Dir,* French Art Colony, Library, Gallipolis OH

McCallister Clark, Ellen, *Dir Library,* The Society of the Cincinnati at Anderson House, Washington DC

McCampbell, Jerry, *Chmn Math & Science,* Idyllwild Arts Academy, Idyllwild CA (S)

McCandaless, Michael, *Theater Instr,* Creighton University, Fine & Performing Arts Dept, Omaha NE (S)

McCandless, Harry, *Treas,* Lancaster County Art Association, Inc, Strasburg PA

McCann, Don, *Pres,* Lahaina Arts Society, Art Organization, Lahaina HI

McCann, Heather, *Librn Urban Studies & Planning,* Massachusetts Institute of Technology, Rotch Library of Architecture & Planning, Cambridge MA

McCarroll Cutshaw, Stacey, *Exposure Ed,* Society for Photographic Education (SPE), SPE Gallery, Cleveland OH

McCarter, John W, *Pres & CEO,* Field Museum, Chicago IL

McCarthy, Christine, *Exec Dir,* Provincetown Art Association & Museum, Provincetown MA

McCarthy, Christine, *Exec Dir,* Provincetown Art Association & Museum, Library, Provincetown MA

McCarthy, David, *Assoc Prof,* Rhodes College, Dept of Art, Memphis TN (S)

McCarthy, Mary, *Pub Rels,* Greenville County Museum of Art, Greenville SC

McCarthy, Paul H, *Dir,* University of Alaska, Elmer E Rasmuson Library, Fairbanks AK

McCarthy, Ted, *Treas,* Pasadena Museum of California Art, Pasadena CA

McCartney, Kevin, *Dir,* Northern Maine Museum of Science, Presque Isle ME

McCarty, Cara, *Cur Dir,* Cooper-Hewitt National Design Museum, Smithsonian Institution, New York NY

McCarty, Laura, *Colls Registrar,* Tufts University, Tufts University Art Gallery, Medford MA

McCarville, Sarah, *Youth Svcs Coordr,* Grand Rapids Public Library, Grand Rapids MI

McCasland, Paul, *Museum & Planetarium Tech,* Lafayette Science Museum & Planetarium, Lafayette LA

McCaslin, Jack, *Prof,* James Madison University, School of Art & Art History, Harrisonburg VA (S)

McCauley, Anne, *Assoc Prof & Dept Chair,* Albion College, Bobbitt Visual Arts Center, Albion MI

McCauley, Anne, *Chmn,* University of Massachusetts - Boston, Art Dept, Boston MA (S)

McCauley, Barbara, *Chmn,* North Florida Community College, Dept Humanities & Art, Madison FL (S)

McCauley, Frank, *Asst Dir & Cur,* Sumter Gallery of Art, Sumter SC

McCauley, Robert N, *Chmn Dept Fine Arts,* Rockford College, Dept of Fine Arts, Rockford IL (S)

McCausland, Peter, *Chmn,* Independence Seaport Museum, Philadelphia PA

McCavley, Eva, *Instr,* University of Waterloo, Fine Arts Dept, Waterloo ON (S)

McCaw, Shana, *Gallery Dir,* Cardinal Stritch University, NM Gallery, Milwaukee WI

McClanahan, Pamela, *MHS Pres,* Minnesota Historical Society, Saint Paul MN

McClanan, Anne, *Asst Prof,* Portland State University, Dept of Art, Portland OR (S)

McClatchy, Ezra J D, *Pres,* American Academy of Arts & Letters, New York NY

McClay, Malcolm, *Lectr,* Southeastern Louisiana University, Dept of Visual Arts, Hammond LA (S)

McCleary, Joan Jeffers, *Dir,* Pacific Grove Art Center, Pacific Grove CA

McCleary, Stephen, *Pres,* Ocean County College, Humanities Dept, Toms River NJ (S)

McClellan, Andrew, *Prof,* Tufts University, Dept of Art & Art History, Medford MA (S)

McClelland, Mary, *Gallery Mgr,* South Shore Arts, Munster IN

McClenney-Brooker, Cheryl, *Dir,* Philadelphia Museum of Art, Main Building, Philadelphia PA

McClenny, Bart, *Dir Develop,* Trust Authority, Museum of the Great Plains, Lawton OK

McCloskey, Barbara, *Assoc Prof,* University of Pittsburgh, Henry Clay Frick Dept History of Art & Architecture, Pittsburgh PA (S)

McCloy, Keenan, *Dir Libraries,* Memphis-Shelby County Public Library & Information Center, Dept of Art, Music & Films, Memphis TN

McClung, Elizabeth, *Exec Dir,* Belle Grove Inc., Belle Grove Plantation, Middletown VA

McClure, Jeff, *Pres,* Whatcom Museum, Library, Bellingham WA

McClure, Michael J, *Asst Prof,* University of Wisconsin, Madison, Dept of Art, Madison WI (S)

McClure, Rachelle, *Chair, Interior Design,* Endicott College, School of Visual & Performing Arts, Beverly MA (S)

McCluskey, Holly, *Dir,* Oglebay Institute, Mansion Museum, Wheeling WV

McClusky, Pamela, *Cur African Art,* Seattle Art Museum, Downtown, Seattle WA

McClusky, Pamela, *Cur African Art,* Seattle Art Museum, Dorothy Stimson Bullitt Library, Seattle WA

McClyment, David, *Project Officer,* Visual Arts Ontario, Toronto ON

Mccoin, Mark, *Asst Prof,* University of Texas at San Antonio, Dept of Art & Art History, San Antonio TX (S)

McColl, Bruce, *Dir Art Center,* The Currier Museum of Art, Manchester NH

McColl, Donald, *Contact,* Washington College, Kohl Gallery, Chestertown MD

McColl, Terrie L, *Dir,* Palisades Park Public Library, Palisades Park NJ

McCollough, Pam, *Pres,* Casa Amesti, Monterey CA

McCollum, Ken, *Asst Prof,* Muskingum College, Art Department, New Concord OH (S)

McComas, Jenny, *Cur 19th & 20th Century Art,* Indiana University, Art Museum, Bloomington IN

McCombs, Bruce, *Prof,* Hope College, Dept of Art & Art History, Holland MI (S)

McCone, John, *Pres,* The Bartlett Museum, Amesbury MA

McConnaughy, James, *Pres,* National Antique & Art Dealers Association of America, Inc, New York NY

McConnell, Angela, *Exec Dir,* Montalvo Center for the Arts, Saratoga CA

McConnell, Brian, *Chair, Assoc Prof Art History & Classical Archaeology,* Florida Atlantic University, D F Schmidt College of Arts & Letters Dept of Visual Arts & Art History, Boca Raton FL (S)

McConnell, Michael, *Prof,* University of New Hampshire, Dept of Arts & Art History, Durham NH (S)

McConnell, Pamela Violante, *Registrar,* United States Capitol, Architect of the Capitol, Washington DC

McConnor, Sean, *Dir Permanent Coll,* Thiel College, Weyers-Sampson Art Gallery, Greenville PA

McConville, Matthew, *Prof,* Goucher College, Art & Art History Dept, Baltimore MD (S)

McConville, Shayna V, *Interim Dir,* Temple University, Tyler School of Art-Galleries, Philadelphia PA

McCord, Keryl, *Dir Resource Devel,* Alternate ROOTS, Inc, Atlanta GA

McCormack, John, *Dir,* INTAR Gallery, New York NY

McCormack, Lynne, *Mus Store Mgr,* The Pennsylvania State University, Palmer Museum of Art, University Park PA

McCormick, Jennifer, *Asst Archivist,* Charleston Museum, Library & Archives, Charleston SC

McCormick, Karen, *Asst Prof,* Mount Mary College, Art & Design Division, Milwaukee WI (S)

McCormick, Kathryn, *Asst Prof Graphic Design,* California Polytechnic State University at San Luis Obispo, Dept of Art & Design, San Luis Obispo CA (S)

McCosker, Jane, *First VPres,* Monmouth Museum & Cultural Center, Lincroft NJ

McCourt, Bonnie, *Publicity Coordr,* Order Sons of Italy in America, Garibaldi & Meucci Museum, Staten Island NY

McCourt, Emer, *Dir Mktg & PR,* Concord Museum, Concord MA

McCourt, Tim, *Assoc Prof,* Mississippi State University, Dept of Art, Starville MS (S)

McCourtney, Perry, *VPres,* Kennebec Valley Art Association, Harlow Gallery, Hallowell ME

McCoy, Claire B, *Asst Prof,* Longwood University, Dept of Art, Farmville VA (S)

McCoy, Dennis, *1st VPres,* Newport Historical Society & Museum of Newport History, Newport RI

McCoy, John, *Media Specialist,* Boston College, McMullen Museum of Art, Chestnut Hill MA

McCoy, Lori, *Treas,* Searchlight Historic Museum & Mining Park, Searchlight NV

McCoy, Paul A, *Prof & Ceramic in Res,* Baylor University - College of Arts and Sciences, Dept of Art, Waco TX (S)

McCracken, Patrick, *Dir & Cur,* Amarillo Art Association, Amarillo Museum of Art, Amarillo TX

McCrane, John, *Dir Finance & Admin,* The Trustees of Reservations, The Mission House, Ipswich MA

McCravey, Sally, *Bd Dir VChmn,* Plains Art Museum, Fargo ND

McCrea, Elizabeth, *Dir Commun Svcs,* Canadian Museum of Nature, Musee Canadien de la Nature, Ottawa ON

McCrea, Judith, *Chmn,* University of Kansas, Dept of Art, Lawrence KS (S)

McCrea, Judith, *Prof,* University of Kansas, The School of the Arts, Dept of Visual Art, Lawrence KS (S)

McCreary, Robert, *Instr,* University of South Carolina at Aiken, Dept of Visual & Performing Arts, Aiken SC (S)

McCrohan, Kay, *Art Chair Rockville,* Montgomery College, Dept of Art, Rockville MD (S)

McCroskey, Nancy, *Assoc Prof,* Indiana-Purdue University, Dept of Fine Arts, Fort Wayne IN (S)

McCue, Donald, *Cur,* Lincoln Memorial Shrine, Redlands CA

McCullagh, Diane, *Dir Human Resources,* Canadian Museum of Nature, Musee Canadien de la Nature, Ottawa ON

McCullagh, Suzanne Folds, *Prince Trust Chair & Cur Prints & Drawings,* The Art Institute of Chicago, Dept of Prints & Drawings, Chicago IL

McCulloch, Judith, *Dir,* Cape Ann Historical Association, Cape Ann Historical Museum, Gloucester MA

McCullogh, Heather Patterson, *Asst Prof,* Colorado Mesa University, Art Dept, Grand Junction CO (S)

McCullough, Ben, *Security Mgr,* Delaware Center for the Contemporary Arts, Wilmington DE

McCullough, Gloria, *Librn,* Wayne County Historical Society, Museum, Honesdale PA

McCullough, Holly K, *Cur Fine Arts & Exhibs,* Telfair Museums' Jepson Center for the Arts Library, Savannah GA

McCullough, James, *Instr,* Oklahoma State University, Graphic Arts Dept, Visual Communications, Okmulgee OK (S)

McCullough, Malcom, *Assoc Prof,* University of Michigan, Ann Arbor, School of Art & Design, Ann Arbor MI (S)

McCullough-Hudson, Mary, *Exec Dir,* Cincinnati Institute of Fine Arts, Cincinnati OH

McCutcheon, Paul, *Librn,* National Postal Museum, Library, Washington DC

McDade, Carrie L, *Head Librn,* Lesley University, College of Art & Design Library, Boston MA

McDade, Elizabeth, *Dir,* State University of New York, College at Brockport, Tower Fine Arts Gallery, Brockport NY

McDade, Marci, *Ed Surface Design Journal,* Surface Design Association, Inc, Sebastopol CA

McDaniel, Anita, *Colls Mgr,* Taos, E.L. Blumenschein Home & Museum & La Hacienda de los Martinez, Taos NM

McDaniel, Sheila, *Deputy Dir, Finance & Admin,* The Studio Museum in Harlem, New York NY

McDaniel, Sue Lynn, *Univ Archivist,* Western Kentucky University, Kentucky Library & Museum, Bowling Green KY

McDaniel, Taylor, *Events Coordr,* The Dallas Contemporary, Dallas Visual Art Center, Dallas TX

McDaniel, Todd, *Preparator,* Cheekwood-Tennessee Botanical Garden & Museum of Art, Nashville TN

McDavid, Stephanie, *Chmn Art Dept & Instr,* Saint Andrews Presbyterian College, Art Program, Laurinburg NC (S)

McDearmon, Nancy, *Registrarial Asst,* Sweet Briar College, Art Collection & Galleries, Sweet Briar VA

McDermott, Amanda, *Gallery Mgr,* Stephen Huneck Gallery at Dog Mountain, Saint Johnsbury VT

McDermott, Georgia, *Mus Store Mgr,* Santa Barbara Museum of Art, Library, Santa Barbara CA

McDermott, Inez, *Assoc Prof,* New England College, Art & Art History, Henniker NH (S)

McDermott, LeRoy, *Prof,* Central Missouri State University, Dept Art & Design, Warrensburg MO (S)

McDermott-Lewis, Melora, *Dir Educ,* Denver Art Museum, Denver CO

McDevitt, Jeannette, *Ast Librn,* Carnegie Mellon University, Hunt Institute for Botanical Documentation, Pittsburgh PA

McDevitt, John, *VPres Opers,* Please Touch Museum, Philadelphia PA

McDole, Amber, *Instr,* Graceland University, Fine Arts Div, Lamoni IA (S)

McDonald, Ann, *Asst Prof,* Northeastern University, Dept of Art & Architecture, Boston MA (S)

McDonald, Claire, *Dept Chmn,* University of Saint Thomas, Fine and Performing Arts Dept, Houston TX (S)

McDonald, Gordon, *Dir,* The Art Gallery of Southwestern Manitoba, Brandon MB

McDonald, Helen, *Registrar,* University of Chicago, Oriental Institute, Chicago IL

McDonald, J P, *Exec Dir,* Museum of East Texas, Lufkin TX

McDonald, Jessica, *Cur Colls,* Visual Studies Workshop, Research Center, Rochester NY (S)

McDonald, Jillian, *Prof,* Pace University, Dyson College of Arts & Sciences, Pleasantville NY (S)

McDonald, Karalee, *Educ,* George A Spiva, Joplin MO

McDonald, Katy, *Deputy Dir External Affairs,* San Diego Museum of Art, San Diego CA

McDonald, Larry, *Theatre Librn,* University of Regina, Education/Fine Arts Library, Regina SK

McDonald, Louisa, *Asst Prof,* University of Nevada, Las Vegas, Dept of Art, Las Vegas NV (S)

McDonald, Mercedes, *Adjunct,* College of the Canyons, Art Dept, Santa Clarita CA (S)

McDonald, Neal, *Asst Prof,* University of Saint Francis, School of Creative Arts, Fort Wayne IN (S)

McDonald, Norman D, *Pres,* Museum of Ossining Historical Society, Ossining NY

McDonald, Robert, *Coordr Art,* Cape Cod Community College, Art Dept, West Barnstable MA (S)

McDonald, Shirley, *Project Coordr,* Frederic Remington, Ogdensburg NY

McDonald, Terry, *Exec Dir,* Roberson Museum & Science Center, Binghamton NY

McDonald, Timothy, *Asst Prof,* Framingham State College, Art Dept, Framingham MA (S)

McDonald-Bell, Sheila, *Dir Events,* Lighthouse ArtCenter Museum & School of Art, Tequesta FL

McDonnell, Patricia, *Dir,* Wichita Art Museum, Wichita KS

McDonnell, Patricia, *Dir,* Wichita Art Museum, Emprise Bank Research Library, Wichita KS

McDonough, Amanda, *Mem & Vis Servs Mgr,* Triton Museum of Art, Santa Clara CA

McDonough, Anne, *Colls Mgr,* Historical Society of Washington DC, The City Museum of Washington DC, Washington DC

McDonough, Anne, *Colls Mgr,* Historical Society of Washington DC, Washington DC

McDonough, Thomas, *Assoc Prof,* State University of New York at Binghamton, Dept of Art History, Binghamton NY (S)

McDougle, Valli Thayer, *4th VPres,* National Watercolor Society, San Pedro CA

McDowell, Bill, *Prof Photog,* Texas A&M University Commerce, Dept of Art, Commerce TX (S)

McDowell, Cassie, *Visitor & Mem Serv,* Appalachian State University, Turchin Center for the Visual Arts, Boone NC

McDowell, Tim, *Prof,* Connecticut College, Dept of Art, New London CT (S)

McDuffie, Lori, *Registrar,* History Museum of Mobile, Mobile AL

McEiwan, Marilyn, *Instr,* University of Indianapolis, Dept Art & Design, Indianapolis IN (S)

McElherne, Linda, *Vis Lectr Art,* North Central College, Dept of Art, Naperville IL (S)

McElhiney, Brian, *Bldgs & Grounds Coordr,* National Trust for Historic Preservation, Chesterwood, Stockbridge MA

McElrath, Susan, *Archives & Spec Coll,* American University, Jack I & Dorothy G Bender Library & Learning Resources Center, New York NY

McElroy, Penny, *Chair Art Dept,* University of Redlands, Peppers Art Gallery, Redlands CA

McElroy, Sherri, *Instr,* Illinois Wesleyan University, School of Art, Bloomington IL (S)

McElvain, Jean, *Asst Cur,* University of Minnesota, Goldstein Museum of Design, Saint Paul MN

McElvaney Coonce, Jane, *VPres,* The Art League Gallery & School, Alexandria VA

McEvoy, Maureen, *Prog Mgr,* Canadian Museum of Contemporary Photography, Ottawa ON

McEvoy, Richard, *Recording Secy,* Pastel Society of America, National Arts Club, Grand Gallery, New York NY

McEwin, Florence, *Head Dept,* Western Wyoming Community College, Art Dept, Rock Springs WY (S)

McFadden, David, *Chief Cur,* Museum of Arts & Design, New York NY

McFadden, Dennis, *Assoc Dir,* Wellesley College, Davis Museum & Cultural Center, Wellesley MA

McFadden, Martin, *Treas,* Artspace, Richmond VA

McFadden, Robert, *Educ,* Pennsylvania Historical & Museum Commission, State Archives Div, Harrisburg PA

McFadden, Theresa, *Asst Prof,* Northern Virginia Community College, Art Dept, Annandale VA (S)

McFall, Tom, *Exec Dir,* Alberta Craft Council, Edmonton AB

McFarland, Felix, *Buildings & Grounds Supv,* Mamie McFaddin Ward, Beaumont TX

McFarland, James, *Prof Art,* Harford Community College, Visual, Performing and Applied Arts Division, Bel Air MD (S)

McFarland, JoAnne, *Dir,* A.I.R. Gallery, Brooklyn NY

McFarland, Thomas, *Chmn,* Union College, Music and Fine Arts Dept, Barbourville KY (S)

McFarlane, James, *Instr,* Wayne Art Center, Wayne PA (S)

McFarlane, Jim, *Pres,* American Watercolor Society, Inc., New York NY

McFarlane, Leesa, *Dir Sales,* State of North Carolina, Battleship North Carolina, Wilmington NC

McFarlane, Suzanne, *Site Supv,* Mississippi Valley Conservation Authority, R Tait McKenzie Memorial Museum, Almonte ON

McFee, Doris, *Asst Librn,* Chappell Memorial Library and Art Gallery, Chappell NE

McGaffin, Terri, *Asst Prof,* Morningside College, Art Dept, Sioux City IA (S)

McGahey, Laurie, *Dir Advanc,* James A Michener, Doylestown PA

McGarry, Joan, *Cur Educ,* Westmoreland Museum of American Art, Greensburg PA

McGarry, Steve, *Pres,* National Cartoonists Society, Winter Park FL

McGeachy, Heather, *Faculty,* Green River Community College, Art Dept, Auburn WA (S)

McGee, Bruce, *Mus Shop Mgr,* Heard Museum, Phoenix AZ

McGee, Gigi, *Chmn Graphic Design,* Moore College of Art & Design, Philadelphia PA (S)

McGee, Jo, *Planning & Exhib,* Lunenburg Art Gallery Society, Lunenburg NS

McGee, Julie L, *Cur African American Art,* University of Delaware, University Museums, Newark DE

McGee, Kelly, *Admin Asst,* Art Association of Harrisburg, School & Galleries, Harrisburg PA

McGee, Mike, *Cur,* California State University, Fullerton, Visual Arts Galleries, Fullerton CA

McGehee, Thomas C, *Dir Mus,* Bellingrath Gardens & Home, Theodore AL

McGehee, Turner, *Chmn Dept,* Hastings College, Art Dept, Hastings NE (S)

McGeough, Michelle, *Mus Studies Dept Faculty,* Institute of American Indian Arts, Museum of Contemporary Native Arts, Santa Fe NM (S)

McGibbon, Phyllis, *Assoc Prof,* Wellesley College, Art Dept, Wellesley MA (S)

McGill, Charles, *Dir,* Arthur M. Berger Art Gallery - Manhattanville College, Purchase NY

McGill, Charles, *Gallery Dir,* Manhattanville College, Brownson Gallery, Purchase NY

McGill, Charles, *Gallery Dir,* Manhattanville College, Arthur M Berger Gallery, Purchase NY

McGill, Dave, *Asst Prof,* Azusa Pacific University, College of Liberal Arts, Art Dept, Azusa CA (S)

McGill, Forrest, *Chief Cur,* Asian Art Museum of San Francisco, Chong-Moon Lee Ctr for Asian Art and Culture, San Francisco CA

McGill, Heather, *Head Sculpture Dept,* Cranbrook Academy of Art, Bloomfield Hills MI (S)

McGinn, Howard, *Dean,* Seton Hall University, Walsh Gallery & Library, South Orange NJ

McGinness, Karin, *Instr,* Century College, Humanities Dept, White Bear Lake MN (S)

McGinnis, George, *Instr,* California State University, San Bernardino, Dept of Art, San Bernardino CA (S)

McGinnis, Helen F, *Slide Cur,* Moore College of Art & Design, Library, Philadelphia PA

McGinnis, Mark, *Prof,* Northern State University, Art Dept, Aberdeen SD (S)

McGivern, Andy, *Cur Exhibs,* Leigh Yawkey Woodson Art Museum, Wausau WI

McGlauflin, Kristen, *Exhib Preparator,* Greenville Museum of Art, Inc, Greenville NC

McGloughlin, Kate, *Instr,* Woodstock School of Art, Inc, Woodstock NY (S)

McLaughlin, Kevin, *Instr,* South Central Technical College, Commercial & Technical Art Dept, North Mankato MN (S)

McLaughlin, Pam, *Cur Educ & Pub Progs,* Everson Museum of Art, Syracuse NY

McLaughlin, Patricia, *Chmn Art Dept,* State University of New York College at Old Westbury, Amelie A Wallace Gallery, Old Westbury NY

McLaughlin, Ursula, *Spec Projects Adminr,* College of William & Mary, Muscarelle Museum of Art, Williamsburg VA

McLean, Carlos, *Asst Dean,* Laney College, Art Dept, Oakland CA (S)

McLean, Dawn, *Grad Adv,* University of Alberta, Dept of Art & Design, Edmonton AB (S)

McLean, Dollie, *Founding Exec Dir,* Artists Collective Inc, Hartford CT

McLean, Jackie, *Founder,* Artists Collective Inc, Hartford CT

McLean, Julie Zappie, *Assoc Educator School & Family Progs,* Smith College, Museum of Art, Northampton MA

McLean, Linda, *Historic Site Mgr,* Olana State Historic Site, Hudson NY

McLean-Cowan, Evelyn, *Instr,* Marian University, Art Dept, Fond Du Lac WI (S)

McLean Ward, Barbara, *Dir & Cur,* The National Society of The Colonial Dames of America in the State of New Hampshire, Moffatt-Ladd House & Garden, Portsmouth NH

McLemore, Mary, *Dean,* Motlow State Community College, Art Dept, Tullahoma TN (S)

McLendon, Kirk, *Graphic Design,* Henry Ford Community College, McKenzie Fine Art Ctr, Dearborn MI (S)

McLendon, Marty, *Chair Visual Arts,* Northeast Mississippi Junior College, Art Dept, Booneville MS (S)

McLennan, Bill, *Mgr Design & Photog,* University of British Columbia, Museum of Anthropology, Vancouver BC

McLeod, Christian, *Asst Cur,* Maslak McLeod Gallery, Toronto ON

McLeod, Joseph, *Cur,* Maslak McLeod Gallery, Toronto ON

McLeod, Kersti, *Asst Cur,* Maslak McLeod Gallery, Toronto ON

McLeod, Nicole, *Dir Mktg & Pub Rels,* Morris Museum of Art, Augusta GA

McLerran, Jennifer, *Cur Mus,* Museum of Northern Arizona, Flagstaff AZ

McLoughlin, Boo, *Exec Dir,* Craft Alliance, Saint Louis MO

McMahan, Evadine, *Deputy Exec Dir,* Tennessee State Museum, Nashville TN

McMahan, Robert, *Prof,* Antelope Valley College, Art Dept, Division of Fine Arts, Lancaster CA (S)

McMahon, Cliff, *Prof,* Delta State University, Dept of Art, Cleveland MS (S)

McMahon, Diane, *Mus Shop Mgr,* Wenham Museum, Timothy Pickering Library, Wenham MA

McMahon, John, *Coll Mgr,* National Portrait Gallery, Smithsonian Institution, Washington DC

McMahon, John, *Dir Artist Svcs,* Idaho Commission on the Arts, Boise ID

McMahon, Maggie, *Prof,* University of Tennessee at Chattanooga, Dept of Art, Chattanooga TN (S)

McMahon, Patrick, *Dir Exhib & Design,* Museum of Fine Arts, Boston MA

McMahon, Sharon, *Chmn,* Saint Mary's University, Dept of Fine Arts, San Antonio TX (S)

McManus, James, *Prof Emeritus,* California State University, Chico, Department of Art & Art History, Chico CA (S)

McManus, James, *Prof Emeritus Art History Research,* California State University, Chico, Janet Turner Print Museum, CSU, Chicago, Chico CA

McManus Zurko, Kitty, *Dir,* The College of Wooster, The College of Wooster Art Museum, Wooster OH

McMaster, Lynn, *Exec VPres,* Please Touch Museum, Philadelphia PA

McMath, Hope, *Dir,* Cummer Museum of Art & Gardens, Museum & Library, Jacksonville FL

McMath, Sheila, *Dir Educator,* Canadian Clay and Glass Gallery, Waterloo ON

McMathon, Janet, *Admin Spec,* Iowa State University, Brunnier Art Museum, Ames IA

McMichael, Luci, *Instr,* University of Missouri, Saint Louis, Dept of Art & Art History, Saint Louis MO (S)

McMillan, Barbara, *Librn,* Mount Vernon Ladies' Association of the Union, Library, Mount Vernon VA

McMillan, David, *Prof,* University of Manitoba, School of Art, Winnipeg MB (S)

McMillan, David, *Security Mgr,* Kimbell Art Foundation, Kimbell Art Museum, Fort Worth TX

McMillan, Edna, *Chmn,* Cameron University, Art Dept, Lawton OK (S)

McMillan, Gillian, *Sr Conservator Colls,* Solomon R Guggenheim, New York NY

McMillan, Melinda, *Mgr Gardens,* Philbrook Museum of Art, Tulsa OK

McMillan, Morgan, *Coll Mgr,* Lehigh Valley Heritage Center, Allentown PA

McMillan, Murray, *Asst Prof,* Biola University, Art Dept, La Mirada CA (S)

McMillen, Jim, *Living History Coord,* West Florida Historic Preservation, Inc/University of West Florida, T T Wentworth, Jr Florida State Museum; Historic Pensacola Village; Pensacola Historical Society & Resource Center, Pensacola FL

McMorris, Lillian, *Pub Rels,* The Walker African American Museum & Research Center, Las Vegas NV

McMullen, Paul, *Asst Prof,* Siena Heights University, Studio Angelico-Art Dept, Adrian MI (S)

McMurrey, Enfys, *Instr,* Indian Hills Community College, Dept of Art, Centerville IA (S)

McNab, Cheryl, *Chief Exec Officer,* Western Colorado Center for the Arts, Library, Grand Junction CO

McNab, Cheryl, *Dir,* Western Colorado Center for the Arts, The Art Center, Grand Junction CO

McNair, Amy, *Assoc Prof,* University of Kansas, Kress Foundation Dept of Art History, Lawrence KS (S)

McNally, Dennis, *Chmn/Prof Painting,* Saint Joseph's University, Art Dept, Philadelphia PA (S)

McNally, Joanne, *Dir Exhib,* Valley Cottage Library, Gallery, Valley Cottage NY

McNally, Ryan, *Asst Cataloger,* Philadelphia Museum of Art, Library & Archives, Philadelphia PA

McNally, Samantha, *Dir Communs,* California Watercolor Association, Gallery Concord, Concord CA

McNally, Sheila J, *Prof,* University of Minnesota, Minneapolis, Art History, Minneapolis MN (S)

McNamara, Brian, *Preparator,* DeCordova Museum & Sculpture Park, DeCordova Museum, Lincoln MA

McNamara, Chris, *Registrar,* Parrish Art Museum, Water Mill NY

McNamara, Jennifer, *Asst Prof,* State University of New York, College at Cortland, Dept Art & Art History, Cortland NY (S)

McNamara, Mary, *Pres & Exec Dir,* The Interchurch Center, Library, New York NY

McNamara, Mary Jo, *Asst Prof,* State University of New York College at Potsdam, Dept of Fine Arts, Potsdam NY (S)

McNamara, Sarah, *Pub Rels & Spec Events,* Rockford Art Museum, Rockford IL

McNamee, AAron, *Vis Artist,* University of New Orleans-Lake Front, Dept of Fine Arts, New Orleans LA (S)

McNamee, Donald W, *Chief Librn,* Natural History Museum of Los Angeles County, Research Library, Los Angeles CA

McNaughton, John, *Prof Emeritus,* University of Southern Indiana, Department of Art, Evansville IN (S)

McNaughton, Mary Davis, *Dir,* Scripps College, Ruth Chandler Williamson Gallery, Claremont CA

McNeer, James B, *Pres,* Richard Bland College, Art Dept, Petersburg VA (S)

McNeil, Courtney, *Cur Art,* Telfair Museums' Jepson Center for the Arts Library, Savannah GA

McNeil, Dan, *Dir Develop,* Figge Art Museum, Davenport IA

McNeil-Kemp, Linda, *Dir Educ,* Cape Cod Museum of Art Inc, Dennis MA

McNeill, Richard, *VPres & Gallery Co Dir,* Sculptor's Society of Canada, Canadian Sculpture Centre, Toronto ON

McNeill, Winifred, *Asst Prof,* New Jersey City University, Art Dept, Jersey City NJ (S)

McNiell, Winifred, *Dept Chair,* New Jersey City University, Courtney Art Gallery & Lemmerman Gallery, Jersey City NJ

McNulty, John, *Retail Mgr,* Tucson Museum of Art and Historic Block, Tucson AZ

McNulty, Neely, *School & Family Programs Coordr,* Dartmouth College, Hood Museum of Art, Hanover NH

McNutt, James, *Adjunct Prof,* Washington & Jefferson College, Art Dept, Washington PA (S)

McNutt, James C, *Pres & CEO,* National Museum of Wildlife Art of the Unites States, Jackson WY

McNutt, James C, *Pres & Exec Dir,* Witte Museum, San Antonio TX

McOstrichZarull, Katherine, *Past Pres,* Canadian Society of Painters In Watercolour, Toronto ON

McPhail, Howard, *Cur Educ,* Mobile Museum of Art, Mobile AL

McPhail, Howard, *Cur Educ,* Mobile Museum of Art, Library, Mobile AL

McPhee, Maureen, *Adjunct,* Feather River Community College, Art Dept, Quincy CA (S)

McPhee, Sarah Collyer, *Prof,* Emory University, Art History Dept, Atlanta GA (S)

McPherson, Heather, *Prof,* University of Alabama at Birmingham, Dept of Art & Art History, Birmingham AL (S)

McPherson, Tina, *Libr Supv,* Art Museum of the University of Houston, William R Jenkins Architecture & Art Library, Houston TX

McQuaid, Matilda, *Cur Textiles,* Cooper-Hewitt National Design Museum, Smithsonian Institution, New York NY

McQuillen, Troy, *Adjunct Instr,* Northern State University, Art Dept, Aberdeen SD (S)

McRainey, D Lynn, *Dir History Educ,* Chicago History Museum, Chicago IL

McRorie, Sharon, *Educ Progs Mgr,* Asheville Art Museum, Asheville NC

McSweeney, Emmett, *Dir,* Silas Bronson, Waterbury CT

McTavish, Lianne, *Coordr History of Art, Design & Visual Culture,* University of Alberta, Dept of Art & Design, Edmonton AB (S)

McTighe, Lake, *Dir Gallery,* College of Santa Fe, Art Dept, Santa Fe NM (S)

McTighe, Monica, *Asst Prof,* Tufts University, Dept of Art & Art History, Medford MA (S)

McTique, Mary, *Exec Dir,* Boston Center for Adult Education, Boston MA (S)

McTyre, Robert, *Asst Chair,* Middle Georgia State College, Humanities Division, Dept of Art - School of Liberal Arts, Dept of Media, Culture & the Arts, Cochran GA (S)

McVaugh, Robert, *Assoc Prof,* Colgate University, Dept of Art & Art History, Hamilton NY (S)

McVay, Desmond, *Lectr,* California State Polytechnic University, Pomona, Department of Art, Pomona CA (S)

McVicker, Charles, *Asst Prof,* The College of New Jersey, School of Arts & Sciences, Ewing NJ (S)

McWeeney, Jim, *Instr,* Joe Kubert, Dover NJ (S)

McWhorter, Mark, *Dept Head,* Indian Hills Community College, Ottumwa Campus, Dept of Art, Ottumwa IA (S)

McWhorter, Mark, *Head Dept,* Indian Hills Community College, Dept of Art, Centerville IA (S)

McWilliams, Curtis, *Pres,* Orlando Museum of Art, Orlando FL

McWilliams, Leighton, *Assoc Prof,* University of Texas at Arlington, Art & Art History Department, Arlington TX (S)

McWillie, Judy, *Prof Drawing & Painting,* University of Georgia, Franklin College of Arts & Sciences, Lamar Dodd School of Art, Athens GA (S)

Meacham, Sue, *Secy,* San Angelo Art Club, Helen King Kendall Memorial Art Gallery, San Angelo TX

Mead, Elizabeth, *Assoc Prof,* Portland State University, Dept of Art, Portland OR (S)

Mead, Jeanine, *Recorder,* Neville Public Museum of Brown County, Research Library, Photo & Film Collection, Green Bay WI

Mead, Taylor, *Artist,* U Gallery, New York NY

Mead-Donaldson, Barbara Young, *Art Svcs Librn,* Miami-Dade Public Library, Miami FL

Meade, James, *Prof,* University of Southern Mississippi, Dept of Art & Design, Hattiesburg MS (S)

Meadows, Andrew, *Deputy Dir,* American Numismatic Society, New York NY

Meadows, Ted, *Adjunct Assoc Prof Art History/Architecture,* Johnson County Community College, Fine Arts Dept & Art History Dept, Overland Park KS (S)

Meadows, Teresa, *Assoc Prof, Film Studies & Visual & Performing Arts,* University of Colorado-Colorado Springs, Visual & Performing Arts Dept (VAPA), Colorado Springs CO (S)

Meadu, Alexander, *Dir Opers,* McMichael Canadian Art Collection, Kleinburg ON

Mealing, Cathleen, *Dir,* Bryant Library, Roslyn NY

Meanley, Jennifer, *Prof,* University of North Carolina at Greensboro, Art Dept, Greensboro NC (S)

Means, Leland, *Sculpture,* Orange Coast College, Visual & Performing Arts Division, Costa Mesa CA (S)

Mear, Margaret, *Prof,* Saint Mary's University of Minnesota, Art & Design Dept, Winona MN (S)

Mearns, Travis, *Pub Rels Coordr,* Southern Alleghenies Museum of Art, Ligonier Valley Facility, Loretto PA

Mears, Patricia, *Deputy Dir,* Fashion Institute of Technology, The Museum at FIT, New York NY

Mechnig, Daniel, *Pres,* Providence Art Club, Providence RI

Mecklenburg, Frank, *Archivist,* Leo Baeck, Library, New York NY

Mecklenburg, Frank, *Chief Archivist,* Leo Baeck, New York NY

Meckstroth, Emelia, *Mktg Mgr,* University of Virginia, The Fralin Museum of Art at the University of Virginia, Charlottesville VA

Mecky, Debra L, *Exec Dir,* Bush-Holley Historic Site & Storehouse Gallery, Greenwich Historical Society/ Bush-Holley House, Cos Cob CT

Meder, Brenda K., *Exec Dir,* Hays Arts Center Gallery, Hays KS

Medford, Amy, *Dir,* Quietude Garden Gallery, East Brunswick NJ

Medina, Christine, *Mgr,* Rice University, Rice Gallery, Houston TX

Medina, Ron, *Instr,* Laramie County Community College, Division of Arts & Humanities, Cheyenne WY (S)

Medinger, Bob, *Dir,* Sitka Historical Society, Sitka Historical Museum, Sitka AK

Medley, Chris, *Asst Prof,* Maryland College of Art & Design, Silver Spring MD (S)

Medrano, Jerry, *Asst Cur,* City of El Paso, El Paso TX

Medua, Maria, *Corporate Art Coordr,* San Francisco Museum of Modern Art, Artist Gallery, San Francisco CA

Medvedow, Jill, *Dir,* Institute of Contemporary Art, Boston MA

Meehan, Brian, *Exec Dir,* Museum London, London ON

Meek, A J, *Prof,* Louisiana State University, School of Art, Baton Rouge LA (S)

Meek, Ken, *Dir,* The Frank Phillips, Woolaroc Museum, Bartlesville OK

Meek, William, *Prof,* Texas State University - San Marcos, Dept of Art and Design, San Marcos TX (S)

Meeker, Cheryl, *Prof Art,* Monmouth College, Dept of Art, Monmouth IL (S)

Meeks, Donna M, *Chmn & Prof,* Lamar University, Art Dept, Beaumont TX (S)

Meeks, Jim, *Registrar,* Oklahoma City Museum of Art, Oklahoma City OK

Meeks, Stephanie, *Pres,* National Trust for Historic Preservation, Washington DC

Meeuwsen, Jeffrey, *Exec Dir,* Urban Institute for Contemporary Arts, Grand Rapids MI

Mehalakes, Elaine, *Cur,* Wellesley College, Davis Museum & Cultural Center, Wellesley MA

Mehlferber, Jon, *Chmn,* Virginia Intermont College, Fine Arts Div, Bristol VA (S)

Mehling, Beth, *Pres,* Big Horn County Historical Museum, Hardin MT

Mehner, Da-ka-xeen, *Asst Prof,* University of Alaska-Fairbanks, Dept of Art, Fairbanks AK (S)

Mehnng, Christine, *Chair,* University of Chicago, Dept of Art History, Chicago IL (S)

Mehran, Laleh, *Assoc Prof Electronic Media Arts & Design,* University of Denver, School of Art & Art History, Denver CO (S)

Mehrhoff, Arthur, *Academic Coordr,* University of Missouri, Museum of Art & Archaeology, Columbia MO

Meier, Carsten, *Asst Prof,* University of Miami, Dept of Art & Art History, Coral Gables FL (S)

Meier, Jan, *Mgr,* Maritz, Inc, Library, Fenton MO

Meier, Scott, *Exhibit Preparator,* University of Michigan, Kelsey Museum of Archaeology, Ann Arbor MI

Meiers, Susanna, *Dir,* El Camino College Art Gallery, Torrance CA

Meijer, Lena, *Prof Art History,* Aquinas College, Art Dept, Grand Rapids MI (S)

Meine, Carol, *Dir,* Mesa Public Library Art Gallery, Los Alamos NM

Meir, Katia, *Asst Dir,* Saidye Bronfman, Liane & Danny Taran Gallery, Montreal PQ

Meissner, Elizabeth, *Contact,* Francis Hardy Gallery, Fish Creek WI

Meister, Clara, *Curatorial Res (2012),* Goethe-Institut New York, Mini/Goethe-Institut Curatorial Residencies Ludlow 38, New York NY

Meister, Pam, *Dir Colls Resources,* Atlanta Historical Society Inc, Atlanta History Center, Atlanta GA

Meixner, Laura L, *Assoc Prof,* Cornell University, Dept of the History of Art & Visual Studies, Ithaca NY (S)

Meizner, Karen, *Registrar,* Sheldon Museum & Cultural Center, Inc, Sheldon Museum & Cultural Center, Haines AK

Mejchar, James D, *Exec Dir,* International Clown Hall of Fame & Research Center, Inc, West Allis WI

Mejer, Robert Lee, *Dir Gallery,* Quincy University, The Gray Gallery, Quincy IL

Mejer, Robert Lee, *Prof Art,* Quincy University, Dept of Art, Quincy IL (S)

Mejia-Krumbein, Beatriz, *Prof,* La Sierra University, Art Dept, Riverside CA (S)

Mekas, Jonas, *Dir & Vol Pres,* Anthology Film Archives, New York NY

Melancon, Joseph, *Instr,* Art Center Sarasota, Sarasota FL (S)

Melandri, Lisa, *Deputy Dir Exhibs & Programming,* Santa Monica Museum of Art, Santa Monica CA

Melberg, Jerald, *Dir,* Jerald Melberg Gallery, Charlotte NC

Melching, Sarah, *Adj Faculty Conservation,* University of Denver, School of Art & Art History, Denver CO (S)

Melching, Sarah, *Dir Conservation,* Denver Art Museum, Denver CO

Melemenis, Lia, *Registrar,* Glenbow Museum, Calgary AB

Melenbrink, Michael, *Bus Mgr,* Flint Institute of Arts, Library, Flint MI

Melenbrink, Michael, *Dir Finance & Admin,* Flint Institute of Arts, Flint MI

Melendez, Tanya, *Educ Cur,* Fashion Institute of Technology, The Museum at FIT, New York NY

Melhem, Yahya, *Aga Khan Cataloger,* Massachusetts Institute of Technology, Rotch Library of Architecture & Planning, Cambridge MA

Melick, Randolph, *Instr,* New York Academy of Art, Graduate School of Figurative Art, New York NY (S)

Melion, Walter S, *Prof,* Emory University, Art History Dept, Atlanta GA (S)

Melis, Rachel, *Asst Prof,* Kansas State University, Art Dept, Manhattan KS (S)

Melius, Mary, *Mgr Traveling Exhibs,* Norman Rockwell Museum, Stockbridge MA

Melkumyan, Marian, *Instr,* South Dakota State University, Dept of Visual Arts, Brookings SD (S)

Mella, Joseph S, *Dir,* Vanderbilt University, Vanderbilt University Fine Arts Gallery, Nashville TN

Mellili, Mary, *Prof,* Salem State University, Art & Design Department, Salem MA (S)

Mellin, Kim, *Dir Educ,* New Canaan Historical Society, New Canaan CT

Mellin, Robert, *Prof,* McGill University, School of Architecture, Montreal PQ (S)

Mello, Emily, *Cur Educ,* Purchase College, Neuberger Museum of Art, Purchase NY

Mello, Sally Dean, *Coordr Educ,* Art Complex Museum, Carl A. Weyerhaeuser Library, Duxbury MA

Mellon, Marc Richard, *Pres,* Artists' Fellowship, Inc, New York NY

Mellone, Allyson, *Colls Mgr,* Queens College, City University of New York, Godwin-Ternbach Museum, Flushing NY

Melloy, Bridget, *Dir.,* Philip Slein Gallery, Saint Louis MO

Melmer, Janeen, *Mus Registrar,* Crazy Horse Memorial, Indian Museum of North America, Native American Educational & Cultural Center & Crazy Horse Memorial Library (Reference), Crazy Horse SD

Melochick, Patricia, *Treas,* Peninsula Fine Arts Center, Newport News VA

Melsner, Robin, *Dir Programs,* Massachusetts Institute of Technology, MIT Museum, Cambridge MA

Melton, Allison, *Asst Prof,* Delta State University, Dept of Art, Cleveland MS (S)

Melton, Laura, *Chmn Music,* Idyllwild Arts Academy, Idyllwild CA (S)

Melton, Matthew, *Chmn,* Lee University, Dept of Communication & the Arts, Cleveland TN (S)

Melton, Maureen, *Dir Library & Archives,* Museum of Fine Arts, William Morris Hunt Memorial Library, Boston MA

Melton, Maureen, *Hilles Dir Libraries & Archives,* Museum of Fine Arts, Boston MA

Melville, Crystal, *Exec Dir,* Visual Arts Nova Scotia, Halifax NS

Melvin, Meg, *Mod & Contemp Specialist,* National Gallery of Art, Department of Image Collections, Washington DC

Melvin, Meghan, *Jean S & Frederic A Sharf Cur Design,* Museum of Fine Arts, Boston MA

Menard, Lloyd, *Prof,* University of South Dakota, Department of Art, College of Fine Arts, Vermillion SD (S)

Menard, Michael J, *Cur Archives & Librn,* Museum of Western Colorado, Museum of the West, Grand Junction CO

Mencini, Susan, *Instr,* Cuyahoga Valley Art Center, Cuyahoga Falls OH (S)

Mendell, Cyndi, *Instr Foundation Art,* The Art Institute of Cincinnati, AIC College of Design, Cincinnati OH (S)

Mendell, Sean M, *Pres,* The Art Institute of Cincinnati, AIC College of Design, Cincinnati OH (S)

Mendenhall, Kathleen, *Adjunct Assoc Prof Art History,* Johnson County Community College, Fine Arts Dept & Art History Dept, Overland Park KS (S)

Mendenhall, Susan, *Dir Resource Develop,* Arts United of Greater Fort Wayne, Fort Wayne IN

Mendez, Ivan, *Cur Archaeology,* University of Puerto Rico, Museum of Anthropology, History & Art, Rio Piedras PR

Mendez, Ivan, *Cur Archaeology,* University of Puerto Rico, Museum of Anthropology, History & Art, Rio Piedras PR

Mendez, Mike, *Dir Exhib,* Shepherd University, Dept of Contemporary Art & Theater, Shepherdstown WV (S)

Mendive, Toni, *Archivist,* Northeastern Nevada Museum, Elko NV

Mendoza, Cora Myers, *Mem Bd Dir,* Hatch-Billops Collection, Inc, New York NY

Mendoza, Mary, *Treas,* Long Beach Art League, Long Beach Library, Long Beach NY

Meng, Micki, *Asst Dir,* California College of the Arts, CCAC Wattis Institute for Contemporary Arts, San Francisco CA

Meng, Micki, *Progs Coordr,* Capp Street Project, Wattis Institute, San Francisco CA

Meng, Sara F, *Chmn Art Dept,* Harrisburg Area Community College, Division of Communications, Humanities & the Arts, Harrisburg PA (S)

Menius, Art, *Exec Dir,* The ArtsCenter, The Nicholson Gallery at the Arts Center, Carrboro NC

Menk, Marty, *Bus Mgr,* The Butler Institute of American Art, Art Museum, Youngstown OH

Menn, Richard J, *Cur,* Carmel Mission & Gift Shop, Carmel CA

Menocal, Narciso G, *Prof,* University of Wisconsin, Madison, Dept of Art History, Madison WI (S)

Menschel, Robert B, *Chmn Emeritus,* Museum of Modern Art, New York NY

Mensching, Bill, *Vice Pres,* National Society of Mural Painters, Inc, New York NY

Menser, Shirley, *Chmn,* Dawson Springs Museum and Art Center, Dawson Springs KY

Mercado, Anita, *Dir Community Empowerment Progs,* Inquilinos Boricuas en Accion, Boston MA

Mercede, Nevin, *Dir,* Antioch College, Noyes & Read Gallery/Herndon Gallery, Yellow Springs OH

Mercede, Nevin, *Prof,* Antioch College, Visual Arts Dept, Yellow Springs OH

Mercer, Clay, *Develop Dir,* Arkansas Arts Center, Museum, Little Rock AR (S)

Mercer, Cynda, *Head Admin,* Museum London, London ON

Mercer, Deborah O, *Pres,* Warwick Museum of Art, Warwick RI

Mercer, John, *Coordr, Photograph Dept,* Phoenix College, Dept of Art & Photography, Phoenix AZ (S)

Mercer, Valerie, *Cur African American Art,* Detroit Institute of Arts, Detroit MI

Merchant, Lynn, *Staff Asst,* Grassroots Art Center, Lucas KS

Mercogliano, Carol, *Bemis Admin Asst,* Colorado Springs Fine Arts Center, Bemis School of Art, Colorado Springs CO

Merdzinski, Marilyn, *Dir Colls & Preservation,* Grand Rapids Public Museum, Public Museum of Grand Rapids, Grand Rapids MI

Meredith, Jane, *Cur,* The Schepis, Louisiana Artists Museum, Columbia LA

Merendino, Mia, *Dir,* Clymer Museum of Art, Ellensburg WA

Mergel, Jennifer, *Robert, Enid & Bruce Beal Sr Cur Contemporary Art,* Museum of Fine Arts, Boston MA

Merker, Mary Ann, *Civic Arts Coordr,* Berkeley Civic Arts Program, Berkeley CA

Merklin, Tillian, *Program Coordr,* Western Sculpture Academy of Meriks, Tucson AZ

Merkt, Donna, *Cur Educ,* Mabee-Gerrer Museum of Art, Shawnee OK

Merkur, Barbara, *Instr & Supv,* Toronto Art Therapy Institute, Toronto ON (S)

Merle, Michel D, *Prof,* Worcester State College, Visual & Performing Arts Dept, Worcester MA (S)

Merline, Mark, *Chair Art Dept,* Marian University, Art Dept, Fond Du Lac WI (S)

Merling, Mitchell, *Paul Mellon Cur & Head Dept European Art,* Virginia Museum of Fine Arts, Richmond VA

Merrill, Yolanda, *Art Librn,* Washington & Lee University, Leyburn Library, Lexington VA

Merriman, Larry, *Asst Prof & Gallery Dir,* Coker College, Art Dept, Hartsville SC (S)

Merriman, Larry, *Dir,* Coker College, Cecelia Coker Bell Gallery, Hartsville SC

Merritt, Keely, *Head Photographer,* The Historic New Orleans Collection, Royal Street Galleries, New Orleans LA

Merritt, Sarah, *Exec Dir,* The Arts Council of Wayne County, Goldsboro NC (S)

Merryday, Michaela, *Asst Prof, Art Hist & Visual Cult,* University of Tulsa, School of Art, Tulsa OK (S)

Mershimer, Frederick, *Instr,* Manhattan Graphics Center, New York NY (S)

Mersmann, Armin, *Mus School Mgr,* Alden B. Dow Museum of Science & Art, Alden B. Dow Museum School, Midland MI (S)

Mersmann, Armin, *Museum School Mgr,* Arts Midland Galleries & School, Alden B. Dow Museum of Science & Art, Midland MI

Mersmann, Armin, *Studio School Coordr & Registrar,* Arts Midland Galleries & School, Midland MI

Mesa, Osvaldo, *Co-Chmn,* Fondo del Sol, Visual Art & Media Center, Washington DC

Mesa-Gaido, Elisabeth, *Prof,* Morehead State University, Art & Design Dept, Morehead KY (S)

Mesa-Gaido, Gary, *Prof,* Morehead State University, Art & Design Dept, Morehead KY (S)

Mesch, Claudia, *Asst Prof,* Cleveland State University, Art Dept, Cleveland OH (S)

Mess, Tamara, *Office Mgr,* New Visions Gallery, Inc, Marshfield WI

Messec, Don, *Asst Prof,* College of Santa Fe, Art Dept, Santa Fe NM (S)

Messer, James, *Instr,* Mitchell Community College, Visual Art Dept, Statesville NC (S)

Messer, Jennifer, *Asst to Dir,* Sweetwater County Library System and School District #1, Community Fine Arts Center, Rock Springs WY

Messerschmidt, Gale, *Cur,* West Florida Historic Preservation, Inc/University of West Florida, T T Wentworth, Jr Florida State Museum; Historic Pensacola Village; Pensacola Historical Society & Resource Center, Pensacola FL

Messersmith, Lynne C, *Gallery Dir,* Carnegie Arts Center, Alliance NE

Messersmith, Mark, *Prof,* Florida State University, Art Dept, Tallahassee FL (S)

Messimer, Susan, *Cur Community Life,* Landis Valley Village and Farm Museum, PA Historical & Museum Commission, Lancaster PA

Messina, Mitchell, *Assoc Prof,* Nazareth College of Rochester, Art Dept, Rochester NY (S)

Messinger, Faye, *Librn,* Monterey History & Art Association, Library, Monterey CA

Metcalf, D, *Librn Asst,* Fort Worth Public Library Arts & Humanities, Fine Arts Section, Fort Worth TX

Metcalf, Michael, *Prof,* Western New Mexico University, Dept of Expressive Arts, Silver City NM (S)

Metcalf, Ned, *State Svcs,* Arkansas Arts Center, Museum, Little Rock AR (S)

Metcalf, Preston, *Chief Cur,* Triton Museum of Art, Santa Clara CA

Metcalf, Susan E, *Cur,* Miracle at Pentecost Foundation, Biblical Arts Center, Dallas TX

Metcalfe, Robin, *Dir & Cur,* St Mary's University, Art Gallery, Halifax NS

Metcoff, Donald, *Chicago Representative,* American Society of Artists, Inc, Palatine IL

Metcoff, Donald, *Librn,* American Society of Artists, Inc, Library Organization, Palatine IL

Metoyer, Priscilla, *Curriculum Specialist,* The Multicultural Center of the South, Shreveport LA

Metraux, M, *Cur,* York University, Fine Arts Phase II Slide Library, Toronto ON

Metrou, Wendy, *Dir Media & Film Relations,* Ford Motor Company, Henry Ford Museum & Greenfield Village, Dearborn MI

Mettala, Teri, *Dir,* Ojai Art Center, Ojai CA

Mette, Alan T, *Exec Assoc Dir, Prof,* University of Illinois, Urbana-Champaign, School of Art & Design, Champaign IL (S)

Mettler, Bonnie, *Instr,* Main Line Art Center, Haverford PA (S)

Metz, Don, *Assoc Dir,* State University of New York College at Buffalo, Buffalo NY

Metz, Katy, *Adult Prog Coordr,* City of Irvine, Irvine Fine Arts Center, Irvine CA

Metzen, Greg, *Chmn,* Ellsworth Community College, Dept of Fine Arts, Iowa Falls IA (S)

Metzger, Megan, *Office Mgr,* Springfield Art Association of Edwards Place, Springfield IL

Metzger, Richard, *Exec Dir,* Troy-Pike Cultural Arts Center, Troy AL

Metzler, Sue, *Dir Develop & Mktg,* Oregon Historical Society, Oregon History Museum, Portland OR

Meuleer, James, *Chief Historian,* Independence National Historical Park, Library, Philadelphia PA

Meunier, Brian A, *Prof,* Swarthmore College, Dept of Art & Art History, Swarthmore PA (S)

Meunier, John, *Dean,* Arizona State University, College of Architecture & Environmental Design, Tempe AZ (S)

Meurer, John, *VPres Admis,* Rocky Mountain College of Art & Design, Lakewood CO (S)

Mew, T J, *Prof & Chmn,* Berry College, Art Dept, Mount Berry GA (S)

Mew, T J, *Prof Art,* Berry College, Memorial Library, Mount Berry GA

Mey, Andree, *Cur Coll,* Lehigh Valley Heritage Center, Allentown PA

Meyer, Diane, *Asst Prof,* Loyola Marymount University, Dept of Art & Art History, Los Angeles CA (S)

Meyer, Elisabeth, *Assoc Prof,* Cornell University, Dept of Art, Ithaca NY (S)

Meyer, Elizabeth, *Vis Reference Librn,* University of Cincinnati, Visual Resource Center, Cincinnati OH

Meyer, Elizabeth, *Visual Resources Librn,* University of Cincinnati, Robert A. Deshon and Karl J. Schlachter Library for Design, Architecture, Art, and Planning, Cincinnati OH

Meyer, Ellen, *Instr,* Edgewood College, Art Dept, Madison WI (S)

Meyer, Ellen L, *Pres,* Watkins College of Art, Design & Film, Brownlee O Currey Gallery, Nashville TN

Meyer, Ellen L, *Pres,* Watkins College of Art, Design & Film, Nashville TN (S)

Meyer, Hugo, *Prof,* Princeton University, Dept of Art & Archaeology, Princeton NJ (S)

Meyer, Jaymie, *Educ Outreach Coordr,* Green Hill Center for North Carolina Art, Greensboro NC

Meyer, Joseph, *Farm & Garden Mgr,* Landis Valley Village and Farm Museum, PA Historical & Museum Commission, Lancaster PA

Meyer, Kara, *Dir External Relations,* Storefront for Art & Architecture, New York NY

Meyer, Kate, *Asst Cur,* University of Kansas, Spencer Museum of Art, Lawrence KS

Meyer, Marilyn, *Exec Dir,* American Indian Services, Sioux Falls SD

Meyer, Mark, *Instr Comp Art,* North Seattle Community College, Art Dept, Seattle WA (S)

Meyer, Nancy, *Instr,* California State University, Chico, Department of Art & Art History, Chico CA (S)

Meyer, Norman, *Instr,* Clark-Atlanta University, School of Arts & Sciences, Atlanta GA (S)

Meyer, R, *Faculty Lectr,* McGill University, Dept of Art History, Montreal PQ (S)

Meyer, Rachel, *Dir,* Palo Alto Junior Museum & Zoo, Palo Alto CA

Meyer, Rudi, *Dir MDes Prog,* Nova Scotia College of Art & Design, Halifax NS (S)

Meyer, Sarah, *Chair, Prof,* California State Polytechnic University, Pomona, Department of Art, Pomona CA (S)

Meyer, Susan, *Assoc Prof,* College of Saint Rose, The Center For Art and Design, Albany NY (S)

Meyer, Susan, *Lectr Foundations,* University of Denver, School of Art & Art History, Denver CO (S)

Meyerer, Kim, *Designer & Digital Facility,* Center for Exploratory & Perceptual Art, CEPA Library, Buffalo NY

Meyer Ernst, Renee, *Asst Prof Art,* Saint Ambrose University, Art Dept, Davenport IA (S)

Meyers, Amy, *Dir,* Yale University, Yale Center for British Art, New Haven CT

Meyers, Buzz, *Pres,* Spectrum Gallery, Toledo OH

Meyers, Carole J, *Pres,* American Color Print Society, Huntingdon Valley PA

Meyers, Christine, *Chief Develop & Corporate Rels Officer,* National Gallery of Art, Washington DC

Meyers, Gifford C, *Prof Ceramic Sculpture,* University of California, Irvine, Studio Art Dept, Irvine CA (S)

Meyers, Jill, *Dir Opers,* Triton Museum of Art, Santa Clara CA

Meyers, Kenneth, *Cur American Art,* Detroit Institute of Arts, Detroit MI

Meyers, Peggy, *Treas,* Northwest Watercolor Society, Woodinville WA

Meyers, Rebecca D, *Permanent Coll,* National Museum of Mexican Art, Chicago IL

Meyrick, Charles, *Instr,* Art Center Sarasota, Sarasota FL (S)

Meza, Alberto, *Prof,* Miami-Dade Community College, Arts & Philosophy Dept, Miami FL (S)

Mezguida, Pavlova, *Supvr Educ Guides,* Museo de las Americas, Viejo San Juan PR

Mezguida, Pavlova, *Supvr Educ Guides,* Museo de las Americas, Viejo San Juan PR

Mhiripiri, John, *Admin Dir & Exhibs Coordr,* Anthology Film Archives, New York NY

Mhiripiri, Julie, *Co-Owner,* Mhiripiri Gallery, Bloomington MN

Mhiripiri, Rex, *Co-Owner,* Mhiripiri Gallery, Bloomington MN

Micas, Nieves, *Assoc Prof,* New York Institute of Technology, Fine Arts Dept, Old Westbury NY (S)

Miccinilli, Gina, *VPres,* Sculptors Guild, Inc, Brooklyn NY

Micelli, Vince, *Pres,* Gallery XII, Wichita KS

Michael, Ronald, *Cur,* Birger Sandzen Memorial Gallery, Lindsborg KS

Michael, Simon, *Head Dept,* Simon Michael, Rockport TX (S)

Michaels, Bonni-Dara, *Cur & Registrar,* Yeshiva University Museum, New York NY

Michaels, Kathleen, *Office Mgr,* Millicent Rogers Museum, Taos NM

Michalak, Kyle, *Dir Gallery,* Firelands Association for the Visual Arts, Oberlin OH

Michalak, Megan, *Asst Prof,* University at Buffalo, State University of New York, Dept of Visual Studies, Buffalo NY (S)

Michalak, Shannon, *Visual Resource Cur,* Wright State University, Visual Resources Center, Department of Art & Art History, Dayton OH

Michalczyk, John, *Chmn,* Boston College, Fine Arts Dept, Chestnut Hill MA (S)

Michaud, Ronald, *Chmn Dept,* University of Massachusetts, Amherst, College of Arts & Sciences, Fine Arts Center, Amherst MA (S)

Michaud, Ronald, *Dir,* University of Massachusetts, Amherst, Art History Program, Amherst MA (S)

Michel, Barbara, *Gallery Dir,* Huntington University, Robert E Wilson Art Gallery, Huntington IN

Michels, Dana, *Assoc Cur,* Iowa State University, Brunnier Art Museum, Ames IA

Michie, Thomas, *Russel B & Andree Beauchamp Stearns Sr Cur DA&S,* Museum of Fine Arts, Boston MA

Mickelson, Duane, *Prof,* Concordia College, Art Dept, Moorhead MN (S)

Mickenberg, David, *Dir,* Wellesley College, Davis Museum & Cultural Center, Wellesley MA

Mickenberg, David, *Exec Dir,* Taubman Museum of Art, Roanoke VA

Mickey, Michelle, *Cur Asst,* The Mint Museum, Mint Museum of Craft & Design, Charlotte NC

Mickie, Jima, *Instr,* Williams Baptist College, Dept of Art, Walnut Ridge AR (S)

Mickle, Katherine, *Prof,* Slippery Rock University of Pennsylvania, Dept of Art, Slippery Rock PA (S)

Mickle Smaczny, Lynne, *Asst to Exec Dir,* Glessner House Museum, Chicago IL

Micklewright, Nancy, *Prof,* University of Victoria, Dept of History in Art, Victoria BC (S)

Middag, Lisa, *Publ & Design Mgr,* Walker Art Center, Minneapolis MN

Middlemass, C, *Mgr Colls,* Vancouver Public Library, Fine Arts & Music Department, Vancouver BC

Midgett, Corinne, *Registrar,* City of High Point, High Point Museum, High Point NC

Midgett, Ed, *Assoc Prof,* Appalachian State University, Dept of Art, Boone NC (S)

Midkiff, David, *Chmn,* Williams Baptist College, Dept of Art, Walnut Ridge AR (S)

Mieczinkowski, Richard, *Chmn Dept,* California University of Pennsylvania, Dept of Art, California PA (S)

Miele Holt, Madeline, *Asst Dir,* Ames Free-Easton's Public Library, North Easton MA

Mierse, William E, *Chmn,* University of Vermont, Dept of Art, Burlington VT (S)

Migdal, Michele, *Mus Shop Mgr,* Williams College, Museum of Art, Williamstown MA

Migiel, Agnieszka, *Asst Librn,* Polish Museum of America, Research Library, Chicago IL

Migliori, Larry, *Head Dept,* Mohawk Valley Community College, Utica NY (S)

Migone, Christof, *Dir & Cur,* University of Toronto at Mississauga, Blackwood Gallery, Mississauga ON

Mihailescu, Adda, *Art Educ & Mgr Pub Progs,* Beaverbrook Art Gallery, Fredericton NB

Mihaly, Sara, *Circ & Student Supvr,* University of Cincinnati, Robert A. Deshon and Karl J. Schlachter Library for Design, Architecture, Art, and Planning, Cincinnati OH

Mihm, Nina, *Pres,* The Society of Layerists in Multi-Media (SLMM), Albuquerque NM

Mikami, Lynn C, *Dir,* The Society of Layerists in Multi-Media (SLMM), Albuquerque NM

Mikelson, Arnold, *Mgr,* Arnold Mikelson Mind & Matter Art Gallery, White Rock BC

Mikelson, Mary, *Pres,* Arnold Mikelson Mind & Matter Art Gallery, White Rock BC

Mikelson, Myra, *Asst Dir,* Arnold Mikelson Mind & Matter Art Gallery, White Rock BC

Mikelson, Sapphire, *Asst Mgr,* Arnold Mikelson Mind & Matter Art Gallery, White Rock BC

Mikkelson, Rick, *Chmn,* State University of New York at Plattsburgh, Art Dept, Plattsburgh NY (S)

Miklas, Lois, *Pub Programs Mgr,* Hershey Museum, Hershey PA

Mikle, Tricia, *Pres,* Nobles County Art Center, Worthington MN

Milad, Jackie, *Cur & Coordr,* University of Maryland, College Park, Stamp Gallery, College Park MD

Milakovich, Jeannie, *Chmn,* Gogebic Community College, Fine Arts Dept, Ironwood MI (S)

Milam, Katherine, *Develop Coordr,* Danville Museum of Fine Arts & History, Danville VA

Milanesi, Betty, *Asst Librn,* Williams College, Sawyer Library, Williamstown MA

Milanowski, Stephanie, *Asst Prof,* Hope College, Dept of Art & Art History, Holland MI (S)

Milburn, Gina, *Sr Mgr Humanities,* Memphis-Shelby County Public Library & Information Center, Dept of Art, Music & Films, Memphis TN

Mileaf, Janine, *Assoc Prof,* Swarthmore College, Dept of Art & Art History, Swarthmore PA (S)

Miles, Carolyn, *Dir,* Atrium Gallery, Saint Louis MO

Miles, Carolyn, *Dir,* Aiken County Historical Museum, Aiken SC

Miles, Christine M, *Dir,* Albany Institute of History & Art, Albany NY

Miles, David, *Prof,* Ohio University-Eastern Campus, Dept Comparative Arts, Saint Clairsville OH (S)

Miles, Ted, *Library Technician,* San Francisco Maritime National Historical Park, Maritime Library, San Francisco CA

Miletic-Vejzovic, Laila, *Head Spec Coll,* University of Central Florida Libraries, Orlando FL

Miley, E J, *Chmn,* Lincoln College, Art Dept, Lincoln IL (S)

Miley, Karen, *Instr Painting & Design,* Lincoln College, Art Dept, Lincoln IL (S)

Miley, Randy B, *Head Art Dept,* Mississippi College, Art Dept, Clinton MS (S)

Milford, Mary-Ann, *Prof,* Mills College, Art Dept, Oakland CA (S)

Milholland, Valerie, *Instr,* University of Evansville, Art Dept, Evansville IN (S)

Milillu, Joey, *Prog Mgr,* Museum of Fine Arts Houston, Bayou Bend Collection & Gardens, Houston TX

Milinkovich, Mary, *Coordr Humanities, Arts & Special Colls,* Milwaukee Public Library, Art, Music & Recreation Dept, Milwaukee WI

Milkie, Jane, *Asst Prof,* Northern Michigan University, Dept of Art & Design, Marquette MI (S)

Milkofsky, Brenda, *Dir,* Wethersfield Historical Society Inc, Museum, Wethersfield CT

Milkova, Liliana, *Cur Acad Progs,* Oberlin College, Allen Memorial Art Museum, Oberlin OH

Mill, Cheryl, *Office Mgr,* Phelps County Historical Society, Donald O. Lindgren Library, Holdrege NE

Mill, Mary, *Dir,* Mill Fine Art, Santa Fe NM

Millan, Jacqueline R, *Dir Art Prog,* PepsiCo Inc, Donald M Kendall Sculpture Garden, Purchase NY

Millan, Nelson, *Prof,* University of Puerto Rico, Dept of Fine Arts, Rio Piedras PR (S)

Millan, Nelson, *Prof,* University of Puerto Rico, Dept of Fine Arts, Rio Piedras PR (S)

Millar, Joyce, *Dir Art Gallery,* Pointe Claire Cultural Centre, Stewart Hall Art Gallery, Pointe Claire PQ

Millar, Norman, *Chmn Architecture,* Woodbury University, Dept of Graphic Design, Burbank CA (S)

Millard, Larry, *Prof Sculpture,* University of Georgia, Franklin College of Arts & Sciences, Lamar Dodd School of Art, Athens GA (S)

Millard, Lee S, *Gallery Assoc,* Bloomsburg University of Pennsylvania, Haas Gallery of Art, Bloomsburg PA

Millard, Sandra, *Asst Dir Library Pub Serv,* University of Delaware, Morris Library, Newark DE

Millard, Wil, *Chief Preparator & Bldg Coordr,* Cornell University, Herbert F Johnson Museum of Art, Ithaca NY

Millard-Mendez, Robert, *Asst Prof,* University of Southern Indiana, Department of Art, Evansville IN (S)

Millarson, Lucille, *Mus Shop Mgr,* New York State Military Museum and Veterans Research Center, Saratoga Springs NY

Miller, Allison, *Prof,* Southwestern University, Sarofim School of Fine Art, Dept of Art & Art History, Georgetown TX (S)

Miller, Andrea, *Asst Mus Shop Mgr,* South Shore Arts, Munster IN

Miller, Anelle, *Dir,* Society of Illustrators, Museum of American Illustration, New York NY

Miller, Anthony, *Mgr,* Atlanta-Fulton Public Library, Central Library Art Gallery, Atlanta GA

Miller, Barbara, *Prof Art History,* Eastern Washington University, Dept of Art, Cheney WA (S)

Miller, Cary, *Instr & Dir Gen Educ & BA Prog,* Watkins College of Art, Design & Film, Nashville TN (S)

Miller, Chelsy, *Office Mgr,* Wilkes Art Gallery, North Wilkesboro NC

Miller, Chris, *Assoc Prof,* Judson University, School of Art, Design & Architecture, Elgin IL (S)

Miller, Christine, *Assoc Prof,* Mohawk Valley Community College, Utica NY (S)

Miller, Craig, *Senior Cur Design Arts,* Indianapolis Museum of Art, Indianapolis IN

Miller, Dana, *Cur Postwar Art,* Whitney Museum of American Art, New York NY

Miller, Darren Lee, *Gallery Dir,* Allegheny College, Bowman, Megahan & Penelec Galleries, Meadville PA

Miller, David, *Conservator in Charge,* Indianapolis Museum of Art, Indianapolis IN

Miller, Debra, *Mgr,* Arts Quest, Bethlehem PA

Miller, Dennis, *Assoc Prof,* University of Michigan, Ann Arbor, School of Art & Design, Ann Arbor MI (S)

Miller, Donna, *Edmonton Branch Chmn,* Alberta Society of Artists, Calgary AB

Miller, Edward C, *Assoc Prof,* Rochester Institute of Technology, School of Design, Rochester NY (S)

Miller, Elizabeth, *Exec Dir,* Allied Arts of Yakima Valley, The Peggy Lewis Gallery, Yakima WA

Miller, Ethelbert, *Pres,* Provisions Library, Provisions Research Center for Arts & Social Change, Fairfax VA

Miller, Fayette, *Cur,* Frontier Gateway Museum, Glendive MT

Miller, Fred, *Vis Asst Prof,* University of Texas at Arlington, Art & Art History Department, Arlington TX (S)

Miller, G Chris, *Photog,* Art Institute of Pittsburgh, Pittsburgh PA (S)

Miller, George, *Dir,* California State University, East Bay, C E Smith Museum of Anthropology, Hayward CA

Miller, Glen, *Asst Prof,* Rochester Institute of Technology, School of Photographic Arts & Sciences, Rochester NY (S)

Miller, Greg, *Asst Prof,* Mount Mary College, Art & Design Division, Milwaukee WI (S)

Miller, Gregory, *Pres,* White Columns, White Columns Curated Artist Registry, New York NY

Miller, J Robert, *Prof,* McMurry University, Art Dept, Abilene TX (S)

Miller, James, *Studio Dir & Master Printer,* Lower East Side Printshop Inc, New York NY (S)

Miller, Jason, *Mus Media Specialist,* University of Memphis, Art Museum, Memphis TN

Miller, Jean, *Secy,* Sonoma Valley Historical Society, Depot Park Museum, Sonoma CA

Miller, Jo, *Treas,* Sonoma Valley Historical Society, Depot Park Museum, Sonoma CA

Miller, Jo Anne, *Mus Store Mgr,* Vero Beach Museum of Art, Vero Beach FL

Miller, Joan, *Mus Shop Mgr & Mus Asst,* Big Horn County Historical Museum, Hardin MT

Miller, John M, *Photog Dept Head,* Johnson State College, Dept Fine & Performing Arts, Dibden Center for the Arts, Johnson VT (S)

Miller, Joseph E, *Dir,* Viterbo University, Art Gallery, La Crosse WI

Miller, Joyce, *Ceramics Prof,* Mount Wachusett Community College, East Wing Gallery, Gardner MA

Miller, Karen, *Admin Asst,* Lafayette Science Museum & Planetarium, Lafayette LA

Miller, Karen, *Exhibitions & Events Coordr,* Dartmouth College, Hood Museum of Art, Hanover NH

Miller, Kathryn, *Drawing,* Pitzer College, Dept of Art, Claremont CA (S)

Miller, Kathy, *Instr,* Wayne Art Center, Wayne PA (S)

Miller, Kevin, *Contact,* Windhover Center for the Arts, Fond Du Lac WI

Miller, Kevin R, *Dir,* Daytona State College, Southeast Museum of Photography, Daytona Beach FL

Miller, Kimberly, *Asst Prof,* Transylvania University, Art Program, Lexington KY (S)

Miller, Kitty, *Asst Prof,* Graceland University, Fine Arts Div, Lamoni IA (S)

Miller, Laura, *Dir Mktg,* Guggenheim Museum Soho, New York NY

Miller, Lenore D, *Dir,* George Washington University, The Dimock Gallery, Washington DC

Miller, Leticia, *Cur Educ,* Polk Museum of Art, Lakeland FL

Miller, Linda, *Graphic Design,* Art Institute of Pittsburgh, Pittsburgh PA (S)

Miller, Lynette, *Cur Art,* Washington State Historical Society, Research Center, Tacoma WA

Miller, Lynn, *Dir HR,* Toledo Museum of Art, Toledo OH

Miller, Lynn, *Office Mgr,* Galesburg Civic Art Center, Galesburg IL

Miller, Margaret A, *Dir,* University of South Florida, Contemporary Art Museum, Tampa FL

Miller, Marie Celeste, *Prof,* Aquinas College, Art Dept, Grand Rapids MI (S)

Miller, Marilyn, *Dir Budget,* California Watercolor Association, Gallery Concord, Concord CA

Miller, Marlene, *Instr,* Bucks County Community College, Fine Arts Dept, Newtown PA (S)

Miller, Mary Jane, *Acting Registrar,* Pennsylvania Historical & Museum Commission, The State Museum of Pennsylvania, Harrisburg PA

Miller, Mary Jane, *Colls Mgr,* Pennsylvania Historical & Museum Commission, The State Museum of Pennsylvania, Harrisburg PA

Miller, Melanie, *Guest Svcs Admin,* Belz Museum of Asian & Judaic Art, Memphis TN

Miller, Michael, *Coordr Grad Progs & Instr Painting,* Texas A&M University Commerce, Dept of Art, Commerce TX (S)

Miller, Michael D, *Head Librn & Dir Arts & Engineering Librs,* University of Michigan, Media Union Library, Ann Arbor MI

Miller, Mike, *CFO,* Delaware Art Museum, Wilmington DE

Miller, Monica, *Asst Dir,* Gallery One Visual Arts Center, Ellensburg WA

Miller, Pamela, *Dir Programs,* California Watercolor Association, Gallery Concord, Concord CA

Miller, Patrick, *Graphic Design,* University of South Alabama, Dept of Art & Art History, Mobile AL (S)

Miller, Patrick, *Assoc Prof,* Mississippi State University, Dept of Art, Starville MS (S)

Miller, Rachel, *Asst Cur,* University of Wyoming, University of Wyoming Art Museum, Laramie WY

Miller, Randall, *Webmaster,* Art Association of Harrisburg, School & Galleries, Harrisburg PA

Miller, Randy, *Cur Geology,* New Brunswick Museum, Saint John NB

Miller, Remy, *Acad Dean & Div Chair Foundation,* Memphis College of Art, Memphis TN (S)

Miller, Remy, *Div Chair Foundations,* Memphis College of Art, Memphis TN (S)

Miller, Richard, *Preparator,* Williams College, Museum of Art, Williamstown MA

Miller, Rob, *Lectr,* University of Wisconsin-Parkside, Art Dept, Kenosha WI (S)

Miller, Robert, *Instr Ceramics & Gallery Dir,* Rio Hondo College, Visual Arts Dept, Whittier CA (S)

Miller, Robert B, *Vis Lect,* Lewis & Clark College, Dept of Art, Portland OR (S)

Miller, Roland, *Photog,* College of Lake County, Art Dept, Grayslake IL (S)

Miller, Ron, *Dir,* World Archaeological Society, Information Center, Library, & Timbertop Studio, Hollister MO

Miller, Ronald A, *Graphic Design,* Art Institute of Pittsburgh, Pittsburgh PA (S)

Miller, Sally, *Adj Instr,* University of West Florida, Dept of Art, Pensacola FL (S)

Miller, Sean, *Asst Prof,* University of Florida, School of Art & Art History, Gainesville FL (S)

Miller, Sean, *Asst Prof Film,* Watkins College of Art, Design & Film, Nashville TN (S)

Miller, Stan, *Treas,* Whatcom Museum, Library, Bellingham WA

Miller, Stephen S, *Dir,* Landis Valley Village and Farm Museum, PA Historical & Museum Commission, Lancaster PA

Miller, Steve, *Assoc Prof,* Palomar Community College, Art Dept, San Marcos CA (S)

Miller, Susan, *Slide Coll Supv,* Syracuse University, Syracuse University Library, Syracuse NY

Miller, Susan, *Electronic Records Archivist,* The Cleveland Museum of Art, Ingalls Library, Cleveland OH

Miller, Tami, *Dir Exhibs & Colls,* Krasl Art Center, Saint Joseph MI

Miller, Tammy, *Ed,* Historical Society of Pennsylvania, Philadelphia PA

Miller, Thomas, *Chmn,* Indiana University South Bend, Fine Arts Dept, South Bend IN (S)

Miller, Tricia, *Head Registrar,* University of Georgia, Georgia Museum of Art, Athens GA

Miller, Valerie, *Coordr Coll,* Red Deer & District Museum & Archives, Red Deer AB

Miller, Victoria, *Asst Librn,* The York County Heritage Trust, Library, York PA

Miller, Walter R, *Pres,* New Haven Museum & Historical Society, New Haven CT

Miller, Wendell, *VPres,* Zigler Art Museum, Jennings LA

MillerAltman, Apryl, *VPres & Artistic Dir,* This Century Art Gallery, Williamsburg VA

Miller Zohn, Kristen, *Cur Coll & Exhib,* Columbus Museum, Columbus GA

Millet, Cristin, *Asst Prof Art (Sculpture),* Pennsylvania State University, University Park, Penn State School of Visual Arts, University Park PA (S)

Milligan, Frank D, *CEO,* Nantucket Historical Association, Historic Nantucket, Nantucket MA

Milliken, Aldy, *Dir & Chief Cur,* Kentucky Museum of Art and Craft, Louisville KY

Millin, Laura J, *CEO & Dir,* Missoula Art Museum, Missoula MT

Millions, Karly, *Gallery Educator,* Estevan National Exhibition Centre Inc, Estevan Art Gallery & Museum, Estevan SK

Millmore, Mark, *Dir MCA Store,* Museum of Contemporary Art, Chicago IL

Mills, Anne, *Sr Staff Asst,* University of Notre Dame, Snite Museum of Art, Notre Dame IN

Mills, Bernadette, *Exec Dir,* Scottsdale Artists' School Library, Scottsdale AZ

Mills, Beth, *Head Reference,* New Rochelle Public Library, Art Section, New Rochelle NY

Mills, Connie, *Libr Coordr,* Western Kentucky University, Kentucky Library & Museum, Bowling Green KY

Mills, Cynthia, *VPres Programs,* Birmingham Bloomfield Art Center, Birmingham MI (S)

Mills, Cynthia K, *VP Progs,* Birmingham Bloomfield Art Center, Art Center, Birmingham MI

Mills, Dan, *Dir,* Bates College, Museum of Art, Lewiston ME

Mills, Don, *Dir Library Svcs,* Mississauga Library System, Mississauga ON

Mills, Don, *Dir Library Svcs,* Mississauga Library System, Central Library, Arts Dept, Mississauga ON

Mills, Emmy, *Admin Asst,* Arts Midland Galleries & School, Midland MI

Mills, Emmy, *Bus & Opers Mgr,* Arts Midland Galleries & School, Alden B. Dow Museum of Science & Art, Midland MI

Mills, Jeanette C, *Dir Visual Svcs,* University of Washington, Art Slide Library, Seattle WA

Mills, Josephine, *Dir & Cur,* University of Lethbridge, Art Gallery, Lethbridge AB

Mills, Kelly, *Instr,* Avila College, Art Division, Dept of Humanities, Kansas City MO (S)

Mills, Lea, *Dean,* College of the Redwoods, Arts & Languages Dept Division, Eureka CA (S)

Mills, Mary Cheek, *Educ Progs Mgr,* Corning Museum of Glass, The Studio, Corning NY

Mills, Richard, *Asst Prof,* C W Post Campus of Long Island University, School of Visual & Performing Arts, Brookville NY (S)

Mills, Ron, *Prof,* Linfield College, Department of Art & Visual Culture, McMinnville OR (S)

Millsap, Gina, *Exec Dir,* Topeka & Shawnee County Public Library, Alice C Sabatini Gallery, Topeka KS

Mills Widener, Joy, *Dir,* Shain Gallery, Charlotte NC

Milne, Joseph W, *Graphic Design & Digital Design,* Art Institute of Pittsburgh, Pittsburgh PA (S)

Milnor, Nancy, *Dir Libr,* Connecticut Historical Society, Hartford CT

Milon, Rachel, *Dir Communs,* Nevada Museum of Art, Reno NV

Milosevich, Joe, *Instr,* Joliet Junior College, Fine Arts Dept, Joliet IL (S)

Milosevich, Joe B, *Dir Gallery,* Joliet Junior College, Laura A Sprague Art Gallery, Joliet IL

Milot, Barbara, *Prof,* Framingham State College, Art Dept, Framingham MA (S)

Milroy, Elizabeth, *Assoc Prof, Dir,* Wesleyan University, Dept of Art & Art History, Middletown CT (S)

Milteer, Blake, *Mus Dir & Cur American Art,* Colorado Springs Fine Arts Center, Taylor Museum, Colorado Springs CO

Milton-Elmore, Kara, *Exec Dir,* Wilkes Art Gallery, North Wilkesboro NC

Mimlitsch-Gray, Myra, *Chmn Art Studio & Art Educ,* State University of New York at New Paltz, Art Education Program, New Paltz NY (S)

Mims, Hazel, *Office Asst,* History Museum of Mobile, Mobile AL

Min, Yong Soon, *Prof Asian American Studies,* University of California, Irvine, Studio Art Dept, Irvine CA (S)

Minchin, Edward, *Instr,* Art Center Sarasota, Sarasota FL (S)

Mindlin, Beth, *Recording Secy,* Halifax Historical Society, Inc, Halifax Historical Museum, Daytona Beach FL

Minegar, Dawn, *Registrar,* Laguna Art Museum, Laguna Beach CA

Miner, Curt, *Acting Cur,* Pennsylvania Historical & Museum Commission, The State Museum of Pennsylvania, Harrisburg PA

Minet, Cynthia, *Asst Prof,* Antelope Valley College, Art Dept, Division of Fine Arts, Lancaster CA (S)

Mingalone, Maria, *Dir Educ & Progs,* Berkshire Museum, Pittsfield MA

Minge, Janet, *Physical Anthropology Cur,* University of Pennsylvania, Museum of Archaeology & Anthropology, Philadelphia PA

Minglu, Gao, *Assoc Prof,* University of Pittsburgh, Henry Clay Frick Dept History of Art & Architecture, Pittsburgh PA (S)

Mingst, Raymond E, *Dir,* Curious Matter, Jersey City NJ

Mink, Pat, *Assoc Prof,* East Tennessee State University, College of Arts and Sciences, Dept of Art & Design, Johnson City TN (S)

Minkkinen, Arno, *Prof,* University of Massachusetts Lowell, Dept of Art, Lowell MA (S)

Minkovski, Beate C, *Exec Dir,* Woman Made Gallery, Chicago IL

Minkowski, Lenka, *Bookstore/Archive Mgr,* Beyond Baroque Foundation, Beyond Baroque Literary Arts Center, Venice CA

Minks, Ronald, *Co-Dir Gallery,* Mississippi Valley State University, Fine Arts Dept, Itta Bena MS (S)

Minnaert, Sarah, *Dir of Exhib,* Carnegie Museums of Pittsburgh, Carnegie Museum of Art, Pittsburgh PA

Minogue, Eileen, *Asst Dir,* Northport-East Northport Public Library, Northport NY

Minogue, Nancy, *Admin & Prog Specialist,* Northern Virginia Community College, Art Dept, Annandale VA (S)

Minor, Lauren, *Mus Shop Mgr,* Silvermine Guild Arts Center, School of Art, New Canaan CT

Minor, Madge, *Dir Fin & Admin & CFO,* Hillwood Museum & Gardens Foundation, Hillwood Estate Museum & Gardens, Washington DC

Mintich, Mary, *Prof,* Winthrop University, Dept of Art & Design, Rock Hill SC (S)

Minton, Jane, *Contact,* IFP MN Center for Media Arts, Saint Paul MN

Minton, Randy, *Instr,* Hinds Community College, Dept of Art, Raymond MS (S)

Minty, Robert, *Cur Asian Art,* Walters Art Museum, Library, Baltimore MD

Mintz, Deborah, *Exec Dir,* Arts Council of Fayetteville-Cumberland County, The Arts Center, Fayetteville NC

Mintz, Robert, *Cur Asian Art,* Walters Art Museum, Baltimore MD

Minushkin, Arlene, *Operations Mgr,* Prescott Fine Arts Association, Gallery, Prescott AZ

Miraglia, Anthony J, *Chmn Fine Art,* University of Massachusetts Dartmouth, College of Visual & Performing Arts, North Dartmouth MA (S)

Miranda, Candida, *VPres Admin,* Museum of Science & Industry, Chicago IL

Mirch, Kijeong Jeon, *Prof,* California State University, Chico, Department of Art & Art History, Chico CA (S)

Mirensky, Gabriela, *Dir Competitions & Exhibs,* American Institute of Graphic Arts, New York NY

Mirrer, Louise, *Pres & CEO,* New-York Historical Society, Museum, New York NY

Misegadis, Lois, *Head Dept,* Hesston College, Art Dept, Hesston KS (S)

Mishler, John, *Asst Prof,* Goshen College, Art Dept, Goshen IN (S)

Mishne, Merle, *Pres & Dir,* Portholes Into the Past, Medina OH

Misite, Phyllis, *School Dir,* Mount Ida College, Chamberlayne School of Design & Merchandising, Boston MA (S)

Miskuly, Mary Helen, *Registrar,* State University of New York College at Buffalo, Buffalo NY

Misner, Mary, *Gallery Dir,* Cambridge Public Library and Gallery, Cambridge ON

Missal, Paul, *Instr,* Pacific Northwest College of Art, Portland OR (S)

Misterka, Halina, *Archivist,* Polish Museum of America, Chicago IL

Misterka, Halina, *Archivist,* Polish Museum of America, Research Library, Chicago IL

Mistick, Barbara K, *Pres & Dir,* Carnegie Museums of Pittsburgh, Carnegie Library of Pittsburgh, Pittsburgh PA

Mitas, William R, *Industrial Design Technology,* Art Institute of Pittsburgh, Pittsburgh PA (S)

Mitchell, Ann, *Dept Chmn,* Long Beach City College, Art & Photography Dept, Long Beach CA (S)

Mitchell, Barbara, *Cur,* Arts and Letters Club of Toronto, Toronto ON

Mitchell, Barbara, *Gift Shop Coordr,* Morris-Jumel Mansion, Inc, New York NY

Mitchell, Beverly, *Art Librn,* Southern Methodist University, Hamon Arts Library, Dallas TX

Mitchell, Brenda, *Assoc Prof,* Indiana University of Pennsylvania, College of Fine Arts, Indiana PA (S)

Mitchell, Bruce, *Chmn Historical Comt,* Wistariahurst Museum, Holyoke MA

Mitchell, Cheryl, *Admin Asst,* Anderson Fine Arts Center, The Anderson Center for the Arts, Anderson IN

Mitchell, Cynthia, *Asst Librn,* Thomas College, Mariner Library, Waterville ME

Mitchell, Deb, *Educ,* Montana Historical Society, Helena MT

Mitchell, Elizabeth, *Cur Prints & Drawings,* Stanford University, Cantor Arts Center at Stanford University, Stanford CA

Mitchell, Elliott, *Instr,* Greenfield Community College, Art Dept, Greenfield MA (S)

Mitchell, Gary A, *Provincial Archivist & Dir,* Royal British Columbia Museum, BC Archives, Victoria BC

Mitchell, Heather, *Exec Dir,* New Hampshire Antiquarian Society, Hopkinton Historical Society, Hopkinton NH

Mitchell, Joann, *Exec Dir,* Blowing Rock Art and History Museum, Blowing Rock NC

Mitchell, Joseph, *Adjunct Prof Art,* Florida Southern College, Melvin Art Gallery, Lakeland FL

Mitchell, Joseph, *Adjunct Prof Art,* Florida Southern College, Department of Art & Art History, Lakeland FL (S)

Mitchell, Lois, *Treas,* Alton Museum of History & Art, Inc, Alton IL

Mitchell, Michelle, *Gallery Coordr,* The APEX Museum, Atlanta GA

Mitchell, Nancy, *Instr,* Sinclair Community College, Division of Fine & Performing Arts, Dayton OH (S)

Mitchell, Nita, *Cur Science Educ,* Louisiana Arts & Science Museum, Baton Rouge LA

Mitchell, Shannon, *Instr,* University of Arkansas, Art Dept, Fayetteville AR (S)

Mitchell, Shelly, *Mgr Finance & Admin,* Kitchener-Waterloo Art Gallery, Kitchener ON

Mitchell, Starr, *Dir Educ,* Historic Arkansas Museum, Little Rock AR

Mitchell, Starr, *Educ Dir,* Historic Arkansas Museum, Library, Little Rock AR

Mitchell, Suzanne, *Prof Emeritus,* University of Louisville, Allen R Hite Art Institute, Louisville KY (S)

Mitchell, Teresa, *Mus Mgr,* Lac du Flambeau Band of Lake Superior Chippewa Indians, George W Brown Jr Ojibwe Museum & Cultural Center, Lac Du Flambeau WI

Mitchell, William J, *Dean,* Massachusetts Institute of Technology, School of Architecture and Planning, Cambridge MA (S)

Mitchell-Innes, Lucy, *Pres,* Art Dealers Association of America, Inc, New York NY

Mitchell-Walker, Kristina, *Dir Educ,* University of Kansas, Spencer Museum of Art, Lawrence KS

Mitigay, Mary, *Exec Dir,* Rutland Area Art Association, Chaffee Art Center, Rutland VT

Mitra, Srimoyee, *Cur,* Art Gallery of Windsor, Windsor ON

Mitrasinovic, Miodrag, *Dean School of Design Strategies,* Parsons The New School for Design, New York NY (S)

Mitten, David Gordon, *Cur Ancient Art,* Harvard University, Arthur M Sackler Museum, Cambridge MA

Mittenberg, Valerie, *Information Access,* State University of New York at New Paltz, Sojourner Truth Library, New Paltz NY

Mittenthal, Cherie, *Exec Dir,* Truro Center for the Arts at Castle Hill, Inc, Truro MA (S)

Mittman, Asa, *Assoc Prof,* California State University, Chico, Department of Art & Art History, Chico CA (S)

Mitton, Maureen, *Asst Prof,* University of Wisconsin-Stout, Dept of Art & Design, Menomonie WI (S)

Mixon, Jamie, *Prof,* Mississippi State University, Dept of Art, Starville MS (S)

Miyagawa, Haruyo, *Head Librn,* Birmingham Public Library, Arts, Literature & Sports Department, Birmingham AL

Miyata, Masako, *Prof,* James Madison University, School of Art & Art History, Harrisonburg VA (S)

Miyata, Wayne A, *Faculty,* Kauai Community College, Dept of Art, Lihue HI (S)

Mizel, Larry, *Chmn Bd,* Mizel Museum, Denver CO

Mizraki, Tracy, *Dir Devel,* Santa Monica Museum of Art, Santa Monica CA

Mladenoff, Nancy, *Assoc Prof,* University of Wisconsin, Madison, Dept of Art, Madison WI (S)

Mo, Charles, *Chief Cur Fine Arts,* The Mint Museum, Art Organization & Library, Charlotte NC

Mo, Charles, *Dir Fine Arts,* The Mint Museum, Charlotte NC

Moak, Mark, *Chmn,* Rocky Mountain College, Art Dept, Billings MT (S)

Moazami, Emily, *Photo Archives Tech,* National Museum of the American Indian, Archives, Washington DC

Mobbs, Leslie, *Dir,* Vancouver City Archives, Vancouver BC

Moberg, David, *Chmn Fine Arts,* Indian River Community College, Fine Arts Dept, Fort Pierce FL (S)

Moberly, Juanita, *Gallery Mgr,* Brown County Art Gallery Foundation, Nashville IN

Mobley, Chuck, *Dir,* San Francisco Camerawork, San Francisco CA

Mobley, Ree, *Librn,* Museum of New Mexico, Bartlett Library, Santa Fe NM

Mocilnikar, Gregory, *Instructional Support Technician,* University Art Gallery at California State University, Dominguez Hills, Carson CA

Mocko, Sarah, *Coordr Pub Programs,* Noah Webster House, Inc, Noah Webster House & West Hartford Historical Society, West Hartford CT

Moderegger, Hajoe, *Assoc Prof,* City College of New York, Art Dept, New York NY (S)

Modiano, Richard, *Exec Dir,* Beyond Baroque Foundation, Beyond Baroque Literary Arts Center, Venice CA

Modine, Austin, *Mktg & Pub Rels Assoc,* Boca Raton Museum of Art, Boca Raton FL

Modler, David, *Coordr Art Educ,* Shepherd University, Dept of Contemporary Art & Theater, Shepherdstown WV (S)

Modrak, Rebekah, *Vis Assoc Prof,* University of Michigan, Ann Arbor, School of Art & Design, Ann Arbor MI (S)

Moeller, Gary E, *Dir,* Rogers State College, Art Dept, Claremore OK (S)

Moeller, Whitney, *Asst Dir,* University of Illinois at Chicago, Gallery 400, Chicago IL

Moffat, Constance, *Prof,* Pierce College, Art Dept, Woodland Hills CA (S)

Moffat, Martha, *Site Supvr,* Ryerss Victorian Museum & Library, Philadelphia PA

Moffatt, Laurie Norton, *Dir,* Norman Rockwell Museum, Stockbridge MA

Moffit, Judy, *Art Hist Instr,* Grand Canyon University, Art Dept, Phoenix AZ (S)

Moffitt, Sally, *Admin Asst,* Oberlin College, Allen Memorial Art Museum, Oberlin OH

Mogayzel, Jeannie, *Museum Shop Mgr,* University of Connecticut, William Benton Museum of Art, Storrs CT

Moggridge, Bill, *Dir,* Cooper-Hewitt National Design Museum, Smithsonian Institution, New York NY

Mogyorody, Veronica, *Prof,* University of Windsor, Visual Arts, Windsor ON (S)

Mohamed, Zeheda, *Project Mgr Nelson Mandela Ctr,* Museum for African Art, New York NY

Mohan, Rajee, *Adjunct Prof Art History,* Johnson County Community College, Fine Arts Dept & Art History Dept, Overland Park KS (S)

Mohar, Karen, *Asst Librn,* Lourdes College, Duns Scotus Library, Sylvania OH

Mohivddin, Rouben, *Asst Prof,* California State University, Chico, Department of Art & Art History, Chico CA (S)

Mohr, Amber, *Cur,* University of Nebraska-Lincoln, Great Plains Art Museum, Lincoln NE

Mohr, Cynthia, *Chair, Dept Design,* University of North Texas, College of Visual Arts & Design, Denton TX (S)

Mohr, Lisa, *Art Coordr & Instr,* Carl Sandburg College, Galesburg IL (S)

Mohsin, Mohammad, *Gallery Dir,* Saint John's University, Dept of Fine Arts, Jamaica NY (S)

Mohsin, Parvez, *Dir Gallery,* Saint John's University, Dr. M.T. Geoffrey Yeh Art Gallery, Queens NY

Moir, Flora, *Dir Educ,* Art Directors Club, New York NY

Moir, Lindsay, *Librn,* Glenbow Museum, Library, Calgary AB

Mojica, Francis J, *Dir,* Centro de Estudios Avanzados, Art Library, Old San Juan PR

Mojica, Francis J, *Dir,* Centro de Estudios Avanzados, Art Library, Old San Juan PR

Mokren, Jennifer, *Asst Prof,* University of Wisconsin-Green Bay, Arts Dept, Green Bay WI (S)

Mola, Geraldine, *VPres,* Passaic County Historical Society, Lambert Castle Museum & Library, Paterson NJ

Mold, David, *Prof Theatre & Chair Fine & Performing Arts,* Marymount Manhattan College, Fine & Performing Arts Div, New York NY (S)

Moldenhauer, Susan, *Dir & Chief Cur,* University of Wyoming, University of Wyoming Art Museum, Laramie WY

Molen, Jan, *Chmn & Dir,* Napa Valley College, Art Dept, Napa CA (S)

Moles, Kathleen, *Cur Art,* Whatcom Museum, Library, Bellingham WA

Molesworth, Helen, *Chief Cur,* Institute of Contemporary Art, Boston MA

Moley, Mary Beth, *Art Instr,* Metropolitan Community College - Penn Valley, Art Dept, Kansas City MO (S)

Molife, Brenda, *Chmn,* Bridgewater State College, Art Dept, Bridgewater MA (S)

Mollett, David, *Dept Chmn & Assoc Prof,* University of Alaska-Fairbanks, Dept of Art, Fairbanks AK (S)

Mollo, Arlene, *Chmn Art Educ,* University of Massachusetts Dartmouth, College of Visual & Performing Arts, North Dartmouth MA (S)

Molloy, Bryan, *Gallery Asst,* Art Association of Harrisburg, School & Galleries, Harrisburg PA

Molnar, Cindy Lou, *Conservator,* National Portrait Gallery, Smithsonian Institution, Washington DC

Molnar, Imre, *Acad Dean,* College for Creative Studies, Detroit MI (S)

Molnar, Mike, *Instr,* Luzerne County Community College, Commercial Art Dept, Nanticoke PA (S)

Molon, Dominic, *Cur,* Contemporary Art Museum St Louis, Saint Louis MO

Moloney, Kate, *Exec Asst,* Pensacola Museum of Art, Pensacola FL

Momin, Shamim, *Branch Dir & Cur Altria,* Whitney Museum of American Art, New York NY

Mompho, Bo, *Registrar,* Wellesley College, Davis Museum & Cultural Center, Wellesley MA

Monaco, Theresa, *Chmn Art Dept,* Emmanuel College, Art Dept, Boston MA (S)

Monahan, Casey, *Educ Asst,* Museum of Fine Arts, Houston, Rienzi Center for European Decorative Arts, Houston TX

Monahan, Rebekah, *Registrar,* Utah Valley University, Woodbury Art Museum, Orem UT

Monath, Marilyn, *Mktg & Develop,* Landis Valley Village and Farm Museum, PA Historical & Museum Commission, Lancaster PA

Monau, Steve, *Assoc Prof,* East Los Angeles College, Art Dept, Monterey Park CA (S)

Monckton, Rachel, *Colls Mgr,* Tom Thomson, Owen Sound ON

Moncur, Shannon, *Chmn,* Moncur Gallery, Boissevain MB

Monday, Elden, *Pres,* The Art Institutes, The Art Institute of Seattle, Seattle WA (S)

Mondi, Annelies, *Deputy Dir,* University of Georgia, Georgia Museum of Art, Athens GA

Mondro, Anne, *Vis Assoc Prof,* University of Michigan, Ann Arbor, School of Art & Design, Ann Arbor MI (S)

Monenerkit, Marcus, *Assoc Registrar,* Heard Museum, Phoenix AZ

Monger, Janice, *Mgr Admin & Vis Svcs,* Brooklyn Historical Society, Brooklyn NY

Monhollen, Kyle, *Preparator,* University of California, Richard L Nelson Gallery & Fine Arts Collection, Davis CA

Monk, Mary, *Art House Coordr,* St Tammany Art Association, Covington LA

Monk, Philip, *Dir & Cur,* York University, Art Gallery of York University, Toronto ON

Monk, Richard, *Coll Mgr (Sciences) & Cur of Coll (Sciences),* Texas Tech University, Museum of Texas Tech University, Lubbock TX

Monk-Hilty, Tamara, *Instr,* Lourdes University, Art Dept, Sylvania OH (S)

Monkhouse, Christopher, *Cur & Chair,* The Art Institute of Chicago, Department of Textiles, Textile Society, Chicago IL

Monnier, Annette, *Outreach Prog Dir,* Clay Studio, Philadelphia PA

Monroe, Dan L, *Exec Dir,* Peabody Essex Museum, Salem MA

Monroe, Dan L, *Exec Dir,* Peabody Essex Museum, Cotting-Smith-Assembly House, Salem MA

Monroe, Gary, *Prof,* Daytona Beach Community College, Dept of Fine Arts & Visual Arts, Daytona Beach FL (S)

Monroe, Mark, *Chair,* Austin College, Ida Green Gallery, Sherman TX

Monroe, Mark, *Prof,* Austin College, Art Dept, Sherman TX (S)

Monroe, Martha, *Cur Exhibs & Coll,* Milwaukee County War Memorial Inc., Villa Terrace Decorative Arts Museum, Milwaukee WI

Monroe, Rose, *Chmn,* Baltimore City Community College, Dept of Fine Arts, Baltimore MD (S)

Montag, Ann, *Finance Mgr,* Shaker Museum & Library, Old Chatham NY

Montague, Benjamin, *Assoc Prof,* Wright State University, Dept of Art & Art History, Dayton OH (S)

Montague, Michele, *Tech Svcs & Circ Coordr,* Grand Rapids Public Library, Grand Rapids MI

Montali, Amy, *Asst Prof,* Rhode Island College, Art Dept, Providence RI (S)

Montalvo, Emmanuel, *Advertising Catalog Production & Photog,* Illustration House Inc, Gallery Auction House, New York NY

Montana, Kelly, *Office Mgr,* Lawndale Art Center, Houston TX

Monteith, Jerry, *Prof, Head Grad Studies & Studio Area Head,* Southern Illinois University, School of Art & Design, Carbondale IL (S)

Montenegro, Diane, *Office Mgr,* Newport Art Museum and Association, Newport RI

Montes, Chemi, *Assoc Prof,* American University, Dept of Art, New York NY (S)

Monteyne, Joseph, *Assoc Prof,* University of British Columbia, Dept of Art History, Visual Art & Theory, Vancouver BC (S)

Montford, Hannah, *Educ Dir,* St. Louis Artists' Guild, Saint Louis MO

Montford, James, *Gallery Dir,* Rhode Island College, Edward M Bannister Gallery, Providence RI

Montgomery, Alexandra, *Exec Dir,* George R Gardiner, Toronto ON

Montgomery, Andrea, *Dean Humanities,* Tougaloo College, Art Dept, Tougaloo MS (S)

Montgomery, Charlotte A, *Chief Fiscal Officer & HR Resources Mgr,* Illinois State Museum, Museum Store, Chicago IL

Montgomery, David, *Prof,* Saint Louis Community College at Meramec, Art Dept, Saint Louis MO (S)

Montgomery, Doris, *Archivist,* Almond Historical Society, Inc, Hagadorn House, The 1800-37 Museum, Almond NY

Montgomery, Edward, *Prof,* Miami University, Dept Fine Arts, Hamilton OH (S)

Montgomery, Florence, *Pres,* Bromfield Art Gallery, Boston MA

Montgomery, Janet, *Instr,* Appalachian State University, Dept of Art, Boone NC (S)

Montgomery, Scott, *Assoc Prof Art History,* University of Denver, School of Art & Art History, Denver CO (S)

Montgomery, Susan, *Adjunct Faculty,* Mount Wachusett Community College, East Wing Gallery, Gardner MA

Monti, Michael J, *Exec Dir,* Association of Collegiate Schools of Architecture, Washington DC

Montileaux, Paulette, *Interim Cur,* Indian Arts & Crafts Board, US Dept of the Interior, Sioux Indian Museum, Rapid City SD

Montley, Pat, *Chmn,* Chatham College, Fine & Performing Arts, Pittsburgh PA (S)

Montoya, Malaquias, *Cooperating Faculty Dept of Art,* University of California, Davis, Dept of Art & Art History, Davis CA (S)

Montrose-Graem, Douglass, *Chmn & CEO,* J.M.W. Turner Museum, Sarasota FL

Moody, Larrie J, *Chairperson,* Pittsburg State University, Art Dept, Pittsburg KS (S)

Moody, Marge, *Asst Prof,* Winthrop University, Dept of Art & Design, Rock Hill SC (S)

Moody, Phil, *Assoc Prof,* Winthrop University, Dept of Art & Design, Rock Hill SC (S)

Moon, Bruce, *Prof,* Mount Mary College, Art & Design Division, Milwaukee WI (S)

Moon, Bruce, *Prog Dir Art Therapy,* Mount Mary College, Marian Gallery, Milwaukee WI

Moon, Susan, *Head Arts Library,* University of California, Santa Barbara, Arts Library, Santa Barbara CA

Moonelis, Judy, *Faculty,* Fairleigh Dickinson University, Fine Arts Dept, Madison NJ (S)

Mooney, Aurel, *Pres,* Yarmouth County Historical Society, Yarmouth County Museum & Archives, Yarmouth NS

Mooney, Karyn, *Educ Coordr,* Queens Historical Society, Kingsland Homestead, Flushing NY

Mooney, Kathleen, *Mem/Communs,* National Watercolor Society, San Pedro CA

Mooney, Tom, *Archivist & Cur,* Cherokee Heritage Center, Library & Archives, Park Hill OK

Mooney, Wanda, *Mgr Opers,* Memorial University of Newfoundland, The Rooms Provincial Art Gallery, Saint John's NF

Moore, Allison, *Asst Prof,* University of South Florida, School The Arts, Tampa FL (S)

Moore, Bernadette, *Dir Mktg,* Piedmont Arts Association, Martinsville VA

Moore, Bobby J, *Coll Mgr,* Southern Alleghenies Museum of Art, Loretto Facility, Loretto PA

Moore, Connie, *Graphic Design,* Art Institute of Pittsburgh, Pittsburgh PA (S)

Moore, Craig, *Assoc Prof,* Taylor University, Visual Art Dept, Upland IN (S)

Moore, Cynthia, *Mktg & Pub Rels,* Virginia Historical Society, Library, Richmond VA

Moore, Dan, *Pres, Dir & Founder,* The APEX Museum, Atlanta GA

Moore, Daryl, *Chmn Art Dept,* Montclair State University, Art Galleries, Upper Montclair NJ

Moore, David G, *Adjunct Asst Prof,* Le Moyne College, Fine Arts Dept, Syracuse NY (S)

Moore, Del, *Reference Librn,* Colonial Williamsburg Foundation, John D Rockefeller, Jr Library, Williamsburg VA

Moore, Donald Everett, *Chmn,* Mitchell Community College, Visual Art Dept, Statesville NC (S)

Moore, Elizabeth, *Asst Cur,* Telfair Museums' Jepson Center for the Arts Library, Telfair Academy of Arts & Sciences Library, Savannah GA

Moore, Elizabeth, *Asst Prof,* Cazenovia College, Center for Art & Design Studies, Cazenovia NY (S)

Moore, Ellen, *Cur Educ,* Roswell Museum & Art Center, Roswell NM

Moore, Gina, *Prof,* Benedict College, School of Humanities, Arts & Social Sciences, Columbia SC (S)

Moore, Ginny, *Secy & Cur,* Alaska Museum of Natural History, Anchorage AK

Moore, Heather, *Registrar,* University of North Carolina at Greensboro, Weatherspoon Art Museum, Greensboro NC

Moore, Janet, *Sr Registrar,* Institute of Contemporary Art, Boston MA

Moore, Janice, *Recording Secy,* Plastic Club, Art Club, Philadelphia PA

Moore, Jason, *VPres,* Artspace, Richmond VA

Moore, Jeanne, *Instr Art History,* Madonna University, College of Arts & Humanities, Livonia MI (S)

Moore, Jenny, *Proj Cur Photo Legacy Prog,* Andy Warhol Foundation for the Visual Arts, New York NY

Moore, Jo-Anna, *Chmn Univ Art & Art Educ,* Temple University, Tyler School of Art, Philadelphia PA (S)

Moore, Joanna, *Past Pres,* Alberta Society of Artists, Calgary AB

Moore, Joe, *Asst Prof,* City College of New York, Art Dept, New York NY (S)

Moore, John, *Prof,* Smith College, Art Dept, Northampton MA (S)

Moore, Kate, *Dir Mktg & Communs,* The Adirondack Historical Association, The Adirondack Museum, Blue Mountain Lake NY

Moore, Kathleen, *Visual Arts Coordr,* Endicott College, School of Visual & Performing Arts, Beverly MA (S)

Moore, Kathleen, *Admin Coordr,* San Francisco Arts Education Project, San Francisco CA

Moore, Kathleen A, *Asst to Librn,* University of Louisville, Margaret M Bridwell Art Library, Louisville KY

Moore, Kathy, *VPres,* North Shore Arts Association, Inc, Gloucester MA

Moore, Kemille, *Prof, Chmn,* University of North Carolina at Wilmington, Dept of Fine Arts - Division of Art, Wilmington NC (S)

Moore, Kyle, *Friends of Lovejoy Librn,* Southern Illinois University, Lovejoy Library, Edwardsville IL

Moore, Linda, *COO,* Morris Museum, Morristown NJ

Moore, Lisa, *Exec Dir,* Georgia Lawyers for the Arts, Atlanta GA

Moore, Lynda, *Dir California Shows,* California Watercolor Association, Gallery Concord, Concord CA

Moore, Mae Frances, *Acquisition Librn,* Laney College Library, Art Section, Oakland CA

Moore, Margaret, *Assoc Dir & Cur,* Egan Institute of Maritime Studies, Nantucket MA

Moore, Mark, *Instr,* Oklahoma State University, Graphic Arts Dept, Visual Communications, Okmulgee OK (S)

Moore, Mary, *Dean,* Arkansas State University-Art Department, Jonesboro, Library, Jonesboro AR

Moore, Mary Ruth, *Lectr Photog,* University of Georgia, Franklin College of Arts & Sciences, Lamar Dodd School of Art, Athens GA (S)

Moore, Richard, *Dir,* Barnard's Mill Art Museum, Glen Rose TX

Moore, Robert, *Asst Prof,* West Virginia University, College of Creative Arts, School of Art & Design, Morgantown WV (S)

Moore, Robyn, *Asst Prof,* Delta State University, Dept of Art, Cleveland MS (S)

Moore, Sandra, *Dir Info Tech,* Toledo Museum of Art, Toledo OH

Moore, Sharon, *Registrar,* Heard Museum, Phoenix AZ

Moore, Stanley, *Speech,* Henry Ford Community College, McKenzie Fine Art Ctr, Dearborn MI (S)

Moore, Stephen A, *Pres,* Susquehanna Art Museum, Harrisburg PA

Moore, Susan, *Instr & Exhib Dir,* Paris Junior College, Visual Art Dept, Paris TX (S)

Moore, Sylvia, *Educ,* Midmarch Associates/Midmarch Arts Press, Midmarch Arts Press and Library, New York NY

Moore, Teri, *Exec Dir,* Yeiser Art Center Inc, Paducah KY

Moore, Tina, *Pres, Exhibits & Awards Chair,* Pastel Society of the West Coast, Sacramento Fine Arts Center, Carmichael CA

Moore, William, *Instr,* Pacific Northwest College of Art, Portland OR (S)

Moorji, Aliza, *Gallery Asst,* Saint John's University, Dr. M.T. Geoffrey Yeh Art Gallery, Queens NY

Moorman, Evette, *Inst,* Grayson County College, Art Dept, Denison TX (S)

Moos, Walter A, *Pres,* Gallery Moos Ltd, Toronto ON

Moose, Nancy, *Assoc Prof,* Dakota State University, College of Liberal Arts, Madison SD (S)

Moppett, Ron, *Dir & Cur,* Alberta College of Art & Design, Illingworth Kerr Gallery, Calgary AB

Moquino, Denise, *Tourism Dir,* Pueblo of San Ildefonso, Maria Martinez Museum, Santa Fe NM

Moralde, Jocelyn, *Coordr,* The Art Institute of Chicago, Teacher Resource Center, Chicago IL

Morales, Raymond, *Prof,* University of Utah, Dept of Art & Art History, Salt Lake City UT (S)

Morales, Reinaldo, *Assoc Prof,* University of Central Arkansas, Department of Art, Conway AR (S)

Morales-Coll, Eduardo, *Pres,* Ateneo Puertorriqueno, Ateneo Gallery, San Juan PR

Morales-Coll, Eduardo, *Pres,* Ateneo Puertorriqueno, Library, San Juan PR

Morales-Coll, Eduardo, *Pres,* Ateneo Puertorriqueno, Ateneo Gallery, San Juan PR

Morales-Coll, Eduardo, *Pres,* Ateneo Puertorriqueno, Library, San Juan PR

Moran, Arturo, *Groundskeeper,* Plaza de la Raza Cultural Center, Los Angeles CA

Moran, Claudia, *Opers Mgr,* Museo De Las Americas, Denver CO

Moran, Diane H, *Prof,* Sweet Briar College, Art History Dept, Sweet Briar VA (S)

Moran, George F, *Treas,* National Hall of Fame for Famous American Indians, Anadarko OK

Moran, James David, *Dir Outreach,* American Antiquarian Society, Worcester MA

Moran, Joe, *Chmn Art Dept,* California State University, San Bernardino, San Bernardino CA

Moran, Joe, *Chmn Dept & Instr,* California State University, San Bernardino, Dept of Art, San Bernardino CA (S)

Moran, Lynda A, *Exec Dir,* Islip Art Museum, East Islip NY

Moran, Susan, *Dir Resource Center,* Art Institute of Pittsburgh, John P. Barclay Memorial Gallery, Pittsburgh PA

Morand, Anne, *Cur,* C M Russell, Great Falls MT

Morandi, Thomas, *Prof,* Oregon State University, Dept of Art, Corvallis OR (S)

Moreau, Andrea, *Bibliographer & Inventory Asst,* Printed Matter, Inc, New York NY

Moreau, Robert, *Asst Prof,* Northwestern State University of Louisiana, School of Creative & Performing Arts - Dept of Fine & Graphic Arts, Natchitoches LA (S)

Morehouse, Dorothy V, *Pres & CEO,* Monmouth Museum & Cultural Center, Lincroft NJ

Morehouse, John, *Treas,* Salmagundi Club, New York NY

Moreland, Catherine, *Exec Dir & CEO,* Delaplaine Visual Arts Education Center, Frederick MD

Morello, Terry, *VP Devel,* Los Angeles County Museum of Art, Los Angeles CA

Moren, Lisa, *Assoc Prof,* University of Maryland, Baltimore County, Imaging & Digital Arts (IMDA), Dept of Visual Arts, Baltimore MD (S)

Moreno, Barry, *Library Technician,* The National Park Service, United States Department of the Interior, Statue of Liberty National Monument & The Ellis Island Immigration Museum, Washington DC

Moreno, Ceareo, *Visual Arts Dir,* National Museum of Mexican Art, Chicago IL

Moreno, Mario, *Instr,* San Joaquin Delta College, Arts & Communication, Stockton CA (S)

Moreno Vega, Dr Marta, *Founder & Bd Pres,* Caribbean Cultural Center, Cultural Arts Organization & Resource Center, New York NY

Morey, Gina, *Dir Prog & Educ,* Anniston Museum of Natural History, Anniston AL

Morey, Mark, *Cur Educ,* Amarillo Art Association, Amarillo Museum of Art, Amarillo TX

Morgan, Anne H, *Pres Bd,* Norman Rockwell Museum, Stockbridge MA

Morgan, Blake, *Asst Prof,* University of Science & Arts of Oklahoma, Arts Dept, Chickasha OK (S)

Morgan, Carol, *Deputy Dir Education,* ArtsConnection Inc, New York NY

Morgan, Clarence, *Chmn Dept,* University of Minnesota, Minneapolis, Dept of Art, Minneapolis MN (S)

Morgan, Dave W, *Mus Dir,* Carlsbad Museum & Art Center, Carlsbad NM

Morgan, David, *Asst Prof,* University of Wisconsin-Stout, Dept of Art & Design, Menomonie WI (S)

Morgan, Donna, *Adjunct Instr,* Davis & Elkins College, Dept of Art, Elkins WV (S)

Morgan, Dylan, *Gallery Mgr,* Museum of Contemporary Craft, Portland OR

Morgan, Jennifer, *Mus Shop Mgr,* Columbus Museum, Columbus GA

Morgan, Jeremy, *Exec Dir,* Saskatchewan Arts Board, Regina SK

Morgan, Julie, *Registrar,* Sawtooth Center for Visual Art, Winston-Salem NC (S)

Morgan, Ken, *Photog Instr,* Locust Street Neighborhood Art Classes, Inc, Buffalo NY (S)

Morgan, Kenneth, *Assoc Prof Studio Art,* Bethany College, Dept of Fine Arts, Bethany WV (S)

Morgan, Laura, *Serials/Architecture,* Chicago Public Library, Harold Washington Library Center, Chicago IL

Morgan, Linda D, *Librn,* University of South Carolina, Slide Library, Columbia SC

Morgan, Mary, *Instr,* Dallas Baptist University, Dept of Art, Dallas TX (S)

Morgan, Melissa, *Dean Acad Affairs,* Hussian School of Art, Commercial Art Dept, Philadelphia PA (S)

Morgan, Melissa, *Exec Dir,* Pensacola Museum of Art, Pensacola FL

Morgan, Rick, *Dir,* Oglebay Institute, Stifel Fine Arts Center, Wheeling WV

Morgan, Robert C, *Prof,* Rochester Institute of Technology, School of Design, Rochester NY (S)

Morgan, Sara, *Assoc Dir,* South Texas Institute for the Arts, Art Museum of South Texas, Corpus Christi TX

Morgan, William, *Prof,* University of Wisconsin-Superior, Programs in the Visual Arts, Superior WI (S)

Morgan, William, *Prof Emeritus,* University of Louisville, Allen R Hite Art Institute, Louisville KY (S)

Morgano, Stephanie, *Pres,* Trenton City Museum, Trenton NJ

Morgan Taylor, Robert, *Adjunct Asst Prof,* College of Staten Island, Performing & Creative Arts Dept, Staten Island NY (S)

Morganti, Mary, *Library Dir,* The California Historical Society, North Baker Research Library, San Francisco CA

Moriarity, Lyn, *Admin Dir,* National Trust for Historic Preservation, Washington DC

Moriarty, John, *Instr,* Springfield College, Dept of Visual & Performing Arts, Springfield MA (S)

Moriarty, Stephen, *Cur,* University of Notre Dame, Snite Museum of Art, Notre Dame IN

Morice, Kit, *Cur Educ,* Eastern Illinois University, Tarble Arts Center, Charleston IL

Morics, Andrea, *Registrar,* San Bernardino County Museum, Fine Arts Institute, Redlands CA

Morihara, Chizu, *Art Librn,* University of California, Santa Barbara, Arts Library, Santa Barbara CA

Morimoto, Ed.D, Dennis, *Dir,* University of Northern Colorado, School of Art & Design, Greeley CO (S)

Morin, Mark, *Treas,* Westfield Athenaeum, Jasper Rand Art Museum, Westfield MA

Morin, Suzanne, *Librn,* The Stewart Museum, Montreal PQ

Morin, Thomas, *Dir,* Rochester Institute of Technology, School for American Craft, Rochester NY (S)

Moriority, Kaleen, *Asst Prof,* Rochester Institute of Technology, School of Photographic Arts & Sciences, Rochester NY (S)

Morita, Linda, *Librn & Archivist,* McMichael Canadian Art Collection, Library & Archives, Kleinburg ON

Moritz, Tom, *Dir Library Servs,* American Museum of Natural History, Library, New York NY

Morlan, Jenny, *Asst Prof,* DePaul University, Dept of Art, Chicago IL (S)

Morley, Alison, *Chair Photog & Photojournalism Prog,* International Center of Photography, School, New York NY (S)

Morley, Janet, *Fashion Merchandising Prog Dir,* Brenau University, Art & Design Dept, Gainesville GA (S)

Morley, Stephen, *Special Asst to Dir,* Academy of the New Church, Glencairn Museum, Bryn Athyn PA

Mornes, Joon, *Library Head,* University of Minnesota, Architecture & Landscape Library, Minneapolis MN

Morningstar, William, *Prof,* Berea College, Art & Art History Program, Berea KY (S)

Moro, Takeshi, *Asst Prof,* Santa Clara University, Dept of Art & Art History, Santa Clara CA (S)

Morphy, Barbara, *Dir Retail Svcs,* Morris Museum of Art, Augusta GA

Morphy, Richard, *Dir,* Minnesota Historical Society, Library, Saint Paul MN

Morr, Lynell, *Dir,* Center for Creative Studies, College of Art & Design Library, Detroit MI

Morrell, John, *Asst Prof,* Georgetown University, Dept of Art & Art History, Washington DC (S)

Morrelli, William P, *VPres,* Tennessee Historical Society, Nashville TN

Morrill, Michael, *Assoc Prof,* University of Pittsburgh, Dept of Studio Arts, Pittsburgh PA (S)

Morrin, Peter, *Adjunct Assoc Prof,* University of Louisville, Allen R Hite Art Institute, Louisville KY (S)

Morris, Amy, *Instr,* Wittenberg University, Art Dept, Springfield OH (S)

Morris, Betsy, *Prof,* Saint Louis Community College at Meramec, Art Dept, Saint Louis MO (S)

Morris, Catherine J, *Cur, Elizabeth A Sackler Center for Feminist Art,* Brooklyn Museum, Brooklyn NY

Morris, Craig, *Sr VPres,* American Museum of Natural History, New York NY

Morris, Curtis, *Exhib Designer,* City of Springdale, Shiloh Museum of Ozark History, Springdale AR

Morris, Elke, *Senior Lectr,* Bates College, Art & Visual Culture, Lewiston ME (S)

Morris, Fae, *Circ,* J T & E J Crumbaugh, Le Roy IL

Morris, James, *Assoc Prof,* State University of New York College at Brockport, Dept of Art, Brockport NY (S)

Morris, Jeffory, *Exhibs Cur,* Arizona Museum For Youth, Mesa AZ

Morris, Jennie, *VPres,* Alaska Watercolor Society, Anchorage AK

Morris, Jerry W, *Chmn,* Miami University, Art Dept, Oxford OH (S)

Morris, Joella, *Pres Emeritus,* Museum of Southern History, Houston TX

Morris, Katherine, *Assoc Prof,* Santa Clara University, Dept of Art & Art History, Santa Clara CA (S)

Morris, Kelly, *Mgr Publ,* High Museum of Art, Atlanta GA

Morris, Laura, *Prog Coordr,* University of Oregon, Aperture Photo Gallery - EMU Art Gallery, Eugene OR

Morris, Mary, *Exec Dir,* Venice Art Center, Venice FL

Morris, Nikki, *Registrar,* Booth Western Art Museum, Cartersville GA

Morris, Paul, *Dir Pub Information & Literature,* Arizona Commission on the Arts, Phoenix AZ

Morris, Stuart, *Asst Prof,* University of Wisconsin-Stevens Point, Dept of Art & Design, Stevens Point WI (S)

Morris, W S, *Chmn & CEO,* Morris Communications Co. LLC, Corporate Collection, Augusta GA

Morris-Cafiero, Haley, *Dir Grad Studies,* Memphis College of Art, Memphis TN (S)

Morris-Hunt, Carolyn, *COO,* State University of New York College at Buffalo, Buffalo NY

Morris-Hunt, Carolyn, *COO,* State University of New York College at Buffalo, Burchfield Penney Art Center, Buffalo NY

Morrisey, Bob, *Prof,* Polk Community College, Art, Letters & Social Sciences, Winter Haven FL (S)

Morrisey, Marena Grant, *Exec Dir,* Orlando Museum of Art, Orlando FL

Morrisey, Marena Grant, *Exec Dir,* Orlando Museum of Art, Orlando Sentinel Library, Orlando FL

Morrish, David, *Prof,* Memorial University of Newfoundland, Division of Fine Arts, Visual Arts Program, Corner Brook NF (S)

Morrish, William, *Dean School of Constructed Environments,* Parsons The New School for Design, New York NY (S)

Morrison, Cindi, *Dir,* College of Central Florida, Appleton Museum of Art, Ocala FL

Morrison, Darrin, *Project Mgr Conservation,* University of British Columbia, Museum of Anthropology, Vancouver BC

Morrison, Elizabeth, *Acting Sr Cur Manuscripts,* Getty Center, The J Paul Getty Museum, Los Angeles CA

Morrison, Ian, *Asst Prof Art, Chair,* Grand Canyon University, Art Dept, Phoenix AZ (S)

Morrison, Jeff, *Asst Prof Theatre,* Marymount Manhattan College, Fine & Performing Arts Div, New York NY (S)

Morrison, Ken, *Thesis Adv,* Toronto Art Therapy Institute, Toronto ON (S)

Morrison, Patrick, *Educ,* Pennsylvania Historical & Museum Commission, Railroad Museum of Pennsylvania, Harrisburg PA

Morrison, Susan, *Prof,* University of Wisconsin-Stevens Point, Dept of Art & Design, Stevens Point WI (S)

Morrison, Virginia, *Exec Dir,* Society for Photographic Education (SPE), SPE Gallery, Cleveland OH

Morrisroe, Julia, *Assoc Prof,* University of Florida, School of Art & Art History, Gainesville FL (S)

Morrissey, Jennifer, *Publ Relations Officer,* Museum of Contemporary Art, San Diego-Downtown, La Jolla CA

Morrissey, T, *Prof,* Community College of Rhode Island, Dept of Art, Warwick RI (S)

Morrissey, Tom, *Dir & Librn,* Community College of Rhode Island, Flanagan Valley Campus Art Gallery, Warwick RI

Morrow, David, *Treas,* Barnard's Mill Art Museum, Glen Rose TX

Morrow, Delores, *Photograph Cur,* Montana Historical Society, Library, Helena MT

Morrow, Kara, *Asst Prof,* The College of Wooster, Dept of Art and Art History, Wooster OH (S)

Morrow, Lisa, *Visual Cur,* Center for Creative Studies, College of Art & Design Library, Detroit MI

Morrow, Nancy, *Asst Prof,* Kansas State University, Art Dept, Manhattan KS (S)

Morrow, William, *Dir,* 21c Museum, Louisville KY

Morse, Anne, *William & Helen Pounds Sr Cur Japanese Art,* Museum of Fine Arts, Boston MA

Morse, Karen W, *Archivist,* Historic Hudson Valley, Pocantico Hills NY

Morse, Karen Walton, *Mgr Library & Archival Servs,* Historic Hudson Valley, Library, Pocantico Hills NY

Morse, Samuel C, *Prof of History of Art & Asian Languages/Civilizaitions,* Amherst College, Dept of Art & the History of Art, Amherst MA (S)

Morse, William, *Asst Prof Art,* Belhaven College, Art Dept, Jackson MS (S)

Morse Majewski, Sally, *Contact Person,* Sterling & Francine Clark, Williamstown MA

Mort, Rhonda, *Children's Librn,* Willard Library, Dept of Fine Arts, Evansville IN

Mortensen, Loring, *Pub & Community Relations,* University of North Carolina at Greensboro, Weatherspoon Art Museum, Greensboro NC

Mortensen, Christian, *Adj Prof,* Augustana College, Art Dept, Rock Island IL (S)

Mortenson, Mark, *Pres & CEO,* Buffalo Museum of Science, Research Library, Buffalo NY

Morton, Christopher, *Registrar,* New York State Military Museum and Veterans Research Center, Saratoga Springs NY

Morton, Elizabeth, *Asst Prof Art History,* Wabash College, Art Dept, Crawfordsville IN (S)

Morton, Ennette, *Dir Mus,* Riverside Metropolitan Museum, Riverside CA

Morton, Janet, *Instr,* Toronto School of Art, Toronto ON (S)

Morton, Jean Pell, *Staff,* Gallery 9, Los Altos CA

Morton, Patricia M, *Chmn & Assoc Prof,* University of California, Riverside, Dept of the History of Art, Riverside CA (S)

Morton, Tracey, *Admin Mgr,* Diverse Works, Houston TX

Moscardini, Gina, *Mus Shop Mgr,* The Bartlett Museum, Amesbury MA

Moscarillo, Mark, *Assoc Prof,* State University of New York at Farmingdale, Visual Communications, Farmingdale NY (S)

Moscovitch, Ruth, *Pres,* Manhattan Graphics Center, New York NY (S)

Moseley, Bill, *Prof,* University of Maine at Augusta, College of Arts & Humanities, Augusta ME (S)

Moseley, W L Tim, *Cur,* Alice Moseley Folk Art and Antique Museum, Bay Saint Louis MS

Mosena, David, *Pres & CEO,* Museum of Science & Industry, Chicago IL

Moser, Gabby, *Commun Specialist,* Oakville Galleries, Centennial Square and Gairloch Gardens, Oakville ON

Moser, Nikki, *Instr,* Keystone College, Fine Arts Dept, LaPlume PA (S)

Moser, Suzy, *Assoc VPres Advancement,* The Huntington Library, Art Collections & Botanical Gardens, San Marino CA

Moser, Suzy, *Assoc VPres Advancement,* The Huntington Library, Art Collections & Botanical Gardens, Library, San Marino CA

Moses, Jennifer, *Asst Prof,* University of New Hampshire, Dept of Arts & Art History, Durham NH (S)

Moses, Kerry, *Accnt & HR Mgr,* Tyler Museum of Art, Tyler TX

Moses, Monica, *Editor in Chief American Craft Mag,* American Craft Council, Minneapolis MN

Mosher, Mike, *Asst Prof,* Saginaw Valley State University, Dept of Art & Design, University Center MI (S)

Mosher, Ted, *Pres,* High Wire Gallery, Philadelphia PA

Moshier, Wendy, *Dir Community Develop,* Salina Art Center, Salina KS

Moskowitz, Anita, *Chair & Prof,* Stony Brook University, College of Arts & Sciences, Dept of Art, Stony Brook NY (S)

Moskowitz, Herb, *Chief Registrar,* The Metropolitan Museum of Art, New York NY

Moskowitz, Mollie, *Admin Asst,* Queens College, City University of New York, Queens College Art Center, Flushing NY

Moskwa, Jessica, *Exec Dir,* Allied Arts of Yakima Valley, The Peggy Lewis Gallery, Yakima WA

Mosley, Kim, *Prof,* Saint Louis Community College at Florissant Valley, Liberal Arts Division, Ferguson MO (S)

Moss, Cris, *Gallery Dir,* Linfield College, Department of Art & Visual Culture, McMinnville OR (S)

Moss, David, *Mng Dir,* Saidye Bronfman, Liane & Danny Taran Gallery, Montreal PQ

Moss, Elizabeth, *Exec Dir,* Hockaday Museum of Art, Kalispell MT

Moss, Jessica, *Asst Cur,* University of Chicago, Smart Museum of Art, Chicago IL

Moss, Kenneth, *Dir,* Morris-Jumel Mansion, Inc, New York NY

Moss, Kent, *Prof,* Midland College, Art Dept, Midland TX (S)

Moss, Nina, *Asst to Dir,* Mississippi Museum of Art, Howorth Library, Jackson MS

Moss, Sedgwick, *Ranger,* Bluemont Historical Railroad Junction, Arlington VA

Moss, Susan, *Prof, chmn dept,* Fort Lewis College, Art Dept, Durango CO (S)

Mossaides Strassfield, Christina, *Mus Dir & Chief Cur,* Guild Hall of East Hampton, Inc, Guild Hall Museum, East Hampton NY

Mosser, Dennis, *Library Technician III,* University of Oklahoma, Fine Arts Library, Norman OK

Most, Gregory P J, *Chief,* National Gallery of Art, Department of Image Collections, Washington DC

Moster, Hilary, *Exec Dir,* Maude Kerns Art Center, Eugene OR

Mote, Cindy, *Admin Asst,* Amarillo Art Association, Amarillo Museum of Art, Amarillo TX

Motes, J Barry, *Fine Art Dept Head,* Jefferson Community College & Technical College, Fine Arts, Louisville KY (S)

Mott, Cathy, *Cur Educ,* Muskegon Museum of Art, Muskegon MI

Mott, Margie, *Vol Coordr,* Delaplaine Visual Arts Education Center, Frederick MD

Mott, Rebecca, *Assoc Prof,* West Shore Community College, Division of Humanities & Fine Arts, Scottville MI (S)

Motte, Stephen, *Cur Coll,* Florence Museum, Florence SC

Motts, Wayne E, *Exec Dir,* Adams County Historical Society, Gettysburg PA

Motyka, Judith, *Develop Officer,* Ellen Noel Art Museum of the Permian Basin, Odessa TX

Moudry, Mary Lou, *Exec Dir,* Crow Wing County Historical Society, Brainerd MN

Moulton, Aaron, *Cur Exhibs,* Salt Lake Art Center, Utah Museum of Contemporary Art, Salt Lake City UT

Mounger, Becky, *Instr,* Oklahoma State University, Graphic Arts Dept, Visual Communications, Okmulgee OK (S)

Mount, Allison, *Dir,* State University of New York College at Cortland, Dowd Fine Arts Gallery, Cortland NY

Moura-Ona, Sylvia, *Asst Dir,* Miami-Dade Public Library, Miami FL

Mouton, Alexander, *Asst Prof,* Seattle University, Dept of Fine Arts, Visual Art Division, Seattle WA (S)

Movahedi-Lankarani, Stephanie, *Library Supv,* The Pennsylvania State University, Architecture & Landscape Architecture Library, University Park PA

Mowat, Janet, *Dir Mktg & Communs,* Art Gallery of Hamilton, Hamilton ON

Mowder, William, *Dean,* Kutztown University, College of Visual & Performing Arts, Kutztown PA (S)

Mowery, Lynn, *Treas,* Cody Country Art League, Cody WY

Mowll Mathews, Nancy, *Cur 19th & 20th Century Art & Art Lect,* Williams College, Museum of Art, Williamstown MA

Mowry, Crystal, *Cur,* Kitchener-Waterloo Art Gallery, Kitchener ON

Mowry, Robert, *Cur Chinese Art,* Harvard University, Arthur M Sackler Museum, Cambridge MA

Moxley, Elizabeth, *Dir & Custodian Holdings,* National Archives of Canada, Art & Photography Archives, Ottawa ON

Moxley, Richard W, *Exec Dir,* Agecroft Association, Agecroft Hall, Richmond VA

Moxley, Richard W, *Exec Dir,* Agecroft Association, Museum, Richmond VA

Moy, James, *VPres & Provost,* Nova Scotia College of Art & Design, Halifax NS (S)

Moy, Jeffrey V, *Archivist,* Newark Museum Association, The Newark Museum, Newark NJ

Moye, Stephanie, *Serials Librn,* National Portrait Gallery, Library, Washington DC

Moyer, Ashleigh, *Prog Dir,* University of Tennessee, Visual Arts Committee, Knoxville TN

Moyer, David, *Cur Estuarine Biology,* Calvert Marine Museum, Solomons MD

Moyer, G Gary, *Exec Dir,* Southern Alleghenies Museum of Art, Loretto Facility, Loretto PA

Moyer, G Gary, *Exec Dir,* Southern Alleghenies Museum of Art, Johnstown Gallery, Loretto PA

Moyer, G Gary, *Exec Dir,* Southern Alleghenies Museum of Art, Altoona Facility, Loretto PA

Moyer, G Gary, *Exec Dir,* Southern Alleghenies Museum of Art, Ligonier Valley Facility, Loretto PA

Moyer, Lydia, *Asst Prof Studio Art,* University of Virginia, McIntire Dept of Art, Charlottesville VA (S)

Moyer, Nancy, *Chmn Dept,* University of Texas Pan American, Art Dept, Edinburg TX (S)

Moyers, Michael, *Assoc Dean,* Yuba College, Fine Arts Division, Marysville CA (S)

Moynahan, Alberta, *Asst Dir,* McDowell House & Apothecary Shop, Danville KY

Moynahan, Karen P, *Assoc Dir,* National Association of Schools of Art & Design, Reston VA

Moyse, Katherine, *Assoc Prof,* Hillsborough Community College, Fine Arts Dept, Tampa FL (S)

Mraovic, Dejan, *Asst Prof,* Campbellsville University, Department of Art, Campbellsville KY (S)

Mroz, Michael, *Exec Dir,* Newburyport Maritime Society, Inc, Custom House Maritime Museum, Newburyport MA

Muccigrosso, John, *Dean,* Drew University, Elizabeth P Korn Gallery, Madison NJ

Muchow, Michael, *Librn,* University of Missouri, Art, Archaeology & Music Collection, Columbia MO

Mudd, Douglas, *Museum Cur,* American Numismatic Association, Edward C. Rochette Money Museum, Colorado Springs CO

Mudd, Jane, *Instr,* William Woods-Westminster Colleges, Art Dept, Fulton MO (S)

Mudd, Peter, *Exec Dir,* C G Jung Center, Evanston IL

Mudrinich, David, *Asst Prof,* Arkansas Tech University, Dept of Art, Russellville AR (S)

Muehlemann, Kathy, *Acting Chmn,* Randolph-Macon Woman's College, Dept of Art, Lynchburg VA (S)

Muehlig, Linda, *Cur Paintings & Sculpture,* Smith College, Museum of Art, Northampton MA

Mueller, Eleanor, *Develop Assoc,* Kitchener-Waterloo Art Gallery, Kitchener ON

Mueller, Jo, *Exec Dir,* George A Spiva, Joplin MO

Mueller, John C, *Prof,* University of Detroit Mercy, School of Architecture, Detroit MI (S)

Mueller, Lyn, *Instr,* Wayne Art Center, Wayne PA (S)

Mueller, Margaret, *Librn,* Riverside County Museum, Library, Cherry Valley CA

Mueller, Mark, *Adj Asst Prof,* University of Texas at Arlington, Art & Art History Department, Arlington TX (S)

Mueller, Marlene, *Prof,* Wayne State College, Nordstrand Visual Arts Dept, Wayne NE

Mueller, Marlene, *Prof,* Wayne State College, Dept Art & Design, Wayne NE (S)

Mueller, Mitzi, *Mus Serv Coordr,* Paine Art Center & Gardens, Oshkosh WI

Mueller, Robert, *Assoc Prof,* University of Florida, School of Art & Art History, Gainesville FL (S)

Muente, Tamera, *Asst Cur,* Taft Museum of Art, Cincinnati OH

Mugavero, C J, *Owner,* The Artful Deposit, Inc., The Artful Deposit Gallery, Bordentown City NJ

Muhammad, Waduda, *Interim Gallery Dir,* Georgia State University, Ernest G Welch Gallery, Atlanta GA

Muhlbauer, Mic, *Asst Prof,* Eastern New Mexico University, Dept of Art, Portales NM (S)

Muhlbauer, Mic, *Prof Art,* Eastern New Mexico University, Runnels Gallery, Golden Library, Portales NM

Muhn, B G, *Assoc Prof,* Georgetown University, Dept of Art & Art History, Washington DC (S)

Muhsam, Armin, *Assoc Prof,* Northwest Missouri State University, Dept of Fine & Performing Arts, Maryville MO (S)

Muir, Linda, *Acting Cur,* Harvard University, Busch-Reisinger Museum, Cambridge MA

Muir, Tom, *Museum Adminr,* Historic Pensacola Preservation Board, T.T. Wentworth Jr. Florida State Museum, Pensacola FL

Muirawski, Michael, *Dir Educ & Pub Rels,* Portland Art Museum, Portland OR

Muirhead, Robert, *Prof,* Hamilton College, Art Dept, Clinton NY (S)

Mukherjee, Sandeep, *Asst Prof,* Pomona College, Dept of Art & Art History, Claremont CA (S)

Mulcahy, Fran, *Cur Educ,* Museum of Art, Fort Lauderdale, Library, Fort Lauderdale FL

Mulcahy, Kevin, *Mem Coordr,* Intuit: The Center for Intuitive & Outsider Art, Chicago IL

Muldavin, Phyllis, *Instr,* Los Angeles City College, Dept of Art, Los Angeles CA (S)

Mulder, Bruce, *Chmn Design Studies,* Kendall College of Art & Design, Grand Rapids MI (S)

Muldowney, Nancy, *Pres,* Glynn Art Association, Saint Simons Island GA

Muldowney, Ryan, *Prof,* Sheridan College, Art Dept, Sheridan WY (S)

Mulford, Hansen, *Cur,* Orlando Museum of Art, Orlando FL

Mulford, Hansen, *Cur,* Orlando Museum of Art, Orlando Sentinel Library, Orlando FL

Mulgrew, John, *Chmn,* Pace University, Dyson College of Arts & Sciences, Pleasantville NY (S)

Mulgrew, John, *Dept Chair,* Pace University Gallery, Art Gallery in Choate House, Pleasantville NY

Mulholland, Sarah, *Media & Communs Officer Mktg & Communs,* OCAD University, Toronto ON (S)

Mulhollen, Jack, *Instr,* Cuyahoga Valley Art Center, Cuyahoga Falls OH (S)

Mulkey, Elly, *Treas/Secy,* Roswell Museum & Art Center, Roswell NM

Mullally, Susan, *Asst Prof,* Baylor University - College of Arts and Sciences, Dept of Art, Waco TX (S)

Mullen, Conor, *Prep,* University of Wyoming, University of Wyoming Art Museum, Laramie WY

Mullen, Denise, *Pres,* Oregon College of Art & Craft, Portland OR (S)

Mullen, Jim, *Prof,* Bowdoin College, Art Dept, Brunswick ME (S)

Mullen, Karen, *Cur Educ,* Laumeier Sculpture Park, Saint Louis MO

Mullen, Sarah, *Dir Annual Giving,* University of Virginia, The Fralin Museum of Art at the University of Virginia, Charlottesville VA

Muller, Arlene, *Gift Shop Mgr,* Eccles Community Art Center, Ogden UT

Muller, Debra, *Asst Dir,* Eccles Community Art Center, Ogden UT

Muller, Jefffrey, *Prof,* Brown University, Dept History of Art & Architecture, Providence RI (S)

Muller, Kristin, *Exec Dir,* Peters Valley Craft Center, Layton NJ

Muller, Martin, *Owner,* Modernism, San Francisco CA

Muller, Nina, *Dir External Affairs,* The Heckscher Museum of Art, Huntington NY

Muller, Priscilla E, *Cur Emeritus,* The Hispanic Society of America, Museum & Library, New York NY

Muller, Sheila, *Prof,* University of Utah, Dept of Art & Art History, Salt Lake City UT (S)

Muller, William, *VPres,* Society of American Historical Artists, Oyster Bay NY

Mullin, Diane, *Cur,* University of Minnesota, Frederick R Weisman Art Museum, Minneapolis MN

Mullin, Timothy, *Dept Head,* Western Kentucky University, Kentucky Library & Museum, Bowling Green KY

Mullineaux, Connie, *Chairperson,* Edinboro University of Pennsylvania, Art Dept, Edinboro PA (S)

Mullings, Ted, *VPres,* Lake County Civic Center Association, Inc, Heritage Museum & Gallery, Leadville CO

Mullins, Barbara, *CFO,* Memphis Brooks Museum of Art, Memphis TN

Mullins, Derek, *Mktg & Sales,* Appalshop Inc, Appalshop, Whitesburg KY

Mullins, Kara, *Dir Develop,* The Phillips Collection, Washington DC

Mullis, Connie, *Pres Commission Bd,* Drew County Historical Society, Museum, Monticello AR

Mulrooney, Melissa, *Dir,* Stamford Museum & Nature Center, Stamford CT

Mulroy, Kevin, *Interim Head,* University of California, Los Angeles, Arts Library, Los Angeles CA

Mulvaney, Rebecca, *Dir Gallery,* Northern State University, Northern Galleries, Aberdeen SD

Mumford, Jessica, *Registrar,* Telfair Museums' Jepson Center for the Arts Library, Savannah GA

Mumford, Jessica, *Registrar,* Telfair Museums' Jepson Center for the Arts Library, Telfair Academy of Arts & Sciences Library, Savannah GA

Mummert, Joan J, *Pres & CEO,* The York County Heritage Trust, York PA

Mundy, James, *Dir,* Vassar College, The Frances Lehman Loeb Art Center, Poughkeepsie NY

Munger, Kari, *Head Librn,* Canajoharie Library & Art Gallery, Arkell Museum of Canajoharie, Canajoharie NY

Munns, Judith, *Cur,* Skagway City Museum & Archives, Skagway AK

Munns, Melanie, *Spec Projects Mgr,* University of Mississippi, University Museum & Historic Houses, Oxford MS

Munoz, Steven, *Contact,* Lee Arts Center, Arlington VA

Munoz, Terresa, *Prof,* Loyola Marymount University, Dept of Art & Art History, Los Angeles CA (S)

Munro, Gale, *Art Coll Cur,* Naval Historical Center, The Navy Museum, Washington DC

Munro, Gale, *Cur,* United States Navy, Art Gallery, Washington DC

Munro, Hilary, *Head Adult Servs,* Medicine Hat Public Library, Medicine Hat AB

Munroe, Alexandra, *Cur Asian Art,* Solomon R Guggenheim, New York NY

Munsch, Anne, *CFO,* Peabody Essex Museum, Salem MA

Murad, Andrew, *Coordr,* McLennan Community College, Visual Arts Dept, Waco TX (S)

Muraoka, Anne, *Asst Prof,* Old Dominion University, Art Dept, Norfolk VA (S)

Murawski, Alex, *Asst Prof Graphic Design,* University of Georgia, Franklin College of Arts & Sciences, Lamar Dodd School of Art, Athens GA (S)

Murawski, Paul, *Dir Retail,* American Museum of Natural History, New York NY

Murback, Mitch, *Prof Chmn,* DePauw University, Art Dept, Greencastle IN (S)

Murch, Anna Valentina, *Prof,* Mills College, Art Dept, Oakland CA (S)

Murchie, John, *Coordr,* Struts Gallery, Sackville NB

Murchinson, Alex, *Instr,* Holland College, Photography & Digital Imaging, Charlottetown PE (S)

Murdoch, Carol, *Reference Librn,* North Central College, Oesterle Library, Naperville IL

Murdoch, John, *Dir Art Coll,* The Huntington Library, Art Collections & Botanical Gardens, San Marino CA

Murdoch, John, *Dir Colls,* The Huntington Library, Art Collections & Botanical Gardens, Library, San Marino CA

Murdoch, Wayne, *Dir Colls Mgmt,* Ministry of Alberta Culture, Provincial Archives of Alberta, Edmonton AB

Murdock, Elena, *Financial Officer,* Portland Museum of Art, Portland ME

Murdock, Ronda, *Library Technical Asst,* French Institute-Alliance Francaise, Library, New York NY

Murdock, Tina, *Music Librn,* J Eric Johnson, Fine Arts Division, Dallas TX

Murney, Kathleen, *Adjunct Instr,* Southern Oregon University, Art & Art History Dept, Ashland OR (S)

Muro, Michelle, *Colls Coordr,* Workman & Temple Family Homestead Museum, City of Industry CA

Murphey, F Warren, *Dir Mus & Historic Preservation,* Jekyll Island Museum, Jekyll Island GA

Murphy, Betty, *Librn,* Heard Museum, Billie Jane Baguley Library and Archives, Phoenix AZ

Murphy, Bridget, *Assoc Prof,* Marymount University, School of Arts & Sciences Div, Arlington VA (S)

Murphy, Camay, *Exec Dir,* Eubie Blake, Baltimore MD

Murphy, Caroline P., *Asst Prof,* Salem State University, Art & Design Department, Salem MA (S)

Murphy, Darin, *Librn,* Museum of Fine Arts, William Morris Hunt Memorial Library, Boston MA

Murphy, Debra E, *Asst Prof,* University of North Florida, Dept of Communications & Visual Arts, Jacksonville FL (S)

Murphy, Felicia, *Admin Secy,* Rocky Mount Arts Center, Rocky Mount NC

Murphy, Greg, *Dean,* Maine College of Art, Portland ME (S)

Murphy, Harold, *Chmn,* Yesteryear Village, West Palm Beach FL

Murphy, Jeff, *Assoc Prof,* University of North Carolina at Charlotte, Dept Art, Charlotte NC (S)

Murphy, John, *VPres,* Belskie Museum, Closter NJ

Murphy, Kevin, *Prof,* City University of New York, PhD Program in Art History, New York NY (S)

Murphy, Laura, *PT Instr,* Adams State College, Dept of Visual Arts, Alamosa CO (S)

Murphy, Margaret, *Exec Dir,* Fine Arts Work Center, Provincetown MA

Murphy, Margaret H, *Chmn,* Alabama Southern Community College, Art Dept, Monroeville AL (S)

Murphy, Marilyn, *Chair,* Vanderbilt University, Dept of Art, Nashville TN (S)

Murphy, Marilyn, *Librn,* Mount Mercy College, Library, Cedar Rapids IA

Murphy, Mary, *Vis Resources Librn,* Savannah College of Art & Design - Atlanta, ACA Library of Atlanta, Atlanta GA

Murphy, Mary Jo, *Dir Develop,* Berkshire Museum, Pittsfield MA

Murphy, Michael, *Exhibits Mgr,* Putnam Museum of History and Natural Science, Davenport IA

Murphy, Michael, *Instr,* California State University, Chico, Department of Art & Art History, Chico CA (S)

Murphy, Nita, *Librn,* Taos, Ernest Blumenschein Home & Studio, Taos NM

Murphy, Nita, *Librn,* Taos, La Hacienda de Los Martinez, Taos NM

Murphy, Patricia, *Pub Rels,* Friends of Historic Kingston, Fred J Johnston House Museum, Kingston NY

Murphy, Vince, *Thesis Adv,* Toronto Art Therapy Institute, Toronto ON (S)

Murphy Milligan, Bridget, *Assoc Prof,* The College of Wooster, Dept of Art and Art History, Wooster OH (S)

Murrah, Molly, *Pres,* Northwest Watercolor Society, Woodinville WA

Murrary, Cassandra, *Mem Mgr,* African American Museum in Philadelphia, Philadelphia PA

Murray, Ann H, *Dir,* Wheaton College, Beard and Weil Galleries, Norton MA

Murray, Barbara, *Exec Dir,* Philadelphia Sketch Club, Philadelphia PA

Murray, Catherine, *Prof, Interim Chair,* East Tennessee State University, College of Arts and Sciences, Dept of Art & Design, Johnson City TN (S)

Murray, David, *Assoc Prof,* Black Hawk College, Art Dept, Moline IL (S)

Murray, Debi, *Dir Research & Archives,* Historical Society of Palm Beach County, The Richard and Pat Johnson Palm Beach County History Museum, West Palm Beach FL

Murray, Donna, *Dir Educ,* Putnam Museum of History and Natural Science, Davenport IA

Murray, Gale, *Assoc Prof,* Colorado College, Dept of Art, Colorado Springs CO (S)

Murray, Holly, *Dir Gallery,* Springfield College, William Blizard Gallery, Springfield MA

Murray, Holly, *Instr,* Springfield College, Dept of Visual & Performing Arts, Springfield MA (S)

Murray, Jan, *Prof,* University of Mississippi, Department of Art, University MS (S)

Murray, Jeffery, *Cur Interpretation,* Wade House Historic Site-Wisconsin Historical Society, Wesley W. Jung Carriage Museum, Greenbush WI

Murray, Jennifer, *Gallery Dir,* Averill and Bernard Leviton A + D Gallery, Chicago IL

Murray, Julia K, *Prof,* University of Wisconsin, Madison, Dept of Art History, Madison WI (S)

Murray, Karin, *Dir Gallery,* Valdosta State University, Art Gallery, Valdosta GA

Murray, Keith, *Programming & Commun Coordr,* Quickdraw Animation Society, Calgary AB

Murray, Mary E, *Cur Modern & Contemporary Art,* Munson-Williams-Proctor Arts Institute, Museum of Art, Utica NY

Murray, Mary M, *Secy,* Second Street Gallery, Charlottesville VA

Murray, Neale, *Chmn Dept,* North Park University, Art Dept, Chicago IL (S)

Murray, Peter J, *Dir,* The National Shrine of the North American Martyrs, Fultonville NY

Murray, Steve, *Asst Dir Admin,* Alabama Department of Archives & History, Museum of Alabama, Montgomery AL

Murray, Tina, *Mgr Vis Servs,* Foosaner Art Museum, Melbourne FL

Murray, Todd, *Photog,* Antonelli Institute, Professional Photography & Commercial Art, Erdenheim PA (S)

Murray Adams, Claire, *Prof,* Malone University, Dept of Art, Canton OH (S)

Murrell, Tracy, *Interim Cur,* Hammonds House Museum, Atlanta GA

Murtaugh, Rebecca, *Assoc Prof,* Hamilton College, Art Dept, Clinton NY (S)

Musca, Robert, *Dir Finance,* Society for Contemporary Craft, Pittsburgh PA

Muscat, Ann, *Exec VPres,* Natural History Museum of Los Angeles County, Los Angeles CA

Muse, Vance, *Pub Rels,* Menil Foundation, Inc, The Menil Collection, Houston TX

Muse-Mclea, Robin, *Dir Educ,* Barnes Foundation, Merion PA

Musgnug, Kristin, *Assoc Prof,* University of Arkansas, Art Dept, Fayetteville AR (S)

Musser, Ann, *Assoc Acad Progs & Pub Educ,* Smith College, Museum of Art, Northampton MA

Musto, Linda, *Gen Educ,* Art Institute of Pittsburgh, Pittsburgh PA (S)

Muto, Iya, *Intern,* New Image Art, West Hollywood CA

Mutter, William, *Adjunct Asst Prof,* Drew University, Art Dept, Madison NJ (S)

Mutza, Amy, *Opers Mgr,* Wildling Art Museum, Solvang CA

Muzikar, Debra, *Exec Dir,* Red Brick Center for the Arts, Aspen CO

Myatt, Doug, *Dir Colls & Exhibs,* Walter Anderson, Ocean Springs MS

Mycue, David J, *Cur Archives & Coll,* Hidalgo County Historical Museum, Edinburg TX

Myers, Derek, *Prof,* Virginia Polytechnic Institute & State University, Dept of Art & Art History, Blacksburg VA (S)

Myers, Frances, *Prof,* University of Wisconsin, Madison, Dept of Art, Madison WI (S)

Myers, Glen, *Cur,* Wells Fargo Bank, Wells Fargo History Museum, San Francisco CA

Myers, Jenny, *Asst Prof Interior Design,* Watkins College of Art, Design & Film, Nashville TN (S)

Myers, Kat, *Assoc Prof,* Western Illinois University, Department of Art, Macomb IL (S)

Myers, Kevin, *Prof Ceramics,* Orange Coast College, Visual & Performing Arts Division, Costa Mesa CA (S)

Myers, Mickey, *Exec Dir,* Bryan Memorial Gallery, Cambridge VT

Myers, Nathan, *Mus Registrar,* Dwight D Eisenhower, Abilene KS

Myers, Pamela L, *Exec Dir,* Asheville Art Museum, Asheville NC

Myers, Susan, *Instr,* Ocean City Arts Center, Ocean City NJ (S)

Myers, Susan, *Prog Mgr,* Fairmount Park Art Association, Philadelphia PA

Myers, Tracy, *Cur Architecture,* Carnegie Museums of Pittsburgh, Carnegie Museum of Art, Pittsburgh PA

Myers, Vickie, *Treas & Dir Finance,* National Watercolor Society, San Pedro CA

Myers, Virginia, *Prof Foil Stamping,* University of Iowa, School of Art & Art History, Iowa City IA (S)

Myers, William, *Preparator,* Smith College, Museum of Art, Northampton MA

Myler, Debby, *VPres,* The Art Museum of Eastern Idaho, Idaho Falls ID

Mynes, Jess, *Coordr, Library Svcs,* Mount Wachusett Community College, La Chance Library, Gardner MA

Myoda, Paul, *Asst Prof,* Brown University, Dept of Visual Art, Providence RI (S)

Myrick, Bryon, *Pres,* Mississippi Art Colony, Stoneville MS

Myrick, Tommy, *Instr,* Southern University in New Orleans, Fine Arts & Philosophy Dept, New Orleans LA (S)

Naab, Michael, *Dir,* City of Ketchikan Museum, Tongass Historical Museum, Ketchikan AK

Naab, Michael, *Dir,* City of Ketchikan Museum Dept, Ketchikan AK

Naab, Michael, *Dir,* City of Ketchikan Museum Dept, Library, Ketchikan AK

Naar, Harry I, *Prof Art & Dir,* Rider University, Art Gallery, Lawrenceville NJ

Nace, Aprille, *Assoc Librn Pub Svcs,* Corning Museum of Glass, Juliette K and Leonard S Rakow Research Library, Corning NY

Nacheman, Elinor, *Catalog/Reference Librn,* Rhode Island School of Design, Fleet Library at RISD, Providence RI

Nachison, Emily, *Fibers,* Oregon College of Art & Craft, Portland OR (S)

Nacke, Bruce, *Assoc Prof Interior Design,* University of North Texas, College of Visual Arts & Design, Denton TX (S)

Nadal, Maria, *Pres Elect,* Inter-Society Color Council, Reston VA

Nadaskay, Chris, *Prof,* Union University, Dept of Art, Jackson TN (S)

Nadeau, Ed, *Adjunct Asst Prof,* University of Maine, Dept of Art, Orono ME (S)

Nadeau, Nils, *Publications & Web Mgr,* Dartmouth College, Hood Museum of Art, Hanover NH

Nadel, Joshua, *Chmn,* University of Maine at Augusta, College of Arts & Humanities, Augusta ME (S)

Nadler, Evelyn, *Bus Mgr,* Green Hill Center for North Carolina Art, Greensboro NC

Nadler, Jeff, *Dir Develop,* Independent Curators International, New York NY

Naef, Weston, *Cur Photographs,* Getty Center, Trust Museum, Los Angeles CA

Naeser, Barbara, *Treas,* Marblehead Arts Association, Inc, Marblehead MA

Naficy, Hamid, *Adjunct Prof,* Northwestern University, Evanston, Dept of Art History, Evanston IL (S)

Nagai, Mona, *Film Coll Mgr,* University of California, Berkeley, Berkeley Art Museum & Pacific Film Archive, Berkeley CA

Nagai, Mona, *Film Coll Mgr,* University of California, Berkeley, Pacific Film Archive, Berkeley CA

Nagar, Deeksha, *Cur Coll,* Indiana University, The Mathers Museum of World Cultures, Bloomington IN

Nagar, Devvrat, *Prof,* La Roche College, Division of Design, Pittsburgh PA (S)

Nagasawa, Nobuho, *Assoc Prof,* Stony Brook University, College of Arts & Sciences, Dept of Art, Stony Brook NY (S)

Nagel, Alexander, *Undergrad Coordr Art History,* University of Toronto, Dept of Fine Art, Toronto ON (S)

Nagel, Brian, *Dir Interpretation,* Genesee Country Village & Museum, John L Wehle Art Gallery, Mumford NY

Nagel, Toni, *Photo Archivist,* Whatcom Museum, Library, Bellingham WA

Nagler, Katherine, *Dir,* Indianapolis Museum of Contemporary Art, Indianapolis IN

Nagy, Jean, *Instr,* Middle Tennessee State University, Art Dept, Murfreesboro TN (S)

Nagy, Rebecca M, *Dir,* University of Florida, Samuel P Harn Museum of Art, Gainesville FL

Nakajima, Takashi, *Faculty Dean Arts, Architecture & Amenagement,* Universite Quebec Cite Universitaire, School of Visual Arts, Quebec PQ (S)

Nakamura, Cayleen, *Dir National Program,* Japanese American National Museum, Los Angeles CA

Nakamura, Kayo, *Asst Prof,* Biola University, Art Dept, La Mirada CA (S)

Nakano, Yuzo, *Artistic Dir,* Kala Institute, Kala Art Institute, Berkeley CA

Nakao, Susan, *Lectr,* Emporia State University, Dept of Art, Emporia KS (S)

Nakashima, Thomas, *Prof,* Catholic University of America, Dept of Art, Washington DC (S)

Nakata, Rory, *Prof 3D Sculpture & Ceramics,* College of San Mateo, Creative Arts Dept, San Mateo CA (S)

Nakoneczny, Michael, *Assoc Prof,* University of Alaska-Fairbanks, Dept of Art, Fairbanks AK (S)

Nam, Yoomi, *Assoc Prof,* University of Kansas, The School of the Arts, Dept of Visual Art, Lawrence KS (S)

Nam, Yun-Dong, *Prof,* University of North Carolina at Chapel Hill, Art Dept, Chapel Hill NC (S)

Nancarrow, Mindy, *Dir Grad Studies Art History,* University of Alabama, Dept of Art, Tuscaloosa AL (S)

Nance, Dennis, *Exhibs & Programming Dir,* Lawndale Art Center, Houston TX

Nance, Glenn, *Sec,* San Francisco African-American Historical & Cultural Society, Library, San Francisco CA

Nanney, Nancy, *Chmn,* West Virginia University at Parkersburg, Art Dept, Parkersburg WV (S)

Naos, Theodore, *Prof,* Catholic University of America, School of Architecture & Planning, Washington DC (S)

Napier, Louise, *Chmn Div*, Wingate University, Art Department, Wingate NC (S)

Napoli, August A, *Deputy Dir & Chief Advancement Officer*, The Cleveland Museum of Art, Cleveland OH

Napoli, Marie, *Mus Shop Mgr*, Taubman Museum of Art, Roanoke VA

Napple, Debbie Strong, *Board Mem*, American Color Print Society, Huntingdon Valley PA

Naragon, Dwain, *Prof*, Eastern Illinois University, Art Dept, Charleston IL (S)

Narauyanan, Neena, *Dir*, Studio Gallery, Washington DC

Narcum-Perez, Patricia, *Bush House Coordr*, Salem Art Association, Archives, Salem OR

Nardi, Brenda, *Dir Develop*, University of Illinois at Urbana-Champaign, Krannert Art Museum and Kinkead Pavilion, Champaign IL

Nardi, Graciela H, *Pres & Founder*, Latino Art Museum, Pomona CA

Nardin, Kate, *Mgr Develop Communs*, University of Chicago, Smart Museum of Art, Chicago IL

Narkiewicz-Laine, Christian K, *Dir & Pres*, Chicago Athenaeum, Museum of Architecture & Design, Galena IL

Naselli, Cheri Reif, *VPres*, ARC Gallery, Chicago IL

Nasgaard, Roald, *Chmn Studio Art*, Florida State University, Art Dept, Tallahassee FL (S)

Nash, Shelia, *Sr Librn*, Los Angeles Public Library, Art, Music, Recreation & Rare Books, Los Angeles CA

Nash, Steven A, *Exec Dir*, Palm Springs Art Museum, Palm Springs CA

Nasisse, Andy, *Grad Coordr*, University of Georgia, Franklin College of Arts & Sciences, Lamar Dodd School of Art, Athens GA (S)

Naskarin, Daniel, *Asst Prof*, University of Victoria, Dept of Visual Arts, Victoria BC (S)

Nasse, Harry, *Dir & Chmn Bd*, Ward-Nasse Gallery, New York NY

Nasse, Leda, *Outreach*, Ward-Nasse Gallery, New York NY

Natale, Marie, *Instr*, Ocean City Arts Center, Ocean City NJ (S)

Natanson, Barbara, *Head Reference Section*, Library of Congress, Prints & Photographs Division, Washington DC

Nathan, Gail, *Exec Dir*, Bronx River Art Center Inc, Gallery, Bronx NY

Nathan, Jacqueline, *Dir Gallery*, Bowling Green State University, School of Art, Bowling Green OH (S)

Nathan, Jacqueline S, *Dir Galleries*, Bowling Green State University, Fine Arts Center Galleries, Bowling Green OH

Nathanson, Marjorie Frankel, *Exec Dir*, Hunterdon Art Museum, Clinton NJ

Natif, Mika, *Asst Prof*, George Washington University, Dept of Art of Fine Arts & Art History, Washington DC (S)

Natsoulas, Donna, *Mus Store Mgr*, Crocker Art Museum, Sacramento CA

Naubert-Riser, Constance, *Instr*, Universite de Montreal, Dept of Art History, Montreal PQ (S)

Nauert, Robert, *VPres Finance*, Chicago History Museum, Chicago IL

Naughton, Amy, *Pub Svcs Librn*, Minneapolis College of Art & Design, Library, Minneapolis MN

Naughton, Christine, *Dir Mus Donor Relations*, Williams College, Museum of Art, Williamstown MA

Naujoks, Robert, *Instr*, Kirkwood Community College, Dept of Arts & Humanities, Cedar Rapids IA (S)

Naujoks, Robert, *Instr*, Mount Mercy College, Art Dept, Cedar Rapids IA (S)

Naulin, Melissa, *Asst Cur*, White House, Washington DC

Nauts, Alan, *Instr*, University of Saint Francis, School of Creative Arts, Fort Wayne IN (S)

Nauyok, Michael, *VPres Exhibs*, Natural History Museum of Los Angeles County, Los Angeles CA

Navaretta, Cynthia, *Exec Dir*, Midmarch Associates/Midmarch Arts Press, Midmarch Arts Press and Library, New York NY

Navarro, Leonard, *Deputy Dir Admin*, Natural History Museum of Los Angeles County, Los Angeles CA

Navarro, Maria, *Co-Chmn*, 1078 Gallery, Chico CA

Navas, Eduardo, *Instr*, Pierce College, Art Dept, Woodland Hills CA (S)

Navas-Nieves, Tariana, *Cur Hispanic & Native American Art*, Colorado Springs Fine Arts Center, Taylor Museum, Colorado Springs CO

Navlty, Rosemary, *Develop Dir*, Springfield Museum of Art, Library, Springfield OH

Nawrocki, Thomas, *Prof*, Mississippi University for Women, Division of Fine & Performing Arts, Columbus MS (S)

Nawrocki, Tom, *Treas*, Kappa Pi International Honorary Art Fraternity, Cleveland MS

Nay, Barbara, *Admin Asst*, Sharon Arts Center, Sharon Arts Center Exhibition Gallery, Peterborough NH

Naylor, Valerie J, *Supt*, Oregon Trail Museum Association, Scotts Bluff National Monument, Gering NE

Nazionale, Nina, *Dir Libr Opers*, New-York Historical Society, Library, New York NY

Neabel, Maureen, *Secy*, Dauphin & District Allied Arts Council, Watson Art Centre, Dauphin MB

Neaderland, Louise, *Dir*, International Society of Copier Artists (ISCA), Brooklyn NY

Neal, Jack, *Pres*, Danville Museum of Fine Arts & History, Danville VA

Neal, Kenneth, *Art Librn*, Mayfield Regional Library, Cuyahoga County Public Library, Mayfield Village OH

Neal, Pat, *Opers Mgr*, Textile Museum of Canada, Toronto ON

Neal, Sheri, *Dir Finance*, Oregon Historical Society, Oregon History Museum, Portland OR

Neale, Maria, *Dir Educ Servs*, Genesee Country Village & Museum, John L Wehle Art Gallery, Mumford NY

Nealis, Sharon, *Exec Dir*, Allegany County Historical Society, Gordon-Roberts House, Cumberland MD

Near, Andrew, *Temp Opers Mgr*, Zanesville Museum of Art, Zanesville OH

Near, Hollis, *Dir Library Svcs*, Cornish College of the Arts, Cornish Library, Seattle WA

Near, Susan R, *Dir Mus Svcs*, Montana Historical Society, Helena MT

Neault, Carolyn, *Cur*, Columbus Historic Foundation, Blewett-Harrison-Lee Museum, Columbus MS

Nebel, Ken, *Dir*, Fuller Lodge Art Center, Los Alamos NM

Necarsulmer, Robert, *Dir & CFO*, Winterthur Museum, Winterthur Museum, Garden & Library, Winterthur DE

Nechis, Barbara, *Instr*, Art Center Sarasota, Sarasota FL (S)

Necowitz, Joel E., *Dir Fin & Admin*, Brandywine Conservancy, Brandywine River Museum, Chadds Ford PA

Nedd, Patrick, *Dir Finance*, Longue Vue House & Gardens, New Orleans LA

Needell, Allan, *Space History Dept*, National Air and Space Museum, Smithsonian Institution, Washington DC

Needham, Gerald, *VPres (Toronto)*, International Association of Art Critics, AICA Canada, Inc, Toronto ON

Neel, Jim, *Art Chair Prof*, Birmingham-Southern College, Art & Art History, Birmingham AL (S)

Neel, Jim, *Prof*, Birmingham Southern College, Doris Wainwright Kennedy Art Center, Birmingham AL

Neeley, Margaret, *Publications & Exhibs Admin*, Boston College, McMullen Museum of Art, Chestnut Hill MA

Neely, John, *Assoc Prof*, Utah State University, Dept of Art, Logan UT (S)

Neely, Linda, *Asst Prof Art Educ*, Lander University, College of Arts & Humanities, Greenwood SC (S)

Neff, Heidi, *Assoc Prof Art*, Harford Community College, Visual, Performing and Applied Arts Division, Bel Air MD (S)

Neff, Jean W, *Cur Educ*, Amherst Museum, Amherst NY

Neff, Mary Kay, *Prog Dir & Assoc Prof*, Seton Hill University, Art Program, Greensburg PA (S)

Negron, Mayra, *Chief Fin & Admin*, Inquilinos Boricuas en Accion, Boston MA

Neidhardt, Jane, *Publications*, Washington University, Mildred Lane Kemper Art Museum, Saint Louis MO

Neil, Daniel, *Preparator*, Auburn University, Julie Collins Smith Museum, Auburn AL

Neil, Erik, *Exec Dir*, Academy Art Museum, Easton MD

Neil, Jonathan T.D., *Exec Ed*, The Drawing Center, New York NY

Neill, Peter, *Pres*, South Street Seaport Museum, New York NY

Neils, Jenifer, *Prof*, Case Western Reserve University, Dept of Art History & Art, Cleveland OH (S)

Neilson, Robert, *Assoc Prof*, Lawrence University, Dept of Art & Art History, Appleton WI (S)

Nell-Smith, Bruce, *Head Dept*, Newberry College, Dept of Art, Newberry SC (S)

Nellermoe, J, *Chmn*, Texas Lutheran University, Dept of Visual Arts, Seguin TX (S)

Nellis, Mike, *Exec Dir*, Austin Children's Museum, Austin TX

Nelly, Benjamin F, *Coll Mgr*, Adams County Historical Society, Gettysburg PA

Nelsen, Ginger, *Admin*, Washington Art Association, Washington Depot CT

Nelson, Amy, *Office Coordr*, Augustana College, Center for Western Studies, Sioux Falls SD

Nelson, Carol, *Staff Asst*, Dawson County Historical Society, Museum, Lexington NE

Nelson, Crystal, *Dir & Cur*, Yankton County Historical Society, Dakota Territorial Museum, Yankton SD

Nelson, Crystal, *Prog Coordr*, 18th Street Arts Complex, Santa Monica CA

Nelson, Dean, *Mus Adminr*, Connecticut State Library, Museum of Connecticut History, Hartford CT

Nelson, Fred, *Coordr Illustration*, Columbia College, Art Dept, Chicago IL (S)

Nelson, Gene, *Asst Dir*, Las Vegas-Clark County Library District, Las Vegas NV

Nelson, Harold, *Dir*, Long Beach Museum of Art Foundation, Long Beach Museum of Art, Long Beach CA

Nelson, Irving, *Librn*, Navajo Nation Library System, Window Rock AZ

Nelson, Julie D, *Exec Dir*, Quincy Art Center, Quincy IL

Nelson, Kelly, *Asst Prof*, Longwood University, Dept of Art, Farmville VA (S)

Nelson, Kristi, *Prof Art History*, University of Cincinnati, School of Art, Cincinnati OH (S)

Nelson, Kyle, *Circ Supv*, University of New Mexico, Fine Arts Library, Albuquerque NM

Nelson, Leona, *Asst Prof*, Mount Mary College, Art & Design Division, Milwaukee WI (S)

Nelson, Leslee, *Prof*, University of Wisconsin, Madison, Dept of Art, Madison WI (S)

Nelson, Linda, *Exec Dir*, North Shore Art League, Winnetka IL

Nelson, Marilyn, *Assoc Prof*, University of Arkansas, Art Dept, Fayetteville AR (S)

Nelson, Mary Carroll, *Founder*, The Society of Layerists in Multi-Media (SLMM), Albuquerque NM

Nelson, Maryann, *Pres*, Douglas Art Association, The Gallery and Gift Shop, Douglas AZ

Nelson, Natalie, *Dir & Cur*, Pence Gallery, Davis CA

Nelson, Nathan, *Dept Chair*, Evangel University, Humanities-Art Dept, Springfield MO (S)

Nelson, Nick, *Cur Educ*, Albany Museum of Art, Albany GA

Nelson, Norman L, *Chmn*, First State Bank, They Also Ran Gallery, Norton KS

Nelson, Paula, *Pres*, Woodstock School of Art, Inc, Woodstock NY (S)

Nelson, Rai, *Audience Serv Mgr*, Painted Bride Art Center Gallery, Philadelphia PA

Nelson, Renee, *Coordr*, Mattawoman Creek Art Center, Marbury MD

Nelson, Ron, *Exec Dir*, Long Beach Museum of Art Foundation, Long Beach CA

Nelson, Sarah, *Cur Educ*, Lehigh Valley Heritage Center, Allentown PA

Nelson, Sarah, *Silversmith*, Worcester Center for Crafts, Worcester MA (S)

Nelson, Sharon, *Exec Dir*, Associated Artists of Winston-Salem, Winston Salem NC

Nelson, Steve, *Assoc Prof & Chmn*, Hope College, Dept of Art & Art History, Holland MI (S)

Nelson, Steve, *Mgr*, Hope College, DePree Art Center & Gallery, Holland MI

Nelson, Susan, *Assoc Prof*, University of Saint Mary, Fine Arts Dept, Leavenworth KS (S)

Nelson, Traci, *Events & Publicity Coordr*, Cheltenham Center for the Arts, Cheltenham PA (S)

Nelson-Haynes, Lisa, *Assoc Dir*, Painted Bride Art Center Gallery, Philadelphia PA

Nelson-Mayson, Lin, *Dir*, University of Minnesota, Goldstein Museum of Design, Saint Paul MN

Nelson Hoyle, Karen, *Cur*, University of Minnesota, Children's Literature Research Collections, Minneapolis MN

Nemcosky, Gary, *Assoc Prof*, Appalachian State University, Dept of Art, Boone NC (S)

Nemec, Vernita, *Dir*, Viridian Artists Inc, New York NY

Nemec, Vernita, *Founder & Exec Dir*, Earthfire, Art from Detritus: Recycling with Imagination, New York NY

Nemiroff, Paul, *1st VPres Progs*, Scottsdale Artists' League, Scottsdale AZ

Nenno, Mardis, *Asst Prof*, Spokane Falls Community College, Fine Arts Dept, Spokane WA (S)

Nero, Irene, *Asst Prof*, Southeastern Louisiana University, Dept of Visual Arts, Hammond LA (S)

Nesbit, Molly, *Prof*, Vassar College, Art Dept, Poughkeepsie NY (S)

Nesbit, Bill, *Cur*, Dundurn Castle, Hamilton ON

Nesbitt, Elizabeth, *Cur Invertebrate Paleontology*, University of Washington, Burke Museum of Natural History and Culture, Seattle WA

Neset, Marjorie, *Exec Dir*, VSA Arts of New Mexico, Very Special Arts Gallery, Albuquerque NM

Nesin, Jeffrey D, *Pres*, Memphis College of Art, G Pillow Lewis Memorial Library, Memphis TN

Nesmith, Joseph, *Progs Mgr*, National YoungArts Foundation, Miami FL

Ness, Gary, *Dir*, Ohio Historical Society, Columbus OH

Ness, Gary C, *CEO*, Ohio Historical Society, National Road-Zane Grey Museum, Columbus OH

Ness, Karla, *Prof*, Concordia University, Art Dept, Saint Paul MN (S)

Nesser-Chu, Janice, *Instr II*, Saint Louis Community College at Florissant Valley, Liberal Arts Division, Ferguson MO (S)

Nesteruk, Janet, *Prof*, Northwestern Connecticut Community College, Fine Arts Dept, Winsted CT (S)

Neszpaul, Susan, *Dir External Affairs*, The Frick Art & Historical Center, Inc, Frick Art Museum, Pittsburgh PA

Netsky, Ron, *Head Dept*, Nazareth College of Rochester, Art Dept, Rochester NY (S)

Netsky, Ron, *Instr*, Woodstock School of Art, Inc, Woodstock NY (S)

Nettles, Stephen, *Co-Gallery Mgr*, Craftsmen's Guild of Mississippi, Inc, Mississippi Crafts Center, Ridgeland MS

Nettleton, John, *Asst Prof*, Oregon State University, Dept of Art, Corvallis OR (S)

Netzer, Nancy, *Dir*, Boston College, McMullen Museum of Art, Chestnut Hill MA

Netzer, Sylvia, *Prof*, City College of New York, Art Dept, New York NY (S)

Neu, Noreen, *Dir*, Regina Public Library, Dunlop Art Gallery, Regina SK

Neu, Wendy, *Bus Mgr*, Kala Institute, Kala Art Institute, Berkeley CA

Neubauer, Joan, *Pres*, Yankton County Historical Society, Dakota Territorial Museum, Yankton SD

Neufeld, Nicole, *Dir Pub Prog*, Kitchener-Waterloo Art Gallery, Kitchener ON

Neugebauer, Kurt, *Assoc Dir*, University of Oregon, Jordan Schnitzer Museum of Art, Eugene OR

Neuhaus, Margie, *Assoc Prof*, The College of New Rochelle, School of Arts & Sciences Art Dept, New Rochelle NY (S)

Neumaier, Joan, *Prof*, Rutgers, The State University of New Jersey, Mason Gross School of the Arts, Visual Arts Dept, New Brunswick NJ (S)

Neuman, Robert M, *Prof*, Florida State University, Art History Dept, Tallahassee FL (S)

Neuman de Vegvar, Carol, *Prof*, Ohio Wesleyan University, Fine Arts Dept, Delaware OH (S)

Neumann, Dietrich, *Prof*, Brown University, Dept History of Art & Architecture, Providence RI (S)

Neumann, Timothy C, *Dir*, Pocumtuck Valley Memorial Association, Memorial Hall Museum, Deerfield MA

Neumer, Marie, *Dir for Develop*, Cornell University, Herbert F Johnson Museum of Art, Ithaca NY

Nevadomi, Kenneth, *Prof*, Cleveland State University, Art Dept, Cleveland OH (S)

Neves, Steve, *Assoc Prof*, Hardin-Simmons University, Art Dept, Abilene TX (S)

Neves, Todd, *Pres Bd*, Visual Arts Center of Northwest Florida, Visual Arts Center Library, Panama City FL

Neveu, Louise, *Registrar*, New Brunswick College of Craft & Design, Gallery, Fredericton NB

Neville, Kristoffer, *Asst Prof*, University of California, Riverside, Dept of the History of Art, Riverside CA (S)

Nevin, Jean, *Dir*, The Society of Layerists in Multi-Media (SLMM), Albuquerque NM

Nevins, Jerome, *Prof Art*, Albertus Magnus College, Visual and Performing Arts, New Haven CT (S)

Nevitt, Stephen, *Chmn*, Columbia College, Dept of Art, Columbia SC (S)

Newberry-Mills, Ashleigh, *Tour & Spec Events Coordr*, R W Norton Art Foundation, R W Norton Art Gallery, Shreveport LA

Newbold, Abby, *Preparator*, Cranbrook Art Museum, Bloomfield Hills MI

Newcomb, Mary, *Co-VP Dir of Classes & Office Mgr*, Greenwich Art Society Inc, Greenwich CT

Newcombe, J'Laine, *Registrar*, Vero Beach Museum of Art, Vero Beach FL

Newell, Aimee, *Dir Coll*, National Heritage Museum, Lexington MA

Newhouse, Kristina, *Cur*, Torrance Art Museum, Torrance CA

Newhouse, Meta, *Asst Prof Graphic Design*, Montana State University, School of Art, Bozeman MT (S)

Newirth, Richard, *Dir Cultural Affairs*, San Francisco City & County Art Commission, San Francisco CA

Newland, Sally, *Librn*, Amerind Foundation, Inc, Fulton-Hayden Memorial Library & Art Gallery, Dragoon AZ

Newlands, Jennifer, *Adjunct Asst Prof Art History*, Johnson County Community College, Fine Arts Dept & Art History Dept, Overland Park KS (S)

Newman, Alan B, *Exec Dir Imaging & Technical Serv*, The Art Institute of Chicago, Chicago IL

Newman, Bernie, *Artist*, Walker's Point Artists Assoc Inc, Gallery 218, Milwaukee WI

Newman, Geoffrey, *Dean*, Montclair State University, Art Galleries, Upper Montclair NJ

Newman, Geoffrey, *Dean*, Montclair State University, Fine Arts Dept, Montclair NJ (S)

Newman, John, *Assoc Prof*, University of Arkansas, Art Dept, Fayetteville AR (S)

Newman, Laura, *Assoc Prof*, Vassar College, Art Dept, Poughkeepsie NY (S)

Newman, Lia, *Dir*, Davidson College, William H Van Every Jr & Edward M Smith Galleries, Davidson NC

Newman, Rebecca, *VPres Mktg*, Rocky Mountain College of Art & Design, Lakewood CO (S)

Newman, Ruth D, *Dir*, New York University, Washington Square East Galleries, New York NY

Newman, Stephanie, *Prof Graphic Design*, Montana State University, School of Art, Bozeman MT (S)

Newman, Todd, *Preparator*, Boise Art Museum, Boise ID

Newman-Goins, Diane, *2nd VPres*, Warwick Museum of Art, Warwick RI

Newport, Mark, *Head Fiber Dept*, Cranbrook Academy of Art, Bloomfield Hills MI (S)

Newquist, Ruth, *Second VPres*, Kent Art Association, Gallery, Kent CT

Newsom, Thomas W, *Pres*, The Art Institute of Dallas, Dallas TX (S)

Newsome, Denise, *Exhibit Design Mgr*, Texas Tech University, Museum of Texas Tech University, Lubbock TX

Newsome, Levi, *Dir*, Danbury Scott-Fanton Museum & Historical Society, Inc, Danbury CT

Newsome, Levi, *Dir*, Danbury Scott-Fanton Museum & Historical Society, Inc, Library, Danbury CT

Newsome, Steven, *Dir*, Anacostia Community Museum, Smithsonian Institution, Washington DC

Newton, Brandi, *Exec Dir*, Willard Arts Center, Carr Gallery, Colonial Theater, Idaho Falls ID

Newton, David, *Prof of Art*, Guilford College, Art Dept, Greensboro NC (S)

Newton, Ian, *Preparator*, Kitchener-Waterloo Art Gallery, Kitchener ON

Newton, Janet, *Prof*, Illinois Central College, Arts & Communication Dept, East Peoria IL (S)

Newton, Tim, *Bd Chmn*, Salmagundi Club, New York NY

Ney, Susan, *Assoc Prof*, Azusa Pacific University, College of Liberal Arts, Art Dept, Azusa CA (S)

Neylan, Callie, *Asst Prof*, University of Maryland, Baltimore County, Imaging & Digital Arts (IMDA), Dept of Visual Arts, Baltimore MD (S)

Ngoc Bich, Nguyen, *Pres*, VICANA (Vietnamese Cultural Association in North America) Library, Springfield VA

Ngoh, Soon Ee, *Assoc Prof*, Mississippi State University, Dept of Art, Starville MS (S)

Nguien-Ouy, Pipo, *Asst Prof*, Oberlin College, Dept of Art, Oberlin OH (S)

Nguyen, Chi, *VPres*, Society of Scribes, Ltd, New York NY

Nguyen, Thuy, *CFO*, Bowers Museum, Santa Ana CA

Nguyen, Trian, *Asst Prof, Chmn*, Bates College, Art & Visual Culture, Lewiston ME (S)

Niamath, Ian, *Pres*, Malaspina College, Nanaimo Art Gallery, Nanaimo BC

Nicandri, David, *Dir*, Washington State Historical Society, Tacoma WA

Nicanor, Maria, *Asst Cur*, Solomon R Guggenheim, New York NY

Nicastro, Kathleen, *Libr Asst*, University of Rochester, Charlotte W Allen Library-Memorial Art Gallery, Rochester NY

Niceley, H T, *Chmn Dept*, Carson-Newman College, Art Dept, Jefferson City TN (S)

Nicholas, Grace, *Admin Asst*, 1890 House-Museum & Center for the Arts, Kellogg Library & Reading Room, Cortland NY

Nicholas, Jamar, *Cur Asst*, Arcadia University Art Gallery, Spruance Fine Arts Center, Glenside PA

Nicholls, Sarah, *Progs Mgr*, Center for Book Arts, New York NY

Nicholls, Susan, *Admin Asst*, East Carolina University, Wellington B Gray Gallery, Greenville NC

Nichols, Angela, *Dir Visual Arts*, Morgan County Foundation, Inc, Madison-Morgan Cultural Center, Madison GA

Nichols, Bill, *Dir Opers & Vis Servs*, The Frick Art & Historical Center, Inc, Frick Art Museum, Pittsburgh PA

Nichols, Charlotte, *Chmn*, Seton Hall University, College of Arts & Sciences, South Orange NJ (S)

Nichols, Charlotte, *Dir*, Seton Hall University, South Orange NJ

Nichols, Cheryl, *Dir Budgeting & Reporting*, The Phillips Collection, Washington DC

Nichols, Elaine, *History Cur*, South Carolina State Museum, Columbia SC

Nichols, Georgina, *Exec Asst Dir*, El Museo del Barrio, New York NY

Nichols, Jeff, *Adjunct Prof Photog*, Johnson County Community College, Fine Arts Dept & Art History Dept, Overland Park KS (S)

Nichols, Jeff, *Dir Educ*, Mark Twain, Hartford CT

Nichols, Kim, *Assoc Paper Conservator*, The Art Institute of Chicago, Dept of Prints & Drawings, Chicago IL

Nichols, Lawrence, *Cur European Painting & Sculpture Before 1900*, Toledo Museum of Art, Toledo OH

Nichols, Mark, *Pres*, National Oil & Acrylic Painters Society, Osage Beach MO

Nichols, Meghan, *Adjunct Prof Photog*, Johnson County Community College, Fine Arts Dept & Art History Dept, Overland Park KS (S)

Nichols, Sue, *Dir Operations*, Atlanta Historical Society Inc, Atlanta History Center, Atlanta GA

Nichols, Susan, *Lunder Educ Chair*, American Art Museum, Smithsonian Institution, Washington DC

Nichols, Susan J, *Chief Admin & Financial Officer*, The Phillips Collection, Washington DC

Nicholson, Joseph, *VPres*, Woodmere Art Museum Inc, Library, Philadelphia PA

Nicholson, Karla, *Exec Dir*, Liberty Hall Historic Site, Liberty Hall Museum, Frankfort KY

Nicholson, Paul, *VPres*, Legacy Ltd, Seattle WA

Nicholson, Robin, *Deputy Dir Exhibs*, Virginia Museum of Fine Arts, Richmond VA

Nickard, Gary, *Asst Prof,* University at Buffalo, State University of New York, Dept of Visual Studies, Buffalo NY (S)

Nickel, Douglas, *Andrea V Rosenthal Prof Modern Art,* Brown University, Dept History of Art & Architecture, Providence RI (S)

Nickel, Lorene, *Prof,* University of Mary Washington, Dept of Art & Art History, Fredericksburg VA (S)

Nickel, Richard, *Assoc Prof,* Old Dominion University, Art Dept, Norfolk VA (S)

Nickel, Richard, *Instr,* Valley City State College, Art Dept, Valley City ND (S)

Nickell, Jeff, *Asst Dir,* Kern County Museum, Bakersfield CA

Nickell, Jeff, *Cur,* Kern County Museum, Library, Bakersfield CA

Nickels, Kim, *Dir Finance,* Putnam Museum of History and Natural Science, Davenport IA

Nickerson, Samantha, *CFO,* Genesee Country Village & Museum, John L Wehle Art Gallery, Mumford NY

Nickeson, Karen, *Theatre Cur,* The New York Public Library, The New York Public Library for the Performing Arts, New York NY

Nickle, Elspeth, *Librn,* Southern Alberta Art Gallery, Library, Lethbridge AB

Nickson, Graham, *Dean,* New York Studio School of Drawing, Painting & Sculpture, Gallery, New York NY

Nickson, Graham, *Dean,* New York Studio School of Drawing, Painting & Sculpture, Library, New York NY

Nickson, Graham, *Dean,* New York Studio School of Drawing, Painting & Sculpture, New York NY (S)

Nicolescu, Alec, *Dir Gallery,* Kean University, James Howe Gallery, Union NJ

Nicolescu, Alec, *Dir Gallery,* Kean University, Fine Arts Dept, Union NJ (S)

Nicoletti, Lisa, *Vis Asst Prof,* Centenary College of Louisiana, Dept of Art, Shreveport LA (S)

Nicoll, Jennifer, *Coll Mgr & Exhib Coordr,* Queen's University, Agnes Etherington Art Centre, Kingston ON

Nicoll, Jessica, *Dir,* Smith College, Museum of Art, Northampton MA

Nideffer, Robert, *Prof Elec Intermedia, Tech & Culture,* University of California, Irvine, Studio Art Dept, Irvine CA (S)

Nied, Renee, *Exec Dir,* Tri-County Arts Council, Inc, Cobleskill NY

Niederstadt, Leah, *Asst Prof Mus Studies/Art History & Cur Permanent Coll,* Wheaton College, Beard and Weil Galleries, Norton MA

Nields, David, *Theatre Dir,* Rocky Mount Arts Center, Rocky Mount NC

Nielsen, Dori, *Conf Mgr,* National Council on Education for the Ceramic Arts (NCECA), Erie CO

Nielsen, Erik, *Chmn,* Texas State University - San Marcos, Dept of Art and Design, San Marcos TX (S)

Nielsen, Kim, *Dir,* Naval Historical Center, The Navy Museum, Washington DC

Nielsen, Mark, *Dir,* University of Michigan, Jean Paul Slusser Gallery, Ann Arbor MI

Nielsen, Matt, *Develop Dir,* University of Minnesota, Frederick R Weisman Art Museum, Minneapolis MN

Nielson, Nancy, *Coll Access,* State University of New York at New Paltz, Sojourner Truth Library, New Paltz NY

Nielson, Sherri, *Exec Dir,* Sawtooth Center for Visual Art, Winston-Salem NC (S)

Niemeyer, Stephenie, *Docent Prog Mgr,* Museum of Fine Arts, Houston, Rienzi Center for European Decorative Arts, Houston TX

Niemier, Carolyn, *Staff Accountant,* University of Notre Dame, Snite Museum of Art, Notre Dame IN

Niepold, Andrea, *Ed,* Germantown Historical Society, Philadelphia PA

Niesar, Sherry, *Program Dir,* Bismarck Art & Galleries Association, Bismarck ND

Nieson, Audrey, *Interpretation Supv,* New York State Office of Parks, Recreation and Historic Preservation, Bureau of Historic Sites, Waterford NY

Nietcr, Gary, *Assoc Prof,* Grace College, Dept of Art, Winona Lake IN (S)

Niewald, Janet, *Prof,* Virginia Polytechnic Institute & State University, Dept of Art & Art History, Blacksburg VA (S)

Nigh, Robin, *Admin,* City of Tampa, Public Art Program, Tampa FL

Nigro, Christie, *Chmn,* Worcester State College, Visual & Performing Arts Dept, Worcester MA (S)

Nigro, Maria, *Educ Mgr,* Bronx River Art Center Inc, Gallery, Bronx NY

Nii, Yuko, *Founder & Artistic Dir,* Williamsburg Art & Historical Center, Brooklyn NY

Niki, Kenji, *Librn,* Saint John's University, Asian Collection, Queens NY

Nikolov, Nikolai, *Asst Prof,* Lehigh University, Dept of Art, Architecture & Design, Bethlehem PA (S)

Nilan, Jeffrey, *Asst Prof,* Ohio Wesleyan University, Fine Arts Dept, Delaware OH (S)

Niles, Fred, *Prof, Chmn Dept,* University of Dayton, Visual Arts Dept, Dayton OH (S)

Niles, Naomi, *Librn,* The Metropolitan Museum of Art, The Nolen Library in the Ruth and Harold D. Uris Center for Education, New York NY

Niles, Richard, *Prof Theatre,* Marymount Manhattan College, Fine & Performing Arts Div, New York NY (S)

Nilson, Craig, *Prof,* Tidewater Community College, Visual Arts Center, Portsmouth VA (S)

Nilson, Robert, *Dir Facilities,* Albany Institute of History & Art, Albany NY

Nisbet, Peter, *Chief Cur,* University of North Carolina at Chapel Hill, Ackland Art Museum, Chapel Hill NC

Nishioka, Reiko, *Dir Educ,* Palm Beach County Parks & Recreation Department, Morikami Museum & Japanese Gardens, Delray Beach FL

Nissenhold, Mark, *Chmn Visual Arts Dept,* Lakehead University, Dept of Visual Arts, Thunder Bay ON (S)

Nitsch, Michael, *Mus Asst,* Miller Art Center Foundation Inc, Miller Art Museum, Sturgeon Bay WI

Niven, Don, *Chmn,* St Lawrence College, Dept of Graphic Design, Kingston ON (S)

Nivens, Charles, *Prof,* Eastern Illinois University, Art Dept, Charleston IL (S)

Nixon, Jennifer, *Mktg Dir,* Arts Place, Inc., Hugh N Ronald Memorial Gallery, Portland IN

Nixon, Nancy H, *Arts Specialist,* Patterson Library & Art Gallery, Westfield NY

Nixon, Rob, *Production Dir,* Golden Isles Arts & Humanities Association, Brunswick GA

Nixon, Sean, *Assoc Prof,* University of Bridgeport, Shintaro Akatsu School of Design, Bridgeport CT (S)

Nixon, Sean, *Prof,* Ulster County Community College/Suny Ulster, Dept of Art, Design, Music, Theatre & Communication, Stone Ridge NY (S)

Nixon, Wally, *Pres,* Historic Arkansas Museum, Little Rock AR

Nixx, Tanja, *Mgr,* Tattoo Art Museum, San Francisco CA

Njah, Doug, *VPrin,* Nutana Collegiate Institute, Memorial Library and Art Gallery, Saskatoon SK

Noble, Bonnie, *Asst Prof,* University of North Carolina at Charlotte, Dept Art, Charlotte NC (S)

Noble, Cynthia, *Asst Prof,* Springfield College, Dept of Visual & Performing Arts, Springfield MA (S)

Noble, Jillian, *Prof,* University of Wisconsin-Stevens Point, Dept of Art & Design, Stevens Point WI (S)

Noble, Joni, *Instr,* University of Louisiana at Monroe, Dept of Art, Monroe LA (S)

Noble, Nancy, *CEO,* Museum of Vancouver, Vancouver BC

Noble, Nancy, *CEO,* Museum of Vancouver, Museum of Vancouver Library, Vancouver BC

Noble, Nancy, *Cataloger,* Maine Historical Society, Library and Museum, Portland ME

Nobles-McDaniel, Deborah, *Mus Registrar,* Morgan State University, James E Lewis Museum of Art, Baltimore MD

Noblett, David, *Prof,* Missouri Southern State University, Dept of Art, Joplin MO (S)

Noblett, Duane, *Head Dept & Prof,* Kansas State University, Art Dept, Manhattan KS (S)

Noblick, Martha, *Asst Librn,* Historic Deerfield, Inc, Henry N Flynt Library, Deerfield MA

Nocom, Rowena, *Admin Asst,* Broward County Board of Commissioners, Cultural Div, Fort Lauderdale FL

Noda, Masaaki, *VPres,* Society of American Graphic Artists, New York NY

Nodelman, Jenny, *Coordr Pub Progs, Info & Mktg,* Nova Scotia Museum, Maritime Museum of the Atlantic, Halifax NS

Nodine, Jane, *Dir Gallery,* University of South Carolina at Spartanburg, Art Gallery, Spartanburg SC

Noe, Lendon H, *Asst Prof,* Lambuth University, Dept of Human Ecology & Visual Arts, Jackson TN (S)

Noeding, Thomas, *Owner,* Bent Museum & Gallery, Taos NM

Noel, Carol, *Dir Develop,* Amon Carter Museum of American Art, Fort Worth TX

Noel, William, *Cur Mss,* Walters Art Museum, Library, Baltimore MD

Noel, William, *Cur Mus & Rare Books,* Walters Art Museum, Baltimore MD

Noga, Joseph L, *Coordr Grad Prog,* Rochester Institute of Technology, School of Printing Management & Sciences, Rochester NY (S)

Nohe, Timothy, *Assoc Prof,* University of Maryland, Baltimore County, Imaging & Digital Arts (IMDA), Dept of Visual Arts, Baltimore MD (S)

Nolan, Carrie, *Mgr,* Ford Motor Company, Henry Ford Museum & Greenfield Village, Dearborn MI

Nolan, John, *Cur,* Bob Jones University Museum & Gallery Inc, Greenville SC

Nolan, Mary, *Asst Dir & Ed,* C G Jung Center, Evanston IL

Nolan, Patricia E, *Spec Arts Services Dir,* American Society of Artists, Inc, Palatine IL

Nolan, Scott, *Dir Develop,* Columbia Museum of Art, Columbia SC

Noland, Lloyd U, *Chmn,* The Mariners' Museum, Newport News VA

Nolan Warren, Gwen, *Mus Shop Mgr,* Harrison County Historical Museum, Marshall TX

Nold, Carl R, *Pres,* Historic New England, Boston MA

Nolen, Lori, *Instr,* Union University, Dept of Art, Jackson TN (S)

Nolf, Richard A, *Dir,* Saint Joseph Museum, Library, Saint Joseph MO

Noll, Steve, *Exec Dir,* Jackson County Historical Society, The 1859 Jail, Marshal's Home & Museum, Independence MO

Noll, Steve, *Exec Dir,* Jackson County Historical Society, Research Library & Archives, Independence MO

Noon, Patrick, *Cur Paintings,* Minneapolis Institute of Arts, Minneapolis MN

Noonan, Jennifer, *Asst Prof,* Caldwell College, Dept of Fine Arts, Caldwell NJ (S)

Norberg, Deborah, *Deputy Dir,* San Jose Museum of Art, San Jose CA

Norbert, Deborah, *Deputy Dir,* San Jose Museum of Art, Library, San Jose CA

Norbut, Irene, *Dir Periodicals Coll,* Balzekas Museum of Lithuanian Culture, Chicago IL

Nordtorp-Madson, Shelly, *Prof,* University of Saint Thomas, Dept of Art History, Saint Paul MN (S)

Nordyke, John, *Asst Prof,* University of Hartford, Hartford Art School, West Hartford CT (S)

Nore, Nano, *Chmn,* William Jewell College, Art Dept, Liberty MO (S)

Noreen, Kirsten, *Asst,* Louisiana State University, School of Art, Baton Rouge LA (S)

Noreen, Kirstin, *Assoc Prof,* Loyola Marymount University, Dept of Art & Art History, Los Angeles CA (S)

Norell, Mark A, *Chmn & Cur Divisio,* American Museum of Natural History, New York NY

Noriega, Ed, *Prof,* Troy State University, Dept of Art & Classics, Troy AL (S)

Noriega, Marcela, *Instr,* Langara College, Department of Design: Design Formation, Vancouver BC (S)

Norley, Mark, *Advising Cur,* Hockaday Museum of Art, Kalispell MT

Norman, Denver, *Gen Asst,* Black American West Museum & Heritage Center, Denver CO

Norman, Gary, *Coll Mgr,* Hartwick College, The Yager Museum, Oneonta NY

Norman, Heather L, *CEO & Archivist,* Galesburg Civic Art Center, Galesburg IL

Norman, Joe, *Assoc Prof Drawing & Painting,* University of Georgia, Franklin College of Arts & Sciences, Lamar Dodd School of Art, Athens GA (S)

Norman, Joyce, *Bus Mgr,* University of Chicago, Smart Museum of Art, Chicago IL

Norman, Lynn, *Commun & Mktg Coordr,* Red Deer & District Museum & Archives, Red Deer AB

Norment, Kate, *Interim Mgr Pubis,* The American Federation of Arts, New York NY

Norris, Andrea, *Dir Mus,* University of Kansas, Kress Foundation Dept of Art History, Lawrence KS (S)

Norris, Joyce Goering, *Librn,* Wichita Art Museum, Emprise Bank Research Library, Wichita KS

Norris, Laura, *Commun Mem Assoc,* Photographic Resource Center at Boston University, Boston MA

Norris, Sarah, *Rental Coordr,* Art Community Center, Art Center of Corpus Christi, Corpus Christi TX

Norris, Tim, *Prog Coordr,* Muskegon Community College, Dept of Creative & Performing Arts, Muskegon MI (S)

North, Holly, *Cur Coll,* Grace Museum, Inc, Abilene TX

North, Kenda, *Prof,* University of Texas at Arlington, Art & Art History Department, Arlington TX (S)

Northerner, Sara, *Assoc Prof,* Utah State University, Dept of Art, Logan UT (S)

Northrop, Eileen, *Dir Admis,* Art Institute of Fort Lauderdale, Fort Lauderdale FL (S)

Northrop, Jennifer, *Communs & Mktg Dir,* Cooper-Hewitt National Design Museum, Smithsonian Institution, New York NY

Northrup, JoAnne, *Chief Cur,* San Jose Museum of Art, San Jose CA

Northrup, JoAnne, *Sr Cur,* San Jose Museum of Art, Library, San Jose CA

Norton, Ann Wood, *Chmn,* Providence College, Art & Art History Dept, Providence RI (S)

Norton, Heidi, *Shop Mgr,* The Currier Museum of Art, Manchester NH

Norton, James, *Instr,* University of Louisiana at Monroe, Dept of Art, Monroe LA (S)

Norton, Jessica A, *Cur,* Amherst Museum, Amherst NY

Norton, Julia, *Admin Asst,* Laumeier Sculpture Park, Saint Louis MO

Norton, M Lewis, *Pres Bd,* R W Norton Art Foundation, R W Norton Art Gallery, Shreveport LA

Norton, Maria, *Educ Coordr,* Muscatine Art Center, Muscatine IA

Norton, Nancy, *VPres,* Blacksburg Regional Art Association, Blacksburg VA

Noss, Maggie, *Acting Dir, School of Art + Design,* Montgomery College, Dept of Art, Rockville MD (S)

Nostrala, Justin, *Asst Prof,* Simpson College, Farnham Gallery, Indianola IA

Notarnicola, Cathy, *Unit Registrar,* Museum of New Mexico, Museum of International Folk Art, Santa Fe NM

Nottage, James H, *VPres & Chief Curatorial Officer,* Eiteljorg Museum of American Indians & Western Art, Indianapolis IN

Nourse, Mike, *Dir Educ,* Hyde Park Art Center, Chicago IL

Novacek, Michael J, *Sr VPres & Pro,* American Museum of Natural History, New York NY

Novak, Alice, *Asst Cur Educ,* Montgomery Museum of Fine Arts, Library, Montgomery AL

Novak, Allen, *Visual Resources Librn,* Ringling College of Art & Design, Verman Kimbrough Memorial Library, Sarasota FL

Novak, Constance, *Supervising Librn,* The New York Public Library, Mid-Manhattan Library, Picture Collection, New York NY

Novak, Gaynor, *Admin Mgr,* University of Regina, MacKenzie Art Gallery, Regina SK

Novak, Martin, *Instr,* University of Utah, Dept of Art & Art History, Salt Lake City UT (S)

Novak, Philip, *Asst Dir,* Stamford Museum & Nature Center, Stamford CT

Novikova, Svetlana, *Adminr,* Gallery Moos Ltd, Toronto ON

Novosel, Michelle, *Visitor Svcs,* Sonoma County Museum, Santa Rosa CA

Novotny, Eric, *Head Arts & Humanities Library,* The Pennsylvania State University, Arts & Humanities Library, University Park PA

Nowak, Monika, *Graphic Art Coll Cur,* Polish Museum of America, Chicago IL

Nowicki, Angie, *Ranger,* Jack London, House of Happy Walls, Glen Ellen CA

Nowicki, Joshua, *Dir Community Rels,* Krasl Art Center, Saint Joseph MI

Nowlan, Gillian, *Music Librn & Film Librn,* University of Regina, Education/Fine Arts Library, Regina SK

Nowlin, Brian, *COO,* California State University, Long Beach Foundation, Long Beach CA

Nowlin, Bridget, *Cur Visual Resources,* Cornish College of the Arts, Cornish Library, Seattle WA

Nowlin, Joyce, *Pres,* Searchlight Historic Museum & Mining Park, Searchlight NV

Nowlin, Stephen, *Dir,* Art Center College of Design, Alyce de Roulet Williamson Gallery, Pasadena CA

Nowling, Margaret, *Dir Jones Gallery,* Bakersfield College, Art Dept, Bakersfield CA (S)

Nowosielski, Rodney, *Assoc Prof,* Saginaw Valley State University, Dept of Art & Design, University Center MI (S)

Noyes, Cecilia, *Instr,* Bakersfield College, Art Dept, Bakersfield CA (S)

Noyes, Julia, *Dir,* Noyes Art Gallery, Lincoln NE

Noyes, Julie, *Instr,* Northeast Community College, Dept of Liberal Arts, Norfolk NE (S)

Noyes, Nicholas, *Dir Library Svcs,* Maine Historical Society, Library and Museum, Portland ME

Noyes, Nick, *Head Library Svcs,* Maine Historical Society, Portland ME

Nozkowski, Thomas, *Assoc Prof,* Rutgers, The State University of New Jersey, Mason Gross School of the Arts, Visual Arts Dept, New Brunswick NJ (S)

Nuell, Christie, *Instr,* Middle Tennessee State University, Art Dept, Murfreesboro TN (S)

Nuell, Lon, *Instr,* Middle Tennessee State University, Art Dept, Murfreesboro TN (S)

Nugent, Marjorie, *Media Relations Mgr,* Minnesota Historical Society, Saint Paul MN

Nugent, Patricia, *Assoc Prof & Dir Gallery,* Rosemont College, Art Program, Rosemont PA (S)

Null, Charleen A, *Instr,* Pearl River Community College, Visual Arts, Dept of Fine Arts & Communication, Poplarville MS (S)

Nunes, Grafton, *Pres,* Cleveland Institute of Art, Reinberger Galleries, Cleveland OH

Nunes, Grafton, *Pres,* Cleveland Institute of Art, Cleveland OH (S)

Nunez, Mercedes, *Prof,* Bridgewater State College, Art Dept, Bridgewater MA (S)

Nunn, Graeme, *Chief Financial & Operating Officer,* Peter & Catharine Whyte Foundation, Whyte Museum of the Canadian Rockies, Banff AB

Nunn, Peggy, *Bus Mgr,* University of South Carolina, McKissick Museum, Columbia SC

Nusbaum, Patricia, *VPres,* LeSueur County Historical Society, Chapter One, Elysian MN

Nussbaum, Margaret, *Instr,* Manhattan Graphics Center, New York NY (S)

Nutt, Molly, *Registrar & Gallery Asst,* Dieu Donne Papermill, Inc, Gallery, New York NY

Nutter, Robin, *Develop Dir,* Pilgrim Society, Pilgrim Hall Museum, Plymouth MA

Nuvayestewa, Grace, *Library Specialist,* Institute of American Indian Arts, College of Contemporary Native Arts Library and Archives, Santa Fe NM

Nyberg, John, *Dir,* Jefferson County Historical Society Museum, Madison IN

Nydorf, Roy, *Prof of Art,* Guilford College, Art Dept, Greensboro NC (S)

Nye, Linda, *Dir,* Cuyahoga Valley Art Center, Cuyahoga Falls OH (S)

Nye, Michelle, *Gallery Coordr,* San Francisco Museum of Modern Art, Artist Gallery, San Francisco CA

Nye, Valerie, *Library Dir,* Institute of American Indian Arts, College of Contemporary Native Arts Library and Archives, Santa Fe NM

Nyerges, Alex, *Dir & CEO,* Virginia Museum of Fine Arts, Richmond VA

Nygard, Travis, *Asst Prof,* Ripon College, Art Dept, Ripon WI (S)

Nyman, Andra, *Arts Educ Mgr,* North Shore Art League, Winnetka IL

Nyman, William, *Asst Prof,* The College of New Jersey, School of Arts & Sciences, Ewing NJ (S)

Nyquist, Lars, *Industrial Design,* Art Institute of Pittsburgh, Pittsburgh PA (S)

NyQuist, Michelle, *Pres,* Dauphin & District Allied Arts Council, Watson Art Centre, Dauphin MB

Oakley, Rochelle L R, *Coll Mgr, Registrar,* Saint Joseph College, Art Gallery, University of Saint Joseph, West Hartford CT

Oaks, Gary, *Asst Prof,* Southern University in New Orleans, Fine Arts & Philosophy Dept, New Orleans LA (S)

Oaks, Martha, *Cur,* Cape Ann Historical Association, Cape Ann Museum, Gloucester MA

Oats, Joclyn, *Architectural-Grad Studies & Coordr Interior Design,* Columbia College, Art Dept, Chicago IL (S)

Obalil, Deborah, *Exec Dir,* Association of Independent Colleges of Art & Design, Providence RI

Obed, Martin, *Dept Chair Humanities,* Kalamazoo Valley Community College, Center for New Media, Kalamazoo MI (S)

Ober, Ingram, *Gallery Dir,* Palomar Community College, Boehm Gallery, San Marcos CA

Ober, Kathy, *Dir Libr Svcs,* Art Institute of Pittsburgh, Resource Center, Pittsburgh PA

Oberkirsch, Marie, *Special Events Mgr,* Laumeier Sculpture Park, Saint Louis MO

Obermeyer, Cheryl, *Dir Information Serv,* Chicago History Museum, Chicago IL

Obershan, Micheal, *Temp Asst Prof,* Georgia Southern University, Dept of Art, Statesboro GA (S)

Obert, Liz, *Assoc Prof,* Linfield College, Department of Art & Visual Culture, McMinnville OR (S)

Obert, Susan, *Develop Officer,* The San Joaquin Pioneer & Historical Society, The Haggin Museum, Stockton CA

Oberweiser, Don, *Staff Artist,* Oshkosh Public Museum, Oshkosh WI

Obetz, Tim, *Chief Preparator,* Institute of Contemporary Art, Boston MA

Obler, Bibiana, *Asst Prof,* George Washington University, Dept of Art of Fine Arts & Art History, Washington DC (S)

Oblinger, Mollie, *Asst Prof,* Ripon College, Art Dept, Ripon WI (S)

O'Bourke, Rosemarie, *Dir,* Gulf Coast Community College, Division of Visual & Performing Arts, Panama City FL (S)

O'Brian, John, *Prof,* University of British Columbia, Dept of Art History, Visual Art & Theory, Vancouver BC (S)

O'Brien, Carol, *Dir Ann & Planned Giving,* Virginia Center for the Creative Arts, Amherst VA

O'Brien, Derek, *Instr,* Lakeland Community College, Fine Arts Department, Kirtland OH (S)

O'Brien, Jennifer, *Data Asst,* National Air and Space Museum, Regional Planetary Image Facility, Washington DC

O'Brien, Liz Hunt, *Dir Arts Prog,* Artists Association of Nantucket, Nantucket MA

O'Brien, Maggie, *Finance Dir,* Nevada Northern Railway Museum, Ely NV

O'Brien, Marie, *Coll Mgr,* Saco Museum, Saco ME

O'Brien, Mary Francis, *Chief Pub Servs,* Boston Public Library, Central Library, Boston MA

O'Brien, Maureen, *Cur Painting & Sculpture,* Rhode Island School of Design, Museum of Art, Providence RI

O'Brien, Patricia, *Pres,* Kennebec Valley Art Association, Harlow Gallery, Hallowell ME

O'Brien, Susan, *Assoc Prof,* University of Wisconsin-Eau Claire, Dept of Art & Design, Eau Claire WI (S)

O'Brien, Susan, *Asst Prof,* Murray State University, Dept of Art, Murray KY (S)

O'Brien, Tim, *Exec VPres,* Society of Illustrators, New York NY

O'Brion, Tara, *Dir Conservation,* Historical Society of Pennsylvania, Philadelphia PA

Obrochta, William, *Dir Educ,* Virginia Historical Society, Library, Richmond VA

O'Callaghan, Thomas A, *Spanish Specialist,* National Gallery of Art, Department of Image Collections, Washington DC

Ocampo, Lisa, *Mus Shop Mgr*, Telfair Museums' Jepson Center for the Arts Library, Telfair Academy of Arts & Sciences Library, Savannah GA

Ocasio, Billy, *CEO & Pres*, Institute of Puerto Rican Arts & Culture, Chicago IL

Occhino, Kristina N, *Dir Gallery*, Rhode Island Watercolor Society, Pawtucket RI

Occhiogrosso, Gina, *Asst Prof*, College of Saint Rose, The Center For Art and Design, Albany NY (S)

Ocello, Claudia, *Cur Educ*, New Jersey Historical Society, Library, Newark NJ

Och, Marjorie, *Asst Prof*, University of Mary Washington, Dept of Art & Art History, Fredericksburg VA (S)

Ochoa, Jody, *Registrar*, Idaho Historical Museum, Boise ID

Ochs, Steven, *Prof*, Southern Arkansas University, Art Dept Gallery & Magale Art Gallery, Magnolia AR

Ochs, Steven, *Prof*, Southern Arkansas University at Magnolia, Dept of Art & Design, Magnolia AR (S)

O'Connell, Bonnie, *Asst Prof*, University of Nebraska at Omaha, Dept of Art & Art History, Omaha NE (S)

O'Connell, Dan, *Circ Librn*, Wentworth Institute of Technology Library, Boston MA

O'Connell, Daniel M, *Commissioner of Cultural Affairs & Artistic Dir*, City of Pittsfield, Berkshire Artisans, Pittsfield MA

O'Connell, John, *Asst Prof*, University of Utah, Dept of Art & Art History, Salt Lake City UT (S)

O'Connell, John, *Instr*, Middle Tennessee State University, Art Dept, Murfreesboro TN (S)

O'Connell, Karen, *Accounting Mgr*, Portraits South, Raleigh NC

O'Connell, Meg, *Pres*, Skaneateles Library Association, Skaneateles NY

O'Conner, Chris, *Dir Educ*, Farmington Valley Arts Center, Avon CT

O'Connor, David, *Deputy Dir*, New York University, Institute of Fine Arts, New York NY (S)

O'Connor, Harold, *Head*, Dunconor Workshops, Salida CO (S)

O'Connor, J Dennis, *Under Secy for Science*, Smithsonian Institution, Washington DC

O'Connor, John, *Asst Prof*, Radford University, Art Dept, Radford VA (S)

O'Connor, Margaret, *Exec Dir*, Gilbert Stuart, Gilbert Stuart Birthplace & Museum, Saunderstown RI

O'Connor, Susan, *Archit Librn*, New Jersey Institute of Technology, Littman Architecture & Design Library, Newark NJ

O'Day, Karen, *Assoc Prof*, University of Wisconsin-Eau Claire, Dept of Art & Design, Eau Claire WI (S)

O'Day, Tom, *Asst Prof*, Spokane Falls Community College, Fine Arts Dept, Spokane WA (S)

Oddo, Shawn, *Culinary Arts & Management*, Art Institute of Pittsburgh, Pittsburgh PA (S)

Odegaard, Jill, *Asst Prof*, Cedar Crest College, Art Dept, Allentown PA (S)

Odel, Bill, *Prof*, University of Massachusetts, Amherst, Art History Program, Amherst MA (S)

Odeleye, Cheryl, *Mem & Vol Coordr*, Hammonds House Museum, Atlanta GA

O'Dell, Kathy, *Assoc Prof & Assoc Dean Coll Arts, Humanities & Soc Sciences*, University of Maryland, Baltimore County, Imaging & Digital Arts (IMDA), Dept of Visual Arts, Baltimore MD (S)

Oden, Fred, *Pres*, Fulton County Historical Society Inc, Fulton County Museum (Tetzlaff Reference Room), Rochester IN

Odence, Janet, *Secy*, Bergen County Historical Society, Steuben House Museum, River Edge NJ

Odita, Donald, *Assoc Prof*, Florida State University, Art Dept, Tallahassee FL (S)

Odom, Anne, *Cur Emerita*, Hillwood Museum & Gardens Foundation, Hillwood Estate Museum & Gardens, Washington DC

O'Donnell, Gail, *Dir External Affairs & Special Projs*, Delaware Art Museum, Wilmington DE

O'Donnell, Hugh, *Prof*, Boston University, School for the Arts, Boston MA (S)

O'Donnell, Mark Stansbury, *Prof*, University of Saint Thomas, Dept of Art History, Saint Paul MN (S)

O'Donnell, Maryann, *Dean of Art*, Manhattan College, School of Arts, Bronx NY (S)

O'Donnell, Rose, *Gallery Dir*, The Art League Gallery & School, Alexandria VA

O'Donnell, Sue, *Asst Prof*, Bloomsburg University, Dept of Art & Art History, Bloomsburg PA (S)

O'Dougherty, Winnie, *Sec*, Hudson Valley Art Association, Brooklyn NY

Oehler, David, *Assoc Prof/Chair*, Northwest Missouri State University, Dept of Fine & Performing Arts, Maryville MO (S)

Oehlke, Vailey, *Multnomah County Libr Dir*, Multnomah County Library, Henry Failing Art & Music Dept, Portland OR

Oelbaum, Brenda, *Pres (2014)*, Women's Caucus For Art, New York NY

Oelkers, Karl, *Facility Mgr*, New Orleans Museum of Art, New Orleans LA

Oerichbauer, Edgar, *Exec Dir*, Koochiching Museums, International Falls MN

Oettinger, Marion, *Dir*, San Antonio Museum of Art, San Antonio TX

Ogar, Ray, *Assoc Prof*, University of Central Arkansas, Department of Art, Conway AR (S)

Ogden, Dale, *Chief Cur Cultural History*, Indiana State Museum, Indianapolis IN

Ogden, Vivian, *Cur*, Kelly-Griggs House Museum, Red Bluff CA

Ogilvie, Cheryl, *Cur*, McDonald's Corporation, Art Collection, Oak Brook IL

Ogilvie, Michael, *Coordr*, Kohler Co, John Michael Kohler Arts Center - Arts/Industry Program, Sheboygan WI

Ogle, Drew, *Exec Dir*, Rose Center & Council for the Arts, Morristown TN

Ogoli, David M, *Asst Prof*, Judson University, School of Art, Design & Architecture, Elgin IL (S)

O'Grady, Sarah, *Educ Coordr*, Mississippi Valley Conservation Authority, R Tait McKenzie Memorial Museum, Almonte ON

O'Grody, Jeannine, *Chief Cur & Cur European Art*, Birmingham Museum of Art, Birmingham AL

O'Grody, Jeannine A, *Cur European Art*, Birmingham Museum of Art, Clarence B Hanson Jr Library, Birmingham AL

Oguz, Cetin, *Asst Prof*, Delta State University, Dept of Art, Cleveland MS (S)

O'Halloran, Therese, *Instr*, Illinois Wesleyan University, School of Art, Bloomington IL (S)

O'Hara, David, *Mus Admin*r, City of Toronto Museum Services, Historic Fort York, Toronto ON

O'Hara, Rita, *Library Technician*, Hirshhorn Museum & Sculpture Garden, Library, Washington DC

O'Hara, Virginia, *Cur Collections*, Brandywine Conservancy, Brandywine River Museum, Chadds Ford PA

O'Hare, Mary Kate, *Cur American Art*, Newark Museum Association, The Newark Museum, Newark NJ

O'Harrow, Sean, *Dir*, Figge Art Museum, Art Reference Library, Davenport IA

O'Harrow, Sean, *Dir*, University of Iowa, University of Iowa Museum of Art, Iowa City IA

Ohira-Rollando, Akemi, *Studio Faculty*, University of Virginia, McIntire Dept of Art, Charlottesville VA (S)

Ohland, Karen, *Assoc Dir Finance & Opers*, Princeton University, Princeton University Art Museum, Princeton NJ

Ohrmann, Bill, *Artist & Owner*, Ohrmann Museum and Gallery, Drummond MT

Oing, Michelle, *Museum Asst*, Museum of Biblical Art, New York NY

Oishei, Judith, *Prog Dir*, Library Association of La Jolla, Athenaeum Music & Arts Library, La Jolla CA

Oja, Vivien, *Prog Assoc*, University of Minnesota, Minneapolis, Split Rock Arts Program, Minneapolis MN (S)

Ojala, Meg, *Assoc Prof*, Saint Olaf College, Art Dept, Northfield MN (S)

Oka, Sara, *Mgr Textile Coll*, Honolulu Museum of Art, Honolulu HI

Okamura, Hideyo, *Mgr Exhibs Design & Planning*, Williams College, Museum of Art, Williamstown MA

O'Kano, Roy, *VPres*, Association of Hawaii Artists, Honolulu HI

Okaya, Michiko, *Dir Gallery*, Lafayette College, Lafayette College Art Galleries, Easton PA

Okazaki, Arthur, *Chmn*, Tulane University, Sophie H Newcomb Memorial College, New Orleans LA (S)

Oke, Ejenobo, *Assoc Prof*, Manchester College, Dept of Art, North Manchester IN (S)

O'Keefe, Barbara, *CEO & Dir*, Coral Springs Museum of Art, Coral Springs FL

O'Keefe, Doris N, *Sr Cataloger Rare Books*, American Antiquarian Society, Worcester MA

O'Keefe, Elizabeth, *Dir Coll Info Systems*, The Morgan Library & Museum, Museum, New York NY

O'Keefe, Michael, *Board Pres*, Cabot's Old Indian Pueblo Museum, Desert Hot Springs CA

O'Keefe, Michael J, *Chmn*, Oklahoma Christian University of Science & Arts, Dept of Art & Design, Oklahoma City OK (S)

O'Keefe, Ruth, *Chmn Art History & Liberal Arts*, Kendall College of Art & Design, Grand Rapids MI (S)

O'Keeffe, Timothy, *Asst Prof*, University of Wisconsin-Stout, Dept of Art & Design, Menomonie WI (S)

Okeke-Agulu, Chika, *Asst Prof*, Pennsylvania State University, University Park, Dept of Art History, University Park PA (S)

Okoruwa, Vassandra, *Sales & Mktg*, City of Lubbock, Buddy Holly Center, Lubbock TX

Okshteyn, Tatyana, *Dir*, Black & White Gallery, Southampton NY

Okuyama, Ken, *Transportation Design Chmn*, Art Center College of Design, Pasadena CA (S)

Oladipe, Jennifer, *Receptionist*, Embroiderers Guild of America, Margaret Parshall Gallery, Louisville KY

O'Laughaire, Niamh, *Dir*, University of Toronto, University of Toronto Art Centre, Toronto ON

Olbrantz, John, *Dir*, Willamette University, Hallie Ford Museum of Art, Salem OR

Oldach, Linda R, *Asst Dean & Library Info Servs*, Mount Wachusett Community College, La Chance Library, Gardner MA

Oldfield, Barney, *Chmn Bd*, Anthology Film Archives, New York NY

Oldham, Terry, *Adjunct Prof*, Missouri Western State University, Art Dept, Saint Joseph MO (S)

Oldham, Terry, *Dir*, The Albrecht-Kemper Museum of Art, Saint Joseph MO

Oldham, Terry, *Dir*, The Albrecht-Kemper Museum of Art, Bradley Art Library, Saint Joseph MO

Oldknow, Tina, *Cur Modern Glass*, Corning Museum of Glass, Museum, Corning NY

Olds, Clifton, *Prof*, Bowdoin College, Art Dept, Brunswick ME (S)

O'Leary, Elizabeth, *Assoc Cur American Art*, Virginia Museum of Fine Arts, Richmond VA

O'Leary, Helen, *Prof Art (Drawing/Painting)*, Pennsylvania State University, University Park, Penn State School of Visual Arts, University Park PA (S)

Olijnyk, Michael, *Bd Mem, Co-Dir*, The Mattress Factory, Pittsburgh PA

Olin, Ferris, *Cur*, Rutgers, The State University of New Jersey, Mary H Dana Women Artists Series, a Partnership of the Institute for Women & Art and the Rutgers University Libraries, New Brunswick NJ

Olivant, David, *Prof*, California State University, Art Dept, Turlock CA (S)

Olive, Nancy, *Chmn*, University of Sioux Falls, Dept of Art, Sioux Falls SD (S)

Oliver, Caroline, *Dir Develop & Mktg*, Kitchener-Waterloo Art Gallery, Kitchener ON

Oliver, Daniela, *Pub Rels*, McNay, San Antonio TX

Oliver, Debbie, *Registrar*, Nicolaysen Art Museum & Discovery Center, Museum, Casper WY

Oliver, James M, *Asst Prof*, Pittsburg State University, Art Dept, Pittsburg KS (S)

Oliver, Judith, *Assoc Prof*, Colgate University, Dept of Art & Art History, Hamilton NY (S)

Oliver, Kurt, *Access Mgr*, Wentworth Institute of Technology Library, Boston MA

Oliver, Mark, *Vis Instr Sculpture*, Florida Atlantic University, D F Schmidt College of Arts & Letters Dept of Visual Arts & Art History, Boca Raton FL (S)

Oliver, Megan, *Asst Librn*, Florida State University, The John and Mable Ringling Museum of Art Library, Sarasota FL

Oliver, Patricia, *Chmn Environmental Design*, Art Center College of Design, Pasadena CA (S)

Oliver, Valerie Cassel, *Sr Cur*, Contemporary Arts Museum Houston, Houston TX

Oliver, Wendy, *Dir Workshops*, California Watercolor Association, Gallery Concord, Concord CA

Oliver-Smith, Kerry, *Cur Contemporary Art*, University of Florida, Samuel P Harn Museum of Art, Gainesville FL

Oliveras, Autumn, *Admin Asst*, Cultural Council of Palm Beach County, Lake Worth FL

Oliveri, Meg, *Cur*, Nassau Community College, Firehouse Art Gallery, Garden City NY

Oliveri, Michael, *Asst Prof Digital Media*, University of Georgia, Franklin College of Arts & Sciences, Lamar Dodd School of Art, Athens GA (S)

Olivette, Daniel, *Dir*, Susquehanna University, Lore Degenstein Gallery, Selinsgrove PA

Olivia, Jack, *Pres*, Lincoln Arts Council, Lincoln NE

Olivier-Salmon, Camille, *Prog Dir*, San Francisco Arts Education Project, San Francisco CA

Olivo, Sandra, *Cur Educ*, Middlebury College, Museum of Art, Middlebury VT

Ollman, Arthur, *Dir*, San Diego State University, School of Art, Design & Art History, San Diego CA (S)

Olmstead, Richard, *Cur Botany*, University of Washington, Burke Museum of Natural History and Culture, Seattle WA

Olney, Kirsten, *Finance Mgr*, Sonoma County Museum, Santa Rosa CA

Olon, Gill, *Asst Prof*, University of Wisconsin-Eau Claire, Dept of Art & Design, Eau Claire WI (S)

O'Loughlin, Meghan, *Cur Educ*, Arnot Art Museum, Elmira NY

Olsen, Charles, *Chmn*, St Francis College, Fine Arts Dept, Loretto PA (S)

Olsen, Denise, *Asst Dir*, Yakima Valley Community College, Larson Gallery, Yakima WA

Olsen, Dennis, *Prof*, University of Texas at San Antonio, Dept of Art & Art History, San Antonio TX (S)

Olsen, Geoffrey, *Grad Prof*, Florida International University, School of Art & Art History, Miami FL (S)

Olsen, Haylee, *Gallery Asst*, Yakima Valley Community College, Larson Gallery, Yakima WA

Olsen, Kathleen, *Dir*, Washington & Lee University, Gallery of DuPont Hall, Lexington VA

Olsen, Mel, *Prof*, University of Wisconsin-Superior, Programs in the Visual Arts, Superior WI (S)

Olsen, Michael, *Bd Dir Chmn*, Plains Art Museum, Fargo ND

Olson, A J, *Prof*, Troy State University, Dept of Art & Classics, Troy AL (S)

Olson, Alan, *Dir Colls*, Dallas Historical Society, Hall of State, Dallas TX

Olson, Alan, *Dir Colls*, Dallas Historical Society, Research Center Library, Dallas TX

Olson, Carrie, *Assoc Prof & Chair*, Denison University, Studio Art Program, Granville OH (S)

Olson, Dennis, *Asst Prof*, Amarillo College, Visual Art Dept, Amarillo TX (S)

Olson, Janis, *Cur Coll*, Whatcom Museum, Bellingham WA

Olson, Janis, *Cur Coll*, Whatcom Museum, Library, Bellingham WA

Olson, Kristina, *Cur*, West Virginia University, Laura & Paul Mesaros Galleries, Morgantown WV

Olson, Kristina, *Prof*, West Virginia University, College of Creative Arts, School of Art & Design, Morgantown WV (S)

Olson, Kyle, *IT Specialist*, Blue Star Contemporary Art Center, San Antonio TX

Olson, Michael, *Instr*, Casper College, Dept of Visual Arts, Casper WY (S)

Olson, Pat, *Assoc Prof*, St. Catherine University, Art & Art History Dept, Saint Paul MN (S)

Olson, Sarah, *Supt*, Roosevelt-Vanderbilt National Historic Sites, Hyde Park NY

Olson, Susan, *Develop Secy*, Iowa State University, Brunnier Art Museum, Ames IA

Olson-Clark, Kim, *Develop Officer*, Evanston Historical Society, Charles Gates Dawes House, Evanston IL

Olson-Janjic, Kathleen, *Assoc Prof*, Washington and Lee University, Div of Art, Lexington VA (S)

Olson-Urtechio, Allen, *Deputy Dir*, Fondo del Sol, Visual Art & Media Center, Washington DC

Olt, Frank, *Assoc Prof*, C W Post Campus of Long Island University, School of Visual & Performing Arts, Brookville NY (S)

Oltjenbruns, Leona, *Secy*, Phillips County Museum, Holyoke CO

Oltvedt, Carl, *Prof*, Minnesota State University-Moorhead, Dept of Art & Design, Moorhead MN (S)

Oltvero, Michelle Lee. *Exec Asst*, Museum of Chinese in America, New York NY

Olvera, John, *Prof*, Winthrop University, Dept of Art & Design, Rock Hill SC (S)

Olvstebo, Solveig, *Dir & Chief Cur*, The Renaissance Society, Chicago IL

Olynyk, Patricia, *Asst Prof*, University of Michigan, Ann Arbor, School of Art & Design, Ann Arbor MI (S)

O'Malley, Jeannette, *Exec Dir*, Pasadena Museum of History, Pasadena CA

O'Malley, Kathleen, *Assoc Registrar*, Dartmouth College, Hood Museum of Art, Hanover NH

O'Malley, Kathleen L, *Pres*, Cohasset Historical Society, Cohasset Maritime Museum, Cohasset MA

O'Malley, Kathleen L, *Pres*, Cohasset Historical Society, Captain John Wilson Historical House, Cohasset MA

O'Malley, Kathleen L, *Pres*, Cohasset Historical Society, Pratt Building (Society Headquarters), Cohasset MA

O'Malley, Kathleen P, *Contact Registrar*, Aidron Duckworth Art Preservation Trust, Aidron Duckworth Art Museum, Meriden NH

O'Malley, Michael, *Assoc Prof*, Pomona College, Dept of Art & Art History, Claremont CA (S)

O'Malley, Tom, *Dept Head*, Worcester Center for Crafts, Worcester MA (S)

Oman, Earl, *Cur Colls (Emeritus)*, Northern Maine Museum of Science, Presque Isle ME

O'Mara, Joan, *Assoc Prof*, Washington and Lee University, Div of Art, Lexington VA (S)

O'Mara, Shawn, *Digital Design*, Art Institute of Pittsburgh, Pittsburgh PA (S)

O'Meara, Nancy G, *Exec Dir*, Philadelphia Museum of Art, Women's Committee, Philadelphia PA

Omogbai, Meme, *Chief Oper Officer*, Newark Museum Association, The Newark Museum, Newark NJ

Ondo, Greg, *Adjunct Asst Prof*, University of Maine, Dept of Art, Orono ME (S)

Ondrizek, Geraldine, *Asst Prof Art*, Reed College, Dept of Art, Portland OR (S)

O'Neal, Jennifer R, *Head Archivist*, National Museum of the American Indian, Archives, Washington DC

O'Neil, Alexandra, *Co-Chair ADAD Dept*, Butte College, Art Gallery, Oroville CA

O'Neil, Brian, *Chmn*, Museum of Biblical Art, New York NY

O'Neil, Karen, *Instr*, Woodstock School of Art, Inc, Woodstock NY (S)

O'Neil, Kevin, *Instr*, Keystone College, Fine Arts Dept, LaPlume PA (S)

O'Neil, Mary Lovelace, *Chair*, University of California, Berkeley, College of Letters & Sciences-Art Practice Dept, Berkeley CA (S)

O'Neil, Maureen, *Instr*, Flagler College, Visual Arts Dept, Saint Augustine FL (S)

O'Neil, Robert, *Asst Prof*, College of Saint Rose, The Center For Art and Design, Albany NY (S)

O'Neill, Cheryl, *Librn*, Art Complex Museum, Carl A. Weyerhaeuser Library, Duxbury MA

O'Neill, Cheryl, *Librn*, Art Complex Museum, Library, Duxbury MA

O'Neill, Ed, *Chmn*, Brookdale Community College, Center for the Visual Arts, Lincroft NJ (S)

O'Neill, John, *Cur Rare Books*, The Hispanic Society of America, Museum & Library, New York NY

O'Neill, John P, *Ed In Chief*, The Metropolitan Museum of Art, New York NY

O'Neill, Kevin, *Dir*, Chatillon-DeMenil House Foundation, Chatillon-DeMenil House, Saint Louis MO

O'Neill, Mark, *Dir Gen Canadian War Mus*, Canadian Museum of Civilization, Gatineau PQ

O'Neill, Morna, *Asst Prof*, Wake Forest University, Dept of Art, Winston-Salem NC (S)

O'Neill, Stephen, *Assoc Cur*, Pilgrim Society, Pilgrim Hall Museum, Plymouth MA

O'Neill, Stephen, *Assoc Dir & Cur*, Pilgrim Society, Library, Plymouth MA

O'Neill, Walt, *Dir*, Education Alliance, Art School & Gallery, New York NY (S)

O'Neill, Yvette, *Instr*, Lower Columbia College, Art Dept, Longview WA (S)

Oney, Danielle, *Events Coord*, North Tonawanda History Museum, North Tonawanda NY

Onofrio, Jennifer, *Prof*, Augusta State University, Dept of Art, Augusta GA (S)

Onyile, Onyile B, *Assoc Prof*, Georgia Southern University, Dept of Art, Statesboro GA (S)

Opalko, Michael N, *Graphic Design*, Art Institute of Pittsburgh, Pittsburgh PA (S)

Opar, Barbara A, *Architecture Librn*, Syracuse University, Syracuse University Library, Syracuse NY

Ophime, Jeff, *Dir*, Colquitt County Arts Center, Moultrie GA

Opoku, kofi, *Asst Prof*, West Virginia University, College of Creative Arts, School of Art & Design, Morgantown WV (S)

Opp, Nathan, *Instr*, Oral Roberts University, Art Dept, Tulsa OK (S)

Oppenheim, Phyllis, *Colls Mgr*, Herrett Center for Arts & Sciences, Jean B King Art Gallery, Twin Falls ID

Oppenhimer, Ann, *Pres*, Folk Art Society of America, Richmond VA

Oppenhimer, William, *Financial Dir*, Folk Art Society of America, Richmond VA

Oppio, Amy, *Deputy Dir & COO*, Nevada Museum of Art, Reno NV

Oppio, Amy, *Deputy Dir*, Nevada Museum of Art, Art Library, Reno NV

Oram, Richard W, *Assoc Dir*, University of Texas at Austin, Harry Ransom Humanities Research Center, Austin TX

Ore, Joyce, *Dir Pub Rels*, Hastings College, Art Dept, Hastings NE (S)

O'Reere, Regina, *Gallery Preparator*, Nebraska Wesleyan University, Elder Gallery, Lincoln NE

O'Reilly, Jack, *Treas*, New Jersey Watercolor Society, Parsippany NJ

O'Reilly, Margaret M, *Cur Fine Art*, New Jersey State Museum, Fine Art Bureau, Trenton NJ

Orenstein, Ellen, *Assoc Prof Theatre*, Marymount Manhattan College, Fine & Performing Arts Div, New York NY (S)

Oring, Sheryl, *Prof*, University of North Carolina at Greensboro, Art Dept, Greensboro NC (S)

Oritsky, Mimi, *Instr*, Main Line Art Center, Haverford PA (S)

Orlando, Fran, *Dir Exhib*, Bucks County Community College, Hicks Art Center, Newtown PA

Orlando, Joe, *Dir Educ*, Art Institute of Houston, Houston TX (S)

Orleans, Sarah, *Exec Dir*, Portland Children's Museum, Portland OR

Orlofsky, Patsy, *Exec Dir*, Textile Conservation Workshop Inc, South Salem NY

Orlovski, Stas, *Instr*, Long Beach City College, Art & Photography Dept, Long Beach CA (S)

Ormai, Ted, *Vice Pres*, New Arts Program, Inc, NAP Museum, Gallery, Resource Library, Kutztown PA

Ormasen, Debbie, *Accnt Mgr*, Frederic Remington, Ogdensburg NY

Orme, Joyce, *Staff Asst III*, College of Central Florida, Appleton Museum of Art, Ocala FL

Ormerod-Glynn, Barbara, *Acting Dir*, Greenwich Library, Greenwich CT

O'Rork, Sunnee D, *Exec Dir*, Arizona Museum For Youth, Mesa AZ

O'Rourke-Kaplan, Marian, *Assoc Prof Fashion Design*, University of North Texas, College of Visual Arts & Design, Denton TX (S)

Orozco, Denise L, *Mktg*, The University of Texas at San Antonio, Institute of Texan Cultures, San Antonio TX

Orozco, Sylvia, *Exec Dir*, MEXIC-ARTE Museum, Austin TX

Orr, Amy, *Asst Prof*, Rosemont College, Art Program, Rosemont PA (S)

Orr, Clint, *Assoc Prof,* Central Missouri State University, Dept Art & Design, Warrensburg MO (S)

Orr, Clint, *Graphic Design,* University of South Alabama, Dept of Art & Art History, Mobile AL (S)

Orr, Estelle, *Painting,* Santa Ana College, Art Dept, Santa Ana CA (S)

Orr, Fred, *Opers Tech,* Zanesville Museum of Art, Zanesville OH

Orr, Heather, *Dept Chair,* Western State College of Colorado, Dept of Art & Industrial Technology, Gunnison CO (S)

Orr, Lynn Federle, *Cur European Art,* Fine Arts Museums of San Francisco, M H de Young Museum, San Francisco CA

Orr, Lynn Federle, *Cur European Art,* Fine Arts Museums of San Francisco, Legion of Honor, San Francisco CA

Orr, Rebecca, *Mem Adminr,* Southern Highland Craft Guild, Folk Art Center, Asheville NC

Orr, Susan, *Registrar,* Hebrew Union College Museum, Jewish Institute of Religion Museum, New York NY

Orr, Vivian, *Commns Coordr,* Saskatchewan Craft Council & Affinity Gallery, Saskatoon SK

Orsic, Maja, *Dir,* Robert Klein Gallery, Boston MA

Orsinger, Marilyn, *Dir Opers,* Delaplaine Visual Arts Education Center, Frederick MD

Ortbals, John, *Assoc Prof,* Saint Louis Community College at Florissant Valley, Liberal Arts Division, Ferguson MO (S)

Ortega, Jean, *Asst Dir,* Bass Museum of Art, Miami Beach FL

Ortega, Lee, *Exec Dir,* Fort Smith Regional Art Museum, Fort Smith AR

Ortiz, Alfredo, *Prof,* University of Puerto Rico, Mayaguez, Dept of Humanities, College of Fine Arts & Theory of Art Programs, Mayaguez PR (S)

Ortiz, Alfredo, *Prof,* University of Puerto Rico, Mayaguez, Dept of Humanities, College of Fine Arts & Theory of Art Programs, Mayaguez PR (S)

Ortiz, Andrew, *Assoc Prof,* University of Texas at Arlington, Art & Art History Department, Arlington TX (S)

Ortiz, Carla, *Admin Asst,* Museum of New Mexico, Palace of Governors, Santa Fe NM

Ortiz, Jose, *Deputy Dir & Chief Admin,* Hirshhorn Museum & Sculpture Garden, Smithsonian Institution, Washington DC

Ortiz, Jose, *Mgr Admin,* The Metropolitan Museum of Art, The Cloisters Museum & Gardens, New York NY

Ortiz, Patty, *Exec Dir,* Guadalupe Cultural Arts Center, San Antonio TX

Ortiz, Raphael, *Prof,* Rutgers, The State University of New Jersey, Mason Gross School of the Arts, Visual Arts Dept, New Brunswick NJ (S)

Ortner, Frederick, *Chmn,* Knox College, Dept of Art, Galesburg IL (S)

Orvick, Jan, *Asst to Dir,* Santa Clara University, de Saisset Museum, Santa Clara CA

Orzel, Robyn P, *Dir Develop,* Vero Beach Museum of Art, Vero Beach FL

O'Sahaugnessy, Maureane, *Dir,* Arts Club of Washington, James Monroe House, Washington DC

Osberg, Kerry K, *Exec Dir,* Visual Arts Minnesota, Saint Cloud MN

Osborn, Nancy, *Theater,* Saint Clair County Community College, Jack R Hennesey Art Dept, Port Huron MI (S)

Osborne, John L, *Prof,* University of Victoria, Dept of History in Art, Victoria BC (S)

Osborne, Josie, *Dir Foundations,* University of Wisconsin-Milwaukee, Peck School of the Arts, Dept of Art & Design, Milwaukee WI (S)

Osbourne, Ginger, *Office Mgr,* Fairmount Park Art Association, Philadelphia PA

Osbourne Bender, Sarah, *Cataloguing & Technical Svcs Librn,* The Phillips Collection, Library, Washington DC

Osepchook, Felicity, *Head, Archives & Research Library,* New Brunswick Museum, Archives & Research Library, Saint John NB

O'Shaughnessey, Mary Ellen, *Exec Asst Dean,* University of Illinois, Urbana-Champaign, College of Fine & Applied Arts, Champaign IL (S)

O'Shaughnessy, David, *Chmn,* Los Angeles Harbor College, Art Dept, Wilmington CA (S)

O'Shaughnessy, Margaret, *Admin,* Fraunces Tavern Museum, New York NY

Oshima, David, *Art Dept Chmn,* Pierce College, Art Dept, Woodland Hills CA (S)

Osler, John C, *Chmn,* Alberta Foundation for the Arts, Edmonton AB

Osmond, Lynn J, *Pres,* Chicago Architecture Foundation, Chicago IL

Oste-Alexander, Pia, *Instr,* Woodstock School of Art, Inc, Woodstock NY (S)

Ostedorf, Eleanor, *Cur Historic House,* Iowa State University, Brunnier Art Museum, Ames IA

Ostendarp, Carl, *Asst Prof,* Cornell University, Dept of Art, Ithaca NY (S)

Osterman, William, *Asst Prof,* Rochester Institute of Technology, School of Photographic Arts & Sciences, Rochester NY (S)

Osthoff, Simone, *Assoc Prof Art (Art Criticism),* Pennsylvania State University, University Park, Penn State School of Visual Arts, University Park PA (S)

Ostman, Jessica, *Prog Dir,* Saint Cloud State University, Atwood Memorial Center Gallery, Saint Cloud MN

Ostrosky, Amelia, *Exec Dir,* Robert & Mary Montgomery Armory Art Center, Armory Art Center, West Palm Beach FL

Ostrow, Steven, *Chmn & Prof,* University of Minnesota, Minneapolis, Art History, Minneapolis MN (S)

Osttinger, April, *Prof,* Goucher College, Art & Art History Dept, Baltimore MD (S)

Ostwald, Don, *Pres Heritage Foundation,* Fort Morgan Heritage Foundation, Fort Morgan CO

Ostwind, Marcia, *Coordr Bd Mem,* Women in the Arts Foundation, Inc, Staten Island NY

Oswald, April, *Educ Dir,* Munson-Williams-Proctor Arts Institute, Museum of Art, Utica NY

Oswell, Mary, *Dir,* Bonita Museum and Cultural Center, Bonita CA

Oszuscik, Philippe, *Art Historian,* University of South Alabama, Dept of Art & Art History, Mobile AL (S)

Otani, Priscilla, *Pres (2013),* Women's Caucus For Art, New York NY

Otis, Jeanine, *Arts in Educ Mgr,* Staten Island Museum, Staten Island NY

Otis, Michaelin, *Faculty,* Grand Marais Art Colony, Grand Marais MN (S)

O'Toole, Judith H, *Dir & CEO,* Westmoreland Museum of American Art, Greensburg PA

O'Toole, Judith H, *Dir & CEO,* Westmoreland Museum of American Art, Art Reference Library, Greensburg PA

O'Toole, Molly, *Dir Commun & Community Engagement,* Contemporary Arts Center, Cincinnati OH

Otremsky, William, *Assoc Prof Art, Chmn Dept Art & Art History, Dir Studio Prog,* Florida Southern College, Melvin Art Gallery, Lakeland FL

Otremsky, William, *Assoc Prof Art, Dept Art & Art History Chair, Dir Studio Programming,* Florida Southern College, Department of Art & Art History, Lakeland FL (S)

Otsuka, Ron, *Adj Faculty Art History,* University of Denver, School of Art & Art History, Denver CO (S)

Otsuka, Ronald, *Dr Joseph De Heer Cur Asian,* Denver Art Museum, Denver CO

Ott, Christine, *Secy,* The Art Museum of Eastern Idaho, Idaho Falls ID

Ott, Lili, *Dir,* Shaker Museum & Library, Old Chatham NY

Ott, William, *Info Sys Mgr,* Grand Rapids Public Library, Grand Rapids MI

Ottaviano, Lillian, *Prof,* Cazenovia College, Center for Art & Design Studies, Cazenovia NY (S)

Otterson, Nathan, *Conservator, Sculpture,* Solomon R Guggenheim, New York NY

Ottesen, Bodil, *Adjunct Faculty,* University of Maryland, Baltimore County, Imaging & Digital Arts (IMDA), Dept of Visual Arts, Baltimore MD (S)

Ottmann, Klaus, *Cur, Robert Lehman,* Parrish Art Museum, Water Mill NY

Otto, Elizabeth, *Asst Prof,* University at Buffalo, State University of New York, Dept of Visual Studies, Buffalo NY (S)

Otto, Martha, *Head Archaeology,* Ohio Historical Society, Columbus OH

Otto, Richard H, *Pres,* American Academy of Art, Chicago IL (S)

Otto-Diniz, Sara, *Cur, Acad Initiatives,* University of New Mexico, University of New Mexico Art Museum, Albuquerque NM

Otto-Miller, Jackie, *Dir,* Valencia Community College - East Campus, Art Dept, Orlando FL (S)

Otts, Dylan, *Site Mgr,* Stone Quarry Hill Art Park, Winner Gallery, Cazenovia NY

Otts, Dylan, *Site Mgr,* Stone Quarry Hill Art Park, Jenny Library, Cazenovia NY

Ouchi, Eugene, *Acad Head Design,* Alberta College of Art & Design, Calgary AB (S)

Ouellet, Line, *Exec Dir,* Musee National des Beaux Arts du Quebec, Quebec PQ

Ouellet, Therese, *VPres,* Institut des Arts au Saguenay, Centre National D'Exposition a Jonquiere, Jonquiere PQ

Ouellette, David, *Dir Galleries,* Florida School of the Arts, Visual Arts, Palatka FL (S)

Ouellette, Gisele, *Prof Painting,* Universite de Moncton, Dept of Visual Arts, Moncton NB (S)

Ouellette, Jonathan, *Financial Officer,* Royal Architectural Institute of Canada, Ottawa ON

Oughton, Linda, *Admin Asst,* American Homing Pigeon Institute, Oklahoma City OK

Oursler, Henry Charles, *Asst Prof Art,* Western Illinois University, Department of Art, Macomb IL (S)

Ousey, Jack, *Instr,* Southeastern Oklahoma State University, Dept of Art, Communication & Theatre, Durant OK (S)

Overall, Scott, *Assoc Dir & Cur,* University Club Library, New York NY

Overbeck, John, *Prof,* State University of New York at Albany, Art Dept, Albany NY (S)

Overbeck Laise, Kristen, *VPres Colls Care Progs,* Heritage Preservation, The National Institute for Conservation, Washington DC

Overbey, Karen, *Asst Prof,* Tufts University, Dept of Art & Art History, Medford MA (S)

Overby, Osmund, *Prof Emeritus,* University of Missouri - Columbia, Art History & Archaeology Dept, Columbia MO (S)

Overcash, Debbie, *Program Dir,* Iredell Museums, Statesville NC

Overmyer, Dwayne, *Prof,* University of Michigan, Ann Arbor, School of Art & Design, Ann Arbor MI (S)

Overstreet, Jennifer, *Asst Prof & Chair Interior Design,* Watkins College of Art, Design & Film, Nashville TN (S)

Overstreet, Joe, *Art Dir,* Kenkeleba House, Inc, Kenkeleba Gallery, New York NY

Overton, Robert, *Assoc Dir,* West Florida Historic Preservation, Inc/University of West Florida, T T Wentworth, Jr Florida State Museum; Historic Pensacola Village; Pensacola Historical Society & Resource Center, Pensacola FL

Overy, Jane Bunker, *Founder,* Searchlight Historic Museum & Mining Park, Searchlight NV

Ovesia, Steluta, *Information Specialist,* Jardin Botanique de Montreal, Bibliotheque, Montreal PQ

Oviedo, Rebecca, *Mus Asst,* La Salle University Art Museum, Philadelphia PA

Ovrebo, Reidun, *Chair,* West Virginia State University, Art Dept, Institute WV (S)

Owcvark, Bob, *Div Chmn,* Pine Manor College, Visual Arts Dept, Chestnut Hill MA (S)

Owczarski, Marian, *Dir,* St Mary's Galeria, Orchard Lake MI

Owen, Dawn, *Asst Cur,* Macdonald Stewart Art Centre, Guelph ON

Owen, Ginger, *Photo/Intermedia,* Western Michigan University, Frostic School of Art, Kalamazoo MI (S)

Owen, Jane, *Exec Dir,* Center for Art & Education, Van Buren AR

Owen, Lisa, *Assoc Prof Art History,* University of North Texas, College of Visual Arts & Design, Denton TX (S)

Owen, Paula, *Pres,* Southwest School of Art, San Antonio TX

Owen, Robert, *Facilities & Spec Events,* Tyler Museum of Art, Tyler TX

Owen, Robert, *Spec Events & Facilities Mgr,* Tyler Museum of Art, Reference Library, Tyler TX

Owen Moss, Eric, *Dir,* Southern California Institute of Architecture, Los Angeles CA (S)

Owens, Beth, *Patron Svcs Librn,* Cleveland Institute of Art, Jessica Gund Memorial Library, Cleveland OH

Owens, Carlotta, *Asst Cur,* National Gallery of Art, Index of American Design, Washington DC

Owens, Chris, *Part-Time Instr,* Oklahoma Baptist University, Art Dept, Shawnee OK (S)

Owens, Eileen, *Mktg Communs Coordr,* Philadelphia Museum of Art, Samuel S Fleisher Art Memorial, Philadelphia PA

Owens, Heather, *CFO,* Cedarhurst Center for the Arts, Mitchell Museum, Mount Vernon IL

Owens, Keith, *Assoc Prof Commun Design,* University of North Texas, College of Visual Arts & Design, Denton TX (S)

Owens, Mike, *Prof,* East Los Angeles College, Art Dept, Monterey Park CA (S)

Owens, Quintin, *Adj Instr,* University of West Florida, Dept of Art, Pensacola FL (S)

Owens, Robert G, *Head Div of Fine Arts & Humanities,* Fayetteville State University, Performing & Fine Arts, Fayetteville NC (S)

Owens, Susan, *Youth Prog Dir,* Birmingham Bloomfield Art Center, Birmingham MI (S)

Owens, Valerie, *Prof,* Texarkana College, Art Dept, Texarkana TX (S)

Owens-Pelton, Lesley, *Mgr,* Stone Quarry Hill Art Park, John & Virginia Winner Memorial Art Gallery, Cazenovia NY

Owensby, Mary, *Exec Asst,* Trust Authority, Museum of the Great Plains, Lawton OK

Owinell, Kim, *Instr,* Art Institute of Southern California, Laguna Beach CA (S)

Oxenberg, Harvey, *Pres Board,* Bakehouse Art Complex, Inc, Miami FL

Oxman, M, *Prof,* American University, Dept of Art, New York NY (S)

Oxman, Ron Haynie, *Assoc Prof,* American University, Dept of Art, New York NY (S)

Oxtoby, Susan, *Sr Film Cur,* University of California, Berkeley, Berkeley Art Museum & Pacific Film Archive, Berkeley CA

Oygur, Sule, *Cur Natural Science,* Newark Museum Association, The Newark Museum, Newark NJ

Ozdogan, Turker, *Prof,* George Washington University, Dept of Art of Fine Arts & Art History, Washington DC (S)

Ozguzer, Selin, *Asst Prof of Computer Art & Design,* Jacksonville University, Dept of Art, Theater, Dance, Jacksonville FL (S)

Ozog, Wallace M, *Chmn,* Polish Museum of America, Research Library, Chicago IL

Ozolis, Auseklis, *Dir Academy,* New Orleans Academy of Fine Arts, Academy Gallery, New Orleans LA

Ozubko, Christopher, *Dir,* University of Washington, School of Art, Seattle WA (S)

Pacaud, Margaret, *Treas,* Revelstoke Visual Arts Centre, Revelstoke BC

Pace, David, *Lectr,* Santa Clara University, Dept of Art & Art History, Santa Clara CA (S)

Pace, Deanna L, *Dir,* 1890 House-Museum & Center for the Arts, Cortland NY

Pace, James R, *Prof,* University of Texas at Tyler, Department of Art, School of Visual & Performing Arts, Tyler TX (S)

Pace, William, *Cultural Affairs Assoc,* School 33 Art Center, Baltimore MD

Pace-Robinson, Jennifer, *VP Experience Develop & Family Learning,* The Children's Museum of Indianapolis, Indianapolis IN

Pacheco, John, *Painting Prof,* Mount Wachusett Community College, East Wing Gallery, Gardner MA

Pacheco, Raoul, *Prof,* Augusta State University, Dept of Art, Augusta GA (S)

Pachikara, Cynthia, *Asst Prof,* University of Michigan, Ann Arbor, School of Art & Design, Ann Arbor MI (S)

Pachikara, Cynthia, *Instr,* Pacific Northwest College of Art, Portland OR (S)

Pachter, Marc, *Interim Dir,* National Museum of American History, Smithsonian Institution, Washington DC

Pacini, Marina, *Cur Educ,* Memphis Brooks Museum of Art, Memphis TN

Pacini, Marina, *Dir & Cur,* Rhodes College, Clough-Hanson Gallery, Memphis TN

Packard, Sally, *Dir School of Art,* Texas Christian University, School of Art, Fort Worth TX (S)

Paddock, Eric, *Cur Photog,* Colorado Historical Society, Colorado History Museum, Denver CO

Paddock, Eric, *Cur Photography,* Denver Art Museum, Denver CO

Padgett, Deborah L, *Media Relations Mgr,* Jamestown-Yorktown Foundation, Jamestown Settlement, Williamsburg VA

Padgett, J Michael, *Cur Ancient Art,* Princeton University, Princeton University Art Museum, Princeton NJ

Padgett, James, *Adv,* Wilberforce University, Art Dept, Wilberforce OH (S)

Padgett, Michael, *Chmn,* University of Wisconsin-River Falls, Art Dept, River Falls WI (S)

Padgett, Michael, *Dir Gallery,* University of Wisconsin, Gallery 101, River Falls WI

Padilla, Aaron, *Cur Educ,* The Contemporary Museum, Honolulu HI

Padilla Virola, Shirley, *Educ Coordr,* Museo de las Americas, Viejo San Juan PR

Padilla Virola, Shirley, *Educ Coordr,* Museo de las Americas, Viejo San Juan PR

Padon, Thomas, *Brandywine River Mus Dir,* Brandywine Conservancy, Brandywine River Museum, Chadds Ford PA

Padulo, Louis, *Exec Dean College & Architecture,* Philadelphia University, Philadelphia PA (S)

Pagani, Catherine, *Chair,* University of Alabama, Dept of Art, Tuscaloosa AL (S)

Pagano, Donna, *Mgr Exhibs,* Staten Island Museum, Staten Island NY

Pagano, Donna, *Mgr Exhibs,* Staten Island Museum, Archives Library, Staten Island NY

Page, Graham, *Chmn Visual Arts,* Red Deer College, Dept of Visual Arts, Red Deer AB (S)

Page, Gregory, *Assoc Prof,* Cornell University, Dept of Art, Ithaca NY (S)

Page, Helen, *Assoc Dir Admin,* Delaware Center for the Contemporary Arts, Wilmington DE

Page, Joe, *Vis Asst Prof Art,* Whitman College, Art Dept, Walla Walla WA (S)

Page, Jutta Annette, *Cur Glass & Decorative Arts,* Toledo Museum of Art, Toledo OH

Page, Kathryn, *Cur Maps & Documents,* Louisiana Department of Culture, Recreation & Tourism, Louisiana Historical Center Library, New Orleans LA

Page, Kelly, *Registrar,* Maine Maritime Museum, Archives Library, Bath ME

Page, Marcia, *Dir Project,* LA County Museum of Art, Los Angeles CA

Page, Mary, *Head of Acquisitions,* University of Central Florida Libraries, Orlando FL

Pagel, Angelika, *Assoc Prof,* Weber State University, Dept of Visual Arts, Ogden UT (S)

Pagel, David, *Chair,* Claremont Graduate University, Art Department, Claremont CA (S)

Paggie, Michael, *Bus Mgr,* Madison Museum of Contemporary Art, Madison WI

Pagh, Barbara, *Pres,* Hera Educational Foundation, Hera Gallery, Wakefield RI

Paglia, Lenora, *Conservator of Art,* Staten Island Museum, Staten Island NY

Pagnucci, Anna, *Head Dept,* Ashford University, Art Dept, Clinton IA (S)

Pahn, Michael, *Media Archivist,* National Museum of the American Indian, Archives, Washington DC

Paice, Kimberly, *Asst Prof Art History,* University of Cincinnati, School of Art, Cincinnati OH (S)

Paier, Daniel, *VPres,* Paier College of Art, Inc, Library, Hamden CT

Paier, Jonathan E, *Pres,* Paier College of Art, Inc, Library, Hamden CT

Paier, Jonathan E, *Pres,* Paier College of Art, Inc, Hamden CT (S)

Pain, Eric, *Supt,* Ringwood Manor House Museum, Ringwood NJ

Paine, Howard, *Div Chair Fine Arts,* Memphis College of Art, Memphis TN (S)

Paine, Pam, *Exec Asst,* Austin Children's Museum, Austin TX

Paine, Peter S, *Pres,* Fort Ticonderoga Association, Ticonderoga NY

Paine, Wesley M, *Dir,* Board of Parks & Recreation, The Parthenon, Nashville TN

Pair, Cassandra, *Accreditation Mgr,* National Architectural Accrediting Board, Inc, Washington DC

Paisley, Leslie, *Paper Conservator & Dept Head,* Williamstown Art Conservation Center, Williamstown MA

Paitz, Kendra, *Cur,* Illinois State University, University Galleries, Normal IL

Paizy, Guy, *Dir,* University of Puerto Rico, Dept of Fine Arts, Rio Piedras PR

Paizy, Guy, *Dir,* University of Puerto Rico, Dept of Fine Arts, Rio Piedras PR (S)

Palanuk, Garth, *Webmaster,* Manitoba Society of Artists, Winnipeg MB

Palatucci, Ernie, *Dir Opers,* Visual Arts Center of New Jersey, Summit NJ

Palazzolo, T, *Prof,* City Colleges of Chicago, Daley College, Chicago IL (S)

Palermo, Frank, *Prof,* Dalhousie University, Faculty of Architecture, Halifax NS (S)

Palermo, Lou, *Educ,* Arkansas Arts Center, Museum, Little Rock AR (S)

Palermo, Louise, *Dir Educ,* Arkansas Arts Center, Little Rock AR

Paletz, Susan, *Prog Dir,* Barbara & Ray Alpert Jewish Community Center, Pauline & Zena Gatov Gallery, Long Beach CA

Paley, Albert, *Prof,* Rochester Institute of Technology, School of Design, Rochester NY (S)

Paley, Valerie, *Historian & VPres Scholarly Progs,* New-York Historical Society, Museum, New York NY

Palijczuk, Wasyl, *Prof,* Western Maryland College, Dept of Art & Art History, Westminster MD (S)

Palisin, B, *Instr,* Sacramento City College, Art Dept, Sacramento CA (S)

Palkovic, Francis, *Art Instr,* Big Bend Community College, Art Dept, Moses Lake WA (S)

Palkovic, Rie, *Dir,* Big Bend Community College, Art Dept, Moses Lake WA (S)

Palladino-Craig, Allys, *Dir & Ed-in-Chief,* Florida State University, Museum of Fine Arts, Tallahassee FL

Pallas, James, *Prof,* Macomb Community College, Art Dept, Warren MI (S)

Pallesen, Ann, *Gallery Dir,* Photo Center NW, Seattle WA

Palm, Nancy, *Asst Prof,* University of North Carolina at Pembroke, Art Dept, Pembroke NC (S)

Palma, Wanda, *Interim Dir Commun & Mktg,* Musee d'art Contemporain de Montreal, Montreal PQ

Palmer, A Laurie, *Chmn Sculpture,* School of the Art Institute of Chicago, Chicago IL (S)

Palmer, Bob E, *Chmn,* University of Central Oklahoma, Dept of Art & Design, Edmond OK (S)

Palmer, Brian, *Div Chair Theater & Dance,* Jacksonville University, Dept of Art, Theater, Dance, Jacksonville FL (S)

Palmer, Cheryl, *Dir Educ,* The Mint Museum, Charlotte NC

Palmer, Doug, *Chair,* Sioux City Art Center, Sioux City IA (S)

Palmer, Erin, *Assoc Prof,* Southern Illinois University, School of Art & Design, Carbondale IL (S)

Palmer, Jon, *VPres,* Searchlight Historic Museum & Mining Park, Searchlight NV

Palmer, Patrick, *Faculty Chair & Studio School Dean,* Museum of Fine Arts, Houston, Glassell School of Art, Houston TX (S)

Palmer, Sharon S, *Exec Dir,* Columbia County Historical Society, 1820 James Vanderpoel House, Kinderhook NY

Palmer, Stephen, *2nd VPres,* South County Art Association, Kingston RI

Palmer, Susan, *Dir Develop,* Toledo Museum of Art, Toledo OH

Palmer, Teri Evans, *Asst Prof,* Texas State University - San Marcos, Dept of Art and Design, San Marcos TX (S)

Palmer, Virginia, *Friends of the Alaska State Mus Pres,* Alaska State Museum, Juneau AK

Palmeri, Mark, *Asst Prof,* Oakton Community College, Language Humanities & Art Divisions, Des Plaines IL (S)

Palmeri, Nancy, *Assoc Prof,* University of Texas at Arlington, Art & Art History Department, Arlington TX (S)

Palmieri, Lynn, *Bus Mgr,* Cayuga Museum of History & Art, Auburn NY

Palmisano, Susan, *Prof,* Indiana University of Pennsylvania, College of Fine Arts, Indiana PA (S)

Palodichule, Dan, *Access Servs Asst,* University of California, Los Angeles, Arts Library, Los Angeles CA

Panczenko, Russell, *Dir,* University of Wisconsin-Madison, Chazen Museum of Art, Madison WI

Pandelis, Judy E, *Office Mgr,* Birmingham-Southern College, Art & Art History, Birmingham AL (S)

Panek, Mary, *Dir Devel,* Grand Rapids Art Museum, Grand Rapids MI

Panhorst, Michael, *Cur Art,* Montgomery Museum of Fine Arts, Montgomery AL

Panhorst, Michael, *Cur Art,* Montgomery Museum of Fine Arts, Library, Montgomery AL

Panitz, Zimra, *Tech Serv/Systems Librn,* Visual Arts Library, New York NY

Pankow, David P, *Asst Prof,* Rochester Institute of Technology, School of Printing Management & Sciences, Rochester NY (S)

Pannafino, James, *Asst Prof Graphic & Interactive Design,* Millersville University, Dept of Art & Design, Millersville PA (S)

Pannen, Richard, *Chmn,* Rochester Institute of Technology, School for American Craft, Rochester NY (S)

Panske, Gail, *Prof,* University of Wisconsin Oshkosh, Dept of Art, Oshkosh WI (S)

Pantano, Nadine, *Adjunct Asst Prof Art History,* Florida Southern College, Melvin Art Gallery, Lakeland FL

Pantano, Nadine, *Adjunct Asst Prof Art History,* Florida Southern College, Department of Art & Art History, Lakeland FL (S)

Panzer, Robert, *Exec Dir,* Visual Artists & Galleries Association (VAGA), New York NY

Paoletta, Donald, *Dept Chair, Prof Art History,* Nebraska Wesleyan University, Art Dept, Lincoln NE (S)

Paoletta, Donald, *Dir,* Nebraska Wesleyan University, Elder Gallery, Lincoln NE

Papadopoulos, Joan, *Treas,* Swedish American Museum Association of Chicago, Chicago IL

Papageorge, Tod, *Prof,* Yale University, School of Art, New Haven CT (S)

Papalambros, Panos, *Prof,* University of Michigan, Ann Arbor, School of Art & Design, Ann Arbor MI (S)

Papanek-Miller, MaryAnn, *Chmn,* Bemidji State University, Visual Arts Dept, Bemidji MN (S)

Papanikolas, Theresa, *Cur Euro & American Art,* Honolulu Museum of Art, Honolulu HI

Papararo, Jenifer, *Cur,* Contemporary Art Gallery Society of British Columbia, Vancouver BC

Papazian, Aline, *Asst Dir,* Passaic County Community College, Division of Humanities, Paterson NJ (S)

Papazian, Aram, *Bd Pres,* Hunterdon Art Museum, Clinton NJ

Pape, Whitney, *Spec Coll Librn,* Redwood Library & Athenaeum, Newport RI

Papenfoth, Mary, *1st VPres,* South County Art Association, Kingston RI

Papenfus, Esther, *Opers Mgr,* Foothills Art Center, Inc, Golden CO

Papier, Maurice A, *Prof,* University of Saint Francis, School of Creative Arts, Fort Wayne IN (S)

Papineau, Karen, *Registrar,* The Currier Museum of Art, Manchester NH

Pappalardo, Anna, *Mgr Admin,* University of British Columbia, Museum of Anthropology, Vancouver BC

Pappas, Andrea, *Assoc Prof,* Santa Clara University, Dept of Art & Art History, Santa Clara CA (S)

Pappenheimer, William, *Prof,* Pace University, Dyson College of Arts & Sciences, Pleasantville NY (S)

Papson, Don, *Interim Dir,* Hershey Museum, Hershey PA

Papuga, Shelby, *Office Mgr,* Safety Harbor Museum of Regional History, Safety Harbor FL

Paquette, Adrian, *Cur,* Slater Mill, Old Slater Mill Association, Pawtucket RI

Paquette, Thomas, *VPres,* Crary Art Gallery Inc, Grary Art Gallery, Warren PA

Paquin, Nycole, *Head Art History,* Universite du Quebec a Montreal, Famille des Arts, Montreal PQ (S)

Paradis, Elisabeth, *Registrar,* OCAD University, Toronto ON (S)

Paratore, Philip, *Prof,* University of Maine at Augusta, College of Arts & Humanities, Augusta ME (S)

Parcell, S, *Assoc Prof,* Dalhousie University, Faculty of Architecture, Halifax NS (S)

Parcon, Dana, *Dir Capital Improvements of Facility Opers,* Museum of African American History, Boston MA

Pardee, Pattie, *Asst to Exec Dir,* The Museum of Arts & Sciences Inc, Daytona Beach FL

Pardee, Pattie, *Dir Develop,* Museum of Florida Art, Deland FL

Pardo, Mary, *Assoc Prof,* University of North Carolina at Chapel Hill, Art Dept, Chapel Hill NC (S)

Pardue, Diana, *Chief Cur,* The National Park Service, United States Department of the Interior, Statue of Liberty National Monument & The Ellis Island Immigration Museum, Washington DC

Pardue, Diana, *Cur Colls,* Heard Museum, Phoenix AZ

Paredes, Liana, *Dir Collections, Chief Cur,* Hillwood Museum & Gardens Foundation, Hillwood Estate Museum & Gardens, Washington DC

Parent, Geraldine, *Dir,* The Penticton Art Gallery, Penticton BC

Paret, Paul, *Asst Prof,* University of Utah, Dept of Art & Art History, Salt Lake City UT (S)

Parham, Annette, *Acquisitions Librn,* Colonial Williamsburg Foundation, John D Rockefeller, Jr Library, Williamsburg VA

Paris, Eric, *Pres,* Shores Memorial Museum, Lyndon Center VT

Paris, Marguerite, *Secy,* DuPage Art League School & Gallery, Wheaton IL

Paris, Robin, *Assoc Prof & Chair Photog,* Watkins College of Art, Design & Film, Nashville TN (S)

Paris, Tiara N, *Exhibs Mgr,* North Carolina Museum of Art, Raleigh NC

Parisien, Diane, *Dir Fin & External Affairs,* Jersey City Museum, Jersey City NJ

Park, Bryan, *Vis Asst Lectr,* Idaho State University, Dept of Art & Pre-Architecture, Pocatello ID (S)

Park, JP, *Asst Prof,* University of California, Riverside, Dept of the History of Art, Riverside CA (S)

Park, Jim, *Asst Prof,* Minnesota State University-Moorhead, Dept of Art & Design, Moorhead MN (S)

Park, Kyong, *Founder,* Storefront for Art & Architecture, New York NY

Park, Maria, *Assoc Prof,* Cornell University, Dept of Art, Ithaca NY (S)

Park, Penny, *Assoc Prof,* Wright State University, Dept of Art & Art History, Dayton OH (S)

Park, So Yeon, *Assoc Prof,* University of Kansas, The School of the Arts, Dept of Visual Art, Lawrence KS (S)

Park, YuJune Gina, *Vis Asst Prof,* Purchase College, State University of New York, School of Art+Design, Purchase NY (S)

Parke-Harrison, Robert, *Assoc Prof,* College of the Holy Cross, Dept of Visual Arts, Worcester MA (S)

Parker, Albert, *Dir Opers,* Buffalo Museum of Science, Research Library, Buffalo NY

Parker, Barbara, *Dir Programs,* Piedmont Arts Association, Martinsville VA

Parker, Belua, *Arts Prog Coordr,* City of Raleigh Arts Commission, Miriam Preston Block Gallery, Raleigh NC

Parker, Carolyn, *Head Dept,* Peace College, Art Dept, Raleigh NC (S)

Parker, Donna, *Exhib Cur,* Western Kentucky University, Kentucky Library & Museum, Bowling Green KY

Parker, Donovan, *Libr Specialist,* Art Museum of the University of Houston, William R Jenkins Architecture & Art Library, Houston TX

Parker, Jeanette, *Serials,* Friends University, Edmund Stanley Library, Wichita KS

Parker, Jennifer, *Architecture Librn,* University of Notre Dame, Architecture Library, Notre Dame IN

Parker, Kathi, *Sec,* First Street Gallery, New York NY

Parker, Kathleen, *Sec,* Morris-Jumel Mansion, Inc, New York NY

Parker, Kristin, *Archivist,* Isabella Stewart Gardner, Isabella Stewart Garden Museum Library & Archives, Boston MA

Parker, Laura, *Instr,* American River College, Dept of Art/Art New Media, Sacramento CA (S)

Parker, Marsha H, *Dean Fine Arts & Performing Arts,* Lindenwood University, Harry D Hendren Gallery, Saint Charles MO

Parker, Martha, *Mem Coordr,* Historical Society of Martin County, Elliott Museum, Stuart FL

Parker, Mary Jo, *Pub Rels & Mem,* Tennessee Valley Art Association, Tuscumbia AL

Parker, Niles, *Chief Cur,* Nantucket Historical Association, Historic Nantucket, Nantucket MA

Parker, Phil, *Coordr Graphic Design,* Florida School of the Arts, Visual Arts, Palatka FL (S)

Parker, Richard (Scott), *Assoc Prof,* Tarrant County College, Art Dept, Hurst TX (S)

Parker, Rod, *Dir, School of Art,* Louisiana State University, School of Art - Glassell Gallery, Baton Rouge LA

Parker, Rosalie, *Develop Coordr,* Johns Hopkins University, Homewood Museum, Baltimore MD

Parker, Shalon, *Asst Prof,* Gonzaga University, Dept of Art, Spokane WA (S)

Parker, Shannon, *Cur Colls,* Art Gallery of Nova Scotia, Halifax NS

Parker, Stephen, *Prof,* Black Hills State University, Art Dept, Spearfish SD (S)

Parker, Stuart, *Acad Head Fine Arts,* Alberta College of Art & Design, Calgary AB (S)

Parker, Susan R, *Exec Dir,* Saint Augustine Historical Society, Library, Saint Augustine FL

Parker, Teresa J, *Cur,* Illinois Benedictine University, Department of Fine Arts, Lisle IL (S)

Parker, Trinity, *Registrar,* University of Arizona, Center for Creative Photography, Tucson AZ

Parker Farris, Teresa, *Mktg Coordr,* Tulane University, Newcomb Art Gallery, New Orleans LA

Parkinson, Carol, *Dir,* Harvestworks, Inc, New York NY

Parkinson, George, *Div Chief & State Archivist,* Ohio Historical Society, Archives-Library Division, Columbus OH

Parkinson, Trude, *Instr,* Marylhurst University, Art Dept, Marylhurst OR (S)

Parks, Aaron, *COO,* The University of Texas at San Antonio, Institute of Texan Cultures, San Antonio TX

Parks, Janet, *Cur Drawings & Archives,* Columbia University, Avery Architectural & Fine Arts Library, New York NY

Parks, Michael, *Admin Asst,* Five Civilized Tribes Museum, Muskogee OK

Parks, Nancy, *Asst Prof Art Educ,* University of Cincinnati, School of Art, Cincinnati OH (S)

Parks, Robert, *Dir Library & Mus Svcs,* The Morgan Library & Museum, Library, New York NY

Parks, Tom, *Chief Security Officer,* Nelda C & H J Lutcher Stark, Stark Museum of Art, Orange TX

Parks, Tonya, *Mem Coordr,* Embroiderers Guild of America, Margaret Parshall Gallery, Louisville KY

Parks-Kirby, Carrie Anne, *Prof, Chmn,* Alma College, Clack Art Center, Dept of Art & Design, Alma MI (S)

Parks Smith, Margaret, *Prof Ceramics Sculpture,* Asbury College, Student Center Gallery, Wilmore KY

Parmal, Pamela, *Dept Head & Logie Cur Textiles & Fashion Arts,* Museum of Fine Arts, Boston MA

Parmenter, Becky, *Educ Coordr,* Gallery One Visual Arts Center, Ellensburg WA

Parmenter, Marian, *Dir,* San Francisco Museum of Modern Art, Artist Gallery, San Francisco CA

Parmigiani, Sara, *Head Cur,* Fleetwood Museum, North Plainfield NJ

Parnes, Laura, *Bd Dir,* Momenta Art, Brooklyn NY

Parr, Doug, *VPres,* Owatonna Arts Center, Owatonna MN

Parr, Ryan, *Colls Asst,* University at Albany, State University of New York, University Art Museum, Albany NY

Parra, Adrian, *Programming Coordr,* The Center for Contemporary Arts of Santa Fe, Santa Fe NM

Parra, Victor, *Preparator,* East Los Angeles College, Vincent Price Art Museum, Monterey Park CA

Parreton, Nicole, *Admin,* Conseil des Arts du Quebec (CATQ), Diagonale, Centre des arts et des fibres du Quebec, Montreal PQ

Parris, Melissa, *Registrar,* College of William & Mary, Muscarelle Museum of Art, Williamsburg VA

Parrott, Frances, *Chmn,* Iowa Western Community College, Art Dept, Council Bluffs IA (S)

Parrott, Karen, *Dir Outreach,* Arts Partnership of Greater Spartanburg, Inc, Chapman Cultural Center, Spartanburg SC

Parrott, Lindsy R, *Dir & Cur,* Neustadt Collection of Tiffany Glass, Long Island City NY

Parry, John, *Exec Dir,* Saskatchewan Association of Architects, Saskatoon SK

Parsley, Myrtie, *Instr,* Campbellsville University, Department of Art, Campbellsville KY (S)

Parson, Del, *Asst Prof,* Dixie College, Art Dept, Saint George UT (S)

Parson, Leon, *Instr,* Ricks College, Dept of Art, Rexburg ID (S)

Parsons, Austin, *Asst Prof,* Dalhousie University, Faculty of Architecture, Halifax NS (S)

Parsons, David, *Dir Finance,* Historic Hudson Valley, Pocantico Hills NY

Parsons, David, *Instr,* California State University, Dominguez Hills, Art & Design Dept, Carson CA (S)

Parsons, Laura, *Pres,* American Folk Art Museum, New York NY

Parsons, Merribell, *Adjunct Cur Decorative Arts,* San Antonio Museum of Art, San Antonio TX

Parsons, Michael, *Prof,* Ohio State University, Dept of Art Education, Columbus OH (S)

Parsons, Sarah, *Secy (Toronto),* International Association of Art Critics, AICA Canada, Inc, Toronto ON

Parsons-O'Keefe, Colby, *Asst Prof,* Texas Woman's University, School of the Arts, Dept of Visual Arts, Denton TX (S)

Partin, Bruce, *Chmn,* Roanoke College, Fine Arts Dept-Art, Salem VA (S)

Partington, Judith, *Head Librn,* The Filson Historical Society, Louisville KY

Partington, Judith, *Librn,* The Filson Historical Society, Reference & Research Library, Louisville KY

Partlow, Gayle, *Prof,* Los Angeles City College, Dept of Art, Los Angeles CA (S)

Parton, Julia, *Pub Rels Dir,* Palos Verdes Art Center/Beverly G. Alpay Center for Arts Education, Rancho Palos Verdes CA

Partovi, Pat, *Dir,* Spokane Public Library, Spokane WA

Partridge, David, *Chmn,* Pasadena Museum of California Art, Pasadena CA

Partridge, Kathleen, *Instr,* Mohawk Valley Community College, Utica NY (S)

Pasas, Anna Liza, *Head Librn & Archivist,* Autry National Center, Braun Research Library, Los Angeles CA

Pascale, Mark, *Cur,* The Art Institute of Chicago, Dept of Prints & Drawings, Chicago IL

Pasch, Anne, *Cur,* Alaska Museum of Natural History, Anchorage AK

Paschal, Mary Lou, *Chmn,* Central Piedmont Community College, Visual & Performing Arts, Charlotte NC (S)

Paschall, W Douglass, *Cur Coll,* Woodmere Art Museum Inc, Library, Philadelphia PA

Paschke, Ed, *Prof,* Northwestern University, Evanston, Dept of Art Theory & Practice, Evanston IL (S)

Pascual, Robert, *Dir Fin,* Bay Area Video Coalition, Inc, San Francisco CA

Pascucci, Marisa, *Cur 20th Century & Contemporary Art,* Boca Raton Museum of Art, Library, Boca Raton FL

Pascucci, Marisa J, *Cur,* Boca Raton Museum of Art, Boca Raton FL

Pasquina, Lavinia, *Asst Prof,* Catholic University of America, School of Architecture & Planning, Washington DC (S)

Pass, Dwayne, *Instr,* Tulsa Community College, Art Dept, Tulsa OK (S)

Passanise, Gary, *Asst Prof,* Webster University, Art Dept, Webster Groves MO (S)

Passey, Erica, *Mgr Mktg,* Milwaukee County War Memorial Inc., Villa Terrace Decorative Arts Museum, Milwaukee WI

Passic, Frank, *Chmn Numismatic,* Balzekas Museum of Lithuanian Culture, Chicago IL

Passlof, Pat, *Coordr Art Prog,* College of Staten Island, Performing & Creative Arts Dept, Staten Island NY (S)

Pastan, Rachel, *Staff Writer,* University of Pennsylvania, Institute of Contemporary Art, Philadelphia PA

Paster, Carol, *Exec Dir,* Creative Arts Center, Pontiac MI

Pasternak, Anne, *Pres & Artistic Dir,* Creative Time, New York NY

Pasternak, Stephanie, *Secy,* Town of Cummington Historical Commission, Kingman Tavern Historical Museum, Cummington MA

Pasti, Sara, *Interim Dir,* State University of New York at New Paltz, Samuel Dorsky Museum of Art, New Paltz NY

Pastore, Andrew, *Exhibit Mgr,* Hartwick College, The Yager Museum, Oneonta NY

Pastore, Heather, *Controller,* Elmhurst Art Museum, Elmhurst IL

Pasture, Randy Good, *Facilities Mgr & Gen Mgr,* American Homing Pigeon Institute, Oklahoma City OK

Patalano, Anna, *Pres & Co-VP Dir of Classes,* Greenwich Art Society Inc, Greenwich CT

Patchell, Chris, *Graphic Design,* Antonelli Institute, Professional Photography & Commercial Art, Erdenheim PA (S)

Patchen, Jeffrey, *Pres & CEO,* The Children's Museum of Indianapolis, Indianapolis IN

Pate, Annette, *Med Adjunct Prof,* Oklahoma Christian University of Science & Arts, Dept of Art & Design, Oklahoma City OK (S)

Patel, Alka, *Asst Prof,* University of Michigan, Ann Arbor, Dept of History of Art, Ann Arbor MI (S)

Patel, Joy, *Chief Library Svcs,* Department of Canadian Heritage, Canadian Conservation Institute, Ottawa ON

Patenaude, Danielle, *Foundation,* Musee d'art Contemporain de Montreal, Montreal PQ

Paterson, James C, *Assoc Prof,* Franklin & Marshall College, Art & Art History Dept, Lancaster PA (S)

Paterson, Pamela, *Cur Asst,* Nevada Museum of Art, Reno NV

Patino, Luis, *VPres Pub Affairs,* MEXIC-ARTE Museum, Austin TX

Patnode, J Scott, *Prof,* Gonzaga University, Dept of Art, Spokane WA (S)

Patrick, Jill, *Dir Library Servs,* OCAD University, Toronto ON (S)

Patrick, Jill, *Dir Library Svcs,* OCAD University, Dorothy H Hoover Library, Toronto ON

Patrick, Stephen, *Cur,* George Washington, Alexandria VA

Patrick, Stephen, *Vol Pub Rels,* Bluemont Historical Railroad Junction, Arlington VA

Patrick, Vernon, *Prof Emeritus,* California State University, Chico, Department of Art & Art History, Chico CA (S)

Patridge, Margaret, *Pub Information,* Walker Art Center, Minneapolis MN

Patt, Stephne, *Instr,* La Sierra University, Art Dept, Riverside CA (S)

Patt, Susan, *Chmn,* La Sierra University, Art Dept, Riverside CA (S)

Patten, Burke, *Commun Mgr,* Northwestern University, Mary & Leigh Block Museum of Art, Evanston IL

Patten, James, *Finance Dir,* Wiscasset, Waterville & Farmington Railway Museum (WW&F), Alna ME

Patterson, Aubrey B, *Pres,* Bancorp South, Art Collection, Tupelo MS

Patterson, Belinda A, *Lectr,* Lambuth University, Dept of Human Ecology & Visual Arts, Jackson TN (S)

Patterson, Brent, *Asst Prof,* West Virginia Wesleyan College, Art Dept, Buckhannon WV (S)

Patterson, Carl, *Adj Faculty Conservation,* University of Denver, School of Art & Art History, Denver CO (S)

Patterson, Carolyn, *Dir IL Artisans Prog,* Illinois State Museum, Illinois Artisans Shop, Chicago IL

Patterson, Carolyn, *Dir ILL Artisans Prog,* Illinois State Museum, Illinois Artisans & Visitors Centers, Chicago IL

Patterson, Chad, *Fine Arts Technician,* University of Lethbridge, Art Gallery, Lethbridge AB

Patterson, Charlene, *Pub Rels Coordr,* Eastern Shore Art Association, Inc, Eastern Shore Art Center, Fairhope AL

Patterson, Jeremiah, *Asst Prof,* University of Hartford, Hartford Art School, West Hartford CT (S)

Patterson, Josie, *Dir Pub Rel & Mktg,* Massachusetts Institute of Technology, MIT Museum, Cambridge MA

Patterson, L Dale, *Archivist,* Archives & History Center of the United Methodist Church, Madison NJ

Patterson, Michelle, *Prof,* North Carolina Central University, Art Dept, Durham NC (S)

Patterson, Nick, *Dir Commun,* Birmingham Museum of Art, Birmingham AL

Patterson, Oscar, *Chmn,* University of North Florida, Dept of Communications & Visual Arts, Jacksonville FL (S)

Patterson, Richard, *Dir,* Old Barracks Museum, Trenton NJ

Patterson, Roy, *Board Mem,* Cambridge Museum, Cambridge NE

Patterson, Vivian, *Cur Coll,* Williams College, Museum of Art, Williamstown MA

Patterson, William C, *Pres,* Philadelphia Sketch Club, Philadelphia PA

Patterson, Zabet, *Asst Prof,* Stony Brook University, College of Arts & Sciences, Dept of Art, Stony Brook NY (S)

Patterson-Tutschka, Andrew, *Instr,* Shasta College, Arts, Communications & Social Sciences Division, Redding CA (S)

Patteson, Rita S, *Dir & Cur Manuscripts,* Baylor University, Armstrong Browning Library, Waco TX

Patton, Andy, *Instr,* Toronto School of Art, Toronto ON (S)

Patton, Larry, *Dean,* Butler County Community College, Art Dept, El Dorado KS (S)

Patton, Rachel, *Mus Shop Mgr,* Olana State Historic Site, Hudson NY

Patton, Tom, *Prof,* California State University, Chico, Department of Art & Art History, Chico CA (S)

Patula, Timothy A, *Dir of Design,* Chicago Athenaeum, Museum of Architecture & Design, Galena IL

Patzlaff, Kris, *Pres,* Society of North American Goldsmiths, Eugene OR

Patzlaff, Kris, *Prof,* Humboldt State University, College of Arts & Humanities, Art Dept, Arcata CA (S)

Pauckner, Jenny, *Asst Prof Art History,* Marian University, Visual Arts Dept, Indianapolis IN (S)

Paul, Chantel, *Curatorial Asst,* Museum of Photographic Arts, Edmund L. and Nancy K Dubois Library, San Diego CA

Paul, Eli, *Dir,* Liberty Memorial Museum & Archives, The National Museum of World War I, Kansas City MO

Paul, Gayle, *Cur,* Portsmouth Museums, Courthouse Galleries, Portsmouth VA

Paul, Janie, *Asst Prof,* University of Michigan, Ann Arbor, School of Art & Design, Ann Arbor MI (S)

Paul, Rob, *Archivist,* University of Saskatchewan, Diefenbaker Canada Centre, Saskatoon SK

Paul, Sylvanus, *Colls Asst,* School for Advanced Research (SAR), Indian Arts Research Center, Santa Fe NM

Paul, Tanya, *Cur European Art,* Philbrook Museum of Art, Tulsa OK

Pauley, Caren, *Mus Vis Svcs Coordr,* The Society of the Cincinnati at Anderson House, Washington DC

Pauley, Ed, *CEO & Exec Dir,* The Cultural Center of Fine Arts, Art Gallery, Parkersburg WV

Pauley, Edward E, *Dir,* Ohio University, Kennedy Museum of Art, Athens OH

Pauley, Steve, *Instr,* North Hennepin Community College, Art Dept, Brooklyn Park MN (S)

Paulin, Luc, *Dir Craft School,* New Brunswick College of Craft & Design, Fredericton NB (S)

Paulin, Luc, *Prin,* New Brunswick College of Craft & Design, Gallery, Fredericton NB

Paulitzky, Barbara, *Trustee,* Brooklyn Historical Society, Brooklyn OH

Paulk, Ann, *Vis Asst Prof,* Hamline University, Dept of Studio Arts & Art History, Saint Paul MN (S)

Paulsen, Richard, *Chmn,* Elmhurst College, Art Dept, Elmhurst IL (S)

Paulson, Alan, *Prof,* Gettysburg College, Dept of Visual Arts, Gettysburg PA (S)

Paulson, Wesley E, *Pres,* Maryland College of Art & Design, Silver Spring MD (S)

Pauly, Lauren, *Mktg & Events Coordr,* Captain Forbes House Museum, Milton MA

Pautler, Charles D, *Historic Site Mgr,* Charles A Lindbergh Historic Site, Little Falls MN

Pavelec, Karen Marie, *Exec Dir,* Maude Kerns, Eugene OR (S)

Pavlock, Paul, *Instr,* Marylhurst University, Art Dept, Marylhurst OR (S)

Pavlos, Laurie, *Mem & Website Mgr,* Lyme Art Association, Inc, Old Lyme CT

Pavlovic, Milutin, *Designer & Preparator,* Telfair Museums' Jepson Center for the Arts Library, Telfair Academy of Arts & Sciences Library, Savannah GA

Pavone, Julia, *Dir & Cur,* Alexey von Schlippe Gallery of Art, Groton CT

Pawloski, Carole, *Visual Resource Librn,* Eastern Michigan University, Art Dept Slide Collection, Ypsilanti MI

Pawlowicz, Peter, *Assoc Prof,* East Tennessee State University, College of Arts and Sciences, Dept of Art & Design, Johnson City TN (S)

Paxton, Sue Ellen, *Deputy Dir of Collections & Programs,* Indianapolis Museum of Art, Indianapolis IN

Payne, Christopher, *Chmn,* Huntingdon College, Dept of Art, Montgomery AL (S)

Payne, Daniel, *Head Reference, Information & Access Svcs,* OCAD University, Dorothy H Hoover Library, Toronto ON

Payne, Darien, *Graphics Instr,* Monterey Peninsula College, Art Dept/Art Gallery, Monterey CA (S)

Payne, Jennifer Cover, *Pres,* Cultural Alliance of Greater Washington, Washington DC

Payne, Suzanne, *Pres,* Minneapolis Institute of Arts, Friends of the Institute, Minneapolis MN

Payne, Thomas, *Dept Head,* Wartburg College, Dept of Art, Waverly IA (S)

Payson, Caroline, *Educ Dir,* Cooper-Hewitt National Design Museum, Smithsonian Institution, New York NY

Pazcoguin, Melissa, *Exec Asst,* The Art School at Old Church, Demarest NJ (S)

Peacock, Jan, *Dir MFA Program,* Nova Scotia College of Art & Design, Halifax NS (S)

Peague, Ed, *Head Librn,* University of Oregon, Architecture & Allied Arts Library, Eugene OR

Peak, Elizabeth, *Assoc Prof,* Georgia Southern University, Dept of Art, Statesboro GA (S)

Peak, Marianne, *Supt,* Adams National Historic Park, Quincy MA

Peak, Pamela, *Chmn,* Charleston Southern University, Dept of Language & Visual Art, Charleston SC (S)

Peake, James, *Educ Coordr,* Firelands Association for the Visual Arts, Oberlin OH

Pear, William H, *Historian,* Nichols House Museum, Inc, Boston MA

Pearce, A Blake, *Acting Head Art Dept,* Valdosta State University, Art Gallery, Valdosta GA

Pearce, A Blake, *Dept Head,* Valdosta State University, Dept of Art, Valdosta GA (S)

Pearce, Anne, *Gallery Dir,* Rockhurst University, Dept of Communication & Fine Arts, Kansas City MO (S)

Pearce, Donald, *VChmn,* Town of Cummington Historical Commission, Kingman Tavern Historical Museum, Cummington MA

Pearce, John N, *Dir,* James Monroe, James Monroe Memorial Library, Fredericksburg VA

Pearce, Michael, *Asst Prof,* California Lutheran University, Art Dept, Thousand Oaks CA (S)

Pearce-Adashkevich, Vladimir, *Workshop Coordr,* Villanova University Art Gallery, The Art Gallery, Villanova PA

Pearlman, Alison, *Assoc Prof,* California State Polytechnic University, Pomona, Department of Art, Pomona CA (S)

Pearlman, Eden Juron, *Cur,* Evanston Historical Society, Charles Gates Dawes House, Evanston IL

Pearlstein, Elinor, *Assoc Cur Chinese Art,* The Art Institute of Chicago, Department of Asian Art, Chicago IL

Pearson, Arla Mae, *Board Mem,* Cambridge Museum, Cambridge NE

Pearson, Barry, *Dir,* Millikin University, Perkinson Gallery, Decatur IL

Pearson, Clifton, *Chmn,* University of Montevallo, College of Fine Arts, Montevallo AL (S)

Pearson, Dana, *Dir Library Svcs,* North Central Texas College, Library, Gainesville TX

Pearson, David, *Deputy Dir,* Columbia River Maritime Museum, Astoria OR

Pearson, Faye, *Treas,* Kings County Historical Society & Museum, Hampton NB

Pearson, Gary, *Assoc Prof (Visual Art),* University of British Columbia Okanagan, Dept of Creative Studies, Kelowna BC (S)

Pearson, Gary, *Instr,* Ricks College, Dept of Art, Rexburg ID (S)

Pearson, James, *Coll Mgr,* Beloit College, Wright Museum of Art, Beloit WI

Pearson, Jason, *Educ Coordr,* Rochester Art Center, Rochester MN

Pearson, Jim, *Prof,* Vincennes University Junior College, Humanities Art Dept, Vincennes IN (S)

Pearson, John, *Prof,* Oberlin College, Dept of Art, Oberlin OH (S)

Pearson, Sally, *VPres Merchandise,* The Metropolitan Museum of Art, New York NY

Pease, Brian, *Historic Site Mgr,* Minnesota Historical Society, Minnesota State Capitol Historic Site, St Paul MN

Pease, Mark, *Asst Prof,* Southern Illinois University, School of Art & Design, Carbondale IL (S)

Pec, Steve, *Librn,* Greene County Historical Society, Bronck Museum, Coxsackie NY

Pecchio, Pamela, *Asst Prof Studio Art,* University of Virginia, McIntire Dept of Art, Charlottesville VA (S)

Pecimon, Sandy, *Bus Mgr,* The Summit County Historical Society of Akron, OH, Akron OH

Peck, Judith, *Prof,* Ramapo College of New Jersey, School of Contemporary Arts, Mahwah NJ (S)

Peck, Kevin, *Events Coordr,* Northern Virginia Fine Arts Association, The Athenaeum, Alexandria VA

Peck, Nathan, *Instr,* Saint Xavier University, Dept of Art & Design, Chicago IL (S)

Peckham, Cynthia, *Cur,* Sandy Bay Historical Society & Museums, Sewall Scripture House-Old Castle, Rockport MA

Peckham, Mark, *Dir,* New York State Office of Parks, Recreation and Historic Preservation, Bureau of Historic Sites, Waterford NY

Peckham Allen, Kathleen, *Mus Educator,* Seattle Art Museum, Dorothy Stimson Bullitt Library, Seattle WA

Peckman, Beth, *Asst Cur,* Temple University, Slide Library, Philadelphia PA

Peden, Susan, *Educ Coordr,* Henry Sheldon Museum of Vermont History and Research Center, Middlebury VT

Pedersen, Jennifer, *Registrar,* National Archives & Records Administration, Herbert Hoover Presidential Library - Museum, West Branch IA

Pedersen, Morrie, *Chmn,* Fort Steilacoom Community College, Fine Arts Dept, Lakewood WA (S)

Pederson, Curt, *Cur,* American Swedish Institute, Minneapolis MN

Pederson, Ron, *Chmn Dept & Prof,* Aquinas College, Art Dept, Grand Rapids MI (S)

Pedone, Francis, *Dir Operations,* Worcester Art Museum, Worcester MA

Pedros, Natasha, *Dir Outreach & Publ,* Niagara Artists' Company, St Catharines ON

Pedroso, Marco, *Assoc Dir,* Roy Boyd, Chicago IL

Peeler, Diedre, *Mus Store Mgr,* Maitland Art Center, Maitland FL

Peeler, Dierdra, *Mus Store Mgr & Receptionist,* Maitland Art Center, Library, Maitland FL

Peer, Charles, *Head Dept,* John Brown University, Art Dept, Siloam Springs AR (S)

Peery, Michael, *Instr,* Woodstock School of Art, Inc, Woodstock NY (S)

Peffer, John, *Assoc Prof Art History,* Ramapo College of New Jersey, School of Contemporary Arts, Mahwah NJ (S)

Peglau, Michael, *Dept Chmn,* Drew University, Art Dept, Madison NJ (S)

Pehler, Jordan, *Educ Dir,* Custer County Art & Heritage Center, Miles City MT

Peihl, Mark, *Archivist,* Historical and Cultural Society of Clay County, Hjemkomst Center, Moorhead MN

Peimer, Jordan, *Prog Dir,* Hebrew Union College, Skirball Cultural Center, Los Angeles CA

Peiser, Judy, *Exec Dir,* Center for Southern Folklore, Memphis TN

Peitz, Doris, *Financial Bus Mgr,* Paine Art Center & Gardens, Oshkosh WI

Pekala, Robert J, *Preparator,* University of Mississippi, University Museum & Historic Houses, Oxford MS

Pekarsky, Melvin H, *Prof,* Stony Brook University, College of Arts & Sciences, Dept of Art, Stony Brook NY (S)

Pelasky Hout, Jacqueline, *Art Image Cur & Developer,* Denison University, Slide Library, Granville OH

Pelfrey, Bob, *Chmn Fine Arts Div & Instr,* Cuesta College, Art Dept, San Luis Obispo CA (S)

Pelizzari, M Antonella, *Prof,* City University of New York, PhD Program in Art History, New York NY (S)

Pelkey, Brenda Francis, *Dir & Prof,* University of Windsor, Visual Arts, Windsor ON (S)

Pell, Rich, *Vis Assoc Prof,* University of Michigan, Ann Arbor, School of Art & Design, Ann Arbor MI (S)

Pellcrito, Marlene, *Instr,* Saginaw Valley State University, Dept of Art & Design, University Center MI (S)

Pellegrin, Maurizio, *Dir School,* National Academy School, New York NY (S)

Pellegrin, Maurizio, *School Dir,* National Academy Museum & School, New York NY

Pellegrino, Karen, *Admin Asst,* York University, Art Gallery of York University, Toronto ON

Pelletier, Carol, *Assoc Prof,* West Virginia Wesleyan College, Art Dept, Buckhannon WV (S)

Pelletier, Carol, *Chair, Fine Arts,* Endicott College, School of Visual & Performing Arts, Beverly MA (S)

Pelletier, Denise, *Vis Asst Prof,* Connecticut College, Dept of Art, New London CT (S)

Pelletier, Michel, *Dir Mktg,* McCord Museum of Canadian History, Montreal PQ

Pelletier, Nicole, *Adminr Asst/Receptionist/Document Orders,* Royal Architectural Institute of Canada, Ottawa ON

Pellum, Frederick, *Asst Prof,* Elizabeth City State University, School of Arts & Humanities, Dept of Art, Elizabeth City NC (S)

Pelrine, Christopher, *Opers Mgr,* Intermuseum Conservation Association, Cleveland OH

Pelrine, Diane, *Assoc Dir Curatorial Services & Cur African & Oceanic Pre-Columbian Art,* Indiana University, Art Museum, Bloomington IN

Peltier, Cynthia, *Operations Mgr,* Bucknell University, Edward & Marthann Samek Art Gallery, Lewisburg PA

Peluso, Robert, *Gen Educ,* Art Institute of Pittsburgh, Pittsburgh PA (S)

Pelvit, Leann, *Admin Asst,* MonDak Heritage Center, History Library, Sidney MT

Pena, Alejandra, *Deputy Dir,* Museo de Arte de Ponce, The Luis A Ferre Foundation Inc, Ponce PR

Pena, Alejandra, *Deputy Dir,* Museo de Arte de Ponce, Library, Ponce PR

Pena, Alejandra, *Deputy Dir,* Museo de Arte de Ponce, The Luis A Ferre Foundation Inc, Ponce PR

Pena, Alejandra, *Deputy Dir,* Museo de Arte de Ponce, Library, Ponce PR

Pena, Annie, *Coll Asst,* Hostos Center for the Arts & Culture, Bronx NY

Penafiel, Guillermo, *Prof,* University of Wisconsin-Stevens Point, Dept of Art & Design, Stevens Point WI (S)

Pena Moskin, Mary, *Museum Shop Mgr,* National Hispanic Cultural Center, Art Museum, Albuquerque NM

Pence, David, *Industrial Design Technology,* Art Institute of Pittsburgh, Pittsburgh PA (S)

Pendell, David, *Prof,* University of Utah, Dept of Art & Art History, Salt Lake City UT (S)

Pender, Michael R, *Trustee,* J.M.W. Turner Museum, Sarasota FL

Pendergrass, Candice, *Dir Mktg & Mem,* Fresno Metropolitan Museum, Fresno CA

Pendergrass, Gayle, *Instr,* Arkansas State University, Dept of Art, State University AR (S)

Pendleton, Belle, *Prof,* Christopher Newport University, Dept of Fine Performing Arts, Newport News VA (S)

Pendleton, Debbie, *Asst Dir Pub Svcs,* Alabama Department of Archives & History, Museum of Alabama, Montgomery AL

Pendleton, Edith, *Head Dept Fine & Performing Arts,* Edison Community College, Gallery of Fine Arts, Fort Myers FL (S)

Pener, Syndey, *Adjunct Prof Fine Art,* Johnson County Community College, Fine Arts Dept & Art History Dept, Overland Park KS (S)

Penfield, Lenore, *Gallery Dir,* Pennsylvania College of Technology, The Gallery at Penn College, Williamsport PA (S)

Penhall, Michele M, *Cur Photographs & Prints,* University of New Mexico, University of New Mexico Art Museum, Albuquerque NM

Penick, Pamela, *Exec Dir,* Arts & Humanities Council of Tuscaloosa, Junior League Gallery, Tuscaloosa AL

Peniston, William, *Librn,* Newark Museum Association, The Newark Museum, Newark NJ

Penman, Evelyn, *Cur,* Saint Bonaventure University, Regina A Quick Center for the Arts, Saint Bonaventure NY

Penn, Beverley, *Prof,* Texas State University - San Marcos, Dept of Art and Design, San Marcos TX (S)

Penn-Goetsch, Christina, *Chmn Dept Art & Lectr in Art,* Cornell College, Peter Paul Luce Gallery, Mount Vernon IA

Penney, David, *Cur Native American Art,* Detroit Institute of Arts, Detroit MI

Pennington, Claudia, *Exec Dir,* Key West Art & Historical Society, East Martello Museum & Gallery, Key West FL

Pennington, Julia, *Cur,* Turtle Bay Exploration Park, Redding CA

Pennington, Robert, *Registrar & Colls Mgr,* University of Tennessee, McClung Museum of Natural History & Culture, Knoxville TN

Penny, John, *Adjunct Faculty,* University of Maryland, Baltimore County, Imaging & Digital Arts (IMDA), Dept of Visual Arts, Baltimore MD (S)

Penny, Simon, *Prof Robotic Sculpture, Critical Theory,* University of California, Irvine, Studio Art Dept, Irvine CA (S)

Pentangelo, John, *Cur,* Naval War College Museum, Newport RI

Penuel, Jaime, *Lectr,* North Dakota State University, Division of Fine Arts, Fargo ND (S)

Peonie, Ann M, *Exec Dir,* Mohawk Valley Heritage Association, Inc, Walter Elwood Museum, Amsterdam NY

Pepall, Rosalynd, *Cur Non-Canadian Decorative Arts,* Montreal Museum of Fine Arts, Montreal PQ

Pepe, Art, *Screen Printing Instr,* Locust Street Neighborhood Art Classes, Inc, Buffalo NY (S)

Pepich, Bruce, *CEO,* Racine Art Museum, Racine WI

Pepich, Bruce W, *Dir,* Wustum Museum Art Association, Racine WI

Pepich, Bruce W, *Dir,* Wustum Museum Art Association, Charles A Wustum Museum of Fine Arts, Racine WI

Pepich, Bruce W, *Dir,* Wustum Museum Art Association, Wustum Art Library, Racine WI

Peppe, Dee, *Vis Asst Prof,* Colby College, Art Dept, Waterville ME (S)

Pepper, James Henry, *Pres & CEO,* Heard Museum, Billie Jane Baguley Library and Archives, Phoenix AZ

Pepper, Jerold L, *Librn,* The Adirondack Historical Association, The Adirondack Museum, Blue Mountain Lake NY

Pepper, Jerold L, *Librn,* The Adirondack Historical Association, Library, Blue Mountain Lake NY

Pepper Henry, James, *Dir,* Anchorage Museum at Rasmuson Center, Anchorage AK

Perakis, Stephen, *Gallery Asst,* Richard M Ross Art Museum at Wesleyan University, Delaware OH

Perbeck, David, *Dir Opers,* Hill-Stead Museum, Farmington CT

Percy, Ann B, *Cur Drawings,* Philadelphia Museum of Art, Main Building, Philadelphia PA

Percy, Ingrid, *Asst Prof,* Memorial University of Newfoundland, Division of Fine Arts, Visual Arts Program, Corner Brook NF (S)

Pereira, Michael, *Artist in Residence,* Fondo del Sol, Visual Art & Media Center, Washington DC

Perera, Diana, *Coordr Sales,* Guilde canadienne des metiers d'art, Canadian Guild of Crafts, Montreal PQ

Peres, Michael, *Chmn Biomedical Photo Communs,* Rochester Institute of Technology, School of Photographic Arts & Sciences, Rochester NY (S)

Perez, Mabel, *Mgr External Relations,* National YoungArts Foundation, Miami FL

Perez, Myrna Z, *Develop Mem,* Museo de Arte de Puerto Rico, San Juan PR

Perez, Myrna Z, *Develop Mem,* Museo de Arte de Puerto Rico, San Juan PR

Perez, Pablo, *European Art Asst Cur,* Museo de Arte de Ponce, The Luis A Ferre Foundation Inc, Ponce PR

Perez, Pablo, *European Art Asst Cur,* Museo de Arte de Ponce, The Luis A Ferre Foundation Inc, Ponce PR

Perez, Pamela, *Admin Dean, Junior School,* Museum of Fine Arts, Houston, Glassell School of Art, Houston TX (S)

Perez, Suzanne, *Instr,* Tarrant County College, Art Dept, Hurst TX (S)

Perez-Gomez, Alberto, *Prof,* McGill University, School of Architecture, Montreal PQ (S)

Perin, Dorothee, *Educ Outreach Coordr,* Tufts University, Tufts University Art Gallery, Medford MA

Perkins, Abigail, *Office Mgr,* Noah Webster House, Inc, Noah Webster House & West Hartford Historical Society, West Hartford CT

Perkins, Allison C, *Exec Dir,* Reynolda House Museum of American Art, Winston-Salem NC

Perkins, Beverly N, *Field Serv Officer,* Balboa Art Conservation Center, San Diego CA

Perkins, Cynthia, *Assoc Prof,* Del Mar College, Art Dept, Corpus Christi TX (S)

Perkins, Douglas, *Admin Opers Mgr,* Middlebury College, Museum of Art, Middlebury VT

Perkins, Frank, *Facilities Mgr,* Staten Island Museum, Staten Island NY

Perkins, Jill, *Interiors Admin,* National Museum of American Illustration, Newport RI

Perkins, Jon, *Treas,* Livingston County Historical Society, Museum, Geneseo NY

Perkins, Kendall, *Educ Mgr,* Lyme Art Association, Inc, Old Lyme CT

Perkins, Phyllis, *VPres,* Southern Lorain County Historical Society, Spirit of '76 Museum, Elyria OH

Perkins, Scott, *Dir Preservation,* Western Pennsylvania Conservancy, Fallingwater, Mill Run PA

Perkins, Stephen, *Acad Cur of Art,* University of Wisconsin, Green Bay, Lawton Gallery, Green Bay WI

Perkins, Stephen, *Exec Dir,* Bennington Museum, Bennington VT

Perkins-McGuinness, Margaret, *Dir External Affairs,* University of Kansas, Spencer Museum of Art, Lawrence KS

Perkinson, Stephen, *Asst Prof,* Bowdoin College, Art Dept, Brunswick ME (S)

Perlin, Alana, *Digital Media Prog,* Merced College, Arts Division, Merced CA (S)

Perlman, Bill, *VPres,* Women's Interart Center, Inc, Interart Gallery, New York NY

Perlman, Liz, *Prog Coordr,* Columbia University, School of the Arts, Division of Visual Arts, New York NY (S)

Perloneo, Marie, *Instr,* Mount Mary College, Art & Design Division, Milwaukee WI (S)

Perlov, Diane, *Deputy Dir Exhib,* California Science Center, Los Angeles CA

Perlus, Barry, *Assoc Dean, Assoc Prof,* Cornell University, Dept of Art, Ithaca NY (S)

Permahos, Susan, *Dir,* Springfield Free Public Library, Donald B Palmer Museum, Springfield NJ

Perrault, Nathalie, *Inter Mag Mgr,* Les Editions Intervention, Inter-Le Lieu, Documentation Center, Quebec PQ

Perret, Marguerite, *Assoc Prof,* Washburn University of Topeka, Dept of Art, Topeka KS (S)

Perrill, Elizabeth, *Prof,* University of North Carolina at Greensboro, Art Dept, Greensboro NC (S)

Perrin, Ralph W, *Dean Div Arts, Commun & Soc Sciences,* Shasta College, Arts, Communications & Social Sciences Division, Redding CA (S)

Perron, Margot, *Dir Educ,* Wave Hill, Bronx NY

Perron, Michel, *Dir,* Societe des Musees Quebecois, Montreal PQ

Perron, Mireille, *Acad Head Liberal Studies,* Alberta College of Art & Design, Calgary AB (S)

Perron, Nicole, *Dir Mus,* Musee des Augustines de l'Hotel Dieu de Quebec, Quebec PQ

Perron, Nicole, *Dir Mus,* Musee des Augustines de l'Hotel Dieu de Quebec, Archive, Quebec PQ

Perron-Croteau, Lise, *Dir Bus Planning,* Department of Canadian Heritage, Canadian Conservation Institute, Ottawa ON

Perry, Adam, *Sr Prog Dir,* Arts Midwest, Minneapolis MN

Perry, Carole, *Exec Dir,* Edward Hopper, Nyack NY

Perry, Elizabeth, *Assoc Prof,* Framingham State College, Art Dept, Framingham MA (S)

Perry, Eve, *Asst Registrar,* Museum for African Art, New York NY

Perry, Frances, *Pres Mus Bd Trustees,* Sheldon Museum & Cultural Center, Inc, Sheldon Museum & Cultural Center, Haines AK

Perry, Karen, *Asst to Dir Admin & Develop,* Hermitage Foundation Museum, Norfolk VA

Perry, Karen, *Asst to Dir Admin & Develop,* Hermitage Foundation Museum, Library, Norfolk VA

Perry, Mary, *Instr,* Appalachian State University, Dept of Art, Boone NC (S)

Perry, Michelle, *Admin Asst,* University of Mississippi, University Museum & Historic Houses, Oxford MS

Perry, Nancy S, *Dir,* Portsmouth Museums, Courthouse Galleries, Portsmouth VA

Perry, Rachel, *Cur Fine Arts,* Indiana State Museum, Indianapolis IN

Perry, Stephanie, *Gen Educ,* Art Institute of Pittsburgh, Pittsburgh PA (S)

Perry, Steven, *Dean,* Ramapo College of New Jersey, School of Contemporary Arts, Mahwah NJ (S)

Perry, Susan L, *Dir,* Mount Holyoke College, Art Library, South Hadley MA

Perry, Wendy, *Dir Devel,* Heritage Museums & Gardens, Sandwich MA

Perryman, Tom, *Instr,* Lenoir Rhyne College, Dept of Art, Hickory NC (S)

Persanti, Heather, *Sr Cur,* The Contemporary Austin, Austin TX

Pershey, Ed, *Dir Mus Servs,* Western Reserve Historical Society, Library, Cleveland OH

Person, Robin Seage, *Exec Dir,* Cottonlandia Museum, Greenwood MS

Pertl, Susan, *Cur,* McDonald's Corporation, Art Collection, Oak Brook IL

Pesanti, Heather, *Cur,* The Buffalo Fine Arts Academy, Albright-Knox Art Gallery, Buffalo NY

Pesenti, Allegra, *Cur,* University of California, Los Angeles, Grunwald Center for the Graphic Arts at Hammer Museum, Los Angeles CA

Pesesky, Jill, *Cur Educ,* Agecroft Association, Museum, Richmond VA

Peshek, Brian, *Instr,* Pierce College, Art Dept, Woodland Hills CA (S)

Pessa, Joanna, *Res Prog Coordr,* Philipse Manor Hall State Historic Site, Yonkers NY

Pestel, Michael, *Asst Prof,* Chatham College, Fine & Performing Arts, Pittsburgh PA (S)

Pestel, Michael, *Dir,* Chatham College, Art Gallery, Pittsburgh PA

Pestrak, Judy, *Exec Dir,* Manitoba Association of Architects, Winnipeg MB

Peter, August, *Preparator & Exhib Designer,* Museum of Wisconsin Art, West Bend WI

Peter, Carolyn, *Dir,* Loyola Marymount University, Laband Art Gallery, Los Angeles CA

Peters, Allison, *Dir Exhibs,* Hyde Park Art Center, Chicago IL

Peters, Belinda A, *Chmn Dept,* Clark-Atlanta University, School of Arts & Sciences, Atlanta GA (S)

Peters, John, *Gallery Coordr,* Augustana College, Eide-Dalrymple Gallery, Sioux Falls SD

Peters, John, *Instr,* Augustana College, Art Dept, Sioux Falls SD (S)

Phillips, Kathryn D, *Librn,* Freer Gallery of Art & Arthur M Sackler Gallery, Library, Washington DC

Phillips, Kathy, *Pres,* Coquille Valley Art Association, Coquille OR

Phillips, Kenneth E, *Aerospace Cur,* California Science Center, Los Angeles CA

Phillips, Larry, *Comm Rel/Spec Proj Officer,* Institute of American Indian Arts, Museum of Contemporary Native Arts, Santa Fe NM

Phillips, Larry, *Spec Proj & Community Relations,* Institute of American Indian Arts, Museum of Contemporary Native Arts, Santa Fe NM (S)

Phillips, Lisa, *Dir,* New Museum of Contemporary Art, The Soho Center Library, New York NY

Phillips, Lynne, *Coll Mgr,* Chesapeake Bay Maritime Museum, Howard I Chapelle Memorial Library, Saint Michaels MD

Phillips, Patricia, *Interim Assoc Provost,* Rhode Island School of Design, Providence RI (S)

Phillips, Patsy, *Dir,* Institute of American Indian Arts, Museum of Contemporary Native Arts, Santa Fe NM

Phillips, Patsy, *Dir,* Institute of American Indian Arts, Museum of Contemporary Native Arts, Santa Fe NM (S)

Phillips, Quitman E, *Prof,* University of Wisconsin, Madison, Dept of Art History, Madison WI (S)

Phillips, Rebecca, *Registrar,* Pine Bluff/Jefferson County Historical Museum, Pine Bluff AR

Phillips, Richard, *Asst Prof Art History,* University of Texas Pan American, Art Dept, Edinburg TX (S)

Phillips, Robert, *Pres Board Trustees,* Roswell Museum & Art Center, Roswell NM

Phillips, Ruth, *Dir & Prof,* University of British Columbia, Museum of Anthropology, Vancouver BC

Phillips, Sandra, *Cur Photog,* San Francisco Museum of Modern Art, San Francisco CA

Phillips, Stephen Bennett, *Dir,* Federal Reserve Board, Art Gallery, Washington DC

Phillips, Susan, *Prof,* Waynesburg College, Dept of Fine Arts, Waynesburg PA (S)

Phillipson, Thomas, *Regional Svcs Coordr,* Portland Art Museum, Northwest Film Center, Portland OR

Philpot, Eloise, *Asst Prof,* Radford University, Art Dept, Radford VA (S)

Phinney, Gail, *Dir Educ Progs,* Palos Verdes Art Center/Beverly G. Alpay Center for Arts Education, Rancho Palos Verdes CA

Phippen, Will, *Dir Mus Coll Svcs,* Peabody Essex Museum, Salem MA

Phipps, Vickie, *Asst Prof,* Augustana College, Art Dept, Rock Island IL (S)

Phong, Ann, *Lectr,* California State Polytechnic University, Pomona, Department of Art, Pomona CA (S)

Piasecki, Jane, *VPres Finance,* Natural History Museum of Los Angeles County, Los Angeles CA

Piasecki, Sara, *Photo Archivist,* Anchorage Museum at Rasmuson Center, Atwood Alaska Resource Center, Anchorage AK

Piasentin, Joe, *Prof,* Pepperdine University, Seaver College, Dept of Art, Malibu CA (S)

Piastuck, Gina, *Dept Head,* East Hampton Library, Long Island Collection, East Hampton NY

Piatt, Margaret, *Pres & CEO,* Piatt Castles, West Liberty OH

Piazza, Paul J, *Controller,* George Eastman, Rochester NY

Picano, John, *Pub Rels,* Yesteryear Village, West Palm Beach FL

Picco, Ronald, *Prof,* College of Santa Fe, Art Dept, Santa Fe NM (S)

Piccolo, Ellen, *Sec,* Prince Street Gallery, New York NY

Piccuirro, Jeneen, *Instr,* American University, Dept of Art, New York NY (S)

Piche, Thomas, *Dir,* Daum Museum of Contemporary Art, Sedalia MO

Pickel, John, *Assoc Prof,* Wake Forest University, Dept of Art, Winston-Salem NC (S)

Pickens, Donna, *Asst Cur Educ,* Montgomery Museum of Fine Arts, Montgomery AL

Pickens, Donna, *Asst Cur Educ,* Montgomery Museum of Fine Arts, Library, Montgomery AL

Pickens, Jeff, *Dir Facilities,* Arts Partnership of Greater Spartanburg, Inc, Chapman Cultural Center, Spartanburg SC

Pickering, Amy, *Visitor Svcs,* State University of New York at New Paltz, Samuel Dorsky Museum of Art, New Paltz NY

Pickering, Robert B, *Sr Cur,* University of Tulsa, Gilcrease Museum, Tulsa OK

Pickering-Carter, Yvonne, *Chairperson & Prof,* University of the District of Columbia, Dept of Mass Media, Visual & Performing Arts, Washington DC (S)

Pickford, Melissa, *Art Gallery Dir,* Monterey Peninsula College, Art Dept/Art Gallery, Monterey CA (S)

Picon, Carlos, *Cur In Charge,* The Metropolitan Museum of Art, New York NY

Piehl, Angela, *Assoc Prof,* Oklahoma State University, Department of Art, Graphic Design and Art History, Stillwater OK (S)

Piehl, Walter, *Art Dept Coordr,* Minot State University, Dept of Art, Division of Humanities, Minot ND (S)

Piejko, Alex, *Asst Prof,* Mohawk Valley Community College, Utica NY (S)

Piepenburg, Robert, *Chmn,* Oakland Community College, Art Dept, Farmington Hills MI (S)

Pier, Gwen P, *Exec Dir,* National Sculpture Society, New York NY

Pierce, Adrienne, *Mus Shop Mgr,* High Museum of Art, Atlanta GA

Pierce, Donna, *Frederick & Jan Mayer Cur Spanish Colonial Art,* Denver Art Museum, Denver CO

Pierce, Frederick S, *Chmn (V),* The American Film Institute, Center for Advanced Film & Television, Los Angeles CA (S)

Pierce, Greg, *Instr,* Columbia Basin College, Esvelt Gallery, Pasco WA (S)

Pierce, Judy, *Mktg Dir,* Cherokee Heritage Center, Park Hill OK

Piersol, Daniel, *Deputy Dir Progs,* Mississippi Museum of Art, Jackson MS

Pierson Ellingson, Susan, *Asst Prof,* Concordia College, Art Dept, Moorhead MN (S)

Pietrangeli, Jason, *Dir Fin & Opers,* Brooklyn Historical Society, Brooklyn NY

Pietsch, Theodore, *Cur Fishes,* University of Washington, Burke Museum of Natural History and Culture, Seattle WA

Piispanen, Ruth, *Dir Arts Educ,* Idaho Commission on the Arts, Boise ID

Pike, Jeffrey C, *Dean School,* Washington University, School of Art, Saint Louis MO (S)

Pike, Kermit J, *COO,* Western Reserve Historical Society, Cleveland OH

Pike, Kermit J, *COO,* Western Reserve Historical Society, Library, Cleveland OH

Pike, Paulita, *Pres,* The Art Institute of Chicago, Auxiliary Board of the Art Institute of Chicago, Chicago IL

Pilachowski, David, *Librn,* Williams College, Sawyer Library, Williamstown MA

Pilar, Jacqueline, *Cur,* Fresno Arts Center & Museum, Fresno CA

Pilatowicz, Grazyna W, *Chmn Interior Design,* Fashion Institute of Technology, Art & Design Division, New York NY (S)

Pilcher, Jerry, *Educ & Fundraising Coordr,* Visual Arts Center of Northwest Florida, Panama City FL

Pilgram, Suzanne, *Assoc Prof,* Georgian Court University, Dept of Art, Lakewood NJ (S)

Pilic, Patty, *Secy,* Mississippi Art Colony, Stoneville MS

Pillar, Marjorie, *Mus Educ Outreach Coordr,* Hofstra University, Hofstra University Museum, Hempstead NY

Pillod, Elizabeth, *Prof,* Oregon State University, Dept of Art, Corvallis OR (S)

Pillote, Lauren, *Dean Design & Communs Art,* Rocky Mountain College of Art & Design, Lakewood CO (S)

Pillow, Kirk, *Provost,* The University of the Arts, Rosenwald-Wolf Gallery, Philadelphia PA

Pillow, Kirk E, *Provost,* University of the Arts, Philadelphia Colleges of Art & Design, Performing Arts & Media & Communication, Philadelphia PA (S)

Pillsbury, Robert, *Pres,* Salmagundi Club, New York NY

Pina, Manuel, *Asst Prof,* University of British Columbia, Dept of Art History, Visual Art & Theory, Vancouver BC (S)

Pinales, Deena, *Mus Educ,* Springfield Museum of Art, Springfield OH

Pinales, Deena, *Mus Educ,* Springfield Museum of Art, Library, Springfield OH

Pinardi, Brenda, *Prof,* University of Massachusetts Lowell, Dept of Art, Lowell MA (S)

Pinckley, Donna, *Assoc Prof,* University of Central Arkansas, Department of Art, Conway AR (S)

Pindell, Howardena, *Prof,* Stony Brook University, College of Arts & Sciences, Dept of Art, Stony Brook NY (S)

Pindle, Arthur, *Instr,* Southern University in New Orleans, Fine Arts & Philosophy Dept, New Orleans LA (S)

Pine, Steven, *Conservator,* Museum of Fine Arts Houston, Bayou Bend Collection & Gardens, Houston TX

Pineau, Alain, *National Dir,* Canadian Conference of the Arts, Ottawa ON

Pinedo, Michelle, *Dir Merchandising & Traveling Progs,* Museum for African Art, New York NY

Pinette, Robert J, *Cur Herbarium,* Northern Maine Museum of Science, Presque Isle ME

Pingree, Nichole, *Finance Mgr,* Riverside Art Museum, Library, Riverside CA

Pingrey, Bradley, *Pres,* Washington County Museum of Fine Arts, Hagerstown MD

Pinkel, Sheila, *Prof,* Pomona College, Dept of Art & Art History, Claremont CA (S)

Pinkham, Ashley Peel, *Asst Dir,* The Print Center, Philadelphia PA

Pinkston, David, *Adjunct Prof,* University of Texas at Arlington, Art & Art History Department, Arlington TX (S)

Pinkston, Dorothy, *Dir Fin,* Staten Island Museum, Staten Island NY

Pinkston, Heidi, *Educ Coordr,* Piedmont Arts Association, Martinsville VA

Pinkston, Howell, *Instr,* Pierce College, Art Dept, Woodland Hills CA (S)

Pintado, Vanessa, *Asst Cur Rare Books & US,* The Hispanic Society of America, Museum & Library, New York NY

Pinto, John, *Prof,* Princeton University, Dept of Art & Archaeology, Princeton NJ (S)

Pinto, Vincent, *Sec,* Federation of Modern Painters & Sculptors, New York NY

Pintz, Joe, *Asst Prof,* University of Missouri - Columbia, Dept of Art, Columbia MO (S)

Piombino, Dante, *Multimedia & Web Design,* Art Institute of Pittsburgh, Pittsburgh PA (S)

Pion-Berlin, David, *Secy,* Latino Art Museum, Pomona CA

Pionati, Francis A, *Media Arts & Animation,* Art Institute of Pittsburgh, Pittsburgh PA (S)

Piper, Andre, *Asst Prof,* Emporia State University, Dept of Art, Emporia KS (S)

Piper, Clinton, *Mus Prog Asst,* Western Pennsylvania Conservancy, Fallingwater, Mill Run PA

Pipman, Mor, *Adj Assoc Prof,* College of Staten Island, Performing & Creative Arts Dept, Staten Island NY (S)

Pires, Wendy, *Cur Educ,* Dickinson College, The Trout Gallery, Carlisle PA

Piribeck, Jan, *Prof Digital & Foundation,* University of Southern Maine, Dept of Art, Gorham ME (S)

Pirosky, Daniel, *Assoc Prof,* Portland State University, Dept of Art, Portland OR (S)

Pirozzolo, Rick, *Exec Dir,* Arnot Art Museum, Elmira NY

Pirraglia, Diane, *Asst Educ Cur,* Sangre de Cristo Arts & Conference Center, Pueblo CO

Pirro, Louis, *Adjunct,* Idaho State University, Dept of Art & Pre-Architecture, Pocatello ID (S)

Pirtle, Kenneth, *Dept Head,* Amarillo College, Visual Art Dept, Amarillo TX (S)

Pisano, Dominick, *Aeronautics Dept,* National Air and Space Museum, Smithsonian Institution, Washington DC

Pisano, Jane, *Pres & Dir,* Natural History Museum of Los Angeles County, Los Angeles CA

Pisciotta, Henry, *Arts & Architecture Librn,* The Pennsylvania State University, Arts & Humanities Library, University Park PA

Pisciotta, Henry, *Arts & Architecture Librn,* The Pennsylvania State University, Architecture & Landscape Architecture Library, University Park PA

Pisha, Nikki, *Fine Arts Prog Asst,* Federal Reserve Board, Art Gallery, Washington DC

Pishkur, Frank, *Prof,* Missouri Southern State University, Dept of Art, Joplin MO (S)

Piskel, Annette, *Vis Instr Graphic Design,* Florida Atlantic University, D F Schmidt College of Arts & Letters Dept of Visual Arts & Art History, Boca Raton FL (S)

Pitard, Wayne, *Dir,* University of Illinois at Urbana-Champaign, Spurlock Museum, Champaign IL

Pitluga, Kurt, *Prof,* Slippery Rock University of Pennsylvania, Dept of Art, Slippery Rock PA (S)

Pitman, Bonnie, *Dir,* Dallas Museum of Art, Dallas TX

Pitman, Brian, *Instr,* Adrian College, Art & Design Dept, Adrian MI (S)

Pitt, Paul, *Prof,* Harding University, Dept of Art & Design, Searcy AR (S)

Pittenger, Charles, *Registrar,* The Speed Art Museum, Louisville KY

Pittman, John, *Chmn,* John Jay College of Criminal Justice, Dept of Art, Music & Philosophy, New York NY (S)

Pittman, Jude, *Prof 2D Art,* College of San Mateo, Creative Arts Dept, San Mateo CA (S)

Pittman, Kate, *Dir Opers,* Contemporary Art Center of Virginia, Virginia Beach VA

Pitts, Angela, *Instr,* Dallas Baptist University, Dept of Art, Dallas TX (S)

Pitts, Terence, *Dir,* Cedar Rapids Museum of Art, Cedar Rapids IA

Pitts, Tom R, *Assoc Prof Art History,* Lander University, College of Arts & Humanities, Greenwood SC (S)

Pivarnyik, Roslyn, *Pres,* Niagara Artists' Company, St Catharines ON

Pivovar, Ronald A, *Chmn Dept,* Thiel College, Dept of Art, Greenville PA (S)

Pixley, Mary, *Cur European & American Art,* University of Missouri, Museum of Art & Archaeology, Columbia MO

Pizer, Alan, *Asst Prof,* Texas State University - San Marcos, Dept of Art and Design, San Marcos TX (S)

Pizzo, Tony, *Exec Dir,* Ships of the Sea Maritime Museum, Savannah GA

Place-Gleason, Michelle, *Secy,* Warwick Museum of Art, Warwick RI

Plakias, Elaine, *Staff Asst,* Art Complex Museum, Carl A. Weyerhaeuser Library, Duxbury MA

Plante, Michael, *Assoc Prof,* Tulane University, Sophie H Newcomb Memorial College, New Orleans LA (S)

Plapler, Dina, *Chief Dev Officer,* Mark Twain, Hartford CT

Plascencia, Gustavo, *Asst Prof,* Lycoming College, Art Dept, Williamsport PA (S)

Platow, Raphaela, *Dir & Chief Cur,* Contemporary Arts Center, Cincinnati OH

Platt, Carol, *Asst Prof,* Brenau University, Art & Design Dept, Gainesville GA (S)

Platt, Melvin, *Dept Chmn & Prof,* University of Missouri - Columbia, Dept of Art, Columbia MO (S)

Platt, Ron, *Cur Modern & Contemporary Art,* Birmingham Museum of Art, Birmingham AL

Plaut, Anthony, *Prof,* Cornell College, Peter Paul Luce Gallery, Mount Vernon IA

Pleasants, Craig, *Artistic Dir,* Virginia Center for the Creative Arts, Amherst VA

Pleasants, Sheila Gully, *Dir Artists' Servs,* Virginia Center for the Creative Arts, Amherst VA

Pleasure, Lashey, *Office Asst,* History Museum of Mobile, Mobile AL

Plesch, Veronique, *Assoc Prof,* Colby College, Art Dept, Waterville ME (S)

Plosky, Charles, *Prof,* New Jersey City University, Art Dept, Jersey City NJ (S)

Plotkin, Edna Hibel, *Exec Trustee,* Edna Hibel, Hibel Museum of Art, Jupiter FL

Plotkin, Helene, *Dir Sales,* Edna Hibel, Hibel Museum of Art, Jupiter FL

Plourd, Katherine, *Dir Coll Svcs,* Chicago History Museum, Chicago IL

Plourde, Nelie, *Exec Dir,* UMLAUF Sculpture Garden & Museum, Austin TX

Plume, Kathy, *Secy,* City of Springdale, Shiloh Museum of Ozark History, Springdale AR

Plumlee, Janie, *Admin Asst & Mus Store Mgr,* Carson County Square House Museum, Panhandle TX

Plummer, Bruce, *Dean Library,* Becker College, William F Ruska Library, Worcester MA

Plummer, Jack, *Prof Emeritus,* University of Texas at Arlington, Art & Art History Department, Arlington TX (S)

Plummer, Johanna, *Dir Educ,* Wadsworth Atheneum Museum of Art, Hartford CT

Plummer Rohloff, Rebecca, *Asst Prof,* Salem State University, Art & Design Department, Salem MA (S)

Plunkett, Stephanie Haboush, *Deputy Dir & Chief Cur,* Norman Rockwell Museum, Stockbridge MA

Plyler, Anne, *Gallery Coordr,* James Prendergast, Jamestown NY

Poce, Patrick E, *Dir,* Eccles Community Art Center, Ogden UT

Pocius, Edward, *Cur Cartography,* Balzekas Museum of Lithuanian Culture, Chicago IL

Pocklington, Tom, *Pres,* Bonita Museum and Cultural Center, Bonita CA

Pockriss, Peter, *Dir Devel,* Historic Hudson Valley, Pocantico Hills NY

Pocock, Dan, *Asst Prof,* Indiana Wesleyan University, School of Arts & Humanities, Division of Art, Marion IN (S)

Poddar, Sandhini, *Asst Cur Asian Art,* Solomon R Guggenheim, New York NY

Podedworny, Carol, *Dir & Chief Cur,* McMaster University, McMaster Museum of Art, Hamilton ON

Podgajny, Stephen, *Dir,* Portland Public Library, Art - Audiovisual Dept, Portland ME

Podmaniczky, Christine B, *Assoc Cur NC Wyeth Collections,* Brandywine Conservancy, Brandywine River Museum, Chadds Ford PA

Poe, Michelle, *Educ Dir,* African American Museum of Iowa, Cedar Rapids IA

Poe, Robert H, *Assoc Prof Art,* Lander University, College of Arts & Humanities, Greenwood SC (S)

Poeschl, Paul, *Activities Coordr,* Oshkosh Public Museum, Oshkosh WI

Pogue, Ed, *Assoc Prof,* Bethany College, Mingenback Art Center, Lindsborg KS

Pogue, Ed, *Asst Prof,* Bethany College, Art Dept, Lindsborg KS (S)

Pohl, Frances, *Chmn & Prof,* Pomona College, Dept of Art & Art History, Claremont CA (S)

Pohlad, Mark, *Asst Prof,* DePaul University, Dept of Art, Chicago IL (S)

Pohle, Peter, *Asst Prof,* John Brown University, Art Dept, Siloam Springs AR (S)

Pohlkamp, Mark, *Lect,* University of Wisconsin-Stevens Point, Dept of Art & Design, Stevens Point WI (S)

Pohlman, Ken, *Designer,* Middlebury College, Museum of Art, Middlebury VT

Pohlman, Lynette, *Dir,* Iowa State University, Brunnier Art Museum, Ames IA

Poindexter, David, *Asst Prof,* University of Texas of Permian Basin, Dept of Art, Odessa TX (S)

Poindexter, Edith, *Cur,* Patrick Henry, Red Hill National Memorial, Brookneal VA

Poire, Danielle, *Conservation & Management Dir,* Musee de l'Amerique Francaise, Quebec PQ

Poirier, Francine, *Dir,* Museum for Textiles, Canada Aviation Museum, Ottawa ON

Poirier, Rose, *Mgr Programming,* New Brunswick Museum, Saint John NB

Poisaant, Margaret, *Pres (V),* Art League of Houston, Houston TX

Polachek, Sarah, *Events & Retail Oper Mgr,* University of Chicago, Smart Museum of Art, Chicago IL

Poland, Barbara, *Research Librn,* Warner Bros Studio Research Library, Burbank CA

Polenberg, Marcia, *Instr,* Barton County Community College, Fine Arts Dept, Great Bend KS (S)

Polesnak, Ronald, *Technical Dir,* State University of New York at Binghamton, Binghamton University Art Museum, Binghamton NY

Poley, Darren, *Head Pub Serv,* Lutheran Theological Seminary, Krauth Memorial Library, Philadelphia PA

Poli, Ed, *Gallery Mgr,* Malaspina College, Nanaimo Art Gallery, Nanaimo BC

Poliakov, Lev, *Asst Prof,* New York Institute of Technology, Fine Arts Dept, Old Westbury NY (S)

Polich, Debra, *Exec Dir,* Artrain, Ann Arbor MI

Poling, Jenna, *Music Dir,* The National Shrine of the North American Martyrs, Fultonville NY

Polirer, Sarah A, *Mgr,* CIGNA Corporation, CIGNA Art Collection, Bloomfield CT

Polishook, Mark, *Prof,* University of Maine at Augusta, College of Arts & Humanities, Augusta ME (S)

Polito, Ronald, *Assoc Prof,* University of Massachusetts - Boston, Art Dept, Boston MA (S)

Polk, May-Lin, *Mus Advisor,* Museums Association of Saskatchewan, Regina SK

Polk, Tom, *Assoc Prof Art History,* University of Georgia, Franklin College of Arts & Sciences, Lamar Dodd School of Art, Athens GA (S)

Pollack, Anat, *Assoc Prof,* University of South Florida, School The Arts, Tampa FL (S)

Pollan, Ellen, *Develop,* Bronx Council on the Arts, Longwood Arts Gallery @ Hostos, Bronx NY

Pollard, Frances, *Dir Lib Services,* Virginia Historical Society, Library, Richmond VA

Pollei, Dane, *Dir and Chief Cur,* Mabee-Gerrer Museum of Art, Shawnee OK

Polley, Brook, *Dir Develop,* Hunterdon Art Museum, Clinton NJ

Pollick, Marilyn, *Dir Devel,* University of Pennsylvania, Institute of Contemporary Art, Philadelphia PA

Pollman, Howard, *Dir External Affairs,* Pennsylvania Historical & Museum Commission, The State Museum of Pennsylvania, Harrisburg PA

Pollock, Janine, *Asst Head,* Free Library of Philadelphia, Rare Book Dept, Philadelphia PA

Polosa, Marina, *Educ & Pub Prog Coordr,* Concordia University, Leonard & Bina Ellen Art Gallery, Montreal PQ

Poloukhine, Olga, *Recording Sec,* New York Society of Women Artists, Inc, Westport CT

Polowy, Barbara, *Librn,* Smith College, Hillyer Art Library, Northampton MA

Polskin, Philippa, *Pres,* Ruder Finn Arts & Communications, Inc, New York NY

Pomeroy, Dan, *Dir Coll,* Tennessee State Museum, Nashville TN

Pomeroy, Dan, *Dir Coll,* Tennessee State Museum, Library, Nashville TN

Pomeroy, Jordana, *Exec Dir,* Louisiana State University, Museum of Art, Baton Rouge LA

Pomeroy Draper, Stacy, *Cur,* Rensselaer County Historical Society, Museum & Library, Troy NY

Pommer, Joyce, *Treas,* New York Society of Women Artists, Inc, Westport CT

Pompelia, Mark, *Visual Resources Librn,* Rhode Island School of Design, Fleet Library at RISD, Providence RI

Pon, Steve, *Exhib Supv,* San Francisco Museum of Modern Art, Artist Gallery, San Francisco CA

Ponce, Audra, *Opers Mgr,* Galeria de la Raza, Studio 24, San Francisco CA

Ponce, Magaly, *Asst Prof,* Bridgewater State College, Art Dept, Bridgewater MA (S)

Ponce de Leon, Carolina, *Dir,* Galeria de la Raza, Studio 24, San Francisco CA

Ponciroli, Susan, *Mus Shop Mgr,* Missouri Historical Society, Missouri History Museum, Saint Louis MO

Pond, Mandy, *Archivist,* Massillon Museum, Massillon OH

Pondelick, Chris, *Exec Dir,* Grants Pass Museum of Art, Grants Pass OR

Ponder, Anita, *Dir Educ,* Tubman African American Museum, Macon GA

Pondone, Marc, *Instr,* Solano Community College, Division of Fine & Applied Art & Behavioral Science, Fairfield CA (S)

Pongetti, Rachael, *Adj Instr,* University of West Florida, Dept of Art, Pensacola FL (S)

Ponikvar, Laura, *Image & Instruc Srvcs Librn,* Cleveland Institute of Art, Jessica Gund Memorial Library, Cleveland OH

Pontance, Rebecca, *Librn,* Museum of New Mexico, New Mexico Museum of Art, Santa Fe NM

Pontenello, Darlene, *Mem Coordr,* Kalamazoo Institute of Arts, Kalamazoo MI

Pontynen, Arthur, *Prof,* University of Wisconsin Oshkosh, Dept of Art, Oshkosh WI (S)

Poole, Barbara, *Treas,* Bromfield Art Gallery, Boston MA

Poole, Bill, *Dir,* Canadian Clay and Glass Gallery, Waterloo ON

Poole, Kristin, *Artistic Dir,* Sun Valley Center for the Arts, Dept of Fine Art, Sun Valley ID (S)

Poole, Mary, *Exec Dir,* Artspace Inc, Raleigh NC

Poole, Richard, *VPres,* Delaware Historical Society, Library, Wilmington DE

Poon, Bonnie, *Mgr Pub Prog,* University of California, Los Angeles, Fowler Museum at UCLA, Los Angeles CA

Poon, Elysia, *Prog Coordr,* School for Advanced Research (SAR), Indian Arts Research Center, Santa Fe NM

Poor, Robert, *Prof,* University of Minnesota, Minneapolis, Art History, Minneapolis MN (S)

Poore, Mark, *Instr,* Glendale Community College, Visual & Performing Arts Div, Glendale CA (S)

Popa, Amy Jo, *Asst Lectr,* Idaho State University, Dept of Art & Pre-Architecture, Pocatello ID (S)

Pope, Jennifer, *Develop Asst,* Montgomery Museum of Fine Arts, Montgomery AL

Pope, Karen, *Sr Lectr,* Baylor University - College of Arts and Sciences, Dept of Art, Waco TX (S)

Pope, Linda, *Dir,* University of California at Santa Cruz, Eloise Pickard Smith Gallery, Santa Cruz CA

Pope, Louise, *Assoc Prof,* Dakota State University, College of Liberal Arts, Madison SD (S)

Pope, Nancy, *Cur,* National Postal Museum, Smithsonian Institution, Washington DC

Popkin, Maggie, *Asst Prof,* Case Western Reserve University, Dept of Art History & Art, Cleveland OH (S)

Poplack, Robert, *Gallery Dir,* Notre Dame de Namur University, Wiegand Gallery, Belmont CA (S)

Poplawski, Tina, *Instr,* Toronto School of Art, Toronto ON (S)

Popovic, Milica, *Art Gallery Mgr,* Herrett Center for Arts & Sciences, Jean B King Art Gallery, Twin Falls ID

Popovich, George, *Dir Theater,* Henry Ford Community College, McKenzie Fine Art Ctr, Dearborn MI (S)

Popp, Zan, *Gallery Assoc,* Topeka & Shawnee County Public Library, Alice C Sabatini Gallery, Topeka KS

Poppenga, Carol, *Educ Dir,* Lewistown Art Center, Lewistown MT

Poppenhouse, Jerry, *Instr,* Oklahoma State University, Graphic Arts Dept, Visual Communications, Okmulgee OK (S)

Poras, E Linda, *Exec Dir,* The Brush Art Gallery & Studios, Lowell MA

Porcari, George, *Acquisitions Librn,* Art Center College of Design, James Lemont Fogg Memorial Library, Pasadena CA

Porch, Whitney, *Assoc Professional Specialist,* Southern Nazarene University, Art & Design Department, Bethany OK (S)

Porps, Ernest O, *Prof,* University of Colorado at Denver, College of Arts & Media Visual Arts Dept, Denver CO (S)

Porsild, Charlene, *Head Librn & Archivist,* Montana Historical Society, Library, Helena MT

Porta, Giogio, *Asst Prof,* Northern Virginia Community College, Art Dept, Annandale VA (S)

Porter, Alberta, *Pres,* Macartney House Museum, Oakland ME

Porter, Amy Jean, *Pub Rels,* Yale University, Yale University Art Gallery, New Haven CT

Porter, Andrea, *Registrar,* University of Pennsylvania, Graduate School of Fine Arts, Philadelphia PA (S)

Porter, Austin, *Vis Asst Prof,* Kenyon College, Art Dept, Gambier OH (S)

Porter, Carolyn, *Asst Dir Develop,* University of Texas, Dept of Art & Art History, Austin TX (S)

Porter, Daphne, *Treas,* Museum of African American Art, Los Angeles CA

Porter, David S, *Assoc Prof,* University of North Florida, Dept of Communications & Visual Arts, Jacksonville FL (S)

Porter, James, *Designer/Preparator,* Wichita State University, Ulrich Museum of Art, Wichita KS

Porter, Jeanne Chenault, *Assoc Prof Emeritus,* Pennsylvania State University, University Park, Dept of Art History, University Park PA (S)

Porter, Jenelle, *Cur,* Artists Space, Irving Sandler Artists File, New York NY

Porter, Jenelle, *Cur,* University of Pennsylvania, Institute of Contemporary Art, Philadelphia PA

Porter, Larry, *Assoc Prof,* Central State University, Dept of Art, Wilberforce OH (S)

Porter, Liz, *VPres,* Livingston County Historical Society, Museum, Geneseo NY

Porter, Marianetta, *Assoc Prof,* University of Michigan, Ann Arbor, School of Art & Design, Ann Arbor MI (S)

Porter, Matt, *Assoc Cur, Educ & School Programs,* Morris Museum of Art, Augusta GA

Porter, Michele, *Cur Coll,* Dacotah Prairie Museum, Ruth Bunker Memorial Library, Aberdeen SD

Porter, Robert F, *Fine Arts Chmn,* Queens College, Fine Arts Dept, Charlotte NC (S)

Porter, Ron, *Sr Lectr,* Vanderbilt University, Dept of Art, Nashville TN (S)

Porter, Stephanie, *Educ Officer,* City of Woodstock, Woodstock Art Gallery, Woodstock ON

Porter, Tom, *Instr,* Bismarck State College, Fine Arts Dept, Bismarck ND (S)

Porter Trubert, Eleanor, *Dir Develop,* Hunterdon Art Museum, Clinton NJ

Portnoy, Deidre, *VPres,* Wellfleet Historical Society & Museum, Inc, Wellfleet MA

Poruchnyk, Alexander, *Assoc Prof,* University of Manitoba, School of Art, Winnipeg MB (S)

Porzan, Robert, *Chm (V),* The Jewish Museum, New York NY

Posey, Laurel, *Dir Performing Arts,* South Carolina Arts Commission, Columbia SC

Poshek, Joe, *Div Dean,* Orange Coast College, Visual & Performing Arts Division, Costa Mesa CA (S)

Posner, Dr David M, *Senior Rabbi,* Congregation Emanu-El, Bernard Judaica Museum, New York NY

Posner, Helaine, *Chief Cur & Deputy Dir Cur Affairs,* Purchase College, Neuberger Museum of Art, Purchase NY

Poss, Sharon, *Office Mgr,* Historical Society of Palm Beach County, The Richard and Pat Johnson Palm Beach County History Museum, West Palm Beach FL

Post, Barbara T, *VPres Prog,* Berks Art Alliance, Reading PA

Post, Stephanie, *Asst Mus Librn,* The Metropolitan Museum of Art, Image Library, New York NY

Post, William, *Cur Ornithology,* Charleston Museum, Charleston SC

Poston, Virginia, *Instr,* University of Southern Indiana, Department of Art, Evansville IN (S)

Potapenko, Tony, *Dir Fin,* Mobile Museum of Art, Mobile AL

Pote, Judy, *Pres,* Philadelphia Museum of Art, Women's Committee, Philadelphia PA

Poteel, Daniel, *Provost,* School of the Museum of Fine Arts, Boston MA (S)

Potochniak, Andrea, *Publicity & Publications Coordr,* Cornell University, Herbert F Johnson Museum of Art, Ithaca NY

Potochnik, Sherry, *Educational Specialist,* The Ohio Historical Society, Inc, Campus Martius Museum & Ohio River Museum, Marietta OH

Potratz, Wayne, *Assoc Prof,* University of Minnesota, Minneapolis, Dept of Art, Minneapolis MN (S)

Potter, Dave, *Assoc Prof,* Keystone College, Fine Arts Dept, LaPlume PA (S)

Potter, Donna, *Admin Asst,* Saskatchewan Craft Council & Affinity Gallery, Saskatoon SK

Potter, Edmund, *Dir Coll,* Woodrow Wilson, Staunton VA

Potter, Edmund, *Dir Coll,* Woodrow Wilson, Woodrow Wilson Presidential Library, Staunton VA

Potter, Elena, *Advertising Asst,* Canadian Art Foundation, Toronto ON

Potter, Joann, *Registrar,* Vassar College, The Frances Lehman Loeb Art Center, Poughkeepsie NY

Potter, Joe, *Instr,* William Woods-Westminster Colleges, Art Dept, Fulton MO (S)

Potter, Leslie, *Exhib & Educ Coordr,* Saskatchewan Craft Council & Affinity Gallery, Saskatoon SK

Potter, Maomi, *Cur,* Banff Centre, Walter Phillips Gallery, Banff AB

Potter, Susan, *Librn,* Springfield Art Museum, Library, Springfield MO

Potter, Susan, *Librn,* Springfield Art Museum, Springfield MO

Potter, Willis, *Exhib Mgr,* Chrysler Museum of Art, Norfolk VA

Pottie, John, *Cur,* National Silk Art Museum, Weston MO

Pottie, Venessa, *Cur,* National Silk Art Museum, Weston MO

Potts, Jennifer, *Colls Mgr,* Delaware Historical Society, Delaware History Museum, Wilmington DE

Potts, Jennifer, *Registrar,* Delaware Historical Society, Library, Wilmington DE

Pottunger, Mark, *Prof,* Manhattan College, School of Arts, Bronx NY (S)

Poueymirou, Frank, *Deputy Dir,* New York University, Grey Art Gallery, New York NY

Poulos, Basilios N, *Prof Emeritus,* Rice University, Visual & Dramatic Arts, Houston TX (S)

Poulson, Jan, *Board Dirs Pres,* Sioux City Art Center, Sioux City IA

Poulter, Jennifer, *Special Facility Mgr,* Baton Rouge Gallery, Center For Contemporary Art, Baton Rouge LA

Poulter, Melissa, *Sales Assoc,* Gene Roncka Willow Point Gallery/Museum, Ashland NE

Poulton, Michael, *Prof,* Dalhousie University, Faculty of Architecture, Halifax NS (S)

Pousanby, Claire, *Dir Mus Opers,* Albin Polasek Museum & Sculpture Gardens, Winter Park FL

Pouwels, J, *Instr,* California State University, Chico, Department of Art & Art History, Chico CA (S)

Povlsen-Jones, Malunda, *Instr,* Whitman College, Art Dept, Walla Walla WA (S)

Povse, Matt, *Chmn,* Marywood University, Art Dept, Scranton PA (S)

Powell, Ann, *Dir Devel,* The Trustees of Reservations, The Mission House, Ipswich MA

Powell, Brandon, *Program Coordr,* Woodbridge Township Cultural Arts Commission, Barron Arts Center, Woodbridge NJ

Powell, Chris, *Prof,* Texas Christian University, School of Art, Fort Worth TX (S)

Powell, Daniel, *Dir Fine & Performing Arts,* Chipola College, Dept of Fine & Performing Arts, Marianna FL (S)

Powell, Earl A, *Dir,* National Gallery of Art, Washington DC

Powell, Edward, *Assoc Prof,* University of Pittsburgh, Dept of Studio Arts, Pittsburgh PA (S)

Powell, Fabienne, *Exhib Coordr,* Sage College of Albany, Opalka Gallery, Albany NY

Powell, Isaac, *Asst Prof,* Northwestern State University of Louisiana, School of Creative & Performing Arts - Dept of Fine & Graphic Arts, Natchitoches LA (S)

Powell, James, *Dir,* Natural History Museum of Los Angeles County, Los Angeles CA

Powell, Janelle, *Dir,* Arts & Science Center for Southeast Arkansas, Pine Bluff AR

Powell, Jennifer, *Admin Secy,* Birmingham Museum of Art, Birmingham AL

Powell, John, *Cur,* Woodrow Wilson, Washington DC

Powell, John, *Cur,* City of Saint Augustine, Saint Augustine FL

Powell, Kimberly, *Asst Prof Art Educ & Curriculum & Instruction,* Pennsylvania State University, University Park, Penn State School of Visual Arts, University Park PA (S)

Powell, Lalana, *Library Technician,* University of Kentucky, Hunter M Adams Architecture Library, Lexington KY

Powell, Mary Ellen, *Registrar,* Frederick R Weisman, Los Angeles CA

Powell, Nancy, *Senior Cur,* National Audubon Society, John James Audubon Center at Mill Grove, Audubon PA

Powell, Sylvie, *Commun & Mem,* Royal Architectural Institute of Canada, Ottawa ON

Powelson, Rosemary, *Chmn,* Lower Columbia College, Art Dept, Longview WA (S)

Power, Nadine, *Colls Mgr,* Simon Fraser University, Simon Fraser University Gallery, Burnaby BC

Power, Peter, *Chmn Printmedia,* School of the Art Institute of Chicago, Chicago IL (S)

Powers, Carol, *Instr,* Mount Mary College, Art & Design Division, Milwaukee WI (S)

Proper, Donna, *Asst Prof*, State University of New York at Farmingdale, Visual Communications, Farmingdale NY (S)

Proper, Hope, *Cur of Exhibs*, Perkins Center for the Arts, Moorestown NJ

Proper, Joann, *Circ Library Asst*, Colonial Williamsburg Foundation, John D Rockefeller, Jr Library, Williamsburg VA

Prosser, Andrea, *Site Mgr*, Hermitage Foundation Museum, Norfolk VA

Prosser, Andrea, *Site Mgr*, Hermitage Foundation Museum, Library, Norfolk VA

Protka, Jacqueline, *Digital Assets & Media Librn*, Corcoran Gallery of Art, Corcoran Library, Washington DC

Proulx, Anne-Marie, *Commun*, Concordia University, Leonard & Bina Ellen Art Gallery, Montreal PQ

Provan, Archibald D, *Assoc Prof*, Rochester Institute of Technology, School of Printing Management & Sciences, Rochester NY (S)

Provan, Jill E, *Librn*, Tucson Museum of Art and Historic Block, Library, Tucson AZ

Provancher, Scott, *Pres*, Arts & Science Council, Charlotte NC

Provence, Dana, *Prof Art*, Adams State College, Dept of Visual Arts, Alamosa CO (S)

Provenzano, Sandra Parker, *Head Cataloger*, Harvard University, Dumbarton Oaks Research Library, Washington DC

Provine, William, *Instr*, John C Calhoun, Department of Fine Arts, Tanner AL (S)

Provo, Dan, *Dir*, Oklahoma Historical Society, State Museum of History, Oklahoma City OK

Provo, Dan, *Okla Mus*, Oklahoma Historical Society, Library Resources Division, Oklahoma City OK

Provost, Elaine, *Treas*, Blackwell Street Center for the Arts, Denville NJ

Provost, Jon C, *Dir Finance & Admin*, Berkshire Museum, Pittsfield MA

Pruden, Sue, *Retail Operations Dir*, Contemporary Arts Museum Houston, Houston TX

Prudhomme, Sue, *Dir*, Twin City Art Foundation, Masur Museum of Art, Monroe LA

Prudic, Nancy, *Asst Prof Visual Art*, Lake Erie College, Fine Arts Dept, Painesville OH (S)

Pruett, Jeff, *Progs Coordr*, Gaston County Museum of Art & History, Dallas NC

Pruitt, Jack, *Dir Develop & External Affairs*, The Historic New Orleans Collection, Royal Street Galleries, New Orleans LA

Pruner, Gary, *Instr*, American River College, Dept of Art/Art New Media, Sacramento CA (S)

Prusa, Carol, *Prof Art, Painting/Drawing*, Florida Atlantic University, D F Schmidt College of Arts & Letters Dept of Visual Arts & Art History, Boca Raton FL (S)

Pry, George, *Pres*, Art Institute of Pittsburgh, Pittsburgh PA (S)

Przybilla, Carrie, *Cur Modern & Contemporary*, High Museum of Art, Atlanta GA

Przybylek, Stephanie, *Dir Mus Divsn*, Delaware Historical Society, Library, Wilmington DE

Puccinelli, Keith, *VPres*, Santa Barbara Contemporary Arts Forum, Santa Barbara CA

Pucker, Gigi Pritzker, *Immediate Past Chmn*, Chicago Children's Museum, Chicago IL

Puckett, Jean L, *Dir Finance*, Jamestown-Yorktown Foundation, Jamestown Settlement, Williamsburg VA

Puckett, Paula, *Chmn*, Kellogg Community College, Arts & Communication Dept, Battle Creek MI (S)

Puckitt, Sarah, *Colls Information Specialist*, Montgomery Museum of Fine Arts, Library, Montgomery AL

Puff, Allison, *Assoc Prof*, State University of New York at Farmingdale, Visual Communications, Farmingdale NY (S)

Puffer, John, *Assoc Prof*, Vincennes University Junior College, Humanities Art Dept, Vincennes IN (S)

Puffer, Wendy, *Asst Prof*, Indiana Wesleyan University, School of Arts & Humanities, Division of Art, Marion IN (S)

Pugh, Mary Jo, *Coll Mgr*, San Francisco Maritime National Historical Park, Maritime Museum, San Francisco CA

Puglisi, Catherine, *Dir Prog & Assoc Prof*, Rutgers, The State University of New Jersey, Graduate Program in Art History, New Brunswick NJ (S)

Pujol, Elliott, *Prof*, Kansas State University, Art Dept, Manhattan KS (S)

Pulido, Lorraine, *Mktg & Pub Rels Dir*, Guadalupe Cultural Arts Center, San Antonio TX

Pulin, Carol, *Dir*, American Print Alliance, Peachtree City GA

Pullen, Reg, *Pres*, Coos County Historical Society Museum, North Bend OR

Puller, Mary, *Exhibs Dir*, Durango Arts Center, Barbara Conrad Art Gallery, Durango CO

Pulling, Thomas L, *Chmn*, Norman Rockwell Museum, Stockbridge MA

Pullini Brown, Ada, *Assoc Prof Painting & Drawing*, Rio Hondo College, Visual Arts Dept, Whittier CA (S)

Puls, Lucy, *Prof Sculpture*, University of California, Davis, Dept of Art & Art History, Davis CA (S)

Pulsifer, Dorothy, *Prof*, Bridgewater State College, Art Dept, Bridgewater MA (S)

Pultz, John, *Assoc Prof*, University of Kansas, Kress Foundation Dept of Art History, Lawrence KS (S)

Pulver, Sara, *Gallery Coordr*, Lansing Art Gallery, Lansing MI

Pumphrey, M Jo, *Prof*, Brevard College, Department of Art, Brevard NC (S)

Pumphrey, Richard, *Prof*, Lynchburg College, Art Dept, Lynchburg VA (S)

Pumputiene, Irena, *Librn*, Balzekas Museum of Lithuanian Culture, Chicago IL

Punch, Walter, *Dir*, Wentworth Institute of Technology Library, Boston MA

Punt, Gerry, *Instr*, Augustana College, Art Dept, Sioux Falls SD (S)

Pura, Bill, *Prof*, University of Manitoba, School of Art, Winnipeg MB (S)

Purcell, Amy Lixi, *Prof*, University of North Carolina at Greensboro, Art Dept, Greensboro NC (S)

Purcell, Carl, *Chmn*, Snow College, Art Dept, Ephraim UT (S)

Purcell, Marilu, *Dir Visual Arts & National Gallery*, Institute of Puerto Rican Culture, National Gallery, San Juan PR

Purcell, Marilu, *Dir Visual Arts & National Gallery*, Institute of Puerto Rican Culture, National Gallery, San Juan PR

Purdy, Jana, *Mktg Mgr*, Museum of Contemporary Art, San Diego-Downtown, La Jolla CA

Purje, Lauren, *Asst to Dir*, Viridian Artists Inc, New York NY

Purkiss, Christine, *Library Asst*, Bryn Mawr College, Rhys Carpenter Library for Art, Archaeology, Classics & Cities, Bryn Mawr PA

Purpura, Allyson, *Cur*, University of Illinois at Urbana-Champaign, Krannert Art Museum and Kinkead Pavilion, Champaign IL

Purrington, Robert H, *Innkeeper*, Longfellow's Wayside Inn Museum, Sudbury MA

Purves, Eric, *Assoc Prof*, Appalachian State University, Dept of Art, Boone NC (S)

Purvis, Alston, *Chmn Graphic Design*, Boston University, School for the Arts, Boston MA (S)

Purvis, Amy, *Assoc Dir Develop*, Museum of Fine Arts, Houston, Houston TX

Putka, Robert, *Instr*, Cuyahoga Valley Art Center, Cuyahoga Falls OH (S)

Putman, Sumi, *Printmaker*, University of South Alabama, Dept of Art & Art History, Mobile AL (S)

Putnam, Carol, *Mng Dir*, Grass Roots Art & Community Effort (GRACE), Firehouse Gallery, Hardwick VT

Putnam, Christy, *Assoc Dir Exhibs*, Whitney Museum of American Art, New York NY

Putnam, Thomas, *Dir*, National Archives & Records Administration, John F Kennedy Presidential Library & Museum, Boston MA

Putney, Carolyn M, *Chief Cur & Cur of Asian Art*, Toledo Museum of Art, Toledo OH

Putney, Claire, *Instr*, Bakersfield College, Art Dept, Bakersfield CA (S)

Puzziferro, Maria, *Pres & Provost*, Rocky Mountain College of Art & Design, Lakewood CO (S)

Pye, Jennifer, *Cur Coll*, Monhegan Museum, Monhegan ME

Pygin, Cynthia, *CFO*, California Science Center, Los Angeles CA

Pylant, Carol, *Prof*, University of Wisconsin, Madison, Dept of Art, Madison WI (S)

Pyle, Aaron, *Mus Tech*, University of Maine, Museum of Art, Bangor ME

Pyle, Dorothy, *Div Chmn*, Maui Community College, Art Program, Kahului HI (S)

Pyra, Greg, *Advocacy Chmn*, Alberta Society of Artists, Calgary AB

Pyrke, Dougla, *Dir Develop*, Hill-Stead Museum, Farmington CT

Pytel, Margaret, *Admin Asst/Accounting*, Maitland Art Center, Library, Maitland FL

Qian, Hong, *Assoc Cur Botany*, Illinois State Museum, Museum Store, Chicago IL

Qibgirne, Joan, *Instr*, Greenfield Community College, Art Dept, Greenfield MA (S)

Qua-Hiansen, Jaclyn, *Gallery Asst*, Art Gallery of Mississauga, Mississauga ON

Quackenbush, Elizabeth, *Assoc Prof Art (Ceramics)*, Pennsylvania State University, University Park, Penn State School of Visual Arts, University Park PA (S)

Quackenbush, Laura, *Cur*, Leelanau Historical Museum, Leland MI

Qualman, Roger, *VPres*, Columbia River Maritime Museum, Astoria OR

Quandt, Kendra, *Dir Develop*, Birmingham Museum of Art, Birmingham AL

Quarcoopome, Nii, *Cur African, Oceanic & New World Cultures Art*, Detroit Institute of Arts, Detroit MI

Quatchak, Pam, *Dir Develop*, Society for Contemporary Craft, Pittsburgh PA

Queen, Bill, *Asst Cur*, University of Montana, Montana Museum of Art & Culture, Missoula MT

Quek, Stanley, *Asst to Exec Dir*, Place des Arts at Heritage Square, Coquitlam BC

Quella, Hillary, *Instr*, Marian University, Art Dept, Fond Du Lac WI (S)

Quick, Betsy, *Educ Dir*, University of California, Los Angeles, Fowler Museum at UCLA, Los Angeles CA

Quick, Jonathan, *Asst Prof*, Ohio Wesleyan University, Fine Arts Dept, Delaware OH (S)

Quigley, Austin, *Dean*, Columbia University, Columbia College, New York NY (S)

Quimby, Sean, *Dir Spec Colls*, Syracuse University, Syracuse University Library, Syracuse NY

Quin, Emma, *Exec Dir*, Ontario Crafts Council, OCC Gallery, Toronto ON

Quin, Langdon, *Asst Prof*, University of New Hampshire, Dept of Arts & Art History, Durham NH (S)

Quinan, John, *Distinguished Prof*, University at Buffalo, State University of New York, Dept of Visual Studies, Buffalo NY (S)

Quincy, Susan, *Environmental Educ*, Osborne Homestead Museum, Derby CT

Quinlan-Brown, Susan, *Mus Store Mgr*, Cahoon Museum of American Art, Cotuit MA

Quinn, Alana, *Sr Prog Assoc*, National Academy of Sciences, Arts in the Academy, Washington DC

Quinn, Ellen, *Asst Prof*, New Jersey City University, Art Dept, Jersey City NJ (S)

Quinn, Karen, *Kristin & Roger Servison Cur Paintings*, Museum of Fine Arts, Boston MA

Quinn, Kristin, *Prof Art*, Saint Ambrose University, Art Dept, Davenport IA (S)

Quinn, Megan, *Prof*, Augustana College, Art Dept, Rock Island IL (S)

Quinn, Tery, *Dir Develop*, The Contemporary Austin, Austin TX

Quinn-Cary, Bridget, *Dir*, Buffalo & Erie County Public Library, Buffalo NY

Quinn-Hensley, Carolyn I, *Prof*, Colorado Mesa University, Art Dept, Grand Junction CO (S)

Quinney, G B, *Security Dir*, Birmingham Museum of Art, Clarence B Hanson Jr Library, Birmingham AL

Quinones-Keber, Eloise, *Prof Emerita*, City University of New York, PhD Program in Art History, New York NY (S)

Quinonez, Gary, *Sculpture Instr*, Monterey Peninsula College, Art Dept/Art Gallery, Monterey CA (S)

Quintana, Frances, *Gift Shop Mgr*, Pueblo of Pojoaque, Poeh Museum, Santa Fe NM

Quintanilla, Faustino, *Adj Asst Prof,* College of Staten Island, Performing & Creative Arts Dept, Staten Island NY (S)

Quintanilla, Faustino, *Dir,* Queensborough Community College, Art Gallery, Bayside NY

Quintanilla, Mimi, *Exec VPres,* Witte Museum, San Antonio TX

Quintanilla, Sonya, *Cur Asian Art,* San Diego Museum of Art, San Diego CA

Quintanilla, Sonya Rhie, *Cur Indian & Southeast Asian Art Dir,* The Cleveland Museum of Art, Cleveland OH

Quintella, Joel, *Maintenance Chief/Security,* San Angelo Museum of Fine Arts, San Angelo TX

Quintero, Miriam B, *Dir Finance & Admin,* Museo de Arte de Ponce, The Luis A Ferre Foundation Inc, Ponce PR

Quintero, Miriam B, *Dir Finance & Admin,* Museo de Arte de Ponce, The Luis A Ferre Foundation Inc, Ponce PR

Quinteros, Alejandro, *Assoc Prof,* University of Puerto Rico, Dept of Fine Arts, Rio Piedras PR (S)

Quinteros, Alejandro, *Assoc Prof,* University of Puerto Rico, Dept of Fine Arts, Rio Piedras PR (S)

Quinto, Carmela, *Cur,* Millicent Rogers Museum, Taos NM

Quinton, Sarah, *Cur Dir,* Textile Museum of Canada, Toronto ON

Quirino, Barbara, *Mus Shop Mgr,* Hancock Shaker Village, Inc, Pittsfield MA

Quirion, Lisa, *Colls Mgr,* The Winnipeg Art Gallery, Winnipeg MB

Quiroga, Mercedes, *Chmn,* Miami-Dade Community College, Wolfson Galleries, Miami FL

Raatz, Heidi, *Visual Resource Librn,* Minneapolis Institute of Arts, Art Research & Reference Library, Minneapolis MN

Rabb, George, *Bd Chmn Ill State Mus Bd,* Illinois State Museum, Museum Store, Chicago IL

Rabb, Lauren, *Cur,* University of Arizona, Museum of Art & Archive of Visual Arts, Tucson AZ

Rabe, Lana, *Asst Direct Publ Coordr,* Quincy Art Center, Quincy IL

Rabe, Michael, *Assoc Prof,* Saint Xavier University, Dept of Art & Design, Chicago IL (S)

Rabenold, Christine, *Asst Prof Art,* North Central College, Dept of Art, Naperville IL (S)

Rabineau, Phyllis, *Deputy Dir Interpretation & Educ,* Chicago History Museum, Chicago IL

Rabinovitch, Victor, *Pres & CEO,* Canadian Museum of Civilization, Gatineau PQ

Rabun, Julie, *Asst Prof,* Carson-Newman College, Art Dept, Jefferson City TN (S)

Raby, Julian, *Dir,* Freer Gallery of Art & Arthur M Sackler Gallery, Freer Gallery of Art, Washington DC

Raby, Julian, *Dir,* Freer Gallery of Art & Arthur M Sackler Gallery, Arthur M Sackler Gallery, Washington DC

Racey, Nicholas, *VPres,* Strasburg Museum, Strasburg VA

Rackow, Marcia, *Coordr,* Aesthetic Realism Foundation, Terrain Gallery, New York NY

Raczka, Laurel, *Exec Dir,* Painted Bride Art Center Gallery, Philadelphia PA

Radan, George, *Prof,* Villanova University, Dept of Theater, Villanova PA (S)

Radandt, Gina, *Cur Collections,* Kenosha Public Museums, Kenosha WI

Radbourne, Ele, *Admin Asst,* Museums Association of Saskatchewan, Regina SK

Radcliffe, Tony, *VPres,* Redlands Art Association, Redlands Art Association Gallery & Art Center, Redlands CA

Rader, Chris, *Dir Pub Rels,* North Central Washington Museum, Wenatchee Valley Museum & Cultural Center, Wenatchee WA

Radford, Michelle Berg, *Instr,* Bob Jones University, School of Fine Arts, Div of Art & Design, Greenville SC (S)

Radke, Don, *Adjunct Assoc Prof,* Texas Woman's University, School of the Arts, Dept of Visual Arts, Denton TX (S)

Radke, Doug, *Chmn,* Blue Mountain Community College, Fine Arts Dept, Pendleton OR (S)

Radke, Gary, *Prof,* Syracuse University, Dept of Fine Arts (Art History), Syracuse NY (S)

Radosh, Sondra M, *Asst Dir, Children's Librn,* Jones Library, Inc, Amherst MA

Radulovlic, Radovan, *Conservator,* The Winnipeg Art Gallery, Winnipeg MB

Radusky, Jan, *Dir Grants,* Cultural Council of Palm Beach County, Lake Worth FL

Radycki, Diane, *Dir,* Moravian College, Payne Gallery, Bethlehem PA

Radycki, Diane, *Dir of Payne Gallery,* Moravian College, Dept of Art, Bethlehem PA (S)

Rafat, Pasha, *Assoc Prof,* University of Nevada, Las Vegas, Dept of Art, Las Vegas NV (S)

Rafferty, Emily K, *Sr VPres Exter,* The Metropolitan Museum of Art, New York NY

Rafferty-Weinisch, Jill, *Dir Performing Arts & Outreach,* The Arts Center of the Capital Region, Troy NY

Ragain, Melissa, *Assoc Prof Art History,* Montana State University, School of Art, Bozeman MT (S)

Ragbir, Lise, *Asst Dir,* Perkins Center for the Arts, Moorestown NJ

Rager, Andrea, *Asst Prof,* Case Western Reserve University, Dept of Art History & Art, Cleveland OH (S)

Rago, Juliet, *Prof Emeritus,* Loyola University of Chicago, Fine Arts Dept, Chicago IL (S)

Ragon, Jan, *Secy I,* University of Oklahoma, Fred Jones Jr Museum of Art, Norman OK

Raguin, Virginia C, *Prof,* College of the Holy Cross, Dept of Visual Arts, Worcester MA (S)

Rahaim, Margaret, *Prof,* Mount Saint Mary's University, Visual & Performing Arts Dept, Emmitsburg MD (S)

Rahe, Diane, *VPres,* Phillips County Museum, Holyoke CO

Rahimi, Dan, *Exec Dir Gallery Devel,* Royal Ontario Museum, Toronto ON

Raia, Nancy, *ABC Project Dir,* Eastern Shore Art Association, Inc, Eastern Shore Art Center, Fairhope AL

Railey, Clayton A, *Dean,* Delaware County Community College, Communications, Art & Humanities, Media PA (S)

Raine, Vicki, *Div Chmn Humanities,* Metropolitan Community College - Penn Valley, Art Dept, Kansas City MO (S)

Rainer, Yvonne, *Prof & Bren Chair,* University of California, Irvine, Studio Art Dept, Irvine CA (S)

Raines, Kevin, *Prof,* College of Notre Dame of Maryland, Art Dept, Baltimore MD (S)

Rains, Jerry, *Chmn,* Northeast Mississippi Junior College, Art Dept, Booneville MS (S)

Rainville, Melanie, *Max Stern Cur,* Concordia University, Leonard & Bina Ellen Art Gallery, Montreal PQ

Raithel, Jan, *Dept Chmn,* Chaffey Community College, Art Dept, Rancho Cucamonga CA (S)

Rajan, Ravi, *Dir,* Purchase College, State University of New York, School of Art+Design, Purchase NY (S)

Rakes, Susan, *Asst Dir,* Art & Culture Center of Hollywood, Art Gallery/Multidisciplinary Cultural Center, Hollywood FL

Rakow, Catherine, *Curatorial Asst,* Boise Art Museum, Boise ID

Raley, Gwendolen, *Mus & Heritage Tourism Dir,* Indiana Landmarks, Morris-Butler House, Indianapolis IN

Ralph, Fran, *Dir Mktg,* The National Shrine of the North American Martyrs, Fultonville NY

Ralph, Thomas F, *Dir Opers,* The National Shrine of the North American Martyrs, Fultonville NY

Rama, Ronnie, *Prof,* Abilene Christian University, Dept of Art & Design, Abilene TX (S)

Ramage, Andrew, *Prof,* Cornell University, Dept of the History of Art & Visual Studies, Ithaca NY (S)

Ramage, Priscilla, *Mus Shop Mgr,* Hill-Stead Museum, Farmington CT

Ramage, William, *Prof,* Castleton State College, Art Dept, Castleton VT (S)

Ramberg, W Dodd, *Prof,* Catholic University of America, School of Architecture & Planning, Washington DC (S)

Rambolina, Madame, *Dir Security,* Fondo del Sol, Visual Art & Media Center, Washington DC

Ramer, Randy, *Dir Exhibs & Publs,* University of Tulsa, Gilcrease Museum, Tulsa OK

Ramirez, Cynthia, *Instr,* Southern University in New Orleans, Fine Arts & Philosophy Dept, New Orleans LA (S)

Ramirez, Dee, *Bookkeeper,* Brownsville Art League, Brownsville Museum of Fine Art, Brownsville TX

Ramirez-Montagut, Monica, *Cur,* Aldrich Museum of Contemporary Art, Ridgefield CT

Ramirez-Weaver, Eric, *Asst Prof, Art History,* University of Virginia, McIntire Dept of Art, Charlottesville VA (S)

Ramljak, Suzanne, *Cur,* The American Federation of Arts, New York NY

Ramon, Art, *Archives,* Deming-Luna Mimbres Museum, Deming NM

Ramoran, Edwin, *Dir Exhibs & Progs,* Aljira Center for Contemporary Art, Newark NJ

Ramos, Jim, *Instr,* Gettysburg College, Dept of Visual Arts, Gettysburg PA (S)

Ramos, Julianne, *Exec Dir,* Rockland Center for the Arts, West Nyack NY

Ramos, Julianne, *Exec Dir,* Rockland Center for the Arts, West Nyack NY (S)

Ramos, Liliane, *Exec Dir,* Institute of Puerto Rican Culture, Dr Jose C Barbosa Museum, San Juan PR

Ramos, Liliane, *Exec Dir,* Institute of Puerto Rican Culture, Dr Jose C Barbosa Museum, San Juan PR

Ramos, Ora, *Exec Dir,* Institute of Puerto Rican Culture, Museo y Parque Historico Ruinas de Caparra, San Juan PR

Ramos, Ora, *Exec Dir,* Institute of Puerto Rican Culture, Museo y Parque Historico Ruinas de Caparra, San Juan PR

Ramos, Rosa, *Mus Adminr,* Islip Art Museum, East Islip NY

Ramos, Wanda, *Hr Dir,* Museo de Arte de Ponce, The Luis A Ferre Foundation Inc, Ponce PR

Ramos, Wanda, *Hr Dir,* Museo de Arte de Ponce, The Luis A Ferre Foundation Inc, Ponce PR

Ramos-Rivas, Lourdes, *Dir,* Museo de Arte de Puerto Rico, San Juan PR

Ramos-Rivas, Lourdes, *Dir,* Museo de Arte de Puerto Rico, San Juan PR

Ramsaran, Helen, *Assoc Prof,* John Jay College of Criminal Justice, Dept of Art, Music & Philosophy, New York NY (S)

Ramsay, Chris, *Prof,* Oklahoma State University, Department of Art, Graphic Design and Art History, Stillwater OK (S)

Ramsay, Ted, *Prof,* University of Michigan, Ann Arbor, School of Art & Design, Ann Arbor MI (S)

Ramsey, Chuck, *Coordr,* Clark College, Art Dept, Vancouver WA (S)

Ramsey, Liz, *Third VPres,* Arizona Watercolor Association, Phoenix AZ

Ran, Shulamit, *VPres Music,* American Academy of Arts & Letters, New York NY

Ranalli, Daniel, *Dir,* Boston University, Graduate Program - Arts Administration, Boston MA (S)

Rancourt, Allan, *Treas,* Waterville Historical Society, Redington Museum, Waterville ME

Rancourt, Lichen, *Head of Info Svcs,* Manchester City Library, Manchester NH

Rand, Anne Gimes, *Deputy Dir,* USS Constitution Museum, Boston MA

Rand, Charles, *Librn/Archivist,* United Society of Shakers, Shaker Museum, New Gloucester ME

Rand, Charles E, *Archivist & Librn,* United Society of Shakers, The Shaker Library, New Gloucester ME

Rand, Erica, *Prof,* Bates College, Art & Visual Culture, Lewiston ME (S)

Rand, Richard, *Cur Mathematics,* Northern Maine Museum of Science, Presque Isle ME

Rand, Richard, *Sr Cur of Paintings & Sculpture,* Sterling & Francine Clark, Williamstown MA

Rand, Valerie, *Dir Housing,* The Illinois Institute of Art - Chicago, Chicago IL (S)

Randall, Anthony, *Pres,* Association of Hawaii Artists, Honolulu HI

Randall, Ross, *Dir,* Frank Lloyd Wright, Mount Vernon VA

Randall, Ross, *Dir,* Woodlawn/The Pope-Leighey, Mount Vernon VA

Randall, Susan, *Instr,* Midland College, Art Dept, Midland TX (S)

Randall, Vaughn, *Asst Prof,* State University of New York, College at Cortland, Dept Art & Art History, Cortland NY (S)

Randel, Melissa, *Instr,* Glendale Community College, Visual & Performing Arts Div, Glendale CA (S)

Randolph, Deborah, *Cur Educ,* Southeastern Center for Contemporary Art, Winston Salem NC

Randolph, Karen, *Prof,* Lubbock Christian University, Dept of Communication & Fine Art, Lubbock TX (S)

Rangel, Gabriela, *Dir Visual Arts,* Americas Society Art Gallery, New York NY

Rank-Beauchamp, Beth, *CEO, Pres,* Sharon Arts Center, Sharon Arts Center Exhibition Gallery, Peterborough NH

Rankin, Jennifer, *Educ Coordr,* Rocky Mount Arts Center, Rocky Mount NC

Rankin, Robin, *Dir,* Kimball Art Center, Park City UT

Rankin, Shan, *Exec Dir,* Hidalgo County Historical Museum, Edinburg TX

Ransom, Brian, *Prof,* Eckerd College, Art Dept, Saint Petersburg FL (S)

Ransom, Marzia, *Adj Instr,* University of West Florida, Dept of Art, Pensacola FL (S)

Rante, Danielle, *Asst Prof,* Wright State University, Dept of Art & Art History, Dayton OH (S)

Rantoul, T Neal, *Assoc Prof,* Northeastern University, Dept of Art & Architecture, Boston MA (S)

Rapp, Karen, *Dir,* East Los Angeles College, Vincent Price Art Museum, Monterey Park CA

Rapp, Karen, *Dir,* University of California, Sweeney Art Gallery, Riverside CA

Rappaport, Deborah, *Pres,* San Jose Museum of Art, Library, San Jose CA

Rappaport, Matt, *Asst Prof,* University of Dayton, Visual Arts Dept, Dayton OH (S)

Rappoport, Eileen, *VPres,* Cultural Alliance of Greater Washington, Washington DC

Rardin, Dori, *Sec,* New Mexico Art League, Gallery & School, Albuquerque NM

Rasbury, Patricia, *Dir Opers,* Tennessee State Museum, Nashville TN

Rashid, Shahida, *Dir Library Svcs,* Sheridan College of Applied Arts and Technology, Trafalgar Campus Library, Oakville ON

Rasic, Alexandra, *Pub Prog Mgr,* Workman & Temple Family Homestead Museum, City of Industry CA

Raskin, David, *Chmn Art History, Theory & Criticism,* School of the Art Institute of Chicago, Chicago IL (S)

Rasmussen, Jack, *Dir & Cur,* American University, Katzen Art Center Gallery, New York NY

Rasmussen, Lisa Anne, *Coordr & Instr,* Walla Walla Community College, Fine Arts Dept, Walla Walla WA (S)

Rasmussen, Mary, *Res Asst Prof,* University of Illinois at Chicago, Biomedical Visualization, Chicago IL (S)

Rasmussen, William, *Cur Art,* Virginia Historical Society, Library, Richmond VA

Rasmussen, William, *Cur of Virginia Art,* Virginia Historical Society, Richmond VA

Rass, Patty, *Instr,* Mount Mary College, Art & Design Division, Milwaukee WI (S)

Rassetti, Mark L, *Dir,* Hutchinson Art Association, Hutchinson Art Center, Hutchinson KS

Rassieur, Thomas, *Cur Prints & Drawings,* Minneapolis Institute of Arts, Minneapolis MN

Rassweiler, Janet, *Prog & Colls Dir,* New Jersey Historical Society, Newark NJ

Rata Stutzbach, Alisa, *Dir,* Southern Methodist University, Hamon Arts Library, Dallas TX

Ratchliflie, Sam, *Head Bywaters Spec Coll,* Southern Methodist University, Hamon Arts Library, Dallas TX

Ratcliff, Douglas, *Dir of Retail,* Museum of Art, Fort Lauderdale, Fort Lauderdale FL

Ratcliff, Gary, *Head,* University of Louisiana at Monroe, Bry Gallery, Monroe LA

Ratcliff, Gary, *Instr,* University of Louisiana at Monroe, Dept of Art, Monroe LA (S)

Rathbone, Eliza, *Chief Cur,* The Phillips Collection, Washington DC

Rathbun, Bob, *Dir,* Sloss Furnaces National Historic Landmark, Birmingham AL

Rathbun, Linda, *Gen Educ,* Art Institute of Pittsburgh, Pittsburgh PA (S)

Rathbun, Nichole, *Commun Dir,* 911 Media Arts Center, Seattle WA

Rather, Susan, *Asst Chair - Art History,* University of Texas, Dept of Art & Art History, Austin TX (S)

Rathje, Terry, *Asst Prof,* Western Illinois University, Department of Art, Macomb IL (S)

Rathwell, Robert, *Vol Coordr,* Craigdarroch Castle Historical Museum Society, Victoria BC

Ratner, Peter, *Asst Prof,* James Madison University, School of Art & Art History, Harrisonburg VA (S)

Ratner, Rhoda, *Librn,* National Museum of American History, Branch Library, Washington DC

Ratte, Christopher, *Assoc Prof,* University of Michigan, Kelsey Museum of Archaeology, Ann Arbor MI

Ratterree, Scott, *Head Preparator,* The Historic New Orleans Collection, Royal Street Galleries, New Orleans LA

Rattner, Carl, *Prof,* Saint Thomas Aquinas College, Art Dept, Sparkill NY (S)

Rau, Sue, *Instr Painting,* Ocean City Arts Center, Ocean City NJ (S)

Rauchbauer, Martin, *Deputy Dir,* Austrian Cultural Forum Gallery, New York NY

Rauder, Lawrence, *Dir,* University of California, Berkeley, Berkeley Art Museum & Pacific Film Archive, Berkeley CA

Rauf, Barb, *Dir,* Thomas More College, Eva G Farris Art Gallery, Crestview KY

Rauf, Barbara, *Assoc Prof,* Thomas More College, Art Dept, Crestview Hills KY (S)

Rauhauser, Andrew, *VPres,* Ages of Man Foundation, Amenia NY

Rauschenbusch, Stephanie, *Pres,* New York Society of Women Artists, Inc, Westport CT

Rauser, Amelia, *Assoc Prof,* Franklin & Marshall College, Art & Art History Dept, Lancaster PA (S)

Rautman, Marcus, *Prof,* University of Missouri - Columbia, Art History & Archaeology Dept, Columbia MO (S)

Ravel Abarbanel, Stacey, *Dir Mktg,* University of California, Los Angeles, Fowler Museum at UCLA, Los Angeles CA

Ravenal, John, *Cur Modern & Contemporary Art,* Virginia Museum of Fine Arts, Richmond VA

Ravenwood, Gregory, *Exhib Coordr,* Boulder Public Library & Gallery, Arts Gallery, Boulder CO

Raverty, Dennis, *Prof,* New Jersey City University, Art Dept, Jersey City NJ (S)

Rawles, Susan J, *Asst Cur American Art,* Virginia Museum of Fine Arts, Richmond VA

Rawlins, Dori, *Cur,* City of Irvine, Irvine Fine Arts Center, Irvine CA (S)

Rawlins, Gary, *Adjunct,* Chemeketa Community College, Dept of Humanities & Communications, Art Program, Salem OR (S)

Rawlins, Kathleen L, *Asst Dir,* Cambridge Historical Commission, Research Library on Architectural Social History of Cambridge, Mass, Cambridge MA

Rawlins, W Scott, *Asst Prof,* Arcadia University, Dept of Fine Arts, Glenside PA (S)

Rawls, James A, *Chmn,* Pearl River Community College, Visual Arts, Dept of Fine Arts & Communication, Poplarville MS (S)

Rawson, Gale, *Mus Registrar,* Pennsylvania Academy of the Fine Arts, Philadelphia PA

Rawson, Kimberly, *Dir Commun,* Berkshire Museum, Pittsfield MA

Rawstern, Sherri, *Cur Educ,* Dacotah Prairie Museum, Lamont Art Gallery, Aberdeen SD

Ray, Alan, *CFO,* California State University, Long Beach Foundation, Long Beach CA

Ray, Cindy, *Coordr,* Mississippi Delta Community College, Dept of Fine Arts, Moorhead MS (S)

Ray, Jeffrey, *Sr Cur,* Philadelphia History Museum, Philadelphia PA

Ray, Lawrence A, *Chmn,* Lambuth University, Dept of Human Ecology & Visual Arts, Jackson TN (S)

Ray, Randy S, *CFO,* Amon Carter Museum of American Art, Fort Worth TX

Ray, Rebekah, *Mgr Opers,* Arts & Science Center for Southeast Arkansas, Pine Bluff AR

Ray, Todd, *Pres,* Hutchinson Art Association, Hutchinson Art Center, Hutchinson KS

Rayca, Brian, *Mus Technician,* United States Military Academy, West Point Museum, West Point NY

Rayen, James W, *Prof,* Wellesley College, Art Dept, Wellesley MA (S)

Rayme, Mary, *Adjunct Instr,* Davis & Elkins College, Dept of Art, Elkins WV (S)

Raymond, Arlys, *Exec Dir,* Bakehouse Art Complex, Inc, Miami FL

Raymond, Christopher, *Cur,* Shores Memorial Museum, Lyndon Center VT

Raymond, Mark Kuaola, *Admin,* Maui Historical Society, Bailey House, Wailuku HI

Raymond, Yasmil, *Cur,* Dia Art Foundation, Beacon NY

Rayne, Angela, *Cur,* Jefferson County Open Space, Hiwan Homestead Museum, Evergreen CO

Raynor, Anne E, *Arts Coordr,* Worthington Arts Council, Columbus OH

Raynor, Rachel, *Dir Registration & Collections Mgr,* University of California, Los Angeles, Fowler Museum at UCLA, Los Angeles CA

Razzore, Lauren, *Asst Prof,* William Paterson University, Dept Arts, Wayne NJ (S)

Re, Peggy, *Assoc Prof,* University of Maryland, Baltimore County, Imaging & Digital Arts (IMDA), Dept of Visual Arts, Baltimore MD (S)

Rea, Douglas F, *Assoc Prof,* Rochester Institute of Technology, School of Photographic Arts & Sciences, Rochester NY (S)

Read, Bob, *Art Dir,* New Mexico Highlands University, The Ray Drew Gallery, Las Vegas NM

Read, Brittney, *Inter-Library Loan Librn,* Bethany College, Wallerstedt Library, Lindsborg KS

Read, Cindy, *Asst Prof,* Marygrove College, Department of Art, Detroit MI (S)

Read, Edith, *Vis Asst Prof,* Assumption College, Dept of Art, Music & Theatre, Worcester MA (S)

Read, Jon, *Opers Mgr,* Diverse Works, Houston TX

Read, Ron, *Librn,* Church of Jesus Christ of Latter-Day Saints, Art Library, Salt Lake City UT

Reading, Christine, *Instr,* Sacramento City College, Art Dept, Sacramento CA (S)

Ready, John, *Gallery Dir,* University of Wisconsin-La Crosse, Center for the Arts, La Crosse WI (S)

Reagan, Pat, *Assoc Prof,* Southeast Missouri State University, Dept of Art, Cape Girardeau MO (S)

Reamer, Melissa, *Colls Mgr,* Daytona State College, Southeast Museum of Photography, Daytona Beach FL

Reardon, Siobhan A, *Library Pres & Dir,* Free Library of Philadelphia, Art Dept, Philadelphia PA

Reas, Casey, *Chmn,* University of California, Los Angeles, Dept of Design & Media Arts, Los Angeles CA (S)

Reaven, Marco, *VPres History Exhibs,* New-York Historical Society, Museum, New York NY

Reaves, James, *Dir of Librn,* United Methodist Historical Society, Lovely Lane Museum, Baltimore MD

Reaves, Sharon C, *Dir Human Resources,* The Cleveland Museum of Art, Cleveland OH

Reaves, Wendy W, *Cur Prints & Drawings,* National Portrait Gallery, Smithsonian Institution, Washington DC

Reba, Kathy, *Asst Prof Visual Arts,* Dowling College, Dept of Visual Arts, Oakdale NY (S)

Rebac, Laurie, *Asst Gallery Mgr,* Sharon Arts Center, Sharon Arts Center Exhibition Gallery, Peterborough NH

Reber, Paul, *Exec Dir,* National Trust for Historic Preservation, Decatur House, Washington DC

Reber, Wally, *Assoc Dir,* Buffalo Bill Memorial Association, Buffalo Bill Historical Center, Cody WY

Reboli, Father John, *Assoc Prof,* College of the Holy Cross, Dept of Visual Arts, Worcester MA (S)

Rebsamen, Werner, *Assoc Prof,* Rochester Institute of Technology, School of Printing Management & Sciences, Rochester NY (S)

Recchia, Marissa, *Instr,* Middle Tennessee State University, Art Dept, Murfreesboro TN (S)

Rech, Leslie, *Asst Prof,* South Carolina State University, Dept of Visual & Performing Arts, Orangeburg SC (S)

Recht, Ray, *Prof Theatre,* Marymount Manhattan College, Fine & Performing Arts Div, New York NY (S)

Rector, Renee, *Arts in Educ Dir,* Creative Arts Guild, Dalton GA

Recuparo, Joan, *Budget Analyst,* Syracuse University, SUArt Galleries, Syracuse NY

Redden, Deborah, *Co-Pres,* Guild of Creative Art, Shrewsbury NJ (S)

Reddig, Deborah, *Dir Mus Advancement*, Pennsylvania Historical & Museum Commission. Railroad Museum of Pennsylvania, Harrisburg PA

Reddin, Jim, *Prof*, Shoreline Community College, Humanities Division, Seattle WA (S)

Redding, Jim, *Prof*, Lansing Community College, Visual Arts & Media Dept, Lansing MI (S)

Redding, Mary Anne, *Photo Archives*, Museum of New Mexico, Palace of Governors, Santa Fe NM

Redding, Shawn, *Dir*, City of Atlanta, Arts Clearinghouse, Atlanta GA

Redington, Andrew, *Assoc Prof*, University of Wisconsin Oshkosh, Dept of Art, Oshkosh WI (S)

Redington, Andrew, *Dir*, University of Wisconsin Oshkosh, Allen R Priebe Gallery, Oshkosh WI

Redman, Elisa, *Asst Dir Preservation Svcs*, Midwest Art Conservation Center, Minneapolis MN

Redman, Scott, *Instr*, Springfield College, Dept of Visual & Performing Arts, Springfield MA (S)

Redmon, Maggie, *COO*, Turtle Bay Exploration Park, Redding CA

Redmond, Michael, *Dean Art & Humanities*, Bergen Community College, Visual Art Dept, Paramus NJ (S)

Redvale, Jolene, *Cur Educ*, San Bernardino County Museum, Fine Arts Institute, Redlands CA

Reece-Hughes, Shirley, *Asst Cur Paintings & Sculpture*, Amon Carter Museum of American Art, Fort Worth TX

Reed, Alan, *Assoc Prof*, Saint John's University, Art Dept, Collegeville MN (S)

Reed, Amanda, *Mgr Mem & Special Events*, Tucson Museum of Art and Historic Block, Tucson AZ

Reed, Amy, *Cur Educ*, City of El Paso, El Paso Museum of Art, El Paso TX

Reed, Barbara E, *Librn*, Dartmouth College, Sherman Art Library, Hanover NH

Reed, Barry, *Security*, Yesteryear Village, West Palm Beach FL

Reed, Carl, *Chmn*, Colorado College, Dept of Art, Colorado Springs CO (S)

Reed, Dennis, *Chmn*, Los Angeles Valley College, Art Dept, Van Nuys CA (S)

Reed, Dennis, *Dean*, Los Angeles Valley College, Art Gallery, Valley Glen CA

Reed, Elizabeth, *Mem Coordr*, College of Charleston School of Arts, Halsey Institute of Contemporary Art, Charleston SC

Reed, Evan, *Dir Gallery*, Georgetown University, Dept of Art & Art History, Washington DC (S)

Reed, Jessica, *Promotions Coordr*, Light Work, Robert B Menschel Photography Gallery, Syracuse NY

Reed, Julia, *Chair*, The Ogden Museum of Southern Art, University of New Orleans, New Orleans LA

Reed, Katharine, *Sr Catalogue Librn*, The Nelson-Atkins Museum of Art, Spencer Art Reference Library, Kansas City MO

Reed, Mike, *Deputy Dir Facilities & Risk Management*, Contemporary Arts Museum Houston, Houston TX

Reed, Pamela, *Art History*, Phoenix College, Dept of Art & Photography, Phoenix AZ (S)

Reed, Richard, *Chmn Humanities*, City Colleges of Chicago, Olive-Harvey College, Chicago IL (S)

Reed, Robert, *Prof*, Yale University, School of Art, New Haven CT (S)

Reed, Roger, *Pres*, Illustration House Inc, Gallery Auction House, New York NY

Reed, Roger, *Prof*, Dakota State University, College of Liberal Arts, Madison SD (S)

Reed, Scott, *Assoc Prof*, Colby College, Art Dept, Waterville ME (S)

Reed, Susan H, *Dir*, Imperial Calcasieu Museum, Lake Charles LA

Reed, Victoria, *Monica S Sadler Cur Provenance*, Museum of Fine Arts, Boston MA

Reed, Walt A, *Founder*, Illustration House Inc, Gallery Auction House, New York NY

Reeder, Deborah, *Dir*, St George Art Museum, Saint George UT

Reeder, Leah, *Registrar*, Fort Wayne Museum of Art, Inc, Fort Wayne IN

Reeder, Ron, *Asst Prof 3D & 2D Design*, Rio Hondo College, Visual Arts Dept, Whittier CA (S)

Reed Sanchez, Pamela, *Dir Develop*, George Eastman, Rochester NY

Reekie, Clara, *Dir*, Five Civilized Tribes Museum, Muskogee OK

Reel, David M, *Dir*, United States Military Academy, West Point Museum, West Point NY

Reep, Amy, *Gallery Adminr*, Wichita Center for the Arts, Wichita KS

Reep, Amy, *Gallery Asst*, Kansas Watercolor Society, The Wichita Center for the Arts, Wichita KS

Reese, Brandon, *Assoc Prof*, Oklahoma State University, Department of Art, Graphic Design and Art History, Stillwater OK (S)

Reese, David, *Dir*, Gunston Hall Plantation, Library, Mason Neck VA

Reeve, Deborah B, *Exec Dir*, National Art Education Association, Reston VA

Reeve, Gordon, *Prof*, University of Manitoba, School of Art, Winnipeg MB (S)

Reeves, Alvin, *Asst Cur Agriculture (Emeritus)*, Northern Maine Museum of Science, Presque Isle ME

Reeves, Betty, *Interior Design Faculty*, Harford Community College, Visual, Performing and Applied Arts Division, Bel Air MD (S)

Reeves, Richard, *Film Production Coordr, Instr (Tour de Film)*, Quickdraw Animation Society, Calgary AB

Reeves, Roger, *Exhibit Designer & Production Coordr*, Columbus Museum, Columbus GA

Reeves, Stockton, *VChmn*, Maitland Art Center, Maitland FL

Reeves, Wayne, *Cur*, City of Toronto Museum Services, Historic Fort York, Toronto ON

Reeves, V I S K, *Pres*, Architects Design Group Inc, Winter Park FL

Reff, Yvonne, *Reference Librn*, Roswell P Flower, Watertown NY

Regalado, Lydia, *Educ Coordr*, The Dallas Contemporary, Dallas Visual Art Center, Dallas TX

Regan, David, *Prof*, The University of Montana Western, Art Program, Dillon MT (S)

Regan, Thomas, *Dean of Arts*, Acadia University, Art Dept, Wolfville NS (S)

Regan, Tom, *Dean*, Texas A&M University, College of Architecture, College Station TX (S)

Regan-Dalzell, Kathie, *Instr*, Main Line Art Center, Haverford PA (S)

Reger, Lawrence L, *Pres*, Heritage Preservation, The National Institute for Conservation, Washington DC

Regina, Kristen, *Head of Research Colls*, Hillwood Museum & Gardens Foundation, Hillwood Estate Museum & Gardens, Washington DC

Regis, Jim, *Pres*, Marblehead Arts Association, Inc, Marblehead MA

Register, Christopher M, *Assoc Prof*, Longwood University, Dept of Art, Farmville VA (S)

Regnier, Suzanne M, *Dir Develop*, Brandywine Conservancy, Brandywine River Museum, Chadds Ford PA

Rehm-Mott, Denise, *Prof*, Eastern Illinois University, Art Dept, Charleston IL (S)

Rehrig, Jeanne, *Program Coordr*, Berkeley Art Center, Berkeley CA

Reibach, Lois, *Head Technical Servs*, Lutheran Theological Seminary, Krauth Memorial Library, Philadelphia PA

Reibe, Denise, *Adjunct Instr Foundations*, Montana State University, School of Art, Bozeman MT (S)

Reich, Dindy, *Gallery Dir*, University of Texas Pan American, Art Dept, Edinburg TX (S)

Reich, Marsha, *Educ Coordr*, Southern Alberta Art Gallery, Library, Lethbridge AB

Reichardt, Peter, *Instr*, South Dakota State University, Dept of Visual Arts, Brookings SD (S)

Reiche, Christopher, *New Music Coordr*, Open Space, Victoria BC

Reichert, Herb, *Instr Visual Arts*, Dowling College, Dept of Visual Arts, Oakdale NY (S)

Reichert, John, *Preparator*, Regina Public Library, Dunlop Art Gallery, Regina SK

Reid, Allison, *Dir Exhibs & Prog*, Cheekwood-Tennessee Botanical Garden & Museum of Art, Nashville TN

Reid, Chris, *Cur*, The Art Gallery of Southwestern Manitoba, Brandon MB

Reid, Dennis, *Chief Cur*, Art Gallery of Ontario, Toronto ON

Reid, Dolores Erikson, *VPres*, North Shore Arts Association, Inc, Gloucester MA

Reid, Graeme, *Dir Colls & Exhibs*, Museum of Wisconsin Art, West Bend WI

Reid, Jacqueline, *Dir*, Duke University Library, Hartman Center for Sales, Advertising & Marketing History, Durham NC

Reid, Joan Elizabeth, *Registrar*, Walters Art Museum, Baltimore MD

Reid, Joan-Elisabeth, *Registrar*, Walters Art Museum, Library, Baltimore MD

Reid, Margaret, *Head*, Guilford Technical Community College, Commercial Art Dept, Jamestown NC (S)

Reid, Mary, *Gallery Dir*, University of Manitoba, School of Art Gallery, Winnipeg MB

Reid, Patricia L, *Tech Svcs Assoc*, Corcoran Gallery of Art, Corcoran Library, Washington DC

Reid, Randal, *Prof*, Texas State University - San Marcos, Dept of Art and Design, San Marcos TX (S)

Reid, Shannon, *Shop Mgr*, Craft Council of Newfoundland & Labrador, Saint John's NF

Reid, Sonja, *Registrar*, University of Texas at Austin, Harry Ransom Humanities Research Center, Austin TX

Reid, Stuart, *Dir*, Tom Thomson, Owen Sound ON

Reid, Stuart, *Dir*, Tom Thomson, Library/Archives, Owen Sound ON

Reid, Theresia, *Rentals Mgr*, Chilliwack Community Arts Council, Community Arts Centre, Chilliwack BC

Reid-Cunningham, Jim, *Chief Conservator*, Library of the Boston Athenaeum, Boston MA

Reidel, Caroline, *Cur*, University of Victoria, The Legacy Art Gallery, Victoria BC

Reiff, Daniel, *Prof*, State University of New York at Fredonia, Dept of Art, Fredonia NY (S)

Reiff, Meghan, *Registrar Asst*, Cornell University, Herbert F Johnson Museum of Art, Ithaca NY

Reiff, Roseanne, *Chair Graphics*, Hudson Valley Art Association, Brooklyn NY

Reifsneider, Jennifer, *Registrar*, Missoula Art Museum, Missoula MT

Reigle, Alexandra, *Library Technician*, Hirshhorn Museum & Sculpture Garden, Library, Washington DC

Reiland, Neal, *Prof*, Salt Lake Community College, Graphic Design Dept, Salt Lake City UT (S)

Reiling Lindell, Joanna, *Cur*, Thrivent Financial for Lutherans, Gallery of Religious Art, Minneapolis MN

Reilly, Ann-Marie, *Registrar*, American Folk Art Museum, New York NY

Reilly, Edwin D, *Pres*, Schenectady County Historical Society, Museum of Schenectady History, Schenectady NY

Reilly, James, *Assoc Prof*, Rochester Institute of Technology, School of Photographic Arts & Sciences, Rochester NY (S)

Reilly, Jerry M, *Instr*, Modesto Junior College, Arts Humanities & Communications Division, Modesto CA (S)

Reilly, Karen, *Assoc Dir*, College of the Holy Cross, Dinand Library, Worcester MA

Reilly, Katie, *Head Publ*, Carnegie Museums of Pittsburgh, Carnegie Museum of Art, Pittsburgh PA

Reilly, Patricia L, *Assoc Provost & Assoc Prof*, Swarthmore College, Dept of Art & Art History, Swarthmore PA (S)

Reily, Shelia, *Deputy Dir Prog*, South Carolina State Museum, Columbia SC

Reimann, Amy, *Exec Dir*, Ella Sharp, Jackson MI

Reimer, Karen, *Publications Dir*, The Renaissance Society, Chicago IL

Reinckens, Sharon, *Deputy Dir*, Anacostia Community Museum, Smithsonian Institution, Washington DC

Reinhardt, Beatrix, *Asst Prof*, College of Staten Island, Performing & Creative Arts Dept, Staten Island NY (S)

Reinhardt, Janine, *Visitor Serv Assoc*, University of Wyoming, University of Wyoming Art Museum, Laramie WY

Reinhardt, Kim, *Mgr*, Nova Scotia Museum, Maritime Museum of the Atlantic, Halifax NS

Reinhardt-Gillis, Giselle, *Exec Asst & Office Mgr*, Blue Star Contemporary Art Center, San Antonio TX

Reinhart, Virginia, *Develop Assoc,* Museum for African Art, New York NY

Reintjes, Brandon, *Cur,* University of Montana, Montana Museum of Art & Culture, Missoula MT

Reis, Jennifer, *Asst Prof,* Morehead State University, Art & Design Dept, Morehead KY (S)

Reis, Jennifer, *Dir,* Morehead State University, Claypool-Young Art Gallery, Morehead KY

Reischmann, Monica, *Dir Develop,* Nassau County Museum of Art, Roslyn Harbor NY

Reising, Christine, *Prof & Chmn,* Siena Heights University, Studio Angelico-Art Dept, Adrian MI (S)

Reisner, Vicki, *Dir Vis Svcs,* Honolulu Museum of Art, Honolulu HI

Reisner, Vicki, *Spec Events,* Honolulu Academy of Arts, The Art Center at Linekona, Honolulu HI (S)

Reiss, Ellen, *Chmn Educ,* Aesthetic Realism Foundation, New York NY

Reiss, Ellen, *Chmn Educ,* Aesthetic Realism Foundation, New York NY

Reist, Inge, *Dir Center for the History of Collecting,* The Frick Collection, Frick Art Reference Library, New York NY

Reiter, Wellington, *School Pres,* The Art Institute of Chicago, Chicago IL

Reitzenstein, Reinhard, *Asst Prof,* University at Buffalo, State University of New York, Dept of Visual Studies, Buffalo NY (S)

Reizen, Sandie, *Mus Shop Mgr,* Rensselaer County Historical Society, Hart-Cluett Mansion, 1827, Troy NY

Rejholec, Joe, *Chmn,* South Suburban College, Art Dept, South Holland IL (S)

Rekedael, Jane, *Adjunct Prof,* Gavilan Community College, Art Dept, Gilroy CA (S)

Reker, Ken, *Assoc Prof,* Salem State University, Art & Design Department, Salem MA (S)

Reller, Tracy, *Assoc Prof,* Hillsborough Community College, Fine Arts Dept, Tampa FL (S)

Relyea, Lane, *Asst Prof,* Northwestern University, Evanston, Dept of Art Theory & Practice, Evanston IL (S)

Relyea, Linda, *PT Instr,* Adams State College, Dept of Visual Arts, Alamosa CO (S)

Remeczki, Paul, *Asst Librn,* Queens College, City University of New York, Art Library, Flushing NY

Remieres, Roberta, *Receptionist,* Rhode Island Watercolor Society, Pawtucket RI

Remington, Lynne, *Exec Dir,* Chicago Art Dealers Association, Chicago IL

Remington, R Roger, *Prof,* Rochester Institute of Technology, School of Design, Rochester NY (S)

Remning-Johnson, John, *Sculpture Tour Coordr,* Western Michigan University, Gwen Frostic School of Art, Kalamazoo MI

Remus, Stephen, *Dir Opers & Programming,* Niagara Artists' Company, St Catharines ON

Renaldi, Beverly, *Properties Mgr,* Lehigh Valley Heritage Center, Allentown PA

Rendon, Joanne, *Librn,* The Society of the Four Arts, Gioconda & Joseph King Library, Palm Beach FL

Reneav, Davie, *Assoc Prof Art,* Campbellsville University, Department of Art, Campbellsville KY (S)

Renfro, Charles, *Pres,* Storefront for Art & Architecture, New York NY

Renfro, Cora, *Instr,* Campbellsville University, Department of Art, Campbellsville KY (S)

Renfro, William, *Prof,* Texas A&M University-Kingsville, Art Dept, Kingsville TX (S)

Renko, Jennifer, *Asst Dean Admis & Cont Ed,* Lyme Academy College of Fine Arts, Old Lyme CT (S)

Renneker, Holly, *Exhib Cur,* Anderson Fine Arts Center, The Anderson Center for the Arts, Anderson IN

Renner, Jennifer, *Dir External Affairs & Develop,* National Portrait Gallery, Smithsonian Institution, Washington DC

Rennie, Mark, *Exec Dir,* Eyes & Ears Foundation, San Francisco CA

Reno, Carolyn, *Coll Mgr,* City of Springdale, Shiloh Museum of Ozark History, Springdale AR

Reno, Kathy, *Dir Mktg & Pub Rels,* Saint Joseph Museum, Saint Joseph MO

Reno, Timothy, *Asst Prof Music,* Siena College, Dept of Creative Arts, Loudonville NY (S)

Renskers, Kim, *Lib Asst,* New York Institute of Technology, Art & Architectural Library, Old Westbury NY

Renz, Kevin, *Assoc Dean Interior Design,* Endicott College, School of Visual & Performing Arts, Beverly MA (S)

Reo, Danielle, *Assoc Dir,* Installation Gallery, San Diego CA

Repice, Jenine, *Prog Coordr,* Greenwich House Pottery, First Floor Gallery, New York NY

Repinski, Robert, *Asst Prof,* University of Minnesota, Duluth, Art Dept, Duluth MN (S)

Reres, Sara, *Dir, Treas & Cur,* Sea Cliff Village Museum, Sea Cliff NY

Resch, Tyler, *Librn,* Bennington Museum, Bennington VT

Resnick, Alyssa, *Sr Library Supvr,* Glendale Public Library, Brand Library & Art Center, Glendale CA

Resnick, Elizabeth, *Chair Commun Design,* Massachusetts College of Art, Boston MA (S)

Resnik, Kim, *Pub Rels Media Contact,* International Fine Arts College, Miami FL (S)

Resnik, Lisa Betson, *COO,* The Speed Art Museum, Louisville KY

Reso-Hickman, Dorothy, *Vol Coordr,* Red Deer & District Museum & Archives, Red Deer AB

Retallack, John, *Assoc Prof,* Rochester Institute of Technology, School of Photographic Arts & Sciences, Rochester NY (S)

Rettew, Robert H, *Librn,* Saint Paul's School, Ohrstrom Library, Concord NH

Rettich, Jon, *Treas,* Federation of Modern Painters & Sculptors, New York NY

Reuter, Laurel J, *Dir & Chief Cur,* North Dakota Museum of Art, Grand Forks ND

Reutter, David, *Registrar,* College of Central Florida, Appleton Museum of Art, Ocala FL

Reville, Patricia, *Pres,* Wesleyan University, Friends of the Davison Art Center, Middletown CT

ReVille, Stephen W, *Owner & CEO,* Portraits South, Raleigh NC

Rexine, John, *Registrar,* Massachusetts Institute of Technology, List Visual Arts Center, Cambridge MA

Rey, Alberto, *Prof,* State University of New York at Fredonia, Dept of Art, Fredonia NY (S)

Reyes, Ann N, *Cur Educ,* Museum of East Texas, Lufkin TX

Reyes, David, *Cur Colls & Exhibs,* Huntsville Museum of Art, Huntsville AL

Reyes, Roman, *Chmn,* Phoenix College, Dept of Art & Photography, Phoenix AZ (S)

Reyman, Johnathan, *Cur Anthropology,* Illinois State Museum, Museum Store, Chicago IL

Reymann, Patrick H, *VPres,* Western Reserve Historical Society, Library, Cleveland OH

Reymond, Rhonda, *Assoc Prof,* West Virginia University, College of Creative Arts, School of Art & Design, Morgantown WV (S)

Reyna, Nazario, *Maintenance,* Hidalgo County Historical Museum, Edinburg TX

Reyner, Justen, *Asst Prof,* Oklahoma State University, Department of Art, Graphic Design and Art History, Stillwater OK (S)

Reynolds, Ben, *Acad Professional Photog,* University of Georgia, Franklin College of Arts & Sciences, Lamar Dodd School of Art, Athens GA (S)

Reynolds, Carol, *Dir,* Congregation Beth Israel's Plotkin Judaica Museum, Scottsdale AZ

Reynolds, Edmond, *Dir,* R L S Silverado Museum, Saint Helena CA

Reynolds, Jock, *Dir,* Yale University, Yale University Art Gallery, New Haven CT

Reynolds, Joclyn L, *Grants Mgr,* Arts Council Of New Orleans, New Orleans LA

Reynolds, John, *Lead Preparator,* Dartmouth College, Hood Museum of Art, Hanover NH

Reynolds, Kathy, *Dir,* Cripple Creek District Museum, Cripple Creek CO

Reynolds, Kimberly, *Cur Manuscripts,* Boston Public Library, Rare Book & Manuscripts Dept, Boston MA

Reynolds, Kimberly, *Dir Commun,* Wadsworth Atheneum Museum of Art, Hartford CT

Reynolds, Lindsey, *Library Asst,* Whitney Museum of American Art, Frances Mulhall Achilles Library, New York NY

Reynolds, Lisa I, *Office Mgr,* National Trust for Historic Preservation, Chesterwood, Stockbridge MA

Reynolds, Lynn, *Chmn,* McNeese State University, Dept of Visual Arts, Lake Charles LA (S)

Reynolds, Mike, *Asst Preparation,* Oberlin College, Allen Memorial Art Museum, Oberlin OH

Reynolds, Pamela, *Pres,* Virginia Museum of Fine Arts, Richmond VA

Reynolds, Rebecca, *Asst Prof,* University of New Orleans-Lake Front, Dept of Fine Arts, New Orleans LA (S)

Reynolds, Ryan, *Asst Prof,* Santa Clara University, Dept of Art & Art History, Santa Clara CA (S)

Reynolds, Tony, *Pres,* Licking County Arts, Art Gallery, Newark OH

Reynolds, Vic, *Prof,* Wayne State College, Dept Art & Design, Wayne NE (S)

Reynolds-Botwin, Virginia, *Corresp Secy,* Miami Watercolor Society, Inc, Miami FL

Reynoso, Rondall, *Dept Coordr,* Louisiana College, Dept of Art, Pineville LA (S)

Reznicek, Laura, *Develop Dir,* University of Nebraska, Lincoln, Sheldon Memorial Art Gallery & Sculpture Garden, Lincoln NE

Rhea, Patty, *Cur,* Rockford Art Museum, Rockford IL

Rheault, Martine, *Dir,* York University, Glendon Gallery, Toronto ON

Rhein, Katrina, *Dir,* College of New Rochelle, Castle Gallery, New Rochelle NY

Rhie, Marylin, *Prof,* Smith College, Art Dept, Northampton MA (S)

Rhinehart, Benjamin, *Assoc Prof,* Lawrence University, Dept of Art & Art History, Appleton WI (S)

Rhinelander, Patty, *Members' Gallery,* Lunenburg Art Gallery Society, Lunenburg NS

Rhoad, Julie, *Exec Dir,* The Names Project Foundation AIDS Memorial Quilt, Atlanta GA

Rhoades, Sara, *Asst Dir,* University of Southern Indiana, New Harmony Gallery of Contemporary Art, New Harmony IN

Rhoads, Beverly, *Prof,* Lynchburg College, Art Dept, Lynchburg VA (S)

Rhoads, Thomas, *Assoc Dir Admin,* Getty Center, The J Paul Getty Museum, Los Angeles CA

Rhoback, Kristie, *Textile Cur,* Amherst Museum, Amherst NY

Rhoda, Lynn, *Comm Arts Develop Dir,* Arts of the Southern Finger Lakes, Corning NY

Rhodes, C T, *Pres,* eMediaLoft.org, New York NY

Rhodes, Che, *Asst Prof,* University of Louisville, Allen R Hite Art Institute, Louisville KY (S)

Rhodes, David, *Pres,* School of Visual Arts, New York NY (S)

Rhodes, Mark, *Assoc Prof,* University of Richmond, Dept of Art and Art History, Richmond VA (S)

Rhodes, Milton, *Pres & CEO,* The Arts Council of Winston-Salem & Forsyth County, Winston Salem NC

Rhodes, Richard, *Ed,* Canadian Art Foundation, Toronto ON

Rhodes, Silas H, *Chmn,* School of Visual Arts, New York NY (S)

Rhodes, Tisha, *Spec Events Coordr,* Montgomery Museum of Fine Arts, Montgomery AL

Rhodes-Ousley, Marjorie, *Assoc Dir,* California State University, East Bay, C E Smith Museum of Anthropology, Hayward CA

Rhodier, Vicki, *Corresp Secy,* Berks Art Alliance, Reading PA

Rhone, Kim, *Instr,* Lycoming College, Art Dept, Williamsport PA (S)

Rhyne, Grace, *Exec Dir,* WomanKraft Art Center, Tucson AZ

Rhyne, Zoe, *Dir Exhibs,* WomanKraft Art Center, Tucson AZ

Rial, Vicki, *Exhib Coordr,* University of Alabama, Sarah Moody Gallery of Art, Tuscaloosa AL

Ribas, Jose, *Preparator,* Bowdoin College, Museum of Art, Brunswick ME

Ribkoff, Natalie, *Cur Art,* Toronto Dominion Bank, Toronto ON

Ribner, Naomi, *Instr,* College of the Holy Cross, Dept of Visual Arts, Worcester MA (S)

Riccardi, Lee-Ann, *Prof Art History,* The College of New Jersey, School of Arts & Sciences, Ewing NJ (S)

Ricci, Pat, *Cur,* Confederate Memorial Hall, Confederate Museum, New Orleans LA

Ricci, Steve, *Pub Rels & Mktg Mgr,* Albany Institute of History & Art, Albany NY

Ricco, Wendy, *Dept Secy,* University of Nevada, Reno, Sheppard Contemporary & University Galleries, Reno NV

Rice, Carol, *Dir Progs,* ArtsConnection Inc, New York NY

Rice, Danielle, *Exec Dir,* Delaware Art Museum, Wilmington DE

Rice, Emily, *Lectr,* Washburn University of Topeka, Dept of Art, Topeka KS (S)

Rice, James, *Chmn Photographic Processing & Finishing Management,* Rochester Institute of Technology, School of Photographic Arts & Sciences, Rochester NY (S)

Rice, Jamie K, *Pub Svcs Librn,* Maine Historical Society, Library and Museum, Portland ME

Rice, Jane, *Dir Institutional Advanc,* Museum of Contemporary Art, San Diego, Geisel Library, La Jolla CA

Rice, Jenna, *Gallery Coordr,* Florida Southern College, Melvin Art Gallery, Lakeland FL

Rice, John Henry, *Assoc Cur, S Asian & Islamic Art,* Virginia Museum of Fine Arts, Richmond VA

Rice, Joseph A, *Chmn,* John Simon Guggenheim, New York NY

Rice, Kevin, *Art Gallery Dir & Cur Hist Art,* Confederation Centre Art Gallery and Museum, Charlottetown PE

Rice, Laura, *Chief Cur,* The Adirondack Historical Association, The Adirondack Museum, Blue Mountain Lake NY

Rice, Noelle, *Asst Cur,* University of South Carolina, McKissick Museum, Columbia SC

Rice, Noelle, *Curatorial Asst,* Columbia Museum of Art, Lee Alexander Lorick Library, Columbia SC

Rice, Ryan, *Chief Cur,* Institute of American Indian Arts, Museum of Contemporary Native Arts, Santa Fe NM

Rice, Ryan, *Chief Cur,* Institute of American Indian Arts, Museum of Contemporary Native Arts, Santa Fe NM (S)

Rice, Tom, *Chmn,* Kalamazoo College, Art Dept, Kalamazoo MI (S)

Rice-Allen, Daphne, *Coordr,* Black American West Museum & Heritage Center, Denver CO

Rich, Harry, *CFO,* Missouri Historical Society, Missouri History Museum, Saint Louis MO

Rich, Sarah, *Assoc Prof,* Pennsylvania State University, University Park, Dept of Art History, University Park PA (S)

Rich-Wulfmeyer, Rebecca, *Chief Librn & Archivist,* Albany Institute of History & Art, Library, Albany NY

Richard, Charles, *Media Chmn,* Riverside Community College, Dept of Art & Mass Media, Riverside CA (S)

Richard, Jack, *Dir,* Jack Richard Gallery, Almond Tea Museum & Jane Williams Galleries, Divisions of Studios of Jack Richard, Cuyahoga Falls OH

Richard, Jack, *Dir,* Studios of Jack Richard, Professional School of Painting & Design, Cuyahoga Falls OH (S)

Richard, Jack, *Owner,* Jack Richard Gallery, Almond Tea Museum & Jane Williams Galleries, Library, Cuyahoga Falls OH

Richard, Lucille, *Vol Secy,* Rangeley Lakes Region Logging Museum, Rangeley ME

Richard, Lynn-Marie, *Registrar,* Nova Scotia Museum, Maritime Museum of the Atlantic, Halifax NS

Richard, Mervin, *Board Chair,* Heritage Preservation, The National Institute for Conservation, Washington DC

Richard, Mervin, *Chief Conservation,* National Gallery of Art, Washington DC

Richard, Rodney C, *Vol Pres & Dir,* Rangeley Lakes Region Logging Museum, Rangeley ME

Richard, Stephen A, *Festival Coordr,* Rangeley Lakes Region Logging Museum, Rangeley ME

Richard, Tom, *Chmn,* University of Arkansas at Monticello, Fine Arts Dept, Monticello AR (S)

Richards, Evann, *Asst Prof,* Saint Louis Community College at Forest Park, Art Dept, Saint Louis MO (S)

Richards, Frank, *Resource Devel,* Bob Jones University Museum & Gallery Inc, Greenville SC

Richards, Janet, *Assoc Cur,* University of Michigan, Kelsey Museum of Archaeology, Ann Arbor MI

Richards, Jennifer, *Develop & Communs Mgr,* Fairmount Park Art Association, Philadelphia PA

Richards, Karen, *Accnt,* The San Joaquin Pioneer & Historical Society, The Haggin Museum, Stockton CA

Richards, Kevin, *Liberal Arts Dept Chair,* Pennsylvania Academy of the Fine Arts, Office of Admission, Philadelphia PA (S)

Richards, Larry, *Coordr, Eric Arthur Gallery,* University of Toronto, Faculty of Architecture, Landscape & Design, Toronto ON (S)

Richards, Nancy, *Cur Coll,* Tryon Palace Historic Sites & Gardens, New Bern NC

Richards, Patricia, *Assoc Prof Photog,* Tarrant County College, Art Dept, Hurst TX (S)

Richards, Ron, *Chief Cur Nat History,* Indiana State Museum, Indianapolis IN

Richards, Rosalyn, *Head Dept,* Bucknell University, Dept of Art, Lewisburg PA (S)

Richardson, Carl, *Asst Prof,* Spokane Falls Community College, Fine Arts Dept, Spokane WA (S)

Richardson, Cassidy, *Asst Cur,* Plug In, Institute of Contemporary Art, Winnipeg MB

Richardson, Courtney, *Museum Educator,* Cape Ann Historical Association, Cape Ann Museum, Gloucester MA

Richardson, Dave, *Asst Prof,* Eastern Illinois University, Art Dept, Charleston IL (S)

Richardson, Debra, *Exec Dir,* Fillmore County Historical Society, Fillmore County History Center, Fountain MN

Richardson, Elvis, *Asst Prof Visual Arts,* Dowling College, Dept of Visual Arts, Oakdale NY (S)

Richardson, Louise, *Cur,* Warner House Association, MacPheadris-Warner House, Portsmouth NH

Richardson, Terry, *Instr,* Rochester Community & Technical College, Art Dept, Rochester MN (S)

Richardson, Tracey, *Assoc Prof,* Silver Lake College, Art Dept, Manitowoc WI (S)

Richardson, Trevor, *Contact,* University of Massachusetts, Amherst, Herter Art Gallery, Amherst MA

Richardson, Vicki, *Dir,* Left of Center Art Gallery & Studio, North Las Vegas NV

Richbourg, Lance, *Assoc Prof,* St Michael's College, Fine Arts Dept, Colchester VT (S)

Richel, Jean Marc, *Artist,* Walker's Point Artists Assoc Inc, Gallery 218, Milwaukee WI

Richelson, Paul W, *Chief Cur,* Mobile Museum of Art, Mobile AL

Richelson, Paul W, *Chief Cur,* Mobile Museum of Art, Library, Mobile AL

Richerson, Jim, *Pres & CEO,* Lakeview Museum of Arts & Sciences, Peoria IL

Richey-Ward, Diane, *Instr,* American River College, Dept of Art/Art New Media, Sacramento CA (S)

Richman, Irwin, *Prof,* Penn State Harrisburg, School of Humanities, Middletown PA (S)

Richman, Martin, *Dir Develop,* Worcester Art Museum, Worcester MA

Richman, Roger, *Prof,* University of Maine at Augusta, College of Arts & Humanities, Augusta ME (S)

Richmond, David, *Head Art Dept,* Simpson College, Farnham Gallery, Indianola IA

Richmond, Jennifer, *Asst Cur,* University of North Texas, Visual Resources Collection, Denton TX

Richmond, Jerl, *Exhib Designer & Chief Preparator,* University of Wisconsin-Madison, Chazen Museum of Art, Madison WI

Richner, Nancy, *Mus Educ Dir,* Hofstra University, Hofstra University Museum, Hempstead NY

Richter, Donald, *Pres,* Vermilion County Museum Society, Library, Danville IL

Richter, Eric, *Co-Chmn,* 1078 Gallery, Chico CA

Richter, Kristen, *Pub Rels Mgr,* City Arts Center at Fair Park, Oklahoma City OK

Richter, Marianne, *Exec Dir,* Swope Art Museum, Terre Haute IN

Richter, Marianne, *Exec Dir,* Swope Art Museum, Research Library, Terre Haute IN

Richter, Susan, *Dir,* Vermilion County Museum Society, Danville IL

Richter, Susan E, *Dir,* Vermilion County Museum Society, Library, Danville IL

Rickard, Jolene, *Assoc Prof,* University at Buffalo, State University of New York, Dept of Visual Studies, Buffalo NY (S)

Rickard, Jolene, *Assoc Prof,* Cornell University, Dept of Art, Ithaca NY (S)

Rickerson, Carla, *Head,* University of Washington, Univ of Washington Libraries, Special Collections, Seattle WA

Rickerson, Irini, *Art History,* Orange Coast College, Visual & Performing Arts Division, Costa Mesa CA (S)

Ricklin, Elaine, *Sec,* Spark Gallery, Denver CO

Ricks-Bates, Anita, *Instr,* Marygrove College, Department of Art, Detroit MI (S)

Riddle, Lola, *Treas,* Fulton County Historical Society Inc, Fulton County Museum (Tetzlaff Reference Room), Rochester IN

Rider, Diane, *Library-LRC Dir,* Art Institute of Fort Lauderdale, Technical Library, Fort Lauderdale FL

Rider, Geoff, *Dir Curatorial,* Canada Science and Technology Museum, Ottawa ON

Ridgway, Holly, *Mem & Events Coordr,* Hockaday Museum of Art, Kalispell MT

Ridgway, Linda, *Admin Coordr,* National Audubon Society, John James Audubon Center at Mill Grove, Audubon PA

Rieben, John, *Prof,* University of Wisconsin, Madison, Dept of Art, Madison WI (S)

Riedel, Walter, *Pres & CEO Stark Foundation,* Nelda C & H J Lutcher Stark, Stark Museum of Art, Orange TX

Rieder, Andrew, *Instr,* Delta College, Art Dept, University Center MI (S)

Riedinger, Robert J, *Correspondence Secy,* Artists' Fellowship, Inc, New York NY

Riefler, Heidi, *Dir Communs,* National Academy Museum & School, New York NY

Rieger, Sonja, *Prof,* University of Alabama at Birmingham, Dept of Art & Art History, Birmingham AL (S)

Rieke Miller, Stephanie, *External Rels Mgr & Sr Writer,* University of Michigan, Museum of Art, Ann Arbor MI

Rieman, Diane, *Asst Prof,* Marygrove College, Department of Art, Detroit MI (S)

Riesby, Mark, *Mus Dir,* University of Southern Mississippi, Dept of Art & Design, Hattiesburg MS (S)

Riese, Tara, *Asst Librn,* The Buffalo Fine Arts Academy, G Robert Strauss Jr Memorial Library, Buffalo NY

Riesenberg, Mindy, *Dir Mktg,* Phoenix Art Museum, Phoenix AZ

Riess, Jonathan, *Prof Art History,* University of Cincinnati, School of Art, Cincinnati OH (S)

Rieth, Sheri, *Chair & Prof,* University of Mississippi, Department of Art, University MS (S)

Rietveld, Rickard, *Chmn,* Valencia Community College - East Campus, Art Dept, Orlando FL (S)

Rietveldt, Bill, *Exhibits Coordr,* North Central Washington Museum, Wenatchee Valley Museum & Cultural Center, Wenatchee WA

Rife, Jerry, *Chmn,* Rider University, Dept of Fine Arts, Lawrenceville NJ (S)

Riffee, Steve, *Asst Dir,* Lynchburg College, Daura Gallery, Lynchburg VA

Riffi, Nadia, ASTED Inc, Montreal QC

Riffle, Brenda, *Librn,* Hampshire County Public Library, Romney WV

Rifkin, Ned, *Dir,* University of Texas at Austin, Blanton Museum of Art, Austin TX

Rigby, Bruce, *Prof,* The College of New Jersey, School of Arts & Sciences, Ewing NJ (S)

Rigby, Casey, *Exhibs Coordr,* Spartanburg Art Museum, Spartanburg SC

Rigby, Ida K, *Dir,* San Diego State University, University Art Gallery, San Diego CA

Rigby, Mary Ellen, *Gift Shop Mgr,* Dartmouth College, Hood Museum of Art, Hanover NH

Rigg, Siobhan, *Asst Prof,* George Washington University, Dept of Art of Fine Arts & Art History, Washington DC (S)

Riggins-Ezzell, Lois, *Exec Dir,* Tennessee State Museum, Nashville TN

Riggle, Shelby, *Mktg & Outreach Coordr,* Saginaw Art Museum, Saginaw MI

Riggleman, Jim, *Treas,* Allegany County Historical Society, Gordon-Roberts House, Cumberland MD

Riggs, Ed, *Chair Commun Art Technology,* Montgomery College, Dept of Art, Rockville MD (S)

Riggs, Timothy, *Cur Colls,* University of North Carolina at Chapel Hill, Ackland Art Museum, Chapel Hill NC

Rigsby, Mark, *Asst Dir,* University of Southern Mississippi, Museum of Art, Hattiesburg MS

Riker, Janet, *Dir,* University at Albany, State University of New York, University Art Museum, Albany NY

Riley, Caroline, *Cur,* Gunston Hall Plantation, Library, Mason Neck VA

Riley, Christine, *Artist in Res, Musical Theatre,* Marymount Manhattan College, Fine & Performing Arts Div, New York NY (S)

Riley, Corrin, *Dir Develop,* Columbus Museum, Columbus GA

Riley, Dixie, *Head Librn,* Chappell Memorial Library and Art Gallery, Chappell NE

Riley, Jill St Clair, *Asst Prof,* Catholic University of America, School of Architecture & Planning, Washington DC (S)

Riley, Lane, *Mem Coordr,* Columbus Museum, Columbus GA

Riley, Lynn, *Mgr,* Delaware Division of Historical & Cultural Affairs, Dover DE

Riley, Megan, *Dir External Affairs,* Bass Museum of Art, Miami Beach FL

Riley, Philip, *Secy,* Association of Hawaii Artists, Honolulu HI

Riley, Wendy, *Instr,* Casper College, Dept of Visual Arts, Casper WY (S)

Rimel, Luanne, *Educ Dir,* Craft Alliance, Saint Louis MO

Rimmer, Cate, *Cur,* Emily Carr Institute of Art & Design, The Charles H Scott Gallery, Vancouver BC

Rimpela, Cindy, *Bus Mgr,* Ashtabula Arts Center, Ashtabula OH

Rinaldi, Tina, *Gallery Dir,* Lane Arts Council, Jacobs Gallery, Eugene OR

Rinaldo, Lisa, *Instr,* Biola University, Art Dept, La Mirada CA (S)

Rindfleisch, Jan, *Dir,* De Anza College, Euphrat Museum of Art, Cupertino CA

Rindlisbacher, David, *Assoc Prof,* West Texas A&M University, Art, Theatre & Dance Dept, Canyon TX (S)

Rindt, Brooke, *Gift Shop coordr,* Historic Columbian Theatre Foundation, Columbian Theatre Museum & Art Center, Wamego KS

Rine, Margie, *Assoc Dir,* University of Texas at Austin, Harry Ransom Humanities Research Center, Austin TX

Rinehart, Jeff, *Instr,* University of New Orleans-Lake Front, Dept of Fine Arts, New Orleans LA (S)

Rinehart, Patrick, *Prog Dir,* Walt Whitman Cultural Arts Center, Inc, Camden NJ

Ringer, Mark, *Prof Theatre,* Marymount Manhattan College, Fine & Performing Arts Div, New York NY (S)

Ringering, Dennis L, *Head Drawing,* Southern Illinois University at Edwardsville, Dept of Art & Design, Edwardsville IL (S)

Ringkvist, Leilani, *Cur Asst,* University of New Mexico, University of New Mexico Art Museum, Albuquerque NM

Ringler, Sara, *Prof,* Cape Cod Community College, Art Dept, West Barnstable MA (S)

Ringler, Tamsie, *Asst Prof,* St. Catherine University, Art & Art History Dept, Saint Paul MN (S)

Rini, David, *Assoc Prof,* Johns Hopkins University, School of Medicine, Dept of Art as Applied to Medicine, Baltimore MD (S)

Rinklin, Cristi, *Asst Prof,* College of the Holy Cross, Dept of Visual Arts, Worcester MA (S)

Riordon, Bernard, *Dir & CEO,* Beaverbrook Art Gallery, Fredericton NB

Rios-Bermudez, Anna, *Cur Colls,* Museum of Ventura County, Ventura CA

Ripepi, Maria, *Asst Prof,* La Roche College, Division of Design, Pittsburgh PA (S)

Ripley, Debra, *Chmn Art History & Sciences,* Milwaukee Institute of Art & Design, Milwaukee WI (S)

Ripley, Richard, *Instructional Aide,* Victor Valley Community College, Art Dept, Victorville CA (S)

Ripley, Robert C, *Capitol Adminr,* Nebraska State Capitol, Lincoln NE

Ripley, Sylvia, *Owner,* Addison/Ripley Fine Art, Washington DC

Rippe, Diane, *Dir Opers,* Key West Art & Historical Society, East Martello Museum & Gallery, Key West FL

Ripperger, Margaret, *Chmn,* Winterset Art Center, Winterset IA

Ripps, Cerise, *Admin Asst,* Frontier Times Museum, Bandera TX

Risatti, Howard, *Prof,* Virginia Commonwealth University, Art History Dept, Richmond VA (S)

Risbeck, Phil, *Chmn,* Colorado State University, Dept of Art, Fort Collins CO (S)

Risberg, Debra, *Cur,* Illinois State University, Museum Library, Normal IL

Riseman, Henry, *Dir,* New England Center for Contemporary Art, Brooklyn CT

Rishel, Joseph, *Cur,* Philadelphia Museum of Art, John G Johnson Collection, Philadelphia PA

Rishel, Joseph, *Cur of Pre-1900 European Painting & Sculpture,* Philadelphia Museum of Art, Rodin Museum of Philadelphia, Philadelphia PA

Riske, Patricia, *Instr,* Biola University, Art Dept, La Mirada CA (S)

Riskin, Seth, *Emerging Technologies Coordr,* Massachusetts Institute of Technology, MIT Museum, Cambridge MA

Risser, Julie, *Prof,* University of Saint Thomas, Dept of Art History, Saint Paul MN (S)

Ritchie, Andrea, *Paints Coordr,* Visual Arts Nova Scotia, Halifax NS

Ritchie, Cathy, *Theater/Film Librn,* J Eric Johnson, Fine Arts Division, Dallas TX

Ritchie, David, *Instr,* Pacific Northwest College of Art, Portland OR (S)

Ritchie, Robert C, *Dir Research,* The Huntington Library, Art Collections & Botanical Gardens, San Marino CA

Ritchie, Robert C, *Dir Research & Educ,* The Huntington Library, Art Collections & Botanical Gardens, Library, San Marino CA

Riter, David, *Chmn,* City Colleges of Chicago, Daley College, Chicago IL (S)

Ritger, Suzanne, *Gallery Dir,* Johnson State College, Dept Fine & Performing Arts, Dibden Center for the Arts, Johnson VT (S)

Ritiger, Scott, *Industrial Design Technology,* Art Institute of Pittsburgh, Pittsburgh PA (S)

Ritson, Kate, *Chmn & Prof,* Trinity University, Dept of Art, San Antonio TX (S)

Rittelmann, Leesa, *Assoc Prof,* Hartwick College, Art Dept, Oneonta NY (S)

Rittenhouse, Cherri, *Prof,* Rock Valley College, Humanities and Fine Arts Division, Rockford IL (S)

Ritter, Connie, *Interpretive Resource Technician,* Mark Twain, State Historic Site Museum, Florida MO

Ritter, Josef, *Prof,* Cazenovia College, Center for Art & Design Studies, Cazenovia NY (S)

Ritter, Shelley, *Dir,* Delta Blues Museum, Clarksdale MS

Rittler, Steve, *Asst Prof,* William Paterson University, Dept Arts, Wayne NJ (S)

Rivard, TJ, *Chmn,* Indiana University-East, Humanities Dept, Richmond IN (S)

Rivera, Diane, *Mus Asst,* Blauvelt Demarest Foundation, Hiram Blauvelt Art Museum, Oradell NJ

Rivera, Frank, *Prof,* Mercer County Community College, Arts, Communication & Engineering Technology, West Windsor NJ (S)

Rivera, George, *Exec Dir & Sr Cur,* Triton Museum of Art, Santa Clara CA

Rivero, Arturo, *Industrial Design Technology,* Art Institute of Pittsburgh, Pittsburgh PA (S)

Rivers, Todd, *Cur Exhibs,* University of Georgia, Georgia Museum of Art, Athens GA

Rix, Marilu, *Store Mgr,* Maricopa County Historical Society, Desert Caballeros Western Museum, Wickenburg AZ

Rizvi, Ahtasham, *Librn Colls Liaison,* Sheridan College of Applied Arts and Technology, Trafalgar Campus Library, Oakville ON

Rizzardi, Nancy, *Instr,* Pierce College, Art Dept, Woodland Hills CA (S)

Rizzo, Mike, *Designer,* National Heritage Museum, Lexington MA

Roan, Joan, *Circ & Interlibrary Loan,* Ames Free-Easton's Public Library, North Easton MA

Robb, Betsy, *Cur Educ,* Honolulu Museum of Art, Honolulu HI

Robb, Jenny E, *Cur,* Ohio State University, Billy Ireland Cartoon Library & Museum, Columbus OH

Robb, Lisa, *Exec Dir,* Pelham Art Center, Pelham NY

Robb, Penny, *School of Art Admin Asst,* Lighthouse ArtCenter Museum & School of Art, Tequesta FL

Robbin, C Roxanne, *Prof,* California State University, Art Dept, Turlock CA (S)

Robbins, Carol, *Cur Arts of the Americas & the Pacific,* Dallas Museum of Art, Dallas TX

Robbins, Carolyn, *Cur Educ,* Scottsdale Cultural Council, Scottsdale Museum of Contemporary Art, Scottsdale AZ

Robbins, Christopher, *Asst Prof,* Purchase College, State University of New York, School of Art+Design, Purchase NY (S)

Robbins, Gay, *Prof,* Emory University, Art History Dept, Atlanta GA (S)

Robbins, Jay, *Exec Dir,* Lincoln County Historical Association, Inc, Pownalborough Courthouse, Wiscasset ME

Robbins, Jay, *Exec Dir,* Lincoln County Historical Association, Inc, 1811 Old Lincoln County Jail & Lincoln County Museum, Wiscasset ME

Robbins, Stephanie, *Co-Coordr Photog,* Shepherd University, Dept of Contemporary Art & Theater, Shepherdstown WV (S)

Roberge, Michele, *Asst Mgr,* Lincoln County Historical Association, Inc, Maine Art Gallery, Wiscasset ME

Roberson, Keith, *Assoc Prof,* Florida State University, Art Dept, Tallahassee FL (S)

Roberson, Robert, *Dir Asst,* Plains Indians & Pioneers Historical Foundation, Museum & Art Center, Woodward OK

Roberson, Tom, *Devel,* Booth Western Art Museum, Cartersville GA

Robert, Brenda, *Dean,* Anoka Ramsey Community College, Art Dept, Coon Rapids MN (S)

Roberts, Anne, *Chmn,* Lake Forest College, Dept of Art, Lake Forest IL (S)

Roberts, Brady, *Chief Cur,* Milwaukee Art Museum, Milwaukee WI

Roberts, Eva, *Prof, Visual Communication Design,* Indiana University-Purdue University, Indianapolis, Herron School of Art & Design, Indianapolis IN (S)

Roberts, Gail, *Dir Finance,* Museum London, London ON

Roberts, Holly, *Spec Events Mng,* Wiregrass Museum of Art, Dothan AL

Roberts, Jill, *Exec Dir,* Dorland Mountain Arts Colony, Temecula CA (S)

Roberts, Jo, *Dir,* The Ella Carothers Dunnegan Gallery of Art, Bolivar MO

Roberts, Joan, *Dir,* Place des Arts at Heritage Square, Coquitlam BC

Roberts, Joshua, *Digital Initiatives & Systems Librn,* The University of the Arts, University Libraries, Philadelphia PA

Roberts, Kelley, *Instr,* Southern University A & M College, School of Architecture, Baton Rouge LA (S)

Roberts, Matt, *Assoc Prof,* Stetson University, Department of Creative Arts, Deland FL (S)

Roberts, Michelle, *Chief Registrar,* Museum of New Mexico, New Mexico Museum of Art, Unit of NM Dept of Cultural Affairs, Santa Fe NM

Roberts, Nita, *Photographer,* New York University, Institute of Fine Arts Visual Resources Collection, New York NY

Roberts, Perri L, *Adjunct Cur Renaissance,* University of Miami, Lowe Art Museum, Coral Gables FL

Roberts, Perri Lee, *Prof,* University of Miami, Dept of Art & Art History, Coral Gables FL (S)

Roberts, Rachel, *Archives Dir,* Dallas Historical Society, Research Center Library, Dallas TX

Roberts, Rey, *Dir,* Meriks American Designers, Inc., Baltimore MD

Roberts, Rhea, *Exec Dir,* Quapaw Quarter Association, Inc, Villa Marre, Little Rock AR

Roberts, Rhea, *Exec Dir,* Quapaw Quarter Association, Inc, Preservation Resource Center/ Historic Cannon Hall, Little Rock AR

Roberts, Susan, *Prof Graphic Design,* University of Georgia, Franklin College of Arts & Sciences, Lamar Dodd School of Art, Athens GA (S)

Roberts-Manganelli, Susan, *Dir Art & Science Leaning Lab,* Stanford University, Cantor Arts Center at Stanford University, Stanford CA

Robertson, Colin, *Cur of Educ,* Nevada Museum of Art, Reno NV

Robertson, D Scott, *Prof,* University of Wisconsin-Eau Claire, Dept of Art & Design, Eau Claire WI (S)

Robertson, Dale, *Pres & CEO,* Grand Rapids Public Museum, Public Museum of Grand Rapids, Grand Rapids MI

Robertson, David Alan, *Dir,* Northwestern University, Mary & Leigh Block Museum of Art, Evanston IL

Robertson, David J, *Prof,* Rochester Institute of Technology, School of Photographic Arts & Sciences, Rochester NY (S)

Robertson, Dennis, *Pres,* Dillman's Creative Arts Foundation, Lac Du Flambeau WI

Robertson, Dennis, *Pres,* Dillman's Creative Arts Foundation, Tom Lynch Resource Center, Lac Du Flambeau WI

Robertson, Donna, *Dean,* Illinois Institute of Technology, College of Architecture, Chicago IL (S)

Robertson, Frank R, *Treas,* Rhode Island Watercolor Society, Pawtucket RI

Robertson, James, *Instr Pottery,* Red Rocks Community College, Arts Dept, Lakewood CO (S)

Robertson, John, *Exec Dir,* Brant Historical Society, Brant Museum & Archives, Brantford ON

Robertson, Karen, *Dir,* Morgan State University, Library, Baltimore MD

Robertson, Lynn, *Dir,* University of South Carolina, McKissick Museum, Columbia SC

Robertson, Lynn, *Gallery Dir,* Capitol Arts Alliance, Houchens Gallery, Bowling Green KY

Robertson, Lynne, *Museum Cur,* Historic Pensacola Preservation Board, T.T. Wentworth Jr. Florida State Museum, Pensacola FL

Robertson, Lynne, *Chief Cur,* West Florida Historic Preservation, Inc/University of West Florida, T T Wentworth, Jr Florida State Museum; Historic Pensacola Village; Pensacola Historical Society & Resource Center, Pensacola FL

Robertson, Roderick, *Prof,* Saint Mary's University of Minnesota, Art & Design Dept, Winona MN (S)

Robertson, Ruthanne, *Adjunct Assoc Prof Fine Art,* Johnson County Community College, Fine Arts Dept & Art History Dept, Overland Park KS (S)

Robertson, Sheila, *Communs Coordr,* Mendel Art Gallery & Civic Conservatory, Saskatoon SK

Robertson, Sue, *VPres,* Dillman's Creative Arts Foundation, Lac Du Flambeau WI

Robertson, Sue, *VPres,* Dillman's Creative Arts Foundation, Tom Lynch Resource Center, Lac Du Flambeau WI

Robertson, Susan, *Exec Dir,* Wiregrass Museum of Art, Dothan AL

Robicheaux, Carol, *Mus Shop Mgr,* Auburn University, Julie Collins Smith Museum, Auburn AL

Robideau, Patrick, *Preparator,* State University of New York College at Buffalo, Buffalo NY

Robin, Madeleine, *Dir Art,* L'Universite Laval, Library, Quebec PQ

Robinacci, Lorraine, *Serials Technician,* Ames Free-Easton's Public Library, North Easton MA

Robinson, Bonnell, *Dir Gallery & Exhib,* Lesley University, Main Gallery, Boston MA

Robinson, Brian, *Art Teacher,* Motlow State Community College, Art Dept, Tullahoma TN (S)

Robinson, Bridget, *Trustee,* J.M.W. Turner Museum, Sarasota FL

Robinson, Cheryl, *Secy of Gallery,* University of Victoria, The Legacy Art Gallery, Victoria BC

Robinson, Chris, *Exec Dir,* Ministry of Alberta Culture, Royal Alberta Museum, Edmonton AB

Robinson, Christie, *Mktg & Progs,* Skokie Public Library, Skokie IL

Robinson, Cory, *Assoc Prof, Chair Fine Arts,* Indiana University-Purdue University, Indianapolis, Herron School of Art & Design, Indianapolis IN (S)

Robinson, Edward, *Facilities Mgr,* Academy Art Museum, Easton MD

Robinson, Franklin W, *Dir,* Cornell University, Herbert F Johnson Museum of Art, Ithaca NY

Robinson, Harry, *Pres & CEO,* African American Museum, Dallas TX

Robinson, Heidi J, *Curatorial Specialist,* Northern Arizona University, Art Museum & Galleries, Flagstaff AZ

Robinson, Jeri L, *Prof Drawing, 2D & Graphic Design,* Millersville University, Dept of Art & Design, Millersville PA (S)

Robinson, Jim, *Jane Weldon Myers Cur Emeritus,* Indianapolis Museum of Art, Indianapolis IN

Robinson, Johanna, *Mgr Appraisals & Programs,* Art Dealers Association of Canada, Toronto ON

Robinson, Joyce Henri, *Cur,* The Pennsylvania State University, Palmer Museum of Art, University Park PA

Robinson, Julia, *Learning Ctr Coordr,* University of Illinois at Urbana-Champaign, Spurlock Museum, Champaign IL

Robinson, Kim, *Collections Mgr,* United States Department of the Interior, Interior Museum, Washington DC

Robinson, Kim, *Office Mgr,* Mennello Museum of American Art, Orlando FL

Robinson, Mary, *Dir,* Five Civilized Tribes Museum, Library, Muskogee OK

Robinson, Mary, *Librn,* Buffalo Bill Memorial Association, Buffalo Bill Historical Center, Cody WY

Robinson, Matt, *Dir,* NAB Gallery, Chicago IL

Robinson, Michelle, *Cur,* Figge Art Museum, Art Reference Library, Davenport IA

Robinson, Mike, *Exec Dir,* Bill Reid Gallery of Northwest Coast Art, Vancouver BC

Robinson, Phillip, *Asst Prof,* University of Missouri, Saint Louis, Dept of Art & Art History, Saint Louis MO (S)

Robinson, Sally, *Secy,* Yukon Historical & Museums Association, Whitehorse YT

Robinson, Scott, *Prof,* North Central Texas College, Division of Communications & Fine Arts, Gainesville TX (S)

Robinson, Shanna, *Dept Contact,* North Central Michigan College, Art Dept, Petoskey MI (S)

Robinson, Sue Ann, *Dir Colls,* Long Beach Museum of Art Foundation, Long Beach CA

Robinson, Susan, *Mus Educ,* Osborne Homestead Museum, Derby CT

Robinson, Veronica, *Cur,* Swedish American Museum Association of Chicago, Chicago IL

Robinson, Vickie, *Pres,* Community Council for the Arts, Kinston NC

Robinson, William, *Cur Modern European Art,* The Cleveland Museum of Art, Cleveland OH

Robinson, William W, *Cur Drawings,* Harvard University, William Hayes Fogg Art Museum, Cambridge MA

Robinson, Yakingma L, *Mktg and Pub Rels,* City of Atlanta, Atlanta Cyclorama & Civil War Museum, Atlanta GA

Robles, Mary Jane, *Mus Shop Mgr,* Polish Museum of America, Research Library, Chicago IL

Robson, Judy, *Pres,* Ashtabula Arts Center, Ashtabula OH

Robtoy, Tim, *Registrar,* Art Museum of Southeast Texas, Beaumont TX

Roby, Thomas, *Chmn,* City Colleges of Chicago, Kennedy-King College, Chicago IL (S)

Roche, James, *Prof,* Florida State University, Art Dept, Tallahassee FL (S)

Roche, Joanne, *Librn,* Yonkers Public Library, Fine Arts Dept, Yonkers NY

Roche, Joanne, *Librn,* Yonkers Public Library, Will Library, Yonkers NY

Roche, Valerie, *Dance Coordr,* Creighton University, Fine & Performing Arts Dept, Omaha NE (S)

Rochester, Susan, *Dir Fine Arts,* Umpqua Community College, Fine & Performing Arts Dept, Roseburg OR (S)

Rochford, Sheri, *Exec Dir,* Durango Arts Center, Barbara Conrad Art Gallery, Durango CO

Rochfort, Desmond, *Pres,* Alberta College of Art & Design, Calgary AB (S)

Rochon, Alain, *Dir,* L'Universite Laval, Ecole des Arts Visuels, Quebec PQ

Rochon, Louise, *Admin Asst,* Canadian Conference of the Arts, Ottawa ON

Rock, Rodney, *Dir,* University of Connecticut, Jorgensen Auditorium, Storrs CT

Rock, Sheri, *Controller,* Taubman Museum of Art, Roanoke VA

Rockenstein, Faith, *Dir Edu & Pub Progs,* Museum of Wisconsin Art, West Bend WI

Rockhill, King, *Pres,* Appaloosa Museum and Heritage Center, Moscow ID

Rockman, Dawn, *Treas,* Wellfleet Historical Society & Museum, Inc, Wellfleet MA

Rod-ari, Melody, *Asst Cur,* Norton Simon, Pasadena CA

Rodda, Jenni, *Cur,* New York University, Institute of Fine Arts Visual Resources Collection, New York NY

Roddenberry, Heather, *Asst Cur & Registrar,* Pensacola Museum of Art, Harry Thornton Library, Pensacola FL

Rode, Meredith, *Prof,* University of the District of Columbia, Dept of Mass Media, Visual & Performing Arts, Washington DC (S)

Rode, Penny, *Assoc Prof,* Indiana University of Pennsylvania, College of Fine Arts, Indiana PA (S)

Rodeiro, Jose, *Prof,* New Jersey City University, Art Dept, Jersey City NJ (S)

Rodemer, Michael, *Assoc Prof,* University of Michigan, Ann Arbor, School of Art & Design, Ann Arbor MI (S)

Rodenbeck, Emily, *Mktg/Commun Mgr,* Laumeier Sculpture Park, Saint Louis MO

Rodenbeck, Judith, *Faculty,* Sarah Lawrence College, Dept of Art History, Bronxville NY (S)

Rodenhauser, Debora, *Instr,* Bakersfield College, Art Dept, Bakersfield CA (S)

Rodgers, Darlene, *Secy,* Glanmore National Historic Site of Canada, Belleville ON

Rodgers, Forrest, *Exec Dir,* Eastern Washington State Historical Society, Northwest Museum of Arts & Culture, Spokane WA

Rodgers, Forrest, *VPres Opers,* High Desert Museum, Bend OR

Rodgers, Kenneth, *Prof, Dir Art Museum,* North Carolina Central University, Art Dept, Durham NC (S)

Rodgers, Kenneth G, *Dir,* North Carolina Central University, NCCU Art Museum, Durham NC

Rodgers, Tim, *Dir,* Scottsdale Cultural Council, Scottsdale Museum of Contemporary Art, Scottsdale AZ

Rodgers, Tommie, *Registrar,* Lauren Rogers, Laurel MS

Rodney, Lee, *Asst Prof Art History & Visual Culture,* University of Windsor, Visual Arts, Windsor ON (S)

Rodney, Winston, *Facilities Mgr,* Museum for African Art, New York NY

Rodrick, Mark, *Brd Trustees-Treas,* Jersey City Museum, Jersey City NJ

Rodrigues, Gemma, *Cur Africa,* University of California, Los Angeles, Fowler Museum at UCLA, Los Angeles CA

Rodriguez, Aida T, *Dir,* Institute of Puerto Rican Culture, Museo de Arte Religioso Porta Coeli, San Juan PR

Rodriguez, Aida T, *Dir,* Institute of Puerto Rican Culture, Museo de Arte Religioso Porta Coeli, San Juan PR

Rodriguez, Frank M, *Dir Develop,* MEXIC-ARTE Museum, Austin TX

Rodriguez, Jennie, *Exec Dir,* Mission Cultural Center for Latino Arts, San Francisco CA

Rodriguez, Kathy, *Instr,* University of New Orleans-Lake Front, Dept of Fine Arts, New Orleans LA (S)

Rodriguez, Klaudio, *Asst Cur,* Florida International University, The Patricia & Phillip Frost Art Museum, Miami FL

Rodriguez, Linda, *Cur Educ,* South Texas Institute for the Arts, Art Museum of South Texas, Corpus Christi TX

Rodriguez, Luis, *Univ Librn,* Kean University, Nancy Thompson Library, Union NJ

Rodriguez, M Teresa Lapid, *Dir,* Montclair State University, Art Galleries, Upper Montclair NJ

Rodriguez, Maria del Carmen, *Coll Supvr,* Museo de las Americas, Viejo San Juan PR

Rodriguez, Maria del Carmen, *Coll Supvr,* Museo de las Americas, Viejo San Juan PR

Rodriguez, Ramiro, *Asst Preparator,* University of Notre Dame, Snite Museum of Art, Notre Dame IN

Rodriguez-Mont, Jacquelina, *Exhibs Mgr,* Museo de Arte de Puerto Rico, San Juan PR

Rodriguez-Mont, Jacquelina, *Exhibs Mgr,* Museo de Arte de Puerto Rico, San Juan PR

Rodriguez A, Rommy, *Outreach Coordr,* Ontario Crafts Council, Craft Resource Centre, Toronto ON

Roe, Betsy Knab, *Gallery Assoc,* Topeka & Shawnee County Public Library, Alice C Sabatini Gallery, Topeka KS

Roe, Bill, *Board Pres,* Pence Gallery, Davis CA

Roe, Daniel, *Dir Educ,* The York County Heritage Trust, York PA

Roe, Ward V, *Prof,* Keystone College, Fine Arts Dept, LaPlume PA (S)

Roeper, Susan, *Librn,* Sterling & Francine Clark, Library, Williamstown MA

Roesch, Rob, *Sculpture Dept Chair,* Pennsylvania Academy of the Fine Arts, Office of Admission, Philadelphia PA (S)

Roese, Ronnie L, *Dir,* Miracle at Pentecost Foundation, Biblical Arts Center, Dallas TX

Roessek, Nadja, *Mus Asst,* City of Nome Alaska, Carrie M McLain Memorial Museum, Nome AK

Roever, James, *VPres,* Missouri Western State University, Gallery 206 Foyer Gallery, Saint Joseph MO

Roff, Mary, *Assoc Dir,* Art Center Manatee, Bradenton FL

Rogal, Maria, *Assoc Prof,* University of Florida, School of Art & Art History, Gainesville FL (S)

Rogan, Clare, *Cur,* Wesleyan University, Davison Art Center, Middletown CT

Rogan, Ed, *VPres Legal,* Belskie Museum, Closter NJ

Rogeberg, Hanneline, *Asst Prof,* Rutgers, The State University of New Jersey, Mason Gross School of the Arts, Visual Arts Dept, New Brunswick NJ (S)

Rogenstein, Steven, *Dir Mktg & Commun,* American Institute of Graphic Arts, New York NY

Roger, Judith, *Acting Dir,* University of Western Ontario, McIntosh Gallery, London ON

Rogerge, Celeste, *Prof,* University of Florida, School of Art & Art History, Gainesville FL (S)

Rogers, Alexis, *Lead Mus Technician,* Daytona State College, Southeast Museum of Photography, Daytona Beach FL

Rogers, Bryan, *Prof,* University of Michigan, Ann Arbor, School of Art & Design, Ann Arbor MI (S)

Rogers, Cathy, *Accnt,* University of North Carolina at Greensboro, Weatherspoon Art Museum, Greensboro NC

Rogers, Dan, *Instr,* Bismarck State College, Fine Arts Dept, Bismarck ND (S)

Rogers, Darlene, *Interpretive Program Dir,* Schuyler Mansion State Historic Site, Albany NY

Rogers, Donald, *Dir Facilities,* Hillwood Museum & Gardens Foundation, Hillwood Estate Museum & Gardens, Washington DC

Rogers, Eric, *Exec Dir,* Arts Place, Inc., Hugh N Ronald Memorial Gallery, Portland IN

Rogers, Geoffrey, *Chmn Science & Math,* Fashion Institute of Technology, Art & Design Division, New York NY (S)

Rogers, James, *Div Fine & Performing Arts Chair, Prof Art History,* Florida Southern College, Department of Art & Art History, Lakeland FL (S)

Rogers, James, *Pres,* Westfield Athenaeum, Jasper Rand Art Museum, Westfield MA

Rogers, James, *Prof Art History & Chmn Div Fine & Performing Arts,* Florida Southern College, Melvin Art Gallery, Lakeland FL

Rogers, June, *Exec Dir,* Fairbanks Arts Association, Bear Gallery, Fairbanks AK

Rogers, Kathy, *Exec Dir,* Piedmont Arts Association, Martinsville VA

Rogers, Nancy M, *Exec Dir,* Wooster Community Art Center, Danbury CT

Rogers, Nancy M, *Exec Dir,* Wooster Community Art Center, Library, Danbury CT

Rogers, Nikyia, *Bus & Bldg Adminr,* University of Pennsylvania, Institute of Contemporary Art, Philadelphia PA

Rogers, Richard L, *Pres,* College for Creative Studies, Detroit MI (S)

Rogers, Robert, *Assoc Prof,* Queensborough Community College, Dept of Art & Photography, Bayside Hills NY (S)

Rogers, Robert, *Cur Antique Auto Mus,* Heritage Museums & Gardens, Sandwich MA

Rogers, Robert Meadows, *Chair,* Concordia College, Art Dept, Moorhead MN (S)

Rogers, Robert W, *Dir,* Maryland Historical Society, Museum of Maryland History, Baltimore MD

Rogers, Sally, *Board Secy,* Cabot's Old Indian Pueblo Museum, Desert Hot Springs CA

Rogers, Sarah J, *Deputy Dir Institutional Develop,* Columbus Museum of Art, Columbus OH

Rogers, William, *Pres,* Canadian Society of Painters In Watercolour, Toronto ON

Rogers-Naff, Shirley, *Store Mgr,* Martin and Osa Johnson, Chanute KS

Rogerson, Lynn K, *Dir & CEO,* Art Services International, Alexandria VA

Roglan, Mark, *Dir,* Southern Methodist University, Meadows Museum, Dallas TX

Rogol, Rachel, *Media & Marketing Coordr & Exec Asst to Dir,* Amherst College, Mead Art Museum, Amherst MA

Rogstad, Mary Labate, *Registrar,* Vermont Historical Society, Museum, Montpelier VT

Roh, Michael, *Dir Facility Opers,* Columbia Museum of Art, Columbia SC

Rohmiller, Ellen, *Librn,* Dayton Art Institute, Library, Dayton OH

Rohn, Mathew, *Assoc Prof,* Saint Olaf College, Art Dept, Northfield MN (S)

Rohovit, Ron, *Deputy Dir Educ,* California Science Center, Los Angeles CA

Rohrbach, John, *Sr Cur Photographs,* Amon Carter Museum of American Art, Fort Worth TX

Rohrer, Judith C, *Assoc Prof,* Emory University, Art History Dept, Atlanta GA (S)

Rohrer, Susan, *Cur Educ,* State Capital Museum, Olympia WA

Rohrer, Thelma S, *Chmn Dept,* Manchester College, Dept of Art, North Manchester IN (S)

Rohwer, Stephanie, *Archivist Cur Asst & Event Coordr,* The National Society of The Colonial Dames of America in the State of New Hampshire, Moffatt-Ladd House & Garden, Portsmouth NH

Roizen, Morrie, *Adjunct,* Gavilan Community College, Art Dept, Gilroy CA (S)

Roizen, Morry, *Chmn,* West Valley College, Art Dept, Saratoga CA (S)

Rojas, Juan, *Chief Preparator,* University of Southern California, USC Fisher Museum of Art, Los Angeles CA

Rojas-Sukkar, Alba, *Dir Devel,* Tucson Museum of Art and Historic Block, Tucson AZ

Rojo, Catalina, *Develop Coordr,* DeCordova Museum & Sculpture Park, DeCordova Museum, Lincoln MA

Rokes, Carla, *Asst Prof & Gallery Dir,* University of North Carolina at Pembroke, Art Dept, Pembroke NC (S)

Roland, Craig, *Assoc Prof,* University of Florida, School of Art & Art History, Gainesville FL (S)

Roland, Marya, *Asst Prof,* Western Carolina University, Dept of Art/College of Arts & Science, Cullowhee NC (S)

Roldan, Deborah, *Asst Dir Exhibs,* Museum of Fine Arts, Houston, Houston TX

Rolla, Maureen, *Deputy Dir,* Carnegie Museums of Pittsburgh, Carnegie Museum of Art, Pittsburgh PA

Rolle, James, *Lectr,* Saint John's University, Art Dept, Collegeville MN (S)

Roller, Anne, *Pub Rels Coordr,* Cliveden, Philadelphia PA

Roller, Terry M, *Prof,* Baylor University - College of Arts and Sciences, Dept of Art, Waco TX (S)

Rollins, Avon William, *Dir & CEO,* Beck Cultural Exchange Center, Inc, Knoxville TN

Rollins, Eleanor, *Admin Asst,* Beaufort County Arts Council, Washington NC

Rollins, Fred, *Mus Aide,* Village of Potsdam, Potsdam Public Museum, Potsdam NY

Rollins, Ken, *Dir,* Tampa Museum of Art, Tampa FL

Rollins, Rich, *Instr,* Marylhurst University, Art Dept, Marylhurst OR (S)

Rollinson, Elizabeth, *Controller,* State of North Carolina, Battleship North Carolina, Wilmington NC

Rollins Stanis, Suzanne, *Dir Heritage Educ & Info,* Indiana Landmarks, Morris-Butler House, Indianapolis IN

Rolnick, Neil, *Chmn,* Rensselaer Polytechnic Institute, Eye Ear Studio Dept of Art, Troy NY (S)

Rolon, Edwin, *Asst Cur Used Books,* The Hispanic Society of America, Museum & Library, New York NY

Rom, Cristine, *Library Dir,* Cleveland Institute of Art, Jessica Gund Memorial Library, Cleveland OH

Romais, Miriam, *Exec Dir,* En Foco, Inc, Bronx NY

Roman, Dulce, *Cur Modern Art,* University of Florida, Samuel P Harn Museum of Art, Gainesville FL

Roman, Julio Cesar, *Dir Youth Progs,* Inquilinos Boricuas en Accion, Boston MA

Romano, Jaime, *Prof,* University of Puerto Rico, Dept of Fine Arts, Rio Piedras PR (S)

Romano, Jaime, *Prof,* University of Puerto Rico, Dept of Fine Arts, Rio Piedras PR (S)

Romano, Pia, *Reference,* Wentworth Institute of Technology Library, Boston MA

Romeo, Joy, *Vol Coordr,* Lockwood-Mathews Mansion Museum, Norwalk CT

Romeo, Louise, *Asst Dean,* New World School of the Arts, Gallery, Miami FL

Romeo, Louise, *Dean,* New World School of the Arts, Miami FL (S)

Romer, Ligla, *Registrar,* Walter Anderson, Ocean Springs MS

Romer, Teresa, *Admin Asst,* Pace University Gallery, Art Gallery in Choate House, Pleasantville NY

Romer Huckaby, Laura, *Coll Mgr,* San Angelo Museum of Fine Arts, San Angelo TX

Romero, Lynda, *Admin Asst,* Pueblo of Pojoaque, Poeh Museum, Santa Fe NM

Romero, Samuel, *Asst Prof Art & Dir Graphic Design Prog,* Florida Southern College, Melvin Art Gallery, Lakeland FL

Romero, Samuel, *Asst Prof Art & Dir Graphic Design Prog,* Florida Southern College, Department of Art & Art History, Lakeland FL (S)

Romnes, Juliana, *Exhib Coordr,* Daytona State College, Southeast Museum of Photography, Daytona Beach FL

Ron, Will, *Art Dept Chmn,* Montana State University-Northern, Humanities & Social Sciences, Havre MT (S)

Ronayne, Natalie, *Exec Dir,* Cleveland Botanical Garden, Eleanor Squire Library, Cleveland OH

Roncka, Gene, *Artist,* Gene Roncka Willow Point Gallery/Museum, Ashland NE

Roncka, Mary, *Gallery Dir,* Gene Roncka Willow Point Gallery/Museum, Ashland NE

Rone, Catherine, *Gift Shop Mgr,* Yuma Fine Arts Association, Yuma Art Center, Yuma AZ

Rood, Warren, *Instr,* Walla Walla Community College, Fine Arts Dept, Walla Walla WA (S)

Roodman, Karen, *Mus Shop Mgr,* St. Louis Artists' Guild, Saint Louis MO

Roof, Beth, *Spec Events Coordr,* Cedar Rapids Museum of Art, Cedar Rapids IA

Rooney, Marsha, *Cur History,* Eastern Washington State Historical Society, Northwest Museum of Arts & Culture, Spokane WA

Rooney, Steve, *Deputy Dir for Adminr,* International Center of Photography, Museum, New York NY

Roos-Brown, Diana, *Visual Arts Coordr,* Real Art Ways (RAW), Hartford CT

Roosa, Rosemary, *Exec Dir,* Walter Anderson, Ocean Springs MS

Roosa, Wayne L, *Prof,* Bethel College, Dept of Art, Saint Paul MN (S)

Root, Linda, *Office Mgr,* Koshare Indian Museum, Inc, La Junta CO

Root, Margaret, *Cur,* University of Michigan, Kelsey Museum of Archaeology, Ann Arbor MI

Root, Margaret, *Prof,* University of Michigan, Ann Arbor, Dept of History of Art, Ann Arbor MI (S)

Root, Patricia, *Head of Reference,* Bronxville Public Library, Bronxville NY

Roper, Tim, *Asst Prof,* Louisiana College, Dept of Art, Pineville LA (S)

Roper, Timothy, *Lectr,* Southeastern Louisiana University, Dept of Visual Arts, Hammond LA (S)

Ropson, Jerry, *Asst Prof,* Mount Allison University, Dept of Fine Arts, Sackville NB (S)

Ror, Ron, *Cur,* Weyburn Arts Council, Allie Griffin Art Gallery, Weyburn SK

Rorech, Joseph, *Deputy Dir Fin & Admin,* The Jewish Museum, New York NY

Rorschach, Kimberly, *Dir,* Duke University, Nasher Museum of Art at Duke University, Durham NC

Rorschach, Kimberly, *Dir,* Seattle Art Museum, Seattle Asian Art Museum, Seattle WA

Rosa, Joseph, *Dir,* University of Michigan, Museum of Art, Ann Arbor MI

Rosal, Marcia L, *Prof,* Florida State University, Art Education Dept, Tallahassee FL (S)

Rosandich, Thomas P, *CEO,* American Sport Art Museum and Archives, Daphne AL

Rosario, Francisco, *Dir Security,* Bronx Museum of the Arts, Bronx NY

Rosas, Carlos, *Assoc Prof Art (New Media),* Pennsylvania State University, University Park, Penn State School of Visual Arts, University Park PA (S)

Rosasco, Betsy J, *Research Cur European Painting & Sculpture,* Princeton University, Princeton University Art Museum, Princeton NJ

Rosata, Nancy, *Assoc Dir,* Regis College, Carney Gallery, Weston MA

Rosati, Lauren, *Asst Cur,* Exit Art, San Leandro CA

Rosati, Tony, *Printmaking Dept Chair,* Pennsylvania Academy of the Fine Arts, Office of Admission, Philadelphia PA (S)

Rose, Barbara, *Prof,* American University, Dept of Art, New York NY (S)

Rose, Brian, *Mediterranean Section Cur,* University of Pennsylvania, Museum of Archaeology & Anthropology, Philadelphia PA

Rose, Corinne, *Mgr Educ,* Columbia College Chicago, Museum of Contemporary Photography, Chicago IL

Rose, Elizabeth, *Libr Dir,* Fairfield Historical Society, Fairfield Museum & History Center, Fairfield CT

Rose, Ellen, *Circ Librn,* Athenaeum of Philadelphia, Library, Philadelphia PA

Rose, Erin, *Asst Cur,* University of Wisconsin, Green Bay, Lawton Gallery, Green Bay WI

Rose, James, *Asst Prof,* Clarion University of Pennsylvania, Dept of Art, Clarion PA (S)

Rose, Joshua, *Prof,* New Mexico State University, Art Dept, Las Cruces NM (S)

Rose, Julia, *Dir,* West Baton Rouge Parish, West Baton Rouge Museum, Port Allen LA

Rose, June, *Gallery Mgr,* Boothbay Region Art Foundation, Boothbay Harbor ME

Rose, Patrice, *Dir Admin & Gift Shop Mgr,* Krasl Art Center, Saint Joseph MI

Rose, Richard, *Chmn Studio,* University of South Carolina, Dept of Art, Columbia SC (S)

Rose, Robert, *Pres,* Artworks, The Visual Art School of Trenton, Trenton NJ

Rose, Robert, *Pres,* Artworks, The Visual Art School of Trenton, Library, Trenton NJ

Rose, Steve, *Pres,* Passaic County Community College, Division of Humanities, Paterson NJ (S)

Rose, Thomas, *Prof,* University of Minnesota, Minneapolis, Dept of Art, Minneapolis MN (S)

Rosedale, Jeff, *Asst Library Dir,* Manhattanville College, Library, Purchase NY

Rosehart, Robert, *Pres,* Wilfrid Laurier University, Robert Langen Art Gallery, Waterloo ON

Rosek, Mary, *Assoc Lect,* University of Wisconsin-Stevens Point, Dept of Art & Design, Stevens Point WI (S)

Roseland, Claire, *Mem & Vol Coordr,* The McKinney Avenue Contemporary (The MAC), Dallas TX

Roselione-Valadez, Juan, *Dir,* Rubell Family Collection and Contemporary Arts Foundation, Miami FL

Rosell, Karen, *Chmn Dept,* Juniata College, Dept of Art, Huntingdon PA (S)

Roselle, David P, *Dir,* Winterthur Museum, Winterthur Museum, Garden & Library, Winterthur DE

Roseman, Harry, *Prof,* Vassar College, Art Dept, Poughkeepsie NY (S)

Rosen, Annabeth, *Prof,* University of California, Davis, Dept of Art & Art History, Davis CA (S)

Rosen, Leila, *Librn,* Aesthetic Realism Foundation, Eli Siegel Collection, New York NY

Rosen, M, *Prof,* City Colleges of Chicago, Daley College, Chicago IL (S)

Rosen, Robert, *Dir,* University of Southern California, Cinema-Television Library & Archives of Performing Arts, Los Angeles CA

Rosenbaum, Arthur, *Wheatley Prof Drawing & Painting,* University of Georgia, Franklin College of Arts & Sciences, Lamar Dodd School of Art, Athens GA (S)

Rosenbaum, Joan H, *Dir,* The Jewish Museum, Library, New York NY

Rosenberg, Eric, *Assoc Prof,* Tufts University, Dept of Art & Art History, Medford MA (S)

Rosenberg, Herbert, *Prof,* New Jersey City University, Art Dept, Jersey City NJ (S)

Rosenberg, Kristina, *Dir Educ,* Timken Museum of Art, San Diego CA

Rosenberg, Ramona, *Communs Coordr,* Bard College, Center for Curatorial Studies and the Hessel Museum of Art, Annandale-on-Hudson NY

Rosenberg, Ronni, *Dean,* Sheridan College, Faculty of Animation, Arts & Design, Oakville ON (S)

Rosenbert, Pam, *Dir Opers,* Indianapolis Art Center, Marilyn K. Glick School of Art, Indianapolis IN

Rosenblum, Paul, *Mng Dir,* Caramoor Center for Music & the Arts, Inc, Rosen House at Caramoor, Katonah NY

Rosenfeld, Andrew, *Prof,* Mount Saint Mary's University, Visual & Performing Arts Dept, Emmitsburg MD (S)

Rosenfeld, Daniel, *Dir,* Colby College, Museum of Art, Waterville ME

Rosenfeld, Jason, *Assoc Prof Art History,* Marymount Manhattan College, Fine & Performing Arts Div, New York NY (S)

Rosenfeld, Susan, *Asst Cur,* University of California, Los Angeles, Visual Resource Collection, Los Angeles CA

Rosengren, James, *Deputy Dir,* Art Museum of the University of Houston, Blaffer Gallery, Houston TX

Rosensaft, Jean Bloch, *Dir,* Hebrew Union College Museum, Jewish Institute of Religion Museum, New York NY

Rosenstveicht, Lisa, *Lectr,* Humboldt State University, College of Arts & Humanities, Art Dept, Arcata CA (S)

Rosenthal, Barbara, *Co-Dir, Cur & Grants Officer,* eMediaLoft.org, New York NY

Rosenthal, Barbara, *FT,* University of Wisconsin Oshkosh, Dept of Art, Oshkosh WI (S)

Rosenthal, Deborah, *Cur,* Miller Art Center Foundation Inc, Miller Art Museum, Sturgeon Bay WI

Rosenthal, Mark, *Adjunct Cur Contemp Art,* Detroit Institute of Arts, Detroit MI

Rosera, Kathy, *Office Mgr,* Neville Public Museum of Brown County, Green Bay WI

Rosette, Arturo, *Prof,* Gavilan Community College, Art Dept, Gilroy CA (S)

Rosetti, Janet, *Mgr Facility Usage,* Worcester Art Museum, Worcester MA

Rosier, Ken, *Chair & Prof,* Del Mar College, Art Dept, Corpus Christi TX (S)

Rosier, Ken, *Chair Art & Drama Dept,* Del Mar College, Joseph A Cain Memorial Art Gallery, Corpus Christi TX

Rosine, Gary, *Chmn,* Boise State University, Art Dept, Boise ID (S)

Rosini, Brook, *Mktg & Communs Mgr,* Hyde Park Art Center, Chicago IL

Roslak, Robyn, *Assoc Prof,* University of Minnesota, Duluth, Art Dept, Duluth MN (S)

Rosler, Martha, *Prof,* Rutgers, The State University of New Jersey, Mason Gross School of the Arts, Visual Arts Dept, New Brunswick NJ (S)

Rosner, Brienne, *Gallery Mgr,* Peters Valley Craft Center, Layton NJ

Rosoff, Nancy, *Andrew W Mellon Cur of the Arts of the Americas,* Brooklyn Museum, Brooklyn NY

Rosol, Chris, *Dir Mem & Develop Opers,* Institute of Contemporary Art, Boston MA

Rospert, Jennifer, *Asst Prof,* University of Central Arkansas, Department of Art, Conway AR (S)

Ross, Alex, *Head Librn,* Stanford University, Art & Architecture Library, Stanford CA

Ross, Alice, *Museum Shop Mgr,* Victoria Mansion - Morse Libby House, Portland ME

Ross, Carol, *Mem Chair,* Pastel Society of the West Coast, Sacramento Fine Arts Center, Carmichael CA

Ross, Charles, *Chair Watercolors,* Hudson Valley Art Association, Brooklyn NY

Ross, Christine, *Chmn,* McGill University, Dept of Art History, Montreal PQ (S)

Ross, Cynthia, *Instr,* Goddard College, Dept of Art, Plainfield VT (S)

Ross, Dan, *Dir Community Develop,* Arts United of Greater Fort Wayne, Fort Wayne IN

Ross, Dave, *Div Chmn,* Rock Valley College, Humanities and Fine Arts Division, Rockford IL (S)

Ross, Diane, *Archivist,* University of Southern Mississippi, McCain Library & Archives, Hattiesburg MS

Ross, Elizabeth, *Assoc Prof,* University of Florida, School of Art & Art History, Gainesville FL (S)

Ross, Frances, *Chmn,* Historic Arkansas Museum, Little Rock AR

Ross, Gary, *Chmn,* Capital University, Fine Arts Dept, Columbus OH (S)

Ross, Gillian, *Educ,* Huronia Museum, Gallery of Historic Huronia, Midland ON

Ross, Ian D, *Exec Dir,* Burlington Art Centre, Burlington ON

Ross, Jerry, *Dir,* New Zone Virtual Gallery, Eugene OR

Ross, John, *Dir,* Fort Hays State University, Forsyth Library, Hays KS

Ross, Lauren, *Cur Modern & Contemp Art,* Philbrook Museum of Art, Tulsa OK

Ross, Linda, *Dir Humanities,* Penn State Harrisburg, School of Humanities, Middletown PA (S)

Ross, Margaret, *Dir,* Chatham College, Fine & Performing Arts, Pittsburgh PA (S)

Ross, Megan, *Preparator,* Averill and Bernard Leviton A + D Gallery, Chicago IL

Ross, Michelle, *Painting,* Oregon College of Art & Craft, Portland OR (S)

Ross, Murray, *Instr Theater,* University of Colorado-Colorado Springs, Visual & Performing Arts Dept (VAPA), Colorado Springs CO (S)

Ross, Nancy, *Instr,* Mary Baldwin College, Dept of Art & Art History, Staunton VA (S)

Ross, Peter, *Dir Devel,* McMichael Canadian Art Collection, Kleinburg ON

Ross, Rita, *Pres,* Kitchener-Waterloo Art Gallery, Kitchener ON

Ross, Robert, *Prof Emeritus,* University of Arkansas, Art Dept, Fayetteville AR (S)

Rosseau, Gwenn, *VP Fin,* Birmingham Bloomfield Art Center, Birmingham MI (S)

Rosseau, Gwenn, *VP Finance,* Birmingham Bloomfield Art Center, Art Center, Birmingham MI

Rossen, Susan F, *Exec Dir Publications,* The Art Institute of Chicago, Chicago IL

Rosser, Kay, *Vol Coordr,* Plaza de la Raza Cultural Center, Los Angeles CA

Rossetti, John, *Colls Assoc Registrar,* Tufts University, Tufts University Art Gallery, Medford MA

Rossiter, Shannon, *Dir,* Mohave Museum of History & Arts, Kingman AZ

Rossman, Jae, *Spec Colls Librn,* Yale University, The Robert B. Haas Family Arts Library, New Haven CT

Rossman, Val, *Instr,* Main Line Art Center, Haverford PA (S)

Rossnagel, Liz, *Dir,* Lethbridge Public Library, Art Gallery, Lethbridge AB

Rossol, Monona, *Pres,* Arts, Craft & Theater Safety, New York NY

Rosson, Lindsay G, *Mem Coordr & Financial Officer,* Asheville Art Museum, Asheville NC

Rossy, Caroline, *Mem & Mktg,* American Swedish Historical Foundation & Museum, American Swedish Historical Museum, Philadelphia PA

Rostkie, Philip, *Assoc Prof,* Seton Hill University, Art Program, Greensburg PA (S)

Rotblatt, Martin, *Exec Dir,* Farmington Valley Arts Center, Avon CT

Rotenberg, Judi, *Pres,* Rockport Art Association, Rockport MA

Roth, Ann, *Dir,* Meredith College, Frankie G Weems Gallery & Rotunda Gallery, Raleigh NC

Roth, Dan, *Cur & Dir,* United States Navy Supply Corps School, US Navy Supply Corps Museum, Newport RI

Roth, Eric, *Dir,* Huguenot Historical Society of New Paltz Galleries, New Paltz NY

Roth, James, *Deputy Dir,* National Archives & Records Administration, John F Kennedy Presidential Library & Museum, Boston MA

Roth, John, *Asst Prof,* Old Dominion University, Art Dept, Norfolk VA (S)

Roth, Linda, *Cur European Decorate Arts,* Wadsworth Atheneum Museum of Art, Hartford CT

Roth, Liz, *Assoc Prof,* Oklahoma State University, Department of Art, Graphic Design and Art History, Stillwater OK (S)

Roth, Moira, *Prof,* Mills College, Art Dept, Oakland CA (S)

Rothermel, Barbara, *Dir,* Lynchburg College, Daura Gallery, Lynchburg VA

Rothermel, Barbara, *Lectr,* Lynchburg College, Art Dept, Lynchburg VA (S)

Rothgeb, Ray, *Pres,* Independence Historical Museum & Art Center, Independence KS

Rothkopf, Katherine, *Sr Cur Painting & Sculpture,* The Baltimore Museum of Art, Baltimore MD

Rothman, Roger, *Art Historian,* Agnes Scott College, Dalton Art Gallery, Decatur GA

Rothrock, Kristin, *Lectr,* University of North Carolina at Charlotte, Dept Art, Charlotte NC (S)

Rothweiler, David, *Adjunct Prof Art,* University of Great Falls, Art Dept, Great Falls MT (S)

Rotondo-McCord, Lisa, *Asst Dir Art & Cur Asian Art,* New Orleans Museum of Art, New Orleans LA

Rouleau, Bishop Reynald, *Dir,* Eskimo Museum, Churchill MB

Rousseau, Jacques, *Dir,* Dalhousie University, Faculty of Architecture, Halifax NS (S)

Rousseaux, Mary, *Instr Studio Art,* Madonna University, College of Arts & Humanities, Livonia MI (S)

Rousso, Gabrielle, *Exec Dir,* The Art Center - TAC, The Art Center of Highland Park (TAC), Highland Park IL

Rouston, Roger, *Asst Prof,* Kansas State University, Art Dept, Manhattan KS (S)

Routley, Keith, *Cur,* Shoreline Historical Museum, Shoreline WA

Rovet, Christine, *Sr Dir Guest Relations & Admin,* Genesee Country Village & Museum, John L Wehle Art Gallery, Mumford NY

Rovine, Victoria, *Assoc Prof,* University of Florida, School of Art & Art History, Gainesville FL (S)

Row, Brian, *Prof,* Texas State University - San Marcos, Dept of Art and Design, San Marcos TX (S)

Rowan, Gerald, *Prog Coordr,* Northampton Community College, Art Dept, Bethlehem PA (S)

Rowars, Lorelei, *Merchandise Mgr,* Newark Museum Association, The Newark Museum, Newark NJ

Rowden, Stephanie, *Asst Prof,* University of Michigan, Ann Arbor, School of Art & Design, Ann Arbor MI (S)

Rowe, Donald, *Dir,* Olivet College, Armstrong Collection, Olivet MI

Rowe, Donald, *Prof,* Olivet College, Art Dept, Olivet MI (S)

Rowe, John, *CEO & Pres,* Chicago History Museum, Chicago IL

Rowe, Libby, *Assoc Prof,* University of Texas at San Antonio, Dept of Art & Art History, San Antonio TX (S)

Rowe, Libby, *Sr Lectr,* Vanderbilt University, Dept of Art, Nashville TN (S)

Rowe, Martha, *Admin Research Assoc,* Old Salem Museums & Gardens, Library and Research Center, Winston Salem NC

Rowe, Martha, *Dir Research Center,* Old Salem Museums & Gardens, Museum of Early Southern Decorative Arts, Winston Salem NC

Rowe, Susan, *Instr,* Olivet College, Art Dept, Olivet MI (S)

Rowe, William Brit, *Chmn,* Ohio Northern University, Dept of Art & Design, Ada OH (S)

Rowe, William H, *Instr,* Arkansas State University, Dept of Art, State University AR (S)

Rowe Berry, Victoria, *Exec Dir & Chief Cur,* Utah State University, Nora Eccles Harrison Museum of Art, Logan UT

Rowland, Ann, *CFO,* Los Angeles County Museum of Art, Los Angeles CA

Rowland, Cynthia, *1st Vice Pres,* New Mexico Art League, Gallery & School, Albuquerque NM

Rowland, Leslie W, *Exec Dir,* Thousand Islands Arts Center - Home of the Handweaving Museum, Clayton NY (S)

Rowlands, J, *Dean & Prof,* Camden County College, Visual & Performing Arts Dept, Blackwood NJ (S)

Rowlett, Jeannette, *Dir,* Kentucky Guild of Artists & Craftsmen Inc, Berea KY

Rowley, Roger, *Gallery Dir & Lectr,* University of Idaho/College of Art & Architecture, Dept of Art & Design, Moscow ID (S)

Roy, Carolyn, *Cur,* Warner House Association, MacPheadris-Warner House, Portsmouth NH

Roy, Denise, *Instr,* Marylhurst University, Art Dept, Marylhurst OR (S)

Roy, John, *VPres,* Rensselaer County Historical Society, Hart-Cluett Mansion, 1827, Troy NY

Roy, Marina, *Assoc Prof,* University of British Columbia, Dept of Art History, Visual Art & Theory, Vancouver BC (S)

Roy, Rob, *Painting,* Montserrat College of Art, Beverly MA (S)

Royall, Richard R, *Managing Dir,* James Dick Foundation, Festival - Institute, Round Top TX

Royce, Amy Cavanaugh, *Exec Dir,* Maryland Art Place, Baltimore MD

Royce, Linden, *Mgr Mus Store,* Museum of Ventura County, Ventura CA

Royer, Catherine M, *Chmn, Assoc Prof,* Adrian College, Art & Design Dept, Adrian MI (S)

Royer, Debra, *Library Dir,* Portland Art Museum, Crumpacker Family Library, Portland OR

Royer, Jennifer, *Cur,* Landis Valley Village and Farm Museum, PA Historical & Museum Commission, Landis Collections Gallery, Lancaster PA

Royer, Randall, *Prof,* Black Hills State University, Art Dept, Spearfish SD (S)

Royse, Stephanie, *Pub Rels,* University of Oklahoma, Fred Jones Jr Museum of Art, Norman OK

Royster, Kenneth, *Coordr Art Dept,* Morgan State University, Dept of Art, Baltimore MD (S)

Royston, Colette Carson, *VPres Board Trustees,* Museum of Contemporary Art, San Diego, La Jolla CA

Royston, Tricia, *Librn,* New London County Historical Society, Shaw Mansion, New London CT

Rozak, Tony, *Assoc Prof,* University at Buffalo, State University of New York, Dept of Visual Studies, Buffalo NY (S)

Rozier, Robert, *Assoc Prof,* Alma College, Clack Art Center, Dept of Art & Design, Alma MI (S)

Rozko, Laurie, *Deputy Dir,* San Bernardino County Museum, Fine Arts Institute, Redlands CA

Rozman, Joseph, *Prof,* Mount Mary College, Art & Design Division, Milwaukee WI (S)

Roznoy, Cynthia, *PhD,* Mattatuck Historical Society, Mattatuck Museum, Waterbury CT

Rozzi Casey, Lynn, *Dir & Cur,* Nassau Community College, Firehouse Art Gallery, Garden City NY

Rubel, William, *Pres,* Children's Art Foundation, Museum of International Children's Art, Santa Cruz CA

Rubenstein, David, *Chmn,* The John F Kennedy, Washington DC

Rubenstein, Elliott, *Assoc Prof,* Rochester Institute of Technology, School of Photographic Arts & Sciences, Rochester NY (S)

Rubin, Jane, *Dir Coll & Exhib,* The Jewish Museum, New York NY

Rubin, Jeff, *Dir Cur Serv,* Louisiana Department of Culture, Recreation & Tourism, Louisiana State Museum, New Orleans LA

Rubin, Patricia, *Judy & Michael Steinhardt Dir,* New York University, Institute of Fine Arts, New York NY (S)

Rubin, Stephen, *Asst Prof Art (Photog),* Pennsylvania State University, University Park, Penn State School of Visual Arts, University Park PA (S)

Rubini, Gail, *Assoc Prof,* Florida State University, Art Dept, Tallahassee FL (S)

Rubinoff, Michael, *Assoc Dean Visual & Performing Arts,* Sheridan College, Faculty of Animation, Arts & Design, Oakville ON (S)

Rubio, Adriana, *Exec Asst,* Museum of Fine Arts, Houston, Rienzi Center for European Decorative Arts, Houston TX

Rubio, Alex, *Studio Mgr & Art Instr,* Blue Star Contemporary Art Center, San Antonio TX

Rubio, Pablo, *Prof,* University of Puerto Rico, Dept of Fine Arts, Rio Piedras PR (S)

Rubio, Pablo, *Prof,* University of Puerto Rico, Dept of Fine Arts, Rio Piedras PR (S)

Ruble, Paula, *Reference Tech,* Maysville, Kentucky Gateway Museum Center, Maysville KY

Ruby, Janet, *Assoc Prof,* Shippensburg University, Art Dept, Shippensburg PA (S)

Ruby, Scott, *Asst Cur Russian & Eastern European Art,* Hillwood Museum & Gardens Foundation, Hillwood Estate Museum & Gardens, Washington DC

Ruckler, Eric, *Coll Specialist,* State University of New York at Plattsburgh, Art Museum, Plattsburgh NY

Ruda, Jeffrey, *Dir Art History,* University of California, Davis, Dept of Art & Art History, Davis CA (S)

Rudd, Jeremy, *Asst Prof Art,* Divine Word College, Father Weyland SVD Gallery, Epworth IA

Rudd, Wayne, *Adjunct,* Idaho State University, Dept of Art & Pre-Architecture, Pocatello ID (S)

Rudder, John, *Spec Projects Mgr,* Mount Vernon Ladies' Association of the Union, Library, Mount Vernon VA

Rudey, Liz, *Prof,* Long Island University, Brooklyn Campus, Art Dept, Brooklyn NY (S)

Rudick, Nancy, *Supv,* Skidmore College, Lucy Scribner Library, Saratoga Springs NY

Rudin, Eric, *Co Chmn,* The Drawing Center, New York NY

Rudin, Vicci, *VChmn,* City of Port Angeles, Port Angeles Fine Arts Center & Webster Woods Art Park, Port Angeles WA

Rudnick, Matthew S, *Asst Gen Mgr,* City of Los Angeles, Cultural Affairs Dept, Los Angeles CA

Rudnicki, Michelle, *Mktg & Develop,* Buffalo Museum of Science, Research Library, Buffalo NY

Rudolf, Scooter, *Dir,* New Image Art, West Hollywood CA

Rudolph, Beth, *Exec Dir,* VSA Arts of New Mexico, Enabled Arts Center, Albuquerque NM (S)

Rudolph, Conrad, *Prof,* University of California, Riverside, Dept of the History of Art, Riverside CA (S)

Rudolph, Jeffrey N, *Pres & CEO,* California Science Center, Los Angeles CA

Rudolph, William Keyse, *Assoc Cur American Art,* Dallas Museum of Art, Dallas TX

Rudy, Carl, *Art Instr,* Indiana Wesleyan University, School of Arts & Humanities, Division of Art, Marion IN (S)

Rudzykte, Rasa, *Dir Intl Prog,* Balzekas Museum of Lithuanian Culture, Chicago IL

Ruedi, Katerina, *Dir School Archit,* University of Illinois at Chicago, College of Architecture, Chicago IL (S)

Ruedy, Don, *Prof,* University of Wisconsin, Center-Barron County, Dept of Art, Rice Lake WI (S)

Ruesch, Andre, *Chair Photog,* Lesley University, College of Art & Design, Boston MA (S)

Rufe, Laurie, *Dir,* Roswell Museum & Art Center, Roswell NM

Ruff, Elizabeth, *Asst Prof,* Newberry College, Dept of Art, Newberry SC (S)

Ruff, Gloria, *Assoc Cur & Registrar,* Valparaiso University, Brauer Museum of Art, Valparaiso IN

Ruff, Joshua, *Dir Coll & Interpretation,* The Long Island Museum of American Art, History & Carriages, Stony Brook NY

Ruff, Joshua, *Dir Colls & Interpretation,* The Long Island Museum of American Art, History & Carriages, Library, Stony Brook NY

Ruffin, Ellen, *Cur,* University of Southern Mississippi, McCain Library & Archives, Hattiesburg MS

Ruffini, Marco, *Adjunct Prof,* Northwestern University, Evanston, Dept of Art History, Evanston IL (S)

Ruffo, Joseph M, *Chmn & Dir,* University of Nebraska, Lincoln, Eisentrager Howard Gallery, Lincoln NE

Ruffolo, Robert E, *Pres,* Princeton Antiques Bookservice, Art Marketing Reference Library, Atlantic City NJ

Rufkahr, Abby, *Prog & Develop Asst,* Kansas City Jewish Museum of Contemporary Art - Epsten Gallery, Overland Park KS

Ruga, Glenn, *Exec Dir,* Photographic Resource Center at Boston University, Boston MA

Ruggerio, Marie, *Mus Shop Mgr,* Bergen County Historical Society, Steuben House Museum, River Edge NJ

Ruggiero, Laurence, *Dir,* Charles Morse, Charles Hosmer Morse Museum of American Art, Winter Park FL

Ruggie Saunders, Cathie, *Assoc Prof,* Saint Xavier University, Dept of Art & Design, Chicago IL (S)

Ruggio, Pamela, *Dir Communs,* Aldrich Museum of Contemporary Art, Ridgefield CT

Ruggles, Janet, *Dir & Chief Paper Conservator,* Balboa Art Conservation Center, San Diego CA

Ruggles, Janet, *Gen Mgr,* Balboa Art Conservation Center, Richard D Buck Memorial Library, San Diego CA

Ruhe, Barnaby, *Artist,* U Gallery, New York NY

Ruhstaller, Tod, *Dir,* The San Joaquin Pioneer & Historical Society, Petzinger Memorial Library & Earl Rowland Art Library, Stockton CA

Ruhstaller, Tod, *Dir & Cur of History,* The San Joaquin Pioneer & Historical Society, The Haggin Museum, Stockton CA

Ruhwald, Anders, *Head Ceramics Dept,* Cranbrook Academy of Art, Bloomfield Hills MI (S)

Ruiz, Amber, *Acting Head, VRC,* Stanford University, Art & Architecture Library, Stanford CA

Rule, Dan, *Asst Prof,* University of New Orleans-Lake Front, Dept of Fine Arts, New Orleans LA (S)

Ruleaux, Don, *Instr,* Chadron State College, Dept of Art, Chadron NE (S)

Rumery, Caitlin, *Assoc Colls Mgr & Registrar,* University of Colorado, CU Art Museum, Boulder CO

Rummel, Lee, *Facilities Mgr,* Southern Alleghenies Museum of Art, Loretto Facility, Loretto PA

Rumold, Danila, *Lectr,* Seattle University, Dept of Fine Arts, Visual Art Division, Seattle WA (S)

Rumrill, Alan, *Exec Dir,* Historical Society of Cheshire County, Keene NH

Rundels, Donna, *Slide Libm,* Center for Creative Studies, College of Art & Design Library, Detroit MI

Runge, Christen, *Asst Cur,* Georgetown University, Art Collection, Washington DC

Runge, Christen, *Asst Cur,* Georgetown University, Lauinger Library-Special Collections Division, Washington DC

Runnells, Jamie, *Assoc Prof,* Mississippi State University, Dept of Art, Starville MS (S)

Ruoff, Maria, *Publicity,* Berks Art Alliance, Reading PA

Rupert, Mark, *Photo,* Oregon College of Art & Craft, Portland OR (S)

Ruppert, John, *Chmn,* University of Maryland, Department of Art, College Park MD (S)

Ruppman, Walter C, *Exec Dir,* Peoria Historical Society, Peoria IL

Rusak, Sandra C, *Deputy Dir Educ & Statewide Partnerships,* Virginia Museum of Fine Arts, Richmond VA

Rusfvold, Georgia, *Prog Coordr,* SVACA - Sheyenne Valley Arts & Crafts Association, Bjarne Ness Gallery at Bear Creek Hall, Fort Ransom ND

Rush, Jon, *Prof,* University of Michigan, Ann Arbor, School of Art & Design, Ann Arbor MI (S)

Rush, Kent, *Prof,* University of Texas at San Antonio, Dept of Art & Art History, San Antonio TX (S)

Rush, Sallee, *Instr,* Main Line Art Center, Haverford PA (S)

Rushing, Jack, *Chmn,* University of Missouri, Saint Louis, Gallery 210, Saint Louis MO

Rushing, Kelly, *Registrar,* Eiteljorg Museum of American Indians & Western Art, Indianapolis IN

Rushing, Kim, *Prof,* Delta State University, Dept of Art, Cleveland MS (S)

Rushing, Mollie Rollins, *Instr,* Delta State University, Dept of Art, Cleveland MS (S)

Rushing, W Jackson, *Chmn,* University of Houston, Dept of Art, Houston TX (S)

Rushton, Edward, *Asst Prof,* Viterbo College, Art Dept, La Crosse WI (S)

Rusinek, Marvin, *Asst Archivist,* American Jewish Historical Society, The Center for Jewish History, New York NY

Rusk, Carol, *Benjamin & Irma Weiss Libm,* Whitney Museum of American Art, Frances Mulhall Achilles Library, New York NY

Rusk, Carol, *Libm & Assoc Cur Spec Coll,* Whitney Museum of American Art, New York NY

Ruskin, Mary, *Accounting Dir,* Laumeier Sculpture Park, Saint Louis MO

Rusnak, Jeff, *Dir Develop,* Art & Culture Center of Hollywood, Art Gallery/Multidisciplinary Cultural Center, Hollywood FL

Russ, Barbara, *Mus Asst,* Department of Economic & Community Development, Eric Sloane Museum, Kent CT

Russ, Charlotte, *Mem Coordr,* Birmingham Museum of Art, Birmingham AL

Russell, Barry, *Instr Dean Fine Arts,* Cerritos Community College, Fine Arts & Communication Div, Norwalk CA (S)

Russell, Christopher, *Vis Asst Prof,* Hamilton College, Art Dept, Clinton NY (S)

Russell, Donald, *Dir & Cur,* Provisions Library, Provisions Research Center for Arts & Social Change, Fairfax VA

Russell, Donald H, *Exec Dir,* Art Resources International, Washington DC

Russell, Douglas, *Gallery Dir,* Oregon State University, Fairbanks Gallery, Corvallis OR

Russell, Douglas, *Sr Research Assoc,* Oregon State University, Dept of Art, Corvallis OR (S)

Russell, John, *Chmn Critical Studies,* Massachusetts College of Art, Boston MA (S)

Russell, Lisa, *Assoc Prof,* Rhode Island College, Art Dept, Providence RI (S)

Russell, Lynn, *Educ Div Head,* National Gallery of Art, Washington DC

Russell, Margaret, *Receptionist,* Sweetwater County Library System and School District #1, Community Fine Arts Center, Rock Springs WY

Russell, Marilyn M, *Cur Educ,* Carnegie Museums of Pittsburgh, Carnegie Museum of Art, Pittsburgh PA

Russell, Melissa, *Accountant,* Tulane University, Newcomb Art Gallery, New Orleans LA

Russell, Pamela, *Head Ed Cur AC Progs,* Amherst College, Mead Art Museum, Amherst MA

Russell, Paul, *Asst Dir,* Plumas County Museum, Quincy CA

Russell, Robert, *Chmn & Assoc Prof Art Educ,* University of Cincinnati, School of Art, Cincinnati OH (S)

Russell, Sandra, *Dept Adminr,* University of Wisconsin, Madison, Dept of Art History, Madison WI (S)

Russell, Sy, *Vis Svcs Mgr,* The California Historical Society, San Francisco CA

Russell, Tiffany, *Spec Event Mgr,* Contemporary Art Center of Virginia, Virginia Beach VA

Russick, David, *Chief Designer,* Indianapolis Museum of Art, Indianapolis IN

Russi Kirshner, Judith, *Dean,* University of Illinois at Chicago, College of Architecture, Chicago IL (S)

Russmann, Ann, *Cur, Egyptian, Classical & Ancient Near Eastern Art,* Brooklyn Museum, Brooklyn NY

Russo, Barbara, *Fine Arts Mgr,* Cypress College, Cypress CA

Russo, Howard, *Instr,* Elgin Community College, Fine Arts Dept, Elgin IL (S)

Russo, Patrice, *Museum Mgr,* Concordia Historical Institute, Saint Louis MO

Russo, Susan, *Chmn,* Youngstown State University, Dept of Art, Youngstown OH (S)

Russolo, Lloyd, *Assoc Provost,* Philadelphia University, Philadelphia PA (S)

Rust, Brian, *Prof,* Augusta State University, Dept of Art, Augusta GA (S)

Rustige, Rona, *Cur,* Glanmore National Historic Site of Canada, Belleville ON

Rutberg, Nicole, *Cur Asst,* Bishop's University, Foreman Art Gallery, Sherbrooke PQ

Ruth, Nicholas, *Chair,* Hobart & William Smith Colleges, Art Dept, Geneva NY (S)

Rutherford, Mary Jane, *Community Rels Officer,* University of Oklahoma, Fred Jones Jr Museum of Art, Norman OK

Rutica, Sofia, *Prog Mgr & Registry Coordr,* Maryland Art Place, Baltimore MD

Rutigliano, Vincenzo, The New York Public Library, Art & Architecture Collection, New York NY

Rutkovsky, Paul, *Assoc Prof,* Florida State University, Art Dept, Tallahassee FL (S)

Rutkowski, Sandra, *Dir Libr Svcs,* Lourdes College, Duns Scotus Library, Sylvania OH

Rutledge, Andrea S, *Exec Dir,* National Architectural Accrediting Board, Inc, Washington DC

Rutledge, Bethany S, *Cur,* Thornton W Burgess, Museum, Sandwich MA

Ruttner, Nancy, *Dir,* Art Institute of Pittsburgh, John P. Barclay Memorial Gallery, Pittsburgh PA

Rux, Sandra, *Cur,* Portsmouth Historical Society, John Paul Jones House & Discover Portsmouth, Portsmouth NH

Ruzicka, Jean, *Secy,* North Country Museum of Arts, Park Rapids MN

Ryan, Amy E, *Pres,* Boston Public Library, Central Library, Boston MA

Ryan, Barbara, *Contact Person,* Broward Community College - A. Hugh Adams Campus, Fine Arts Gallery, Davie FL

Ryan, Chris, *Assoc Prof, Dept Chair,* Hiram College, Art Dept, Hiram OH (S)

Ryan, David, *Preparator,* Cornell University, Herbert F Johnson Museum of Art, Ithaca NY

Ryan, Debora, *Sr Cur,* Everson Museum of Art, Syracuse NY

Ryan, Donna B, *Newsletter Ed/Sec,* Almond Historical Society, Inc, Hagadorn House, The 1800-37 Museum, Almond NY

Ryan, Jennifer, *Develop Admin Asst & Mem Coordr,* Cornell University, Herbert F Johnson Museum of Art, Ithaca NY

Ryan, Joleen, *Asst Cur Children's Mus,* Sangre de Cristo Arts & Conference Center, Pueblo CO

Ryan, Kathy, *Prog Coordr,* McMaster University, School of Art, Drama & Music, Hamilton ON (S)

Ryan, Lee A, *Pres,* Almond Historical Society, Inc, Hagadorn House, The 1800-37 Museum, Almond NY

Ryan, Linda Lee, *Prog Dir,* Casper College, Dept of Visual Arts, Casper WY (S)

Ryan, Margaret, *Secy,* Mystic Art Association, Inc, Mystic Arts Center, Mystic CT

Ryan, Mark, *VP Coll,* Plains Art Museum, Fargo ND

Ryan, Maureen, *Assoc Prof,* University of British Columbia, Dept of Art History, Visual Art & Theory, Vancouver BC (S)

Ryan, Paul, *Assoc Prof,* Mary Baldwin College, Dept of Art & Art History, Staunton VA (S)

Ryan, Raymund, *Cur Architecture,* Carnegie Museums of Pittsburgh, Carnegie Museum of Art, Pittsburgh PA

Ryan, Susan, *Asst,* Louisiana State University, School of Art, Baton Rouge LA (S)

Ryan, Tim, *Special Projects Mgr,* Delaplaine Visual Arts Education Center, Frederick MD

Ryan-Cook, Joelle, *Deputy Dir,* Columbia Museum of Art, Columbia SC

Ryan Kelley, Heather, *Dir,* Abercrombie Gallery, Lake Charles LA

Rychlak, Bonnie, *Cur,* Isamu Noguchi, Isamu Noguchi Garden Museum, Long Island City NY

Ryckbosch, Bart, *Archivist,* The Art Institute of Chicago, Ryerson & Burnham Libraries, Chicago IL

Rydell, Christine, *Instr,* Solano Community College, Division of Fine & Applied Art & Behavioral Science, Fairfield CA (S)

Ryden, Michelle, *Registrar,* City of El Paso, El Paso Museum of Art, El Paso TX

Ryder, Brigid, *Shop Mgr,* Prince George Art Gallery, Prince George BC

Ryder-O'Malley, Grace, *Educ Asst,* Provincetown Art Association & Museum, Provincetown MA

Rye, Leigh, *Sec,* Reading Public Museum, Reading PA

Rykels, Sam, *Mus Dir,* Louisiana Department of Culture, Recreation & Tourism, Louisiana State Museum, New Orleans LA

Ryker-Crawford, Jessie, *Mus Studies Dept Chair,* Institute of American Indian Arts, Museum of Contemporary Native Arts, Santa Fe NM (S)

Rylance, Keli E, *Head,* Tulane University, Southeastern Architectural Archive, New Orleans LA

Ryley, Bryan, *Assoc Prof (Visual Art),* University of British Columbia Okanagan, Dept of Creative Studies, Kelowna BC (S)

Rzoska, Linda, *Coordr Ctr for New Media,* Kalamazoo Valley Community College, Center for New Media, Kalamazoo MI (S)

Saaby, Lynn, *VPres House & Grounds,* Edward Hopper, Nyack NY

Saarnio, Robert, *Cur,* Peabody Essex Museum, Peirce-Nichols House, Salem MA

Saarnio, Robert, *Dir,* University of Mississippi, University Museum & Historic Houses, Oxford MS

Sabatini, Jenna, *Mgr Special Events, Guest Servs & Mem,* Museum of Florida Art, Deland FL

Sablow, Mark, *Prof,* Florida Community College at Jacksonville, South Campus, Art Dept, Jacksonville FL (S)

Sabol, Robert, *Dept Chair (art & design),* Purdue University, West Lafayette, Patti and Rusty Rueff School of Visual & Performing Arts, Art & Design Dept, West Lafayette IN (S)

Sacandiz, Paul, *Assoc Prof,* University of Wisconsin, Madison, Dept of Art, Madison WI (S)

Sachs, Sid, *Dir Exhibs,* The University of the Arts, Rosenwald-Wolf Gallery, Philadelphia PA

Sack, Bill, *Tech Dir,* Hallwalls Contemporary Arts Center, Buffalo NY

Sack, Jessica, *Cur Educ,* Yale University, Yale University Art Gallery, New Haven CT

Sackel, Matthew, *Art Hist Librn,* University of Wisconsin-Stevens Point, Dept of Art & Design, Stevens Point WI (S)

Sackett, Margot Magee, *Dir,* Ross Memorial Museum, Saint Andrews NB

Sackman, Elmer, *Librn,* Fort Worth Public Library Arts & Humanities, Fine Arts Section, Fort Worth TX

Sackrey, Ponteir, *Dir Develop & Mktg,* National Museum of Wildlife Art of the Unites States, Jackson WY

Sade, Marianne, *Instructional Librn,* Maryland Institute, Decker Library, Baltimore MD

Sadler, Cody, *Co-Dir,* Canadian Wildlife & Wilderness Art Museum, Ottawa ON

Sadler, Cody, *Co-Dir,* Canadian Wildlife & Wilderness Art Museum, Library, Ottawa ON

Sadler, Donna, *Chmn Art Dept,* Agnes Scott College, Dalton Art Gallery, Decatur GA

Sadler, Ginna, *Prof,* Abilene Christian University, Dept of Art & Design, Abilene TX (S)

Sadler, Laura M, *Sr VPres Mus Enterprises,* Field Museum, Chicago IL

Saenger, Allana, *Cur Exhibits,* Riley County Historical Society & Museum, Riley County Historical Museum, Manhattan KS

Saenger, Allana, *Exhibits,* Riley County Historical Society & Museum, Seaton Library, Manhattan KS

Saenz, Marisela, *Admin Asst,* Hidalgo County Historical Museum, Edinburg TX

Safiran, Ed, *Asst Site Mgr,* Illinois Historic Preservation Agency, Bishop Hill State Historic Site, Bishop Hill IL

Saganic, Livio, *Prof,* Drew University, Art Dept, Madison NJ (S)

Sage, Colleen, *Human Resources Mgr,* The Adirondack Historical Association, The Adirondack Museum, Blue Mountain Lake NY

Sager, Judy, *Owner,* Sager Studios, Fort Worth TX (S)

Saggus, Frank, *Instr,* Brenau University, Art & Design Dept, Gainesville GA (S)

Sahdana-Melber, Soledad, *Educ Dir,* Pacific Northwest Art School, Gallery at the Wharf, Coupeville WA

Sahlstrand, James, *Dir Art Gallery,* Central Washington University, Sarah Spurgeon Gallery, Ellensburg WA

Saidel, Alice, *Ref Librn,* Dayton Art Institute, Library, Dayton OH

Saidpour, Massoud, *Cur Performing Arts, Music & Film,* The Cleveland Museum of Art, Cleveland OH

Said Schuler, Tania, *Cur Educ,* Ball State University, Museum of Art, Muncie IN

Saikai, Paul, *Coordr, Graphic Design,* York College of Pennsylvania, Dept of Music, Art & Speech Communications, York PA (S)

Sailor, Rebecca, *Assoc Cur Educ,* Gibbes Museum of Art, Charleston SC (S)

Sain, Jennifer George, *Dir,* William Woods University, Cox Gallery, Fulton MO

Sajet, Kim, *Dir,* National Portrait Gallery, Smithsonian Institution, Washington DC

Sakoulas, Thomas, *Instr,* State University of New York College at Oneonta, Dept of Art, Oneonta NY (S)

Saks, Dawn, *Instr,* Century College, Humanities Dept, White Bear Lake MN (S)

Sakurai, Motoatsu, *Pres Japan Society,* Japan Society, Inc, Japan Society Gallery, New York NY

Salam, Halide, *Prof,* Radford University, Art Dept, Radford VA (S)

Salamah, Stephanie, *Dir Develop,* Las Vegas Art Museum, Las Vegas NV

Sala Pomeranz, Christine, *Chmn International Trade,* Fashion Institute of Technology, Art & Design Division, New York NY (S)

Salas, Rafael, *Dir,* Ripon College Caestecker Art Gallery, Ripon WI

Salas, Rafael, *Chmn,* Ripon College, Art Dept, Ripon WI (S)

Salazar, Carolina, *Dir,* Miami-Dade Community College, Wolfson Galleries, Miami FL

Salazar, Jim Bob, *Asst Prof,* Sul Ross State University, Dept of Fine Arts & Communications, Alpine TX (S)

Salazar, Maribel, *Santa Fe Shop,* Chicago Architecture Foundation, Chicago IL

Salazar, Roberto, *HR & Admin Mgr,* University of California, Los Angeles, Fowler Museum at UCLA, Los Angeles CA

Salazar, Rosemarie, *Supv Ranger,* Mesa Verde National Park, Research Library, Mesa Verde National Park CO

Salberg, Lester, *Prof,* Rock Valley College, Humanities and Fine Arts Division, Rockford IL (S)

Salcedo, Zinnia, *Exhib & Prog Mgr,* Blue Star Contemporary Art Center, San Antonio TX

Sale, Gregory, *Visual Arts Dir,* Arizona Commission on the Arts, Phoenix AZ

Sale, Tom, *Dir,* Navarro College, Art Dept, Corsicana TX (S)

Sale-Hook, Joanne, *Preparator,* Vernon Art Gallery, Vernon BC

Salerno, Dawn, *Dir Educ,* Mystic Art Association, Inc, Mystic Arts Center, Mystic CT

Salerno, Robert, *CFO,* Museum of Arts & Design, New York NY

Salesses, John J, *Pres,* Newport Historical Society & Museum of Newport History, Newport RI

Saliga, Pauline, *Exec Dir,* Society of Architectural Historians, Chicago IL

Saliklis, Ruta, *Exhib & Develop Dir,* San Luis Obispo Museum of Art, San Luis Obispo CA

Salinas, Juan Carlos, *Educ Dir,* Jamaica Center for Arts & Learning (JCAL), Jamaica NY

Salinas, Vickie, *Pres,* Fusion: The Ontario Clay & Glass Association, Fusion Clay & Glass Association, Toronto ON

Salisbury, Anne, *Instr,* Saint John's University, Art Dept, Collegeville MN (S)

Salisbury, Rachael, *Asst Registrar,* University of Virginia, The Fralin Museum of Art at the University of Virginia, Charlottesville VA

Sallee, Roberta, *Pres,* Blacksburg Regional Art Association, Blacksburg VA

Sallinger, Joan, *Foundations,* Orange Coast College, Visual & Performing Arts Division, Costa Mesa CA (S)

Salm, Judy, *Reference Librn,* Fort Hays State University, Forsyth Library, Hays KS

Salmon, Henry A, *Chmn Board,* Staten Island Museum, Staten Island NY

Salmon, Patricia, *Cur History,* Staten Island Museum, Staten Island NY

Salmon, Ray, *Instr,* Solano Community College, Division of Fine & Applied Art & Behavioral Science, Fairfield CA (S)

Salmond, Wendy, *Prof,* Chapman University, Art Dept, Orange CA (S)

Salomon, Colleen, *Digital Specialist,* Scripps College, Ruth Chandler Williamson Gallery, Claremont CA

Salomon, Nanette, *Prof,* College of Staten Island, Performing & Creative Arts Dept, Staten Island NY (S)

Salomon, Peter, *Bus Mgr,* Laguna Art Museum, Laguna Beach CA

Salomon, Suzanne, *Chair Art Comt,* New Canaan Library, H. Pelham Curtis Gallery, New Canaan CT

Salpeter, Ellen, *Deputy Dir External,* The Jewish Museum, New York NY

Salsbury, Kathleen, *Library Asst,* Munson-Williams-Proctor Arts Institute, Art Reference Library, Utica NY

Saltonstall, G West, *Chmn, VPres,* USS Constitution Museum, Boston MA

Saltz, Ina, *Prof,* City College of New York, Art Dept, New York NY (S)

Saltz, Laura, *Asst Prof,* Colby College, Art Dept, Waterville ME (S)

Saluti, Andrew, *Designer & Preparator,* Syracuse University, SUArt Galleries, Syracuse NY

Salvator, Marilee, *Asst Prof,* Bloomsburg University, Dept of Art & Art History, Bloomsburg PA (S)

Salvayon, Leon L, *Multimedia & Web Design,* Art Institute of Pittsburgh, Pittsburgh PA (S)

Salveson, Douglas, *Prof,* University of Findlay, Art Program, Findlay OH (S)

Salvest, John J, *Assoc Prof,* Arkansas State University, Dept of Art, State University AR (S)

Salzillo, William, *Prof,* Hamilton College, Art Dept, Clinton NY (S)

Salzman, Kevin, *Asst Prof,* Wittenberg University, Art Dept, Springfield OH (S)

Samaras, Connie, *Prof Photog & Media Theory,* University of California, Irvine, Studio Art Dept, Irvine CA (S)

Sametz, Peter, *Dir Operations,* Saskatchewan Arts Board, Regina SK

Sammon, Christine E, *Library Dir,* Alberta College of Art & Design, Luke Lindoe Library, Calgary AB

Sammons, Richard, *Assoc Prof,* Bismarck State College, Fine Arts Dept, Bismarck ND (S)

Sammons, Tania J, *Cur (Owens-Thomas House),* Telfair Museums' Jepson Center for the Arts Library, Savannah GA

Samoylova, Anastasia, *Asst Prof,* Illinois Central College, Arts & Communication Dept, East Peoria IL (S)

Samples-Davis, Olga, *Dir Educ,* San Antonio Museum of Art, San Antonio TX

Sampson, Cherie, *Assoc Prof (Environmental Sculpture, Video & Performance),* University of Missouri - Columbia, Dept of Art, Columbia MO (S)

Sampson, Debra, *Dir,* Academy of Art, University Library, San Francisco CA

Sampson, George, *Lectr Arts Admin,* University of Virginia, McIntire Dept of Art, Charlottesville VA (S)

Samson, Carl, *Chmn,* American Society of Portrait Artists (ASOPA), Montgomery AL

Samson, Helene, *Cur Notman Photog Archives,* McCord Museum of Canadian History, Montreal PQ

Samuel, Meika, *Dir Educ Progs,* South Carolina State Museum, Columbia SC

Samuels, Allen, *Prof,* University of Michigan, Ann Arbor, School of Art & Design, Ann Arbor MI (S)

Samuels, Clifford, *Dir,* Trova Foundation, Philip Samuels Fine Art, Saint Louis MO

Samuels, Philip, *Pres,* Trova Foundation, Philip Samuels Fine Art, Saint Louis MO

Samuelson, Claire, *Cur,* Headquarters Fort Monroe, Dept of Army, Casemate Museum, Hampton VA

Samuelson, Jerry, *Dean School of Arts,* California State University, Fullerton, Art Dept, Fullerton CA (S)

Samuelson, Laura, *Dir,* City of Nome Alaska, Carrie M McLain Memorial Museum, Nome AK

Sanborn, Reilly, *Exec Dir,* Foothills Art Center, Inc, Golden CO

Sanchez, Jacquelyn Roesch, *Dir,* Montclair Art Museum, Yard School of Art, Montclair NJ (S)

Sanchez, Jesse, *Pres,* New Rochelle Public Library, New Rochelle Art Association, New Rochelle NY

Sanchez, Marisa, *Asst Cur Modern Art,* Seattle Art Museum, Downtown, Seattle WA

Sanchez, Nereida, *Exec Sec,* New York Society of Architects, New York NY

Sanchez, Pamela Reed, *Develop,* George Eastman, Museum, Rochester NY

Sanchez-Dallam, Marta, *Adj Prof,* Saint Joseph's University, Art Dept, Philadelphia PA (S)

Sanchez Villarreal, Ernesto, *Head, Exhibit Design & Reg,* Oklahoma City Museum of Art, Oklahoma City OK

Sanchis, Frank E, *Sr VP,* Municipal Art Society of New York, New York NY

Sandals, Leah, *Assoc Ed,* Canadian Art Foundation, Toronto ON

Sandberg, Emmet, *Asst Prof,* University of Wisconsin Oshkosh, Dept of Art, Oshkosh WI (S)

Sandberg, Sharon, *Adjunct Assoc Prof Painting,* Aquinas College, Art Dept, Grand Rapids MI (S)

Sanders, Albert E, *Cur Natural History*, Charleston Museum, Charleston SC

Sanders, Cynthia, *Center Supv*, Baton Rouge Gallery, Center For Contemporary Art, Baton Rouge LA

Sanders, Debra, *Office Mgr*, Hambidge Center for Creative Arts & Sciences, Rabun Gap GA

Sanders, Frank, *Maintenance*, American Swedish Historical Foundation & Museum, American Swedish Historical Museum, Philadelphia PA

Sanders, Jan, *Dir*, Pasadena Public Library, Fine Arts Dept, Pasadena CA

Sanders, Jean, *Assoc Prof Art (Printmaking & New Media)*, Pennsylvania State University, University Park, Penn State School of Visual Arts, University Park PA (S)

Sanders, Joe, *Assoc Prof Printmaking*, University of Georgia, Franklin College of Arts & Sciences, Lamar Dodd School of Art, Athens GA (S)

Sanders, Mary, *Instr*, Cuyahoga Valley Art Center, Cuyahoga Falls OH (S)

Sanders, Philip, *Asst Prof*, The College of New Jersey, School of Arts & Sciences, Ewing NJ (S)

Sanders, Rebecca, *Dir Art School*, Boca Raton Museum of Art, Boca Raton FL

Sanders, Susan L, *Colls Cur*, University of Memphis, Visual Resource Collection, Memphis TN

Sanders, Tom, *Site Mgr*, Jeffers Petroglyphs Historic Site, Comfrey MN

Sanders, William, *Instr*, Surry Community College, Art Dept, Dobson NC (S)

Sanderson, Brandon, *Asst Prof*, University of North Carolina at Pembroke, Art Dept, Pembroke NC (S)

Sanderson, Doug, *Asst Prof*, Oberlin College, Dept of Art, Oberlin OH (S)

Sanderson, Natalie, *Chief Cur*, University of California, Santa Barbara, University Art Museum, Santa Barbara CA

Sanderson, Sheri, *Events, Gift Shop*, LeMoyne Art Foundation, Center for the Visual Arts, Tallahassee FL

Sandiford, Vickie, *Mgr Retail Operations*, The Adirondack Historical Association, The Adirondack Museum, Blue Mountain Lake NY

Sandino, Margarita, *Cur Educ*, The Dixon Gallery & Gardens, Memphis TN

Sandkulher, Iris, *Temp Asst Prof*, Georgia Southern University, Dept of Art, Statesboro GA (S)

Sandler, Irving, *Prof Emeritus*, Purchase College, State University of New York, School of Art+Design, Purchase NY (S)

Sandlin, Diane, *Exec Dir*, Surface Design Association, Inc, Sebastopol CA

Sandman, Keith, *Prof*, Munson-Williams-Proctor Arts Institute, Pratt MWP College of Art, Utica NY (S)

Sandone, Corinne, *Assoc Prof*, Johns Hopkins University, School of Medicine, Dept of Art as Applied to Medicine, Baltimore MD (S)

Sandoval, Angelica, *Adjunct Assoc Prof Fine Art*, Johnson County Community College, Fine Arts Dept & Art History Dept, Overland Park KS (S)

Sandoval, Claudia, *Coordr*, City of Brea, Art Gallery, Brea CA

Sands, Craig, *Adjunct Asst Prof Photog*, Johnson County Community College, Fine Arts Dept & Art History Dept, Overland Park KS (S)

Sanford, Claire, *Pres*, Haystack Mountain School of Crafts, Deer Isle ME

Sanford, Eva, *Adult Librn*, Willard Library, Dept of Fine Arts, Evansville IN

Sanftner, Patricia, *Co-1st Vice Regent*, Schuyler-Hamilton House, Morristown NJ

Sanftner, Phyllis, *Cur*, Schuyler-Hamilton House, Morristown NJ

Sangelo, Trish, *Gallery Coordr*, Arapahoe Community College, Colorado Gallery of the Arts, Littleton CO

Sanger, Erika, *Dir Educ*, Albany Institute of History & Art, Albany NY

Saniat, Christine, *Registrar*, University of Illinois at Urbana-Champaign, Krannert Art Museum and Kinkead Pavilion, Champaign IL

Sanidad, Michelle, *CFO*, United Indians of All Tribes Foundation, Daybreak Star Center Gallery, Seattle WA

Sankey, Gretchen, *Instr*, Toronto School of Art, Toronto ON (S)

San Miguel, Carmen Febo, *Exec Dir*, Taller Puertorriqueno Inc, Lorenzo Homar Gallery, Philadelphia PA

Sanpei, Sandra, *Dept Head*, Honolulu Community College, Commercial Art Dept, Honolulu HI (S)

Sansalone, Nancy A, *COO & CFO*, Special Libraries Association, Alexandria VA

Sansom, Helen, *Sec*, American Society of Portrait Artists (ASOPA), Montgomery AL

Sansone, Bettielee, *Dir*, Pine Castle Center of the Arts, Orlando FL

Sansone, Kristina Lamour, *Chair Design*, Lesley University, College of Art & Design, Boston MA (S)

Santamaria, Jose, *Dir & Cur*, Tellus Northwest Georgia Science Museum, Cartersville GA

Santana, Nil, *Prof*, Abilene Christian University, Dept of Art & Design, Abilene TX (S)

Santangelo, Mark, *Chief Librn*, Mount Vernon Ladies' Association of the Union, The Fred W Smith National Library for the Study of George Washington, Mount Vernon VA

Santee, Ruth, *Instr*, San Joaquin Delta College, Arts & Communication, Stockton CA (S)

Santelli, Thomas, *Asst Prof*, College of Saint Rose, The Center For Art and Design, Albany NY (S)

Santiago, Fernando, *Auxiliary Prof*, Inter American University of Puerto Rico, Dept of Art, San German PR (S)

Santiago, Fernando, *Auxiliary Prof*, Inter American University of Puerto Rico, Dept of Art, San German PR (S)

Santiago, Raymond, *Dir*, Miami-Dade Public Library, Miami FL

Santina, Adrianne, *Instr*, Linfield College, Department of Art & Visual Culture, McMinnville OR (S)

Santmyers, Stephanie, *Chmn*, North Carolina Agricultural & Technical State University, Visual Arts Dept, Greensboro NC (S)

Santoro, Geraldine, *Cur Coll*, The National Park Service, United States Department of the Interior, Statue of Liberty National Monument & The Ellis Island Immigration Museum, Washington DC

Santos, Dan, *Educ Mgr*, Rhode Island Historical Society, John Brown House, Providence RI

Santos, Lori, *Prof*, University of Nebraska, Kearney, Dept of Art & Art History, Kearney NE (S)

Santos, Owen, *Opers Mgr*, Henry Gallery Association, Henry Art Gallery, Seattle WA

Santos, Tammy, *Prog Coordr*, Allied Arts Council of St Joseph, Saint Joseph MO

Santoso, Dee, *Deputy Dir*, Manchester City Library, Manchester NH

Sanyal, Bish, *Urban Studies & Planning*, Massachusetts Institute of Technology, School of Architecture and Planning, Cambridge MA (S)

Sapp, Aimee, *Chmn Arts & Humanities*, William Woods University, Cox Gallery, Fulton MO

Sapp, Aimee, *Instr*, William Woods-Westminster Colleges, Art Dept, Fulton MO (S)

Sapp, David, *Prof Art*, Bowling Green State University, Firelands College, Humanities Dept, Huron OH (S)

Sapp, Rocky, *Assoc Prof Sculpture*, University of Georgia, Franklin College of Arts & Sciences, Lamar Dodd School of Art, Athens GA (S)

Sargent, Denis, *Dir Grad Studies*, University of Wisconsin-Milwaukee, Peck School of the Arts, Dept of Art & Design, Milwaukee WI (S)

Sargent, Shannon, *Exhib & Coll Coordr*, Sioux City Art Center, Sioux City IA (S)

Sargent, Shannon, *Instr*, Morningside College, Art Dept, Sioux City IA (S)

Sarjeant-Jenkins, Rachel, *Chief Librn*, Medicine Hat Public Library, Medicine Hat AB

Sarnacki, Michael, *Dir*, Detroit Focus, Royal Oak MI

Sarno, Lisa, *Asst Gen Mgr*, El Pueblo de Los Angeles Historical Monument, Los Angeles CA

Sarns, Mary, *Dept Chair*, Willoughby School of Fine Arts, Visual Arts Dept, Willoughby OH (S)

Sarofim, Louisa S, *Chmn*, Menil Foundation, Inc, The Menil Collection, Houston TX

Sarre, Camille, *Assoc Prof*, Murray State University, Dept of Art, Murray KY (S)

Sarris, Rita, *Gallery Dir*, Arts & Crafts Association of Meriden Inc, Gallery 53, Meriden CT

Sartor, Curtis, *Dean*, Judson University, School of Art, Design & Architecture, Elgin IL (S)

Sartori, Dean, *Conservator*, Kirkland Museum of Fine & Decorative Art, Denver CO

Sartwell, Crispin, *Assoc Prof*, Dickinson College, Dept of Art & Art History, Carlisle PA (S)

Sarver, Jennifer, *Dir Educ*, Cedarhurst Center for the Arts, Mitchell Museum, Mount Vernon IL

Sarver, Jill, *Visual Arts Coordr*, Westport Arts Center, Westport CT

Sasaki, Jon, *Exhib Tech*, Mercer Union, A Centre for Contemporary Art, Toronto ON

Saslow, James, *Chmn*, Queens College, Art Dept, Flushing NY (S)

Saslow, James M, *Prof*, City University of New York, PhD Program in Art History, New York NY (S)

Sass, Diane, *Deputy Dir*, Dubuque Museum of Art, Dubuque IA

Sassa, Reiko, *Dir*, Japan Society, Inc, C.V. Starr Library, New York NY

Sasse, Julie, *Chief Cur & Cur Modern & Contemporary Art*, Tucson Museum of Art and Historic Block, Tucson AZ

Sasser, Teiko, *Instr*, Sacramento City College, Art Dept, Sacramento CA (S)

Sasso, Paul, *Prof*, Murray State University, Dept of Art, Murray KY (S)

Satake, Shoji, *Assoc Prof*, West Virginia University, College of Creative Arts, School of Art & Design, Morgantown WV (S)

Satalino, Jennifer, *Dir Enrol*, Pacific Northwest College of Art, Portland OR (S)

Satchell, Ernest R, *Coordr Art Educ*, University of Maryland Eastern Shore, Art & Technology Dept, Princess Anne MD (S)

Satoda, Ikuko, *Deputy Dir Admin & Finance*, San Francisco Museum of Modern Art, San Francisco CA

Satterfield, Debra, *Assoc Prof*, Arkansas State University, Dept of Art, State University AR (S)

Satterfield, Debra, *Coordr Graphic Design*, Iowa State University, Dept of Art & Design, Ames IA (S)

Satterlee, Craig, *Assoc Prof*, Northwest Community College, Dept of Art, Powell WY (S)

Satterlee, Joy, *Exec Dir*, Art & Culture Center of Hollywood, Art Gallery/Multidisciplinary Cultural Center, Hollywood FL

Sauder, Molly, *Archivist & Librn*, The Old Jail Art Center, Albany TX

Sauder, Molly, *Archivist/Librn*, The Old Jail Art Center, Green Research Library, Albany TX

Sauer, Stacy, *Educ Coordr & Mus Asst*, Rockford Art Museum, Rockford IL

Saui, Elisa, *Assoc Cur*, George R Gardiner, Toronto ON

Saul, Rachel, *Studio Prog Coordr*, Society for Contemporary Craft, Pittsburgh PA

Sauls, Allison, *Chmn Dept*, Missouri Western State University, Art Dept, Saint Joseph MO (S)

Sauls, Allison, *Chmn Dept Art*, Missouri Western State University, Gallery 206 Foyer Gallery, Saint Joseph MO

Saumders, Gregory, *Adj Instr*, University of West Florida, Dept of Art, Pensacola FL (S)

Saunders, Kathy, *Comp*, Huntington Museum of Art, Huntington WV

Saunders, Preston, *Asst Prof*, Bridgewater State College, Art Dept, Bridgewater MA (S)

Saunders, Richard, *Dir*, Middlebury College, Museum of Art, Middlebury VT

Saunders, Richard, *Dir College Museum*, Middlebury College, History of Art & Architecture Dept, Middlebury VT (S)

Saunders, Susanna T, *Instr*, Main Line Art Center, Haverford PA (S)

Saupe, Ted, *Assoc Prof Ceramics*, University of Georgia, Franklin College of Arts & Sciences, Lamar Dodd School of Art, Athens GA (S)

Saurer, John, *Asst Prof*, Saint Olaf College, Art Dept, Northfield MN (S)

Sautman, Anne, *Dir Educ*, University of Illinois at Urbana-Champaign, Krannert Art Museum and Kinkead Pavilion, Champaign IL

Savage, Beth, *Colls Coordr*, Andy Warhol Foundation for the Visual Arts, New York NY

Savage, Cort, *Prof*, Davidson College, Art Dept, Davidson NC (S)

Savage, J Thomas, *Dir Museum Affairs*, Winterthur Museum, Winterthur Museum, Garden & Library, Winterthur DE

Savage, Kirk, *Chmn,* University of Pittsburgh, Henry Clay Frick Dept History of Art & Architecture, Pittsburgh PA (S)

Savage, Sheree, *Media Rels,* Saint Paul Public Library, Central Adult Public Services, Saint Paul MN

Saviello, Debbie, *Mus Shop Mgr,* The Barnum Museum, Bridgeport CT

Saville, Jennifer, *Cur Western Art,* Honolulu Academy of Arts, The Art Center at Linekona, Honolulu HI (S)

Savini, Richard, *Prof,* California State University, Art Dept, Turlock CA (S)

Savory, Kathy, *Develop Officer,* Henry Gallery Association, Henry Art Gallery, Seattle WA

Savu, Cristina, *Registra,* Massillon Museum, Massillon OH

Saw, James T, *Assoc Prof,* Palomar Community College, Art Dept, San Marcos CA (S)

Sawada, Naomi, *Prog Coordr,* University of British Columbia, Morris & Helen Belkin Art Gallery, Vancouver BC

Sawchuk, Michele, *Reference & Coll Develop Librn - Fine Arts & Archit,* University of Waterloo, Dana Porter Library, Waterloo ON

Sawicki, Nicholas, *Asst Prof,* Lehigh University, Dept of Art, Architecture & Design, Bethlehem PA (S)

Sawicz, Darcey, *Registrar,* University of Pennsylvania, Institute of Contemporary Art, Philadelphia PA

Sawkins, AnneMarie, *Assoc Cur,* Marquette University, Haggerty Museum of Art, Milwaukee WI

Sawyer, Janet, *Secy,* Blue Mountain Gallery, New York NY

Sawyer, Tamra, *Instr,* Dallas Baptist University, Dept of Art, Dallas TX (S)

Saxon, Mark, *Instr,* Milwaukee Area Technical College, School of Media & Creative Arts, Milwaukee WI (S)

Sayre, Amanda, *Vis Svcs Mgr,* Plains Art Museum, Fargo ND

Sayre, Henry, *Prof,* Oregon State University, Dept of Art, Corvallis OR (S)

Sayre, Roger, *Prof,* Pace University, Dyson College of Arts & Sciences, Pleasantville NY (S)

Sbarge, Suzanne, *Exec Dir,* 516 ARTS, Albuquerque NM

Sbicca, Penny, *Gallery Asst,* The Art Spirit Gallery, Coeur D Alene ID

Scala, Joseph A, *Exec Dir,* Stone Quarry Hill Art Park, Jenny Library, Cazenovia NY

Scala, Laura, *Sr Dir Develop,* Genesee Country Village & Museum, John L Wehle Art Gallery, Mumford NY

Scalera, Michelle, *Chief Conservator,* Florida State University, John & Mable Ringling Museum of Art, Sarasota FL

Scallen, Catherine, *Assoc Prof, Dept Chmn,* Case Western Reserve University, Dept of Art History & Art, Cleveland OH (S)

Scally, Amie, *Deputy Dir & Cur,* White Columns, White Columns Curated Artist Registry, New York NY

Scalora, Salvatore, *Dir,* University of Connecticut, William Benton Museum of Art, Storrs CT

Scamahorn, Dru, *Librn,* Amarillo Art Association, Library, Amarillo TX

Scandaliato, Lisa, *Admin Asst,* Queensborough Community College, Art Gallery, Bayside NY

Scanlon, James, *Pres,* Missouri Western State University, Gallery 206 Foyer Gallery, Saint Joseph MO

Scaramella, Julie, *Dir,* Boston Sculptors at Chapel Gallery, West Newton MA

Scarborough, Don, *Pres,* Anson County Historical Society, Inc, Wadesboro NC

Scarborough, Janet, *Dir Fin & Admin,* Gibbes Museum of Art, Charleston SC (S)

Scarborough, Klare, *Dir,* La Salle University Art Museum, Philadelphia PA

Scarlato, William, *Prof,* Illinois Benedictine University, Department of Fine Arts, Lisle IL (S)

Scarpitta, Salvatore, *Faculty,* Maryland Institute, Mount Royal School of Art, Baltimore MD (S)

Scarvelis, Elaine, *First VPres,* Toledo Artists' Club, Toledo Artists' Club & Gallery, Toledo OH

Scary, Rocio, *Adjunct Prof,* College of Saint Elizabeth, Art Dept, Morristown NJ (S)

Scavone, Jennifer, *Instr,* Illinois Benedictine University, Department of Fine Arts, Lisle IL (S)

Scearce, Geraldine, *Office Mgr,* Danville Museum of Fine Arts & History, Danville VA

Sceiford, Richard, *VPres,* North Carolina Museums Council, Raleigh NC

Scerbo, Drusiano, *Prof,* Elizabeth City State University, School of Arts & Humanities, Dept of Art, Elizabeth City NC (S)

Scerbo, Jean, *Mus Store Mgr,* Saint Augustine Historical Society, Oldest House Museum Complex, Saint Augustine FL

Schaad, Dee, *Chair,* University of Indianapolis, Dept Art & Design, Indianapolis IN (S)

Schaad, Dee, *Chmn,* University of Indianapolis, Christel DeHaan Fine Arts Gallery, Indianapolis IN

Schaar, Raja, *Educ Dir,* Atlanta International Museum of Art & Design, Museum of Design Atlanta, Atlanta GA

Schaber, Ken, *Instr,* Lake Michigan College, Dept of Art & Science, Benton Harbor MI (S)

Schaber, Todd, *Traveling Exhib Cur,* Prairie Art Gallery, Grande Prairie AB

Schachter, Ruth, *Libr Dir,* Art Institute of Philadelphia Library, Philadelphia PA

Schackai, Hilairie, *Community Initiatives,* Longue Vue House & Gardens, New Orleans LA

Schaefer, Mary, *Fin Mgr,* Boise Art Museum, Boise ID

Schaefer, Matt, *Reference Archivist,* National Archives & Records Administration, Herbert Hoover Presidential Library - Museum, West Branch IA

Schaefer, Scott, *Cur Paintings & Drawings,* Getty Center, Trust Museum, Los Angeles CA

Schaefer, Scott, *Sr Cur Paintings,* Getty Center, The J Paul Getty Museum, Los Angeles CA

Schaefer, Susan, *Asst Gallery Mgr,* Sharon Arts Center, Sharon Arts Center Exhibition Gallery, Peterborough NH

Schaeffer, Christine, *Dir Grad Adult Studies,* Seton Hill University, Art Program, Greensburg PA (S)

Schaeffer, Ron, *Archivist,* Bernice Pauahi Bishop, Library, Honolulu HI

Schaeffer, Ron, *Archivist,* Bernice Pauahi Bishop, Archives, Honolulu HI

Schafer, Carl, *Assoc Dir,* Ball State University, Museum of Art, Muncie IN

Schafer, Chris, *Head of Pub Servs,* South Dakota State University, Hilton M. Briggs Library, Brookings SD

Schafer, Michael I, *Pres,* Mohawk Valley Community College, Utica NY (S)

Schafer, Shelby, *Mgr Food Svcs,* Kimbell Art Foundation, Kimbell Art Museum, Fort Worth TX

Schafer, Sheldon, *VPres Educ,* Lakeview Museum of Arts & Sciences, Peoria IL

Schaffer, Dale E, *Owner,* Gloridale Partnership, National Museum of Woodcarving, Custer SD

Schaffer, Marcy, *Historic Site Mgr,* Schuyler Mansion State Historic Site, Albany NY

Schaffner, Ingrid, *Grad Comt,* Bard College, Center for Curatorial Studies Graduate Program, Annandale-on-Hudson NY (S)

Schaffner, Ingrid, *Sr Cur,* University of Pennsylvania, Institute of Contemporary Art, Philadelphia PA

Schaffner, Wesley, *Preparator,* Santa Ana College, Art Gallery, Santa Ana CA

Schafroth, Colleen, *Dir,* Maryhill Museum of Art, Goldendale WA

Schaller, Arthur, *Asst Prof,* Norwich University, Dept of Architecture and Art, Northfield VT (S)

Schaller, Hydee, *Dir,* St John's College, Elizabeth Myers Mitchell Art Gallery, Annapolis MD

Schaming, Corinna, *Assoc Dir,* University at Albany, State University of New York, University Art Museum, Albany NY

Schaming, Mark, *Dir Exhibits,* New York State Museum, Albany NY

Schantz, Michael W, *CEO, Dir & Cur,* Woodmere Art Museum Inc, Library, Philadelphia PA

Schantz, Michael W, *Dir,* Woodmere Art Museum Inc, Philadelphia PA

Schantz, Michael W, *Exec Dir & CEO,* The Heckscher Museum of Art, Huntington NY

Schapp, Rebecca M, *Dir,* Santa Clara University, de Saisset Museum, Santa Clara CA

Schar, Stuart, *Dean,* University of Hartford, Hartford Art School, West Hartford CT (S)

Scharf, Carrie, *Circ Asst,* National Gallery of Art, Department of Image Collections, Washington DC

Scharf, Emily, *Instruction & Liaison ServLibrn,* Webster University, Emerson Library, Webster Groves MO

Scharfberg, Vicki, *Sr Dir Communs,* Milwaukee Art Museum, Milwaukee WI

Scharlock, Jodi, *Controller,* Bellevue Arts Museum, Bellevue WA

Schartow, Christianna, *Asst Dir,* Northwood University, Alden B Dow Creativity Center, Midland MI (S)

Schatz, Cara, *Dir Pub Rels,* Special Libraries Association, Alexandria VA

Schatz, Charlotte, *Instr,* Bucks County Community College, Fine Arts Dept, Newtown PA (S)

Schatz, Doug, *Instr,* Middle Tennessee State University, Art Dept, Murfreesboro TN (S)

Schaub, Becca, *Mgr Youth Programs,* Urban Institute for Contemporary Arts, Grand Rapids MI

Schaunam, Lora, *Cur Exhib,* Dacotah Prairie Museum, Lamont Art Gallery, Aberdeen SD

Schechan, Kevin, *Librn,* Maritime Museum of San Diego, San Diego CA

Scheele, Christie, *Instr,* Woodstock School of Art, Inc, Woodstock NY (S)

Scheer, Elaine, *Prof,* University of Wisconsin, Madison, Dept of Art, Madison WI (S)

Scheer, Stephen, *Assoc Prof Photog,* University of Georgia, Franklin College of Arts & Sciences, Lamar Dodd School of Art, Athens GA (S)

Scheetz, Jennifer, *Archivist,* Charleston Museum, Library & Archives, Charleston SC

Schefcik, Jerry, *Dir,* University of Nevada, Las Vegas, Donna Beam Fine Art Gallery, Las Vegas NV

Scheffer, Jamie, *Bus Mgr,* Owensboro Museum of Fine Art, Owensboro KY

Scheibraur, Kim, *Office Mgr,* Santa Cruz Art League, Inc, Center for the Arts, Santa Cruz CA

Scheid, Ann, *Archivist,* University of Southern California/The Gamble House, Greene & Greene Archives, San Marino CA

Scheidt, Diana, *Dir,* Big Horn County Historical Museum, Hardin MT

Schelemanow, Amy, *Exposure Designer,* Society for Photographic Education (SPE), SPE Gallery, Cleveland OH

Schelemanow, Amy, *Mgr Publications,* George Eastman, Rochester NY

Schell, Edwin, *Exec Secy,* United Methodist Historical Society, Lovely Lane Museum, Baltimore MD

Schell, Edwin, *Secy,* United Methodist Historical Society, Library, Baltimore MD

Schell, William H, *Dir,* Martin Memorial Library, York PA

Schenck, Marvin, *Cur,* City of Ukiah, Grace Hudson Museum & The Sun House, Ukiah CA

Schenk, Joe, *Dir,* South Texas Institute for the Arts, Art Museum of South Texas, Corpus Christi TX

Schenk, Joe, *Dir,* South Texas Institute for the Arts, Art Museum of South Texas, Corpus Christi TX

Schenk, Mary Jane, *Exec Dir,* Arts Council of Southwestern Indiana, The Bower-Suhrheinrich Foundation Gallery, Evansville IN

Schenker, Beth, *Dir Programming,* Spertus Institute of Jewish Studies, Chicago IL

Scher, Anne J, *Dir Communs,* The Jewish Museum, New York NY

Scherer, Brooke, *Prof,* University of Tampa, College of Arts & Letters, Tampa FL (S)

Schermerhorn, Gretchen, *Artistic Dir,* Pyramid Atlantic, Silver Spring MD

Scherpereel, Richard, *Prof,* Texas A&M University-Kingsville, Art Dept, Kingsville TX (S)

Schertz, Peter J, *Cur Ancient Art,* Virginia Museum of Fine Arts, Richmond VA

Schery, Matthew, *Curatorial Asst,* The Long Island Museum of American Art, History & Carriages, Library, Stony Brook NY

Schick, Marjorie K, *Prof,* Pittsburg State University, Art Dept, Pittsburg KS (S)

Schiemann, Larry, *Dir,* Ashland College Arts & Humanities Gallery, The Coburn Gallery, Ashland OH

Schienbaum, David, *Asst Prof,* College of Santa Fe, Art Dept, Santa Fe NM (S)

Schiesser, Paul, *Acting Supvr Librn, Branches,* Oakland Public Library, Art, Music, History & Literature Section, Oakland CA

Schiever, Lawrence, *Treas,* Amerind Foundation, Inc, Amerind Museum, Fulton-Hayden Memorial Art Gallery, Dragoon AZ

Schiff, Andre, *Technical Dir,* Regis College, Carney Gallery, Weston MA

Schiff, Jeffrey, *Assoc Prof,* Wesleyan University, Dept of Art & Art History, Middletown CT (S)

Schiffer, Tim, *Exec Dir,* Museum of Ventura County, Ventura CA

Schifferdecker, Patrick, *Site Mgr,* Minnesota Historical Society, North West Company Fur Post, Saint Paul MN

Schildkrout, Enid, *Chmn & Cur Divisio,* American Museum of Natural History, New York NY

Schillemat, Katharine, *Admin Asst,* Historical Society of Cheshire County, Keene NH

Schiller, Barbara, *Pres,* American Society of Contemporary Artists (ASCA), Yorktown Heights NY

Schiller, Lauren, *Asst Prof,* Utah State University, Dept of Art, Logan UT (S)

Schilling, Eugene, *Prof Art,* Adams State College, Dept of Visual Arts, Alamosa CO (S)

Schillinger, Jakob, *Curatorial Res (2013),* Goethe-Institut New York, Mini/Goethe-Institut Curatorial Residencies Ludlow 38, New York NY

Schillings, Chuck, *Exec Dir,* Omniplex Science Museum, Oklahoma City OK

Schillizzi, Chris, *Chief Interpretation,* Independence National Historical Park, Library, Philadelphia PA

Schillo, Deb, *Librn,* Southern Highland Craft Guild, Folk Art Center, Asheville NC

Schimke, Susan, *Instr & Gallery Dir,* Shasta College, Arts, Communications & Social Sciences Division, Redding CA (S)

Schimmelman, Janice, *Prof,* Oakland University, Dept of Art & Art History, Rochester MI (S)

Schindel, Terri, *Cur Costumes,* Boulder History Museum, Museum of History, Boulder CO

Schindler, Leona Lopez, *Adjunct Asst Prof,* Spokane Falls Community College, Fine Arts Dept, Spokane WA (S)

Schipporeit, George, *Assoc Prof,* Illinois Institute of Technology, College of Architecture, Chicago IL (S)

Schirm, David, *Chmn, Prof,* University at Buffalo, State University of New York, Dept of Visual Studies, Buffalo NY (S)

Schisla, Gretchen, *Assoc Prof,* University of Missouri, Saint Louis, Dept of Art & Art History, Saint Louis MO (S)

Schitinger, Jim, *Dir Gall,* Millikin University, Perkinson Gallery, Decatur IL

Schlafly, David, *Chmn Bd Trustees,* Laumeier Sculpture Park, Saint Louis MO

Schlagenhauff, Annette, *Cur, Assoc for Research,* Indianapolis Museum of Art, Indianapolis IN

Schlaikjer, Tia, *Treas,* Essex Historical Society and Shipbuilding Museum, Essex MA

Schlanger, Gregg, *Assoc Prof,* Austin Peay State University, Dept of Art, Clarksville TN (S)

Schlanger, Gregg, *Dept Chair,* Austin Peay State University, Art Dept Library, Clarksville TN

Schlanzky, Gerhard, *Dir Exhib,* New-York Historical Society, Museum, New York NY

Schlatter, N Elizabeth, *Deputy Dir,* University of Richmond, University Museums, Richmond VA

Schlawin, Judy, *Prof,* Winona State University, Dept of Art, Winona MN (S)

Schlegel, Amy Ingrid, *Dir,* Tufts University, Tufts University Art Gallery, Medford MA

Schleh, Karoline, *Gallery Dir,* Collins C. Diboll Art Gallery, New Orleans LA

Schleicher, Marissa, *Dir & Cur,* R L S Silverado Museum, Reference Library, Saint Helena CA

Schlesier, Douglas, *Prof Art,* Clarke College, Dept of Art, Dubuque IA (S)

Schlesinger, Allison, *Dir Communs,* Western Pennsylvania Conservancy, Fallingwater, Mill Run PA

Schlichting, Eunice, *Chief Cur,* Putnam Museum of History and Natural Science, Davenport IA

Schlimmer, Alexa, *Asst Prof,* High Point University, Fine Arts Dept, High Point NC (S)

Schlinger, Robin, *CFO,* American Folk Art Museum, New York NY

Schlink, John-Mark, *Dir Soeffker Gallery & Permanent Coll, Lectr,* Hamline University, Dept of Studio Arts & Art History, Saint Paul MN

Schlink, John-Mark T, *Dir Exhibs,* Hamline University Studio Arts & Art History Depts, Gallery, Saint Paul MN

Schlinke, John, *Architecture Art Librn,* Roger Williams University, Architecture Library, Bristol RI

Schlitt, Melinda, *Prof,* Dickinson College, Dept of Art & Art History, Carlisle PA (S)

Schloder, John E, *Interim Cur Educ,* Museum of Fine Arts, Saint Petersburg, Florida, Inc, Saint Petersburg FL

Schlorff, Cara, *Mgr ILL Artisans Shop,* Illinois State Museum, Illinois Artisans Shop, Chicago IL

Schloss, Lauren, *Dir Educ,* The Queens Museum of Art, Flushing NY

Schlosser, Herbert S, *Chmn Bd Trustees,* American Museum of the Moving Image, Astoria NY

Schlosser, Tom, *Chmn Dept,* College of Saint Mary, Art Dept, Omaha NE (S)

Schmeichler, Daniel, *Co-Ed,* En Foco, Inc, Bronx NY

Schmelzer, John, *Pres,* Graphic Artists Guild, New York NY

Schmidd, Robert, *Prof,* Norwich University, Dept of Architecture and Art, Northfield VT (S)

Schmidlapp, Don, *Assoc Prof,* Winona State University, Dept of Art, Winona MN (S)

Schmidt, Araan, *Asst Prof,* Colorado Mesa University, Art Dept, Grand Junction CO (S)

Schmidt, Brady, *Develop Assoc,* Oakville Galleries, Centennial Square and Gairloch Gardens, Oakville ON

Schmidt, Brady, *Exec Dir,* Art Dealers Association of Canada, Toronto ON

Schmidt, Brian, *VPres,* New Haven Paint & Clay Club, Inc, New Haven CT

Schmidt, Carolyn, *Deputy Dir,* Saint Louis Art Museum, Saint Louis MO

Schmidt, Damewe, *Dir Events,* Creative Time, New York NY

Schmidt, Edward, *Bd Dir,* Grand River Museum, Lemmon SD

Schmidt, Edward, *Instr,* New York Academy of Art, Graduate School of Figurative Art, New York NY (S)

Schmidt, Eike, *Cur Decorative Arts, Textiles & Sculpture,* Minneapolis Institute of Arts, Minneapolis MN

Schmidt, Elaine, *VPres,* Brooklyn Historical Society, Brooklyn OH

Schmidt, Eleanore, *Dir Libr Servs,* Long Beach Public Library, Long Beach CA

Schmidt, Ferne, *Second VPres,* San Bernardino Art Association, Inc, Sturges Fine Arts Center, San Bernardino CA

Schmidt, Jan, *Cur Dance,* The New York Public Library, The New York Public Library for the Performing Arts, New York NY

Schmidt, Jan, *Dir Human Resources,* Milwaukee Art Museum, Milwaukee WI

Schmidt, Kenneth, *Prof,* Concordia University, Art Dept, Seward NE (S)

Schmidt, Kristen, *Registrar,* University of Arizona, Museum of Art & Archive of Visual Arts, Tucson AZ

Schmidt, Liana, *Office Mgr,* Canadian Art Foundation, Toronto ON

Schmidt, Lisa, *Bd Dir,* Grand River Museum, Lemmon SD

Schmidt, Lorraine, *Assoc Chair,* Corcoran School of Art, Washington DC (S)

Schmidt, Mary, *FT Lectr,* University of Michigan, Ann Arbor, School of Art & Design, Ann Arbor MI (S)

Schmidt, Maurice, *Prof,* Texas A&M University-Kingsville, Art Dept, Kingsville TX (S)

Schmidt, Patrick T, *Asst Prof,* Washington & Jefferson College, Art Dept, Washington PA (S)

Schmidt, Peter, *Opers Dir,* The Art School at Old Church, Demarest NJ (S)

Schmidt, Phyllis, *Bd Dir,* Grand River Museum, Lemmon SD

Schmidt, Rolf D, *Immediate Past Chair,* Reading Public Museum, Reading PA

Schmidt, Sherrie, *Univ Librn,* Arizona State University, ASU Library, Tempe AZ

Schmidt, Stuart, *Pres, Bd Dir,* Grand River Museum, Lemmon SD

Schmidt, Susan S, *Assoc Prof,* College of the Holy Cross, Dept of Visual Arts, Worcester MA (S)

Schmidt, Teresa Tempero, *Prof,* Kansas State University, Art Dept, Manhattan KS (S)

Schmierbach, Amy, *Assoc Prof,* Fort Hays State University, Dept of Art & Design, Hays KS (S)

Schmitt, Helmut, *Dir,* Merritt College, Art Dept, Oakland CA (S)

Schmitt, Jenn, *Cur Dept Asst,* DeCordova Museum & Sculpture Park, Sculpture Park, Lincoln MA

Schmitt, Jessie, *Exhibs Asst,* The Exhibition Alliance, Hamilton NY

Schmitt, Julia, *Asst Prof,* Stetson University, Department of Creative Arts, Deland FL (S)

Schmitt, Larry, *Dir Properties,* Chicago History Museum, Chicago IL

Schmitz, Robert, *Prof,* Rochester Institute of Technology, School of Design, Rochester NY (S)

Schmoldt, Robin, *Art Advisor & Art Coll Mgr,* University of Wisconsin-Madison, Wisconsin Union Galleries, Madison WI

Schmuckli, Claudia, *Dir & Chief Cur,* Art Museum of the University of Houston, Blaffer Gallery, Houston TX

Schnabel, JoAnn, *Prof,* University of Northern Iowa, Dept of Art, Cedar Falls IA (S)

Schneider, Emery E, *Chmn Design Composition Division,* Rochester Institute of Technology, School of Printing Management & Sciences, Rochester NY (S)

Schneider, Erika, *Asst Prof,* Framingham State College, Art Dept, Framingham MA (S)

Schneider, Gary, *Artist in Res,* Stony Brook University, College of Arts & Sciences, Dept of Art, Stony Brook NY (S)

Schneider, Gary, *Deputy Dir,* Montclair Art Museum, Montclair NJ

Schneider, John, *Dir Opers,* Newport Art Museum and Association, Newport RI

Schneider, Karen, *Librn,* The Phillips Collection, Library, Washington DC

Schneider, Keith, *Prof,* Humboldt State University, College of Arts & Humanities, Art Dept, Arcata CA (S)

Schneider, Laurie, *Prof,* John Jay College of Criminal Justice, Dept of Art, Music & Philosophy, New York NY (S)

Schneider, Nicholas, *Asst Prof Art,* Marymount Manhattan College, Fine & Performing Arts Div, New York NY (S)

Schneider, Richard, *Assoc Prof,* Cleveland State University, Art Dept, Cleveland OH (S)

Schneider, Sabine, *Community Experience Mgr,* Prairie Art Gallery, Grande Prairie AB

Schneider, Zoe, *Visual & Media Arts Asst,* Organization of Saskatchewan Arts Councils (OSAC), Regina SK

Schneiderman, Kara, *Asst Dir,* University of Miami, Lowe Art Museum, Coral Gables FL

Schneidermann, Cheryl, *Instr,* Marylhurst University, Art Dept, Marylhurst OR (S)

Schnell, Eric, *Instr,* Brazosport College, Art Dept, Lake Jackson TX (S)

Schnell, Ron, *Dir,* Tougaloo College, Art Collection, Tougaloo MS

Schneph, Scott, *Chmn,* University of New Hampshire, Dept of Arts & Art History, Durham NH (S)

Schnepp, Travis, *Exec Dir,* Maui Historical Society, Bailey House, Wailuku HI

Schnupp, Amy, *Patrons' Serv & Vol Coordr,* Pensacola Museum of Art, Pensacola FL

Schnur, Melissa, *Develop Dir,* Sherwin Miller Museum of Jewish Art, Tulsa OK

Schoeben, Jan, *Pres,* Tubac Center of the Arts, Santa Cruz Valley Art Association, Tubac AZ

Schoelwer, Susan, *Cur,* Mount Vernon Ladies' Association of the Union, Mount Vernon VA

Schoelwer, Susan P, *Dir Mus Colls,* Connecticut Historical Society, Hartford CT

Schoen, Stacy, *Prof,* Harding University, Dept of Art & Design, Searcy AR (S)

Schoenbaum, Mark, *Instr,* University of Evansville, Art Dept, Evansville IN (S)

Schoenfielder, Lisa, *Chmn,* Viterbo College, Art Dept, La Crosse WI (S)

Schoepp, Cameron, *Prof,* Texas Christian University, School of Art, Fort Worth TX (S)

Schoff, Soren, *Circ/Reserves,* University of Wisconsin-Madison, Kohler Art Library, Madison WI

Schofield, Woodburn T, *Deputy Dir Opers & Special Progs,* California African-American Museum, Los Angeles CA

Scholder, Laurence, *Prof,* Southern Methodist University, Division of Art, Dallas TX (S)

Scholl, Debbie, *Security Mgr,* Indiana University, Art Museum, Bloomington IN

Scholten, Lisa, *Cur Coll,* South Dakota State University, South Dakota Art Museum, Brookings SD

Scholz, Zeenie, *Dir Digital Communs,* National Museum of Wildlife Art of the Unites States, Jackson WY

Schon, Miguel A, *Asst Prof,* Johns Hopkins University, School of Medicine, Dept of Art as Applied to Medicine, Baltimore MD (S)

Schonholtz, Gleniss, *Interim CEO,* The Interchurch Center, Galleries at the Interchurch Center, New York NY

Schoonmaker, Trevor, *Cur Contemporary Art,* Duke University, Nasher Museum of Art at Duke University, Durham NC

Schorr, Annalee, *Treas,* Spark Gallery, Denver CO

Schorr, David, *Prof,* Wesleyan University, Dept of Art & Art History, Middletown CT (S)

Schorr, Elizabeth A, *Registrar,* City of El Paso, El Paso TX

Schorr, Laurie, *Outreach Coordr,* The Light Factory Contemporary Museum of Photography and Film, Charlotte NC

Schott, Daniel, *Sr Mgr Leadership Svcs,* National Alliance for Media Arts & Culture, San Francisco CA

Schott, Gene A, *Dir,* Heritage Museums & Gardens, Sandwich MA

Schott, Joseph, *Heirloom Seed Project,* Landis Valley Village and Farm Museum, PA Historical & Museum Commission, Lancaster PA

Schousen, Steve, *Prof,* Aquinas College, Art Dept, Grand Rapids MI (S)

Schoyer, Elizabeth, *Studio Faculty,* University of Virginia, McIntire Dept of Art, Charlottesville VA (S)

Schrager, Tim, *Board Pres,* Atlanta Contemporary Art Center, Atlanta GA

Schramm, Catherine, *Cur Educ,* National Trust for Historic Preservation, Shadows-on-the-Teche, New Iberia LA

Schramm, Chrissy, *Develop Mgr,* Hickory Museum of Art, Inc, Hickory NC

Schranom, Harry, *Pres (V),* The Cultural Center of Fine Arts, Art Gallery, Parkersburg WV

Schriber, Stephanie, *Pres,* Santa Cruz Art League, Inc, Center for the Arts, Santa Cruz CA

Schrock, Eileen, *VPres,* Phelps County Historical Society, Nebraska Prairie Museum, Holdrege NE

Schrock, Peggy, *Asst Prof,* Murray State University, Dept of Art, Murray KY (S)

Schroeder, Beth, *Dir Devel,* The Arts Center of the Capital Region, Troy NY

Schroeder, Elaine, *Admin Asst,* Rahr-West Art Museum, Manitowoc WI

Schroeder, Euniu, *Music Librn,* University of California, Santa Barbara, Arts Library, Santa Barbara CA

Schroeder, George, *Prof,* Hiram College, Art Dept, Hiram OH (S)

Schroeder, Ivy, *Chmn Dept,* Southern Illinois University at Edwardsville, Dept of Art & Design, Edwardsville IL (S)

Schroepfer, Dave, *Financial Officer,* Rockford Art Museum, Rockford IL

Schroth, Adella, *Cur Anthropology,* San Bernardino County Museum, Fine Arts Institute, Redlands CA

Schryer, Chantel, *VPres Pub Affairs & Publishing,* Canadian Museum of Civilization, Gatineau PQ

Schube, Lee, *Develop Dir,* Social & Public Art Resource Center, (SPARC), Venice CA

Schuessler, Richard, *Asst Prof,* University of Nebraska, Kearney, Dept of Art & Art History, Kearney NE (S)

Schuetz, Michael, *Asst Dir,* Eastern Illinois University, Tarble Arts Center, Charleston IL

Schuh, Randall T, *Chm & Cur Divisio,* American Museum of Natural History, New York NY

Schulenberg, Melissa, *Assoc Prof,* St Lawrence University, Dept of Fine Arts, Canton NY (S)

Schuler, Jane, *Prof,* York College of the City University of New York, Fine & Performing Arts, Jamaica NY (S)

Schuller, Brant D, *Chair & Assoc Prof Printmaking,* Millersville University, Dept of Art & Design, Millersville PA (S)

Schulman, Gail, *Treas,* American Artists Professional League, Inc, New York NY

Schulte, Elizabeth, *Board Vice Chair,* Heritage Preservation, The National Institute for Conservation, Washington DC

Schulte, Greg, *Assoc Prof,* Utah State University, Dept of Art, Logan UT (S)

Schulte, Michelle, *Cur Educ,* Morris Museum of Art, Augusta GA

Schultz, Donna, *Admin Asst,* Queens College, City University of New York, Art Library, Flushing NY

Schultz, Kathryn, *Dir,* Cambridge Art Association, Cambridge MA

Schultz, Kurt, *Div Head Design,* Northern Illinois University, School of Art, DeKalb IL (S)

Schultz, Nick, *Pres,* Jefferson County Historical Society Museum, Madison IN

Schultz, Robert, *Asst Dir,* Mesa Arts Center, Mesa Contemporary Arts Museum, Mesa AZ

Schultz, Robert, *Instr,* Northwest Missouri State University, Dept of Fine & Performing Arts, Maryville MO (S)

Schultz, Rosslyn, *Exec Dir,* Grassroots Art Center, Lucas KS

Schultz, Susan, *Grants Financial Analyst,* Broward County Board of Commissioners, Cultural Div, Fort Lauderdale FL

Schulz, Barbara, *Bldg Contact,* Brown University, Annmary Brown Memorial, Providence RI

Schulz, Cornelia, *Prof Painting,* University of California, Davis, Dept of Art & Art History, Davis CA (S)

Schulz, Emily L, *Deputy Dir & Cur,* The Society of the Cincinnati at Anderson House, Washington DC

Schulz, Roswitha, *Bd Dir, VChmn,* Plumas County Museum, Museum Archives, Quincy CA

Schumacher, Diane, *Dir Mktg & Spec Events,* University of Illinois at Urbana-Champaign, Krannert Art Museum and Kinkead Pavilion, Champaign IL

Schumacher, Sheila, *Asst Prof Art,* Grand Canyon University, Art Dept, Phoenix AZ (S)

Schumacher, Walt, *Gallery Dir,* The Huntsville Art League (HAL), Gallery & Visual Arts Center, Huntsville AL

Schumaker, Julie, *Prog Mgr,* Boulder History Museum, Museum of History, Boulder CO

Schumann, Elka, *Mgr,* Bread & Puppet Theater, Bread & Puppet Museum, Barton VT

Schumann, Max, *Assoc Dir,* Printed Matter, Inc, New York NY

Schumann, Peter, *Artist,* Bread & Puppet Theater, Bread & Puppet Museum, Barton VT

Schurmacher, Judy, *Bus Mgr,* Hammond Museum & Japanese Stroll Garden, Cross-Cultural Center, North Salem NY

Schussheim-Anderson, Rowen, *Chair,* Augustana College, Art Dept, Rock Island IL (S)

Schuster, Barbara R, *Registrar,* Bradford Brinton, Big Horn WY

Schuster, Helmut, *Art Dir,* World Erotic Art Museum, Miami Beach FL

Schuster, Kenneth L, *Dir & Chief Cur,* Bradford Brinton, Big Horn WY

Schuster, Sarah, *Assoc Prof,* Oberlin College, Dept of Art, Oberlin OH (S)

Schuweiler, Suzanne, *Assoc Prof & Coordr Art History,* Converse College, School of the Arts, Dept of Art & Design, Spartanburg SC (S)

Schuyler, Robert L, *Historical Arch Assoc Cur,* University of Pennsylvania, Museum of Archaeology & Anthropology, Philadelphia PA

Schuyler-King, Lynn, *Financial Officer,* San Jose Museum of Art, Library, San Jose CA

Schwab, Ben, *Asst Prof,* College of Saint Rose, The Center For Art and Design, Albany NY (S)

Schwab, Michael C, *Media Arts & Animation,* Art Institute of Pittsburgh, Pittsburgh PA (S)

Schwab, Norman, *Chmn,* Los Angeles City College, Dept of Art, Los Angeles CA (S)

Schwab, Steve, *Dir Educ,* Art Institute of Fort Lauderdale, Fort Lauderdale FL (S)

Schwab, Tim, *Dir Opers,* Laguna Art Museum, Laguna Beach CA

Schwabach, James Bruce, *Assoc Prof,* Herkimer County Community College, Humanities Social Services, Herkimer NY (S)

Schwager, Michael, *Art Chmn,* Sonoma State University, Art & Art History Dept, Rohnert Park CA (S)

Schwager, Michael, *Dir,* Sonoma State University, University Art Gallery, Rohnert Park CA

Schwain, Kristin, *Assoc Prof,* University of Missouri - Columbia, Art History & Archaeology Dept, Columbia MO (S)

Schwarm, Larry, *Prof,* Emporia State University, Dept of Art, Emporia KS (S)

Schwarting, Paulette, *Dir Tech Services,* Virginia Historical Society, Library, Richmond VA

Schwartz, Alexandra, *Cur Contemporary Art,* Montclair Art Museum, Montclair NJ

Schwartz, Amy, *Dir Devel, Educ & The Studio,* Corning Museum of Glass, The Studio, Corning NY

Schwartz, Carole, *Dept Head,* Jacksonville Public Library, Fine Arts & Recreation Dept, Jacksonville FL

Schwartz, Deanna, *Dir Exhibs,* The Dairy Barn Arts Center, Athens OH

Schwartz, Deborah, *Pres,* Brooklyn Historical Society, Brooklyn NY

Schwartz, Laura, *Head Librn,* University of Texas at Austin, Fine Arts Library, Austin TX

Schwartz, Melanie, *Prof,* Southwestern Oregon Community College, Visual Arts Dept, Coos Bay OR (S)

Schwartz, Michael, *Prof,* Augusta State University, Dept of Art, Augusta GA (S)

Schwartz, Robin, *Asst Prof,* William Paterson University, Dept Arts, Wayne NJ (S)

Schwartz, Tom, *Library Dir,* National Archives & Records Administration, Herbert Hoover Presidential Library - Museum, West Branch IA

Schwartzbaum, Paul, *Conservator,* Guggenheim Museum Soho, New York NY

Schwarz, Gregory, *Chief Ranger,* Saint-Gaudens National Historic Site, Cornish NH

Schwarz, Gregory C, *Supv Interpretation,* Saint-Gaudens National Historic Site, Library, Cornish NH

Schwarz, Kerry, *Dir Educ,* Essex Historical Society and Shipbuilding Museum, Essex MA

Schwarzer, Lynn, *Assoc Prof,* Colgate University, Dept of Art & Art History, Hamilton NY (S)

Schweiger, Christy, *Educ Coordr,* Moose Jaw Art Museum, Inc, Art & History Museum, Moose Jaw SK

Schweiger, Rebecca, *Founder, Dir & Instr,* The Art Studio New York, New York NY (S)

Schweigert, Scott A, *Cur Arts & Civilization,* Reading Public Museum, Reading PA

Schweitzer, Rob, *Dir Pub Rels,* Historic Hudson Valley, Pocantico Hills NY

Schweitzer, Tricia, *Coordr,* University of Minnesota, The Studio/Larson Gallery, Minneapolis MN

Schweitzer, Tricia, *Gallery Mgr,* University of Minnesota, Paul Whitney Larson Gallery, Saint Paul MN

Schweizer, Paul D, *Dir Emeritus,* Munson-Williams-Proctor Arts Institute, Museum of Art, Utica NY

Schwender, Judy, *Cur & Registrar,* The National Quilt Museum, Paducah KY

Schwertley, Mark, *Chmn Humanities,* City Colleges of Chicago, Malcolm X College, Chicago IL (S)

Schwetman, Sondra, *Assoc Prof,* Humboldt State University, College of Arts & Humanities, Art Dept, Arcata CA (S)

Schwitz, Fred, *Vol Pres,* St Mary Landmarks, Grevemberg House Museum, Franklin LA

Semivan, Douglas, *Chmn Art Dept*, Madonna University, College of Arts & Humanities, Livonia MI (S)

Semler, Jerry, *Pres*, Hoosier Salon Patrons Association, Inc, Art Gallery & Membership Organization, Indianapolis IN

Semowich, Charles, *VPres & Cur*, Print Club of Albany, Albany NY

Senat, Simone, *Instr*, Butte College, Dept of Fine Arts and Communication Tech, Oroville CA (S)

Senecal, Denise, *Treas*, Fitchburg Art Museum, Fitchburg MA

Senf, Rebecca, *Assoc Cur*, University of Arizona, Center for Creative Photography, Tucson AZ

Seng, Yvonne, *Cur Art*, Holter Museum of Art, Helena MT

Sengoku, Noriko, *Mem Bd Dir*, Hatch-Billops Collection, Inc, New York NY

Senie, Harriet, *Dir Mus Studies*, City College of New York, Art Dept, New York NY (S)

Senie, Harriet, *Prof*, City University of New York, PhD Program in Art History, New York NY (S)

Senior, Gordon, *Chmn Dept*, California State University, Art Dept, Turlock CA (S)

Senior, Gordon, *Dept Chair*, California State University Stanislaus, University Art Gallery, Turlock CA

Senior, Heidi, *Reference Librn*, University of Portland, Wilson W Clark Memorial Library, Portland OR

Seniuk, Jake, *Bd Trustees*, City of Port Angeles, Port Angeles Fine Arts Center & Webster Woods Art Park, Port Angeles WA

Senn, Carol Johnson, *Dir*, McDowell House & Apothecary Shop, Danville KY

Senn, Greg, *Prof Art*, Eastern New Mexico University, Runnels Gallery, Golden Library, Portales NM

Senn, Kurt, *Dir*, Missouri Department of Natural Resources, Elizabeth Rozier Gallery, Jefferson City MO

Senn, Kurt, *Mus Dir*, Missouri Department of Natural Resources, Missouri State Museum, Jefferson City MO

Senne, Saundie, *Educ Asst*, Tucson Museum of Art and Historic Block, Tucson AZ

Sennefeld, Jacques, *Webmaster*, J.M.W. Turner Museum, Sarasota FL

Sennett, Menique, *Pub Rels*, Art Museum of Southeast Texas, Beaumont TX

Sensabaugh, David, *Asian*, Yale University, Yale University Art Gallery, New Haven CT

Seo, Sang-Duok, *Asst Prof*, University of Nevada, Las Vegas, Dept of Art, Las Vegas NV (S)

Serbert, Peter, *Ed*, Millicent Rogers Museum, Taos NM

Serebrennikov, Nina, *Prof*, Davidson College, Art Dept, Davidson NC (S)

Serenco, Henry, *Assoc Prof*, University of Nebraska at Omaha, Dept of Art & Art History, Omaha NE (S)

Sergejeff, Nadine, *Librn*, Newark Public Library, Reference, Newark NJ

Serio, Alexis, *Asst Prof*, University of Texas at Tyler, Department of Art, School of Visual & Performing Arts, Tyler TX (S)

Serio, Faye, *Assoc Prof*, St Lawrence University, Dept of Fine Arts, Canton NY (S)

Serlin, Fran, *Dir Pub Progs*, Milwaukee Art Museum, Milwaukee WI

Serran, Jamie, *Archivist*, Yarmouth County Historical Society, Yarmouth County Museum & Archives, Yarmouth NS

Serratore, Nick, *Gallery Mgr*, Rehoboth Art League, Inc, Rehoboth Beach DE

Serroes, Richard, *Instr*, Modesto Junior College, Arts Humanities & Communications Division, Modesto CA (S)

Sersland, Peggy, *Mem Mgr*, Vesterheim Norwegian-American Museum, Decorah IA

Sertic, Allison, *Opers Mgr*, Sierra Arts Foundation, Sierra Arts Gallery, Reno NV

Servant, Lise, *Cur Slide Library*, Jardin Botanique de Montreal, Bibliotheque, Montreal PQ

Servantes, Raul, *Gardner & Asst Facilities*, Saginaw Art Museum, Saginaw MI

Servantez, Leslie, *Registrar*, Wichita Art Museum, Wichita KS

Servantez, Leslie, *Registrar*, Wichita Art Museum, Emprise Bank Research Library, Wichita KS

Sessions, Billie, *Instr*, California State University, San Bernardino, Dept of Art, San Bernardino CA (S)

Sessions, Susan, *Prog Dir*, Adirondack Lakes Center for the Arts, Blue Mountain Lake NY

Setford, David, *Dir*, Hyde Collection Trust, Glens Falls NY

Sethem, Brian, *Asst Prof*, California Lutheran University, Art Dept, Thousand Oaks CA (S)

Setter, Suzanne, *Librn*, East Hampton Library, Long Island Collection, East Hampton NY

Settle, Hillary, *Dir Develop*, Cedarhurst Center for the Arts, Mitchell Museum, Mount Vernon IL

Settle-Cooney, Mary, *Exec Dir*, Tennessee Valley Art Association, Tuscumbia AL

Settles, Dana, *Educ*, Mount Vernon Hotel Museum & Garden, New York NY

Sever, Ziya, *Chmn Art*, Western Nebraska Community College, Division of Language & Arts, Scottsbluff NE (S)

Severe, Milton, *Exhib Designer*, Grinnell College, Faulconer Gallery, Grinnell IA

Severino, Michelle A, *Exec Dir*, Heritage Museum Association, Inc, The Heritage Museum of Northwest Florida, Valparaiso FL

Severstad, Jami, *Cur*, Bergstrom-Mahler Museum, Neenah WI

Sewell, Dennita, *Cur Fashion Design*, Phoenix Art Museum, Phoenix AZ

Sewell, Nika, *Mus Shop Mgr*, The Walker African American Museum & Research Center, Las Vegas NV

Sexton, Norma, *Dir Devel*, Columbus Museum of Art, Columbus OH

Sexton, Randall, *Chmn Dept of Design*, San Jose State University, School of Art & Design, San Jose CA (S)

Sexton, Rives, *Interim Dir*, Albany Museum of Art, Albany GA

Seybt, Teri Keener, *Mgr Human Resources*, Columbia Museum of Art, Columbia SC

Seydl, Jon, *Cur Euorpean Painting & Sculpture*, The Cleveland Museum of Art, Cleveland OH

Seydler-Hepworth, Betty Lee, *Asst Dean*, Lawrence Technological University, College of Architecture, Southfield MI (S)

Seymour, Gayle, *Prof*, University of Central Arkansas, Department of Art, Conway AR (S)

Seymour, Griff, *Recording Secy*, Salmagundi Club, New York NY

Sfirri, Mark, *Instr*, Bucks County Community College, Fine Arts Dept, Newtown PA (S)

Shaarhan, Jeff, *Prof*, Concordia University, Division of Performing & Visual Arts, Mequon WI (S)

Shabout, Nada, *Assoc Prof Art History*, University of North Texas, College of Visual Arts & Design, Denton TX (S)

Shackelford, David, *Dir*, National Society of Colonial Dames of America in the State of Maryland, Mount Clare Museum House, Baltimore MD

Shackelford, George TM, *Deputy Dir*, Kimbell Art Foundation, Kimbell Art Museum, Fort Worth TX

Shada, Mary, *Office Support Specialist*, Loveland Museum/Gallery, Loveland CO

Shady, Ronald L, *Prof*, University of North Alabama, Dept of Art, Florence AL (S)

Shaefer, Jessica, *Mktg Assoc*, Creative Time, New York NY

Shafer, Phyllis, *Painting Instr*, Lake Tahoe Community College, Art Dept, South Lake Tahoe CA (S)

Shaffer, Travis, *Asst Tchg Prof*, University of Missouri - Columbia, Dept of Art, Columbia MO (S)

Shafik, Adel, *Prof Art*, Bakersfield College, Art Dept, Bakersfield CA (S)

Shah, Bijal, *Dir Asst*, Southern California Institute of Architecture, Los Angeles CA (S)

Shah, Monica, *Dir Colls*, Anchorage Museum at Rasmuson Center, Anchorage AK

Shailer, Kathryn, *Dean Liberal Studies*, OCAD University, Toronto ON (S)

Shaiman, Jason, *Chief Cur Exhibs*, University of South Carolina, McKissick Museum, Columbia SC

Shain-Bryson, Gabrielle, *Owner*, Shain Gallery, Charlotte NC

Shainin, Christopher, *Exec Dir*, Kirkland Arts Center, Kirkland WA

Shainin, Christopher, *Exec Dir*, Museum of Northwest Art, La Conner WA

Shaken, Andy, *Asst Prof*, Oberlin College, Dept of Art, Oberlin OH (S)

Shaker, Andrea, *Asst Prof*, Saint John's University, Art Dept, Collegeville MN (S)

Shaker, Andrea, *Asst Prof*, College of Saint Benedict, Art Dept, Saint Joseph MN (S)

Shalom, Karen, *Admin Dir*, The Art School at Old Church, Demarest NJ (S)

Sham, James, *Asst Prof*, George Washington University, Dept of Art of Fine Arts & Art History, Washington DC (S)

Shambarger, Sara, *Dir Krasl Art Fair on the Bluff & Special Events*, Krasl Art Center, Saint Joseph MI

Shamblin, Barbara, *Chmn*, Salve Regina University, Art Dept, Newport RI (S)

Shames, Susan, *Decorative Arts Librn*, Colonial Williamsburg Foundation, John D Rockefeller, Jr Library, Williamsburg VA

Shamir, Adi, *Exec Dir*, Van Alen Institute, New York NY

Shamro, Joyce, *Prof*, Bluefield State College, Division of Arts & Sciences, Bluefield WV (S)

Shanahan, Carl, *Chmn*, State University of New York College at Geneseo, Dept of Art, Geneseo NY (S)

Shanberg, Ariel, *Exec Dir*, Center for Photography at Woodstock Inc, Woodstock NY

Shand, Rachel, *Asst Registrar*, Tucson Museum of Art and Historic Block, Tucson AZ

Shand, Rhona E, *Asst Prof*, Pittsburg State University, Art Dept, Pittsburg KS (S)

Shane, Janicanne, *Program Coordr & Visual Arts Comt Advisor*, Duke University Union, Louise Jones Brown Gallery, Durham NC

Shane, Robert, *Assit Prof*, College of Saint Rose, The Center For Art and Design, Albany NY (S)

Shanfeld, Raymond, *VPres*, American Society of Contemporary Artists (ASCA), Yorktown Heights NY

Shang, Xuhong, *Prof*, Southern Illinois University, School of Art & Design, Carbondale IL (S)

Shanis, Carole Price, *Pres*, Philadelphia Art Alliance, Philadelphia PA

Shank, Nick, *Dir*, University of Minnesota, Katherine E Nash Gallery, Minneapolis MN

Shankle, Kent, *Cur*, Waterloo Center of the Arts, Waterloo IA

Shanks, Bradlee, *Assoc Prof*, University of South Florida, School The Arts, Tampa FL (S)

Shannon, Anna-Maria, *Assoc. Dir*, Washington State University, Museum of Art, Pullman WA

Shannon, Jenkins, *Exec Dir*, Pasadena Museum of California Art, Pasadena CA

Shannon, Lucia M, *Head Adult Serv*, Brockton Public Library System, Joseph A Driscoll Art Gallery, Brockton MA

Shannon, Mary Kay, *Cur Educ*, Branigan Cultural Center, Las Cruces NM

Shannon, Nancy, *Dir Devel*, Visual Arts Center of New Jersey, Summit NJ

Shannon-Miller, Joan, *Gallery Dir*, University of Northern Colorado, School of Art and Design, Mariani Gallery, Greeley CO

Shapero, Janet, *Assoc Prof*, Utah State University, Dept of Art, Logan UT (S)

Shapiro, Babe, *Faculty*, Maryland Institute, Mount Royal School of Art, Baltimore MD (S)

Shapiro, Cara, *Dir Educ*, Louisa May Alcott Memorial Association, Orchard House, Concord MA

Shapiro, Chaya, *Asst to Dir*, Howard Community College, The Rouse Company Foundation Gallery, Columbia MD

Shapiro, David, *Prof*, William Paterson University, Dept Arts, Wayne NJ (S)

Shapiro, Denise, *District Gallery Dir*, Las Vegas-Clark County Library District, Las Vegas NV

Shapiro, Denise, *District Gallery Mgr*, Las Vegas-Clark County Library District, Flamingo Gallery, Las Vegas NV

Shapiro, Eben, *Prog Coordr*, Franklin Furnace Archive, Inc, Brooklyn NY

Shapiro, Keith, *Asst Prof Integrative Art & Art (Photog)*, Pennsylvania State University, University Park, Penn State School of Visual Arts, University Park PA (S)

Shapiro, Laura, *Vol Coordr*, Wing Luke Asian Museum, Seattle WA

Shapiro, Martin, *Coll Develop Librn*, American University, Jack I & Dorothy G Bender Library & Learning Resources Center, New York NY

Shapiro, Michael E, *Dir,* High Museum of Art, Atlanta GA

Sharafy, Azyz, *Assoc Prof,* Washburn University of Topeka, Dept of Art, Topeka KS (S)

Sharbaugh, Kathryn, *Develop Dir,* Flint Institute of Arts, Flint MI

Sharer, Cory, *Asst Dir,* Cooperstown Art Association, Cooperstown NY

Sharer, Robert, *American Sections Cur,* University of Pennsylvania, Museum of Archaeology & Anthropology, Philadelphia PA

Sharman, George T, *Pres,* Frontier Times Museum, Bandera TX

Sharp, Alison, *Coordr Pub Rels,* Dartmouth College, Hood Museum of Art, Hanover NH

Sharp, Avery, *Coordr,* Baylor University, Armstrong Browning Library, Waco TX

Sharp, Bert, *Chief Preparator,* Memphis Brooks Museum of Art, Memphis TN

Sharp, Kevin, *Dir,* The Dixon Gallery & Gardens, Memphis TN

Sharp, Megan, *Dir,* Plainsman Museum, Aurora NE

Sharpe, David, *Assoc Prof,* Illinois Institute of Technology, College of Architecture, Chicago IL (S)

Sharpe, Linda, *Librn,* Turtle Bay Exploration Park, Shasta Historical Society Research Library, Redding CA

Sharpe, Yolanda, *Instr,* State University of New York College at Oneonta, Dept of Art, Oneonta NY (S)

Sharps, David, *Pres & CEO,* Waterfront Museum, Brooklyn NY

Sharps, Nancy, *Instr,* Chadron State College, Dept of Art, Chadron NE (S)

Shaskan, Isabel, *Instr,* Sacramento City College, Art Dept, Sacramento CA (S)

Shastal, Belinda, *Secy,* Chicago Athenaeum, Museum of Architecture & Design, Galena IL

Shauck, Barry, *Chmn Art Educ,* Boston University, School for the Arts, Boston MA (S)

Shaughnessy, Michael, *Prof Sculpture,* University of Southern Maine, Dept of Art, Gorham ME (S)

Shaughnessy, Sandy, *Dir,* Florida Department of State, Division of Cultural Affairs, Florida Council on Arts & Culture, Tallahassee FL

Shaul, David, *Instr,* Middle Tennessee State University, Art Dept, Murfreesboro TN (S)

Shaver, Jana, *Secy,* Independence Historical Museum & Art Center, Independence KS

Shaw, Cameron, *Preparator,* Brown University, David Winton Bell Gallery, Providence RI

Shaw, Catherine Elliot, *Cur & Educ Dir,* University of Western Ontario, McIntosh Gallery, London ON

Shaw, DeAnn, *Bd Mem,* Coquille Valley Art Association, Coquille OR

Shaw, Frank, *Asst Prof,* Bethany College, Mingenback Art Center, Lindsborg KS

Shaw, Frank, *Asst Prof,* Bethany College, Art Dept, Lindsborg KS (S)

Shaw, Judy, *Assoc Dir External Relations,* Norman Rockwell Museum, Stockbridge MA

Shaw, Lindsay, *Librn,* Providence Athenaeum, Library, Providence RI

Shaw, Meg, *Librn,* The Art Museum at the University of Kentucky, Lucille Little Fine Arts Library, Lexington KY

Shaw, Richard, *Grad & undergrad faculty adv,* University of California, Berkeley, College of Letters & Sciences-Art Practice Dept, Berkeley CA (S)

Shaw, Tate, *Dir,* Visual Studies Workshop, Rochester NY (S)

Shawhan, Jeffrey, *Gallery Dir,* Concordia University Wisconsin, Fine Art Gallery, Mequon WI

Shawn, Doug, *Deputy Dir Exhibs,* Art Services International, Alexandria VA

Shay, Robert, *Dean,* University of Kentucky, Dept of Art, Lexington KY (S)

Shaykett, Jessica, *Librn,* American Craft Council, Library, Minneapolis MN

Shea, Ann, *Librn,* California African-American Museum, Research Library, Los Angeles CA

Shea, Beth, *Educ Chair,* Illinois State Museum, Museum Store, Chicago IL

Shea, Elizabeth A, *Admin Coordr,* La Centrale Powerhouse Gallery, Montreal PQ

Shea, Josephine, *Cur,* Edsel & Eleanor Ford, Grosse Pointe Shores MI

Shea, Norman, *Pres,* Hagerstown Junior College, Art Dept, Hagerstown MD (S)

Shea-Pelletier, Hamish, *Monitor/Display Provider,* McMaster University, McMaster Museum of Art, Hamilton ON

Sheahan, Kim, *Asst Educator,* University of Illinois at Urbana-Champaign, Spurlock Museum, Champaign IL

Sheakoski, Renee, *Mus Shop Mgr,* The Butler Institute of American Art, Art Museum, Youngstown OH

Sheaks, Barclay, *Assoc Prof,* Virginia Wesleyan College, Art Dept of the Humanities Div, Norfolk VA (S)

Shealy, Tony, *Deputy Dir Admin,* South Carolina State Museum, Columbia SC

Shearer, Christine, *Develop Dir,* Canton Museum of Art, Art Library, Canton OH

Shearer, Lee Ann, *Contact,* First State Bank, They Also Ran Gallery, Norton KS

Shear Jr, T Leslie, *Prof,* Princeton University, Dept of Art & Archaeology, Princeton NJ (S)

Sheary, Patrick, *Cur Historic Furnishings,* DAR Museum, Library, Washington DC

Shedro, Michelle, *Educ Dir,* Think 360 Art Complete Education, Colo Chapter, Denver CO

Sheehan, Kathryn, *Registrar,* Rensselaer County Historical Society, Hart-Cluett Mansion, 1827, Troy NY

Sheehan, Kathryn, *Registrar,* Rensselaer County Historical Society, Museum & Library, Troy NY

Sheehy, Carolyn A, *Dir,* North Central College, Oesterle Library, Naperville IL

Sheehy, Colleen, *Educ Dir,* University of Minnesota, Frederick R Weisman Art Museum, Minneapolis MN

Sheer, Doug, *Chmn Bd of Dir,* Artists Talk on Art, New York NY

Sheesley, Peter, *Instr,* Judson University, School of Art, Design & Architecture, Elgin IL (S)

Sheesley, Timothy, *Gallery Dir,* State University of New York College at Oneonta, Martin - Mullen Art Gallery, Oneonta NY

Sheets, Allen, *Prof,* Minnesota State University-Moorhead, Dept of Art & Design, Moorhead MN (S)

Sheets, Luke, *Asst Prof Art,* Ohio Northern University, Dept of Art & Design, Ada OH (S)

Sheffer, Beth, *Cur Coll,* National Museum of Racing, Reference Library, Saratoga Springs NY

Sheffera, Beth, *Cur Coll,* National Museum of Racing, National Museum of Racing & Hall of Fame, Saratoga Springs NY

Sheffield, Ellen, *Coordr,* Kenyon College, Olin Art Gallery, Gambier OH

Sheffield, Ellen, *Instr,* Kenyon College, Art Dept, Gambier OH (S)

Sheffield, Lin, *Asst Dir,* Colquitt County Arts Center, Moultrie GA

Shefner, Christine, *Prof,* Shoreline Community College, Humanities Division, Seattle WA (S)

Sheih, Annie, *Adj Prof,* Saint Thomas Aquinas College, Art Dept, Sparkill NY (S)

Shein, Rich, *CFO,* New-York Historical Society, Museum, New York NY

Shekore, Mark, *Prof,* Northern State University, Art Dept, Aberdeen SD (S)

Shelburne, Brian, *Visual Resources Cur,* Virginia Polytechnic Institute & State University, Art & Architecture Library, Blacksburg VA

Shell, Andrew, *Adjunct Asst Prof Fine Art,* Johnson County Community College, Fine Arts Dept & Art History Dept, Overland Park KS (S)

Shell, Martin, *Asst Prof,* Springfield College, Dept of Visual & Performing Arts, Springfield MA (S)

Shelley, Matthew, *Instr,* Moravian College, Dept of Art, Bethlehem PA (S)

Shelly, Diane, *Exec Dir,* Florida Craftsmen Gallery, Saint Petersburg FL

Shelnot-Hendrick, Stacey, *Dir Educ,* Crocker Art Museum, Research Library, Sacramento CA

Shelnut-Hendrick, Stacy, *Educ Dir,* Crocker Art Museum, Sacramento CA

Shelnutt, Greg, *Chair, Art Dept,* Clemson University, College of Architecture, Arts & Humanities, Art Dept, Clemson SC (S)

Shelton, Barbara, *Photographer,* Keystone Gallery, Scott City KS

Shelton, Betty, *Dean Fine Arts,* Art Institute of Southern California, Laguna Beach CA (S)

Shelton, Tom, *Photo Archivist,* The University of Texas at San Antonio, Institute of Texan Cultures, San Antonio TX

Shen, Richard, *Adjunct Asst Prof,* New York Institute of Technology, Fine Arts Dept, Old Westbury NY (S)

Shepard, Heidi, *Acad Dept Asst,* Connecticut College, Dept of Art, New London CT (S)

Shepard, Lee, *VPres Coll,* Virginia Historical Society, Library, Richmond VA

Sheperd, Lindy, *Media Coordr,* Mennello Museum of American Art, Orlando FL

Shephard, Charles A, *Dir,* Fort Wayne Museum of Art, Inc, Fort Wayne IN

Shepherd, Murray, *Univ Librn,* University of Waterloo, Dana Porter Library, Waterloo ON

Shepherd, Roxanne, *Campaign Dir,* Corporate Council for the Arts/Arts Fund, Seattle WA

Shepherd, Terry, *Artist in Res,* Western Colorado Center for the Arts, The Art Center, Grand Junction CO

Shepp, James G, *CEO & Exec Dir,* Maitland Art Center, Maitland FL

Shepp, James G, *Dir,* Maitland Art Center, Library, Maitland FL

Sheppard, Adrian, *Prof,* McGill University, School of Architecture, Montreal PQ (S)

Sheppard, Heather, *Librn,* Cornish College of the Arts, Cornish Library, Seattle WA

Sherard, Tyler, *Develop Coordr,* Latitude 53 Contemporary Visual Culture, Edmonton AB

Sherer, Aaron, *Exec Dir,* Paine Art Center & Gardens, George P Nevitt Library, Oshkosh WI

Sherer, Scott, *Assoc Prof,* University of Texas at San Antonio, Dept of Art & Art History, San Antonio TX (S)

Sheridan, Clare, *Librn,* American Textile History Museum, Lowell MA

Sheridan, Clare, *Librn,* American Textile History Museum, Library, Lowell MA

Sheridan, Ginger, *Asst Prof Photog,* Jacksonville University, Dept of Art, Theater, Dance, Jacksonville FL (S)

Sheridan, Phil, *Pub Affairs Officer,* Independence National Historical Park, Library, Philadelphia PA

Sheriff, Mary, *Chm & Prof,* University of North Carolina at Chapel Hill, Art Dept, Chapel Hill NC (S)

Sherin, Kathleen, *Dir Gallery,* Niagara County Community College, Art Gallery, Sanborn NY

Sherk, Scott, *Assoc Prof,* Muhlenberg College, Dept of Art, Allentown PA (S)

Sherman, Dagan, *Instr,* Midland College, Art Dept, Midland TX (S)

Sherman, Gordon, *Prof,* Fort Hays State University, Dept of Art & Design, Hays KS (S)

Sherman, Paul T, *Admin Svcs Librn,* New York City Technical College, Ursula C Schwerin Library, Brooklyn NY

Sherman, Todd, *Prof,* University of Alaska-Fairbanks, Dept of Art, Fairbanks AK (S)

Sherman, Ziti, *Financial Mgr,* National Architectural Accrediting Board, Inc, Washington DC

Shermantine, Ray, *Facilities Supt,* The San Joaquin Pioneer & Historical Society, The Haggin Museum, Stockton CA

Shermer, James, *Grants Admin,* Broward County Board of Commissioners, Cultural Div, Fort Lauderdale FL

Sherrard, Jeanette, *Dir Sales,* Ward-Nasse Gallery, New York NY

Sherrell, Steve, *Instr,* Joliet Junior College, Fine Arts Dept, Joliet IL (S)

Sherrill, Martine, *Visual Resources Librn,* Wake Forest University, A Lewis Aycock Visual Resource Library, Winston Salem NC

Sherrock, Roger, *CEO,* Clark County Historical Society, Heritage Center of Clark County, Springfield OH

Sherrock, Roger, *Dir Opers & Personnel,* Clark County Historical Society, Library, Springfield OH

Sherry, Christopher R, *Interior Design Prog Dir,* Brenau University, Art & Design Dept, Gainesville GA (S)

Sherry, James, *Pres,* Segue Foundation, Reading Room-Archive, New York NY

Sherry, Karen, *Asst Cur, American ARt,* Brooklyn Museum, Brooklyn NY

Sherry, Karen, *Chief Cur,* Portland Museum of Art, Portland ME

Sherwin, Michael, *Assoc Prof,* West Virginia University, College of Creative Arts, School of Art & Design, Morgantown WV (S)

Sherwood, Katherine, *Grad & undergrad faculty adv,* University of California, Berkeley, College of Letters & Sciences-Art Practice Dept, Berkeley CA (S)

Shewchuk, Diane, *Cur,* Columbia County Historical Society, Columbia County Museum and Library, Kinderhook NY

Shewchuk, Diane, *Cur,* Columbia County Historical Society, Luykas Van Alen House, Kinderhook NY

Shieh, Suewhei T, *Dir,* Towson University, Asian Arts & Culture Center, Towson MD

Shields, Alissa, *Asst Dir,* Chautauqua Center for the Visual Arts, Chautauqua NY

Shields, Ann, *Dir,* The Pennsylvania State University, HUB Robeson Galleries, University Park PA

Shields, Christopher, *Archivist,* Bush-Holley Historic Site & Storehouse Gallery, Greenwich Historical Society/ Bush-Holley House, Cos Cob CT

Shields, David, *Prof,* Texas State University - San Marcos, Dept of Art and Design, San Marcos TX (S)

Shields, Holly, *Assoc Prof,* Texas State University - San Marcos, Dept of Art and Design, San Marcos TX (S)

Shields, Paul M, *Asst Prof,* York College, Art Dept, York NE (S)

Shields, Scott, *Chief Cur & Assoc Dir,* Crocker Art Museum, Sacramento CA

Shields, Sharon, *Admin Mgr,* Toronto School of Art, Toronto ON (S)

Shields, Tom, *Asst Prof,* Augustana College, Art Dept, Sioux Falls SD (S)

Shields, Van W, *Exec Dir,* Museum of York County, Rock Hill SC

Shields, Wendy, *Dir,* City of Irvine, Irvine Fine Arts Center, Irvine CA

Shier, Kara, *Dir Admin,* Putnam County Historical Society, Foundry School Museum, Cold Spring NY

Shiffler, Meg, *Gallery Dir,* San Francisco Arts Commission, Gallery, San Francisco CA

Shifman, Barry, *Cur Decorative Arts 1890 to Present,* Virginia Museum of Fine Arts, Richmond VA

Shifrin, Susan, *Assoc Dir Educ,* Ursinus College, Philip & Muriel Berman Museum of Art, Collegeville PA

Shigekawa, Joan, *Sr Deputy Chmn,* National Endowment for the Arts, Washington DC

Shih, Chia-Chun, *Librn,* Kimbell Art Foundation, Kimbell Art Museum, Fort Worth TX

Shih, Chia-Chun, *Librn,* Kimbell Art Foundation, Library, Fort Worth TX

Shilkoff, Jacqueline, *Assoc Cur New Media & Digital Mus,* Purchase College, Neuberger Museum of Art, Purchase NY

Shill, Marion, *VPres Central Servs,* Glenbow Museum, Calgary AB

Shillabeer, S L, *Asst Prof,* Troy State University, Dept of Art & Classics, Troy AL (S)

Shilliam, Nicola, *Western Bibliographer,* Princeton University, Marquand Library of Art & Archaeology, Princeton NJ

Shillieto, Sadie, *Art Adv Bd Fellow,* Mount Holyoke College, Art Museum, South Hadley MA

Shimiza, Yoshiaki, *Dir Prog Chinese & Japanese Art & Archaeology,* Princeton University, Dept of Art & Archaeology, Princeton NJ (S)

Shimon, J, *Assoc Prof,* Lawrence University, Dept of Art & Art History, Appleton WI (S)

Shin, Roberta, *Exec Asst,* Dartmouth College, Hood Museum of Art, Hanover NH

Shin-tsu Tai, Susan, *Cur Asian Art,* Santa Barbara Museum of Art, Library, Santa Barbara CA

Shindler, Kelly, *Asst Cur,* Contemporary Art Museum St Louis, Saint Louis MO

Shinkle, Bradford, *Pres,* Museum of Russian Art, Minneapolis MN

Shinn, Nancy, *Sec,* Coquille Valley Art Association, Coquille OR

Shinners, Jackie, *Art Historian,* Northwestern Michigan College, Art Dept, Traverse City MI (S)

Shipley, Anne, *Chmn,* Sierra Nevada College, Fine Arts Dept, Incline Village NV (S)

Shipman, Jen, *Mem Mgr,* Akron Art Museum, Akron OH

Shipman, John, *Dir,* University of Maryland, College Park, The Art Gallery, College Park MD

Shipp, Rebecca, *Tour Admin,* Liberty Hall Historic Site, Liberty Hall Museum, Frankfort KY

Shipp, Tony, *Prof,* Sam Houston State University, Art Dept, Huntsville TX (S)

Shippert-Meyers, Beth, *Performing Arts Mgr & Mem Coordr,* Contemporary Arts Center, New Orleans LA

Shiras, Susan, *Librn,* Brooks Institute of Photography, Santa Barbara CA (S)

Shires, Christopher, *Dir Interpretation & Progs,* Edsel & Eleanor Ford, Grosse Pointe Shores MI

Shires, James, *Educ Coordr,* Maysville, Kentucky Gateway Museum Center, Maysville KY

Shires, Jeanette, *Dir,* Northwest Florida State College, Mattie Kelly Arts Center Galleries, Niceville FL (S)

Shirey, David, *Ceramic Studio Mgr,* The Art School at Old Church, Demarest NJ (S)

Shirey, Heather, *Prof,* University of Saint Thomas, Dept of Art History, Saint Paul MN (S)

Shirley, Donna, *Dir,* Science Fiction Museum and Hall of Fame, Seattle WA

Shirley, Margaret, *Instr,* Marylhurst University, Art Dept, Marylhurst OR (S)

Shirley, Trey, *Asst Prof,* Wayland Baptist University, Dept of Art, School of Fine Art, Plainview TX (S)

Shkurti, Gjergji, *Producer,* Storefront for Art & Architecture, New York NY

Shmalo, Marlene, *Gen Educ,* The Art Institute of Cincinnati, AIC College of Design, Cincinnati OH (S)

Shockley, Darlas, *Dean Arts & Sciences,* Indian Hills Community College, Ottumwa Campus, Dept of Art, Ottumwa IA (S)

Shockley, Evelyn, *Prog Mgr,* Xerox Corporation, Art Collection, Norwalk CT

Shockley, Susan, *Cur,* Board of Parks & Recreation, The Parthenon, Nashville TN

Shockley, Teresa, *Exec Dir,* The Community Education Center, Philadelphia PA

Shoe, Ross, *Instr,* Bob Jones University, School of Fine Arts, Div of Art & Design, Greenville SC (S)

Shoemaker, Edward C, *Dir Library Resources Div,* Oklahoma Historical Society, Library Resources Division, Oklahoma City OK

Shoemaker, Innis, *Sr Cur Prints, Drawings & Photographs,* Philadelphia Museum of Art, Main Building, Philadelphia PA

Shoemaker, Marla, *Cur Educ,* Philadelphia Museum of Art, Main Building, Philadelphia PA

Shoger, Jan, *Assoc Prof,* Saint Olaf College, Art Dept, Northfield MN (S)

Shomale, Lu, *Exec Dir,* Schoolhouse History & Art Center, Colstrip MT

Shook, Jim, *Pres Chilkat Valley Historical Society,* Sheldon Museum & Cultural Center, Inc, Sheldon Museum & Cultural Center, Haines AK

Shook, Kevin, *Asst Prof,* Birmingham-Southern College, Art & Art History, Birmingham AL (S)

Shook, Langley, *Pres,* Chesapeake Bay Maritime Museum, Saint Michaels MD

Shook, Melissa, *Assoc Prof,* University of Massachusetts - Boston, Art Dept, Boston MA (S)

Shopsis, Mari, *Dir Educ,* Rensselaer County Historical Society, Museum & Library, Troy NY

Shor-Cohen, Inez, *Dir,* Mechanics' Institute, San Francisco CA

Shore, Bob, *VChmn,* Kern County Museum, Library, Bakersfield CA

Shore, Bob, *VPres,* Manhattan Graphics Center, New York NY (S)

Shore, Don, *Chmn Animation,* Mount San Antonio College, Art Dept, Walnut CA (S)

Shore, Francine, *Instr,* Main Line Art Center, Haverford PA (S)

Shore, Jeff, *Preparator,* Contemporary Arts Museum Houston, Houston TX

Shorlemer, Beth, *Art Coll Develop Specialist,* Central Library, Dept of Fine Arts, San Antonio TX

Short, Frank, *Coordr,* Montgomery County Community College, Art Center, Blue Bell PA (S)

Short, Georgianna, *Asst Prof,* Ohio State University, Dept of Art Education, Columbus OH (S)

Short, Janet, *Librn,* Bernice Pauahi Bishop, Library, Honolulu HI

Short, John D, *Bd Pres,* National Art Museum of Sport, Indianapolis IN

Short, Sherry, *Asst Prof,* Minnesota State University-Moorhead, Dept of Art & Design, Moorhead MN (S)

Shortridge, Katherine, *Asst Prof,* Roanoke College, Fine Arts Dept-Art, Salem VA (S)

Shorts, Katie, *Events Mgr,* Milwaukee County War Memorial Inc., Villa Terrace Decorative Arts Museum, Milwaukee WI

Shortslef, Lisa M, *Admin Aide,* State University of New York at Oswego, Tyler Art Gallery, Oswego NY

Shortt, A J (Fred), *Cur,* Museum for Textiles, Canada Aviation Museum, Ottawa ON

Shostak, Anthony, *Educ Cur,* Bates College, Museum of Art, Lewiston ME

Shott, Cynthia, *Pres (V),* Missoula Art Museum, Missoula MT

Shotwell, Camille, *Librn,* Spertus Institute of Jewish Studies, Asher Library, Chicago IL

Shoup, Libby, *Comm Coordr,* Salina Art Center, Salina KS

Show, H E (Skip), *Deputy Exec Dir,* The Heckscher Museum of Art, Huntington NY

Showers, Norman, *Pres,* Alton Museum of History & Art, Inc, Alton IL

Shrack, Marsha, *Art Instr,* Pratt Community College, Art Dept, Pratt KS (S)

Shrenk, Lisa, *Architectural History,* Norwich University, Dept of Architecture and Art, Northfield VT (S)

Shrewder, Susan, *Mus Shop Mgr,* Philbrook Museum of Art, Tulsa OK

Shriver, Totem, *Instr,* Linfield College, Department of Art & Visual Culture, McMinnville OR (S)

Shteynberg, Catherine, *Asst Cur,* University of Tennessee, McClung Museum of Natural History & Culture, Knoxville TN

Shtromberg, Elena, *Asst Prof,* University of Utah, Dept of Art & Art History, Salt Lake City UT (S)

Shuemake, Steve, *Asst Dir Opers,* Montgomery Museum of Fine Arts, Montgomery AL

Shuemake, Steve, *Asst Dir Opers,* Montgomery Museum of Fine Arts, Library, Montgomery AL

Shuey Altamirano, Noelle, *Coll Cur,* Palm Beach County Parks & Recreation Department, Donald B Gordon Memorial Library, Delray Beach FL

Shuflat, Michael S, *Capital Projects Admin,* Jamestown-Yorktown Foundation, Jamestown Settlement, Williamsburg VA

Shugart, Sanford, *Pres,* Valencia Community College, Art Gallery-East Campus, Orlando FL

Shulman, Randy, *Asst VPres Advancement,* The Huntington Library, Art Collections & Botanical Gardens, San Marino CA

Shultes, Steph, *Mus Shop Mgr,* Iroquois Indian Museum, Howes Cave NY

Shultis, Eric, *Assoc Prof,* Saint Louis Community College at Florissant Valley, Liberal Arts Division, Ferguson MO (S)

Shults, Belinda, *Pres,* Arkansas Arts Center, Museum, Little Rock AR (S)

Shultz, Jay, *Assoc Prof,* Palomar Community College, Art Dept, San Marcos CA (S)

Shultz, Mike, *Library Dir,* The University of Montana - Western, Lucy Carson Memorial Library, Dillon MT

Shultz, Randy, *Exhibs Dir,* Besser Museum for Northeast Michigan, Philip M Park Library, Alpena MI

Shumaker, Rhonda, *Dir,* South County Art Association, Kingston RI

Shum Allen, Irene, *Cur & Colls Mgr,* Philip Johnson Glass House, National Trust for Historic Preservation, New Canaan CT

Shumard, Ann, *Cur Photographs,* National Portrait Gallery, Smithsonian Institution, Washington DC

Shumate, Michael, *Gallery Coordr,* St Lawrence College, Art Gallery, Kingston ON

Shumow, Lynne, *Cur Educ,* Marquette University, Haggerty Museum of Art, Milwaukee WI

Shumway, John, *Asst Prof,* Slippery Rock University of Pennsylvania, Dept of Art, Slippery Rock PA (S)

Shunk, Hal, *Chmn,* Wilmington College, Art Dept, Wilmington OH (S)

Shurley-Olivas, Laura, *Adjunct,* College of the Canyons, Art Dept, Santa Clarita CA (S)

Shurter, James, *Asst Prof,* Mott Community College, Fine Arts & Social Sciences Division, Flint MI (S)

Shurtleff, Carol B, *Staff Coordr,* Maitland Art Center, Maitland FL

Shust, Maria, *Dir,* The Ukrainian Museum, New York NY

Shust, Maria, *Dir,* The Ukrainian Museum, Library, New York NY

Shutte, Sue, *Historic Site Admin,* Ringwood Manor House Museum, Ringwood NJ

Shuttleworth, Erica, *Instr,* Toronto School of Art, Toronto ON (S)

Shynkaruk, Wil, *Assoc Prof,* Minnesota State University-Moorhead, Dept of Art & Design, Moorhead MN (S)

Siano, Mary Ann, *Grants Officer,* Lehman College Art Gallery, Bronx NY

Sias, James H, *Prof,* Rochester Institute of Technology, School of Design, Rochester NY (S)

Sibbison, Diane, *Exhibits Mgr,* Delaplaine Visual Arts Education Center, Frederick MD

Sicko, Barbara, *Registrar,* Bob Jones University Museum & Gallery Inc, Greenville SC

Sicola, Kimberly, *Coll Mgr,* County of Henrico, Meadow Farm Museum, Glen Allen VA

Sicotte, Etienne, *Graphic/Web Designer/Coordr,* Royal Architectural Institute of Canada, Ottawa ON

Siddons, Louise, *Asst Prof,* Oklahoma State University, Department of Art, Graphic Design and Art History, Stillwater OK (S)

Sides, Wayne, *Prof,* University of North Alabama, Dept of Art, Florence AL (S)

Sido, Barb, *Exec Dir,* Pewabic Society Inc, Pewabic Pottery, Detroit MI

Sido, Lee, *Asst Dir,* Northern Illinois University, School of Art, DeKalb IL (S)

Sidor, Christian, *Cur Vertebrate Paleontology,* University of Washington, Burke Museum of Natural History and Culture, Seattle WA

Sieber, Ellen, *Cur Educ,* Indiana University, The Mathers Museum of World Cultures, Bloomington IN

Sieber, Matthew, *Co-cur of Exhibits,* Indiana University, The Mathers Museum of World Cultures, Bloomington IN

Sieber, Richard, *Asst Reader Svc Librn,* Philadelphia Museum of Art, Library & Archives, Philadelphia PA

Siebert, Muriel, *Treas,* Guild Hall of East Hampton, Inc, Guild Hall Museum, East Hampton NY

Sieboda, Sedor, *Adjunct Prof,* Wilkes University, Dept of Art, Wilkes-Barre PA (S)

Siefmund, Tom, *Asst Prof,* Tidewater Community College, Visual Arts Center, Portsmouth VA (S)

Siegal, Robert L Rabin, *Dir,* Institute of Puerto Rican Culture, Museo Fuerte Conde de Mirasol, Vieques PR

Siegal, Robert L Rabin, *Dir,* Institute of Puerto Rican Culture, Museo Fuerte Conde de Mirasol, Vieques PR

Siegel, Cheryl, *Librn,* Vancouver Art Gallery, Vancouver BC

Siegel, Cheryl A, *Librn,* Vancouver Art Gallery, Library, Vancouver BC

Siegesmund, Richard, *Asst Prof Art Educ,* University of Georgia, Franklin College of Arts & Sciences, Lamar Dodd School of Art, Athens GA (S)

Siegfried, Clifford, *Dir & Asst Commissioner,* New York State Museum, Albany NY

Siegfried, Jay, *Chmn,* Middlesex County College, Visual Arts Dept, Edison NJ (S)

Siegle, Peggy, *Bd Mem,* Kennebec Valley Art Association, Harlow Gallery, Hallowell ME

Siem, Katie, *VPres,* St Mary Landmarks, Grevemberg House Museum, Franklin LA

Sierpinski, Cort, *Dept Head,* Southern Connecticut State University, Dept of Art, New Haven CT (S)

Sierpinski, Cort, *Dir,* Southern Connecticut State University, Art Dept, New Haven CT

Siesling, Jan, *Dir,* University of Southern Mississippi, Museum of Art, Hattiesburg MS

Sietz, Phillip, *Cur History,* Cliveden, Philadelphia PA

Sievers, Ann H, *Dir, Cur,* Saint Joseph College, Art Gallery, University of Saint Joseph, West Hartford CT

Siewert, John, *Chmn,* The College of Wooster, Dept of Art and Art History, Wooster OH (S)

Sigala, Patricia, *Outreach Educator,* Museum of New Mexico, Museum of International Folk Art, Santa Fe NM

Sigel, Deborah S, *Assoc Prof Ceramics,* Millersville University, Dept of Art & Design, Millersville PA (S)

Sigel, Milt, *Instr,* Bucks County Community College, Fine Arts Dept, Newtown PA (S)

Sigerson, Marge, *Librn,* The Museum of Arts & Sciences Inc, Library, Daytona Beach FL

Sigler, Doug, *Prof,* Rochester Institute of Technology, School of Design, Rochester NY (S)

Signi, Holly, *Cur Exhibs,* San Bernardino County Museum, Fine Arts Institute, Redlands CA

Sigre-Lewis, Chris, *Painting & Drawing,* Asbury College, Student Center Gallery, Wilmore KY

Sijpkes, Pieter, *Prof,* McGill University, School of Architecture, Montreal PQ (S)

Siker, Nancy, *Asst Dir, Library Serv,* Milwaukee Institute of Art & Design, Library, Milwaukee WI

Silagy Benedek, Nelly, *Dir School Family,* The Jewish Museum, New York NY

Silas, Anna, *Dir,* Hopi Cultural Center Museum, Second Mesa AZ

Silber, Loren, *Dir Educ,* Morris-Jumel Mansion, Inc, New York NY

Silberg, Nicholas, *Asst Prof,* Savannah State University, Dept of Fine Arts, Savannah GA (S)

Silberman, Jeffrey, *Chmn Textile Develop & Mktg,* Fashion Institute of Technology, Art & Design Division, New York NY (S)

Silberman, Rebecca, *Prog Coordr,* College of Charleston School of Arts, Halsey Institute of Contemporary Art, Charleston SC

Silberman, Robert, *Prof,* University of Minnesota, Minneapolis, Art History, Minneapolis MN (S)

Silcox, Sharon, *Library Asst,* North Carolina State University, Harrye Lyons Design Library, Raleigh NC

Silet, Emily, *Cur Educ,* DeCordova Museum & Sculpture Park, DeCordova Museum, Lincoln MA

Silitch, Suzanne, *Dir Commns & Strategy,* Williams College, Museum of Art, Williamstown MA

Silk, Gerald, *Chmn Art History,* Temple University, Tyler School of Art, Philadelphia PA (S)

Silkworth, Cynthia, *Admin,* Rensselaer County Historical Society, Hart-Cluett Mansion, 1827, Troy NY

Sill, Diane, *Gallery Mgr,* Gilpin County Arts Association, Central City CO

Sill, Robert, *Asst Dir,* Illinois State Museum, ISM Lockport Gallery, Chicago Gallery & Southern Illinois Art Gallery, Springfield IL

Sill, Robert, *Asst Dir Art,* Illinois State Museum, Museum Store, Chicago IL

Silliman, Mark, *Dean,* Leeward Community College, Arts & Humanities Division, Pearl City HI (S)

Sills, Pamela, *Develop,* Louisiana Arts & Science Museum, Baton Rouge LA

Sills, Susan, *Pres,* Viridian Artists Inc, New York NY

Silva, Luis, *Asst Prof,* American University, Dept of Art, New York NY (S)

Silva, Robin, *Cataloger,* Portsmouth Athenaeum, Joseph Copley Research Library, Portsmouth NH

Silva, Timothy, *Lectr,* Southeastern Louisiana University, Dept of Visual Arts, Hammond LA (S)

Silva, Tom, *Asst Prof Art,* Tusculum College, Fine Arts Dept, Greeneville TN (S)

Silver, Nancy, *Gen Mgr,* Arts Council of Fayetteville-Cumberland County, The Arts Center, Fayetteville NC

Silveria, Kristine, *Shop Mgr,* Carmel Mission & Gift Shop, Carmel CA

Silverio, Jo-Ann B, *Admin Asst,* Farmington Village Green & Library Association, Stanley-Whitman House, Farmington CT

Silverman, Camille, *Educ & Exhib Cur,* Western Colorado Center for the Arts, The Art Center, Grand Junction CO

Silverman, David, *Egyptian Section Cur,* University of Pennsylvania, Museum of Archaeology & Anthropology, Philadelphia PA

Silverman, Peggy, *Mission Coordr,* Buehler Challenger & Science Center, Paramus NJ

Silverman, Robert, *Asst Prof,* Louisiana State University, School of Art, Baton Rouge LA (S)

Silverman, Robert, *Dean,* Queen's University, Dept of Art, Kingston ON (S)

Silverson, Lauren, *Registrar,* Portland Museum of Art, Portland ME

Silverstein, Dan, *Mgr Exhibs & Facilities,* Northwestern University, Mary & Leigh Block Museum of Art, Evanston IL

Silverstein, Romy, *Dir,* Addison/Ripley Fine Art, Washington DC

Silverthorne, Jeanette, *Asst Dir,* Columbia University, Miriam & Ira D Wallach Art Gallery, New York NY

Silvis, Gregg, *Asst Dir Library Computing Systems,* University of Delaware, Morris Library, Newark DE

Sim, Richard, *Prof,* Antelope Valley College, Art Dept, Division of Fine Arts, Lancaster CA (S)

Simak, Ellen, *Chief Cur,* Hunter Museum of American Art, Chattanooga TN

Simard, Claire, *Gen Dir,* Musee de l'Amerique Francaise, Quebec PQ

Simard, Claire, *Secy,* Institut des Arts au Saguenay, Centre National D'Exposition a Jonquiere, Jonquiere PQ

Simard, Jim, *Librn, Head Historical Coll,* Alaska State Library, Alaska Historical Collections, Juneau AK

Simcoe, Barbara, *Prof,* University of Nebraska at Omaha, Dept of Art & Art History, Omaha NE (S)

Simcox, Andrew, *Placement, Faculty,* Antonelli Institute, Professional Photography & Commercial Art, Erdenheim PA (S)

Simile, Robert, *Head Dept,* West Virginia Institute of Technology, Creative Arts Dept, Montgomery WV (S)

Simkin, Phillips, *Coordr Fine Arts,* York College of the City University of New York, Fine & Performing Arts, Jamaica NY (S)

Simkin, Steven, *VPres,* Dahesh Museum of Art, Greenwich CT

Simmonds, Beth, *Special Events Coordr,* National Postal Museum, Smithsonian Institution, Washington DC

Simmons, Byron, *Facilities Mgr & Security,* Hammonds House Museum, Atlanta GA

Simmons, David, *Dir,* Wade House Historic Site-Wisconsin Historical Society, Wesley W. Jung Carriage Museum, Greenbush WI

Simmons, Ellen, *Mgr Art & Literature Dept,* Detroit Public Library, Art & Literature Dept, Detroit MI

Simmons, Katherine, *Pres,* Lyme Art Association, Inc, Old Lyme CT

Simmons, Michael, *Prof Emeritus,* California State University, Chico, Department of Art & Art History, Chico CA (S)

Simmons, Pam, *Develop Dir,* The Winnipeg Art Gallery, Winnipeg MB

Simmons, Seymour, *Assoc Prof,* Winthrop University, Dept of Art & Design, Rock Hill SC (S)

Simms, Jennifer, *Instr,* Greenfield Community College, Art Dept, Greenfield MA (S)

Simon, Ann, *Instr,* Main Line Art Center, Haverford PA (S)

Simon, Anne, *Accounting Asst,* Buffalo Arts Studio, Art Gallery, Buffalo NY

Simon, David, *Prof,* Colby College, Art Dept, Waterville ME (S)

Simon, Gladys, *Operations Mgr,* The Museum of Western Art, Kerrville TX

Simon, Jane, *Exhib Cur,* Madison Museum of Contemporary Art, Madison WI

Simon, Janice, *Assoc Prof Art History,* University of Georgia, Franklin College of Arts & Sciences, Lamar Dodd School of Art, Athens GA (S)

Simon, Joshua, *Exec Dir,* East Bay Asian Local Development Corp (EBALDC), Asian Resource Gallery, Oakland CA

Simon, Lisa, *Asst Prof,* Jefferson Community College & Technical College, Fine Arts, Louisville KY (S)

Simon, Meryl, *Librn,* Aesthetic Realism Foundation, Eli Siegel Collection, New York NY

Simon, Nancy, *Dir,* Denver Art Museum, Library, Denver CO

Simon, Patricia, *Assoc Prof Theatre,* Marymount Manhattan College, Fine & Performing Arts Div, New York NY (S)

Simon, Robert, *Chmn Dept,* Holy Names College, Art Dept, Oakland CA (S)

Simona, Lauti, *Chmn Board Trustees,* Jean P Haydon, Pago Pago, American Samoa PI

Simoneau, Christiane, *Dir,* Galerie d'Art du Parc-Manoir de Tonnancour, Manoir de Tonnancour, Trois Rivieres PQ

Simonov, Russell, *Dir Operations,* Nevada Museum of Art, Art Library, Reno NV

Simons, Chris, *Prof,* Shoreline Community College, Humanities Division, Seattle WA (S)

Simons, Patricia, *Assoc Prof,* University of Michigan, Ann Arbor, Dept of History of Art, Ann Arbor MI (S)

Simons, Rachel, *Instr,* American University, Dept of Art, New York NY (S)

Simons, Sheri, *Prof,* California State University, Chico, Department of Art & Art History, Chico CA (S)

Simons, Yvonne, *VPres,* South Street Seaport Museum, New York NY

Simonsen, Garric, *Asst Prof,* Spokane Falls Community College, Fine Arts Dept, Spokane WA (S)

Simonsen, Oliver, *Pres of Board,* Canajoharie Library & Art Gallery, Arkell Museum of Canajoharie, Canajoharie NY

Simonsen, Oliver, *Pres of Board,* Canajoharie Library & Art Gallery, Library, Canajoharie NY

Simor, Suzanna, *Dir,* Queens College, City University of New York, Queens College Art Center, Flushing NY

Simor, Suzanna, *Head,* Queens College, City University of New York, Art Library, Flushing NY

Simpkins, Wayne, *Chmn Asst,* University of Memphis, Art Dept, Memphis TN (S)

Simpson, Alan, *Chmn,* Buffalo Bill Memorial Association, Buffalo Bill Historical Center, Cody WY

Simpson, Barbara, *Dir Library Svcs,* Kean University, Nancy Thompson Library, Union NJ

Simpson, Erion, *Exec Dir,* Taos Art Museum, Taos NM

Simpson, Gail, *Assoc Prof,* University of Wisconsin, Madison, Dept of Art, Madison WI (S)

Simpson, Jane, *Visual Arts Dir,* Colquitt County Arts Center, Moultrie GA

Simpson, Janet F, *Exec Dir,* Kansas City Artists Coalition, Kansas City MO

Simpson, Janice, *Dir Grad Prog,* Michigan State University, Dept of Art & Art History, East Lansing MI (S)

Simpson, John, *Media Arts & Animation,* Art Institute of Pittsburgh, Pittsburgh PA (S)

Simpson, Kathleen, *Dir Museum Educ & Institutional Advancement,* Springfield Museums, Springfield Science Museum, Springfield MA

Simpson, Kathleen, *VPres,* Springfield Museums, Michele & Donald D'Amour Museum of Fine Arts, Springfield MA

Simpson, Larry, *Chmn & Graphic Design,* University of South Alabama, Dept of Art & Art History, Mobile AL (S)

Simpson, Larry, *Pres,* Culberson County Historical Museum, Van Horn TX

Simpson, Larry L, *Chmn,* University of South Alabama, Ethnic American Slide Library, Mobile AL

Simpson, Laurence, *VChmn,* Fraunces Tavern Museum, New York NY

Simpson, Leland, *Bd Mem,* Coquille Valley Art Association, Coquille OR

Simpson, Leslie T, *Dir,* Winfred L & Elizabeth C Post, Post Memorial Art Reference Library, Joplin MO

Simpson, Lisa A, *Dir,* Louisa May Alcott Memorial Association, Orchard House, Concord MA

Simpson, Mary, *Asst Prof,* Eastern Illinois University, Art Dept, Charleston IL (S)

Simpson, Mary Caroline, *Prof,* University of Nebraska at Omaha, Dept of Art & Art History, Omaha NE (S)

Simpson, Michael, *Lectr,* University of North Carolina at Charlotte, Dept Art, Charlotte NC (S)

Simpson, Pamela, *Chmn Dept Art,* Washington & Lee University, Gallery of DuPont Hall, Lexington VA

Simpson, Pamela H, *Prof,* Washington and Lee University, Div of Art, Lexington VA (S)

Simpson, Shannon, *Cur,* Ellis County Museum Inc, Waxahachie TX

Simpson, Vicki, *Develop Coordr,* City of Cedar Falls, Iowa, James & Meryl Hearst Center for the Arts & Sculpture Garden, Cedar Falls IA

Simpson Bear, Phoebe, *Printed Art Conservation Librn,* Rhode Island Historical Society, Library, Providence RI

Simpson Darden, Barbara, *Dean Library Serv,* Kutztown University, Rohrbach Library, Kutztown PA

Simpson Voth, Karrie, *Prof,* Fort Hays State University, Dept of Art & Design, Hays KS (S)

Sims, Arlie, *Head Ref & Instruction,* Columbia College Chicago, Library, Chicago IL

Sims, Jessica, *Pres,* Artspace, Richmond VA

Sims, Judith, *Art School Dir,* The Contemporary Austin, Austin TX

Sims, Lowery Stokes, *Adjunct Cur,* The Studio Museum in Harlem, New York NY

Sims, Nathan, *Instr,* Waynesburg College, Dept of Fine Arts, Waynesburg PA (S)

Sims, Richard, *Dir,* Montana Historical Society, Helena MT

Sinchak, Kenneth, *CFO,* Cleveland Botanical Garden, Eleanor Squire Library, Cleveland OH

Sinclair, Jane, *Prof,* Chapman University, Art Dept, Orange CA (S)

Sinclair, Joel, *Councilor at Large,* Alberta Society of Artists, Calgary AB

Sincox, Kim Robinson, *Mus Services Dir,* State of North Carolina, Battleship North Carolina, Wilmington NC

Sindelar, Norma, *Archivist,* Saint Louis Art Museum, Richardson Memorial Library, Saint Louis MO

Sindile, Sandu, *Cur,* Homer Watson, Kitchener ON

Sinfield, Ann, *Registrar,* University of Wisconsin-Madison, Chazen Museum of Art, Madison WI

Sing, Susan, *Instr,* Glendale Community College, Visual & Performing Arts Div, Glendale CA (S)

Singer, Christian Bernard, *Cur,* Canadian Clay and Glass Gallery, Waterloo ON

Singer, Dana, *Exec Dir,* Society of North American Goldsmiths, Eugene OR

Singer, Gerald R, *Gen Counsel,* American Museum of Natural History, New York NY

Singer, Kimberly, *Mktg,* Washington University, Mildred Lane Kemper Art Museum, Saint Louis MO

Singer, Marijane, *Dir,* Blauvelt Demarest Foundation, Hiram Blauvelt Art Museum, Oradell NJ

Singh, Juanita, *Admin Asst,* Northeast Document Conservation Center, Inc, Andover MA

Singh-Bischofberger, Surana, *Assoc Prof,* East Los Angeles College, Art Dept, Monterey Park CA (S)

Singhoff, Andrea, *Gift Shop Mgr,* Walter Anderson, Ocean Springs MS

Singleton, Carolyn, *Dir,* Carnegie Arts Center, Leavenworth KS

Singleton, David, *Deputy Dir,* Philbrook Museum of Art, Tulsa OK

Singleton, Pamela, *Treas,* Artists' Fellowship, Inc, New York NY

Sinha, Ajay, *Art History,* Mount Holyoke College, Art Dept, South Hadley MA (S)

Sink, Bruce, *Treas,* Arizona Watercolor Association, Phoenix AZ

Sinsheimer, Karen, *Cur Photo,* Santa Barbara Museum of Art, Santa Barbara CA

Sinsheimer, Karen, *Cur Photography,* Santa Barbara Museum of Art, Library, Santa Barbara CA

Sio, Elizabeth M, *Sec,* John D Barrow, Skaneateles NY

Sioblom, Jill S, *Cur of Educ,* Eccles Community Art Center, Ogden UT

Siokalo, Zorianne, *Cur Pub Progs,* James A Michener, Doylestown PA

Sipiorski, Dennis, *Art Dept Head,* Nicholls State University, Dept of Art, Thibodaux LA (S)

Sipp, Geo, *Prof,* Missouri Western State University, Art Dept, Saint Joseph MO (S)

Sippel, Jeffrey, *Assoc Prof,* University of Missouri, Saint Louis, Dept of Art & Art History, Saint Louis MO (S)

Sipple, Laurie, *Programs Coordr,* University of Nebraska, Lincoln, Sheldon Memorial Art Gallery & Sculpture Garden, Lincoln NE

Sirman, Robert, *Dir,* Canada Council for the Arts, Conseil des Arts du Canada, Ottawa ON

Sirmans, Barbara, *Dir,* Birmingham Public Library, Arts, Literature & Sports Department, Birmingham AL

Sirmons, Franklin, *Grad Comt,* Bard College, Center for Curatorial Studies Graduate Program, Annandale-on-Hudson NY (S)

Sirna, Jessie, *Prof,* Mott Community College, Fine Arts & Social Sciences Division, Flint MI (S)

Siry, Joseph, *Chair,* Wesleyan University, Dept of Art & Art History, Middletown CT (S)

Sissen, Melissa M, *Pub Servs Librn,* Siena Heights College, Art Library, Adrian MI

Sisson, Mark, *Prof,* Oklahoma State University, Department of Art, Graphic Design and Art History, Stillwater OK (S)

Sivulich, Ken, *Dir,* Jacksonville Public Library, Fine Arts & Recreation Dept, Jacksonville FL

Six, Dean, *Exec Dir,* Museum of American Glass in WV, Weston WV

Sizer, Nancy, *Exec Dir,* Detroit Artists Market, Detroit MI

Sjogren, Margaret, *Dept Chmn,* Southern Oregon University, Art & Art History Dept, Ashland OR (S)

Sjoholm, Karen, *Chair,* John F Kennedy, Department of Arts & Consciousness, Pleasant Hill CA (S)

Sjosten, David, *Deputy Dir Admin,* Worcester Art Museum, Worcester MA

Sjovold, Erling, *Asst Prof,* University of Richmond, Dept of Art and Art History, Richmond VA (S)

Skaggs, Dale, *Dir Horticulture,* The Dixon Gallery & Gardens, Memphis TN

Skaggs, Steve, *Prof,* University of Louisville, Allen R Hite Art Institute, Louisville KY (S)

Skeele, Devon, *Librn & Archivist,* Museum of New Mexico, New Mexico Museum of Art, Unit of NM Dept of Cultural Affairs, Santa Fe NM

Skeen, Geneva, *Prog Coordr,* LACE (Los Angeles Contemporary Exhibitions), Los Angeles CA

Skeeter, Anita, *Gallery Cur & Educ Dir,* Embroiderers Guild of America, Margaret Parshall Gallery, Louisville KY

Skinner, Arthur, *Prof,* Eckerd College, Art Dept, Saint Petersburg FL (S)

Skinner, Bill, *Chmn Div of Communs & Arts,* North Arkansas Community-Technical College, Art Dept, Harrison AR (S)

Skinner, Ellie, *Events Coordr,* History Museum of Mobile, Mobile AL

Skinner, Jaineth, *Asst Prof,* Bemidji State University, Visual Arts Dept, Bemidji MN (S)

Sklaver, Ellen, *Librn Mgr,* Suffolk University, New England School of Art & Design Library, Boston MA

Skoglund, Margaret, *Assoc Prof,* University of Southern Indiana, Department of Art, Evansville IN (S)

Skonieczka, Angelina, *Office Mgr,* University of New Mexico, University of New Mexico Art Museum, Albuquerque NM

Skove, Margaret, *Dir,* Blanden Memorial Art Museum, Fort Dodge IA

Skove, Margaret A, *Dir,* Huntington Museum of Art, Huntington WV

Skowronski, Nancy, *Library Dir,* Detroit Public Library, Art & Literature Dept, Detroit MI

Skroch, Diana P, *Div Chair,* Valley City State College, Art Dept, Valley City ND (S)

Skrzynski, Jackie, *Asst Prof Drawing & Painting,* Ramapo College of New Jersey, School of Contemporary Arts, Mahwah NJ (S)

Skubinna, Bradd, *Adjunct asst Prof,* Spokane Falls Community College, Fine Arts Dept, Spokane WA (S)

Skupin, Marinta, *Cur Educ,* Laguna Art Museum, Laguna Beach CA

Skuratofsky, Carol, *Mgr,* Prudential Art Program, Newark NJ

Skurkis, Barry, *Chair Art Dept, Assoc Prof,* North Central College, Dept of Art, Naperville IL (S)

Skvarla, Diane, *Cur,* United States Senate Commission on Art, Washington DC

Skwerski, Thomas, *Mus Cur,* Springfield Museum of Art, Library, Springfield OH

Slade, Alex, *Asst Chmn,* Otis College of Art & Design, Fine Arts, Los Angeles CA (S)

Slade, Debbie, *Interim Dir,* Rodman Hall Arts Centre, Saint Catharines ON

Slade, Terry, *Asst Prof,* Hartwick College, Art Dept, Oneonta NY (S)

Slagell, Jeff H, *Asst Dir,* Delta State University, Roberts LaForge Library, Cleveland MS

Slagle, Nancy, *Assoc Dir & Assoc Prof,* Texas Tech University, Dept of Art, Lubbock TX (S)

Slane, Kathleen, *Prof,* University of Missouri - Columbia, Art History & Archaeology Dept, Columbia MO (S)

Slaney, Deborah, *Cur History,* Albuquerque Museum of Art & History, Albuquerque NM

Slania, Heather, *Dir of Libr & Res Ctr,* National Museum of Women in the Arts, Library & Research Center, Washington DC

Slania, Heather, *Dir of Library & Research Center,* National Museum of Women in the Arts, Washington DC

Slater, Kaiti, *Assoc Prof,* University of Utah, Dept of Art & Art History, Salt Lake City UT (S)

Slater, Sandra, *Genealogy Librn,* Phelps County Historical Society, Nebraska Prairie Museum, Holdrege NE

Slater, Sandra, *Genealogy Librn,* Phelps County Historical Society, Donald O. Lindgren Library, Holdrege NE

Slater-Tanner, Susan, *Asst Prof Arts & Communs,* Orange County Community College, Arts & Communication, Middletown NY (S)

Slatery, W Patrick, *Art Dept Chmn,* Palm Beach Community College, Dept of Art, Lake Worth FL (S)

Slatkin, Wendy E, *Lectr,* California State Polytechnic University, Pomona, Department of Art, Pomona CA (S)

Slattery, Michael, *Studio Dept Head,* Bob Jones University, School of Fine Arts, Div of Art & Design, Greenville SC (S)

Slatton, Ralph, *Prof,* East Tennessee State University, College of Arts and Sciences, Dept of Art & Design, Johnson City TN (S)

Slaughter, Alan, *2nd VPres,* Historical Society of Bloomfield, Bloomfield NJ

Slaughter, Rebecca, *Asst Mgr,* Branigan Cultural Center, Las Cruces NM

Slautterback, Catharina, *Cur Prints & Photos,* Library of the Boston Athenaeum, Boston MA

Slavick, Elin O, *Prof,* University of North Carolina at Chapel Hill, Art Dept, Chapel Hill NC (S)

Slavik, Barbara, *Educ Dir,* City of Port Angeles, Port Angeles Fine Arts Center & Webster Woods Art Park, Port Angeles WA

Slavik, John, *Adjunct Prof,* North Central College, Dept of Art, Naperville IL (S)

Slavin, Ruth, *Dir Educ,* University of Michigan, Museum of Art, Ann Arbor MI

Slawson, Brian, *Assoc Prof,* University of Florida, School of Art & Art History, Gainesville FL (S)

Slaymaker, Samuel C, *Exec Dir,* Rock Ford Foundation, Inc, Rock Ford Plantation, Lancaster PA

Sledd, Michael, *Instr,* Columbia College, Art Dept, Columbia MO (S)

Sledge, Sarah, *Dir Commun,* Cedarhurst Center for the Arts, Mitchell Museum, Mount Vernon IL

Slein, Alison, *Prof,* Virginia Polytechnic Institute & State University, Dept of Art & Art History, Blacksburg VA (S)

Slein, Philip, *Owner,* Philip Slein Gallery, Saint Louis MO

Slemmons, Rod, *Dir,* Columbia College Chicago, Museum of Contemporary Photography, Chicago IL

Slepitza, Ron, *Pres,* Avila University, Thornhill Art Gallery, Kansas City MO

Slider, HJ, *Adjunct Asst Prof Art Educ,* Aquinas College, Art Dept, Grand Rapids MI (S)

Slimon, Gary, *Dir,* Canadian Wildlife & Wilderness Art Museum, Ottawa ON

Slimon, Gary, *Dir,* Canadian Wildlife & Wilderness Art Museum, Library, Ottawa ON

Sloan, David, *Chmn,* Whittier College, Dept of Art, Whittier CA (S)

Sloan, Katherine, *Pres,* Massachusetts College of Art, Boston MA (S)

Sloan, Mark, *Gallery Dir,* College of Charleston School of Arts, Halsey Institute of Contemporary Art, Charleston SC

Sloane, Kim, *Asst Prof,* Cedar Crest College, Art Dept, Allentown PA (S)

Sloane, Robert, *Head Art Information Center,* Chicago Public Library, Harold Washington Library Center, Chicago IL

Sloane, Ruragna, *Mus Shop Mgr,* Van Cortlandt House Museum, Bronx NY

Sloat, Caroline F, *Dir Scholarly Publications,* American Antiquarian Society, Worcester MA

Slobe, Gennie, *Progs Coordr,* Workman & Temple Family Homestead Museum, City of Industry CA

Sloboda, Stacey, *Assoc Prof,* Southern Illinois University, School of Art & Design, Carbondale IL (S)

Slorck, Lonnie, *Prof Photog,* Central Wyoming College, Art Center, Riverton WY (S)

Sloss, Katie, *Music Dir,* Kaji Aso Studio, Gallery Nature & Temptation, Boston MA

Sloss, Tencha, *Admin Dir,* Brownsville Art League, Brownsville Museum of Fine Art, Brownsville TX

Slouffman, James, *Dept Head Commercial Arts,* Antonelli College, Cincinnati OH (S)

Slovin, Rochelle, *Dir,* American Museum of the Moving Image, Astoria NY

Slowik, Theresa, *Publ Chief,* American Art Museum, Smithsonian Institution, Washington DC

Sluterbeck, Kay R, *Admin Asst,* Wassenberg Art Center, Van Wert OH

Slyfield, Donna, *Adult Servs,* Helen M Plum, Lombard IL

Small, Arlene, *Dir Mktg & Communs,* Art Gallery of Ontario, Toronto ON

Small, Carol, *Asst Prof,* Gettysburg College, Dept of Visual Arts, Gettysburg PA (S)

Small, Cindy, *Faculty,* Green River Community College, Art Dept, Auburn WA (S)

Small, Jocelyn, *Prof,* Rutgers, The State University of New Jersey, Graduate Program in Art History, New Brunswick NJ (S)

Small, Lawrence, *Secy,* Smithsonian Institution, Washington DC

Small, Lisa, *Cur, Exhibs,* Brooklyn Museum, Brooklyn NY

Smalley, Camille, *Programs & Educ Mgr,* Saco Museum, Saco ME

Smalley, David, *Prof,* Connecticut College, Dept of Art, New London CT (S)

Smalley, Gail, *Office Mgr,* Lynnwood Arts Centre, Simcoe ON

Smalls, James, *Prof,* University of Maryland, Baltimore County, Imaging & Digital Arts (IMDA), Dept of Visual Arts, Baltimore MD (S)

Smallwood, Donnely, *Instr,* Toronto School of Art, Toronto ON (S)

Smart, Tom, *Exec Dir & CEO,* McMichael Canadian Art Collection, Kleinburg ON

Smart Martin, Ann, *Assoc Prof,* University of Wisconsin, Madison, Dept of Art History, Madison WI (S)

Smeland, Celeste, *Dir Develop,* Kala Institute, Kala Art Institute, Berkeley CA

Smelko, James J, *Interior Design,* Art Institute of Pittsburgh, Pittsburgh PA (S)

Smetak, Robert, *Dir Financial Services,* The Illinois Institute of Art - Chicago, Chicago IL (S)

Smetana, David, *Chmn Art Comt,* North Canton Public Library, The Little Art Gallery, North Canton OH

Smetana, Zbynek, *Lectr,* Murray State University, Dept of Art, Murray KY (S)

Smigocki, Stephen, *Prof,* Fairmont State College, Div of Fine Arts, Fairmont WV (S)

Smiley, Kristen, *Develop Assoc,* Cultural Council of Palm Beach County, Lake Worth FL

Smilkovich, Cora, *Exec Dir,* The Art Cafe, Davison MI

Smit, David, *Assoc Prof,* Illinois Central College, Arts & Communication Dept, East Peoria IL (S)

Smith, Allison, *Assoc Prof Art History & Chair Art History,* Johnson County Community College, Fine Arts Dept & Art History Dept, Overland Park KS (S)

Smith, Ann, *Chmn Dept Art,* Howard Payne University, Dept of Art, Brownwood TX (S)

Smith, Ann, *Cur,* Mattatuck Historical Society, Library, Waterbury CT

Smith, Arthur, *Library Mgr,* Royal Ontario Museum, Library & Archives, Toronto ON

Smith, B J, *Dir,* Oklahoma State University, Gardiner Art Gallery, Stillwater OK

Smith, Barb, *Preparator,* University of Missouri, Museum of Art & Archaeology, Columbia MO

Smith, Bob, *Contact,* Buena Vista Museum of Natural History, Bakersfield CA

Smith, Brad, *Assoc Prof,* University of Michigan, Ann Arbor, School of Art & Design, Ann Arbor MI (S)

Smith, Bradley, *Cur,* Pennsylvania Historical & Museum Commission, Railroad Museum of Pennsylvania, Harrisburg PA

Smith, Bradley K, *Cur Adminr,* Pennsylvania Historical & Museum Commission, The State Museum of Pennsylvania, Harrisburg PA

Smith, Brena, *Reference & Instruction Librn,* California Institute of the Arts Library, Santa Clarita CA

Smith, Brenda, *Conservator,* University of Regina, MacKenzie Art Gallery, Regina SK

Smith, Brian, *Photo Lab Technician,* Trust Authority, Museum of the Great Plains, Lawton OK

Smith, C, *Prof,* Community College of Rhode Island, Dept of Art, Warwick RI (S)

Smith, C Martin, *Product Design Chmn,* Art Center College of Design, Pasadena CA (S)

Smith, C Shaw, *Chmn,* Davidson College, Art Dept, Davidson NC (S)

Smith, Carmen, *Dir Educ,* Southern Methodist University, Meadows Museum, Dallas TX

Smith, Carol, *Sr Librn,* Jacksonville Public Library, Fine Arts & Recreation Dept, Jacksonville FL

Smith, Carol, *VPres,* Carteret County Historical Society, The History Place, Morehead City NC

Smith, Carolyn, *Librn,* Johns Hopkins University, George Peabody Library, Baltimore MD

Smith, Catherine, *Pres,* Mattatuck Historical Society, Mattatuck Museum, Waterbury CT

Smith, Catherine Howett, *Assoc Dir,* Emory University, Michael C Carlos Museum, Atlanta GA

Smith, Charles, *Instr,* Southern University A & M College, School of Architecture, Baton Rouge LA (S)

Smith, Christy, *Student Svcs,* Maine Photographic Workshops, The International T.V. & Film Workshops & Rockport College, Rockport ME (S)

Smith, Clare M, *Dir,* Morven Museum & Garden, Princeton NJ

Smith, Claude, *Prof,* Western New Mexico University, Dept of Expressive Arts, Silver City NM (S)

Smith, Claudia, *Prof,* University of Wisconsin-Stout, Dept of Art & Design, Menomonie WI (S)

Smith, Corrine, *Adj Prof,* Augustana College, Art Dept, Rock Island IL (S)

Smith, Craig, *Assoc Prof,* University of Florida, School of Art & Art History, Gainesville FL (S)

Smith, Craig, *Instr,* American River College, Dept of Art/Art New Media, Sacramento CA (S)

Smith, Curtis, *Instr Music,* University of Colorado-Colorado Springs, Visual & Performing Arts Dept (VAPA), Colorado Springs CO (S)

Smith, Cynthia, *Cur,* Cooper-Hewitt National Design Museum, Smithsonian Institution, New York NY

Smith, Darold, *Prof,* West Texas A&M University, Art, Theatre & Dance Dept, Canyon TX (S)

Smith, David, *Assoc Prof,* University of New Hampshire, Dept of Arts & Art History, Durham NH (S)

Smith, David, *Assoc Prof,* Edgewood College, Art Dept, Madison WI (S)

Smith, David, *Exhib Mgr,* Contemporary Art Museum St Louis, Saint Louis MO

Smith, David, *Pres,* Nova Scotia College of Art and Design, Anna Leonowens Gallery, Halifax NS

Smith, David, *Pres,* Brewton-Parker College, Visual Arts, Mount Vernon GA (S)

Smith, David J B, *Pres,* Nova Scotia College of Art & Design, Halifax NS (S)

Smith, Debbie Williamson, *Communs Mgr,* University of Oregon, Jordan Schnitzer Museum of Art, Eugene OR

Smith, Diane, *Chmn Acad Studies Dept,* Art Academy of Cincinnati, Cincinnati OH (S)

Smith, Dickson K, *Dean Arts & Scis,* Cardinal Stritch University, Art Dept, Milwaukee WI (S)

Smith, Don, *Dean,* Maryland College of Art & Design, Silver Spring MD (S)

Smith, Doug, *Instr,* Modesto Junior College, Arts Humanities & Communications Division, Modesto CA (S)

Smith, Edward, *Asst,* Louisiana State University, School of Art, Baton Rouge LA (S)

Smith, Elise, *Chmn,* Millsaps College, Dept of Art, Jackson MS (S)

Smith, Elizabeth, *Exec Dir,* Sharon Arts Center, Sharon Arts Center Exhibition Gallery, Peterborough NH

Smith, Elizabeth B, *Assoc Prof,* Pennsylvania State University, University Park, Dept of Art History, University Park PA (S)

Smith, Emily, *Exec Dir,* 1708 Gallery, Richmond VA

Smith, Emily, *Research Fel Modern & Contemporary Art,* Virginia Museum of Fine Arts, Richmond VA

Smith, Frederick M R, *Treas,* Aperture Foundation, New York NY

Smith, Gary T, *Dir,* Hartnell College Gallery, Salinas CA

Smith, George, *Asst Prof,* University of the District of Columbia, Dept of Mass Media, Visual & Performing Arts, Washington DC (S)

Smith, George, *Prof Emeritus,* Rice University, Visual & Dramatic Arts, Houston TX (S)

Smith, Gil R, *Chmn,* Eastern Kentucky University, Art Dept, Richmond KY (S)

Smith, Greg, *Dir Info & Tech Svcs,* Canadian Museum of Nature, Musee Canadien de la Nature, Ottawa ON

Smith, Gregory, *VPres,* Society for Commercial Archeology, Little AR

Smith, Gregory A, *Pres,* Art Academy of Cincinnati, Cincinnati OH (S)

Smith, Gregory Allgiire, *Exec Dir,* Virginia Center for the Creative Arts, Amherst VA

Smith, Gregory Jay, *Prep,* Williams College, Museum of Art, Williamstown MA

Smith, Greta, *Library Asst,* Old Colony Historical Society, Library, Taunton MA

Smith, Heather, *Cur,* Moose Jaw Art Museum, Inc, Art & History Museum, Moose Jaw SK

Smith, Howard, *Adj Asst Prof,* College of Staten Island, Performing & Creative Arts Dept, Staten Island NY (S)

Smith, Ian, *Pres Bd Dir,* Santa Barbara Contemporary Arts Forum, Santa Barbara CA

Smith, Jack, *VPres,* Westmoreland Museum of American Art, Art Reference Library, Greensburg PA

Smith, James F, *Registrar,* Carleton College, Art Gallery, Northfield MN

Smith, Jeanette, *Mus Shop Mgr,* Cape Ann Historical Association, Cape Ann Museum, Gloucester MA

Smith, Jeff, *Cur,* Columbia River Maritime Museum, Astoria OR

Smith, Jeff, *Cur,* Columbia River Maritime Museum, Library, Astoria OR

Smith, Jennifer, *Assoc Cur,* Washington County Museum of Fine Arts, Hagerstown MD

Smith, Jerry, *Cur American & Western Art,* Phoenix Art Museum, Phoenix AZ

Smith, Jessica, *Cur American Art,* The Huntington Library, Art Collections & Botanical Gardens, San Marino CA

Smith, Jessica, *Publicity,* Ellen Noel Art Museum of the Permian Basin, Odessa TX

Smith, Jessie Carney, *Univ Librn,* Fisk University, Library, Nashville TN

Smith, Jill, *Develop Officer,* Urbanglass, Robert Lehman Gallery, Brooklyn NY

Smith, Jo, *Office Mgr, Dir,* Marin Society of Artists Inc, Ross CA

Smith, John, *Dir,* Archives of American Art, Smithsonian Institution, Washington DC

Smith, John O, *Prof,* University of Wisconsin-Stevens Point, Dept of Art & Design, Stevens Point WI (S)

Smith, Joseph, *Studio Chmn,* Mount Holyoke College, Art Dept, South Hadley MA (S)

Smith, Joseph E, *Prof,* Oakland City University, Division of Fine Arts, Oakland City IN (S)

Smith, Josh, *Asst Prof,* Asbury University, Art Dept, Wilmore KY (S)

Smith, Joshua, *Gallery Mgr,* Salina Art Center, Salina KS

Smith, Judith, *Pres,* Gallery West Ltd, Alexandria VA

Smith, Jury, *Prof Ceramics,* Saint Joseph's University, Art Dept, Philadelphia PA (S)

Smith, Karen Burgess, *VPres Acad Affairs,* New Hampshire Institute of Art, Manchester NH

Smith, Katherine, *Facilities Coordr,* African American Museum of Iowa, Cedar Rapids IA

Smith, Kathy, *Admin Dir,* Riverside Art Museum, Library, Riverside CA

Smith, Kendall, *Dir,* Art Museum of Greater Lafayette, Lafayette IN

Smith, Kent, *Dir Art,* Illinois State Museum, Museum Store, Chicago IL

Smith, Kevin, *Instr,* Langara College, Department of Design: Design Formation, Vancouver BC (S)

Smith, Kevin P, *Deputy Dir & Cur,* Brown University, Haffenreffer Museum of Anthropology, Providence RI

Smith, Kimberly, *Assoc Prof,* Southwestern University, Sarofim School of Fine Art, Dept of Art & Art History, Georgetown TX (S)

Smith, Laura, *Mus Academy Dir,* Huntsville Museum of Art, Huntsville AL

Smith, Laura S, *Chief Advancement Officer,* National Assembly of State Arts Agencies, Washington DC

Smith, Leah, *Serials & Acquisitions Technician,* National Air and Space Museum, Archives, Washington DC

Smith, Leah, *Tour Coordr,* Academy of the New Church, Glencairn Museum, Bryn Athyn PA

Smith, Letitia, *Grad Program Admin,* Bard College, Center for Curatorial Studies and the Hessel Museum of Art, Annandale-on-Hudson NY

Smith, Lisa Deanne, *Asst Coordr,* OCAD University, Student Gallery, Toronto ON

Smith, Lisa Deanne, *Co-Dir,* YYZ Artists' Outlet, Toronto ON

Smith, Liz, *Assoc Prof,* University of Central Arkansas, Department of Art, Conway AR (S)

Smith, Lucy, *Develop Dir,* Hockaday Museum of Art, Kalispell MT

Smith, Luther, *Prof,* Texas Christian University, School of Art, Fort Worth TX (S)

Smith, Lyn, *Dir Educ,* The Dairy Barn Arts Center, Athens OH

Smith, Lynn, *A/V Archivist,* National Archives & Records Administration, Herbert Hoover Presidential Library - Museum, West Branch IA

Smith, Maie, *Group Tour Mgr,* Delta Blues Museum, Clarksdale MS

Smith, Malcolm, *Assoc Prof,* Indiana University, Bloomington, Henry Radford Hope School of Fine Arts, Bloomington IN (S)

Smith, Marcee, *Human Resources Mgr & Mus Store Coordr,* Oklahoma City Museum of Art, Oklahoma City OK

Smith, Margaret Park, *Instr,* Asbury University, Art Dept, Wilmore KY (S)

Smith, Mariann, *Cur Educ,* The Buffalo Fine Arts Academy, Albright-Knox Art Gallery, Buffalo NY

Smith, Marilyn, *Dir,* Southern Alberta Art Gallery, Lethbridge AB

Smith, Marilyn, *Dir,* Southern Alberta Art Gallery, Library, Lethbridge AB

Smith, Marilyn, *Prof,* Appalachian State University, Dept of Art, Boone NC (S)

Smith, Mark, *Mgr Mktg, Commun & Events,* African American Museum, Dallas TX

Smith, Mark, *Prof,* Austin College, Art Dept, Sherman TX (S)

Smith, Mark Addison, *Asst Prof,* City College of New York, Art Dept, New York NY (S)

Smith, Martie, *Art,* Union County Public Library Union Room, Monroe NC

Smith, Mary Ruth, *Prof,* Baylor University - College of Arts and Sciences, Dept of Art, Waco TX (S)

Smith, Maureen, *Bus & Progs Coordr,* University of Toronto, University of Toronto Art Centre, Toronto ON

Smith, Megan, *Exhibs Coordr,* Grolier Club Library, New York NY

Smith, Melinda K, *Assoc Dir,* United States Senate Commission on Art, Washington DC

Smith, Michael, *CFO,* The Mint Museum, Art Organization & Library, Charlotte NC

Smith, Michael, *Dir Finance & Admin,* The Mint Museum, Charlotte NC

Smith, Michael, *Facility Mgr,* New Britain Museum of American Art, New Britain CT

Smith, Michael, *Prof,* East Tennessee State University, College of Arts and Sciences, Dept of Art & Design, Johnson City TN (S)

Smith, Michael V, *Asst Prof (creative writing),* University of British Columbia Okanagan, Dept of Creative Studies, Kelowna BC (S)

Smith, Michele L, *Exec Dir,* Wassenberg Art Center, Van Wert OH

Smith, Mike, *Artist,* Walker's Point Artists Assoc Inc, Gallery 218, Milwaukee WI

Smith, Mirenda, *Exec Dir & Cur,* Bergstrom-Mahler Museum, Library, Neenah WI

Smith, Monica, *Conservator,* Vancouver Art Gallery, Vancouver BC

Smith, Morgan, *Exec Dir,* Bainbridge Island Arts Council, Bainbridge Island WA

Smith, Nan, *Prof,* University of Florida, School of Art & Art History, Gainesville FL (S)

Smith, Nelson, *Chmn & Asst Prof,* Marygrove College, Department of Art, Detroit MI (S)

Smith, Patricia F, *Vol Chmn,* Sea Cliff Village Museum, Sea Cliff NY

Smith, Patrick, *Cur,* Connecticut State Library, Museum of Connecticut History, Hartford CT

Smith, Paul, *Preparator,* Southern Alberta Art Gallery, Lethbridge AB

Smith, Paul, *Tech Supvr,* Concordia University, Leonard & Bina Ellen Art Gallery, Montreal PQ

Smith, Philip, *Asst Dir,* University of Tennessee, Visual Arts Committee, Knoxville TN

Smith, Rachel, *Assoc Prof, Gilkison Family Chair in Art History,* Taylor University, Visual Art Dept, Upland IN (S)

Smith, Rae, *Pres,* Pastel Society of America, National Arts Club, Grand Gallery, New York NY

Smith, Rebecca, *Secy,* Marcella Sembrich Memorial Association Inc, Marcella Sembrich Opera Museum, Bolton Landing NY

Smith, Rene, *Adj Prof,* Saint Thomas Aquinas College, Art Dept, Sparkill NY (S)

Smith, Renee, *Asst Dir,* Louisiana State University School of Art, Alfred C Glassell Jr Exhibition Gallery, Baton Rouge LA

Smith, Renee, *Bd Pres,* Yuma Fine Arts Association, Yuma Art Center, Yuma AZ

Smith, Rhonda, *Admin Dir,* Morgan County Foundation, Inc, Madison-Morgan Cultural Center, Madison GA

Smith, Rhonda, *Chair & Coordr Non-Toxic Printmaking,* Shepherd University, Dept of Contemporary Art & Theater, Shepherdstown WV (S)

Smith, Richard E, *Prof & Studio Area Head,* Southern Illinois University, School of Art & Design, Carbondale IL (S)

Smith, Rob, *Dir,* Lachenmeyer Arts Center, Art Resource Library, Cushing OK

Smith, Robert, *Chmn Fine Arts,* Milwaukee Institute of Art & Design, Milwaukee WI (S)

Smith, Robert Michael, *Pres,* Sculptors Guild, Inc, Brooklyn NY

Smith, Robert W, *Caretaker,* 1890 House-Museum & Center for the Arts, Cortland NY

Smith, Robynn, *Painting Instr,* Monterey Peninsula College, Art Dept/Art Gallery, Monterey CA (S)

Smith, Ronni, *Galleria & Visitor Serv Mgr,* Hickory Museum of Art, Inc, Hickory NC

Smith, Roxanne E, *Tourism Supvr,* Nebraska State Capitol, Lincoln NE

Smith, Sabrina, *Mktg Communs Dir,* Exploratorium, San Francisco CA

Smith, Sarah, *Dir Mktg & Communs,* Reynolda House Museum of American Art, Winston-Salem NC

Smith, Scott, *Asst Prof,* Alabama A & M University, Art & Art Education Dept, Normal AL (S)

Smith, Sharon, *Prof Emeritus,* California State University, Chico, Department of Art & Art History, Chico CA (S)

Smith, Shelby B, *Cur & Gallery Mgr,* Volcano Art Center Gallery, Hawaii Volcanoes National Park HI

Smith, Sherri, *Prof,* University of Michigan, Ann Arbor, School of Art & Design, Ann Arbor MI (S)

Smith, Stephanie, *Deputy Dir & Chief Cur,* University of Chicago, Smart Museum of Art, Chicago IL

Smith, Stephanie, *Instr,* Ouachita Baptist University, Dept of Visual Art, Arkadelphia AR (S)

Smith, Sterling, *Chief Prep,* University of Wyoming, University of Wyoming Art Museum, Laramie WY

Smith, Susan, *Treas,* New Mexico Art League, Gallery & School, Albuquerque NM

Smith, T'Ai, *Asst Prof,* University of British Columbia, Dept of Art History, Visual Art & Theory, Vancouver BC (S)

Smith, Tamytha, *Educ Coordr,* Southern Methodist University, Meadows Museum, Dallas TX

Smith, Tara, *Cur Asst,* California Center for the Arts, Escondido Museum, Escondido CA

Smith, Terence, *Mellon Prof,* University of Pittsburgh, Henry Clay Frick Dept History of Art & Architecture, Pittsburgh PA (S)

Smith, Terry, *Assoc Dir Fin,* Norman Rockwell Museum, Stockbridge MA

Smith, Thomas, *Dir Petrie Institute of Western American Art,* Denver Art Museum, Denver CO

Smith, Thomas H, *Asst Prof,* Park University, Dept of Art & Design, Parkville MO (S)

Smith, Thomas O, *Chmn,* Grambling State University, Art Dept, Grambling LA (S)

Smith, Timothy B, *Asst Prof,* Birmingham-Southern College, Art & Art History, Birmingham AL (S)

Smith, Timothy H, *Research Asst,* Adams County Historical Society, Gettysburg PA

Smith, Tina, *Museum Educ,* Wake Forest University, Museum of Anthropology, Winston Salem NC

Smith, Virginia, *Chmn,* Bernard M Baruch College of the City University of New York, Art Dept, New York NY (S)

Smith, Ya'Ke, *Asst Prof,* University of Texas at Arlington, Art & Art History Department, Arlington TX (S)

Smith-Abbott, Katherine, *Vis Asst Prof,* Middlebury College, History of Art & Architecture Dept, Middlebury VT (S)

Smith-Bove, Holly, *CFO,* Springfield Museums, Springfield Science Museum, Springfield MA

Smith-Bove, Holly, *Pres,* Springfield Museums, Michele & Donald D'Amour Museum of Fine Arts, Springfield MA

Smith-Ferri, Sherrie, *Dir,* City of Ukiah, Grace Hudson Museum & The Sun House, Ukiah CA

Smith-Hunter, Susan, *Chmn,* Green Mountain College, Dept of Art, Poultney VT (S)

Smith-Talbott, Monica, *Instr,* Harrisburg Area Community College, Division of Communications, Humanities & the Arts, Harrisburg PA (S)

Smith de Tarnowsky, Andrea, *Cur,* T C Steele, Nashville IN

Smith Lake, Kendal, *Pub Information Officer,* Modern Art Museum, Fort Worth TX

Smith Shafts, Karen, *Asst Keeper of Prints,* Boston Public Library, Albert H Wiggin Gallery & Print Department, Boston MA

Smithson, Sandra, *Instr,* Millsaps College, Dept of Art, Jackson MS (S)

Smits, Kathy, *Shop Mgr,* Bergstrom-Mahler Museum, Library, Neenah WI

Smoak, Janet, *Dir,* Besser Museum for Northeast Michigan, Alpena MI

Smogor, Robert, *Registrar,* University of Notre Dame, Snite Museum of Art, Notre Dame IN

Smoke, Joe, *Cultural Grant Prog Dir,* City of Los Angeles, Cultural Affairs Dept, Los Angeles CA

Smolinsky, Matthew, *Instr,* University of Maine, Dept of Art, Orono ME (S)

Smotherman, Ann, *Art Teacher,* Motlow State Community College, Art Dept, Tullahoma TN (S)

Smotrich, Hannah, *Asst Prof,* University of Michigan, Ann Arbor, School of Art & Design, Ann Arbor MI (S)

Smotrich, Keri, *Comm Coord,* James A Michener, Doylestown PA

Smutko, Paul, *Coll Mgr,* Museum of New Mexico, Museum of International Folk Art, Santa Fe NM

Smyrnios, Arleigh, *Dir Fine Art,* Kalamazoo Valley Community College, Center for New Media, Kalamazoo MI (S)

Smyth, Colleen, *Dir Educ,* Indiana State Museum, Indianapolis IN

Smyth, Mimi, *Develop Coordr,* Grass Roots Art & Community Effort (GRACE), Firehouse Gallery, Hardwick VT

Smythe, Dan, *Sr Media Rels Officer,* Canadian Museum of Nature, Musee Canadien de la Nature, Ottawa ON

Smythe, Elaine, *Head Special Colls,* Louisiana State University, Middleton Library, Baton Rouge LA

Smythe, James E, *Prof,* Western Carolina University, Dept of Art/College of Arts & Science, Cullowhee NC (S)

Snail, Mike, *Planetarium Producer,* Louisiana Arts & Science Museum, Baton Rouge LA

Snapp, Brian, *Assoc Prof,* University of Utah, Dept of Art & Art History, Salt Lake City UT (S)

Snelgrove, Sheila, *Exec Asst,* George R Gardiner, Toronto ON

Snell, Shawana, *Circ Mgr,* Corcoran Gallery of Art, Corcoran Library, Washington DC

Snell, Walter, *VPres,* Halifax Historical Society, Inc, Halifax Historical Museum, Daytona Beach FL

Snellenburg, Jonathan, *2nd VPres,* National Antique & Art Dealers Association of America, Inc, New York NY

Snibbe, Robert, *Pres,* Napoleonic Society of America, Museum & Library, Saint Helena CA

Snider, Karen, *Deputy Dir Exhibits,* Children's Museum of Manhattan, New York NY

Snoddy, Suzie, *Admin,* Museum of Southern History, Houston TX

Snoddy, Suzie, *Dir,* Houston Baptist University, Museum of American Architecture and Decorative Arts, Houston TX

Snodgrass, Susan, *Pres,* Gilpin County Arts Association, Central City CO

Snook, Randy, *Instr,* Sierra Community College, Art Dept, Rocklin CA (S)

Snouffer, Karen F, *Prof,* Kenyon College, Art Dept, Gambier OH (S)

Snow, Maryly, *Librn,* University of California, Berkeley, Architecture Visual Resources Library, Berkeley CA

Snowden, Gilda, *Chmn Fine Arts,* College for Creative Studies, Detroit MI (S)

Snowden, Gilda, *Gallery Dir,* Detroit Repertory Theatre Gallery, Detroit MI

Snowman, Tracy, *Instr,* Spoon River College, Art Dept, Canton IL (S)

Snyder, Barry, *Prof,* Fairmont State College, Div of Fine Arts, Fairmont WV (S)

Snyder, Charlie, *Dir Communs,* Colorado Springs Fine Arts Center, Taylor Museum, Colorado Springs CO

Snyder, Gerry, *Chmn,* College of Santa Fe, Art Dept, Santa Fe NM (S)

Snyder, Jackie, *Exec Dir,* Design Commission of the City of New York, New York NY

Snyder, Janet, *Prof,* West Virginia University, College of Creative Arts, School of Art & Design, Morgantown WV (S)

Snyder, Jennifer, *Admin,* Fetherston Foundation, Packwood House Museum, Lewisburg PA

Snyder, Jill, *Dir,* Museum of Contemporary Art Cleveland, Library, Cleveland OH

Snyder, Jill, *Exec Dir,* Museum of Contemporary Art Cleveland, Cleveland OH

Snyder, Kimberly, *Develop Dir,* Grace Museum, Inc, Abilene TX

Snyder, Mark, *Asst Prof,* University of Hartford, Hartford Art School, West Hartford CT (S)

Snyder, Monica, *Gallery Asst,* Buckham Fine Arts Project, Gallery, Flint MI

Snyder, Nicole, *Pres Bd Trustees,* Boise Art Museum, Boise ID

Snyder, Patricia, *Exec Dir,* East End Arts & Humanities Council, Riverhead NY

Snyder, Randy, *Chmn Fine Arts Dept,* San Jacinto College-North, Art Dept, Houston TX (S)

Snyder, Richard, *Pres,* Hendricks Hill Museum, Southport ME

Snyder, Robin D, *Chmn,* Samford University, Art Dept, Birmingham AL (S)

Snyder, Sheryl, *Admin Asst,* Adams County Historical Society, Gettysburg PA

Snyder, Stephanie, *Dir,* Reed College, Douglas F Cooley Memorial Art Gallery, Portland OR

Snyder-Grenier, Ellen, *Cur, Murtogh D Guinness Coll,* Morris Museum, Morristown NJ

Snyder-Grenier, Ellen, *Dir Spec Projects,* New Jersey Historical Society, Newark NJ

Soave, Sergio, *Chmn,* Ohio State University, Dept of Art, Columbus OH (S)

Sobiech-Munson, Ann, *Coordr Core Prog,* Iowa State University, Dept of Art & Design, Ames IA (S)

Sobolik, Bonnie, *Dir Develop,* North Dakota Museum of Art, Grand Forks ND

Sobral, Luis de Moura, *Instr,* Universite de Montreal, Dept of Art History, Montreal PQ (S)

Sobre, Judith, *Prof,* University of Texas at San Antonio, Dept of Art & Art History, San Antonio TX (S)

Sobsey, Leah, *Lectr,* University of North Carolina at Greensboro, Art Dept, Greensboro NC (S)

Sodaev, Rahatbek, *Instr,* Kirkwood Community College, Dept of Arts & Humanities, Cedar Rapids IA (S)

Sodervick, Bruce, *Assoc Prof,* Rochester Institute of Technology, School of Design, Rochester NY (S)

Soehner, Kenneth, *Arthur K Watson C,* The Metropolitan Museum of Art, New York NY

Soehner, Kenneth, *Chief Librn,* The Metropolitan Museum of Art, Museum Libraries, New York NY

Soenksen, Virginia, *Docent Coordr,* University of Virginia, The Fralin Museum of Art at the University of Virginia, Charlottesville VA

Softie, Tanja, *Assoc Prof,* University of Richmond, Dept of Art and Art History, Richmond VA (S)

Sogard, Carol, *Assoc Prof,* University of Utah, Dept of Art & Art History, Salt Lake City UT (S)

Sohi, Marilyn, *Registrar,* Madison Museum of Contemporary Art, Madison WI

Sojka, Nancy, *Cur Prints, Drawings & Photographs,* Detroit Institute of Arts, Detroit MI

Sok, Lisa, *Admin Coordr,* Brandywine Workshop, Center for the Visual Arts, Philadelphia PA

Sokochoff, Shari, *Mgr Finance & Opers,* University of Regina, MacKenzie Art Gallery, Regina SK

Sokol, David, *Chmn Dept Art & Art History,* University of Illinois at Chicago, College of Architecture, Chicago IL (S)

Sokoloff, Emily, *Trustee,* Miami Watercolor Society, Inc, Miami FL

Sokolove, Deborah, *Dir,* Wesley Theological Seminary, Henry Luce III Center for the Arts & Religion, Dadian Gallery, Washington DC

Sokolove, Nancy, *Instr,* Appalachian State University, Dept of Art, Boone NC (S)

Sokolowski, Thomas, *Dir,* The Andy Warhol Museum, Museum, Pittsburgh PA

Sole, Matthew, *Dir Bus Devel,* Pyramid Atlantic, Silver Spring MD

Solensky, Jeanne, *Librn Joseph Downs Coll of Manuscripts & Printed Ephemera,* Winterthur Museum, Garden & Library, Library, Winterthur DE

Soles, Kathleen A, *Assoc Prof,* Emmanuel College, Art Dept, Boston MA (S)

Soles, Teresa, *Instr,* West Shore Community College, Division of Humanities & Fine Arts, Scottville MI (S)

Solge, James, *Supt,* The Nemours Foundatioin, Nemours Mansion & Gardens, Wilmington DE

Solien, T L, *Prof,* University of Wisconsin, Madison, Dept of Art, Madison WI (S)

Solimon, Ron, *Pres & CEO,* Indian Pueblo Cultural Center, Albuquerque NM

Solis, Claudia, *Exec Dir,* Art League of Houston, Houston TX

Sollenberger, Emily, *Develop Mgr,* Maryland Art Place, Baltimore MD

Soller, Helaine, *Coordr Bd Mem,* Women in the Arts Foundation, Inc, Staten Island NY

Solno, Dave, *Interactive Instr,* The Art Institute of Cincinnati, AIC College of Design, Cincinnati OH (S)

Solomon, Ginger, *Art Appreciation,* Western Michigan University, Frostic School of Art, Kalamazoo MI (S)

Solomon, Mary Karen, *Chair,* Colorado Northwestern Community College, Art Dept, Rangely CO (S)

Solomon, Rachel, *Exec Asst Office Artistic Dir & Cur,* Museum of Contemporary Canadian Art, Toronto ON

Solomon-Kiefer, C, *Asst Prof,* McGill University, Dept of Art History, Montreal PQ (S)

Solomon Marino, Beth, *Gallery Dir & Art Instr,* Fullerton College Art Gallery, Fullerton CA

Solon, Lisa, *Adjunct Asst Prof,* Drew University, Art Dept, Madison NJ (S)

Solowan, Barbara, *Art Dir,* Canadian Art Foundation, Toronto ON

Soloway, Lynn, *Prof,* Concordia University, Art Dept, Seward NE (S)

Solt, Mary, *Exec Dir of Museum Reg,* The Art Institute of Chicago, Chicago IL

Somaio, Theresa, *Visual Resource Assoc,* Skidmore College, Lucy Scribner Library, Saratoga Springs NY

Somerdin, Steven, *Reference Librn & Adult Svcs,* Ames Free-Easton's Public Library, North Easton MA

Somers, David, *Cur,* Art Gallery of Peel, Peel Heritage Complex, Brampton ON

Somers, David, *Cur,* Art Gallery of Peel, Archives, Brampton ON

Somers, Eric, *Dir,* Dutchess Community College, Dept of Visual Arts, Poughkeepsie NY (S)

Somerson, Rosanne, *Interim Provost,* Rhode Island School of Design, Providence RI (S)

Somma, Rachel, *Communs Coordr,* Staten Island Museum, Staten Island NY

Sommer, Karen, *Bus Mgr,* University of Connecticut, William Benton Museum of Art, Storrs CT

Sommer, Lucia, *Assoc Ed Afterimage,* Visual Studies Workshop, Rochester NY (S)

Sommers, Lynda J, *Dir Gallery,* Alverno College Gallery, Art and Cultures Gallery, Milwaukee WI

Somone, Kay, *Instr,* The Art Institute of Cincinnati, AIC College of Design, Cincinnati OH (S)

Somple, Michael, *Registrar & Exhib Mgr,* Munson-Williams-Proctor Arts Institute, Museum of Art, Utica NY

Sonderman, Karen, *Library Dir,* North Canton Public Library, The Little Art Gallery, North Canton OH

Sonders, Carter S, *Chief Develop Officer,* Jamestown-Yorktown Foundation, Jamestown Settlement, Williamsburg VA

Song, Felicia, *Adult Svcs Coordr,* Lake Forest Library, Fine Arts Dept, Lake Forest IL

Songhurst-Thonet, Sarah, *Cur,* Art Gallery of Calgary, Calgary AB

Sonnema, Roy, *Art Dept Chmn,* University of Southern Colorado, College of Liberal & Fine Arts, Pueblo CO

Sonnema, Roy, *Chmn,* University of Southern Colorado, Dept of Art, Pueblo CO (S)

Sonnema, Roy B, *Assoc Prof,* Georgia Southern University, Dept of Art, Statesboro GA (S)

Sonnichsen, Michael, *Instr,* University of North Carolina at Chapel Hill, Art Dept, Chapel Hill NC (S)

Sookrah, Andrew, *VPres Exhibs,* Society of Canadian Artists, Toronto ON

Soorikian, Diana, *Dir,* Fairleigh Dickinson University, Edward Williams Gallery, Hackensack NJ

Sopotiuk, Owen, *Preparator & Colls Mgr,* University of British Columbia, Morris & Helen Belkin Art Gallery, Vancouver BC

Sorel, Paul, *Assoc Dir,* New England Center for Contemporary Art, Brooklyn CT

Sorensen, Lee, *Art Librn,* Duke University, Lilly Art Library, Durham NC

Sorenson-Clem, Sherri, *Asst Cur, Photographs, & Prints,* University of New Mexico, University of New Mexico Art Museum, Albuquerque NM

Soriano, Irene, *Co-Chair,* Santa Ana College, Art Dept, Santa Ana CA (S)

Sorrell, Robert, *Asst Prof,* College of Santa Fe, Art Dept, Santa Fe NM (S)

Sorrell, Sonia, *Assoc Prof,* Pepperdine University, Seaver College, Dept of Art, Malibu CA (S)

Sorrell, Thomas, *Pres,* Toledo Artists' Club, Toledo Artists' Club & Gallery, Toledo OH

Sotelo, Melissa, *Coll Coordr,* University of Illinois at Urbana-Champaign, Spurlock Museum, Champaign IL

Soucek, Priscilla P, *Deputy Dir,* New York University, Institute of Fine Arts, New York NY (S)

Soule, Debora Thaxton, *Dir,* Sweetwater County Library System and School District #1, Community Fine Arts Center, Rock Springs WY

Sourakli, Judy, *Cur Coll,* Henry Gallery Association, Henry Art Gallery, Seattle WA

Sourakli, Judy, *Cur Coll,* University of Washington, Henry Art Gallery, Seattle WA

Soussloff, Catherine, *Prof,* University of British Columbia, Dept of Art History, Visual Art & Theory, Vancouver BC (S)

South, Jessamy, *Youth & Family Programs Coordr,* Columbus Museum, Columbus GA

South, Will, *Chief Cur,* Dayton Art Institute, Dayton OH

Southall, Thomas, *Cur Photography,* University of Florida, Samuel P Harn Museum of Art, Gainesville FL

Southall, Tom, *Cur Photography,* High Museum of Art, Atlanta GA

Souther, Rita, *Progs Coordr,* California College of the Arts, CCAC Wattis Institute for Contemporary Arts, San Francisco CA

Southworth, Michael, *Chmn City & Regional Planning,* University of California, Berkeley, College of Environmental Design, Berkeley CA (S)

Southworth, Michael, *Instr,* University of South Carolina at Aiken, Dept of Visual & Performing Arts, Aiken SC (S)

Southworth, Miles F, *Prof,* Rochester Institute of Technology, School of Printing Management & Sciences, Rochester NY (S)

Sovern, Michael I, *Chmn,* American Academy in Rome, New York NY (S)

Sowd, Laurie, *Assoc VPres Operations,* The Huntington Library, Art Collections & Botanical Gardens, Library, San Marino CA

Sowd, Laurie, *Assoc VPres Opers,* The Huntington Library, Art Collections & Botanical Gardens, San Marino CA

Sowden, Alison, *VPres Financial Affairs,* The Huntington Library, Art Collections & Botanical Gardens, San Marino CA

Sowder, Cheryl, *Assoc Prof Art Hist,* Jacksonville University, Dept of Art, Theater, Dance, Jacksonville FL (S)

Sowiak, Christine, *Cur Art,* University of Calgary, Nickle Galleries, Calgary AB

Sowinski, Larry, *Dir,* Knights of Columbus Supreme Council, Knights of Columbus Museum, New Haven CT

Sowiski, Peter, *Chmn,* State University of New York College at Buffalo, Fine Arts Dept, Buffalo NY (S)

Soyka, Ed, *Chmn Fashion Illustrations,* Fashion Institute of Technology, Art & Design Division, New York NY (S)

Spadafora, David, *Pres & Librn,* Newberry Library, Chicago IL

Spadafora, Tracy, *Adj Instruc,* Quincy College, Art Dept, Quincy MA (S)

Spadaro, Barbara, *Treas,* High Wire Gallery, Philadelphia PA

Spagnol, Natalie, *Dir Opers,* Stephen Bulger Gallery, Toronto ON

Spagnolo, Francesco, *Cur Coll,* University of California, Berkeley, The Magnes Collection of Jewish Art & Life, Berkeley CA

Spahr, P Andrew, *Cur,* The Currier Museum of Art, Manchester NH

Spahr, Stephanie, *Curatorial Asst,* El Museo del Barrio, New York NY

Spaid, Gregory P, *Prof,* Kenyon College, Art Dept, Gambier OH (S)

Spain, Stacey, *Prog Mgr,* Sierra Arts Foundation, Sierra Arts Gallery, Reno NV (S)

Spalatin, Ivana, *Instr Art History,* Texas A&M University Commerce, Dept of Art, Commerce TX (S)

Spalding, Ann E, *Educ Coordr,* Maitland Art Center, Maitland FL

Spalding, Sherea, *Operations Dir,* Colorado Photographic Arts Center, Denver CO

Spallina, Emily, *Registrar,* Canajoharie Library & Art Gallery, Arkell Museum of Canajoharie, Canajoharie NY

Spanbauer, Trisha, *Office & Prog Mgr,* Lincoln Arts Council, Lincoln NE

Spangenberg, Kristin L, *Cur Prints & Drawings,* Cincinnati Art Museum, Cincinnati Art Museum, Cincinnati OH

Spangler, Bonnie, *Educ Dir,* Michelson Museum of Art, Marshall TX

Spangler, Cindy, *Registrar,* University of Tennessee, Ewing Gallery of Art and Architecture, Knoxville TN

Spangler, David R, *Pres,* St Martins College, Humanities Dept, Lacey WA (S)

Spangler, Gary, *Chmn Visual Arts,* Malone University, Dept of Art, Canton OH (S)

Spangler, Shawn, *Asst Prof Art,* Western Illinois University, Department of Art, Macomb IL (S)

Spanich, Deborah, *Registrar,* Randolph College, Maier Museum of Art, Lynchburg VA

Spanich, John, *Mus Preparator,* Randolph College, Maier Museum of Art, Lynchburg VA

Sparagana, John, *Prof,* Rice University, Visual & Dramatic Arts, Houston TX (S)

Sparklin, Sophia, *Adjunct Prof Art,* University of Great Falls, Art Dept, Great Falls MT (S)

Sparks, Rhonda, *Librn,* Cedarhurst Center for the Arts, Cedar Hurst Library, Mount Vernon IL

Sparrow, James, *Exec Dir,* Arts United of Greater Fort Wayne, Fort Wayne IN

Spataro, Peter, *Instr,* Art Center Sarasota, Sarasota FL (S)

Spatz-Rabinowitz, Elaine, *Assoc Prof,* Wellesley College, Art Dept, Wellesley MA (S)

Spaulding, Daniel, *Cur Collections,* Anniston Museum of Natural History, Anniston AL

Spaulding, Fred, *Adjunct Prof,* University of Texas at Arlington, Art & Art History Department, Arlington TX (S)

Spaulding, Fred, *Prof,* Victoria College, Fine Arts Dept, Victoria TX (S)

Spaulding, Karen Lee, *Deputy Dir,* The Buffalo Fine Arts Academy, Albright-Knox Art Gallery, Buffalo NY

Spear, Ellen, *Pres,* Hancock Shaker Village, Inc, Pittsfield MA

Spears, Dolores, *Cur,* Zigler Art Museum, Jennings LA

Spears, Kimberly, *Exec Dir,* Anderson County Arts Council, Anderson SC

Spears, Leslie, *Communs Mgr,* Oklahoma City Museum of Art, Oklahoma City OK

Spears, Susan, *Dir,* Michelson Museum of Art, Marshall TX

Specht, Andrea, *Exec Dir,* Bloomington Theatre & Art Center, Inez Greenberg Gallery, Bloomington MN

Speck, Erin, *Dept Chmn,* George Washington University, School of Interior Design, Washington DC (S)

Speck, Lawrence, *Dean,* University of Texas, School of Architecture, Austin TX (S)

Specter, David, *Bd Pres,* Neustadt Collection of Tiffany Glass, Long Island City NY

Specter, Patricia, *Treas,* Neustadt Collection of Tiffany Glass, Long Island City NY

Spector, Jack J, *Prof,* Rutgers, The State University of New Jersey, Graduate Program in Art History, New Brunswick NJ (S)

Spector, Nancy, *Deputy Dir & Chief Cur,* Solomon R Guggenheim, New York NY

Speed, Bonnie, *Dir,* Emory University, Michael C Carlos Museum, Atlanta GA

Speight, Jerry, *Prof,* Murray State University, Dept of Art, Murray KY (S)

Speigle, Elizabeth K, *Cur,* Yesteryear Village, West Palm Beach FL

Spellman-Grimes, Diane, *Art Lectr & Prog Coordr,* Burlington County College, Humanities & Fine Art Div, Pemberton NJ (S)

Spellman-Grimes, Diane, *Coordr, Asst Prof,* Cumberland County College, Humanities Div, Vineland NJ (S)

Spence, Catherine, *Library Asst,* University of Toronto, Fine Art Library, Toronto ON

Spence, Margaret, *Librn,* Arts and Letters Club of Toronto, Library, Toronto ON

Spence, Muneera U, *Asst Prof,* Oregon State University, Dept of Art, Corvallis OR (S)

Spence, Rachel, *Educ & Outreach,* Beck Center for the Arts, Lakewood OH

Spence, Scott, *Artistic Dir,* Beck Center for the Arts, Lakewood OH

Spencer, Amy, *Prog Coordr/Cur,* Pro Arts, Oakland CA

Spencer, Christina, *Educ Coordr,* Owatonna Arts Center, Owatonna MN

Spencer, Deirdre, *Head Fine Arts Library, Head Librn,* University of Michigan, Fine Arts Library, Ann Arbor MI

Spencer, Elizabeth, *1st VPres,* Salmagundi Club, New York NY

Stangeland, Bruce, *Pres,* California Watercolor Association, Gallery Concord, Concord CA

Stanger, Alexa, *Educ Dir,* The Art Museum of Eastern Idaho, Idaho Falls ID

Stanger, David, *Instr,* Seton Hill University, Art Program, Greensburg PA (S)

Stangl, Denise, *Asst to Dir,* Lehigh University Art Galleries, Museum Operation, Bethlehem PA

Stanicky, Paul, *Board Dirs,* Ukrainian Cultural & Educational Centre, Gallery, Winnipeg MB

Stanicky, Paul, *Pres Board Dirs,* Ukrainian Cultural & Educational Centre, Winnipeg MB

Stanicky, Paul, *Pres Board Dirs,* Ukrainian Cultural & Educational Centre, Library & Archives, Winnipeg MB

Stanionis, Lin, *Prof,* University of Kansas, The School of the Arts, Dept of Visual Art, Lawrence KS (S)

Stanis, Suzanne, *Educ & Information Dir,* Indiana Landmarks, Information Center Library, Indianapolis IN

Stanislow, Gail, *Coll Librn,* Brandywine Conservancy, Library, Chadds Ford PA

Stanitz, Mark, *Prof,* Rochester Institute of Technology, School of Design, Rochester NY (S)

Stankiewicz, Mary Ann, *Prof Art Educ,* Pennsylvania State University, University Park, Penn State School of Visual Arts, University Park PA (S)

Stanko, John, *Asst Prof,* Graceland University, Fine Arts Div, Lamoni IA (S)

Stanko, John, *Asst Prof,* University of Nebraska, Kearney, Dept of Art & Art History, Kearney NE (S)

Stanley, Annie, *Educ Coordr,* Ellen Noel Art Museum of the Permian Basin, Odessa TX

Stanley, B, *Dir,* District of Columbia Arts Center (DCAC), Washington DC

Stanley, Bruce, *Graphic Design Coordr,* Nossi College of Art, Nashville TN (S)

Stanley, Chris, *Assoc Prof,* University of Texas of Permian Basin, Dept of Art, Odessa TX (S)

Stanley, Diane, *Cur,* Southern Lorain County Historical Society, Spirit of '76 Museum, Elyria OH

Stanley, Eric, *Cur Exhibs & Collections,* Sonoma County Museum, Santa Rosa CA

Stanley, Janet L, *Librn,* National Museum of African Art, Warren M Robbins Library, Washington DC

Stanley, Jared, *Instr,* Bob Jones University, School of Fine Arts, Div of Art & Design, Greenville SC (S)

Stanley, Kathi, *Assoc Librn,* New York State Library, Manuscripts & Special Collections, Albany NY

Stanley, Lynn, *Educ Coordr,* Provincetown Art Association & Museum, Provincetown MA

Stanley, R Brent, *VPres Finance,* Americans for the Arts, New York NY

Stanley, Robert A, *Asst Prof,* Ashland University, Art Dept, Ashland OH (S)

Stanley, Susie, *Prof,* Lansing Community College, Visual Arts & Media Dept, Lansing MI (S)

Stanley, Tamar, *Dir,* Ravalli County Museum, Hamilton MT

Stanley, Teresa, *Chmn,* Humboldt State University, College of Arts & Humanities, Art Dept, Arcata CA (S)

Stanley, Tom, *Dir,* Winthrop University Galleries, Rock Hill SC

Stansberry, Tammy, *Mus Store Mgr,* Amerind Foundation, Inc, Amerind Museum, Fulton-Hayden Memorial Art Gallery, Dragoon AZ

Stanton, Anne Rudloff, *Chmn,* University of Missouri - Columbia, Art History & Archaeology Dept, Columbia MO (S)

Stanton, Edward, *Mgr Soc Independent Artists,* Archives of MOCA (Museum of Conceptual Art), Society of Independent Artists, San Francisco CA

Stanton, Meridith Z, *Dir,* United States Department of the Interior, Indian Arts & Crafts Board, Washington DC

Stanton, Susan, *Dir Access & Pres Servs,* Ministry of Alberta Culture, Provincial Archives of Alberta, Edmonton AB

Staples, Wayne, *Chmn & Prof,* Acadia University, Art Dept, Wolfville NS (S)

Stapleton, Doug, *Preparations & Asst Cur,* Illinois State Museum, Chicago Gallery, Chicago IL

Stapleton, Douglas, *Assoc Cur ISM Chicago Gallery,* Illinois State Museum, ISM Lockport Gallery, Chicago Gallery & Southern Illinois Art Gallery, Springfield IL

Starck, Sandra, *Assoc Prof,* University of Wisconsin-Eau Claire, Dept of Art & Design, Eau Claire WI (S)

Starett, Leanne, *Adminstr Asst,* Hockaday Museum of Art, Kalispell MT

Stark, Bonnie, *Asst Dir,* Big Horn County Historical Museum, Hardin MT

Stark, Johnnie, *Assoc Prof Interior Design,* University of North Texas, College of Visual Arts & Design, Denton TX (S)

Stark, Kathy, *Exhib Dir,* Grass Roots Art & Community Effort (GRACE), Firehouse Gallery, Hardwick VT

Stark, Mary, *Fine Arts Librn,* Beverly Hills Public Library, Fine Arts Library, Beverly Hills CA

Stark, Robert, *Dir,* Susquehanna Studio, Susquehanna Studio, Union Dale PA

Stark, Sonia, *Pres,* National Association of Women Artists, Inc, N.A.W.A. Gallery, New York NY

Stark, William, *Admin/Deputy Dir,* Mamie McFaddin Ward, Beaumont TX

Starkey, Sherri, *Operations Coordr,* Arizona State University, Deer Valley Rock Art Center, Phoenix AZ

Starkey, Willow, *Curatorial Asst,* California State University, Chico, Janet Turner Print Museum, CSU, Chicago, Chico CA

Starks, Beverly, *Librn,* Watkins College of Art, Design & Film, Library, Nashville TN

Starling, Anna, *Develop Dir,* Art in General, New York NY

Starling, Zoe, *Cur Educ,* North Carolina State University, Gregg Museum of Art & Design, Raleigh NC

Starr, Daniel, *Assoc Chief Librn,* The Metropolitan Museum of Art, Museum Libraries, New York NY

Starr, Lori, *Exec Dir,* Koffler Centre of the Arts, Koffler Gallery, Toronto ON

Starr, Tom, *Assoc Prof,* Northeastern University, Dept of Art & Architecture, Boston MA (S)

Starr, Tyler, *Prof,* Davidson College, Art Dept, Davidson NC (S)

Starrels, Josine Ianco, *Cur,* Southern Oregon University, Schneider Museum of Art, Ashland OR

Starrett, Judy L, *Owner,* Louisiana Pottery, Sorrento LA

Stasiak, Marilyn, *Cur Art,* Neville Public Museum of Brown County, Green Bay WI

Statham, Stephanie, *Library Technical Asst,* North Carolina State University, Harrye Lyons Design Library, Raleigh NC

Statlander, Raymond, *Assoc Prof,* New Jersey City University, Art Dept, Jersey City NJ (S)

Statz, Brian, *VP Opers & Gen Counsel,* The Children's Museum of Indianapolis, Indianapolis IN

Stauber, Jacob, *Operations Mgr,* Kirkland Museum of Fine & Decorative Art, Denver CO

St Aubyn, Jacklyn, *College Asst Prof,* New Mexico State University, Art Dept, Las Cruces NM (S)

Stauffer, George B, *Dean,* Rutgers, The State University of New Jersey, Mason Gross School of the Arts, Visual Arts Dept, New Brunswick NJ (S)

Stauffer, Randall, *Chmn Interior Design,* Woodbury University, Dept of Graphic Design, Burbank CA (S)

Staum, Sonja, *Dir,* Indiana University - Purdue University at Indianapolis, Herron School of Art Library, Indianapolis IN

Stausland, Lillian, *Instr,* Wagner College, Arts Administration Dept, Staten Island NY (S)

Staveloz, Auntaneshia, *Secy,* Association of African American Museums, Washington DC

Stavitsky, Gail, *Chief Cur,* Montclair Art Museum, Montclair NJ

Stavrinos, Tom, *Dir Opers,* Society of Illustrators, Museum of American Illustration, New York NY

Stayrook, Chad, *Gallery Dir,* Bronx River Art Center Inc, Gallery, Bronx NY

Stayton, Kevin, *Chief Cur,* Brooklyn Museum, Brooklyn NY

Steadman, Allison, *Asst Prof of Theatre,* Jacksonville University, Dept of Art, Theater, Dance, Jacksonville FL (S)

Steadman, Amanda, *Asst Cur,* Erie Art Museum, Erie PA

Steadman, Kandace, *Dir,* Museum of Utah Art & History, Salt Lake City UT

Steadman, Thomas, *Prof,* Georgia Southern University, Dept of Art, Statesboro GA (S)

Stealey, Jo, *Prof (Fibers),* University of Missouri - Columbia, Dept of Art, Columbia MO (S)

Stearns, Emily, *Dir,* Wenham Museum, Wenham MA

Stebbins, Joan, *Cur,* Southern Alberta Art Gallery, Library, Lethbridge AB

Stebbins, Joan, *Cur Spec Projects,* Southern Alberta Art Gallery, Lethbridge AB

Stebich, Stephanie, *Dir,* Tacoma Art Museum, Tacoma WA

Stechschulte, Brian, *Gallery Dir,* National Institute of Art & Disabilities (NIAD), Florence Ludins-Katz Gallery, Richmond CA

Steck, Stuart, *Chair Art History,* Lesley University, College of Art & Design, Boston MA (S)

Steedle, Bill, *Assoc Prof,* State University of New York at Farmingdale, Visual Communications, Farmingdale NY (S)

Steel, James, *Exec Dir,* Sunbury Shores Arts & Nature Centre, Inc, Gallery, Saint Andrews NB

Steel, Virginia Oberlin, *Dir & Cur,* Rutgers University, Stedman Art Gallery, Camden NJ

Steele, Curtis, *Assoc Prof,* Arkansas State University, Dept of Art, State University AR (S)

Steele, Curtis, *Chair Art Dept,* Arkansas State University-Art Department, Jonesboro, Fine Arts Center Gallery, Jonesboro AR

Steele, Jonathan, *Dean,* Saint Petersburg College, Fine & Applied Arts at Clearwater Campus, Clearwater FL (S)

Steele, Kelly, *Historic Preservation Off,* United States Senate Commission on Art, Washington DC

Steele, Keri, *Admin Asst,* Art Center of Battle Creek, Battle Creek MI

Steele, Keri, *Office Mgr,* Art Center of Battle Creek, Michigan Art & Artist Archives, Battle Creek MI

Steele, Linda, *Dir Community Rels,* The Art Institute of Chicago, Chicago IL

Steele, Lisa, *Assoc Chmn Visual Studies,* University of Toronto, Dept of Fine Arts, Toronto ON (S)

Steele, Michael, *Prof Head Dept,* South Dakota State University, Dept of Visual Arts, Brookings SD (S)

Steele, Priscilla, *Adjunct,* Coe College, Dept of Art, Cedar Rapids IA (S)

Steele, Susan, *Advertising & Publicity,* Society of Scribes, Ltd, New York NY

Steele, Valerie, *Dir,* Fashion Institute of Technology, The Museum at FIT, New York NY

Steele-Hamme, Nancy, *Chair,* Midwestern State University, Lamar D. Fain College of Fine Arts, Wichita Falls TX (S)

Steen, Bill, *Treas,* North Country Museum of Arts, Park Rapids MN

Steen, Karen, *Assoc Prof,* Cazenovia College, Center for Art & Design Studies, Cazenovia NY (S)

Steenburg, Nancy, *Pres,* New London County Historical Society, Shaw Mansion, New London CT

Steever, Lasley, *Prog & Events Mgr,* Gibbes Museum of Art, Charleston SC (S)

Steeves, Dan, *Lectr,* Mount Allison University, Dept of Fine Arts, Sackville NB (S)

Stefani, Robert, *Pres,* The National Art League, Douglaston NY

Steffen, Pam, *Prog Dir Interior Design,* Mount Mary College, Marian Gallery, Milwaukee WI

Steffen, Pamela, *Assoc Prof,* Mount Mary College, Art & Design Division, Milwaukee WI (S)

Steffensen, Jared, *Educ Dir,* Salt Lake Art Center, Utah Museum of Contemporary Art, Salt Lake City UT

Stefl, Bob, *Assoc Prof,* Lincoln College, Art Dept, Lincoln IL (S)

Steggles, Mary Ann, *Prof,* University of Manitoba, School of Art, Winnipeg MB (S)

Steglitz, Marc, *Sr Deputy Dir COO,* Solomon R Guggenheim, New York NY

Stein, Betty R, *Mus Shop Mgr,* Woodmere Art Museum Inc, Library, Philadelphia PA

Stein, Gil, *Dir,* University of Chicago, Oriental Institute, Chicago IL

Stein, Joan, *Head of Access Services,* Carnegie Mellon University, Hunt Library, Pittsburgh PA

Stein, Julie, *Dir,* University of Washington, Burke Museum of Natural History and Culture, Seattle WA

Stein, Lynn, *Artistic Dir,* Rockland Center for the Arts, West Nyack NY

Stein, Lynn, *Artistic Dir,* Rockland Center for the Arts, West Nyack NY (S)

Stein, Michael, *Faculty,* Housatonic Community College, Art Dept, Bridgeport CT (S)

Stein, Raymond, *Adjunct Asst Prof,* Drew University, Art Dept, Madison NJ (S)

Stein, Renata, *Art Cur,* Leo Baeck, New York NY

Stein, Renata, *Cur,* Leo Baeck, Library, New York NY

Stein, Rob, *Chief Information Officer, Dir of MIS,* Indianapolis Museum of Art, Indianapolis IN

Steinat, Rose, *Data Mgr,* National Air and Space Museum, Regional Planetary Image Facility, Washington DC

Steinbach, Ken, *Prof,* Bethel College, Dept of Art, Saint Paul MN (S)

Steinberg, Barbara, *Slide Librn,* University of New Hampshire, Dept of the Arts Slide Library, Durham NH

Steinberg, Bryan E, *Assoc Prof,* Rhode Island College, Art Dept, Providence RI (S)

Steinbrenner, Paul, *Treas,* Newport Historical Society & Museum of Newport History, Newport RI

Steinbrink, Nate, *Cur Exhibs,* Southern Illinois University Carbondale, University Museum, Carbondale IL

Steiner, Frederick, *Chmn Planning,* Arizona State University, College of Architecture & Environmental Design, Tempe AZ (S)

Steiner, Suzanne, *Assoc Chmn,* Carlow College, Art Dept, Pittsburgh PA (S)

Steinert, Elissa, *Sr Office Asst,* Texas Tech University, School of Art Visual Resource Center, Lubbock TX

Steinkeller, Piotr, *Cur Cuneiform Coll,* Harvard University, Semitic Museum, Cambridge MA

Steinle, John, *Adminr,* Jefferson County Open Space, Hiwan Homestead Museum, Evergreen CO

Steinmetz, Angela, *Registrar Loans & Exhib,* University of Chicago, Smart Museum of Art, Chicago IL

Steinway, Kate, *Deputy Dir Interpretation,* Connecticut Historical Society, Hartford CT

Steirnagle, Michael, *Assoc Prof,* Palomar Community College, Art Dept, San Marcos CA (S)

Stejer, Carl, *Instr,* Whitworth College, Art Dept, Spokane WA (S)

Stelioeswills, Alex, *Cur,* Mississippi University for Women, Fine Arts Gallery, Columbus MS

Stella, Dante, *Chmn Bd Dir,* Detroit Artists Market, Detroit MI

Stelzer, Stuart, *Library Dir,* University of the Ozarks, Robson Library, Clarksville AR

Stemwedel, Mark, *Instr,* South Dakota State University, Dept of Visual Arts, Brookings SD (S)

Stene, Larry M, *Prof,* Washington and Lee University, Div of Art, Lexington VA (S)

Stenhouse, Douglas, *Dir Bldg,* National Watercolor Society, San Pedro CA

Stenner, Jack, *Assoc Prof,* University of Florida, School of Art & Art History, Gainesville FL (S)

Stensaas, Starla, *Prof,* Dana College, Art Dept, Blair NE (S)

Stenstrom, Kurt, *Instr,* Oklahoma State University, Graphic Arts Dept, Visual Communications, Okmulgee OK (S)

Stentaford, Karen, *Lectr,* Mount Allison University, Dept of Fine Arts, Sackville NB (S)

Stentzel, Allen, *Adjunct,* Feather River Community College, Art Dept, Quincy CA (S)

Stenzel, Steve, *Vis Asst Prof,* Hamline University, Dept of Studio Arts & Art History, Saint Paul MN (S)

Stepanek, Stephanie, *Cur Prints & Drawings,* Museum of Fine Arts, Boston MA

Stephan, Mariam, *Prof,* University of North Carolina at Greensboro, Art Dept, Greensboro NC (S)

Stephanian, Charles, *Media Dir,* San Francisco Art Institute, Anne Bremer Memorial Library, San Francisco CA

Stephens, Carolyn, *Dept Chmn,* Spokane Falls Community College, Fine Arts Dept, Spokane WA (S)

Stephens, Dennis, *Coll Develop Officer,* University of Alaska, Elmer E Rasmuson Library, Fairbanks AK

Stephens, Harold, *Dir Finance,* Walters Art Museum, Library, Baltimore MD

Stephens, Jessica, *Educ Progs Mgr,* Morris Museum of Art, Augusta GA

Stephens, Mary, *CEO,* California State University, Long Beach Foundation, Long Beach CA

Stephens, Robert, *Assoc Prof,* Graceland University, Fine Arts Div, Lamoni IA (S)

Stephens, Sandra, *Asst Prof,* Munson-Williams-Proctor Arts Institute, Pratt MWP College of Art, Utica NY (S)

Stephenson, Carol Ann, *Office Mgr,* Harriet Beecher Stowe, Hartford CT

Stephenson, Kay, *Shop Mgr,* Wayne County Historical Society, Museum, Honesdale PA

Stephenson, Warren, *Library Technical Asst,* University of Maryland, College Park, Art Library, College Park MD

Stepic, Barbara, *Pres,* Brooklyn Historical Society, Brooklyn OH

Sterling, Susan Fisher, *Dir,* National Museum of Women in the Arts, Washington DC

Sterman, Chris, *Interpretive Progs & Tours,* Missouri Department of Natural Resources, Missouri State Museum, Jefferson City MO

Stern, Barry, *Dir,* C W Post Campus of Long Island University, Hillwood Art Museum, Brookville NY

Stern, Emily, *Chair,* The College of New Rochelle, School of Arts & Sciences Art Dept, New Rochelle NY (S)

Stern, Jean, *Exec Dir,* Irvine Museum, Irvine CA

Stern, John P, *Pres,* Storm King Art Center, Mountainville NY

Stern, Lindsay A, *Educ Coordr,* Center for Photography at Woodstock Inc, Woodstock NY

Stern, Robert, *Dean,* Yale University, School of Architecture, New Haven CT (S)

Stern, Selma, *Program Dir,* Long Beach Art League, Long Beach Library, Long Beach NY

Stern, Stacey P, *Office Mgr,* R L S Silverado Museum, Reference Library, Saint Helena CA

Stern, Ted, *Prof Music,* Glendale Community College, Visual & Performing Arts Div, Glendale CA (S)

Sternberger, Paul, *Deputy Chair,* Rutgers University, Newark, Arts, Culture & Media, Newark NJ (S)

Sterngold, Katherine, *Instr,* Lycoming College, Art Dept, Williamsport PA (S)

Sterrett, Jill, *Dir Conservation & Colls,* San Francisco Museum of Modern Art, San Francisco CA

Sterritt, Colleen, *Instr,* Long Beach City College, Art & Photography Dept, Long Beach CA (S)

Stetson, Carla, *Asst Prof,* Ithaca College, Fine Art Dept, Ithaca NY (S)

Stetson, Daniel, *Exec Dir,* Polk Museum of Art, Lakeland FL

Stevanov, Zoran, *Prof,* Fort Hays State University, Dept of Art & Design, Hays KS (S)

Steven, Moira, *Libr Dir,* Maine College of Art, Joanne Waxman Library, Portland ME

Steven, Robert, *Exec Dir & Cur,* Prairie Art Gallery, Grande Prairie AB

Stevens, Andrew, *Cur Prints, Drawings, Photos,* University of Wisconsin-Madison, Chazen Museum of Art, Madison WI

Stevens, Ann, *Exposure Copyeditor,* Society for Photographic Education (SPE), SPE Gallery, Cleveland OH

Stevens, Christopher, *Dir Develop,* Walker Art Center, Minneapolis MN

Stevens, Clark, *Secy,* Cincinnati Art Club, Cincinnati OH

Stevens, Dennis, *Dean College Liberal Arts,* University of Findlay, Art Program, Findlay OH (S)

Stevens, Don, *IT Tech/Mem Secy,* Sonoma Valley Historical Society, Depot Park Museum, Sonoma CA

Stevens, Edward B, *Chmn Emeritus,* American Textile History Museum, Lowell MA

Stevens, Grant, *Develop Dir,* African American Museum of Iowa, Cedar Rapids IA

Stevens, Harold, *Sr Dir Admin,* Walters Art Museum, Baltimore MD

Stevens, Jane, *Asst Dir Art ISM Chicago Gallery,* Illinois State Museum, ISM Lockport Gallery, Chicago Gallery & Southern Illinois Art Gallery, Springfield IL

Stevens, Jane Alden, *Prof Fine Arts,* University of Cincinnati, School of Art, Cincinnati OH (S)

Stevens, John, *Prof,* Manchester Community College, Fine Arts Dept, Manchester CT (S)

Stevens, Joslin, *Adjunct Faculty,* Mount Wachusett Community College, East Wing Gallery, Gardner MA

Stevens, Karen, *Archivist,* Independence National Historical Park, Library, Philadelphia PA

Stevens, Kathy, *Exec Dir,* Octagon Center for the Arts, Ames IA

Stevens, Lawrence, *Cur Ecology & Conservation,* Museum of Northern Arizona, Flagstaff AZ

Stevens, N Lee, *Sr Cur Art,* Pennsylvania Historical & Museum Commission, The State Museum of Pennsylvania, Harrisburg PA

Stevens, Rachel, *Assoc Prof,* New Mexico State University, Art Dept, Las Cruces NM (S)

Stevens, Scott, *Head of Security,* University of Minnesota Duluth, Tweed Museum of Art, Duluth MN

Stevens, Vivian Lea, *Cur,* Old Barracks Museum, Trenton NJ

Stevenson, Ann, *Coll Mgr,* University of British Columbia, Museum of Anthropology, Vancouver BC

Stevenson, Jill, *Asst Prof Theatre,* Marymount Manhattan College, Fine & Performing Arts Div, New York NY (S)

Stevenson, Kathleen (K), *Prof,* Weber State University, Dept of Visual Arts, Ogden UT (S)

Stevenson, Ron, *Dir,* Witter Gallery, Storm Lake IA

Stevenson, Sara, *Prog Cur,* Goethe-Institut New York, Mini/Goethe-Institut Curatorial Residencies Ludlow 38, New York NY

Stevenson, Susan, *Assoc Prof,* Central Missouri State University, Dept Art & Design, Warrensburg MO (S)

Steward, James, *Dir,* Princeton University, Princeton University Art Museum, Princeton NJ

Steward, James, *Dir Museum Art,* University of Michigan, Ann Arbor, Dept of History of Art, Ann Arbor MI (S)

Steward, James, *Prof,* University of Michigan, Ann Arbor, School of Art & Design, Ann Arbor MI (S)

Steward, Meredith, *Prog Dir,* Grand Prairie Arts Council, Inc, Arts Center of the Grand Prairie, Stuttgart AR

Steward Heon, Laura, *Phillips Dir,* SITE Santa Fe, Santa Fe NM

Stewart, Allyn, *Asst Prof,* Cazenovia College, Center for Art & Design Studies, Cazenovia NY (S)

Stewart, Amy, *Prof,* Jefferson Community College & Technical College, Fine Arts, Louisville KY (S)

Stewart, Andrew, *Dir Licensing & Repr,* Barnes Foundation, Merion PA

Stewart, Bridget, *Adjunct Assoc Prof Fine Art,* Johnson County Community College, Fine Arts Dept & Art History Dept, Overland Park KS (S)

Stewart, Callie, *Colls Mgr,* Bennington Museum, Bennington VT

Stewart, Charles Anthony, *Asst Prof,* University of Saint Thomas, Fine and Performing Arts Dept, Houston TX (S)

Stewart, Chris, *Dept Dir,* Tyler Junior College, Art Program, Tyler TX (S)

Stewart, Dan, *Adjunct Prof Art,* Monroe County Community College, Humanities Division, Monroe MI (S)

Stewart, David, *Prof,* University of Alabama in Huntsville, Dept of Art and Art History, Huntsville AL (S)

Stewart, Deborah, *Byzantine Studies Librn,* Harvard University, Dumbarton Oaks Research Library, Washington DC

Stewart, Gaylen, *Assoc Prof Art,* Grand Canyon University, Art Dept, Phoenix AZ (S)

Stewart, Gene, *Dept Chair,* Regis University, Fine Arts Dept, Denver CO (S)

Stewart, James W, *Pres,* Utah Lawyers for the Arts, Salt Lake City UT

Stewart, Janice, *Instr,* Mount Mary College, Art & Design Division, Milwaukee WI (S)

Stewart, John, *Prof Fine Arts,* University of Cincinnati, School of Art, Cincinnati OH (S)

Stewart, Kristen, *Office Asst,* Arts of the Southern Finger Lakes, Corning NY

Stewart, Laura, *Dir Gallery,* Georgetown College Gallery, Georgetown KY

Stewart, Laura, *Gallery Dir & Cur Coll,* Georgetown College, Art Dept, Georgetown KY (S)

Stewart, Lorelei, *Dir,* University of Illinois at Chicago, Gallery 400, Chicago IL

Stewart, Lynn, *Studio Supv,* Palo Alto Art Center, Palo Alto CA

Stewart, Mark, *Dir Commercial Activities,* Art Gallery of Hamilton, Hamilton ON

Stewart, Mary Lou, *Asst Prof,* Elmhurst College, Art Dept, Elmhurst IL (S)

Stewart, Regina, *Exec Dir,* New York Artists Equity Association, Inc, New York NY

Stewart, Rick, *Sr Cur Western Paintings & Sculpture,* Amon Carter Museum of American Art, Fort Worth TX

Stewart, Robarth, *Dir Admin,* Boca Raton Museum of Art, Library, Boca Raton FL

Stewart, Roberta, *Dir Admin,* Boca Raton Museum of Art, Boca Raton FL

Stewart, Ruth, *Fine Arts Librn,* Long Beach Public Library, Long Beach CA

Stewart, Sara, *Gallery Coordr,* University of Pennsylvania, Arthur Ross Gallery, Philadelphia PA

Stewart, Susan, *Dean Faculty of Art & Culture & Community,* Emily Carr University of Art + Design, Vancouver BC (S)

Steyaert, John, *Assoc Prof,* University of Minnesota, Minneapolis, Art History, Minneapolis MN (S)

Steylen, Traci, *Office Mgr,* Mount Saint Vincent University, MSVU Art Gallery, Halifax NS

St Hilaire, Nancy, *Mgr Admin,* Alberta Craft Council, Edmonton AB

Sticha, Denise, *Reference & Pub Servs Librn,* Seton Hill College, Reeves Memorial Library, Greensburg PA

Stickney, Laura, *Dir JAC Educ,* Cultural Affairs Department City of Los Angeles/Barnsdall Art Centers/Junior Arts Center, Library, Los Angeles CA

Stickney, Laura, *Teacher Outreach Coordr,* Cultural Affairs Department City of Los Angeles/Barnsdall Art Centers/Junior Arts Center, Los Angeles CA

Stidham, Jane, *Assoc Prof Design,* University of North Texas, College of Visual Arts & Design, Denton TX (S)

Stidsen, Donald, *Mgr Exhibs,* Massachusetts Institute of Technology, MIT Museum, Cambridge MA

Stier, David, *Dir,* Springfield Museums, Springfield Science Museum, Springfield MA

Stieve, Janet, *Mus Shop Mgr,* Dallas Museum of Art, Dallas TX

Stiffler, Kmberley, *Develop Asst,* Virginia Center for the Creative Arts, Amherst VA

Stiger, Lucille, *Registrar,* Oberlin College, Allen Memorial Art Museum, Oberlin OH

Stigora, Alison, *Adj Prof,* Saint Joseph's University, Art Dept, Philadelphia PA (S)

Stiles, Kenton, *Asst Prof,* Indiana Wesleyan University, School of Arts & Humanities, Division of Art, Marion IN (S)

Still, Todd, *Dir of Youth,* Dunedin Fine Art Center, Dunedin FL (S)

Stiller, Dalia, *Pres,* Boca Raton Museum of Art, Boca Raton FL

Stillions, Wanda, *Bus Mgr,* Scottsdale Artists' School Library, Scottsdale AZ

Stillman, Waddell, *Pres,* Historic Hudson Valley, Pocantico Hills NY

Stillwell, Kim, *Registrar,* Museum of Contemporary Art, North Miami FL

Stinchcomb, Donna, *Cur Children's Mus,* Sangre de Cristo Arts & Conference Center, Pueblo CO

Stindt, Henry, *Prof,* Lenoir Community College, Dept of Visual Art, Kinston NC (S)

Stingam, Susannah, *Dir Mktg & Commun,* Fine Arts Museums of San Francisco, Legion of Honor, San Francisco CA

Stinnett, Hester, *Pres,* The Print Center, Philadelphia PA

Stinnett, Hester, *Vice Dean,* Temple University, Tyler School of Art, Philadelphia PA (S)

Stinson, Debby, *Media/PR Mgr,* Washington State University, Museum of Art, Pullman WA

Stinson, Jim, *VPres Finance & Treas,* Kitchener-Waterloo Art Gallery, Kitchener ON

Stinson, Lisa, *Asst Prof,* Appalachian State University, Dept of Art, Boone NC (S)

Stip, Patricia, *Exec Asst,* Burlington County Historical Society, Burlington NJ

Stirton-Broad, Carol, *Instr,* Main Line Art Center, Haverford PA (S)

Stiso Mullins, Kathleen, *Pres,* Edsel & Eleanor Ford, Grosse Pointe Shores MI

St Laurent, Beatrice, *Asst Prof,* Bridgewater State College, Art Dept, Bridgewater MA (S)

St Martin, Francois, *Communs Agent,* Shawinigan Art Center, Shawinigan PQ

St Michael, Sean, *Exec Dir Develop,* Art Gallery of Ontario, Toronto ON

Stock, Joan, *Art Cur,* State Historical Society of Missouri, Gallery and Library, Columbia MO

Stock, Matthew, *Fine & Applied Arts Librn,* University of Oklahoma, Architecture Library, Norman OK

Stock, Matthew, *Fine & Applied Arts Librn,* University of Oklahoma, Fine Arts Library, Norman OK

Stockert, Rebecca, *Gallery & Educ Coordr,* Artlink, Inc, Auer Center for Arts & Culture, Fort Wayne IN

Stocki, Robert, *Instr,* Milwaukee Area Technical College, School of Media & Creative Arts, Milwaukee WI (S)

Stockstill, Patrick, *Prog Mgr for Artist Res & Classes,* Kala Institute, Kala Art Institute, Berkeley CA

Stockwell, Ross, *Instr,* San Diego Mesa College, Fine Arts Dept, San Diego CA (S)

Stockwell, Todd, *Cur Agriculture, Industry & Technology,* Indiana State Museum, Indianapolis IN

Stoddard, Brooks, *Assoc Prof,* University of Maine at Augusta, College of Arts & Humanities, Augusta ME (S)

Stoddard, Pamela, *Gallery Coordr,* Michigan Guild of Artists & Artisans, Michigan Guild Gallery, Ann Arbor MI

Stoffel, Jennifer, *Acting Asst Dir External Affairs,* Saint Louis Art Museum, Saint Louis MO

Stohn, Franz, *Asst Chmn of Art,* Edinboro University of Pennsylvania, Art Dept, Edinboro PA (S)

Stojanovic, Jelena, *Dir,* Ithaca College, Handwerker Gallery of Art, Ithaca NY

Stokall, Krista, *Assoc Dir Admin,* Okanagan Heritage Museum, Kelowna BC

Stoker, E, *Prof,* University of the Incarnate Word, Art Dept, San Antonio TX (S)

Stokes, David, *Assoc Prof,* Winthrop University, Dept of Art & Design, Rock Hill SC (S)

Stokes, Hunter, *VChmn,* Florence Museum, Florence SC

Stokes, Jeff, *Dir,* Individual Artists of Oklahoma, Oklahoma City OK

Stokes, Julie, *Treas,* Madison County Historical Society, Cottage Lawn, Oneida NY

Stokes, Sally Sims, *Librn,* University of Maryland, College Park, National Trust for Historic Preservation Library Collection, College Park MD

Stokes, Vicki, *VPres,* Florence Museum, Florence SC

Stokstad, Marilyn, *Prof,* University of Kansas, Kress Foundation Dept of Art History, Lawrence KS (S)

Stollhans, Cindy, *Chmn,* Saint Louis University, Fine & Performing Arts Dept, Saint Louis MO (S)

Stoltze, Ginger, *Pres,* Edward Hopper, Nyack NY

Stolzer, Rob, *Prof,* University of Wisconsin-Stevens Point, Dept of Art & Design, Stevens Point WI (S)

Stomberg, John, *Deputy Dir, Chief Cur & Lect Art,* Williams College, Museum of Art, Williamstown MA

Stone, Carla, *Exhib Coordr,* Sonoma State University, University Art Gallery, Rohnert Park CA

Stone, Caroline, *Cur,* Memorial University of Newfoundland, The Rooms Provincial Art Gallery, Saint John's NF

Stone, Cindy, *Dir,* Historic Newton, Newton MA

Stone, Clint, *Artistic Dir,* City Arts Center at Fair Park, Oklahoma City OK

Stone, Denise, *Assoc Prof,* University of Kansas, The School of the Arts, Dept of Visual Art, Lawrence KS (S)

Stone, Denise, *Asst Prof,* University of Kansas, Dept of Art & Music Education & Music Therapy, Lawrence KS (S)

Stone, Elizabeth, *Pres,* Wenham Museum, Wenham MA

Stone, Ellen, *Dir, Develop & Mem,* North Carolina Museum of Art, Raleigh NC

Stone, Joan, *Dean,* Rochester Institute of Technology, School of Printing Management & Sciences, Rochester NY (S)

Stone, Joan, *Dean,* Rochester Institute of Technology, School for American Craft, Rochester NY (S)

Stone, Joan, *Dean Col,* Rochester Institute of Technology, College of Imaging Arts & Sciences, Rochester NY (S)

Stone, Joy, *Asst Prof,* University of New Hampshire, Dept of Arts & Art History, Durham NH (S)

Stone, Kenneth H, *Deputy Dir Finance,* Buffalo & Erie County Public Library, Buffalo NY

Stone, Linda, *Cur Art,* The Frank Phillips, Woolaroc Museum, Bartlesville OK

Stone, Martha, *Gallery Monitor,* Arthur Griffin Center for Photographic Art, Griffin Museum of Photography, Winchester MA

Stone, Millard, *Treas,* Spectrum Gallery, Toledo OH

Stone, Rebecca R, *Assoc Prof,* Emory University, Art History Dept, Atlanta GA (S)

Stone, Robin, *Chmn,* Hannibal La Grange College, Art Dept, Hannibal MO (S)

Stone, Sara, *Dir Develop,* Cleveland Botanical Garden, Eleanor Squire Library, Cleveland OH

Stone, Shelby, *Co-Pres,* Los Angeles Center for Photographic Studies, Los Angeles CA

Stone, Thelma, *Unit Mgr,* Fort Worth Public Library Arts & Humanities, Fine Arts Section, Fort Worth TX

Stone, Yuri, *Mktg Dir,* The Renaissance Society, Chicago IL

Stone-Ferrier, Linda, *Dept Chair,* University of Kansas, Kress Foundation Dept of Art History, Lawrence KS (S)

Stone-Street, Nancy, *Instr,* Mississippi Delta Community College, Dept of Fine Arts, Moorhead MS (S)

Stonehouse, Fred, *Asst Prof,* University of Wisconsin, Madison, Dept of Art, Madison WI (S)

Stoner, Kathy, *Asst Cur,* City of Fayette, Alabama, Fayette Art Museum, Fayette AL

Stoner, Kevin, *Interim Chair Visual Arts,* The Sage Colleges, Dept Visual Arts, Albany NY (S)

Stoner, Richard, *Instr,* Seton Hill University, Art Program, Greensburg PA (S)

Stoner, Roger, *Assoc Dean Summer School,* Missouri State University, Dept of Art & Design, Springfield MO (S)

Stonesanders, Rebecca, *Asst Prof,* Lincoln University, Dept Visual and Performing Arts, Jefferson City MO (S)

Stonewall, Charles, *Adjunct Asst Prof Photog,* Johnson County Community College, Fine Arts Dept & Art History Dept, Overland Park KS (S)

St Onge, Stan, *Secy & Dir,* The New England Museum of Telephony, Inc., The Telephone Museum, Ellsworth ME

Stoops, Susan, *Cur Contemporary Art,* Worcester Art Museum, Worcester MA

Stopka, Christina, *Deputy Dir Opers,* Texas Ranger Hall of Fame & Museum, Waco TX

Stopka, Christina, *Head,* Texas Ranger Hall of Fame & Museum, Texas Ranger Research Center, Waco TX

Stoppel, Joel, *Instr,* North Central Michigan College, Art Dept, Petoskey MI (S)

Storer, Gail, *Library Dir,* Columbus College of Art & Design, Packard Library, Columbus OH

Storey, Kate, *Mgr,* Ford Motor Company, Henry Ford Museum & Greenfield Village, Dearborn MI

Storhoff, Timothy, *Arts Admin,* Florida Department of State, Division of Cultural Affairs, Florida Council on Arts & Culture, Tallahassee FL

Story, Elizabeth, *Sr Libr Assoc,* Ohio University, Fine Arts Library, Athens OH

Stott, Annette, *Prof Art History,* University of Denver, School of Art & Art History, Denver CO (S)

Stout, Andrew, *Asst Dir Grad,* University of Oklahoma, School of Art, Norman OK (S)

Stout, Andrew R, *Dir,* Florence Museum, Florence SC

Stout, Nancy, *Assoc Dir Institutional Advancement,* Princeton University, Princeton University Art Museum, Princeton NJ

Stout, Paul, *Asst Prof,* University of Utah, Dept of Art & Art History, Salt Lake City UT (S)

Stout, Scotland, *Assoc Prof,* Southern Arkansas University at Magnolia, Dept of Art & Design, Magnolia AR (S)

Stout, Scotland, *Chmn Art Dept,* Southern Arkansas University, Art Dept Gallery & Magale Art Gallery, Magnolia AR

Stovall, Alisha, *Registrar,* Kirkland Museum of Fine & Decorative Art, Denver CO

Stover Quarles, Valorie, *Prof Film,* Watkins College of Art, Design & Film, Nashville TN (S)

Stowe, Tim, *Museum Shop Mgr,* Danville Museum of Fine Arts & History, Danville VA

Stowell, Greg, *Installation Asst,* Organization of Independent Artists, Inc, Brooklyn NY

Stowers, Robert, *Prof,* University of Wisconsin-Stevens Point, Dept of Art & Design, Stevens Point WI (S)

Stowman, Annetta T, *Asst Dir,* Villanova University Art Gallery, The Art Gallery, Villanova PA

Strachan, Sue, *Pub Relations,* The Ogden Museum of Southern Art, University of New Orleans, New Orleans LA

Strackbein, Davidde, *Chmn,* Bush-Holley Historic Site & Storehouse Gallery, Greenwich Historical Society/ Bush-Holley House, Cos Cob CT

Strain, David, *Chmn,* University of the Ozarks, Dept of Art, Clarksville AR (S)

Straka, Keri, *Asst Prof,* Framingham State College, Art Dept, Framingham MA (S)

Strand, Chris, *Dir Garden & Estate,* Winterthur Museum, Winterthur Museum, Garden & Library, Winterthur DE

Strand, Eric, *Treas,* Marion Art Center, Cecil Clark Davis Gallery, Marion MA

Strand, Laura, *Head Fiber & Fabric,* Southern Illinois University at Edwardsville, Dept of Art & Design, Edwardsville IL (S)

Strandberg, Kevin, *Instr,* Illinois Wesleyan University, School of Art, Bloomington IL (S)

Stranges, Robert, *Instr,* Adrian College, Art & Design Dept, Adrian MI (S)

Stranges, Robert, *Instr,* Siena Heights University, Studio Angelico-Art Dept, Adrian MI (S)

Strangfeld, Robin, *Asst Prof,* Southern Oregon University, Art & Art History Dept, Ashland OR (S)

Strano, Susan, *Mktg & Pub Rels,* Bennington Museum, Bennington VT

Strassberg, Roy, *Chmn,* Mankato State University, Art Dept, Mankato MN (S)

Strassberg, Roy, *Prof & Chair,* University of North Carolina at Charlotte, Dept Art, Charlotte NC (S)

Straszheim, Heather, *Cur,* Octagon Center for the Arts, Ames IA

Stratford, Linda, *Instr,* Asbury University, Art Dept, Wilmore KY (S)

Stratford, Linda, *Prof Art History,* Asbury College, Student Center Gallery, Wilmore KY

Stratford, Marguerite, *Dir Strategic Initiatives & Corp Secy,* McCord Museum of Canadian History, Montreal PQ

Stratis, Harriet, *Paper Conservator,* The Art Institute of Chicago, Dept of Prints & Drawings, Chicago IL

Stratton, David, *Prof Fine Arts,* Brescia University, Art Dept, Owensboro KY (S)

Stratton, David, *Prof of Art & Gallery Dir,* Brescia University, Anna Eaton Stout Memorial Art Gallery, Owensboro KY

Stratton, Donald, *Prof,* University of Maine at Augusta, College of Arts & Humanities, Augusta ME (S)

Straub, Jim, *Pres,* Galesburg Civic Art Center, Galesburg IL

Strauch-Nelson, Wendy, *Assoc Prof,* University of Wisconsin Oshkosh, Dept of Art, Oshkosh WI (S)

Straughn, Celka, *Dir Acad Progs,* University of Kansas, Spencer Museum of Art, Lawrence KS

Straus, Melville, *Chmn,* Guild Hall of East Hampton, Inc, Guild Hall Museum, East Hampton NY

Strauss, Candace, *Dir Develop,* Montana State University, Museum of the Rockies, Bozeman MT

Strauss, Carol Kahn, *Dir,* Leo Baeck, Library, New York NY

Strauss, Carol Kahn, *Exec Dir,* Leo Baeck, New York NY

Strauss, David, *Dir External Affairs,* The Queens Museum of Art, Flushing NY

Strauss, Haila, *Assoc Prof Dance,* Marymount Manhattan College, Fine & Performing Arts Div, New York NY (S)

Strauss, Linda, *Instr,* St Lawrence University, Dept of Fine Arts, Canton NY (S)

Strauss, Matt, *VPres Board Trustees,* Museum of Contemporary Art, San Diego, La Jolla CA

Strauss, Samara, *Arts Coordr,* Northwood University, Jeannette Hare Art Gallery, West Palm Beach FL

Strawbridge, Simone, *Chmn,* Mississippi Delta Community College, Dept of Fine Arts, Moorhead MS (S)

Strawder, Maxine, *Head Librn,* Memphis College of Art, G Pillow Lewis Memorial Library, Memphis TN

Strean, Heidi, *Dir Exhibs & Publs,* The Cleveland Museum of Art, Cleveland OH

Strean, Jeffrey, *Dir Design & Architecture,* The Cleveland Museum of Art, Cleveland OH

Streeter, Anita, *Exec Dir,* Embroiderers Guild of America, Margaret Parshall Gallery, Louisville KY

Streetman, John W, *Dir,* Evansville Museum of Arts, History & Science, Evansville IN

Strehlke, Carl B, *Adjunct Cur,* Philadelphia Museum of Art, John G Johnson Collection, Philadelphia PA

Streich, Amy, *Mktg Dir,* Octagon Center for the Arts, Ames IA

Streifel, Renae, *Mem Mgr,* Plains Art Museum, Fargo ND

Streifler, Leesa, *Head,* University of Regina, Visual Arts Dept, Regina SK (S)

Streit, Jessica, *Vis Asst Prof,* Hamline University, Dept of Studio Arts & Art History, Saint Paul MN (S)

Stremsterfer, Joanne, *Pres,* St. Louis Artists' Guild, Saint Louis MO

Stremsterfer, Marianne, *Instr,* Springfield College in Illinois, Dept of Art, Springfield IL (S)

Streng, Kay, *Technical Svcs Librn,* Minneapolis College of Art & Design, Library, Minneapolis MN

Streu, Karin, *Gallery Asst,* Plug In, Institute of Contemporary Art, Winnipeg MB

Strevy, Samantha, *Admin Asst,* Saratoga County Historical Society, Brookside Museum, Ballston Spa NY

Strickland, Barbour, *Exec Dir,* Greenville Museum of Art, Inc, Reference Library, Greenville NC

Strickland, Karla, *Visual Resources Cur,* Memphis College of Art, G Pillow Lewis Memorial Library, Memphis TN

Strickland, Ken, *Assoc Prof Emeritus,* Purchase College, State University of New York, School of Art+Design, Purchase NY (S)

Strickland, Ken, *Dean,* Memphis College of Art, G Pillow Lewis Memorial Library, Memphis TN

Strickland, Rod, *Instr,* University of Windsor, Visual Arts, Windsor ON (S)

Strickler, Susan, *Dir,* The Currier Museum of Art, Manchester NH

Stricklin, Linda, *Asst Prof,* McMurry University, Art Dept, Abilene TX (S)

Stricklin, Tracy, *Security,* University of Mississippi, University Museum & Historic Houses, Oxford MS

Strider, Thomas, *Registrar Univ Colls,* Tulane University, Newcomb Art Gallery, New Orleans LA

Striegel, Rita, *Office Mgr,* Balzekas Museum of Lithuanian Culture, Chicago IL

Stringam, Susannah, *Dir Mktg & Commun,* Fine Arts Museums of San Francisco, M H de Young Museum, San Francisco CA

Stringari, Carol, *Deputy Dir & Chief Conservator,* Solomon R Guggenheim, New York NY

Stringer, Candace, *Instr,* Wayne Art Center, Wayne PA (S)

Stringer, Howard, *Chmn Bd Trustees,* The American Film Institute, Center for Advanced Film & Television, Los Angeles CA (S)

Strobel, Hillary, *Mktg & Commun,* Longue Vue House & Gardens, New Orleans LA

Strohl-Morgan, Janet, *Assoc Dir Information & Technology,* Princeton University, Princeton University Art Museum, Princeton NJ

Strohm, Robert, *COO, Assoc Dir,* Virginia Historical Society, Richmond VA

Strohmeyer, Beverly, *Exec Dir,* Missouri Arts Council, Saint Louis MO

Stroker, Robert, *Interim Dean,* Temple University, Tyler School of Art-Galleries, Philadelphia PA

Stroker, Robert, *Interim Dean,* Temple University, Tyler School of Art, Temple Gallery, Philadelphia PA

Stroker, Robert, *Interim Dean,* Temple University, Tyler School of Art, Philadelphia PA (S)

Strom, Christine, *Communs Mgr,* University of Minnesota Duluth, Tweed Museum of Art, Duluth MN

Strom, Jordan, *Cur,* Surrey Art Gallery, Surrey BC

Strom, Jordan, *Cur Exhib & Coll,* Surrey Art Gallery, Library, Surrey BC

Strom, Jordan, *Interim Cur,* Kamloops Art Gallery, Kamloops BC

Strom, Kristen, *Assoc Prof,* Grand Valley State University, Art & Design Dept, Allendale MI (S)

Stromberg, Caroline, *Cur Paleobotany,* University of Washington, Burke Museum of Natural History and Culture, Seattle WA

Stromberg, Linda, *Opers Mgr,* Northern Arizona University, Art Museum & Galleries, Flagstaff AZ

Strombotne, James S, *Prof,* University of California, Riverside, Dept of Art, Riverside CA (S)

Stromquist, Susan, *Exhib Chair,* Plastic Club, Art Club, Philadelphia PA

Stronach, Tami, *Asst Prof Dance,* Marymount Manhattan College, Fine & Performing Arts Div, New York NY (S)

Strong, Barbara, *Instr,* College of the Sequoias, Art Dept, Visalia CA (S)

Strong, Belinda, *Develop Mem,* The Walker African American Museum & Research Center, Las Vegas NV

Strong, Dan, *Assoc Dir,* Grinnell College, Faulconer Gallery, Grinnell IA

Strong, John, *Dir,* Lake George Arts Project, Courthouse Gallery, Lake George NY

Strong, Marjorie, *Asst Librn,* Vermont Historical Society, Library, Montpelier VT

Strong, Peter, *Dir,* Heritage Center, Inc, Pine Ridge SD

Strong, Scott M, *Admin,* United States Senate Commission on Art, Washington DC

Stroud, James, *Assoc Dir,* University of Texas at Austin, Harry Ransom Humanities Research Center, Austin TX

Stroud, Marion Boulton, *Dir,* The Fabric Workshop & Museum, Philadelphia PA

Strozza, Sarah, *Dir Special Events,* Laguna Art Museum, Laguna Beach CA

Struble, Joe, *Archivist,* George Eastman, Museum, Rochester NY

Strudwick, Gilbert, *VPres Commun,* Society of Canadian Artists, Toronto ON

Struever, Sally, *Mus Shop Mgr,* Portland Museum of Art, Portland ME

Strunsky, Mark, *Chair,* Orange County Community College, Arts & Communication, Middletown NY (S)

Struss, Sonny, *Instr,* Appalachian State University, Dept of Art, Boone NC (S)

Struve, Carol, *Asst Prof,* Bemidji State University, Visual Arts Dept, Bemidji MN (S)

Struve, Sue, *Commun Mgr,* National Assembly of State Arts Agencies, Washington DC

Stuart, Chris, *Pres,* Peninsula Fine Arts Center, Newport News VA

Stuart, Daniel, *Adjunct Instr Art,* Monroe County Community College, Fine Arts Council, Monroe MI

Stuart, Nancy, *Assoc Dir,* Rochester Institute of Technology, School of Photographic Arts & Sciences, Rochester NY (S)

Stuart, Sandra, *Asst Mgr,* Houston Public Library, Houston TX

Stuart-Hill, Vickie, *Art Cur,* Marine Corps University, National Museum of the Marine Corps, Triangle VA

Stubbs, Judy, *Cur Asian Art,* Indiana University, Art Museum, Bloomington IN

Stuber, Vicki, *Bus Mgr,* University of California, Santa Barbara, University Art Museum, Santa Barbara CA

Stuckenbruck, Corky, *Dir,* Texas Woman's University Art Gallery, Denton TX

Stuckenbruck, Linda, *Prof,* Texas Woman's University, School of the Arts, Dept of Visual Arts, Denton TX (S)

Stuckey, James P, *Pres,* Design Commission of the City of New York, New York NY

Stucky, John, *Librn,* Asian Art Museum of San Francisco, Chong-Moon Lee Ctr for Asian Art and Culture, San Francisco CA

Stucky, John Carl, *Librn,* Asian Art Museum of San Francisco, C Laan Chun Library, San Francisco CA

Stueber, Casey, *Art Instr,* Crowder College, Longwell Museum/Art Department, Neosho MO (S)

Stueve, Clint, *Exec Dir,* Historic Columbian Theatre Foundation, Columbian Theatre Museum & Art Center, Wamego KS

Stuhlman, Rachel, *Librn,* George Eastman, Museum, Rochester NY

Stuhlman, Theresa, *Site Supvr,* Ryerss Victorian Museum & Library, Philadelphia PA

Stuhr, Patricia, *Prof,* Ohio State University, Dept of Art Education, Columbus OH (S)

Stukator, Angela, *Assoc Dean Animation & Game Design,* Sheridan College, Faculty of Animation, Arts & Design, Oakville ON (S)

Stula, Nancy, *Dir & Cur,* Lyman Allyn Art Museum, New London CT

Stull, Staci, *Slide Cur,* Massachusetts College of Art, Morton R Godine Library, Boston MA

Stull, Will, *Instr,* Butte College, Dept of Fine Arts and Communication Tech, Oroville CA (S)

Stulpz, Larry, *Dean,* Art Institute of Atlanta, Atlanta GA (S)

Stultz, Rick, *Preparator Asst,* Marquette University, Haggerty Museum of Art, Milwaukee WI

Stuppier, Barry, *Pres,* American Numismatic Association, Edward C. Rochette Money Museum, Colorado Springs CO

Sturgeon, John, *Prof,* University of Maryland, Baltimore County, Imaging & Digital Arts (IMDA), Dept of Visual Arts, Baltimore MD (S)

Sturgeon, Mary C, *Prof,* University of North Carolina at Chapel Hill, Art Dept, Chapel Hill NC (S)

Sturgeon, Willie, *Security/Facilities Technician,* Ellen Noel Art Museum of the Permian Basin, Odessa TX

Sturges, Molly, *Educ Dir,* The Center for Contemporary Arts of Santa Fe, Santa Fe NM

Sturgess, Louise, *Exec Dir,* Pittsburgh History & Landmarks Foundation, James D Van Trump Library, Pittsburgh PA

Sturhahn, Kelly, *Asst Prof Art & Dir Foundation Prog,* Florida Southern College, Melvin Art Gallery, Lakeland FL

Sturhahn, Kelly, *Asst Prof Art & Dir Foundation Prog,* Florida Southern College, Department of Art & Art History, Lakeland FL (S)

Sturm, Kathryn, *Dir Progs,* Society of Architectural Historians, Chicago IL

Sturnick, Helena, *Pres,* Montserrat College of Art, Beverly MA (S)

Sturrock, Sherrod A, *Deputy Dir,* Calvert Marine Museum, Solomons MD

Sturtevant, Sue, *Dir & CEO,* Hill-Stead Museum, Farmington CT

Stusse, Bryan, *Asst Registrar,* Washington University, Mildred Lane Kemper Art Museum, Saint Louis MO

Stwyer, Aurolyn, *Chmn,* Atlatl, Phoenix AZ

Styers, Jeffrey, *Media Arts & Animation,* Art Institute of Pittsburgh, Pittsburgh PA (S)

Styka, Wanda Magdeleine, *Archivist,* National Trust for Historic Preservation, Chesterwood Museum Archives, Stockbridge MA

Style, Christine, *Assoc Prof,* University of Wisconsin-Green Bay, Arts Dept, Green Bay WI (S)

Styles, Bonnie W, *Dir,* Illinois State Museum, ISM Lockport Gallery, Chicago Gallery & Southern Illinois Art Gallery, Springfield IL

Styles, Bonnie W, *Mus Dir,* Illinois State Museum, Museum Store, Chicago IL

Styron, Thomas W, *Dir,* Greenville County Museum of Art, Greenville SC

Su, Lin-Lang, *Frame Shop Mgr,* Erie Art Museum, Erie PA

Suarez, Mayra, *Educ,* Miami Art Museum, Miami FL

Suarez, Will, *Adjunct Prof,* College of Saint Elizabeth, Art Dept, Morristown NJ (S)

Subler, Craig, *Dir,* University of Missouri-Kansas City, Gallery of Art, Kansas City MO

Sublett, Dyan, *Sr VPres Advancement,* Natural History Museum of Los Angeles County, Los Angeles CA

Subota, Irene, *Treas,* Ukrainian National Museum & Library, Chicago IL

Suderburg, Erika, *Chmn,* University of California, Riverside, Dept of Art, Riverside CA (S)

Sueda, Jon, *Designer,* California College of the Arts, CCAC Wattis Institute for Contemporary Arts, San Francisco CA

Suelflow, Jennifer, *Exec Asst,* Museum of Wisconsin Art, West Bend WI

Suffolk, Randall, *Dir,* Hyde Collection Trust, Library, Glens Falls NY

Suffolk, Randall, *Dir & Pres,* Philbrook Museum of Art, Tulsa OK

Sugden, Sarah, *Cur,* Waterville Historical Society, Redington Museum, Waterville ME

Suggs, Marianne, *Prof,* Appalachian State University, Dept of Art, Boone NC (S)

Sugimoto, Lisa, *Instr,* Avila College, Art Division, Dept of Humanities, Kansas City MO (S)

Sugita, Lisa, *Shop Supervisor,* Museum of Fine Arts Houston, Bayou Bend Collection & Gardens, Houston TX

Suh, Eun-Kyung, *Asst Prof,* University of Minnesota, Duluth, Art Dept, Duluth MN (S)

Suhoza, Rebecca, *Gen Educ,* Art Institute of Pittsburgh, Pittsburgh PA (S)

Suhre, Terry, *Asst Prof,* University of Missouri, Saint Louis, Dept of Art & Art History, Saint Louis MO (S)

Suhre, Terry, *Dir,* University of Missouri, Saint Louis, Gallery 210, Saint Louis MO

Sujdak, Andrew, *Graphic Design, Media Arts & Animation,* Art Institute of Pittsburgh, Pittsburgh PA (S)

Suk, Ian, *Assoc Prof,* Johns Hopkins University, School of Medicine, Dept of Art as Applied to Medicine, Baltimore MD (S)

Sulazar, Maruca, *Exec Dir,* Museo De Las Americas, Denver CO

Sulka, Arlie, *Secy,* National Antique & Art Dealers Association of America, Inc, New York NY

Sulkin, Robert, *Prof & Chair,* Hollins University, Art Dept, Roanoke VA (S)

Sullivan, Alice, *Research Asst,* City of Nome Alaska, Carrie M McLain Memorial Museum, Nome AK

Sullivan, Andrea, *Reference Librn,* Daemen College, Marian Library, Amherst NY

Sullivan, Anne, *Registrar,* Arizona State University, ASU Art Museum, Tempe AZ

Sullivan, Catherine, *Cur, Head of Colls,* California State University, Chico, Janet Turner Print Museum, CSU, Chicago, Chico CA

Sullivan, Charles M, *Exec Dir,* Cambridge Historical Commission, Research Library on Architectural Social History of Cambridge, Mass, Cambridge MA

Sullivan, Christine M, *Dir,* Captain Forbes House Museum, Milton MA

Sullivan, Eileen, *Assoc Mus Librn,* The Metropolitan Museum of Art, Image Library, New York NY

Sullivan, Gary, *Chmn,* Wagner College, Arts Administration Dept, Staten Island NY (S)

Sullivan, Jay, *Chair,* Southern Methodist University, Division of Art, Dallas TX (S)

Sullivan, Joan, *VPres Mktg,* Wilmington Trust Company, Wilmington DE

Sullivan, John, *Assoc Prof,* Arkansas Tech University, Dept of Art, Russellville AR (S)

Sullivan, John, *Dean Acad Affairs,* Watkins College of Art, Design & Film, Brownlee O Currey Gallery, Nashville TN

Sullivan, John M, *Chmn,* Jackson State University, Dept of Art, Jackson MS (S)

Sullivan, John M, *Dean, VPres Acad Affairs,* Watkins College of Art, Design & Film, Nashville TN (S)

Sullivan, Karen, *Lectr,* California State Polytechnic University, Pomona, Department of Art, Pomona CA (S)

Sullivan, Katherine, *Assoc Prof,* Hope College, Dept of Art & Art History, Holland MI (S)

Sullivan, Kendra, *Admin,* Center for Book Arts, New York NY

Sullivan, Mark, *Asst Prof,* Villanova University, Dept of Theater, Villanova PA (S)

Sullivan, Megan, *Vol Coordr,* Kirkland Museum of Fine & Decorative Art, Denver CO

Sullivan, Melissa L, *Advancement & Communs,* Historical Society of Palm Beach County, The Richard and Pat Johnson Palm Beach County History Museum, West Palm Beach FL

Sullivan, Michael, *Asst Prof,* Fontbonne University, Fine Art Dept, Saint Louis MO (S)

Sullivan, Pat, *Pub Prog Officer,* Queen's University, Agnes Etherington Art Centre, Kingston ON

Sullivan, Sarah, *Dir Develop,* The Museum of Contemporary Art (MOCA), Moca Grand Avenue, Los Angeles CA

Sullivan, Scott, *Dean of Fine Arts,* Texas Christian University, School of Art, Fort Worth TX (S)

Sullivan, Shane, *Undergrad Coordr,* University of Texas, Dept of Art & Art History, Austin TX (S)

Sullivan, Sheila, *Assoc Lectr,* University of Wisconsin-Stevens Point, Dept of Art & Design, Stevens Point WI (S)

Sullivan, Stephanie, *Installation Asst,* Smith College, Museum of Art, Northampton MA

Sullivan, Will, *Museum Shop Mgr,* The Metropolitan Museum of Art, New York NY

Sullivan, William J, *Mgr Opers,* ArtSpace/Lima, Lima OH

Sultan, Terrie, *Cur Contemporary Art,* Corcoran Gallery of Art, Washington DC

Sultan, Terrie, *Dir,* Parrish Art Museum, Water Mill NY

Sumberg, Bobbie, *Cur Textiles & Costumes,* Museum of New Mexico, Museum of International Folk Art, Santa Fe NM

Summers, Candace, *Dir Educ,* McLean County Historical Society, McLean County Museum of History, Bloomington IL

Summers, Cherie, *Registrar,* Santa Barbara Museum of Art, Santa Barbara CA

Summers, Cherie, *Registrar,* Santa Barbara Museum of Art, Library, Santa Barbara CA

Summers, David, *Prof,* University of Virginia, McIntire Dept of Art, Charlottesville VA (S)

Summers, George, *Retail Gallery Mgr,* The Society of Arts & Crafts, Boston MA

Summers, Karen, *Accounting Mgr,* Amherst College, Mead Art Museum, Amherst MA

Summers, Ruth, *Dir,* Southern Highland Craft Guild, Folk Art Center, Asheville NC

Summerville, Christie, *Coordr of Arts,* University of New Haven, Dept of Visual & Performing Arts & Philosophy, West Haven CT (S)

Sumner, Andrew, *Secy,* The Art Cafe, Davison MI

Sumner, Karen, *Develop Dir,* Honolulu Museum of Art, Honolulu HI

Sumner, Kent, *Dir,* Oregon State University, Memorial Union Art Gallery, Corvallis OR

Sumner, Wil, *Performing Arts Librn,* Chicago Public Library, Harold Washington Library Center, Chicago IL

Sumrall, Bradley, *Cur,* The Ogden Museum of Southern Art, University of New Orleans, New Orleans LA

Sumrall, Robert F, *Cur Ship Models,* United States Naval Academy, USNA Museum, Annapolis MD

Sumrall, Robert F, *Cur of Ship Models,* United States Naval Academy, Naval Academy Museum, Annapolis MD

Sun, Leon, *Graphic Design,* Western Michigan University, Frostic School of Art, Kalamazoo MI (S)

Sun, Yan John, *Chmn,* Muskingum College, Art Department, New Concord OH (S)

Sund, Judy, *Prof,* City University of New York, PhD Program in Art History, New York NY (S)

Sundahl, Steve, *Asst Prof,* Bemidji State University, Visual Arts Dept, Bemidji MN (S)

Sundberg, Beth, *Web & Office Mgr,* Davistown Museum, Liberty Location, Liberty ME

Sundby, Mel, *Instr,* Century College, Humanities Dept, White Bear Lake MN (S)

Sundell, Christa, *Admin Asst,* Heritage Preservation, The National Institute for Conservation, Washington DC

Sundgrenz, Evangelina, *Conf & Prog Outreach Mgr,* Society of North American Goldsmiths, Eugene OR

Sundstrom, K, *Cur,* The Currier Museum of Art, Manchester NH

Sundt, Christine L, *Visual Resources Cur,* University of Oregon, Architecture & Allied Arts Library, Eugene OR

Sung, Hou-mei, *Cur Asian Art,* Cincinnati Art Museum, Cincinnati Art Museum, Cincinnati OH

Sung, Lillian, *Instr,* Stephens College, Art Dept, Columbia MO (S)

Suominen Guyas, Anniina, *Prof,* Florida State University, Art Education Dept, Tallahassee FL (S)

Suppa, Stephen, *Pres,* Wiscasset, Waterville & Farmington Railway Museum (WW&F), Alna ME

Sura, Heidi, *Gallery Svcs Coordr,* Museum London, London ON

Sures, Lynn, *Interim Chair, Fine Art,* Corcoran School of Art, Washington DC (S)

Surkamer, Suzette, *Pres,* National Assembly of State Arts Agencies, Washington DC

Surkin, Elliot M, *Chmn (V)*, The Trustees of Reservations, The Mission House, Ipswich MA

Surratt, Catherine, *Dir Auxiliary Serv*, The Cleveland Museum of Art, Cleveland OH

Surratt, Monte, *Instr Dept Head*, Cochise College, Art Dept, Douglas AZ (S)

Sussman, Elisabeth, *Cur Photography*, Whitney Museum of American Art, New York NY

Sussman, Wendy, *Grad & undergrad faculty adv*, University of California, Berkeley, College of Letters & Sciences-Art Practice Dept, Berkeley CA (S)

Susstrink, Sabrine, *Asst Prof*, Rochester Institute of Technology, School of Photographic Arts & Sciences, Rochester NY (S)

Sutcliffe, Nina, *Adjunct Assoc Prof*, University of Maine, Dept of Art, Orono ME (S)

Sutherland, Cara A, *Exec Dir*, Everhart Museum, Scranton PA

Sutherland, Daniel, *Asst Chair - Studio Art*, University of Texas, Dept of Art & Art History, Austin TX (S)

Sutherland, Doug, *Prof*, University of Tampa, College of Arts & Letters, Tampa FL (S)

Sutherland, Lesley, *Bookkeeper*, Saskatchewan Craft Council & Affinity Gallery, Saskatoon SK

Sutherland, Ross, *Bush House Mus Dir*, Salem Art Association, Bush House Museum, Salem OR

Sutinen, Paul, *Dir*, Marylhurst University, Art Dept, Marylhurst OR (S)

Sutley, Beverly, *Registrar*, The Pennsylvania State University, Palmer Museum of Art, University Park PA

Sutley, Kate, *Develop Coordr*, Pensacola Museum of Art, Pensacola FL

Sutor, Nancy, *Asst Prof*, College of Santa Fe, Art Dept, Santa Fe NM (S)

Sutter MFA, James, *Prof*, State University of New York College at Potsdam, Dept of Fine Arts, Potsdam NY (S)

Sutton, Elizabeth, *Asst Prof*, University of Northern Iowa, Dept of Art, Cedar Falls IA (S)

Sutton, Judith, *Deputy Dir*, Public Library of Charlotte & Mecklenburg County, Charlotte NC

Sutton, Lory, *Pub Rels*, Minnesota Historical Society, Saint Paul MN

Sutton, Peter C, *Exec Dir*, Bruce Museum, Inc, Greenwich CT

Sutton, Raina, *Asst to Pres*, Museum for African Art, New York NY

Sutton, Randy, *Chmn Board Trustees*, Contemporary Art Center of Virginia, Virginia Beach VA

Suzio, Peggy, *Instr*, Marylhurst University, Art Dept, Marylhurst OR (S)

Suzor, Mary, *Dir Colls Management*, The Cleveland Museum of Art, Cleveland OH

Svarckopf, Jennifer, *Descriptive Servs Section*, National Archives of Canada, Art & Photography Archives, Ottawa ON

Svendson, Erin, *Educ Coordr*, Springfield Art Association of Edwards Place, Springfield IL

Svenson, Jessica, *Prog Mgr*, Dieu Donne Papermill, Inc, Gallery, New York NY

Svoboda, Stephen, *Exec Dir*, Adirondack Lakes Center for the Arts, Blue Mountain Lake NY

Swacker, Sharon, *Dir Technical Servs*, New York City Technical College, Ursula C Schwerin Library, Brooklyn NY

Swail, Barbara, *Treas*, South Peace Art Society, Dawson Creek Art Gallery, Dawson Creek BC

Swaim, Dawn, *Instr*, North Central Michigan College, Art Dept, Petoskey MI (S)

Swain, Adrian, *Cur*, Morehead State University, Kentucky Folk Art Center, Morehead KY

Swain, Darlene, *Instr*, Mesa Community College, Dept of Art, Mesa AZ (S)

Swain, Kristin A, *Dir*, The Rockwell Museum of Western Art, Corning NY

Swain, Tim, *Exhib Cur*, Anderson Fine Arts Center, The Anderson Center for the Arts, Anderson IN

Swales, Janna, *VPres*, Yukon Historical & Museums Association, Whitehorse YT

Swallow, Nancy, *Registrar*, Corcoran Gallery of Art, Washington DC

Swan, Claudia, *Chmn, Assoc Prof*, Northwestern University, Evanston, Dept of Art History, Evanston IL (S)

Swan, Nancy, *Dir Newsletter*, National Watercolor Society, San Pedro CA

Swanbeck, Gayle, *Dir School of Arts*, WomanKraft Art Center, Tucson AZ

Swanepoel, Kevin, *Pres*, The One Club, New York NY

Swangstu, Holly, *Managing Dir*, Leedy-Voulkos Art Center, Kansas City MO

Swanson, Ann, *Coll Mgr*, Rome Historical Society, Museum & Archives, Rome NY

Swanson, Ann, *Coll Mgr*, Rome Historical Society, William E Scripture Memorial Library, Rome NY

Swanson, Catherine, *Archivist*, National Heritage Museum, Lexington MA

Swanson, Don, *Chief, Coll Preservation*, The Frick Collection, Frick Art Reference Library, New York NY

Swanson, James, *Assoc Prof*, Dakota State University, College of Liberal Arts, Madison SD (S)

Swanson, Jennie, *Mgr Mem & Mus Servs*, Laumeier Sculpture Park, Saint Louis MO

Swanson, John, *VPres*, Springfield Art & Historical Society, The Miller Art Center, Springfield VT

Swanson, Kenneth J, *Museum Adminr*, Idaho Historical Museum, Boise ID

Swanson, Kristina, *Grants Admin*, Historical Museum at Fort Missoula, Missoula MT

Swanson, Kyra, *Asst Cur & Registrar*, University of Mary Washington, University of Mary Washington Galleries, Fredericksburg VA

Swanson, Lealan, *Assoc Prof*, Jackson State University, Dept of Art, Jackson MS (S)

Swanson, Linda, *Adjunct Assoc*, College of Santa Fe, Art Dept, Santa Fe NM (S)

Swanson, Mark, *Librn & AV Production Mgr*, C G Jung Center, Evanston IL

Swanson, Michael, *Chmn Dept*, Franklin College, Art Dept, Franklin IN (S)

Swanson, Richard, *Develop Dir*, Historical Society of Cheshire County, Keene NH

Swanson, Roy, *Prof*, Hutchinson Community College, Visual Arts Dept, Hutchinson KS (S)

Swanson, Vern, *Dir*, Springville Museum of Art, Springville UT

Swarez, Bibiana, *Assoc Prof*, DePaul University, Dept of Art, Chicago IL (S)

Swart, Paula, *Cur Asian Studies*, Museum of Vancouver, Vancouver BC

Swartwood, Larry, *Asst Prof*, University of Arkansas, Art Dept, Fayetteville AR (S)

Swartz, Kate, *Pub Rels*, C M Russell, Great Falls MT

Swarz, Priscilla, *Lectr*, Oklahoma State University, Department of Art, Graphic Design and Art History, Stillwater OK (S)

Sweeney, Dennis F, *Mgr Bldgs & Secy*, Frick Collection, New York NY

Sweeney, Elena, *Asst Dir*, Museum of New Mexico, Museum of International Folk Art, Santa Fe NM

Sweeney, Kathy, *Dir Educ*, Wichita Center for the Arts, Wichita KS

Sweeney, Lisa, *Head of GIS*, Massachusetts Institute of Technology, Rotch Library of Architecture & Planning, Cambridge MA

Sweeney, Maureen, *Office Mgr*, Napa Valley Museum, Yountville CA

Sweeney, Robert T, *Head of Studio, Wm R Mead Prof of Art*, Amherst College, Dept of Art & the History of Art, Amherst MA (S)

Sweeney O'Bryan, Judith, *Asst Prof Graphic Design*, Watkins College of Art, Design & Film, Nashville TN (S)

Sweeters, Jim, *Dir*, California State University, Northridge, Art Galleries, Northridge CA

Sweetland, Theresa, *Exec & Artistic Dir*, Intermedia Arts Minnesota, Minneapolis MN

Sweigart, Wendy, *Dir Outreach Educ*, Susquehanna Art Museum, Harrisburg PA

Sweigart, Wendy, *Exhibs Coordr*, Pennsylvania Department of Education, Arts in Education Program, Harrisburg PA

Sweigert, Lawrence, *Dir*, Rehoboth Art League, Inc, Rehoboth Beach DE

Swenson, David, *Lectr*, North Dakota State University, Division of Fine Arts, Fargo ND (S)

Swenson, Dean, *Adjunct*, North Iowa Area Community College, Dept of Art, Mason City IA (S)

Swenson, Kirsten, *Asst Prof*, University of Nevada, Las Vegas, Dept of Art, Las Vegas NV (S)

Swenson-Wolsey, Sonja, *Chmn*, Taft College, Art Department, Taft CA (S)

Swensson, Lise C, *Exec Dir*, Hickory Museum of Art, Inc, Hickory NC

Swetcharnik, Sara Morris, *Project Coordr & Artist*, Swetcharnik Art Studio, Mount Airy MD

Swetcharnik, William, *Dir & Artist*, Swetcharnik Art Studio, Mount Airy MD

Swiatek, Kathryn, *Mem & Mktg Mgr*, Association of Collegiate Schools of Architecture, Washington DC

Swick, Deane, *Lectr*, California State Polytechnic University, Pomona, Department of Art, Pomona CA (S)

Swickard, Kelly, *Catalog Librn*, Maryland Institute, Decker Library, Baltimore MD

Swider, Bougdon, *Prof*, Colorado College, Dept of Art, Colorado Springs CO (S)

Swiderski, Christine, *Exhibitions Coordr*, OCAD University, Student Gallery, Toronto ON

Swierenga, Heidi, *Conservator*, University of British Columbia, Museum of Anthropology, Vancouver BC

Swift, J Charles, *Exec Dir*, Gibson Society, Inc, Gibson House Museum, Boston MA

Swindell, Jon, *Prof*, University of Kansas, The School of the Arts, Dept of Visual Art, Lawrence KS (S)

Swindull, Laurie, *Instr*, American University, Dept of Art, New York NY (S)

Swing, Michael, *Instr*, Guilford Technical Community College, Commercial Art Dept, Jamestown NC (S)

Swisher, Michael, *Chmn Humanities*, City Colleges of Chicago, Truman College, Chicago IL (S)

Switzer, Terri, *Chair Art Dept & Prof Art History*, Saint Ambrose University, Art Dept, Davenport IA (S)

Swoboda, Michael, *Prof*, Saint Louis Community College at Meramec, Art Dept, Saint Louis MO (S)

Swonger, Denny, *Dean Arts & Sciences*, Eastern Oregon University, School of Arts & Science, La Grande OR (S)

Swopes, Thomas, *Assoc Prof*, Saint Mary-of-the-Woods College, Art Dept, Saint Mary of the Woods IN (S)

Syct, Sarah, *Mus Educ*, Andover Historical Society, Andover MA

Sydenstricker, Janet, *Pub Rels Specialist*, Tidewater Community College, Visual Arts Center, Portsmouth VA (S)

Sykora, Christine, *Coordr Vis Svcs & Educational Programming*, Nova Scotia Museum, Maritime Museum of the Atlantic, Halifax NS

Sylvester, Beverly, *Dept Adminr Asst*, Williams College, Dept of Art, Williamstown MA (S)

Sylvester, Cindy, *Dir*, San Jose Museum of Art, Library, San Jose CA

Sylvester, Judith, *Conservator*, Indiana University, The Mathers Museum of World Cultures, Bloomington IN

Sylwester, Laurie, *Instr*, Columbia College, Fine Arts, Sonora CA (S)

Symmes, Edwin C, *Pres*, Symmes Systems, Photographic Investments Gallery, Atlanta GA

Symmes, Marilyn, *Cur Prints and Drawings*, Rutgers, The State University of New Jersey, Zimmerli Art Museum, Rutgers University, New Brunswick NJ

Synder, Fred, *Dir & Consultant*, National Native American Co-Operative, North American Indian Information & Trade Center, Tucson AZ

Sypher, Jodi, *Cur Educ*, University of Miami, Lowe Art Museum, Coral Gables FL

Szabla, Joanne, *Prof*, Rochester Institute of Technology, School of Design, Rochester NY (S)

Szabo, Joyce, *Chmn*, University of New Mexico, Dept of Art & Art History, Albuquerque NM (S)

Szakacs, Dennis, *Dir*, Orange County Museum of Art, Newport Beach CA

Szavuly, Erin Palmer, *Assoc Prof*, Lourdes University, Art Dept, Sylvania OH (S)

Szepe, Helena, *Assoc Prof*, University of South Florida, School The Arts, Tampa FL (S)

Szmagaj, Kenneth, *Prof*, James Madison University, School of Art & Art History, Harrisonburg VA (S)

Szoke, Andrew, *Asst Prof*, Northampton Community College, Art Dept, Bethlehem PA (S)

Szpila, Kathleen, *Slide Cur*, Temple University, Slide Library, Philadelphia PA

Szwaczkowski, Daniel, *Preparator*, University of Texas at El Paso, Stanlee & Gerald Rubin Center for the Visual Arts, El Paso TX

Szycher, Lawrence, *Prof,* Caldwell College, Dept of Fine Arts, Caldwell NJ (S)

Szymanski, Tim, *CFO,* Toledo Museum of Art, Toledo OH

Szynkowski, Stan, *Asst Chair,* University of Alberta, Dept of Art & Design, Edmonton AB (S)

Taaffe, Ranee, *Cur Educ,* Missoula Art Museum, Missoula MT

Taaffe, Susan, *Preparator,* University of North Carolina at Greensboro, Weatherspoon Art Museum, Greensboro NC

Tab, Winston, *Dir,* Johns Hopkins University, Homewood Museum, Baltimore MD

Tabaha, Kathy, *Mus Tech,* National Park Service, Hubbell Trading Post National Historic Site, Ganado AZ

Taber, Norman, *Assoc Prof Pharmacy Practice,* Southwestern Oklahoma State University, Art Dept, Weatherford OK (S)

Taber-Conova, Rebecca, *Mus Shop Mgr,* Old State House, Hartford CT

Tacang, Lee, *Instr,* De Anza College, Creative Arts Division, Cupertino CA (S)

Tachora, Jerry, *Interim Exec Dir,* Hendersonville Arts Council, Monthaven Mansion, Hendersonville TN

Tacks, Melissa, *Librn/Archivist,* Schenectady County Historical Society, Library, Schenectady NY

Taddie, Dan, *Chmn,* Maryville College, Dept of Fine Arts, Maryville TN (S)

Tadie, Elizabeth, *Pub Rels Coordr,* Louisiana Arts & Science Museum, Baton Rouge LA

Taft, Dudley S, *VChmn,* Cincinnati Institute of Fine Arts, Cincinnati OH

Taft, Stan, *Assoc Prof,* Cornell University, Dept of Art, Ithaca NY (S)

Tagg, John, *Assoc Prof,* State University of New York at Binghamton, Dept of Art History, Binghamton NY (S)

Tai, Susan, *Cur Asian Art,* Santa Barbara Museum of Art, Santa Barbara CA

Tait Glover, Deanna, *Cur,* Kanab Heritage Museum & Juniper Fine Arts Gallery, Kanab UT

Takach, Bonnie Sadler, *Coordr Visual Communs Design,* University of Alberta, Dept of Art & Design, Edmonton AB (S)

Takahara, Takeshi, *Prof,* University of Michigan, Ann Arbor, School of Art & Design, Ann Arbor MI (S)

Takahashi, Satoru, *Asst Prof,* University of Michigan, Ann Arbor, School of Art & Design, Ann Arbor MI (S)

Takechi, K, *Prof,* Shoreline Community College, Humanities Division, Seattle WA (S)

Takei, George, *VChmn,* Japanese American National Museum, Los Angeles CA

Takekawa, Beth, *Assoc Dir,* Wing Luke Asian Museum, Governor Gary Locke Library and Community Heritage Center, Seattle WA

Takemori, Lianne, *Asst Cur Educ,* Mississippi Museum of Art, Howorth Library, Jackson MS

Takeuchi, Arthur, *Assoc Prof,* Illinois Institute of Technology, College of Architecture, Chicago IL (S)

Taki, Elga, *Sec,* Saint Peter's College, Art Gallery, Jersey City NJ

Talaga, Sally, *Dir,* Wayne County Historical Society, Museum, Honesdale PA

Talalay, Lauren E, *Assoc Dir & Assoc Cur Educ,* University of Michigan, Kelsey Museum of Archaeology, Ann Arbor MI

Talasek, JD, *Dir,* National Academy of Sciences, Arts in the Academy, Washington DC

Talbert, Hope C, *Dir,* Santarella Museum & Gardens, Tyringham MA

Talbot, Randall, *Councilor at Large,* Alberta Society of Artists, Calgary AB

Talbott, Jennifer Neuburger, *Dir Internal Opers,* University of Kansas, Spencer Museum of Art, Lawrence KS

Talbott, Page, *Interim Pres,* Historical Society of Pennsylvania, Philadelphia PA

Talbott, Ronald, *Instr,* Harrisburg Area Community College, Division of Communications, Humanities & the Arts, Harrisburg PA (S)

Talbott, Susan Lubowsky, *Exec Dir,* Wadsworth Atheneum Museum of Art, Hartford CT

Talebi, Marjaneh, *Instr,* Harrisburg Area Community College, Division of Communications, Humanities & the Arts, Harrisburg PA (S)

Talkington, John, *Deputy Dir Fin & Opers,* The Contemporary Museum, Honolulu HI

Tallent, Tony, *Dir Library,* Boulder Public Library & Gallery, Arts Gallery, Boulder CO

Tallon, Andrew, *Asst Prof,* Vassar College, Art Dept, Poughkeepsie NY (S)

Talmon, Renee, *Dir Admissions,* San Francisco Art Institute, San Francisco CA (S)

Tam, Herb, *Assoc Cur,* Exit Art, San Leandro CA

Tam, Herb, *Cur & Dir Exhib,* Museum of Chinese in America, New York NY

Tammen, Hans, *Dep Dir,* Harvestworks, Inc, New York NY

Tamony, Katie, *Dir Mktg & Audience Strategy,* San Francisco Museum of Modern Art, San Francisco CA

Tanaka, Maiko, *Cur in Res,* University of Toronto, Justina M Barnicke Gallery, Toronto ON

Tanber, Joel, *Asst Prof,* Wake Forest University, Dept of Art, Winston-Salem NC (S)

Tancig, Amy, *Business Dir,* Metropolitan State University of Denver, Center for Visual Art, Denver CO

Tancin, Charlotte, *Librn,* Carnegie Mellon University, Hunt Institute for Botanical Documentation, Pittsburgh PA

Tander, David, *Adjunct Instr,* Quincy College, Art Dept, Quincy MA (S)

Tang, Serena, *Graphics Instr,* Tucson Museum of Art and Historic Block, Tucson AZ

Tanglao, Fatima, *Circ & Reference Asst,* New York University, Institute of Fine Arts Visual Resources Collection, New York NY

Taniguchi, Dennis, *Exec Dir,* Japantown Art & Media Workshop, San Francisco CA

Tankersley, Janice, *Librn,* The Dixon Gallery & Gardens, Library, Memphis TN

Tankersley, Jenna, *Outreach Educ Coordr,* Morris Museum of Art, Augusta GA

Tannen, Jason, *Chmn,* California State University, Chico, University Art Gallery, Chico CA

Tannen, Jason, *Instr,* California State University, Chico, Department of Art & Art History, Chico CA (S)

Tannenbaum, Barbara, *Cur Photog,* The Cleveland Museum of Art, Cleveland OH

Tannenbaum, Barbara, *Dir Cur Affairs,* Akron Art Museum, Martha Stecher Reed Art Library, Akron OH

Tannenbaum, Barbara, *Dir Curatorial Affairs,* Akron Art Museum, Akron OH

Tannenbaum, Judith, *Cur Contemporary Art,* Rhode Island School of Design, Museum of Art, Providence RI

Tannenbaum, Marilyn, *Instr,* Solano Community College, Division of Fine & Applied Art & Behavioral Science, Fairfield CA (S)

Tannenbaum, Toby, *Asst Dir Educ,* Getty Center, The J Paul Getty Museum, Los Angeles CA

Tanner, David, *Assoc Dir Admin,* Indiana University, Art Museum, Bloomington IN

Tanner, Jim, *Assoc Prof (Visual Art),* University of British Columbia Okanagan, Dept of Creative Studies, Kelowna BC (S)

Tanner, Richard, *Prof,* Rochester Institute of Technology, School of Design, Rochester NY (S)

Tanze, Don, *Asst Prof,* Seattle Central Community College, Humanities - Social Sciences Division, Seattle WA (S)

Tapahonso, Cherie, *Accounting Specialist,* University of Kansas, Spencer Museum of Art, Lawrence KS

Tarallo, Donald, *Asst Prof,* Bridgewater State College, Art Dept, Bridgewater MA (S)

Tarapor, Mahrukh, *Assoc Dir Exhibition,* The Metropolitan Museum of Art, New York NY

Tardella, Sally S, *Spec Instr,* Oakland University, Dept of Art & Art History, Rochester MI (S)

Tardif, Mark, *Pub Rels Dir,* Thomas College, Art Gallery, Waterville ME

Tarions, Cheyanne, *Shop Mgr,* Art Metropole, Toronto ON

Tarmann Lynch, Anastasia, *Librn, Cur Colls,* Alaska State Library, Alaska Historical Collections, Juneau AK

Tarnow, Terry, *Museum Shop Mgr,* Northwestern Michigan College, Dennos Museum Center, Traverse City MI

Tarnowski, Tom, *Prof Photog & Photog Dept Coordr,* Johnson County Community College, Fine Arts Dept & Art History Dept, Overland Park KS (S)

Tarplee, Cork, *Dir,* Old Island Restoration Foundation Inc, Oldest House in Key West, Key West FL

Tarr, Blair, *Cur of Decorative Art,* Kansas State Historical Society, Kansas Museum of History, Topeka KS

Tarrell, Robert, *Prof,* Edgewood College, Art Dept, Madison WI (S)

Tarver, Paul, *Registrar & Cur Native American & Pre-Columbian Art,* New Orleans Museum of Art, New Orleans LA

Tasaka, Sharon, *Assoc Dir,* University of Hawaii at Manoa, Art Gallery, Honolulu HI

Tassone, Rachel U, *Assoc Registrar,* Williams College, Museum of Art, Williamstown MA

Tate, Alan, *Head Landscape Archit,* University of Manitoba, Faculty of Architecture, Winnipeg MB (S)

Tate, Barbara, *Dir,* Henry Street Settlement Arts for Living Center, New York NY (S)

Tate, Belinda, *Dir, Cur, Develop & Registrar,* Winston-Salem State University, Diggs Gallery, Winston Salem NC

Tate, Jamie, *Art Consultant,* National League of American Pen Women, Washington DC

Tate, Jamie, *Dir,* Mississippi Art Colony, Stoneville MS

Tate, Valerie, *Mem Mgr,* Laguna Art Museum, Laguna Beach CA

Tate, William, *Asst Prof,* James Madison University, School of Art & Art History, Harrisonburg VA (S)

Tateishi, Cheryl, *Deputy Dir Admin,* California Science Center, Los Angeles CA

Tatge, Jean, *Exec VP Devel,* Municipal Art Society of New York, New York NY

Tation, Carol, *Reference Librn,* Providence Athenaeum, Library, Providence RI

Tatman, Sandra L, *Dir,* Athenaeum of Philadelphia, Philadelphia PA

Tatro, Amy M, *Asst to Dir,* Williams College, Museum of Art, Williamstown MA

Tatum, James, *Prof,* Lincoln University, Dept Visual and Performing Arts, Jefferson City MO (S)

Tatum, Kandace, *Mktg Dir,* Lexington Art League, Inc, Lexington KY

Tatum, Marcolm, *Graphic Designer,* Columbus Museum, Columbus GA

Taub, Peter, *Dir of Performance Prog,* Museum of Contemporary Art, Chicago IL

Tauben, Evelyn, *Head Progs & Exhib,* Koffler Centre of the Arts, Koffler Gallery, Toronto ON

Taubenberger, Michael, *Dir Fin & Opers,* Institute of Contemporary Art, Boston MA

Taugner, Julia, *Asst Prof,* University of Indianapolis, Dept Art & Design, Indianapolis IN (S)

Taugner, Stephanie, *Instr,* Art Institute of Southern California, Laguna Beach CA (S)

Taulbee, Ann, *Dir,* Hiestand Galleries, Oxford OH

Taurins, Irene, *Registrar,* Philadelphia Museum of Art, Main Building, Philadelphia PA

Tavani, Robert, *Asst Prof,* Mercyhurst College, Dept of Art, Erie PA (S)

Tavani, Robert, *Gallery Dir,* DePaul University, Dept of Art, Chicago IL (S)

Tavares, Shirley A, *Institutional Researcher,* Escuela de Artes Plasticas de Puerto Rico, San Juan PR (S)

Tavares, Shirley A, *Institutional Researcher,* Escuela de Artes Plasticas de Puerto Rico, San Juan PR (S)

Tavenner, Irene, *Facilities Mgr,* Contemporary Art Center of Virginia, Virginia Beach VA

Taxgenson, Mark, *Instr,* Judson University, School of Art, Design & Architecture, Elgin IL (S)

Tayes, Debra, *Dir ISM Southern IL Art Gallery,* Illinois State Museum, ISM Lockport Gallery, Chicago Gallery & Southern Illinois Art Gallery, Springfield IL

Tayler, Felicity, *Information Specialist,* Artexte Information Centre, Documentation Centre, Montreal PQ

Taylor, Adams, *Historic Sites & Colls Mgr,* Newport Historical Society & Museum of Newport History, Newport RI

Taylor, Aletha, *Children's Librn,* Mexico-Audrain County Library, Mexico MO

Taylor, Andrew, *Dir,* University of Wisconsin, Madison, Graduate School of Business, Bolz Center for Arts Administration, Madison WI (S)

Taylor, Barbara, *Exhibits Specialist,* Fort George G Meade Museum, Fort Meade MD

Taylor, Beth, *Asst Cur Entomology,* Northern Maine Museum of Science, Presque Isle ME

Taylor, Bethany, *Asst Prof,* University of Florida, School of Art & Art History, Gainesville FL (S)

Taylor, Bonnie, *Pres,* Manitoba Society of Artists, Winnipeg MB

Taylor, Brian, *Chmn Dept of Art,* San Jose State University, School of Art & Design, San Jose CA (S)

Taylor, Brian, *Co-Chair,* Shorter College, Art Dept, Rome GA (S)

Taylor, Brook, *Educ Prog Coordr,* University of Illinois at Urbana-Champaign, Spurlock Museum, Champaign IL

Taylor, Bruce, *Prof & Chmn,* University of Waterloo, Fine Arts Dept, Waterloo ON (S)

Taylor, Bruce T, *VPres,* National Museum of Ceramic Art & Glass, Baltimore MD

Taylor, Charlene, *Instr,* Lourdes University, Art Dept, Sylvania OH (S)

Taylor, Christine M, *Prog Dir,* Arts Midwest, Minneapolis MN

Taylor, Christopher, *Pres,* Clay Studio, Philadelphia PA

Taylor, Colleen, *Secy,* Fort Hays State University, Moss-Thorns Gallery of Arts, Hays KS

Taylor, Darrell, *Dir,* University of Northern Iowa, UNI Gallery of Art, Cedar Falls IA

Taylor, David, *Photo Dir,* New Mexico State University, Art Dept, Las Cruces NM (S)

Taylor, Diane, *Exec Asst,* Birmingham Bloomfield Art Center, Birmingham MI (S)

Taylor, Elmer, *Regents Prof,* University of North Texas, College of Visual Arts & Design, Denton TX (S)

Taylor, Glenda, *Art Prof Chmn,* Washburn University of Topeka, Dept of Art, Topeka KS (S)

Taylor, Hollis, *Cur,* Barnard's Mill Art Museum, Glen Rose TX

Taylor, Howard J, *Dir,* San Angelo Museum of Fine Arts, San Angelo TX

Taylor, Jeffrey, *Collections Mgr,* Norton Simon, Pasadena CA

Taylor, Judith, *Asst Prof,* Arcadia University, Dept of Fine Arts, Glenside PA (S)

Taylor, Kathryn T, *Dir,* Westerly Public Library, Hoxie Gallery, Westerly RI

Taylor, Kathy, *Asst Registrar,* Indiana University, Art Museum, Bloomington IN

Taylor, Larry, *Instr,* South Dakota State University, Dept of Visual Arts, Brookings SD (S)

Taylor, Lee, *Pub Rels Coordr,* African American Museum, Dallas TX

Taylor, Marc, *Planetarium Coordr,* The Hudson River Museum, Yonkers NY

Taylor, Marcia, *Assoc Prof,* The College of New Jersey, School of Arts & Sciences, Ewing NJ (S)

Taylor, Marilyn S, *Cur Ethnology,* Saint Joseph Museum, Saint Joseph MO

Taylor, Mark A, *Graphic Design Prog Dir,* Brenau University, Art & Design Dept, Gainesville GA (S)

Taylor, Mary, *Pres,* San Angelo Art Club, Helen King Kendall Memorial Art Gallery, San Angelo TX

Taylor, Mary Diane, *Chair, Div Fine Art,* Brescia University, Anna Eaton Stout Memorial Art Gallery, Owensboro KY

Taylor, Mary Diane, *Chmn,* Brescia University, Art Dept, Owensboro KY (S)

Taylor, Michael, *Assoc Prof,* Lewis & Clark College, Dept of Art, Portland OR (S)

Taylor, Michael, *Chmn Art History,* University of Massachusetts Dartmouth, College of Visual & Performing Arts, North Dartmouth MA (S)

Taylor, Michael, *Prof,* Rochester Institute of Technology, School of Design, Rochester NY (S)

Taylor, Mona Lee, *Rec Sec,* Allegany County Historical Society, Gordon-Roberts House, Cumberland MD

Taylor, Pam, *Asst Prof Art Educ,* University of Georgia, Franklin College of Arts & Sciences, Lamar Dodd School of Art, Athens GA (S)

Taylor, Rebecca, *Asst Prof Journalism,* Siena College, Dept of Creative Arts, Loudonville NY (S)

Taylor, Richard, *Pres,* National Museum of Ceramic Art & Glass, Baltimore MD

Taylor, Robin, *Librn,* Philmont Scout Ranch, Philmont Museum - Seton Memorial Library, Cimarron NM

Taylor, Rod A, *Head Dept,* Norfolk State University, Fine Arts Dept, Norfolk VA (S)

Taylor, Ron, *Pres,* Merced College, Arts Division, Merced CA (S)

Taylor, Rose, *Mem/Mktg Dir,* Salisbury University, Ward Museum of Wildfowl Art, Salisbury MD

Taylor, Ruth, *Acquisitions Librn,* Mexico-Audrain County Library, Mexico MO

Taylor, Saddler, *Cur Folk Art & Research,* University of South Carolina, McKissick Museum, Columbia SC

Taylor, Shea, *Head Reference Div,* City College of the City University of New York, Morris Raphael Cohen Library, New York NY

Taylor, Stephanie, *Asst Prof,* New Mexico State University, Art Dept, Las Cruces NM (S)

Taylor, Stephanie, *Interim Dir Gallery,* New Mexico State University, Art Gallery, Las Cruces NM

Taylor, Steve, *Pres,* Second Street Gallery, Charlottesville VA

Taylor, Steven J, *Treas,* Morris-Jumel Mansion, Inc, New York NY

Taylor, Sue, *Assoc Prof,* Portland State University, Dept of Art, Portland OR (S)

Taylor, Susan M, *Dir,* New Orleans Museum of Art, New Orleans LA

Taylor, Tom, *Coordr Fine Arts,* Columbia College, Art Dept, Chicago IL (S)

Taylor-Gore, Victoria, *Instr,* Amarillo College, Visual Art Dept, Amarillo TX (S)

Teagle, Rachel, *Cur,* Museum of Contemporary Art, San Diego, Geisel Library, La Jolla CA

Teague, Gypsey, *Branch Head,* Clemson University, Emery A Gunnin Architectural Library, Clemson SC

Teague, Patrick G, *Human Resources Mgr,* Jamestown-Yorktown Foundation, Jamestown Settlement, Williamsburg VA

Teahan, John W, *Librn,* Wadsworth Atheneum Museum of Art, Auerbach Art Library, Hartford CT

Teal, Randall, *Instr,* Southern University A & M College, School of Architecture, Baton Rouge LA (S)

Teasley, Sarah, *Instr,* Hinds Community College, Dept of Art, Raymond MS (S)

Teasley, Stephanie, *Registrar,* Wichita State University, Ulrich Museum of Art, Wichita KS

Tebo, Ginger, *Children's Librn,* Roswell P Flower, Watertown NY

Tebon, Elizabeth, *Prof,* Northern Virginia Community College, Art Dept, Annandale VA (S)

Tebow, Duncan, *Chmn,* Northern Virginia Community College, Art Dept, Annandale VA (S)

Teczar, Steven, *Prof,* Maryville University of Saint Louis, Art & Design Program, Saint Louis MO (S)

Tederick, Lydia, *Asst Cur,* White House, Washington DC

Tedeschi, Martha, *Cur Prints & Drawings,* The Art Institute of Chicago, Chicago IL

Tedeschi, Martha, *Pres,* Print Council of America, Chicago IL

Teeters-Eichacker, Mary Jane, *Cur Social History,* Indiana State Museum, Indianapolis IN

Tegge, Susan, *Head Reference Dept,* Springfield Free Public Library, Donald B Palmer Museum, Springfield NJ

Teilhet-Fisk, Jehnne, *Prof,* Florida State University, Art History Dept, Tallahassee FL (S)

Teipel, Juliet S, *Librn,* The Illinois Institute of Art - Chicago, Chicago IL (S)

Teitelbaum, Matthew, *Dir & CEO,* Art Gallery of Ontario, Toronto ON

Teixeira, Jose, *Assoc Vis Prof,* Case Western Reserve University, Dept of Art History & Art, Cleveland OH (S)

Teixeira-Gomes, Daniel, *Dir Tech,* Bay Area Video Coalition, Inc, San Francisco CA

Teixido, Mercedes, *Assoc Prof,* Pomona College, Dept of Art & Art History, Claremont CA (S)

Teixido, Sara Monserrat, *Dir Mktg & Communs,* Delaware Center for the Contemporary Arts, Wilmington DE

Tejada, Susana, *Head Research Resources,* The Buffalo Fine Arts Academy, Albright-Knox Art Gallery, Buffalo NY

Telander, Tristan, *Graphic Designer,* University of Kansas, Spencer Museum of Art, Lawrence KS

Telfair, Tula, *Assoc Prof, Dir,* Wesleyan University, Dept of Art & Art History, Middletown CT (S)

Telford, John, *Chmn,* Brigham Young University, Dept of Visual Arts, Provo UT (S)

Telford, Rachel, *Archive Asst,* National Museum of the American Indian, Archives, Washington DC

Teller, Kelly, *Dir Develop,* Indianapolis Art Center, Marilyn K. Glick School of Art, Indianapolis IN

Tellier, Cassandra Lee, *Dir,* Capital University, Schumacher Gallery, Columbus OH

Temple, Daniel, *VPres Library,* Kenyon College, Olin Art Gallery, Gambier OH

Temple, Harold, *Prof,* Wayland Baptist University, Dept of Art, School of Fine Art, Plainview TX (S)

Temple, Paula, *Prof,* University of Mississippi, Department of Art, University MS (S)

Temple, Steve, *Dir,* Gadsden Museum of Fine Arts, Inc, Gadsden Museum of Art and History, Gadsden AL

Templer, Peggy, *Exec Dir,* Mendocino Art Center, Gallery & School, Mendocino CA

Templer, Peggy, *Exec Dir,* Mendocino Art Center, Mendocino CA (S)

Templer, Peggy, *Exec Dir,* Mendocino Art Center, Library, Mendocino CA

Templeton, Amy, *Deputy Dir,* Birmingham Museum of Art, Birmingham AL

Templeton, Amy W, *Dir of Develop,* Birmingham Museum of Art, Clarence B Hanson Jr Library, Birmingham AL

Templeton, Ed, *Dir,* New Image Art, West Hollywood CA

Templeton, Kimberly, *Dir External Affairs,* Taubman Museum of Art, Roanoke VA

Templeton, Rijn, *Head Librn,* University of Iowa, Art Library, Iowa City IA

Templeton, Tracy, *Asst Prof,* Southern Oregon University, Art & Art History Dept, Ashland OR (S)

Tenabe, Gabriel S, *Dir & Cur,* Morgan State University, James E Lewis Museum of Art, Baltimore MD

Tennant, Andy, *Asst Dir,* Auburn University, Julie Collins Smith Museum, Auburn AL

Tennant, Brad, *Dir,* Wein Gallery, Aberdeen SD

Tennant, Carolyn, *Media Cur,* Hallwalls Contemporary Arts Center, Buffalo NY

Tennen, Steve, *Exec Dir,* ArtsConnection Inc, New York NY

Tenney, Kim, *Cur Arts Dept,* Boston Public Library, Arts Reference Department, Boston MA

Tenney, Kimberly, *Cur the Arts,* Boston Public Library, Central Library, Boston MA

Tenny, Elissa, *Dean,* New School University, Adult Education Division, New York NY (S)

Tent, Lauren, *Educ Coordr,* Center for Exploratory & Perceptual Art, CEPA Library, Buffalo NY

Tent, Lauren, *Educ Dir,* Center for Exploratory & Perceptual Art, CEPA Gallery, Buffalo NY

Teramoto, John, *Asst Prof,* University of Kansas, Kress Foundation Dept of Art History, Lawrence KS (S)

Teramoto, John, *Cur, Asian Art,* Indianapolis Museum of Art, Indianapolis IN

teRiele-Karkoski, Heidi, *Cur Landscape,* Fort Ticonderoga Association, Ticonderoga NY

ter Kuile, Jacqueline, *Registrar,* Grounds for Sculpture, Hamilton NJ

Terpstra, Jennifer Williams, *Chmn,* University of Wisconsin-La Crosse, Center for the Arts, La Crosse WI (S)

Terrano, Robert A, *Dean,* Mercer County Community College, Arts, Communication & Engineering Technology, West Windsor NJ (S)

Terrasi, Tore, *Asst Prof,* University of Texas at Arlington, Art & Art History Department, Arlington TX (S)

Terratas, Angela, *Mus Asst,* United States Figure Skating Association, World Figure Skating Museum & Hall of Fame, Colorado Springs CO

Terrell, James, *Chmn,* Northeastern State University, College of Arts & Letters, Tahlequah OK (S)

Terrell, Krista, *VP Pub Rels & Communs,* Arts & Science Council, Charlotte NC

Terrell, Richard, *Head Dept,* Doane College, Dept of Art, Crete NE (S)

Terrenato, Nicholas, *Assoc Prof,* University of Michigan, Kelsey Museum of Archaeology, Ann Arbor MI

Terreri, Taylor, *Office Mgr,* Warwick Museum of Art, Warwick RI

Terrono, Evie, *Lectr,* Randolph-Macon College, Dept of the Arts, Ashland VA (S)

Terry, Carol, *Dir,* Rhode Island School of Design, Fleet Library at RISD, Providence RI

Terry, Christopher, *Assoc Prof,* Utah State University, Dept of Art, Logan UT (S)

Terry, James H, *Chair,* Stephens College, Art Dept, Columbia MO (S)

Terry, Meghan, *Grad Advisor,* University of Tennessee, Visual Arts Committee, Knoxville TN

Tersteeg, William, *Prof,* Keystone College, Fine Arts Dept, LaPlume PA (S)

Terzia, Louise, *Develop Dir,* Historic Arkansas Museum, Little Rock AR

Terzia, Louise, *Develop Dir,* Historic Arkansas Museum, Library, Little Rock AR

Tesner, Linda, *Dir,* Ronna and Eric Hoffman Gallery of Contemporary Art, Portland OR

Tesso, Jane B, *Consulting Cur,* Federal Reserve Bank of Cleveland, Cleveland OH

Tesson, Brian, *Pres,* Copper Village Museum & Arts Center, Anaconda MT

Tetenbaum, Barb, *Book Arts,* Oregon College of Art & Craft, Portland OR (S)

Teter, Jennifer, *Dir Educ,* Quincy Art Center, Quincy IL

Teter, Marcia, *Mus Coordr,* Daum Museum of Contemporary Art, Sedalia MO

Teterenko, Paul, *Pres,* Ukrainian Canadian Archives & Museum of Alberta, Edmonton AB

Tetkowski, Neil, *Dir Gallery,* Kean University, James Howe Gallery, Union NJ

Teunis, Janet, *Managing Dir,* Urban Institute for Contemporary Arts, Grand Rapids MI

Teverow, Lee, *Reference Librn,* Rhode Island Historical Society, Library, Providence RI

Tewell, Tanya, *Instr,* Middle Tennessee State University, Art Dept, Murfreesboro TN (S)

Thacker, Terry, *Prof Fine Art,* Watkins College of Art, Design & Film, Nashville TN (S)

Thaler, Janice M, *Bd Mem,* French Art Colony, Gallipolis OH

Thalhuber, Margaret, *Dept Mgr,* University of California, Berkeley, College of Letters & Sciences-Art Practice Dept, Berkeley CA (S)

Thames, Charles, *Cur, Art Coll,* 3M, Art Collection, Maplewood MN

Thau, Sheila, *Dir,* Quietude Garden Gallery, East Brunswick NJ

Thaxton-Ward, Vanessa, *Cur Colls,* Hampton University, University Museum, Hampton VA

Thayer, Laura, *Mus Programs Mgr,* Eastern Washington State Historical Society, Northwest Museum of Arts & Culture, Spokane WA

Thayer, Preston, *Dir Gallery,* Augustana College, Augustana College Art Museum, Rock Island IL

Thayer, Tom, *Lectr,* City College of New York, Art Dept, New York NY (S)

Theaman, Jessica, *Devel,* Archives of American Art, Smithsonian Institution, Washington DC

Theilking, Kristin, *Asst Prof,* University of Wisconsin-Stevens Point, Dept of Art & Design, Stevens Point WI (S)

Thein, John, *Instr,* Creighton University, Fine & Performing Arts Dept, Omaha NE (S)

Theis, Leah, *Slide Librn,* University of California, Art Dept Library, Davis CA

Theisen, Nate, *Asst Prof of Art,* Belhaven College, Art Dept, Jackson MS (S)

Theo, Christos, *Chmn,* University of Wisconsin-Eau Claire, Dept of Art & Design, Eau Claire WI (S)

Theodore, Wiebke, *Vis Asst Prof,* Bowdoin College, Art Dept, Brunswick ME (S)

Theoret, Yves, *Managing Dir,* Museum of Contemporary Canadian Art, Toronto ON

Theriault, Michele, *Dir,* Concordia University, Leonard & Bina Ellen Art Gallery, Montreal PQ

Thesen, Sharon, *Assoc Prof (Creative Writing),* University of British Columbia Okanagan, Dept of Creative Studies, Kelowna BC (S)

Thesing, Claudia, *Dir Develop,* New Britain Museum of American Art, New Britain CT

Thibault, Barbara, *Dir,* Gibson Society, Inc, Gibson House Museum, Boston MA

Thibault, Nathalie, *Documentary & Archives Mngmt,* Musee National des Beaux Arts du Quebec, Bibliotheque, Quebec PQ

Thibodean, Marianne, *Asst Dir,* Wentworth Institute of Technology Library, Boston MA

Thiesen, Barbara A, *Librn,* Bethel College, Mennonite Library & Archives, North Newton KS

Thiesen, John D, *Archivist,* Bethel College, Mennonite Library & Archives, North Newton KS

Thi Hoi, Dao, *Librn,* VICANA (Vietnamese Cultural Association in North America) Library, Springfield VA

Thistle, Paul, *Dir,* Dawson City Museum & Historical Society, Dawson City YT

Thistlethwaite, Mark, *Prof,* Texas Christian University, School of Art, Fort Worth TX (S)

Thom, Ian, *Sr Cur,* Vancouver Art Gallery, Vancouver BC

Thom, Laine, *Naturalist,* Grand Teton National Park Service, Colter Bay Indian Arts Museum, Moose WY

Thomas, Ally, *Educ Coordr,* Erie Art Museum, Erie PA

Thomas, Andrew L, *American Specialist,* National Gallery of Art, Department of Image Collections, Washington DC

Thomas, Angela, *Dir Mktg,* Knoxville Museum of Art, Knoxville TN

Thomas, Ann, *Cur, Photography,* National Gallery of Canada, Ottawa ON

Thomas, Ben, *Educ & Outreach Coordr,* Archaeological Institute of America, Boston MA

Thomas, Bruce, *Assoc,* Lehigh University, Dept of Art, Architecture & Design, Bethlehem PA (S)

Thomas, Bruce, *Vis Asst Prof,* Hamline University, Dept of Studio Arts & Art History, Saint Paul MN (S)

Thomas, C David, *Prof,* Emmanuel College, Art Dept, Boston MA (S)

Thomas, Charles, *Trustee,* L D Brinkman, Kerrville TX

Thomas, Christopher, *Asst Prof,* University of Victoria, Dept of History in Art, Victoria BC (S)

Thomas, Christopher, *Lectr,* University of North Carolina at Greensboro, Art Dept, Greensboro NC (S)

Thomas, Dana, *Donor & Guest Relations Liaison & Educ Cur,* Rollins College, George D & Harriet W Cornell Fine Arts Museum, Winter Park FL

Thomas, Delesha, *Pub Rels,* Carnegie Center for Art & History, New Albany IN

Thomas, Elaine, *Pub Relations,* The Sandwich Historical Society, Inc & Sandwich Glass Museum, Sandwich Glass Museum, Sandwich MA

Thomas, Elizabeth, *Matrix Cur,* University of California, Berkeley, Berkeley Art Museum & Pacific Film Archive, Berkeley CA

Thomas, Erin, *Educ Dir,* Cedar Rapids Museum of Art, Cedar Rapids IA

Thomas, Floyd, *Acting Dir,* Ohio Historical Society, National Afro-American Museum & Cultural Center, Wilberforce OH

Thomas, Gary, *Prof,* Culver-Stockton College, Art Dept, Canton MO (S)

Thomas, Jack, *Information Technology,* University of Illinois at Urbana-Champaign, Spurlock Museum, Champaign IL

Thomas, Jacob, *Dir of Arboretum,* Barnes Foundation, Merion PA

Thomas, James E, *Prof,* Rochester Institute of Technology, School of Design, Rochester NY (S)

Thomas, Janet, *Technical Servs Librn,* Ringling College of Art & Design, Verman Kimbrough Memorial Library, Sarasota FL

Thomas, Joan, *Supervisory Cur Art,* Marine Corps University, National Museum of the Marine Corps, Triangle VA

Thomas, Joe, *Assoc Prof,* Clarion University of Pennsylvania, Dept of Art, Clarion PA (S)

Thomas, Joe, *Chmn,* Clarion University, Hazel Sandford Gallery, Clarion PA

Thomas, Julie Bledsoe, *Treas,* North Carolina Museums Council, Raleigh NC

Thomas, Kristi, *Educ Asst,* Augustana College, Center for Western Studies, Sioux Falls SD

Thomas, Kristy, *Gallery Cur,* The Center for Visual Artists - Greensboro, Greensboro NC

Thomas, Kurtis, *Cur Coll,* Mobile Museum of Art, Mobile AL

Thomas, Kurtis, *Cur Collections,* Mobile Museum of Art, Library, Mobile AL

Thomas, Larry, *Prof & Chair Fine Art,* Johnson County Community College, Fine Arts Dept & Art History Dept, Overland Park KS (S)

Thomas, Leigh, *Asst Dir,* Norwich Free Academy, Slater Memorial Museum, Norwich CT

Thomas, Linda, *Asst Dir Exhib & Coll,* Saint Louis Art Museum, Saint Louis MO

Thomas, Lorelle, *Prof,* Grand Valley State University, Art & Design Dept, Allendale MI (S)

Thomas, Mark, *Prof,* Art Academy of Cincinnati, Cincinnati OH (S)

Thomas, Michele M, *Gen Educ,* Art Institute of Pittsburgh, Pittsburgh PA (S)

Thomas, Nancy, *Deputy Dir Cur Admin,* Los Angeles County Museum of Art, Los Angeles CA

Thomas, Paul, *Assoc Prof,* Illinois Institute of Technology, College of Architecture, Chicago IL (S)

Thomas, Prince, *Assoc Prof,* Lamar University, Art Dept, Beaumont TX (S)

Thomas, Robert, *Deputy Dir,* Oklahoma Historical Society, Library Resources Division, Oklahoma City OK

Thomas, Steve, *Educ Cur,* Riverside Art Museum, Riverside CA

Thomas, Susan, *Adjunct Prof Art,* University of Great Falls, Art Dept, Great Falls MT (S)

Thomas, Susanne, *Lectr,* University of North Carolina at Greensboro, Art Dept, Greensboro NC (S)

Thomas, Sylvia Lynn, *Exec Dir,* Dawson Springs Museum and Art Center, Dawson Springs KY

Thomas, Tara, *Dir Educ,* Colorado Springs Fine Arts Center, Taylor Museum, Colorado Springs CO

Thomas, Tara, *Dir Educ,* Colorado Springs Fine Arts Center, Bemis School of Art, Colorado Springs CO

Thomas, Ted, *Treas,* Berks Art Alliance, Reading PA

Thomas, Thelma, *Assoc Prof,* University of Michigan, Ann Arbor, Dept of History of Art, Ann Arbor MI (S)

Thomas, Troy, *Assoc Prof,* Penn State Harrisburg, School of Humanities, Middletown PA (S)

Thomas, William, *Grounds & Maint,* Art Complex Museum, Carl A. Weyerhaeuser Library, Duxbury MA

Thomas, William G, *Supt,* San Francisco Maritime National Historical Park, Maritime Museum, San Francisco CA

Thomas-Clark, Jill, *Rights & Reproductions Mgr,* Corning Museum of Glass, Juliette K and Leonard S Rakow Research Library, Corning NY

Thomas-McGee, Gina, *Assoc Educator,* Akron Art Museum, Akron OH

Thomas-Vickory, Stacy, *Printmaking,* Montserrat College of Art, Beverly MA (S)

Thomason, Barbara, *Lectr,* California State Polytechnic University, Pomona, Department of Art, Pomona CA (S)

Thompson, Amanda, *Registrar,* Museum for African Art, New York NY

Thompson, Ann, *Instr,* Appalachian State University, Dept of Art, Boone NC (S)

Thompson, Calla, *Asst Prof,* University of Maryland, Baltimore County, Imaging & Digital Arts (IMDA), Dept of Visual Arts, Baltimore MD (S)

Thompson, Carol, *Cur African Art,* High Museum of Art, Atlanta GA

Thompson, Carolyn, *Educ Asst,* Historical Museum at Fort Missoula, Missoula MT

Thompson, Cheryl, *Dir Admin,* Dawson City Museum & Historical Society, Dawson City YT

Thompson, Cheryl, *Mus Aide,* City of Nome Alaska, Carrie M McLain Memorial Museum, Nome AK

Thompson, Christine, *Prof Art Educ,* Pennsylvania State University, University Park, Penn State School of Visual Arts, University Park PA (S)

Thompson, Christy, *Dir,* Redhead Gallery, Toronto ON

Thompson, Daren, *Cur Educ,* Honolulu Academy of Arts, The Art Center at Linekona, Honolulu HI (S)

Thompson, Dave, *Finance Dir,* The New England Museum of Telephony, Inc., The Telephone Museum, Ellsworth ME

Thompson, Dolie, *Instr,* Morningside College, Art Dept, Sioux City IA (S)

Tingley, Charles, *Library Dir,* Saint Augustine Historical Society, Library, Saint Augustine FL

Tingley, Charles, *Library Mgr,* Saint Augustine Historical Society, Oldest House Museum Complex, Saint Augustine FL

Tinker, William, *Treas,* Wichita Center for the Arts, Wichita KS

Tinney, Harle, *Exec Dir,* Royal Arts Foundation, Belcourt Castle, Newport RI

Tinsley, Maggi, *Mktg & Media,* Visual Arts Center of Richmond, Richmond VA

Tinterow, Gary, *Dir,* Museum of Fine Arts, Houston, Houston TX

Tio, Teresa, *Prof,* University of Puerto Rico, Dept of Fine Arts, Rio Piedras PR (S)

Tio, Teresa, *Prof,* University of Puerto Rico, Dept of Fine Arts, Rio Piedras PR (S)

Tippit, Mike, *Mus Shop Mgr,* Oklahoma Historical Society, Library Resources Division, Oklahoma City OK

Tisdale, Jane, *Fine Art Conservator,* Mount Allison University, Owens Art Gallery, Sackville NB

Tisdale, Rainey, *Dir The Old State House Museum,* The Bostonian Society, Old State House Museum, Boston MA

Tisdale, Shelby, *Dir,* Museum of New Mexico, New Mexico Museum of Art, Santa Fe NM

Tite, Winston, *Assoc Prof,* University of North Carolina at Charlotte, Dept Art, Charlotte NC (S)

Titman, Allison, *Asst Dir & Cur,* Hammond-Harwood House Association, Inc, Hammond-Harwood House, Annapolis MD

Titmus, Wilma, *Office Mgr,* Herrett Center for Arts & Sciences, Jean B King Art Gallery, Twin Falls ID

Titus, Harry B, *Prof,* Wake Forest University, Dept of Art, Winston-Salem NC (S)

Titus, Jack, *Prof,* Oklahoma State University, Department of Art, Graphic Design and Art History, Stillwater OK (S)

Titus, Katherin Canton, *Admin Gallery Coordr,* Pro Arts, Oakland CA

Tkaczuk, Lydia, *VPres,* Ukrainian National Museum & Library, Chicago IL

Tobias, Harvey, *Treas,* San Bernardino Art Association, Inc, Sturges Fine Arts Center, San Bernardino CA

Tobias, Jennifer, *Librn, Collection Develop,* Museum of Modern Art, Library and Museum Archives, New York NY

Tobier, Nick, *Asst Prof,* University of Michigan, Ann Arbor, School of Art & Design, Ann Arbor MI (S)

Tobkin, Donna, *Dir Finance,* Triton Museum of Art, Santa Clara CA

Tocci, Alison, *Vol,* Waterfront Museum, Brooklyn NY

Todd, Andrea, *Mktg Dir,* Willard Arts Center, Carr Gallery, Colonial Theater, Idaho Falls ID

Todd, Gui, *Instr,* Modesto Junior College, Arts Humanities & Communications Division, Modesto CA (S)

Todd, Mark, *Prof,* Texas State University - San Marcos, Dept of Art and Design, San Marcos TX (S)

Todd, Melody, *Asst Prof,* Mount Mary College, Art & Design Division, Milwaukee WI (S)

Todd, Sandy, *Exec Asst,* Rollins College, George D & Harriet W Cornell Fine Arts Museum, Winter Park FL

Todenhoff, Mary, *Adjunct,* York College of Pennsylvania, Dept of Music, Art & Speech Communications, York PA (S)

Todoroff, Rhonda, *Asst Prof,* Tidewater Community College, Visual Arts Center, Portsmouth VA (S)

Toensing, Robert E, *Instr,* Anoka Ramsey Community College, Art Dept, Coon Rapids MN (S)

Toffle, Sommer, *Ligonier Valley Coordr,* Southern Alleghenies Museum of Art, Ligonier Valley Facility, Loretto PA

Tofolo, Robert, *Dir Retail & Wholesale,* Whitney Museum of American Art, New York NY

Tognarelli, Paula, *Exec Dir,* Arthur Griffin Center for Photographic Art, Griffin Museum of Photography, Winchester MA

Togneri, Carol, *Chief Cur,* Norton Simon, Pasadena CA

Toivaner, Kati, *Chmn,* University of Missouri-Kansas City, Dept of Art & Art History, Kansas City MO (S)

Toker, Franklin, *Prof,* University of Pittsburgh, Henry Clay Frick Dept History of Art & Architecture, Pittsburgh PA (S)

Toku, Masami, *Prof,* California State University, Chico, Department of Art & Art History, Chico CA (S)

Tolan, Ron, *Facility Mgr,* Indiana State Museum, Indianapolis IN

Tolbert, Javier, *Instr,* Clark-Atlanta University, School of Arts & Sciences, Atlanta GA (S)

Toler, James, *Mgr Security,* Indiana State Museum, Indianapolis IN

Toler, Joey, *Prog Dir,* Beaufort County Arts Council, Washington NC

Toll, Carmen, *Exec Dir,* The Dalles Art Association, The Dalles Art Center, The Dalles OR

Tolmie, Kris, *Asst Prof,* College of Saint Rose, The Center For Art and Design, Albany NY (S)

Tolnick, Judith, *Galleries Dir,* University of Rhode Island, Fine Arts Center Galleries, Kingston RI

Tolstedt, Lowell, *Dean,* Columbus College of Art & Design, Fine Arts Dept, Columbus OH (S)

Toluse, Joe, *Cur,* Idaho Historical Museum, Boise ID

Tom, Gregory, *Dir Gallery,* Eastern Michigan University, Ford Gallery, Ypsilanti MI

Tomasch, Otto, *Asst Prof,* York College of Pennsylvania, Dept of Music, Art & Speech Communications, York PA (S)

Tomasello, Terry, *Exec Dir,* Creative Arts Guild, Dalton GA

Tombarge, John, *Head Librn,* Washington & Lee University, Leyburn Library, Lexington VA

Tomberlin, Pat, *Museum Shop Mgr,* Montgomery Museum of Fine Arts, Montgomery AL

Tomczak, Catherine, *Operations,* Organization of Saskatchewan Arts Councils (OSAC), Regina SK

Tomczak, Pat, *Dean of Library,* Quincy University, Brenner Library, Quincy IL

Tomio, Ken, *Cur & Head Educ,* Tyler Museum of Art, Reference Library, Tyler TX

Tomio, Ken, *Head Educ Cur,* Tyler Museum of Art, Tyler TX

Tomio, Kimberley Bush, *Dir,* Tyler Museum of Art, Tyler TX

Tomio, Kimberley Bush, *Dir,* Tyler Museum of Art, Reference Library, Tyler TX

Tomko, Monika, *Registrar,* Carnegie Museums of Pittsburgh, Carnegie Museum of Art, Pittsburgh PA

Tomlin, Terry, *Chmn Fine Arts,* University of Texas at Brownsville & Texas Southmost College, Fine Arts Dept, Brownsville TX (S)

Tomlinson, Janis A, *Dir,* University of Delaware, University Museums, Newark DE

Tomor, Michael A, *Dir,* City of El Paso, El Paso TX

Tompkins, Andi, *Mus School Mgr,* Arkansas Arts Center, Museum, Little Rock AR (S)

Tompkins, Jack D, *VPres,* Lincoln Memorial Shrine, Redlands CA

Tompkins-Baldwin, Linda, *Library Dir,* The Baltimore Museum of Art, E Kirkbride Miller Art Library, Baltimore MD

Tompkins-Baldwin, Linda, *Librn,* The Baltimore Museum of Art, Baltimore MD

Tomsic, Walt, *Assoc Prof,* Pacific Lutheran University, Dept of Art, Tacoma WA (S)

Tonelli, Laura, *Dean,* Montserrat College of Art, Beverly MA (S)

Tonetti, Charles, *Chief Architect,* Independence National Historical Park, Library, Philadelphia PA

Tong, Darlene, *Art Librn,* San Francisco State University, J Paul Leonard Library, San Francisco CA

Tonkovich, Jennifer, *Cur Drawings & Prints,* The Morgan Library & Museum, Museum, New York NY

Tonz, Sandra, *Instr,* Mount Mary College, Art & Design Division, Milwaukee WI (S)

Tooker, David, *Exec Dir,* Scottsdale Artists' School, Scottsdale AZ

Tooley, Billie, *Exec Dir,* New Hampshire Art Association, Portsmouth NH

Toon, Richard, *Dir,* Arizona State University, Deer Valley Rock Art Center, Phoenix AZ

Toone, Thomas, *Assoc Prof,* Utah State University, Dept of Art, Logan UT (S)

Tootle, Ann, *Registrar,* The Albrecht-Kemper Museum of Art, Saint Joseph MO

Topfer, Stephen, *Coll Mgr,* Art Gallery of Greater Victoria, Victoria BC

Toplovich, Ann, *CEO,* Tennessee Historical Society, Nashville TN

Topolski, Allen C, *Chmn,* University of Rochester, Dept of Art & Art History, Rochester NY (S)

Topping, Holly, *Instr Life Draw,* Orange Coast College, Visual & Performing Arts Division, Costa Mesa CA (S)

Topping, Karin, *Co-Dir,* Tubac Center of the Arts, Santa Cruz Valley Art Association, Tubac AZ

Torano, Vince, *Painting,* Western Michigan University, Frostic School of Art, Kalamazoo MI (S)

Torchia, Richard, *Gallery Dir,* Arcadia University Art Gallery, Spruance Fine Arts Center, Glenside PA

Torcoletti, Enzo, *Prof,* Flagler College, Visual Arts Dept, Saint Augustine FL (S)

Torgerson, Kari, *COO,* Colorado Springs Fine Arts Center, Taylor Museum, Colorado Springs CO

Torinus, Sigi, *Prof,* University of Windsor, Visual Arts, Windsor ON (S)

Torke, Ann, *Assoc Prof,* University of Massachusetts - Boston, Art Dept, Boston MA (S)

Tornheim, N, *Instr,* Golden West College, Visual Art Dept, Huntington Beach CA (S)

Tornquist, Kristi, *Chief Univ Librn,* South Dakota State University, Hilton M. Briggs Library, Brookings SD

Torrance, Joshua C, *Exec Dir,* Hancock County Trustees of Public Reservations, Woodlawn: Museum, Gardens & Park, Ellsworth ME

Torre, Mike, *Instr,* Northwestern Michigan College, Art Dept, Traverse City MI (S)

Torreano, John, *MFA Prog Co-Dir & BFA Proj,* New York University, Dept of Art & Art Professions, New York NY (S)

Torrenti, Raymond, *Mem & Spec Events Mgr,* Williams College, Museum of Art, Williamstown MA

Torres, Bernadette, *Art Instr/Gallery Dir,* Metropolitan Community College - Penn Valley, Art Dept, Kansas City MO (S)

Torres, Harold, *Tourism Asst,* Pueblo of San Ildefonso, Maria Martinez Museum, Santa Fe NM

Torres, Javier, *Contact,* Villa Victoria Center for the Arts, Boston MA

Torres, Jennifer, *Assoc Prof,* University of Southern Mississippi, Dept of Art & Design, Hattiesburg MS (S)

Torres, Manuel, *Prof,* Florida International University, School of Art & Art History, Miami FL (S)

Torrey, Charles, *Researcher,* History Museum of Mobile, Mobile AL

Torri, Erika, *Exec Dir,* Library Association of La Jolla, Athenaeum Music & Arts Library, La Jolla CA

Tortolero, Carlos, *Exec Dir,* National Museum of Mexican Art, Chicago IL

Toscan, Richard, *Dean,* Virginia Commonwealth University, School of the Arts, Richmond VA (S)

Tosczak, Frank, *Restoration Mgr,* Craigdarroch Castle Historical Museum Society, Victoria BC

Tosten, Erik, *Adjunct Prof,* University of Texas at Arlington, Art & Art History Department, Arlington TX (S)

Tosti, Sally, *Assoc Prof,* Keystone College, Fine Arts Dept, LaPlume PA (S)

Toth, John Michael, *Interior Design,* Art Institute of Pittsburgh, Pittsburgh PA (S)

Toth, Myra, *Chmn,* Ventura College, Fine Arts Dept, Ventura CA (S)

Tottis, James W, *Dir Colls,* Museum of the City of New York, Research Room, New York NY

Totton, Mary-Louise, *Art History,* Western Michigan University, Frostic School of Art, Kalamazoo MI (S)

Toub, Jim, *Assoc Prof,* Appalachian State University, Dept of Art, Boone NC (S)

Toubes, Xavier, *Chmn Ceramics,* School of the Art Institute of Chicago, Chicago IL (S)

Touchine, Maxine Armstrong, *Museum Specialist,* Red Rock Park, Library, Church Rock NM

Toumani, Monica, *Dir Fin,* Arts Council Silicon Valley, San Jose CA

Tourdot, Kelly, *Tech Svcs,* University of Wisconsin-Madison, Kohler Art Library, Madison WI

Tournear, Libby, *Exhibs Prep,* Quincy Art Center, Quincy IL

Tourtillotte, Bill, *Chief Cur,* South Bend Regional Museum of Art, South Bend IN

Tourtillotte, Julie, *Chmn,* Saint Mary's College, Dept of Art, Notre Dame IN (S)

Tousignant, Serge, *Instr*, Universite de Montreal, Dept of Art History, Montreal PQ (S)

Towers, Debbie, *Admin Assoc*, Palm Beach County Parks & Recreation Department, Morikami Museum & Japanese Gardens, Delray Beach FL

Towers, Joel, *Exec Dean*, Parsons The New School for Design, New York NY (S)

Towers, Matthew, *Asst Prof*, University of Hartford, Hartford Art School, West Hartford CT (S)

Towle, Evan, *Librn Reader Svcs*, Philadelphia Museum of Art, Library & Archives, Philadelphia PA

Towle-Hilt, Mary, *Coll Mgr*, Henry Sheldon Museum of Vermont History and Research Center, Middlebury VT

Towler, Patty, *Treas*, San Angelo Art Club, Helen King Kendall Memorial Art Gallery, San Angelo TX

Towne, Marian, *Asst Prof Art Therapy*, Albertus Magnus College, Visual and Performing Arts, New Haven CT (S)

Towner, Mark, *Dean*, Endicott College, School of Visual & Performing Arts, Beverly MA (S)

Towns, Carole, *Bus Admin*, Northwestern University, Mary & Leigh Block Museum of Art, Evanston IL

Townsend, Allen, *Dir*, Yale University, The Robert B. Haas Family Arts Library, New Haven CT

Townsend, Belinda, *Secy*, Maitland Art Center, Maitland FL

Townsend, Dabney, *Secy-Treas*, American Society for Aesthetics, Pooler GA

Townsend, Gavin, *Prof*, University of Tennessee at Chattanooga, Dept of Art, Chattanooga TN (S)

Townsend, Lisa, *VP Mktg & External Rels*, The Children's Museum of Indianapolis, Indianapolis IN

Townsend, Melanie, *Cur Contemporary Art & Head Exhibitions and Collections*, Museum London, London ON

Townsend, Pat O'Brien, *Vol Pres*, Three Forks Area Historical Society, Headwaters Heritage Museum, Three Forks MT

Townsend, Rhys, *Chmn*, Clark University, Dept of Visual & Performing Arts, Worcester MA (S)

Townsend, Richard, *Vol Secy*, Three Forks Area Historical Society, Headwaters Heritage Museum, Three Forks MT

Townsend, Richard F, *Cur Africa, Oceania & the Americas*, The Art Institute of Chicago, Chicago IL

Townsend-Gault, Charlotte, *Prof*, University of British Columbia, Dept of Art History, Visual Art & Theory, Vancouver BC (S)

Toy, Lyda, *Adj Instr*, University of West Florida, Dept of Art, Pensacola FL (S)

Tracey, Lenore, *CFO*, Higgins Armory Museum, Worcester MA

Trachtenberg, Mara, *VPres*, Hera Educational Foundation, Hera Gallery, Wakefield RI

Tracy, Bob, *Prof*, University of Nevada, Las Vegas, Dept of Art, Las Vegas NV (S)

Tracy, Jamie, *Prof*, State College of Florida Manatee - Sarasota, Art, Design, Humanities, Bradenton FL (S)

Tracy, Paul, *Asst Preparator*, Memphis Brooks Museum of Art, Memphis TN

Tracz, Tim, *Chmn*, Austin College, Art Dept, Sherman TX (S)

Traetto, Michela, *Dir*, Order Sons of Italy in America, Garibaldi & Meucci Museum, Staten Island NY

Trafton, Carolyn, *Asst Dir*, Red River Valley Museum, Vernon TX

Trafton, Robin, *Cur*, Commerce Bancshares, Inc, Fine Art Collection, Kansas City MO

Trager, Neil C, *Dir*, State University of New York at New Paltz, Samuel Dorsky Museum of Art, New Paltz NY

Trager, Ruth, *Pres*, Halifax Historical Society, Inc, Halifax Historical Museum, Daytona Beach FL

Trager, Warren, *VPres*, Halifax Historical Society, Inc, Halifax Historical Museum, Daytona Beach FL

Trahan, Eric, *Dir*, Canajoharie Library & Art Gallery, Arkell Museum of Canajoharie, Canajoharie NY

Trahan, Eric, *Dir Library*, Canajoharie Library & Art Gallery, Library, Canajoharie NY

Trainor, Jon, *Dir Develop*, Akron Art Museum, Akron OH

Trainor-Bruzzese, Mavourneen, *Instr*, Lakehead University, Dept of Visual Arts, Thunder Bay ON (S)

Trammell, Mary, *Instr*, Oklahoma State University, Graphic Arts Dept, Visual Communications, Okmulgee OK (S)

Tran, Howard, *Asst Prof*, Lycoming College, Art Dept, Williamsport PA (S)

Traudt, Miranda, *Prog Dir*, Schweinfurth Art Center, Auburn NY

Traugott, Joseph, *Cur 20th Century Painting*, Museum of New Mexico, New Mexico Museum of Art, Unit of NM Dept of Cultural Affairs, Santa Fe NM

Trautman, Charlotte, *Cur*, Mount Vernon Hotel Museum & Garden, New York NY

Trautman, Patricia, *Mus Shop Mgr*, New Orleans Museum of Art, New Orleans LA

Traver, Michelle, *Dir Exhib*, Peoria Art Guild, Peoria IL

Travers, Cindy, *VPres*, Fairfield Art Association, Fairfield IA

Travers, Jason, *Lectr*, Lehigh University, Dept of Art, Architecture & Design, Bethlehem PA (S)

Travis, David, *Cur Photography*, The Art Institute of Chicago, Chicago IL

Travis, Julie, *Asst Mgr*, J Eric Johnson, Fine Arts Division, Dallas TX

Travis, Sven, *Dean School of Art, Media & Tech*, Parsons The New School for Design, New York NY (S)

Traylor, Margaret, *Head of Ref*, Laney College Library, Art Section, Oakland CA

Treadwell, Jaime, *Prof*, Delaware County Community College, Communications, Art & Humanities, Media PA (S)

Trebilcock, Evelyn, *Chief Cur*, Olana State Historic Site, Hudson NY

Trebilcock, Evelyn, *Cur*, Olana State Historic Site, Library, Hudson NY

Trechsel, Gail A, *R Hugh Daniel Dir*, Birmingham Museum of Art, Clarence B Hanson Jr Library, Birmingham AL

Trecker, Stan, *Dean*, Lesley University, College of Art & Design, Boston MA (S)

Tredway, Cherry, *Assoc Prof*, Oklahoma Christian University of Science & Arts, Dept of Art & Design, Oklahoma City OK (S)

Treinen, Wendy, *Dir Communs*, Kentucky Derby Museum, Louisville KY

Tremblay, Manon, *Library Technician*, Montreal Museum of Fine Arts, Library, Montreal PQ

Tremblay, Matthew, *Exhibition Designer/Preparator*, Kamloops Art Gallery, Kamloops BC

Tremble, Steve, *Managing Dir*, Center on Contemporary Art, Seattle WA

Trend, David, *Prof Visual Studies, Culture*, University of California, Irvine, Studio Art Dept, Irvine CA (S)

Trendler, Amy, *Librn*, Ball State University, Architecture Library, Muncie IN

Trenholm, Marjorie, *Office Mgr*, Stanley Museum, Inc, Kingfield ME

Trentham, Rod, *Prog Coordr*, Red Deer & District Museum & Archives, Red Deer AB

Trepanier, Peter, *Head Reader Serv*, National Gallery of Canada, Library, Ottawa ON

Trepp, George, *Dir*, Long Beach Public Library, Long Beach NY

Tresner, Cliff, *Asst Prof*, University of Louisiana at Monroe, Dept of Art, Monroe LA (S)

Tresner, Cliff, *Gallery Dir*, University of Louisiana at Monroe, Bry Gallery, Monroe LA

Trevethan, Shannon, *Dir*, Deines Cultural Center, Russell KS

Trevino, Rene, *Exhibs Coordr*, School 33 Art Center, Baltimore MD

Trickey, Karen, *Prof*, Nazareth College of Rochester, Art Dept, Rochester NY (S)

Triff, Michael, *Communs*, The Trustees of Reservations, The Mission House, Ipswich MA

Trim, Delaynna, *Cur Collections*, Mabee-Gerrer Museum of Art, Shawnee OK

Trim, Delaynna, *Part-Time Instr*, Oklahoma Baptist University, Art Dept, Shawnee OK (S)

Trim, Sheryl, *Dir Finance*, Mississippi Museum of Art, Howorth Library, Jackson MS

Trimble, Brian, *Cur Educ*, California State University, Long Beach, University Art Museum, Long Beach CA

Trimble, Sandy, *Instr*, Seton Hill University, Art Program, Greensburg PA (S)

Trimble, Stephen, *VPres*, Alaska Museum of Natural History, Anchorage AK

Trimmer, Jason, *Cur Educ*, Oberlin College, Allen Memorial Art Museum, Oberlin OH

Triplett, Jayson, *Lectr*, Mississippi State University, Dept of Art, Starville MS (S)

Tripman, Holly, *Registrar*, Cameron Art Museum, Wilmington NC

Tripp, Lauren, *Head Jewelry Dept*, Kalamazoo Institute of Arts, KIA School, Kalamazoo MI (S)

Trippel, Andrew, *Assoc Dir Develop*, Memphis Brooks Museum of Art, Memphis TN

Trippett, Lorraine, *Controller*, LA County Museum of Art, Los Angeles CA

Trisoliere, Robert, *Exhib Fabricator*, Arizona Museum For Youth, Mesa AZ

Trissel, James, *Prof*, Colorado College, Dept of Art, Colorado Springs CO (S)

Tritel, Lynette, *Museum Store*, George Phippen, Phippen Museum - Art of the American West, Prescott AZ

Troccoli, Joan C, *Sr Scholar*, Petrie Institute of Western American Art, Denver Art Museum, Denver CO

Troemner, Deborah W, *Admin Asst*, Philadelphia Museum of Art, Mount Pleasant, Philadelphia PA

Troffkin, Eric, *Dir Grad Studies*, Washington University, School of Art, Saint Louis MO (S)

Tromble, Bill, *Interim Dir Devel*, Colorado Springs Fine Arts Center, Taylor Museum, Colorado Springs CO

Tronzo, Bill, *Prof*, Tulane University, Sophie H Newcomb Memorial College, New Orleans LA (S)

Trosko, Mariella, *Dir Educ*, Hershey Museum, Hershey PA

Trotman, Nat, *Assoc Cur*, Solomon R Guggenheim, New York NY

Trotter, Ruth, *Dept Chmn, Prof Art*, University of La Verne, Dept of Art, La Verne CA (S)

Trotty, Sarah, *Assoc Prof*, Texas Southern University, College of Liberal Arts & Behavioral Sciences, Houston TX (S)

Trousdale, Deborah, *Instr*, Chemeketa Community College, Dept of Humanities & Communications, Art Program, Salem OR (S)

Trouse, Marilyn, *Instr*, West Hills Community College, Fine Arts Dept, Coalinga CA (S)

Trousil, Carrie, *Communs Mgr*, Milwaukee Public Museum, Milwaukee WI

Trout, Katherine, *Admin Asst*, Springfield Museum of Art, Springfield OH (S)

Trovell, Robert, *Instr*, Harrisburg Area Community College, Division of Communications, Humanities & the Arts, Harrisburg PA (S)

Trowbridge, Kyle, *Instr*, University of Miami, Dept of Art & Art History, Coral Gables FL (S)

Troy, John, *Instr*, Joe Kubert, Dover NJ (S)

Troy, V, *Asst Prof*, Berry College, Art Dept, Mount Berry GA (S)

Trubridge, Mark, *Assoc Prof*, Marymount University, School of Arts & Sciences Div, Arlington VA (S)

Trudeau, Marcelle, *Asst to Dir*, Le Musee Marc-Aurele Fortin, Montreal PQ

Trudel, Jean, *Instr*, Universite de Montreal, Dept of Art History, Montreal PQ (S)

True, Marion, *Cur Antiquities*, Getty Center, Trust Museum, Los Angeles CA

True, Rich, *Chmn*, Clackamas Community College, Art Dept, Oregon City OR (S)

Trujillo, Arthur, *Asst Prof*, New Mexico Highlands University, Dept of Communications & Fine Arts, Las Vegas NM (S)

Trulock, Sue, *Dir*, Pine Bluff/Jefferson County Historical Museum, Pine Bluff AR

Truly, Gabriella, *Cir Collections Mgmt*, Dallas Museum of Art, Dallas TX

Truman-McGlohon, Susan, *Temp Asst Prof*, University of Alabama in Huntsville, Dept of Art and Art History, Huntsville AL (S)

Trumble, Angus, *Sr Cur Paintings & Sculpture*, Yale University, Yale Center for British Art, New Haven CT

Trumble, Edward P, *Founder*, Leanin' Tree Museum & Sculpture Garden of Western Art, Boulder CO

Trumble, Kathryn, *Develop Officer*, Montgomery Museum of Fine Arts, Library, Montgomery AL

Trumble, Tom, *Pres*, Leanin' Tree Museum & Sculpture Garden of Western Art, Boulder CO

Trumpey, Joe, *Assoc Prof,* University of Michigan, Ann Arbor, School of Art & Design, Ann Arbor MI (S)

Trumps, Patricia, *Dir Educ,* Ohio State University, Wexner Center for the Arts, Columbus OH

Trumpy, Sigrid, *Cur Robinson Coll,* United States Naval Academy, USNA Museum, Annapolis MD

Trumpy, Sigrid, *Cur of Beverley R Robinson Collection,* United States Naval Academy, Naval Academy Museum, Annapolis MD

Trumpy, Sigrid, *Dir Exhibs,* Maryland Hall for the Creative Arts, Chaney Gallery, Annapolis MD

Trumpy, Sigrid, *Exhibit Preparator,* St John's College, Elizabeth Myers Mitchell Art Gallery, Annapolis MD

Truong, Lien, *Lectr,* Humboldt State University, College of Arts & Humanities, Art Dept, Arcata CA (S)

Trupin, Deborah, *Chief Conservator,* New York State Office of Parks, Recreation and Historic Preservation, Bureau of Historic Sites, Waterford NY

Trutty-Coohill, Patricia, *Chair & Prof Art History,* Siena College, Dept of Creative Arts, Loudonville NY (S)

Tsai, Eugenie, *John & Barbara Vogelstein Cur, Contemporary Art,* Brooklyn Museum, Brooklyn NY

Tsai, Joyce, *Asst Prof,* University of Florida, School of Art & Art History, Gainesville FL (S)

Tsang, Chui L, *Interim Pres,* San Jose City College, School of Fine Arts, San Jose CA (S)

Tsao, Calvin, *Pres,* Architectural League of New York, New York NY

Tsao, Hsingyuan, *Asst Prof,* University of British Columbia, Dept of Art History, Visual Art & Theory, Vancouver BC (S)

Tsatos, Irene, *Dir Gallery Progs,* Armory Center for the Arts, Pasadena CA

Tschernisch, Sergei, *Pres,* Cornish College of the Arts, Art Dept, Seattle WA (S)

Tschinkel, Paul, *Prof,* Queensborough Community College, Dept of Art & Photography, Bayside Hills NY (S)

Tschumi, Bernard, *Dean Architectural Planning,* Columbia University, Graduate School of Architecture, Planning & Preservation, New York NY (S)

Tselentis, Jason, *Lectr,* University of North Carolina at Charlotte, Dept Art, Charlotte NC (S)

Tselos, George, *Supervisory Archivist,* The National Park Service, United States Department of the Interior, Statue of Liberty National Monument & The Ellis Island Immigration Museum, Washington DC

Tso, Kwok-Pong (Bobby), *Instr,* Northwest Missouri State University, Dept of Fine & Performing Arts, Maryville MO (S)

Tsolakis, Alkis, *Chmn,* Drury College, Art & Art History Dept, Springfield MO (S)

Tsuji, Bill, *Dean Humanities,* Sierra Community College, Art Dept, Rocklin CA (S)

Tsukashima, Rodney, *Instr,* Long Beach City College, Art & Photography Dept, Long Beach CA (S)

Tubbs, Lyllian, *Mus Shop Mgr,* Cottonlandia Museum, Greenwood MS

Tubutis, Todd J, *Exec Dir,* Blue Sky Gallery, Oregon Center for the Photographic Arts, Portland OR

Tucci, Judy, *Instr,* Northeast Mississippi Junior College, Art Dept, Booneville MS (S)

Tuccillo, Anita, *Asst Prof,* Illinois Central College, Arts & Communication Dept, East Peoria IL (S)

Tuccillo, John, *Prof,* Illinois Central College, Arts & Communication Dept, East Peoria IL (S)

Tuck, David, *Co-Dir,* Wynick Tuck Gallery, Toronto ON

Tucke, Bethany, *Deputy Dir,* The Andy Warhol Museum, Museum, Pittsburgh PA

Tucker, Ben, *Co-Chmn Music,* Western New Mexico University, Dept of Expressive Arts, Silver City NM (S)

Tucker, Brenda, *Dir Communications,* California College of the Arts, CCAC Wattis Institute for Contemporary Arts, San Francisco CA

Tucker, Brenda, *Dir Pub Rels,* Capp Street Project, Wattis Institute, San Francisco CA

Tucker, Brian, *Gallery Dir,* Pasadena City College, Art Gallery, Pasadena CA

Tucker, Buffie, *Mems Council Coordr,* University of Iowa, University of Iowa Museum of Art, Iowa City IA

Tucker, Gary, *Gallery Dir,* Kaji Aso Studio, Gallery Nature & Temptation, Boston MA

Tucker, Kevin W, *Cur Decorative Arts & Design,* Dallas Museum of Art, Dallas TX

Tucker, LC, *Chief Preparator,* Mississippi Museum of Art, Howorth Library, Jackson MS

Tucker, Linda L, *Asst,* Black River Academy Museum & Historical Society, Black River Academy Museum, Ludlow VT

Tucker, Paul, *Prof,* University of Massachusetts - Boston, Art Dept, Boston MA (S)

Tucker, Susan, *Dir,* Ormond Memorial Art Museum and Gardens, Ormond Beach FL

Tucker, Tracy, *Exec Dir,* Association of Medical Illustrators, Lexington KY

Tudor, William-John, *Exhib & Tech Dir, Ctr for Art, Design & Visual Culture,* University of Maryland, Baltimore County, Imaging & Digital Arts (IMDA), Dept of Visual Arts, Baltimore MD (S)

Tuffy, Eiliesh, *Preservation Adminr,* Cambridge Historical Commission, Research Library on Architectural Social History of Cambridge, Mass, Cambridge MA

Tugwell, Maurice, *Asst Dean of Arts,* Acadia University, Art Dept, Wolfville NS (S)

Tukey, Phillip A, *VPres Devel,* Brookgreen Gardens, Murrells Inlet SC

Tullis, Linda, *Exec Dir,* Lewistown Art Center, Lewistown MT

Tully, Inger, *Cur,* The Contemporary Museum at First Hawaiian Center, Honolulu HI

Tully, Inger, *Cur Exhibs,* The Contemporary Museum, Honolulu HI

Tulovsky, Julia, *Assoc Cur Russian & Soviet Art,* Rutgers, The State University of New Jersey, Zimmerli Art Museum, Rutgers University, New Brunswick NJ

Tuma, Gary, *Exec Dir,* Walker's Point Center for the Arts, Milwaukee WI

Tuma, Mary, *Assoc Prof,* University of North Carolina at Charlotte, Dept Art, Charlotte NC (S)

Tuman, Donna, *Asst Prof,* C W Post Campus of Long Island University, School of Visual & Performing Arts, Brookville NY (S)

Tung, Lisa, *Dir,* Massachusetts College of Art, Bakalar & Paine Galleries, Boston MA

Tunstall, Arnold, *Colls Mgr,* Akron Art Museum, Akron OH

Tupa, Dana Chapman, *Div Chair Art,* Jacksonville University, Dept of Art, Theater, Dance, Jacksonville FL (S)

Tupper, Jon, *Dir,* Art Gallery of Greater Victoria, Victoria BC

Turbide, Chantal, *Museum Cur,* Saint Joseph's Oratory, Museum, Montreal PQ

Turk, Christopher, *Prof,* East Los Angeles College, Art Dept, Monterey Park CA (S)

Turk, Gloria, *Librn,* San Jose Museum of Art, Library, San Jose CA

Turkovic, Dana, *Cur Exhib,* Laumeier Sculpture Park, Saint Louis MO

Turley, G Pasha, *Gallery Dir,* Southwestern College, Art Gallery, Chula Vista CA

Turley, Lindsay, *Librn,* Whitney Museum of American Art, New York NY

Turlington, Matthew, *Photog Instr,* Southwestern Community College, Advertising & Graphic Design, Sylva NC (S)

Turlington, Patricia, *Instr,* Wayne Community College, Liberal Arts Dept, Goldsboro NC (S)

Turmel, Jean, *Admin Asst,* Hermitage Foundation Museum, Norfolk VA

Turner, Anderson, *Galleries Dir,* Kent State University, School of Art Galleries, Kent OH

Turner, Anderson, *Dir Galleries,* Kent State University, School of Art, Kent OH (S)

Turner, Becky, *Chmn Board,* Wichita Center for the Arts, Wichita KS

Turner, Carlton, *Exec Dir,* Alternate ROOTS, Inc, Atlanta GA

Turner, Cindy, *Visual Resources Cur,* Ball State University, Architecture Library, Muncie IN

Turner, Colin D, *Exec Dir,* Midwest Art Conservation Center, Minneapolis MN

Turner, Elizabeth, *Univ Prof,* University of Virginia, McIntire Dept of Art, Charlottesville VA (S)

Turner, Eric, *Events Coordr,* Salisbury University, Ward Museum of Wildfowl Art, Salisbury MD

Turner, Frank M, *Prof,* Yale University, Beinecke Rare Book & Manuscript Library, New Haven CT

Turner, James, *Instr,* Bethany College, Art Dept, Lindsborg KS (S)

Turner, Jeff, *Asst Prof,* Maryville College, Dept of Fine Arts, Maryville TN (S)

Turner, Jim, *Instr,* Bethany College, Mingenback Art Center, Lindsborg KS

Turner, John D, *Prof,* University of North Alabama, Dept of Art, Florence AL (S)

Turner, Judith, *Dir,* Art Instruction Schools, Education Dept, Minneapolis MN (S)

Turner, Kevin, *Assoc Prof,* Indiana University of Pennsylvania, College of Fine Arts, Indiana PA (S)

Turner, Kevin, *Instr (3-D),* Mississippi Gulf Coast Community College-Jackson County Campus, Art Dept, Gautier MS (S)

Turner, Laurel, *Cur Exhibitions,* Charles Allis Art Museum, Milwaukee WI

Turner, Lynn M, *Colls Mgr & Registrar,* United States Department of State, Diplomatic Reception Rooms, Washington DC

Turner, Marietta, *Instr,* Bismarck State College, Fine Arts Dept, Bismarck ND (S)

Turner, Michele, *Librn,* The Currier Museum of Art, Library, Manchester NH

Turner, Nancy, *Dir Community Relations,* Columbus Museum of Art, Columbus OH

Turner, Richard, *Prof,* Chapman University, Art Dept, Orange CA (S)

Turner, Shannon M, *Mgr Progs & Svcs,* Alternate ROOTS, Inc, Atlanta GA

Turner, Sylvia, *Dean of Fine & Performing Arts,* Santa Ana College, Art Dept, Santa Ana CA (S)

Turner, Tom, *Chmn,* Pacific Union College, Art Dept, Angwin CA (S)

Turner-Ingham, Dianne, *Educ Specialist,* Ohio Historical Society, National Afro-American Museum & Cultural Center, Wilberforce OH

Turner-Lowe, Susan, *VPres Communs,* The Huntington Library, Art Collections & Botanical Gardens, San Marino CA

Turner-Lowe, Susan, *VPres Communs,* The Huntington Library, Art Collections & Botanical Gardens, Library, San Marino CA

Turner-Rahman, Gregory, *Assoc Prof,* University of Idaho/College of Art & Architecture, Dept of Art & Design, Moscow ID (S)

Turnock, Elizabeth, *Exec Dir,* Garrison Art Center, Garrison NY

Turnock, Jack, *Assoc Prof of Art,* Jacksonville University, Dept of Art, Theater, Dance, Jacksonville FL (S)

Turnock, Jack, *Dir,* Jacksonville University, Alexander Brest Museum & Gallery, Jacksonville FL

Turnure, James, *Prof,* Bucknell University, Dept of Art, Lewisburg PA (S)

Turounet, Paul, *Dept Chair,* Grossmont Community College, Hyde Art Gallery, El Cajon CA

Turpin, David, *Pres,* University of Victoria, The Legacy Art Gallery, Victoria BC

Turri, Scott, *Instr,* Clarion University of Pennsylvania, Dept of Art, Clarion PA (S)

Turrill, Catherine, *Chmn,* California State University, Sacramento, Dept of Art, Sacramento CA (S)

Turschman, Rick, *Asst Mgr Security & Guest Servs,* Smith College, Museum of Art, Northampton MA

Turtell, Neal, *Chief Librn,* National Gallery of Art, Washington DC

Turtell, Neal, *Exec Librn,* National Gallery of Art, Library, Washington DC

Turvey, Joyce Clarke, *Owner & Mgr,* The John L. Clarke Western Art Gallery & Memorial Museum, East Glacier Park MT

Tuscano, *Prof,* Lynn University, Art & Design Dept, Boca Raton FL (S)

Tush, Peter, *Cur Educ,* Salvador Dali, Library, Saint Petersburg FL

Tusman, Lee, *Adult Educ Cur,* Riverside Art Museum, Library, Riverside CA

Tustin, Kerry, *Asst Prof,* Flagler College, Visual Arts Dept, Saint Augustine FL (S)

Tuttle, David, *Reparator/Registrar,* Art Gallery of Swift Current, Swift Current SK

Tuttle, Gail, *Dir & Cur,* Memorial University of Newfoundland, Sir Wilfred Grenfell College Art Gallery, Corner Brook NF

Tuttle, Judith, *Consultant,* Tattoo Art Museum, San Francisco CA

Tuttle, Kevin, *Instr,* Muhlenberg College, Dept of Art, Allentown PA (S)

Tuttle, Lyle, *Dir,* Tattoo Art Museum, San Francisco CA

Tuzzeo, Suzanne, *Adj Instr,* University of West Florida, Dept of Art, Pensacola FL (S)

Tveekrem, Susan, *Mng Dir,* Bard College, Milton Avery Graduate School of the Arts, Annandale-on-Hudson NY (S)

Twa, Lindsay, *Dir,* Augustana College, Eide-Dalrymple Gallery, Sioux Falls SD

Twachtmann, Jeannette, *Museum Relations,* University of Tampa, Henry B Plant Museum, Tampa FL

Tweedy, Joan, *Asst Prof,* University of North Carolina at Charlotte, Dept Art, Charlotte NC (S)

Tweten, Emily, *Event Mgr,* Rochester Art Center, Rochester MN

Twiss-Houting, Beth, *Dir Progs,* Historical Society of Pennsylvania, Philadelphia PA

Tyler, James, *Dir,* GAGA Arts Center, Garnerville NY

Tyler, Ron, *Dir,* Amon Carter Museum of American Art, Fort Worth TX

Tymas-Jones, Raymond, *Dean,* University of Utah, Dept of Art & Art History, Salt Lake City UT (S)

Tymchuk, Kerry, *Exec Dir,* Oregon Historical Society, Oregon History Museum, Portland OR

Tynemouth, Brian, *Librn,* Suffolk University, New England School of Art & Design Library, Boston MA

Tyneski, Frank, *Exec Dir,* Industrial Designers Society of America, Herndon VA

Tyre, William, *Exec Dir & Cur,* Glessner House Museum, Chicago IL

Tyree, Morgan, *Asst Prof,* Northwest Community College, Dept of Art, Powell WY (S)

Tyrer, Nancy, *Asst Dir,* Heritage Museums & Gardens, Sandwich MA

Tyrrell, Kimberly, *Studio Mgr,* Clayworks Gallery, Charlotte NC

Tyson, Neil Degrasse, *Frederick P Rose D,* American Museum of Natural History, New York NY

Tyson, Rhonda R, *Exhib & Design Mgr,* Jamestown-Yorktown Foundation, Jamestown Settlement, Williamsburg VA

Uchin, Andrew, *Mus Store Mgr,* Norton Simon, Pasadena CA

Udechukwu, Obiora, *Prof,* St Lawrence University, Dept of Fine Arts, Canton NY (S)

Udesen, Britt, *Dir Educ,* Sun Valley Center for the Arts, Dept of Fine Art, Sun Valley ID (S)

Udick, James, *Coll Admin,* Hockaday Museum of Art, Kalispell MT

Uduehi, Joseph, *Assoc Prof,* University of Southern Indiana, Department of Art, Evansville IN (S)

Uetz, M Katherine, *Dir,* Xavier University, Art Gallery, Cincinnati OH

Uhde, Jan, *Prof,* University of Waterloo, Fine Arts Dept, Waterloo ON (S)

Uhlein, Thomas, *Asst Prof,* William Paterson University, Dept Arts, Wayne NJ (S)

Uhlenbrock, Jaimee, *Assoc Cur of Coll,* State University of New York at New Paltz, Samuel Dorsky Museum of Art, New Paltz NY

Uithol, Ruthann, *Asst Dir of Colls & Colls Mgr,* Hillwood Museum & Gardens Foundation, Hillwood Estate Museum & Gardens, Washington DC

Ujczo, Anne, *Facilities Planner,* Federal Reserve Bank of Cleveland, Cleveland OH

Ulacia, Marietta, *Dir Develop & Dir Theater Progs,* Museum for African Art, New York NY

Ulibarri, Nadine, *Cur,* Pueblo of Pojoaque, Poeh Museum, Santa Fe NM

Ulinskas, Moriah, *Dir Next Gen Progs,* Bay Area Video Coalition, Inc, San Francisco CA

Ulivo, Christopher, *Vis Asst Prof,* Purchase College, State University of New York, School of Art+Design, Purchase NY (S)

Ullmann, Katya, *Receptionist,* American Folk Art Museum, New York NY

Ulloa, Derby, *Prof,* Florida Community College at Jacksonville, South Campus, Art Dept, Jacksonville FL (S)

Ullrich, Maren, *Traveling Exhibits Coordr,* International Center of Photography, Museum, New York NY

Ulmer, Sean, *Cur,* Cedar Rapids Museum of Art, Cedar Rapids IA

Ulrich, David, *Art Dept Chair,* Cornish College of the Arts, Art Dept, Seattle WA (S)

Ulrich, Helen, *Asst Librn,* Ball State University, Architecture Library, Muncie IN

Ulrich, Jim, *Painting Dept,* Alberta College of Art & Design, Calgary AB (S)

Ulry, James E, *Acad Dir,* Johnson Atelier Technical Institute of Sculpture, Trenton NJ (S)

Ultan, Deborah K, *Arts, Architecture & Landscape Architecture Librn,* University of Minnesota, Arts & Architecture Collections, Minneapolis MN

Um, Nancy, *Assoc Prof,* State University of New York at Binghamton, Dept of Art History, Binghamton NY (S)

Umana, Pedro, *Pastor,* Mission San Miguel Museum, San Miguel CA

Umberger, Leslie, *Cur,* Sheboygan Arts Foundation, Inc, John Michael Kohler Arts Center, Sheboygan WI

Umlah, Christine, *Publicity & Gallery Mgr,* Lunenburg Art Gallery Society, Lunenburg NS

Umlauf, Karl, *Prof & Artist in Res,* Baylor University - College of Arts and Sciences, Dept of Art, Waco TX (S)

Unander, Lisa, *Dir Educ,* The Long Island Museum of American Art, History & Carriages, Stony Brook NY

Unchester, Robert, *Exhib Mgr,* Cameron Art Museum, Wilmington NC

Underhill, Jane, *First VPres,* Arizona Watercolor Association, Phoenix AZ

Underhill, Kristin, *Admin,* Hope College, DePree Art Center & Gallery, Holland MI

Underhill, Michael, *Dir Archit,* Arizona State University, College of Architecture & Environmental Design, Tempe AZ (S)

Underwood, Barry, *Dept Head Photog,* Cleveland Institute of Art, Cleveland OH (S)

Underwood, Candace, *Cur,* Colquitt County Arts Center, Moultrie GA

Underwood, David, *Assoc Prof & Second Dept Chmn,* Carson-Newman College, Art Dept, Jefferson City TN (S)

Underwood, Jeremy, *Cur Exhibs,* Center for Puppetry Arts, Atlanta GA

Underwood, Tut, *Dir,* South Carolina State Museum, Columbia SC

Unger, Fred, *Pres Bd Trustees,* Beck Center for the Arts, Lakewood OH

Unger, Geri, *Dir Educ,* Cleveland Botanical Garden, Eleanor Squire Library, Cleveland OH

Unger, Howard, *Prof,* Ocean County College, Humanities Dept, Toms River NJ (S)

Ungerman, Temmi, *Instr,* Toronto Art Therapy Institute, Toronto ON (S)

Uno, Allan, *Bldgs & Grounds Supv,* Tucson Museum of Art and Historic Block, Tucson AZ

Unterschultz, Judy, *Exec Dir,* Multicultural Heritage Centre, Public Art Gallery, Stony Plain AB

Unterschulz, Cheryl, *Asst Prof,* Lincoln University, Dept Visual and Performing Arts, Jefferson City MO (S)

Unvir, Amira, *Dir Library,* College of Saint Elizabeth, Mahoney Library, Morristown NJ

Unwin-Barkley, Pam, *VPres,* Warwick Museum of Art, Warwick RI

Updike Walker, Janis, *Dir Develop,* Philbrook Museum of Art, Tulsa OK

Uphoff, Joseph A, *Dir & Ed in Chief, Journal of Regional Criticism,* Arjuna Library, Digital Visual Dream Laboratory & Acoustic Studio, Colorado Springs CO

Upton, Joel M, *Prof Fine Arts,* Amherst College, Dept of Art & the History of Art, Amherst MA (S)

Uraneck, Joan, *Instr,* Maine College of Art, Portland ME (S)

Uranz, Rebecca, *Asst Librn,* New York School of Interior Design, New York School of Interior Design Library, New York NY

Urban, Erin, *Dir,* The Noble Maritime Collection, Staten Island NY

Urbanelli, Lora, *Dir,* Montclair Art Museum, Montclair NJ

Urbanick, Paul, *Chmn Humanities,* City Colleges of Chicago, Harold Washington College, Chicago IL (S)

Urbanik, Markus, *Ceramics,* Central Wyoming College, Art Center, Riverton WY (S)

Urbanz, Angela, *Midwest Arts Conference Dir,* Arts Midwest, Minneapolis MN

Urbizu, William, *Asst Dir,* Miami-Dade Public Library, Miami FL

Ure, Maureen O'Hara, *Asst Prof Lectr,* University of Utah, Dept of Art & Art History, Salt Lake City UT (S)

Urgo, John, *Collections Mgr,* New Britain Museum of American Art, New Britain CT

Urian, Edward A, *Media Arts & Animation,* Art Institute of Pittsburgh, Pittsburgh PA (S)

Urness, Janine, *Office Mgr,* Avila University, Thornhill Art Gallery, Kansas City MO

Uroskie, Andrew, *Asst Prof,* Stony Brook University, College of Arts & Sciences, Dept of Art, Stony Brook NY (S)

Ursillo, Linda, *Dir Finance,* Boca Raton Museum of Art, Boca Raton FL

Urso, Len, *Prof,* Rochester Institute of Technology, School of Design, Rochester NY (S)

Usai, Paab Cherchi, *Cur,* George Eastman, Museum, Rochester NY

Usai, Paolo Cherchi, *Cur Motion Picture Coll,* George Eastman, Rochester NY

Ushenko, Audrey, *Prof,* Indiana-Purdue University, Dept of Fine Arts, Fort Wayne IN (S)

Usherwood, Ron, *Exec Dir,* Taos Center for the Arts, Stables Gallery, Taos NM

Uslaner, Diane, *Dir Cultural Programming, Mktg & Develop,* Koffler Center of the Arts, School of Visual Art, Toronto ON (S)

Usrey, Angela, *Dir,* Tanner Hill Gallery, Chattanooga TN

Ussler, Christine, *Prof Practice,* Lehigh University, Dept of Art, Architecture & Design, Bethlehem PA (S)

Usui, Emiko, *Dir MFA Publs,* Museum of Fine Arts, Boston MA

Uyekawa, Jim, *Prof,* East Los Angeles College, Art Dept, Monterey Park CA (S)

Vaccaro, Kathleen, *Adj Prof,* Saint Joseph's University, Art Dept, Philadelphia PA (S)

Vaccaro, Mary, *Assoc Prof,* University of Texas at Arlington, Art & Art History Department, Arlington TX (S)

Vaccaro, Sal, *Mktg Mgr,* Caramoor Center for Music & the Arts, Inc, Rosen House at Caramoor, Katonah NY

Vachon, Christian, *Head Coll Mgmt,* McCord Museum of Canadian History, Montreal PQ

Vachon, Renee, *Admin Asst,* Shawinigan Art Center, Shawinigan PQ

Vadeboncoeur, Guy, *Dir & Chief Cur,* The Stewart Museum, Montreal PQ

Vadeboncoeur, Guy, *Exec Dir & Chief Cur,* The Stewart Museum, Library, Montreal PQ

Vaigardson, Val, *Asst Prof,* Rhodes College, Dept of Art, Memphis TN (S)

Vail, Karole, *Asst Cur,* Solomon R Guggenheim, New York NY

Vail, Marguerite K, *VPres Develop,* The Mariners' Museum, Newport News VA

Vail, Mita, *VPres Develop,* The Mariners' Museum, Newport News VA

Vaitkute, Karile, *Dir Educ & Edit,* Balzekas Museum of Lithuanian Culture, Chicago IL

Vajracharya, Gautama, *Instr,* University of Wisconsin, Madison, Dept of Art History, Madison WI (S)

Valand, Roger, *Asst Prof,* Spring Arbor College, Art Dept, Spring Arbor MI (S)

Valandani, Jasmine, *Educ Dir,* Museum of Northwest Art, La Conner WA

Valavanis, Liz, *Pres,* South Shore Arts, Munster IN

Valderrama, Tonito, *Mus Educator,* C W Post Campus of Long Island University, Hillwood Art Museum, Brookville NY

Valdes, Juana, *Asst Prof Art, Printmaking,* Florida Atlantic University, D F Schmidt College of Arts &

Letters Dept of Visual Arts & Art History, Boca Raton FL (S)

Valencia, Romolo, *Instr Graphic Arts,* Honolulu Community College, Commercial Art Dept, Honolulu HI (S)

Valenti, Thomas, *Pres,* The Allied Artists of America, Inc, New York NY

Valenti-Protas, Jodi, *Sch Progs Coordr,* Buffalo Museum of Science, Research Library, Buffalo NY

Valentin, Noel, *Permanent Coll Mgr,* El Museo del Barrio, New York NY

Valentin, Velky, *Sr Acct,* Museum for African Art, New York NY

Valentine, Christina, *Instr,* Biola University, Art Dept, La Mirada CA (S)

Valentine, John, *Asst Prof,* Southeastern Louisiana University, Dept of Visual Arts, Hammond LA (S)

Valentine, Terry, *Prof,* Concordia University, Division of Performing & Visual Arts, Mequon WI (S)

Valerio, James, *Prof,* Northwestern University, Evanston, Dept of Art Theory & Practice, Evanston IL (S)

Valero, Meghan, *Admin,* Artists Association of Nantucket, Nantucket MA

Valiquette, Carol, *Exec Asst Finance & Admin,* United Westurne Inc, Art Collection, Montreal PQ

Valiquette, Sharon, *Pres,* Rensselaer Newman Foundation Chapel + Cultural Center, The Gallery at the Chapel & Cultural Center, Troy NY

Valladao, Roxanne, *Instr,* Feather River Community College, Art Dept, Quincy CA (S)

Valle, Chris, *Prof,* University of Tampa, College of Arts & Letters, Tampa FL (S)

Valleau, Steven, *Carver-in-Residence,* Wendell Gilley, Southwest Harbor ME

Vallee, Francois, *Gen Coordr,* La Chambre Blanche, Quebec PQ

Valley, Derek R, *Dir,* State Capital Museum, Olympia WA

Vallieres, Nicole, *Dir Coll, Res & Progs,* McCord Museum of Canadian History, Montreal PQ

Vallila, Marja, *Assoc Prof,* State University of New York at Albany, Art Dept, Albany NY (S)

Valmestad, Liv, *Reference Librn,* University of Manitoba, Architecture & Fine Arts Library, Winnipeg MB

van Aalst, Kirsten, *Asst Prof,* Norwich University, Dept of Architecture and Art, Northfield VT (S)

van Alfen, Peter, *Cur,* American Numismatic Society, New York NY

VanAllen, David, *Asst Prof,* Mount Mercy College, Art Dept, Cedar Rapids IA (S)

Van Allen, David, *Dir,* Mount Mercy College, White Gallery, Cedar Rapids IA

Van Allen, Katherine, *Mng Dir Mus Svcs,* Missouri Historical Society, Missouri History Museum, Saint Louis MO

Van Alphen, Jan, *Dir Exhibs, Colls & Research,* Rubin Museum of Art, New York NY

VanAntwerp, Deb, *Dir Vols,* McLean County Historical Society, McLean County Museum of History, Bloomington IL

Van Antwerp, Randy, *Interim Dir,* Grand Rapids Art Museum, Grand Rapids MI

Van Arnam, Barbara, *Dir,* Gallery 25, Art Gallery, Fresno CA

Vanausdall, John, *Pres & CEO,* Eiteljorg Museum of American Indians & Western Art, Indianapolis IN

Van Ausdall, Kristen, *Assoc Prof,* Kenyon College, Art Dept, Gambier OH (S)

Van Balgooy, Max, *Dir Interpretation,* National Trust for Historic Preservation, Washington DC

Van Beke, Timothy, *Asst Prof,* Southeastern Louisiana University, Dept of Visual Arts, Hammond LA (S)

Van Benscheten, Elijah, *Instr,* Adrian College, Art & Design Dept, Adrian MI (S)

Van Benschoten, Elijah, *Instr,* South Dakota State University, Dept of Visual Arts, Brookings SD (S)

van Boekel, Maria, *Asst,* Ohio State University, Fine Arts Library, Columbus OH

Van Brunt, Carl, *Gallery Dir,* Woodstock Artists Association & Museum, Woodstock NY

Van Buren, David, *Chmn,* University of Wisconsin-Platteville, Dept of Fine Art, Platteville WI (S)

Vance, Alex, *Exec Dir,* Bergstrom-Mahler Museum, Neenah WI

Vance, Cindy, *Coll Coordr,* University of Victoria, The Legacy Art Gallery, Victoria BC

Vance, Steve, *Instr,* University of Wisconsin-Platteville, Dept of Fine Art, Platteville WI (S)

Vanche, Sheri, *Registrar,* Eastern Shore Art Association, Inc, Eastern Shore Art Center, Fairhope AL

Van Cleave, Richard H, *Cur Coll,* City of Ketchikan Museum, Tongass Historical Museum, Ketchikan AK

Vanco, John, *Dir,* Erie Art Museum, Erie PA

VandenBerg, Eli, *Gallery Store Mgr,* The Print Center, Philadelphia PA

Vanderbrug, Kelly, *Asst Prof,* North Park University, Art Dept, Chicago IL (S)

Vanderhill, Rein, *Rotation Exhib Coordr,* Northwestern College, Te Paske Gallery, Orange City IA

Vanderhoff, Darci, *Chief Information Officer,* The Phillips Collection, Washington DC

VanderHoff, Kerri, *Dir Mktg & Pub Rels,* Grand Rapids Art Museum, Grand Rapids MI

VanderKaay, Cody, *Asst Prof,* Oakland University, Dept of Art & Art History, Rochester MI (S)

VanderKamp, Joel, *Preparator,* University of North Carolina at Greensboro, Weatherspoon Art Museum, Greensboro NC

Van Der Leer, David, *Asst Cur Architecture & Design,* Solomon R Guggenheim, New York NY

van der Plas, Claire, *Asst Prof Art,* Adams State College, Dept of Visual Arts, Alamosa CO (S)

Vanderpool, Guy C, *Dir,* Panhandle-Plains Historical Museum, Canyon TX

VanDerpool, Karen, *Prof Emeritus,* California State University, Chico, Department of Art & Art History, Chico CA (S)

Vanderslice, Karen, *Tour Coordr,* The Nemours Foundation, Nemours Mansion & Gardens, Wilmington DE

Vanderup, Sarah, *Chair & Assoc Prof,* California State University, Bakersfield, Dept of Art, Bakersfield CA (S)

Vanderway, Richard, *Educ Coordr,* Whatcom Museum, Library, Bellingham WA

Vandest, Bill, *Theater Coordr,* Creighton University, Fine & Performing Arts Dept, Omaha NE (S)

Van Deursen, Lyndi, *Mktg & Mem,* The Art Museum at the University of Kentucky, Lexington KY

Van Deusen, Mimi, *Dir & Cur,* Village of Potsdam, Potsdam Public Museum, Potsdam NY

Vandeville, Denise, *Dean,* Finlandia Univ, International School of Art and Design, Hancock MI (S)

Van Donand, Mark, *Instr,* Judson University, School of Art, Design & Architecture, Elgin IL (S)

Van Dorp, Dale, *Mgr Performing Arts,* Henry Ford Community College, McKenzie Fine Art Ctr, Dearborn MI (S)

Van Dorston, Teri, *Registrar,* Cedar Rapids Museum of Art, Cedar Rapids IA

Van Duesen, Patrick, *Prof,* Daytona Beach Community College, Dept of Fine Arts & Visual Arts, Daytona Beach FL (S)

Van Duyne, Sue, *Instr,* Ocean City Arts Center, Ocean City NJ (S)

Van Dyk, Stephen H, *Librn,* Cooper-Hewitt National Design Museum, Doris & Henry Dreyfuss Memorial Study Center Library & Archive, New York NY

Van Dyke, Benjamin, *Asst Prof,* University at Buffalo, State University of New York, Dept of Visual Studies, Buffalo NY (S)

Van Dyke, Dan R, *Exec Dir,* Phelps County Historical Society, Donald O. Lindgren Library, Holdrege NE

VanDyke, Fred, *Prof,* Salt Lake Community College, Graphic Design Dept, Salt Lake City UT (S)

van Dyke, James, *Dean Arts, Humanities & Letters,* Marian University, Art Dept, Fond Du Lac WI (S)

Van Dyke, Lissa, *Librn,* Lyman Allyn Art Museum, Hendel Library, New London CT

Van Evera, Margie, *Store Asst,* Morris Museum of Art, Augusta GA

Van Gelderen, Annie, *Pres & CEO,* Birmingham Bloomfield Art Center, Art Center, Birmingham MI

Van Gelderen, Annie, *Pres & Ceo,* Birmingham Bloomfield Art Center, Birmingham MI (S)

Van Gent, Elona, *Vis Assoc Prof,* University of Michigan, Ann Arbor, School of Art & Design, Ann Arbor MI (S)

Van Heerden, Peter, *Exec Dir,* Westport Arts Center, Westport CT

Van Hook, Bailey, *Art Chair & Interim Staff Dir,* Virginia Polytechnic Institute & State University, Armory Art Gallery, Blacksburg VA

Van Hook, L Bailey, *Head Dept,* Virginia Polytechnic Institute & State University, Dept of Art & Art History, Blacksburg VA (S)

Van Hooser, Karen, *Exec Adminr,* The Society of Layerists in Multi-Media (SLMM), Albuquerque NM

Van Hooten, Joan, *Exec Dir,* Arts Council for Long Beach, 350 Elm Ave. CA

VanHorn, Wendy, *Dir Educ,* Museum of Ventura County, Ventura CA

Van Horne, John C, *Dir & CEO,* Library Company of Philadelphia, Philadelphia PA

Van Hoy, Karen, *Dir,* West Hills Unitarian Fellowship, Doll Gardner Art Gallery, Portland OR

Van Huffel, Hana, *Mus Resources Coordr,* Boise Art Museum, Boise ID

Van Keuren, Francis, *Prof Art History,* University of Georgia, Franklin College of Arts & Sciences, Lamar Dodd School of Art, Athens GA (S)

VanKeuren, Philip, *Dir,* Southern Methodist University, Division of Art, Dallas TX (S)

Van Kleek, Shauna, *Mus Store Mgr,* Boise Art Museum, Boise ID

Van Lusk, Kyle, *Instr,* Appalachian State University, Dept of Art, Boone NC (S)

vanMeenen, Karen, *Ed Afterimage,* Visual Studies Workshop, Rochester NY (S)

Van Meter, Kay, *Assoc Mgr,* ArtSpace/Lima, Lima OH

Van Meter, Peggy, *Cataloger,* Fulton County Historical Society Inc, Fulton County Museum (Tetzlaff Reference Room), Rochester IN

Van Miegroet, Hans J, *Chair & Prof,* Duke University, Dept of Art, Art History & Visual Studies, Durham NC (S)

Van Ness, Venus, *Archivist,* Norman Rockwell Museum, Library, Stockbridge MA

Van Nort, Sydney, *Archivist,* City College of the City University of New York, Morris Raphael Cohen Library, New York NY

Van Nostrand, Jess, *Exhibition Cur,* Cornish College of the Arts, Fisher Gallery, Seattle WA

Vannoy, Alonita, *Bus Mgr,* Historical Society of Washington DC, The City Museum of Washington DC, Washington DC

Vannoy, Alonita, *Bus Mgr,* Historical Society of Washington DC, Washington DC

van Osnabrugge, William, *Pres,* Art Center Sarasota, Sarasota FL (S)

Vanouse, Paul, *Assoc Prof,* University at Buffalo, State University of New York, Dept of Visual Studies, Buffalo NY (S)

Van Rooyen, Robin, *Art Gallery Dir,* Grand Rapids Community College, Visual Art Dept, Grand Rapids MI (S)

Van Schaack, Eric, *Prof,* Colgate University, Dept of Art & Art History, Hamilton NY (S)

Van Sickle, Delene, *Admin Asst,* Washburn University, Mulvane Art Museum, Topeka KS

Van Slyck, Abigail, *First VPres,* Society of Architectural Historians, Chicago IL

Van Strander, Kitren, *Dir,* Rochester Institute of Technology, Corporate Education & Training, Rochester NY

Van Suchtelen, Adrian, *Prof,* Utah State University, Dept of Art, Logan UT (S)

Van Tassel, Rhoda, *Instr,* Muskingum College, Art Department, New Concord OH (S)

Van Tomme, Niel, *Dir Arts & Media,* Provisions Library, Provisions Research Center for Arts & Social Change, Fairfax VA

Vantz, Mickel, *Cur,* Cherokee Heritage Center, Park Hill OK

Van Wagenberg, Anke, *Cur,* Academy Art Museum, Easton MD

Van Went, Sherri, *Gallery Shop & Art Rental & Sales Mgr,* The Winnipeg Art Gallery, Winnipeg MB

Van Wey, Ken, *Program Support Specialist,* United States Department of the Interior, Indian Arts & Crafts Board, Washington DC

Van Winkle, Sarah, *Prog Coordr,* University of South Carolina Beaufort Art Gallery, Beaufort SC

Vidarte, Juan Ignacio, *Deputy Dir & Chief Officer Global Strategies,* Solomon R Guggenheim, New York NY

Vidaurri, Polly, *Dir Finance & Admin,* San Antonio Museum of Art, San Antonio TX

Vidergar, Stephanie, *Assoc Mktg & Commun,* San Jose Museum of Art, Library, San Jose CA

Viditz-Ward, Vera, *Prof,* Bloomsburg University, Dept of Art & Art History, Bloomsburg PA (S)

Vidler, Anthony, *Dept Chmn,* University of California, Los Angeles, Dept Art History, Los Angeles CA (S)

Viebranz, Curt, *Pres & CEO,* Mount Vernon Ladies' Association of the Union, Mount Vernon VA

Vielbig, Bernadette, *Asst Prof,* Spokane Falls Community College, Fine Arts Dept, Spokane WA (S)

Vienneau, Larry, *Instr,* Century College, Humanities Dept, White Bear Lake MN (S)

Viens, Katheryn P, *Dir,* Old Colony Historical Society, Library, Taunton MA

Viens, Katheryn P, *Dir, CEO,* Old Colony Historical Society, Museum, Taunton MA

Viera, Ricardo, *Dir Exhib & Coll,* Lehigh University Art Galleries, Museum Operation, Bethlehem PA

Viera, Ricardo, *Prof,* Lehigh University, Dept of Art, Architecture & Design, Bethlehem PA (S)

Vierra, Marie, *Asst to Dir,* University of California, Santa Barbara, University Art Museum, Santa Barbara CA

Vierus, Jenny, *Admin Asst & Shop Mgr,* Sandwich Historical Society, Center Sandwich NH

Vieter, Rosemary, *Pres,* Bowne House Historical Society, Flushing NY

Vigier, Janique, *Admin & Events Coordr,* Plug In, Institute of Contemporary Art, Winnipeg MB

Vigilante, Amy, *Assoc Instr,* University of Florida, School of Art & Art History, Gainesville FL (S)

Vigilante, Amy, *Dir,* University of Florida, University Gallery, Gainesville FL

Vigiletti, Christine, *Asst Registrar,* Los Angeles County Museum of Art, Robert Gore Rifkind Center for German Expressionist Studies, Los Angeles CA

Vigo, John, *Fin Mgr,* Arts Council Of New Orleans, New Orleans LA

Vigueras, Carlos, *Contact,* Casasola Museum, El Paso TX

Vikan, Gary, *Dir,* Walters Art Museum, Baltimore MD

Vikan, Gary, *Dir,* Walters Art Museum, Library, Baltimore MD

Vilella, Maria Angela Lopez, *Exec Dir,* Museo de las Americas, Viejo San Juan PR

Vilella, Maria Angela Lopez, *Exec Dir,* Museo de las Americas, Viejo San Juan PR

Vilkas, Elliott, *VPres,* New York Society of Architects, New York NY

Villalelobos, Patricia, *Printmaking,* Western Michigan University, Frostic School of Art, Kalamazoo MI (S)

Villalonga, Yuneikys, *Asst Cur,* Lehman College Art Gallery, Bronx NY

Villalpando, Kim, *Dir,* George Phippen, Phippen Museum - Art of the American West, Prescott AZ

Villanueva, Isabela, *Asst Cur Visual Arts,* Americas Society Art Gallery, New York NY

Villarreal, Raul, *Adjunct Prof,* College of Saint Elizabeth, Art Dept, Morristown NJ (S)

Villela, Khristaan, *Asst Prof,* College of Santa Fe, Art Dept, Santa Fe NM (S)

Villeneuve, Line, *Head Exhib,* McCord Museum of Canadian History, Montreal PQ

Villeneuve, Pat, *Assoc Prof,* Florida State University, Art Education Dept, Tallahassee FL (S)

Villmagna, Robert, *Assoc Prof,* West Liberty State College, Div Art, West Liberty WV (S)

Vincelli, Deborah, *Electronic Resource Librn,* The Metropolitan Museum of Art, Museum Libraries, New York NY

Vincent, Christine J, *Pres,* Maine College of Art, Portland ME (S)

Vincent, Haideh, *Accnt,* Creative Growth Art Center, Oakland CA

Vincent, Marc, *Chmn Div,* Baldwin-Wallace College, Dept of Art, Berea OH (S)

Vincent, Michael, *Dean,* Northern Arizona University, College of Arts & Letters, Flagstaff AZ (S)

Vinci, Sarah G, *Pub Relations Dir,* California State University, Long Beach, University Art Museum, Long Beach CA

Vinokurov, Bryce, *Asst Prof,* Worcester State College, Visual & Performing Arts Dept, Worcester MA (S)

Vinovich, Jennifer, *Spec Projects Mgr,* South Shore Arts, Munster IN

Vinski, Joe, *Weekend Attendant,* Art Gallery of Mississauga, Mississauga ON

Vinson, Mary, *Asst Dir,* Tellus Northwest Georgia Science Museum, Cartersville GA

Vinyard, Jordan, *Asst Prof,* University of Science & Arts of Oklahoma, Arts Dept, Chickasha OK (S)

Virden, Walter, *Pres,* Arlington Museum of Art, Arlington TX

Virgin, Louise, *Cur Asian Art,* Worcester Art Museum, Worcester MA

Virgint, Dwayne, *COO,* Indian Pueblo Cultural Center, Albuquerque NM

Viscardi, Anthony, *Prof,* Lehigh University, Dept of Art, Architecture & Design, Bethlehem PA (S)

Vissat, Maureen, *Asst Prof,* Seton Hill University, Art Program, Greensburg PA (S)

Visser, Mary, *Prof,* Southwestern University, Sarofim School of Fine Art, Dept of Art & Art History, Georgetown TX (S)

Visser, Susan R, *Exec Dir,* South Bend Regional Museum of Art, South Bend IN

Visser, Susan R, *Exec Dir,* South Bend Regional Museum of Art, Library, South Bend IN

Vitale, James, *Instr,* Mohawk Valley Community College, Utica NY (S)

Vitale, Thomas Jewell, *Assoc Prof,* Loras College, Dept of Art, Dubuque IA (S)

Vitale, Whitney, *Assoc Dir,* Boston Architectural College, Library, Boston MA

Vito, Kimberly, *Prof,* Wright State University, Dept of Art & Art History, Dayton OH (S)

Vitrano, Sandy, *Exec Asst,* Houston Center For Photography, Houston TX

Viverette, Lee B, *Reference Librn,* Virginia Museum of Fine Arts, Margaret R & Robert M Freeman Library, Richmond VA

Vivero, Michaela, *Assoc Prof,* Denison University, Studio Art Program, Granville OH (S)

Viviano, Norwood, *Asst Prof,* Grand Valley State University, Art & Design Dept, Allendale MI (S)

Voce, Yolanda, *VPres, Acting Pres,* San Bernardino Art Association, Inc, Sturges Fine Arts Center, San Bernardino CA

Voci, Donna, *Adjunct Asst Prof,* New York Institute of Technology, Fine Arts Dept, Old Westbury NY (S)

Voci, Peter, *Chmn,* New York Institute of Technology, Gallery, Old Westbury NY

Voci, Peter, *Chmn & Assoc Prof,* New York Institute of Technology, Fine Arts Dept, Old Westbury NY (S)

Voduarka, Frank, *Assoc Prof,* Loyola University of Chicago, Fine Arts Dept, Chicago IL (S)

Voelkel, David, *Cur,* James Monroe, James Monroe Memorial Library, Fredericksburg VA

Voelkel, David B, *Cur,* James Monroe, Fredericksburg VA

Voelker, Jim, *Head Dept,* Bluefield State College, Division of Arts & Sciences, Bluefield WV (S)

Voelkle, William M, *Cur & Dept Head Medieval & Renaissance Manuscripts,* The Morgan Library & Museum, Museum, New York NY

Voellinger, David, *Dir Develop,* Lehigh Valley Heritage Center, Allentown PA

Vogel, Alan, *Assoc Prof,* Rochester Institute of Technology, School of Photographic Arts & Sciences, Rochester NY (S)

Vogel, Barbara, *VPres,* Royal Canadian Academy of Arts, Toronto ON

Vogel, Jerry, *Special Adv to Pres,* Museum for African Art, New York NY

Vogel, Stephan P, *Dean,* University of Detroit Mercy, School of Architecture, Detroit MI (S)

Vogel, Theodore, *Asst Prof,* Lewis & Clark College, Dept of Art, Portland OR (S)

Vogelsong, Diana, *Assoc University Librn,* American University, Jack I & Dorothy G Bender Library & Learning Resources Center, New York NY

Vogt, Allie, *Dept Chmn,* North Idaho College, Art Dept, Coeur D'Alene ID (S)

Voight, Robert, *Asst Prof,* College of Mount Saint Joseph, Art Dept, Cincinnati OH (S)

Voinot, Andrea, *Art Sls Mgr,* Kala Institute, Kala Art Institute, Berkeley CA

Voinot, Andrea, *Gallery Mgr,* San Francisco Museum of Modern Art, Artist Gallery, San Francisco CA

Voit, Irene, *Bus Serv,* Las Vegas-Clark County Library District, Las Vegas NV

Vokt Ziemba, Emily, *Coll Mgr,* The Art Institute of Chicago, Dept of Prints & Drawings, Chicago IL

Volk, John, *Asst Prof,* Minnesota State University-Moorhead, Dept of Art & Design, Moorhead MN (S)

Volland, Patti, *Internship Coordr,* University of Southern Maine, Dept of Art, Gorham ME (S)

Volmar, Michael, *Cur,* Fruitlands Museum, Inc, Harvard MA

Volmar, Michael A, *Cur,* Fruitlands Museum, Inc, Library, Harvard MA

Voloshin, Metro, *Cur Music,* Boston Public Library, Central Library, Boston MA

Voloshin, Metro, *Cur Music,* Boston Public Library, Arts Reference Department, Boston MA

Volpacchio, John, *Prof,* Salem State University, Art & Design Department, Salem MA (S)

Volz, Robert L, *Custodian,* Williams College, Chapin Library, Williamstown MA

Vonada, Wayne, *Sr Preparator,* Florida State University, Museum of Fine Arts, Tallahassee FL

Von Barghahn, Barbara, *Prof,* George Washington University, Dept of Art of Fine Arts & Art History, Washington DC (S)

Von Bloomberg, Randell, *Gallery Dir,* New World School of the Arts, Gallery, Miami FL

Von Bothmer, Dietrich, *Distinguished Research,* The Metropolitan Museum of Art, New York NY

von Dassanowsky, Robert, *Prof & Dir Film Studies,* University of Colorado-Colorado Springs, Visual & Performing Arts Dept (VAPA), Colorado Springs CO (S)

Vondras, Barbara, *Dir,* Dawson County Historical Society, Museum, Lexington NE

von Haeger, Arden, *Illustration Coordr,* Nossi College of Art, Nashville TN (S)

Vonier, Pascale, *Commun Mgr,* Association of Collegiate Schools of Architecture, Washington DC

Von Kann, Lisa, *Library Dir,* Saint Johnsbury Athenaeum, Saint Johnsbury VT

Vonkeman, Anine, *Head Pub Rels,* Southern Alberta Art Gallery, Library, Lethbridge AB

Vonkeman, Anine, *Mktg & Commun,* City of Lethbridge, Sir Alexander Galt Museum, Lethbridge AB

Vonkeman, Anine, *Pub Prog Cur,* Southern Alberta Art Gallery, Lethbridge AB

Von Kessler, Caroline, *Dir Develop,* Hunter Museum of American Art, Chattanooga TN

von Lates, Adrienne, *Dir Educ,* Bass Museum of Art, Miami Beach FL

von Lates, Adrienne, *Educ Cur,* Museum of Contemporary Art, North Miami FL

Von Martin, Christaan, *Sr Preparator,* Riverside Art Museum, Riverside CA

Von Rosk, Laura, *Gallery Dir,* Lake George Arts Project, Courthouse Gallery, Lake George NY

Von Schlegell, Mark, *Circ Supv,* Art Center College of Design, James Lemont Fogg Memorial Library, Pasadena CA

Von Sonnenburg, Hubert, *Sherman Fairchild Chmn,* The Metropolitan Museum of Art, New York NY

von Stuelpnagel, Anne, *Dir Exhibitions,* Bruce Museum, Inc, Greenwich CT

VonVoetcsch, Kurt, *Gallery Mgr,* Niagara University, Castellani Art Museum, Niagara NY

von Wettberg, Rachel, *Registrar,* Bard College, Center for Curatorial Studies and the Hessel Museum of Art, Annandale-on-Hudson NY

Von Wolffersdorff, Joy, *Adjunct,* College of the Canyons, Art Dept, Santa Clarita CA (S)

Vookles, Laura, *Chief Cur Collections,* The Hudson River Museum, Yonkers NY

Vorhaus, Kate, *Projects Mgr,* National Council on Education for the Ceramic Arts (NCECA), Erie CO

Vorys, Jay, *Pres,* Columbus Museum of Art, Columbus OH

Vosikas, Anne, *Dir Library & Spec Colls,* The Bostonian Society, Library, Boston MA

Vosikas, Anne, *Dir Research Center,* The Bostonian Society, Old State House Museum, Boston MA

Vowels, Courtney, *Dir Educ*, Tacoma Art Museum, Tacoma WA

Vroom, Steven Michael, *Exec Dir*, 911 Media Arts Center, Seattle WA

Vrotsus, Susan, *Dir Sales & Rental*, Cambridge Art Association, Cambridge MA

Vruwink, J, *Chmn*, Central College, Art Dept, Pella IA (S)

Vuchetich, Jill, *Archivist*, Walker Art Center, Staff Reference Library, Minneapolis MN

Vuwigh, James, *Assoc Prof*, University of Indianapolis, Dept Art & Design, Indianapolis IN (S)

Waala, Andrea, *Registrar*, Museum of Wisconsin Art, West Bend WI

Waale, Kim, *Assoc Prof*, Cazenovia College, Center for Art & Design Studies, Cazenovia NY (S)

Wabnitz, Robert, *Prof*, Rochester Institute of Technology, School of Design, Rochester NY (S)

Wachna, Pamela, *Cur*, City of Toronto Culture, The Market Gallery, Toronto ON

Wachs, Joel, *Pres*, Andy Warhol Foundation for the Visual Arts, New York NY

Wacker, Kelly, *Gallery Dir*, University of Montevallo, The Gallery, Montevallo AL

Wactman, Lynne, *Admis Dir*, Hussian School of Art, Commercial Art Dept, Philadelphia PA (S)

Wada, W, *Prof Painting*, Ramapo College of New Jersey, School of Contemporary Arts, Mahwah NJ (S)

Waddell, Wayne, *Dir*, Louisiana State Exhibit Museum, Shreveport LA

Wade, Cara, *Asst Prof*, University of Saint Francis, School of Creative Arts, Fort Wayne IN (S)

Wade, Karen Graham, *Dir*, Workman & Temple Family Homestead Museum, City of Industry CA

Wade, Ken, *Security*, Booth Western Art Museum, Cartersville GA

Wadley, William, *Head*, Texas A&M University Commerce, Dept of Art, Commerce TX (S)

Wadsworth, David, *Historian*, Cohasset Historical Society, Pratt Building (Society Headquarters), Cohasset MA

Wadsworth, David H, *Historian*, Cohasset Historical Society, Cohasset Maritime Museum, Cohasset MA

Wagan, Sixto, *Co-Dir*, Diverse Works, Houston TX

Wagener, Thomas, *Dir*, University of Wisconsin-Eau Claire, Foster Gallery, Eau Claire WI

Wagener, Tom, *Dir Foster Gallery Woodshop Supv*, University of Wisconsin-Eau Claire, Dept of Art & Design, Eau Claire WI (S)

Wagenet, Hal, *Pres*, Arts Council of Mendocino County, Ukiah CA

Waggoner, Jean, *Treas*, Coquille Valley Art Association, Coquille OR

Waggoner, Lynda, *Dir*, Western Pennsylvania Conservancy, Fallingwater, Mill Run PA

Wagner, Ann Prentice, *Cur Drawings*, Arkansas Arts Center, Little Rock AR

Wagner, Betty L, *Librn*, University of Washington, Architecture-Urban Planning Library, Seattle WA

Wagner, Beverly, *Admin Secy*, Texas A&M University, J Wayne Stark University Center Galleries, College Station TX

Wagner, Bob, *Preparator*, State University of New York at New Paltz, Samuel Dorsky Museum of Art, New Paltz NY

Wagner, Catherine F, *Prof*, Mills College, Art Dept, Oakland CA (S)

Wagner, Denise, *Secy*, Hartwick College, The Yager Museum, Oneonta NY

Wagner, Eva, *Educ Coordr*, University of Maine, Museum of Art, Bangor ME

Wagner, Jasmine, *Mem Coordr*, Real Art Ways (RAW), Hartford CT

Wagner, Jill, *Asst Prof Graphic Design*, Kansas Wesleyan University, Art Dept, Salina KS (S)

Wagner, Karen, *Archivist*, Nebraska State Capitol, Lincoln NE

Wagner, Lois, *Pres*, Lois Wagner Fine Arts, New York NY

Wagner, Margaret, *Asst Prof*, University of Massachusetts - Boston, Art Dept, Boston MA (S)

Wagner, Mary, *Admin Asst*, Marquette University, Haggerty Museum of Art, Milwaukee WI

Wagner, Sarah, *Conserv*, National Gallery of Art, Department of Image Collections, Washington DC

Wagner, Teri, *Asst Prof*, Cardinal Stritch University, Art Dept, Milwaukee WI (S)

Wagoner, Phillip, *Assoc Prof*, Wesleyan University, Dept of Art & Art History, Middletown CT (S)

Wagoner, Scott Bishop, *Educ Cur*, Auburn University, Julie Collins Smith Museum, Auburn AL

Wahamaki, Sheila, *Dept Chmn*, Muskegon Community College, Dept of Creative & Performing Arts, Muskegon MI (S)

Wahl, Gary, *Vis Asst Prof*, Albion College, Bobbitt Visual Arts Center, Albion MI

Wahl, Sonja, *Cur*, Thousand Islands Arts Center - Home of the Handweaving Museum, Clayton NY (S)

Wahl, Val, *Cur of Collections*, Eastern Washington State Historical Society, Northwest Museum of Arts & Culture, Spokane WA

Wahlgren, Kay, *VPres Educ & Pres Emeritus*, DuPage Art League School & Gallery, Wheaton IL

Wahlmann, Susan, *Performing Arts & Arts in Educ Dir*, Quad City Arts Inc, Rock Island IL

Wahnee, B J, *Instr*, Haskell Indian Nations University, Art Dept, Lawrence KS (S)

Waide, Blaine, *Folk Arts Coordr*, Florida Folklife Programs, Library, Tallahassee FL

Wainright, Carolyn, *Office Mgr*, Rosemount Museum, Inc, Pueblo CO

Wait, Tamara, *Pub Historian*, Clark County Historical Society, Library, Springfield OH

Waite Bunker, Lisa, *Research Librn*, Tucson Museum of Art and Historic Block, Tucson AZ

Wakajima, Ryuta, *Asst Prof*, University of Minnesota, Minneapolis, Dept of Art, Minneapolis MN (S)

Wakeford, Elizabeth, *Cur Asst*, Dundurn Castle, Hamilton ON

Wakeham, Duane, *2nd VPres*, Pastel Society of America, National Arts Club, Grand Gallery, New York NY

Wakeling, Melissa, *Educ*, Glanmore National Historic Site of Canada, Belleville ON

Walcek Averett, Erin, *Gallery Dir*, Creighton University, Lied Art Gallery, Omaha NE

Walde, Paul, *Cur Pub Programs*, Museum London, London ON

Walden, Jerry, *Chmn*, Winthrop University, Dept of Art & Design, Rock Hill SC (S)

Walder, Penelope, *Gallery Adminr*, Allied Arts Association, Allied Arts Center & Gallery, Richland WA

Walders, Katie, *Pub Rels*, Library Association of La Jolla, Athenaeum Music & Arts Library, La Jolla CA

Waldman, Arthur, *Prof*, Ocean County College, Humanities Dept, Toms River NJ (S)

Waldman, Mila, *Study Room Supv*, Amherst College, Mead Art Museum, Amherst MA

Waldner, Tibor, *Chief Design & Production*, National Portrait Gallery, Smithsonian Institution, Washington DC

Waldrep, Lee W, *Assoc Exec Dir*, National Architectural Accrediting Board, Inc, Washington DC

Waldrep, Lee W, *Asst Dean Student Affairs*, Illinois Institute of Technology, College of Architecture, Chicago IL (S)

Waldrop, Tim, *Asst Prof*, Western Illinois University, Department of Art, Macomb IL (S)

Wale, George, *Dir Programs*, Burlington Art Centre, Burlington ON

Waletzky, Lucy R, *Chair State Council Parks, Recreation & Historic Preservation*, New York Office of Parks, Recreation & Historic Preservation, Natural Heritage Trust, Albany NY

Walford, E John, *Chmn*, Wheaton College, Dept of Art, Wheaton IL (S)

Walia, Christine, *Mgr Exhibs & Progs*, Aljira Center for Contemporary Art, Newark NJ

Walk, Deborah, *Cur Circus Mus & Archivist*, Florida State University, John & Mable Ringling Museum of Art, Sarasota FL

Walker, Andrew, *Asst Dir Curatorial Affairs*, Saint Louis Art Museum, Saint Louis MO

Walker, Beth, *Prin Librn & Information Access Servs*, Pasadena Public Library, Fine Arts Dept, Pasadena CA

Walker, Beth, *Reference Librn*, Center for Creative Studies, College of Art & Design Library, Detroit MI

Walker, Betsy, *Interim Educ Coordr*, Pensacola Museum of Art, Pensacola FL

Walker, Bev, *Asst Dir*, Cumberland Theatre, Lobby for the Arts Gallery, Cumberland MD

Walker, Bobbi, *Dir*, Walker Fine Art, Denver CO

Walker, Celia, *Chief Cur*, Cheekwood-Tennessee Botanical Garden & Museum of Art, Nashville TN

Walker, Celia, *Cur Coll*, Cheekwood Nashville's Home of Art & Gardens, Education Dept, Nashville TN (S)

Walker, Cynthia, *Assoc Dir & Cur*, Brick Store Museum, Kennebunk ME

Walker, Dan, *Dean Instruction*, Butte College, Dept of Fine Arts and Communication Tech, Oroville CA (S)

Walker, Daniel, *Pritzker Chmn Asian Art & Cur Islamic Art*, The Art Institute of Chicago, Department of Asian Art, Chicago IL

Walker, David B, *Exec Dir & CEO*, Nevada Museum of Art, Reno NV

Walker, David B, *Exec Dir & CEO*, Nevada Museum of Art, Art Library, Reno NV

Walker, Denise, *Admin Dir*, Visual Arts Center of Northwest Florida, Panama City FL

Walker, Doug, *Chmn*, College of the Desert, Art Dept, Palm Desert CA (S)

Walker, Edwin G, *Chmn Art Dept*, Millikin University, Art Dept, Decatur IL (S)

Walker, Grant, *Research Assoc*, United States Naval Academy, USNA Museum, Annapolis MD

Walker, Gwendolyn, *Founder & Cur*, The Walker African American Museum & Research Center, Las Vegas NV

Walker, Hamza, *Educ Dir & Assoc Cur*, The Renaissance Society, Chicago IL

Walker, Jeffrey, *Instr*, Campbellsville University, Department of Art, Campbellsville KY (S)

Walker, Jeffry, *Dir*, Trinity College, Austin Arts Center, Widener Gallery, Hartford CT

Walker, Jennifer, *Operations Mgr*, Kirkland Art Center, Clinton NY

Walker, John, *Prof*, Boston University, School for the Arts, Boston MA (S)

Walker, Josh, *Security*, American Sport Art Museum and Archives, Daphne AL

Walker, Juanita, *Treas*, The Walker African American Museum & Research Center, Las Vegas NV

Walker, Kenneth D, *Head Bldgs & Grounds*, The Buffalo Fine Arts Academy, Albright-Knox Art Gallery, Buffalo NY

Walker, Lanke, *Mktg & Develop Mgr*, Sonoma Valley Museum of Art, Sonoma CA

Walker, Leslie, *VPres Community Progs*, Please Touch Museum, Philadelphia PA

Walker, Lulen, *Art Coll Cur*, Georgetown University, Lauinger Library-Special Collections Division, Washington DC

Walker, Lulen, *Cur*, Georgetown University, Art Collection, Washington DC

Walker, Maggie, *Pres Bd*, Seattle Art Museum, Downtown, Seattle WA

Walker, Mara, *Chief Planning Officer*, Americans for the Arts, New York NY

Walker, Martha, *Fine Arts Librn*, Cornell University, Fine Arts Library, Ithaca NY

Walker, Matthew, *Photog*, Illustration House Inc, Gallery Auction House, New York NY

Walker, Melissa, *Dir Educ*, Perkins Center for the Arts, Moorestown NJ

Walker, Melveta, *Library Dir*, Eastern New Mexico University, Golden Library/Runnels Gallery, Portales NM

Walker, Myra, *Prof Fashion Design*, University of North Texas, College of Visual Arts & Design, Denton TX (S)

Walker, Pat, *Dir Educ*, Danforth Museum of Art, Danforth Museum of Art, Framingham MA

Walker, Pat, *Mus Educ*, Danforth Museum of Art, Library, Framingham MA

Walker, Patricia, *Asst Prof*, Georgia Southern University, Dept of Art, Statesboro GA (S)

Walker, Patricia, *Dir*, Danforth Museum of Art School, Framingham MA (S)

Walker, Robert, *Instr*, College of the Canyons, Art Dept, Santa Clarita CA (S)

Walker, Roslyn A, *Sr Cur Arts of Africa, Pacific & Americas*, Dallas Museum of Art, Dallas TX

Walker, Sarah, *Assoc Prof,* Clark University, Dept of Visual & Performing Arts, Worcester MA (S)

Walker, Susan B, *Assoc Cur,* New York State Office of Parks, Recreation and Historic Preservation, Bureau of Historic Sites, Waterford NY

Walker, Sydney, *Assoc Prof,* Ohio State University, Dept of Art Education, Columbus OH (S)

Walker-Millar, Kathy, *Head Dept,* McMurry University, Art Dept, Abilene TX (S)

Walker Powell, Patrice, *Dep Chmn Progs & Partnerships,* National Endowment for the Arts, Washington DC

Wall, Brent, *Assoc Prof,* Saint Xavier University, Dept of Art & Design, Chicago IL (S)

Wall, Deborah, *Lectr,* University of North Carolina at Charlotte, Dept Art, Charlotte NC (S)

Wall, Kay L, *Dir,* University of Southern Mississippi, McCain Library & Archives, Hattiesburg MS

Wall, Pam, *Cur Exhibs,* Gibbes Museum of Art, Charleston SC (S)

Wall, Rick, *Chair, Foundation,* Corcoran School of Art, Washington DC (S)

Wall, Susan, *Interim Dir Develop,* Montclair Art Museum, Montclair NJ

Wallace, Alan, *Asst Prof,* Chattanooga State Technical Community College, Advertising Arts Dept, Chattanooga TN (S)

Wallace, Andrea, *Artistic Dir,* Anderson Ranch Arts Center, Snowmass Village CO

Wallace, Brian, *Cur,* State University of New York at New Paltz, Samuel Dorsky Museum of Art, New Paltz NY

Wallace, Brian, *Dir Exhib & Chief Cur,* International Center of Photography, Museum, New York NY

Wallace, Charles, *Dir,* Pump House Center for the Arts, Chillicothe OH

Wallace, Danielle, *Prog Dir,* State of North Carolina, Battleship North Carolina, Wilmington NC

Wallace, Ellen, *Mktg & Pub Rels Mgr,* Southeastern Center for Contemporary Art, Winston Salem NC

Wallace, Kevin, *Dir,* Beatrice Wood Center for the Arts, Ojai CA

Wallace, Margaret, *Registrar,* Middlebury College, Museum of Art, Middlebury VT

Wallace, Mary, *Accnt,* Art Complex Museum, Carl A. Weyerhaeuser Library, Duxbury MA

Wallace, Matt, *Asst Dir Educ,* North Dakota Museum of Art, Grand Forks ND

Wallace, Richard W, *Prof,* Wellesley College, Art Dept, Wellesley MA (S)

Wallace, Robin, *Assoc Cur Art, Photos & Prints,* The Filson Historical Society, Louisville KY

Wallace, Scott, *Prof,* South Dakota State University, Dept of Visual Arts, Brookings SD (S)

Wallace, Sheila, *Library Dir,* Emily Carr Institute of Art & Design, Library, Vancouver BC

Wallace, Tammy, *Sr Asst,* Richard M Ross Art Museum at Wesleyan University, Delaware OH

Wallach, Alan, *Ralph H Wark Prof Art & Art History,* College of William & Mary, Dept of Fine Arts, Williamsburg VA (S)

Wallach, Nancy, *Dir Curatorial Affairs,* Katonah Museum of Art, Katonah NY

Wallach, Ruth, *Reference Center,* University of Southern California, Helen Topping Architecture & Fine Arts Library, Los Angeles CA

Waller, Diane, *Financial Coordr,* Women in the Arts Foundation, Inc, Staten Island NY

Waller, Richard, *Dir,* University of Richmond, University Museums, Richmond VA

Waller, Richard, *Exec Dir Univ Mus,* University of Richmond, Dept of Art and Art History, Richmond VA (S)

Waller, Susan, *Asst Prof,* University of Missouri, Saint Louis, Dept of Art & Art History, Saint Louis MO (S)

Waller, Sydney, *Exec Dir,* Sculpture Space, Inc, Utica NY

Wallestad, Tom, *Assoc Prof,* Marian University, Art Dept, Fond Du Lac WI (S)

Wallin, Scott, *Designer,* Whatcom Museum, Library, Bellingham WA

Wallin, Scott, *Exhib Designer,* Whatcom Museum, Bellingham WA

Walline, Lucy, *Librn,* Bethany College, Wallerstedt Library, Lindsborg KS

Wallis, Jonathan, *Chmn Liberal Arts,* Moore College of Art & Design, Philadelphia PA (S)

Walls, Adam, *Asst Prof,* University of North Carolina at Pembroke, Art Dept, Pembroke NC (S)

Walls, Lucinda, *Librn,* Queen's University, Stauffer Library Art Collection, Kingston ON

Walls, Nancy, *Dir,* Edna Hibel, Hibel Museum of Art, Jupiter FL

Walls, Nancy, *Dir,* Edna Hibel, Hibel Museum Gallery, Jupiter FL

Wallsmith, Matt, *Fin Dir,* Yesteryear Village, West Palm Beach FL

Walmsley, William, *Prof Emeritus,* Florida State University, Art Dept, Tallahassee FL (S)

Walsh, Anne, *Dir Finance,* Henry Gallery Association, Henry Art Gallery, Seattle WA

Walsh, Anne, *Dir Finance,* University of Washington, Henry Art Gallery, Seattle WA

Walsh, David, *Gallery Cur,* Valencia Community College, Art Gallery-East Campus, Orlando FL

Walsh, Jack, *Co-Dir,* National Alliance for Media Arts & Culture, San Francisco CA

Walsh, Johnathon, *Asst Prof,* South Carolina State University, Dept of Visual & Performing Arts, Orangeburg SC (S)

Walsh, Joseph, *Assoc Prof,* Amarillo College, Visual Art Dept, Amarillo TX (S)

Walsh, Krista, *Vis Asst Prof,* Hamline University, Dept of Studio Arts & Art History, Saint Paul MN (S)

Walsh, Marguerite, *Prof,* New England College, Art & Art History, Henniker NH (S)

Walsh, Michael, *Artist in Residence Coordr,* Bunnell Street AAS Center, Bunnell Street Arts Center, Homer AK

Walsh, Penny, *Dir Mktg,* Confederation Centre Art Gallery and Museum, Charlottetown PE

Walsh, Stacey, *Coll Mgr,* University of Nebraska, Lincoln, Sheldon Memorial Art Gallery & Sculpture Garden, Lincoln NE

Walsh, Stephen, *Environmental & Studio Tech,* University of Southern Maine, Dept of Art, Gorham ME (S)

Walsh, Timothy F, *Head Dept,* Otero Junior College, Dept of Arts, La Junta CO (S)

Walsh-Piper, Kathleen, *Dir,* The Art Museum at the University of Kentucky, Lexington KY

Walter, Barbara, *Interim Dir,* Syracuse University, College of Visual & Performing Arts, Syracuse NY (S)

Walter, Charles Thomas, *Assoc Prof,* Bloomsburg University, Dept of Art & Art History, Bloomsburg PA (S)

Walter, Robert, *Artist,* U Gallery, New York NY

Walter, Wendy R, *Gallery Dir & Registrar,* San Luis Obispo Museum of Art, San Luis Obispo CA

Walter-Frojen, Rhonda, *Assoc Dir,* Dickinson State University, Art Gallery, Dickinson ND

Walters, Bruce, *Prof,* Western Illinois University, Department of Art, Macomb IL (S)

Walters, Dallas, *Prof,* Indiana Wesleyan University, School of Arts & Humanities, Division of Art, Marion IN (S)

Walters, Daniel, *Dir,* Las Vegas-Clark County Library District, Las Vegas NV

Walters, David M, *Media Arts & Animation,* Art Institute of Pittsburgh, Pittsburgh PA (S)

Walters, Elizabeth J, *Assoc Prof,* Pennsylvania State University, University Park, Dept of Art History, University Park PA (S)

Walters, Jamie, *Co-Dir,* Carnegie Mellon University, The Frame, Pittsburgh PA

Walters, Jo Ann, *Assoc Prof,* Purchase College, State University of New York, School of Art+Design, Purchase NY (S)

Walters, Kim, *Ahmanson Cur of Native American History & Culture,* Autry National Center, Southwest Museum of the American Indian, Mt. Washington Campus, Los Angeles CA

Walters, Maura, *Asst to Dir/Exhibs,* Library Association of La Jolla, Athenaeum Music & Arts Library, La Jolla CA

Walthall, Nina, *Asst Cur Educ,* Illinois State Museum, Museum Store, Chicago IL

Walton, Amy, *Dir Develop,* Contemporary Art Center of Virginia, Virginia Beach VA

Walton, Dan, *Dir Operations,* San Antonio Museum of Art, San Antonio TX

Walton, Jim, *Exec Dir,* Beck Center for the Arts, Lakewood OH

Walton, Lee, *Prof,* University of North Carolina at Greensboro, Art Dept, Greensboro NC (S)

Walton, Peter, *CFO,* Museum of Contemporary Art, Chicago IL

Walton, Thomas, *Assoc Prof,* Catholic University of America, School of Architecture & Planning, Washington DC (S)

Waltz, Liz, *Art Studios Mgr,* Charles B Goddard, Ardmore OK

Walz, Jonathan F, *Cur,* Rollins College, George D & Harriet W Cornell Fine Arts Museum, Winter Park FL

Walzer, Barbara, *Exec Dir,* Worcester Center for Crafts, Krikorian Gallery, Worcester MA

Wamhoff, Meryl, *Fine Arts Div Dean,* San Joaquin Delta College, Arts & Communication, Stockton CA (S)

Wanamaker, Monty, *Southern Standard Staff Reporter,* Southern Museum & Galleries of Photography, Mc Minnville TN

Wanberg, Kate, *Preparator,* University of Wisconsin-Madison, Chazen Museum of Art, Madison WI

Wandrei, Jason, *Mus Security Officer,* Williams College, Museum of Art, Williamstown MA

Wang, Jenny, *Cataloging Librn,* Savannah College of Art & Design - Atlanta, ACA Library of Atlanta, Atlanta GA

Wang, Kirk, *Prof,* Eckerd College, Art Dept, Saint Petersburg FL (S)

Wang, Santy, *Registrar,* Santa Monica Museum of Art, Santa Monica CA

Wang, Susan, *Mem & Bookstore Assoc,* Pasadena Museum of California Art, Pasadena CA

Wang, Victor, *Assoc Prof,* Fontbonne University, Fine Art Dept, Saint Louis MO (S)

Wang, Ye, *Asst Prof,* Washburn University of Topeka, Dept of Art, Topeka KS (S)

Wanless, Mary Dorsey, *Asst Prof,* Washburn University of Topeka, Dept of Art, Topeka KS (S)

Wanserski, Martin, *Assoc Prof,* University of South Dakota, Department of Art, College of Fine Arts, Vermillion SD (S)

Wanzel, J Grant, *Prof,* Dalhousie University, Faculty of Architecture, Halifax NS (S)

Warcup, Stacy, *Mem Coordr,* North Dakota Museum of Art, Grand Forks ND

Ward, Alf, *Prof,* Winthrop University, Dept of Art & Design, Rock Hill SC (S)

Ward, Carla, *Dir & Owner,* Tinkertown Museum, Sandia Park NM

Ward, Charles, *Asst Prof Art,* Middle Georgia State College, Humanities Division, Dept of Art - School of Liberal Arts, Dept of Media, Culture & the Arts, Cochran GA (S)

Ward, Dawn, *Instr,* Northeastern State University, College of Arts & Letters, Tahlequah OK (S)

Ward, Elizabeth, *Asst Prof,* Trinity University, Dept of Art, San Antonio TX (S)

Ward, Ellie, *Librn,* Akron Art Museum, Akron OH

Ward, Ellie, *Librn,* Akron Art Museum, Martha Stecher Reed Art Library, Akron OH

Ward, Erica M, *Archivist/Cur,* Coachella Valley History Museum, Indio CA

Ward, Frazer, *Assoc Prof,* Smith College, Art Dept, Northampton MA (S)

Ward, Gerry, *Bldg & Grounds Supt,* R W Norton Art Foundation, R W Norton Art Gallery, Shreveport LA

Ward, James, *Event Coordr,* George Phippen, Phippen Museum - Art of the American West, Prescott AZ

Ward, Jennifer, *Exhib Coordr,* Foto Fest International, Houston TX

Ward, Karen, *Chmn,* Hampton University, Dept of Fine & Performing Arts, Hampton VA (S)

Ward, Linda, *Instr,* University of Louisiana at Monroe, Dept of Art, Monroe LA (S)

Ward, Neidra, *Progs Coordr,* National YoungArts Foundation, Miami FL

Ward, R D, *Prof,* Randolph-Macon College, Dept of the Arts, Ashland VA (S)

Ward, Robert, *Coordr Gallery Dir,* Bowie State University, Fine & Performing Arts Dept, Bowie MD (S)

Watson, Tom, *Chmn,* Columbia College, Art Dept, Columbia MO (S)

Watson, Wendy, *Interim Dir & Cur,* Mount Holyoke College, Art Museum, South Hadley MA

Watson-Mauro, Sharon, *Lib Dir,* Moore College of Art & Design, Library, Philadelphia PA

Watt, Ambert, *Educ Coordr,* Southern Alberta Art Gallery, Lethbridge AB

Watt, Kelly, *Asst Prof,* Washburn University of Topeka, Dept of Art, Topeka KS (S)

Watters, Clare, *Sales Gallery Mgr,* Southwest School of Art, San Antonio TX

Watters, Tom, *Dir,* National Air and Space Museum, Regional Planetary Image Facility, Washington DC

Watts, Angela, *Coll Mgr,* University of Kansas, Spencer Museum of Art, Lawrence KS

Watts, Barbara, *Assoc Prof,* Florida International University, School of Art & Art History, Miami FL (S)

Watts, Bronwen, *Mem Sec,* College of William & Mary, Muscarelle Museum of Art, Williamsburg VA

Watts, Greg, *Chmn,* Metropolitan State University of Denver, Art Dept, Denver CO (S)

Watts, Greg, *Exec Dir,* Metropolitan State University of Denver, Center for Visual Art, Denver CO

Watts, Michael, *Dir,* Eastern Illinois University, Tarble Arts Center, Charleston IL

Watts, Mitra, *Dean Acad Affairs,* Art Institute of Colorado, Denver CO (S)

Watts, Steve, *Coordr,* University of Charleston, Carleton Varney Dept of Art & Design, Charleston WV (S)

Watts, Tracy, *Asst Prof,* State University of New York College at Potsdam, Dept of Fine Arts, Potsdam NY (S)

Watts Pope, Elizabeth, *Reference Librn,* American Antiquarian Society, Worcester MA

Waugaman, Linda, *Vis Arts Dir,* Indian River Community College, Fine Arts Dept, Fort Pierce FL (S)

Waugh, Michael, *Resource Dir,* Momenta Art, Brooklyn NY

Wavrat, Dennis, *Prof,* University of South Dakota, Department of Art, College of Fine Arts, Vermillion SD (S)

Waxman, Marcia, *Pres,* Congregation Emanu-El, Bernard Judaica Museum, New York NY

Waxter, Dorsey, *VPres,* Art Dealers Association of America, Inc, New York NY

Way, Catherine A, *Dir,* James Prendergast, Jamestown NY

Way, Cynthia, *Dir Educ & Visitor Experience,* Williams College, Museum of Art, Williamstown MA

Way, Jennifer, *Assoc Prof Art History,* University of North Texas, College of Visual Arts & Design, Denton TX (S)

Way, William, *Chair Bd Trustee,* Phoenix Art Museum, Phoenix AZ

Wayman, Adele, *Prof of Art, Dept Chair,* Guilford College, Art Dept, Greensboro NC (S)

Wazwaz, Maysoun, *Exhibs Progs Mgr,* Southern Exposure, San Francisco CA

Weakland, Cindy, *Supvr Pub Progs,* The Rockwell Museum of Western Art, Corning NY

Weand-Kilkenny, Betsy, *Develop Dir,* Abington Art Center, Jenkintown PA

Weander-Gaster, Kara, *Exec Dir,* Norfolk Arts Center, Norfolk NE

Wear, Beth, *Site Mgr,* Longfellow National Historic Site, Longfellow House - Washington's Headquarters, Cambridge MA

Wear, Lisa, *Dir,* Horizons Unlimited Supplementary Educational Center, Science Museum, Salisbury NC

Wear, Lori, *Cur,* Kern County Museum, Bakersfield CA

Wearth, Pat, *Mus Shop Mgr,* Kemp Center for the Arts, Wichita Falls TX

Weatherley, Glynn, *Lectr,* Lambuth University, Dept of Human Ecology & Visual Arts, Jackson TN (S)

Weathers, Dennis, *Area Dir,* College of the Siskiyous, Theatre Dept, Weed CA (S)

Weathers, Marion, *Registrar,* Rocky Mount Arts Center, Rocky Mount NC

Weatherwax, Sarah, *Cur Prints,* Library Company of Philadelphia, Philadelphia PA

Weaver, Angela, *Librn,* University of Washington, Art Library, Seattle WA

Weaver, Christy, *Staff Asst,* Grassroots Art Center, Lucas KS

Weaver, David, *Exec Dir,* St. Louis Artists' Guild, Saint Louis MO

Weaver, Henry C, *Pres, Cur & Sculpture,* John Weaver Sculpture Collection, Hope BC

Weaver, Herb, *Head Dept,* Bethany College, Dept of Fine Arts, Bethany WV (S)

Weaver, James, *Dir Institutional Advancement Opers,* Heard Museum, Billie Jane Baguley Library and Archives, Phoenix AZ

Weaver, Joyce, *Librn,* The Mint Museum, Charlotte NC

Weaver, Melanie, *Assoc Prof,* Azusa Pacific University, College of Liberal Arts, Art Dept, Azusa CA (S)

Weaver, Noni, *Exec Asst,* John Weaver Sculpture Collection, Hope BC

Weaver, Patsy, *Bd Mem,* Coquille Valley Art Association, Coquille OR

Weaver, Suzanne, *Assoc Cur Contemporary Art,* Dallas Museum of Art, Dallas TX

Weaver, Timothy, *Assoc Prof Electronic Media Arts & Design,* University of Denver, School of Art & Art History, Denver CO (S)

Weaver, Victoria, *Asst Grad Prof Art Educ,* Millersville University, Dept of Art & Design, Millersville PA (S)

Weaver, Victoria, *Cur Educ,* Daum Museum of Contemporary Art, Sedalia MO

Webb, Ann, *Exec Dir & Interim Publr,* Canadian Art Foundation, Toronto ON

Webb, Ashley, *Colls Mgr,* Longwood Center for the Visual Arts, Farmville VA

Webb, Deborah, *Library Supv,* University of Notre Dame, Architecture Library, Notre Dame IN

Webb, Dixie, *Dean College Arts & Letters,* Austin Peay State University, Art Dept Library, Clarksville TN

Webb, Duncan J, *Dir Educ,* American Academy of Art, Chicago IL (S)

Webb, Frank, *Instr,* Art Center Sarasota, Sarasota FL (S)

Webb, Greg, *Instr,* Joe Kubert, Dover NJ (S)

Webb, Hugh, *Dir,* Portland Community College, North View Gallery, Portland OR

Webb, Jennifer, *Communs Mgr,* University of British Columbia, Museum of Anthropology, Vancouver BC

Webb, Lanny, *Prof Graphic Design,* University of Georgia, Franklin College of Arts & Sciences, Lamar Dodd School of Art, Athens GA (S)

Webb, Nicole, *Cur Colls,* Historical Museum at Fort Missoula, Missoula MT

Webb, Ron, *Dean,* Huntington College, Art Dept, Huntington IN (S)

Webber, Barry C, *Pres,* Norfolk Historical Society Inc, Museum, Norfolk CT

Webber, David, *Asst Prof,* Coe College, Dept of Art, Cedar Rapids IA (S)

Webber, Nancy E, *Asst Prof,* Los Angeles Harbor College, Art Dept, Wilmington CA (S)

Webber, Sandra, *Paintings Conservator,* Williamstown Art Conservation Center, Williamstown MA

Weber, Bruce, *Sr Cur Nineteenth Century Art,* National Academy Museum & School, Archives, New York NY

Weber, Camille, *Grants & Corporate Support,* Plains Art Museum, Fargo ND

Weber, Chela Scot, *Dir Library & Archives,* Brooklyn Historical Society, Othmer Library, Brooklyn NY

Weber, Deborah, *Exec Dir,* Lincoln Arts Council, Lincoln NE

Weber, Heather, *Dir,* Northeastern Illinois University, Gallery, Chicago IL

Weber, Jean M, *Exec Dir,* Nantucket Historical Association, Historic Nantucket, Nantucket MA

Weber, Joan, *VPres,* Washington Sculptors Group, Washington DC

Weber, John, *Prof,* Elmhurst College, Art Dept, Elmhurst IL (S)

Weber, Joseph A, *Art Educ,* Southern Illinois University at Edwardsville, Dept of Art & Design, Edwardsville IL (S)

Weber, Matthew, *Instr,* Middlesex Community College, Fine Arts Div, Middletown CT (S)

Weber, Megan, *Prog Asst,* Think 360 Art Complete Education, Colo Chapter, Denver CO

Weber, Robin, *Dir,* Museum of Northern British Columbia, Library, Prince Rupert BC

Weber-Byer, Kayleigh, *Admin Asst,* Midwest Museum of American Art, Elkhart IN

Webster, Christine, *VPres,* Arts & Crafts Association of Meriden Inc, Gallery 53, Meriden CT

Webster, Drew, *Prof, Photog,* State College of Florida Manatee - Sarasota, Art, Design, Humanities, Bradenton FL (S)

Webster, Helen, *Graphic Design, Media Arts & Animation,* Art Institute of Pittsburgh, Pittsburgh PA (S)

Webster, James D, *Chmn Div Physical,* American Museum of Natural History, New York NY

Webster, Lynn, *Assoc Prof Art,* The College of Idaho, Rosenthal Art Gallery, Caldwell ID

Webster, Maryann, *Instr,* University of Utah, Dept of Art & Art History, Salt Lake City UT (S)

Webster, Rebecca, *Commissioner,* United States Department of the Interior, Indian Arts & Crafts Board, Washington DC

Webster, Sally, *Prof Emerita,* City University of New York, PhD Program in Art History, New York NY (S)

Webster, Stephen, *Dir Mktg,* Vancouver Art Gallery, Vancouver BC

Weckel, Eric, *Chmn,* Abington Art Center, Jenkintown PA

Wedderspoon, Craig, *Dir Grad Studies Studio Art,* University of Alabama, Dept of Art, Tuscaloosa AL (S)

Weddle, Wayneath, *Instr,* East Central University, School of Fine Arts, Ada OK (S)

Wedel, Pam, *Instr,* Oklahoma State University, Graphic Arts Dept, Visual Communications, Okmulgee OK (S)

Wedig, Dale, *Prof,* Northern Michigan University, Dept of Art & Design, Marquette MI (S)

Weech, Michael, *Curatorial Asst,* Heritage Museum Association, Inc, The Heritage Museum of Northwest Florida, Valparaiso FL

Weed, Rahila, *Asst Prof,* Central Missouri State University, Dept Art & Design, Warrensburg MO (S)

Weedman, Kenneth R, *Chmn,* Cumberland College, Dept of Art, Williamsburg KY (S)

Weekly, Nancy, *Head Colls & Charles Cary Rumsey Cur,* State University of New York College at Buffalo, Buffalo NY

Weeks, Chris Chang, *Dir Develop,* Triton Museum of Art, Santa Clara CA

Weeks, Christopher W, *Assoc Prof,* Hillsborough Community College, Fine Arts Dept, Tampa FL (S)

Weeks, Jason, *Exec Dir,* Cambridge Arts Council, CAC Gallery, Cambridge MA

Weeks, John, *Dir,* University of Pennsylvania, Museum Library, Philadelphia PA

Weeks, William, *V Chmn,* North Country Museum of Arts, Park Rapids MN

Weems, Jason, *Asst Prof,* University of California, Riverside, Dept of the History of Art, Riverside CA (S)

Weese, Cynthia, *Dean School,* Washington University, School of Architecture, Saint Louis MO (S)

Weese, Judy, *Bus Mgr,* Landis Valley Village and Farm Museum, PA Historical & Museum Commission, Lancaster PA

Weg, Carol L, *VPres,* Wendell Gilley, Southwest Harbor ME

Wegman, Jay, *Dir,* Henry Street Settlement, Abrons Art Center, New York NY

Wegman, Jay D, *Reverend Canon,* Cathedral of Saint John the Divine, New York NY

Wegner, Susan, *Dir Art History,* Bowdoin College, Art Dept, Brunswick ME (S)

Weich, George, *VPres Horticulture & Conservation,* Brookgreen Gardens, Murrells Inlet SC

Weickart, Joseph G, *Exec Dir,* Amherst Museum, Amherst NY

Weida, Wendy S, *Exec Dir,* Moravian Historical Society, Whitefield House Museum, Nazareth PA

Weidel, Deb, *Asst Cur Exhibs,* Columbus Museum, Columbus GA

Weider, Greg, *Media Arts & Animation,* Art Institute of Pittsburgh, Pittsburgh PA (S)

Weidl, Beverly, *Cur,* Hopewell Museum, Hopewell NJ

Weidman, James F, *Pres,* Arts & Education Council of Greater Saint Louis, Saint Louis MO

Wenzel, Ashley, *Collec Mgr & Registrar,* Laumeier Sculpture Park, Saint Louis MO

Wenzel, Duane, *Head Librn,* Bernice Pauahi Bishop, Library, Honolulu HI

Wepler, Bill, *Cur Historic Archaeology,* Indiana State Museum, Indianapolis IN

Werbel, Amy, *Asst Prof,* St Michael's College, Fine Arts Dept, Colchester VT (S)

Werfel, Gina, *Chmn Art Studio,* University of California, Davis, Dept of Art & Art History, Davis CA (S)

Werhan, Lee, *Mus Shop Mgr,* Phoenix Art Museum, Phoenix AZ

Werhane, David, *Dir,* Philmont Scout Ranch, Philmont Museum - Seton Memorial Library, Cimarron NM

Werle, Thomas, *Prof,* Capitol Community Technical College, Humanities Division & Art Dept, Hartford CT (S)

Werline, Dee, *Pres,* Maysville, Kentucky Gateway Museum Center, Maysville KY

Werlink, Joy, *Asst Cur Photo,* Washington State Historical Society, Research Center, Tacoma WA

Werner, Charlotte, *Faculty,* University of Manitoba, School of Art, Winnipeg MB (S)

Werner, Lisa, *Dir Opers,* Centrum Arts & Creative Education, Port Townsend WA

Werner, Michael, *Assoc Prof,* State University of New York at Albany, Art Dept, Albany NY (S)

Werness, Hope, *Prof,* California State University, Art Dept, Turlock CA (S)

Wertheimer, Gary, *Chmn,* Olivet College, Art Dept, Olivet MI (S)

Wertz, Sandra, *Chmn Media Arts,* University of South Carolina, Dept of Art, Columbia SC (S)

Wesaw Sloan, Sallie, *Graphic Designer,* Institute of American Indian Arts, Museum of Contemporary Native Arts, Santa Fe NM

Weselmann, Mona, *Registrar,* Saint Olaf College, Flaten Art Museum, Northfield MN

Wesley, John, *Photo Instr,* Bellevue Community College, Art Dept, Bellevue WA (S)

Wesley, Nashie, *Admin Asst,* Okefenokee Heritage Center, Inc, Waycross GA

Wesley, Richard, *Interim Chmn,* University of Pennsylvania, Dept of Architecture, Philadelphia PA (S)

Wessel, Frederick, *Prof,* University of Hartford, Hartford Art School, West Hartford CT (S)

Wessel, Mary, *Adjunct Prof Photog,* Johnson County Community College, Fine Arts Dept & Art History Dept, Overland Park KS (S)

West, Arleen, *Gift Shop Mgr,* San Antonio Museum of Art, San Antonio TX

West, Barbara J, *Pres,* Alberta Society of Artists, Calgary AB

West, Bruce, *Vis Lect,* Lewis & Clark College, Dept of Art, Portland OR (S)

West, Carolyn, *Prog Facilitator,* Central Florida Community College, Humanities Dept, Ocala FL (S)

West, Christine Jelson, *Exec Dir,* Lawndale Art Center, Houston TX

West, Claire, *Performing Art Dir,* Arizona Commission on the Arts, Phoenix AZ

West, Coleen, *Exec Dir,* Howard County Arts Council, Ellicott City MD

West, Edward, *Prof,* University of Michigan, Ann Arbor, School of Art & Design, Ann Arbor MI (S)

West, Margy, *3rd VPres,* National Watercolor Society, San Pedro CA

West, Mark, *Chmn Transportation Design,* College for Creative Studies, Detroit MI (S)

West, Matt, *Instr,* Laramie County Community College, Division of Arts & Humanities, Cheyenne WY (S)

West, Ruth, *Instr,* Springfield College, Dept of Visual & Performing Arts, Springfield MA (S)

West, W Richard, *Dir,* National Museum of the American Indian, Smithsonian Institution, Washington DC

West, W Richard, *Interim Dir,* The Textile Museum, Washington DC

West, William, *Adjunct Asst Prof,* Le Moyne College, Fine Arts Dept, Syracuse NY (S)

Westbrook, Lindsey, *Managing Ed,* California College of the Arts, CCAC Wattis Institute for Contemporary Arts, San Francisco CA

Westbrook, Paul, *Asst Dean,* Northeastern State University, College of Arts & Letters, Tahlequah OK (S)

Westcott-Sykes, Sheena, *Colls Mgr,* Orillia Museum of Art & History, Orillia ON

Westerbeck, Colin, *Cur Photography,* The Art Institute of Chicago, Chicago IL

Westerbeck, Colin, *Dir,* University of California, California Museum of Photography, Riverside CA

Westergard, Gina, *Assoc Prof,* University of Kansas, The School of the Arts, Dept of Visual Art, Lawrence KS (S)

Westerman, Shannon, *Exec Dir,* Louisville Visual Art Association, Louisville KY

Westfall, Stephen, *Asst Prof,* Rutgers, The State University of New Jersey, Mason Gross School of the Arts, Visual Arts Dept, New Brunswick NJ (S)

Westkaemper, Kathleen, *Adminr,* Artspace, Richmond VA

Westlake, Richard, *Theatre Arts Instr,* Edison Community College, Gallery of Fine Arts, Fort Myers FL (S)

Westmacott, Jean, *Cur, Arts Management Prog Dir,* Brenau University, Art & Design Dept, Gainesville GA (S)

Westman, Barbara, *Prof,* Slippery Rock University of Pennsylvania, Dept of Art, Slippery Rock PA (S)

Westman, Hans, *Media Arts & Animation,* Art Institute of Pittsburgh, Pittsburgh PA (S)

Westmark, Michelle, *Asst Prof,* Bethel College, Dept of Art, Saint Paul MN (S)

Westmoreland, La Monte, *Prof,* Los Angeles City College, Dept of Art, Los Angeles CA (S)

Westmorland, Lamont, *Dir,* California State University, Los Angeles, Fine Arts Gallery, Los Angeles CA

Weston, Laura, *Digitization Specialist,* Mount Holyoke College, Art Museum, South Hadley MA

Weston, Robert, *VPres,* Long Branch Historical Museum, Long Branch NJ

Weston, Victoria, *Asst Prof,* University of Massachusetts - Boston, Art Dept, Boston MA (S)

Westphal, Rebecca, *Dir Communs, Mktg & Customer Serv,* Grand Rapids Public Museum, Public Museum of Grand Rapids, Grand Rapids MI

Westwood, Dan, *Pres,* Southern Alberta Art Gallery, Lethbridge AB

Westwood, Lyn, *Instr,* Toronto Art Therapy Institute, Toronto ON (S)

Wetenhall, John, *Exec Dir,* Florida State University, John & Mable Ringling Museum of Art, Sarasota FL

Wetherington, Mark V, *Dir,* The Filson Historical Society, Louisville KY

Wetherwell, Leslie, *CFO,* Maryhill Museum of Art, Goldendale WA

Wethli, Mark, *Chair,* Bowdoin College, Art Dept, Brunswick ME (S)

Wetmore, Joan, *Dir Develop,* Hillwood Museum & Gardens Foundation, Hillwood Estate Museum & Gardens, Washington DC

Wetmore, Laura, *Cur Collections,* Arnot Art Museum, Elmira NY

Wetson, Joan, *Dir Admis & Financial Aid,* University of Pennsylvania, Graduate School of Fine Arts, Philadelphia PA (S)

Wetta, Frank, *Dean,* Daytona Beach Community College, Dept of Fine Arts & Visual Arts, Daytona Beach FL (S)

Wetzel, Anita, *Develop Dir,* Women's Studio Workshop, Inc, Rosendale NY

Wetzel, David, *Dir Research & Publications,* Colorado Historical Society, Colorado History Museum, Denver CO

Wetzel, Jean, *Assoc Prof Art History,* California Polytechnic State University at San Luis Obispo, Dept of Art & Design, San Luis Obispo CA (S)

Wetzig, Jeffrey, *Assoc Prof,* Bethel College, Dept of Art, Saint Paul MN (S)

Wexler, Geoff, *Library Mgr,* Oregon Historical Society, Oregon History Museum, Portland OR

Wexler, Jessica, *Asst Prof,* Purchase College, State University of New York, School of Art+Design, Purchase NY (S)

Weyerhaeuser, Charles, *Dir,* Art Complex Museum, Library, Duxbury MA

Weyerhaeuser, Charles A, *Dir & CEO,* Art Complex Museum, Carl A. Weyerhaeuser Library, Duxbury MA

Weygandt, Virginia, *Cur,* Clark County Historical Society, Library, Springfield OH

Weygandt, Virginia, *Dir Coll,* Clark County Historical Society, Heritage Center of Clark County, Springfield OH

Weyhrich, Denise, *Prof,* Chapman University, Art Dept, Orange CA (S)

Weymouth, George A, *Chmn (V),* Brandywine Conservancy, Brandywine River Museum, Chadds Ford PA

Whalen, Connie, *Cur,* Wells Fargo, Wells Fargo History Museum, Phoenix AZ

Whalen, Mary, *Chair Photog & Digital Media,* Kalamazoo Institute of Arts, KIA School, Kalamazoo MI (S)

Whalen, Wickie, *Prof,* Miami-Dade Community College, Arts & Philosophy Dept, Miami FL (S)

Whalert, Mark D, *Exec Dir,* Dubuque Museum of Art, Dubuque IA

Whatford, Mark, *Librn,* Gunston Hall Plantation, Library, Mason Neck VA

Wheeler, Adrienne, *Asst Coordr,* Society of Photographers & Artists Representatives, New York NY

Wheeler, Barbara, *Dir,* Roswell P Flower, Watertown NY

Wheeler, Bonnie, *Registrar,* Dundas Valley School of Art, DVSA Gallery, Dundas ON (S)

Wheeler, Elizabeth, *Dir of Vol Services,* Georgia Lawyers for the Arts, Atlanta GA

Wheeler, Ken, *Vol Chmn,* River Heritage Museum, Paducah KY

Wheeler, Lawrence J, *Dir,* North Carolina Museum of Art, Raleigh NC

Wheeler, Linda, *Staff Coordr,* Cedarhurst Center for the Arts, Mitchell Museum, Mount Vernon IL

Wheeler, Lisa, *Educ,* Booth Western Art Museum, Cartersville GA

Wheeler, Stephen, *Fine Art,* San Diego Public Library, Art, Music & Recreation, San Diego CA

Wheelock, Arthur, *Cur Northern Baroque Painting,* National Gallery of Art, Washington DC

Wheelock, Scott, *Instr,* Main Line Art Center, Haverford PA (S)

Whelan, Agnieszka, *Instr,* Old Dominion University, Art Dept, Norfolk VA (S)

Whelan, Jeff, *Asst Prof,* Elizabeth City State University, School of Arts & Humanities, Dept of Art, Elizabeth City NC (S)

Whelan, John, *Instr,* Saint Mary's University of Minnesota, Art & Design Dept, Winona MN (S)

Wheless, Andrea, *Chmn,* High Point University, Fine Arts Dept, High Point NC (S)

Whetstone, Jeff, *Asst Prof,* University of North Carolina at Chapel Hill, Art Dept, Chapel Hill NC (S)

Whiffen, Lorraine, *Develop Assoc,* The Long Island Museum of American Art, History & Carriages, Stony Brook NY

Whight, Ian, *Acting Head Dept City Planning,* University of Manitoba, Faculty of Architecture, Winnipeg MB (S)

Whipking, Jean, *Coll Mgr,* Buffalo Museum of Science, Research Library, Buffalo NY

Whipple, Sally, *Dir,* Old State House, Hartford CT

Whisenhunt, Brian Lee, *Exec Dir,* Museum of the Southwest, Midland TX

Whisman, Beth, *Dir Develop,* McLean County Historical Society, McLean County Museum of History, Bloomington IL

Whisman, Evelyn, *Asst Cur,* Plumas County Museum, Museum Archives, Quincy CA

Whistler, Debbie, *Interim Chmn Dept,* Hanover College, Dept of Art, Hanover IN (S)

Whitaker, Jayne, *Asst Prof,* University of Dayton, Visual Arts Dept, Dayton OH (S)

Whitaker, Joel, *Asst Prof,* University of Dayton, Visual Arts Dept, Dayton OH (S)

Whitaker, Marilyn, *Registrar,* Scottsdale Artists' School Library, Scottsdale AZ

Whitaker, Martha, *Instr Interior Design,* Maryville University of Saint Louis, Art & Design Program, Saint Louis MO (S)

Wiedemeyer, Ruth, *Shop Mgr,* Octagon Center for the Arts, Ames IA

Wiedenbaum, Marlene, *Recording Sec,* New York Society of Women Artists, Inc, Westport CT

Wiederspahn, Peter, *Asst Prof,* Northeastern University, Dept of Art & Architecture, Boston MA (S)

Wiegmann, Richard, *Prof,* Concordia University, Art Dept, Seward NE (S)

Wier, Alyssum, *Exec Dir,* Arts Council of Mendocino County, Ukiah CA

Wierich, Jochen, *Cur,* Cheekwood-Tennessee Botanical Garden & Museum of Art, Museum of Art, Nashville TN

Wiersema, Juliet, *Asst Prof,* University of Texas at San Antonio, Dept of Art & Art History, San Antonio TX (S)

Wiertz, Michael, *Dir Visitor Svcs,* Wave Hill, Bronx NY

Wieske, Ellen, *Asst Dir,* Haystack Mountain School of Crafts, Center for Community Programs Gallery, Deer Isle ME

Wiggers, Namita Gupta, *Cur,* Museum of Contemporary Craft, Portland OR

Wiggins, Amelia, *Educ Studio & Family Progs,* Nelda C & H J Lutcher Stark, Stark Museum of Art, Orange TX

Wiggins, Denise, *Cur Archaeology,* Wisconsin Historical Society, Wisconsin Historical Museum, Madison WI

Wiggins, Ginger, *Gallery Coordr,* Associated Artists of Winston-Salem, Winston Salem NC

Wiggins, Mike, *Prof,* Abilene Christian University, Dept of Art & Design, Abilene TX (S)

Wiggins, Suzanne, *Contact,* Paint Cree Center for the Arts, Rochester MI

Wight, Darlene Coward, *Cur Inuit Art,* The Winnipeg Art Gallery, Winnipeg MB

Wight, Karol, *Sr Cur Antiquities,* Getty Center, The J Paul Getty Museum, Los Angeles CA

Wightman, Jan, *Treas,* Dawson County Historical Society, Museum, Lexington NE

Wightman, Lisa Gregg, *Prof,* Munson-Williams-Proctor Arts Institute, Pratt MWP College of Art, Utica NY (S)

Wigle, Hannah, *Asst Cur,* Southern Alberta Art Gallery, Lethbridge AB

Wiklund, Ann, *Adjunct Prof Art History,* Johnson County Community College, Fine Arts Dept & Art History Dept, Overland Park KS (S)

Wilbers, Tim, *Assoc Prof,* University of Dayton, Visual Arts Dept, Dayton OH (S)

Wilbur, Kathy, *Bookkeeper,* Vesterheim Norwegian-American Museum, Decorah IA

Wilburn, Hugh, *Librn,* Harvard University, Frances Loeb Library, Cambridge MA

Wilburn, Karen, *Dir Finance & Bus Serv,* Grand Rapids Public Museum, Public Museum of Grand Rapids, Grand Rapids MI

Wilcox, David R, *Sr Research Anthropologist,* Museum of Northern Arizona, Flagstaff AZ

Wilcox, Jeffrey, *Registrar,* University of Missouri, Museum of Art & Archaeology, Columbia MO

Wilcox, Ken, *Treas,* Pioneer Historical Museum of South Dakota, Hot Springs SD

Wilcox, Lawrence, *Instr,* New Mexico Junior College, Arts & Sciences, Hobbs NM (S)

Wilcox, Scott, *Chief Cur Art Colls, Information & Access & Sr Cur Prints & Drawings,* Yale University, Yale Center for British Art, New Haven CT

Wilcoxen, Jessa, *Asst Prof,* Greenville College, Art Dept, Greenville IL (S)

Wilcoxson, Shirlie Bowers, *Chmn & Prof Emerita,* Saint Gregory's University, Dept of Art, Shawnee OK (S)

Wilczek, Ronald, *Prof,* Roger Williams University, Visual Art Dept, Bristol RI (S)

Wild, Gail, *COO,* Akron Art Museum, Akron OH

Wild, Jami, *Controller,* Museum of Wisconsin Art, West Bend WI

Wild, Jane, *Educ & Prog Coordr,* Art Gallery of Peterborough, Peterborough ON

Wilde, Douglas, *Admin Officer,* American Art Museum, Smithsonian Institution, Washington DC

Wilde, Robert, *Instr,* College of Saint Benedict, Art Dept, Saint Joseph MN (S)

Wilde, Robert, *Lectr,* Saint John's University, Art Dept, Collegeville MN (S)

Wilde, Wilson, *VChmn,* Connecticut Historical Society, Hartford CT

Wilder, Wendy, *Bookkeeper,* Vermilion County Museum Society, Danville IL

Wildey, Al, *Chmn Dept,* Central Michigan University, Dept of Art, Mount Pleasant MI (S)

Wildey, Sharon A, *Legal Affairs Adv to Bd,* Brown County Art Gallery Foundation, Nashville IN

Wilds, Alexander, *Assoc Prof,* Benedict College, School of Humanities, Arts & Social Sciences, Columbia SC (S)

Wiley, Francis, *Gallery Mgr,* Redlands Art Association, Redlands Art Association Gallery & Art Center, Redlands CA

Wiley, Jenny, *Coordr Communs,* Heritage Preservation, The National Institute for Conservation, Washington DC

Wiley, Karen, *Exec Dir,* Louise Hopkins Underwood Center for the Arts, Lubbock TX

Wilfong, Terry, *Assoc Cur,* University of Michigan, Kelsey Museum of Archaeology, Ann Arbor MI

Wilhelm, Elliot, *Cur Film,* Detroit Institute of Arts, Detroit MI

Wilhoit, Sarah, *Asst Prof,* Harding University, Dept of Art & Design, Searcy AR (S)

Wilk, Elizabeth, *Registrar,* Wheaton Arts & Cultural Center, Museum of American Glass, Millville NJ

Wilk, Joseph, *Instr,* Antonelli Institute, Professional Photography & Commercial Art, Erdenheim PA (S)

Wilke, Amanda, *Educ Dir,* LeMoyne Art Foundation, Center for the Visual Arts, Tallahassee FL

Wilken, Marilyn, *Art Gallery Chmn & Secy,* Iroquois County Historical Society Museum, Old Courthouse Museum, Watseka IL

Wilkes, Peggy, *Lectr,* Texas A&M University-Kingsville, Art Dept, Kingsville TX (S)

Wilkes, Pegi, *Dir,* Southern Ohio Museum Corporation, Southern Ohio Museum, Portsmouth OH

Wilkie, Jane J, *Treas,* Plastic Club, Art Club, Philadelphia PA

Wilkins, Cary, *Librn & Archivist,* Morris Museum of Art, Augusta GA

Wilkins, Catherine, *Dir,* University of Western Ontario, The D B Weldon Library, London ON

Wilkins, David, *Prof Emeritus,* University of Pittsburgh, Henry Clay Frick Dept History of Art & Architecture, Pittsburgh PA (S)

Wilkins, Laura, *Dir Mktg and Outreach,* Carnegie Center for Art & History, New Albany IN

Wilkins, Mark, *Exec Dir,* Chatham Historical Society, The Atwood House Museum, Chatham MA

Wilkins, Nancy, *Instr,* Marylhurst University, Art Dept, Marylhurst OR (S)

Wilkins, Rebecca, *Asst Mgr,* Queens Borough Public Library, Fine Arts & Recreation Division, Jamaica NY

Wilkins, Will K, *Exec Dir,* Real Art Ways (RAW), Hartford CT

Wilkinson, Carlton, *Sr Lectr,* Vanderbilt University, Dept of Art, Nashville TN (S)

Wilkinson, Lonnie, *Instr,* Southern University A & M College, School of Architecture, Baton Rouge LA (S)

Wilkinson, MaryAnn, *Cur Modern Art,* Detroit Institute of Arts, Detroit MI

Wilkinson, Sean, *Prof,* University of Dayton, Visual Arts Dept, Dayton OH (S)

Wilks, Barbara, *Dir,* Pyramid Hill Sculpture Park & Museum, Hamilton OH

Wilks, Harry T, *Trustee,* Pyramid Hill Sculpture Park & Museum, Hamilton OH

Wilks, Molly, *Instr,* South Dakota State University, Dept of Visual Arts, Brookings SD (S)

Will, Vernon, *Head Conservation,* Ohio Historical Society, Archives-Library Division, Columbus OH

Willard, Shirley, *Pres Emerita,* Fulton County Historical Society Inc, Fulton County Museum (Tetzlaff Reference Room), Rochester IN

Willcox, Christine, *Asst Prof,* Macalester College, Art Dept, Saint Paul MN (S)

Willeke, Linda, *Educ Coordr,* City of Mason City, Charles H MacNider Museum, Mason City IA

Willens, Ann, *Admin Dir,* Palos Verdes Art Center/Beverly G Alpay Center for Arts Education, Rancho Palos Verdes CA

Willers, Karl Emil, *Dir,* Nassau County Museum of Art, Roslyn Harbor NY

Willet, E Crosby, *Pres,* Willet Hauser Architectural Glass Inc, Philadelphia PA

Willet, Jennifer, *Prof,* University of Windsor, Visual Arts, Windsor ON (S)

Willett, Catherine, *Develop Officer,* Buffalo Arts Studio, Art Gallery, Buffalo NY

Willey, Christina, *Prof,* Central Missouri State University, Dept Art & Design, Warrensburg MO (S)

Williamon, Scott, *Facilities Mgr,* Anniston Museum of Natural History, Anniston AL

Williams, Al, *Pres,* San Francisco African-American Historical & Cultural Society, San Francisco CA

Williams, Alfred, *Pres,* San Francisco African-American Historical & Cultural Society, Library, San Francisco CA

Williams, Annette, *Instr,* Southern University A & M College, School of Architecture, Baton Rouge LA (S)

Williams, Barbara, *Dir & Owner,* The Mather Homestead Museum, Library & Memorial Park, Wellsville NY

Williams, Benjamin, *Librn & Spec Coll Librn,* Field Museum, Library, Chicago IL

Williams, Brad, *Pres,* Wellfleet Historical Society & Museum, Inc, Wellfleet MA

Williams, Brandon, *Lectr,* Savannah State University, Dept of Fine Arts, Savannah GA (S)

Williams, Brian, *VP Devel,* The Children's Museum of Indianapolis, Indianapolis IN

Williams, Caitlin, *Cur Art,* Art Museum of Southeast Texas, Beaumont TX

Williams, Cecil, *Instr,* Claflin College, Dept of Art, Orangeburg SC (S)

Williams, Charles, *Treas,* Charles B Goddard, Ardmore OK

Williams, Ed, *Dir Photo,* Art Institute of Fort Lauderdale, Fort Lauderdale FL (S)

Williams, Glen, *Assoc Prof,* Northwest Missouri State University, Dept of Fine & Performing Arts, Maryville MO (S)

Williams, Gloria, *Cur,* Norton Simon, Pasadena CA

Williams, Greg, *Asst Dir,* Colby College, Museum of Art, Waterville ME

Williams, Harry R, *Dir,* Brockton Public Library System, Joseph A Driscoll Art Gallery, Brockton MA

Williams, Heather, *Dir,* Gertrude Herbert, Augusta GA

Williams, Heidi, *Coordr,* University of Notre Dame, Snite Museum of Art, Notre Dame IN

Williams, Inessa, *Events Coordr,* Museum of New Mexico, Palace of Governors, Santa Fe NM

Williams, J Dustin, *Archivist,* Carnegie Mellon University, Hunt Institute for Botanical Documentation, Pittsburgh PA

Williams, James, *Graphic Designer,* Birmingham Museum of Art, Birmingham AL

Williams, James, *Pres, Chmn,* Old State House, Hartford CT

Williams, Jane, *Agent,* Jack Richard Gallery, Almond Tea Museum & Jane Williams Galleries, Divisions of Studios of Jack Richard, Cuyahoga Falls OH

Williams, Jay, *Cur Coll & Exhibs,* Vero Beach Museum of Art, Vero Beach FL

Williams, Jay, *Pres & CEO,* Milwaukee Public Museum, Milwaukee WI

Williams, Jay, *Art Cur,* The Museum of Arts & Sciences Inc, Daytona Beach FL

Williams, Jennifer F, *VPres,* American Society of Portrait Artists (ASOPA), Montgomery AL

Williams, Jere, *Instr,* Brenau University, Art & Design Dept, Gainesville GA (S)

Williams, Jim, *Prof Fine Arts,* University of Cincinnati, School of Art, Cincinnati OH (S)

Williams, Jim, *Ranch Mgr,* Will Rogers Memorial Museum & Birthplace Ranch, Claremore OK

Williams, John, *Lectr,* Longwood University, Dept of Art, Farmville VA (S)

Williams, John A, *Mem Bd Dir,* Hatch-Billops Collection, Inc, New York NY

Williams, Jovani, *Cur Tolson Ctr,* Langston University, Melvin B Tolson Black Heritage Center, Langston OK

Wilson, Paul, *Accounts & Opers Mgr,* Ontario Crafts Council, OCC Gallery, Toronto ON

Wilson, Pierre, *Dir,* Musee des Maitres et Artisans du Quebec, Montreal PQ

Wilson, Ric, *Assoc Prof (Graphic Design, Interactive Media),* University of Missouri - Columbia, Dept of Art, Columbia MO (S)

Wilson, Roger D (Sam), *Prof,* University of Utah, Dept of Art & Art History, Salt Lake City UT (S)

Wilson, Sheila, *Asst Prof,* Denison University, Studio Art Program, Granville OH (S)

Wilson, Sheilah, *Res Dir,* Santa Fe Arts Institute, Santa Fe NM (S)

Wilson, Sidney, *Chmn,* Black American West Museum & Heritage Center, Denver CO

Wilson, Siona, *Asst Prof,* College of Staten Island, Performing & Creative Arts Dept, Staten Island NY (S)

Wilson, Ted, *Registrar,* National Postal Museum, Smithsonian Institution, Washington DC

Wilson, Wallace, *Dir,* University of South Florida, School The Arts, Tampa FL (S)

Wilson, Wayne, *Dir & Cur,* Okanagan Heritage Museum, Kelowna BC

Wilson, Wesley, *Chief State Library Resource Center,* Enoch Pratt, Baltimore MD

Wilson, Will, *Asst Prof,* Oberlin College, Dept of Art, Oberlin OH (S)

Wilson, William L, *Pres,* Philadelphia Art Commission, Philadelphia PA

Wilson-McKee, Marie, *Dir,* Wyoming State Museum, Cheyenne WY

Wilson-Pauwels, Linda, *Pres,* Association of Medical Illustrators, Lexington KY

Wilson Aden, Patricia, *VPres Opers,* African American Museum in Philadelphia, Philadelphia PA

Wilson Hoge, Robert, *Cur,* American Numismatic Society, New York NY

Wilt, Larry, *Dir,* Albin O Kuhn Library & Gallery, Baltimore MD

Wilt, Matt, *Ceramics,* Sam Houston State University, Art Dept, Huntsville TX (S)

Wilton, John, *Prof,* Daytona Beach Community College, Dept of Fine Arts & Visual Arts, Daytona Beach FL (S)

Wiltrout, Douglas, *Pres,* National Society of Painters in Casein & Acrylic, Inc, Whitehall PA

Wiltse, Terri, *Opers Mgr,* League of New Hampshire Craftsmen, Grodin Permanent Collection Museum, Concord NH

Wilzig, Naomi, *Owner, Cur,* World Erotic Art Museum, Miami Beach FL

Wimberly, Dexter, *Dir Communs,* Museum for African Art, New York NY

Wimbley, Jessica, *Mus Coordr,* The Pomona College, Claremont CA

Wimer, Rod, *Senior Design Consultant,* Providence Gallery, Charlotte NC

Wimpfheimer, Lisa, *Horticulturist,* Tryon Palace Historic Sites & Gardens, New Bern NC

Winchester, Juti, *Cur Buffalo Bill Mus,* Buffalo Bill Memorial Association, Buffalo Bill Historical Center, Cody WY

Winder, Kaye, *Instr,* University of Wisconsin-Platteville, Dept of Fine Art, Platteville WI (S)

Windham, Joshua, *Library Technician,* Tulane University, Architecture Library, New Orleans LA

Windsor-Liscombe, Rhodri, *Prof,* University of British Columbia, Dept of Art History, Visual Art & Theory, Vancouver BC (S)

Wine, Bonnie Sue, *Financial Dir,* Virginia Center for the Creative Arts, Amherst VA

Winegar, Joshua, *Asst Prof,* Weber State University, Dept of Visual Arts, Ogden UT (S)

Wines, Claudia, *Dir,* Northeastern Nevada Museum, Elko NV

Winfield, Charles, *Prof,* University of Maine at Augusta, College of Arts & Humanities, Augusta ME (S)

Winfree, Bob, *Pres,* Alaska Watercolor Society, Anchorage AK

Wing, Ethan, *Chmn,* Center on Contemporary Art, Seattle WA

Wing, Qiang, *Asst Prof,* University of Michigan, Ann Arbor, Dept of History of Art, Ann Arbor MI (S)

Wingard, Susan, *Lectr,* Southeastern Louisiana University, Dept of Visual Arts, Hammond LA (S)

Wingert-Playdon, Kate, *Prog Dir Architecture,* Temple University, Tyler School of Art, Philadelphia PA (S)

Wingertzahn, Marianne, *Head of Circ,* Bronxville Public Library, Bronxville NY

Wingood, Harold, *Dean Admissions,* Clark University, Dept of Visual & Performing Arts, Worcester MA (S)

Winingear, Sara, *Asst Dir,* Westminster College, Winston Churchill Memorial & Library in the United States, Fulton MO

Wink, Jon D, *Chmn,* Stephen F Austin State University, Art Dept, Nacogdoches TX (S)

Winkenweder, Brian, *Chmn Dept,* Linfield College, Department of Art & Visual Culture, McMinnville OR (S)

Winkler, Alan, *Cur,* Wabaunsee County Historical Museum, Alma KS

Winkler, Eugene, *Pres,* Oshkosh Public Museum, Oshkosh WI

Winkler, Judith, *Slide Cur,* University of Nebraska, Lincoln, Architecture Library, Lincoln NE

Winninger, Bonnie, *Educ Dir,* Waterloo Center of the Arts, Waterloo IA

Winningham, Geoffrey, *Prof,* Rice University, Visual & Dramatic Arts, Houston TX (S)

Winograde, Edie, *Bd Chair,* Colorado Photographic Arts Center, Denver CO

Winshel, Deborah, *Sr VPres & CF,* The Metropolitan Museum of Art, New York NY

Winship, Andrew, *Prof, Dir Grad Progs,* Indiana University-Purdue University, Indianapolis, Herron School of Art & Design, Indianapolis IN (S)

Winship, John, *Instr,* Gettysburg College, Dept of Visual Arts, Gettysburg PA (S)

Winslow, B B, *Dir,* Arts Midland Galleries & School, Midland MI

Winslow, B B, *Dir,* Alden B. Dow Museum of Science & Art, Alden B. Dow Museum School, Midland MI (S)

Winslow, Bruce, *Dir,* Arts Midland Galleries & School, Alden B. Dow Museum of Science & Art, Midland MI

Winslow, John, *Chmn Dept,* Catholic University of America, Dept of Art, Washington DC (S)

Winsor, Amber, *Deputy Dir Finance & Admin,* Contemporary Arts Museum Houston, Houston TX

Winston, Patrick, *Assoc Prof,* Montgomery County Community College, Art Center, Blue Bell PA (S)

Wintemberg, Tim, *Dir Exhib,* Newark Museum Association, The Newark Museum, Newark NJ

Winter, Amy, *Dir & Cur,* Queens College, City University of New York, Godwin-Ternbach Museum, Flushing NY

Winter, Heather, *Archivist & Librn,* Milwaukee Art Museum, George Peckham Miller Art Research Library, Milwaukee WI

Winter, Heather, *Librn & Archivist,* Milwaukee Art Museum, Milwaukee WI

Winter, Heidi, *Dir Develop,* Museum of Wisconsin Art, West Bend WI

Winter, Robert, *Chmn Dept,* Lenoir Rhyne College, Dept of Art, Hickory NC (S)

Winterick, Douglas E, *CEO,* Burlington County Historical Society, Burlington NJ

Winterrowd, Scott, *Asst Cur Educ,* Southern Methodist University, Meadows Museum, Dallas TX

Winters, Laurie, *Dir Exhibs & Sr Cur European Art,* Milwaukee Art Museum, Milwaukee WI

Winters, Laurie, *Exec Dir & CEO,* Museum of Wisconsin Art, West Bend WI

Winters, Susie, *Instr,* Appalachian State University, Dept of Art, Boone NC (S)

Winton, Georgina, *Museum Shop Mgr,* Nantucket Historical Association, Historic Nantucket, Nantucket MA

Winton, Jane, *Librn,* Boston Public Library, Albert H Wiggin Gallery & Print Department, Boston MA

Winzenz, Karon, *Prof,* University of Wisconsin-Green Bay, Arts Dept, Green Bay WI (S)

Wisbey, Peter, *Cur Colls,* Genesee Country Village & Museum, John L Wehle Art Gallery, Mumford NY

Wisch, Barbara, *Prof,* State University of New York, College at Cortland, Dept Art & Art History, Cortland NY (S)

Wise, Annette, *Cataloger,* Fulton County Historical Society Inc, Fulton County Museum (Tetzlaff Reference Room), Rochester IN

Wise, JoAnn, *Treas & Exec Dir,* Western Art Association, Ellensburg WA

Wise, Marie, *Hill Archive Proj Mgr,* Museum of Fine Arts Houston, Bayou Bend Collection & Gardens, Houston TX

Wise, Meg, *Dir Develop & Fin,* Philadelphia Museum of Art, Samuel S Fleisher Art Memorial, Philadelphia PA

Wiseman, Sarah-Jane, *Mktg Develop Coordr,* Sonoma County Museum, Santa Rosa CA

Wisgerhof, Mary, *Bd Chair,* Pewabic Society Inc, Pewabic Pottery, Detroit MI

Wishart, Kimberly, *Chinese Art Specialist,* Princeton University, Marquand Library of Art & Archaeology, Princeton NJ

Wisotzki, Paula, *Assoc Prof,* Loyola University of Chicago, Fine Arts Dept, Chicago IL (S)

Wisotzki, Paula, *Pres,* Midwest Art History Society, Waco TX

Wisse, Jacob, *Asst Prof,* Adelphi University, Dept of Art & Art History, Garden City NY (S)

Wisse, Jacob, *Dir,* Yeshiva University Museum, New York NY

Wissinger, Charles, *Asst Prof Ceramics,* University of Texas Pan American, Art Dept, Edinburg TX (S)

Wissler-Thomas, Carrie, *Pres,* Art Association of Harrisburg, School & Galleries, Harrisburg PA

Wist, Rona, *Sr VP Policy & Advocacy,* Municipal Art Society of New York, New York NY

Witcombe, Christopher, *Chmn,* Sweet Briar College, Art History Dept, Sweet Briar VA (S)

Witek, Joseph, *Prof,* Stetson University, Department of Creative Arts, Deland FL (S)

Withelder, Barbara, *Pres,* Mesquite Fine Arts Center & Gallery, Mesquite NV

Witkes, Michael, *Exec Dir,* Jewish Community Center of Greater Washington, Jane L & Robert H Weiner Judaic Museum, Rockville MD

Witte, Rex, *Exhibs Coordr,* Arizona Museum For Youth, Mesa AZ

Witten, Morris, *Educator,* Taos, La Hacienda de Los Martinez, Taos NM

Wittenbraker, Paul, *Assoc Prof,* Grand Valley State University, Art & Design Dept, Allendale MI (S)

Witter, Craig, *Preparator,* The Pennsylvania State University, Palmer Museum of Art, University Park PA

Witter, Karen A, *Assoc Dir,* Illinois State Museum, Museum Store, Chicago IL

Wittershiem, John, *Prof,* Siena Heights University, Studio Angelico-Art Dept, Adrian MI (S)

Wittkopp, Greg, *Dir,* Cranbrook Art Museum, Bloomfield Hills MI

Wittmer, Marcilene, *Adjunct Cur African Art,* University of Miami, Lowe Art Museum, Coral Gables FL

Wittstruck, Martha, *Art Coordr,* Normandale Community College, Art Dept, Bloomington MN (S)

Witty, Anne, *Asst Cur,* Bowdoin College, Peary-MacMillan Arctic Museum, Brunswick ME

Witulski, Christine, *Dir,* Besser Museum for Northeast Michigan, Philip M Park Library, Alpena MI

Witzel, Michael, *Preparator,* The Art Museum at the University of Kentucky, Lexington KY

Witzling, Mara, *Assoc Prof,* University of New Hampshire, Dept of Arts & Art History, Durham NH (S)

Wixom, Rachel, *Dir Publs,* Whitney Museum of American Art, New York NY

Wobido, Steve, *Dir,* The Children's Aid Society, Visual Arts Program of the Philip Coltoff Center at Green Arts and After School Program, New York NY (S)

Wodehouse, Kate, *Coll Librn,* Providence Athenaeum, Library, Providence RI

Woermke, Laura, *Exec Dir & Cur,* St Thomas-Elgin Public Art Centre, Saint Thomas ON

Woesneer, Tiffany, *Educ Coordr,* Visual Arts Center of Northwest Florida, Visual Arts Center Library, Panama City FL

Woffard, Tobias, *Asst Prof,* Santa Clara University, Dept of Art & Art History, Santa Clara CA (S)

Wofford, Barbara, *Pres,* Houston Museum of Decorative Arts, Chattanooga TN

Woods Rosner, Jennifer, *Chief Conservation,* Library Company of Philadelphia, Philadelphia PA

Woodward, David, *Dir,* Yuma Fine Arts Association, Yuma Art Center, Yuma AZ

Woodward, Judith L, *Fin Mgr,* Franklin Furnace Archive, Inc, Brooklyn NY

Woodward, Kristen, *Chmn,* Albright College, Dept of Art, Reading PA (S)

Woodward, Richard B, *Cur African Art,* Virginia Museum of Fine Arts, Richmond VA

Woodward, Roland H, *Exec Dir,* Chester County Historical Society, West Chester PA

Woodward, Tilly, *Cur Acad & Community Outreach,* Grinnell College, Faulconer Gallery, Grinnell IA

Woodward-Detrich, Denise, *Dir,* Clemson University, Rudolph E Lee Gallery, Clemson SC

Woodworth, Patricia, *Exec VPres Admin Affairs,* The Art Institute of Chicago, Chicago IL

Woodworth, Robin, *Dir Develop,* Museum of Ventura County, Ventura CA

Wooff, Annette, *Adminr,* University of British Columbia, Morris & Helen Belkin Art Gallery, Vancouver BC

Woofon-Bonner, Tamara, *Dir Exhibs & Publs,* Dallas Museum of Art, Dallas TX

Woolery, Reggie, *Cur Educ,* University of California, California Museum of Photography, Riverside CA

Woolever, Mary, *Architecture Librn,* The Art Institute of Chicago, Ryerson & Burnham Libraries, Chicago IL

Woolf, David, *Assoc Prof,* Norwich University, Dept of Architecture and Art, Northfield VT (S)

Woollard, Dave, *John Hancock Shop,* Chicago Architecture Foundation, Chicago IL

Woolley, Lois, *Instr,* Woodstock School of Art, Inc, Woodstock NY (S)

Woolsey, Ann, *Interim Dir,* Rhode Island School of Design, Museum of Art, Providence RI

Wooster, Liz, *Dir Institutional Advancement,* Bruce Museum, Inc, Greenwich CT

Wopecka, Camila, *Mus Store,* Morris Museum of Art, Augusta GA

Worden, Fred, *Assoc Prof,* University of Maryland, Baltimore County, Imaging & Digital Arts (IMDA), Dept of Visual Arts, Baltimore MD (S)

Workman, Bob, *Dir,* Wichita State University, Ulrich Museum of Art, Wichita KS

Workman, Mary Jo, *Art Div,* Lane Community College, Art & Applied Design Dept, Eugene OR (S)

Workneh, Sarah, *Exec Dir Prog,* Skowhegan School of Painting & Sculpture, New York NY (S)

Worrell, Philip, *Visual Resource Cur,* Texas Tech University, School of Art Visual Resource Center, Lubbock TX

Worrington, Susan, *Art Instr,* Phillips Community College at The University of Arkansas, Dept of English & Fine Arts, Helena AR (S)

Worteck, Ed, *Prof,* Goucher College, Art & Art History Dept, Baltimore MD (S)

Wortheimer, Gary, *Chmn Arts & Comm Depts,* Olivet College, Armstrong Collection, Olivet MI

Worthen, W B, *Dir,* Historic Arkansas Museum, Library, Little Rock AR

Worthen, William B, *Dir & CEO,* Historic Arkansas Museum, Little Rock AR

Worthing, Katie, *Site Mgr/Educ Asst,* Victoria Mansion - Morse Libby House, Portland ME

Worthley, Martha, *Young Artist Proj Prog Mgr,* Centrum Arts & Creative Education, Port Townsend WA

Wray, Jessica, *Library Assoc,* Miami University, Wertz Art & Architecture Library, Oxford OH

Wrega, Marek, *Mgr Finance & Admin,* Art Services International, Alexandria VA

Wren, Linnea, *Chmn,* Gustavus Adolphus College, Art & Art History Dept, Saint Peter MN (S)

Wride, Tim, *Cur Photography,* Norton Museum of Art, West Palm Beach FL

Wright, Astri, *Assoc Prof,* University of Victoria, Dept of History in Art, Victoria BC (S)

Wright, Audrey, *Chmn,* Seattle Central Community College, Humanities - Social Sciences Division, Seattle WA (S)

Wright, Beth, *Prof,* University of Texas at Arlington, Art & Art History Department, Arlington TX (S)

Wright, Brianna, *Cur,* African American Museum of Iowa, Cedar Rapids IA

Wright, Bruce, *Chair,* Vancouver Art Gallery, Vancouver BC

Wright, Cathy, *Dir,* Albuquerque Museum of Art & History, Albuquerque NM

Wright, Charles, *Chair Dept of Art & Prof,* Western Illinois University, Department of Art, Macomb IL (S)

Wright, Charlie, *Chmn Bd,* Seattle Art Museum, Downtown, Seattle WA

Wright, Craig, *Archivist,* National Archives & Records Administration, Herbert Hoover Presidential Library - Museum, West Branch IA

Wright, Denise, *Lectr,* Colorado Mesa University, Art Dept, Grand Junction CO (S)

Wright, Elizabeth, *Dir Develop,* University of Virginia, The Fralin Museum of Art at the University of Virginia, Charlottesville VA

Wright, Erin, *Assoc Prof,* University of Alabama at Birmingham, Dept of Art & Art History, Birmingham AL (S)

Wright, Gene, *Asst Prof Scientific Illustration,* University of Georgia, Franklin College of Arts & Sciences, Lamar Dodd School of Art, Athens GA (S)

Wright, Holly, *Archives Asst,* The Nelson-Atkins Museum of Art, Spencer Art Reference Library, Kansas City MO

Wright, J Franklin, *Prof,* George Washington University, Dept of Art of Fine Arts & Art History, Washington DC (S)

Wright, Jerri, *Admin,* Fremont Center for the Arts, Canon City CO

Wright, Jimmy, *Treas,* Pastel Society of America, National Arts Club, Grand Gallery, New York NY

Wright, John, *Dir,* University of Calgary, Nickle Galleries, Calgary AB

Wright, John, *Photographer,* Tougaloo College, Art Collection, Tougaloo MS

Wright, Joseph, *Exec Dir,* French Art Colony, Gallipolis OH

Wright, Joy, *Lib & Archivist,* Laumeier Sculpture Park, Saint Louis MO

Wright, Larry, *Managing Dir,* Bellevue Arts Museum, Bellevue WA

Wright, Lesley, *Dir,* Grinnell College, Faulconer Gallery, Grinnell IA

Wright, Lori, *Asst Prof of Art Dept Chair,* Kansas Wesleyan University, Art Dept, Salina KS (S)

Wright, Lorri, *Museum Store Mgr,* Modern Art Museum, Fort Worth TX

Wright, Mary A, *Dept Head,* Central Library, Dept of Fine Arts, San Antonio TX

Wright, Mary C, *Dir,* Xochipilli Art Gallery, Birmingham MI

Wright, Maya, *Mktg & Commun Mgr,* Kirkland Museum of Fine & Decorative Art, Denver CO

Wright, Megan, *Assoc Prof Art,* Marian University, Visual Arts Dept, Indianapolis IN (S)

Wright, Philip, *Chmn,* Warner House Association, MacPheadris-Warner House, Portsmouth NH

Wright, Pope, *Lectr,* University of Wisconsin-Superior, Programs in the Visual Arts, Superior WI (S)

Wright, Robert, *Assoc Dean, Dir Prog in Landscape Architecture,* University of Toronto, Programme in Landscape Architecture, Toronto ON (S)

Wright, Robin, *Cur Native American Art,* University of Washington, Burke Museum of Natural History and Culture, Seattle WA

Wright, Ron, *Prof,* Marietta College, Art Dept, Marietta OH (S)

Wright, Sharyl, *Instr,* Avila College, Art Division, Dept of Humanities, Kansas City MO (S)

Wright, Suzanne, *Dir Educ,* The Phillips Collection, Washington DC

Wright, Tony, *Head Design & Installation,* Modern Art Museum, Fort Worth TX

Wright, Ursula, *Research Libr,* Portsmouth Athenaeum, Joseph Copley Research Library, Portsmouth NH

Wright, Vicki, *Dir Colls & Exhibs,* Kalamazoo Institute of Arts, The Mary & Edwin Meader Fine Arts Library, Kalamazoo MI

Wright, Vincent, *Asst Prof,* C W Post Campus of Long Island University, School of Visual & Performing Arts, Brookville NY (S)

Wright, Wayne W, *Head Librn,* New York State Historical Association, Research Library, Cooperstown NY

Wright, Welynda, *Asst Prof Interior Design,* University of Georgia, Franklin College of Arts & Sciences, Lamar Dodd School of Art, Athens GA (S)

Wrigley, LaVaine, *Coll Coordr,* Historical Society of Martin County, Elliott Museum, Stuart FL

Wrinn, Mariann, *Assoc Prof,* Herkimer County Community College, Humanities Social Services, Herkimer NY (S)

Wrobewski, Peter, *VPres,* Artists' Cooperative Gallery, Omaha NE

Wroble, Stephen, *Prof,* Schoolcraft College, Dept of Art & Design, Livonia MI (S)

Wu, Ina, *Instr,* Olympic College, Social Sciences & Humanities Div, Bremerton WA (S)

Wu, Jialu, *Gen Educ,* Art Institute of Pittsburgh, Pittsburgh PA (S)

Wu, Xiaojin, *Cur Japanese & Korean Art,* Seattle Art Museum, Seattle Asian Art Museum, Seattle WA

Wu, Yan, *Registrar,* Art Metropole, Toronto ON

Wunder, Amanda, *Prof,* City University of New York, PhD Program in Art History, New York NY (S)

Wuorinen, Charles, *Treas,* American Academy of Arts & Letters, New York NY

Wurdinger, Deborah, *Mus Technician,* United States Department of the Interior, Interior Museum, Washington DC

Wurmfeld, Sanford, *Chmn Art Dept,* Hunter College, Art Dept, New York NY (S)

Wyatt, Jeffrey, *VPres,* Santa Barbara Contemporary Arts Forum, Santa Barbara CA

Wyatt, Judy, *Library Asst,* Kansas State University, Paul Weigel Library of Architecture Planning & Design, Manhattan KS

Wyatt, Thelma W, *Treas,* Miles B Carpenter Folk Art Museum, Waverly VA

Wyatt, Victoria, *Assoc Prof,* University of Victoria, Dept of History in Art, Victoria BC (S)

Wyckoff, Elizabeth, *Cur,* Wellesley College, Davis Museum & Cultural Center, Wellesley MA

Wyer, Sue, *Prof,* State College of Florida Manatee - Sarasota, Art, Design, Humanities, Bradenton FL (S)

Wykes, Andrew, *Assoc Prof,* Hamline University, Dept of Studio Arts & Art History, Saint Paul MN (S)

Wylde, Nanette, *Assoc Prof,* California State University, Chico, Department of Art & Art History, Chico CA (S)

Wylder, Viki D, *Cur Educ,* Florida State University, Museum of Fine Arts, Tallahassee FL

Wylie, Caroline, *Develop Officer,* Tyler Museum of Art, Reference Library, Tyler TX

Wylie, Charles, *Cur Contemporary Art,* Dallas Museum of Art, Dallas TX

Wylie, Lyndsey, *Cur Asst,* San Jose Museum of Art, Library, San Jose CA

Wylie, William, *Studio Faculty,* University of Virginia, McIntire Dept of Art, Charlottesville VA (S)

Wyllie, Nancy, *Prof,* Community College of Rhode Island, Dept of Art, Warwick RI (S)

Wylly, Barbara, *Exec Dir,* Center for Puppetry Arts, Atlanta GA

Wylly, Bill, *Exec Dir,* Center for Puppetry Arts, Atlanta GA

Wyly, Mary, *Librn,* Newberry Library, Chicago IL

Wyman, Sara, *Instr,* Walla Walla Community College, Fine Arts Dept, Walla Walla WA (S)

Wyngaard, Susan E, *Head Librn,* Ohio State University, Fine Arts Library, Columbus OH

Wynick, Lynne, *Co-Dir,* Wynick Tuck Gallery, Toronto ON

Wynn, Nancy, *Asst Prof,* University of Hartford, Hartford Art School, West Hartford CT (S)

Wynne, Alan, *Pres,* South County Art Association, Kingston RI

Wynne, Stephen, *Artistic Dir for School of Dance,* Sangre de Cristo Arts & Conference Center, Pueblo CO

Wyrick, Gabrielle, *Cur Educ,* Museum of Contemporary Art, San Diego, La Jolla CA

Wyshak, Robin, *Adjunct Faculty,* Southern Oregon University, Art & Art History Dept, Ashland OR (S)

Wyszomirski, Margaret, *Prof,* Ohio State University, Dept of Art Education, Columbus OH (S)

Xiao, Peter, *Prof,* Augustana College, Art Dept, Rock Island IL (S)

Xiong, Lihui, *Asian Catalogue Asst,* The Nelson-Atkins Museum of Art, Spencer Art Reference Library, Kansas City MO

Xu, Gan, *Instr,* Maine College of Art, Portland ME (S)

Xu, Jay, *Cur Asian Art,* The Art Institute of Chicago, Chicago IL

Xu, Jay, *Dir,* Asian Art Museum of San Francisco, Chong-Moon Lee Ctr for Asian Art and Culture, San Francisco CA

Yackulic, Evelyn, *Finance Officer,* City of Lethbridge, Sir Alexander Galt Museum, Lethbridge AB

Yaghdjian, Ed, *VPres Mem,* Society of Canadian Artists, Toronto ON

Yahnke, David, *Instr,* Mohawk Valley Community College, Utica NY (S)

Yakel, Norm, *Chair Arts Educ Prog,* University of Regina, Art Education Program, Regina SK (S)

Yakstis, Gary, *Operations Dir,* University of Connecticut, Jorgensen Auditorium, Storrs CT

Yakunovich, Jennifer, *Mus Educator,* Manchester Historic Association, Millyard Museum, Manchester NH

Yakunovich, Jennifer, *Mus Educator,* Manchester Historic Association, Library, Manchester NH

Yale-Read, Barbara, *Assoc Prof,* Appalachian State University, Dept of Art, Boone NC (S)

Yamamoto, Audrey, *Exec Dir,* Zeum, San Francisco CA

Yamamoto, Koichi, *Asst Prof,* Utah State University, Dept of Art, Logan UT (S)

Yanari-Rizzo, Sachi, *Cur of Colls,* Fort Wayne Museum of Art, Inc, Fort Wayne IN

Yancey, John, *Chair,* University of Texas, Dept of Art & Art History, Austin TX (S)

Yancey, Shirley S, *Pres,* Miles B Carpenter Folk Art Museum, Waverly VA

Yanero, Susan, *Instr,* American University, Dept of Art, New York NY (S)

Yang, Christina, *Assoc Dir Educ Pub Progs,* Solomon R Guggenheim, New York NY

Yang, Xiaoneng, *Cur Asian Art,* Stanford University, Cantor Arts Center at Stanford University, Stanford CA

Yanik, John V, *Prof,* Catholic University of America, School of Architecture & Planning, Washington DC (S)

Yank, Paul, *Art Dir,* Wisconsin Fine Arts Association, Inc, Ozaukee Art Center, Cedarburg WI

Yankavskas, Raye, *Library Asst,* Lesley University, College of Art & Design Library, Boston MA

Yankowski, Michael, *Prof,* Northwestern State University of Louisiana, School of Creative & Performing Arts - Dept of Fine & Graphic Arts, Natchitoches LA (S)

Yannopoulos, Kimon, *Jewelry & Silversmithing Studio Mgr,* DeCordova Museum School, Lincoln MA (S)

Yanow, Elaine, *Admin Asst,* Williams College, Chapin Library, Williamstown MA

Yanto, Paul, *Asst Prof,* Oberlin College, Dept of Art, Oberlin OH (S)

Yapelli, Tina, *Gallery Dir,* San Diego State University, University Art Gallery, San Diego CA

Yarber, Robert, *Distinguished Prof Art (Drawing/Painting),* Pennsylvania State University, University Park, Penn State School of Visual Arts, University Park PA (S)

Yarborough, Bert, *Assoc Prof,* Colby-Sawyer College, Dept of Fine & Performing Arts, New London NH (S)

Yard, Sally, *Dir,* University of San Diego, Founders' Gallery, San Diego CA

Yarlow, Loretta, *Dir,* University of Massachusetts, Amherst, University Gallery, Amherst MA

Yarnall, James, *Newsletter Ed,* Newport Historical Society & Museum of Newport History, Newport RI

Yarrington, Kathryn Jo, *Prof, Chmn,* Fairfield University, Visual & Performing Arts, Fairfield CT (S)

Yassin, Robert A, *Exec Dir,* Palos Verdes Art Center/Beverly G. Alpay Center for Arts Education, Rancho Palos Verdes CA

Yasuda, Kim, *Chmn Dept,* University of California, Santa Barbara, Dept of Art Studio, Santa Barbara CA (S)

Yasuda, Robert, *Prof,* C W Post Campus of Long Island University, School of Visual & Performing Arts, Brookville NY (S)

Yates, Joey, *Assoc Cur,* Kentucky Museum of Art and Craft, Louisville KY

Yates, Sam, *Dir,* University of Tennessee, Ewing Gallery of Art and Architecture, Knoxville TN

Yatt, Barry D, *Assoc Prof,* Catholic University of America, School of Architecture & Planning, Washington DC (S)

Yau, Esther, *Prof,* Occidental College, Dept of Art History & Visual Arts, Los Angeles CA (S)

Yaukey, Margaret, *Asst Prof,* Appalachian State University, Dept of Art, Boone NC (S)

Yay, John, *Assoc Prof,* Rutgers, The State University of New Jersey, Mason Gross School of the Arts, Visual Arts Dept, New Brunswick NJ (S)

Yeager, Raymond, *Chmn Art Dept,* MacMurray College, Art Dept, Jacksonville IL (S)

Yeaworth, David, *Pres,* Allied Arts of Seattle, Seattle WA

Yeboah, Tony, *Instr,* Judson University, School of Art, Design & Architecture, Elgin IL (S)

Yedinak, James, *Industrial Design,* Art Institute of Pittsburgh, Pittsburgh PA (S)

Yee, Kay, *Acting Area Head Jewelry,* Pasadena City College, Visual Arts and Media Studies Division, Pasadena CA (S)

Yee, Shirley, *Graphic Design,* Art Institute of Pittsburgh, Pittsburgh PA (S)

Yeh, John, *Technical Dir,* Maryland-National Capital Park & Planning Commission, Montpelier Arts Center, Laurel MD

Yelen, Alice, *Asst Dir Educ,* New Orleans Museum of Art, New Orleans LA

Yerdon, Lawrence J, *Pres,* Hancock Shaker Village, Inc, Pittsfield MA

Yerkes, Carolyn, *Cur Avery Classics,* Columbia University, Avery Architectural & Fine Arts Library, New York NY

Yerkovich, Sally, *Pres & CEO,* New Jersey Historical Society, Library, Newark NJ

Yes, Phyllis, *Prof,* Lewis & Clark College, Dept of Art, Portland OR (S)

Yesner, David, *Cur,* Alaska Museum of Natural History, Anchorage AK

Yetter, George, *Assoc Cur Architecture Coll,* Colonial Williamsburg Foundation, John D Rockefeller, Jr Library, Williamsburg VA

Yevich, Courtney C, *Asst Librn,* Virginia Museum of Fine Arts, Margaret R & Robert M Freeman Library, Richmond VA

Yi, Hyewon, *Gallery Dir,* State University of New York College at Old Westbury, Amelie A Wallace Gallery, Old Westbury NY

Yi, Jason, *Chmn Foundations,* Milwaukee Institute of Art & Design, Milwaukee WI (S)

Yiengpruksawan, Mimi, *Prof,* Yale University, Dept of the History of Art, New Haven CT (S)

Yingst, Dawn, *Admin,* The Art Institute of Chicago, Antiquarian Society of the Art Institute of Chicago, Chicago IL

Yiu, Josh, *Foster Foundation Cur Chinese Art,* Seattle Art Museum, Seattle Asian Art Museum, Seattle WA

Yoakum, Sherillyn, *Exec Dir,* Red River Valley Museum, Vernon TX

Yobbi, Charmain, *Publ Relations & Community Partnership Mgr,* Art & Culture Center of Hollywood, Art Gallery/Multidisciplinary Cultural Center, Hollywood FL

Yocom, Margaret, *Vol Mus Folklorist, Cur & Archivist,* Rangeley Lakes Region Logging Museum, Rangeley ME

Yoder, Julie, *Asst Dir Educ,* Kentucky Museum of Art and Craft, Louisville KY

Yokley, Shirley, *Instr,* Middle Tennessee State University, Art Dept, Murfreesboro TN (S)

Yolleck, Frima, *Bookkeeper,* Visual Arts Ontario, Toronto ON

Yonan, Michael, *Asst Prof,* University of Missouri - Columbia, Art History & Archaeology Dept, Columbia MO (S)

Yonemoto, Bruce, *Prof Video, Film Theory, Exper Media,* University of California, Irvine, Studio Art Dept, Irvine CA (S)

Yontz, Terri, *Publicist,* Xavier University, Art Gallery, Cincinnati OH

Yonz, Barbara, *Assoc Prof,* Saint Thomas Aquinas College, Art Dept, Sparkill NY (S)

Yoo, Jeanna, *Chief Advancement Officer,* Museum of Contemporary Art, San Diego, La Jolla CA

Yoo, Jeanna, *Chief Advancement Officer,* Museum of Contemporary Art San Diego, San Diego CA

Yood, James, *Lectr,* Northwestern University, Evanston, Dept of Art Theory & Practice, Evanston IL (S)

Yoon, Sang, *Assoc Prof,* James Madison University, School of Art & Art History, Harrisonburg VA (S)

Yorba, Jonathan L, *CEO,* Mexican Museum, San Francisco CA

York, Bev, *Site Admin,* Nathan Hale Homestead Museum, Coventry CT

York, Hildreth, *Pres Bd Trustees,* Hunterdon Art Museum, Clinton NJ

York, Karen, *Cur,* Sherwin Miller Museum of Jewish Art, Tulsa OK

York, Robert, *Instr of Art,* Edison Community College, Gallery of Fine Arts, Fort Myers FL (S)

Yoshihara, Lisa, *Dir,* University of Hawaii at Manoa, Art Gallery, Honolulu HI

Yoshimine-Webster, Carol, *Assoc Prof,* Centenary College, Humanities Dept, Hackettstown NJ (S)

Yoshimoto, Midori, *Art History Prof,* New Jersey City University, Art Dept, Jersey City NJ (S)

Yoshimura, Reiko, *Head Librn,* Freer Gallery of Art & Arthur M Sackler Gallery, Library, Washington DC

Yoshimura, Reiko, *Librn,* Freer Gallery of Art & Arthur M Sackler Gallery, Library, Washington DC

Youds, Robert, *Prof,* University of Victoria, Dept of Visual Arts, Victoria BC (S)

Young, Alice D, *Cur Educ,* Agecroft Association, Agecroft Hall, Richmond VA

Young, Allyson C, *Pres,* Twin City Art Foundation, Masur Museum of Art, Monroe LA

Young, Amy Nelson, *Dir Grants & Community Assets,* The Art Museum at the University of Kentucky, Lexington KY

Young, Ann, *Dir Visitor Servs,* Pilgrim Society, Pilgrim Hall Museum, Plymouth MA

Young, Anne, *Bd Mem,* Kennebec Valley Art Association, Harlow Gallery, Hallowell ME

Young, Barrie, *Pres,* Pilgrim Society, Pilgrim Hall Museum, Plymouth MA

Young, Beth, *Adjunct Instr,* Mary Baldwin College, Dept of Art & Art History, Staunton VA (S)

Young, Brad, *Chief of Security,* University of North Carolina at Greensboro, Weatherspoon Art Museum, Greensboro NC

Young, Brent, *Dept Head Glass,* Cleveland Institute of Art, Cleveland OH (S)

Young, David, *Asst Prof,* University of Tennessee at Chattanooga, Dept of Art, Chattanooga TN (S)

Young, David, *Exec Dir,* Cliveden, Philadelphia PA

Young, Dodi Michelle, *Pres & Gallery Co Dir,* Sculptor's Society of Canada, Canadian Sculpture Centre, Toronto ON

Young, Gary, *Gallery Cur,* University of Saskatchewan, Gordon Snelgrove Art Gallery, Saskatoon SK

Young, J, *Treas,* Sculptor's Society of Canada, Canadian Sculpture Centre, Toronto ON

Young, Jane, *Dir & Owner,* Chase Young Gallery, Boston MA

Young, Jean, *Fiscal Officer & Registrar,* Florida State University, Museum of Fine Arts, Tallahassee FL

Young, Jeff, *Chair, Assoc Prof,* University of Central Arkansas, Department of Art, Conway AR (S)

Young, Joan, *Assoc Cur Contemporary Art & Mgr Cur Affairs,* Solomon R Guggenheim, New York NY

Young, Judi Michelle, *Pres Emeritus & Gallery Co Dir,* Sculptor's Society of Canada, Canadian Sculpture Centre, Toronto ON

Young, Karen S, *Dir,* Taos, Taos NM

Young, Karen S, *Dir,* Taos, Ernest Blumenschein Home & Studio, Taos NM

Young, Karen S, *Dir,* Taos, La Hacienda de Los Martinez, Taos NM

Young, Lisa, *Exhibs Dir,* Museum of Northwest Art, La Conner WA

Young, Marjorie, *Team Leader Bibliographic Access,* State University of New York at New Paltz, Sojourner Truth Library, New Paltz NY

Young, Mary, *ArtQuest & Educ Dir,* Green Hill Center for North Carolina Art, Greensboro NC

Young, Megan K, *Dir,* Lamar University, Dishman Art Museum, Beaumont TX

Young, Patience, *Cur Educ,* Stanford University, Cantor Arts Center at Stanford University, Stanford CA

Young, Phil, *Prof*, Hartwick College, Art Dept, Oneonta NY (S)

Young, Quala Lynn, *Cur Educ*, The Contemporary Museum, J Russell & Charlotte McLean Cades Library, Honolulu HI

Young, Roy, *Cur Educ*, Western Pennsylvania Conservancy, Fallingwater, Mill Run PA

Young, Shea Patterson, *Cur*, University of North Texas Health Science Center Fort Worth, Atrium Gallery, Fort Worth TX

Young, Susan, *Outreach Coordr*, City of Springdale, Shiloh Museum of Ozark History, Springdale AR

Young, Tara, *Asst Cur Modern Art*, Seattle Art Museum, Dorothy Stimson Bullitt Library, Seattle WA

Young, Thomas E, *Librn*, Philbrook Museum of Art, H.A. & Mary K Chapman Library, Tulsa OK

Young, Thomas E, *Librn*, Philbrook Museum of Art, Eugene B Adkins Study Center, Tulsa OK

Young, Timothy, *Assoc Prof*, Grace College, Dept of Art, Winona Lake IN (S)

Young, Tom, *Prof*, Greenfield Community College, Art Dept, Greenfield MA (S)

Young, Tyvonia, *Secy*, Morgan State University, James E Lewis Museum of Art, Baltimore MD

Young, Victoria, *Prof*, University of Saint Thomas, Dept of Art History, Saint Paul MN (S)

Young, Zenida, *Architecture & Interior Design Chmn*, Palm Beach Community College, Dept of Art, Lake Worth FL (S)

Young-Sanchez, Margaret, *Chief Cur & Frederick & Jan Mayer Cur Pre-Columbian Art*, Denver Art Museum, Denver CO

Younger, Dan, *Chmn*, University of Missouri, Saint Louis, Dept of Art & Art History, Saint Louis MO (S)

Younger, Erin, *Assoc Dir*, University of Washington, Burke Museum of Natural History and Culture, Seattle WA

Youngers, Peter L, *Instr*, Northeastern Junior College, Art Department, Sterling CO (S)

Younghans-Haug, Samantha, *Prog Dir*, University of California, Irvine, Beall Center for Art + Technology, and University Art Gallery, Irvine CA

Younginger, Jennifer, *Dir Exhib & Coll*, Heritage Museums & Gardens, Sandwich MA

Youngquist, Stephanie, *Registrar*, Northeastern Nevada Museum, Elko NV

Youngs, Christopher, *Lectr*, Albright College, Dept of Art, Reading PA (S)

Young Schoenthal, Rebecca, *Exec Dir*, Second Street Gallery, Charlottesville VA

Yount, Katherine, *Dir Tour Progs*, Sid W Richardson, Sid Richardson Museum, Fort Worth TX

Yount, Sylvia, *Chief Cur Designate & Cur American Art*, Virginia Museum of Fine Arts, Richmond VA

Yount, Sylvia, *Cur Am Art*, High Museum of Art, Atlanta GA

Yourman, Judy, *Asst Prof*, Saint Olaf College, Art Dept, Northfield MN (S)

Yow, Janice, *Pres*, Coppini Academy of Fine Arts, Elizabeth di Barbieri, San Antonio TX

Yox, David, *Prof*, Delaware County Community College, Communications, Art & Humanities, Media PA (S)

Yrrizarry, Gina, *Advertising & Promotion*, Fine Arts Museums of San Francisco, M H de Young Museum, San Francisco CA

Yrrizarry, Gina, *Advertising & Promotion*, Fine Arts Museums of San Francisco, Legion of Honor, San Francisco CA

Yslas, Alfredo, *Maintenance*, Museum of Western Colorado, Museum of the West, Grand Junction CO

Yu, Shuishan, *Asst Prof*, Oakland University, Dept of Art & Art History, Rochester MI (S)

Yuan, Juliana, *Sr Lectr*, University of Missouri, Saint Louis, Dept of Art & Art History, Saint Louis MO (S)

Yuars Petruccia, Breta, *Art Historian*, Greenfield Community College, Art Dept, Greenfield MA (S)

Yuen, Alyssa, *Mem, Publicity & Events Coordr*, University of Mississippi, University Museum & Historic Houses, Oxford MS

Yuen, Cileia Miranda, *Contact*, Belas Artes Multicultural Center, Art Gallery, Saint Louis MO

Yuhas, Louise, *Chmn*, Occidental College, Dept of Art History & Visual Arts, Los Angeles CA (S)

Yurchak, Lorraine, *Pres*, Passaic County Historical Society, Lambert Castle Museum & Library, Paterson NJ

Yurkanin, Sharon, *Mus Shop Mgr*, Allentown Art Museum, Allentown PA

Yuskaitis, Evin Nederbrook, *Prog & Exhib Mgr*, Photographic Resource Center at Boston University, Boston MA

Yust, Alex, *Chief Preparator*, Academy of Motion Picture Arts & Sciences, The Academy Gallery, Beverly Hills CA

Yuzha, Jake, *Pub Progs*, Museum of Arts & Design, New York NY

Yzzi, Nicholas, *Cur Coll*, Woodmere Art Museum Inc, Philadelphia PA

Zabalotney, Bonne, *Dean Faculty of Design & Dynamic Media*, Emily Carr University of Art + Design, Vancouver BC (S)

Zabel, Craig, *Assoc Prof & Dept Head*, Pennsylvania State University, University Park, Dept of Art History, University Park PA (S)

Zaborowski, Dennis, *Prof*, University of North Carolina at Chapel Hill, Art Dept, Chapel Hill NC (S)

Zaccerras, Carmen, *Dir*, Taos, E.L. Blumenschein Home & Museum & La Hacienda de los Martinez, Taos NM

Zacharias, David, *Assoc Prof & Coordr Studio Art*, Converse College, School of the Arts, Dept of Art & Design, Spartanburg SC (S)

Zacharias, James, *Cur History & Science*, The Museum of Arts & Sciences Inc, Daytona Beach FL

Zacher, Kevin, *Registrar*, Museum London, London ON

Zacher, Melinda, *Dir Visual Arts*, Interlochen Center for the Arts, Interlochen Arts Academy, Dept of Visual Art, Interlochen MI (S)

Zadov, Irina, *Dir Prog & Experience*, Zeum, San Francisco CA

Zafran, Eric, *Cur European Art*, Wadsworth Atheneum Museum of Art, Hartford CT

Zahabl, Liese, *Asst Prof*, Weber State University, Dept of Visual Arts, Ogden UT (S)

Zaharis, Kay, *Dir*, Cortland Free Library, Cortland NY

Zahid, Amira, *VPres, Sec & Treas*, Dahesh Museum of Art, Greenwich CT

Zahid, Mervat, *Pres*, Dahesh Museum of Art, Greenwich CT

Zahner, Mary, *Assoc Prof*, University of Dayton, Visual Arts Dept, Dayton OH (S)

Zajda, Darlene, *Mem Coordr*, Arizona Museum For Youth, Mesa AZ

Zalaznick, Betsy, *Dir Educ*, Hunterdon Art Museum, Clinton NJ

Zaloom, Lorraine, *Communs*, The Art School at Old Church, Demarest NJ (S)

Zalucky, Juliana, *Curatorial Asst*, University of Toronto at Mississauga, Blackwood Gallery, Mississauga ON

Zalut, Lauren, *Educ Mgr*, American Swedish Historical Foundation & Museum, American Swedish Historical Museum, Philadelphia PA

Zamagias, James D, *Chmn*, Allegany Community College, Art Dept, Cumberland MD (S)

Zamora, Frank, *Instr*, Sacramento City College, Art Dept, Sacramento CA (S)

Zandler, Richard, *Dir*, Maryland-National Capital Park & Planning Commission, Montpelier Arts Center, Laurel MD

Zanetti, Maria, *Office Mgr*, Oakville Galleries, Centennial Square and Gairloch Gardens, Oakville ON

Zapata, Beverly, *Auxiliary Prof*, Pontifical Catholic University of Puerto Rico, Dept of Fine Arts, Ponce PR (S)

Zapata, Beverly, *Auxiliary Prof*, Pontifical Catholic University of Puerto Rico, Dept of Fine Arts, Ponce PR (S)

Zapata, Felix, *Prof*, University of Puerto Rico, Mayaguez, Dept of Humanities, College of Fine Arts & Theory of Art Programs, Mayaguez PR (S)

Zapata, Felix, *Prof*, University of Puerto Rico, Mayaguez, Dept of Humanities, College of Fine Arts & Theory of Art Programs, Mayaguez PR (S)

Zapico, Mark, *Chair Advertising Design*, College for Creative Studies, Detroit MI (S)

Zapolis, Frank, *Cur Folk Art*, Balzekas Museum of Lithuanian Culture, Chicago IL

Zapton, Steve, *Prof*, James Madison University, School of Art & Art History, Harrisonburg VA (S)

Zardini, Mirko, *Dir*, Canadian Centre for Architecture, Library, Montreal PQ

Zaretsky, Barbara, *Exhibit Coordr*, C G Jung Center, Evanston IL

Zarich, Katie, *Dep Dir Pub Affairs*, Indianapolis Museum of Art, Indianapolis IN

Zaros, Christa, *Coll Mgr*, The Long Island Museum of American Art, History & Carriages, Stony Brook NY

Zaros, Christa, *Colls Mgr*, The Long Island Museum of American Art, History & Carriages, Library, Stony Brook NY

Zarr, Gary, *Sr VPres Com*, American Museum of Natural History, New York NY

Zarriw, Laura J, *Dean & VP Acad Affairs*, Lyme Academy College of Fine Arts, Old Lyme CT (S)

Zarrow, Laura, *Dean & VP Acad Affairs*, Lyme Academy College of Fine Arts, Krieble Library, Old Lyme CT

Zarrow, Laura, *Dean & VP Acad Affairs*, Lyme Academy College of Fine Arts, Chauncy Stillman Gallery, Old Lyme CT

Zarubica, Karyn, *Traveling Exhibs Dir*, University of California, Los Angeles, Fowler Museum at UCLA, Los Angeles CA

Zarucchi, Jeanne Morgan, *Prof*, University of Missouri, Saint Louis, Dept of Art & Art History, Saint Louis MO (S)

Zarur, Elizabeth, *Assoc Prof*, New Mexico State University, Art Dept, Las Cruces NM (S)

Zaszlavik, Katalin, *Asst Prof*, Grand Valley State University, Art & Design Dept, Allendale MI (S)

Zaugg, Elwood, *Dean*, Salt Lake Community College, Graphic Design Dept, Salt Lake City UT (S)

Zavala, Adriana, *Assoc Prof*, Tufts University, Dept of Art & Art History, Medford MA (S)

Zawacki, Andrew, *Conservator*, Historic Arkansas Museum, Little Rock AR

Zawada, Elizabeth, *Dir*, Greenwich House Pottery, First Floor Gallery, New York NY

Zawada, Elizabeth, *Dir*, Greenwich House Inc, Greenwich House Pottery, New York NY (S)

Zawora, Ed, *Graphic Design*, Antonelli Institute, Professional Photography & Commercial Art, Erdenheim PA (S)

Zayatz, Matthew, *Preparator*, Dartmouth College, Hood Museum of Art, Hanover NH

Zea, Philip, *Pres*, Historic Deerfield, Inc, Deerfield MA

Zebot, George, *Instr*, Art Institute of Southern California, Laguna Beach CA (S)

Zee, Rosa, *Vol Coordr*, Pacific - Asia Museum, Pasadena CA

Zeftel, Julie, *Mus Librn*, The Metropolitan Museum of Art, Image Library, New York NY

Zeh, Roger, *Interim Mus Dir*, Museum of Fine Arts, Saint Petersburg, Florida, Inc, Saint Petersburg FL

Zehner, Jeffrey, *Media Arts & Animation*, Art Institute of Pittsburgh, Pittsburgh PA (S)

Zeidberg, David, *Dir Library*, The Huntington Library, Art Collections & Botanical Gardens, San Marino CA

Zeidberg, David, *Dir Library*, The Huntington Library, Art Collections & Botanical Gardens, Library, San Marino CA

Zeigler, Barbara, *Assoc Prof*, University of British Columbia, Dept of Art History, Visual Art & Theory, Vancouver BC (S)

Zeile, Kirche, *Asst Prof Theatre*, Marymount Manhattan College, Fine & Performing Arts Div, New York NY (S)

Zeits, Rae Ellen, *Bookkeeper*, Hockaday Museum of Art, Kalispell MT

Zela, Sara B, *Interim Dir*, Phillips Exeter Academy, Frederick R. Mayer Art Center, Lamont Gallery, Exeter NH

Zeleski, Lynn, *Vol Coord*, Hastings Museum of Natural & Cultural History, Hastings NE

Zelevansky, Lynn, *Dir*, Carnegie Museums of Pittsburgh, Carnegie Museum of Art, Pittsburgh PA

Zell, Valerie, *Adjunct Asst Prof Art History*, Johnson County Community College, Fine Arts Dept & Art History Dept, Overland Park KS (S)

Zella, Robbin, *Dir*, Housatonic Community College, Housatonic Museum of Art, Bridgeport CT

Zelleke, Ghenete, *Cur European Decorative Arts & Sculpture,* The Art Institute of Chicago, Chicago IL

Zeller, Emily, *Vis Asst Prof,* Kenyon College, Art Dept, Gambier OH (S)

Zeller, Joyce, *Pres,* Catharine Lorillard Wolfe, New York NY

Zeller, Linda, *Mus Gift Shop Mgr,* Wiscasset, Waterville & Farmington Railway Museum (WW&F), Alna ME

Zellers, Mark, *Dept Chmn & Asst Prof,* Community College of Rhode Island, Dept of Art, Warwick RI (S)

Zellmer, Ginny, *Youth Educator,* Hickory Museum of Art, Inc, Hickory NC

Zellner, Susan M, *Dir Devel,* Delaware Art Museum, Wilmington DE

Zellner Neal, Donna, *Dir,* North Tonawanda History Museum, North Tonawanda NY

Zelonis, Mark, *Ruth Lilly Dir Environmental & Historic Preservation,* Indianapolis Museum of Art, Indianapolis IN

Zemancik, Lisa, *Educ Coordr,* Wayne Center for the Arts, Wooster OH

Zeng, Li, *Asst Prof,* University of Central Arkansas, Department of Art, Conway AR (S)

Zenhari, Ellie, *Asst Prof,* California State University, Dominguez Hills, Art & Design Dept, Carson CA (S)

Zeppetelli, John, *Dir & Chief Cur,* Musee d'art Contemporain de Montreal, Montreal PQ

Zercher, Wendel, *Cur,* Heritage Center of Lancaster County Museum, Lancaster PA

Zerendow, Chris, *Cur,* University of Wisconsin-Stout, J Furlong Gallery, Menomonie WI

Zerner, Catherine, *Prof,* Brown University, Dept History of Art & Architecture, Providence RI (S)

Zervigon, Andres, *Asst Prof Art History,* University of La Verne, Dept of Art, La Verne CA (S)

Zettle-Sterling, Renee, *Assoc Prof,* Grand Valley State University, Art & Design Dept, Allendale MI (S)

Zettler, Richard, *Near East Section Assoc Cur,* University of Pennsylvania, Museum of Archaeology & Anthropology, Philadelphia PA

Zetzman, Frank, *Prof,* University of Wisconsin College - Marinette, Art Dept, Marinette WI (S)

Zhang, Fan, *Freeman/McPherson Post-Doc Fel & Lectr Art,* Smith College, Museum of Art, Northampton MA

Zhang, He, *Asst Prof,* William Paterson University, Dept Arts, Wayne NJ (S)

Zhang, Hong Nian, *Instr,* Woodstock School of Art, Inc, Woodstock NY (S)

Zhang, Jessica, *Sr Acquisitions Librn,* The Nelson-Atkins Museum of Art, Spencer Art Reference Library, Kansas City MO

Zhang, Naijun, *Prof,* West Virginia University, College of Creative Arts, School of Art & Design, Morgantown WV (S)

Zhang, Shaoqian, *Asst Prof,* Oklahoma State University, Department of Art, Graphic Design and Art History, Stillwater OK (S)

Zhang, Yue, *Coordr,* University of Florida, University Gallery, Gainesville FL

Zhou, Yan, *Adjunct Asst Prof,* Kenyon College, Art Dept, Gambier OH (S)

Zic, Virginia F, *Prof,* Sacred Heart University, Dept of Art, Fairfield CT (S)

Zicterman, Karen, *Admin,* Art Museum of the University of Houston, Blaffer Gallery, Houston TX

Zidek, Al, *Instr,* Solano Community College, Division of Fine & Applied Art & Behavioral Science, Fairfield CA (S)

Ziebell, Sarah, *Cur Recordings,* The New York Public Library, The New York Public Library for the Performing Arts, New York NY

Ziegler, Arthur P, *Pres,* Pittsburgh History & Landmarks Foundation, James D Van Trump Library, Pittsburgh PA

Ziegler, David, *Dir,* University of California, Los Angeles, Visual Resource Collection, Los Angeles CA

Ziegler, Georgianna, *Head of Ref,* Folger Shakespeare, Washington DC

Ziegler, Janice, *Dir Educ,* Western Reserve Historical Society, Library, Cleveland OH

Ziegler, Joanna, *Prof,* College of the Holy Cross, Dept of Visual Arts, Worcester MA (S)

Zielinski, Henrietta, *Bibliographer,* School of the Art Institute of Chicago, John M Flaxman Library, Chicago IL

Ziellnski, Angie, *Instr,* Idaho State University, Dept of Art & Pre-Architecture, Pocatello ID (S)

Zierden, Martha, *Cur Historic Archaeology,* Charleston Museum, Charleston SC

Zies, Daniel, *Vis Servs Coordr,* Ellen Noel Art Museum of the Permian Basin, Odessa TX

Zietz, Myrta, *Bus Asst,* The Art Museum of Eastern Idaho, Idaho Falls ID

Zietz, Stephen, *Head Spec Colls,* Cleveland Public Library, Fine Arts & Special Collections Dept, Cleveland OH

Zilber, Emily, *Asst Cur,* Cranbrook Art Museum, Bloomfield Hills MI

Zilber, Emily, *Ronald & Anita Wornick Cur Contemporary Decorative Arts,* Museum of Fine Arts, Boston MA

Zill, Anne B, *Dir,* Art Gallery at the University of New England, Portland ME

Zimiles, Murray, *Prof,* Purchase College, State University of New York, School of Art+Design, Purchase NY (S)

Zimlich, Robert, *Cur,* American Sport Art Museum and Archives, Daphne AL

Zimmer, Jim, *Dir Art,* Illinois State Museum, Chicago Gallery, Chicago IL

Zimmer, Jim, *Dir Art,* Illinois State Museum, ISM Lockport Gallery, Chicago Gallery & Southern Illinois Art Gallery, Springfield IL

Zimmer, Tom, *Controller,* Colorado Historical Society, Colorado History Museum, Denver CO

Zimmerer, Kathy, *Gallery Dir,* University Art Gallery at California State University, Dominguez Hills, Carson CA

Zimmerlink, PJ, *Preparator,* Westmoreland Museum of American Art, Greensburg PA

Zimmerlink, PJ, *Preparator,* Westmoreland Museum of American Art, Art Reference Library, Greensburg PA

Zimmerman, Jerome, *Chmn & Prof,* C W Post Campus of Long Island University, School of Visual & Performing Arts, Brookville NY (S)

Zimmerman, Jim, *Archivist & Preparator,* Provincetown Art Association & Museum, Provincetown MA

Zimmerman, Luke, *Instr,* Linfield College, Department of Art & Visual Culture, McMinnville OR (S)

Zimmerman, Randy, *Instr Computer Graphics,* The Art Institute of Cincinnati, AIC College of Design, Cincinnati OH (S)

Zimmermann, Philip, *Prof Emeritus,* Purchase College, State University of New York, School of Art+Design, Purchase NY (S)

Zimpel, Jim, *Assoc Prof Sculpture,* Montana State University, School of Art, Bozeman MT (S)

Zimprich, Shirley, *Dir,* LeSueur County Historical Society, Collections Library, Elysian MN

Zimprich, Shirley, *Genealogist,* LeSueur County Historical Society, Chapter One, Elysian MN

Zinkham, Helena, *Chief Prints & Photograph,* Library of Congress, Prints & Photographs Division, Washington DC

Zinn, Nancy E, *Assoc Dir,* Walters Art Museum, Baltimore MD

Zinz, Kasia, *Secy,* Pioneer Town, Pioneer Museum of Western Art, Wimberley TX

Ziolkowski, Jan M, *Dir,* Harvard University, Museum & Garden, Washington DC

Ziolkowski, Ruth, *CEO & Pres,* Crazy Horse Memorial, Indian Museum of North America, Native American Educational & Cultural Center & Crazy Horse Memorial Library (Reference), Crazy Horse SD

Zipay, Terry, *Chmn,* Wilkes University, Dept of Art, Wilkes-Barre PA (S)

Zippay, Lori, *Exec Dir,* Electronic Arts Intermix (EAI), New York NY

Zirkle, Merle W, *Prof,* Grinnell College, Dept of Art, Grinnell IA (S)

Ziun, Nancy, *Assoc Dir Colls & Exhibs,* Walters Art Museum, Library, Baltimore MD

Zivich, Matthew, *Prof,* Saginaw Valley State University, Dept of Art & Design, University Center MI (S)

Zivkovich, Kay M, *Asst Dir & Prof,* Southern Illinois University, School of Art & Design, Carbondale IL (S)

Zlock, Colleen, *Visitor Ctr Mgr,* Storm King Art Center, Mountainville NY

Zobel, James W, *Archivist,* MacArthur Memorial, Norfolk VA

Zobel, James W, *Archivist,* MacArthur Memorial, Library & Archives, Norfolk VA

Zoe, Vivian, *Dir,* Norwich Free Academy, Slater Memorial Museum, Norwich CT

Zolghadr, Tirdad, *Grad Comt,* Bard College, Center for Curatorial Studies Graduate Program, Annandale-on-Hudson NY (S)

Zoller, Guy, *Instr,* American University, Dept of Art, New York NY (S)

Zollinger, Wendy, *Exhib Coordr,* VSA Arts of New Mexico, Enabled Arts Center, Albuquerque NM (S)

Zona, Louis A, *Dir & Chief Cur,* The Butler Institute of American Art, Art Museum, Youngstown OH

Zonker, Kenneth L, *Assoc Prof,* Sam Houston State University, Art Dept, Huntsville TX (S)

Zorn, David, *Pres,* Art Institute of Colorado, Denver CO (S)

Zortea, Flavia, *Graphic Design, Media Arts & Animation,* Art Institute of Pittsburgh, Pittsburgh PA (S)

Zotovich Phillips, Devon, *Prog Dir,* Bainbridge Island Arts Council, Bainbridge Island WA

Zoualalian, Val, *Instr,* Toronto Art Therapy Institute, Toronto ON (S)

Zrebiec, Alice, *Cur Textile Art,* Denver Art Museum, Denver CO

Zsako, Julius, *Prof,* Seton Hall University, College of Arts & Sciences, South Orange NJ (S)

Zserdin, Carmelle, *Assoc Prof,* Clarke College, Dept of Art, Dubuque IA (S)

Zuccari, Frank, *Exec Dir Conservation,* The Art Institute of Chicago, Chicago IL

Zucco, Doug, *Instr,* Moravian College, Dept of Art, Bethlehem PA (S)

Zucker, Heather, *Program Dir,* Hillel Foundation, Hillel Jewish Student Center Gallery, Cincinnati OH

Zucker, Mark, *Prof,* Louisiana State University, School of Art, Baton Rouge LA (S)

Zuckerman, Art, *Historian,* Bronx Community College (CUNY), Hall of Fame for Great Americans, Bronx NY

Zuckerman, Susan, *Dir & Historian,* Bronx Community College (CUNY), Hall of Fame for Great Americans, Bronx NY

Zuckerman Jacobson, Heidi, *Dir & Chief Cur,* Aspen Art Museum, Aspen CO

Zugazagoitia, Julian, *CEO & Cur,* The Nelson-Atkins Museum of Art, Creative Arts Center, Kansas City MO

Zugazagoitia, Julian, *Dir & CEO,* The Nelson-Atkins Museum of Art, Kansas City MO

Zuhlke, Christy, *Mem & Admin,* Rochester Historical Society, Rochester NY

Zuidema, Richard, *1st VChmn,* Reading Public Museum, Reading PA

Zuk, Radoslav, *Prof (Emeritus),* McGill University, School of Architecture, Montreal PQ (S)

Zukowsky, John, *Cur Architecture,* The Art Institute of Chicago, Chicago IL

Zumeta, Jay, *Instr,* Art Academy of Cincinnati, Cincinnati OH (S)

Zuniga, Yvette, *Coordr,* California State University, Chico, BMU Art Gallery, Chico CA

Zupnick, Matthew, *Prof,* Central Missouri State University, Dept Art & Design, Warrensburg MO (S)

Zuraw, Shelley, *Assoc Dir,* University of Georgia, Franklin College of Arts & Sciences, Lamar Dodd School of Art, Athens GA (S)

Zurawski, Simone, *Assoc Prof,* DePaul University, Dept of Art, Chicago IL (S)

Zurcher, Becky, *Mgr Admin & Operations,* University of Oklahoma, Fred Jones Jr Museum of Art, Norman OK

Zurier, Rebecca, *Asst Prof,* University of Michigan, Ann Arbor, Dept of History of Art, Ann Arbor MI (S)

Zurinsky, Suzanne D, *Assoc Prof,* University of North Alabama, Dept of Art, Florence AL (S)

Zuris, Kathleen, *Research Specialist,* Danbury Scott-Fanton Museum & Historical Society, Inc, Danbury CT

Zuris, Kathleen, *Research Specialist,* Danbury Scott-Fanton Museum & Historical Society, Inc, Library, Danbury CT

Zurko, Walter, *Prof,* The College of Wooster, Dept of Art and Art History, Wooster OH (S)

Zust, Mark, *Chmn Design Studies,* Bowling Green State University, School of Art, Bowling Green OH (S)

Zuver, W Marc, *Chief Cur, Dir,* Fondo del Sol, Visual Art & Media Center, Washington DC

Zver, Jodi, *CFO,* Confederation Centre Art Gallery and Museum, Charlottetown PE

Zwart, Joel, *Dir Exhibs,* Calvin College, Center Art Gallery, Grand Rapids MI

Zwerneman, Jane, *Prog Asst,* University of California, San Diego, Stuart Collection, La Jolla CA

Zwicker, Marianne, *Office Mgr,* National Society of the Colonial Dames of America in The Commonwealth of Virginia, Wilton House Museum, Richmond VA

Zwieback, Nancy, *Controller,* Seattle Art Museum, Downtown, Seattle WA

Zwierciadlowski, Donna, *Librn,* Emily Carr Institute of Art & Design, Library, Vancouver BC

Organization Index

Schools are indicated by "S".

Arthur Ross Gallery, see University of Pennsylvania, Philadelphia PA

Art Information Center, Inc, New York NY (A)

Art in General, New York NY (A)

Art Institute of Atlanta, Atlanta GA (S)

The Art Institute of Chicago, Chicago IL (A,L,M)

The Art Institute of Cincinnati, AIC College of Design, Cincinnati OH (S)

Art Institute of Colorado, Denver CO (S)

The Art Institute of Dallas, Dallas TX (S)

Art Institute of Fort Lauderdale, Fort Lauderdale FL (S)

Art Institute of Fort Lauderdale, Technical Library, Fort Lauderdale FL (L)

Art Institute of Houston, Houston TX (S)

Art Institute of Philadelphia, Philadelphia PA (S)

Art Institute of Philadelphia Library, Philadelphia PA (L)

Art Institute of Pittsburgh, Pittsburgh PA (S)

Art Institute of Pittsburgh, John P. Barclay Memorial Gallery, Pittsburgh PA (M,L)

Art Institute of Southern California, Laguna Beach CA (S)

Art Institutes International at Portland, Portland OR (L)

The Art Institutes, The Art Institute of Seattle, Seattle WA (S)

Art Instruction Schools, Education Dept, Minneapolis MN (S)

Artists' Cooperative Gallery, Omaha NE (M)

Artists' Fellowship, Inc, New York NY (O)

Artists Association of Nantucket, Nantucket MA (A)

Artists Collective Inc, Hartford CT (A)

Artists in Stained Glass, see Ontario Crafts Council, Toronto ON

Artists Space, New York NY (A,M,L)

Artists Talk on Art, New York NY (A)

The Art League Gallery & School, Alexandria VA (A)

Art League of Houston, Houston TX (A)

The Art League of Long Island, Stevenson Academy Program, Dix Hills NY (S)

Artlink, Inc, Auer Center for Arts & Culture, Fort Wayne IN (M)

Art Metropole, Toronto ON (M)

Art Museum, see State University of New York at Plattsburgh, Plattsburgh NY

The Art Museum at the University of Kentucky, Lexington KY (M,L)

The Art Museum of Eastern Idaho, Idaho Falls ID (M)

Art Museum of Greater Lafayette, Lafayette IN (M)

Art Museum of Southeast Texas, Beaumont TX (M)

Art Museum of the Americas, Washington DC (M,L)

Art Museum of the University of Houston, Blaffer Gallery, Houston TX (M,L)

Art PAC, Washington DC (A)

Artrain, Inc, Ann Arbor MI (A)

Art Resources International, Washington DC (A)

Arts & Crafts Association of Meriden Inc, Gallery 53, Meriden CT (A,L)

Arts & Education Council of Greater Saint Louis, Saint Louis MO (A)

Arts & Humanities Council of Tuscaloosa, Junior League Gallery, Tuscaloosa AL (A)

Arts & Media Division Carnegie Gallery, see Columbus Metropolitan Library, Columbus OH

Arts & Science Center for Southeast Arkansas, Pine Bluff AR (A)

Arts & Science Council, Charlotte NC (A)

Arts, Craft & Theater Safety, New York NY (A)

Arts, Recreation & Literature Dept, see Seattle Public Library, Seattle WA

Art Saint Louis, Saint Louis MO (M)

Arts and Letters Club of Toronto, Toronto ON (A,L)

The Arts Center, see Arts Council of Fayetteville-Cumberland County, Fayetteville NC

The Arts Center, Inc, see Associates for Community Development, Martinsburg WV

Arts Center in Orange, Orange VA (M)

The Arts Center of the Capital Region, Troy NY (A)

The ArtsCenter, The Nicholson Gallery at the Arts Center, Carrboro NC (M)

The Art School at Old Church, Demarest NJ (S)

Arts Clearinghouse, see City of Atlanta, Atlanta GA

The Arts Club of Chicago, Chicago IL (A,L)

Arts Club of Washington, James Monroe House, Washington DC (M)

ArtsConnection Inc, New York NY (A)

Arts Council for Long Beach, 350 Elm Ave. CA (A)

Arts Council of Fayetteville-Cumberland County, The Arts Center, Fayetteville NC (A)

Arts Council of Greater Kingsport, Renaissance Center Main Gallery, Kingsport TN (A)

Arts Council of Mendocino County, Ukiah CA (A)

Arts Council Of New Orleans, New Orleans LA (A)

Arts Council of Southwestern Indiana, The Bower-Suhrheinrich Foundation Gallery, Evansville IN (A)

The Arts Council of Wayne County, Goldsboro NC (S)

The Arts Council of Winston-Salem & Forsyth County, Winston Salem NC (A)

Arts Council Silicon Valley, San Jose CA (A)

Art Services International, Alexandria VA (O)

Arts Extension Service, Amherst MA (O)

Arts Midland Galleries & School, Midland MI (A)

Arts Midland Galleries & School, Alden B. Dow Museum of Science & Art, Midland MI (M)

Arts Midwest, Minneapolis MN (A)

Arts of the Southern Finger Lakes, Corning NY (A)

Arts on the Park, Lakeland Center for Creative Arts, Lakeland FL (M)

Artspace, Richmond VA (M)

Artspace Inc, Raleigh NC (A)

ArtSpace/Lima, Lima OH (M)

Arts Partnership of Greater Spartanburg, Inc, Chapman Cultural Center, Spartanburg SC (A)

The Art Spirit Gallery, Coeur D Alene ID (M)

Arts Place, Inc., Hugh N Ronald Memorial Gallery, Portland IN (M)

Arts Quest, Bethlehem PA (M)

Art Students League of New York, New York NY (S)

Art Students League of New York, New York NY (A,L)

The Art Studio Inc, Beaumont TX (A)

The Art Studio New York, New York NY (S)

Arts United of Greater Fort Wayne, Fort Wayne IN (A)

Art Without Walls Inc, New York NY (M)

Artworks!, New Bedford MA (A)

Artworks, The Visual Art School of Trenton, Trenton NJ (A,L)

Asbury College, Student Center Gallery, Wilmore KY (M)

Asbury University, Art Dept, Wilmore KY (S)

Ascension Lutheran Church Library, Milwaukee WI (L)

Ashby-Hodge Gallery of American Art, see Central Methodist University, Fayette MO

Asher Library, see Spertus Institute of Jewish Studies, Chicago IL

Asheville Art Museum, Asheville NC (M)

Ashford Hollow Foundation for Visual & Performing Arts, Griffis Sculpture Park, East Otto NY (A)

Ashford University, Art Dept, Clinton IA (S)

The Ashland Academy of Art, Haiku HI (S)

Ashland College Arts & Humanities Gallery, The Coburn Gallery, Ashland OH (M)

Ashland Inc, Ashland KY (C)

Ashland University, Art Dept, Ashland OH (S)

Ashtabula Arts Center, Ashtabula OH (A)

Asian American Arts Centre, New York NY (A)

Asian Art Museum of San Francisco, Chong-Moon Lee Ctr for Asian Art and Culture, San Francisco CA (M,L)

Asian Collection, see Saint John's University, Queens NY

Asian Resource Gallery, see East Bay Asian Local Development Corp (EBALDC), Oakland CA

The Asia Society Museum, New York NY (M)

A Space, Toronto ON (A)

Aspen Art Museum, Aspen CO (M)

Associated Artists of Pittsburgh, Pittsburgh PA (A)

Associated Artists of Winston-Salem, Winston Salem NC (A)

Associates for Community Development, The Arts Center, Inc, Martinsburg WV (M)

Associates of the Art Commission, Inc, see Design Commission of the City of New York, New York NY

Association des Musees Canadiens, see Canadian Museums Association, Ottawa ON

Association des Musees Canadiens, see Canadian Museums Association, Ottawa ON

Association of African American Museums, Washington DC (O)

Association of Art Museum Directors, New York NY (O)

Association of Collegiate Schools of Architecture, Washington DC (O)

Association of Hawaii Artists, Honolulu HI (A)

Association of Independent Colleges of Art & Design, Providence RI (O)

Association of Medical Illustrators, Lexington KY (O)

Association professionnelle des designers d'interieur du Quebec, Montreal PQ (A)

Assumption College, Dept of Art, Music & Theatre, Worcester MA (S)

ASTED Inc, Montreal PQ

ASTED Inc, Montreal QC (O)

ASU Library, see Arizona State University, Tempe AZ

Ataloa Lodge Museum, Muskogee OK (M)

Ateneo Puertorriqueno, Ateneo Gallery, San Juan PR (M,L)

Ateneo Puertorriqueno, Ateneo Gallery, San Juan PR (M,L)

The Athenaeum, see Northern Virginia Fine Arts Association, Alexandria VA

Athenaeum Music & Arts Library, see Library Association of La Jolla, La Jolla CA

Athenaeum of Philadelphia, Philadelphia PA (M,L)

Atlanta Contemporary Art Center, Atlanta GA (M)

Atlanta Cyclorama & Civil War Museum, see City of Atlanta, Atlanta GA

Atlanta-Fulton Public Library, Central Library Art Gallery, Atlanta GA (L)

Atlanta Historical Society Inc, Atlanta History Center, Atlanta GA (M)

Atlanta History Center, see Atlanta Historical Society Inc, Atlanta GA

Atlanta International Museum of Art & Design, Museum of Design Atlanta, Atlanta GA (M)

Atlanta Technical Institute, Visual Communications Class, Atlanta GA (S)

Atlantic City Art Center, Atlantic City NJ (M)

Atlantic Gallery, New York NY (M)

Atlatl, Phoenix AZ (O)

Atrium Gallery, see University of North Texas Health Science Center Fort Worth, Fort Worth TX

Atrium Gallery, Saint Louis MO (M)

Attleboro Arts Museum, Attleboro MA (M)

The Atwood House Museum, see Chatham Historical Society, Chatham MA

Auburn University, Dept of Art, Auburn AL (S)

Auburn University, Julie Collins Smith Museum, Auburn AL (M)

Auburn University Montgomery, Dept of Fine Arts, Montgomery AL (S)

Audrain County Historical Society, Graceland Museum & American Saddlehorse Museum, Mexico MO (M)

Auerbach Art Library, see Wadsworth Atheneum Museum of Art, Hartford CT

Augsburg College, Art Dept, Minneapolis MN (S)

Augustana College, Art Dept, Rock Island IL (S)

Augustana College, Art Dept, Sioux Falls SD (S)

Augustana College, Augustana College Art Museum, Rock Island IL (M)

Augustana College, Center for Western Studies, Sioux Falls SD (A)

Augustana College, Eide-Dalrymple Gallery, Sioux Falls SD (M)

Augusta State University, Dept of Art, Augusta GA (S)

Aurora Regional Fire Museum, Aurora IL (M)

Aurora University, Art Dept, Aurora IL (S)

Aurora University, Schingoethe Center for Native American Cultures & The Schingoethe Art Gallery, Aurora IL (M)

Austin Arts Center, Widener Gallery, see Trinity College, Hartford CT

Austin Children's Museum, Austin TX (M)

Austin College, Art Dept, Sherman TX (S)

Austin College, Ida Green Gallery, Sherman TX (M)

Austin Community College, Dept of Commercial Art, North Ridge Campus, Austin TX (S)

Austin Peay State University, Dept of Art, Clarksville TN (S)

Austin Peay State University, Margaret Fort Trahern Gallery, Clarksville TN (M,L)

Austrian Cultural Forum Gallery, New York NY (M)

Autozone, Autozone Corporation Collection, Memphis TN (C)

Autozone Corporation Collection, see Autozone, Memphis TN

Autry National Center, Museum of the American West, Griffith Park, Los Angeles CA (M,L)

Avampato Discovery Museum, The Clay Center for Arts & Sciences, Charleston WV (M)

Averett College, Art Dept, Danville VA (S)

Avery Architectural & Fine Arts Library, see Columbia University, New York NY

Milton Avery Graduate School of the Arts, see Bard College, Annandale-on-Hudson NY

Avila College, Art Division, Dept of Humanities, Kansas City MO (S)

Avila University, Thornhill Art Gallery, Kansas City MO (M)

Azusa Pacific University, College of Liberal Arts, Art Dept, Azusa CA (S)

B'nai B'rith International, B'nai B'rith Klutznick National Jewish Museum, Washington DC (M)

B'nai B'rith Klutznick National Jewish Museum, see B'nai B'rith International, Washington DC

Leo Baeck, New York NY (A,L)

Bailey House, see Maui Historical Society, Wailuku HI

Bainbridge Arts & Crafts Gallery, Bainbridge Island WA (M)

Bainbridge Island Arts Council, Bainbridge Island WA (A)
Bakehouse Art Complex, Inc, Miami FL (M)
Baker Arts Center, Liberal KS (M)
Bakersfield Art Foundation, Bakersfield Museum of Art, Bakersfield CA (M)
Bakersfield College, Art Dept, Bakersfield CA (S)
Bakersfield Museum of Art, see Bakersfield Art Foundation, Bakersfield CA
Baker University, Dept of Mass Media & Visual Arts, Baldwin City KS (S)
Baker University, Old Castle Museum, Baldwin City KS (M)
Balboa Art Conservation Center, San Diego CA (A,L)
Allan C Balch Art Research Library, see Los Angeles County Museum of Art, Los Angeles CA
Baldwin Gallery, Aspen CO (M)
Baldwin Historical Society Museum, Baldwin NY (M)
Baldwin Hotel Museum Annex, see Klamath County Museum, Klamath Falls OR
Baldwin Photographic Gallery, see Middle Tennessee State University, Murfreesboro TN
Baldwin-Wallace College, Dept of Art, Berea OH (S)
Baldwin-Wallace College, Fawick Art Gallery, Berea OH (M)
Ball State University, Dept of Art, Muncie IN (S)
Ball State University, Museum of Art, Muncie IN (M,L)
Baltimore City Community College, Art Gallery, Baltimore MD (M)
Baltimore City Community College, Dept of Fine Arts, Baltimore MD (S)
The Baltimore Museum of Art, Baltimore MD (M,L)
Balzekas Museum of Lithuanian Culture, Chicago IL (M,L)
BanCorp South, Art Collection, Tupelo MS (C)
Banff Centre, Banff AB (S)
Banff Centre, Walter Phillips Gallery, Banff AB (M,L)
Banfill-Locke Center for the Arts, Fridley MN (M)
Bank of NY Mellon Corporation, Pittsburgh PA (C)
Bank of Oklahoma NA, Art Collection, Tulsa OK (C)
Bank One Arizona, Phoenix AZ (C)
Bank One Fort Worth, Fort Worth TX (C)
Bank One Wisconsin, Milwaukee WI (C)
Edward M Bannister Gallery, see Rhode Island College, Providence RI
Barbara & Ray Alpert Jewish Community Center, Pauline & Zena Gatov Gallery, Long Beach CA (M)
Bard College at Simon's Rock, Hillman-Jackson Gallery, Great Barrington MA (M,L)
Bard College, Milton Avery Graduate School of the Arts, Annandale-on-Hudson NY (S)
Bard College, Center for Curatorial Studies and the Hessel Museum of Art, Annandale-on-Hudson NY (M,L)
Bard College, Center for Curatorial Studies Graduate Program, Annandale-on-Hudson NY (S)
Bard College, Fisher Art Center, Annandale-on-Hudson NY (M)
Barker Character, Comic and Cartoon Museum, Cheshire CT (M)
Barnard College, see Columbia University, New York NY
Barnard's Mill Art Museum, Glen Rose TX (M)
Barnes Foundation, Merion PA (M)
Barn Gallery, Ogunquit ME (M)
The Barnum Museum, Bridgeport CT (M)
Barr Colony Heritage Cultural Centre, Lloydminster SK (A)
Pete & Susan Barrett Art Gallery, see Santa Monica College, Santa Monica CA
Barron Arts Center, see Woodbridge Township Cultural Arts Commission, Woodbridge NJ
John D Barrow, Skaneateles NY (M)
Barry University, Dept of Fine Arts, Miami Shores FL (S)
The Bartlett Museum, Amesbury MA (M)
Barton College, Art & Design Dept, Wilson NC (S)
Barton College, Barton Museum - Virginia Graves Gallery - Lula E Rackley Gallery, Wilson NC (M,L)
Barton County Community College, Fine Arts Dept, Great Bend KS (S)
Barton Museum - Virginia Graves Gallery - Lula E Rackley Gallery, see Barton College, Wilson NC
Bartow-Pell Mansion Museum & Gardens, Bronx NY (M)
Baruch College of the City University of New York, Sidney Mishkin Gallery, New York NY (M)
The Bascomb, Highlands NC (M)
Bass Museum of Art, Miami Beach FL (M)
Bates College, Art & Visual Culture, Lewiston ME (S)
Bates College, Museum of Art, Lewiston ME (M)
Baton Rouge Gallery, Center For Contemporary Art, Baton Rouge LA (M)

Bau-Xi Gallery, Toronto ON (M)
Bay Area Video Coalition, Inc, San Francisco CA (A)
Bay Arts, Inc., Bay Village OH (A)
Bay County Historical Society, Historical Museum of Bay County, Bay City MI (M)
Baycrest Centre for Geriatric Care, The Morris & Sally Justein of Baycrest Heritage Museum, Toronto ON (M)
Bay De Noc Community College, Art Dept, Escanaba MI (S)
Baylor University - College of Arts and Sciences, Dept of Art, Waco TX (S)
Baylor University, Martin Museum of Art, Waco TX (M,L)
Bayonne Free Public Library, Cultural Center, Bayonne NJ (L)
Bay Path College, Dept of Art, Longmeadow MA (S)
Donna Beam Fine Art Gallery, see University of Nevada, Las Vegas, Las Vegas NV
Beard and Weil Galleries, see Wheaton College, Norton MA
Beaufort County Arts Council, Washington NC (A)
Beaumont Art League, Beaumont TX (M)
Beaverbrook Art Gallery, Fredericton NB (M,L)
Bechtler Museum of Modern Art, Charlotte NC (M)
Beck Center for the Arts, Lakewood OH (A)
Beck Cultural Exchange Center, Inc, Knoxville TN (M)
Becker College, William F Ruska Library, Worcester MA (L)
Bede Art Gallery, Yankton SD (M)
Bedford Gallery, see Dean Lesher, Walnut Creek CA
Beinecke Rare Book & Manuscript Library, see Yale University, New Haven CT
Belas Artes Multicultural Center, Art Gallery, Saint Louis MO (M)
Belger Arts Center, Kansas City MO (M)
Belhaven College, Art Dept, Jackson MS (S)
Bellagio Resort & Casino, Bellagio Gallery of Fine Art, Las Vegas NV (M)
Cecelia Coker Bell Gallery, see Coker College, Hartsville SC
Belle Grove Inc., Belle Grove Plantation, Middletown VA (M)
Bellevue Arts Museum, Bellevue WA (M)
Bellevue College, Art Dept, Bellevue NE (S)
Bellevue Community College, Art Dept, Bellevue WA (S)
Bellingrath Gardens & Home, Theodore AL (M)
The Bell Museum of Natural History, see University of Minnesota, Minneapolis MN
Joseph Bellows Gallery, La Jolla CA (M)
Beloit College, Wright Museum of Art, Beloit WI (M)
Belskie Museum, Closter NJ (M)
Belton Center for the Arts, Belton SC (M)
Belz Museum of Asian & Judaic Art, Memphis TN (M)
Bemidji State University, Visual Arts Dept, Bemidji MN (S)
Bemis Center for Contemporary Arts, Omaha NE (M)
Benedict College, School of Humanities, Arts & Social Sciences, Columbia SC (S)
Benedictine College, Art Dept, Atchison KS (S)
The Benini Foundation & Sculpture Ranch, Johnson City TX (M)
W A C Bennett Library, see Simon Fraser University, Burnaby BC
Bennington College, Visual Arts Division, Bennington VT (S)
Bennington Museum, Bennington VT (M)
Ben Shahn Art Galleries, see William Paterson University, Wayne NJ
Bent Museum & Gallery, Taos NM (M)
Berea College, Art & Art History Program, Berea KY (S)
Berea College, Ulmann Doris Galleries, Berea KY (M)
Bergen Community College, Visual Art Dept, Paramus NJ (S)
Bergen County Historical Society, Steuben House Museum, River Edge NJ (M)
Bergstrom-Mahler Museum, Neenah WI (M,L)
Berkeley Art Center, Berkeley CA (A)
Berkeley Civic Arts Program, Berkeley CA (A)
Berkeley Heights Free Public Library, Berkeley Heights NJ (L)
Berkeley Public Library, Berkeley CA (L)
Berks Art Alliance, Reading PA (A)
Berkshire Artisans, see City of Pittsfield, Pittsfield MA
Berkshire Athenaeum, Reference Dept, Pittsfield MA (L)
Berkshire Community College, Dept of Fine Arts, Pittsfield MA (S)
Berkshire Museum, Pittsfield MA (M)
Berman Museum, Anniston AL (M)

Philip & Muriel Berman Museum of Art, see Ursinus College, Collegeville PA
Bernard Judaica Museum, see Congregation Emanu-El, New York NY
Bernard M Baruch College of the City University of New York, Art Dept, New York NY (S)
Berry College, Art Dept, Mount Berry GA (S)
Berry College, Moon Gallery, Mount Berry GA (M,L)
Bert Gallery, Providence RI (M)
Bertha V B Lederer Fine Arts Gallery-Suny Geneseo, Bertha V B Lederer Fine Arts Gallery, Geneseo NY (M)
Bertha V B Lederer Gallery, see State University of New York at Geneseo, Geneseo NY
Besser Museum for Northeast Michigan, Alpena MI (M,L)
Bethany College, Art Dept, Lindsborg KS (S)
Bethany College, Dept of Fine Arts, Bethany WV (S)
Bethany College, Mingenback Art Center, Lindsborg KS (M,L)
Bethany Lutheran College, Art Dept, Mankato MN (S)
Bethel College, Dept of Art, North Newton KS (S)
Bethel College, Dept of Art, Saint Paul MN (S)
Bethel College, Mennonite Library & Archives, North Newton KS (L)
Beverly Hills Public Library, Fine Arts Library, Beverly Hills CA (L)
Beverly Historical Society, Cabot, Hale & Balch House Museums, Beverly MA (M,L)
Beyond Baroque Foundation, Beyond Baroque Literary Arts Center, Venice CA (A)
Bicentennial Art Center & Museum, Paris IL (M)
Big Bend Community College, Art Dept, Moses Lake WA (S)
Biggs Museum of American Art, Dover DE (M)
Big Horn County Historical Museum, Hardin MT (M)
Big Horn Galleries, Cody WY (M)
Big Red Barn Gallery, see Ucross Foundation, Clearmont WY
Billings Meriks Sculptors Society, Billings MT (O)
Biola University, Art Dept, La Mirada CA (S)
Birger Sandzen Memorial Gallery, Lindsborg KS (M)
Birmingham Bloomfield Art Center, Birmingham MI (S)
Birmingham Bloomfield Art Center, Art Center, Birmingham MI (A)
Birmingham Museum of Art, Birmingham AL (M,L)
Birmingham Public Library, Arts, Literature & Sports Department, Birmingham AL (L)
Birmingham-Southern College, Art & Art History, Birmingham AL (S)
Birmingham Southern College, Doris Wainwright Kennedy Art Center, Birmingham AL (M)
Bisbee Arts & Humanities Council, Lemuel Shattuck Memorial Library, Bisbee AZ (L)
Bishop's University, Foreman Art Gallery, Sherbrooke PQ (L)
Bernice Pauahi Bishop, Honolulu HI (M,L)
Bishop Hill State Historic Site, see Illinois Historic Preservation Agency, Bishop Hill IL
Bismarck Art & Galleries Association, Bismarck ND (A)
Bismarck State College, Fine Arts Dept, Bismarck ND (S)
Bixler Art & Music Library, see Colby College, Waterville ME
Black & White Gallery, Southampton NY (M)
Black American West Museum & Heritage Center, Denver CO (M)
Black Bear Bosin Resource Center, see Mid-America All-Indian Center, Wichita KS
Blackburn College, Dept of Art, Carlinville IL (S)
Black Cultural Center for Nova Scotia, see Society for the Protection & Preservation of Black Culture in Nova Scotia, Dartmouth NS
Black Hawk College, Art Dept, Moline IL (S)
Black Hills State University, Art Dept, Spearfish SD (S)
Black Hills State University, Ruddell Gallery, Spearfish SD (M,L)
Black River Academy Museum & Historical Society, Black River Academy Museum, Ludlow VT (M)
BlackRock Center for the Arts, Germantown MD (M)
Blacksburg Regional Art Association, Blacksburg VA (A)
Blackwell Library, see Salisbury University, Salisbury MD
Blackwell Street Center for the Arts, Denville NJ (A)
Blackwood Gallery, see University of Toronto at Mississauga, Mississauga ON
Blaffer Gallery, see Art Museum of the University of Houston, Houston TX
Eubie Blake, Baltimore MD (M)
Blanden Memorial Art Museum, Fort Dodge IA (M)
Blanton Museum of Art, see University of Texas at Austin, Austin TX

Blauvelt Demarest Foundation, Hiram Blauvelt Art Museum, Oradell NJ (M)

Hiram Blauvelt Art Museum, see Blauvelt Demarest Foundation, Oradell NJ

Blewett-Harrison-Lee Museum, see Columbus Historic Foundation, Columbus MS

Mary & Leigh Block Museum of Art, see Northwestern University, Evanston IL

Bloomington Theatre & Art Center, Inez Greenberg Gallery, Bloomington MN (M)

Bloomsburg University, Dept of Art & Art History, Bloomsburg PA (S)

Bloomsburg University of Pennsylvania, Haas Gallery of Art, Bloomsburg PA (M)

Eleanor Blossom Memorial Library, see Maricopa County Historical Society, Wickenburg AZ

Blount-Bridgers House, Hobson Pittman Memorial Gallery, see Edgecombe County Cultural Arts Council, Inc, Tarboro NC

Blowing Rock Art and History Museum, Blowing Rock NC (M)

Bluefield State College, Division of Arts & Sciences, Bluefield WV (S)

Blue Lake Fine Arts Camp, Art Dept, Twin Lake MI (S)

Bluemont Historical Railroad Junction, Arlington VA (M)

Blue Mountain College, Art Dept, Blue Mountain MS (S)

Blue Mountain Community College, Fine Arts Dept, Pendleton OR (S)

Blue Mountain Gallery, New York NY (M)

Blue Sky Gallery, Oregon Center for the Photographic Arts, Portland OR (M)

Blue Star Contemporary Art Center, San Antonio TX (M)

Bluff Country Artists Gallery, Spring Grove MN (M)

Bluffton University, Art Dept, Bluffton OH (S)

Ernest Blumenschein Home & Studio, see Taos, Taos NM

Blumenthal Rare Book & Manuscript Library, see University of California, Berkeley, Berkeley CA

Board of Parks & Recreation, The Parthenon, Nashville TN (M)

Bobbitt Visual Arts Center, see Albion College, Albion MI

Boca Raton Museum of Art, Boca Raton FL (A,L)

The Richard W Bock Sculpture Collection & Art Library, see Greenville College, Greenville IL

Bodley-Bullock House Museum, Lexington KY (M)

Boehm Gallery, see Palomar Community College, San Marcos CA

Boise Art Museum, Boise ID (M)

Boise State University, Art Dept, Boise ID (S)

Bone Creek Museum of Agrarian Art, David City NE (M)

William Bonifas, Alice Powers Art Gallery, Escanaba MI (M)

Bonita Museum and Cultural Center, Bonita CA (M)

Boothbay Region Art Foundation, Boothbay Harbor ME (A)

Booth Western Art Museum, Cartersville GA (M)

Bose Pacia, Brooklyn NY (M)

Boston Architectural College, McCormick Gallery, Boston MA (A,L)

Boston Center for Adult Education, Boston MA (S)

Boston College, Fine Arts Dept, Chestnut Hill MA (S)

Boston College, McMullen Museum of Art, Chestnut Hill MA (M)

The Bostonian Society, Old State House Museum, Boston MA (M,L)

The Boston Printmakers, Boston MA (A)

Boston Properties LLC, San Francisco CA (C)

Boston Public Library, Central Library, Boston MA (L,M)

Boston Sculptors at Chapel Gallery, West Newton MA (M)

Boston University, Graduate Program - Arts Administration, Boston MA (S)

Boston University, School for the Arts, Boston MA (S)

Muriel Isabel Bostwick Library, see Art Gallery of Hamilton, Hamilton ON

Botanic Hall Library, see Cheekwood-Tennessee Botanical Garden & Museum of Art, Nashville TN

Boulder History Museum, Museum of History, Boulder CO (A)

Boulder Museum of Contemporary Art, Boulder CO (A)

Boulder Public Library & Gallery, Arts Gallery, Boulder CO (L)

Bowdoin College, Art Dept, Brunswick ME (S)

Bowdoin College, Peary-MacMillan Arctic Museum, Brunswick ME (M)

Bowers Museum, Santa Ana CA (M)

Bowie Arts Center, Due West SC (M)

Bowie State University, Fine & Performing Arts Dept, Bowie MD (S)

Bowling Green State University, Firelands College, Humanities Dept, Huron OH (S)

Bowling Green State University, Fine Arts Center Galleries, Bowling Green OH (M)

Bowling Green State University, School of Art, Bowling Green OH (S)

Bowman, Megahan & Penelec Galleries, see Allegheny College, Meadville PA

Bowman Arts Center, see Allied Arts Council of Lethbridge, Lethbridge AB

Bowne House Historical Society, Flushing NY (A)

The Dwight Frederick Boyden Gallery, see St Mary's College of Maryland, St Mary's City MD

Roy Boyd, Chicago IL (M)

The Bradford Group, Niles IL (M)

Bradley University, Dept of Art, Peoria IL (S)

Bradley University, Heuser Art Center, Peoria IL (M)

Braithwaite Fine Arts Gallery, see Southern Utah University, Cedar City UT

Brandeis University, Dept of Fine Arts, Waltham MA (S)

Brandon Public Library, see The Art Gallery of Southwestern Manitoba, Brandon MB

Brandywine Battlefield Park, see Pennsylvania Historical & Museum Commission, Harrisburg PA

Brandywine Conservancy, Brandywine River Museum, Chadds Ford PA (M,L)

Brandywine Workshop, Center for the Visual Arts, Philadelphia PA (A)

Branigan Cultural Center, Las Cruces NM (M)

Brant Historical Society, Brant Museum & Archives, Brantford ON (M,L)

Brattleboro Museum & Art Center, Brattleboro VT (M)

Brauer Museum of Art, see Valparaiso University, Valparaiso IN

Braun Research Library, see Autry National Center, Los Angeles CA

Brazosport College, Art Dept, Lake Jackson TX (S)

Bread & Puppet Theater, Bread & Puppet Museum, Barton VT (M)

Anne Bremer Memorial Library, see San Francisco Art Institute, San Francisco CA

Brenau University, Art & Design Dept, Gainesville GA (S)

Brenner Library, see Quincy University, Quincy IL

Brentwood Art Center, Los Angeles CA (S)

Brescia University, Anna Eaton Stout Memorial Art Gallery, Owensboro KY (M)

Brescia University, Art Dept, Owensboro KY (S)

Alexander Brest Museum & Gallery, see Jacksonville University, Jacksonville FL

Brevard College, Department of Art, Brevard NC (S)

Brevard College, Spiers Gallery, Brevard NC (M,L)

Brewton-Parker College, Visual Arts, Mount Vernon GA (S)

Briar Cliff University, Art Dept, Sioux City IA (S)

BRIC - Brooklyn Information & Culture, Rotunda Gallery, Brooklyn NY (M)

Brick Store Museum, Kennebunk ME (A)

Brickton Art Center, Park Ridge IL (M)

Bridgewater College, Art Dept, Bridgewater VA (S)

Bridgewater State College, Art Dept, Bridgewater MA (S)

Margaret M Bridwell Art Library, see University of Louisville, Louisville KY

Hilton M. Briggs Library, see South Dakota State University, Brookings SD

Brigham City Corporation, Brigham City Museum & Gallery, Brigham City UT (M)

Brigham Young University, Hawaii Campus, Division of Fine Arts, Laie HI (S)

Brigham Young University, Dept of Visual Arts, Provo UT (S)

Brigham Young University, B F Larsen Gallery, Provo UT (M,L)

L D Brinkman, Kerrville TX (M)

Bradford Brinton, Big Horn WY (M)

British Columbia Museums Association, Victoria BC (A)

Broadway, LRC, and Hamilton Club Galleries, see Passaic County Community College, Paterson NJ

Brockton Public Library System, Joseph A Driscoll Art Gallery, Brockton MA (L)

Bromfield Art Gallery, Boston MA (M)

Bronck Museum, see Greene County Historical Society, Coxsackie NY

Saidye Bronfman, Liane & Danny Taran Gallery, Montreal PQ (A)

Silas Bronson, Waterbury CT (L)

Bronx Community College (CUNY), Hall of Fame for Great Americans, Bronx NY (M)

Bronx Community College, Music & Art Dept, Bronx NY (S)

Bronx Council on the Arts, Longwood Arts Gallery @ Hostos, Bronx NY (M)

Bronx Museum of the Arts, Bronx NY (M)

Bronx River Art Center Inc, Gallery, Bronx NY (M)

Bronxville Public Library, Bronxville NY (L)

Brookdale Community College, Center for the Visual Arts, Lincroft NJ (S)

Brookfield Craft Center, Inc, Gallery, Brookfield CT (M)

Brookgreen Gardens, Murrells Inlet SC (M,L)

Brooklyn Arts Council, BAC Gallery, Brooklyn NY (A)

Brooklyn Botanic Garden, Steinhardt Conservatory Gallery, Brooklyn NY (M)

Brooklyn College, Art Dept, Brooklyn NY (S)

Brooklyn Historical Society, Brooklyn NY (A,L)

Brooklyn Historical Society, Brooklyn OH (M)

Brooklyn Museum, Brooklyn NY (M,L)

Brooklyn Public Library, Art & Music Division, Brooklyn NY (L)

Brookside Museum, see Saratoga County Historical Society, Ballston Spa NY

Brooks Institute of Photography, Santa Barbara CA (S)

Broward Community College - A. Hugh Adams Campus, Fine Arts Gallery, Davie FL (M)

Broward Community College - South Campus, Art Gallery, Pembroke Pines FL (M)

Broward County Board of Commissioners, Cultural Div, Fort Lauderdale FL (A)

Annmary Brown Memorial, see Brown University, Providence RI

Brown County Art Gallery Foundation, Nashville IN (A)

George W Brown Jr Ojibwe Museum & Cultural Center, see Lac du Flambeau Band of Lake Superior Chippewa Indians, Lac Du Flambeau WI

Armstrong Browning Library, see Baylor University, Waco TX

Browning Arts, Grand Forks ND (M)

John Brown House, see Rhode Island Historical Society, Providence RI

Orlando Brown House, see Liberty Hall Historic Site, Frankfort KY

Brownson Gallery, see Manhattanville College, Purchase NY

Brownsville Art League, Brownsville Museum of Fine Art, Brownsville TX (M)

Brown University, David Winton Bell Gallery, Providence RI (M,L)

Brown University, Dept History of Art & Architecture, Providence RI (S)

Bruce Museum, Inc, Greenwich CT (M)

Brunnier Art Museum, see Iowa State University, Ames IA

The Brush Art Gallery & Studios, Lowell MA (M)

Bryan Memorial Gallery, Cambridge VT (M)

Bryant Library, Roslyn NY (L)

Bry Gallery, see University of Louisiana at Monroe, Monroe LA

Bryn Mawr College, Dept of the History of Art, Bryn Mawr PA (S)

Bryn Mawr College, Rhys Carpenter Library for Art, Archaeology, Classics & Cities, Bryn Mawr PA (L)

Buckham Fine Arts Project, Gallery, Flint MI (M)

Buckley Center Gallery, see University of Portland, Portland OR

Bucknell University, Dept of Art, Lewisburg PA (S)

Bucknell University, Edward & Marthann Samek Art Gallery, Lewisburg PA (M)

Richard D Buck Memorial Library, see Balboa Art Conservation Center, San Diego CA

Bucks County Community College, Fine Arts Dept, Newtown PA (S)

Bucks County Community College, Hicks Art Center, Newtown PA (M)

Bucks County Historical Society, Mercer Museum, Doylestown PA (M,L)

Buehler Challenger & Science Center, Paramus NJ (M)

Buena Vista Museum of Natural History, Bakersfield CA (M)

Buffalo & Erie County Public Library, Buffalo NY (L)

Buffalo Arts Studio, Art Gallery, Buffalo NY (M)

Buffalo Bill Memorial Association, Buffalo Bill Historical Center, Cody WY (A,L)

The Buffalo Fine Arts Academy, Albright-Knox Art Gallery, Buffalo NY (M,L)

Buffalo Museum of Science, Research Library, Buffalo NY (L)

Bullion Plaza Cultural Center & Museum, Miami AZ (M)

Ruth Bunker Memorial Library, see Dacotah Prairie Museum, Aberdeen SD

Bunnell Street AAS Center, Bunnell Street Arts Center, Homer AK (M)

Bunte Gallery, Dublin OH (M)

Carving Studio and Sculpture Center, West Rutland VT (M)

Casa Amesti, Monterey CA (M)

Casasola Museum, El Paso TX (M)

Cascade County Historical Society, The History Museum, Great Falls MT (M)

Casemate Museum, see Headquarters Fort Monroe, Dept of Army, Hampton VA

Case Western Reserve University, Dept of Art History & Art, Cleveland OH (S)

Casper College, Dept of Visual Arts, Casper WY (S)

Caspers, Inc, Art Collection, Tampa FL (C)

Castellani Art Museum, see Niagara University, Niagara NY

Castle Gallery, see College of New Rochelle, New Rochelle NY

Castleton State College, Art Dept, Castleton VT (S)

Catfish Capital Visitors Center and Museum, Belzoni MS (M)

Catharine B Mitchell Museum, see Stratford Historical Society, Stratford CT

Cathedral of Saint John the Divine, New York NY (M,L)

Catholic University of America, Humanities Library, Mullen Library, Washington DC (L)

Catholic University of America, School of Architecture & Planning, Washington DC (L)

Cathy and Jesse Marion Art Gallery, see State University of New York College at Fredonia, Fredonia NY

Cavalry-Armor Foundation, Patton Museum of Cavalry & Armor, Fort Knox KY (M)

Cayuga Museum of History & Art, Auburn NY (M)

Cazenovia College, Center for Art & Design Studies, Cazenovia NY (S)

Cazenovia College, Chapman Art Center Gallery, Cazenovia NY (M)

CCAC Wattis Institute for Contemporary Arts, see California College of the Arts, San Francisco CA

Cedar Crest College, Art Dept, Allentown PA (S)

Cedar Grove, see Philadelphia Museum of Art, Philadelphia PA

Cedarhurst Center for the Arts, Mitchell Museum, Mount Vernon IL (M,L)

Cedar Hurst Library, see Cedarhurst Center for the Arts, Mount Vernon IL

Cedar Rapids Museum of Art, Cedar Rapids IA (M,L)

Cedar Ridge Creative Centre, see City of Scarborough, Scarborough ON

Centaur Art Galleries, Las Vegas NV (M)

Centenary College, Humanities Dept, Hackettstown NJ (S)

Centenary College of Louisiana, Dept of Art, Shreveport LA (S)

Centenary College of Louisiana, Meadows Museum of Art, Shreveport LA (M)

Center-Barron County, Dept of Art, see University of Wisconsin, Rice Lake WI

Center for Advanced Film & Television, see The American Film Institute, Los Angeles CA

Center for Art & Education, Van Buren AR (M)

Center for Art Design and Visual Culture, Baltimore MD (M)

Center for Art Design and Visual Culture, Baltimore MD (M)

Center for Book Arts, New York NY (M)

Center For Contemporary Art, see Baton Rouge Gallery, Baton Rouge LA

Center for Contemporary Arts, Abilene TX (M)

The Center for Contemporary Arts of Santa Fe, Santa Fe NM (A)

Center for Creative Photography, see University of Arizona, Tucson AZ

Center for Creative Studies, College of Art & Design Library, Detroit MI (L)

Center for Exploratory & Perceptual Art, CEPA Gallery, Buffalo NY (M,L)

Center for Fine Art Photography, Fort Collins CO (M)

The Center for Intuitive and Outside Art, Chicago IL

Center for Photography at Woodstock Inc, Woodstock NY (A)

Center for Puppetry Arts, Atlanta GA (M,L)

Center for Southern Folklore, Memphis TN (A)

Center for the Arts Piper Gallery, Crested Butte CO (M)

Center for the Visual Arts, Gallery, Wausau WI (M)

The Center for Visual Artists - Greensboro, Greensboro NC (A)

Center of Creative Arts (COCA), Millstone Gallery, Saint Louis MO (M)

Center on Contemporary Art, Seattle WA (M)

Center on Contemporary Art, Seattle WA (A)

Central College, Art Dept, Pella IA (S)

Central Community College - Columbus Campus, Business & Arts Cluster, Columbus NE (S)

Central Connecticut State University, Art Dept Museum, New Britain CT (M)

Central Connecticut State University, Dept of Art, New Britain CT (S)

Central Florida Community College, Humanities Dept, Ocala FL (S)

Central Iowa Art Association, Inc, Marshalltown IA (A,L)

Central Library, Dept of Fine Arts, San Antonio TX (L)

Central Methodist University, Ashby-Hodge Gallery of American Art, Fayette MO (M)

Central Michigan University, Dept of Art, Mount Pleasant MI (S)

Central Michigan University, University Art Gallery, Mount Pleasant MI (M)

Central Missouri State University, Dept Art & Design, Warrensburg MO (S)

Central Oregon Community College, Dept of Art, Bend OR (S)

Central Piedmont Community College, Visual & Performing Arts, Charlotte NC (S)

Central State University, Dept of Art, Wilberforce OH (S)

Central United Methodist Church, Swords Into Plowshares Peace Center & Gallery, Detroit MI (M)

Central Washington University, Dept of Art, Ellensburg WA (S)

Central Washington University, Sarah Spurgeon Gallery, Ellensburg WA (M)

Central Wyoming College, Art Center, Riverton WY (S)

Centre National d'Exposition, see Le Musee Regional de Rimouski, Rimouski PQ

Centre National D'Exposition a Jonquiere, see Institut des Arts au Saguenay, Jonquiere PQ

Centro Cultural Aztlan, San Antonio TX (A)

Centro Cultural De La Raza, San Diego CA (M)

Centro de Estudios Avanzados, Art Library, Old San Juan PR (A)

Centro de Estudios Avanzados, Art Library, Old San Juan PR (L)

Centrum Arts & Creative Education, Port Townsend WA (A)

Century College, Humanities Dept, White Bear Lake MN (S)

Century Gallery, see County of Los Angeles, Sylmar CA

CEPA Gallery, see Center for Exploratory & Perceptual Art, Buffalo NY

Cerritos Community College, Fine Arts & Communication Div, Norwalk CA (S)

C G Jung Center, Evanston IL (L)

Chabot College, Humanities Division, San Leandro CA (S)

Chadron State College, Dept of Art, Chadron NE (S)

Chadron State College, Memorial Hall Main Gallery & Memorial Hall 239, Chadron NE (M)

Chaffee Art Center, see Rutland Area Art Association, Rutland VT

Chaffey Community College, Art Dept, Rancho Cucamonga CA (S)

Chalet of the Golden Fleece, New Glarus WI (M)

Billie Trimble Chandler, Texas State Museum of Asian Cultures, Corpus Christi TX (M)

Chaney Gallery, see Maryland Hall for the Creative Arts, Annapolis MD

Channel Islands Maritime Museum, Oxnard CA (M)

Stephen Chan Library of Fine Arts, see New York University, New York NY

Chapel Gallery, see Muskoka Arts & Crafts Inc, Bracebridge ON

Howard I Chapelle Memorial Library, see Chesapeake Bay Maritime Museum, Saint Michaels MD

Chapin Library, see Williams College, Williamstown MA

Chapman Art Center Gallery, see Cazenovia College, Cazenovia NY

Chapman Cultural Center, see Arts Partnership of Greater Spartanburg, Inc, Spartanburg SC

Chapman University, Art Dept, Orange CA (S)

Chapman University Guggenheim Gallery, Orange CA (M)

Chappell Memorial Library and Art Gallery, Chappell NE (L)

Charles A Lindbergh Historic Site, Little Falls MN (M)

Charles Allis Art Museum, Milwaukee WI (M)

Charles Bruce Davis Museum of Art, History & Science, Yadkinville NC (M)

Charles City Arts Center, Charles City IA (M)

Charles City Library, Mooney Art Collection, Charles City IA (M)

Charles River School, Creative Arts Program, Dover MA (S)

Charleston Museum, Charleston SC (M,L)

Charleston Southern University, Dept of Language & Visual Art, Charleston SC (S)

Charter Oak Cultural Center, Hartford CT (M)

Chase Home Museum of Utah Folk Arts, see Utah Arts Council, Salt Lake City UT

Chasen Galleries of Fine Art, Richmond VA (M)

Chase Young Gallery, Boston MA (M)

Chassie Meriks Academy of Performance Art, Wilmington DE (S)

Chastain Arts Center & Gallery, see City of Atlanta, Atlanta GA

Chateau Ramezay Museum, Montreal PQ (M,L)

Chatham College, Art Gallery, Pittsburgh PA (M)

Chatham College, Fine & Performing Arts, Pittsburgh PA (S)

Chatham Historical Society, The Atwood House Museum, Chatham MA (M)

Chatillon-DeMenil House, see Chatillon-DeMenil House Foundation, Saint Louis MO

Chatillon-DeMenil House Foundation, Chatillon-DeMenil House, Saint Louis MO (M)

Chattanooga-Hamilton County Bicentennial Library, Fine Arts Dept, Chattanooga TN (L)

Chattanooga State Technical Community College, Advertising Arts Dept, Chattanooga TN (S)

Chautauqua Center for the Visual Arts, Chautauqua NY (M)

Chautauqua Institution, School of Art, Chautauqua NY (S)

Fray Angelico Chavez History Library, see Museum of New Mexico, Santa Fe NM

Chazen Museum of Art, see University of Wisconsin-Madison, Madison WI

Cheekwood Nashville's Home of Art & Gardens, Education Dept, Nashville TN (S)

Cheekwood-Tennessee Botanical Garden & Museum of Art, Nashville TN (M,L)

Chelan County Public Utility District, Rocky Reach Dam, Wenatchee WA (M)

Chelsea Art Museum, New York NY (M)

Cheltenham Center for the Arts, Cheltenham PA (S)

Chemeketa Community College, Dept of Humanities & Communications, Art Program, Salem OR (S)

Cherokee Heritage Center, Park Hill OK (A,L)

Chesapeake Bay Maritime Museum, Saint Michaels MD (M,L)

Chester County Historical Society, West Chester PA (A)

Chesterton Art Center, Chesterton IN (M)

Chesterwood, see National Trust for Historic Preservation, Stockbridge MA

Cheyney University of Pennsylvania, Dept of Art, Cheyney PA (S)

Chicago Architecture Foundation, Chicago IL (M)

Chicago Art Dealers Association, Chicago IL (A)

Chicago Artists' Coalition, Coalition Gallery, Chicago IL (M)

Chicago Athenaeum, Museum of Architecture & Design, Galena IL (M)

Chicago Children's Museum, Chicago IL (M)

Chicago Gallery, see Illinois State Museum, Chicago IL

Chicago History Museum, Chicago IL (A,L)

Chicago Public Library, Harold Washington Library Center, Chicago IL (L)

Chicago State University - President's Gallery, Chicago IL (M)

Chief Plenty Coups Museum State Park, Pryor MT (M)

The Children's Aid Society, Visual Arts Program of the Philip Coltoff Center at Green Arts and After School Program, New York NY (A)

Children's Art Carnival, New York NY (A)

Children's Art Foundation, Museum of International Children's Art, Santa Cruz CA (A)

The Children's Museum of Indianapolis, Indianapolis IN (M)

Children's Museum of Manhattan, New York NY (M)

Chilliwack Community Arts Council, Community Arts Centre, Chilliwack BC (A)

China Institute Gallery, see China Institute in America, New York NY

China Institute in America, China Institute Gallery, New York NY (M)

Chinati Foundation, Marfa TX (M)

Chinese-American Arts Council, New York NY (A)

Chinese Culture Foundation, Center Gallery, San Francisco CA (M)

Chinese Information & Culture Center Library, see Taipei Economic & Cultural Office, New York NY

Chipola College, Dept of Fine & Performing Arts, Marianna FL (S)

Chong-Moon Lee Ctr for Asian Art and Culture, see Asian Art Museum of San Francisco, San Francisco CA

Chowan College, Division of Art, Murfreesboro NC (S)

Christina Cultural Arts Center, Inc, Wilmington DE (A)

Christopher Newport University, Dept of Fine Performing Arts, Newport News VA (S)

Jean Outland Chrysler Library, see Chrysler Museum of Art, Norfolk VA

Chrysler Museum of Art, Norfolk VA (M,L)

Winston Churchill Memorial & Library in the United States, see Westminster College, Fulton MO

Church of Jesus Christ of Latter-Day Saints, Mormon Visitors' Center, Independence MO (M)

Church of Jesus Christ of Latter-Day Saints, Museum of Church History & Art, Salt Lake City UT (M,L)

CIGNA Corporation, CIGNA Art Collection, Bloomfield CT (C)

Cincinnati Art Club, Cincinnati OH (A)

Cincinnati Art Museum, see Cincinnati Art Museum, Cincinnati OH

Cincinnati Art Museum, Cincinnati Art Museum, Cincinnati OH (M,L)

Cincinnati Institute of Fine Arts, Cincinnati OH (A)

Citizens for the Arts in Pennsylvania, Harrisburg PA (A)

Citrus College, Art Dept, Glendora CA (S)

City Arts Center at Fair Park, Oklahoma City OK (M)

City Art Works, Pratt Fine Arts Center, Seattle WA (S)

City College of New York, Art Dept, New York NY (S)

City College of San Francisco, Art Dept, San Francisco CA (S)

City College of the City University of New York, Morris Raphael Cohen Library, New York NY (L)

City Colleges of Chicago, Daley College, Chicago IL (S)

City Gallery East, see City of Atlanta, Atlanta GA

City Lights Gallery, Bridgeport CT (M)

The City Museum of Washington DC, see Historical Society of Washington DC, Washington DC

City of Atlanta, Office of Cultural Affairs, Atlanta GA (A,M,L)

City of Austin Parks & Recreation Department, Julia C Butridge Gallery, Austin TX (M)

City of Austin Parks & Recreation, O. Henry Museum, Austin TX (M)

City of Brea, Art Gallery, Brea CA (M)

City of Cedar Falls, Iowa, James & Meryl Hearst Center for the Arts & Sculpture Garden, Cedar Falls IA (M)

City of Charleston, City Hall Council Chamber Gallery, Charleston SC (M)

City of El Paso, El Paso TX (M,L)

City of Fayette, Alabama, Fayette Art Museum, Fayette AL (M)

City of Fremont, Olive Hyde Art Gallery, Fremont CA (M)

City of Gainesville, Thomas Center Galleries - Cultural Affairs, Gainesville FL (M)

City of Hampton, Hampton Arts Commission, Hampton VA (A)

City of High Point, High Point Museum, High Point NC (M)

City of Irvine, Irvine Fine Arts Center, Irvine CA (S)

City of Irvine, Irvine Fine Arts Center, Irvine CA (M)

City of Ketchikan Museum Dept, Ketchikan AK (M,L)

City of Ketchikan Museum, Tongass Historical Museum, Ketchikan AK (M)

City of Lethbridge, Sir Alexander Galt Museum, Lethbridge AB (M)

City of Los Angeles, Cultural Affairs Dept, Los Angeles CA (M)

City of Lubbock, Buddy Holly Center, Lubbock TX (M)

City of Mason City, Charles H MacNider Museum, Mason City IA (M)

City of New York Parks & Recreation, Arsenal Gallery, New York NY (M)

City of Nome Alaska, Carrie M McLain Memorial Museum, Nome AK (M)

The City of Petersburg Museums, Petersburg VA (M)

City of Pittsfield, Berkshire Artisans, Pittsfield MA (M)

City of Port Angeles, Port Angeles Fine Arts Center & Webster Woods Art Park, Port Angeles WA (M)

City of Providence Parks Department, Roger Williams Park Museum of Natural History, Providence RI (M,L)

City of Raleigh Arts Commission, Miriam Preston Block Gallery, Raleigh NC (A)

City of Saint Augustine, Saint Augustine FL (A)

City of San Antonio, San Antonio TX (M)

City of San Rafael, Falkirk Cultural Center, San Rafael CA (M)

City of Scarborough, Cedar Ridge Creative Centre, Scarborough ON (M)

City of Springdale, Shiloh Museum of Ozark History, Springdale AR (M)

City of Tampa, Public Art Program, Tampa FL (A)

City of Toronto Culture, The Market Gallery, Toronto ON (M)

City of Toronto Museum Services, Historic Fort York, Toronto ON (A)

City of Ukiah, Grace Hudson Museum & The Sun House, Ukiah CA (M)

City of Woodstock, Woodstock Art Gallery, Woodstock ON (M)

City University of New York, PhD Program in Art History, New York NY (S)

Clackamas Community College, Art Dept, Oregon City OR (S)

Clack Art Center, Dept of Art & Design, see Alma College, Alma MI

Claflin College, Dept of Art, Orangeburg SC (S)

Clarion University of Pennsylvania, Dept of Art, Clarion PA (S)

Clarion University, Hazel Sandford Gallery, Clarion PA (M)

Clark-Atlanta University, School of Arts & Sciences, Atlanta GA (S)

Clark College, Archer Gallery/Gaiser Hall, Vancouver WA (M)

Clark College, Art Dept, Vancouver WA (S)

Clark County Historical Society, Heritage Center of Clark County, Springfield OH (M,L)

Clark County Historical Society, Pioneer - Krier Museum, Ashland KS (M)

Clarke College, Dept of Art, Dubuque IA (S)

Henry B Clarke, Chicago IL (M)

Clark Humanities Museum, see Scripps College, Claremont CA

Sterling & Francine Clark, Williamstown MA (M,L)

Clark University, Dept of Visual & Performing Arts, Worcester MA (S)

Clark University, The Schiltkamp Gallery/Traina Center for the Arts, Worcester MA (M)

Wilson W Clark Memorial Library, see University of Portland, Portland OR

Clay House Museum, Madison AL (M)

Claypool-Young Art Gallery, see Morehead State University, Morehead KY

Clay Studio, Philadelphia PA (M)

Clayworks Gallery, Charlotte NC (M)

Clear Creek History Park, Golden CO (M)

Clear Lake Arts Center, Clear Lake IA (M)

Clemson University, College of Architecture, Arts & Humanities, Art Dept, Clemson SC (S)

Clemson University, Rudolph E Lee Gallery, Clemson SC (M,L)

Cleveland Art Association, see Cleveland Institute of Art, Cleveland OH

Cleveland Botanical Garden, Eleanor Squire Library, Cleveland OH (L)

Cleveland Institute of Art, Cleveland OH (S)

Cleveland Institute of Art, Reinberger Galleries, Cleveland OH (M,L,A)

The Cleveland Museum of Art, Cleveland OH (M,L,A)

Cleveland Public Library, Fine Arts & Special Collections Dept, Cleveland OH (L)

Cleveland State Community College, Dept of Art, Cleveland TN (S)

Cleveland State University, Art Dept, Cleveland OH (S)

Clinch Valley College of the University of Virginia, Visual & Performing Arts Dept, Wise VA (S)

Clinton Art Association, River Arts Center, Clinton IA (M)

Clinton Community College, Art Dept, Plattsburgh NY (S)

Clinton County Historical Association, Clinton County Historical Museum, Plattsburgh NY (M)

Cliveden, Philadelphia PA (M)

The Cloisters Museum & Gardens, see The Metropolitan Museum of Art, New York NY

Clough-Hanson Gallery, see Rhodes College, Memphis TN

Clymer Museum of Art, Ellensburg WA (M)

CMCA-Center for Maine Contemporary Art, Art Gallery, Rockport ME (A)

Coachella Valley History Museum, Indio CA (M)

Coahoma Community College, Art Education & Fine Arts Dept, Clarksdale MS (S)

Coastal Arts League Museum, Half Moon Bay CA (M)

Cochise College, Art Dept, Douglas AZ (S)

Cochise College, Charles Di Peso Library, Douglas AZ (L)

Cody Country Art League, Cody WY (A)

Coe College, Dept of Art, Cedar Rapids IA (S)

Coe College, Eaton-Buchan Gallery & Marvin Cone Gallery, Cedar Rapids IA (M)

Coffeyville Community College, Art Dept, Coffeyville KS (S)

Cohasset Historical Society, Pratt Building (Society Headquarters), Cohasset MA (M)

Cohasset Maritime Museum, see Cohasset Historical Society, Cohasset MA

Morris Raphael Cohen Library, see City College of the City University of New York, New York NY

Coker College, Art Dept, Hartsville SC (S)

Coker College, Cecelia Coker Bell Gallery, Hartsville SC (M)

Francis Colburn Gallery, see University of Vermont, Burlington VT

Colby College, Art Dept, Waterville ME (S)

Colby College, Museum of Art, Waterville ME (M,L)

Colby Community College, Visual Arts Dept, Colby KS (S)

Colby-Sawyer College, Dept of Fine & Performing Arts, New London NH (S)

Coleman Library, see Tougaloo College, Tougaloo MS

Colgate University, Dept of Art & Art History, Hamilton NY (S)

Colgate University, Picker Art Gallery, Hamilton NY (M)

College Art Association, New York NY (O)

College for Creative Studies, Detroit MI (S)

College of Arts and Crafts, Faculty of Fine Arts, see University of Lucknow, Lucknow UP

College of Central Florida, Appleton Museum of Art, Ocala FL (M)

College of Central Florida, Appleton Museum of Art, Ocala FL (M)

College of Charleston School of Arts, Halsey Institute of Contemporary Art, Charleston SC (M)

College of Eastern Utah, Gallery East, Price UT (M)

The College of Idaho, Rosenthal Art Gallery, Caldwell ID (M)

College of Lake County, Art Dept, Grayslake IL (S)

College of Marin, Art Gallery, Kentfield CA (M)

College of Marin, Dept of Art, Kentfield CA (S)

College of Mount Saint Joseph, Art Dept, Cincinnati OH (S)

College of Mount Saint Joseph, Studio San Giuseppe, Cincinnati OH (M,L)

College of Mount Saint Vincent, Fine Arts Dept, Riverdale NY (S)

College of New Jersey, Art Gallery, Ewing NJ (M)

The College of New Jersey, School of Arts & Sciences, Ewing NJ (S)

College of New Rochelle, Castle Gallery, New Rochelle NY (M)

The College of New Rochelle, School of Arts & Sciences Art Dept, New Rochelle NY (S)

College of Notre Dame of Maryland, Art Dept, Baltimore MD (S)

College of Saint Benedict, Art Dept, Saint Joseph MN (S)

College of Saint Benedict, Gorecki Gallery & Gallery Lounge, Saint Joseph MN (M)

College of Saint Elizabeth, Art Dept, Morristown NJ (S)

College of Saint Elizabeth, Mahoney Library, Morristown NJ (L)

College of Saint Mary, Art Dept, Omaha NE (S)

College of Saint Rose, Art Gallery, Albany NY (M)

College of Saint Rose, The Center For Art and Design, Albany NY (S)

College of San Mateo, Creative Arts Dept, San Mateo CA (S)

College of Santa Fe, Art Dept, Santa Fe NM (S)

College of Southern Idaho, Art Dept, Twin Falls ID (S)

College of Staten Island, Performing & Creative Arts Dept, Staten Island NY (S)

College of the Canyons, Art Dept, Santa Clarita CA (S)

College of the Desert, Art Dept, Palm Desert CA (S)

College of the Holy Cross, Dept of Visual Arts, Worcester MA (S)

College of the Holy Cross, Dinand Library, Worcester MA (L)

College of the Ozarks, Dept of Art, Point Lookout MO (S)

College of the Redwoods, Arts & Languages Dept Division, Eureka CA (S)

College of the Sequoias, Art Dept, Visalia CA (S)

College of the Siskiyous, Theatre Dept, Weed CA (S)

College of Visual & Performing Arts, see Kutztown University, Kutztown PA

College of William & Mary, Dept of Fine Arts, Williamsburg VA (S)

College of William & Mary, Muscarelle Museum of Art, Williamsburg VA (M)

The College of Wooster, Dept of Art and Art History, Wooster OH (S)
The College of Wooster, The College of Wooster Art Museum, Wooster OH (M)
Collins C. Diboll Art Gallery, New Orleans LA (M)
Colonial Williamsburg Foundation, Williamsburg VA (M,A,L)
Colorado College, Dept of Art, Colorado Springs CO (S)
Colorado Gallery of the Arts, see Arapahoe Community College, Littleton CO
Colorado Historical Society, Colorado History Museum, Denver CO (M,L)
Colorado Mesa University, Art Dept, Grand Junction CO (S)
Colorado Mountain College, Fine Arts Gallery, Breckenridge CO (M)
Colorado Northwestern Community College, Art Dept, Rangely CO (S)
Colorado Photographic Arts Center, Denver CO (M)
Colorado Springs Fine Arts Center, Taylor Museum, Colorado Springs CO (M)
Colorado State University, Curfman Gallery, Fort Collins CO (M)
Colorado State University, Dept of Art, Fort Collins CO (S)
Colorado Watercolor Society, Denver CO (A)
Color Association of the US, New York NY (O)
Color Association of the US, New York NY
Colquitt County Arts Center, Moultrie GA (M)
Colter Bay Indian Arts Museum, see Grand Teton National Park Service, Moose WY
Columbia Basin College, Esvelt Gallery, Pasco WA (S)
Columbia College, see Columbia University, New York NY
Columbia College, Art Dept, Chicago IL (S)
Columbia College, Art Dept, Columbia MO (S)
Columbia College Chicago, Museum of Contemporary Photography, Chicago IL (M,L)
Columbia College, Dept of Art, Columbia SC (S)
Columbia College, Fine Arts, Sonora CA (S)
Columbia County Historical Society, Columbia County Museum and Library, Kinderhook NY (M)
Columbia Museum of Art, Columbia SC (M,L)
Columbia River Maritime Museum, Astoria OR (M,L)
Columbia State Community College, Dept of Art, Columbia TN (S)
Columbia University, Avery Architectural & Fine Arts Library, New York NY (L,M)
Columbia University, Graduate School of Architecture, Planning & Preservation, New York NY (M)
Columbus Chapel & Boal Mansion Museum, Boalsburg PA (M)
Columbus College of Art & Design, Fine Arts Dept, Columbus OH (S)
Columbus College of Art & Design, Packard Library, Columbus OH (L)
Columbus Cultural Arts Center, Columbus OH (M)
Columbus Historic Foundation, Blewett-Harrison-Lee Museum, Columbus MS (M)
Columbus Metropolitan Library, Arts & Media Division Carnegie Gallery, Columbus OH (L)
Columbus Museum, Columbus GA (M)
Columbus Museum of Art, Columbus OH (M)
Columbus State University, Dept of Art, Fine Arts Hall, Columbus GA (S)
Columbus State University, Norman Shannon and Emmy Lou P Illges Gallery, Columbus GA (M)
Commerce Bancshares, Inc, Fine Art Collection, Kansas City MO (C)
Communications and History Museum of Sutton, Sutton PQ (M)
Community Arts Council of Vancouver, Vancouver BC (A)
The Community Arts Project Gallery, Cornelius NC (M)
Community College of Allegheny County, Boyce Campus, Art Dept, Monroeville PA (S)
Community College of Allegheny County, Fine Arts Dept, West Mifflin PA (S)
Community College of Baltimore County, Art Dept, Catonsville MD (S)
Community College of Rhode Island, Dept of Art, Warwick RI (S)
Community College of Rhode Island, Knight Campus Art Gallery, Warwick RI (M)
Community Council for the Arts, Kinston NC (A)
The Community Education Center, Philadelphia PA (A)
Community Fine Arts Center, see Sweetwater County Library System and School District #1, Rock Springs WY
Comox Valley Art Gallery, Courtenay BC (M)
Compton Community College, Art Dept, Compton CA (S)
Concord College, Fine Art Division, Athens WV (S)

Concordia College, Art Dept, Bronxville NY (S)
Concordia College, Art Dept, Moorhead MN (S)
Concordia Historical Institute, Saint Louis MO (M)
Concordia University, Art Dept, Saint Paul MN (S)
Concordia University, Art Dept, Seward NE (S)
Concordia University, Dept of Fine Arts, Austin TX (S)
Concordia University, Division of Performing & Visual Arts, Mequon WI (S)
Concordia University, Leonard & Bina Ellen Art Gallery, Montreal PQ (M)
Concordia University, Faculty of Fine Arts, Montreal PQ (S)
Concordia University, Marxhausen Art Gallery, Seward NE (M)
Concordia University Wisconsin, Fine Art Gallery, Mequon WI (M)
Concord Museum, Concord MA (M)
Conejo Valley Art Museum, Thousand Oaks CA (M)
Confederate Memorial Hall, Confederate Museum, New Orleans LA (A)
Confederate Museum, see Confederate Memorial Hall, New Orleans LA
Confederation Centre Art Gallery and Museum, Charlottetown PE (M,L)
Congregation Beth Israel's Plotkin Judaica Museum, Scottsdale AZ (M)
Congregation Emanu-El, Bernard Judaica Museum, New York NY (M)
Connecticut College, Dept of Art, New London CT (S)
Connecticut Historical Society, Hartford CT (A,L)
Connecticut State Library, Museum of Connecticut History, Hartford CT (L)
Conrad-Caldwell House Museum, Louisville KY (M)
Conseil des Arts du Canada, see Canada Council for the Arts, Ottawa ON
Conseil des Arts du Quebec (CATQ), Diagonale, Centre des arts et des fibres du Quebec, Montreal PQ (L)
Conservation Center for Art & Historic Artifacts, Philadelphia PA (A)
Contemporary Art Center, Peoria IL (M)
Contemporary Art Center of Virginia, Virginia Beach VA (A)
Contemporary Art Gallery, Vancouver BC (M)
Contemporary Art Gallery Society of British Columbia, Vancouver BC (M)
Contemporary Art Museum St Louis, Saint Louis MO (A)
Contemporary Arts Center, Cincinnati OH (M,L)
Contemporary Arts Center, New Orleans LA (A)
Contemporary Arts Museum Houston, Houston TX (M)
The Contemporary Austin, Austin TX (M)
The Contemporary Museum, Honolulu HI (M,L)
The Contemporary Museum at First Hawaiian Center, Honolulu HI (M)
Contra Costa Community College, Dept of Art, San Pablo CA (S)
Converse College, Milliken Art Gallery, Spartanburg SC (M)
Converse College, School of the Arts, Dept of Art & Design, Spartanburg SC (S)
Cookeville Art Gallery, see Cumberland Art Society Inc, Cookeville TN
Douglas F Cooley Memorial Art Gallery, see Reed College, Portland OR
Cooper-Hewitt National Design Museum, Smithsonian Institution, New York NY (M,L)
Cooperstown Art Association, Cooperstown NY (A)
Cooper Union, School of Art, New York NY (S)
Coos Art Museum, Coos Bay OR (S)
Coos Art Museum, Coos Bay OR (M)
Coos County Historical Society Museum, North Bend OR (M)
Helen E Copeland Gallery, see Montana State University, Bozeman MT
Copper Village Museum & Arts Center, Anaconda MT (A,L)
Coppini Academy of Fine Arts, Elizabeth di Barbieri, San Antonio TX (A,L)
Coppin State College, Dept Fine & Communication Arts, Baltimore MD (S)
Coquille Valley Art Association, Coquille OR (A,L)
Coral Springs Museum of Art, Coral Springs FL (M)
Corbin Art Center, Spokane WA (A)
Corbit-Calloway Memorial Library, Odessa DE (L)
Corcoran Gallery of Art, Washington DC (M,L)
Corcoran School of Art, Washington DC (S)
Core, New Art Space, Denver CO (M)
Cornell College, Peter Paul Luce Gallery, Mount Vernon IA (M)
George D & Harriet W Cornell Fine Arts Museum, see Rollins College, Winter Park FL
Cornell Museum of Art and American Culture, Delray Beach FL (M)

Cornell University, Dept of Art, Ithaca NY (S)
Cornell University, Herbert F Johnson Museum of Art, Ithaca NY (M,L)
Corning Center for the Fine Arts, Corning IA (M)
Corning Community College, Division of Humanities, Corning NY (S)
Corning Museum of Glass, Museum, Corning NY (M,L)
Cornish College of the Arts, Art Dept, Seattle WA (S)
Cornish College of the Arts, Fisher Gallery, Seattle WA (M,L)
Cornwall Gallery Society, Cornwall Regional Art Gallery, Cornwall ON (M)
Cornwall Regional Art Gallery, see Cornwall Gallery Society, Cornwall ON
Corporate Council for the Arts/Arts Fund, Seattle WA (A)
Cortland Free Library, Cortland NY (L)
Corvallis Art Center, Corvallis OR (M)
Cottage Lawn, see Madison County Historical Society, Oneida NY
Cottey College, Art Dept, Nevada MO (S)
Cotting-Smith-Assembly House, see Peabody Essex Museum, Salem MA
Cottonlandia Museum, Greenwood MS (M)
Cotuit Center for the Arts, Cotuit MA (M)
County College of Morris, Art Dept, Randolph NJ (S)
County of Henrico, Meadow Farm Museum, Glen Allen VA (M,L)
County of Los Angeles, Century Gallery, Sylmar CA (M)
Courthouse Galleries, see Portsmouth Museums, Portsmouth VA
Courtney Art Gallery & Lemmerman Gallery, see New Jersey City University, Jersey City NJ
Coutts Museum of Art, Inc, El Dorado KS (M)
Craft Alliance, Saint Louis MO (A)
Craft and Folk Art Museum (CAFAM), Los Angeles CA (M)
Craft Council of Newfoundland & Labrador, Saint John's NF (A)
Craftsmen's Guild of Mississippi, Inc, Agriculture & Forestry Museum, Ridgeland MS (M)
Craftsmen's Guild of Mississippi, Inc, Mississippi Crafts Center, Ridgeland MS (M)
Craigdarroch Castle Historical Museum Society, Victoria BC (M)
Cranbrook Academy of Art, Bloomfield Hills MI (S)
Cranbrook Art Museum, Bloomfield Hills MI (M,L)
Crane Collection, Gallery of American Painting and Sculpture, Magnolia MA (M)
Cranford Historical Society, Cranford NJ (M)
Crary Art Gallery Inc, Grary Art Gallery, Warren PA (M)
Crazy Bone Gallery, Eureka Springs AR (M)
Crazy Horse Memorial, Indian Museum of North America, Native American Educational & Cultural Center & Crazy Horse Memorial Library (Reference), Crazy Horse SD (M)
Creative Art Center-North Oakland County, Pontiac MI (S)
Creative Arts Center, Pontiac MI (A)
Creative Arts Guild, Dalton GA (A)
Creative Growth Art Center, Oakland CA (M)
Creative Time, New York NY (A)
Creek Council House Museum, Okmulgee OK (M,L)
Creighton University, Fine & Performing Arts Dept, Omaha NE (S)
Creighton University, Lied Art Gallery, Omaha NE (M)
Cress Gallery of Art, see University of Tennessee at Chattanooga, Chattanooga TN
Crestar Bank, Art Collection, Richmond VA (C)
Cripple Creek District Museum, Cripple Creek CO (M)
Crocker Art Museum, Sacramento CA (M,L)
Crook County Museum & Art Gallery, Sundance WY (M)
Crooked Tree Arts Council, Virginia M McCune Community Arts Center, Petoskey MI (M)
Crossman Gallery, see University of Wisconsin-Whitewater, Whitewater WI
Crossroads Art Center Gallery, Richmond VA (M)
Crowder College, Longwell Museum/Art Department, Neosho MO (S)
Crowley Art Association, The Gallery, Crowley LA (A)
Crow Wing County Historical Society, Brainerd MN (M)
J T & E J Crumbaugh, Le Roy IL (L)
Crumpacker Family Library, see Portland Art Museum, Portland OR
Crystal Bridges Museum of American Art, Bentonville AR (M)
John M Cuelenaere, Grace Campbell Gallery, Prince Albert SK (M)

Lamar Dodd Art Center Museum, see LaGrange College, LaGrange GA

Lamar Dodd Art Center Museum, see LaGrange College, LaGrange GA

George J Doizaki Gallery, see Japanese American Cultural & Community Center, Los Angeles CA

Dominican College of Blauvelt, Art Dept, Orangeburg NY (S)

Dominican College of San Rafael, Art Dept, San Rafael CA (S)

Doris & Henry Dreyfuss Memorial Study Center Library & Archive, see Cooper-Hewitt National Design Museum, New York NY

Dorland Mountain Arts Colony, Temecula CA (S)

Dorothy Babcock Memorial Library, see Embroiderers Guild of America, Louisville KY

Dorsky Gallery, Dorsky Gallery Curatorial Programs, Long Island City NY (M)

Samuel Dorsky Museum of Art, see State University of New York at New Paltz, New Paltz NY

Dorval Cultural Centre, Dorval PQ (A)

Douglas Art Association, The Gallery and Gift Shop, Douglas AZ (M)

Mabel Smith Douglass Library, see Rutgers, The State University of New Jersey, New Brunswick NJ

Alden B Dow Creativity Center, see Northwood University, Midland MI

Dowd Fine Arts Gallery, see State University of New York College at Cortland, Cortland NY

Grace A Dow, Fine Arts Dept, Midland MI (L)

Dowling College, Dept of Visual Arts, Oakdale NY (S)

Dr. M.T. Geoffrey Yeh Art Gallery, see Saint John's University, Queens NY

Dr. Martin Luther King Jr. Library, see San Jose State University, San Jose CA

Drake University, Dept Art & Design, Des Moines IA (S)

The Drawing Center, New York NY (A)

Drew County Historical Society, Museum, Monticello AR (M)

Drew University, Art Dept, Madison NJ (S)

Drew University, Elizabeth P Korn Gallery, Madison NJ (M,L)

Drexel University, Drexel Collection, Philadelphia PA (M)

Felix J Dreyfous Library, see New Orleans Museum of Art, New Orleans LA

Joseph A Driscoll Art Gallery, see Brockton Public Library System, Brockton MA

Dr Jose C Barbosa Museum, see Institute of Puerto Rican Culture, San Juan PR

Dr Jose C Barbosa Museum, see Institute of Puerto Rican Culture, San Juan PR

Jose Drudis-Biada Art Gallery, see Mount Saint Mary's College, Los Angeles CA

Drury College, Art & Art History Dept, Springfield MO (S)

Dublin-Laurens Museum, see Laurens County Historical Society, Dublin GA

Dubuque Museum of Art, Dubuque IA (M)

Duke University, Dept of Art, Art History & Visual Studies, Durham NC (S)

Duke University Library, Hartman Center for Sales, Advertising & Marketing History, Durham NC (L)

Duke University, Nasher Museum of Art at Duke University, Durham NC (M,L)

Duke University Union, Louise Jones Brown Gallery, Durham NC (M)

Duley-Jones Gallery, Paradise Valley AZ (M)

Duncan-McAshan Visual Arts Center, see Hill Country Arts Foundation, Ingram TX

Dunconor Workshops, Salida CO (S)

Dundas Valley School of Art, DVSA Gallery, Dundas ON (S)

Dundurn Castle, Hamilton ON (M)

Dunedin Fine Art Center, Dunedin FL (S)

Dunlop Art Gallery, see Regina Public Library, Regina SK

Duns Scotus Library, see Lourdes College, Sylvania OH

DuPage Art League School & Gallery, Wheaton IL (A)

Durango Arts Center, Barbara Conrad Art Gallery, Durango CO (M)

Durham Art Gallery, Durham ON (M)

Durham Art Guild, Durham NC (M)

DuSable Museum of African American History, Chicago IL (M)

Dutchess Community College, Dept of Visual Arts, Poughkeepsie NY (S)

Dutchess County Arts Council, Poughkeepsie NY (M)

Dyson College of Arts & Sciences, see Pace University, Pleasantville NY

Earlham College, Art Dept, Richmond IN (S)

Earlham College, Leeds Gallery, Richmond IN (M)

Earthfire, Art from Detritus: Recycling with Imagination, New York NY (M)

East Bay Asian Local Development Corp (EBALDC), Asian Resource Gallery, Oakland CA (M)

East Carolina University, Wellington B Gray Gallery, Greenville NC (M,L)

East Carolina University, School of Art & Design, Greenville NC (S)

East Central College, Art Dept, Union MO (S)

East Central Community College, Art Dept, Decatur MS (S)

East Central University, School of Fine Arts, Ada OK (S)

East End Arts & Humanities Council, Riverhead NY (A)

Eastern Arizona College, Art Dept, Thatcher AZ (S)

Eastern Connecticut State University, Fine Arts Dept, Willimantic CT (S)

Eastern Illinois University, Art Dept, Charleston IL (S)

Eastern Illinois University, Tarble Arts Center, Charleston IL (M)

Eastern Iowa Community College, Clinton Community College, Clinton IA (S)

Eastern Kentucky University, Art Dept, Richmond KY (S)

Eastern Mennonite University, Art Dept, Harrisonburg VA (S)

Eastern Michigan University, Dept of Art, Ypsilanti MI (S)

Eastern Michigan University, Ford Gallery, Ypsilanti MI (M,L)

Eastern New Mexico University, Dept of Art, Portales NM (S)

Eastern New Mexico University, Runnels Gallery, Golden Library, Portales NM (M,L)

Eastern Oregon University, School of Arts & Science, La Grande OR (S)

Eastern Shore Art Association, Inc, Eastern Shore Art Center, Fairhope AL (A)

Eastern Shore Art Center, see Eastern Shore Art Association, Inc, Fairhope AL

Eastern Washington State Historical Society, Northwest Museum of Arts & Culture, Spokane WA (M)

Eastern Washington University, Dept of Art, Cheney WA (S)

Eastern Wyoming College, Art Dept, Torrington WY (S)

Eastfield College, Humanities Division, Art Dept, Mesquite TX (S)

East Hampton Library, Long Island Collection, East Hampton NY (L)

East Los Angeles College, Art Dept, Monterey Park CA (S)

East Los Angeles College, Vincent Price Art Museum, Monterey Park CA (M)

George Eastman, Rochester NY (M,L)

East Martello Museum & Gallery, see Key West Art & Historical Society, Key West FL

East Stroudsburg University, Fine Arts Center, East Stroudsburg PA (S)

East Tennessee State University, College of Arts and Sciences, Dept of Art & Design, Johnson City TN (S)

East Tennessee State University, The Reece Museum, Johnson City TN (M)

Eaton-Buchan Gallery & Marvin Cone Gallery, see Coe College, Cedar Rapids IA

Eccles Community Art Center, Ogden UT (A)

Eckerd College, Art Dept, Saint Petersburg FL (S)

Ecole des Arts Visuels, see L'Universite Laval, Quebec PQ

Edgecombe County Cultural Arts Council, Inc, Blount-Bridgers House, Hobson Pittman Memorial Gallery, Tarboro NC (M)

Edgewood College, Art Dept, Madison WI (S)

Edgewood College, DeRicci Gallery, Madison WI (M)

Edina Art Center, Margaret Foss Gallery, Edina MN (M)

Edinboro University of Pennsylvania, Art Dept, Edinboro PA (S)

Edison Community College, Gallery of Fine Arts, Fort Myers FL (S)

Edison State College, Bob Rauschenberg Gallery, Fort Myers FL (M)

Edith R Wyle Research Library of The Craft & Folk Art Museum, see LA County Museum of Art, Los Angeles CA

Edmundson Art Foundation, Inc, Des Moines Art Center, Des Moines IA (M,L)

Education Alliance, Art School & Gallery, New York NY (S)

Edward-Dean Museum & Gardens, see Riverside County Museum, Cherry Valley CA

Egan Institute of Maritime Studies, Nantucket MA (M)

Eide-Dalrymple Gallery, see Augustana College, Sioux Falls SD

1890 House-Museum & Center for the Arts, Cortland NY (M,L)

18th Street Arts Complex, Santa Monica CA (A)

800 Gallery & Rotary Ice House Gallery, West Long Branch NJ (M)

Dwight D Eisenhower, Abilene KS (L)

Eiteljorg Museum of American Indians & Western Art, Indianapolis IN (M)

Ekstrom Library Photographic Archives, see University of Louisville, Louisville KY

El Camino College Art Gallery, Torrance CA (M)

El Camino College, Division of Fine Arts, Torrance CA (S)

Elder Gallery, Charlotte NC (M)

Elder Gallery, see Nebraska Wesleyan University, Lincoln NE

Eleanor Squire Library, see Cleveland Botanical Garden, Cleveland OH

Electronic Arts Intermix (EAI), New York NY (A)

Elgin Community College, Fine Arts Dept, Elgin IL (S)

Elizabeth City State University, School of Arts & Humanities, Dept of Art, Elizabeth City NC (S)

The Ella Carothers Dunnegan Gallery of Art, Bolivar MO (M)

Leonard & Bina Ellen Art Gallery, see Concordia University, Montreal PQ

Ellen Noel Art Museum of the Permian Basin, Odessa TX (M)

Elliott Museum, see Historical Society of Martin County, Stuart FL

Ellis County Museum Inc, Waxahachie TX (M)

Ellsworth Community College, Dept of Fine Arts, Iowa Falls IA (S)

Elmhurst Art Museum, Elmhurst IL (M)

Elmhurst College, Art Dept, Elmhurst IL (S)

Elmira College, Art Dept, Elmira NY (S)

Elmira College, George Waters Gallery, Elmira NY (M)

El Museo del Barrio, New York NY (M)

El Museo Latino, Omaha NE (M)

El Paso Museum of Archaeology, see City of El Paso, El Paso TX

El Pueblo de Los Angeles Historical Monument, Los Angeles CA (A)

Elverhoj Museum of History and Art, Solvang CA (M)

Walter Elwood Museum, see Mohawk Valley Heritage Association, Inc, Amsterdam NY

Embroiderers Guild of America, Margaret Parshall Gallery, Louisville KY (A,L)

eMediaLoft.org, New York NY (M)

Emerald Empire Art Association, Emerald Art Center, Springfield OR (A)

Emerson Gallery, see Hamilton College, Clinton NY

Emily Carr Institute of Art & Design, The Charles H Scott Gallery, Vancouver BC (M,L)

Emily Carr University of Art + Design, Vancouver BC (S)

Emmanuel College, Art Dept, Boston MA (S)

Emmanuel Gallery, Denver CO (M)

Emma Willard School, Dept of Visual & Performing Arts, Troy NY (S)

Emory University, Art History Dept, Atlanta GA (S)

Emory University, Michael C Carlos Museum, Atlanta GA (M)

Emporia State University, Dept of Art, Emporia KS (S)

Emporia State University, Norman R Eppink Art Gallery, Emporia KS (M)

Emprise Bank Research Library, see Wichita Art Museum, Wichita KS

Enabled Arts Center, see VSA Arts of New Mexico, Albuquerque NM

Endicott College, School of Visual & Performing Arts, Beverly MA (S)

En Foco, Inc, Bronx NY (M)

Englewood Library, Fine Arts Dept, Englewood NJ (L)

Amos Eno, Brooklyn NY (M)

Environic Foundation International Library, South Bend IN (L)

Environment Canada - Parks Canada, Laurier House, National Historic Site, Ottawa ON (M)

Norman R Eppink Art Gallery, see Emporia State University, Emporia KS

Max Epstein Archive, see University of Chicago, Chicago IL

Eric Sloane Museum, see Department of Economic & Community Development, Kent CT

Erie Art Museum, Erie PA (M)

Erie County Historical Society, Erie PA (M)

The Erman B. White Gallery, El Dorado KS (M)

Escuela de Artes Plasticas de Puerto Rico, San Juan PR (S)

Escuela de Artes Plasticas de Puerto Rico, San Juan PR (S)

Wharton Esherick, Paoli PA (M,L)

Eskimo Museum, Churchill MB (M,L)

Esplanade Arts & Heritage Centre, Medicine Hat AB (M)

Essex Art Association, Inc, Essex CT (A)

Essex Art Center, Lawrence MA (M)

Essex Historical Society and Shipbuilding Museum, Essex MA (M)

Estevan National Exhibition Centre Inc, Estevan Art Gallery & Museum, Estevan SK (M)

Esvelt Gallery, see Columbia Basin College, Pasco WA

The Ethel Wright Mohamed Stitchery Museum, Belzoni MS (M)

Agnes Etherington Art Centre, see Queen's University, Kingston ON

Ethnic American Slide Library, see University of South Alabama, Mobile AL

Eula Mae Edwards Museum & Gallery, Clovis NM (M)

Euphrat Museum of Art, see De Anza College, Cupertino CA

Eureka Fine Art Gallery, Eureka Springs AR (M)

Eva G Farris Art Gallery, see Thomas More College, Crestview KY

Evangel University, Humanities-Art Dept, Springfield MO (S)

Evanston Art Center, Evanston IL (A)

Evanston Historical Society, Charles Gates Dawes House, Evanston IL (M)

Evansville Museum of Arts, History & Science, Evansville IN (M,L)

Everett Community College, Art Dept, Everett WA (S)

Evergreen Museum & Library, see Johns Hopkins University, Baltimore MD

Evergreen State College, Evergreen Gallery, Olympia WA (M)

Everhart Museum, Scranton PA (M)

Everson Museum of Art, Syracuse NY (M)

Ewing Gallery of Art and Architecture, see University of Tennessee, Knoxville TN

The Exhibition Alliance, Hamilton NY (A)

Exit Art, San Leandro CA (M)

Exploratorium, San Francisco CA (A)

Eye Level Gallery, Halifax NS (M)

Eyes & Ears Foundation, San Francisco CA (A)

The Fabric Workshop & Museum, Philadelphia PA (M)

Henry Failing Art & Music Dept, see Multnomah County Library, Portland OR

Fairbanks Arts Association, Bear Gallery, Fairbanks AK (A)

Fairbanks Museum & Planetarium, Saint Johnsbury VT (M)

Fairfield Art Association, Fairfield IA (L)

Fairfield Historical Society, Fairfield Museum & History Center, Fairfield CT (A,L)

Fairfield University, Visual & Performing Arts, Fairfield CT (S)

Fairfield University, Thomas J Walsh Art Gallery, Fairfield CT (M)

Fairleigh Dickinson University, Edward Williams Gallery, Hackensack NJ (M)

Fairleigh Dickinson University, Fine Arts Dept, Madison NJ (S)

Fairmont State College, Div of Fine Arts, Fairmont WV (S)

Fairmount Park Art Association, Philadelphia PA (A)

Falkirk Cultural Center, see City of San Rafael, San Rafael CA

Fallingwater, see Western Pennsylvania Conservancy, Mill Run PA

Fall River Historical Society, Fall River MA (M)

Famille des Arts, see Universite du Quebec a Montreal, Montreal PQ

Farmington Valley Arts Center, Avon CT (A)

Farmington Village Green & Library Association, Stanley-Whitman House, Farmington CT (M)

Farnham Gallery, see Simpson College, Indianola IA

William A Farnsworth, Museum, Rockland ME (M,L)

Fashion Institute of Technology, Art & Design Division, New York NY (S)

Fashion Institute of Technology, The Museum at FIT, New York NY (M,L)

Father Weyland SVD Gallery, see Divine Word College, Epworth IA

James H Faulkner, Art Dept, Bay Minette AL (S)

Faulkner Memorial Art Wing, see Santa Barbara Public Central Library, Santa Barbara CA

Favell Museum of Western Art & Indian Artifacts, Klamath Falls OR (M)

Fawick Art Gallery, see Baldwin-Wallace College, Berea OH

Fayette Art Museum, see City of Fayette, Alabama, Fayette AL

Fayetteville State University, Performing & Fine Arts, Fayetteville NC (S)

Feather River Community College, Art Dept, Quincy CA (S)

Harriet FeBland, New York NY (S)

Federal Reserve Bank of Cleveland, Cleveland OH (C)

Federal Reserve Bank of Minneapolis, Minneapolis MN (C)

Federal Reserve Board, Art Gallery, Washington DC (M)

Federation of Modern Painters & Sculptors, New York NY (O)

Fellowship of the Pennsylvania Academy of the Fine Arts, see Pennsylvania Academy of the Fine Arts, Philadelphia PA

Fellows of Contemporary Art, Los Angeles CA (A)

Ferguson Library, Stamford CT (L)

Ferris State University, Visual Communication Dept, Big Rapids MI (S)

Festival - Institute, see James Dick Foundation, Round Top TX

Fetherston Foundation, Packwood House Museum, Lewisburg PA (M)

Field Museum, Chicago IL (M,L)

The Fields Sculpture Park at Omi International Arts Center, Ghent NY (M)

55 Mercer Gallery, New York NY (M)

Figge Art Museum, Davenport IA (M,L)

Fillmore County Historical Society, Fillmore County History Center, Fountain MN (L)

The Filson Historical Society, Louisville KY (A,L)

Fine Arts Association, School of Fine Arts, Willoughby OH (A)

Fine Arts Center for the New River Valley, Pulaski VA (M)

The Fine Arts Center of Hot Springs, Hot Springs AR (M)

Fine Arts Museums of San Francisco, M H de Young Museum, San Francisco CA (M)

Fine Arts Work Center, Provincetown MA (A)

Finger Lakes Community College, Visual & Performing Arts Dept, Canandaigua NY (S)

Finlandia Univ, International School of Art and Design, Hancock MI (S)

Firehouse Art Center, Norman OK (M)

Firehouse Art Gallery, see Nassau Community College, Garden City NY

Firehouse Center & Gallery, Bainbridge GA (M)

Firehouse Gallery, see Martha's Vineyard Center for the Visual Arts, Oak Bluffs MA

Firelands Association for the Visual Arts, Oberlin OH (A)

Fireweed Gallery, Homer AK (M)

First Horizon National Corp, First Tennessee Heritage Collection, Memphis TN (C)

The First National Bank of Chicago, Art Collection, Chicago IL (C)

First State Bank, They Also Ran Gallery, Norton KS (C)

First Street Gallery, New York NY (M)

First Tennessee Bank, Memphis TN (C)

First Tennessee Heritage Collection, see First Horizon National Corp, Memphis TN

Fisher Art Center, see Bard College, Annandale-on-Hudson NY

Fisher Art Gallery, Marshalltown IA (M)

Fisher Gallery, see Cornish College of the Arts, Seattle WA

Jonathan Fisher Memorial, Inc, see Parson Fisher House, Blue Hill ME

Fisher Landau Center for Art, Long Island City NY (M)

Fishkill Historical Society, Van Wyck Homestead Museum, Fishkill NY (M)

Fisk University, Art Dept, Nashville TN (S)

Fisk University, Carl Van Vechten Gallery, Nashville TN (M,L)

Fitchburg Art Museum, Fitchburg MA (M)

Fitton Center for Creative Arts, Hamilton OH (S)

Fitton Center for Creative Arts, Hamilton OH (M)

Five Civilized Tribes Museum, Muskogee OK (M,L)

Flag House & 1812 Museum, see Star-Spangled Banner Flag House Association, Baltimore MD

Flagler College, Visual Arts Dept, Saint Augustine FL (S)

Flamingo Gallery, see Las Vegas-Clark County Library District, Las Vegas NV

Flanagan Valley Campus Art Gallery, see Community College of Rhode Island, Warwick RI

Flashpoint, Washington DC (M)

Flaten Art Museum, see Saint Olaf College, Northfield MN

John M Flaxman Library, see School of the Art Institute of Chicago, Chicago IL

Paul D Fleck Library & Archives, see Banff Centre, Banff AB

Fleet Boston Financial, Gallery, Boston MA (C)

Fleetwood Museum, North Plainfield NJ (M)

Samuel S Fleisher Art Memorial, see Philadelphia Museum of Art, Philadelphia PA

Samuel S Fleisher, Philadelphia PA (S)

Robert Hull Fleming Museum, see University of Vermont, Burlington VT

Flint Hills Gallery, Cottonwood Falls KS (M)

Flint Institute of Arts, Flint MI (M,L)

Flippo Gallery, Ashland VA (M)

Florence & Chafetz Hillel House at Boston University, Boston University Art Gallery at the Stone Gallery, Boston MA (M)

Florence Museum, Florence SC (M)

Florida A & M University, Dept of Visual Arts, Humanities & Theatre, Tallahassee FL (S)

Florida Atlantic University, D F Schmidt College of Arts & Letters Dept of Visual Arts & Art History, Boca Raton FL (S)

Florida Atlantic University, University Galleries/Ritter Art Gallery/Schmidt Center Gallery, Boca Raton FL (M)

Florida College, Division of Art, Temple Terrace FL (S)

Florida Community College at Jacksonville, South Campus, Art Dept, Jacksonville FL (S)

Florida Council on Arts & Culture, see Florida Department of State, Division of Cultural Affairs, Tallahassee FL

Florida Craftsmen Gallery, Saint Petersburg FL (M)

Florida Department of Environmental Protection, Stephen Foster Folk Culture Center State Park, White Springs FL (M)

Florida Department of State, Division of Cultural Affairs, Florida Council on Arts & Culture, Tallahassee FL (A)

Florida Folklife Programs, Tallahassee FL (A,L)

Florida Gateway College, Liberal Art Dept, Lake City FL (S)

Florida International University, School of Art & Art History, Miami FL (S)

Florida International University, The Patricia & Phillip Frost Art Museum, Miami FL (M)

Florida Keys Community College, Fine Arts Div, Key West FL (S)

Florida Museum of Women Artists, Deland FL (M)

Florida School of the Arts, Visual Arts, Palatka FL (S)

Florida Southern College, Department of Art & Art History, Lakeland FL (S)

Florida Southern College, Melvin Art Gallery, Lakeland FL (M)

Florida State College at Jacksonville, South Gallery, Jacksonville FL (M)

Florida State University, Art Dept, Tallahassee FL (S)

Florida State University, Museum of Fine Arts, Tallahassee FL (M)

Florida State University, John & Mable Ringling Museum of Art, Sarasota FL (M,L)

Roswell P Flower, Watertown NY (M)

James Lemont Fogg Memorial Library, see Art Center College of Design, Pasadena CA

William Hayes Fogg Art Museum, see Harvard University, Cambridge MA

Folger Shakespeare, Washington DC (L)

Folk Art Society of America, Richmond VA (M)

Fondo del Sol, Visual Art & Media Center, Washington DC (M)

Fontbonne University, Fine Art Dept, Saint Louis MO (S)

Foosaner Art Museum, Melbourne FL (M)

Foothill College, Fine Arts & Communications Div, Los Altos Hills CA (S)

Foothills Art Center, Inc, Golden CO (A)

Forbes Library, Northampton MA (L)

Forbes Magazine, Inc, Forbes Collection, New York NY (C)

Edsel & Eleanor Ford, Grosse Pointe Shores MI (M)

Ford Gallery, see Eastern Michigan University, Ypsilanti MI

Hallie Ford Museum of Art, see Willamette University, Salem OR

Fordham University, Art Dept, New York NY (S)

Henry Ford Museum & Greenfield Village, see Ford Motor Company, Dearborn MI

Ford Motor Company, Henry Ford Museum & Greenfield Village, Dearborn MI (C)

Foreman Gallery, see Hartwick College, Oneonta NY

Forest Hills Adult and Youth Center, Forest Hills NY (S)

Forest Lawn Museum, Glendale CA (M)

Forges du Saint-Maurice National Historic Site, Trois Rivieres PQ (M)

Forsyth Library, see Fort Hays State University, Hays KS

Glendale Community College, Visual & Performing Arts Div, Glendale CA (S)

Glendale Public Library, Brand Library & Art Center, Glendale CA (M)

Glendon Gallery, see York University, Toronto ON

Glenhyrst Art Gallery of Brant, Brantford ON (M)

Glenville State College, Dept of Fine Arts, Glenville WV (S)

Glenwood Center for the Arts, Glenwood Springs CO (M)

Glessner House Museum, Chicago IL (M)

Gloridale Partnership, National Museum of Woodcarving, Custer SD (M)

Gloucester County College, Liberal Arts Dept, Sewell NJ (S)

Glynn Art Association, Saint Simons Island GA (A)

Go Antiques, Inc, Atlanta GA (A)

Charles B Goddard, Ardmore OK (A)

Goddard College, Dept of Art, Plainfield VT (S)

Godwin-Ternbach Museum, see Queens College, City University of New York, Flushing NY

Goethe-Institut New York, Mini/Goethe-Institut Curatorial Residencies Ludlow 38, New York NY (M)

Gogebic Community College, Fine Arts Dept, Ironwood MI (S)

Golden Isles Arts & Humanities Association, Brunswick GA (A)

Golden State Mutual Life Insurance Company, Afro-American Art Collection, Los Angeles CA (C)

Golden West College, Visual Art Dept, Huntington Beach CA (S)

Fanette Goldman & Carolyn Greenfield Gallery, see Daemen College, Amherst NY

Goldstein Museum of Design, see University of Minnesota, Saint Paul MN

Gonzaga University, Art Gallery, Spokane WA (M)

Gonzaga University, Dept of Art, Spokane WA (S)

Gaston T Gooch Library & Learning Resource Center, see Navarro College, Corsicana TX

Gordon College, Dept of Fine Arts, Barnesville GA (S)

Donald B Gordon Memorial Library, see Palm Beach County Parks & Recreation Department, Delray Beach FL

Goshen College, Art Dept, Goshen IN (S)

Goshen Historical Society, Goshen CT (M)

Goucher College, Art & Art History Dept, Baltimore MD (S)

Goucher College, Rosenberg Gallery, Baltimore MD (M)

Governors State University, College of Arts & Science, Art Dept, University Park IL (S)

Grace College, Dept of Art, Winona Lake IN (S)

Graceland Museum & American Saddlehorse Museum, see Audrain County Historical Society, Mexico MO

Graceland University, Fine Arts Div, Lamoni IA (S)

Grace Museum, Inc, Abilene TX (M)

Grambling State University, Art Dept, Grambling LA (S)

Grand Canyon University, Art Dept, Phoenix AZ (S)

Grand Marais Art Colony, Grand Marais MN (S)

Grand Prairie Arts Council, Inc, Arts Center of the Grand Prairie, Stuttgart AR (A)

Grand Rapids Art Museum, Grand Rapids MI (M,L)

Grand Rapids Community College, Visual Art Dept, Grand Rapids MI (S)

Grand Rapids Public Library, Grand Rapids MI (L)

Grand Rapids Public Museum, Public Museum of Grand Rapids, Grand Rapids MI (M)

Grand River Museum, Lemmon SD (M)

Grand Teton National Park Service, Colter Bay Indian Arts Museum, Moose WY (A)

Grand Valley State University, Art & Design Dept, Allendale MI (S)

Grand View College, Art Dept, Des Moines IA (S)

Grants Pass Museum of Art, Grants Pass OR (M)

Grant Wood Memorial Park & Gallery, see Paint 'N Palette Club, Anamosa IA

Graphic Artists Guild, New York NY (A)

The Graphic Eye Gallery, Port Washington NY (M)

Grass Roots Art & Community Effort (GRACE), Firehouse Gallery, Hardwick VT (M)

Grassroots Art Center, Lucas KS (M)

The Gray Gallery, see Quincy University, Quincy IL

Grayson County College, Art Dept, Denison TX (S)

Wellington B Gray Gallery, see East Carolina University, Greenville NC

Great Lakes Historical Society, Inland Seas Maritime Museum, Vermilion OH (M)

Great Plains Art Museum, see University of Nebraska-Lincoln, Lincoln NE

Greene & Greene Archives, see University of Southern California/The Gamble House, San Marino CA

Greene County Historical Society, Xenia OH (A)

Greene County Historical Society, Bronck Museum, Coxsackie NY (M)

Greenfield Community College, Art Dept, Greenfield MA (S)

Green Hill Center for North Carolina Art, Greensboro NC (A)

Ida Green Gallery, see Austin College, Sherman TX

Green Mountain College, Dept of Art, Poultney VT (S)

Green Mountain Fine Art Gallery, Stowe VT (M)

Green Research Library, see The Old Jail Art Center, Albany TX

Green River Community College, Art Dept, Auburn WA (S)

Greensboro College, Irene Cullis Gallery, Greensboro NC (M)

Greensboro College, Dept of Art, Division of Fine Arts, Greensboro NC (S)

Greenville College, Art Dept, Greenville IL (S)

Greenville College, Richard W Bock Sculpture Collection, Almira College House, Greenville IL (M,L)

Greenville County Museum of Art, Greenville SC (M)

Greenville County Museum of Art Center for Museum Education, Greenville SC (S)

Greenville Museum of Art, Inc, Greenville NC (A,L)

Greenville Technical College, Visual Arts Dept, Greenville SC (S)

Greenwich Art Society Inc, Greenwich CT (A,M)

Greenwich Historical Society/ Bush-Holley House, see Bush-Holley Historic Site & Storehouse Gallery, Cos Cob CT

Greenwich House Inc, Greenwich House Pottery, New York NY (S)

Greenwich House Pottery, First Floor Gallery, New York NY (M,L)

Greenwich Library, Greenwich CT (L)

Sir Wilfred Grenfell College Art Gallery, see Memorial University of Newfoundland, Corner Brook NF

Allie Griffin Art Gallery, see Weyburn Arts Council, Weyburn SK

Griffis Sculpture Park, see Ashford Hollow Foundation for Visual & Performing Arts, East Otto NY

Grinnell College, Dept of Art, Grinnell IA (S)

Grinnell College, Faulconer Gallery, Grinnell IA (M)

Florence Griswold Museum, see Lyme Historical Society, Old Lyme CT

Grodin Permanent Collection Museum, see League of New Hampshire Craftsmen, Concord NH

Grohmann Museum, Milwaukee WI (M)

Grolier Club Library, New York NY (L)

Grossmont College, Art Dept, El Cajon CA (S)

Grossmont Community College, Hyde Art Gallery, El Cajon CA (M)

The Renee & Chaim Gross Foundation, Chaim Gross Studio, New York NY (M)

Grounds for Sculpture, Hamilton NJ (M)

Grunwald Center for the Graphic Arts at Hammer Museum, see University of California, Los Angeles, Los Angeles CA

Emile A Gruppe Gallery, Jericho VT (M)

Guadalupe Cultural Arts Center, San Antonio TX (A)

Guadalupe Historic Foundation, Santuario de Guadalupe, Santa Fe NM (A)

John Simon Guggenheim, New York NY (A)

Guggenheim Museum Soho, New York NY (M)

Solomon R Guggenheim, New York NY (M,L)

Guild Arts Center, Silvermine, New Canaan CT (S)

Guilde canadienne des metiers d'art, Canadian Guild of Crafts, Montreal PQ (A)

Guild Hall of East Hampton, Inc, Guild Hall Museum, East Hampton NY (M)

Guild of Book Workers, New York NY (O,L)

The Guild of Boston Artists, Boston MA (A)

Guild of Creative Art, Shrewsbury NJ (S)

Guilford College, Art Dept, Greensboro NC (S)

Guilford College, Art Gallery, Greensboro NC (M)

Guilford Technical Community College, Commercial Art Dept, Jamestown NC (S)

Gulf Beach Art Center, Indian Rocks Beach FL (M)

Gulf Coast Community College, Division of Visual & Performing Arts, Panama City FL (S)

GumTree Museum of Art, Tupelo MS (M)

Jessica Gund Memorial Library, see Cleveland Institute of Art, Cleveland OH

Emery A Gunnin Architectural Library, see Clemson University, Clemson SC

Gunnison Arts Center, Gunnison CO (M)

Gunston Hall Plantation, Mason Neck VA (M,L)

George Gustav Heye Center, see National Museum of the American Indian, New York NY

Gustavus Adolphus College, Art & Art History Dept, Saint Peter MN (S)

H.A. & Mary K Chapman Library, see Philbrook Museum of Art, Tulsa OK

Haas Gallery of Art, see Bloomsburg University of Pennsylvania, Bloomsburg PA

Haffenreffer Museum of Anthropology, see Brown University, Providence RI

Hagadorn House, The 1800-37 Museum, see Almond Historical Society, Inc, Almond NY

Hagerstown Junior College, Art Dept, Hagerstown MD (S)

Haggerty Museum of Art, see Marquette University, Milwaukee WI

The Haggin Museum, see The San Joaquin Pioneer & Historical Society, Stockton CA

Halifax Historical Society, Inc, Halifax Historical Museum, Daytona Beach FL (M)

Hallmark Cards, Inc, Hallmark Art Collection, Kansas City MO (C,L)

Hall of Fame for Great Americans, see Bronx Community College (CUNY), Bronx NY

Hall of State, see Dallas Historical Society, Dallas TX

Hallwalls Contemporary Arts Center, Buffalo NY (M)

Halsey Institute of Contemporary Art, see College of Charleston School of Arts, Charleston SC

Hambidge Center for Creative Arts & Sciences, Rabun Gap GA (M)

Hamilton College, Art Dept, Clinton NY (S)

Hamilton College, Emerson Gallery, Clinton NY (M)

Hamline University, Dept of Studio Arts & Art History, Saint Paul MN (S)

Hamline University Studio Arts & Art History Depts, Gallery, Saint Paul MN (M)

Hammond Castle Museum, Gloucester MA (M)

Hammond-Harwood House Association, Inc, Hammond-Harwood House, Annapolis MD (M)

Hammond Museum & Japanese Stroll Garden, Cross-Cultural Center, North Salem NY (M)

Hammonds House Museum, Atlanta GA (M)

Hampden-Booth Theatre Library, New York NY (L)

Hampden-Sydney College, Fine Arts Dept, Hampden Sydney VA (S)

Hampshire County Public Library, Romney WV (L)

Hampton Arts Commission, see City of Hampton, Hampton VA

Hampton University, Dept of Fine & Performing Arts, Hampton VA (S)

Hampton University, University Museum, Hampton VA (M)

Hancock County Trustees of Public Reservations, Woodlawn: Museum, Gardens & Park, Ellsworth ME (M)

Hancock Shaker Village, Inc, Pittsfield MA (M)

Handforth Gallery, see Tacoma Public Library, Tacoma WA

Handweavers Guild of America, Suwanee GA (A)

Handwerker Gallery of Art, see Ithaca College, Ithaca NY

Hannibal La Grange College, Art Dept, Hannibal MO (S)

Hanover College, Dept of Art, Hanover IN (S)

Dane G Hansen, Logan KS (M)

Clarence B Hanson Jr Library, see Birmingham Museum of Art, Birmingham AL

Harbourfront Centre, The Power Plant Contemporary Art Gallery, Toronto ON (M)

Harcourt House Arts Centre, see Where Edmonton Community Artists Network Society, Edmonton AB

Harcum College, Fashion Design, Bryn Mawr PA (S)

Harding University, Dept of Art & Design, Searcy AR (S)

Hardin-Simmons University, Art Dept, Abilene TX (S)

Francis Hardy Gallery, Fish Creek WI (M)

Jeannette Hare Art Gallery, see Northwood University, West Palm Beach FL

Harford Community College, Visual, Performing and Applied Arts Division, Bel Air MD (S)

Harlin Museum, West Plains MO (M)

Harlow Gallery, see Kennebec Valley Art Association, Hallowell ME

Harness Racing Museum & Hall of Fame, Goshen NY (M)

Samuel P Harn Museum of Art, see University of Florida, Gainesville FL

Harold Washington College, see City Colleges of Chicago, Chicago IL

Harrington College of Design, Design Library, Chicago IL (L)

Harrington Institute of Interior Design, Chicago IL (S)

Mark Harrington Library, see San Fernando Valley Historical Society, Mission Hills CA

Harrisburg Area Community College, Division of Communications, Humanities & the Arts, Harrisburg PA (S)

Harrison County Historical Museum, Marshall TX (M)

Harry & Laura Nohr Gallery, see University of Wisconsin - Platteville, Platteville WI

Hart-Cluett Mansion, 1827, see Rensselaer County Historical Society, Troy NY

Hopper Resource Library, see The Butler Institute of American Art, Youngstown OH

Horizons Unlimited Supplementary Educational Center, Science Museum, Salisbury NC (M)

Hostos Center for the Arts & Culture, Bronx NY (A)

Hot Shops Art Center, Omaha NE (M)

Houchens Gallery, see Capitol Arts Alliance, Bowling Green KY

Houghton College, Art Dept, Houghton NY (S)

Housatonic Community College, Art Dept, Bridgeport CT (S)

Housatonic Community College, Housatonic Museum of Art, Bridgeport CT (M,L)

House of Happy Walls, see Jack London, Glen Ellen CA

Houston Baptist University, Dept of Art, Houston TX (S)

Houston Baptist University, Museum of American Architecture and Decorative Arts, Houston TX (M)

Houston Center For Photography, Houston TX (A)

Houston Museum of Decorative Arts, Chattanooga TN (M)

Houston Public Library, Houston TX (L)

Howard College, Art Dept, Big Spring TX (S)

Howard Community College, The Rouse Company Foundation Gallery, Columbia MD (M)

Howard County Arts Council, Ellicott City MD (A)

Howard Payne University, Dept of Art, Brownwood TX (S)

Howard University, Gallery of Art, Washington DC (M,L)

James Howe Gallery, see Kean University, Union NJ

Hoxie Gallery, see Westerly Public Library, Westerly RI

Hoyt Center for the Arts, New Castle PA (M)

Anna & Harlan Hubbard Gallery, see Frankfort Community Public Library, Frankfort IN

Hubbell Trading Post National Historic Site, see National Park Service, Ganado AZ

HUB Robeson Galleries, see The Pennsylvania State University, University Park PA

Grace Hudson Museum & The Sun House, see City of Ukiah, Ukiah CA

Hudson Guild Gallery, see Hudson Guild, New York NY

Hudson Guild, Hudson Guild Gallery, New York NY (M)

The Hudson River Museum, Yonkers NY (M)

Hudson River Reference Collection, see Alice Curtis Desmond, Garrison NY

Hudson Valley Art Association, Brooklyn NY (A)

Hughes Fine Arts Center-Col Eugene Myers Art Gallery, see University of North Dakota, Grand Forks ND

Huguenot Historical Society of New Paltz Galleries, New Paltz NY (M)

Hui No'eau Visual Arts Center, Gallery and Gift Shop, Makawao Maui HI (M)

Marie Hull Gallery, see Hinds Community College District, Raymond MS

Hulsey Gallery-Norick Art Center, see Oklahoma City University, Oklahoma City OK

Humber College of Applied Arts & Technology, The School of Media Studies, Toronto ON (S)

Humboldt Arts Council, Morris Graves Museum of Art, Eureka CA (A)

Humboldt State University, College of Arts & Humanities, Art Dept, Arcata CA (S)

Stephen Huneck Gallery at Dog Mountain, Saint Johnsbury VT (M)

Cecille R Hunt Gallery, see Webster University, Webster Groves MO

Hunter College, Art Dept, New York NY (S)

Hunterdon Art Museum, Clinton NJ (A)

Hunter Museum of American Art, Chattanooga TN (M,L)

H A Hunt Memorial Library, see Fort Valley State College, Fort Valley GA

Huntingdon College, Dept of Art, Montgomery AL (S)

Huntington Beach Art Center, Huntington Beach CA (M)

Huntington College, Art Dept, Huntington IN (S)

The Huntington Library, Art Collections & Botanical Gardens, San Marino CA (M,L)

Huntington Museum of Art, Huntington WV (M)

Huntington University, Robert E Wilson Art Gallery, Huntington IN (M)

Hunt Institute for Botanical Documentation, see Carnegie Mellon University, Pittsburgh PA

Hunt Library, see Carnegie Mellon University, Pittsburgh PA

The Huntsville Art League (HAL), Gallery & Visual Arts Center, Huntsville AL (A)

Huntsville Museum of Art, Huntsville AL (M,L)

Huronia Museum, Gallery of Historic Huronia, Midland ON (M)

Hussian School of Art, Commercial Art Dept, Philadelphia PA (S)

Hutchinson Art Association, Hutchinson Art Center, Hutchinson KS (A)

Hutchinson Community College, Visual Arts Dept, Hutchinson KS (S)

Hyde Art Gallery, see Grossmont Community College, El Cajon CA

Hyde Collection Trust, Glens Falls NY (M,L)

Olive Hyde Art Gallery, see City of Fremont, Fremont CA

Hyde Park Art Center, Chicago IL (M)

Stan Hywet, Akron OH (M)

Idaho Commission on the Arts, Boise ID (A)

Idaho Historical Museum, Boise ID (M)

Idaho State University, John B Davis Gallery of Fine Art, Pocatello ID (M)

Idaho State University, Dept of Art & Pre-Architecture, Pocatello ID (S)

Idyllwild Arts Academy, Idyllwild CA (S)

IFP MN Center for Media Arts, Saint Paul MN (M)

Illinois Alliance for Arts Education (IAAE), DeKalb IL (A)

Illinois Artisans & Visitors Centers, see Illinois State Museum, Chicago IL

Illinois Artisans Shop, see Illinois State Museum, Chicago IL

Illinois Benedictine University, Department of Fine Arts, Lisle IL (S)

Illinois Central College, Arts & Communication Dept, East Peoria IL (S)

Illinois Historic Preservation Agency, Bishop Hill State Historic Site, Bishop Hill IL (M)

The Illinois Institute of Art - Chicago, Chicago IL (S)

Illinois Institute of Technology, College of Architecture, Chicago IL (S)

Illinois State Museum, Chicago Gallery, Chicago IL (M)

Illinois State Museum, ISM Lockport Gallery, Chicago Gallery & Southern Illinois Art Gallery, Springfield IL (M,L)

Illinois State University, College of Fine Arts, Normal IL (S)

Illinois State University, University Galleries, Normal IL (M,L)

Illinois Valley Community College, Division of Humanities & Fine Arts, Oglesby IL (S)

Illinois Wesleyan University, Merwin & Wakeley Galleries, Bloomington IL (M,L)

Illinois Wesleyan University, School of Art, Bloomington IL (S)

Illustration House Inc, Gallery Auction House, New York NY (M)

Imago Galleries, Palm Desert CA (M)

Imhoff Art Gallery, Alberta SK (M)

Imperato Collection of West African Artifacts, see Martin and Osa Johnson, Chanute KS

Imperial Calcasieu Museum, Lake Charles LA (M,L)

Imperial Valley College, Art Dept, Imperial CA (S)

Independence Historical Museum & Art Center, Independence KS (M)

Independence National Historical Park, Philadelphia PA (M,L)

Independence Seaport Museum, Philadelphia PA (M,L)

Independent Curators International, New York NY (A)

Index of American Design, see National Gallery of Art, Washington DC

Indiana Landmarks, Morris-Butler House, Indianapolis IN (M,L)

Indianapolis Art Center, Marilyn K. Glick School of Art, Indianapolis IN (A)

Indianapolis Marion County Public Library, Central Library, Indianapolis IN (L)

Indianapolis Museum of Art, Indianapolis IN (M,L)

Indianapolis Museum of Contemporary Art, Indianapolis IN (M)

Indiana-Purdue University, Dept of Fine Arts, Fort Wayne IN (S)

Indian Arts & Crafts Association, Albuquerque NM (A)

Indian Arts & Crafts Board, see United States Department of the Interior, Washington DC

Indian Arts & Crafts Board, US Dept of the Interior, Sioux Indian Museum, Rapid City SD (M)

Indiana State Museum, Indianapolis IN (M)

Indiana State University, Dept of Art, Terre Haute IN (S)

Indiana State University, University Art Gallery, Terre Haute IN (M)

Indiana University, Bloomington, Henry Radford Hope School of Fine Arts, Bloomington IN (S)

Indiana University, Art Museum, Bloomington IN (M)

Indiana University-East, Humanities Dept, Richmond IN (S)

Indiana University, Fine Arts Library, Bloomington IN (L)

Indiana University of Pennsylvania, College of Fine Arts, Indiana PA (S)

Indiana University of Pennsylvania, Kipp Gallery, Indiana PA (M)

Indiana University-Purdue University, Indianapolis, Herron School of Art & Design, Indianapolis IN (S)

Indiana University - Purdue University at Indianapolis, Herron Galleries, Indianapolis IN (M)

Indiana University South Bend, Fine Arts Dept, South Bend IN (S)

Indiana University-Southeast, Fine Arts Dept, New Albany IN (S)

Indiana Wesleyan University, School of Arts & Humanities, Division of Art, Marion IN (S)

Indian Center Museum, see Mid-America All-Indian Center, Wichita KS

Indian Hills Community College, Ottumwa Campus, Dept of Art, Ottumwa IA (S)

Indian Hills Community College, Dept of Art, Centerville IA (S)

Indian Museum of Lake County, Ohio, see Archaeological Society of Ohio, Willoughby OH

Indian Museum of North America, Native American Educational & Cultural Center & Crazy Horse Memorial Library (Reference), see Crazy Horse Memorial, Crazy Horse SD

Indian Pueblo Cultural Center, Albuquerque NM (M)

Indian River Community College, Fine Arts Dept, Fort Pierce FL (S)

Individual Artists of Oklahoma, Oklahoma City OK (M)

Industrial Designers Society of America, Herndon VA (O)

Ingalls Library, see The Cleveland Museum of Art, Cleveland OH

Ingraham Memorial Research Library, see Litchfield History Museum, Litchfield CT

Inland Seas Maritime Museum, see Great Lakes Historical Society, Vermilion OH

Inner-City Arts, Los Angeles CA (S)

Inquilinos Boricuas en Accion, Boston MA (A)

Installation Gallery, San Diego CA (A)

Institut des Arts au Saguenay, Centre National D'Exposition a Jonquiere, Jonquiere PQ (M)

Institute for Arts & Humanities Education, New Jersey Summer Arts Institute, Staten Island NY (S)

Institute of American Indian Arts, Museum of Contemporary Native Arts, Santa Fe NM (S)

Institute of American Indian Arts, Museum of Contemporary Native Arts, Santa Fe NM (M,L)

Institute of Contemporary Art, Boston MA (M)

The Institute of Contemporary Art, see Maine College of Art, Portland ME

Institute of Fine Arts Visual Resources Collection, see New York University, New York NY

Institute of Puerto Rican Arts & Culture, Chicago IL (M)

Institute of Puerto Rican Culture, Instituto de Cultura Puertorriquena, San Juan PR (M,A,L)

Institute of Puerto Rican Culture, Instituto de Cultura Puertorriquena, San Juan PR (M,A,L)

Institute of Puerto Rican Culture, Museo Fuerte Conde de Mirasol, Vieques PR (M)

Institute of Puerto Rican Culture, Museo Fuerte Conde de Mirasol, Vieques PR (M)

Institute of Texan Cultures, see The University of Texas at San Antonio, San Antonio TX

INTAR Gallery, New York NY (M)

Interact Studio, Inside Out Gallery, Minneapolis MN (M)

Inter American University of Puerto Rico, Dept of Art, San German PR (S)

Inter American University of Puerto Rico, Dept of Art, San German PR (S)

The Interchurch Center, Galleries at the Interchurch Center, New York NY (M,L)

Interlochen Center for the Arts, Interlochen MI (L)

Interlochen Center for the Arts, Interlochen Arts Academy, Dept of Visual Art, Interlochen MI (S)

Intermedia Arts Minnesota, Minneapolis MN (M)

Intermuseum Conservation Association, Cleveland OH (O)

International Association of Art Critics, AICA Canada, Inc, Toronto ON (O)

International Center of Medieval Art, New York NY (A)

International Center of Photography, Museum, New York NY (M,L)

International Center of Photography, School, New York NY (S)

International Clown Hall of Fame & Research Center, Inc, West Allis WI (M)

International Council for Cultural Exchange (ICCE), Brookhaven NY (S)

International Fine Arts College, Miami FL (S)

International Foundation for Art Research, Inc (IFAR), New York NY (O)

International Museum of Art, El Paso TX (M)

International Museum of Art & Science, McAllen TX (M)

International Sculpture Center, Hamilton NJ (M)

International Society of Copier Artists (ISCA), Brooklyn NY (O)

International Society of Marine Painters, Puryear TN (A)

Intersection for the Arts, San Francisco CA (A)

Inter-Society Color Council, Reston VA (O)

Intuit: The Center for Intuitive & Outsider Art, Chicago IL (M)

Iowa Central Community College, Dept of Art, Fort Dodge IA (S)

Iowa Great Lakes Maritime Museum, Arnolds Park IA (M)

Iowa Lakes Community College, Dept of Art, Estherville IA (S)

Iowa State University, Brunnier Art Museum, Ames IA (M)

Iowa State University, Dept of Art & Design, Ames IA (S)

Iowa Wesleyan College, Art Dept, Mount Pleasant IA (S)

Iowa Western Community College, Art Dept, Council Bluffs IA (S)

Iredell Museums, Statesville NC (M)

Iroquois County Historical Society Museum, Old Courthouse Museum, Watseka IL (M)

Iroquois Indian Museum, Howes Cave NY (M)

Irvine Fine Arts Center, see City of Irvine, Irvine CA

Irvine Fine Arts Center, see City of Irvine, Irvine CA

Irvine Museum, Irvine CA (M)

Irving Arts Center, Galleries & Sculpture Garden, Irving TX (M)

Irving Sandler Artists File, see Artists Space, New York NY

Island Gallery West, Holmes Beach FL (M)

Islip Art Museum, East Islip NY (M)

ISM Lockport Gallery, Chicago Gallery & Southern Illinois Art Gallery, see Illinois State Museum, Springfield IL

Ithaca College, Fine Art Dept, Ithaca NY (S)

Ithaca College, Handwerker Gallery of Art, Ithaca NY (M)

J.M.W. Turner Museum, Sarasota FL (M)

Jack I & Dorothy G Bender Library & Learning Resources Center, see American University, New York NY

Jackson County Historical Society, The 1859 Jail, Marshal's Home & Museum, Independence MO (M,L)

Jackson Hall Gallery, see Kentucky State University, Frankfort KY

Sheldon Jackson Museum, see Alaska Department of Education, Division of Libraries, Archives & Museums, Sitka AK

Jackson State University, Dept of Art, Jackson MS (S)

Jacksonville Public Library, Fine Arts & Recreation Dept, Jacksonville FL (L)

Jacksonville State University, Art Dept, Jacksonville AL (S)

Jacksonville University, Alexander Brest Museum & Gallery, Jacksonville FL (M)

Jacksonville University, Dept of Art, Theater, Dance, Jacksonville FL (S)

Jacobs Gallery, see Lane Arts Council, Eugene OR

Jailhouse Galleries, see Burke Arts Council, Morganton NC

Jamaica Center for Arts & Learning (JCAL), Jamaica NY (M)

James & Meryl Hearst Center for the Arts & Sculpture Garden, see City of Cedar Falls, Iowa, Cedar Falls IA

James Dick Foundation, Festival - Institute, Round Top TX (M)

James Madison University, Sawhill Gallery, Harrisonburg VA (M)

James Madison University, School of Art & Art History, Harrisonburg VA (S)

Jamestown College, Art Dept, Jamestown ND (S)

Jamestown Community College, Arts, Humanities & Health Sciences Division, Jamestown NY (S)

Jamestown Community College, The Weeks, Jamestown NY (M)

Jamestown-Yorktown Foundation, Jamestown Settlement, Williamsburg VA (M)

Janet Turner Print Museum, CSU, Chicago, see California State University, Chico, Chico CA

Japanese American Cultural & Community Center, George J Doizaki Gallery, Los Angeles CA (M)

Japanese American National Museum, Los Angeles CA (M)

Japan Society, Inc, Japan Society Gallery, New York NY (M,L)

Japantown Art & Media Workshop, San Francisco CA (A)

The Jaques Art Center, Aitkin MN (M)

Jardin Botanique de Montreal, Bibliotheque, Montreal PQ (L)

Jay I Kislak Foundation, Miami Lakes FL (M)

John Jay Homestead State Historic Site, see New York State Office of Parks Recreation & Historic Preservation, Katonah NY

Jean B King Art Gallery, see Herrett Center for Arts & Sciences, Twin Falls ID

Jean Paul Slusser Gallery, see University of Michigan, Ann Arbor MI

Jefferson College, Dept of Art, Hillsboro MO (S)

Jefferson Community College & Technical College, Fine Arts, Louisville KY (S)

Jefferson Community College, Art Dept, Watertown NY (S)

Jefferson County Historical Society Museum, Madison IN (M)

Jefferson County Open Space, Hiwan Homestead Museum, Evergreen CO (M)

Jefferson Davis Community College, Art Dept, Brewton AL (S)

Thomas Jefferson, Monticello, Charlottesville VA (M)

Jeffers Petroglyphs Historic Site, Comfrey MN (M)

Jekyll Island Museum, Jekyll Island GA (M)

Jenison-Meacham Memorial Art Center & Museum, Belmond IA (M)

William R Jenkins Architecture & Art Library, see Art Museum of the University of Houston, Houston TX

Jenny Library, see Stone Quarry Hill Art Park, Cazenovia NY

Jericho Historical Society, Jericho VT (A)

J Eric Johnson, Fine Arts Division, Dallas TX (L)

Jersey City Museum, Jersey City NJ (M)

Jessie Ball duPont Library, see University of the South, Sewanee TN

Jewett Hall Gallery, see University of Maine at Augusta, Augusta ME

Jewish Community Center of Greater Washington, Jane L & Robert H Weiner Judaic Museum, Rockville MD (M)

Jewish Institute of Religion Museum, see Hebrew Union College Museum, New York NY

The Jewish Museum, New York NY (M,L)

Joe Gish's Old West Museum, Fredericksburg TX (M)

John B Aird Gallery, Toronto ON (M)

John Brown University, Art Dept, Siloam Springs AR (S)

John Carroll University, Dept of Art History & Humanities, University Heights OH (S)

John F Kennedy Presidential Library & Museum, see National Archives & Records Administration, Boston MA

John Jay College of Criminal Justice, Dept of Art, Music & Philosophy, New York NY (S)

The John J McDonough Museum of Art, see Youngstown State University, Youngstown OH

The John L. Clarke Western Art Gallery & Memorial Museum, East Glacier Park MT (M)

John L Wehle Art Gallery, see Genesee Country Village & Museum, Mumford NY

John Michael Kohler Arts Center - Arts/Industry Program, see Kohler Co, Sheboygan WI

John Orne Johnson Frost Gallery, see Marblehead Museum & Historical Society, Marblehead MA

John Paul Jones House & Discover Portsmouth, see Portsmouth Historical Society, Portsmouth NH

John P Weatherford Gallery & Lupke Gallery, see University of Saint Francis, School of Creative Arts, Fort Wayne IN

Johns Hopkins University, Archaeological Collection, Baltimore MD (M,L)

Johns Hopkins University, Dept of the History of Art, Baltimore MD (S)

Johnson Atelier Technical Institute of Sculpture, Trenton NJ (S)

Johnson Atelier Technical Institute of Sculpture, Johnson Atelier Library, Mercerville NJ (L)

Johnson Collection of Photographs, Movies & Memorabilia, see Martin and Osa Johnson, Chanute KS

Johnson County Community College, Fine Arts Dept & Art History Dept, Overland Park KS (S)

Herbert F Johnson Museum of Art, see Cornell University, Ithaca NY

Johnson-Humrickhouse Museum, Coshocton OH (M)

John G Johnson Collection, see Philadelphia Museum of Art, Philadelphia PA

Johnson State College, Dept Fine & Performing Arts, Dibden Center for the Arts, Johnson VT (S)

John Weaver Sculpture Collection, Hope BC (M)

Joliet Junior College, Fine Arts Dept, Joliet IL (S)

Joliet Junior College, Laura A Sprague Art Gallery, Joliet IL (M)

Bob Jones University Museum & Gallery Inc, Greenville SC (M)

Bob Jones University, School of Fine Arts, Div of Art & Design, Greenville SC (S)

Jones County Junior College, Art Dept, Ellisville MS (S)

James A Jones Library, see Brevard College, Brevard NC

Jones Library, Inc, Amherst MA (L)

Jones Memorial Library, Lynchburg VA (L)

Jordan Historical Museum of The Twenty, Jordan ON (M)

Jorgensen Auditorium, see University of Connecticut, Storrs CT

Joseloff Gallery, see University of Hartford, West Hartford CT

Joslyn Art Museum, Omaha NE (M)

The JPMorgan Chase, Art Collection, New York NY (C)

J Sargeant Reynolds Community College, Humanities & Social Science Division, Richmond VA (S)

Judiciary History Center, Honolulu HI (M)

Judson College, Division of Fine and Performing Arts, Marion AL (S)

Judson University, School of Art, Design & Architecture, Elgin IL (S)

Juliette K and Leonard S Rakow Research Library, see Corning Museum of Glass, Corning NY

Junction City Arts Council Gallery, Junction City KS (M)

Jundt Art Museum, Spokane WA (M)

Juniata College, Dept of Art, Huntingdon PA (S)

Juniata College Museum of Art, Huntingdon PA (M)

The Morris & Sally Justein of Baycrest Heritage Museum, see Baycrest Centre for Geriatric Care, Toronto ON

Juxtaposition Arts, Minneapolis MN (M)

Kaji Aso Studio, Gallery Nature & Temptation, Boston MA (M)

Kala Institute, Kala Art Institute, Berkeley CA (A)

Kalamazoo College, Art Dept, Kalamazoo MI (S)

Kalamazoo Institute of Arts, Kalamazoo MI (M,L)

Kalamazoo Institute of Arts, KIA School, Kalamazoo MI (S)

Kalamazoo Valley Community College, Center for New Media, Kalamazoo MI (S)

Kamloops Art Gallery, Kamloops BC (M)

Kanab Heritage Museum & Juniper Fine Arts Gallery, Kanab UT (M)

Kansas City Art Institute, Kansas City MO (S)

Kansas City Artists Coalition, Kansas City MO (M)

Kansas City Jewish Museum of Contemporary Art - Epsten Gallery, Overland Park KS (M)

Kansas City Municipal Art Commission, Kansas City MO (A)

Kansas City Public Library, Kansas City MO (L)

Kansas Museum of History, see Kansas State Historical Society, Topeka KS

Kansas State Historical Society, Kansas Museum of History, Topeka KS (M)

Kansas State University, Art Dept, Manhattan KS (S)

Kansas State University, Paul Weigel Library of Architecture Planning & Design, Manhattan KS (L)

Kansas Watercolor Society, The Wichita Center for the Arts, Wichita KS (A)

Kansas Wesleyan University, Art Dept, Salina KS (S)

Kapiolani Community College, see University of Hawaii, Honolulu HI

Kappa Pi International Honorary Art Fraternity, Cleveland MS (O)

Karl Drerup Art Gallery, see Plymouth State University, Plymouth NH

Kateri Tekakwitha Shrine/St. Francis Xavier Mission, Kahnawake PQ (M)

Katherine & Tom Belk Visual Arts Center, see Davidson College, Davidson NC

Katherine W Dumke Architecture Library, Marriott Library, see University of Utah, Salt Lake City UT

Katonah Museum of Art, Katonah NY (M)

Katzen Art Center Gallery, see American University, New York NY

Kauai Community College, Dept of Art, Lihue HI (S)

Kauai Museum Association, Ltd., Lihue HI (M)

Kauffman Gallery, see Shippensburg University, Shippensburg PA

Kean University, Fine Arts Dept, Union NJ (S)

Kean University, James Howe Gallery, Union NJ (M,L)

Keene State College, Thorne-Sagendorph Art Gallery, Keene NH (M)

Keil Resource Center, see Tubman African American Museum, Macon GA

Kellogg Community College, Arts & Communication Dept, Battle Creek MI (S)

Kellogg Library & Reading Room, see 1890 House-Museum & Center for the Arts, Cortland NY

Kelly-Griggs House Museum, Red Bluff CA (M)

Kelsey Museum of Archaeology, see University of Michigan, Ann Arbor MI

Kemp Center for the Arts, Wichita Falls TX (M)

Kendall College of Art & Design, Grand Rapids MI (S)

Kendall College of Art & Design, Kendall Gallery, Grand Rapids MI (L)

Donald M Kendall Sculpture Garden, see PepsiCo Inc, Purchase NY

Kendall Gallery, see Kendall College of Art & Design, Grand Rapids MI

Helen King Kendall Memorial Art Gallery, see San Angelo Art Club, San Angelo TX

Kenkeleba House, Inc, Kenkeleba Gallery, New York NY (A)

Kennebec Valley Art Association, Harlow Gallery, Hallowell ME (A)

Doris Wainwright Kennedy Art Center, see Birmingham Southern College, Birmingham AL

Kennedy Galleries, Kennedy Galleries, Inc, New York NY (M)

John F Kennedy, Department of Arts & Consciousness, Pleasant Hill CA (S)

Kennedy-King College, see City Colleges of Chicago, Chicago IL

Kennedy Museum of Art, see Ohio University, Athens OH

The John F Kennedy, Washington DC (A,L)

Kenosha Public Museums, Kenosha WI (M)

Kent Art Association, Gallery, Kent CT (A)

Kent Library, see Southeast Missouri State University, Cape Girardeau MO

Kent State University, School of Art, Kent OH (S)

Kent State University, School of Art Galleries, Kent OH (M)

Kentuck Museum Association, Inc., Kentuck Art Center & Festival of the Arts, Northport AL (M)

Kentucky Derby Museum, Louisville KY (M)

Kentucky Folk Art Center, see Morehead State University, Morehead KY

Kentucky Guild of Artists & Craftsmen Inc, Berea KY (A)

Kentucky Historical Society, Old State Capitol & Annex, Frankfort KY (M,L)

Kentucky Library & Museum, see Western Kentucky University, Bowling Green KY

Kentucky Museum of Art and Craft, Louisville KY (M)

Kentucky New State Capitol, Division of Historic Properties, Frankfort KY (M)

Kentucky State University, Jackson Hall Gallery, Frankfort KY (M)

Kentucky Wesleyan College, Dept Art, Owensboro KY (S)

Kenyon College, Art Dept, Gambier OH (S)

Kenyon College, Olin Art Gallery, Gambier OH (M)

Keokuk Art Center, Keokuk IA (A)

Kern County Museum, Bakersfield CA (M,L)

Illingworth Kerr Gallery, see Alberta College of Art & Design, Calgary AB

Keystone College, Fine Arts Dept, LaPlume PA (S)

Keystone Gallery, Scott City KS (M)

Key West Art & Historical Society, East Martello Museum & Gallery, Key West FL (M)

Kiehle Gallery, see Saint Cloud State University, Saint Cloud MN

Kilgore College, Visual Arts Dept, Kilgore TX (S)

Kimball Art Center, Park City UT (A)

Fiske Kimball Fine Arts Library, see University of Virginia, Charlottesville VA

Kimball Jenkins Estate, Concord NH (M)

Kimbell Art Foundation, Kimbell Art Museum, Fort Worth TX (M,L)

Kimbell Art Museum, see Kimbell Art Foundation, Fort Worth TX

Verman Kimbrough Memorial Library, see Ringling College of Art & Design, Sarasota FL

Kimmel-Harding-Nelson Center for the Arts, Nebraska City NE (M)

Emma B King Library, see Shaker Museum & Library, Old Chatham NY

Gioconda & Joseph King Library, see The Society of the Four Arts, Palm Beach FL

Kingman Tavern Historical Museum, see Town of Cummington Historical Commission, Cummington MA

Kingsborough Community College, CUNY, Art Gallery, Brooklyn NY (M)

Kingsborough Community College, Dept of Art, Brooklyn NY (S)

Kings County Historical Society & Museum, Hampton NB (M)

Kinkead Contemporary, Los Angeles CA (M)

Kipp Gallery, see Indiana University of Pennsylvania, Indiana PA

Kirkland Art Center, Clinton NY (A)

Kirkland Arts Center, Kirkland WA

Kirkland Museum of Fine & Decorative Art, Denver CO (A)

Kirkwood Community College, Dept of Arts & Humanities, Cedar Rapids IA (S)

Kishwaukee College, Art Dept, Malta IL (S)

The Kitchen, New York NY (M)

Kitchener-Waterloo Art Gallery, Kitchener ON (M)

Kittredge Art Gallery, see University of Puget Sound, Tacoma WA

Klamath Art Association, Klamath Falls OR (A)

Klamath County Museum, Klamath Falls OR (M,L)

Klein Museum, Mobridge SD (M)

Robert Klein Gallery, Boston MA (M)

Klemm Gallery, Studio Angelico, see Siena Heights College, Adrian MI

Knights of Columbus Supreme Council, Knights of Columbus Museum, New Haven CT (M)

M Knoedler, Library, New York NY (L)

Knox College, Dept of Art, Galesburg IL (S)

Knoxville Museum of Art, Knoxville TN (M)

Koffler Center of the Arts, School of Visual Art, Toronto ON (S)

Koffler Centre of the Arts, Koffler Gallery, Toronto ON (M)

Koffler Gallery, see Koffler Centre of the Arts, Toronto ON

Kohler Art Library, see University of Wisconsin-Madison, Madison WI

Kohler Co, John Michael Kohler Arts Center - Arts/Industry Program, Sheboygan WI (C)

John Michael Kohler Arts Center, see Sheboygan Arts Foundation, Inc, Sheboygan WI

Michael Kohn Gallery, Los Angeles CA (M)

Koochiching Museums, International Falls MN (M)

Elizabeth P Korn Gallery, see Drew University, Madison NJ

Koshare Indian Museum, Inc, La Junta CO (M,L)

Koucky Gallery, Charlevoix MI (M)

Kraft Education Center/Museum Education, see The Art Institute of Chicago, Chicago IL

Krannert Art Museum and Kinkead Pavilion, see University of Illinois at Urbana-Champaign, Champaign IL

Krannert Gallery & Peterson Gallery, see University of Evansville, Evansville IN

Krasl Art Center, Saint Joseph MI (M)

Krauth Memorial Library, see Lutheran Theological Seminary, Philadelphia PA

Kress Foundation Dept of Art History, see University of Kansas, Lawrence KS

Joe Kubert, Dover NJ (S)

Kutztown University, College of Visual & Performing Arts, Kutztown PA (S)

Kutztown University, The Martin & Regina Miller Gallery, Kutztown PA (M,L)

L'Universite Laval, Ecole des Arts Visuels, Quebec PQ (M,L)

The Lab, San Francisco CA (M)

Laband Art Gallery, see Loyola Marymount University, Los Angeles CA

John Labatt Visual Arts Centre, see University of Western Ontario, London ON

Lac du Flambeau Band of Lake Superior Chippewa Indians, George W Brown Jr Ojibwe Museum & Cultural Center, Lac Du Flambeau WI (M)

LACE (Los Angeles Contemporary Exhibitions), Los Angeles CA (M)

La Centrale Powerhouse Gallery, Montreal PQ (M)

La Chambre Blanche, Quebec PQ (M)

Lachenmeyer Arts Center, Art Resource Library, Cushing OK (L)

Lackawanna College, Fine Arts Dept, Scranton PA (S)

LA County Museum of Art, Los Angeles CA (M,L)

Lafayette College Art Galleries, see Lafayette College, Easton PA

Lafayette College, Dept of Art, Easton PA (S)

Lafayette College, Lafayette College Art Galleries, Easton PA (M)

Lafayette Museum Association, Lafayette Museum-Alexandre Mouton House, Lafayette LA (M)

Lafayette Science Museum & Planetarium, Lafayette LA (M)

LaGrange Art Museum, LaGrange GA (M)

LaGrange College, Lamar Dodd Art Center Museum, LaGrange GA (S)

LaGrange College, Lamar Dodd Art Center Museum, LaGrange GA (M)

Laguna Art Museum, Laguna Beach CA (M)

Laguna College of Art & Design, Dennis & Leslie Power Library, Laguna Beach CA (L)

La Hacienda de Los Martinez, see Taos, Taos NM

Lahaina Arts Society, Art Organization, Lahaina HI (A)

Lake County Civic Center Association, Inc, Heritage Museum & Gallery, Leadville CO (A)

Lake Erie College, Fine Arts Dept, Painesville OH (S)

Lake Forest College, Dept of Art, Lake Forest IL (S)

Lake Forest Library, Fine Arts Dept, Lake Forest IL (L)

Lake George Arts Project, Courthouse Gallery, Lake George NY (M)

Lakehead University, Dept of Visual Arts, Thunder Bay ON (S)

Lakeland Community College, Fine Arts Department, Kirtland OH (S)

Lake Michigan College, Dept of Art & Science, Benton Harbor MI (S)

Lake Pontchartrain Basin Maritime Museum, Madisonville LA

Lakeside Studio, Lakeside MI (M)

Lake Tahoe Community College, Art Dept, South Lake Tahoe CA (S)

Lakeview Museum of Arts & Sciences, Peoria IL (M)

Lake Wales Arts Center, Lake Wales FL (M)

Lamama La Galleria, New York NY (M)

Lamar University, Art Dept, Beaumont TX (S)

Lamar University, Dishman Art Museum, Beaumont TX (M)

Lambuth University, Dept of Human Ecology & Visual Arts, Jackson TN (S)

Lamont Art Gallery, see Dacotah Prairie Museum, Aberdeen SD

Lamont Gallery, see Phillips Exeter Academy, Frederick R. Mayer Art Center, Exeter NH

La Napoule Art Foundation, Chateau de la Napoule, Portsmouth NH (A)

Lancaster County Art Association, Inc, Strasburg PA (A)

Lancaster Museum of Art, Lancaster PA (M)

Lancaster Quilt & Textile Museum, Lancaster PA (M)

Clara Lander Library, see The Winnipeg Art Gallery, Winnipeg MB

Lander University, College of Arts & Humanities, Greenwood SC (S)

Landis Valley Village and Farm Museum, PA Historical & Museum Commission, Lancaster PA (M,L)

Landmark Society of Western New York, Inc, The Campbell-Whittlesey House Museum, Rochester NY (M,L)

Lane Arts Council, Jacobs Gallery, Eugene OR (M)

Lane Community College, Art & Applied Design Dept, Eugene OR (S)

Lane Community College, Art Dept Gallery, Eugene OR (M)

Lanesboro Arts Center, Lanesboro MN (M)

Laney College, Art Dept, Oakland CA (S)

Laney College Library, Art Section, Oakland CA (L)

Langara College, Department of Design: Design Formation, Vancouver BC (S)

Robert Langen Art Gallery, see Wilfrid Laurier University, Waterloo ON

Langston University, Melvin B Tolson Black Heritage Center, Langston OK (A)

Lannan Foundation, Santa Fe NM (O)

Lansing Art Gallery, Lansing MI (M)

Lansing Community College, Visual Arts & Media Dept, Lansing MI (S)

Laramie County Community College, Division of Arts & Humanities, Cheyenne WY (S)

La Raza-Galeria Posada, Sacramento CA (M)

Laredo Center for the Arts, Laredo TX (M)

La Roche College, Division of Design, Pittsburgh PA (S)

Mabel Larsen Fine Arts Gallery, see Austin Peay State University, Clarksville TN

Larson Gallery, see Yakima Valley Community College, Yakima WA

Paul Whitney Larson Gallery, see University of Minnesota, Saint Paul MN

La Salle University Art Museum, Philadelphia PA (M)

La Salle University, Dept of Art, Philadelphia PA (S)

La Sierra University, Art Dept, Riverside CA (S)

Las Vegas Art Museum, Las Vegas NV (M)

Las Vegas-Clark County Library District, Las Vegas NV (L,M)

Las Vegas Natural History Museum, Las Vegas NV (M)

Latino Art Museum, Pomona CA (M)

Latitude 53 Contemporary Visual Culture, Edmonton AB (A)

Lauinger Library-Special Collections Division, see Georgetown University, Washington DC

Laumeier Sculpture Park, Saint Louis MO (M)

McColl Fine Art Gallery, Charlotte NC (M)
Alameda McCollough Library, see Tippecanoe County Historical Association, Lafayette IN
McCord Museum of Canadian History, Montreal PQ (M)
Harold McCracken Research Library, see Buffalo Bill Memorial Association, Cody WY
Virginia M McCune Community Arts Center, see Crooked Tree Arts Council, Petoskey MI
McDaniel College, Esther Prangley Rice Gallery, Westminster MD (M)
McDonald's Corporation, Art Collection, Oak Brook IL (C)
McDowell House & Apothecary Shop, Danville KY (M)
McGill University, Blackader-Lauterman Library of Architecture and Art, Montreal PQ (L)
McGill University, Dept of Art History, Montreal PQ (S)
McGroarty Cultural Art Center, Tujunga CA (S)
McIntire Dept of Art, see University of Virginia, Charlottesville VA
McIntosh Gallery, see University of Western Ontario, London ON
The McKinney Avenue Contemporary (The MAC), Dallas TX (M)
McKissick Museum, see University of South Carolina, Columbia SC
The Robert McLaughlin, Oshawa ON (M,L)
McLean County Art Association, McLean County Arts Center, Bloomington IL (A)
McLean County Arts Center, see McLean County Art Association, Bloomington IL
McLean County Historical Society, McLean County Museum of History, Bloomington IL (M)
McLean County Museum of History, see McLean County Historical Society, Bloomington IL
McLennan Community College, Visual Arts Dept, Waco TX (S)
McMaster University, McMaster Museum of Art, Hamilton ON (M)
McMaster University, School of Art, Drama & Music, Hamilton ON (S)
McMichael Canadian Art Collection, Kleinburg ON (M,L)
McMullen Museum of Art, see Boston College, Chestnut Hill MA
McMurry University, Art Dept, Abilene TX (S)
McMurry University, Ryan Fine Arts Center, Abilene TX (M)
McNay, San Antonio TX (M,L)
McNeese State University, Dept of Visual Arts, Lake Charles LA (S)
McPherson College, Art Dept, McPherson KS (S)
McPherson College Gallery, McPherson KS (M)
McPherson Museum and Arts Foundation, McPherson KS (M)
Mead Art Museum, see Amherst College, Amherst MA
Meadow Farm Museum, see County of Henrico, Glen Allen VA
Meadows Museum, see Southern Methodist University, Dallas TX
Meadows Museum of Art, see Centenary College of Louisiana, Shreveport LA
Meadville Council on the Arts, Meadville PA (A)
Mechanics' Institute, San Francisco CA (L)
Medicine Hat Public Library, Medicine Hat AB (L)
Medina Railroad Museum, Medina NY (M)
Jerald Melberg Gallery, Charlotte NC (M)
Melvin Art Gallery, see Florida Southern College, Lakeland FL
Memorial Library, see Berry College, Mount Berry GA
Memorial Union Art Gallery, see Oregon State University, Corvallis OR
Memorial Union Gallery, see Arizona State University, Tempe AZ
Memorial University of Newfoundland, Division of Fine Arts, Visual Arts Program, Corner Brook NF (S)
Memorial University of Newfoundland, Sir Wilfred Grenfell College Art Gallery, Corner Brook NF (M)
Memorial University of Newfoundland, The Rooms Provincial Art Gallery, Saint John's NF (M)
Memphis Brooks Museum of Art, Memphis TN (M,L)
Memphis College of Art, Memphis TN (S)
Memphis College of Art, G Pillow Lewis Memorial Library, Memphis TN (L)
Memphis-Shelby County Public Library & Information Center, Dept of Art, Music & Films, Memphis TN (L)
Mendel Art Gallery & Civic Conservatory, Saskatoon SK (M,L)
Mendocino Art Center, Mendocino CA (S)

Mendocino Art Center, Gallery & School, Mendocino CA (A,L)
Menil Foundation, Inc, The Menil Collection, Houston TX (M)
Mennello Museum of American Art, Orlando FL (M)
Mennonite Library & Archives, see Bethel College, North Newton KS
Robert B Menschel Photography Gallery, see Light Work, Syracuse NY
Merced College, Arts Division, Merced CA (S)
Mercer County Community College, Arts, Communication & Engineering Technology, West Windsor NJ (S)
Mercer County Community College, The Gallery, West Windsor NJ (M,L)
Mercer Museum, see Bucks County Historical Society, Doylestown PA
Mercer Museum Library, see Bucks County Historical Society, Doylestown PA
Mercer Union, A Centre for Contemporary Art, Toronto ON (M)
Mercer University, Art Dept, Macon GA (S)
Mercyhurst College, Dept of Art, Erie PA (S)
Meredith College, Art Dept, Raleigh NC (S)
Meredith College, Frankie G Weems Gallery & Rotunda Gallery, Raleigh NC (M)
Meredith Gallery, Baltimore MD (M)
Meriam Library, see California State University, Chico, Chico CA
Meridian International Center, Cafritz Galleries, Washington DC (M)
Meridian Museum of Art, Meridian MS (M)
Meriks American Designers, Inc., Baltimore MD (O)
Merrick Art Gallery, New Brighton PA (M)
Merritt College, Art Dept, Oakland CA (S)
Merwin & Wakeley Galleries, see Illinois Wesleyan University, Bloomington IL
Mesa Arts Center, Mesa Contemporary Arts Museum, Mesa AZ (M)
Mesa Community College, Dept of Art, Mesa AZ (S)
Mesa Contemporary Arts Museum, see Mesa Arts Center, Mesa AZ
Mesa Public Library Art Gallery, Los Alamos NM (M)
Laura & Paul Mesaros Galleries, see West Virginia University, Morgantown WV
Mesa Verde National Park, Research Library, Mesa Verde National Park CO (L)
Mesquite Fine Arts Center & Gallery, Mesquite NV (M)
Metamora Museum of Ethnographic Art, Metamora IN (M)
Metcalf Art Gallery, see Taylor University, Upland IN
Methodist College, Art Dept, Fayetteville NC (S)
Metropolitan Center for Public Arts, see Regional Arts & Culture Council, Portland OR
Metropolitan Community College - Penn Valley, Art Dept, Kansas City MO (S)
The Metropolitan Museum of Art, New York NY (M,L)
Metropolitan State University of Denver, Art Dept, Denver CO (S)
Metropolitan State University of Denver, Center for Visual Art, Denver CO (M)
Mexican Museum, San Francisco CA (M)
MEXIC-ARTE Museum, Austin TX (A)
Mexico-Audrain County Library, Mexico MO (L)
Mhiripiri Gallery, Bloomington MN (M)
MHS Museum, see Maine Historical Society, Portland ME
Miami Art Museum, Miami FL (M)
Miami-Dade College, Kendal Campus, Art Gallery, Miami FL (M)
Miami-Dade Community College, Arts & Philosophy Dept, Miami FL (S)
Miami Dade County Dept of Cultural Affairs, see South Florida Cultural Consortium, Miami FL
Miami-Dade Public Library, Miami FL (L)
Miami University, Art Dept, Oxford OH (S)
Miami University, Art Museum, Oxford OH (M,L)
Miami University, Dept Fine Arts, Hamilton OH (S)
Miami Watercolor Society, Inc, Miami FL (A)
Simon Michael, Rockport TX (S)
Michelson Museum of Art, Marshall TX (M)
James A Michener, Doylestown PA (M)
Michigan Art & Artist Archives, see Art Center of Battle Creek, Battle Creek MI
Michigan Guild Gallery, see Michigan Guild of Artists & Artisans, Ann Arbor MI
Michigan Guild of Artists & Artisans, Michigan Guild Gallery, Ann Arbor MI (A)
Michigan State University, Dept of Art & Art History, East Lansing MI (S)
Mid-America All-Indian Center, Indian Center Museum, Wichita KS (M,L)
Mid America Arts Alliance & Exhibits USA, Kansas City MO (O)

Middle Border Museum & Oscar Howe Art Center, Mitchell SD (M)
Middlebury College, History of Art & Architecture Dept, Middlebury VT (S)
Middlebury College, Museum of Art, Middlebury VT (M)
Middle Georgia State College, Humanities Division, Dept of Art - School of Liberal Arts, Dept of Media, Culture & the Arts, Cochran GA (S)
Middlesex Community College, Fine Arts Div, Middletown CT (S)
Middlesex County College, Visual Arts Dept, Edison NJ (S)
Middlesex County Cultural & Heritage Commission, New Brunswick NJ (A)
Middle Tennessee State University, Art Dept, Murfreesboro TN (S)
Middle Tennessee State University, Baldwin Photographic Gallery, Murfreesboro TN (M)
Middletown Arts Center, Middletown OH (A,L)
Midland College, Art Dept, Midland TX (S)
Midmarch Arts Press and Library, see Midmarch Associates/Midmarch Arts Press, New York NY
Midmarch Associates/Midmarch Arts Press, Midmarch Arts Press and Library, New York NY (L)
Midtown Art Center, Houston TX (M)
Midway College, Art Dept, Midway KY (S)
Midwest Art Conservation Center, Minneapolis MN (A)
Midwest Art History Society, Waco TX (O)
Midwestern State University, Lamar D. Fain College of Fine Arts, Wichita Falls TX (S)
Midwest Museum of American Art, Elkhart IN (M)
Mildred R & Frederick M Mayer Library, see Dallas Museum of Art, Dallas TX
Miles B Carpenter Folk Art Museum, Waverly VA (M)
Miles Community College, Dept of Fine Arts & Humanities, Miles City MT (S)
Millard Sheets Art Center-Williamson Gallery, see Scripps College, Claremont CA
Miller Art Center Foundation Inc, Miller Art Museum, Sturgeon Bay WI (M)
Miller Art Museum, see Miller Art Center Foundation Inc, Sturgeon Bay WI
E Kirkbride Miller Art Library, see The Baltimore Museum of Art, Baltimore MD
Millersville University, Dept of Art & Design, Millersville PA (S)
Mill Fine Art, Santa Fe NM (M)
Millicent Rogers Museum, Taos NM (M)
Milliken Art Gallery, see Converse College, Spartanburg SC
Millikin University, Art Dept, Decatur IL (S)
Millikin University, Perkinson Gallery, Decatur IL (M)
Millsaps College, Dept of Art, Jackson MS (S)
Mills College, Art Dept, Oakland CA (S)
Mills College Art Museum, Oakland CA (M)
Mills Gallery - Boston Center for the Arts, Boston MA (M)
Milwaukee Area Technical College, School of Media & Creative Arts, Milwaukee WI (S)
Milwaukee Art Museum, Milwaukee WI (M,L)
Milwaukee County War Memorial Inc., Villa Terrace Decorative Arts Museum, Milwaukee WI (M)
Milwaukee Institute of Art & Design, Milwaukee WI (S)
Milwaukee Institute of Art & Design, Library, Milwaukee WI (L)
Milwaukee Public Library, Art, Music & Recreation Dept, Milwaukee WI (L)
Milwaukee Public Museum, Milwaukee WI (M)
Mingenback Art Center, see Bethany College, Lindsborg KS
Mini/Goethe-Institut Curatorial Residencies Ludlow 38, see Goethe-Institut New York, New York NY
Ministry of Alberta Culture, Royal Alberta Museum, Edmonton AB (M,L)
Minneapolis College of Art & Design, Minneapolis MN (S)
Minneapolis College of Art & Design, Library, Minneapolis MN (L)
Minneapolis Institute of Arts, Minneapolis MN (M,L,A)
Minnesota Historical Society, Saint Paul MN (A,L,M)
Minnesota Historical Society, Minnesota State Capitol Historic Site, St Paul MN (M)
Minnesota Museum of American Art, Saint Paul MN (M)
Minnesota State University, Mankato, Mankato MN (M)
Minnesota State University-Moorhead, Dept of Art & Design, Moorhead MN (S)
Minnetonka Center for the Arts, Wayzata MN (M)
Minot State University, Dept of Art, Division of Humanities, Minot ND (S)

Niagara County Community College, Fine Arts Division, Sanborn NY (S)

Niagara University, Castellani Art Museum, Niagara NY (M)

Niagara University, Fine Arts Dept, Niagara Falls NY (S)

Nicholls State University, Dept of Art, Thibodaux LA (S)

Nichols House Museum, Inc, Boston MA (M)

Nickle Galleries, see University of Calgary, Calgary AB

Nicolaysen Art Museum & Discovery Center, Children's Discovery Center, Casper WY (M,L)

Niederlander Research Library, see Amherst Museum, Amherst NY

911 Media Arts Center, Seattle WA (A)

The Nippon Gallery at the Nippon Club, New York NY (A)

Noah Webster House, Inc, Noah Webster House & West Hartford Historical Society, West Hartford CT (M)

Noah Webster House & West Hartford Historical Society, see Noah Webster House, Inc, West Hartford CT

The Noble Maritime Collection, Staten Island NY (M)

Nobles County Art Center, Worthington MN (A)

Isamu Noguchi Garden Museum, see Isamu Noguchi, Long Island City NY

Isamu Noguchi, Isamu Noguchi Garden Museum, Long Island City NY (M)

The Nolen Library in the Ruth and Harold D. Uris Center for Education, see The Metropolitan Museum of Art, New York NY

No Man's Land Historical Society, No Man's Land Museum, Goodwell OK (M)

Nordstrand Visual Arts Gallery, see Wayne State College, Wayne NE

Norfolk Arts Center, Norfolk NE (M)

Norfolk Historical Society Inc, Museum, Norfolk CT (M)

Norfolk State University, Fine Arts Dept, Norfolk VA (S)

Norick Art Center, see Oklahoma City University, Oklahoma City OK

Norman and Sarah Brown Art Gallery, Baltimore MD (M)

Normandale Community College, Art Dept, Bloomington MN (S)

Norman Rockwell Museum, Stockbridge MA (M,L)

Norman Rockwell Museum of Vermont, Rutland VT (M)

North American Indian Information & Trade Center, see National Native American Co-Operative, Tucson AZ

Northampton Center for the Arts, Northampton MA (M)

Northampton Community College, Art Dept, Bethlehem PA (S)

North Arkansas Community-Technical College, Art Dept, Harrison AR (S)

North Canton Public Library, The Little Art Gallery, North Canton OH (L)

North Carolina Agricultural & Technical State University, Visual Arts Dept, Greensboro NC (S)

North Carolina Central University, Art Dept, Durham NC (S)

North Carolina Central University, NCCU Art Museum, Durham NC (M)

North Carolina Museum of Art, Raleigh NC (M,L)

North Carolina Museums Council, Raleigh NC (A)

North Carolina State University at Raleigh, School of Design, Raleigh NC (S)

North Carolina State University, Harrye Lyons Design Library, Raleigh NC (L,M)

North Carolina Wesleyan College, Dept of Visual & Performing Arts, Rocky Mount NC (S)

North Central Arkansas Art Gallery, Fairfield Bay AR

North Central College, Dept of Art, Naperville IL (S)

North Central College, Oesterle Library, Naperville IL (L)

North Central Michigan College, Art Dept, Petoskey MI (S)

North Central Texas College, Division of Communications & Fine Arts, Gainesville TX (S)

North Central Texas College, Library, Gainesville TX (L)

North Central Washington Museum, Wenatchee Valley Museum & Cultural Center, Wenatchee WA (M)

North Country Museum of Arts, Park Rapids MN (M)

Northcutt Steele Gallery, see Montana State University at Billings, Billings MT

North Dakota Museum of Art, Grand Forks ND (M)

North Dakota State College of Science, Dept of Graphic Arts, Wahpeton ND (S)

North Dakota State University, Division of Fine Arts, Fargo ND (S)

North Dakota State University, Memorial Union Gallery, Fargo ND (M)

Northeast Community College, Dept of Liberal Arts, Norfolk NE (S)

Northeast Document Conservation Center, Inc, Andover MA (A)

Northeastern Illinois University, Art Dept, Chicago IL (S)

Northeastern Illinois University, Gallery, Chicago IL (M)

Northeastern Junior College, Art Department, Sterling CO (S)

Northeastern Nevada Museum, Elko NV (M)

Northeastern Oklahoma A & M College, Art Dept, Miami OK (S)

Northeastern State University, College of Arts & Letters, Tahlequah OK (S)

Northeastern University, Dept of Art & Architecture, Boston MA (S)

Northeast Kingdom Artisans Guild, Saint Johnsbury VT (M)

Northeast Louisiana Children's Museum, Monroe LA (M)

Northeast Mississippi Junior College, Art Dept, Booneville MS (S)

Northeast Ohio Areawide Coordinating Agency (NOACA), Information Resource Center, Cleveland OH (L)

North End Gallery, Leonardtown MD (M)

Northern Arizona University, Art Museum & Galleries, Flagstaff AZ (M)

Northern Arizona University, College of Arts & Letters, Flagstaff AZ (S)

Northern Galleries, see Northern State University, Aberdeen SD

Northern Illinois University, NIU Art Museum, DeKalb IL (M,L)

Northern Illinois University, School of Art, DeKalb IL (S)

Northern Kentucky University, Dept of Visual Arts, Highland Heights KY (S)

Northern Kentucky University, Galleries, Highland Heights KY (M)

Northern Lights Art Gallery, see Mayville State University, Mayville ND

Northern Maine Museum of Science, Presque Isle ME (M)

Northern Michigan University, Dept of Art & Design, Marquette MI (S)

Northern Michigan University, De Vos Art Museum, Marquette MI (M)

Northern State University, Art Dept, Aberdeen SD (S)

Northern State University, Northern Galleries, Aberdeen SD (M)

Northern Virginia Community College, Art Dept, Annandale VA (S)

Northern Virginia Fine Arts Association, The Athenaeum, Alexandria VA (A)

Northfield Arts Guild, Northfield MN (A)

North Florida Community College, Dept Humanities & Art, Madison FL (S)

North Fourth Art Center & Gallery, Albuquerque NM (M)

North Georgia College & State University, Fine Arts Dept, Dahlonega GA (S)

North Hennepin Community College, Art Dept, Brooklyn Park MN (S)

North Hennepin Community College, Joseph Gazzuolo Fine Arts Gallery, Brooklyn Park MN (M)

North Idaho College, Art Dept, Coeur D'Alene ID (S)

North Iowa Area Community College, Dept of Art, Mason City IA (S)

Northland Pioneer College, Art Dept, Holbrook AZ (S)

North Light Gallery, Millinocket ME (M)

North Park University, Art Dept, Chicago IL (S)

North Park University, Carlson Tower Gallery, Chicago IL (M)

Northport-East Northport Public Library, Northport NY (L)

North Seattle Community College, Art Dept, Seattle WA (S)

North Shore Art League, Winnetka IL (S)

North Shore Art League, Winnetka IL (A)

North Shore Arts Association, Inc, Gloucester MA (A)

North Tonawanda History Museum, North Tonawanda NY (M)

North View Gallery, see Portland Community College, Portland OR

Northwest Art Center, see Minot State University, Minot ND

Northwest Community College, Dept of Art, Powell WY (S)

Northwestern College, Art Dept, Orange City CA (S)

Northwestern College, Te Paske Gallery, Orange City IA (M)

Northwestern Connecticut Community College, Fine Arts Dept, Winsted CT (S)

Northwestern Michigan College, Art Dept, Traverse City MI (S)

Northwestern Michigan College, Dennos Museum Center, Traverse City MI (M)

Northwestern State University of Louisiana, School of Creative & Performing Arts - Dept of Fine & Graphic Arts, Natchitoches LA (S)

Northwestern University, Evanston, Dept of Art Theory & Practice, Evanston IL (S)

Northwestern University, Mary & Leigh Block Museum of Art, Evanston IL (M,L)

Northwest Florida State College, Mattie Kelly Arts Center Galleries, Niceville FL (S)

Northwest Missouri State University, DeLuce Art Gallery, Maryville MO (M)

Northwest Missouri State University, Dept of Fine & Performing Arts, Maryville MO (S)

Northwest Museum of Arts & Culture, see Eastern Washington State Historical Society, Spokane WA

Northwest Nazarene College, Art Dept, Nampa ID (S)

Northwest Pastel Society (NPS), Dallas OR (A)

Northwest Watercolor Society, Woodinville WA (A)

Northwind Arts Center, Port Townsend WA (M)

Northwood University, Alden B Dow Creativity Center, Midland MI (A)

Northwood University, Jeannette Hare Art Gallery, West Palm Beach FL (M)

Norton Museum of Art, West Palm Beach FL (M)

Norwich Free Academy, Slater Memorial Museum, Norwich CT (M)

Norwich University, Dept of Architecture and Art, Northfield VT (S)

Nossi College of Art, Nashville TN (S)

Notre Dame de Namur University, Wiegand Gallery, Belmont CA (M)

Nova Scotia Association of Architects, Halifax NS (A)

Nova Scotia Centre for Craft & Design, Mary E Black Gallery, Halifax NS (S)

Nova Scotia College of Art & Design, Halifax NS (S)

Nova Scotia College of Art and Design, Anna Leonowens Gallery, Halifax NS (M,L)

Nova Scotia Museum, Maritime Museum of the Atlantic, Halifax NS (M)

Noyes & Read Gallery/Herndon Gallery, see Antioch College, Yellow Springs OH

Noyes Art Gallery, Lincoln NE (M)

The Noyes Museum of Art, Oceanville NJ (M)

Nutana Collegiate Institute, Memorial Library and Art Gallery, Saskatoon SK (L)

Nuveen Community Center for the Arts, Montague MI (M)

O. Henry Museum, see City of Austin Parks & Recreation, Austin TX

Oakland City University, Division of Fine Arts, Oakland City IN (S)

Oakland Community College, Art Dept, Farmington Hills MI (S)

Oakland Museum of California, Art Dept, Oakland CA (M,L)

Oakland Public Library, Art, Music, History & Literature Section, Oakland CA (L)

Oakland University Art Gallery, see Oakland University, Rochester MI

Oakland University, Dept of Art & Art History, Rochester MI (S)

Oakland University, Oakland University Art Gallery, Rochester MI (M)

Oak Ridge Art Center, Oak Ridge TN (A,L)

Oakton Community College, Language Humanities & Art Divisions, Des Plaines IL (S)

Oakville Galleries, Centennial Square and Gairloch Gardens, Oakville ON (M)

Oatlands Plantation, Leesburg VA (M)

Oberlin College, Allen Memorial Art Museum, Oberlin OH (M,L)

Oberlin College, Dept of Art, Oberlin OH (S)

OCAD University, Toronto ON (S)

OCAD University, Student Gallery, Toronto ON (M,L)

OCC Gallery, see Ontario Crafts Council, Toronto ON

Occidental College, Dept of Art History & Visual Arts, Los Angeles CA (S)

Occidental College, Weingart Galleries, Los Angeles CA (M)

Ocean City Art Center, Ocean City NJ (A)

Ocean City Arts Center, Ocean City NJ (S)

Ocean County College, Humanities Dept, Toms River NJ (S)

Oceanside Gallery, Belmar NJ (M)

Octagon Center for the Arts, Ames IA (A)

Oesterle Library, see North Central College, Naperville IL

Office of Cultural Affairs, see City of Atlanta, Atlanta GA

Riley County Historical Society & Museum, Riley County Historical Museum, Manhattan KS (M,L)

Rinehart School of Sculpture, see Maryland Institute, Baltimore MD

Riney Fine Arts Center Gallery, see Friends University, Wichita KS

Ringling College of Art & Design, Verman Kimbrough Memorial Library, Sarasota FL (L)

Ringling College of Art & Design, Selby Gallery, Sarasota FL (M)

John & Mable Ringling Museum of Art, see Florida State University, Sarasota FL

Ringling School of Art & Design, Sarasota FL (S)

Ringwood Manor House Museum, Ringwood NJ (M)

Rio Hondo College Art Gallery, Whittier CA (M)

Rio Hondo College, Visual Arts Dept, Whittier CA (S)

Ripon College, Art Dept, Ripon WI (S)

Ripon College Caestecker Art Gallery, Ripon WI (M)

River Arts, Arts Gallery, Damariscotta ME (M)

River Arts Center, see Clinton Art Association, Clinton IA

Tomas Rivera Library, see University of California, Riverside CA

Riverfront Renaissance Center for the Arts, Millville NJ (M)

River Heritage Museum, Paducah KY (M)

Riverside, the Farnsley-Moremen Landing, Louisville KY (M)

Riverside Art Museum, Riverside CA (M,L)

Riverside Arts Center, Riverside IL (S)

Riverside Community College, Dept of Art & Mass Media, Riverside CA (S)

Riverside County Museum, Edward-Dean Museum & Gardens, Cherry Valley CA (M,L)

Riverside Metropolitan Museum, Riverside CA (M)

Rivier College, Art Dept, Nashua NH (S)

Roanoke College, Fine Arts Dept-Art, Salem VA (S)

Roberson Museum & Science Center, Binghamton NY (M)

Robert Allerton Art Library, see Honolulu Museum of Art, Honolulu HI

Robert Graves Gallery, see Wenatchee Valley College, Wenatchee WA

Robert N & Peggy Sears Gallery, see Dixie State College, Saint George UT

Robert Paul Gallery, Stowe VT (M)

Roberts County Museum, Miami TX (M)

Roberts Wesleyan College, Art Dept, Rochester NY (S)

Robson Library, see University of the Ozarks, Clarksville AR

Rochester Art Center, Rochester MN (A)

Rochester Community & Technical College, Art Dept, Rochester MN (S)

Rochester Contemporary, Art Center, Rochester NY (M)

Rochester Historical Society, Rochester NY (A)

Rochester Institute of Technology, College of Imaging Arts & Sciences, Rochester NY (S)

Rochester Institute of Technology, Corporate Education & Training, Rochester NY (L)

John D Rockefeller, Jr Library, see Colonial Williamsburg Foundation, Williamsburg VA

Rockford Art Museum, Rockford IL (A)

Rockford College Art Gallery, Rockford IL (M)

Rockford College, Dept of Fine Arts, Rockford IL (S)

Rock Ford Foundation, Inc, Rock Ford Plantation, Lancaster PA (M)

Rock Ford Plantation, see Rock Ford Foundation, Inc, Lancaster PA

Rockhurst University, Dept of Communication & Fine Arts, Kansas City MO (S)

Rockland Center for the Arts, West Nyack NY (S)

Rockland Center for the Arts, West Nyack NY (M)

Rockland Community College, Graphic Arts & Advertising Tech Dept, Suffern NY (S)

Rockport Art Association, Rockport MA (A)

Rock Valley College, Humanities and Fine Arts Division, Rockford IL (S)

The Rockwell Museum of Western Art, Corning NY (M,L)

Rocky Mountain College, Art Dept, Billings MT (S)

Rocky Mountain College of Art & Design, Lakewood CO (S)

Rocky Mountain Museum of Military History, Missoula MT (M)

Rocky Mount Arts Center, Rocky Mount NC (A)

Rocky Reach Dam, see Chelan County Public Utility District, Wenatchee WA

Rodin Museum of Philadelphia, see Philadelphia Museum of Art, Philadelphia PA

Rodman Hall Arts Centre, Saint Catharines ON (A,L)

Nicholas Roerich, New York NY (M)

Lauren Rogers, Laurel MS (M,L)

Rogers State College, Art Dept, Claremore OK (S)

Will Rogers Memorial Museum & Birthplace Ranch, Claremore OK (M,L)

Roger Williams University, Architecture Library, Bristol RI (L)

Roger Williams University, Visual Art Dept, Bristol RI (S)

Rogue Community College, Wiseman Gallery - FireHouse Gallery, Grants Pass OR (M)

Rogue Valley Art Association, Rogue Gallery & Art Center, Medford OR (A)

Rohrbach Library, see Kutztown University, Kutztown PA

Rokeby Museum, Ferrisburgh VT (A)

Rollins College, George D & Harriet W Cornell Fine Arts Museum, Winter Park FL (M)

Rollins College, Dept of Art, Main Campus, Winter Park FL (S)

Rome Art & Community Center, Rome NY (A)

Rome Historical Society, Museum & Archives, Rome NY (M,L)

Hugh N Ronald Memorial Gallery, see Arts Place, Inc., Portland IN

The Rooms Corporation of Newfoundland & Labrador, Saint John's NF (M)

Franklin D Roosevelt Museum, see National Archives & Records Administration, Hyde Park NY

Franklin D Roosevelt Library, see National Archives & Records Administration, Hyde Park NY

Roosevelt-Vanderbilt National Historic Sites, Hyde Park NY (M)

The Stephanie Ann Roper Gallery, see Frostburg State University, Frostburg MD

Rose Center & Council for the Arts, Morristown TN (A)

Rose Lehrman Art Gallery, Harrisburg PA (M)

Rosemont College, Art Program, Rosemont PA (S)

Rosemount Museum, Inc, Pueblo CO (M)

The Rosenbach Museum & Library, Philadelphia PA (M)

Rosenberg Gallery, see Goucher College, Baltimore MD

Rosenberg Library, Galveston TX (L)

Rosenthal Art Gallery, see The College of Idaho, Caldwell ID

Rosicrucian Egyptian Museum & Planetarium, Rosicrucian Order, A.M.O.R.C., San Jose CA (M)

Ross Memorial Museum, Saint Andrews NB (M)

Roswell Artist-in-Residence Foundation, Anderson Museum of Contemporary Art, Roswell NM (M)

Roswell Museum & Art Center, Roswell NM (M,L)

Rotch Library of Architecture & Planning, see Massachusetts Institute of Technology, Cambridge MA

Rothmans, Benson & Hedges, Art Collection, Don Mills ON (C)

Rotunda Gallery, see BRIC - Brooklyn Information & Culture, Brooklyn NY

Rowan University, Dept of Art, Glassboro NJ (S)

Royal Alberta Museum, see Ministry of Alberta Culture, Edmonton AB

Royal Architectural Institute of Canada, Ottawa ON (O,L)

Royal Arts Foundation, Belcourt Castle, Newport RI (M)

Royal British Columbia Museum, BC Archives, Victoria BC (L)

Royal Canadian Academy of Arts, Toronto ON (O)

Royal Ontario Museum, Toronto ON (M,L)

Elizabeth Rozier Gallery, see Missouri Department of Natural Resources, Jefferson City MO

R Tait McKenzie Memorial Museum, see Mississippi Valley Conservation Authority, Almonte ON

The Rubelle & Norman Schafler Gallery, see Pratt Institute, Brooklyn NY

Rubell Family Collection and Contemporary Arts Foundation, Miami FL (M)

Rubin Museum of Art, New York NY (M)

Ruddell Gallery, see Black Hills State University, Spearfish SD

Ruder Finn Arts & Communications, Inc, New York NY (C)

William F Ruska Library, see Becker College, Worcester MA

C M Russell, Great Falls MT (M,L)

Russell Day Gallery, see Everett WA (M)

Russell Sage College, Visual & Performing Arts Dept, Troy NY (S)

Rutgers, The State University of New Jersey, Mason Gross School of the Arts, Visual Arts Dept, New Brunswick NJ (S)

Rutgers, The State University of New Jersey, Zimmerli Art Museum, Rutgers University, New Brunswick NJ (M,L)

Rutgers University, Camden, Art Dept, Camden NJ (S)

Rutgers University, Newark, Arts, Culture & Media, Newark NJ (S)

Rutgers University, Stedman Art Gallery, Camden NJ (M)

Ruthmere Museum, Robert B. Beardsley Arts Reference Library, Elkhart IN (L)

Rutland Area Art Association, Chaffee Art Center, Rutland VT (A)

R W Norton Art Foundation, R W Norton Art Gallery, Shreveport LA (M,L)

Ryan Fine Arts Center, see McMurry University, Abilene TX

Ryerson & Burnham Libraries, see The Art Institute of Chicago, Chicago IL

Ryerson University, Ryerson University Library, Toronto ON (L)

Ryerss Victorian Museum & Library, Philadelphia PA (M)

Alice C Sabatini Gallery, see Topeka & Shawnee County Public Library, Topeka KS

Sackler Art Gallery, Stamford CT (M)

Arthur M Sackler Museum, see Harvard University, Cambridge MA

Arthur M Sackler Gallery, see Freer Gallery of Art & Arthur M Sackler Gallery, Washington DC

Arthur M Sackler Gallery, see Smithsonian Institution, Washington DC

Saco Museum, Saco ME (M)

Sacramento City College, Art Dept, Sacramento CA (S)

Sacramento Fine Arts Center, see Pastel Society of the West Coast, Carmichael CA

Sacred Heart University, Dept of Art, Fairfield CT (S)

Sacred Heart University, Gallery of Contemporary Art, Fairfield CT (M)

Safety Harbor Museum of Regional History, Safety Harbor FL (M)

Sage College of Albany, Opalka Gallery, Albany NY (M)

The Sage Colleges, Dept Visual Arts, Albany NY (S)

Sager Creek Arts Center, Siloam Springs AR (M)

Sager Studios, Fort Worth TX (S)

Saginaw Art Museum, Saginaw MI (M)

Saginaw Valley State University, Dept of Art & Design, University Center MI (S)

Saint Ambrose University, Art Dept, Davenport IA (S)

Saint Andrews Presbyterian College, Art Program, Laurinburg NC (S)

Saint Anselm College, Alva de Mars Megan Chapel Art Center, Manchester NH (M)

Saint Anselm College, Dept of Fine Arts, Manchester NH (S)

Saint Augustine Art Association and Art Gallery, Saint Augustine FL (A)

Saint Augustine Historical Society, Oldest House Museum Complex, Saint Augustine FL (M,L)

Saint Bonaventure University, Regina A Quick Center for the Arts, Saint Bonaventure NY (M)

Saint Clair County Community College, Jack R Hennesey Art Dept, Port Huron MI (S)

Saint Clair County Community College, Jack R Hennesey Art Galleries, Port Huron MI (M)

Saint Cloud State University, Atwood Memorial Center Gallery, Saint Cloud MN (M)

Saint Cloud State University, Dept of Art, Saint Cloud MN (S)

Saint Edward's University, Fine Arts Gallery, Austin TX (M)

St Francis College, Fine Arts Dept, Loretto PA (S)

St Francis Xavier University, Fine Arts Dept, Antigonish NS (S)

Saint-Gaudens National Historic Site, Cornish NH (M,L)

Saint Gregory's University, Dept of Art, Shawnee OK (S)

St John's College, Elizabeth Myers Mitchell Art Gallery, Annapolis MD (M)

Saint John's University, Art Dept, Collegeville MN (S)

Saint John's University, Dept of Fine Arts, Jamaica NY (S)

Saint John's University, Dr. M.T. Geoffrey Yeh Art Gallery, Queens NY (M)

Saint Johnsbury Athenaeum, Saint Johnsbury VT (M)

Saint Joseph's Oratory, Museum, Montreal PQ (M,L)

Saint Joseph's University, Art Dept, Philadelphia PA (S)

Saint Joseph College, Art Gallery, University of Saint Joseph, West Hartford CT (M)

Saint Joseph Museum, Saint Joseph MO (M,L)

St Lawrence College, Art Gallery, Kingston ON (M)

St Lawrence College, Dept of Graphic Design, Kingston ON (S)

St Lawrence University, Dept of Fine Arts, Canton NY (S)

Saint Louis Art Museum, Saint Louis MO (M,L)

Saint Louis Community College at Florissant Valley, Liberal Arts Division, Ferguson MO (S)

Scripps College, Clark Humanities Museum, Claremont CA (M)

Scripps College, Millard Sheets Art Center-Williamson Gallery, Claremont CA (S)

Scripps College, Ruth Chandler Williamson Gallery, Claremont CA (S)

William E Scripture Memorial Library, see Rome Historical Society, Rome NY

Sculptor's Society of Canada, Canadian Sculpture Centre, Toronto ON (O)

Sculptors Guild, Inc, Brooklyn NY (O)

Sculpture Center, Long Island City NY (M)

Sculpture Center School, Studios & Gallery, Long Island City NY (S)

Sculpture Space, Inc, Utica NY (M)

Sea Cliff Village Museum, Sea Cliff NY (M)

Searchlight Historic Museum & Mining Park, Searchlight NV (M)

Seaton Library, see Riley County Historical Society & Museum, Manhattan KS

Seattle Art Museum, Downtown, Seattle WA (M,L)

Seattle Central Community College, Humanities - Social Sciences Division, Seattle WA (S)

Seattle Pacific University, Art Dept, Seattle WA (S)

Seattle Public Library, Arts, Recreation & Literature Dept, Seattle WA (L)

Seattle University, Dept of Fine Arts, Visual Art Division, Seattle WA (S)

Second Street Gallery, Charlottesville VA (M)

See Science Center, Manchester NH (M)

Segue Foundation, Reading Room-Archive, New York NY (A)

Seigfred Gallery, see Ohio University, Athens OH

Selby Gallery, see Ringling College of Art & Design, Sarasota FL

Self Help Graphics, Los Angeles CA (A)

Selsor Art Gallery, see Martin and Osa Johnson, Chanute KS

Marcella Sembrich Opera Museum, see Marcella Sembrich Memorial Association Inc, Bolton Landing NY

Semitic Museum, see Harvard University, Cambridge MA

Senate House State Historic Site, see New York State Office of Parks: Recreation and Historic Preservation, Kingston NY

Seneca Falls Historical Society Museum, Seneca Falls NY (M)

Seneca-Iroquois National Museum, Salamanca NY (M)

Mary Porter Sesnon Art Gallery, see University of California at Santa Cruz, Santa Cruz CA

Seton Hall University, South Orange NJ (M)

Seton Hall University, College of Arts & Sciences, South Orange NJ (S)

Seton Hill College, Reeves Memorial Library, Greensburg PA (L)

Seton Hill University, Art Program, Greensburg PA (S)

1708 Gallery, Richmond VA (M)

Sewall Scripture House-Old Castle, see Sandy Bay Historical Society & Museums, Rockport MA

Seward County Community College, Art Dept, Liberal KS (S)

SFA Galleries, see Stephen F Austin State University, Nacogdoches TX

Shadows-on-the-Teche, see National Trust for Historic Preservation, New Iberia LA

Shain Gallery, Charlotte NC (M)

The Shaker Library, see United Society of Shakers, New Gloucester ME

Shaker Museum, see United Society of Shakers, New Gloucester ME

Shaker Museum & Library, Old Chatham NY (M,L)

Shaker Village of Pleasant Hill, Harrodsburg KY (M)

Shakespeare Ghost Town, Lordsburg NM (M)

Sharon Arts Center, School Arts & Crafts, Sharon NH (S)

Sharon Arts Center, Sharon Arts Center Exhibition Gallery, Peterborough NH (M)

Ella Sharp, Jackson MI (M)

Shasta College, Arts, Communications & Social Sciences Division, Redding CA (S)

Shasta Historical Society Research Library, see Turtle Bay Exploration Park, Redding CA

Lemuel Shattuck Memorial Library, see Bisbee Arts & Humanities Council, Bisbee AZ

Shawinigan Art Center, Shawinigan PQ (A)

Sheboygan Arts Foundation, Inc, John Michael Kohler Arts Center, Sheboygan WI (A)

Sheean Library, see Illinois Wesleyan University, Bloomington IL

Millard Sheets Library, see Otis College of Art & Design, Los Angeles CA

Shelburne Museum, Museum, Shelburne VT (M,L)

Sheldon Art Galleries, Saint Louis MO (M)

Sheldon Museum & Cultural Center, see Sheldon Museum & Cultural Center, Inc, Haines AK

Sheldon Museum & Cultural Center, Inc, Sheldon Museum & Cultural Center, Haines AK (M)

Shell Canada Ltd, Calgary AB (C)

Shepherd University, Dept of Contemporary Art & Theater, Shepherdstown WV (S)

Sheppard Contemporary & University Galleries, see University of Nevada, Reno, Reno NV

Sheridan College, Art Dept, Sheridan WY (S)

Sheridan College, Faculty of Animation, Arts & Design, Oakville ON (S)

Sheridan College of Applied Arts and Technology, Trafalgar Campus Library, Oakville ON (L)

Sherman Art Library, see Dartmouth College, Hanover NH

Sherwin Miller Museum of Jewish Art, Tulsa OK (M)

Shiawassee Arts Center, Owosso MI (M)

Shiloh Museum of Ozark History, see City of Springdale, Springdale AR

Shippensburg University, Art Dept, Shippensburg PA (S)

Shippensburg University, Kauffman Gallery, Shippensburg PA (M)

Ships of the Sea Maritime Museum, Savannah GA (M)

Shirley Plantation Foundation, Charles City VA (M)

Shoreline Community College, Humanities Division, Seattle WA (S)

Shoreline Historical Museum, Shoreline WA (M)

Shores Memorial Museum, Lyndon Center VT (M)

Shorncliffe Park Improvement Assoc, Prairie Panorama Museum, Czar AB (M)

Shorter College, Art Dept, Rome GA (S)

Shoshone Bannock Tribes, Shoshone Bannock Tribal Museum, Fort Hall ID (M)

Side Street Projects, Pasadena CA (M)

Eli Siegel Collection, see Aesthetic Realism Foundation, New York NY

Siena College, Dept of Creative Arts, Loudonville NY (S)

Siena Heights College, Klemm Gallery, Studio Angelico, Adrian MI (M,L)

Siena Heights University, Studio Angelico-Art Dept, Adrian MI (S)

Sierra Arts Foundation, Sierra Arts Gallery, Reno NV (A)

Sierra Community College, Art Dept, Rocklin CA (S)

Sierra Nevada College, Fine Arts Dept, Incline Village NV (S)

R L S Silverado Museum, Saint Helena CA (M,L)

Silver Eye Center for Photography, Pittsburgh PA (A)

Silver Lake College, Art Dept, Manitowoc WI (S)

Silvermine Guild Arts Center, Silvermine Galleries, New Canaan CT (M,L)

Simon's Rock College of Bard, Visual Arts Dept, Great Barrington MA (S)

Simon Fraser University Gallery, see Simon Fraser University, Burnaby BC

Simon Fraser University, Simon Fraser University Gallery, Burnaby BC (M,L)

Norton Simon, Pasadena CA (M)

Simpson College, Farnham Gallery, Indianola IA (M)

Simpson Gallagher Gallery, Cody WY (M)

Sinclair Community College, Division of Fine & Performing Arts, Dayton OH (S)

Sioux City Art Center, Sioux City IA (S)

Sioux City Art Center, Sioux City IA (A,L)

Sioux Indian Museum, see Indian Arts & Crafts Board, US Dept of the Interior, Rapid City SD

SITE Santa Fe, Santa Fe NM (M)

Sitka Historical Museum, see Sitka Historical Society, Sitka AK

Sitka Historical Society, Sitka Historical Museum, Sitka AK (M)

Skagit Valley College, Dept of Art, Mount Vernon WA (S)

Skagway City Museum & Archives, Skagway AK (M)

Skaneateles Library Association, Skaneateles NY (A)

Skidmore College, Dept of Art & Art History, Saratoga Springs NY (S)

Skidmore College, Schick Art Gallery, Saratoga Springs NY (M,L)

Skirball Cultural Center, see Hebrew Union College, Los Angeles CA

Skirball Museum Cincinnati, see Hebrew Union College - Jewish Institute of Religion, Cincinnati OH

Skokie Public Library, Skokie IL (L)

Skowhegan School of Painting & Sculpture, New York NY (S)

Slater Memorial Museum, see Norwich Free Academy, Norwich CT

Slater Mill, Old Slater Mill Association, Pawtucket RI (M)

Philip Slein Gallery, Saint Louis MO (M)

Slippery Rock University of Pennsylvania, Dept of Art, Slippery Rock PA (S)

Joseph Curtis Sloane Art Library, see University of North Carolina at Chapel Hill, Chapel Hill NC

Helen Farr Sloan Library, see Delaware Art Museum, Wilmington DE

Sloss Furnaces National Historic Landmark, Birmingham AL (M)

Smart Museum of Art, see University of Chicago, Chicago IL

C E Smith Museum of Anthropology, see California State University, East Bay, Hayward CA

Smith College, Art Dept, Northampton MA (S)

Smith College, Museum of Art, Northampton MA (M,L)

Smithsonian Institution, see National Museum of African Art, Washington DC

Smithsonian Institution, Washington DC (M)

Snake River Heritage Center, Weiser ID (M)

Gordon Snelgrove Art Gallery, see University of Saskatchewan, Saskatoon SK

Snite Museum of Art, see University of Notre Dame, Notre Dame IN

Snow College, Art Dept, Ephraim UT (S)

Snow College Art Gallery, Ephraim UT (M)

Snug Harbor Cultural Center, Newhouse Center for Contemporary Art, Staten Island NY (M)

Soap Factory, Minneapolis MN (M)

Social & Public Art Resource Center, (SPARC), Venice CA (A)

Societe des Musees Quebecois, Montreal PQ (A)

Society for Commercial Archeology, Little AR

Society for Contemporary Craft, Pittsburgh PA (M)

Society for Contemporary Photography, Kansas City MO (M)

Society for Photographic Education (SPE), SPE Gallery, Cleveland OH (A)

Society for the Protection & Preservation of Black Culture in Nova Scotia, Black Cultural Center for Nova Scotia, Dartmouth NS (L)

Society of American Graphic Artists, New York NY (O)

Society of American Historical Artists, Oyster Bay NY (O)

Society of Architectural Historians, Chicago IL (O)

The Society of Arts & Crafts, Boston MA (A)

Society of Canadian Artists, Toronto ON (O)

Society of Decorative Painters, Inc, Decorative Arts Collection Museum, Atlanta GA (A)

Society of Illustrators, New York NY (O)

Society of Illustrators, Museum of American Illustration, New York NY (M)

The Society of Layerists in Multi-Media (SLMM), Albuquerque NM (A)

Society of North American Goldsmiths, Eugene OR (O)

Society of Photographers & Artists Representatives, New York NY (O)

Society of Scribes, Ltd, New York NY (A)

The Society of the Cincinnati at Anderson House, Washington DC (M)

The Society of the Four Arts, Palm Beach FL (A,L)

Socrates Sculpture Park, Long Island City NY (M)

The Soho Center Library, see New Museum of Contemporary Art, New York NY

Soho 20 Gallery, New York NY (M)

Soka University, Founders Hall Art Gallery, Aliso Viejo CA (M)

Solano Community College, Division of Fine & Applied Art & Behavioral Science, Fairfield CA (S)

Sonoma County Museum, Santa Rosa CA (M)

Sonoma State University, Art & Art History Dept, Rohnert Park CA (S)

Sonoma State University, University Art Gallery, Rohnert Park CA (M)

Sonoma Valley Historical Society, Depot Park Museum, Sonoma CA (M)

Sonoma Valley Museum of Art, Sonoma CA (M)

Sooke Region Museum & Art Gallery, Sooke BC (M)

Soo Visual Arts Center, Minneapolis MN (M)

Sophie H Newcomb Memorial College, see Tulane University, New Orleans LA

Sordoni Art Gallery, see Wilkes University, Wilkes-Barre PA

Southampton Art Society, Southampton Art School, Southampton ON (S)

Southampton College of Long Island University, Arts & Media Division, Riverhead NY (S)

South Arkansas Arts Center, El Dorado AR (A)

South Bend Regional Museum of Art, South Bend IN (A,L)

South Carolina Artisans Center, Walterboro SC (M)

South Carolina Arts Commission, Columbia SC (A,L)

South Carolina State Museum, Columbia SC (M)

South Carolina State University, Dept of Visual & Performing Arts, Orangeburg SC (S)

State University of New York College at Old Westbury, Visual Arts Dept, Old Westbury NY (S)

State University of New York College at Old Westbury, Amelie A Wallace Gallery, Old Westbury NY (M)

State University of New York College at Oneonta, Dept of Art, Oneonta NY (S)

State University of New York College at Oneonta, Martin - Mullen Art Gallery, Oneonta NY (M)

State University of New York College at Potsdam, Dept of Fine Arts, Potsdam NY (S)

State University of West Georgia, Art Dept, Carrollton GA (S)

Stauth Foundation & Museum, Stauth Memorial Museum, Montezuma KS (M)

Staunton Augusta Art Center, Staunton VA (A)

Stedman Art Gallery, see Rutgers University, Camden NJ

T C Steele, Nashville IN (M)

Steep & Brew Gallery, Madison WI (M)

Ste Genevieve Museum, Sainte Genevieve MO (M)

Steinhardt Conservatory Gallery, see Brooklyn Botanic Garden, Brooklyn NY

Stephen Bulger Gallery, Toronto ON (M)

Stephen F Austin State University, Art Dept, Nacogdoches TX (S)

Stephen F Austin State University, SFA Galleries, Nacogdoches TX (M)

Stephen Foster Folk Culture Center State Park, see Florida Department of Environmental Protection, White Springs FL

Stephen Phillips Memorial Library, see Penobscot Marine Museum, Searsport ME

Stephens College, Art Dept, Columbia MO (S)

Stephens College, Lewis James & Nellie Stratton Davis Art Gallery, Columbia MO (M)

Sterling College, Art Dept, Sterling KS (S)

Stetson University, Department of Creative Arts, Deland FL (S)

Steuben House Museum, see Bergen County Historical Society, River Edge NJ

Stewart Hall Art Gallery, see Pointe Claire Cultural Centre, Pointe Claire PQ

Stewart Memorial Library & Gallery, see Coe College, Cedar Rapids IA

The Stewart Museum, Montreal PQ (M,L)

St George Art Museum, Saint George UT (M)

Stillman College, Stillman Art Gallery & Art Dept, Tuscaloosa AL (S)

Stone Quarry Hill Art Park, John & Virginia Winner Memorial Art Gallery, Cazenovia NY (M,L)

Stony Brook University, College of Arts & Sciences, Dept of Art, Stony Brook NY (S)

Storefront for Art & Architecture, New York NY (M)

Storm King Art Center, Mountainville NY (M)

Stout Reference Library, see Indianapolis Museum of Art, Indianapolis IN

Harriet Beecher Stowe, Hartford CT (L)

Stoxen Library, see Dickinson State University, Dickinson ND

Strasburg Museum, Strasburg VA (M)

Stratford Historical Society, Catharine B Mitchell Museum, Stratford CT (L)

G Robert Strauss Jr Memorial Library, see The Buffalo Fine Arts Academy, Buffalo NY

Stremmel Gallery, Reno NV (M)

Struts Gallery, Sackville NB (M)

Stuart Collection, see University of California, San Diego, La Jolla CA

Gilbert Stuart, Gilbert Stuart Birthplace & Museum, Saunderstown RI (M)

The Studio/Larson Gallery, see University of Minnesota, Minneapolis MN

Studio 24, see Galeria de la Raza, San Francisco CA

Studio Channel Islands Art Center, Camarillo CA (M)

Studio Gallery, Washington DC (M)

The Studio Museum in Harlem, New York NY (M)

Studio Place Arts, Barre VT (M)

Studio San Giuseppe, see College of Mount Saint Joseph, Cincinnati OH

Stumptown Art Studio, Whitefish Gallery, Whitefish MT (M)

Sturdivant Museum Association, Sturdivant Museum, Selma AL (M)

Sturges Fine Arts Center, see San Bernardino Art Association, Inc, San Bernardino CA

Suffolk County Community College, Art Dept, Selden NY (S)

Suffolk University, New England School of Art & Design Library, Boston MA (L)

Sullivan County Community College, Division of Commercial Art & Photography, Loch Sheldrake NY (S)

Sul Ross State University, Dept of Fine Arts & Communications, Alpine TX (S)

The Summit County Historical Society of Akron, OH, Akron OH (M)

Sumter Gallery of Art, Sumter SC (M)

SunAmerica, Inc, The SunAmerica Collection, Los Angeles CA (C)

The SunAmerica Collection, see SunAmerica, Inc, Los Angeles CA

Sunbury Shores Arts & Nature Centre, Inc, Gallery, Saint Andrews NB (A,L)

Sun Gallery, Hayward CA (M)

Sun Valley Center for the Arts, Dept of Fine Art, Sun Valley ID (S)

Supreme Court of the United States, Office of the Curator, Washington DC (M)

Surface Design Association, Inc, Sebastopol CA (A)

Surrey Art Gallery, Surrey BC (M,L)

Surry Community College, Art Dept, Dobson NC (S)

Susquehanna Art Museum, Harrisburg PA (A)

Susquehanna Studio, Susquehanna Studio, Union Dale PA (A)

Susquehanna University, Lore Degenstein Gallery, Selinsgrove PA (M)

SVACA - Sheyenne Valley Arts & Crafts Association, Bjarne Ness Gallery at Bear Creek Hall, Fort Ransom ND (M,A)

Swarthmore College, Dept of Art & Art History, Swarthmore PA (S)

Swarthmore College, Friends Historical Library of Swarthmore College, Swarthmore PA (L)

Swedish American Museum Association of Chicago, Chicago IL (M)

Sweet Briar College, Art History Dept, Sweet Briar VA (S)

Sweet Briar College, Mary Helen Cochran Library, Sweet Briar VA (L,M)

Sweet Mabel Folk Arts & Fine Craft Gallery, Narberth PA (A)

Sweetwater County Library System and School District #1, Community Fine Arts Center, Rock Springs WY (A)

Swetcharnik Art Studio, Mount Airy MD (M)

Swiss Institute, New York NY (M)

Switzerland County Historical Society Inc, Life on the Ohio: River History Museum, Vevay IN (M)

Swope Art Museum, Terre Haute IN (M,L)

Swords Into Plowshares Peace Center & Gallery, see Central United Methodist Church, Detroit MI

Symmes Systems, Photographic Investments Gallery, Atlanta GA (M)

Synagogue Art & Architectural Library, see Union for Reformed Judaism, New York NY

Syracuse University, College of Visual & Performing Arts, Syracuse NY (S)

Syracuse University, SUArt Galleries, Syracuse NY (M,L)

Tabor Opera House Museum, Leadville CO (M)

Tacoma Art Museum, Tacoma WA (M)

Tacoma Community College, Art Dept, Tacoma WA (S)

Tacoma Public Library, Handforth Gallery, Tacoma WA (L)

Taft College, Art Department, Taft CA (S)

Lorado Taft Midway Studios, see University of Chicago, Chicago IL

Taft Museum of Art, Cincinnati OH (M)

Taipei Economic & Cultural Office, Chinese Information & Culture Center Library, New York NY (L)

Tallahassee Community College, Art Dept, Tallahassee FL (S)

Tallahassee Museum of History & Natural Science, Tallahassee FL (M,L)

Taller Puertorriqueno Inc, Lorenzo Homar Gallery, Philadelphia PA (A)

Tamarind Institute, see University of New Mexico, Albuquerque NM

Tampa Museum of Art, Tampa FL (M,L)

Tanner Hill Gallery, Chattanooga TN (M)

Taos Art Museum, Taos NM (M)

Taos Center for the Arts, Stables Gallery, Taos NM (A)

Taos, Taos NM (M,L)

Taos Public Library, Fine Art Collection, Taos NM (L)

Tarble Arts Center, see Eastern Illinois University, Charleston IL

Tarrant County College, Art Dept, Hurst TX (S)

Tattoo Art Museum, San Francisco CA (M)

Lillian & Coleman Taube Museum of Art, Minot ND (M)

Taubman Museum of Art, Roanoke VA (M)

Edward P Taylor Research Library & Archives, see Art Gallery of Ontario, Toronto ON

Elizabeth Prewitt Taylor Memorial Library, see Arkansas Arts Center, Little Rock AR

Taylor University, Metcalf Art Gallery, Upland IN (M)

Taylor University, Visual Art Dept, Upland IN (S)

Telfair Museums' Jepson Center for the Arts Library, Savannah GA (M)

Tellus Northwest Georgia Science Museum, Cartersville GA (M)

Temiskaming Art Gallery, Haileybury ON (M)

Temple College, Art Dept, Temple TX (S)

Temple Gallery, see Temple University, Tyler School of Art, Philadelphia PA

The Temple-Tifereth Israel, The Temple Museum of Religious Art, Beachwood OH (M)

Temple University, Tyler School of Art, Temple Gallery, Philadelphia PA (M)

Temple University, Tyler School of Art, Philadelphia PA (S)

Temple University, Tyler School of Art-Galleries, Philadelphia PA (M,L)

Tennessee Historical Society, Nashville TN (A)

Tennessee State Museum, Nashville TN (M,L)

Tennessee Tech University, Appalachian Center for Craft, Smithville TN (S)

Tennessee Valley Art Association, Tuscumbia AL (A)

1078 Gallery, Chico CA (M)

Te Paske Gallery, see Northwestern College, Orange City IA

Terrain Gallery, see Aesthetic Realism Foundation, New York NY

Sandor Teszler Library Gallery, see Wofford College, Spartanburg SC

Texarkana College, Art Dept, Texarkana TX (S)

Texas A&M University, Art Gallery, Kingsville TX (M)

Texas A&M University, College of Architecture, College Station TX (S)

Texas A&M University Commerce, Dept of Art, Commerce TX (S)

Texas A&M University - Commerce, University Gallery, Commerce TX (M)

Texas A&M University-Corpus Christi, Weil Art Gallery, Corpus Christi TX (A)

Texas A&M University-Kingsville, Art Dept, Kingsville TX (S)

Texas A&M University, J Wayne Stark University Center Galleries, College Station TX (M,A)

Texas Christian University, School of Art, Fort Worth TX (S)

Texas Christian University, University Art Gallery, Fort Worth TX (M)

Texas Lutheran University, Dept of Visual Arts, Seguin TX (S)

Texas Ranger Hall of Fame & Museum, Waco TX (M,L)

Texas Ranger Research Center, see Texas Ranger Hall of Fame & Museum, Waco TX

Texas Southern University, College of Liberal Arts & Behavioral Sciences, Houston TX (S)

Texas State Museum of Asian Cultures, see Billie Trimble Chandler, Corpus Christi TX

Texas State University - San Marcos, Dept of Art and Design, San Marcos TX (S)

Texas Tech University, Dept of Art, Lubbock TX (S)

Texas Tech University, Museum of Texas Tech University, Lubbock TX (M,L)

Texas Wesleyan University, Dept of Art, Fort Worth TX (S)

Texas Woman's University Art Gallery, Denton TX (M)

Texas Woman's University, School of the Arts, Dept of Visual Arts, Denton TX (S)

Textile Conservation Workshop Inc, South Salem NY (A)

The Textile Museum, Washington DC (M,L)

Textile Museum of Canada, Toronto ON (M)

Thames Art Gallery, Chatham ON (A)

Thiel College, Dept of Art, Greenville PA (S)

Thiel College, Weyers-Sampson Art Gallery, Greenville PA (M)

Think 360 Art Complete Education, Colo Chapter, Denver CO (A)

This Century Art Gallery, Williamsburg VA (M)

Thomas Center Galleries - Cultural Affairs, see City of Gainesville, Gainesville FL

Thomas College, Art Gallery, Waterville ME (M,L)

Thomas Jefferson University, Eakins Gallery, Philadelphia PA (M)

Thomas More College, Art Dept, Crestview Hills KY (S)

Thomas More College, Eva G Farris Art Gallery, Crestview KY (M)

Thomas University, Humanities Division, Thomasville GA (S)

Nancy Thompson Library, see Kean University, Union NJ

Tom Thomson, Owen Sound ON (M,L)

Thorne-Sagendorph Art Gallery, see Keene State College, Keene NH

University of Toronto at Mississauga, Blackwood Gallery, Mississauga ON (M)

University of Toronto, Justina M Barnicke Gallery, Toronto ON (M,L)

University of Toronto, Dept of Fine Art, Toronto ON (S)

University of Toronto, University of Toronto Art Centre, Toronto ON (M)

University of Tulsa, Gilcrease Museum, Tulsa OK (M,L)

University of Tulsa, Alexandre Hogue Gallery, Tulsa OK (M)

University of Tulsa, School of Art, Tulsa OK (S)

University of Utah, Dept of Art & Art History, Salt Lake City UT (S)

University of Utah, Utah Museum of Fine Arts, Salt Lake City UT (M,L)

University of Vermont, Dept of Art, Burlington VT (S)

University of Vermont, Robert Hull Fleming Museum, Burlington VT (M)

University of Victoria, Dept of Visual Arts, Victoria BC (S)

University of Victoria, The Legacy Art Gallery, Victoria BC (M)

University of Virginia, McIntire Dept of Art, Charlottesville VA (S)

University of Virginia, The Fralin Museum of Art at the University of Virginia, Charlottesville VA (M,L)

University of Washington, Henry Art Gallery, Seattle WA (M,L)

University of Washington, School of Art, Seattle WA (S)

University of Waterloo, Fine Arts Dept, Waterloo ON (S)

University of Waterloo, University of Waterloo Art Gallery, Waterloo ON (M,L)

University of West Alabama, Division of Fine Arts, Livingston AL (S)

University of Western Ontario, John Labatt Visual Arts Centre, London ON (S)

University of Western Ontario, McIntosh Gallery, London ON (M,L)

University of West Florida, Art Gallery, Pensacola FL (M,L)

University of West Florida, Dept of Art, Pensacola FL (S)

University of Windsor, Visual Arts, Windsor ON (S)

University of Wisconsin, Green Bay, Lawton Gallery, Green Bay WI (M)

University of Wisconsin, Madison, Dept of Art, Madison WI (S)

University of Wisconsin, Center-Barron County, Dept of Art, Rice Lake WI (S)

University of Wisconsin College - Marinette, Art Dept, Marinette WI (S)

University of Wisconsin-Eau Claire, Dept of Art & Design, Eau Claire WI (S)

University of Wisconsin-Eau Claire, Foster Gallery, Eau Claire WI (M)

University of Wisconsin, Gallery 101, River Falls WI (M)

University of Wisconsin-Green Bay, Arts Dept, Green Bay WI (S)

University of Wisconsin, Institute of Visual Arts, (INOVA), Milwaukee WI (M)

University of Wisconsin-La Crosse, Center for the Arts, La Crosse WI (S)

University of Wisconsin-Madison, Wisconsin Union Galleries, Madison WI (M,L)

University of Wisconsin-Milwaukee, Peck School of the Arts, Dept of Art & Design, Milwaukee WI (S)

University of Wisconsin Oshkosh, Dept of Art, Oshkosh WI (S)

University of Wisconsin Oshkosh, Allen R Priebe Gallery, Oshkosh WI (M)

University of Wisconsin-Parkside, Art Dept, Kenosha WI (S)

University of Wisconsin-Platteville, Dept of Fine Art, Platteville WI (S)

University of Wisconsin - Platteville, Harry & Laura Nohr Gallery, Platteville WI (M)

University of Wisconsin-River Falls, Art Dept, River Falls WI (S)

University of Wisconsin-Stevens Point, Carlsten Art Gallery, Stevens Point WI (M)

University of Wisconsin-Stevens Point, Dept of Art & Design, Stevens Point WI (S)

University of Wisconsin-Stout, Dept of Art & Design, Menomonie WI (S)

University of Wisconsin-Stout, J Furlong Gallery, Menomonie WI (M)

University of Wisconsin-Superior, Programs in the Visual Arts, Superior WI (S)

University of Wisconsin-Whitewater, Art Dept, Whitewater WI (S)

University of Wisconsin-Whitewater, Crossman Gallery, Whitewater WI (M)

University of Wyoming, Dept of Art, Laramie WY (S)

University of Wyoming, University of Wyoming Art Museum, Laramie WY (M)

The Upper Room Chapel & Museum, see General Board of Discipleship, The United Methodist Church, Nashville TN

UrbanArts Institute at Massachusetts College of Art, Boston MA (A)

Urbanglass, Robert Lehman Gallery, Brooklyn NY (A)

Urban Institute for Contemporary Arts, Grand Rapids MI (M)

Ursinus College, Philip & Muriel Berman Museum of Art, Collegeville PA (M)

USC Fisher Museum of Art, see University of Southern California, Los Angeles CA

US Navy Supply Corps Museum, see United States Navy Supply Corps School, Newport RI

USS Constitution Museum, Boston MA (M)

Utah Arts Council, Chase Home Museum of Utah Folk Arts, Salt Lake City UT (M)

Utah Department of Natural Resources, Division of Parks & Recreation, Territorial Statehouse State Park Museum, Fillmore UT (M)

Utah Lawyers for the Arts, Salt Lake City UT (A)

Utah Museum of Fine Arts, see University of Utah, Salt Lake City UT

Utah State University, Dept of Landscape Architecture Environmental Planning, Logan UT (S)

Utah State University, Nora Eccles Harrison Museum of Art, Logan UT (M)

Utah Valley University, Woodbury Art Museum, Orem UT (M)

Utica College of Syracuse University, Division of Art & Science, Utica NY (S)

Valdosta State University, Art Gallery, Valdosta GA (M)

Valdosta State University, Dept of Art, Valdosta GA (S)

Valencia Community College, Art Gallery-East Campus, Orlando FL (M)

Valencia Community College - East Campus, Art Dept, Orlando FL (S)

Valentine Richmond History Center, Richmond VA (M,L)

Valley Art Center Inc, Clarkston WA (A)

Valley Art Gallery, Forest Grove OR (M)

Valley City State College, Art Dept, Valley City ND (S)

Valley Cottage Library, Gallery, Valley Cottage NY (L)

Valparaiso University, Brauer Museum of Art, Valparaiso IN (M)

Van Alen Institute, New York NY (O)

Van Cortlandt House Museum, Bronx NY (M)

Vancouver Art Gallery, Vancouver BC (M,L)

Vancouver City Archives, Vancouver BC (L)

Vancouver Public Library, Fine Arts & Music Department, Vancouver BC (M)

Vanderbilt University, Dept of Art, Nashville TN (S)

Vanderbilt University, Vanderbilt University Fine Arts Gallery, Nashville TN (M)

William H Van Every Jr & Edward M Smith Galleries, see Davidson College, Davidson NC

Van Ingel Fine Arts Center, Gainey Gallery, Byron Center MI (M)

James D Van Trump Library, see Pittsburgh History & Landmarks Foundation, Pittsburgh PA

Van Wyck Homestead Museum, see Fishkill Historical Society, Fishkill NY

Carleton Varney Dept of Art & Design, see University of Charleston, Charleston WV

Vassar College, Art Dept, Poughkeepsie NY (S)

Vassar College, The Frances Lehman Loeb Art Center, Poughkeepsie NY (M,L)

Venice Art Center, Venice FL (M)

Ventura College, Art Galleries, Ventura CA (M)

Ventura College, Fine Arts Dept, Ventura CA (S)

Vermilion Community College, Art Dept, Ely MN (S)

Vermilion County Museum Society, Danville IL (M,L)

Vermont Historical Society, Museum, Montpelier VT (M,L)

Vermont State Craft Center at Frog Hollow, Burlington VT (M)

Vermont Studio Center, Red Mill Gallery, Johnson VT (M)

Vernon Art Gallery, Vernon BC (M)

Vero Beach Museum of Art, Vero Beach FL (M)

Vesterheim Norwegian-American Museum, Decorah IA (M)

VICANA (Vietnamese Cultural Association in North America) Library, Springfield VA (L)

Victor Heritage Museum, Victor MT (M)

Victoria College, Fine Arts Dept, Victoria TX (S)

Victoria Mansion - Morse Libby House, Portland ME (M)

Michael Victor II Art Library, see Springfield Art Association of Edwards Place, Springfield IL

Victor Valley Community College, Art Dept, Victorville CA (S)

Viking Union Gallery, see Western Washington University, Bellingham WA

Village of Potsdam, Potsdam Public Museum, Potsdam NY (M)

Villa Maria College of Buffalo, Art Dept, Buffalo NY (S)

Villa Marre, see Quapaw Quarter Association, Inc, Little Rock AR

Villanova University Art Gallery, The Art Gallery, Villanova PA (M)

Villanova University, Dept of Theater, Villanova PA (S)

Villa Victoria Center for the Arts, Boston MA (M)

Vincennes University Junior College, Humanities Art Dept, Vincennes IN (S)

Vincent Price Art Museum, see East Los Angeles College, Monterey Park CA

Virginia Center for the Creative Arts, Amherst VA (O)

Virginia Commonwealth University, Anderson Gallery, Richmond VA (M)

Virginia Commonwealth University, Art History Dept, Richmond VA (S)

Virginia Dept Historic Resources, Research Library, Richmond VA (L)

Virginia Historical Society, Richmond VA (A,L)

Virginia Intermont College, Fine Arts Div, Bristol VA (S)

Virginia Museum of Fine Arts, Richmond VA (M,L)

Virginia Polytechnic Institute & State University, Armory Art Gallery, Blacksburg VA (M,L)

Virginia Polytechnic Institute & State University, Dept of Art & Art History, Blacksburg VA (S)

Virginia Quilt Museum, Harrisonburg VA

Virginia State University, Department of Art & Design, Petersburg VA (S)

Virginia Wesleyan College, Art Dept of the Humanities Div, Norfolk VA (S)

Virginia Western Community College, Communication Design, Fine Art & Photography, Roanoke VA (S)

Viridian Artists Inc, New York NY (A)

Visual Art Exchange, Raleigh NC (A)

Visual Artists & Galleries Association (VAGA), New York NY (O)

Visual Arts Center of New Jersey, Summit NJ (A)

Visual Arts Center of Northwest Florida, Panama City FL (M,L)

Visual Arts Center of Richmond, Richmond VA (A)

Visual Arts Library, New York NY (L)

Visual Arts Minnesota, Saint Cloud MN (A)

Visual Arts Nova Scotia, Halifax NS (A)

Visual Arts Ontario, Toronto ON (A)

Visual Studies Workshop, Rochester NY (S)

Viterbo College, Art Dept, La Crosse WI (S)

Viterbo University, Art Gallery, La Crosse WI (M)

Vizcaya Museum & Gardens, Miami FL (M,L)

Volcano Art Center Gallery, Hawaii Volcanoes National Park HI (M)

Volunteer Lawyers for the Arts of Massachusetts Inc, Boston MA (A)

VSA Arts of New Mexico, Enabled Arts Center, Albuquerque NM (S)

VSA Arts of New Mexico, Very Special Arts Gallery, Albuquerque NM (M)

VU Centre De Diffusion Et De Production De La Photographie, Quebec PQ (M)

Wabash College, Art Dept, Crawfordsville IN (S)

Wabaunsee County Historical Museum, Alma KS (M)

Wade House Historic Site-Wisconsin Historical Society, Wesley W. Jung Carriage Museum, Greenbush WI (M)

Wadsworth Atheneum Museum of Art, Hartford CT (M,L)

Wadsworth-Longfellow House, see Maine Historical Society, Portland ME

Wagner College, Arts Administration Dept, Staten Island NY (S)

Wailoa Arts & Cultural Center, Hilo HI (M)

Wake Forest University, A Lewis Aycock Visual Resource Library, Winston Salem NC (L,M)

Wake Forest University, Dept of Art, Winston-Salem NC (S)

Waldorf College, Art Dept, Forest City IA (S)

Walker's Point Artists Assoc Inc, Gallery 218, Milwaukee WI (A)

Walker's Point Center for the Arts, Milwaukee WI (M)

The Walker African American Museum & Research Center, Las Vegas NV (M)

Walker Art Center, Minneapolis MN (M,L)

Jacob Walker Art Gallery, Johnson VT (M)

Walker Fine Art, Denver CO (M)